THE SPORT AMERICANA®

Baseball Card

PRICE GUIDE

By

DR. JAMES BECKETT

NUMBER 14

EDGEWATER BOOK COMPANY • CLEVELAND

SPORT AMERICANA is a registered trademark of

EDGEWATER BOOK COMPANY
P.O. BOX 40238
CLEVELAND, OHIO 44140

Manufactured in the United States of America.

First Printing

Library of Congress catalog card number: 79-643474

ISBN 0-937424-58-7

Acknowledgments

A great deal of diligence, hard work, and dedicated effort went into this year's volume. However, the high standards to which we hold ourselves could not have been met without the expert input and generous amount of time contributed by many people. Our sincere thanks are extended to each and every one of you.

Those who have worked closely with us on this and many other books have again proven themselves invaluable — Frank and Vivian Barning (*Baseball Hobby News*), Chris Benjamin, Sy Berger (Topps), Card Collectors Co., Peter Brennan, Cartophilium (Andrew Pywowarczuk), Ira Cetron, Barry Colla, Mike Cramer (Pacific Trading Cards), Bill and Diane Dodge, Doubleheaders (Wayne Varner, Mike Wheat, and Bill Zimpleman), Fleer Corporation (Paul Mullen, Vincent Murray, and Jeff Massien), Steve Freedman, Gervise Ford, Larry and Jeff Fritsch, Tony Galovich (American Card Exchange), Georgia Music and Sports (Dick DeCourcey), Dick Gilkeson, Steve Gold (AU Sports), Bill Goodwin (St. Louis Baseball Cards), Mike and Howard Gordon, George Grauer, John Greenwald, Wayne Grove, Bill Haber, Bill Henderson, Jay and Mary Kasper, Allan Kaye (*Baseball Card News*), Rick Keplinger, Michael Keyton, David Kohler (SportsCards Plus), Don Lepore, Paul Lewicki, Neil Lewis (Leaf), Lew Lipset, Norman and Ken Liss (Topps), Mark Macrae, Bill Madden, Major League Marketing (Dan Shedrick, Tom Day, and Julie Haddon), Mid-Atlantic Sports Cards (Bill Bossert), Dick Millerd, Brian Morris, B.A. Murry, Ralph Nozaki, Oldies and Goodies (Nigel Spill), Optigraphics/Score Group (Ed Fick), Jack Pollard, Jeff Prillaman, Gavin Riley, Alan Rosen (Mr. Mint), Clifton Rouse, John Rumierz, San Diego Sport Collectibles (Bill Goepner and Nacho Arredondo), Kevin Savage (Sports Gallery), Mike Schechter, Barry Sloate, John Spalding, Phil Spector (Scoreboard, Inc.), Sports Collectors Store, Frank Steele, Murvin Sterling, Lee Temanson, Ed Twombly (New England Bullpen), Gary Walter, Bill Wesslund (Portland Sports Card Co.), Craig Williamson, Scott Williard, Kit Young, and Ted Zanidakis. Of special help on this edition was B.A. Murry, who in early 1991 laid the groundwork for our Technical Services department before becoming our Senior Pricing Consultant. Finally we give a special acknowledgment to Dennis W. Eckes, "Mr. Sport Americana," whose untimely passing last year was a real loss to the hobby and to me

personally. The success of the *Beckett Price Guides* has always been the result of a team effort.

I believe this year's Price Guide is our best yet. For that, you can thank all of the contributors nationwide (listed above and below) as well as our staff here in Dallas. Our company now boasts a substantial Technical Services team which has made (and is continuing to make) direct and important contributions to this work. Technical Services capably handled numerous technical details and provided able assistance in pricing for this edition of the annual guide. That effort was directed by Technical Services managers Jay Johnson and Pepper Hastings. They were assisted by Technical Services coordinator Mary Gregory, price guide analysts Theo Chen, Mike Hersh, Dan Hitt, Mary Huston, Rich Klein, Allan Muir, Grant Sandground and Dave Sliepka. Also contributing to our Technical Services functions were Jana Threatt, Wendy Jewell, Peter Tepp and Scott Layton, whose special assistance was invaluable in making this project a success. The price gathering and analytical talents of this fine group of hobbyists has helped make our Beckett team stronger, while making this guide and its companion monthly price guides even more widely recognized as the hobby's most reliable and relied upon sources of pricing information.

It is very difficult to be "accurate" — one can only do one's best. But this job is especially difficult since we're shooting at a moving target: Prices are fluctuating all the time. Having several full-time pricing experts has definitely proven to be better than just one, and I thank all of them for working together to provide you, our readers, with the most accurate prices possible.

Many people have provided price input, illustrative material, checklist verifications, errata, and/or background information. We should like to individually thank AbD Cards (Dale Wesolewski), Robert Abel, Carl Abrams, Dave Acker, Jeremy Ackerman, Jerry Adamic, Michael Adams, Ron Adelson, Tony Adkins, Andrew R. Aebi, A.J.'s Sport Stop, R.J. Albanese, Bob Alexander, Mike Alexander, Will Allison, All Star Sports Collectibles, J. Almeda, David Anderson, Dennis Anderson, Jason Anderson, T.M. Angell, Graham Anthony, Jim Anthony, Tom Antonowicz, Ric Apter, Jason Arasate, Mark Argo (Olde South Cards), William Arkell, Burl Armstrong, Neil Armstrong (World Series Cards), Brian Ashbach, Lester H. Auclair Jr., Robert August, Charles Austin, B & B Sales Co., B & F Sports Cards (Bill Bryda), Jeff Baas, Robert Baker, Ball Four Cards, John Barbier,

MasterCard   **VISA**

BILL HENDERSON'S CARDS
"King of the Commons"

"ALWAYS BUYING"
Call or Write
for Quote

2320 RUGER AVE. PG14
JANESVILLE, WISCONSIN 53545
1-608-755-0922

"ALWAYS BUYING"
Call or Write
for Quote

	EX/MT TO MINT CONDITION HI # OR SEMI HI SCARCE SERIES	PRICE PER COMMON CARD	COMMON EACH	EX/MT TO MINT CONDITION OTHER SERIES	PRICE PER COMMON CARD	50 Diff.	100 Diff.	200 Asst.	300 Asst.	500 Asst.	50	100	200
						GROUP LOTS FOR SALE / MY CHOICE OF CARDS					VG+ to EX Condition Different		
1948 BOWMAN (37-48)		30.00	25.00										
1949 BOWMAN (145-240)		80.00	16.00			720.					480.		
50-51 BOWMAN 50 (1-72) 51 (253-324)		60.00	16.00	51 (2-36)	25.00	720.					480.		
1952 TOPPS (311-407)		P.O.R.	30.00	(2-80)	60.00	1350.					900.		
1952 BOWMAN (217-252)		30.00	16.00	(2-36)	20.00	720.					480.		
1953 TOPPS (220-280)		80.00	20.00	(2-165)	30.00	900.					600.		
1953 BOWMAN (129-160)		40.00	35.00	(113-128)	50.00	1575.					950.		
1954 TOPPS			15.00	(51-75)	30.00	675.					400.		
1954 BOWMAN			10.00	(129-224)	15.00	450.	850.				270.	510.	
1955 TOPPS (161-210)		30.00	10.00	(151-160)	20.00	450.					270.		
1955 BOWMAN (225-320)	18-.30. Umps	8.00	(2-96)	8.50	360.	700.				210.	400.		
1956 TOPPS (261-340)		12.00	10.00	(181-260)	15.00	450.					270.	510.	
1957 TOPPS (265-352)		20.00	7.00	(1-88)	8.50	320.	600.				190.	360.	
1958 TOPPS (111-198)		5.00	4.50	(1-110)	7.50	205.	400.	775.	1020.		125.	230.	
1959 TOPPS (507-572)		15.00	4.00	(1-110)	6.00	190.	370.	720.	1000.		115.	220.	430.
1960 TOPPS (441-506) 5.00 (507-572) 15.00		3.50	(287-440)	4.00	165.	320.	620.	900.		100.	190.	370.	
1961 TOPPS (447-522) 5.00 (523-589) 30.00		3.00	(371-446)	4.00	140.	270.	530.	765.		85.	100.	310.	
1962 TOPPS (371-522) 4.50 (523-590) 15.00		2.50	(284-370)	3.00	115.	220.				70.	130.	250.	
1963 TOPPS (447-522) 13.00 (523-573) 10.00		2.50	(284-446)	4.50	115.	220.				70.	130.		
1964 TOPPS (371-522) 4.50 (523)-587) 8.50		2.00	(197-370)	3.00	90.	175.	*340.			60.	110.	210.	
1965 TOPPS (447-522) 5.00 (523-598) 6.00		2.00	(284-446)	3.00	90.	175.				60.	110.	210.	
1966 TOPPS (447-522) 6.00 (523-598) 15.00		1.50	(371-446)	3.50	65.	125.	*240.			45.	85.	160.	
1967 TOPPS (458-533) 6.00 (534-609) 20.00		1.50	(284-457)	3.00	65.	125.	*240.			45.	85.	160.	
1968 TOPPS (534-598)		3.50	1.50	(458-533)	3.00	60.	115.	*220.			37.	70.	130.
1969 TOPPS (589-664)		2.00	1.25	(219-327)	2.00	60.	115.	*220.			30.	55.	105.
1970 TOPPS (547-633) 3.00 (634-720) 6.00		1.00	(460-546)	1.50	45.	88.	*170.	250.	400.	27.	52.	100.	
1971 TOPPS (524-643) 3.50 (644-752) 6.00		1.00	(394-523)	1.50	45.	88.	*170.	250.	400.	27.	52.	100.	
1972 TOPPS (526-656) 3.00 (657-787) 6.00		.75	(395-525)	1.50	35.	68.	*130.	*190.	300.	21.	40.	78.	
1973 TOPPS (529-660)		3.00	.50	(397-528)	1.50	23.	45.	*85.	*125.	200.	14.	27.	50.
1974 TOPPS			.40			18.	35.	*68.	*100.	*170.		22.	40.
1975 TOPPS (8-132)		.50	.40			18.	35.	*68.	*100.			22.	40.
1976-77 TOPPS & 84 DONRUS			.25			23.	*44.	*65.	*100.		15.	28.	
1978-1980 TOPPS			.15			13.	*25.	*38.	*65.		8.	15.	
1981 thru 1991 Topps, Fleer, or Donrus except those listed separately (specify year & co.)			.10			9. Per Yr.	*17. Per Yr.	*26. Per Yr.	*40. Per Yr.				
1985-86 DONRUS, 1984-86 FLEER			.15			13.	*25.	*38.	*65.				

* Group Lots are all different

SPECIAL IN VG+ to EX
CONDITION-POSTPAID
Equal Distribution
of Each Year

250	58-62	450.00
500	58-62	850.00
250	60-69	270.00
500	60-69	520.00
1000	60-69	1000.00
250	70-79	60.00
500	70-79	110.00
1000	70-79	200.00
250	80-84	15.00
500	80-84	28.00
1000	80-84	55.00

Special 1 Different from each year 1949-80 EX/MT - $150.00, VG-EX $110.00
Special 100 Different from each year 1956-80 EX/MT - $3000.00, VG-EX $2100.00
Special 10 Different from each year 1956-80 EX/MT - $310.00, VG-EX $220.00

All lot groups are my choice only.

All assorted lots will contain as many different as possible.
Please list alternates whenever possible.
Send your want list and I will fill them at the above price for commons. High numbers,
specials, scarce series, and stars are priced at current Beckett.
You can use your Master Card or Visa to charge your purchases.
Minimum order $7.50 - Postage and handling .50 per 100 cards (minimum $1.75)

ANY CARD NOT LISTED ON PRICE SHEET IS PRICED AT CURRENT BECKETT MONTHLY HIGH COLUMN

SETS AVAILABLE
Topps 1988, 1989, 1990, 1991,
1992
22.95 ea. + 2.50 UPS
6 for 22.95 ea. + 9.00 UPS
18 for 22.35 ea. + 20.00 UPS
MIX OR MATCH

George Barkwell, Youssef Barnetche, Joe Barney, Brent Barnhill, Ed Barry (Ed's Collectibles), Bob Bartosz (Baseball Card Shop), Nathan Basford, Nick Basso, David Bauers, Baxter's Cards, Bay State Cards (Lenny DeAngelico), Fred Beck, Andy Beisel, Joey Beland, Dennis Joe Belk, Scott Bell, Nick Belletto, Peter S. Bennett, Graham Benyman, Carl Berg, Ken Berg, Dave Berman, Bernie's Bullpen, Mildred Berteau, Beulah Sports, Seth Bienstock, Brian Bigelow, Josh Bird, Jack Bishop, Robert Bittner, Scott Bixby, Helga E. Blackford, Gilbert Blakey, Jim Bland, Karry and Levi Bleam, Brad Bliek, Steven Blosser, Bob Boffa, Bill Boiani, Cortland Bolles, Tim Bond (Tim's Cards & Comics), Jim Bosecker, Charlie Botello, Holly Bott, Andy Bowen, Chivous Bradley, Todd Brammer, Bill Brandt, Scott Brandt, Josh Brann, Brian Brannen, Shawn Bratt, Jim Braun, Jeff Breitenfield, James Brennan, Michael Brennan, Bob Bresnahan, Wes Brewer, John Brigandi, Chidozie Bright, William Brislin, Corey Broeckling, Philip Bronikowski, Chuck Brooks, Richard Brown, Dan Bruner, David Bryant, Brad Buchta, Ngoc Bui, Steve Burchett, Gerald Burkett, T.J. Burner, Virgil Burns, Benjamin Burrell, Gary Bursae, Justin Bush, Patrick Buss, Jason Butler, Jim Butler, Al Cady, California Card Co., Allen Capeloto, Card Capital USA, The Card Mart, Danny Cariseo, Eric Carlson, Jim Carr, Patrick Carroll, Dale Cartwright, Carves Cards, Ray Castelluccio Sr., Hector Castro, Joe Cavallo, Sandy Chan, Dwight Chapin, Ray Cherry, Peter Childs, Mike Chmielewski, Tim Chrisp, Bigg Wayne Christian, Dick Cianciotto, Cincinnati Baseball Cards, David Clark, Derrick Clark, Justin Clark, Clay Clement, Richard Clement, Nathanael Clemons, Bill Cochran, Ronald Coleman, Collectibles Unlimited (John Alward and Deb Ingram), Collection de Sport AZ (Ronald Villaneuve), The Collectory, Andrew T. Collier, Dan Collins, Ryan Collins, Jason T. Commerford, Joe Conkle, Charles Cook, Aaron Cooper, Curt and Steven Cooter, Pedro Cortes, Lou Costanzo (Champion Sports), Adam Cota, Michael Cotter, Tom Cox, Paul and Ryan Crabb, Steven C. Crane, Taylor Crane, Chad Cripe, James Critzer, Darrin Crow, Paul Curran, Allen Custer;

Ryan Dahlstrom, Gene Dalager, Dave Dame, Brett Daniel, Jason Daniel, William J. Danley, Jeff Daub, Brian David, James Davis, Roy Dawes, James Day, Travis Deaton, Gus DeLaFuente, Dakota Derr, Eric Devine, Diamond Jack's Sportcards, Gilberto Diaz, John Diaz, David DiGrezio, Ken Dinerman (California Cruizers), Discount Dorothy, Richard Dolloff (Dolloff Coin Center), Greg Douglass, Jon Dresher, Bobby Drumm, Richard Duglin (Baseball Cards-n-More), Rob Dunkel, Robert Dunn Jr., Gerald Dupire, F.J. Durkin, Mike Durr, Bill Dyer, Alan John Dykshorn, Bill Eddy, Ron Edge, Ken Edick (Home Plate of Utah), Adrian Edler, Danny Eggleston, John Ehm, Michael L. Ellis, David Elstein, Kevin Erhart, Leigh Erickson, Dallas Erle, Dave Estes, Cameron Evans, Doak Ewing, Bryan Failing, John Fales, Richard Faletti, Juan Faunce, Don Ferguson, Chris Ferreira, Robert Ferrell, Chuck Ferrero, Angela Festa, David Festberg, The Fieldhouse, Anthony Fillizola, Financial Dynamics Corporation, Jay Finglass, Ross Fishman, Dan Foley, Fremont Fong, Perry Fong, Forever Young Sports Cards, Vern Forthun, Robert Fortney, Adam Foust, Ryan Fout, Clinton Fox, Linda Fox, Tommy Francavilla, Craig Frank, Walter Franklin, Frank's Comics, John Franzatti, Gary and Marilyn Frazier, Edward Freeland Sr., Matthew Fullerton, Bill Furman, Richard Galasso, Robert Gallagher, Stephen Gamblin, Glenn Garber, David Garzy, Bob Gavin, R. Genova, Willie George, Georgetown Card Exchange, Matt Gerig, Don Germaise, Tom Gerstmann, Larry Gevert, Randy Giefer, Mario Giordano, Mike Giovannoni, Herbert Gladhill, Bob Glassman, Patrick Gobble, Dick Goddard, Greg Goldstein (Dragon's Den), Jeff Goldstein, Ron Gomez, Jacob Goodman, Chris Goodrum, David Goss, Stephen J. Grauf, Bryan Greaves, Kenneth Greer Jr., Glen Gregson, Matt Griffin, Cameron Grimard, Bo Grimes, George Griswold, David Grogan, Bruce Gross, Mike Gunderson;

Michael Hagoe, LaRue Haigleratt, Hall's Nostalgia, Michael Hamel, Josh Hammer, Hershell Hanks, Joel Hansen, Gregg Hara, Zac Hargis, Mike Harper, Robert Harris, R. Winston Harris, Bryan and Renee Hart, Danny Hatchell, Pat Haven, Jacob Hawkins, Michael Head, Lucas Heck, Kevin Heimbigner, Jeremy W. Hekter, Joel Hellman, Rick Helmle, Chris Hendriksen, Gary Henry, Jim Hester, Scott Heuer, Kevin P. Hickey, Jonathan Hill, Ryan Hiney, Mary Hoagland, Robert Hodges, Ron Hodges, Ben Hodnett, Jason Hoffmann, C. Robert Hofheinz, Gary Holcomb, Peter Holzhauer, Stephen Honsinger, Daniel R. Horn II, Frank Horrath, Reed Houchens, Bill House, Scott Howell, Dennis Hughes, Greg Hunt, Thomas Hurley, Rob Huscher, James Hwang, Shawn Ilg, Tom Imboden, Vern Isenberg, Steve Isler, Zachary Jacobs, Dave Janelt, Paul Jastrzembski, Forrest Jay, Nathan Jeffries, Donn Jennings Cards, Adam

Jeske, JJ's Budget Baseball Cards, Chuck Johnson, June Johnson, Scott Johnson, Jason Johnston, Stewart W. Jones, W.L. Jordan, Dave Jurgensmeier, John Just;

Bruce Kalin, Drew Kalina, Doug Kane, Sam Kane, Max Kanter, Wayne Kardel, Bijan Karkouki, Jay Kasper, Frank Katen, Jerry I. Katz, Neil Katz, Bill Kaval, Gregory Keil, Karl Kelch, Nick Kerimi, Kevin's Kards, Tom Kladovasilakis, Jay Klippstein, Jeremy Knochel, Ernie Kohlstruk, Koinz and Kards (Tom Zmuda), Peter Kolch, Keith Komorny, Joshua Kouma, Ray Kramer, Stephen Krauss, Joe Krieger, Justin Krile, Neil Krohn, Greg Kroll, Jeff Kroll, Thomas Kunnecke, Danny Kyle, John Kyranos, Beau Lalonde, Howard Landrum, Adam Laneuster, Jason Langham, Jason Lassic, Allan Latawiec, Adalbert Lavature, Dan Lavin, William Lawrence, Tom Layberger, Tim Leatherwood, Brian Lee, Morley Leeking, Tommy Leffler, Mike Lehman, Tricia Leifhott, Cynthia Lemieux, William Lenhart, Irv Lerner, David Levy, Caleb and Ben Lewis, Frank Liao, Kevin Lichtsinn, Dan Lindamood, Wade Lindsey, Bernice Lines, Andrew Ling, Leon Lipkovich, Mel Litroff, Litteral's, David Lloyd, Louie Locke, David Logsdon, Mike London, Ralph Long, Damian Lopez, Paul Lopresti Jr., Brett Love, Allan Lowenberg, David Loy, LSG Promotions, Bob Luce, Alan Lynn, Dan Mabey, David Macaray, Jim Macie, Shane Maerdele, Magoo's Sports Cards, John Mainor, Patrick Manary, Paul Marchant, Randy Mardus, Mark Twain Card Shop, Steve Marlin, Angelo Martignetti, Ernest Martinez, Tom Mason, Tony Mastrianni, Bill Mastro, Eric Mathison, Harold Matlock, Paul Mazeika, Jack McAnlis, Pat McAulay (River City Trading Cards), Dr. William McAvoy, Dan McCrory, McDag Productions Inc., Michael McDonald (The Sports Page), Terry McFarland, Jim McGee, Branson H. McKay, Scott McKevitt, Tony McLaughlin, Bill McMahon, Mendal Mearkle, Ken Melanson, Jeff Melaragno, Stephanie Melton, William Mendel, Marc Mendoza, Eric Meredith, Beverly Merry, Denise Merry, Randy Messel, Jeff Messler, Blake Meyer (Lone Star Sportscards), John Meyer, Keith Meyer, Joe Michalowicz, Elie Michaud Jr., Barry Miller, Cary Miller, Dan Miller, David (Otis) Miller, George Miller, Wayne Miller, Mitchell's Baseball Cards, Perry Miyashita, Douglas Mo, Peter Molick, Greg Mollo, George Moore, Rick Moore, Bruce Morehouse, Robert Morelli, Roger Morey, Jason Morgan, Ben Morrison, Dale Moseley, Jordan Moskovitz, Jeremy L. Muncy, Richard A. Muncy, Sandra J. Muncy, Bill Munn, Brian Murphy, Mark Murphy, John Musacchio,

Jude Muses, Billy Myers, Michael Myers;

Andrew de Naray, Stephen Nardiello, National Sportscard Exchange, Edward Nazzaro (The Collector), Jeffrey Neumann, New England Card Promotions, William D. Newhand, New York Card Company, Royal Norman, Andrew Nunnally, Bud Obermeyer, Mark Obert, Bob O'Brien, Mike O'Brien, John O'Hara, Keith Olbermann, Michael Oldham, Ryan Ollila, Patrick O'Neill, Tim Oord, Donovan Orbon, John Osborne, Ron Oser, Ed Osheskie, Brian Oster, Shawn Otterson, Federico Palazuelos, L.G. Pangle II, Mervin Parker, John Pash, Clay Pasternack, Eric Pauly, John Pawleska, Gary Pecherkiewicz Jr., Michael Perrotta, Doug and Trevor Perry, Russ Perry, Brian Peterson, Jon Peterson, Tom Pfirrmann, Lam Pham, Roger Pierce, Daniel Piscopo, Brian Pittman, David Pollack, Seth Poppel, Chris Port, Don Prestia, Eric Porteous, Kathleen Porter, Steve Pozgay, Andrew Prescott, J.P. Pritchard, Rich Pugh, Chris Quigley, Justin Quintana, Marco Quintana, Michael I. Raff, Bob Ragonese, Brighton Rain, Carol Ramstedt, Richard H. Ranck, Octavio Ranzola, Rick Rapa and Barry Sanders (Atlanta Sports Cards), Joe Raque, Jamie Ratliff, R.W. Ray, Brian Reed, Phil Regli, Paul Reichl, Tom Reid, John Revell, Barry Rickert, Stephen J. Riggins, Dave Ring, Greg Ritzer, Louis Rivers, Jeremy Robbins, Chad Roberts, Nathan Roberts, Dee Robinson, Matt Robinson, Bill Rodman, Doug Rodman, Michael Roedema, Fred Romanski, Steven J. Rondorf, Michael H. Rosen, Jerry Rosensewaike, Adam Rothans, Alan Rubenstein, Joseph A. Rushlaw, George Rusnak, Rust Inc.;

Terry Sack, Paul Sadows, Joe Sak, Jennifer Salems, Andrew Sanchez, Jon Sands, Charles Santee Jr., Merrill Santy, Reggie Sapida, Larry Saucier, Eric Saulnier, Kevin Savage, Gary Sawatzki, Joe Schaub, Rudy Scheithauer, Vince Schielack, A.J. Schmidt, Scott Schoeneberger, Aron Schor, Jack Schultz, Bruce Schwartz, Brian Schweitzer, Charlie Seaver, Michael N. Seikel, John Selsam, Rob Serfass, Jeff Sharp, Mary A. Shea, Paul Sheehan, Richard Sheldon, Travis Sheldon, Michael Shepherd, Craig Sherman, Nicholas Shiftan, Marcia Shipwash, Bob Sipos, Eugene Siuda, Randy Small, Art Smith, Eric Smith, Ray Smith, Fred M. Snyder, David Solka, Harry Sommer, Jim Sorensen, Paul Sorensen, Darrel Spalding, C. Specht, Jim Spickelmire, Sports Unlimited Card Company, Milton Spurlock, Adam Squiller, R. Dauer Stackpole, Charles Stahr, Dewayne Stanford, Joe Staviscak, Bob Stern, Ben Stodghill, Kelly Stohr, Robert Stone, Robert J. Stone, Sam Stone, Tim

Strandberg (East Texas Sports Cards), Edward Strauss, Frankie Strigare, Richard Strobino, Eric Stubbs, Alan Sugahara, Scott Sullivan, Superior Sport Card, Jamie Sutherell, Gerry Swain, Richard Swales, Dusty Swenson, Roger Syferd, Josh Taft, David Talton, Maury Tasem, Ian Taylor, Norma Taylor, Lyle Telfer, Daniel Temmesfeld, Sam Tessier, John Thayer, Jason Thomas, Dave Thompson, Gerry Thompson, Jim D. Thompson, Carl Thrower, Al Tom, Patrick Tomberlin, Bud Tompkins (Minnesota Connection), Lenny Tonozzi, Gregory Torres, Doug Traverso, Harold Trieb, Dr. Ralph Triplette, Tom Tsaldaris, Eric Unplanb, G.M. Vernidis Jr., Larry Paul Vonckx, Brian Wagoner, Geoff Waidelich, G.E. Walker, Bob Wallace, Ed Wallar, Gary Walter, John and Lori Ward, Matt Ward, Michael Ward, Mary Wassil, Scott Weberpal, Jack Welch, Richard West, David Westman, Bill White, Dave White, John White, Dan Whitehouse, Liz Wiechern, Wild Pitch, Judd Wildman, Brandon W. Wilkins, John Willenborg, Ed Willett, Brandon Williams, Jeff Williams, Mark Willis, Brandon Willoughby, Michael Wilson, James Winner, Opry Winston, David Withers, Gary Wittman, John H. Wolf Jr., Jay Wolt (Cavalcade of Sports), John Wood, William Wood, Pete Wooten, Mike Worley, Jeff Wright, Frank Wunder, Steve Wymer, Lotay Yang, Yesterday's Heroes, Charles Yezak Jr., Joey Young, Wes Young, Robert Zanze, Mike Zinniel and Gary Zold.

Every year we make active solicitations for expert input. We are particularly appreciative of help (however extensive or cursory) provided for this volume. We receive many inquiries, comments and questions regarding material within this book. In fact, each and every one is read and digested. Time constraints, however, prevent us from personally replying. But keep sharing your knowledge. Your letters and input are part of the "big picture" of hobby information we can pass along to readers in our books and magazines. Even though we cannot respond to each letter, you are making significant contributions to the hobby through your interest and comments.

In the years since this guide debuted, *Beckett Publications* has grown beyond any rational expectation. A great many talented and hard working individuals have been instrumental in this growth and success. Our whole team is to be congratulated for what we together have accomplished. Our *Beckett Publications* team is led by Associate Publisher Claire Backus, Vice Presidents Joe Galindo and Fred Reed, and Director of Marketing Jeff Amano. They are

ably assisted by Fernando Albieri, Theresa Anderson, Gena Andrews, Jeff Anthony, Patricia Bales, Airey Baringer II (special thanks to Airey for his late-night typesetting excellence), Barbara Barry, Nancy Bassi, Therese Bellar, Louise Bird, Wendy Bird, Cathryn Black, Terry Bloom, Lisa Borden, Amy Brougher, Chris Calandro, Mary Campana, Renata Campos, Sammy Cantrell, Susan Catka, Deana Chapman, Theo Chen, Lynne Chinn, Catherine Colbert, Tommy Collins, Belinda Cross, Billy Culbert, Randy Cummings, Patrick Cunningham, Gail Docekal, Andrew Drago, Louise Ebaugh, Mila Egusquiza, Susan Elliott, Daniel Evans, Bruce Felps, Jorge Field, Sara Field, Jean Paul Figari, Jeany Finch, Robson Fonseca, Kim Ford, Eric Ford, Gayle Gasperin, Anita Gonzalez, Mary Gonzalez-Davis, Jeff Greer, Mary Gregory, Julie Grove, Marcio Guimaraes, Karen Hall, Carmen Hand, Lori Harmeyer, Beth Harwell, Jenny Harwell, Mark Harwell, Pepper Hastings, Joanna Hayden, Mike Hersh, Barbara Hinkle, Tracy Hinton, Dan Hitt, Charlie Hodges, Heather Holland, E.J. Hradek, Rex Hudson, Rhonda Hughes, Mary Huston, Don James, Marion Jarrell, Sara Jenks, Julia Jernigan, Wendy Jewell, Jay Johnson, Michael Johnson Jr., Matt Keifer, Fran Keng, Monte King, Debbie Kingsbury, Amy Kirk, Rudy Klancnik, Rich Klein, Frances Knight, Jane Layton, Scott Layton, Tom Liggitt, Lori Lindsey, Mark Manning, Louis Marroquin, Kaki Matheson, Teri McGahey, Kirk McKinney, Omar Mediano, Edras Mendez, Stephen Moore, Glen Morante, Elizabeth Morris, Daniel Moscoso, Daniel Moscoso Jr., Mike Moss, Randy Mosty, Allan Muir, Hugh Murphy, Wendy Neumann, Allen Neumann, LaQuita Norton, Robert Norton, Lisa O'Neill, Rich Olivieri, Abraham Pacheco, Guillermo Pacheco, Mike Payne, Suzee Payton, Ronda Pearson, Karen Penhollow, Julie Polomis, Reed Poole, Karen Quinn, Linda Rainwater, Roberto Ramirez, Nikki Renshaw, Patrick Richard, Jamile Romero, Grant Sandground, Gary Santaniello, Gabriel Santos, Maggie Seward, Carol Slawson, Steve Slawson, Dave Sliepka, Judi Smalling, Lisa Spaight, Mark Stokes, Cindy Struble, Peter Tepp, Jim Tereschuk, Christiann Thomas, Kimberly Thompson, Jana Threatt, Brett Tulloss, Valerie Voigt, Kim Whitesell, Mark Whitesell, Steve Wilson, Carol Ann Wurster, Robert Yearby. The whole *Beckett Publications* team has my thanks for jobs well done. Thank you, everyone.

I also thank my family, especially my wife, Patti, and daughters, Christina, Rebecca, and Melissa, for putting up with me again.

The Sport Americana Baseball Card Price Guide
Table Of Contents

Preface

Isn't it great? Every year this book gets bigger and bigger with all the new sets coming out. But even more exciting is that every year there are more collectors, more shows, more stores, and more interest in the cards we love so much. This edition has been enhanced and expanded from the previous edition. The cards you collect — who they are, what they look like, where they are from, and (most important to many of you) what their current values are — are enumerated within. Many of the features contained in the other Beckett Price Guides have been incorporated into this volume since condition grading, nomenclature, and many other aspects of collecting are common to the card hobby in general. We hope you find the book both interesting and useful in your collecting pursuits.

The Beckett Guide has been successful where other attempts have failed because it is complete, current, and valid. This Price Guide contains not just one, but three prices by condition for all the baseball cards listed. These account for almost all the baseball cards in existence. The prices were added to the card lists just prior to printing and reflect not the author's opinions or desires but the going retail prices for each card, based on the marketplace (sports memorabilia conventions and shows, sports card shops, hobby papers, current mail order catalogs, local club meetings, auction results, and other firsthand reportings of actually realized prices).

What is the **best** price guide available (on the market) today? Of course card sellers will prefer the price guide with the highest prices as the best — while card buyers will naturally prefer the one with the lowest prices. Accuracy, however, is the true test. The price guide is used by more collectors and dealers than all the others combined. Look for the Beckett name. I won't put my name on anything I won't stake my reputation on. Not the lowest and not the highest — but the most accurate, with integrity.

To facilitate your use of this book, read the complete introductory section in the pages following before going to the pricing pages. Every collectible field has its own terminology; we've tried to capture most of these terms and definitions in our glossary. Please read carefully the section on grading and the condition of your cards, as you will not be able to determine which price column is appropriate for a given card without first knowing its condition.

Welcome to the world of baseball cards.

Sincerely, Dr. James Beckett

Introduction

Welcome to the exciting world of baseball card collecting, America's fastest-growing avocation. You have made a good choice in buying this book, since it will open up to you the entire panorama of this field in the simplest, most concise way.

It is estimated that a third of a million different baseball cards have been issued during the past century. And the number of total cards put out by all manufacturers last year has been estimated at several billion, with an initial retail value of more than $500 million. Sales of older cards by dealers may account for a like amount. With all that cardboard available in the marketplace, it should be no surprise that several million sports fans like you collect baseball cards today, and that number is growing by hundreds of thousands each year.

The growth of *Beckett Baseball Card Monthly* is another indication of this rising crescendo of popularity for baseball cards. Founded in 1984 by Dr. James Beckett, the author of this Price Guide, *Beckett Baseball Card Monthly* has grown to the pinnacle of the baseball card hobby with more than a million readers anxiously awaiting each enjoyable issue.

So collecting baseball cards — while still pursued as a hobby with youthful exuberance by kids in the neighborhood — has also taken on the trappings of an industry, with thousands of full- and part-time card dealers, as well as vendors of supplies, clubs and conventions. In fact, each year since 1980 thousands of hobbyists have assembled for a National Sports Collectors Convention, at which hundreds of dealers have displayed their wares, seminars have been conducted, autographs penned by sports notables, and millions of cards changed hands. These colossal affairs have been staged in Los Angeles, Detroit, St. Louis, Chicago, New York, Anaheim, Arlington (TX), San Francisco, Atlantic City, Chicago, Arlington (TX), Anaheim, and this year in Atlanta. So baseball card collecting really is national in scope!

This increasing interest has been reflected in card values. As more collectors compete for available supplies, card prices (especially for premium-grade cards) rise. A national publication indicated a "very strong advance" in baseball card prices during the past decade, and a quick perusal of prices in this book compared to the figures in earlier editions of this Price Guide will quickly confirm this. Which brings us back around again to the book you have in your hands. It is the best annual guide available to this exciting world of baseball cards. Read it and use it. May your enjoyment and your card collection increase in the coming months and years.

WANTED

Advanced collector seeking singles, lots, accumulations and sets of pre-1948 baseball cards. Of special interest are "E" Cards (Early Gum and Candy), "T" Cards (20th Century Tobacco), "N" Cards (19th Century Tobacco), 1930's Gum Cards, with an extra emphasis on Pacific Coast League items (Zeenuts, Obaks,etc.).

Unlike some dealers who accept only Mint or Excellent cards, I will consider all recognizable grades (Poor-Mint). While I cannot promise "The Absolute Gem Mint Untouchable Top Offer Guaranteed" I will submit a competitive and fair offer on any collection; as I have since 1972. Please feel free to write or call advising me of your holdings.

Thanks.

Mark Macrae
Box 2111
Castro Valley, CA 94546
510-538-6245
Fax: 510-538-4645

Send $1 (check or stamps) for my latest "Old Card" listing.

How to Collect

Each collection is personal and reflects the individuality of its owner. There are no set rules on how to collect cards. Since card collecting is a hobby or leisure pastime, what you collect, how much you collect, and how much time and money you spend collecting are entirely up to you. The funds you have available for collecting and your own personal taste should determine how you collect. Information and ideas presented here are intended to help you get the most enjoyment from this hobby.

It is impossible to collect every card ever produced. Therefore, beginners as well as intermediate and advanced collectors usually specialize in some way. One of the reasons this hobby is popular is that individual collectors can define and tailor their collecting methods to match their own tastes. To give you some ideas of the various approaches to collecting, we will list some of the more popular areas of specialization.

Many collectors select complete sets from particular years. For example, they may concentrate on assembling complete sets from all the years since their birth or since they became avid sports fans. They may try to collect a card for every player during that specified period of time. Many others wish to acquire only certain players. Usually such players are the superstars of the sport, but occasionally collectors will specialize in all the cards of players who attended a particular college or came from a certain town. Some collectors are only interested in the first cards or Rookie Cards of certain players. A handy guide for collectors interested in pursuing the hobby this way is the *Sport Americana Alphabetical Checklist No. 5.*

Another fun way to collect cards is by team. Most fans have a favorite team, and it is natural for that loyalty to be translated into a desire for cards of the players on that favorite team. For most of the recent years, team sets (all the cards from a given team for that year) are readily available at a reasonable price. The *Sport Americana Team Baseball Card Checklist* will open up this field to the collector.

Obtaining Cards

Several avenues are open to card collectors. Cards can be purchased in the traditional way at the local candy, grocery, or drug stores, with the bubble gum or other products included. For many years it has been possible to purchase complete sets of baseball cards through mail order advertisers found in traditional sports media publications, such as *The Sporting News, Baseball Digest, Street & Smith* yearbooks, and others. These sets are also advertised in the card collecting periodicals. Many collectors will begin by subscribing to at least one of the hobby periodicals, all with good up-to-date information. In fact, subscription offers can be found in the advertising section of this book. In addition, a great variety of cards (typically from all eras and all sports) can be obtained at the growing number of hobby retail stores dedicated to sports cards and memorabilia around the country.

Most serious card collectors obtain old (and new) cards from one or more of several main sources: (1) trading or buying from other collectors or dealers; (2) responding to sale or auction ads in the hobby publications; (3) buying at a local hobby store; and/or (4) attending sports collectibles shows or conventions.

We advise that you try all four methods since each has its own distinct advantages: (1) trading is a great way to make new friends; (2) hobby periodicals help you keep up with what's going on in the hobby (including when and where the conventions are happening); (3) stores provide the opportunity for considering (any day of the week) a great diversity of material in a relaxed sports-oriented atmosphere that most fans love; and (4) shows provide enjoyment and the opportunity to view millions of collectibles under one roof, in addition to meeting some of the hundreds or even thousands of other collectors with similar interests who also attend the shows.

Preserving Your Cards

Cards are fragile. They must be handled properly in order to retain their value. Careless handling can easily result in creased or bent cards. It is, however, not recommended that tweezers or tongs be used to pick up your cards since such utensils might mar or indent card surfaces and thus reduce those cards' conditions and values. In general, your cards should be handled directly as little as possible. This is sometimes easier to say than to do. Although there are still many who use custom boxes, storage trays, or even shoe boxes, plastic sheets are the preferred method of storing cards. A collection stored in plastic pages in a three-ring album allows you to view your collection at any time without the need to touch the card itself. Cards can also be kept in single holders (of various types and thickness) designed for the enjoyment of each card individually. For a large collection, some collectors may use a combination of the above methods.

When purchasing plastic sheets for your cards, be sure that you find the pocket size that fits the cards snugly. Don't put your 1951 Bowmans in a sheet designed to fit 1981 Topps. Most hobby and collectibles shops and virtually all collectors' conventions will have these plastic pages available in quantity for the various sizes offered or you can purchase them directly from the advertisers in this book. Also remember that pocket size isn't the only factor to consider when looking for plastic sheets. Some collectors concerned with long-term storage of their cards in plastic sheets are cautious to avoid sheets containing PVC and request non-PVC sheets from their dealer.

Damp, sunny and/or hot conditions — no, this is not a weather forecast — are three elements to avoid in extremes if you are interested in preserving your collection. Too much (or too little) humidity can cause gradual deterioration of a card. Direct, bright sun (or fluorescent light) over time will bleach out the color of a card. Extreme heat accelerates the decomposition of the card. On the other hand, many cards have lasted more than 50 years without much scientific intervention. So be cautious, even if the above factors typically present a problem only when present in the extreme. It never hurts to be prudent.

Collecting vs. Investing

Collecting individual players and collecting complete sets are both popular vehicles for investment and speculation. Most investors and speculators stock up on complete sets or on quantities of players they think have good investment potential. There is obviously no guarantee in this book, or anywhere else for that matter, that cards will outperform the stock market or other investment alternatives in the future. After all, baseball cards do not pay quarterly dividends and cards cannot be sold at their "current values" as easily as stocks or bonds. Nevertheless, investors have noticed a favorable long-term trend in the past performance of baseball and other sports collectibles, and certain cards and sets have outperformed just about any other investment in some years. Many hobbyists maintain that the best investment is and always will be the building of a collection, which traditionally has held up better than outright speculation.

Some of the obvious questions are: Which cards? When to buy? When to sell? The best investment you can make is in your own education. The more you know about your collection and the hobby, the more informed the decisions you will be able to make. We're not selling investment tips. We're selling information about the current value of baseball cards. It's up to you to use that information to your best advantage.

Nomenclature

Each hobby has its own language to describe its area of interest. The nomenclature traditionally used for trading cards is derived from the *American Card Catalog*, published in 1960 by Nostalgia Press. That catalog, written by Jefferson Burdick (who is called the "Father of Card Collecting" for his pioneering work), uses letter and number designations for each separate set of cards.

The letter used in the ACC designation refers to the generic type of card. While both sport and non-sport issues are classified in the ACC, we shall confine ourselves to the sport issues. The following list defines the letters and their meanings as used by the *American Card Catalog*.

(none) or N - 19th Century U.S. Tobacco
B - Blankets
D - Bakery Inserts Including Bread
E - Early Candy and Gum
F - Food Inserts
H - Advertising
M - Periodicals
PC - Postcards
R - Candy and Gum Cards 1930 to Present
T - 20th Century U.S. Tobacco
UO - Gas and Oil Inserts
V - Canadian Candy
W - Exhibits, Strip Cards, Team Issues

Following the letter prefix and an optional hyphen are one-, two-, or three-digit numbers, 1-999. These typically represent the company or entity issuing the cards. In several cases, the ACC number is extended by an additional hyphen and another one- or two-digit numerical suffix. For example, the 1957 Topps regular series baseball card issue carries an ACC designation of R414-11. The "R" indicates a Candy or Gum card produced since 1930. The "414" is the ACC designation for Topps Chewing Gum baseball card issues, and the "11" is the ACC designation for the 1957 regular issue (Topps' eleventh baseball set).

Like other traditional methods of identification, this system provides order to the process of cataloging cards; however, most serious collectors learn the ACC designation of the popular sets by repetition and familiarity, rather than by attempting to "figure out" what they might or should be.

From 1948 forward, collectors and dealers commonly refer to all sets by their year, maker, type of issue, and any other distinguishing characteristic. For example, such a characteristic could be an unusual issue or one of several regular issues put out by a specific maker in a single year. Regional issues are usually referred to by year, maker, and sometimes by title or theme of the set.

Glossary/Legend

Our glossary defines terms frequently used in the card collecting hobby. Many of these terms are also common to other types of sports memorabilia collecting. Some terms may have several meanings depending on use.

AAS - Action All Stars, a postcard-size set issued by Donruss during the mid-1980s.

ACC - Acronym for American Card Catalog.

ALP - Alphabetical checklist.

ANN - Announcer.

AS - All-Star card. A card portraying an All-Star Player of the previous year that says "All-Star" on its face.

ATG - All-Time Great card.

ATL - All-Time Leaders card.

AU - With autograph.

BC - Bonus Card (Used by Donruss for their team MVP bonus sets from 1988 through 1991).

BL - Blue letters.

BLANKET - A felt square (normally 5 to 6 inches) portraying a baseball player.

BOX - Card issued on a box or a card depicting a Boxer.

BRICK - A group of 50 or more cards having common characteristics that is intended to be bought, sold or traded as a unit.

CABINETS - Popular and highly valuable photographs on thick card stock produced in the 19th and early 20th century.

CHECKLIST - A list of the cards contained in a particular set. The list is always in numerical order if the cards are numbered. Some unnumbered sets are artificially numbered in alphabetical order, by team and alphabetically within the team, or by uniform number for convenience.

CL - Checklist card. A card that lists in order the cards and players in the set or series. Older checklist cards in Mint condition that have not been marked are very desirable and command premiums.

CO - Abbreviation for Coach.

COIN - A small disc of metal or plastic portraying a player in its center.

COLLECTOR - A person who engages in the hobby of collecting cards primarily for his own enjoyment, with any profit motive being secondary.

Brian Morris

102 Watchung Ave.
Montclair, NJ 07042
201-746-9697

Always buying and selling any and all issues
listed in this book in top conditions prior to 1976.
I specialize in unopened material, scarce, rare and
unusual sets and single cards, as well as Topps,
Bowmans, Play Balls, Goudeys and Tobacco Cards.
Whether you are buying or selling, do it with confidence,
with one of the hobby's leading dealers.

COLLECTOR ISSUE - A set produced for the sake of the card itself with no product or service sponsor. It derives its name from the fact that most of these sets are produced for sale directly to the hobby market.

COM - Card issued by the Post Cereal Company through their mail-in offer.

COMBINATION CARD - A single card depicting two or more players (but not a team card).

COMM - Commissioner.

COMMON CARD - The typical card of any set; it has no premium value accruing from subject matter, numerical scarcity, popular demand, or anomaly.

CONVENTION - A large weekend gathering of dealers and collectors at a single location for the purpose of buying, selling, and sometimes trading sports memorabilia items. Conventions are open to the public and sometimes feature autograph guests, door prizes, contests, seminars, etc. They are frequently referred to simply as "shows."

CONVENTION ISSUE - A set produced in conjunction with a sports collectibles convention to commemorate or promote the show.

COR - Corrected card.

COUPON - See Tab.

CREASE - A wrinkle on the card, usually caused by bending the card. Creases are a common (and serious) defect resulting from careless handling.

CY - Cy Young Award.

DC - Draft Choice.

DEALER - A person who engages in buying, selling, and trading sports collectibles or supplies. A dealer may also be a collector, but as a dealer, his main goal is to earn a profit.

DIE-CUT - A card with part of its stock partially cut, allowing one or more parts to be folded or removed. After removal or appropriate folding, the remaining part of the card can frequently be made to stand up.

DISC - A circular-shaped card.

DISPLAY CARD - A sheet, usually containing three to nine cards, that is printed and used by the manufacturer to advertise and/or display the packages containing his products and cards. The backs of display cards are blank or contain advertisements.

DK - Diamond King (artwork produced by Perez-Steele for Donruss).

DP - Double Print (a card that was printed in double the quantity compared to the other cards in the same series).

DT - Dream Team (produced by Score in 1990, 1991 and 1992).

EP - Elite Performer (1991 Fleer Ultra).

ERA - Earned Run Average.

ERR - Error card. A card with erroneous information, spelling, or depiction on either side of the card. Most errors are not corrected by the producing card company.

EXHIBIT - The generic name given to thick-stock, postcard-size cards with single color obverse pictures. The name is derived from the Exhibit Supply Co. of Chicago, the principal manufacturer of this type of card. These are also known as Arcade cards since they were found in many arcades.

FDP - First Draft Pick.

FOIL - Foil embossed stamp on card.

FRAN - The Franchise card (1991 Score).

FS - Father/son card.

FULL SHEET - A complete sheet of cards that has not been cut up into individual cards by the manufacturer. Also called an uncut sheet.

GL - Green letters.

HIGH NUMBER - The cards in the last series of numbers in a year in which such higher-numbered cards were printed or distributed in significantly lesser amounts than the lower-numbered cards. The high-number designation refers to a scarcity of the high-numbered cards. Not all years have high numbers in terms of this definition.

HL - Highlight card.

HOF - Hall of Fame, or a card that portrays a Hall of Famer (HOFer).

HOR - Horizontal pose on card as opposed to the standard vertical orientation found on most cards.

IA - In Action card.

IF - Infielder.

INSERT - A card of a different type or any other sports collectible (typically a poster or sticker) contained and sold in the same package along with a card or cards of a major set. An insert card is either unnumbered or not numbered in the same sequence as the major set. Sometimes the inserts are randomly distributed and are not found in every pack.

ISSUE - Synonymous with set, but usually used in conjunction with a manufacturer, e.g., a Topps issue.

K - Strikeout.

KM - K-Man (1991 Score).

KP - Kid Picture (a subset issued in the Topps Baseball sets of 1972 and 1973).

LAYERING - The separation or peeling of one or more layers of the card stock, usually at the corner of the card.

LEGITIMATE ISSUE - A set produced to promote or boost sales of a product or service,

e.g., bubble gum, cereal, cigarettes, etc. Most collector issues are not legitimate issues in this sense.

LHP - Lefthanded pitcher.

LID - A circular-shaped card (possibly with tab) that forms the top of the container for the product being promoted.

LL - League leaders card or large letters on card.

MAJOR SET - A set produced by a national manufacturer of cards containing a large number of cards. Usually 100 or more different cards comprise a major set.

MB - Master Blaster (1991 Score).

MEM - Memorial card. For example, the 1990 Donruss and Topps Bart Giamatti cards.

MG - Manager.

MINI - A small card; for example, a 1975 Topps card of identical design but smaller dimensions than the regular Topps issue of 1975.

ML - Major League.

MVP - Most Valuable Player.

NAU - No autograph on card.

NH - No-Hitter card.

NNOF - No Name on Front (1949 Bowman).

NOF - Name on Front (1949 Bowman).

NON-SPORT CARD - A card from a set whose major theme is a subject other than a sports subject. A card of a sports figure or event that is part of a non-sport set is still a non-sport card; e.g., while the "Look 'N' See" non-sport card set contains a card of Babe Ruth, a sports figure, that card is a non-sport card.

NOTCHING - The grooving of the card, usually caused by fingernails, rubber bands, or bumping card edges against other objects.

OBVERSE - The front, face, or pictured side of the card.

OF - Outfield or Outfielder.

OLY - Olympics (see the 1985 Topps and 1988 Topps Traded sets; the members of the U.S. Olympic Baseball teams were featured subsets in both of these sets).

ORG - Organist.

P - Pitcher or Pitching pose.

P1 - First Printing.

P2 - Second Printing.

P3 - Third Printing.

PANEL - An extended card that is composed of two or more individual cards. Often the panel forms the back part of the container for the product being promoted, e.g., a Hostess panel, a Bazooka panel, an Esskay Meat panel.

PCL - Pacific Coast League.

PLASTIC SHEET - A clear, plastic page that is punched for insertion into a binder (with standard three-ring spacing) containing pockets

for displaying cards. Many different styles of sheets exist with pockets of varying sizes to hold the many differing card formats. Also called a display sheet or storage sheet.

PREMIUM - A card, sometimes on photographic stock, that is purchased or obtained in conjunction with, or redemption for, another card or product. The premium is not packaged in the same unit as the primary item.

PUZZLE CARD - A card whose back contains a part of a picture which, when joined correctly with other puzzle cards, forms the completed picture.

PUZZLE PIECE - A die-cut piece designed to interlock with similar pieces.

PVC - Polyvinyl Chloride, a substance used to make many of the popular card display protective sheets. Non-PVC sheets are considered preferable for long-term storage of cards.

RARE - A card or series of cards of very limited availability. Unfortunately, "rare" is a subjective term frequently used indiscriminately to hype value. "Rare" cards are harder to obtain than "scarce" cards.

RB - Record Breaker card.

REGIONAL - A card or set of cards issued and distributed only in a limited geographical area of the country.

REVERSE - The back or narrative side of the card.

RHP - Righthanded pitcher.

RIF - Rifleman (1991 Score).

ROY - Rookie of the Year.

RP - Relief pitcher.

RR - Rated Rookies (a subset featured in Donruss sets).

SA - Super Action card.

SASE - Self-Addressed, Stamped Envelope.

SB - Stolen Bases.

SCARCE - A card or series of cards of limited availability. This subjective term is sometimes used indiscriminately to hype value. "Scarce" cards are not as difficult to obtain as "rare" cards.

SCR - Script name on back (1949 Bowman).

SEMI-HIGH - A card from the next to last series of a sequentially issued set. It has more value than an average card and generally less value than a high number. A card is not called a semi-high unless the next to last series in which it exists has an additional premium attached to it.

SERIES - The entire set of cards issued by a particular producer in a particular year, e.g., the 1971 Topps series. Also, within a particular set, series can refer to a group of (consecutively numbered) cards printed at the same time, e.g.,

If you're vacationing in New York or if you're just escaping the city, then **THE DRAGON'S DEN** is the place to visit. Located in the heart of Westchester's finest shopping area, **THE DRAGON'S DEN** is only thirty minutes from midtown Manhattan and easily accessible to all major New York roadways. Check out our enormous inventory of collectibles, including:

- **Baseball, football, basketball & hockey stars, sets & unopened material from 1909 to present**
- **Plastic sheets, binders, lucites, cases & boxes**
- **Over 1,000,000 back issue Marvel, D.C. & alternate comics**
- **All New comic releases**
- **Comic bags, boxes and mylars**
- **Fantasy role playing games and figures**

Along with our impressive inventory, we have a veteran staff that will be happy to assist you in your selection. We accept all major credit cards and we're even open every day. What more could you ask for? Convenient parking? We have that too!

NOW 2 GREAT LOCATIONS!

THE
DRAGON'S
DEN

2614 CENTRAL PK. AVE.
YONKERS, NY 10710
(914) 793-4630

43 GREENWICH AVE.
GREENWICH, CT 06830
(203) 622-1171

the first series of the 1957 Topps issue (#1-#88).

SET - One each of the entire run of cards of the same type produced by a particular manufacturer during a single year. In other words, if you have a complete set of 1976 Topps then you have every card from #1 up to and including #660, i.e., all of the different cards that were produced.

SKIP-NUMBERED - A set that has many unissued card numbers between the lowest number in the set and the highest number in the set, e.g., the 1948 Leaf baseball set contains 98 cards skip-numbered from #1 to #168. A major set in which a few numbers were not printed is not considered to be skip-numbered.

SLUG - Silver Slugger card (1991 Bowman).

SP - Single or Short Print (a card which was printed in lesser quantity compared to the other cards in the same series; see also DP and TP).

SPECIAL CARD - A card that portrays something other than a single player or team, for example, a card that portrays the previous year's statistical leaders or the results from the previous year's World Series.

SS - Shortstop.

STAMP - Adhesive-backed papers depicting a player. The stamp may be individual or in a sheet of many stamps. Moisture must be applied to the adhesive in order for the stamp to be attached to another surface.

STAR CARD - A card that portrays a player of some repute, usually determined by his ability; however, sometimes referring to sheer popularity.

STICKER - A card with a removable layer that can be affixed to (stuck onto) another surface.

STOCK - The cardboard or paper on which the card is printed.

STRIP CARDS - A sheet or strip of cards, particularly popular in the 1920s and 1930s, with the individual cards usually separated by broken or dotted lines.

SUPERSTAR CARD - A card that portrays a superstar, e.g., a Hall of Famer or player with strong Hall of Fame potential.

SV - Super Veteran (see 1982 Topps).

TAB - A card portion set off from the rest of the card, usually with perforations, that may be removed without damaging the central character or event depicted by the card.

TBC - Turn Back the Clock cards.

TC - Team Checklist card.

TEAM CARD - A card that depicts an entire team.

TEST SET - A set, usually containing a small number of cards, issued by a national card producer and distributed in a limited section or sections of the country. Presumably, the purpose of a test set is to test market appeal for a particular type of card.

TL - Team Leader card.

TP - Triple Print (a card that was printed in triple the quantity compared to the other cards in the same series).

TRIMMED - A card cut down from its original size. Trimmed cards are undesirable to most collectors.

UER - Uncorrected Error.

UMP - Umpire.

USA - Team USA cards (see the 1991 Topps Traded set).

VAR - Variation card. One of two or more cards from the same series with the same number (or player with identical pose if the series is unnumbered) differing from one another by some aspect, the different feature stemming from the printing or stock of the card. This can be caused when the manufacturer of the cards notices an error in one or more of the cards, makes the changes, and then resumes the print run. In this case there will be two versions or variations of the same card. Sometimes one of the variations is relatively scarce.

VERT - Vertical pose on card.

WAS - Washington National League (1974 Topps).

WS - World Series card.

YL - Yellow Letters (1958 Topps).

YT - Yellow Team (1958 Topps).

Business of Baseball Card Collecting

Determining Value

Why are some cards more valuable than others? Obviously, the economic laws of supply and demand are applicable to card collecting just as they are to any other field where a commodity is bought, sold or traded in a free, unregulated market.

Supply (the number of cards available on the market) is less than the total number of cards originally produced since attrition diminishes that original quantity. Each year a percentage of cards is typically thrown away, destroyed or otherwise lost to collectors. This percentage is much smaller today than it was in the past because more and more people have become increasingly aware of the value of their cards.

For those who collect only Mint condition cards, the supply of older cards can be quite small indeed. Until recently, collectors were not so conscious of the need to preserve the condition of their cards. For this reason, it is difficult to know exactly how many 1953 Topps are currently available, Mint or otherwise. It is generally accepted that there are fewer 1953 Topps available than 1963, 1973 or 1983 Topps cards. If demand were equal for each of these sets, the law of supply and demand would increase the price for the least available sets. Demand, however, is never equal for all sets, so price correlations can be complicated.

The demand for a card is influenced by many factors. These include: (1) the age of the card; (2) the number of cards printed; (3) the player(s) portrayed on the card; (4) the attractiveness and popularity of the set; and perhaps most important, (5) the physical condition of the card.

In general, (1) the older the card, (2) the fewer the number of the cards printed, (3) the more famous the player, (4) the more attractive and popular the set, or (5) the better the condition of the card, the higher the value of the card will be. There are exceptions to all but one of these factors: the condition of the card. Given two cards similar in all respects except condition, the one in the best condition will **always** be valued higher.

While there are certain guidelines that help to establish the value of a card, the exceptions and peculiarities make any simple, direct mathematical formula to determine card values impossible.

Regional Variation

Two types of price variations exist among the sections of the country where a card is bought or sold. The first is the general price variation on all cards bought and sold in one geographical area as compared to another. Card prices are slightly higher on the East and West coasts, and slightly lower in the middle of the country. Although prices may vary from the East to the West, or from the Southwest to the Midwest, the prices listed in this guide are nonetheless presented as a consensus of all sections of this large and diverse country.

Still, prices for a particular player's cards may well be higher in his home team's area than in other regions. This exhibits the second type of regional price variation in which local players are favored over those from distant areas. For example, an Al Kaline card would be valued higher in Detroit than in Cincinnati because Kaline played in Detroit; therefore, the demand there for Al Kaline cards is higher than it is in Cincinnati. On the other hand, a Johnny Bench card would be priced higher in Cincinnati, where he played, than in Detroit for similar reasons. Frequently, even common player cards command such a premium from hometown collectors.

Set Prices

A somewhat paradoxical situation exists in the price of a complete set versus the combined cost of the individual cards in the set. In nearly every case, the sum of the prices for the individual cards is higher than the cost for the complete set. This is especially prevalent in the cards of the past few years. The reasons for this apparent anomaly stem from the habits of collectors and from the carrying costs to dealers. Today, each card in a set is normally produced in the same quantity as all others in its set.

However, many collectors pick up only stars, superstars and particular teams. As a result, the dealer is left with a shortage of certain player cards and an abundance of others. He therefore incurs an expense in simply "carrying" these less desirable cards in stock. On the other hand, if he sells a complete set, he gets rid of large numbers of cards at one time. For this reason, he generally is willing to receive less money for a complete set. By doing this, he recovers all of his costs and also makes a profit.

The disparity between the price of the complete set and that for the sum of the individual cards also has been influenced by the fact that the major manufacturers now are pre-collating card sets. Since "pulling" individual cards from

EARLY BASEBALL MEMORABILIA WANTED

- Quality 19th century photographic material, especially CDV's, tintypes and cabinets.
- All early display and advertising pieces, scorecards, programs and autographs.
- All 19th century Tobacco cards, especially Allen & Ginter, Old Judge, Gypsy Queen, Kalamazoo Bats, Goodwin Champion & Duke.
- All 20th century Tobacco cards, especially T-202, T-205, & T-206.
- All quality Candy and Gum cards, especially E90-1, Cracker Jack, Goudey, Diamond Star & Playball.

- All cards of Hall of Famers, especially Ruth, Gehrig, Cobb, DiMaggio, Mantle & Wagner.
- We will also sell your collection for you on a consignment basis. Call or write for details.
- All transactions handled confidentially and professionally. We have over nine years full-time hobby experience.

BARRY SLOATE
231 Clinton St.
Brooklyn, NY 11201
(718) 855-7513

Krause Publications
CUSTOMER SERVICE AWARD

HIGHEST PRICES PAID
FOR BASEBALL, FOOTBALL & BASKETBALL CARDS AND MEMORABILIA

I LET MY MONEY DO THE TALKING.

SEND LIST OR CALL

BRIAN WANG
28 YACHT CLUB COVE
STATEN ISLAND, N.Y. 10308
(718) 356-4502 evenings
(718) 948-2223 days

the sets of all the manufacturers involves a specific type of labor (and cost), the singles or star card market is not affected significantly by pre-collation.

Set prices also do not include rare card varieties, unless specifically stated. Of course, the prices for sets do include one example of each type for the given set, but this is the least expensive variety.

Scarce Series

Scarce series occur because cards issued before 1974 were made available to the public each year in several series of finite numbers of cards, rather than all cards of the set being available for purchase at one time. At some point during the year, usually toward the end of the baseball season, interest in current year baseball cards waned. Consequently, the manufacturers produced smaller numbers of these later series of cards.

Nearly all nationwide issues from post-World War II manufacturers (1948 to 1973) exhibit these series variations. In the past, Topps, for example, may have issued series consisting of many different numbers of cards, including 55, 66, 80, 88 and others. Recently Topps has settled on what is now their standard sheet size of 132 cards, six of which comprise its 792-card set.

While the number of cards within a given series is usually the same as the number of cards on one printed sheet, this is not always the case. For example, Bowman used 36 cards on its standard printed sheets, but in 1948 substituted 12 cards during later print runs of that year's baseball cards. Twelve of the cards from the initial sheet of 36 cards were removed and replaced by 12 different cards giving, in effect, a first series of 36 cards and a second series of 12 new cards. This replacement produced a scarcity of 24 cards — the 12 cards removed from the original sheet and the 12 new cards added to the sheet. A full sheet of 1948 Bowman cards (second printing) shows that card numbers 37 through 48 have replaced 12 of the cards on the first printing sheet.

The Topps Company also has created scarcities and/or excesses of certain cards in many of their sets. Topps, however, has most frequently gone the other direction by double printing some of the cards. Double printing causes an abundance of cards of the players who are on the same sheet more than one time. During the years from 1978 to 1981, Topps double printed 66 cards out of their large 726-card set. The Topps practice of double printing cards in earlier years is the most logical explanation for the known scarcities of particular cards in some of these Topps sets.

From 1988 through 1990, Donruss short printed or double printed certain cards in its major sets. Ostensibly this was because of its addition of bonus team MVP cards in its regular-issue wax packs.

We are always looking for information or photographs of printing sheets of cards for research. Each year we try to update the hobby's knowledge of distribution anomalies. Please let us know at the address in this book if you have first-hand knowledge that would be helpful in this pursuit.

SPORTSCARDS

Always Buying

Highest Percent of Catalogue Paid

Specialists in Pre-1976 Topps and
Bowman Baseball Sets, Stars,
Commons and Starter Sets
in All Grades

**WANT
LISTS
FILLED**

707 Sportscards
P.O. Box 707
Plumsteadville, PA 18949
Phone (215) 249-0976
Karry & Levi Bleam

Office Address For
Federal Express and UPS
707 Sportscards
875 N. Easton Rd. Suite 11
Doylestown, PA 18901
M-F 9-5 (215) 230-9080
OR
Phone (215) 249-0976

24 HOUR FAX
(215) 230-9082

**BUY
SELL
TRADE**

See Our Weekly Advertisements in the
SPORTS COLLECTORS DIGEST
Financing and Lay-Away Available

We Carry A Full Line of
Allstate Display Cases

Phone, Write or Fax for Complete Price List

MASTER CARD	VISA
DISCOVER	AMERICAN EXPRESS

Grading Your Cards

Each hobby has its own grading terminology — stamps, coins, comic books, beer cans, etc. Collectors of sports cards are no exception. The one invariable criterion for determining the value of a card is its condition: the better the condition of the card, the more valuable it is. However, condition grading is very subjective. Individual card dealers and collectors differ in the strictness of their grading, but the stated condition of a card should be determined without regard to whether it is being bought or sold.

The physical defects which lower the condition of a card are usually quite apparent, but each individual places his own estimation (negative value in this case) on these defects. We present the condition guide for use in determining values listed in this Price Guide in the hopes that excess subjectivity can be minimized.

The defects listed in the condition guide below are those either placed in the card at the time of printing — uneven borders, focus — or those defects that can occur to a card under normal handling — corner sharpness, gloss, edge wear, light creases — and finally, environmental conditions — browning. Other defects to cards are caused by human carelessness and in all cases should be noted separately and in addition to the condition grade. Among the more common alterations are heavy creases, tape, tape stains, rubber band marks, water damage, severe warping, smoke damage, trimming, paste, tears, writing, pin or tack holes, any back damage, and missing parts (tabs, tops, coupons, backgrounds).

Centering

It is important to define in words and pictures what is meant by certain frequently used hobby terms relating to grading cards. The adjacent pictures portray various stages of centering. Centering can range from well-centered to slightly off-center to off-center to badly off-center to miscut.

Slightly Off-Center (60/40): A slightly off-center card is one which upon close inspection is found to have one border bigger than the opposite border. This degree once was only offensive to purists, but now some hobbyists try to avoid cards that are anything other than perfectly centered.

Off-Center (70/30): An off-center card has one border which is noticeably more than twice as wide as the opposite border.

Badly Off-Center (80/20 or worse): A badly off-center card has virtually no border on one side of the card.

Miscut: A miscut card actually shows part of the adjacent card in its larger border and consequently a corresponding amount of its card is cut off.

Corner Wear

Degrees of corner wear generate several common terms useful to accurate grading. The wear on card corners can be expressed as fuzzy corners, corner wear or slightly rounded corners, rounded corners, badly rounded corners.

Fuzzy Corners: Fuzzy corners still come to a right angle (to a point) but the point has begun to fray slightly.

Corner Wear or Slightly Rounded Corners: The slight fraying of the corners has increased to where there is no longer a point to the corner. Nevertheless the corner is still reasonably sharp. There may be evidence of some slight loss of color in the corner also.

Rounded Corners: The corner is definitely no longer sharp but is not badly rounded.

Badly Rounded Corners: The corner is rounded to an objectionable degree. Excessive wear and rough handling are evident.

Creases

A third common defect is the crease. The degree of creasing in a card is very difficult to show in a drawing or picture. On giving the specific condition of an expensive card for sale, the seller should note any creases additionally. Creases can be categorized as to severity according to the following scale.

Light Crease: A light crease is a crease that is barely noticeable on close inspection. In fact when cards are in plastic sheets or holders, a light crease may not be seen (until the card is taken out of the holder). A light crease on the front is much more serious than a light crease on the card back only.

Medium Crease: A medium crease is noticeable when held and studied at arm's length by the naked eye, but does not overly detract from the appearance of the card. It is an obvious crease, but not one that breaks the picture surface of the card.

Heavy Crease: A heavy crease is one that has torn or broken through the card's picture surface, e.g., puts a tear in the photo surface.

Centering

Well-centered

Slightly Off-centered

Off-centered

Badly Off-centered

Miscut

Alterations

Deceptive Trimming: This occurs when someone alters the card in order (1) to shave off edge wear, (2) to improve the sharpness of the corners, or (3) to improve centering — obviously their objective is to falsely increase the perceived value of the card to an unsuspecting buyer. The shrinkage is usually only evident if the trimmed card is compared to an adjacent full-sized card or if the trimmed card is itself measured.

Obvious Trimming: Obvious trimming is noticeable and unfortunate. It usually is performed by non-collectors who give no thought to the present or future value of their cards.

Deceptively Retouched Borders: This occurs when the borders (especially on those cards with dark borders) with edges and corners with magic marker of appropriate color in order to make the card appear to be Mint.

Categorization of Defects

A "Micro Defect" would be fuzzy corners, slight off-centering, printers' lines, printers' spots, slightly out of focus, or slight loss of original gloss. A NrMt card may have one micro defect. An ExMt card may have two or more micro defects.

A "Minor Defect" would be corner wear or slight rounding, off-centering, light crease on back, wax or gum stains on reverse, loss of original gloss, writing or tape marks on back, or rubber band marks. An Excellent card may have minor defects.

A "Major Defect" would be rounded corner(s), badly off-centering, crease(s), deceptive trimming, deceptively retouched borders, pin hole, staple hole, incidental writing or tape marks on front, severe warping, water stains, medium crease(s), or sun fading. A Vg card may have one major defect. A Good card may have two or more major defects.

A "Catastrophic Defect" is the worst kind of defect and would include such defects as badly rounded corner(s), miscutting, heavy crease(s), obvious trimming, punch hole, tack hole, tear(s), corner missing or clipped, destructive writing on front. A Fair card may have one catastrophic defect. A Poor card has two or more catastrophic defects.

Corner Wear

The partial cards shown at the right have been photographed at 300%. This was done in order to magnify each card's corner wear to such a degree that differences could be shown on a printed page.

The 1962 Topps Mickey Mantle card definitely has a rounded corner. Some may say that this corner is badly rounded, but that is a judgment call.

The 1962 Topps Hank Aaron card has a slightly rounded corner. Note that there is definite corner wear evident by the fraying and that there is no longer a sharp point to which the corner converges.

The 1962 Topps Gil Hodges card has corner wear; it is slightly better than the Aaron card above. Nevertheless some collectors might classify this Hodges corner as slightly rounded.

The 1962 Topps Manager's Dream card showing Mantle and Mays has slight corner wear. This is not a fuzzy corner as very slight wear is noticeable on the card's photo surface.

The 1962 Topps Don Mossi card has very slight corner wear such that it might be called a fuzzy corner. A close look at the original card shows that the corner is not perfect, but almost. However, note that corner wear is somewhat academic on this card. As you can plainly see, the heavy crease going across his name breaks through the photo surface.

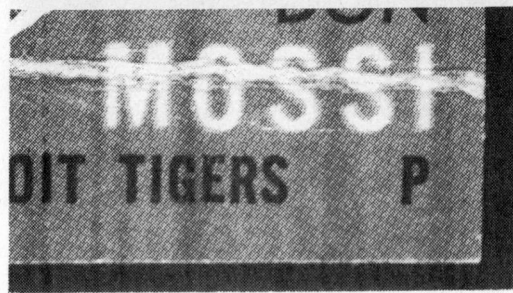

Condition Guide

Mint (Mt) - A card with no defects. The card has sharp corners, even borders, original gloss or shine on the surface, sharp focus of the picture, smooth edges, no signs of wear, and white borders. A Mint card does NOT have printers' lines or other printing defects or other serious quality control problems that should have been discovered by the card company before distribution. Note also that there is no allowance made for the age of the card.

Near Mint (NrMt) - A card with a micro defect. Any of the following would be sufficient to lower the grade of a card from Mint to the Near Mint category: layering at some of the corners (fuzzy corners), a very small amount of the original gloss lost, very minor wear on the edges, slightly off-center borders, slight wear visible only on close inspection, slight off-whiteness of the borders.

Excellent to Mint (ExMt) - A card with micro defects, but no minor defects. Two or three of the following would be sufficient to lower the grade of a card from Mint to the ExMt category: layering at some of the corners (fuzzy corners), a very small amount of the original gloss lost, minor wear on the edges, slightly off-center borders, slight wear visible only on close inspection, slight off-whiteness of the borders.

Excellent (Ex) - A card with minor defects. Any of the following would be sufficient to lower the grade of a card from Mint to the Excellent category: slight rounding at some of the corners, a small amount of the original gloss lost, minor wear on the edges, off-center borders, wear visible only on close inspection; off-whiteness of the borders.

Very Good (Vg) - A card that has been handled but not abused. Some rounding at all corners, slight layering or scuffing at one or two corners, slight notching on edges, gloss lost from the surface but not scuffed, borders might be somewhat uneven but some white is visible on all borders, noticeable yellowing or browning of borders, light crease(s), pictures may be slightly off focus.

Good (G) - A well-handled card, rounding and some layering at the corners, scuffing at the corners and minor scuffing on the face, borders noticeably uneven and browning, loss of gloss on the face, medium crease(s), notching on the edges.

Fair (F) - Round and layering corners, brown and dirty borders, frayed edges, noticeable scuffing on the face, white not visible on one or more borders, medium to heavy creases, cloudy focus.

Poor (P) - An abused card: The lowest grade of card, frequently some major physical alteration has been performed on the card, collectible only as a filler until a better-condition replacement can be obtained.

Categories between these major condition grades are used frequently, such as Very Good to Excellent (VgEx), Fair to Good (F-G), etc. Such grades indicate a card with all qualities at least in the lower of the two categories, but with several qualities in the higher of the two categories. In the case of ExMt, it essentially refers to a card which is halfway between Excellent and Mint.

Unopened packs, boxes and factory-collated sets are considered Mint in their unknown (and presumed perfect) state. However, once opened or broken out, each of these cards is graded (and valued) in its own right by taking into account any quality control defects (such as off-centering, printers' lines, machine creases, or gum stains) that may be present in spite of the fact that the card has never been handled.

Cards before 1980 that are priced in the Price Guide in a top condition of NrMt are obviously worth an additional premium when offered in strict Mint condition. This additional premium increases relative to the age and scarcity of the card. For example, Mint cards from the late '70s may bring only a 10 percent premium for Mint (above NrMt), whereas high demand (or condition rarity) cards from early vintage sets can be sold for as much as double (and occasionally even more) the NrMt price when offered in strict Mint condition.

Cards before 1946 that are priced in the Price Guide in a top condition of ExMt are obviously worth an additional premium when offered in strict Near Mint or better condition. This additional premium increases relative to the age and scarcity of the card.

Selling Your Cards

Just about every collector sells cards or will sell cards eventually. Someday you may be interested in selling your duplicates or maybe even your whole collection. You may sell to other collectors, friends or dealers. You may even sell cards you purchased from a certain dealer back to that same dealer. In any event, it helps to know some of the mechanics of the typical transaction between buyer and seller.

Dealers will buy cards in order to resell them to other collectors who are interested in the cards. Dealers will always pay a higher percentage for items that (in their opinion) can be resold quickly, and a much lower percentage for those items that are perceived as having low demand and hence are slow moving. In either case, dealers must buy at a price that allows for the expense of doing business and a margin for profit.

If you have cards for sale, the best advice we can give is that you get several offers for your cards — either from card shops or at a card show — and take the best offer, all things considered. Note, the "best" offer may not be the one for the highest amount. And remember, if a dealer really wants your cards, he won't let you get away without making his best competitive offer. Another alternative is to place your cards in an auction as one or several lots.

Many people think nothing of going into a department store and paying $15 for an item of clothing for which the store paid $5. But if you were selling your $15 card to a dealer and he offered you only $5 for it, you might think his markup unreasonable. To complete the analogy: most department stores (and card dealers) that consistently pay $10 for $15 items eventually go out of business. An exception is when the dealer has lined up a willing buyer for the item(s) you are attempting to sell, or if the cards are so Hot that it's likely he'll only have to hold the cards for a short period of time.

In those cases, an offer of up to 75 percent of book value still will allow the dealer to make a reasonable profit considering the short time he will need to hold the merchandise. In general, however, most cards and collections will bring offers in the range of 25 to 50 percent of retail price. Also consider that most material from the past five to 10 years is very plentiful. If that's what you're selling, don't be surprised if your best offer is well below that range.

Interesting Notes

The first card numerically of an issue is the single card most likely to obtain excessive wear. Consequently, you will typically find the price on the #1 card (in NrMt or Mint condition) somewhat higher than might otherwise be the case. Similarly, but to a lesser extent (because normally the less important, reverse side of the card is the one exposed), the last card numerically in an issue also is prone to abnormal wear. This extra wear and tear occurs because the first and last cards are exposed to the elements (human element included) more than any other cards. They are generally end cards in any brick formations, rubber bandings, stackings on wet surfaces, and like activities.

Sports cards have no intrinsic value. The value of a card, like the value of other collectibles, can be determined only by you and your enjoyment in viewing and possessing these cardboard swatches.

Remember, the buyer ultimately determines the price of each baseball card. You are the determining price factor because you have the ability to say "No" to the price of any card by not exchanging your hard-earned money for a given card. When the cost of a trading card exceeds the enjoyment you will receive from it, your answer should be "No." We assess and report the prices. You set them!

We are always interested in receiving the price input of collectors and dealers from around the country. We happily credit major contributors. We welcome your opinions, since your contributions assist us in ensuring a better guide each year. If you would like to join our survey list for the next editions of this book and others authored by Dr. Beckett, please send your name and address to Dr. James Beckett, 4887 Alpha Road, Suite 200, Dallas, Texas 75244.

Advertising

Within this Price Guide you will find advertisements for sports memorabilia material, mail order, and retail sports collectibles establishments. All advertisements were accepted in good faith based on the reputation of the advertiser; however, neither the author, the publisher, the distributors, nor the other advertisers in this Price Guide accept any responsibility for any particular advertiser not complying with the terms of his or her ad.

Readers should also be aware that prices in advertisements are subject to change over the annual period before a new edition of this volume is issued each spring. When replying to an advertisement late in the baseball year, the reader should take this into account, and contact the dealer by phone or in writing for up-to-date price information. Should you come into contact with any of the advertisers in this guide as a result of their advertisement herein, please mention to them this source as your contact.

Additional Reading

With the increase in popularity of the hobby in recent years, there has been a corresponding increase in available literature. Below is a list of the books and periodicals that receive our highest recommendation and which we hope will further advance your knowledge and enjoyment of our great hobby.

The Official Price Guide to Baseball Cards by Dr. James Beckett (Eleventh Edition, $5.95, released 1991, published by The House of Collectibles) — an abridgement of the Sport Americana Price Guide in a convenient and economical pocket-size format providing Dr. Beckett's pricing of the major baseball sets since 1948.

The Sport Americana Price Guide to Baseball Collectibles by Dr. James Beckett (Second Edition, $12.95, released 1988, published by Edgewater Book Company) — the complete guide/checklist with up-to-date values for box cards, coins, labels, Canadian cards, stamps, stickers, pins, etc.

The Sport Americana Football Card Price Guide by Dr. James Beckett (Eighth Edition, $14.95, released 1991, published by Edgewater Book Company) — the most comprehensive Price Guide and checklist ever issued on football cards. No serious football card hobbyist should be without it.

The Official Price Guide to Football Cards by Dr. James Beckett (Eleventh Edition, $5.99, released 1991, published by The House of Collectibles) — an abridgement of the Sport Americana Price Guide listed above in a convenient and economical pocket-size format providing Dr. Beckett's pricing of the major football sets since 1948.

The Sport Americana Hockey Card Price Guide by Dr. James Beckett (First Edition, $12.95, released 1991, published by Edgewater Book Company) — the most comprehensive Price Guide and checklist ever issued on hockey cards.

The Official Price Guide to Hockey Cards by Dr. James Beckett (First Edition, $5.99, released 1991, published by The House of Collectibles) — an abridgement of the Sport Americana Price Guide listed above in a convenient and economical pocket-size format providing Dr. Beckett's pricing of the major hockey sets since 1951.

The Sport Americana Basketball Card Price Guide and Alphabetical Checklist by Dr. James Beckett (First Edition, $12.95, released 1991, published by Edgewater Book Company) — the most comprehensive combination Price Guide and alphabetical checklist ever issued on basketball cards.

The Official Price Guide to Basketball Cards by Dr. James Beckett (First Edition, $5.99, released 1991, published by The House of Collectibles) — an abridgement of the Sport Americana Price Guide listed above in a convenient and economical pocket-size format providing Dr. Beckett's pricing of the major basketball sets since 1948.

The Sport Americana Alphabetical Baseball Card Checklist by Dr. James Beckett (Fourth Edition, $12.95, released 1990, published by Edgewater Book Company) — an alphabetical listing, by the last name of the player portrayed on the card, of virtually all baseball cards (Major League and Minor League) produced up through the 1990 major sets.

The Sport Americana Price Guide to the Non-Sports Cards by Christopher Benjamin and Dennis W. Eckes (Third Edition [Part Two], $12.95, released 1988, published by Edgewater Book Company) — the definitive guide to all popular non-sports American tobacco and bubble gum cards. In addition to cards, illustrations and prices for wrappers are also included. Part Two covers non-sports cards from 1961 through 1987.

The Sport Americana Price Guide to the Non-Sports Cards 1930-1960 by Christopher Benjamin and Dennis W. Eckes ($14.95, released

1991, published by Edgewater Book Company) — the definitive guide to virtually all popular non-sports American tobacco and bubble gum cards issued between 1930 and 1960. In addition to cards, illustrations and prices for wrappers are also included.

The Sport Americana Baseball Address List by Jack Smalling and Dennis W. Eckes (Sixth Edition, $12.95, released 1990, published by Edgewater Book Company) — the definitive guide for autograph hunters, giving addresses and deceased information for virtually all major league baseball players past and present.

The Sport Americana Baseball Card Team Checklist by Jeff Fritsch and Dennis W. Eckes (Fifth Edition, $12.95, released 1990, published by Edgwater Book Company) — includes all Topps, Bowman, Donruss, Fleer, Score, Play Ball, Goudey and Upper Deck cards, with the players portrayed on the cards listed with the teams for which they played. The book is invaluable to the collector who specializes in an individual team because it is the most complete baseball card team checklist available.

The Encyclopedia of Baseball Cards, Volume I: 19th Century Cards by Lew Lipset ($11.95, released 1983, published by the author) — everything you ever wanted to know about 19th century cards.

The Encyclopedia of Baseball Cards, Volume II: Early Gum and Candy Cards by Lew Lipset ($10.95, released 1984, published by the author) — everything you ever wanted to know about Early Candy and Gum cards.

The Encyclopedia of Baseball Cards, Volume III: 20th Century Tobacco Cards, 1909-1932 by Lew Lipset ($12.95, released 1986, published by the author) — everything you ever wanted to know about old tobacco cards.

Beckett Baseball Card Monthly authored and edited by Dr. James Beckett — contains the most extensive and accepted monthly Price Guide, feature articles, "who's hot and who's not" section, convention calendar, and numerous letters to and responses from the editor. Published 12 times annually, it is the hobby's largest paid circulation periodical. *Beckett Football Card Monthly, Beckett Basketball Monthly, Beckett Hockey Monthly* and *Beckett Focus on Future Stars* are all similar to *Beckett Baseball Card Monthly* in style and content.

Errata

There are thousands of names, close to a half million prices, and untold other words in this book. There are going to be a few typographical errors, a few misspellings, and possibly, a number or two out of place. If you catch a blooper, drop me a note directly or in care of the publisher, and we will fix it up in the next year's edition.

Prices in this Guide

Prices found in this guide reflect current retail rates just prior to the printing of this book. They do not reflect the FOR SALE prices of the author, the publisher, the distributors, the advertisers, or any card dealers associated with this guide. No one is obligated in any way to buy, sell or trade his or her cards based on these prices. The price listings were compiled by the author from actual buy/sell transactions at sports conventions, sports card shops, buy/sell advertisements in the hobby papers, for sale prices from dealer catalogs and price lists, and discussions with leading hobbyists in the U.S. and Canada. All prices are in U.S. dollars.

1988 Action Packed Test

The 1988 Action Packed Test set contains six standard-size (2 1/2" by 3 1/2") cards with slightly rounded corners. This apparently was the set of cards that Action Packed produced to show their technique to Major League Baseball and the Major League Baseball Players Association in their unsuccessful attempt to seek a baseball card license in 1988. The embossed color player photos on the fronts are bordered in gold. In black lettering, the player's name appears on a gold plaque above the picture, and the team name on a gold plaque beneath the picture. The card backs have the same design as Score issues, with a color head shot, team logo, biography, and major league batting or pitching statistics, again inside a gold border. The face on the front photo of the Ozzie Smith card was apparently considered too dark and thus reportedly not submitted. The cards are unnumbered and checklisted below in alphabetical order.

	MINT	EXC	G-VG
COMPLETE SET (6)	400.00	180.00	60.00
COMMON PLAYER (1-6)	50.00	22.50	7.50
☐ 1 Wade Boggs	75.00	34.00	11.25
☐ 2 Andre Dawson	50.00	22.50	7.50
☐ 3 Dwight Gooden	60.00	27.00	9.00
☐ 4 Carney Lansford	50.00	22.50	7.50
☐ 5 Don Mattingly	75.00	34.00	11.25
☐ 6 Ozzie Smith	125.00	57.50	18.75

1962 American Tract Society

These cards are quite attractive and feature the "pure card" concept that is always popular with collectors, i.e., no borders or anything else on the card front to detract from the color photo. The cards are numbered on the back and are actually part of a much larger set with a Christian theme. The set features Christian ballplayers giving first-person testimonies on the card backs telling how Jesus Christ has changed their lives. These cards are sometimes referred to as "Tracards." The cards measure approximately 2 3/4" by 3 1/2". The set price below refers to only one of each player, not including any variations.

	NRMT	VG-E	GOOD
COMPLETE SET (4)	21.00	9.00	3.00
COMMON PLAYER	5.00	2.25	.50
☐ 43A Bobby Richardson (black print on back)	10.00	4.50	1.25
☐ 43B Bobby Richardson (blue print on back)	10.00	4.50	1.25
☐ 43C Bobby Richardson (black print on back with Play Ball in red)	10.00	4.50	1.25
☐ 43D Bobby Richardson (black print on back with exclamation point after Play Ball)	10.00	4.50	1.25
☐ 51A Jerry Kindall (portrait from chest up, black print on back)	5.00	2.25	.50
☐ 51B Jerry Kindall (on one knee with bat, blue print on back)	5.00	2.25	.50
☐ 52A Felipe Alou (on one knee looking up, black print on back)	7.50	3.25	.75
☐ 52B Felipe Alou (on one knee looking up, blue print on back)	7.50	3.25	.75
☐ 52C Felipe Alou (batting pose)	7.50	3.25	.75
☐ 66 Al Worthington (black print on back)	5.00	2.25	.50

1991 Arena Holograms

The 1991 Arena hologram cards were distributed through hobby dealers and feature famous football, basketball, and baseball players. Supposedly production quantities were limited to 250,000 of each card. The cards measure the standard size (2 1/2" by 3 1/2") and display holograms on the fronts. The horizontally oriented backs have a color photo of the player in a tuxedo on the right portion, while the left portion presents player profile in white lettering on black. The cards are numbered on the back.

	MINT	EXC	G-VG
COMPLETE SET (5)	10.00	4.50	1.25
COMMON PLAYER (1-5)	2.50	1.00	.25
☐ 1 Joe Montana	2.50	1.00	.25
☐ 2 Ken Griffey Jr.	2.50	1.00	.25
☐ 3 Frank Thomas	2.50	1.00	.25
☐ 4 Barry Sanders	2.50	1.00	.25
☐ 5 David Robinson	2.50	1.00	.25

1948 Babe Ruth Story

The 1948 Babe Ruth Story set of 28 black and white numbered cards (measuring 2" by 2 1/2") was issued by the Philadelphia Chewing Gum Company to commemorate the 1949 movie of the same name starring William Bendix, Claire Trevor, and Charles Bickford. Babe Ruth himself appears on several cards. The last 12 cards (17 to 28) are more difficult to obtain than other cards in the set and are also more desirable in that most picture actual players as well as actors from the movie. Supposedly these last 12 cards were issued much later after the first 16 cards had already been released and distributed. The last seven cards (22-28) in the set are subtitled "The Babe Ruth Story in the Making" at the top of each reverse. The bottom of every card says "Swell Bubble Gum, Philadelphia Chewing Gum Corporation." The catalog designation for this set is R421.

	NRMT	VG-E	GOOD
COMPLETE SET (28)	1250.00	550.00	175.00
COMMON PLAYER (1-16)	15.00	6.50	2.15
COMMON PLAYER (17-24)	45.00	20.00	6.75
COMMON PLAYER (25-28)	135.00	60.00	20.00
☐ 1 The Babe Ruth Story In the Making (Babe Ruth shown with William Bendix)	150.00	25.00	5.00
☐ 2 Bat Boy Becomes the Babe (Facsimile autographed by William Bendix)	15.00	6.50	2.15
☐ 3 Claire Hodgson played by Claire Trevor	15.00	6.50	2.15
☐ 4 Babe Ruth played by William Bendix; Claire Hodgson played by Claire Trevor	15.00	6.50	2.15
☐ 5 Brother Matthias played by Charles Bickford	15.00	6.50	2.15
☐ 6 Phil Conrad played by Sam Levene	15.00	6.50	2.15
☐ 7 Night Club Singer played by Gertrude Niesen	15.00	6.50	2.15
☐ 8 Baseball's Famous Deal	15.00	6.50	2.15
☐ 9 Babe Ruth played by William Bendix; Mrs.Babe Ruth played by Claire Trevor	15.00	6.50	2.15
☐ 10 Actors for Babe Ruth, Mrs. Babe Ruth, and Brother Matthias	15.00	6.50	2.15
☐ 11 Babe Ruth played by William Bendix; Miller Huggins played by Fred Lightner	15.00	6.50	2.15
☐ 12 Babe Ruth played by William Bendix; Johnny Sylvester played by George Marshall	15.00	6.50	2.15
☐ 13 Actors for Mr., Mrs. and Johnny Sylvester	15.00	6.50	2.15
☐ 14 When A Feller Needs A Friend	15.00	6.50	2.15
☐ 15 Dramatic Home Run	15.00	6.50	2.15
☐ 16 The Homer That Set the Record	15.00	6.50	2.15
☐ 17 The Slap That Started Baseball's Most Famous Career	45.00	20.00	6.75
☐ 18 The Babe Plays Santa Claus	45.00	20.00	6.75
☐ 19 Actors for Ed Barrow, Jacob Ruppert, and Miller Huggins	45.00	20.00	6.75
☐ 20 Broken Window Paid Off	45.00	20.00	6.75
☐ 21 Regardless of the Generation/ Babe Ruth (Bendix shown getting mobbed by crowd)	45.00	20.00	6.75
☐ 22 Ted Lyons and William Bendix	60.00	27.00	9.00
☐ 23 Charley Grimm and William Bendix	45.00	20.00	6.75
☐ 24 Lefty Gomez, William Bendix, and Bucky Harris	75.00	34.00	11.25
☐ 25 Babe Ruth and William Bendix (Babe Ruth pictured with ball)	135.00	60.00	20.00
☐ 26 Babe Ruth and William Bendix (Babe Ruth pictured with bat)	135.00	60.00	20.00
☐ 27 Babe Ruth and Claire Trevor	135.00	60.00	20.00
☐ 28 William Bendix, Babe Ruth, Claire Trevor (Babe Ruth pictured autographing ball)	135.00	60.00	20.00

1990 Baseball Wit

The 1990 Baseball Wit set was issued in complete set form only. This set was dedicated to and featured several ex-members of the Little Leagues. This 108-card, standard-size (2 1/2" by 3 1/2") set was available primarily in retail and chain outlets. Most of the older (retired) players in the set are shown in black and white. The card backs typically give three trivia questions with answers following. The object of the game is to collect points by correctly answering any one of the questions on the back of each card or identifying the picture on the front. The first printing of 10,000 sets had several errors, and the cards were not numbered. The second printing corrected these errors and numbered the cards.

	MINT	VG-E	F-G
COMPLETE SET (108)	10.00	4.50	1.25
COMMON PLAYER (1-108)	.08	.03	.01
☐ 1 Orel Hershiser	.15	.06	.01
☐ 2 Tony Gwynn	.20	.08	.02
☐ 3 Mickey Mantle	.65	.25	.06
☐ 4 Willie Stargell	.15	.06	.01
☐ 5 Don Baylor	.08	.03	.01
☐ 6 Hank Aaron	.25	.10	.02
☐ 7 Don Larsen	.08	.03	.01
☐ 8 Lee Mazzilli	.08	.03	.01
☐ 9 John"Boog" Powell	.08	.03	.01

		EX-MT	VG-E	GOOD
☐ 10	Little League World Series	.08	.03	.01
☐ 11	Jose Canseco	.40	.16	.04
☐ 12	Mike Scott	.08	.03	.01
☐ 13	Bob Feller	.12	.05	.01
☐ 14	Ron Santo	.08	.03	.01
☐ 15A	Mel Stottlemyer ERR (sic, Stottlmyre)	.12	.05	.01
☐ 15B	Mel Stottlemyer COR	.12	.05	.01
☐ 16	Shea Stadium	.08	.03	.01
☐ 17	Brooks Robinson	.12	.05	.01
☐ 18	Willie Mays	.25	.10	.02
☐ 19	Ernie Banks	.15	.06	.01
☐ 20	Keith Hernandez	.08	.03	.01
☐ 21	Bret Saberhagen	.12	.05	.01
☐ 22	Baseball Hall of Fame	.08	.03	.01
☐ 23	Luis Aparicio	.12	.05	.01
☐ 24	Yogi Berra	.15	.06	.01
☐ 25	Manny Mota	.08	.03	.01
☐ 26	Steve Garvey	.12	.05	.01
☐ 27	Bill Shea	.08	.03	.01
☐ 28	Fred Lynn	.08	.03	.01
☐ 29	Todd Worrell	.08	.03	.01
☐ 30	Roy Campanella	.15	.06	.01
☐ 31	Bob Gibson	.12	.05	.01
☐ 32	Gary Carter	.12	.05	.01
☐ 33	Jim Palmer	.15	.06	.01
☐ 34	Carl Yastrzemski	.15	.06	.01
☐ 35	Dwight Gooden	.15	.06	.01
☐ 36	Stan Musial	.25	.10	.02
☐ 37	Rickey Henderson	.35	.15	.03
☐ 38	Dale Murphy	.15	.06	.01
☐ 39	Mike Schmidt	.25	.10	.02
☐ 40	Gaylord Perry	.12	.05	.01
☐ 41	Ozzie Smith	.15	.06	.01
☐ 42	Reggie Jackson	.25	.10	.02
☐ 43	Steve Carlton	.15	.06	.01
☐ 44	Jim Perry	.08	.03	.01
☐ 45	Vince Coleman	.12	.05	.01
☐ 46	Tom Seaver	.25	.10	.02
☐ 47	Marty Marion	.08	.03	.01
☐ 48	Frank Robinson	.12	.05	.01
☐ 49	Joe DiMaggio	.45	.18	.04
☐ 50	Ted Williams	.35	.15	.03
☐ 51	Rollie Fingers	.12	.05	.01
☐ 52	Jackie Robinson	.35	.15	.03
☐ 53	Victor Raschi	.08	.03	.01
☐ 54	Johnny Bench	.20	.08	.02
☐ 55	Nolan Ryan	.60	.25	.06
☐ 56	Ty Cobb	.45	.18	.04
☐ 57	Harry Steinfeldt	.08	.03	.01
☐ 58	James O'Rourke	.08	.03	.01
☐ 59	John McGraw	.12	.05	.01
☐ 60	Candy Cummings	.08	.03	.01
☐ 61	Jimmie Foxx	.12	.05	.01
☐ 62	Walter Johnson	.12	.05	.01
☐ 63	1903 World Series	.08	.03	.01
☐ 64	Satchel Paige	.15	.06	.01
☐ 65	Bobby Wallace	.08	.03	.01
☐ 66	Cap Anson	.12	.05	.01
☐ 67	Hugh Duffy	.08	.03	.01
☐ 68	William(Buck) Ewing	.08	.03	.01
☐ 69	Bobo Holloman	.08	.03	.01
☐ 70	Ed Delahanty	.08	.03	.01
☐ 71	Dizzy Dean	.15	.06	.01
☐ 72	Tris Speaker	.12	.05	.01
☐ 73	Lou Gehrig	.45	.18	.04
☐ 74	Wee Willie Keeler	.08	.03	.01
☐ 75	Cal Hubbard	.08	.03	.01
☐ 76	Eddie Collins	.08	.03	.01
☐ 77	Chris Von Der Ahe	.08	.03	.01
☐ 78	Sam Crawford	.08	.03	.01
☐ 79	Cy Young	.15	.06	.01
☐ 80	Johnny Vander Meer	.08	.03	.01
☐ 81	Joey Jay	.08	.03	.01
☐ 82	Zack Wheat	.08	.03	.01
☐ 83	Jim Bottomley	.08	.03	.01
☐ 84	Honus Wagner	.25	.10	.02
☐ 85	Casey Stengel	.15	.06	.01
☐ 86	Babe Ruth	.65	.25	.06
☐ 87	John Lindemuth/Carl	.08	.03	.01
☐ 88	Max Carey	.08	.03	.01
☐ 89	Mordecai Brown	.08	.03	.01
☐ 90	1869 Cincinnati Red Stockings	.08	.03	.01
☐ 91	Rube Marquard	.08	.03	.01
☐ 92	Charles Radbourne (Horse)	.08	.03	.01
☐ 93	Hack Wilson	.08	.03	.01
☐ 94	Lefty Grove	.12	.05	.01
☐ 95	Carl Hubbell	.08	.03	.01
☐ 96	A.J. Cartwright	.08	.03	.01
☐ 97	Roger Hornsby	.15	.06	.01
☐ 98	Ernest Thayer	.08	.03	.01
☐ 99	Connie Mack	.12	.05	.01
☐ 100	1939 Centennial Celebration	.08	.03	.01
☐ 101	Branch Rickey	.12	.05	.01
☐ 102	Dan Brouthers	.08	.03	.01
☐ 103	First Baseball Uniform	.08	.03	.01
☐ 104	Christy Mathewson	.15	.06	.01
☐ 105	Joe Nuxhall	.08	.03	.01
☐ 106	1939 Centennial Celebration	.08	.03	.01
☐ 107	President Taft	.08	.03	.01
☐ 108	Abner Doubleday	.08	.03	.01

1934-36 Batter-Up

The 1934-36 Batter-Up set issued by National Chicle contains 192 blank-backed die-cut cards. Numbers 1 to 80 are 2 3/8" by 3 1/4" in size while 81 to 192 are 2 3/8" by 3". The latter are more difficult to find than the former. The pictures come in basic black and white or in tints of blue, brown, green, purple, red, or sepia. There are three combination cards (each featuring two players per card) in the high series (98, 111, and 115). The catalog designation for the set is R318. Cards with backs removed are graded fair at best.

		EX-MT	VG-E	GOOD
COMPLETE SET (192)		22500.00	9500.00	2500.00
COMMON PLAYER (1-80)		50.00	22.50	7.50
COMMON PLAYER (81-192)		100.00	45.00	15.00
☐ 1	Wally Berger	100.00	45.00	15.00
☐ 2	Ed Brandt	50.00	22.50	7.50
☐ 3	Al Lopez	120.00	55.00	18.00
☐ 4	Dick Bartell	50.00	22.50	7.50
☐ 5	Carl Hubbell	175.00	80.00	27.00
☐ 6	Bill Terry	175.00	80.00	27.00
☐ 7	Pepper Martin	75.00	34.00	11.25
☐ 8	Jim Bottomley	120.00	55.00	18.00
☐ 9	Tom Bridges	60.00	27.00	9.00
☐ 10	Rick Ferrell	120.00	55.00	18.00
☐ 11	Ray Benge	50.00	22.50	7.50
☐ 12	Wes Ferrell	60.00	27.00	9.00
☐ 13	Chalmer Cissell	50.00	22.50	7.50
☐ 14	Pie Traynor	175.00	80.00	27.00
☐ 15	Leroy Mahaffey	50.00	22.50	7.50
☐ 16	Chick Hafey	120.00	55.00	18.00
☐ 17	Lloyd Waner	120.00	55.00	18.00
☐ 18	Jack Burns	50.00	22.50	7.50
☐ 19	Buddy Myer	50.00	22.50	7.50
☐ 20	Bob Johnson	60.00	27.00	9.00
☐ 21	Arky Vaughan	120.00	55.00	18.00
☐ 22	Red Rolfe	60.00	27.00	9.00
☐ 23	Lefty Gomez	175.00	80.00	27.00
☐ 24	Earl Averill	120.00	55.00	18.00
☐ 25	Mickey Cochrane	175.00	80.00	27.00
☐ 26	Van Lingle Mungo	60.00	27.00	9.00
☐ 27	Mel Ott	200.00	90.00	30.00
☐ 28	Jimmy Foxx	200.00	90.00	30.00
☐ 29	Jimmy Dykes	60.00	27.00	9.00
☐ 30	Bill Dickey	200.00	90.00	30.00
☐ 31	Lefty Grove	200.00	90.00	30.00
☐ 32	Joe Cronin	175.00	80.00	27.00
☐ 33	Frank Frisch	175.00	80.00	27.00
☐ 34	Al Simmons	150.00	67.50	22.50
☐ 35	Rogers Hornsby	200.00	90.00	30.00

☐ 36	Ted Lyons	120.00	55.00	18.00
☐ 37	Rabbit Maranville	120.00	55.00	18.00
☐ 38	Jimmy Wilson	50.00	22.50	7.50
☐ 39	Willie Kamm	50.00	22.50	7.50
☐ 40	Bill Hallahan	50.00	22.50	7.50
☐ 41	Gus Suhr	50.00	22.50	7.50
☐ 42	Charlie Gehringer	150.00	67.50	22.50
☐ 43	Joe Heving	50.00	22.50	7.50
☐ 44	Adam Comorosky	50.00	22.50	7.50
☐ 45	Tony Lazzeri	120.00	55.00	18.00
☐ 46	Sam Leslie	50.00	22.50	7.50
☐ 47	Bob Smith	50.00	22.50	7.50
☐ 48	Willis Hudlin	50.00	22.50	7.50
☐ 49	Carl Reynolds	50.00	22.50	7.50
☐ 50	Fred Schulte	50.00	22.50	7.50
☐ 51	Cookie Lavagetto	60.00	27.00	9.00
☐ 52	Hal Schumacher	50.00	22.50	7.50
☐ 53	Roger Cramer	60.00	27.00	9.00
☐ 54	Sylvester Johnson	50.00	22.50	7.50
☐ 55	Ollie Bejma	50.00	22.50	7.50
☐ 56	Sam Byrd	50.00	22.50	7.50
☐ 57	Hank Greenberg	200.00	90.00	30.00
☐ 58	Bill Knickerbocker	50.00	22.50	7.50
☐ 59	Bill Urbanski	50.00	22.50	7.50
☐ 60	Eddie Morgan	50.00	22.50	7.50
☐ 61	Rabbit McNair	50.00	22.50	7.50
☐ 62	Ben Chapman	60.00	27.00	9.00
☐ 63	Roy Johnson	50.00	22.50	7.50
☐ 64	Dizzy Dean	375.00	165.00	55.00
☐ 65	Zeke Bonura	50.00	22.50	7.50
☐ 66	Fred Marberry	50.00	22.50	7.50
☐ 67	Gus Mancuso	50.00	22.50	7.50
☐ 68	Joe Vosmik	50.00	22.50	7.50
☐ 69	Earl Grace	50.00	22.50	7.50
☐ 70	Tony Piet	50.00	22.50	7.50
☐ 71	Rollie Hemsley	50.00	22.50	7.50
☐ 72	Fred Fitzsimmons	50.00	22.50	7.50
☐ 73	Hack Wilson	175.00	80.00	27.00
☐ 74	Chick Fullis	50.00	22.50	7.50
☐ 75	Fred Frankhouse	50.00	22.50	7.50
☐ 76	Ethan Allen	50.00	22.50	7.50
☐ 77	Heine Manush	120.00	55.00	18.00
☐ 78	Rip Collins	50.00	22.50	7.50
☐ 79	Tony Cuccinello	50.00	22.50	7.50
☐ 80	Joe Kuhel	50.00	22.50	7.50
☐ 81	Tom Bridges	120.00	55.00	18.00
☐ 82	Clint Brown	100.00	45.00	15.00
☐ 83	Albert Blanche	100.00	45.00	15.00
☐ 84	Boze Berger	100.00	45.00	15.00
☐ 85	Goose Goslin	200.00	90.00	30.00
☐ 86	Lefty Gomez	325.00	150.00	50.00
☐ 87	Joe Glenn	100.00	45.00	15.00
☐ 88	Cy Blanton	100.00	45.00	15.00
☐ 89	Tom Carey	100.00	45.00	15.00
☐ 90	Ralph Birkofer	100.00	45.00	15.00
☐ 91	Fred Gabler	100.00	45.00	15.00
☐ 92	Dick Coffman	100.00	45.00	15.00
☐ 93	Ollie Bejma	100.00	45.00	15.00
☐ 94	Leroy Parmelee	100.00	45.00	15.00
☐ 95	Carl Reynolds	100.00	45.00	15.00
☐ 96	Ben Cantwell	100.00	45.00	15.00
☐ 97	Curtis Davis	100.00	45.00	15.00
☐ 98	Webb and Wally Moses	120.00	55.00	18.00
☐ 99	Ray Benge	100.00	45.00	15.00
☐ 100	Pie Traynor	225.00	100.00	33.00
☐ 101	Phil Cavarretta	120.00	55.00	18.00
☐ 102	Pep Young	100.00	45.00	15.00
☐ 103	Willis Hudlin	100.00	45.00	15.00
☐ 104	Mickey Haslin	100.00	45.00	15.00
☐ 105	Oswald Bluege	100.00	45.00	15.00
☐ 106	Paul Andrews	100.00	45.00	15.00
☐ 107	Ed Brandt	100.00	45.00	15.00
☐ 108	Don Taylor	100.00	45.00	15.00
☐ 109	Thornton Lee	100.00	45.00	15.00
☐ 110	Hal Schumacher	100.00	45.00	15.00
☐ 111	Hayes and Ted Lyons	175.00	80.00	27.00
☐ 112	Odell Hale	100.00	45.00	15.00
☐ 113	Earl Averill	200.00	90.00	30.00
☐ 114	Italo Chelini	100.00	45.00	15.00
☐ 115	Andrews and Jim Bottomley	175.00	80.00	27.00
☐ 116	Bill Walker	100.00	45.00	15.00
☐ 117	Bill Dickey	350.00	160.00	52.50
☐ 118	Gerald Walker	100.00	45.00	15.00
☐ 119	Ted Lyons	200.00	90.00	30.00
☐ 120	Eldon Auker	100.00	45.00	15.00
☐ 121	Bill Hallahan	100.00	45.00	15.00
☐ 122	Fred Lindstrom	200.00	90.00	30.00
☐ 123	Oral Hildebrand	100.00	45.00	15.00
☐ 124	Luke Appling	225.00	100.00	33.00
☐ 125	Pepper Martin	135.00	60.00	20.00
☐ 126	Rick Ferrell	200.00	90.00	30.00
☐ 127	Ival Goodman	100.00	45.00	15.00
☐ 128	Joe Kuhel	100.00	45.00	15.00
☐ 129	Ernie Lombardi	200.00	90.00	30.00

☐ 130	Charlie Gehringer	300.00	135.00	45.00
☐ 131	Van Lingle Mungo	120.00	55.00	18.00
☐ 132	Larry French	100.00	45.00	15.00
☐ 133	Buddy Myer	100.00	45.00	15.00
☐ 134	Mel Harder	135.00	60.00	20.00
☐ 135	Augie Galan	100.00	45.00	15.00
☐ 136	Gabby Hartnett	200.00	90.00	30.00
☐ 137	Stan Hack	120.00	55.00	18.00
☐ 138	Billy Herman	200.00	90.00	30.00
☐ 139	Bill Jurges	100.00	45.00	15.00
☐ 140	Bill Lee	100.00	45.00	15.00
☐ 141	Zeke Bonura	100.00	45.00	15.00
☐ 142	Tony Piet	100.00	45.00	15.00
☐ 143	Paul Dean	135.00	60.00	20.00
☐ 144	Jimmy Foxx	450.00	200.00	67.50
☐ 145	Joe Medwick	250.00	110.00	37.50
☐ 146	Rip Collins	100.00	45.00	15.00
☐ 147	Mel Almada	100.00	45.00	15.00
☐ 148	Allan Cooke	100.00	45.00	15.00
☐ 149	Moe Berg	175.00	80.00	27.00
☐ 150	Dolph Camilli	100.00	45.00	15.00
☐ 151	Oscar Melillo	100.00	45.00	15.00
☐ 152	Bruce Campbell	100.00	45.00	15.00
☐ 153	Lefty Grove	350.00	160.00	52.50
☐ 154	Johnny Murphy	120.00	55.00	18.00
☐ 155	Luke Sewell	120.00	55.00	18.00
☐ 156	Leo Durocher	250.00	110.00	37.50
☐ 157	Lloyd Waner	200.00	90.00	30.00
☐ 158	Gus Bush	100.00	45.00	15.00
☐ 159	Jimmy Dykes	120.00	55.00	18.00
☐ 160	Steve O'Neill	100.00	45.00	15.00
☐ 161	General Crowder	100.00	45.00	15.00
☐ 162	Joe Cascarella	100.00	45.00	15.00
☐ 163	Daniel (Bud) Hafey	100.00	45.00	15.00
☐ 164	Gilly Campbell	100.00	45.00	15.00
☐ 165	Ray Hayworth	100.00	45.00	15.00
☐ 166	Frank Demaree	100.00	45.00	15.00
☐ 167	John Babich	100.00	45.00	15.00
☐ 168	Marvin Owen	100.00	45.00	15.00
☐ 169	Ralph Kress	100.00	45.00	15.00
☐ 170	Mule Haas	100.00	45.00	15.00
☐ 171	Frank Higgins	100.00	45.00	15.00
☐ 172	Wally Berger	120.00	55.00	18.00
☐ 173	Frank Frisch	225.00	100.00	33.00
☐ 174	Wes Ferrell	120.00	55.00	18.00
☐ 175	Pete Fox	100.00	45.00	15.00
☐ 176	John Vergez	100.00	45.00	15.00
☐ 177	Billy Rogell	100.00	45.00	15.00
☐ 178	Don Brennan	100.00	45.00	15.00
☐ 179	Jim Bottomley	200.00	90.00	30.00
☐ 180	Travis Jackson	200.00	90.00	30.00
☐ 181	Red Rolfe	100.00	45.00	15.00
☐ 182	Frank Crosetti	150.00	67.50	22.50
☐ 183	Joe Cronin	200.00	90.00	30.00
☐ 184	Schoolboy Rowe	100.00	45.00	15.00
☐ 185	Chuck Klein	225.00	100.00	33.00
☐ 186	Lon Warneke	120.00	55.00	18.00
☐ 187	Gus Suhr	100.00	45.00	15.00
☐ 188	Ben Chapman	120.00	55.00	18.00
☐ 189	Clint Brown	100.00	45.00	15.00
☐ 190	Paul Derringer	135.00	60.00	20.00
☐ 191	John Burns	100.00	45.00	15.00
☐ 192	John Broaca	150.00	67.50	22.50

1988 Bazooka

There are 22 cards in the set; cards are standard size, 2 1/2" by 3 1/2". The cards have extra thick white borders. Card backs are printed in blue and red on white card stock. Some sets can also be found with gray backs. Cards are numbered on the back; they were numbered by Topps alphabetically. The word "Bazooka" only appears faintly as background for the statistics on the back of the card. Cards were available inside specially marked boxes of Bazooka gum retailing between 59 cents and 99 cents. The emphasis in the player selection for this set is on the young stars of baseball.

		MINT	EXC	G-VG
	COMPLETE SET (22)	10.00	4.50	1.25
	COMMON PLAYER (1-22)	.35	.15	.03
☐ 1	George Bell	.45	.18	.04
☐ 2	Wade Boggs	1.00	.40	.10
☐ 3	Jose Canseco	1.25	.50	.12
☐ 4	Roger Clemens	1.25	.50	.12
☐ 5	Vince Coleman	.60	.25	.06

		MINT	EXC	G-VG
☐ 6	Eric Davis	.75	.30	.07
☐ 7	Tony Fernandez	.35	.15	.03
☐ 8	Dwight Gooden	.75	.30	.07
☐ 9	Tony Gwynn	.75	.30	.07
☐ 10	Wally Joyner	.45	.18	.04
☐ 11	Don Mattingly	1.00	.40	.10
☐ 12	Willie McGee	.35	.15	.03
☐ 13	Mark McGwire	.75	.30	.07
☐ 14	Kirby Puckett	1.00	.40	.10
☐ 15	Tim Raines	.45	.18	.04
☐ 16	Dave Righetti	.35	.15	.03
☐ 17	Cal Ripken	1.25	.50	.12
☐ 18	Juan Samuel	.35	.15	.03
☐ 19	Ryne Sandberg	1.00	.40	.10
☐ 20	Benny Santiago	.45	.18	.04
☐ 21	Darryl Strawberry	1.00	.40	.10
☐ 22	Todd Worrell	.35	.15	.03

1989 Bazooka Shining Stars

The 1989 Bazooka Shining Stars set contains 22 standard-size (2 1/2 by 3 1/2 inch) cards. The fronts have white borders and a large yellow stripe; the vertically-oriented backs are pink, red and white and have career stats. The cards were inserted one per box of Bazooka Gum.

		MINT	EXC	G-VG
COMPLETE SET (22)		9.00	4.00	.90
COMMON PLAYER (1-22)		.35	.15	.03
☐ 1	Tim Belcher	.35	.15	.03
☐ 2	Damon Berryhill	.35	.15	.03
☐ 3	Wade Boggs	1.00	.40	.10
☐ 4	Jay Buhner	.45	.18	.04
☐ 5	Jose Canseco	1.25	.50	.12
☐ 6	Vince Coleman	.60	.25	.06
☐ 7	Cecil Espy	.35	.15	.03
☐ 8	Dave Gallagher	.35	.15	.03
☐ 9	Ron Gant	1.00	.40	.10
☐ 10	Kirk Gibson	.45	.18	.04
☐ 11	Paul Gibson	.35	.15	.03
☐ 12	Mark Grace	1.00	.40	.10
☐ 13	Tony Gwynn	.75	.30	.07
☐ 14	Rickey Henderson	1.00	.40	.10
☐ 15	Orel Hershiser	.60	.25	.06
☐ 16	Gregg Jefferies	.75	.30	.07
☐ 17	Ricky Jordan	.45	.18	.04
☐ 18	Chris Sabo	.60	.25	.06
☐ 19	Gary Sheffield	.60	.25	.06
☐ 20	Darryl Strawberry	1.00	.40	.10
☐ 21	Frank Viola	.45	.18	.04
☐ 22	Walt Weiss	.45	.18	.04

1990 Bazooka Shining Stars

The 1990 Bazooka Shining Stars set contains 22 cards with a mix of award winners, league leaders, and young stars. This standard-size (2 1/2 by 3 1/2") set was issued by Topps using the Bazooka name. Card backs were printed in blue and red on white card stock. Cards are numbered on the back; they were numbered by Topps alphabetically. The word "Bazooka" appears faintly as background for the statistics on the back of the card as well as appearing prominently on the front of each card.

		MINT	EXC	G-VG
COMPLETE SET (22)		8.00	3.50	.80
COMMON PLAYER (1-22)		.30	.12	.03
☐ 1	Kevin Mitchell	.50	.20	.05
☐ 2	Robin Yount	.50	.20	.05
☐ 3	Mark Davis	.30	.12	.03
☐ 4	Bret Saberhagen	.50	.20	.05
☐ 5	Fred McGriff	.50	.20	.05
☐ 6	Tony Gwynn	.60	.25	.06
☐ 7	Kirby Puckett	.75	.30	.07
☐ 8	Vince Coleman	.50	.20	.05
☐ 9	Rickey Henderson	.90	.40	.09
☐ 10	Ben McDonald	.75	.30	.07
☐ 11	Gregg Olson	.40	.16	.04
☐ 12	Todd Zeile	.50	.20	.05
☐ 13	Carlos Martinez	.30	.12	.03
☐ 14	Gregg Jefferies	.60	.25	.06
☐ 15	Craig Worthington	.30	.12	.03
☐ 16	Gary Sheffield	.40	.16	.04
☐ 17	Greg Briley	.30	.12	.03
☐ 18	Ken Griffey Jr.	1.50	.60	.15
☐ 19	Jerome Walton	.50	.20	.05
☐ 20	Bob Geren	.30	.12	.03
☐ 21	Tom Gordon	.40	.16	.04
☐ 22	Jim Abbott	.75	.30	.07

1991 Bazooka Shining Stars

The 1991 Bazooka Shining Stars set contains 22 cards featuring league leaders and rookie sensations. The standard-size (2 1/2 by 3 1/2") cards were produced by Topps for Bazooka. One card was inserted in each box of Bazooka Bubble Gum. The fronts are similar to the Topps regular issue, only that the "Shining Star" emblem appears at the card top and the Bazooka logo overlays the lower right corner of the picture. In a blue and red design on white card stock, the backs have statistics and biography. The cards are numbered on the back.

	MINT	EXC	G-VG
COMPLETE SET (22)	12.50	5.50	1.65
COMMON PLAYER (1-22)	.35	.15	.03
☐ 1 Barry Bonds	.75	.30	.07
☐ 2 Rickey Henderson	1.00	.40	.10
☐ 3 Bob Welch	.35	.15	.03
☐ 4 Doug Drabek	.35	.15	.03
☐ 5 Alex Fernandez	.45	.18	.04
☐ 6 Jose Offerman	.45	.18	.04
☐ 7 Frank Thomas	3.00	1.25	.30
☐ 8 Cecil Fielder	.75	.30	.07
☐ 9 Ryne Sandberg	1.00	.40	.10
☐ 10 George Brett	.60	.25	.06
☐ 11 Willie McGee	.45	.18	.04
☐ 12 Vince Coleman	.45	.18	.04
☐ 13 Hal Morris	.60	.25	.06
☐ 14 Delino DeShields	.45	.18	.04
☐ 15 Robin Ventura	1.00	.40	.10
☐ 16 Jeff Huson	.35	.15	.03
☐ 17 Felix Jose	.60	.25	.06
☐ 18 Dave Justice	2.00	.80	.20
☐ 19 Larry Walker	.45	.18	.04
☐ 20 Sandy Alomar Jr.	.60	.25	.06
☐ 21 Kevin Appier	.35	.15	.03
☐ 22 Scott Radinsky	.35	.15	.03

1958 Bell Brand

The 1958 Bell Brand Potato Chips set of 10 unnumbered cards features members of the Los Angeles Dodgers exclusively. Each card has a 1/4" dark green border, and the Gino Cimoli, Johnny Podres, and Duke Snider cards are more difficult to find; they are marked with an SP (short printed) in the checklist below. The cards measure 3" by 4". This set marks the first year for the Dodgers in Los Angeles and includes a Campanella card despite the fact that he never played for the team in California. The catalog designation is F339-1. Cards found still inside the original cellophane wrapper are valued at 50 percent more than the prices below.

	NRMT	VG-E	GOOD
COMPLETE SET (10)	1250.00	550.00	135.00
COMMON PLAYER (1-10)	45.00	20.00	6.75
☐ 1 Roy Campanella	150.00	67.50	22.50
☐ 2 Gino Cimoli SP	150.00	67.50	22.50
☐ 3 Don Drysdale	110.00	50.00	16.50
☐ 4 Jim Gilliam	45.00	20.00	6.75
☐ 5 Gil Hodges	90.00	40.00	13.50
☐ 6 Sandy Koufax	175.00	80.00	27.00
☐ 7 Johnny Podres SP	150.00	67.50	22.50
☐ 8 Pee Wee Reese	110.00	50.00	16.50
☐ 9 Duke Snider SP	300.00	135.00	45.00
☐ 10 Don Zimmer	45.00	20.00	6.75

1960 Bell Brand

The 1960 Bell Brand Potato Chips set of 20 full color, numbered cards features Los Angeles Dodgers only. Because these cards, measuring approximately 2 1/2" by 3 1/2", were issued in packages of potato chips, many cards suffered from stains. Clem Labine, Johnny Klippstein, and Walter Alston are somewhat more difficult to obtain than other cards in the set; they are marked with SP (short printed) in the checklist below. The catalog designation for this set is F339-2.

	NRMT	VG-E	GOOD
COMPLETE SET (20)	900.00	400.00	135.00
COMMON PLAYER (1-20)	18.00	7.50	2.50
☐ 1 Norm Larker	18.00	7.50	2.50
☐ 2 Duke Snider	90.00	40.00	13.50
☐ 3 Danny McDevitt	18.00	7.50	2.50
☐ 4 Jim Gilliam	22.00	9.50	3.15
☐ 5 Rip Repulski	18.00	7.50	2.50
☐ 6 Clem Labine SP	100.00	45.00	15.00
☐ 7 John Roseboro	18.00	7.50	2.50
☐ 8 Carl Furillo	27.00	12.00	4.00
☐ 9 Sandy Koufax	135.00	60.00	20.00
☐ 10 Joe Pignatano	18.00	7.50	2.50
☐ 11 Chuck Essegian	18.00	7.50	2.50
☐ 12 John Klippstein SP	100.00	45.00	15.00
☐ 13 Ed Roebuck	18.00	7.50	2.50
☐ 14 Don Demeter	18.00	7.50	2.50
☐ 15 Roger Craig	27.00	12.00	4.00
☐ 16 Stan Williams	18.00	7.50	2.50
☐ 17 Don Zimmer	22.00	9.50	3.15
☐ 18 Walt Alston SP	150.00	67.50	22.50
☐ 19 Johnny Podres	27.00	12.00	4.00
☐ 20 Maury Wills	45.00	20.00	6.75

1961 Bell Brand

The 1961 Bell Brand Potato Chips set of 20 full color cards features Los Angeles Dodger players only and is numbered by the uniform numbers of the players. The cards are slightly smaller (2 7/16" by 3 1/2") than the 1960 Bell Brand cards and are on thinner paper stock. The catalog designation is F339-3.

	NRMT	VG-E	GOOD
COMPLETE SET (20)	450.00	200.00	67.50
COMMON PLAYER	12.50	5.50	1.65
☐ 3 Willie Davis	15.00	6.50	2.15
☐ 4 Duke Snider	65.00	29.00	9.75
☐ 5 Norm Larker	12.50	5.50	1.65
☐ 8 John Roseboro	12.50	5.50	1.65
☐ 9 Wally Moon	12.50	5.50	1.65
☐ 11 Bob Lillis	12.50	5.50	1.65
☐ 12 Tom Davis	15.00	6.50	2.15
☐ 14 Gil Hodges	30.00	13.50	4.50
☐ 16 Don Demeter	12.50	5.50	1.65
☐ 19 Jim Gilliam .	15.00	6.50	2.15
☐ 22 John Podres	15.00	6.50	2.15
☐ 24 Walt Alston MG	25.00	11.00	3.50
☐ 30 Maury Wills	25.00	11.00	3.50
☐ 32 Sandy Koufax	110.00	50.00	16.50
☐ 34 Norm Sherry	12.50	5.50	1.65
☐ 37 Ed Roebuck	12.50	5.50	1.65
☐ 38 Roger Craig	18.00	7.50	2.50
☐ 40 Stan Williams	12.50	5.50	1.65
☐ 43 Charlie Neal	12.50	5.50	1.65
☐ 51 Larry Sherry	12.50	5.50	1.65

1962 Bell Brand

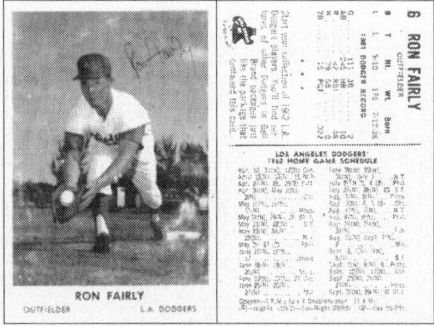

RON FAIRLY
OUTFIELDER   L.A. DODGERS

The 1962 Bell Brand Potato Chips set of 20 full color cards features Los Angeles Dodger players only and is numbered by the uniform numbers of the players. These cards were printed on a high quality glossy paper, much better than the previous two years, virtually eliminating the grease stains. This set is distinguished by a 1962 Home schedule on the backs of the cards. The cards measure 2 7/16" by 3 1/2", the same size as the year before. The catalog designation is F339-4.

	NRMT	VG-E	GOOD
COMPLETE SET (20)	450.00	200.00	67.50
COMMON PLAYER	12.50	5.50	1.65
☐ 3 Willie Davis	15.00	6.50	2.15
☐ 4 Duke Snider	65.00	29.00	9.75
☐ 6 Ron Fairly	12.50	5.50	1.65
☐ 8 John Roseboro	12.50	5.50	1.65
☐ 9 Wally Moon	12.50	5.50	1.65
☐ 12 Tom Davis	15.00	6.50	2.15
☐ 16 Ron Perranoski	12.50	5.50	1.65
☐ 19 Jim Gilliam	15.00	6.50	2.15
☐ 20 Daryl Spencer	12.50	5.50	1.65
☐ 22 John Podres	15.00	6.50	2.15
☐ 24 Walt Alston MG	25.00	11.00	3.50
☐ 25 Frank Howard	15.00	6.50	2.15
☐ 30 Maury Wills	25.00	11.00	3.50
☐ 32 Sandy Koufax	110.00	50.00	16.50
☐ 34 Norm Sherry	12.50	5.50	1.65
☐ 37 Ed Roebuck	12.50	5.50	1.65
☐ 40 Stan Williams	12.50	5.50	1.65
☐ 51 Larry Sherry	12.50	5.50	1.65
☐ 53 Don Drysdale	45.00	20.00	6.75
☐ 56 Lee Walls	12.50	5.50	1.65

1951 Berk Ross

HIT PARADE OF CHAMPIONS
1951
Trade Mark Reg. U.S. Pat. Off.
RICHIE ASHBURN
Outfield, Philadelphia Phillies
Member of Philadelphia Phillies
National League Champions
Born March 19, 1927
Tilden, Nebraska
Height 5-11, Weight 170
Throws Right, Bats Left
1950 Hit .303 in 151 Games
No. 1-9   © Berk Ross Inc., New York, N.Y.

The 1951 Berk Ross set consists of 72 cards (each measuring 2 1/16" by 2 1/2") with tinted photographs, divided evenly into four series (designated in the checklist as A, B, C and D). The cards were marketed in boxes containing two card panels, without gum, and the set includes stars of other sports as well as baseball players. Intact panels are worth 20 percent more than the sum of the individual cards. The catalog designation is W532-1. In every series the first ten cards are baseball players; the set has a heavy emphasis on Yankees and Phillies players as they were in the World Series the year before.

		NRMT	VG-E	GOOD
COMPLETE SET (72)		900.00	400.00	135.00
COMMON BASEBALL		8.00	3.50	.80
COMMON FOOTBALL		8.00	3.50	.80
COMMON OTHERS		5.00	2.25	.50
☐ A1	Al Rosen	12.00	5.25	1.50
☐ A2	Bob Lemon	16.50	7.00	2.35
☐ A3	Phil Rizzuto	21.00	9.00	3.00
☐ A4	Hank Bauer	12.00	5.25	1.50
☐ A5	Billy Johnson	8.00	3.50	.80
☐ A6	Jerry Coleman	8.00	3.50	.80
☐ A7	Johnny Mize	21.00	9.00	3.00
☐ A8	Dom DiMaggio	12.00	5.25	1.50
☐ A9	Richie Ashburn	15.00	6.50	2.15
☐ A10	Del Ennis	8.00	3.50	.80
☐ A11	Bob Cousy	80.00	36.00	12.00
☐ A12	Dick Schnittker	5.00	2.25	.50
☐ A13	Ezzard Charles	8.00	3.50	.80
☐ A14	Leon Hart	10.00	4.50	1.25
☐ A15	James Martin	8.00	3.50	.80
☐ A16	Ben Hogan	10.00	4.50	1.25
☐ A17	Bill Durnan	12.00	5.25	1.50
☐ A18	Bill Quackenbush	8.00	3.50	.80
☐ B1	Stan Musial	80.00	36.00	12.00
☐ B2	Warren Spahn	27.00	12.00	4.00
☐ B3	Tom Henrich	12.00	5.25	1.50
☐ B4	Yogi Berra	60.00	27.00	9.00
☐ B5	Joe DiMaggio	125.00	57.50	18.75
☐ B6	Bobby Brown	12.00	5.25	1.50
☐ B7	Granny Hamner	8.00	3.50	.80
☐ B8	Willie Jones	8.00	3.50	.80
☐ B9	Stan Lopata	8.00	3.50	.80
☐ B10	Mike Goliat	8.00	3.50	.80
☐ B11	Sherman White	8.00	3.50	.80
☐ B12	Joe Maxim	6.00	2.50	.60
☐ B13	Ray Robinson	21.00	9.00	3.00
☐ B14	Doak Walker	15.00	6.50	2.15
☐ B15	Emil Sitko	5.00	2.25	.50
☐ B16	Jack Stewart	5.00	2.25	.50
☐ B17	Dick Button	8.00	3.50	.80
☐ B18	Melvin Patton	5.00	2.25	.50
☐ C1	Ralph Kiner	21.00	9.00	3.00
☐ C2	Bill Goodman	8.00	3.50	.80
☐ C3	Allie Reynolds	12.00	5.25	1.50
☐ C4	Vic Raschi	12.00	5.25	1.50
☐ C5	Joe Page	10.00	4.50	1.25
☐ C6	Eddie Lopat	12.00	5.25	1.50
☐ C7	Andy Seminick	8.00	3.50	.80
☐ C8	Dick Sisler	8.00	3.50	.80
☐ C9	Eddie Waitkus	8.00	3.50	.80
☐ C10	Ken Heintzelman	8.00	3.50	.80
☐ C11	Paul Unruh	5.00	2.25	.50
☐ C12	Jake LaMotta	16.50	7.00	2.35
☐ C13	Ike Williams	5.00	2.25	.50
☐ C14	Wade Walker	5.00	2.25	.50
☐ C15	Rodney Franz	5.00	2.25	.50

		NRMT	VG-E	GOOD
☐	C16 Sid Abel	12.00	5.25	1.50
☐	C17 Claire Sherman	5.00	2.25	.50
☐	C18 Jesse Owens	15.00	6.50	2.15
☐	D1 Gene Woodling	10.00	4.50	1.25
☐	D2 Cliff Mapes	8.00	3.50	.80
☐	D3 Fred Sanford	8.00	3.50	.80
☐	D4 Tommy Byrne	8.00	3.50	.80
☐	D5 Whitey Ford	27.00	12.00	4.00
☐	D6 Jim Konstanty	8.00	3.50	.80
☐	D7 Russ Meyer	8.00	3.50	.80
☐	D8 Robin Roberts	21.00	9.00	3.00
☐	D9 Curt Simmons	10.00	4.50	1.25
☐	D10 Sam Jethroe	8.00	3.50	.80
☐	D11 Bill Sharman	15.00	6.50	2.15
☐	D12 Sandy Saddler	5.00	2.25	.50
☐	D13 Margaret DuPont	5.00	2.25	.50
☐	D14 Arnold Galiffa	10.00	4.50	1.25
☐	D15 Charlie Justice	15.00	6.50	2.15
☐	D16 Glen Cunningham	6.00	2.50	.60
☐	D17 Gregory Rice	5.00	2.25	.50
☐	D18 Harrison Dillard	6.00	2.50	.60

1952 Berk Ross

The 1952 Berk Ross set of 72 unnumbered, tinted photocards, each measuring 2" by 3", seems to have been patterned after the highly successful 1951 Bowman set. The reverses of Ewell Blackwell and Nellie Fox are transposed while Phil Rizzuto comes with two different poses. There is a card of Joe DiMaggio even though he retired after the 1951 season. The catalog designation for this set is W532-2, and the cards have been assigned numbers in the alphabetical checklist below.

		NRMT	VG-E	GOOD
	COMPLETE SET (72)	4500.00	2000.00	500.00
	COMMON PLAYER (1-71)	13.50	6.00	1.85
☐	1 Richie Ashburn	40.00	18.00	6.00
☐	2 Hank Bauer	20.00	8.50	2.75
☐	3 Yogi Berra	150.00	67.50	22.50
☐	4 Ewell Blackwell UER	22.50	9.75	3.25
	(photo actually Nellie Fox)			
☐	5 Bobby Brown	20.00	8.50	2.75
☐	6 Jim Busby	13.50	6.00	1.85
☐	7 Roy Campanella	150.00	67.50	22.50
☐	8 Chico Carrasquel	13.50	6.00	1.85
☐	9 Jerry Coleman	13.50	6.00	1.85
☐	10 Joe Collins	13.50	6.00	1.85
☐	11 Alvin Dark	16.50	7.00	2.35
☐	12 Dom DiMaggio	20.00	8.50	2.75
☐	13 Joe DiMaggio	750.00	325.00	110.00
☐	14 Larry Doby	22.50	9.75	3.25
☐	15 Bobby Doerr	45.00	20.00	6.75
☐	16 Bob Elliott	13.50	6.00	1.85
☐	17 Del Ennis	13.50	6.00	1.85
☐	18 Ferris Fain	13.50	6.00	1.85
☐	19 Bob Feller	90.00	40.00	13.50
☐	20 Nellie Fox UER	22.50	9.75	3.25
	(photo actually Ewell Blackwell)			
☐	21 Ned Garver	13.50	6.00	1.85
☐	22 Clint Hartung	13.50	6.00	1.85
☐	23 Jim Hearn	13.50	6.00	1.85

☐	24 Gil Hodges	45.00	20.00	6.75
☐	25 Monte Irvin	45.00	20.00	6.75
☐	26 Larry Jansen	13.50	6.00	1.85
☐	27 Sheldon Jones	13.50	6.00	1.85
☐	28 George Kell	40.00	18.00	6.00
☐	29 Monte Kennedy	13.50	6.00	1.85
☐	30 Ralph Kiner	50.00	22.50	7.50
☐	31 Dave Koslo	13.50	6.00	1.85
☐	32 Bob Kuzava	13.50	6.00	1.85
☐	33 Bob Lemon	40.00	18.00	6.00
☐	34 Whitey Lockman	13.50	6.00	1.85
☐	35 Ed Lopat	22.50	9.75	3.25
☐	36 Sal Maglie	18.00	7.50	2.50
☐	37 Mickey Mantle	1250.00	500.00	150.00
☐	38 Billy Martin	50.00	22.50	7.50
☐	39 Willie Mays	425.00	190.00	63.00
☐	40 Gil McDougald	20.00	8.50	2.75
☐	41 Minnie Minoso	22.50	9.75	3.25
☐	42 Johnny Mize	50.00	22.50	7.50
☐	43 Tom Morgan	13.50	6.00	1.85
☐	44 Don Mueller	13.50	6.00	1.85
☐	45 Stan Musial	250.00	110.00	37.50
☐	46 Don Newcombe	22.50	9.75	3.25
☐	47 Ray Noble	13.50	6.00	1.85
☐	48 Joe Ostrowski	13.50	6.00	1.85
☐	49 Mel Parnell	16.50	7.00	2.35
☐	50 Vic Raschi	18.00	7.50	2.50
☐	51 Pee Wee Reese	75.00	34.00	11.25
☐	52 Allie Reynolds	22.50	9.75	3.25
☐	53 Bill Rigney	13.50	6.00	1.85
☐	54A Phil Rizzuto	50.00	22.50	7.50
	(bunting)			
☐	54B Phil Rizzuto	50.00	22.50	7.50
	(swinging)			
☐	55 Robin Roberts	45.00	20.00	6.75
☐	56 Eddie Robinson	13.50	6.00	1.85
☐	57 Jackie Robinson	250.00	110.00	37.50
☐	58 Preacher Roe	18.00	7.50	2.50
☐	59 Johnny Sain	22.50	9.75	3.25
☐	60 Red Schoendienst	45.00	20.00	6.75
☐	61 Duke Snider	150.00	67.50	22.50
☐	62 George Spencer	13.50	6.00	1.85
☐	63 Eddie Stanky	16.50	7.00	2.35
☐	64 Hank Thompson	13.50	6.00	1.85
☐	65 Bobby Thomson	20.00	8.50	2.75
☐	66 Vic Wertz	13.50	6.00	1.85
☐	67 Wally Westlake	13.50	6.00	1.85
☐	68 Wes Westrum	13.50	6.00	1.85
☐	69 Ted Williams	350.00	160.00	52.50
☐	70 Gene Woodling	16.50	7.00	2.35
☐	71 Gus Zernial	13.50	6.00	1.85

1986 Big League Chew

This 12-card set was produced by Big League Chew and was inserted in with their packages of chewing gum, which were shaped and styled after a pouch of chewing tobacco. The cards were found one per pouch of shredded chewing gum or were available through a mail-in offer of two coupons and $2.00 for a complete set. The players featured are members of the 500 career home run club. The backs are printed in blue ink on white card stock. The cards are standard size, 2 1/2" by 3 1/2" and are subtitled "Home Run Legends." The front of each card shows a year inside a small flag; the year is the year that player passed 500 homers.

	MINT	EXC	G-VG
COMPLETE SET (12)	5.00	2.25	.50
COMMON PLAYER (1-12)	.35	.15	.03
☐ 1 Hank Aaron	.75	.30	.07
☐ 2 Babe Ruth	1.25	.50	.12
☐ 3 Willie Mays	.75	.30	.07
☐ 4 Frank Robinson	.50	.20	.05
☐ 5 Harmon Killebrew	.35	.15	.03
☐ 6 Mickey Mantle	1.25	.50	.12
☐ 7 Jimmie Foxx	.35	.15	.03
☐ 8 Ted Williams	.75	.30	.07
☐ 9 Ernie Banks	.50	.20	.05
☐ 10 Eddie Mathews	.35	.15	.03
☐ 11 Mel Ott	.35	.15	.03
☐ 12 500 HR Members	.35	.15	.03

1991 Bleachers 23K Frank Thomas

These three 23-karat gold cards were produced by Bleachers and measure the standard size (2 1/2" by 3 1/2"). On a gold card front, posed color player photos are enframed by different color borders (1-blue; 2-black; 3-red). The top of each photo is extended by a small semi-circle that is intersected by two border stripes. The player's name, team name, and position are printed in white lettering in the border beneath the picture. On gray, yellow, white, and red stripes, the back has the player's name, biography, statistics, highlights, and the serial number (1 of 10,000), inside a black border. It is reported that the production run was limited to 10,000 sets and 1,500 uncut numbered strips. The player's signature, team name, and jersey number are written in gold at the bottom of the card. The cards are numbered on the back.

	MINT	EXC	G-VG
COMPLETE SET (3)	20.00	8.50	2.75
COMMON PLAYER (1-3)	8.00	3.50	.80
☐ 1 Frank Thomas Auburn Tigers	8.00	3.50	.80
☐ 2 Frank Thomas Sarasota White Sox	8.00	3.50	.80
☐ 3 Frank Thomas Birmingham Barons	8.00	3.50	.80

1987 Boardwalk and Baseball

This 33-card set was produced by Topps for distribution by the "Boardwalk and Baseball" Theme Park located near Orlando, Florida. The cards are standard size, 2 1/2" by 3 1/2", and come in a custom blue collector box. The full-color fronts are surrounded by a pink and black frame border. The card backs are

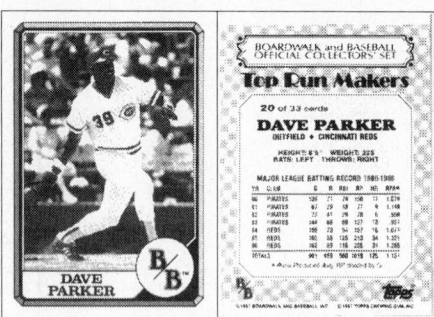

printed in pink and black on white card stock. The set is subtitled "Top Run Makers." Hence no pitchers are included in the set. The checklist for the set is given on the back panel of the box.

	MINT	EXC	G-VG
COMPLETE SET (33)	5.00	2.25	.50
COMMON PLAYER (1-33)	.12	.05	.01
☐ 1 Mike Schmidt	.75	.30	.07
☐ 2 Eddie Murray	.50	.20	.05
☐ 3 Dale Murphy	.40	.16	.04
☐ 4 Dave Winfield	.30	.12	.03
☐ 5 Jim Rice	.20	.08	.02
☐ 6 Cecil Cooper	.12	.05	.01
☐ 7 Dwight Evans	.15	.06	.01
☐ 8 Rickey Henderson	.75	.30	.07
☐ 9 Robin Yount	.50	.20	.05
☐ 10 Andre Dawson	.40	.16	.04
☐ 11 Gary Carter	.20	.08	.02
☐ 12 Keith Hernandez	.15	.06	.01
☐ 13 George Brett	.40	.16	.04
☐ 14 Bill Buckner	.12	.05	.01
☐ 15 Tony Armas	.12	.05	.01
☐ 16 Harold Baines	.15	.06	.01
☐ 17 Don Baylor	.12	.05	.01
☐ 18 Steve Garvey	.20	.08	.02
☐ 19 Lance Parrish	.15	.06	.01
☐ 20 Dave Parker	.15	.06	.01
☐ 21 Buddy Bell	.12	.05	.01
☐ 22 Cal Ripken	.75	.30	.07
☐ 23 Bob Horner	.12	.05	.01
☐ 24 Tim Raines	.25	.10	.02
☐ 25 Jack Clark	.15	.06	.01
☐ 26 Leon Durham	.12	.05	.01
☐ 27 Pedro Guerrero	.15	.06	.01
☐ 28 Kent Hrbek	.20	.08	.02
☐ 29 Kirk Gibson	.25	.10	.02
☐ 30 Ryne Sandberg	.75	.30	.07
☐ 31 Wade Boggs	.60	.25	.06
☐ 32 Don Mattingly	.60	.25	.06
☐ 33 Darryl Strawberry	.75	.30	.07

1987 Bohemian Padres

The Bohemian Hearth Bread Company issued this 22-card set of San Diego Padres. The cards measure 2 1/2" by 3 1/2" and feature a distinctive yellow border on the front of the cards. Card backs provide career year-by-year statistics and are numbered.

	MINT	EXC	G-VG
COMPLETE SET (22)	45.00	20.00	6.75
COMMON PLAYER (1-22)	.75	.30	.07
☐ 1 Garry Templeton	1.00	.40	.10
☐ 4 Joe Cora	1.00	.40	.10
☐ 5 Randy Ready	1.00	.40	.10
☐ 6 Steve Garvey	6.00	2.50	.60
☐ 7 Kevin Mitchell	9.00	4.00	.90
☐ 8 John Kruk	2.50	1.00	.25
☐ 9 Benito Santiago	6.00	2.50	.60
☐ 10 Larry Bowa MG	1.00	.40	.10
☐ 11 Tim Flannery	.75	.30	.07
☐ 14 Carmelo Martinez	1.00	.40	.10
☐ 16 Marvell Wynne	.75	.30	.07
☐ 19 Tony Gwynn	15.00	6.50	2.15

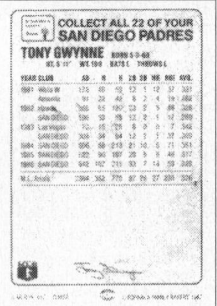

☐ 7	Profile with glove in front of head; facsimile autograph) DP	300.00	135.00	45.00
☐ 8	Leaping over second base, ready to throw	600.00	270.00	90.00
☐ 9	Portrait, holding glove over head	600.00	270.00	90.00
☐ 10	Portrait, holding bat perpendicular to body	600.00	270.00	90.00
☐ 11	Reaching for throw, glove near ankle	600.00	270.00	90.00
☐ 12	Leaping for throw, no scoreboard in background	600.00	270.00	90.00
☐ 13	Portrait, holding bat parallel to body	600.00	270.00	90.00

☐ 21	James Steels	.75	.30	.07
☐ 22	Stan Jefferson	.75	.30	.07
☐ 30	Eric Show	1.00	.40	.10
☐ 31	Ed Whitson	1.00	.40	.10
☐ 34	Storm Davis	1.50	.60	.15
☐ 37	Craig Lefferts	1.00	.40	.10
☐ 40	Andy Hawkins	1.00	.40	.10
☐ 41	Lance McCullers	.90	.40	.09
☐ 43	Dave Dravecky	2.50	1.00	.25
☐ 54	Rich Gossage	2.50	1.00	.25

1947 Bond Bread

The 1947 Bond Bread Jackie Robinson set features 13 unnumbered cards of Jackie in different action or portrait poses; each card measures approximately 2 1/4" by 3 1/2". Card number 7, which is the only card in the set to contain a facsimile autograph, was apparently issued in greater quantity than other cards in the set. Several of the cards have a horizontal format; these are marked in the checklist below by HOR. The catalog designation is D302.

	NRMT	VG-E	GOOD
COMPLETE SET (13)	7000.00	2800.00	900.00
COMMON PLAYER (1-13)	600.00	270.00	90.00

☐ 1	Sliding into base, cap, ump in photo, HOR	600.00	270.00	90.00
☐ 2	Running down 3rd base line	600.00	270.00	90.00
☐ 3	Batting, bat behind head, facing camera	600.00	270.00	90.00
☐ 4	Moving towards second, throw almost to glove, HOR	600.00	270.00	90.00
☐ 5	Taking throw at first, HOR	600.00	270.00	90.00
☐ 6	Jumping high in the air for ball	600.00	270.00	90.00

1948 Bowman

The 48-card Bowman set of 1948 was the first major set of the post-war period. Each 2 1/16" by 2 1/2" card had a black and white photo of a current player, with his biographical information printed in black ink on a gray back. Due to the printing process and the 36-card sheet size upon which Bowman was then printing, the 12 cards marked with an SP in the checklist are scarcer numerically, as they were removed from the printing sheet in order to make room for the 12 high numbers (37-48). Many cards are found with over-printed, transposed, or blank backs. The set features the Rookie Cards of Hall of Famers Yogi Berra, Ralph Kiner, Stan Musial, Red Schoendienst, and Warren Spahn. Half of the cards in the set feature New York players (Yankees or Giants).

	NRMT	VG-E	GOOD
COMPLETE SET (48)	3500.00	1500.00	350.00
COMMON PLAYER (1-36)	21.00	9.00	3.00
COMMON PLAYER (37-48)	28.00	12.50	4.00
COMMON PLAYER SP	35.00	15.75	5.25

☐ 1	Bob Elliott	95.00	15.00	3.00
☐ 2	Ewell Blackwell	42.00	18.00	5.00
☐ 3	Ralph Kiner	160.00	72.00	24.00
☐ 4	Johnny Mize	100.00	45.00	15.00
☐ 5	Bob Feller	225.00	100.00	33.00
☐ 6	Yogi Berra	525.00	225.00	75.00
☐ 7	Pete Reiser SP	56.00	26.00	6.00
☐ 8	Phil Rizzuto SP	240.00	100.00	30.00
☐ 9	Walker Cooper	21.00	9.00	3.00
☐ 10	Buddy Rosar	21.00	9.00	3.00
☐ 11	Johnny Lindell	21.00	9.00	3.00
☐ 12	Johnny Sain	50.00	22.50	7.50
☐ 13	Willard Marshall SP	36.00	16.25	5.50
☐ 14	Allie Reynolds	50.00	22.50	7.50
☐ 15	Eddie Joost	21.00	9.00	3.00
☐ 16	Jack Lohrke SP	36.00	16.25	5.50
☐ 17	Enos Slaughter	100.00	45.00	15.00
☐ 18	Warren Spahn	275.00	120.00	40.00
☐ 19	Tommy Henrich	28.00	12.50	4.00
☐ 20	Buddy Kerr SP	36.00	16.25	5.50
☐ 21	Ferris Fain	24.00	10.50	3.50
☐ 22	Floyd Bevens SP	38.00	17.00	4.50
☐ 23	Larry Jansen	24.00	10.50	3.50
☐ 24	Dutch Leonard SP	38.00	17.00	4.50

☐ 25	Barney McCosky	21.00	9.00	3.00
☐ 26	Frank Shea SP	36.00	16.25	5.50
☐ 27	Sid Gordon	21.00	9.00	3.00
☐ 28	Emil Verban SP	36.00	16.25	5.50
☐ 29	Joe Page SP	45.00	20.00	6.75
☐ 30	Whitey Lockman SP	42.00	18.00	5.25
☐ 31	Bill McCahan	21.00	9.00	3.00
☐ 32	Bill Rigney	24.00	10.50	3.50
☐ 33	Bill Johnson	21.00	9.00	3.00
☐ 34	Sheldon Jones SP	36.00	16.25	5.50
☐ 35	Snuffy Stirnweiss	24.00	10.50	3.50
☐ 36	Stan Musial	825.00	375.00	90.00
☐ 37	Clint Hartung	33.00	15.00	5.00
☐ 38	Red Schoendienst	150.00	67.50	22.50
☐ 39	Augie Galan	28.00	12.50	4.00
☐ 40	Marty Marion	75.00	34.00	11.25
☐ 41	Rex Barney	33.00	15.00	5.00
☐ 42	Ray Poat	28.00	12.50	4.00
☐ 43	Bruce Edwards	28.00	12.50	4.00
☐ 44	Johnny Wyrostek	28.00	12.50	4.00
☐ 45	Hank Sauer	40.00	18.00	6.00
☐ 46	Herman Wehmeier	28.00	12.50	4.00
☐ 47	Bobby Thomson	75.00	34.00	11.25
☐ 48	Dave Koslo	65.00	15.00	3.00

1949 Bowman

JOHNNY VANDER MEER

The cards in this 240-card set measure 2 1/16" by 2 1/2". In 1949 Bowman took an intermediate step between black and white and full color with this set of tinted photos on colored backgrounds. Collectors should note the series price variations, which reflect some inconsistencies in the printing process. There are four major varieties in name printing, which are noted in the checklist below: NOF: name on front; NNOF: no name on front; PR: printed name on back; and SCR: script name on back. These variations resulted when Bowman used twelve of the lower numbers to fill out the last press sheet of 36 cards, adding to numbers 217-240. Cards 1-3 and 5-73 can be found with either gray or white backs. The set features the Rookie Cards of Hall of Famers Roy Campanella, Bob Lemon, Robin Roberts, Duke Snider, and Early Wynn as well as Rookie Cards of Richie Ashburn and Gil Hodges.

	NRMT	VG-E	GOOD
COMPLETE SET (240)	16000.00	7000.00	1750.00
COMMON CARD 1-3/5-36	17.00	7.25	2.50
COMMON CARD (37-72)	20.00	8.50	2.75
COMMON CARD (4/74-108)	17.00	7.25	2.50
COMMON CARD (109-144)	14.50	6.50	1.75
COMMON CARD (145-180)	90.00	40.00	13.50
COMMON CARD (181-216)	80.00	36.00	12.00
COMMON CARD (217-240)	80.00	36.00	12.00

☐ 1	Vern Bickford	80.00	12.00	2.00
☐ 2	Whitey Lockman	20.00	8.50	2.75
☐ 3	Bob Porterfield	17.00	7.25	2.50
☐ 4A	Jerry Priddy NNOF	17.00	7.25	2.50
☐ 4B	Jerry Priddy NOF	40.00	18.00	6.00
☐ 5	Hank Sauer	20.00	8.50	2.75
☐ 6	Phil Cavarretta	22.00	9.50	3.15
☐ 7	Joe Dobson	17.00	7.25	2.50
☐ 8	Murry Dickson	17.00	7.25	2.50
☐ 9	Ferris Fain	20.00	8.50	2.75
☐ 10	Ted Gray	17.00	7.25	2.50
☐ 11	Lou Boudreau MG	60.00	27.00	9.00

☐ 12	Cass Michaels	17.00	7.25	2.50
☐ 13	Bob Chesnes	17.00	7.25	2.50
☐ 14	Curt Simmons	27.00	12.00	4.00
☐ 15	Ned Garver	17.00	7.25	2.50
☐ 16	Al Kozar	17.00	7.25	2.50
☐ 17	Earl Torgeson	17.00	7.25	2.50
☐ 18	Bobby Thomson	30.00	13.50	4.50
☐ 19	Bobby Brown	50.00	22.50	7.50
☐ 20	Gene Hermanski	17.00	7.25	2.50
☐ 21	Frank Baumholtz	17.00	7.25	2.50
☐ 22	Peanuts Lowrey	17.00	7.25	2.50
☐ 23	Bobby Doerr	65.00	29.00	9.75
☐ 24	Stan Musial	500.00	225.00	75.00
☐ 25	Carl Scheib	17.00	7.25	2.50
☐ 26	George Kell	50.00	22.50	7.50
☐ 27	Bob Feller	160.00	72.00	24.00
☐ 28	Don Kolloway	17.00	7.25	2.50
☐ 29	Ralph Kiner	90.00	40.00	13.50
☐ 30	Andy Seminick	17.00	7.25	2.50
☐ 31	Dick Kokos	17.00	7.25	2.50
☐ 32	Eddie Yost	22.00	9.50	3.15
☐ 33	Warren Spahn	170.00	75.00	25.00
☐ 34	Dave Koslo	17.00	7.25	2.50
☐ 35	Vic Raschi	50.00	22.50	7.50
☐ 36	Pee Wee Reese	210.00	80.00	25.00
☐ 37	Johnny Wyrostek	20.00	8.50	2.75
☐ 38	Emil Verban	20.00	8.50	2.75
☐ 39	Billy Goodman	22.00	9.50	3.15
☐ 40	Red Munger	20.00	8.50	2.75
☐ 41	Lou Brissie	20.00	8.50	2.75
☐ 42	Hoot Evers	20.00	8.50	2.75
☐ 43	Dale Mitchell	22.00	9.50	3.15
☐ 44	Dave Philley	20.00	8.50	2.75
☐ 45	Wally Westlake	20.00	8.50	2.75
☐ 46	Robin Roberts	275.00	120.00	40.00
☐ 47	Johnny Sain	33.00	15.00	5.00
☐ 48	Willard Marshall	20.00	8.50	2.75
☐ 49	Frank Shea	20.00	8.50	2.75
☐ 50	Jackie Robinson	750.00	325.00	110.00
☐ 51	Herman Wehmeier	20.00	8.50	2.75
☐ 52	Johnny Schmitz	20.00	8.50	2.75
☐ 53	Jack Kramer	20.00	8.50	2.75
☐ 54	Marty Marion	27.00	12.00	4.00
☐ 55	Eddie Joost	20.00	8.50	2.75
☐ 56	Pat Mullin	20.00	8.50	2.75
☐ 57	Gene Bearden	22.00	9.50	3.15
☐ 58	Bob Elliott	22.00	9.50	3.15
☐ 59	Jack Lohrke	20.00	8.50	2.75
☐ 60	Yogi Berra	300.00	135.00	45.00
☐ 61	Rex Barney	20.00	8.50	2.75
☐ 62	Grady Hatton	20.00	8.50	2.75
☐ 63	Andy Pafko	22.00	9.50	3.15
☐ 64	Dom DiMaggio	27.00	12.00	4.00
☐ 65	Enos Slaughter	80.00	36.00	12.00
☐ 66	Elmer Valo	20.00	8.50	2.75
☐ 67	Alvin Dark	33.00	15.00	5.00
☐ 68	Sheldon Jones	20.00	8.50	2.75
☐ 69	Tommy Henrich	27.00	12.00	4.00
☐ 70	Carl Furillo	60.00	27.00	9.00
☐ 71	Vern Stephens	22.00	9.50	3.15
☐ 72	Tommy Holmes	22.00	9.50	3.15
☐ 73	Billy Cox	32.00	14.25	4.75
☐ 74	Tom McBride	17.00	7.25	2.50
☐ 75	Eddie Mayo	17.00	7.25	2.50
☐ 76	Bill Nicholson	20.00	8.50	2.75
☐ 77	Ernie Bonham	17.00	7.25	2.50
☐ 78A	Sam Zoldak NNOF	17.00	7.25	2.50
☐ 78B	Sam Zoldak NOF	40.00	18.00	6.00
☐ 79	Ron Northey	17.00	7.25	2.50
☐ 80	Bill McCahan	17.00	7.25	2.50
☐ 81	Virgil Stallcup	17.00	7.25	2.50
☐ 82	Joe Page	24.00	10.50	3.50
☐ 83A	Bob Scheffing NNOF	17.00	7.25	2.50
☐ 83B	Bob Scheffing NOF	40.00	18.00	6.00
☐ 84	Roy Campanella	675.00	300.00	90.00
☐ 85A	Johnny Mize NNOF	75.00	34.00	11.25
☐ 85B	Johnny Mize NOF	135.00	60.00	20.00
☐ 86	Johnny Pesky	24.00	10.50	3.50
☐ 87	Randy Gumpert	17.00	7.25	2.50
☐ 88A	Bill Salkeld NNOF	17.00	7.25	2.50
☐ 88B	Bill Salkeld NOF	40.00	18.00	6.00
☐ 89	Mizell Platt	17.00	7.25	2.50
☐ 90	Gil Coan	17.00	7.25	2.50
☐ 91	Dick Wakefield	17.00	7.25	2.50
☐ 92	Willie Jones	17.00	7.25	2.50
☐ 93	Ed Stevens	17.00	7.25	2.50
☐ 94	Mickey Vernon	32.00	14.25	4.75
☐ 95	Howie Pollet	20.00	8.50	2.75
☐ 96	Taft Wright	17.00	7.25	2.50
☐ 97	Danny Litwhiler	17.00	7.25	2.50
☐ 98A	Phil Rizzuto NNOF	100.00	45.00	15.00
☐ 98B	Phil Rizzuto NOF	200.00	90.00	30.00
☐ 99	Frank Gustine	17.00	7.25	2.50
☐ 100	Gil Hodges	210.00	80.00	25.00

☐	101	Sid Gordon	17.00	7.25	2.50
☐	102	Stan Spence	17.00	7.25	2.50
☐	103	Joe Tipton	17.00	7.25	2.50
☐	104	Eddie Stanky	27.00	12.00	4.00
☐	105	Bill Kennedy	17.00	7.25	2.50
☐	106	Jake Early	17.00	7.25	2.50
☐	107	Eddie Lake	17.00	7.25	2.50
☐	108	Ken Heintzelman	17.00	7.25	2.50
☐	109A	Ed Fitzgerald SCR	14.50	6.50	1.75
☐	109B	Ed Fitzgerald PR	36.00	16.25	5.50
☐	110	Early Wynn	125.00	57.50	18.75
☐	111	Red Schoendienst	75.00	34.00	11.25
☐	112	Sam Chapman	14.50	6.50	1.75
☐	113	Ray LaManno	14.50	6.50	1.75
☐	114	Allie Reynolds	30.00	13.50	4.50
☐	115	Dutch Leonard	14.50	6.50	1.75
☐	116	Joe Hatton	14.50	6.50	1.75
☐	117	Walker Cooper	14.50	6.50	1.75
☐	118	Sam Mele	14.50	6.50	1.75
☐	119	Floyd Baker	14.50	6.50	1.75
☐	120	Cliff Fannin	14.50	6.50	1.75
☐	121	Mark Christman	14.50	6.50	1.75
☐	122	George Vico	14.50	6.50	1.75
☐	123	Johnny Blatnick	14.50	6.50	1.75
☐	124A	Danny Murtaugh SCR	14.50	6.50	1.75
☐	124B	Danny Murtaugh PR	36.00	16.25	5.50
☐	125	Ken Keltner	14.50	6.50	1.75
☐	126A	Al Brazle SCR	14.50	6.50	1.75
☐	126B	Al Brazle PR	36.00	16.25	5.50
☐	127A	Hank Majeski SCR	14.50	6.50	1.75
☐	127B	Hank Majeski PR	36.00	16.25	5.50
☐	128	Johnny VanderMeer	25.00	11.00	3.50
☐	129	Bill Johnson	14.50	6.50	1.75
☐	130	Harry Walker	14.50	6.50	1.75
☐	131	Paul Lehner	14.50	6.50	1.75
☐	132A	Al Evans SCR	14.50	6.50	1.75
☐	132B	Al Evans PR	36.00	16.25	5.50
☐	133	Aaron Robinson	14.50	6.50	1.75
☐	134	Hank Borowy	14.50	6.50	1.75
☐	135	Stan Rojek	14.50	6.50	1.75
☐	136	Hank Edwards	14.50	6.50	1.75
☐	137	Ted Wilks	14.50	6.50	1.75
☐	138	Buddy Rosar	14.50	6.50	1.75
☐	139	Hank Arft	14.50	6.50	1.75
☐	140	Ray Scarborough	14.50	6.50	1.75
☐	141	Ulysses Lupien	14.50	6.50	1.75
☐	142	Eddie Waitkus	18.00	7.50	2.50
☐	143A	Bob Dillinger SCR	14.50	6.50	1.75
☐	143B	Bob Dillinger PR	36.00	16.25	5.50
☐	144	Mickey Haefner	14.50	6.50	1.75
☐	145	Sylvester Donnelly	90.00	40.00	13.50
☐	146	Mike McCormick	90.00	40.00	13.50
☐	147	Bert Singleton	90.00	40.00	13.50
☐	148	Bob Swift	90.00	40.00	13.50
☐	149	Roy Partee	90.00	40.00	13.50
☐	150	Allie Clark	90.00	40.00	13.50
☐	151	Mickey Harris	90.00	40.00	13.50
☐	152	Clarence Maddern	90.00	40.00	13.50
☐	153	Phil Masi	90.00	40.00	13.50
☐	154	Clint Hartung	90.00	40.00	13.50
☐	155	Mickey Guerra	90.00	40.00	13.50
☐	156	Al Zarilla	90.00	40.00	13.50
☐	157	Walt Masterson	90.00	40.00	13.50
☐	158	Harry Brecheen	100.00	45.00	15.00
☐	159	Glen Moulder	90.00	40.00	13.50
☐	160	Jim Blackburn	90.00	40.00	13.50
☐	161	Jocko Thompson	90.00	40.00	13.50
☐	162	Preacher Roe	140.00	63.00	21.00
☐	163	Clyde McCullough	90.00	40.00	13.50
☐	164	Vic Wertz	100.00	45.00	15.00
☐	165	Snuffy Stirnweiss	100.00	45.00	15.00
☐	166	Mike Tresh	90.00	40.00	13.50
☐	167	Babe Martin	90.00	40.00	13.50
☐	168	Doyle Lade	90.00	40.00	13.50
☐	169	Jeff Heath	90.00	40.00	13.50
☐	170	Bill Rigney	100.00	45.00	15.00
☐	171	Dick Fowler	90.00	40.00	13.50
☐	172	Eddie Pellagrini	90.00	40.00	13.50
☐	173	Eddie Stewart	90.00	40.00	13.50
☐	174	Terry Moore	115.00	50.00	15.00
☐	175	Luke Appling	135.00	60.00	20.00
☐	176	Ken Raffensberger	90.00	40.00	13.50
☐	177	Stan Lopata	90.00	40.00	13.50
☐	178	Tom Brown	90.00	40.00	13.50
☐	179	Hugh Casey	100.00	45.00	15.00
☐	180	Connie Berry	90.00	40.00	13.50
☐	181	Gus Niarhos	80.00	36.00	12.00
☐	182	Hal Peck	80.00	36.00	12.00
☐	183	Lou Stringer	80.00	36.00	12.00
☐	184	Bob Chipman	80.00	36.00	12.00
☐	185	Pete Reiser	100.00	45.00	15.00
☐	186	Buddy Kerr	80.00	36.00	12.00
☐	187	Phil Marchildon	80.00	36.00	12.00
☐	188	Karl Drews	80.00	36.00	12.00
☐	189	Earl Wooten	80.00	36.00	12.00
☐	190	Jim Hearn	80.00	36.00	12.00
☐	191	Joe Haynes	80.00	36.00	12.00
☐	192	Harry Gumbert	80.00	36.00	12.00
☐	193	Ken Trinkle	80.00	36.00	12.00
☐	194	Ralph Branca	110.00	50.00	16.50
☐	195	Eddie Bockman	80.00	36.00	12.00
☐	196	Fred Hutchinson	100.00	45.00	15.00
☐	197	Johnny Lindell	80.00	36.00	12.00
☐	198	Steve Gromek	80.00	36.00	12.00
☐	199	Tex Hughson	80.00	36.00	12.00
☐	200	Jess Dobernic	80.00	36.00	12.00
☐	201	Sibby Sisti	80.00	36.00	12.00
☐	202	Larry Jansen	90.00	40.00	13.50
☐	203	Barney McCosky	80.00	36.00	12.00
☐	204	Bob Savage	80.00	36.00	12.00
☐	205	Dick Sisler	80.00	36.00	12.00
☐	206	Bruce Edwards	80.00	36.00	12.00
☐	207	Johnny Hopp	90.00	40.00	13.50
☐	208	Dizzy Trout	90.00	40.00	13.50
☐	209	Charlie Keller	110.00	50.00	16.50
☐	210	Joe Gordon	110.00	50.00	16.50
☐	211	Boo Ferriss	80.00	36.00	12.00
☐	212	Ralph Hamner	80.00	36.00	12.00
☐	213	Red Barrett	80.00	36.00	12.00
☐	214	Richie Ashburn	500.00	225.00	75.00
☐	215	Kirby Higbe	80.00	36.00	12.00
☐	216	Schoolboy Rowe	90.00	40.00	13.50
☐	217	Marino Pieretti	80.00	36.00	12.00
☐	218	Dick Kryhoski	80.00	36.00	12.00
☐	219	Virgil Fire Trucks	90.00	40.00	13.50
☐	220	Johnny McCarthy	80.00	36.00	12.00
☐	221	Bob Muncrief	80.00	36.00	12.00
☐	222	Alex Kellner	80.00	36.00	12.00
☐	223	Bobby Hofman	80.00	36.00	12.00
☐	224	Satchell Paige	1200.00	500.00	125.00
☐	225	Gerry Coleman	100.00	45.00	15.00
☐	226	Duke Snider	1100.00	500.00	125.00
☐	227	Fritz Ostermueller	80.00	36.00	12.00
☐	228	Jackie Mayo	80.00	36.00	12.00
☐	229	Ed Lopat	140.00	63.00	21.00
☐	230	Augie Galan	80.00	36.00	12.00
☐	231	Earl Johnson	80.00	36.00	12.00
☐	232	George McQuinn	80.00	36.00	12.00
☐	233	Larry Doby	175.00	80.00	27.00
☐	234	Rip Sewell	80.00	36.00	12.00
☐	235	Jim Russell	80.00	36.00	12.00
☐	236	Fred Sanford	80.00	36.00	12.00
☐	237	Monte Kennedy	80.00	36.00	12.00
☐	238	Bob Lemon	260.00	110.00	32.00
☐	239	Frank McCormick	90.00	40.00	13.50
☐	240	Babe Young UER	150.00	50.00	10.00
		(photo actually			
		Bobby Young)			

1950 Bowman

The cards in this 252-card set measure 2 1/16" by 2 1/2". This set, marketed in 1950 by Bowman, represented a major improvement in terms of quality over their previous efforts. Each card was a beautifully colored line drawing developed from a simple photograph. The first 72 cards are the scarcest in the set, while the final 72 cards may be found with or without the copyright line. This was the only Bowman sports set to carry the famous "5-Star" logo. Key rookies in this set are Hank Bauer, Don Newcombe, and Al Rosen.

	NRMT	VG-E	GOOD
COMPLETE SET (252)	9600.00	4500.00	1000.00
COMMON PLAYER (1-72)	55.00	25.00	8.25
COMMON PLAYER (73-216)	18.00	7.50	2.50
COMMON PLAYER (217-252)	20.00	8.50	2.75
☐ 1 Mel Parnell	200.00	30.00	6.00
☐ 2 Vern Stephens	60.00	27.00	9.00
☐ 3 Dom DiMaggio	65.00	29.00	9.75
☐ 4 Gus Zernial	65.00	29.00	9.75
☐ 5 Bob Kuzava	55.00	25.00	8.25
☐ 6 Bob Feller	180.00	80.00	27.00
☐ 7 Jim Hegan	60.00	27.00	9.00
☐ 8 George Kell	95.00	42.00	12.00
☐ 9 Vic Wertz	60.00	27.00	9.00
☐ 10 Tommy Henrich	65.00	29.00	9.75
☐ 11 Phil Rizzuto	165.00	70.00	22.00
☐ 12 Joe Page	65.00	29.00	9.75
☐ 13 Ferris Fain	60.00	27.00	9.00
☐ 14 Alex Kellner	55.00	25.00	8.25
☐ 15 Al Kozar	55.00	25.00	8.25
☐ 16 Roy Sievers	65.00	29.00	9.75
☐ 17 Sid Hudson	55.00	25.00	8.25
☐ 18 Eddie Robinson	55.00	25.00	8.25
☐ 19 Warren Spahn	210.00	85.00	27.00
☐ 20 Bob Elliott	60.00	27.00	9.00
☐ 21 Pee Wee Reese	210.00	85.00	27.00
☐ 22 Jackie Robinson	650.00	300.00	100.00
☐ 23 Don Newcombe	130.00	60.00	20.00
☐ 24 Johnny Schmitz	55.00	25.00	8.25
☐ 25 Hank Sauer	60.00	27.00	9.00
☐ 26 Grady Hatton	55.00	25.00	8.25
☐ 27 Herman Wehmeier	55.00	25.00	8.25
☐ 28 Bobby Thomson	65.00	29.00	9.75
☐ 29 Eddie Stanky	60.00	27.00	9.00
☐ 30 Eddie Waitkus	55.00	25.00	8.25
☐ 31 Del Ennis	65.00	29.00	9.75
☐ 32 Robin Roberts	140.00	63.00	21.00
☐ 33 Ralph Kiner	125.00	57.50	18.75
☐ 34 Murry Dickson	55.00	25.00	8.25
☐ 35 Enos Slaughter	125.00	57.50	18.75
☐ 36 Eddie Kazak	55.00	25.00	8.25
☐ 37 Luke Appling	75.00	34.00	11.25
☐ 38 Bill Wight	55.00	25.00	8.25
☐ 39 Larry Doby	70.00	32.00	10.50
☐ 40 Bob Lemon	110.00	50.00	16.50
☐ 41 Hoot Evers	55.00	25.00	8.25
☐ 42 Art Houtteman	55.00	25.00	8.25
☐ 43 Bobby Doerr	95.00	40.00	12.00
☐ 44 Joe Dobson	55.00	25.00	8.25
☐ 45 Al Zarilla	55.00	25.00	8.25
☐ 46 Yogi Berra	350.00	160.00	52.50
☐ 47 Jerry Coleman	65.00	29.00	9.75
☐ 48 Lou Brissie	55.00	25.00	8.25
☐ 49 Elmer Valo	55.00	25.00	8.25
☐ 50 Dick Kokos	55.00	25.00	8.25
☐ 51 Ned Garver	55.00	25.00	8.25
☐ 52 Sam Mele	55.00	25.00	8.25
☐ 53 Clyde Vollmer	55.00	25.00	8.25
☐ 54 Gil Coan	55.00	25.00	8.25
☐ 55 Buddy Kerr	55.00	25.00	8.25
☐ 56 Del Crandall	70.00	32.00	10.50
☐ 57 Vern Bickford	55.00	25.00	8.25
☐ 58 Carl Furillo	70.00	32.00	10.50
☐ 59 Ralph Branca	65.00	29.00	9.75
☐ 60 Andy Pafko	60.00	27.00	9.00
☐ 61 Bob Rush	55.00	25.00	8.25
☐ 62 Ted Kluszewski	90.00	40.00	13.50
☐ 63 Ewell Blackwell	60.00	27.00	9.00
☐ 64 Alvin Dark	65.00	29.00	9.75
☐ 65 Dave Koslo	55.00	25.00	8.25
☐ 66 Larry Jansen	60.00	27.00	9.00
☐ 67 Willie Jones	55.00	25.00	8.25
☐ 68 Curt Simmons	60.00	27.00	9.00
☐ 69 Wally Westlake	55.00	25.00	8.25
☐ 70 Bob Chesnes	55.00	25.00	8.25
☐ 71 Red Schoendienst	110.00	50.00	16.50
☐ 72 Howie Pollet	55.00	25.00	8.25
☐ 73 Willard Marshall	18.00	7.50	2.50
☐ 74 Johnny Antonelli	30.00	13.50	4.50
☐ 75 Roy Campanella	280.00	115.00	39.00
☐ 76 Rex Barney	18.00	7.50	2.50
☐ 77 Duke Snider	280.00	115.00	39.00
☐ 78 Mickey Owen	20.00	8.50	2.75
☐ 79 Johnny VanderMeer	26.00	11.50	3.75
☐ 80 Howard Fox	18.00	7.50	2.50
☐ 81 Ron Northey	18.00	7.50	2.50
☐ 82 Whitey Lockman	20.00	8.50	2.75
☐ 83 Sheldon Jones	18.00	7.50	2.50
☐ 84 Richie Ashburn	100.00	45.00	15.00
☐ 85 Ken Heintzelman	18.00	7.50	2.50
☐ 86 Stan Rojek	18.00	7.50	2.50
☐ 87 Bill Werle	18.00	7.50	2.50
☐ 88 Marty Marion	24.00	10.50	3.50
☐ 89 Red Munger	18.00	7.50	2.50
☐ 90 Harry Brecheen	20.00	8.50	2.75
☐ 91 Cass Michaels	18.00	7.50	2.50
☐ 92 Hank Majeski	18.00	7.50	2.50
☐ 93 Gene Bearden	20.00	8.50	2.75
☐ 94 Lou Boudreau	50.00	22.50	7.50
☐ 95 Aaron Robinson	18.00	7.50	2.50
☐ 96 Virgil Trucks	20.00	8.50	2.75
☐ 97 Maurice McDermott	18.00	7.50	2.50
☐ 98 Ted Williams	700.00	315.00	105.00
☐ 99 Billy Goodman	20.00	8.50	2.75
☐ 100 Vic Raschi	30.00	13.50	4.50
☐ 101 Bobby Brown	32.00	14.25	4.75
☐ 102 Billy Johnson	18.00	7.50	2.50
☐ 103 Eddie Joost	18.00	7.50	2.50
☐ 104 Sam Chapman	18.00	7.50	2.50
☐ 105 Bob Dillinger	18.00	7.50	2.50
☐ 106 Cliff Fannin	18.00	7.50	2.50
☐ 107 Sam Dente	18.00	7.50	2.50
☐ 108 Ray Scarborough	18.00	7.50	2.50
☐ 109 Sid Gordon	18.00	7.50	2.50
☐ 110 Tommy Holmes	20.00	8.50	2.75
☐ 111 Walker Cooper	18.00	7.50	2.50
☐ 112 Gil Hodges	100.00	45.00	15.00
☐ 113 Gene Hermanski	18.00	7.50	2.50
☐ 114 Wayne Terwilliger	20.00	8.50	2.75
☐ 115 Roy Smalley	18.00	7.50	2.50
☐ 116 Virgil Stallcup	18.00	7.50	2.50
☐ 117 Bill Rigney	18.00	7.50	2.50
☐ 118 Clint Hartung	18.00	7.50	2.50
☐ 119 Dick Sisler	18.00	7.50	2.50
☐ 120 John Thompson	18.00	7.50	2.50
☐ 121 Andy Seminick	18.00	7.50	2.50
☐ 122 Johnny Hopp	20.00	8.50	2.75
☐ 123 Dino Restelli	18.00	7.50	2.50
☐ 124 Clyde McCullough	18.00	7.50	2.50
☐ 125 Del Rice	18.00	7.50	2.50
☐ 126 Al Brazle	18.00	7.50	2.50
☐ 127 Dave Philley	18.00	7.50	2.50
☐ 128 Phil Masi	18.00	7.50	2.50
☐ 129 Joe Gordon	22.00	9.50	3.15
☐ 130 Dale Mitchell	20.00	8.50	2.75
☐ 131 Steve Gromek	18.00	7.50	2.50
☐ 132 Mickey Vernon	22.00	9.50	3.15
☐ 133 Don Kolloway	18.00	7.50	2.50
☐ 134 Paul Trout	18.00	7.50	2.50
☐ 135 Pat Mullin	18.00	7.50	2.50
☐ 136 Warren Rosar	18.00	7.50	2.50
☐ 137 Johnny Pesky	20.00	8.50	2.75
☐ 138 Allie Reynolds	30.00	13.50	4.50
☐ 139 Johnny Mize	70.00	32.00	10.50
☐ 140 Pete Suder	18.00	7.50	2.50
☐ 141 Joe Coleman	18.00	7.50	2.50
☐ 142 Sherm Lollar	24.00	10.50	3.50
☐ 143 Eddie Stewart	18.00	7.50	2.50
☐ 144 Al Evans	18.00	7.50	2.50
☐ 145 Jack Graham	18.00	7.50	2.50
☐ 146 Floyd Baker	18.00	7.50	2.50
☐ 147 Mike Garcia	24.00	10.50	3.50
☐ 148 Early Wynn	65.00	29.00	9.75
☐ 149 Bob Swift	18.00	7.50	2.50
☐ 150 George Vico	18.00	7.50	2.50
☐ 151 Fred Hutchinson	22.00	9.50	3.15
☐ 152 Ellis Kinder	18.00	7.50	2.50
☐ 153 Walt Masterson	18.00	7.50	2.50
☐ 154 Gus Niarhos	18.00	7.50	2.50
☐ 155 Frank Shea	18.00	7.50	2.50
☐ 156 Fred Sanford	18.00	7.50	2.50
☐ 157 Mike Guerra	18.00	7.50	2.50
☐ 158 Paul Lehner	18.00	7.50	2.50
☐ 159 Joe Tipton	18.00	7.50	2.50
☐ 160 Mickey Harris	18.00	7.50	2.50
☐ 161 Sherry Robertson	18.00	7.50	2.50
☐ 162 Eddie Yost	20.00	8.50	2.75
☐ 163 Earl Torgeson	18.00	7.50	2.50
☐ 164 Sibby Sisti	18.00	7.50	2.50
☐ 165 Bruce Edwards	18.00	7.50	2.50
☐ 166 Joe Hatton	18.00	7.50	2.50
☐ 167 Preacher Roe	30.00	13.50	4.50
☐ 168 Bob Scheffing	18.00	7.50	2.50
☐ 169 Hank Edwards	18.00	7.50	2.50
☐ 170 Dutch Leonard	20.00	8.50	2.75
☐ 171 Harry Gumbert	18.00	7.50	2.50
☐ 172 Peanuts Lowrey	18.00	7.50	2.50
☐ 173 Lloyd Merriman	18.00	7.50	2.50
☐ 174 Hank Thompson	22.00	9.50	3.15
☐ 175 Monte Kennedy	18.00	7.50	2.50
☐ 176 Sylvester Donnelly	18.00	7.50	2.50
☐ 177 Hank Borowy	18.00	7.50	2.50
☐ 178 Ed Fitzgerald	18.00	7.50	2.50
☐ 179 Chuck Diering	18.00	7.50	2.50
☐ 180 Harry Walker	18.00	7.50	2.50
☐ 181 Marino Pieretti	18.00	7.50	2.50
☐ 182 Sam Zoldak	18.00	7.50	2.50
☐ 183 Mickey Haefner	18.00	7.50	2.50
☐ 184 Randy Gumpert	18.00	7.50	2.50

		NRMT	VG-E	GOOD
☐	185 Howie Judson	18.00	7.50	2.50
☐	186 Ken Keltner	20.00	8.50	2.75
☐	187 Lou Stringer	18.00	7.50	2.50
☐	188 Earl Johnson	18.00	7.50	2.50
☐	189 Owen Friend	18.00	7.50	2.50
☐	190 Ken Wood	18.00	7.50	2.50
☐	191 Dick Starr	18.00	7.50	2.50
☐	192 Bob Chipman	18.00	7.50	2.50
☐	193 Pete Reiser	22.00	9.50	3.15
☐	194 Billy Cox	22.00	9.50	3.15
☐	195 Phil Cavarretta	20.00	8.50	2.75
☐	196 Doyle Lade	18.00	7.50	2.50
☐	197 Johnny Wyrostek	18.00	7.50	2.50
☐	198 Danny Litwhiler	18.00	7.50	2.50
☐	199 Jack Kramer	18.00	7.50	2.50
☐	200 Kirby Higbe	18.00	7.50	2.50
☐	201 Pete Castiglione	18.00	7.50	2.50
☐	202 Cliff Chambers	18.00	7.50	2.50
☐	203 Danny Murtaugh	18.00	7.50	2.50
☐	204 Granny Hamner	22.00	9.50	3.15
☐	205 Mike Goliat	18.00	7.50	2.50
☐	206 Stan Lopata	18.00	7.50	2.50
☐	207 Max Lanier	18.00	7.50	2.50
☐	208 Jim Hearn	18.00	7.50	2.50
☐	209 Johnny Lindell	18.00	7.50	2.50
☐	210 Ted Gray	18.00	7.50	2.50
☐	211 Charley Keller	22.00	9.50	3.15
☐	212 Jerry Priddy	18.00	7.50	2.50
☐	213 Carl Scheib	18.00	7.50	2.50
☐	214 Dick Fowler	18.00	7.50	2.50
☐	215 Ed Lopat	30.00	13.50	4.50
☐	216 Bob Porterfield	18.00	7.50	2.50
☐	217 Casey Stengel MG	125.00	57.50	18.75
☐	218 Cliff Mapes	22.00	9.50	3.15
☐	219 Hank Bauer	75.00	34.00	11.25
☐	220 Leo Durocher MG	60.00	27.00	9.00
☐	221 Don Mueller	33.00	15.00	5.00
☐	222 Bobby Morgan	20.00	8.50	2.75
☐	223 Jim Russell	20.00	8.50	2.75
☐	224 Jack Banta	20.00	8.50	2.75
☐	225 Eddie Sawyer MG	22.00	9.50	3.15
☐	226 Jim Konstanty	33.00	15.00	5.00
☐	227 Bob Miller	20.00	8.50	2.75
☐	228 Bill Nicholson	20.00	8.50	2.75
☐	229 Frank Frisch	45.00	20.00	6.75
☐	230 Bill Serena	20.00	8.50	2.75
☐	231 Preston Ward	20.00	8.50	2.75
☐	232 Al Rosen	60.00	27.00	9.00
☐	233 Allie Clark	20.00	8.50	2.75
☐	234 Bobby Shantz	27.00	12.00	4.00
☐	235 Harold Gilbert	20.00	8.50	2.75
☐	236 Bob Cain	20.00	8.50	2.75
☐	237 Bill Salkeld	20.00	8.50	2.75
☐	238 Vernal Jones	20.00	8.50	2.75
☐	239 Bill Howerton	20.00	8.50	2.75
☐	240 Eddie Lake	20.00	8.50	2.75
☐	241 Neil Berry	20.00	8.50	2.75
☐	242 Dick Kryhoski	20.00	8.50	2.75
☐	243 Johnny Groth	20.00	8.50	2.75
☐	244 Dale Coogan	20.00	8.50	2.75
☐	245 Al Papai	20.00	8.50	2.75
☐	246 Walt Dropo	27.00	12.00	4.00
☐	247 Irv Noren	22.00	9.50	3.15
☐	248 Sam Jethroe	22.00	9.50	3.15
☐	249 Snuffy Stirnweiss	22.00	9.50	3.15
☐	250 Ray Coleman	20.00	8.50	2.75
☐	251 John Moss	20.00	8.50	2.75
☐	252 Billy DeMars	85.00	15.00	3.00

1951 Bowman

The cards in this 324-card set measure 2 1/16" by 3 1/8". Many of the obverses of the cards appearing in the 1951 Bowman set are enlargements of those appearing in the previous year. The high number series (253-324) is highly valued and contains the true "Rookie" cards of Mickey Mantle and Willie Mays. Card number 195 depicts Paul Richards in caricature. George Kell's card (number 46) incorrectly lists him as being in the "1941" Bowman series. Player names are found printed in a panel on the front of the card. These cards were supposedly also sold in sheets in variety stores in the Philadelphia area.

	NRMT	VG-E	GOOD
COMPLETE SET (324)	19000.00	8250.00	2000.00
COMMON PLAYER (1-36)	22.00	9.50	3.15
COMMON PLAYER (37-72)	18.00	7.50	2.50

		NRMT	VG-E	GOOD
	COMMON PLAYER (73-252)	14.00	6.25	2.00
	COMMON PLAYER (253-324)	65.00	29.00	9.75
☐	1 Whitey Ford	1300.00	300.00	60.00
☐	2 Yogi Berra	450.00	200.00	67.50
☐	3 Robin Roberts	80.00	36.00	12.00
☐	4 Del Ennis	27.00	12.00	4.00
☐	5 Dale Mitchell	25.00	11.00	3.50
☐	6 Don Newcombe	40.00	18.00	6.00
☐	7 Gil Hodges	80.00	36.00	12.00
☐	8 Paul Lehner	22.00	9.50	3.15
☐	9 Sam Chapman	22.00	9.50	3.15
☐	10 Red Schoendienst	75.00	34.00	11.25
☐	11 Red Munger	22.00	9.50	3.15
☐	12 Hank Majeski	22.00	9.50	3.15
☐	13 Eddie Stanky	25.00	11.00	3.50
☐	14 Alvin Dark	27.00	12.00	4.00
☐	15 Johnny Pesky	25.00	11.00	3.50
☐	16 Maurice McDermott	22.00	9.50	3.15
☐	17 Pete Castiglione	22.00	9.50	3.15
☐	18 Gil Coan	22.00	9.50	3.15
☐	19 Sid Gordon	22.00	9.50	3.15
☐	20 Del Crandell UER	25.00	11.00	3.50
	(sic, Crandall)			
☐	21 Snuffy Stirnweiss	25.00	11.00	3.50
☐	22 Hank Sauer	25.00	11.00	3.50
☐	23 Hoot Evers	22.00	9.50	3.15
☐	24 Ewell Blackwell	27.00	12.00	4.00
☐	25 Vic Raschi	32.00	14.25	4.75
☐	26 Phil Rizzuto	100.00	45.00	15.00
☐	27 Jim Konstanty	25.00	11.00	3.50
☐	28 Eddie Waitkus	22.00	9.50	3.15
☐	29 Allie Clark	22.00	9.50	3.15
☐	30 Bob Feller	130.00	60.00	20.00
☐	31 Roy Campanella	275.00	120.00	40.00
☐	32 Duke Snider	250.00	110.00	37.50
☐	33 Bob Hooper	22.00	9.50	3.15
☐	34 Marty Marion	27.00	12.00	4.00
☐	35 Al Zarilla	22.00	9.50	3.15
☐	36 Joe Dobson	22.00	9.50	3.15
☐	37 Whitey Lockman	20.00	8.50	2.75
☐	38 Al Evans	18.00	7.50	2.50
☐	39 Ray Scarborough	18.00	7.50	2.50
☐	40 Gus Bell	27.00	12.00	4.00
☐	41 Eddie Yost	18.00	7.50	2.50
☐	42 Vern Bickford	18.00	7.50	2.50
☐	43 Billy DeMars	18.00	7.50	2.50
☐	44 Roy Smalley	18.00	7.50	2.50
☐	45 Art Houtteman	18.00	7.50	2.50
☐	46 George Kell 1941 UER	50.00	22.50	7.50
☐	47 Grady Hatton	18.00	7.50	2.50
☐	48 Ken Raffensberger	18.00	7.50	2.50
☐	49 Jerry Coleman	20.00	8.50	2.75
☐	50 Johnny Mize	55.00	25.00	8.25
☐	51 Andy Seminick	18.00	7.50	2.50
☐	52 Dick Sisler	18.00	7.50	2.50
☐	53 Bob Lemon	50.00	22.50	7.50
☐	54 Ray Boone	22.00	9.50	3.15
☐	55 Gene Hermanski	18.00	7.50	2.50
☐	56 Ralph Branca	27.00	12.00	4.00
☐	57 Alex Kellner	18.00	7.50	2.50
☐	58 Enos Slaughter	55.00	25.00	8.25
☐	59 Randy Gumpert	18.00	7.50	2.50
☐	60 Chico Carrasquel	18.00	7.50	2.50
☐	61 Jim Hearn	18.00	7.50	2.50
☐	62 Lou Boudreau	45.00	20.00	6.75
☐	63 Bob Dillinger	18.00	7.50	2.50
☐	64 Bill Werle	18.00	7.50	2.50
☐	65 Mickey Vernon	20.00	8.50	2.75
☐	66 Bob Elliott	20.00	8.50	2.75
☐	67 Roy Sievers	20.00	8.50	2.75

☐ 68	Dick Kokos	18.00	7.50	2.50	☐ 163	Monte Kennedy	14.00	6.25	2.00
☐ 69	Johnny Schmitz	18.00	7.50	2.50	☐ 164	Bill Wight	14.00	6.25	2.00
☐ 70	Ron Northey	18.00	7.50	2.50	☐ 165	Ted Williams	600.00	270.00	90.00
☐ 71	Jerry Priddy	18.00	7.50	2.50	☐ 166	Stan Rojek	14.00	6.25	2.00
☐ 72	Lloyd Merriman	18.00	7.50	2.50	☐ 167	Murry Dickson	14.00	6.25	2.00
☐ 73	Tommy Byrne	16.00	6.75	2.25	☐ 168	Sam Mele	14.00	6.25	2.00
☐ 74	Billy Johnson	16.00	6.75	2.25	☐ 169	Sid Hudson	14.00	6.25	2.00
☐ 75	Russ Meyer	14.00	6.25	2.00	☐ 170	Sibby Sisti	14.00	6.25	2.00
☐ 76	Stan Lopata	14.00	6.25	2.00	☐ 171	Buddy Kerr	14.00	6.25	2.00
☐ 77	Mike Goliat	14.00	6.25	2.00	☐ 172	Ned Garver	14.00	6.25	2.00
☐ 78	Early Wynn	48.00	22.00	5.50	☐ 173	Hank Arft	14.00	6.25	2.00
☐ 79	Jim Hegan	16.00	6.75	2.25	☐ 174	Mickey Owen	16.00	6.75	2.25
☐ 80	Pee Wee Reese	145.00	65.00	18.00	☐ 175	Wayne Terwilliger	14.00	6.25	2.00
☐ 81	Carl Furillo	35.00	15.75	5.25	☐ 176	Vic Wertz	16.00	6.75	2.25
☐ 82	Joe Tipton	14.00	6.25	2.00	☐ 177	Charlie Keller	16.00	6.75	2.25
☐ 83	Carl Scheib	14.00	6.25	2.00	☐ 178	Ted Gray	14.00	6.25	2.00
☐ 84	Barney McCosky	14.00	6.25	2.00	☐ 179	Danny Litwhiler	14.00	6.25	2.00
☐ 85	Eddie Kazak	14.00	6.25	2.00	☐ 180	Howie Fox	14.00	6.25	2.00
☐ 86	Harry Brecheen	16.00	6.75	2.25	☐ 181	Casey Stengel MG	100.00	45.00	15.00
☐ 87	Floyd Baker	14.00	6.25	2.00	☐ 182	Tom Ferrick	14.00	6.25	2.00
☐ 88	Eddie Robinson	14.00	6.25	2.00	☐ 183	Hank Bauer	28.00	12.50	4.00
☐ 89	Hank Thompson	16.00	6.75	2.25	☐ 184	Eddie Sawyer MG	16.00	6.75	2.25
☐ 90	Dave Koslo	14.00	6.25	2.00	☐ 185	Jimmy Bloodworth	14.00	6.25	2.00
☐ 91	Clyde Vollmer	14.00	6.25	2.00	☐ 186	Richie Ashburn	60.00	27.00	9.00
☐ 92	Vern Stephens	16.00	6.75	2.25	☐ 187	Al Rosen	28.00	12.50	4.00
☐ 93	Danny O'Connell	14.00	6.25	2.00	☐ 188	Bobby Avila	18.00	7.50	2.50
☐ 94	Clyde McCullough	14.00	6.25	2.00	☐ 189	Erv Palica	14.00	6.25	2.00
☐ 95	Sherry Robertson	14.00	6.25	2.00	☐ 190	Joe Hatton	14.00	6.25	2.00
☐ 96	Sandy Consuegra	14.00	6.25	2.00	☐ 191	Billy Hitchcock	14.00	6.25	2.00
☐ 97	Bob Kuzava	14.00	6.25	2.00	☐ 192	Hank Wyse	14.00	6.25	2.00
☐ 98	Willard Marshall	14.00	6.25	2.00	☐ 193	Ted Wilks	14.00	6.25	2.00
☐ 99	Earl Torgeson	14.00	6.25	2.00	☐ 194	Peanuts Lowrey	14.00	6.25	2.00
☐ 100	Sherm Lollar	16.00	6.75	2.25	☐ 195	Paul Richards	18.00	7.50	2.50
☐ 101	Owen Friend	14.00	6.25	2.00		(caricature)			
☐ 102	Dutch Leonard	16.00	6.75	2.25	☐ 196	Billy Pierce	30.00	13.50	4.50
☐ 103	Andy Pafko	16.00	6.75	2.25	☐ 197	Bob Cain	14.00	6.25	2.00
☐ 104	Virgil Trucks	16.00	6.75	2.25	☐ 198	Monte Irvin	110.00	50.00	16.50
☐ 105	Don Kolloway	14.00	6.25	2.00	☐ 199	Sheldon Jones	14.00	6.25	2.00
☐ 106	Pat Mullin	14.00	6.25	2.00	☐ 200	Jack Kramer	14.00	6.25	2.00
☐ 107	Johnny Wyrostek	14.00	6.25	2.00	☐ 201	Steve O'Neill	14.00	6.25	2.00
☐ 108	Virgil Stallcup	14.00	6.25	2.00	☐ 202	Mike Guerra	14.00	6.25	2.00
☐ 109	Allie Reynolds	30.00	13.50	4.50	☐ 203	Vernon Law	25.00	11.00	3.50
☐ 110	Bobby Brown	30.00	13.50	4.50	☐ 204	Vic Lombardi	14.00	6.25	2.00
☐ 111	Curt Simmons	16.00	6.75	2.25	☐ 205	Mickey Grasso	14.00	6.25	2.00
☐ 112	Willie Jones	14.00	6.25	2.00	☐ 206	Conrado Marrero	14.00	6.25	2.00
☐ 113	Bill Nicholson	14.00	6.25	2.00	☐ 207	Billy Southworth	14.00	6.25	2.00
☐ 114	Sam Zoldak	14.00	6.25	2.00	☐ 208	Blix Donnelly	14.00	6.25	2.00
☐ 115	Steve Gromek	14.00	6.25	2.00	☐ 209	Ken Wood	14.00	6.25	2.00
☐ 116	Bruce Edwards	14.00	6.25	2.00	☐ 210	Les Moss	14.00	6.25	2.00
☐ 117	Eddie Miksis	14.00	6.25	2.00	☐ 211	Hal Jeffcoat	14.00	6.25	2.00
☐ 118	Preacher Roe	28.00	12.50	4.00	☐ 212	Bob Rush	14.00	6.25	2.00
☐ 119	Eddie Joost	14.00	6.25	2.00	☐ 213	Neil Berry	14.00	6.25	2.00
☐ 120	Joe Coleman	14.00	6.25	2.00	☐ 214	Bob Swift	14.00	6.25	2.00
☐ 121	Jerry Staley	14.00	6.25	2.00	☐ 215	Ken Peterson	14.00	6.25	2.00
☐ 122	Joe Garagiola	150.00	67.50	22.50	☐ 216	Connie Ryan	14.00	6.25	2.00
☐ 123	Howie Judson	14.00	6.25	2.00	☐ 217	Joe Page	20.00	8.50	2.75
☐ 124	Gus Niarhos	14.00	6.25	2.00	☐ 218	Ed Lopat	28.00	12.50	4.00
☐ 125	Bill Rigney	14.00	6.25	2.00	☐ 219	Gene Woodling	33.00	15.00	5.00
☐ 126	Bobby Thomson	32.00	14.25	4.75	☐ 220	Bob Miller	14.00	6.25	2.00
☐ 127	Sal Maglie	48.00	22.00	5.50	☐ 221	Dick Whitman	14.00	6.25	2.00
☐ 128	Ellis Kinder	14.00	6.25	2.00	☐ 222	Thurman Tucker	14.00	6.25	2.00
☐ 129	Matt Batts	14.00	6.25	2.00	☐ 223	Johnny VanderMeer	24.00	10.50	3.50
☐ 130	Tom Saffell	14.00	6.25	2.00	☐ 224	Billy Cox	16.00	6.75	2.25
☐ 131	Cliff Chambers	14.00	6.25	2.00	☐ 225	Dan Bankhead	16.00	6.75	2.25
☐ 132	Cass Michaels	14.00	6.25	2.00	☐ 226	Jimmy Dykes	16.00	6.75	2.25
☐ 133	Sam Dente	14.00	6.25	2.00	☐ 227	Bobby Schantz UER	18.00	7.50	2.50
☐ 134	Warren Spahn	120.00	55.00	18.00		(sic, Shantz)			
☐ 135	Walker Cooper	14.00	6.25	2.00	☐ 228	Cloyd Boyer	16.00	6.75	2.25
☐ 136	Ray Coleman	14.00	6.25	2.00	☐ 229	Bill Howerton	14.00	6.25	2.00
☐ 137	Dick Starr	14.00	6.25	2.00	☐ 230	Max Lanier	14.00	6.25	2.00
☐ 138	Phil Cavarretta	16.00	6.75	2.25	☐ 231	Luis Aloma	14.00	6.25	2.00
☐ 139	Doyle Lade	14.00	6.25	2.00	☐ 232	Nelson Fox	135.00	60.00	20.00
☐ 140	Eddie Lake	14.00	6.25	2.00	☐ 233	Leo Durocher MG	50.00	22.50	7.50
☐ 141	Fred Hutchinson	16.00	6.75	2.25	☐ 234	Clint Hartung	14.00	6.25	2.00
☐ 142	Aaron Robinson	14.00	6.25	2.00	☐ 235	Jack Lohrke	14.00	6.25	2.00
☐ 143	Ted Kluszewski	35.00	15.75	5.25	☐ 236	Warren Rosar	14.00	6.25	2.00
☐ 144	Herman Wehmeier	14.00	6.25	2.00	☐ 237	Billy Goodman	16.00	6.75	2.25
☐ 145	Fred Sanford	14.00	6.25	2.00	☐ 238	Pete Reiser	18.00	7.50	2.50
☐ 146	Johnny Hopp	16.00	6.75	2.25	☐ 239	Bill MacDonald	14.00	6.25	2.00
☐ 147	Ken Heintzelman	14.00	6.25	2.00	☐ 240	Joe Haynes	14.00	6.25	2.00
☐ 148	Granny Hamner	14.00	6.25	2.00	☐ 241	Irv Noren	16.00	6.75	2.25
☐ 149	Bubba Church	14.00	6.25	2.00	☐ 242	Sam Jethroe	16.00	6.75	2.25
☐ 150	Mike Garcia	16.00	6.75	2.25	☐ 243	Johnny Antonelli	16.00	6.75	2.25
☐ 151	Larry Doby	30.00	13.50	4.50	☐ 244	Cliff Fannin	14.00	6.25	2.00
☐ 152	Cal Abrams	14.00	6.25	2.00	☐ 245	John Berardino	24.00	10.50	3.50
☐ 153	Rex Barney	14.00	6.25	2.00	☐ 246	Bill Serena	14.00	6.25	2.00
☐ 154	Pete Suder	14.00	6.25	2.00	☐ 247	Bob Ramazotti	14.00	6.25	2.00
☐ 155	Lou Brissie	14.00	6.25	2.00	☐ 248	Johnny Klippstein	14.00	6.25	2.00
☐ 156	Del Rice	14.00	6.25	2.00	☐ 249	Johnny Groth	14.00	6.25	2.00
☐ 157	Al Brazle	14.00	6.25	2.00	☐ 250	Hank Borowy	14.00	6.25	2.00
☐ 158	Chuck Diering	14.00	6.25	2.00	☐ 251	Willard Ramsdell	14.00	6.25	2.00
☐ 159	Eddie Stewart	14.00	6.25	2.00	☐ 252	Dixie Howell	14.00	6.25	2.00
☐ 160	Phil Masi	14.00	6.25	2.00	☐ 253	Mickey Mantle	7000.00	2750.00	750.00
☐ 161	Wes Westrum	18.00	7.50	2.50	☐ 254	Jackie Jensen	140.00	63.00	21.00
☐ 162	Larry Jansen	16.00	6.75	2.25	☐ 255	Milo Candini	65.00	29.00	9.75

☐	256	Ken Sylvestri	65.00	29.00	9.75
☐	257	Birdie Tebbetts	70.00	32.00	10.50
☐	258	Luke Easter	70.00	32.00	10.50
☐	259	Chuck Dressen MG	75.00	34.00	11.25
☐	260	Carl Erskine	120.00	55.00	18.00
☐	261	Wally Moses	70.00	32.00	10.50
☐	262	Gus Zernial	70.00	32.00	10.50
☐	263	Howie Pollet	65.00	29.00	9.75
☐	264	Don Richmond	65.00	29.00	9.75
☐	265	Steve Bilko	65.00	29.00	9.75
☐	266	Harry Dorish	65.00	29.00	9.75
☐	267	Ken Holcombe	65.00	29.00	9.75
☐	268	Don Mueller	70.00	32.00	10.50
☐	269	Ray Noble	65.00	29.00	9.75
☐	270	Willard Nixon	65.00	29.00	9.75
☐	271	Tommy Wright	65.00	29.00	9.75
☐	272	Billy Meyer MG	65.00	29.00	9.75
☐	273	Danny Murtaugh	65.00	29.00	9.75
☐	274	George Metkovich	65.00	29.00	9.75
☐	275	Bucky Harris MG	80.00	36.00	12.00
☐	276	Frank Quinn	65.00	29.00	9.75
☐	277	Roy Hartsfield	65.00	29.00	9.75
☐	278	Norman Roy	65.00	29.00	9.75
☐	279	Jim Delsing	65.00	29.00	9.75
☐	280	Frank Overmire	65.00	29.00	9.75
☐	281	Al Widmar	65.00	29.00	9.75
☐	282	Frank Frisch	100.00	45.00	15.00
☐	283	Walt Dubiel	65.00	29.00	9.75
☐	284	Gene Bearden	70.00	32.00	10.50
☐	285	Johnny Lipon	65.00	29.00	9.75
☐	286	Bob Usher	65.00	29.00	9.75
☐	287	Jim Blackburn	65.00	29.00	9.75
☐	288	Bobby Adams	65.00	29.00	9.75
☐	289	Cliff Mapes	70.00	32.00	10.50
☐	290	Bill Dickey CO	175.00	80.00	27.00
☐	291	Tommy Henrich CO	75.00	34.00	11.25
☐	292	Eddie Pellegrini	65.00	29.00	9.75
☐	293	Ken Johnson	65.00	29.00	9.75
☐	294	Jocko Thompson	65.00	29.00	9.75
☐	295	Al Lopez MG	110.00	50.00	16.50
☐	296	Bob Kennedy	70.00	32.00	10.50
☐	297	Dave Philley	65.00	29.00	9.75
☐	298	Joe Astroth	65.00	29.00	9.75
☐	299	Clyde King	70.00	32.00	10.50
☐	300	Hal Rice	65.00	29.00	9.75
☐	301	Tommy Glaviano	65.00	29.00	9.75
☐	302	Jim Busby	65.00	29.00	9.75
☐	303	Marv Rotblatt	65.00	29.00	9.75
☐	304	Al Gettell	65.00	29.00	9.75
☐	305	Willie Mays	2700.00	1000.00	250.00
☐	306	Jim Piersall	120.00	55.00	18.00
☐	307	Walt Masterson	65.00	29.00	9.75
☐	308	Ted Beard	65.00	29.00	9.75
☐	309	Mel Queen	65.00	29.00	9.75
☐	310	Erv Dusak	65.00	29.00	9.75
☐	311	Mickey Harris	65.00	29.00	9.75
☐	312	Gene Mauch	80.00	36.00	12.00
☐	313	Ray Mueller	65.00	29.00	9.75
☐	314	Johnny Sain	80.00	36.00	12.00
☐	315	Zack Taylor	65.00	29.00	9.75
☐	316	Duane Pillette	65.00	29.00	9.75
☐	317	Smoky Burgess	90.00	40.00	13.50
☐	318	Warren Hacker	65.00	29.00	9.75
☐	319	Red Rolfe	70.00	32.00	10.50
☐	320	Hal White	65.00	29.00	9.75
☐	321	Earl Johnson	65.00	29.00	9.75
☐	322	Luke Sewell	70.00	32.00	10.50
☐	323	Joe Adcock	100.00	45.00	15.00
☐	324	Johnny Pramesa	120.00	40.00	8.00

1952 Bowman

The cards in this 252-card set measure 2 1/16" by 3 1/8". While the Bowman set of 1952 retained the card size introduced in 1951, it employed a modification of color tones from the two preceding years. The cards also appeared with a facsimile autograph on the front and, for the first time since 1949, premium advertising on the back. The 1952 set was sold in sheets as well as in gum packs. Artwork for 15 cards that were never issued was recently discovered. Notable rookies in this set are Lew Burdette, Gil McDougald, and Minnie Minoso.

	NRMT	VG-E	GOOD
COMPLETE SET (252)	9000.00	4200.00	1000.00
COMMON PLAYER (1-36)	20.00	8.50	2.75
COMMON PLAYER (37-72)	18.00	7.50	2.50

COMMON PLAYER (73-108)	15.00	6.50	2.15
COMMON PLAYER (109-144)	15.00	6.50	2.15
COMMON PLAYER (145-180)	14.00	6.25	2.00
COMMON PLAYER (181-216)	13.00	5.75	1.75
COMMON PLAYER (217-252)	30.00	13.50	4.50

☐	1	Yogi Berra	600.00	150.00	30.00
☐	2	Bobby Thomson	32.00	14.25	4.75
☐	3	Fred Hutchinson	24.00	10.50	3.50
☐	4	Robin Roberts	65.00	29.00	9.75
☐	5	Minnie Minoso	100.00	45.00	15.00
☐	6	Virgil Stallcup	20.00	8.50	2.75
☐	7	Mike Garcia	22.00	9.50	3.15
☐	8	Pee Wee Reese	110.00	50.00	16.50
☐	9	Vern Stephens	22.00	9.50	3.15
☐	10	Bob Hooper	20.00	8.50	2.75
☐	11	Ralph Kiner	60.00	27.00	9.00
☐	12	Max Surkont	20.00	8.50	2.75
☐	13	Cliff Mapes	20.00	8.50	2.75
☐	14	Cliff Chambers	20.00	8.50	2.75
☐	15	Sam Mele	20.00	8.50	2.75
☐	16	Turk Lown	20.00	8.50	2.75
☐	17	Ed Lopat	33.00	15.00	5.00
☐	18	Don Mueller	22.00	9.50	3.15
☐	19	Bob Cain	20.00	8.50	2.75
☐	20	Willie Jones	20.00	8.50	2.75
☐	21	Nellie Fox	42.00	18.00	5.00
☐	22	Willard Ramsdell	20.00	8.50	2.75
☐	23	Bob Lemon	55.00	25.00	8.25
☐	24	Carl Furillo	35.00	15.75	5.25
☐	25	Mickey McDermott	20.00	8.50	2.75
☐	26	Eddie Joost	20.00	8.50	2.75
☐	27	Joe Garagiola	75.00	34.00	11.25
☐	28	Roy Hartsfield	20.00	8.50	2.75
☐	29	Ned Garver	20.00	8.50	2.75
☐	30	Red Schoendienst	65.00	29.00	9.75
☐	31	Eddie Yost	20.00	8.50	2.75
☐	32	Eddie Miksis	20.00	8.50	2.75
☐	33	Gil McDougald	65.00	29.00	9.75
☐	34	Alvin Dark	24.00	10.50	3.50
☐	35	Granny Hamner	20.00	8.50	2.75
☐	36	Cass Michaels	20.00	8.50	2.75
☐	37	Vic Raschi	24.00	10.50	3.50
☐	38	Whitey Lockman	20.00	8.50	2.75
☐	39	Vic Wertz	20.00	8.50	2.75
☐	40	Bubba Church	18.00	7.50	2.50
☐	41	Chico Carrasquel	18.00	7.50	2.50
☐	42	Johnny Wyrostek	18.00	7.50	2.50
☐	43	Bob Feller	110.00	50.00	16.50
☐	44	Roy Campanella	210.00	85.00	27.00
☐	45	Johnny Pesky	22.00	9.50	3.15
☐	46	Carl Scheib	18.00	7.50	2.50
☐	47	Pete Castiglione	18.00	7.50	2.50
☐	48	Vern Bickford	18.00	7.50	2.50
☐	49	Jim Hearn	18.00	7.50	2.50
☐	50	Jerry Staley	18.00	7.50	2.50
☐	51	Gil Coan	18.00	7.50	2.50
☐	52	Phil Rizzuto	80.00	36.00	12.00
☐	53	Richie Ashburn	55.00	25.00	8.25
☐	54	Billy Pierce	24.00	10.50	3.50
☐	55	Ken Raffensberger	18.00	7.50	2.50
☐	56	Clyde King	18.00	7.50	2.50
☐	57	Clyde Vollmer	18.00	7.50	2.50
☐	58	Hank Majeski	18.00	7.50	2.50
☐	59	Murry Dickson	18.00	7.50	2.50
☐	60	Sid Gordon	18.00	7.50	2.50
☐	61	Tommy Byrne	18.00	7.50	2.50
☐	62	Joe Presko	18.00	7.50	2.50
☐	63	Irv Noren	20.00	8.50	2.75
☐	64	Roy Smalley	18.00	7.50	2.50
☐	65	Hank Bauer	27.00	12.00	4.00

☐ 66	Sal Maglie	24.00	10.50	3.50
☐ 67	Johnny Groth	18.00	7.50	2.50
☐ 68	Jim Busby	18.00	7.50	2.50
☐ 69	Joe Adcock	24.00	10.50	3.50
☐ 70	Carl Erskine	27.00	12.00	4.00
☐ 71	Vernon Law	20.00	8.50	2.75
☐ 72	Earl Torgeson	18.00	7.50	2.50
☐ 73	Gerry Coleman	20.00	8.50	2.75
☐ 74	Wes Westrum	18.00	7.50	2.50
☐ 75	George Kell	42.00	18.00	5.00
☐ 76	Del Ennis	20.00	8.50	2.75
☐ 77	Eddie Robinson	15.00	6.50	2.15
☐ 78	Lloyd Merriman	15.00	6.50	2.15
☐ 79	Lou Brissie	15.00	6.50	2.15
☐ 80	Gil Hodges	65.00	29.00	9.75
☐ 81	Billy Goodman	18.00	7.50	2.50
☐ 82	Gus Zernial	18.00	7.50	2.50
☐ 83	Howie Pollet	15.00	6.50	2.15
☐ 84	Sam Jethroe	15.00	6.50	2.15
☐ 85	Marty Marion CO	20.00	8.50	2.75
☐ 86	Cal Abrams	15.00	6.50	2.15
☐ 87	Mickey Vernon	18.00	7.50	2.50
☐ 88	Bruce Edwards	15.00	6.50	2.15
☐ 89	Billy Hitchcock	15.00	6.50	2.15
☐ 90	Larry Jansen	18.00	7.50	2.50
☐ 91	Don Kolloway	15.00	6.50	2.15
☐ 92	Eddie Waitkus	15.00	6.50	2.15
☐ 93	Paul Richards	18.00	7.50	2.50
☐ 94	Luke Sewell	18.00	7.50	2.50
☐ 95	Luke Easter	18.00	7.50	2.50
☐ 96	Ralph Branca	20.00	8.50	2.75
☐ 97	Willard Marshall	15.00	6.50	2.15
☐ 98	Jimmy Dykes	18.00	7.50	2.50
☐ 99	Clyde McCullough	15.00	6.50	2.15
☐ 100	Sibby Sisti	15.00	6.50	2.15
☐ 101	Mickey Mantle	2000.00	800.00	200.00
☐ 102	Peanuts Lowrey	15.00	6.50	2.15
☐ 103	Joe Haynes	15.00	6.50	2.15
☐ 104	Hal Jeffcoat	15.00	6.50	2.15
☐ 105	Bobby Brown	25.00	11.00	3.50
☐ 106	Randy Gumpert	15.00	6.50	2.15
☐ 107	Del Rice	15.00	6.50	2.15
☐ 108	George Metkovich	15.00	6.50	2.15
☐ 109	Tom Morgan	15.00	6.50	2.15
☐ 110	Max Lanier	15.00	6.50	2.15
☐ 111	Hoot Evers	15.00	6.50	2.15
☐ 112	Smoky Burgess	18.00	7.50	2.50
☐ 113	Al Zarilla	15.00	6.50	2.15
☐ 114	Frank Hiller	15.00	6.50	2.15
☐ 115	Larry Doby	24.00	10.50	3.50
☐ 116	Duke Snider	190.00	85.00	28.50
☐ 117	Bill Wight	15.00	6.50	2.15
☐ 118	Ray Murray	15.00	6.50	2.15
☐ 119	Bill Howerton	15.00	6.50	2.15
☐ 120	Chet Nichols	15.00	6.50	2.15
☐ 121	Al Corwin	15.00	6.50	2.15
☐ 122	Billy Johnson	18.00	7.50	2.50
☐ 123	Sid Hudson	15.00	6.50	2.15
☐ 124	Birdie Tebbetts	18.00	7.50	2.50
☐ 125	Howie Fox	15.00	6.50	2.15
☐ 126	Phil Cavarretta	18.00	7.50	2.50
☐ 127	Dick Sisler	15.00	6.50	2.15
☐ 128	Don Newcombe	28.00	12.50	4.00
☐ 129	Gus Niarhos	15.00	6.50	2.15
☐ 130	Allie Clark	15.00	6.50	2.15
☐ 131	Bob Swift	15.00	6.50	2.15
☐ 132	Dave Cole	15.00	6.50	2.15
☐ 133	Dick Kryhoski	15.00	6.50	2.15
☐ 134	Al Brazle	15.00	6.50	2.15
☐ 135	Mickey Harris	15.00	6.50	2.15
☐ 136	Gene Hermanski	15.00	6.50	2.15
☐ 137	Stan Rojek	15.00	6.50	2.15
☐ 138	Ted Wilks	15.00	6.50	2.15
☐ 139	Jerry Priddy	15.00	6.50	2.15
☐ 140	Ray Scarborough	15.00	6.50	2.15
☐ 141	Hank Edwards	15.00	6.50	2.15
☐ 142	Early Wynn	45.00	20.00	6.75
☐ 143	Sandy Consuegra	15.00	6.50	2.15
☐ 144	Joe Hatton	15.00	6.50	2.15
☐ 145	Johnny Mize	50.00	22.50	7.50
☐ 146	Leo Durocher MG	42.00	18.00	5.00
☐ 147	Marlin Stuart	14.00	6.25	2.00
☐ 148	Ken Heintzelman	14.00	6.25	2.00
☐ 149	Howie Judson	14.00	6.25	2.00
☐ 150	Herman Wehmeier	14.00	6.25	2.00
☐ 151	Al Rosen	22.00	9.50	3.15
☐ 152	Billy Cox	18.00	7.50	2.50
☐ 153	Fred Hatfield	14.00	6.25	2.00
☐ 154	Ferris Fain	16.00	6.75	2.25
☐ 155	Billy Meyer	14.00	6.25	2.00
☐ 156	Warren Spahn	100.00	45.00	15.00
☐ 157	Jim Delsing	14.00	6.25	2.00
☐ 158	Bucky Harris MG	27.00	12.00	4.00
☐ 159	Dutch Leonard	16.00	6.75	2.25
☐ 160	Eddie Stanky	18.00	7.50	2.50
☐ 161	Jackie Jensen	30.00	13.50	4.50
☐ 162	Monte Irvin	45.00	20.00	6.75
☐ 163	Johnny Lipon	14.00	6.25	2.00
☐ 164	Connie Ryan	14.00	6.25	2.00
☐ 165	Saul Rogovin	14.00	6.25	2.00
☐ 166	Bobby Adams	14.00	6.25	2.00
☐ 167	Bobby Avila	16.00	6.75	2.25
☐ 168	Preacher Roe	27.00	12.00	4.00
☐ 169	Walt Dropo	16.00	6.75	2.25
☐ 170	Joe Astroth	14.00	6.25	2.00
☐ 171	Mel Queen	14.00	6.25	2.00
☐ 172	Ebba St.Claire	14.00	6.25	2.00
☐ 173	Gene Bearden	16.00	6.75	2.25
☐ 174	Mickey Grasso	14.00	6.25	2.00
☐ 175	Randy Jackson	14.00	6.25	2.00
☐ 176	Harry Brecheen	16.00	6.75	2.25
☐ 177	Gene Woodling	20.00	8.50	2.75
☐ 178	Dave Williams	18.00	7.50	2.50
☐ 179	Pete Suder	14.00	6.25	2.00
☐ 180	Ed Fitzgerald	14.00	6.25	2.00
☐ 181	Joe Collins	18.00	7.50	2.50
☐ 182	Dave Koslo	13.00	5.75	1.75
☐ 183	Pat Mullin	13.00	5.75	1.75
☐ 184	Curt Simmons	16.00	6.75	2.25
☐ 185	Eddie Stewart	13.00	5.75	1.75
☐ 186	Frank Smith	13.00	5.75	1.75
☐ 187	Jim Hegan	15.00	6.50	2.15
☐ 188	Charlie Dressen MG	16.00	6.75	2.25
☐ 189	Jim Piersall	20.00	8.50	2.75
☐ 190	Dick Fowler	13.00	5.75	1.75
☐ 191	Bob Friend	25.00	11.00	3.50
☐ 192	John Cusick	13.00	5.75	1.75
☐ 193	Bobby Young	13.00	5.75	1.75
☐ 194	Bob Porterfield	13.00	5.75	1.75
☐ 195	Frank Baumholtz	13.00	5.75	1.75
☐ 196	Stan Musial	500.00	225.00	75.00
☐ 197	Charlie Silvera	16.00	6.75	2.25
☐ 198	Chuck Diering	13.00	5.75	1.75
☐ 199	Ted Gray	13.00	5.75	1.75
☐ 200	Ken Silvestri	13.00	5.75	1.75
☐ 201	Ray Coleman	13.00	5.75	1.75
☐ 202	Harry Perkowski	13.00	5.75	1.75
☐ 203	Steve Gromek	13.00	5.75	1.75
☐ 204	Andy Pafko	15.00	6.50	2.15
☐ 205	Walt Masterson	13.00	5.75	1.75
☐ 206	Elmer Valo	13.00	5.75	1.75
☐ 207	George Strickland	13.00	5.75	1.75
☐ 208	Walker Cooper	13.00	5.75	1.75
☐ 209	Dick Littlefield	13.00	5.75	1.75
☐ 210	Archie Wilson	13.00	5.75	1.75
☐ 211	Paul Minner	13.00	5.75	1.75
☐ 212	Solly Hemus	13.00	5.75	1.75
☐ 213	Monte Kennedy	13.00	5.75	1.75
☐ 214	Ray Boone	15.00	6.50	2.15
☐ 215	Sheldon Jones	13.00	5.75	1.75
☐ 216	Matt Batts	13.00	5.75	1.75
☐ 217	Casey Stengel MG	165.00	72.00	20.00
☐ 218	Willie Mays	1000.00	400.00	100.00
☐ 219	Neil Berry	30.00	13.50	4.50
☐ 220	Russ Meyer	30.00	13.50	4.50
☐ 221	Lou Kretlow	30.00	13.50	4.50
☐ 222	Dixie Howell	30.00	13.50	4.50
☐ 223	Harry Simpson	30.00	13.50	4.50
☐ 224	Johnny Schmitz	30.00	13.50	4.50
☐ 225	Del Wilber	30.00	13.50	4.50
☐ 226	Alex Kellner	30.00	13.50	4.50
☐ 227	Clyde Sukeforth	30.00	13.50	4.50
☐ 228	Bob Chipman	30.00	13.50	4.50
☐ 229	Hank Arft	30.00	13.50	4.50
☐ 230	Frank Shea	30.00	13.50	4.50
☐ 231	Dee Fondy	30.00	13.50	4.50
☐ 232	Enos Slaughter	85.00	38.00	12.75
☐ 233	Bob Kuzava	30.00	13.50	4.50
☐ 234	Fred Fitzsimmons	30.00	13.50	4.50
☐ 235	Steve Souchock	30.00	13.50	4.50
☐ 236	Tommy Brown	30.00	13.50	4.50
☐ 237	Sherm Lollar	33.00	15.00	5.00
☐ 238	Roy McMillan	35.00	15.75	5.25
☐ 239	Dale Mitchell	33.00	15.00	5.00
☐ 240	Billy Loes	37.50	16.00	5.25
☐ 241	Mel Parnell	33.00	15.00	5.00
☐ 242	Everett Kell	30.00	13.50	4.50
☐ 243	Red Munger	30.00	13.50	4.50
☐ 244	Lew Burdette	60.00	27.00	9.00
☐ 245	George Schmees	30.00	13.50	4.50
☐ 246	Jerry Snyder	30.00	13.50	4.50
☐ 247	Johnny Pramesa	30.00	13.50	4.50
☐ 248	Bill Werle	30.00	13.50	4.50
☐ 249	Hank Thompson	33.00	15.00	5.00
☐ 250	Ike Delock	30.00	13.50	4.50
☐ 251	Jack Lohrke	30.00	13.50	4.50
☐ 252	Frank Crosetti CO	160.00	50.00	10.00

1953 Bowman Color

The cards in this 160-card set measure 2 1/2" by 3 3/4". The 1953 Bowman Color set, considered by many to be the best looking set of the modern era, contains Kodachrome photographs with no names or facsimile autographs on the face. Numbers 113 to 160 are somewhat more difficult to obtain. There are two cards of Al Corwin (126 and 149). There are no key rookie cards in this set.

	NRMT	VG-E	GOOD
COMPLETE SET (160)	11000.00	4500.00	1000.00
COMMON PLAYER (1-96)	33.00	15.00	5.00
COMMON PLAYER (97-112)	36.00	16.25	5.50
COMMON PLAYER (113-128)	55.00	25.00	8.25
COMMON PLAYER (129-160)	42.00	18.00	5.50

		NRMT	VG-E	GOOD
☐	1 Dave Williams	100.00	20.00	4.00
☐	2 Vic Wertz	36.00	16.25	5.50
☐	3 Sam Jethroe	33.00	15.00	5.00
☐	4 Art Houtteman	33.00	15.00	5.00
☐	5 Sid Gordon	33.00	15.00	5.00
☐	6 Joe Ginsberg	33.00	15.00	5.00
☐	7 Harry Chiti	33.00	15.00	5.00
☐	8 Al Rosen	45.00	20.00	6.75
☐	9 Phil Rizzuto	110.00	50.00	16.50
☐	10 Richie Ashburn	90.00	40.00	13.50
☐	11 Bobby Shantz	36.00	16.25	5.50
☐	12 Carl Erskine	42.00	18.00	5.50
☐	13 Gus Zernial	36.00	16.25	5.50
☐	14 Billy Loes	36.00	16.25	5.50
☐	15 Jim Busby	33.00	15.00	5.00
☐	16 Bob Friend	36.00	16.25	5.50
☐	17 Jerry Staley	33.00	15.00	5.00
☐	18 Nellie Fox	65.00	29.00	9.75
☐	19 Alvin Dark	36.00	16.25	5.50
☐	20 Don Lenhardt	33.00	15.00	5.00
☐	21 Joe Garagiola	80.00	36.00	12.00
☐	22 Bob Porterfield	33.00	15.00	5.00
☐	23 Herman Wehmeier	33.00	15.00	5.00
☐	24 Jackie Jensen	40.00	18.00	6.00
☐	25 Hoot Evers	33.00	15.00	5.00
☐	26 Roy McMillan	33.00	15.00	5.00
☐	27 Vic Raschi	40.00	18.00	6.00
☐	28 Smoky Burgess	36.00	16.25	5.50
☐	29 Bobby Avila	36.00	16.25	5.50
☐	30 Phil Cavarretta	36.00	16.25	5.50
☐	31 Jimmy Dykes	36.00	16.25	5.50
☐	32 Stan Musial	500.00	225.00	75.00
☐	33 Pee Wee Reese HOR	425.00	190.00	63.00
☐	34 Gil Coan	33.00	15.00	5.00
☐	35 Maurice McDermott	33.00	15.00	5.00
☐	36 Minnie Minoso	60.00	27.00	9.00
☐	37 Jim Wilson	33.00	15.00	5.00
☐	38 Harry Byrd	33.00	15.00	5.00
☐	39 Paul Richards MG	36.00	16.25	5.50
☐	40 Larry Doby	45.00	20.00	6.75
☐	41 Sammy White	33.00	15.00	5.00
☐	42 Tommy Brown	33.00	15.00	5.00
☐	43 Mike Garcia	36.00	16.25	5.50
☐	44 Berra/Bauer/Mantle	425.00	190.00	63.00
☐	45 Walt Dropo	36.00	16.25	5.50
☐	46 Roy Campanella	240.00	110.00	35.00
☐	47 Ned Garver	33.00	15.00	5.00
☐	48 Hank Sauer	36.00	16.25	5.50
☐	49 Eddie Stanky	36.00	16.25	5.50
☐	50 Lou Kretlow	33.00	15.00	5.00
☐	51 Monte Irvin	60.00	27.00	9.00
☐	52 Marty Marion	40.00	18.00	6.00
☐	53 Del Rice	33.00	15.00	5.00
☐	54 Chico Carrasquel	33.00	15.00	5.00
☐	55 Leo Durocher MG	60.00	27.00	9.00
☐	56 Bob Cain	33.00	15.00	5.00
☐	57 Lou Boudreau MG	50.00	22.50	7.50
☐	58 Willard Marshall	33.00	15.00	5.00
☐	59 Mickey Mantle	1750.00	700.00	200.00
☐	60 Granny Hamner	33.00	15.00	5.00
☐	61 George Kell	60.00	27.00	9.00
☐	62 Ted Kluszewski	60.00	27.00	9.00
☐	63 Gil McDougald	60.00	27.00	9.00
☐	64 Curt Simmons	36.00	16.25	5.50
☐	65 Robin Roberts	75.00	34.00	11.25
☐	66 Mel Parnell	36.00	16.25	5.50
☐	67 Mel Clark	33.00	15.00	5.00
☐	68 Allie Reynolds	45.00	20.00	6.75
☐	69 Charlie Grimm MG	36.00	16.25	5.50
☐	70 Clint Courtney	33.00	15.00	5.00
☐	71 Paul Minner	33.00	15.00	5.00
☐	72 Ted Gray	33.00	15.00	5.00
☐	73 Billy Pierce	40.00	18.00	6.00
☐	74 Don Mueller	36.00	16.25	5.50
☐	75 Saul Rogovin	33.00	15.00	5.00
☐	76 Jim Hearn	33.00	15.00	5.00
☐	77 Mickey Grasso	33.00	15.00	5.00
☐	78 Carl Furillo	50.00	22.50	7.50
☐	79 Ray Boone	36.00	16.25	5.50
☐	80 Ralph Kiner	80.00	36.00	12.00
☐	81 Enos Slaughter	75.00	34.00	11.25
☐	82 Joe Astroth	33.00	15.00	5.00
☐	83 Jack Daniels	33.00	15.00	5.00
☐	84 Hank Bauer	50.00	22.50	7.50
☐	85 Solly Hemus	33.00	15.00	5.00
☐	86 Harry Simpson	33.00	15.00	5.00
☐	87 Harry Perkowski	33.00	15.00	5.00
☐	88 Joe Dobson	33.00	15.00	5.00
☐	89 Sandy Consuegra	33.00	15.00	5.00
☐	90 Joe Nuxhall	36.00	16.25	5.50
☐	91 Steve Souchock	33.00	15.00	5.00
☐	92 Gil Hodges	120.00	55.00	18.00
☐	93 Phil Rizzuto and Billy Martin	210.00	90.00	27.00
☐	94 Bob Addis	33.00	15.00	5.00
☐	95 Wally Moses	36.00	16.25	5.50
☐	96 Sal Maglie	42.00	18.00	5.50
☐	97 Eddie Mathews	175.00	80.00	27.00
☐	98 Hector Rodriguez	36.00	16.25	5.50
☐	99 Warren Spahn	150.00	67.50	22.50
☐	100 Bill Wight	36.00	16.25	5.50
☐	101 Red Schoendienst	85.00	38.00	12.75
☐	102 Jim Hegan	40.00	18.00	6.00
☐	103 Del Ennis	40.00	18.00	6.00
☐	104 Luke Easter	40.00	18.00	6.00
☐	105 Eddie Joost	36.00	16.25	5.50
☐	106 Ken Raffensberger	36.00	16.25	5.50
☐	107 Alex Kellner	36.00	16.25	5.50
☐	108 Bobby Adams	36.00	16.25	5.50
☐	109 Ken Wood	36.00	16.25	5.50
☐	110 Bob Rush	36.00	16.25	5.50
☐	111 Jim Dyck	36.00	16.25	5.50
☐	112 Toby Atwell	36.00	16.25	5.50
☐	113 Karl Drews	55.00	25.00	8.25
☐	114 Bob Feller	300.00	135.00	45.00
☐	115 Cloyd Boyer	60.00	27.00	9.00
☐	116 Eddie Yost	60.00	27.00	9.00
☐	117 Duke Snider	550.00	240.00	80.00
☐	118 Billy Martin	300.00	135.00	45.00
☐	119 Dale Mitchell	60.00	27.00	9.00
☐	120 Marlin Stuart	55.00	25.00	8.25
☐	121 Yogi Berra	550.00	240.00	80.00
☐	122 Bill Serena	55.00	25.00	8.25
☐	123 Johnny Lipon	55.00	25.00	8.25
☐	124 Charlie Dressen MG	60.00	27.00	9.00
☐	125 Fred Hatfield	55.00	25.00	8.25
☐	126 Al Corwin	55.00	25.00	8.25
☐	127 Dick Kryhoski	55.00	25.00	8.25
☐	128 Whitey Lockman	60.00	27.00	9.00
☐	129 Russ Meyer	42.00	18.00	5.50
☐	130 Cass Michaels	42.00	18.00	5.50
☐	131 Connie Ryan	42.00	18.00	5.50
☐	132 Fred Hutchinson	45.00	20.00	6.75
☐	133 Willie Jones	42.00	18.00	5.50
☐	134 Johnny Pesky	45.00	20.00	6.75
☐	135 Bobby Morgan	42.00	18.00	5.50
☐	136 Jim Brideweser	42.00	18.00	5.50
☐	137 Sam Dente	42.00	18.00	5.50
☐	138 Bubba Church	42.00	18.00	5.50
☐	139 Pete Runnels	45.00	20.00	6.75
☐	140 Al Brazle	42.00	18.00	5.50
☐	141 Frank Shea	42.00	18.00	5.50
☐	142 Larry Miggins	42.00	18.00	5.50
☐	143 Al Lopez MG	65.00	29.00	9.75
☐	144 Warren Hacker	42.00	18.00	5.50

			NRMT	VG-E	GOOD
☐	145	George Shuba	45.00	20.00	6.75
☐	146	Early Wynn	120.00	55.00	18.00
☐	147	Clem Koshorek	42.00	18.00	5.50
☐	148	Billy Goodman	45.00	20.00	6.75
☐	149	Al Corwin	42.00	18.00	5.50
☐	150	Carl Scheib	42.00	18.00	5.50
☐	151	Joe Adcock	50.00	22.50	7.50
☐	152	Clyde Vollmer	42.00	18.00	5.50
☐	153	Whitey Ford	450.00	200.00	67.50
☐	154	Turk Lown	42.00	18.00	5.50
☐	155	Allie Clark	42.00	18.00	5.50
☐	156	Max Surkont	42.00	18.00	5.50
☐	157	Sherm Lollar	45.00	20.00	6.75
☐	158	Howard Fox	42.00	18.00	5.50
☐	159	Mickey Vernon UER (photo actually Floyd Baker)	45.00	20.00	6.75
☐	160	Cal Abrams	90.00	25.00	5.00

1953 Bowman B/W

The cards in this 64-card set measure 2 1/2" by 3 3/4". Some collectors believe that the high cost of producing the 1953 color series forced Bowman to issue this set in black and white, since the two sets are identical in design except for the element of color. This set was also produced in fewer numbers than its color counterpart, and is popular among collectors for the challenge involved in completing it. There are no key rookie cards in this set.

			NRMT	VG-E	GOOD
		COMPLETE SET (64)	2500.00	1000.00	275.00
		COMMON PLAYER (1-64)	35.00	15.75	5.25
☐	1	Gus Bell	125.00	25.00	5.00
☐	2	Willard Nixon	35.00	15.75	5.25
☐	3	Bill Rigney	35.00	15.75	5.25
☐	4	Pat Mullin	35.00	15.75	5.25
☐	5	Dee Fondy	35.00	15.75	5.25
☐	6	Ray Murray	35.00	15.75	5.25
☐	7	Andy Seminick	35.00	15.75	5.25
☐	8	Pete Suder	35.00	15.75	5.25
☐	9	Walt Masterson	35.00	15.75	5.25
☐	10	Dick Sisler	35.00	15.75	5.25
☐	11	Dick Gernert	35.00	15.75	5.25
☐	12	Randy Jackson	35.00	15.75	5.25
☐	13	Joe Tipton	35.00	15.75	5.25
☐	14	Bill Nicholson	35.00	15.75	5.25
☐	15	Johnny Mize	130.00	60.00	20.00
☐	16	Stu Miller	40.00	18.00	6.00
☐	17	Virgil Trucks	40.00	18.00	6.00
☐	18	Billy Hoeft	35.00	15.75	5.25
☐	19	Paul LaPalme	35.00	15.75	5.25
☐	20	Eddie Robinson	35.00	15.75	5.25
☐	21	Clarence Podbielan	35.00	15.75	5.25
☐	22	Matt Batts	35.00	15.75	5.25
☐	23	Wilmer Mizell	35.00	15.75	5.25
☐	24	Del Wilber	35.00	15.75	5.25
☐	25	Johnny Sain	55.00	25.00	8.25
☐	26	Preacher Roe	55.00	25.00	8.25
☐	27	Bob Lemon	130.00	60.00	20.00
☐	28	Hoyt Wilhelm	130.00	60.00	20.00
☐	29	Sid Hudson	35.00	15.75	5.25

			NRMT	VG-E	GOOD
☐	30	Walker Cooper	35.00	15.75	5.25
☐	31	Gene Woodling	48.00	22.00	6.50
☐	32	Rocky Bridges	35.00	15.75	5.25
☐	33	Bob Kuzava	35.00	15.75	5.25
☐	34	Ebba St.Claire	35.00	15.75	5.25
☐	35	Johnny Wyrostek	35.00	15.75	5.25
☐	36	Jim Piersall	48.00	22.00	6.50
☐	37	Hal Jeffcoat	35.00	15.75	5.25
☐	38	Dave Cole	35.00	15.75	5.25
☐	39	Casey Stengel MG	325.00	150.00	50.00
☐	40	Larry Jansen	35.00	15.75	5.25
☐	41	Bob Ramazotti	35.00	15.75	5.25
☐	42	Howie Judson	35.00	15.75	5.25
☐	43	Hal Bevan	35.00	15.75	5.25
☐	44	Jim Delsing	35.00	15.75	5.25
☐	45	Irv Noren	35.00	15.75	5.25
☐	46	Bucky Harris	55.00	25.00	8.25
☐	47	Jack Lohrke	35.00	15.75	5.25
☐	48	Steve Ridzik	35.00	15.75	5.25
☐	49	Floyd Baker	35.00	15.75	5.25
☐	50	Dutch Leonard	35.00	15.75	5.25
☐	51	Lou Burdette	48.00	22.00	6.50
☐	52	Ralph Branca	40.00	18.00	6.00
☐	53	Morrie Martin	35.00	15.75	5.25
☐	54	Bill Miller	35.00	15.75	5.25
☐	55	Don Johnson	35.00	15.75	5.25
☐	56	Roy Smalley	35.00	15.75	5.25
☐	57	Andy Pafko	35.00	15.75	5.25
☐	58	Jim Konstanty	40.00	18.00	6.00
☐	59	Duane Pillette	35.00	15.75	5.25
☐	60	Billy Cox	40.00	18.00	6.00
☐	61	Tom Gorman	35.00	15.75	5.25
☐	62	Keith Thomas	35.00	15.75	5.25
☐	63	Steve Gromek	35.00	15.75	5.25
☐	64	Andy Hansen	50.00	20.00	4.00

1954 Bowman

The cards in this 224-card set measure 2 1/2" by 3 3/4". A contractual problem apparently resulted in the deletion of the number 66 Ted Williams card from this Bowman set, thereby creating a scarcity that is highly valued among collectors. The set price below does NOT include number 66 Williams. Many errors in players' statistics exist (and some were corrected) while a few players' names were printed on the front, instead of appearing as a facsimile autograph. The notable rookie cards in this set are Harvey Kuenn and Don Larsen.

			NRMT	VG-E	GOOD
		COMPLETE SET (224)	4500.00	1800.00	475.00
		COMMON PLAYER (1-128)	10.00	4.50	1.25
		COMMON PLAYER (129-224)	14.00	6.25	2.00
☐	1	Phil Rizzuto	135.00	35.00	7.00
☐	2	Jackie Jensen	15.00	6.50	2.15
☐	3	Marion Fricano	10.00	4.50	1.25
☐	4	Bob Hooper	10.00	4.50	1.25
☐	5	Billy Hunter	10.00	4.50	1.25
☐	6	Nellie Fox	25.00	11.00	3.50
☐	7	Walt Dropo	12.00	5.25	1.50
☐	8	Jim Busby	10.00	4.50	1.25
☐	9	Davey Williams	10.00	4.50	1.25
☐	10	Carl Erskine	15.00	6.50	2.15
☐	11	Sid Gordon	10.00	4.50	1.25

No.	Player			
☐ 12	Roy McMillan	10.00	4.50	1.25
☐ 13	Paul Minner	10.00	4.50	1.25
☐ 14	Jerry Staley	10.00	4.50	1.25
☐ 15	Richie Ashburn	30.00	13.50	4.50
☐ 16	Jim Wilson	10.00	4.50	1.25
☐ 17	Tom Gorman	10.00	4.50	1.25
☐ 18	Hoot Evers	10.00	4.50	1.25
☐ 19	Bobby Shantz	12.00	5.25	1.50
☐ 20	Art Houtteman	10.00	4.50	1.25
☐ 21	Vic Wertz	12.00	5.25	1.50
☐ 22	Sam Mele	10.00	4.50	1.25
☐ 23	Harvey Kuenn	28.00	12.50	4.00
☐ 24	Bob Porterfield	10.00	4.50	1.25
☐ 25	Wes Westrum	10.00	4.50	1.25
☐ 26	Billy Cox	12.00	5.25	1.50
☐ 27	Dick Cole	10.00	4.50	1.25
☐ 28	Jim Greengrass	10.00	4.50	1.25
☐ 29	Johnny Klippstein	10.00	4.50	1.25
☐ 30	Del Rice	10.00	4.50	1.25
☐ 31	Smoky Burgess	12.00	5.25	1.50
☐ 32	Del Crandall	12.00	5.25	1.50
☐ 33A	Vic Raschi (no mention of trade on back)	18.00	7.50	2.50
☐ 33B	Vic Raschi (traded to St.Louis)	30.00	13.50	4.50
☐ 34	Sammy White	10.00	4.50	1.25
☐ 35	Eddie Joost	10.00	4.50	1.25
☐ 36	George Strickland	10.00	4.50	1.25
☐ 37	Dick Kokos	10.00	4.50	1.25
☐ 38	Minnie Minoso	20.00	8.50	2.75
☐ 39	Ned Garver	10.00	4.50	1.25
☐ 40	Gil Coan	10.00	4.50	1.25
☐ 41	Alvin Dark	12.00	5.25	1.50
☐ 42	Billy Loes	12.00	5.25	1.50
☐ 43	Bob Friend	12.00	5.25	1.50
☐ 44	Harry Perkowski	10.00	4.50	1.25
☐ 45	Ralph Kiner	42.00	18.00	5.50
☐ 46	Rip Repulski	10.00	4.50	1.25
☐ 47	Granny Hamner	10.00	4.50	1.25
☐ 48	Jack Dittmer	10.00	4.50	1.25
☐ 49	Harry Byrd	10.00	4.50	1.25
☐ 50	George Kell	28.00	12.50	4.00
☐ 51	Alex Kellner	10.00	4.50	1.25
☐ 52	Joe Ginsberg	10.00	4.50	1.25
☐ 53	Don Lenhardt	10.00	4.50	1.25
☐ 54	Chico Carrasquel	10.00	4.50	1.25
☐ 55	Jim Delsing	10.00	4.50	1.25
☐ 56	Maurice McDermott	10.00	4.50	1.25
☐ 57	Hoyt Wilhelm	28.00	12.50	4.00
☐ 58	Pee Wee Reese	70.00	32.00	10.50
☐ 59	Bob Schultz	10.00	4.50	1.25
☐ 60	Fred Baczewski	10.00	4.50	1.25
☐ 61	Eddie Miksis	10.00	4.50	1.25
☐ 62	Enos Slaughter	42.00	18.00	5.50
☐ 63	Earl Torgeson	10.00	4.50	1.25
☐ 64	Eddie Mathews	65.00	29.00	9.75
☐ 65	Mickey Mantle	850.00	375.00	125.00
☐ 66A	Ted Williams	4000.00	1500.00	300.00
☐ 66B	Jim Piersall	100.00	45.00	15.00
☐ 67	Carl Scheib	10.00	4.50	1.25
☐ 68	Bobby Avila	10.00	4.50	1.25
☐ 69	Clint Courtney	10.00	4.50	1.25
☐ 70	Willard Marshall	10.00	4.50	1.25
☐ 71	Ted Gray	10.00	4.50	1.25
☐ 72	Eddie Yost	10.00	4.50	1.25
☐ 73	Don Mueller	12.00	5.25	1.50
☐ 74	Jim Gilliam	20.00	8.50	2.75
☐ 75	Max Surkont	10.00	4.50	1.25
☐ 76	Joe Nuxhall	12.00	5.25	1.50
☐ 77	Bob Rush	10.00	4.50	1.25
☐ 78	Sal Yvars	10.00	4.50	1.25
☐ 79	Curt Simmons	12.00	5.25	1.50
☐ 80	Johnny Logan	12.00	5.25	1.50
☐ 81	Jerry Coleman	12.00	5.25	1.50
☐ 82	Billy Goodman	12.00	5.25	1.50
☐ 83	Ray Murray	10.00	4.50	1.25
☐ 84	Larry Doby	15.00	6.50	2.15
☐ 85	Jim Dyck	10.00	4.50	1.25
☐ 86	Harry Dorish	10.00	4.50	1.25
☐ 87	Don Lund	10.00	4.50	1.25
☐ 88	Tom Umphlett	10.00	4.50	1.25
☐ 89	Willie Mays	350.00	160.00	52.50
☐ 90	Roy Campanella	135.00	60.00	20.00
☐ 91	Cal Abrams	10.00	4.50	1.25
☐ 92	Ken Raffensberger	10.00	4.50	1.25
☐ 93	Bill Serena	10.00	4.50	1.25
☐ 94	Solly Hemus	10.00	4.50	1.25
☐ 95	Robin Roberts	36.00	16.25	5.50
☐ 96	Joe Adcock	12.00	5.25	1.50
☐ 97	Gil McDougald	18.00	7.50	2.50
☐ 98	Ellis Kinder	10.00	4.50	1.25
☐ 99	Pete Suder	10.00	4.50	1.25
☐ 100	Mike Garcia	12.00	5.25	1.50
☐ 101	Don Larsen	35.00	15.75	5.25
☐ 102	Billy Pierce	12.00	5.25	1.50
☐ 103	Steve Souchock	10.00	4.50	1.25
☐ 104	Frank Shea	10.00	4.50	1.25
☐ 105	Sal Maglie	15.00	6.50	2.15
☐ 106	Clem Labine	12.00	5.25	1.50
☐ 107	Paul LaPalme	10.00	4.50	1.25
☐ 108	Bobby Adams	10.00	4.50	1.25
☐ 109	Roy Smalley	10.00	4.50	1.25
☐ 110	Red Schoendienst	36.00	16.25	5.50
☐ 111	Murry Dickson	10.00	4.50	1.25
☐ 112	Andy Pafko	12.00	5.25	1.50
☐ 113	Allie Reynolds	18.00	7.50	2.50
☐ 114	Willard Nixon	10.00	4.50	1.25
☐ 115	Don Bollweg	10.00	4.50	1.25
☐ 116	Luke Easter	10.00	4.50	1.25
☐ 117	Dick Kryhoski	10.00	4.50	1.25
☐ 118	Bob Boyd	10.00	4.50	1.25
☐ 119	Fred Hatfield	10.00	4.50	1.25
☐ 120	Mel Hoderlein	10.00	4.50	1.25
☐ 121	Ray Katt	10.00	4.50	1.25
☐ 122	Carl Furillo	20.00	8.50	2.75
☐ 123	Toby Atwell	10.00	4.50	1.25
☐ 124	Gus Bell	12.00	5.25	1.50
☐ 125	Warren Hacker	10.00	4.50	1.25
☐ 126	Cliff Chambers	10.00	4.50	1.25
☐ 127	Del Ennis	12.00	5.25	1.50
☐ 128	Ebba St.Claire	10.00	4.50	1.25
☐ 129	Hank Bauer	21.00	9.00	3.00
☐ 130	Milt Bolling	14.00	6.25	2.00
☐ 131	Joe Astroth	14.00	6.25	2.00
☐ 132	Bob Feller	90.00	40.00	13.50
☐ 133	Duane Pillette	14.00	6.25	2.00
☐ 134	Luis Aloma	14.00	6.25	2.00
☐ 135	Johnny Pesky	16.00	6.75	2.25
☐ 136	Clyde Vollmer	14.00	6.25	2.00
☐ 137	Al Corwin	14.00	6.25	2.00
☐ 138	Gil Hodges	65.00	29.00	9.75
☐ 139	Preston Ward	14.00	6.25	2.00
☐ 140	Saul Rogovin	14.00	6.25	2.00
☐ 141	Joe Garagiola	48.00	22.00	6.00
☐ 142	Al Brazle	14.00	6.25	2.00
☐ 143	Willie Jones	14.00	6.25	2.00
☐ 144	Ernie Johnson	18.00	7.50	2.50
☐ 145	Billy Martin	70.00	32.00	10.50
☐ 146	Dick Gernert	14.00	6.25	2.00
☐ 147	Joe DeMaestri	14.00	6.25	2.00
☐ 148	Dale Mitchell	16.00	6.75	2.25
☐ 149	Bob Young	14.00	6.25	2.00
☐ 150	Cass Michaels	14.00	6.25	2.00
☐ 151	Pat Mullin	14.00	6.25	2.00
☐ 152	Mickey Vernon	16.00	6.75	2.25
☐ 153	Whitey Lockman	16.00	6.75	2.25
☐ 154	Don Newcombe	24.00	10.50	3.50
☐ 155	Frank Thomas	18.00	7.50	2.50
☐ 156	Rocky Bridges	14.00	6.25	2.00
☐ 157	Turk Lown	14.00	6.25	2.00
☐ 158	Stu Miller	16.00	6.75	2.25
☐ 159	Johnny Lindell	14.00	6.25	2.00
☐ 160	Danny O'Connell	14.00	6.25	2.00
☐ 161	Yogi Berra	175.00	80.00	27.00
☐ 162	Ted Lepcio	14.00	6.25	2.00
☐ 163A	Dave Philley (no mention of trade on back)	16.00	6.75	2.25
☐ 163B	Dave Philley (traded to Cleveland)	24.00	10.50	3.50
☐ 164	Early Wynn	42.00	18.00	5.75
☐ 165	Johnny Groth	14.00	6.25	2.00
☐ 166	Sandy Consuegra	14.00	6.25	2.00
☐ 167	Billy Hoeft	14.00	6.25	2.00
☐ 168	Ed Fitzgerald	14.00	6.25	2.00
☐ 169	Larry Jansen	16.00	6.75	2.25
☐ 170	Duke Snider	150.00	67.50	22.50
☐ 171	Carlos Bernier	14.00	6.25	2.00
☐ 172	Andy Seminick	14.00	6.25	2.00
☐ 173	Dee Fondy	14.00	6.25	2.00
☐ 174	Pete Castiglione	14.00	6.25	2.00
☐ 175	Mel Clark	14.00	6.25	2.00
☐ 176	Vern Bickford	14.00	6.25	2.00
☐ 177	Whitey Ford	100.00	45.00	15.00
☐ 178	Del Wilber	14.00	6.25	2.00
☐ 179	Morrie Martin	14.00	6.25	2.00
☐ 180	Joe Tipton	14.00	6.25	2.00
☐ 181	Les Moss	14.00	6.25	2.00
☐ 182	Sherm Lollar	16.00	6.75	2.25
☐ 183	Matt Batts	14.00	6.25	2.00
☐ 184	Mickey Grasso	14.00	6.25	2.00
☐ 185	Daryl Spencer	14.00	6.25	2.00
☐ 186	Russ Meyer	14.00	6.25	2.00
☐ 187	Vernon Law	16.00	6.75	2.25
☐ 188	Frank Smith	14.00	6.25	2.00
☐ 189	Randy Jackson	14.00	6.25	2.00
☐ 190	Joe Presko	14.00	6.25	2.00
☐ 191	Karl Drews	14.00	6.25	2.00

		NRMT	VG-E	GOOD
☐ 192	Lou Burdette	18.00	7.50	2.50
☐ 193	Eddie Robinson	14.00	6.25	2.00
☐ 194	Sid Hudson	14.00	6.25	2.00
☐ 195	Bob Cain	14.00	6.25	2.00
☐ 196	Bob Lemon	36.00	16.25	5.50
☐ 197	Lou Kretlow	14.00	6.25	2.00
☐ 198	Virgil Trucks	16.00	6.75	2.25
☐ 199	Steve Gromek	14.00	6.25	2.00
☐ 200	Conrado Marrero	14.00	6.25	2.00
☐ 201	Bobby Thomson	18.00	7.50	2.50
☐ 202	George Shuba	18.00	7.50	2.50
☐ 203	Vic Janowicz	16.00	6.75	2.25
☐ 204	Jack Collum	14.00	6.25	2.00
☐ 205	Hal Jeffcoat	14.00	6.25	2.00
☐ 206	Steve Bilko	14.00	6.25	2.00
☐ 207	Stan Lopata	14.00	6.25	2.00
☐ 208	Johnny Antonelli	16.00	6.75	2.25
☐ 209	Gene Woodling	16.00	6.75	2.25
☐ 210	Jim Piersall	18.00	7.50	2.50
☐ 211	Al Robertson	14.00	6.25	2.00
☐ 212	Owen Friend	14.00	6.25	2.00
☐ 213	Dick Littlefield	14.00	6.25	2.00
☐ 214	Ferris Fain	16.00	6.75	2.25
☐ 215	Johnny Bucha	14.00	6.25	2.00
☐ 216	Jerry Snyder	14.00	6.25	2.00
☐ 217	Hank Thompson	16.00	6.75	2.25
☐ 218	Preacher Roe	18.00	7.50	2.50
☐ 219	Hal Rice	14.00	6.25	2.00
☐ 220	Hobie Landrith	14.00	6.25	2.00
☐ 221	Frank Baumholtz	14.00	6.25	2.00
☐ 222	Memo Luna	14.00	6.25	2.00
☐ 223	Steve Ridzik	14.00	6.25	2.00
☐ 224	Bill Bruton	42.00	9.00	2.00

1955 Bowman

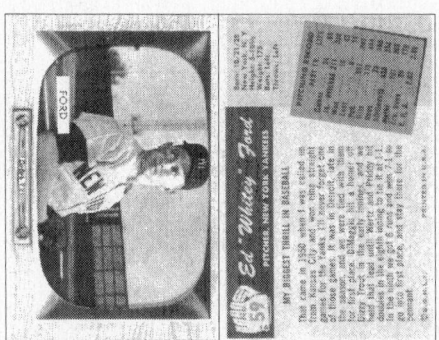

The cards in this 320-card set measure 2 1/2" by 3 3/4". The Bowman set of 1955 is known as the "TV set" because each player photograph is cleverly shown within a television set design. The set contains umpire cards, some transposed pictures (e.g., Johnsons and Bollings), an incorrect spelling for Harvey Kuenn, and a traded line for Palica (all of which are noted in the checklist below). Some three-card advertising strips exist, the backs of these panels contain advertising for Bowman products. Advertising panels seen include Nellie Fox/Carl Furillo/ Carl Erskine and a panel including Early Wynn and Pee Wee Reese. The notable rookie cards in this set are Elston Howard and Don Zimmer.

	NRMT	VG-E	GOOD
COMPLETE SET (320)	5250.00	2350.00	550.00
COMMON PLAYER (1-96)	8.00	3.50	.80
COMMON PLAYER (97-224)	7.00	3.00	.70
COMMON PLAYER (225-320)	16.50	7.00	2.35
COMMON UMPIRES (225-320)	30.00	13.50	4.50

☐ 1	Hoyt Wilhelm	100.00	15.00	3.00
☐ 2	Alvin Dark	11.00	5.00	1.35
☐ 3	Joe Coleman	8.00	3.50	.80
☐ 4	Eddie Waitkus	8.00	3.50	.80
☐ 5	Jim Robertson	8.00	3.50	.80
☐ 6	Pete Suder	8.00	3.50	.80

☐ 7	Gene Baker	8.00	3.50	.80
☐ 8	Warren Hacker	8.00	3.50	.80
☐ 9	Gil McDougald	16.00	6.75	2.25
☐ 10	Phil Rizzuto	50.00	22.50	7.50
☐ 11	Bill Bruton	9.00	4.00	.90
☐ 12	Andy Pafko	9.00	4.00	.90
☐ 13	Clyde Vollmer	8.00	3.50	.80
☐ 14	Gus Keriazakos	8.00	3.50	.80
☐ 15	Frank Sullivan	8.00	3.50	.80
☐ 16	Jim Piersall	11.00	5.00	1.35
☐ 17	Del Ennis	9.00	4.00	.90
☐ 18	Stan Lopata	8.00	3.50	.80
☐ 19	Bobby Avila	8.00	3.50	.80
☐ 20	Al Smith	8.00	3.50	.80
☐ 21	Don Hoak	9.00	4.00	.90
☐ 22	Roy Campanella	110.00	50.00	16.50
☐ 23	Al Kaline	140.00	63.00	21.00
☐ 24	Al Aber	8.00	3.50	.80
☐ 25	Minnie Minoso	16.00	6.75	2.25
☐ 26	Virgil Trucks	9.00	4.00	.90
☐ 27	Preston Ward	8.00	3.50	.80
☐ 28	Dick Cole	8.00	3.50	.80
☐ 29	Red Schoendienst	27.00	12.00	4.00
☐ 30	Bill Sarni	8.00	3.50	.80
☐ 31	Johnny Temple	10.00	4.50	1.25
☐ 32	Wally Post	9.00	4.00	.90
☐ 33	Nellie Fox	22.00	9.50	3.15
☐ 34	Clint Courtney	8.00	3.50	.80
☐ 35	Bill Tuttle	8.00	3.50	.80
☐ 36	Wayne Belardi	8.00	3.50	.80
☐ 37	Pee Wee Reese	70.00	32.00	10.50
☐ 38	Early Wynn	27.00	12.00	4.00
☐ 39	Bob Darnell	8.00	3.50	.80
☐ 40	Vic Wertz	9.00	4.00	.90
☐ 41	Mel Clark	8.00	3.50	.80
☐ 42	Bob Greenwood	8.00	3.50	.80
☐ 43	Bob Buhl	9.00	4.00	.90
☐ 44	Danny O'Connell	8.00	3.50	.80
☐ 45	Tom Umphlett	8.00	3.50	.80
☐ 46	Mickey Vernon	9.00	4.00	.90
☐ 47	Sammy White	8.00	3.50	.80
☐ 48A	Milt Bolling ERR (name on back is Frank Bolling)	10.00	4.50	1.25
☐ 48B	Milt Bolling COR	25.00	11.00	3.50
☐ 49	Jim Greengrass	8.00	3.50	.80
☐ 50	Hobie Landrith	8.00	3.50	.80
☐ 51	Elvin Tappe	8.00	3.50	.80
☐ 52	Hal Rice	8.00	3.50	.80
☐ 53	Alex Kellner	8.00	3.50	.80
☐ 54	Don Bollweg	8.00	3.50	.80
☐ 55	Cal Abrams	8.00	3.50	.80
☐ 56	Billy Cox	9.00	4.00	.90
☐ 57	Bob Friend	9.00	4.00	.90
☐ 58	Frank Thomas	10.00	4.50	1.25
☐ 59	Whitey Ford	70.00	32.00	10.50
☐ 60	Enos Slaughter	27.00	12.00	4.00
☐ 61	Paul LaPalme	8.00	3.50	.80
☐ 62	Royce Lint	8.00	3.50	.80
☐ 63	Irv Noren	9.00	4.00	.90
☐ 64	Curt Simmons	9.00	4.00	.90
☐ 65	Don Zimmer	30.00	13.50	4.50
☐ 66	George Shuba	9.00	4.00	.90
☐ 67	Don Larsen	16.00	6.75	2.25
☐ 68	Elston Howard	65.00	29.00	9.75
☐ 69	Billy Hunter	8.00	3.50	.80
☐ 70	Lou Burdette	10.00	4.50	1.25
☐ 71	Dave Jolly	8.00	3.50	.80
☐ 72	Chet Nichols	8.00	3.50	.80
☐ 73	Eddie Yost	8.00	3.50	.80
☐ 74	Jerry Snyder	8.00	3.50	.80
☐ 75	Brooks Lawrence	8.00	3.50	.80
☐ 76	Tom Poholsky	8.00	3.50	.80
☐ 77	Jim McDonald	8.00	3.50	.80
☐ 78	Gil Coan	8.00	3.50	.80
☐ 79	Willie Miranda	8.00	3.50	.80
☐ 80	Lou Limmer	8.00	3.50	.80
☐ 81	Bobby Morgan	8.00	3.50	.80
☐ 82	Lee Walls	8.00	3.50	.80
☐ 83	Max Surkont	8.00	3.50	.80
☐ 84	George Freese	8.00	3.50	.80
☐ 85	Cass Michaels	8.00	3.50	.80
☐ 86	Ted Gray	8.00	3.50	.80
☐ 87	Randy Jackson	8.00	3.50	.80
☐ 88	Steve Bilko	8.00	3.50	.80
☐ 89	Lou Boudreau MG	22.00	9.50	3.15
☐ 90	Art Ditmar	8.00	3.50	.80
☐ 91	Dick Marlowe	8.00	3.50	.80
☐ 92	George Zuverink	8.00	3.50	.80
☐ 93	Andy Seminick	8.00	3.50	.80
☐ 94	Hank Thompson	9.00	4.00	.90
☐ 95	Sal Maglie	12.00	5.25	1.50
☐ 96	Ray Narleski	8.00	3.50	.80
☐ 97	Johnny Podres	16.00	6.75	2.25
☐ 98	Jim Gilliam	16.00	6.75	2.25

#	Player			
☐ 99	Jerry Coleman	9.00	4.00	.90
☐ 100	Tom Morgan	8.00	3.50	.80
☐ 101A	Don Johnson ERR (photo actually Ernie Johnson)	10.00	4.50	1.25
☐ 101B	Don Johnson COR	21.00	9.00	3.00
☐ 102	Bobby Thomson	11.00	5.00	1.35
☐ 103	Eddie Mathews	50.00	22.50	7.50
☐ 104	Bob Porterfield	7.00	3.00	.70
☐ 105	Johnny Schmitz	7.00	3.00	.70
☐ 106	Del Rice	7.00	3.00	.70
☐ 107	Solly Hemus	7.00	3.00	.70
☐ 108	Lou Kretlow	7.00	3.00	.70
☐ 109	Vern Stephens	8.00	3.50	.80
☐ 110	Bob Miller	7.00	3.00	.70
☐ 111	Steve Ridzik	7.00	3.00	.70
☐ 112	Granny Hamner	7.00	3.00	.70
☐ 113	Bob Hall	7.00	3.00	.70
☐ 114	Vic Janowicz	8.00	3.50	.80
☐ 115	Roger Bowman	7.00	3.00	.70
☐ 116	Sandy Consuegra	7.00	3.00	.70
☐ 117	Johnny Groth	7.00	3.00	.70
☐ 118	Bobby Adams	7.00	3.00	.70
☐ 119	Joe Astroth	7.00	3.00	.70
☐ 120	Ed Burtschy	7.00	3.00	.70
☐ 121	Rufus Crawford	7.00	3.00	.70
☐ 122	Al Corwin	7.00	3.00	.70
☐ 123	Marv Grissom	7.00	3.00	.70
☐ 124	Johnny Antonelli	9.00	4.00	.90
☐ 125	Paul Giel	7.00	3.00	.70
☐ 126	Billy Goodman	8.00	3.50	.80
☐ 127	Hank Majeski	7.00	3.00	.70
☐ 128	Mike Garcia	8.00	3.50	.80
☐ 129	Hal Naragon	7.00	3.00	.70
☐ 130	Richie Ashburn	24.00	10.50	3.50
☐ 131	Willard Marshall	7.00	3.00	.70
☐ 132A	Harvey Kueen ERR (sic, Kuenn)	11.00	5.00	1.35
☐ 132B	Harvey Kuenn COR	27.00	12.00	4.00
☐ 133	Charles King	7.00	3.00	.70
☐ 134	Bob Feller	60.00	27.00	9.00
☐ 135	Lloyd Merriman	7.00	3.00	.70
☐ 136	Rocky Bridges	7.00	3.00	.70
☐ 137	Bob Talbot	7.00	3.00	.70
☐ 138	Davey Williams	8.00	3.50	.80
☐ 139	Shantz Brothers Wilmer and Bobby	9.00	4.00	.90
☐ 140	Bobby Shantz	9.00	4.00	.90
☐ 141	Wes Westrum	7.00	3.00	.70
☐ 142	Rudy Regalado	7.00	3.00	.70
☐ 143	Don Newcombe	17.00	7.25	2.50
☐ 144	Art Houtteman	7.00	3.00	.70
☐ 145	Bob Nieman	7.00	3.00	.70
☐ 146	Don Liddle	7.00	3.00	.70
☐ 147	Sam Mele	7.00	3.00	.70
☐ 148	Bob Chakales	7.00	3.00	.70
☐ 149	Cloyd Boyer	7.00	3.00	.70
☐ 150	Billy Klaus	7.00	3.00	.70
☐ 151	Jim Brideweser	7.00	3.00	.70
☐ 152	Johnny Klippstein	7.00	3.00	.70
☐ 153	Eddie Robinson	7.00	3.00	.70
☐ 154	Frank Lary	10.00	4.50	1.25
☐ 155	Jerry Staley	7.00	3.00	.70
☐ 156	Jim Hughes	7.00	3.00	.70
☐ 157A	Ernie Johnson ERR (photo actually Don Johnson)	10.00	4.50	1.25
☐ 157B	Ernie Johnson COR	21.00	9.00	3.00
☐ 158	Gil Hodges	40.00	18.00	6.00
☐ 159	Harry Byrd	8.00	3.50	.80
☐ 160	Bill Skowron	22.00	9.50	3.15
☐ 161	Matt Batts	7.00	3.00	.70
☐ 162	Charlie Maxwell	8.00	3.50	.80
☐ 163	Sid Gordon	7.00	3.00	.70
☐ 164	Toby Atwell	7.00	3.00	.70
☐ 165	Maurice McDermott	7.00	3.00	.70
☐ 166	Jim Busby	7.00	3.00	.70
☐ 167	Bob Grim	12.00	5.25	1.50
☐ 168	Yogi Berra	95.00	42.00	12.00
☐ 169	Carl Furillo	16.00	6.75	2.25
☐ 170	Carl Erskine	15.00	6.50	2.15
☐ 171	Robin Roberts	25.00	11.00	3.50
☐ 172	Willie Jones	7.00	3.00	.70
☐ 173	Chico Carrasquel	7.00	3.00	.70
☐ 174	Sherm Lollar	8.00	3.50	.80
☐ 175	Wilmer Shantz	7.00	3.00	.70
☐ 176	Joe DeMaestri	7.00	3.00	.70
☐ 177	Willard Nixon	7.00	3.00	.70
☐ 178	Tom Brewer	7.00	3.00	.70
☐ 179	Hank Aaron	225.00	100.00	33.00
☐ 180	Johnny Logan	8.00	3.50	.80
☐ 181	Eddie Miksis	7.00	3.00	.70
☐ 182	Bob Rush	7.00	3.00	.70
☐ 183	Ray Katt	7.00	3.00	.70
☐ 184	Willie Mays	225.00	100.00	33.00
☐ 185	Vic Raschi	10.00	4.50	1.25
☐ 186	Alex Grammas	7.00	3.00	.70
☐ 187	Fred Hatfield	7.00	3.00	.70
☐ 188	Ned Garver	7.00	3.00	.70
☐ 189	Jack Collum	7.00	3.00	.70
☐ 190	Fred Baczewski	7.00	3.00	.70
☐ 191	Bob Lemon	25.00	11.00	3.50
☐ 192	George Strickland	7.00	3.00	.70
☐ 193	Howie Judson	7.00	3.00	.70
☐ 194	Joe Nuxhall	8.00	3.50	.80
☐ 195A	Erv Palica (without trade)	8.00	3.50	.80
☐ 195B	Erv Palica (with trade)	20.00	8.50	2.75
☐ 196	Russ Meyer	7.00	3.00	.70
☐ 197	Ralph Kiner	28.00	12.50	4.00
☐ 198	Dave Pope	7.00	3.00	.70
☐ 199	Vernon Law	8.00	3.50	.80
☐ 200	Dick Littlefield	7.00	3.00	.70
☐ 201	Allie Reynolds	15.00	6.50	2.15
☐ 202	Mickey Mantle	450.00	200.00	67.50
☐ 203	Steve Gromek	7.00	3.00	.70
☐ 204A	Frank Bolling ERR (name on back is Milt Bolling)	9.00	4.00	.90
☐ 204B	Frank Bolling COR	21.00	9.00	3.00
☐ 205	Rip Repulski	7.00	3.00	.70
☐ 206	Ralph Beard	7.00	3.00	.70
☐ 207	Frank Shea	7.00	3.00	.70
☐ 208	Ed Fitzgerald	7.00	3.00	.70
☐ 209	Smoky Burgess	9.00	4.00	.90
☐ 210	Earl Torgeson	7.00	3.00	.70
☐ 211	Sonny Dixon	7.00	3.00	.70
☐ 212	Jack Dittmer	7.00	3.00	.70
☐ 213	George Kell	20.00	8.50	2.75
☐ 214	Billy Pierce	10.00	4.50	1.25
☐ 215	Bob Kuzava	7.00	3.00	.70
☐ 216	Preacher Roe	12.00	5.25	1.50
☐ 217	Del Crandall	8.00	3.50	.80
☐ 218	Joe Adcock	9.00	4.00	.90
☐ 219	Whitey Lockman	8.00	3.50	.80
☐ 220	Jim Hearn	7.00	3.00	.70
☐ 221	Hector Brown	7.00	3.00	.70
☐ 222	Russ Kemmerer	7.00	3.00	.70
☐ 223	Hal Jeffcoat	7.00	3.00	.70
☐ 224	Dee Fondy	7.00	3.00	.70
☐ 225	Paul Richards	20.00	8.50	2.75
☐ 226	W. McKinley UMP	30.00	13.50	4.50
☐ 227	Frank Baumholtz	16.50	7.00	2.35
☐ 228	John Phillips	16.50	7.00	2.35
☐ 229	Jim Brosnan	20.00	8.50	2.75
☐ 230	Al Brazle	16.50	7.00	2.35
☐ 231	Jim Konstanty	20.00	8.50	2.75
☐ 232	Birdie Tebbetts	18.00	7.50	2.50
☐ 233	Bill Serena	16.50	7.00	2.35
☐ 234	Dick Bartell	18.00	7.50	2.50
☐ 235	J. Paparella UMP	30.00	13.50	4.50
☐ 236	Murry Dickson	16.50	7.00	2.35
☐ 237	Johnny Wyrostek	16.50	7.00	2.35
☐ 238	Eddie Stanky	20.00	8.50	2.75
☐ 239	Edwin Rommel UMP	30.00	13.50	4.50
☐ 240	Billy Loes	18.00	7.50	2.50
☐ 241	Johnny Pesky	18.00	7.50	2.50
☐ 242	Ernie Banks	350.00	160.00	52.50
☐ 243	Gus Bell	18.00	7.50	2.50
☐ 244	Duane Pillette	16.50	7.00	2.35
☐ 245	Bill Miller	16.50	7.00	2.35
☐ 246	Hank Bauer	36.00	16.25	5.50
☐ 247	Dutch Leonard	18.00	7.50	2.50
☐ 248	Harry Dorish	16.50	7.00	2.35
☐ 249	Billy Gardner	18.00	7.50	2.50
☐ 250	Larry Napp UMP	30.00	13.50	4.50
☐ 251	Stan Jok	16.50	7.00	2.35
☐ 252	Roy Smalley	16.50	7.00	2.35
☐ 253	Jim Wilson	16.50	7.00	2.35
☐ 254	Bennett Flowers	16.50	7.00	2.35
☐ 255	Pete Runnels	18.00	7.50	2.50
☐ 256	Owen Friend	16.50	7.00	2.35
☐ 257	Tom Alston	16.50	7.00	2.35
☐ 258	John Stevens UMP	30.00	13.50	4.50
☐ 259	Don Mossi	22.00	9.50	3.15
☐ 260	Edwin Hurley UMP	30.00	13.50	4.50
☐ 261	Walt Moryn	16.50	7.00	2.35
☐ 262	Jim Lemon	20.00	8.50	2.75
☐ 263	Eddie Joost	16.50	7.00	2.35
☐ 264	Bill Henry	16.50	7.00	2.35
☐ 265	Albert Barlick UMP	80.00	36.00	12.00
☐ 266	Mike Fornieles	16.50	7.00	2.35
☐ 267	Jim Honochick UMP	70.00	32.00	10.50
☐ 268	Roy Lee Hawes	16.50	7.00	2.35
☐ 269	Joe Amalfitano	16.50	7.00	2.35
☐ 270	Chico Fernandez	16.50	7.00	2.35
☐ 271	Bob Hooper	16.50	7.00	2.35
☐ 272	John Flaherty UMP	30.00	13.50	4.50
☐ 273	Bubba Church	16.50	7.00	2.35

		MINT	EXC	G-VG
☐ 274	Jim Delsing	16.50	7.00	2.35
☐ 275	William Grieve UMP	30.00	13.50	4.50
☐ 276	Ike Delock	16.50	7.00	2.35
☐ 277	Ed Runge UMP	35.00	15.75	5.25
☐ 278	Charlie Neal	30.00	13.50	4.50
☐ 279	Hank Soar UMP	30.00	13.50	4.50
☐ 280	Clyde McCullough	16.50	7.00	2.35
☐ 281	Charles Berry UMP	30.00	13.50	4.50
☐ 282	Phil Cavarretta	18.00	7.50	2.50
☐ 283	Nestor Chylak UMP	30.00	13.50	4.50
☐ 284	Bill Jackowski UMP	30.00	13.50	4.50
☐ 285	Walt Dropo	18.00	7.50	2.50
☐ 286	Frank Secory UMP	30.00	13.50	4.50
☐ 287	Ron Mrozinski	16.50	7.00	2.35
☐ 288	Dick Smith	16.50	7.00	2.35
☐ 289	Arthur Gore UMP	30.00	13.50	4.50
☐ 290	Hershell Freeman	16.50	7.00	2.35
☐ 291	Frank Dascoli UMP	30.00	13.50	4.50
☐ 292	Marv Blaylock	16.50	7.00	2.35
☐ 293	Thomas Gorman UMP	35.00	15.75	5.25
☐ 294	Wally Moses	18.00	7.50	2.50
☐ 295	Lee Ballanfant UMP	30.00	13.50	4.50
☐ 296	Bill Virdon	35.00	15.75	5.25
☐ 297	Dusty Boggess UMP	30.00	13.50	4.50
☐ 298	Charlie Grimm	18.00	7.50	2.50
☐ 299	Lon Warneke UMP	35.00	15.75	5.25
☐ 300	Tommy Byrne	18.00	7.50	2.50
☐ 301	William Engeln UMP	30.00	13.50	4.50
☐ 302	Frank Malzone	30.00	13.50	4.50
☐ 303	Jocko Conlan UMP	100.00	45.00	15.00
☐ 304	Harry Chiti	16.50	7.00	2.35
☐ 305	Frank Umont UMP	30.00	13.50	4.50
☐ 306	Bob Cerv	24.00	10.50	3.50
☐ 307	Babe Pinelli UMP	35.00	15.75	5.25
☐ 308	Al Lopez MG	45.00	20.00	6.75
☐ 309	Hal Dixon UMP	30.00	13.50	4.50
☐ 310	Ken Lehman	16.50	7.00	2.35
☐ 311	Lawrence Goetz UMP	30.00	13.50	4.50
☐ 312	Bill Wight	16.50	7.00	2.35
☐ 313	Augie Donatelli UMP	35.00	15.75	5.25
☐ 314	Dale Mitchell	18.00	7.50	2.50
☐ 315	Cal Hubbard UMP	85.00	38.00	12.75
☐ 316	Marion Fricano	16.50	7.00	2.35
☐ 317	William Summers UMP	30.00	13.50	4.50
☐ 318	Sid Hudson	16.50	7.00	2.35
☐ 319	Al Schroll	16.50	7.00	2.35
☐ 320	George Susce Jr.	50.00	10.00	2.00

1989 Bowman

The 1989 Bowman set, which was actually produced by Topps, contains 484 cards measuring 2 1/2" by 3 3/4". The fronts have white-bordered color photos with facsimile autographs and small Bowman logos. The backs are scarlet and feature charts detailing 1988 player performances vs. each team. The cards are checklisted below alphabetically according to teams in the AL and NL as follows: Baltimore Orioles (1-18), Boston Red Sox (19-36), California Angels (37-54), Chicago White Sox (55-72), Cleveland Indians (73-91), Detroit Tigers (92-109), Kansas City Royals (110-128), Milwaukee Brewers (129-146), Minnesota Twins (147-164), New York Yankees (165-183), Oakland Athletics (184-202), Seattle Mariners (203-220), Texas Rangers

(221-238), Toronto Blue Jays (239-257), Atlanta Braves (262-279), Chicago Cubs (280-298), Cincinnati Reds (299-316), Houston Astros (317-334), Los Angeles Dodgers (335-352), Montreal Expos (353-370), New York Mets (371-389), Philadelphia Phillies (390-408), Pittsburgh Pirates (409-426), St. Louis Cardinals (427-444), San Diego Padres (445-462), and San Francisco Giants (463-480). Cards 258-261 form a father\son subset. The player selection is concentrated on prospects and "name" players. The cards were released in midseason 1989 in wax, rack, and cello pack formats. The key rookie cards in this set are Jim Abbott, Steve Avery, Ken Griffey Jr., Tino Martinez, and Jerome Walton. Topps also produced a limited Bowman "Tiffany" set with supposedly only 6,000 sets being produced. This Tiffany version is valued at approximately five times the values listed below.

		MINT	EXC	G-VG
	COMPLETE SET (484)	17.00	7.25	2.50
	COMMON PLAYER (1-484)	.03	.01	.00
☐ 1	Oswald Peraza	.06	.02	.00
☐ 2	Brian Holton	.03	.01	.00
☐ 3	Jose Bautista	.06	.02	.00
☐ 4	Pete Harnisch	.17	.07	.01
☐ 5	Dave Schmidt	.03	.01	.00
☐ 6	Gregg Olson	.40	.16	.04
☐ 7	Jeff Ballard	.06	.02	.00
☐ 8	Bob Melvin	.03	.01	.00
☐ 9	Cal Ripken	.30	.12	.03
☐ 10	Randy Milligan	.08	.03	.01
☐ 11	Juan Bell	.08	.03	.01
☐ 12	Billy Ripken	.03	.01	.00
☐ 13	Jim Traber	.03	.01	.00
☐ 14	Pete Stanicek	.03	.01	.00
☐ 15	Steve Finley	.25	.10	.02
☐ 16	Larry Sheets	.03	.01	.00
☐ 17	Phil Bradley	.03	.01	.00
☐ 18	Brady Anderson	.08	.03	.01
☐ 19	Lee Smith	.08	.03	.01
☐ 20	Tom Fischer	.06	.02	.00
☐ 21	Mike Boddicker	.03	.01	.00
☐ 22	Rob Murphy	.03	.01	.00
☐ 23	Wes Gardner	.03	.01	.00
☐ 24	John Dopson	.08	.03	.01
☐ 25	Bob Stanley	.03	.01	.00
☐ 26	Roger Clemens	.25	.10	.02
☐ 27	Rich Gedman	.03	.01	.00
☐ 28	Marty Barrett	.03	.01	.00
☐ 29	Luis Rivera	.03	.01	.00
☐ 30	Jody Reed	.06	.02	.00
☐ 31	Nick Esasky	.03	.01	.00
☐ 32	Wade Boggs	.18	.08	.01
☐ 33	Jim Rice	.08	.03	.01
☐ 34	Mike Greenwell	.12	.05	.01
☐ 35	Dwight Evans	.08	.03	.01
☐ 36	Ellis Burks	.12	.05	.01
☐ 37	Chuck Finley	.10	.04	.01
☐ 38	Kirk McCaskill	.03	.01	.00
☐ 39	Jim Abbott	.90	.40	.09
☐ 40	Bryan Harvey	.20	.08	.02
☐ 41	Bert Blyleven	.08	.03	.01
☐ 42	Mike Witt	.03	.01	.00
☐ 43	Bob McClure	.03	.01	.00
☐ 44	Bill Schroeder	.03	.01	.00
☐ 45	Lance Parrish	.08	.03	.01
☐ 46	Dick Schofield	.03	.01	.00
☐ 47	Wally Joyner	.10	.04	.01
☐ 48	Jack Howell	.03	.01	.00
☐ 49	Johnny Ray	.03	.01	.00
☐ 50	Chili Davis	.06	.02	.00
☐ 51	Tony Armas	.03	.01	.00
☐ 52	Claudell Washington	.03	.01	.00
☐ 53	Brian Downing	.03	.01	.00
☐ 54	Devon White	.08	.03	.01
☐ 55	Bobby Thigpen	.08	.03	.01
☐ 56	Bill Long	.03	.01	.00
☐ 57	Jerry Reuss	.03	.01	.00
☐ 58	Shawn Hillegas	.03	.01	.00
☐ 59	Melido Perez	.06	.02	.00
☐ 60	Jeff Bittiger	.06	.02	.00
☐ 61	Jack McDowell	.15	.06	.01
☐ 62	Carlton Fisk	.12	.05	.01
☐ 63	Steve Lyons	.03	.01	.00
☐ 64	Ozzie Guillen	.06	.02	.00
☐ 65	Robin Ventura	1.00	.40	.10
☐ 66	Fred Manrique	.03	.01	.00
☐ 67	Dan Pasqua	.03	.01	.00
☐ 68	Ivan Calderon	.06	.02	.00
☐ 69	Ron Kittle	.06	.02	.00
☐ 70	Daryl Boston	.03	.01	.00

☐ 71	Dave Gallagher	.08	.03	.01
☐ 72	Harold Baines	.08	.03	.01
☐ 73	Charles Nagy	.20	.08	.02
☐ 74	John Farrell	.03	.01	.00
☐ 75	Kevin Wickander	.06	.02	.00
☐ 76	Greg Swindell	.06	.02	.00
☐ 77	Mike Walker	.08	.03	.01
☐ 78	Doug Jones	.03	.01	.00
☐ 79	Rich Yett	.03	.01	.00
☐ 80	Tom Candiotti	.06	.02	.00
☐ 81	Jesse Orosco	.03	.01	.00
☐ 82	Bud Black	.03	.01	.00
☐ 83	Andy Allanson	.03	.01	.00
☐ 84	Pete O'Brien	.03	.01	.00
☐ 85	Jerry Browne	.03	.01	.00
☐ 86	Brook Jacoby	.03	.01	.00
☐ 87	Mark Lewis	.35	.15	.03
☐ 88	Luis Aguayo	.03	.01	.00
☐ 89	Cory Snyder	.06	.02	.00
☐ 90	Oddibe McDowell	.03	.01	.00
☐ 91	Joe Carter	.10	.04	.01
☐ 92	Frank Tanana	.06	.02	.00
☐ 93	Jack Morris	.10	.04	.01
☐ 94	Doyle Alexander	.03	.01	.00
☐ 95	Steve Searcy	.08	.03	.01
☐ 96	Randy Bockus	.03	.01	.00
☐ 97	Jeff Robinson	.03	.01	.00
☐ 98	Mike Henneman	.03	.01	.00
☐ 99	Paul Gibson	.03	.01	.00
☐ 100	Frank Williams	.03	.01	.00
☐ 101	Matt Nokes	.06	.02	.00
☐ 102	Rico Brogna UER	.35	.15	.03
	(Misspelled Ricco on card back)			
☐ 103	Lou Whitaker	.08	.03	.01
☐ 104	Al Pedrique	.03	.01	.00
☐ 105	Alan Trammell	.12	.05	.01
☐ 106	Chris Brown	.03	.01	.00
☐ 107	Pat Sheridan	.03	.01	.00
☐ 108	Chet Lemon	.03	.01	.00
☐ 109	Keith Moreland	.03	.01	.00
☐ 110	Mel Stottlemyre Jr.	.06	.02	.00
☐ 111	Bret Saberhagen	.10	.04	.01
☐ 112	Floyd Bannister	.03	.01	.00
☐ 113	Jeff Montgomery	.06	.02	.00
☐ 114	Steve Farr	.03	.01	.00
☐ 115	Tom Gordon UER	.17	.07	.01
	(front shows autograph of Don Gordon)			
☐ 116	Charlie Leibrandt	.03	.01	.00
☐ 117	Mark Gubicza	.06	.02	.00
☐ 118	Mike Macfarlane	.10	.04	.01
☐ 119	Bob Boone	.06	.02	.00
☐ 120	Kurt Stillwell	.03	.01	.00
☐ 121	George Brett	.12	.05	.01
☐ 122	Frank White	.03	.01	.00
☐ 123	Kevin Seitzer	.06	.02	.00
☐ 124	Willie Wilson	.06	.02	.00
☐ 125	Pat Tabler	.03	.01	.00
☐ 126	Bo Jackson	.40	.16	.04
☐ 127	Hugh Walker	.08	.03	.01
☐ 128	Danny Tartabull	.10	.04	.01
☐ 129	Teddy Higuera	.03	.01	.00
☐ 130	Don August	.03	.01	.00
☐ 131	Juan Nieves	.03	.01	.00
☐ 132	Mike Birkbeck	.03	.01	.00
☐ 133	Dan Plesac	.03	.01	.00
☐ 134	Chris Bosio	.03	.01	.00
☐ 135	Bill Wegman	.03	.01	.00
☐ 136	Chuck Crim	.03	.01	.00
☐ 137	B.J. Surhoff	.06	.02	.00
☐ 138	Joey Meyer	.03	.01	.00
☐ 139	Dale Sveum	.03	.01	.00
☐ 140	Paul Molitor	.08	.03	.01
☐ 141	Jim Gantner	.03	.01	.00
☐ 142	Gary Sheffield	.25	.10	.02
☐ 143	Greg Brock	.03	.01	.00
☐ 144	Robin Yount	.12	.05	.01
☐ 145	Glenn Braggs	.03	.01	.00
☐ 146	Rob Deer	.06	.02	.00
☐ 147	Fred Toliver	.03	.01	.00
☐ 148	Jeff Reardon	.08	.03	.01
☐ 149	Allan Anderson	.03	.01	.00
☐ 150	Frank Viola	.08	.03	.01
☐ 151	Shane Rawley	.03	.01	.00
☐ 152	Juan Berenguer	.03	.01	.00
☐ 153	Johnny Ard	.12	.05	.01
☐ 154	Tim Laudner	.03	.01	.00
☐ 155	Brian Harper	.06	.02	.00
☐ 156	Al Newman	.03	.01	.00
☐ 157	Kent Hrbek	.08	.03	.01
☐ 158	Gary Gaetti	.06	.02	.00
☐ 159	Wally Backman	.03	.01	.00
☐ 160	Gene Larkin	.03	.01	.00
☐ 161	Greg Gagne	.03	.01	.00
☐ 162	Kirby Puckett	.25	.10	.02
☐ 163	Dan Gladden	.03	.01	.00
☐ 164	Randy Bush	.03	.01	.00
☐ 165	Dave LaPoint	.03	.01	.00
☐ 166	Andy Hawkins	.03	.01	.00
☐ 167	Dave Righetti	.06	.02	.00
☐ 168	Lance McCullers	.03	.01	.00
☐ 169	Jimmy Jones	.03	.01	.00
☐ 170	Al Leiter	.03	.01	.00
☐ 171	John Candelaria	.03	.01	.00
☐ 172	Don Slaught	.03	.01	.00
☐ 173	Jamie Quirk	.03	.01	.00
☐ 174	Rafael Santana	.03	.01	.00
☐ 175	Mike Pagliarulo	.03	.01	.00
☐ 176	Don Mattingly	.20	.08	.02
☐ 177	Ken Phelps	.03	.01	.00
☐ 178	Steve Sax	.08	.03	.01
☐ 179	Dave Winfield	.10	.04	.01
☐ 180	Stan Jefferson	.03	.01	.00
☐ 181	Rickey Henderson	.30	.12	.03
☐ 182	Bob Brower	.03	.01	.00
☐ 183	Roberto Kelly	.12	.05	.01
☐ 184	Curt Young	.03	.01	.00
☐ 185	Gene Nelson	.03	.01	.00
☐ 186	Bob Welch	.08	.03	.01
☐ 187	Rick Honeycutt	.03	.01	.00
☐ 188	Dave Stewart	.08	.03	.01
☐ 189	Mike Moore	.06	.02	.00
☐ 190	Dennis Eckersley	.08	.03	.01
☐ 191	Eric Plunk	.03	.01	.00
☐ 192	Storm Davis	.03	.01	.00
☐ 193	Terry Steinbach	.06	.02	.00
☐ 194	Ron Hassey	.03	.01	.00
☐ 195	Stan Royer	.12	.05	.01
☐ 196	Walt Weiss	.08	.03	.01
☐ 197	Mark McGwire	.12	.05	.01
☐ 198	Carney Lansford	.06	.02	.00
☐ 199	Glenn Hubbard	.03	.01	.00
☐ 200	Dave Henderson	.08	.03	.01
☐ 201	Jose Canseco	.45	.18	.04
☐ 202	Dave Parker	.08	.03	.01
☐ 203	Scott Bankhead	.06	.02	.00
☐ 204	Tom Niedenfuer	.03	.01	.00
☐ 205	Mark Langston	.08	.03	.01
☐ 206	Erik Hanson	.40	.16	.04
☐ 207	Mike Jackson	.03	.01	.00
☐ 208	Dave Valle	.03	.01	.00
☐ 209	Scott Bradley	.03	.01	.00
☐ 210	Harold Reynolds	.06	.02	.00
☐ 211	Tino Martinez	.60	.25	.06
☐ 212	Rich Renteria	.06	.02	.00
☐ 213	Rey Quinones	.03	.01	.00
☐ 214	Jim Presley	.03	.01	.00
☐ 215	Alvin Davis	.06	.02	.00
☐ 216	Edgar Martinez	.15	.06	.01
☐ 217	Darnell Coles	.03	.01	.00
☐ 218	Jeffrey Leonard	.03	.01	.00
☐ 219	Jay Buhner	.15	.06	.01
☐ 220	Ken Griffey Jr.	5.00	2.25	.50
☐ 221	Drew Hall	.03	.01	.00
☐ 222	Bobby Witt	.06	.02	.00
☐ 223	Jamie Moyer	.03	.01	.00
☐ 224	Charlie Hough	.03	.01	.00
☐ 225	Nolan Ryan	.45	.18	.04
☐ 226	Jeff Russell	.03	.01	.00
☐ 227	Jim Sundberg	.03	.01	.00
☐ 228	Julio Franco	.10	.04	.01
☐ 229	Buddy Bell	.06	.02	.00
☐ 230	Scott Fletcher	.03	.01	.00
☐ 231	Jeff Kunkel	.03	.01	.00
☐ 232	Steve Buechele	.03	.01	.00
☐ 233	Monty Fariss	.25	.10	.02
☐ 234	Rick Leach	.03	.01	.00
☐ 235	Ruben Sierra	.20	.08	.02
☐ 236	Cecil Espy	.06	.02	.00
☐ 237	Rafael Palmeiro	.12	.05	.01
☐ 238	Pete Incaviglia	.06	.02	.00
☐ 239	Dave Stieb	.08	.03	.01
☐ 240	Jeff Musselman	.03	.01	.00
☐ 241	Mike Flanagan	.06	.02	.00
☐ 242	Todd Stottlemyre	.12	.05	.01
☐ 243	Jimmy Key	.08	.03	.01
☐ 244	Tony Castillo	.08	.03	.01
☐ 245	Alex Sanchez	.08	.03	.01
☐ 246	Tom Henke	.06	.02	.00
☐ 247	John Cerutti	.03	.01	.00
☐ 248	Ernie Whitt	.03	.01	.00
☐ 249	Bob Brenly	.03	.01	.00
☐ 250	Rance Mulliniks	.03	.01	.00
☐ 251	Kelly Gruber	.08	.03	.01
☐ 252	Ed Sprague	.25	.10	.02
☐ 253	Fred McGriff	.15	.06	.01
☐ 254	Tony Fernandez	.06	.02	.00
☐ 255	Tom Lawless	.03	.01	.00
☐ 256	George Bell	.10	.04	.01

	#	Name			
☐	257	Jesse Barfield	.08	.03	.01
☐	258	Roberto Alomar w/Dad	.20	.08	.02
☐	259	Ken Griffey Jr./Sr.	1.00	.40	.10
☐	260	Cal Ripken Jr./Sr.	.10	.04	.01
☐	261	M.Stottlemyre Jr./Sr.	.06	.02	.00
☐	262	Zane Smith	.06	.02	.00
☐	263	Charlie Puleo	.03	.01	.00
☐	264	Derek Lilliquist	.08	.03	.01
☐	265	Paul Assenmacher	.03	.01	.00
☐	266	John Smoltz	.45	.18	.04
☐	267	Tom Glavine	.35	.15	.03
☐	268	Steve Avery	1.50	.60	.15
☐	269	Pete Smith	.06	.02	.00
☐	270	Jody Davis	.03	.01	.00
☐	271	Bruce Benedict	.03	.01	.00
☐	272	Andres Thomas	.03	.01	.00
☐	273	Gerald Perry	.03	.01	.00
☐	274	Ron Gant	.35	.15	.03
☐	275	Darrell Evans	.06	.02	.00
☐	276	Dale Murphy	.10	.04	.01
☐	277	Dion James	.03	.01	.00
☐	278	Lonnie Smith	.06	.02	.00
☐	279	Geronimo Berroa	.03	.01	.00
☐	280	Steve Wilson	.08	.03	.01
☐	281	Rick Sutcliffe	.06	.02	.00
☐	282	Kevin Coffman	.03	.01	.00
☐	283	Mitch Williams	.03	.01	.00
☐	284	Greg Maddux	.08	.03	.01
☐	285	Paul Kilgus	.03	.01	.00
☐	286	Mike Harkey	.10	.04	.01
☐	287	Lloyd McClendon	.03	.01	.00
☐	288	Damon Berryhill	.06	.02	.00
☐	289	Ty Griffin	.08	.03	.01
☐	290	Ryne Sandberg	.30	.12	.03
☐	291	Mark Grace	.25	.10	.02
☐	292	Curt Wilkerson	.03	.01	.00
☐	293	Vance Law	.03	.01	.00
☐	294	Shawon Dunston	.08	.03	.01
☐	295	Jerome Walton	.35	.15	.03
☐	296	Mitch Webster	.03	.01	.00
☐	297	Dwight Smith	.10	.04	.01
☐	298	Andre Dawson	.12	.05	.01
☐	299	Jeff Sellers	.03	.01	.00
☐	300	Jose Rijo	.08	.03	.01
☐	301	John Franco	.03	.01	.00
☐	302	Rick Mahler	.03	.01	.00
☐	303	Ron Robinson	.03	.01	.00
☐	304	Danny Jackson	.06	.02	.00
☐	305	Rob Dibble	.20	.08	.02
☐	306	Tom Browning	.06	.02	.00
☐	307	Bo Diaz	.03	.01	.00
☐	308	Manny Trillo	.03	.01	.00
☐	309	Chris Sabo	.50	.20	.05
☐	310	Ron Oester	.03	.01	.00
☐	311	Barry Larkin	.12	.05	.01
☐	312	Todd Benzinger	.03	.01	.00
☐	313	Paul O'Neill	.08	.03	.01
☐	314	Kal Daniels	.08	.03	.01
☐	315	Joel Youngblood	.03	.01	.00
☐	316	Eric Davis	.10	.04	.01
☐	317	Dave Smith	.03	.01	.00
☐	318	Mark Portugal	.03	.01	.00
☐	319	Brian Meyer	.06	.02	.00
☐	320	Jim Deshaies	.03	.01	.00
☐	321	Juan Agosto	.03	.01	.00
☐	322	Mike Scott	.08	.03	.01
☐	323	Rick Rhoden	.03	.01	.00
☐	324	Jim Clancy	.03	.01	.00
☐	325	Larry Andersen	.03	.01	.00
☐	326	Alex Trevino	.03	.01	.00
☐	327	Alan Ashby	.03	.01	.00
☐	328	Craig Reynolds	.03	.01	.00
☐	329	Bill Doran	.03	.01	.00
☐	330	Rafael Ramirez	.03	.01	.00
☐	331	Glenn Davis	.08	.03	.01
☐	332	Willie Ansley	.15	.06	.01
☐	333	Gerald Young	.03	.01	.00
☐	334	Cameron Drew	.03	.01	.00
☐	335	Jay Howell	.03	.01	.00
☐	336	Tim Belcher	.08	.03	.01
☐	337	Fernando Valenzuela	.08	.03	.01
☐	338	Ricky Horton	.03	.01	.00
☐	339	Tim Leary	.06	.02	.00
☐	340	Bill Bene	.03	.01	.00
☐	341	Orel Hershiser	.08	.03	.01
☐	342	Mike Scioscia	.03	.01	.00
☐	343	Rick Dempsey	.03	.01	.00
☐	344	Willie Randolph	.06	.02	.00
☐	345	Alfredo Griffin	.03	.01	.00
☐	346	Eddie Murray	.10	.04	.01
☐	347	Mickey Hatcher	.03	.01	.00
☐	348	Mike Sharperson	.03	.01	.00
☐	349	John Shelby	.03	.01	.00
☐	350	Mike Marshall	.06	.02	.00
☐	351	Kirk Gibson	.08	.03	.01
☐	352	Mike Davis	.03	.01	.00
☐	353	Bryn Smith	.03	.01	.00
☐	354	Pascual Perez	.03	.01	.00
☐	355	Kevin Gross	.03	.01	.00
☐	356	Andy McGaffigan	.03	.01	.00
☐	357	Brian Holman	.15	.06	.01
☐	358	Dave Wainhouse	.08	.03	.01
☐	359	Dennis Martinez	.06	.02	.00
☐	360	Tim Burke	.03	.01	.00
☐	361	Nelson Santovenia	.08	.03	.01
☐	362	Tim Wallach	.06	.02	.00
☐	363	Spike Owen	.03	.01	.00
☐	364	Rex Hudler	.06	.02	.00
☐	365	Andres Galarraga	.06	.02	.00
☐	366	Otis Nixon	.06	.02	.00
☐	367	Hubie Brooks	.06	.02	.00
☐	368	Mike Aldrete	.03	.01	.00
☐	369	Tim Raines	.08	.03	.01
☐	370	Dave Martinez	.06	.02	.00
☐	371	Bob Ojeda	.03	.01	.00
☐	372	Ron Darling	.06	.02	.00
☐	373	Wally Whitehurst	.08	.03	.01
☐	374	Randy Myers	.03	.01	.00
☐	375	David Cone	.08	.03	.01
☐	376	Dwight Gooden	.12	.05	.01
☐	377	Sid Fernandez	.06	.02	.00
☐	378	Dave Proctor	.08	.03	.01
☐	379	Gary Carter	.08	.03	.01
☐	380	Keith Miller	.03	.01	.00
☐	381	Gregg Jefferies	.25	.10	.02
☐	382	Tim Teufel	.03	.01	.00
☐	383	Kevin Elster	.03	.01	.00
☐	384	Dave Magadan	.08	.03	.01
☐	385	Keith Hernandez	.08	.03	.01
☐	386	Mookie Wilson	.03	.01	.00
☐	387	Darryl Strawberry	.30	.12	.03
☐	388	Kevin McReynolds	.08	.03	.01
☐	389	Mark Carreon	.06	.02	.00
☐	390	Jeff Parrett	.03	.01	.00
☐	391	Mike Maddux	.03	.01	.00
☐	392	Don Carman	.03	.01	.00
☐	393	Bruce Ruffin	.03	.01	.00
☐	394	Ken Howell	.03	.01	.00
☐	395	Steve Bedrosian	.06	.02	.00
☐	396	Floyd Youmans	.03	.01	.00
☐	397	Larry McWilliams	.03	.01	.00
☐	398	Pat Combs	.10	.04	.01
☐	399	Steve Lake	.03	.01	.00
☐	400	Dickie Thon	.03	.01	.00
☐	401	Ricky Jordan	.12	.05	.01
☐	402	Mike Schmidt	.25	.10	.02
☐	403	Tom Herr	.03	.01	.00
☐	404	Chris James	.03	.01	.00
☐	405	Juan Samuel	.06	.02	.00
☐	406	Von Hayes	.06	.02	.00
☐	407	Ron Jones	.08	.03	.01
☐	408	Curt Ford	.03	.01	.00
☐	409	Bob Walk	.03	.01	.00
☐	410	Jeff Robinson	.03	.01	.00
☐	411	Jim Gott	.03	.01	.00
☐	412	Scott Medvin	.08	.03	.01
☐	413	John Smiley	.08	.03	.01
☐	414	Bob Kipper	.03	.01	.00
☐	415	Brian Fisher	.03	.01	.00
☐	416	Doug Drabek	.08	.03	.01
☐	417	Mike LaValliere	.03	.01	.00
☐	418	Ken Oberkfell	.03	.01	.00
☐	419	Sid Bream	.03	.01	.00
☐	420	Austin Manahan	.10	.04	.01
☐	421	Jose Lind	.03	.01	.00
☐	422	Bobby Bonilla	.17	.07	.01
☐	423	Glenn Wilson	.03	.01	.00
☐	424	Andy Van Slyke	.10	.04	.01
☐	425	Gary Redus	.03	.01	.00
☐	426	Barry Bonds	.20	.08	.02
☐	427	Don Heinkel	.03	.01	.00
☐	428	Ken Dayley	.03	.01	.00
☐	429	Todd Worrell	.06	.02	.00
☐	430	Brad DuVall	.08	.03	.01
☐	431	Jose DeLeon	.03	.01	.00
☐	432	Joe Magrane	.06	.02	.00
☐	433	John Ericks	.12	.05	.01
☐	434	Frank DiPino	.03	.01	.00
☐	435	Tony Pena	.06	.02	.00
☐	436	Ozzie Smith	.10	.04	.00
☐	437	Terry Pendleton	.08	.03	.01
☐	438	Jose Oquendo	.03	.01	.00
☐	439	Tim Jones	.06	.02	.00
☐	440	Pedro Guerrero	.08	.03	.01
☐	441	Milt Thompson	.03	.01	.00
☐	442	Willie McGee	.08	.03	.01
☐	443	Vince Coleman	.08	.03	.01
☐	444	Tom Brunansky	.06	.02	.00

		MINT	EXC	G-VG
☐ 445	Walt Terrell	.03	.01	.00
☐ 446	Eric Show	.03	.01	.00
☐ 447	Mark Davis	.06	.02	.00
☐ 448	Andy Benes	.45	.18	.04
☐ 449	Ed Whitson	.03	.01	.00
☐ 450	Dennis Rasmussen	.03	.01	.00
☐ 451	Bruce Hurst	.06	.02	.00
☐ 452	Pat Clements	.03	.01	.00
☐ 453	Benito Santiago	.08	.03	.01
☐ 454	Sandy Alomar Jr.	.35	.15	.03
☐ 455	Garry Templeton	.06	.02	.00
☐ 456	Jack Clark	.08	.03	.01
☐ 457	Tim Flannery	.03	.01	.00
☐ 458	Roberto Alomar	.40	.16	.04
☐ 459	Carmelo Martinez	.03	.01	.00
☐ 460	John Kruk	.03	.01	.00
☐ 461	Tony Gwynn	.15	.06	.01
☐ 462	Jerald Clark	.17	.07	.01
☐ 463	Don Robinson	.03	.01	.00
☐ 464	Craig Lefferts	.03	.01	.00
☐ 465	Kelly Downs	.03	.01	.00
☐ 466	Rick Reuschel	.06	.02	.00
☐ 467	Scott Garrelts	.03	.01	.00
☐ 468	Wil Tejada	.03	.01	.00
☐ 469	Kirt Manwaring	.03	.01	.00
☐ 470	Terry Kennedy	.03	.01	.00
☐ 471	Jose Uribe	.03	.01	.00
☐ 472	Royce Clayton	.45	.18	.04
☐ 473	Robby Thompson	.03	.01	.00
☐ 474	Kevin Mitchell	.15	.06	.01
☐ 475	Ernie Riles	.03	.01	.00
☐ 476	Will Clark	.40	.16	.04
☐ 477	Donell Nixon	.03	.01	.00
☐ 478	Candy Maldonado	.06	.02	.00
☐ 479	Tracy Jones	.03	.01	.00
☐ 480	Brett Butler	.08	.03	.01
☐ 481	Checklist Card	.06	.01	.00
☐ 482	Checklist Card	.06	.01	.00
☐ 483	Checklist Card	.06	.01	.00
☐ 484	Checklist Card	.06	.01	.00

1989 Bowman Reprint Inserts

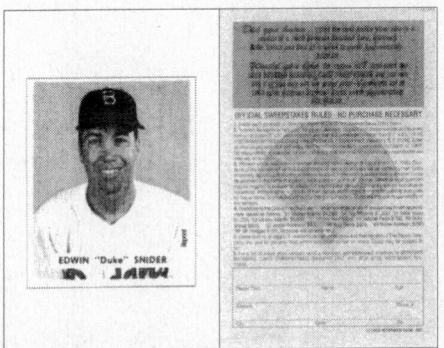

The 1989 Bowman Reprint Inserts set contains 11 cards measuring 2 1/2" by 3 3/4". The fronts depict reproduced actual size "classic" Bowman cards, which are noted as reprints. The backs are devoted to a sweepstakes entry form. One of these reprint cards was included in each 1989 Bowman wax pack thus making these "reprints" quite easy to find. Since the cards are unnumbered, they are ordered below in alphabetical order by player's name and year within player.

		MINT	EXC	G-VG
	COMPLETE SET (11)	2.00	.80	.20
	COMMON PLAYER (1-11)	.15	.06	.01
☐ 1	Richie Ashburn '49	.15	.06	.01
☐ 2	Yogi Berra '48	.25	.10	.02
☐ 3	Whitey Ford '51	.20	.08	.02
☐ 4	Gil Hodges '49	.15	.06	.01
☐ 5	Mickey Mantle '51	.30	.12	.03
☐ 6	Mickey Mantle '53	.30	.12	.03
☐ 7	Willie Mays '51	.25	.10	.02

		MINT	EXC	G-VG
☐ 8	Satchel Paige '49	.25	.10	.02
☐ 9	Jackie Robinson '50	.25	.10	.02
☐ 10	Duke Snider '49	.20	.08	.02
☐ 11	Ted Williams '54	.25	.10	.02

1990 Bowman

The 1990 Bowman set was issued in the standard card size of 2 1/2" by 3 1/2". This was the second issue by Topps using the Bowman name. The set consists of 528 cards, increased from 1989's edition of 484 cards. The cards feature a white border with the player's photo inside and the Bowman logo on top. Again, the Bowman cards were issued with the backs featuring team by team statistics. The card numbering is in team order with the teams themselves being ordered alphabetically within each league. The set numbering is as follows: Atlanta Braves (1-20), Chicago Cubs (21-40), Cincinnati Reds (41-60), Houston Astros (61-81), Los Angeles Dodgers (82-101), Montreal Expos (102-121), New York Mets (122-142), Philadelphia Phillies (143-162), Pittsburgh Pirates (163-182), St. Louis Cardinals (183-202), San Diego Padres (203-222), San Francisco Giants (223-242), Baltimore Orioles (243-262), Boston Red Sox (263-282), California Angels (283-302), Chicago White Sox (303-322), Cleveland Indians (323-342), Detroit Tigers (343-362), Kansas City Royals (363-383), Milwaukee Brewers (384-404), Minnesota Twins (405-424), New York Yankees (425-444), Oakland A's (445-464), Seattle Mariners (465-484), Texas Rangers (485-503), and Toronto Blue Jays (504-524). The key rookie cards in this set are Travis Fryman, Juan Gonzalez, Chuck Knoblauch, Ray Lankford, Kevin Maas, Ben McDonald, Jose Offerman, John Olerud, Frank Thomas, and Maurice Vaughn. Topps also produced a Bowman Tiffany glossy set. Production of these Tiffany Bowmans was reported to be approximately 3,000 sets. These Tiffany versions are valued at approximately eight times the values listed below.

		MINT	EXC	G-VG
	COMPLETE SET (528)	17.00	7.25	2.50
	COMMON PLAYER (1-528)	.03	.01	.00
☐ 1	Tommy Greene	.30	.10	.02
☐ 2	Tom Glavine	.15	.06	.01
☐ 3	Andy Nezelek	.03	.01	.00
☐ 4	Mike Stanton	.10	.04	.01
☐ 5	Rick Luecken	.08	.03	.01
☐ 6	Kent Mercker	.15	.06	.01
☐ 7	Derek Lilliquist	.03	.01	.00
☐ 8	Charlie Leibrandt	.03	.01	.00
☐ 9	Steve Avery	.50	.20	.05
☐ 10	John Smoltz	.17	.07	.01
☐ 11	Mark Lemke	.06	.02	.00
☐ 12	Lonnie Smith	.06	.02	.00
☐ 13	Oddibe McDowell	.03	.01	.00
☐ 14	Tyler Houston	.10	.04	.01
☐ 15	Jeff Blauser	.03	.01	.00
☐ 16	Ernie Whitt	.03	.01	.00
☐ 17	Alexis Infante	.06	.02	.00
☐ 18	Jim Presley	.03	.01	.00

☐ 19 Dale Murphy	.10	.04	.01
☐ 20 Nick Esasky	.03	.01	.00
☐ 21 Rick Sutcliffe	.06	.02	.00
☐ 22 Mike Bielecki	.03	.01	.00
☐ 23 Steve Wilson	.03	.01	.00
☐ 24 Kevin Blankenship	.03	.01	.00
☐ 25 Mitch Williams	.03	.01	.00
☐ 26 Dean Wilkins	.08	.03	.01
☐ 27 Greg Maddux	.08	.03	.01
☐ 28 Mike Harkey	.08	.03	.01
☐ 29 Mark Grace	.10	.04	.01
☐ 30 Ryne Sandberg	.25	.10	.02
☐ 31 Greg Smith	.08	.03	.01
☐ 32 Dwight Smith	.06	.02	.00
☐ 33 Damon Berryhill	.03	.01	.00
☐ 34 Earl Cunningham UER	.12	.05	.01
(errant * by the			
word "in")			
☐ 35 Jerome Walton	.08	.03	.01
☐ 36 Lloyd McClendon	.03	.01	.00
☐ 37 Ty Griffin	.06	.02	.00
☐ 38 Shawon Dunston	.08	.03	.01
☐ 39 Andre Dawson	.10	.04	.01
☐ 40 Luis Salazar	.03	.01	.00
☐ 41 Tim Layana	.10	.04	.01
☐ 42 Rob Dibble	.08	.03	.01
☐ 43 Tom Browning	.06	.02	.00
☐ 44 Danny Jackson	.06	.02	.00
☐ 45 Jose Rijo	.08	.03	.01
☐ 46 Scott Scudder	.10	.04	.01
☐ 47 Randy Myers UER	.03	.01	.00
(Career ERA .274,			
should be 2.74)			
☐ 48 Brian Lane	.08	.03	.01
☐ 49 Paul O'Neill	.08	.03	.01
☐ 50 Barry Larkin	.10	.04	.01
☐ 51 Reggie Jefferson	.40	.16	.04
☐ 52 Jeff Branson	.10	.04	.01
☐ 53 Chris Sabo	.10	.04	.01
☐ 54 Joe Oliver	.08	.03	.01
☐ 55 Todd Benzinger	.03	.01	.00
☐ 56 Rolando Roomes	.03	.01	.00
☐ 57 Hal Morris	.35	.15	.03
☐ 58 Eric Davis	.10	.04	.01
☐ 59 Scott Bryant	.12	.05	.01
☐ 60 Ken Griffey Sr.	.08	.03	.01
☐ 61 Darryl Kile	.17	.07	.01
☐ 62 Dave Smith	.03	.01	.00
☐ 63 Mark Portugal	.03	.01	.00
☐ 64 Jeff Juden	.30	.12	.03
☐ 65 Bill Gullickson	.06	.02	.00
☐ 66 Danny Darwin	.03	.01	.00
☐ 67 Larry Andersen	.03	.01	.00
☐ 68 Jose Cano	.08	.03	.01
☐ 69 Dan Schatzeder	.03	.01	.00
☐ 70 Jim Deshaies	.03	.01	.00
☐ 71 Mike Scott	.08	.03	.01
☐ 72 Gerald Young	.03	.01	.00
☐ 73 Ken Caminiti	.03	.01	.00
☐ 74 Ken Oberkfell	.03	.01	.00
☐ 75 Dave Rohde	.08	.03	.01
☐ 76 Bill Doran	.03	.01	.00
☐ 77 Andujar Cedeno	.50	.20	.05
☐ 78 Craig Biggio	.08	.03	.01
☐ 79 Karl Rhodes	.12	.05	.01
☐ 80 Glenn Davis	.08	.03	.01
☐ 81 Eric Anthony	.17	.07	.01
☐ 82 John Wetteland	.08	.03	.01
☐ 83 Jay Howell	.03	.01	.00
☐ 84 Orel Hershiser	.08	.03	.01
☐ 85 Tim Belcher	.06	.02	.00
☐ 86 Kiki Jones	.15	.06	.01
☐ 87 Mike Hartley	.12	.05	.01
☐ 88 Ramon Martinez	.25	.10	.02
☐ 89 Mike Scioscia	.03	.01	.00
☐ 90 Willie Randolph	.06	.02	.00
☐ 91 Juan Samuel	.06	.02	.00
☐ 92 Jose Offerman	.20	.08	.02
☐ 93 Dave Hansen	.20	.08	.02
☐ 94 Jeff Hamilton	.03	.01	.00
☐ 95 Alfredo Griffin	.03	.01	.00
☐ 96 Tom Goodwin	.25	.10	.02
☐ 97 Kirk Gibson	.08	.03	.01
☐ 98 Jose Vizcaino	.10	.04	.01
☐ 99 Kal Daniels	.08	.03	.01
☐ 100 Hubie Brooks	.06	.02	.00
☐ 101 Eddie Murray	.10	.04	.01
☐ 102 Dennis Boyd	.03	.01	.00
☐ 103 Tim Burke	.03	.01	.00
☐ 104 Bill Sampen	.10	.04	.01
☐ 105 Brett Gideon	.03	.01	.00
☐ 106 Mark Gardner	.12	.05	.01
☐ 107 Howard Farmer	.10	.04	.01
☐ 108 Mel Rojas	.08	.03	.01
☐ 109 Kevin Gross	.03	.01	.00
☐ 110 Dave Schmidt	.03	.01	.00
☐ 111 Denny Martinez	.06	.02	.00
☐ 112 Jeff Goff	.06	.02	.00
☐ 113 Andres Galarraga	.06	.02	.00
☐ 114 Tim Wallach	.06	.02	.00
☐ 115 Marquis Grissom	.40	.16	.04
☐ 116 Spike Owen	.03	.01	.00
☐ 117 Larry Walker	.20	.08	.02
☐ 118 Tim Raines	.08	.03	.01
☐ 119 Delino DeShields	.40	.16	.04
☐ 120 Tom Foley	.03	.01	.00
☐ 121 Dave Martinez	.03	.01	.00
☐ 122 Frank Viola UER	.08	.03	.01
(Career ERA .384,			
should be 3.84)			
☐ 123 Julio Valera	.10	.04	.01
☐ 124 Alejandro Pena	.06	.02	.00
☐ 125 David Cone	.08	.03	.01
☐ 126 Dwight Gooden	.10	.04	.01
☐ 127 Kevin D. Brown	.10	.04	.01
☐ 128 John Franco	.03	.01	.00
☐ 129 Terry Bross	.10	.04	.01
☐ 130 Blaine Beatty	.10	.04	.01
☐ 131 Sid Fernandez	.06	.02	.00
☐ 132 Mike Marshall	.06	.02	.00
☐ 133 Howard Johnson	.08	.03	.01
☐ 134 Jaime Roseboro	.12	.05	.01
☐ 135 Alan Zinter	.08	.03	.01
☐ 136 Keith Miller	.03	.01	.00
☐ 137 Kevin Elster	.03	.01	.00
☐ 138 Kevin McReynolds	.08	.03	.01
☐ 139 Barry Lyons	.03	.01	.00
☐ 140 Gregg Jefferies	.10	.04	.01
☐ 141 Darryl Strawberry	.20	.08	.02
☐ 142 Todd Hundley	.30	.12	.03
☐ 143 Scott Service	.06	.02	.00
☐ 144 Chuck Malone	.08	.03	.01
☐ 145 Steve Ontiveros	.03	.01	.00
☐ 146 Roger McDowell	.03	.01	.00
☐ 147 Ken Howell	.03	.01	.00
☐ 148 Pat Combs	.08	.03	.01
☐ 149 Jeff Parrett	.03	.01	.00
☐ 150 Chuck McElroy	.10	.04	.01
☐ 151 Jason Grimsley	.10	.04	.01
☐ 152 Len Dykstra	.08	.03	.01
☐ 153 Mickey Morandini	.15	.06	.01
☐ 154 John Kruk	.03	.01	.00
☐ 155 Dickie Thon	.03	.01	.00
☐ 156 Ricky Jordan	.08	.03	.01
☐ 157 Jeff Jackson	.10	.04	.01
☐ 158 Darren Daulton	.03	.01	.00
☐ 159 Tom Herr	.03	.01	.00
☐ 160 Von Hayes	.06	.02	.00
☐ 161 Dave Hollins	.25	.10	.02
☐ 162 Carmelo Martinez	.03	.01	.00
☐ 163 Bob Walk	.03	.01	.00
☐ 164 Doug Drabek	.08	.03	.01
☐ 165 Walt Terrell	.03	.01	.00
☐ 166 Bill Landrum	.03	.01	.00
☐ 167 Scott Ruskin	.10	.04	.01
☐ 168 Bob Patterson	.03	.01	.00
☐ 169 Bobby Bonilla	.12	.05	.01
☐ 170 Jose Lind	.03	.01	.00
☐ 171 Andy Van Slyke	.08	.03	.01
☐ 172 Mike LaValliere	.03	.01	.00
☐ 173 Willie Greene	.12	.05	.01
☐ 174 Jay Bell	.03	.01	.00
☐ 175 Sid Bream	.03	.01	.00
☐ 176 Tom Prince	.03	.01	.00
☐ 177 Wally Backman	.03	.01	.00
☐ 178 Moises Alou	.10	.04	.01
☐ 179 Steve Carter	.08	.03	.01
☐ 180 Gary Redus	.03	.01	.00
☐ 181 Barry Bonds	.15	.06	.01
☐ 182 Don Slaught UER	.03	.01	.00
(Card back shows			
headings for a pitcher)			
☐ 183 Joe Magrane	.03	.01	.00
☐ 184 Bryn Smith	.03	.01	.00
☐ 185 Todd Worrell	.03	.01	.00
☐ 186 Jose DeLeon	.03	.01	.00
☐ 187 Frank DiPino	.03	.01	.00
☐ 188 John Tudor	.06	.02	.00
☐ 189 Howard Hilton	.10	.04	.01
☐ 190 John Ericks	.06	.02	.00
☐ 191 Ken Dayley	.03	.01	.00
☐ 192 Ray Lankford	.75	.30	.07
☐ 193 Todd Zeile	.30	.12	.03
☐ 194 Willie McGee	.08	.03	.01
☐ 195 Ozzie Smith	.10	.04	.01
☐ 196 Milt Thompson	.03	.01	.00
☐ 197 Terry Pendleton	.08	.03	.01
☐ 198 Vince Coleman	.08	.03	.01
☐ 199 Paul Coleman	.15	.06	.01
☐ 200 Jose Oquendo	.03	.01	.00

☐ 201	Pedro Guerrero	.08	.03	.01
☐ 202	Tom Brunansky	.06	.02	.00
☐ 203	Roger Smithberg	.10	.04	.01
☐ 204	Eddie Whitson	.03	.01	.00
☐ 205	Dennis Rasmussen	.03	.01	.00
☐ 206	Craig Lefferts	.03	.01	.00
☐ 207	Andy Benes	.15	.06	.01
☐ 208	Bruce Hurst	.06	.02	.00
☐ 209	Eric Show	.03	.01	.00
☐ 210	Rafael Valdez	.10	.04	.01
☐ 211	Joey Cora	.03	.01	.00
☐ 212	Thomas Howard	.12	.05	.01
☐ 213	Rob Nelson	.03	.01	.00
☐ 214	Jack Clark	.08	.03	.01
☐ 215	Garry Templeton	.03	.01	.00
☐ 216	Fred Lynn	.08	.03	.01
☐ 217	Tony Gwynn	.12	.05	.01
☐ 218	Benito Santiago	.08	.03	.01
☐ 219	Mike Pagliarulo	.03	.01	.00
☐ 220	Joe Carter	.10	.04	.01
☐ 221	Roberto Alomar	.12	.05	.01
☐ 222	Bip Roberts	.06	.02	.00
☐ 223	Rick Reuschel	.06	.02	.00
☐ 224	Russ Swan	.10	.04	.01
☐ 225	Eric Gunderson	.12	.05	.01
☐ 226	Steve Bedrosian	.06	.02	.00
☐ 227	Mike Remlinger	.12	.05	.01
☐ 228	Scott Garrelts	.03	.01	.00
☐ 229	Ernie Camacho	.03	.01	.00
☐ 230	Andres Santana	.20	.08	.02
☐ 231	Will Clark	.25	.10	.02
☐ 232	Kevin Mitchell	.10	.04	.01
☐ 233	Robby Thompson	.03	.01	.00
☐ 234	Bill Bathe	.03	.01	.00
☐ 235	Tony Perezchica	.03	.01	.00
☐ 236	Gary Carter	.08	.03	.01
☐ 237	Brett Butler	.08	.03	.01
☐ 238	Matt Williams	.15	.06	.01
☐ 239	Earnie Riles	.03	.01	.00
☐ 240	Kevin Bass	.03	.01	.00
☐ 241	Terry Kennedy	.03	.01	.00
☐ 242	Steve Hosey	.15	.06	.01
☐ 243	Ben McDonald	.60	.25	.06
☐ 244	Jeff Ballard	.03	.01	.00
☐ 245	Joe Price	.03	.01	.00
☐ 246	Curt Schilling	.03	.01	.00
☐ 247	Pete Harnisch	.06	.02	.00
☐ 248	Mark Williamson	.03	.01	.00
☐ 249	Gregg Olson	.10	.04	.01
☐ 250	Chris Myers	.10	.04	.01
☐ 251A	David Segui ERR (missing vital stats at top of card back under name)	.15	.06	.01
☐ 251B	David Segui COR	.15	.06	.01
☐ 252	Joe Orsulak	.03	.01	.00
☐ 253	Craig Worthington	.03	.01	.00
☐ 254	Mickey Tettleton	.06	.02	.00
☐ 255	Cal Ripken	.25	.10	.02
☐ 256	Billy Ripken	.03	.01	.00
☐ 257	Randy Milligan	.06	.02	.00
☐ 258	Brady Anderson	.03	.01	.00
☐ 259	Chris Hoiles	.20	.08	.02
☐ 260	Mike Devereaux	.03	.01	.00
☐ 261	Phil Bradley	.03	.01	.00
☐ 262	Leo Gomez	.40	.16	.04
☐ 263	Lee Smith	.06	.02	.00
☐ 264	Mike Rochford	.03	.01	.00
☐ 265	Jeff Reardon	.06	.02	.00
☐ 266	Wes Gardner	.03	.01	.00
☐ 267	Mike Boddicker	.03	.01	.00
☐ 268	Roger Clemens	.25	.10	.02
☐ 269	Rob Murphy	.03	.01	.00
☐ 270	Mickey Pina	.10	.04	.01
☐ 271	Tony Pena	.06	.02	.00
☐ 272	Jody Reed	.06	.02	.00
☐ 273	Kevin Romine	.03	.01	.00
☐ 274	Mike Greenwell	.12	.05	.01
☐ 275	Maurice Vaughn	.90	.40	.09
☐ 276	Danny Heep	.03	.01	.00
☐ 277	Scott Cooper	.30	.12	.03
☐ 278	Greg Blosser	.15	.06	.01
☐ 279	Dwight Evans UER (* by "1990 Team Breakdown")	.08	.03	.01
☐ 280	Ellis Burks	.08	.03	.01
☐ 281	Wade Boggs	.12	.05	.01
☐ 282	Marty Barrett	.03	.01	.00
☐ 283	Kirk McCaskill	.03	.01	.00
☐ 284	Mark Langston	.08	.03	.01
☐ 285	Bert Blyleven	.06	.02	.00
☐ 286	Mike Fetters	.08	.03	.01
☐ 287	Kyle Abbott	.20	.08	.02
☐ 288	Jim Abbott	.15	.06	.01
☐ 289	Chuck Finley	.08	.03	.01
☐ 290	Gary DiSarcina	.10	.04	.01
☐ 291	Dick Schofield	.03	.01	.00
☐ 292	Devon White	.06	.02	.00
☐ 293	Bobby Rose	.10	.04	.01
☐ 294	Brian Downing	.03	.01	.00
☐ 295	Lance Parrish	.08	.03	.01
☐ 296	Jack Howell	.03	.01	.00
☐ 297	Claudell Washington	.03	.01	.00
☐ 298	John Orton	.08	.03	.01
☐ 299	Wally Joyner	.10	.04	.01
☐ 300	Lee Stevens	.15	.06	.01
☐ 301	Chili Davis	.06	.02	.00
☐ 302	Johnny Ray	.03	.01	.00
☐ 303	Greg Hibbard	.15	.06	.01
☐ 304	Eric King	.03	.01	.00
☐ 305	Jack McDowell	.12	.05	.01
☐ 306	Bobby Thigpen	.08	.03	.01
☐ 307	Adam Peterson	.03	.01	.00
☐ 308	Scott Radinsky	.12	.05	.01
☐ 309	Wayne Edwards	.08	.03	.01
☐ 310	Melido Perez	.03	.01	.00
☐ 311	Robin Ventura	.45	.18	.04
☐ 312	Sammy Sosa	.20	.08	.02
☐ 313	Dan Pasqua	.03	.01	.00
☐ 314	Carlton Fisk	.12	.05	.01
☐ 315	Ozzie Guillen	.06	.02	.00
☐ 316	Ivan Calderon	.06	.02	.00
☐ 317	Daryl Boston	.03	.01	.00
☐ 318	Craig Grebeck	.08	.03	.01
☐ 319	Scott Fletcher	.03	.01	.00
☐ 320	Frank Thomas	3.50	1.50	.35
☐ 321	Steve Lyons	.08	.03	.01
☐ 322	Carlos Martinez	.08	.03	.01
☐ 323	Joe Skalski	.06	.02	.00
☐ 324	Tom Candiotti	.06	.02	.00
☐ 325	Greg Swindell	.06	.02	.00
☐ 326	Steve Olin	.08	.03	.01
☐ 327	Kevin Wickander	.03	.01	.00
☐ 328	Doug Jones	.03	.01	.00
☐ 329	Jeff Shaw	.10	.04	.01
☐ 330	Kevin Bearse	.08	.03	.01
☐ 331	Dion James	.03	.01	.00
☐ 332	Jerry Browne	.03	.01	.00
☐ 333	Joey Belle	.50	.20	.05
☐ 334	Felix Fermin	.03	.01	.00
☐ 335	Candy Maldonado	.06	.02	.00
☐ 336	Cory Snyder	.06	.02	.00
☐ 337	Sandy Alomar Jr.	.10	.04	.01
☐ 338	Mark Lewis	.17	.07	.01
☐ 339	Carlos Baerga	.35	.15	.03
☐ 340	Chris James	.03	.01	.00
☐ 341	Brook Jacoby	.03	.01	.00
☐ 342	Keith Hernandez	.06	.02	.00
☐ 343	Frank Tanana	.06	.02	.00
☐ 344	Scott Aldred	.15	.06	.01
☐ 345	Mike Henneman	.03	.01	.00
☐ 346	Steve Wapnick	.08	.03	.01
☐ 347	Greg Gohr	.15	.06	.01
☐ 348	Eric Stone	.10	.04	.01
☐ 349	Brian DuBois	.08	.03	.01
☐ 350	Kevin Ritz	.08	.03	.01
☐ 351	Rico Brogna	.12	.05	.01
☐ 352	Mike Heath	.03	.01	.00
☐ 353	Alan Trammell	.08	.03	.01
☐ 354	Chet Lemon	.03	.01	.00
☐ 355	Dave Bergman	.03	.01	.00
☐ 356	Lou Whitaker	.06	.02	.00
☐ 357	Cecil Fielder UER (* by "1990 Team Breakdown")	.35	.15	.03
☐ 358	Milt Cuyler	.30	.12	.03
☐ 359	Tony Phillips	.03	.01	.00
☐ 360	Travis Fryman	1.00	.40	.10
☐ 361	Ed Romero	.03	.01	.00
☐ 362	Lloyd Moseby	.03	.01	.00
☐ 363	Mark Gubicza	.06	.02	.00
☐ 364	Bret Saberhagen	.08	.03	.01
☐ 365	Tom Gordon	.08	.03	.01
☐ 366	Steve Farr	.03	.01	.00
☐ 367	Kevin Appier	.15	.06	.01
☐ 368	Storm Davis	.03	.01	.00
☐ 369	Mark Davis	.06	.02	.00
☐ 370	Jeff Montgomery	.03	.01	.00
☐ 371	Frank White	.03	.01	.00
☐ 372	Brent Mayne	.17	.07	.01
☐ 373	Bob Boone	.06	.02	.00
☐ 374	Jim Eisenreich	.03	.01	.00
☐ 375	Danny Tartabull	.10	.04	.01
☐ 376	Kurt Stillwell	.03	.01	.00
☐ 377	Bill Pecota	.03	.01	.00
☐ 378	Bo Jackson	.35	.15	.03
☐ 379	Bob Hamelin	.10	.04	.01
☐ 380	Kevin Seitzer	.06	.02	.00
☐ 381	Rey Palacios	.03	.01	.00
☐ 382	George Brett	.10	.04	.01

☐ 383	Gerald Perry	.03	.01	.00	
☐ 384	Teddy Higuera	.03	.01	.00	
☐ 385	Tom Filer	.03	.01	.00	
☐ 386	Dan Plesac	.03	.01	.00	
☐ 387	Cal Eldred	.10	.04	.01	
☐ 388	Jaime Navarro	.08	.03	.01	
☐ 389	Chris Bosio	.03	.01	.00	
☐ 390	Randy Veres	.06	.02	.00	
☐ 391	Gary Sheffield	.08	.03	.01	
☐ 392	George Canale	.10	.04	.01	
☐ 393	B.J. Surhoff	.03	.01	.00	
☐ 394	Tim McIntosh	.12	.05	.01	
☐ 395	Greg Brock	.03	.01	.00	
☐ 396	Greg Vaughn	.40	.16	.04	
☐ 397	Darryl Hamilton	.08	.03	.01	
☐ 398	Dave Parker	.08	.03	.01	
☐ 399	Paul Molitor	.08	.03	.01	
☐ 400	Jim Gantner	.03	.01	.00	
☐ 401	Rob Deer	.06	.02	.00	
☐ 402	Billy Spiers	.08	.03	.01	
☐ 403	Glenn Braggs	.03	.01	.00	
☐ 404	Robin Yount	.10	.04	.01	
☐ 405	Rick Aguilera	.06	.02	.00	
☐ 406	Johnny Ard	.06	.02	.00	
☐ 407	Kevin Tapani	.25	.10	.02	
☐ 408	Park Pittman	.10	.04	.01	
☐ 409	Allan Anderson	.03	.01	.00	
☐ 410	Juan Berenguer	.03	.01	.00	
☐ 411	Willie Banks	.30	.12	.03	
☐ 412	Rich Yett	.03	.01	.00	
☐ 413	Dave West	.03	.01	.00	
☐ 414	Greg Gagne	.03	.01	.00	
☐ 415	Chuck Knoblauch	1.25	.50	.12	
☐ 416	Randy Bush	.03	.01	.00	
☐ 417	Gary Gaetti	.06	.02	.00	
☐ 418	Kent Hrbek	.08	.03	.01	
☐ 419	Al Newman	.03	.01	.00	
☐ 420	Danny Gladden	.03	.01	.00	
☐ 421	Paul Sorrento	.10	.04	.01	
☐ 422	Derek Parks	.10	.04	.01	
☐ 423	Scott Leius	.20	.08	.02	
☐ 424	Kirby Puckett	.18	.08	.01	
☐ 425	Willie Smith	.10	.04	.01	
☐ 426	Dave Righetti	.06	.02	.00	
☐ 427	Jeff Robinson	.03	.01	.00	
☐ 428	Alan Mills	.10	.04	.01	
☐ 429	Tim Leary	.06	.02	.00	
☐ 430	Pascual Perez	.03	.01	.00	
☐ 431	Alvaro Espinoza	.03	.01	.00	
☐ 432	Dave Winfield	.10	.04	.01	
☐ 433	Jesse Barfield	.08	.03	.01	
☐ 434	Randy Velarde	.03	.01	.00	
☐ 435	Rick Cerone	.03	.01	.00	
☐ 436	Steve Balboni	.03	.01	.00	
☐ 437	Mel Hall	.03	.01	.00	
☐ 438	Bob Geren	.06	.02	.00	
☐ 439	Bernie Williams	.35	.15	.03	
☐ 440	Kevin Maas	1.25	.50	.12	
☐ 441	Mike Blowers	.10	.04	.01	
☐ 442	Steve Sax	.08	.03	.01	
☐ 443	Don Mattingly	.20	.08	.02	
☐ 444	Roberto Kelly	.08	.03	.01	
☐ 445	Mike Moore	.06	.02	.00	
☐ 446	Reggie Harris	.12	.05	.01	
☐ 447	Scott Sanderson	.06	.02	.00	
☐ 448	Dave Otto	.03	.01	.00	
☐ 449	Dave Stewart	.08	.03	.01	
☐ 450	Rick Honeycutt	.03	.01	.00	
☐ 451	Dennis Eckersley	.08	.03	.01	
☐ 452	Carney Lansford	.06	.02	.00	
☐ 453	Scott Hemond	.10	.04	.01	
☐ 454	Mark McGwire	.12	.05	.01	
☐ 455	Felix Jose	.20	.08	.02	
☐ 456	Terry Steinbach	.06	.02	.00	
☐ 457	Rickey Henderson	.25	.10	.02	
☐ 458	Dave Henderson	.08	.03	.01	
☐ 459	Mike Gallego	.03	.01	.00	
☐ 460	Jose Canseco	.35	.15	.03	
☐ 461	Walt Weiss	.06	.02	.00	
☐ 462	Ken Phelps	.03	.01	.00	
☐ 463	Darren Lewis	.35	.15	.03	
☐ 464	Ron Hassey	.03	.01	.00	
☐ 465	Roger Salkeld	.45	.18	.04	
☐ 466	Scott Bankhead	.03	.01	.00	
☐ 467	Keith Comstock	.03	.01	.00	
☐ 468	Randy Johnson	.12	.05	.01	
☐ 469	Erik Hanson	.08	.03	.01	
☐ 470	Mike Schooler	.06	.02	.00	
☐ 471	Gary Eave	.08	.03	.01	
☐ 472	Jeffrey Leonard	.03	.01	.00	
☐ 473	Dave Valle	.03	.01	.00	
☐ 474	Omar Vizquel	.03	.01	.00	
☐ 475	Pete O'Brien	.03	.01	.00	
☐ 476	Henry Cotto	.03	.01	.00	
☐ 477	Jay Buhner	.10	.04	.01	
☐ 478	Harold Reynolds	.06	.02	.00	
☐ 479	Alvin Davis	.06	.02	.00	
☐ 480	Darnell Coles	.03	.01	.00	
☐ 481	Ken Griffey Jr.	1.50	.60	.15	
☐ 482	Greg Briley	.06	.02	.00	
☐ 483	Scott Bradley	.03	.01	.00	
☐ 484	Tino Martinez	.35	.15	.03	
☐ 485	Jeff Russell	.03	.01	.00	
☐ 486	Nolan Ryan	.40	.16	.04	
☐ 487	Robb Nen	.10	.04	.01	
☐ 488	Kevin Brown	.06	.02	.00	
☐ 489	Brian Bohanon	.10	.04	.01	
☐ 490	Ruben Sierra	.17	.07	.01	
☐ 491	Pete Incaviglia	.06	.02	.00	
☐ 492	Juan Gonzalez	1.50	.60	.15	
☐ 493	Steve Buechele	.03	.01	.00	
☐ 494	Scott Coolbaugh	.08	.03	.01	
☐ 495	Geno Petralli	.03	.01	.00	
☐ 496	Rafael Palmeiro	.10	.04	.01	
☐ 497	Julio Franco	.08	.03	.01	
☐ 498	Gary Pettis	.03	.01	.00	
☐ 499	Donald Harris	.10	.04	.01	
☐ 500	Monty Fariss	.06	.02	.00	
☐ 501	Harold Baines	.08	.03	.01	
☐ 502	Cecil Espy	.03	.01	.00	
☐ 503	Jack Daugherty	.06	.02	.00	
☐ 504	Willie Blair	.06	.02	.00	
☐ 505	Dave Stieb	.08	.03	.01	
☐ 506	Tom Henke	.06	.02	.00	
☐ 507	John Cerutti	.03	.01	.00	
☐ 508	Paul Kilgus	.03	.01	.00	
☐ 509	Jimmy Key	.06	.02	.00	
☐ 510	John Olerud	.75	.30	.07	
☐ 511	Ed Sprague	.10	.04	.01	
☐ 512	Manny Lee	.03	.01	.00	
☐ 513	Fred McGriff	.10	.04	.01	
☐ 514	Glenallen Hill	.08	.03	.01	
☐ 515	George Bell	.08	.03	.01	
☐ 516	Mookie Wilson	.03	.01	.00	
☐ 517	Luis Sojo	.10	.04	.01	
☐ 518	Nelson Liriano	.03	.01	.00	
☐ 519	Kelly Gruber	.08	.03	.01	
☐ 520	Greg Myers	.03	.01	.00	
☐ 521	Pat Borders	.06	.02	.00	
☐ 522	Junior Felix	.08	.03	.01	
☐ 523	Eddie Zosky	.20	.08	.02	
☐ 524	Tony Fernandez	.06	.02	.00	
☐ 525	Checklist 1-132 UER (no copyright mark on the back)	.06	.01	.00	
☐ 526	Checklist 133-264	.06	.01	.00	
☐ 527	Checklist 265-396	.06	.01	.00	
☐ 528	Checklist 397-528	.08	.01	.00	

1990 Bowman Inserts

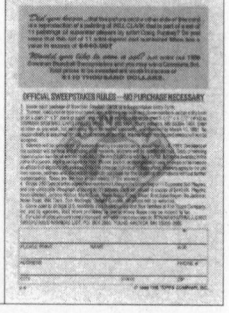

These 2 1/2" by 3 1/2" cards were an insert in every 1990 Bowman pack. This set, which consists of 11 superstars, depicts drawings by Craig Pursley with the backs being descriptions of the 1990 Bowman sweepstakes. We have checklisted the set alphabetically by player. All the cards in this set can be found with either one asterisk or two on the back.

	MINT	EXC	G-VG
COMPLETE SET (11)	2.00	.80	.20
COMMON PLAYER (1-11)	.10	.04	.01

			MINT	EXC	G-VG
☐	1	Will Clark	.30	.12	.03
☐	2	Mark Davis	.10	.04	.01
☐	3	Dwight Gooden	.20	.08	.02
☐	4	Bo Jackson	.50	.20	.05
☐	5	Don Mattingly	.25	.10	.02
☐	6	Kevin Mitchell	.20	.08	.02
☐	7	Gregg Olson	.15	.06	.01
☐	8	Nolan Ryan	.50	.20	.05
☐	9	Bret Saberhagen	.20	.08	.02
☐	10	Jerome Walton	.15	.06	.01
☐	11	Robin Yount	.20	.08	.02

1991 Bowman

This 704-card standard size (2 1/2" by 3 1/2") set marked the third straight year that Topps issued a set using the Bowman name. The cards are arranged in team order by division as follows: AL East, AL West, NL East, and NL West. Some of the specials in the set include cards made for all the 1990 MVP's in each minor league, the leader sluggers by position (Silver Sluggers), and special cards commemorating long-time baseball figure Jimmie Reese, General Colin Powell, newly inducted Hall of Famer Rod Carew and Rickey Henderson's 938th Stolen Base. The cards themselves are designed just like the 1990 Bowman set while the backs again feature the innovative team by team breakdown of how the player did the previous year against a green background. The set numbering is as follows: Toronto Blue Jays (6-30), Milwaukee Brewers (31-56), Cleveland Indians (57-82), Baltimore Orioles (83-106), Boston Red Sox (107-130), Detroit Tigers (131-154), New York Yankees (155-179), California Angels (187-211), Oakland Athletics (212-238), Seattle Mariners (239-264), Texas Rangers (265-290), Kansas City Royals (291-316), Minnesota Twins (317-341), Chicago White Sox (342-366), St. Louis Cardinals (385-409), Chicago Cubs (411-433), Montreal Expos (434-459), New York Mets (460-484), Philadelphia Phillies (485-508), Pittsburgh Pirates (509-532), Houston Astros (539-565), Atlanta Braves (566-590), Los Angles Dodgers (591-615), San Fransico Giants (616-641), San Diego Padres (642-665), and Cincinnati Reds (666-691). Special subsets feature AL Silver Sluggers (367-375) and NL Silver Sluggers (376-384). The key rookie cards in this set are Jeff Bagwell, Jeromy Burnitz, Ryan Klesko, Phil Plantier, Ivan Rodriguez, and Todd Van Poppel.

		MINT	EXC	G-VG
COMPLETE SET (704)		18.00	7.50	2.50
COMMON PLAYER (1-704)		.03	.01	.00

☐	1	Rod Carew I	.15	.05	.01
☐	2	Rod Carew II	.10	.04	.01
☐	3	Rod Carew III	.10	.04	.01
☐	4	Rod Carew IV	.10	.04	.01
☐	5	Rod Carew V	.10	.04	.01
☐	6	Willie Fraser	.03	.01	.00
☐	7	John Olerud	.10	.04	.01
☐	8	William Suero	.12	.05	.01
☐	9	Roberto Alomar	.10	.04	.01
☐	10	Todd Stottlemyre	.06	.02	.00

☐	11	Joe Carter	.10	.04	.01
☐	12	Steve Karsay	.20	.08	.02
☐	13	Mark Whiten	.17	.07	.01
☐	14	Pat Borders	.06	.02	.00
☐	15	Mike Timlin	.12	.05	.01
☐	16	Tom Henke	.06	.02	.00
☐	17	Eddie Zosky	.06	.02	.00
☐	18	Kelly Gruber	.08	.03	.01
☐	19	Jimmy Key	.06	.02	.00
☐	20	Jerry Schunk	.08	.03	.01
☐	21	Manny Lee	.03	.01	.00
☐	22	Dave Stieb	.06	.02	.00
☐	23	Pat Hentgen	.10	.04	.01
☐	24	Glenallen Hill	.06	.02	.00
☐	25	Rene Gonzales	.03	.01	.00
☐	26	Ed Sprague	.08	.03	.01
☐	27	Ken Dayley	.03	.01	.00
☐	28	Pat Tabler	.03	.01	.00
☐	29	Denis Boucher	.10	.04	.01
☐	30	Devon White	.06	.02	.00
☐	31	Dante Bichette	.03	.01	.00
☐	32	Paul Molitor	.08	.03	.01
☐	33	Greg Vaughn	.08	.03	.01
☐	34	Dan Plesac	.03	.01	.00
☐	35	Chris George	.08	.03	.01
☐	36	Tim McIntosh	.03	.01	.00
☐	37	Franklin Stubbs	.03	.01	.00
☐	38	Bo Dodson	.17	.07	.01
☐	39	Ron Robinson	.03	.01	.00
☐	40	Ed Nunez	.03	.01	.00
☐	41	Greg Brock	.03	.01	.00
☐	42	Jaime Navarro	.03	.01	.00
☐	43	Chris Bosio	.03	.01	.00
☐	44	B.J. Surhoff	.03	.01	.00
☐	45	Chris Johnson	.10	.04	.01
☐	46	Willie Randolph	.06	.02	.00
☐	47	Narciso Elvira	.08	.03	.01
☐	48	Jim Gantner	.03	.01	.00
☐	49	Kevin Brown	.03	.01	.00
☐	50	Julio Machado	.03	.01	.00
☐	51	Chuck Crim	.03	.01	.00
☐	52	Gary Sheffield	.08	.03	.01
☐	53	Angel Miranda	.03	.01	.00
☐	54	Teddy Higuera	.03	.01	.00
☐	55	Robin Yount	.10	.04	.01
☐	56	Cal Eldred	.06	.02	.00
☐	57	Sandy Alomar Jr.	.08	.03	.01
☐	58	Greg Swindell	.06	.02	.00
☐	59	Brook Jacoby	.03	.01	.00
☐	60	Efrain Valdez	.08	.03	.01
☐	61	Ever Magallanes	.08	.03	.01
☐	62	Tom Candiotti	.06	.02	.00
☐	63	Eric King	.03	.01	.00
☐	64	Alex Cole	.08	.03	.01
☐	65	Charles Nagy	.08	.03	.01
☐	66	Mitch Webster	.03	.01	.00
☐	67	Chris James	.03	.01	.00
☐	68	Jim Thome	.35	.15	.03
☐	69	Carlos Baerga	.10	.04	.01
☐	70	Mark Lewis	.10	.04	.01
☐	71	Jerry Browne	.03	.01	.00
☐	72	Jesse Orosco	.03	.01	.00
☐	73	Mike Huff	.03	.01	.00
☐	74	Jose Escobar	.08	.03	.01
☐	75	Jeff Manto	.06	.02	.00
☐	76	Turner Ward	.10	.04	.01
☐	77	Doug Jones	.03	.01	.00
☐	78	Bruce Egloff	.08	.03	.01
☐	79	Tim Costo	.20	.08	.02
☐	80	Beau Allred	.08	.03	.01
☐	81	Albert Belle	.12	.05	.01
☐	82	John Farrell	.03	.01	.00
☐	83	Glenn Davis	.08	.03	.01
☐	84	Joe Orsulak	.03	.01	.00
☐	85	Mark Williamson	.03	.01	.00
☐	86	Ben McDonald	.08	.03	.01
☐	87	Billy Ripken	.03	.01	.00
☐	88	Leo Gomez	.10	.04	.01
☐	89	Bob Melvin	.03	.01	.00
☐	90	Jeff Robinson	.03	.01	.00
☐	91	Jose Mesa	.03	.01	.00
☐	92	Gregg Olson	.08	.03	.01
☐	93	Mike Devereaux	.03	.01	.00
☐	94	Luis Mercedes	.25	.10	.02
☐	95	Arthur Rhodes	.20	.08	.02
☐	96	Juan Bell	.03	.01	.00
☐	97	Mike Mussina	.30	.12	.03
☐	98	Jeff Ballard	.03	.01	.00
☐	99	Chris Hoiles	.06	.02	.00
☐	100	Brady Anderson	.03	.01	.00
☐	101	Bob Milacki	.03	.01	.00
☐	102	David Segui	.08	.03	.01
☐	103	Dwight Evans	.06	.02	.00
☐	104	Cal Ripken	.17	.07	.01
☐	105	Mike Linskey	.08	.03	.01

☐ 106 Jeff Tackett	.10	.04	.01	☐ 195 Wally Joyner	.08	.03	.01
☐ 107 Jeff Reardon	.06	.02	.00	☐ 196 Chuck Finley	.08	.03	.01
☐ 108 Dana Kiecker	.06	.02	.00	☐ 197 Luis Sojo	.03	.01	.00
☐ 109 Ellis Burks	.08	.03	.01	☐ 198 Jeff Richardson	.08	.03	.01
☐ 110 Dave Owen	.08	.03	.01	☐ 199 Dave Parker	.08	.03	.01
☐ 111 Danny Darwin	.03	.01	.00	☐ 200 Jim Abbott	.10	.04	.01
☐ 112 Mo Vaughn	.20	.08	.02	☐ 201 Junior Felix	.03	.01	.00
☐ 113 Jeff McNeely	.35	.15	.03	☐ 202 Mark Langston	.06	.02	.00
☐ 114 Tom Bolton	.03	.01	.00	☐ 203 Tim Salmon	.25	.10	.02
☐ 115 Greg Blosser	.10	.04	.01	☐ 204 Cliff Young	.06	.02	.00
☐ 116 Mike Greenwell	.10	.04	.01	☐ 205 Scott Bailes	.03	.01	.00
☐ 117 Phil Plantier	1.25	.50	.12	☐ 206 Bobby Rose	.03	.01	.00
☐ 118 Roger Clemens	.15	.06	.01	☐ 207 Gary Gaetti	.06	.02	.00
☐ 119 John Marzano	.03	.01	.00	☐ 208 Ruben Amaro	.12	.05	.01
☐ 120 Jody Reed	.06	.02	.00	☐ 209 Luis Polonia	.03	.01	.00
☐ 121 Scott Taylor	.10	.04	.01	☐ 210 Dave Winfield	.08	.03	.01
☐ 122 Jack Clark	.08	.03	.01	☐ 211 Bryan Harvey	.06	.02	.00
☐ 123 Derek Livernois	.10	.04	.01	☐ 212 Mike Moore	.06	.02	.00
☐ 124 Tony Pena	.06	.02	.00	☐ 213 Rickey Henderson	.20	.08	.02
☐ 125 Tom Brunansky	.06	.02	.00	☐ 214 Steve Chitren	.08	.03	.01
☐ 126 Carlos Quintana	.06	.02	.00	☐ 215 Bob Welch	.06	.02	.00
☐ 127 Tim Naehring	.10	.04	.01	☐ 216 Terry Steinbach	.03	.01	.00
☐ 128 Matt Young	.03	.01	.00	☐ 217 Earnest Riles	.03	.01	.00
☐ 129 Wade Boggs	.12	.05	.01	☐ 218 Todd Van Poppel	1.00	.40	.10
☐ 130 Kevin Morton	.10	.04	.01	☐ 219 Mike Gallego	.03	.01	.00
☐ 131 Pete Incaviglia	.06	.02	.00	☐ 220 Curt Young	.03	.01	.00
☐ 132 Rob Deer	.06	.02	.00	☐ 221 Todd Burns	.03	.01	.00
☐ 133 Bill Gullickson	.06	.02	.00	☐ 222 Vance Law	.03	.01	.00
☐ 134 Rico Brogna	.10	.04	.01	☐ 223 Eric Show	.03	.01	.00
☐ 135 Lloyd Moseby	.03	.01	.00	☐ 224 Don Peters	.12	.05	.01
☐ 136 Cecil Fielder	.15	.06	.01	☐ 225 Dave Stewart	.08	.03	.01
☐ 137 Tony Phillips	.03	.01	.00	☐ 226 Dave Henderson	.08	.03	.01
☐ 138 Mark Leiter	.10	.04	.01	☐ 227 Jose Canseco	.25	.10	.02
☐ 139 John Cerutti	.03	.01	.00	☐ 228 Walt Weiss	.06	.02	.00
☐ 140 Mickey Tettleton	.06	.02	.00	☐ 229 Dann Howitt	.08	.03	.01
☐ 141 Milt Cuyler	.08	.03	.01	☐ 230 Willie Wilson	.06	.02	.00
☐ 142 Greg Gohr	.06	.02	.00	☐ 231 Harold Baines	.06	.02	.00
☐ 143 Tony Bernazard	.03	.01	.00	☐ 232 Scott Hemond	.06	.02	.00
☐ 144 Dan Gakeler	.08	.03	.01	☐ 233 Joe Slusarski	.08	.03	.01
☐ 145 Travis Fryman	.20	.08	.02	☐ 234 Mark McGwire	.10	.04	.01
☐ 146 Dan Petry	.03	.01	.00	☐ 235 Kirk Dressendorfer	.20	.08	.02
☐ 147 Scott Aldred	.03	.01	.00	☐ 236 Craig Paquette	.15	.06	.01
☐ 148 John DeSilva	.10	.04	.01	☐ 237 Dennis Eckersley	.08	.03	.01
☐ 149 Rusty Meacham	.10	.04	.01	☐ 238 Dana Allison	.12	.05	.01
☐ 150 Lou Whitaker	.06	.02	.00	☐ 239 Scott Bradley	.03	.01	.00
☐ 151 Dave Haas	.08	.03	.01	☐ 240 Brian Holman	.03	.01	.00
☐ 152 Luis de los Santos	.03	.01	.00	☐ 241 Mike Schooler	.03	.01	.00
☐ 153 Ivan Cruz	.10	.04	.01	☐ 242 Rich DeLucia	.12	.05	.01
☐ 154 Alan Trammell	.08	.03	.01	☐ 243 Edgar Martinez	.08	.03	.01
☐ 155 Pat Kelly	.25	.10	.02	☐ 244 Henry Cotto	.03	.01	.00
☐ 156 Carl Everett	.25	.10	.02	☐ 245 Omar Vizquel	.03	.01	.00
☐ 157 Greg Cadaret	.03	.01	.00	☐ 246 Ken Griffey Jr.	.75	.30	.07
☐ 158 Kevin Maas	.15	.06	.01	(See also 255)			
☐ 159 Jeff Johnson	.15	.06	.01	☐ 247 Jay Buhner	.08	.03	.01
☐ 160 Willie Smith	.06	.02	.00	☐ 248 Bill Krueger	.03	.01	.00
☐ 161 Gerald Williams	.25	.10	.02	☐ 249 Dave Fleming	.10	.04	.01
☐ 162 Mike Humphreys	.15	.06	.01	☐ 250 Patrick Lennon	.20	.08	.02
☐ 163 Alvaro Espinoza	.03	.01	.00	☐ 251 Dave Valle	.03	.01	.00
☐ 164 Matt Nokes	.06	.02	.00	☐ 252 Harold Reynolds	.06	.02	.00
☐ 165 Wade Taylor	.12	.05	.01	☐ 253 Randy Johnson	.06	.02	.00
☐ 166 Roberto Kelly	.08	.03	.01	☐ 254 Scott Bankhead	.03	.01	.00
☐ 167 John Habyan	.03	.01	.00	☐ 255 Ken Griffey Sr. UER	.08	.03	.01
☐ 168 Steve Farr	.03	.01	.00	(Card number is 246)			
☐ 169 Jesse Barfield	.06	.02	.00	☐ 256 Greg Briley	.03	.01	.00
☐ 170 Steve Sax	.06	.02	.00	☐ 257 Tino Martinez	.12	.05	.01
☐ 171 Jim Leyritz	.06	.02	.00	☐ 258 Alvin Davis	.06	.02	.00
☐ 172 Robert Eenhoorn	.10	.04	.01	☐ 259 Pete O'Brien	.03	.01	.00
☐ 173 Bernie Williams	.12	.05	.01	☐ 260 Erik Hanson	.06	.02	.00
☐ 174 Scott Lusader	.03	.01	.00	☐ 261 Bret Boone	.15	.06	.01
☐ 175 Torey Lovullo	.03	.01	.00	☐ 262 Roger Salkeld	.15	.06	.01
☐ 176 Chuck Cary	.03	.01	.00	☐ 263 Dave Burba	.10	.04	.01
☐ 177 Scott Sanderson	.03	.01	.00	☐ 264 Kerry Woodson	.10	.04	.01
☐ 178 Don Mattingly	.12	.05	.01	☐ 265 Julio Franco	.08	.03	.01
☐ 179 Mel Hall	.06	.02	.00	☐ 266 Dan Peltier	.10	.04	.01
☐ 180 Juan Gonzalez	.30	.12	.03	☐ 267 Jeff Russell	.03	.01	.00
☐ 181 Hensley Meulens	.06	.02	.00	☐ 268 Steve Buechele	.03	.01	.00
Minor League MVP				☐ 269 Donald Harris	.06	.02	.00
☐ 182 Jose Offerman	.08	.03	.01	☐ 270 Robb Nen	.03	.01	.00
Minor League MVP				☐ 271 Rich Gossage	.06	.02	.00
☐ 183 Jeff Bagwell	1.50	.60	.15	☐ 272 Ivan Rodriguez	1.50	.60	.15
Minor League MVP				☐ 273 Jeff Huson	.03	.01	.00
☐ 184 Jeff Conine	.10	.04	.01	☐ 274 Kevin Brown	.06	.02	.00
Minor League MVP				☐ 275 Dan Smith	.10	.04	.01
☐ 185 Henry Rodriguez	.15	.06	.01	☐ 276 Gary Pettis	.03	.01	.00
Minor League MVP				☐ 277 Jack Daugherty	.03	.01	.00
☐ 186 Jimmie Reese	.03	.01	.00	☐ 278 Mike Jeffcoat	.03	.01	.00
☐ 187 Kyle Abbott	.06	.02	.00	☐ 279 Brad Arnsberg	.03	.01	.00
☐ 188 Lance Parrish	.06	.02	.00	☐ 280 Nolan Ryan	.30	.12	.03
☐ 189 Rafael Montalvo	.08	.03	.01	☐ 281 Eric McCray	.10	.04	.01
☐ 190 Floyd Bannister	.03	.01	.00	☐ 282 Scott Chiamparino	.06	.02	.00
☐ 191 Dick Schofield	.03	.01	.00	☐ 283 Ruben Sierra	.12	.05	.01
☐ 192 Scott Lewis	.08	.03	.01	☐ 284 Geno Petralli	.03	.01	.00
☐ 193 Jeff Robinson	.03	.01	.00	☐ 285 Monty Fariss	.06	.02	.00
☐ 194 Kent Anderson	.03	.01	.00	☐ 286 Rafael Palmeiro	.08	.03	.01
				☐ 287 Bobby Witt	.06	.02	.00

#	Player			
☐ 288	Dean Palmer UER (Photo actually Dan Peltier)	.30	.12	.03
☐ 289	Tony Scruggs	.10	.04	.01
☐ 290	Kenny Rogers	.03	.01	.00
☐ 291	Bret Saberhagen	.08	.03	.01
☐ 292	Brian McRae	.35	.15	.03
☐ 293	Storm Davis	.03	.01	.00
☐ 294	Danny Tartabull	.08	.03	.01
☐ 295	David Howard	.10	.04	.01
☐ 296	Mike Boddicker	.03	.01	.00
☐ 297	Joel Johnston	.15	.06	.01
☐ 298	Tim Spehr	.15	.06	.01
☐ 299	Hector Wagner	.08	.03	.01
☐ 300	George Brett	.10	.04	.01
☐ 301	Mike Macfarlane	.03	.01	.00
☐ 302	Kirk Gibson	.08	.03	.01
☐ 303	Harvey Pulliam	.12	.05	.01
☐ 304	Jim Eisenreich	.03	.01	.00
☐ 305	Kevin Seitzer	.06	.02	.00
☐ 306	Mark Davis	.06	.02	.00
☐ 307	Kurt Stillwell	.03	.01	.00
☐ 308	Jeff Montgomery	.03	.01	.00
☐ 309	Kevin Appier	.06	.02	.00
☐ 310	Bob Hamelin	.03	.01	.00
☐ 311	Tom Gordon	.06	.02	.00
☐ 312	Kerwin Moore	.15	.06	.01
☐ 313	Hugh Walker	.03	.01	.00
☐ 314	Terry Shumpert	.06	.02	.00
☐ 315	Warren Cromartie	.03	.01	.00
☐ 316	Gary Thurman	.03	.01	.00
☐ 317	Steve Bedrosian	.03	.01	.00
☐ 318	Danny Gladden	.03	.01	.00
☐ 319	Jack Morris	.08	.03	.01
☐ 320	Kirby Puckett	.12	.05	.01
☐ 321	Kent Hrbek	.06	.02	.00
☐ 322	Kevin Tapani	.06	.02	.00
☐ 323	Denny Neagle	.30	.12	.03
☐ 324	Rich Garces	.10	.04	.01
☐ 325	Larry Casian	.08	.03	.01
☐ 326	Shane Mack	.06	.02	.00
☐ 327	Allan Anderson	.03	.01	.00
☐ 328	Junior Ortiz	.03	.01	.00
☐ 329	Paul Abbott	.08	.03	.01
☐ 330	Chuck Knoblauch	.20	.08	.02
☐ 331	Chili Davis	.06	.02	.00
☐ 332	Todd Ritchie	.15	.06	.01
☐ 333	Brian Harper	.06	.02	.00
☐ 334	Rick Aguilera	.06	.02	.00
☐ 335	Scott Erickson	.60	.25	.06
☐ 336	Pedro Munoz	.20	.08	.02
☐ 337	Scott Leius	.06	.02	.00
☐ 338	Greg Gagne	.03	.01	.00
☐ 339	Mike Pagliarulo	.03	.01	.00
☐ 340	Terry Leach	.03	.01	.00
☐ 341	Willie Banks	.08	.03	.01
☐ 342	Bobby Thigpen	.06	.02	.00
☐ 343	Roberto Hernandez	.15	.06	.01
☐ 344	Melido Perez	.03	.01	.00
☐ 345	Carlton Fisk	.10	.04	.01
☐ 346	Norberto Martin	.10	.04	.01
☐ 347	Johnny Ruffin	.10	.04	.01
☐ 348	Jeff Carter	.10	.04	.01
☐ 349	Lance Johnson	.03	.01	.00
☐ 350	Sammy Sosa	.08	.03	.01
☐ 351	Alex Fernandez	.17	.07	.01
☐ 352	Jack McDowell	.08	.03	.01
☐ 353	Bob Wickman	.08	.03	.01
☐ 354	Wilson Alvarez	.10	.04	.01
☐ 355	Charlie Hough	.03	.01	.00
☐ 356	Ozzie Guillen	.06	.02	.00
☐ 357	Cory Snyder	.06	.02	.00
☐ 358	Robin Ventura	.20	.08	.02
☐ 359	Scott Fletcher	.03	.01	.00
☐ 360	Cesar Bernhardt	.10	.04	.01
☐ 361	Dan Pasqua	.03	.01	.00
☐ 362	Tim Raines	.08	.03	.01
☐ 363	Brian Drahman	.08	.03	.01
☐ 364	Wayne Edwards	.03	.01	.00
☐ 365	Scott Radinsky	.06	.02	.00
☐ 366	Frank Thomas	.75	.30	.07
☐ 367	Cecil Fielder SLUG	.10	.04	.01
☐ 368	Julio Franco SLUG	.08	.03	.01
☐ 369	Kelly Gruber SLUG	.08	.03	.01
☐ 370	Alan Trammell SLUG	.08	.03	.01
☐ 371	Rickey Henderson SLUG	.12	.05	.01
☐ 372	Jose Canseco SLUG	.15	.06	.01
☐ 373	Ellis Burks SLUG	.08	.03	.01
☐ 374	Lance Parrish SLUG	.06	.02	.00
☐ 375	Dave Parker SLUG	.08	.03	.01
☐ 376	Eddie Murray SLUG	.08	.03	.01
☐ 377	Ryne Sandberg SLUG	.12	.05	.01
☐ 378	Matt Williams SLUG	.08	.03	.01
☐ 379	Barry Larkin SLUG	.08	.03	.01
☐ 380	Barry Bonds SLUG	.08	.03	.01
☐ 381	Bobby Bonilla SLUG	.08	.03	.01
☐ 382	Darryl Strawberry SLUG	.10	.04	.01
☐ 383	Benny Santiago SLUG	.08	.03	.01
☐ 384	Don Robinson SLUG	.03	.01	.00
☐ 385	Paul Coleman	.06	.02	.00
☐ 386	Milt Thompson	.03	.01	.00
☐ 387	Lee Smith	.06	.02	.00
☐ 388	Ray Lankford	.15	.06	.01
☐ 389	Tom Pagnozzi	.03	.01	.00
☐ 390	Ken Hill	.03	.01	.00
☐ 391	Jamie Moyer	.03	.01	.00
☐ 392	Greg Carmona	.10	.04	.01
☐ 393	John Ericks	.06	.02	.00
☐ 394	Bob Tewksbury	.03	.01	.00
☐ 395	Jose Oquendo	.03	.01	.00
☐ 396	Rheal Cormier	.35	.15	.03
☐ 397	Mike Milchin	.10	.04	.01
☐ 398	Ozzie Smith	.08	.03	.01
☐ 399	Aaron Holbert	.12	.05	.01
☐ 400	Jose DeLeon	.03	.01	.00
☐ 401	Felix Jose	.10	.04	.01
☐ 402	Juan Agosto	.03	.01	.00
☐ 403	Pedro Guerrero	.08	.03	.01
☐ 404	Todd Zeile	.10	.04	.01
☐ 405	Gerald Perry	.03	.01	.00
☐ 406	Donovan Osborne UER (Card number is 410)	.12	.05	.01
☐ 407	Bryn Smith	.03	.01	.00
☐ 408	Bernard Gilkey	.15	.06	.01
☐ 409	Rex Hudler	.03	.01	.00
☐ 410	Thomson/Branca Shot Bobby Thomson Ralph Branca (See also 406)	.08	.03	.01
☐ 411	Lance Dickson	.17	.07	.01
☐ 412	Danny Jackson	.03	.01	.00
☐ 413	Jerome Walton	.08	.03	.01
☐ 414	Sean Cheetham	.10	.04	.01
☐ 415	Joe Girardi	.03	.01	.00
☐ 416	Ryne Sandberg	.15	.06	.01
☐ 417	Mike Harkey	.06	.02	.00
☐ 418	George Bell	.08	.03	.01
☐ 419	Rick Wilkins	.17	.07	.01
☐ 420	Earl Cunningham	.06	.02	.00
☐ 421	Heathcliff Slocumb	.08	.03	.01
☐ 422	Mike Bielecki	.03	.01	.00
☐ 423	Jessie Hollins	.08	.03	.01
☐ 424	Shawon Dunston	.06	.02	.00
☐ 425	Dave Smith	.03	.01	.00
☐ 426	Greg Maddux	.06	.02	.00
☐ 427	Jose Vizcaino	.06	.02	.00
☐ 428	Luis Salazar	.03	.01	.00
☐ 429	Andre Dawson	.10	.04	.01
☐ 430	Rick Sutcliffe	.06	.02	.00
☐ 431	Paul Assenmacher	.03	.01	.00
☐ 432	Erik Pappas	.08	.03	.01
☐ 433	Mark Grace	.08	.03	.01
☐ 434	Dennis Martinez	.06	.02	.00
☐ 435	Marquis Grissom	.10	.04	.01
☐ 436	Wilfredo Cordero	.25	.10	.02
☐ 437	Tim Wallach	.06	.02	.00
☐ 438	Brian Barnes	.12	.05	.01
☐ 439	Barry Jones	.03	.01	.00
☐ 440	Ivan Calderon	.06	.02	.00
☐ 441	Stan Spencer	.10	.04	.01
☐ 442	Larry Walker	.06	.02	.00
☐ 443	Chris Haney	.12	.05	.01
☐ 444	Hector Rivera	.10	.04	.01
☐ 445	Delino DeShields	.08	.03	.01
☐ 446	Andres Galarraga	.06	.02	.00
☐ 447	Gilberto Reyes	.03	.01	.00
☐ 448	Willie Greene	.06	.02	.00
☐ 449	Greg Colbrunn	.12	.05	.01
☐ 450	Rondell White	.30	.12	.03
☐ 451	Steve Frey	.08	.03	.01
☐ 452	Shane Andrews	.15	.06	.01
☐ 453	Mike Fitzgerald	.03	.01	.00
☐ 454	Spike Owen	.03	.01	.00
☐ 455	Dave Martinez	.03	.01	.00
☐ 456	Dennis Boyd	.03	.01	.00
☐ 457	Eric Bullock	.03	.01	.00
☐ 458	Reid Cornelius	.20	.08	.02
☐ 459	Chris Nabholz	.08	.03	.01
☐ 460	David Cone	.06	.02	.00
☐ 461	Hubie Brooks	.06	.02	.00
☐ 462	Sid Fernandez	.06	.02	.00
☐ 463	Doug Simons	.08	.03	.01
☐ 464	Howard Johnson	.08	.03	.01
☐ 465	Chris Donnels	.20	.08	.02
☐ 466	Anthony Young	.20	.08	.02
☐ 467	Todd Hundley	.10	.04	.01
☐ 468	Rick Cerone	.03	.01	.00
☐ 469	Kevin Elster	.03	.01	.00
☐ 470	Wally Whitehurst	.03	.01	.00
☐ 471	Vince Coleman	.08	.03	.01

☐ 472	Dwight Gooden	.08	.03	.01
☐ 473	Charlie O'Brien	.03	.01	.00
☐ 474	Jeromy Burnitz	.60	.25	.06
☐ 475	John Franco	.03	.01	.00
☐ 476	Daryl Boston	.03	.01	.00
☐ 477	Frank Viola	.08	.03	.01
☐ 478	D.J. Dozier	.10	.04	.01
☐ 479	Kevin McReynolds	.06	.02	.00
☐ 480	Tom Herr	.03	.01	.00
☐ 481	Gregg Jefferies	.08	.03	.01
☐ 482	Pete Schourek	.10	.04	.01
☐ 483	Ron Darling	.06	.02	.00
☐ 484	Dave Magadan	.06	.02	.00
☐ 485	Andy Ashby	.10	.04	.01
☐ 486	Dale Murphy	.08	.03	.01
☐ 487	Von Hayes	.06	.02	.00
☐ 488	Kim Batiste	.10	.04	.01
☐ 489	Tony Longmire	.20	.08	.02
☐ 490	Wally Backman	.03	.01	.00
☐ 491	Jeff Jackson	.06	.02	.00
☐ 492	Mickey Morandini	.08	.03	.01
☐ 493	Darrel Akerfelds	.03	.01	.00
☐ 494	Ricky Jordan	.06	.02	.00
☐ 495	Randy Ready	.03	.01	.00
☐ 496	Darrin Fletcher	.06	.02	.00
☐ 497	Chuck Malone	.03	.01	.00
☐ 498	Pat Combs	.06	.02	.00
☐ 499	Dickie Thon	.03	.01	.00
☐ 500	Roger McDowell	.03	.01	.00
☐ 501	Len Dykstra	.06	.02	.00
☐ 502	Joe Boever	.03	.01	.00
☐ 503	John Kruk	.03	.01	.00
☐ 504	Terry Mulholland	.06	.02	.00
☐ 505	Wes Chamberlain	.40	.16	.04
☐ 506	Mike Lieberthal	.12	.05	.01
☐ 507	Darren Daulton	.03	.01	.00
☐ 508	Charlie Hayes	.03	.01	.00
☐ 509	John Smiley	.06	.02	.00
☐ 510	Gary Varsho	.03	.01	.00
☐ 511	Curt Wilkerson	.03	.01	.00
☐ 512	Orlando Merced	.35	.15	.03
☐ 513	Barry Bonds	.10	.04	.01
☐ 514	Mike LaValliere	.03	.01	.00
☐ 515	Doug Drabek	.06	.02	.00
☐ 516	Gary Redus	.03	.01	.00
☐ 517	William Pennyfeather	.15	.06	.01
☐ 518	Randy Tomlin	.15	.06	.01
☐ 519	Mike Zimmerman	.08	.03	.01
☐ 520	Jeff King	.06	.02	.00
☐ 521	Kurt Miller	.15	.06	.01
☐ 522	Jay Bell	.03	.01	.00
☐ 523	Bill Landrum	.03	.01	.00
☐ 524	Zane Smith	.06	.02	.00
☐ 525	Bobby Bonilla	.10	.04	.01
☐ 526	Bob Walk	.03	.01	.00
☐ 527	Austin Manahan	.06	.02	.00
☐ 528	Joe Ausanio	.08	.03	.01
☐ 529	Andy Van Slyke	.08	.03	.01
☐ 530	Jose Lind	.03	.01	.00
☐ 531	Carlos Garcia	.08	.03	.01
☐ 532	Don Slaught	.03	.01	.00
☐ 533	Colin Powell	.12	.05	.01
☐ 534	Frank Bolick	.17	.07	.01
☐ 535	Gary Scott	.25	.10	.02
☐ 536	Nikco Riesgo	.35	.15	.03
☐ 537	Reggie Sanders	.40	.16	.04
☐ 538	Tim Howard	.20	.08	.02
☐ 539	Ryan Bowen	.15	.06	.01
☐ 540	Eric Anthony	.08	.03	.01
☐ 541	Jim Deshaies	.03	.01	.00
☐ 542	Tom Nevers	.15	.06	.01
☐ 543	Ken Caminiti	.03	.01	.00
☐ 544	Karl Rhodes	.06	.02	.00
☐ 545	Xavier Hernandez	.06	.02	.00
☐ 546	Mike Scott	.06	.02	.00
☐ 547	Jeff Juden	.08	.03	.01
☐ 548	Darryl Kile	.03	.01	.00
☐ 549	Willie Ansley	.06	.02	.00
☐ 550	Luis Gonzalez	.40	.16	.04
☐ 551	Mike Simms	.12	.05	.01
☐ 552	Mark Portugal	.03	.01	.00
☐ 553	Jimmy Jones	.03	.01	.00
☐ 554	Jim Clancy	.03	.01	.00
☐ 555	Pete Harnisch	.06	.02	.00
☐ 556	Craig Biggio	.08	.03	.01
☐ 557	Eric Yelding	.03	.01	.00
☐ 558	Dave Rohde	.03	.01	.00
☐ 559	Casey Candaele	.03	.01	.00
☐ 560	Curt Schilling	.03	.01	.00
☐ 561	Steve Finley	.06	.02	.00
☐ 562	Javier Ortiz	.08	.03	.01
☐ 563	Andujar Cedeno	.20	.08	.02
☐ 564	Rafael Ramirez	.03	.01	.00
☐ 565	Kenny Lofton	.20	.08	.02
☐ 566	Steve Avery	.30	.12	.03
☐ 567	Lonnie Smith	.06	.02	.00
☐ 568	Kent Mercker	.03	.01	.00
☐ 569	Chipper Jones	.30	.12	.03
☐ 570	Terry Pendleton	.08	.03	.01
☐ 571	Otis Nixon	.06	.02	.00
☐ 572	Juan Berenguer	.03	.01	.00
☐ 573	Charlie Leibrandt	.03	.01	.00
☐ 574	David Justice	.40	.16	.04
☐ 575	Keith Mitchell	.35	.15	.03
☐ 576	Tom Glavine	.12	.05	.01
☐ 577	Greg Olson	.06	.02	.00
☐ 578	Rafael Belliard	.03	.01	.00
☐ 579	Ben Rivera	.08	.03	.01
☐ 580	John Smoltz	.10	.04	.01
☐ 581	Tyler Houston	.06	.02	.00
☐ 582	Mark Wohlers	.40	.16	.04
☐ 583	Ron Gant	.12	.05	.01
☐ 584	Ramon Caraballo	.08	.03	.01
☐ 585	Sid Bream	.03	.01	.00
☐ 586	Jeff Treadway	.03	.01	.00
☐ 587	Javier Lopez	.08	.03	.01
☐ 588	Deion Sanders	.08	.03	.01
☐ 589	Mike Heath	.03	.01	.00
☐ 590	Ryan Klesko	1.25	.50	.12
☐ 591	Bob Ojeda	.03	.01	.00
☐ 592	Alfredo Griffin	.03	.01	.00
☐ 593	Raul Mondesi	.20	.08	.02
☐ 594	Greg Smith	.03	.01	.00
☐ 595	Orel Hershiser	.08	.03	.01
☐ 596	Juan Samuel	.06	.02	.00
☐ 597	Brett Butler	.06	.02	.00
☐ 598	Gary Carter	.08	.03	.01
☐ 599	Stan Javier	.03	.01	.00
☐ 600	Kal Daniels	.06	.02	.00
☐ 601	Jamie McAndrew	.12	.05	.01
☐ 602	Mike Sharperson	.03	.01	.00
☐ 603	Jay Howell	.03	.01	.00
☐ 604	Eric Karros	.40	.16	.04
☐ 605	Tim Belcher	.06	.02	.00
☐ 606	Dan Opperman	.10	.04	.01
☐ 607	Lenny Harris	.03	.01	.00
☐ 608	Tom Goodwin	.06	.02	.00
☐ 609	Darryl Strawberry	.15	.06	.01
☐ 610	Ramon Martinez	.10	.04	.01
☐ 611	Kevin Gross	.03	.01	.00
☐ 612	Zakary Shinall	.08	.03	.01
☐ 613	Mike Scioscia	.03	.01	.00
☐ 614	Eddie Murray	.10	.04	.01
☐ 615	Ronnie Walden	.10	.04	.01
☐ 616	Will Clark	.20	.08	.02
☐ 617	Adam Hyzdu	.12	.05	.01
☐ 618	Matt Williams	.08	.03	.01
☐ 619	Don Robinson	.03	.01	.00
☐ 620	Jeff Brantley	.03	.01	.00
☐ 621	Greg Litton	.03	.01	.00
☐ 622	Steve Decker	.25	.10	.02
☐ 623	Robby Thompson	.03	.01	.00
☐ 624	Mark Leonard	.10	.04	.01
☐ 625	Kevin Bass	.03	.01	.00
☐ 626	Scott Garrelts	.03	.01	.00
☐ 627	Jose Uribe	.03	.01	.00
☐ 628	Eric Gunderson	.06	.02	.00
☐ 629	Steve Hosey	.06	.02	.00
☐ 630	Trevor Wilson	.03	.01	.00
☐ 631	Terry Kennedy	.03	.01	.00
☐ 632	Dave Righetti	.06	.02	.00
☐ 633	Kelly Downs	.03	.01	.00
☐ 634	Johnny Ard	.06	.02	.00
☐ 635	Eric Christopherson	.08	.03	.01
☐ 636	Kevin Mitchell	.10	.04	.01
☐ 637	John Burkett	.03	.01	.00
☐ 638	Kevin Rogers	.10	.04	.01
☐ 639	Bud Black	.03	.01	.00
☐ 640	Willie McGee	.08	.03	.01
☐ 641	Royce Clayton	.12	.05	.01
☐ 642	Tony Fernandez	.06	.02	.00
☐ 643	Ricky Bones	.10	.04	.01
☐ 644	Thomas Howard	.03	.01	.00
☐ 645	Dave Staton	.15	.06	.01
☐ 646	Jim Presley	.03	.01	.00
☐ 647	Tony Gwynn	.12	.05	.01
☐ 648	Marty Barrett	.03	.01	.00
☐ 649	Scott Coolbaugh	.03	.01	.00
☐ 650	Craig Lefferts	.03	.01	.00
☐ 651	Eddie Whitson	.03	.01	.00
☐ 652	Oscar Azocar	.06	.02	.00
☐ 653	Wes Gardner	.03	.01	.00
☐ 654	Bip Roberts	.03	.01	.00
☐ 655	Robbie Beckett	.10	.04	.01
☐ 656	Benito Santiago	.08	.03	.01
☐ 657	Greg W.Harris	.03	.01	.00
☐ 658	Jerald Clark	.03	.01	.00
☐ 659	Fred McGriff	.08	.03	.01
☐ 660	Larry Andersen	.03	.01	.00
☐ 661	Bruce Hurst	.06	.02	.00

☐ 662	Steve Martin	.10	.04	.01
☐ 663	Rafael Valdez	.03	.01	.00
☐ 664	Paul Faries	.08	.03	.01
☐ 665	Andy Benes	.06	.02	.00
☐ 666	Randy Myers	.03	.01	.00
☐ 667	Rob Dibble	.06	.02	.00
☐ 668	Glenn Sutko	.08	.03	.01
☐ 669	Glenn Braggs	.03	.01	.00
☐ 670	Billy Hatcher	.06	.02	.00
☐ 671	Joe Oliver	.03	.01	.00
☐ 672	Freddy Benavides	.08	.03	.01
☐ 673	Barry Larkin	.08	.03	.01
☐ 674	Chris Sabo	.08	.03	.01
☐ 675	Mariano Duncan	.03	.01	.00
☐ 676	Chris Jones	.15	.06	.01
☐ 677	Gino Minutelli	.15	.06	.01
☐ 678	Reggie Jefferson	.10	.04	.01
☐ 679	Jack Armstrong	.06	.02	.00
☐ 680	Chris Hammond	.08	.03	.01
☐ 681	Jose Rijo	.06	.02	.00
☐ 682	Bill Doran	.03	.01	.00
☐ 683	Terry Lee	.10	.04	.01
☐ 684	Tom Browning	.06	.02	.00
☐ 685	Paul O'Neill	.06	.02	.00
☐ 686	Eric Davis	.10	.04	.01
☐ 687	Dan Wilson	.15	.06	.01
☐ 688	Ted Power	.03	.01	.00
☐ 689	Tim Layana	.03	.01	.00
☐ 690	Norm Charlton	.03	.01	.00
☐ 691	Hal Morris	.08	.03	.01
☐ 692	Rickey Henderson	.15	.06	.01
☐ 693	Sam Militello Minor League MVP	.20	.08	.02
☐ 694	Matt Mieske Minor League MVP	.45	.18	.04
☐ 695	Paul Russo Minor League MVP	.15	.06	.01
☐ 696	Domingo Mota Minor League MVP	.20	.08	.02
☐ 697	Todd Guggiana Minor League MVP	.15	.06	.01
☐ 698	Marc Newfield Minor League MVP	.75	.30	.07
☐ 699	Checklist 1	.06	.01	.00
☐ 700	Checklist 2	.06	.01	.00
☐ 701	Checklist 3	.06	.01	.00
☐ 702	Checklist 4	.06	.01	.00
☐ 703	Checklist 5	.06	.01	.00
☐ 704	Checklist 6	.06	.01	.00

1989 Brewers Yearbook

This 18-card standard size, 2 1/2" by 3 1/2" set was issued as an insert in the 1989 Milwaukee Brewer Yearbooks. The yearbook itself had a suggested retail price of 4.95. The card set features 17 of the Brewers and their manager. The cards are dominated by a full-color photo of the player on the top two-thirds of the cards along with the uniform number name and position underneath the player. There is also a large logo on the bottom right of the card commemorating the twentieth anniversary of the Brewers in Milwaukee. The backs only contain the player's name and their career statistics. The set is checklisted below by uniform numbers.

		MINT	EXC	G-VG
COMPLETE SET (18)		7.00	3.00	.70
COMMON PLAYER (1-18)		.35	.15	.03
☐ 1	Gary Sheffield	.75	.30	.07
☐ 4	Paul Molitor	.90	.40	.09
☐ 5	B.J. Surhoff	.45	.18	.04
☐ 7	Dale Sveum	.35	.15	.03
☐ 9	Greg Brock	.35	.15	.03
☐ 17	Jim Gantner	.35	.15	.03
☐ 19	Robin Yount	1.00	.40	.10
☐ 20	Juan Nieves	.35	.15	.03
☐ 26	Glenn Braggs	.35	.15	.03
☐ 29	Chris Bosio	.45	.18	.04
☐ 32	Chuck Crim	.35	.15	.03
☐ 37	Dan Plesac	.35	.15	.03
☐ 38	Don August	.35	.15	.03
☐ 40	Mike Birkbeck	.35	.15	.03
☐ 42	Tom Trebelhorn MG	.35	.15	.03
☐ 45	Rob Deer	.45	.18	.04
☐ 46	Bill Wegman	.45	.18	.04
☐ 49	Ted Higuera	.60	.25	.06

1990 Brewers Miller Brewing

This 32-card set and a plastic binder were sponsored by Miller Brewing Co. and given away to the first 25,000 adults (21 years and older) attending the Brewers' home game against the White Sox on August 4th. The cards measure the standard size (2 1/2" by 3 1/2"). The fronts have either action or posed color player photos, with the player's name and position given in white lettering on a black stripe at the bottom of the card face. The backs have biographical information and player statistics. The cards are unnumbered and checklisted below in alphabetical order.

		MINT	EXC	G-VG
COMPLETE SET (32)		12.00	5.25	1.50
COMMON PLAYER (1-32)		.30	.12	.03
☐ 1	Chris Bosio	.40	.16	.04
☐ 2	Greg Brock	.30	.12	.03
☐ 3	Chuck Crim	.30	.12	.03
☐ 4	Rob Deer	.50	.20	.05
☐ 5	Edgar Diaz	.30	.12	.03
☐ 6	Tom Edens	.30	.12	.03
☐ 7	Mike Felder	.30	.12	.03
☐ 8	Tom Filer	.30	.12	.03
☐ 9	Jim Gantner	.40	.16	.04
☐ 10	Darryl Hamilton	.50	.20	.05
☐ 11	Teddy Higuera	.50	.20	.05
☐ 12	Mark Knudson	.40	.16	.04
☐ 13	Bill Krueger	.40	.16	.04
☐ 14	Paul Mirabella	.30	.12	.03
☐ 15	Paul Molitor	.90	.40	.09
☐ 16	Jaime Navarro	.40	.16	.04
☐ 17	Charlie O'Brien	.30	.12	.03
☐ 18	Dave Parker	.75	.30	.07
☐ 19	Dan Plesac	.30	.12	.03
☐ 20	Dennis Powell	.30	.12	.03
☐ 21	Ron Robinson	.40	.16	.04
☐ 22	Bob Sebra	.30	.12	.03
☐ 23	Gary Sheffield	.60	.25	.06
☐ 24	Bill Spiers	.40	.16	.04

		MINT	EXC	G-VG
☐ 25	B.J. Surhoff	.40	.16	.04
☐ 26	Dale Sveum	.30	.12	.03
☐ 27	Tom Trebelhorn MG	.30	.12	.03
☐ 28	Greg Vaughn	.75	.30	.07
☐ 29	Randy Veres	.30	.12	.03
☐ 30	Bill Wegman	.40	.16	.04
☐ 31	Robin Yount	1.00	.40	.10
☐ 32	Coaches Card	.30	.12	.03
	Don Baylor			
	Ray Burris			
	Duffy Dyer			
	Andy Etchebarren			
	Larry Haney			

☐ 29	Greg Vaughn	.75	.30	.07
☐ 30	Bill Wegman	.40	.16	.04
☐ 31	Robin Yount	1.00	.40	.10
☐ 32	Coaches Card	.30	.12	.03
	Don Baylor			
	Fred Stanley			
	Duffy Dyer			
	Larry Haney			
	Andy Etchebarren			
	Ray Burris			

1991 Brewers Miller Brewing

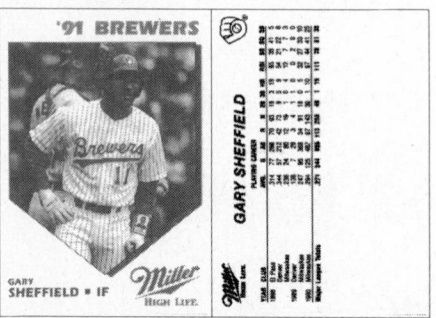

This 32-card set was sponsored by the Miller Brewing Company, and the company logo appears in red lettering at the lower right corner of the front. The sets were given away at the Brewers' home game against the Baltimore Orioles on August 17. The standard size (2 1/2" by 3 1/2") cards feature on the fronts color action player photos inside a pentagonal-shaped design. A black border on the right side of the pentagon creates the impression of a shadow. The words "'91 Brewers" appears in bluish-purple lettering above the photo, with player information given in black lettering in the lower left corner of the card face. The backs are printed in black and present complete Major League statistics. The cards are unnumbered and checklisted below in alphabetical order, with the coaches' card listed at the end.

		MINT	EXC	G-VG
COMPLETE SET (32)		10.00	4.50	1.25
COMMON PLAYER (1-32)		.30	.12	.03
☐ 1	Don August	.30	.12	.03
☐ 2	James Austin	.30	.12	.03
☐ 3	Dante Bichette	.40	.16	.04
☐ 4	Chris Bosio	.40	.16	.04
☐ 5	Kevin Brown	.40	.16	.04
☐ 6	Chuck Crim	.30	.12	.03
☐ 7	Rick Dempsey	.30	.12	.03
☐ 8	Jim Gantner	.40	.16	.04
☐ 9	Darryl Hamilton	.40	.16	.04
☐ 10	Teddy Higuera	.40	.16	.04
☐ 11	Darren Holmes	.30	.12	.03
☐ 12	Jim Hunter	.40	.16	.04
☐ 13	Mark Knudson	.40	.16	.04
☐ 14	Mark Lee	.30	.12	.03
☐ 15	Julio Machado	.40	.16	.04
☐ 16	Candy Maldonado	.40	.16	.04
☐ 17	Paul Molitor	.90	.40	.09
☐ 18	Jaime Navarro	.40	.16	.04
☐ 19	Edwin Nunez	.30	.12	.03
☐ 20	Dan Plesac	.30	.12	.03
☐ 21	Willie Randolph	.40	.16	.04
☐ 22	Ron Robinson	.30	.12	.03
☐ 23	Gary Sheffield	.50	.20	.05
☐ 24	Bill Spiers	.40	.16	.04
☐ 25	Franklin Stubbs	.40	.16	.04
☐ 26	B.J. Surhoff	.40	.16	.04
☐ 27	Dale Sveum	.30	.12	.03
☐ 28	Tom Trebelhorn MG	.30	.12	.03

1977 Burger King Yankees

The cards in this 24-card set measure 2 1/2" by 3 1/2". The cards in this set marked with an asterisk have different poses than those cards in the regular 1977 Topps set. The checklist card is unnumbered and the Piniella card was issued subsequent to the original printing. The complete set price below refers to all 24 cards listed, including Piniella.

		NRMT	VG-E	GOOD
COMPLETE SET (24)		40.00	18.00	6.00
COMMON PLAYER (1-24)		.35	.15	.03
☐ 1	Yankees Team	1.25	.50	.12
	Billy Martin MG			
☐ 2	Thurman Munson * UER	7.50	3.25	.75
	(facsimile autograph misspelled)			
☐ 3	Fran Healy	.35	.15	.03
☐ 4	Jim Hunter	3.00	1.25	.30
☐ 5	Ed Figueroa	.35	.15	.03
☐ 6	Don Gullett *	.75	.30	.07
	(mouth closed)			
☐ 7	Mike Torrez *	.60	.25	.06
☐ 8	Ken Holtzman	.35	.15	.03
☐ 9	Dick Tidrow	.35	.15	.03
☐ 10	Sparky Lyle	.50	.20	.05
☐ 11	Ron Guidry	2.00	.80	.20
☐ 12	Chris Chambliss	.50	.20	.05
☐ 13	Willie Randolph *	1.50	.60	.15
	(no rookie trophy)			
☐ 14	Bucky Dent *	1.50	.60	.15
	(shown as White Sox in 1977 Topps)			
☐ 15	Graig Nettles *	1.50	.60	.15
	(closer photo than in 1977 Topps)			
☐ 16	Fred Stanley	.35	.15	.03
☐ 17	Reggie Jackson *	9.00	4.00	.90
	(looking up with bat)			
☐ 18	Mickey Rivers	.50	.20	.05
☐ 19	Roy White	.35	.15	.03
☐ 20	Jim Wynn *	.75	.30	.07
	(shown as Brave in 1977 Topps)			
☐ 21	Paul Blair *	.75	.30	.07
	(shown as Oriole in 1977 Topps)			
☐ 22	Carlos May *	.50	.20	.05
☐ 23	Lou Piniella	18.00	7.50	2.50
☐ xx	Checklist Card TP	.15	.06	.01
	(unnumbered)			

1978 Burger King Astros

JESUS ALOU

The cards in this 23-card set measure 2 1/2" by 3 1/2". Released in local Houston Burger King outlets during the 1978 season, this Houston Astros series contains the standard 22 numbered player cards and one unnumbered checklist. The player poses found to differ from the regular Topps issue are marked with astericks.

		NRMT	VG-E	GOOD
COMPLETE SET (23)		11.00	5.00	1.35
COMMON PLAYER (1-23)		.35	.15	.03
☐ 1	Bill Virdon MG	.60	.25	.06
☐ 2	Joe Ferguson	.35	.15	.03
☐ 3	Ed Herrmann	.35	.15	.03
☐ 4	J.R. Richard	.90	.40	.09
☐ 5	Joe Niekro	1.00	.40	.10
☐ 6	Floyd Bannister	.90	.40	.09
☐ 7	Joaquin Andujar	.90	.40	.09
☐ 8	Ken Forsch	.45	.18	.04
☐ 9	Mark Lemongello	.35	.15	.03
☐ 10	Joe Sambito	.45	.18	.04
☐ 11	Gene Pentz	.35	.15	.03
☐ 12	Bob Watson	.75	.30	.07
☐ 13	Julio Gonzales	.35	.15	.03
☐ 14	Enos Cabell	.35	.15	.03
☐ 15	Roger Metzger	.35	.15	.03
☐ 16	Art Howe	.75	.30	.07
☐ 17	Jose Cruz	.90	.40	.09
☐ 18	Cesar Cedeno	.75	.30	.07
☐ 19	Terry Puhl	.60	.25	.06
☐ 20	Wilbur Howard	.35	.15	.03
☐ 21	Dave Bergman *	.45	.18	.04
☐ 22	Jesus Alou *	.45	.18	.04
☐ 23	Checklist Card TP (unnumbered)	.05	.02	.00

1978 Burger King Rangers

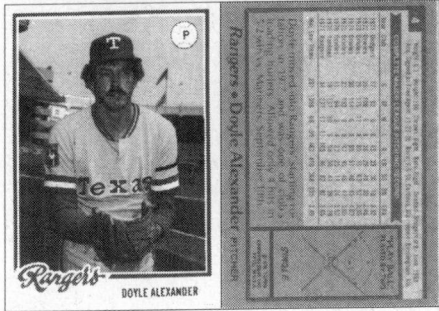

DOYLE ALEXANDER

The cards in this 23-card set measure 2 1/2" by 3 1/2". This set of 22 numbered player cards (featuring the Texas Rangers) and

one unnumbered checklist was issued regionally by Burger King in 1978. Astericks denote poses different from those found in the regular Topps cards of this year.

		NRMT	VG-E	GOOD
COMPLETE SET (23)		11.00	5.00	1.35
COMMON PLAYER (1-23)		.35	.15	.03
☐ 1	Billy Hunter MG	.35	.15	.03
☐ 2	Jim Sundberg	.60	.25	.06
☐ 3	John Ellis	.35	.15	.03
☐ 4	Doyle Alexander	.60	.25	.06
☐ 5	Jon Matlack *	.60	.25	.06
☐ 6	Dock Ellis	.35	.15	.03
☐ 7	Doc Medich	.45	.18	.04
☐ 8	Fergie Jenkins *	2.00	.80	.20
☐ 9	Len Barker	.35	.15	.03
☐ 10	Reggie Cleveland *	.35	.15	.03
☐ 11	Mike Hargrove	.75	.30	.07
☐ 12	Bump Wills	.35	.15	.03
☐ 13	Toby Harrah	.75	.30	.07
☐ 14	Bert Campaneris	.60	.25	.06
☐ 15	Sandy Alomar	.35	.15	.03
☐ 16	Kurt Bevacqua	.35	.15	.03
☐ 17	Al Oliver *	1.00	.40	.10
☐ 18	Juan Beniquez	.45	.18	.04
☐ 19	Claudell Washington	.75	.30	.07
☐ 20	Richie Zisk	.45	.18	.04
☐ 21	John Lowenstein *	.35	.15	.03
☐ 22	Bobby Thompson *	.35	.15	.03
☐ xx	Checklist Card TP (unnumbered)	.05	.02	.00

1978 Burger King Tigers

STEVE DILLARD

The cards in this 23-card set measure 2 1/2" by 3 1/2". Twenty-three color cards, 22 players and one numbered checklist, comprise the 1978 Burger King Tigers set issued in the Detroit area. The cards marked with an asterisk contain photos different from those appearing on the Topps regular issue cards of that year. For example, Jack Morris, Alan Trammell, and Lou Whitaker (in the 1978 Topps regular issue cards) each appear on rookie prospect cards with three other young players; whereas in this Burger King set, each has his own individual card.

		NRMT	VG-E	GOOD
COMPLETE SET (23)		50.00	22.50	7.50
COMMON PLAYER (1-23)		.35	.15	.03
☐ 1	Ralph Houk MG	.60	.25	.06
☐ 2	Milt May	.35	.15	.03
☐ 3	John Wockenfuss	.35	.15	.03
☐ 4	Mark Fidrych	1.00	.40	.10
☐ 5	Dave Rozema	.35	.15	.03
☐ 6	Jack Billingham *	.35	.15	.03
☐ 7	Jim Slaton *	.35	.15	.03
☐ 8	Jack Morris	15.00	6.50	2.15
☐ 9	John Hiller	.60	.25	.06
☐ 10	Steve Foucault	.35	.15	.03
☐ 11	Milt Wilcox	.35	.15	.03
☐ 12	Jason Thompson	.60	.25	.06
☐ 13	Lou Whitaker *	12.00	5.25	1.50
☐ 14	Aurelio Rodriguez	.35	.15	.03
☐ 15	Alan Trammell *	22.00	9.50	3.15

			NRMT	VG-E	GOOD
☐	16	Steve Dillard *	.35	.15	.03
☐	17	Phil Mankowski	.35	.15	.03
☐	18	Steve Kemp	.60	.25	.06
☐	19	Ron LeFlore	.45	.18	.04
☐	20	Tim Corcoran	.35	.15	.03
☐	21	Mickey Stanley	.45	.18	.04
☐	22	Rusty Staub	1.00	.40	.10
☐	xx	Checklist Card TP (unnumbered)	.05	.02	.00

1978 Burger King Yankees

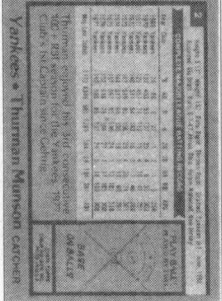

THURMAN MUNSON

The cards in this 23-card set measure 2 1/2" by 3 1/2". These cards were distributed in packs of three players plus a checklist at Burger King's New York area outlets. Cards with an asterisk have different poses than those in the Topps regular issue.

			NRMT	VG-E	GOOD
		COMPLETE SET (23)	13.50	6.00	1.85
		COMMON PLAYER (1-23)	.25	.10	.02
☐	1	Billy Martin MG	.75	.30	.07
☐	2	Thurman Munson	3.50	1.50	.35
☐	3	Cliff Johnson	.25	.10	.02
☐	4	Ron Guidry	1.25	.50	.12
☐	5	Ed Figueroa	.25	.10	.02
☐	6	Dick Tidrow	.25	.10	.02
☐	7	Jim Hunter	1.50	.60	.15
☐	8	Don Gullett	.35	.15	.03
☐	9	Sparky Lyle	.50	.20	.05
☐	10	Rich Gossage *	1.25	.50	.12
☐	11	Rawly Eastwick *	.25	.10	.02
☐	12	Chris Chambliss	.50	.20	.05
☐	13	Willie Randolph	.75	.30	.07
☐	14	Graig Nettles	.75	.30	.07
☐	15	Bucky Dent	.60	.25	.06
☐	16	Jim Spencer *	.25	.10	.02
☐	17	Fred Stanley	.25	.10	.02
☐	18	Lou Piniella	.75	.30	.07
☐	19	Roy White	.35	.15	.03
☐	20	Mickey Rivers	.35	.15	.03
☐	21	Reggie Jackson	5.00	2.25	.50
☐	22	Paul Blair	.25	.10	.02
☐	xx	Checklist Card TP (unnumbered)	.05	.02	.00

1979 Burger King Phillies

The cards in this 23-card set measure 2 1/2" by 3 1/2". The 1979 Burger King Phillies set follows the regular format of 22 player cards and one unnumbered checklist card. The asterisk indicates where the pose differs from the Topps card of that year.

			NRMT	VG-E	GOOD
		COMPLETE SET (23)	9.00	4.00	.90
		COMMON PLAYER (1-23)	.15	.06	.01
☐	1	Danny Ozark MG *	.15	.06	.01
☐	2	Bob Boone	.50	.20	.05

PETE ROSE 1B
N.L. ALL-STAR
PHILLIES

			NRMT	VG-E	GOOD
☐	3	Tim McCarver	.50	.20	.05
☐	4	Steve Carlton	2.25	.90	.22
☐	5	Larry Christenson	.15	.06	.01
☐	6	Dick Ruthven	.15	.06	.01
☐	7	Ron Reed	.15	.06	.01
☐	8	Randy Lerch	.15	.06	.01
☐	9	Warren Brusstar	.15	.06	.01
☐	10	Tug McGraw	.35	.15	.03
☐	11	Nino Espinosa *	.15	.06	.01
☐	12	Doug Bird *	.15	.06	.01
☐	13	Pete Rose *	3.00	1.25	.30
☐	14	Manny Trillo *	.15	.06	.01
☐	15	Larry Bowa	.35	.15	.03
☐	16	Mike Schmidt	3.50	1.50	.35
☐	17	Pete Mackanin *	.15	.06	.01
☐	18	Jose Cardenal	.15	.06	.01
☐	19	Greg Luzinski	.35	.15	.03
☐	20	Garry Maddox	.15	.06	.01
☐	21	Bake McBride	.15	.06	.01
☐	22	Greg Gross *	.15	.06	.01
☐	xx	Checklist Card TP (unnumbered)	.05	.02	.00

1979 Burger King Yankees

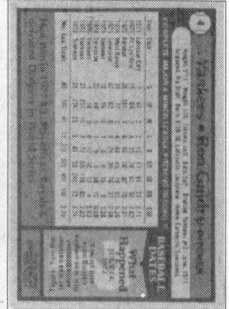

RON GUIDRY P.
YANKEES

The cards in this 23-card set measure 2 1/2" by 3 1/2". There are 22 numbered cards and one unnumbered checklist in the 1979 Burger King Yankee set. The poses of Guidry, Tiant, John and Beniquez, each marked with an asterisk below, are different from their poses appearing in the regular Topps issue. The team card has a picture of Lemon rather than Martin.

			NRMT	VG-E	GOOD
		COMPLETE SET (23)	9.00	4.00	.90
		COMMON PLAYER (1-23)	.15	.06	.01
☐	1	Yankees Team: Bob Lemon MG *	.75	.30	.07
☐	2	Thurman Munson	2.50	1.00	.25
☐	3	Cliff Johnson	.15	.06	.01
☐	4	Ron Guidry *	1.25	.50	.12
☐	5	Jay Johnstone	.35	.15	.03
☐	6	Jim Hunter	1.25	.50	.12

		MINT	EXC	G-VG
☐ 7	Jim Beattie	.15	.06	.01
☐ 8	Luis Tiant *	.35	.15	.03
☐ 9	Tommy John *	1.00	.40	.10
☐ 10	Rich Gossage	.75	.30	.07
☐ 11	Ed Figueroa	.15	.06	.01
☐ 12	Chris Chambliss	.30	.12	.03
☐ 13	Willie Randolph	.50	.20	.05
☐ 14	Bucky Dent	.40	.16	.04
☐ 15	Graig Nettles	.50	.20	.05
☐ 16	Fred Stanley	.15	.06	.01
☐ 17	Jim Spencer	.15	.06	.01
☐ 18	Lou Piniella	.60	.25	.06
☐ 19	Roy White	.25	.10	.02
☐ 20	Mickey Rivers	.25	.10	.02
☐ 21	Reggie Jackson	3.50	1.50	.35
☐ 22	Juan Beniquez *	.25	.10	.02
☐ xx	Checklist Card TP	.05	.02	.00
	(unnumbered)			

1980 Burger King Phillies

The cards in this 23-card set measure 2 1/2" by 3 1/2". The 1980 edition of Burger King Phillies follows the established pattern of 22 numbered player cards and one unnumbered checklist. Cards marked with astericks contain poses different from those found in the regular 1980 Topps cards. This was the first Burger King set to carry the Burger King logo and hence does not generate the same confusion that the three previous years do for collectors trying to distinguish Burger King cards from the very similar Topps cards of the same years. Keith Moreland's card predates his rookie cards by one year as he did not appear on a regular issue card until 1981.

		MINT	EXC	G-VG
COMPLETE SET (23)		8.00	3.50	.80
COMMON PLAYER (1-23)		.15	.06	.01
☐ 1	Dallas Green MG *	.35	.15	.03
☐ 2	Bob Boone	.40	.16	.04
☐ 3	Keith Moreland *	.60	.25	.06
☐ 4	Pete Rose	3.00	1.25	.30
☐ 5	Manny Trillo	.15	.06	.01
☐ 6	Mike Schmidt	3.50	1.50	.35
☐ 7	Larry Bowa	.35	.15	.03
☐ 8	John Vukovich *	.15	.06	.01
☐ 9	Bake McBride	.15	.06	.01
☐ 10	Garry Maddox	.15	.06	.01
☐ 11	Greg Luzinski	.35	.15	.03
☐ 12	Greg Gross	.15	.06	.01
☐ 13	Del Unser	.15	.06	.01
☐ 14	Lonnie Smith *	.90	.40	.09
☐ 15	Steve Carlton	2.00	.80	.20
☐ 16	Larry Christenson	.15	.06	.01
☐ 17	Nino Espinosa	.15	.06	.01
☐ 18	Randy Lerch	.15	.06	.01
☐ 19	Dick Ruthven	.15	.06	.01
☐ 20	Tug McGraw	.35	.15	.03
☐ 21	Ron Reed	.15	.06	.01
☐ 22	Kevin Saucier *	.15	.06	.01
☐ xx	Checklist Card TP	.05	.02	.00
	(unnumbered)			

1980 Burger King Pitch/Hit/Run

The cards in this 34-card set measure 2 1/2" by 3 1/2". The "Pitch, Hit, and Run" set was a promotion introduced by Burger King in 1980. The cards carry a Burger King logo on the front and those marked by an asterisk in the checklist contain a different photo from that found in the regularly issued Topps series. For example, Nolan Ryan was shown as a California Angel and Joe Morgan was a Cincinnati Red in the 1980 Topps regular set. Cards 1-11 are pitchers, 12-22 are hitters, and 23-33 are speedsters. Within each subgroup, the players are numbered corresponding to the alphabetical order of their names. The unnumbered checklist card was triple printed and is the least valuable card in the set.

		MINT	EXC	G-VG
COMPLETE SET (34)		21.00	8.50	2.75
COMMON PLAYER (1-34)		.15	.06	.01
☐ 1	Vida Blue *	.15	.06	.01
☐ 2	Steve Carlton	2.00	.80	.20
☐ 3	Rollie Fingers	1.25	.50	.12
☐ 4	Ron Guidry *	.40	.16	.04
☐ 5	Jerry Koosman *	.25	.10	.02
☐ 6	Phil Niekro	.75	.30	.07
☐ 7	Jim Palmer *	1.75	.60	.15
☐ 8	J.R. Richard	.15	.06	.01
☐ 9	Nolan Ryan *	8.00	3.25	.75
	Houston Astros			
☐ 10	Tom Seaver *	3.00	1.00	.25
☐ 11	Bruce Sutter	.15	.06	.01
☐ 12	Don Baylor	.15	.06	.01
☐ 13	George Brett	1.75	.70	.17
☐ 14	Rod Carew	1.25	.50	.12
☐ 15	George Foster	.15	.06	.01
☐ 16	Keith Hernandez *	.50	.20	.05
☐ 17	Reggie Jackson *	3.00	1.00	.25
☐ 18	Fred Lynn *	.20	.08	.02
☐ 19	Dave Parker	.35	.15	.03
☐ 20	Jim Rice	.35	.15	.03
☐ 21	Pete Rose	2.50	1.00	.25
☐ 22	Dave Winfield *	1.75	.60	.15
☐ 23	Bobby Bonds *	.15	.06	.01
☐ 24	Enos Cabell	.15	.06	.01
☐ 25	Cesar Cedeno *	.15	.06	.01
☐ 26	Julio Cruz	.15	.06	.01
☐ 27	Ron LeFlore *	.15	.06	.01
☐ 28	Dave Lopes	.15	.06	.01
☐ 29	Omar Moreno *	.15	.06	.01
☐ 30	Joe Morgan *	1.75	.60	.15
	Houston Astros			
☐ 31	Bill North	.15	.06	.01
☐ 32	Frank Taveras	.15	.06	.01
☐ 33	Willie Wilson	.20	.08	.02
☐ 34	Checklist Card TP	.05	.02	.00
	(unnumbered)			

1982 Burger King Indians

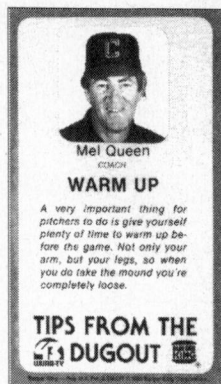

The cards in this 12-card set measure 3" by 5". Tips From The Dugout is the series title of this set issued on a one card per week basis by the Burger King chain in the Cleveland area. Each card contains a black and white photo of manager Dave Garcia or coaches Goryl, McCraw, Queen and Sommers, under whom appears a paragraph explaining some aspect of inside baseball. The photo and "Tip" are set upon a large yellow area surrounded by green borders. The cards are not numbered and are blank-backed. The logos of Burger King and WUAB-TV appear at the base of the card.

	MINT	EXC	G-VG
COMPLETE SET (12)	5.00	2.25	.50
COMMON PLAYER (1-12)	.50	.20	.05
☐ 1 Dave Garcia: Be in the Game	.50	.20	.05
☐ 2 Dave Garcia: Sportsmanship	.50	.20	.05
☐ 3 Johnny Goryl: Rounding Bases	.50	.20	.05
☐ 4 Johnny Goryl: 3B Running	.50	.20	.05
☐ 5 Tom McCraw: Follow Thru	.50	.20	.05
☐ 6 Tom McCraw: Selecting a Bat	.50	.20	.05
☐ 7 Tom McCraw: Watch the Ball	.50	.20	.05
☐ 8 Mel Queen: Master One Pitch	.50	.20	.05
☐ 9 Mel Queen: Warm Up	.50	.20	.05
☐ 10 Dennis Sommers: Protect Fingers	.50	.20	.05
☐ 11 Dennis Sommers: Tagging 1st Base	.50	.20	.05
☐ 12 Dennis Sommers	.50	.20	.05

1986 Burger King All-Pro

This 20-card set was distributed in Burger King restaurants across the country. They were produced as panels of three where the middle card was actually a special discount coupon card. The folded panel was given with the purchase of a Whopper. Each individual card measures 2 1/2" by 3 1/2". The team logos have been airbrushed from the pictures. The cards are numbered on the front at the top.

	MINT	EXC	G-VG
COMPLETE SET (20)	6.00	2.50	.60
COMMON PLAYER (1-20)	.20	.08	.02

☐ 1 Tony Pena	.20	.08	.02
☐ 2 Dave Winfield	.40	.16	.04
☐ 3 Fernando Valenzuela	.25	.10	.02
☐ 4 Pete Rose	.80	.35	.08
☐ 5 Mike Schmidt	1.00	.40	.10
☐ 6 Steve Carlton	.50	.20	.05
☐ 7 Glenn Wilson	.20	.08	.02
☐ 8 Jim Rice	.25	.10	.02
☐ 9 Wade Boggs	.75	.30	.07
☐ 10 Juan Samuel	.20	.08	.02
☐ 11 Dale Murphy	.50	.20	.05
☐ 12 Reggie Jackson	.80	.35	.08
☐ 13 Kirk Gibson	.30	.12	.03
☐ 14 Eddie Murray	.60	.25	.06
☐ 15 Cal Ripken	1.00	.40	.10
☐ 16 Willie McGee	.25	.10	.02
☐ 17 Dwight Gooden	.50	.20	.05
☐ 18 Steve Garvey	.35	.15	.03
☐ 19 Don Mattingly	.80	.35	.08
☐ 20 George Brett	.80	.35	.08

1987 Burger King All-Pro

This 20-card set consists of 10 panels of two cards each joined together along with a promotional coupon. Individual cards measure 2 1/2" by 3 1/2" whereas the panels measure approximately 3 1/2" by 7 5/8". MSA (Mike Schechter Associates produced the cards for Burger King; there are no Major League logos on the cards. The cards are numbered on the front. The set card numbering is almost (but not quite) in alphabetical order by player's name.

	MINT	EXC	G-VG
COMPLETE SET (20)	5.00	2.25	.50
COMMON PLAYER (1-20)	.20	.08	.02
☐ 1 Wade Boggs	.75	.30	.07
☐ 2 Gary Carter	.40	.16	.04
☐ 3 Will Clark	1.00	.40	.10
☐ 4 Roger Clemens	1.00	.40	.10
☐ 5 Steve Garvey	.35	.15	.03
☐ 6 Ron Darling	.20	.08	.02
☐ 7 Pedro Guerrero	.25	.10	.02
☐ 8 Von Hayes	.20	.08	.02

			MINT	EXC	G-VG
☐	9	Rickey Henderson	.90	.40	.09
☐	10	Keith Hernandez	.30	.12	.03
☐	11	Wally Joyner	.45	.18	.04
☐	12	Mike Krukow	.20	.08	.02
☐	13	Don Mattingly	.75	.30	.07
☐	14	Ozzie Smith	.45	.18	.04
☐	15	Tony Pena	.20	.08	.02
☐	16	Jim Rice	.25	.10	.02
☐	17	Mike Schmidt	1.00	.40	.10
☐	18	Ryne Sandberg	1.00	.40	.10
☐	19	Darryl Strawberry	.90	.40	.09
☐	20	Fernando Valenzuela	.25	.10	.02

1956 Carling Black Label Indians

CARLING Black Label BEER
and
THE CLEVELAND INDIANS

This 10-card, approximately 8 1/2" by 12", set was issued by Carling Beer and celebrated members of the (then) perennial contending Cleveland Indians. These cards feature a black and white photo with the printed name of the player inserted in the photo. Underneath the photo is a joint advertisement for Carling Black Label Beer and The Cleveland Indians. The set looks like it could be easily replicated and may indeed have been reprinted. The checklist for this unnumbered set is ordered alphabetically.

			MINT	EXC	G-VG
	COMPLETE SET (10)		75.00	34.00	11.25
	COMMON PLAYER (1-10)		5.00	2.25	.50
☐	1	Bob Feller	27.00	12.00	4.00
☐	2	Mike Garcia	6.00	2.50	.60
☐	3	Jim Hegan	5.00	2.25	.50
☐	4	Art Houtteman	5.00	2.25	.50
☐	5	Bob Lemon	15.00	6.50	2.15
☐	6	Al Rosen	10.00	4.50	1.25
☐	7	Herb Score	10.00	4.50	1.25
☐	8	Al Smith	5.00	2.25	.50
☐	9	George Strickland	5.00	2.25	.50
☐	10	Early Wynn	15.00	6.50	2.15

1987 Champion Phillies

This four-card set which measured approximately 3" by 4 3/4" (with scratch-off tab) is unusual in that there is no way to determine the player's identity other than knowing and recognizing whose photo it is. The top part of the card has a color photo of the player surrounded in the upper left hand corner with a Champion spark plug logo. The Philadelphia Phillies logo is in the upper right hand part of the card. A Pep Boys ad is in the lower left hand corner of the photo and the WIP Philadelphia Sports Radio promo is in the lower right hand corner of the photo. The set is checklisted alphabetically by subject since the cards are unnumbered.

	MINT	EXC	G-VG
COMPLETE SET (4)	17.50	8.00	2.25
COMMON PLAYER (1-4)	1.25	.50	.12

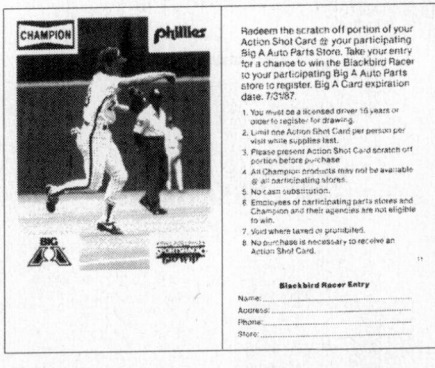

			MINT	EXC	G-VG
☐	1	Von Hayes	2.50	1.00	.25
☐	2	Steve Jeltz	1.25	.50	.12
☐	3	Juan Samuel	2.50	1.00	.25
☐	4	Mike Schmidt	12.50	5.50	1.65

1988 Chef Boyardee

MIKE SCOTT
HOUSTON ASTROS
PITCHER

This 24-card set was distributed as a perforated sheet of four rows and six columns of cards in return for ten proofs of purchase of Chef Boyardeee products and $1.50 for postage and handling. The card photos on the fronts are in full color with a light blue border but are not shown with team logos. The card backs are numbered and printed in red and blue on gray card stock. Individual cards measure approximately 2 1/2" by 3 1/2" and show the Chef Boyardee logo in the upper right corner of the obverse. Card backs feature year-by-year season statistics since 1984. There is no additional premium for having the sheet intact as opposed to having individual cards neatly cut.

			MINT	EXC	G-VG
	COMPLETE SET (24)		11.00	5.00	1.35
	COMMON PLAYER (1-24)		.40	.16	.04
☐	1	Mark McGwire	.75	.30	.07
☐	2	Eric Davis	.75	.30	.07
☐	3	Jack Morris	.60	.25	.06
☐	4	George Bell	.50	.20	.05
☐	5	Ozzie Smith	.60	.25	.06
☐	6	Tony Gwynn	.90	.40	.09
☐	7	Cal Ripken	1.00	.40	.10
☐	8	Todd Worrell	.40	.16	.04
☐	9	Larry Parrish	.40	.16	.04
☐	10	Gary Carter	.50	.20	.05
☐	11	Ryne Sandberg	1.00	.40	.10
☐	12	Keith Hernandez	.50	.20	.05
☐	13	Kirby Puckett	1.00	.40	.10
☐	14	Mike Schmidt	1.25	.50	.12
☐	15	Frank Viola	.50	.20	.05
☐	16	Don Mattingly	1.00	.40	.10
☐	17	Dale Murphy	.75	.30	.07

		MINT	EXC	G-VG
☐ 18	Andre Dawson	.75	.30	.07
☐ 19	Mike Scott	.40	.16	.04
☐ 20	Rickey Henderson	1.00	.40	.10
☐ 21	Jim Rice	.50	.20	.05
☐ 22	Wade Boggs	.90	.40	.09
☐ 23	Roger Clemens	1.00	.40	.10
☐ 24	Fernando Valenzuela	.50	.20	.05

1985 CIGNA Phillies

 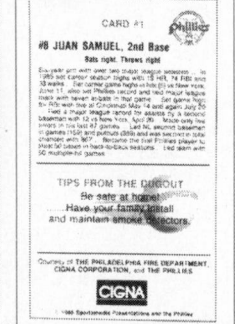

This colorful 16-card set (measuring 2 5/8" by 4 1/8") features the Philadelphia Phillies and was also sponsored by CIGNA Corporation. Cards are numbered on the back and contain a safety tip as such the set is frequently categorized and referenced as a safety set. Cards are also numbered by uniform number on the front.

		MINT	EXC	G-VG
COMPLETE SET (16)		8.00	3.50	.80
COMMON PLAYER (1-16)		.25	.10	.02
☐ 1	Juan Samuel	.50	.20	.05
☐ 2	Von Hayes	.50	.20	.05
☐ 3	Ozzie Virgil	.35	.15	.03
☐ 4	Mike Schmidt	3.00	1.25	.30
☐ 5	Greg Gross	.25	.10	.02
☐ 6	Tim Corcoran	.25	.10	.02
☐ 7	Jerry Koosman	.50	.20	.05
☐ 8	Jeff Stone	.25	.10	.02
☐ 9	Glenn Wilson	.35	.15	.03
☐ 10	Steve Jeltz	.25	.10	.02
☐ 11	Garry Maddox	.35	.15	.03
☐ 12	Steve Carlton	1.75	.70	.17
☐ 13	John Denny	.35	.15	.03
☐ 14	Kevin Gross	.35	.15	.03
☐ 15	Shane Rawley	.35	.15	.03
☐ 16	Charlie Hudson	.25	.10	.02

1986 CIGNA Phillies

This 16-card set was sponsored by CIGNA Corp. and was given away by the Philadelphia area Fire Departments. Cards measure 2 3/4" by 4 1/8" and feature full color fronts. The card backs are printed in maroon and black on white card stock. Although the uniform numbers are given on the front of the card, the cards are numbered on the back in the order listed below.

		MINT	EXC	G-VG
COMPLETE SET (16)		7.00	3.00	.70
COMMON PLAYER (1-16)		.25	.10	.02
☐ 1	Juan Samuel	.50	.20	.05
☐ 2	Don Carman	.35	.15	.03
☐ 3	Von Hayes	.50	.20	.05
☐ 4	Kent Tekulve	.35	.15	.03
☐ 5	Greg Gross	.25	.10	.02
☐ 6	Shane Rawley	.35	.15	.03

 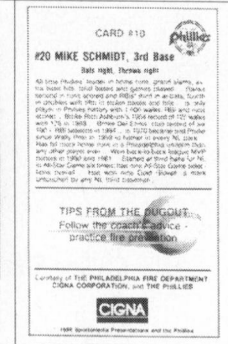

		MINT	EXC	G-VG
☐ 7	Darren Daulton	.60	.25	.06
☐ 8	Kevin Gross	.35	.15	.03
☐ 9	Steve Jeltz	.25	.10	.02
☐ 10	Mike Schmidt	3.00	1.25	.30
☐ 11	Steve Bedrosian	.60	.25	.06
☐ 12	Gary Redus	.35	.15	.03
☐ 13	Charles Hudson	.25	.10	.02
☐ 14	John Russell	.25	.10	.02
☐ 15	Fred Toliver	.25	.10	.02
☐ 16	Glenn Wilson	.35	.15	.03

1985 Circle K

 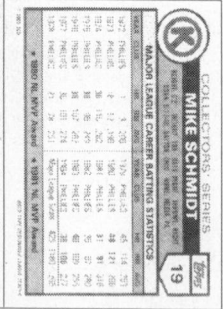

The cards in this 33-card set measure 2 1/2" by 3 1/2" and were issued with accompanying box. In 1985, Topps produced this set for Circle K; cards were printed in Ireland. Cards are numbered on the back according to each player's rank on the all-time career Home Run list. The backs are printed in blue and red on white card stock. The card fronts are glossy and each player is named in the lower left corner. Most of the obverses are in color, although the older vintage players are pictured in black and white. Joe DiMaggio was not included in the set; card number 31 does not exist. It was intended to be DiMaggio but he apparently would not consent to be included in the set.

		MINT	EXC	G-VG
COMPLETE SET (33)		5.00	2.25	.50
COMMON PLAYER (1-34)		.10	.04	.01
☐ 1	Hank Aaron	.60	.25	.06
☐ 2	Babe Ruth	1.00	.40	.10
☐ 3	Willie Mays	.60	.25	.06
☐ 4	Frank Robinson	.20	.08	.02
☐ 5	Harmon Killebrew	.15	.06	.01
☐ 6	Mickey Mantle	1.00	.40	.10
☐ 7	Jimmie Foxx	.15	.06	.01
☐ 8	Willie McCovey	.20	.08	.02
☐ 9	Ted Williams	.50	.20	.05
☐ 10	Ernie Banks	.20	.08	.02

☐	11	Eddie Mathews	.15	.06	.01	☐	22	Mike Pagliarulo	.25	.10	.02

☐ 11	Eddie Mathews	.15	.06	.01
☐ 12	Mel Ott	.15	.06	.01
☐ 13	Reggie Jackson	.50	.20	.05
☐ 14	Lou Gehrig	.60	.25	.06
☐ 15	Stan Musial	.35	.15	.03
☐ 16	Willie Stargell	.20	.08	.02
☐ 17	Carl Yastrzemski	.40	.16	.04
☐ 18	Billy Williams	.15	.06	.01
☐ 19	Mike Schmidt	.60	.25	.06
☐ 20	Duke Snider	.30	.12	.03
☐ 21	Al Kaline	.25	.10	.02
☐ 22	Johnny Bench	.35	.15	.03
☐ 23	Frank Howard	.10	.04	.01
☐ 24	Orlando Cepeda	.10	.04	.01
☐ 25	Norm Cash	.10	.04	.01
☐ 26	Dave Kingman	.10	.04	.01
☐ 27	Rocky Colavito	.10	.04	.01
☐ 28	Tony Perez	.15	.06	.01
☐ 29	Gil Hodges	.10	.04	.01
☐ 30	Ralph Kiner	.10	.04	.01
☐ 31	Joe DiMaggio	.00	.00	.00
	(not included in set, card does not exist)			
☐ 32	Johnny Mize	.15	.06	.01
☐ 33	Yogi Berra	.30	.12	.03
☐ 34	Lee May	.10	.04	.01

1987 Classic Game

Steve Garvey

This 100-card set was actually distributed as part of a trivia board game. The card backs contain several trivia questions (and answers) which are used to play the game. A dark green border frames the full-color photo. The games were produced by Game Time, Ltd. and were available in toy stores as well as from card dealers. According to the producers of this game, only 75,000 sets were distributed. The cards are standard size, 2 1/2" by 3 1/2".

	MINT	EXC	G-VG
COMPLETE SET (100)	150.00	67.50	22.50
COMMON PLAYER (1-100)	.25	.10	.02

☐ 1	Pete Rose	2.50	1.00	.25
☐ 2	Len Dykstra	.90	.40	.09
☐ 3	Darryl Strawberry	3.00	1.25	.30
☐ 4	Keith Hernandez	.50	.20	.05
☐ 5	Gary Carter	.60	.25	.06
☐ 6	Wally Joyner	2.00	.80	.20
☐ 7	Andres Thomas	.25	.10	.02
☐ 8	Pat Dodson	.25	.10	.02
☐ 9	Kirk Gibson	.50	.20	.05
☐ 10	Don Mattingly	2.50	1.00	.25
☐ 11	Dave Winfield	.75	.30	.07
☐ 12	Rickey Henderson	4.00	1.75	.40
☐ 13	Dan Pasqua	.25	.10	.02
☐ 14	Don Baylor	.35	.15	.03
☐ 15	Bo Jackson	75.00	34.00	11.25
	(swinging bat in Auburn FB uniform)			
☐ 16	Pete Incaviglia	.75	.30	.07
☐ 17	Kevin Bass	.25	.10	.02
☐ 18	Barry Larkin	3.50	1.50	.35
☐ 19	Dave Magadan	1.50	.60	.15
☐ 20	Steve Sax	.50	.20	.05
☐ 21	Eric Davis	1.50	.60	.15

☐ 22	Mike Pagliarulo	.25	.10	.02
☐ 23	Fred Lynn	.35	.15	.03
☐ 24	Reggie Jackson	1.50	.60	.15
☐ 25	Larry Parrish	.25	.10	.02
☐ 26	Tony Gwynn	2.00	.80	.20
☐ 27	Steve Garvey	1.00	.40	.10
☐ 28	Glenn Davis	.75	.30	.07
☐ 29	Tim Raines	.75	.30	.07
☐ 30	Vince Coleman	.75	.30	.07
☐ 31	Willie McGee	.60	.25	.06
☐ 32	Ozzie Smith	.75	.30	.07
☐ 33	Dave Parker	.50	.20	.05
☐ 34	Tony Pena	.35	.15	.03
☐ 35	Ryne Sandberg	4.00	1.75	.40
☐ 36	Brett Butler	.35	.15	.03
☐ 37	Dale Murphy	1.00	.40	.10
☐ 38	Bob Horner	.35	.15	.03
☐ 39	Pedro Guerrero	.50	.20	.05
☐ 40	Brook Jacoby	.25	.10	.02
☐ 41	Carlton Fisk	1.00	.40	.10
☐ 42	Harold Baines	.35	.15	.03
☐ 43	Rob Deer	.35	.15	.03
☐ 44	Robin Yount	1.50	.60	.15
☐ 45	Paul Molitor	.50	.20	.05
☐ 46	Jose Canseco	25.00	11.00	3.50
☐ 47	George Brett	1.50	.60	.15
☐ 48	Jim Presley	.25	.10	.02
☐ 49	Rich Gedman	.25	.10	.02
☐ 50	Lance Parrish	.35	.15	.03
☐ 51	Eddie Murray	1.25	.50	.12
☐ 52	Cal Ripken	4.00	1.75	.40
☐ 53	Kent Hrbek	.60	.25	.06
☐ 54	Gary Gaetti	.50	.20	.05
☐ 55	Kirby Puckett	2.50	1.00	.25
☐ 56	George Bell	.50	.20	.05
☐ 57	Tony Fernandez	.35	.15	.03
☐ 58	Jesse Barfield	.35	.15	.03
☐ 59	Jim Rice	.50	.20	.05
☐ 60	Wade Boggs	2.50	1.00	.25
☐ 61	Marty Barrett	.25	.10	.02
☐ 62	Mike Schmidt	3.50	1.50	.35
☐ 63	Von Hayes	.35	.15	.03
☐ 64	Jeff Leonard	.25	.10	.02
☐ 65	Chris Brown	.25	.10	.02
☐ 66	Dave Smith	.25	.10	.02
☐ 67	Mike Krukow	.25	.10	.02
☐ 68	Ron Guidry	.35	.15	.03
☐ 69	Rob Woodward	.25	.10	.02
☐ 70	Rob Murphy	.25	.10	.02
☐ 71	Andres Galarraga	.50	.20	.05
☐ 72	Dwight Gooden	1.00	.40	.10
☐ 73	Bob Ojeda	.35	.15	.03
☐ 74	Sid Fernandez	.35	.15	.03
☐ 75	Jesse Orosco	.25	.10	.02
☐ 76	Roger McDowell	.35	.15	.03
☐ 77	John Tudor UER	.35	.15	.03
	(misspelled Tutor)			
☐ 78	Tom Browning	.35	.15	.03
☐ 79	Rick Aguilera	.25	.10	.02
☐ 80	Lance McCullers	.25	.10	.02
☐ 81	Mike Scott	.35	.15	.03
☐ 82	Nolan Ryan	7.50	3.25	.75
☐ 83	Bruce Hurst	.35	.15	.03
☐ 84	Roger Clemens	4.00	1.75	.40
☐ 85	Oil Can Boyd	.25	.10	.02
☐ 86	Dave Righetti	.35	.15	.03
☐ 87	Dennis Rasmussen	.25	.10	.02
☐ 88	Bret Saberhagen	.90	.40	.09
☐ 89	Mark Langston	.50	.20	.05
☐ 90	Jack Morris	.75	.30	.07
☐ 91	Fernando Valenzuela	.50	.20	.05
☐ 92	Orel Hershiser	.75	.30	.07
☐ 93	Rick Honeycutt	.25	.10	.02
☐ 94	Jeff Reardon	.50	.20	.05
☐ 95	John Habyan	.25	.10	.02
☐ 96	Goose Gossage	.35	.15	.03
☐ 97	Todd Worrell	.35	.15	.03
☐ 98	Floyd Youmans	.25	.10	.02
☐ 99	Don Aase	.25	.10	.02
☐ 100	John Franco	.35	.15	.03

1987 Classic Update Yellow

This 50-card set was actually distributed as part of an update to a trivia board game, but (unlike the original Classic game) was sold without the game. The set is sometimes referred to as the "Travel Edition" of the game. The card backs contain several

Kevin Seitzer

1988 Classic Red

Don Mattingly

trivia questions (and answers) which are used to play the game. A yellow border frames the full-color photo. The games were produced by Game Time, Ltd. and were available in toy stores as well as from card dealers. Cards are numbered beginning with 101, as they are an extension of the original set. According to the set's producers, supposedly about 1/3 of the 150,000 sets printed were error sets in that they had green backs instead of yellow backs. This "green back" variation/error set is valued at approximately double the prices listed below. The cards are standard size, 2 1/2" by 3 1/2".

	MINT	EXC	G-VG
COMPLETE SET (50)	22.50	9.75	3.25
COMMON PLAYER (101-150)	.15	.06	.01
☐ 101 Mike Schmidt	1.75	.70	.17
☐ 102 Eric Davis	1.00	.40	.10
☐ 103 Pete Rose	1.50	.60	.15
☐ 104 Don Mattingly	1.50	.60	.15
☐ 105 Wade Boggs	1.50	.60	.15
☐ 106 Dale Murphy	.60	.25	.06
☐ 107 Glenn Davis	.50	.20	.05
☐ 108 Wally Joyner	1.00	.40	.10
☐ 109 Bo Jackson	5.00	2.25	.50
☐ 110 Cory Snyder	.25	.10	.02
☐ 111 Jim Lindeman	.15	.06	.01
☐ 112 Kirby Puckett	1.50	.60	.15
☐ 113 Barry Bonds	3.50	1.50	.35
☐ 114 Roger Clemens	2.00	.80	.20
☐ 115 Oddibe McDowell	.15	.06	.01
☐ 116 Bret Saberhagen	.50	.20	.05
☐ 117 Joe Magrane	.15	.06	.01
☐ 118 Scott Fletcher	.15	.06	.01
☐ 119 Mark McLemore	.15	.06	.01
☐ 120 Who Me (Joe Niekro)	.20	.08	.02
☐ 121 Mark McGwire	1.25	.50	.12
☐ 122 Darryl Strawberry	1.50	.60	.15
☐ 123 Mike Scott	.25	.10	.02
☐ 124 Andre Dawson	.50	.20	.05
☐ 125 Jose Canseco	3.50	1.50	.35
☐ 126 Kevin McReynolds	.35	.15	.03
☐ 127 Joe Carter	.75	.30	.07
☐ 128 Casey Candaele	.15	.06	.01
☐ 129 Matt Nokes	.35	.15	.03
☐ 130 Kal Daniels	.45	.18	.04
☐ 131 Pete Incaviglia	.35	.15	.03
☐ 132 Benito Santiago	1.00	.40	.10
☐ 133 Barry Larkin	1.00	.40	.10
☐ 134 Gary Pettis	.15	.06	.01
☐ 135 B.J. Surhoff	.25	.10	.02
☐ 136 Juan Nieves	.15	.06	.01
☐ 137 Jim Deshaies	.15	.06	.01
☐ 138 Pete O'Brien	.15	.06	.01
☐ 139 Kevin Seitzer	.35	.15	.03
☐ 140 Devon White	.35	.15	.03
☐ 141 Rob Deer	.20	.08	.02
☐ 142 Kurt Stillwell	.20	.08	.02
☐ 143 Edwin Correa	.15	.06	.01
☐ 144 Dion James	.15	.06	.01
☐ 145 Danny Tartabull	.75	.30	.07
☐ 146 Jerry Browne	.15	.06	.01
☐ 147 Ted Higuera	.25	.10	.02
☐ 148 Jack Clark	.25	.10	.02
☐ 149 Ruben Sierra	4.00	1.75	.40
☐ 150 McGwire/Eric Davis	.75	.30	.07

This 50-card red-bordered set was actually distributed as part of an update to a trivia board game, but (unlike the original Classic game) was sold without the game. The card backs contain several trivia questions (and answers) which are used to play the game. A red border frames the full color photo. The games were produced by Game Time, Ltd. and were available in toy stores as well as from card dealers. Cards are numbered beginning with 151 as they are an extension of the original sets. The cards are standard size, 2 1/2" by 3 1/2".

	MINT	EXC	G-VG
COMPLETE SET (50)	13.50	6.00	1.85
COMMON PLAYER (151-200)	.12	.05	.01
☐ 151 Mark McGwire and Don Mattingly	1.00	.40	.10
☐ 152 Don Mattingly	1.00	.40	.10
☐ 153 Mark McGwire	.75	.30	.07
☐ 154 Eric Davis	.60	.25	.06
☐ 155 Wade Boggs	1.00	.40	.10
☐ 156 Dale Murphy	.50	.20	.05
☐ 157 Andre Dawson	.40	.16	.04
☐ 158 Roger Clemens	1.50	.60	.15
☐ 159 Kevin Seitzer	.20	.08	.02
☐ 160 Benito Santiago	.50	.20	.05
☐ 161 Kal Daniels	.30	.12	.03
☐ 162 John Kruk	.12	.05	.01
☐ 163 Bill Ripken	.20	.08	.02
☐ 164 Kirby Puckett	1.00	.40	.10
☐ 165 Jose Canseco	1.75	.70	.17
☐ 166 Matt Nokes	.20	.08	.02
☐ 167 Mike Schmidt	1.25	.50	.12
☐ 168 Tim Raines	.30	.12	.03
☐ 169 Ryne Sandberg	1.50	.60	.15
☐ 170 Dave Winfield	.60	.25	.06
☐ 171 Dwight Gooden	.50	.20	.05
☐ 172 Bret Saberhagen	.40	.16	.04
☐ 173 Willie McGee	.35	.15	.03
☐ 174 Jack Morris	.35	.15	.03
☐ 175 Jeff Leonard	.12	.05	.01
☐ 176 Cal Ripken	1.75	.70	.17
☐ 177 Pete Incaviglia	.20	.08	.02
☐ 178 Devon White	.25	.10	.02
☐ 179 Nolan Ryan	3.00	1.25	.30
☐ 180 Ruben Sierra	1.25	.50	.12
☐ 181 Todd Worrell	.20	.08	.02
☐ 182 Glenn Davis	.30	.12	.03
☐ 183 Frank Viola	.30	.12	.03
☐ 184 Cory Snyder	.20	.08	.02
☐ 185 Tracy Jones	.12	.05	.01
☐ 186 Terry Steinbach	.20	.08	.02
☐ 187 Julio Franco	.35	.15	.03
☐ 188 Larry Sheets	.12	.05	.01
☐ 189 John Marzano	.12	.05	.01
☐ 190 Kevin Elster	.20	.08	.02
☐ 191 Vicente Palacios	.20	.08	.02
☐ 192 Kent Hrbek	.30	.12	.03
☐ 193 Eric Bell	.12	.05	.01
☐ 194 Kelly Downs	.20	.08	.02
☐ 195 Jose Lind	.20	.08	.02
☐ 196 Dave Stewart	.35	.15	.03
☐ 197 Mark McGwire and Jose Canseco	1.00	.40	.10
☐ 198 Phil Niekro Cleveland Indians	.20	.08	.02

		MINT	EXC	G-VG
☐ 199	Phil Niekro	.20	.08	.02
	Toronto Blue Jays			
☐ 200	Phil Niekro	.20	.08	.02
	Atlanta Braves			

1988 Classic Blue

Tony Gwynn

This 50-card blue-bordered set was actually distributed as part of an update to a trivia board game, but (unlike the original Classic game) was sold without the game. The card backs contain several trivia questions (and answers) which are used to play the game. A blue border frames the full color photo. The games were produced by Game Time, Ltd. and were available in toy stores as well as from card dealers. Cards are numbered beginning with 201 as they are an extension of the original sets. The cards are standard size, 2 1/2" by 3 1/2".

		MINT	EXC	G-VG
COMPLETE SET (50)		16.00	6.75	2.25
COMMON PLAYER (201-250)		.12	.05	.01
☐ 201	Eric Davis and	.50	.20	.05
	Dale Murphy			
☐ 202	B.J. Surhoff	.20	.08	.02
☐ 203	John Kruk	.12	.05	.01
☐ 204	Sam Horn	.20	.08	.02
☐ 205	Jack Clark	.20	.08	.02
☐ 206	Wally Joyner	.40	.16	.04
☐ 207	Matt Nokes	.25	.10	.02
☐ 208	Bo Jackson	3.00	1.25	.30
☐ 209	Darryl Strawberry	1.00	.40	.10
☐ 210	Ozzie Smith	.45	.18	.04
☐ 211	Don Mattingly	1.00	.40	.10
☐ 212	Mark McGwire	.75	.30	.07
☐ 213	Eric Davis	.60	.25	.06
☐ 214	Wade Boggs	1.00	.40	.10
☐ 215	Dale Murphy	.50	.20	.05
☐ 216	Andre Dawson	.40	.16	.04
☐ 217	Roger Clemens	1.50	.60	.15
☐ 218	Kevin Seitzer	.20	.08	.02
☐ 219	Benito Santiago	.45	.18	.04
☐ 220	Tony Gwynn	.90	.40	.09
☐ 221	Mike Scott	.20	.08	.02
☐ 222	Steve Bedrosian	.12	.05	.01
☐ 223	Vince Coleman	.35	.15	.03
☐ 224	Rick Sutcliffe	.20	.08	.02
☐ 225	Will Clark	5.00	2.25	.50
☐ 226	Pete Rose	1.25	.50	.12
☐ 227	Mike Greenwell	.90	.40	.09
☐ 228	Ken Caminiti	.25	.10	.02
☐ 229	Ellis Burks	1.00	.40	.10
☐ 230	Dave Magadan	.25	.10	.02
☐ 231	Alan Trammell	.35	.15	.03
☐ 232	Paul Molitor	.30	.12	.03
☐ 233	Gary Gaetti	.20	.08	.02
☐ 234	Rickey Henderson	2.00	.80	.20
☐ 235	Danny Tartabull UER	.50	.20	.05
	(photo actually			
	Hal McRae)			
☐ 236	Bobby Bonilla	1.50	.60	.15
☐ 237	Mike Dunne	.12	.05	.01
☐ 238	Al Leiter	.12	.05	.01
☐ 239	John Farrell	.12	.05	.01
☐ 240	Joe Magrane	.20	.08	.02
☐ 241	Mike Henneman	.20	.08	.02

☐ 242	George Bell	.35	.15	.03
☐ 243	Gregg Jefferies	1.25	.50	.12
☐ 244	Jay Buhner	.40	.16	.04
☐ 245	Todd Benzinger	.20	.08	.02
☐ 246	Matt Williams	2.00	.80	.20
☐ 247	Mark McGwire and	1.00	.40	.10
	Don Mattingly			
	(unnumbered; game			
	instructions on back)			
☐ 248	George Brett	.90	.40	.09
☐ 249	Jimmy Key	.20	.08	.02
☐ 250	Mark Langston	.20	.08	.02

1989 Classic Light Blue

Orel Hershiser

The 1989 Classic set contains 100 standard-size (2 1/2" by 3 1/2") cards. The fronts of these cards have light blue borders. The backs feature 1988 and lifetime stats. The cards were distributed with a baseball boardgame. Supposedly there were 150,000 sets produced.

		MINT	EXC	G-VG
COMPLETE SET (100)		25.00	11.00	3.50
COMMON PLAYER (1-100)		.10	.04	.01
☐ 1	Orel Hershiser	.35	.15	.03
☐ 2	Wade Boggs	.75	.30	.07
☐ 3	Jose Canseco	1.50	.60	.15
☐ 4	Mark McGwire	.60	.25	.06
☐ 5	Don Mattingly	1.00	.40	.10
☐ 6	Gregg Jefferies	.75	.30	.07
☐ 7	Dwight Gooden	.45	.18	.04
☐ 8	Darryl Strawberry	1.00	.40	.10
☐ 9	Eric Davis	.50	.20	.05
☐ 10	Joey Meyer	.10	.04	.01
☐ 11	Joe Carter	.35	.15	.03
☐ 12	Paul Molitor	.20	.08	.02
☐ 13	Mark Grace	1.25	.50	.12
☐ 14	Kurt Stillwell	.15	.06	.01
☐ 15	Kirby Puckett	1.00	.40	.10
☐ 16	Keith Miller	.10	.04	.01
☐ 17	Glenn Davis	.25	.10	.02
☐ 18	Will Clark	1.50	.60	.15
☐ 19	Cory Snyder	.15	.06	.01
☐ 20	Jose Lind	.10	.04	.01
☐ 21	Andres Thomas	.10	.04	.01
☐ 22	Dave Smith	.10	.04	.01
☐ 23	Mike Scott	.15	.06	.01
☐ 24	Kevin McReynolds	.20	.08	.02
☐ 25	B.J. Surhoff	.15	.06	.01
☐ 26	Mackey Sasser	.15	.06	.01
☐ 27	Chad Kreuter	.10	.04	.01
☐ 28	Hal Morris	1.00	.40	.10
☐ 29	Wally Joyner	.35	.15	.03
☐ 30	Tony Gwynn	.75	.30	.07
☐ 31	Kevin Mitchell	.90	.40	.09
☐ 32	Dave Winfield	.35	.15	.03
☐ 33	Billy Bean	.10	.04	.01
☐ 34	Steve Bedrosian	.10	.04	.01
☐ 35	Ron Gant	1.50	.60	.15
☐ 36	Len Dykstra	.30	.12	.03
☐ 37	Andre Dawson	.40	.16	.04
☐ 38	Brett Butler	.15	.06	.01
☐ 39	Rob Deer	.15	.06	.01
☐ 40	Tommy John	.20	.08	.02
☐ 41	Gary Gaetti	.15	.06	.01

☐ 42	Tim Raines	.25	.10	.02
☐ 43	George Bell	.25	.10	.02
☐ 44	Dwight Evans	.20	.08	.02
☐ 45	Dennis Martinez	.15	.06	.01
☐ 46	Andres Galarraga	.20	.08	.02
☐ 47	George Brett	.75	.30	.07
☐ 48	Mike Schmidt	1.25	.50	.12
☐ 49	Dave Stieb	.20	.08	.02
☐ 50	Rickey Henderson	1.50	.60	.15
☐ 51	Craig Biggio	.50	.20	.05
☐ 52	Mark Lemke	.15	.06	.01
☐ 53	Chris Sabo	1.00	.40	.10
☐ 54	Jeff Treadway	.10	.04	.01
☐ 55	Kent Hrbek	.20	.08	.02
☐ 56	Cal Ripken	1.50	.60	.15
☐ 57	Tim Belcher	.20	.08	.02
☐ 58	Ozzie Smith	.30	.12	.03
☐ 59	Keith Hernandez	.20	.08	.02
☐ 60	Pedro Guerrero	.20	.08	.02
☐ 61	Greg Swindell	.15	.06	.01
☐ 62	Bret Saberhagen	.40	.16	.04
☐ 63	John Tudor	.15	.06	.01
☐ 64	Gary Carter	.20	.08	.02
☐ 65	Kevin Seitzer	.15	.06	.01
☐ 66	Jesse Barfield	.15	.06	.01
☐ 67	Luis Medina	.15	.06	.01
☐ 68	Walt Weiss	.20	.08	.02
☐ 69	Terry Steinbach	.15	.06	.01
☐ 70	Barry Larkin	.50	.20	.05
☐ 71	Pete Rose	1.00	.40	.10
☐ 72	Luis Salazar	.10	.04	.01
☐ 73	Benito Santiago	.30	.12	.03
☐ 74	Kal Daniels	.25	.10	.02
☐ 75	Kevin Elster	.15	.06	.01
☐ 76	Rob Dibble	.35	.15	.03
☐ 77	Bobby Witt	.30	.12	.03
☐ 78	Steve Searcy	.10	.04	.01
☐ 79	Sandy Alomar Jr.	1.00	.40	.10
☐ 80	Chili Davis	.15	.06	.01
☐ 81	Alvin Davis	.10	.04	.01
☐ 82	Charlie Leibrandt	.10	.04	.01
☐ 83	Robin Yount	.75	.30	.07
☐ 84	Mark Carreon	.10	.04	.01
☐ 85	Pascual Perez	.15	.06	.01
☐ 86	Dennis Rasmussen	.10	.04	.01
☐ 87	Ernie Riles	.10	.04	.01
☐ 88	Melido Perez	.15	.06	.01
☐ 89	Doug Jones	.15	.06	.01
☐ 90	Dennis Eckersley	.25	.10	.02
☐ 91	Bob Welch	.20	.08	.02
☐ 92	Bob Milacki	.15	.06	.01
☐ 93	Jeff Robinson	.10	.04	.01
☐ 94	Mike Henneman	.10	.04	.01
☐ 95	Randy Johnson	.35	.15	.03
☐ 96	Ron Jones	.15	.06	.01
☐ 97	Jack Armstrong	.25	.10	.02
☐ 98	Willie McGee	.20	.08	.02
☐ 99	Ryne Sandberg	1.25	.50	.12
☐ 100	David Cone and Danny Jackson	.25	.10	.02

1989 Classic Travel Orange

Roger Clemens

The 1989 Classic Travel Orange set contains 50 standard-size (2 1/2" by 3 1/2") cards. The fronts of the cards have orange borders. The backs feature 1988 and lifetime stats. This subset of cards were distributed as a set in blister packs as "Travel Update I" subsets. Supposedly there were 150,000 sets produced.

		MINT	EXC	G-VG
COMPLETE SET (50)		15.00	6.50	2.15
COMMON PLAYER (101-150)		.10	.04	.01
☐ 101	Gary Sheffield	.50	.20	.05
☐ 102	Wade Boggs	.75	.30	.07
☐ 103	Jose Canseco	1.25	.50	.12
☐ 104	Mark McGwire	.60	.25	.06
☐ 105	Orel Hershiser	.25	.10	.02
☐ 106	Don Mattingly	.75	.30	.07
☐ 107	Dwight Gooden	.40	.16	.04
☐ 108	Darryl Strawberry	.75	.30	.07
☐ 109	Eric Davis	.45	.18	.04
☐ 110	Hensley Meulens UER (listed on card as Bam Bam Muelens)	.45	.18	.04
☐ 111	Andy Van Slyke	.15	.06	.01
☐ 112	Al Leiter	.10	.04	.01
☐ 113	Matt Nokes	.15	.06	.01
☐ 114	Mike Krukow	.10	.04	.01
☐ 115	Tony Fernandez	.15	.06	.01
☐ 116	Fred McGriff	.60	.25	.06
☐ 117	Barry Bonds	.60	.25	.06
☐ 118	Gerald Perry	.10	.04	.01
☐ 119	Roger Clemens	1.00	.40	.10
☐ 120	Kirk Gibson	.20	.08	.02
☐ 121	Greg Maddux	.15	.06	.01
☐ 122	Bo Jackson	1.50	.60	.15
☐ 123	Danny Jackson	.15	.06	.01
☐ 124	Dale Murphy	.35	.15	.03
☐ 125	David Cone	.25	.10	.02
☐ 126	Tom Browning	.15	.06	.01
☐ 127	Roberto Alomar	.75	.30	.07
☐ 128	Alan Trammell	.25	.10	.02
☐ 129	Ricky Jordan UER (misspelled Jordon on card back)	.15	.06	.01
☐ 130	Ramon Martinez	1.25	.50	.12
☐ 131	Ken Griffey Jr.	7.50	3.25	.75
☐ 132	Gregg Olson	.50	.20	.05
☐ 133	Carlos Quintana	.40	.16	.04
☐ 134	Dave West	.15	.06	.01
☐ 135	Cameron Drew	.10	.04	.01
☐ 136	Teddy Higuera	.15	.06	.01
☐ 137	Sil Campusano	.10	.04	.01
☐ 138	Mark Gubicza	.10	.04	.01
☐ 139	Mike Boddicker	.10	.04	.01
☐ 140	Paul Gibson	.10	.04	.01
☐ 141	Jose Rijo	.25	.10	.02
☐ 142	John Costello	.10	.04	.01
☐ 143	Cecil Espy	.10	.04	.01
☐ 144	Frank Viola	.20	.08	.02
☐ 145	Erik Hanson	.40	.16	.04
☐ 146	Juan Samuel	.15	.06	.01
☐ 147	Harold Reynolds	.15	.06	.01
☐ 148	Joe Magrane	.15	.06	.01
☐ 149	Mike Greenwell	.35	.15	.03
☐ 150	Darryl Strawberry and Will Clark	.75	.30	.07

1989 Classic Travel Purple

The 1989 Classic "Travel Update II" set contains 50 standard-size (2 1/2" by 3 1/2") cards. The fronts have purple (and gray) borders. The set features "two sport" cards of Bo Jackson and Deion Sanders. The cards were distributed as a set in blister packs.

		MINT	EXC	G-VG
COMPLETE SET (50)		12.00	5.25	1.50
COMMON PLAYER (151-200)		.10	.04	.01
☐ 151	Jim Abbott	1.00	.40	.10
☐ 152	Ellis Burks	.35	.15	.03
☐ 153	Mike Schmidt	1.00	.40	.10
☐ 154	Gregg Jefferies	.35	.15	.03
☐ 155	Mark Grace	.40	.16	.04
☐ 156	Jerome Walton	.35	.15	.03
☐ 157	Bo Jackson	1.50	.60	.15
☐ 158	Jack Clark	.15	.06	.01
☐ 159	Tom Glavine	.50	.20	.05
☐ 160	Eddie Murray	.35	.15	.03

Kevin Mitchell

Will Clark

			MINT	EXC	G-VG
☐	161	John Dopson	.10	.04	.01
☐	162	Ruben Sierra	.40	.16	.04
☐	163	Rafael Palmeiro	.35	.15	.03
☐	164	Nolan Ryan	1.50	.60	.15
☐	165	Barry Larkin	.35	.15	.03
☐	166	Tommy Herr	.10	.04	.01
☐	167	Roberto Kelly	.50	.20	.05
☐	168	Glenn Davis	.20	.08	.02
☐	169	Glenn Braggs	.15	.06	.01
☐	170	Juan Bell	.10	.04	.01
☐	171	Todd Burns	.10	.04	.01
☐	172	Derek Lilliquist	.10	.04	.01
☐	173	Orel Hershiser	.25	.10	.02
☐	174	John Smoltz	.60	.25	.06
☐	175	O.Guillen/E.Burks	.35	.15	.03
☐	176	Kirby Puckett	.75	.30	.07
☐	177	Robin Ventura	1.00	.40	.10
☐	178	Allan Anderson	.10	.04	.01
☐	179	Steve Sax	.15	.06	.01
☐	180	Will Clark	1.00	.40	.10
☐	181	Mike Devereaux	.10	.04	.01
☐	182	Tom Gordon	.25	.10	.02
☐	183	Rob Murphy	.10	.04	.01
☐	184	Pete O'Brien	.10	.04	.01
☐	185	Cris Carpenter	.10	.04	.01
☐	186	Tom Brunansky	.15	.06	.01
☐	187	Bob Boone	.15	.06	.01
☐	188	Lou Whitaker	.20	.08	.02
☐	189	Dwight Gooden	.40	.16	.04
☐	190	Mark McGwire	.50	.20	.05
☐	191	John Smiley	.20	.08	.02
☐	192	Tommy Gregg	.10	.04	.01
☐	193	Ken Griffey Jr.	3.50	1.50	.35
☐	194	Bruce Hurst	.10	.04	.01
☐	195	Greg Swindell	.15	.06	.01
☐	196	Nelson Liriano	.10	.04	.01
☐	197	Randy Myers	.15	.06	.01
☐	198	Kevin Mitchell	.40	.16	.04
☐	199	Dante Bichette	.10	.04	.01
☐	200	Deion Sanders	.60	.25	.06

1990 Classic Blue

The 1990 Classic Blue (Game) set contains 150 standard-size (2 1/2" by 3 1/2") cards, the largest Classic set to date in terms of player selection. The front borders are blue with magenta splotches. The backs feature 1989 and career total stats. The cards were distributed as a set in blister packs. According to distributors of the set, supposedly there were 200,000 sets produced. Supposedly the Sanders "correction" was made at Sanders own request; less than 10 percent of the sets contain the first version and hence it has the higher value in the checklist below. The complete set price below does not include any of the more difficult variation cards.

	MINT	EXC	G-VG
COMPLETE SET (150)	20.00	8.50	2.75
COMMON PLAYER (1-150)	.10	.04	.01

			MINT	EXC	G-VG
☐	1	Nolan Ryan	1.50	.60	.15
☐	2	Bo Jackson	1.25	.50	.12
☐	3	Gregg Olson	.30	.12	.03
☐	4	Tom Gordon	.20	.08	.02
☐	5	Robin Ventura	.50	.20	.05
☐	6	Will Clark	1.00	.40	.10
☐	7	Ruben Sierra	.40	.16	.04
☐	8	Mark Grace	.35	.15	.03
☐	9	Luis De Los Santos	.10	.04	.01
☐	10	Bernie Williams	.75	.30	.07
☐	11	Eric Davis	.35	.15	.03
☐	12	Carney Lansford	.15	.06	.01
☐	13	John Smoltz	.35	.15	.03
☐	14	Gary Sheffield	.25	.10	.02
☐	15	Kent Mercker	.15	.06	.01
☐	16	Don Mattingly	.75	.30	.07
☐	17	Tony Gwynn	.50	.20	.05
☐	18	Ozzie Smith	.25	.10	.02
☐	19	Fred McGriff	.35	.15	.03
☐	20	Ken Griffey Jr.	2.00	.80	.20
☐	21A	Deion Sanders	7.50	3.25	.75
		(Identified only as "Prime Time" on front)			
☐	21B	Deion Sanders	.90	.40	.09
		(Identified as Deion "Prime Time" Sanders on front of card)			
☐	22	Jose Canseco	1.00	.40	.10
☐	23	Mitch Williams	.15	.06	.01
☐	24	Cal Ripken UER	1.00	.40	.10
		(Misspelled Ripkin on the card back)			
☐	25	Bob Geren	.15	.06	.01
☐	26	Wade Boggs	.60	.25	.06
☐	27	Ryne Sandberg	.90	.40	.09
☐	28	Kirby Puckett	.50	.20	.05
☐	29	Mike Scott	.15	.06	.01
☐	30	Dwight Smith	.15	.06	.01
☐	31	Craig Worthington	.10	.04	.01
☐	32A	Ricky Jordan ERR	4.00	1.75	.40
		(Misspelled Jordon on card back)			
☐	32B	Ricky Jordan COR	.25	.10	.02
☐	33	Darryl Strawberry	.75	.30	.07
☐	34	Jerome Walton	.25	.10	.02
☐	35	John Olerud	1.00	.40	.10
☐	36	Tom Glavine	.35	.15	.03
☐	37	Rickey Henderson	1.00	.40	.10
☐	38	Rolando Roomes	.10	.04	.01
☐	39	Mickey Tettleton	.15	.06	.01
☐	40	Jim Abbott	.35	.15	.03
☐	41	Dave Righetti	.15	.06	.01
☐	42	Mike LaValliere	.10	.04	.01
☐	43	Rob Dibble	.20	.08	.02
☐	44	Pete Harnisch	.15	.06	.01
☐	45	Jose Offerman	.35	.15	.03
☐	46	Walt Weiss	.15	.06	.01
☐	47	Mike Greenwell	.30	.12	.03
☐	48	Barry Larkin	.30	.12	.03
☐	49	Dave Gallagher	.15	.06	.01
☐	50	Junior Felix	.20	.08	.02
☐	51	Roger Clemens	1.00	.40	.10
☐	52	Lonnie Smith	.15	.06	.01
☐	53	Jerry Browne	.10	.04	.01
☐	54	Greg Briley	.10	.04	.01
☐	55	Delino Deshields	.45	.18	.04
☐	56	Carmelo Martinez	.10	.04	.01
☐	57	Craig Biggio	.25	.10	.02
☐	58	Dwight Gooden	.35	.15	.03
☐	59A	Bo/Rubin/Mark	7.50	3.25	.75
		Bo Jackson			
		Ruben Sierra			
		Mark McGwire			

☐ 59B	A.L. Fence Busters	.90	.40	.09
	Bo Jackson			
	Ruben Sierra			
	Mark McGwire			
☐ 60	Greg Vaughn	.75	.30	.07
☐ 61	Roberto Alomar	.35	.15	.03
☐ 62	Steve Bedrosian	.10	.04	.01
☐ 63	Devon White	.15	.06	.01
☐ 64	Kevin Mitchell	.35	.15	.03
☐ 65	Marquis Grissom	.45	.18	.04
☐ 66	Brian Holman	.15	.06	.01
☐ 67	Julio Franco	.25	.10	.02
☐ 68	Dave West	.15	.06	.01
☐ 69	Harold Baines	.15	.06	.01
☐ 70	Eric Anthony	.25	.10	.02
☐ 71	Glenn Davis	.20	.08	.02
☐ 72	Mark Langston	.15	.06	.01
☐ 73	Matt Williams	.45	.18	.04
☐ 74	Rafael Palmeiro	.30	.12	.03
☐ 75	Pete Rose Jr.	.25	.10	.02
☐ 76	Ramon Martinez	.35	.15	.03
☐ 77	Dwight Evans	.15	.06	.01
☐ 78	Mackey Sasser	.15	.06	.01
☐ 79	Mike Schooler	.15	.06	.01
☐ 80	Dennis Cook	.10	.04	.01
☐ 81	Orel Hershiser	.25	.10	.02
☐ 82	Barry Bonds	.40	.16	.04
☐ 83	Geronimo Berroa	.10	.04	.01
☐ 84	George Bell	.20	.08	.02
☐ 85	Andre Dawson	.30	.12	.03
☐ 86	John Franco	.15	.06	.01
☐ 87A	Clark/Gwynn	4.00	1.75	.40
	Will Clark			
	Tony Gwynn			
☐ 87B	N.L. Hit Kings	.60	.25	.06
	Will Clark			
	Tony Gwynn			
☐ 88	Glenallen Hill	.20	.08	.02
☐ 89	Jeff Ballard	.10	.04	.01
☐ 90	Todd Zeile	.75	.30	.07
☐ 91	Frank Viola	.20	.08	.02
☐ 92	Ozzie Guillen	.15	.06	.01
☐ 93	Jeffrey Leonard	.10	.04	.01
☐ 94	Dave Smith	.10	.04	.01
☐ 95	Dave Parker	.20	.08	.02
☐ 96	Jose Gonzalez	.10	.04	.01
☐ 97	Dave Stieb	.20	.08	.02
☐ 98	Charlie Hayes	.15	.06	.01
☐ 99	Jesse Barfield	.15	.06	.01
☐ 100	Joey Belle	.60	.25	.06
☐ 101	Jeff Reardon	.20	.08	.02
☐ 102	Bruce Hurst	.15	.06	.01
☐ 103	Luis Medina	.15	.06	.01
☐ 104	Mike Moore	.15	.06	.01
☐ 105	Vince Coleman	.25	.10	.02
☐ 106	Alan Trammell	.25	.10	.02
☐ 107	Randy Myers	.15	.06	.01
☐ 108	Frank Tanana	.10	.04	.01
☐ 109	Craig Lefferts	.10	.04	.01
☐ 110	John Wetteland	.20	.08	.02
☐ 111	Chris Gwynn	.10	.04	.01
☐ 112	Mark Carreon	.10	.04	.01
☐ 113	Von Hayes	.15	.06	.01
☐ 114	Doug Jones	.10	.04	.01
☐ 115	Andres Galarraga	.20	.08	.02
☐ 116	Carlton Fisk UER	.50	.20	.05
	(Bellows Falls mis-			
	spelled as Bellow			
	Falls on back)			
☐ 117	Paul O'Neill	.20	.08	.02
☐ 118	Tim Raines	.20	.08	.02
☐ 119	Tom Brunansky	.15	.06	.01
☐ 120	Andy Benes	.50	.20	.05
☐ 121	Mark Portugal	.10	.04	.01
☐ 122	Willie Randolph	.15	.06	.01
☐ 123	Jeff Blauser	.10	.04	.01
☐ 124	Don August	.10	.04	.01
☐ 125	Chuck Cary	.10	.04	.01
☐ 126	John Smiley	.20	.08	.02
☐ 127	Terry Mulholland	.10	.04	.01
☐ 128	Harold Reynolds	.15	.06	.01
☐ 129	Hubie Brooks	.15	.06	.01
☐ 130	Ben McDonald	.75	.30	.07
☐ 131	Kevin Ritz	.15	.06	.01
☐ 132	Luis Quinones	.10	.04	.01
☐ 133A	Hensley Meulens ERR	10.00	4.50	1.25
	(misspelled Muelens			
	on card front)			
☐ 133B	Hensley Meulens COR	.50	.20	.05
☐ 134	Bill Spiers UER	.15	.06	.01
	(Orangeburg misspelled			
	as Orangburg on back)			
☐ 135	Andy Hawkins	.10	.04	.01
☐ 136	Alvin Davis	.15	.06	.01

☐ 137	Lee Smith	.20	.08	.02
☐ 138	Joe Carter	.30	.12	.03
☐ 139	Bret Saberhagen	.25	.10	.02
☐ 140	Sammy Sosa	.35	.15	.03
☐ 141	Matt Nokes	.15	.06	.01
☐ 142	Bert Blyleven	.15	.06	.01
☐ 143	Bobby Bonilla	.35	.15	.03
☐ 144	Howard Johnson	.25	.10	.02
☐ 145	Joe Magrane	.10	.04	.01
☐ 146	Pedro Guerrero	.20	.08	.02
☐ 147	Robin Yount	.50	.20	.05
☐ 148	Dan Gladden	.10	.04	.01
☐ 149	Steve Sax	.15	.06	.01
☐ 150A	Clark/Mitchell	4.00	1.75	.40
	Will Clark			
	Kevin Mitchell			
☐ 150B	Bay Bombers	.50	.20	.05
	Will Clark			
	Kevin Mitchell			

1990 Classic Update

Len Dykstra

The 1990 Classic Update set was the second set issued by the Classic Game company in 1990. Sometimes referenced as Classic Pink or Red, this set included a Kevin Maas card. This 50-card, standard-size (2 1/2" by 3 1/2") set was issued in late June of 1990.

		MINT	EXC	G-VG
COMPLETE SET (50)		10.00	4.50	1.25
COMMON PLAYER (T1-T49)		.10	.04	.01
☐ T1	Gregg Jefferies	.25	.10	.02
☐ T2	Steve Adkins	.15	.06	.01
☐ T3	Sandy Alomar Jr.	.25	.10	.02
☐ T4	Steve Avery	1.00	.40	.10
☐ T5	Mike Blowers	.15	.06	.01
☐ T6	George Brett	.50	.20	.05
☐ T7	Tom Browning	.10	.04	.01
☐ T8	Ellis Burks	.30	.12	.03
☐ T9	Joe Carter	.25	.10	.02
☐ T10	Jerald Clark	.15	.06	.01
☐ T11	Hot Corners HOR	.50	.20	.05
	Matt Williams			
	Will Clark			
☐ T12	Pat Combs	.15	.06	.01
☐ T13	Scott Cooper	.30	.12	.03
☐ T14	Mark Davis	.10	.04	.01
☐ T15	Storm Davis	.10	.04	.01
☐ T16	Larry Walker	.25	.10	.02
☐ T17	Brian DuBois	.10	.04	.01
☐ T18	Len Dykstra	.15	.06	.01
☐ T19	John Franco	.15	.06	.01
☐ T20	Kirk Gibson	.20	.08	.02
☐ T21	Juan Gonzalez	1.50	.60	.15
☐ T22	Tommy Greene	.20	.08	.02
☐ T23	Kent Hrbek	.15	.06	.01
☐ T24	Mike Huff	.15	.06	.01
☐ T25	Bo Jackson	1.00	.40	.10
☐ T26	Nolan Ryan	3.00	1.25	.30
	(Nolan Knows Bo)			
☐ T27	Roberto Kelly	.25	.10	.02
☐ T28	Mark Langston	.15	.06	.01
☐ T29	Ray Lankford	.75	.30	.07
☐ T30	Kevin Maas	1.00	.40	.10

		MINT	EXC	G-VG
☐ T31	Julio Machado	.10	.04	.01
☐ T32	Greg Maddux	.15	.06	.01
☐ T33	Mark McGwire	.35	.15	.03
☐ T34	Paul Molitor	.15	.06	.01
☐ T35	Hal Morris	.30	.12	.03
☐ T36	Dale Murphy	.30	.12	.03
☐ T37	Eddie Murray	.35	.15	.03
☐ T38	Jaime Navarro	.15	.06	.01
☐ T39	Dean Palmer	.40	.16	.04
☐ T40	Derek Parks	.20	.08	.02
☐ T41	Bobby Rose	.15	.06	.01
☐ T42	Wally Joyner	.25	.10	.02
☐ T43	Chris Sabo	.25	.10	.02
☐ T44	Benito Santiago	.25	.10	.02
☐ T45	Mike Stanton	.15	.06	.01
☐ T46	Terry Steinbach UER	.15	.06	.01
	(Career BA .725)			
☐ T47	Dave Stewart	.20	.08	.02
☐ T48	Greg Swindell	.15	.06	.01
☐ T49	Jose Vizcaino	.15	.06	.01
☐ NNO	Royal Flush	.20	.08	.02
	Mark Davis			
	Bret Saberhagen			
	(unnnumbered; game			
	instructions on back)			

1990 Classic III

Ruben Sierra

The 1990 Classic III set is also referenced as Classic Yellow. This set also featured number one draft picks of the current year mixed with the other Classic cards. This 100-card set was issued in standard size (2 1/2" by 3 1/2") and also contained a special Nolan Ryan commemorative card, Texas Heat.

		MINT	EXC	G-VG
COMPLETE SET (100)		12.50	5.50	1.65
COMMON PLAYER (T1-T100)		.10	.04	.01
☐ T1	Ken Griffey Jr.	1.25	.50	.12
☐ T2	John Tudor	.10	.04	.01
☐ T3	John Kruk	.10	.04	.01
☐ T4	Mark Gardner	.15	.06	.01
☐ T5	Scott Radinsky	.15	.06	.01
☐ T6	John Burkett	.15	.06	.01
☐ T7	Will Clark	.75	.30	.07
☐ T8	Not issued	.00	.00	.00
☐ T9	Ted Higuera	.15	.06	.01
☐ T10	Dave Parker	.20	.08	.02
☐ T11	Dante Bichette	.15	.06	.01
☐ T12	Don Mattingly	.50	.20	.05
☐ T13	Greg Harris	.10	.04	.01
☐ T14	Dave Hollins	.20	.08	.02
☐ T15	Matt Nokes	.15	.06	.01
☐ T16	Kevin Tapani	.20	.08	.02
☐ T17	Shane Mack	.20	.08	.02
☐ T18	Randy Myers	.10	.04	.01
☐ T19	Greg Olson	.15	.06	.01
☐ T20	Shane Abner	.10	.04	.01
☐ T21	Jim Presley	.10	.04	.01
☐ T22	Randy Johnson	.20	.08	.02
☐ T23	Edgar Martinez	.25	.10	.02
☐ T24	Scott Coolbaugh	.15	.06	.01
☐ T25	Jeff Treadway	.10	.04	.01
☐ T26	Joe Klink	.10	.04	.01
☐ T27	Rickey Henderson	.75	.30	.07
☐ T28	Sam Horn	.10	.04	.01

		MINT	EXC	G-VG
☐ T29	Kurt Stillwell	.10	.04	.01
☐ T30	Andy Van Slyke	.15	.06	.01
☐ T31	Willie Banks	.25	.10	.02
☐ T32	Jose Canseco	.75	.30	.07
☐ T33	Felix Jose	.35	.15	.03
☐ T34	Candy Maldonado	.10	.04	.01
☐ T35	Carlos Baerga	.30	.12	.03
☐ T36	Keith Hernandez	.15	.06	.01
☐ T37	Frank Viola	.15	.06	.01
☐ T38	Pete O'Brien	.10	.04	.01
☐ T39	Pat Borders	.15	.06	.01
☐ T40	Mike Heath	.10	.04	.01
☐ T41	Kevin Brown	.15	.06	.01
☐ T42	Chris Bosio	.15	.06	.01
☐ T43	Shawn Boskie	.15	.06	.01
☐ T44	Carlos Quintana	.20	.08	.02
☐ T45	Juan Samuel	.15	.06	.01
☐ T46	Tim Layana	.15	.06	.01
☐ T47	Mike Harkey	.20	.08	.02
☐ T48	Gerald Perry	.10	.04	.01
☐ T49	Mike Witt	.10	.04	.01
☐ T50	Joe Orsulak	.10	.04	.01
☐ T51	Not issued	.00	.00	.00
☐ T52	Willie Blair	.10	.04	.01
☐ T53	Gene Larkin	.10	.04	.01
☐ T54	Jody Reed	.15	.06	.01
☐ T55	Jeff Reardon	.20	.08	.02
☐ T56	Kevin McReynolds	.20	.08	.02
☐ T57	Mike Marshall	.15	.06	.01
	(unnumbered; game			
	instructions on back)			
☐ T58	Eric Yelding	.15	.06	.01
☐ T59	Fred Lynn	.15	.06	.01
☐ T60	Jim Leyritz	.10	.04	.01
☐ T61	John Orton	.15	.06	.01
☐ T62	Mike Lieberthal	.25	.10	.02
☐ T63	Mike Hartley	.15	.06	.01
☐ T64	Kal Daniels	.20	.08	.02
☐ T65	Terry Shumpert	.10	.04	.01
☐ T66	Sil Campusano	.10	.04	.01
☐ T67	Tony Pena	.15	.06	.01
☐ T68	Barry Bonds	.35	.15	.03
☐ T69	Roger McDowell	.10	.04	.01
☐ T70	Kelly Gruber	.20	.08	.02
☐ T71	Willie Randolph	.15	.06	.01
☐ T72	Rick Parker	.10	.04	.01
☐ T73	Bobby Bonilla	.30	.12	.03
☐ T74	Jack Armstrong	.15	.06	.01
☐ T75	Hubie Brooks	.15	.06	.01
☐ T76	Sandy Alomar Jr.	.25	.10	.02
☐ T77	Ruben Sierra	.35	.15	.03
☐ T78	Eric Hanson	.20	.08	.02
☐ T79	Tony Phillips	.10	.04	.01
☐ T80	Rondell White	.45	.18	.04
☐ T81	Bobby Thigpen	.20	.08	.02
☐ T82	Ron Walden	.20	.08	.02
☐ T83	Don Peters	.15	.06	.01
☐ T84	Nolan Ryan 6th	1.00	.40	.10
☐ T85	Lance Dickson	.25	.10	.02
☐ T86	Ryne Sandberg	.75	.30	.07
☐ T87	Eric Christopherson	.20	.08	.02
☐ T88	Shane Andrews	.30	.12	.03
☐ T89	Marc Newfield	1.00	.40	.10
☐ T90	Adam Hyzdu	.35	.15	.03
☐ T91	Texas Heat	1.50	.60	.15
	Nolan Ryan			
	Reid Ryan			
☐ T92	Chipper Jones	.50	.20	.05
☐ T93	Frank Thomas	3.00	1.25	.30
☐ T94	Cecil Fielder	.50	.20	.05
☐ T95	Delino DeShields	.25	.10	.02
☐ T96	John Olerud	.40	.16	.04
☐ T97	Dave Justice	1.75	.70	.17
☐ T98	Joe Oliver	.15	.06	.01
☐ T99	Alex Fernandez	.40	.16	.04
☐ T100	Todd Hundley	.20	.08	.02
☐ NNO	Micro Players	.35	.15	.03
	Frank Viola			
	Texas Heat			
	Don Mattingly			
	Chipper Jones			
	(blue blank back)			

1990 Classic Draft Picks

The 1990 Classic Draft Pick set is a standard-size (2 1/2" by 3 1/2"), 26-card set honoring the number one (first round) draft picks of 1990. According to the producer, the printing on this set was limited to 150,000 of each card. This was the first Classic set to not be a game or trivia set. Card numbers 2 and 22 were not issued.

	MINT	EXC	G-VG
COMPLETE SET (25)	14.00	6.25	2.00
COMMON PLAYER (1-26)	.25	.10	.02
☐ 1 Chipper Jones	1.25	.50	.12
☐ 2 Not issued	.00	.00	.00
☐ 3 Mike Lieberthal	.45	.18	.04
☐ 4 Alex Fernandez	.75	.30	.07
☐ 5 Kurt Miller	.45	.18	.04
☐ 6 Marc Newfield	2.25	.90	.22
☐ 7 Dan Wilson	.45	.18	.04
☐ 8 Tim Costo	.60	.25	.06
☐ 9 Ron Walden	.35	.15	.03
☐ 10 Carl Everett UER	.45	.18	.04
(misspelled Evertt on card front)			
☐ 11 Shane Andrews	.35	.15	.03
☐ 12 Todd Ritchie	.35	.15	.03
☐ 13 Donovan Osborne	.25	.10	.02
☐ 14 Todd Van Poppel	3.75	1.60	.37
☐ 15 Adam Hyzdu	.60	.25	.06
☐ 16 Dan Smith	.35	.15	.03
☐ 17 Jeromy Burnitz	1.50	.60	.15
☐ 18 Aaron Holbert	.25	.10	.02
☐ 19 Eric Christopherson	.35	.15	.03
☐ 20 Mike Mussina	1.00	.40	.10
☐ 21 Tom Nevers	.45	.18	.04
☐ 22 Not issued	.00	.00	.00
☐ 23 Lance Dickson	.75	.30	.07
☐ 24 Rondell White	.75	.30	.07
☐ 25 Robbie Beckett	.35	.15	.03
☐ 26 Don Peters	.35	.15	.03
☐ NNO Future Stars HOR	.35	.15	.03
Chipper Jones Rondell White (unnumbered; checklist on back)			

1991 Classic Game 200

The 1991 Classic Baseball Collector's Edition board game is Classic's first Big Game issue since the 1989 Big Game. Only 100,000 games were produced, and each one included a board game, action spinner, eight stand-up baseball player pieces, action scoreboard, eight-page picture book with tips from five great baseball players (Carew, Spahn, Schmidt, Brock, and Aaron), 200 player cards, and a certificate of limited edition. The standard-size (2 1/2" by 3 1/2") cards have on the fronts glossy color action photos bordered in purple. The backs are purple and white and have biography, statistics, five trivia questions, and an autograph slot. The cards are numbered on the back.

	MINT	EXC	G-VG
COMPLETE SET (200)	30.00	13.50	4.50
COMMON PLAYER (1-200)	.10	.04	.01
☐ 1 Frank Viola	.15	.06	.01
☐ 2 Tim Wallach	.15	.06	.01
☐ 3 Lou Whitaker	.15	.06	.01
☐ 4 Brett Butler	.15	.06	.01
☐ 5 Jim Abbott	.35	.15	.03
☐ 6 Jack Armstrong	.15	.06	.01
☐ 7 Craig Biggio	.15	.06	.01
☐ 8 Brian Barnes	.15	.06	.01
☐ 9 Dennis(Oil Can) Boyd	.10	.04	.01
☐ 10 Tom Browning	.15	.06	.01
☐ 11 Tom Brunansky	.15	.06	.01
☐ 12 Ellis Burks	.30	.12	.03
☐ 13 Harold Baines	.15	.06	.01
☐ 14 Kal Daniels	.15	.06	.01
☐ 15 Mark Davis	.10	.04	.01
☐ 16 Storm Davis	.10	.04	.01
☐ 17 Tom Glavine	.25	.10	.02
☐ 18 Mike Greenwell	.30	.12	.03
☐ 19 Kelly Gruber	.20	.08	.02
☐ 20 Mark Gubicza	.10	.04	.01
☐ 21 Pedro Guerrero	.15	.06	.01
☐ 22 Mike Harkey	.15	.06	.01
☐ 23 Orel Hershiser	.20	.08	.02
☐ 24 Ted Higuera	.10	.04	.01
☐ 25 Von Hayes	.15	.06	.01
☐ 26 Andre Dawson	.30	.12	.03
☐ 27 Shawon Dunston	.15	.06	.01
☐ 28 Roberto Kelly	.25	.10	.02
☐ 29 Joe Magrane	.10	.04	.01
☐ 30 Dennis Martinez	.15	.06	.01
☐ 31 Kevin McReynolds	.20	.08	.02
☐ 32 Matt Nokes	.15	.06	.01
☐ 33 Dan Plesac	.10	.04	.01
☐ 34 Dave Parker	.15	.06	.01
☐ 35 Randy Johnson	.15	.06	.01
☐ 36 Bret Saberhagen	.25	.10	.02
☐ 37 Mackey Sasser	.15	.06	.01
☐ 38 Mike Scott	.15	.06	.01
☐ 39 Ozzie Smith	.25	.10	.02
☐ 40 Kevin Seitzer	.15	.06	.01
☐ 41 Ruben Sierra	.30	.12	.03
☐ 42 Kevin Tapani	.20	.08	.02
☐ 43 Danny Tartabull	.30	.12	.03
☐ 44 Robby Thompson	.10	.04	.01
☐ 45 Andy Van Slyke	.15	.06	.01
☐ 46 Greg Vaughn	.20	.08	.02
☐ 47 Harold Reynolds	.15	.06	.01
☐ 48 Will Clark	.50	.20	.05
☐ 49 Gary Gaetti	.15	.06	.01
☐ 50 Joe Grahe	.15	.06	.01
☐ 51 Carlton Fisk	.25	.10	.02
☐ 52 Robin Ventura	.30	.12	.03
☐ 53 Ozzie Guillen	.15	.06	.01
☐ 54 Tom Candiotti	.15	.06	.01
☐ 55 Doug Jones	.10	.04	.01
☐ 56 Eric King	.10	.04	.01
☐ 57 Kirk Gibson	.15	.06	.01
☐ 58 Tim Costo	.25	.10	.02
☐ 59 Robin Yount	.35	.15	.03
☐ 60 Sammy Sosa	.20	.08	.02
☐ 61 Jesse Barfield	.15	.06	.01
☐ 62 Marc Newfield	.60	.25	.06
☐ 63 Jimmy Key	.15	.06	.01
☐ 64 Felix Jose	.25	.10	.02
☐ 65 Mark Whiten	.25	.10	.02
☐ 66 Tommy Greene	.15	.06	.01
☐ 67 Kent Mercker	.15	.06	.01
☐ 68 Greg Maddux	.15	.06	.01

☐ 69	Danny Jackson	.10	.04	.01
☐ 70	Reggie Sanders	.40	.16	.04
☐ 71	Eric Yelding	.15	.06	.01
☐ 72	Karl Rhodes	.15	.06	.01
☐ 73	Fernando Valenzuela	.15	.06	.01
☐ 74	Chris Nabholz	.15	.06	.01
☐ 75	Andres Galarraga	.15	.06	.01
☐ 76	Howard Johnson	.25	.10	.02
☐ 77	Hubie Brooks	.15	.06	.01
☐ 78	Terry Mulholland	.15	.06	.01
☐ 79	Paul Molitor	.20	.08	.02
☐ 80	Roger McDowell	.10	.04	.01
☐ 81	Darren Daulton	.15	.06	.01
☐ 82	Zane Smith	.10	.04	.01
☐ 83	Ray Lankford	.30	.12	.03
☐ 84	Bruce Hurst	.15	.06	.01
☐ 85	Andy Benes	.25	.10	.02
☐ 86	John Burkett	.15	.06	.01
☐ 87	Dave Righetti	.15	.06	.01
☐ 88	Steve Karsay	.25	.10	.02
☐ 89	D.J. Dozier	.25	.10	.02
☐ 90	Jeff Bagwell	1.50	.60	.15
☐ 91	Joe Carter	.25	.10	.02
☐ 92	Wes Chamberlain	.50	.20	.05
☐ 93	Vince Coleman	.20	.08	.02
☐ 94	Pat Combs	.10	.04	.01
☐ 95	Jerome Walton	.20	.08	.02
☐ 96	Jeff Conine	.20	.08	.02
☐ 97	Alan Trammell	.20	.08	.02
☐ 98	Don Mattingly	.50	.20	.05
☐ 99	Ramon Martinez	.35	.15	.03
☐ 100	Dave Magadan	.15	.06	.01
☐ 101	Greg Swindell UER	.15	.06	.01
	misnumbered as T10			
☐ 102	Dave Stewart	.20	.08	.02
☐ 103	Gary Sheffield	.25	.10	.02
☐ 104	George Bell	.25	.10	.02
☐ 105	Mark Grace	.25	.10	.02
☐ 106	Steve Sax	.15	.06	.01
☐ 107	Ryne Sandberg	.50	.20	.05
☐ 108	Chris Sabo	.25	.10	.02
☐ 109	Jose Rijo	.15	.06	.01
☐ 110	Cal Ripken	.60	.25	.06
☐ 111	Kirby Puckett	.35	.15	.03
☐ 112	Eddie Murray	.30	.12	.03
☐ 113	Roberto Alomar	.30	.12	.03
☐ 114	Randy Myers	.15	.06	.01
☐ 115	Rafael Palmeiro	.25	.10	.02
☐ 116	John Olerud	.30	.12	.03
☐ 117	Gregg Jefferies	.25	.10	.02
☐ 118	Kent Hrbek	.15	.06	.01
☐ 119	Marquis Grissom	.20	.08	.02
☐ 120	Ken Griffey Jr.	1.25	.50	.12
☐ 121	Dwight Gooden	.25	.10	.02
☐ 122	Juan Gonzalez	.50	.20	.05
☐ 123	Ron Gant	.40	.16	.04
☐ 124	Travis Fryman	.75	.30	.07
☐ 125	John Franco	.15	.06	.01
☐ 126	Dennis Eckersley	.15	.06	.01
☐ 127	Cecil Fielder	.35	.15	.03
☐ 128	Phil Plantier	1.25	.50	.12
☐ 129	Kevin Mitchell	.35	.15	.03
☐ 130	Kevin Maas	.35	.15	.03
☐ 131	Mark McGwire	.35	.15	.03
☐ 132	Ben McDonald	.35	.15	.03
☐ 133	Len Dykstra	.15	.06	.01
☐ 134	Delino DeShields	.20	.08	.02
☐ 135	Jose Canseco	.50	.20	.05
☐ 136	Eric Davis	.25	.10	.02
☐ 137	George Brett	.30	.12	.03
☐ 138	Steve Avery	.40	.16	.04
☐ 139	Eric Anthony	.20	.08	.02
☐ 140	Bobby Thigpen	.15	.06	.01
☐ 141	Ken Griffey Sr.	.15	.06	.01
☐ 142	Barry Larkin	.20	.08	.02
☐ 143	Jeff Brantley	.15	.06	.01
☐ 144	Bobby Bonilla	.25	.10	.02
☐ 145	Jose Offerman	.20	.08	.02
☐ 146	Mike Mussina	.40	.16	.04
☐ 147	Erik Hanson	.15	.06	.01
☐ 148	Dale Murphy	.30	.12	.03
☐ 149	Roger Clemens	.50	.20	.05
☐ 150	Tino Martinez	.30	.12	.03
☐ 151	Todd Van Poppel	1.00	.40	.10
☐ 152	Mo Vaughn	.75	.30	.07
☐ 153	Derrick May	.25	.10	.02
☐ 154	Jack Clark	.15	.06	.01
☐ 155	Dave Hansen	.15	.06	.01
☐ 156	Tony Gwynn	.40	.16	.04
☐ 157	Brian McRae	.40	.16	.04
☐ 158	Matt Williams	.30	.12	.03
☐ 159	Kirk Dressendorfer	.30	.12	.03
☐ 160	Scott Erickson	.75	.30	.07
☐ 161	Tony Fernandez	.15	.06	.01

☐ 162	Willie McGee	.15	.06	.01
☐ 163	Fred McGriff	.25	.10	.02
☐ 164	Leo Gomez	.40	.16	.04
☐ 165	Bernard Gilkey	.30	.12	.03
☐ 166	Bobby Witt	.15	.06	.01
☐ 167	Doug Drabek	.15	.06	.01
☐ 168	Rob Dibble	.15	.06	.01
☐ 169	Glenn Davis	.20	.08	.02
☐ 170	Danny Darwin	.10	.04	.01
☐ 171	Eric Karros	.30	.12	.03
☐ 172	Eddie Zosky	.20	.08	.02
☐ 173	Todd Zeile	.30	.12	.03
☐ 174	Tim Raines	.20	.08	.02
☐ 175	Benito Santiago	.20	.08	.02
☐ 176	Dan Peltier	.20	.08	.02
☐ 177	Darryl Strawberry	.50	.20	.05
☐ 178	Hal Morris	.25	.10	.02
☐ 179	Hensley Meulens	.20	.08	.02
☐ 180	John Smoltz	.20	.08	.02
☐ 181	Frank Thomas	1.50	.60	.15
☐ 182	Dave Staton	.30	.12	.03
☐ 183	Scott Chiamparino	.15	.06	.01
☐ 184	Alex Fernandez	.25	.10	.02
☐ 185	Mark Lewis	.30	.12	.03
☐ 186	Bo Jackson	1.00	.40	.10
☐ 187	Mickey Morandini UER	.20	.08	.02
	Photo is actually			
	Darren Daulton			
☐ 188	Cory Snyder	.15	.06	.01
☐ 189	Rickey Henderson	.50	.20	.05
☐ 190	Junior Felix	.15	.06	.01
☐ 191	Milt Cuyler	.30	.12	.03
☐ 192	Wade Boggs	.40	.16	.04
☐ 193	Dave Justice	1.00	.40	.10
	Justice Prevails			
☐ 194	Sandy Alomar Jr.	.20	.08	.02
☐ 195	Barry Bonds	.35	.15	.03
☐ 196	Nolan Ryan	1.00	.40	.10
☐ 197	Rico Brogna	.30	.12	.03
☐ 198	Steve Decker	.30	.12	.03
☐ 199	Bob Welch	.15	.06	.01
☐ 200	Andujar Cedeno	.40	.16	.04

1991 Classic I

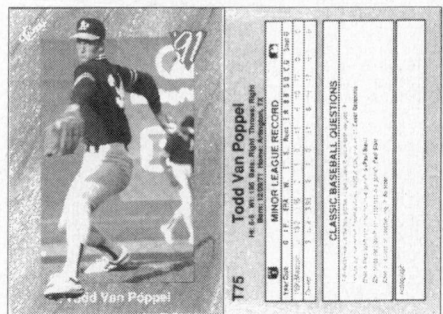

This 100-card set features many of the most popular players in the game of baseball as well as some of the more exciting prospects. The set measures the standard size, 2 1/2" by 3 1/2" and includes trivia questions on the backs of the cards. For the most part the set is arranged alphabetically by team and then alphabetically by players within that team.

		MINT	EXC	G-VG
COMPLETE SET (100)		12.00	5.25	1.50
COMMON PLAYER (1-99)		.10	.04	.01
☐ T1	John Olerud	.30	.12	.03
☐ T2	Tino Martinez	.25	.10	.02
☐ T3	Ken Griffey Jr.	1.00	.40	.10
☐ T4	Jeromy Burnitz	.75	.30	.07
☐ T5	Ron Gant	.35	.15	.03
☐ T6	Mike Benjamin	.10	.04	.01
☐ T7	Steve Decker	.25	.10	.02
☐ T8	Matt Williams	.25	.10	.02
☐ T9	Rafael Novoa	.15	.06	.01

☐ T10	Kevin Mitchell	.25	.10	.02
☐ T11	Dave Justice	.75	.30	.07
☐ T12	Leo Gomez	.35	.15	.03
☐ T13	Chris Hoiles	.20	.08	.02
☐ T14	Ben McDonald	.25	.10	.02
☐ T15	David Segui	.15	.06	.01
☐ T16	Anthony Telford	.10	.04	.01
☐ T17	Mike Mussina	.40	.16	.04
☐ T18	Roger Clemens	.50	.20	.05
☐ T19	Wade Boggs	.40	.16	.04
☐ T20	Tim Naehring	.20	.08	.02
☐ T21	Joe Carter	.25	.10	.02
☐ T22	Phil Plantier	1.00	.40	.10
☐ T23	Rob Dibble	.15	.06	.01
☐ T24	Maurice Vaughn	.75	.30	.07
☐ T25	Lee Stevens	.30	.12	.03
☐ T26	Chris Sabo	.25	.10	.02
☐ T27	Mark Grace	.25	.10	.02
☐ T28	Derrick May	.25	.10	.02
☐ T29	Ryne Sandberg	.50	.20	.05
☐ T30	Matt Stark	.25	.10	.02
☐ T31	Bobby Thigpen	.15	.06	.01
☐ T32	Frank Thomas	1.25	.50	.12
☐ T33	Don Mattingly	.50	.20	.05
☐ T34	Eric Davis	.30	.12	.03
☐ T35	Reggie Jefferson	.45	.18	.04
☐ T36	Alex Cole	.25	.10	.02
☐ T37	Mark Lewis	.35	.15	.03
☐ T38	Tim Costo	.35	.15	.03
☐ T39	Sandy Alomar Jr.	.25	.10	.02
☐ T40	Travis Fryman	.60	.25	.06
☐ T41	Cecil Fielder	.35	.15	.03
☐ T42	Milt Cuyler	.35	.15	.03
☐ T43	Andujar Cedeno	.45	.18	.04
☐ T44	Danny Darwin	.10	.04	.01
☐ T45	Randy Hennis	.15	.06	.01
☐ T46	George Brett	.35	.15	.03
☐ T47	Jeff Conine	.20	.08	.02
☐ T48	Bo Jackson	.90	.40	.09
☐ T49	Brian McRae	.50	.20	.05
☐ T50	Brent Mayne	.25	.10	.02
☐ T51	Eddie Murray	.30	.12	.03
☐ T52	Ramon Martinez	.35	.15	.03
☐ T53	Jim Neidlinger	.15	.06	.01
☐ T54	Jim Poole	.15	.06	.01
☐ T55	Tim McIntosh	.15	.06	.01
☐ T56	Randy Veres	.15	.06	.01
☐ T57	Kirby Puckett	.35	.15	.03
☐ T58	Todd Ritchie	.25	.10	.02
☐ T59	Rich Garces	.15	.06	.01
☐ T60	Moises Alou	.15	.06	.01
☐ T61	Delino DeShields	.20	.08	.02
☐ T62	Oscar Azocar	.15	.06	.01
☐ T63	Kevin Maas	.40	.16	.04
☐ T64	Alan Mills	.15	.06	.01
☐ T65	John Franco	.15	.06	.01
☐ T66	Chris Jelic	.25	.10	.02
☐ T67	Dave Magadan	.15	.06	.01
☐ T68	Darryl Strawberry	.45	.18	.04
☐ T69	Hensley Meulens	.15	.06	.01
☐ T70	Juan Gonzalez	.75	.30	.07
☐ T71	Reggie Harris	.15	.06	.01
☐ T72	Rickey Henderson	.50	.20	.05
☐ T73	Mark McGwire	.30	.12	.03
☐ T74	Willie McGee	.20	.08	.02
☐ T75	Todd Van Poppel	1.00	.40	.10
☐ T76	Bob Welch	.15	.06	.01
☐ T77	Future Aces	1.50	.60	.15
	Todd Van Poppel			
	Don Peters			
	David Zancanaro			
	Kirk Dressendorfer			
☐ T78	Len Dykstra	.15	.06	.01
☐ T79	Mickey Morandini	.20	.08	.02
☐ T80	Wes Chamberlain	.45	.18	.04
☐ T81	Barry Bonds	.35	.15	.03
☐ T82	Doug Drabek	.15	.06	.01
☐ T83	Randy Tomlin	.20	.08	.02
☐ T84	Scott Chiamparino	.15	.06	.01
☐ T85	Rafael Palmiero	.20	.08	.02
☐ T86	Nolan Ryan	1.00	.40	.10
☐ T87	Bobby Witt	.15	.06	.01
☐ T88	Fred McGriff	.25	.10	.02
☐ T89	Dave Stieb	.15	.06	.01
☐ T90	Ed Sprague	.20	.08	.02
☐ T91	Vince Coleman	.20	.08	.02
☐ T92	Rod Brewer	.10	.04	.01
☐ T93	Bernard Gilkey	.30	.12	.03
☐ T94	Roberto Alomar	.25	.10	.02
☐ T95	Chuck Finley	.15	.06	.01
☐ T96	Dale Murphy	.25	.10	.02
☐ T97	Jose Rijo	.15	.06	.01
☐ T98	Hal Morris	.25	.10	.02
☐ T99	Friendly Foes	.35	.15	.03

	Darryl Strawberry			
	Dwight Gooden			
	(instructions on back)			
☐ NNO	Todd Van Poppel	.75	.30	.07
	Dave Justice			
	Ryne Sandberg			
	Kevin Maas			
	(blank back)			

1991 Classic II

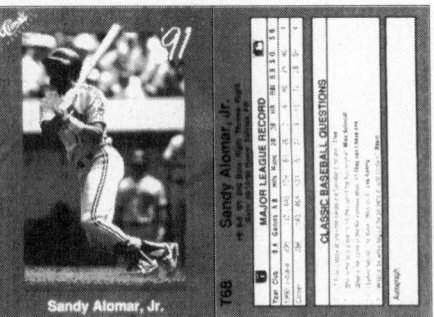

Sandy Alomar, Jr.

This second issue of the 1991 Classic baseball trivia game contains a small gameboard, accessories, 99 player cards with trivia questions on the backs, and one "4-in-1" micro player card. The cards measure the standard size (2 1/2" by 3 1/2") and have on the fronts glossy color action photos with cranberry red borders. The backs are cranberry and white and have biography, statistics, five trivia questions, and an autograph slot. The cards are numbered on the back.

		MINT	EXC	G-VG
COMPLETE SET (100)		11.00	5.00	1.35
COMMON PLAYER (1-100)		.10	.04	.01
☐ T1	Ken Griffey Jr.	.75	.30	.07
☐ T2	Wilfredo Cordero	.30	.12	.03
☐ T3	Cal Ripken	.50	.20	.05
☐ T4	D.J. Dozier	.20	.08	.02
☐ T5	Darrin Fletcher	.15	.06	.01
☐ T6	Glenn Davis	.15	.06	.01
☐ T7	Alex Fernandez	.25	.10	.02
☐ T8	Cory Snyder	.15	.06	.01
☐ T9	Tim Raines	.15	.06	.01
☐ T0	Greg Swindell	.15	.06	.01
☐ T11	Mark Lewis	.25	.10	.02
☐ T12	Rico Brogna	.25	.10	.02
☐ T13	Gary Sheffield	.20	.08	.02
☐ T14	Paul Molitor	.15	.06	.01
☐ T15	Kent Hrbek	.15	.06	.01
☐ T16	Scott Erickson	.60	.25	.06
☐ T17	Steve Sax	.15	.06	.01
☐ T18	Dennis Eckersley	.15	.06	.01
☐ T19	Jose Canseco	.50	.20	.05
☐ T20	Kirk Dressendorfer	.30	.12	.03
☐ T21	Ken Griffey Sr.	.15	.06	.01
☐ T22	Erik Hanson	.15	.06	.01
☐ T23	Dan Peltier	.15	.06	.01
☐ T24	John Olerud	.25	.10	.02
☐ T25	Eddie Zosky	.15	.06	.01
☐ T26	Steve Avery	.30	.12	.03
☐ T27	John Smoltz	.20	.08	.02
☐ T28	Frank Thomas	1.00	.40	.10
☐ T29	Jerome Walton	.15	.06	.01
☐ T30	George Bell	.20	.08	.02
☐ T31	Jose Rijo	.15	.06	.01
☐ T32	Randy Myers	.10	.04	.01
☐ T33	Barry Larkin	.20	.08	.02
☐ T34	Eric Anthony	.20	.08	.02
☐ T35	Dave Hansen	.15	.06	.01
☐ T36	Eric Karros	.30	.12	.03
☐ T37	Jose Offerman	.20	.08	.02
☐ T38	Marquis Grissom	.20	.08	.02
☐ T39	Dwight Gooden	.25	.10	.02
☐ T40	Gregg Jefferies	.25	.10	.02
☐ T41	Pat Combs	.15	.06	.01

☐ T42	Todd Zeile	.25	.10	.02
☐ T43	Benito Santiago	.20	.08	.02
☐ T44	Dave Staton	.25	.10	.02
☐ T45	Tony Fernandez	.15	.06	.01
☐ T46	Fred McGriff	.20	.08	.02
☐ T47	Jeff Brantley	.10	.04	.01
☐ T48	Junior Felix	.15	.06	.01
☐ T49	Jack Morris	.20	.08	.02
☐ T50	Chris George	.15	.06	.01
☐ T51	Henry Rodriguez	.25	.10	.02
☐ T52	Paul Marak	.15	.06	.01
☐ T53	Ryan Klesko	1.25	.50	.12
☐ T54	Darren Lewis	.20	.08	.02
☐ T55	Lance Dickson	.15	.06	.01
☐ T56	Anthony Young	.25	.10	.02
☐ T57	Willie Banks	.15	.06	.01
☐ T58	Mike Bordick	.10	.04	.01
☐ T59	Roger Salkeld	.40	.16	.04
☐ T60	Steve Karsay	.25	.10	.02
☐ T61	Bernie Williams	.30	.12	.03
☐ T62	Mickey Tettleton	.15	.06	.01
☐ T63	Dave Justice	.75	.30	.07
☐ T64	Steve Decker	.25	.10	.02
☐ T65	Roger Clemens	.50	.20	.05
☐ T66	Phil Plantier	.75	.30	.07
☐ T67	Ryne Sandberg	.50	.20	.05
☐ T68	Sandy Alomar Jr.	.20	.08	.02
☐ T69	Cecil Fielder	.35	.15	.03
☐ T70	George Brett	.30	.12	.03
☐ T71	Delino DeShields	.20	.08	.02
☐ T72	Dave Magadan	.15	.06	.01
☐ T73	Darryl Strawberry	.50	.20	.05
☐ T74	Juan Gonzalez	.50	.20	.05
☐ T75	Rickey Henderson	.50	.20	.05
☐ T76	Willie McGee	.15	.06	.01
☐ T77	Todd Van Poppel	.75	.30	.07
☐ T78	Barry Bonds	.30	.12	.03
☐ T79	Doug Drabek	.15	.06	.01
☐ T80	Nolan Ryan	.90	.40	.09
	300 Game Winner			
☐ T81	Roberto Alomar	.25	.10	.02
☐ T82	Ivan Rodriguez	1.25	.50	.12
☐ T83	Dan Opperman	.20	.08	.02
☐ T84	Jeff Bagwell	1.25	.50	.12
☐ T85	Braulio Castillo	.35	.15	.03
☐ T86	Doug Simons	.15	.06	.01
☐ T87	Wade Taylor	.15	.06	.01
☐ T88	Gary Scott	.25	.10	.02
☐ T89	Dave Stewart	.15	.06	.01
☐ T90	Mike Simms	.20	.08	.02
☐ T91	Luis Gonzalez	.50	.20	.05
☐ T92	Bobby Bonilla	.25	.10	.02
☐ T93	Tony Gwynn	.35	.15	.03
☐ T94	Will Clark	.50	.20	.05
☐ T95	Rich Rowland	.15	.06	.01
☐ T96	Alan Trammell	.20	.08	.02
☐ T97	Strikeout Kings	.90	.40	.09
	Nolan Ryan			
	Roger Clemens			
☐ T98	Joe Carter	.25	.10	.02
☐ T99	Jack Clark	.15	.06	.01
☐ T100	Steve Decker	.25	.10	.02

1991 Classic III

Scott Erickson

The third issue of the 1991 Classic baseball trivia game contains a small gameboard, accessories, 99 player cards with trivia questions on the backs, and one "4-in-1" micro player card. The cards measure the standard size (2 1/2" by 3 1/2") and have on the fronts glossy color action photos with grayish-green borders. In a horizontal format, the backs feature biography, statistics, and five trivia questions. This information is superimposed over the team logo. The card numbers on the back appear in a green stripe. With few exceptions, the cards are arranged in alphabetical order.

		MINT	EXC	G-VG
COMPLETE SET (100)		11.00	5.00	1.35
COMMON PLAYER (1-99)		.10	.04	.01
☐ T1	Jim Abbott	.30	.12	.03
☐ T2	Craig Biggio	.20	.08	.02
☐ T3	Wade Boggs	.40	.16	.04
☐ T4	Bobby Bonilla	.30	.12	.03
☐ T5	Ivan Calderon	.15	.06	.01
☐ T6	Jose Canseco	.50	.20	.05
☐ T7	Andy Benes	.25	.10	.02
☐ T8	Wes Chamberlain	.30	.12	.03
☐ T9	Will Clark	.50	.20	.05
☐ T10	Royce Clayton	.30	.12	.03
☐ T11	Gerald Alexander	.15	.06	.01
☐ T12	Chili Davis	.15	.06	.01
☐ T13	Eric Davis	.25	.10	.02
☐ T14	Andre Dawson	.25	.10	.02
☐ T15	Rob Dibble	.15	.06	.01
☐ T16	Chris Donnels	.25	.10	.02
☐ T17	Scott Erickson	.50	.20	.05
☐ T18	Monty Fariss	.20	.08	.02
☐ T19	Ruben Amaro Jr.	.15	.06	.01
☐ T20	Chuck Finley	.15	.06	.01
☐ T21	Carlton Fisk	.25	.10	.02
☐ T22	Carlos Baerga	.25	.10	.02
☐ T23	Ron Gant	.35	.15	.03
☐ T24	Dave Justice	.75	.30	.07
	and Ron Gant			
☐ T25	Mike Gardiner	.15	.06	.01
☐ T26	Tom Glavine	.25	.10	.02
☐ T27	Joe Grahe	.15	.06	.01
☐ T28	Derek Bell	.50	.20	.05
☐ T29	Mike Greenwell	.25	.10	.02
☐ T30	Ken Griffey Jr.	.75	.30	.07
☐ T31	Leo Gomez	.20	.08	.02
☐ T32	Tom Goodwin	.20	.08	.02
☐ T33	Tony Gwynn	.35	.15	.03
☐ T34	Mel Hall	.10	.04	.01
☐ T35	Brian Harper	.10	.04	.01
☐ T36	Dave Henderson	.15	.06	.01
☐ T37	Albert Belle	.25	.10	.02
☐ T38	Orel Hershiser	.20	.08	.02
☐ T39	Brian Hunter	.50	.20	
☐ T40	Howard Johnson	.20	.08	
☐ T41	Felix Jose	.20	.08	.02
☐ T42	Wally Joyner	.20	.08	.02
☐ T43	Jeff Juden	.35	.15	.03
☐ T44	Pat Kelly	.50	.20	.05
☐ T45	Jimmy Key	.15	.06	.01
☐ T46	Chuck Knoblauch	.75	.30	.07
☐ T47	John Kruk	.10	.04	.01
☐ T48	Ray Lankford	.25	.10	.02
☐ T49	Cedric Landrum	.15	.06	.01
☐ T50	Scott Livingstone	.15	.06	.01
☐ T51	Kevin Maas	.25	.10	.02
☐ T52	Greg Maddux	.15	.06	.01
☐ T53	Dennis Martinez	.10	.04	.01
☐ T54	Edgar Martinez	.20	.08	.02
☐ T55	Pedro Martinez	.75	.30	.07
☐ T56	Don Mattingly	.50	.20	.05
☐ T57	Orlando Merced	.30	.12	.03
☐ T58	Keith Mitchell	.40	.16	.04
☐ T59	Kevin Mitchell	.25	.10	.02
☐ T60	Paul Molitor	.15	.06	.01
☐ T61	Jack Morris	.20	.08	.02
☐ T62	Hal Morris	.25	.10	.02
☐ T63	Kevin Morton	.15	.06	.01
☐ T64	Pedro Munoz	.25	.10	.02
☐ T65	Eddie Murray	.25	.10	.02
☐ T66	Jack McDowell	.20	.08	.02
☐ T67	Jeff McNeely	.35	.15	.03
☐ T68	Brian McRae	.25	.10	.02
☐ T69	Kevin McReynolds	.15	.06	.01
☐ T70	Gregg Olson	.15	.06	.01
☐ T71	Rafael Palmeiro	.20	.08	.02
☐ T72	Dean Palmer	.30	.12	.03
☐ T73	Tony Phillips	.10	.04	.01
☐ T74	Kirby Puckett	.35	.15	.03
☐ T75	Carlos Quintana	.15	.06	.01
☐ T76	Pat Rice	.15	.06	.01
☐ T77	Cal Ripken	.50	.20	.05
☐ T78	Ivan Rodriguez	.75	.30	.07

		MINT	EXC	G-VG
☐ T79	Nolan Ryan Number 7	.75	.30	.07
☐ T80	Bret Saberhagen	.20	.08	.02
☐ T81	Tim Salmon	.25	.10	.02
☐ T82	Juan Samuel	.15	.06	.01
☐ T83	Ruben Sierra	.30	.12	.03
☐ T84	Heathcliff Slocumb	.15	.06	.01
☐ T85	Joe Slusarski	.20	.08	.02
☐ T86	John Smiley	.15	.06	.01
☐ T87	Dave Smith	.10	.04	.01
☐ T88	Ed Sprague	.15	.06	.01
☐ T89	Todd Stottlemyre	.15	.06	.01
☐ T90	Mike Timlin	.15	.06	.01
☐ T91	Greg Vaughn	.25	.10	.02
☐ T92	Frank Viola	.15	.06	.01
☐ T93	Chico Walker	.15	.06	.01
☐ T94	Devon White	.15	.06	.01
☐ T95	Matt Williams	.25	.10	.02
☐ T96	Rick Wilkins	.15	.06	.01
☐ T97	Bernie Williams	.25	.10	.02
☐ T98	Starter and Stopper	.60	.25	.06
	Nolan Ryan			
	Goose Gossage			
☐ T99	Gerald Williams	.50	.20	.05
☐ NNO	4-in-1 Card	.50	.20	.05
	Bobby Bonilla			
	Will Clark			
	Cal Ripken			
	Scott Erickson			

1991 Classic Draft Picks

#2 Mike Kelly

The premier edition of the 1991 Classic Draft Picks set contains 50 standard size (2 1/2" by 3 1/2") cards, plus a bonus card featuring Frankie Rodriguez. The production run was distributed between 330,000 hobby sets, 165,000 non-hobby sets, and 1,500 test sets. Each set includes a certificate of limited edition with a unique set number. The fronts display glossy color player photos, with maroon borders and a gray card face. The draft pick number, player's name, and position appear in the maroon border at the bottom of the picture. The horizontally oriented backs have biography and maroon border stripes intersecting at the upper corner. Also high school or college statistics and player profile are printed over a washed-out picture of a batter and catcher at home plate. The cards are numbered on the back. This set includes Brien Taylor, the first pick of the '91 draft. The Frankie Rodriguez bonus card was only included in hobby sets.

		MINT	EXC	G-VG
COMPLETE SET (51)		12.00	5.25	1.50
COMMON PLAYER (1-50)		.10	.04	.01
☐ 1	Brien Taylor	2.50	1.00	.25
☐ 2	Mike Kelly	2.25	.90	.22
☐ 3	David McCarty	1.50	.60	.15
☐ 4	Dmitri Young	1.50	.60	.15
☐ 5	Joe Vitiello	1.00	.40	.10
☐ 6	Mark Smith	.60	.25	.06
☐ 7	Tyler Green	.60	.25	.06
☐ 8	Shawn Estes	.30	.12	.03
☐ 9	Doug Glanville	.60	.25	.06
☐ 10	Manny Ramirez	1.00	.40	.10
☐ 11	Cliff Floyd	.60	.25	.06

		MINT	EXC	G-VG
☐ 12	Tyrone Hill	.25	.10	.02
☐ 13	Eduardo Perez	1.00	.40	.10
☐ 14	Al Shirley	.75	.30	.07
☐ 15	Benji Gil	.60	.25	.06
☐ 16	Calvin Reese	.30	.12	.03
☐ 17	Allen Watson	.25	.10	.02
☐ 18	Brian Barber	.20	.08	.02
☐ 19	Aaron Sele	.30	.12	.03
☐ 20	John Farrell	.30	.12	.03
☐ 21	Scott Ruffcorn	.30	.12	.03
☐ 22	Brent Gates	.40	.16	.04
☐ 23	Scott Stahoviak	.30	.12	.03
☐ 24	Tom McKinnon	.20	.08	.02
☐ 25	Shawn Livsey	.25	.10	.02
☐ 26	Jason Pruitt	.20	.08	.02
☐ 27	Greg Anthony	.20	.08	.02
☐ 28	Justin Thompson	.25	.10	.02
☐ 29	Steve Whitaker	.20	.08	.02
☐ 30	Jorge Fabregas	.25	.10	.02
☐ 31	Jeff Ware	.30	.12	.03
☐ 32	Bobby Jones	.30	.12	.03
☐ 33	J.J. Johnson	.20	.08	.02
☐ 34	Mike Rossiter	.20	.08	.02
☐ 35	Dan Cholowsky	.20	.08	.02
☐ 36	Jimmy Gonzalez	.20	.08	.02
☐ 37	Trevor Miller	.25	.10	.02
☐ 38	Scott Hatteberg	.25	.10	.02
☐ 39	Mike Groppuso	.20	.08	.02
☐ 40	Ryan Long	.10	.04	.01
☐ 41	Eddie Williams	.30	.12	.03
☐ 42	Mike Durant	.25	.10	.02
☐ 43	Buck McNabb	.10	.04	.01
☐ 44	Jimmy Lewis	.10	.04	.01
☐ 45	Eddie Ramos	.10	.04	.01
☐ 46	Terry Horn	.20	.08	.02
☐ 47	Jon Barnes	.10	.04	.01
☐ 48	Shawn Curran	.10	.04	.01
☐ 49	Tommy Adams	.30	.12	.03
☐ 50	Trevor Mallory	.20	.08	.02
☐ NNO	Frankie Rodriguez	1.50	.60	.15
	Bonus card			

1992 Classic I

KEVIN MITCHELL

The first issue of the 1992 Classic baseball trivia game contains a small gameboard, accessories, 99 player cards with trivia questions on the backs, one "4-in-1" micro player card, and 4 micro player pieces. The cards measure the standard size (2 1/2" by 3 1/2") and have on the fronts glossy color action photos bordered in white. A red, gray, and purple stripe with the year "1992" traverses the top of the card. In a horizontal format, the backs feature biography, statistics, and five trivia questions, printed on a ghosted image of the 26 major league city skylines. The cards are numbered on the back and basically arranged in alphabetical order.

		MINT	EXC	G-VG
COMPLETE SET (100)		12.00	5.25	1.50
COMMON PLAYER (1-99)		.10	.04	.01
☐ T1	Jim Abbott	.30	.12	.03
☐ T2	Kyle Abbott	.20	.08	.02
☐ T3	Scott Aldred	.15	.06	.01

		MINT	EXC	G-VG
☐ T4	Roberto Alomar	.25	.10	.02
☐ T5	Wilson Alvarez	.15	.06	.01
☐ T6	Andy Ashby	.15	.06	.01
☐ T7	Steve Avery	.25	.10	.02
☐ T8	Jeff Bagwell	.50	.20	.05
☐ T9	Bret Barberie	.30	.12	.03
☐ T10	Kim Batiste	.15	.06	.01
☐ T11	Derek Bell	.25	.10	.02
☐ T12	Jay Bell	.10	.04	.01
☐ T13	Albert Belle	.20	.08	.02
☐ T14	Andy Benes	.20	.08	.02
☐ T15	Sean Berry	.15	.06	.01
☐ T16	Barry Bonds	.25	.10	.02
☐ T17	Ryan Bowen	.20	.08	.02
☐ T18	Trifecta	.15	.06	.01
	Alejandro Pena			
	Mark Wohlers			
	Kent Mercker			
☐ T19	Scott Brosius	.15	.06	.01
☐ T20	Jay Buhner	.20	.08	.02
☐ T21	David Burba	.15	.06	.01
☐ T22	Jose Canseco	.45	.18	.04
☐ T23	Andujar Cedeno	.25	.10	.02
☐ T24	Will Clark	.45	.18	.04
☐ T25	Royce Clayton	.25	.10	.02
☐ T26	Roger Clemens	.45	.18	.04
☐ T27	David Cone	.15	.06	.01
☐ T28	Scott Cooper	.20	.08	.02
☐ T29	Chris Cron	.20	.08	.02
☐ T30	Len Dykstra	.15	.06	.01
☐ T31	Cal Eldred	.15	.06	.01
☐ T32	Hector Fajardo	.20	.08	.02
☐ T33	Cecil Fielder	.25	.10	.02
☐ T34	Dave Fleming	.15	.06	.01
☐ T35	Steve Foster	.15	.06	.01
☐ T36	Julio Franco	.20	.08	.02
☐ T37	Carlos Garcia	.15	.06	.01
☐ T38	Tom Glavine	.20	.08	.02
☐ T39	Tom Goodwin	.20	.08	.02
☐ T40	Ken Griffey Jr.	.75	.30	.07
☐ T41	Chris Haney	.20	.08	.02
☐ T42	Bryan Harvey	.15	.06	.01
☐ T43	Rickey Henderson 939	.45	.18	.04
☐ T44	Carlos Hernandez	.20	.08	.02
☐ T45	Roberto Hernandez	.20	.08	.02
☐ T46	Brook Jacoby	.10	.04	.01
☐ T47	Howard Johnson	.20	.08	.02
☐ T48	Pat Kelly	.20	.08	.02
☐ T49	Darryl Kile	.15	.06	.01
☐ T50	Chuck Knoblauch	.40	.16	.04
☐ T51	Ray Lankford	.25	.10	.02
☐ T52	Mark Leiter	.15	.06	.01
☐ T53	Darren Lewis	.20	.08	.02
☐ T54	Scott Livingstone	.15	.06	.01
☐ T55	Shane Mack	.15	.06	.01
☐ T56	Chito Martinez	.30	.12	.03
☐ T57	Dennis Martinez	.15	.06	.01
	The Perfect Game			
☐ T58	Don Mattingly	.40	.16	.04
☐ T59	Paul McClellan	.20	.08	.02
☐ T60	Chuck McElroy	.15	.06	.01
☐ T61	Fred McGriff	.20	.08	.02
☐ T62	Orlando Merced	.20	.08	.02
☐ T63	Luis Mercedes	.25	.10	.02
☐ T64	Kevin Mitchell	.25	.10	.02
☐ T65	Hal Morris	.20	.08	.02
☐ T66	Jack Morris	.15	.06	.01
☐ T67	Mike Mussina	.25	.10	.02
☐ T68	Denny Neagle	.30	.12	.03
☐ T69	Tom Pagnozzi	.10	.04	.01
☐ T70	Terry Pendleton	.15	.06	.01
☐ T71	Phil Plantier	.35	.15	.03
☐ T72	Kirby Puckett	.30	.12	.03
☐ T73	Carlos Quintana	.15	.06	.01
☐ T74	Willie Randolph	.10	.04	.01
☐ T75	Arthur Rhodes	.25	.10	.02
☐ T76	Cal Ripken	.45	.18	.04
☐ T77	Ivan Rodriguez	.45	.18	.04
☐ T78	Nolan Ryan	.75	.30	.07
☐ T79	Ryne Sandberg	.45	.18	.04
☐ T80	Deion Sanders	.25	.10	.02
	Deion Drops In			
☐ T81	Reggie Sanders	.20	.08	.02
☐ T82	Mo Sanford	.20	.08	.02
☐ T83	Terry Shumpert	.10	.04	.01
☐ T84	Tim Spehr	.15	.06	.01
☐ T85	Lee Stevens	.15	.06	.01
☐ T86	Darryl Strawberry	.40	.16	.04
☐ T87	Kevin Tapani	.15	.06	.01
☐ T88	Danny Tartabull	.25	.10	.02
☐ T89	Frank Thomas	.75	.30	.07
☐ T90	Jim Thome	.50	.20	.05
☐ T91	Todd Van Poppel	.50	.20	.05
☐ T92	Andy Van Slyke	.15	.06	.01
☐ T93	John Wehner	.20	.08	.02
☐ T94	John Wetteland	.15	.06	.01
☐ T95	Devon White	.15	.06	.01
☐ T96	Brian Williams	.20	.08	.02
☐ T97	Mark Wohlers	.25	.10	.02
☐ T98	Robin Yount	.30	.12	.03
☐ T99	Eddie Zosky	.15	.06	.01
☐ NNO	4-in-1 Card	.50	.20	.05
	Barry Bonds			
	Roger Clemens			
	Steve Avery			
	Nolan Ryan			

1988 CMC Don Mattingly

This 20-card set featuring Don Mattingly was distributed as part of a Collecting Kit produced by Collector's Marketing Corp. The cards themselves measure approximately 2 1/2" by 3 1/2" and have a light blue border. The card backs describe some aspect of Mattingly's career. Also in the kit were plastic sheets, a small album, a record, a booklet, and information on how to join Don's Fan Club. The set price below is for the whole kit as well as the cards.

		MINT	EXC	G-VG
COMPLETE SET (20)		9.00	4.00	.90
COMMON PLAYER (1-20)		.60	.25	.06
☐ 1	Game Face	.60	.25	.06
☐ 2	Columbus Clippers	.60	.25	.06
☐ 3	1983 Spring Camp	.60	.25	.06
☐ 4	AL Batting Crown	.60	.25	.06
☐ 5	1981 All-Star	.60	.25	.06
	Outfielder			
☐ 6	The Batting Tee	.60	.25	.06
☐ 7	AL MVP Honors	.60	.25	.06
☐ 8	Gold Glove Winner	.60	.25	.06
☐ 9	Batting Practice	.60	.25	.06
☐ 10	Yankee Records	.60	.25	.06
☐ 11	Baseball On His Mind	.60	.25	.06
☐ 12	Big Home Runs	.60	.25	.06
☐ 13	Hustle and	.60	.25	.06
	Determination			
☐ 14	Delivering In The	.60	.25	.06
	Clutch			
☐ 15	A Slick First Baseman	.60	.25	.06
☐ 16	Keep Playing Hard	.60	.25	.06
☐ 17	Mattingly's Eight-	.60	.25	.06
	Game Streak			
☐ 18	The Textbook Swing	.60	.25	.06
☐ 19	It's Time To Go	.60	.25	.06
	Forward			
☐ 20	Surehanded First	.60	.25	.06
	Baseman			

1989 CMC Jose Canseco

1989 CMC Mickey Mantle

The 1989 CMC Jose Canseco Collector's Kit set contains 20 numbered standard-size (2 1/2 by 3 1/2 inch) cards. The front borders are Oakland A's green and yellow. The backs are green and white, and feature narratives and facsimile signatures. The cards were distributed as a set in a box along with an album and a booklet as well as other elements by CMC, Collectors Marketing Corporation. Since all the cards in the set feature the same player, cards in the checklist below are differentiated by some other characteristic of the particular card.

	MINT	EXC	G-VG
COMPLETE SET (20)	9.00	4.00	.90
COMMON PLAYER (1-20)	.60	.25	.06
☐ 1 Looking up with .... yellow jersey	.60	.25	.06
☐ 2 Posing with bat from .... the waist up	.60	.25	.06
☐ 3 Portrait with green .... cap	.60	.25	.06
☐ 4 Follow-through on .... swing (catcher visible)	.60	.25	.06
☐ 5 Running the bases	.60	.25	.06
☐ 6 Warming up with bat .... over head	.60	.25	.06
☐ 7 Sitting in dugout .... holding bat	.60	.25	.06
☐ 8 Standing in outfield .... with sunglasses up	.60	.25	.06
☐ 9 Batting stance ready .... for pitch	.60	.25	.06
☐ 10 Taking a lead off .... first base	.60	.25	.06
☐ 11 Looking to the side .... (elephant logo on left shoulder)	.60	.25	.06
☐ 12 Bashing with Mark .... McGwire after homer	.60	.25	.06
☐ 13 Looking up witrh green .... batting glove in foreground	.60	.25	.06
☐ 14 Stretching to catch .... fly ball	.60	.25	.06
☐ 15 Follow through on .... swing (no catcher visible)	.60	.25	.06
☐ 16 Standing at plate .... glaring at pitcher	.60	.25	.06
☐ 17 Follow through on .... swing (stain on pants)	.60	.25	.06
☐ 18 Signing autographs .... for the fans at the ballpark	.60	.25	.06
☐ 19 Waiting at first base .... with hands on hips	.60	.25	.06
☐ 20 Admiring his hit at .... plate with tongue out	.60	.25	.06

The 1989 CMC Mickey Mantle Collector's Kit set contains 20 numbered standard-size (2 1/2 by 3 1/2 inch) cards. The fronts and backs are white, red and navy. The backs feature narratives and facsimile signatures. The cards were distributed as a set in a box along with an album and a booklet as well as other elements by CMC, Collectors Marketing Corporation. Since all the cards in the set feature the same player, cards in the checklist below are differentiated by some other characteristic of the particular card. Some of the cards in this set are sepia-tone photos as the action predates the widespread use of color film.

	MINT	EXC	G-VG
COMPLETE SET (20)	9.00	4.00	.90
COMMON PLAYER (1-20)	.60	.25	.06
☐ 1 Standing with bat on .... left shoulder	.60	.25	.06
☐ 2 Batting stance lefty .... (back to camera)	.60	.25	.06
☐ 3 Looking intense in .... the field (waist up)	.60	.25	.06
☐ 4 Follow through on .... lefty swing	.60	.25	.06
☐ 5 Half smile (head and .... shoulders)	.60	.25	.06
☐ 6 Posing with bat .... alongside Roger Maris	.60	.25	.06
☐ 7 Holding up his 1962 .... contract (wearing suit and tie)	.60	.25	.06
☐ 8 Receiving 1962 MVP .... form Joe Cronin	.60	.25	.06
☐ 9 Batting stance lefty .... (catcher's glove in picture)	.60	.25	.06
☐ 10 Posing with Roger .... Maris and Yogi Berra	.60	.25	.06
☐ 11 Looking away with eyes .... closed, holding bat	.60	.25	.06
☐ 12 Swinging righty at .... pitch	.60	.25	.06
☐ 13 Starting to run to .... first base	.60	.25	.06
☐ 14 Mickey Mantle Day, ... September 18, 1965	.60	.25	.06
☐ 15 Shaking hands with .... Joe DiMaggio at Yankee Stadium	.60	.25	.06
☐ 16 Giving speech at .... Yankee Stadium	.60	.25	.06
☐ 17 Backing away from .... plate after pitch	.60	.25	.06
☐ 18 Getting ready at .... plate with bat in right hand	.60	.25	.06
☐ 19 Holding bat in both .... hands parallel to ground	.60	.25	.06
☐ 20 Waiting for pitch with .... bat on shoulder (lefty)	.60	.25	.06

1989 CMC Babe Ruth

1981 Coke Team Sets

The 1989 CMC Babe Ruth Collector's Kit set contains 20 numbered standard-size (2 1/2" by 3 1/2") cards. The front borders are white, red and navy. The backs are blue and white, and feature narratives and facsimile signatures. The cards were distributed as a set in a box along with an album and a booklet as well as other elements by CMC, Collectors Marketing Corporation. Since all the cards in the set feature the same player, cards in the checklist below are differentiated by some other characteristic of the particular card. All of the cards in this set are sepia-tone photos as the action predates the widespread use of color film.

	MINT	EXC	G-VG
COMPLETE SET (20)	9.00	4.00	.90
COMMON PLAYER (1-20)	.60	.25	.06
☐ 1 Smiling holding three bats	.60	.25	.06
☐ 2 Posing in Red Sox uniform (head and shoulders)	.60	.25	.06
☐ 3 Looking up (waist up)	.60	.25	.06
☐ 4 Holding nine bats in front of him	.60	.25	.06
☐ 5 Golfing swing follow through	.60	.25	.06
☐ 6 Oldtimers' game photo holding two bats	.60	.25	.06
☐ 7 Follow through looking up (in Japan)	.60	.25	.06
☐ 8 Looking dapper in fur coat	.60	.25	.06
☐ 9 Babe Ruth Day, April 27, 1947	.60	.25	.06
☐ 10 Bust photo with no background	.60	.25	.06
☐ 11 Practicing swing (photo from knees up)	.60	.25	.06
☐ 12 Watching his hit after swing (knees up)	.60	.25	.06
☐ 13 Follow through on swing, starting to first base	.60	.25	.06
☐ 14 Practice swing with photographers in background	.60	.25	.06
☐ 15 Posing with Jacob Ruppert	.60	.25	.06
☐ 16 Follow through from waist up	.60	.25	.06
☐ 17 Shaking hands with Miller Huggins	.60	.25	.06
☐ 18 Signing autographs for the kids	.60	.25	.06
☐ 19 Sitting wearing Braves uniform	.60	.25	.06
☐ 20 Hall of Fame Plaque	.60	.25	.06

The cards in this 132-card set measure 2 1/2" by 3 1/2". In 1981, Topps produced 11 sets of 12 cards each for the Coca-Cola Company. Each set features 11 star players for a particular team plus an advertising card with the team name on the front. Although the cards are numbered in the upper right corner of the back from 1 to 11, they are re-numbered below within team, i.e., Boston Red Sox (1-12), Chicago Cubs (13-24), Chicago White Sox (25-36), Cincinnati Reds (37-48), Detroit Tigers (49-60), Houston Astros (61-72), Kansas City Royals (73-84), New York Mets (85-96), Philadelphia Phillies (97-108), Pittsburgh Pirates (109-120), and St. Louis Cardinals (121-132). Within each team the player actually numbered number 1 (on the card back) is the first player below and the player numbered number 11 is the last in that team's list. These player cards are quite similar to the 1981 Topps issue but feature a Coca-Cola logo on both the front and the back. The advertising card for each team features, on its back, an offer for obtaining an uncut sheet of 1981 Topps cards. These promotional cards were actually issued by Coke in only a few of the cities, and most of these cards have reached collectors hands through dealers who have purchased the cards through suppliers.

	MINT	EXC	G-VG
COMPLETE SET (132)	35.00	15.75	5.25
COMMON PLAYER (1-132)	.08	.03	.01
COMMON CHECKLIST	.03	.01	.00
☐ 1 Tom Burgmeier	.08	.03	.01
☐ 2 Dennis Eckersley	1.25	.50	.12
☐ 3 Dwight Evans	.60	.25	.06
☐ 4 Bob Stanley	.12	.05	.01
☐ 5 Glenn Hoffman	.08	.03	.01
☐ 6 Carney Lansford	.50	.20	.05
☐ 7 Frank Tanana	.20	.08	.02
☐ 8 Tony Perez	1.00	.40	.10
☐ 9 Jim Rice	.90	.40	.09
☐ 10 Dave Stapleton	.08	.03	.01
☐ 11 Carl Yastrzemski	2.50	1.00	.25
☐ 12 Red Sox Checklist (unnumbered)	.03	.01	.00
☐ 13 Tim Blackwell	.08	.03	.01
☐ 14 Bill Buckner	.20	.08	.02
☐ 15 Ivan DeJesus	.08	.03	.01
☐ 16 Leon Durham	.12	.05	.01
☐ 17 Steve Henderson	.08	.03	.01
☐ 18 Mike Krukow	.12	.05	.01
☐ 19 Ken Reitz	.08	.03	.01
☐ 20 Rick Reuschel	.25	.10	.02
☐ 21 Scot Thompson	.08	.03	.01
☐ 22 Dick Tidrow	.08	.03	.01
☐ 23 Mike Tyson	.08	.03	.01
☐ 24 Cubs Checklist (unnumbered)	.03	.01	.00
☐ 25 Britt Burns	.15	.06	.01
☐ 26 Todd Cruz	.08	.03	.01
☐ 27 Rich Dotson	.15	.06	.01
☐ 28 Jim Essian	.08	.03	.01
☐ 29 Ed Farmer	.08	.03	.01
☐ 30 Lamar Johnson	.08	.03	.01
☐ 31 Ron LeFlore	.12	.05	.01
☐ 32 Chet Lemon	.12	.05	.01

		MINT	EXC	G-VG
☐ 33	Bob Molinaro	.08	.03	.01
☐ 34	Jim Morrison	.08	.03	.01
☐ 35	Wayne Nordhagen	.08	.03	.01
☐ 36	White Sox Checklist	.03	.01	.00
	(unnumbered)			
☐ 37	Johnny Bench	2.25	.90	.22
☐ 38	Dave Collins	.12	.05	.01
☐ 39	Dave Concepcion	.30	.12	.03
☐ 40	Dan Driessen	.08	.03	.01
☐ 41	George Foster	.40	.16	.04
☐ 42	Ken Griffey	.40	.16	.04
☐ 43	Tom Hume	.08	.03	.01
☐ 44	Ray Knight	.20	.08	.02
☐ 45	Ron Oester	.12	.05	.01
☐ 46	Tom Seaver	3.00	1.25	.30
☐ 47	Mario Soto	.12	.05	.01
☐ 48	Reds Checklist	.03	.01	.00
	(unnumbered)			
☐ 49	Champ Summers	.08	.03	.01
☐ 50	Al Cowens	.08	.03	.01
☐ 51	Rich Hebner	.08	.03	.01
☐ 52	Steve Kemp	.12	.05	.01
☐ 53	Aurelio Lopez	.08	.03	.01
☐ 54	Jack Morris	1.50	.60	.15
☐ 55	Lance Parrish	1.00	.40	.10
☐ 56	Johnny Wockenfuss	.08	.03	.01
☐ 57	Alan Trammell	1.75	.70	.17
☐ 58	Lou Whitaker	1.25	.50	.12
☐ 59	Kirk Gibson	2.50	1.00	.25
☐ 60	Tigers Checklist	.03	.01	.00
	(unnumbered)			
☐ 61	Alan Ashby	.08	.03	.01
☐ 62	Cesar Cedeno	.12	.05	.01
☐ 63	Jose Cruz	.15	.06	.01
☐ 64	Art Howe	.15	.06	.01
☐ 65	Rafael Landestoy	.08	.03	.01
☐ 66	Joe Niekro	.20	.08	.02
☐ 67	Terry Puhl	.12	.05	.01
☐ 68	J.R. Richard	.15	.06	.01
☐ 69	Nolan Ryan	7.50	3.25	.75
☐ 70	Joe Sambito	.12	.05	.01
☐ 71	Don Sutton	1.25	.50	.12
☐ 72	Astros Checklist	.03	.01	.00
	(unnumbered)			
☐ 73	Willie Aikens	.10	.04	.01
☐ 74	George Brett	3.00	1.25	.30
☐ 75	Larry Gura	.12	.05	.01
☐ 76	Dennis Leonard	.12	.05	.01
☐ 77	Hal McRae	.20	.08	.02
☐ 78	Amos Otis	.20	.08	.02
☐ 79	Dan Quisenberry	.30	.12	.03
☐ 80	U.L. Washington	.08	.03	.01
☐ 81	John Wathan	.15	.06	.01
☐ 82	Frank White	.20	.08	.02
☐ 83	Willie Wilson	.25	.10	.02
☐ 84	Royals Checklist	.03	.01	.00
	(unnumbered)			
☐ 85	Neil Allen	.12	.05	.01
☐ 86	Doug Flynn	.08	.03	.01
☐ 87	Dave Kingman	.25	.10	.02
☐ 88	Randy Jones	.08	.03	.01
☐ 89	Pat Zachry	.08	.03	.01
☐ 90	Lee Mazzilli	.12	.05	.01
☐ 91	Rusty Staub	.25	.10	.02
☐ 92	Craig Swan	.08	.03	.01
☐ 93	Frank Taveras	.08	.03	.01
☐ 94	Alex Trevino	.08	.03	.01
☐ 95	Joel Youngblood	.08	.03	.01
☐ 96	Mets Checklist	.03	.01	.00
	(unnumbered)			
☐ 97	Bob Boone	.30	.12	.03
☐ 98	Larry Bowa	.25	.10	.02
☐ 99	Steve Carlton	1.50	.60	.15
☐ 100	Greg Luzinski	.20	.08	.02
☐ 101	Garry Maddox	.12	.05	.01
☐ 102	Bake McBride	.08	.03	.01
☐ 103	Tug McGraw	.25	.10	.02
☐ 104	Pete Rose	2.00	.80	.20
☐ 105	Mike Schmidt	3.25	1.35	.32
☐ 106	Lonnie Smith	.30	.12	.03
☐ 107	Manny Trillo	.08	.03	.01
☐ 108	Phillies Checklist	.03	.01	.00
	(unnumbered)			
☐ 109	Jim Bibby	.08	.03	.01
☐ 110	John Candelaria	.12	.05	.01
☐ 111	Mike Easler	.12	.05	.01
☐ 112	Tim Foli	.08	.03	.01
☐ 113	Phil Garner	.15	.06	.01
☐ 114	Bill Madlock	.20	.08	.02
☐ 115	Omar Moreno	.08	.03	.01
☐ 116	Ed Ott	.08	.03	.01
☐ 117	Dave Parker	1.00	.40	.10
☐ 118	Willie Stargell	1.00	.40	.10
☐ 119	Kent Tekulve	.12	.05	.01

		MINT	EXC	G-VG
☐ 120	Pirates Checklist	.03	.01	.00
	(unnumbered)			
☐ 121	Bob Forsch	.12	.05	.01
☐ 122	George Hendrick	.12	.05	.01
☐ 123	Keith Hernandez	.75	.30	.07
☐ 124	Tom Herr	.15	.06	.01
☐ 125	Sixto Lezcano	.08	.03	.01
☐ 126	Ken Oberkfell	.08	.03	.01
☐ 127	Darrell Porter	.12	.05	.01
☐ 128	Tony Scott	.08	.03	.01
☐ 129	Lary Sorensen	.08	.03	.01
☐ 130	Bruce Sutter	.30	.12	.03
☐ 131	Garry Templeton	.12	.05	.01
☐ 132	Cardinals Checklist	.03	.01	.00
	(unnumbered)			

1982 Coke Red Sox

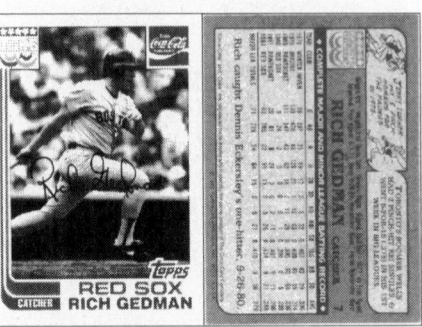

The cards in this 23-card set measure 2 1/2" by 3 1/2". This set of Boston Red Sox ballplayers was issued locally in the Boston area as a joint promotion by Brigham's Ice Cream Stores and Coca-Cola. The pictures are identical to those in the Topps regular 1982 issue, except that the colors are brighter and the Brigham and Coke logos appear inside the frame line. The reverses are done in red, black and gray, in contrast to the Topps set, and the number appears to the right of the position listing. The cards were initally distributed in three-card cello packs with an ice cream or Coca-Cola purchase but later became available as sets within the hobby. The unnumbered title or advertising card carries a premium offer on the reverse.

		MINT	EXC	G-VG
COMPLETE SET (23)		7.50	3.25	.75
COMMON PLAYER (1-23)		.08	.03	.01
☐ 1	Gary Allenson	.08	.03	.01
☐ 2	Tom Burgmeier	.08	.03	.01
☐ 3	Mark Clear	.12	.05	.01
☐ 4	Steve Crawford	.08	.03	.01
☐ 5	Dennis Eckersley	1.25	.50	.12
☐ 6	Dwight Evans	.75	.30	.07
☐ 7	Rich Gedman	.35	.15	.03
☐ 8	Garry Hancock	.08	.03	.01
☐ 9	Glen Hoffman	.08	.03	.01
☐ 10	Carney Lansford	.50	.20	.05
☐ 11	Rick Miller	.08	.03	.01
☐ 12	Reid Nichols	.08	.03	.01
☐ 13	Bob Ojeda	.35	.15	.03
☐ 14	Tony Perez	.90	.40	.09
☐ 15	Chuck Rainey	.08	.03	.01
☐ 16	Jerry Remy	.08	.03	.01
☐ 17	Jim Rice	.90	.40	.09
☐ 18	Bob Stanley	.15	.06	.01
☐ 19	Dave Stapleton	.08	.03	.01
☐ 20	Mike Torrez	.12	.05	.01
☐ 21	John Tudor	.40	.16	.04
☐ 22	Carl Yastrzemski	3.25	1.35	.32
☐ 23	Title Card	.03	.01	.00
	(unnumbered)			

1982 Coke Reds

JOHNNY BENCH

The cards in this 23-card set measure 2 1/2" by 3 1/2". The 1982 Coca-Cola Cincinnati Reds set, issued in conjunction with Topps, contains 22 cards of current Reds players. Although the cards of 15 players feature the exact photo used in the Topps' regular issue, the Coke photos have better coloration and appear sharper than their Topps counterparts. Six players, Cedeno, Harris, Hurdle, Kern, Krenchicki, and Trevino are new to the Redleg uniform via trades, while Paul Householder had formerly appeared on the Reds' 1982 Topps "Future Stars" card. The cards are numbered 1 to 22 on the red and gray reverse, and the Coke logo appears on both sides of the card. There is an unnumbered title card which contains a premium offer on the reverse.

		MINT	EXC	G-VG
COMPLETE SET (23)		7.50	3.25	.75
COMMON PLAYER (1-23)		.08	.03	.01
☐ 1	Johnny Bench	2.75	1.10	.27
☐ 2	Bruce Berenyi	.08	.03	.01
☐ 3	Larry Biittner	.08	.03	.01
☐ 4	Cesar Cedeno	.15	.06	.01
☐ 5	Dave Concepcion	.30	.12	.03
☐ 6	Dan Driessen	.12	.05	.01
☐ 7	Greg Harris	.30	.12	.03
☐ 8	Paul Householder	.08	.03	.01
☐ 9	Tom Hume	.08	.03	.01
☐ 10	Clint Hurdle	.12	.05	.01
☐ 11	Jim Kern	.08	.03	.01
☐ 12	Wayne Krenchicki	.08	.03	.01
☐ 13	Rafael Landestoy	.08	.03	.01
☐ 14	Charlie Leibrandt	.30	.12	.03
☐ 15	Mike O'Berry	.08	.03	.01
☐ 16	Ron Oester	.12	.05	.01
☐ 17	Frank Pastore	.08	.03	.01
☐ 18	Joe Price	.08	.03	.01
☐ 19	Tom Seaver	3.50	1.50	.35
☐ 20	Mario Soto	.15	.06	.01
☐ 21	Alex Trevino	.08	.03	.01
☐ 22	Mike Vail	.08	.03	.01
☐ 23	Title Card	.03	.01	.00
	(unnumbered)			

1985 Coke Dodgers Postcards

This 34-card set was sponsored by Coke, and the company logo appears on the back of the cards. These oversized cards measure approximately 3 1/2" by 5 1/2". The front design features glossy color player photos, bordered in white and with the player's name below the pictures. Except for the sponsor's logo, the backs are blank. The cards are unnumbered and checklisted below in alphabetical order.

	MINT	EXC	G-VG
COMPLETE SET (34)	15.00	6.50	2.15
COMMON PLAYER (1-34)	.40	.16	.04

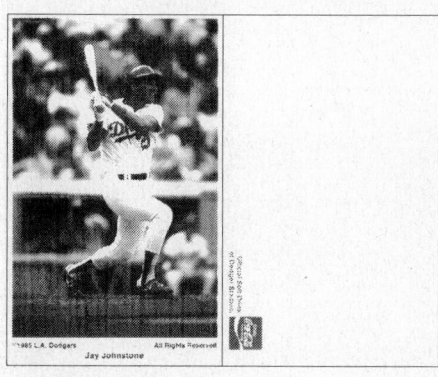

'1985 L.A. Dodgers   All Rights Reserved

Jay Johnstone

☐ 1	Joe Amalfitano CO	.40	.16	.04
☐ 2	Dave Anderson	.50	.20	.05
☐ 3	Bob Bailor	.40	.16	.04
☐ 4	Monty Basgall CO	.40	.16	.04
☐ 5	Tom Brennan	.40	.16	.04
☐ 6	Greg Brock	.40	.16	.04
☐ 7	Bobby Castillo	.40	.16	.04
☐ 8	Mark Cresse CO	.40	.16	.04
☐ 9	Carlos Diaz	.40	.16	.04
☐ 10	Mariano Duncan	.50	.20	.05
☐ 11	Pedro Guerrero	1.00	.40	.10
☐ 12	Orel Hershiser	2.50	1.00	.25
☐ 13	Rick Honeycutt	.50	.20	.05
☐ 14	Steve Howe	.40	.16	.04
☐ 15	Ken Howell	.40	.16	.04
☐ 16	Jay Johnstone	.50	.20	.05
☐ 17	Ken Landreaux	.40	.16	.04
☐ 18	Tom Lasorda MG	.75	.30	.07
☐ 19	Candy Maldonado	.50	.20	.05
☐ 20	Mike Marshall	.50	.20	.05
☐ 21	Manny Mota CO	.50	.20	.05
☐ 22	Tom Niedenfuer	.40	.16	.04
☐ 23	Al Oliver	.50	.20	.05
☐ 24	Alejandro Pena	.60	.25	.06
☐ 25	Ron Perranoski CO	.50	.20	.05
☐ 26	Jerry Reuss	.40	.16	.04
☐ 27	R.J. Reynolds	.40	.16	.04
☐ 28	Bill Russell	.50	.20	.05
☐ 29	Steve Sax	.75	.30	.07
☐ 30	Mike Scioscia	.50	.20	.05
☐ 31	Fernando Valenzuela	.75	.30	.07
☐ 32	Bob Welch	.75	.30	.07
☐ 33	Terry Whitfield	.40	.16	.04
☐ 34	Steve Yeager	.50	.20	.05

1985 Coke White Sox

This 30-card set features present and past Chicago White Sox players and personnel. Cards measure 2 5/8" by 4 1/8" and feature a red band at the bottom of the card. Within the red band are the White Sox logo, the player's name, position, uniform number, and a small oval portrait of an all-time White Sox Great at a similar position. The cards were available two at a time on Tuesday night White Sox home games or as a complete set through membership in the Coca-Cola White Sox Fan Club. The cards below are numbered by uniform number; the last three cards are unnumbered.

	MINT	EXC	G-VG
COMPLETE SET (30)	12.00	5.25	1.50
COMMON PLAYER	.35	.15	.03
☐ 0 Oscar Gamble	.35	.15	.03
Zeke Bonura			
☐ 1 Scott Fletcher	.60	.25	.06
Luke Appling			
☐ 3 Harold Baines	.90	.40	.09
Bill Melton			
☐ 5 Luis Salazar	.35	.15	.03
Chico Carrasquel			

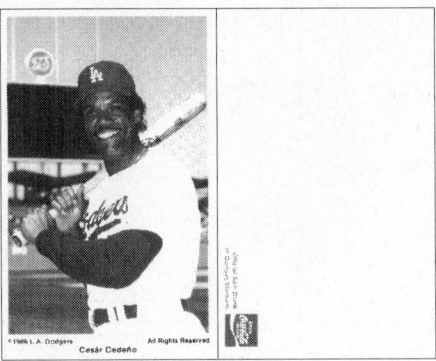

Cesar Cedeño

			MINT	EXC	G-VG
☐	7	Marc Hill	.35	.15	.03
		Sherm Lollar			
☐	8	Daryl Boston	.45	.18	.04
		Jim Landis			
☐	10	Tony LaRussa	.90	.40	.09
		Al Lopez			
☐	12	Julio Cruz	.45	.18	.04
		Nellie Fox			
☐	13	Ozzie Guillen	2.00	.80	.20
		Luis Aparicio			
☐	17	Jerry Hairston	.35	.15	.03
		Smoky Burgess			
☐	20	Joe DeSa	.35	.15	.03
		Carlos May			
☐	22	Joel Skinner	.35	.15	.03
		J.C. Martin			
☐	23	Rudy Law	.35	.15	.03
		Bill Skowron			
☐	24	Floyd Bannister	.45	.18	.04
		Red Faber			
☐	29	Greg Walker	.60	.25	.06
		Dick Allen			
☐	30	Gene Nelson	.60	.25	.06
		Early Wynn			
☐	32	Tim Hulett	.35	.15	.03
		Pete Ward			
☐	34	Richard Dotson	.45	.18	.04
		Ed Walsh			
☐	37	Dan Spillner	.35	.15	.03
		Thornton Lee			
☐	40	Britt Burns	.35	.15	.03
		Gary Peters			
☐	41	Tom Seaver	2.50	1.00	.25
		Ted Lyons			
☐	42	Ron Kittle	.60	.25	.06
		Minnie Minoso			
☐	43	Bob James	.45	.18	.04
		Hoyt Wilhelm			
☐	44	Tom Paciorek	.45	.18	.04
		Eddie Collins			
☐	46	Tim Lollar	.35	.15	.03
		Billy Pierce			
☐	50	Juan Agosto	.35	.15	.03
		Wilbur Wood			
☐	72	Carlton Fisk	2.00	.80	.20
		Ray Schalk			
☐	xx	Comiskey Park	.35	.15	.03
		(unnumbered)			
☐	xx	Nancy Faust	.35	.15	.03
		(park organist)			
		(unnumbered)			
☐	xx	Ribbie and Roobarb	.35	.15	.03
		(unnumbered)			

1986 Coke Dodgers Postcards

This 33-card Dodger set was sponsored by Coke, and the company logo appears on the back of the cards. The oversized cards measure approximately 3 1/2" by 5 1/2". The front design features glossy color player photos (mostly action), bordered in white and with the player's name below the picture. The backs

are blank. The cards are unnumbered and checklisted below in alphabetical order.

			MINT	EXC	G-VG
		COMPLETE SET (33)	12.50	5.50	1.65
		COMMON PLAYER (1-33)	.35	.15	.03
☐	1	Joe Amalfitano CO	.35	.15	.03
☐	2	Dave Anderson	.35	.15	.03
☐	3	Monty Basgall CO	.35	.15	.03
☐	4	Greg Brock	.35	.15	.03
☐	5	Enos Cabell	.35	.15	.03
☐	6	Cesar Cedeno	.45	.18	.04
☐	7	Mark Cresse CO	.35	.15	.03
☐	8	Mariano Duncan	.45	.18	.04
☐	9	Carlos Diaz	.35	.15	.03
☐	10	Pedro Guerrero	.75	.30	.07
☐	11	Orel Hershiser	1.00	.40	.10
☐	12	Ben Hines TR	.35	.15	.03
☐	13	Rick Honeycutt	.35	.15	.03
☐	14	Ken Howell	.35	.15	.03
☐	15	Ken Landreaux	.35	.15	.03
☐	16	Tom Lasorda MG	.60	.25	.06
☐	17	Bill Madlock	.45	.18	.04
☐	18	Mike Marshall	.45	.18	.04
☐	19	Len Matuszek	.35	.15	.03
☐	20	Manny Mota CO	.45	.18	.04
☐	21	Tom Niedenfuer	.35	.15	.03
☐	22	Alejandro Pena	.45	.18	.04
☐	23	Ron Perranoski CO	.45	.18	.04
☐	24	Dennis Powell	.35	.15	.03
☐	25	Jerry Reuss	.35	.15	.03
☐	26	Bill Russell	.45	.18	.04
☐	27	Steve Sax	.75	.30	.07
☐	28	Mike Scioscia	.45	.18	.04
☐	29	Alex Trevino	.35	.15	.03
☐	30	Fernando Valenzuela	.60	.25	.06
☐	31	Ed VandeBerg	.35	.15	.03
☐	32	Bob Welch	.60	.25	.06
☐	33	Terry Whitfield	.35	.15	.03

1986 Coke White Sox

This colorful 30-card set features a borderless photo on top of a blue-on-white name, position, and uniform number. Card backs provide complete major and minor season-by-season career statistical information. Since the cards are unnumbered, they are numbered below according to uniform number. The cards measure approximately 2 5/8" by 4". The five unnumbered non-player cards are listed at the end of the checklist below.

			MINT	EXC	G-VG
		COMPLETE SET (30)	13.50	6.00	1.85
		COMMON PLAYER	.35	.15	.03
☐	1	Wayne Tolleson	.35	.15	.03
☐	3	Harold Baines	1.00	.40	.10
☐	7	Marc Hill	.35	.15	.03
☐	8	Daryl Boston	.45	.18	.04
☐	12	Julio Cruz	.35	.15	.03

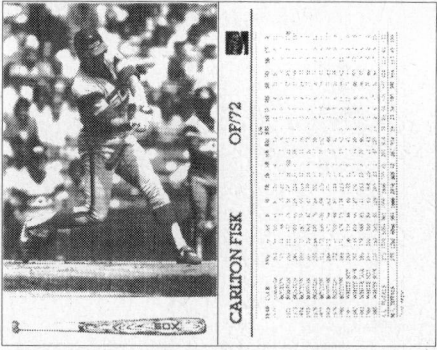

		MINT	EXC	G-VG
COMPLETE SET (18)		6.50	2.75	.65
COMMON PLAYER (1-18)		.30	.12	.03
☐ 1	Kirk Gibson	.75	.30	.07
☐ 2	Larry Herndon	.30	.12	.03
☐ 3	Walt Terrell	.40	.16	.04
☐ 4	Alan Trammell	1.00	.40	.10
☐ 5	Frank Tanana	.50	.20	.05
☐ 6	Pat Sheridan	.30	.12	.03
☐ 7	Jack Morris	.75	.30	.07
☐ 8	Mike Heath	.30	.12	.03
☐ 9	Dave Bergman	.30	.12	.03
☐ 10	Chet Lemon	.40	.16	.04
☐ 11	Dwight Lowry	.30	.12	.03
☐ 12	Dan Petry	.40	.16	.04
☐ 13	Darrell Evans	.40	.16	.04
☐ 14	Darnell Coles	.30	.12	.03
☐ 15	Willie Hernandez	.40	.16	.04
☐ 16	Lou Whitaker	.75	.30	.07
☐ 17	Tom Brookens	.30	.12	.03
☐ 18	John Grubb	.30	.12	.03

standard 2 1/2" by 3 1/2" and were produced by MSA, Mike Schechter Associates.

☐ 13	Ozzie Guillen	1.00	.40	.10
☐ 17	Jerry Hairston	.35	.15	.03
☐ 19	Floyd Bannister	.45	.18	.04
☐ 20	Reid Nichols	.35	.15	.03
☐ 22	Joel Skinner	.35	.15	.03
☐ 24	Dave Schmidt	.45	.18	.04
☐ 26	Bobby Bonilla	5.00	2.25	.50
☐ 29	Greg Walker	.45	.18	.04
☐ 30	Gene Nelson	.45	.18	.04
☐ 32	Tim Hulett	.35	.15	.03
☐ 33	Neil Allen	.45	.18	.04
☐ 34	Richard Dotson	.45	.18	.04
☐ 40	Joe Cowley	.35	.15	.03
☐ 41	Tom Seaver	2.00	.80	.20
☐ 42	Ron Kittle	.60	.25	.06
☐ 43	Bob James	.35	.15	.03
☐ 44	John Cangelosi	.35	.15	.03
☐ 50	Juan Agosto	.35	.15	.03
☐ 52	Joel Davis	.35	.15	.03
☐ 72	Carlton Fisk	1.50	.60	.15
☐ xx	Nancy Faust ORG (unnumbered)	.35	.15	.03
☐ xx	Ken"Hawk" Harrelson (unnumbered)	.45	.18	.04
☐ xx	Tony LaRussa MG (unnumbered)	.45	.18	.04
☐ xx	Minnie Minoso CO (unnumbered)	.45	.18	.04
☐ xx	Ribbie and Roobarb (unnumbered)	.35	.15	.03

1987 Coke Tigers

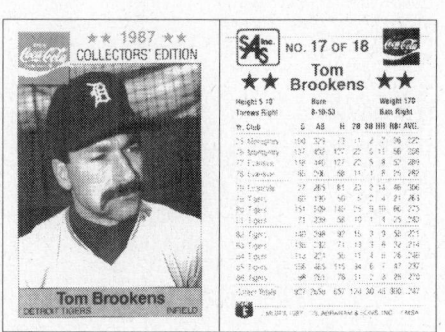

Coca-Cola in collaboration with S. Abraham and Sons issued a set of 18 cards featuring the Detroit Tigers. The cards are numbered on the back. The cards are distinguished by the bright yellow border framing the full-color picture of the player on the front. The cards were issued in panels of four: three player cards and a team logo card. The cards measure the

1987 Coke White Sox

This colorful 30-card set features a card front with a blue-bordered photo and name, position, and uniform number. Card backs provide complete major and minor season-by-season career statistical information. Since the cards are unnumbered, they are numbered below in uniform number order. The cards measure approximately 2 5/8" by 4". The three unnumbered non-player cards are listed at the end. The card set, sponsored by Coca-Cola, is an exclusive for fan club members who join (for 10.00) in 1987.

		MINT	EXC	G-VG
COMPLETE SET (30)		10.00	4.50	1.25
COMMON PLAYER (1-30)		.25	.10	.02
☐ 1	Jerry Royster 1	.25	.10	.02
☐ 2	Harold Baines 3	.75	.30	.07
☐ 3	Ron Karkovice 5	.35	.15	.03
☐ 4	Daryl Boston 8	.35	.15	.03
☐ 5	Fred Manrique 10	.25	.10	.02
☐ 6	Steve Lyons 12	.35	.15	.03
☐ 7	Ozzie Guillen 13	.75	.30	.07
☐ 8	Russ Morman 14	.25	.10	.02
☐ 9	Donnie Hill 15	.25	.10	.02
☐ 10	Jim Fregosi MG 16	.35	.15	.03
☐ 11	Jerry Hairston 17	.25	.10	.02
☐ 12	Floyd Bannister 19	.35	.15	.03
☐ 13	Gary Redus 21	.35	.15	.03
☐ 14	Ivan Calderon 22	.75	.30	.07
☐ 15	Ron Hassey 25	.35	.15	.03
☐ 16	Jose DeLeon 26	.35	.15	.03
☐ 17	Greg Walker 29	.50	.20	.05
☐ 18	Tim Hulett 32	.25	.10	.02
☐ 19	Neil Allen 33	.35	.15	.03
☐ 20	Richard Dotson 34	.35	.15	.03

		MINT	EXC	G-VG
☐ 21	Ray Searage 36	.25	.10	.02
☐ 22	Bobby Thigpen 37	1.25	.50	.12
☐ 23	Jim Winn 40	.25	.10	.02
☐ 24	Bob James 43	.25	.10	.02
☐ 25	Joel McKeon 50	.25	.10	.02
☐ 26	Joel Davis 52	.25	.10	.02
☐ 27	Carlton Fisk 72	1.50	.60	.15
☐ 28	Nancy Faust ORG (unnumbered)	.25	.10	.02
☐ 29	Minnie Minoso (unnumbered)	.35	.15	.03
☐ 30	Robbie and Roobarb (unnumbered)	.25	.10	.02

1988 Coke Padres

These cards were actually issued as two separate promotions. The first eight cards were issued as a perforated sheet (approximately 7 1/2" by 10 1/2") as a Coca Cola Junior Padres Club promotion. The other 12 cards were issued later on specific game days to members of the Junior Padres Club. All the cards are standard size, 2 1/2" by 3 1/2" and are unnumbered. Cards that were on the perforated panel are indicated by PAN in the checklist below. Since the cards are unnumbered, they are listed below by uniform number, which is featured prominently on the card fronts.

		MINT	EXC	G-VG
COMPLETE SET (21)		35.00	15.75	5.25
COMMON PANEL PLAYER		.50	.20	.05
COMMON NON-PAN PLAYER (1-21)		1.25	.50	.12
☐ 1	Garry Templeton PAN	.50	.20	.05
☐ 5	Randy Ready PAN	.50	.20	.05
☐ 7	Keith Moreland	1.25	.50	.12
☐ 8	John Kruk	2.00	.80	.20
☐ 9	Benito Santiago	6.00	2.50	.60
☐ 10	Larry Bowa MG PAN	.50	.20	.05
☐ 11	Tim Flannery PAN	.50	.20	.05
☐ 14	Carmelo Martinez	1.25	.50	.12
☐ 15	Jack McKeon MG	1.25	.50	.12
☐ 19	Tony Gwynn	12.50	5.50	1.65
☐ 22	Stan Jefferson	1.50	.60	.15
☐ 27	Mark Parent	1.25	.50	.12
☐ 30	Eric Show	1.50	.60	.15
☐ 31	Eddie Whitson	1.75	.70	.17
☐ 35	Chris Brown PAN	.50	.20	.05
☐ 41	Lance McCullers	1.50	.60	.15
☐ 45	Jimmy Jones PAN	.50	.20	.05
☐ 48	Mark Davis PAN	1.50	.60	.15
☐ 51	Greg Booker	1.25	.50	.12
☐ 55	Mark Grant PAN	.50	.20	.05
☐ xx	Padres Logo PAN (program explanation on reverse)	.50	.20	.05

1988 Coke White Sox

This colorful 30-card set features a card front with a red-bordered photo and name and position. Card backs provide a narrative without any statistical tables. Since the cards are unnumbered, they are numbered below in alphabetical order according to the subject's name or card's title. The cards measure approximately 2 5/8" by 3 1/2". The card set, sponsored by Coca-Cola, was for fan club members who join (for 10.00) in 1988. The cards were also given out at the May 22nd game at Comiskey Park. These cards do not even list the player's uniform number anywhere on the card. Card backs are printed in black and gray on thin white card stock.

		MINT	EXC	G-VG
COMPLETE SET (30)		6.50	2.75	.65
COMMON PLAYER (1-30)		.15	.06	.01
☐ 1	Harold Baines	.50	.20	.05
☐ 2	Daryl Boston	.25	.10	.02
☐ 3	Ivan Calderon	.50	.20	.05
☐ 4	Comiskey Park	.15	.06	.01
☐ 5	John Davis	.25	.10	.02
☐ 6	Nancy Faust (organist)	.15	.06	.01
☐ 7	Jim Fregosi MG	.25	.10	.02
☐ 8	Carlton Fisk	.90	.40	.09
☐ 9	Ozzie Guillen	.60	.25	.06
☐ 10	Donnie Hill	.15	.06	.01
☐ 11	Ricky Horton	.25	.10	.02
☐ 12	Lance Johnson	.25	.10	.02
☐ 13	Dave LaPoint	.25	.10	.02
☐ 14	Bill Long	.15	.06	.01
☐ 15	Steve Lyons	.25	.10	.02
☐ 16	Jack McDowell	.50	.20	.05
☐ 17	Fred Manrique	.15	.06	.01
☐ 18	Minnie Minoso	.35	.15	.03
☐ 19	Dan Pasqua	.25	.10	.02
☐ 20	John Pawlowski	.15	.06	.01
☐ 21	Melido Perez	.35	.15	.03
☐ 22	Billy Pierce	.25	.10	.02
☐ 23	Jerry Reuss	.25	.10	.02
☐ 24	Gary Redus	.25	.10	.02
☐ 25	Ribbie and Roobarb	.15	.06	.01
☐ 26	Mark Salas	.15	.06	.01
☐ 27	Jose Segura	.25	.10	.02
☐ 28	Bobby Thigpen	.60	.25	.06
☐ 29	Greg Walker	.35	.15	.03
☐ 30	Kenny Williams	.25	.10	.02

1989 Coke Padres

These cards were actually issued as two separate promotions. The first nine cards were issued as a perforated sheet (approximately 7 1/2" by 10 1/2") as a Coca Cola Junior Padres Club promotion. The other 12 cards were issued later on specific game days to members of the Junior Padres Club. All the cards are standard size, 2 1/2" by 3 1/2" and are unnumbered. Cards that were on the perforated panel are indicated by PAN in the checklist below. Since the cards are unnumbered, they are listed below in alphabetical order by subject. Marvell Wynne was planned for the set but was not issued since he was traded before the set was released; Walt Terrell also is tougher to find due to his mid-season trade.

		MINT	EXC	G-VG
COMPLETE SET (21)		32.00	14.25	4.75
COMMON PLAYER (1-21)		1.25	.50	.12
COMMON PLAYER PAN		.50	.20	.05
☐ 1	Roberto Alomar PAN	1.25	.50	.12
☐ 2	Jack Clark	2.50	1.00	.25
☐ 3	Mark Davis	2.50	1.00	.25
☐ 4	Tim Flannery	1.25	.50	.12
☐ 5	Mark Grant	1.25	.50	.12
☐ 6	Tony Gwynn	11.00	5.00	1.35
☐ 7	Bruce Hurst	2.50	1.00	.25
☐ 8	Chris James	1.75	.70	.17
☐ 9	Carmelo Martinez PAN	.50	.20	.05
☐ 10	Jack McKeon MG PAN	.50	.20	.05
☐ 11	Mark Parent	1.25	.50	.12
☐ 12	Dennis Rasmussen PAN	.50	.20	.05
☐ 13	Randy Ready PAN	.50	.20	.05
☐ 14	Leon Bip Roberts	1.75	.70	.17
☐ 15	Luis Salazar	1.25	.50	.12
☐ 16	Benito Santiago	4.00	1.75	.40
☐ 17	Eric Show PAN	.60	.25	.06
☐ 18	Gary Templeton PAN	.60	.25	.06
☐ 19	Walt Terrell SP	6.50	2.75	.65
☐ 20	Ed Whitson PAN	.60	.25	.06
☐ xx	Padres Logo PAN	.50	.20	.05

1989 Coke White Sox

The 1989 Coke Chicago White Sox set contains 30 cards measuring 2 5/8" by 3 1/2". The players in the set represent the White Sox opening day roster. The fronts are blue. The horizontally oriented backs are gray and white, and feature biographical information. The set was a promotional give-away August 10, 1989 at the Baseball Card Night game against the Oakland A's to the first 15,000 fans. The set includes a special

"New Comiskey Park, 1991" card. The complete set was also available with (10.00) membership in the Chi-Sox Fan Club. The cards in the set are numbered on the backs in the lower right corner in very small print.

		MINT	EXC	G-VG
COMPLETE SET (30)		6.50	2.75	.65
COMMON PLAYER (1-30)		.15	.06	.01
☐ 1	New Comiskey Park 1991	.25	.10	.02
☐ 2	Comiskey Park	.15	.06	.01
☐ 3	Jeff Torborg MG	.25	.10	.02
☐ 4	Coaching Staff	.25	.10	.02
☐ 5	Harold Baines	.50	.20	.05
☐ 6	Daryl Boston	.25	.10	.02
☐ 7	Ivan Calderon	.45	.18	.04
☐ 8	Carlton Fisk	1.00	.40	.10
☐ 9	Dave Gallagher	.25	.10	.02
☐ 10	Ozzie Guillen	.50	.20	.05
☐ 11	Shawn Hillegas	.15	.06	.01
☐ 12	Barry Jones	.25	.10	.02
☐ 13	Ron Karkovice	.15	.06	.01
☐ 14	Eric King	.25	.10	.02
☐ 15	Ron Kittle	.25	.10	.02
☐ 16	Bill Long	.15	.06	.01
☐ 17	Steve Lyons	.25	.10	.02
☐ 18	Donn Pall	.15	.06	.01
☐ 19	Dan Pasqua	.25	.10	.02
☐ 20	Ken Patterson	.15	.06	.01
☐ 21	Melido Perez	.25	.10	.02
☐ 22	Jerry Reuss	.15	.06	.01
☐ 23	Billy Joe Robidoux	.15	.06	.01
☐ 24	Steve Rosenberg	.15	.06	.01
☐ 25	Jeff Schaefer	.15	.06	.01
☐ 26	Bobby Thigpen	.50	.20	.05
☐ 27	Greg Walker	.25	.10	.02
☐ 28	Eddie Williams	.15	.06	.01
☐ 29	Nancy Faust (organist)	.15	.06	.01
☐ 30	Minnie Minoso	.25	.10	.02

1990 Coke Padres

These standard-size cards (2 1/2" by 3 1/2") were issued in two forms: a 7 1/2" by 10 5/8" perforated sheet featuring eight player cards and the Padre logo card (marked by PAN below) as well as 12 individual player cards. The sheet was issued to Coca-Cola Junior Padres Club Members as a starter set, and club members who attended the first six Junior Padres Club games received two additional cards per game. The fronts have color action player photos, with two-toned brown borders on a beige card face. The team logo appears in the upper right corner, and the lower left corner of each picture is cut out to provide space for the player's number and position. In dark brown lettering, the horizontally oriented backs present biography, statistics, and career highlights. The cards are unnumbered and checklisted below in alphabetical order, with the team logo card listed at the end.

		MINT	EXC	G-VG
	COMPLETE SET (21)	20.00	8.50	2.75
	COMMON PLAYER PAN (1-21)	.40	.16	.04
	COMMON PLAYER NON-PAN	1.00	.40	.10
☐ 1	Roberto Alomar	4.00	1.75	.40
☐ 2	Andy Benes PAN	.60	.25	.06
☐ 3	Joe Carter	3.00	1.25	.30
☐ 4	Jack Clark	2.00	.80	.20
☐ 5	Mark Grant PAN	.40	.16	.04
☐ 6	Tony Gwynn	6.00	2.50	.60
☐ 7	Greg Harris	1.25	.50	.12
☐ 8	Bruce Hurst	1.50	.60	.15
☐ 9	Craig Lefferts	1.25	.50	.12
☐ 10	Fred Lynn	1.25	.50	.12
☐ 11	Jack McKeon MG PAN	.40	.16	.04
☐ 12	Mike Pagliarulo	1.00	.40	.10
☐ 13	Mark Parent PAN	.40	.16	.04
☐ 14	Dennis Rasmussen PAN	.40	.16	.04
☐ 15	Bip Roberts PAN	.50	.20	.05
☐ 16	Benito Santiago	2.50	1.00	.25
☐ 17	Calvin Schiraldi	1.00	.40	.10
☐ 18	Eric Show PAN	.40	.16	.04
☐ 19	Garry Templeton	1.00	.40	.10
☐ 20	Ed Whitson PAN	.40	.16	.04
☐ xx	Padres Logo PAN	.40	.16	.04

1990 Coke/Kroger Tigers

(45) CECIL FIELDER
Infielder

The 1990 Coke/Kroger Detroit Tigers set contains 28 cards, measuring approximately 2 7/8" by 4 1/4", which was used as a giveaway at the July 14th Detroit Tigers home game. The player photo is surrounded by green borders with complete career statistical information printed on the back of each card. This set is checklisted alphabetically in the listings below.

		MINT	EXC	G-VG
	COMPLETE SET (28)	7.50	3.25	.75
	COMMON PLAYER (1-28)	.25	.10	.02
☐ 1	Sparky Anderson MG	.35	.15	.03
☐ 2	Dave Bergman	.25	.10	.02
☐ 3	Brian DuBois	.35	.15	.03
☐ 4	Cecil Fielder	1.25	.50	.12
☐ 5	Paul Gibson	.35	.15	.03
☐ 6	Jerry Don Gleaton	.25	.10	.02
☐ 7	Mike Heath	.25	.10	.02
☐ 8	Mike Henneman	.35	.15	.03
☐ 9	Tracy Jones	.25	.10	.02
☐ 10	Chet Lemon	.35	.15	.03
☐ 11	Urbano Lugo	.25	.10	.02
☐ 12	Jack Morris	.75	.30	.07
☐ 13	Lloyd Moseby	.35	.15	.03
☐ 14	Matt Nokes	.45	.18	.04
☐ 15	Edwin Nunez	.25	.10	.02
☐ 16	Dan Petry	.35	.15	.03
☐ 17	Tony Phillips	.35	.15	.03
☐ 18	Kevin Ritz	.35	.15	.03
☐ 19	Jeff Robinson	.35	.15	.03
☐ 20	Ed Romero	.25	.10	.02
☐ 21	Mark Salas	.25	.10	.02
☐ 22	Larry Sheets	.25	.10	.02
☐ 23	Frank Tanana	.35	.15	.03
☐ 24	Alan Trammell	1.00	.40	.10
☐ 25	Gary Ward	.25	.10	.02

☐ 26	Lou Whitaker	.60	.25	.06
☐ 27	Ken Williams	.25	.10	.02
☐ 28	Tigers Coaches UER	.25	.10	.02
	Billy Consolo			
	Alex Grammas			
	Billy Muffet			
	(sic, Muffett)			
	Vada Pinson			
	Dick Tracewski			

1990 Coke White Sox

IVAN CALDERON • 22

The 1990 Coca Cola White Sox set contains 30 cards. The set is a beautiful full-color set commemorating the 1990 White Sox who were celebrating the eightieth and last season played in old Comiskey Park. This (approximately) 2 5/8" by 3 1/2" set has a Comiskey Park logo on the front with 1989 statistics and a brief biography on the back. The set is checklisted alphabetically and notated by the uniform number on the front of the card.

		MINT	EXC	G-VG
	COMPLETE SET (30)	7.50	3.25	.75
	COMMON PLAYER (1-30)	.25	.10	.02
☐ 1	Ivan Calderon 22	.60	.25	.06
☐ 2	Wayne Edwards 45	.35	.15	.03
☐ 3	Carlton Fisk 72	1.00	.40	.10
☐ 4	Scott Fletcher 7	.25	.10	.02
☐ 5	Dave Gallagher 17	.25	.10	.02
☐ 6	Craig Grebeck 14	.35	.15	.03
☐ 7	Ozzie Guillen 13	.50	.20	.05
☐ 8	Greg Hibbard 27	.35	.15	.03
☐ 9	Lance Johnson 1	.35	.15	.03
☐ 10	Barry Jones 50	.35	.15	.03
☐ 11	Ron Karkovice 20	.35	.15	.03
☐ 12	Eric King 36	.35	.15	.03
☐ 13	Ron Kittle 42	.35	.15	.03
☐ 14	Jerry Kutzler 52	.25	.10	.02
☐ 15	Steve Lyons 12	.35	.15	.03
☐ 16	Carlos Martinez 24	.35	.15	.03
☐ 17	Jack McDowell 29	.60	.25	.06
☐ 18	Donn Pall 30	.25	.10	.02
☐ 19	Dan Pasqua 44	.35	.15	.03
☐ 20	Ken Patterson 34	.25	.10	.02
☐ 21	Melido Perez 33	.35	.15	.03
☐ 22	Scott Radinsky 31	.35	.15	.03
☐ 23	Sammy Sosa 25	.60	.25	.06
☐ 24	Bobby Thigpen 37	.60	.25	.06
☐ 25	Frank Thomas	4.00	1.75	.40
☐ 26	Jeff Torborg MG 10	.35	.15	.03
☐ 27	Robin Ventura 23	1.00	.40	.10
☐ 28	Rookies: Jerry Kutzler	.50	.20	.05
	Wayne Edwards			
	Craig Grebeck			
	Scott Radinsky			
	Robin Ventura			
☐ 29	Captains: Ozzie	.50	.20	.05
	Guillen and			
	Carlton Fisk			
☐ 30	Coaches: Barry Foote	.25	.10	.02
	Sammy Ellis			
	Walt Hriniak			
	Terry Bevington			
	Dave LaRoche			
	Joe Nossek			
	Ron Clark			

1991 Coke Don Mattingly

This 15-card set was sponsored by Coca-Cola and measures the standard size (2 1/2" by 3 1/2"). The front design features mostly color action player photos on a white and blue pinstripe card face. Each card has a year number on the top edge of the picture, and the Coke logo is superimposed at the lower left corner. In a horizontal format the backs are printed in blue and red, and present career highlights and statistics. The cards are numbered on the back.

		MINT	EXC	G-VG
COMPLETE SET (15)		6.00	2.50	.60
COMMON PLAYER (1-15)		.60	.25	.06
☐ 1	Don Mattingly 1978	.60	.25	.06
☐ 2	Don Mattingly 1979	.60	.25	.06
☐ 3	Don Mattingly 1980	.60	.25	.06
☐ 4	Don Mattingly 1981 (black and white)	.60	.25	.06
☐ 5	Don Mattingly 1982	.60	.25	.06
☐ 6	Don Mattingly 1983	.60	.25	.06
☐ 7	Don Mattingly 1983-84 (black and white)	.60	.25	.06
☐ 8	Don Mattingly 1984	.60	.25	.06
☐ 9	Don Mattingly 1985	.60	.25	.06
☐ 10	Don Mattingly 1986	.60	.25	.06
☐ 11	Don Mattingly 1987	.60	.25	.06
☐ 12	Don Mattingly 1990	.60	.25	.06
☐ 13	Don Mattingly 1991 (Photo)	.60	.25	.06
☐ 14	Don Mattingly 1991 (Drawing)	.60	.25	.06
☐ 15	Don Mattingly 1991 (Career statistics)	.60	.25	.06

1991 Coke/Kroger Tigers

The 1991 Coke/Kroger Tigers set contains 27 cards measuring 2 7/8" by 4 1/4". The fronts feature a mix of action or posed color player photos with white borders. The player's name is written vertically in a purple stripe on the right side of the picture, and the player's number appears in an inverted orange triangle toward the bottom of the stripe. In a horizontal format the back has the sponsors' logos and presents complete statistical information. The set is skip-numbered by uniform number and checklisted below accordingly.

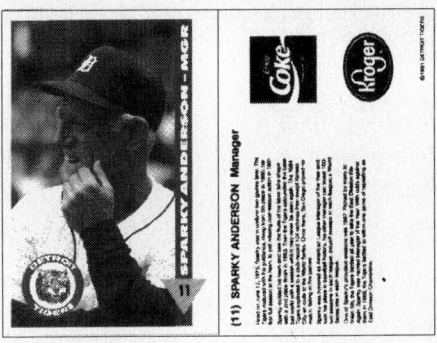

		MINT	EXC	G-VG
COMPLETE SET (27)		7.00	3.00	.70
COMMON PLAYER		.25	.10	.02
☐ 1	Lou Whitaker	.60	.25	.06
☐ 3	Alan Trammell	1.00	.40	.10
☐ 4	Tony Phillips	.35	.15	.03
☐ 10	Andy Allanson	.25	.10	.02
☐ 11	Sparky Anderson MG	.35	.15	.03
☐ 14	Dave Bergman	.25	.10	.02
☐ 15	Lloyd Moseby	.35	.15	.03
☐ 19	Jerry Don Gleaton	.25	.10	.02
☐ 20	Mickey Tettleton	.45	.18	.04
☐ 22	Milt Cuyler	.45	.18	.04
☐ 23	Mark Leiter	.35	.15	.03
☐ 24	Travis Fryman	1.25	.50	.12
☐ 25	John Shelby	.25	.10	.02
☐ 26	Frank Tanana	.35	.15	.03
☐ 27	Mark Salas	.25	.10	.02
☐ 29	Pete Incaviglia	.35	.15	.03
☐ 31	Kevin Ritz	.25	.10	.02
☐ 35	Walt Terrell	.25	.10	.02
☐ 36	Bill Gullickson	.35	.15	.03
☐ 39	Mike Henneman	.35	.15	.03
☐ 44	Rob Deer	.35	.15	.03
☐ 45	Cecil Fielder	1.00	.40	.10
☐ 46	Dan Petry	.35	.15	.03
☐ 48	Paul Gibson	.35	.15	.03
☐ 49	Steve Searcy	.25	.10	.02
☐ 55	John Cerutti	.25	.10	.02
☐ xx	Coaches Card	.25	.10	.02
	Billy Consolo			
	Jim Davenport			
	Alex Grammas			
	Billy Muffett			
	Vada Pinson			
	Dick Tracewski			

1990 Colla Jose Canseco

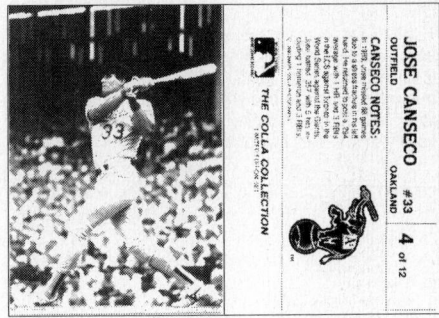

This 12-card set, issued by noted photographer Barry Colla, measures the standard size 2 1/2" by 3 1/2" and features Jose Canseco in various poses. The fronts are beautiful full-color photos while the backs contain notes about Canseco. According to the back of the first card in the set, 20,000 numbered sets were issued.

	MINT	EXC	G-VG
COMPLETE SET (12)	10.00	4.50	1.25
COMMON PLAYER (1-12)	1.00	.40	.10
☐ 1 Jose Canseco (Portrait)	1.00	.40	.10
☐ 2 Jose Canseco (Follow-Through, Bat at Waist)	1.00	.40	.10
☐ 3 Jose Canseco (Follow-Through, Bat at Shoulders)	1.00	.40	.10
☐ 4 Jose Canseco (Follow-Through, Helmetless)	1.00	.40	.10
☐ 5 Jose Canseco (Dugout Portrait)	1.00	.40	.10
☐ 6 Jose Canseco (Profile, Bat on Shoulder)	1.00	.40	.10
☐ 7 Jose Canseco (Batting Cage Pose)	1.00	.40	.10
☐ 8 Jose Canseco (Follow-Through, ready to run)	1.00	.40	.10
☐ 9 Jose Canseco (Portrait, Kneeling)	1.00	.40	.10
☐ 10 Jose Canseco (Portrait, bat under shoulder)	1.00	.40	.10
☐ 11 Jose Canseco (At Bat-rack)	1.00	.40	.10
☐ 12 Jose Canseco (Running Bases)	1.00	.40	.10

1990 Colla Will Clark

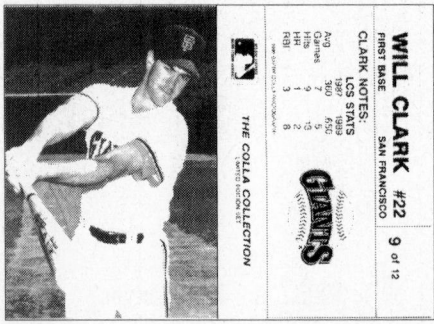

This 12-card set again features the beautiful photography of Barry Colla; this time Will Clark is the featured player. Each card in the set measures the standard size, 2 1/2" by 3 1/2". Again the fronts are borderless photos while the back contains notes about Will Clark. According to card number one, 15,000 numbered sets were produced.

	MINT	EXC	G-VG
COMPLETE SET (12)	12.50	5.50	1.65
COMMON PLAYER (1-12)	1.25	.50	.12
☐ 1 Will Clark (Batting Pose, Gray Shirt)	1.25	.50	.12
☐ 2 Will Clark (Bat at Shoulder, Short Sleeves)	1.25	.50	.12
☐ 3 Will Clark (Smiling)	1.25	.50	.12
☐ 4 Will Clark (Ball in Glove)	1.25	.50	.12
☐ 5 Will Clark	1.25	.50	.12
☐ 6 Will Clark (Batting Pose, Long Sleeves)	1.25	.50	.12
☐ 7 Will Clark (Follow-Through, bat over head)	1.25	.50	.12
☐ 8 Will Clark (Follow-Through, hand released)	1.25	.50	.12
☐ 9 Will Clark (Standing, bat on ground)	1.25	.50	.12
☐ 10 Will Clark (Pose with bat at waist)	1.25	.50	.12
☐ 11 Will Clark (Portrait with Bat)	1.25	.50	.12
☐ 12 Will Clark (Kneeling with Glove)	1.25	.50	.12
(Preparing to Field)			

1990 Colla Kevin Maas

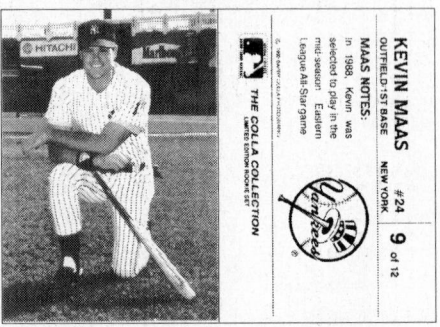

This extremely attractive 12-card standard size 2 1/2" by 3 1/2" card set was produced by photographer Barry Colla. The set was limited to 7,500 made and each card has some facts relevant to Maas' career on the back of the card. The set was produced to be sold in its own special box and the boxes were issued 24 sets to each bigger box. All of the boxes were produced in the team's colors.

	MINT	EXC	G-VG
COMPLETE SET (12)	9.00	4.00	.90
COMMON PLAYER (1-12)	1.00	.40	.10
☐ 1 Kevin Maas (Batting Pose)	1.00	.40	.10
☐ 2 Kevin Maas (Sitting on Dugout Steps)	1.00	.40	.10
☐ 3 Kevin Maas (Taking a lead on basepaths)	1.00	.40	.10
☐ 4 Kevin Maas (Close-Up)	1.00	.40	.10
☐ 5 Kevin Maas (Standing in Dugout)	1.00	.40	.10
☐ 6 Kevin Maas (Kneeling with bat)	1.00	.40	.10
☐ 7 Kevin Maas (Fielding Pose)	1.00	.40	.10
☐ 8 Kevin Maas (Follow Through 24 showing)	1.00	.40	.10
☐ 9 Kevin Maas (Portrait with Bat)	1.00	.40	.10
☐ 10 Kevin Maas (Follow Through)	1.00	.40	.10
☐ 11 Kevin Maas (Side Portrait)	1.00	.40	.10
☐ 12 Kevin Maas (Taking Batting Practice)	1.00	.40	.10

1990 Colla Don Mattingly

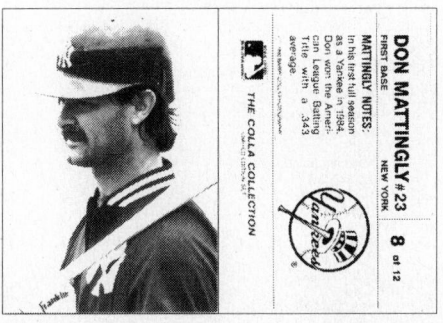

This 13-card set features the photography of Barry Colla as he features Don Mattingly in various poses. Each card in the set measures the standard size, 2 1/2" by 3 1/2". The set was limited to 15,000 numbered sets and feature full-color photographs on the borderless fronts along with notes about Mattingly on the back.

	MINT	EXC	G-VG
COMPLETE SET (13)	9.00	4.00	.90
COMMON PLAYER (1-13)	1.00	.40	.10
☐ 1 Don Mattingly (Head-On Portrait)	1.00	.40	.10
☐ 2 Don Mattingly (Preparing to Swing)	1.00	.40	.10
☐ 3 Don Mattingly (Running Bases)	1.00	.40	.10
☐ 4 Don Mattingly (Portrait with glove in hand)	1.00	.40	.10
☐ 5 Don Mattingly (Backhanding a Ball)	1.00	.40	.10
☐ 6 Don Mattingly (Follow-Through, Bat Pointing Up)	1.00	.40	.10
☐ 7 Don Mattingly (Follow-Through, bat to be released)	1.00	.40	.10
☐ 8 Don Mattingly (Facing left, bat on shoulder)	1.00	.40	.10
☐ 9 Don Mattingly (Portrait, facing right)	1.00	.40	.10
☐ 10 Don Mattingly (Practice Swing, bat at waist)	1.00	.40	.10
☐ 11 Don Mattingly (Preparing to field ball)	1.00	.40	.10
☐ 12 Don Mattingly (Kneeling)	1.00	.40	.10
☐ 13 Promo Card	1.00	.40	.10

1991 Colla Roberto Alomar

This 13-card standard size (2 1/2" by 3 1/2") set features colorful photos of Roberto Alomar by noted photographer Barry Colla. The high gloss borderless color photos were packed in a full color collector's box. Only 7,500 sets were produced, with 24 sets per display carton. The first card of each set bears the registration number. In black lettering on a light gray background, the horizontally oriented backs feature facts about Alomar. The cards are numbered on the back.

	MINT	EXC	G-VG
COMPLETE SET (13)	10.00	4.50	1.25
COMMON PLAYER (1-12)	1.00	.40	.10
☐ 1 Roberto Alomar (Headshot)	1.00	.40	.10
☐ 2 Roberto Alomar (In mid-air at 2nd preparing to throw)	1.00	.40	.10
☐ 3 Roberto Alomar (In mid-air at 2nd throwing ball)	1.00	.40	.10
☐ 4 Roberto Alomar (Pose showing right shoulder)	1.00	.40	.10
☐ 5 Roberto Alomar (Pose showing left shoulder)	1.00	.40	.10
☐ 6 Roberto Alomar (Watching ball after hit)	1.00	.40	.10
☐ 7 Roberto Alomar (Follow through, hands at waist)	1.00	.40	.10
☐ 8 Roberto Alomar (Headshot, bat on shoulder)	1.00	.40	.10
☐ 9 Roberto Alomar (Posed kneeling)	1.00	.40	.10
☐ 10 Roberto Alomar (Follow through, hands at chest)	1.00	.40	.10
☐ 11 Roberto Alomar (Posed with bat on left shoulder)	1.00	.40	.10
☐ 12 Roberto Alomar (Posed with left shoulder forward and bat on right shoulder)	1.00	.40	.10
☐ xx Roberto Alomar (Posed with bat on right shoulder)	1.00	.40	.10

1991 Colla Barry Bonds

This 13-card standard size (2 1/2" by 3 1/2") set features colorful photos of Barry Bonds by noted photographer Barry Colla. The high gloss borderless color photos were packed in a full color collector's box. Only 7,500 were produced, with 24 sets per display carton. The first card of each set bears the registration number. In black lettering on a gray background, the horizontally oriented backs feature facts about Bonds. The cards are numbered on the back. This set was issued so late in 1991 that it was actually January 1992 before the set was in general distribution.

	MINT	EXC	G-VG
COMPLETE SET (13)	10.00	4.50	1.25
COMMON PLAYER (1-12)	1.00	.40	.10
☐ 1 Barry Bonds (Posed with bat behind head)	1.00	.40	.10

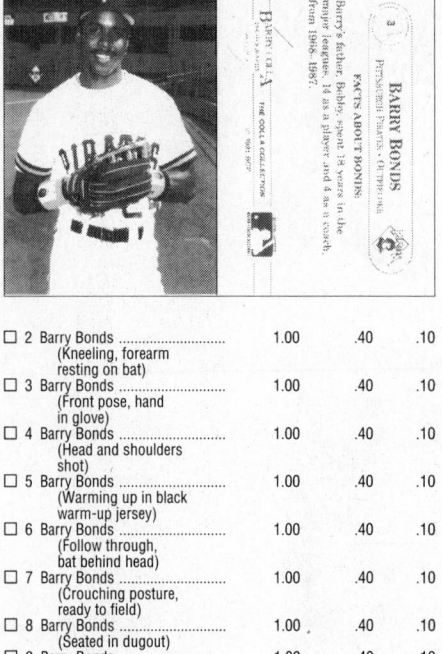

registration number. In black lettering on a light gray background, the horizontally oriented backs feature facts about Carter. The cards are numbered on the back.

	MINT	EXC	G-VG
COMPLETE SET (13)	10.00	4.50	1.25
COMMON PLAYER (1-12)	1.00	.40	.10
☐ 1 Joe Carter .... (Posed, bat above shoulder)	1.00	.40	.10
☐ 2 Joe Carter .... (Kneeling pose, arm on bat)	1.00	.40	.10
☐ 3 Joe Carter .... (Head and shoulders pose)	1.00	.40	.10
☐ 4 Joe Carter .... (Posed, bat on right shoulder)	1.00	.40	.10
☐ 5 Joe Carter .... (Kneeling pose, close up)	1.00	.40	.10
☐ 6 Joe Carter .... (Ready to throw from outfield)	1.00	.40	.10
☐ 7 Joe Carter .... (After throw from outfield)	1.00	.40	.10
☐ 8 Joe Carter .... (Watching fly ball after hit)	1.00	.40	.10
☐ 9 Joe Carter .... (Bat on shoulder in blue uniform)	1.00	.40	.10
☐ 10 Joe Carter .... (Batting helmet in hand)	1.00	.40	.10
☐ 11 Joe Carter .... (Posed in blue uni- form and sunglasses)	1.00	.40	.10
☐ 12 Joe Carter .... (Posed with bat on shoulder, from waist up)	1.00	.40	.10
☐ xx Joe Carter .... Title card (Front pose, bat on right shoulder)	1.00	.40	.10

☐ 2 Barry Bonds .... (Kneeling, forearm resting on bat)	1.00	.40	.10
☐ 3 Barry Bonds .... (Front pose, hand in glove)	1.00	.40	.10
☐ 4 Barry Bonds .... (Head and shoulders shot)	1.00	.40	.10
☐ 5 Barry Bonds .... (Warming up in black warm-up jersey)	1.00	.40	.10
☐ 6 Barry Bonds .... (Follow through, bat behind head)	1.00	.40	.10
☐ 7 Barry Bonds .... (Crouching posture, ready to field)	1.00	.40	.10
☐ 8 Barry Bonds .... (Seated in dugout)	1.00	.40	.10
☐ 9 Barry Bonds .... (Right shoulder forward, bat on shoulder)	1.00	.40	.10
☐ 10 Barry Bonds .... (Front pose, glove in front of chest)	1.00	.40	.10
☐ 11 Barry Bonds .... (Right shoulder forward, batting pose)	1.00	.40	.10
☐ 12 Barry Bonds .... (Front pose, arms crossed)	1.00	.40	.10
☐ xx Title card .... (Close-up pose, forearm resting on bat)	1.00	.40	.10

1991 Colla Dwight Gooden

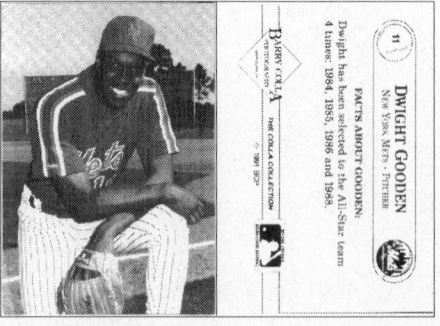

This 13-card standard size (2 1/2" by 3 1/2") set features colorful photos of Dwight Gooden by noted photographer Barry Colla. The high gloss borderless color photos were packed in a full color collector's box. Only 15,000 sets were produced, with 24 sets per display carton. The first card of each set bears the registration number. In black lettering on a light gray background, the horizontally oriented backs feature facts about Gooden. The cards are numbered on the back.

1991 Colla Joe Carter

This 13-card standard size (2 1/2" by 3 1/2") set features colorful photos of Joe Carter by noted photographer Barry Colla. The high gloss borderless color photos were packed in a full color collector's box. Only 7,500 sets were produced, with 24 sets per display carton. The first card of each set bears the

	MINT	EXC	G-VG
COMPLETE SET (13)	10.00	4.50	1.25
COMMON PLAYER (1-12)	1.00	.40	.10
☐ 1 Dwight Gooden .... (Head and shoulders pose)	1.00	.40	.10
☐ 2 Dwight Gooden .... (Pitching, arm behind back)	1.00	.40	.10
☐ 3 Dwight Gooden .... (Pitching, arm above head)	1.00	.40	.10
☐ 4 Dwight Gooden .... (Posed with glove)	1.00	.40	.10
☐ 5 Dwight Gooden .... (Kneeling, glove on knee)	1.00	.40	.10
☐ 6 Dwight Gooden .... (Posed, blue uniform)	1.00	.40	.10
☐ 7 Dwight Gooden .... (Pitching, just after release)	1.00	.40	.10
☐ 8 Dwight Gooden .... (Pose with glove, left shoulder forward)	1.00	.40	.10
☐ 9 Dwight Gooden .... (Posed in dugout)	1.00	.40	.10
☐ 10 Dwight Gooden .... (Head and shoulders pose, blue uniform)	1.00	.40	.10
☐ 11 Dwight Gooden .... (Kneeling, arms on left knee)	1.00	.40	.10
☐ 12 Dwight Gooden .... (Left shoulder pose)	1.00	.40	.10
☐ xx Dwight Gooden .... Title Card (Front pose)	1.00	.40	.10

1991 Colla Ken Griffey Jr.

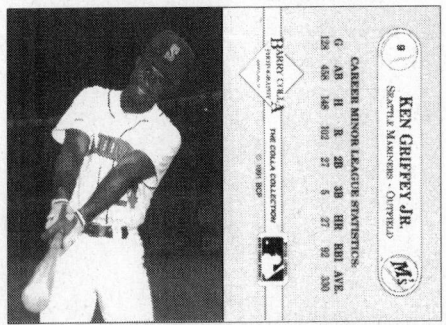

This 12-card standard size (2 1/2" by 3 1/2") set features colorful photos of Ken Griffey Jr. by noted photographer Barry Colla. The high gloss borderless color photos were packed in a full color collector's box. Only 15,000 sets were produced, with 24 sets per display carton. The first card of each set bears the registration number. In black lettering on a light gray background, the horizontally oriented backs feature facts about Ken Griffey. The cards are numbered on the back.

	MINT	EXC	G-VG
COMPLETE SET (12)	10.00	4.50	1.25
COMMON PLAYER (1-12)	1.00	.40	.10
☐ 1 Ken Griffey Jr. .... (Bat on shoulder, right side)	1.00	.40	.10
☐ 2 Ken Griffey Jr. .... (Bat on shoulder, straight on)	1.00	.40	.10
☐ 3 Ken Griffey Jr. .... (Follow-through)	1.00	.40	.10

	MINT	EXC	G-VG
☐ 4 Ken Griffey Jr. .... (Beside batting cage)	1.00	.40	.10
☐ 5 Ken Griffey Jr. .... (In dugout)	1.00	.40	.10
☐ 6 Ken Griffey Jr. .... (Batting pose)	1.00	.40	.10
☐ 7 Ken Griffey Jr. .... (Adjusting hat)	1.00	.40	.10
☐ 8 Ken Griffey Jr. .... (Swinging bat)	1.00	.40	.10
☐ 9 Ken Griffey Jr. .... (Pose, middle of swing)	1.00	.40	.10
☐ 10 Ken Griffey Jr. .... (Bat at waist)	1.00	.40	.10
☐ 11 Ken Griffey Jr. .... (Middle of swing)	1.00	.40	.10
☐ 12 Ken Griffey Jr. .... (Hitting fly ball)	1.00	.40	.10

1991 Colla Dave Justice

This 13-card standard size (2 1/2" by 3 1/2") set features colorful photos of Dave Justice by noted photographer Barry Colla. The high gloss borderless color photos were packed in a full color collector's box. Only 15,000 sets were produced, with 24 sets per display carton. The first card of each set bears the registration number. In black lettering on a light gray background, the horizontally oriented backs feature facts about Justice. The cards are numbered on the back.

	MINT	EXC	G-VG
COMPLETE SET (13)	10.00	4.50	1.25
COMMON PLAYER (1-12)	1.00	.40	.10
☐ 1 Dave Justice .... (Bat on shoulder, White jersey)	1.00	.40	.10
☐ 2 Dave Justice .... (Leaning on bat)	1.00	.40	.10
☐ 3 Dave Justice .... (Running in outfield)	1.00	.40	.10
☐ 4 Dave Justice .... (Throwing from the outfield)	1.00	.40	.10
☐ 5 Dave Justice .... (Bat over shoulder)	1.00	.40	.10
☐ 6 Dave Justice .... (Looking through batting cage)	1.00	.40	.10
☐ 7 Dave Justice .... (After ball thrown)	1.00	.40	.10
☐ 8 Dave Justice .... (Just before batting)	1.00	.40	.10
☐ 9 Dave Justice .... (Watching hit ball)	1.00	.40	.10
☐ 10 Dave Justice .... (Running to first)	1.00	.40	.10
☐ 11 Dave Justice .... (Warm-up exercises Stretching)	1.00	.40	.10

		MINT	EXC	G-VG
☐ 12	Dave Justice .... (Bat on shoulder, Squatting posture)	1.00	.40	.10
☐ xx	Title card .... (Bat on shoulder, Blue jersey)	1.00	.40	.10

1991 Colla Ryne Sandberg

This 13-card standard size (2 1/2" by 3 1/2") set features colorful photos of Ryne Sandberg by noted photographer Barry Colla. The high gloss borderless color photos were packed in a full color collector's box. Only 15,000 sets were produced, with 24 sets per display carton. The first card of each set bears the registration number. In black lettering on a light gray background, the horizontally oriented backs feature facts about Ryne Sandberg. The cards are numbered on the back.

		MINT	EXC	G-VG
COMPLETE SET (13)		10.00	4.50	1.25
COMMON PLAYER (1-12)		1.00	.40	.10
☐ 1	Ryne Sandberg .... (Follow-through, bat in motion)	1.00	.40	.10
☐ 2	Ryne Sandberg .... (Preparing to field blue uniform)	1.00	.40	.10
☐ 3	Ryne Sandberg .... (Awaiting throw)	1.00	.40	.10
☐ 4	Ryne Sandberg .... (Follow-Through facing left close up)	1.00	.40	.10
☐ 5	Ryne Sandberg .... (Holding bat behind back)	1.00	.40	.10
☐ 6	Ryne Sandberg .... (Pivoting at second)	1.00	.40	.10
☐ 7	Ryne Sandberg .... (Ready to throw)	1.00	.40	.10
☐ 8	Ryne Sandberg .... (Left profile shot)	1.00	.40	.10
☐ 9	Ryne Sandberg .... (Holding bat at waist)	1.00	.40	.10
☐ 10	Ryne Sandberg .... (Awaiting pitch)	1.00	.40	.10
☐ 11	Ryne Sandberg .... (Follow-through, bat at shoulders)	1.00	.40	.10
☐ 12	Ryne Sandberg .... (Batting Cage Pose)	1.00	.40	.10
☐ xx	Ryne Sandberg .... (Header card)	1.00	.40	.10

1991 Colla Darryl Strawberry

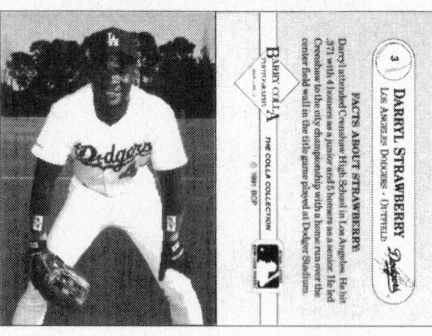

This 13-card standard size (2 1/2" by 3 1/2") set features colorful photos of Darryl Strawberry by noted photographer Barry Colla. The high gloss borderless color photos were packed in a full color collector's box. Only 15,000 sets were produced, with 24 sets per display carton. The first card of each set bears the registration number. In black lettering on a light gray background, the horizontally oriented backs feature facts about Strawberry. The cards are numbered on the back.

		MINT	EXC	G-VG
COMPLETE SET (13)		10.00	4.50	1.25
COMMON PLAYER (1-12)		1.00	.40	.10
☐ 1	Darryl Strawberry .... (Posed follow through)	1.00	.40	.10
☐ 2	Darryl Strawberry .... (Bat on shoulder)	1.00	.40	.10
☐ 3	Darryl Strawberry .... (Posed with glove)	1.00	.40	.10
☐ 4	Darryl Strawberry .... (Kneeling with bat)	1.00	.40	.10
☐ 5	Darryl Strawberry .... (Head shot with flip-up sunglasses)	1.00	.40	.10
☐ 6	Darryl Strawberry .... (Ready to run in base path)	1.00	.40	.10
☐ 7	Darryl Strawberry .... (Awaiting fly ball)	1.00	.40	.10
☐ 8	Darryl Strawberry .... (Head shot with batting helmet)	1.00	.40	.10
☐ 9	Darryl Strawberry .... (Follow through after hit)	1.00	.40	.10
☐ 10	Darryl Strawberry .... (Watching hit ball)	1.00	.40	.10
☐ 11	Darryl Strawberry .... (Waiting for at bat)	1.00	.40	.10
☐ 12	Darryl Strawberry .... (Running bases)	1.00	.40	.10
☐ xx	Title card .... (Two bats on shoulder)	1.00	.40	.10

1990 Collect-A-Books

The 1990 Collect-A-Books set was issued by CMC (Collectors marketing Corp.) in three different sets (boxes) of 12 players apiece. The sets (boxes) were distinguishable by color, red, yellow, or green. The Collect-A-Books were in the style of the 1970 Topps Comic Book inserts but were much more profesionally made. The cards all fit into a 9-pocket sheet (since they are standard size, 2 1/2" by 3 1/2") even though they can be expanded. The set contains an interesting mixture of retired and current players.

		MINT	EXC	G-VG
	COMPLETE SET (36)	8.00	3.50	.80
	COMMON PLAYER (1-36)	.20	.08	.02
☐ 1	Bo Jackson	.75	.30	.07
☐ 2	Dwight Gooden	.40	.16	.04
☐ 3	Ken Griffey Jr.	.90	.40	.09
☐ 4	Will Clark	.50	.20	.05
☐ 5	Ozzie Smith	.30	.12	.03
☐ 6	Orel Hershiser	.25	.10	.02
☐ 7	Ruben Sierra	.30	.12	.03
☐ 8	Rickey Henderson	.50	.20	.05
☐ 9	Robin Yount	.30	.12	.03
☐ 10	Babe Ruth	.50	.20	.05
☐ 11	Ernie Banks	.25	.10	.02
☐ 12	Carl Yastrzemski	.30	.12	.03
☐ 13	Don Mattingly	.75	.30	.07
☐ 14	Nolan Ryan	.90	.40	.09
☐ 15	Jerome Walton	.25	.10	.02
☐ 16	Kevin Mitchell	.25	.10	.02
☐ 17	Tony Gwynn	.35	.15	.03
☐ 18	Dave Stewart	.20	.08	.02
☐ 19	Roger Clemens	.60	.25	.06
☐ 20	Darryl Strawberry	.50	.20	.05
☐ 21	George Brett	.35	.15	.03
☐ 22	Hank Aaron	.40	.16	.04
☐ 23	Ted Williams	.40	.16	.04
☐ 24	Warren Spahn	.20	.08	.02
☐ 25	Jose Canseco	.75	.30	.07
☐ 26	Wade Boggs	.50	.20	.05
☐ 27	Jim Abbott	.35	.15	.03
☐ 28	Eric Davis	.45	.18	.04
☐ 29	Ryne Sandberg	.90	.40	.09
☐ 30	Bret Saberhagen	.20	.08	.02
☐ 31	Mark Grace	.40	.16	.04
☐ 32	Gregg Olson	.25	.10	.02
☐ 33	Kirby Puckett	.50	.20	.05
☐ 34	Lou Gehrig	.50	.20	.05
☐ 35	Roberto Clemente	.35	.15	.03
☐ 36	Bob Feller	.25	.10	.02

Marketing Corp., the 1990 Collect-a-Book producer, was a division within the Impel Corporation. This 1991 set was issued under Impel's Line Drive brand. Each book consists of eight pages and fits into a standard size plastic sheet. The set features 27 active stars and nine famous retired stars. An action shot of the player is pictured on the first two pages. The next four pages has textual information broken down into biographical information, two pages of more detailed personal information, and a page of statistics. The inside back cover has a quote from the player pictured while the back cover has an attractive drawing of the player. Unlike the 1990 issue, the Collect-A-Books were issued in random packs.

		MINT	EXC	G-VG
	COMPLETE SET (36)	8.00	3.50	.80
	COMMON PLAYER (1-36)	.20	.08	.02
☐ 1	Roger Clemens	.60	.25	.06
☐ 2	Cal Ripken	.75	.30	.07
☐ 3	Nolan Ryan	.90	.40	.09
☐ 4	Ken Griffey Jr.	.90	.40	.09
☐ 5	Bob Welch	.20	.08	.02
☐ 6	Kevin Mitchell	.40	.16	.04
☐ 7	Kirby Puckett	.50	.20	.05
☐ 8	Len Dykstra	.20	.08	.02
☐ 9	Ben McDonald	.30	.12	.03
☐ 10	Don Drysdale	.30	.12	.03
☐ 11	Lou Brock	.30	.12	.03
☐ 12	Ralph Kiner	.30	.12	.03
☐ 13	Jose Canseco	.75	.30	.07
☐ 14	Cecil Fielder	.50	.20	.05
☐ 15	Ryne Sandberg	.75	.30	.07
☐ 16	Wade Boggs	.50	.20	.05
☐ 17	Dwight Gooden	.40	.16	.04
☐ 18	Ramon Martinez	.40	.16	.04
☐ 19	Tony Gwynn	.40	.16	.04
☐ 20	Mark Grace	.30	.12	.03
☐ 21	Kevin Maas	.30	.12	.03
☐ 22	Thurman Munson	.30	.12	.03
☐ 23	Bob Gibson	.30	.12	.03
☐ 24	Bill Mazeroski	.20	.08	.02
☐ 25	Rickey Henderson	.75	.30	.07
☐ 26	Barry Bonds	.40	.16	.04
☐ 27	Jose Rijo	.20	.08	.02
☐ 28	George Brett	.40	.16	.04
☐ 29	Doug Drabek	.20	.08	.02
☐ 30	Matt Williams	.35	.15	.03
☐ 31	Barry Larkin	.30	.12	.03
☐ 32	Dave Stewart	.20	.08	.02
☐ 33	Dave Justice	.60	.25	.06
☐ 34	Harmon Killebrew	.30	.12	.03
☐ 35	Yogi Berra	.35	.15	.03
☐ 36	Billy Williams	.25	.10	.02

1983 Conlon Marketcom

1991 Collect-A-Books

This 36-card set, which measures the standard 2 1/2" by 3 1/2", was issued by Impel for the second consecutive year. Collectors

This set of 60 Charles Martin Conlon photo cards was produced by Marketcom in conjunction with The Sporting News. The cards are large size, approximately 4 1/2" by 6 1/8" and are in a sepia tone. The players selected for the set are members of the 1933 American and National League All-Star teams as well as

Negro League All-Stars. These cards are numbered at the bottom of each reverse. The set numbering is American League (1-24), National League (25-48), and Negro League (49-60). In the upper right corner of each card's obverse is printed "1933 American (National or Negro League as appropriate) All Stars." Each obverse also features a facsimile autograph of the player pictured.

	MINT	EXC	G-VG
COMPLETE SET (60)	20.00	8.50	2.75
COMMON PLAYER (1-24)	.25	.10	.02
COMMON PLAYER (25-48)	.25	.10	.02
COMMON PLAYER (49-60)	.35	.15	.03

		MINT	EXC	G-VG
☐	1 James Emory Foxx	.50	.20	.05
☐	2 Heinie Manush	.25	.10	.02
☐	3 Lou Gehrig	1.00	.40	.10
☐	4 Al Simmons	.25	.10	.02
☐	5 Charlie Gehringer	.35	.15	.03
☐	6 Luke Appling	.35	.15	.03
☐	7 Mickey Cochrane	.45	.18	.04
☐	8 Joe Kuhel	.25	.10	.02
☐	9 Bill Dickey	.45	.18	.04
☐	10 Pinky Higgins	.25	.10	.02
☐	11 Roy Johnson	.25	.10	.02
☐	12 Ben Chapman	.25	.10	.02
☐	13 Urban Hodapp	.25	.10	.02
☐	14 Joe Cronin	.35	.15	.03
☐	15 Evar Swanson	.25	.10	.02
☐	16 Earl Averill	.25	.10	.02
☐	17 Babe Ruth	1.50	.60	.15
☐	18 Tony Lazzeri	.35	.15	.03
☐	19 Alvin Crowder	.25	.10	.02
☐	20 Lefty Grove	.45	.18	.04
☐	21 Earl Whitehill	.25	.10	.02
☐	22 Lefty Gomez	.45	.18	.04
☐	23 Mel Harder	.25	.10	.02
☐	24 Tommy Bridges	.25	.10	.02
☐	25 Chuck Klein	.35	.15	.03
☐	26 Spud Davis	.25	.10	.02
☐	27 Riggs Stephenson	.25	.10	.02
☐	28 Tony Piet	.25	.10	.02
☐	29 Bill Terry	.35	.15	.03
☐	30 Wes Schulmerich	.25	.10	.02
☐	31 Pepper Martin	.25	.10	.02
☐	32 Arky Vaughan	.35	.15	.03
☐	33 Wally Berger	.25	.10	.02
☐	34 Ripper Collins	.25	.10	.02
☐	35 Fred Lindstrom	.25	.10	.02
☐	36 Chick Fullis	.25	.10	.02
☐	37 Paul Waner	.35	.15	.03
☐	38 Johnny Frederick	.25	.10	.02
☐	39 Joe Medwick	.35	.15	.03
☐	40 Pie Traynor	.35	.15	.03
☐	41 Frankie Frisch	.35	.15	.03
☐	42 Chick Hafey	.25	.10	.02
☐	43 Carl Hubbell	.35	.15	.03
☐	44 Guy Bush	.25	.10	.02
☐	45 Dizzy Dean	.60	.25	.06
☐	46 Hal Schumacher	.25	.10	.02
☐	47 Larry French	.25	.10	.02
☐	48 Lon Warneke	.25	.10	.02
☐	49 Cool Papa Bell	.60	.25	.06
☐	50 Oscar Charleston	.60	.25	.06
☐	51 Josh Gibson	.75	.30	.07
☐	52 Satch Paige	.75	.30	.07
☐	53 Dave Malarcher	.35	.15	.03
☐	54 John Henry Lloyd	.60	.25	.06
☐	55 Rube Foster	.60	.25	.06
☐	56 Buck Leonard	.60	.25	.06
☐	57 Smoky Joe Williams	.35	.15	.03
☐	58 Willie Wells	.35	.15	.03
☐	59 Judy Johnson	.60	.25	.06
☐	60 Martin DiHigo	.60	.25	.06

1986 Conlon Series 1

This 60-card set was produced from the black and white photos in the Charles Martin Conlon collection. Each set comes with a special card which contains the number of that set out of the 12,000 sets which were produced. The cards measure 2 1/2" by 3 1/2" and are printed in sepia tones. The cards are individually numbered on the back.

	MINT	EXC	G-VG
COMPLETE SET (60)	15.00	6.50	2.15
COMMON PLAYER (1-60)	.25	.10	.02

		MINT	EXC	G-VG
☐	1 Henry Louis Gehrig	1.00	.40	.10
☐	2 Tyrus Raymond Cobb	.90	.40	.09
☐	3 Grover C. Alexander	.35	.15	.03
☐	4 Walter Perry Johnson	.60	.25	.06
☐	5 William Joseph Klem	.40	.16	.04
☐	6 Tyrus Raymond Cobb	.90	.40	.09
☐	7 Gordon S. Cochrane	.35	.15	.03
☐	8 Paul Glee Waner	.25	.10	.02
☐	9 Joseph Edward Cronin	.25	.10	.02
☐	10 Jay Hanna Dean	.60	.25	.06
☐	11 Leo Ernest Durocher	.35	.15	.03
☐	12 James Emory Foxx	.35	.15	.03
☐	13 George Herman Ruth	1.50	.60	.15
☐	14 Miguel Angel Gonzalez	.25	.10	.02
	Frank Francis Frisch			
	Clyde Ellsworth Wares			
☐	15 Carl Owen Hubbell	.35	.15	.03
☐	16 Miller James Huggins	.25	.10	.02
☐	17 Henry Louis Gehrig	.90	.40	.09
☐	18 Connie McGillicuddy	.35	.15	.03
☐	19 Henry Emmett Manush	.25	.10	.02
☐	20 George Herman Ruth	1.50	.60	.15
☐	22 John L.R. Martin	.25	.10	.02
☐	23 Christopher Mathewson	.60	.25	.06
☐	24 Tyrus Raymond Cobb	.90	.40	.09
☐	25 Stanley R. Harris	.25	.10	.02
☐	26 Waite Charles Hoyt	.25	.10	.02
☐	27 Richard W. Marquard	.25	.10	.02
☐	28 Joseph V. McCarthy	.25	.10	.02
☐	29 John Joseph McGraw	.25	.10	.02
☐	30 Tristram Speaker	.35	.15	.03
☐	31 William Harold Terry	.35	.15	.03
☐	32 Christopher Mathewson	.60	.25	.06
☐	33 Charles D. Stengel	.60	.25	.06
☐	34 Robert William Meusel	.25	.10	.02
☐	35 George Edward Waddell	.25	.10	.02
☐	36 Melvin Thomas Ott	.35	.15	.03
☐	37 Roger T. Peckinpaugh	.25	.10	.02
☐	38 Harold Joseph Traynor	.25	.10	.02
☐	39 Charles Albert Bender	.25	.10	.02
☐	40 John Wesley Coombs	.25	.10	.02
☐	41 Tyrus Raymond Cobb	.90	.40	.09
☐	42 Harry Edwin Heilmann	.25	.10	.02
☐	43 Charles L. Gehringer	.35	.15	.03
☐	44 Rogers Hornsby	.60	.25	.06
☐	45 Vernon Gomez	.45	.18	.04
☐	46 Christopher Mathewson	.60	.25	.06
☐	47 Robert Moses Grove	.45	.18	.04
☐	48 George Herman Ruth	1.50	.60	.15
☐	49 Frederick C. Merkle	.25	.10	.02
☐	50 George Herman Ruth	1.50	.60	.15
☐	51 Herbert J. Pennock	.25	.10	.02
☐	52 Henry Louis Gehrig	.90	.40	.09
☐	53 Fred Clifford Clarke	.25	.10	.02
☐	54 George Herman Ruth	1.50	.60	.15
☐	55 John Peter Wagner	.60	.25	.06
☐	56 Lewis Robert Wilson	.35	.15	.03
☐	57 Henry Louis Gehrig	.90	.40	.09
☐	58 Lloyd James Waner	.25	.10	.02
☐	59 Charles Martin Conlon	.25	.10	.02
☐	60 Conlon and Margie	.25	.10	.02
☐	xx Set Number Card	.25	.10	.02
	(unnumbered)			

1987 Conlon Series 2

The second series of 60 Charles Martin Conlon photo cards was produced by World Wide Sports in conjunction with The Sporting News. The cards are standard size, 2 1/2" by 3 1/2" and are in a sepia tone. Supposedly 12,000 sets were produced. The photos were selected and background information written by Paul MacFarlane of The Sporting News. The cards are individually numbered on the back.

	MINT	EXC	G-VG
COMPLETE SET (60)	11.00	5.00	1.35
COMMON PLAYER (1-60)	.25	.10	.02
☐ 1 Henry Gehrig	1.00	.40	.10
☐ 2 Vernon Gomez	.40	.16	.04
☐ 3 Christopher Mathewson	.60	.25	.06
☐ 4 Grover Alexander	.35	.15	.03
☐ 5 Tyrus Cobb	.90	.40	.09
☐ 6 Walter Johnson	.60	.25	.06
☐ 7 Charles Adams	.25	.10	.02
☐ 8 Nicholas Altrock	.25	.10	.02
☐ 9 Al Schacht	.25	.10	.02
☐ 10 Hugh Critz	.25	.10	.02
☐ 11 Henry Cullop	.25	.10	.02
☐ 12 Jacob Daubert	.25	.10	.02
☐ 13 William Donovan	.25	.10	.02
☐ 14 Charles Hafey	.25	.10	.02
☐ 15 William Hallahan	.25	.10	.02
☐ 16 Fred Haney	.25	.10	.02
☐ 17 Charles Hartnett	.25	.10	.02
☐ 18 Walter Henline	.25	.10	.02
☐ 19 Edwin Rommel	.25	.10	.02
☐ 20 Ralph Pinelli	.25	.10	.02
☐ 21 Robert Meusel	.25	.10	.02
☐ 22 Emil Meusel	.25	.10	.02
☐ 23 Smead Jolley	.25	.10	.02
☐ 24 Isaac Boone	.25	.10	.02
☐ 25 Earl Webb	.25	.10	.02
☐ 26 Charles Comiskey	.35	.15	.03
☐ 27 Edward Collins	.35	.15	.03
☐ 28 George Weaver	.35	.15	.03
☐ 29 Edward Cicotte	.35	.15	.03
☐ 30 Samuel Crawford	.25	.10	.02
☐ 31 Charles Dressen	.25	.10	.02
☐ 32 Arthur Fletcher	.25	.10	.02
☐ 33 Hugh Duffy	.35	.15	.03
☐ 34 Ira Flagstead	.25	.10	.02
☐ 35 Harry Hooper	.25	.10	.02
☐ 36 George Lewis	.25	.10	.02
☐ 37 James Dykes	.25	.10	.02
☐ 38 Leon Goslin	.25	.10	.02
☐ 39 Henry Gowdy	.25	.10	.02
☐ 40 Charles Grimm	.25	.10	.02
☐ 41 Mark Koenig	.25	.10	.02
☐ 42 James Hogan	.25	.10	.02
☐ 43 William Jacobson	.25	.10	.02
☐ 44 Fielder Jones	.25	.10	.02
☐ 45 George Kelly	.25	.10	.02
☐ 46 Adolpho Luque	.25	.10	.02
☐ 47 Walter Maranville	.25	.10	.02
☐ 48 Carl Mays	.25	.10	.02
☐ 49 Edward Plank	.35	.15	.03
☐ 50 Hubert Pruett	.25	.10	.02
☐ 51 John Quinn	.25	.10	.02
☐ 52 Charles Rhem	.25	.10	.02
☐ 53 Amos Rusie	.35	.15	.03
☐ 54 Edd Roush	.25	.10	.02
☐ 55 Raymond Schalk	.35	.15	.03
☐ 56 Ernest Shore	.25	.10	.02
☐ 57 Joe Wood	.25	.10	.02
☐ 58 George Sisler	.35	.15	.03
☐ 59 James Thorpe	1.50	.60	.15
☐ 60 Earl Whitehill	.25	.10	.02

1988 Conlon Series 3

This third series of 30 Charles Martin Conlon photo cards was produced by World Wide Sports in conjunction with The Sporting News. The cards are standard size, 2 1/2" by 3 1/2" and are in a sepia tone. The photos were selected and background information written by Paul MacFarlane of The Sporting News. These cards are unnumbered and hence are listed below in alphabetical order. Series 3 is indicated in the lower right corner of each card's reverse. A black and white logo for the "Baseball Immortals" and The Conlon Collection is over-printed in the lower left corner of each obverse.

	MINT	EXC	G-VG
COMPLETE SET (30)	6.00	2.50	.60
COMMON PLAYER (1-30)	.25	.10	.02
☐ 1 Ace Adams	.25	.10	.02
☐ 2 Grover C. Alexander	.35	.15	.03
☐ 3 Elden Auker	.25	.10	.02
☐ 4 Jack Barry	.25	.10	.02
☐ 5 Wally Berger	.25	.10	.02
☐ 6 Ben Chapman	.25	.10	.02
☐ 7 Mickey Cochrane	.35	.15	.03
☐ 8 Frankie Crosetti	.30	.12	.03
☐ 9 Paul Dean	.30	.12	.03
☐ 10 Leo Durocher	.45	.18	.04
☐ 11 Wes Ferrell	.25	.10	.02
☐ 12 Hank Gowdy	.25	.10	.02
☐ 13 Andy High	.25	.10	.02
☐ 14 Rogers Hornsby	.40	.16	.04
☐ 15 Carl Hubbell	.35	.15	.03
☐ 16 Joe Judge	.25	.10	.02
☐ 17 Tony Lazzeri	.35	.15	.03
☐ 18 Pepper Martin	.30	.12	.03
☐ 19 Lee Meadows	.25	.10	.02
☐ 20 Johnny Murphy	.25	.10	.02
☐ 21 Steve O'Neil	.25	.10	.02
☐ 22 Ed Plank	.35	.15	.03
☐ 23 Jack"Picus" Quinn	.25	.10	.02
☐ 24 Charley Root	.25	.10	.02
☐ 25 Babe Ruth	1.50	.60	.15
☐ 26 Fred Snodgrass	.25	.10	.02
☐ 27 Tris Speaker	.35	.15	.03
☐ 28 Bill Terry	.35	.15	.03
☐ 29 Jeff Tesreau	.25	.10	.02
☐ 30 George Toporcer	.25	.10	.02

1988 Conlon Series 4

This fourth series of 30 Charles Martin Conlon photo cards was produced by World Wide Sports in conjunction with The Sporting News. The cards are standard size, 2 1/2" by 3 1/2" and are in a sepia tone. The photos were selected and background information written by Paul MacFarlane of The Sporting News. These cards are unnumbered and hence are listed below in alphabetical order. Series 4 is indicated in the lower right corner of each card's reverse. A black and white logo for the "Baseball Immortals" and The Conlon Collection is over-printed in the lower left corner of each obverse.

	MINT	EXC	G-VG
COMPLETE SET (30)	6.00	2.50	.60
COMMON PLAYER (1-30)	.25	.10	.02

		MINT	EXC	G-VG
☐ 1	Dale Alexander	.25	.10	.02
☐ 2	Morris Badgro	.25	.10	.02
☐ 3	Dick Bartell	.25	.10	.02
☐ 4	Max Bishop	.25	.10	.02
☐ 5	Hal Chase	.25	.10	.02
☐ 6	Ty Cobb	.90	.40	.09
☐ 7	Nick Cullop	.25	.10	.02
☐ 8	Dizzy Dean	.50	.20	.05
☐ 9	Charlie Dressen	.25	.10	.02
☐ 10	Jimmy Dykes	.25	.10	.02
☐ 11	Art Fletcher	.25	.10	.02
☐ 12	Charlie Grimm	.25	.10	.02
☐ 13	Lefty Grove	.40	.16	.04
☐ 14	Baby Doll Jacobson	.25	.10	.02
☐ 15	Bill Klem	.40	.16	.04
☐ 16	Mark Koenig	.25	.10	.02
☐ 17	Duffy Lewis	.25	.10	.02
☐ 18	Carl Mays	.25	.10	.02
☐ 19	Fred Merkle	.25	.10	.02
☐ 20	Greasy Neale	.25	.10	.02
☐ 21	Mel Ott	.40	.16	.04
☐ 22	Babe Pinelli	.25	.10	.02
☐ 23	Flint Rhem	.25	.10	.02
☐ 24	Slim Sallee UER	.25	.10	.02
	(Misspelled Salee on card back)			
☐ 25	Al Simmons	.35	.15	.03
☐ 26	George Sisler	.35	.15	.03
☐ 27	Riggs Stephenson	.25	.10	.02
☐ 28	Jim Thorpe	1.50	.60	.15
☐ 29	Bill Wambsganss	.25	.10	.02
☐ 30	Cy Young	.40	.16	.04

1988 Conlon Series 5

This fifth series of 30 Charles Martin Conlon photo cards was produced by World Wide Sports in conjunction with The Sporting News. The cards are standard size, 2 1/2" by 3 1/2" and are in a sepia tone. The photos were selected and background information written by Paul MacFarlane of The Sporting News. These cards are unnumbered and hence are listed below in alphabetical order. Series 5 is indicated in the lower right corner

of each card's reverse. A black and white logo for the "Baseball Immortals" and The Conlon Collection is over-printed in the lower left corner of each obverse.

	MINT	EXC	G-VG
COMPLETE SET (30)	5.00	2.25	.50
COMMON PLAYER (1-30)	.25	.10	.02

		MINT	EXC	G-VG
☐ 1	Nick Altrock	.25	.10	.02
☐ 2	Del Baker	.25	.10	.02
☐ 3	Moe Berg	.35	.15	.03
☐ 4	Zeke Bonura	.25	.10	.02
☐ 5	Eddie Collins	.35	.15	.03
☐ 6	Hughie Critz	.25	.10	.02
☐ 7	George Dauss	.25	.10	.02
☐ 8	Joe Dugan	.25	.10	.02
☐ 9	Howard Ehmke	.25	.10	.02
☐ 10	James Emory Foxx	.40	.16	.04
☐ 11	Frankie Frisch	.35	.15	.03
☐ 12	Lou Gehrig	.90	.40	.09
☐ 13	Charlie Gehringer	.40	.16	.04
☐ 14	Kid Gleason	.25	.10	.02
☐ 15	Lefty Gomez	.40	.16	.04
☐ 16	Babe Herman	.25	.10	.02
☐ 17	Bill James	.25	.10	.02
☐ 18	Joe Kuhel	.25	.10	.02
☐ 19	Dolf Luque	.25	.10	.02
☐ 20	John McGraw	.35	.15	.03
☐ 21	Stuffy McInnis	.25	.10	.02
☐ 22	Bob Meusel	.25	.10	.02
☐ 23	Lefty O'Doul	.25	.10	.02
☐ 24	Hub Pruett	.25	.10	.02
☐ 25	Paul Richards	.25	.10	.02
☐ 26	Bob Shawkey	.25	.10	.02
☐ 27	Gabby Street	.25	.10	.02
☐ 28	Johnny Tobin	.25	.10	.02
☐ 29	Rube Waddell	.35	.15	.03
☐ 30	Billy Werber	.25	.10	.02

1988 Conlon American All-Stars

This set of 24 Charles Martin Conlon photo cards was produced by World Wide Sports in conjunction with The Sporting News. The cards are standard size, 2 1/2" by 3 1/2" and are in a sepia tone. The photos (members of the 1933 American League All-Star team) were selected and background information written by Paul MacFarlane of The Sporting News. These cards are unnumbered and hence are listed below in alphabetical order. American League is indicated in the lower right corner of each card's reverse. In the upper right corner of each card's obverse is printed "1933 American All Stars."

	MINT	EXC	G-VG
COMPLETE SET (24)	5.00	2.25	.50
COMMON PLAYER (1-24)	.25	.10	.02

		MINT	EXC	G-VG
☐ 1	Luke Appling	.35	.15	.03
☐ 2	Earl Averill	.35	.15	.03
☐ 3	Tommy Bridges	.25	.10	.02
☐ 4	Ben Chapman	.25	.10	.02
☐ 5	Mickey Cochrane	.35	.15	.03
☐ 6	Joe Cronin	.35	.15	.03

			MINT	EXC	G-VG
☐	8	Frankie Frisch	.35	.15	.03
☐	9	Chick Fullis	.25	.10	.02
☐	10	Chick Hafey	.35	.15	.03
☐	11	Carl Hubbell	.40	.16	.04
☐	12	Chuck Klein	.35	.15	.03
☐	13	Fred Lindstrom	.35	.15	.03
☐	14	Pepper Martin	.25	.10	.02
☐	15	Joe Medwick	.35	.15	.03
☐	16	Tony Piet	.25	.10	.02
☐	17	Wes Schulmerich	.25	.10	.02
☐	18	Hal Schumacher	.25	.10	.02
☐	19	Riggs Stephenson	.25	.10	.02
☐	20	Bill Terry	.40	.16	.04
☐	21	Pie Traynor	.35	.15	.03
☐	22	Arky Vaughan	.35	.15	.03
☐	23	Paul Waner	.35	.15	.03
☐	24	Lon Warneke	.25	.10	.02

			MINT	EXC	G-VG
☐	7	Alvin Crowder	.25	.10	.02
☐	8	Bill Dickey	.40	.16	.04
☐	9	James Emory Foxx	.40	.16	.04
☐	10	Lou Gehrig	.90	.40	.09
☐	11	Charlie Gehringer	.35	.15	.03
☐	12	Lefty Gomez	.35	.15	.03
☐	13	Lefty Grove	.40	.16	.04
☐	14	Mel Harder	.25	.10	.02
☐	15	Pinky Higgins	.25	.10	.02
☐	16	Urban Hodapp	.25	.10	.02
☐	17	Roy Johnson	.25	.10	.02
☐	18	Joe Kuhel	.25	.10	.02
☐	19	Tony Lazzeri	.35	.15	.03
☐	20	Heinie Manush	.25	.10	.02
☐	21	Babe Ruth	1.50	.60	.15
☐	22	Al Simmons	.35	.15	.03
☐	23	Evar Swanson	.25	.10	.02
☐	24	Earl Whitehill	.25	.10	.02

1988 Conlon National All-Stars

This set of 24 Charles Martin Conlon photo cards was produced by World Wide Sports in conjunction with The Sporting News. The cards are standard size, 2 1/2" by 3 1/2" and are in a sepia tone. The photos (members of the 1933 National League All-Star team) were selected and background information written by Paul MacFarlane of The Sporting News. These cards are unnumbered and hence are listed below in alphabetical order. American League is indicated in the lower right corner of each card's reverse. In the upper right corner of each card's obverse is printed "1933 National All Stars."

			MINT	EXC	G-VG
COMPLETE SET (24)			5.00	2.25	.50
COMMON PLAYER (1-24)			.25	.10	.02
☐	1	Wally Berger	.25	.10	.02
☐	2	Guy Bush	.25	.10	.02
☐	3	Ripper Collins	.25	.10	.02
☐	4	Spud Davis	.25	.10	.02
☐	5	Dizzy Dean	.50	.20	.05
☐	6	Johnny Frederick	.25	.10	.02
☐	7	Larry French	.25	.10	.02

1988 Conlon Negro All-Stars

This set of 12 photo cards was produced by World Wide Sports in conjunction with The Sporting News. The cards are standard size, 2 1/2" by 3 1/2" and are in a sepia tone. The photos (Negro League All Stars from 1933) were selected and background information written by Paul MacFarlane of The Sporting News. Despite the similarity of this set with the other Conlon sets, the photos for this set were not taken by Charles Martin Conlon. These cards are unnumbered and hence are listed below in alphabetical order. Negro League is indicated in the lower right corner of each card's reverse. In the upper right corner of each card's obverse is printed "1933 Negro All Stars." The photo quality on some of the cards is very poor suggesting that the original photo or negative may have been enlarged to an excessive degree.

			MINT	EXC	G-VG
COMPLETE SET (12)			4.00	1.75	.40
COMMON PLAYER (1-12)			.35	.15	.03
☐	1	Cool Papa Bell	.50	.20	.05
☐	2	Oscar Charleston	.50	.20	.05
☐	3	Martin DiHigo	.50	.20	.05
☐	4	Rube Foster	.50	.20	.05
☐	5	Josh Gibson	.75	.30	.07
☐	6	Judy Johnson	.50	.20	.05
☐	7	Buck Leonard	.50	.20	.05
☐	8	John Henry Lloyd	.50	.20	.05
☐	9	Dave Malarcher	.35	.15	.03
☐	10	Satch Paige	.60	.25	.06
☐	11	Willie Wells	.35	.15	.03
☐	12	Smoky Joe Williams	.35	.15	.03

1988 Conlon Hardee's/Coke

This six-card set was issued in 18 central Indiana Hardee's restaurants over a six-week period, a different card per purchase per week. The set features the vintage photography of Charles Martin Conlon, except for the Cool Papa Bell photo which was not shot by Conlon. The cards are sepia tone and are standard size, 2 1/2" by 3 1/2". The card backs contain biographical information, Hardee's logo, and a Coca Cola Classic logo. The cards are also copyrighted by The Sporting News.

	MINT	EXC	G-VG
COMPLETE SET (6)	4.00	1.75	.40
COMMON PLAYER (1-6)	.50	.20	.05
☐ 1 James Bell (Cool Papa)	.50	.20	.05
☐ 2 Tyrus Raymond Cobb (Georgia Peach)	1.50	.60	.15
☐ 3 Henry Louis Gehrig (Iron Horse)	1.50	.60	.15
☐ 4 Cornelius McGillicuddy (Connie Mack)	.50	.20	.05
☐ 5 Charles Dillon Stengel (Casey)	.75	.30	.07
☐ 6 George Edward Waddell (Rube)	.50	.20	.05

1991 Conlon Sporting News

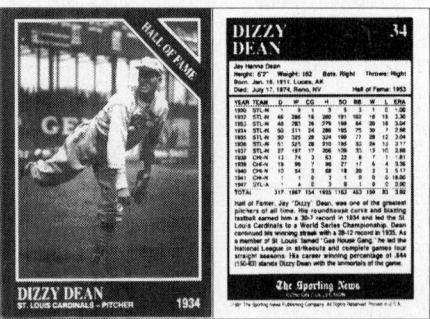

This 330-card set issued in black and white again featured the photography of Charles Conlon. The set was produced by MegaCards in conjunction with The Sporting News. The set features standard size, 2 1/2" by 3 1/2", cards with black and white borders surrounded by black borders. The card backs contain pertinent information relevant to the front of the cards whether it is career statistics or all-time leaders format or the special cards commemorating the great teams of the first part

of the twentieth century.

	MINT	EXC	G-VG
COMPLETE SET (330)	20.00	8.50	2.75
COMMON PLAYER (1-330)	.10	.04	.01
☐ 1 HOF: Hornsby	.30	.12	.03
☐ 2 HOF: Foxx	.30	.12	.03
☐ 3 HOF: Dean	.35	.15	.03
☐ 4 HOF: Maranville	.20	.08	.02
☐ 5 HOF: P.Waner	.20	.08	.02
☐ 6 HOF: L.Waner	.20	.08	.02
☐ 7 HOF: Mel Ott	.25	.10	.02
☐ 8 HOF: Wagner	.35	.15	.03
☐ 9 HOF: W.Johnson	.30	.12	.03
☐ 10 HOF: Hubbell	.20	.08	.02
☐ 11 HOF: Frisch	.20	.08	.02
☐ 12 HOF: Cuyler	.20	.08	.02
☐ 13 HOF: Ruffing	.20	.08	.02
☐ 14 HOF: Greenberg	.30	.12	.03
☐ 15 HOF: Evers	.20	.08	.02
☐ 16 HOF: Jennings	.20	.08	.02
☐ 17 HOF: Bancroft	.20	.08	.02
☐ 18 HOF: Medwick	.20	.08	.02
☐ 19 HOF: Lyons	.20	.08	.02
☐ 20 HOF: Bender	.20	.08	.02
☐ 21 HOF: Collins	.20	.08	.02
☐ 22 HOF: Bottomley	.20	.08	.02
☐ 23 HOF: Grove	.30	.12	.03
☐ 24 HOF: Carey	.20	.08	.02
☐ 25 HOF: Grimes	.20	.08	.02
☐ 26 HOF: Youngs	.20	.08	.02
☐ 27 HOF: Lombardi	.20	.08	.02
☐ 28 HOF: McCarthy	.20	.08	.02
☐ 29 HOF: Wilson	.30	.12	.03
☐ 30 HOF: Klein	.20	.08	.02
☐ 31 HOF: Averill	.20	.08	.02
☐ 32 HOF: Alexander	.20	.08	.02
☐ 33 HOF: Hafey	.20	.08	.02
☐ 34 HOF: McKechnie	.20	.08	.02
☐ 35 HOF: Feller	.30	.12	.03
☐ 36 HOF: Traynor	.20	.08	.02
☐ 37 HOF: Stengel	.30	.12	.03
☐ 38 HOF: Vaughan	.20	.08	.02
☐ 39 HOF: Rixey	.20	.08	.02
☐ 40 HOF: Sewell	.20	.08	.02
☐ 41 HOF: Faber	.20	.08	.02
☐ 42 HOF: Jackson	.20	.08	.02
☐ 43 HOF: Haines	.20	.08	.02
☐ 44 HOF: Speaker	.20	.08	.02
☐ 45 HOF: Mack	.20	.08	.02
☐ 46 HOF: Mack	.20	.08	.02
☐ 47 HOF: Mack	.20	.08	.02
☐ 48 HOF: Schalk	.20	.08	.02
☐ 49 HOF: Simmons	.20	.08	.02
☐ 50 HOF: Cronin	.20	.08	.02
☐ 51 HOF: Cochrane	.20	.08	.02
☐ 52 HOF: Heilmann	.20	.08	.02
☐ 53 HOF: Mize	.20	.08	.02
☐ 54 HOF: Rice	.20	.08	.02
☐ 55 HOF: Roush	.20	.08	.02
☐ 56 HOF: Slaughter	.20	.08	.02
☐ 57 HOF: Mathewson	.35	.15	.03
☐ 58 HOF: Lindstrom	.20	.08	.02
☐ 59 HOF: Hartnett	.20	.08	.02
☐ 60 HOF: Kelly	.20	.08	.02
☐ 61 HOF: Harris	.20	.08	.02
☐ 62 HOF: Goslin	.20	.08	.02
☐ 63 HOF: Manush	.20	.08	.02
☐ 64 HOF: Terry	.20	.08	.02
☐ 65 HOF: McGraw	.20	.08	.02
☐ 66 HOF: Sisler	.20	.08	.02
☐ 67 HOF: Gomez	.20	.08	.02
☐ 68 Joe Judge	.10	.04	.01
☐ 69 Tommy Thevenow	.10	.04	.01
☐ 70 Charlie Gelbert	.10	.04	.01
☐ 71 Jackie Hayes	.10	.04	.01
☐ 72 Bob Fothergill	.10	.04	.01
☐ 73 Adam Comorosky	.10	.04	.01
☐ 74 Earl Smith	.10	.04	.01
☐ 75 Sam Gray	.10	.04	.01
☐ 76 Pete Appleton	.10	.04	.01
☐ 77 Gene Moore	.10	.04	.01
☐ 78 Art Jorgens	.10	.04	.01
☐ 79 Bill Knickerbocker	.10	.04	.01
☐ 80 Carl Reynolds	.10	.04	.01
☐ 81 Ski Melillo	.10	.04	.01
☐ 82 Johnny Burnett	.10	.04	.01
☐ 83 Jake Powell	.10	.04	.01
☐ 84 Johnny Murphy	.10	.04	.01
☐ 85 Roy Parmelee	.10	.04	.01
☐ 86 Jimmy Ripple	.10	.04	.01
☐ 87 Gee Walker	.10	.04	.01
☐ 88 George Earnshaw	.10	.04	.01

#	Player			
☐ 89	Billy Southworth	.10	.04	.01
☐ 90	Wally Moses	.10	.04	.01
☐ 91	Rube Walberg	.10	.04	.01
☐ 92	Jimmy Dykes	.10	.04	.01
☐ 93	Charlie Root	.10	.04	.01
☐ 94	Johnny Cooney	.10	.04	.01
☐ 95	Charlie Grimm	.10	.04	.01
☐ 96	Bob Johnson	.10	.04	.01
☐ 97	Jack Scott	.10	.04	.01
☐ 98	Rip Radcliff	.10	.04	.01
☐ 99	Fritz Ostermueller	.10	.04	.01
☐ 100	'27NY: Wera	.10	.04	.01
☐ 101	'27NY: Huggins	.20	.08	.02
☐ 102	'27NY: Morehart	.10	.04	.01
☐ 103	'27NY: Bengough	.10	.04	.01
☐ 104	'27NY: Ruether	.10	.04	.01
☐ 105	'27NY: Combs	.20	.08	.02
☐ 106	'27NY: Thomas	.10	.04	.01
☐ 107	'27NY: Paschal	.10	.04	.01
☐ 108	'27NY: Durst	.10	.04	.01
☐ 109	'27NY: Moore	.10	.04	.01
☐ 110	'27NY: Ruth	.75	.30	.07
☐ 111	'27NY: Gehrig	.50	.20	.05
☐ 112	'27NY: Dugan	.10	.04	.01
☐ 113	'27NY: Lazzeri	.25	.10	.02
☐ 114	'27NY: Shocker	.10	.04	.01
☐ 115	'27NY: Hoyt	.20	.08	.02
☐ 116	'27NY: O'Leary	.10	.04	.01
☐ 117	'27NY: Fletcher	.10	.04	.01
☐ 118	'27NY: Collins	.10	.04	.01
☐ 119	'27NY: Giard	.10	.04	.01
☐ 120	'27NY: Pennock	.20	.08	.02
☐ 121	'27NY: Gazella	.10	.04	.01
☐ 122	'27NY: Meusel	.10	.04	.01
☐ 123	'27NY: Pipgras	.10	.04	.01
☐ 124	'27NY: Grabowski	.10	.04	.01
☐ 125	'27NY: Koenig	.10	.04	.01
☐ 126	Stan Hack	.10	.04	.01
☐ 127	Earl Whitehill	.10	.04	.01
☐ 128	Bill Lee	.10	.04	.01
☐ 129	Gus Mancuso	.10	.04	.01
☐ 130	Ray Blades	.10	.04	.01
☐ 131	Jack Burns	.10	.04	.01
☐ 132	Clint Brown	.10	.04	.01
☐ 133	Bill Dietrich	.10	.04	.01
☐ 134	Cy Blanton	.10	.04	.01
☐ 135	'16Champs: Hooper	.20	.08	.02
☐ 136	'16Champs: Shorten	.10	.04	.01
☐ 137	'16Champs: Walker	.10	.04	.01
☐ 138	'16Champs: Foster	.10	.04	.01
☐ 139	'16Champs: Barry	.10	.04	.01
☐ 140	'16Champs: Jones	.10	.04	.01
☐ 141	'16Champs: Shore	.10	.04	.01
☐ 142	'16Champs: Leonard	.10	.04	.01
☐ 143	'16Champs: Pennock	.20	.08	.02
☐ 144	'16Champs: Janvrin	.10	.04	.01
☐ 145	'16Champs: Ruth	.75	.30	.07
☐ 146	'16Champs: Lewis	.10	.04	.01
☐ 147	'16Champs: Gardner	.10	.04	.01
☐ 148	'16Champs: Hoblitzel	.10	.04	.01
☐ 149	'16Champs: Scott	.10	.04	.01
☐ 150	'16Champs: Mays	.10	.04	.01
☐ 151	'16LL: Niehoff	.10	.04	.01
☐ 152	'16LL: Shotton	.10	.04	.01
☐ 153	'16LL: Ames	.10	.04	.01
☐ 154	'16LL: Williams	.10	.04	.01
☐ 155	'16LL: Hinchman	.10	.04	.01
☐ 156	'16LL: Shawkey	.10	.04	.01
☐ 157	'16LL: Pipp	.15	.06	.01
☐ 158	'16LL: Geo.J.Burns	.10	.04	.01
☐ 159	'16LL: Veach	.10	.04	.01
☐ 160	'16LL: Chase	.10	.04	.01
☐ 161	'16LL: Hughes	.10	.04	.01
☐ 162	'16LL: Pratt	.10	.04	.01
☐ 163	'16LL: Groh	.10	.04	.01
☐ 164	'16LL: Wheat	.20	.08	.02
☐ 165	Story: O'Doul	.10	.04	.01
☐ 166	Story: Kamm	.10	.04	.01
☐ 167	Story: P.Waner	.20	.08	.02
☐ 168	Story: Snodgrass	.10	.04	.01
☐ 169	Story: Herman	.20	.08	.02
☐ 170	Story: Bridwell	.10	.04	.01
☐ 171	Story: Meyers	.10	.04	.01
☐ 172	Story: Lobert	.10	.04	.01
☐ 173	Story: Bressler	.10	.04	.01
☐ 174	Story: Jones	.10	.04	.01
☐ 175	Story: O'Farrell	.10	.04	.01
☐ 176	Story: Toporcer	.10	.04	.01
☐ 177	Story: Earl McNeely	.10	.04	.01
☐ 178	Story: Jack Knott	.10	.04	.01
☐ 179	Heinie Mueller	.10	.04	.01
☐ 180	Tommy Bridges	.10	.04	.01
☐ 181	Lloyd Brown	.10	.04	.01
☐ 182	Larry Benton	.10	.04	.01
☐ 183	Max Bishop	.10	.04	.01
☐ 184	Moe Berg	.20	.08	.02
☐ 185	Cy Perkins	.10	.04	.01
☐ 186	Steve O'Neill	.10	.04	.01
☐ 187	Glenn Myatt	.10	.04	.01
☐ 188	Joe Kuhel	.10	.04	.01
☐ 189	Marty McManus	.10	.04	.01
☐ 190	Red Lucas	.10	.04	.01
☐ 191	Stuffy McInnis	.10	.04	.01
☐ 192	Bing Miller	.10	.04	.01
☐ 193	Luke Sewell	.10	.04	.01
☐ 194	Bill Sherdel	.10	.04	.01
☐ 195	Hal Rhyne	.10	.04	.01
☐ 196	Guy Bush	.10	.04	.01
☐ 197	Pete Fox	.10	.04	.01
☐ 198	Wes Ferrell	.10	.04	.01
☐ 199	Roy Johnson	.10	.04	.01
☐ 200	Tr.Play: Wambsganss	.10	.04	.01
☐ 201	Tr.Play: G.H.Burns	.10	.04	.01
☐ 202	Tr.Play: Mitchell	.10	.04	.01
☐ 203	Tr.Play: Ball	.10	.04	.01
☐ 204	Tr.Play: Neun	.10	.04	.01
☐ 205	Tr.Play: Summa	.10	.04	.01
☐ 206	Tr.Play: Padgett	.10	.04	.01
☐ 207	Tr.Play: Holke	.10	.04	.01
☐ 208	Tr.Play: Wright	.10	.04	.01
☐ 209	Hank Gowdy	.10	.04	.01
☐ 210	Zack Taylor	.10	.04	.01
☐ 211	Ben Cantwell	.10	.04	.01
☐ 212	Frank Demaree	.10	.04	.01
☐ 213	Paul Derringer	.10	.04	.01
☐ 214	Bill Hallahan	.10	.04	.01
☐ 215	Danny MacFayden	.10	.04	.01
☐ 216	Harry Rice	.10	.04	.01
☐ 217	Bob Smith	.10	.04	.01
☐ 218	Riggs Stephenson	.10	.04	.01
☐ 219	Pat Malone	.10	.04	.01
☐ 220	Bennie Tate	.10	.04	.01
☐ 221	Joe Vosmik	.10	.04	.01
☐ 222	George Watkins	.10	.04	.01
☐ 223	Jimmie Wilson	.10	.04	.01
☐ 224	George Uhle	.10	.04	.01
☐ 225	Trivia: Ott	.20	.08	.02
☐ 226	Trivia: Altrock	.10	.04	.01
☐ 227	Trivia: Ruffing	.20	.08	.02
☐ 228	Trivia: Krakauskas	.10	.04	.01
☐ 229	Trivia: Berger	.10	.04	.01
☐ 230	Bobo Newsom	.10	.04	.01
☐ 231	Lon Warneke	.10	.04	.01
☐ 232	Frank Snyder	.10	.04	.01
☐ 233	Myril Hoag	.10	.04	.01
☐ 234	Mel Almada	.10	.04	.01
☐ 235	Ivey Wingo	.10	.04	.01
☐ 236	Jimmy Austin	.10	.04	.01
☐ 237	Zeke Bonura	.10	.04	.01
☐ 238	Russ Wrightstone	.10	.04	.01
☐ 239	Al Todd	.10	.04	.01
☐ 240	Rabbit Warstler	.10	.04	.01
☐ 241	Sammy West	.10	.04	.01
☐ 242	Art Reinhart	.10	.04	.01
☐ 243	Lefty Stewart	.10	.04	.01
☐ 244	Johnny Gooch	.10	.04	.01
☐ 245	Bubbles Hargrave	.10	.04	.01
☐ 246	George Harper	.10	.04	.01
☐ 247	Sarge Connally	.10	.04	.01
☐ 248	Garland Braxton	.10	.04	.01
☐ 249	Wally Schang	.10	.04	.01
☐ 250	ATL: Cobb	.50	.20	.05
☐ 251	ATL: Hornsby	.30	.12	.03
☐ 252	ATL: Marquard	.20	.08	.02
☐ 253	ATL: Hubbell	.20	.08	.02
☐ 254	ATL: Wood	.20	.08	.02
☐ 255	ATL: Grove	.30	.12	.03
☐ 256	ATL: Rowe	.10	.04	.01
☐ 257	ATL: Crowder	.10	.04	.01
☐ 258	ATL: Johnson	.10	.04	.01
☐ 259	ATL: Hafey	.20	.08	.02
☐ 260	ATL: Fitzsimmons	.10	.04	.01
☐ 261	ATL: Webb	.10	.04	.01
☐ 262	ATL: Combs	.20	.08	.02
☐ 263	ATL: Konetchy	.10	.04	.01
☐ 264	ATL: Douthit	.10	.04	.01
☐ 265	ATL: L.Waner	.20	.08	.02
☐ 266	ATL: Cochrane	.20	.08	.02
☐ 267	ATL: Wilson	.20	.08	.02
☐ 268	ATL: Traynor	.20	.08	.02
☐ 269	ATL: Davis	.10	.04	.01
☐ 270	ATL: Manush	.20	.08	.02
☐ 271	ATL: Higgins	.10	.04	.01
☐ 272	ATL: Joss	.20	.08	.02
☐ 273	ATL: Walsh	.20	.08	.02
☐ 274	ATL: Martin	.20	.08	.02
☐ 275	ATL: Sewell	.20	.08	.02
☐ 276	ATL: Leonard	.10	.04	.01

☐ 277	ATL: Cravath	.10	.04	.01
☐ 278	Oral Hildebrand	.10	.04	.01
☐ 279	Ray Kremer	.10	.04	.01
☐ 280	Frankie Pytlak	.10	.04	.01
☐ 281	Sammy Byrd	.10	.04	.01
☐ 282	Curt Davis	.10	.04	.01
☐ 283	Lew Fonseca	.10	.04	.01
☐ 284	Muddy Ruel	.10	.04	.01
☐ 285	Moose Solters	.10	.04	.01
☐ 286	Fred Schulte	.10	.04	.01
☐ 287	Jack Quinn	.10	.04	.01
☐ 288	Pinky Whitney	.10	.04	.01
☐ 289	John Stone	.10	.04	.01
☐ 290	Hughie Critz	.10	.04	.01
☐ 291	Ira Flagstead	.10	.04	.01
☐ 292	George Grantham	.10	.04	.01
☐ 293	Sammy Hale	.10	.04	.01
☐ 294	Shanty Hogan	.10	.04	.01
☐ 295	Ossie Bluege	.10	.04	.01
☐ 296	Debs Garms	.10	.04	.01
☐ 297	Barney Friberg	.10	.04	.01
☐ 298	Ed Brandt	.10	.04	.01
☐ 299	Rollie Hemsley	.10	.04	.01
☐ 300	MVP: Klein	.20	.08	.02
☐ 301	MVP: Cooper	.10	.04	.01
☐ 302	MVP: Bottomley	.20	.08	.02
☐ 303	MVP: Foxx	.30	.12	.03
☐ 304	MVP: Schulte	.10	.04	.01
☐ 305	MVP: Frisch	.20	.08	.02
☐ 306	MVP: McCormick	.10	.04	.01
☐ 307	MVP: Daubert	.10	.04	.01
☐ 308	MVP: Peckinpaugh	.10	.04	.01
☐ 309	MVP: Geo.H.Burns	.10	.04	.01
☐ 310	MVP: Gehrig	.50	.20	.05
☐ 311	MVP: Simmons	.20	.08	.02
☐ 312	MVP: Collins	.20	.08	.02
☐ 313	MVP: Hartnett	.20	.08	.02
☐ 314	MVP: Cronin	.20	.08	.02
☐ 315	MVP: P.Waner	.20	.08	.02
☐ 316	MVP: O'Farrell	.10	.04	.01
☐ 317	MVP: Doyle	.10	.04	.01
☐ 318	Lyn Lary	.10	.04	.01
☐ 319	Jakie May	.10	.04	.01
☐ 320	Roy Spencer	.10	.04	.01
☐ 321	Dick Coffman	.10	.04	.01
☐ 322	Pete Donohue	.10	.04	.01
☐ 323	Mule Haas	.10	.04	.01
☐ 324	Doc Farrell	.10	.04	.01
☐ 325	Flint Rhem	.10	.04	.01
☐ 326	Firpo Marberry	.10	.04	.01
☐ 327	Charles Conlon	.10	.04	.01
☐ 328	Checklist 1-110	.10	.02	.00
☐ 329	Checklist 111-220	.10	.02	.00
☐ 330	Checklist 221-330	.10	.02	.00

1992 Conlon Sporting News

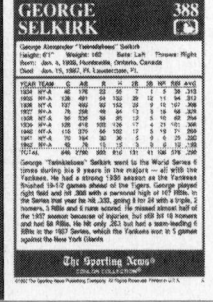

This 330-card set is numbered in continuation of the previous year's issue and again features the photography of Charles Conlon. The standard-size cards (2 1/2" by 3 1/2") have on the fronts either posed or action black , white player photos, enframed by a white line on a black card face. A caption in a diagonal stripe cuts across the upper right corner of the picture. The player's name, team, position, and year the photos were taken appear below the pictures in white lettering. The back has

biography, statistics, and career summary. The cards are numbered on the back. Special subsets include No-Hitters (331-372), Two Sports (393-407), Great Stories (421-440), Why Not in Hall of Fame (441-450), Hall of Fame (459-474), 75 Years Ago Highlights (483-492), Triple Crown Winners (525-537), Everyday Heroes (538-550), Nicknames (551-566), Trivia (581-601), and St. Louis Cardinals 1892-1992 (618-657).

		MINT	EXC	G-VG
COMPLETE SET (330)		20.00	8.50	2.75
COMMON PLAYER (331-660)		.10	.04	.01

☐ 331	Christy Mathewson	.30	.12	.03
☐ 332	Hooks Wiltse	.10	.04	.01
☐ 333	Nap Rucker	.10	.04	.01
☐ 334	Red Ames	.10	.04	.01
☐ 335	Chief Bender	.20	.08	.02
☐ 336	Smoky Joe Wood	.15	.06	.01
☐ 337	Ed Walsh	.20	.08	.02
☐ 338	George Mullin	.10	.04	.01
☐ 339	Earl Hamilton	.10	.04	.01
☐ 340	Jeff Tesreau	.10	.04	.01
☐ 341	Jim Scott	.10	.04	.01
☐ 342	Rube Marquard	.20	.08	.02
☐ 343	Claude Hendrix	.10	.04	.01
☐ 344	Jimmy Lavender	.10	.04	.01
☐ 345	Joe Bush	.10	.04	.01
☐ 346	Dutch Leonard	.10	.04	.01
☐ 347	Fred Toney	.10	.04	.01
☐ 348	Hippo Vaughn	.10	.04	.01
☐ 349	Ernie Koob	.10	.04	.01
☐ 350	Bob Groom	.10	.04	.01
☐ 351	Ernie Shore	.10	.04	.01
☐ 352	Hod Eller	.10	.04	.01
☐ 353	Walter Johnson	.35	.15	.03
☐ 354	Charles Robertson	.10	.04	.01
☐ 355	Jesse Barnes	.10	.04	.01
☐ 356	Sad Sam Jones	.10	.04	.01
☐ 357	Howard Ehmke	.10	.04	.01
☐ 358	Jesse Haines	.20	.08	.02
☐ 359	Ted Lyons	.20	.08	.02
☐ 360	Carl Hubbell	.25	.10	.02
☐ 361	Wes Ferrell	.10	.04	.01
☐ 362	Bobby Burke	.10	.04	.01
☐ 363	Daffy Dean	.15	.06	.01
☐ 364	Bobo Newsom	.10	.04	.01
☐ 365	Vern Kennedy	.10	.04	.01
☐ 366	Bill Dietrich	.10	.04	.01
☐ 367	Johnny Vander Meer	.15	.06	.01
☐ 368	Johnny Vander Meer	.15	.06	.01
☐ 369	Monte Pearson	.10	.04	.01
☐ 370	Bob Feller	.30	.12	.03
☐ 371	Lon Warneke	.10	.04	.01
☐ 372	Jim Tobin	.10	.04	.01
☐ 373	Earl Moore	.10	.04	.01
☐ 374	Bill Dineen	.10	.04	.01
☐ 375	Mal Eason	.10	.04	.01
☐ 376	George Mogridge	.10	.04	.01
☐ 377	Dazzy Vance	.20	.08	.02
☐ 378	Tex Carleton	.10	.04	.01
☐ 379	Clyde Shoun	.10	.04	.01
☐ 380	Frankie Hayes	.10	.04	.01
☐ 381	Benny Frey	.10	.04	.01
☐ 382	Hank Johnson	.10	.04	.01
☐ 383	Red Kress	.10	.04	.01
☐ 384	Johnny Allen	.10	.04	.01
☐ 385	Hal Trosky	.10	.04	.01
☐ 386	Gene Robertson	.10	.04	.01
☐ 387	Pep Young	.10	.04	.01
☐ 388	George Selkirk	.10	.04	.01
☐ 389	Ed Wells	.10	.04	.01
☐ 390	Jim Weaver	.10	.04	.01
☐ 391	George McQuinn	.10	.04	.01
☐ 392	Hans Lobert	.10	.04	.01
☐ 393	Evar Swanson	.10	.04	.01
☐ 394	Ernie Nevers	.20	.08	.02
☐ 395	Jim Levey	.10	.04	.01
☐ 396	Hugo Bezdek	.10	.04	.01
☐ 397	Walt French	.10	.04	.01
☐ 398	Charlie Berry	.10	.04	.01
☐ 399	Frank Grube	.10	.04	.01
☐ 400	Chuck Dressen	.10	.04	.01
☐ 401	Greasy Neale	.10	.04	.01
☐ 402	Ernie Vick	.10	.04	.01
☐ 403	Jim Thorpe	.75	.30	.07
☐ 404	Wally Gilbert	.10	.04	.01
☐ 405	Luke Urban	.10	.04	.01
☐ 406	Pid Purdy	.10	.04	.01
☐ 407	Ab Wright	.10	.04	.01
☐ 408	Billy Urbanski	.10	.04	.01
☐ 409	Carl Fischer	.10	.04	.01
☐ 410	Jack Warner	.10	.04	.01

#	Player				#	Player			
☐ 411	Bill Cissell	.10	.04	.01	☐ 505	Cliff Bolton	.10	.04	.01
☐ 412	Merv Shea	.10	.04	.01	☐ 506	Dixie Walker	.10	.04	.01
☐ 413	Dolf Luque	.10	.04	.01	☐ 507	Jack Smith	.10	.04	.01
☐ 414	Johnny Bassler	.10	.04	.01	☐ 508	Bump Hadley	.10	.04	.01
☐ 415	Odell Hale	.10	.04	.01	☐ 509	Buck Crouse	.10	.04	.01
☐ 416	Larry French	.10	.04	.01	☐ 510	Joe Glenn	.10	.04	.01
☐ 417	Curt Walker	.10	.04	.01	☐ 511	Chad Kimsey	.10	.04	.01
☐ 418	Dusty Cooke	.10	.04	.01	☐ 512	Lou Finney	.10	.04	.01
☐ 419	Phil Todt	.10	.04	.01	☐ 513	Roxie Lawson	.10	.04	.01
☐ 420	Poison Andrews	.10	.04	.01	☐ 514	Chuck Fullis	.10	.04	.01
☐ 421	Billy Herman	.20	.08	.02	☐ 515	Earl Sheely	.10	.04	.01
☐ 422	Tris Speaker	.30	.12	.03	☐ 516	George Gibson	.10	.04	.01
☐ 423	Al Simmons	.20	.08	.02	☐ 517	Johnny Broaca	.10	.04	.01
☐ 424	Hack Wilson	.25	.10	.02	☐ 518	Bibb Falk	.10	.04	.01
☐ 425	Ty Cobb	.50	.20	.05	☐ 519	Don Hurst	.10	.04	.01
☐ 426	Babe Ruth	.75	.30	.07	☐ 520	Grover Hartley	.10	.04	.01
☐ 427	Ernie Lombardi	.20	.08	.02	☐ 521	Don Heffner	.10	.04	.01
☐ 428	Dizzy Dean	.40	.16	.04	☐ 522	Harvey Hendrick	.10	.04	.01
☐ 429	Lloyd Waner	.20	.08	.02	☐ 523	Allen Sothoron	.10	.04	.01
☐ 430	Hank Greenberg	.30	.12	.03	☐ 524	Tony Piet	.10	.04	.01
☐ 431	Lefty Grove	.30	.12	.03	☐ 525	Ty Cobb	.50	.20	.05
☐ 432	Mickey Cochrane	.25	.10	.02	☐ 526	Jimmie Foxx	.35	.15	.03
☐ 433	Burleigh Grimes	.20	.08	.02	☐ 527	Rogers Hornsby	.35	.15	.03
☐ 434	Pie Traynor	.20	.08	.02	☐ 528	Nap Lajoie	.35	.15	.03
☐ 435	Johnny Mize	.25	.10	.02	☐ 529	Lou Gehrig	.50	.20	.05
☐ 436	Sam Rice	.20	.08	.02	☐ 530	Heinie Zimmerman	.10	.04	.01
☐ 437	Goose Goslin	.20	.08	.02	☐ 531	Chuck Klein	.20	.08	.02
☐ 438	Chuck Klein	.20	.08	.02	☐ 532	Hugh Duffy	.20	.08	.02
☐ 439	Connie Mack	.25	.10	.02	☐ 533	Lefty Grove	.30	.12	.03
☐ 440	Jim Bottomley	.20	.08	.02	☐ 534	Grover C. Alexander	.30	.12	.03
☐ 441	Riggs Stephenson	.10	.04	.01	☐ 535	Amos Rusie	.20	.08	.02
☐ 442	Ken Williams	.15	.06	.01	☐ 536	Lefty Gomez	.30	.12	.03
☐ 443	Babe Adams	.10	.04	.01	☐ 537	Bucky Walters	.10	.04	.01
☐ 444	Joe Jackson	.50	.20	.05	☐ 538	Johnny Hodapp	.10	.04	.01
☐ 445	Hal Newhouser	.15	.06	.01	☐ 539	Bruce Campbell	.10	.04	.01
☐ 446	Wes Ferrell	.10	.04	.01	☐ 540	Hod Lisenbee	.10	.04	.01
☐ 447	Lefty O'Doul	.10	.04	.01	☐ 541	Jack Fournier	.10	.04	.01
☐ 448	Wally Schang	.10	.04	.01	☐ 542	Jim Tabor	.10	.04	.01
☐ 449	Sherry Magee	.10	.04	.01	☐ 543	Johnny Burnett	.10	.04	.01
☐ 450	Mike Donlin	.10	.04	.01	☐ 544	Roy Hartzell	.10	.04	.01
☐ 451	Doc Cramer	.10	.04	.01	☐ 545	Doc Gautreau	.10	.04	.01
☐ 452	Dick Bartell	.10	.04	.01	☐ 546	Emil Yde	.10	.04	.01
☐ 453	Earle Mack	.10	.04	.01	☐ 547	Bob Johnson	.10	.04	.01
☐ 454	Jumbo Brown	.10	.04	.01	☐ 548	Joe Hauser	.10	.04	.01
☐ 455	Johnnie Heving	.10	.04	.01	☐ 549	Ed Reulbach	.10	.04	.01
☐ 456	Percy Jones	.10	.04	.01	☐ 550	Mel Almada	.10	.04	.01
☐ 457	Ted Blankenship	.10	.04	.01	☐ 551	Mickey Cochrane	.25	.10	.02
☐ 458	Al Wingo	.10	.04	.01	☐ 552	Carl Hubbell	.25	.10	.02
☐ 459	Roger Bresnahan	.20	.08	.02	☐ 553	Charlie Gehringer	.25	.10	.02
☐ 460	Bill Klem	.25	.10	.02	☐ 554	Al Simmons	.20	.08	.02
☐ 461	Charlie Gehringer	.25	.10	.02	☐ 555	Mordecai Brown	.20	.08	.02
☐ 462	Stan Coveleski	.20	.08	.02	☐ 556	Hughie Jennings	.20	.08	.02
☐ 463	Eddie Plank	.25	.10	.02	☐ 557	Kid Elberfeld	.10	.04	.01
☐ 464	Clark Griffith	.20	.08	.02	☐ 558	Casey Stengel	.30	.12	.03
☐ 465	Herb Pennock	.20	.08	.02	☐ 559	Al Schacht	.15	.06	.01
☐ 466	Earle Combs	.20	.08	.02	☐ 560	Jimmie Foxx	.35	.15	.03
☐ 467	Bobby Doerr	.25	.10	.02	☐ 561	George Kelly	.20	.08	.02
☐ 468	Waite Hoyt	.20	.08	.02	☐ 562	Lloyd Waner	.20	.08	.02
☐ 469	Tommy Connolly	.10	.04	.01	☐ 563	Paul Waner	.20	.08	.02
☐ 470	Harry Hooper	.20	.08	.02	☐ 564	Walter Johnson	.35	.15	.03
☐ 471	Rick Ferrell	.20	.08	.02	☐ 565	Home Run Baker	.20	.08	.02
☐ 472	Billy Evans	.10	.04	.01	☐ 566	Roy Hughes	.10	.04	.01
☐ 473	Billy Herman	.20	.08	.02	☐ 567	Lew Riggs	.10	.04	.01
☐ 474	Bill Dickey	.30	.12	.03	☐ 568	John Whitehead	.10	.04	.01
☐ 475	Luke Appling	.25	.10	.02	☐ 569	Elam Vangilder	.10	.04	.01
☐ 476	Babe Pinelli	.10	.04	.01	☐ 570	Billy Zitzmann	.10	.04	.01
☐ 477	Eric McNair	.10	.04	.01	☐ 571	Walter Schmidt	.10	.04	.01
☐ 478	Sherriff Blake	.10	.04	.01	☐ 572	Jackie Tavener	.10	.04	.01
☐ 479	Val Picinich	.10	.04	.01	☐ 573	Joe Genewich	.10	.04	.01
☐ 480	Fred Heimach	.10	.04	.01	☐ 574	Johnny Marcum	.10	.04	.01
☐ 481	Jack Graney	.10	.04	.01	☐ 575	Fred Hofmann	.10	.04	.01
☐ 482	Reb Russell	.10	.04	.01	☐ 576	Red Rolfe	.10	.04	.01
☐ 483	Red Faber	.20	.08	.02	☐ 577	Vic Sorrell	.10	.04	.01
☐ 484	Benny Kauff	.10	.04	.01	☐ 578	Pete Scott	.10	.04	.01
☐ 485	Pants Rowland	.10	.04	.01	☐ 579	Tommy Thomas	.10	.04	.01
☐ 486	Bobby Veach	.10	.04	.01	☐ 580	Al Smith	.10	.04	.01
☐ 487	Jim Bagby Sr.	.10	.04	.01	☐ 581	Butch Henline	.10	.04	.01
☐ 488	Pol Perritt	.10	.04	.01	☐ 582	Eddie Collins	.20	.08	.02
☐ 489	Buck Herzog	.10	.04	.01	☐ 583	Earle Combs	.20	.08	.02
☐ 490	Art Fletcher	.10	.04	.01	☐ 584	John McGraw	.20	.08	.02
☐ 491	Walter Holke	.10	.04	.01	☐ 585	Hack Wilson	.20	.08	.02
☐ 492	Art Nehf	.10	.04	.01	☐ 586	Gabby Hartnett	.20	.08	.02
☐ 493	Fresco Thompson	.10	.04	.01	☐ 587	Kiki Cuyler	.20	.08	.02
☐ 494	Jimmy Welsh	.10	.04	.01	☐ 588	Bill Terry	.25	.10	.02
☐ 495	Ossie Vitt	.10	.04	.01	☐ 589	Joe McCarthy	.20	.08	.02
☐ 496	Ownie Carroll	.10	.04	.01	☐ 590	Hank Greenberg	.30	.12	.03
☐ 497	Ken O'Dea	.10	.04	.01	☐ 591	Tris Speaker	.30	.12	.03
☐ 498	Fred Frankhouse	.10	.04	.01	☐ 592	Bucky McKechnie	.20	.08	.02
☐ 499	Jewel Ens	.10	.04	.01	☐ 593	Bucky Harris	.20	.08	.02
☐ 500	Morrie Arnovich	.10	.04	.01	☐ 594	Herb Pennock	.20	.08	.02
☐ 501	Wally Gerber	.10	.04	.01	☐ 595	George Sisler	.20	.08	.02
☐ 502	Kiddo Davis	.10	.04	.01	☐ 596	Freddie Lindstrom	.20	.08	.02
☐ 503	Buddy Myer	.10	.04	.01	☐ 597	Earl Averill	.20	.08	.02
☐ 504	Sam Leslie	.10	.04	.01	☐ 598	Dave Bancroft	.20	.08	.02

□ 599	Connie Mack	.25	.10	.02
□ 600	Joe Cronin	.20	.08	.02
□ 601	Ken Ash	.10	.04	.01
□ 602	Al Spohrer	.10	.04	.01
□ 603	Roy Mahaffey	.10	.04	.01
□ 604	Frank O'Rourke	.10	.04	.01
□ 605	Lil Stoner	.10	.04	.01
□ 606	Frank Gabler	.10	.04	.01
□ 607	Tom Padden	.10	.04	.01
□ 608	Art Shires	.10	.04	.01
□ 609	Sherry Smith	.10	.04	.01
□ 610	Phil Weintraub	.10	.04	.01
□ 611	Russ Van Atta	.10	.04	.01
□ 612	Jo-Jo White	.10	.04	.01
□ 613	Cliff Melton	.10	.04	.01
□ 614	Jimmy Ring	.10	.04	.01
□ 615	Heinie Sand	.10	.04	.01
□ 616	Dale Alexander	.10	.04	.01
□ 617	Kent Greenfield	.10	.04	.01
□ 618	Eddie Dyer	.10	.04	.01
□ 619	Bill Sherdel	.10	.04	.01
□ 620	Max Lanier	.10	.04	.01
□ 621	Bob O'Farrell	.10	.04	.01
□ 622	Rogers Hornsby	.30	.12	.03
□ 623	Bill Beckman	.10	.04	.01
□ 624	Mort Cooper	.10	.04	.01
□ 625	Bill DeLancey	.10	.04	.01
□ 626	Marty Marion	.15	.06	.01
□ 627	Billy Southworth	.10	.04	.01
□ 628	Johnny Mize	.25	.10	.02
□ 629	Joe Medwick	.20	.08	.02
□ 630	Grover C. Alexander	.30	.12	.03
□ 631	Daffy Dean	.15	.06	.01
□ 632	Hi Bell	.10	.04	.01
□ 633	Walker Cooper	.10	.04	.01
□ 634	Frankie Frisch	.20	.08	.02
□ 635	Dizzy Dean	.40	.16	.04
□ 636	Don Gutteridge	.10	.04	.01
□ 637	Pepper Martin	.15	.06	.01
□ 638	Ed Konetchy	.10	.04	.01
□ 639	Bill Hallahan	.10	.04	.01
□ 640	Lon Warneke	.10	.04	.01
□ 641	Terry Moore	.10	.04	.01
□ 642	Enos Slaughter	.25	.10	.02
□ 643	Heinie Mueller	.10	.04	.01
□ 644	Specs Toporcer	.10	.04	.01
□ 645	Ed Bottomley	.10	.04	.01
□ 646	Ray Blades	.10	.04	.01
□ 647	Jesse Haines	.20	.08	.02
□ 648	Andy High	.10	.04	.01
□ 649	Miller Huggins	.20	.08	.02
□ 650	Ernie Orsatti	.10	.04	.01
□ 651	Les Bell	.10	.04	.01
□ 652	Gabby Street	.10	.04	.01
□ 653	Wally Roettger	.10	.04	.01
□ 654	Syl Johnson	.10	.04	.01
□ 655	Mike Gonzalez	.10	.04	.01
□ 656	Ripper Collins	.10	.04	.01
□ 657	Chick Hafey	.20	.08	.02
□ 658	Checklist 331-440	.10	.02	.00
□ 659	Checklist 441-550	.10	.02	.00
□ 660	Checklist 551-660	.10	.02	.00

1991 Country Hearth Mariners

This 29-card set was sponsored and produced by the Country Hearth Breads and Langendorf Baking Company, and individual cards were inserted unprotected in specially marked loaves of Country Hearth. In addition, the cards (ten at a time) were given away to fans attending the Mariners home game at the Seattle Kingdome on August 17th. The cards measure the standard size (2 1/2" by 3 1/2"). The fronts have either a horizontal or vertical orientation and feature glossy color player photos with thin white borders. The player's name and team appear in small white lettering toward the top of the card face. In black print on a light gray background, the horizontally oriented backs present biography, statistics, or career highlights. The cards are numbered on the back. According to sources, only 20,000 sets were produced, and all cards were produced in equal quantities.

		MINT	EXC	G-VG
COMPLETE SET (29)		17.50	7.50	2.25
COMMON PLAYER (1-29)		.40	.16	.04
□ 1	Jim Lefebvre MG	.40	.16	.04
□ 2	Jeff Schaefer	.50	.20	.05
□ 3	Harold Reynolds	.50	.20	.05
□ 4	Greg Briley	.50	.20	.05
□ 5	Scott Bradley	.40	.16	.04
□ 6	Dave Valle	.40	.16	.04
□ 7	Edgar Martinez	.75	.30	.07
□ 8	Pete O'Brien	.50	.20	.05
□ 9	Omar Vizquel	.40	.16	.04
□ 10	Tino Martinez	1.00	.40	.10
□ 11	Scott Bankhead	.50	.20	.05
□ 12	Bill Swift	.50	.20	.05
□ 13	Jay Buhner	.75	.30	.07
□ 14	Alvin Davis	.60	.25	.06
□ 15	Ken Griffey Jr. (Ready to swing)	4.50	2.00	.45
□ 16	Tracy Jones	.40	.16	.04
□ 17	Brent Knackert	.50	.20	.05
□ 18	Henry Cotto	.40	.16	.04
□ 19	Ken Griffey Sr. (Watching ball after hit)	.60	.25	.06
□ 20	Keith Comstock	.40	.16	.04
□ 21	Brian Holman	.60	.25	.06
□ 22	Russ Swan	.40	.16	.04
□ 23	Mike Jackson	.50	.20	.05
□ 24	Erik Hanson	.75	.30	.07
□ 25	Mike Schooler	.60	.25	.06
□ 26	Randy Johnson	.50	.20	.05
□ 27	Rich DeLucia	.40	.16	.04
□ 28	Ken Griffey Jr./Sr. (Both on same card)	2.25	.90	.22
□ 29	Mariner Moose Mascot	.40	.16	.04

1914 Cracker Jack

The cards in this 144-card set measure approximately 2 1/4" by 3". This "Series of colored pictures of Famous Ball Players and Managers" was issued in packages of Cracker Jack in 1914. The cards have tinted photos set against red backgrounds and many are found with caramel stains. The set also contains Federal League players. The company claims to have printed 15 million cards. The 1914 series can be distinguished from the 1915 issue by the advertising found on the back of the cards. The catalog number for this set is E145-1.

		EX-MT	VG-E	GOOD
	COMPLETE SET (144)	40000.00	16000.00	4000.00
	COMMON PLAYER (1-144)	150.00	67.50	22.50
☐ 1	Otto Knabe	150.00	67.50	22.50
☐ 2	Frank Baker	375.00	165.00	55.00
☐ 3	Joe Tinker	300.00	135.00	45.00
☐ 4	Larry Doyle	150.00	67.50	22.50
☐ 5	Ward Miller	150.00	67.50	22.50
☐ 6	Eddie Plank	400.00	180.00	60.00
	(Phila. AL)			
☐ 7	Eddie Collins	400.00	180.00	60.00
	(Phila. AL)			
☐ 8	Rube Oldring	150.00	67.50	22.50
☐ 9	Artie Hoffman	150.00	67.50	22.50
☐ 10	John McInnis	175.00	80.00	27.00
☐ 11	George Stovall	150.00	67.50	22.50
☐ 12	Connie Mack	450.00	200.00	67.50
☐ 13	Art Wilson	150.00	67.50	22.50
☐ 14	Sam Crawford	300.00	135.00	45.00
☐ 15	Reb Russell	150.00	67.50	22.50
☐ 16	Howie Camnitz	150.00	67.50	22.50
☐ 17	Roger Bresnahan	325.00	150.00	50.00
	(Catcher)			
☐ 18	Johnny Evers	300.00	135.00	45.00
☐ 19	Chief Bender	400.00	180.00	60.00
	(Phila. AL)			
☐ 20	Cy Falkenberg	150.00	67.50	22.50
☐ 21	Heine Zimmerman	150.00	67.50	22.50
☐ 22	Joe Wood	200.00	90.00	30.00
☐ 23	Charles Comiskey	325.00	150.00	50.00
☐ 24	George Mullen	150.00	67.50	22.50
☐ 25	Michael Simon	150.00	67.50	22.50
☐ 26	James Scott	150.00	67.50	22.50
☐ 27	Bill Carrigan	150.00	67.50	22.50
☐ 28	Jack Barry	150.00	67.50	22.50
☐ 29	Vean Gregg	175.00	80.00	27.00
	(Cleveland)			
☐ 30	Ty Cobb	5000.00	2000.00	500.00
☐ 31	Heine Wagner	150.00	67.50	22.50
☐ 32	Mordecai Brown	300.00	135.00	45.00
☐ 33	Amos Strunk	150.00	67.50	22.50
☐ 34	Ira Thomas	150.00	67.50	22.50
☐ 35	Harry Hooper	300.00	135.00	45.00
☐ 36	Ed Walsh	300.00	135.00	45.00
☐ 37	Grover Alexander	600.00	270.00	90.00
☐ 38	Red Dooin	175.00	80.00	27.00
	(Phila. NL)			
☐ 39	Chick Gandil	225.00	100.00	33.00
☐ 40	Jimmy Austin	175.00	80.00	27.00
	(St.L. AL)			
☐ 41	Tommy Leach	150.00	67.50	22.50
☐ 42	Al Bridwell	150.00	67.50	22.50
☐ 43	Rube Marquard	350.00	160.00	52.50
	(NY NL)			
☐ 44	Charles Tesreau	150.00	67.50	22.50
☐ 45	Fred Luderus	150.00	67.50	22.50
☐ 46	Bob Groom	150.00	67.50	22.50
☐ 47	Josh Devore	175.00	80.00	27.00
	(Phila. NL)			
☐ 48	Harry Lord	250.00	110.00	37.50
☐ 49	John Miller	150.00	67.50	22.50
☐ 50	John Hummell	150.00	67.50	22.50
☐ 51	Nap Rucker	150.00	67.50	22.50
☐ 52	Zach Wheat	300.00	135.00	45.00
☐ 53	Otto Miller	150.00	67.50	22.50
☐ 54	Marty O'Toole	150.00	67.50	22.50
☐ 55	Dick Hoblitzel	175.00	80.00	27.00
	(Cinc.)			
☐ 56	Clyde Milan	150.00	67.50	22.50
☐ 57	Walter Johnson	1250.00	500.00	125.00
☐ 58	Wally Schang	150.00	67.50	22.50
☐ 59	Harry Gessler	150.00	67.50	22.50
☐ 60	Rollie Zeider	200.00	90.00	30.00
☐ 61	Ray Schalk	350.00	160.00	52.50
☐ 62	Jay Cashion	250.00	110.00	37.50
☐ 63	Babe Adams	150.00	67.50	22.50
☐ 64	Jimmy Archer	150.00	67.50	22.50
☐ 65	Tris Speaker	600.00	270.00	90.00
☐ 66	Napoleon Lajoie	750.00	325.00	110.00
	(Cleve.)			
☐ 67	Otis Crandall	150.00	67.50	22.50
☐ 68	Honus Wagner	1250.00	500.00	125.00
☐ 69	John McGraw	375.00	165.00	55.00
☐ 70	Fred Clarke	300.00	135.00	45.00
☐ 71	Chief Meyers	150.00	67.50	22.50
☐ 72	John Boehling	150.00	67.50	22.50
☐ 73	Max Carey	300.00	135.00	45.00
☐ 74	Frank Owens	150.00	67.50	22.50
☐ 75	Miller Huggins	300.00	135.00	45.00
☐ 76	Claude Hendrix	150.00	67.50	22.50
☐ 77	Hugh Jennings	300.00	135.00	45.00
☐ 78	Fred Merkle	175.00	80.00	27.00
☐ 79	Ping Bodie	150.00	67.50	22.50
☐ 80	Ed Ruelbach	150.00	67.50	22.50
☐ 81	J.C. Delehanty	150.00	67.50	22.50
☐ 82	Gavvy Cravath	175.00	80.00	27.00
☐ 83	Russ Ford	150.00	67.50	22.50
☐ 84	E.E. Knetzer	150.00	67.50	22.50
☐ 85	Buck Herzog	150.00	67.50	22.50
☐ 86	Burt Shotten	150.00	67.50	22.50
☐ 87	Forrest Cady	150.00	67.50	22.50
☐ 88	Christy Mathewson	1500.00	600.00	150.00
	(Pitching)			
☐ 89	Lawrence Cheney	150.00	67.50	22.50
☐ 90	Frank Smith	150.00	67.50	22.50
☐ 91	Roger Peckinpaugh	150.00	67.50	22.50
☐ 92	Al Demaree (N.Y. NL)	175.00	80.00	27.00
☐ 93	Derrill Pratt	225.00	100.00	33.00
	(Throwing)			
☐ 94	Eddie Cicotte	200.00	90.00	30.00
☐ 95	Ray Keating	150.00	67.50	22.50
☐ 96	Beals Becker	150.00	67.50	22.50
☐ 97	John (Rube) Benton	150.00	67.50	22.50
☐ 98	Frank LaPorte	150.00	67.50	22.50
☐ 99	Frank Chance	1000.00	400.00	100.00
☐ 100	Thomas Seaton	150.00	67.50	22.50
☐ 101	Frank Schulte	150.00	67.50	22.50
☐ 102	Ray Fisher	150.00	67.50	22.50
☐ 103	Joe Jackson	6000.00	2400.00	600.00
☐ 104	Vic Saier	150.00	67.50	22.50
☐ 105	James Lavender	150.00	67.50	22.50
☐ 106	Joe Birmingham	150.00	67.50	22.50
☐ 107	Tom Downey	150.00	67.50	22.50
☐ 108	Sherwood Magee	175.00	80.00	27.00
	(Phila. NL)			
☐ 109	Fred Blanding	150.00	67.50	22.50
☐ 110	Bob Bescher	150.00	67.50	22.50
☐ 111	Jim Callahan	250.00	110.00	37.50
☐ 112	Ed Sweeney	150.00	67.50	22.50
☐ 113	George Suggs	150.00	67.50	22.50
☐ 114	Geo. J. Moriarty	150.00	67.50	22.50
☐ 115	Addison Brennan	150.00	67.50	22.50
☐ 116	Rollie Zeider	150.00	67.50	22.50
☐ 117	Ted Easterly	150.00	67.50	22.50
☐ 118	Ed Konetchy	175.00	80.00	27.00
	(Pittsburgh)			
☐ 119	George Perring	150.00	67.50	22.50
☐ 120	Mike Doolan	150.00	67.50	22.50
☐ 121	Perdue (Boston NL)	175.00	80.00	27.00
☐ 122	Owen Bush	150.00	67.50	22.50
☐ 123	Slim Sallee	150.00	67.50	22.50
☐ 124	Earl Moore	150.00	67.50	22.50
☐ 125	Bert Niehoff	175.00	80.00	27.00
☐ 126	Walter Blair	150.00	67.50	22.50
☐ 127	Butch Schmidt	150.00	67.50	22.50
☐ 128	Steve Evans	150.00	67.50	22.50
☐ 129	Ray Caldwell	150.00	67.50	22.50
☐ 130	Ivy Wingo	150.00	67.50	22.50
☐ 131	George Baumgardner	150.00	67.50	22.50
☐ 132	Les Nunamaker	150.00	67.50	22.50
☐ 133	Branch Rickey	400.00	180.00	60.00
☐ 134	Armando Marsans	175.00	80.00	27.00
	(Cincinnati)			
☐ 135	Bill Killefer	150.00	67.50	22.50
☐ 136	Rabbit Maranville	300.00	135.00	45.00
☐ 137	William Rariden	150.00	67.50	22.50
☐ 138	Hank Gowdy	150.00	67.50	22.50
☐ 139	Rebel Oakes	150.00	67.50	22.50
☐ 140	Danny Murphy	150.00	67.50	22.50
☐ 141	Cy Barger	150.00	67.50	22.50
☐ 142	Eugene Packard	150.00	67.50	22.50
☐ 143	Jake Daubert	175.00	80.00	27.00
☐ 144	James C. Walsh	175.00	80.00	27.00

1915 Cracker Jack

The cards in this 176-card set measure approximately 2 1/4" by 3". When turned over in a lateral motion, a 1915 "series of 176" Cracker Jack card shows the back printing upside-down. Cards were available in boxes of Cracker Jack or from the company for "100 Cracker Jack coupons, or one coupon and 25 cents." An album was available for "50 coupons or one coupon and 10 cents." Because of this send-in offer, the 1915 Cracker Jack cards are noticeably easier to find than the 1914 Cracker Jack cards, although obviously neither set is plentiful. The set essentially duplicates E145-1 (1914 Cracker Jack) except for some additional cards and new poses. Players in the Federal League are indicated by FED in the checklist below. The catalog designation for the set is E145-2.

106

Joseph Birmingham, manager of the Cleveland American League team, was born in Elmira, N. Y., August 6, 1884. He played on local nines in 1901 and with the Mercersburg, Pa., Preparatory School team during 1902 and 1903. In 1906 he played baseball professionally with the A. J. G. Club of the New York State League, and was secured by Cleveland in August of the same year.

This is one of a series of pictures of famous Ball Players and Managers in the American, National and Federal Leagues, given Free with Cracker Jack, "The Famous Popcorn Confection," one card in each package. Send 100 Cracker Jack Coupons, or 1 Coupon and 50c. to CHICAGO OFFICE for complete set of 176 Pictures. Handsome Album is held full set of pictures sent postpaid for 50 Coupons or 1 Coupon and 10c. in coin or stamps.

RUECKHEIM BROS. & ECKSTEIN
Brooklyn, N. Y.   Chicago, Ill.

BIRMINGHAM, Cleveland - Americans

		EX-MT	VG-E	GOOD
COMPLETE SET (176)		32500.00	14000.00	3500.00
COMMON PLAYER (1-144)		100.00	45.00	15.00
COMMON PLAYER (145-176)		125.00	57.50	18.75
☐ 1	Otto Knabe	100.00	45.00	15.00
☐ 2	Frank Baker	250.00	110.00	37.50
☐ 3	Joe Tinker	200.00	90.00	30.00
☐ 4	Larry Doyle	100.00	45.00	15.00
☐ 5	Ward Miller	100.00	45.00	15.00
☐ 6	Eddie Plank (St.L. FED)	300.00	135.00	45.00
☐ 7	Eddie Collins (Chicago AL)	300.00	135.00	45.00
☐ 8	Rube Oldring	100.00	45.00	15.00
☐ 9	Artie Hoffman	100.00	45.00	15.00
☐ 10	John McInnis	125.00	57.50	18.75
☐ 11	George Stovall	100.00	45.00	15.00
☐ 12	Connie Mack	325.00	150.00	50.00
☐ 13	Art Wilson	100.00	45.00	15.00
☐ 14	Sam Crawford	200.00	90.00	30.00
☐ 15	Reb Russell	100.00	45.00	15.00
☐ 16	Howie Camnitz	100.00	45.00	15.00
☐ 17	Roger Bresnahan	225.00	100.00	33.00
☐ 18	Johnny Evers	200.00	90.00	30.00
☐ 19	Chief Bender (Baltimore FED)	300.00	135.00	45.00
☐ 20	Cy Falkenberg	100.00	45.00	15.00
☐ 21	Heine Zimmerman	100.00	45.00	15.00
☐ 22	Joe Wood	150.00	67.50	22.50
☐ 23	Charles Comiskey	225.00	100.00	33.00
☐ 24	George Mullen	100.00	45.00	15.00
☐ 25	Michael Simon	100.00	45.00	15.00
☐ 26	James Scott	100.00	45.00	15.00
☐ 27	Bill Carrigan	100.00	45.00	15.00
☐ 28	Jack Barry	100.00	45.00	15.00
☐ 29	Vean Gregg (Boston AL)	125.00	57.50	18.75
☐ 30	Ty Cobb	4000.00	1600.00	400.00
☐ 31	Heine Wagner	100.00	45.00	15.00
☐ 32	Mordecai Brown	200.00	90.00	30.00
☐ 33	Amos Strunk	100.00	45.00	15.00
☐ 34	Ira Thomas	100.00	45.00	15.00
☐ 35	Harry Hooper	200.00	90.00	30.00
☐ 36	Ed Walsh	200.00	90.00	30.00
☐ 37	Grover C. Alexander	425.00	190.00	63.00
☐ 38	Red Dooin (Cincinnati)	125.00	57.50	18.75
☐ 39	Chick Gandil	175.00	80.00	27.00
☐ 40	Jimmy Austin (Pitts. FED)	125.00	57.50	18.75
☐ 41	Tommy Leach	100.00	45.00	15.00
☐ 42	Al Bridwell	100.00	45.00	15.00
☐ 43	Rube Marquard (Brooklyn FED)	275.00	120.00	40.00
☐ 44	Charles Tesreau	100.00	45.00	15.00
☐ 45	Fred Luderus	100.00	45.00	15.00
☐ 46	Bob Groom	100.00	45.00	15.00
☐ 47	Josh Devore (Boston NL)	125.00	57.50	18.75
☐ 48	Steve O'Neill	125.00	57.50	18.75
☐ 49	John Miller	100.00	45.00	15.00
☐ 50	John Hummell	100.00	45.00	15.00
☐ 51	Nap Rucker	100.00	45.00	15.00
☐ 52	Zach Wheat	200.00	90.00	30.00
☐ 53	Otto Miller	100.00	45.00	15.00
☐ 54	Marty O'Toole	100.00	45.00	15.00
☐ 55	Dick Hoblitzel (Boston AL)	125.00	57.50	18.75
☐ 56	Clyde Milan	100.00	45.00	15.00
☐ 57	Walter Johnson	1000.00	400.00	100.00
☐ 58	Wally Schang	100.00	45.00	15.00
☐ 59	Harry Gessler	100.00	45.00	15.00
☐ 60	Oscar Dugey	125.00	57.50	18.75
☐ 61	Ray Schalk	225.00	100.00	33.00
☐ 62	Willie Mitchell	125.00	57.50	18.75
☐ 63	Babe Adams	100.00	45.00	15.00
☐ 64	Jimmy Archer	100.00	45.00	15.00
☐ 65	Tris Speaker	425.00	190.00	63.00
☐ 66	Napoleon Lajoie (Phila. AL)	525.00	225.00	75.00
☐ 67	Otis Crandall	100.00	45.00	15.00
☐ 68	Honus Wagner	1000.00	400.00	100.00
☐ 69	John McGraw	250.00	110.00	37.50
☐ 70	Fred Clarke	200.00	90.00	30.00
☐ 71	Chief Meyers	100.00	45.00	15.00
☐ 72	John Boehling	100.00	45.00	15.00
☐ 73	Max Carey	200.00	90.00	30.00
☐ 74	Frank Owens	100.00	45.00	15.00
☐ 75	Miller Huggins	200.00	90.00	30.00
☐ 76	Claude Hendrix	100.00	45.00	15.00
☐ 77	Hugh Jennings	200.00	90.00	30.00
☐ 78	Fred Merkle	125.00	57.50	18.75
☐ 79	Ping Bodie	100.00	45.00	15.00
☐ 80	Ed Ruelbach	100.00	45.00	15.00
☐ 81	J.C. Delehanty	100.00	45.00	15.00
☐ 82	Gavvy Cravath	125.00	57.50	18.75
☐ 83	Russ Ford	100.00	45.00	15.00
☐ 84	E.E. Knetzer	100.00	45.00	15.00
☐ 85	Buck Herzog	100.00	45.00	15.00
☐ 86	Burt Shotten	100.00	45.00	15.00
☐ 87	Forrest Cady	100.00	45.00	15.00
☐ 88	Christy Mathewson (Portrait)	1250.00	500.00	125.00
☐ 89	Lawrence Cheney	100.00	45.00	15.00
☐ 90	Frank Smith	100.00	45.00	15.00
☐ 91	Roger Peckinpaugh	100.00	45.00	15.00
☐ 92	Al Demaree (Phila. NL)	125.00	57.50	18.75
☐ 93	Derrill Pratt (Portrait)	150.00	67.50	22.50
☐ 94	Eddie Cicotte	150.00	67.50	22.50
☐ 95	Ray Keating	100.00	45.00	15.00
☐ 96	Beals Becker	100.00	45.00	15.00
☐ 97	John (Rube) Benton	100.00	45.00	15.00
☐ 98	Frank LaPorte	100.00	45.00	15.00
☐ 99	Hal Chase	250.00	110.00	37.50
☐ 100	Thomas Seaton	100.00	45.00	15.00
☐ 101	Frank Schulte	100.00	45.00	15.00
☐ 102	Ray Fisher	100.00	45.00	15.00
☐ 103	Joe Jackson	4500.00	1800.00	450.00
☐ 104	Vic Saier	100.00	45.00	15.00
☐ 105	James Lavender	100.00	45.00	15.00
☐ 106	Joe Birmingham	100.00	45.00	15.00
☐ 107	Thomas Downey	100.00	45.00	15.00
☐ 108	Sherwood Magee (Boston NL)	125.00	57.50	18.75
☐ 109	Fred Blanding	100.00	45.00	15.00
☐ 110	Bob Bescher	100.00	45.00	15.00
☐ 111	Herbie Moran	125.00	57.50	18.75
☐ 112	Ed Sweeney	100.00	45.00	15.00
☐ 113	George Suggs	100.00	45.00	15.00
☐ 114	Geo. J. Moriarty	100.00	45.00	15.00
☐ 115	Addison Brennan	100.00	45.00	15.00
☐ 116	Rollie Zeider	100.00	45.00	15.00
☐ 117	Ted Easterly	100.00	45.00	15.00
☐ 118	Ed Konetchy (Pitts. FED)	125.00	57.50	18.75
☐ 119	George Perring	100.00	45.00	15.00
☐ 120	Mike Doolan	100.00	45.00	15.00
☐ 121	Perdue (St.L. NL)	125.00	57.50	18.75
☐ 122	Owen Bush	100.00	45.00	15.00
☐ 123	Slim Sallee	100.00	45.00	15.00
☐ 124	Earl Moore	100.00	45.00	15.00
☐ 125	Bert Niehoff (Phila. NL)	125.00	57.50	18.75
☐ 126	Walter Blair	100.00	45.00	15.00
☐ 127	Butch Schmidt	100.00	45.00	15.00
☐ 128	Steve Evans	100.00	45.00	15.00
☐ 129	Ray Caldwell	100.00	45.00	15.00
☐ 130	Ivy Wingo	100.00	45.00	15.00
☐ 131	Geo. Baumgardner	100.00	45.00	15.00
☐ 132	Les Nunamaker	100.00	45.00	15.00
☐ 133	Branch Rickey	275.00	120.00	40.00
☐ 134	Armando Marsans (St.L. FED)	125.00	57.50	18.75
☐ 135	William Killefer	100.00	45.00	15.00
☐ 136	Rabbit Maranville	200.00	90.00	30.00
☐ 137	William Rariden	100.00	45.00	15.00
☐ 138	Hank Gowdy	100.00	45.00	15.00
☐ 139	Rebel Oakes	100.00	45.00	15.00
☐ 140	Danny Murphy	100.00	45.00	15.00
☐ 141	Cy Barger	100.00	45.00	15.00
☐ 142	Eugene Packard	100.00	45.00	15.00
☐ 143	Jake Daubert	125.00	57.50	18.75
☐ 144	James C. Walsh	100.00	45.00	15.00
☐ 145	Ted Cather	125.00	57.50	18.75

			MINT	EXC	G-VG
☐	146	George Tyler	125.00	57.50	18.75
☐	147	Lee Magee	125.00	57.50	18.75
☐	148	Owen Wilson	125.00	57.50	18.75
☐	149	Hal Janvrin	125.00	57.50	18.75
☐	150	Doc Johnston	125.00	57.50	18.75
☐	151	George Whitted	125.00	57.50	18.75
☐	152	George McQuillen	125.00	57.50	18.75
☐	153	Bill James	125.00	57.50	18.75
☐	154	Dick Rudolph	125.00	57.50	18.75
☐	155	Joe Connolly	125.00	57.50	18.75
☐	156	Jean Dubuc	125.00	57.50	18.75
☐	157	George Kaiserling	125.00	57.50	18.75
☐	158	Fritz Maisel	125.00	57.50	18.75
☐	159	Heine Groh	125.00	57.50	18.75
☐	160	Benny Kauff	125.00	57.50	18.75
☐	161	Ed Rousch	275.00	120.00	40.00
☐	162	George Stallings	125.00	57.50	18.75
☐	163	Bert Whaling	125.00	57.50	18.75
☐	164	Bob Shawkey	125.00	57.50	18.75
☐	165	Eddie Murphy	125.00	57.50	18.75
☐	166	Joe Bush	150.00	67.50	22.50
☐	167	Clark Griffith	250.00	110.00	37.50
☐	168	Vin Campbell	125.00	57.50	18.75
☐	169	Raymond Collins	125.00	57.50	18.75
☐	170	Hans Lobert	125.00	57.50	18.75
☐	171	Earl Hamilton	125.00	57.50	18.75
☐	172	Erskine Mayer	125.00	57.50	18.75
☐	173	Tilly Walker	125.00	57.50	18.75
☐	174	Robert Veach	125.00	57.50	18.75
☐	175	Joseph Benz	125.00	57.50	18.75
☐	176	Jim Vaughn	150.00	67.50	22.50

1982 Cracker Jack

The cards in this 16-card set measure 2 1/2" by 3 1/2"; cards came in two sheets of eight cards, plus an advertising card with a title in the center, which measured approximately 7 1/2" by 10 1/2". Cracker Jack reentered the baseball card market for the first time since 1915 to promote the first "Old Timers Baseball Classic" held July 19, 1982. The color player photos have a Cracker Jack border and have either green (NL) or red (AL) frame lines and name panels. The Cracker Jack logo appears on both sides of each card, with AL players numbered 1-8 and NL players numbered 9-16. Of the 16 ballplayers pictured, five did not appear at the game. At first, the two sheets were available only through the mail but are now commonly found in hobby circles. The set was prepared for Cracker Jack by Topps. The prices below reflect individual card prices; the price for complete panels would be about the same as the sum of the card prices for those players on the panel due to the easy availability of uncut sheets.

		MINT	EXC	G-VG
COMPLETE SET (16)		8.00	3.50	.80
COMMON PLAYER (1-16)		.20	.08	.02
☐ 1	Larry Doby	.20	.08	.02
☐ 2	Bob Feller	.75	.30	.07
☐ 3	Whitey Ford	.75	.30	.07
☐ 4	Al Kaline	.75	.30	.07
☐ 5	Harmon Killebrew	.50	.20	.05
☐ 6	Mickey Mantle	2.00	.80	.20
☐ 7	Tony Oliva	.20	.08	.02

			MINT	EXC	G-VG
☐	8	Brooks Robinson	.75	.30	.07
☐	9	Hank Aaron	1.00	.40	.10
☐	10	Ernie Banks	.75	.30	.07
☐	11	Ralph Kiner	.45	.18	.04
☐	12	Ed Mathews	.35	.15	.03
☐	13	Willie Mays	1.00	.40	.10
☐	14	Robin Roberts	.35	.15	.03
☐	15	Duke Snider	.75	.30	.07
☐	16	Warren Spahn	.50	.20	.05

1991 Crown Orioles

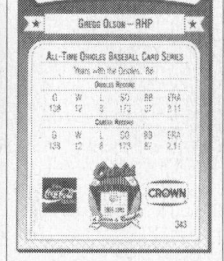

This 501-card set was produced by the Baltimore Orioles in conjunction with Crown Gasoline Stations and Coca-Cola. The cards measure approximately 2 1/2" by 3 1/8" and feature every Oriole player in the team's modern history (1954-1991). The cards were issued in four series, with ten twelve-card sheets per set. The front features a black and white head shot of the player, with a green border and an orange picture frame. The player's name and position appear above the picture, while the Orioles' team logo is superimposed at the lower left corner. In a similar design to the front, the back is printed in black and gray, and presents the player's Orioles statistics and Major League statistics. The sponsors' logos adorn the bottom of the card back, with the card number in the lower right hand corner. The first set was given away at the Orioles May 17th game against the California Angels, and the following day the set went on sale at Baltimore area Crown gasoline stations for $1.99 with an eight gallon fill-up. The second set was given away at the Orioles June 28th game against the Boston Red Sox, and again it went on sale the following day at Crown gasoline stations. The third set was given away at the Orioles August 11th game against the Chicago White Sox and went on sale on the same day. The fourth set went on sale at Crown gasoline stations on September 16. The cards are arranged alphabetically by player and checklisted below accordingly.

		MINT	EXC	G-VG
COMPLETE SET (501)		35.00	15.75	5.25
COMMON PLAYER (1-360)		.10	.04	.01
COMMON PLAYER (361-501)		.10	.04	.01
☐ 1	Don Aase	.15	.06	.01
☐ 2	Cal Abrams	.10	.04	.01
☐ 3	Jerry Adair	.10	.04	.01
☐ 4	Bobby Adams	.10	.04	.01
☐ 5	Mike Adamson	.10	.04	.01
☐ 6	Jay Aldrich	.10	.04	.01
☐ 7	Bob Alexander	.10	.04	.01
☐ 8	Doyle Alexander	.15	.06	.01
☐ 9	Brady Anderson	.10	.04	.01
☐ 10	John Anderson	.10	.04	.01
☐ 11	Mike Anderson	.10	.04	.01
☐ 12	Luis Aparicio	.30	.12	.03
☐ 13	Tony Arnold	.10	.04	.01
☐ 14	Bobby Avila	.10	.04	.01
☐ 15	Benny Ayala	.10	.04	.01
☐ 16	Bob Bailor	.10	.04	.01
☐ 17	Frank Baker	.10	.04	.01

☐ 18	Jeff Ballard	.10	.04	.01
☐ 19	George Bamberger	.10	.04	.01
☐ 20	Steve Barber	.10	.04	.01
☐ 21	Ray(Buddy) Barker	.10	.04	.01
☐ 22	Ed Barnowski	.10	.04	.01
☐ 23	Jose Bautista	.10	.04	.01
☐ 24	Don Baylor	.20	.08	.02
☐ 25	Charlie Beamon	.10	.04	.01
☐ 26	Fred Beene	.10	.04	.01
☐ 27	Mark Belanger	.20	.08	.02
☐ 28	Eric Bell	.10	.04	.01
☐ 29	Juan Bell	.10	.04	.01
☐ 30	Juan Beniquez	.10	.04	.01
☐ 31	Neil Berry	.10	.04	.01
☐ 32	Frank Bertaina	.10	.04	.01
☐ 33	Fred Besana	.10	.04	.01
☐ 34	Vern Bickford	.10	.04	.01
☐ 35	Babe Birrer	.10	.04	.01
☐ 36	Paul Blair	.15	.06	.01
☐ 37	Curt Blefary	.15	.06	.01
☐ 38	Mike Blyzka	.10	.04	.01
☐ 39	Mike Boddicker	.15	.06	.01
☐ 40	Juan Bonilla	.10	.04	.01
☐ 41	Bob Bonner	.10	.04	.01
☐ 42	Dan Boone	.10	.04	.01
☐ 43	Rich Bordi	.10	.04	.01
☐ 44	Dave Boswell	.10	.04	.01
☐ 45	Sam Bowens	.10	.04	.01
☐ 46	Bob Boyd	.10	.04	.01
☐ 47	Gene Brabender	.10	.04	.01
☐ 48	Phil Bradley	.15	.06	.01
☐ 49	Jackie Brandt	.10	.04	.01
☐ 50	Marv Breeding	.10	.04	.01
☐ 51	Jim Brideweser	.10	.04	.01
☐ 52	Nellie Briles	.15	.06	.01
☐ 53	Dick Brown	.10	.04	.01
☐ 54	Hal Brown	.10	.04	.01
☐ 55	Larry Brown	.10	.04	.01
☐ 56	Mark Brown	.10	.04	.01
☐ 57	Marty Brown	.10	.04	.01
☐ 58	George Brunet	.10	.04	.01
☐ 59	Don Buford	.15	.06	.01
☐ 60	Al Bumbry	.10	.04	.01
☐ 61	Wally Bunker	.15	.06	.01
☐ 62	Leo Burke	.10	.04	.01
☐ 63	Rick Burleson	.15	.06	.01
☐ 64	Pete Burnside	.10	.04	.01
☐ 65	Jim Busby	.10	.04	.01
☐ 66	John Buzhardt	.10	.04	.01
☐ 67	Harry Byrd	.10	.04	.01
☐ 68	Enos Cabell	.10	.04	.01
☐ 69	Chico Carrasquel	.10	.04	.01
☐ 70	Camilo Carreon	.10	.04	.01
☐ 71	Foster Castleman	.10	.04	.01
☐ 72	Wayne Causey	.10	.04	.01
☐ 73	Art Ceccarelli	.10	.04	.01
☐ 74	Bob Chakales	.10	.04	.01
☐ 75	Tony Chevez	.10	.04	.01
☐ 76	Tom Chism	.10	.04	.01
☐ 77	Gino Cimoli	.10	.04	.01
☐ 78	Gil Coan	.10	.04	.01
☐ 79	Rich Coggins	.10	.04	.01
☐ 80	Joe Coleman	.10	.04	.01
☐ 81	Rip Coleman	.10	.04	.01
☐ 82	Fritz Connally	.10	.04	.01
☐ 83	Sandy Consuegra	.10	.04	.01
☐ 84	Doug Corbett	.10	.04	.01
☐ 85	Mark Corey	.10	.04	.01
☐ 86	Clint Courtney	.10	.04	.01
☐ 87	Billy Cox	.10	.04	.01
☐ 88	Dave Criscione	.10	.04	.01
☐ 89	Terry Crowley	.10	.04	.01
☐ 90	Todd Cruz	.10	.04	.01
☐ 91	Mike Cuellar	.20	.08	.02
☐ 92	Angie Dagres	.10	.04	.01
☐ 93	Clay Dalrymple	.10	.04	.01
☐ 94	Rich Dauer	.10	.04	.01
☐ 95	Jerry DaVanon	.10	.04	.01
☐ 96	Butch Davis	.10	.04	.01
☐ 97	Storm Davis	.15	.06	.01
☐ 98	Tommy Davis	.15	.06	.01
☐ 99	Doug DeCinces	.20	.08	.02
☐ 100	Luis DeLeon	.10	.04	.01
☐ 101	Ike Delock	.10	.04	.01
☐ 102	Rick Dempsey	.15	.06	.01
☐ 103	Mike Devereaux	.15	.06	.01
☐ 104	Chuck Diering	.10	.04	.01
☐ 105	Gordon Dillard	.10	.04	.01
☐ 106	Bill Dillman	.10	.04	.01
☐ 107	Mike Dimmel	.10	.04	.01
☐ 108	Ken Dixon	.10	.04	.01
☐ 109	Pat Dobson	.15	.06	.01
☐ 110	Tom Dodd	.10	.04	.01
☐ 111	Harry Dorish	.10	.04	.01
☐ 112	Moe Drabowsky	.15	.06	.01
☐ 113	Dick Drago	.10	.04	.01
☐ 114	Walt Dropo	.15	.06	.01
☐ 115	Tom Dukes	.10	.04	.01
☐ 116	Dave Duncan	.10	.04	.01
☐ 117	Ryne Duren	.20	.08	.02
☐ 118	Joe Durham	.10	.04	.01
☐ 119	Jim Dwyer	.10	.04	.01
☐ 120	Jim Dyck	.10	.04	.01
☐ 121	Mike Epstein	.15	.06	.01
☐ 122	Chuck Essegian	.10	.04	.01
☐ 123	Chuck Estrada	.15	.06	.01
☐ 124	Andy Etchebarren	.15	.06	.01
☐ 125	Hoot Evers	.10	.04	.01
☐ 126	Ed Farmer	.10	.04	.01
☐ 127	Chico Fernandez	.10	.04	.01
☐ 128	Don Ferrarese	.10	.04	.01
☐ 129	Jim Finigan	.10	.04	.01
☐ 130	Steve Finley	.15	.06	.01
☐ 131	Mike Fiore	.10	.04	.01
☐ 132	Eddie Fisher	.10	.04	.01
☐ 133	Jack Fisher	.10	.04	.01
☐ 134	Tom Fisher	.10	.04	.01
☐ 135	Mike Flanagan	.20	.08	.02
☐ 136	John Flinn	.10	.04	.01
☐ 137	Bobby Floyd	.10	.04	.01
☐ 138	Hank Foiles	.10	.04	.01
☐ 139	Dan Ford	.10	.04	.01
☐ 140	Dave Ford	.10	.04	.01
☐ 141	Mike Fornieles	.10	.04	.01
☐ 142	Howie Fox	.10	.04	.01
☐ 143	Tito Francona	.15	.06	.01
☐ 144	Joe Frazier	.10	.04	.01
☐ 145	Roger Freed	.10	.04	.01
☐ 146	Jim Fridley	.10	.04	.01
☐ 147	Jim Fuller	.10	.04	.01
☐ 148	Joe Gaines	.10	.04	.01
☐ 149	Vinicio(Chico) Garcia	.10	.04	.01
☐ 150	Kiko Garcia	.10	.04	.01
☐ 151	Billy Gardner	.10	.04	.01
☐ 152	Wayne Garland	.10	.04	.01
☐ 153	Tommy Gastall	.10	.04	.01
☐ 154	Jim Gentile	.15	.06	.01
☐ 155	Ken Gerhart	.10	.04	.01
☐ 156	Paul Gilliford	.10	.04	.01
☐ 157	Joe Ginsberg	.10	.04	.01
☐ 158	Leo Gomez	.25	.10	.02
☐ 159	Rene Gonzales	.10	.04	.01
☐ 160	Billy Goodman	.15	.06	.01
☐ 161	Dan Graham	.10	.04	.01
☐ 162	Ted Gray	.10	.04	.01
☐ 163	Gene Green	.10	.04	.01
☐ 164	Lenny Green	.10	.04	.01
☐ 165	Bobby Grich	.20	.08	.02
☐ 166	Nuje Griffin	.10	.04	.01
☐ 167	Ross Grimsley	.10	.04	.01
☐ 168	Wayne Gross	.10	.04	.01
☐ 169	Glenn Gulliver	.10	.04	.01
☐ 170	Jackie Guttierrez	.10	.04	.01
☐ 171	John Habyan	.10	.04	.01
☐ 172	Harvey Haddix	.15	.06	.01
☐ 173	Bob Hale	.10	.04	.01
☐ 174	Dick Hall	.10	.04	.01
☐ 175	Bert Hamric	.10	.04	.01
☐ 176	Larry Haney	.10	.04	.01
☐ 177	Ron Hansen	.15	.06	.01
☐ 178	Jim Hardin	.10	.04	.01
☐ 179	Larry Harlow	.10	.04	.01
☐ 180	Pete Harnisch	.15	.06	.01
☐ 181	Tommy Harper	.15	.06	.01
☐ 182	Bob Harrison	.10	.04	.01
☐ 183	Roric Harrison	.10	.04	.01
☐ 184	Jack Harshman	.10	.04	.01
☐ 185	Mike Hart	.10	.04	.01
☐ 186	Pete Hartzell	.10	.04	.01
☐ 187	Grady Hatton	.10	.04	.01
☐ 188	Brad Havens	.10	.04	.01
☐ 189	Drungo Hazewood	.10	.04	.01
☐ 190	Jehosie Heard	.10	.04	.01
☐ 191	Mel Held	.10	.04	.01
☐ 192	Woodie Held	.15	.06	.01
☐ 193	Ellie Hendricks	.15	.06	.01
☐ 194	Leo Hernandez	.10	.04	.01
☐ 195	Whitey Herzog	.20	.08	.02
☐ 196	Kevin Hickey	.10	.04	.01
☐ 197	Billy Hoeft	.15	.06	.01
☐ 198	Chris Hoiles	.20	.08	.02
☐ 199	Fred Holdsworth	.10	.04	.01
☐ 200	Brian Holton	.10	.04	.01
☐ 201	Ken Holtzman	.15	.06	.01
☐ 202	Don Hood	.10	.04	.01
☐ 203	Sam Horn	.20	.08	.02
☐ 204	Art Houtteman	.10	.04	.01
☐ 205	Bruce Howard	.10	.04	.01

#	Name				#	Name			
☐ 206	Rex Hudler	.15	.06	.01	☐ 300	Bill Miller	.10	.04	.01
☐ 207	Phil Huffman	.10	.04	.01	☐ 301	Dyar Miller	.10	.04	.01
☐ 208	Keith Hughes	.10	.04	.01	☐ 302	John Miller	.10	.04	.01
☐ 209	Mark Huismann	.10	.04	.01	☐ 303	Randy Miller	.10	.04	.01
☐ 210	Tim Hulett	.10	.04	.01	☐ 304	Stu Miller	.15	.06	.01
☐ 211	Billy Hunter	.15	.06	.01	☐ 305	Randy Milligan	.20	.08	.02
☐ 212	Dave Huppert	.10	.04	.01	☐ 306	Paul Mirabella	.10	.04	.01
☐ 213	Jim Hutto	.10	.04	.01	☐ 307	Willie Miranda	.10	.04	.01
☐ 214	Dick Hyde	.10	.04	.01	☐ 308	John Mitchell	.10	.04	.01
☐ 215	Grant Jackson	.15	.06	.01	☐ 309	Paul Mitchell	.10	.04	.01
☐ 216	Lou Jackson	.15	.06	.01	☐ 310	Ron Moeller	.10	.04	.01
☐ 217	Reggie Jackson	.60	.25	.06	☐ 311	Bob Molinaro	.10	.04	.01
☐ 218	Ron Jackson	.10	.04	.01	☐ 312	Ray Moore	.10	.04	.01
☐ 219	Jesse Jefferson	.10	.04	.01	☐ 313	Andres Mora	.10	.04	.01
☐ 220	Stan Jefferson	.10	.04	.01	☐ 314	Jose Morales	.10	.04	.01
☐ 221	Bob Johnson	.10	.04	.01	☐ 315	Keith Moreland	.10	.04	.01
☐ 222	Connie Johnson	.10	.04	.01	☐ 316	Mike Morgan	.15	.06	.01
☐ 223	Darrell Johnson	.10	.04	.01	☐ 317	Dan Morogiello	.10	.04	.01
☐ 224	Dave Johnson	.10	.04	.01	☐ 318	John Morris	.10	.04	.01
☐ 225	Davey Johnson	.20	.08	.02	☐ 319	Les Moss	.10	.04	.01
☐ 226	David Johnson	.10	.04	.01	☐ 320	Curt Motton	.10	.04	.01
☐ 227	Don Johnson	.10	.04	.01	☐ 321	Eddie Murray	.35	.15	.03
☐ 228	Ernie Johnson	.15	.06	.01	☐ 322	Ray Murray	.10	.04	.01
☐ 229	Gordon Jones	.10	.04	.01	☐ 323	Tony Muser	.10	.04	.01
☐ 230	Ricky Jones	.10	.04	.01	☐ 324	Buster Narum	.10	.04	.01
☐ 231	O'Dell Jones	.10	.04	.01	☐ 325	Bob Nelson	.10	.04	.01
☐ 232	Sam Jones	.15	.06	.01	☐ 326	Roger Nelson	.10	.04	.01
☐ 233	George Kell	.30	.12	.03	☐ 327	Carl Nichols	.10	.04	.01
☐ 234	Frank Kellert	.10	.04	.01	☐ 328	Dave Nicholson	.10	.04	.01
☐ 235	Pat Kelly	.15	.06	.01	☐ 329	Tim Niedenfuer	.10	.04	.01
☐ 236	Bob Kennedy	.15	.06	.01	☐ 330	Bob Nieman	.10	.04	.01
☐ 237	Terry Kennedy	.15	.06	.01	☐ 331	Donell Nixon	.10	.04	.01
☐ 238	Joe Kerrigan	.10	.04	.01	☐ 332	Joe Nolan	.10	.04	.01
☐ 239	Mike Kinnunen	.10	.04	.01	☐ 333	Dickie Noles	.10	.04	.01
☐ 240	Willie Kirkland	.15	.06	.01	☐ 334	Tim Nordbrook	.10	.04	.01
☐ 241	Ron Kittle	.10	.04	.01	☐ 335	Jim Northrup	.15	.06	.01
☐ 242	Billy Klaus	.10	.04	.01	☐ 336	Jack O'Connor	.10	.04	.01
☐ 243	Ray Knight	.20	.08	.02	☐ 337	Billy O'Dell	.10	.04	.01
☐ 244	Darold Knowles	.10	.04	.01	☐ 338	John O'Donoghue	.10	.04	.01
☐ 245	Dick Kokos	.10	.04	.01	☐ 339	Tom O'Malley	.10	.04	.01
☐ 246	Brad Komminsk	.10	.04	.01	☐ 340	Johnny Oates	.20	.08	.02
☐ 247	Dave Koslo	.10	.04	.01	☐ 341	Chuck Oertel	.10	.04	.01
☐ 248	Wayne Krenchicki	.10	.04	.01	☐ 342	Bob Oliver	.10	.04	.01
☐ 249	Lou Kretlow	.10	.04	.01	☐ 343	Gregg Olson	.30	.12	.03
☐ 250	Dick Kryhoski	.10	.04	.01	☐ 344	John Orsino	.10	.04	.01
☐ 251	Bob Kuzava	.10	.04	.01	☐ 345	Joe Orsulak	.10	.04	.01
☐ 252	Lee Lacy	.10	.04	.01	☐ 346	John Pacella	.10	.04	.01
☐ 253	Hobie Landrith	.10	.04	.01	☐ 347	Dave Pagan	.10	.04	.01
☐ 254	Tito Landrum	.10	.04	.01	☐ 348	Erv Palica	.10	.04	.01
☐ 255	Don Larsen	.20	.08	.02	☐ 349	Jim Palmer	.50	.20	.05
☐ 256	Charlie Lau	.15	.06	.01	☐ 350	John Papa	.10	.04	.01
☐ 257	Jim Lehew	.10	.04	.01	☐ 351	Milt Pappas	.15	.06	.01
☐ 258	Ken Lehman	.10	.04	.01	☐ 352	Al Pardo	.10	.04	.01
☐ 259	Don Lenhardt	.10	.04	.01	☐ 353	Kelly Paris	.10	.04	.01
☐ 260	Dave Leonard	.10	.04	.01	☐ 354	Mike Parrott	.10	.04	.01
☐ 261	Don Leppert	.10	.04	.01	☐ 355	Tom Patton	.10	.04	.01
☐ 262	Dick Littlefield	.10	.04	.01	☐ 356	Albie Pearson	.10	.04	.01
☐ 263	Charlie Locke	.10	.04	.01	☐ 357	Orlando Pena	.10	.04	.01
☐ 264	Whitey Lockman	.15	.06	.01	☐ 358	Oswaldo Peraza	.10	.04	.01
☐ 265	Billy Loes	.15	.06	.01	☐ 359	Buddy Peterson	.10	.04	.01
☐ 266	Ed Lopat	.20	.08	.02	☐ 360	Dave Philley	.10	.04	.01
☐ 267	Carlos Lopez	.10	.04	.01	☐ 361	Tom Phoebus	.10	.04	.01
☐ 268	Marcelino Lopez	.10	.04	.01	☐ 362	Al Pilarcik	.10	.04	.01
☐ 269	John Lowenstein	.10	.04	.01	☐ 363	Duane Pillette	.10	.04	.01
☐ 270	Steve Luebber	.10	.04	.01	☐ 364	Lou Piniella	.20	.08	.02
☐ 271	Dick Luebke	.10	.04	.01		(Pictured wearing			
☐ 272	Fred Lynn	.20	.08	.02		a KC Royals cap)			
☐ 273	Bobby Mabe	.10	.04	.01	☐ 365	Dave Pope	.10	.04	.01
☐ 274	Elliott Maddox	.10	.04	.01	☐ 366	Arnie Portocarrero	.10	.04	.01
☐ 275	Hank Majeski	.10	.04	.01	☐ 367	Boog Powell	.25	.10	.02
☐ 276	Roger Marquis	.10	.04	.01	☐ 368	Johnny Powers	.10	.04	.01
☐ 277	Freddie Marsh	.10	.04	.01	☐ 369	Carl Powis	.10	.04	.01
☐ 278	Jim Marshall	.10	.04	.01	☐ 370	Joe Price	.10	.04	.01
☐ 279	Morrie Martin	.10	.04	.01	☐ 371	Jim Pyburn	.10	.04	.01
☐ 280	Dennis Martinez	.20	.08	.02	☐ 372	Art Quirk	.10	.04	.01
☐ 281	Tippy Martinez	.10	.04	.01	☐ 373	Jamie Quirk	.10	.04	.01
☐ 282	Tom Matchick	.10	.04	.01	☐ 374	Allan Ramirez	.10	.04	.01
☐ 283	Charlie Maxwell	.10	.04	.01	☐ 375	Floyd Rayford	.10	.04	.01
☐ 284	Dave May	.10	.04	.01	☐ 376	Mike Reinbach	.10	.04	.01
☐ 285	Lee May	.15	.06	.01	☐ 377	Merv Rettenmund	.10	.04	.01
☐ 286	Rudy May	.10	.04	.01	☐ 378	Bob Reynolds	.10	.04	.01
☐ 287	Mike McCormick	.15	.06	.01	☐ 379	Del Rice	.10	.04	.01
☐ 288	Ben McDonald	.30	.12	.03	☐ 380	Pete Richert	.10	.04	.01
☐ 289	Jim McDonald	.10	.04	.01	☐ 381	Jeff Rineer	.10	.04	.01
☐ 290	Scott McGregor	.15	.06	.01	☐ 382	Bill Ripken	.15	.06	.01
☐ 291	Mickey McGuire	.10	.04	.01	☐ 383	Cal Ripken	.75	.30	.07
☐ 292	Jeff McKnight	.10	.04	.01	☐ 384	Robin Roberts	.30	.12	.03
☐ 293	Dave McNally	.20	.08	.02	☐ 385	Brooks Robinson	.60	.25	.06
☐ 294	Sam Mele	.10	.04	.01	☐ 386	Earl Robinson	.10	.04	.01
☐ 295	Francisco Melendez	.10	.04	.01	☐ 387	Eddie Robinson	.10	.04	.01
☐ 296	Bob Melvin	.10	.04	.01	☐ 388	Frank Robinson	.50	.20	.05
☐ 297	Jose Mesa	.10	.04	.01	☐ 389	Sergio Robles	.10	.04	.01
☐ 298	Eddie Miksis	.10	.04	.01	☐ 390	Aurelio Rodriguez	.10	.04	.01
☐ 299	Bob Milacki	.15	.06	.01	☐ 391	Vic Rodriguez	.10	.04	.01

☐ 392	Gary Roenicke	.15	.06	.01
☐ 393	Saul Rogovin	.10	.04	.01
☐ 394	Wade Rowdon	.10	.04	.01
☐ 395	Ken Rowe	.10	.04	.01
☐ 396	Willie Royster	.10	.04	.01
☐ 397	Vic Roznovsky	.10	.04	.01
☐ 398	Ken Rudolph	.10	.04	.01
☐ 399	Lenn Sakata	.10	.04	.01
☐ 400	Chico Salmon	.10	.04	.01
☐ 401	Orlando Sanchez	.10	.04	.01
	(Pictured wearing St. Louis Cardinals cap)			
☐ 402	Bob Saverine	.10	.04	.01
☐ 403	Art Schallock	.10	.04	.01
☐ 404	Bill Scherrer	.10	.04	.01
☐ 405	Curt Schilling	.10	.04	.01
☐ 406	Dave Schmidt	.10	.04	.01
☐ 407	Johnny Schmitz	.10	.04	.01
☐ 408	Jeff Schneider	.10	.04	.01
☐ 409	Rick Schu	.10	.04	.01
☐ 410	Mickey Scott	.10	.04	.01
☐ 411	Kal Segrist	.10	.04	.01
☐ 412	David Segui	.15	.06	.01
☐ 413	Al Severinsen	.10	.04	.01
☐ 414	Larry Sheets	.15	.06	.01
☐ 415	John Shelby	.10	.04	.01
☐ 416	Barry Shetrone	.10	.04	.01
☐ 417	Tom Shopay	.10	.04	.01
☐ 418	Bill Short	.15	.06	.01
☐ 419	Norm Siebern	.15	.06	.01
☐ 420	Nelson Simmons	.10	.04	.01
☐ 421	Ken Singleton	.20	.08	.02
☐ 422	Doug Sisk	.10	.04	.01
☐ 423	Dave Skaggs	.10	.04	.01
☐ 424	Lou Sleater	.10	.04	.01
☐ 425	Al Smith	.15	.06	.01
☐ 426	Billy Smith	.10	.04	.01
☐ 427	Hal Smith	.10	.04	.01
☐ 428	Mike(Texas) Smith	.10	.04	.01
☐ 429	Nate Smith	.10	.04	.01
☐ 430	Nate Snell	.10	.04	.01
☐ 431	Russ Snyder	.10	.04	.01
☐ 432	Don Stanhouse	.15	.06	.01
☐ 433	Pete Stanicek	.10	.04	.01
☐ 434	Herm Starrette	.10	.04	.01
☐ 435	John Stefero	.10	.04	.01
☐ 436	Gene Stephens	.10	.04	.01
☐ 437	Vern Stephens	.15	.06	.01
☐ 438	Earl Stephenson	.10	.04	.01
☐ 439	Sammy Stewart	.10	.04	.01
☐ 440	Royle Stillman	.10	.04	.01
☐ 441	Wes Stock	.15	.06	.01
☐ 442	Tim Stoddard	.10	.04	.01
☐ 443	Dean Stone	.10	.04	.01
☐ 444	Jeff Stone	.10	.04	.01
☐ 445	Steve Stone	.15	.06	.01
☐ 446	Marlin Stuart	.10	.04	.01
☐ 447	Gordie Sundin	.10	.04	.01
☐ 448	Bill Swaggerty	.10	.04	.01
☐ 449	Willie Tasby	.10	.04	.01
☐ 450	Joe Taylor	.10	.04	.01
☐ 451	Dorn Taylor	.10	.04	.01
☐ 452	Anthony Telford	.15	.06	.01
☐ 453	Johnny Temple	.15	.06	.01
☐ 454	Mickey Tettleton	.20	.08	.02
☐ 455	Valmy Thomas	.10	.04	.01
☐ 456	Bobby Thomson	.15	.06	.01
☐ 457	Marv Throneberry	.20	.08	.02
☐ 458	Mark Thurmond	.10	.04	.01
☐ 459	Jay Tibbs	.10	.04	.01
☐ 460	Mike Torrez	.15	.06	.01
☐ 461	Jim Traber	.10	.04	.01
☐ 462	Gus Triandos	.20	.08	.02
☐ 463	Paul(Dizzy) Trout	.15	.06	.01
☐ 464	Bob Turley	.20	.08	.02
☐ 465	Tom Underwood	.10	.04	.01
☐ 466	Fred Valentine	.10	.04	.01
☐ 467	Dave Van Gorder	.10	.04	.01
☐ 468	Dave Vineyard	.10	.04	.01
☐ 469	Ozzie Virgil	.15	.06	.01
☐ 470	Eddie Waitkus	.15	.06	.01
☐ 471	Greg Walker	.10	.04	.01
☐ 472	Jerry Walker	.10	.04	.01
☐ 473	Pete Ward	.10	.04	.01
☐ 474	Carl Warwick	.10	.04	.01
☐ 475	Ron Washington	.10	.04	.01
☐ 476	Eddie Watt	.10	.04	.01
☐ 477	Don Welchel	.10	.04	.01
☐ 478	George Werley	.10	.04	.01
☐ 479	Vic Wertz	.15	.06	.01
☐ 480	Wally Westlake	.10	.04	.01
☐ 481	Mickey Weston	.10	.04	.01
☐ 482	Alan Wiggins	.10	.04	.01
☐ 483	Bill Wight	.10	.04	.01

☐ 484	Hoyt Wilhelm	.30	.12	.03
☐ 485	Dallas Williams	.10	.04	.01
☐ 486	Dick Williams	.15	.06	.01
☐ 487	Earl Williams	.10	.04	.01
☐ 488	Mark Williamson	.10	.04	.01
☐ 489	Jim Wilson	.10	.04	.01
☐ 490	Gene Woodling	.15	.06	.01
☐ 491	Craig Worthington	.15	.06	.01
☐ 492	Bobby Young	.10	.04	.01
☐ 493	Mike Young	.10	.04	.01
☐ 494	Frank Zupo	.10	.04	.01
☐ 495	George Zuverink	.10	.04	.01
☐ 496	Glenn Davis	.30	.12	.03
☐ 497	Dwight Evans	.20	.08	.02
☐ 498	Dave Gallagher	.10	.04	.01
☐ 499	Paul Kilgus	.10	.04	.01
☐ 500	Jeff Robinson	.10	.04	.01
☐ 501	Ernie Whitt	.10	.04	.01

1982 Cubs Red Lobster

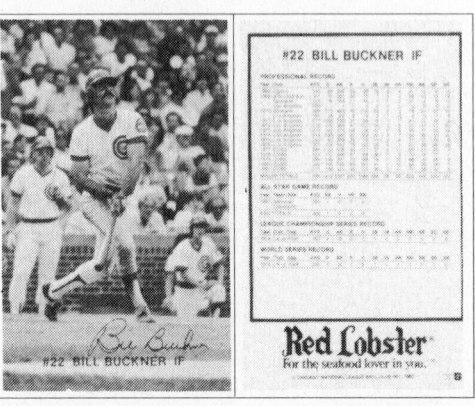

The cards in this 28-card set measure 2 1/4" by 3 1/2". This set of Chicago Cubs players was co-produced by the Cubs and Chicago-area Red Lobster restaurants and was introduced as a promotional giveaway on August 20, 1982, at Wrigley Field. The cards contain borderless color photos of 25 players, manager Lee Elia, the coaching staff, and a team picture. A facsimile autograph appears on the front, and the cards run in sequence by uniform number. While the coaches have a short biographical sketch on back, the player cards simply list the individual's professional record. The key card in the set is obviously Ryne Sandberg's as it predates his Donruss, Fleer, and Topps rookie cards by one year.

		MINT	EXC	G-VG
	COMPLETE SET (28)	75.00	34.00	11.25
	COMMON PLAYER	.70	.30	.07
☐ 1	Larry Bowa	1.00	.40	.10
☐ 4	Lee Elia MG	.75	.30	.07
☐ 6	Keith Moreland	.90	.40	.09
☐ 7	Jody Davis	.90	.40	.09
☐ 10	Leon Durham	.90	.40	.09
☐ 15	Junior Kennedy	.75	.30	.07
☐ 17	Bump Wills	.75	.30	.07
☐ 18	Scot Thompson	.75	.30	.07
☐ 21	Jay Johnstone	.90	.40	.09
☐ 22	Bill Buckner	1.00	.40	.10
☐ 23	Ryne Sandberg	50.00	22.50	7.50
☐ 24	Jerry Morales	.75	.30	.07
☐ 25	Gary Woods	.75	.30	.07
☐ 28	Steve Henderson	.75	.30	.07
☐ 29	Bob Molinaro	.75	.30	.07
☐ 31	Fergie Jenkins	3.00	1.25	.30
☐ 33	Al Ripley	.75	.30	.07
☐ 34	Randy Martz	.75	.30	.07
☐ 36	Mike Proly	.75	.30	.07
☐ 37	Ken Kravec	.75	.30	.07
☐ 38	Willie Hernandez	.90	.40	.09

		MINT	EXC	G-VG
☐	39 Bill Campbell	.75	.30	.07
☐	41 Dick Tidrow	.75	.30	.07
☐	46 Lee Smith	2.25	.90	.22
☐	47 Doug Bird	.75	.30	.07
☐	48 Dickie Noles	.75	.30	.07
☐	xx Team Picture (unnumbered)	1.00	.40	.10
☐	xx Coaches Card (unnumbered)	.75	.30	.07

1983 Cubs Thorn Apple Valley

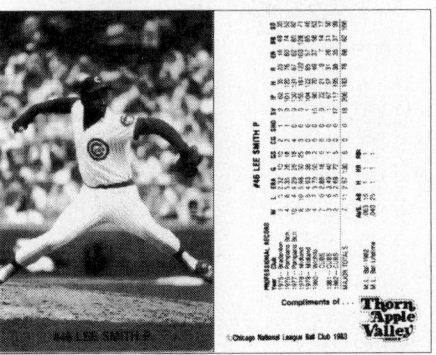

This set of 27 Chicago Cubs features full-color action photos on the front and was sponsored by Thorn Apple Valley. The cards measure approximately 2 1/4" by 3 1/2". The backs provide year-by-year statistics. The cards are unnumbered except for uniform number; they are listed below by uniform with the special cards listed at the end. The card of Joe Carter predates his Donruss rookie card by one year.

		MINT	EXC	G-VG
	COMPLETE SET (27)	20.00	8.50	2.75
	COMMON PLAYER	.45	.18	.04
☐	1 Larry Bowa	.75	.30	.07
☐	6 Keith Moreland	.60	.25	.06
☐	7 Jody Davis	.60	.25	.06
☐	10 Leon Durham	.60	.25	.06
☐	11 Ron Cey	.75	.30	.07
☐	16 Steve Lake	.45	.18	.04
☐	20 Thad Bosley	.45	.18	.04
☐	21 Jay Johnstone	.60	.25	.06
☐	22 Bill Buckner	.75	.30	.07
☐	23 Ryne Sandberg	7.50	3.25	.75
☐	24 Jerry Morales	.45	.18	.04
☐	25 Gary Woods	.45	.18	.04
☐	27 Mel Hall	1.00	.40	.10
☐	29 Tom Veryzer	.45	.18	.04
☐	30 Chuck Rainey	.45	.18	.04
☐	31 Fergie Jenkins	1.50	.60	.15
☐	32 Craig Lefferts	.60	.25	.06
☐	33 Joe Carter	7.50	3.25	.75
☐	34 Steve Trout	.45	.18	.04
☐	36 Mike Proly	.45	.18	.04
☐	39 Bill Campbell	.45	.18	.04
☐	41 Warren Brusstar	.45	.18	.04
☐	44 Dick Ruthven	.45	.18	.04
☐	46 Lee Smith	.90	.40	.09
☐	48 Dickie Noles	.45	.18	.04
☐	xx Manager/Coaches Lee Elia MG Ruben Amaro Billy Connors Duffy Dyer Fred Koenig John Vukovich	.45	.18	.04
☐	xx Team Photo (unnumbered)	.45	.18	.04

1984 Cubs Seven-Up

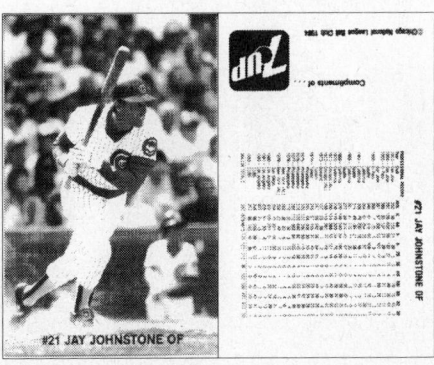

#21 JAY JOHNSTONE OF

This 28-card set was sponsored by 7-Up. The cards are in full color and measure 2 1/4" by 3 1/2". The card backs are printed in black on white card stock. This set is tougher to find than the other similar Cubs sets since the Cubs were more successful (on the field) in 1984 winning their division, that is, virtually all of the cards printed were distributed during the "Baseball Card Day" promotion (August 12th) which was much better attended that year. There actually were two additional cards produced (in limited quantities) later which some collectors consider part of this set; these late issue cards show four Cubs rookies on each card.

		MINT	EXC	G-VG
	COMPLETE SET (28)	20.00	8.50	2.75
	COMMON PLAYER	.60	.25	.06
☐	1 Larry Bowa	.90	.40	.09
☐	6 Keith Moreland	.75	.30	.07
☐	7 Jody Davis	.75	.30	.07
☐	10 Leon Durham	.75	.30	.07
☐	11 Ron Cey	.90	.40	.09
☐	15 Ron Hassey	.60	.25	.06
☐	18 Richie Hebner	.60	.25	.06
☐	19 Dave Owen	.60	.25	.06
☐	20 Bob Dernier	.60	.25	.06
☐	21 Jay Johnstone	.75	.30	.07
☐	23 Ryne Sandberg	6.00	2.50	.60
☐	24 Scott Sanderson	.90	.40	.09
☐	25 Gary Woods	.60	.25	.06
☐	27 Thad Bosley	.60	.25	.06
☐	28 Henry Cotto	.60	.25	.06
☐	34 Steve Trout	.60	.25	.06
☐	36 Gary Matthews	.75	.30	.07
☐	39 George Frazier	.60	.25	.06
☐	40 Rick Sutcliffe	1.00	.40	.10
☐	41 Warren Brusstar	.60	.25	.06
☐	42 Rich Bordi	.60	.25	.06
☐	43 Dennis Eckersley	1.50	.60	.15
☐	44 Dick Ruthven	.60	.25	.06
☐	46 Lee Smith	1.25	.50	.12
☐	47 Rick Reuschel	.90	.40	.09
☐	49 Tim Stoddard	.60	.25	.06
☐	xx Coaches Card (unnumbered)	.60	.25	.06
☐	xx Jim Frey MG (unnumbered)	.60	.25	.06

1985 Cubs Seven-Up

This 28-card set was distributed on August 14th at Wrigley Field for the game against the Expos. The cards measure 2 1/2" by 3 1/2" and were distributed wrapped in cellophane. The cards are unnumbered except for uniform number. The card backs are printed in black on white with a 7-Up logo in the upper right hand corner.

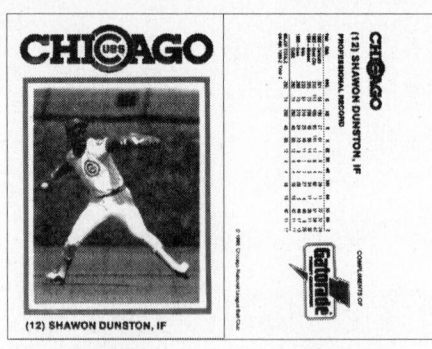

	MINT	EXC	G-VG
COMPLETE SET (28)	9.00	4.00	.90
COMMON PLAYER	.20	.08	.02
☐ 1 Larry Bowa	.40	.16	.04
☐ 6 Keith Moreland	.30	.12	.03
☐ 7 Jody Davis	.30	.12	.03
☐ 10 Leon Durham	.30	.12	.03
☐ 11 Ron Cey	.40	.16	.04
☐ 15 Davey Lopes	.30	.12	.03
☐ 16 Steve Lake	.20	.08	.02
☐ 18 Rich Hebner	.20	.08	.02
☐ 20 Bob Dernier	.20	.08	.02
☐ 21 Scott Sanderson	.30	.12	.03
☐ 22 Billy Hatcher	.40	.16	.04
☐ 23 Ryne Sandberg	3.75	1.60	.37
☐ 24 Brian Dayett	.20	.08	.02
☐ 25 Gary Woods	.20	.08	.02
☐ 27 Thad Bosley	.20	.08	.02
☐ 28 Chris Speier	.20	.08	.02
☐ 31 Ray Fontenot	.20	.08	.02
☐ 34 Steve Trout	.20	.08	.02
☐ 36 Gary Matthews	.30	.12	.03
☐ 39 George Frazier	.20	.08	.02
☐ 40 Rick Sutcliffe	.50	.20	.05
☐ 41 Warren Brusstar	.20	.08	.02
☐ 42 Lary Sorensen	.20	.08	.02
☐ 43 Dennis Eckersley	.75	.30	.07
☐ 44 Dick Ruthven	.20	.08	.02
☐ 46 Lee Smith	.60	.25	.06
☐ xx Jim Frey MG	.20	.08	.02
(unnumbered)			
☐ xx Cubs Coaching Staff	.20	.08	.02
Ruben Amaro			
Billy Connors			
Johnny Oates			
John Vukovich			
Don Zimmer			
(unnumbered)			

	MINT	EXC	G-VG
☐ 21 Scott Sanderson	.30	.12	.03
☐ 22 Jerry Mumphrey	.20	.08	.02
☐ 23 Ryne Sandberg	3.00	1.25	.30
☐ 27 Thad Bosley	.20	.08	.02
☐ 28 Chris Speier	.20	.08	.02
☐ 29 Steve Lake	.20	.08	.02
☐ 31 Ray Fontenot	.20	.08	.02
☐ 34 Steve Trout	.20	.08	.02
☐ 36 Gary Matthews	.30	.12	.03
☐ 39 George Frazier	.20	.08	.02
☐ 40 Rick Sutcliffe	.40	.16	.04
☐ 43 Dennis Eckersley	.75	.30	.07
☐ 46 Lee Smith	.50	.20	.05
☐ 48 Jay Baller	.20	.08	.02
☐ 49 Jamie Moyer	.20	.08	.02
☐ 50 Guy Hoffman	.20	.08	.02
☐ xx Coaches Card	.20	.08	.02
(unnumbered)			

1986 Cubs Unocal

1986 Cubs Gatorade

This 28-card set was given out at Wrigley Field on the Cubs' special "baseball card" promotion held July 17th for the game against the Giants. The set was sponsored by Gatorade. The cards are unnumbered except for uniform number. Card backs feature blue print on white card stock. The cards measure 2 7/8" by 4 1/4" and are in full color.

	MINT	EXC	G-VG
COMPLETE SET (28)	9.00	4.00	.90
COMMON PLAYER	.20	.08	.02
☐ 4 Gene Michael MG	.30	.12	.03
☐ 6 Keith Moreland	.30	.12	.03
☐ 7 Jody Davis	.30	.12	.03
☐ 10 Leon Durham	.30	.12	.03
☐ 11 Ron Cey	.30	.12	.03
☐ 12 Shawon Dunston	1.00	.40	.10
☐ 15 Davey Lopes	.30	.12	.03
☐ 16 Terry Francona	.20	.08	.02
☐ 18 Steve Christmas	.20	.08	.02
☐ 19 Manny Trillo	.20	.08	.02
☐ 20 Bob Dernier	.20	.08	.02

This set of 20 color action player photos was sponsored by Unocal 76. They are bordered in black and are printed on (approximately) 8 1/2" by 11" glossy paper sheets. A color headshot is superimposed on each front. The backs contain extensive player information, including biography, performance in the 1985 season, complete Major League statistics, and career summary. The player photos are unnumbered and checklisted below in alphabetical order.

	MINT	EXC	G-VG
COMPLETE SET (20)	8.00	3.50	.80
COMMON PLAYER (1-20)	.30	.12	.03
☐ 1 Jay Baller	.30	.12	.03
☐ 2 Thad Bosley	.30	.12	.03
☐ 3 Ron Cey	.50	.20	.05
☐ 4 Jody Davis	.40	.16	.04
☐ 5 Bob Dernier	.30	.12	.03
☐ 6 Shawon Dunston	.75	.30	.07
☐ 7 Leon Durham	.40	.16	.04
☐ 8 Dennis Eckersley	.75	.30	.07
☐ 9 Ray Fontenot	.30	.12	.03
☐ 10 George Frazier	.30	.12	.03

		MINT	EXC	G-VG
☐ 11	Davey Lopes	.40	.16	.04
☐ 12	Gary Matthews	.40	.16	.04
☐ 13	Keith Moreland	.40	.16	.04
☐ 14	Jerry Mumphrey	.30	.12	.03
☐ 15	Ryne Sandberg	3.00	1.25	.30
☐ 16	Scott Sanderson	.40	.16	.04
☐ 17	Lee Smith	.60	.25	.06
☐ 18	Rick Sutcliffe	.50	.20	.05
☐ 19	Manny Trillo	.30	.12	.03
☐ 20	Steve Trout	.30	.12	.03

1987 Cubs David Berg

This 26-card set was given out at Wrigley Field on the Cubs' special "baseball card" promotion held July 29th. The set was sponsored by David Berg Pure Beef Hot Dogs. The cards are unnumbered except for uniform number. Card backs feature red and blue print on white card stock. The cards measure 2 7/8" by 4 1/4" and are in full color.

		MINT	EXC	G-VG
	COMPLETE SET (26)	9.00	4.00	.90
	COMMON PLAYER	.20	.08	.02
☐ 1	Dave Martinez	.40	.16	.04
☐ 4	Gene Michael MG	.30	.12	.03
☐ 6	Keith Moreland	.30	.12	.03
☐ 7	Jody Davis	.30	.12	.03
☐ 8	Andre Dawson	1.50	.60	.15
☐ 10	Leon Durham	.30	.12	.03
☐ 11	Jim Sundberg	.20	.08	.02
☐ 12	Shawon Dunston	.75	.30	.07
☐ 19	Manny Trillo	.20	.08	.02
☐ 20	Bob Dernier	.20	.08	.02
☐ 21	Scott Sanderson	.30	.12	.03
☐ 22	Jerry Mumphrey	.20	.08	.02
☐ 23	Ryne Sandberg	2.50	1.00	.25
☐ 24	Brian Dayett	.20	.08	.02
☐ 29	Chico Walker	.30	.12	.03
☐ 31	Greg Maddux	.75	.30	.07
☐ 33	Frank DiPino	.20	.08	.02
☐ 34	Steve Trout	.20	.08	.02
☐ 36	Gary Matthews	.30	.12	.03
☐ 37	Ed Lynch	.20	.08	.02
☐ 39	Ron Davis	.20	.08	.02
☐ 40	Rick Sutcliffe	.40	.16	.04
☐ 46	Lee Smith	.50	.20	.05
☐ 47	Dickie Noles	.20	.08	.02
☐ 49	Jamie Moyer	.20	.08	.02
☐ xx	Coaching Staff	.20	.08	.02

1988 Cubs David Berg

This 27-card set was given out at Wrigley Field with every paid admission on the Cubs' special "baseball card" promotion held August 24th. The set was sponsored by David Berg Pure Beef Hot Dogs and the Venture store chain. The cards are unnumbered except for uniform number. Card backs feature primarily black

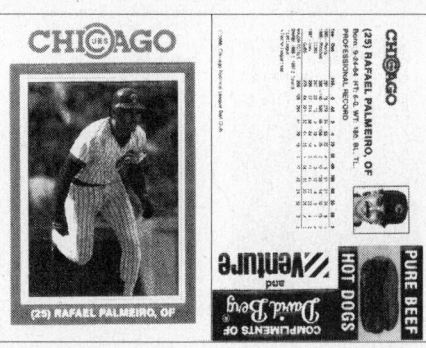

print on white card stock. The cards measure approximately 2 7/8" by 4 1/4" and are in full color.

		MINT	EXC	G-VG
	COMPLETE SET (27)	9.00	4.00	.90
	COMMON PLAYER	.20	.08	.02
☐ 2	Vance Law	.30	.12	.03
☐ 4	Don Zimmer MG	.30	.12	.03
☐ 7	Jody Davis	.30	.12	.03
☐ 8	Andre Dawson	1.25	.50	.12
☐ 9	Damon Berryhill	.40	.16	.04
☐ 12	Shawon Dunston	.50	.20	.05
☐ 17	Mark Grace	1.25	.50	.12
☐ 18	Angel Salazar	.20	.08	.02
☐ 19	Manny Trillo	.20	.08	.02
☐ 21	Scott Sanderson	.30	.12	.03
☐ 22	Jerry Mumphrey	.20	.08	.02
☐ 23	Ryne Sandberg	1.50	.60	.15
☐ 24	Gary Varsho	.30	.12	.03
☐ 25	Rafael Palmeiro	1.25	.50	.12
☐ 28	Mitch Webster	.30	.12	.03
☐ 30	Darrin Jackson	.30	.12	.03
☐ 31	Greg Maddux	.50	.20	.05
☐ 32	Calvin Schiraldi	.20	.08	.02
☐ 33	Frank DiPino	.20	.08	.02
☐ 37	Pat Perry	.20	.08	.02
☐ 40	Rick Sutcliffe	.40	.16	.04
☐ 41	Jeff Pico	.20	.08	.02
☐ 45	Al Nipper	.20	.08	.02
☐ 49	Jamie Moyer	.20	.08	.02
☐ 50	Les Lancaster	.20	.08	.02
☐ 54	Rich Gossage	.40	.16	.04
☐ xx	Cubs Coaching Staff	.20	.08	.02
	Joe Altobelli CO			
	Chuck Cottier CO			
	Larry Cox CO			
	Jose Martinez CO			
	Dick Pole CO			

1989 Cubs Marathon

The 1989 Marathon Cubs set features 25 cards measuring 2 3/4" by 4 1/4". The fronts are green and white, and feature facsimile autographs. The backs show black and white mug shots and career stats. The set was given away at the August 10, 1989 Cubs home game. The cards are numbered by the players' uniform numbers.

		MINT	EXC	G-VG
	COMPLETE SET (25)	13.50	6.00	1.85
	COMMON PLAYER	.35	.15	.03
☐ 2	Vance Law	.45	.18	.04
☐ 4	Don Zimmer MG	.45	.18	.04
☐ 7	Joe Girardi	.45	.18	.04
☐ 8	Andre Dawson	1.00	.40	.10
☐ 9	Damon Berryhill	.45	.18	.04
☐ 10	Lloyd McClendon	.35	.15	.03
☐ 12	Shawon Dunston	.90	.40	.09
☐ 15	Domingo Ramos	.35	.15	.03
☐ 17	Mark Grace	1.25	.50	.12
☐ 18	Dwight Smith	.60	.25	.06
☐ 19	Curt Wilkerson	.35	.15	.03

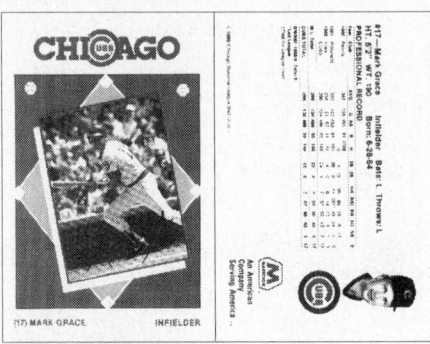

(17) MARK GRACE   INFIELDER

		.90	.40	.09
☐	20 Jerome Walton	.90	.40	.09
☐	21 Scott Sanderson	.45	.18	.04
☐	23 Ryne Sandberg	2.00	.80	.20
☐	28 Mitch Williams	.60	.25	.06
☐	31 Greg Maddux	.60	.25	.06
☐	32 Calvin Schiraldi	.35	.15	.03
☐	33 Mitch Webster	.35	.15	.03
☐	36 Mike Bielecki	.45	.18	.04
☐	39 Paul Kilgus	.35	.15	.03
☐	40 Rick Sutcliffe	.45	.18	.04
☐	41 Jeff Pico	.35	.15	.03
☐	44 Steve Wilson	.45	.18	.04
☐	50 Les Lancaster	.45	.18	.04
☐	xx Cubs Coaches	.35	.15	.03

1990 Cubs Marathon

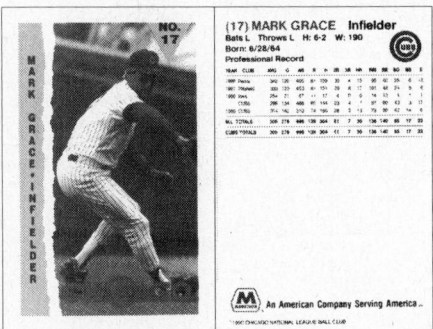

The Marathon Oil Chicago Cubs set contains 28 cards measuring 2 7/8" by 4 1/4" which was given away at the August 17th Cub game. This set is checklisted alphabetically below with the uniform number next to the players name.

		MINT	EXC	G-VG
	COMPLETE SET (28)	10.00	4.50	1.25
	COMMON PLAYER (1-28)	.35	.15	.03
☐	1 Paul Assenmacher 45	.35	.15	.03
☐	2 Mike Bielecki 36	.45	.18	.04
☐	3 Shawn Boskie 47	.45	.18	.04
☐	4 Dave Clark 30	.35	.15	.03
☐	5 Doug Dascenzo 29	.35	.15	.03
☐	6 Andre Dawson 8	.90	.40	.09
☐	7 Shawon Dunston 12	.60	.25	.06
☐	8 Joe Girardi 7	.45	.18	.04
☐	9 Mark Grace 17	1.00	.40	.10
☐	10 Mike Harkey 22	.75	.30	.07
☐	11 Les Lancaster 50	.35	.15	.03
☐	12 Bill Long 37	.35	.15	.03
☐	13 Greg Maddux 31	.60	.25	.06
☐	14 Lloyd McClendon 10	.35	.15	.03
☐	15 Jeff Pico 41	.35	.15	.03

☐	16 Domingo Ramos 15	.35	.15	.03
☐	17 Luis Salazar 11	.35	.15	.03
☐	18 Ryne Sandberg 23	1.50	.60	.15
☐	19 Dwight Smith 18	.45	.18	.04
☐	20 Rick Sutcliffe 40	.45	.18	.04
☐	21 Hector Villanueva 32	.45	.18	.04
☐	22 Jerome Walton 20	.60	.25	.06
☐	23 Curtis Wilkerson 19	.35	.15	.03
☐	24 Mitch Williams 28	.45	.18	.04
☐	25 Steve Wilson 44	.35	.15	.03
☐	26 Marvell Wynne 25	.35	.15	.03
☐	27 Don Zimmer 4 MG	.35	.15	.03
☐	28 Cubs Coaches	.35	.15	.03
	Joe Altobelli			
	Jose Martinez			
	Phil Roof			
	Chuck Cottier			
	Dick Pole			

1991 Cubs Marathon

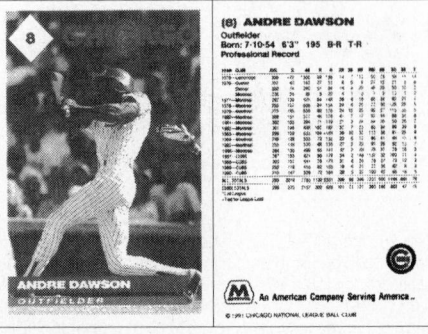

This 28-card set was produced by Marathon Oil, and its company logo appears at the bottom of card back. The cards were given away at the Cubs' home game against Montreal Expos on August 14, 1991. The oversized cards measure approximately 2 7/8" by 4 1/4" and feature on the fronts color action player photos with white borders. The card number inside a white diamond and the words "Chicago Cubs" overlay the top portion of the photo. The player's name and position appear in the blue and red stripes traversing the bottom of the card face. The backs are printed in blue, red, and black on a white background and present biographical and statistical information. The cards are skip-numbered by uniform number and checklisted below accordingly.

		MINT	EXC	G-VG
	COMPLETE SET (28)	8.00	3.50	.80
	COMMON PLAYER	.25	.10	.02
☐	7 Joe Girardi	.35	.15	.03
☐	8 Andre Dawson	.75	.30	.07
☐	9 Damon Berryhill	.35	.15	.03
☐	10 Luis Salazar	.25	.10	.02
☐	11 George Bell	.45	.18	.04
☐	12 Shawon Dunston	.45	.18	.04
☐	16 Jose Vizcaino	.35	.15	.03
☐	17 Mark Grace	.75	.30	.07
☐	18 Dwight Smith	.35	.15	.03
☐	19 Hector Villanueva	.35	.15	.03
☐	20 Jerome Walton	.45	.18	.04
☐	22 Mike Harkey	.45	.18	.04
☐	23 Ryne Sandberg	1.00	.40	.10
☐	24 Chico Walker	.35	.15	.03
☐	29 Doug Dascenzo	.25	.10	.02
☐	30 Bob Scanlan	.25	.10	.02
☐	31 Greg Maddux	.45	.18	.04
☐	32 Danny Jackson	.35	.15	.03
☐	33 Chuck McElroy	.35	.15	.03
☐	36 Mike Bielecki	.35	.15	.03
☐	40 Rick Sutcliffe	.35	.15	.03
☐	41 Jim Essian MG	.25	.10	.02
☐	42 Dave Smith	.35	.15	.03
☐	45 Paul Assenmacher	.25	.10	.02

☐ 47	Shawn Boskie	.35	.15	.03
☐ 50	Les Lancaster	.25	.10	.02
☐ 51	Heathcliff Slocumb	.25	.10	.02
☐ xx	Coaches Card	.25	.10	.02

Joe Altobelli
Chuck Cottier
Jose Martinez
Billy Connors
Phil Roof
Richie Zisk

1954 Dan Dee

The cards in this 29-card set measure 2 1/2" by 3 5/8". Most of the cards marketed by Dan Dee in bags of potato chips in 1954 depict players from the Indians or Pirates. The Pirate players in the set are much tougher to find than the Cleveland Indians players. The pictures used for Yankee players were also employed in the Briggs and Stahl-Meyer sets. Dan Dee cards have a waxed surface, but are commonly found with product stains. Paul Smith and Walker Cooper are considered the known scarcities. The catalog designation for this set is F342.

		NRMT	VG-E	GOOD
	COMPLETE SET (29)	4000.00	1800.00	400.00
	COMMON PLAYER (1-29)	50.00	22.50	7.50
	COMMON PIRATE PLAYER	75.00	34.00	11.25
☐ 1	Bobby Avila	50.00	22.50	7.50
☐ 2	Hank Bauer	75.00	34.00	11.25
☐ 3	Walker Cooper	325.00	150.00	50.00
	Pittsburgh Pirates			
☐ 4	Larry Doby	60.00	27.00	9.00
☐ 5	Luke Easter	50.00	22.50	7.50
☐ 6	Bob Feller	225.00	100.00	33.00
☐ 7	Bob Friend	100.00	45.00	15.00
	Pittsburgh Pirates			
☐ 8	Mike Garcia	60.00	27.00	9.00
☐ 9	Sid Gordon	75.00	34.00	11.25
	Pittsburgh Pirates			
☐ 10	Jim Hegan	50.00	22.50	7.50
☐ 11	Gil Hodges	165.00	75.00	22.50
☐ 12	Art Houtteman	50.00	22.50	7.50
☐ 13	Monte Irvin	110.00	50.00	16.50
☐ 14	Paul LaPalme	75.00	34.00	11.25
	Pittsburgh Pirates			
☐ 15	Bob Lemon	125.00	57.50	18.75
☐ 16	Al Lopez	110.00	50.00	16.50
☐ 17	Mickey Mantle	1000.00	400.00	100.00
☐ 18	Dale Mitchell	50.00	22.50	7.50
☐ 19	Phil Rizzuto	165.00	75.00	22.50
☐ 20	Curt Roberts	75.00	34.00	11.25
	Pittsburgh Pirates			
☐ 21	Al Rosen	75.00	34.00	11.25
☐ 22	Red Schoendienst	150.00	67.50	22.50
☐ 23	Paul Smith	450.00	200.00	67.50
	Pittsburgh Pirates			
☐ 24	Duke Snider	225.00	100.00	33.00
☐ 25	George Strickland	50.00	22.50	7.50
☐ 26	Max Surkont	75.00	34.00	11.25
	Pittsburgh Pirates			
☐ 27	Frank Thomas	125.00	57.50	18.75
	Pittsburgh Pirates			
☐ 28	Wally Westlake	50.00	22.50	7.50
☐ 29	Early Wynn	125.00	57.50	18.75

1933 Delong

The cards in this 24-card set measures 2" by 3". The 1933 Delong Gum set of 24 multi-colored cards was, along with the 1933 Goudey Big League series, one of the first baseball card sets issued with chewing gum. It was the only card set issued by this company. The reverse text was written by Austen Lake, who also wrote the sports tips found on the Diamond Stars series which began in 1934, leading to speculation that Delong was bought out by National Chicle. The catalog designation for this set is R333.

		EX-MT	VG-E	GOOD
	COMPLETE SET (24)	10000.00	4000.00	1000.00
	COMMON PLAYER (1-24)	200.00	90.00	30.00
☐ 1	Marty McManus	200.00	90.00	30.00
☐ 2	Al Simmons	325.00	150.00	50.00
☐ 3	Oscar Melillo	200.00	90.00	30.00
☐ 4	William Terry	400.00	180.00	60.00
☐ 5	Charlie Gehringer	400.00	180.00	60.00
☐ 6	Mickey Cochrane	400.00	180.00	60.00
☐ 7	Lou Gehrig	3250.00	1400.00	325.00
☐ 8	Kiki Cuyler	325.00	150.00	50.00
☐ 9	Bill Urbanski	200.00	90.00	30.00
☐ 10	Lefty O'Doul	225.00	100.00	33.00
☐ 11	Fred Lindstrom	325.00	150.00	50.00
☐ 12	Pie Traynor	375.00	165.00	55.00
☐ 13	Rabbit Maranville	325.00	150.00	50.00
☐ 14	Lefty Gomez	400.00	180.00	60.00
☐ 15	Riggs Stephenson	225.00	100.00	33.00
☐ 16	Lon Warneke	200.00	90.00	30.00
☐ 17	Pepper Martin	225.00	100.00	33.00
☐ 18	Jim Dykes	200.00	90.00	30.00
☐ 19	Chick Hafey	325.00	150.00	50.00
☐ 20	Joe Vosmik	200.00	90.00	30.00
☐ 21	Jimmie Foxx	650.00	300.00	100.00
☐ 22	Chuck Klein	375.00	165.00	55.00
☐ 23	Lefty Grove	500.00	225.00	75.00
☐ 24	Goose Goslin	325.00	150.00	50.00

1991 Denny's Grand Slam

The 1991 Denny's Grand Slam hologram baseball card set was produced by Upper Deck. The 26-card set contains one player from each major league team, who was selected on the basis of the number and circumstances of his grand slam home runs. These standard size (2 1/2" by 3 1/2") cards were available at Denny's only with the purchase of a meal from the restaurant's Grand Slam menu; each card came sealed in a plastic bag that prevents prior identification. It is estimated that two million cards were printed. The 3-D cards alternate between silver and full color, and the player appears to stand apart from a background of exploding fireworks. A stripe at the top of the card has the player's name and team, while the Upper Deck and Denny's logos appear toward the bottom of the card face. The back has a descriptive account of the player's grand slams. The cards are numbered on the front.

		MINT	EXC	G-VG
	COMPLETE SET (26)	60.00	27.00	9.00
	COMMON PLAYER (1-26)	2.00	.80	.20
☐ 1	Ellis Burks	3.00	1.25	.30
☐ 2	Cecil Fielder	5.00	2.25	.50
☐ 3	Will Clark	6.00	2.50	.60
☐ 4	Eric Davis	3.50	1.50	.35
☐ 5	Dave Parker	2.50	1.00	.25
☐ 6	Kelly Gruber	2.00	.80	.20
☐ 7	Kent Hrbek	2.00	.80	.20
☐ 8	Don Mattingly	5.00	2.25	.50
☐ 9	Brook Jacoby	2.00	.80	.20
☐ 10	Mark McGwire	3.50	1.50	.35
☐ 11	Howard Johnson	2.50	1.00	.25
☐ 12	Tim Wallach	2.00	.80	.20
☐ 13	Ricky Jordan	2.00	.80	.20
☐ 14	Andre Dawson	3.50	1.50	.35
☐ 15	Eddie Murray	3.50	1.50	.35
☐ 16	Danny Tartabull	3.50	1.50	.35
☐ 17	Bobby Bonilla	3.50	1.50	.35
☐ 18	Benito Santiago	2.50	1.00	.25
☐ 19	Alvin Davis	2.00	.80	.20
☐ 20	Cal Ripken	6.00	2.50	.60
☐ 21	Ruben Sierra	4.00	1.75	.40
☐ 22	Pedro Guerrero	2.00	.80	.20
☐ 23	Wally Joyner	2.50	1.00	.25
☐ 24	Craig Biggio	2.00	.80	.20
☐ 25	Dave Justice	6.00	2.50	.60
☐ 26	Tim Raines	2.00	.80	.20

1981 Detroit News

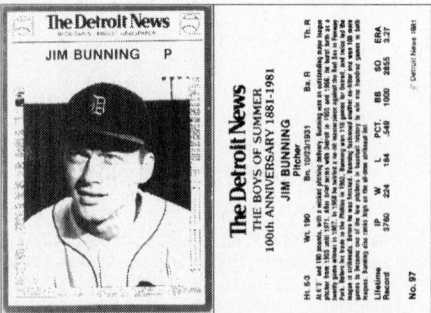

This 135-card, standard-size, 2 1/2" by 3 1/2" set was issued in 1981 to celebrate the centennial of professional baseball in Detroit. This set features black and white photos surrounded by solid red borders, while the back provides information about either the player or event featured on the front of the card. This set was issued by the Detroit newspaper, the Detroit News and

covered players from the nineteenth century right up to players and other personnel active at the time of issue.

		MINT	EXC	G-VG
	COMPLETE SET (135)	15.00	6.50	2.15
	COMMON PLAYER (1-135)	.10	.04	.01
☐ 1	Detroit's Boys of Summer 100th Anniversary	.20	.08	.02
☐ 2	Charles W. Bennett C	.10	.04	.01
☐ 3	Mickey Cochrane C	.30	.12	.03
☐ 4	Harry Heilmann, OF	.30	.12	.03
☐ 5	Walter O. Briggs, Owner	.10	.04	.01
☐ 6	Mark Fidrych P	.20	.08	.02
☐ 7	1887 Tigers	.15	.06	.01
☐ 8	Tiger Stadium	.10	.04	.01
☐ 9	Rudy York 1B	.10	.04	.01
☐ 10	George Kell 3B	.20	.08	.02
☐ 11	Steve O'Neill MG	.10	.04	.01
☐ 12	John Hiller P	.10	.04	.01
☐ 13	1934 Tigers	.15	.06	.01
☐ 14	Charlie Gehringer 2B	.30	.12	.03
☐ 15	Denny McLain P	.20	.08	.02
☐ 16	Billy Rogell SS	.10	.04	.01
☐ 17	Ty Cobb OF	1.00	.40	.10
☐ 18	Sparky Anderson MG	.20	.08	.02
☐ 19	Davy Jones OF	.10	.04	.01
☐ 20	Kirk Gibson OF	.15	.06	.01
☐ 21	Pat Mullin OF	.10	.04	.01
☐ 22	1972 Tigers	.15	.06	.01
☐ 23	What A Night	.10	.04	.01
☐ 24	Doc Cramer OF	.10	.04	.01
☐ 25	Mickey Stanley OF	.10	.04	.01
☐ 26	John Lipon SS	.10	.04	.01
☐ 27	Jo Jo White OF	.10	.04	.01
☐ 28	Recreation Park	.10	.04	.01
☐ 29	Wild Bill Donovan P	.10	.04	.01
☐ 30	Ray Oyler SS	.10	.04	.01
☐ 31	Earl Whitehill P	.10	.04	.01
☐ 32	Billy Hoeft P	.10	.04	.01
☐ 33	Johnny Groth OF	.10	.04	.01
☐ 34	Hughie Jennings SS/Mgr.	.30	.12	.03
☐ 35	Mayo Smith MG	.10	.04	.01
☐ 36	Bennett Park	.10	.04	.01
☐ 37	Tigers Win	.10	.04	.01
☐ 38	Donie Bush SS/Mgr.	.10	.04	.01
☐ 39	Harry Coveleski P	.10	.04	.01
☐ 40	Paul Richards C	.10	.04	.01
☐ 41	Jonathon Stone OF	.10	.04	.01
☐ 42	Bob Swift C	.10	.04	.01
☐ 43	Roy Cullenbine OF	.10	.04	.01
☐ 44	Hoot Evers OF	.10	.04	.01
☐ 45	Tigers Win Series	.15	.06	.01
☐ 46	Art Houtteman P	.10	.04	.01
☐ 47	Aurelio Rodriguez 3B	.10	.04	.01
☐ 48	Fred Hutchinson P/Mgr.	.15	.06	.01
☐ 49	Don Mossi P	.10	.04	.01
☐ 50	Lou Gehrig Streak Ends in Detroit At 2130 Games	.20	.08	.02
☐ 51	Earl Wilson P	.10	.04	.01
☐ 52	Jim Northrup OF	.10	.04	.01
☐ 53	1907 Tigers	.10	.04	.01
☐ 54	Hank Hits 2 Homers to Draw Even with Ruth	.30	.12	.03
☐ 55	Mickey Lolich P	.20	.08	.02
☐ 56	Tommy Bridges P	.10	.04	.01
☐ 57	Al Benton P	.10	.04	.01
☐ 58	Del Baker MG	.10	.04	.01
☐ 59	Lou Whitaker 2B	.20	.08	.02
☐ 60	Navin Field	.10	.04	.01
☐ 61	1945 Tigers	.15	.06	.01
☐ 62	Ernie Harwell, Announcer	.20	.08	.02
☐ 63	Tigers League Champs	.15	.06	.01
☐ 64	Bobo Newsom P	.10	.04	.01
☐ 65	Don Wert 3B	.10	.04	.01
☐ 66	Ed Summers P	.10	.04	.01
☐ 67	Billy Martin MG	.30	.12	.03
☐ 68	Alan Trammell SS	.35	.15	.03
☐ 69	Dale Alexander 1B	.10	.04	.01
☐ 70	Ed Brinkman SS	.10	.04	.01
☐ 71	Right Man in Right Place in Right Park Wins Game	.15	.06	.01
☐ 72	Bill Freehan C	.20	.08	.02
☐ 73	Norm Cash 1B	.20	.08	.02
☐ 74	George Dauss P	.10	.04	.01

		NRMT	VG-E	GOOD
☐ 75	Aurelio Lopez P	.10	.04	.01
☐ 76	Charlie Maxwell OF	.10	.04	.01
☐ 77	Ed Barrow MG	.20	.08	.02
☐ 78	Willie Horton OF	.15	.06	.01
☐ 79	Denny Sets Record 31 Wins	.15	.06	.01
☐ 80	Dan Brouthers 1B	.30	.12	.03
☐ 81	John E. Fetzer, Owner	.10	.04	.01
☐ 82	Heinie Manush OF	.20	.08	.02
☐ 83	1935 Tigers	.15	.06	.01
☐ 84	Ray Boone INF	.10	.04	.01
☐ 85	Bob Fothergill OF	.10	.04	.01
☐ 86	Steve Kemp OF	.15	.06	.01
☐ 87	Ed Killian P	.10	.04	.01
☐ 88	Giebell Is Ineligible for Series But	.10	.04	.01
☐ 89	Pinky Higgins 3B	.10	.04	.01
☐ 90	Lance Parrish C	.20	.08	.02
☐ 91	Eldon Auker P	.10	.04	.01
☐ 92	Birdie Tebbetts C	.10	.04	.01
☐ 93	Schoolboy Rowe P	.15	.06	.01
☐ 94	Tiger rally gives McLain 30	.15	.06	.01
☐ 95	1909 Tigers	.15	.06	.01
☐ 96	Harvey Kuenn SS/OF	.20	.08	.02
☐ 97	Jim Bunning P	.20	.08	.02
☐ 98	1940 Tigers	.15	.06	.01
☐ 99	Rocky Colavito OF	.25	.10	.02
☐ 100	Kaline Enters Hall Of Fame	.35	.15	.03
☐ 101	Billy Bruton OF	.10	.04	.01
☐ 102	Germany Schaefer 2B	.10	.04	.01
☐ 103	Frank Bolling 2B	.10	.04	.01
☐ 104	Briggs Stadium	.10	.04	.01
☐ 105	Bucky Harris 2B/Mgr.	.15	.06	.01
☐ 106	Gates Brown OF	.10	.04	.01
☐ 107	Billy Martin made the difference	.20	.08	.02
☐ 108	1908 Tigers	.15	.06	.01
☐ 109	Gee Walker OF	.10	.04	.01
☐ 110	Pete Fox OF	.10	.04	.01
☐ 111	Virgil Trucks P	.10	.04	.01
☐ 112	1968 Tigers	.20	.08	.02
☐ 113	Dizzy Trout P	.10	.04	.01
☐ 114	Barney McCosky OF	.10	.04	.01
☐ 115	Lu Blue 1B	.10	.04	.01
☐ 116	Hal Newhouser P	.20	.08	.02
☐ 117	Tigers Are Home To Prepare For World's Championship Series	.10	.04	.01
☐ 118	Bobby Veach OF	.10	.04	.01
☐ 119	George Mullin P	.10	.04	.01
☐ 120	Reggie's super homer ignites A.L.	.20	.08	.02
☐ 121	Sam Crawford OF	.20	.08	.02
☐ 122	Hank Aguirre P	.10	.04	.01
☐ 123	Vic Wertz 1B	.10	.04	.01
☐ 124	Goose Goslin OF	.20	.08	.02
☐ 125	Frank Lary P	.15	.06	.01
☐ 126	Joe Coleman P	.10	.04	.01
☐ 127	Ed Katalinas Scout	.10	.04	.01
☐ 128	Jack Morris P	.30	.12	.03
☐ 129	Tigers Picked As Winners Of Pirate Battle	.10	.04	.01
☐ 130	James A. Campbell GM	.15	.06	.01
☐ 131	Ted Gray P	.10	.04	.01
☐ 132	Al Kaline OF	.60	.25	.06
☐ 133	Hank Greenberg 1B	.35	.15	.03
☐ 134	Dick McAuliffe INF	.10	.04	.01
☐ 135	Ozzie Virgil INF	.10	.04	.01

1968 Dexter Press

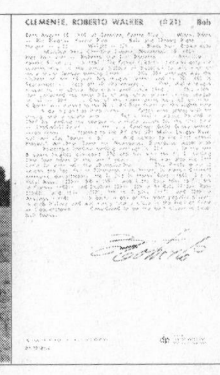

This 77-card set, which measures approximately 3 1/2" by 5 1/2", has beautiful full-color photos on the front of the card with biographical and career information on the back of the card. There are no year by year statistical lines on the back of the card. Dexter Press is another name for cards which the Coca-Cola Company helped to distribute during the mid sixties. The backs of the cards have a facsimile autograph. Dexter Press was located in West Nyack, New York.

	NRMT	VG-E	GOOD
COMPLETE SET (77)	400.00	180.00	60.00
COMMON PLAYER (1-77)	2.50	1.00	.25

		NRMT	VG-E	GOOD
☐ 1	Hank Aaron	35.00	15.75	5.25
☐ 2	Jerry Adair	2.50	1.00	.25
☐ 3	Richie Allen	4.00	1.75	.40
☐ 4	Bob Allison	2.50	1.00	.25
☐ 5	Felipe Alou	3.00	1.25	.30
☐ 6	Jesus Alou	2.50	1.00	.25
☐ 7	Mike Andrews	2.50	1.00	.25
☐ 8	Bob Aspromonte	2.50	1.00	.25
☐ 9	Johnny Bateman	2.50	1.00	.25
☐ 10	Mark Belanger	3.00	1.25	.30
☐ 11	Gary Bell	2.50	1.00	.25
☐ 12	Paul Blair	2.50	1.00	.25
☐ 13	Curt Blefary	2.50	1.00	.25
☐ 14	Bobby Bolin	2.50	1.00	.25
☐ 15	Ken Boswell	2.50	1.00	.25
☐ 16	Clete Boyer	3.00	1.25	.30
☐ 17	Ron Brand	2.50	1.00	.25
☐ 18	Darrell Brandon	2.50	1.00	.25
☐ 19	Don Buford	2.50	1.00	.25
☐ 20	Rod Carew	30.00	13.50	4.50
☐ 21	Clay Carroll	2.50	1.00	.25
☐ 22	Rico Carty	3.00	1.25	.30
☐ 23	Dean Chance	2.50	1.00	.25
☐ 24	Roberto Clemente	35.00	15.75	5.25
☐ 25	Tony Cloninger	2.50	1.00	.25
☐ 26	Mike Cuellar	3.00	1.25	.30
☐ 27	Jim Davenport	2.50	1.00	.25
☐ 28	Ron Davis	2.50	1.00	.25
☐ 29	Moe Drabowsky	2.50	1.00	.25
☐ 30	Dick Ellsworth	2.50	1.00	.25
☐ 31	Andy Etchebarren	2.50	1.00	.25
☐ 32	Joe Foy	2.50	1.00	.25
☐ 33	Bill Freehan	3.00	1.25	.30
☐ 34	Jim Fregosi	3.00	1.25	.30
☐ 35	Julio Gotay	2.50	1.00	.25
☐ 36	Dave Giusti	2.50	1.00	.25
☐ 37	Jim Ray Hart	2.50	1.00	.25
☐ 38	Jack Hiatt	2.50	1.00	.25
☐ 39	Ron Hunt	2.50	1.00	.25
☐ 40	Sonny Jackson	2.50	1.00	.25
☐ 41	Pat Jarvis	2.50	1.00	.25
☐ 42	Dave Johnson	3.00	1.25	.30
☐ 43	Ken Johnson	2.50	1.00	.25
☐ 44	Dalton Jones	2.50	1.00	.25
☐ 45	Jim Kaat	5.00	2.25	.50
☐ 46	Harmon Killebrew	18.00	7.50	2.50
☐ 47	Denny Lemaster	2.50	1.00	.25
☐ 48	Frank Linzy	2.50	1.00	.25
☐ 49	Jim Lonborg	3.00	1.25	.30
☐ 50	Juan Marichal	15.00	6.50	2.15
☐ 51	Willie Mays	35.00	15.75	5.25
☐ 52	Bill Mazeroski	4.00	1.75	.40
☐ 53	Mike McCormick	3.00	1.25	.30
☐ 54	Dave McNally	3.00	1.25	.30
☐ 55	Denis Menke	2.50	1.00	.25
☐ 56	Joe Morgan	18.00	7.50	2.50
☐ 57	Dave Morehead	2.50	1.00	.25
☐ 58	Phil Niekro	12.00	5.25	1.50
☐ 59	Russ Nixon	2.50	1.00	.25
☐ 60	Tony Oliva	6.00	2.50	.60
☐ 61	Gaylord Perry	15.00	6.50	2.15
☐ 62	Rico Petrocelli	3.00	1.25	.30
☐ 63	Tom Phoebus	2.50	1.00	.25
☐ 64	Boog Powell	4.00	1.75	.40
☐ 65	Brooks Robinson	20.00	8.50	2.75
☐ 66	Frank Robinson	18.00	7.50	2.50
☐ 67	Rich Rollins	2.50	1.00	.25
☐ 68	John Roseboro	2.50	1.00	.25
☐ 69	Ray Sadecki	2.50	1.00	.25
☐ 70	George Scott	3.00	1.25	.30
☐ 71	Rusty Staub	5.00	2.25	.50

		EX-MT	VG-E	GOOD
☐ 72	Cesar Tovar	2.50	1.00	.25
☐ 73	Joe Torre	6.00	2.50	.60
☐ 74	Ted Uhlaender	2.50	1.00	.25
☐ 75	Woody Woodward	2.50	1.00	.25
☐ 76	John Wyatt	2.50	1.00	.25
☐ 77	Jimmy Wynn	3.50	1.50	.35

1934-36 Diamond Stars

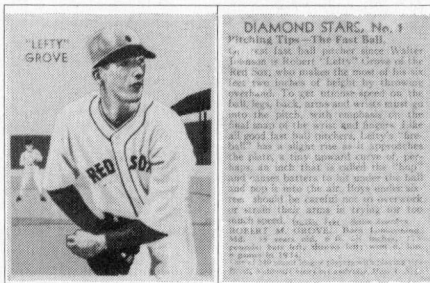

The cards in this 119-card set measure approximately 2 3/8" by 2 7/8". The Diamond Stars set produced by National Chicle from 1934-36 is also commonly known by its catalog designation, R327. The year of production can be determined by the statistics contained on the back of the card. There are at least 168 possible front/back combinations counting blue (B) and green (G) backs over all three years. The last twelve cards are repeat players and are quite scarce. The checklist below lists the year(s) and back color(s) for the cards. Cards 32 through 72 were issued only in 1935 with green ink on back. Cards 73 through 84 were issued three ways: 35B, 35G, and 36B. Card numbers 85 through 108 were issued only in 1936 with blue ink on back. The complete set price below refers to the set of all variations listed explicitly below. A blank backed proof sheet of 12 additional (never-issued) cards was discovered in 1980.

	EX-MT	VG-E	GOOD
COMPLETE SET (119)	17500.00	7500.00	1750.00
COMMON PLAYER (1-31)	50.00	22.50	7.50
COMMON PLAYER (32-72)	60.00	27.00	9.00
COMMON PLAYER (73-84)	60.00	27.00	9.00
COMMON PLAYER (85-96)	120.00	55.00	18.00
COMMON PLAYER (97-108)	350.00	160.00	52.50

		EX-MT	VG-E	GOOD
☐ 1	Lefty Grove	900.00	100.00	20.00
	(34G, 35G)			
☐ 2A	Al Simmons	150.00	67.50	22.50
	(34G, 35G)			
	(Sox on uniform)			
☐ 2B	Al Simmons	225.00	100.00	33.00
	(36B)			
	(No name on uniform)			
☐ 3	Rabbit Maranville	125.00	57.50	18.75
	(34G, 35G)			
☐ 4	Buddy Myer	50.00	22.50	7.50
	(34G, 35G, 36B)			
☐ 5	Tommy Bridges	50.00	22.50	7.50
	(34G, 35G, 36B)			
☐ 6	Max Bishop	50.00	22.50	7.50
	(34G, 35G)			
☐ 7	Lew Fonseca	50.00	22.50	7.50
	(34G, 35G)			
☐ 8	Joe Vosmik	50.00	22.50	7.50
	(34G, 35G, 36B)			
☐ 9	Mickey Cochrane	150.00	67.50	22.50
	(34G, 35G, 36B)			
☐ 10A	Leroy Mahaffey	50.00	22.50	7.50
	(34G, 35G)			
	(A's on uniform)			
☐ 10B	Leroy Mahaffey	100.00	45.00	15.00
	(36B)			
	(No name on uniform)			
☐ 11	Bill Dickey	225.00	100.00	33.00
	(34G, 35G)			
☐ 12A	F. Walker (34G)	75.00	34.00	11.25
	(Ruth retires			

		EX-MT	VG-E	GOOD
	mentioned on back)			
☐ 12B	F. Walker (35G)	60.00	27.00	9.00
	(Ruth to Boston			
	mentioned on back)			
☐ 12C	F. Walker (36B)	100.00	45.00	15.00
☐ 13	George Blaeholder	50.00	22.50	7.50
	(34G, 35G)			
☐ 14	Bill Terry	150.00	67.50	22.50
	(34G, 35G)			
☐ 15A	Dick Bartell (34G)	75.00	34.00	11.25
	(Philadelphia Phillies			
	on card back)			
☐ 15B	Dick Bartell (35G)	60.00	27.00	9.00
	(New York Giants			
	on card back)			
☐ 16	Lloyd Waner	125.00	57.50	18.75
	(34G, 35G, 36B)			
☐ 17	Frank Frisch	150.00	67.50	22.50
	(34G, 35G)			
☐ 18	Chick Hafey	125.00	57.50	18.75
	(34G, 35G)			
☐ 19	Van Lingle Mungo	50.00	22.50	7.50
	(34G, 35G)			
☐ 20	Frank Hogan	50.00	22.50	7.50
	(34G, 35G)			
☐ 21A	Johnny Vergez (34G)	75.00	34.00	11.25
	(New York Giants			
	on card back)			
☐ 21B	Johnny Vergez (35G)	60.00	27.00	9.00
	(Philadelphia Phillies			
	on card back)			
☐ 22	Jimmy Wilson	50.00	22.50	7.50
	(34G, 35G, 36B)			
☐ 23	Bill Hallahan	50.00	22.50	7.50
	(34G, 35G)			
☐ 24	Earl Adams	50.00	22.50	7.50
	(34G, 35G)			
☐ 25	Wally Berger	60.00	27.00	9.00
	(35G)			
☐ 26	Pepper Martin	75.00	34.00	11.25
	35G, 36B)			
☐ 27	Pie Traynor (35G)	175.00	80.00	27.00
☐ 28	Al Lopez (35G)	150.00	67.50	22.50
☐ 29	Red Rolfe (35G)	75.00	34.00	11.25
☐ 30A	Heine Manush	150.00	67.50	22.50
	(35G)			
	(W on sleeve)			
☐ 30B	Heine Manush	225.00	100.00	33.00
	(36B)			
	(No W on sleeve)			
☐ 31A	Kiki Cuyler (35G)	125.00	57.50	18.75
	(Chicago Cubs)			
☐ 31B	Kiki Cuyler (36B)	175.00	80.00	27.00
	(Cincinnati Reds)			
☐ 32	Sam Rice	125.00	57.50	18.75
☐ 33	Schoolboy Rowe	60.00	27.00	9.00
☐ 34	Stan Hack	60.00	27.00	9.00
☐ 35	Earl Averill	125.00	57.50	18.75
☐ 36A	"Earnie" Lombardi	300.00	135.00	45.00
	(sic, Ernie)			
☐ 36B	"Ernie" Lombardi	125.00	57.50	18.75
☐ 37	Billy Urbanski	60.00	27.00	9.00
☐ 38	Ben Chapman	75.00	34.00	11.25
☐ 39	Carl Hubbell	150.00	67.50	22.50
☐ 40	Blondy Ryan	60.00	27.00	9.00
☐ 41	Harvey Hendrick	60.00	27.00	9.00
☐ 42	Jimmy Dykes	75.00	34.00	11.25
☐ 43	Ted Lyons	125.00	57.50	18.75
☐ 44	Rogers Hornsby	350.00	160.00	52.50
☐ 45	Jo Jo White	60.00	27.00	9.00
☐ 46	Red Lucas	60.00	27.00	9.00
☐ 47	Bob Bolton	60.00	27.00	9.00
☐ 48	Rick Ferrell	125.00	57.50	18.75
☐ 49	Buck Jordan	60.00	27.00	9.00
☐ 50	Mel Ott	250.00	110.00	37.50
☐ 51	Burgess Whitehead	60.00	27.00	9.00
☐ 52	Tuck Stainback	60.00	27.00	9.00
☐ 53	Oscar Melillo	60.00	27.00	9.00
☐ 54A	"Hank" Greenburg	500.00	225.00	75.00
	(sic, Greenberg)			
☐ 54B	"Hank" Greenberg	250.00	110.00	37.50
☐ 55	Tony Cuccinello	60.00	27.00	9.00
☐ 56	Gus Suhr	60.00	27.00	9.00
☐ 57	Cy Blanton	60.00	27.00	9.00
☐ 58	Glenn Myatt	60.00	27.00	9.00
☐ 59	Jim Bottomley	125.00	57.50	18.75
☐ 60	Red Ruffing	150.00	67.50	22.50
☐ 61	Bill Werber	60.00	27.00	9.00
☐ 62	Fred Frankhouse	60.00	27.00	9.00
☐ 63	Travis Jackson	125.00	57.50	18.75
☐ 64	Jimmy Foxx	400.00	180.00	60.00
☐ 65	Zeke Bonura	60.00	27.00	9.00
☐ 66	Ducky Medwick	150.00	67.50	22.50
☐ 67	Marvin Owen	60.00	27.00	9.00

		MINT	EXC	G-VG
☐ 68	Sam Leslie	60.00	27.00	9.00
☐ 69	Earl Grace	60.00	27.00	9.00
☐ 70	Hal Trosky	75.00	34.00	11.25
☐ 71	Ossie Bluege	60.00	27.00	9.00
☐ 72	Tony Piet	60.00	27.00	9.00
☐ 73	Fritz Ostermueller	60.00	27.00	9.00
☐ 74	Tony Lazzeri	125.00	57.50	18.75
☐ 75	Jack Burns	60.00	27.00	9.00
☐ 76	Billy Rogell	60.00	27.00	9.00
☐ 77	Charlie Gehringer	150.00	67.50	22.50
☐ 78	Joe Kuhel	60.00	27.00	9.00
☐ 79	Willis Hudlin	60.00	27.00	9.00
☐ 80	Lou Chiozza	60.00	27.00	9.00
☐ 81	Bill Delancey	60.00	27.00	9.00
☐ 82A	Johnny Babich (Dodgers on uniform; 35G, 35B)	60.00	27.00	9.00
☐ 82B	Johnny Babich (No name on uniform; 36B)	125.00	57.50	18.75
☐ 83	Paul Waner	150.00	67.50	22.50
☐ 84	Sam Byrd	60.00	27.00	9.00
☐ 85	Moose Solters	120.00	55.00	18.00
☐ 86	Frank Crosetti	150.00	67.50	22.50
☐ 87	Steve O'Neill	120.00	55.00	18.00
☐ 88	George Selkirk	150.00	67.50	22.50
☐ 89	Joe Stripp	120.00	55.00	18.00
☐ 90	Ray Hayworth	120.00	55.00	18.00
☐ 91	Bucky Harris	200.00	90.00	30.00
☐ 92	Ethan Allen	120.00	55.00	18.00
☐ 93	General Crowder	120.00	55.00	18.00
☐ 94	Wes Ferrell	150.00	67.50	22.50
☐ 95	Luke Appling	250.00	110.00	37.50
☐ 96	Lew Riggs	120.00	55.00	18.00
☐ 97	Al Lopez	600.00	270.00	90.00
☐ 98	Schoolboy Rowe	400.00	180.00	60.00
☐ 99	Pie Traynor	650.00	300.00	100.00
☐ 100	Earl Averill	600.00	270.00	90.00
☐ 101	Dick Bartell	350.00	160.00	52.50
☐ 102	Van Lingle Mungo	350.00	160.00	52.50
☐ 103	Bill Dickey	900.00	400.00	135.00
☐ 104	Red Rolfe	350.00	160.00	52.50
☐ 105	Ernie Lombardi	600.00	270.00	90.00
☐ 106	Red Lucas	350.00	160.00	52.50
☐ 107	Stan Hack	350.00	160.00	52.50
☐ 108	Wally Berger	400.00	180.00	60.00

1988 Domino's Tigers

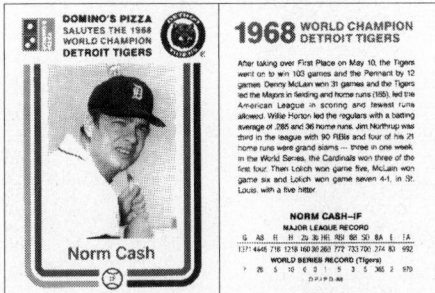

This rather unattractive set commemorates the 20th anniversary of the Detroit Tigers' World Championship season in 1968. The card stock used is rather thin. The cards measure approximately 2 1/2" by 3 1/2". There are a number of errors in the set including biographical errors, misspellings, and photo misidentification. Players are pictured in black and white inside a red and blue horseshoe. The numerous factual errors in the set detract from the set's collectibility in the eyes of many collectors.

		MINT	EXC	G-VG
COMPLETE SET (28)		6.00	2.50	.60
COMMON PLAYER (1-28)		.15	.06	.01
☐ 1	Gates Brown	.15	.06	.01
☐ 2	Norm Cash	.40	.16	.04
☐ 3	Wayne Comer	.15	.06	.01
☐ 4	Pat Dobson	.15	.06	.01

		MINT	EXC	G-VG
☐ 5	Bill Freehan	.40	.16	.04
☐ 6	Ernie Harwell (announcer)	.30	.12	.03
☐ 7	John Hiller	.25	.10	.02
☐ 8	Willie Horton	.25	.10	.02
☐ 9	Al Kaline	1.25	.50	.12
☐ 10	Fred Lasher	.15	.06	.01
☐ 11	Mickey Lolich	.40	.16	.04
☐ 12	Tom Matchick	.15	.06	.01
☐ 13	Ed Mathews	1.00	.40	.10
☐ 14	Dick McAuliffe	.25	.10	.02
☐ 15	Denny McLain	.40	.16	.04
☐ 16	Don McMahon	.15	.06	.01
☐ 17	Jim Northrup	.15	.06	.01
☐ 18	Ray Oyler	.15	.06	.01
☐ 19	Daryl Patterson	.15	.06	.01
☐ 20	Jim Price	.15	.06	.01
☐ 21	Joe Sparma	.15	.06	.01
☐ 22	Mickey Stanley	.25	.10	.02
☐ 23	Dick Tracewski	.15	.06	.01
☐ 24	Jon Warden	.15	.06	.01
☐ 25	Don Wert	.15	.06	.01
☐ 26	Earl Wilson	.15	.06	.01
☐ 27	Pizza Buck Coupon	.15	.06	.01
☐ 28	Title Card	.15	.06	.01
	Old Timers Game 1988			

1981 Donruss

The cards in this 605-card set measure 2 1/2" by 3 1/2". In 1981 Donruss launched itself into the baseball card market with a set containing 600 numbered cards and five unnumbered checklists. Even though the five checklist cards are unnumbered, they are numbered below (601-605) for convenience in reference. The cards are printed on thin stock and more than one pose exists for several popular players. The numerous errors of the first print run were later corrected by the company. These are marked P1 and P2 in the checklist below. The key rookie cards in this set are Tim Raines and Jeff Reardon.

		MINT	EXC	G-VG
COMPLETE SET (605)		60.00	27.00	9.00
COMMON PLAYER (1-605)		.05	.02	.00
☐ 1	Ozzie Smith	2.50	.75	.15
☐ 2	Rollie Fingers	.75	.30	.07
☐ 3	Rick Wise	.05	.02	.00
☐ 4	Gene Richards	.05	.02	.00
☐ 5	Alan Trammell	1.00	.40	.10
☐ 6	Tom Brookens	.05	.02	.00
☐ 7A	Duffy Dyer P1 (980 batting average has decimal point)	.10	.04	.01
☐ 7B	Duffy Dyer P2 (980 batting average has no decimal point)	.10	.04	.01
☐ 8	Mark Fidrych	.15	.06	.01
☐ 9	Dave Rozema	.05	.02	.00
☐ 10	Ricky Peters	.05	.02	.00
☐ 11	Mike Schmidt	2.50	1.00	.25
☐ 12	Willie Stargell	.60	.25	.06
☐ 13	Tim Foli	.05	.02	.00
☐ 14	Manny Sanguillen	.10	.04	.01
☐ 15	Grant Jackson	.05	.02	.00
☐ 16	Eddie Solomon	.05	.02	.00

☐ 17 Omar Moreno	.05	.02	.00
☐ 18 Joe Morgan	.75	.30	.07
☐ 19 Rafael Landestoy	.05	.02	.00
☐ 20 Bruce Bochy	.05	.02	.00
☐ 21 Joe Sambito	.05	.02	.00
☐ 22 Manny Trillo	.05	.02	.00
☐ 23A Dave Smith P1	.40	.16	.04
(Line box around stats is not complete)			
☐ 23B Dave Smith P2	.40	.16	.04
(Box totally encloses stats at top)			
☐ 24 Terry Puhl	.05	.02	.00
☐ 25 Bump Wills	.05	.02	.00
☐ 26A John Ellis P1 ERR	.50	.20	.05
(Photo on front shows Danny Walton)			
☐ 26B John Ellis P2 COR	.10	.04	.01
☐ 27 Jim Kern	.05	.02	.00
☐ 28 Richie Zisk	.05	.02	.00
☐ 29 John Mayberry	.10	.04	.01
☐ 30 Bob Davis	.05	.02	.00
☐ 31 Jackson Todd	.05	.02	.00
☐ 32 Alvis Woods	.05	.02	.00
☐ 33 Steve Carlton	1.25	.50	.12
☐ 34 Lee Mazzilli	.05	.02	.00
☐ 35 John Stearns	.05	.02	.00
☐ 36 Roy Lee Jackson	.05	.02	.00
☐ 37 Mike Scott	.50	.20	.05
☐ 38 Lamar Johnson	.05	.02	.00
☐ 39 Kevin Bell	.05	.02	.00
☐ 40 Ed Farmer	.05	.02	.00
☐ 41 Ross Baumgarten	.05	.02	.00
☐ 42 Leo Sutherland	.05	.02	.00
☐ 43 Dan Meyer	.05	.02	.00
☐ 44 Ron Reed	.05	.02	.00
☐ 45 Mario Mendoza	.05	.02	.00
☐ 46 Rick Honeycutt	.05	.02	.00
☐ 47 Glenn Abbott	.05	.02	.00
☐ 48 Leon Roberts	.05	.02	.00
☐ 49 Rod Carew	1.50	.60	.15
☐ 50 Bert Campaneris	.10	.04	.01
☐ 51A Tom Donahue P1 ERR	.10	.04	.01
(Name on front misspelled Donahue)			
☐ 51B Tom Donohue P2 COR	.10	.04	.01
☐ 52 Dave Frost	.05	.02	.00
☐ 53 Ed Halicki	.05	.02	.00
☐ 54 Dan Ford	.05	.02	.00
☐ 55 Garry Maddox	.05	.02	.00
☐ 56A Steve Garvey P1	1.00	.40	.10
("Surpassed 25 HR")			
☐ 56B Steve Garvey P2	.75	.30	.07
("Surpassed 21 HR")			
☐ 57 Bill Russell	.10	.04	.01
☐ 58 Don Sutton	.50	.20	.05
☐ 59 Reggie Smith	.10	.04	.01
☐ 60 Rick Monday	.10	.04	.01
☐ 61 Ray Knight	.10	.04	.01
☐ 62 Johnny Bench	1.50	.60	.15
☐ 63 Mario Soto	.10	.04	.01
☐ 64 Doug Bair	.05	.02	.00
☐ 65 George Foster	.20	.08	.02
☐ 66 Jeff Burroughs	.05	.02	.00
☐ 67 Keith Hernandez	.35	.15	.03
☐ 68 Tom Herr	.10	.04	.01
☐ 69 Bob Forsch	.05	.02	.00
☐ 70 John Fulgham	.05	.02	.00
☐ 71A Bobby Bonds P1 ERR	.30	.12	.03
(986 lifetime HR)			
☐ 71B Bobby Bonds P2 COR	.15	.06	.01
(326 lifetime HR)			
☐ 72A Rennie Stennett P1	.10	.04	.01
("breaking broke leg")			
☐ 72B Rennie Stennett P2	.10	.04	.01
(Word "broke" deleted)			
☐ 73 Joe Strain	.05	.02	.00
☐ 74 Ed Whitson	.10	.04	.01
☐ 75 Tom Griffin	.05	.02	.00
☐ 76 Billy North	.05	.02	.00
☐ 77 Gene Garber	.05	.02	.00
☐ 78 Mike Hargrove	.10	.04	.01
☐ 79 Dave Rosello	.05	.02	.00
☐ 80 Ron Hassey	.10	.04	.01
☐ 81 Sid Monge	.05	.02	.00
☐ 82A Joe Charboneau P1	.10	.04	.01
('78 highlights, "For some reason")			
☐ 82B Joe Charboneau P2	.10	.04	.01
(Phrase "For some reason" deleted)			
☐ 83 Cecil Cooper	.15	.06	.01
☐ 84 Sal Bando	.10	.04	.01
☐ 85 Moose Haas	.05	.02	.00

☐ 86 Mike Caldwell	.05	.02	.00
☐ 87A Larry Hisle P1	.10	.04	.01
('77 highlights, line ends with "28 RBI")			
☐ 87B Larry Hisle P2	.10	.04	.01
(Correct line "28 HR")			
☐ 88 Luis Gomez	.05	.02	.00
☐ 89 Larry Parrish	.05	.02	.00
☐ 90 Gary Carter	.90	.40	.09
☐ 91 Bill Gullickson	.50	.20	.05
☐ 92 Fred Norman	.05	.02	.00
☐ 93 Tommy Hutton	.05	.02	.00
☐ 94 Carl Yastrzemski	1.50	.60	.15
☐ 95 Glenn Hoffman	.05	.02	.00
☐ 96 Dennis Eckersley	.60	.25	.06
☐ 97A Tom Burgmeier P1	.10	.04	.01
ERR (Throws: Right)			
☐ 97B Tom Burgmeier P2	.10	.04	.01
COR (Throws: Left)			
☐ 98 Win Remmerswaal	.05	.02	.00
☐ 99 Bob Horner	.10	.04	.01
☐ 100 George Brett	2.50	1.00	.25
☐ 101 Dave Chalk	.05	.02	.00
☐ 102 Dennis Leonard	.05	.02	.00
☐ 103 Renie Martin	.05	.02	.00
☐ 104 Amos Otis	.10	.04	.01
☐ 105 Graig Nettles	.15	.06	.01
☐ 106 Eric Soderholm	.05	.02	.00
☐ 107 Tommy John	.20	.08	.02
☐ 108 Tom Underwood	.05	.02	.00
☐ 109 Lou Piniella	.15	.06	.01
☐ 110 Mickey Klutts	.05	.02	.00
☐ 111 Bobby Murcer	.15	.06	.01
☐ 112 Eddie Murray	2.50	1.00	.25
☐ 113 Rick Dempsey	.05	.02	.00
☐ 114 Scott McGregor	.05	.02	.00
☐ 115 Ken Singleton	.10	.04	.01
☐ 116 Gary Roenicke	.05	.02	.00
☐ 117 Dave Revering	.05	.02	.00
☐ 118 Mike Norris	.05	.02	.00
☐ 119 Rickey Henderson	18.00	7.50	2.50
☐ 120 Mike Heath	.05	.02	.00
☐ 121 Dave Cash	.05	.02	.00
☐ 122 Randy Jones	.05	.02	.00
☐ 123 Eric Rasmussen	.05	.02	.00
☐ 124 Jerry Mumphrey	.05	.02	.00
☐ 125 Richie Hebner	.05	.02	.00
☐ 126 Mark Wagner	.05	.02	.00
☐ 127 Jack Morris	1.00	.40	.10
☐ 128 Dan Petry	.10	.04	.01
☐ 129 Bruce Robbins	.05	.02	.00
☐ 130 Champ Summers	.05	.02	.00
☐ 131A Pete Rose P1	2.00	.80	.20
(Last line ends with "see card 251")			
☐ 131B Pete Rose P2	1.75	.70	.17
(Last line corrected "see card 371")			
☐ 132 Willie Stargell	.60	.25	.06
☐ 133 Ed Ott	.05	.02	.00
☐ 134 Jim Bibby	.05	.02	.00
☐ 135 Bert Blyleven	.25	.10	.02
☐ 136 Dave Parker	.60	.25	.06
☐ 137 Bill Robinson	.10	.04	.01
☐ 138 Enos Cabell	.05	.02	.00
☐ 139 Dave Bergman	.05	.02	.00
☐ 140 J.R. Richard	.10	.04	.01
☐ 141 Ken Forsch	.05	.02	.00
☐ 142 Larry Bowa UER	.15	.06	.01
(Shortshop on front)			
☐ 143 Frank LaCorte UER	.05	.02	.00
(photo actually Randy Niemann)			
☐ 144 Denny Walling	.05	.02	.00
☐ 145 Buddy Bell	.10	.04	.01
☐ 146 Ferguson Jenkins	.50	.20	.05
☐ 147 Danny Darwin	.10	.04	.01
☐ 148 John Grubb	.05	.02	.00
☐ 149 Alfredo Griffin	.10	.04	.01
☐ 150 Jerry Garvin	.05	.02	.00
☐ 151 Paul Mirabella	.05	.02	.00
☐ 152 Rick Bosetti	.05	.02	.00
☐ 153 Dick Ruthven	.05	.02	.00
☐ 154 Frank Taveras	.05	.02	.00
☐ 155 Craig Swan	.05	.02	.00
☐ 156 Jeff Reardon	3.50	1.50	.35
☐ 157 Steve Henderson	.05	.02	.00
☐ 158 Jim Morrison	.05	.02	.00
☐ 159 Glenn Borgmann	.05	.02	.00
☐ 160 LaMarr Hoyt	.15	.06	.01
☐ 161 Rich Wortham	.05	.02	.00
☐ 162 Thad Bosley	.05	.02	.00
☐ 163 Julio Cruz	.05	.02	.00
☐ 164A Del Unser P1	.10	.04	.01

	(No "3B" heading)			
☐	164B Del Unser P2	.10	.04	.01
	(Batting record on back corrected ("3B")			
☐	165 Jim Anderson	.05	.02	.00
☐	166 Jim Beattie	.05	.02	.00
☐	167 Shane Rawley	.05	.02	.00
☐	168 Joe Simpson	.05	.02	.00
☐	169 Rod Carew	1.50	.60	.15
☐	170 Fred Patek	.05	.02	.00
☐	171 Frank Tanana	.10	.04	.01
☐	172 Alfredo Martinez	.05	.02	.00
☐	173 Chris Knapp	.05	.02	.00
☐	174 Joe Rudi	.10	.04	.01
☐	175 Greg Luzinski	.15	.06	.01
☐	176 Steve Garvey	.75	.30	.07
☐	177 Joe Ferguson	.05	.02	.00
☐	178 Bob Welch	.50	.20	.05
☐	179 Dusty Baker	.10	.04	.01
☐	180 Rudy Law	.05	.02	.00
☐	181 Dave Concepcion	.20	.08	.02
☐	182 Johnny Bench	1.50	.60	.15
☐	183 Mike LaCoss	.05	.02	.00
☐	184 Ken Griffey	.30	.12	.03
☐	185 Dave Collins	.05	.02	.00
☐	186 Brian Asselstine	.05	.02	.00
☐	187 Garry Templeton	.10	.04	.01
☐	188 Mike Phillips	.05	.02	.00
☐	189 Pete Vuckovich	.05	.02	.00
☐	190 John Urrea	.05	.02	.00
☐	191 Tony Scott	.05	.02	.00
☐	192 Darrell Evans	.15	.06	.01
☐	193 Milt May	.05	.02	.00
☐	194 Bob Knepper	.05	.02	.00
☐	195 Randy Moffitt	.05	.02	.00
☐	196 Larry Herndon	.05	.02	.00
☐	197 Rick Camp	.05	.02	.00
☐	198 Andre Thornton	.10	.04	.01
☐	199 Tom Veryzer	.05	.02	.00
☐	200 Gary Alexander	.05	.02	.00
☐	201 Rick Waits	.05	.02	.00
☐	202 Rick Manning	.05	.02	.00
☐	203 Paul Molitor	.60	.25	.06
☐	204 Jim Gantner	.05	.02	.00
☐	205 Paul Mitchell	.05	.02	.00
☐	206 Reggie Cleveland	.05	.02	.00
☐	207 Sixto Lezcano	.05	.02	.00
☐	208 Bruce Benedict	.05	.02	.00
☐	209 Rodney Scott	.05	.02	.00
☐	210 John Tamargo	.05	.02	.00
☐	211 Bill Lee	.05	.02	.00
☐	212 Andre Dawson UER	1.75	.70	.17
	(Middle name Fernando, should be Nolan)			
☐	213 Rowland Office	.05	.02	.00
☐	214 Carl Yastrzemski	1.50	.60	.15
☐	215 Jerry Remy	.05	.02	.00
☐	216 Mike Torrez	.05	.02	.00
☐	217 Skip Lockwood	.05	.02	.00
☐	218 Fred Lynn	.20	.08	.02
☐	219 Chris Chambliss	.10	.04	.01
☐	220 Willie Aikens	.05	.02	.00
☐	221 John Wathan	.10	.04	.01
☐	222 Dan Quisenberry	.25	.10	.02
☐	223 Willie Wilson	.20	.08	.02
☐	224 Clint Hurdle	.05	.02	.00
☐	225 Bob Watson	.05	.02	.00
☐	226 Jim Spencer	.05	.02	.00
☐	227 Ron Guidry	.25	.10	.02
☐	228 Reggie Jackson	2.50	1.00	.25
☐	229 Oscar Gamble	.05	.02	.00
☐	230 Jeff Cox	.05	.02	.00
☐	231 Luis Tiant	.10	.04	.01
☐	232 Rich Dauer	.05	.02	.00
☐	233 Dan Graham	.05	.02	.00
☐	234 Mike Flanagan	.10	.04	.01
☐	235 John Lowenstein	.05	.02	.00
☐	236 Benny Ayala	.05	.02	.00
☐	237 Wayne Gross	.05	.02	.00
☐	238 Rick Langford	.05	.02	.00
☐	239 Tony Armas	.05	.02	.00
☐	240A Bob Lacy P1 ERR	.20	.08	.02
	(Name misspelled Bob "Lacy")			
☐	240B Bob Lacey P2 COR	.10	.04	.01
☐	241 Gene Tenace	.10	.04	.01
☐	242 Bob Shirley	.05	.02	.00
☐	243 Gary Lucas	.05	.02	.00
☐	244 Jerry Turner	.05	.02	.00
☐	245 John Wockenfuss	.05	.02	.00
☐	246 Stan Papi	.05	.02	.00
☐	247 Milt Wilcox	.05	.02	.00
☐	248 Dan Schatzeder	.05	.02	.00
☐	249 Steve Kemp	.05	.02	.00
☐	250 Jim Lentine	.05	.02	.00
☐	251 Pete Rose	1.75	.70	.17
☐	252 Bill Madlock	.15	.06	.01
☐	253 Dale Berra	.05	.02	.00
☐	254 Kent Tekulve	.10	.04	.01
☐	255 Enrique Romo	.05	.02	.00
☐	256 Mike Easler	.05	.02	.00
☐	257 Chuck Tanner MG	.05	.02	.00
☐	258 Art Howe	.10	.04	.01
☐	259 Alan Ashby	.05	.02	.00
☐	260 Nolan Ryan	6.25	2.75	.60
☐	261A Vern Ruhle P1 ERR	.50	.20	.05
	(Photo on front actually Ken Forsch)			
☐	261B Vern Ruhle P2 COR	.10	.04	.01
☐	262 Bob Boone	.15	.06	.01
☐	263 Cesar Cedeno	.10	.04	.01
☐	264 Jeff Leonard	.10	.04	.01
☐	265 Pat Putnam	.05	.02	.00
☐	266 Jon Matlack	.05	.02	.00
☐	267 Dave Rajsich	.05	.02	.00
☐	268 Billy Sample	.05	.02	.00
☐	269 Damaso Garcia	.05	.02	.00
☐	270 Tom Buskey	.05	.02	.00
☐	271 Joey McLaughlin	.05	.02	.00
☐	272 Barry Bonnell	.05	.02	.00
☐	273 Tug McGraw	.15	.06	.01
☐	274 Mike Jorgensen	.05	.02	.00
☐	275 Pat Zachry	.05	.02	.00
☐	276 Neil Allen	.05	.02	.00
☐	277 Joel Youngblood	.05	.02	.00
☐	278 Greg Pryor	.05	.02	.00
☐	279 Britt Burns	.10	.04	.01
☐	280 Rich Dotson	.15	.06	.01
☐	281 Chet Lemon	.05	.02	.00
☐	282 Rusty Kuntz	.05	.02	.00
☐	283 Ted Cox	.05	.02	.00
☐	284 Sparky Lyle	.15	.06	.01
☐	285 Larry Cox	.05	.02	.00
☐	286 Floyd Bannister	.05	.02	.00
☐	287 Byron McLaughlin	.05	.02	.00
☐	288 Rodney Craig	.05	.02	.00
☐	289 Bobby Grich	.10	.04	.01
☐	290 Dickie Thon	.15	.06	.01
☐	291 Mark Clear	.05	.02	.00
☐	292 Dave Lemanczyk	.05	.02	.00
☐	293 Jason Thompson	.05	.02	.00
☐	294 Rick Miller	.05	.02	.00
☐	295 Lonnie Smith	.35	.15	.03
☐	296 Ron Cey	.15	.06	.01
☐	297 Steve Yeager	.05	.02	.00
☐	298 Bobby Castillo	.05	.02	.00
☐	299 Manny Mota	.10	.04	.01
☐	300 Jay Johnstone	.10	.04	.01
☐	301 Dan Driessen	.05	.02	.00
☐	302 Joe Nolan	.05	.02	.00
☐	303 Paul Householder	.05	.02	.00
☐	304 Harry Spilman	.05	.02	.00
☐	305 Cesar Geronimo	.05	.02	.00
☐	306A Gary Mathews P1 ERR	.20	.08	.02
	(Name misspelled)			
☐	306B Gary Matthews P2 COR	.10	.04	.01
☐	307 Ken Reitz	.05	.02	.00
☐	308 Ted Simmons	.20	.08	.02
☐	309 John Littlefield	.05	.02	.00
☐	310 George Frazier	.05	.02	.00
☐	311 Dane Iorg	.05	.02	.00
☐	312 Mike Ivie	.05	.02	.00
☐	313 Dennis Littlejohn	.05	.02	.00
☐	314 Gary Lavelle	.05	.02	.00
☐	315 Jack Clark	.25	.10	.02
☐	316 Jim Wohlford	.05	.02	.00
☐	317 Rick Matula	.05	.02	.00
☐	318 Toby Harrah	.05	.02	.00
☐	319A Dwane Kuiper P1 ERR	.10	.04	.01
	(Name misspelled)			
☐	319B Duane Kuiper P2 COR	.10	.04	.01
☐	320 Len Barker	.05	.02	.00
☐	321 Victor Cruz	.05	.02	.00
☐	322 Dell Alston	.05	.02	.00
☐	323 Robin Yount	2.50	1.00	.25
☐	324 Charlie Moore	.05	.02	.00
☐	325 Lary Sorensen	.05	.02	.00
☐	326A Gorman Thomas P1	.20	.08	.02
	(2nd line on back: "30 HR mark 4th")			
☐	326B Gorman Thomas P2	.10	.04	.01
	("30 HR mark 3rd")			
☐	327 Bob Rodgers MG	.05	.02	.00
☐	328 Phil Niekro	.50	.20	.05
☐	329 Chris Speier	.05	.02	.00
☐	330A Steve Rodgers P1	.20	.08	.02
	ERR (Name misspelled)			
☐	330B Steve Rogers P2 COR	.10	.04	.01

☐ 331	Woodie Fryman	.05	.02	.00
☐ 332	Warren Cromartie	.05	.02	.00
☐ 333	Jerry White	.05	.02	.00
☐ 334	Tony Perez	.35	.15	.03
☐ 335	Carlton Fisk	1.50	.60	.15
☐ 336	Dick Drago	.05	.02	.00
☐ 337	Steve Renko	.05	.02	.00
☐ 338	Jim Rice	.25	.10	.02
☐ 339	Jerry Royster	.05	.02	.00
☐ 340	Frank White	.10	.04	.01
☐ 341	Jamie Quirk	.05	.02	.00
☐ 342A	Paul Spittorff P1 ERR (Name misspelled)	.10	.04	.01
☐ 342B	Paul Splittorff P2 COR	.10	.04	.01
☐ 343	Marty Pattin	.05	.02	.00
☐ 344	Pete LaCock	.05	.02	.00
☐ 345	Willie Randolph	.15	.06	.01
☐ 346	Rick Cerone	.05	.02	.00
☐ 347	Rich Gossage	.20	.08	.02
☐ 348	Reggie Jackson	2.50	1.00	.25
☐ 349	Ruppert Jones	.05	.02	.00
☐ 350	Dave McKay	.05	.02	.00
☐ 351	Yogi Berra CO	.25	.10	.02
☐ 352	Doug DeCinces	.05	.02	.00
☐ 353	Jim Palmer	1.00	.40	.10
☐ 354	Tippy Martinez	.05	.02	.00
☐ 355	Al Bumbry	.05	.02	.00
☐ 356	Earl Weaver MG	.10	.04	.01
☐ 357A	Bob Picciolo P1 ERR (Name misspelled)	.10	.04	.01
☐ 357B	Rob Picciolo P2 COR	.10	.04	.01
☐ 358	Matt Keough	.05	.02	.00
☐ 359	Dwayne Murphy	.05	.02	.00
☐ 360	Brian Kingman	.05	.02	.00
☐ 361	Bill Fahey	.05	.02	.00
☐ 362	Steve Mura	.05	.02	.00
☐ 363	Dennis Kinney	.05	.02	.00
☐ 364	Dave Winfield	1.25	.50	.12
☐ 365	Lou Whitaker	.60	.25	.06
☐ 366	Lance Parrish	.40	.16	.04
☐ 367	Tim Corcoran	.05	.02	.00
☐ 368	Pat Underwood	.05	.02	.00
☐ 369	Al Cowens	.05	.02	.00
☐ 370	Sparky Anderson MG	.10	.04	.01
☐ 371	Pete Rose	1.75	.70	.17
☐ 372	Phil Garner	.10	.04	.01
☐ 373	Steve Nicosia	.05	.02	.00
☐ 374	John Candelaria	.10	.04	.01
☐ 375	Don Robinson	.05	.02	.00
☐ 376	Lee Lacy	.05	.02	.00
☐ 377	John Milner	.05	.02	.00
☐ 378	Craig Reynolds	.05	.02	.00
☐ 379A	Luis Pujois P1 ERR (Name misspelled)	.10	.04	.01
☐ 379B	Luis Pujols P2 COR	.10	.04	.01
☐ 380	Joe Niekro	.10	.04	.01
☐ 381	Joaquin Andujar	.10	.04	.01
☐ 382	Keith Moreland	.15	.06	.01
☐ 383	Jose Cruz	.10	.04	.01
☐ 384	Bill Virdon MG	.05	.02	.00
☐ 385	Jim Sundberg	.05	.02	.00
☐ 386	Doc Medich	.05	.02	.00
☐ 387	Al Oliver	.10	.04	.01
☐ 388	Jim Norris	.05	.02	.00
☐ 389	Bob Bailor	.05	.02	.00
☐ 390	Ernie Whitt	.05	.02	.00
☐ 391	Otto Velez	.05	.02	.00
☐ 392	Roy Howell	.05	.02	.00
☐ 393	Bob Walk	.25	.10	.02
☐ 394	Doug Flynn	.05	.02	.00
☐ 395	Pete Falcone	.05	.02	.00
☐ 396	Tom Hausman	.05	.02	.00
☐ 397	Elliott Maddox	.05	.02	.00
☐ 398	Mike Squires	.05	.02	.00
☐ 399	Marvis Foley	.05	.02	.00
☐ 400	Steve Trout	.05	.02	.00
☐ 401	Wayne Nordhagen	.05	.02	.00
☐ 402	Tony LaRussa MG	.10	.04	.01
☐ 403	Bruce Bochte	.05	.02	.00
☐ 404	Bake McBride	.05	.02	.00
☐ 405	Jerry Narron	.05	.02	.00
☐ 406	Rob Dressler	.05	.02	.00
☐ 407	Dave Heaverlo	.05	.02	.00
☐ 408	Tom Paciorek	.05	.02	.00
☐ 409	Carney Lansford	.15	.06	.01
☐ 410	Brian Downing	.10	.04	.01
☐ 411	Don Aase	.05	.02	.00
☐ 412	Jim Barr	.05	.02	.00
☐ 413	Don Baylor	.15	.06	.01
☐ 414	Jim Fregosi	.05	.02	.00
☐ 415	Dallas Green MG	.05	.02	.00
☐ 416	Dave Lopes	.10	.04	.01
☐ 417	Jerry Reuss	.05	.02	.00
☐ 418	Rick Sutcliffe	.15	.06	.01
☐ 419	Derrel Thomas	.05	.02	.00
☐ 420	Tom Lasorda MG	.10	.04	.01
☐ 421	Charles Leibrandt	.50	.20	.05
☐ 422	Tom Seaver	1.50	.60	.15
☐ 423	Ron Oester	.05	.02	.00
☐ 424	Junior Kennedy	.05	.02	.00
☐ 425	Tom Seaver	1.50	.60	.15
☐ 426	Bobby Cox MG	.05	.02	.00
☐ 427	Leon Durham	.15	.06	.01
☐ 428	Terry Kennedy	.10	.04	.01
☐ 429	Silvio Martinez	.05	.02	.00
☐ 430	George Hendrick	.05	.02	.00
☐ 431	Red Schoendienst MG	.15	.06	.01
☐ 432	Johnnie LeMaster	.05	.02	.00
☐ 433	Vida Blue	.10	.04	.01
☐ 434	John Montefusco	.05	.02	.00
☐ 435	Terry Whitfield	.05	.02	.00
☐ 436	Dave Bristol MG	.05	.02	.00
☐ 437	Dale Murphy	1.00	.40	.10
☐ 438	Jerry Dybzinski	.05	.02	.00
☐ 439	Jorge Orta	.05	.02	.00
☐ 440	Wayne Garland	.05	.02	.00
☐ 441	Miguel Dilone	.05	.02	.00
☐ 442	Dave Garcia MG	.05	.02	.00
☐ 443	Don Money	.05	.02	.00
☐ 444A	Buck Martinez P1 ERR (reverse negative)	.10	.04	.01
☐ 444B	Buck Martinez P2 COR	.10	.04	.01
☐ 445	Jerry Augustine	.05	.02	.00
☐ 446	Ben Oglivie	.05	.02	.00
☐ 447	Jim Slaton	.05	.02	.00
☐ 448	Doyle Alexander	.05	.02	.00
☐ 449	Tony Bernazard	.05	.02	.00
☐ 450	Scott Sanderson	.10	.04	.01
☐ 451	David Palmer	.05	.02	.00
☐ 452	Stan Bahnsen	.05	.02	.00
☐ 453	Dick Williams MG	.05	.02	.00
☐ 454	Rick Burleson	.10	.04	.01
☐ 455	Gary Allenson	.05	.02	.00
☐ 456	Bob Stanley	.05	.02	.00
☐ 457A	John Tudor P1 ERR (Lifetime W-L "9.7")	.50	.20	.05
☐ 457B	John Tudor P2 COR (Corrected "9-7")	.50	.20	.05
☐ 458	Dwight Evans	.35	.15	.03
☐ 459	Glenn Hubbard	.05	.02	.00
☐ 460	U.L. Washington	.05	.02	.00
☐ 461	Larry Gura	.05	.02	.00
☐ 462	Rich Gale	.05	.02	.00
☐ 463	Hal McRae	.15	.06	.01
☐ 464	Jim Frey MG	.05	.02	.00
☐ 465	Bucky Dent	.10	.04	.01
☐ 466	Dennis Werth	.05	.02	.00
☐ 467	Ron Davis	.05	.02	.00
☐ 468	Reggie Jackson UER (32 HR in 1970, should be 23)	2.50	1.00	.25
☐ 469	Bobby Brown	.05	.02	.00
☐ 470	Mike Davis	.15	.06	.01
☐ 471	Gaylord Perry	.50	.20	.05
☐ 472	Mark Belanger	.10	.04	.01
☐ 473	Jim Palmer	1.00	.40	.10
☐ 474	Sammy Stewart	.05	.02	.00
☐ 475	Tim Stoddard	.05	.02	.00
☐ 476	Steve Stone	.05	.02	.00
☐ 477	Jeff Newman	.05	.02	.00
☐ 478	Steve McCatty	.05	.02	.00
☐ 479	Billy Martin MG	.20	.08	.02
☐ 480	Mitchell Page	.05	.02	.00
☐ 481	Cy Young Winner 1980 Steve Carlton	.50	.20	.05
☐ 482	Bill Buckner	.10	.04	.01
☐ 483A	Ivan DeJesus P1 ERR (Lifetime hits "702")	.10	.04	.01
☐ 483B	Ivan DeJesus P2 COR (Lifetime hits "642")	.10	.04	.01
☐ 484	Cliff Johnson	.05	.02	.00
☐ 485	Lenny Randle	.05	.02	.00
☐ 486	Larry Milbourne	.05	.02	.00
☐ 487	Roy Smalley	.05	.02	.00
☐ 488	John Castino	.05	.02	.00
☐ 489	Ron Jackson	.05	.02	.00
☐ 490A	Dave Roberts P1 (Career Highlights: "Showed pop in")	.10	.04	.01
☐ 490B	Dave Roberts P2 ("Declared himself")	.10	.04	.01
☐ 491	MVP: George Brett	1.50	.60	.15
☐ 492	Mike Cubbage	.05	.02	.00
☐ 493	Rob Wilfong	.05	.02	.00
☐ 494	Danny Goodwin	.05	.02	.00
☐ 495	Jose Morales	.05	.02	.00
☐ 496	Mickey Rivers	.10	.04	.01
☐ 497	Mike Edwards	.05	.02	.00

☐ 498	Mike Sadek	.05	.02	.00
☐ 499	Lenn Sakata	.05	.02	.00
☐ 500	Gene Michael MG	.05	.02	.00
☐ 501	Dave Roberts	.05	.02	.00
☐ 502	Steve Dillard	.05	.02	.00
☐ 503	Jim Essian	.10	.04	.01
☐ 504	Rance Mulliniks	.05	.02	.00
☐ 505	Darrell Porter	.05	.02	.00
☐ 506	Joe Torre MG	.15	.06	.01
☐ 507	Terry Crowley	.05	.02	.00
☐ 508	Bill Travers	.05	.02	.00
☐ 509	Nelson Norman	.05	.02	.00
☐ 510	Bob McClure	.05	.02	.00
☐ 511	Steve Howe	.10	.04	.01
☐ 512	Dave Rader	.05	.02	.00
☐ 513	Mick Kelleher	.05	.02	.00
☐ 514	Kiko Garcia	.05	.02	.00
☐ 515	Larry Biittner	.05	.02	.00
☐ 516A	Willie Norwood P1 (Career Highlights "Spent most of")	.10	.04	.01
☐ 516B	Willie Norwood P2 ("Traded to Seattle")	.10	.04	.01
☐ 517	Bo Diaz	.05	.02	.00
☐ 518	Juan Beniquez	.05	.02	.00
☐ 519	Scot Thompson	.05	.02	.00
☐ 520	Jim Tracy	.05	.02	.00
☐ 521	Carlos Lezcano	.05	.02	.00
☐ 522	Joe Amalfitano MG	.05	.02	.00
☐ 523	Preston Hanna	.05	.02	.00
☐ 524A	Ray Burris P1 (Career Highlights: "Went on ...")	.10	.04	.01
☐ 524B	Ray Burris P2 ("Drafted by ...")	.10	.04	.01
☐ 525	Broderick Perkins	.05	.02	.00
☐ 526	Mickey Hatcher	.10	.04	.01
☐ 527	John Goryl MG	.05	.02	.00
☐ 528	Dick Davis	.05	.02	.00
☐ 529	Butch Wynegar	.05	.02	.00
☐ 530	Sal Butera	.05	.02	.00
☐ 531	Jerry Koosman	.10	.04	.01
☐ 532A	Geoff Zahn P1 (Career Highlights: "Was 2nd in")	.10	.04	.01
☐ 532B	Geoff Zahn P2 ("Signed a 3 year")	.10	.04	.01
☐ 533	Dennis Martinez	.20	.08	.02
☐ 534	Gary Thomasson	.05	.02	.00
☐ 535	Steve Macko	.05	.02	.00
☐ 536	Jim Kaat	.20	.08	.02
☐ 537	Best Hitters George Brett Rod Carew	2.00	.80	.20
☐ 538	Tim Raines	5.50	2.50	.55
☐ 539	Keith Smith	.05	.02	.00
☐ 540	Ken Macha	.05	.02	.00
☐ 541	Burt Hooton	.05	.02	.00
☐ 542	Butch Hobson	.10	.04	.01
☐ 543	Bill Stein	.05	.02	.00
☐ 544	Dave Stapleton	.05	.02	.00
☐ 545	Bob Pate	.05	.02	.00
☐ 546	Doug Corbett	.05	.02	.00
☐ 547	Darrell Jackson	.05	.02	.00
☐ 548	Pete Redfern	.05	.02	.00
☐ 549	Roger Erickson	.05	.02	.00
☐ 550	Al Hrabosky	.05	.02	.00
☐ 551	Dick Tidrow	.05	.02	.00
☐ 552	Dave Ford	.05	.02	.00
☐ 553	Dave Kingman	.15	.06	.01
☐ 554A	Mike Vail P1 (Career Highlights: "After two ...")	.10	.04	.01
☐ 554B	Mike Vail P2 ("Traded to ...")	.10	.04	.01
☐ 555A	Jerry Martin P1 (Career Highlights: "Overcame a ...")	.10	.04	.01
☐ 555B	Jerry Martin P2 ("Traded to ...")	.10	.04	.01
☐ 556A	Jesus Figueroa P1 (Career Highlights: "Had an ...")	.10	.04	.01
☐ 556B	Jesus Figueroa P2 ("Traded to ...")	.10	.04	.01
☐ 557	Don Stanhouse	.05	.02	.00
☐ 558	Barry Foote	.05	.02	.00
☐ 559	Tim Blackwell	.05	.02	.00
☐ 560	Bruce Sutter	.20	.08	.02
☐ 561	Rick Reuschel	.15	.06	.01
☐ 562	Lynn McGlothen	.05	.02	.00
☐ 563A	Bob Owchinko P1 (Career Highlights: "Traded to ...")	.10	.04	.01

☐ 563B	Bob Owchinko P2 ("Involved in a ...")	.10	.04	.01
☐ 564	John Verhoeven	.05	.02	.00
☐ 565	Ken Landreaux	.05	.02	.00
☐ 566A	Glen Adams P1 ERR (Name misspelled)	.10	.04	.01
☐ 566B	Glenn Adams P2 COR	.10	.04	.01
☐ 567	Hosken Powell	.05	.02	.00
☐ 568	Dick Noles	.05	.02	.00
☐ 569	Danny Ainge	1.00	.40	.10
☐ 570	Bobby Mattick MG	.05	.02	.00
☐ 571	Joe Lefebvre	.05	.02	.00
☐ 572	Bobby Clark	.05	.02	.00
☐ 573	Dennis Lamp	.05	.02	.00
☐ 574	Randy Lerch	.05	.02	.00
☐ 575	Mookie Wilson	.60	.25	.06
☐ 576	Ron LeFlore	.05	.02	.00
☐ 577	Jim Dwyer	.05	.02	.00
☐ 578	Bill Castro	.05	.02	.00
☐ 579	Greg Minton	.05	.02	.00
☐ 580	Mark Littell	.05	.02	.00
☐ 581	Andy Hassler	.05	.02	.00
☐ 582	Dave Stieb	.60	.25	.06
☐ 583	Ken Oberkfell	.05	.02	.00
☐ 584	Larry Bradford	.05	.02	.00
☐ 585	Fred Stanley	.05	.02	.00
☐ 586	Bill Caudill	.05	.02	.00
☐ 587	Doug Capilla	.05	.02	.00
☐ 588	George Riley	.05	.02	.00
☐ 589	Willie Hernandez	.10	.04	.01
☐ 590	MVP: Mike Schmidt	1.50	.60	.15
☐ 591	Cy Young Winner 1980: Steve Stone	.05	.02	.00
☐ 592	Rick Sofield	.05	.02	.00
☐ 593	Bombo Rivera	.05	.02	.00
☐ 594	Gary Ward	.05	.02	.00
☐ 595A	Dave Edwards P1 (Career Highlights: "Sidelined the")	.10	.04	.01
☐ 595B	Dave Edwards P2 ("Traded to ...")	.10	.04	.01
☐ 596	Mike Proly	.05	.02	.00
☐ 597	Tommy Boggs	.05	.02	.00
☐ 598	Greg Gross	.05	.02	.00
☐ 599	Elias Sosa	.05	.02	.00
☐ 600	Pat Kelly	.05	.02	.00
☐ 601A	Checklist 1 P1 ERR unnumbered (51 Donahue)	.15	.02	.00
☐ 601B	Checklist 1 P2 COR unnumbered (51 Donohue)	.75	.07	.01
☐ 602	Checklist 2 unnumbered	.15	.02	.00
☐ 603A	Checklist 3 P1 ERR unnumbered (306 Mathews)	.15	.02	.00
☐ 603B	Checklist 3 P2 COR unnumbered (306 Matthews)	.15	.02	.00
☐ 604A	Checklist 4 P1 ERR unnumbered (379 Pujois)	.15	.02	.00
☐ 604B	Checklist 4 P2 COR unnumbered (379 Pujols)	.15	.02	.00
☐ 605A	Checklist 5 P1 ERR unnumbered (566 Glen Adams)	.15	.02	.00
☐ 605B	Checklist 5 P2 COR unnumbered (566 Glenn Adams)	.15	.02	.00

1982 Donruss

The 1982 Donruss set contains 653 numbered cards and the seven unnumbered checklists; each card measures 2 1/2" by 3 1/2". The first 26 cards of this set are entitled Donruss Diamond Kings (DK) and feature the artwork of Dick Perez of Perez-Steele Galleries. The set was marketed with puzzle pieces rather than with bubble gum. There are 63 pieces to the puzzle, which, when put together, make a collage of Babe Ruth entitled "Hall of Fame Diamond King." The card stock in this year's Donruss cards is considerably thicker than that of the 1981 cards. The seven unnumbered checklist cards are arbitrarily assigned numbers 654 through 660 and are listed at the end of the list below. The key rookie cards in this set are George Bell, Cal Ripken Jr., Steve Sax, Lee Smith, and Dave Stewart.

	MINT	EXC	G-VG
COMPLETE SET (660)	80.00	36.00	12.00
COMMON PLAYER (1-660)	.05	.02	.00

		MINT	EXC	G-VG
☐ 1	Pete Rose DK	1.50	.50	.10
☐ 2	Gary Carter DK	.35	.15	.03
☐ 3	Steve Garvey DK	.40	.16	.04
☐ 4	Vida Blue DK	.10	.04	.01
☐ 5A	Alan Trammel DK ERR (name misspelled)	1.50	.60	.15
☐ 5B	Alan Trammell DK COR	.40	.16	.04
☐ 6	Len Barker DK	.10	.04	.01
☐ 7	Dwight Evans DK	.15	.06	.01
☐ 8	Rod Carew DK	.60	.25	.06
☐ 9	George Hendrick DK	.10	.04	.01
☐ 10	Phil Niekro DK	.20	.08	.02
☐ 11	Richie Zisk DK	.10	.04	.01
☐ 12	Dave Parker DK	.30	.12	.03
☐ 13	Nolan Ryan DK	2.75	1.10	.27
☐ 14	Ivan DeJesus DK	.10	.04	.01
☐ 15	George Brett DK	.85	.35	.08
☐ 16	Tom Seaver DK	.70	.30	.07
☐ 17	Dave Kingman DK	.10	.04	.01
☐ 18	Dave Winfield DK	.55	.22	.05
☐ 19	Mike Norris DK	.10	.04	.01
☐ 20	Carlton Fisk DK	.70	.30	.07
☐ 21	Ozzie Smith DK	.75	.30	.07
☐ 22	Roy Smalley DK	.10	.04	.01
☐ 23	Buddy Bell DK	.10	.04	.01
☐ 24	Ken Singleton DK	.10	.04	.01
☐ 25	John Mayberry DK	.10	.04	.01
☐ 26	Gorman Thomas DK	.10	.04	.01
☐ 27	Earl Weaver MG	.10	.04	.01
☐ 28	Rollie Fingers	.50	.20	.05
☐ 29	Sparky Anderson MG	.10	.04	.01
☐ 30	Dennis Eckersley	.50	.20	.05
☐ 31	Dave Winfield	1.00	.40	.10
☐ 32	Burt Hooton	.05	.02	.00
☐ 33	Rick Waits	.05	.02	.00
☐ 34	George Brett	2.00	.80	.20
☐ 35	Steve McCatty	.05	.02	.00
☐ 36	Steve Rogers	.05	.02	.00
☐ 37	Bill Stein	.05	.02	.00
☐ 38	Steve Renko	.05	.02	.00
☐ 39	Mike Squires	.05	.02	.00
☐ 40	George Hendrick	.05	.02	.00
☐ 41	Bob Knepper	.05	.02	.00
☐ 42	Steve Carlton	1.00	.40	.10
☐ 43	Larry Biittner	.05	.02	.00
☐ 44	Chris Welsh	.05	.02	.00
☐ 45	Steve Nicosia	.05	.02	.00
☐ 46	Jack Clark	.25	.10	.02
☐ 47	Chris Chambliss	.10	.04	.01
☐ 48	Ivan DeJesus	.05	.02	.00
☐ 49	Lee Mazzilli	.05	.02	.00
☐ 50	Julio Cruz	.05	.02	.00
☐ 51	Pete Redfern	.05	.02	.00
☐ 52	Dave Stieb	.35	.15	.03
☐ 53	Doug Corbett	.05	.02	.00
☐ 54	Jorge Bell	8.00	3.50	.80
☐ 55	Joe Simpson	.05	.02	.00
☐ 56	Rusty Staub	.15	.06	.01
☐ 57	Hector Cruz	.05	.02	.00
☐ 58	Claudell Washington	.05	.02	.00
☐ 59	Enrique Romo	.05	.02	.00
☐ 60	Gary Lavelle	.05	.02	.00
☐ 61	Tim Flannery	.05	.02	.00
☐ 62	Joe Nolan	.05	.02	.00
☐ 63	Larry Bowa	.10	.04	.01
☐ 64	Sixto Lezcano	.05	.02	.00
☐ 65	Joe Sambito	.05	.02	.00
☐ 66	Bruce Kison	.05	.02	.00
☐ 67	Wayne Nordhagen	.05	.02	.00
☐ 68	Woodie Fryman	.05	.02	.00
☐ 69	Billy Sample	.05	.02	.00
☐ 70	Amos Otis	.05	.02	.00
☐ 71	Matt Keough	.05	.02	.00
☐ 72	Toby Harrah	.05	.02	.00
☐ 73	Dave Righetti	1.25	.50	.12
☐ 74	Carl Yastrzemski	1.25	.50	.12
☐ 75	Bob Welch	.35	.15	.03
☐ 76A	Alan Trammel ERR (name misspelled)	1.75	.70	.17
☐ 76B	Alan Trammell COR	.60	.25	.06
☐ 77	Rick Dempsey	.05	.02	.00
☐ 78	Paul Molitor	.50	.20	.05
☐ 79	Dennis Martinez	.15	.06	.01
☐ 80	Jim Slaton	.05	.02	.00
☐ 81	Champ Summers	.05	.02	.00
☐ 82	Carney Lansford	.15	.06	.01
☐ 83	Barry Foote	.05	.02	.00
☐ 84	Steve Garvey	.60	.25	.06
☐ 85	Rick Manning	.05	.02	.00
☐ 86	John Wathan	.05	.02	.00
☐ 87	Brian Kingman	.05	.02	.00
☐ 88	Andre Dawson UER (Middle name Fernando, should be Nolan)	1.25	.50	.12
☐ 89	Jim Kern	.05	.02	.00
☐ 90	Bobby Grich	.10	.04	.01
☐ 91	Bob Forsch	.05	.02	.00
☐ 92	Art Howe	.10	.04	.01
☐ 93	Marty Bystrom	.05	.02	.00
☐ 94	Ozzie Smith	1.50	.60	.15
☐ 95	Dave Parker	.50	.20	.05
☐ 96	Doyle Alexander	.05	.02	.00
☐ 97	Al Hrabosky	.05	.02	.00
☐ 98	Frank Taveras	.05	.02	.00
☐ 99	Tim Blackwell	.05	.02	.00
☐ 100	Floyd Bannister	.05	.02	.00
☐ 101	Alfredo Griffin	.05	.02	.00
☐ 102	Dave Engle	.05	.02	.00
☐ 103	Mario Soto	.05	.02	.00
☐ 104	Ross Baumgarten	.05	.02	.00
☐ 105	Ken Singleton	.10	.04	.01
☐ 106	Ted Simmons	.15	.06	.01
☐ 107	Jack Morris	.60	.25	.06
☐ 108	Bob Watson	.05	.02	.00
☐ 109	Dwight Evans	.25	.10	.02
☐ 110	Tom Lasorda MG	.10	.04	.01
☐ 111	Bert Blyleven	.25	.10	.02
☐ 112	Dan Quisenberry	.15	.06	.01
☐ 113	Rickey Henderson	6.00	2.50	.60
☐ 114	Gary Carter	.50	.20	.05
☐ 115	Brian Downing	.10	.04	.01
☐ 116	Al Oliver	.10	.04	.01
☐ 117	LaMarr Hoyt	.05	.02	.00
☐ 118	Cesar Cedeno	.10	.04	.01
☐ 119	Keith Moreland	.05	.02	.00
☐ 120	Bob Shirley	.05	.02	.00
☐ 121	Terry Kennedy	.05	.02	.00
☐ 122	Frank Pastore	.05	.02	.00
☐ 123	Gene Garber	.05	.02	.00
☐ 124	Tony Pena	.35	.15	.03
☐ 125	Allen Ripley	.05	.02	.00
☐ 126	Randy Martz	.05	.02	.00
☐ 127	Richie Zisk	.05	.02	.00
☐ 128	Mike Scott	.25	.10	.02
☐ 129	Lloyd Moseby	.15	.06	.01
☐ 130	Rob Wilfong	.05	.02	.00
☐ 131	Tim Stoddard	.05	.02	.00
☐ 132	Gorman Thomas	.10	.04	.01
☐ 133	Dan Petry	.05	.02	.00
☐ 134	Bob Stanley	.05	.02	.00
☐ 135	Lou Piniella	.10	.04	.01
☐ 136	Pedro Guerrero	.40	.16	.04
☐ 137	Len Barker	.05	.02	.00
☐ 138	Rich Gale	.05	.02	.00
☐ 139	Wayne Gross	.05	.02	.00
☐ 140	Tim Wallach	1.25	.50	.12
☐ 141	Gene Mauch MG	.05	.02	.00
☐ 142	Doc Medich	.05	.02	.00
☐ 143	Tony Bernazard	.05	.02	.00
☐ 144	Bill Virdon MG	.05	.02	.00
☐ 145	John Littlefield	.05	.02	.00
☐ 146	Dave Bergman	.05	.02	.00
☐ 147	Dick Davis	.05	.02	.00
☐ 148	Tom Seaver	1.25	.50	.12
☐ 149	Matt Sinatro	.05	.02	.00

#	Name			
☐ 150	Chuck Tanner MG	.05	.02	.00
☐ 151	Leon Durham	.05	.02	.00
☐ 152	Gene Tenace	.10	.04	.01
☐ 153	Al Bumbry	.05	.02	.00
☐ 154	Mark Brouhard	.05	.02	.00
☐ 155	Rick Peters	.05	.02	.00
☐ 156	Jerry Remy	.05	.02	.00
☐ 157	Rick Reuschel	.10	.04	.01
☐ 158	Steve Howe	.05	.02	.00
☐ 159	Alan Bannister	.05	.02	.00
☐ 160	U.L. Washington	.05	.02	.00
☐ 161	Rick Langford	.05	.02	.00
☐ 162	Bill Gullickson	.10	.04	.01
☐ 163	Mark Wagner	.05	.02	.00
☐ 164	Geoff Zahn	.05	.02	.00
☐ 165	Ron LeFlore	.05	.02	.00
☐ 166	Dane Iorg	.05	.02	.00
☐ 167	Joe Niekro	.10	.04	.01
☐ 168	Pete Rose	1.50	.60	.15
☐ 169	Dave Collins	.05	.02	.00
☐ 170	Rick Wise	.05	.02	.00
☐ 171	Jim Bibby	.05	.02	.00
☐ 172	Larry Herndon	.05	.02	.00
☐ 173	Bob Horner	.10	.04	.01
☐ 174	Steve Dillard	.05	.02	.00
☐ 175	Mookie Wilson	.10	.04	.01
☐ 176	Dan Meyer	.05	.02	.00
☐ 177	Fernando Arroyo	.05	.02	.00
☐ 178	Jackson Todd	.05	.02	.00
☐ 179	Darrell Jackson	.05	.02	.00
☐ 180	Alvis Woods	.05	.02	.00
☐ 181	Jim Anderson	.05	.02	.00
☐ 182	Dave Kingman	.15	.06	.01
☐ 183	Steve Henderson	.05	.02	.00
☐ 184	Brian Asselstine	.05	.02	.00
☐ 185	Rod Scurry	.05	.02	.00
☐ 186	Fred Breining	.05	.02	.00
☐ 187	Danny Boone	.05	.02	.00
☐ 188	Junior Kennedy	.05	.02	.00
☐ 189	Sparky Lyle	.10	.04	.01
☐ 190	Whitey Herzog MG	.10	.04	.01
☐ 191	Dave Smith	.10	.04	.01
☐ 192	Ed Ott	.05	.02	.00
☐ 193	Greg Luzinski	.10	.04	.01
☐ 194	Bill Lee	.05	.02	.00
☐ 195	Don Zimmer MG	.05	.02	.00
☐ 196	Hal McRae	.10	.04	.01
☐ 197	Mike Norris	.05	.02	.00
☐ 198	Duane Kuiper	.05	.02	.00
☐ 199	Rick Cerone	.05	.02	.00
☐ 200	Jim Rice	.25	.10	.02
☐ 201	Steve Yeager	.05	.02	.00
☐ 202	Tom Brookens	.05	.02	.00
☐ 203	Jose Morales	.05	.02	.00
☐ 204	Roy Howell	.05	.02	.00
☐ 205	Tippy Martinez	.05	.02	.00
☐ 206	Moose Haas	.05	.02	.00
☐ 207	Al Cowens	.05	.02	.00
☐ 208	Dave Stapleton	.05	.02	.00
☐ 209	Bucky Dent	.10	.04	.01
☐ 210	Ron Cey	.10	.04	.01
☐ 211	Jorge Orta	.05	.02	.00
☐ 212	Jamie Quirk	.05	.02	.00
☐ 213	Jeff Jones	.05	.02	.00
☐ 214	Tim Raines	1.25	.50	.12
☐ 215	Jon Matlack	.05	.02	.00
☐ 216	Rod Carew	1.25	.50	.12
☐ 217	Jim Kaat	.15	.06	.01
☐ 218	Joe Pittman	.05	.02	.00
☐ 219	Larry Christenson	.05	.02	.00
☐ 220	Juan Bonilla	.05	.02	.00
☐ 221	Mike Easler	.05	.02	.00
☐ 222	Vida Blue	.10	.04	.01
☐ 223	Rick Camp	.05	.02	.00
☐ 224	Mike Jorgensen	.05	.02	.00
☐ 225	Jody Davis	.15	.06	.01
☐ 226	Mike Parrott	.05	.02	.00
☐ 227	Jim Clancy	.05	.02	.00
☐ 228	Hosken Powell	.05	.02	.00
☐ 229	Tom Hume	.05	.02	.00
☐ 230	Britt Burns	.05	.02	.00
☐ 231	Jim Palmer	.90	.40	.09
☐ 232	Bob Rodgers MG	.05	.02	.00
☐ 233	Milt Wilcox	.05	.02	.00
☐ 234	Dave Revering	.05	.02	.00
☐ 235	Mike Torrez	.05	.02	.00
☐ 236	Robert Castillo	.05	.02	.00
☐ 237	Von Hayes	.60	.25	.06
☐ 238	Renie Martin	.05	.02	.00
☐ 239	Dwayne Murphy	.05	.02	.00
☐ 240	Rodney Scott	.05	.02	.00
☐ 241	Fred Patek	.05	.02	.00
☐ 242	Mickey Rivers	.10	.04	.01
☐ 243	Steve Trout	.05	.02	.00
☐ 244	Jose Cruz	.10	.04	.01
☐ 245	Manny Trillo	.05	.02	.00
☐ 246	Lary Sorensen	.05	.02	.00
☐ 247	Dave Edwards	.05	.02	.00
☐ 248	Dan Driessen	.05	.02	.00
☐ 249	Tommy Boggs	.05	.02	.00
☐ 250	Dale Berra	.05	.02	.00
☐ 251	Ed Whitson	.05	.02	.00
☐ 252	Lee Smith	3.00	1.25	.30
☐ 253	Tom Paciorek	.05	.02	.00
☐ 254	Pat Zachry	.05	.02	.00
☐ 255	Luis Leal	.05	.02	.00
☐ 256	John Castino	.05	.02	.00
☐ 257	Rich Dauer	.05	.02	.00
☐ 258	Cecil Cooper	.15	.06	.01
☐ 259	Dave Rozema	.05	.02	.00
☐ 260	John Tudor	.10	.04	.01
☐ 261	Jerry Mumphrey	.05	.02	.00
☐ 262	Jay Johnstone	.10	.04	.01
☐ 263	Bo Diaz	.05	.02	.00
☐ 264	Dennis Leonard	.05	.02	.00
☐ 265	Jim Spencer	.05	.02	.00
☐ 266	John Milner	.05	.02	.00
☐ 267	Don Aase	.05	.02	.00
☐ 268	Jim Sundberg	.05	.02	.00
☐ 269	Lamar Johnson	.05	.02	.00
☐ 270	Frank LaCorte	.05	.02	.00
☐ 271	Barry Evans	.05	.02	.00
☐ 272	Enos Cabell	.05	.02	.00
☐ 273	Del Unser	.05	.02	.00
☐ 274	George Foster	.15	.06	.01
☐ 275	Brett Butler	2.00	.80	.20
☐ 276	Lee Lacy	.05	.02	.00
☐ 277	Ken Reitz	.05	.02	.00
☐ 278	Keith Hernandez	.25	.10	.02
☐ 279	Doug DeCinces	.05	.02	.00
☐ 280	Charlie Moore	.05	.02	.00
☐ 281	Lance Parrish	.30	.12	.03
☐ 282	Ralph Houk MG	.05	.02	.00
☐ 283	Rich Gossage	.20	.08	.02
☐ 284	Jerry Reuss	.05	.02	.00
☐ 285	Mike Stanton	.05	.02	.00
☐ 286	Frank White	.05	.02	.00
☐ 287	Bob Owchinko	.05	.02	.00
☐ 288	Scott Sanderson	.10	.04	.01
☐ 289	Bump Wills	.05	.02	.00
☐ 290	Dave Frost	.05	.02	.00
☐ 291	Chet Lemon	.05	.02	.00
☐ 292	Tito Landrum	.05	.02	.00
☐ 293	Vern Ruhle	.05	.02	.00
☐ 294	Mike Schmidt	2.50	1.00	.25
☐ 295	Sam Mejias	.05	.02	.00
☐ 296	Gary Lucas	.05	.02	.00
☐ 297	John Candelaria	.05	.02	.00
☐ 298	Jerry Martin	.05	.02	.00
☐ 299	Dale Murphy	1.00	.40	.10
☐ 300	Mike Lum	.05	.02	.00
☐ 301	Tom Hausman	.05	.02	.00
☐ 302	Glenn Abbott	.05	.02	.00
☐ 303	Roger Erickson	.05	.02	.00
☐ 304	Otto Velez	.05	.02	.00
☐ 305	Danny Goodwin	.05	.02	.00
☐ 306	John Mayberry	.10	.04	.01
☐ 307	Lenny Randle	.05	.02	.00
☐ 308	Bob Bailor	.05	.02	.00
☐ 309	Jerry Morales	.05	.02	.00
☐ 310	Rufino Linares	.05	.02	.00
☐ 311	Kent Tekulve	.10	.04	.01
☐ 312	Joe Morgan	.60	.25	.06
☐ 313	John Urrea	.05	.02	.00
☐ 314	Paul Householder	.05	.02	.00
☐ 315	Garry Maddox	.05	.02	.00
☐ 316	Mike Ramsey	.05	.02	.00
☐ 317	Alan Ashby	.05	.02	.00
☐ 318	Bob Clark	.05	.02	.00
☐ 319	Tony LaRussa MG	.10	.04	.01
☐ 320	Charlie Lea	.05	.02	.00
☐ 321	Danny Darwin	.05	.02	.00
☐ 322	Cesar Geronimo	.05	.02	.00
☐ 323	Tom Underwood	.05	.02	.00
☐ 324	Andre Thornton	.10	.04	.01
☐ 325	Rudy May	.05	.02	.00
☐ 326	Frank Tanana	.10	.04	.01
☐ 327	Dave Lopes	.10	.04	.01
☐ 328	Richie Hebner	.05	.02	.00
☐ 329	Mike Flanagan	.10	.04	.01
☐ 330	Mike Caldwell	.05	.02	.00
☐ 331	Scott McGregor	.05	.02	.00
☐ 332	Jerry Augustine	.05	.02	.00
☐ 333	Stan Papi	.05	.02	.00
☐ 334	Rick Miller	.05	.02	.00
☐ 335	Graig Nettles	.15	.06	.01
☐ 336	Dusty Baker	.10	.04	.01
☐ 337	Dave Garcia MG	.05	.02	.00

☐	338 Larry Gura	.05	.02	.00
☐	339 Cliff Johnson	.05	.02	.00
☐	340 Warren Cromartie	.05	.02	.00
☐	341 Steve Comer	.05	.02	.00
☐	342 Rick Burleson	.10	.04	.01
☐	343 John Martin	.05	.02	.00
☐	344 Craig Reynolds	.05	.02	.00
☐	345 Mike Proly	.05	.02	.00
☐	346 Ruppert Jones	.05	.02	.00
☐	347 Omar Moreno	.05	.02	.00
☐	348 Greg Minton	.05	.02	.00
☐	349 Rick Mahler	.15	.06	.01
☐	350 Alex Trevino	.05	.02	.00
☐	351 Mike Krukow	.05	.02	.00
☐	352A Shane Rawley ERR (photo actually Jim Anderson)	.75	.30	.07
☐	352B Shane Rawley COR	.10	.04	.01
☐	353 Garth Iorg	.05	.02	.00
☐	354 Pete Mackanin	.05	.02	.00
☐	355 Paul Moskau	.05	.02	.00
☐	356 Richard Dotson	.05	.02	.00
☐	357 Steve Stone	.05	.02	.00
☐	358 Larry Hisle	.05	.02	.00
☐	359 Aurelio Lopez	.05	.02	.00
☐	360 Oscar Gamble	.05	.02	.00
☐	361 Tom Burgmeier	.05	.02	.00
☐	362 Terry Forster	.10	.04	.01
☐	363 Joe Charboneau	.05	.02	.00
☐	364 Ken Brett	.05	.02	.00
☐	365 Tony Armas	.05	.02	.00
☐	366 Chris Speier	.05	.02	.00
☐	367 Fred Lynn	.20	.08	.02
☐	368 Buddy Bell	.10	.04	.01
☐	369 Jim Essian	.10	.04	.01
☐	370 Terry Puhl	.05	.02	.00
☐	371 Greg Gross	.05	.02	.00
☐	372 Bruce Sutter	.15	.06	.01
☐	373 Joe Lefebvre	.05	.02	.00
☐	374 Ray Knight	.10	.04	.01
☐	375 Bruce Benedict	.05	.02	.00
☐	376 Tim Foli	.05	.02	.00
☐	377 Al Holland	.05	.02	.00
☐	378 Ken Kravec	.05	.02	.00
☐	379 Jeff Burroughs	.05	.02	.00
☐	380 Pete Falcone	.05	.02	.00
☐	381 Ernie Whitt	.05	.02	.00
☐	382 Brad Havens	.05	.02	.00
☐	383 Terry Crowley	.05	.02	.00
☐	384 Don Money	.05	.02	.00
☐	385 Dan Schatzeder	.05	.02	.00
☐	386 Gary Allenson	.05	.02	.00
☐	387 Yogi Berra CO	.25	.10	.02
☐	388 Ken Landreaux	.05	.02	.00
☐	389 Mike Hargrove	.10	.04	.01
☐	390 Darryl Motley	.05	.02	.00
☐	391 Dave McKay	.05	.02	.00
☐	392 Stan Bahnsen	.05	.02	.00
☐	393 Ken Forsch	.05	.02	.00
☐	394 Mario Mendoza	.05	.02	.00
☐	395 Jim Morrison	.05	.02	.00
☐	396 Mike Ivie	.05	.02	.00
☐	397 Broderick Perkins	.05	.02	.00
☐	398 Darrell Evans	.15	.06	.01
☐	399 Ron Reed	.05	.02	.00
☐	400 Johnny Bench	1.25	.50	.12
☐	401 Steve Bedrosian	.50	.20	.05
☐	402 Bill Robinson	.10	.04	.01
☐	403 Bill Buckner	.10	.04	.01
☐	404 Ken Oberkfell	.05	.02	.00
☐	405 Cal Ripken Jr.	48.00	20.00	5.00
☐	406 Jim Gantner	.05	.02	.00
☐	407 Kirk Gibson	1.25	.50	.12
☐	408 Tony Perez	.25	.10	.02
☐	409 Tommy John UER (Text says 52-56 as Yankee, should be 52-26)	.20	.08	.02
☐	410 Dave Stewart	5.50	2.50	.55
☐	411 Dan Spillner	.05	.02	.00
☐	412 Willie Aikens	.05	.02	.00
☐	413 Mike Heath	.05	.02	.00
☐	414 Ray Burris	.05	.02	.00
☐	415 Leon Roberts	.05	.02	.00
☐	416 Mike Witt	.25	.10	.02
☐	417 Bob Molinaro	.05	.02	.00
☐	418 Steve Braun	.05	.02	.00
☐	419 Nolan Ryan UER (Nisnumbering of Nolan's no-hitters on card back)	5.75	2.50	.55
☐	420 Tug McGraw	.15	.06	.01
☐	421 Dave Concepcion	.15	.06	.01
☐	422A Juan Eichelberger ERR (photo actually Gary Lucas)	.75	.30	.07
☐	422B Juan Eichelberger COR	.10	.04	.01
☐	423 Rick Rhoden	.05	.02	.00
☐	424 Frank Robinson MG	.25	.10	.02
☐	425 Eddie Miller	.05	.02	.00
☐	426 Bill Caudill	.05	.02	.00
☐	427 Doug Flynn	.05	.02	.00
☐	428 Larry Andersen UER (misspelled Anderson on card front)	.05	.02	.00
☐	429 Al Williams	.05	.02	.00
☐	430 Jerry Garvin	.05	.02	.00
☐	431 Glenn Adams	.05	.02	.00
☐	432 Barry Bonnell	.05	.02	.00
☐	433 Jerry Narron	.05	.02	.00
☐	434 John Stearns	.05	.02	.00
☐	435 Mike Tyson	.05	.02	.00
☐	436 Glenn Hubbard	.05	.02	.00
☐	437 Eddie Solomon	.05	.02	.00
☐	438 Jeff Leonard	.05	.02	.00
☐	439 Randy Bass	.05	.02	.00
☐	440 Mike LaCoss	.05	.02	.00
☐	441 Gary Matthews	.05	.02	.00
☐	442 Mark Littell	.05	.02	.00
☐	443 Don Sutton	.40	.16	.04
☐	444 John Harris	.05	.02	.00
☐	445 Vada Pinson CO	.10	.04	.01
☐	446 Elias Sosa	.05	.02	.00
☐	447 Charlie Hough	.10	.04	.01
☐	448 Willie Wilson	.15	.06	.01
☐	449 Fred Stanley	.05	.02	.00
☐	450 Tom Veryzer	.05	.02	.00
☐	451 Ron Davis	.05	.02	.00
☐	452 Mark Clear	.05	.02	.00
☐	453 Bill Russell	.10	.04	.01
☐	454 Lou Whitaker	.40	.16	.04
☐	455 Dan Graham	.05	.02	.00
☐	456 Reggie Cleveland	.05	.02	.00
☐	457 Sammy Stewart	.05	.02	.00
☐	458 Pete Vuckovich	.05	.02	.00
☐	459 John Wockenfuss	.05	.02	.00
☐	460 Glenn Hoffman	.05	.02	.00
☐	461 Willie Randolph	.10	.04	.01
☐	462 Fernando Valenzuela	.60	.25	.06
☐	463 Ron Hassey	.05	.02	.00
☐	464 Paul Splittorff	.05	.02	.00
☐	465 Rob Picciolo	.05	.02	.00
☐	466 Larry Parrish	.05	.02	.00
☐	467 Johnny Grubb	.05	.02	.00
☐	468 Dan Ford	.05	.02	.00
☐	469 Silvio Martinez	.05	.02	.00
☐	470 Kiko Garcia	.05	.02	.00
☐	471 Bob Boone	.10	.04	.01
☐	472 Luis Salazar	.10	.04	.01
☐	473 Randy Niemann	.05	.02	.00
☐	474 Tom Griffin	.05	.02	.00
☐	475 Phil Niekro	.40	.16	.04
☐	476 Hubie Brooks	.60	.25	.06
☐	477 Dick Tidrow	.05	.02	.00
☐	478 Jim Beattie	.05	.02	.00
☐	479 Damaso Garcia	.05	.02	.00
☐	480 Mickey Hatcher	.05	.02	.00
☐	481 Joe Price	.05	.02	.00
☐	482 Ed Farmer	.05	.02	.00
☐	483 Eddie Murray	1.50	.60	.15
☐	484 Ben Oglivie	.05	.02	.00
☐	485 Kevin Saucier	.05	.02	.00
☐	486 Bobby Murcer	.10	.04	.01
☐	487 Bill Campbell	.05	.02	.00
☐	488 Reggie Smith	.10	.04	.01
☐	489 Wayne Garland	.05	.02	.00
☐	490 Jim Wright	.05	.02	.00
☐	491 Billy Martin MG	.20	.08	.02
☐	492 Jim Fanning MG	.05	.02	.00
☐	493 Don Baylor	.15	.06	.01
☐	494 Rick Honeycutt	.05	.02	.00
☐	495 Carlton Fisk	1.25	.50	.12
☐	496 Denny Walling	.05	.02	.00
☐	497 Bake McBride	.05	.02	.00
☐	498 Darrell Porter	.05	.02	.00
☐	499 Gene Richards	.05	.02	.00
☐	500 Ron Oester	.05	.02	.00
☐	501 Ken Dayley	.15	.06	.01
☐	502 Jason Thompson	.05	.02	.00
☐	503 Milt May	.05	.02	.00
☐	504 Doug Bird	.05	.02	.00
☐	505 Bruce Bochte	.05	.02	.00
☐	506 Neil Allen	.05	.02	.00
☐	507 Joey McLaughlin	.05	.02	.00
☐	508 Butch Wynegar	.05	.02	.00
☐	509 Gary Roenicke	.05	.02	.00
☐	510 Robin Yount	2.00	.80	.20
☐	511 Dave Tobik	.05	.02	.00

☐ 512	Rich Gedman	.20	.08	.02
☐ 513	Gene Nelson	.05	.02	.00
☐ 514	Rick Monday	.05	.02	.00
☐ 515	Miguel Dilone	.05	.02	.00
☐ 516	Clint Hurdle	.05	.02	.00
☐ 517	Jeff Newman	.05	.02	.00
☐ 518	Grant Jackson	.05	.02	.00
☐ 519	Andy Hassler	.05	.02	.00
☐ 520	Pat Putnam	.05	.02	.00
☐ 521	Greg Pryor	.05	.02	.00
☐ 522	Tony Scott	.05	.02	.00
☐ 523	Steve Mura	.05	.02	.00
☐ 524	Johnnie LeMaster	.05	.02	.00
☐ 525	Dick Ruthven	.05	.02	.00
☐ 526	John McNamara MG	.05	.02	.00
☐ 527	Larry McWilliams	.05	.02	.00
☐ 528	Johnny Ray	.20	.08	.02
☐ 529	Pat Tabler	.20	.08	.02
☐ 530	Tom Herr	.10	.04	.01
☐ 531A	San Diego Chicken COR .... (with TM)	1.00	.40	.10
☐ 531B	San Diego Chicken ERR .... (without TM)	1.00	.40	.10
☐ 532	Sal Butera	.05	.02	.00
☐ 533	Mike Griffin	.05	.02	.00
☐ 534	Kelvin Moore	.05	.02	.00
☐ 535	Reggie Jackson	1.75	.70	.17
☐ 536	Ed Romero	.05	.02	.00
☐ 537	Derrel Thomas	.05	.02	.00
☐ 538	Mike O'Berry	.05	.02	.00
☐ 539	Jack O'Connor	.05	.02	.00
☐ 540	Bob Ojeda	.50	.20	.05
☐ 541	Roy Lee Jackson	.05	.02	.00
☐ 542	Lynn Jones	.05	.02	.00
☐ 543	Gaylord Perry	.40	.16	.04
☐ 544A	Phil Garner ERR (reverse negative)	.75	.30	.07
☐ 544B	Phil Garner COR	.10	.04	.01
☐ 545	Garry Templeton	.10	.04	.01
☐ 546	Rafael Ramirez	.05	.02	.00
☐ 547	Jeff Reardon	.75	.30	.07
☐ 548	Ron Guidry	.25	.10	.02
☐ 549	Tim Laudner	.10	.04	.01
☐ 550	John Henry Johnson	.05	.02	.00
☐ 551	Chris Bando	.05	.02	.00
☐ 552	Bobby Brown	.05	.02	.00
☐ 553	Larry Bradford	.05	.02	.00
☐ 554	Scott Fletcher	.25	.10	.02
☐ 555	Jerry Royster	.05	.02	.00
☐ 556	Shooty Babitt UER (spelled Babbitt on front)	.05	.02	.00
☐ 557	Kent Hrbek	3.00	1.25	.30
☐ 558	Yankee Winners Ron Guidry Tommy John	.15	.06	.01
☐ 559	Mark Bomback	.05	.02	.00
☐ 560	Julio Valdez	.05	.02	.00
☐ 561	Buck Martinez	.05	.02	.00
☐ 562	Mike Marshall (Dodger hitter)	.35	.15	.03
☐ 563	Rennie Stennett	.05	.02	.00
☐ 564	Steve Crawford	.05	.02	.00
☐ 565	Bob Babcock	.05	.02	.00
☐ 566	Johnny Podres CO	.10	.04	.01
☐ 567	Paul Serna	.05	.02	.00
☐ 568	Harold Baines	1.50	.60	.15
☐ 569	Dave LaRoche	.05	.02	.00
☐ 570	Lee May	.05	.02	.00
☐ 571	Gary Ward	.05	.02	.00
☐ 572	John Denny	.05	.02	.00
☐ 573	Roy Smalley	.05	.02	.00
☐ 574	Bob Brenly	.10	.04	.01
☐ 575	Bronx Bombers Reggie Jackson Dave Winfield	.90	.40	.09
☐ 576	Luis Pujols	.05	.02	.00
☐ 577	Butch Hobson	.10	.04	.01
☐ 578	Harvey Kuenn MG	.10	.04	.01
☐ 579	Cal Ripken Sr. CO	.15	.06	.01
☐ 580	Juan Berenguer	.05	.02	.00
☐ 581	Benny Ayala	.05	.02	.00
☐ 582	Vance Law	.10	.04	.01
☐ 583	Rick Leach	.05	.02	.00
☐ 584	George Frazier	.05	.02	.00
☐ 585	Phillies Finest Pete Rose Mike Schmidt	1.00	.40	.10
☐ 586	Joe Rudi	.10	.04	.01
☐ 587	Juan Beniquez	.05	.02	.00
☐ 588	Luis DeLeon	.05	.02	.00
☐ 589	Craig Swan	.05	.02	.00
☐ 590	Dave Chalk	.05	.02	.00
☐ 591	Billy Gardner MG	.05	.02	.00
☐ 592	Sal Bando	.10	.04	.01
☐ 593	Bert Campaneris	.10	.04	.01
☐ 594	Steve Kemp	.05	.02	.00
☐ 595A	Randy Lerch ERR (Braves)	.75	.30	.07
☐ 595B	Randy Lerch COR (Brewers)	.10	.04	.01
☐ 596	Bryan Clark	.05	.02	.00
☐ 597	Dave Ford	.05	.02	.00
☐ 598	Mike Scioscia	.40	.16	.04
☐ 599	John Lowenstein	.05	.02	.00
☐ 600	Rene Lachemann MG	.05	.02	.00
☐ 601	Mick Kelleher	.05	.02	.00
☐ 602	Ron Jackson	.05	.02	.00
☐ 603	Jerry Koosman	.10	.04	.01
☐ 604	Dave Goltz	.05	.02	.00
☐ 605	Ellis Valentine	.05	.02	.00
☐ 606	Lonnie Smith	.25	.10	.02
☐ 607	Joaquin Andujar	.10	.04	.01
☐ 608	Garry Hancock	.05	.02	.00
☐ 609	Jerry Turner	.05	.02	.00
☐ 610	Bob Bonner	.05	.02	.00
☐ 611	Jim Dwyer	.05	.02	.00
☐ 612	Terry Bulling	.05	.02	.00
☐ 613	Joel Youngblood	.05	.02	.00
☐ 614	Larry Milbourne	.05	.02	.00
☐ 615	Gene Roof UER (name on front is Phil Roof)	.05	.02	.00
☐ 616	Keith Drumwright	.05	.02	.00
☐ 617	Dave Rosello	.05	.02	.00
☐ 618	Rickey Keeton	.05	.02	.00
☐ 619	Dennis Lamp	.05	.02	.00
☐ 620	Sid Monge	.05	.02	.00
☐ 621	Jerry White	.05	.02	.00
☐ 622	Luis Aguayo	.05	.02	.00
☐ 623	Jamie Easterly	.05	.02	.00
☐ 624	Steve Sax	3.50	1.50	.35
☐ 625	Dave Roberts	.05	.02	.00
☐ 626	Rick Bosetti	.05	.02	.00
☐ 627	Terry Francona	.05	.02	.00
☐ 628	Pride of Reds Tom Seaver Johnny Bench	.90	.40	.09
☐ 629	Paul Mirabella	.05	.02	.00
☐ 630	Rance Mulliniks	.05	.02	.00
☐ 631	Kevin Hickey	.05	.02	.00
☐ 632	Reid Nichols	.05	.02	.00
☐ 633	Dave Geisel	.05	.02	.00
☐ 634	Ken Griffey	.25	.10	.02
☐ 635	Bob Lemon MG	.10	.04	.01
☐ 636	Orlando Sanchez	.05	.02	.00
☐ 637	Bill Almon	.05	.02	.00
☐ 638	Danny Ainge	.35	.15	.03
☐ 639	Willie Stargell	.50	.20	.05
☐ 640	Bob Sykes	.05	.02	.00
☐ 641	Ed Lynch	.05	.02	.00
☐ 642	John Ellis	.05	.02	.00
☐ 643	Ferguson Jenkins	.40	.16	.04
☐ 644	Lenn Sakata	.05	.02	.00
☐ 645	Julio Gonzalez	.05	.02	.00
☐ 646	Jesse Orosco	.05	.02	.00
☐ 647	Jerry Dybzinski	.05	.02	.00
☐ 648	Tommy Davis CO	.10	.04	.01
☐ 649	Ron Gardenhire	.05	.02	.00
☐ 650	Felipe Alou CO	.10	.04	.01
☐ 651	Harvey Haddix CO	.05	.02	.00
☐ 652	Willie Upshaw	.05	.02	.00
☐ 653	Bill Madlock	.10	.04	.01
☐ 654A	DK Checklist ERR (unnumbered) (with Trammel)	.50	.10	.02
☐ 654B	DK Checklist COR (unnumbered) (with Trammell)	.15	.02	.00
☐ 655	Checklist 1 (unnumbered)	.15	.02	.00
☐ 656	Checklist 2 (unnumbered)	.15	.02	.00
☐ 657	Checklist 3 (unnumbered)	.15	.02	.00
☐ 658	Checklist 4 (unnumbered)	.15	.02	.00
☐ 659	Checklist 5 (unnumbered)	.15	.02	.00
☐ 660	Checklist 6 (unnumbered)	.15	.02	.00

1983 Donruss

The cards in this 660-card set measure 2 1/2" by 3 1/2". The 1983 Donruss baseball set, issued with a 63-piece Diamond King puzzle, again leads off with a 26-card Diamond Kings (DK) series. Of the remaining 634 cards, two are combination cards, one portrays the San Diego Chicken, one shows the completed Ty Cobb puzzle, and seven are unnumbered checklist cards. The seven unnumbered checklist cards are arbitrarily assigned numbers 654 through 660 and are listed at the end of the list below. The Donruss logo and the year of issue are shown in the upper left corner of the obverse. The card backs have black print on yellow and white and are numbered on a small ball design. The complete set price below includes only the more common of each variation pair. The key rookie cards in this set are Wade Boggs, Julio Franco, Tony Gwynn, Howard Johnson, Willie McGee, Ryne Sandberg, and Frank Viola.

	MINT	EXC	G-VG
COMPLETE SET (660)	120.00	55.00	18.00
COMMON PLAYER (1-660)	.05	.02	.00

		MINT	EXC	G-VG
☐ 1	Fernando Valenzuela DK	.25	.08	.02
☐ 2	Rollie Fingers DK	.20	.08	.02
☐ 3	Reggie Jackson DK	.65	.25	.06
☐ 4	Jim Palmer DK	.50	.20	.05
☐ 5	Jack Morris DK	.30	.12	.03
☐ 6	George Foster DK	.15	.06	.01
☐ 7	Jim Sundberg DK	.10	.04	.01
☐ 8	Willie Stargell DK	.30	.12	.03
☐ 9	Dave Stieb DK	.15	.06	.01
☐ 10	Joe Niekro DK	.10	.04	.01
☐ 11	Rickey Henderson DK	2.00	.80	.20
☐ 12	Dale Murphy DK	.45	.18	.04
☐ 13	Toby Harrah DK	.10	.04	.01
☐ 14	Bill Buckner DK	.10	.04	.01
☐ 15	Willie Wilson DK	.10	.04	.01
☐ 16	Steve Carlton DK	.50	.20	.05
☐ 17	Ron Guidry DK	.15	.06	.01
☐ 18	Steve Rogers DK	.10	.04	.01
☐ 19	Kent Hrbek DK	.30	.12	.03
☐ 20	Keith Hernandez DK	.15	.06	.01
☐ 21	Floyd Bannister DK	.10	.04	.01
☐ 22	Johnny Bench DK	.65	.25	.06
☐ 23	Britt Burns DK	.10	.04	.01
☐ 24	Joe Morgan DK	.30	.12	.03
☐ 25	Carl Yastrzemski DK	.60	.25	.06
☐ 26	Terry Kennedy DK	.10	.04	.01
☐ 27	Gary Roenicke	.05	.02	.00
☐ 28	Dwight Bernard	.05	.02	.00
☐ 29	Pat Underwood	.05	.02	.00
☐ 30	Gary Allenson	.05	.02	.00
☐ 31	Ron Guidry	.25	.10	.02
☐ 32	Burt Hooton	.05	.02	.00
☐ 33	Chris Bando	.05	.02	.00
☐ 34	Vida Blue	.10	.04	.01
☐ 35	Rickey Henderson	5.00	2.25	.50
☐ 36	Ray Burris	.05	.02	.00
☐ 37	John Butcher	.05	.02	.00
☐ 38	Don Aase	.05	.02	.00
☐ 39	Jerry Koosman	.10	.04	.01
☐ 40	Bruce Sutter	.15	.06	.01
☐ 41	Jose Cruz	.10	.04	.01
☐ 42	Pete Rose	1.25	.50	.12
☐ 43	Cesar Cedeno	.10	.04	.01
☐ 44	Floyd Chiffer	.05	.02	.00
☐ 45	Larry McWilliams	.05	.02	.00
☐ 46	Alan Fowlkes	.05	.02	.00
☐ 47	Dale Murphy	.75	.30	.07
☐ 48	Doug Bird	.05	.02	.00
☐ 49	Hubie Brooks	.25	.10	.02
☐ 50	Floyd Bannister	.05	.02	.00
☐ 51	Jack O'Connor	.05	.02	.00
☐ 52	Steve Senteney	.05	.02	.00
☐ 53	Gary Gaetti	1.00	.40	.10
☐ 54	Damaso Garcia	.05	.02	.00
☐ 55	Gene Nelson	.05	.02	.00
☐ 56	Mookie Wilson	.10	.04	.01
☐ 57	Allen Ripley	.05	.02	.00
☐ 58	Bob Horner	.10	.04	.01
☐ 59	Tony Pena	.10	.04	.01
☐ 60	Gary Lavelle	.05	.02	.00
☐ 61	Tim Lollar	.05	.02	.00
☐ 62	Frank Pastore	.05	.02	.00
☐ 63	Garry Maddox	.05	.02	.00
☐ 64	Bob Forsch	.05	.02	.00
☐ 65	Harry Spilman	.05	.02	.00
☐ 66	Geoff Zahn	.05	.02	.00
☐ 67	Salome Barojas	.05	.02	.00
☐ 68	David Palmer	.05	.02	.00
☐ 69	Charlie Hough	.05	.02	.00
☐ 70	Dan Quisenberry	.10	.04	.01
☐ 71	Tony Armas	.05	.02	.00
☐ 72	Rick Sutcliffe	.15	.06	.01
☐ 73	Steve Balboni	.05	.02	.00
☐ 74	Jerry Remy	.05	.02	.00
☐ 75	Mike Scioscia	.10	.04	.01
☐ 76	John Wockenfuss	.05	.02	.00
☐ 77	Jim Palmer	.75	.30	.07
☐ 78	Rollie Fingers	.45	.18	.04
☐ 79	Joe Nolan	.05	.02	.00
☐ 80	Pete Vuckovich	.05	.02	.00
☐ 81	Rick Leach	.05	.02	.00
☐ 82	Rick Miller	.05	.02	.00
☐ 83	Graig Nettles	.10	.04	.01
☐ 84	Ron Cey	.10	.04	.01
☐ 85	Miguel Dilone	.05	.02	.00
☐ 86	John Wathan	.05	.02	.00
☐ 87	Kelvin Moore	.05	.02	.00
☐ 88A	Byrn Smith ERR	.20	.08	.02
	(sic, Bryn)			
☐ 88B	Bryn Smith COR	.60	.25	.06
☐ 89	Dave Hostetler	.05	.02	.00
☐ 90	Rod Carew	1.00	.40	.10
☐ 91	Lonnie Smith	.15	.06	.01
☐ 92	Bob Knepper	.05	.02	.00
☐ 93	Marty Bystrom	.05	.02	.00
☐ 94	Chris Welsh	.05	.02	.00
☐ 95	Jason Thompson	.05	.02	.00
☐ 96	Tom O'Malley	.05	.02	.00
☐ 97	Phil Niekro	.35	.15	.03
☐ 98	Neil Allen	.05	.02	.00
☐ 99	Bill Buckner	.10	.04	.01
☐ 100	Ed VandeBerg	.05	.02	.00
☐ 101	Jim Clancy	.05	.02	.00
☐ 102	Robert Castillo	.05	.02	.00
☐ 103	Bruce Berenyi	.05	.02	.00
☐ 104	Carlton Fisk	1.00	.40	.10
☐ 105	Mike Flanagan	.10	.04	.01
☐ 106	Cecil Cooper	.10	.04	.01
☐ 107	Jack Morris	.60	.25	.06
☐ 108	Mike Morgan	.10	.04	.01
☐ 109	Luis Aponte	.05	.02	.00
☐ 110	Pedro Guerrero	.35	.15	.03
☐ 111	Len Barker	.05	.02	.00
☐ 112	Willie Wilson	.10	.04	.01
☐ 113	Dave Beard	.05	.02	.00
☐ 114	Mike Gates	.05	.02	.00
☐ 115	Reggie Jackson	1.25	.50	.12
☐ 116	George Wright	.05	.02	.00
☐ 117	Vance Law	.10	.04	.01
☐ 118	Nolan Ryan	5.25	2.25	.50
☐ 119	Mike Krukow	.05	.02	.00
☐ 120	Ozzie Smith	1.25	.50	.12
☐ 121	Broderick Perkins	.05	.02	.00
☐ 122	Tom Seaver	1.00	.40	.10
☐ 123	Chris Chambliss	.10	.04	.01
☐ 124	Chuck Tanner MG	.05	.02	.00
☐ 125	Johnnie LeMaster	.05	.02	.00
☐ 126	Mel Hall	.10	.04	.01
☐ 127	Bruce Bochte	.05	.02	.00
☐ 128	Charlie Puleo	.05	.02	.00
☐ 129	Luis Leal	.05	.02	.00
☐ 130	John Pacella	.05	.02	.00
☐ 131	Glenn Gulliver	.05	.02	.00
☐ 132	Don Money	.05	.02	.00
☐ 133	Dave Rozema	.05	.02	.00
☐ 134	Bruce Hurst	.40	.16	.04
☐ 135	Rudy May	.05	.02	.00

□	#	Name			
□	136	Tom Lasorda MG	.10	.04	.01
□	137	Dan Spillner UER	.10	.04	.01
		(photo actually			
		Ed Whitson)			
□	138	Jerry Martin	.05	.02	.00
□	139	Mike Norris	.05	.02	.00
□	140	Al Oliver	.10	.04	.01
□	141	Daryl Sconiers	.05	.02	.00
□	142	Lamar Johnson	.05	.02	.00
□	143	Harold Baines	.50	.20	.05
□	144	Alan Ashby	.05	.02	.00
□	145	Garry Templeton	.10	.04	.01
□	146	Al Holland	.05	.02	.00
□	147	Bo Diaz	.05	.02	.00
□	148	Dave Concepcion	.10	.04	.01
□	149	Rick Camp	.05	.02	.00
□	150	Jim Morrison	.05	.02	.00
□	151	Randy Martz	.05	.02	.00
□	152	Keith Hernandez	.25	.10	.02
□	153	John Lowenstein	.05	.02	.00
□	154	Mike Caldwell	.05	.02	.00
□	155	Milt Wilcox	.05	.02	.00
□	156	Rich Gedman	.05	.02	.00
□	157	Rich Gossage	.15	.06	.01
□	158	Jerry Reuss	.05	.02	.00
□	159	Ron Hassey	.05	.02	.00
□	160	Larry Gura	.05	.02	.00
□	161	Dwayne Murphy	.05	.02	.00
□	162	Woodie Fryman	.05	.02	.00
□	163	Steve Comer	.05	.02	.00
□	164	Ken Forsch	.05	.02	.00
□	165	Dennis Lamp	.05	.02	.00
□	166	David Green	.05	.02	.00
□	167	Terry Puhl	.05	.02	.00
□	168	Mike Schmidt	2.00	.80	.20
		(wearing 37			
		rather than 20)			
□	169	Eddie Milner	.05	.02	.00
□	170	John Curtis	.05	.02	.00
□	171	Don Robinson	.05	.02	.00
□	172	Rich Gale	.05	.02	.00
□	173	Steve Bedrosian	.10	.04	.01
□	174	Willie Hernandez	.05	.02	.00
□	175	Ron Gardenhire	.05	.02	.00
□	176	Jim Beattie	.05	.02	.00
□	177	Tim Laudner	.05	.02	.00
□	178	Buck Martinez	.05	.02	.00
□	179	Kent Hrbek	.50	.20	.05
□	180	Alfredo Griffin	.05	.02	.00
□	181	Larry Andersen	.05	.02	.00
□	182	Pete Falcone	.05	.02	.00
□	183	Jody Davis	.05	.02	.00
□	184	Glenn Hubbard	.05	.02	.00
□	185	Dale Berra	.05	.02	.00
□	186	Greg Minton	.05	.02	.00
□	187	Gary Lucas	.05	.02	.00
□	188	Dave Van Gorder	.05	.02	.00
□	189	Bob Dernier	.05	.02	.00
□	190	Willie McGee	3.50	1.50	.35
□	191	Dickie Thon	.10	.04	.01
□	192	Bob Boone	.10	.04	.01
□	193	Britt Burns	.05	.02	.00
□	194	Jeff Reardon	.50	.20	.05
□	195	Jon Matlack	.05	.02	.00
□	196	Don Slaught	.35	.15	.03
□	197	Fred Stanley	.05	.02	.00
□	198	Rick Manning	.05	.02	.00
□	199	Dave Righetti	.25	.10	.02
□	200	Dave Stapleton	.05	.02	.00
□	201	Steve Yeager	.05	.02	.00
□	202	Enos Cabell	.05	.02	.00
□	203	Sammy Stewart	.05	.02	.00
□	204	Moose Haas	.05	.02	.00
□	205	Lenn Sakata	.05	.02	.00
□	206	Charlie Moore	.05	.02	.00
□	207	Alan Trammell	.60	.25	.06
□	208	Jim Rice	.25	.10	.02
□	209	Roy Smalley	.05	.02	.00
□	210	Bill Russell	.10	.04	.01
□	211	Andre Thornton	.05	.02	.00
□	212	Willie Aikens	.05	.02	.00
□	213	Dave McKay	.05	.02	.00
□	214	Tim Blackwell	.05	.02	.00
□	215	Buddy Bell	.10	.04	.01
□	216	Doug DeCinces	.10	.04	.01
□	217	Tom Herr	.10	.04	.01
□	218	Frank LaCorte	.05	.02	.00
□	219	Steve Carlton	1.00	.40	.10
□	220	Terry Kennedy	.05	.02	.00
□	221	Mike Easler	.05	.02	.00
□	222	Jack Clark	.25	.10	.02
□	223	Gene Garber	.05	.02	.00
□	224	Scott Holman	.05	.02	.00
□	225	Mike Proly	.05	.02	.00
□	226	Terry Bulling	.05	.02	.00
□	227	Jerry Garvin	.05	.02	.00
□	228	Ron Davis	.05	.02	.00
□	229	Tom Hume	.05	.02	.00
□	230	Marc Hill	.05	.02	.00
□	231	Dennis Martinez	.10	.04	.01
□	232	Jim Gantner	.05	.02	.00
□	233	Larry Pashnick	.05	.02	.00
□	234	Dave Collins	.05	.02	.00
□	235	Tom Burgmeier	.05	.02	.00
□	236	Ken Landreaux	.05	.02	.00
□	237	John Denny	.05	.02	.00
□	238	Hal McRae	.10	.04	.01
□	239	Matt Keough	.05	.02	.00
□	240	Doug Flynn	.05	.02	.00
□	241	Fred Lynn	.20	.08	.02
□	242	Billy Sample	.05	.02	.00
□	243	Tom Paciorek	.05	.02	.00
□	244	Joe Sambito	.05	.02	.00
□	245	Sid Monge	.05	.02	.00
□	246	Ken Oberkfell	.05	.02	.00
□	247	Joe Pittman UER	.10	.04	.01
		(photo actually			
		Juan Eichelberger)			
□	248	Mario Soto	.05	.02	.00
□	249	Claudell Washington	.05	.02	.00
□	250	Rick Rhoden	.05	.02	.00
□	251	Darrell Evans	.10	.04	.01
□	252	Steve Henderson	.05	.02	.00
□	253	Manny Castillo	.05	.02	.00
□	254	Craig Swan	.05	.02	.00
□	255	Joey McLaughlin	.05	.02	.00
□	256	Pete Redfern	.05	.02	.00
□	257	Ken Singleton	.10	.04	.01
□	258	Robin Yount	1.50	.60	.15
□	259	Elias Sosa	.05	.02	.00
□	260	Bob Ojeda	.10	.04	.01
□	261	Bobby Murcer	.10	.04	.01
□	262	Candy Maldonado	.50	.20	.05
□	263	Rick Waits	.05	.02	.00
□	264	Greg Pryor	.05	.02	.00
□	265	Bob Owchinko	.05	.02	.00
□	266	Chris Speier	.05	.02	.00
□	267	Bruce Kison	.05	.02	.00
□	268	Mark Wagner	.05	.02	.00
□	269	Steve Kemp	.05	.02	.00
□	270	Phil Garner	.10	.04	.01
□	271	Gene Richards	.05	.02	.00
□	272	Renie Martin	.05	.02	.00
□	273	Dave Roberts	.05	.02	.00
□	274	Dan Driessen	.05	.02	.00
□	275	Rufino Linares	.05	.02	.00
□	276	Lee Lacy	.05	.02	.00
□	277	Ryne Sandberg	35.00	15.75	5.25
□	278	Darrell Porter	.05	.02	.00
□	279	Cal Ripken	12.50	5.50	1.65
□	280	Jamie Easterly	.05	.02	.00
□	281	Bill Fahey	.05	.02	.00
□	282	Glenn Hoffman	.05	.02	.00
□	283	Willie Randolph	.10	.04	.01
□	284	Fernando Valenzuela	.25	.10	.02
□	285	Alan Bannister	.05	.02	.00
□	286	Paul Splittorff	.05	.02	.00
□	287	Joe Rudi	.10	.04	.01
□	288	Bill Gullickson	.10	.04	.01
□	289	Danny Darwin	.05	.02	.00
□	290	Andy Hassler	.05	.02	.00
□	291	Ernesto Escarrega	.05	.02	.00
□	292	Steve Mura	.05	.02	.00
□	293	Tony Scott	.05	.02	.00
□	294	Manny Trillo	.05	.02	.00
□	295	Greg Harris	.05	.02	.00
□	296	Luis DeLeon	.05	.02	.00
□	297	Kent Tekulve	.05	.02	.00
□	298	Atlee Hammaker	.05	.02	.00
□	299	Bruce Benedict	.05	.02	.00
□	300	Fergie Jenkins	.35	.15	.03
□	301	Dave Kingman	.15	.06	.01
□	302	Bill Caudill	.05	.02	.00
□	303	John Castino	.05	.02	.00
□	304	Ernie Whitt	.05	.02	.00
□	305	Randy Johnson	.05	.02	.00
□	306	Garth Iorg	.05	.02	.00
□	307	Gaylord Perry	.35	.15	.03
□	308	Ed Lynch	.05	.02	.00
□	309	Keith Moreland	.05	.02	.00
□	310	Rafael Ramirez	.05	.02	.00
□	311	Bill Madlock	.10	.04	.01
□	312	Milt May	.05	.02	.00
□	313	John Montefusco	.05	.02	.00
□	314	Wayne Krenchicki	.05	.02	.00
□	315	George Vukovich	.05	.02	.00
□	316	Joaquin Andujar	.10	.04	.01
□	317	Craig Reynolds	.05	.02	.00

☐ 318	Rick Burleson	.05	.02	.00
☐ 319	Richard Dotson	.05	.02	.00
☐ 320	Steve Rogers	.05	.02	.00
☐ 321	Dave Schmidt	.10	.04	.01
☐ 322	Bud Black	.40	.16	.04
☐ 323	Jeff Burroughs	.05	.02	.00
☐ 324	Von Hayes	.15	.06	.01
☐ 325	Butch Wynegar	.05	.02	.00
☐ 326	Carl Yastrzemski	1.00	.40	.10
☐ 327	Ron Roenicke	.05	.02	.00
☐ 328	Howard Johnson	10.00	4.50	1.25
☐ 329	Rick Dempsey UER (posing as a left-handed batter)	.05	.02	.00
☐ 330A	Jim Slaton (bio printed black on white)	.10	.04	.01
☐ 330B	Jim Slaton (bio printed black on yellow)	.15	.06	.01
☐ 331	Benny Ayala	.05	.02	.00
☐ 332	Ted Simmons	.10	.04	.01
☐ 333	Lou Whitaker	.35	.15	.03
☐ 334	Chuck Rainey	.05	.02	.00
☐ 335	Lou Piniella	.10	.04	.01
☐ 336	Steve Sax	.50	.20	.05
☐ 337	Toby Harrah	.05	.02	.00
☐ 338	George Brett	1.50	.60	.15
☐ 339	Dave Lopes	.10	.04	.01
☐ 340	Gary Carter	.40	.16	.04
☐ 341	John Grubb	.05	.02	.00
☐ 342	Tim Foli	.05	.02	.00
☐ 343	Jim Kaat	.15	.06	.01
☐ 344	Mike LaCoss	.05	.02	.00
☐ 345	Larry Christenson	.05	.02	.00
☐ 346	Juan Bonilla	.05	.02	.00
☐ 347	Omar Moreno	.05	.02	.00
☐ 348	Chili Davis	.60	.25	.06
☐ 349	Tommy Boggs	.05	.02	.00
☐ 350	Rusty Staub	.15	.06	.01
☐ 351	Bump Wills	.05	.02	.00
☐ 352	Rick Sweet	.05	.02	.00
☐ 353	Jim Gott	.20	.08	.02
☐ 354	Terry Felton	.05	.02	.00
☐ 355	Jim Kern	.05	.02	.00
☐ 356	Bill Almon UER (Expos/Mets in 1983, not Padres/Mets)	.05	.02	.00
☐ 357	Tippy Martinez	.05	.02	.00
☐ 358	Roy Howell	.05	.02	.00
☐ 359	Dan Petry	.05	.02	.00
☐ 360	Jerry Mumphrey	.05	.02	.00
☐ 361	Mark Clear	.05	.02	.00
☐ 362	Mike Marshall	.10	.04	.01
☐ 363	Lary Sorensen	.05	.02	.00
☐ 364	Amos Otis	.10	.04	.01
☐ 365	Rick Langford	.05	.02	.00
☐ 366	Brad Mills	.05	.02	.00
☐ 367	Brian Downing	.10	.04	.01
☐ 368	Mike Richardt	.05	.02	.00
☐ 369	Aurelio Rodriguez	.05	.02	.00
☐ 370	Dave Smith	.05	.02	.00
☐ 371	Tug McGraw	.10	.04	.01
☐ 372	Doug Bair	.05	.02	.00
☐ 373	Ruppert Jones	.05	.02	.00
☐ 374	Alex Trevino	.05	.02	.00
☐ 375	Ken Dayley	.05	.02	.00
☐ 376	Rod Scurry	.05	.02	.00
☐ 377	Bob Brenly	.05	.02	.00
☐ 378	Scot Thompson	.05	.02	.00
☐ 379	Julio Cruz	.05	.02	.00
☐ 380	John Stearns	.05	.02	.00
☐ 381	Dale Murray	.05	.02	.00
☐ 382	Frank Viola	4.50	2.00	.45
☐ 383	Al Bumbry	.05	.02	.00
☐ 384	Ben Oglivie	.05	.02	.00
☐ 385	Dave Tobik	.05	.02	.00
☐ 386	Bob Stanley	.05	.02	.00
☐ 387	Andre Robertson	.05	.02	.00
☐ 388	Jorge Orta	.05	.02	.00
☐ 389	Ed Whitson	.05	.02	.00
☐ 390	Don Hood	.05	.02	.00
☐ 391	Tom Underwood	.05	.02	.00
☐ 392	Tim Wallach	.20	.08	.02
☐ 393	Steve Renko	.05	.02	.00
☐ 394	Mickey Rivers	.05	.02	.00
☐ 395	Greg Luzinski	.10	.04	.01
☐ 396	Art Howe	.10	.04	.01
☐ 397	Alan Wiggins	.05	.02	.00
☐ 398	Jim Barr	.05	.02	.00
☐ 399	Ivan DeJesus	.05	.02	.00
☐ 400	Tom Lawless	.05	.02	.00
☐ 401	Bob Walk	.05	.02	.00
☐ 402	Jimmy Smith	.05	.02	.00
☐ 403	Lee Smith	.60	.25	.06
☐ 404	George Hendrick	.05	.02	.00
☐ 405	Eddie Murray	1.25	.50	.12
☐ 406	Marshall Edwards	.05	.02	.00
☐ 407	Lance Parrish	.25	.10	.02
☐ 408	Carney Lansford	.10	.04	.01
☐ 409	Dave Winfield	.75	.30	.07
☐ 410	Bob Welch	.25	.10	.02
☐ 411	Larry Milbourne	.05	.02	.00
☐ 412	Dennis Leonard	.05	.02	.00
☐ 413	Dan Meyer	.05	.02	.00
☐ 414	Charlie Lea	.05	.02	.00
☐ 415	Rick Honeycutt	.05	.02	.00
☐ 416	Mike Witt	.05	.02	.00
☐ 417	Steve Trout	.05	.02	.00
☐ 418	Glenn Brummer	.05	.02	.00
☐ 419	Denny Walling	.05	.02	.00
☐ 420	Gary Matthews	.05	.02	.00
☐ 421	Charlie Leibrandt UER (Liebrandt on front of card)	.10	.04	.01
☐ 422	Juan Eichelberger UER (photo actually Joe Pittman)	.05	.02	.00
☐ 423	Cecilio Guante UER (listed as Matt on card)	.05	.02	.00
☐ 424	Bill Laskey	.05	.02	.00
☐ 425	Jerry Royster	.05	.02	.00
☐ 426	Dickie Noles	.05	.02	.00
☐ 427	George Foster	.15	.06	.01
☐ 428	Mike Moore	.90	.40	.09
☐ 429	Gary Ward	.05	.02	.00
☐ 430	Barry Bonnell	.05	.02	.00
☐ 431	Ron Washington	.05	.02	.00
☐ 432	Rance Mulliniks	.05	.02	.00
☐ 433	Mike Stanton	.05	.02	.00
☐ 434	Jesse Orosco	.05	.02	.00
☐ 435	Larry Bowa	.10	.04	.01
☐ 436	Biff Pocoroba	.05	.02	.00
☐ 437	Johnny Ray	.05	.02	.00
☐ 438	Joe Morgan	.50	.20	.05
☐ 439	Eric Show	.15	.06	.01
☐ 440	Larry Biittner	.05	.02	.00
☐ 441	Greg Gross	.05	.02	.00
☐ 442	Gene Tenace	.10	.04	.01
☐ 443	Danny Heep	.05	.02	.00
☐ 444	Bobby Clark	.05	.02	.00
☐ 445	Kevin Hickey	.05	.02	.00
☐ 446	Scott Sanderson	.10	.04	.01
☐ 447	Frank Tanana	.10	.04	.01
☐ 448	Cesar Geronimo	.05	.02	.00
☐ 449	Jimmy Sexton	.05	.02	.00
☐ 450	Mike Hargrove	.05	.02	.00
☐ 451	Doyle Alexander	.05	.02	.00
☐ 452	Dwight Evans	.25	.10	.02
☐ 453	Terry Forster	.05	.02	.00
☐ 454	Tom Brookens	.05	.02	.00
☐ 455	Rich Dauer	.05	.02	.00
☐ 456	Rob Picciolo	.05	.02	.00
☐ 457	Terry Crowley	.05	.02	.00
☐ 458	Ned Yost	.05	.02	.00
☐ 459	Kirk Gibson	.50	.20	.05
☐ 460	Reid Nichols	.05	.02	.00
☐ 461	Oscar Gamble	.05	.02	.00
☐ 462	Dusty Baker	.10	.04	.01
☐ 463	Jack Perconte	.05	.02	.00
☐ 464	Frank White	.05	.02	.00
☐ 465	Mickey Klutts	.05	.02	.00
☐ 466	Warren Cromartie	.05	.02	.00
☐ 467	Larry Parrish	.05	.02	.00
☐ 468	Bobby Grich	.10	.04	.01
☐ 469	Dane Iorg	.05	.02	.00
☐ 470	Joe Niekro	.10	.04	.01
☐ 471	Ed Farmer	.05	.02	.00
☐ 472	Tim Flannery	.05	.02	.00
☐ 473	Dave Parker	.40	.16	.04
☐ 474	Jeff Leonard	.05	.02	.00
☐ 475	Al Hrabosky	.05	.02	.00
☐ 476	Ron Hodges	.05	.02	.00
☐ 477	Leon Durham	.05	.02	.00
☐ 478	Jim Essian	.05	.02	.00
☐ 479	Roy Lee Jackson	.05	.02	.00
☐ 480	Brad Havens	.05	.02	.00
☐ 481	Joe Price	.05	.02	.00
☐ 482	Tony Bernazard	.05	.02	.00
☐ 483	Scott McGregor	.05	.02	.00
☐ 484	Paul Molitor	.40	.16	.04
☐ 485	Mike Ivie	.05	.02	.00
☐ 486	Ken Griffey	.25	.10	.02
☐ 487	Dennis Eckersley	.40	.16	.04
☐ 488	Steve Garvey	.50	.20	.05
☐ 489	Mike Fischlin	.05	.02	.00
☐ 490	U.L. Washington	.05	.02	.00

☐ 491	Steve McCatty	.05	.02	.00
☐ 492	Roy Johnson	.05	.02	.00
☐ 493	Don Baylor	.10	.04	.01
☐ 494	Bobby Johnson	.05	.02	.00
☐ 495	Mike Squires	.05	.02	.00
☐ 496	Bert Roberge	.05	.02	.00
☐ 497	Dick Ruthven	.05	.02	.00
☐ 498	Tito Landrum	.05	.02	.00
☐ 499	Sixto Lezcano	.05	.02	.00
☐ 500	Johnny Bench	1.00	.40	.10
☐ 501	Larry Whisenton	.05	.02	.00
☐ 502	Manny Sarmiento	.05	.02	.00
☐ 503	Fred Breining	.05	.02	.00
☐ 504	Bill Campbell	.05	.02	.00
☐ 505	Todd Cruz	.05	.02	.00
☐ 506	Bob Bailor	.05	.02	.00
☐ 507	Dave Stieb	.25	.10	.02
☐ 508	Al Williams	.05	.02	.00
☐ 509	Dan Ford	.05	.02	.00
☐ 510	Gorman Thomas	.10	.04	.01
☐ 511	Chet Lemon	.05	.02	.00
☐ 512	Mike Torrez	.05	.02	.00
☐ 513	Shane Rawley	.05	.02	.00
☐ 514	Mark Belanger	.10	.04	.01
☐ 515	Rodney Craig	.05	.02	.00
☐ 516	Onix Concepcion	.05	.02	.00
☐ 517	Mike Heath	.05	.02	.00
☐ 518	Andre Dawson UER	1.25	.50	.12
	(Middle name Fernando, should be Nolan)			
☐ 519	Luis Sanchez	.05	.02	.00
☐ 520	Terry Bogener	.05	.02	.00
☐ 521	Rudy Law	.05	.02	.00
☐ 522	Ray Knight	.10	.04	.01
☐ 523	Joe Lefebvre	.05	.02	.00
☐ 524	Jim Wohlford	.05	.02	.00
☐ 525	Julio Franco	10.00	4.50	1.25
☐ 526	Ron Oester	.05	.02	.00
☐ 527	Rick Mahler	.05	.02	.00
☐ 528	Steve Nicosia	.05	.02	.00
☐ 529	Junior Kennedy	.05	.02	.00
☐ 530A	Whitey Herzog MG	.10	.04	.01
	(bio printed black on white)			
☐ 530B	Whitey Herzog MG	.10	.04	.01
	(bio printed black on yellow)			
☐ 531A	Don Sutton	.35	.15	.03
	(blue border on photo)			
☐ 531B	Don Sutton	.35	.15	.03
	(green border on photo)			
☐ 532	Mark Brouhard	.05	.02	.00
☐ 533A	Sparky Anderson MG	.10	.04	.01
	(bio printed black on white)			
☐ 533B	Sparky Anderson MG	.10	.04	.01
	(bio printed black on yellow)			
☐ 534	Roger LaFrancois	.05	.02	.00
☐ 535	George Frazier	.05	.02	.00
☐ 536	Tom Niedenfuer	.05	.02	.00
☐ 537	Ed Glynn	.05	.02	.00
☐ 538	Lee May	.05	.02	.00
☐ 539	Bob Kearney	.05	.02	.00
☐ 540	Tim Raines	.60	.25	.06
☐ 541	Paul Mirabella	.05	.02	.00
☐ 542	Luis Tiant	.10	.04	.01
☐ 543	Ron LeFlore	.05	.02	.00
☐ 544	Dave LaPoint	.10	.04	.01
☐ 545	Randy Moffitt	.05	.02	.00
☐ 546	Luis Aguayo	.05	.02	.00
☐ 547	Brad Lesley	.05	.02	.00
☐ 548	Luis Salazar	.05	.02	.00
☐ 549	John Candelaria	.05	.02	.00
☐ 550	Dave Bergman	.05	.02	.00
☐ 551	Bob Watson	.05	.02	.00
☐ 552	Pat Tabler	.05	.02	.00
☐ 553	Brent Gaff	.05	.02	.00
☐ 554	Al Cowens	.05	.02	.00
☐ 555	Tom Brunansky	.40	.16	.04
☐ 556	Lloyd Moseby	.10	.04	.01
☐ 557A	Pascual Perez ERR	2.00	.80	.20
	(Twins in glove)			
☐ 557B	Pascual Perez COR	.10	.04	.01
	(Braves in glove)			
☐ 558	Willie Upshaw	.05	.02	.00
☐ 559	Richie Zisk	.05	.02	.00
☐ 560	Pat Zachry	.05	.02	.00
☐ 561	Jay Johnstone	.10	.04	.01
☐ 562	Carlos Diaz	.05	.02	.00
☐ 563	John Tudor	.10	.04	.01
☐ 564	Frank Robinson MG	.20	.08	.02
☐ 565	Dave Edwards	.05	.02	.00
☐ 566	Paul Householder	.05	.02	.00
☐ 567	Ron Reed	.05	.02	.00
☐ 568	Mike Ramsey	.05	.02	.00
☐ 569	Kiko Garcia	.05	.02	.00
☐ 570	Tommy John	.15	.06	.01
☐ 571	Tony LaRussa MG	.10	.04	.01
☐ 572	Joel Youngblood	.05	.02	.00
☐ 573	Wayne Tolleson	.10	.04	.01
☐ 574	Keith Creel	.05	.02	.00
☐ 575	Billy Martin MG	.15	.06	.01
☐ 576	Jerry Dybzinski	.05	.02	.00
☐ 577	Rick Cerone	.05	.02	.00
☐ 578	Tony Perez	.30	.12	.03
☐ 579	Greg Brock	.10	.04	.01
☐ 580	Glenn Wilson	.10	.04	.01
☐ 581	Tim Stoddard	.05	.02	.00
☐ 582	Bob McClure	.05	.02	.00
☐ 583	Jim Dwyer	.05	.02	.00
☐ 584	Ed Romero	.05	.02	.00
☐ 585	Larry Herndon	.05	.02	.00
☐ 586	Wade Boggs	24.00	10.50	3.50
☐ 587	Jay Howell	.10	.04	.01
☐ 588	Dave Stewart	.75	.30	.07
☐ 589	Bert Blyleven	.20	.08	.02
☐ 590	Dick Howser MG	.05	.02	.00
☐ 591	Wayne Gross	.05	.02	.00
☐ 592	Terry Francona	.05	.02	.00
☐ 593	Don Werner	.05	.02	.00
☐ 594	Bill Stein	.05	.02	.00
☐ 595	Jesse Barfield	.40	.16	.04
☐ 596	Bob Molinaro	.05	.02	.00
☐ 597	Mike Vail	.05	.02	.00
☐ 598	Tony Gwynn	23.00	10.00	3.35
☐ 599	Gary Rajsich	.05	.02	.00
☐ 600	Jerry Ujdur	.05	.02	.00
☐ 601	Cliff Johnson	.05	.02	.00
☐ 602	Jerry White	.05	.02	.00
☐ 603	Bryan Clark	.05	.02	.00
☐ 604	Joe Ferguson	.05	.02	.00
☐ 605	Guy Sularz	.05	.02	.00
☐ 606A	Ozzie Virgil	.10	.04	.01
	(green border on photo)			
☐ 606B	Ozzie Virgil	.10	.04	.01
	(orange border on photo)			
☐ 607	Terry Harper	.05	.02	.00
☐ 608	Harvey Kuenn MG	.05	.02	.00
☐ 609	Jim Sundberg	.05	.02	.00
☐ 610	Willie Stargell	.50	.20	.05
☐ 611	Reggie Smith	.10	.04	.01
☐ 612	Rob Wilfong	.05	.02	.00
☐ 613	The Niekro Brothers	.20	.08	.02
	Joe Niekro Phil Niekro			
☐ 614	Lee Elia MG	.05	.02	.00
☐ 615	Mickey Hatcher	.05	.02	.00
☐ 616	Jerry Hairston	.05	.02	.00
☐ 617	John Martin	.05	.02	.00
☐ 618	Wally Backman	.10	.04	.01
☐ 619	Storm Davis	.25	.10	.02
☐ 620	Alan Knicely	.05	.02	.00
☐ 621	John Stuper	.05	.02	.00
☐ 622	Matt Sinatro	.05	.02	.00
☐ 623	Geno Petralli	.10	.04	.01
☐ 624	Duane Walker	.05	.02	.00
☐ 625	Dick Williams MG	.05	.02	.00
☐ 626	Pat Corrales MG	.05	.02	.00
☐ 627	Vern Ruhle	.05	.02	.00
☐ 628	Joe Torre MG	.10	.04	.01
☐ 629	Anthony Johnson	.05	.02	.00
☐ 630	Steve Howe	.05	.02	.00
☐ 631	Gary Woods	.05	.02	.00
☐ 632	LaMarr Hoyt	.05	.02	.00
☐ 633	Steve Swisher	.05	.02	.00
☐ 634	Terry Leach	.10	.04	.01
☐ 635	Jeff Newman	.05	.02	.00
☐ 636	Brett Butler	.40	.16	.04
☐ 637	Gary Gray	.05	.02	.00
☐ 638	Lee Mazzilli	.05	.02	.00
☐ 639A	Ron Jackson ERR	14.00	6.25	2.00
	(A's in glove)			
☐ 639B	Ron Jackson COR	.10	.04	.01
	(Angels in glove, red border on photo)			
☐ 639C	Ron Jackson COR	.50	.20	.05
	(Angels in glove, green border on photo)			
☐ 640	Juan Beniquez	.05	.02	.00
☐ 641	Dave Rucker	.05	.02	.00
☐ 642	Luis Pujols	.05	.02	.00

			MINT	EXC	G-VG
☐	643	Rick Monday	.05	.02	.00
☐	644	Hosken Powell	.05	.02	.00
☐	645	The Chicken	.25	.10	.02
☐	646	Dave Engle	.05	.02	.00
☐	647	Dick Davis	.05	.02	.00
☐	648	Frank Robinson	.30	.12	.03
		Vida Blue			
		Joe Morgan			
☐	649	Al Chambers	.05	.02	.00
☐	650	Jesus Vega	.05	.02	.00
☐	651	Jeff Jones	.05	.02	.00
☐	652	Marvis Foley	.05	.02	.00
☐	653	Ty Cobb Puzzle Card	.05	.02	.00
☐	654A	Dick Perez/Diamond King Checklist (unnumbered) (word "checklist" omitted from back)	.35	.05	.01
☐	654B	Dick Perez/Diamond King Checklist (unnumbered) (word "checklist" is on back)	.35	.05	.01
☐	655	Checklist 1 (unnumbered)	.15	.02	.00
☐	656	Checklist 2 (unnumbered)	.15	.02	.00
☐	657	Checklist 3 (unnumbered)	.15	.02	.00
☐	658	Checklist 4 (unnumbered)	.15	.02	.00
☐	659	Checklist 5 (unnumbered)	.15	.02	.00
☐	660	Checklist 6 (unnumbered)	.15	.02	.00

☐	10	Greg Minton	.07	.03	.01
☐	11	Terry Kennedy	.07	.03	.01
☐	12	Phil Niekro	.20	.08	.02
☐	13	Willie Wilson	.10	.04	.01
☐	14	Johnny Bench	.40	.16	.04
☐	15	Ron Guidry	.10	.04	.01
☐	16	Hal McRae	.10	.04	.01
☐	17	Damaso Garcia	.07	.03	.01
☐	18	Gary Ward	.07	.03	.01
☐	19	Cecil Cooper	.10	.04	.01
☐	20	Keith Hernandez	.15	.06	.01
☐	21	Ron Cey	.07	.03	.01
☐	22	Rickey Henderson	1.00	.40	.10
☐	23	Nolan Ryan	1.50	.60	.15
☐	24	Steve Carlton	.35	.15	.03
☐	25	John Stearns	.07	.03	.01
☐	26	Jim Sundberg	.07	.03	.01
☐	27	Joaquin Andujar	.07	.03	.01
☐	28	Gaylord Perry	.20	.08	.02
☐	29	Jack Clark	.20	.08	.02
☐	30	Bill Madlock	.07	.03	.01
☐	31	Pete Rose	.75	.30	.07
☐	32	Mookie Wilson	.07	.03	.01
☐	33	Rollie Fingers	.25	.10	.02
☐	34	Lonnie Smith	.10	.04	.01
☐	35	Tony Pena	.07	.03	.01
☐	36	Dave Winfield	.25	.10	.02
☐	37	Tim Lollar	.07	.03	.01
☐	38	Rod Carew	.35	.15	.03
☐	39	Toby Harrah	.07	.03	.01
☐	40	Buddy Bell	.07	.03	.01
☐	41	Bruce Sutter	.10	.04	.01
☐	42	George Brett	.50	.20	.05
☐	43	Carlton Fisk	.50	.20	.05
☐	44	Carl Yastrzemski	.75	.30	.07
☐	45	Dale Murphy	.40	.16	.04
☐	46	Bob Horner	.10	.04	.01
☐	47	Dave Concepcion	.10	.04	.01
☐	48	Dave Stieb	.15	.06	.01
☐	49	Kent Hrbek	.15	.06	.01
☐	50	Lance Parrish	.15	.06	.01
☐	51	Joe Niekro	.10	.04	.01
☐	52	Cal Ripken	1.00	.40	.10
☐	53	Fernando Valenzuela	.20	.08	.02
☐	54	Richie Zisk	.07	.03	.01
☐	55	Leon Durham	.07	.03	.01
☐	56	Robin Yount	.50	.20	.05
☐	57	Mike Schmidt	1.00	.40	.10
☐	58	Gary Carter	.30	.12	.03
☐	59	Fred Lynn	.10	.04	.01
☐	60	Checklist Card	.07	.03	.01

1983 Donruss Action All-Stars

The cards in this 60-card set measure approximately 3 1/2" by 5". The 1983 Action All-Stars series depicts 60 major leagers in a distinctive new style. Each card contains a large close-up on the left and an action photo on the right. Team affiliations appear as part of the background design, and the cards have cranberry color borders. The backs contain the card number, the player's major league line record, and biographical material. A 63-piece Mickey Mantle puzzle (three pieces on one card per pack) was marketed as an insert premium.

		MINT	EXC	G-VG
		7.50	3.25	.75
COMPLETE SET (60)		7.50	3.25	.75
COMMON PLAYER (1-60)		.07	.03	.01
☐	1 Eddie Murray	.40	.16	.04
☐	2 Dwight Evans	.15	.06	.01
☐	3A Reggie Jackson ERR (Red screen on back covers some stats)	1.25	.50	.12
☐	3B Reggie Jackson COR	.75	.30	.07
☐	4 Greg Luzinski	.10	.04	.01
☐	5 Larry Herndon	.07	.03	.01
☐	6 Al Oliver	.10	.04	.01
☐	7 Bill Buckner	.10	.04	.01
☐	8 Jason Thompson	.07	.03	.01
☐	9 Andre Dawson	.40	.16	.04

1983 Donruss HOF Heroes

The cards in this 44-card set measure 2 1/2" by 3 1/2". Although it was issued with the same Mantle puzzle as the Action All Stars set, the Donruss Hall of Fame Heroes set is completely different in content and design. Of the 44 cards in the set, 42 are Dick Perez artwork portraying Hall of Fame members, while one card depicts the completed Mantle puzzle and the last card is a checklist. The red, white, and blue backs contain the card number and a short player biography. The cards were packaged eight cards plus one puzzle card (three pieces) for 30 cents in the summer of 1983.

	MINT	EXC	G-VG
COMPLETE SET (44)	5.00	2.25	.50
COMMON PLAYER (1-44)	.06	.02	.00

		MINT	EXC	G-VG
☐ 1	Ty Cobb	.60	.25	.06
☐ 2	Walter Johnson	.20	.08	.02
☐ 3	Christy Mathewson	.20	.08	.02
☐ 4	Josh Gibson	.25	.10	.02
☐ 5	Honus Wagner	.25	.10	.02
☐ 6	Jackie Robinson	.25	.10	.02
☐ 7	Mickey Mantle	1.00	.40	.10
☐ 8	Luke Appling	.06	.02	.00
☐ 9	Ted Williams	.25	.10	.02
☐ 10	Johnny Mize	.06	.02	.00
☐ 11	Satchel Paige	.15	.06	.01
☐ 12	Lou Boudreau	.06	.02	.00
☐ 13	Jimmie Foxx	.10	.04	.01
☐ 14	Duke Snider	.20	.08	.02
☐ 15	Monte Irvin	.06	.02	.00
☐ 16	Hank Greenberg	.10	.04	.01
☐ 17	Roberto Clemente	.25	.10	.02
☐ 18	Al Kaline	.15	.06	.01
☐ 19	Frank Robinson	.15	.06	.01
☐ 20	Joe Cronin	.06	.02	.00
☐ 21	Burleigh Grimes	.06	.02	.00
☐ 22	The Waner Brothers	.06	.02	.00
	Paul Waner			
	Lloyd Waner			
☐ 23	Grover Alexander	.10	.04	.01
☐ 24	Yogi Berra	.20	.08	.02
☐ 25	Cool Papa Bell	.06	.02	.00
☐ 26	Bill Dickey	.10	.04	.01
☐ 27	Cy Young	.15	.06	.01
☐ 28	Charlie Gehringer	.06	.02	.00
☐ 29	Dizzy Dean	.20	.08	.02
☐ 30	Bob Lemon	.06	.02	.00
☐ 31	Red Ruffing	.06	.02	.00
☐ 32	Stan Musial	.20	.08	.02
☐ 33	Carl Hubbell	.10	.04	.01
☐ 34	Hank Aaron	.30	.12	.03
☐ 35	John McGraw	.06	.02	.00
☐ 36	Bob Feller	.15	.06	.01
☐ 37	Casey Stengel	.10	.04	.01
☐ 38	Ralph Kiner	.10	.04	.01
☐ 39	Roy Campanella	.20	.08	.02
☐ 40	Mel Ott	.10	.04	.01
☐ 41	Robin Roberts	.10	.04	.01
☐ 42	Early Wynn	.06	.02	.00
☐ 43	Mantle Puzzle Card	.10	.04	.01
☐ 44	Checklist Card	.06	.02	.00

1984 Donruss

KEITH HERNANDEZ 1B

The 1984 Donruss set contains a total of 660 cards, each measuring 2 1/2" by 3 1/2"; however, only 658 are numbered. The first 26 cards in the set are again Diamond Kings (DK), although the drawings this year were styled differently and are easily differentiated from other DK issues. A new feature, Rated Rookies (RR), was introduced with this set with Bill Madden's 20 selections comprising numbers 27 through 46. Two "Living Legend" cards designated A (featuring Gaylord Perry and Rollie Fingers) and B (featuring Johnny Bench and Carl Yastrzemski) were issued as bonus cards in wax packs, but were not issued in the vending sets sold to hobby dealers. The seven unnumbered checklist cards are arbitrarily assigned numbers 652 through

658 and are listed at the end of the list below. The designs on the fronts of the Donruss cards changed considerably from the past two years. The backs contain statistics and are printed in green and black ink. The cards were distributed with a 63-piece puzzle of Duke Snider. There are no extra variation cards included in the complete set price below. The variation cards apparently resulted from a different printing for the factory sets as the Darling and Stenhouse no number variations as well as the Perez-Steel errors were corrected in the factory sets which were released later in the year. The key rookie cards in this set are Joe Carter, Ron Darling, Sid Fernandez, Tony Fernandez, Don Mattingly, Kevin McReynolds, Darryl Strawberry, and Andy Van Slyke.

	MINT	EXC	G-VG
COMPLETE SET (658)	350.00	160.00	52.50
COMMON PLAYER (1-658)	.14	.06	.01

		MINT	EXC	G-VG
☐ 1A	Robin Yount DK ERR (Perez Steel)	2.25	.75	.15
☐ 1B	Robin Yount DK COR	3.00	1.00	.20
☐ 2A	Dave Concepcion DK ERR (Perez Steel)	.25	.10	.02
☐ 2B	Dave Concepcion DK COR	.35	.15	.03
☐ 3A	Dwayne Murphy DK ERR (Perez Steel)	.20	.08	.02
☐ 3B	Dwayne Murphy DK COR	.30	.12	.03
☐ 4A	John Castino DK ERR (Perez Steel)	.20	.08	.02
☐ 4B	John Castino DK COR	.30	.12	.03
☐ 5A	Leon Durham DK ERR (Perez Steel)	.20	.08	.02
☐ 5B	Leon Durham DK COR	.30	.12	.03
☐ 6A	Rusty Staub DK ERR (Perez Steel)	.20	.08	.02
☐ 6B	Rusty Staub DK COR	.30	.12	.03
☐ 7A	Jack Clark DK ERR (Perez Steel)	.25	.10	.02
☐ 7B	Jack Clark DK COR	.35	.15	.03
☐ 8A	Dave Dravecky DK ERR (Perez Steel)	.20	.08	.02
☐ 8B	Dave Dravecky DK COR	.30	.12	.03
☐ 9A	Al Oliver DK ERR (Perez Steel)	.20	.08	.02
☐ 9B	Al Oliver DK COR	.30	.12	.03
☐ 10A	Dave Righetti DK ERR (Perez Steel)	.20	.08	.02
☐ 10B	Dave Righetti DK COR	.30	.12	.03
☐ 11A	Hal McRae DK ERR (Perez Steel)	.20	.08	.02
☐ 11B	Hal McRae DK COR	.30	.12	.03
☐ 12A	Ray Knight DK ERR (Perez Steel)	.20	.08	.02
☐ 12B	Ray Knight DK COR	.30	.12	.03
☐ 13A	Bruce Sutter DK ERR (Perez Steel)	.20	.08	.02
☐ 13B	Bruce Sutter DK COR	.30	.12	.03
☐ 14A	Bob Horner DK ERR (Perez Steel)	.20	.08	.02
☐ 14B	Bob Horner DK COR	.30	.12	.03
☐ 15A	Lance Parrish DK ERR (Perez Steel)	.35	.15	.03
☐ 15B	Lance Parrish DK COR	.50	.20	.05
☐ 16A	Matt Young DK ERR (Perez Steel)	.20	.08	.02
☐ 16B	Matt Young DK COR	.30	.12	.03
☐ 17A	Fred Lynn DK ERR (Perez Steel) (A's logo on back)	.25	.10	.02
☐ 17B	Fred Lynn DK COR	.35	.15	.03
☐ 18A	Ron Kittle DK ERR (Perez Steel)	.20	.08	.02
☐ 18B	Ron Kittle DK COR	.30	.12	.03
☐ 19A	Jim Clancy DK ERR	.20	.08	.02
☐ 19B	Jim Clancy DK COR	.30	.12	.03
☐ 20A	Bill Madlock DK ERR (Perez Steel)	.20	.08	.02
☐ 20B	Bill Madlock DK COR	.30	.12	.03
☐ 21A	Larry Parrish DK ERR (Perez Steel)	.20	.08	.02
☐ 21B	Larry Parrish DK COR	.30	.12	.03
☐ 22A	Eddie Murray DK ERR (Perez Steel)	1.25	.50	.12

22B	Eddie Murray DK COR	1.75	.70	.17
23A	Mike Schmidt DK ERR (Perez Steel)	2.50	1.00	.25
23B	Mike Schmidt DK COR	3.50	1.50	.35
24A	Pedro Guerrero DK ERR (Perez Steel)	.35	.15	.03
24B	Pedro Guerrero DK COR	.50	.20	.05
25A	Andre Thornton DK ERR (Perez Steel)	.20	.08	.02
25B	Andre Thornton DK COR	.30	.12	.03
26A	Wade Boggs DK ERR (Perez Steel)	3.50	1.50	.35
26B	Wade Boggs DK COR	4.50	2.00	.45
27	Joel Skinner RR	.20	.08	.02
28	Tommy Dunbar RR	.14	.06	.01
29A	Mike Stenhouse RR ERR (no number on back)	.20	.08	.02
29B	Mike Stenhouse RR COR (numbered on back)	2.50	1.00	.25
30A	Ron Darling RR ERR (no number on back)	3.00	1.25	.30
30B	Ron Darling RR COR (numbered on back)	18.00	7.50	2.50
31	Dion James RR	.20	.08	.02
32	Tony Fernandez RR	6.00	2.50	.60
33	Angel Salazar RR	.14	.06	.01
34	Kevin McReynolds RR	8.00	3.50	.80
35	Dick Schofield RR	.40	.16	.04
36	Brad Komminsk RR	.20	.08	.02
37	Tim Teufel RR	.50	.20	.05
38	Doug Frobel RR	.14	.06	.01
39	Greg Gagne RR	.75	.30	.07
40	Mike Fuentes RR	.14	.06	.01
41	Joe Carter RR	32.00	14.25	4.75
42	Mike Brown RR (Angels OF)	.14	.06	.01
43	Mike Jeffcoat RR	.20	.08	.02
44	Sid Fernandez RR	4.00	1.75	.40
45	Brian Dayett RR	.14	.06	.01
46	Chris Smith RR	.14	.06	.01
47	Eddie Murray	4.00	1.75	.40
48	Robin Yount	4.50	2.00	.45
49	Lance Parrish	.75	.30	.07
50	Jim Rice	.45	.18	.04
51	Dave Winfield	2.75	1.10	.27
52	Fernando Valenzuela	.50	.20	.05
53	George Brett	4.50	2.00	.45
54	Rickey Henderson	15.00	6.50	2.15
55	Gary Carter	1.25	.50	.12
56	Buddy Bell	.20	.08	.02
57	Reggie Jackson	4.00	1.75	.40
58	Harold Baines	.90	.40	.09
59	Ozzie Smith	3.25	1.35	.32
60	Nolan Ryan	17.00	7.25	2.50
61	Pete Rose	3.50	1.50	.35
62	Ron Oester	.14	.06	.01
63	Steve Garvey	1.25	.50	.12
64	Jason Thompson	.14	.06	.01
65	Jack Clark	.40	.16	.04
66	Dale Murphy	2.50	1.00	.25
67	Leon Durham	.14	.06	.01
68	Darryl Strawberry	65.00	29.00	9.75
69	Richie Zisk	.14	.06	.01
70	Kent Hrbek	.85	.35	.08
71	Dave Stieb	.60	.25	.06
72	Ken Schrom	.14	.06	.01
73	George Bell	3.00	1.25	.30
74	John Moses	.20	.08	.02
75	Ed Lynch	.14	.06	.01
76	Chuck Rainey	.14	.06	.01
77	Biff Pocoroba	.14	.06	.01
78	Cecilio Guante	.14	.06	.01
79	Jim Barr	.14	.06	.01
80	Kurt Bevacqua	.14	.06	.01
81	Tom Foley	.14	.06	.01
82	Joe Lefebvre	.14	.06	.01
83	Andy Van Slyke	7.00	3.00	.70
84	Bob Lillis MG	.14	.06	.01
85	Ricky Adams	.14	.06	.01
86	Jerry Hairston	.14	.06	.01
87	Bob James	.14	.06	.01
88	Joe Altobelli MG	.14	.06	.01
89	Ed Romero	.14	.06	.01
90	John Grubb	.14	.06	.01
91	John Henry Johnson	.14	.06	.01
92	Juan Espino	.14	.06	.01
93	Candy Maldonado	.30	.12	.03
94	Andre Thornton	.14	.06	.01
95	Onix Concepcion	.14	.06	.01
96	Donnie Hill UER (listed as P, should be 2B)	.25	.10	.02
97	Andre Dawson UER (wrong middle name, should be Nolan)	4.00	1.75	.40
98	Frank Tanana	.20	.08	.02
99	Curt Wilkerson	.14	.06	.01
100	Larry Gura	.14	.06	.01
101	Dwayne Murphy	.14	.06	.01
102	Tom Brennan	.14	.06	.01
103	Dave Righetti	.40	.16	.04
104	Steve Sax	.80	.35	.08
105	Dan Petry	.14	.06	.01
106	Cal Ripken	20.00	8.50	2.75
107	Paul Molitor UER ('83 stats should say .270 BA, 608 AB, and 164 hits)	.90	.40	.09
108	Fred Lynn	.35	.15	.03
109	Neil Allen	.14	.06	.01
110	Joe Niekro	.20	.08	.02
111	Steve Carlton	3.25	1.35	.32
112	Terry Kennedy	.14	.06	.01
113	Bill Madlock	.20	.08	.02
114	Chili Davis	.30	.12	.03
115	Jim Gantner	.14	.06	.01
116	Tom Seaver	5.25	2.25	.50
117	Bill Buckner	.20	.08	.02
118	Bill Caudill	.14	.06	.01
119	Jim Clancy	.14	.06	.01
120	John Castino	.14	.06	.01
121	Dave Concepcion	.30	.12	.03
122	Greg Luzinski	.20	.08	.02
123	Mike Boddicker	.20	.08	.02
124	Pete Ladd	.14	.06	.01
125	Juan Berenguer	.14	.06	.01
126	John Montefusco	.14	.06	.01
127	Ed Jurak	.14	.06	.01
128	Tom Niedenfuer	.14	.06	.01
129	Bert Blyleven	.45	.18	.04
130	Bud Black	.25	.10	.02
131	Gorman Heimueller	.14	.06	.01
132	Dan Schatzeder	.14	.06	.01
133	Ron Jackson	.14	.06	.01
134	Tom Henke	1.25	.50	.12
135	Kevin Hickey	.14	.06	.01
136	Mike Scott	.40	.16	.04
137	Bo Diaz	.14	.06	.01
138	Glenn Brummer	.14	.06	.01
139	Sid Monge	.14	.06	.01
140	Rich Gale	.14	.06	.01
141	Brett Butler	.75	.30	.07
142	Brian Harper	1.50	.60	.15
143	John Rabb	.14	.06	.01
144	Gary Woods	.14	.06	.01
145	Pat Putnam	.14	.06	.01
146	Jim Acker	.20	.08	.02
147	Mickey Hatcher	.14	.06	.01
148	Todd Cruz	.14	.06	.01
149	Tom Tellmann	.14	.06	.01
150	John Wockenfuss	.14	.06	.01
151	Wade Boggs	15.00	6.50	2.15
152	Don Baylor	.20	.08	.02
153	Bob Welch	.50	.20	.05
154	Alan Bannister	.14	.06	.01
155	Willie Aikens	.14	.06	.01
156	Jeff Burroughs	.14	.06	.01
157	Bryan Little	.14	.06	.01
158	Bob Boone	.25	.10	.02
159	Dave Hostetler	.14	.06	.01
160	Jerry Dybzinski	.14	.06	.01
161	Mike Madden	.14	.06	.01
162	Luis DeLeon	.14	.06	.01
163	Willie Hernandez	.20	.08	.02
164	Frank Pastore	.14	.06	.01
165	Rick Camp	.14	.06	.01
166	Lee Mazzilli	.14	.06	.01
167	Scot Thompson	.14	.06	.01
168	Bob Forsch	.14	.06	.01
169	Mike Flanagan	.20	.08	.02
170	Rick Manning	.14	.06	.01
171	Chet Lemon	.14	.06	.01
172	Jerry Remy	.14	.06	.01
173	Ron Guidry	.40	.16	.04
174	Pedro Guerrero	.60	.25	.06
175	Willie Wilson	.20	.08	.02
176	Carney Lansford	.20	.08	.02
177	Al Oliver	.20	.08	.02
178	Jim Sundberg	.14	.06	.01
179	Bobby Grich	.20	.08	.02
180	Rich Dotson	.14	.06	.01
181	Joaquin Andujar	.20	.08	.02
182	Jose Cruz	.20	.08	.02
183	Mike Schmidt	13.00	5.75	1.75
184	Gary Redus	.60	.25	.06
185	Garry Templeton	.20	.08	.02

☐ 186	Tony Pena	.25	.10	.02
☐ 187	Greg Minton	.14	.06	.01
☐ 188	Phil Niekro	.90	.40	.09
☐ 189	Ferguson Jenkins	.90	.40	.09
☐ 190	Mookie Wilson	.20	.08	.02
☐ 191	Jim Beattie	.14	.06	.01
☐ 192	Gary Ward	.14	.06	.01
☐ 193	Jesse Barfield	.45	.18	.04
☐ 194	Pete Filson	.14	.06	.01
☐ 195	Roy Lee Jackson	.14	.06	.01
☐ 196	Rick Sweet	.14	.06	.01
☐ 197	Jesse Orosco	.14	.06	.01
☐ 198	Steve Lake	.14	.06	.01
☐ 199	Ken Dayley	.14	.06	.01
☐ 200	Manny Sarmiento	.14	.06	.01
☐ 201	Mark Davis	.30	.12	.03
☐ 202	Tim Flannery	.14	.06	.01
☐ 203	Bill Scherrer	.14	.06	.01
☐ 204	Al Holland	.14	.06	.01
☐ 205	Dave Von Ohlen	.14	.06	.01
☐ 206	Mike LaCoss	.14	.06	.01
☐ 207	Juan Beniquez	.14	.06	.01
☐ 208	Juan Agosto	.20	.08	.02
☐ 209	Bobby Ramos	.14	.06	.01
☐ 210	Al Bumbry	.14	.06	.01
☐ 211	Mark Brouhard	.14	.06	.01
☐ 212	Howard Bailey	.14	.06	.01
☐ 213	Bruce Hurst	.30	.12	.03
☐ 214	Bob Shirley	.14	.06	.01
☐ 215	Pat Zachry	.14	.06	.01
☐ 216	Julio Franco	5.00	2.25	.50
☐ 217	Mike Armstrong	.14	.06	.01
☐ 218	Dave Beard	.14	.06	.01
☐ 219	Steve Rogers	.14	.06	.01
☐ 220	John Butcher	.14	.06	.01
☐ 221	Mike Smithson	.14	.06	.01
☐ 222	Frank White	.14	.06	.01
☐ 223	Mike Heath	.14	.06	.01
☐ 224	Chris Bando	.14	.06	.01
☐ 225	Roy Smalley	.14	.06	.01
☐ 226	Dusty Baker	.20	.08	.02
☐ 227	Lou Whitaker	.90	.40	.09
☐ 228	John Lowenstein	.14	.06	.01
☐ 229	Ben Oglivie	.14	.06	.01
☐ 230	Doug DeCinces	.20	.08	.02
☐ 231	Lonnie Smith	.30	.12	.03
☐ 232	Ray Knight	.20	.08	.02
☐ 233	Gary Matthews	.14	.06	.01
☐ 234	Juan Bonilla	.14	.06	.01
☐ 235	Rod Scurry	.14	.06	.01
☐ 236	Atlee Hammaker	.14	.06	.01
☐ 237	Mike Caldwell	.14	.06	.01
☐ 238	Keith Hernandez	.50	.20	.05
☐ 239	Larry Bowa	.20	.08	.02
☐ 240	Tony Bernazard	.14	.06	.01
☐ 241	Damaso Garcia	.14	.06	.01
☐ 242	Tom Brunansky	.35	.15	.03
☐ 243	Dan Driessen	.14	.06	.01
☐ 244	Ron Kittle	.30	.12	.03
☐ 245	Tim Stoddard	.14	.06	.01
☐ 246	Bob L. Gibson (Brewers Pitcher)	.14	.06	.01
☐ 247	Marty Castillo	.14	.06	.01
☐ 248	Don Mattingly UER ("traiing" on back)	60.00	27.00	9.00
☐ 249	Jeff Newman	.14	.06	.01
☐ 250	Alejandro Pena	.90	.40	.09
☐ 251	Toby Harrah	.14	.06	.01
☐ 252	Cesar Geronimo	.14	.06	.01
☐ 253	Tom Underwood	.14	.06	.01
☐ 254	Doug Flynn	.14	.06	.01
☐ 255	Andy Hassler	.14	.06	.01
☐ 256	Odell Jones	.14	.06	.01
☐ 257	Rudy Law	.14	.06	.01
☐ 258	Harry Spilman	.14	.06	.01
☐ 259	Marty Bystrom	.14	.06	.01
☐ 260	Dave Rucker	.14	.06	.01
☐ 261	Ruppert Jones	.14	.06	.01
☐ 262	Jeff R. Jones (Reds OF)	.14	.06	.01
☐ 263	Gerald Perry	.60	.25	.06
☐ 264	Gene Tenace	.20	.08	.02
☐ 265	Brad Wellman	.14	.06	.01
☐ 266	Dickie Noles	.14	.06	.01
☐ 267	Jamie Allen	.14	.06	.01
☐ 268	Jim Gott	.20	.08	.02
☐ 269	Ron Davis	.14	.06	.01
☐ 270	Benny Ayala	.14	.06	.01
☐ 271	Ned Yost	.14	.06	.01
☐ 272	Dave Rozema	.14	.06	.01
☐ 273	Dave Stapleton	.14	.06	.01
☐ 274	Lou Piniella	.25	.10	.02
☐ 275	Jose Morales	.14	.06	.01
☐ 276	Broderick Perkins	.14	.06	.01
☐ 277	Butch Davis	.14	.06	.01

☐ 278	Tony Phillips	1.25	.50	.12
☐ 279	Jeff Reardon	.90	.40	.09
☐ 280	Ken Forsch	.14	.06	.01
☐ 281	Pete O'Brien	.90	.40	.09
☐ 282	Tom Paciorek	.14	.06	.01
☐ 283	Frank LaCorte	.14	.06	.01
☐ 284	Tim Lollar	.14	.06	.01
☐ 285	Greg Gross	.14	.06	.01
☐ 286	Alex Trevino	.14	.06	.01
☐ 287	Gene Garber	.14	.06	.01
☐ 288	Dave Parker	1.25	.50	.12
☐ 289	Lee Smith	.90	.40	.09
☐ 290	Dave LaPoint	.14	.06	.01
☐ 291	John Shelby	.40	.16	.04
☐ 292	Charlie Moore	.14	.06	.01
☐ 293	Alan Trammell	2.50	1.00	.25
☐ 294	Tony Armas	.14	.06	.01
☐ 295	Shane Rawley	.14	.06	.01
☐ 296	Greg Brock	.20	.08	.02
☐ 297	Hal McRae	.20	.08	.02
☐ 298	Mike Davis	.14	.06	.01
☐ 299	Tim Raines	1.25	.50	.12
☐ 300	Bucky Dent	.20	.08	.02
☐ 301	Tommy John	.35	.15	.03
☐ 302	Carlton Fisk	3.25	1.35	.32
☐ 303	Darrell Porter	.14	.06	.01
☐ 304	Dickie Thon	.20	.08	.02
☐ 305	Garry Maddox	.14	.06	.01
☐ 306	Cesar Cedeno	.20	.08	.02
☐ 307	Gary Lucas	.14	.06	.01
☐ 308	Johnny Ray	.14	.06	.01
☐ 309	Andy McGaffigan	.14	.06	.01
☐ 310	Claudell Washington	.20	.08	.02
☐ 311	Ryne Sandberg	25.00	11.00	3.50
☐ 312	George Foster	.35	.15	.03
☐ 313	Spike Owen	.50	.20	.05
☐ 314	Gary Gaetti	.40	.16	.04
☐ 315	Willie Upshaw	.14	.06	.01
☐ 316	Al Williams	.14	.06	.01
☐ 317	Jorge Orta	.14	.06	.01
☐ 318	Orlando Mercado	.14	.06	.01
☐ 319	Junior Ortiz	.14	.06	.01
☐ 320	Mike Proly	.14	.06	.01
☐ 321	Randy Johnson UER ('72-'82 stats are from one Randy Johnson (Twins), '83 stats are from the other (Braves)	.14	.06	.01
☐ 322	Jim Morrison	.14	.06	.01
☐ 323	Max Venable	.14	.06	.01
☐ 324	Tony Gwynn	12.50	5.50	1.65
☐ 325	Duane Walker	.14	.06	.01
☐ 326	Ozzie Virgil	.14	.06	.01
☐ 327	Jeff Lahti	.14	.06	.01
☐ 328	Bill Dawley	.14	.06	.01
☐ 329	Rob Wilfong	.14	.06	.01
☐ 330	Marc Hill	.14	.06	.01
☐ 331	Ray Burris	.14	.06	.01
☐ 332	Allan Ramirez	.14	.06	.01
☐ 333	Chuck Porter	.14	.06	.01
☐ 334	Wayne Krenchicki	.14	.06	.01
☐ 335	Gary Allenson	.14	.06	.01
☐ 336	Bobby Meacham	.14	.06	.01
☐ 337	Joe Beckwith	.14	.06	.01
☐ 338	Rick Sutcliffe	.25	.10	.02
☐ 339	Mark Huismann	.20	.08	.02
☐ 340	Tim Conroy	.14	.06	.01
☐ 341	Scott Sanderson	.20	.08	.02
☐ 342	Larry Biittner	.14	.06	.01
☐ 343	Dave Stewart	1.75	.70	.17
☐ 344	Darryl Motley	.14	.06	.01
☐ 345	Chris Codiroli	.14	.06	.01
☐ 346	Rich Behenna	.14	.06	.01
☐ 347	Andre Robertson	.14	.06	.01
☐ 348	Mike Marshall	.25	.10	.02
☐ 349	Larry Herndon	.14	.06	.01
☐ 350	Rich Dauer	.14	.06	.01
☐ 351	Cecil Cooper	.20	.08	.02
☐ 352	Rod Carew	3.50	1.50	.35
☐ 353	Willie McGee	1.25	.50	.12
☐ 354	Phil Garner	.20	.08	.02
☐ 355	Joe Morgan	1.50	.60	.15
☐ 356	Luis Salazar	.14	.06	.01
☐ 357	John Candelaria	.14	.06	.01
☐ 358	Bill Laskey	.14	.06	.01
☐ 359	Bob McClure	.14	.06	.01
☐ 360	Dave Kingman	.25	.10	.02
☐ 361	Ron Cey	.20	.08	.02
☐ 362	Matt Young	.20	.08	.02
☐ 363	Lloyd Moseby	.20	.08	.02
☐ 364	Frank Viola	2.00	.80	.20
☐ 365	Eddie Milner	.14	.06	.01
☐ 366	Floyd Bannister	.14	.06	.01
☐ 367	Dan Ford	.14	.06	.01
☐ 368	Moose Haas	.14	.06	.01

☐ 369 Doug Bair	.14	.06	.01
☐ 370 Ray Fontenot	.14	.06	.01
☐ 371 Luis Aponte	.14	.06	.01
☐ 372 Jack Fimple	.14	.06	.01
☐ 373 Neal Heaton	.40	.16	.04
☐ 374 Greg Pryor	.14	.06	.01
☐ 375 Wayne Gross	.14	.06	.01
☐ 376 Charlie Lea	.14	.06	.01
☐ 377 Steve Lubratich	.14	.06	.01
☐ 378 Jon Matlack	.14	.06	.01
☐ 379 Julio Cruz	.14	.06	.01
☐ 380 John Mizerock	.14	.06	.01
☐ 381 Kevin Gross	.50	.20	.05
☐ 382 Mike Ramsey	.14	.06	.01
☐ 383 Doug Gwosdz	.14	.06	.01
☐ 384 Kelly Paris	.14	.06	.01
☐ 385 Pete Falcone	.14	.06	.01
☐ 386 Milt May	.14	.06	.01
☐ 387 Fred Breining	.14	.06	.01
☐ 388 Craig Lefferts	.50	.20	.05
☐ 389 Steve Henderson	.14	.06	.01
☐ 390 Randy Moffitt	.14	.06	.01
☐ 391 Ron Washington	.14	.06	.01
☐ 392 Gary Roenicke	.14	.06	.01
☐ 393 Tom Candiotti	1.25	.50	.12
☐ 394 Larry Pashnick	.14	.06	.01
☐ 395 Dwight Evans	.60	.25	.06
☐ 396 Goose Gossage	.35	.15	.03
☐ 397 Derrel Thomas	.14	.06	.01
☐ 398 Juan Eichelberger	.14	.06	.01
☐ 399 Leon Roberts	.14	.06	.01
☐ 400 Dave Lopes	.20	.08	.02
☐ 401 Bill Gullickson	.20	.08	.02
☐ 402 Geoff Zahn	.14	.06	.01
☐ 403 Billy Sample	.14	.06	.01
☐ 404 Mike Squires	.14	.06	.01
☐ 405 Craig Reynolds	.14	.06	.01
☐ 406 Eric Show	.20	.08	.02
☐ 407 John Denny	.14	.06	.01
☐ 408 Dann Bilardello	.14	.06	.01
☐ 409 Bruce Benedict	.14	.06	.01
☐ 410 Kent Tekulve	.14	.06	.01
☐ 411 Mel Hall	.50	.20	.05
☐ 412 John Stuper	.14	.06	.01
☐ 413 Rick Dempsey	.14	.06	.01
☐ 414 Don Sutton	.90	.40	.09
☐ 415 Jack Morris	1.50	.60	.15
☐ 416 John Tudor	.30	.12	.03
☐ 417 Willie Randolph	.25	.10	.02
☐ 418 Jerry Reuss	.14	.06	.01
☐ 419 Don Slaught	.20	.08	.02
☐ 420 Steve McCatty	.14	.06	.01
☐ 421 Tim Wallach	.35	.15	.03
☐ 422 Larry Parrish	.14	.06	.01
☐ 423 Brian Downing	.20	.08	.02
☐ 424 Britt Burns	.14	.06	.01
☐ 425 David Green	.14	.06	.01
☐ 426 Jerry Mumphrey	.14	.06	.01
☐ 427 Ivan DeJesus	.14	.06	.01
☐ 428 Mario Soto	.14	.06	.01
☐ 429 Gene Richards	.14	.06	.01
☐ 430 Dale Berra	.14	.06	.01
☐ 431 Darrell Evans	.20	.08	.02
☐ 432 Glenn Hubbard	.14	.06	.01
☐ 433 Jody Davis	.14	.06	.01
☐ 434 Danny Heep	.14	.06	.01
☐ 435 Ed Nunez	.25	.10	.02
☐ 436 Bobby Castillo	.14	.06	.01
☐ 437 Ernie Whitt	.14	.06	.01
☐ 438 Scott Ullger	.14	.06	.01
☐ 439 Doyle Alexander	.14	.06	.01
☐ 440 Domingo Ramos	.14	.06	.01
☐ 441 Craig Swan	.14	.06	.01
☐ 442 Warren Brusstar	.14	.06	.01
☐ 443 Len Barker	.14	.06	.01
☐ 444 Mike Easler	.14	.06	.01
☐ 445 Renie Martin	.14	.06	.01
☐ 446 Dennis Rasmussen	.60	.25	.06
☐ 447 Ted Power	.20	.08	.02
☐ 448 Charles Hudson	.20	.08	.02
☐ 449 Danny Cox	.25	.10	.02
☐ 450 Kevin Bass	.20	.08	.02
☐ 451 Daryl Sconiers	.14	.06	.01
☐ 452 Scott Fletcher	.20	.08	.02
☐ 453 Bryn Smith	.20	.08	.02
☐ 454 Jim Dwyer	.14	.06	.01
☐ 455 Rob Picciolo	.14	.06	.01
☐ 456 Enos Cabell	.14	.06	.01
☐ 457 Dennis Boyd	.50	.20	.05
☐ 458 Butch Wynegar	.14	.06	.01
☐ 459 Burt Hooton	.14	.06	.01
☐ 460 Ron Hassey	.14	.06	.01
☐ 461 Danny Jackson	1.00	.40	.10
☐ 462 Bob Kearney	.14	.06	.01
☐ 463 Terry Francona	.14	.06	.01
☐ 464 Wayne Tolleson	.14	.06	.01
☐ 465 Mickey Rivers	.14	.06	.01
☐ 466 John Wathan	.14	.06	.01
☐ 467 Bill Almon	.14	.06	.01
☐ 468 George Vukovich	.14	.06	.01
☐ 469 Steve Kemp	.14	.06	.01
☐ 470 Ken Landreaux	.14	.06	.01
☐ 471 Milt Wilcox	.14	.06	.01
☐ 472 Tippy Martinez	.14	.06	.01
☐ 473 Ted Simmons	.20	.08	.02
☐ 474 Tim Foli	.14	.06	.01
☐ 475 George Hendrick	.14	.06	.01
☐ 476 Terry Puhl	.14	.06	.01
☐ 477 Von Hayes	.30	.12	.03
☐ 478 Bobby Brown	.14	.06	.01
☐ 479 Lee Lacy	.14	.06	.01
☐ 480 Joel Youngblood	.14	.06	.01
☐ 481 Jim Slaton	.14	.06	.01
☐ 482 Mike Fitzgerald	.14	.06	.01
☐ 483 Keith Moreland	.14	.06	.01
☐ 484 Ron Roenicke	.14	.06	.01
☐ 485 Luis Leal	.14	.06	.01
☐ 486 Bryan Oelkers	.14	.06	.01
☐ 487 Bruce Berenyi	.14	.06	.01
☐ 488 LaMarr Hoyt	.14	.06	.01
☐ 489 Joe Nolan	.14	.06	.01
☐ 490 Marshall Edwards	.14	.06	.01
☐ 491 Mike Laga	.14	.06	.01
☐ 492 Rick Cerone	.14	.06	.01
☐ 493 Rick Miller UER	.14	.06	.01
(listed as Mike on card front)			
☐ 494 Rick Honeycutt	.14	.06	.01
☐ 495 Mike Hargrove	.14	.06	.01
☐ 496 Joe Simpson	.14	.06	.01
☐ 497 Keith Atherton	.14	.06	.01
☐ 498 Chris Welsh	.14	.06	.01
☐ 499 Bruce Kison	.14	.06	.01
☐ 500 Bobby Johnson	.14	.06	.01
☐ 501 Jerry Koosman	.20	.08	.02
☐ 502 Frank DiPino	.14	.06	.01
☐ 503 Tony Perez	.65	.25	.06
☐ 504 Ken Oberkfell	.14	.06	.01
☐ 505 Mark Thurmond	.14	.06	.01
☐ 506 Joe Price	.14	.06	.01
☐ 507 Pascual Perez	.30	.12	.03
☐ 508 Marvell Wynne	.20	.08	.02
☐ 509 Mike Krukow	.14	.06	.01
☐ 510 Dick Ruthven	.14	.06	.01
☐ 511 Al Cowens	.14	.06	.01
☐ 512 Cliff Johnson	.14	.06	.01
☐ 513 Randy Bush	.25	.10	.02
☐ 514 Sammy Stewart	.14	.06	.01
☐ 515 Bill Schroeder	.14	.06	.01
☐ 516 Aurelio Lopez	.14	.06	.01
☐ 517 Mike Brown	.14	.06	.01
(Red Sox pitcher)			
☐ 518 Graig Nettles	.25	.10	.02
☐ 519 Dave Sax	.14	.06	.01
☐ 520 Jerry Willard	.20	.08	.02
☐ 521 Paul Splittorff	.14	.06	.01
☐ 522 Tom Burgmeier	.14	.06	.01
☐ 523 Chris Speier	.14	.06	.01
☐ 524 Bobby Clark	.14	.06	.01
☐ 525 George Wright	.14	.06	.01
☐ 526 Dennis Lamp	.14	.06	.01
☐ 527 Tony Scott	.14	.06	.01
☐ 528 Ed Whitson	.14	.06	.01
☐ 529 Ron Reed	.14	.06	.01
☐ 530 Charlie Puleo	.14	.06	.01
☐ 531 Jerry Royster	.14	.06	.01
☐ 532 Don Robinson	.14	.06	.01
☐ 533 Steve Trout	.14	.06	.01
☐ 534 Bruce Sutter	.30	.12	.03
☐ 535 Bob Horner	.25	.10	.02
☐ 536 Pat Tabler	.20	.08	.02
☐ 537 Chris Chambliss	.20	.08	.02
☐ 538 Bob Ojeda	.25	.10	.02
☐ 539 Alan Ashby	.14	.06	.01
☐ 540 Jay Johnstone	.20	.08	.02
☐ 541 Bob Dernier	.14	.06	.01
☐ 542 Brook Jacoby	1.00	.40	.10
☐ 543 U.L. Washington	.14	.06	.01
☐ 544 Danny Darwin	.14	.06	.01
☐ 545 Kiko Garcia	.14	.06	.01
☐ 546 Vance Law UER	.14	.06	.01
(listed as P on card front)			
☐ 547 Tug McGraw	.25	.10	.02
☐ 548 Dave Smith	.14	.06	.01
☐ 549 Len Matuszek	.14	.06	.01
☐ 550 Tom Hume	.14	.06	.01
☐ 551 Dave Dravecky	.45	.18	.04

☐ 552	Rick Rhoden	.14	.06	.01
☐ 553	Duane Kuiper	.14	.06	.01
☐ 554	Rusty Staub	.25	.10	.02
☐ 555	Bill Campbell	.14	.06	.01
☐ 556	Mike Torrez	.14	.06	.01
☐ 557	Dave Henderson	1.75	.70	.17
☐ 558	Len Whitehouse	.14	.06	.01
☐ 559	Barry Bonnell	.14	.06	.01
☐ 560	Rick Lysander	.14	.06	.01
☐ 561	Garth Iorg	.14	.06	.01
☐ 562	Bryan Clark	.14	.06	.01
☐ 563	Brian Giles	.14	.06	.01
☐ 564	Vern Ruhle	.14	.06	.01
☐ 565	Steve Bedrosian	.25	.10	.02
☐ 566	Larry McWilliams	.14	.06	.01
☐ 567	Jeff Leonard UER (listed as P on card front)	.20	.08	.02
☐ 568	Alan Wiggins	.14	.06	.01
☐ 569	Jeff Russell	.65	.25	.06
☐ 570	Salome Barojas	.14	.06	.01
☐ 571	Dane Iorg	.14	.06	.01
☐ 572	Bob Knepper	.14	.06	.01
☐ 573	Gary Lavelle	.14	.06	.01
☐ 574	Gorman Thomas	.20	.08	.02
☐ 575	Manny Trillo	.14	.06	.01
☐ 576	Jim Palmer	3.00	1.25	.30
☐ 577	Dale Murray	.14	.06	.01
☐ 578	Tom Brookens	.14	.06	.01
☐ 579	Rich Gedman	.14	.06	.01
☐ 580	Bill Doran	.90	.40	.09
☐ 581	Steve Yeager	.14	.06	.01
☐ 582	Dan Spillner	.14	.06	.01
☐ 583	Dan Quisenberry	.25	.10	.02
☐ 584	Rance Mulliniks	.14	.06	.01
☐ 585	Storm Davis	.20	.08	.02
☐ 586	Dave Schmidt	.14	.06	.01
☐ 587	Bill Russell	.20	.08	.02
☐ 588	Pat Sheridan	.20	.08	.02
☐ 589	Rafael Ramirez UER (A's on front)	.20	.08	.02
☐ 590	Bud Anderson	.14	.06	.01
☐ 591	George Frazier	.14	.06	.01
☐ 592	Lee Tunnell	.14	.06	.01
☐ 593	Kirk Gibson	1.25	.50	.12
☐ 594	Scott McGregor	.14	.06	.01
☐ 595	Bob Bailor	.14	.06	.01
☐ 596	Tommy Herr	.20	.08	.02
☐ 597	Luis Sanchez	.14	.06	.01
☐ 598	Dave Engle	.14	.06	.01
☐ 599	Craig McMurtry	.14	.06	.01
☐ 600	Carlos Diaz	.14	.06	.01
☐ 601	Tom O'Malley	.14	.06	.01
☐ 602	Nick Esasky	.40	.16	.04
☐ 603	Ron Hodges	.14	.06	.01
☐ 604	Ed VandeBerg	.14	.06	.01
☐ 605	Alfredo Griffin	.14	.06	.01
☐ 606	Glenn Hoffman	.14	.06	.01
☐ 607	Hubie Brooks	.40	.16	.04
☐ 608	Richard Barnes UER (photo actually Neal Heaton)	.14	.06	.01
☐ 609	Greg Walker	.25	.10	.02
☐ 610	Ken Singleton	.20	.08	.02
☐ 611	Mark Clear	.14	.06	.01
☐ 612	Buck Martinez	.14	.06	.01
☐ 613	Ken Griffey	.35	.15	.03
☐ 614	Reid Nichols	.14	.06	.01
☐ 615	Doug Sisk	.14	.06	.01
☐ 616	Bob Brenly	.14	.06	.01
☐ 617	Joey McLaughlin	.14	.06	.01
☐ 618	Glenn Wilson	.14	.06	.01
☐ 619	Bob Stoddard	.14	.06	.01
☐ 620	Lenn Sakata UER (listed as Len on card front)	.14	.06	.01
☐ 621	Mike Young	.20	.08	.02
☐ 622	John Stefero	.14	.06	.01
☐ 623	Carmelo Martinez	.25	.10	.02
☐ 624	Dave Bergman	.14	.06	.01
☐ 625	Runnin' Reds UER (sic, Redbirds) David Green Willie McGee Lonnie Smith Ozzie Smith	.60	.25	.06
☐ 626	Rudy May	.14	.06	.01
☐ 627	Matt Keough	.14	.06	.01
☐ 628	Jose DeLeon	.50	.20	.05
☐ 629	Jim Essian	.20	.08	.02
☐ 630	Darnell Coles	.25	.10	.02
☐ 631	Mike Warren	.14	.06	.01
☐ 632	Del Crandall MG	.14	.06	.01
☐ 633	Dennis Martinez	.25	.10	.02
☐ 634	Mike Moore	.40	.16	.04
☐ 635	Lary Sorensen	.14	.06	.01
☐ 636	Ricky Nelson	.14	.06	.01
☐ 637	Omar Moreno	.14	.06	.01
☐ 638	Charlie Hough	.14	.06	.01
☐ 639	Dennis Eckersley	1.25	.50	.12
☐ 640	Walt Terrell	.40	.16	.04
☐ 641	Denny Walling	.14	.06	.01
☐ 642	Dave Anderson	.25	.10	.02
☐ 643	Jose Oquendo	.40	.16	.04
☐ 644	Bob Stanley	.14	.06	.01
☐ 645	Dave Geisel	.14	.06	.01
☐ 646	Scott Garrelts	.50	.20	.05
☐ 647	Gary Pettis	.40	.16	.04
☐ 648	Duke Snider Puzzle Card	.20	.08	.02
☐ 649	Johnnie LeMaster	.14	.06	.01
☐ 650	Dave Collins	.14	.06	.01
☐ 651	The Chicken	.35	.15	.03
☐ 652	DK Checklist (unnumbered)	.20	.02	.00
☐ 653	Checklist 1-130 (unnumbered)	.20	.02	.00
☐ 654	Checklist 131-234 (unnumbered)	.20	.02	.00
☐ 655	Checklist 235-338 (unnumbered)	.20	.02	.00
☐ 656	Checklist 339-442 (unnumbered)	.20	.02	.00
☐ 657	Checklist 443-546 (unnumbered)	.20	.02	.00
☐ 658	Checklist 547-651 (unnumbered)	.20	.02	.00
☐ A	Living Legends A Gaylord Perry Rollie Fingers	5.50	2.50	.55
☐ B	Living Legends B Carl Yastrzemski Johnny Bench	8.50	3.75	.85

1984 Donruss Action All-Stars

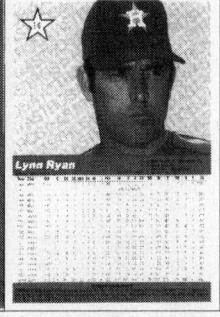

The cards in this 60-card set measure approximately 3 1/2" by 5". For the second year in a row, Donruss issued a postcard-size card set. The set was distributed with a 63-piece Ted Williams puzzle. Unlike last year, when the fronts of the cards contained both an action and a portrait shot of the player, the fronts of this year's cards contain only an action photo. On the backs, the top section contains the card number and a full-color portrait of the player pictured on the front. The bottom half features the player's career statistics.

		MINT	EXC	G-VG
	COMPLETE SET (60)	7.50	3.25	.75
	COMMON PLAYER (1-60)	.07	.03	.01
☐ 1	Gary Lavelle	.07	.03	.01
☐ 2	Willie McGee	.20	.08	.02
☐ 3	Tony Pena	.07	.03	.01
☐ 4	Lou Whitaker	.15	.06	.01
☐ 5	Robin Yount	.50	.20	.05
☐ 6	Doug DeCinces	.07	.03	.01
☐ 7	John Castino	.07	.03	.01
☐ 8	Terry Kennedy	.07	.03	.01

☐ 9	Rickey Henderson	1.00	.40	.10
☐ 10	Bob Horner	.15	.06	.01
☐ 11	Harold Baines	.15	.06	.01
☐ 12	Buddy Bell	.07	.03	.01
☐ 13	Fernando Valenzuela	.15	.06	.01
☐ 14	Nolan Ryan	1.25	.50	.12
☐ 15	Andre Thornton	.07	.03	.01
☐ 16	Gary Redus	.07	.03	.01
☐ 17	Pedro Guerrero	.15	.06	.01
☐ 18	Andre Dawson	.40	.16	.04
☐ 19	Dave Stieb	.10	.04	.01
☐ 20	Cal Ripken	1.00	.40	.10
☐ 21	Ken Griffey	.15	.06	.01
☐ 22	Wade Boggs	1.00	.40	.10
☐ 23	Keith Hernandez	.15	.06	.01
☐ 24	Steve Carlton	.35	.15	.03
☐ 25	Hal McRae	.10	.04	.01
☐ 26	John Lowenstein	.07	.03	.01
☐ 27	Fred Lynn	.10	.04	.01
☐ 28	Bill Buckner	.10	.04	.01
☐ 29	Chris Chambliss	.07	.03	.01
☐ 30	Richie Zisk	.07	.03	.01
☐ 31	Jack Clark	.15	.06	.01
☐ 32	George Hendrick	.07	.03	.01
☐ 33	Bill Madlock	.07	.03	.01
☐ 34	Lance Parrish	.20	.08	.02
☐ 35	Paul Molitor	.30	.12	.03
☐ 36	Reggie Jackson	.75	.30	.07
☐ 37	Kent Hrbek	.15	.06	.01
☐ 38	Steve Garvey	.35	.15	.03
☐ 39	Carney Lansford	.10	.04	.01
☐ 40	Dale Murphy	.45	.18	.04
☐ 41	Greg Luzinski	.10	.04	.01
☐ 42	Larry Parrish	.07	.03	.01
☐ 43	Ryne Sandberg	1.00	.40	.10
☐ 44	Dickie Thon	.07	.03	.01
☐ 45	Bert Blyleven	.15	.06	.01
☐ 46	Ron Oester	.07	.03	.01
☐ 47	Dusty Baker	.07	.03	.01
☐ 48	Steve Rogers	.07	.03	.01
☐ 49	Jim Clancy	.07	.03	.01
☐ 50	Eddie Murray	.40	.16	.04
☐ 51	Ron Guidry	.20	.08	.02
☐ 52	Jim Rice	.20	.08	.02
☐ 53	Tom Seaver	.75	.30	.07
☐ 54	Pete Rose	.75	.30	.07
☐ 55	George Brett	.50	.20	.05
☐ 56	Dan Quisenberry	.10	.04	.01
☐ 57	Mike Schmidt	1.00	.40	.10
☐ 58	Ted Simmons	.10	.04	.01
☐ 59	Dave Righetti	.15	.06	.01
☐ 60	Checklist Card	.07	.03	.01

1984 Donruss Champions

The cards in this 60-card set measure approximately 3 1/2" by 5". The 1984 Donruss Champions set is a hybrid photo/artwork issue. Grand Champions, listed GC in the checklist below, feature the artwork of Dick Perez of Perez-Steele Galleries. Current players in the set feature photographs. The theme of this postcard-size set features a Grand Champion and those current players that are directly behind him in a baseball statistical category, for example, Season Home Runs (1-7), Career Home Runs (8-13), Season Batting Average (14-19),

Career Batting Average (20-25), Career Hits (26-30), Career Victories (31-36), Career Strikeouts (37-42), Most Valuable Players (43-49), World Series stars (50-54), and All-Star heroes (55-59). The cards were issued in cello packs with pieces of the Duke Snider puzzle.

		MINT	EXC	G-VG
COMPLETE SET (60)		7.50	3.25	.75
COMMON PLAYER (1-60)		.07	.03	.01
☐ 1	Babe Ruth GC	1.00	.40	.10
☐ 2	George Foster	.10	.04	.01
☐ 3	Dave Kingman	.10	.04	.01
☐ 4	Jim Rice	.15	.06	.01
☐ 5	Gorman Thomas	.07	.03	.01
☐ 6	Ben Oglivie	.07	.03	.01
☐ 7	Jeff Burroughs	.07	.03	.01
☐ 8	Hank Aaron GC	.35	.15	.03
☐ 9	Reggie Jackson	.60	.25	.06
☐ 10	Carl Yastrzemski	.50	.20	.05
☐ 11	Mike Schmidt	1.00	.40	.10
☐ 12	Graig Nettles	.10	.04	.01
☐ 13	Greg Luzinski	.07	.03	.01
☐ 14	Ted Williams GC	.50	.20	.05
☐ 15	George Brett	.45	.18	.04
☐ 16	Wade Boggs	.75	.30	.07
☐ 17	Hal McRae	.10	.04	.01
☐ 18	Bill Buckner	.10	.04	.01
☐ 19	Eddie Murray	.40	.16	.04
☐ 20	Rogers Hornsby GC	.10	.04	.01
☐ 21	Rod Carew	.35	.15	.03
☐ 22	Bill Madlock	.07	.03	.01
☐ 23	Lonnie Smith	.10	.04	.01
☐ 24	Cecil Cooper	.10	.04	.01
☐ 25	Ken Griffey	.10	.04	.01
☐ 26	Ty Cobb GC	.50	.20	.05
☐ 27	Pete Rose	.60	.25	.06
☐ 28	Rusty Staub	.07	.03	.01
☐ 29	Tony Perez	.20	.08	.02
☐ 30	Al Oliver	.10	.04	.01
☐ 31	Cy Young GC	.15	.06	.01
☐ 32	Gaylord Perry	.20	.08	.02
☐ 33	Ferguson Jenkins	.20	.08	.02
☐ 34	Phil Niekro	.20	.08	.02
☐ 35	Jim Palmer	.30	.12	.03
☐ 36	Tommy John	.10	.04	.01
☐ 37	Walter Johnson GC	.20	.08	.02
☐ 38	Steve Carlton	.30	.12	.03
☐ 39	Nolan Ryan	1.00	.40	.10
☐ 40	Tom Seaver	.60	.25	.06
☐ 41	Don Sutton	.15	.06	.01
☐ 42	Bert Blyleven	.15	.06	.01
☐ 43	Frank Robinson GC	.15	.06	.01
☐ 44	Joe Morgan	.25	.10	.02
☐ 45	Rollie Fingers	.25	.10	.02
☐ 46	Keith Hernandez	.15	.06	.01
☐ 47	Robin Yount	.40	.16	.04
☐ 48	Cal Ripken	.90	.40	.09
☐ 49	Dale Murphy	.35	.15	.03
☐ 50	Mickey Mantle GC	1.00	.40	.10
☐ 51	Johnny Bench	.45	.18	.04
☐ 52	Carlton Fisk	.45	.18	.04
☐ 53	Tug McGraw	.07	.03	.01
☐ 54	Paul Molitor	.15	.06	.01
☐ 55	Carl Hubbell GC	.10	.04	.01
☐ 56	Steve Garvey	.30	.12	.03
☐ 57	Dave Parker	.20	.08	.02
☐ 58	Gary Carter	.20	.08	.02
☐ 59	Fred Lynn	.10	.04	.01
☐ 60	Checklist Card	.07	.03	.01

1985 Donruss

The cards in this 660-card set measure 2 1/2" by 3 1/2". The 1985 Donruss regular issue cards have fronts that feature jet black borders on which orange lines have been placed. The fronts contain the standard team logo, player's name, position, and Donruss logo. The cards were distributed with puzzle pieces from a Dick Perez rendition of Lou Gehrig. The first 26 cards of the set feature Diamond Kings (DK), for the fourth year in a row; the artwork on the Diamond Kings was again produced by the Perez-Steele Galleries. Cards 27-46 feature Rated Rookies (RR). The unnumbered checklist cards are arbitrarily numbered below as numbers 654 through 660. This set is noted for

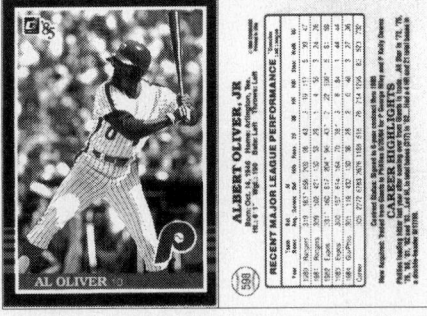

containing the Rookie Cards of Roger Clemens, Alvin Davis, Eric Davis, Shawon Dunston, Dwight Gooden, Orel Hershiser, Jimmy Key, Mark Langston, Terry Pendleton, Kirby Puckett, Jose Rijo, Bret Saberhagen, and Danny Tartabull.

	MINT	EXC	G-VG
COMPLETE SET (660)	180.00	80.00	27.00
COMMON PLAYER (1-660)	.08	.03	.01

		MINT	EXC	G-VG
☐ 1	Ryne Sandberg DK	3.00	.75	.15
☐ 2	Doug DeCinces DK	.12	.05	.01
☐ 3	Richard Dotson DK	.12	.05	.01
☐ 4	Bert Blyleven DK	.15	.06	.01
☐ 5	Lou Whitaker DK	.17	.07	.01
☐ 6	Dan Quisenberry DK	.15	.06	.01
☐ 7	Don Mattingly DK	3.50	1.50	.35
☐ 8	Carney Lansford DK	.12	.05	.01
☐ 9	Frank Tanana DK	.12	.05	.01
☐ 10	Willie Upshaw DK	.12	.05	.01
☐ 11	Claudell Washington DK	.12	.05	.01
☐ 12	Mike Marshall DK	.12	.05	.01
☐ 13	Joaquin Andujar DK	.12	.05	.01
☐ 14	Cal Ripken DK	3.00	1.25	.30
☐ 15	Jim Rice DK	.17	.07	.01
☐ 16	Don Sutton DK	.17	.07	.01
☐ 17	Frank Viola DK	.30	.12	.03
☐ 18	Alvin Davis DK	.35	.15	.03
☐ 19	Mario Soto DK	.12	.05	.01
☐ 20	Jose Cruz DK	.12	.05	.01
☐ 21	Charlie Lea DK	.12	.05	.01
☐ 22	Jesse Orosco DK	.12	.05	.01
☐ 23	Juan Samuel DK	.25	.10	.02
☐ 24	Tony Pena DK	.12	.05	.01
☐ 25	Tony Gwynn DK	1.25	.50	.12
☐ 26	Bob Brenly DK	.12	.05	.01
☐ 27	Danny Tartabull RR	7.50	3.25	.75
☐ 28	Mike Bielecki RR	.40	.16	.04
☐ 29	Steve Lyons RR	.35	.15	.03
☐ 30	Jeff Reed RR	.12	.05	.01
☐ 31	Tony Brewer RR	.08	.03	.01
☐ 32	John Morris RR	.15	.06	.01
☐ 33	Daryl Boston RR	.45	.18	.04
☐ 34	Al Pulido RR	.08	.03	.01
☐ 35	Steve Kiefer RR	.08	.03	.01
☐ 36	Larry Sheets RR	.15	.06	.01
☐ 37	Scott Bradley RR	.17	.07	.01
☐ 38	Calvin Schiraldi RR	.15	.06	.01
☐ 39	Shawon Dunston RR	5.50	2.50	.55
☐ 40	Charlie Mitchell RR	.08	.03	.01
☐ 41	Billy Hatcher RR	.90	.40	.09
☐ 42	Russ Stephans RR	.08	.03	.01
☐ 43	Alejandro Sanchez RR	.08	.03	.01
☐ 44	Steve Jeltz RR	.12	.05	.01
☐ 45	Jim Traber RR	.15	.06	.01
☐ 46	Doug Loman RR	.08	.03	.01
☐ 47	Eddie Murray	1.25	.50	.12
☐ 48	Robin Yount	1.50	.60	.15
☐ 49	Lance Parrish	.25	.10	.02
☐ 50	Jim Rice	.20	.08	.02
☐ 51	Dave Winfield	.85	.35	.08
☐ 52	Fernando Valenzuela	.17	.07	.01
☐ 53	George Brett	1.50	.60	.15
☐ 54	Dave Kingman	.15	.06	.01
☐ 55	Gary Carter	.40	.16	.04
☐ 56	Buddy Bell	.12	.05	.01
☐ 57	Reggie Jackson	1.25	.50	.12
☐ 58	Harold Baines	.35	.15	.03
☐ 59	Ozzie Smith	1.00	.40	.10
☐ 60	Nolan Ryan	6.50	2.75	.65
☐ 61	Mike Schmidt	3.50	1.50	.35
☐ 62	Dave Parker	.35	.15	.03
☐ 63	Tony Gwynn	4.25	1.75	.42
☐ 64	Tony Pena	.12	.05	.01
☐ 65	Jack Clark	.25	.10	.02
☐ 66	Dale Murphy	.75	.30	.07
☐ 67	Ryne Sandberg	7.00	3.00	.70
☐ 68	Keith Hernandez	.25	.10	.02
☐ 69	Alvin Davis	1.75	.70	.17
☐ 70	Kent Hrbek	.35	.15	.03
☐ 71	Willie Upshaw	.08	.03	.01
☐ 72	Dave Engle	.08	.03	.01
☐ 73	Alfredo Griffin	.08	.03	.01
☐ 74A	Jack Perconte (Career Highlights takes four lines)	.12	.05	.01
☐ 74B	Jack Perconte (Career Highlights takes three lines)	.12	.05	.01
☐ 75	Jesse Orosco	.08	.03	.01
☐ 76	Jody Davis	.08	.03	.01
☐ 77	Bob Horner	.12	.05	.01
☐ 78	Larry McWilliams	.08	.03	.01
☐ 79	Joel Youngblood	.08	.03	.01
☐ 80	Alan Wiggins	.08	.03	.01
☐ 81	Ron Oester	.08	.03	.01
☐ 82	Ozzie Virgil	.08	.03	.01
☐ 83	Ricky Horton	.15	.06	.01
☐ 84	Bill Doran	.15	.06	.01
☐ 85	Rod Carew	1.00	.40	.10
☐ 86	LaMarr Hoyt	.08	.03	.01
☐ 87	Tim Wallach	.15	.06	.01
☐ 88	Mike Flanagan	.12	.05	.01
☐ 89	Jim Sundberg	.08	.03	.01
☐ 90	Chet Lemon	.08	.03	.01
☐ 91	Bob Stanley	.08	.03	.01
☐ 92	Willie Randolph	.12	.05	.01
☐ 93	Bill Russell	.12	.05	.01
☐ 94	Julio Franco	1.25	.50	.12
☐ 95	Dan Quisenberry	.12	.05	.01
☐ 96	Bill Caudill	.08	.03	.01
☐ 97	Bill Gullickson	.12	.05	.01
☐ 98	Danny Darwin	.08	.03	.01
☐ 99	Curtis Wilkerson	.08	.03	.01
☐ 100	Bud Black	.12	.05	.01
☐ 101	Tony Phillips	.08	.03	.01
☐ 102	Tony Bernazard	.08	.03	.01
☐ 103	Jay Howell	.12	.05	.01
☐ 104	Burt Hooton	.08	.03	.01
☐ 105	Milt Wilcox	.08	.03	.01
☐ 106	Rich Dauer	.08	.03	.01
☐ 107	Don Sutton	.35	.15	.03
☐ 108	Mike Witt	.08	.03	.01
☐ 109	Bruce Sutter	.15	.06	.01
☐ 110	Enos Cabell	.08	.03	.01
☐ 111	John Denny	.08	.03	.01
☐ 112	Dave Dravecky	.15	.06	.01
☐ 113	Marvell Wynne	.08	.03	.01
☐ 114	Johnnie LeMaster	.08	.03	.01
☐ 115	Chuck Porter	.08	.03	.01
☐ 116	John Gibbons	.08	.03	.01
☐ 117	Keith Moreland	.08	.03	.01
☐ 118	Darnell Coles	.08	.03	.01
☐ 119	Dennis Lamp	.08	.03	.01
☐ 120	Ron Davis	.08	.03	.01
☐ 121	Nick Esasky	.12	.05	.01
☐ 122	Vance Law	.08	.03	.01
☐ 123	Gary Roenicke	.08	.03	.01
☐ 124	Bill Schroeder	.08	.03	.01
☐ 125	Dave Rozema	.08	.03	.01
☐ 126	Bobby Meacham	.08	.03	.01
☐ 127	Marty Barrett	.12	.05	.01
☐ 128	R.J. Reynolds	.20	.08	.02
☐ 129	Ernie Camacho UER (photo actually Rich Thompson)	.08	.03	.01
☐ 130	Jorge Orta	.08	.03	.01
☐ 131	Lary Sorensen	.08	.03	.01
☐ 132	Terry Francona	.08	.03	.01
☐ 133	Fred Lynn	.17	.07	.01
☐ 134	Bob Jones	.08	.03	.01
☐ 135	Jerry Hairston	.08	.03	.01
☐ 136	Kevin Bass	.12	.05	.01
☐ 137	Garry Maddox	.08	.03	.01
☐ 138	Dave LaPoint	.08	.03	.01
☐ 139	Kevin McReynolds	.90	.40	.09
☐ 140	Wayne Krenchicki	.08	.03	.01
☐ 141	Rafael Ramirez	.08	.03	.01
☐ 142	Rod Scurry	.08	.03	.01
☐ 143	Greg Minton	.08	.03	.01
☐ 144	Tim Stoddard	.08	.03	.01
☐ 145	Steve Henderson	.08	.03	.01
☐ 146	George Bell	.90	.40	.09
☐ 147	Dave Meier	.08	.03	.01
☐ 148	Sammy Stewart	.08	.03	.01
☐ 149	Mark Brouhard	.08	.03	.01
☐ 150	Larry Herndon	.08	.03	.01
☐ 151	Oil Can Boyd	.12	.05	.01

☐ 152	Brian Dayett	.08	.03	.01
☐ 153	Tom Niedenfuer	.08	.03	.01
☐ 154	Brook Jacoby	.15	.06	.01
☐ 155	Onix Concepcion	.08	.03	.01
☐ 156	Tim Conroy	.08	.03	.01
☐ 157	Joe Hesketh	.30	.12	.03
☐ 158	Brian Downing	.12	.05	.01
☐ 159	Tommy Dunbar	.08	.03	.01
☐ 160	Marc Hill	.08	.03	.01
☐ 161	Phil Garner	.12	.05	.01
☐ 162	Jerry Davis	.08	.03	.01
☐ 163	Bill Campbell	.08	.03	.01
☐ 164	John Franco	1.50	.60	.15
☐ 165	Len Barker	.08	.03	.01
☐ 166	Benny Distefano	.08	.03	.01
☐ 167	George Frazier	.08	.03	.01
☐ 168	Tito Landrum	.08	.03	.01
☐ 169	Cal Ripken	7.00	3.00	.70
☐ 170	Cecil Cooper	.12	.05	.01
☐ 171	Alan Trammell	.60	.25	.06
☐ 172	Wade Boggs	5.00	2.25	.50
☐ 173	Don Baylor	.15	.06	.01
☐ 174	Pedro Guerrero	.25	.10	.02
☐ 175	Frank White	.08	.03	.01
☐ 176	Rickey Henderson	5.00	2.25	.50
☐ 177	Charlie Lea	.08	.03	.01
☐ 178	Pete O'Brien	.12	.05	.01
☐ 179	Doug DeCinces	.08	.03	.01
☐ 180	Ron Kittle	.12	.05	.01
☐ 181	George Hendrick	.08	.03	.01
☐ 182	Joe Niekro	.12	.05	.01
☐ 183	Juan Samuel	1.00	.40	.10
☐ 184	Mario Soto	.08	.03	.01
☐ 185	Goose Gossage	.15	.06	.01
☐ 186	Johnny Ray	.08	.03	.01
☐ 187	Bob Brenly	.08	.03	.01
☐ 188	Craig McMurtry	.08	.03	.01
☐ 189	Leon Durham	.08	.03	.01
☐ 190	Dwight Gooden	13.00	5.75	1.75
☐ 191	Barry Bonnell	.08	.03	.01
☐ 192	Tim Teufel	.12	.05	.01
☐ 193	Dave Stieb	.17	.07	.01
☐ 194	Mickey Hatcher	.08	.03	.01
☐ 195	Jesse Barfield	.17	.07	.01
☐ 196	Al Cowens	.08	.03	.01
☐ 197	Hubie Brooks	.15	.06	.01
☐ 198	Steve Trout	.08	.03	.01
☐ 199	Glenn Hubbard	.08	.03	.01
☐ 200	Bill Madlock	.12	.05	.01
☐ 201	Jeff Robinson	.15	.06	.01
	(Giants pitcher)			
☐ 202	Eric Show	.08	.03	.01
☐ 203	Dave Concepcion	.12	.05	.01
☐ 204	Ivan DeJesus	.08	.03	.01
☐ 205	Neil Allen	.08	.03	.01
☐ 206	Jerry Mumphrey	.08	.03	.01
☐ 207	Mike Brown	.08	.03	.01
	(Angels OF)			
☐ 208	Carlton Fisk	1.00	.40	.10
☐ 209	Bryn Smith	.12	.05	.01
☐ 210	Tippy Martinez	.08	.03	.01
☐ 211	Dion James	.08	.03	.01
☐ 212	Willie Hernandez	.08	.03	.01
☐ 213	Mike Easler	.08	.03	.01
☐ 214	Ron Guidry	.17	.07	.01
☐ 215	Rick Honeycutt	.08	.03	.01
☐ 216	Brett Butler	.25	.10	.02
☐ 217	Larry Gura	.08	.03	.01
☐ 218	Ray Burris	.08	.03	.01
☐ 219	Steve Rogers	.08	.03	.01
☐ 220	Frank Tanana UER	.12	.05	.01
	(Bats Left listed twice on card back)			
☐ 221	Ned Yost	.08	.03	.01
☐ 222	Bret Saberhagen UER	8.00	3.50	.80
	(18 career IP on back)			
☐ 223	Mike Davis	.08	.03	.01
☐ 224	Bert Blyleven	.25	.10	.02
☐ 225	Steve Kemp	.08	.03	.01
☐ 226	Jerry Reuss	.08	.03	.01
☐ 227	Darrell Evans UER	.15	.06	.01
	(80 homers in 1980)			
☐ 228	Wayne Gross	.08	.03	.01
☐ 229	Jim Gantner	.08	.03	.01
☐ 230	Bob Boone	.12	.05	.01
☐ 231	Lonnie Smith	.15	.06	.01
☐ 232	Frank DiPino	.08	.03	.01
☐ 233	Jerry Koosman	.12	.05	.01
☐ 234	Graig Nettles	.15	.06	.01
☐ 235	John Tudor	.15	.06	.01
☐ 236	John Rabb	.08	.03	.01
☐ 237	Rick Manning	.08	.03	.01
☐ 238	Mike Fitzgerald	.08	.03	.01
☐ 239	Gary Matthews	.08	.03	.01
☐ 240	Jim Presley	.20	.08	.02
☐ 241	Dave Collins	.08	.03	.01
☐ 242	Gary Gaetti	.15	.06	.01
☐ 243	Dann Bilardello	.08	.03	.01
☐ 244	Rudy Law	.08	.03	.01
☐ 245	John Lowenstein	.08	.03	.01
☐ 246	Tom Tellmann	.08	.03	.01
☐ 247	Howard Johnson	2.75	1.10	.27
☐ 248	Ray Fontenot	.08	.03	.01
☐ 249	Tony Armas	.08	.03	.01
☐ 250	Candy Maldonado	.15	.06	.01
☐ 251	Mike Jeffcoat	.12	.05	.01
☐ 252	Dane Iorg	.08	.03	.01
☐ 253	Bruce Bochte	.08	.03	.01
☐ 254	Pete Rose	1.25	.50	.12
☐ 255	Don Aase	.08	.03	.01
☐ 256	George Wright	.08	.03	.01
☐ 257	Britt Burns	.08	.03	.01
☐ 258	Mike Scott	.20	.08	.02
☐ 259	Len Matuszek	.08	.03	.01
☐ 260	Dave Rucker	.08	.03	.01
☐ 261	Craig Lefferts	.12	.05	.01
☐ 262	Jay Tibbs	.08	.03	.01
☐ 263	Bruce Benedict	.08	.03	.01
☐ 264	Don Robinson	.08	.03	.01
☐ 265	Gary Lavelle	.08	.03	.01
☐ 266	Scott Sanderson	.12	.05	.01
☐ 267	Matt Young	.08	.03	.01
☐ 268	Ernie Whitt	.08	.03	.01
☐ 269	Houston Jimenez	.08	.03	.01
☐ 270	Ken Dixon	.08	.03	.01
☐ 271	Pete Ladd	.08	.03	.01
☐ 272	Juan Berenguer	.08	.03	.01
☐ 273	Roger Clemens	37.50	15.00	4.00
☐ 274	Rick Cerone	.08	.03	.01
☐ 275	Dave Anderson	.08	.03	.01
☐ 276	George Vukovich	.08	.03	.01
☐ 277	Greg Pryor	.08	.03	.01
☐ 278	Mike Warren	.08	.03	.01
☐ 279	Bob James	.08	.03	.01
☐ 280	Bobby Grich	.12	.05	.01
☐ 281	Mike Mason	.08	.03	.01
☐ 282	Ron Reed	.08	.03	.01
☐ 283	Alan Ashby	.08	.03	.01
☐ 284	Mark Thurmond	.08	.03	.01
☐ 285	Joe Lefebvre	.08	.03	.01
☐ 286	Ted Power	.08	.03	.01
☐ 287	Chris Chambliss	.12	.05	.01
☐ 288	Lee Tunnell	.08	.03	.01
☐ 289	Rich Bordi	.08	.03	.01
☐ 290	Glenn Brummer	.08	.03	.01
☐ 291	Mike Boddicker	.08	.03	.01
☐ 292	Rollie Fingers	.35	.15	.03
☐ 293	Lou Whitaker	.35	.15	.03
☐ 294	Dwight Evans	.25	.10	.02
☐ 295	Don Mattingly	11.00	5.00	1.35
☐ 296	Mike Marshall	.12	.05	.01
☐ 297	Willie Wilson	.12	.05	.01
☐ 298	Mike Heath	.08	.03	.01
☐ 299	Tim Raines	.40	.16	.04
☐ 300	Larry Parrish	.08	.03	.01
☐ 301	Geoff Zahn	.08	.03	.01
☐ 302	Rich Dotson	.08	.03	.01
☐ 303	David Green	.08	.03	.01
☐ 304	Jose Cruz	.12	.05	.01
☐ 305	Steve Carlton	.90	.40	.09
☐ 306	Gary Redus	.12	.05	.01
☐ 307	Steve Garvey	.50	.20	.05
☐ 308	Jose DeLeon	.08	.03	.01
☐ 309	Randy Lerch	.08	.03	.01
☐ 310	Claudell Washington	.08	.03	.01
☐ 311	Lee Smith	.40	.16	.04
☐ 312	Darryl Strawberry	12.50	5.50	1.65
☐ 313	Jim Beattie	.08	.03	.01
☐ 314	John Butcher	.08	.03	.01
☐ 315	Damaso Garcia	.08	.03	.01
☐ 316	Mike Smithson	.08	.03	.01
☐ 317	Luis Leal	.08	.03	.01
☐ 318	Ken Phelps	.12	.05	.01
☐ 319	Wally Backman	.08	.03	.01
☐ 320	Ron Cey	.12	.05	.01
☐ 321	Brad Komminsk	.08	.03	.01
☐ 322	Jason Thompson	.08	.03	.01
☐ 323	Frank Williams	.08	.03	.01
☐ 324	Tim Lollar	.08	.03	.01
☐ 325	Eric Davis	13.50	6.00	1.85
☐ 326	Von Hayes	.15	.06	.01
☐ 327	Andy Van Slyke	.90	.40	.09
☐ 328	Craig Reynolds	.08	.03	.01
☐ 329	Dick Schofield	.12	.05	.01
☐ 330	Scott Fletcher	.08	.03	.01
☐ 331	Jeff Reardon	.40	.16	.04
☐ 332	Rick Dempsey	.08	.03	.01
☐ 333	Ben Oglivie	.08	.03	.01

☐ 334	Dan Petry	.08	.03	.01
☐ 335	Jackie Gutierrez	.08	.03	.01
☐ 336	Dave Righetti	.15	.06	.01
☐ 337	Alejandro Pena	.15	.06	.01
☐ 338	Mel Hall	.17	.07	.01
☐ 339	Pat Sheridan	.08	.03	.01
☐ 340	Keith Atherton	.08	.03	.01
☐ 341	David Palmer	.08	.03	.01
☐ 342	Gary Ward	.08	.03	.01
☐ 343	Dave Stewart	.60	.25	.06
☐ 344	Mark Gubicza	.75	.30	.07
☐ 345	Carney Lansford	.15	.06	.01
☐ 346	Jerry Willard	.08	.03	.01
☐ 347	Ken Griffey	.17	.07	.01
☐ 348	Franklin Stubbs	.50	.20	.05
☐ 349	Aurelio Lopez	.08	.03	.01
☐ 350	Al Bumbry	.08	.03	.01
☐ 351	Charlie Moore	.08	.03	.01
☐ 352	Luis Sanchez	.08	.03	.01
☐ 353	Darrell Porter	.08	.03	.01
☐ 354	Bill Dawley	.08	.03	.01
☐ 355	Charles Hudson	.08	.03	.01
☐ 356	Garry Templeton	.12	.05	.01
☐ 357	Cecilio Guante	.08	.03	.01
☐ 358	Jeff Leonard	.08	.03	.01
☐ 359	Paul Molitor	.40	.16	.04
☐ 360	Ron Gardenhire	.08	.03	.01
☐ 361	Larry Bowa	.12	.05	.01
☐ 362	Bob Kearney	.08	.03	.01
☐ 363	Garth Iorg	.08	.03	.01
☐ 364	Tom Brunansky	.15	.06	.01
☐ 365	Brad Gulden	.08	.03	.01
☐ 366	Greg Walker	.08	.03	.01
☐ 367	Mike Young	.08	.03	.01
☐ 368	Rick Waits	.08	.03	.01
☐ 369	Doug Bair	.08	.03	.01
☐ 370	Bob Shirley	.08	.03	.01
☐ 371	Bob Ojeda	.12	.05	.01
☐ 372	Bob Welch	.20	.08	.02
☐ 373	Neal Heaton	.08	.03	.01
☐ 374	Danny Jackson UER	.15	.06	.01
	(photo actually			
	Frank Wills)			
☐ 375	Donnie Hill	.08	.03	.01
☐ 376	Mike Stenhouse	.08	.03	.01
☐ 377	Bruce Kison	.08	.03	.01
☐ 378	Wayne Tolleson	.08	.03	.01
☐ 379	Floyd Bannister	.08	.03	.01
☐ 380	Vern Ruhle	.08	.03	.01
☐ 381	Tim Corcoran	.08	.03	.01
☐ 382	Kurt Kepshire	.08	.03	.01
☐ 383	Bobby Brown	.08	.03	.01
☐ 384	Dave Van Gorder	.08	.03	.01
☐ 385	Rick Mahler	.08	.03	.01
☐ 386	Lee Mazzilli	.08	.03	.01
☐ 387	Bill Laskey	.08	.03	.01
☐ 388	Thad Bosley	.08	.03	.01
☐ 389	Al Chambers	.08	.03	.01
☐ 390	Tony Fernandez	.60	.25	.06
☐ 391	Ron Washington	.08	.03	.01
☐ 392	Bill Swaggerty	.08	.03	.01
☐ 393	Bob L. Gibson	.08	.03	.01
☐ 394	Marty Castillo	.08	.03	.01
☐ 395	Steve Crawford	.08	.03	.01
☐ 396	Clay Christiansen	.08	.03	.01
☐ 397	Bob Bailor	.08	.03	.01
☐ 398	Mike Hargrove	.08	.03	.01
☐ 399	Charlie Leibrandt	.08	.03	.01
☐ 400	Tom Burgmeier	.08	.03	.01
☐ 401	Razor Shines	.08	.03	.01
☐ 402	Rob Wilfong	.08	.03	.01
☐ 403	Tom Henke	.17	.07	.01
☐ 404	Al Jones	.08	.03	.01
☐ 405	Mike LaCoss	.08	.03	.01
☐ 406	Luis DeLeon	.08	.03	.01
☐ 407	Greg Gross	.08	.03	.01
☐ 408	Tom Hume	.08	.03	.01
☐ 409	Rick Camp	.08	.03	.01
☐ 410	Milt May	.08	.03	.01
☐ 411	Henry Cotto	.15	.06	.01
☐ 412	David Von Ohlen	.08	.03	.01
☐ 413	Scott McGregor	.08	.03	.01
☐ 414	Ted Simmons	.12	.05	.01
☐ 415	Jack Morris	.60	.25	.06
☐ 416	Bill Buckner	.12	.05	.01
☐ 417	Butch Wynegar	.08	.03	.01
☐ 418	Steve Sax	.35	.15	.03
☐ 419	Steve Balboni	.08	.03	.01
☐ 420	Dwayne Murphy	.08	.03	.01
☐ 421	Andre Dawson	1.00	.40	.10
☐ 422	Charlie Hough	.08	.03	.01
☐ 423	Tommy John	.17	.07	.01
☐ 424A	Tom Seaver ERR	1.25	.50	.12
	(photo actually			

	Floyd Bannister)			
☐ 424B	Tom Seaver COR	25.00	11.00	3.50
☐ 425	Tommy Herr	.12	.05	.01
☐ 426	Terry Puhl	.08	.03	.01
☐ 427	Al Holland	.08	.03	.01
☐ 428	Eddie Milner	.08	.03	.01
☐ 429	Terry Kennedy	.08	.03	.01
☐ 430	John Candelaria	.08	.03	.01
☐ 431	Manny Trillo	.08	.03	.01
☐ 432	Ken Oberkfell	.08	.03	.01
☐ 433	Rick Sutcliffe	.12	.05	.01
☐ 434	Ron Darling	.30	.12	.03
☐ 435	Spike Owen	.08	.03	.01
☐ 436	Frank Viola	.60	.25	.06
☐ 437	Lloyd Moseby	.12	.05	.01
☐ 438	Kirby Puckett	30.00	13.50	4.50
☐ 439	Jim Clancy	.08	.03	.01
☐ 440	Mike Moore	.12	.05	.01
☐ 441	Doug Sisk	.08	.03	.01
☐ 442	Dennis Eckersley	.40	.16	.04
☐ 443	Gerald Perry	.12	.05	.01
☐ 444	Dale Berra	.08	.03	.01
☐ 445	Dusty Baker	.12	.05	.01
☐ 446	Ed Whitson	.08	.03	.01
☐ 447	Cesar Cedeno	.12	.05	.01
☐ 448	Rick Schu	.12	.05	.01
☐ 449	Joaquin Andujar	.12	.05	.01
☐ 450	Mark Bailey	.08	.03	.01
☐ 451	Ron Romanick	.08	.03	.01
☐ 452	Julio Cruz	.08	.03	.01
☐ 453	Miguel Dilone	.08	.03	.01
☐ 454	Storm Davis	.08	.03	.01
☐ 455	Jaime Cocanower	.08	.03	.01
☐ 456	Barbaro Garbey	.08	.03	.01
☐ 457	Rich Gedman	.08	.03	.01
☐ 458	Phil Niekro	.30	.12	.03
☐ 459	Mike Scioscia	.12	.05	.01
☐ 460	Pat Tabler	.08	.03	.01
☐ 461	Darryl Motley	.08	.03	.01
☐ 462	Chris Codiroli	.08	.03	.01
☐ 463	Doug Flynn	.08	.03	.01
☐ 464	Billy Sample	.08	.03	.01
☐ 465	Mickey Rivers	.08	.03	.01
☐ 466	John Wathan	.08	.03	.01
☐ 467	Bill Krueger	.08	.03	.01
☐ 468	Andre Thornton	.12	.05	.01
☐ 469	Rex Hudler	.30	.12	.03
☐ 470	Sid Bream	.75	.30	.07
☐ 471	Kirk Gibson	.40	.16	.04
☐ 472	John Shelby	.08	.03	.01
☐ 473	Moose Haas	.08	.03	.01
☐ 474	Doug Corbett	.08	.03	.01
☐ 475	Willie McGee	.60	.25	.06
☐ 476	Bob Knepper	.08	.03	.01
☐ 477	Kevin Gross	.08	.03	.01
☐ 478	Carmelo Martinez	.08	.03	.01
☐ 479	Kent Tekulve	.08	.03	.01
☐ 480	Chili Davis	.20	.08	.02
☐ 481	Bobby Clark	.08	.03	.01
☐ 482	Mookie Wilson	.12	.05	.01
☐ 483	Dave Owen	.08	.03	.01
☐ 484	Ed Nunez	.08	.03	.01
☐ 485	Rance Mulliniks	.08	.03	.01
☐ 486	Ken Schrom	.08	.03	.01
☐ 487	Jeff Russell	.12	.05	.01
☐ 488	Tom Paciorek	.08	.03	.01
☐ 489	Dan Ford	.08	.03	.01
☐ 490	Mike Caldwell	.08	.03	.01
☐ 491	Scottie Earl	.08	.03	.01
☐ 492	Jose Rijo	2.50	1.00	.25
☐ 493	Bruce Hurst	.15	.06	.01
☐ 494	Ken Landreaux	.08	.03	.01
☐ 495	Mike Fischlin	.08	.03	.01
☐ 496	Don Slaught	.08	.03	.01
☐ 497	Steve McCatty	.08	.03	.01
☐ 498	Gary Lucas	.08	.03	.01
☐ 499	Gary Pettis	.12	.05	.01
☐ 500	Marvis Foley	.08	.03	.01
☐ 501	Mike Squires	.08	.03	.01
☐ 502	Jim Pankovits	.08	.03	.01
☐ 503	Luis Aguayo	.08	.03	.01
☐ 504	Ralph Citarella	.08	.03	.01
☐ 505	Bruce Bochy	.08	.03	.01
☐ 506	Bob Owchinko	.08	.03	.01
☐ 507	Pascual Perez	.12	.05	.01
☐ 508	Lee Lacy	.08	.03	.01
☐ 509	Atlee Hammaker	.08	.03	.01
☐ 510	Bob Dernier	.08	.03	.01
☐ 511	Ed VandeBerg	.08	.03	.01
☐ 512	Cliff Johnson	.08	.03	.01
☐ 513	Len Whitehouse	.08	.03	.01
☐ 514	Dennis Martinez	.12	.05	.01
☐ 515	Ed Romero	.08	.03	.01
☐ 516	Rusty Kuntz	.08	.03	.01

☐ 517 Rick Miller	.08	.03	.01
☐ 518 Dennis Rasmussen	.12	.05	.01
☐ 519 Steve Yeager	.08	.03	.01
☐ 520 Chris Bando	.08	.03	.01
☐ 521 U.L. Washington	.08	.03	.01
☐ 522 Curt Young	.15	.06	.01
☐ 523 Angel Salazar	.08	.03	.01
☐ 524 Curt Kaufman	.08	.03	.01
☐ 525 Odell Jones	.08	.03	.01
☐ 526 Juan Agosto	.08	.03	.01
☐ 527 Denny Walling	.08	.03	.01
☐ 528 Andy Hawkins	.15	.06	.01
☐ 529 Sixto Lezcano	.08	.03	.01
☐ 530 Skeeter Barnes	.15	.06	.01
☐ 531 Randy Johnson	.08	.03	.01
☐ 532 Jim Morrison	.08	.03	.01
☐ 533 Warren Brusstar	.08	.03	.01
☐ 534A Jeff Pendleton ERR	4.50	2.00	.45
(wrong first name)			
☐ 534B Terry Pendleton COR	12.00	5.25	1.50
☐ 535 Vic Rodriguez	.12	.05	.01
☐ 536 Bob McClure	.08	.03	.01
☐ 537 Dave Bergman	.08	.03	.01
☐ 538 Mark Clear	.08	.03	.01
☐ 539 Mike Pagliarulo	.75	.30	.07
☐ 540 Terry Whitfield	.08	.03	.01
☐ 541 Joe Beckwith	.08	.03	.01
☐ 542 Jeff Burroughs	.08	.03	.01
☐ 543 Dan Schatzeder	.08	.03	.01
☐ 544 Donnie Scott	.08	.03	.01
☐ 545 Jim Slaton	.08	.03	.01
☐ 546 Greg Luzinski	.12	.05	.01
☐ 547 Mark Salas	.08	.03	.01
☐ 548 Dave Smith	.08	.03	.01
☐ 549 John Wockenfuss	.08	.03	.01
☐ 550 Frank Pastore	.08	.03	.01
☐ 551 Tim Flannery	.08	.03	.01
☐ 552 Rick Rhoden	.08	.03	.01
☐ 553 Mark Davis	.15	.06	.01
☐ 554 Jeff Dedmon	.08	.03	.01
☐ 555 Gary Woods	.08	.03	.01
☐ 556 Danny Heep	.08	.03	.01
☐ 557 Mark Langston	4.50	2.00	.45
☐ 558 Darrell Brown	.08	.03	.01
☐ 559 Jimmy Key	2.00	.80	.20
☐ 560 Rick Lysander	.08	.03	.01
☐ 561 Doyle Alexander	.08	.03	.01
☐ 562 Mike Stanton	.08	.03	.01
☐ 563 Sid Fernandez	.35	.15	.03
☐ 564 Richie Hebner	.08	.03	.01
☐ 565 Alex Trevino	.08	.03	.01
☐ 566 Brian Harper	.30	.12	.03
☐ 567 Dan Gladden	.60	.25	.06
☐ 568 Luis Salazar	.08	.03	.01
☐ 569 Tom Foley	.08	.03	.01
☐ 570 Larry Andersen	.08	.03	.01
☐ 571 Danny Cox	.08	.03	.01
☐ 572 Joe Sambito	.08	.03	.01
☐ 573 Juan Beniquez	.08	.03	.01
☐ 574 Joel Skinner	.08	.03	.01
☐ 575 Randy St.Claire	.08	.03	.01
☐ 576 Floyd Rayford	.08	.03	.01
☐ 577 Roy Howell	.08	.03	.01
☐ 578 John Grubb	.08	.03	.01
☐ 579 Ed Jurak	.08	.03	.01
☐ 580 John Montefusco	.08	.03	.01
☐ 581 Orel Hershiser	5.00	2.25	.50
☐ 582 Tom Waddell	.08	.03	.01
☐ 583 Mark Huismann	.08	.03	.01
☐ 584 Joe Morgan	.40	.16	.04
☐ 585 Jim Wohlford	.08	.03	.01
☐ 586 Dave Schmidt	.08	.03	.01
☐ 587 Jeff Kunkel	.08	.03	.01
☐ 588 Hal McRae	.12	.05	.01
☐ 589 Bill Almon	.08	.03	.01
☐ 590 Carmen Castillo	.08	.03	.01
☐ 591 Omar Moreno	.08	.03	.01
☐ 592 Ken Howell	.15	.06	.01
☐ 593 Tom Brookens	.08	.03	.01
☐ 594 Joe Nolan	.08	.03	.01
☐ 595 Willie Lozado	.08	.03	.01
☐ 596 Tom Nieto	.08	.03	.01
☐ 597 Walt Terrell	.08	.03	.01
☐ 598 Al Oliver	.12	.05	.01
☐ 599 Shane Rawley	.08	.03	.01
☐ 600 Denny Gonzalez	.08	.03	.01
☐ 601 Mark Grant	.08	.03	.01
☐ 602 Mike Armstrong	.08	.03	.01
☐ 603 George Foster	.15	.06	.01
☐ 604 Dave Lopes	.12	.05	.01
☐ 605 Salome Barojas	.08	.03	.01
☐ 606 Roy Lee Jackson	.08	.03	.01
☐ 607 Pete Filson	.08	.03	.01
☐ 608 Duane Walker	.08	.03	.01

☐ 609 Glenn Wilson	.08	.03	.01
☐ 610 Rafael Santana	.15	.06	.01
☐ 611 Roy Smith	.12	.05	.01
☐ 612 Ruppert Jones	.08	.03	.01
☐ 613 Joe Cowley	.08	.03	.01
☐ 614 Al Nipper UER	.12	.05	.01
(photo actually			
Mike Brown)			
☐ 615 Gene Nelson	.08	.03	.01
☐ 616 Joe Carter	5.50	2.50	.55
☐ 617 Ray Knight	.12	.05	.01
☐ 618 Chuck Rainey	.08	.03	.01
☐ 619 Dan Driessen	.08	.03	.01
☐ 620 Daryl Sconiers	.08	.03	.01
☐ 621 Bill Stein	.08	.03	.01
☐ 622 Roy Smalley	.08	.03	.01
☐ 623 Ed Lynch	.08	.03	.01
☐ 624 Jeff Stone	.12	.05	.01
☐ 625 Bruce Berenyi	.08	.03	.01
☐ 626 Kelvin Chapman	.08	.03	.01
☐ 627 Joe Price	.08	.03	.01
☐ 628 Steve Bedrosian	.12	.05	.01
☐ 629 Vic Mata	.08	.03	.01
☐ 630 Mike Krukow	.08	.03	.01
☐ 631 Phil Bradley	.35	.15	.03
☐ 632 Jim Gott	.08	.03	.01
☐ 633 Randy Bush	.08	.03	.01
☐ 634 Tom Browning	1.75	.70	.17
☐ 635 Lou Gehrig	.15	.06	.01
Puzzle Card			
☐ 636 Reid Nichols	.08	.03	.01
☐ 637 Dan Pasqua	.75	.30	.07
☐ 638 German Rivera	.08	.03	.01
☐ 639 Don Schulze	.08	.03	.01
☐ 640A Mike Jones	.12	.05	.01
(Career Highlights,			
takes five lines)			
☐ 640B Mike Jones	.12	.05	.01
(Career Highlights,			
takes four lines)			
☐ 641 Pete Rose	1.25	.50	.12
☐ 642 Wade Rowdon	.08	.03	.01
☐ 643 Jerry Narron	.08	.03	.01
☐ 644 Darrell Miller	.12	.05	.01
☐ 645 Tim Hulett	.12	.05	.01
☐ 646 Andy McGaffigan	.08	.03	.01
☐ 647 Kurt Bevacqua	.08	.03	.01
☐ 648 John Russell	.12	.05	.01
☐ 649 Ron Robinson	.20	.08	.02
☐ 650 Donnie Moore	.08	.03	.01
☐ 651A Two for the Title	4.00	1.75	.40
Dave Winfield			
Don Mattingly			
(yellow letters)			
☐ 651B Two for the Title	9.00	4.00	.90
Dave Winfield			
Don Mattingly			
(white letters)			
☐ 652 Tim Laudner	.08	.03	.01
☐ 653 Steve Farr	.40	.16	.04
☐ 654 DK Checklist 1-26	.15	.02	.00
(unnumbered)			
☐ 655 Checklist 27-130	.15	.02	.00
(unnumbered)			
☐ 656 Checklist 131-234	.15	.02	.00
(unnumbered)			
☐ 657 Checklist 235-338	.15	.02	.00
(unnumbered)			
☐ 658 Checklist 339-442	.15	.02	.00
(unnumbered)			
☐ 659 Checklist 443-546	.15	.02	.00
(unnumbered)			
☐ 660 Checklist 547-653	.15	.02	.00
(unnumbered)			

1985 Donruss Wax Box Cards

The boxes of the 1985 Donruss regular issue baseball cards, in which the wax packs were contained, featured four baseball cards, with backs. The complete set price of the regular issue set does not include these cards; they are considered a separate set. The cards measure the standard 2 1/2" by 3 1/2" and are styled the same as the regular Donruss cards. The cards are numbered but with the prefix PC before the number. The value of the panel uncut is slightly greater, perhaps by 25 percent greater, than the value of the individual cards cut up carefully.

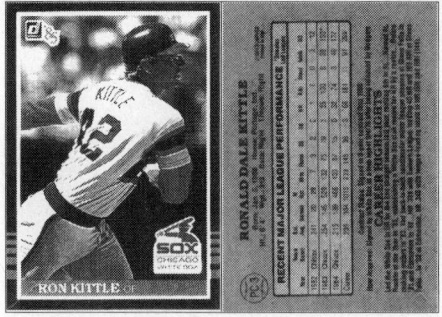

	MINT	EXC	G-VG
COMPLETE SET (4)	6.00	2.50	.60
COMMON PLAYER	.05	.02	.00
☐ PC1 Dwight Gooden	4.50	2.00	.45
☐ PC2 Ryne Sandberg	2.25	.90	.22
☐ PC3 Ron Kittle	.15	.06	.01
☐ PUZ Lou Gehrig Puzzle Card	.05	.02	.00

1985 Donruss Super DK's

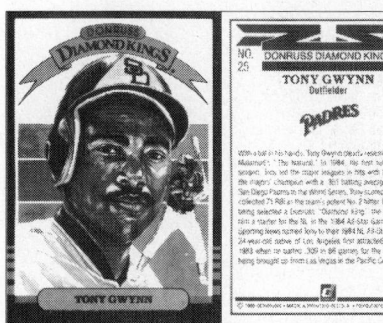

The cards in this 28-card set measure 4 15/16 by 6 3/4". The 1985 Donruss Diamond Kings Supers set contains enlarged cards of the first 26 cards of the Donruss regular set of this year. In addition, the Diamond Kings checklist card, a card of artist Dick Perez, and a Lou Gehrig puzzle card are included in the set. The set was the brain-child of the Perez-Steele Galleries and could be obtained via a write-in offer on the wrappers of the Donruss regular cards of this year. The Gehrig puzzle card is actually a 12-piece jigsaw puzzle. The back of the checklist card is blank; however, the Dick Perez card back gives a short history of Dick Perez and the Perez-Steele Galleries. The offer for obtaining this set was detailed on the wax pack wrappers; three wrappers plus $9.00 was required for this mail-in offer.

	MINT	EXC	G-VG
COMPLETE SET (28)	12.00	5.25	1.50
COMMON PLAYER (1-28)	.25	.10	.02
☐ 1 Ryne Sandberg	3.00	1.25	.30
☐ 2 Doug DeCinces	.25	.10	.02
☐ 3 Richard Dotson	.25	.10	.02
☐ 4 Bert Blyleven	.35	.15	.03
☐ 5 Lou Whitaker	.50	.20	.05
☐ 6 Dan Quisenberry	.35	.15	.03
☐ 7 Don Mattingly	3.00	1.25	.30
☐ 8 Carney Lansford	.35	.15	.03
☐ 9 Frank Tanana	.25	.10	.02
☐ 10 Willie Upshaw	.25	.10	.02
☐ 11 Claudell Washington	.25	.10	.02

	MINT	EXC	G-VG
☐ 12 Mike Marshall	.35	.15	.03
☐ 13 Joaquin Andujar	.25	.10	.02
☐ 14 Cal Ripken	3.00	1.25	.30
☐ 15 Jim Rice	.45	.18	.04
☐ 16 Don Sutton	.45	.18	.04
☐ 17 Frank Viola	.60	.25	.06
☐ 18 Alvin Davis	.60	.25	.06
☐ 19 Mario Soto	.25	.10	.02
☐ 20 Jose Cruz	.25	.10	.02
☐ 21 Charlie Lea	.25	.10	.02
☐ 22 Jesse Orosco	.25	.10	.02
☐ 23 Juan Samuel	.35	.15	.03
☐ 24 Tony Pena	.25	.10	.02
☐ 25 Tony Gwynn	2.00	.80	.20
☐ 26 Bob Brenly	.25	.10	.02
☐ 27 Checklist Card (unnumbered)	.25	.10	.02
☐ 28 Dick Perez (unnumbered) (History of DK's)	.25	.10	.02

1985 Donruss Action All-Stars

The cards in this 60-card set measure approximately 3 1/2" by 5". For the third year in a row, Donruss issued a set of Action All-Stars. This set features action photos on the obverse which also contains a portrait inset of the player. The backs, unlike the year before, do not contain a full color picture of the player but list, if space is available, full statistical data, biographical data, career highlights, and acquisition and contract status. The cards were issued with a Lou Gehrig puzzle card.

	MINT	EXC	G-VG
COMPLETE SET (60)	7.50	3.25	.75
COMMON PLAYER (1-60)	.07	.03	.01
☐ 1 Tim Raines	.30	.12	.03
☐ 2 Jim Gantner	.07	.03	.01
☐ 3 Mario Soto	.07	.03	.01
☐ 4 Spike Owen	.07	.03	.01
☐ 5 Lloyd Moseby	.07	.03	.01
☐ 6 Damaso Garcia	.07	.03	.01
☐ 7 Cal Ripken	.90	.40	.09
☐ 8 Dan Quisenberry	.10	.04	.01
☐ 9 Eddie Murray	.35	.15	.03
☐ 10 Tony Pena	.10	.04	.01
☐ 11 Buddy Bell	.10	.04	.01
☐ 12 Dave Winfield	.25	.10	.02
☐ 13 Ron Kittle	.10	.04	.01
☐ 14 Rich Gossage	.15	.06	.01
☐ 15 Dwight Evans	.15	.06	.01
☐ 16 Alvin Davis	.10	.04	.01
☐ 17 Mike Schmidt	.90	.40	.09
☐ 18 Pascual Perez	.10	.04	.01
☐ 19 Tony Gwynn	.60	.25	.06
☐ 20 Nolan Ryan	1.25	.50	.12
☐ 21 Robin Yount	.50	.20	.05
☐ 22 Mike Marshall	.10	.04	.01
☐ 23 Brett Butler	.15	.06	.01
☐ 24 Ryne Sandberg	.90	.40	.09
☐ 25 Dale Murphy	.50	.20	.05
☐ 26 George Brett	.50	.20	.05
☐ 27 Jim Rice	.20	.08	.02
☐ 28 Ozzie Smith	.35	.15	.03

☐ 29	Larry Parrish	.07	.03	.01
☐ 30	Jack Clark	.15	.06	.01
☐ 31	Manny Trillo	.07	.03	.01
☐ 32	Dave Kingman	.10	.04	.01
☐ 33	Geoff Zahn	.07	.03	.01
☐ 34	Pedro Guerrero	.15	.06	.01
☐ 35	Dave Parker	.15	.06	.01
☐ 36	Rollie Fingers	.20	.08	.02
☐ 37	Fernando Valenzuela	.15	.06	.01
☐ 38	Wade Boggs	.60	.25	.06
☐ 39	Reggie Jackson	.60	.25	.06
☐ 40	Kent Hrbek	.20	.08	.02
☐ 41	Keith Hernandez	.15	.06	.01
☐ 42	Lou Whitaker	.15	.06	.01
☐ 43	Tom Herr	.07	.03	.01
☐ 44	Alan Trammell	.25	.10	.02
☐ 45	Butch Wynegar	.07	.03	.01
☐ 46	Leon Durham	.07	.03	.01
☐ 47	Dwight Gooden	.90	.40	.09
☐ 48	Don Mattingly	.90	.40	.09
☐ 49	Phil Niekro	.20	.08	.02
☐ 50	Johnny Ray	.07	.03	.01
☐ 51	Doug DeCinces	.07	.03	.01
☐ 52	Willie Upshaw	.07	.03	.01
☐ 53	Lance Parrish	.10	.04	.01
☐ 54	Jody Davis	.07	.03	.01
☐ 55	Steve Carlton	.35	.15	.03
☐ 56	Juan Samuel	.10	.04	.01
☐ 57	Gary Carter	.20	.08	.02
☐ 58	Harold Baines	.10	.04	.01
☐ 59	Eric Show	.07	.03	.01
☐ 60	Checklist Card	.07	.03	.01

1985 Donruss Highlights

This 56-card set features the players and pitchers of the month for each league as well as a number of highlight cards commemorating the 1985 season. The Donruss Company dedicated the last two cards to their own selections for Rookies of the Year (ROY). This set proved to be more popular than the Donruss Company had predicted, as their first and only print run was exhausted before card dealers' initial orders were filled.

		MINT	EXC	G-VG
	COMPLETE SET (56)	27.00	12.00	4.00
	COMMON PLAYER (1-56)	.12	.05	.01
☐ 1	Tom Seaver: Sets Opening Day Record	.75	.30	.07
☐ 2	Rollie Fingers: Sets AL Save Mark	.35	.15	.03
☐ 3	Mike Davis: AL Player April	.12	.05	.01
☐ 4	Charlie Leibrandt: AL Pitcher April	.12	.05	.01
☐ 5	Dale Murphy: NL Player April	.65	.25	.06
☐ 6	Fernando Valenzuela: NL Pitcher April	.20	.08	.02
☐ 7	Larry Bowa: NL Shortstop Leader	.12	.05	.01
☐ 8	Dave Concepcion: Joins Reds' 2000 Hit Club	.12	.05	.01
☐ 9	Tony Perez: Eldest Grand Slammer	.25	.10	.02

☐ 10	Pete Rose: NL Career Run Leader	1.00	.40	.10
☐ 11	George Brett: AL Player May	.80	.35	.08
☐ 12	Dave Stieb: AL Pitcher May	.20	.08	.02
☐ 13	Dave Parker: NL Player May	.20	.08	.02
☐ 14	Andy Hawkins: NL Pitcher May	.12	.05	.01
☐ 15	Andy Hawkins: Records 11th Straight Win	.12	.05	.01
☐ 16	Von Hayes: Two Homers in First Inning	.12	.05	.01
☐ 17	Rickey Henderson: AL Player June	1.00	.40	.10
☐ 18	Jay Howell: AL Pitcher June	.12	.05	.01
☐ 19	Pedro Guerrero: NL Player June	.20	.08	.02
☐ 20	John Tudor: NL Pitcher June	.12	.05	.01
☐ 21	Hernandez/Carter: Marathon Game Iron Men	.25	.10	.02
☐ 22	Nolan Ryan: Records 4000th K	2.00	.80	.20
☐ 23	LaMarr Hoyt: All-Star Game MVP	.12	.05	.01
☐ 24	Oddibe McDowell: 1st Ranger to Hit for Cycle	.20	.08	.02
☐ 25	George Brett: AL Player July	.80	.35	.08
☐ 26	Bret Saberhagen: AL Pitcher July	1.00	.40	.10
☐ 27	Keith Hernandez: NL Player July	.20	.08	.02
☐ 28	Fernando Valenzuela: NL Pitcher July	.20	.08	.02
☐ 29	W.McGee/V.Coleman: Record Setting Base Stealers	.80	.35	.08
☐ 30	Tom Seaver: Notches 300th Career Win	.50	.20	.05
☐ 31	Rod Carew: Strokes 3000th Hit	.40	.16	.04
☐ 32	Dwight Gooden: Establishes Met Record	1.00	.40	.10
☐ 33	Dwight Gooden: Achieves Strikeout Milestone	1.00	.40	.10
☐ 34	Eddie Murray: Explodes for 9 RBI	.50	.20	.05
☐ 35	Don Baylor: AL Career HBP Leader	.20	.08	.02
☐ 36	Don Mattingly: AL Player August	1.50	.60	.15
☐ 37	Dave Righetti: AL Pitcher August	.20	.08	.02
☐ 38	Willie McGee: NL Player August	.25	.10	.02
☐ 39	Shane Rawley: NL Pitcher August	.12	.05	.01
☐ 40	Pete Rose: Ty-Breaking Hit	1.25	.50	.12
☐ 41	Andre Dawson: Hits 3 HR's Drives in 8 Runs	.40	.16	.04
☐ 42	Rickey Henderson: Sets Yankee Theft Mark	1.25	.50	.12
☐ 43	Tom Browning: 20 Wins in Rookie Season	.20	.08	.02
☐ 44	Don Mattingly: Yankee Milestone for Hits	1.50	.60	.15
☐ 45	Don Mattingly: AL Player September	1.50	.60	.15
☐ 46	Charlie Leibrandt: AL Pitcher September	.12	.05	.01
☐ 47	Gary Carter: NL Player September	.30	.12	.03
☐ 48	Dwight Gooden: NL Pitcher September	1.00	.40	.10
☐ 49	Wade Boggs: Major League Record Setter	1.25	.50	.12
☐ 50	Phil Niekro: Hurls Shutout for 300th Win	.25	.10	.02
☐ 51	Darrell Evans: Venerable HR King	.12	.05	.01
☐ 52	Willie McGee: NL Switch-Hitting Record	.20	.08	.02
☐ 53	Dave Winfield: Equals DiMaggio Feat	.35	.15	.03

Don Mattingly

American League Player of the Month August

Don Mattingly established his Most Valuable Player credentials early in '85, but in August he had his biggest surge. The New York Yankee first baseman batted .390 for the month (46-for-118) with eight doubles, 11 homers and 87 total bases. His production numbers for the month included 28 runs and 26 RBI. Capping his player of the month stats was a .737 slugging percentage and a .447 on-base percentage.

NO. 36

DON MATTINGLY A.L.
PLAYER OF THE MONTH AUGUST

© 1985 LEAF/DONRUSS   MADE & PRINTED IN U.S.A.

			MINT	EXC	G-VG
☐	54	Vince Coleman:	2.00	.80	.20
		Donruss NL ROY			
☐	55	Ozzie Guillen:	.75	.30	.07
		Donruss AL ROY			
☐	56	Checklist Card	.12	.05	.01
		(unnumbered)			

1986 Donruss

The cards in this 660-card set measure 2 1/2" by 3 1/2". The 1986 Donruss regular issue cards have fronts that feature blue borders. The fronts contain the standard team logo, player's name, position, and Donruss logo. The cards were distributed with puzzle pieces from a Dick Perez rendition of Hank Aaron. The first 26 cards of the set are Diamond Kings (DK), for the fifth year in a row; the artwork on the Diamond Kings was again produced by the Perez-Steele Galleries. Cards 27-46 again feature Rated Rookies (RR); Danny Tartabull is included in this subset for the second year in a row. The unnumbered checklist cards are arbitrarily numbered below as numbers 654 through 660. The key rookie cards in this set are Jose Canseco, Vince Coleman, Kal Daniels, Cecil Fielder, Fred McGriff, and Paul O'Neill.

			MINT	EXC	G-VG
	COMPLETE SET (660)		180.00	80.00	27.00
	COMMON PLAYER (1-660)		.07	.03	.01
☐	1	Kirk Gibson DK	.30	.08	.02
☐	2	Goose Gossage DK	.15	.06	.01
☐	3	Willie McGee DK	.15	.06	.01
☐	4	George Bell DK	.20	.08	.02
☐	5	Tony Armas DK	.10	.04	.01
☐	6	Chili Davis DK	.15	.06	.01
☐	7	Cecil Cooper DK	.12	.05	.01
☐	8	Mike Boddicker DK	.10	.04	.01
☐	9	Dave Lopes DK	.10	.04	.01
☐	10	Bill Doran DK	.10	.04	.01
☐	11	Bret Saberhagen DK	.40	.16	.04
☐	12	Brett Butler DK	.15	.06	.01
☐	13	Harold Baines DK	.15	.06	.01
☐	14	Mike Davis DK	.10	.04	.01
☐	15	Tony Perez DK	.15	.06	.01
☐	16	Willie Randolph DK	.12	.05	.01
☐	17	Bob Boone DK	.12	.05	.01
☐	18	Orel Hershiser DK	.35	.15	.03
☐	19	Johnny Ray DK	.10	.04	.01
☐	20	Gary Ward DK	.10	.04	.01
☐	21	Rick Mahler DK	.10	.04	.01
☐	22	Phil Bradley DK	.10	.04	.01
☐	23	Jerry Koosman DK	.12	.05	.01
☐	24	Tom Brunansky DK	.12	.05	.01
☐	25	Andre Dawson DK	.35	.15	.03
☐	26	Dwight Gooden DK	.65	.25	.06
☐	27	Kal Daniels RR	3.25	1.35	.32
☐	28	Fred McGriff RR	22.00	9.50	3.15
☐	29	Cory Snyder RR	.50	.20	.05
☐	30	Jose Guzman RR	.35	.15	.03
☐	31	Ty Gainey RR	.10	.04	.01
☐	32	Johnny Abrego RR	.07	.03	.01
☐	33A	Andres Galarraga RR	1.00	.40	.10
		(no accent)			
☐	33B	Andre's Galarraga RR	2.00	.80	.20
		(accent over e)			

☐	34	Dave Shipanoff RR	.07	.03	.01
☐	35	Mark McLemore RR	.10	.04	.01
☐	36	Marty Clary RR	.10	.04	.01
☐	37	Paul O'Neill RR	3.25	1.35	.32
☐	38	Danny Tartabull RR	1.25	.50	.12
☐	39	Jose Canseco RR	80.00	36.00	12.00
☐	40	Juan Nieves RR	.12	.05	.01
☐	41	Lance McCullers RR	.12	.05	.01
☐	42	Rick Surhoff RR	.10	.04	.01
☐	43	Todd Worrell RR	.17	.07	.01
☐	44	Bob Kipper RR	.12	.05	.01
☐	45	John Habyan RR	.10	.04	.01
☐	46	Mike Woodard RR	.07	.03	.01
☐	47	Mike Boddicker	.07	.03	.01
☐	48	Robin Yount	.85	.35	.08
☐	49	Lou Whitaker	.25	.10	.02
☐	50	Oil Can Boyd	.07	.03	.01
☐	51	Rickey Henderson	2.50	1.00	.25
☐	52	Mike Marshall	.10	.04	.01
☐	53	George Brett	.85	.35	.08
☐	54	Dave Kingman	.12	.05	.01
☐	55	Hubie Brooks	.12	.05	.01
☐	56	Oddibe McDowell	.10	.04	.01
☐	57	Doug DeCinces	.07	.03	.01
☐	58	Britt Burns	.07	.03	.01
☐	59	Ozzie Smith	.75	.30	.07
☐	60	Jose Cruz	.10	.04	.01
☐	61	Mike Schmidt	2.50	1.00	.25
☐	62	Pete Rose	.80	.35	.08
☐	63	Steve Garvey	.35	.15	.03
☐	64	Tony Pena	.10	.04	.01
☐	65	Chili Davis	.15	.06	.01
☐	66	Dale Murphy	.50	.20	.05
☐	67	Ryne Sandberg	3.75	1.60	.37
☐	68	Gary Carter	.35	.15	.03
☐	69	Alvin Davis	.15	.06	.01
☐	70	Kent Hrbek	.20	.08	.02
☐	71	George Bell	.50	.20	.05
☐	72	Kirby Puckett	7.00	3.00	.70
☐	73	Lloyd Moseby	.10	.04	.01
☐	74	Bob Kearney	.07	.03	.01
☐	75	Dwight Gooden	2.25	.90	.22
☐	76	Gary Matthews	.07	.03	.01
☐	77	Rick Mahler	.07	.03	.01
☐	78	Benny Distefano	.07	.03	.01
☐	79	Jeff Leonard	.07	.03	.01
☐	80	Kevin McReynolds	.35	.15	.03
☐	81	Ron Oester	.07	.03	.01
☐	82	John Russell	.07	.03	.01
☐	83	Tommy Herr	.10	.04	.01
☐	84	Jerry Mumphrey	.07	.03	.01
☐	85	Ron Romanick	.07	.03	.01
☐	86	Daryl Boston	.10	.04	.01
☐	87	Andre Dawson	.75	.30	.07
☐	88	Eddie Murray	.75	.30	.07
☐	89	Dion James	.07	.03	.01
☐	90	Chet Lemon	.07	.03	.01
☐	91	Bob Stanley	.07	.03	.01
☐	92	Willie Randolph	.10	.04	.01
☐	93	Mike Scioscia	.10	.04	.01
☐	94	Tom Waddell	.07	.03	.01
☐	95	Danny Jackson	.10	.04	.01
☐	96	Mike Davis	.07	.03	.01
☐	97	Mike Fitzgerald	.07	.03	.01
☐	98	Gary Ward	.07	.03	.01
☐	99	Pete O'Brien	.07	.03	.01
☐	100	Bret Saberhagen	1.00	.40	.10
☐	101	Alfredo Griffin	.07	.03	.01
☐	102	Brett Butler	.15	.06	.01
☐	103	Ron Guidry	.15	.06	.01
☐	104	Jerry Reuss	.07	.03	.01
☐	105	Jack Morris	.40	.16	.04
☐	106	Rick Dempsey	.07	.03	.01
☐	107	Ray Burris	.07	.03	.01
☐	108	Brian Downing	.10	.04	.01
☐	109	Willie McGee	.25	.10	.02
☐	110	Bill Doran	.10	.04	.01
☐	111	Kent Tekulve	.07	.03	.01
☐	112	Tony Gwynn	2.00	.80	.20
☐	113	Marvell Wynne	.07	.03	.01
☐	114	David Green	.07	.03	.01
☐	115	Jim Gantner	.07	.03	.01
☐	116	George Foster	.12	.05	.01
☐	117	Steve Trout	.07	.03	.01
☐	118	Mark Langston	.60	.25	.06
☐	119	Tony Fernandez	.20	.08	.02
☐	120	John Butcher	.07	.03	.01
☐	121	Ron Robinson	.07	.03	.01
☐	122	Dan Spillner	.07	.03	.01
☐	123	Mike Young	.07	.03	.01
☐	124	Paul Molitor	.25	.10	.02
☐	125	Kirk Gibson	.25	.10	.02
☐	126	Ken Griffey	.15	.06	.01
☐	127	Tony Armas	.07	.03	.01
☐	128	Mariano Duncan	.35	.15	.03

#	Player			
☐ 129	Pat Tabler	.07	.03	.01
☐ 130	Frank White	.07	.03	.01
☐ 131	Carney Lansford	.10	.04	.01
☐ 132	Vance Law	.07	.03	.01
☐ 133	Dick Schofield	.07	.03	.01
☐ 134	Wayne Tolleson	.07	.03	.01
☐ 135	Greg Walker	.07	.03	.01
☐ 136	Denny Walling	.07	.03	.01
☐ 137	Ozzie Virgil	.07	.03	.01
☐ 138	Ricky Horton	.07	.03	.01
☐ 139	LaMarr Hoyt	.07	.03	.01
☐ 140	Wayne Krenchicki	.07	.03	.01
☐ 141	Glenn Hubbard	.07	.03	.01
☐ 142	Cecilio Guante	.07	.03	.01
☐ 143	Mike Krukow	.07	.03	.01
☐ 144	Lee Smith	.35	.15	.03
☐ 145	Edwin Nunez	.07	.03	.01
☐ 146	Dave Stieb	.15	.06	.01
☐ 147	Mike Smithson	.07	.03	.01
☐ 148	Ken Dixon	.07	.03	.01
☐ 149	Danny Darwin	.07	.03	.01
☐ 150	Chris Pittaro	.07	.03	.01
☐ 151	Bill Buckner	.10	.04	.01
☐ 152	Mike Pagliarulo	.10	.04	.01
☐ 153	Bill Russell	.10	.04	.01
☐ 154	Brook Jacoby	.10	.04	.01
☐ 155	Pat Sheridan	.07	.03	.01
☐ 156	Mike Gallego	.07	.03	.01
☐ 157	Jim Wohlford	.07	.03	.01
☐ 158	Gary Pettis	.07	.03	.01
☐ 159	Toby Harrah	.07	.03	.01
☐ 160	Richard Dotson	.07	.03	.01
☐ 161	Bob Knepper	.07	.03	.01
☐ 162	Dave Dravecky	.10	.04	.01
☐ 163	Greg Gross	.07	.03	.01
☐ 164	Eric Davis	2.50	1.00	.25
☐ 165	Gerald Perry	.10	.04	.01
☐ 166	Rick Rhoden	.07	.03	.01
☐ 167	Keith Moreland	.07	.03	.01
☐ 168	Jack Clark	.17	.07	.01
☐ 169	Storm Davis	.07	.03	.01
☐ 170	Cecil Cooper	.10	.04	.01
☐ 171	Alan Trammell	.45	.18	.04
☐ 172	Roger Clemens	8.00	3.50	.80
☐ 173	Don Mattingly	4.00	1.75	.40
☐ 174	Pedro Guerrero	.20	.08	.02
☐ 175	Willie Wilson	.12	.05	.01
☐ 176	Dwayne Murphy	.07	.03	.01
☐ 177	Tim Raines	.35	.15	.03
☐ 178	Larry Parrish	.07	.03	.01
☐ 179	Mike Witt	.07	.03	.01
☐ 180	Harold Baines	.25	.10	.02
☐ 181	Vince Coleman UER (BA 2.67 on back)	6.00	2.50	.60
☐ 182	Jeff Heathcock	.07	.03	.01
☐ 183	Steve Carlton	.60	.25	.06
☐ 184	Mario Soto	.07	.03	.01
☐ 185	Goose Gossage	.15	.06	.01
☐ 186	Johnny Ray	.07	.03	.01
☐ 187	Dan Gladden	.10	.04	.01
☐ 188	Bob Horner	.12	.05	.01
☐ 189	Rick Sutcliffe	.12	.05	.01
☐ 190	Keith Hernandez	.17	.07	.01
☐ 191	Phil Bradley	.10	.04	.01
☐ 192	Tom Brunansky	.10	.04	.01
☐ 193	Jesse Barfield	.15	.06	.01
☐ 194	Frank Viola	.35	.15	.03
☐ 195	Willie Upshaw	.07	.03	.01
☐ 196	Jim Beattie	.07	.03	.01
☐ 197	Darryl Strawberry	4.75	2.00	.45
☐ 198	Ron Cey	.10	.04	.01
☐ 199	Steve Bedrosian	.10	.04	.01
☐ 200	Steve Kemp	.07	.03	.01
☐ 201	Manny Trillo	.07	.03	.01
☐ 202	Garry Templeton	.10	.04	.01
☐ 203	Dave Parker	.25	.10	.02
☐ 204	John Denny	.07	.03	.01
☐ 205	Terry Pendleton	.75	.30	.07
☐ 206	Terry Puhl	.07	.03	.01
☐ 207	Bobby Grich	.10	.04	.01
☐ 208	Ozzie Guillen	1.25	.50	.12
☐ 209	Jeff Reardon	.35	.15	.03
☐ 210	Cal Ripken	4.00	1.75	.40
☐ 211	Bill Schroeder	.07	.03	.01
☐ 212	Dan Petry	.07	.03	.01
☐ 213	Jim Rice	.15	.06	.01
☐ 214	Dave Righetti	.12	.05	.01
☐ 215	Fernando Valenzuela	.15	.06	.01
☐ 216	Julio Franco	.75	.30	.07
☐ 217	Darryl Motley	.07	.03	.01
☐ 218	Dave Collins	.07	.03	.01
☐ 219	Tim Wallach	.10	.04	.01
☐ 220	George Wright	.07	.03	.01
☐ 221	Tommy Dunbar	.07	.03	.01
☐ 222	Steve Balboni	.07	.03	.01
☐ 223	Jay Howell	.07	.03	.01
☐ 224	Joe Carter	1.25	.50	.12
☐ 225	Ed Whitson	.07	.03	.01
☐ 226	Orel Hershiser	.75	.30	.07
☐ 227	Willie Hernandez	.07	.03	.01
☐ 228	Lee Lacy	.07	.03	.01
☐ 229	Rollie Fingers	.30	.12	.03
☐ 230	Bob Boone	.12	.05	.01
☐ 231	Joaquin Andujar	.10	.04	.01
☐ 232	Craig Reynolds	.07	.03	.01
☐ 233	Shane Rawley	.07	.03	.01
☐ 234	Eric Show	.07	.03	.01
☐ 235	Jose DeLeon	.07	.03	.01
☐ 236	Jose Uribe	.20	.08	.02
☐ 237	Moose Haas	.07	.03	.01
☐ 238	Wally Backman	.07	.03	.01
☐ 239	Dennis Eckersley	.30	.12	.03
☐ 240	Mike Moore	.10	.04	.01
☐ 241	Damaso Garcia	.07	.03	.01
☐ 242	Tim Teufel	.07	.03	.01
☐ 243	Dave Concepcion	.12	.05	.01
☐ 244	Floyd Bannister	.07	.03	.01
☐ 245	Fred Lynn	.15	.06	.01
☐ 246	Charlie Moore	.07	.03	.01
☐ 247	Walt Terrell	.07	.03	.01
☐ 248	Dave Winfield	.60	.25	.06
☐ 249	Dwight Evans	.15	.06	.01
☐ 250	Dennis Powell	.07	.03	.01
☐ 251	Andre Thornton	.07	.03	.01
☐ 252	Onix Concepcion	.07	.03	.01
☐ 253	Mike Heath	.07	.03	.01
☐ 254A	David Palmer ERR (position 2B)	.10	.04	.01
☐ 254B	David Palmer COR (position P)	.60	.25	.06
☐ 255	Donnie Moore	.07	.03	.01
☐ 256	Curtis Wilkerson	.07	.03	.01
☐ 257	Julio Cruz	.07	.03	.01
☐ 258	Nolan Ryan	4.25	1.75	.42
☐ 259	Jeff Stone	.07	.03	.01
☐ 260	John Tudor	.10	.04	.01
☐ 261	Mark Thurmond	.07	.03	.01
☐ 262	Jay Tibbs	.07	.03	.01
☐ 263	Rafael Ramirez	.07	.03	.01
☐ 264	Larry McWilliams	.07	.03	.01
☐ 265	Mark Davis	.10	.04	.01
☐ 266	Bob Dernier	.07	.03	.01
☐ 267	Matt Young	.07	.03	.01
☐ 268	Jim Clancy	.07	.03	.01
☐ 269	Mickey Hatcher	.07	.03	.01
☐ 270	Sammy Stewart	.07	.03	.01
☐ 271	Bob L. Gibson	.07	.03	.01
☐ 272	Nelson Simmons	.07	.03	.01
☐ 273	Rich Gedman	.07	.03	.01
☐ 274	Butch Wynegar	.07	.03	.01
☐ 275	Ken Howell	.07	.03	.01
☐ 276	Mel Hall	.12	.05	.01
☐ 277	Jim Sundberg	.07	.03	.01
☐ 278	Chris Codiroli	.07	.03	.01
☐ 279	Herm Winningham	.07	.03	.01
☐ 280	Rod Carew	.75	.30	.07
☐ 281	Don Slaught	.07	.03	.01
☐ 282	Scott Fletcher	.07	.03	.01
☐ 283	Bill Dawley	.07	.03	.01
☐ 284	Andy Hawkins	.07	.03	.01
☐ 285	Glenn Wilson	.07	.03	.01
☐ 286	Nick Esasky	.10	.04	.01
☐ 287	Claudell Washington	.07	.03	.01
☐ 288	Lee Mazzilli	.07	.03	.01
☐ 289	Jody Davis	.07	.03	.01
☐ 290	Darrell Porter	.07	.03	.01
☐ 291	Scott McGregor	.07	.03	.01
☐ 292	Ted Simmons	.10	.04	.01
☐ 293	Aurelio Lopez	.07	.03	.01
☐ 294	Marty Barrett	.07	.03	.01
☐ 295	Dale Berra	.07	.03	.01
☐ 296	Greg Brock	.07	.03	.01
☐ 297	Charlie Leibrandt	.07	.03	.01
☐ 298	Bill Krueger	.07	.03	.01
☐ 299	Bryn Smith	.07	.03	.01
☐ 300	Burt Hooton	.07	.03	.01
☐ 301	Stu Cliburn	.07	.03	.01
☐ 302	Luis Salazar	.07	.03	.01
☐ 303	Ken Dayley	.07	.03	.01
☐ 304	Frank DiPino	.07	.03	.01
☐ 305	Von Hayes	.12	.05	.01
☐ 306	Gary Redus	.07	.03	.01
☐ 307	Craig Lefferts	.07	.03	.01
☐ 308	Sammy Khalifa	.07	.03	.01
☐ 309	Scott Garrelts	.10	.04	.01
☐ 310	Rick Cerone	.07	.03	.01
☐ 311	Shawon Dunston	.75	.30	.07
☐ 312	Howard Johnson	.90	.40	.09

#	Player				#	Player			
313	Jim Presley	.10	.04	.01	407	Garry Maddox	.07	.03	.01
314	Gary Gaetti	.15	.06	.01	408	Ted Power	.07	.03	.01
315	Luis Leal	.07	.03	.01	409	Len Barker	.07	.03	.01
316	Mark Salas	.07	.03	.01	410	Denny Gonzalez	.07	.03	.01
317	Bill Caudill	.07	.03	.01	411	George Frazier	.07	.03	.01
318	Dave Henderson	.35	.15	.03	412	Andy Van Slyke	.35	.15	.03
319	Rafael Santana	.07	.03	.01	413	Jim Dwyer	.07	.03	.01
320	Leon Durham	.07	.03	.01	414	Paul Householder	.07	.03	.01
321	Bruce Sutter	.12	.05	.01	415	Alejandro Sanchez	.07	.03	.01
322	Jason Thompson	.07	.03	.01	416	Steve Crawford	.07	.03	.01
323	Bob Brenly	.07	.03	.01	417	Dan Pasqua	.15	.06	.01
324	Carmelo Martinez	.07	.03	.01	418	Enos Cabell	.07	.03	.01
325	Eddie Milner	.07	.03	.01	419	Mike Jones	.07	.03	.01
326	Juan Samuel	.25	.10	.02	420	Steve Kiefer	.07	.03	.01
327	Tom Nieto	.07	.03	.01	421	Tim Burke	.20	.08	.02
328	Dave Smith	.07	.03	.01	422	Mike Mason	.07	.03	.01
329	Urbano Lugo	.07	.03	.01	423	Ruppert Jones	.07	.03	.01
330	Joel Skinner	.07	.03	.01	424	Jerry Hairston	.07	.03	.01
331	Bill Gullickson	.10	.04	.01	425	Tito Landrum	.07	.03	.01
332	Floyd Rayford	.07	.03	.01	426	Jeff Calhoun	.07	.03	.01
333	Ben Oglivie	.07	.03	.01	427	Don Carman	.15	.06	.01
334	Lance Parrish	.17	.07	.01	428	Tony Perez	.25	.10	.02
335	Jackie Gutierrez	.07	.03	.01	429	Jerry Davis	.07	.03	.01
336	Dennis Rasmussen	.07	.03	.01	430	Bob Walk	.07	.03	.01
337	Terry Whitfield	.07	.03	.01	431	Brad Wellman	.07	.03	.01
338	Neal Heaton	.07	.03	.01	432	Terry Forster	.07	.03	.01
339	Jorge Orta	.07	.03	.01	433	Billy Hatcher	.15	.06	.01
340	Donnie Hill	.07	.03	.01	434	Clint Hurdle	.07	.03	.01
341	Joe Hesketh	.12	.05	.01	435	Ivan Calderon	2.00	.80	.20
342	Charlie Hough	.07	.03	.01	436	Pete Filson	.07	.03	.01
343	Dave Rozema	.07	.03	.01	437	Tom Henke	.12	.05	.01
344	Greg Pryor	.07	.03	.01	438	Dave Engle	.07	.03	.01
345	Mickey Tettleton	1.25	.50	.12	439	Tom Filer	.07	.03	.01
346	George Vukovich	.07	.03	.01	440	Gorman Thomas	.10	.04	.01
347	Don Baylor	.12	.05	.01	441	Rick Aguilera	.90	.40	.09
348	Carlos Diaz	.07	.03	.01	442	Scott Sanderson	.10	.04	.01
349	Barbaro Garbey	.07	.03	.01	443	Jeff Dedmon	.07	.03	.01
350	Larry Sheets	.07	.03	.01	444	Joe Orsulak	.35	.15	.03
351	Ted Higuera	.45	.18	.04	445	Atlee Hammaker	.07	.03	.01
352	Juan Beniquez	.07	.03	.01	446	Jerry Royster	.07	.03	.01
353	Bob Forsch	.07	.03	.01	447	Buddy Bell	.10	.04	.01
354	Mark Bailey	.07	.03	.01	448	Dave Rucker	.07	.03	.01
355	Larry Andersen	.07	.03	.01	449	Ivan DeJesus	.07	.03	.01
356	Terry Kennedy	.07	.03	.01	450	Jim Pankovits	.07	.03	.01
357	Don Robinson	.07	.03	.01	451	Jerry Narron	.07	.03	.01
358	Jim Gott	.07	.03	.01	452	Bryan Little	.07	.03	.01
359	Earnie Riles	.17	.07	.01	453	Gary Lucas	.07	.03	.01
360	John Christensen	.07	.03	.01	454	Dennis Martinez	.10	.04	.01
361	Ray Fontenot	.07	.03	.01	455	Ed Romero	.07	.03	.01
362	Spike Owen	.07	.03	.01	456	Bob Melvin	.10	.04	.01
363	Jim Acker	.07	.03	.01	457	Glenn Hoffman	.07	.03	.01
364	Ron Davis	.07	.03	.01	458	Bob Shirley	.07	.03	.01
365	Tom Hume	.07	.03	.01	459	Bob Welch	.15	.06	.01
366	Carlton Fisk	.75	.30	.07	460	Carmen Castillo	.07	.03	.01
367	Nate Snell	.07	.03	.01	461	Dave Leeper	.07	.03	.01
368	Rick Manning	.07	.03	.01		(outfielder)			
369	Darrell Evans	.10	.04	.01	462	Tim Birtsas	.10	.04	.01
370	Ron Hassey	.07	.03	.01	463	Randy St.Claire	.07	.03	.01
371	Wade Boggs	2.50	1.00	.25	464	Chris Welsh	.07	.03	.01
372	Rick Honeycutt	.07	.03	.01	465	Greg Harris	.07	.03	.01
373	Chris Bando	.07	.03	.01	466	Lynn Jones	.07	.03	.01
374	Bud Black	.10	.04	.01	467	Dusty Baker	.10	.04	.01
375	Steve Henderson	.07	.03	.01	468	Roy Smith	.07	.03	.01
376	Charlie Lea	.07	.03	.01	469	Andre Robertson	.07	.03	.01
377	Reggie Jackson	.90	.40	.09	470	Ken Landreaux	.07	.03	.01
378	Dave Schmidt	.07	.03	.01	471	Dave Bergman	.07	.03	.01
379	Bob James	.07	.03	.01	472	Gary Roenicke	.07	.03	.01
380	Glenn Davis	2.25	.90	.22	473	Pete Vuckovich	.07	.03	.01
381	Tim Corcoran	.07	.03	.01	474	Kirk McCaskill	.30	.12	.03
382	Danny Cox	.07	.03	.01	475	Jeff Lahti	.07	.03	.01
383	Tim Flannery	.07	.03	.01	476	Mike Scott	.15	.06	.01
384	Tom Browning	.25	.10	.02	477	Darren Daulton	.35	.15	.03
385	Rick Camp	.07	.03	.01	478	Graig Nettles	.12	.05	.01
386	Jim Morrison	.07	.03	.01	479	Bill Almon	.07	.03	.01
387	Dave LaPoint	.07	.03	.01	480	Greg Minton	.07	.03	.01
388	Dave Lopes	.10	.04	.01	481	Randy Ready	.10	.04	.01
389	Al Cowens	.07	.03	.01	482	Len Dykstra	2.50	1.00	.25
390	Doyle Alexander	.07	.03	.01	483	Thad Bosley	.07	.03	.01
391	Tim Laudner	.07	.03	.01	484	Harold Reynolds	.90	.40	.09
392	Don Aase	.07	.03	.01	485	Al Oliver	.12	.05	.01
393	Jaime Cocanower	.07	.03	.01	486	Roy Smalley	.07	.03	.01
394	Randy O'Neal	.07	.03	.01	487	John Franco	.15	.06	.01
395	Mike Easler	.07	.03	.01	488	Juan Agosto	.07	.03	.01
396	Scott Bradley	.07	.03	.01	489	Al Pardo	.07	.03	.01
397	Tom Niedenfuer	.07	.03	.01	490	Bill Wegman	.25	.10	.02
398	Jerry Willard	.07	.03	.01	491	Frank Tanana	.10	.04	.01
399	Lonnie Smith	.12	.05	.01	492	Brian Fisher	.10	.04	.01
400	Bruce Bochte	.07	.03	.01	493	Mark Clear	.07	.03	.01
401	Terry Francona	.07	.03	.01	494	Len Matuszek	.07	.03	.01
402	Jim Slaton	.07	.03	.01	495	Ramon Romero	.07	.03	.01
403	Bill Stein	.07	.03	.01	496	John Wathan	.07	.03	.01
404	Tim Hulett	.07	.03	.01	497	Rob Picciolo	.07	.03	.01
405	Alan Ashby	.07	.03	.01	498	U.L. Washington	.07	.03	.01
406	Tim Stoddard	.07	.03	.01	499	John Candelaria	.07	.03	.01

☐ 500 Duane Walker	.07	.03	.01
☐ 501 Gene Nelson	.07	.03	.01
☐ 502 John Mizerock	.07	.03	.01
☐ 503 Luis Aguayo	.07	.03	.01
☐ 504 Kurt Kepshire	.07	.03	.01
☐ 505 Ed Wojna	.07	.03	.01
☐ 506 Joe Price	.07	.03	.01
☐ 507 Milt Thompson	.25	.10	.02
☐ 508 Junior Ortiz	.07	.03	.01
☐ 509 Vida Blue	.10	.04	.01
☐ 510 Steve Engel	.07	.03	.01
☐ 511 Karl Best	.07	.03	.01
☐ 512 Cecil Fielder	24.00	10.50	3.50
☐ 513 Frank Eufemia	.07	.03	.01
☐ 514 Tippy Martinez	.07	.03	.01
☐ 515 Billy Jo Robidoux	.07	.03	.01
☐ 516 Bill Scherrer	.07	.03	.01
☐ 517 Bruce Hurst	.10	.04	.01
☐ 518 Rich Bordi	.07	.03	.01
☐ 519 Steve Yeager	.07	.03	.01
☐ 520 Tony Bernazard	.07	.03	.01
☐ 521 Hal McRae	.10	.04	.01
☐ 522 Jose Rijo	.35	.15	.03
☐ 523 Mitch Webster	.17	.07	.01
☐ 524 Jack Howell	.15	.06	.01
☐ 525 Alan Bannister	.07	.03	.01
☐ 526 Ron Kittle	.10	.04	.01
☐ 527 Phil Garner	.10	.04	.01
☐ 528 Kurt Bevacqua	.07	.03	.01
☐ 529 Kevin Gross	.07	.03	.01
☐ 530 Bo Diaz	.07	.03	.01
☐ 531 Ken Oberkfell	.07	.03	.01
☐ 532 Rick Reuschel	.10	.04	.01
☐ 533 Ron Meridith	.07	.03	.01
☐ 534 Steve Braun	.07	.03	.01
☐ 535 Wayne Gross	.07	.03	.01
☐ 536 Ray Searage	.07	.03	.01
☐ 537 Tom Brookens	.07	.03	.01
☐ 538 Al Nipper	.07	.03	.01
☐ 539 Billy Sample	.07	.03	.01
☐ 540 Steve Sax	.25	.10	.02
☐ 541 Dan Quisenberry	.12	.05	.01
☐ 542 Tony Phillips	.10	.04	.01
☐ 543 Floyd Youmans	.10	.04	.01
☐ 544 Steve Buechele	.75	.30	.07
☐ 545 Craig Gerber	.07	.03	.01
☐ 546 Joe DeSa	.07	.03	.01
☐ 547 Brian Harper	.25	.10	.02
☐ 548 Kevin Bass	.10	.04	.01
☐ 549 Tom Foley	.07	.03	.01
☐ 550 Dave Van Gorder	.07	.03	.01
☐ 551 Bruce Bochy	.07	.03	.01
☐ 552 R.J. Reynolds	.07	.03	.01
☐ 553 Chris Brown	.10	.04	.01
☐ 554 Bruce Benedict	.07	.03	.01
☐ 555 Warren Brusstar	.07	.03	.01
☐ 556 Danny Heep	.07	.03	.01
☐ 557 Darnell Coles	.07	.03	.01
☐ 558 Greg Gagne	.12	.05	.01
☐ 559 Ernie Whitt	.07	.03	.01
☐ 560 Ron Washington	.07	.03	.01
☐ 561 Jimmy Key	.30	.12	.03
☐ 562 Billy Swift	.15	.06	.01
☐ 563 Ron Darling	.15	.06	.01
☐ 564 Dick Ruthven	.07	.03	.01
☐ 565 Zane Smith	.40	.16	.04
☐ 566 Sid Bream	.07	.03	.01
☐ 567A Joel Youngblood ERR (position P)	.10	.04	.01
☐ 567B Joel Youngblood COR (position IF)	.60	.25	.06
☐ 568 Mario Ramirez	.07	.03	.01
☐ 569 Tom Runnells	.15	.06	.01
☐ 570 Rick Schu	.07	.03	.01
☐ 571 Bill Campbell	.07	.03	.01
☐ 572 Dickie Thon	.10	.04	.01
☐ 573 Al Holland	.07	.03	.01
☐ 574 Reid Nichols	.07	.03	.01
☐ 575 Bert Roberge	.07	.03	.01
☐ 576 Mike Flanagan	.10	.04	.01
☐ 577 Tim Leary	.15	.06	.01
☐ 578 Mike Laga	.07	.03	.01
☐ 579 Steve Lyons	.07	.03	.01
☐ 580 Phil Niekro	.25	.10	.02
☐ 581 Gilberto Reyes	.20	.08	.02
☐ 582 Jamie Easterly	.07	.03	.01
☐ 583 Mark Gubicza	.15	.06	.01
☐ 584 Stan Javier	.25	.10	.02
☐ 585 Bill Laskey	.07	.03	.01
☐ 586 Jeff Russell	.10	.04	.01
☐ 587 Dickie Noles	.07	.03	.01
☐ 588 Steve Farr	.10	.04	.01
☐ 589 Steve Ontiveros	.07	.03	.01
☐ 590 Mike Hargrove	.07	.03	.01
☐ 591 Marty Bystrom	.07	.03	.01
☐ 592 Franklin Stubbs	.10	.04	.01
☐ 593 Larry Herndon	.07	.03	.01
☐ 594 Bill Swaggerty	.07	.03	.01
☐ 595 Carlos Ponce	.07	.03	.01
☐ 596 Pat Perry	.07	.03	.01
☐ 597 Ray Knight	.10	.04	.01
☐ 598 Steve Lombardozzi	.07	.03	.01
☐ 599 Brad Havens	.07	.03	.01
☐ 600 Pat Clements	.07	.03	.01
☐ 601 Joe Niekro	.10	.04	.01
☐ 602 Hank Aaron Puzzle Card	.10	.04	.01
☐ 603 Dwayne Henry	.15	.06	.01
☐ 604 Mookie Wilson	.10	.04	.01
☐ 605 Buddy Biancalana	.07	.03	.01
☐ 606 Rance Mulliniks	.07	.03	.01
☐ 607 Alan Wiggins	.07	.03	.01
☐ 608 Joe Cowley	.07	.03	.01
☐ 609A Tom Seaver (green borders on name)	1.00	.40	.10
☐ 609B Tom Seaver (yellow borders on name)	2.25	.90	.22
☐ 610 Neil Allen	.07	.03	.01
☐ 611 Don Sutton	.25	.10	.02
☐ 612 Fred Toliver	.10	.04	.01
☐ 613 Jay Baller	.07	.03	.01
☐ 614 Marc Sullivan	.07	.03	.01
☐ 615 John Grubb	.07	.03	.01
☐ 616 Bruce Kison	.07	.03	.01
☐ 617 Bill Madlock	.10	.04	.01
☐ 618 Chris Chambliss	.10	.04	.01
☐ 619 Dave Stewart	.35	.15	.03
☐ 620 Tim Lollar	.07	.03	.01
☐ 621 Gary Lavelle	.07	.03	.01
☐ 622 Charles Hudson	.07	.03	.01
☐ 623 Joel Davis	.10	.04	.01
☐ 624 Joe Johnson	.10	.04	.01
☐ 625 Sid Fernandez	.17	.07	.01
☐ 626 Dennis Lamp	.07	.03	.01
☐ 627 Terry Harper	.07	.03	.01
☐ 628 Jack Lazorko	.07	.03	.01
☐ 629 Roger McDowell	.35	.15	.03
☐ 630 Mark Funderburk	.07	.03	.01
☐ 631 Ed Lynch	.07	.03	.01
☐ 632 Rudy Law	.07	.03	.01
☐ 633 Roger Mason	.10	.04	.01
☐ 634 Mike Felder	.25	.10	.02
☐ 635 Ken Schrom	.07	.03	.01
☐ 636 Bob Ojeda	.10	.04	.01
☐ 637 Ed VandeBerg	.07	.03	.01
☐ 638 Bobby Meacham	.07	.03	.01
☐ 639 Cliff Johnson	.07	.03	.01
☐ 640 Garth Iorg	.07	.03	.01
☐ 641 Dan Driessen	.07	.03	.01
☐ 642 Mike Brown OF	.07	.03	.01
☐ 643 John Shelby	.07	.03	.01
☐ 644 Pete Rose (Ty-Breaking)	.40	.16	.04
☐ 645 The Knuckle Brothers Phil Niekro Joe Niekro	.12	.05	.01
☐ 646 Jesse Orosco	.07	.03	.01
☐ 647 Billy Beane	.10	.04	.01
☐ 648 Cesar Cedeno	.10	.04	.01
☐ 649 Bert Blyleven	.15	.06	.01
☐ 650 Max Venable	.07	.03	.01
☐ 651 Fleet Feet Vince Coleman Willie McGee	.50	.20	.05
☐ 652 Calvin Schiraldi	.07	.03	.01
☐ 653 King of Kings (Pete Rose)	.75	.30	.07
☐ 654 CL: Diamond Kings (unnumbered)	.15	.02	.00
☐ 655A CL 1: 27-130 (unnumbered) (45 Beane ERR)	.15	.02	.00
☐ 655B CL 1: 27-130 (unnumbered) (45 Habyan COR)	.50	.10	.02
☐ 656 CL 2: 131-234 (unnumbered)	.15	.02	.00
☐ 657 CL 3: 235-338 (unnumbered)	.15	.02	.00
☐ 658 CL 4: 339-442 (unnumbered)	.15	.02	.00
☐ 659 CL 5: 443-546 (unnumbered)	.15	.02	.00
☐ 660 CL 6: 547-653 (unnumbered)	.15	.02	.00

1986 Donruss Wax Box Cards

The cards in this four-card set measure the standard 2 1/2" by 3 1/2". Cards have essentially the same design as the 1986 Donruss regular issue set. The cards were printed on the bottoms of the regular issue wax pack boxes. The four cards (PC4 to PC6 plus a Hank Aaron puzzle card) are considered a separate set in their own right and are not typically included in a complete set of the regular issue 1986 Donruss cards. The value of the panel uncut is slightly greater, perhaps by 25 percent greater, than the value of the individual cards cut up carefully.

	MINT	EXC	G-VG
COMPLETE SET (4)	.60	.25	.06
COMMON PLAYERS	.05	.02	.00
☐ PC4 Kirk Gibson	.50	.20	.05
☐ PC5 Willie Hernandez	.10	.04	.01
☐ PC6 Doug DeCinces	.10	.04	.01
☐ PUZ Hank Aaron Puzzle Card	.05	.02	.00

1986 Donruss All-Stars

The cards in this 60-card set measure approximately 3 1/2" by 5". Players featured were involved in the 1985 All-Star game played in Minnesota. Cards are very similar in design to the 1986 Donruss regular issue set. The backs give each player's All-Star game statistics and have an orange-yellow border.

	MINT	EXC	G-VG
COMPLETE SET (60)	7.50	3.25	.75
COMMON PLAYERS (1-60)	.07	.03	.01
☐ 1 Tony Gwynn	.50	.20	.05
☐ 2 Tommy Herr	.07	.03	.01

☐ 3 Steve Garvey	.30	.12	.03
☐ 4 Dale Murphy	.45	.18	.04
☐ 5 Darryl Strawberry	.75	.30	.07
☐ 6 Graig Nettles	.10	.04	.01
☐ 7 Terry Kennedy	.07	.03	.01
☐ 8 Ozzie Smith	.30	.12	.03
☐ 9 LaMarr Hoyt	.07	.03	.01
☐ 10 Rickey Henderson	1.00	.40	.10
☐ 11 Lou Whitaker	.15	.06	.01
☐ 12 George Brett	.45	.18	.04
☐ 13 Eddie Murray	.40	.16	.04
☐ 14 Cal Ripken	1.00	.40	.10
☐ 15 Dave Winfield	.25	.10	.02
☐ 16 Jim Rice	.20	.08	.02
☐ 17 Carlton Fisk	.40	.16	.04
☐ 18 Jack Morris	.25	.10	.02
☐ 19 Jose Cruz	.07	.03	.01
☐ 20 Tim Raines	.20	.08	.02
☐ 21 Nolan Ryan	1.25	.50	.12
☐ 22 Tony Pena	.07	.03	.01
☐ 23 Jack Clark	.15	.06	.01
☐ 24 Dave Parker	.15	.06	.01
☐ 25 Tim Wallach	.07	.03	.01
☐ 26 Ozzie Virgil	.07	.03	.01
☐ 27 Fernando Valenzuela	.15	.06	.01
☐ 28 Dwight Gooden	.60	.25	.06
☐ 29 Glenn Wilson	.07	.03	.01
☐ 30 Garry Templeton	.07	.03	.01
☐ 31 Goose Gossage	.15	.06	.01
☐ 32 Ryne Sandberg	1.00	.40	.10
☐ 33 Jeff Reardon	.20	.08	.02
☐ 34 Pete Rose	.90	.40	.09
☐ 35 Scott Garrelts	.07	.03	.01
☐ 36 Willie McGee	.15	.06	.01
☐ 37 Ron Darling	.10	.04	.01
☐ 38 Dick Williams MG	.07	.03	.01
☐ 39 Paul Molitor	.20	.08	.02
☐ 40 Damaso Garcia	.07	.03	.01
☐ 41 Phil Bradley	.07	.03	.01
☐ 42 Dan Petry	.07	.03	.01
☐ 43 Willie Hernandez	.10	.04	.01
☐ 44 Tom Brunansky	.10	.04	.01
☐ 45 Alan Trammell	.25	.10	.02
☐ 46 Donnie Moore	.07	.03	.01
☐ 47 Wade Boggs	.90	.40	.09
☐ 48 Ernie Whitt	.07	.03	.01
☐ 49 Harold Baines	.10	.04	.01
☐ 50 Don Mattingly	.75	.30	.07
☐ 51 Gary Ward	.07	.03	.01
☐ 52 Bert Blyleven	.15	.06	.01
☐ 53 Jimmy Key	.10	.04	.01
☐ 54 Cecil Cooper	.10	.04	.01
☐ 55 Dave Stieb	.10	.04	.01
☐ 56 Rich Gedman	.07	.03	.01
☐ 57 Jay Howell	.07	.03	.01
☐ 58 Sparky Anderson MG	.07	.03	.01
☐ 59 Minneapolis Metrodome	.07	.03	.01
☐ 60 Checklist Card (unnumbered)	.07	.03	.01

1986 Donruss All-Star Box

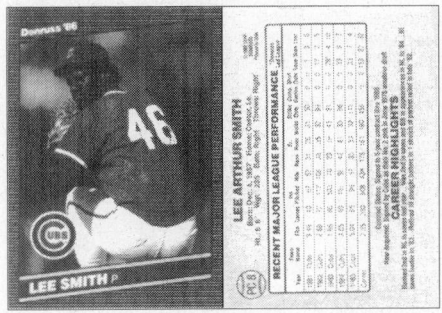

The cards in this four-card set measure the standard 2 1/2" by 3 1/2" in spite of the fact that they form the bottom of the wax pack box for the larger Donruss All-Star cards. These box cards have essentially the same design as the 1986 Donruss regular issue set. The cards were printed on the bottoms of the Donruss All-Star (3 1/2" by 5") wax pack boxes. The four cards (PC7 to PC9 plus a Hank Aaron puzzle card) are considered a separate set in their own right and are not typically included in a complete set of the regular issue 1986 Donruss All-Star (or regular) cards. The value of the panel uncut is slightly greater, perhaps by 25 percent greater, than the value of the individual cards cut up carefully.

	MINT	EXC	G-VG
COMPLETE SET (4)	1.25	.50	.12
COMMON PLAYERS	.05	.02	.00
☐ PC7 Wade Boggs	1.25	.50	.12
☐ PC8 Lee Smith	.35	.15	.03
☐ PC9 Cecil Cooper	.10	.04	.01
☐ PUZ Hank Aaron Puzzle Card	.05	.02	.00

1986 Donruss Pop-Ups

This set is the companion of the 1986 Donruss All-Star (60) set; as such it features the first 18 cards of that set (the All-Star starting line-ups) in a pop-up, die-cut type of card. These cards (measuring (2 1/2" by 5") can be "popped up" to feature a standing card showing the player in action in front of the Metrodome ballpark background. Although this set is unnumbered it is numbered in the same order as its companion set, presumably according to the respective batting orders of the starting line-ups. The first nine numbers below are National Leaguers and the last nine are American Leaguers. See also the Donruss All-Star checklist card which contains a checklist for the Pop-Ups as well.

	MINT	EXC	G-VG
COMPLETE SET (18)	4.00	1.75	.40
COMMON PLAYERS (1-18)	.10	.04	.01
☐ 1 Tony Gwynn	.50	.20	.05
☐ 2 Tommy Herr	.10	.04	.01
☐ 3 Steve Garvey	.35	.15	.03
☐ 4 Dale Murphy	.40	.16	.04
☐ 5 Darryl Strawberry	.75	.30	.07
☐ 6 Graig Nettles	.10	.04	.01
☐ 7 Terry Kennedy	.10	.04	.01
☐ 8 Ozzie Smith	.25	.10	.02
☐ 9 LaMarr Hoyt	.10	.04	.01
☐ 10 Rickey Henderson	1.00	.40	.10
☐ 11 Lou Whitaker	.20	.08	.02
☐ 12 George Brett	.60	.25	.06
☐ 13 Eddie Murray	.45	.18	.04
☐ 14 Cal Ripken	1.00	.40	.10
☐ 15 Dave Winfield	.25	.10	.02
☐ 16 Jim Rice	.20	.08	.02

☐ 17 Carlton Fisk	.35	.15	.03
☐ 18 Jack Morris	.25	.10	.02

1986 Donruss Super DK's

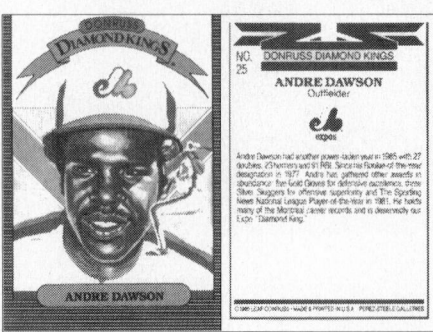

This 29-card set of large Diamond Kings features the full-color artwork of Dick Perez. The set could be obtained from Perez-Steele Galleries by sending three Donruss wrappers and $9.00. The cards measure 4 7/8" by 6 13/16" and are identical in design to the Diamond King cards in the Donruss regular issue.

	MINT	EXC	G-VG
COMPLETE SET (29)	9.00	4.00	.90
COMMON PLAYER (1-27)	.20	.08	.02
☐ 1 Kirk Gibson	.50	.20	.05
☐ 2 Goose Gossage	.40	.16	.04
☐ 3 Willie McGee	.40	.16	.04
☐ 4 George Bell	.50	.20	.05
☐ 5 Tony Armas	.20	.08	.02
☐ 6 Chili Davis	.30	.12	.03
☐ 7 Cecil Cooper	.30	.12	.03
☐ 8 Mike Boddicker	.20	.08	.02
☐ 9 Dave Lopes	.20	.08	.02
☐ 10 Bill Doran	.20	.08	.02
☐ 11 Bret Saberhagen	.75	.30	.07
☐ 12 Brett Butler	.30	.12	.03
☐ 13 Harold Baines	.30	.12	.03
☐ 14 Mike Davis	.20	.08	.02
☐ 15 Tony Perez	.40	.16	.04
☐ 16 Willie Randolph	.30	.12	.03
☐ 17 Bob Boone	.30	.12	.03
☐ 18 Orel Hershiser	.75	.30	.07
☐ 19 Johnny Ray	.20	.08	.02
☐ 20 Gary Ward	.20	.08	.02
☐ 21 Rick Mahler	.20	.08	.02
☐ 22 Phil Bradley	.20	.08	.02
☐ 23 Jerry Koosman	.30	.12	.03
☐ 24 Tom Brunansky	.30	.12	.03
☐ 25 Andre Dawson	.60	.25	.06
☐ 26 Dwight Gooden	1.00	.40	.10
☐ 27 Pete Rose King of Kings	1.00	.40	.10
☐ 28 Checklist Card (unnumbered)	.20	.08	.02
☐ 29 Aaron Large Puzzle (unnumbered)	.20	.08	.02

1986 Donruss Rookies

The 1986 Donruss "The Rookies" set features 56 cards plus a 15-piece puzzle of Hank Aaron. Cards are in full color and are standard size, 2 1/2" by 3 1/2". The set was distributed in a small green box with gold lettering. Although the set was wrapped in cellophane, the top card was number 1 Joyner, resulting in a percentage of the Joyner cards arriving in less than perfect condition. Donruss fixed the problem after it was called to their attention and even went so far as to include a customer service phone number in their second printing. Card fronts are similar in design to the 1986 Donruss regular issue except for the presence of "The Rookies" logo in the lower left corner and a bluish green border instead of a blue border. The key (extended) rookie cards in this set are Barry Bonds, Bobby Bonilla, Will Clark, Bo Jackson, Wally Joyner, Kevin Mitchell, and Ruben Sierra.

		MINT	EXC	G-VG
COMPLETE SET (56)		60.00	27.00	9.00
COMMON PLAYER (1-56)		.12	.05	.01
☐ 1	Wally Joyner	3.25	1.25	.25
☐ 2	Tracy Jones	.20	.08	.02
☐ 3	Allan Anderson	.20	.08	.02
☐ 4	Ed Correa	.12	.05	.01
☐ 5	Reggie Williams	.12	.05	.01
☐ 6	Charlie Kerfeld	.12	.05	.01
☐ 7	Andres Galarraga	.50	.20	.05
☐ 8	Bob Tewksbury	.20	.08	.02
☐ 9	Al Newman	.20	.08	.02
☐ 10	Andres Thomas	.20	.08	.02
☐ 11	Barry Bonds	8.50	3.75	.85
☐ 12	Juan Nieves	.20	.08	.02
☐ 13	Mark Eichhorn	.20	.08	.02
☐ 14	Dan Plesac	.20	.08	.02
☐ 15	Cory Snyder	.25	.10	.02
☐ 16	Kelly Gruber	2.50	1.00	.25
☐ 17	Kevin Mitchell	6.00	2.50	.60
☐ 18	Steve Lombardozzi	.20	.08	.02
☐ 19	Mitch Williams	.40	.16	.04
☐ 20	John Cerutti	.20	.08	.02
☐ 21	Todd Worrell	.20	.08	.02
☐ 22	Jose Canseco	12.00	5.25	1.50
☐ 23	Pete Incaviglia	.75	.30	.07
☐ 24	Jose Guzman	.25	.10	.02
☐ 25	Scott Bailes	.20	.08	.02
☐ 26	Greg Mathews	.12	.05	.01
☐ 27	Eric King	.20	.08	.02
☐ 28	Paul Assenmacher	.20	.08	.02
☐ 29	Jeff Sellers	.12	.05	.01
☐ 30	Bobby Bonilla	7.50	3.25	.75
☐ 31	Doug Drabek	1.50	.60	.15
☐ 32	Will Clark UER	13.50	6.00	1.85
	(Listed as throwing right, should be left)			
☐ 33	Bip Roberts	.60	.25	.06
☐ 34	Jim Deshaies	.20	.08	.02
☐ 35	Mike LaValliere	.30	.12	.03
☐ 36	Scott Bankhead	.20	.08	.02
☐ 37	Dale Sveum	.20	.08	.02
☐ 38	Bo Jackson	11.00	5.00	1.35
☐ 39	Robby Thompson	.45	.18	.04
☐ 40	Eric Plunk	.20	.08	.02
☐ 41	Bill Bathe	.12	.05	.01
☐ 42	John Kruk	.45	.18	.04
☐ 43	Andy Allanson	.20	.08	.02
☐ 44	Mark Portugal	.25	.10	.02
☐ 45	Danny Tartabull	1.00	.40	.10
☐ 46	Bob Kipper	.20	.08	.02
☐ 47	Gene Walter	.20	.08	.02
☐ 48	Rey Quinones	.12	.05	.01
☐ 49	Bobby Witt	.60	.25	.06
☐ 50	Bill Mooneyham	.12	.05	.01
☐ 51	John Cangelosi	.12	.05	.01
☐ 52	Ruben Sierra	11.00	5.00	1.35
☐ 53	Rob Woodward	.12	.05	.01
☐ 54	Ed Hearn	.12	.05	.01
☐ 55	Joel McKeon	.12	.05	.01
☐ 56	Checklist Card	.12	.02	.00

1986 Donruss Highlights

Donruss' second edition of Highlights was released late in 1986. These glossy-coated cards are standard size, measuring 2 1/2" by 3 1/2". Cards commemorate events during the 1986 season, as well as players and pitchers of the month from each league. The set was distributed in its own red, white, blue, and gold box along with a small Hank Aaron puzzle. Card fronts are similar to the regular 1986 Donruss issue except that the Highlights logo is positioned in the lower left-hand corner and the borders are in gold instead of blue. The backs are printed in black and gold on white card stock.

		MINT	EXC	G-VG
COMPLETE SET (56)		9.00	4.00	.90
COMMON PLAYER (1-56)		.06	.02	.00
☐ 1	Will Clark	1.25	.50	.12
	Homers in First At-Bat			
☐ 2	Jose Rijo	.30	.12	.03
	Oakland Milestone for Strikeouts			
☐ 3	George Brett	.30	.12	.03
	Royals' All-Time Hit Man			
☐ 4	Mike Schmidt	.75	.30	.07
	Phillies RBI Leader			
☐ 5	Roger Clemens	.60	.25	.06
	KKKKKKKKKK KKKKKKKKKK			
☐ 6	Roger Clemens	.60	.25	.06
	AL Pitcher April			
☐ 7	Kirby Puckett	.60	.25	.06
	AL Player April			
☐ 8	Dwight Gooden	.35	.15	.03
	NL Pitcher April			
☐ 9	Johnny Ray	.06	.02	.00
	NL Player April			
☐ 10	Reggie Jackson	.40	.16	.04
	Eclipses Mantle HR Record			
☐ 11	Wade Boggs	.60	.25	.06
	First Five Hit Game of Career			
☐ 12	Don Aase	.06	.02	.00
	AL Pitcher May			
☐ 13	Wade Boggs	.60	.25	.06
	AL Player May			
☐ 14	Jeff Reardon	.15	.06	.01
	NL Pitcher May			
☐ 15	Hubie Brooks	.06	.02	.00
	NL Player May			
☐ 16	Don Sutton	.15	.06	.01
	Notches 300th			
☐ 17	Roger Clemens	.60	.25	.06
	Starts 14-0			
☐ 18	Roger Clemens	.60	.25	.06
	AL Pitcher June			
☐ 19	Kent Hrbek	.15	.06	.01
	AL Player June			
☐ 20	Rick Rhoden	.06	.02	.00
	NL Pitcher June			
☐ 21	Kevin Bass	.06	.02	.00
	NL Player June			

☐ 22	Bob Horner Blasts four HRs in one Game	.10	.04	.01
☐ 23	Wally Joyner Starting All-Star Rookie	.60	.25	.06
☐ 24	Darryl Strawberry Starts Third Straight All-Star Game	.60	.25	.06
☐ 25	Fernando Valenzuela Ties All-Star Game Record	.15	.06	.01
☐ 26	Roger Clemens All-Star Game MVP	.60	.25	.06
☐ 27	Jack Morris AL Pitcher July	.20	.08	.02
☐ 28	Scott Fletcher AL Player July	.06	.02	.00
☐ 29	Todd Worrell NL Pitcher July	.10	.04	.01
☐ 30	Eric Davis NL Player July	.60	.25	.06
☐ 31	Bert Blyleven Records 3000th Strikeout	.15	.06	.01
☐ 32	Bobby Doerr '86 HOF Inductee	.15	.06	.01
☐ 33	Ernie Lombardi '86 HOF Inductee	.15	.06	.01
☐ 34	Willie McCovey '86 HOF Inductee	.25	.10	.02
☐ 35	Steve Carlton Notches 4000th K	.25	.10	.02
☐ 36	Mike Schmidt Surpasses DiMaggio Record	.75	.30	.07
☐ 37	Juan Samuel Records 3rd "Quadruple Double"	.10	.04	.01
☐ 38	Mike Witt AL Pitcher August	.06	.02	.00
☐ 39	Doug DeCinces AL Player August	.06	.02	.00
☐ 40	Bill Gullickson NL Pitcher August	.10	.04	.01
☐ 41	Dale Murphy NL Player August	.30	.12	.03
☐ 42	Joe Carter Sets Tribe Offensive Record	.25	.10	.02
☐ 43	Bo Jackson Longest HR in Royals Stadium	1.50	.60	.15
☐ 44	Joe Cowley Majors 1st No- Hitter in 2 Years	.06	.02	.00
☐ 45	Jim Deshaies Sets ML Strikeout Record	.06	.02	.00
☐ 46	Mike Scott No Hitter Clinches Division	.10	.04	.01
☐ 47	Bruce Hurst AL Pitcher September	.10	.04	.01
☐ 48	Don Mattingly AL Player September	.75	.30	.07
☐ 49	Mike Krukow NL Pitcher September	.06	.02	.00
☐ 50	Steve Sax NL Player September	.15	.06	.01
☐ 51	John Cangelosi AL Rookie Steals Record	.10	.04	.01
☐ 52	Dave Righetti ML Save Mark	.10	.04	.01
☐ 53	Don Mattingly Yankee Record for Hits and Doubles	.75	.30	.07
☐ 54	Todd Worrell Donruss NL ROY	.15	.06	.01
☐ 55	Jose Canseco Donruss AL ROY	1.50	.60	.15
☐ 56	Checklist Card	.06	.02	.00

1987 Donruss

This 660-card set was distributed along with a puzzle of Roberto Clemente. The checklist cards are numbered throughout

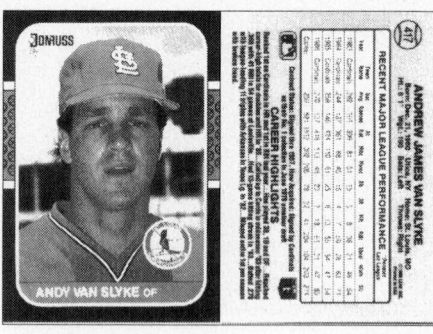

the set as multiples of 100. The wax pack boxes again contain four separate cards printed on the bottom of the box. Cards measure 2 1/2" by 3 1/2" and feature a black and gold border on the front; the backs are also done in black and gold on white card stock. The popular Diamond King subset returns for the sixth consecutive year. Some of the Diamond King (1-26) selections are repeats from prior years; Perez-Steele Galleries has indicated that a five-year rotation will be maintained in order to avoid depleting the pool of available worthy "kings" on some of the teams. Three of the Diamond Kings have a variation (on the reverse) where the yellow strip behind the words "Donruss Diamond Kings" is not printed and, hence, the background is white. The key rookie cards in this set are Barry Bonds, Bobby Bonilla, Will Clark, David Cone, Chuck Finley, Mike Greenwell, Bo Jackson, Wally Joyner, Barry Larkin, Dave Magadan, Kevin Mitchell, Rafael Palmiero, and Ruben Sierra. The backs of the cards in the factory sets are oriented differently than cards taken from wax packs, giving the appearance that one version or the other is upside down when sorting from the card backs.

		MINT	EXC	G-VG
	COMPLETE SET (660)	65.00	27.00	3.00
	COMMON PLAYER (1-660)	.05	.02	.00
☐ 1	Wally Joyner DK	.35	.15	.03
☐ 2	Roger Clemens DK	.65	.25	.06
☐ 3	Dale Murphy DK	.15	.06	.01
☐ 4	Darryl Strawberry DK	.50	.20	.05
☐ 5	Ozzie Smith DK	.15	.06	.01
☐ 6	Jose Canseco DK	1.25	.50	.12
☐ 7	Charlie Hough DK	.08	.03	.01
☐ 8	Brook Jacoby DK	.08	.03	.01
☐ 9	Fred Lynn DK	.12	.05	.01
☐ 10	Rick Rhoden DK	.08	.03	.01
☐ 11	Chris Brown DK	.08	.03	.01
☐ 12	Von Hayes DK	.10	.04	.01
☐ 13	Jack Morris DK	.15	.06	.01
☐ 14A	Kevin McReynolds DK ERR (Yellow strip missing on back)	.50	.20	.05
☐ 14B	Kevin McReynolds DK COR	.12	.05	.01
☐ 15	George Brett DK	.25	.10	.02
☐ 16	Ted Higuera DK	.08	.03	.01
☐ 17	Hubie Brooks DK	.08	.03	.01
☐ 18	Mike Scott DK	.10	.04	.01
☐ 19	Kirby Puckett DK	.50	.20	.05
☐ 20	Dave Winfield DK	.20	.08	.02
☐ 21	Lloyd Moseby DK	.08	.03	.01
☐ 22A	Eric Davis DK ERR (Yellow strip missing on back)	1.00	.40	.10
☐ 22B	Eric Davis DK COR	.25	.10	.02
☐ 23	Jim Presley DK	.08	.03	.01
☐ 24	Keith Moreland DK	.08	.03	.01
☐ 25A	Greg Walker DK ERR (Yellow strip missing on back)	.45	.18	.04
☐ 25B	Greg Walker DK COR	.10	.04	.01
☐ 26	Steve Sax DK	.12	.05	.01
☐ 27	DK Checklist 1-26	.07	.03	.01
☐ 28	B.J. Surhoff RR	.25	.10	.02
☐ 29	Randy Myers RR	.25	.10	.02
☐ 30	Ken Gerhart RR	.05	.02	.00
☐ 31	Benito Santiago RR	1.25	.50	.12
☐ 32	Greg Swindell RR	.75	.30	.07

#	Player			
☐ 33	Mike Birkbeck RR	.10	.04	.01
☐ 34	Terry Steinbach RR	.40	.16	.04
☐ 35	Bo Jackson RR	7.50	3.25	.75
☐ 36	Greg Maddux RR	1.25	.50	.12
☐ 37	Jim Lindeman RR	.08	.03	.01
☐ 38	Devon White RR	.90	.40	.09
☐ 39	Eric Bell RR	.08	.03	.01
☐ 40	Willie Fraser RR	.08	.03	.01
☐ 41	Jerry Browne RR	.20	.08	.02
☐ 42	Chris James RR	.35	.15	.03
☐ 43	Rafael Palmeiro RR	6.00	2.50	.60
☐ 44	Pat Dodson RR	.08	.03	.01
☐ 45	Duane Ward RR	.30	.12	.03
☐ 46	Mark McGwire RR	5.00	2.25	.50
☐ 47	Bruce Fields RR UER (photo actually Darnell Coles)	.08	.03	.01
☐ 48	Eddie Murray	.40	.16	.04
☐ 49	Ted Higuera	.08	.03	.01
☐ 50	Kirk Gibson	.17	.07	.01
☐ 51	Oil Can Boyd	.05	.02	.00
☐ 52	Don Mattingly	1.00	.40	.10
☐ 53	Pedro Guerrero	.15	.06	.01
☐ 54	George Brett	.40	.16	.04
☐ 55	Jose Rijo	.17	.07	.01
☐ 56	Tim Raines	.20	.08	.02
☐ 57	Ed Correa	.05	.02	.00
☐ 58	Mike Witt	.05	.02	.00
☐ 59	Greg Walker	.05	.02	.00
☐ 60	Ozzie Smith	.35	.15	.03
☐ 61	Glenn Davis	.25	.10	.02
☐ 62	Glenn Wilson	.05	.02	.00
☐ 63	Tom Browning	.08	.03	.01
☐ 64	Tony Gwynn	.70	.30	.07
☐ 65	R.J. Reynolds	.05	.02	.00
☐ 66	Will Clark	10.00	4.50	1.25
☐ 67	Ozzie Virgil	.05	.02	.00
☐ 68	Rick Sutcliffe	.08	.03	.01
☐ 69	Gary Carter	.20	.08	.02
☐ 70	Mike Moore	.08	.03	.01
☐ 71	Bert Blyleven	.10	.04	.01
☐ 72	Tony Fernandez	.12	.05	.01
☐ 73	Kent Hrbek	.15	.06	.01
☐ 74	Lloyd Moseby	.05	.02	.00
☐ 75	Alvin Davis	.10	.04	.01
☐ 76	Keith Hernandez	.12	.05	.01
☐ 77	Ryne Sandberg	1.25	.50	.12
☐ 78	Dale Murphy	.30	.12	.03
☐ 79	Sid Bream	.05	.02	.00
☐ 80	Chris Brown	.05	.02	.00
☐ 81	Steve Garvey	.25	.10	.02
☐ 82	Mario Soto	.05	.02	.00
☐ 83	Shane Rawley	.05	.02	.00
☐ 84	Willie McGee	.12	.05	.01
☐ 85	Jose Cruz	.08	.03	.01
☐ 86	Brian Downing	.08	.03	.01
☐ 87	Ozzie Guillen	.15	.06	.01
☐ 88	Hubie Brooks	.10	.04	.01
☐ 89	Cal Ripken	1.50	.60	.15
☐ 90	Juan Nieves	.05	.02	.00
☐ 91	Lance Parrish	.10	.04	.01
☐ 92	Jim Rice	.12	.05	.01
☐ 93	Ron Guidry	.12	.05	.01
☐ 94	Fernando Valenzuela	.10	.04	.01
☐ 95	Andy Allanson	.05	.02	.00
☐ 96	Willie Wilson	.10	.04	.01
☐ 97	Jose Canseco	8.00	3.50	.80
☐ 98	Jeff Reardon	.12	.05	.01
☐ 99	Bobby Witt	.50	.20	.05
☐ 100	Checklist Card	.10	.01	.00
☐ 101	Jose Guzman	.08	.03	.01
☐ 102	Steve Balboni	.05	.02	.00
☐ 103	Tony Phillips	.05	.02	.00
☐ 104	Brook Jacoby	.08	.03	.01
☐ 105	Dave Winfield	.30	.12	.03
☐ 106	Orel Hershiser	.20	.08	.02
☐ 107	Lou Whitaker	.15	.06	.01
☐ 108	Fred Lynn	.12	.05	.01
☐ 109	Bill Wegman	.08	.03	.01
☐ 110	Donnie Moore	.05	.02	.00
☐ 111	Jack Clark	.15	.06	.01
☐ 112	Bob Knepper	.05	.02	.00
☐ 113	Von Hayes	.10	.04	.01
☐ 114	Bip Roberts	.40	.16	.04
☐ 115	Tony Pena	.08	.03	.01
☐ 116	Scott Garrelts	.05	.02	.00
☐ 117	Paul Molitor	.15	.06	.01
☐ 118	Darryl Strawberry	1.25	.50	.12
☐ 119	Shawon Dunston	.20	.08	.02
☐ 120	Jim Presley	.05	.02	.00
☐ 121	Jesse Barfield	.10	.04	.01
☐ 122	Gary Gaetti	.10	.04	.01
☐ 123	Kurt Stillwell	.20	.08	.02
☐ 124	Joel Davis	.05	.02	.00
☐ 125	Mike Boddicker	.05	.02	.00
☐ 126	Robin Yount	.45	.18	.04
☐ 127	Alan Trammell	.25	.10	.02
☐ 128	Dave Righetti	.10	.04	.01
☐ 129	Dwight Evans	.15	.06	.01
☐ 130	Mike Scioscia	.05	.02	.00
☐ 131	Julio Franco	.35	.15	.03
☐ 132	Bret Saberhagen	.30	.12	.03
☐ 133	Mike Davis	.05	.02	.00
☐ 134	Joe Hesketh	.08	.03	.01
☐ 135	Wally Joyner	2.00	.80	.20
☐ 136	Don Slaught	.05	.02	.00
☐ 137	Daryl Boston	.05	.02	.00
☐ 138	Nolan Ryan	2.00	.80	.20
☐ 139	Mike Schmidt	1.00	.40	.10
☐ 140	Tommy Herr	.05	.02	.00
☐ 141	Garry Templeton	.08	.03	.01
☐ 142	Kal Daniels	.20	.08	.02
☐ 143	Billy Sample	.05	.02	.00
☐ 144	Johnny Ray	.05	.02	.00
☐ 145	Rob Thompson	.25	.10	.02
☐ 146	Bob Dernier	.05	.02	.00
☐ 147	Danny Tartabull	.25	.10	.02
☐ 148	Ernie Whitt	.05	.02	.00
☐ 149	Kirby Puckett	1.75	.70	.17
☐ 150	Mike Young	.05	.02	.00
☐ 151	Ernest Riles	.05	.02	.00
☐ 152	Frank Tanana	.08	.03	.01
☐ 153	Rich Gedman	.05	.02	.00
☐ 154	Willie Randolph	.08	.03	.01
☐ 155	Bill Madlock	.08	.03	.01
☐ 156	Joe Carter	.50	.20	.05
☐ 157	Danny Jackson	.08	.03	.01
☐ 158	Carney Lansford	.10	.04	.01
☐ 159	Bryn Smith	.05	.02	.00
☐ 160	Gary Pettis	.05	.02	.00
☐ 161	Oddibe McDowell	.08	.03	.01
☐ 162	John Cangelosi	.05	.02	.00
☐ 163	Mike Scott	.10	.04	.01
☐ 164	Eric Show	.05	.02	.00
☐ 165	Juan Samuel	.15	.06	.01
☐ 166	Nick Esasky	.08	.03	.01
☐ 167	Zane Smith	.10	.04	.01
☐ 168	Mike Brown (Pirates OF)	.05	.02	.00
☐ 169	Keith Moreland	.05	.02	.00
☐ 170	John Tudor	.08	.03	.01
☐ 171	Ken Dixon	.05	.02	.00
☐ 172	Jim Gantner	.05	.02	.00
☐ 173	Jack Morris	.25	.10	.02
☐ 174	Bruce Hurst	.10	.04	.01
☐ 175	Dennis Rasmussen	.05	.02	.00
☐ 176	Mike Marshall	.08	.03	.01
☐ 177	Dan Quisenberry	.10	.04	.01
☐ 178	Eric Plunk	.05	.02	.00
☐ 179	Tim Wallach	.10	.04	.01
☐ 180	Steve Buechele	.08	.03	.01
☐ 181	Don Sutton	.15	.06	.01
☐ 182	Dave Schmidt	.05	.02	.00
☐ 183	Terry Pendleton	.20	.08	.02
☐ 184	Jim Deshaies	.15	.06	.01
☐ 185	Steve Bedrosian	.08	.03	.01
☐ 186	Pete Rose	.50	.20	.05
☐ 187	Dave Dravecky	.10	.04	.01
☐ 188	Rick Reuschel	.08	.03	.01
☐ 189	Dan Gladden	.05	.02	.00
☐ 190	Rick Mahler	.05	.02	.00
☐ 191	Thad Bosley	.05	.02	.00
☐ 192	Ron Darling	.10	.04	.01
☐ 193	Matt Young	.05	.02	.00
☐ 194	Tom Brunansky	.10	.04	.01
☐ 195	Dave Stieb	.10	.04	.01
☐ 196	Frank Viola	.20	.08	.02
☐ 197	Tom Henke	.08	.03	.01
☐ 198	Karl Best	.05	.02	.00
☐ 199	Dwight Gooden	.50	.20	.05
☐ 200	Checklist Card	.10	.01	.00
☐ 201	Steve Trout	.05	.02	.00
☐ 202	Rafael Ramirez	.05	.02	.00
☐ 203	Bob Walk	.05	.02	.00
☐ 204	Roger Mason	.05	.02	.00
☐ 205	Terry Kennedy	.05	.02	.00
☐ 206	Ron Oester	.05	.02	.00
☐ 207	John Russell	.05	.02	.00
☐ 208	Greg Mathews	.08	.03	.01
☐ 209	Charlie Kerfeld	.05	.02	.00
☐ 210	Reggie Jackson	.40	.16	.04
☐ 211	Floyd Bannister	.05	.02	.00
☐ 212	Vance Law	.05	.02	.00
☐ 213	Rich Bordi	.05	.02	.00
☐ 214	Dan Plesac	.15	.06	.01
☐ 215	Dave Collins	.05	.02	.00
☐ 216	Bob Stanley	.05	.02	.00
☐ 217	Joe Niekro	.08	.03	.01

☐ 218	Tom Niedenfuer	.05	.02	.00
☐ 219	Brett Butler	.12	.05	.01
☐ 220	Charlie Leibrandt	.05	.02	.00
☐ 221	Steve Ontiveros	.05	.02	.00
☐ 222	Tim Burke	.05	.02	.00
☐ 223	Curtis Wilkerson	.05	.02	.00
☐ 224	Pete Incaviglia	.35	.15	.03
☐ 225	Lonnie Smith	.10	.04	.01
☐ 226	Chris Codiroli	.05	.02	.00
☐ 227	Scott Bailes	.08	.03	.01
☐ 228	Rickey Henderson	1.00	.40	.10
☐ 229	Ken Howell	.05	.02	.00
☐ 230	Darnell Coles	.05	.02	.00
☐ 231	Don Aase	.05	.02	.00
☐ 232	Tim Leary	.10	.04	.01
☐ 233	Bob Boone	.10	.04	.01
☐ 234	Ricky Horton	.05	.02	.00
☐ 235	Mark Bailey	.05	.02	.00
☐ 236	Kevin Gross	.05	.02	.00
☐ 237	Lance McCullers	.05	.02	.00
☐ 238	Cecilio Guante	.05	.02	.00
☐ 239	Bob Melvin	.05	.02	.00
☐ 240	Billy Jo Robidoux	.05	.02	.00
☐ 241	Roger McDowell	.05	.02	.00
☐ 242	Leon Durham	.05	.02	.00
☐ 243	Ed Nunez	.05	.02	.00
☐ 244	Jimmy Key	.12	.05	.01
☐ 245	Mike Smithson	.05	.02	.00
☐ 246	Bo Diaz	.05	.02	.00
☐ 247	Carlton Fisk	.35	.15	.03
☐ 248	Larry Sheets	.05	.02	.00
☐ 249	Juan Castillo	.05	.02	.00
☐ 250	Eric King	.15	.06	.01
☐ 251	Doug Drabek	1.25	.50	.12
☐ 252	Wade Boggs	.75	.30	.07
☐ 253	Mariano Duncan	.08	.03	.01
☐ 254	Pat Tabler	.05	.02	.00
☐ 255	Frank White	.05	.02	.00
☐ 256	Alfredo Griffin	.05	.02	.00
☐ 257	Floyd Youmans	.05	.02	.00
☐ 258	Rob Wilfong	.05	.02	.00
☐ 259	Pete O'Brien	.05	.02	.00
☐ 260	Tim Hulett	.05	.02	.00
☐ 261	Dickie Thon	.05	.02	.00
☐ 262	Darren Daulton	.10	.04	.01
☐ 263	Vince Coleman	.50	.20	.05
☐ 264	Andy Hawkins	.05	.02	.00
☐ 265	Eric Davis	.50	.20	.05
☐ 266	Andres Thomas	.10	.04	.01
☐ 267	Mike Diaz	.05	.02	.00
☐ 268	Chili Davis	.10	.04	.01
☐ 269	Jody Davis	.05	.02	.00
☐ 270	Phil Bradley	.05	.02	.00
☐ 271	George Bell	.25	.10	.02
☐ 272	Keith Atherton	.05	.02	.00
☐ 273	Storm Davis	.05	.02	.00
☐ 274	Rob Deer	.15	.06	.01
☐ 275	Walt Terrell	.05	.02	.00
☐ 276	Roger Clemens	2.00	.80	.20
☐ 277	Mike Easler	.05	.02	.00
☐ 278	Steve Sax	.15	.06	.01
☐ 279	Andre Thornton	.05	.02	.00
☐ 280	Jim Sundberg	.05	.02	.00
☐ 281	Bill Bathe	.05	.02	.00
☐ 282	Jay Tibbs	.05	.02	.00
☐ 283	Dick Schofield	.05	.02	.00
☐ 284	Mike Mason	.05	.02	.00
☐ 285	Jerry Hairston	.05	.02	.00
☐ 286	Bill Doran	.05	.02	.00
☐ 287	Tim Flannery	.05	.02	.00
☐ 288	Gary Redus	.05	.02	.00
☐ 289	John Franco	.10	.04	.01
☐ 290	Paul Assenmacher	.05	.02	.00
☐ 291	Joe Orsulak	.08	.03	.01
☐ 292	Lee Smith	.15	.06	.01
☐ 293	Mike Laga	.05	.02	.00
☐ 294	Rick Dempsey	.05	.02	.00
☐ 295	Mike Felder	.08	.03	.01
☐ 296	Tom Brookens	.05	.02	.00
☐ 297	Al Nipper	.05	.02	.00
☐ 298	Mike Pagliarulo	.05	.02	.00
☐ 299	Franklin Stubbs	.08	.03	.01
☐ 300	Checklist Card	.10	.01	.00
☐ 301	Steve Farr	.08	.03	.01
☐ 302	Bill Mooneyham	.05	.02	.00
☐ 303	Andres Galarraga	.10	.04	.01
☐ 304	Scott Fletcher	.05	.02	.00
☐ 305	Jack Howell	.05	.02	.00
☐ 306	Russ Morman	.05	.02	.00
☐ 307	Todd Worrell	.10	.04	.01
☐ 308	Dave Smith	.05	.02	.00
☐ 309	Jeff Stone	.05	.02	.00
☐ 310	Ron Robinson	.05	.02	.00
☐ 311	Bruce Bochy	.05	.02	.00
☐ 312	Jim Winn	.05	.02	.00
☐ 313	Mark Davis	.08	.03	.01
☐ 314	Jeff Dedmon	.05	.02	.00
☐ 315	Jamie Moyer	.08	.03	.01
☐ 316	Wally Backman	.05	.02	.00
☐ 317	Ken Phelps	.05	.02	.00
☐ 318	Steve Lombardozzi	.05	.02	.00
☐ 319	Rance Mulliniks	.05	.02	.00
☐ 320	Tim Laudner	.05	.02	.00
☐ 321	Mark Eichhorn	.10	.04	.01
☐ 322	Lee Guetterman	.12	.05	.01
☐ 323	Sid Fernandez	.12	.05	.01
☐ 324	Jerry Mumphrey	.05	.02	.00
☐ 325	David Palmer	.05	.02	.00
☐ 326	Bill Almon	.05	.02	.00
☐ 327	Candy Maldonado	.08	.03	.01
☐ 328	John Kruk	.40	.16	.04
☐ 329	John Denny	.05	.02	.00
☐ 330	Milt Thompson	.08	.03	.01
☐ 331	Mike LaValliere	.25	.10	.02
☐ 332	Alan Ashby	.05	.02	.00
☐ 333	Doug Corbett	.05	.02	.00
☐ 334	Ron Karkovice	.08	.03	.01
☐ 335	Mitch Webster	.05	.02	.00
☐ 336	Lee Lacy	.05	.02	.00
☐ 337	Glenn Braggs	.30	.12	.03
☐ 338	Dwight Lowry	.05	.02	.00
☐ 339	Don Baylor	.08	.03	.01
☐ 340	Brian Fisher	.05	.02	.00
☐ 341	Reggie Williams	.05	.02	.00
☐ 342	Tom Candiotti	.10	.04	.01
☐ 343	Rudy Law	.05	.02	.00
☐ 344	Curt Young	.05	.02	.00
☐ 345	Mike Fitzgerald	.05	.02	.00
☐ 346	Ruben Sierra	8.50	3.75	.85
☐ 347	Mitch Williams	.30	.12	.03
☐ 348	Jorge Orta	.05	.02	.00
☐ 349	Mickey Tettleton	.15	.06	.01
☐ 350	Ernie Camacho	.05	.02	.00
☐ 351	Ron Kittle	.08	.03	.01
☐ 352	Ken Landreaux	.05	.02	.00
☐ 353	Chet Lemon	.05	.02	.00
☐ 354	John Shelby	.05	.02	.00
☐ 355	Mark Clear	.05	.02	.00
☐ 356	Doug DeCinces	.08	.03	.01
☐ 357	Ken Dayley	.05	.02	.00
☐ 358	Phil Garner	.08	.03	.01
☐ 359	Steve Jeltz	.05	.02	.00
☐ 360	Ed Whitson	.05	.02	.00
☐ 361	Barry Bonds	6.00	2.50	.60
☐ 362	Vida Blue	.08	.03	.01
☐ 363	Cecil Cooper	.08	.03	.01
☐ 364	Bob Ojeda	.05	.02	.00
☐ 365	Dennis Eckersley	.15	.06	.01
☐ 366	Mike Morgan	.08	.03	.01
☐ 367	Willie Upshaw	.05	.02	.00
☐ 368	Allan Anderson	.17	.07	.01
☐ 369	Bill Gullickson	.08	.03	.01
☐ 370	Bobby Thigpen	1.00	.40	.10
☐ 371	Juan Beniquez	.05	.02	.00
☐ 372	Charlie Moore	.05	.02	.00
☐ 373	Dan Petry	.05	.02	.00
☐ 374	Rod Scurry	.05	.02	.00
☐ 375	Tom Seaver	.45	.18	.04
☐ 376	Ed VandeBerg	.05	.02	.00
☐ 377	Tony Bernazard	.05	.02	.00
☐ 378	Greg Pryor	.05	.02	.00
☐ 379	Dwayne Murphy	.05	.02	.00
☐ 380	Andy McGaffigan	.05	.02	.00
☐ 381	Kirk McCaskill	.05	.02	.00
☐ 382	Greg Harris	.05	.02	.00
☐ 383	Rich Dotson	.05	.02	.00
☐ 384	Craig Reynolds	.05	.02	.00
☐ 385	Greg Gross	.05	.02	.00
☐ 386	Tito Landrum	.05	.02	.00
☐ 387	Craig Lefferts	.05	.02	.00
☐ 388	Dave Parker	.17	.07	.01
☐ 389	Bob Horner	.10	.04	.01
☐ 390	Pat Clements	.05	.02	.00
☐ 391	Jeff Leonard	.05	.02	.00
☐ 392	Chris Speier	.05	.02	.00
☐ 393	John Moses	.05	.02	.00
☐ 394	Garth Iorg	.05	.02	.00
☐ 395	Greg Gagne	.05	.02	.00
☐ 396	Nate Snell	.05	.02	.00
☐ 397	Bryan Clutterbuck	.05	.02	.00
☐ 398	Darrell Evans	.08	.03	.01
☐ 399	Steve Crawford	.05	.02	.00
☐ 400	Checklist Card	.10	.01	.00
☐ 401	Phil Lombardi	.08	.03	.01
☐ 402	Rick Honeycutt	.05	.02	.00
☐ 403	Ken Schrom	.05	.02	.00
☐ 404	Bud Black	.05	.02	.00
☐ 405	Donnie Hill	.05	.02	.00

☐ 406	Wayne Krenchicki	.05	.02	.00
☐ 407	Chuck Finley	2.00	.80	.20
☐ 408	Toby Harrah	.05	.02	.00
☐ 409	Steve Lyons	.05	.02	.00
☐ 410	Kevin Bass	.05	.02	.00
☐ 411	Marvell Wynne	.05	.02	.00
☐ 412	Ron Roenicke	.05	.02	.00
☐ 413	Tracy Jones	.12	.05	.01
☐ 414	Gene Garber	.05	.02	.00
☐ 415	Mike Bielecki	.10	.04	.01
☐ 416	Frank DiPino	.05	.02	.00
☐ 417	Andy Van Slyke	.20	.08	.02
☐ 418	Jim Dwyer	.05	.02	.00
☐ 419	Ben Oglivie	.05	.02	.00
☐ 420	Dave Bergman	.05	.02	.00
☐ 421	Joe Sambito	.05	.02	.00
☐ 422	Bob Tewksbury	.08	.03	.01
☐ 423	Len Matuszek	.05	.02	.00
☐ 424	Mike Kingery	.08	.03	.01
☐ 425	Dave Kingman	.10	.04	.01
☐ 426	Al Newman	.08	.03	.01
☐ 427	Gary Ward	.05	.02	.00
☐ 428	Ruppert Jones	.05	.02	.00
☐ 429	Harold Baines	.15	.06	.01
☐ 430	Pat Perry	.05	.02	.00
☐ 431	Terry Puhl	.05	.02	.00
☐ 432	Don Carman	.05	.02	.00
☐ 433	Eddie Milner	.05	.02	.00
☐ 434	LaMarr Hoyt	.05	.02	.00
☐ 435	Rick Rhoden	.05	.02	.00
☐ 436	Jose Uribe	.05	.02	.00
☐ 437	Ken Oberkfell	.05	.02	.00
☐ 438	Ron Davis	.05	.02	.00
☐ 439	Jesse Orosco	.05	.02	.00
☐ 440	Scott Bradley	.05	.02	.00
☐ 441	Randy Bush	.05	.02	.00
☐ 442	John Cerutti	.12	.05	.01
☐ 443	Roy Smalley	.05	.02	.00
☐ 444	Kelly Gruber	2.00	.80	.20
☐ 445	Bob Kearney	.05	.02	.00
☐ 446	Ed Hearn	.05	.02	.00
☐ 447	Scott Sanderson	.08	.03	.01
☐ 448	Bruce Benedict	.05	.02	.00
☐ 449	Junior Ortiz	.05	.02	.00
☐ 450	Mike Aldrete	.08	.03	.01
☐ 451	Kevin McReynolds	.15	.06	.01
☐ 452	Rob Murphy	.12	.05	.01
☐ 453	Kent Tekulve	.05	.02	.00
☐ 454	Curt Ford	.05	.02	.00
☐ 455	Dave Lopes	.08	.03	.01
☐ 456	Bob Grich	.08	.03	.01
☐ 457	Jose DeLeon	.05	.02	.00
☐ 458	Andre Dawson	.40	.16	.04
☐ 459	Mike Flanagan	.08	.03	.01
☐ 460	Joey Meyer	.10	.04	.01
☐ 461	Chuck Cary	.10	.04	.01
☐ 462	Bill Buckner	.08	.03	.01
☐ 463	Bob Shirley	.05	.02	.00
☐ 464	Jeff Hamilton	.10	.04	.01
☐ 465	Phil Niekro	.17	.07	.01
☐ 466	Mark Gubicza	.10	.04	.01
☐ 467	Jerry Willard	.05	.02	.00
☐ 468	Bob Sebra	.08	.03	.01
☐ 469	Larry Parrish	.05	.02	.00
☐ 470	Charlie Hough	.05	.02	.00
☐ 471	Hal McRae	.08	.03	.01
☐ 472	Dave Leiper	.05	.02	.00
☐ 473	Mel Hall	.10	.04	.01
☐ 474	Dan Pasqua	.08	.03	.01
☐ 475	Bob Welch	.10	.04	.01
☐ 476	Johnny Grubb	.05	.02	.00
☐ 477	Jim Traber	.05	.02	.00
☐ 478	Chris Bosio	.25	.10	.02
☐ 479	Mark McLemore	.05	.02	.00
☐ 480	John Morris	.05	.02	.00
☐ 481	Billy Hatcher	.08	.03	.01
☐ 482	Dan Schatzeder	.05	.02	.00
☐ 483	Rich Gossage	.10	.04	.01
☐ 484	Jim Morrison	.05	.02	.00
☐ 485	Bob Brenly	.05	.02	.00
☐ 486	Bill Schroeder	.05	.02	.00
☐ 487	Mookie Wilson	.08	.03	.01
☐ 488	Dave Martinez	.40	.16	.04
☐ 489	Harold Reynolds	.10	.04	.01
☐ 490	Jeff Hearron	.05	.02	.00
☐ 491	Mickey Hatcher	.05	.02	.00
☐ 492	Barry Larkin	3.50	1.50	.35
☐ 493	Bob James	.05	.02	.00
☐ 494	John Habyan	.05	.02	.00
☐ 495	Jim Adduci	.05	.02	.00
☐ 496	Mike Heath	.05	.02	.00
☐ 497	Tim Stoddard	.05	.02	.00
☐ 498	Tony Armas	.05	.02	.00
☐ 499	Dennis Powell	.05	.02	.00
☐ 500	Checklist Card	.10	.01	.00
☐ 501	Chris Bando	.05	.02	.00
☐ 502	David Cone	2.25	.90	.22
☐ 503	Jay Howell	.05	.02	.00
☐ 504	Tom Foley	.05	.02	.00
☐ 505	Ray Chadwick	.05	.02	.00
☐ 506	Mike Loynd	.05	.02	.00
☐ 507	Neil Allen	.05	.02	.00
☐ 508	Danny Darwin	.05	.02	.00
☐ 509	Rick Schu	.05	.02	.00
☐ 510	Jose Oquendo	.05	.02	.00
☐ 511	Gene Walter	.05	.02	.00
☐ 512	Terry McGriff	.08	.03	.01
☐ 513	Ken Griffey	.12	.05	.01
☐ 514	Benny Distefano	.05	.02	.00
☐ 515	Terry Mulholland	.40	.16	.04
☐ 516	Ed Lynch	.05	.02	.00
☐ 517	Bill Swift	.08	.03	.01
☐ 518	Manny Lee	.05	.02	.00
☐ 519	Andre David	.05	.02	.00
☐ 520	Scott McGregor	.05	.02	.00
☐ 521	Rick Manning	.05	.02	.00
☐ 522	Willie Hernandez	.05	.02	.00
☐ 523	Marty Barrett	.05	.02	.00
☐ 524	Wayne Tolleson	.05	.02	.00
☐ 525	Jose Gonzalez	.10	.04	.01
☐ 526	Cory Snyder	.12	.05	.01
☐ 527	Buddy Biancalana	.05	.02	.00
☐ 528	Moose Haas	.05	.02	.00
☐ 529	Wilfredo Tejada	.05	.02	.00
☐ 530	Stu Cliburn	.05	.02	.00
☐ 531	Dale Mohorcic	.08	.03	.01
☐ 532	Ron Hassey	.05	.02	.00
☐ 533	Ty Gainey	.05	.02	.00
☐ 534	Jerry Royster	.05	.02	.00
☐ 535	Mike Maddux	.10	.04	.01
☐ 536	Ted Power	.05	.02	.00
☐ 537	Ted Simmons	.10	.04	.01
☐ 538	Rafael Belliard	.25	.10	.02
☐ 539	Chico Walker	.10	.04	.01
☐ 540	Bob Forsch	.05	.02	.00
☐ 541	John Stefero	.05	.02	.00
☐ 542	Dale Sveum	.08	.03	.01
☐ 543	Mark Thurmond	.05	.02	.00
☐ 544	Jeff Sellers	.08	.03	.01
☐ 545	Joel Skinner	.05	.02	.00
☐ 546	Alex Trevino	.05	.02	.00
☐ 547	Randy Kutcher	.05	.02	.00
☐ 548	Joaquin Andujar	.05	.02	.00
☐ 549	Casey Candaele	.08	.03	.01
☐ 550	Jeff Russell	.08	.03	.01
☐ 551	John Candelaria	.05	.02	.00
☐ 552	Joe Cowley	.05	.02	.00
☐ 553	Danny Cox	.05	.02	.00
☐ 554	Denny Walling	.05	.02	.00
☐ 555	Bruce Ruffin	.10	.04	.01
☐ 556	Buddy Bell	.08	.03	.01
☐ 557	Jimmy Jones	.15	.06	.01
☐ 558	Bobby Bonilla	5.50	2.50	.55
☐ 559	Jeff Robinson (Giants pitcher)	.08	.03	.01
☐ 560	Ed Olwine	.05	.02	.00
☐ 561	Glenallen Hill	.30	.12	.03
☐ 562	Lee Mazzilli	.05	.02	.00
☐ 563	Mike Brown (pitcher)	.05	.02	.00
☐ 564	George Frazier	.05	.02	.00
☐ 565	Mike Sharperson	.08	.03	.01
☐ 566	Mark Portugal	.15	.06	.01
☐ 567	Rick Leach	.05	.02	.00
☐ 568	Mark Langston	.25	.10	.02
☐ 569	Rafael Santana	.05	.02	.00
☐ 570	Manny Trillo	.05	.02	.00
☐ 571	Cliff Speck	.05	.02	.00
☐ 572	Bob Kipper	.05	.02	.00
☐ 573	Kelly Downs	.15	.06	.01
☐ 574	Randy Asadoor	.05	.02	.00
☐ 575	Dave Magadan	.75	.30	.07
☐ 576	Marvin Freeman	.08	.03	.01
☐ 577	Jeff Lahti	.05	.02	.00
☐ 578	Jeff Calhoun	.05	.02	.00
☐ 579	Gus Polidor	.05	.02	.00
☐ 580	Gene Nelson	.05	.02	.00
☐ 581	Tim Teufel	.05	.02	.00
☐ 582	Odell Jones	.05	.02	.00
☐ 583	Mark Ryal	.05	.02	.00
☐ 584	Randy O'Neal	.05	.02	.00
☐ 585	Mike Greenwell	6.00	2.50	.60
☐ 586	Ray Knight	.08	.03	.01
☐ 587	Ralph Bryant	.08	.03	.01
☐ 588	Carmen Castillo	.05	.02	.00
☐ 589	Ed Wojna	.05	.02	.00
☐ 590	Stan Javier	.08	.03	.01
☐ 591	Jeff Musselman	.08	.03	.01

☐ 592	Mike Stanley	.12	.05	.01
☐ 593	Darrell Porter	.05	.02	.00
☐ 594	Drew Hall	.05	.02	.00
☐ 595	Rob Nelson	.10	.04	.01
☐ 596	Bryan Oelkers	.05	.02	.00
☐ 597	Scott Nielsen	.10	.04	.01
☐ 598	Brian Holton	.10	.04	.01
☐ 599	Kevin Mitchell	5.00	2.25	.50
☐ 600	Checklist Card	.10	.01	.00
☐ 601	Jackie Gutierrez	.05	.02	.00
☐ 602	Barry Jones	.12	.05	.01
☐ 603	Jerry Narron	.05	.02	.00
☐ 604	Steve Lake	.05	.02	.00
☐ 605	Jim Pankovits	.05	.02	.00
☐ 606	Ed Romero	.05	.02	.00
☐ 607	Dave LaPoint	.05	.02	.00
☐ 608	Don Robinson	.05	.02	.00
☐ 609	Mike Krukow	.05	.02	.00
☐ 610	Dave Valle	.05	.02	.00
☐ 611	Len Dykstra	.30	.12	.03
☐ 612	Roberto Clemente Puzzle Card	.10	.04	.01
☐ 613	Mike Trujillo	.05	.02	.00
☐ 614	Damaso Garcia	.05	.02	.00
☐ 615	Neal Heaton	.05	.02	.00
☐ 616	Juan Berenguer	.05	.02	.00
☐ 617	Steve Carlton	.35	.15	.03
☐ 618	Gary Lucas	.05	.02	.00
☐ 619	Geno Petralli	.05	.02	.00
☐ 620	Rick Aguilera	.15	.06	.01
☐ 621	Fred McGriff	3.50	1.50	.35
☐ 622	Dave Henderson	.15	.06	.01
☐ 623	Dave Clark	.12	.05	.01
☐ 624	Angel Salazar	.05	.02	.00
☐ 625	Randy Hunt	.05	.02	.00
☐ 626	John Gibbons	.05	.02	.00
☐ 627	Kevin Brown	.50	.20	.05
☐ 628	Bill Dawley	.05	.02	.00
☐ 629	Aurelio Lopez	.05	.02	.00
☐ 630	Charles Hudson	.05	.02	.00
☐ 631	Ray Soff	.05	.02	.00
☐ 632	Ray Hayward	.05	.02	.00
☐ 633	Spike Owen	.05	.02	.00
☐ 634	Glenn Hubbard	.05	.02	.00
☐ 635	Kevin Elster	.15	.06	.01
☐ 636	Mike LaCoss	.05	.02	.00
☐ 637	Dwayne Henry	.05	.02	.00
☐ 638	Rey Quinones	.05	.02	.00
☐ 639	Jim Clancy	.05	.02	.00
☐ 640	Larry Andersen	.05	.02	.00
☐ 641	Calvin Schiraldi	.05	.02	.00
☐ 642	Stan Jefferson	.08	.03	.01
☐ 643	Marc Sullivan	.05	.02	.00
☐ 644	Mark Grant	.05	.02	.00
☐ 645	Cliff Johnson	.05	.02	.00
☐ 646	Howard Johnson	.40	.16	.04
☐ 647	Dave Sax	.05	.02	.00
☐ 648	Dave Stewart	.20	.08	.02
☐ 649	Danny Heep	.05	.02	.00
☐ 650	Joe Johnson	.05	.02	.00
☐ 651	Bob Brower	.08	.03	.01
☐ 652	Rob Woodward	.05	.02	.00
☐ 653	John Mizerock	.05	.02	.00
☐ 654	Tim Pyznarski	.05	.02	.00
☐ 655	Luis Aquino	.05	.02	.00
☐ 656	Mickey Brantley	.08	.03	.01
☐ 657	Doyle Alexander	.05	.02	.00
☐ 658	Sammy Stewart	.05	.02	.00
☐ 659	Jim Acker	.05	.02	.00
☐ 660	Pete Ladd	.08	.03	.01

1987 Donruss Wax Box Cards

The cards in this four-card set measure the standard 2 1/2" by 3 1/2". Cards have essentially the same design as the 1987 Donruss regular issue set. The cards were printed on the bottoms of the regular issue wax pack boxes. The four cards (PC10 to PC12 plus a Roberto Clemente puzzle card) are considered a separate set in their own right and are not typically included in a complete set of the regular issue 1987 Donruss cards. The value of the panel uncut is slightly greater, perhaps by 25 percent greater, than the value of the individual cards cut up carefully.

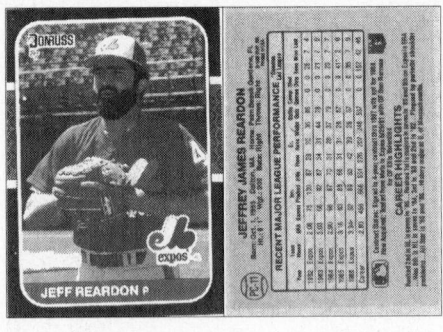

	MINT	EXC	G-VG
COMPLETE SET (4)	2.25	.90	.22
COMMON PLAYER	.05	.02	.00
☐ PC10 Dale Murphy	.35	.15	.03
☐ PC11 Jeff Reardon	.25	.10	.02
☐ PC12 Jose Canseco	2.00	.80	.20
☐ PUZ Roberto Clemente (Puzzle Card)	.05	.02	.00

1987 Donruss Super DK's

This 28-card set was available through a mail-in offer detailed on the wax packs. The set was sent in return for 8.00 and three wrappers plus 1.50 postage and handling. The set features the popular Diamond King subseries in large (approximately 4 7/8" by 6 13/16") form. Dick Perez of Perez-Steele Galleries did another outstanding job on the artwork. The cards are essentially a large version of the Donruss regular issue Diamond Kings.

	MINT	EXC	G-VG
COMPLETE SET (28)	11.00	5.00	1.35
COMMON PLAYER (1-26)	.20	.08	.02
☐ 1 Wally Joyner	.75	.30	.07
☐ 2 Roger Clemens	1.00	.40	.10
☐ 3 Dale Murphy	.50	.20	.05
☐ 4 Darryl Strawberry	.90	.40	.09
☐ 5 Ozzie Smith	.40	.16	.04
☐ 6 Jose Canseco	1.75	.70	.17
☐ 7 Charlie Hough	.20	.08	.02
☐ 8 Brook Jacoby	.20	.08	.02
☐ 9 Fred Lynn	.30	.12	.03
☐ 10 Rick Rhoden	.20	.08	.02
☐ 11 Chris Brown	.20	.08	.02
☐ 12 Von Hayes	.30	.12	.03
☐ 13 Jack Morris	.40	.16	.04
☐ 14 Kevin McReynolds	.50	.20	.05
☐ 15 George Brett	.75	.30	.07
☐ 16 Ted Higuera	.30	.12	.03
☐ 17 Hubie Brooks	.30	.12	.03
☐ 18 Mike Scott	.30	.12	.03
☐ 19 Kirby Puckett	1.00	.40	.10

			MINT	EXC	G-VG
☐	20	Dave Winfield	.50	.20	.05
☐	21	Lloyd Moseby	.20	.08	.02
☐	22	Eric Davis	.75	.30	.07
☐	23	Jim Presley	.20	.08	.02
☐	24	Keith Moreland	.20	.08	.02
☐	25	Greg Walker	.20	.08	.02
☐	26	Steve Sax	.30	.12	.03
☐	27	DK Checklist 1-26	.20	.08	.02
☐	28	Roberto Clemente Large Puzzle (unnumbered)	.30	.12	.03

1987 Donruss All-Stars

This 60-card set features cards measuring approximately 3 1/2" by 5". Card fronts are in full color with a black border. The card backs are printed in black and blue on white card stock. Cards are numbered on the back. Card backs feature statistical information about the player's performance in past All-Star games. The set was distributed in packs which also contained a Pop-Up.

			MINT	EXC	G-VG
		COMPLETE SET (60)	7.50	3.25	.75
		COMMON PLAYER (1-60)	.07	.03	.01
☐	1	Wally Joyner	.50	.20	.05
☐	2	Dave Winfield	.30	.12	.03
☐	3	Lou Whitaker	.15	.06	.01
☐	4	Kirby Puckett	.60	.25	.06
☐	5	Cal Ripken	.75	.30	.07
☐	6	Rickey Henderson	.75	.30	.07
☐	7	Wade Boggs	.60	.25	.06
☐	8	Roger Clemens	.75	.30	.07
☐	9	Lance Parrish	.10	.04	.01
☐	10	Dick Howser MG	.07	.03	.01
☐	11	Keith Hernandez	.10	.04	.01
☐	12	Darryl Strawberry	.60	.25	.06
☐	13	Ryne Sandberg	.75	.30	.07
☐	14	Dale Murphy	.35	.15	.03
☐	15	Ozzie Smith	.30	.12	.03
☐	16	Tony Gwynn	.45	.18	.04
☐	17	Mike Schmidt	.75	.30	.07
☐	18	Dwight Gooden	.50	.20	.05
☐	19	Gary Carter	.25	.10	.02
☐	20	Whitey Herzog MG	.07	.03	.01
☐	21	Jose Canseco	.90	.40	.09
☐	22	John Franco	.10	.04	.01
☐	23	Jesse Barfield	.10	.04	.01
☐	24	Rick Rhoden	.07	.03	.01
☐	25	Harold Baines	.10	.04	.01
☐	26	Sid Fernandez	.10	.04	.01
☐	27	George Brett	.45	.18	.04
☐	28	Steve Sax	.15	.06	.01
☐	29	Jim Presley	.07	.03	.01
☐	30	Dave Smith	.07	.03	.01
☐	31	Eddie Murray	.30	.12	.03
☐	32	Mike Scott	.10	.04	.01
☐	33	Don Mattingly	.75	.30	.07
☐	34	Dave Parker	.20	.08	.02
☐	35	Tony Fernandez	.15	.06	.01
☐	36	Tim Raines	.25	.10	.02
☐	37	Brook Jacoby	.07	.03	.01
☐	38	Chili Davis	.10	.04	.01
☐	39	Rich Gedman	.07	.03	.01
☐	40	Kevin Bass	.07	.03	.01

			MINT	EXC	G-VG
☐	41	Frank White	.07	.03	.01
☐	42	Glenn Davis	.20	.08	.02
☐	43	Willie Hernandez	.07	.03	.01
☐	44	Chris Brown	.07	.03	.01
☐	45	Jim Rice	.15	.06	.01
☐	46	Tony Pena	.07	.03	.01
☐	47	Don Aase	.07	.03	.01
☐	48	Hubie Brooks	.07	.03	.01
☐	49	Charlie Hough	.07	.03	.01
☐	50	Jody Davis	.07	.03	.01
☐	51	Mike Witt	.07	.03	.01
☐	52	Jeff Reardon	.20	.08	.02
☐	53	Ken Schrom	.07	.03	.01
☐	54	Fernando Valenzuela	.15	.06	.01
☐	55	Dave Righetti	.15	.06	.01
☐	56	Shane Rawley	.07	.03	.01
☐	57	Ted Higuera	.10	.04	.01
☐	58	Mike Krukow	.07	.03	.01
☐	59	Lloyd Moseby	.07	.03	.01
☐	60	Checklist Card	.07	.03	.01

1987 Donruss All-Star Box

The cards in this 4-card set measure the standard 2 1/2" by 3 1/2" in spite of the fact that they form the bottom of the wax pack box for the larger Donruss All-Star cards. These box cards have essentially the same design as the 1987 Donruss regular issue set. The cards were printed on the bottoms of the Donruss All-Star (3 1/2" by 5") wax pack boxes. The four cards (PC13 to PC15 plus a Roberto Clemente puzzle card) are considered a separate set in their own right and are not typically included in a complete set of the 1987 Donruss All-Star (or regular) cards. The value of the panel uncut is slightly greater, perhaps by 25 percent greater, than the value of the individual cards cut up carefully.

			MINT	EXC	G-VG
		COMPLETE SET (4)	1.50	.60	.15
		COMMON PLAYERS	.05	.02	.00
☐	PC13	Mike Scott	.30	.12	.03
☐	PC14	Roger Clemens	1.25	.50	.12
☐	PC15	Mike Krukow	.10	.04	.01
☐	PUZ	Roberto Clemente Puzzle Card	.05	.02	.00

1987 Donruss Pop-Ups

This 20-card set features "fold-out" cards measuring 2 1/2" by 5". Card fronts are in full color. Cards are unnumbered but are listed in the same order as the Donruss All-Stars on the All-Star checklist card. Card backs present essentially no information about the player. The set was distributed in packs which also contained All-Star cards (3 1/2" by 5").

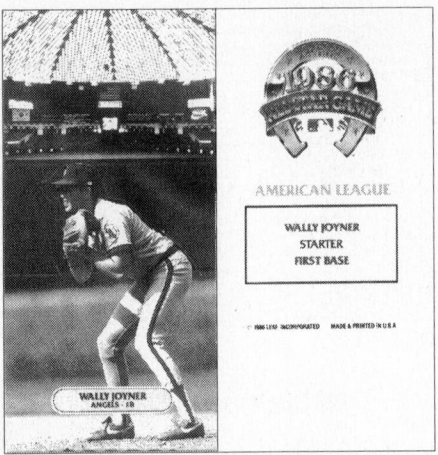

	MINT	EXC	G-VG
COMPLETE SET (20)	4.00	1.75	.40
COMMON PLAYER (1-20)	.10	.04	.01

		MINT	EXC	G-VG
☐	1 Wally Joyner	.50	.20	.05
☐	2 Dave Winfield	.30	.12	.03
☐	3 Lou Whitaker	.15	.06	.01
☐	4 Kirby Puckett	.60	.25	.06
☐	5 Cal Ripken	.75	.30	.07
☐	6 Rickey Henderson	.75	.30	.07
☐	7 Wade Boggs	.60	.25	.06
☐	8 Roger Clemens	.75	.30	.07
☐	9 Lance Parrish	.10	.04	.01
☐	10 Dick Howser MG	.10	.04	.01
☐	11 Keith Hernandez	.15	.06	.01
☐	12 Darryl Strawberry	.60	.25	.06
☐	13 Ryne Sandberg	.75	.30	.07
☐	14 Dale Murphy	.35	.15	.03
☐	15 Ozzie Smith	.30	.12	.03
☐	16 Tony Gwynn	.45	.18	.04
☐	17 Mike Schmidt	.75	.30	.07
☐	18 Dwight Gooden	.50	.20	.05
☐	19 Gary Carter	.25	.10	.02
☐	20 Whitey Herzog MG	.10	.04	.01

1987 Donruss Opening Day

This innovative set of 272 cards features a card for each of the players in the starting line-ups of all the teams on Opening Day 1987. Cards are the standard size, 2 1/2" by 3 1/2", and are packaged as a complete set in a specially designed box. Cards are very similar in design to the 1987 regular Donruss issue except that these "OD" cards have a maroon border instead of a black border. The set features the first card in a Major League uniform of Joey Cora, Mark Davidson, Donnell Nixon, Bob

Patterson, and Alonzo Powell. Teams in the same city share a checklist card. A 15-piece puzzle of Roberto Clemente is also included with every complete set. The error on Barry Bonds was corrected very early in the press run; supposedly less than one percent of the sets have the error.

	MINT	EXC	G-VG
COMPLETE SET (272)	20.00	8.50	2.75
COMMON PLAYER (1-248)	.05	.02	.00
COMMON LOGO (249-272)	.03	.01	.00

		MINT	EXC	G-VG
☐	1 Doug DeCinces	.10	.04	.01
☐	2 Mike Witt	.05	.02	.00
☐	3 George Hendrick	.05	.02	.00
☐	4 Dick Schofield	.05	.02	.00
☐	5 Devon White	.50	.20	.05
☐	6 Butch Wynegar	.05	.02	.00
☐	7 Wally Joyner	1.00	.40	.10
☐	8 Mark McLemore	.05	.02	.00
☐	9 Brian Downing	.05	.02	.00
☐	10 Gary Pettis	.05	.02	.00
☐	11 Bill Doran	.10	.04	.01
☐	12 Phil Garner	.10	.04	.01
☐	13 Jose Cruz	.10	.04	.01
☐	14 Kevin Bass	.05	.02	.00
☐	15 Mike Scott	.15	.06	.01
☐	16 Glenn Davis	.30	.12	.03
☐	17 Alan Ashby	.05	.02	.00
☐	18 Billy Hatcher	.15	.06	.01
☐	19 Craig Reynolds	.05	.02	.00
☐	20 Carney Lansford	.10	.04	.01
☐	21 Mike Davis	.05	.02	.00
☐	22 Reggie Jackson	.75	.30	.07
☐	23 Mickey Tettleton	.20	.08	.02
☐	24 Jose Canseco	3.00	1.25	.30
☐	25 Rob Nelson	.05	.02	.00
☐	26 Tony Phillips	.10	.04	.01
☐	27 Dwayne Murphy	.05	.02	.00
☐	28 Alfredo Griffin	.05	.02	.00
☐	29 Curt Young	.05	.02	.00
☐	30 Willie Upshaw	.05	.02	.00
☐	31 Mike Sharperson	.05	.02	.00
☐	32 Rance Mulliniks	.05	.02	.00
☐	33 Ernie Whitt	.05	.02	.00
☐	34 Jesse Barfield	.15	.06	.01
☐	35 Tony Fernandez	.15	.06	.01
☐	36 Lloyd Moseby	.05	.02	.00
☐	37 Jimmy Key	.10	.04	.01
☐	38 Fred McGriff	1.50	.60	.15
☐	39 George Bell	.30	.12	.03
☐	40 Dale Murphy	.35	.15	.03
☐	41 Rick Mahler	.05	.02	.00
☐	42 Ken Griffey	.10	.04	.01
☐	43 Andres Thomas	.05	.02	.00
☐	44 Dion James	.05	.02	.00
☐	45 Ozzie Virgil	.05	.02	.00
☐	46 Ken Oberkfell	.05	.02	.00
☐	47 Gary Roenicke	.05	.02	.00
☐	48 Glenn Hubbard	.05	.02	.00
☐	49 Bill Schroeder	.05	.02	.00
☐	50 Greg Brock	.05	.02	.00
☐	51 Billy Jo Robidoux	.05	.02	.00
☐	52 Glenn Braggs	.20	.08	.02
☐	53 Jim Gantner	.05	.02	.00
☐	54 Paul Molitor	.20	.08	.02
☐	55 Dale Sveum	.10	.04	.01
☐	56 Ted Higuera	.10	.04	.01
☐	57 Rob Deer	.10	.04	.01
☐	58 Robin Yount	.50	.20	.05
☐	59 Jim Lindeman	.05	.02	.00
☐	60 Vince Coleman	.35	.15	.03
☐	61 Tommy Herr	.05	.02	.00
☐	62 Terry Pendleton	.25	.10	.02
☐	63 John Tudor	.10	.04	.01
☐	64 Tony Pena	.10	.04	.01
☐	65 Ozzie Smith	.30	.12	.03
☐	66 Tito Landrum	.05	.02	.00
☐	67 Jack Clark	.15	.06	.01
☐	68 Bob Dernier	.05	.02	.00
☐	69 Rick Sutcliffe	.10	.04	.01
☐	70 Andre Dawson	.35	.15	.03
☐	71 Keith Moreland	.05	.02	.00
☐	72 Jody Davis	.05	.02	.00
☐	73 Brian Dayett	.05	.02	.00
☐	74 Leon Durham	.05	.02	.00
☐	75 Ryne Sandberg	1.25	.50	.12
☐	76 Shawon Dunston	.35	.15	.03
☐	77 Mike Marshall	.10	.04	.01
☐	78 Bill Madlock	.05	.02	.00
☐	79 Orel Hershiser	.45	.18	.04
☐	80 Mike Ramsey	.10	.04	.01
☐	81 Ken Landreaux	.05	.02	.00
☐	82 Mike Scioscia	.05	.02	.00

☐	83	Franklin Stubbs	.10	.04	.01
☐	84	Mariano Duncan	.10	.04	.01
☐	85	Steve Sax	.15	.06	.01
☐	86	Mitch Webster	.05	.02	.00
☐	87	Reid Nichols	.05	.02	.00
☐	88	Tim Wallach	.10	.04	.01
☐	89	Floyd Youmans	.05	.02	.00
☐	90	Andres Galarraga	.25	.10	.02
☐	91	Hubie Brooks	.10	.04	.01
☐	92	Jeff Reed	.05	.02	.00
☐	93	Alonzo Powell	.15	.06	.01
☐	94	Vance Law	.05	.02	.00
☐	95	Bob Brenly	.05	.02	.00
☐	96	Will Clark	3.00	1.25	.30
☐	97	Chili Davis	.15	.06	.01
☐	98	Mike Krukow	.05	.02	.00
☐	99	Jose Uribe	.05	.02	.00
☐	100	Chris Brown	.05	.02	.00
☐	101	Robby Thompson	.10	.04	.01
☐	102	Candy Maldonado	.10	.04	.01
☐	103	Jeff Leonard	.05	.02	.00
☐	104	Tom Candiotti	.10	.04	.01
☐	105	Chris Bando	.05	.02	.00
☐	106	Cory Snyder	.15	.06	.01
☐	107	Pat Tabler	.05	.02	.00
☐	108	Andre Thornton	.05	.02	.00
☐	109	Joe Carter	.50	.20	.05
☐	110	Tony Bernazard	.05	.02	.00
☐	111	Julio Franco	.35	.15	.03
☐	112	Brook Jacoby	.10	.04	.01
☐	113	Brett Butler	.15	.06	.01
☐	114	Donnell Nixon	.10	.04	.01
☐	115	Alvin Davis	.15	.06	.01
☐	116	Mark Langston	.25	.10	.02
☐	117	Harold Reynolds	.10	.04	.01
☐	118	Ken Phelps	.05	.02	.00
☐	119	Mike Kingery	.05	.02	.00
☐	120	Dave Valle	.05	.02	.00
☐	121	Rey Quinones	.05	.02	.00
☐	122	Phil Bradley	.05	.02	.00
☐	123	Jim Presley	.05	.02	.00
☐	124	Keith Hernandez	.15	.06	.01
☐	125	Kevin McReynolds	.20	.08	.02
☐	126	Rafael Santana	.05	.02	.00
☐	127	Bob Ojeda	.10	.04	.01
☐	128	Darryl Strawberry	1.00	.40	.10
☐	129	Mookie Wilson	.05	.02	.00
☐	130	Gary Carter	.20	.08	.02
☐	131	Tim Teufel	.05	.02	.00
☐	132	Howard Johnson	.30	.12	.03
☐	133	Cal Ripken	1.00	.40	.10
☐	134	Rick Burleson	.05	.02	.00
☐	135	Fred Lynn	.10	.04	.01
☐	136	Eddie Murray	.30	.12	.03
☐	137	Ray Knight	.10	.04	.01
☐	138	Alan Wiggins	.05	.02	.00
☐	139	John Shelby	.05	.02	.00
☐	140	Mike Boddicker	.05	.02	.00
☐	141	Ken Gerhart	.05	.02	.00
☐	142	Terry Kennedy	.05	.02	.00
☐	143	Steve Garvey	.30	.12	.03
☐	144	Marvell Wynne	.05	.02	.00
☐	145	Kevin Mitchell	1.50	.60	.15
☐	146	Tony Gwynn	.75	.30	.07
☐	147	Joey Cora	.15	.06	.01
☐	148	Benito Santiago	.90	.40	.09
☐	149	Eric Show	.05	.02	.00
☐	150	Garry Templeton	.05	.02	.00
☐	151	Carmelo Martinez	.05	.02	.00
☐	152	Von Hayes	.10	.04	.01
☐	153	Lance Parrish	.15	.06	.01
☐	154	Milt Thompson	.05	.02	.00
☐	155	Mike Easler	.05	.02	.00
☐	156	Juan Samuel	.15	.06	.01
☐	157	Steve Jeltz	.05	.02	.00
☐	158	Glenn Wilson	.05	.02	.00
☐	159	Shane Rawley	.05	.02	.00
☐	160	Mike Schmidt	1.00	.40	.10
☐	161	Andy Van Slyke	.25	.10	.02
☐	162	Johnny Ray	.10	.04	.01
☐	163A	Barry Bonds ERR (photo actually Johnny Ray)	200.00	90.00	30.00
☐	163B	Barry Bonds COR	1.25	.50	.12
☐	164	Junior Ortiz	.05	.02	.00
☐	165	Rafael Belliard	.10	.04	.01
☐	166	Bob Patterson	.15	.06	.01
☐	167	Bobby Bonilla	1.00	.40	.10
☐	168	Sid Bream	.05	.02	.00
☐	169	Jim Morrison	.05	.02	.00
☐	170	Jerry Browne	.10	.04	.01
☐	171	Scott Fletcher	.05	.02	.00
☐	172	Ruben Sierra	2.25	.90	.22
☐	173	Larry Parrish	.05	.02	.00
☐	174	Pete O'Brien	.05	.02	.00
☐	175	Pete Incaviglia	.20	.08	.02
☐	176	Don Slaught	.05	.02	.00
☐	177	Oddibe McDowell	.05	.02	.00
☐	178	Charlie Hough	.05	.02	.00
☐	179	Steve Buechele	.10	.04	.01
☐	180	Bob Stanley	.05	.02	.00
☐	181	Wade Boggs	1.00	.40	.10
☐	182	Jim Rice	.20	.08	.02
☐	183	Bill Buckner	.10	.04	.01
☐	184	Dwight Evans	.15	.06	.01
☐	185	Spike Owen	.05	.02	.00
☐	186	Don Baylor	.10	.04	.01
☐	187	Marc Sullivan	.05	.02	.00
☐	188	Marty Barrett	.05	.02	.00
☐	189	Dave Henderson	.15	.06	.01
☐	190	Bo Diaz	.05	.02	.00
☐	191	Barry Larkin	1.25	.50	.12
☐	192	Kal Daniels	.50	.20	.05
☐	193	Terry Francona	.05	.02	.00
☐	194	Tom Browning	.15	.06	.01
☐	195	Ron Oester	.05	.02	.00
☐	196	Buddy Bell	.10	.04	.01
☐	197	Eric Davis	.90	.40	.09
☐	198	Dave Parker	.20	.08	.02
☐	199	Steve Balboni	.05	.02	.00
☐	200	Danny Tartabull	.50	.20	.05
☐	201	Ed Hearn	.05	.02	.00
☐	202	Buddy Biancalana	.05	.02	.00
☐	203	Danny Jackson	.10	.04	.01
☐	204	Frank White	.10	.04	.01
☐	205	Bo Jackson	2.50	1.00	.25
☐	206	George Brett	.50	.20	.05
☐	207	Kevin Seitzer	.35	.15	.03
☐	208	Willie Wilson	.10	.04	.01
☐	209	Orlando Mercado	.05	.02	.00
☐	210	Darrell Evans	.10	.04	.01
☐	211	Larry Herndon	.05	.02	.00
☐	212	Jack Morris	.25	.10	.02
☐	213	Chet Lemon	.05	.02	.00
☐	214	Mike Heath	.05	.02	.00
☐	215	Darnell Coles	.05	.02	.00
☐	216	Alan Trammell	.30	.12	.03
☐	217	Terry Harper	.05	.02	.00
☐	218	Lou Whitaker	.15	.06	.01
☐	219	Gary Gaetti	.10	.04	.01
☐	220	Tom Nieto	.05	.02	.00
☐	221	Kirby Puckett	1.00	.40	.10
☐	222	Tom Brunansky	.10	.04	.01
☐	223	Greg Gagne	.05	.02	.00
☐	224	Dan Gladden	.05	.02	.00
☐	225	Mark Davidson	.10	.04	.01
☐	226	Bert Blyleven	.15	.06	.01
☐	227	Steve Lombardozzi	.05	.02	.00
☐	228	Kent Hrbek	.20	.08	.02
☐	229	Gary Redus	.05	.02	.00
☐	230	Ivan Calderon	.25	.10	.02
☐	231	Tim Hulett	.05	.02	.00
☐	232	Carlton Fisk	.45	.18	.04
☐	233	Greg Walker	.10	.04	.01
☐	234	Ron Karkovice	.05	.02	.00
☐	235	Ozzie Guillen	.20	.08	.02
☐	236	Harold Baines	.15	.06	.01
☐	237	Donnie Hill	.05	.02	.00
☐	238	Rich Dotson	.05	.02	.00
☐	239	Mike Pagliarulo	.10	.04	.01
☐	240	Joel Skinner	.05	.02	.00
☐	241	Don Mattingly	1.00	.40	.10
☐	242	Gary Ward	.05	.02	.00
☐	243	Dave Winfield	.30	.12	.03
☐	244	Dan Pasqua	.15	.06	.01
☐	245	Wayne Tolleson	.05	.02	.00
☐	246	Willie Randolph	.10	.04	.01
☐	247	Dennis Rasmussen	.10	.04	.01
☐	248	Rickey Henderson	1.00	.40	.10
☐	249	Angels Logo	.03	.01	.00
☐	250	Astros Logo	.03	.01	.00
☐	251	A's Logo	.03	.01	.00
☐	252	Blue Jays Logo	.03	.01	.00
☐	253	Braves Logo	.03	.01	.00
☐	254	Brewers Logo	.03	.01	.00
☐	255	Cardinals Logo	.03	.01	.00
☐	256	Dodgers Logo	.03	.01	.00
☐	257	Expos Logo	.03	.01	.00
☐	258	Giants Logo	.03	.01	.00
☐	259	Indians Logo	.03	.01	.00
☐	260	Mariners Logo	.03	.01	.00
☐	261	Orioles Logo	.03	.01	.00
☐	262	Padres Logo	.03	.01	.00
☐	263	Phillies Logo	.03	.01	.00
☐	264	Pirates Logo	.03	.01	.00
☐	265	Rangers Logo	.03	.01	.00
☐	266	Red Sox Logo	.03	.01	.00
☐	267	Reds Logo	.03	.01	.00
☐	268	Royals Logo	.03	.01	.00
☐	269	Tigers Logo	.03	.01	.00

		MINT	EXC	G-VG
☐ 270	Twins Logo	.03	.01	.00
☐ 271	Chicago Logos	.03	.01	.00
☐ 272	New York Logos	.03	.01	.00

1987 Donruss Rookies

The 1987 Donruss "The Rookies" set features 56 cards plus a 15-piece puzzle of Roberto Clemente. Cards are in full color and are standard size, 2 1/2" by 3 1/2". The set was distributed in a small green and black box with gold lettering. Card fronts are similar in design to the 1987 Donruss regular issue except for the presence of "The Rookies" logo in the lower left corner and a green border instead of a black border. The key (extended) rookie cards in this set are Ellis Burks, John Smiley, and Matt Williams.

		MINT	EXC	G-VG
	COMPLETE SET (56)	20.00	8.50	2.75
	COMMON PLAYER (1-56)	.07	.03	.01
☐ 1	Mark McGwire	2.00	.80	.20
☐ 2	Eric Bell	.07	.03	.01
☐ 3	Mark Williamson	.15	.06	.01
☐ 4	Mike Greenwell	2.50	1.00	.25
☐ 5	Ellis Burks	2.50	1.00	.25
☐ 6	DeWayne Buice	.10	.04	.01
☐ 7	Mark McLemore	.07	.03	.01
☐ 8	Devon White	.40	.16	.04
☐ 9	Willie Fraser	.07	.03	.01
☐ 10	Les Lancaster	.15	.06	.01
☐ 11	Ken Williams	.15	.06	.01
☐ 12	Matt Nokes	.60	.25	.06
☐ 13	Jeff Robinson	.12	.05	.01
	(Tigers pitcher)			
☐ 14	Bo Jackson	3.50	1.50	.35
☐ 15	Kevin Seitzer	.20	.08	.02
☐ 16	Billy Ripken	.20	.08	.02
☐ 17	B.J. Surhoff	.15	.06	.01
☐ 18	Chuck Crim	.10	.04	.01
☐ 19	Mike Birkbeck	.07	.03	.01
☐ 20	Chris Bosio	.15	.06	.01
☐ 21	Les Straker	.10	.04	.01
☐ 22	Mark Davidson	.10	.04	.01
☐ 23	Gene Larkin	.25	.10	.02
☐ 24	Ken Gerhart	.07	.03	.01
☐ 25	Luis Polonia	.60	.25	.06
☐ 26	Terry Steinbach	.25	.10	.02
☐ 27	Mickey Brantley	.10	.04	.01
☐ 28	Mike Stanley	.10	.04	.01
☐ 29	Jerry Browne	.10	.04	.01
☐ 30	Todd Benzinger	.40	.16	.04
☐ 31	Fred McGriff	2.50	1.00	.25
☐ 32	Mike Henneman	.35	.15	.03
☐ 33	Casey Candaele	.10	.04	.01
☐ 34	Dave Magadan	.35	.15	.03
☐ 35	David Cone	.75	.30	.07
☐ 36	Mike Jackson	.25	.10	.02
☐ 37	John Mitchell	.10	.04	.01
☐ 38	Mike Dunne	.10	.04	.01
☐ 39	John Smiley	1.25	.50	.12
☐ 40	Joe Magrane	.20	.08	.02
☐ 41	Jim Lindeman	.10	.04	.01
☐ 42	Shane Mack	.30	.12	.03
☐ 43	Stan Jefferson	.10	.04	.01
☐ 44	Benito Santiago	.50	.20	.05

		MINT	EXC	G-VG
☐ 45	Matt Williams	5.50	2.50	.55
☐ 46	Dave Meads	.10	.04	.01
☐ 47	Rafael Palmeiro	2.50	1.00	.25
☐ 48	Bill Long	.12	.05	.01
☐ 49	Bob Brower	.10	.04	.01
☐ 50	James Steels	.07	.03	.01
☐ 51	Paul Noce	.07	.03	.01
☐ 52	Greg Maddux	.75	.30	.07
☐ 53	Jeff Musselman	.10	.04	.01
☐ 54	Brian Holton	.10	.04	.01
☐ 55	Chuck Jackson	.10	.04	.01
☐ 56	Checklist Card	.07	.01	.00

1987 Donruss Highlights

Donruss' third (and last) edition of Highlights was released late in 1987. The cards are standard size, measuring 2 1/2" by 3 1/2", and are glossy in appearance. Cards commemorate events during the 1987 season, as well as players and pitchers of the month from each league. The set was distributed in its own red, black, blue, and gold box along with a small Roberto Clemente puzzle. Card fronts are similar to the regular 1987 Donruss issue except that the Highlights logo is positioned in the lower right-hand corner and the borders are in blue instead of black. The backs are printed in black and gold on white card stock.

		MINT	EXC	G-VG
	COMPLETE SET (56)	7.00	3.00	.70
	COMMON PLAYER (1-56)	.06	.02	.00
☐ 1	Juan Nieves	.06	.02	.00
	First No-Hitter			
☐ 2	Mike Schmidt	.45	.18	.04
	Hits 500th Homer			
☐ 3	Eric Davis	.30	.12	.03
	NL Player April			
☐ 4	Sid Fernandez	.10	.04	.01
	NL Pitcher April			
☐ 5	Brian Downing	.06	.02	.00
	AL Player April			
☐ 6	Bret Saberhagen	.25	.10	.02
	AL Pitcher April			
☐ 7	Tim Raines	.15	.06	.01
	Free Agent Returns			
☐ 8	Eric Davis	.30	.12	.03
	NL Player May			
☐ 9	Steve Bedrosian	.06	.02	.00
	NL Pitcher May			
☐ 10	Larry Parrish	.06	.02	.00
	AL Player May			
☐ 11	Jim Clancy	.06	.02	.00
	AL Pitcher May			
☐ 12	Tony Gwynn UER	.35	.15	.03
	NL Player June			
	ERR (over "20" hits)			
☐ 13	Orel Hershiser	.25	.10	.02
	NL Pitcher June			
☐ 14	Wade Boggs	.45	.18	.04
	AL Player June			
☐ 15	Steve Ontiveros	.06	.02	.00
	AL Pitcher June			
☐ 16	Tim Raines	.15	.06	.01
	All Star Game Hero			

		MINT	EXC	G-VG
☐ 17	Don Mattingly Consecutive Game Homerun Streak	.60	.25	.06
☐ 18	Ray Dandridge 1987 HOF Inductee	.15	.06	.01
☐ 19	Jim"Catfish" Hunter 1987 HOF Inductee	.15	.06	.01
☐ 20	Billy Williams 1987 HOF Inductee	.15	.06	.01
☐ 21	Bo Diaz NL Player July	.06	.02	.00
☐ 22	Floyd Youmans NL Pitcher July	.06	.02	.00
☐ 23	Don Mattingly AL Player July	.60	.25	.06
☐ 24	Frank Viola AL Pitcher July	.15	.06	.01
☐ 25	Bobby Witt Strikes Out Four Batters in One Inning	.15	.06	.01
☐ 26	Kevin Seitzer Ties AL 9-Inning Game Hit Mark	.25	.10	.02
☐ 27	Mark McGwire Sets Rookie HR Record	.75	.30	.07
☐ 28	Andre Dawson Sets Cubs' 1st Year Homer Mark	.30	.12	.03
☐ 29	Paul Molitor Hits in 39 Straight Games	.20	.08	.02
☐ 30	Kirby Puckett Record Weekend	.60	.25	.06
☐ 31	Andre Dawson NL Player August	.30	.12	.03
☐ 32	Doug Drabek NL Pitcher August	.35	.15	.03
☐ 33	Dwight Evans AL Player August	.10	.04	.01
☐ 34	Mark Langston AL Pitcher August	.15	.06	.01
☐ 35	Wally Joyner 100 RBI in 1st Two Major League Seasons	.25	.10	.02
☐ 36	Vince Coleman 100 SB in 1st Three Major League Seasons	.30	.12	.03
☐ 37	Eddie Murray Orioles' All Time Homer King	.30	.12	.03
☐ 38	Cal Ripken Ends Consecutive Innings Streak	.75	.30	.07
☐ 39	Blue Jays Hit Record 10 Homers In One Game (McGriff/Ducey/Whitt)	.06	.02	.00
☐ 40	McGwire/Canseco Equal A's RBI Marks	.75	.30	.07
☐ 41	Bob Boone Sets All-Time Catching Record	.10	.04	.01
☐ 42	Darryl Strawberry Sets Mets' One-Season Home Run Mark	.45	.18	.04
☐ 43	Howard Johnson NL's All-Time Switchhit HR King	.20	.08	.02
☐ 44	Wade Boggs Five Straight 200 Hit Seasons	.45	.18	.04
☐ 45	Benito Santiago Eclipses Rookie Game Hitting Streak	.35	.15	.03
☐ 46	Mark McGwire Eclipses Jackson's A's HR Record	.75	.30	.07
☐ 47	Kevin Seitzer 13th Rookie to Collect 200 Hits	.25	.10	.02
☐ 48	Don Mattingly Sets Slam Record	.75	.30	.07
☐ 49	Darryl Strawberry NL Player September	.45	.18	.04
☐ 50	Pascual Perez NL Pitcher September	.10	.04	.01
☐ 51	Alan Trammell AL Player September	.15	.06	.01
☐ 52	Doyle Alexander AL Pitcher September	.06	.02	.00
☐ 53	Nolan Ryan Strikeout King Again	1.25	.50	.12
☐ 54	Mark McGwire Donruss AL ROY	.75	.30	.07
☐ 55	Benito Santiago Donruss NL ROY	.40	.16	.04
☐ 56	Checklist Card	.06	.02	.00

1988 Donruss

This 660-card set was distributed along with a puzzle of Stan Musial. The six regular checklist cards are numbered throughout the set as multiples of 100. Cards measure 2 1/2" by 3 1/2" and feature a distinctive black and blue border on the front. The popular Diamond King subset returns for the seventh consecutive year. Rated Rookies are featured again as cards 28-47. Cards marked as SP (short printed) from 648-660 are more difficult to find than the other 13 SP's in the lower 600s. These 26 cards listed as SP were apparently pulled from the printing sheet to make room for the 26 Bonus MVP cards. Six of the checklist cards were done two different ways to reflect the inclusion or exclusion of the Bonus MVP cards in the wax packs. In the checklist below, the A variations (for the checklist cards) are from the wax packs and the B variations are from the factory-collated sets. The key rookie cards in this set are Roberto Alomar, Ellis Burks, Ron Gant, Tom Glavine, Mark Grace, Gregg Jefferies, Roberto Kelly, and Matt Williams. There was also a Kirby Puckett card issued as the package back of Donruss blister packs; it uses a different photo from both of Kirby's regular and Bonus MVP cards and is unnumbered on the back.

		MINT	EXC	G-VG
	COMPLETE SET (660)	18.00	7.50	2.50
	COMMON PLAYER (1-647)	.03	.01	.00
	COMMON PLAYER (648-660)	.06	.02	.00
☐ 1	MarkMcGwireD	.1	.0	.0
☐ 2	Tim Raines DK	.08	.03	.01
☐ 3	Benito Santiago DK	.08	.03	.01
☐ 4	Alan Trammell DK	.10	.04	.01
☐ 5	Danny Tartabull DK	.10	.04	.01
☐ 6	Ron Darling DK	.08	.03	.01
☐ 7	Paul Molitor DK	.08	.03	.01
☐ 8	Devon White DK	.08	.03	.01
☐ 9	Andre Dawson DK	.10	.04	.01
☐ 10	Julio Franco DK	.10	.04	.01
☐ 11	Scott Fletcher DK	.06	.02	.00
☐ 12	Tony Fernandez DK	.08	.03	.01
☐ 13	Shane Rawley DK	.06	.02	.00
☐ 14	Kal Daniels DK	.08	.03	.01
☐ 15	Jack Clark DK	.08	.03	.01
☐ 16	Dwight Evans DK	.08	.03	.01
☐ 17	Tommy John DK	.08	.03	.01
☐ 18	Andy Van Slyke DK	.08	.03	.01
☐ 19	Gary Gaetti DK	.06	.02	.00
☐ 20	Mark Langston DK	.08	.03	.01
☐ 21	Will Clark DK	.25	.10	.02
☐ 22	Glenn Hubbard DK	.06	.02	.00
☐ 23	Billy Hatcher DK	.06	.02	.00
☐ 24	Bob Welch DK	.08	.03	.01
☐ 25	Ivan Calderon DK	.06	.02	.00
☐ 26	Cal Ripken DK	.20	.08	.02

☐ 27 DK Checklist 1-26	.06	.01	.00
☐ 28 Mackey Sasser RR	.15	.06	.01
☐ 29 Jeff Treadway RR	.20	.08	.02
☐ 30 Mike Campbell RR	.06	.02	.00
☐ 31 Lance Johnson RR	.15	.06	.01
☐ 32 Nelson Liriano RR	.08	.03	.01
☐ 33 Shawn Abner RR	.06	.02	.00
☐ 34 Roberto Alomar RR	3.00	1.25	.30
☐ 35 Shawn Hillegas RR	.08	.03	.01
☐ 36 Joey Meyer RR	.06	.02	.00
☐ 37 Kevin Elster RR	.06	.02	.00
☐ 38 Jose Lind RR	.20	.08	.02
☐ 39 Kirt Manwaring RR	.10	.04	.01
☐ 40 Mark Grace RR	1.50	.60	.15
☐ 41 Jody Reed RR	.30	.12	.03
☐ 42 John Farrell RR	.08	.03	.01
☐ 43 Al Leiter RR	.08	.03	.01
☐ 44 Gary Thurman RR	.10	.04	.01
☐ 45 Vicente Palacios RR	.10	.04	.01
☐ 46 Eddie Williams RR	.06	.02	.00
☐ 47 Jack McDowell RR	.50	.20	.05
☐ 48 Ken Dixon	.03	.01	.00
☐ 49 Mike Birkbeck	.03	.01	.00
☐ 50 Eric King	.03	.01	.00
☐ 51 Roger Clemens	.35	.15	.03
☐ 52 Pat Clements	.03	.01	.00
☐ 53 Fernando Valenzuela	.08	.03	.01
☐ 54 Mark Gubicza	.06	.02	.00
☐ 55 Jay Howell	.03	.01	.00
☐ 56 Floyd Youmans	.03	.01	.00
☐ 57 Ed Correa	.03	.01	.00
☐ 58 DeWayne Buice	.03	.01	.00
☐ 59 Jose DeLeon	.03	.01	.00
☐ 60 Danny Cox	.03	.01	.00
☐ 61 Nolan Ryan	.45	.18	.04
☐ 62 Steve Bedrosian	.06	.02	.00
☐ 63 Tom Browning	.06	.02	.00
☐ 64 Mark Davis	.06	.02	.00
☐ 65 R.J. Reynolds	.03	.01	.00
☐ 66 Kevin Mitchell	.25	.10	.02
☐ 67 Ken Oberkfell	.03	.01	.00
☐ 68 Rick Sutcliffe	.06	.02	.00
☐ 69 Dwight Gooden	.17	.07	.01
☐ 70 Scott Bankhead	.06	.02	.00
☐ 71 Bert Blyleven	.08	.03	.01
☐ 72 Jimmy Key	.08	.03	.01
☐ 73 Les Straker	.03	.01	.00
☐ 74 Jim Clancy	.03	.01	.00
☐ 75 Mike Moore	.06	.02	.00
☐ 76 Ron Darling	.08	.03	.01
☐ 77 Ed Lynch	.03	.01	.00
☐ 78 Dale Murphy	.15	.06	.01
☐ 79 Doug Drabek	.12	.05	.01
☐ 80 Scott Garrelts	.03	.01	.00
☐ 81 Ed Whitson	.03	.01	.00
☐ 82 Rob Murphy	.03	.01	.00
☐ 83 Shane Rawley	.03	.01	.00
☐ 84 Greg Mathews	.03	.01	.00
☐ 85 Jim Deshaies	.03	.01	.00
☐ 86 Mike Witt	.03	.01	.00
☐ 87 Donnie Hill	.03	.01	.00
☐ 88 Jeff Reed	.03	.01	.00
☐ 89 Mike Boddicker	.03	.01	.00
☐ 90 Ted Higuera	.06	.02	.00
☐ 91 Walt Terrell	.03	.01	.00
☐ 92 Bob Stanley	.03	.01	.00
☐ 93 Dave Righetti	.08	.03	.01
☐ 94 Orel Hershiser	.10	.04	.01
☐ 95 Chris Bando	.03	.01	.00
☐ 96 Bret Saberhagen	.12	.05	.01
☐ 97 Curt Young	.03	.01	.00
☐ 98 Tim Burke	.03	.01	.00
☐ 99 Charlie Hough	.03	.01	.00
☐ 100A Checklist 28-137	.06	.01	.00
☐ 100B Checklist 28-133	.06	.01	.00
☐ 101 Bobby Witt	.08	.03	.01
☐ 102 George Brett	.20	.08	.02
☐ 103 Mickey Tettleton	.08	.03	.01
☐ 104 Scott Bailes	.03	.01	.00
☐ 105 Mike Pagliarulo	.03	.01	.00
☐ 106 Mike Scioscia	.03	.01	.00
☐ 107 Tom Brookens	.03	.01	.00
☐ 108 Ray Knight	.06	.02	.00
☐ 109 Dan Plesac	.03	.01	.00
☐ 110 Wally Joyner	.15	.06	.01
☐ 111 Bob Forsch	.03	.01	.00
☐ 112 Mike Scott	.08	.03	.01
☐ 113 Kevin Gross	.03	.01	.00
☐ 114 Benito Santiago	.12	.05	.01
☐ 115 Bob Kipper	.03	.01	.00
☐ 116 Mike Krukow	.03	.01	.00
☐ 117 Chris Bosio	.06	.02	.00
☐ 118 Sid Fernandez	.08	.03	.01
☐ 119 Jody Davis	.03	.01	.00
☐ 120 Mike Morgan	.06	.02	.00
☐ 121 Mark Eichhorn	.03	.01	.00
☐ 122 Jeff Reardon	.10	.04	.01
☐ 123 John Franco	.06	.02	.00
☐ 124 Richard Dotson	.03	.01	.00
☐ 125 Eric Bell	.03	.01	.00
☐ 126 Juan Nieves	.03	.01	.00
☐ 127 Jack Morris	.12	.05	.01
☐ 128 Rick Rhoden	.03	.01	.00
☐ 129 Rich Gedman	.03	.01	.00
☐ 130 Ken Howell	.03	.01	.00
☐ 131 Brook Jacoby	.03	.01	.00
☐ 132 Danny Jackson	.06	.02	.00
☐ 133 Gene Nelson	.03	.01	.00
☐ 134 Neal Heaton	.03	.01	.00
☐ 135 Willie Fraser	.03	.01	.00
☐ 136 Jose Guzman	.06	.02	.00
☐ 137 Ozzie Guillen	.08	.03	.01
☐ 138 Bob Knepper	.03	.01	.00
☐ 139 Mike Jackson	.10	.04	.01
☐ 140 Joe Magrane	.12	.05	.01
☐ 141 Jimmy Jones	.06	.02	.00
☐ 142 Ted Power	.03	.01	.00
☐ 143 Ozzie Virgil	.03	.01	.00
☐ 144 Felix Fermin	.03	.01	.00
☐ 145 Kelly Downs	.03	.01	.00
☐ 146 Shawon Dunston	.10	.04	.01
☐ 147 Scott Bradley	.03	.01	.00
☐ 148 Dave Stieb	.08	.03	.01
☐ 149 Frank Viola	.10	.04	.01
☐ 150 Terry Kennedy	.03	.01	.00
☐ 151 Bill Wegman	.03	.01	.00
☐ 152 Matt Nokes	.25	.10	.02
☐ 153 Wade Boggs	.30	.12	.03
☐ 154 Wayne Tolleson	.03	.01	.00
☐ 155 Mariano Duncan	.03	.01	.00
☐ 156 Julio Franco	.15	.06	.01
☐ 157 Charlie Leibrandt	.03	.01	.00
☐ 158 Terry Steinbach	.08	.03	.01
☐ 159 Mike Fitzgerald	.03	.01	.00
☐ 160 Jack Lazorko	.03	.01	.00
☐ 161 Mitch Williams	.06	.02	.00
☐ 162 Greg Walker	.03	.01	.00
☐ 163 Alan Ashby	.03	.01	.00
☐ 164 Tony Gwynn	.25	.10	.02
☐ 165 Bruce Ruffin	.03	.01	.00
☐ 166 Ron Robinson	.03	.01	.00
☐ 167 Zane Smith	.08	.03	.01
☐ 168 Junior Ortiz	.03	.01	.00
☐ 169 Jamie Moyer	.03	.01	.00
☐ 170 Tony Pena	.06	.02	.00
☐ 171 Cal Ripken	.45	.18	.04
☐ 172 B.J. Surhoff	.06	.02	.00
☐ 173 Lou Whitaker	.10	.04	.01
☐ 174 Ellis Burks	.60	.25	.06
☐ 175 Ron Guidry	.08	.03	.01
☐ 176 Steve Sax	.10	.04	.01
☐ 177 Danny Tartabull	.15	.06	.01
☐ 178 Carney Lansford	.08	.03	.01
☐ 179 Casey Candaele	.03	.01	.00
☐ 180 Scott Fletcher	.03	.01	.00
☐ 181 Mark McLemore	.03	.01	.00
☐ 182 Ivan Calderon	.08	.03	.01
☐ 183 Jack Clark	.08	.03	.01
☐ 184 Glenn Davis	.10	.04	.01
☐ 185 Luis Aguayo	.03	.01	.00
☐ 186 Bo Diaz	.03	.01	.00
☐ 187 Stan Jefferson	.03	.01	.00
☐ 188 Sid Bream	.03	.01	.00
☐ 189 Bob Brenly	.03	.01	.00
☐ 190 Dion James	.03	.01	.00
☐ 191 Leon Durham	.03	.01	.00
☐ 192 Jesse Orosco	.03	.01	.00
☐ 193 Alvin Davis	.06	.02	.00
☐ 194 Gary Gaetti	.08	.03	.01
☐ 195 Fred McGriff	.30	.12	.03
☐ 196 Steve Lombardozzi	.03	.01	.00
☐ 197 Rance Mulliniks	.03	.01	.00
☐ 198 Rey Quinones	.03	.01	.00
☐ 199 Gary Carter	.08	.03	.01
☐ 200A Checklist 138-247	.06	.01	.00
☐ 200B Checklist 134-239	.06	.01	.00
☐ 201 Keith Moreland	.03	.01	.00
☐ 202 Ken Griffey	.10	.04	.01
☐ 203 Tommy Gregg	.08	.03	.01
☐ 204 Will Clark	.75	.30	.07
☐ 205 John Kruk	.06	.02	.00
☐ 206 Buddy Bell	.06	.02	.00
☐ 207 Von Hayes	.08	.03	.01
☐ 208 Tommy Herr	.03	.01	.00
☐ 209 Craig Reynolds	.03	.01	.00
☐ 210 Gary Pettis	.03	.01	.00
☐ 211 Harold Baines	.08	.03	.01
☐ 212 Vance Law	.03	.01	.00

#	Player				#	Player			
☐ 213	Ken Gerhart	.03	.01	.00	☐ 305	Bob Boone	.06	.02	.00
☐ 214	Jim Gantner	.03	.01	.00	☐ 306	Bill Long	.03	.01	.00
☐ 215	Chet Lemon	.03	.01	.00	☐ 307	Willie McGee	.08	.03	.01
☐ 216	Dwight Evans	.08	.03	.01	☐ 308	Ken Caminiti	.17	.07	.01
☐ 217	Don Mattingly	.25	.10	.02	☐ 309	Darren Daulton	.03	.01	.00
☐ 218	Franklin Stubbs	.03	.01	.00	☐ 310	Tracy Jones	.03	.01	.00
☐ 219	Pat Tabler	.03	.01	.00	☐ 311	Greg Booker	.03	.01	.00
☐ 220	Bo Jackson	.60	.25	.06	☐ 312	Mike LaValliere	.03	.01	.00
☐ 221	Tony Phillips	.03	.01	.00	☐ 313	Chili Davis	.06	.02	.00
☐ 222	Tim Wallach	.06	.02	.00	☐ 314	Glenn Hubbard	.03	.01	.00
☐ 223	Ruben Sierra	.35	.15	.03	☐ 315	Paul Noce	.03	.01	.00
☐ 224	Steve Buechele	.03	.01	.00	☐ 316	Keith Hernandez	.08	.03	.01
☐ 225	Frank White	.03	.01	.00	☐ 317	Mark Langston	.10	.04	.01
☐ 226	Alfredo Griffin	.03	.01	.00	☐ 318	Keith Atherton	.03	.01	.00
☐ 227	Greg Swindell	.08	.03	.01	☐ 319	Tony Fernandez	.08	.03	.01
☐ 228	Willie Randolph	.06	.02	.00	☐ 320	Kent Hrbek	.10	.04	.01
☐ 229	Mike Marshall	.08	.03	.01	☐ 321	John Cerutti	.03	.01	.00
☐ 230	Alan Trammell	.15	.06	.01	☐ 322	Mike Kingery	.03	.01	.00
☐ 231	Eddie Murray	.15	.06	.01	☐ 323	Dave Magadan	.08	.03	.01
☐ 232	Dale Sveum	.03	.01	.00	☐ 324	Rafael Palmeiro	.30	.12	.03
☐ 233	Dick Schofield	.03	.01	.00	☐ 325	Jeff Dedmon	.03	.01	.00
☐ 234	Jose Oquendo	.03	.01	.00	☐ 326	Barry Bonds	.35	.15	.03
☐ 235	Bill Doran	.03	.01	.00	☐ 327	Jeffrey Leonard	.03	.01	.00
☐ 236	Milt Thompson	.03	.01	.00	☐ 328	Tim Flannery	.03	.01	.00
☐ 237	Marvell Wynne	.03	.01	.00	☐ 329	Dave Concepcion	.08	.03	.01
☐ 238	Bobby Bonilla	.30	.12	.03	☐ 330	Mike Schmidt	.35	.15	.03
☐ 239	Chris Speier	.03	.01	.00	☐ 331	Bill Dawley	.03	.01	.00
☐ 240	Glenn Braggs	.03	.01	.00	☐ 332	Larry Andersen	.03	.01	.00
☐ 241	Wally Backman	.03	.01	.00	☐ 333	Jack Howell	.03	.01	.00
☐ 242	Ryne Sandberg	.35	.15	.03	☐ 334	Ken Williams	.06	.02	.00
☐ 243	Phil Bradley	.03	.01	.00	☐ 335	Bryn Smith	.03	.01	.00
☐ 244	Kelly Gruber	.15	.06	.01	☐ 336	Billy Ripken	.12	.05	.01
☐ 245	Tom Brunansky	.08	.03	.01	☐ 337	Greg Brock	.03	.01	.00
☐ 246	Ron Oester	.03	.01	.00	☐ 338	Mike Heath	.03	.01	.00
☐ 247	Bobby Thigpen	.10	.04	.01	☐ 339	Mike Greenwell	.20	.08	.02
☐ 248	Fred Lynn	.08	.03	.01	☐ 340	Claudell Washington	.03	.01	.00
☐ 249	Paul Molitor	.10	.04	.01	☐ 341	Jose Gonzalez	.03	.01	.00
☐ 250	Darrell Evans	.08	.03	.01	☐ 342	Mel Hall	.08	.03	.01
☐ 251	Gary Ward	.03	.01	.00	☐ 343	Jim Eisenreich	.06	.02	.00
☐ 252	Bruce Hurst	.06	.02	.00	☐ 344	Tony Bernazard	.03	.01	.00
☐ 253	Bob Welch	.08	.03	.01	☐ 345	Tim Raines	.10	.04	.01
☐ 254	Joe Carter	.17	.07	.01	☐ 346	Bob Brower	.03	.01	.00
☐ 255	Willie Wilson	.06	.02	.00	☐ 347	Larry Parrish	.03	.01	.00
☐ 256	Mark McGwire	.20	.08	.02	☐ 348	Thad Bosley	.03	.01	.00
☐ 257	Mitch Webster	.03	.01	.00	☐ 349	Dennis Eckersley	.10	.04	.01
☐ 258	Brian Downing	.06	.02	.00	☐ 350	Cory Snyder	.08	.03	.01
☐ 259	Mike Stanley	.03	.01	.00	☐ 351	Rick Cerone	.03	.01	.00
☐ 260	Carlton Fisk	.17	.07	.01	☐ 352	John Shelby	.03	.01	.00
☐ 261	Billy Hatcher	.06	.02	.00	☐ 353	Larry Herndon	.03	.01	.00
☐ 262	Glenn Wilson	.03	.01	.00	☐ 354	John Habyan	.03	.01	.00
☐ 263	Ozzie Smith	.17	.07	.01	☐ 355	Chuck Crim	.03	.01	.00
☐ 264	Randy Ready	.03	.01	.00	☐ 356	Gus Polidor	.03	.01	.00
☐ 265	Kurt Stillwell	.06	.02	.00	☐ 357	Ken Dayley	.03	.01	.00
☐ 266	David Palmer	.03	.01	.00	☐ 358	Danny Darwin	.03	.01	.00
☐ 267	Mike Diaz	.03	.01	.00	☐ 359	Lance Parrish	.08	.03	.01
☐ 268	Robby Thompson	.03	.01	.00	☐ 360	James Steels	.03	.01	.00
☐ 269	Andre Dawson	.15	.06	.01	☐ 361	Al Pedrique	.03	.01	.00
☐ 270	Lee Guetterman	.03	.01	.00	☐ 362	Mike Aldrete	.03	.01	.00
☐ 271	Willie Upshaw	.03	.01	.00	☐ 363	Juan Castillo	.03	.01	.00
☐ 272	Randy Bush	.03	.01	.00	☐ 364	Len Dykstra	.08	.03	.01
☐ 273	Larry Sheets	.03	.01	.00	☐ 365	Luis Quinones	.03	.01	.00
☐ 274	Rob Deer	.06	.02	.00	☐ 366	Jim Presley	.03	.01	.00
☐ 275	Kirk Gibson	.08	.03	.01	☐ 367	Lloyd Moseby	.03	.01	.00
☐ 276	Marty Barrett	.03	.01	.00	☐ 368	Kirby Puckett	.30	.12	.03
☐ 277	Rickey Henderson	.25	.10	.02	☐ 369	Eric Davis	.15	.06	.01
☐ 278	Pedro Guerrero	.08	.03	.01	☐ 370	Gary Redus	.03	.01	.00
☐ 279	Brett Butler	.08	.03	.01	☐ 371	Dave Schmidt	.03	.01	.00
☐ 280	Kevin Seitzer	.08	.03	.01	☐ 372	Mark Clear	.03	.01	.00
☐ 281	Mike Davis	.03	.01	.00	☐ 373	Dave Bergman	.03	.01	.00
☐ 282	Andres Galarraga	.08	.03	.01	☐ 374	Charles Hudson	.03	.01	.00
☐ 283	Devon White	.10	.04	.01	☐ 375	Calvin Schiraldi	.03	.01	.00
☐ 284	Pete O'Brien	.03	.01	.00	☐ 376	Alex Trevino	.03	.01	.00
☐ 285	Jerry Hairston	.03	.01	.00	☐ 377	Tom Candiotti	.06	.02	.00
☐ 286	Kevin Bass	.03	.01	.00	☐ 378	Steve Farr	.03	.01	.00
☐ 287	Carmelo Martinez	.03	.01	.00	☐ 379	Mike Gallego	.03	.01	.00
☐ 288	Juan Samuel	.06	.02	.00	☐ 380	Andy McGaffigan	.03	.01	.00
☐ 289	Kal Daniels	.08	.03	.01	☐ 381	Kirk McCaskill	.03	.01	.00
☐ 290	Albert Hall	.03	.01	.00	☐ 382	Oddibe McDowell	.03	.01	.00
☐ 291	Andy Van Slyke	.10	.04	.01	☐ 383	Floyd Bannister	.03	.01	.00
☐ 292	Lee Smith	.10	.04	.01	☐ 384	Denny Walling	.03	.01	.00
☐ 293	Vince Coleman	.10	.04	.01	☐ 385	Don Carman	.03	.01	.00
☐ 294	Tom Niedenfuer	.03	.01	.00	☐ 386	Todd Worrell	.06	.02	.00
☐ 295	Robin Yount	.20	.08	.02	☐ 387	Eric Show	.03	.01	.00
☐ 296	Jeff Robinson	.08	.03	.01	☐ 388	Dave Parker	.10	.04	.01
	(Tigers pitcher)				☐ 389	Rick Mahler	.03	.01	.00
☐ 297	Todd Benzinger	.20	.08	.02	☐ 390	Mike Dunne	.03	.01	.00
☐ 298	Dave Winfield	.15	.06	.01	☐ 391	Candy Maldonado	.06	.02	.00
☐ 299	Mickey Hatcher	.03	.01	.00	☐ 392	Bob Dernier	.03	.01	.00
☐ 300A	Checklist 248-357	.06	.01	.00	☐ 393	Dave Valle	.03	.01	.00
☐ 300B	Checklist 240-345	.06	.01	.00	☐ 394	Ernie Whitt	.03	.01	.00
☐ 301	Bud Black	.03	.01	.00	☐ 395	Juan Berenguer	.03	.01	.00
☐ 302	Jose Canseco	.75	.30	.07	☐ 396	Mike Young	.03	.01	.00
☐ 303	Tom Foley	.03	.01	.00	☐ 397	Mike Felder	.03	.01	.00
☐ 304	Pete Incaviglia	.08	.03	.01	☐ 398	Willie Hernandez	.03	.01	.00

399 Jim Rice	.08	.03	.01
400A Checklist 358-467	.06	.01	.00
400B Checklist 346-451	.06	.01	.00
401 Tommy John	.08	.03	.01
402 Brian Holton	.03	.01	.00
403 Carmen Castillo	.03	.01	.00
404 Jamie Quirk	.03	.01	.00
405 Dwayne Murphy	.03	.01	.00
406 Jeff Parrett	.06	.02	.00
407 Don Sutton	.10	.04	.01
408 Jerry Browne	.03	.01	.00
409 Jim Winn	.03	.01	.00
410 Dave Smith	.03	.01	.00
411 Shane Mack	.10	.04	.01
412 Greg Gross	.03	.01	.00
413 Nick Esasky	.03	.01	.00
414 Damaso Garcia	.03	.01	.00
415 Brian Fisher	.03	.01	.00
416 Brian Dayett	.03	.01	.00
417 Curt Ford	.03	.01	.00
418 Mark Williamson	.08	.03	.01
419 Bill Schroeder	.03	.01	.00
420 Mike Henneman	.15	.06	.01
421 John Marzano	.03	.01	.00
422 Ron Kittle	.06	.02	.00
423 Matt Young	.03	.01	.00
424 Steve Balboni	.03	.01	.00
425 Luis Polonia	.25	.10	.02
426 Randy St.Claire	.03	.01	.00
427 Greg Harris	.03	.01	.00
428 Johnny Ray	.03	.01	.00
429 Ray Searage	.03	.01	.00
430 Ricky Horton	.03	.01	.00
431 Gerald Young	.08	.03	.01
432 Rick Schu	.03	.01	.00
433 Paul O'Neill	.10	.04	.01
434 Rich Gossage	.08	.03	.01
435 John Cangelosi	.03	.01	.00
436 Mike LaCoss	.03	.01	.00
437 Gerald Perry	.03	.01	.00
438 Dave Martinez	.06	.02	.00
439 Darryl Strawberry	.35	.15	.03
440 John Moses	.03	.01	.00
441 Greg Gagne	.03	.01	.00
442 Jesse Barfield	.08	.03	.01
443 George Frazier	.03	.01	.00
444 Garth Iorg	.03	.01	.00
445 Ed Nunez	.03	.01	.00
446 Rick Aguilera	.06	.02	.00
447 Jerry Mumphrey	.03	.01	.00
448 Rafael Ramirez	.03	.01	.00
449 John Smiley	.45	.18	.04
450 Atlee Hammaker	.03	.01	.00
451 Lance McCullers	.03	.01	.00
452 Guy Hoffman	.03	.01	.00
453 Chris James	.08	.03	.01
454 Terry Pendleton	.12	.05	.01
455 Dave Meads	.04	.02	.00
456 Bill Buckner	.06	.02	.00
457 John Pawlowski	.04	.02	.00
458 Bob Sebra	.03	.01	.00
459 Jim Dwyer	.03	.01	.00
460 Jay Aldrich	.03	.01	.00
461 Frank Tanana	.06	.02	.00
462 Oil Can Boyd	.03	.01	.00
463 Dan Pasqua	.06	.02	.00
464 Tim Crews	.10	.04	.01
465 Andy Allanson	.03	.01	.00
466 Bill Pecota	.08	.03	.01
467 Steve Ontiveros	.03	.01	.00
468 Hubie Brooks	.08	.03	.01
469 Paul Kilgus	.06	.02	.00
470 Dale Mohorcic	.03	.01	.00
471 Dan Quisenberry	.08	.03	.01
472 Dave Stewart	.08	.03	.01
473 Dave Clark	.03	.01	.00
474 Joel Skinner	.03	.01	.00
475 Dave Anderson	.03	.01	.00
476 Dan Petry	.03	.01	.00
477 Carl Nichols	.03	.01	.00
478 Ernest Riles	.03	.01	.00
479 George Hendrick	.03	.01	.00
480 John Morris	.03	.01	.00
481 Manny Hernandez	.03	.01	.00
482 Jeff Stone	.03	.01	.00
483 Chris Brown	.03	.01	.00
484 Mike Bielecki	.06	.02	.00
485 Dave Dravecky	.08	.03	.01
486 Rick Manning	.03	.01	.00
487 Bill Almon	.03	.01	.00
488 Jim Sundberg	.03	.01	.00
489 Ken Phelps	.03	.01	.00
490 Tom Henke	.06	.02	.00
491 Dan Gladden	.03	.01	.00
492 Barry Larkin	.20	.08	.02

493 Fred Manrique	.06	.02	.00
494 Mike Griffin	.03	.01	.00
495 Mark Knudson	.10	.04	.01
496 Bill Madlock	.06	.02	.00
497 Tim Stoddard	.03	.01	.00
498 Sam Horn	.15	.06	.01
499 Tracy Woodson	.08	.03	.01
500A Checklist 468-577	.06	.01	.00
500B Checklist 452-557	.06	.01	.00
501 Ken Schrom	.03	.01	.00
502 Angel Salazar	.03	.01	.00
503 Eric Plunk	.03	.01	.00
504 Joe Hesketh	.06	.02	.00
505 Greg Minton	.03	.01	.00
506 Geno Petralli	.03	.01	.00
507 Bob James	.03	.01	.00
508 Robbie Wine	.03	.01	.00
509 Jeff Calhoun	.03	.01	.00
510 Steve Lake	.03	.01	.00
511 Mark Grant	.03	.01	.00
512 Frank Williams	.03	.01	.00
513 Jeff Blauser	.17	.07	.01
514 Bob Walk	.03	.01	.00
515 Craig Lefferts	.03	.01	.00
516 Manny Trillo	.03	.01	.00
517 Jerry Reed	.03	.01	.00
518 Rick Leach	.03	.01	.00
519 Mark Davidson	.08	.03	.01
520 Jeff Ballard	.08	.03	.01
521 Dave Stapleton	.03	.01	.00
522 Pat Sheridan	.03	.01	.00
523 Al Nipper	.03	.01	.00
524 Steve Trout	.03	.01	.00
525 Jeff Hamilton	.03	.01	.00
526 Tommy Hinzo	.03	.01	.00
527 Lonnie Smith	.08	.03	.01
528 Greg Cadaret	.10	.04	.01
529 Bob McClure UER ("Rob" on front)	.03	.01	.00
530 Chuck Finley	.15	.06	.01
531 Jeff Russell	.03	.01	.00
532 Steve Lyons	.03	.01	.00
533 Terry Puhl	.03	.01	.00
534 Eric Nolte	.06	.02	.00
535 Kent Tekulve	.03	.01	.00
536 Pat Pacillo	.06	.02	.00
537 Charlie Puleo	.03	.01	.00
538 Tom Prince	.06	.02	.00
539 Greg Maddux	.15	.06	.01
540 Jim Lindeman	.03	.01	.00
541 Pete Stanicek	.03	.01	.00
542 Steve Kiefer	.03	.01	.00
543A Jim Morrison ERR (no decimal before lifetime average)	.25	.10	.02
543B Jim Morrison COR	.06	.02	.00
544 Spike Owen	.03	.01	.00
545 Jay Buhner	.40	.16	.04
546 Mike Devereaux	.15	.06	.01
547 Jerry Don Gleaton	.03	.01	.00
548 Jose Rijo	.08	.03	.01
549 Dennis Martinez	.06	.02	.00
550 Mike Loynd	.03	.01	.00
551 Darrell Miller	.03	.01	.00
552 Dave LaPoint	.03	.01	.00
553 John Tudor	.06	.02	.00
554 Rocky Childress	.03	.01	.00
555 Wally Ritchie	.03	.01	.00
556 Terry McGriff	.03	.01	.00
557 Dave Leiper	.03	.01	.00
558 Jeff Robinson (Pirates pitcher)	.06	.02	.00
559 Jose Uribe	.03	.01	.00
560 Ted Simmons	.08	.03	.01
561 Les Lancaster	.08	.03	.01
562 Keith Miller (New York Mets)	.12	.05	.01
563 Harold Reynolds	.06	.02	.00
564 Gene Larkin	.12	.05	.01
565 Cecil Fielder	.35	.15	.03
566 Roy Smalley	.03	.01	.00
567 Duane Ward	.03	.01	.00
568 Bill Wilkinson	.06	.02	.00
569 Howard Johnson	.15	.06	.01
570 Frank DiPino	.03	.01	.00
571 Pete Smith	.08	.03	.01
572 Darnell Coles	.03	.01	.00
573 Don Robinson	.03	.01	.00
574 Rob Nelson UER (Career 0 RBI, but 1 RBI in '87)	.03	.01	.00
575 Dennis Rasmussen	.03	.01	.00
576 Steve Jeltz UER (Photo actually Juan Samuel; Samuel noted	.06	.02	.00

for one batting glove
and black bat)

☐ 577	Tom Pagnozzi	.12	.05	.01
☐ 578	Ty Gainey	.03	.01	.00
☐ 579	Gary Lucas	.03	.01	.00
☐ 580	Ron Hassey	.03	.01	.00
☐ 581	Herm Winningham	.03	.01	.00
☐ 582	Rene Gonzales	.06	.02	.00
☐ 583	Brad Komminsk	.03	.01	.00
☐ 584	Doyle Alexander	.03	.01	.00
☐ 585	Jeff Sellers	.03	.01	.00
☐ 586	Bill Gullickson	.06	.02	.00
☐ 587	Tim Belcher	.12	.05	.01
☐ 588	Doug Jones	.12	.05	.01
☐ 589	Melido Perez	.15	.06	.01
☐ 590	Rick Honeycutt	.03	.01	.00
☐ 591	Pascual Perez	.03	.01	.00
☐ 592	Curt Wilkerson	.03	.01	.00
☐ 593	Steve Howe	.03	.01	.00
☐ 594	John Davis	.06	.02	.00
☐ 595	Storm Davis	.03	.01	.00
☐ 596	Sammy Stewart	.03	.01	.00
☐ 597	Neil Allen	.03	.01	.00
☐ 598	Alejandro Pena	.06	.02	.00
☐ 599	Mark Thurmond	.03	.01	.00
☐ 600A	Checklist 578-BC26	.06	.01	.00
☐ 600B	Checklist 558-660	.06	.01	.00
☐ 601	Jose Mesa	.08	.03	.01
☐ 602	Don August	.03	.01	.00
☐ 603	Terry Leach SP	.06	.02	.00
☐ 604	Tom Newell	.03	.01	.00
☐ 605	Randall Byers SP	.10	.04	.01
☐ 606	Jim Gott	.03	.01	.00
☐ 607	Harry Spilman	.03	.01	.00
☐ 608	John Candelaria	.03	.01	.00
☐ 609	Mike Brumley	.08	.03	.01
☐ 610	Mickey Brantley	.03	.01	.00
☐ 611	Jose Nunez SP	.08	.03	.01
☐ 612	Tom Nieto	.03	.01	.00
☐ 613	Rick Reuschel	.06	.02	.00
☐ 614	Lee Mazzilli SP	.06	.02	.00
☐ 615	Scott Lusader	.06	.02	.00
☐ 616	Bobby Meacham	.03	.01	.00
☐ 617	Kevin McReynolds SP	.10	.04	.01
☐ 618	Gene Garber	.03	.01	.00
☐ 619	Barry Lyons SP	.10	.04	.01
☐ 620	Randy Myers	.06	.02	.00
☐ 621	Donnie Moore	.03	.01	.00
☐ 622	Domingo Ramos	.03	.01	.00
☐ 623	Ed Romero	.03	.01	.00
☐ 624	Greg Myers	.10	.04	.01
☐ 625	Ripken Family	.17	.07	.01
☐ 626	Pat Perry	.03	.01	.00
☐ 627	Andres Thomas SP	.06	.02	.00
☐ 628	Matt Williams SP	1.75	.70	.17
☐ 629	Dave Hengel	.06	.02	.00
☐ 630	Jeff Musselman SP	.06	.02	.00
☐ 631	Tim Laudner	.03	.01	.00
☐ 632	Bob Ojeda SP	.06	.02	.00
☐ 633	Rafael Santana	.03	.01	.00
☐ 634	Wes Gardner	.08	.03	.01
☐ 635	Roberto Kelly SP	.75	.30	.07
☐ 636	Mike Flanagan SP	.06	.02	.00
☐ 637	Jay Bell	.30	.12	.03
☐ 638	Bob Melvin	.03	.01	.00
☐ 639	Damon Berryhill UER (Bats: Switchd)	.10	.04	.01
☐ 640	David Wells SP	.20	.08	.02
☐ 641	Puzzle Card (Stan Musial)	.06	.02	.00
☐ 642	Doug Sisk	.03	.01	.00
☐ 643	Keith Hughes	.06	.02	.00
☐ 644	Tom Glavine	.90	.40	.09
☐ 645	Al Newman	.03	.01	.00
☐ 646	Scott Sanderson	.06	.02	.00
☐ 647	Scott Terry	.06	.02	.00
☐ 648	Tim Teufel SP	.06	.02	.00
☐ 649	Garry Templeton SP	.06	.02	.00
☐ 650	Manny Lee SP	.06	.02	.00
☐ 651	Roger McDowell SP	.06	.02	.00
☐ 652	Mookie Wilson SP	.06	.02	.00
☐ 653	David Cone SP	.20	.08	.02
☐ 654	Ron Gant SP	3.50	1.50	.35
☐ 655	Joe Price SP	.06	.02	.00
☐ 656	George Bell SP	.15	.06	.01
☐ 657	Gregg Jefferies SP	1.50	.60	.15
☐ 658	Todd Stottlemyre SP	.50	.20	.05
☐ 659	Geronimo Berroa SP	.15	.06	.01
☐ 660	Jerry Royster SP	.08	.03	.01

1988 Donruss Bonus MVP's

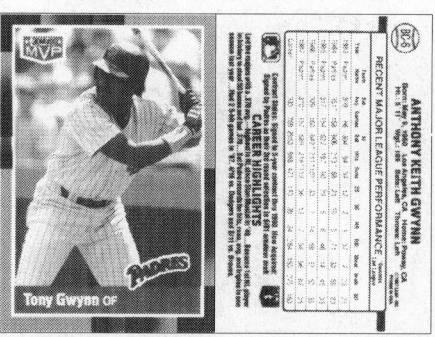

This 26-card set was distributed along with the regular 1988 Donruss issue as random inserts with the rack and wax packs. These bonus cards are numbered with the prefix BC for bonus cards and were supposedly produced in the same quantities as the other 660 regular issue cards. The "most valuable" player was selected from each of the 26 teams. Cards measure 2 1/2" by 3 1/2" and feature the same distinctive black and blue border on the front as the regular issue. The cards are distinguished by the MVP logo in the upper left corner of the obverse. The last 13 cards numerically are considered to be somewhat tougher to find than the first 13 cards.

		MINT	EXC	G-VG
	COMPLETE SET (26)	3.00	1.25	.30
	COMMON CARD (BC1-BC13)	.04	.02	.00
	COMMON CARD (BC14-BC26)	.06	.02	.00
☐ BC1	Cal Ripken	.25	.10	.02
☐ BC2	Eric Davis	.08	.03	.01
☐ BC3	Paul Molitor	.08	.03	.01
☐ BC4	Mike Schmidt	.15	.06	.01
☐ BC5	Ivan Calderon	.04	.02	.00
☐ BC6	Tony Gwynn	.12	.05	.01
☐ BC7	Wade Boggs	.12	.05	.01
☐ BC8	Andy Van Slyke	.08	.03	.01
☐ BC9	Joe Carter	.08	.03	.01
☐ BC10	Andre Dawson	.10	.04	.01
☐ BC11	Alan Trammell	.10	.04	.01
☐ BC12	Mike Scott	.06	.02	.00
☐ BC13	Wally Joyner	.10	.04	.01
☐ BC14	Dale Murphy	.10	.04	.01
☐ BC15	Kirby Puckett	.20	.08	.02
☐ BC16	Pedro Guerrero	.08	.03	.01
☐ BC17	Kevin Seitzer	.08	.03	.01
☐ BC18	Tim Raines	.10	.04	.01
☐ BC19	George Bell	.12	.05	.01
☐ BC20	Darryl Strawberry	.25	.10	.02
☐ BC21	Don Mattingly	.20	.08	.02
☐ BC22	Ozzie Smith	.12	.05	.01
☐ BC23	Mark McGwire	.15	.06	.01
☐ BC24	Will Clark	.30	.12	.03
☐ BC25	Alvin Davis	.06	.02	.00
☐ BC26	Ruben Sierra	.25	.10	.02

1988 Donruss Super DK's

This 26-player card set was available through a mail-in offer detailed on the wax packs. The set was sent in return for $8.00 and three wrappers plus $1.50 postage and handling. The set features the popular Diamond King subseries in large (approximately 4 7/8" by 6 13/16") form. Dick Perez of Perez-Steele Galleries did another outstanding job on the artwork. The cards are essentially a large version of the Donruss regular issue Diamond Kings.

	MINT	EXC	G-VG
COMPLETE SET (26)	9.00	4.00	.90
COMMON PLAYER (1-26)	.20	.08	.02

		MINT	EXC	G-VG
☐ 1	Mark McGwire DK	.75	.30	.07
☐ 2	Tim Raines DK	.35	.15	.03
☐ 3	Benito Santiago DK	.40	.16	.04
☐ 4	Alan Trammell DK	.40	.16	.04
☐ 5	Danny Tartabull DK	.50	.20	.05
☐ 6	Ron Darling DK	.25	.10	.02
☐ 7	Paul Molitor DK	.30	.12	.03
☐ 8	Devon White DK	.40	.16	.04
☐ 9	Andre Dawson DK	.45	.18	.04
☐ 10	Julio Franco DK	.40	.16	.04
☐ 11	Scott Fletcher DK	.20	.08	.02
☐ 12	Tony Fernandez DK	.25	.10	.02
☐ 13	Shane Rawley DK	.20	.08	.02
☐ 14	Kal Daniels DK	.35	.15	.03
☐ 15	Jack Clark DK	.30	.12	.03
☐ 16	Dwight Evans DK	.30	.12	.03
☐ 17	Tommy John DK	.30	.12	.03
☐ 18	Andy Van Slyke DK	.30	.12	.03
☐ 19	Gary Gaetti DK	.30	.12	.03
☐ 20	Mark Langston DK	.35	.15	.03
☐ 21	Will Clark DK	1.00	.40	.10
☐ 22	Glenn Hubbard DK	.20	.08	.02
☐ 23	Billy Hatcher DK	.25	.10	.02
☐ 24	Bob Welch DK	.35	.15	.03
☐ 25	Ivan Calderon DK	.30	.12	.03
☐ 26	Cal Ripken Jr. DK	1.00	.40	.10

1988 Donruss All-Stars

This 64-card set features cards measuring standard size, 2 1/2" by 3 1/2". Card fronts are in full color with a solid blue and black border. The card backs are printed in black and blue on white card stock. Cards are numbered on the back inside a blue star in the upper right hand corner. Card backs feature statistical information about the player's performance in past All-Star games. The set was distributed in packs which also contained a Pop-Up. The AL Checklist card number 32 has two uncorrected

errors on it, Wade Boggs is erroneously listed as the AL Leftfielder and Dan Plesac is erroneously listed as being on the Tigers.

	MINT	EXC	G-VG
COMPLETE SET (64)	8.00	3.50	.80
COMMON PLAYER (1-64)	.10	.04	.01

		MINT	EXC	G-VG
☐ 1	Don Mattingly	.60	.25	.06
☐ 2	Dave Winfield	.30	.12	.03
☐ 3	Willie Randolph	.15	.06	.01
☐ 4	Rickey Henderson	.75	.30	.07
☐ 5	Cal Ripken	.75	.30	.07
☐ 6	George Bell	.20	.08	.02
☐ 7	Wade Boggs	.60	.25	.06
☐ 8	Bret Saberhagen	.30	.12	.03
☐ 9	Terry Kennedy	.10	.04	.01
☐ 10	John McNamara MG	.10	.04	.01
☐ 11	Jay Howell	.10	.04	.01
☐ 12	Harold Baines	.15	.06	.01
☐ 13	Harold Reynolds	.10	.04	.01
☐ 14	Bruce Hurst	.15	.06	.01
☐ 15	Kirby Puckett	.60	.25	.06
☐ 16	Matt Nokes	.15	.06	.01
☐ 17	Pat Tabler	.10	.04	.01
☐ 18	Dan Plesac	.10	.04	.01
☐ 19	Mark McGwire	.50	.20	.05
☐ 20	Mike Witt	.10	.04	.01
☐ 21	Larry Parrish	.10	.04	.01
☐ 22	Alan Trammell	.25	.10	.02
☐ 23	Dwight Evans	.15	.06	.01
☐ 24	Jack Morris	.25	.10	.02
☐ 25	Tony Fernandez	.15	.06	.01
☐ 26	Mark Langston	.15	.06	.01
☐ 27	Kevin Seitzer	.20	.08	.02
☐ 28	Tom Henke	.10	.04	.01
☐ 29	Dave Righetti	.15	.06	.01
☐ 30	Oakland Stadium	.10	.04	.01
☐ 31	Wade Boggs	.60	.25	.06
☐ 32	AL Checklist UER	.10	.04	.01
☐ 33	Jack Clark	.15	.06	.01
☐ 34	Darryl Strawberry	.45	.18	.04
☐ 35	Ryne Sandberg	.75	.30	.07
☐ 36	Andre Dawson	.35	.15	.03
☐ 37	Ozzie Virgil	.30	.12	.03
☐ 38	Eric Davis	.40	.16	.04
☐ 39	Mike Schmidt	.75	.30	.07
☐ 40	Mike Scott	.15	.06	.01
☐ 41	Gary Carter	.20	.08	.02
☐ 42	Davey Johnson MG	.10	.04	.01
☐ 43	Rick Sutcliffe	.10	.04	.01
☐ 44	Willie McGee	.15	.06	.01
☐ 45	Hubie Brooks	.10	.04	.01
☐ 46	Dale Murphy	.30	.12	.03
☐ 47	Bo Diaz	.10	.04	.01
☐ 48	Pedro Guerrero	.15	.06	.01
☐ 49	Keith Hernandez	.20	.08	.02
☐ 50	Ozzie Virgil UER (Phillies logo on card back, wrong birth year)	.10	.04	.01
☐ 51	Tony Gwynn	.45	.18	.04
☐ 52	Rick Reuschel UER (Pirates logo on card back)	.10	.04	.01
☐ 53	John Franco	.15	.06	.01
☐ 54	Jeffrey Leonard	.10	.04	.01
☐ 55	Juan Samuel	.15	.06	.01
☐ 56	Orel Hershiser	.35	.15	.03
☐ 57	Tim Raines	.20	.08	.02
☐ 58	Sid Fernandez	.15	.06	.01
☐ 59	Tim Wallach	.10	.04	.01
☐ 60	Lee Smith	.20	.08	.02
☐ 61	Steve Bedrosian	.10	.04	.01
☐ 62	Tim Raines	.20	.08	.02
☐ 63	Ozzie Smith	.25	.10	.02
☐ 64	NL Checklist	.10	.04	.01

1988 Donruss Pop-Ups

This 20-card set features "fold-out" cards measuring standard size, 2 1/2" by 3 1/2". Card fronts are in full color. Cards are unnumbered but are listed in the same order as the Donruss All-Stars on the All-Star checklist card. Card backs present essentially no information about the player. The set was distributed in packs which also contained All-Star cards. In

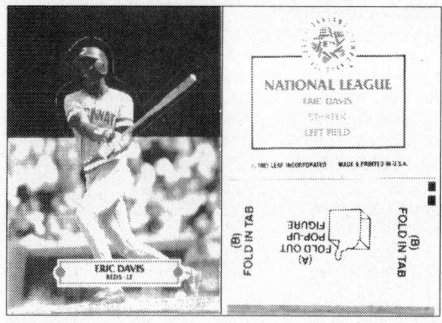

order to remain in mint condition, the cards should not be popped up.

	MINT	EXC	G-VG
COMPLETE SET (20)	4.00	1.75	.40
COMMON PLAYER (1-20)	.10	.04	.01
☐ 1 Don Mattingly	.60	.25	.06
☐ 2 Dave Winfield	.30	.12	.03
☐ 3 Willie Randolph	.15	.06	.01
☐ 4 Rickey Henderson	.75	.30	.07
☐ 5 Cal Ripken	.75	.30	.07
☐ 6 George Bell	.20	.08	.02
☐ 7 Wade Boggs	.60	.25	.06
☐ 8 Bret Saberhagen	.30	.12	.03
☐ 9 Terry Kennedy	.10	.04	.01
☐ 10 John McNamara MG	.10	.04	.01
☐ 11 Jack Clark	.15	.06	.01
☐ 12 Darryl Strawberry	.45	.18	.04
☐ 13 Ryne Sandberg	.75	.30	.07
☐ 14 Andre Dawson	.35	.15	.03
☐ 15 Ozzie Smith	.30	.12	.03
☐ 16 Eric Davis	.40	.16	.04
☐ 17 Mike Schmidt	.75	.30	.07
☐ 18 Mike Scott	.15	.06	.01
☐ 19 Gary Carter	.20	.08	.02
☐ 20 Davey Johnson MG	.10	.04	.01

1988 Donruss Rookies

The 1988 Donruss "The Rookies" set features 56 cards plus a 15-piece puzzle of Stan Musial. Cards are in full color and are standard size, 2 1/2" by 3 1/2". The set was distributed in a small green and black box with gold lettering. Card fronts are similar in design to the 1988 Donruss regular issue except for the presence of "The Rookies" logo in the lower right corner and a green and black border instead of a blue and black border on the fronts. The key rookies in this set are ROY's, Chris Sabo and Walt Weiss.

	MINT	EXC	G-VG
COMPLETE SET (56)	12.00	5.25	1.50
COMMON PLAYER (1-56)	.07	.03	.01
☐ 1 Mark Grace	2.25	.75	.15
☐ 2 Mike Campbell	.07	.03	.01
☐ 3 Todd Frohwirth	.10	.04	.01
☐ 4 Dave Stapleton	.07	.03	.01
☐ 5 Shawn Abner	.10	.04	.01
☐ 6 Jose Cecena	.07	.03	.01
☐ 7 Dave Gallagher	.10	.04	.01
☐ 8 Mark Parent	.10	.04	.01
☐ 9 Cecil Espy	.12	.05	.01
☐ 10 Pete Smith	.10	.04	.01
☐ 11 Jay Buhner	.40	.16	.04
☐ 12 Pat Borders	.30	.12	.03
☐ 13 Doug Jennings	.12	.05	.01
☐ 14 Brady Anderson	.10	.04	.01
☐ 15 Pete Stanicek	.07	.03	.01
☐ 16 Roberto Kelly	.60	.25	.06
☐ 17 Jeff Treadway	.20	.08	.02
☐ 18 Walt Weiss	.25	.10	.02
☐ 19 Paul Gibson	.10	.04	.01
☐ 20 Tim Crews	.10	.04	.01
☐ 21 Melido Perez	.10	.04	.01
☐ 22 Steve Peters	.10	.04	.01
☐ 23 Craig Worthington	.10	.04	.01
☐ 24 John Trautwein	.07	.03	.01
☐ 25 DeWayne Vaughn	.07	.03	.01
☐ 26 David Wells	.12	.05	.01
☐ 27 Al Leiter	.10	.04	.01
☐ 28 Tim Belcher	.12	.05	.01
☐ 29 Johnny Paredes	.10	.04	.01
☐ 30 Chris Sabo	2.00	.80	.20
☐ 31 Damon Berryhill	.10	.04	.01
☐ 32 Randy Milligan	.35	.15	.03
☐ 33 Gary Thurman	.10	.04	.01
☐ 34 Kevin Elster	.12	.05	.01
☐ 35 Roberto Alomar	3.50	1.50	.35
☐ 36 Edgar Martinez UER (photo actually Edwin Nunez)	1.00	.40	.10
☐ 37 Todd Stottlemyre	.35	.15	.03
☐ 38 Joey Meyer	.10	.04	.01
☐ 39 Carl Nichols	.07	.03	.01
☐ 40 Jack McDowell	.45	.18	.04
☐ 41 Jose Bautista	.10	.04	.01
☐ 42 Sil Campusano	.12	.05	.01
☐ 43 John Dopson	.10	.04	.01
☐ 44 Jody Reed	.25	.10	.02
☐ 45 Darrin Jackson	.20	.08	.02
☐ 46 Mike Capel	.10	.04	.01
☐ 47 Ron Gant	2.25	.90	.22
☐ 48 John Davis	.07	.03	.01
☐ 49 Kevin Coffman	.07	.03	.01
☐ 50 Cris Carpenter	.20	.08	.02
☐ 51 Mackey Sasser	.15	.06	.01
☐ 52 Luis Alicea	.10	.04	.01
☐ 53 Bryan Harvey	.60	.25	.06
☐ 54 Steve Ellsworth	.10	.04	.01
☐ 55 Mike Macfarlane	.15	.06	.01
☐ 56 Checklist Card	.07	.01	.00

1988 Donruss Athletics Book

The 1988 Donruss Athletics Team Book set features 27 cards (three pages with nine cards on each page) plus a large full-page puzzle of Stan Musial. Cards are in full color and are standard size, 2 1/2" by 3 1/2". The set was distributed as a four-page book; although the puzzle page was perforated, the card pages were not. The cover of the "Team Collection" book is primarily bright red. Card fronts are very similar in design to the 1988 Donruss regular issue. The card numbers on the backs are the same for those players that are the same as in the regular Donruss set; the new players pictured are numbered on the back as "NEW." In fact 1988 A.L. Rookie of the Year Walt Weiss makes his first Donruss appearance in this set as a "NEW" card. The book is usually sold intact. When cut from the book into individual cards, these cards are distinguishable from the regular 1988 Donruss cards since these have a 1988 copyright on the back whereas the regular issue has a 1987 copyright on the back.

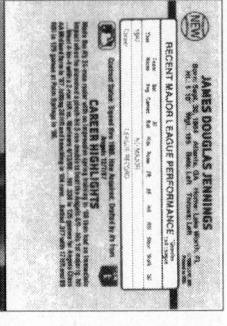

1988 Donruss regular issue. The card numbers on the backs are the same for those players that are the same as in the regular Donruss set; the new players pictured are numbered on the back as "NEW." The book is usually sold intact. When cut from the book into individual cards, these cards are distinguishable from the regular 1988 Donruss cards since these have a 1988 copyright on the back whereas the regular issue has a 1987 copyright on the back.

	MINT	EXC	G-VG
COMPLETE SET (27)	5.00	2.25	.50
COMMON PLAYER	.10	.04	.01
☐ 40 Mark Grace	1.50	.60	.15
☐ 68 Rick Sutcliffe	.15	.06	.01
☐ 119 Jody Davis	.10	.04	.01
☐ 146 Shawon Dunston	.30	.12	.03
☐ 169 Jamie Moyer	.10	.04	.01
☐ 191 Leon Durham	.10	.04	.01
☐ 242 Ryne Sandberg	.75	.30	.07
☐ 269 Andre Dawson	.45	.18	.04
☐ 315 Paul Noce	.15	.06	.01
☐ 324 Rafael Palmeiro	.75	.30	.07
☐ 438 Dave Martinez	.15	.06	.01
☐ 447 Jerry Mumphrey	.10	.04	.01
☐ 488 Jim Sundberg	.10	.04	.01
☐ 516 Manny Trillo	.10	.04	.01
☐ 539 Greg Maddux	.35	.15	.03
☐ 561 Les Lancaster	.10	.04	.01
☐ 570 Frank DiPino	.10	.04	.01
☐ 639 Damon Berryhill	.25	.10	.02
☐ 646 Scott Sanderson	.15	.06	.01
☐ NEW Mike Bielecki	.25	.10	.02
☐ NEW Rich Gossage	.25	.10	.02
☐ NEW Drew Hall	.15	.06	.01
☐ NEW Darrin Jackson	.25	.10	.02
☐ NEW Vance Law	.10	.04	.01
☐ NEW Al Nipper	.10	.04	.01
☐ NEW Angel Salazar	.10	.04	.01
☐ NEW Calvin Schiraldi	.10	.04	.01

	MINT	EXC	G-VG
COMPLETE SET (27)	5.00	2.25	.50
COMMON PLAYER	.10	.04	.01
☐ 97 Curt Young	.10	.04	.01
☐ 133 Gene Nelson	.10	.04	.01
☐ 158 Terry Steinbach	.20	.08	.02
☐ 178 Carney Lansford	.15	.06	.01
☐ 221 Tony Phillips	.15	.06	.01
☐ 256 Mark McGwire	.75	.30	.07
☐ 302 Jose Canseco	1.25	.50	.12
☐ 349 Dennis Eckersley	.40	.16	.04
☐ 379 Mike Gallego	.10	.04	.01
☐ 425 Luis Polonia	.10	.04	.01
☐ 467 Steve Ontiveros	.10	.04	.01
☐ 472 Dave Stewart	.40	.16	.04
☐ 503 Eric Plunk	.10	.04	.01
☐ 528 Greg Cadaret	.10	.04	.01
☐ 590 Rick Honeycutt	.10	.04	.01
☐ 595 Storm Davis	.15	.06	.01
☐ NEW Don Baylor UER (career stats are incorrect)	.25	.10	.02
☐ NEW Ron Hassey	.10	.04	.01
☐ NEW Dave Henderson	.30	.12	.03
☐ NEW Glenn Hubbard	.10	.04	.01
☐ NEW Stan Javier	.10	.04	.01
☐ NEW Doug Jennings	.25	.10	.02
☐ NEW Edward Jurak	.10	.04	.01
☐ NEW Dave Parker	.30	.12	.03
☐ NEW Walt Weiss	1.00	.40	.10
☐ NEW Bob Welch	.35	.15	.03
☐ NEW Matt Young	.10	.04	.01

1988 Donruss Cubs Team Book

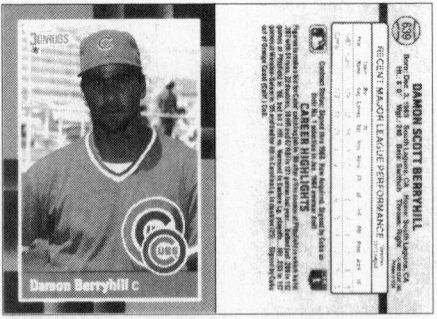

The 1988 Donruss Cubs Team Book set features 27 cards (three pages with nine cards on each page) plus a large full-page puzzle of Stan Musial. Cards are in full color and are standard size, 2 1/2" by 3 1/2". The set was distributed as a four-page book; although the puzzle page was perforated, the card pages were not. The cover of the "Team Collection" book is primarily bright red. Card fronts are very similar in design to the

1988 Donruss Mets Team Book

The 1988 Donruss Mets Team Book set features 27 cards (three pages with nine cards on each page) plus a large full-page puzzle of Stan Musial. Cards are in full color and are standard size, 2 1/2" by 3 1/2". The set was distributed as a four-page book; although the puzzle page was perforated, the card pages were not. The cover of the "Team Collection" book is primarily bright red. Card fronts are very similar in design to the 1988 Donruss regular issue. The card numbers on the backs are the same for those players that are the same as in the regular Donruss set; the new players pictured are numbered on the back as "NEW." The book is usually sold intact. When cut from the book into individual cards, these cards are distinguishable from the regular 1988 Donruss cards since these have a 1988 copyright on the back whereas the regular issue has a 1987 copyright on the back.

	MINT	EXC	G-VG
COMPLETE SET (27)	5.00	2.25	.50
COMMON PLAYER	.10	.04	.01
☐ 37 Kevin Elster	.15	.06	.01
☐ 69 Dwight Gooden	.45	.18	.04
☐ 76 Ron Darling	.20	.08	.02
☐ 118 Sid Fernandez	.20	.08	.02
☐ 199 Gary Carter	.25	.10	.02
☐ 241 Wally Backman	.10	.04	.01
☐ 316 Keith Hernandez	.25	.10	.02
☐ 323 Dave Magadan	.30	.12	.03
☐ 364 Lee Dykstra	.30	.12	.03
☐ 439 Darryl Strawberry	.75	.30	.07
☐ 446 Rick Aguilera	.20	.08	.02
☐ 562 Keith Miller	.15	.06	.01
☐ 569 Howard Johnson	.30	.12	.03
☐ 603 Terry Leach	.10	.04	.01
☐ 614 Lee Mazzilli	.10	.04	.01
☐ 617 Kevin McReynolds	.20	.08	.02
☐ 619 Barry Lyons	.10	.04	.01
☐ 620 Randy Myers	.20	.08	.02
☐ 632 Bob Ojeda	.15	.06	.01
☐ 648 Tim Teufel	.10	.04	.01
☐ 651 Roger McDowell	.15	.06	.01
☐ 652 Mookie Wilson	.15	.06	.01
☐ 653 David Cone	.40	.16	.04
☐ 657 Gregg Jefferies	1.25	.50	.12
☐ NEW Jeff Innis	.20	.08	.02
☐ NEW Mackey Sasser	.25	.10	.02
☐ NEW Gene Walter	.10	.04	.01

	MINT	EXC	G-VG
☐ 276 Marty Barrett	.10	.04	.01
☐ 297 Todd Benzinger	.20	.08	.02
☐ 339 Mike Greenwell	.90	.40	.09
☐ 399 Jim Rice	.20	.08	.02
☐ 421 John Marzano	.10	.04	.01
☐ 462 Oil Can Boyd	.10	.04	.01
☐ 498 Sam Horn	.20	.08	.02
☐ 544 Spike Owen	.10	.04	.01
☐ 585 Jeff Sellers	.10	.04	.01
☐ 623 Ed Romero	.10	.04	.01
☐ 634 Wes Gardner	.15	.06	.01
☐ NEW Brady Anderson	.25	.10	.02
☐ NEW Rick Cerone	.10	.04	.01
☐ NEW Steve Ellsworth	.15	.06	.01
☐ NEW Dennis Lamp	.10	.04	.01
☐ NEW Kevin Romine	.10	.04	.01
☐ NEW Lee Smith	.25	.10	.02
☐ NEW Mike Smithson	.10	.04	.01
☐ NEW John Trautwein	.15	.06	.01

1988 Donruss Yankees Team Book

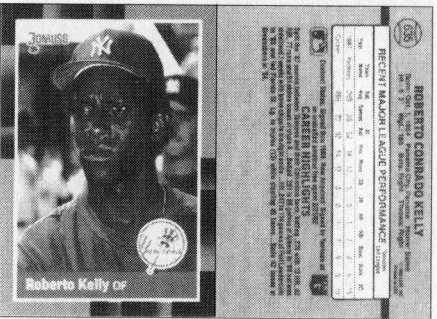

Roberto Kelly OF

The 1988 Donruss Yankees Team Book set features 27 cards (three pages with nine cards on each page) plus a large full-page puzzle of Stan Musial. Cards are in full color and are standard size, 2 1/2" by 3 1/2". The set was distributed as a four-page book; although the puzzle page was perforated, the card pages were not. The cover of the "Team Collection" book is primarily bright red. Card fronts are very similar in design to the 1988 Donruss regular issue. The card numbers on the backs are the same for those players that are the same as in the regular Donruss set; the new players pictured are numbered on the back as "NEW." The book is usually sold intact. When cut from the book into individual cards, these cards are distinguishable from the regular 1988 Donruss cards since these have a 1988 copyright on the back whereas the regular issue has a 1987 copyright on the back.

	MINT	EXC	G-VG
COMPLETE SET (27)	5.00	2.25	.50
COMMON PLAYER	.10	.04	.01
☐ 43 Al Leiter	.15	.06	.01
☐ 93 Dave Righetti	.20	.08	.02
☐ 105 Mike Pagliarulo	.15	.06	.01
☐ 128 Rick Rhoden	.10	.04	.01
☐ 175 Ron Guidry	.25	.10	.02
☐ 217 Don Mattingly	.90	.40	.09
☐ 228 Willie Randolph	.15	.06	.01
☐ 251 Gary Ward	.10	.04	.01
☐ 277 Rickey Henderson	1.00	.40	.10
☐ 278 Dave Winfield	.40	.16	.04
☐ 340 Claudell Washington	.15	.06	.01
☐ 374 Charles Hudson	.10	.04	.01
☐ 401 Tommy John	.20	.08	.02
☐ 474 Joel Skinner	.10	.04	.01
☐ 497 Tim Stoddard	.10	.04	.01
☐ 545 Jay Buhner	.45	.18	.04
☐ 616 Bobby Meacham	.10	.04	.01
☐ 635 Roberto Kelly	1.00	.40	.10
☐ NEW John Candelaria	.20	.08	.02
☐ NEW Jack Clark	.40	.16	.04

1988 Donruss Red Sox Team Book

Brady Anderson OF

The 1988 Donruss Red Sox Team Book set features 27 cards (three pages with nine cards on each page) plus a large full-page puzzle of Stan Musial. Cards are in full color and are standard size, 2 1/2" by 3 1/2". The set was distributed as a four-page book; although the puzzle page was perforated, the card pages were not. The cover of the "Team Collection" book is primarily bright red. Card fronts are very similar in design to the 1988 Donruss regular issue. The card numbers on the backs are the same for those players that are the same as in the regular Donruss set; the new players pictured are numbered on the back as "NEW." The book is usually sold intact. When cut from the book into individual cards, these cards are distinguishable from the regular 1988 Donruss cards since these have a 1988 copyright on the back whereas the regular issue has a 1987 copyright on the back.

	MINT	EXC	G-VG
COMPLETE SET (27)	5.00	2.25	.50
COMMON PLAYER	.10	.04	.01
☐ 41 Jody Reed	.25	.10	.02
☐ 51 Roger Clemens	.75	.30	.07
☐ 92 Bob Stanley	.10	.04	.01
☐ 129 Rich Gedman	.10	.04	.01
☐ 153 Wade Boggs	.75	.30	.07
☐ 174 Ellis Burks	.90	.40	.09
☐ 216 Dwight Evans	.20	.08	.02
☐ 252 Bruce Hurst	.20	.08	.02

		MINT	EXC	G-VG
☐ NEW	Jose Cruz	.15	.06	.01
☐ NEW	Richard Dotson	.15	.06	.01
☐ NEW	Cecilo Guante	.10	.04	.01
☐ NEW	Lee Guetterman	.15	.06	.01
☐ NEW	Rafael Santana	.10	.04	.01
☐ NEW	Steve Shields	.10	.04	.01
☐ NEW	Don Slaught	.10	.04	.01

1988 Donruss Baseball's Best

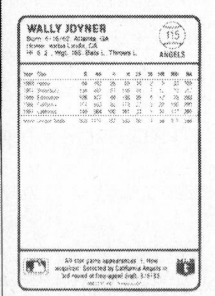

Wally Joyner 1B

This innovative set of 336 cards was released by Donruss very late in the 1988 season to be sold in large national retail chains as a complete packaged set. Cards are the standard size, 2 1/2" by 3 1/2", and are packaged as a complete set in a specially designed box. Cards are very similar in design to the 1988 regular Donruss issue except that these cards have orange and black borders instead of blue and black borders. The set is also sometimes referred to as the Halloween set because of the orange box and design of the cards. Six (2 1/2" by 3 1/2") 15-piece puzzles of Stan Musial are also included with every complete set.

	MINT	EXC	G-VG
COMPLETE SET (336)	18.00	7.50	2.50
COMMON PLAYER (1-336)	.04	.02	.00

		MINT	EXC	G-VG
☐ 1	Don Mattingly	.75	.30	.07
☐ 2	Ron Gant	1.25	.50	.12
☐ 3	Bob Boone	.10	.04	.01
☐ 4	Mark Grace	1.00	.40	.10
☐ 5	Andy Allanson	.04	.02	.00
☐ 6	Kal Daniels	.10	.04	.01
☐ 7	Floyd Bannister	.04	.02	.00
☐ 8	Alan Ashby	.04	.02	.00
☐ 9	Marty Barrett	.04	.02	.00
☐ 10	Tim Belcher	.10	.04	.01
☐ 11	Harold Baines	.10	.04	.01
☐ 12	Hubie Brooks	.07	.03	.01
☐ 13	Doyle Alexander	.04	.02	.00
☐ 14	Gary Carter	.20	.08	.02
☐ 15	Glenn Braggs	.07	.03	.01
☐ 16	Steve Bedrosian	.04	.02	.00
☐ 17	Barry Bonds	.75	.30	.07
☐ 18	Bert Blyleven	.10	.04	.01
☐ 19	Tom Brunansky	.07	.03	.01
☐ 20	John Candelaria	.04	.02	.00
☐ 21	Shawn Abner	.07	.03	.01
☐ 22	Jose Canseco	1.25	.50	.12
☐ 23	Brett Butler	.10	.04	.01
☐ 24	Scott Bradley	.04	.02	.00
☐ 25	Ivan Calderon	.10	.04	.01
☐ 26	Rich Gossage	.10	.04	.01
☐ 27	Brian Downing	.04	.02	.00
☐ 28	Jim Rice	.15	.06	.01
☐ 29	Dion James	.04	.02	.00
☐ 30	Terry Kennedy	.04	.02	.00
☐ 31	George Bell	.20	.08	.02
☐ 32	Scott Fletcher	.04	.02	.00
☐ 33	Bobby Bonilla	.75	.30	.07
☐ 34	Tim Burke	.04	.02	.00
☐ 35	Darrell Evans	.07	.03	.01
☐ 36	Mike Davis	.04	.02	.00
☐ 37	Shawon Dunston	.20	.08	.02

		MINT	EXC	G-VG
☐ 38	Kevin Bass	.04	.02	.00
☐ 39	George Brett	.30	.12	.03
☐ 40	David Cone	.30	.12	.03
☐ 41	Ron Darling	.10	.04	.01
☐ 42	Roberto Alomar	1.50	.60	.15
☐ 43	Dennis Eckersley	.20	.08	.02
☐ 44	Vince Coleman	.20	.08	.02
☐ 45	Sid Bream	.04	.02	.00
☐ 46	Gary Gaetti	.07	.03	.01
☐ 47	Phil Bradley	.04	.02	.00
☐ 48	Jim Clancy	.04	.02	.00
☐ 49	Jack Clark	.15	.06	.01
☐ 50	Mike Krukow	.04	.02	.00
☐ 51	Henry Cotto	.04	.02	.00
☐ 52	Rich Dotson	.04	.02	.00
☐ 53	Jim Gantner	.04	.02	.00
☐ 54	John Franco	.07	.03	.01
☐ 55	Pete Incaviglia	.10	.04	.01
☐ 56	Joe Carter	.25	.10	.02
☐ 57	Roger Clemens	.75	.30	.07
☐ 58	Gerald Perry	.04	.02	.00
☐ 59	Jack Howell	.04	.02	.00
☐ 60	Vance Law	.04	.02	.00
☐ 61	Jay Bell	.04	.02	.00
☐ 62	Eric Davis	.40	.16	.04
☐ 63	Gene Garber	.04	.02	.00
☐ 64	Glenn Davis	.15	.06	.01
☐ 65	Wade Boggs	.60	.25	.06
☐ 66	Kirk Gibson	.15	.06	.01
☐ 67	Carlton Fisk	.30	.12	.03
☐ 68	Casey Candaele	.04	.02	.00
☐ 69	Mike Heath	.04	.02	.00
☐ 70	Kevin Elster	.07	.03	.01
☐ 71	Greg Brock	.04	.02	.00
☐ 72	Don Carman	.04	.02	.00
☐ 73	Doug Drabek	.20	.08	.02
☐ 74	Greg Gagne	.04	.02	.00
☐ 75	Danny Cox	.04	.02	.00
☐ 76	Rickey Henderson	.75	.30	.07
☐ 77	Chris Brown	.04	.02	.00
☐ 78	Terry Steinbach	.07	.03	.01
☐ 79	Will Clark	1.25	.50	.12
☐ 80	Mickey Brantley	.07	.03	.01
☐ 81	Ozzie Guillen	.10	.04	.01
☐ 82	Greg Maddux	.15	.06	.01
☐ 83	Kirk McCaskill	.04	.02	.00
☐ 84	Dwight Evans	.15	.06	.01
☐ 85	Ozzie Virgil	.04	.02	.00
☐ 86	Mike Morgan	.07	.03	.01
☐ 87	Tony Fernandez	.10	.04	.01
☐ 88	Jose Guzman	.07	.03	.01
☐ 89	Mike Dunne	.04	.02	.00
☐ 90	Andres Galarraga	.20	.08	.02
☐ 91	Mike Henneman	.07	.03	.01
☐ 92	Alfredo Griffin	.04	.02	.00
☐ 93	Rafael Palmeiro	.50	.20	.05
☐ 94	Jim Deshaies	.04	.02	.00
☐ 95	Mark Gubicza	.10	.04	.01
☐ 96	Dwight Gooden	.45	.18	.04
☐ 97	Howard Johnson	.25	.10	.02
☐ 98	Mark Davis	.15	.06	.01
☐ 99	Dave Stewart	.25	.10	.02
☐ 100	Joe Magrane	.10	.04	.01
☐ 101	Brian Fisher	.04	.02	.00
☐ 102	Kent Hrbek	.15	.06	.01
☐ 103	Kevin Gross	.04	.02	.00
☐ 104	Tom Henke	.07	.03	.01
☐ 105	Mike Pagliarulo	.07	.03	.01
☐ 106	Kelly Downs	.04	.02	.00
☐ 107	Alvin Davis	.10	.04	.01
☐ 108	Willie Randolph	.07	.03	.01
☐ 109	Rob Deer	.10	.04	.01
☐ 110	Bo Diaz	.04	.02	.00
☐ 111	Paul Kilgus	.04	.02	.00
☐ 112	Tom Candiotti	.07	.03	.01
☐ 113	Dale Murphy	.30	.12	.03
☐ 114	Rick Mahler	.04	.02	.00
☐ 115	Wally Joyner	.35	.15	.03
☐ 116	Ryne Sandberg	.75	.30	.07
☐ 117	John Farrell	.07	.03	.01
☐ 118	Nick Esasky	.07	.03	.01
☐ 119	Bo Jackson	1.25	.50	.12
☐ 120	Bill Doran	.04	.02	.00
☐ 121	Ellis Burks	.90	.40	.09
☐ 122	Pedro Guerrero	.10	.04	.01
☐ 123	Dave LaPoint	.04	.02	.00
☐ 124	Neal Heaton	.04	.02	.00
☐ 125	Willie Hernandez	.03	.01	.00
☐ 126	Roger McDowell	.04	.01	.00
☐ 127	Ted Higuera	.07	.03	.01
☐ 128	Von Hayes	.07	.03	.01
☐ 129	Mike LaValliere	.04	.02	.00
☐ 130	Dan Gladden	.04	.02	.00
☐ 131	Willie McGee	.10	.04	.01

☐	132	Al Leiter	.07	.03	.01
☐	133	Mark Grant	.04	.02	.00
☐	134	Bob Welch	.15	.06	.01
☐	135	Dave Dravecky	.10	.04	.01
☐	136	Mark Langston	.15	.06	.01
☐	137	Dan Pasqua	.07	.03	.01
☐	138	Rick Sutcliffe	.07	.03	.01
☐	139	Dan Petry	.04	.02	.00
☐	140	Rich Gedman	.04	.02	.00
☐	141	Ken Griffey Sr.	.10	.04	.01
☐	142	Eddie Murray	.25	.10	.02
☐	143	Jimmy Key	.10	.04	.01
☐	144	Dale Mohorcic	.04	.02	.00
☐	145	Jose Lind	.07	.03	.01
☐	146	Dennis Martinez	.07	.03	.01
☐	147	Chet Lemon	.04	.02	.00
☐	148	Orel Hershiser	.25	.10	.02
☐	149	Dave Martinez	.07	.03	.01
☐	150	Billy Hatcher	.10	.04	.01
☐	151	Charlie Leibrandt	.07	.03	.01
☐	152	Keith Hernandez	.15	.06	.01
☐	153	Kevin McReynolds	.20	.08	.02
☐	154	Tony Gwynn	.40	.16	.04
☐	155	Stan Javier	.04	.02	.00
☐	156	Tony Pena	.07	.03	.01
☐	157	Andy Van Slyke	.15	.06	.01
☐	158	Gene Larkin	.07	.03	.01
☐	159	Chris James	.07	.03	.01
☐	160	Fred McGriff	.60	.25	.06
☐	161	Rick Rhoden	.04	.02	.00
☐	162	Scott Garrelts	.07	.03	.01
☐	163	Mike Campbell	.04	.02	.00
☐	164	Dave Righetti	.10	.04	.01
☐	165	Paul Molitor	.15	.06	.01
☐	166	Danny Jackson	.10	.04	.01
☐	167	Pete O'Brien	.07	.03	.01
☐	168	Julio Franco	.25	.10	.02
☐	169	Mark McGwire	.75	.30	.07
☐	170	Zane Smith	.10	.04	.01
☐	171	Johnny Ray	.07	.03	.01
☐	172	Lester Lancaster	.07	.03	.01
☐	173	Mel Hall	.10	.04	.01
☐	174	Tracy Jones	.07	.03	.01
☐	175	Kevin Seitzer	.20	.08	.02
☐	176	Bob Knepper	.04	.02	.00
☐	177	Mike Greenwell	.75	.30	.07
☐	178	Mike Marshall	.07	.03	.01
☐	179	Melido Perez	.15	.06	.01
☐	180	Tim Raines	.20	.08	.02
☐	181	Jack Morris	.20	.08	.02
☐	182	Darryl Strawberry	.60	.25	.06
☐	183	Robin Yount	.40	.16	.04
☐	184	Lance Parrish	.10	.04	.01
☐	185	Darnell Coles	.04	.02	.00
☐	186	Kirby Puckett	.60	.25	.06
☐	187	Terry Pendleton	.04	.02	.00
☐	188	Don Slaught	.04	.02	.00
☐	189	Jimmy Jones	.07	.03	.01
☐	190	Dave Parker	.15	.06	.01
☐	191	Mike Aldrete	.04	.02	.00
☐	192	Mike Moore	.07	.03	.01
☐	193	Greg Walker	.07	.03	.01
☐	194	Calvin Schiraldi	.04	.02	.00
☐	195	Dick Schofield	.04	.02	.00
☐	196	Jody Reed	.15	.06	.01
☐	197	Pete Smith	.07	.03	.01
☐	198	Cal Ripken	.75	.30	.07
☐	199	Lloyd Moseby	.07	.03	.01
☐	200	Ruben Sierra	.75	.30	.07
☐	201	R.J. Reynolds	.04	.02	.00
☐	202	Bryn Smith	.04	.02	.00
☐	203	Gary Pettis	.04	.02	.00
☐	204	Steve Sax	.15	.06	.01
☐	205	Frank DiPino	.04	.02	.00
☐	206	Mike Scott UER	.10	.04	.01
		(1977 Jackson losses			
		say 1.10, should be 1)			
☐	207	Kurt Stillwell	.07	.03	.01
☐	208	Mookie Wilson	.07	.03	.01
☐	209	Lee Mazzilli	.04	.02	.00
☐	210	Lance McCullers	.04	.02	.00
☐	211	Rick Honeycutt	.04	.02	.00
☐	212	John Tudor	.07	.03	.01
☐	213	Jim Gott	.04	.02	.00
☐	214	Frank Viola	.15	.06	.01
☐	215	Juan Samuel	.10	.04	.01
☐	216	Jesse Barfield	.10	.04	.01
☐	217	Claudell Washington	.07	.03	.01
☐	218	Rick Reuschel	.07	.03	.01
☐	219	Jim Presley	.04	.02	.00
☐	220	Tommy John	.15	.06	.01
☐	221	Dan Plesac	.04	.02	.00
☐	222	Barry Larkin	.35	.15	.03
☐	223	Mike Stanley	.04	.02	.00
☐	224	Cory Snyder	.10	.04	.01
☐	225	Andre Dawson	.25	.10	.02
☐	226	Ken Oberkfell	.04	.02	.00
☐	227	Devon White	.15	.06	.01
☐	228	Jamie Moyer	.04	.02	.00
☐	229	Brook Jacoby	.04	.02	.00
☐	230	Rob Murphy	.04	.02	.00
☐	231	Bret Saberhagen	.25	.10	.02
☐	232	Nolan Ryan	1.25	.50	.12
☐	233	Bruce Hurst	.10	.04	.01
☐	234	Jesse Orosco	.04	.02	.00
☐	235	Bobby Thigpen	.20	.08	.02
☐	236	Pascual Perez	.07	.03	.01
☐	237	Matt Nokes	.10	.04	.01
☐	238	Bob Ojeda	.07	.03	.01
☐	239	Joey Meyer	.07	.03	.01
☐	240	Shane Rawley	.04	.02	.00
☐	241	Jeff Robinson	.07	.03	.01
☐	242	Jeff Reardon	.15	.06	.01
☐	243	Ozzie Smith	.20	.08	.02
☐	244	Dave Winfield	.25	.10	.02
☐	245	John Kruk	.10	.04	.01
☐	246	Carney Lansford	.10	.04	.01
☐	247	Candy Maldonado	.07	.03	.01
☐	248	Ken Phelps	.04	.02	.00
☐	249	Ken Williams	.04	.02	.00
☐	250	Al Nipper	.04	.02	.00
☐	251	Mark McLemore	.04	.02	.00
☐	252	Lee Smith	.15	.06	.01
☐	253	Albert Hall	.04	.02	.00
☐	254	Billy Ripken	.07	.03	.01
☐	255	Kelly Gruber	.20	.08	.02
☐	256	Charlie Hough	.04	.02	.00
☐	257	John Smiley	.20	.08	.02
☐	258	Tim Wallach	.10	.04	.01
☐	259	Frank Tanana	.07	.03	.01
☐	260	Mike Scioscia	.04	.02	.00
☐	261	Damon Berryhill	.10	.04	.01
☐	262	Dave Smith	.04	.02	.00
☐	263	Willie Wilson	.07	.03	.01
☐	264	Len Dykstra	.15	.06	.01
☐	265	Randy Myers	.07	.03	.01
☐	266	Keith Moreland	.04	.02	.00
☐	267	Eric Plunk	.04	.02	.00
☐	268	Todd Worrell	.10	.04	.01
☐	269	Bob Walk	.04	.02	.00
☐	270	Keith Atherton	.04	.02	.00
☐	271	Mike Schmidt	.60	.25	.06
☐	272	Mike Flanagan	.04	.02	.00
☐	273	Rafael Santana	.04	.02	.00
☐	274	Robby Thompson	.07	.03	.01
☐	275	Rey Quinones	.04	.02	.00
☐	276	Cecilio Guante	.04	.02	.00
☐	277	B.J. Surhoff	.10	.04	.01
☐	278	Chris Sabo	.75	.30	.07
☐	279	Mitch Williams	.10	.04	.01
☐	280	Greg Swindell	.15	.06	.01
☐	281	Alan Trammell	.20	.08	.02
☐	282	Storm Davis	.07	.03	.01
☐	283	Chuck Finley	.25	.10	.02
☐	284	Dave Stieb	.15	.06	.01
☐	285	Scott Bailes	.04	.02	.00
☐	286	Larry Sheets	.04	.02	.00
☐	287	Danny Tartabull	.30	.12	.03
☐	288	Checklist Card	.04	.02	.00
☐	289	Todd Benzinger	.10	.04	.01
☐	290	John Shelby	.04	.02	.00
☐	291	Steve Lyons	.04	.02	.00
☐	292	Mitch Webster	.04	.02	.00
☐	293	Walt Terrell	.04	.02	.00
☐	294	Pete Stanicek	.04	.02	.00
☐	295	Chris Bosio	.07	.03	.01
☐	296	Milt Thompson	.04	.02	.00
☐	297	Fred Lynn	.10	.04	.01
☐	298	Juan Berenguer	.04	.02	.00
☐	299	Ken Dayley	.04	.02	.00
☐	300	Joel Skinner	.04	.02	.00
☐	301	Benito Santiago	.35	.15	.03
☐	302	Ron Hassey	.04	.02	.00
☐	303	Jose Uribe	.04	.02	.00
☐	304	Harold Reynolds	.07	.03	.01
☐	305	Dale Sveum	.04	.02	.00
☐	306	Glenn Wilson	.04	.02	.00
☐	307	Mike Witt	.04	.02	.00
☐	308	Ron Robinson	.04	.02	.00
☐	309	Denny Walling	.04	.02	.00
☐	310	Joe Orsulak	.04	.02	.00
☐	311	David Wells	.07	.03	.01
☐	312	Steve Buechele	.07	.03	.01
☐	313	Jose Oquendo	.04	.02	.00
☐	314	Floyd Youmans	.04	.02	.00
☐	315	Lou Whitaker	.10	.04	.01
☐	316	Fernando Valenzuela	.15	.06	.01
☐	317	Mike Boddicker	.07	.03	.01

		MINT	EXC	G-VG
☐ 318	Gerald Young	.07	.03	.01
☐ 319	Frank White	.07	.03	.01
☐ 320	Bill Wegman	.04	.02	.00
☐ 321	Tom Niedenfuer	.04	.02	.00
☐ 322	Ed Whitson	.07	.03	.01
☐ 323	Curt Young	.04	.02	.00
☐ 324	Greg Mathews	.04	.02	.00
☐ 325	Doug Jones	.10	.04	.01
☐ 326	Tommy Herr	.07	.03	.01
☐ 327	Kent Tekulve	.04	.02	.00
☐ 328	Rance Mulliniks	.04	.02	.00
☐ 329	Checklist Card	.04	.02	.00
☐ 330	Craig Lefferts	.07	.03	.01
☐ 331	Franklin Stubbs	.07	.03	.01
☐ 332	Rick Cerone	.04	.02	.00
☐ 333	Dave Schmidt	.04	.02	.00
☐ 334	Larry Parrish	.04	.02	.00
☐ 335	Tom Browning	.10	.04	.01
☐ 336	Checklist Card	.04	.02	.00

1989 Donruss

This 660-card set was distributed along with a puzzle of Warren Spahn. The six regular checklist cards are numbered throughout the set as multiples of 100. Cards measure 2 1/2" by 3 1/2" and feature a distinctive black side border with an alternating coating. The popular Diamond King subset returns for the eighth consecutive year. Rated Rookies are featured again as cards 28-47. The Donruss '89 logo appears in the lower left corner of every obverse. There are two variations that occur throughout most of the set. On the card backs "Denotes Led League" can be found with one asterisk to the left or with an asterisk on each side. On the card fronts the horizontal lines on the left and right borders can be glossy or non-glossy. Since both of these variation types are relatively minor and seem equally common, there is no premium value for either type. Rather than short-printing 26 cards in order to make room for printing the Bonus MVP's this year, Donruss apparently chose to double print 106 cards. These double prints are listed below by DP. The key rookie cards in this set are Sandy Alomar Jr., Ken Griffey Jr., Felix Jose, Ramon Martinez, Hal Morris, and Gary Sheffield.

	MINT	EXC	G-VG
COMPLETE SET (660)	17.00	7.25	2.50
COMMON PLAYER (1-660)	.03	.01	.00

		MINT	EXC	G-VG
☐ 1	Mike Greenwell DK	.08	.03	.01
☐ 2	Bobby Bonilla DK DP	.08	.03	.01
☐ 3	Pete Incaviglia DK	.06	.02	.00
☐ 4	Chris Sabo DK DP	.08	.03	.01
☐ 5	Robin Yount DK	.10	.04	.01
☐ 6	Tony Gwynn DK DP	.10	.04	.01
☐ 7	Carlton Fisk DK	.10	.04	.01
	(OF on back)			
☐ 8	Cory Snyder DK	.06	.02	.00
☐ 9	David Cone DK UER	.08	.03	.01
	(sic, "hurdlers")			
☐ 10	Kevin Seitzer DK	.06	.02	.00
☐ 11	Rick Reuschel DK	.06	.02	.00

		MINT	EXC	G-VG
☐ 12	Johnny Ray DK	.06	.02	.00
☐ 13	Dave Schmidt DK	.06	.02	.00
☐ 14	Andres Galarraga DK	.06	.02	.00
☐ 15	Kirk Gibson DK	.08	.03	.01
☐ 16	Fred McGriff DK	.10	.04	.01
☐ 17	Mark Grace DK	.12	.05	.01
☐ 18	Jeff Robinson DT DK	.06	.02	.00
☐ 19	Vince Coleman DK DP	.08	.03	.01
☐ 20	Dave Henderson DK	.06	.02	.00
☐ 21	Harold Reynolds DK	.06	.02	.00
☐ 22	Gerald Perry DK	.06	.02	.00
☐ 23	Frank Viola DK	.08	.03	.01
☐ 24	Steve Bedrosian DK	.06	.02	.00
☐ 25	Glenn Davis DK	.08	.03	.01
☐ 26	Don Mattingly DK UER	.12	.05	.01
	(doesn't mention Don's previous DK in 1985)			
☐ 27	DK Checklist DP	.06	.01	.00
☐ 28	Sandy Alomar Jr. RR	.40	.16	.04
☐ 29	Steve Searcy RR	.08	.03	.01
☐ 30	Cameron Drew RR	.03	.01	.00
☐ 31	Gary Sheffield RR	.30	.12	.03
☐ 32	Erik Hanson RR	.50	.20	.05
☐ 33	Ken Griffey Jr. RR	6.00	2.50	.60
☐ 34	Greg Harris RR	.15	.06	.01
	San Diego Padres			
☐ 35	Gregg Jefferies RR	.30	.12	.03
☐ 36	Luis Medina RR	.08	.03	.01
☐ 37	Carlos Quintana RR	.25	.10	.02
☐ 38	Felix Jose RR	.75	.30	.07
☐ 39	Cris Carpenter RR	.10	.04	.01
☐ 40	Ron Jones RR	.08	.03	.01
☐ 41	Dave West RR	.12	.05	.01
☐ 42	Randy Johnson RR	.35	.15	.03
☐ 43	Mike Harkey RR	.12	.05	.01
☐ 44	Pete Harnisch RR DP	.17	.07	.01
☐ 45	Tom Gordon RR DP	.17	.07	.01
☐ 46	Gregg Olson RR DP	.40	.16	.04
☐ 47	Alex Sanchez RR DP	.08	.03	.01
☐ 48	Ruben Sierra	.25	.10	.02
☐ 49	Rafael Palmeiro	.15	.06	.01
☐ 50	Ron Gant	.45	.18	.04
☐ 51	Cal Ripken	.35	.15	.03
☐ 52	Wally Joyner	.12	.05	.01
☐ 53	Gary Carter	.08	.03	.01
☐ 54	Andy Van Slyke	.10	.04	.01
☐ 55	Robin Yount	.15	.06	.01
☐ 56	Pete Incaviglia	.06	.02	.00
☐ 57	Greg Brock	.03	.01	.00
☐ 58	Melido Perez	.06	.02	.00
☐ 59	Craig Lefferts	.03	.01	.00
☐ 60	Gary Pettis	.03	.01	.00
☐ 61	Danny Tartabull	.10	.04	.01
☐ 62	Guillermo Hernandez	.03	.01	.00
☐ 63	Ozzie Smith	.12	.05	.01
☐ 64	Gary Gaetti	.06	.02	.00
☐ 65	Mark Davis	.06	.02	.00
☐ 66	Lee Smith	.08	.03	.01
☐ 67	Dennis Eckersley	.08	.03	.01
☐ 68	Wade Boggs	.20	.08	.02
☐ 69	Mike Scott	.08	.03	.01
☐ 70	Fred McGriff	.15	.06	.01
☐ 71	Tom Browning	.06	.02	.00
☐ 72	Claudell Washington	.03	.01	.00
☐ 73	Mel Hall	.06	.02	.00
☐ 74	Don Mattingly	.20	.08	.02
☐ 75	Steve Bedrosian	.06	.02	.00
☐ 76	Juan Samuel	.06	.02	.00
☐ 77	Mike Scioscia	.03	.01	.00
☐ 78	Dave Righetti	.06	.02	.00
☐ 79	Alfredo Griffin	.03	.01	.00
☐ 80	Eric Davis UER	.10	.04	.01
	(165 games in 1988, should be 135)			
☐ 81	Juan Berenguer	.03	.01	.00
☐ 82	Todd Worrell	.06	.02	.00
☐ 83	Joe Carter	.12	.05	.01
☐ 84	Steve Sax	.10	.04	.01
☐ 85	Frank White	.03	.01	.00
☐ 86	John Kruk	.03	.01	.00
☐ 87	Rance Mulliniks	.03	.01	.00
☐ 88	Alan Ashby	.03	.01	.00
☐ 89	Charlie Leibrandt	.03	.01	.00
☐ 90	Frank Tanana	.06	.02	.00
☐ 91	Jose Canseco	.50	.20	.05
☐ 92	Barry Bonds	.25	.10	.02
☐ 93	Harold Reynolds	.06	.02	.00
☐ 94	Mark McLemore	.03	.01	.00
☐ 95	Mark McGwire	.12	.05	.01
☐ 96	Eddie Murray	.12	.05	.01
☐ 97	Tim Raines	.10	.04	.01
☐ 98	Robby Thompson	.03	.01	.00
☐ 99	Kevin McReynolds	.08	.03	.01
☐ 100	Checklist Card	.06	.01	.00

#	Player			
☐ 101	Carlton Fisk	.15	.06	.01
☐ 102	Dave Martinez	.03	.01	.00
☐ 103	Glenn Braggs	.03	.01	.00
☐ 104	Dale Murphy	.12	.05	.01
☐ 105	Ryne Sandberg	.35	.15	.03
☐ 106	Dennis Martinez	.06	.02	.00
☐ 107	Pete O'Brien	.03	.01	.00
☐ 108	Dick Schofield	.03	.01	.00
☐ 109	Henry Cotto	.03	.01	.00
☐ 110	Mike Marshall	.06	.02	.00
☐ 111	Keith Moreland	.03	.01	.00
☐ 112	Tom Brunansky	.06	.02	.00
☐ 113	Kelly Gruber UER	.10	.04	.01
	(wrong birthdate)			
☐ 114	Brook Jacoby	.03	.01	.00
☐ 115	Keith Brown	.06	.02	.00
☐ 116	Matt Nokes	.06	.02	.00
☐ 117	Keith Hernandez	.08	.03	.01
☐ 118	Bob Forsch	.03	.01	.00
☐ 119	Bert Blyleven UER	.08	.03	.01
	(... 3000 strikeouts in 1987, should be 1986)			
☐ 120	Willie Wilson	.08	.03	.01
☐ 121	Tommy Gregg	.03	.01	.00
☐ 122	Jim Rice	.08	.03	.01
☐ 123	Bob Knepper	.03	.01	.00
☐ 124	Danny Jackson	.06	.02	.00
☐ 125	Eric Plunk	.03	.01	.00
☐ 126	Brian Fisher	.03	.01	.00
☐ 127	Mike Pagliarulo	.03	.01	.00
☐ 128	Tony Gwynn	.17	.07	.01
☐ 129	Lance McCullers	.03	.01	.00
☐ 130	Andres Galarraga	.06	.02	.00
☐ 131	Jose Uribe	.03	.01	.00
☐ 132	Kirk Gibson UER	.08	.03	.01
	(wrong birthdate)			
☐ 133	David Palmer	.03	.01	.00
☐ 134	R.J. Reynolds	.03	.01	.00
☐ 135	Greg Walker	.03	.01	.00
☐ 136	Kirk McCaskill UER	.03	.01	.00
	(wrong birthdate)			
☐ 137	Shawon Dunston	.08	.03	.01
☐ 138	Andy Allanson	.03	.01	.00
☐ 139	Rob Murphy	.03	.01	.00
☐ 140	Mike Aldrete	.03	.01	.00
☐ 141	Terry Kennedy	.03	.01	.00
☐ 142	Scott Fletcher	.03	.01	.00
☐ 143	Steve Balboni	.03	.01	.00
☐ 144	Bret Saberhagen	.10	.04	.01
☐ 145	Ozzie Virgil	.03	.01	.00
☐ 146	Dale Sveum	.03	.01	.00
☐ 147	Darryl Strawberry	.30	.12	.03
☐ 148	Harold Baines	.08	.03	.01
☐ 149	George Bell	.10	.04	.01
☐ 150	Dave Parker	.08	.03	.01
☐ 151	Bobby Bonilla	.20	.08	.02
☐ 152	Mookie Wilson	.03	.01	.00
☐ 153	Ted Power	.03	.01	.00
☐ 154	Nolan Ryan	.50	.20	.05
☐ 155	Jeff Reardon	.08	.03	.01
☐ 156	Tim Wallach	.06	.02	.00
☐ 157	Jamie Moyer	.03	.01	.00
☐ 158	Rich Gossage	.08	.03	.01
☐ 159	Dave Winfield	.12	.05	.01
☐ 160	Von Hayes	.06	.02	.00
☐ 161	Willie McGee	.08	.03	.01
☐ 162	Rich Gedman	.03	.01	.00
☐ 163	Tony Pena	.06	.02	.00
☐ 164	Mike Morgan	.06	.02	.00
☐ 165	Charlie Hough	.03	.01	.00
☐ 166	Mike Stanley	.03	.01	.00
☐ 167	Andre Dawson	.12	.05	.01
☐ 168	Joe Boever	.06	.02	.00
☐ 169	Pete Stanicek	.03	.01	.00
☐ 170	Bob Boone	.06	.02	.00
☐ 171	Ron Darling	.06	.02	.00
☐ 172	Bob Walk	.03	.01	.00
☐ 173	Bob Deer	.06	.02	.00
☐ 174	Steve Buechele	.03	.01	.00
☐ 175	Ted Higuera	.03	.01	.00
☐ 176	Ozzie Guillen	.06	.02	.00
☐ 177	Candy Maldonado	.06	.02	.00
☐ 178	Doyle Alexander	.03	.01	.00
☐ 179	Mark Gubicza	.06	.02	.00
☐ 180	Alan Trammell	.12	.05	.01
☐ 181	Vince Coleman	.10	.04	.01
☐ 182	Kirby Puckett	.25	.10	.02
☐ 183	Chris Brown	.03	.01	.00
☐ 184	Marty Barrett	.03	.01	.00
☐ 185	Stan Javier	.03	.01	.00
☐ 186	Mike Greenwell	.15	.06	.01
☐ 187	Billy Hatcher	.06	.02	.00
☐ 188	Jimmy Key	.06	.02	.00
☐ 189	Nick Esasky	.03	.01	.00
☐ 190	Don Slaught	.03	.01	.00
☐ 191	Cory Snyder	.06	.02	.00
☐ 192	John Candelaria	.03	.01	.00
☐ 193	Mike Schmidt	.35	.15	.03
☐ 194	Kevin Gross	.03	.01	.00
☐ 195	John Tudor	.06	.02	.00
☐ 196	Neil Allen	.03	.01	.00
☐ 197	Orel Hershiser	.08	.03	.01
☐ 198	Kal Daniels	.08	.03	.01
☐ 199	Kent Hrbek	.08	.03	.01
☐ 200	Checklist Card	.06	.01	.00
☐ 201	Joe Magrane	.06	.02	.00
☐ 202	Scott Bailes	.03	.01	.00
☐ 203	Tim Belcher	.06	.02	.00
☐ 204	George Brett	.15	.06	.01
☐ 205	Benito Santiago	.08	.03	.01
☐ 206	Tony Fernandez	.06	.02	.00
☐ 207	Gerald Young	.03	.01	.00
☐ 208	Bo Jackson	.50	.20	.05
☐ 209	Chet Lemon	.03	.01	.00
☐ 210	Storm Davis	.03	.01	.00
☐ 211	Doug Drabek	.08	.03	.01
☐ 212	Mickey Brantley UER	.06	.02	.00
	(photo actually Nelson Simmons)			
☐ 213	Devon White	.06	.02	.00
☐ 214	Dave Stewart	.08	.03	.01
☐ 215	Dave Schmidt	.03	.01	.00
☐ 216	Bryn Smith	.03	.01	.00
☐ 217	Brett Butler	.08	.03	.01
☐ 218	Bob Ojeda	.03	.01	.00
☐ 219	Steve Rosenberg	.08	.03	.01
☐ 220	Hubie Brooks	.06	.02	.00
☐ 221	B.J. Surhoff	.06	.02	.00
☐ 222	Rick Mahler	.03	.01	.00
☐ 223	Rick Sutcliffe	.06	.02	.00
☐ 224	Neal Heaton	.03	.01	.00
☐ 225	Mitch Williams	.03	.01	.00
☐ 226	Chuck Finley	.08	.03	.01
☐ 227	Mark Langston	.08	.03	.01
☐ 228	Jesse Orosco	.03	.01	.00
☐ 229	Ed Whitson	.03	.01	.00
☐ 230	Terry Pendleton	.10	.04	.01
☐ 231	Lloyd Moseby	.03	.01	.00
☐ 232	Greg Swindell	.06	.02	.00
☐ 233	John Franco	.06	.02	.00
☐ 234	Jack Morris	.10	.04	.01
☐ 235	Howard Johnson	.12	.05	.01
☐ 236	Glenn Davis	.08	.03	.01
☐ 237	Frank Viola	.08	.03	.01
☐ 238	Kevin Seitzer	.06	.02	.00
☐ 239	Gerald Perry	.03	.01	.00
☐ 240	Dwight Evans	.08	.03	.01
☐ 241	Jim Deshaies	.03	.01	.00
☐ 242	Bo Diaz	.03	.01	.00
☐ 243	Carney Lansford	.06	.02	.00
☐ 244	Mike LaValliere	.03	.01	.00
☐ 245	Rickey Henderson	.35	.15	.03
☐ 246	Roberto Alomar	.45	.18	.04
☐ 247	Jimmy Jones	.03	.01	.00
☐ 248	Pascual Perez	.03	.01	.00
☐ 249	Will Clark	.40	.16	.04
☐ 250	Fernando Valenzuela	.08	.03	.01
☐ 251	Shane Rawley	.03	.01	.00
☐ 252	Sid Bream	.03	.01	.00
☐ 253	Steve Lyons	.03	.01	.00
☐ 254	Brian Downing	.03	.01	.00
☐ 255	Mark Grace	.25	.10	.02
☐ 256	Tom Candiotti	.06	.02	.00
☐ 257	Barry Larkin	.15	.06	.01
☐ 258	Mike Krukow	.03	.01	.00
☐ 259	Billy Ripken	.03	.01	.00
☐ 260	Cecilio Guante	.03	.01	.00
☐ 261	Scott Bradley	.03	.01	.00
☐ 262	Floyd Bannister	.03	.01	.00
☐ 263	Pete Smith	.03	.01	.00
☐ 264	Jim Gantner UER	.03	.01	.00
	(wrong birtdate)			
☐ 265	Roger McDowell	.03	.01	.00
☐ 266	Bobby Thigpen	.08	.03	.01
☐ 267	Jim Clancy	.03	.01	.00
☐ 268	Terry Steinbach	.06	.02	.00
☐ 269	Mike Dunne	.03	.01	.00
☐ 270	Dwight Gooden	.10	.04	.01
☐ 271	Mike Heath	.03	.01	.00
☐ 272	Dave Smith	.03	.01	.00
☐ 273	Keith Atherton	.03	.01	.00
☐ 274	Tim Burke	.03	.01	.00
☐ 275	Damon Berryhill	.06	.02	.00
☐ 276	Vance Law	.03	.01	.00
☐ 277	Rich Dotson	.03	.01	.00
☐ 278	Lance Parrish	.08	.03	.01
☐ 279	Denny Walling	.03	.01	.00
☐ 280	Roger Clemens	.30	.12	.03

☐ 281	Greg Mathews	.03	.01	.00
☐ 282	Tom Niedenfuer	.03	.01	.00
☐ 283	Paul Kilgus	.03	.01	.00
☐ 284	Jose Guzman	.03	.01	.00
☐ 285	Calvin Schiraldi	.03	.01	.00
☐ 286	Charlie Puleo UER	.03	.01	.00
	(career ERA 4.24,			
	should be 4.23)			
☐ 287	Joe Orsulak	.03	.01	.00
☐ 288	Jack Howell	.03	.01	.00
☐ 289	Kevin Elster	.03	.01	.00
☐ 290	Jose Lind	.03	.01	.00
☐ 291	Paul Molitor	.10	.04	.01
☐ 292	Cecil Espy	.03	.01	.00
☐ 293	Bill Wegman	.03	.01	.00
☐ 294	Dan Pasqua	.06	.02	.00
☐ 295	Scott Garrelts UER	.06	.02	.00
	(wrong birthdate)			
☐ 296	Walt Terrell	.03	.01	.00
☐ 297	Ed Hearn	.03	.01	.00
☐ 298	Lou Whitaker	.08	.03	.01
☐ 299	Ken Dayley	.03	.01	.00
☐ 300	Checklist Card	.06	.01	.00
☐ 301	Tommy Herr	.03	.01	.00
☐ 302	Mike Brumley	.03	.01	.00
☐ 303	Ellis Burks	.15	.06	.01
☐ 304	Curt Young UER	.03	.01	.00
	(wrong birthdate)			
☐ 305	Jody Reed	.08	.03	.01
☐ 306	Bill Doran	.03	.01	.00
☐ 307	David Wells	.06	.02	.00
☐ 308	Ron Robinson	.03	.01	.00
☐ 309	Rafael Santana	.03	.01	.00
☐ 310	Julio Franco	.10	.04	.01
☐ 311	Jack Clark	.08	.03	.01
☐ 312	Chris James	.03	.01	.00
☐ 313	Milt Thompson	.03	.01	.00
☐ 314	John Shelby	.03	.01	.00
☐ 315	Al Leiter	.03	.01	.00
☐ 316	Mike Davis	.03	.01	.00
☐ 317	Chris Sabo	.60	.25	.06
☐ 318	Greg Gagne	.03	.01	.00
☐ 319	Jose Oquendo	.03	.01	.00
☐ 320	John Farrell	.03	.01	.00
☐ 321	Franklin Stubbs	.03	.01	.00
☐ 322	Kurt Stillwell	.03	.01	.00
☐ 323	Shawn Abner	.03	.01	.00
☐ 324	Mike Flanagan	.03	.01	.00
☐ 325	Kevin Bass	.03	.01	.00
☐ 326	Pat Tabler	.03	.01	.00
☐ 327	Mike Henneman	.03	.01	.00
☐ 328	Rick Honeycutt	.03	.01	.00
☐ 329	John Smiley	.06	.02	.00
☐ 330	Rey Quinones	.03	.01	.00
☐ 331	Johnny Ray	.03	.01	.00
☐ 332	Bob Welch	.08	.03	.01
☐ 333	Larry Sheets	.03	.01	.00
☐ 334	Jeff Parrett	.03	.01	.00
☐ 335	Rick Reuschel UER	.06	.02	.00
	(for Don Robinson,			
	should be Jeff)			
☐ 336	Randy Myers	.06	.02	.00
☐ 337	Ken Williams	.03	.01	.00
☐ 338	Andy McGaffigan	.03	.01	.00
☐ 339	Joey Meyer	.03	.01	.00
☐ 340	Dion James	.03	.01	.00
☐ 341	Les Lancaster	.03	.01	.00
☐ 342	Tom Foley	.03	.01	.00
☐ 343	Geno Petralli	.03	.01	.00
☐ 344	Dan Petry	.03	.01	.00
☐ 345	Alvin Davis	.06	.02	.00
☐ 346	Mickey Hatcher	.03	.01	.00
☐ 347	Marvell Wynne	.03	.01	.00
☐ 348	Danny Cox	.03	.01	.00
☐ 349	Dave Stieb	.08	.03	.01
☐ 350	Jay Bell	.06	.02	.00
☐ 351	Jeff Treadway	.06	.02	.00
☐ 352	Luis Salazar	.03	.01	.00
☐ 353	Len Dykstra	.08	.03	.01
☐ 354	Juan Agosto	.03	.01	.00
☐ 355	Gene Larkin	.06	.02	.00
☐ 356	Steve Farr	.03	.01	.00
☐ 357	Paul Assenmacher	.03	.01	.00
☐ 358	Todd Benzinger	.03	.01	.00
☐ 359	Larry Andersen	.03	.01	.00
☐ 360	Paul O'Neill	.08	.03	.01
☐ 361	Ron Hassey	.03	.01	.00
☐ 362	Jim Gott	.03	.01	.00
☐ 363	Ken Phelps	.03	.01	.00
☐ 364	Tim Flannery	.03	.01	.00
☐ 365	Randy Ready	.03	.01	.00
☐ 366	Nelson Santovenia	.08	.03	.01
☐ 367	Kelly Downs	.03	.01	.00
☐ 368	Danny Heep	.03	.01	.00

☐ 369	Phil Bradley	.03	.01	.00
☐ 370	Jeff Robinson	.03	.01	.00
	Pittsburgh Pirates			
☐ 371	Ivan Calderon	.06	.02	.00
☐ 372	Mike Witt	.03	.01	.00
☐ 373	Greg Maddux	.08	.03	.01
☐ 374	Carmen Castillo	.03	.01	.00
☐ 375	Jose Rijo	.08	.03	.01
☐ 376	Joe Price	.03	.01	.00
☐ 377	Rene C. Gonzales	.03	.01	.00
☐ 378	Oddibe McDowell	.03	.01	.00
☐ 379	Jim Presley	.03	.01	.00
☐ 380	Brad Wellman	.03	.01	.00
☐ 381	Tom Glavine	.35	.15	.03
☐ 382	Dan Plesac	.03	.01	.00
☐ 383	Wally Backman	.03	.01	.00
☐ 384	Dave Gallagher	.08	.03	.01
☐ 385	Tom Henke	.06	.02	.00
☐ 386	Luis Polonia	.08	.03	.01
☐ 387	Junior Ortiz	.03	.01	.00
☐ 388	David Cone	.08	.03	.01
☐ 389	Dave Bergman	.03	.01	.00
☐ 390	Danny Darwin	.03	.01	.00
☐ 391	Dan Gladden	.03	.01	.00
☐ 392	John Dopson	.08	.03	.01
☐ 393	Frank DiPino	.03	.01	.00
☐ 394	Al Nipper	.03	.01	.00
☐ 395	Willie Randolph	.06	.02	.00
☐ 396	Don Carman	.03	.01	.00
☐ 397	Scott Terry	.03	.01	.00
☐ 398	Rick Cerone	.03	.01	.00
☐ 399	Tom Pagnozzi	.03	.01	.00
☐ 400	Checklist Card	.06	.01	.00
☐ 401	Mickey Tettleton	.06	.02	.00
☐ 402	Curtis Wilkerson	.03	.01	.00
☐ 403	Jeff Russell	.03	.01	.00
☐ 404	Pat Perry	.03	.01	.00
☐ 405	Jose Alvarez	.06	.02	.00
☐ 406	Rick Schu	.03	.01	.00
☐ 407	Sherman Corbett	.03	.01	.00
☐ 408	Dave Magadan	.08	.03	.01
☐ 409	Bob Kipper	.03	.01	.00
☐ 410	Don August	.03	.01	.00
☐ 411	Bob Brower	.03	.01	.00
☐ 412	Chris Bosio	.03	.01	.00
☐ 413	Jerry Reuss	.03	.01	.00
☐ 414	Atlee Hammaker	.03	.01	.00
☐ 415	Jim Walewander	.03	.01	.00
☐ 416	Mike Macfarlane	.10	.04	.01
☐ 417	Pat Sheridan	.03	.01	.00
☐ 418	Pedro Guerrero	.08	.03	.01
☐ 419	Allan Anderson	.03	.01	.00
☐ 420	Mark Parent	.08	.03	.01
☐ 421	Bob Stanley	.03	.01	.00
☐ 422	Mike Gallego	.03	.01	.00
☐ 423	Bruce Hurst	.06	.02	.00
☐ 424	Dave Meads	.03	.01	.00
☐ 425	Jesse Barfield	.08	.03	.01
☐ 426	Rob Dibble	.25	.10	.02
☐ 427	Joel Skinner	.03	.01	.00
☐ 428	Ron Kittle	.06	.02	.00
☐ 429	Rick Rhoden	.03	.01	.00
☐ 430	Bob Dernier	.03	.01	.00
☐ 431	Steve Jeltz	.03	.01	.00
☐ 432	Rick Dempsey	.03	.01	.00
☐ 433	Roberto Kelly	.12	.05	.01
☐ 434	Dave Anderson	.03	.01	.00
☐ 435	Herm Winningham	.03	.01	.00
☐ 436	Al Newman	.03	.01	.00
☐ 437	Jose DeLeon	.03	.01	.00
☐ 438	Doug Jones	.03	.01	.00
☐ 439	Brian Holton	.03	.01	.00
☐ 440	Jeff Montgomery	.06	.02	.00
☐ 441	Dickie Thon	.03	.01	.00
☐ 442	Cecil Fielder	.30	.12	.03
☐ 443	John Fishel	.03	.01	.00
☐ 444	Jerry Don Gleaton	.03	.01	.00
☐ 445	Paul Gibson	.03	.01	.00
☐ 446	Walt Weiss	.08	.03	.01
☐ 447	Glenn Wilson	.03	.01	.00
☐ 448	Mike Moore	.06	.02	.00
☐ 449	Chili Davis	.06	.02	.00
☐ 450	Dave Henderson	.08	.03	.01
☐ 451	Jose Bautista	.08	.03	.01
☐ 452	Rex Hudler	.06	.02	.00
☐ 453	Bob Brenly	.03	.01	.00
☐ 454	Mackey Sasser	.06	.02	.00
☐ 455	Daryl Boston	.03	.01	.00
☐ 456	Mike Fitzgerald	.03	.01	.00
	Montreal Expos			
☐ 457	Jeffrey Leonard	.03	.01	.00
☐ 458	Bruce Sutter	.08	.03	.01
☐ 459	Mitch Webster	.03	.01	.00
☐ 460	Joe Hesketh	.06	.02	.00

☐ 461	Bobby Witt	.06	.02	.00
☐ 462	Stew Cliburn	.03	.01	.00
☐ 463	Scott Bankhead	.06	.02	.00
☐ 464	Ramon Martinez	1.25	.50	.12
☐ 465	Dave Leiper	.03	.01	.00
☐ 466	Luis Alicea	.03	.01	.00
☐ 467	John Cerutti	.03	.01	.00
☐ 468	Ron Washington	.03	.01	.00
☐ 469	Jeff Reed	.03	.01	.00
☐ 470	Jeff Robinson	.06	.02	.00
	Detroit Tigers			
☐ 471	Sid Fernandez	.06	.02	.00
☐ 472	Terry Puhl	.03	.01	.00
☐ 473	Charlie Lea	.03	.01	.00
☐ 474	Israel Sanchez	.06	.02	.00
☐ 475	Bruce Benedict	.03	.01	.00
☐ 476	Oil Can Boyd	.03	.01	.00
☐ 477	Craig Reynolds	.03	.01	.00
☐ 478	Frank Williams	.03	.01	.00
☐ 479	Greg Cadaret	.03	.01	.00
☐ 480	Randy Kramer	.08	.03	.01
☐ 481	Dave Eiland	.08	.03	.01
☐ 482	Eric Show	.03	.01	.00
☐ 483	Garry Templeton	.06	.02	.00
☐ 484	Wallace Johnson	.03	.01	.00
☐ 485	Kevin Mitchell	.15	.06	.01
☐ 486	Tim Crews	.03	.01	.00
☐ 487	Mike Maddux	.03	.01	.00
☐ 488	Dave LaPoint	.03	.01	.00
☐ 489	Fred Manrique	.03	.01	.00
☐ 490	Greg Minton	.03	.01	.00
☐ 491	Doug Dascenzo UER	.10	.04	.01
	(photo actually			
	Damon Berryhill)			
☐ 492	Willie Upshaw	.03	.01	.00
☐ 493	Jack Armstrong	.10	.04	.01
☐ 494	Kirt Manwaring	.03	.01	.00
☐ 495	Jeff Ballard	.03	.01	.00
☐ 496	Jeff Kunkel	.03	.01	.00
☐ 497	Mike Campbell	.03	.01	.00
☐ 498	Gary Thurman	.03	.01	.00
☐ 499	Zane Smith	.06	.02	.00
☐ 500	Checklist Card DP	.06	.01	.00
☐ 501	Mike Birkbeck	.03	.01	.00
☐ 502	Terry Leach	.03	.01	.00
☐ 503	Shawn Hillegas	.03	.01	.00
☐ 504	Manny Lee	.03	.01	.00
☐ 505	Doug Jennings	.06	.02	.00
☐ 506	Ken Oberkfell	.03	.01	.00
☐ 507	Tim Teufel	.03	.01	.00
☐ 508	Tom Brookens	.03	.01	.00
☐ 509	Rafael Ramirez	.03	.01	.00
☐ 510	Fred Toliver	.03	.01	.00
☐ 511	Brian Holman	.15	.06	.01
☐ 512	Mike Bielecki	.03	.01	.00
☐ 513	Jeff Pico	.06	.02	.00
☐ 514	Charles Hudson	.03	.01	.00
☐ 515	Bruce Ruffin	.03	.01	.00
☐ 516	Larry McWilliams UER	.03	.01	.00
	(New Richland, should			
	be North Richland)			
☐ 517	Jeff Sellers	.03	.01	.00
☐ 518	John Costello	.06	.02	.00
☐ 519	Brady Anderson	.08	.03	.01
☐ 520	Craig McMurtry	.03	.01	.00
☐ 521	Ray Hayward DP	.03	.01	.00
☐ 522	Drew Hall DP	.03	.01	.00
☐ 523	Mark Lemke DP	.17	.07	.01
☐ 524	Oswald Peraza DP	.06	.02	.00
☐ 525	Bryan Harvey DP	.17	.07	.01
☐ 526	Rick Aguilera DP	.03	.01	.00
☐ 527	Tom Prince DP	.03	.01	.00
☐ 528	Mark Clear DP	.03	.01	.00
☐ 529	Jerry Browne DP	.03	.01	.00
☐ 530	Juan Castillo DP	.03	.01	.00
☐ 531	Jack McDowell DP	.08	.03	.01
☐ 532	Chris Speier DP	.03	.01	.00
☐ 533	Darrell Evans DP	.06	.02	.00
☐ 534	Luis Aquino DP	.03	.01	.00
☐ 535	Eric King DP	.03	.01	.00
☐ 536	Ken Hill DP	.15	.06	.01
☐ 537	Randy Bush DP	.03	.01	.00
☐ 538	Shane Mack DP	.06	.02	.00
☐ 539	Tom Bolton DP	.06	.02	.00
☐ 540	Gene Nelson DP	.03	.01	.00
☐ 541	Wes Gardner DP	.03	.01	.00
☐ 542	Ken Caminiti DP	.03	.01	.00
☐ 543	Duane Ward DP	.03	.01	.00
☐ 544	Norm Charlton DP	.10	.04	.01
☐ 545	Hal Morris DP	.75	.30	.07
☐ 546	Rich Yett DP	.03	.01	.00
☐ 547	Hensley Meulens DP	.25	.10	.02
☐ 548	Greg Harris DP	.03	.01	.00
	Philadelphia Phillies			

☐ 549	Darren Daulton DP	.06	.02	.00
	(posing as right-			
	handed hitter)			
☐ 550	Jeff Hamilton DP	.03	.01	.00
☐ 551	Luis Aguayo DP	.03	.01	.00
☐ 552	Tim Leary DP	.06	.02	.00
	(resembles M.Marshall)			
☐ 553	Ron Oester DP	.03	.01	.00
☐ 554	Steve Lombardozzi DP	.03	.01	.00
☐ 555	Tim Jones DP	.06	.02	.00
☐ 556	Bud Black DP	.03	.01	.00
☐ 557	Alejandro Pena DP	.03	.01	.00
☐ 558	Jose DeJesus DP	.10	.04	.01
☐ 559	Dennis Rasmussen DP	.03	.01	.00
☐ 560	Pat Borders DP	.10	.04	.01
☐ 561	Craig Biggio DP	.30	.12	.03
☐ 562	Luis De Los Santos DP	.08	.03	.01
☐ 563	Fred Lynn DP	.06	.02	.00
☐ 564	Todd Burns DP	.08	.03	.01
☐ 565	Felix Fermin DP	.03	.01	.00
☐ 566	Darnell Coles DP	.03	.01	.00
☐ 567	Willie Fraser DP	.03	.01	.00
☐ 568	Glenn Hubbard DP	.03	.01	.00
☐ 569	Craig Worthington DP	.08	.03	.01
☐ 570	Johnny Paredes DP	.08	.03	.01
☐ 571	Don Robinson DP	.03	.01	.00
☐ 572	Barry Lyons DP	.03	.01	.00
☐ 573	Bill Long DP	.03	.01	.00
☐ 574	Tracy Jones DP	.03	.01	.00
☐ 575	Juan Nieves DP	.03	.01	.00
☐ 576	Andres Thomas DP	.03	.01	.00
☐ 577	Rolando Roomes DP	.08	.03	.01
☐ 578	Luis Rivera UER DP	.03	.01	.00
	(wrong birthdate)			
☐ 579	Chad Kreuter DP	.08	.03	.01
☐ 580	Tony Armas DP	.03	.01	.00
☐ 581	Jay Buhner	.15	.06	.01
☐ 582	Ricky Horton DP	.03	.01	.00
☐ 583	Andy Hawkins DP	.03	.01	.00
☐ 584	Sil Campusano	.10	.04	.01
☐ 585	Dave Clark	.03	.01	.00
☐ 586	Van Snider DP	.08	.03	.01
☐ 587	Todd Frohwirth DP	.03	.01	.00
☐ 588	Puzzle Card DP	.06	.02	.00
	Warren Spahn			
☐ 589	William Brennan	.06	.02	.00
☐ 590	German Gonzalez	.06	.02	.00
☐ 591	Ernie Whitt DP	.03	.01	.00
☐ 592	Jeff Blauser	.03	.01	.00
☐ 593	Spike Owen DP	.03	.01	.00
☐ 594	Matt Williams	.20	.08	.02
☐ 595	Lloyd McClendon DP	.03	.01	.00
☐ 596	Steve Ontiveros	.03	.01	.00
☐ 597	Scott Medvin	.08	.03	.01
☐ 598	Hipolito Pena DP	.06	.02	.00
☐ 599	Jerald Clark DP	.15	.06	.01
☐ 600A	Checklist Card DP	.30	.10	.02
	635 Kurt Schilling			
☐ 600B	Checklist Card DP	.06	.01	.00
	635 Curt Schilling			
	(MVP's not listed			
	on checklist card)			
☐ 600C	Checklist Card DP	.06	.01	.00
	635 Curt Schilling			
	(MVP's listed			
	following 660)			
☐ 601	Carmelo Martinez DP	.03	.01	.00
☐ 602	Mike LaCoss	.03	.01	.00
☐ 603	Mike Devereaux	.06	.02	.00
☐ 604	Alex Madrid DP	.06	.02	.00
☐ 605	Gary Redus DP	.03	.01	.00
☐ 606	Lance Johnson	.03	.01	.00
☐ 607	Terry Clark DP	.06	.02	.00
☐ 608	Manny Trillo DP	.03	.01	.00
☐ 609	Scott Jordan	.08	.03	.01
☐ 610	Jay Howell DP	.03	.01	.00
☐ 611	Francisco Melendez	.08	.03	.01
☐ 612	Mike Boddicker	.03	.01	.00
☐ 613	Kevin Brown DP	.08	.03	.01
☐ 614	Dave Valle	.03	.01	.00
☐ 615	Tim Laudner DP	.03	.01	.00
☐ 616	Andy Nezelek UER	.08	.03	.01
	(wrong birthdate)			
☐ 617	Chuck Crim	.03	.01	.00
☐ 618	Jack Savage DP	.06	.02	.00
☐ 619	Adam Peterson	.06	.02	.00
☐ 620	Todd Stottlemyre	.15	.06	.01
☐ 621	Lance Blankenship	.08	.03	.01
☐ 622	Miguel Garcia DP	.08	.03	.01
☐ 623	Keith Miller DP	.03	.01	.00
	New York Mets			
☐ 624	Ricky Jordan DP	.10	.04	.01
☐ 625	Ernest Riles DP	.03	.01	.00
☐ 626	John Moses DP	.03	.01	.00

		MINT	EXC	G-VG
☐ 627	Nelson Liriano DP	.03	.01	.00
☐ 628	Mike Smithson DP	.03	.01	.00
☐ 629	Scott Sanderson	.06	.02	.00
☐ 630	Dale Mohorcic	.03	.01	.00
☐ 631	Marvin Freeman DP	.03	.01	.00
☐ 632	Mike Young DP	.03	.01	.00
☐ 633	Dennis Lamp	.03	.01	.00
☐ 634	Dante Bichette DP	.15	.06	.01
☐ 635	Curt Schilling DP	.08	.03	.01
☐ 636	Scott May DP	.08	.03	.01
☐ 637	Mike Schooler	.12	.05	.01
☐ 638	Rick Leach	.03	.01	.00
☐ 639	Tom Lampkin UER (Throws Left, should be Throws Right)	.08	.03	.01
☐ 640	Brian Meyer	.08	.03	.01
☐ 641	Brian Harper	.06	.02	.00
☐ 642	John Smoltz	.50	.20	.05
☐ 643	Jose: 40/40 Club (Jose Canseco)	.20	.08	.02
☐ 644	Bill Schroeder	.03	.01	.00
☐ 645	Edgar Martinez	.20	.08	.02
☐ 646	Dennis Cook	.10	.04	.01
☐ 647	Barry Jones	.03	.01	.00
☐ 648	Orel: 59 & Counting (Orel Hershiser)	.08	.03	.01
☐ 649	Rod Nichols	.06	.02	.00
☐ 650	Jody Davis	.03	.01	.00
☐ 651	Bob Milacki	.15	.06	.01
☐ 652	Mike Jackson	.03	.01	.00
☐ 653	Derek Lilliquist	.08	.03	.01
☐ 654	Paul Mirabella	.03	.01	.00
☐ 655	Mike Diaz	.03	.01	.00
☐ 656	Jeff Musselman	.03	.01	.00
☐ 657	Jerry Reed	.03	.01	.00
☐ 658	Kevin Blankenship	.06	.02	.00
☐ 659	Wayne Tolleson	.03	.01	.00
☐ 660	Eric Hetzel	.08	.03	.01

		MINT	EXC	G-VG
☐ BC7	George Brett	.12	.05	.01
☐ BC8	Andre Dawson	.10	.04	.01
☐ BC9	Paul Molitor UER (Brewers logo missing the word Milwaukee)	.08	.03	.01
☐ BC10	Andy Van Slyke	.08	.03	.01
☐ BC11	Dave Winfield	.10	.04	.01
☐ BC12	Kevin Gross	.05	.02	.00
☐ BC13	Mike Greenwell	.08	.03	.01
☐ BC14	Ozzie Smith	.10	.04	.01
☐ BC15	Cal Ripken	.15	.06	.01
☐ BC16	Andres Galarraga	.08	.03	.01
☐ BC17	Alan Trammell	.10	.04	.01
☐ BC18	Kal Daniels	.08	.03	.01
☐ BC19	Fred McGriff	.10	.04	.01
☐ BC20	Tony Gwynn	.12	.05	.01
☐ BC21	Wally Joyner DP	.08	.03	.01
☐ BC22	Will Clark DP	.15	.06	.01
☐ BC23	Ozzie Guillen	.05	.02	.00
☐ BC24	Gerald Perry DP	.05	.02	.00
☐ BC25	Alvin Davis DP	.05	.02	.00
☐ BC26	Ruben Sierra	.12	.05	.01

1989 Donruss Super DK's

This 26-player card set was available through a mail-in offer detailed on the wax packs. The set was sent in return for 8.00 and three wrappers plus 2.00 postage and handling. The set features the popular Diamond King subseries in large (approximately 4 7/8" by 6 13/16") form. Dick Perez of Perez-Steele Galleries did another outstanding job on the artwork. The cards are essentially a large version of the Donruss regular issue Diamond Kings.

1989 Donruss Bonus MVP's

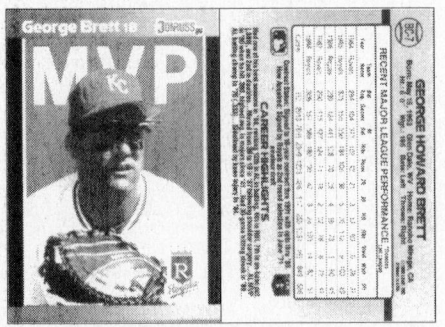

This 26-card set was distributed along with the regular 1989 Donruss issue as random inserts with the rack and wax packs. These bonus cards are numbered with the prefix BC for bonus cards and were supposedly produced in the same quantities as the other 660 regular issue cards. The "most valuable" player was selected from each of the 26 teams. Cards measure 2 1/2" by 3 1/2" and feature the same distinctive side border as the regular issue. The cards are distinguished by the bold MVP logo in the upper background of the obverse. Four of these cards were double printed with respect to the other cards in the set; these four are denoted by DP in the checklist below.

	MINT	EXC	G-VG
COMPLETE SET (26)	2.50	1.00	.25
COMMON CARD (BC1-BC26)	.05	.02	.00

		MINT	EXC	G-VG
☐ BC1	Kirby Puckett	.15	.06	.01
☐ BC2	Mike Scott	.08	.03	.01
☐ BC3	Joe Carter	.08	.03	.01
☐ BC4	Orel Hershiser	.08	.03	.01
☐ BC5	Jose Canseco	.20	.08	.02
☐ BC6	Darryl Strawberry	.15	.06	.01

	MINT	EXC	G-VG
COMPLETE SET (26)	9.00	4.00	.90
COMMON PLAYER (1-26)	.20	.08	.02

		MINT	EXC	G-VG
☐ 1	Mike Greenwell DK	.75	.30	.07
☐ 2	Bobby Bonilla DK	.60	.25	.06
☐ 3	Pete Incaviglia DK	.30	.12	.03
☐ 4	Chris Sabo DK	.75	.30	.07
☐ 5	Robin Yount DK	.60	.25	.06
☐ 6	Tony Gwynn DK	.75	.30	.07
☐ 7	Carlton Fisk DK	.50	.20	.05
☐ 8	Cory Snyder DK	.30	.12	.03
☐ 9	David Cone DK	.40	.16	.04
☐ 10	Kevin Seitzer DK	.30	.12	.03
☐ 11	Rick Reuschel DK	.20	.08	.02
☐ 12	Johnny Ray DK	.20	.08	.02
☐ 13	Dave Schmidt DK	.20	.08	.02
☐ 14	Andres Galarraga DK	.30	.12	.03
☐ 15	Kirk Gibson DK	.30	.12	.03
☐ 16	Fred McGriff DK	.50	.20	.05
☐ 17	Mark Grace DK	.75	.30	.07
☐ 18	Jeff Robinson DT DK	.20	.08	.02
☐ 19	Vince Coleman DK	.35	.15	.03
☐ 20	Dave Henderson DK	.30	.12	.03
☐ 21	Harold Reynolds DK	.25	.10	.02
☐ 22	Gerald Perry DK	.20	.08	.02
☐ 23	Frank Viola DK	.40	.16	.04
☐ 24	Steve Bedrosian DK	.20	.08	.02
☐ 25	Glenn Davis DK	.40	.16	.04
☐ 26	Don Mattingly DK	.75	.30	.07

1989 Donruss All-Stars

These All-Stars are standard size, 2 1/2" by 3 1/2" and very similar in design to the regular issue of 1989 Donruss. The set is distinguished by the presence of the respective League logos in the lower right corner of each obverse. The cards are numbered on the backs. The players chosen for the set are essentially the participants at the previous year's All-Star Game. Individual wax packs of All Stars (suggested retail price of 35 cents) contained one Pop-Up, five All-Star cards, and a Warren Spahn puzzle card.

	MINT	EXC	G-VG
COMPLETE SET (64)	8.00	3.50	.80
COMMON PLAYER (1-64)	.07	.03	.01
□ 1 Mark McGwire	.50	.20	.05
□ 2 Jose Canseco	.90	.40	.09
□ 3 Paul Molitor	.15	.06	.01
□ 4 Rickey Henderson	.75	.30	.07
□ 5 Cal Ripken	.75	.30	.07
□ 6 Dave Winfield	.25	.10	.02
□ 7 Wade Boggs	.60	.25	.06
□ 8 Frank Viola	.15	.06	.01
□ 9 Terry Steinbach	.10	.04	.01
□ 10 Tom Kelly MG	.07	.03	.01
□ 11 George Brett	.40	.16	.04
□ 12 Doyle Alexander	.07	.03	.01
□ 13 Gary Gaetti	.10	.04	.01
□ 14 Roger Clemens	.75	.30	.07
□ 15 Mike Greenwell	.60	.25	.06
□ 16 Dennis Eckersley	.20	.08	.02
□ 17 Carney Lansford	.10	.04	.01
□ 18 Mark Gubicza	.10	.04	.01
□ 19 Tim Laudner	.07	.03	.01
□ 20 Doug Jones	.10	.04	.01
□ 21 Don Mattingly	.75	.30	.07
□ 22 Dan Plesac	.10	.04	.01
□ 23 Kirby Puckett	.60	.25	.06
□ 24 Jeff Reardon	.20	.08	.02
□ 25 Johnny Ray	.07	.03	.01
□ 26 Jeff Russell	.07	.03	.01
□ 27 Harold Reynolds	.10	.04	.01
□ 28 Dave Stieb	.15	.06	.01
□ 29 Kurt Stillwell	.10	.04	.01
□ 30 Jose Canseco	.90	.40	.09
□ 31 Terry Steinbach	.10	.04	.01
□ 32 AL Checklist	.07	.03	.01
□ 33 Will Clark	1.00	.40	.10
□ 34 Darryl Strawberry	.75	.30	.07
□ 35 Ryne Sandberg	.75	.30	.07
□ 36 Andre Dawson	.35	.15	.03
□ 37 Ozzie Smith	.30	.12	.03
□ 38 Vince Coleman	.20	.08	.02
□ 39 Bobby Bonilla	.45	.18	.04
□ 40 Dwight Gooden	.45	.18	.04
□ 41 Gary Carter	.25	.10	.02
□ 42 Whitey Herzog MG	.07	.03	.01
□ 43 Shawon Dunston	.25	.10	.02
□ 44 David Cone	.35	.15	.03
□ 45 Andres Galarraga	.20	.08	.02
□ 46 Mark Davis	.07	.03	.01
□ 47 Barry Larkin	.35	.15	.03
□ 48 Kevin Gross	.07	.03	.01
□ 49 Vance Law	.07	.03	.01
□ 50 Orel Hershiser	.35	.15	.03
□ 51 Willie McGee	.15	.06	.01
□ 52 Danny Jackson	.10	.04	.01
□ 53 Rafael Palmeiro	.35	.15	.03
□ 54 Bob Knepper	.07	.03	.01
□ 55 Lance Parrish	.10	.04	.01
□ 56 Greg Maddux	.15	.06	.01
□ 57 Gerald Perry	.07	.03	.01
□ 58 Bob Walk	.07	.03	.01
□ 59 Chris Sabo	.45	.18	.04
□ 60 Todd Worrell	.15	.06	.01
□ 61 Andy Van Slyke	.15	.06	.01
□ 62 Ozzie Smith	.30	.12	.03
□ 63 Riverfront Stadium	.07	.03	.01
□ 64 NL Checklist	.07	.03	.01

1989 Donruss Pop-Ups

These Pop-Ups are borderless and standard size, 2 1/2" by 3 1/2". The cards are unnumbered; however the All Star checklist card lists the same numbers as the All Star cards. Those numbers are used below for reference. The players chosen for the set are essentially the starting lineups for the previous year's All-Star Game. Individual wax packs of All Stars (suggested retail price of 35 cents) contained one Pop-Up, five All-Star cards, and a puzzle card.

	MINT	EXC	G-VG
COMPLETE SET (20)	4.00	1.75	.40
COMMON PLAYER	.10	.04	.01
□ 1 Mark McGwire	.50	.20	.05
□ 2 Jose Canseco	.90	.40	.09
□ 3 Paul Molitor	.15	.06	.01
□ 4 Rickey Henderson	.75	.30	.07
□ 5 Cal Ripken	.75	.30	.07
□ 6 Dave Winfield	.25	.10	.02
□ 7 Wade Boggs	.60	.25	.06
□ 8 Frank Viola	.15	.06	.01
□ 9 Terry Steinbach	.10	.04	.01
□ 10 Tom Kelly MG	.10	.04	.01
□ 33 Will Clark	1.00	.40	.10
□ 34 Darryl Strawberry	.75	.30	.07
□ 35 Ryne Sandberg	.75	.30	.07
□ 36 Andre Dawson	.35	.15	.03
□ 37 Ozzie Smith	.30	.12	.03
□ 38 Vince Coleman	.20	.08	.02
□ 39 Bobby Bonilla	.45	.18	.04
□ 40 Dwight Gooden	.45	.18	.04
□ 41 Gary Carter	.25	.10	.02
□ 42 Whitey Herzog MG	.10	.04	.01

1989 Donruss Traded

The 1989 Donruss Traded set contains 56 standard-size (2 1/2" by 3 1/2") cards. The fronts have yellowish-orange borders; the backs are yellow and feature recent statistics. The cards were distributed as a boxed set. The set was never very popular with collectors since it included (as the name implies) only traded players rather than rookies.

	MINT	EXC	G-VG
COMPLETE SET (56)	4.00	1.75	.40
COMMON PLAYER (1-55)	.05	.02	.00

		MINT	EXC	G-VG
☐	1 Jeffrey Leonard	.10	.04	.01
☐	2 Jack Clark	.20	.08	.02
☐	3 Kevin Gross	.05	.02	.00
☐	4 Tommy Herr	.10	.04	.01
☐	5 Bob Boone	.15	.06	.01
☐	6 Rafael Palmeiro	.50	.20	.05
☐	7 John Dopson	.05	.02	.00
☐	8 Willie Randolph	.10	.04	.01
☐	9 Chris Brown	.05	.02	.00
☐	10 Wally Backman	.05	.02	.00
☐	11 Steve Ontiveros	.05	.02	.00
☐	12 Eddie Murray	.30	.12	.03
☐	13 Lance McCullers	.05	.02	.00
☐	14 Spike Owen	.05	.02	.00
☐	15 Rob Murphy	.05	.02	.00
☐	16 Pete O'Brien	.05	.02	.00
☐	17 Ken Williams	.05	.02	.00
☐	18 Nick Esasky	.10	.04	.01
☐	19 Nolan Ryan	2.00	.80	.20
☐	20 Brian Holton	.05	.02	.00
☐	21 Mike Moore	.10	.04	.01
☐	22 Joel Skinner	.05	.02	.00
☐	23 Steve Sax	.15	.06	.01
☐	24 Rick Mahler	.05	.02	.00
☐	25 Mike Aldrete	.05	.02	.00
☐	26 Jesse Orosco	.05	.02	.00
☐	27 Dave LaPoint	.05	.02	.00
☐	28 Walt Terrell	.05	.02	.00
☐	29 Eddie Williams	.05	.02	.00
☐	30 Mike Devereaux	.05	.02	.00
☐	31 Julio Franco	.25	.10	.02
☐	32 Jim Clancy	.05	.02	.00
☐	33 Felix Fermin	.05	.02	.00
☐	34 Curt Wilkerson	.05	.02	.00
☐	35 Bert Blyleven	.15	.06	.01
☐	36 Mel Hall	.15	.06	.01
☐	37 Eric King	.10	.04	.01
☐	38 Mitch Williams	.15	.06	.01
☐	39 Jamie Moyer	.05	.02	.00
☐	40 Rick Rhoden	.05	.02	.00
☐	41 Phil Bradley	.10	.04	.01
☐	42 Paul Kilgus	.05	.02	.00
☐	43 Milt Thompson	.05	.02	.00
☐	44 Jerry Browne	.10	.04	.01
☐	45 Bruce Hurst	.10	.04	.01
☐	46 Claudell Washington	.10	.04	.01
☐	47 Todd Benzinger	.10	.04	.01
☐	48 Steve Balboni	.05	.02	.00
☐	49 Oddibe McDowell	.10	.04	.01
☐	50 Charles Hudson	.05	.02	.00
☐	51 Ron Kittle	.10	.04	.01
☐	52 Andy Hawkins	.05	.02	.00
☐	53 Tom Brookens	.05	.02	.00
☐	54 Tom Niedenfuer	.05	.02	.00
☐	55 Jeff Parrett	.05	.02	.00
☐	56 Checklist Card	.05	.02	.00

1989 Donruss Grand Slammers

The 1989 Donruss Grand Slammers set contains 12 standard-size (2 1/2" by 3 1/2") cards. Each card in the set can be found with five different colored border combinations, but no color combination of borders appears to be scarcer than any other. The set includes cards for each player who hit one or more grand slams in 1988. The backs detail the players' grand slams. The cards were distributed one per cello pack as well as an insert (complete) set in each factory set.

		MINT	EXC	G-VG
	COMPLETE SET (12)	2.50	1.00	.25
	COMMON PLAYER (1-12)	.10	.04	.01
☐	1 Jose Canseco	.90	.40	.09
☐	2 Mike Marshall	.15	.06	.01
☐	3 Walt Weiss	.15	.06	.01
☐	4 Kevin McReynolds	.20	.08	.02
☐	5 Mike Greenwell	.35	.15	.03
☐	6 Dave Winfield	.30	.12	.03
☐	7 Mark McGwire	.60	.25	.06
☐	8 Keith Hernandez	.15	.06	.01
☐	9 Franklin Stubbs	.10	.04	.01
☐	10 Danny Tartabull	.35	.15	.03
☐	11 Jesse Barfield	.15	.06	.01
☐	12 Ellis Burks	.30	.12	.03

1989 Donruss Baseball's Best

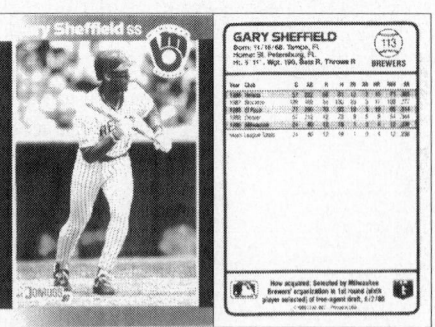

The 1989 Donruss Baseball's Best set contains 336 standard-size (2 1/2" by 3 1/2") glossy cards. The fronts are green and yellow, and the backs feature career highlight information. The backs are green, and feature vertically oriented career stats. The cards were distributed as a set in a blister pack through various retail and department store chains.

		MINT	EXC	G-VG
	COMPLETE SET (336)	18.00	7.50	2.50
	COMMON PLAYER (1-336)	.04	.02	.00
☐	1 Don Mattingly	.75	.30	.07
☐	2 Tom Glavine	.50	.20	.05
☐	3 Bert Blyleven	.10	.04	.01
☐	4 Andre Dawson	.25	.10	.02
☐	5 Pete O'Brien	.04	.02	.00

☐ 6 Eric Davis	.40	.16	.04
☐ 7 George Brett	.40	.16	.04
☐ 8 Glenn Davis	.20	.08	.02
☐ 9 Ellis Burks	.30	.12	.03
☐ 10 Kirk Gibson	.20	.08	.02
☐ 11 Carlton Fisk	.30	.12	.03
☐ 12 Andres Galarraga	.20	.08	.02
☐ 13 Alan Trammell	.20	.08	.02
☐ 14 Dwight Gooden	.35	.15	.03
☐ 15 Paul Molitor	.15	.06	.01
☐ 16 Roger McDowell	.04	.02	.00
☐ 17 Doug Drabek	.10	.04	.01
☐ 18 Kent Hrbek	.10	.04	.01
☐ 19 Vince Coleman	.20	.08	.02
☐ 20 Steve Sax	.15	.06	.01
☐ 21 Roberto Alomar	.35	.15	.03
☐ 22 Carney Lansford	.10	.04	.01
☐ 23 Will Clark	.90	.40	.09
☐ 24 Alvin Davis	.07	.03	.01
☐ 25 Bobby Thigpen	.10	.04	.01
☐ 26 Ryne Sandberg	.75	.30	.07
☐ 27 Devon White	.10	.04	.01
☐ 28 Mike Greenwell	.30	.12	.03
☐ 29 Dale Murphy	.30	.12	.03
☐ 30 Jeff Ballard	.07	.03	.01
☐ 31 Kelly Gruber	.07	.03	.01
☐ 32 Julio Franco	.15	.06	.01
☐ 33 Bobby Bonilla	.30	.12	.03
☐ 34 Tim Wallach	.07	.03	.01
☐ 35 Lou Whitaker	.10	.04	.01
☐ 36 Jay Howell	.07	.03	.01
☐ 37 Greg Maddux	.10	.04	.01
☐ 38 Bill Doran	.04	.02	.00
☐ 39 Danny Tartabull	.25	.10	.02
☐ 40 Darryl Strawberry	.50	.20	.05
☐ 41 Ron Darling	.10	.04	.01
☐ 42 Tony Gwynn	.40	.16	.04
☐ 43 Mark McGwire	.50	.20	.05
☐ 44 Ozzie Smith	.25	.10	.02
☐ 45 Andy Van Slyke	.10	.04	.01
☐ 46 Juan Berenguer	.04	.02	.00
☐ 47 Von Hayes	.07	.03	.01
☐ 48 Tony Fernandez	.07	.03	.01
☐ 49 Eric Plunk	.04	.02	.00
☐ 50 Ernest Riles	.04	.02	.00
☐ 51 Harold Reynolds	.07	.03	.01
☐ 52 Andy Hawkins	.04	.02	.00
☐ 53 Robin Yount	.40	.16	.04
☐ 54 Danny Jackson	.07	.03	.01
☐ 55 Nolan Ryan	1.25	.50	.12
☐ 56 Joe Carter	.25	.10	.02
☐ 57 Jose Canseco	.90	.40	.09
☐ 58 Jody Davis	.04	.02	.00
☐ 59 Lance Parrish	.10	.04	.01
☐ 60 Mitch Williams	.07	.03	.01
☐ 61 Brook Jacoby	.07	.03	.01
☐ 62 Tom Browning	.07	.03	.01
☐ 63 Kurt Stillwell	.07	.03	.01
☐ 64 Rafael Ramirez	.04	.02	.00
☐ 65 Roger Clemens	.75	.30	.07
☐ 66 Mike Scioscia	.04	.02	.00
☐ 67 Dave Gallagher	.04	.02	.00
☐ 68 Mark Langston	.15	.06	.01
☐ 69 Chet Lemon	.04	.02	.00
☐ 70 Kevin McReynolds	.10	.04	.01
☐ 71 Rob Deer	.07	.03	.01
☐ 72 Tommy Herr	.07	.03	.01
☐ 73 Barry Bonds	.60	.25	.06
☐ 74 Frank Viola	.15	.06	.01
☐ 75 Pedro Guerrero	.15	.06	.01
☐ 76 Dave Righetti UER	.10	.04	.01
(ML total of 7			
wins incorrect)			
☐ 77 Bruce Hurst	.07	.03	.01
☐ 78 Rickey Henderson	.75	.30	.07
☐ 79 Robby Thompson	.04	.02	.00
☐ 80 Randy Johnson	.10	.04	.01
☐ 81 Harold Baines	.10	.04	.01
☐ 82 Calvin Schiraldi	.04	.02	.00
☐ 83 Kirk McCaskill	.04	.02	.00
☐ 84 Lee Smith	.15	.06	.01
☐ 85 John Smoltz	.30	.12	.03
☐ 86 Mickey Tettleton	.10	.04	.01
☐ 87 Jimmy Key	.10	.04	.01
☐ 88 Rafael Palmeiro	.25	.10	.02
☐ 89 Sid Bream	.04	.02	.00
☐ 90 Dennis Martinez	.07	.03	.01
☐ 91 Frank Tanana	.07	.03	.01
☐ 92 Eddie Murray	.30	.12	.03
☐ 93 Shawon Dunston	.20	.08	.02
☐ 94 Mike Scott	.10	.04	.01
☐ 95 Bret Saberhagen	.25	.10	.02
☐ 96 David Cone	.20	.08	.02
☐ 97 Kevin Elster	.04	.02	.00
☐ 98 Jack Clark	.15	.06	.01
☐ 99 Dave Stewart	.20	.08	.02
☐ 100 Jose Oquendo	.04	.02	.00
☐ 101 Jose Lind	.04	.02	.00
☐ 102 Gary Gaetti	.07	.03	.01
☐ 103 Ricky Jordan	.15	.06	.01
☐ 104 Fred McGriff	.40	.16	.04
☐ 105 Don Slaught	.04	.02	.00
☐ 106 Jose Uribe	.04	.02	.00
☐ 107 Jeffrey Leonard	.04	.02	.00
☐ 108 Lee Guetterman	.04	.02	.00
☐ 109 Chris Bosio	.07	.03	.01
☐ 110 Barry Larkin	.25	.10	.02
☐ 111 Ruben Sierra	.45	.18	.04
☐ 112 Greg Swindell	.10	.04	.01
☐ 113 Gary Sheffield	.35	.15	.03
☐ 114 Lonnie Smith	.07	.03	.01
☐ 115 Chili Davis	.07	.03	.01
☐ 116 Damon Berryhill	.07	.03	.01
☐ 117 Tom Candiotti	.07	.03	.01
☐ 118 Kal Daniels	.10	.04	.01
☐ 119 Mark Gubicza	.07	.03	.01
☐ 120 Jim Deshaies	.04	.02	.00
☐ 121 Dwight Evans	.10	.04	.01
☐ 122 Mike Morgan	.07	.03	.01
☐ 123 Dan Pasqua	.07	.03	.01
☐ 124 Bryn Smith	.04	.02	.00
☐ 125 Doyle Alexander	.04	.02	.00
☐ 126 Howard Johnson	.15	.06	.01
☐ 127 Chuck Crim	.04	.02	.00
☐ 128 Darren Daulton	.10	.04	.01
☐ 129 Jeff Robinson	.07	.03	.01
☐ 130 Kirby Puckett	.45	.18	.04
☐ 131 Joe Magrane	.07	.03	.01
☐ 132 Jesse Barfield	.07	.03	.01
☐ 133 Mark Davis UER	.15	.06	.01
(photo actually			
Dave Leiper)			
☐ 134 Dennis Eckersley	.20	.08	.02
☐ 135 Mike Krukow	.04	.02	.00
☐ 136 Jay Buhner	.20	.08	.02
☐ 137 Ozzie Guillen	.10	.04	.01
☐ 138 Rick Sutcliffe	.07	.03	.01
☐ 139 Wally Joyner	.20	.08	.02
☐ 140 Wade Boggs	.45	.18	.04
☐ 141 Jeff Treadway	.07	.03	.01
☐ 142 Cal Ripken	.60	.25	.06
☐ 143 Dave Stieb	.10	.04	.01
☐ 144 Pete Incaviglia	.10	.04	.01
☐ 145 Bob Walk	.04	.02	.00
☐ 146 Nelson Santovenia	.07	.03	.01
☐ 147 Mike Heath	.04	.02	.00
☐ 148 Willie Randolph	.07	.03	.01
☐ 149 Paul Kilgus	.04	.02	.00
☐ 150 Billy Hatcher	.07	.03	.01
☐ 151 Steve Farr	.04	.02	.00
☐ 152 Gregg Jefferies	.50	.20	.05
☐ 153 Randy Myers	.07	.03	.01
☐ 154 Garry Templeton	.04	.02	.00
☐ 155 Walt Weiss	.15	.06	.01
☐ 156 Terry Pendleton	.15	.06	.01
☐ 157 John Smiley	.15	.06	.01
☐ 158 Greg Gagne	.04	.02	.00
☐ 159 Len Dykstra	.15	.06	.01
☐ 160 Nelson Liriano	.04	.02	.00
☐ 161 Alvaro Espinoza	.04	.02	.00
☐ 162 Rick Reuschel	.10	.04	.01
☐ 163 Omar Vizquel UER	.15	.06	.01
(photo actually			
Darnell Coles)			
☐ 164 Clay Parker	.07	.03	.01
☐ 165 Dan Plesac	.07	.03	.01
☐ 166 John Franco	.07	.03	.01
☐ 167 Scott Fletcher	.04	.02	.00
☐ 168 Cory Snyder	.10	.04	.01
☐ 169 Bo Jackson	1.25	.50	.12
☐ 170 Tommy Gregg	.07	.03	.01
☐ 171 Jim Abbott	1.00	.40	.10
☐ 172 Jerome Walton	.50	.20	.05
☐ 173 Doug Jones	.04	.02	.00
☐ 174 Todd Benzinger	.04	.02	.00
☐ 175 Frank White	.04	.02	.00
☐ 176 Craig Biggio	.25	.10	.02
☐ 177 John Dopson	.04	.02	.00
☐ 178 Alfredo Griffin	.04	.02	.00
☐ 179 Melido Perez	.07	.03	.01
☐ 180 Tim Burke	.04	.02	.00
☐ 181 Matt Nokes	.10	.04	.01
☐ 182 Gary Carter	.20	.08	.02
☐ 183 Ted Higuera	.07	.03	.01
☐ 184 Ken Howell	.04	.02	.00
☐ 185 Rey Quinones	.04	.02	.00
☐ 186 Wally Backman	.04	.02	.00
☐ 187 Tom Brunansky	.07	.03	.01

☐ 188	Steve Balboni	.04	.02	.00
☐ 189	Marvell Wynne	.04	.02	.00
☐ 190	Dave Henderson	.10	.04	.01
☐ 191	Don Robinson	.04	.02	.00
☐ 192	Ken Griffey Jr.	3.50	1.50	.35
☐ 193	Ivan Calderon	.07	.03	.01
☐ 194	Mike Bielecki	.04	.02	.00
☐ 195	Johnny Ray	.04	.02	.00
☐ 196	Rob Murphy	.04	.02	.00
☐ 197	Andres Thomas	.04	.02	.00
☐ 198	Phil Bradley	.07	.03	.01
☐ 199	Junior Felix	.25	.10	.02
☐ 200	Jeff Russell	.04	.02	.00
☐ 201	Mike LaValliere	.04	.02	.00
☐ 202	Kevin Gross	.04	.02	.00
☐ 203	Keith Moreland	.04	.02	.00
☐ 204	Mike Marshall	.07	.03	.01
☐ 205	Dwight Smith	.25	.10	.02
☐ 206	Jim Clancy	.04	.02	.00
☐ 207	Kevin Seitzer	.10	.04	.01
☐ 208	Keith Hernandez	.15	.06	.01
☐ 209	Bob Ojeda	.07	.03	.01
☐ 210	Ed Whitson	.07	.03	.01
☐ 211	Tony Phillips	.07	.03	.01
☐ 212	Milt Thompson	.04	.02	.00
☐ 213	Randy Kramer	.04	.02	.00
☐ 214	Randy Bush	.04	.02	.00
☐ 215	Randy Ready	.04	.02	.00
☐ 216	Duane Ward	.04	.02	.00
☐ 217	Jimmy Jones	.07	.03	.01
☐ 218	Scott Garrelts	.07	.03	.01
☐ 219	Scott Bankhead	.07	.03	.01
☐ 220	Lance McCullers	.04	.02	.00
☐ 221	B.J. Surhoff	.07	.03	.01
☐ 222	Chris Sabo	.20	.08	.02
☐ 223	Steve Buechele	.07	.03	.01
☐ 224	Joel Skinner	.04	.02	.00
☐ 225	Orel Hershiser	.20	.08	.02
☐ 226	Derek Lilliquist	.10	.04	.01
☐ 227	Claudell Washington	.07	.03	.01
☐ 228	Lloyd McClendon	.04	.02	.00
☐ 229	Felix Fermin	.04	.02	.00
☐ 230	Paul O'Neill	.15	.06	.01
☐ 231	Charlie Leibrandt	.07	.03	.01
☐ 232	Dave Smith	.04	.02	.00
☐ 233	Bob Stanley	.04	.02	.00
☐ 234	Tim Belcher	.10	.04	.01
☐ 235	Eric King	.07	.03	.01
☐ 236	Spike Owen	.04	.02	.00
☐ 237	Mike Henneman	.07	.03	.01
☐ 238	Juan Samuel	.10	.04	.01
☐ 239	Greg Brock	.04	.02	.00
☐ 240	John Kruk	.10	.04	.01
☐ 241	Glenn Wilson	.04	.02	.00
☐ 242	Jeff Reardon	.15	.06	.01
☐ 243	Todd Worrell	.10	.04	.01
☐ 244	Dave LaPoint	.04	.02	.00
☐ 245	Walt Terrell	.04	.02	.00
☐ 246	Mike Moore	.07	.03	.01
☐ 247	Kelly Downs	.04	.02	.00
☐ 248	Dave Valle	.04	.02	.00
☐ 249	Ron Kittle	.10	.04	.01
☐ 250	Steve Wilson	.07	.03	.01
☐ 251	Dick Schofield	.04	.02	.00
☐ 252	Marty Barrett	.04	.02	.00
☐ 253	Dion James	.04	.02	.00
☐ 254	Bob Milacki	.10	.04	.01
☐ 255	Ernie Whitt	.04	.02	.00
☐ 256	Kevin Brown	.10	.04	.01
☐ 257	R.J. Reynolds	.04	.02	.00
☐ 258	Tim Raines	.15	.06	.01
☐ 259	Frank Williams	.04	.02	.00
☐ 260	Jose Gonzalez	.04	.02	.00
☐ 261	Mitch Webster	.04	.02	.00
☐ 262	Ken Caminiti	.04	.02	.00
☐ 263	Bob Boone	.07	.03	.01
☐ 264	Dave Magadan	.15	.06	.01
☐ 265	Rick Aguilera	.04	.02	.00
☐ 266	Chris James	.07	.03	.01
☐ 267	Bob Welch	.15	.06	.01
☐ 268	Ken Dayley	.04	.02	.00
☐ 269	Junior Ortiz	.04	.02	.00
☐ 270	Allan Anderson	.04	.02	.00
☐ 271	Steve Jeltz	.04	.02	.00
☐ 272	George Bell	.20	.08	.02
☐ 273	Roberto Kelly	.35	.15	.03
☐ 274	Brett Butler	.10	.04	.01
☐ 275	Mike Schooler	.15	.06	.01
☐ 276	Ken Phelps	.04	.02	.00
☐ 277	Glenn Braggs	.07	.03	.01
☐ 278	Jose Rijo	.15	.06	.01
☐ 279	Bobby Witt	.10	.04	.01
☐ 280	Jerry Browne	.04	.02	.00
☐ 281	Kevin Mitchell	.40	.16	.04

☐ 282	Craig Worthington	.10	.04	.01
☐ 283	Greg Minton	.04	.02	.00
☐ 284	Nick Esasky	.07	.03	.01
☐ 285	John Farrell	.04	.02	.00
☐ 286	Rick Mahler	.04	.02	.00
☐ 287	Tom Gordon	.25	.10	.02
☐ 288	Gerald Young	.07	.03	.01
☐ 289	Jody Reed	.10	.04	.01
☐ 290	Jeff Hamilton	.04	.02	.00
☐ 291	Gerald Perry	.04	.02	.00
☐ 292	Hubie Brooks	.07	.03	.01
☐ 293	Bo Diaz	.04	.02	.00
☐ 294	Terry Puhl	.04	.02	.00
☐ 295	Jim Gantner	.04	.02	.00
☐ 296	Jeff Parrett	.04	.02	.00
☐ 297	Mike Boddicker	.04	.02	.00
☐ 298	Dan Gladden	.04	.02	.00
☐ 299	Tony Pena	.07	.03	.01
☐ 300	Checklist Card	.04	.02	.00
☐ 301	Tom Henke	.07	.03	.01
☐ 302	Pascual Perez	.07	.03	.01
☐ 303	Steve Bedrosian	.04	.02	.00
☐ 304	Ken Hill	.10	.04	.01
☐ 305	Jerry Reuss	.04	.02	.00
☐ 306	Jim Eisenreich	.07	.03	.01
☐ 307	Jack Howell	.04	.02	.00
☐ 308	Rick Cerone	.04	.02	.00
☐ 309	Tim Leary	.07	.03	.01
☐ 310	Joe Orsulak	.04	.02	.00
☐ 311	Jim Dwyer	.04	.02	.00
☐ 312	Geno Petralli	.04	.02	.00
☐ 313	Rick Honeycutt	.04	.02	.00
☐ 314	Tom Foley	.04	.02	.00
☐ 315	Kenny Rogers	.04	.02	.00
☐ 316	Mike Flanagan	.07	.03	.01
☐ 317	Bryan Harvey	.30	.12	.03
☐ 318	Billy Ripken	.04	.02	.00
☐ 319	Jeff Montgomery	.10	.04	.01
☐ 320	Erik Hanson	.10	.04	.01
☐ 321	Brian Downing	.04	.02	.00
☐ 322	Gregg Olson	.45	.18	.04
☐ 323	Terry Steinbach	.10	.04	.01
☐ 324	Sammy Sosa	.45	.18	.04
☐ 325	Gene Harris	.15	.06	.01
☐ 326	Mike Devereaux	.07	.03	.01
☐ 327	Dennis Cook	.07	.03	.01
☐ 328	David Wells	.07	.03	.01
☐ 329	Checklist Card	.04	.02	.00
☐ 330	Kirt Manwaring	.07	.03	.01
☐ 331	Jim Presley	.04	.02	.00
☐ 332	Checklist Card	.04	.02	.00
☐ 333	Chuck Finley	.15	.06	.01
☐ 334	Rob Dibble	.20	.08	.02
☐ 335	Cecil Espy	.07	.03	.01
☐ 336	Dave Parker	.15	.06	.01

1989 Donruss Rookies

The 1989 Donruss Rookies set contains 56 standard-size (2 1/2"
by 3 1/2") cards. The fronts have green and black borders; the
backs are green and feature career highlights. The cards were
distributed as a boxed set through the Donruss Dealer Network.
The key rookie cards in this set are Jim Abbott, Junior Felix, Deion
Sanders, and Jerome Walton.

	MINT	EXC	G-VG
COMPLETE SET (56)	13.50	6.00	1.85
COMMON PLAYER (1-56)	.05	.02	.00
☐ 1 Gary Sheffield	.30	.12	.03
☐ 2 Gregg Jefferies	.30	.12	.03
☐ 3 Ken Griffey Jr.	7.50	3.25	.75
☐ 4 Tom Gordon	.25	.10	.02
☐ 5 Billy Spiers	.12	.05	.01
☐ 6 Deion Sanders	.60	.25	.06
☐ 7 Donn Pall	.08	.03	.01
☐ 8 Steve Carter	.08	.03	.01
☐ 9 Francisco Oliveras	.08	.03	.01
☐ 10 Steve Wilson	.08	.03	.01
☐ 11 Bob Geren	.08	.03	.01
☐ 12 Tony Castillo	.08	.03	.01
☐ 13 Kenny Rogers	.10	.04	.01
☐ 14 Carlos Martinez	.15	.06	.01
☐ 15 Edgar Martinez	.20	.08	.02
☐ 16 Jim Abbott	1.25	.50	.12
☐ 17 Torey Lovullo	.08	.03	.01
☐ 18 Mark Carreon	.08	.03	.01
☐ 19 Geronimo Berroa	.08	.03	.01
☐ 20 Luis Medina	.10	.04	.01
☐ 21 Sandy Alomar Jr.	.40	.16	.04
☐ 22 Bob Milacki	.15	.06	.01
☐ 23 Joe Girardi	.10	.04	.01
☐ 24 German Gonzalez	.08	.03	.01
☐ 25 Craig Worthington	.08	.03	.01
☐ 26 Jerome Walton	.40	.16	.04
☐ 27 Gary Wayne	.10	.04	.01
☐ 28 Tim Jones	.08	.03	.01
☐ 29 Dante Bichette	.08	.03	.01
☐ 30 Alexis Infante	.08	.03	.01
☐ 31 Ken Hill	.10	.04	.01
☐ 32 Dwight Smith	.12	.05	.01
☐ 33 Luis de los Santos	.08	.03	.01
☐ 34 Eric Yelding	.12	.05	.01
☐ 35 Gregg Olson	.45	.18	.04
☐ 36 Phil Stephenson	.08	.03	.01
☐ 37 Ken Patterson	.08	.03	.01
☐ 38 Rick Wrona	.08	.03	.01
☐ 39 Mike Brumley	.05	.02	.00
☐ 40 Cris Carpenter	.08	.03	.01
☐ 41 Jeff Brantley	.20	.08	.02
☐ 42 Ron Jones	.08	.03	.01
☐ 43 Randy Johnson	.10	.04	.01
☐ 44 Kevin Brown	.08	.03	.01
☐ 45 Ramon Martinez	1.25	.50	.12
☐ 46 Greg W.Harris	.10	.04	.01
☐ 47 Steve Finley	.35	.15	.03
☐ 48 Randy Kramer	.05	.02	.00
☐ 49 Erik Hanson	.45	.18	.04
☐ 50 Matt Merullo	.10	.04	.01
☐ 51 Mike Devereaux	.08	.03	.01
☐ 52 Clay Parker	.08	.03	.01
☐ 53 Omar Vizquel	.08	.03	.01
☐ 54 Derek Lilliquist	.05	.02	.00
☐ 55 Junior Felix	.15	.06	.01
☐ 56 Checklist Card	.05	.01	.00

1990 Donruss Preview

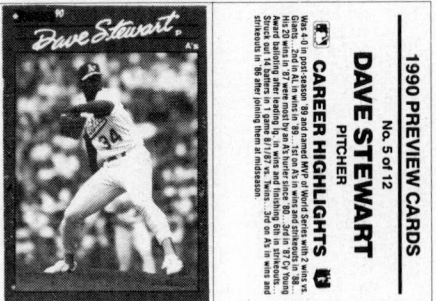

The 1990 Donruss Preview set contains 12 standard-size (2 1/2" by 3 1/2") cards. The bright red borders are exactly like the regular 1990 Donruss cards, but many of the photos are different. The horizontally-oriented backs are plain white with career highlights in black lettering. Two cards were sent to each dealer in the Donruss dealer network thus making it quite difficult to put together a set.

	MINT	EXC	G-VG
COMPLETE SET (12)	600.00	200.00	50.00
COMMON PLAYER (1-12)	25.00	11.00	3.50
☐ 1 Todd Zeile	60.00	22.50	7.50
(Not shown as Rated Rookie on front)			
☐ 2 Ben McDonald	60.00	22.50	7.50
☐ 3 Bo Jackson	125.00	45.00	15.00
☐ 4 Will Clark	125.00	45.00	15.00
☐ 5 Dave Stewart	25.00	11.00	3.50
☐ 6 Kevin Mitchell	50.00	18.00	6.00
☐ 7 Nolan Ryan	150.00	57.50	18.75
☐ 8 Howard Johnson	35.00	13.50	4.50
☐ 9 Tony Gwynn	75.00	27.00	9.00
☐ 10 Jerome Walton	30.00	13.50	4.50
(Shown ready to bunt)			
☐ 11 Wade Boggs	75.00	27.00	9.00
☐ 12 Kirby Puckett	75.00	27.00	9.00

1990 Donruss

The 1990 Donruss set contains 716 standard-size (2 1/2" by 3 1/2") cards. The front borders are bright red. The horizontally-oriented backs are amber. Cards numbered 1-26 are Diamond Kings; cards numbered 28-47 are Rated Rookies (RR). Card number 716 was added to the set shortly after the set's initial production, necessitating the checklist variation on card number 700. The set was the largest ever produced by Donruss, unfortunately it also had a large number of errors which were corrected after the cards were released. Every All-Star selection in the set has two versions, the statistical heading on the back is either "Recent Major League Performance" or "All-Star Game Performance." There are a number of cards that have been discovered to have minor printing flaws, which are insignificant variations, that collectors have found unworthy of price differentials. These very minor variations include numbers 1, 18, 154, 168, 206, 270, 321, 347, 405, 408, 425, 583, 585, 619, 637, 639, 699, 701, and 716. The factory sets were distributed without the Bonus Cards; thus there were again new checklist cards printed to reflect the exclusion of the Bonus Cards. These factory set checklist cards are the B variations below (except for 700C). The key rookie cards in this set are Delino DeShields, Juan Gonzalez, Marquis Grissom, Dave Justice, Ben McDonald, John Olerud, and Dean Palmer. The unusual number of cards in the set (716 plus 26 BC's, i.e., not divisible by 132) apparently led to 50 double-printed numbers, which are indicated in the checklists below (1990 Donruss and 1990 Donruss Bonus MVP's) by DP.

	MINT	EXC	G-VG
COMPLETE SET (716)	18.00	7.50	2.50

COMMON PLAYER (1-716)		.03	.01	.00
☐ 1	Bo Jackson DK	.30	.12	.03
☐ 2	Steve Sax DK	.06	.02	.00
☐ 3A	Ruben Sierra DK ERR	1.00	.40	.10
	(no small line on top border on card back)			
☐ 3B	Ruben Sierra DK COR	.10	.04	.01
☐ 4	Ken Griffey Jr. DK	.60	.25	.06
☐ 5	Mickey Tettleton DK	.06	.02	.00
☐ 6	Dave Stewart DK	.08	.03	.01
☐ 7	Jim Deshaies DK DP	.06	.02	.00
☐ 8	John Smoltz DK	.08	.03	.01
☐ 9	Mike Bielecki DK	.06	.02	.00
☐ 10A	Brian Downing DK ERR	.65	.25	.06
	(reverse neg-ative on card front)			
☐ 10B	Brian Downing DK COR	.08	.03	.01
☐ 11	Kevin Mitchell DK	.08	.03	.01
☐ 12	Kelly Gruber DK	.08	.03	.01
☐ 13	Joe Magrane DK	.06	.02	.00
☐ 14	John Franco DK	.06	.02	.00
☐ 15	Ozzie Guillen DK	.06	.02	.00
☐ 16	Lou Whitaker DK	.06	.02	.00
☐ 17	John Smiley DK	.06	.02	.00
☐ 18	Howard Johnson DK	.08	.03	.01
☐ 19	Willie Randolph DK	.06	.02	.00
☐ 20	Chris Bosio DK	.06	.02	.00
☐ 21	Tommy Herr DK DP	.06	.02	.00
☐ 22	Dan Gladden DK	.06	.02	.00
☐ 23	Ellis Burks DK	.08	.03	.01
☐ 24	Pete O'Brien DK	.06	.02	.00
☐ 25	Bryn Smith DK	.06	.02	.00
☐ 26	Ed Whitson DK DP	.06	.02	.00
☐ 27	DK Checklist DP	.06	.01	.00
	(comments on Perez-Steele on back)			
☐ 28	Robin Ventura RR	.65	.25	.06
☐ 29	Todd Zeile RR	.35	.15	.03
☐ 30	Sandy Alomar Jr. RR	.10	.04	.01
☐ 31	Kent Mercker RR	.15	.06	.01
☐ 32	Ben McDonald RR	.75	.30	.07
☐ 33A	Juan Gonzalez RR ERR	4.00	1.75	.40
	(reverse negative)			
☐ 33B	Juan Gonzalez RR COR	2.00	.80	.20
☐ 34	Eric Anthony RR	.17	.07	.01
☐ 35	Mike Fetters RR	.08	.03	.01
☐ 36	Marquis Grissom RR	.45	.18	.04
☐ 37	Greg Vaughn RR	.50	.20	.05
☐ 38	Brian Dubois RR	.10	.04	.01
☐ 39	Steve Avery RR UER	.90	.40	.09
	(born in MI not NJ)			
☐ 40	Mark Gardner RR	.17	.07	.01
☐ 41	Andy Benes RR	.17	.07	.01
☐ 42	Delino DeShields RR	.40	.16	.04
☐ 43	Scott Coolbaugh RR	.10	.04	.01
☐ 44	Pat Combs RR DP	.06	.02	.00
☐ 45	Alex Sanchez RR DP	.06	.02	.00
☐ 46	Kelly Mann RR DP	.06	.02	.00
☐ 47	Julio Machado RR DP	.06	.02	.00
☐ 48	Pete Incaviglia	.06	.02	.00
☐ 49	Shawon Dunston	.08	.03	.01
☐ 50	Jeff Treadway	.03	.01	.00
☐ 51	Jeff Ballard	.03	.01	.00
☐ 52	Claudell Washington	.03	.01	.00
☐ 53	Juan Samuel	.06	.02	.00
☐ 54	John Smiley	.06	.02	.00
☐ 55	Rob Deer	.06	.02	.00
☐ 56	Geno Petralli	.03	.01	.00
☐ 57	Chris Bosio	.03	.01	.00
☐ 58	Carlton Fisk	.12	.05	.01
☐ 59	Kirt Manwaring	.03	.01	.00
☐ 60	Chet Lemon	.03	.01	.00
☐ 61	Bo Jackson	.40	.16	.04
☐ 62	Doyle Alexander	.03	.01	.00
☐ 63	Pedro Guerrero	.08	.03	.01
☐ 64	Allan Anderson	.03	.01	.00
☐ 65	Greg Harris	.03	.01	.00
☐ 66	Mike Greenwell	.12	.05	.01
☐ 67	Walt Weiss	.06	.02	.00
☐ 68	Wade Boggs	.15	.06	.01
☐ 69	Jim Clancy	.03	.01	.00
☐ 70	Junior Felix	.06	.02	.00
☐ 71	Barry Larkin	.12	.05	.01
☐ 72	Dave LaPoint	.03	.01	.00
☐ 73	Joel Skinner	.03	.01	.00
☐ 74	Jesse Barfield	.06	.02	.00
☐ 75	Tommy Herr	.03	.01	.00
☐ 76	Ricky Jordan	.06	.02	.00
☐ 77	Eddie Murray	.10	.04	.01
☐ 78	Steve Sax	.06	.02	.00
☐ 79	Tim Belcher	.06	.02	.00
☐ 80	Danny Jackson	.03	.01	.00
☐ 81	Kent Hrbek	.08	.03	.01
☐ 82	Milt Thompson	.03	.01	.00
☐ 83	Brook Jacoby	.03	.01	.00
☐ 84	Mike Marshall	.06	.02	.00
☐ 85	Kevin Seitzer	.06	.02	.00
☐ 86	Tony Gwynn	.15	.06	.01
☐ 87	Dave Stieb	.08	.03	.01
☐ 88	Dave Smith	.03	.01	.00
☐ 89	Bret Saberhagen	.08	.03	.01
☐ 90	Alan Trammell	.08	.03	.01
☐ 91	Tony Phillips	.03	.01	.00
☐ 92	Doug Drabek	.08	.03	.01
☐ 93	Jeffrey Leonard	.03	.01	.00
☐ 94	Wally Joyner	.08	.03	.01
☐ 95	Carney Lansford	.06	.02	.00
☐ 96	Cal Ripken	.30	.12	.03
☐ 97	Andres Galarraga	.06	.02	.00
☐ 98	Kevin Mitchell	.10	.04	.01
☐ 99	Howard Johnson	.08	.03	.01
☐ 100A	Checklist Card	.06	.01	.00
	(28-129)			
☐ 100B	Checklist Card	.06	.01	.00
	(28-125)			
☐ 101	Melido Perez	.03	.01	.00
☐ 102	Spike Owen	.03	.01	.00
☐ 103	Paul Molitor	.08	.03	.01
☐ 104	Geronimo Berroa	.03	.01	.00
☐ 105	Ryne Sandberg	.30	.12	.03
☐ 106	Bryn Smith	.03	.01	.00
☐ 107	Steve Buechele	.03	.01	.00
☐ 108	Jim Abbott	.17	.07	.01
☐ 109	Alvin Davis	.06	.02	.00
☐ 110	Lee Smith	.06	.02	.00
☐ 111	Roberto Alomar	.15	.06	.01
☐ 112	Rick Reuschel	.06	.02	.00
☐ 113A	Kelly Gruber ERR	.10	.04	.01
	(born 2/22)			
☐ 113B	Kelly Gruber COR	.10	.04	.01
	(born 2/26; corrected in factory sets)			
☐ 114	Joe Carter	.10	.04	.01
☐ 115	Jose Rijo	.08	.03	.01
☐ 116	Greg Minton	.03	.01	.00
☐ 117	Bob Ojeda	.03	.01	.00
☐ 118	Glenn Davis	.08	.03	.01
☐ 119	Jeff Reardon	.06	.02	.00
☐ 120	Kurt Stillwell	.03	.01	.00
☐ 121	John Smoltz	.15	.06	.01
☐ 122	Dwight Evans	.06	.02	.00
☐ 123	Eric Yelding	.06	.02	.00
☐ 124	John Franco	.03	.01	.00
☐ 125	Jose Canseco	.40	.16	.04
☐ 126	Barry Bonds	.17	.07	.01
☐ 127	Lee Guetterman	.03	.01	.00
☐ 128	Jack Clark	.08	.03	.01
☐ 129	Dave Valle	.03	.01	.00
☐ 130	Hubie Brooks	.06	.02	.00
☐ 131	Ernest Riles	.03	.01	.00
☐ 132	Mike Morgan	.06	.02	.00
☐ 133	Steve Jeltz	.03	.01	.00
☐ 134	Jeff Robinson	.03	.01	.00
☐ 135	Ozzie Guillen	.06	.02	.00
☐ 136	Chili Davis	.06	.02	.00
☐ 137	Mitch Webster	.03	.01	.00
☐ 138	Jerry Browne	.03	.01	.00
☐ 139	Bo Diaz	.03	.01	.00
☐ 140	Robby Thompson	.03	.01	.00
☐ 141	Craig Worthington	.03	.01	.00
☐ 142	Julio Franco	.08	.03	.01
☐ 143	Brian Holman	.03	.01	.00
☐ 144	George Brett	.12	.05	.01
☐ 145	Tom Glavine	.20	.08	.02
☐ 146	Robin Yount	.12	.05	.01
☐ 147	Gary Carter	.08	.03	.01
☐ 148	Ron Kittle	.06	.02	.00
☐ 149	Tony Fernandez	.06	.02	.00
☐ 150	Dave Stewart	.08	.03	.01
☐ 151	Gary Gaetti	.06	.02	.00
☐ 152	Kevin Elster	.03	.01	.00
☐ 153	Gerald Perry	.03	.01	.00
☐ 154	Jesse Orosco	.03	.01	.00
☐ 155	Wally Backman	.03	.01	.00
☐ 156	Dennis Martinez	.06	.02	.00
☐ 157	Rick Sutcliffe	.06	.02	.00
☐ 158	Greg Maddux	.06	.02	.00
☐ 159	Andy Hawkins	.03	.01	.00
☐ 160	John Kruk	.03	.01	.00
☐ 161	Jose Oquendo	.03	.01	.00
☐ 162	John Dopson	.03	.01	.00
☐ 163	Joe Magrane	.03	.01	.00
☐ 164	Bill Ripken	.03	.01	.00
☐ 165	Fred Manrique	.03	.01	.00
☐ 166	Nolan Ryan UER	.50	.20	.05
	(Did not lead NL in K's in '89 as he was			

in AL in '89)

#	Player			
☐ 167	Damon Berryhill	.03	.01	.00
☐ 168	Dale Murphy	.10	.04	.01
☐ 169	Mickey Tettleton	.06	.02	.00
☐ 170A	Kirk McCaskill ERR	.06	.02	.00
	(born 4/19)			
☐ 170B	Kirk McCaskill COR	.06	.02	.00
	(born 4/9; corrected			
	in factory sets)			
☐ 171	Dwight Gooden	.10	.04	.01
☐ 172	Jose Lind	.03	.01	.00
☐ 173	B.J. Surhoff	.03	.01	.00
☐ 174	Ruben Sierra	.20	.08	.02
☐ 175	Dan Plesac	.03	.01	.00
☐ 176	Dan Pasqua	.03	.01	.00
☐ 177	Kelly Downs	.03	.01	.00
☐ 178	Matt Nokes	.06	.02	.00
☐ 179	Luis Aquino	.03	.01	.00
☐ 180	Frank Tanana	.06	.02	.00
☐ 181	Tony Pena	.06	.02	.00
☐ 182	Dan Gladden	.03	.01	.00
☐ 183	Bruce Hurst	.06	.02	.00
☐ 184	Roger Clemens	.30	.12	.03
☐ 185	Mark McGwire	.15	.06	.01
☐ 186	Rob Murphy	.03	.01	.00
☐ 187	Jim Deshaies	.03	.01	.00
☐ 188	Fred McGriff	.12	.05	.01
☐ 189	Rob Dibble	.06	.02	.00
☐ 190	Don Mattingly	.20	.08	.02
☐ 191	Felix Fermin	.03	.01	.00
☐ 192	Roberto Kelly	.08	.03	.01
☐ 193	Dennis Cook	.03	.01	.00
☐ 194	Darren Daulton	.06	.02	.00
☐ 195	Alfredo Griffin	.03	.01	.00
☐ 196	Eric Plunk	.03	.01	.00
☐ 197	Orel Hershiser	.08	.03	.01
☐ 198	Paul O'Neill	.06	.02	.00
☐ 199	Randy Bush	.03	.01	.00
☐ 200A	Checklist Card	.06	.01	.00
	(130-231)			
☐ 200B	Checklist Card	.06	.01	.00
	(126-223)			
☐ 201	Ozzie Smith	.12	.05	.01
☐ 202	Pete O'Brien	.03	.01	.00
☐ 203	Jay Howell	.03	.01	.00
☐ 204	Mark Gubicza	.06	.02	.00
☐ 205	Ed Whitson	.03	.01	.00
☐ 206	George Bell	.08	.03	.01
☐ 207	Mike Scott	.08	.03	.01
☐ 208	Charlie Leibrandt	.03	.01	.00
☐ 209	Mike Heath	.03	.01	.00
☐ 210	Dennis Eckersley	.08	.03	.01
☐ 211	Mike LaValliere	.03	.01	.00
☐ 212	Darnell Coles	.03	.01	.00
☐ 213	Lance Parrish	.06	.02	.00
☐ 214	Mike Moore	.06	.02	.00
☐ 215	Steve Finley	.10	.04	.01
☐ 216	Tim Raines	.08	.03	.01
☐ 217A	Scott Garrelts ERR	.06	.02	.00
	(born 10/20)			
☐ 217B	Scott Garrelts COR	.06	.02	.00
	(born 10/30; corrected			
	in factory sets)			
☐ 218	Kevin McReynolds	.08	.03	.01
☐ 219	Dave Gallagher	.03	.01	.00
☐ 220	Tim Wallach	.06	.02	.00
☐ 221	Chuck Crim	.03	.01	.00
☐ 222	Lonnie Smith	.06	.02	.00
☐ 223	Andre Dawson	.10	.04	.01
☐ 224	Nelson Santovenia	.03	.01	.00
☐ 225	Rafael Palmeiro	.12	.05	.01
☐ 226	Devon White	.06	.02	.00
☐ 227	Harold Reynolds	.06	.02	.00
☐ 228	Ellis Burks	.08	.03	.01
☐ 229	Mark Parent	.03	.01	.00
☐ 230	Will Clark	.30	.12	.03
☐ 231	Jimmy Key	.06	.02	.00
☐ 232	John Farrell	.03	.01	.00
☐ 233	Eric Davis	.10	.04	.01
☐ 234	Johnny Ray	.03	.01	.00
☐ 235	Darryl Strawberry	.25	.10	.02
☐ 236	Bill Doran	.03	.01	.00
☐ 237	Greg Gagne	.03	.01	.00
☐ 238	Jim Eisenreich	.03	.01	.00
☐ 239	Tommy Gregg	.03	.01	.00
☐ 240	Marty Barrett	.03	.01	.00
☐ 241	Rafael Ramirez	.03	.01	.00
☐ 242	Chris Sabo	.10	.04	.01
☐ 243	Dave Henderson	.06	.02	.00
☐ 244	Andy Van Slyke	.08	.03	.01
☐ 245	Alvaro Espinoza	.03	.01	.00
☐ 246	Garry Templeton	.03	.01	.00
☐ 247	Gene Harris	.06	.02	.00
☐ 248	Kevin Gross	.03	.01	.00
☐ 249	Brett Butler	.08	.03	.01
☐ 250	Willie Randolph	.06	.02	.00
☐ 251	Roger McDowell	.03	.01	.00
☐ 252	Rafael Belliard	.03	.01	.00
☐ 253	Steve Rosenberg	.03	.01	.00
☐ 254	Jack Howell	.03	.01	.00
☐ 255	Marvell Wynne	.03	.01	.00
☐ 256	Tom Candiotti	.06	.02	.00
☐ 257	Todd Benzinger	.03	.01	.00
☐ 258	Don Robinson	.03	.01	.00
☐ 259	Phil Bradley	.03	.01	.00
☐ 260	Cecil Espy	.03	.01	.00
☐ 261	Scott Bankhead	.06	.02	.00
☐ 262	Frank White	.03	.01	.00
☐ 263	Andres Thomas	.03	.01	.00
☐ 264	Glenn Braggs	.03	.01	.00
☐ 265	David Cone	.06	.02	.00
☐ 266	Bobby Thigpen	.08	.03	.01
☐ 267	Nelson Liriano	.03	.01	.00
☐ 268	Terry Steinbach	.06	.02	.00
☐ 269	Kirby Puckett UER	.20	.08	.02
	(back doesn't consider			
	Joe Torre's .363 in '71)			
☐ 270	Gregg Jefferies	.10	.04	.01
☐ 271	Jeff Blauser	.03	.01	.00
☐ 272	Cory Snyder	.06	.02	.00
☐ 273	Roy Smith	.03	.01	.00
☐ 274	Tom Foley	.03	.01	.00
☐ 275	Mitch Williams	.03	.01	.00
☐ 276	Paul Kilgus	.03	.01	.00
☐ 277	Don Slaught	.03	.01	.00
☐ 278	Von Hayes	.06	.02	.00
☐ 279	Vince Coleman	.08	.03	.01
☐ 280	Mike Boddicker	.03	.01	.00
☐ 281	Ken Dayley	.03	.01	.00
☐ 282	Mike Devereaux	.03	.01	.00
☐ 283	Kenny Rogers	.06	.02	.00
☐ 284	Jeff Russell	.03	.01	.00
☐ 285	Jerome Walton	.08	.03	.01
☐ 286	Derek Lilliquist	.03	.01	.00
☐ 287	Joe Orsulak	.03	.01	.00
☐ 288	Dick Schofield	.03	.01	.00
☐ 289	Ron Darling	.06	.02	.00
☐ 290	Bobby Bonilla	.15	.06	.01
☐ 291	Jim Gantner	.03	.01	.00
☐ 292	Bobby Witt	.06	.02	.00
☐ 293	Greg Brock	.03	.01	.00
☐ 294	Ivan Calderon	.06	.02	.00
☐ 295	Steve Bedrosian	.03	.01	.00
☐ 296	Mike Henneman	.03	.01	.00
☐ 297	Tom Gordon	.08	.03	.01
☐ 298	Lou Whitaker	.08	.03	.01
☐ 299	Terry Pendleton	.08	.03	.01
☐ 300A	Checklist Card	.06	.01	.00
	(232-333)			
☐ 300B	Checklist Card	.06	.01	.00
	(224-321)			
☐ 301	Juan Berenguer	.03	.01	.00
☐ 302	Mark Davis	.06	.02	.00
☐ 303	Nick Esasky	.03	.01	.00
☐ 304	Rickey Henderson	.25	.10	.02
☐ 305	Rick Cerone	.03	.01	.00
☐ 306	Craig Biggio	.10	.04	.01
☐ 307	Duane Ward	.03	.01	.00
☐ 308	Tom Browning	.06	.02	.00
☐ 309	Walt Terrell	.03	.01	.00
☐ 310	Greg Swindell	.06	.02	.00
☐ 311	Dave Righetti	.06	.02	.00
☐ 312	Mike Maddux	.03	.01	.00
☐ 313	Len Dykstra	.08	.03	.01
☐ 314	Jose Gonzalez	.03	.01	.00
☐ 315	Steve Balboni	.03	.01	.00
☐ 316	Mike Scioscia	.03	.01	.00
☐ 317	Ron Oester	.03	.01	.00
☐ 318	Gary Wayne	.06	.02	.00
☐ 319	Todd Worrell	.03	.01	.00
☐ 320	Doug Jones	.03	.01	.00
☐ 321	Jeff Hamilton	.03	.01	.00
☐ 322	Danny Tartabull	.08	.03	.01
☐ 323	Chris James	.03	.01	.00
☐ 324	Mike Flanagan	.03	.01	.00
☐ 325	Gerald Young	.03	.01	.00
☐ 326	Bob Boone	.06	.02	.00
☐ 327	Frank Williams	.03	.01	.00
☐ 328	Dave Parker	.08	.03	.01
☐ 329	Sid Bream	.03	.01	.00
☐ 330	Mike Schooler	.03	.01	.00
☐ 331	Bert Blyleven	.08	.03	.01
☐ 332	Bob Welch	.08	.03	.01
☐ 333	Bob Milacki	.03	.01	.00
☐ 334	Tim Burke	.03	.01	.00
☐ 335	Jose Uribe	.03	.01	.00
☐ 336	Randy Myers	.03	.01	.00
☐ 337	Eric King	.03	.01	.00

☐ 338	Mark Langston	.08	.03	.01
☐ 339	Teddy Higuera	.03	.01	.00
☐ 340	Oddibe McDowell	.03	.01	.00
☐ 341	Lloyd McClendon	.03	.01	.00
☐ 342	Pascual Perez	.03	.01	.00
☐ 343	Kevin Brown	.06	.02	.00
	(signed is misspelled			
	as signeed on back)			
☐ 344	Chuck Finley	.08	.03	.01
☐ 345	Erik Hanson	.08	.03	.01
☐ 346	Rich Gedman	.03	.01	.00
☐ 347	Bip Roberts	.03	.01	.00
☐ 348	Matt Williams	.15	.06	.01
☐ 349	Tom Henke	.06	.02	.00
☐ 350	Brad Komminsk	.03	.01	.00
☐ 351	Jeff Reed	.03	.01	.00
☐ 352	Brian Downing	.03	.01	.00
☐ 353	Frank Viola	.08	.03	.01
☐ 354	Terry Puhl	.03	.01	.00
☐ 355	Brian Harper	.06	.02	.00
☐ 356	Steve Farr	.03	.01	.00
☐ 357	Joe Boever	.03	.01	.00
☐ 358	Danny Heep	.03	.01	.00
☐ 359	Larry Andersen	.03	.01	.00
☐ 360	Rolando Roomes	.03	.01	.00
☐ 361	Mike Gallego	.03	.01	.00
☐ 362	Bob Kipper	.03	.01	.00
☐ 363	Clay Parker	.03	.01	.00
☐ 364	Mike Pagliarulo	.03	.01	.00
☐ 365	Ken Griffey Jr. UER	1.50	.60	.15
	(signed through 1990,			
	should be 1991)			
☐ 366	Rex Hudler	.03	.01	.00
☐ 367	Pat Sheridan	.03	.01	.00
☐ 368	Kirk Gibson	.08	.03	.01
☐ 369	Jeff Parrett	.03	.01	.00
☐ 370	Bob Walk	.03	.01	.00
☐ 371	Ken Patterson	.03	.01	.00
☐ 372	Bryan Harvey	.03	.01	.00
☐ 373	Mike Bielecki	.03	.01	.00
☐ 374	Tom Magrann	.08	.03	.01
☐ 375	Rick Mahler	.03	.01	.00
☐ 376	Craig Lefferts	.03	.01	.00
☐ 377	Gregg Olson	.12	.05	.01
☐ 378	Jamie Moyer	.03	.01	.00
☐ 379	Randy Johnson	.06	.02	.00
☐ 380	Jeff Montgomery	.03	.01	.00
☐ 381	Marty Clary	.03	.01	.00
☐ 382	Bill Spiers	.06	.02	.00
☐ 383	Dave Magadan	.06	.02	.00
☐ 384	Greg Hibbard	.15	.06	.01
☐ 385	Ernie Whitt	.03	.01	.00
☐ 386	Rick Honeycutt	.03	.01	.00
☐ 387	Dave West	.03	.01	.00
☐ 388	Keith Hernandez	.06	.02	.00
☐ 389	Jose Alvarez	.03	.01	.00
☐ 390	Joey Belle	.60	.25	.06
☐ 391	Rick Aguilera	.06	.02	.00
☐ 392	Mike Fitzgerald	.03	.01	.00
☐ 393	Dwight Smith	.06	.02	.00
☐ 394	Steve Wilson	.06	.02	.00
☐ 395	Bob Geren	.06	.02	.00
☐ 396	Randy Ready	.03	.01	.00
☐ 397	Ken Hill	.03	.01	.00
☐ 398	Jody Reed	.06	.02	.00
☐ 399	Tom Brunansky	.06	.02	.00
☐ 400A	Checklist Card	.06	.01	.00
	(334-435)			
☐ 400B	Checklist Card	.06	.01	.00
	(322-419)			
☐ 401	Rene Gonzales	.03	.01	.00
☐ 402	Harold Baines	.08	.03	.01
☐ 403	Cecilio Guante	.03	.01	.00
☐ 404	Joe Girardi	.06	.02	.00
☐ 405A	Sergio Valdez ERR	.30	.12	.03
	(card front shows			
	black line crossing			
	S in Sergio)			
☐ 405B	Sergio Valdez COR	.10	.04	.01
☐ 406	Mark Williamson	.03	.01	.00
☐ 407	Glenn Hoffman	.03	.01	.00
☐ 408	Jeff Innis	.08	.03	.01
☐ 409	Randy Kramer	.03	.01	.00
☐ 410	Charlie O'Brien	.03	.01	.00
☐ 411	Charlie Hough	.03	.01	.00
☐ 412	Gus Polidor	.03	.01	.00
☐ 413	Ron Karkovice	.03	.01	.00
☐ 414	Trevor Wilson	.10	.04	.01
☐ 415	Kevin Ritz	.10	.04	.01
☐ 416	Gary Thurman	.03	.01	.00
☐ 417	Jeff Robinson	.03	.01	.00
☐ 418	Scott Terry	.03	.01	.00
☐ 419	Tim Laudner	.03	.01	.00
☐ 420	Dennis Rasmussen	.03	.01	.00
☐ 421	Luis Rivera	.03	.01	.00
☐ 422	Jim Corsi	.03	.01	.00
☐ 423	Dennis Lamp	.03	.01	.00
☐ 424	Ken Caminiti	.03	.01	.00
☐ 425	David Wells	.03	.01	.00
☐ 426	Norm Charlton	.03	.01	.00
☐ 427	Deion Sanders	.15	.06	.01
☐ 428	Dion James	.03	.01	.00
☐ 429	Chuck Cary	.03	.01	.00
☐ 430	Ken Howell	.03	.01	.00
☐ 431	Steve Lake	.03	.01	.00
☐ 432	Kal Daniels	.06	.02	.00
☐ 433	Lance McCullers	.03	.01	.00
☐ 434	Lenny Harris	.06	.02	.00
☐ 435	Scott Scudder	.12	.05	.01
☐ 436	Gene Larkin	.03	.01	.00
☐ 437	Dan Quisenberry	.06	.02	.00
☐ 438	Steve Olin	.08	.03	.01
☐ 439	Mickey Hatcher	.03	.01	.00
☐ 440	Willie Wilson	.06	.02	.00
☐ 441	Mark Grant	.03	.01	.00
☐ 442	Mookie Wilson	.03	.01	.00
☐ 443	Alex Trevino	.03	.01	.00
☐ 444	Pat Tabler	.03	.01	.00
☐ 445	Dave Bergman	.03	.01	.00
☐ 446	Todd Burns	.03	.01	.00
☐ 447	R.J. Reynolds	.03	.01	.00
☐ 448	Jay Buhner	.08	.03	.01
☐ 449	Lee Stevens	.15	.06	.01
☐ 450	Ron Hassey	.03	.01	.00
☐ 451	Bob Melvin	.03	.01	.00
☐ 452	Dave Martinez	.03	.01	.00
☐ 453	Greg Litton	.06	.02	.00
☐ 454	Mark Carreon	.03	.01	.00
☐ 455	Scott Fletcher	.03	.01	.00
☐ 456	Otis Nixon	.06	.02	.00
☐ 457	Tony Fossas	.03	.01	.00
☐ 458	John Russell	.03	.01	.00
☐ 459	Paul Assenmacher	.03	.01	.00
☐ 460	Zane Smith	.06	.02	.00
☐ 461	Jack Daugherty	.06	.02	.00
☐ 462	Rich Monteleone	.06	.02	.00
☐ 463	Greg Briley	.06	.02	.00
☐ 464	Mike Smithson	.03	.01	.00
☐ 465	Benito Santiago	.08	.03	.01
☐ 466	Jeff Brantley	.08	.03	.01
☐ 467	Jose Nunez	.03	.01	.00
☐ 468	Scott Bailes	.03	.01	.00
☐ 469	Ken Griffey Sr.	.08	.03	.01
☐ 470	Bob McClure	.03	.01	.00
☐ 471	Mackey Sasser	.03	.01	.00
☐ 472	Glenn Wilson	.03	.01	.00
☐ 473	Kevin Tapani	.30	.12	.03
☐ 474	Bill Buckner	.06	.02	.00
☐ 475	Ron Gant	.25	.10	.02
☐ 476	Kevin Romine	.03	.01	.00
☐ 477	Juan Agosto	.03	.01	.00
☐ 478	Herm Winningham	.03	.01	.00
☐ 479	Storm Davis	.03	.01	.00
☐ 480	Jeff King	.06	.02	.00
☐ 481	Kevin Mmahat	.10	.04	.01
☐ 482	Carmelo Martinez	.03	.01	.00
☐ 483	Omar Vizquel	.03	.01	.00
☐ 484	Jim Dwyer	.03	.01	.00
☐ 485	Bob Knepper	.03	.01	.00
☐ 486	Dave Anderson	.03	.01	.00
☐ 487	Ron Jones	.03	.01	.00
☐ 488	Jay Bell	.03	.01	.00
☐ 489	Sammy Sosa	.25	.10	.02
☐ 490	Kent Anderson	.06	.02	.00
☐ 491	Domingo Ramos	.03	.01	.00
☐ 492	Dave Clark	.03	.01	.00
☐ 493	Tim Birtsas	.03	.01	.00
☐ 494	Ken Oberkfell	.03	.01	.00
☐ 495	Larry Sheets	.03	.01	.00
☐ 496	Jeff Kunkel	.03	.01	.00
☐ 497	Jim Presley	.03	.01	.00
☐ 498	Mike Macfarlane	.03	.01	.00
☐ 499	Pete Smith	.03	.01	.00
☐ 500A	Checklist Card DP	.06	.01	.00
	(436-537)			
☐ 500B	Checklist Card	.06	.01	.00
	(420-517)			
☐ 501	Gary Sheffield	.08	.03	.01
☐ 502	Terry Bross	.10	.04	.01
☐ 503	Jerry Kutzler	.08	.03	.01
☐ 504	Lloyd Moseby	.03	.01	.00
☐ 505	Curt Young	.03	.01	.00
☐ 506	Al Newman	.03	.01	.00
☐ 507	Keith Miller	.03	.01	.00
☐ 508	Mike Stanton	.08	.03	.01
☐ 509	Rich Yett	.03	.01	.00
☐ 510	Tim Drummond	.08	.03	.01
☐ 511	Joe Hesketh	.06	.02	.00

#	Player			
☐ 512	Rick Wrona	.06	.02	.00
☐ 513	Luis Salazar	.03	.01	.00
☐ 514	Hal Morris	.25	.10	.02
☐ 515	Terry Mulholland	.06	.02	.00
☐ 516	John Morris	.03	.01	.00
☐ 517	Carlos Quintana	.08	.03	.01
☐ 518	Frank DiPino	.03	.01	.00
☐ 519	Randy Milligan	.06	.02	.00
☐ 520	Chad Kreuter	.03	.01	.00
☐ 521	Mike Jeffcoat	.03	.01	.00
☐ 522	Mike Harkey	.06	.02	.00
☐ 523A	Andy Nezelek ERR (wrong birth year)	.17	.07	.01
☐ 523B	Andy Nezelek COR (finally corrected in factory sets)	.06	.02	.00
☐ 524	Dave Schmidt	.03	.01	.00
☐ 525	Tony Armas	.03	.01	.00
☐ 526	Barry Lyons	.03	.01	.00
☐ 527	Rick Reed	.08	.03	.01
☐ 528	Jerry Reuss	.03	.01	.00
☐ 529	Dean Palmer	.75	.30	.07
☐ 530	Jeff Peterek	.10	.04	.01
☐ 531	Carlos Martinez	.06	.02	.00
☐ 532	Atlee Hammaker	.03	.01	.00
☐ 533	Mike Brumley	.03	.01	.00
☐ 534	Terry Leach	.03	.01	.00
☐ 535	Doug Strange	.08	.03	.01
☐ 536	Jose DeLeon	.03	.01	.00
☐ 537	Shane Rawley	.03	.01	.00
☐ 538	Joey Cora	.03	.01	.00
☐ 539	Eric Hetzel	.03	.01	.00
☐ 540	Gene Nelson	.03	.01	.00
☐ 541	Wes Gardner	.03	.01	.00
☐ 542	Mark Portugal	.03	.01	.00
☐ 543	Al Leiter	.03	.01	.00
☐ 544	Jack Armstrong	.06	.02	.00
☐ 545	Greg Cadaret	.03	.01	.00
☐ 546	Rod Nichols	.03	.01	.00
☐ 547	Luis Polonia	.03	.01	.00
☐ 548	Charlie Hayes	.06	.02	.00
☐ 549	Dickie Thon	.03	.01	.00
☐ 550	Tim Crews	.03	.01	.00
☐ 551	Dave Winfield	.10	.04	.01
☐ 552	Mike Davis	.03	.01	.00
☐ 553	Ron Robinson	.03	.01	.00
☐ 554	Carmen Castillo	.03	.01	.00
☐ 555	John Costello	.03	.01	.00
☐ 556	Bud Black	.03	.01	.00
☐ 557	Rick Dempsey	.03	.01	.00
☐ 558	Jim Acker	.03	.01	.00
☐ 559	Eric Show	.03	.01	.00
☐ 560	Pat Borders	.03	.01	.00
☐ 561	Danny Darwin	.03	.01	.00
☐ 562	Rick Luecken	.08	.03	.01
☐ 563	Edwin Nunez	.03	.01	.00
☐ 564	Felix Jose	.20	.08	.02
☐ 565	John Cangelosi	.03	.01	.00
☐ 566	Bill Swift	.03	.01	.00
☐ 567	Bill Schroeder	.03	.01	.00
☐ 568	Stan Javier	.03	.01	.00
☐ 569	Jim Traber	.03	.01	.00
☐ 570	Wallace Johnson	.03	.01	.00
☐ 571	Donell Nixon	.03	.01	.00
☐ 572	Sid Fernandez	.06	.02	.00
☐ 573	Lance Johnson	.03	.01	.00
☐ 574	Andy McGaffigan	.03	.01	.00
☐ 575	Mark Knudson	.03	.01	.00
☐ 576	Tommy Greene	.25	.10	.02
☐ 577	Mark Grace	.12	.05	.01
☐ 578	Larry Walker	.25	.10	.02
☐ 579	Mike Stanley	.03	.01	.00
☐ 580	Mike Witt DP	.03	.01	.00
☐ 581	Scott Bradley	.03	.01	.00
☐ 582	Greg Harris	.03	.01	.00
☐ 583A	Kevin Hickey ERR	.17	.07	.01
☐ 583B	Kevin Hickey COR	.06	.02	.00
☐ 584	Lee Mazzilli	.03	.01	.00
☐ 585	Jeff Pico	.03	.01	.00
☐ 586	Joe Oliver	.08	.03	.01
☐ 587	Willie Fraser DP	.03	.01	.00
☐ 588	Carl Yastrzemski PUZ Puzzle Card DP	.06	.02	.00
☐ 589	Kevin Bass DP	.03	.01	.00
☐ 590	John Moses DP	.03	.01	.00
☐ 591	Tom Pagnozzi DP	.03	.01	.00
☐ 592	Tony Castillo DP	.03	.01	.00
☐ 593	Jerald Clark DP	.03	.01	.00
☐ 594	Dan Schatzeder	.03	.01	.00
☐ 595	Luis Quinones DP	.03	.01	.00
☐ 596	Pete Harnisch DP	.03	.01	.00
☐ 597	Gary Redus	.03	.01	.00
☐ 598	Mel Hall	.06	.02	.00
☐ 599	Rick Schu	.03	.01	.00
☐ 600A	Checklist Card (538-639)	.06	.01	.00
☐ 600B	Checklist Card (518-617)	.06	.01	.00
☐ 601	Mike Kingery DP	.03	.01	.00
☐ 602	Terry Kennedy DP	.03	.01	.00
☐ 603	Mike Sharperson DP	.03	.01	.00
☐ 604	Don Carman DP	.03	.01	.00
☐ 605	Jim Gott	.03	.01	.00
☐ 606	Donn Pall DP	.03	.01	.00
☐ 607	Rance Mulliniks	.03	.01	.00
☐ 608	Curt Wilkerson DP	.03	.01	.00
☐ 609	Mike Felder DP	.03	.01	.00
☐ 610	Guillermo Hernandez DP	.03	.01	.00
☐ 611	Candy Maldonado DP	.03	.01	.00
☐ 612	Mark Thurmond DP	.03	.01	.00
☐ 613	Rick Leach DP	.03	.01	.00
☐ 614	Jerry Reed DP	.03	.01	.00
☐ 615	Franklin Stubbs	.03	.01	.00
☐ 616	Billy Hatcher DP	.03	.01	.00
☐ 617	Don August DP	.03	.01	.00
☐ 618	Tim Teufel	.03	.01	.00
☐ 619	Shawn Hillegas DP	.03	.01	.00
☐ 620	Manny Lee	.03	.01	.00
☐ 621	Ward Ward DP	.03	.01	.00
☐ 622	Mark Guthrie DP	.06	.02	.00
☐ 623	Jeff Musselman DP	.03	.01	.00
☐ 624	Mark Lemke DP	.06	.02	.00
☐ 625	Fernando Valenzuela	.08	.03	.01
☐ 626	Paul Sorrento DP	.10	.04	.01
☐ 627	Glenallen Hill DP	.06	.02	.00
☐ 628	Les Lancaster DP	.03	.01	.00
☐ 629	Vance Law DP	.03	.01	.00
☐ 630	Randy Velarde DP	.03	.01	.00
☐ 631	Todd Frohwirth DP	.03	.01	.00
☐ 632	Willie McGee	.08	.03	.01
☐ 633	Dennis Boyd DP	.03	.01	.00
☐ 634	Cris Carpenter DP	.03	.01	.00
☐ 635	Brian Holton	.03	.01	.00
☐ 636	Tracy Jones DP	.03	.01	.00
☐ 637A	Terry Steinbach AS (Recent Major League Performance)	.10	.04	.01
☐ 637B	Terry Steinbach AS (All-Star Game Performance)	.06	.02	.00
☐ 638	Brady Anderson	.03	.01	.00
☐ 639A	Jack Morris ERR (card front shows black line crossing J in Jack)	.30	.12	.03
☐ 639B	Jack Morris COR	.08	.03	.01
☐ 640	Jaime Navarro	.08	.03	.01
☐ 641	Darrin Jackson	.06	.02	.00
☐ 642	Mike Dyer	.10	.04	.01
☐ 643	Mike Schmidt	.25	.10	.02
☐ 644	Henry Cotto	.03	.01	.00
☐ 645	John Cerutti	.03	.01	.00
☐ 646	Francisco Cabrera	.10	.04	.01
☐ 647	Scott Sanderson	.03	.01	.00
☐ 648	Brian Meyer	.03	.01	.00
☐ 649	Ray Searage	.03	.01	.00
☐ 650A	Bo Jackson AS (Recent Major League Performance)	.30	.12	.03
☐ 650B	Bo Jackson AS (All-Star Game Performance)	.17	.07	.01
☐ 651	Steve Lyons	.03	.01	.00
☐ 652	Mike LaCoss	.03	.01	.00
☐ 653	Ted Power	.03	.01	.00
☐ 654A	Howard Johnson AS (Recent Major League Performance)	.12	.05	.01
☐ 654B	Howard Johnson AS (All-Star Game Performance)	.08	.03	.01
☐ 655	Mauro Gozzo	.10	.04	.01
☐ 656	Mike Blowers	.10	.04	.01
☐ 657	Paul Gibson	.03	.01	.00
☐ 658	Neal Heaton	.03	.01	.00
☐ 659A	Nolan Ryan 5000K (665 King of Kings back) ERR	6.00	2.50	.60
☐ 659B	Nolan Ryan 5000K COR (still an error as Ryan did not lead AL in K's in '75)	.75	.30	.07
☐ 660A	Harold Baines AS (black line through star on front; Recent Major League Performance)	4.00	1.75	.40
☐ 660B	Harold Baines AS	6.00	2.50	.60

(black line through star on front; All-Star Game Performance)			
☐ 660C Harold Baines AS (black line behind star on front; Recent Major League Performance)	2.00	.80	.20
☐ 660D Harold Baines AS (black line behind star on front; All-Star Game Performance)	.08	.03	.01
☐ 661 Gary Pettis	.03	.01	.00
☐ 662 Clint Zavaras	.08	.03	.01
☐ 663A Rick Reuschel AS (Recent Major League Performance)	.10	.04	.01
☐ 663B Rick Reuschel AS (All-Star Game Performance)	.06	.02	.00
☐ 664 Alejandro Pena	.06	.02	.00
☐ 665A Nolan Ryan KING (659 5000 K back) ERR	6.00	2.50	.60
☐ 665B Nolan Ryan KING COR	.75	.30	.07
☐ 665C Nolan Ryan KING ERR (no number on back; in factory sets)	2.50	1.00	.25
☐ 666 Ricky Horton	.03	.01	.00
☐ 667 Curt Schilling	.03	.01	.00
☐ 668 Bill Landrum	.03	.01	.00
☐ 669 Todd Stottlemyre	.08	.03	.01
☐ 670 Tim Leary	.06	.02	.00
☐ 671 John Wetteland	.08	.03	.01
☐ 672 Calvin Schiraldi	.03	.01	.00
☐ 673A Ruben Sierra AS (Recent Major League Performance)	.17	.07	.01
☐ 673B Ruben Sierra AS (All-Star Game Performance)	.12	.05	.01
☐ 674A Pedro Guerrero AS (Recent Major League Performance)	.10	.04	.01
☐ 674B Pedro Guerrero AS (All-Star Game Performance)	.06	.02	.00
☐ 675 Ken Phelps	.03	.01	.00
☐ 676A Cal Ripken AS (Recent Major League Performance)	.25	.10	.02
☐ 676B Cal Ripken AS (All-Star Game Performance)	.15	.06	.01
☐ 677 Denny Walling	.03	.01	.00
☐ 678 Goose Gossage	.06	.02	.00
☐ 679 Gary Mielke	.08	.03	.01
☐ 680 Bill Bathe	.03	.01	.00
☐ 681 Tom Lawless	.03	.01	.00
☐ 682 Xavier Hernandez	.08	.03	.01
☐ 683A Kirby Puckett AS (Recent Major League Performance)	.17	.07	.01
☐ 683B Kirby Puckett AS (All-Star Game Performance)	.12	.05	.01
☐ 684 Mariano Duncan	.03	.01	.00
☐ 685 Ramon Martinez	.25	.10	.02
☐ 686 Tim Jones	.03	.01	.00
☐ 687 Tom Filer	.03	.01	.00
☐ 688 Steve Lombardozzi	.03	.01	.00
☐ 689 Bernie Williams	.50	.20	.05
☐ 690 Chip Hale	.08	.03	.01
☐ 691 Beau Allred	.12	.05	.01
☐ 692A Ryne Sandberg AS (Recent Major League Performance)	.20	.08	.02
☐ 692B Ryne Sandberg AS (All-Star Game Performance)	.15	.06	.01
☐ 693 Jeff Huson	.08	.03	.01
☐ 694 Curt Ford	.03	.01	.00
☐ 695A Eric Davis AS (Recent Major League Performance)	.15	.06	.01
☐ 695B Eric Davis AS (All-Star Game Performance)	.10	.04	.01
☐ 696 Scott Lusader	.03	.01	.00
☐ 697A Mark McGwire AS (Recent Major League Performance)	.15	.06	.01

☐ 697B Mark McGwire AS (All-Star Game Performance)	.10	.04	.01
☐ 698 Steve Cummings	.08	.03	.01
☐ 699 George Canale	.10	.04	.01
☐ 700A Checklist Card (640-715/BC1-BC26)	.50	.10	.02
☐ 700B Checklist Card (640-716/BC1-BC26)	.10	.01	.00
☐ 700C Checklist Card (618-716)	.10	.01	.00
☐ 701A Julio Franco AS (Recent Major League Performance)	.12	.05	.01
☐ 701B Julio Franco AS (All-Star Game Performance)	.08	.03	.01
☐ 702 Dave Johnson (P)	.08	.03	.01
☐ 703A Dave Stewart AS (Recent Major League Performance)	.10	.04	.01
☐ 703B Dave Stewart AS (All-Star Game Performance)	.06	.02	.00
☐ 704 Dave Justice	2.50	1.00	.25
☐ 705A Tony Gwynn AS (Recent Major League Performance)	.17	.07	.01
☐ 705B Tony Gwynn AS (All-Star Game Performance)	.12	.05	.01
☐ 706 Greg Myers	.03	.01	.00
☐ 707A Will Clark AS (Recent Major League Performance)	.25	.10	.02
☐ 707B Will Clark AS (All-Star Game Performance)	.15	.06	.01
☐ 708A Benito Santiago AS (Recent Major League Performance)	.10	.04	.01
☐ 708B Benito Santiago AS (All-Star Game Performance)	.06	.02	.00
☐ 709 Larry McWilliams	.03	.01	.00
☐ 710A Ozzie Smith AS (Recent Major League Performance)	.12	.05	.01
☐ 710B Ozzie Smith AS (All-Star Game Performance)	.08	.03	.01
☐ 711 John Olerud	1.00	.40	.10
☐ 712A Wade Boggs AS (Recent Major League Performance)	.17	.07	.01
☐ 712B Wade Boggs AS (All-Star Game Performance)	.12	.05	.01
☐ 713 Gary Eave	.08	.03	.01
☐ 714 Bob Tewksbury	.03	.01	.00
☐ 715A Kevin Mitchell AS (Recent Major League Performance)	.12	.05	.01
☐ 715B Kevin Mitchell AS (All-Star Game Performance)	.08	.03	.01
☐ 716 Bart Giamatti	.15	.06	.01

1990 Donruss Bonus MVP's

The 1990 Donruss Bonus MVP's set contains 26 standard-size (2 1/2" by 3 1/2") cards. The front borders are bright red. The horizontally oriented backs are amber. These cards were randomly distributed in all 1990 Donruss unopened pack formats. The selection of players in the set is Donruss' opinion of each team's MVP. The complete price below does not include any variation cards. These Bonus MVP cards were printed with and distributed with the Donruss regular issue cards.

	MINT	EXC	G-VG
COMPLETE SET (26)	2.50	1.00	.25
COMMON CARD (BC1-BC26)	.05	.02	.00

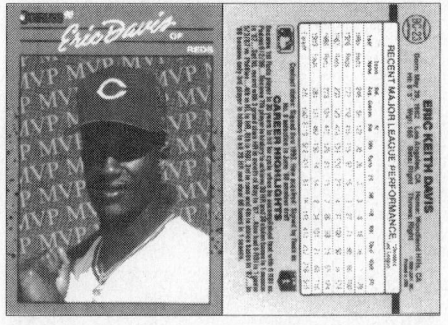

☐ 1	Matt Williams	.30	.12	.03
☐ 2	Jeffrey Leonard	.10	.04	.01
☐ 3	Chris James	.10	.04	.01
☐ 4	Mark McGwire	.50	.20	.05
☐ 5	Dwight Evans	.15	.06	.01
☐ 6	Will Clark	.75	.30	.07
☐ 7	Mike Scioscia	.10	.04	.01
☐ 8	Todd Benzinger	.10	.04	.01
☐ 9	Fred McGriff	.30	.12	.03
☐ 10	Kevin Bass	.10	.04	.01
☐ 11	Jack Clark	.20	.08	.02
☐ 12	Bo Jackson	.90	.40	.09

1990 Donruss Super DK's

☐ BC1	Bo Jackson	.25	.10	.02
☐ BC2	Howard Johnson	.08	.03	.01
☐ BC3	Dave Stewart	.08	.03	.01
☐ BC4	Tony Gwynn	.10	.04	.01
☐ BC5	Orel Hershiser	.08	.03	.01
☐ BC6	Pedro Guerrero	.08	.03	.01
☐ BC7	Tim Raines	.08	.03	.01
☐ BC8	Kirby Puckett	.10	.04	.01
☐ BC9	Alvin Davis	.05	.02	.00
☐ BC10	Ryne Sandberg	.12	.05	.01
☐ BC11	Kevin Mitchell	.08	.03	.01
☐ BC12A	John Smoltz ERR	.25	.10	.02
	(photo actually			
	Tom Glavine)			
☐ BC12B	John Smoltz COR	1.00	.40	.10
☐ BC13	George Bell	.08	.03	.01
☐ BC14	Julio Franco	.08	.03	.01
☐ BC15	Paul Molitor	.08	.03	.01
☐ BC16	Bobby Bonilla	.10	.04	.01
☐ BC17	Mike Greenwell	.08	.03	.01
☐ BC18	Cal Ripken	.15	.06	.01
☐ BC19	Carlton Fisk	.08	.03	.01
☐ BC20	Chili Davis	.05	.02	.00
☐ BC21	Glenn Davis	.08	.03	.01
☐ BC22	Steve Sax	.08	.03	.01
☐ BC23	Eric Davis DP	.08	.03	.01
☐ BC24	Greg Swindell DP	.05	.02	.00
☐ BC25	Von Hayes DP	.05	.02	.00
☐ BC26	Alan Trammell	.08	.03	.01

1990 Donruss Grand Slammers

This 12-card standard size 2 1/2" by 3 1/2" set was in the 1990 Donruss set as a special card deliniating each 55-card section of the 1990 Factory Set. This set honors those players who connected for grand slam homers during the 1989 season. The cards are in the 1990 Donruss design and the back describes the grand slam homer hit by each player.

	MINT	EXC	G-VG
COMPLETE SET (12)	2.50	1.00	.25
COMMON PLAYER (1-12)	.10	.04	.01

This 26-player card set was available through a mail-in offer detailed on the wax packs. The set was sent in return for 10.00 and three wrappers plus 2.00 postage and handling. The set features the popular Diamond King subseries in large (approximately 4 7/8" by 6 13/16") form. Dick Perez of Perez-Steele Galleries did another outstanding job on the artwork. The cards are essentially a large version of the Donruss regular issue Diamond Kings.

	MINT	EXC	G-VG
COMPLETE SET (26)	9.00	4.00	.90
COMMON PLAYER (1-26)	.20	.08	.02

☐ 1	Bo Jackson DK	1.00	.40	.10
☐ 2	Steve Sax DK	.35	.15	.03
☐ 3	Ruben Sierra DK	.60	.25	.06
☐ 4	Ken Griffey Jr. DK	1.50	.60	.15
☐ 5	Mickey Tettleton DK	.30	.12	.03
☐ 6	Dave Stewart DK	.30	.12	.03
☐ 7	Jim Deshaies DK	.20	.08	.02
☐ 8	John Smoltz DK	.40	.16	.04
☐ 9	Mike Bielecki DK	.20	.08	.02
☐ 10	Brian Downing DK	.20	.08	.02
☐ 11	Kevin Mitchell DK	.45	.18	.04
☐ 12	Kelly Gruber DK	.35	.15	.03
☐ 13	Joe Magrane DK	.25	.10	.02
☐ 14	John Franco DK	.25	.10	.02
☐ 15	Ozzie Guillen DK	.30	.12	.03
☐ 16	Lou Whitaker DK	.30	.12	.03
☐ 17	John Smiley DK	.30	.12	.03
☐ 18	Howard Johnson DK	.35	.15	.03
☐ 19	Willie Randolph DK	.20	.08	.02
☐ 20	Chris Bosio DK	.20	.08	.02
☐ 21	Tommy Herr DK	.20	.08	.02
☐ 22	Dan Gladden DK	.20	.08	.02
☐ 23	Ellis Burks DK	.45	.18	.04
☐ 24	Pete O'Brien DK	.20	.08	.02
☐ 25	Bryn Smith DK	.20	.08	.02
☐ 26	Ed Whitson DK	.20	.08	.02

1990 Donruss Learning Series

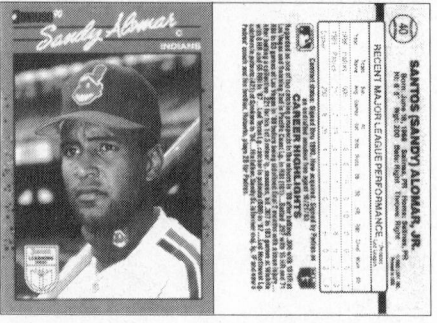

The 1990 Donruss Learning Series consists of 55 standard-size (2 1/2" by 3 1/2") cards that served as part of an educational packet for elementary and middle school students. The cards were issued in two formats. Grades 3 and 4 received the cards, a historical timeline that relates events in baseball to major historical events, additional Donruss cards from wax packs, and a teacher's guide that focused on several academic subjects. Grades 5 through 8 received the cards, a teacher's guide designed for older students, and a 14-minute video shot at Chicago's Wrigley Field. The fronts feature color head shots of the players and bright red borders. The horizontally oriented backs are amber and present biography, statistics, and career highlights. The cards are numbered on the back.

	MINT	EXC	G-VG
COMPLETE SET (55)	90.00	40.00	12.00
COMMON PLAYER (1-55)	.50	.20	.05
☐ 1 George Brett DK	3.00	1.20	.30
☐ 2 Kevin Mitchell	2.50	1.00	.25
☐ 3 Andy Van Slyke	.75	.30	.07
☐ 4 Benito Santiago	1.00	.40	.07
☐ 5 Gary Carter	1.00	.40	.07
☐ 6 Jose Canseco	7.50	3.00	.75
☐ 7 Rickey Henderson	7.50	3.00	.75
☐ 8 Ken Griffey Jr.	13.50	5.50	.90
☐ 9 Ozzie Smith	2.50	1.00	.20
☐ 10 Dwight Gooden	2.50	1.00	.20
☐ 11 Ryne Sandberg DK	6.00	2.50	.50
☐ 12 Don Mattingly	5.00	2.00	.45
☐ 13 Ozzie Guillen	.60	.25	.06
☐ 14 Dave Righetti	.60	.25	.06
☐ 15 Rick Dempsey	.50	.20	.05
☐ 16 Tom Herr	.50	.20	.05
☐ 17 Julio Franco	.75	.30	.07
☐ 18 Von Hayes	.60	.25	.06
☐ 19 Cal Ripken	7.50	3.00	.65
☐ 20 Alan Trammell	1.50	.60	.12
☐ 21 Wade Boggs	5.00	2.00	.45
☐ 22 Glenn Davis	1.00	.40	.10
☐ 23 Will Clark	7.50	3.00	.65
☐ 24 Nolan Ryan	16.00	6.50	1.75
☐ 25 George Bell	1.00	.40	.08
☐ 26 Cecil Fielder	4.00	1.75	.35
☐ 27 Gregg Olson	1.00	.40	.08
☐ 28 Tim Wallach	.50	.20	.05
☐ 29 Ron Darling	.50	.20	.05
☐ 30 Kelly Gruber	.75	.30	.07
☐ 31 Shawn Boskie	.50	.20	.05
☐ 32 Mike Greenwell	2.50	1.00	.25
☐ 33 Dave Parker	1.00	.40	.08
☐ 34 Joe Magrane	.50	.20	.05
☐ 35 Dave Stewart	1.00	.40	.08
☐ 36 Kent Hrbek	.60	.25	.06
☐ 37 Robin Yount	3.00	1.20	.30
☐ 38 Bo Jackson	7.50	3.00	.75
☐ 39 Fernando Valenzuela	.60	.25	.06
☐ 40 Sandy Alomar Jr.	1.00	.40	.10
☐ 41 Lance Parrish	.60	.25	.06
☐ 42 Candy Maldonado	.50	.20	.05
☐ 43 Mike LaValliere	.50	.20	.05
☐ 44 Jim Abbott	2.00	.80	.20
☐ 45 Edgar Martinez	.75	.30	.07
☐ 46 Kirby Puckett	4.00	1.75	.35
☐ 47 Delino DeShields	1.00	.40	.08
☐ 48 Tony Gwynn	4.00	1.75	.35
☐ 49 Carlton Fisk	2.00	.80	.20
☐ 50 Mike Scott	.60	.25	.06
☐ 51 Barry Larkin	2.00	.80	.20
☐ 52 Andre Dawson	2.00	.80	.20
☐ 53 Tom Glavine	1.50	.60	.15
☐ 54 Tom Browning	.60	.25	.06
☐ 55 Checklist Card	.50	.20	.05

1990 Donruss Rookies

The 1990 Donruss Rookies set marked the fifth consecutive year that Donruss issued a boxed set honoring the best rookies of the season. This set, which used the 1990 Donruss design but featured a green border, was issued exclusively through the Donruss dealer network to hobby dealers. This 56-card, standard size, 2 1/2" by 3 1/2" set came in its own box and the words "The Rookies" are featured prominently on the front of the cards. The key rookie card in this set is Carlos Baerga.

	MINT	EXC	G-VG
COMPLETE SET (56)	9.00	4.00	.90
COMMON PLAYER (1-56)	.05	.02	.00
☐ 1 Sandy Alomar Jr. UER (No stitches on base- ball on Donruss logo on card front)	.10	.04	.01
☐ 2 John Olerud	1.00	.40	.10
☐ 3 Pat Combs	.08	.03	.01
☐ 4 Brian Dubois	.08	.03	.01
☐ 5 Felix Jose	.20	.08	.02
☐ 6 Delino DeShields	.40	.16	.04
☐ 7 Mike Stanton	.08	.03	.01
☐ 8 Mike Munoz	.10	.04	.01
☐ 9 Craig Grebeck	.10	.04	.01
☐ 10 Joe Kraemer	.10	.04	.01
☐ 11 Jeff Huson	.08	.03	.01
☐ 12 Bill Sampen	.12	.05	.01
☐ 13 Brian Bohanon	.12	.05	.01
☐ 14 Dave Justice	2.50	1.00	.25
☐ 15 Robin Ventura	.65	.25	.06
☐ 16 Greg Vaughn	.50	.20	.05
☐ 17 Wayne Edwards	.10	.04	.01
☐ 18 Shawn Boskie	.12	.05	.01
☐ 19 Carlos Baerga	.40	.16	.04
☐ 20 Mark Gardner	.20	.08	.02
☐ 21 Kevin Appier	.20	.08	.02
☐ 22 Mike Harkey	.10	.04	.01
☐ 23 Tim Layana	.10	.04	.01
☐ 24 Glenallen Hill	.08	.03	.01
☐ 25 Jerry Kutzler	.08	.03	.01
☐ 26 Mike Blowers	.10	.04	.01
☐ 27 Scott Ruskin	.12	.05	.01
☐ 28 Dana Kiecker	.10	.04	.01
☐ 29 Willie Blair	.08	.03	.01
☐ 30 Ben McDonald	.75	.30	.07
☐ 31 Todd Zeile	.40	.16	.04
☐ 32 Scott Coolbaugh	.10	.04	.01
☐ 33 Xavier Hernandez	.05	.02	.00
☐ 34 Mike Hartley	.15	.06	.01
☐ 35 Kevin Tapani	.30	.12	.03
☐ 36 Kevin Wickander	.05	.02	.00

		MINT	EXC	G-VG
☐ 37	Carlos Hernandez	.10	.04	.01
☐ 38	Brian Traxler	.10	.04	.01
☐ 39	Marty Brown	.05	.02	.00
☐ 40	Scott Radinsky	.12	.05	.01
☐ 41	Julio Machado	.05	.02	.00
☐ 42	Steve Avery	.90	.40	.09
☐ 43	Mark Lemke	.10	.04	.01
☐ 44	Alan Mills	.10	.04	.01
☐ 45	Marquis Grissom	.45	.18	.04
☐ 46	Greg Olson	.20	.08	.02
☐ 47	Dave Hollins	.35	.15	.03
☐ 48	Jerald Clark	.08	.03	.01
☐ 49	Eric Anthony	.20	.08	.02
☐ 50	Tim Drummond	.10	.04	.01
☐ 51	John Burkett	.15	.06	.01
☐ 52	Brent Knackert	.12	.05	.01
☐ 53	Jeff Shaw	.10	.04	.01
☐ 54	John Orton	.10	.04	.01
☐ 55	Terry Shumpert	.12	.05	.01
☐ 56	Checklist Card	.05	.01	.00

1990 Donruss Best AL

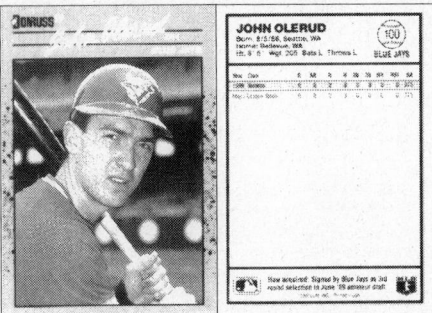

The 1990 Donruss Best of the American League set consists of 144 cards in the standard card size of 2 1/2" by 3 1/2". This was Donruss' latest version of what had been titled the previous two years as Baseball's Best. In 1990, the sets were split into National and American League and marketed separately. The front design was similar to the regular issue Donruss set except for the front borders being blue while the backs have complete major and minor league statistics as compared to the regular Donruss cards which only cover the past five major-league seasons.

		MINT	EXC	G-VG
COMPLETE SET (144)		10.00	4.50	1.25
COMMON PLAYER (1-144)		.04	.02	.00
☐ 1	Ken Griffey Jr.	1.25	.50	.12
☐ 2	Bob Milacki	.04	.02	.00
☐ 3	Mike Boddicker	.04	.02	.00
☐ 4	Bert Blyleven	.10	.04	.01
☐ 5	Carlton Fisk	.20	.08	.02
☐ 6	Greg Swindell	.07	.03	.01
☐ 7	Alan Trammell	.15	.06	.01
☐ 8	Mark Davis	.04	.02	.00
☐ 9	Chris Bosio	.04	.02	.00
☐ 10	Gary Gaetti	.07	.03	.01
☐ 11	Matt Nokes	.07	.03	.01
☐ 12	Dennis Eckersley	.15	.06	.01
☐ 13	Kevin Brown	.07	.03	.01
☐ 14	Tom Henke	.07	.03	.01
☐ 15	Mickey Tettleton	.07	.03	.01
☐ 16	Jody Reed	.07	.03	.01
☐ 17	Mark Langston	.10	.04	.01
☐ 18	Melido Perez UER	.07	.03	.01
	(listed as an Expo rather than White Sox)			
☐ 19	John Farrell	.04	.02	.00
☐ 20	Tony Phillips	.04	.02	.00
☐ 21	Bret Saberhagen	.15	.06	.01
☐ 22	Robin Yount	.25	.10	.02
☐ 23	Kirby Puckett	.30	.12	.03
☐ 24	Steve Sax	.10	.04	.01
☐ 25	Dave Stewart	.10	.04	.01
☐ 26	Alvin Davis	.04	.02	.00
☐ 27	Geno Petralli	.04	.02	.00
☐ 28	Mookie Wilson	.07	.03	.01
☐ 29	Jeff Ballard	.04	.02	.00
☐ 30	Ellis Burks	.15	.06	.01
☐ 31	Wally Joyner	.15	.06	.01
☐ 32	Bobby Thigpen	.10	.04	.01
☐ 33	Keith Hernandez	.15	.06	.01
☐ 34	Jack Morris	.15	.06	.01
☐ 35	George Brett	.25	.10	.02
☐ 36	Dan Plesac	.04	.02	.00
☐ 37	Brian Harper	.07	.03	.01
☐ 38	Don Mattingly	.60	.25	.06
☐ 39	Dave Henderson	.10	.04	.01
☐ 40	Scott Bankhead UER	.07	.03	.01
	Asheboro misspelled as Ashboro on card)			
☐ 41	Rafael Palmeiro	.20	.08	.02
☐ 42	Jimmy Key	.07	.03	.01
☐ 43	Gregg Olson	.15	.06	.01
☐ 44	Tony Pena	.07	.03	.01
☐ 45	Jack Howell	.04	.02	.00
☐ 46	Eric King	.04	.02	.00
☐ 47	Cory Snyder	.10	.04	.01
☐ 48	Frank Tanana	.07	.03	.01
☐ 49	Nolan Ryan	.90	.40	.09
☐ 50	Bob Boone	.07	.03	.01
☐ 51	Dave Parker	.15	.06	.01
☐ 52	Allan Anderson	.04	.02	.00
☐ 53	Tim Leary	.07	.03	.01
☐ 54	Mark McGwire	.40	.16	.04
☐ 55	Dave Valle	.04	.02	.00
☐ 56	Fred McGriff	.25	.10	.02
☐ 57	Cal Ripken	.60	.25	.06
☐ 58	Roger Clemens	.50	.20	.05
☐ 59	Lance Parrish	.10	.04	.01
☐ 60	Robin Ventura	.50	.20	.05
☐ 61	Doug Jones	.07	.03	.01
☐ 62	Lloyd Moseby	.04	.02	.00
☐ 63	Bo Jackson	.90	.40	.09
☐ 64	Paul Molitor	.10	.04	.01
☐ 65	Kent Hrbek	.10	.04	.01
☐ 66	Mel Hall	.07	.03	.01
☐ 67	Bob Welch	.15	.06	.01
☐ 68	Erik Hanson	.20	.08	.02
☐ 69	Harold Baines	.10	.04	.01
☐ 70	Junior Felix	.15	.06	.01
☐ 71	Craig Worthington	.07	.03	.01
☐ 72	Jeff Reardon	.15	.06	.01
☐ 73	Johnny Ray	.04	.02	.00
☐ 74	Ozzie Guillen	.10	.04	.01
☐ 75	Brook Jacoby	.04	.02	.00
☐ 76	Chet Lemon	.04	.02	.00
☐ 77	Mark Gubicza	.07	.03	.01
☐ 78	B.J. Surhoff	.07	.03	.01
☐ 79	Rick Aguilera	.07	.03	.01
☐ 80	Pascual Perez	.07	.03	.01
☐ 81	Jose Canseco	.75	.30	.07
☐ 82	Mike Schooler	.07	.03	.01
☐ 83	Jeff Huson	.04	.02	.00
☐ 84	Kelly Gruber	.15	.06	.01
☐ 85	Randy Milligan	.15	.06	.01
☐ 86	Wade Boggs	.40	.16	.04
☐ 87	Dave Winfield	.25	.10	.02
☐ 88	Scott Fletcher	.04	.02	.00
☐ 89	Tom Candiotti	.07	.03	.01
☐ 90	Mike Heath	.04	.02	.00
☐ 91	Kevin Seitzer	.10	.04	.01
☐ 92	Ted Higuera	.07	.03	.01
☐ 93	Kevin Tapani	.20	.08	.02
☐ 94	Roberto Kelly	.20	.08	.02
☐ 95	Walt Weiss	.10	.04	.01
☐ 96	Checklist Card	.04	.02	.00
☐ 97	Sandy Alomar Jr.	.35	.15	.03
☐ 98	Pete O'Brien	.04	.02	.00
☐ 99	Jeff Russell	.04	.02	.00
☐ 100	John Olerud	.90	.40	.09
☐ 101	Pete Harnisch	.04	.02	.00
☐ 102	Dwight Evans	.10	.04	.01
☐ 103	Chuck Finley	.10	.04	.01
☐ 104	Sammy Sosa	.25	.10	.02
☐ 105	Mike Henneman	.04	.02	.00
☐ 106	Kurt Stillwell	.07	.03	.01
☐ 107	Greg Vaughn	.40	.16	.04
☐ 108	Dan Gladden	.04	.02	.00
☐ 109	Jesse Barfield	.10	.04	.01
☐ 110	Willie Randolph	.07	.03	.01
☐ 111	Randy Johnson	.10	.04	.01
☐ 112	Julio Franco	.15	.06	.01
☐ 113	Tony Fernandez	.10	.04	.01
☐ 114	Ben McDonald	.50	.20	.05
☐ 115	Mike Greenwell	.20	.08	.02
☐ 116	Luis Polonia	.04	.02	.00

		MINT	EXC	G-VG
☐ 117	Carney Lansford	.07	.03	.01
☐ 118	Bud Black	.04	.02	.00
☐ 119	Lou Whitaker	.10	.04	.01
☐ 120	Jim Eisenreich	.04	.02	.00
☐ 121	Gary Sheffield	.25	.10	.02
☐ 122	Shane Mack	.07	.03	.01
☐ 123	Alvaro Espinoza	.04	.02	.00
☐ 124	Rickey Henderson	.45	.18	.04
☐ 125	Jeffrey Leonard	.04	.02	.00
☐ 126	Gary Pettis	.04	.02	.00
☐ 127	Dave Stieb	.10	.04	.01
☐ 128	Danny Tartabull	.20	.08	.02
☐ 129	Joe Orsulak	.04	.02	.00
☐ 130	Tom Brunansky	.07	.03	.01
☐ 131	Dick Schofield	.04	.02	.00
☐ 132	Candy Maldonado	.07	.03	.01
☐ 133	Cecil Fielder	.40	.16	.04
☐ 134	Terry Shumpert	.10	.04	.01
☐ 135	Greg Gagne	.04	.02	.00
☐ 136	Dave Righetti	.10	.04	.01
☐ 137	Terry Steinbach	.07	.03	.01
☐ 138	Harold Reynolds	.07	.03	.01
☐ 139	George Bell	.15	.06	.01
☐ 140	Carlos Quintana	.10	.04	.01
☐ 141	Ivan Calderon	.07	.03	.01
☐ 142	Greg Brock	.04	.02	.00
☐ 143	Ruben Sierra	.25	.10	.02
☐ 144	Checklist Card	.04	.02	.00

1990 Donruss Best NL

The 1990 Donruss Best of the National League set consists of 144 cards in the standard card size of 2 1/2" by 3 1/2". This was Donruss' latest version of what had been titled the previous two years as Baseball's Best. In 1990, the sets were split into National and American League and marketed separately. The front design was similar to the regular issue Donruss set except for the front borders being blue while the backs have complete major and minor league statistics as compared to the regular Donruss cards which only cover the past five major-league seasons.

	MINT	EXC	G-VG
COMPLETE SET (144)	10.00	4.50	1.25
COMMON PLAYER (1-144)	.04	.02	.00

☐ 1	Eric Davis	.25	.10	.02
☐ 2	Tom Glavine	.25	.10	.02
☐ 3	Mike Bielecki	.04	.02	.00
☐ 4	Jim Deshaies	.04	.02	.00
☐ 5	Mike Scioscia	.04	.02	.00
☐ 6	Spike Owen	.04	.02	.00
☐ 7	Dwight Gooden	.20	.08	.02
☐ 8	Ricky Jordan	.10	.04	.01
☐ 9	Doug Drabek	.10	.04	.01
☐ 10	Bryn Smith	.04	.02	.00
☐ 11	Tony Gwynn	.25	.10	.02
☐ 12	John Burkett	.15	.06	.01
☐ 13	Nick Esasky	.07	.03	.01
☐ 14	Greg Maddux	.10	.04	.01
☐ 15	Joe Oliver	.10	.04	.01
☐ 16	Mike Scott	.10	.04	.01
☐ 17	Tim Belcher	.10	.04	.01
☐ 18	Kevin Gross	.04	.02	.00

☐ 19	Howard Johnson	.15	.06	.01
☐ 20	Darren Daulton	.07	.03	.01
☐ 21	John Smiley	.10	.04	.01
☐ 22	Ken Dayley	.04	.02	.00
☐ 23	Craig Lefferts	.07	.03	.01
☐ 24	Will Clark	.50	.20	.05
☐ 25	Greg Olson	.20	.08	.02
☐ 26	Ryne Sandberg	.40	.16	.04
☐ 27	Tom Browning	.07	.03	.01
☐ 28	Eric Anthony	.25	.10	.02
☐ 29	Juan Samuel	.07	.03	.01
☐ 30	Dennis Martinez	.07	.03	.01
☐ 31	Kevin Elster	.04	.02	.00
☐ 32	Tom Herr	.04	.02	.00
☐ 33	Sid Bream	.04	.02	.00
☐ 34	Terry Pendleton	.15	.06	.01
☐ 35	Roberto Alomar	.25	.10	.02
☐ 36	Kevin Bass	.04	.02	.00
☐ 37	Jim Presley	.04	.02	.00
☐ 38	Les Lancaster	.04	.02	.00
☐ 39	Paul O'Neill	.10	.04	.01
☐ 40	Dave Smith	.04	.02	.00
☐ 41	Kirk Gibson	.10	.04	.01
☐ 42	Tim Burke	.04	.02	.00
☐ 43	David Cone	.10	.04	.01
☐ 44	Ken Howell	.04	.02	.00
☐ 45	Barry Bonds	.35	.15	.03
☐ 46	Joe Magrane	.04	.02	.00
☐ 47	Andy Benes	.20	.08	.02
☐ 48	Gary Carter	.10	.04	.01
☐ 49	Pat Combs	.07	.03	.01
☐ 50	John Smoltz	.15	.06	.01
☐ 51	Mark Grace	.30	.12	.03
☐ 52	Barry Larkin	.15	.06	.01
☐ 53	Danny Darwin	.04	.02	.00
☐ 54	Orel Hershiser	.15	.06	.01
☐ 55	Tim Wallach	.07	.03	.01
☐ 56	Dave Magadan	.10	.04	.01
☐ 57	Roger McDowell	.04	.02	.00
☐ 58	Bill Landrum	.04	.02	.00
☐ 59	Jose DeLeon	.04	.02	.00
☐ 60	Bip Roberts	.07	.03	.01
☐ 61	Matt Williams	.20	.08	.02
☐ 62	Dale Murphy	.20	.08	.02
☐ 63	Dwight Smith	.10	.04	.01
☐ 64	Chris Sabo	.15	.06	.01
☐ 65	Glenn Davis	.15	.06	.01
☐ 66	Jay Howell	.04	.02	.00
☐ 67	Andres Galarraga	.10	.04	.01
☐ 68	Frank Viola	.15	.06	.01
☐ 69	John Kruk	.04	.02	.00
☐ 70	Bobby Bonilla	.20	.08	.02
☐ 71	Todd Zeile	.30	.12	.03
☐ 72	Joe Carter	.20	.08	.02
☐ 73	Robby Thompson	.04	.02	.00
☐ 74	Jeff Blauser	.04	.02	.00
☐ 75	Mitch Williams	.07	.03	.01
☐ 76	Rob Dibble	.10	.04	.01
☐ 77	Rafael Ramirez	.04	.02	.00
☐ 78	Eddie Murray	.20	.08	.02
☐ 79	Dave Martinez	.04	.02	.00
☐ 80	Darryl Strawberry	.35	.15	.03
☐ 81	Dickie Thon	.04	.02	.00
☐ 82	Jose Lind	.04	.02	.00
☐ 83	Ozzie Smith	.15	.06	.01
☐ 84	Bruce Hurst	.07	.03	.01
☐ 85	Kevin Mitchell	.20	.08	.02
☐ 86	Lonnie Smith	.07	.03	.01
☐ 87	Joe Girardi	.07	.03	.01
☐ 88	Randy Myers	.07	.03	.01
☐ 89	Craig Biggio	.07	.03	.01
☐ 90	Fernando Valenzuela	.10	.04	.01
☐ 91	Larry Walker	.20	.08	.02
☐ 92	John Franco	.07	.03	.01
☐ 93	Dennis Cook	.07	.03	.01
☐ 94	Bob Walk	.04	.02	.00
☐ 95	Pedro Guerrero	.10	.04	.01
☐ 96	Checklist Card	.04	.02	.00
☐ 97	Andre Dawson	.20	.08	.02
☐ 98	Ed Whitson	.04	.02	.00
☐ 99	Steve Bedrosian	.04	.02	.00
☐ 100	Oddibe McDowell	.04	.02	.00
☐ 101	Todd Benzinger	.04	.02	.00
☐ 102	Bill Doran	.04	.02	.00
☐ 103	Alfredo Griffin	.04	.02	.00
☐ 104	Tim Raines	.15	.06	.01
☐ 105	Sid Fernandez	.07	.03	.01
☐ 106	Charlie Hayes	.07	.03	.01
☐ 107	Mike Lavalliere	.04	.02	.00
☐ 108	Jose Oquendo	.04	.02	.00
☐ 109	Jack Clark	.15	.06	.01
☐ 110	Scott Garrelts	.04	.02	.00
☐ 111	Ron Gant	.30	.12	.03
☐ 112	Shawon Dunston	.15	.06	.01

		MINT	EXC	G-VG
☐ 113	Mariano Duncan	.07	.03	.01
☐ 114	Eric Yelding	.07	.03	.01
☐ 115	Hubie Brooks	.07	.03	.01
☐ 116	Delino DeShields	.35	.15	.03
☐ 117	Gregg Jefferies	.20	.08	.02
☐ 118	Len Dykstra	.10	.04	.01
☐ 119	Andy Van Slyke	.10	.04	.01
☐ 120	Lee Smith	.10	.04	.01
☐ 121	Benito Santiago	.15	.06	.01
☐ 122	Jose Uribe	.04	.02	.00
☐ 123	Jeff Treadway	.04	.02	.00
☐ 124	Jerome Walton	.15	.06	.01
☐ 125	Billy Hatcher	.07	.03	.01
☐ 126	Ken Caminiti	.04	.02	.00
☐ 127	Kal Daniels	.10	.04	.01
☐ 128	Marquis Grissom	.30	.12	.03
☐ 129	Kevin McReynolds	.10	.04	.01
☐ 130	Wally Backman	.04	.02	.00
☐ 131	Willie McGee	.10	.04	.01
☐ 132	Terry Kennedy	.04	.02	.00
☐ 133	Garry Templeton	.04	.02	.00
☐ 134	Lloyd McClendon	.04	.02	.00
☐ 135	Daryl Boston	.04	.02	.00
☐ 136	Jay Bell	.04	.02	.00
☐ 137	Mike Pagliarulo	.04	.02	.00
☐ 138	Vince Coleman	.15	.06	.01
☐ 139	Brett Butler	.07	.03	.01
☐ 140	Von Hayes	.07	.03	.01
☐ 141	Ramon Martinez	.35	.15	.03
☐ 142	Jack Armstrong	.10	.04	.01
☐ 143	Franklin Stubbs	.07	.03	.01
☐ 144	Checklist Card	.04	.02	.00

1991 Donruss Preview

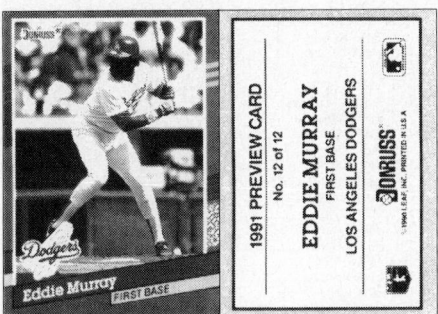

This 12-card set was issued by Donruss for hobby dealers as examples of what the 1991 Donruss cards would look like. This standard size, 2 1/2" by 3 1/2", set had the 1991 Donruss design on the front; the back merely says 1991 Preview card and identifies the player and the team.

		MINT	EXC	G-VG
	COMPLETE SET (12)	350.00	160.00	52.50
	COMMON PLAYER (1-12)	15.00	6.50	2.15
☐ 1	Dave Justice	75.00	34.00	11.25
☐ 2	Doug Drabek	15.00	6.50	2.15
☐ 3	Scott Chiamparino	15.00	6.50	2.15
☐ 4	Ken Griffey Jr.	90.00	40.00	13.50
☐ 5	Bob Welch	15.00	6.50	2.15
☐ 6	Tino Martinez	25.00	11.00	3.50
☐ 7	Nolan Ryan	90.00	40.00	13.50
☐ 8	Dwight Gooden	35.00	15.75	5.25
☐ 9	Ryne Sandberg	45.00	20.00	6.75
☐ 10	Barry Bonds	40.00	18.00	6.00
☐ 11	Jose Canseco	75.00	34.00	11.25
☐ 12	Eddie Murray	25.00	11.00	3.50

1991 Donruss

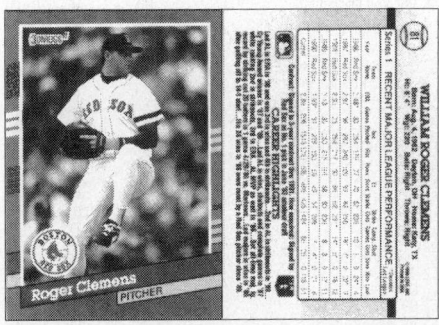

The 1991 Donruss set was issued in two separate series of 396 cards each. This set marked the first time Donruss has issued their cards in series. The cards feature a blue border with some stripes and the players name in white against a red background. The cards measure the standard size of 2 1/2" by 3 1/2". Series I contained 386 cards (numbered 1-386) and another ten cards numbered BC1-BC10. The cards again feature the artwork of Dick Perez drawing each team's Diamond King, which comprise the first 26 cards of the set. The first series also contains 20 Rated Rookie (RR) cards and nine All-Star cards (the AS cards are all American Leaguers in this first series). On cards 60, 70, 127, 182, 239, 294, 355, 368, and 377, the border stripes are red and yellow. As a separate promotion wax packs were also given away with six and 12-packs of Coke and Diet Coke. The key rookie cards in the first series are Wes Chamberlain, Brian McRae, and Phil Plantier. The second series was issued approximately three months after the first series was issued. This series features the 26 MVP cards which Donruss had issued for the three previous years as their Bonus Cards, twenty more rated rookie cards and nine All-Star Cards (National Leaguers in this series). There were also special cards to honor the award winners and the heroes of the World Series. The 11 Bonus Cards pick up in time beginning with Valenzuela's no-hitter through the end of the season.

		MINT	EXC	G-VG
	COMPLETE SET (792)	17.00	7.25	2.50
	COMMON PLAYER (1-386)	.03	.01	.00
	COMMON PLAYER (387-770)	.03	.01	.00
	COMMON PLAYER (BC1-BC10)	.05	.02	.00
	COMMON PLAYER (BC11-BC22)	.05	.02	.00
☐ 1	Dave Stieb DK	.06	.02	.00
☐ 2	Craig Biggio DK	.06	.02	.00
☐ 3	Cecil Fielder DK	.10	.04	.01
☐ 4	Barry Bonds DK	.08	.03	.01
☐ 5	Barry Larkin DK	.08	.03	.01
☐ 6	Dave Parker DK	.06	.02	.00
☐ 7	Len Dykstra DK	.06	.02	.00
☐ 8	Bobby Thigpen DK	.06	.02	.00
☐ 9	Roger Clemens DK	.10	.04	.01
☐ 10	Ron Gant DK UER	.08	.03	.01
	(no trademark on			
	team logo on back)			
☐ 11	Delino DeShields DK	.08	.03	.01
☐ 12	Roberto Alomar DK UER	.08	.03	.01
	(no trademark on			
	team logo on back)			
☐ 13	Sandy Alomar Jr. DK	.06	.02	.00
☐ 14	Ryne Sandberg DK UER	.12	.05	.01
	(was DK in '85, not			
	'83 as shown)			
☐ 15	Ramon Martinez DK	.08	.03	.01
☐ 16	Edgar Martinez DK	.06	.02	.00
☐ 17	Dave Magadan DK	.06	.02	.00
☐ 18	Matt Williams DK	.08	.03	.01
☐ 19	Rafael Palmeiro DK	.08	.03	.01
	UER (no trademark on			
	team logo on back)			
☐ 20	Bob Welch DK	.06	.02	.00

☐	21	Dave Righetti DK	.06	.02	.00
☐	22	Brian Harper DK	.06	.02	.00
☐	23	Gregg Olson DK	.06	.02	.00
☐	24	Kurt Stillwell DK	.06	.02	.00
☐	25	Pedro Guerrero DK UER	.06	.02	.00
		(no trademark on			
		team logo on back)			
☐	26	Chuck Finley DK UER	.06	.02	.00
		(no trademark on			
		team logo on back)			
☐	27	DK Checklist	.06	.01	.00
☐	28	Tino Martinez RR	.15	.06	.01
☐	29	Mark Lewis RR	.20	.08	.02
☐	30	Bernard Gilkey RR	.15	.06	.01
☐	31	Hensley Meulens RR	.08	.03	.01
☐	32	Derek Bell RR	.35	.15	.03
☐	33	Jose Offerman RR	.10	.04	.01
☐	34	Terry Bross RR	.06	.02	.00
☐	35	Leo Gomez RR	.25	.10	.02
☐	36	Derrick May RR	.08	.03	.01
☐	37	Kevin Morton RR	.15	.06	.01
☐	38	Moises Alou RR	.08	.03	.01
☐	39	Julio Valera RR	.08	.03	.01
☐	40	Milt Cuyler RR	.15	.06	.01
☐	41	Phil Plantier RR	1.25	.50	.12
☐	42	Scott Chiamparino RR	.08	.03	.01
☐	43	Ray Lankford RR	.35	.15	.03
☐	44	Mickey Morandini RR	.10	.04	.01
☐	45	Dave Hansen RR	.10	.04	.01
☐	46	Kevin Belcher RR	.10	.04	.01
☐	47	Darrin Fletcher RR	.08	.03	.01
☐	48	Steve Sax AS	.06	.02	.00
☐	49	Ken Griffey Jr. AS	.30	.12	.03
☐	50	Jose Canseco AS UER	.15	.06	.01
		(team in stat box			
		should be AL not A's)			
☐	51	Sandy Alomar AS	.08	.03	.01
☐	52	Cal Ripken AS	.12	.05	.01
☐	53	Rickey Henderson AS	.12	.05	.01
☐	54	Bob Welch AS	.06	.02	.00
☐	55	Wade Boggs AS	.10	.04	.01
☐	56	Mark McGwire AS	.08	.03	.01
☐	57	Jack McDowell UER	.08	.03	.01
		(career stats do			
		not include 1990)			
☐	58	Jose Lind	.03	.01	.00
☐	59	Alex Fernandez	.20	.08	.02
☐	60	Pat Combs	.03	.01	.00
☐	61	Mike Walker	.06	.02	.00
☐	62	Juan Samuel	.06	.02	.00
☐	63	Mike Blowers UER	.06	.02	.00
		(Last line has			
		aseball, not baseball)			
☐	64	Mark Guthrie	.03	.01	.00
☐	65	Mark Salas	.03	.01	.00
☐	66	Tim Jones	.03	.01	.00
☐	67	Tim Leary	.06	.02	.00
☐	68	Andres Galarraga	.06	.02	.00
☐	69	Bob Milacki	.03	.01	.00
☐	70	Tim Belcher	.06	.02	.00
☐	71	Todd Zeile	.10	.04	.01
☐	72	Jerome Walton	.08	.03	.01
☐	73	Kevin Seitzer	.06	.02	.00
☐	74	Jerald Clark	.03	.01	.00
☐	75	John Smoltz UER	.10	.04	.01
		(Born in Detroit,			
		not Warren)			
☐	76	Mike Henneman	.03	.01	.00
☐	77	Ken Griffey Jr.	.75	.30	.07
☐	78	Jim Abbott	.10	.04	.01
☐	79	Gregg Jefferies	.08	.03	.01
☐	80	Kevin Reimer	.08	.03	.01
☐	81	Roger Clemens	.15	.06	.01
☐	82	Mike Fitzgerald	.03	.01	.00
☐	83	Bruce Hurst UER	.06	.02	.00
		(Middle name is			
		Lee, not Vee)			
☐	84	Eric Davis	.10	.04	.01
☐	85	Paul Molitor	.08	.03	.01
☐	86	Will Clark	.20	.08	.02
☐	87	Mike Bielecki	.03	.01	.00
☐	88	Bret Saberhagen	.08	.03	.01
☐	89	Nolan Ryan	.35	.15	.03
☐	90	Bobby Thigpen	.06	.02	.00
☐	91	Dickie Thon	.03	.01	.00
☐	92	Duane Ward	.03	.01	.00
☐	93	Luis Polonia	.03	.01	.00
☐	94	Terry Kennedy	.03	.01	.00
☐	95	Kent Hrbek	.06	.02	.00
☐	96	Danny Jackson	.03	.01	.00
☐	97	Sid Fernandez	.06	.02	.00
☐	98	Jimmy Key	.06	.02	.00
☐	99	Franklin Stubbs	.03	.01	.00
☐	100	Checklist Card	.06	.01	.00
☐	101	R.J. Reynolds	.03	.01	.00
☐	102	Dave Stewart	.08	.03	.01
☐	103	Dan Pasqua	.03	.01	.00
☐	104	Dan Plesac	.03	.01	.00
☐	105	Mark McGwire	.10	.04	.01
☐	106	John Farrell	.03	.01	.00
☐	107	Don Mattingly	.12	.05	.01
☐	108	Carlton Fisk	.10	.04	.01
☐	109	Ken Oberkfell	.03	.01	.00
☐	110	Darrel Akerfelds	.03	.01	.00
☐	111	Gregg Olson	.08	.03	.01
☐	112	Mike Scioscia	.03	.01	.00
☐	113	Bryn Smith	.03	.01	.00
☐	114	Bob Geren	.03	.01	.00
☐	115	Tom Candiotti	.06	.02	.00
☐	116	Kevin Tapani	.06	.02	.00
☐	117	Jeff Treadway	.03	.01	.00
☐	118	Alan Trammell	.08	.03	.01
☐	119	Pete O'Brien	.03	.01	.00
		(Blue shading goes			
		through stats)			
☐	120	Joel Skinner	.03	.01	.00
☐	121	Mike LaValliere	.03	.01	.00
☐	122	Dwight Evans	.06	.02	.00
☐	123	Jody Reed	.06	.02	.00
☐	124	Lee Guetterman	.03	.01	.00
☐	125	Tim Burke	.03	.01	.00
☐	126	Dave Johnson	.03	.01	.00
☐	127	Fernando Valenzuela UER	.06	.02	.00
		(Lower large stripe			
		in yellow instead			
		of blue)			
☐	128	Jose DeLeon	.03	.01	.00
☐	129	Andre Dawson	.10	.04	.01
☐	130	Gerald Perry	.03	.01	.00
☐	131	Greg Harris	.03	.01	.00
☐	132	Tom Glavine	.08	.03	.01
☐	133	Lance McCullers	.03	.01	.00
☐	134	Randy Johnson	.03	.01	.00
☐	135	Lance Parrish UER	.06	.02	.00
		(Born in McKeesport,			
		not Clairton)			
☐	136	Mackey Sasser	.03	.01	.00
☐	137	Geno Petralli	.03	.01	.00
☐	138	Dennis Lamp	.03	.01	.00
☐	139	Dennis Martinez	.06	.02	.00
☐	140	Mike Pagliarulo	.03	.01	.00
☐	141	Hal Morris	.10	.04	.01
☐	142	Dave Parker	.08	.03	.01
☐	143	Brett Butler	.06	.02	.00
☐	144	Paul Assenmacher	.03	.01	.00
☐	145	Mark Gubicza	.06	.02	.00
☐	146	Charlie Hough	.03	.01	.00
☐	147	Sammy Sosa	.08	.03	.01
☐	148	Randy Ready	.03	.01	.00
☐	149	Kelly Gruber	.08	.03	.01
☐	150	Devon White	.06	.02	.00
☐	151	Gary Carter	.08	.03	.01
☐	152	Gene Larkin	.03	.01	.00
☐	153	Chris Sabo	.08	.03	.01
☐	154	David Cone	.06	.02	.00
☐	155	Todd Stottlemyre	.06	.02	.00
☐	156	Glenn Wilson	.03	.01	.00
☐	157	Bob Walk	.03	.01	.00
☐	158	Mike Gallego	.03	.01	.00
☐	159	Greg Hibbard	.03	.01	.00
☐	160	Chris Bosio	.03	.01	.00
☐	161	Mike Moore	.06	.02	.00
☐	162	Jerry Browne UER	.03	.01	.00
		(Born Christiansted,			
		should be St. Croix)			
☐	163	Steve Sax UER	.06	.02	.00
		(No asterisk next to			
		his 1989 At Bats)			
☐	164	Melido Perez	.03	.01	.00
☐	165	Danny Darwin	.03	.01	.00
☐	166	Roger McDowell	.03	.01	.00
☐	167	Bill Ripken	.03	.01	.00
☐	168	Mike Sharperson	.03	.01	.00
☐	169	Lee Smith	.06	.02	.00
☐	170	Matt Nokes	.06	.02	.00
☐	171	Jesse Orosco	.03	.01	.00
☐	172	Rick Aguilera	.06	.02	.00
☐	173	Jim Presley	.03	.01	.00
☐	174	Lou Whitaker	.06	.02	.00
☐	175	Harold Reynolds	.06	.02	.00
☐	176	Brook Jacoby	.03	.01	.00
☐	177	Wally Backman	.03	.01	.00
☐	178	Wade Boggs	.12	.05	.01
☐	179	Chuck Cary	.03	.01	.00
		(Comma after DOB,			
		not on other cards)			
☐	180	Tom Foley	.03	.01	.00
☐	181	Pete Harnisch	.03	.01	.00

☐ 182	Mike Morgan	.06	.02	.00
☐ 183	Bob Tewksbury	.03	.01	.00
☐ 184	Joe Girardi	.03	.01	.00
☐ 185	Storm Davis	.03	.01	.00
☐ 186	Ed Whitson	.03	.01	.00
☐ 187	Steve Avery UER	.30	.12	.03
	(Born in New Jersey, should be Michigan)			
☐ 188	Lloyd Moseby	.03	.01	.00
☐ 189	Scott Bankhead	.03	.01	.00
☐ 190	Mark Langston	.06	.02	.00
☐ 191	Kevin McReynolds	.06	.02	.00
☐ 192	Julio Franco	.08	.03	.01
☐ 193	John Dopson	.03	.01	.00
☐ 194	Oil Can Boyd	.03	.01	.00
☐ 195	Bip Roberts	.03	.01	.00
☐ 196	Billy Hatcher	.03	.01	.00
☐ 197	Edgar Diaz	.06	.02	.00
☐ 198	Greg Litton	.03	.01	.00
☐ 199	Mark Grace	.08	.03	.01
☐ 200	Checklist Card	.06	.01	.00
☐ 201	George Brett	.10	.04	.01
☐ 202	Jeff Russell	.03	.01	.00
☐ 203	Ivan Calderon	.06	.02	.00
☐ 204	Ken Howell	.03	.01	.00
☐ 205	Tom Henke	.06	.02	.00
☐ 206	Bryan Harvey	.06	.02	.00
☐ 207	Steve Bedrosian	.03	.01	.00
☐ 208	Al Newman	.03	.01	.00
☐ 209	Randy Myers	.03	.01	.00
☐ 210	Daryl Boston	.03	.01	.00
☐ 211	Manny Lee	.03	.01	.00
☐ 212	Dave Smith	.03	.01	.00
☐ 213	Don Slaught	.03	.01	.00
☐ 214	Walt Weiss	.06	.02	.00
☐ 215	Donn Pall	.03	.01	.00
☐ 216	Jaime Navarro	.03	.01	.00
☐ 217	Willie Randolph	.06	.02	.00
☐ 218	Rudy Seanez	.10	.04	.01
☐ 219	Jim Leyritz	.08	.03	.01
☐ 220	Ron Karkovice	.03	.01	.00
☐ 221	Ken Caminiti	.03	.01	.00
☐ 222	Von Hayes	.06	.02	.00
☐ 223	Cal Ripken	.20	.08	.02
☐ 224	Lenny Harris	.03	.01	.00
☐ 225	Milt Thompson	.03	.01	.00
☐ 226	Alvaro Espinoza	.03	.01	.00
☐ 227	Chris James	.03	.01	.00
☐ 228	Dan Gladden	.03	.01	.00
☐ 229	Jeff Blauser	.03	.01	.00
☐ 230	Mike Heath	.03	.01	.00
☐ 231	Omar Vizquel	.03	.01	.00
☐ 232	Doug Jones	.03	.01	.00
☐ 233	Jeff King	.03	.01	.00
☐ 234	Luis Rivera	.03	.01	.00
☐ 235	Ellis Burks	.08	.03	.01
☐ 236	Greg Cadaret	.03	.01	.00
☐ 237	Dave Martinez	.03	.01	.00
☐ 238	Mark Williamson	.03	.01	.00
☐ 239	Stan Javier	.03	.01	.00
☐ 240	Ozzie Smith	.10	.04	.01
☐ 241	Shawn Boskie	.06	.02	.00
☐ 242	Tom Gordon	.06	.02	.00
☐ 243	Tony Gwynn	.12	.05	.01
☐ 244	Tommy Gregg	.03	.01	.00
☐ 245	Jeff Robinson	.03	.01	.00
☐ 246	Keith Comstock	.03	.01	.00
☐ 247	Jack Howell	.03	.01	.00
☐ 248	Keith Miller	.03	.01	.00
☐ 249	Bobby Witt	.06	.02	.00
☐ 250	Rob Murphy UER	.03	.01	.00
	(shown as on Reds in '89 in stats, should be Red Sox)			
☐ 251	Spike Owen	.03	.01	.00
☐ 252	Garry Templeton	.03	.01	.00
☐ 253	Glenn Braggs	.03	.01	.00
☐ 254	Ron Robinson	.03	.01	.00
☐ 255	Kevin Mitchell	.10	.04	.01
☐ 256	Les Lancaster	.03	.01	.00
☐ 257	Mel Stottlemyre Jr.	.03	.01	.00
☐ 258	Kenny Rogers UER	.03	.01	.00
	(IP listed as 171, should be 172)			
☐ 259	Lance Johnson	.03	.01	.00
☐ 260	John Kruk	.03	.01	.00
☐ 261	Fred McGriff	.08	.03	.01
☐ 262	Dick Schofield	.03	.01	.00
☐ 263	Trevor Wilson	.03	.01	.00
☐ 264	David West	.03	.01	.00
☐ 265	Scott Scudder	.06	.02	.00
☐ 266	Dwight Gooden	.10	.04	.01
☐ 267	Willie Blair	.03	.01	.00
☐ 268	Mark Portugal	.03	.01	.00
☐ 269	Doug Drabek	.06	.02	.00
☐ 270	Dennis Eckersley	.08	.03	.01
☐ 271	Eric King	.03	.01	.00
☐ 272	Robin Yount	.10	.04	.01
☐ 273	Carney Lansford	.06	.02	.00
☐ 274	Carlos Baerga	.10	.04	.01
☐ 275	Dave Righetti	.06	.02	.00
☐ 276	Scott Fletcher	.03	.01	.00
☐ 277	Eric Yelding	.03	.01	.00
☐ 278	Charlie Hayes	.03	.01	.00
☐ 279	Jeff Ballard	.03	.01	.00
☐ 280	Orel Hershiser	.06	.02	.00
☐ 281	Jose Oquendo	.03	.01	.00
☐ 282	Mike Witt	.03	.01	.00
☐ 283	Mitch Webster	.03	.01	.00
☐ 284	Greg Gagne	.03	.01	.00
☐ 285	Greg Olson	.06	.02	.00
☐ 286	Tony Phillips UER	.03	.01	.00
	(Born 4/15, should be 4/25)			
☐ 287	Scott Bradley	.03	.01	.00
☐ 288	Cory Snyder UER	.06	.02	.00
	(In text, led is re-peated and Inglewood is misspelled as Englewood)			
☐ 289	Jay Bell UER	.03	.01	.00
	(Born in Pensacola, not Eglin AFB)			
☐ 290	Kevin Romine	.03	.01	.00
☐ 291	Jeff Robinson	.03	.01	.00
☐ 292	Steve Frey UER	.06	.02	.00
	(Bats left, should be right)			
☐ 293	Craig Worthington	.03	.01	.00
☐ 294	Tim Crews	.03	.01	.00
☐ 295	Joe Magrane	.03	.01	.00
☐ 296	Hector Villanueva	.03	.01	.00
☐ 297	Terry Shumpert	.03	.01	.00
☐ 298	Joe Carter	.08	.03	.01
☐ 299	Kent Mercker UER	.06	.02	.00
	(IP listed as 53, should be 52)			
☐ 300	Checklist Card	.06	.01	.00
☐ 301	Chet Lemon	.03	.01	.00
☐ 302	Mike Schooler	.03	.01	.00
☐ 303	Dante Bichette	.03	.01	.00
☐ 304	Kevin Elster	.03	.01	.00
☐ 305	Jeff Huson	.03	.01	.00
☐ 306	Greg Harris	.03	.01	.00
☐ 307	Marquis Grissom UER	.10	.04	.01
	(Middle name Deon, should be Dean)			
☐ 308	Calvin Schiraldi	.03	.01	.00
☐ 309	Mariano Duncan	.03	.01	.00
☐ 310	Bill Spiers	.03	.01	.00
☐ 311	Scott Garrelts	.03	.01	.00
☐ 312	Mitch Williams	.03	.01	.00
☐ 313	Mike Macfarlane	.03	.01	.00
☐ 314	Kevin Brown	.03	.01	.00
☐ 315	Robin Ventura	.20	.08	.02
☐ 316	Darren Daulton	.03	.01	.00
☐ 317	Pat Borders	.03	.01	.00
☐ 318	Mark Eichhorn	.03	.01	.00
☐ 319	Jeff Brantley	.03	.01	.00
☐ 320	Shane Mack	.06	.02	.00
☐ 321	Rob Dibble	.06	.02	.00
☐ 322	John Franco	.03	.01	.00
☐ 323	Junior Felix	.06	.02	.00
☐ 324	Casey Candaele	.03	.01	.00
☐ 325	Bobby Bonilla	.10	.04	.01
☐ 326	Dave Henderson	.06	.02	.00
☐ 327	Wayne Edwards	.03	.01	.00
☐ 328	Mark Knudson	.03	.01	.00
☐ 329	Terry Steinbach	.03	.01	.00
☐ 330	Colby Ward UER	.08	.03	.01
	(No comma between city and state)			
☐ 331	Oscar Azocar	.08	.03	.01
☐ 332	Scott Radinsky	.06	.02	.00
☐ 333	Eric Anthony	.08	.03	.01
☐ 334	Steve Lake	.03	.01	.00
☐ 335	Bob Melvin	.03	.01	.00
☐ 336	Kal Daniels	.06	.02	.00
☐ 337	Tom Pagnozzi	.03	.01	.00
☐ 338	Alan Mills	.03	.01	.00
☐ 339	Steve Olin	.03	.01	.00
☐ 340	Juan Berenguer	.03	.01	.00
☐ 341	Francisco Cabrera	.06	.02	.00
☐ 342	Dave Bergman	.03	.01	.00
☐ 343	Henry Cotto	.03	.01	.00
☐ 344	Sergio Valdez	.03	.01	.00
☐ 345	Bob Patterson	.03	.01	.00
☐ 346	John Marzano	.03	.01	.00
☐ 347	Dana Kiecker	.03	.01	.00

☐ 348	Dion James	.03	.01	.00
☐ 349	Hubie Brooks	.06	.02	.00
☐ 350	Bill Landrum	.03	.01	.00
☐ 351	Bill Sampen	.03	.01	.00
☐ 352	Greg Briley	.03	.01	.00
☐ 353	Paul Gibson	.03	.01	.00
☐ 354	Dave Eiland	.03	.01	.00
☐ 355	Steve Finley	.06	.02	.00
☐ 356	Bob Boone	.06	.02	.00
☐ 357	Steve Buechele	.03	.01	.00
☐ 358	Chris Hoiles	.10	.04	.01
☐ 359	Larry Walker	.06	.02	.00
☐ 360	Frank DiPino	.03	.01	.00
☐ 361	Mark Grant	.03	.01	.00
☐ 362	Dave Magadan	.06	.02	.00
☐ 363	Robby Thompson	.03	.01	.00
☐ 364	Lonnie Smith	.06	.02	.00
☐ 365	Steve Farr	.03	.01	.00
☐ 366	Dave Valle	.03	.01	.00
☐ 367	Tim Naehring	.10	.04	.01
☐ 368	Jim Acker	.03	.01	.00
☐ 369	Jeff Reardon UER (Born in Pittsfield, not Dalton)	.06	.02	.00
☐ 370	Tim Teufel	.03	.01	.00
☐ 371	Juan Gonzalez	.30	.12	.03
☐ 372	Luis Salazar	.03	.01	.00
☐ 373	Rick Honeycutt	.03	.01	.00
☐ 374	Greg Maddux	.06	.02	.00
☐ 375	Jose Uribe UER (Middle name Elta, should be Alta)	.03	.01	.00
☐ 376	Donnie Hill	.03	.01	.00
☐ 377	Don Carman	.03	.01	.00
☐ 378	Craig Grebeck	.03	.01	.00
☐ 379	Willie Fraser	.03	.01	.00
☐ 380	Glenallen Hill	.06	.02	.00
☐ 381	Joe Oliver	.03	.01	.00
☐ 382	Randy Bush	.03	.01	.00
☐ 383	Alex Cole	.08	.03	.01
☐ 384	Norm Charlton	.03	.01	.00
☐ 385	Gene Nelson	.03	.01	.00
☐ 386	Checklist Card	.06	.01	.00
☐ 387	Rickey Henderson MVP	.12	.05	.01
☐ 388	Lance Parrish MVP	.06	.02	.00
☐ 389	Fred McGriff MVP	.08	.03	.01
☐ 390	Dave Parker MVP	.08	.03	.01
☐ 391	Candy Maldonado MVP	.06	.02	.00
☐ 392	Ken Griffey Jr. MVP	.30	.12	.03
☐ 393	Gregg Olson MVP	.06	.02	.00
☐ 394	Rafael Palmeiro MVP	.08	.03	.01
☐ 395	Roger Clemens MVP	.10	.04	.01
☐ 396	George Brett MVP	.10	.04	.01
☐ 397	Cecil Fielder MVP	.10	.04	.01
☐ 398	Brian Harper MVP UER (Major League Performance, should be Career)	.03	.01	.00
☐ 399	Bobby Thigpen MVP	.06	.02	.00
☐ 400	Roberto Kelly MVP UER (Second Base on front and OF on back)	.06	.02	.00
☐ 401	Danny Darwin MVP	.03	.01	.00
☐ 402	Dave Justice MVP	.25	.10	.02
☐ 403	Lee Smith MVP	.06	.02	.00
☐ 404	Ryne Sandberg MVP	.12	.05	.01
☐ 405	Eddie Murray MVP	.08	.03	.01
☐ 406	Tim Wallach MVP	.06	.02	.00
☐ 407	Kevin Mitchell MVP	.08	.03	.01
☐ 408	Darryl Strawberry MVP	.10	.04	.01
☐ 409	Joe Carter MVP	.08	.03	.01
☐ 410	Len Dykstra MVP	.06	.02	.00
☐ 411	Doug Drabek MVP	.06	.02	.00
☐ 412	Chris Sabo MVP	.06	.02	.00
☐ 413	Paul Marak RR	.10	.04	.01
☐ 414	Tim McIntosh RR	.08	.03	.01
☐ 415	Brian Barnes RR	.10	.04	.01
☐ 416	Eric Gunderson RR	.08	.03	.01
☐ 417	Mike Gardiner RR	.15	.06	.01
☐ 418	Steve Carter RR	.03	.01	.00
☐ 419	Gerald Alexander RR	.10	.04	.01
☐ 420	Rich Garces RR	.10	.04	.01
☐ 421	Chuck Knoblauch RR	.40	.16	.04
☐ 422	Scott Aldred RR	.08	.03	.01
☐ 423	Wes Chamberlain RR	.45	.18	.04
☐ 424	Lance Dickson RR	.17	.07	.01
☐ 425	Greg Colbrunn RR	.12	.05	.01
☐ 426	Rich Delucia RR	.15	.06	.01
☐ 427	Jeff Conine RR	.15	.06	.01
☐ 428	Steve Decker RR	.25	.10	.02
☐ 429	Turner Ward RR	.15	.06	.01
☐ 430	Mo Vaughn RR	.50	.20	.05
☐ 431	Steve Chitren RR	.10	.04	.01
☐ 432	Mike Benjamin RR	.08	.03	.01
☐ 433	Ryne Sandberg AS	.12	.05	.01
☐ 434	Len Dykstra AS	.06	.02	.00
☐ 435	Andre Dawson AS	.08	.03	.01
☐ 436A	Mike Scioscia AS (White star by name)	.03	.01	.00
☐ 436B	Mike Scioscia AS (Yellow star by name)	.03	.01	.00
☐ 437	Ozzie Smith AS	.08	.03	.01
☐ 438	Kevin Mitchell AS	.08	.03	.01
☐ 439	Jack Armstrong AS	.03	.01	.00
☐ 440	Chris Sabo AS	.06	.02	.00
☐ 441	Will Clark AS	.12	.05	.01
☐ 442	Mel Hall	.06	.02	.00
☐ 443	Mark Gardner	.03	.01	.00
☐ 444	Mike Devereaux	.03	.01	.00
☐ 445	Kirk Gibson	.06	.02	.00
☐ 446	Terry Pendleton	.08	.03	.01
☐ 447	Mike Harkey	.06	.02	.00
☐ 448	Jim Eisenreich	.03	.01	.00
☐ 449	Benito Santiago	.08	.03	.01
☐ 450	Oddibe McDowell	.03	.01	.00
☐ 451	Cecil Fielder	.15	.06	.01
☐ 452	Ken Griffey Sr.	.06	.02	.00
☐ 453	Bert Blyleven	.06	.02	.00
☐ 454	Howard Johnson	.08	.03	.01
☐ 455	Monty Farris	.10	.04	.01
☐ 456	Tony Pena	.06	.02	.00
☐ 457	Tim Raines	.08	.03	.01
☐ 458	Dennis Rasmussen	.03	.01	.00
☐ 459	Luis Quinones	.03	.01	.00
☐ 460	B.J. Surhoff	.03	.01	.00
☐ 461	Ernest Riles	.03	.01	.00
☐ 462	Rick Sutcliffe	.06	.02	.00
☐ 463	Danny Tartabull	.08	.03	.01
☐ 464	Pete Incaviglia	.06	.02	.00
☐ 465	Carlos Martinez	.03	.01	.00
☐ 466	Ricky Jordan	.06	.02	.00
☐ 467	John Cerutti	.03	.01	.00
☐ 468	Dave Winfield	.10	.04	.01
☐ 469	Francisco Oliveras	.03	.01	.00
☐ 470	Roy Smith	.03	.01	.00
☐ 471	Barry Larkin	.08	.03	.01
☐ 472	Ron Darling	.06	.02	.00
☐ 473	David Wells	.03	.01	.00
☐ 474	Glenn Davis	.08	.03	.01
☐ 475	Neal Heaton	.03	.01	.00
☐ 476	Ron Hassey	.03	.01	.00
☐ 477	Frank Thomas	1.25	.50	.12
☐ 478	Greg Vaughn	.10	.04	.01
☐ 479	Todd Burns	.03	.01	.00
☐ 480	Candy Maldonado	.03	.01	.00
☐ 481	Dave LaPoint	.03	.01	.00
☐ 482	Alvin Davis	.06	.02	.00
☐ 483	Mike Scott	.06	.02	.00
☐ 484	Dale Murphy	.10	.04	.01
☐ 485	Ben McDonald	.10	.04	.01
☐ 486	Jay Howell	.03	.01	.00
☐ 487	Vince Coleman	.08	.03	.01
☐ 488	Alfredo Griffin	.03	.01	.00
☐ 489	Sandy Alomar Jr.	.08	.03	.01
☐ 490	Kirby Puckett	.12	.05	.01
☐ 491	Andres Thomas	.03	.01	.00
☐ 492	Jack Morris	.08	.03	.01
☐ 493	Matt Young	.03	.01	.00
☐ 494	Greg Myers	.03	.01	.00
☐ 495	Barry Bonds	.12	.05	.01
☐ 496	Scott Cooper UER (No BA for 1990 and career)	.17	.07	.01
☐ 497	Dan Schatzeder	.03	.01	.00
☐ 498	Jesse Barfield	.06	.02	.00
☐ 499	Jerry Goff	.08	.03	.01
☐ 500	Checklist Card	.06	.01	.00
☐ 501	Anthony Telford	.08	.03	.01
☐ 502	Eddie Murray	.10	.04	.01
☐ 503	Omar Olivares	.10	.04	.01
☐ 504	Ryne Sandberg	.20	.08	.02
☐ 505	Jeff Montgomery	.03	.01	.00
☐ 506	Mark Parent	.03	.01	.00
☐ 507	Ron Gant	.12	.05	.01
☐ 508	Frank Tanana	.06	.02	.00
☐ 509	Jay Buhner	.06	.02	.00
☐ 510	Max Venable	.03	.01	.00
☐ 511	Wally Whitehurst	.03	.01	.00
☐ 512	Gary Pettis	.03	.01	.00
☐ 513	Tom Brunansky	.06	.02	.00
☐ 514	Tim Wallach	.06	.02	.00
☐ 515	Craig Lefferts	.03	.01	.00
☐ 516	Tim Layana	.03	.01	.00
☐ 517	Darryl Hamilton	.08	.03	.01
☐ 518	Rick Reuschel	.06	.02	.00
☐ 519	Steve Wilson	.03	.01	.00
☐ 520	Kurt Stillwell	.03	.01	.00
☐ 521	Rafael Palmeiro	.08	.03	.01

#	Player				#	Player			
☐ 522	Ken Patterson	.03	.01	.00	☐ 614	John Wetteland	.06	.02	.00
☐ 523	Len Dykstra	.06	.02	.00	☐ 615	Mike Perez	.10	.04	.01
☐ 524	Tony Fernandez	.06	.02	.00	☐ 616	Dave Clark	.03	.01	.00
☐ 525	Kent Anderson	.03	.01	.00	☐ 617	Brent Mayne	.08	.03	.01
☐ 526	Mark Leonard	.10	.04	.01	☐ 618	Jack Clark	.06	.02	.00
☐ 527	Allan Anderson	.03	.01	.00	☐ 619	Marvin Freeman	.03	.01	.00
☐ 528	Tom Browning	.06	.02	.00	☐ 620	Edwin Nunez	.03	.01	.00
☐ 529	Frank Viola	.08	.03	.01	☐ 621	Russ Swan	.08	.03	.01
☐ 530	John Olerud	.12	.05	.01	☐ 622	Johnny Ray	.03	.01	.00
☐ 531	Juan Agosto	.03	.01	.00	☐ 623	Charlie O'Brien	.03	.01	.00
☐ 532	Zane Smith	.06	.02	.00	☐ 624	Joe Bitker	.08	.03	.01
☐ 533	Scott Sanderson	.03	.01	.00	☐ 625	Mike Marshall	.06	.02	.00
☐ 534	Barry Jones	.03	.01	.00	☐ 626	Otis Nixon	.06	.02	.00
☐ 535	Mike Felder	.03	.01	.00	☐ 627	Andy Benes	.08	.03	.01
☐ 536	Jose Canseco	.25	.10	.02	☐ 628	Ron Oester	.03	.01	.00
☐ 537	Felix Fermin	.03	.01	.00	☐ 629	Ted Higuera	.03	.01	.00
☐ 538	Roberto Kelly	.08	.03	.01	☐ 630	Kevin Bass	.03	.01	.00
☐ 539	Brian Holman	.03	.01	.00	☐ 631	Damon Berryhill	.03	.01	.00
☐ 540	Mark Davidson	.03	.01	.00	☐ 632	Bo Jackson	.25	.10	.02
☐ 541	Terry Mulholland	.03	.01	.00	☐ 633	Brad Arnsberg	.03	.01	.00
☐ 542	Randy Milligan	.06	.02	.00	☐ 634	Jerry Willard	.03	.01	.00
☐ 543	Jose Gonzalez	.03	.01	.00	☐ 635	Tommy Greene	.06	.02	.00
☐ 544	Craig Wilson	.10	.04	.01	☐ 636	Bob MacDonald	.10	.04	.01
☐ 545	Mike Hartley	.03	.01	.00	☐ 637	Kirk McCaskill	.03	.01	.00
☐ 546	Greg Swindell	.06	.02	.00	☐ 638	John Burkett	.06	.02	.00
☐ 547	Gary Gaetti	.06	.02	.00	☐ 639	Paul Abbott	.08	.03	.01
☐ 548	Dave Justice	.50	.20	.05	☐ 640	Todd Benzinger	.03	.01	.00
☐ 549	Steve Searcy	.03	.01	.00	☐ 641	Todd Hundley	.10	.04	.01
☐ 550	Erik Hansen	.06	.02	.00	☐ 642	George Bell	.08	.03	.01
☐ 551	Dave Stieb	.06	.02	.00	☐ 643	Javier Ortiz	.08	.03	.01
☐ 552	Andy Van Slyke	.08	.03	.01	☐ 644	Sid Bream	.03	.01	.00
☐ 553	Mike Greenwell	.10	.04	.01	☐ 645	Bob Welch	.06	.02	.00
☐ 554	Kevin Maas	.17	.07	.01	☐ 646	Phil Bradley	.03	.01	.00
☐ 555	Delino DeShields	.10	.04	.01	☐ 647	Bill Krueger	.03	.01	.00
☐ 556	Curt Schilling	.03	.01	.00	☐ 648	Rickey Henderson	.20	.08	.02
☐ 557	Ramon Martinez	.10	.04	.01	☐ 649	Kevin Wickander	.03	.01	.00
☐ 558	Pedro Guerrero	.06	.02	.00	☐ 650	Steve Balboni	.03	.01	.00
☐ 559	Dwight Smith	.03	.01	.00	☐ 651	Gene Harris	.03	.01	.00
☐ 560	Mark Davis	.03	.01	.00	☐ 652	Jim Deshaies	.03	.01	.00
☐ 561	Shawn Abner	.03	.01	.00	☐ 653	Jason Grimsley	.08	.03	.01
☐ 562	Charlie Leibrandt	.03	.01	.00	☐ 654	Joe Orsulak	.03	.01	.00
☐ 563	John Shelby	.03	.01	.00	☐ 655	Jim Poole	.08	.03	.01
☐ 564	Bill Swift	.03	.01	.00	☐ 656	Felix Jose	.10	.04	.01
☐ 565	Mike Fetters	.03	.01	.00	☐ 657	Denis Cook	.03	.01	.00
☐ 566	Alejandro Pena	.06	.02	.00	☐ 658	Tom Brookens	.03	.01	.00
☐ 567	Ruben Sierra	.12	.05	.01	☐ 659	Junior Ortiz	.03	.01	.00
☐ 568	Carlos Quintana	.06	.02	.00	☐ 660	Jeff Parrett	.03	.01	.00
☐ 569	Kevin Gross	.03	.01	.00	☐ 661	Jerry Don Gleaton	.03	.01	.00
☐ 570	Derek Lilliquist	.03	.01	.00	☐ 662	Brent Knackert	.06	.02	.00
☐ 571	Jack Armstrong	.06	.02	.00	☐ 663	Rance Mulliniks	.03	.01	.00
☐ 572	Greg Brock	.03	.01	.00	☐ 664	John Smiley	.06	.02	.00
☐ 573	Mike Kingery	.03	.01	.00	☐ 665	Larry Andersen	.03	.01	.00
☐ 574	Greg Smith	.06	.02	.00	☐ 666	Willie McGee	.08	.03	.01
☐ 575	Brian McRae	.45	.18	.04	☐ 667	Chris Nabholz	.10	.04	.01
☐ 576	Jack Daugherty	.03	.01	.00	☐ 668	Brady Anderson	.03	.01	.00
☐ 577	Ozzie Guillen	.06	.02	.00	☐ 669	Darren Holmes UER	.08	.03	.01
☐ 578	Joe Boever	.03	.01	.00		(19 CG's, should be 0)			
☐ 579	Luis Sojo	.08	.03	.01	☐ 670	Ken Hill	.03	.01	.00
☐ 580	Chili Davis	.06	.02	.00	☐ 671	Gary Varsho	.03	.01	.00
☐ 581	Don Robinson	.03	.01	.00	☐ 672	Bill Pecota	.03	.01	.00
☐ 582	Brian Harper	.06	.02	.00	☐ 673	Fred Lynn	.06	.02	.00
☐ 583	Paul O'Neill	.06	.02	.00	☐ 674	Kevin Brown	.03	.01	.00
☐ 584	Bob Ojeda	.03	.01	.00	☐ 675	Dan Petry	.03	.01	.00
☐ 585	Mookie Wilson	.03	.01	.00	☐ 676	Mike Jackson	.03	.01	.00
☐ 586	Rafael Ramirez	.03	.01	.00	☐ 677	Wally Joyner	.08	.03	.01
☐ 587	Gary Redus	.03	.01	.00	☐ 678	Danny Jackson	.03	.01	.00
☐ 588	Jamie Quirk	.03	.01	.00	☐ 679	Bill Haselman	.08	.03	.01
☐ 589	Shawn Hillegas	.03	.01	.00	☐ 680	Mike Boddicker	.03	.01	.00
☐ 590	Tom Edens	.08	.03	.01	☐ 681	Mel Rojas	.08	.03	.01
☐ 591	Joe Klink	.06	.02	.00	☐ 682	Roberto Alomar	.10	.04	.01
☐ 592	Charles Nagy	.10	.04	.01	☐ 683	Dave Justice ROY	.30	.12	.03
☐ 593	Eric Plunk	.03	.01	.00	☐ 684	Chuck Crim	.03	.01	.00
☐ 594	Tracy Jones	.03	.01	.00	☐ 685	Matt Williams	.10	.04	.01
☐ 595	Craig Biggio	.06	.02	.00	☐ 686	Shawon Dunston	.06	.02	.00
☐ 596	Jose DeJesus	.03	.01	.00	☐ 687	Jeff Schulz	.08	.03	.01
☐ 597	Mickey Tettleton	.06	.02	.00	☐ 688	John Barfield	.08	.03	.01
☐ 598	Chris Gwynn	.03	.01	.00	☐ 689	Gerald Young	.03	.01	.00
☐ 599	Rex Hudler	.03	.01	.00	☐ 690	Luis Gonzalez	.45	.18	.04
☐ 600	Checklist Card	.06	.01	.00	☐ 691	Frank Wills	.06	.02	.00
☐ 601	Jim Gott	.03	.01	.00	☐ 692	Chuck Finley	.06	.02	.00
☐ 602	Jeff Manto	.06	.02	.00	☐ 693	Sandy Alomar Jr. ROY	.08	.03	.01
☐ 603	Nelson Liriano	.03	.01	.00	☐ 694	Tim Drummond	.03	.01	.00
☐ 604	Mark Lemke	.06	.02	.00	☐ 695	Herm Winningham	.03	.01	.00
☐ 605	Clay Parker	.03	.01	.00	☐ 696	Darryl Strawberry	.15	.06	.01
☐ 606	Edgar Martinez	.06	.02	.00	☐ 697	Al Leiter	.03	.01	.00
☐ 607	Mark Whiten	.20	.08	.02	☐ 698	Karl Rhodes	.08	.03	.01
☐ 608	Ted Power	.03	.01	.00	☐ 699	Stan Belinda	.08	.03	.01
☐ 609	Tom Bolton	.03	.01	.00	☐ 700	Checklist Card	.06	.01	.00
☐ 610	Tom Herr	.03	.01	.00	☐ 701	Lance Blankenship	.03	.01	.00
☐ 611	Andy Hawkins UER	.03	.01	.00	☐ 702	Willie Stargell PUZ	.06	.02	.00
	(Pitched No-Hitter					Puzzle Card			
	on 7/1, not 7/2)				☐ 703	Jim Gantner	.03	.01	.00
☐ 612	Scott Ruskin	.03	.01	.00	☐ 704	Reggie Harris	.08	.03	.01
☐ 613	Ron Kittle	.06	.02	.00	☐ 705	Rob Ducey	.06	.02	.00

☐ 706	Tim Hulett	.03	.01	.00
☐ 707	Atlee Hammaker	.03	.01	.00
☐ 708	Xavier Hernandez	.03	.01	.00
☐ 709	Chuck McElroy	.06	.02	.00
☐ 710	John Mitchell	.03	.01	.00
☐ 711	Carlos Hernandez	.03	.01	.00
☐ 712	Geronimo Pena	.06	.02	.00
☐ 713	Jim Neidlinger	.10	.04	.01
☐ 714	John Orton	.06	.02	.00
☐ 715	Terry Leach	.03	.01	.00
☐ 716	Mike Stanton	.03	.01	.00
☐ 717	Walt Terrell	.03	.01	.00
☐ 718	Luis Aquino	.03	.01	.00
☐ 719	Bud Black UER	.03	.01	.00
	(Blue Jays uniform, but Giants logo)			
☐ 720	Bob Kipper	.03	.01	.00
☐ 721	Jeff Gray	.08	.03	.01
☐ 722	Jose Rijo	.06	.02	.00
☐ 723	Curt Young	.03	.01	.00
☐ 724	Jose Vizcaino	.06	.02	.00
☐ 725	Randy Tomlin	.20	.08	.02
☐ 726	Junior Noboa	.06	.02	.00
☐ 727	Bob Welch CY	.06	.02	.00
☐ 728	Gary Ward	.03	.01	.00
☐ 729	Rob Deer UER	.06	.02	.00
	(Brewers uniform, but Tigers logo)			
☐ 730	David Segui	.08	.03	.01
☐ 731	Mark Carreon	.03	.01	.00
☐ 732	Vicente Palacios	.03	.01	.00
☐ 733	Sam Horn	.06	.02	.00
☐ 734	Howard Farmer	.08	.03	.01
☐ 735	Ken Dayley UER	.03	.01	.00
	(Cardinals uniform, but Blue Jays logo)			
☐ 736	Kelly Mann	.03	.01	.00
☐ 737	Joe Grahe	.08	.03	.01
☐ 738	Kelly Downs	.03	.01	.00
☐ 739	Jimmy Kremers	.08	.03	.01
☐ 740	Kevin Appier	.03	.01	.00
☐ 741	Jeff Reed	.03	.01	.00
☐ 742	Jose Rijo WS	.06	.02	.00
☐ 743	Dave Rohde	.06	.02	.00
☐ 744	Dr.Dirt/Mr.Clean UER	.06	.02	.00
	Len Dykstra Dale Murphy (No '91 Donruss logo on card front)			
☐ 745	Paul Sorrento	.03	.01	.00
☐ 746	Thomas Howard	.08	.03	.01
☐ 747	Matt Stark	.12	.05	.01
☐ 748	Harold Baines	.06	.02	.00
☐ 749	Doug Dascenzo	.03	.01	.00
☐ 750	Doug Drabek CY	.06	.02	.00
☐ 751	Gary Sheffield	.08	.03	.01
☐ 752	Terry Lee	.10	.04	.01
☐ 753	Jim Vatcher	.08	.03	.01
☐ 754	Lee Stevens	.08	.03	.01
☐ 755	Randy Veres	.08	.03	.01
☐ 756	Bill Doran	.03	.01	.00
☐ 757	Gary Wayne	.03	.01	.00
☐ 758	Pedro Munoz	.17	.07	.01
☐ 759	Chris Hammond	.08	.03	.01
☐ 760	Checklist Card	.06	.01	.00
☐ 761	Rickey Henderson MVP	.12	.05	.01
☐ 762	Barry Bonds MVP	.08	.03	.01
☐ 763	Billy Hatcher WS UER	.03	.01	.00
	(Line 13, on should be one)			
☐ 764	Julio Machado	.03	.01	.00
☐ 765	Jose Mesa	.03	.01	.00
☐ 766	Willie Randolph WS	.03	.01	.00
☐ 767	Scott Erickson	.75	.30	.07
☐ 768	Travis Fryman	.45	.18	.04
☐ 769	Rich Rodriguez	.08	.03	.01
☐ 770	Checklist Card	.06	.01	.00
☐ BC1	Langston/Witt	.05	.02	.00
	No-Hits Mariners			
☐ BC2	Randy Johnson	.05	.02	.00
	No-Hits Tigers			
☐ BC3	Nolan Ryan	.15	.06	.01
	No-Hits A's			
☐ BC4	Dave Stewart	.08	.03	.01
	No-Hits Blue Jays			
☐ BC5	Cecil Fielder	.10	.04	.01
	50 Homer Club			
☐ BC6	Carlton Fisk	.08	.03	.01
	Record Home Run			
☐ BC7	Ryne Sandberg	.10	.04	.01
	Sets Fielding Records			
☐ BC8	Gary Carter	.08	.03	.01
	Breaks Catching Mark			
☐ BC9	Mark McGwire UER	.10	.04	.01
	Home Run Milestone (Back says First Baseman, others say only base)			
☐ BC10	Bo Jackson	.15	.06	.01
	Four Consecutive HR's			
☐ BC11	Fernando Valenzuela	.08	.03	.01
	No Hits Cardinals			
☐ BC12A	Andy Hawkins ERR	1.00	.40	.10
	Pitcher			
☐ BC12B	Andy Hawkins COR	.05	.02	.00
	No Hits White Sox			
☐ BC13	Melido Perez	.05	.02	.00
	No Hits Yankees			
☐ BC14	Terry Mulholland UER	.05	.02	.00
	No Hits Giants (Charlie Hayes is called Chris Hayes)			
☐ BC15	Nolan Ryan	.15	.06	.01
	300th Win			
☐ BC16	Delino DeShields	.08	.03	.01
	4 Hits in Debut			
☐ BC17	Cal Ripken	.12	.05	.01
	Errorless Games			
☐ BC18	Eddie Murray	.08	.03	.01
	Switch Hit Homers			
☐ BC19	George Brett	.08	.03	.01
	3 Decade Champ			
☐ BC20	Bobby Thigpen	.05	.02	.00
	Shatters Save Mark			
☐ BC21	Dave Stieb	.05	.02	.00
	No Hits Indians			
☐ BC22	Willie McGee	.08	.03	.01
	NL Batting Champ			

1991 Donruss Elite

These special cards were inserted in the 1991 Donruss first series wax packs. Production was limited to a maximum of 10,000 cards for each card in the Elite series, and lesser production for the Sandberg Signature (5,000) and Ryan Legend (7,500) cards. The regular Elite cards are photos enclosed in a bronze marble borders which surround an evenly squared photo of the players. The Sandberg Signature card has a green marble border and is signed in a blue sharpie. The Nolan Ryan Legend card is a Dick Perez drawing with silver borders. The cards are all numbered on the back, 1 out of 10,000, etc. All of these special cards measure the standard, 2 1/2" by 3 1/2".

		MINT	EXC	G-VG
COMPLETE SET (10)		1650.00	750.00	175.00
COMMON PLAYER (1-8)		80.00	36.00	12.00
☐ E1	Barry Bonds	120.00	55.00	18.00
☐ E2	George Brett	135.00	60.00	20.00
☐ E3	Jose Canseco	175.00	80.00	27.00
☐ E4	Andre Dawson	100.00	45.00	15.00
☐ E5	Doug Drabek	80.00	36.00	12.00
☐ E6	Cecil Fielder	120.00	55.00	18.00
☐ E7	Rickey Henderson	175.00	80.00	27.00
☐ E8	Matt Williams	100.00	45.00	15.00
☐ L1	Nolan Ryan (Legend)	450.00	200.00	67.50
☐ S1	Ryne Sandberg	450.00	200.00	67.50
	(Signature Series)			

1991 Donruss Super DK's

For the seventh consecutive year Donruss has issued a card set featuring the players used in the current year's Diamond King subset in a larger size, approximately 5" by 7". The set again features the art work of famed sports artist Dick Perez and is available through a postpaid mail-in offer detailed on the 1991 Donruss wax packs involving 14.00 and three wax wrappers.

	MINT	EXC	G-VG
COMPLETE SET (26)	12.00	5.25	1.50
COMMON PLAYER (1-26)	.30	.12	.03

		MINT	EXC	G-VG
☐ 1	Dave Stieb DK	.40	.16	.04
☐ 2	Craig Biggio DK	.40	.16	.04
☐ 3	Cecil Fielder DK	.60	.25	.06
☐ 4	Barry Bonds DK	.60	.25	.06
☐ 5	Barry Larkin DK	.50	.20	.05
☐ 6	Dave Parker DK	.40	.16	.04
☐ 7	Len Dykstra DK	.40	.16	.04
☐ 8	Bobby Thigpen DK	.40	.16	.04
☐ 9	Roger Clemens DK	.90	.40	.09
☐ 10	Ron Gant DK	.60	.25	.06
☐ 11	Delino DeShields DK	.60	.25	.06
☐ 12	Roberto Alomar DK	.60	.25	.06
☐ 13	Sandy Alomar Jr. DK	.50	.20	.05
☐ 14	Ryne Sandberg DK	.90	.40	.09
☐ 15	Ramon Martinez DK	.75	.30	.07
☐ 16	Edgar Martinez DK	.50	.20	.05
☐ 17	Dave Magadan DK	.50	.20	.05
☐ 18	Matt Williams DK	.60	.25	.06
☐ 19	Rafael Palmeiro DK	.60	.25	.06
☐ 20	Bob Welch DK	.40	.16	.04
☐ 21	Dave Righetti DK	.40	.16	.04
☐ 22	Brian Harper DK	.40	.16	.04
☐ 23	Gregg Olson DK	.50	.20	.05
☐ 24	Kurt Stillwell DK	.40	.16	.04
☐ 25	Pedro Guerrero DK	.50	.20	.05
☐ 26	Chuck Finley DK	.50	.20	.05

1991 Donruss Grand Slammers

This 14-card set commemorates players who hit grand slams in 1990. The cards measure the standard size (2 1/2" by 3 1/2") and feature on the fronts color player photos on a computer-generated background design, enframed by white borders on a green card face crisscrossed by different color diagonal stripes. The player's name is given in a color stripe below the picture. Inside pale green borders, the back recounts grand slam homers by the player. The cards are numbered on the back and include a checklist at the bottom.

	MINT	EXC	G-VG
COMPLETE SET (14)	2.50	1.00	.25
COMMON PLAYER (1-14)	.10	.04	.01

		MINT	EXC	G-VG
☐ 1	Joe Carter	.25	.10	.02
☐ 2	Bobby Bonilla	.30	.12	.03
☐ 3	Kal Daniels	.15	.06	.01

		MINT	EXC	G-VG
☐ 4	Jose Canseco	.75	.30	.07
☐ 5	Barry Bonds	.25	.10	.02
☐ 6	Jay Buhner	.20	.08	.02
☐ 7	Cecil Fielder	.35	.15	.03
☐ 8	Matt Williams	.20	.08	.02
☐ 9	Andres Galarraga	.15	.06	.01
☐ 10	Luis Polonia	.10	.04	.01
☐ 11	Mark McGwire	.30	.12	.03
☐ 12	Ron Karkovice	.10	.04	.01
☐ 13	Darryl Strawbery UER (Todd Hundley is called Randy)	.50	.20	.05
☐ 14	Mike Greenwell	.25	.10	.02

1991 Donruss Rookies

The 1991 Donruss Rookies set is a boxed set issued to honor the best rookies of the season. The cards measure the standard size (2 1/2" by 3 1/2"), and a mini puzzle featuring Hall of Famer Willie Stargell was included with the set. The fronts feature color action player photos, with white and red borders. Yellow and green stripes cut across the bottom of the card face, presenting the player's name and position. The words "The Rookies" and a baseball icon appear in the lower left corner of the picture. The horizontally oriented backs are printed in black on a green and white background, and present biography, statistics, and career highlights. The cards are numbered on the back. Outstanding rookies showcased in the set are Jeff Bagwell, Chito Martinez, Orlando Merced, Dean Palmer, Ivan Rodriguez, Todd Van Poppel, and Mo Vaughn.

	MINT	EXC	G-VG
COMPLETE SET (56)	8.50	3.75	.85
COMMON PLAYER (1-56)	.05	.02	.00

		MINT	EXC	G-VG
☐ 1	Pat Kelly	.30	.10	.02
☐ 2	Rich DeLucia	.10	.04	.01
☐ 3	Wes Chamberlain	.30	.12	.03
☐ 4	Scott Leius	.15	.06	.01
☐ 5	Darryl Kile	.15	.06	.01

		MINT	EXC	G-VG
☐ 6	Milt Cuyler	.12	.05	.01
☐ 7	Todd Van Poppel	1.00	.40	.10
☐ 8	Ray Lankford	.25	.10	.02
☐ 9	Brian Hunter	.75	.30	.07
☐ 10	Tony Perezchica	.05	.02	.00
☐ 11	Ced Landrum	.17	.07	.01
☐ 12	Dave Burba	.10	.04	.01
☐ 13	Ramon Garcia	.10	.04	.01
☐ 14	Ed Sprague	.10	.04	.01
☐ 15	Warren Newson	.20	.08	.02
☐ 16	Paul Faries	.10	.04	.01
☐ 17	Luis Gonzales	.30	.12	.03
☐ 18	Charles Nagy	.10	.04	.01
☐ 19	Chris Hammond	.08	.03	.01
☐ 20	Frank Castillo	.15	.06	.01
☐ 21	Pedro Munoz	.20	.08	.02
☐ 22	Orlando Merced	.35	.15	.03
☐ 23	Jose Melendez	.12	.05	.01
☐ 24	Kirk Dressendorfer	.20	.08	.02
☐ 25	Heathcliff Slocumb	.10	.04	.01
☐ 26	Doug Simons	.12	.05	.01
☐ 27	Mike Timlin	.15	.06	.01
☐ 28	Jeff Fassaro	.15	.06	.01
☐ 29	Mark Leiter	.12	.05	.01
☐ 30	Jeff Bagwell	3.00	1.25	.30
☐ 31	Brian McRae	.35	.15	.03
☐ 32	Mark Whiten	.20	.08	.02
☐ 33	Ivan Rodriguez	2.00	.80	.20
☐ 34	Wade Taylor	.17	.07	.01
☐ 35	Darren Lewis	.17	.07	.01
☐ 36	Mo Vaughn	.45	.18	.04
☐ 37	Mike Remlinger	.12	.05	.01
☐ 38	Rick Wilkins	.17	.07	.01
☐ 39	Chuck Knoblauch	.40	.16	.04
☐ 40	Kevin Morton	.10	.04	.01
☐ 41	Carlos Rodriguez	.15	.06	.01
☐ 42	Mark Lewis	.20	.08	.02
☐ 43	Brent Mayne	.10	.04	.01
☐ 44	Chris Haney	.15	.06	.01
☐ 45	Denis Boucher	.15	.06	.01
☐ 46	Mike Gardiner	.10	.04	.01
☐ 47	Jeff Johnson	.20	.08	.02
☐ 48	Dean Palmer	.35	.15	.03
☐ 49	Chuck McElroy	.08	.03	.01
☐ 50	Chris Jones	.17	.07	.01
☐ 51	Scott Kamieniecki	.17	.07	.01
☐ 52	Al Osuna	.15	.06	.01
☐ 53	Rusty Meacham	.12	.05	.01
☐ 54	Chito Martinez	.50	.20	.05
☐ 55	Reggie Jefferson	.35	.15	.03
☐ 56	Checklist Card	.05	.01	.00

1992 Donruss Preview

This 12-card preview set was available only to Donruss dealers. The standard-size (2 1/2" by 3 1/2") cards feature the same glossy color player photos on the fronts and player information on the backs as the regular series issue. The statistics only go through the 1990 season. Only the numbering of the cards on the back is different.

	MINT	EXC	G-VG
COMPLETE SET (12)	250.00	110.00	37.50
COMMON PLAYER (1-12)	15.00	6.50	2.15

		MINT	EXC	G-VG
☐ 1	Wade Boggs	35.00	15.75	5.25
☐ 2	Barry Bonds	35.00	15.75	5.25
☐ 3	Will Clark	45.00	20.00	6.75
☐ 4	Andre Dawson	25.00	11.00	3.50
☐ 5	Dennis Eckersley	20.00	8.50	2.75
☐ 6	Robin Ventura	25.00	11.00	3.50
☐ 7	Ken Griffey Jr.	75.00	34.00	11.25
☐ 8	Kelly Gruber	15.00	6.50	2.15
☐ 9	Ryan Klesko	60.00	27.00	9.00
☐ 10	Cal Ripken	45.00	20.00	6.75
☐ 11	Nolan Ryan	60.00	27.00	9.00
☐ 12	Todd Van Poppel	35.00	15.75	5.25

1992 Donruss I

The 1992 Donruss Series I contains 396 cards, measuring the standard size (2 1/2" by 3 1/2"). The front design features glossy color player photos with white borders. Two-toned blue stripes overlay the top and bottom of the picture, with the player's name printed in silver-and-black lettering above the bottom stripe. The horizontally oriented backs have a color headshot of the player (except on subset cards listed below), biography, career highlights, and recent Major League performance statistics (no earlier than 1987). The set includes 20 Rated Rookies (1-20), ten All-Stars (21-30), five Highlight cards (33, 94, 154, 215, 276), and a puzzle of Hall of Famer Rod Carew. The cards are numbered on the back and checklisted below accordingly. Thirteen Diamond Kings cards featuring the artwork of Dick Perez are randomly inserted in foil packs. Also inserted in Series 1 and 2 foil and rack packs are 5,000 Cal Ripken autographed cards, 7,500 Legend cards of Rickey Henderson, and 10,000 Elite cards each of Wade Boggs, Joe Carter, Will Clark, Dwight Gooden, Ken Griffey Jr., Tony Gwynn, Howard Johnson, Terry Pendleton, Kirby Puckett, and Frank Thomas.

	MINT	EXC	G-VG
COMPLETE SET (396)	24.00	10.50	3.50
COMMON PLAYER (1-396)	.04	.02	.00

		MINT	EXC	G-VG
☐ 1	Mark Wohlers RR	.40	.16	.04
☐ 2	Wilfredo Cordero RR	.25	.10	.02
☐ 3	Kyle Abbott RR	.15	.06	.01
☐ 4	Dave Nilsson RR	.60	.25	.06
☐ 5	Kenny Lofton RR	.35	.15	.03
☐ 6	Luis Mercedes RR	.30	.12	.03
☐ 7	Roger Salkeld RR	.30	.12	.03
☐ 8	Eddie Zosky RR	.15	.06	.01
☐ 9	Todd Van Poppel RR	.75	.30	.07
☐ 10	Frank Seminara RR	.15	.06	.01
☐ 11	Andy Ashby RR	.10	.04	.01
☐ 12	Reggie Jefferson RR	.25	.10	.02
☐ 13	Ryan Klesko RR	2.00	.80	.20
☐ 14	Carlos Garcia RR	.07	.03	.01
☐ 15	John Ramos RR	.18	.08	.01
☐ 16	Eric Karros RR	.35	.15	.03
☐ 17	Patrick Lennon RR	.30	.12	.03
☐ 18	Eddie Taubensee RR	.25	.10	.02
☐ 19	Roberto Hernandez RR	.18	.08	.01
☐ 20	D.J. Dozier RR	.12	.05	.01
☐ 21	Dave Henderson AS	.07	.03	.01

#	Player			
☐ 22	Cal Ripken AS	.18	.08	.01
☐ 23	Wade Boggs AS	.12	.05	.01
☐ 24	Ken Griffey Jr. AS	.30	.12	.03
☐ 25	Jack Morris AS	.07	.03	.01
☐ 26	Danny Tartabull AS	.07	.03	.01
☐ 27	Cecil Fielder AS	.12	.05	.01
☐ 28	Roberto Alomar AS	.10	.04	.01
☐ 29	Sandy Alomar Jr. AS	.07	.03	.01
☐ 30	Rickey Henderson AS	.15	.06	.01
☐ 31	Ken Hill	.04	.02	.00
☐ 32	John Habyan	.04	.02	.00
☐ 33	Otis Nixon HL	.07	.03	.01
☐ 34	Tim Wallach	.07	.03	.01
☐ 35	Cal Ripken	.40	.16	.04
☐ 36	Gary Carter	.10	.04	.01
☐ 37	Juan Agosto	.04	.02	.00
☐ 38	Doug Dascenzo	.04	.02	.00
☐ 39	Kirk Gibson	.10	.04	.01
☐ 40	Benito Santiago	.10	.04	.01
☐ 41	Otis Nixon	.07	.03	.01
☐ 42	Andy Allanson	.04	.02	.00
☐ 43	Brian Holman	.04	.02	.00
☐ 44	Dick Schofield	.04	.02	.00
☐ 45	Dave Magadan	.07	.03	.01
☐ 46	Rafael Palmeiro	.12	.05	.01
☐ 47	Jody Reed	.07	.03	.01
☐ 48	Ivan Calderon	.07	.03	.01
☐ 49	Greg Harris	.04	.02	.00
☐ 50	Chris Sabo	.10	.04	.01
☐ 51	Paul Molitor	.10	.04	.01
☐ 52	Robby Thompson	.04	.02	.00
☐ 53	Dave Smith	.04	.02	.00
☐ 54	Mark Davis	.07	.03	.01
☐ 55	Kevin Brown	.07	.03	.01
☐ 56	Donn Pall	.04	.02	.00
☐ 57	Lenny Dykstra	.07	.03	.01
☐ 58	Roberto Alomar	.15	.06	.01
☐ 59	Jeff Robinson	.04	.02	.00
☐ 60	Willie McGee	.10	.04	.01
☐ 61	Jay Buhner	.07	.03	.01
☐ 62	Mike Pagliarulo	.04	.02	.00
☐ 63	Paul O'Neill	.07	.03	.01
☐ 64	Hubie Brooks	.07	.03	.01
☐ 65	Kelly Gruber	.10	.04	.01
☐ 66	Ken Caminiti	.07	.03	.01
☐ 67	Gary Redus	.04	.02	.00
☐ 68	Harold Baines	.07	.03	.01
☐ 69	Charlie Hough	.04	.02	.00
☐ 70	B.J. Surhoff	.07	.03	.01
☐ 71	Walt Weiss	.07	.03	.01
☐ 72	Shawn Hillegas	.04	.02	.00
☐ 73	Roberto Kelly	.10	.04	.01
☐ 74	Jeff Ballard	.04	.02	.00
☐ 75	Craig Biggio	.10	.04	.01
☐ 76	Pat Combs	.04	.02	.00
☐ 77	Jeff Robinson	.04	.02	.00
☐ 78	Tim Belcher	.07	.03	.01
☐ 79	Cris Carpenter	.04	.02	.00
☐ 80	Checklist Card	.07	.03	.01
☐ 81	Steve Avery	.30	.12	.03
☐ 82	Chris James	.04	.02	.00
☐ 83	Brian Harper	.04	.02	.00
☐ 84	Charlie Leibrandt	.04	.02	.00
☐ 85	Mickey Tettleton	.07	.03	.01
☐ 86	Pete O'Brien	.04	.02	.00
☐ 87	Danny Darwin	.04	.02	.00
☐ 88	Bob Walk	.04	.02	.00
☐ 89	Jeff Reardon	.07	.03	.01
☐ 90	Bobby Rose	.04	.02	.00
☐ 91	Danny Jackson	.04	.02	.00
☐ 92	John Morris	.04	.02	.00
☐ 93	Bud Black	.04	.02	.00
☐ 94	Tommy Greene HL	.07	.03	.01
☐ 95	Rick Aguilera	.04	.02	.00
☐ 96	Gary Gaetti	.07	.03	.01
☐ 97	David Cone	.10	.04	.01
☐ 98	John Olerud	.15	.06	.01
☐ 99	Joel Skinner	.04	.02	.00
☐ 100	Jay Bell	.04	.02	.00
☐ 101	Bob Milacki	.04	.02	.00
☐ 102	Norm Charlton	.04	.02	.00
☐ 103	Chuck Crim	.04	.02	.00
☐ 104	Terry Steinbach	.07	.03	.01
☐ 105	Juan Samuel	.07	.03	.01
☐ 106	Steve Howe	.04	.02	.00
☐ 107	Rafael Belliard	.04	.02	.00
☐ 108	Joey Cora	.04	.02	.00
☐ 109	Tommy Greene	.10	.04	.01
☐ 110	Gregg Olson	.10	.04	.01
☐ 111	Frank Tanana	.07	.03	.01
☐ 112	Lee Smith	.07	.03	.01
☐ 113	Greg Harris	.04	.02	.00
☐ 114	Dwayne Henry	.04	.02	.00
☐ 115	Chili Davis	.07	.03	.01
☐ 116	Kent Mercker	.07	.03	.01
☐ 117	Brian Barnes	.04	.02	.00
☐ 118	Rich DeLucia	.04	.02	.00
☐ 119	Andre Dawson	.12	.05	.01
☐ 120	Carlos Baerga	.12	.05	.01
☐ 121	Mike LaValliere	.04	.02	.00
☐ 122	Jeff Gray	.04	.02	.00
☐ 123	Bruce Hurst	.07	.03	.01
☐ 124	Alvin Davis	.07	.03	.01
☐ 125	John Candelaria	.04	.02	.00
☐ 126	Matt Nokes	.07	.03	.01
☐ 127	George Bell	.10	.04	.01
☐ 128	Bret Saberhagen	.10	.04	.01
☐ 129	Jeff Russell	.04	.02	.00
☐ 130	Jim Abbott	.12	.05	.01
☐ 131	Bill Gullickson	.04	.02	.00
☐ 132	Todd Zeile	.12	.05	.01
☐ 133	Dave Winfield	.12	.05	.01
☐ 134	Wally Whitehurst	.04	.02	.00
☐ 135	Matt Williams	.12	.05	.01
☐ 136	Tom Browning	.07	.03	.01
☐ 137	Marquis Grissom	.10	.04	.01
☐ 138	Erik Hanson	.07	.03	.01
☐ 139	Rob Dibble	.07	.03	.01
☐ 140	Don August	.04	.02	.00
☐ 141	Tom Henke	.04	.02	.00
☐ 142	Dan Pasqua	.04	.02	.00
☐ 143	George Brett	.15	.06	.01
☐ 144	Jerald Clark	.04	.02	.00
☐ 145	Robin Ventura	.30	.12	.03
☐ 146	Dale Murphy	.12	.05	.01
☐ 147	Dennis Eckersley	.10	.04	.01
☐ 148	Eric Yelding	.04	.02	.00
☐ 149	Mario Diaz	.04	.02	.00
☐ 150	Casey Candaele	.04	.02	.00
☐ 151	Steve Olin	.04	.02	.00
☐ 152	Luis Salazar	.04	.02	.00
☐ 153	Kevin Maas	.18	.08	.01
☐ 154	Nolan Ryan HL	.35	.15	.03
☐ 155	Barry Jones	.04	.02	.00
☐ 156	Chris Hoiles	.07	.03	.01
☐ 157	Bobby Ojeda	.04	.02	.00
☐ 158	Pedro Guerrero	.10	.04	.01
☐ 159	Paul Assenmacher	.04	.02	.00
☐ 160	Checklist Card	.07	.03	.01
☐ 161	Mike Macfarlane	.04	.02	.00
☐ 162	Craig Lefferts	.04	.02	.00
☐ 163	Brian Hunter	.60	.25	.06
☐ 164	Alan Trammell	.10	.04	.01
☐ 165	Ken Griffey Jr.	.75	.30	.07
☐ 166	Lance Parrish	.07	.03	.01
☐ 167	Brian Downing	.04	.02	.00
☐ 168	John Barfield	.04	.02	.00
☐ 169	Jack Clark	.07	.03	.01
☐ 170	Chris Nabholz	.04	.02	.00
☐ 171	Tim Teufel	.04	.02	.00
☐ 172	Chris Hammond	.07	.03	.01
☐ 173	Robin Yount	.15	.06	.01
☐ 174	Dave Righetti	.07	.03	.01
☐ 175	Joe Girardi	.04	.02	.00
☐ 176	Mike Boddicker	.04	.02	.00
☐ 177	Dean Palmer	.25	.10	.02
☐ 178	Greg Hibbard	.04	.02	.00
☐ 179	Randy Ready	.04	.02	.00
☐ 180	Devon White	.07	.03	.01
☐ 181	Mark Eichhorn	.04	.02	.00
☐ 182	Mike Felder	.04	.02	.00
☐ 183	Joe Klink	.04	.02	.00
☐ 184	Steve Bedrosian	.04	.02	.00
☐ 185	Barry Larkin	.12	.05	.01
☐ 186	John Franco	.04	.02	.00
☐ 187	Ed Sprague	.10	.04	.01
☐ 188	Mark Portugal	.04	.02	.00
☐ 189	Jose Lind	.04	.02	.00
☐ 190	Bob Welch	.07	.03	.01
☐ 191	Alex Fernandez	.12	.05	.01
☐ 192	Gary Sheffield	.10	.04	.01
☐ 193	Rickey Henderson	.25	.10	.02
☐ 194	Rod Nichols	.04	.02	.00
☐ 195	Scott Kamieniecki	.10	.04	.01
☐ 196	Mike Flanagan	.07	.03	.01
☐ 197	Steve Finley	.07	.03	.01
☐ 198	Darren Daulton	.04	.02	.00
☐ 199	Leo Gomez	.15	.06	.01
☐ 200	Mike Morgan	.07	.03	.01
☐ 201	Bob Tewksbury	.04	.02	.00
☐ 202	Sid Bream	.04	.02	.00
☐ 203	Sandy Alomar Jr.	.10	.04	.01
☐ 204	Greg Gagne	.04	.02	.00
☐ 205	Juan Berenguer	.04	.02	.00
☐ 206	Cecil Fielder	.20	.08	.02
☐ 207	Randy Johnson	.07	.03	.01
☐ 208	Tony Pena	.07	.03	.01
☐ 209	Doug Drabek	.07	.03	.01

☐ 210	Wade Boggs	.20	.08	.02
☐ 211	Bryan Harvey	.07	.03	.01
☐ 212	Jose Vizcaino	.04	.02	.00
☐ 213	Alonzo Powell	.10	.04	.01
☐ 214	Will Clark	.25	.10	.02
☐ 215	Rickey Henderson HL	.15	.06	.01
☐ 216	Jack Morris	.10	.04	.01
☐ 217	Junior Felix	.07	.03	.01
☐ 218	Vince Coleman	.10	.04	.01
☐ 219	Jimmy Key	.07	.03	.01
☐ 220	Alex Cole	.07	.03	.01
☐ 221	Bill Landrum	.04	.02	.00
☐ 222	Randy Milligan	.04	.02	.00
☐ 223	Jose Rijo	.07	.03	.01
☐ 224	Greg Vaughn	.12	.05	.01
☐ 225	Dave Stewart	.10	.04	.01
☐ 226	Lenny Harris	.04	.02	.00
☐ 227	Scott Sanderson	.04	.02	.00
☐ 228	Jeff Blauser	.04	.02	.00
☐ 229	Ozzie Guillen	.07	.03	.01
☐ 230	John Kruk	.04	.02	.00
☐ 231	Bob Melvin	.04	.02	.00
☐ 232	Milt Cuyler	.12	.05	.01
☐ 233	Felix Jose	.15	.06	.01
☐ 234	Ellis Burks	.10	.04	.01
☐ 235	Pete Harnisch	.07	.03	.01
☐ 236	Kevin Tapani	.10	.04	.01
☐ 237	Terry Pendleton	.10	.04	.01
☐ 238	Mark Gardner	.04	.02	.00
☐ 239	Harold Reynolds	.04	.02	.00
☐ 240	Checklist Card	.07	.03	.01
☐ 241	Mike Harkey	.04	.02	.00
☐ 242	Felix Fermin	.04	.02	.00
☐ 243	Barry Bonds	.18	.08	.01
☐ 244	Roger Clemens	.25	.10	.02
☐ 245	Dennis Rasmussen	.04	.02	.00
☐ 246	Jose DeLeon	.04	.02	.00
☐ 247	Orel Hershiser	.10	.04	.01
☐ 248	Mel Hall	.07	.03	.01
☐ 249	Rick Wilkins	.10	.04	.01
☐ 250	Tom Gordon	.07	.03	.01
☐ 251	Kevin Reimer	.07	.03	.01
☐ 252	Luis Polonia	.07	.03	.01
☐ 253	Mike Henneman	.04	.02	.00
☐ 254	Tom Pagnozzi	.04	.02	.00
☐ 255	Chuck Finley	.10	.04	.01
☐ 256	Mackey Sasser	.04	.02	.00
☐ 257	John Burkett	.04	.02	.00
☐ 258	Hal Morris	.12	.05	.01
☐ 259	Larry Walker	.07	.03	.01
☐ 260	Billy Swift	.04	.02	.00
☐ 261	Joe Oliver	.04	.02	.00
☐ 262	Julio Machado	.04	.02	.00
☐ 263	Todd Stottlemyre	.07	.03	.01
☐ 264	Matt Merullo	.04	.02	.00
☐ 265	Brent Mayne	.10	.04	.01
☐ 266	Thomas Howard	.04	.02	.00
☐ 267	Lance Johnson	.04	.02	.00
☐ 268	Terry Mulholland	.04	.02	.00
☐ 269	Rick Honeycutt	.04	.02	.00
☐ 270	Luis Gonzalez	.18	.08	.01
☐ 271	Jose Guzman	.04	.02	.00
☐ 272	Jimmy Jones	.04	.02	.00
☐ 273	Mark Lewis	.18	.08	.01
☐ 274	Rene Gonzales	.04	.02	.00
☐ 275	Jeff Johnson	.10	.04	.01
☐ 276	Dennis Martinez HL	.07	.03	.01
☐ 277	Delino DeShields	.10	.04	.01
☐ 278	Sam Horn	.04	.02	.00
☐ 279	Kevin Gross	.04	.02	.00
☐ 280	Jose Oquendo	.04	.02	.00
☐ 281	Mark Grace	.10	.04	.01
☐ 282	Mark Gubicza	.07	.03	.01
☐ 283	Fred McGriff	.12	.05	.01
☐ 284	Ron Gant	.15	.06	.01
☐ 285	Lou Whitaker	.07	.03	.01
☐ 286	Edgar Martinez	.10	.04	.01
☐ 287	Ron Tingley	.04	.02	.00
☐ 288	Kevin McReynolds	.10	.04	.01
☐ 289	Ivan Rodriguez	1.00	.40	.10
☐ 290	Mike Gardiner	.10	.04	.01
☐ 291	Chris Haney	.10	.04	.01
☐ 292	Darrin Jackson	.04	.02	.00
☐ 293	Bill Doran	.04	.02	.00
☐ 294	Ted Higuera	.04	.02	.00
☐ 295	Jeff Brantley	.04	.02	.00
☐ 296	Les Lancaster	.04	.02	.00
☐ 297	Jim Eisenreich	.04	.02	.00
☐ 298	Ruben Sierra	.20	.08	.02
☐ 299	Scott Radinsky	.04	.02	.00
☐ 300	Jose DeJesus	.04	.02	.00
☐ 301	Mike Timlin	.10	.04	.01
☐ 302	Luis Sojo	.04	.02	.00
☐ 303	Kelly Downs	.04	.02	.00
☐ 304	Scott Bankhead	.04	.02	.00
☐ 305	Pedro Munoz	.15	.06	.01
☐ 306	Scott Scudder	.04	.02	.00
☐ 307	Kevin Elster	.04	.02	.00
☐ 308	Duane Ward	.04	.02	.00
☐ 309	Darryl Kile	.10	.04	.01
☐ 310	Orlando Merced	.20	.08	.02
☐ 311	Dave Henderson	.10	.04	.01
☐ 312	Tim Raines	.10	.04	.01
☐ 313	Mark Lee	.10	.04	.01
☐ 314	Mike Gallego	.04	.02	.00
☐ 315	Charles Nagy	.07	.03	.01
☐ 316	Jesse Barfield	.07	.03	.01
☐ 317	Todd Frohwirth	.04	.02	.00
☐ 318	Al Osuna	.04	.02	.00
☐ 319	Darrin Fletcher	.04	.02	.00
☐ 320	Checklist Card	.07	.03	.01
☐ 321	David Segui	.07	.03	.01
☐ 322	Stan Javier	.04	.02	.00
☐ 323	Bryn Smith	.04	.02	.00
☐ 324	Jeff Treadway	.04	.02	.00
☐ 325	Mark Whiten	.15	.06	.01
☐ 326	Kent Hrbek	.07	.03	.01
☐ 327	Dave Justice	.50	.20	.05
☐ 328	Tony Phillips	.04	.02	.00
☐ 329	Rob Murphy	.04	.02	.00
☐ 330	Kevin Morton	.10	.04	.01
☐ 331	John Smiley	.07	.03	.01
☐ 332	Luis Rivera	.04	.02	.00
☐ 333	Wally Joyner	.10	.04	.01
☐ 334	Heathcliff Slocumb	.04	.02	.00
☐ 335	Rick Cerone	.04	.02	.00
☐ 336	Mike Remlinger	.04	.02	.00
☐ 337	Mike Moore	.07	.03	.01
☐ 338	Lloyd McClendon	.04	.02	.00
☐ 339	Al Newman	.04	.02	.00
☐ 340	Kirk McCaskill	.04	.02	.00
☐ 341	Howard Johnson	.12	.05	.01
☐ 342	Greg Myers	.04	.02	.00
☐ 343	Kal Daniels	.10	.04	.01
☐ 344	Bernie Williams	.25	.10	.02
☐ 345	Shane Mack	.07	.03	.01
☐ 346	Gary Thurman	.04	.02	.00
☐ 347	Dante Bichette	.04	.02	.00
☐ 348	Mark McGwire	.15	.06	.01
☐ 349	Travis Fryman	.25	.10	.02
☐ 350	Ray Lankford	.17	.07	.01
☐ 351	Mike Jeffcoat	.04	.02	.00
☐ 352	Jack McDowell	.10	.04	.01
☐ 353	Mitch Williams	.07	.03	.01
☐ 354	Mike Devereaux	.04	.02	.00
☐ 355	Andres Galarraga	.07	.03	.01
☐ 356	Henry Cotto	.04	.02	.00
☐ 357	Scott Bailes	.04	.02	.00
☐ 358	Jeff Bagwell	1.50	.60	.15
☐ 359	Scott Leius	.07	.03	.01
☐ 360	Zane Smith	.04	.02	.00
☐ 361	Bill Pecota	.04	.02	.00
☐ 362	Tony Fernandez	.07	.03	.01
☐ 363	Glenn Braggs	.04	.02	.00
☐ 364	Bill Spiers	.04	.02	.00
☐ 365	Vicente Palacios	.04	.02	.00
☐ 366	Tim Burke	.04	.02	.00
☐ 367	Randy Tomlin	.10	.04	.01
☐ 368	Kenny Rogers	.04	.02	.00
☐ 369	Brett Butler	.07	.03	.01
☐ 370	Pat Kelly	.15	.06	.01
☐ 371	Bip Roberts	.04	.02	.00
☐ 372	Gregg Jefferies	.10	.04	.01
☐ 373	Kevin Bass	.04	.02	.00
☐ 374	Ron Karkovice	.04	.02	.00
☐ 375	Paul Gibson	.04	.02	.00
☐ 376	Bernard Gilkey	.12	.05	.01
☐ 377	Dave Gallagher	.04	.02	.00
☐ 378	Bill Wegman	.04	.02	.00
☐ 379	Pat Borders	.04	.02	.00
☐ 380	Ed Whitson	.04	.02	.00
☐ 381	Gilberto Reyes	.04	.02	.00
☐ 382	Russ Swan	.04	.02	.00
☐ 383	Andy Van Slyke	.10	.04	.01
☐ 384	Wes Chamberlain	.20	.08	.02
☐ 385	Steve Chitren	.04	.02	.00
☐ 386	Greg Olson	.04	.02	.00
☐ 387	Brian McRae	.18	.08	.01
☐ 388	Rich Rodriguez	.04	.02	.00
☐ 389	Steve Decker	.17	.07	.01
☐ 390	Chuck Knoblauch	.35	.15	.03
☐ 391	Bobby Witt	.07	.03	.01
☐ 392	Eddie Murray	.15	.06	.01
☐ 393	Juan Gonzalez	.40	.16	.04
☐ 394	Scott Ruskin	.04	.02	.00
☐ 395	Jay Howell	.04	.02	.00
☐ 396	Checklist Card	.07	.03	.01

1992 Donruss Diamond Kings

These standard-size (2 1/2" by 3 1/2") cards were randomly inserted in 1992 Donruss I foil packs (cards 1-13 and the checklist only). The fronts feature player portraits by noted sports artist Dick Perez. The words "Donruss Diamond Kings" are superimposed at the card top in a gold-trimmed blue and black banner, with the player's name in a similarly designed black stripe at the card bottom. On a white background with a dark blue border, the backs present career summary. The cards are numbered on the back.

	MINT	EXC	G-VG
COMPLETE SET (27)	70.00	32.00	10.50
COMMON PLAYER (1-13)	2.00	.80	.20
COMMON PLAYER (14-26)	2.00	.80	.20

		MINT	EXC	G-VG
☐ DK1	Paul Molitor	2.25	.90	.22
☐ DK2	Will Clark	5.00	2.25	.50
☐ DK3	Joe Carter	2.50	1.00	.25
☐ DK4	Julio Franco	2.25	.90	.22
☐ DK5	Cal Ripken	6.00	2.50	.60
☐ DK6	Dave Justice	9.00	4.00	.90
☐ DK7	George Bell	2.25	.90	.22
☐ DK8	Frank Thomas	13.50	6.00	1.85
☐ DK9	Wade Boggs	4.00	1.75	.40
☐ DK10	Scott Sanderson	2.00	.80	.20
☐ DK11	Jeff Bagwell	7.50	3.25	.75
☐ DK12	John Kruk	2.00	.80	.20
☐ DK13	Felix Jose	2.50	1.00	.25
☐ DK14	Harold Baines	2.00	.80	.20
☐ DK15	Dwight Gooden	2.50	1.00	.25
☐ DK16	Brian McRae	3.00	1.25	.30
☐ DK17	Jay Bell	2.00	.80	.20
☐ DK18	Brett Butler	2.00	.80	.20
☐ DK19	Hal Morris	2.25	.90	.22
☐ DK20	Mark Langston	2.00	.80	.20
☐ DK21	Scott Erickson	4.00	1.75	.40
☐ DK22	Randy Johnson	2.00	.80	.20
☐ DK23	Greg Swindell	2.00	.80	.20
☐ DK24	Dennis Martinez	2.00	.80	.20
☐ DK25	Tony Phillips	2.00	.80	.20
☐ DK26	Fred McGriff	2.50	1.00	.25
☐ DK27	Checklist Card	2.00	.80	.20

1992 Donruss II

This 396-card set was the second series released by Donruss in 1992. The standard-size (2 1/2" by 3 1/2") cards have the same design as those in the first series. Special cards in the set focus on Rated Rookies (397-421), All-Stars (422-431), and Highlights (434, 495, 555, 616, 677). The cards are numbered on the back.

	MINT	EXC	G-VG
COMPLETE SET (396)	24.00	10.50	3.50
COMMON PLAYER (397-784)	.04	.02	.00
COMMON PLAYER (BC1-BC8)	.04	.02	.00

☐ 397	Royce Clayton RR	.25	.10	.02
☐ 398	John Jaha RR	.40	.16	.04
☐ 399	Dan Wilson RR	.12	.05	.01
☐ 400	Archie Corbin RR	.20	.08	.02
☐ 401	Barry Manuel RR	.20	.08	.02
☐ 402	Kim Batiste RR	.12	.05	.01
☐ 403	Pat Mahomes RR	.45	.18	.04
☐ 404	Dave Fleming RR	.30	.12	.03
☐ 405	Jeff Juden RR	.20	.08	.02
☐ 406	Jim Thome RR	.60	.25	.06
☐ 407	Sam Militello RR	.25	.10	.02
☐ 408	Jeff Nelson RR	.18	.08	.01
☐ 409	Anthony Young RR	.18	.08	.01
☐ 410	Tino Martinez RR	.15	.06	.01
☐ 411	Jeff Mutis RR	.20	.08	.02
☐ 412	Rey Sanchez RR	.12	.05	.01
☐ 413	Chris Gardner RR	.30	.12	.03
☐ 414	John VanderWal RR	.25	.10	.02
☐ 415	Reggie Sanders RR	.25	.10	.02
☐ 416	Brian Williams RR	.25	.10	.02
☐ 417	Mo Sanford RR	.20	.08	.02
☐ 418	David Weathers RR	.20	.08	.02
☐ 419	Hector Fajardo RR	.25	.10	.02
☐ 420	Steve Foster RR	.20	.08	.02
☐ 421	Lance Dickson RR	.07	.03	.01
☐ 422	Andre Dawson AS	.07	.03	.01
☐ 423	Ozzie Smith AS	.07	.03	.01
☐ 424	Chris Sabo AS	.07	.03	.01
☐ 425	Tony Gwynn AS	.10	.04	.01
☐ 426	Tom Glavine AS	.07	.03	.01
☐ 427	Bobby Bonilla AS	.10	.04	.01
☐ 428	Will Clark AS	.15	.06	.01
☐ 429	Ryne Sandberg AS	.15	.06	.01
☐ 430	Benito Santiago AS	.07	.03	.01
☐ 431	Ivan Calderon AS	.07	.03	.01
☐ 432	Ozzie Smith	.12	.05	.01
☐ 433	Tim Leary	.07	.03	.01
☐ 434	Bret Saberhagen HL	.07	.03	.01
☐ 435	Mel Rojas	.07	.03	.01
☐ 436	Ben McDonald	.10	.04	.01
☐ 437	Tim Crews	.04	.02	.00
☐ 438	Rex Hudler	.04	.02	.00
☐ 439	Chico Walker	.04	.02	.00
☐ 440	Kurt Stillwell	.04	.02	.00
☐ 441	Tony Gwynn	.20	.08	.02
☐ 442	John Smoltz	.10	.04	.01
☐ 443	Lloyd Moseby	.04	.02	.00
☐ 444	Mike Schooler	.04	.02	.00
☐ 445	Joe Grahe	.07	.03	.01
☐ 446	Dwight Gooden	.12	.05	.01
☐ 447	Oil Can Boyd	.04	.02	.00
☐ 448	John Marzano	.04	.02	.00
☐ 449	Bret Barberie	.15	.06	.01
☐ 450	Mike Maddux	.04	.02	.00
☐ 451	Jeff Reed	.04	.02	.00
☐ 452	Dale Sveum	.04	.02	.00
☐ 453	Jose Uribe	.04	.02	.00
☐ 454	Bob Scanlan	.04	.02	.00
☐ 455	Kevin Appier	.07	.03	.01
☐ 456	Jeff Huson	.04	.02	.00
☐ 457	Ken Patterson	.04	.02	.00
☐ 458	Ricky Jordan	.07	.03	.01
☐ 459	Tom Candiotti	.07	.03	.01
☐ 460	Lee Stevens	.10	.04	.01
☐ 461	Rod Beck	.15	.06	.01
☐ 462	Dave Valle	.04	.02	.00
☐ 463	Scott Erickson	.45	.18	.04
☐ 464	Chris Jones	.07	.03	.01
☐ 465	Mark Carreon	.04	.02	.00
☐ 466	Rob Ducey	.04	.02	.00
☐ 467	Jim Corsi	.04	.02	.00
☐ 468	Jeff King	.04	.02	.00
☐ 469	Curt Young	.04	.02	.00
☐ 470	Bo Jackson	.35	.15	.03
☐ 471	Chris Bosio	.04	.02	.00
☐ 472	Jamie Quirk	.04	.02	.00
☐ 473	Jesse Orosco	.04	.02	.00
☐ 474	Alvaro Espinoza	.04	.02	.00
☐ 475	Joe Orsulak	.04	.02	.00
☐ 476	Checklist Card	.07	.03	.01
☐ 477	Gerald Young	.04	.02	.00
☐ 478	Wally Backman	.04	.02	.00
☐ 479	Juan Bell	.04	.02	.00
☐ 480	Mike Scioscia	.04	.02	.00
☐ 481	Omar Olivares	.07	.03	.01
☐ 482	Francisco Cabrera	.04	.02	.00
☐ 483	Greg Swindell	.07	.03	.01
☐ 484	Terry Leach	.04	.02	.00
☐ 485	Tommy Gregg	.04	.02	.00
☐ 486	Scott Aldred	.04	.02	.00
☐ 487	Greg Briley	.04	.02	.00
☐ 488	Phil Plantier	.75	.30	.07
☐ 489	Curtis Wilkerson	.04	.02	.00
☐ 490	Tom Brunansky	.07	.03	.01
☐ 491	Mike Fetters	.04	.02	.00

□	No.	Name			
□	492	Frank Castillo	.07	.03	.01
□	493	Joe Boever	.04	.02	.00
□	494	Kirt Manwaring	.04	.02	.00
□	495	Wilson Alvarez HL	.07	.03	.01
□	496	Gene Larkin	.04	.02	.00
□	497	Gary DiSarcina	.04	.02	.00
□	498	Frank Viola	.07	.03	.01
□	499	Manuel Lee	.04	.02	.00
□	500	Albert Belle	.15	.06	.01
□	501	Stan Belinda	.04	.02	.00
□	502	Dwight Evans	.07	.03	.01
□	503	Eric Davis	.12	.05	.01
□	504	Darren Holmes	.07	.03	.01
□	505	Mike Bordick	.07	.03	.01
□	506	Dave Hansen	.07	.03	.01
□	507	Lee Guetterman	.04	.02	.00
□	508	Keith Mitchell	.25	.10	.02
□	509	Melido Perez	.04	.02	.00
□	510	Dickie Thon	.07	.03	.01
□	511	Mark Williamson	.04	.02	.00
□	512	Mark Salas	.04	.02	.00
□	513	Milt Thompson	.04	.02	.00
□	514	Mo Vaughn	.35	.15	.03
□	515	Jim Deshaies	.04	.02	.00
□	516	Rich Garces	.04	.02	.00
□	517	Lonnie Smith	.07	.03	.01
□	518	Spike Owen	.04	.02	.00
□	519	Tracy Jones	.04	.02	.00
□	520	Greg Maddux	.07	.03	.01
□	521	Carlos Martinez	.04	.02	.00
□	522	Neal Heaton	.04	.02	.00
□	523	Mike Greenwell	.12	.05	.01
□	524	Andy Benes	.07	.03	.01
□	525	Jeff Schaefer	.04	.02	.00
□	526	Mike Sharperson	.04	.02	.00
□	527	Wade Taylor	.07	.03	.01
□	528	Jerome Walton	.07	.03	.01
□	529	Storm Davis	.04	.02	.00
□	530	Jose Hernandez	.18	.08	.01
□	531	Mark Langston	.07	.03	.01
□	532	Rob Deer	.04	.02	.00
□	533	Geronimo Pena	.04	.02	.00
□	534	Juan Guzman	.65	.25	.06
□	535	Pete Schourek	.07	.03	.01
□	536	Todd Benzinger	.04	.02	.00
□	537	Billy Hatcher	.07	.03	.01
□	538	Tom Foley	.04	.02	.00
□	539	Dave Cochrane	.04	.02	.00
□	540	Mariano Duncan	.04	.02	.00
□	541	Edwin Nunez	.04	.02	.00
□	542	Rance Mulliniks	.04	.02	.00
□	543	Carlton Fisk	.12	.05	.01
□	544	Luis Aquino	.04	.02	.00
□	545	Ricky Bones	.07	.03	.01
□	546	Craig Grebeck	.04	.02	.00
□	547	Charlie Hayes	.04	.02	.00
□	548	Jose Canseco	.35	.15	.03
□	549	Andujar Cedeno	.20	.08	.02
□	550	Geno Petralli	.04	.02	.00
□	551	Javier Ortiz	.04	.02	.00
□	552	Rudy Seanez	.04	.02	.00
□	553	Rich Gedman	.04	.02	.00
□	554	Eric Plunk	.04	.02	.00
□	555	Nolan Ryan HL	.30	.12	.03
		Rich Gossage			
□	556	Checklist Card	.07	.03	.01
□	557	Greg Colbrunn	.07	.03	.01
□	558	Chito Martinez	.35	.15	.03
□	559	Darryl Strawberry	.25	.10	.02
□	560	Luis Alicea	.04	.02	.00
□	561	Dwight Smith	.07	.03	.01
□	562	Terry Shumpert	.04	.02	.00
□	563	Jim Vatcher	.04	.02	.00
□	564	Deion Sanders	.10	.04	.01
□	565	Walt Terrell	.04	.02	.00
□	566	Dave Burba	.04	.02	.00
□	567	Dave Howard	.07	.03	.01
□	568	Todd Hundley	.10	.04	.01
□	569	Jack Daugherty	.04	.02	.00
□	570	Scott Cooper	.15	.06	.01
□	571	Bill Sampen	.04	.02	.00
□	572	Jose Melendez	.07	.03	.01
□	573	Freddie Benavides	.04	.02	.00
□	574	Jim Gantner	.04	.02	.00
□	575	Trevor Wilson	.04	.02	.00
□	576	Ryne Sandberg	.30	.12	.03
□	577	Kevin Seitzer	.07	.03	.01
□	578	Gerald Alexander	.04	.02	.00
□	579	Mike Huff	.04	.02	.00
□	580	Von Hayes	.07	.03	.01
□	581	Derek Bell	.30	.12	.03
□	582	Mike Stanley	.04	.02	.00
□	583	Kevin Mitchell	.10	.04	.01
□	584	Mike Jackson	.04	.02	.00
□	585	Dan Gladden	.04	.02	.00
□	586	Ted Power	.04	.02	.00
□	587	Jeff Innis	.04	.02	.00
□	588	Bob MacDonald	.07	.03	.01
□	589	Jose Tolentino	.12	.05	.01
□	590	Bob Patterson	.04	.02	.00
□	591	Scott Brosius	.15	.06	.01
□	592	Frank Thomas	1.25	.50	.12
□	593	Darryl Hamilton	.07	.03	.01
□	594	Kirk Dressendorfer	.12	.05	.01
□	595	Jeff Shaw	.04	.02	.00
□	596	Don Mattingly	.20	.08	.02
□	597	Glenn Davis	.07	.03	.01
□	598	Andy Mota	.10	.04	.01
□	599	Jason Grimsley	.04	.02	.00
□	600	Jimmy Poole	.07	.03	.01
□	601	Jim Gott	.04	.02	.00
□	602	Stan Royer	.07	.03	.01
□	603	Marvin Freeman	.04	.02	.00
□	604	Denis Boucher	.07	.03	.01
□	605	Denny Neagle	.25	.10	.02
□	606	Mark Lemke	.07	.03	.01
□	607	Jerry Don Gleaton	.04	.02	.00
□	608	Brent Knackert	.04	.02	.00
□	609	Carlos Quintana	.07	.03	.01
□	610	Bobby Bonilla	.15	.06	.01
□	611	Joe Hesketh	.04	.02	.00
□	612	Daryl Boston	.04	.02	.00
□	613	Shawon Dunston	.07	.03	.01
□	614	Danny Cox	.04	.02	.00
□	615	Darren Lewis	.15	.06	.01
□	616	Alejandro Pena HL	.12	.05	.01
		Kent Mercker			
		Mark Wohlers			
□	617	Kirby Puckett	.20	.08	.02
□	618	Franklin Stubbs	.04	.02	.00
□	619	Chris Donnels	.15	.06	.01
□	620	David Wells	.04	.02	.00
□	621	Mike Aldrete	.04	.02	.00
□	622	Bob Kipper	.04	.02	.00
□	623	Anthony Telford	.04	.02	.00
□	624	Randy Myers	.04	.02	.00
□	625	Willie Randolph	.04	.02	.00
□	626	Joe Slusarski	.07	.03	.01
□	627	John Wetteland	.04	.02	.00
□	628	Greg Cadaret	.04	.02	.00
□	629	Tom Glavine	.10	.04	.01
□	630	Wilson Alvarez	.12	.05	.01
□	631	Wally Ritchie	.04	.02	.00
□	632	Mike Mussina	.20	.08	.02
□	633	Mark Leiter	.07	.03	.01
□	634	Gerald Perry	.04	.02	.00
□	635	Matt Young	.04	.02	.00
□	636	Checklist Card	.07	.03	.01
□	637	Scott Hemond	.04	.02	.00
□	638	David West	.04	.02	.00
□	639	Jim Clancy	.04	.02	.00
□	640	Doug Piatt	.10	.04	.01
□	641	Omar Vizquel	.04	.02	.00
□	642	Rick Sutcliffe	.07	.03	.01
□	643	Glenallen Hill	.07	.03	.01
□	644	Gary Varsho	.04	.02	.00
□	645	Tony Fossas	.04	.02	.00
□	646	Jack Howell	.04	.02	.00
□	647	Jim Campanis	.10	.04	.01
□	648	Chris Gwynn	.04	.02	.00
□	649	Jim Leyritz	.04	.02	.00
□	650	Chuck McElroy	.04	.02	.00
□	651	Sean Berry	.07	.03	.01
□	652	Donald Harris	.10	.04	.01
□	653	Don Slaught	.04	.02	.00
□	654	Rusty Meacham	.10	.04	.01
□	655	Scott Terry	.04	.02	.00
□	656	Ramon Martinez	.15	.06	.01
□	657	Keith Miller	.04	.02	.00
□	658	Ramon Garcia	.07	.03	.01
□	659	Milt Hill	.12	.05	.01
□	660	Steve Frey	.04	.02	.00
□	661	Bob McClure	.04	.02	.00
□	662	Ced Landrum	.10	.04	.01
□	663	Doug Henry	.25	.10	.02
□	664	Candy Maldonado	.04	.02	.00
□	665	Carl Willis	.04	.02	.00
□	666	Jeff Montgomery	.04	.02	.00
□	667	Craig Shipley	.12	.05	.01
□	668	Warren Newson	.12	.05	.01
□	669	Mickey Morandini	.07	.03	.01
□	670	Brook Jacoby	.04	.02	.00
□	671	Ryan Bowen	.12	.05	.01
□	672	Bill Krueger	.04	.02	.00
□	673	Rob Mallicoat	.04	.02	.00
□	674	Doug Jones	.04	.02	.00
□	675	Scott Livingstone	.18	.08	.01
□	676	Danny Tartabull	.10	.04	.01

☐ 677	Joe Carter HL	.07	.03	.01
☐ 678	Cecil Espy	.04	.02	.00
☐ 679	Randy Velarde	.04	.02	.00
☐ 680	Bruce Ruffin	.04	.02	.00
☐ 681	Ted Wood	.30	.12	.03
☐ 682	Dan Plesac	.04	.02	.00
☐ 683	Eric Bullock	.04	.02	.00
☐ 684	Junior Ortiz	.04	.02	.00
☐ 685	Dave Hollins	.04	.02	.00
☐ 686	Dennis Martinez	.07	.03	.01
☐ 687	Larry Andersen	.04	.02	.00
☐ 688	Doug Simons	.04	.02	.00
☐ 689	Tim Spehr	.10	.04	.01
☐ 690	Calvin Jones	.15	.06	.01
☐ 691	Mark Guthrie	.04	.02	.00
☐ 692	Alfredo Griffin	.04	.02	.00
☐ 693	Joe Carter	.12	.05	.01
☐ 694	Terry Mathews	.10	.04	.01
☐ 695	Pascual Perez	.04	.02	.00
☐ 696	Gene Nelson	.04	.02	.00
☐ 697	Gerald Williams	.25	.10	.02
☐ 698	Chris Cron	.15	.06	.01
☐ 699	Steve Buechele	.07	.03	.01
☐ 700	Paul McClellan	.07	.03	.01
☐ 701	Jim Lindeman	.04	.02	.00
☐ 702	Francisco Oliveras	.04	.02	.00
☐ 703	Rob Maurer	.35	.15	.03
☐ 704	Pat Hentgen	.10	.04	.01
☐ 705	Jaime Navarro	.04	.02	.00
☐ 706	Mike Magnante	.15	.06	.01
☐ 707	Nolan Ryan	.50	.20	.05
☐ 708	Bobby Thigpen	.07	.03	.01
☐ 709	John Cerutti	.04	.02	.00
☐ 710	Steve Wilson	.04	.02	.00
☐ 711	Hensley Meulens	.07	.03	.01
☐ 712	Rheal Cormier	.25	.10	.02
☐ 713	Scott Bradley	.04	.02	.00
☐ 714	Mitch Webster	.04	.02	.00
☐ 715	Roger Mason	.04	.02	.00
☐ 716	Checklist Card	.07	.03	.01
☐ 717	Jeff Fassero	.07	.03	.01
☐ 718	Cal Eldred	.04	.02	.00
☐ 719	Sid Fernandez	.07	.03	.01
☐ 720	Bob Zupcic	.20	.08	.02
☐ 721	Jose Offerman	.07	.03	.01
☐ 722	Cliff Brantley	.20	.08	.02
☐ 723	Ron Darling	.07	.03	.01
☐ 724	Dave Stieb	.07	.03	.01
☐ 725	Hector Villanueva	.07	.03	.01
☐ 726	Mike Hartley	.04	.02	.00
☐ 727	Arthur Rhodes	.20	.08	.02
☐ 728	Randy Bush	.04	.02	.00
☐ 729	Steve Sax	.07	.03	.01
☐ 730	Dave Otto	.04	.02	.00
☐ 731	John Wehner	.20	.08	.02
☐ 732	Dave Martinez	.04	.02	.00
☐ 733	Ruben Amaro	.10	.04	.01
☐ 734	Billy Ripken	.04	.02	.00
☐ 735	Steve Farr	.04	.02	.00
☐ 736	Shawn Abner	.04	.02	.00
☐ 737	Gil Heredia	.12	.05	.01
☐ 738	Ron Jones	.04	.02	.00
☐ 739	Tony Castillo	.04	.02	.00
☐ 740	Sammy Sosa	.07	.03	.01
☐ 741	Julio Franco	.07	.03	.01
☐ 742	Tim Naehring	.07	.03	.01
☐ 743	Steve Wapnick	.10	.04	.01
☐ 744	Craig Wilson	.07	.03	.01
☐ 745	Darrin Chapin	.15	.06	.01
☐ 746	Chris George	.15	.06	.01
☐ 747	Mike Simms	.07	.03	.01
☐ 748	Rosario Rodriguez	.07	.03	.01
☐ 749	Skeeter Barnes	.04	.02	.00
☐ 750	Roger McDowell	.04	.02	.00
☐ 751	Dann Howitt	.04	.02	.00
☐ 752	Paul Sorrento	.04	.02	.00
☐ 753	Braulio Castillo	.35	.15	.03
☐ 754	Yorkis Perez	.15	.06	.01
☐ 755	Willie Fraser	.04	.02	.00
☐ 756	Jeremy Hernandez	.20	.08	.02
☐ 757	Curt Schilling	.04	.02	.00
☐ 758	Steve Lyons	.04	.02	.00
☐ 759	Dave Anderson	.04	.02	.00
☐ 760	Willie Banks	.15	.06	.01
☐ 761	Mark Leonard	.04	.02	.00
☐ 762	Jack Armstrong	.07	.03	.01
☐ 763	Scott Servais	.07	.03	.01
☐ 764	Ray Stephens	.07	.03	.01
☐ 765	Junior Noboa	.04	.02	.00
☐ 766	Jim Olander	.18	.08	.01
☐ 767	Joe Magrane	.07	.03	.01
☐ 768	Lance Blankenship	.04	.02	.00
☐ 769	Mike Humphreys	.07	.03	.01
☐ 770	Jarvis Brown	.15	.06	.01
☐ 771	Damon Berryhill	.04	.02	.00
☐ 772	Alejandro Pena	.07	.03	.01
☐ 773	Jose Mesa	.04	.02	.00
☐ 774	Gary Cooper	.15	.06	.01
☐ 775	Carney Lansford	.07	.03	.01
☐ 776	Mike Bielecki	.04	.02	.00
☐ 777	Charlie O'Brien	.04	.02	.00
☐ 778	Carlos Hernandez	.04	.02	.00
☐ 779	Howard Farmer	.04	.02	.00
☐ 780	Mike Stanton	.04	.02	.00
☐ 781	Reggie Harris	.04	.02	.00
☐ 782	Xavier Hernandez	.04	.02	.00
☐ 783	Bryan Hickerson	.17	.07	.01
☐ 784	Checklist Card	.07	.03	.01
☐ BC1	Cal Ripken MVP	.15	.06	.01
☐ BC2	Terry Pendleton MVP	.07	.03	.01
☐ BC3	Roger Clemens CY	.15	.06	.01
☐ BC4	Tom Glavine CY	.07	.03	.01
☐ BC5	Chuck Knoblauch ROY	.15	.06	.01
☐ BC6	Jeff Bagwell ROY	.45	.18	.04
☐ BC7	Colorado Rockies	.15	.06	.01
☐ BC8	Florida Marlins	.15	.06	.01

1992 Donruss Elite

These cards were random inserts in 1992 Donruss foil packs. The numbering on the Elite cards is essentially a continuation of the series started the year before. The Signature Series Cal Ripken card was inserted in 1992 Donruss foil packs. Only 5,000 Ripken Signature Series cards were printed. The Rickey Henderson Legends Series card was inserted in 1992 Donruss foil packs; only 7,500 Henderson Legends cards were printed. All of these special limited cards are standard size, 2 1/2" by 3 1/2".

		MINT	EXC	G-VG
COMPLETE SET (12)		1500.00	600.00	175.00
COMMON ELITE (9-18)		75.00	34.00	11.25
☐ E9	Wade Boggs	125.00	57.50	18.75
☐ E10	Joe Carter	90.00	40.00	13.50
☐ E11	Will Clark	175.00	80.00	27.00
☐ E12	Dwight Gooden	90.00	40.00	13.50
☐ E13	Ken Griffey Jr.	300.00	135.00	45.00
☐ E14	Tony Gwynn	125.00	57.50	18.75
☐ E15	Howard Johnson	90.00	40.00	13.50
☐ E16	Terry Pendleton	75.00	34.00	11.25
☐ E17	Kirby Puckett	150.00	67.50	22.50
☐ E18	Frank Thomas	300.00	135.00	45.00
☐ L1	Rickey Henderson (Legend Series)	350.00	160.00	52.50
☐ S1	Cal Ripken (Signature Series)	400.00	180.00	60.00

1986 Dorman's Cheese

This 20-card set was issued in panels of two cards. The individual cards measure 1 1/2" by 2" whereas the panels measure 3" by 2". Team logos have been removed from the photos as these cards were not licensed by Major League Baseball (team owners). The backs contain a minimum of information.

		MINT	EXC	G-VG
COMPLETE SET (20)		18.00	7.50	2.50
COMMON PLAYER (1-20)		.75	.30	.07

		EX-MT	VG-E	GOOD
☐ 1	George Brett	1.25	.50	.12
☐ 2	Jack Morris	.90	.40	.09
☐ 3	Gary Carter	.90	.40	.09
☐ 4	Cal Ripken	1.50	.60	.15
☐ 5	Dwight Gooden	1.00	.40	.10
☐ 6	Kent Hrbek	.90	.40	.09
☐ 7	Rickey Henderson	1.50	.60	.15
☐ 8	Mike Schmidt	1.50	.60	.15
☐ 9	Keith Hernandez	.90	.40	.09
☐ 10	Dale Murphy	1.00	.40	.10
☐ 11	Reggie Jackson	1.00	.40	.10
☐ 12	Eddie Murray	1.00	.40	.10
☐ 13	Don Mattingly	1.50	.60	.15
☐ 14	Ryne Sandberg	1.50	.60	.15
☐ 15	Willie McGee	.90	.40	.09
☐ 16	Robin Yount	1.25	.50	.12
☐ 17	Rick Sutcliffe	.75	.30	.07
☐ 18	Wade Boggs	1.25	.50	.12
☐ 19	Dave Winfield	1.00	.40	.10
☐ 20	Jim Rice	.90	.40	.09

1941 Double Play

GERALD WALKER
CLEVELAND INDIANS. Left fielder. Born March 19, 1909. Bats right. Throws right. Ht. 5 ft. 11 in. Wt. 185 lbs. Batted .794.
No. 135 Double Play

JOE HEVING
CLEVELAND INDIANS. Pitcher. Born Sept. 2, 1901. Bats and throws right. Ht. 6 ft. 1 in. Wt. 175 lbs. Won 7. Lost 7 with Red Sox.
No. 136 Double Play

The cards in this 75-card set measure 2 1/2" by 3 1/8". The 1941 Double Play set, listed as R330 in the American Card Catalog, was a blank-backed issue distributed by Gum Products. It consists of 75 numbered cards (two consecutive numbers per card), each depicting two players in sepia tone photographs. Cards 81-100 contain action poses, and the last 50 numbers of the set are slightly harder to find. Cards that have been cut in half to form "singles" have a greatly reduced value.

	EX-MT	VG-E	GOOD
COMPLETE SET (150)	4500.00	2000.00	450.00
COMMON PAIRS (1-100)	30.00	13.50	4.50
COMMON PAIRS (101-150)	35.00	15.75	5.25

		EX-MT	VG-E	GOOD
☐ 1	Larry French and 2 Vance Page	30.00	13.50	4.50
☐ 3	Billy Herman and 4 Stan Hack	40.00	18.00	6.00
☐ 5	Lonnie Frey and 6 Johnny VanderMeer	35.00	15.75	5.25
☐ 7	Paul Derringer and 8 Bucky Walters	40.00	18.00	6.00
☐ 9	Frank McCormick and 10 Bill Werber	30.00	13.50	4.50
☐ 11	Jimmy Ripple and 12 Ernie Lombardi	40.00	18.00	6.00
☐ 13	Alex Kampouris and 14 Whitlow Wyatt	30.00	13.50	4.50
☐ 15	Mickey Owen and 16 Paul Waner	40.00	18.00	6.00
☐ 17	Cookie Lavagetto and 18 Pete Reiser	30.00	13.50	4.50
☐ 19	James Wasdell and 20 Dolf Camilli	30.00	13.50	4.50
☐ 21	Dixie Walker and 22 Joe Medwick	40.00	18.00	6.00
☐ 23	Pee Wee Reese and 24 Kirby Higbe	150.00	67.50	22.50
☐ 25	Harry Danning and 26 Cliff Melton	30.00	13.50	4.50

		EX-MT	VG-E	GOOD
☐ 27	Harry Gumbert and 28 Burgess Whitehead	30.00	13.50	4.50
☐ 29	Joe Orengo and 30 Joe Moore	30.00	13.50	4.50
☐ 31	Mel Ott and 32 Norman Young	90.00	40.00	13.50
☐ 33	Lee Handley and 34 Arky Vaughan	40.00	18.00	6.00
☐ 35	Bob Klinger and 36 Stanley Brown	30.00	13.50	4.50
☐ 37	Terry Moore and 38 Gus Mancuso	30.00	13.50	4.50
☐ 39	Johnny Mize and 40 Enos Slaughter	150.00	67.50	22.50
☐ 41	Johnny Cooney and 42 Sibby Sisti	30.00	13.50	4.50
☐ 43	Max West and 44 Carvel Rowell	30.00	13.50	4.50
☐ 45	Danny Litwhiler and 46 Merrill May	30.00	13.50	4.50
☐ 47	Frank Hayes and 48 Al Brancato	30.00	13.50	4.50
☐ 49	Bob Johnson and 50 Bill Nagel	30.00	13.50	4.50
☐ 51	Buck Newsom and 52 Hank Greenberg	60.00	27.00	9.00
☐ 53	Barney McCosky and 54 Charlie Gehringer	60.00	27.00	9.00
☐ 55	Mike Higgins and 56 Dick Bartell	30.00	13.50	4.50
☐ 57	Ted Williams and 58 Jim Tabor	400.00	180.00	60.00
☐ 59	Joe Cronin and 60 Jimmie Foxx	200.00	90.00	30.00
☐ 61	Lefty Gomez and 62 Phil Rizzuto	250.00	110.00	37.50
☐ 63	Joe DiMaggio and 64 Charlie Keller	700.00	315.00	105.00
☐ 65	Red Rolfe and 66 Bill Dickey	125.00	57.50	18.75
☐ 67	Joe Gordon and 68 Red Ruffing	90.00	40.00	13.50
☐ 69	Mike Tresh and 70 Luke Appling	50.00	22.50	7.50
☐ 71	Moose Solters and 72 Johnny Rigney	30.00	13.50	4.50
☐ 73	Buddy Myer and 74 Ben Chapman	30.00	13.50	4.50
☐ 75	Cecil Travis and 76 George Case	30.00	13.50	4.50
☐ 77	Joe Krakauskas and 78 Bob Feller	125.00	57.50	18.75
☐ 79	Ken Keltner and 80 Hal Trosky	30.00	13.50	4.50
☐ 81	Ted Williams and 82 Joe Cronin	500.00	225.00	75.00
☐ 83	Joe Gordon and 84 Charlie Keller	40.00	18.00	6.00
☐ 85	Hank Greenberg and 86 Red Ruffing	200.00	90.00	30.00
☐ 87	Hal Trosky and 88 George Case	30.00	13.50	4.50
☐ 89	Mel Ott and 90 Burgess Whitehead	90.00	40.00	13.50
☐ 91	Harry Danning and 92 Harry Gumbert	30.00	13.50	4.50
☐ 93	Norman Young and 94 Cliff Melton	30.00	13.50	4.50
☐ 95	Jimmy Ripple and 96 Bucky Walters	30.00	13.50	4.50
☐ 97	Stanley Jack and 98 Bob Klinger	30.00	13.50	4.50
☐ 99	Johnny Mize and 100 Dan Litwhiler	60.00	27.00	9.00
☐ 101	Dom Dallesandro and 102 Augie Galan	35.00	15.75	5.25
☐ 103	Bill Lee and 104 Phil Cavarretta	40.00	18.00	6.00
☐ 105	Lefty Grove and 106 Bobby Doerr	200.00	90.00	30.00
☐ 107	Frank Pytlak and 108 Dom DiMaggio	40.00	18.00	6.00
☐ 109	Jerry Priddy and 110 Johnny Murphy	35.00	15.75	5.25
☐ 111	Tommy Henrich and 112 Marius Russo	50.00	22.50	7.50
☐ 113	Frank Crosetti and 114 John Sturm	50.00	22.50	7.50
☐ 115	Ival Goodman and 116 Myron McCormick	35.00	15.75	5.25
☐ 117	Eddie Joost and 118 Ernie Koy	35.00	15.75	5.25
☐ 119	Lloyd Waner and 120 Hank Majeski	50.00	22.50	7.50

			NRMT	VG-E	GOOD
☐ 121	Buddy Hassett and 122 Eugene Moore		35.00	15.75	5.25
☐ 123	Nick Etten and 124 John Rizzo		35.00	15.75	5.25
☐ 125	Sam Chapman and 126 Wally Moses		35.00	15.75	5.25
☐ 127	Johnny Babich and 128 Dick Siebert		35.00	15.75	5.25
☐ 129	Nelson Potter and 130 Benny McCoy		35.00	15.75	5.25
☐ 131	Clarence Campbell and 132 Lou Boudreau		60.00	27.00	9.00
☐ 133	Rollie Hemsley and 134 Mel Harder		45.00	20.00	6.75
☐ 135	Gerald Walker and 136 Joe Heving		35.00	15.75	5.25
☐ 137	Johnny Rucker and 138 Ace Adams		35.00	15.75	5.25
☐ 139	Morris Arnovich and 140 Carl Hubbell		90.00	40.00	13.50
☐ 141	Lew Riggs and 142 Leo Durocher		60.00	27.00	9.00
☐ 143	Fred Fitzsimmons and 144 Joe Vosmik		35.00	15.75	5.25
☐ 145	Frank Crespi and 146 Jim Brown		35.00	15.75	5.25
☐ 147	Don Heffner and 148 Harland Clift		35.00	15.75	5.25
☐ 149	Debs Garms and 150 Elbert Fletcher		35.00	15.75	5.25

1950 Drake's

The cards in this 36-card set measure approximately 2 1/2"
by 2 1/2". The 1950 Drake's Cookies set contains numbered
black and white cards. The players are pictured inside a
simulated television screen and the caption "TV Baseball
Series" appears on the cards. The players selected for this
set show a heavy representation of players from New York
teams. The catalog designation for this set is D358.

		NRMT	VG-E	GOOD
	COMPLETE SET (36)	3750.00	1750.00	375.00
	COMMON PLAYER (1-36)	60.00	27.00	9.00
☐ 1	Preacher Roe	75.00	34.00	11.25
☐ 2	Clint Hartung	60.00	27.00	9.00
☐ 3	Earl Torgeson	60.00	27.00	9.00
☐ 4	Lou Brissie	60.00	27.00	9.00
☐ 5	Duke Snider	300.00	135.00	45.00
☐ 6	Roy Campanella	375.00	165.00	55.00
☐ 7	Sheldon Jones	60.00	27.00	9.00
☐ 8	Whitey Lockman	60.00	27.00	9.00
☐ 9	Bobby Thomson	75.00	34.00	11.25
☐ 10	Dick Sisler	60.00	27.00	9.00
☐ 11	Gil Hodges	175.00	80.00	27.00
☐ 12	Eddie Waitkus	60.00	27.00	9.00
☐ 13	Bobby Doerr	125.00	57.50	18.75
☐ 14	Warren Spahn	225.00	100.00	33.00
☐ 15	Buddy Kerr	60.00	27.00	9.00
☐ 16	Sid Gordon	60.00	27.00	9.00
☐ 17	Willard Marshall	60.00	27.00	9.00
☐ 18	Carl Furillo	90.00	40.00	13.50
☐ 19	Pee Wee Reese	225.00	100.00	33.00
☐ 20	Alvin Dark	75.00	34.00	11.25
☐ 21	Del Ennis	60.00	27.00	9.00
☐ 22	Ed Stanky	75.00	34.00	11.25
☐ 23	Tom Henrich	75.00	34.00	11.25
☐ 24	Yogi Berra	375.00	165.00	55.00
☐ 25	Phil Rizzuto	200.00	90.00	30.00
☐ 26	Jerry Coleman	60.00	27.00	9.00

☐ 27	Joe Page	75.00	34.00	11.25
☐ 28	Allie Reynolds	90.00	40.00	13.50
☐ 29	Ray Scarborough	60.00	27.00	9.00
☐ 30	Birdie Tebbetts	60.00	27.00	9.00
☐ 31	Maurice McDermott	60.00	27.00	9.00
☐ 32	Johnny Pesky	60.00	27.00	9.00
☐ 33	Dom DiMaggio	90.00	40.00	13.50
☐ 34	Vern Stephens	60.00	27.00	9.00
☐ 35	Bob Elliott	60.00	27.00	9.00
☐ 36	Enos Slaughter	200.00	90.00	30.00

1981 Drake's

The cards in this 33-card set measure 2 1/2" by 3 1/2". The 1981
Drake's Bakeries set contains National and American League
stars. Produced in conjunction with Topps and released to the
public in Drake's Cakes, this set features red frames for
American League players and blue frames for National League
players. A Drake's Cakes logo with the words "Big Hitters"
appears on the lower front of each card. The backs are quite
similar to the 1981 Topps backs but contain the Drake's logo,
a different card number, and a short paragraph entitled "What
Makes a Big Hitter" at the top of the card.

		MINT	EXC	G-VG
	COMPLETE SET (33)	8.00	3.50	.80
	COMMON PLAYER (1-33)	.06	.02	.00
☐ 1	Carl Yastrzemski	1.00	.40	.10
☐ 2	Rod Carew	.75	.30	.07
☐ 3	Pete Rose	1.00	.40	.10
☐ 4	Dave Parker	.30	.12	.03
☐ 5	George Brett	.75	.30	.07
☐ 6	Eddie Murray	.75	.30	.07
☐ 7	Mike Schmidt	1.00	.40	.10
☐ 8	Jim Rice	.25	.10	.02
☐ 9	Fred Lynn	.15	.06	.01
☐ 10	Reggie Jackson	.90	.40	.09
☐ 11	Steve Garvey	.45	.18	.04
☐ 12	Ken Singleton	.06	.02	.00
☐ 13	Bill Buckner	.06	.02	.00
☐ 14	Dave Winfield	.35	.15	.03
☐ 15	Jack Clark	.20	.08	.02
☐ 16	Cecil Cooper	.10	.04	.01
☐ 17	Bob Horner	.10	.04	.01
☐ 18	George Foster	.15	.06	.01
☐ 19	Dave Kingman	.10	.04	.01
☐ 20	Cesar Cedeno	.06	.02	.00
☐ 21	Joe Charboneau	.06	.02	.00
☐ 22	George Hendrick	.06	.02	.00
☐ 23	Gary Carter	.25	.10	.02
☐ 24	Al Oliver	.10	.04	.01
☐ 25	Bruce Bochte	.06	.02	.00
☐ 26	Jerry Mumphrey	.06	.02	.00
☐ 27	Steve Kemp	.06	.02	.00
☐ 28	Bob Watson	.06	.02	.00
☐ 29	John Castino	.06	.02	.00
☐ 30	Tony Armas	.06	.02	.00
☐ 31	John Mayberry	.06	.02	.00
☐ 32	Carlton Fisk	.40	.16	.04
☐ 33	Lee Mazzilli	.06	.02	.00

1982 Drake's

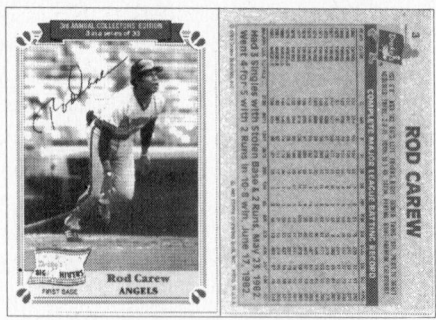

The cards in this 33-card set measure 2 1/2" by 3 1/2". The 1982 Drake's Big Hitters series cards each has the title "2nd Annual Collectors' Edition" in a ribbon design at the top of the picture area. Each color player photo has "photo mount" designs in the corners, red for the AL and green for the NL. The reverses are green and blue, the same as the regular 1982 Topps format, and the photos are larger than those of the previous year. Of the 33 hitters featured, 19 represent the National League. There are 21 returnees from the 1981 set and only one photo, that of Kennedy, is the same as that appearing in the regular Topps issue. The Drake's logo appears centered in the bottom border on the obverse. This set's card numbering is essentially in alphabetical order by the player's name.

	MINT	EXC	G-VG
COMPLETE SET (33)	8.00	3.50	.80
COMMON PLAYER (1-33)	.06	.02	.00
□ 1 Tony Armas	.06	.02	.00
□ 2 Buddy Bell	.10	.04	.01
□ 3 Johnny Bench	.75	.30	.07
□ 4 George Brett	.75	.30	.07
□ 5 Bill Buckner	.06	.02	.00
□ 6 Rod Carew	.75	.30	.07
□ 7 Gary Carter	.30	.12	.03
□ 8 Jack Clark	.20	.08	.02
□ 9 Cecil Cooper	.10	.04	.01
□ 10 Jose Cruz	.06	.02	.00
□ 11 Dwight Evans	.15	.06	.01
□ 12 Carlton Fisk	.40	.16	.04
□ 13 George Foster	.15	.06	.01
□ 14 Steve Garvey	.40	.16	.04
□ 15 Kirk Gibson	.35	.15	.03
□ 16 Mike Hargrove	.10	.04	.01
□ 17 George Hendrick	.06	.02	.00
□ 18 Bob Horner	.15	.06	.01
□ 19 Reggie Jackson	.90	.40	.09
□ 20 Terry Kennedy	.06	.02	.00
□ 21 Dave Kingman	.10	.04	.01
□ 22 Greg Luzinski	.10	.04	.01
□ 23 Bill Madlock	.06	.02	.00
□ 24 John Mayberry	.06	.02	.00
□ 25 Eddie Murray	.75	.30	.07
□ 26 Graig Nettles	.10	.04	.01
□ 27 Jim Rice	.25	.10	.02
□ 28 Pete Rose	1.00	.40	.10
□ 29 Mike Schmidt	1.00	.40	.10
□ 30 Ken Singleton	.06	.02	.00
□ 31 Dave Winfield	.35	.15	.03
□ 32 Butch Wynegar	.06	.02	.00
□ 33 Richie Zisk	.06	.02	.00

1983 Drake's

The cards in this 33-card series measure 2 1/2" by 3 1/2". For the third year in a row, Drake's Cakes, in conjunction with Topps, issued a set entitled Big Hitters. The fronts appear very

similar to those of the previous two years with slight variations on the framelines and player identification sections. The backs are the same as the Topps backs of this year except for the card number and the Drake's logo. This set's card numbering is essentially in alphabetical order by the player's name.

	MINT	EXC	G-VG
COMPLETE SET (33)	7.00	3.00	.70
COMMON PLAYER (1-33)	.06	.02	.00
□ 1 Don Baylor	.10	.04	.01
□ 2 Bill Buckner	.10	.04	.01
□ 3 Rod Carew	.75	.30	.07
□ 4 Gary Carter	.30	.12	.03
□ 5 Jack Clark	.20	.08	.02
□ 6 Cecil Cooper	.10	.04	.01
□ 7 Dwight Evans	.15	.06	.01
□ 8 George Foster	.15	.06	.01
□ 9 Pedro Guerrero	.20	.08	.02
□ 10 George Hendrick	.06	.02	.00
□ 11 Bob Horner	.15	.06	.01
□ 12 Reggie Jackson	.90	.40	.09
□ 13 Steve Kemp	.06	.02	.00
□ 14 Dave Kingman	.10	.04	.01
□ 15 Bill Madlock	.06	.02	.00
□ 16 Gary Matthews	.06	.02	.00
□ 17 Hal McRae	.10	.04	.01
□ 18 Dale Murphy	.60	.25	.06
□ 19 Eddie Murray	.75	.30	.07
□ 20 Ben Oglivie	.06	.02	.00
□ 21 Al Oliver	.10	.04	.01
□ 22 Jim Rice	.25	.10	.02
□ 23 Cal Ripken	1.00	.40	.10
□ 24 Pete Rose	1.00	.40	.10
□ 25 Mike Schmidt	1.00	.40	.10
□ 26 Ken Singleton	.06	.02	.00
□ 27 Gorman Thomas	.06	.02	.00
□ 28 Jason Thompson	.06	.02	.00
□ 29 Mookie Wilson	.10	.04	.01
□ 30 Willie Wilson	.10	.04	.01
□ 31 Dave Winfield	.40	.16	.04
□ 32 Carl Yastrzemski	1.00	.40	.10
□ 33 Robin Yount	.75	.30	.07

1984 Drake's

The cards in this 33-card set measure 2 1/2" by 3 1/2". The Fourth Annual Collectors Edition of baseball cards produced by Drake's Cakes in conjunction with Topps continued this now annual set entitled Big Hitters. As in previous years, the front contains a frameline in which the title of the set, the Drake's logo, and the player's name, his team, and position appear. The cards all feature the player in a batting action pose. While the cards fronts are different from the Topps fronts of this year, the backs differ only in the card number and the use of the Drake's logo instead of the Topps logo. This set's card numbering is essentially in alphabetical order by the player's name.

	MINT	EXC	G-VG
COMPLETE SET (33)	8.00	3.50	.80
COMMON PLAYER (1-33)	.06	.02	.00

		MINT	EXC	G-VG
COMPLETE SET (44)		13.50	6.00	1.85
COMMON PLAYER (1-33)		.06	.02	.00
COMMON PLAYER (34-44)		.10	.04	.01
☐ 1	Tony Armas	.06	.02	.00
☐ 2	Harold Baines	.10	.04	.01
☐ 3	Don Baylor	.10	.04	.01
☐ 4	George Brett	.75	.30	.07
☐ 5	Gary Carter	.30	.12	.03
☐ 6	Ron Cey	.06	.02	.00
☐ 7	Jose Cruz	.06	.02	.00
☐ 8	Alvin Davis	.10	.04	.01
☐ 9	Chili Davis	.10	.04	.01
☐ 10	Dwight Evans	.15	.06	.01
☐ 11	Steve Garvey	.40	.16	.04
☐ 12	Kirk Gibson	.35	.15	.03
☐ 13	Pedro Guerrero	.20	.08	.02
☐ 14	Tony Gwynn	.75	.30	.07
☐ 15	Keith Hernandez	.20	.08	.02
☐ 16	Kent Hrbek	.20	.08	.02
☐ 17	Reggie Jackson	.90	.40	.09
☐ 18	Gary Matthews	.06	.02	.00
☐ 19	Don Mattingly	.90	.40	.09
☐ 20	Dale Murphy	.60	.25	.06
☐ 21	Eddie Murray	.60	.25	.06
☐ 22	Dave Parker	.20	.08	.02
☐ 23	Lance Parrish	.10	.04	.01
☐ 24	Tim Raines	.25	.10	.02
☐ 25	Jim Rice	.20	.08	.02
☐ 26	Cal Ripken	1.00	.40	.10
☐ 27	Juan Samuel	.15	.06	.01
☐ 28	Ryne Sandberg	1.00	.40	.10
☐ 29	Mike Schmidt	1.00	.40	.10
☐ 30	Darryl Strawberry	1.00	.40	.10
☐ 31	Alan Trammell	.25	.10	.02
☐ 32	Dave Winfield	.35	.15	.03
☐ 33	Robin Yount	.60	.25	.06
☐ 34	Mike Boddicker	.10	.04	.01
☐ 35	Steve Carlton	.40	.16	.04
☐ 36	Dwight Gooden	.90	.40	.09
☐ 37	Willie Hernandez	.10	.04	.01
☐ 38	Mark Langston	.25	.10	.02
☐ 39	Dan Quisenberry	.15	.06	.01
☐ 40	Dave Righetti	.15	.06	.01
☐ 41	Tom Seaver	.75	.30	.07
☐ 42	Bob Stanley	.10	.04	.01
☐ 43	Rick Sutcliffe	.10	.04	.01
☐ 44	Bruce Sutter	.15	.06	.01

☐ 1	Don Baylor	.10	.04	.01
☐ 2	Wade Boggs	1.00	.40	.10
☐ 3	George Brett	.75	.30	.07
☐ 4	Bill Buckner	.06	.02	.00
☐ 5	Rod Carew	.75	.30	.07
☐ 6	Gary Carter	.30	.12	.03
☐ 7	Ron Cey	.06	.02	.00
☐ 8	Cecil Cooper	.10	.04	.01
☐ 9	Andre Dawson	.35	.15	.03
☐ 10	Steve Garvey	.40	.16	.04
☐ 11	Pedro Guerrero	.20	.08	.02
☐ 12	George Hendrick	.06	.02	.00
☐ 13	Keith Hernandez	.20	.08	.02
☐ 14	Bob Horner	.15	.06	.01
☐ 15	Reggie Jackson	.90	.40	.09
☐ 16	Steve Kemp	.06	.02	.00
☐ 17	Ron Kittle	.10	.04	.01
☐ 18	Greg Luzinski	.10	.04	.01
☐ 19	Fred Lynn	.10	.04	.01
☐ 20	Bill Madlock	.06	.02	.00
☐ 21	Gary Matthews	.06	.02	.00
☐ 22	Dale Murphy	.60	.25	.06
☐ 23	Eddie Murray	.75	.30	.07
☐ 24	Al Oliver	.10	.04	.01
☐ 25	Jim Rice	.20	.08	.02
☐ 26	Cal Ripken	1.00	.40	.10
☐ 27	Pete Rose	1.00	.40	.10
☐ 28	Mike Schmidt	1.00	.40	.10
☐ 29	Darryl Strawberry	1.50	.60	.15
☐ 30	Alan Trammell	.25	.10	.02
☐ 31	Mookie Wilson	.06	.02	.00
☐ 32	Dave Winfield	.35	.15	.03
☐ 33	Robin Yount	.75	.30	.07

of the cards. The complete set could be obtained directly from the company by sending 2.95 with four proofs of purchase.

1985 Drake's

The cards in this 44-card set measure 2 1/2" by 3 1/2". The Fifth Annual Collectors Edition of baseball cards produced by Drake's Cakes in conjunction with Topps continued this apparently annual set with a new twist, for the first time, 11 pitchers were included. The "Big Hitters" are numbered 1-33 and the pitchers are numbered 34-44; each subgroup is ordered alphabetically. The cards are numbered in the upper right corner of the backs

1986 Drake's

This set of 37 cards was distributed as back panels of various Drake's snack products. Each individual card measures 2 1/2" by 3 1/2". Each specially marked package features two, three, or four cards on the back. The set is easily recognized by the Drake's logo and "6th Annual Collector's Edition" at the top of the obverse. Cards are numbered on the front and the back. Cards below are coded based on the product upon which they appeared, for example, Apple Pies (AP), Cherry Pies (CP), Chocolate Donut Delites (CDD), Coffee Cake Jr. (CCJ), Creme

Shortcakes (CS), Devil Dogs (DD), Fudge Brownies (FUD), Funny Bones (FB), Peanut Butter Squares (PBS), Powdered Sugar Donut Delites (PSDD), Ring Ding Jr. (RDJ), Sunny Doodles (SD), Swiss Rolls (SR), Yankee Doodles (YD), and Yodels (Y). The last nine cards are pitchers. Complete panels would be valued approximately 25 percent higher than the individual card prices listed below.

	MINT	EXC	G-VG
COMPLETE SET (37)	33.00	15.00	5.00
COMMON PLAYER (1-37)	.35	.15	.03
☐ 1 Gary Carter Y	.60	.25	.06
☐ 2 Dwight Evans Y	.45	.18	.04
☐ 3 Reggie Jackson SR	1.25	.50	.12
☐ 4 Dave Parker SR	.60	.25	.06
☐ 5 Rickey Henderson FB	1.75	.70	.17
☐ 6 Pedro Guerrero FB	.45	.18	.04
☐ 7 Don Mattingly YD	1.50	.60	.15
☐ 8 Mike Marshall YD	.45	.18	.04
☐ 9 Keith Moreland YD	.35	.15	.03
☐ 10 Keith Hernandez CS	.60	.25	.06
☐ 11 Cal Ripken CS	1.75	.70	.17
☐ 12 Dale Murphy RDJ	1.00	.40	.10
☐ 13 Jim Rice RDJ	.45	.18	.04
☐ 14 George Brett CCJ	1.00	.40	.10
☐ 15 Tim Raines CCJ	.60	.25	.06
☐ 16 Darryl Strawberry DD	1.50	.60	.15
☐ 17 Bill Buckner DD	.35	.15	.03
☐ 18 Dave Winfield AP	.60	.25	.06
☐ 19 Ryne Sandberg AP	1.50	.60	.15
☐ 20 Steve Balboni AP	.35	.15	.03
☐ 21 Tommy Herr AP	.35	.15	.03
☐ 22 Pete Rose CP	1.50	.60	.15
☐ 23 Willie McGee CP	.45	.18	.04
☐ 24 Harold Baines CP	.45	.18	.04
☐ 25 Eddie Murray CP	1.00	.40	.10
☐ 26 Mike Schmidt SD/FUD	2.00	.80	.20
☐ 27 Wade Boggs SD/FUD	1.50	.60	.15
☐ 28 Kirk Gibson SD/FUD	.60	.25	.06
☐ 29 Bret Saberhagen PBS	.75	.30	.07
☐ 30 John Tudor PBS	.45	.18	.04
☐ 31 Orel Hershiser PBS	.75	.30	.07
☐ 32 Ron Guidry CDD	.45	.18	.04
☐ 33 Nolan Ryan CDD	3.50	1.50	.35
☐ 34 Dave Stieb CDD	.45	.18	.04
☐ 35 Dwight Gooden SDD	.90	.40	.09
☐ 36 Fern.Valenzuela SDD	.60	.25	.06
☐ 37 Tom Browning SDD	.45	.18	.04

1987 Drake's

This 33-card set features 25 top hitters and eight top pitchers. Cards were printed in groups of two, three, or four on the backs of Drake's bakery products. Individual cards measure 2 1/2" by 3 1/2" and tout the 7th annual edition. Card backs feature year-by-year season statistics. The cards are numbered such that the pitchers are listed numerically last. Complete panels would be valued approximately 25 percent higher than the individual card prices listed below.

	MINT	EXC	G-VG
COMPLETE SET (33)	30.00	13.50	4.50
COMMON PLAYER (1-33)	.35	.15	.03
☐ 1 Darryl Strawberry	1.50	.60	.15
☐ 2 Wally Joyner	1.00	.40	.10
☐ 3 Von Hayes	.45	.18	.04
☐ 4 Jose Canseco	3.00	1.25	.30
☐ 5 Dave Winfield	.75	.30	.07
☐ 6 Cal Ripken	1.50	.60	.15
☐ 7 Keith Moreland	.35	.15	.03
☐ 8 Don Mattingly	1.50	.60	.15
☐ 9 Willie McGee	.45	.18	.04
☐ 10 Keith Hernandez	.60	.25	.06
☐ 11 Tony Gwynn	1.25	.50	.12
☐ 12 Rickey Henderson	1.50	.60	.15
☐ 13 Dale Murphy	1.00	.40	.10
☐ 14 George Brett	1.00	.40	.10
☐ 15 Jim Rice	.60	.25	.06
☐ 16 Wade Boggs	1.50	.60	.15
☐ 17 Kevin Bass	.35	.15	.03
☐ 18 Dave Parker	.60	.25	.06
☐ 19 Kirby Puckett	1.25	.50	.12
☐ 20 Gary Carter	.60	.25	.06
☐ 21 Ryne Sandberg	1.50	.60	.15
☐ 22 Harold Baines	.45	.18	.04
☐ 23 Mike Schmidt	2.00	.80	.20
☐ 24 Eddie Murray	1.00	.40	.10
☐ 25 Steve Sax	.45	.18	.04
☐ 26 Dwight Gooden	.75	.30	.07
☐ 27 Jack Morris	.60	.25	.06
☐ 28 Ron Darling	.45	.18	.04
☐ 29 Fernando Valenzuela	.60	.25	.06
☐ 30 John Tudor	.45	.18	.04
☐ 31 Roger Clemens	1.50	.60	.15
☐ 32 Nolan Ryan	2.50	1.00	.25
☐ 33 Mike Scott	.45	.18	.04

1988 Drake's

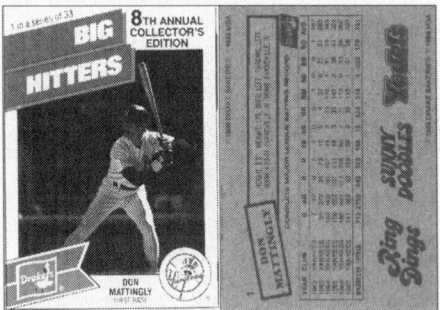

This 33-card set features 27 top hitters and six top pitchers. Cards were printed in groups of two, three, or four on the backs of Drake's bakery products. Individual cards measure approximately 2 1/2 by 3 1/2" and tout the 8th annual edition. Card backs feature year-by-year season statistics. The cards are numbered such that the pitchers are listed numerically last. The product affiliations are as follows, 1-2 Ring Dings, 3-4 Devil Dogs, 5-6 Coffee Cakes, 7-9 Yankee Doodles, 10-11 Funny Bones, 12-14 Fudge Brownies, 15-18 Cherry Pies, 19-21 Sunny Doodles, 22-24 Powdered Sugar Donuts, 25-27 Chocolate Donuts, 28-29 Yodels, and 30-33 Apple Pies. Complete panels would be valued approximately 25 percent higher than the individual card prices listed below.

	MINT	EXC	G-VG
COMPLETE SET (33)	30.00	13.50	4.50
COMMON PLAYER (1-33)	.35	.15	.03
☐ 1 Don Mattingly	1.50	.60	.15
☐ 2 Tim Raines	.60	.25	.06
☐ 3 Darryl Strawberry	1.50	.60	.15
☐ 4 Wade Boggs	1.50	.60	.15
☐ 5 Keith Hernandez	.60	.25	.06

☐ 6	Mark McGwire	1.00	.40	.10
☐ 7	Rickey Henderson	1.75	.70	.17
☐ 8	Mike Schmidt	2.00	.80	.20
☐ 9	Dwight Evans	.45	.18	.04
☐ 10	Gary Carter	.60	.25	.06
☐ 11	Paul Molitor	.60	.25	.06
☐ 12	Dave Winfield	.75	.30	.07
☐ 13	Alan Trammell	.60	.25	.06
☐ 14	Tony Gwynn	1.25	.50	.12
☐ 15	Dale Murphy	1.00	.40	.10
☐ 16	Andre Dawson	.75	.30	.07
☐ 17	Von Hayes	.45	.18	.04
☐ 18	Willie Randolph	.35	.15	.03
☐ 19	Kirby Puckett	1.25	.50	.12
☐ 20	Juan Samuel	.45	.18	.04
☐ 21	Eddie Murray	1.00	.40	.10
☐ 22	George Bell	.60	.25	.06
☐ 23	Larry Sheets	.35	.15	.03
☐ 24	Eric Davis	1.00	.40	.10
☐ 25	Cal Ripken	1.50	.60	.15
☐ 26	Pedro Guerrero	.45	.18	.04
☐ 27	Will Clark	2.00	.80	.20
☐ 28	Dwight Gooden	.90	.40	.09
☐ 29	Frank Viola	.60	.25	.06
☐ 30	Roger Clemens	1.50	.60	.15
☐ 31	Rick Sutcliffe	.45	.18	.04
☐ 32	Jack Morris	.60	.25	.06
☐ 33	John Tudor	.45	.18	.04

☐ 39	Bob Veale	.75	.30	.07
☐ 43	Don Cardwell	.45	.18	.04
☐ 45	Gene Michael	.60	.25	.06

1990 Elite Senior League

The 1990 Elite Senior Pro League Set was a 126-card set issued after the conclusion of the first Senior League season. The card stock was essentially the same type of card stock used by Upper Deck. The set featured full-color fronts and had complete Senior League stats on the back. This set is standard size, 2 1/2" by 3 1/2". It has been reported that there were 5,000 cases of these cards produced. Prior to the debut of the set, Elite also passed out (to prospective dealers) two promo cards for the set, Earl Weaver (numbered 120 rather than 91) and Mike Easler (numbered 1 rather than 19).

		MINT	EXC	G-VG
COMPLETE SET (126)		9.00	4.00	.90
COMMON PLAYER (1-126)		.08	.03	.01
☐ 1	Curt Flood (commissioner)	.40	.16	.04
☐ 2	Bob Tolan	.12	.05	.01
☐ 3	Dick Bosman	.08	.03	.01
☐ 4	Ivan DeJesus	.08	.03	.01
☐ 5	Dock Ellis	.08	.03	.01
☐ 6	Roy Howell	.08	.03	.01
☐ 7	Lamar Johnson	.08	.03	.01
☐ 8	Steve Kemp	.12	.05	.01
☐ 9	Ken Landreaux	.12	.05	.01
☐ 10	Randy Lerch	.08	.03	.01
☐ 11	Jon Matlack	.12	.05	.01
☐ 12	Gary Rajsich	.08	.03	.01
☐ 13	Lenny Randle	.08	.03	.01
☐ 14	Elias Sosa	.08	.03	.01
☐ 15	Ozzie Virgil	.08	.03	.01
☐ 16	Milt Wilcox	.08	.03	.01
☐ 17	Steve Henderson 3X	.12	.05	.01
☐ 18	Ray Burris	.12	.05	.01
☐ 19	Mike Easler	.08	.03	.01
☐ 20	Juan Eichelberger	.08	.03	.01
☐ 21	Rollie Fingers	1.25	.50	.12
☐ 22	Toby Harrah	.12	.05	.01
☐ 23	Randy Johnson	.08	.03	.01
☐ 24	Dave Kingman	.40	.16	.04
☐ 25	Lee Lacy	.08	.03	.01
☐ 26	Tito Landrum	.12	.05	.01
☐ 27	Paul Mirabella	.08	.03	.01
☐ 28	Mickey Rivers	.15	.06	.01
☐ 29	Rodney Scott	.08	.03	.01
☐ 30	Tim Stoddard	.08	.03	.01
☐ 31	Ron Washington	.08	.03	.01
☐ 32	Jerry White	.08	.03	.01
☐ 33	Dick Williams MG	.12	.05	.01
☐ 34	Clete Boyer	.12	.05	.01
☐ 35	Steve Dillard	.08	.03	.01
☐ 36	Garth Iorg	.08	.03	.01
☐ 37	Bruce Kison	.08	.03	.01
☐ 38	Wayne Krenchicki	.08	.03	.01
☐ 39	Ron LeFlore	.12	.05	.01
☐ 40	Tippy Martinez	.08	.03	.01
☐ 41	Omar Moreno	.08	.03	.01
☐ 42	Jim Morrison	.08	.03	.01

1966 East Hills Pirates

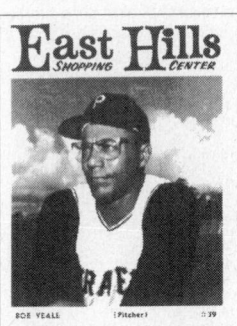

The 1966 East Hills Pirates set consists of 25 large (approximately 3 1/4" by 4 1/4"), full color photos of Pittsburgh Pirate ballplayers. These blank-backed cards are numbered in the lower right corner according to the uniform number of the individual depicted. The set was distributed by various stores located in the East Hills Shopping Center. The catalog number for this set is F405.

		NRMT	VG-E	GOOD
COMPLETE SET (25)		35.00	15.75	5.25
COMMON PLAYER		.45	.18	.04
☐ 3	Harry Walker MG	.60	.25	.06
☐ 7	Bob Bailey	.45	.18	.04
☐ 8	Willie Stargell	9.00	4.00	.90
☐ 9	Bill Mazeroski	2.50	1.00	.25
☐ 10	Jim Pagliaroni	.45	.18	.04
☐ 11	Jose Pagan	.45	.18	.04
☐ 12	Jerry May	.45	.18	.04
☐ 14	Gene Alley	.75	.30	.07
☐ 15	Manny Mota	.75	.30	.07
☐ 16	Andy Rodgers	.45	.18	.04
☐ 17	Donn Clendenon	.75	.30	.07
☐ 18	Matty Alou	1.00	.40	.10
☐ 19	Pete Mikkelsen	.45	.18	.04
☐ 20	Jesse Gonder	.45	.18	.04
☐ 21	Bob Clemente	18.00	7.50	2.50
☐ 22	Woody Fryman	.45	.18	.04
☐ 24	Jerry Lynch	.45	.18	.04
☐ 25	Tommie Sisk	.45	.18	.04
☐ 26	Roy Face	1.25	.50	.12
☐ 28	Steve Blass	.75	.30	.07
☐ 32	Vernon Law	1.00	.40	.10
☐ 34	Al McBean	.45	.18	.04

☐ 43	Graig Nettles	.25	.10	.02
☐ 44	Jim Nettles	.08	.03	.01
☐ 45	Wayne Nordhagen	.08	.03	.01
☐ 46	Al Oliver	.25	.10	.02
☐ 47	Jerry Royster	.08	.03	.01
☐ 48	Sammy Stewart	.08	.03	.01
☐ 49	Randy Bass	.15	.06	.01
☐ 50	Vida Blue	.15	.06	.01
☐ 51	Bruce Bochy	.08	.03	.01
☐ 52	Doug Corbett	.08	.03	.01
☐ 53	Jose Cruz	.15	.06	.01
☐ 54	Jamie Easterly	.08	.03	.01
☐ 55	Pete Falcone	.08	.03	.01
☐ 56	Bob Galasso	.08	.03	.01
☐ 57	Johnny Grubb	.08	.03	.01
☐ 58	Bake McBride	.08	.03	.01
☐ 59	Dyar Miller	.08	.03	.01
☐ 60	Tom Paciorek	.08	.03	.01
☐ 61	Ken Reitz	.08	.03	.01
☐ 62	U.L. Washington	.08	.03	.01
☐ 63	Alan Ashby	.08	.03	.01
☐ 64	Pat Dobson	.12	.05	.01
☐ 65	Doug Bird	.08	.03	.01
☐ 66	Marty Castillo	.08	.03	.01
☐ 67	Dan Driessen	.12	.05	.01
☐ 68	Wayne Garland	.08	.03	.01
☐ 69	Tim Ireland	.08	.03	.01
☐ 70	Ron Jackson	.08	.03	.01
☐ 71	Bobby Jones	.08	.03	.01
☐ 72	Dennis Leonard	.12	.05	.01
☐ 73	Rick Manning	.08	.03	.01
☐ 74	Amos Otis	.15	.06	.01
☐ 75	Pat Putnam	.08	.03	.01
☐ 76	Eric Rasmussen	.08	.03	.01
☐ 77	Paul Blair	.12	.05	.01
☐ 78	Bert Campaneris	.12	.05	.01
☐ 79	Cesar Cedeno	.15	.06	.01
☐ 80	Ed Figueroa	.08	.03	.01
☐ 81	Ross Grimsley	.08	.03	.01
☐ 82	George Hendrick	.12	.05	.01
☐ 83	Cliff Johnson	.08	.03	.01
☐ 84	Mike Kekich	.08	.03	.01
☐ 85	Rafael Landestoy	.08	.03	.01
☐ 86	Larry Milbourne	.08	.03	.01
☐ 87	Bobby Molinaro	.08	.03	.01
☐ 88	Sid Monge	.08	.03	.01
☐ 89	Rennie Stennett	.08	.03	.01
☐ 90	Derrell Thomas	.08	.03	.01
☐ 91	Earl Weaver	.25	.10	.02
☐ 92	Gary Allenson	.08	.03	.01
☐ 93	Pedro Borbon	.08	.03	.01
☐ 94	Al Bumbry	.12	.05	.01
☐ 95	Bill Campbell	.08	.03	.01
☐ 96	Bernie Carbo	.08	.03	.01
☐ 97	Fergie Jenkins	1.00	.40	.10
☐ 98	Pete LaCock	.08	.03	.01
☐ 99	Bill Lee	.12	.05	.01
☐ 100	Tommy McMillan	.08	.03	.01
☐ 101	Joe Pittman	.08	.03	.01
☐ 102	Gene Richards	.08	.03	.01
☐ 103	Leon Roberts	.08	.03	.01
☐ 104	Tony Scott	.08	.03	.01
☐ 105	Doug Simunic	.08	.03	.01
☐ 106	Rick Wise	.12	.05	.01
☐ 107	Willie Aikens	.12	.05	.01
☐ 108	Juan Beniquez	.12	.05	.01
☐ 109	Bobby Bonds	.30	.12	.03
☐ 110	Sergio Ferrer	.08	.03	.01
☐ 111	Chuck Ficks	.08	.03	.01
☐ 112	George Foster	.25	.10	.02
☐ 113	Dave Hilton	.08	.03	.01
☐ 114	Al Holland	.08	.03	.01
☐ 115	Clint Hurdle	.12	.05	.01
☐ 116	Bill Madlock	.20	.08	.02
☐ 117	Steve Ontiveros	.08	.03	.01
☐ 118	Roy Thomas	.08	.03	.01
☐ 119	Luis Tiant	.20	.08	.02
☐ 120	Walt Williams	.15	.06	.01
☐ 121	Vida Blue	.15	.06	.01
☐ 122	Bobby Bonds	.30	.12	.03
☐ 123	Rollie Fingers	1.25	.50	.12
☐ 124	George Foster	.40	.16	.04
☐ 125	Fergie Jenkins	1.00	.40	.10
☐ 126	Dave Kingman	.40	.16	.04

1959 Fleer

Ted's Hitting Fundamentals #1

The cards in this 80-card set measure 2 1/2" by 3 1/2". The 1959 Fleer set, with a catalog designation of R418-1, portrays the life of Ted Williams. The wording of the wrapper, "Baseball's Greatest Series," has led to speculation that Fleer contemplated similar sets honoring other baseball immortals, but chose to develop instead the format of the 1960 and 1961 issues. Card number 68, which was withdrawn early in production, is considered scarce and has even been counterfeited; the fake has a rosy coloration and a cross-hatch pattern visible over the picture area.

		NRMT	VG-E	GOOD
COMPLETE SET (80)		1100.00	500.00	110.00
COMMON CARDS (1-80)		6.00	2.50	.60
☐ 1	The Early Years	35.00	5.00	1.00
☐ 2	Ted's Idol Babe Ruth	30.00	13.50	4.50
☐ 3	Practice Makes Perfect	6.00	2.50	.60
☐ 4	Learns Fine Points	6.00	2.50	.60
☐ 5	Ted's Fame Spreads	6.00	2.50	.60
☐ 6	Ted Turns Pro	6.00	2.50	.60
☐ 7	From Mound to Plate	6.00	2.50	.60
☐ 8	1937 First Full Season	6.00	2.50	.60
☐ 9	First Step to Majors	6.00	2.50	.60
☐ 10	Gunning as Pastime	6.00	2.50	.60
☐ 11	First Spring Training (with Jimmie Foxx)	12.50	5.50	1.65
☐ 12	Burning Up Minors	6.00	2.50	.60
☐ 13	1939 Shows Will Stay	6.00	2.50	.60
☐ 14	Outstanding Rookie '39	6.00	2.50	.60
☐ 15	Licks Sophomore Jinx	6.00	2.50	.60
☐ 16	1941 Greatest Year	6.00	2.50	.60
☐ 17	How Ted Hit .400	6.00	2.50	.60
☐ 18	1941 All Star Hero	6.00	2.50	.60
☐ 19	Ted Wins Triple Crown	6.00	2.50	.60
☐ 20	On to Naval Training	6.00	2.50	.60
☐ 21	Honors for Williams	6.00	2.50	.60
☐ 22	1944 Ted Solos	6.00	2.50	.60
☐ 23	Williams Wins Wings	6.00	2.50	.60
☐ 24	1945 Sharpshooter	6.00	2.50	.60
☐ 25	Ted Discharged	6.00	2.50	.60
☐ 26	Off to Flying Start	6.00	2.50	.60
☐ 27	7/9/46 One Man Show	6.00	2.50	.60
☐ 28	The Williams Shift	6.00	2.50	.60
☐ 29	Ted Hits for Cycle	6.00	2.50	.60
☐ 30	Beating Williams Shift	6.00	2.50	.60
☐ 31	Sox Lose Series	6.00	2.50	.60
☐ 32	Most Valuable Player	6.00	2.50	.60
☐ 33	Another Triple Crown	6.00	2.50	.60
☐ 34	Runs Scored Record	6.00	2.50	.60
☐ 35	Sox Miss Pennant	6.00	2.50	.60
☐ 36	Banner Year for Ted	6.00	2.50	.60
☐ 37	1949 Sox Miss Again	6.00	2.50	.60
☐ 38	1949 Power Rampage	6.00	2.50	.60
☐ 39	1950 Great Start	6.00	2.50	.60
☐ 40	Ted Crashes into Wall	6.00	2.50	.60
☐ 41	1950 Ted Recovers	6.00	2.50	.60
☐ 42	Slowed by Injury	6.00	2.50	.60
☐ 43	Double Play Lead	6.00	2.50	.60
☐ 44	Back to Marines	6.00	2.50	.60
☐ 45	Farewell to Baseball	6.00	2.50	.60

			NRMT	VG-E	GOOD
☐	46	Ready for Combat	6.00	2.50	.60
☐	47	Ted Crash Lands Jet	6.00	2.50	.60
☐	48	1953 Ted Returns	6.00	2.50	.60
☐	49	Smash Return	6.00	2.50	.60
☐	50	1954 Spring Injury	6.00	2.50	.60
☐	51	Ted is Patched Up	6.00	2.50	.60
☐	52	1954 Ted's Comeback	6.00	2.50	.60
☐	53	Comeback is Success	6.00	2.50	.60
☐	54	Ted Hooks Big One	6.00	2.50	.60
☐	55	Retirement "No Go"	6.00	2.50	.60
☐	56	2000th Hit	6.00	2.50	.60
☐	57	400th Homer	6.00	2.50	.60
☐	58	Williams Hits .388	6.00	2.50	.60
☐	59	Hot September for Ted	6.00	2.50	.60
☐	60	More Records for Ted	6.00	2.50	.60
☐	61	1957 Outfielder Ted	6.00	2.50	.60
☐	62	1958 Sixth Batting Title	6.00	2.50	.60
☐	63	Ted's All-Star Record	6.00	2.50	.60
☐	64	Daughter and Daddy	6.00	2.50	.60
☐	65	1958 August 30	6.00	2.50	.60
☐	66	1958 Powerhouse	6.00	2.50	.60
☐	67	Two Famous Fishermen	12.50	5.50	1.65
☐	68	Ted Signs for 1959	625.00	250.00	75.00
☐	69	A Future Ted Williams	6.00	2.50	.60
☐	70	Williams and Thorpe	15.00	6.50	2.15
☐	71	Hitting Fund. 1	6.00	2.50	.60
☐	72	Hitting Fund. 2	6.00	2.50	.60
☐	73	Hitting Fund. 3	6.00	2.50	.60
☐	74	Here's How	6.00	2.50	.60
☐	75	Williams' Value to Sox	6.00	2.50	.60
☐	76	On Base Record	6.00	2.50	.60
☐	77	Ted Relaxes	6.00	2.50	.60
☐	78	Honors for Williams	6.00	2.50	.60
☐	79	Where Ted Stands	6.00	2.50	.60
☐	80	Ted's Goals for 1959	15.00	5.00	1.00

1960 Fleer

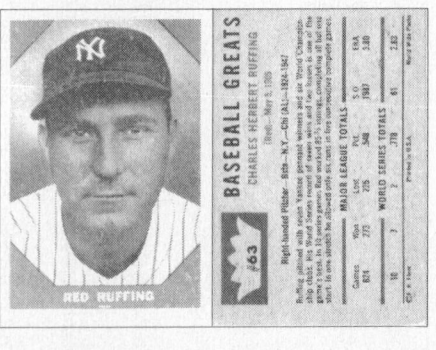

The cards in this 79-card set measure 2 1/2" by 3 1/2". The cards from the 1960 Fleer series of Baseball Greats are sometimes mistaken for 1930s cards by collectors not familiar with this set. The cards each contain a tinted photo of a baseball immortal, and were issued in one series. There are no known scarcities, although a number 80 card (Pepper Martin reverse with either Eddie Collins or Lefty Grove obverse) exists (this is not considered part of the set). The catalog designation for 1960 Fleer is R418-2. The cards were printed on a 96-card sheet with 17 double prints. These are noted in the checklist below by DP. On the sheet the second Eddie Collins card is typically found in the number 80 position.

		NRMT	VG-E	GOOD
COMPLETE SET (79)		400.00	180.00	60.00
COMMON PLAYER (1-79)		3.00	1.25	.30
COMMON PLAYER DP		2.25	.90	.22

☐	1	Napoleon Lajoie DP	15.00	3.00	.60
☐	2	Christy Mathewson	9.00	4.00	.90
☐	3	George H. Ruth	75.00	34.00	11.25
☐	4	Carl Hubbell	5.00	2.25	.50
☐	5	Grover Alexander	5.00	2.25	.50

☐	6	Walter Johnson DP	6.00	2.50	.60
☐	7	Charles A. Bender	3.00	1.25	.30
☐	8	Roger P. Bresnahan	3.00	1.25	.30
☐	9	Mordecai P. Brown	3.00	1.25	.30
☐	10	Tristram Speaker	5.00	2.25	.50
☐	11	Arky Vaughan DP	2.25	.90	.22
☐	12	Zachariah Wheat	3.00	1.25	.30
☐	13	George Sisler	3.00	1.25	.30
☐	14	Connie Mack	5.00	2.25	.50
☐	15	Clark C. Griffith	3.00	1.25	.30
☐	16	Louis Boudreau DP	5.00	2.25	.50
☐	17	Ernest Lombardi	3.00	1.25	.30
☐	18	Henry Manush	3.00	1.25	.30
☐	19	Martin Marion	3.00	1.25	.30
☐	20	Edward Collins DP	2.25	.90	.22
☐	21	James Maranville DP	2.25	.90	.22
☐	22	Joseph Medwick	3.00	1.25	.30
☐	23	Edward Barrow	3.00	1.25	.30
☐	24	Gordon Cochrane	4.00	1.75	.40
☐	25	James J. Collins	3.00	1.25	.30
☐	26	Robert Feller DP	10.00	4.50	1.25
☐	27	Lucius Appling	5.00	2.25	.50
☐	28	Lou Gehrig	40.00	18.00	6.00
☐	29	Charles Hartnett	3.00	1.25	.30
☐	30	Charles Klein	3.00	1.25	.30
☐	31	Anthony Lazzeri DP	3.00	1.25	.30
☐	32	Aloysius Simmons	3.00	1.25	.30
☐	33	Wilbert Robinson	3.00	1.25	.30
☐	34	Edgar Rice	3.00	1.25	.30
☐	35	Herbert Pennock	3.00	1.25	.30
☐	36	Melvin Ott DP	4.00	1.75	.40
☐	37	Frank O'Doul	3.00	1.25	.30
☐	38	John Mize	6.00	2.50	.60
☐	39	Edmund Miller	3.00	1.25	.30
☐	40	Joseph Tinker	3.00	1.25	.30
☐	41	John Baker DP	2.25	.90	.22
☐	42	Tyrus Cobb	40.00	18.00	6.00
☐	43	Paul Derringer	3.00	1.25	.30
☐	44	Adrian Anson	3.00	1.25	.30
☐	45	James Bottomley	3.00	1.25	.30
☐	46	Edward S. Plank DP	3.00	1.25	.30
☐	47	Denton (Cy) Young	7.50	3.25	.75
☐	48	Hack Wilson	5.00	2.25	.50
☐	49	Edward Walsh UER (photo actually Ed Walsh Jr.)	3.00	1.25	.30
☐	50	Frank Chance	3.00	1.25	.30
☐	51	Arthur Vance DP	2.25	.90	.22
☐	52	William Terry	5.00	2.25	.50
☐	53	James Foxx	6.50	2.75	.65
☐	54	Vernon Gomez	5.00	2.25	.50
☐	55	Branch Rickey	3.00	1.25	.30
☐	56	Raymond Schalk DP	2.25	.90	.22
☐	57	John Evers	3.00	1.25	.30
☐	58	Charles Gehringer	5.00	2.25	.50
☐	59	Burleigh Grimes	3.00	1.25	.30
☐	60	Robert (Lefty) Grove	6.00	2.50	.60
☐	61	George Waddell DP	2.25	.90	.22
☐	62	John (Honus) Wagner	9.00	4.00	.90
☐	63	Charles(Red) Ruffing	3.00	1.25	.30
☐	64	Kenesaw M. Landis	3.00	1.25	.30
☐	65	Harry Heilmann	3.00	1.25	.30
☐	66	John McGraw DP	3.00	1.25	.30
☐	67	Hugh Jennings	3.00	1.25	.30
☐	68	Harold Newhouser	3.00	1.25	.30
☐	69	Waite Hoyt	3.00	1.25	.30
☐	70	Louis(Bobo) Newsom	3.00	1.25	.30
☐	71	Earl Averill DP	2.25	.90	.22
☐	72	Theodore Williams	60.00	27.00	9.00
☐	73	Warren Giles	3.00	1.25	.30
☐	74	Ford Frick	3.00	1.25	.30
☐	75	Hazen (Kiki) Cuyler	3.00	1.25	.30
☐	76	Paul Waner DP	2.25	.90	.22
☐	77	Harold(Pie) Traynor	3.00	1.25	.30
☐	78	Lloyd Waner	3.00	1.25	.30
☐	79	Ralph Kiner	7.50	3.25	.75
☐	80A	Pepper Martin SP (Eddie Collins pictured on obverse)	1000.00	400.00	100.00
☐	80B	Pepper Martin SP (Lefty Grove pictured on obverse)	1000.00	400.00	100.00

1961 Fleer

The cards in this 154-card set measure 2 1/2" by 3 1/2". In 1961, Fleer continued its Baseball Greats format by issuing this series of cards. The set was released in two distinct series, 1-88 and

89-154 (of which the latter is more difficult to obtain). The players within each series are conveniently numbered in alphabetical order. It appears that this set continued to be issued the following year by Fleer. The catalog number for this set is F418-3. In each first series pack Fleer inserted a Major League team decal and a pennant sticker honoring past World Series winners.

		NRMT	VG-E	GOOD
	COMPLETE SET (154)	800.00	350.00	120.00
	COMMON PLAYER (1-88)	2.50	1.00	.25
	COMMON PLAYER (89-154)	5.00	2.25	.50
☐ 1	Baker/Cobb/Wheat	25.00	5.00	1.00
	(checklist back)			
☐ 2	Grover C. Alexander	5.00	2.25	.50
☐ 3	Nick Altrock	2.50	1.00	.25
☐ 4	Cap Anson	2.50	1.00	.25
☐ 5	Earl Averill	2.50	1.00	.25
☐ 6	Frank Baker	2.50	1.00	.25
☐ 7	Dave Bancroft	2.50	1.00	.25
☐ 8	Chief Bender	2.50	1.00	.25
☐ 9	Jim Bottomley	2.50	1.00	.25
☐ 10	Roger Bresnahan	2.50	1.00	.25
☐ 11	Mordecai Brown	2.50	1.00	.25
☐ 12	Max Carey	2.50	1.00	.25
☐ 13	Jack Chesbro	2.50	1.00	.25
☐ 14	Ty Cobb	35.00	15.75	5.25
☐ 15	Mickey Cochrane	4.00	1.75	.40
☐ 16	Eddie Collins	2.50	1.00	.25
☐ 17	Earle Combs	2.50	1.00	.25
☐ 18	Charles Comiskey	2.50	1.00	.25
☐ 19	Kiki Cuyler	2.50	1.00	.25
☐ 20	Paul Derringer	2.50	1.00	.25
☐ 21	Howard Ehmke	2.50	1.00	.25
☐ 22	W. Evans	2.50	1.00	.25
☐ 23	Johnny Evers	2.50	1.00	.25
☐ 24	Urban Faber	2.50	1.00	.25
☐ 25	Bob Feller	9.00	4.00	.90
☐ 26	Wes Ferrell	2.50	1.00	.25
☐ 27	Lew Fonseca	2.50	1.00	.25
☐ 28	Jimmy Foxx	6.00	2.50	.60
☐ 29	Ford Frick	2.50	1.00	.25
☐ 30	Frank Frisch	4.00	1.75	.40
☐ 31	Lou Gehrig	35.00	15.75	5.25
☐ 32	Charlie Gehringer	4.00	1.75	.40
☐ 33	Warren Giles	2.50	1.00	.25
☐ 34	Lefty Gomez	4.00	1.75	.40
☐ 35	Goose Goslin	2.50	1.00	.25
☐ 36	Clark Griffith	2.50	1.00	.25
☐ 37	Burleigh Grimes	2.50	1.00	.25
☐ 38	Lefty Grove	5.00	2.25	.50
☐ 39	Chick Hafey	2.50	1.00	.25
☐ 40	Jesse Haines	2.50	1.00	.25
☐ 41	Gabby Hartnett	2.50	1.00	.25
☐ 42	Harry Heilmann	2.50	1.00	.25
☐ 43	Rogers Hornsby	6.00	2.50	.60
☐ 44	Waite Hoyt	2.50	1.00	.25
☐ 45	Carl Hubbell	4.00	1.75	.40
☐ 46	Miller Huggins	2.50	1.00	.25
☐ 47	Hugh Jennings	2.50	1.00	.25
☐ 48	Ban Johnson	2.50	1.00	.25
☐ 49	Walter Johnson	9.00	4.00	.90
☐ 50	Ralph Kiner	6.00	2.50	.60
☐ 51	Chuck Klein	2.50	1.00	.25
☐ 52	Johnny Kling	2.50	1.00	.25
☐ 53	K.M. Landis	2.50	1.00	.25
☐ 54	Tony Lazzeri	2.50	1.00	.25
☐ 55	Ernie Lombardi	2.50	1.00	.25
☐ 56	Dolf Luque	2.50	1.00	.25
☐ 57	Heine Manush	2.50	1.00	.25
☐ 58	Marty Marion	2.50	1.00	.25
☐ 59	Christy Mathewson	9.00	4.00	.90
☐ 60	John McGraw	4.00	1.75	.40
☐ 61	Joe Medwick	2.50	1.00	.25
☐ 62	E. (Bing) Miller	2.50	1.00	.25
☐ 63	Johnny Mize	5.00	2.25	.50
☐ 64	John Mostil	2.50	1.00	.25
☐ 65	Art Nehf	2.50	1.00	.25
☐ 66	Hal Newhouser	2.50	1.00	.25
☐ 67	D. (Bobo) Newsom	2.50	1.00	.25
☐ 68	Mel Ott	4.00	1.75	.40
☐ 69	Allie Reynolds	2.50	1.00	.25
☐ 70	Sam Rice	2.50	1.00	.25
☐ 71	Eppa Rixey	2.50	1.00	.25
☐ 72	Edd Roush	2.50	1.00	.25
☐ 73	Schoolboy Rowe	2.50	1.00	.25
☐ 74	Red Ruffing	2.50	1.00	.25
☐ 75	Babe Ruth	70.00	32.00	10.50
☐ 76	Joe Sewell	2.50	1.00	.25
☐ 77	Al Simmons	2.50	1.00	.25
☐ 78	George Sisler	2.50	1.00	.25
☐ 79	Tris Speaker	5.00	2.25	.50
☐ 80	Fred Toney	2.50	1.00	.25
☐ 81	Dazzy Vance	2.50	1.00	.25
☐ 82	Jim Vaughn	2.50	1.00	.25
☐ 83	Ed Walsh	2.50	1.00	.25
☐ 84	Lloyd Waner	2.50	1.00	.25
☐ 85	Paul Waner	2.50	1.00	.25
☐ 86	Zack Wheat	2.50	1.00	.25
☐ 87	Hack Wilson	4.00	1.75	.40
☐ 88	Jimmy Wilson	2.50	1.00	.25
☐ 89	Sisler and Traynor	20.00	5.00	1.00
	(checklist back)			
☐ 90	Babe Adams	5.00	2.25	.50
☐ 91	Dale Alexander	5.00	2.25	.50
☐ 92	Jim Bagby	5.00	2.25	.50
☐ 93	Ossie Bluege	5.00	2.25	.50
☐ 94	Lou Boudreau	9.00	4.00	.90
☐ 95	Tom Bridges	5.00	2.25	.50
☐ 96	Donie Bush	5.00	2.25	.50
☐ 97	Dolph Camilli	5.00	2.25	.50
☐ 98	Frank Chance	7.50	3.25	.75
☐ 99	Jimmy Collins	7.50	3.25	.75
☐ 100	Stan Coveleskie	7.50	3.25	.75
☐ 101	Hugh Critz	5.00	2.25	.50
☐ 102	Alvin Crowder	5.00	2.25	.50
☐ 103	Joe Dugan	5.00	2.25	.50
☐ 104	Bibb Falk	5.00	2.25	.50
☐ 105	Rick Ferrell	7.50	3.25	.75
☐ 106	Art Fletcher	5.00	2.25	.50
☐ 107	Dennis Galehouse	5.00	2.25	.50
☐ 108	Chick Galloway	5.00	2.25	.50
☐ 109	Mule Haas	5.00	2.25	.50
☐ 110	Stan Hack	5.00	2.25	.50
☐ 111	Bump Hadley	5.00	2.25	.50
☐ 112	Billy B. Hamilton	7.50	3.25	.75
☐ 113	Joe Hauser	5.00	2.25	.50
☐ 114	Babe Herman	5.00	2.25	.50
☐ 115	Travis Jackson	9.00	4.00	.90
☐ 116	Eddie Joost	5.00	2.25	.50
☐ 117	Addie Joss	9.00	4.00	.90
☐ 118	Joe Judge	5.00	2.25	.50
☐ 119	Joe Kuhel	5.00	2.25	.50
☐ 120	Napoleon Lajoie	12.00	5.25	1.50
☐ 121	Dutch Leonard	5.00	2.25	.50
☐ 122	Ted Lyons	7.50	3.25	.75
☐ 123	Connie Mack	12.00	5.25	1.50
☐ 124	Rabbit Maranville	7.50	3.25	.75
☐ 125	Fred Marberry	5.00	2.25	.50
☐ 126	Joe McGinnity	9.00	4.00	.90
☐ 127	Oscar Melillo	5.00	2.25	.50
☐ 128	Ray Mueller	5.00	2.25	.50
☐ 129	Kid Nichols	7.50	3.25	.75
☐ 130	Lefty O'Doul	5.00	2.25	.50
☐ 131	Bob O'Farrell	5.00	2.25	.50
☐ 132	Roger Peckinpaugh	5.00	2.25	.50
☐ 133	Herb Pennock	7.50	3.25	.75
☐ 134	George Pipgras	5.00	2.25	.50
☐ 135	Eddie Plank	9.00	4.00	.90
☐ 136	Ray Schalk	7.50	3.25	.75
☐ 137	Hal Schumacher	5.00	2.25	.50
☐ 138	Luke Sewell	5.00	2.25	.50
☐ 139	Bob Shawkey	5.00	2.25	.50
☐ 140	Riggs Stephenson	5.00	2.25	.50
☐ 141	Billy Sullivan	5.00	2.25	.50
☐ 142	Bill Terry	12.00	5.25	1.50
☐ 143	Joe Tinker	7.50	3.25	.75
☐ 144	Pie Traynor	9.00	4.00	.90
☐ 145	Hal Trosky	5.00	2.25	.50
☐ 146	George Uhle	5.00	2.25	.50
☐ 147	Johnny VanderMeer	7.50	3.25	.75
☐ 148	Arky Vaughan	7.50	3.25	.75

☐	149	Rube Waddell	7.50	3.25	.75
☐	150	Honus Wagner	35.00	15.75	5.25
☐	151	Dixie Walker	5.00	2.25	.50
☐	152	Ted Williams	70.00	32.00	10.50
☐	153	Cy Young	20.00	8.50	2.75
☐	154	Ross Young	15.00	5.00	1.00

1963 Fleer

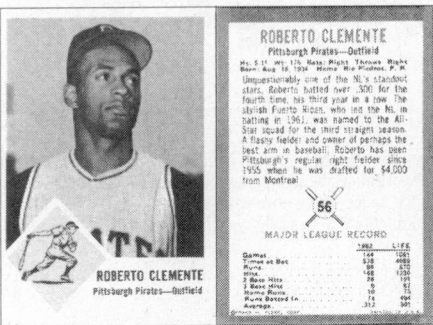

The cards in this 66-card set measure 2 1/2" by 3 1/2". The Fleer set of current baseball players was marketed in 1963 in a gum card-style waxed wrapper package which contained a cherry cookie instead of gum. The cards were printed in sheets of 66 with the scarce card of Adcock apparently being replaced by the unnumbered checklist card for the final press run. The complete set price includes the checklist card. The catalog designation for this set is R418-4. The key rookie card in this set is Maury Wills.

		NRMT	VG-E	GOOD
COMPLETE SET (67)		1100.00	500.00	100.00
COMMON PLAYER (1-66)		7.00	3.00	.70

☐	1	Steve Barber	10.00	4.00	.80
☐	2	Ron Hansen	7.00	3.00	.70
☐	3	Milt Pappas	8.00	3.50	.80
☐	4	Brooks Robinson	42.00	18.00	5.50
☐	5	Willie Mays	90.00	40.00	13.50
☐	6	Lou Clinton	7.00	3.00	.70
☐	7	Bill Monbouquette	7.00	3.00	.70
☐	8	Carl Yastrzemski	90.00	40.00	13.50
☐	9	Ray Herbert	7.00	3.00	.70
☐	10	Jim Landis	7.00	3.00	.70
☐	11	Dick Donovan	7.00	3.00	.70
☐	12	Tito Francona	7.00	3.00	.70
☐	13	Jerry Kindall	7.00	3.00	.70
☐	14	Frank Lary	8.00	3.50	.80
☐	15	Dick Howser	8.00	3.50	.80
☐	16	Jerry Lumpe	7.00	3.00	.70
☐	17	Norm Siebern	7.00	3.00	.70
☐	18	Don Lee	7.00	3.00	.70
☐	19	Albie Pearson	7.00	3.00	.70
☐	20	Bob Rodgers	8.00	3.50	.80
☐	21	Leon Wagner	7.00	3.00	.70
☐	22	Jim Kaat	11.00	5.00	1.35
☐	23	Vic Power	7.00	3.00	.70
☐	24	Rich Rollins	8.00	3.50	.80
☐	25	Bobby Richardson	12.00	5.25	1.50
☐	26	Ralph Terry	8.00	3.50	.80
☐	27	Tom Cheney	7.00	3.00	.70
☐	28	Chuck Cottier	7.00	3.00	.70
☐	29	Jim Piersall	9.00	4.00	.90
☐	30	Dave Stenhouse	7.00	3.00	.70
☐	31	Glen Hobbie	7.00	3.00	.70
☐	32	Ron Santo	11.00	5.00	1.35
☐	33	Gene Freese	7.00	3.00	.70
☐	34	Vada Pinson	11.00	5.00	1.35
☐	35	Bob Purkey	7.00	3.00	.70
☐	36	Joe Amalfitano	7.00	3.00	.70
☐	37	Bob Aspromonte	7.00	3.00	.70
☐	38	Dick Farrell	7.00	3.00	.70
☐	39	Al Spangler	7.00	3.00	.70
☐	40	Tommy Davis	9.00	4.00	.90
☐	41	Don Drysdale	33.00	15.00	5.00

☐	42	Sandy Koufax	110.00	50.00	16.50
☐	43	Maury Wills	60.00	27.00	9.00
☐	44	Frank Bolling	7.00	3.00	.70
☐	45	Warren Spahn	30.00	13.50	4.50
☐	46	Joe Adcock SP	140.00	63.00	21.00
☐	47	Roger Craig	10.00	4.50	1.25
☐	48	Al Jackson	7.00	3.00	.70
☐	49	Rod Kanehl	7.00	3.00	.70
☐	50	Ruben Amaro	7.00	3.00	.70
☐	51	Johnny Callison	8.00	3.50	.80
☐	52	Clay Dalrymple	7.00	3.00	.70
☐	53	Don Demeter	7.00	3.00	.70
☐	54	Art Mahaffey	7.00	3.00	.70
☐	55	Smoky Burgess	8.00	3.50	.80
☐	56	Roberto Clemente	90.00	40.00	13.50
☐	57	Roy Face	9.00	4.00	.90
☐	58	Vern Law	8.00	3.50	.80
☐	59	Bill Mazeroski	11.00	5.00	1.35
☐	60	Ken Boyer	14.00	6.25	2.00
☐	61	Bob Gibson	32.00	14.25	4.75
☐	62	Gene Oliver	7.00	3.00	.70
☐	63	Bill White	12.00	5.25	1.50
☐	64	Orlando Cepeda	14.00	6.25	2.00
☐	65	Jim Davenport	7.00	3.00	.70
☐	66	Billy O'Dell	9.00	4.00	.80
☐	xx	Checklist card (unnumbered)	350.00	75.00	15.00

1970 Fleer World Series

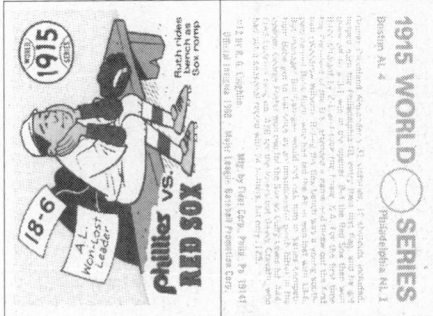

This set of 66 cards was distributed by Fleer. The cards are standard size, 2 1/2" by 3 1/2", and are in crude color on the front with light blue printing on white card stock on the back. All the years are represented except for 1904 when no World Series was played. In the list below, the winning series team is listed first. The year of the Series on the obverse is inside a white baseball. The original art for the cards in this set was drawn by sports artist, R.G. Laughlin.

		NRMT	VG-E	GOOD
COMPLETE SET (66)		40.00	18.00	6.00
COMMON PLAYER (1-66)		.50	.20	.05

☐	1	1903 Red Sox/Pirates	.50	.20	.05
☐	2	1905 Giants/A's (Christy Mathewson)	.75	.30	.07
☐	3	1906 White Sox/Cubs	.50	.20	.05
☐	4	1907 Cubs/Tigers	.50	.20	.05
☐	5	1908 Cubs/Tigers (Tinker/Evers/Chance)	.75	.30	.07
☐	6	1909 Pirates/Tigers (Wagner/Cobb)	1.00	.40	.10
☐	7	1910 A's/Cubs (Bender/Coombs)	.50	.20	.05
☐	8	1911 A's/Giants (John McGraw)	.75	.30	.07
☐	9	1912 Red Sox/Giants	.50	.20	.05
☐	10	1913 A's/Giants	.50	.20	.05
☐	11	1914 Braves/A's	.50	.20	.05
☐	12	1915 Red Sox/Phillies (Babe Ruth)	1.25	.50	.12
☐	13	1916 Red Sox/Dodgers (Babe Ruth)	1.25	.50	.12
☐	14	1917 White Sox/Giants	.50	.20	.05

☐ 15 1918 Red Sox/Cubs	.50	.20	.05
☐ 16 1919 Reds/White Sox	.50	.20	.05
☐ 17 1920 Indians/Dodgers	.50	.20	.05
(Stan Coveleski)			
☐ 18 1921 Giants/Yankees	.50	.20	.05
(Commissioner Landis)			
☐ 19 1922 Giants/Yankees	.50	.20	.05
☐ 20 1923 Yankees/Giants	1.25	.50	.12
(Babe Ruth)			
☐ 21 1924 Senators/Giants	.75	.30	.07
(John McGraw)			
☐ 22 1925 Pirates/Senators	.90	.40	.09
(Walter Johnson)			
☐ 23 1926 Cardinals/Yankees	.75	.30	.07
(Alexander/Lazzeri)			
☐ 24 1927 Yankees/Pirates	.50	.20	.05
☐ 25 1928 Yankees/Cardinals	1.25	.50	.12
(Ruth/Gehrig)			
☐ 26 1929 A's/Cubs	.50	.20	.05
☐ 27 1930 A's/Cardinals	.50	.20	.05
☐ 28 1931 Cardinals/A's	.50	.20	.05
(Pepper Martin)			
☐ 29 1932 Yankees/Cubs	1.25	.50	.12
(Ruth/Gehrig)			
☐ 30 1933 Giants/Senators	.75	.30	.07
(Mel Ott)			
☐ 31 1934 Cardinals/Tigers	.50	.20	.05
☐ 32 1935 Tigers/Cubs	.75	.30	.07
(Gehringer/Bridges)			
☐ 33 1936 Yankees/Giants	.50	.20	.05
☐ 34 1937 Yankees/Giants	.75	.30	.07
(Carl Hubbell)			
☐ 35 1938 Yankees/Cubs	1.00	.40	.10
(Lou Gehrig)			
☐ 36 1939 Yankees/Reds	.50	.20	.05
☐ 37 1940 Reds/Tigers	.50	.20	.05
☐ 38 1941 Yankees/Dodgers	.50	.20	.05
☐ 39 1942 Cardinals/Yankees	.50	.20	.05
☐ 40 1943 Yankees/Cardinals	.50	.20	.05
☐ 41 1944 Cardinals/Browns	.50	.20	.05
☐ 42 1945 Tigers/Cubs	.75	.30	.07
(Hank Greenberg)			
☐ 43 1946 Cardinals/Red Sox	.75	.30	.07
(Enos Slaughter)			
☐ 44 1947 Yankees/Dodgers	.50	.20	.05
(Al Gionfriddo)			
☐ 45 1948 Indians/Braves	.50	.20	.05
☐ 46 1949 Yankees/Dodgers	.50	.20	.05
(Reynolds/Roe)			
☐ 47 1950 Yankees/Phillies	.50	.20	.05
☐ 48 1951 Yankees/Giants	.50	.20	.05
☐ 49 1952 Yankees/Dodgers	1.00	.40	.10
(Mize/Snider)			
☐ 50 1953 Yankees/Dodgers	.50	.20	.05
(Carl Erskine)			
☐ 51 1954 Giants/Indians	.50	.20	.05
(Johnny Antonelli)			
☐ 52 1955 Dodgers/Yankees	.50	.20	.05
(Johnny Podres)			
☐ 53 1956 Yankees/Dodgers	.50	.20	.05
☐ 54 1957 Braves/Yankees	.50	.20	.05
(Lew Burdette)			
☐ 55 1958 Yankees/Braves	.50	.20	.05
(Bob Turley)			
☐ 56 1959 Dodgers/Wh.Sox	.50	.20	.05
(Chuck Essegian)			
☐ 57 1960 Pirates/Yankees	.50	.20	.05
☐ 58 1961 Yankees/Reds	.75	.30	.07
(Whitey Ford)			
☐ 59 1962 Yankees/Giants	.50	.20	.05
☐ 60 1963 Dodgers/Yankees	.50	.20	.05
(Moose Skowron)			
☐ 61 1964 Cardinals/Yankees	.75	.30	.07
(Bobby Richardson)			
☐ 62 1965 Dodgers/Twins	.50	.20	.05
☐ 63 1966 Orioles/Dodgers	.50	.20	.05
☐ 64 1967 Cardinals/Red Sox	.50	.20	.05
☐ 65 1968 Tigers/Cardinals	.50	.20	.05
☐ 66 1969 Mets/Orioles	.60	.25	.06

1971 Fleer World Series

This set of 68 cards was distributed by Fleer. The cards are standard size, 2 1/2" by 3 1/2" and are in crude color on the front with brown printing on white card stock on the back. All the years since 1903 are represented in this set including 1904, when no World Series was played. That year is represented by

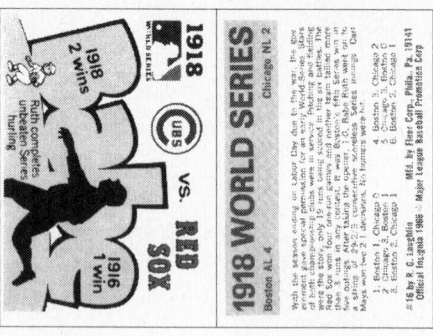

a card explaining why there was no World Series that year. In the list below, the winning series team is listed first. The year of the Series on the obverse is inside a white square over the official World Series logo.

	NRMT	VG-E	GOOD
COMPLETE SET (68)	40.00	18.00	6.00
COMMON PLAYER (1-68)	.50	.20	.05
☐ 1 1903 Red Sox/Pirates	.75	.30	.07
(Cy Young)			
☐ 2 1904 NO Series	.75	.30	.07
(John McGraw)			
☐ 3 1905 Giants/A's	.75	.30	.07
(Mathewson, Bender,			
and McGinnity)			
☐ 4 1906 White Sox/Cubs	.50	.20	.05
☐ 5 1907 Cubs/Tigers	.50	.20	.05
☐ 6 1908 Cubs/Tigers	1.00	.40	.10
(Ty Cobb)			
☐ 7 1909 Pirates/Tigers	.50	.20	.05
☐ 8 1910 A's/Cubs	.75	.30	.07
(Eddie Collins)			
☐ 9 1911 A's/Giants	.75	.30	.07
(Home Run Baker)			
☐ 10 1912 Red Sox/Giants	.50	.20	.05
☐ 11 1913 A's/Giants	.75	.30	.07
(Christy Mathewson)			
☐ 12 1914 Braves/A's	.50	.20	.05
☐ 13 1915 Red Sox/Phillies	.75	.30	.07
(Grover Alexander)			
☐ 14 1916 Red Sox/Dodgers	.50	.20	.05
☐ 15 1917 White Sox/Giants	.50	.20	.05
(Red Faber)			
☐ 16 1918 Red Sox/Cubs	1.25	.50	.12
(Babe Ruth)			
☐ 17 1919 Reds/White Sox	.50	.20	.05
☐ 18 1920 Indians/Dodgers	.50	.20	.05
☐ 19 1921 Giants/Yankees	.75	.30	.07
(Waite Hoyt)			
☐ 20 1922 Giants/Yankees	.50	.20	.05
☐ 21 1923 Yankees/Giants	.75	.30	.07
(Herb Pennock)			
☐ 22 1924 Senators/Giants	.75	.30	.07
(Walter Johnson)			
☐ 23 1925 Pirates/Senators	.75	.30	.07
(Cuyler/W.Johnson)			
☐ 24 1926 Cardinals/Yankees	.75	.30	.07
(Rogers Hornsby)			
☐ 25 1927 Yankees/Pirates	.50	.20	.05
☐ 26 1928 Yankees/Cardinals	1.00	.40	.10
(Lou Gehrig)			
☐ 27 1929 A's/Cubs	.50	.20	.05
☐ 28 1930 A's/Cardinals	.75	.30	.07
(Jimmie Foxx)			
☐ 29 1931 Cardinals/A's	.50	.20	.05
(Pepper Martin)			
☐ 30 1932 Yankees/Cubs	1.25	.50	.12
(Babe Ruth)			
☐ 31 1933 Giants/Senators	.75	.30	.07
(Carl Hubbell)			
☐ 32 1934 Cardinals/Tigers	.50	.20	.05
☐ 33 1935 Tigers/Cubs	.75	.30	.07
(Mickey Cochrane)			
☐ 34 1936 Yankees/Giants	.50	.20	.05
(Red Rolfe)			
☐ 35 1937 Yankees/Giants	.75	.30	.07
(Tony Lazzeri)			
☐ 36 1938 Yankees/Cubs	.50	.20	.05
☐ 37 1939 Yankees/Reds	.50	.20	.05

☐ 38	1940 Reds/Tigers	.50	.20	.05
☐ 39	1941 Yankees/Dodgers	.50	.20	.05
☐ 40	1942 Cardinals/Yankees	.50	.20	.05
☐ 41	1943 Yankees/Cardinals	.50	.20	.05
☐ 42	1944 Cardinals/Browns	.50	.20	.05
☐ 43	1945 Tigers/Cubs (Hank Greenberg)	.75	.30	.07
☐ 44	1946 Cardinals/Red Sox (Enos Slaughter)	.75	.30	.07
☐ 45	1947 Yankees/Dodgers	.50	.20	.05
☐ 46	1948 Indians/Braves	.50	.20	.05
☐ 47	1949 Yankees/Dodgers (Preacher Roe)	.50	.20	.05
☐ 48	1950 Yankees/Phillies (Allie Reynolds)	.50	.20	.05
☐ 49	1951 Yankees/Giants (Ed Lopat)	.50	.20	.05
☐ 50	1952 Yankees/Dodgers (Johnny Mize)	.75	.30	.07
☐ 51	1953 Yankees/Dodgers	.50	.20	.05
☐ 52	1954 Giants/Indians	.50	.20	.05
☐ 53	1955 Dodgers/Yankees (Duke Snider)	.75	.30	.07
☐ 54	1956 Yankees/Dodgers	.50	.20	.05
☐ 55	1957 Braves/Yankees	.50	.20	.05
☐ 56	1958 Yankees/Braves (Hank Bauer)	.50	.20	.05
☐ 57	1959 Dodgers/Wh.Sox (Duke Snider)	.75	.30	.07
☐ 58	1960 Pirates/Yankees	.50	.20	.05
☐ 59	1961 Yankees/Reds (Whitey Ford)	.75	.30	.07
☐ 60	1962 Yankees/Giants	.50	.20	.05
☐ 61	1963 Dodgers/Yankees	.50	.20	.05
☐ 62	1964 Cardinals/Yankees	.50	.20	.05
☐ 63	1965 Dodgers/Twins	.50	.20	.05
☐ 64	1966 Orioles/Dodgers	.50	.20	.05
☐ 65	1967 Cardinals/Red Sox	.50	.20	.05
☐ 66	1968 Tigers/Cardinals	.50	.20	.05
☐ 67	1969 Mets/Orioles	.50	.20	.05
☐ 68	1970 Orioles/Reds	.50	.20	.05

☐ 8	Walter Johnson	.90	.40	.09
☐ 9	Hack Wilson	.60	.25	.06
☐ 10	Wilbert Robinson	.50	.20	.05
☐ 11	Cy Young	.70	.30	.07
☐ 12	Rudy York	.50	.20	.05
☐ 13	Grover C. Alexander	.60	.25	.06
☐ 14	Fred Toney and Hippo Vaughan	.50	.20	.05
☐ 15	Ty Cobb	1.25	.50	.12
☐ 16	Jimmie Foxx	.90	.40	.09
☐ 17	Hub Leonard	.50	.20	.05
☐ 18	Eddie Collins	.50	.20	.05
☐ 19	Joe Oeschger and Leon Cadore	.50	.20	.05
☐ 20	Babe Ruth	1.75	.70	.17
☐ 21	Honus Wagner	.90	.40	.09
☐ 22	Red Rolfe	.50	.20	.05
☐ 23	Ed Walsh	.50	.20	.05
☐ 24	Paul Waner	.50	.20	.05
☐ 25	Mel Ott	.70	.30	.07
☐ 26	Eddie Plank	.60	.25	.06
☐ 27	Sam Crawford	.50	.20	.05
☐ 28	Napoleon Lajoie	.70	.30	.07
☐ 29	Ed Reulbach	.50	.20	.05
☐ 30	Pinky Higgins	.50	.20	.05
☐ 31	Bill Klem	.60	.25	.06
☐ 32	Tris Speaker	.70	.30	.07
☐ 33	Hank Gowdy	.50	.20	.05
☐ 34	Lefty O'Doul	.50	.20	.05
☐ 35	Lloyd Waner	.50	.20	.05
☐ 36	Chuck Klein	.50	.20	.05
☐ 37	Deacon Phillippe	.50	.20	.05
☐ 38	Ed Delahanty	.50	.20	.05
☐ 39	Jack Chesbro	.50	.20	.05
☐ 40	Willie Keeler	.50	.20	.05

1972 Fleer Famous Feats

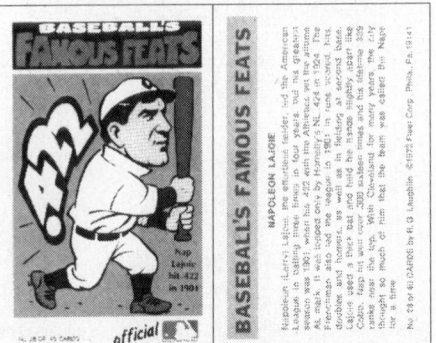

This Fleer set of 40 cards features the artwork of sports artist R.G. Laughlin. The set is titled "Baseball's Famous Feats." The cards are numbered both on the front and back. The backs are printed in light blue on white card stock. The cards measure approximately 2 1/2" by 4". This set was licensed by Major League Baseball.

	NRMT	VG-E	GOOD
COMPLETE SET (40)	20.00	8.50	2.75
COMMON PLAYER (1-40)	.50	.20	.05
☐ 1 Joe McGinnity	.50	.20	.05
☐ 2 Rogers Hornsby	.90	.40	.09
☐ 3 Christy Mathewson	.90	.40	.09
☐ 4 Dazzy Vance	.50	.20	.05
☐ 5 Lou Gehrig	1.25	.50	.12
☐ 6 Jim Bottomley	.50	.20	.05
☐ 7 Johnny Evers	.50	.20	.05

1973 Fleer Wildest Days

This Fleer set of 42 cards is titled "Baseball's Wildest Days and Plays" and features the artwork of sports artist R.G. Laughlin. The cards are numbered on the back. The backs are printed in dark red on white card stock. The cards measure approximately 2 1/2" by 4". This set was not licensed by Major League Baseball.

	NRMT	VG-E	GOOD
COMPLETE SET (42)	18.00	7.50	2.50
COMMON PLAYER (1-42)	.50	.20	.05
☐ 1 Cubs and Phillies Score 49 Runs in Game	.50	.20	.05
☐ 2 Frank Chance Five HBP's in One Day	.50	.20	.05
☐ 3 Jim Thorpe Homered into 3 States	1.25	.50	.12
☐ 4 Eddie Gaedel Midget in Majors	.75	.30	.07
☐ 5 Most Tied Game Ever	.50	.20	.05
☐ 6 Seven Errors in One Inning	.50	.20	.05
☐ 7 Four 20-Game Winners But No Pennant	.50	.20	.05
☐ 8 Dummy Hoy Umpires Signal Strikes	.75	.30	.07

☐ 9	Fourteeen Hits in One Inning	.50	.20	.05
☐ 10	Yankees Not Shut Out For Two Years	.50	.20	.05
☐ 11	Buck Weaver 17 Straight Fouls	.60	.25	.06
☐ 12	George Sisler Greatest Thrill Was as a Pitcher	.50	.20	.05
☐ 13	Wrong-Way Baserunner	.50	.20	.05
☐ 14	Kiki Cuyler Sits Out Series	.50	.20	.05
☐ 15	Grounder Climbed Wall	.50	.20	.05
☐ 16	Gabby Street Washington Monument	.50	.20	.05
☐ 17	Mel Ott Ejected Twice	.75	.30	.07
☐ 18	Shortest Pitching Career	.50	.20	.05
☐ 19	Three Homers in One Inning	.50	.20	.05
☐ 20	Bill Byron Singing Umpire	.50	.20	.05
☐ 21	Fred Clarke Walking Steal of Home	.50	.20	.05
☐ 22	Christy Mathewson 373rd Win Discovered	.75	.30	.07
☐ 23	Hitting Through the Unglaub Arc	.50	.20	.05
☐ 24	Jim O'Rourke Catching at 52	.50	.20	.05
☐ 25	Fired for Striking Out in Series	.50	.20	.05
☐ 26	Eleven Run Inning on One Hit	.50	.20	.05
☐ 27	58 Innings in 3 Days	.50	.20	.05
☐ 28	Homer on Warm-Up Pitch	.50	.20	.05
☐ 29	Giants Win 26 Straight But Finish Fourth	.50	.20	.05
☐ 30	Player Who Stole First Base	.50	.20	.05
☐ 31	Ernie Shore Perfect Game in Relief	.50	.20	.05
☐ 32	Greatest Comeback	.50	.20	.05
☐ 33	All-Time Flash- In-The-Pan	.50	.20	.05
☐ 34	Pruett Fanned Ruth 19 out of 31	.75	.30	.07
☐ 35	Fixed Batting Race Cobb/Lajoie	.90	.40	.09
☐ 36	Wild-Pitch Rebound Play	.50	.20	.05
☐ 37	17 Straight Scoring Innings	.50	.20	.05
☐ 38	Wildest Opening Day	.50	.20	.05
☐ 39	Baseball's Strike One	.50	.20	.05
☐ 40	Opening Day No Hitter That Didn't Count	.50	.20	.05
☐ 41	Jimmie Foxx Six Straight Walks in One Game	.75	.30	.07
☐ 42	Entire Team Hit and Scored in Inning	.50	.20	.05

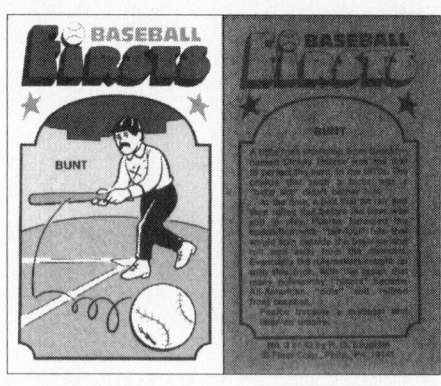

☐ 9	Players Association	.25	.10	.02
☐ 10	Knuckleball	.25	.10	.02
☐ 11	Player With Glasses	.25	.10	.02
☐ 12	Baseball Cards	1.25	.50	.12
☐ 13	Standardized Rules	.25	.10	.02
☐ 14	Grand Slam	.25	.10	.02
☐ 15	Player Fined	.25	.10	.02
☐ 16	Presidential Opener	.25	.10	.02
☐ 17	Player Transaction	.25	.10	.02
☐ 18	All-Star Game	.25	.10	.02
☐ 19	Scoreboard	.25	.10	.02
☐ 20	Cork Center Ball	.25	.10	.02
☐ 21	Scorekeeping	.25	.10	.02
☐ 22	Domed Stadium	.25	.10	.02
☐ 23	Batting Helmet	.25	.10	.02
☐ 24	Fatality	.25	.10	.02
☐ 25	Unassisted Triple Play	.25	.10	.02
☐ 26	Home Run At Night	.20	.08	.02
☐ 27	Black Major Leaguer	.40	.16	.04
☐ 28	Pinch Hitter	.25	.10	.02
☐ 29	Million-Dollar World Series	.25	.10	.02
☐ 30	Tarpaulin	.25	.10	.02
☐ 31	Team Initials	.25	.10	.02
☐ 32	Pennant Playoff	.25	.10	.02
☐ 33	Glove	.25	.10	.02
☐ 34	Curve Ball	.25	.10	.02
☐ 35	Night Game	.25	.10	.02
☐ 36	Admission Charge	.25	.10	.02
☐ 37	Farm System	.25	.10	.02
☐ 38	Telecast	.25	.10	.02
☐ 39	Commissioner	.25	.10	.02
☐ 40	.400 Hitter	.25	.10	.02
☐ 41	World Series	.25	.10	.02
☐ 42	Player Into Service	.25	.10	.02

1974 Fleer Baseball Firsts

This Fleer set of 42 cards is titled "Baseball Firsts" and features the artwork of sports artist R.G. Laughlin. The cards are numbered on the back. The backs are printed in black on gray card stock. The cards measure approximately 2 1/2" by 4". This set was not licensed by Major League Baseball.

	NRMT	VG-E	GOOD
COMPLETE SET (42)	9.00	4.00	.90
COMMON PLAYER (1-42)	.25	.10	.02

☐ 1	Slide	.25	.10	.02
☐ 2	Spring Training	.25	.10	.02
☐ 3	Bunt	.25	.10	.02
☐ 4	Catcher's Mask	.25	.10	.02
☐ 5	Four Straight Homers (Lou Gehrig)	1.00	.40	.10
☐ 6	Radio Broadcast	.25	.10	.02
☐ 7	Numbered Uniforms	.25	.10	.02
☐ 8	Shin Guards	.25	.10	.02

1975 Fleer Pioneers

This 28-card set of brown and white sepia-toned photos of old timers is subtitled "Pioneers of Baseball." The graphics artwork was done by R.G. Laughlin. The cards measure 2 1/2" by 4". The card backs are a narrative about the particular player. The cards are numbered on the back at the bottom.

	NRMT	VG-E	GOOD
COMPLETE SET (28)	12.50	5.50	1.65
COMMON PLAYER (1-28)	.50	.20	.05

☐ 1	Cap Anson	.75	.30	.07
☐ 2	Harry Wright	.60	.25	.06
☐ 3	Buck Ewing	.60	.25	.06
☐ 4	A.G. Spalding	.60	.25	.06
☐ 5	Old Hoss Radbourn	.60	.25	.06
☐ 6	Dan Brouthers	.60	.25	.06
☐ 7	Roger Bresnahan	.50	.20	.05
☐ 8	Mike Kelly	.60	.25	.06
☐ 9	Ned Hanlon	.50	.20	.05
☐ 10	Ed Delahanty	.60	.25	.06
☐ 11	Pud Galvin	.60	.25	.06
☐ 12	Amos Rusie	.60	.25	.06
☐ 13	Tommy McCarthy	.60	.25	.06
☐ 14	Ty Cobb	1.25	.50	.12

HAL CHASE

First Base   1905-1919

☐ 15 John McGraw	.60	.25	.06
☐ 16 Home Run Baker	.60	.25	.06
☐ 17 Johnny Evers	.50	.20	.05
☐ 18 Nap Lajoie	.75	.30	.07
☐ 19 Cy Young	.75	.30	.07
☐ 20 Eddie Collins	.60	.25	.06
☐ 21 John Glasscock	.50	.20	.05
☐ 22 Hal Chase	.50	.20	.05
☐ 23 Mordecai Brown	.50	.20	.05
☐ 24 Jake Daubert	.50	.20	.05
☐ 25 Mike Donlin	.50	.20	.05
☐ 26 John Clarkson	.60	.25	.06
☐ 27 Buck Herzog	.50	.20	.05
☐ 28 Art Nehf	.50	.20	.05

1981 Fleer

The cards in this 660-card set measure 2 1/2" by 3 1/2". This issue of cards marks Fleer's first entry into the current player baseball card market since 1963. Players from the same team are conveniently grouped together by number in the set. The teams are ordered (by 1980 standings) as follows: Philadelphia (1-27), Kansas City (28-50), Houston (51-78), New York Yankees (79-109), Los Angeles (110-141), Montreal (142-168), Baltimore (169-195), Cincinnati (196-220), Boston (221-241), Atlanta (242-267), California (268-290), Chicago Cubs (291-315), New York Mets (316-338), Chicago White Sox (339-350 and 352-359), Pittsburgh (360-386), Cleveland (387-408), Toronto (409-431), San Francisco (432-458), Detroit (459-483), San Diego (484-506), Milwaukee (507-527), St. Louis (528-550), Minnesota (551-571), Oakland (351 and 572-594), Seattle (595-616), and Texas (617-637). Cards 638-660 feature specials and checklists. The cards of pitchers in this set erroneously show a heading (on the card backs) of "Batting Record" over their career pitching statistics. There were three distinct printings: the two following the primary run were designed to correct numerous errors. The variations caused by these multiple printings are noted in the checklist below (P1, P2, or P3). The C. Nettles variation was corrected before the end of the first printing and thus is not included in the complete set consideration. The key rookie cards in this set are Kirk Gibson, Jeff Reardon, and Fernando Valenzuela, whose first name was erroneously spelled Fernand on the card front.

	MINT	EXC	G-VG
COMPLETE SET (660)	60.00	27.00	9.00
COMMON PLAYER (1-660)	.05	.02	.00
☐ 1 Pete Rose UER	2.00	.50	.10
(270 hits in '63, should be 170)			
☐ 2 Larry Bowa	.15	.06	.01
☐ 3 Manny Trillo	.05	.02	.00
☐ 4 Bob Boone	.15	.06	.01
☐ 5 Mike Schmidt	2.50	1.00	.25
See also 640A			
☐ 6A Steve Carlton P1	1.25	.50	.12
Pitcher of Year			
See also 660A			
Back "1066 Cardinals"			
☐ 6B Steve Carlton P2	1.25	.50	.12
Pitcher of Year			
Back "1066 Cardinals"			
☐ 6C Steve Carlton P3	2.00	.80	.20
"1966 Cardinals"			
☐ 7 Tug McGraw	.15	.06	.01
See 657A			
☐ 8 Larry Christenson	.05	.02	.00
☐ 9 Bake McBride	.05	.02	.00
☐ 10 Greg Luzinski	.15	.06	.01
☐ 11 Ron Reed	.05	.02	.00
☐ 12 Dickie Noles	.05	.02	.00
☐ 13 Keith Moreland	.15	.06	.01
☐ 14 Bob Walk	.25	.10	.02
☐ 15 Lonnie Smith	.35	.15	.03
☐ 16 Dick Ruthven	.05	.02	.00
☐ 17 Sparky Lyle	.15	.06	.01
☐ 18 Greg Gross	.05	.02	.00
☐ 19 Garry Maddox	.05	.02	.00
☐ 20 Nino Espinosa	.05	.02	.00
☐ 21 George Vukovich	.05	.02	.00
☐ 22 John Vukovich	.05	.02	.00
☐ 23 Ramon Aviles	.05	.02	.00
☐ 24A Ken Saucier P1	.05	.02	.00
(Name on back "Ken")			
☐ 24B Ken Saucier P2	.05	.02	.00
(Name on back "Ken")			
☐ 24C Kevin Saucier P3	.25	.10	.02
(Name on back "Kevin")			
☐ 25 Randy Lerch	.05	.02	.00
☐ 26 Del Unser	.05	.02	.00
☐ 27 Tim McCarver	.15	.06	.01
☐ 28 George Brett	2.50	1.00	.25
See also 655A			
☐ 29 Willie Wilson	.20	.08	.02
See also 653A			
☐ 30 Paul Splittorff	.05	.02	.00
☐ 31 Dan Quisenberry	.25	.10	.02
☐ 32A Amos Otis P1	.15	.06	.01
Batting Pose			
"Outfield"			
(32 on back)			
☐ 32B Amos Otis P2	.15	.06	.01
"Series Starter"			
(483 on back)			
☐ 33 Steve Busby	.10	.04	.01
☐ 34 U.L. Washington	.05	.02	.00
☐ 35 Dave Chalk	.05	.02	.00
☐ 36 Darrell Porter	.05	.02	.00
☐ 37 Marty Pattin	.05	.02	.00
☐ 38 Larry Gura	.05	.02	.00
☐ 39 Renie Martin	.05	.02	.00
☐ 40 Rich Gale	.05	.02	.00
☐ 41A Hal McRae P1	.50	.20	.05
"Royals" on front in black letters			
☐ 41B Hal McRae P2	.15	.06	.01
"Royals" on front in blue letters			
☐ 42 Dennis Leonard	.05	.02	.00
☐ 43 Willie Aikens	.05	.02	.00
☐ 44 Frank White	.10	.04	.01
☐ 45 Clint Hurdle	.05	.02	.00
☐ 46 John Wathan	.10	.04	.01
☐ 47 Pete LaCock	.05	.02	.00
☐ 48 Rance Mulliniks	.05	.02	.00

☐ 49	Jeff Twitty	.05	.02	.00
☐ 50	Jamie Quirk	.05	.02	.00
☐ 51	Art Howe	.10	.04	.01
☐ 52	Ken Forsch	.05	.02	.00
☐ 53	Vern Ruhle	.05	.02	.00
☐ 54	Joe Niekro	.10	.04	.01
☐ 55	Frank LaCorte	.05	.02	.00
☐ 56	J.R. Richard	.10	.04	.01
☐ 57	Nolan Ryan	6.25	2.75	.60
☐ 58	Enos Cabell	.05	.02	.00
☐ 59	Cesar Cedeno	.10	.04	.01
☐ 60	Jose Cruz	.10	.04	.01
☐ 61	Bill Virdon MG	.05	.02	.00
☐ 62	Terry Puhl	.05	.02	.00
☐ 63	Joaquin Andujar	.10	.04	.01
☐ 64	Alan Ashby	.05	.02	.00
☐ 65	Joe Sambito	.05	.02	.00
☐ 66	Denny Walling	.05	.02	.00
☐ 67	Jeff Leonard	.10	.04	.01
☐ 68	Luis Pujols	.05	.02	.00
☐ 69	Bruce Bochy	.05	.02	.00
☐ 70	Rafael Landestoy	.05	.02	.00
☐ 71	Dave Smith	.40	.16	.04
☐ 72	Danny Heep	.15	.06	.01
☐ 73	Julio Gonzalez	.05	.02	.00
☐ 74	Craig Reynolds	.05	.02	.00
☐ 75	Gary Woods	.05	.02	.00
☐ 76	Dave Bergman	.05	.02	.00
☐ 77	Randy Niemann	.05	.02	.00
☐ 78	Joe Morgan	.75	.30	.07
☐ 79	Reggie Jackson (See also 650A)	2.50	1.00	.25
☐ 80	Bucky Dent	.10	.04	.01
☐ 81	Tommy John	.20	.08	.02
☐ 82	Luis Tiant	.10	.04	.01
☐ 83	Rick Cerone	.05	.02	.00
☐ 84	Dick Howser MG	.05	.02	.00
☐ 85	Lou Piniella	.15	.06	.01
☐ 86	Ron Davis	.05	.02	.00
☐ 87A	Craig Nettles P1ERR (Name on back misspelled "Craig")	11.00	5.00	1.35
☐ 87B	Graig Nettles P2 COR "Graig"	.35	.15	.03
☐ 88	Ron Guidry	.25	.10	.02
☐ 89	Rich Gossage	.20	.08	.02
☐ 90	Rudy May	.05	.02	.00
☐ 91	Gaylord Perry	.50	.20	.05
☐ 92	Eric Soderholm	.05	.02	.00
☐ 93	Bob Watson	.05	.02	.00
☐ 94	Bobby Murcer	.15	.06	.01
☐ 95	Bobby Brown	.05	.02	.00
☐ 96	Jim Spencer	.05	.02	.00
☐ 97	Tom Underwood	.05	.02	.00
☐ 98	Oscar Gamble	.05	.02	.00
☐ 99	Johnny Oates	.10	.04	.01
☐ 100	Fred Stanley	.05	.02	.00
☐ 101	Ruppert Jones	.05	.02	.00
☐ 102	Dennis Werth	.05	.02	.00
☐ 103	Joe Lefebvre	.05	.02	.00
☐ 104	Brian Doyle	.05	.02	.00
☐ 105	Aurelio Rodriguez	.05	.02	.00
☐ 106	Doug Bird	.05	.02	.00
☐ 107	Mike Griffin	.05	.02	.00
☐ 108	Tim Lollar	.05	.02	.00
☐ 109	Willie Randolph	.15	.06	.01
☐ 110	Steve Garvey	.75	.30	.07
☐ 111	Reggie Smith	.10	.04	.01
☐ 112	Don Sutton	.35	.15	.03
☐ 113	Burt Hooton	.05	.02	.00
☐ 114A	Dave Lopes P1 Small hand on back	.50	.20	.05
☐ 114B	Dave Lopes P2 No hand	.10	.04	.01
☐ 115	Dusty Baker	.10	.04	.01
☐ 116	Tom Lasorda MG	.10	.04	.01
☐ 117	Bill Russell	.10	.04	.01
☐ 118	Jerry Reuss	.10	.04	.01
☐ 119	Terry Forster	.10	.04	.01
☐ 120A	Bob Welch P1 Name on back is "Bob"	.50	.20	.05
☐ 120B	Bob Welch P2 Name on back is "Robert"	.50	.20	.05
☐ 121	Don Stanhouse	.05	.02	.00
☐ 122	Rick Monday	.10	.04	.01
☐ 123	Derrel Thomas	.05	.02	.00
☐ 124	Joe Ferguson	.05	.02	.00
☐ 125	Rick Sutcliffe	.15	.06	.01
☐ 126A	Ron Cey P1 Small hand on back	.50	.20	.05
☐ 126B	Ron Cey P2 No hand	.15	.06	.01
☐ 127	Dave Goltz	.05	.02	.00
☐ 128	Jay Johnstone	.10	.04	.01
☐ 129	Steve Yeager	.05	.02	.00
☐ 130	Gary Weiss	.05	.02	.00
☐ 131	Mike Scioscia	1.00	.40	.10
☐ 132	Vic Davalillo	.05	.02	.00
☐ 133	Doug Rau	.05	.02	.00
☐ 134	Pepe Frias	.05	.02	.00
☐ 135	Mickey Hatcher	.05	.02	.00
☐ 136	Steve Howe	.10	.04	.01
☐ 137	Robert Castillo	.05	.02	.00
☐ 138	Gary Thomasson	.05	.02	.00
☐ 139	Rudy Law	.05	.02	.00
☐ 140	Fernand Valenzuela UER (sic, Fernando)	2.75	1.10	.27
☐ 141	Manny Mota	.10	.04	.01
☐ 142	Gary Carter	.90	.40	.09
☐ 143	Steve Rogers	.05	.02	.00
☐ 144	Warren Cromartie	.05	.02	.00
☐ 145	Andre Dawson	1.75	.70	.17
☐ 146	Larry Parrish	.05	.02	.00
☐ 147	Rowland Office	.05	.02	.00
☐ 148	Ellis Valentine	.05	.02	.00
☐ 149	Dick Williams MG	.05	.02	.00
☐ 150	Bill Gullickson	.50	.20	.05
☐ 151	Elias Sosa	.05	.02	.00
☐ 152	John Tamargo	.05	.02	.00
☐ 153	Chris Speier	.05	.02	.00
☐ 154	Ron LeFlore	.05	.02	.00
☐ 155	Rodney Scott	.05	.02	.00
☐ 156	Stan Bahnsen	.05	.02	.00
☐ 157	Bill Lee	.05	.02	.00
☐ 158	Fred Norman	.05	.02	.00
☐ 159	Woodie Fryman	.05	.02	.00
☐ 160	David Palmer	.05	.02	.00
☐ 161	Jerry White	.05	.02	.00
☐ 162	Roberto Ramos	.05	.02	.00
☐ 163	John D'Acquisto	.05	.02	.00
☐ 164	Tommy Hutton	.05	.02	.00
☐ 165	Charlie Lea	.15	.06	.01
☐ 166	Scott Sanderson	.15	.06	.01
☐ 167	Ken Macha	.05	.02	.00
☐ 168	Tony Bernazard	.05	.02	.00
☐ 169	Jim Palmer	1.00	.40	.10
☐ 170	Steve Stone	.05	.02	.00
☐ 171	Mike Flanagan	.10	.04	.01
☐ 172	Al Bumbry	.05	.02	.00
☐ 173	Doug DeCinces	.05	.02	.00
☐ 174	Scott McGregor	.05	.02	.00
☐ 175	Mark Belanger	.10	.04	.01
☐ 176	Tim Stoddard	.05	.02	.00
☐ 177A	Rick Dempsey P1 Small hand on front	.50	.20	.05
☐ 177B	Rick Dempsey P2 No hand	.10	.04	.01
☐ 178	Earl Weaver MG	.10	.04	.01
☐ 179	Tippy Martinez	.05	.02	.00
☐ 180	Dennis Martinez	.20	.08	.02
☐ 181	Sammy Stewart	.05	.02	.00
☐ 182	Rich Dauer	.05	.02	.00
☐ 183	Lee May	.10	.04	.01
☐ 184	Eddie Murray	2.25	.90	.22
☐ 185	Benny Ayala	.05	.02	.00
☐ 186	John Lowenstein	.05	.02	.00
☐ 187	Gary Roenicke	.05	.02	.00
☐ 188	Ken Singleton	.10	.04	.01
☐ 189	Dan Graham	.05	.02	.00
☐ 190	Terry Crowley	.05	.02	.00
☐ 191	Kiko Garcia	.05	.02	.00
☐ 192	Dave Ford	.05	.02	.00
☐ 193	Mark Corey	.05	.02	.00
☐ 194	Lenn Sakata	.05	.02	.00
☐ 195	Doug DeCinces	.05	.02	.00
☐ 196	Johnny Bench	1.50	.60	.15
☐ 197	Dave Concepcion	.20	.08	.02
☐ 198	Ray Knight	.10	.04	.01
☐ 199	Ken Griffey	.30	.12	.03
☐ 200	Tom Seaver	1.50	.60	.15
☐ 201	Dave Collins	.05	.02	.00
☐ 202A	George Foster P1 Slugger Number on back 216	.20	.08	.02
☐ 202B	George Foster P2 Slugger Number on back 202	.20	.08	.02
☐ 203	Junior Kennedy	.05	.02	.00
☐ 204	Frank Pastore	.05	.02	.00
☐ 205	Dan Driessen	.05	.02	.00
☐ 206	Hector Cruz	.05	.02	.00
☐ 207	Paul Moskau	.05	.02	.00
☐ 208	Charlie Leibrandt	.50	.20	.05
☐ 209	Harry Spilman	.05	.02	.00
☐ 210	Joe Price	.05	.02	.00
☐ 211	Tom Hume	.05	.02	.00

☐ 212 Joe Nolan	.05	.02	.00
☐ 213 Doug Bair	.05	.02	.00
☐ 214 Mario Soto	.10	.04	.01
☐ 215A Bill Bonham P1	.50	.20	.05
Small hand on back			
☐ 215B Bill Bonham P2	.10	.04	.01
No hand			
☐ 216 George Foster	.20	.08	.02
(See 202)			
☐ 217 Paul Householder	.05	.02	.00
☐ 218 Ron Oester	.05	.02	.00
☐ 219 Sam Mejias	.05	.02	.00
☐ 220 Sheldon Burnside	.05	.02	.00
☐ 221 Carl Yastrzemski	1.50	.60	.15
☐ 222 Jim Rice	.25	.10	.02
☐ 223 Fred Lynn	.20	.08	.02
☐ 224 Carlton Fisk	1.50	.60	.15
☐ 225 Rick Burleson	.10	.04	.01
☐ 226 Dennis Eckersley	.60	.25	.06
☐ 227 Butch Hobson	.10	.04	.01
☐ 228 Tom Burgmeier	.05	.02	.00
☐ 229 Garry Hancock	.05	.02	.00
☐ 230 Don Zimmer MG	.05	.02	.00
☐ 231 Steve Renko	.05	.02	.00
☐ 232 Dwight Evans	.35	.15	.03
☐ 233 Mike Torrez	.05	.02	.00
☐ 234 Bob Stanley	.05	.02	.00
☐ 235 Jim Dwyer	.05	.02	.00
☐ 236 Dave Stapleton	.05	.02	.00
☐ 237 Glen Hoffman	.05	.02	.00
☐ 238 Jerry Remy	.05	.02	.00
☐ 239 Dick Drago	.05	.02	.00
☐ 240 Bill Campbell	.05	.02	.00
☐ 241 Tony Perez	.35	.15	.03
☐ 242 Phil Niekro	.50	.20	.05
☐ 243 Dale Murphy	1.00	.40	.10
☐ 244 Bob Horner	.10	.04	.01
☐ 245 Jeff Burroughs	.05	.02	.00
☐ 246 Rick Camp	.05	.02	.00
☐ 247 Bobby Cox MG	.05	.02	.00
☐ 248 Bruce Benedict	.05	.02	.00
☐ 249 Gene Garber	.05	.02	.00
☐ 250 Jerry Royster	.05	.02	.00
☐ 251A Gary Matthews P1	.50	.20	.05
Small hand on back			
☐ 251B Gary Matthews P2	.10	.04	.01
No hand			
☐ 252 Chris Chambliss	.10	.04	.01
☐ 253 Luis Gomez	.05	.02	.00
☐ 254 Bill Nahorodny	.05	.02	.00
☐ 255 Doyle Alexander	.05	.02	.00
☐ 256 Brian Asselstine	.05	.02	.00
☐ 257 Biff Pocoroba	.05	.02	.00
☐ 258 Mike Lum	.05	.02	.00
☐ 259 Charlie Spikes	.05	.02	.00
☐ 260 Glenn Hubbard	.05	.02	.00
☐ 261 Tommy Boggs	.05	.02	.00
☐ 262 Al Hrabosky	.05	.02	.00
☐ 263 Rick Matula	.05	.02	.00
☐ 264 Preston Hanna	.05	.02	.00
☐ 265 Larry Bradford	.05	.02	.00
☐ 266 Rafael Ramirez	.15	.06	.01
☐ 267 Larry McWilliams	.05	.02	.00
☐ 268 Rod Carew	1.50	.60	.15
☐ 269 Bobby Grich	.10	.04	.01
☐ 270 Carney Lansford	.15	.06	.01
☐ 271 Don Baylor	.15	.06	.01
☐ 272 Joe Rudi	.10	.04	.01
☐ 273 Dan Ford	.05	.02	.00
☐ 274 Jim Fregosi	.05	.02	.00
☐ 275 Dave Frost	.05	.02	.00
☐ 276 Frank Tanana	.10	.04	.01
☐ 277 Dickie Thon	.15	.06	.01
☐ 278 Jason Thompson	.05	.02	.00
☐ 279 Rick Miller	.05	.02	.00
☐ 280 Bert Campaneris	.10	.04	.01
☐ 281 Tom Donohue	.05	.02	.00
☐ 282 Brian Downing	.10	.04	.01
☐ 283 Fred Patek	.05	.02	.00
☐ 284 Bruce Kison	.05	.02	.00
☐ 285 Dave LaRoche	.05	.02	.00
☐ 286 Don Aase	.05	.02	.00
☐ 287 Jim Barr	.05	.02	.00
☐ 288 Alfredo Martinez	.05	.02	.00
☐ 289 Larry Harlow	.05	.02	.00
☐ 290 Andy Hassler	.05	.02	.00
☐ 291 Dave Kingman	.15	.06	.01
☐ 292 Bill Buckner	.10	.04	.01
☐ 293 Rick Reuschel	.15	.06	.01
☐ 294 Bruce Sutter	.20	.08	.02
☐ 295 Jerry Martin	.05	.02	.00
☐ 296 Scot Thompson	.05	.02	.00
☐ 297 Ivan DeJesus	.05	.02	.00
☐ 298 Steve Dillard	.05	.02	.00
☐ 299 Dick Tidrow	.05	.02	.00
☐ 300 Randy Martz	.05	.02	.00
☐ 301 Lenny Randle	.05	.02	.00
☐ 302 Lynn McGlothen	.05	.02	.00
☐ 303 Cliff Johnson	.05	.02	.00
☐ 304 Tim Blackwell	.05	.02	.00
☐ 305 Dennis Lamp	.05	.02	.00
☐ 306 Bill Caudill	.05	.02	.00
☐ 307 Carlos Lezcano	.05	.02	.00
☐ 308 Jim Tracy	.05	.02	.00
☐ 309 Doug Capilla UER	.05	.02	.00
(Cubs on front but			
Braves on back)			
☐ 310 Willie Hernandez	.10	.04	.01
☐ 311 Mike Vail	.05	.02	.00
☐ 312 Mike Krukow	.05	.02	.00
☐ 313 Barry Foote	.05	.02	.00
☐ 314 Larry Biittner	.05	.02	.00
☐ 315 Mike Tyson	.05	.02	.00
☐ 316 Lee Mazzilli	.05	.02	.00
☐ 317 John Stearns	.05	.02	.00
☐ 318 Alex Trevino	.05	.02	.00
☐ 319 Craig Swan	.05	.02	.00
☐ 320 Frank Taveras	.05	.02	.00
☐ 321 Steve Henderson	.05	.02	.00
☐ 322 Neil Allen	.05	.02	.00
☐ 323 Mark Bomback	.05	.02	.00
☐ 324 Mike Jorgensen	.05	.02	.00
☐ 325 Joe Torre MG	.10	.04	.01
☐ 326 Elliott Maddox	.05	.02	.00
☐ 327 Pete Falcone	.05	.02	.00
☐ 328 Ray Burris	.05	.02	.00
☐ 329 Claudell Washington	.05	.02	.00
☐ 330 Doug Flynn	.05	.02	.00
☐ 331 Joel Youngblood	.05	.02	.00
☐ 332 Bill Almon	.05	.02	.00
☐ 333 Tom Hausman	.05	.02	.00
☐ 334 Pat Zachry	.05	.02	.00
☐ 335 Jeff Reardon	3.50	1.50	.35
☐ 336 Wally Backman	.30	.12	.03
☐ 337 Dan Norman	.05	.02	.00
☐ 338 Jerry Morales	.05	.02	.00
☐ 339 Ed Farmer	.05	.02	.00
☐ 340 Bob Molinaro	.05	.02	.00
☐ 341 Todd Cruz	.05	.02	.00
☐ 342A Britt Burns P1	.50	.20	.05
(Small hand on front)			
☐ 342B Britt Burns P2	.15	.06	.01
(No hand)			
☐ 343 Kevin Bell	.05	.02	.00
☐ 344 Tony LaRussa MG	.10	.04	.01
☐ 345 Steve Trout	.05	.02	.00
☐ 346 Harold Baines	3.00	1.25	.30
☐ 347 Richard Wortham	.05	.02	.00
☐ 348 Wayne Nordhagen	.05	.02	.00
☐ 349 Mike Squires	.05	.02	.00
☐ 350 Lamar Johnson	.05	.02	.00
☐ 351 Rickey Henderson	10.00	4.50	1.25
(Most Stolen Bases AL)			
☐ 352 Francisco Barrios	.05	.02	.00
☐ 353 Thad Bosley	.05	.02	.00
☐ 354 Chet Lemon	.05	.02	.00
☐ 355 Bruce Kimm	.05	.02	.00
☐ 356 Richard Dotson	.15	.06	.01
☐ 357 Jim Morrison	.05	.02	.00
☐ 358 Mike Proly	.05	.02	.00
☐ 359 Greg Pryor	.05	.02	.00
☐ 360 Dave Parker	.60	.25	.06
☐ 361 Omar Moreno	.05	.02	.00
☐ 362A Kent Tekulve P1	.15	.06	.01
(Back "1071 Waterbury"			
and "1078 Pirates")			
☐ 362B Kent Tekulve P2	.10	.04	.01
("1971 Waterbury" and			
"1978 Pirates")			
☐ 363 Willie Stargell	.60	.25	.06
☐ 364 Phil Garner	.10	.04	.01
☐ 365 Ed Ott	.05	.02	.00
☐ 366 Don Robinson	.05	.02	.00
☐ 367 Chuck Tanner MG	.05	.02	.00
☐ 368 Jim Rooker	.05	.02	.00
☐ 369 Dale Berra	.05	.02	.00
☐ 370 Jim Bibby	.05	.02	.00
☐ 371 Steve Nicosia	.05	.02	.00
☐ 372 Mike Easler	.05	.02	.00
☐ 373 Bill Robinson	.10	.04	.01
☐ 374 Lee Lacy	.05	.02	.00
☐ 375 John Candelaria	.10	.04	.01
☐ 376 Manny Sanguillen	.10	.04	.01
☐ 377 Rick Rhoden	.05	.02	.00
☐ 378 Grant Jackson	.05	.02	.00
☐ 379 Tim Foli	.05	.02	.00
☐ 380 Rod Scurry	.05	.02	.00
☐ 381 Bill Madlock	.10	.04	.01

☐ 382A	Kurt Bevacqua P1 ERR (P on cap backwards)	.20	.08	.02
☐ 382B	Kurt Bevacqua P2 COR	.10	.04	.01
☐ 383	Bert Blyleven	.25	.10	.02
☐ 384	Eddie Solomon	.05	.02	.00
☐ 385	Enrique Romo	.05	.02	.00
☐ 386	John Milner	.05	.02	.00
☐ 387	Mike Hargrove	.10	.04	.01
☐ 388	Jorge Orta	.05	.02	.00
☐ 389	Toby Harrah	.05	.02	.00
☐ 390	Tom Veryzer	.05	.02	.00
☐ 391	Miguel Dilone	.05	.02	.00
☐ 392	Dan Spillner	.05	.02	.00
☐ 393	Jack Brohamer	.05	.02	.00
☐ 394	Wayne Garland	.05	.02	.00
☐ 395	Sid Monge	.05	.02	.00
☐ 396	Rick Waits	.05	.02	.00
☐ 397	Joe Charboneau	.10	.04	.01
☐ 398	Gary Alexander	.05	.02	.00
☐ 399	Jerry Dybzinski	.05	.02	.00
☐ 400	Mike Stanton	.05	.02	.00
☐ 401	Mike Paxton	.05	.02	.00
☐ 402	Gary Gray	.05	.02	.00
☐ 403	Rick Manning	.05	.02	.00
☐ 404	Bo Diaz	.05	.02	.00
☐ 405	Ron Hassey	.10	.04	.01
☐ 406	Ross Grimsley	.05	.02	.00
☐ 407	Victor Cruz	.05	.02	.00
☐ 408	Len Barker	.05	.02	.00
☐ 409	Bob Bailor	.05	.02	.00
☐ 410	Otto Velez	.05	.02	.00
☐ 411	Ernie Whitt	.05	.02	.00
☐ 412	Jim Clancy	.05	.02	.00
☐ 413	Barry Bonnell	.05	.02	.00
☐ 414	Dave Stieb	.60	.25	.06
☐ 415	Damaso Garcia	.10	.04	.01
☐ 416	John Mayberry	.10	.04	.01
☐ 417	Roy Howell	.05	.02	.00
☐ 418	Danny Ainge	1.00	.40	.10
☐ 419A	Jesse Jefferson P1 Back says Pirates	.10	.04	.01
☐ 419B	Jesse Jefferson P2 Back says Pirates	.10	.04	.01
☐ 419C	Jesse Jefferson P3 Back says Blue Jays	.25	.10	.02
☐ 420	Joey McLaughlin	.05	.02	.00
☐ 421	Lloyd Moseby	.35	.15	.03
☐ 422	Alvis Woods	.05	.02	.00
☐ 423	Garth Iorg	.05	.02	.00
☐ 424	Doug Ault	.05	.02	.00
☐ 425	Ken Schrom	.05	.02	.00
☐ 426	Mike Willis	.05	.02	.00
☐ 427	Steve Braun	.05	.02	.00
☐ 428	Bob Davis	.05	.02	.00
☐ 429	Jerry Garvin	.05	.02	.00
☐ 430	Alfredo Griffin	.10	.04	.01
☐ 431	Bob Mattick MG	.05	.02	.00
☐ 432	Vida Blue	.10	.04	.01
☐ 433	Jack Clark	.25	.10	.02
☐ 434	Willie McCovey	.75	.30	.07
☐ 435	Mike Ivie	.05	.02	.00
☐ 436A	Darrel Evans P1 ERR Name on front "Darrel"	.40	.16	.04
☐ 436B	Darrell Evans P2 COR Name on front "Darrell"	.15	.06	.01
☐ 437	Terry Whitfield	.05	.02	.00
☐ 438	Rennie Stennett	.05	.02	.00
☐ 439	John Montefusco	.05	.02	.00
☐ 440	Jim Wohlford	.05	.02	.00
☐ 441	Bill North	.05	.02	.00
☐ 442	Milt May	.05	.02	.00
☐ 443	Max Venable	.05	.02	.00
☐ 444	Ed Whitson	.05	.02	.00
☐ 445	Al Holland	.05	.02	.00
☐ 446	Randy Moffitt	.05	.02	.00
☐ 447	Bob Knepper	.05	.02	.00
☐ 448	Gary Lavelle	.05	.02	.00
☐ 449	Greg Minton	.05	.02	.00
☐ 450	Johnnie LeMaster	.05	.02	.00
☐ 451	Larry Herndon	.05	.02	.00
☐ 452	Rich Murray	.05	.02	.00
☐ 453	Joe Pettini	.05	.02	.00
☐ 454	Allen Ripley	.05	.02	.00
☐ 455	Dennis Littlejohn	.05	.02	.00
☐ 456	Tom Griffin	.05	.02	.00
☐ 457	Alan Hargesheimer	.05	.02	.00
☐ 458	Joe Strain	.05	.02	.00
☐ 459	Steve Kemp	.05	.02	.00
☐ 460	Sparky Anderson MG	.10	.04	.01
☐ 461	Alan Trammell	1.00	.40	.10
☐ 462	Mark Fidrych	.10	.04	.01
☐ 463	Lou Whitaker	.60	.25	.06
☐ 464	Dave Rozema	.05	.02	.00
☐ 465	Milt Wilcox	.05	.02	.00
☐ 466	Champ Summers	.05	.02	.00
☐ 467	Lance Parrish	.40	.16	.04
☐ 468	Dan Petry	.10	.04	.01
☐ 469	Pat Underwood	.05	.02	.00
☐ 470	Rick Peters	.05	.02	.00
☐ 471	Al Cowens	.05	.02	.00
☐ 472	John Wockenfuss	.05	.02	.00
☐ 473	Tom Brookens	.05	.02	.00
☐ 474	Richie Hebner	.05	.02	.00
☐ 475	Jack Morris	1.00	.40	.10
☐ 476	Jim Lentine	.05	.02	.00
☐ 477	Bruce Robbins	.05	.02	.00
☐ 478	Mark Wagner	.05	.02	.00
☐ 479	Tim Corcoran	.05	.02	.00
☐ 480A	Stan Papi P1 Front as Pitcher	.15	.06	.01
☐ 480B	Stan Papi P2 Front as Shortstop	.10	.04	.01
☐ 481	Kirk Gibson	3.50	1.50	.35
☐ 482	Dan Schatzeder	.05	.02	.00
☐ 483A	Amos Otis P1 See card 32	.10	.04	.01
☐ 483B	Amos Otis P2 See card 32	.10	.04	.01
☐ 484	Dave Winfield	1.25	.50	.12
☐ 485	Rollie Fingers	.75	.30	.07
☐ 486	Gene Richards	.05	.02	.00
☐ 487	Randy Jones	.05	.02	.00
☐ 488	Ozzie Smith	2.50	1.00	.25
☐ 489	Gene Tenace	.10	.04	.01
☐ 490	Bill Fahey	.05	.02	.00
☐ 491	John Curtis	.05	.02	.00
☐ 492	Dave Cash	.05	.02	.00
☐ 493A	Tim Flannery P1 Batting right	.15	.06	.01
☐ 493B	Tim Flannery P2 Batting left	.10	.04	.01
☐ 494	Jerry Mumphrey	.05	.02	.00
☐ 495	Bob Shirley	.05	.02	.00
☐ 496	Steve Mura	.05	.02	.00
☐ 497	Eric Rasmussen	.05	.02	.00
☐ 498	Broderick Perkins	.05	.02	.00
☐ 499	Barry Evans	.05	.02	.00
☐ 500	Chuck Baker	.05	.02	.00
☐ 501	Luis Salazar	.15	.06	.01
☐ 502	Gary Lucas	.05	.02	.00
☐ 503	Mike Armstrong	.05	.02	.00
☐ 504	Jerry Turner	.05	.02	.00
☐ 505	Dennis Kinney	.05	.02	.00
☐ 506	Willie Montanez	.05	.02	.00
☐ 507	Gorman Thomas	.10	.04	.01
☐ 508	Ben Oglivie	.05	.02	.00
☐ 509	Larry Hisle	.05	.02	.00
☐ 510	Sal Bando	.10	.04	.01
☐ 511	Robin Yount	2.50	1.00	.25
☐ 512	Mike Caldwell	.05	.02	.00
☐ 513	Sixto Lezcano	.05	.02	.00
☐ 514A	Bill Travers P1 ERR "Jerry Augustine" with Augustine back	.20	.08	.02
☐ 514B	Bill Travers P2 COR	.10	.04	.01
☐ 515	Paul Molitor	.60	.25	.06
☐ 516	Moose Haas	.05	.02	.00
☐ 517	Bill Castro	.05	.02	.00
☐ 518	Jim Slaton	.05	.02	.00
☐ 519	Lary Sorensen	.05	.02	.00
☐ 520	Bob McClure	.05	.02	.00
☐ 521	Charlie Moore	.05	.02	.00
☐ 522	Jim Gantner	.05	.02	.00
☐ 523	Reggie Cleveland	.05	.02	.00
☐ 524	Don Money	.05	.02	.00
☐ 525	Bill Travers	.05	.02	.00
☐ 526	Buck Martinez	.05	.02	.00
☐ 527	Dick Davis	.05	.02	.00
☐ 528	Ted Simmons	.20	.08	.02
☐ 529	Garry Templeton	.10	.04	.01
☐ 530	Ken Reitz	.05	.02	.00
☐ 531	Tony Scott	.05	.02	.00
☐ 532	Ken Oberkfell	.05	.02	.00
☐ 533	Bob Sykes	.05	.02	.00
☐ 534	Keith Smith	.05	.02	.00
☐ 535	John Littlefield	.05	.02	.00
☐ 536	Jim Kaat	.20	.08	.02
☐ 537	Bob Forsch	.05	.02	.00
☐ 538	Mike Phillips	.05	.02	.00
☐ 539	Terry Landrum	.05	.02	.00
☐ 540	Leon Durham	.15	.06	.01
☐ 541	Terry Kennedy	.10	.04	.01
☐ 542	George Hendrick	.05	.02	.00
☐ 543	Dane Iorg	.05	.02	.00
☐ 544	Mark Littell	.05	.02	.00

☐ 545 Keith Hernandez	.35	.15	.03
☐ 546 Silvio Martinez	.05	.02	.00
☐ 547A Don Hood P1 ERR	.20	.08	.02
"Pete Vuckovich"			
with Vuckovich back			
☐ 547B Don Hood P2 COR	.10	.04	.01
☐ 548 Bobby Bonds	.15	.06	.01
☐ 549 Mike Ramsey	.05	.02	.00
☐ 550 Tom Herr	.15	.06	.01
☐ 551 Roy Smalley	.05	.02	.00
☐ 552 Jerry Koosman	.10	.04	.01
☐ 553 Ken Landreaux	.05	.02	.00
☐ 554 John Castino	.05	.02	.00
☐ 555 Doug Corbett	.05	.02	.00
☐ 556 Bombo Rivera	.05	.02	.00
☐ 557 Ron Jackson	.05	.02	.00
☐ 558 Butch Wynegar	.05	.02	.00
☐ 559 Hosken Powell	.05	.02	.00
☐ 560 Pete Redfern	.05	.02	.00
☐ 561 Roger Erickson	.05	.02	.00
☐ 562 Glenn Adams	.05	.02	.00
☐ 563 Rick Sofield	.05	.02	.00
☐ 564 Geoff Zahn	.05	.02	.00
☐ 565 Pete Mackanin	.05	.02	.00
☐ 566 Mike Cubbage	.05	.02	.00
☐ 567 Darrell Jackson	.05	.02	.00
☐ 568 Dave Edwards	.05	.02	.00
☐ 569 Rob Wilfong	.05	.02	.00
☐ 570 Sal Butera	.05	.02	.00
☐ 571 Jose Morales	.05	.02	.00
☐ 572 Rick Langford	.05	.02	.00
☐ 573 Mike Norris	.05	.02	.00
☐ 574 Rickey Henderson	15.00	6.50	2.15
☐ 575 Tony Armas	.05	.02	.00
☐ 576 Dave Revering	.05	.02	.00
☐ 577 Jeff Newman	.05	.02	.00
☐ 578 Bob Lacey	.05	.02	.00
☐ 579 Brian Kingman	.05	.02	.00
☐ 580 Mitchell Page	.05	.02	.00
☐ 581 Billy Martin MG	.20	.08	.02
☐ 582 Rob Picciolo	.05	.02	.00
☐ 583 Mike Heath	.05	.02	.00
☐ 584 Mickey Klutts	.05	.02	.00
☐ 585 Orlando Gonzalez	.05	.02	.00
☐ 586 Mike Davis	.15	.06	.01
☐ 587 Wayne Gross	.05	.02	.00
☐ 588 Matt Keough	.05	.02	.00
☐ 589 Steve McCatty	.05	.02	.00
☐ 590 Dwayne Murphy	.05	.02	.00
☐ 591 Mario Guerrero	.05	.02	.00
☐ 592 Dave McKay	.05	.02	.00
☐ 593 Jim Essian	.10	.04	.01
☐ 594 Dave Heaverlo	.05	.02	.00
☐ 595 Maury Wills MG	.10	.04	.01
☐ 596 Juan Beniquez	.05	.02	.00
☐ 597 Rodney Craig	.05	.02	.00
☐ 598 Jim Anderson	.05	.02	.00
☐ 599 Floyd Bannister	.05	.02	.00
☐ 600 Bruce Bochte	.05	.02	.00
☐ 601 Julio Cruz	.05	.02	.00
☐ 602 Ted Cox	.05	.02	.00
☐ 603 Dan Meyer	.05	.02	.00
☐ 604 Larry Cox	.05	.02	.00
☐ 605 Bill Stein	.05	.02	.00
☐ 606 Steve Garvey	.75	.30	.07
☐ 607 Dave Roberts	.05	.02	.00
☐ 608 Leon Roberts	.05	.02	.00
☐ 609 Reggie Walton	.05	.02	.00
☐ 610 Dave Edler	.05	.02	.00
☐ 611 Larry Milbourne	.05	.02	.00
☐ 612 Kim Allen	.05	.02	.00
☐ 613 Mario Mendoza	.05	.02	.00
☐ 614 Tom Paciorek	.05	.02	.00
☐ 615 Glenn Abbott	.05	.02	.00
☐ 616 Joe Simpson	.05	.02	.00
☐ 617 Mickey Rivers	.10	.04	.01
☐ 618 Jim Kern	.05	.02	.00
☐ 619 Jim Sundberg	.05	.02	.00
☐ 620 Richie Zisk	.05	.02	.00
☐ 621 Jon Matlack	.05	.02	.00
☐ 622 Ferguson Jenkins	.50	.20	.05
☐ 623 Pat Corrales MG	.05	.02	.00
☐ 624 Ed Figueroa	.05	.02	.00
☐ 625 Buddy Bell	.10	.04	.01
☐ 626 Al Oliver	.10	.04	.01
☐ 627 Doc Medich	.05	.02	.00
☐ 628 Bump Wills	.05	.02	.00
☐ 629 Rusty Staub	.15	.06	.01
☐ 630 Pat Putnam	.05	.02	.00
☐ 631 John Grubb	.05	.02	.00
☐ 632 Danny Darwin	.10	.04	.01
☐ 633 Ken Clay	.05	.02	.00
☐ 634 Jim Norris	.05	.02	.00
☐ 635 John Butcher	.05	.02	.00
☐ 636 Dave Roberts	.05	.02	.00
☐ 637 Billy Sample	.05	.02	.00
☐ 638 Carl Yastrzemski	1.50	.60	.15
☐ 639 Cecil Cooper	.15	.06	.01
☐ 640A Mike Schmidt P1	2.00	.80	.20
(Portrait)			
"Third Base"			
(number on back 5)			
☐ 640B Mike Schmidt P2	2.00	.80	.20
"1980 Home Run King"			
(640 on back)			
☐ 641A CL: Phils/Royals P1	.15	.02	.00
41 is Hal McRae			
☐ 641B CL: Phils/Royals P2	.15	.02	.00
41 is Hal McRae,			
Double Threat			
☐ 642 CL: Astros/Yankees	.15	.02	.00
☐ 643 CL: Expos/Dodgers	.15	.02	.00
☐ 644A CL: Reds/Orioles P1	.15	.02	.00
202 is George Foster			
☐ 644B CL: Reds/Orioles P2	.15	.02	.00
202 is Foster Slugger			
☐ 645A Rose/Bowa/Schmidt	2.00	.80	.20
Triple Threat P1			
(No number on back)			
☐ 645B Rose/Bowa/Schmidt	1.25	.50	.12
Triple Threat P2			
(Back numbered 645)			
☐ 646 CL: Braves/Red Sox	.15	.02	.00
☐ 647 CL: Cubs/Angels	.15	.02	.00
☐ 648 CL: Mets/White Sox	.15	.02	.00
☐ 649 CL: Indians/Pirates	.15	.02	.00
☐ 650A Reggie Jackson	2.00	.80	.20
Mr. Baseball P1			
Number on back 79			
☐ 650B Reggie Jackson	2.00	.80	.20
Mr. Baseball P2			
Number on back 650			
☐ 651 CL: Giants/Blue Jays	.15	.02	.00
☐ 652A CL: Tigers/Padres P1	.15	.02	.00
483 is listed			
☐ 652B CL: Tigers/Padres P2	.15	.02	.00
483 is deleted			
☐ 653A Willie Wilson P1	.20	.08	.02
Most Hits Most Runs			
Number on back 29			
☐ 653B Willie Wilson P2	.20	.08	.02
Most Hits Most Runs			
Number on back 653			
☐ 654A CL:Brewers/Cards P1	.15	.02	.00
514 Jerry Augustine			
547 Pete Vuckovich			
☐ 654B CL:Brewers/Cards P2	.15	.02	.00
514 Billy Travers			
547 Don Hood			
☐ 655A George Brett P1	1.75	.70	.17
.390 Average			
Number on back 28			
☐ 655B George Brett P2	1.75	.70	.17
.390 Average			
Number on back 655			
☐ 656 CL: Twins/Oakland A's	.15	.02	.00
☐ 657A Tug McGraw P1	.15	.06	.01
Game Saver			
Number on back 7			
☐ 657B Tug McGraw P2	.15	.06	.01
Game Saver			
Number on back 657			
☐ 658 CL: Rangers/Mariners	.15	.02	.00
☐ 659A Checklist P1	.15	.02	.00
of Special Cards			
Last lines on front			
Wilson Most Hits			
☐ 659B Checklist P2	.15	.02	.00
of Special Cards			
Last lines on front			
Otis Series Starter			
☐ 660A Steve Carlton P1	1.25	.50	.12
Golden Arm			
Back "1066 Cardinals"			
Number on back 6			
☐ 660B Steve Carlton P2	1.25	.50	.12
Golden Arm			
Number on back 660			
Back "1066 Cardinals"			
☐ 660C Steve Carlton P3	2.00	.80	.20
Golden Arm			
"1966 Cardinals"			

1981 Fleer Sticker Cards

The stickers in this 128-sticker set measure 2 1/2" by 3 1/2". The 1981 Fleer Baseball Star Stickers consist of numbered cards with peelable, full-color sticker fronts and three unnumbered checklists. The backs of the numbered player cards are the same as the 1981 Fleer regular issue cards except for the numbers, while the checklist cards (cards 126-128 below) have sticker fronts of Jackson (1-42), Brett (43-83), and Schmidt (84-125).

		MINT	EXC	G-VG
	COMPLETE SET (128)	50.00	22.50	7.50
	COMMON PLAYER (1-128)	.15	.06	.01
☐ 1	Steve Garvey	2.00	.80	.20
☐ 2	Ron LeFlore	.15	.06	.01
☐ 3	Ron Cey	.20	.08	.02
☐ 4	Dave Revering	.15	.06	.01
☐ 5	Tony Armas	.15	.06	.01
☐ 6	Mike Norris	.15	.06	.01
☐ 7	Steve Kemp	.15	.06	.01
☐ 8	Bruce Bochte	.15	.06	.01
☐ 9	Mike Schmidt	4.50	2.00	.45
☐ 10	Scott McGregor	.15	.06	.01
☐ 11	Buddy Bell	.20	.08	.02
☐ 12	Carney Lansford	.30	.12	.03
☐ 13	Carl Yastrzemski	3.00	1.25	.30
☐ 14	Ben Oglivie	.15	.06	.01
☐ 15	Willie Stargell	1.50	.60	.15
☐ 16	Cecil Cooper	.20	.08	.02
☐ 17	Gene Richards	.15	.06	.01
☐ 18	Jim Kern	.15	.06	.01
☐ 19	Jerry Koosman	.20	.08	.02
☐ 20	Larry Bowa	.25	.10	.02
☐ 21	Kent Tekulve	.15	.06	.01
☐ 22	Dan Driessen	.15	.06	.01
☐ 23	Phil Niekro	1.00	.40	.10
☐ 24	Dan Quisenberry	.25	.10	.02
☐ 25	Dave Winfield	1.75	.70	.17
☐ 26	Dave Parker	1.00	.40	.10
☐ 27	Rick Langford	.15	.06	.01
☐ 28	Amos Otis	.20	.08	.02
☐ 29	Bill Buckner	.20	.08	.02
☐ 30	Al Bumbry	.15	.06	.01
☐ 31	Bake McBride	.15	.06	.01
☐ 32	Mickey Rivers	.15	.06	.01
☐ 33	Rick Burleson	.15	.06	.01
☐ 34	Dennis Eckersley	.90	.40	.09
☐ 35	Cesar Cedeno	.20	.08	.02
☐ 36	Enos Cabell	.15	.06	.01
☐ 37	Johnny Bench	3.00	1.25	.30
☐ 38	Robin Yount	3.50	1.50	.35
☐ 39	Mark Belanger	.15	.06	.01
☐ 40	Rod Carew	2.50	1.00	.25
☐ 41	George Foster	.60	.25	.06
☐ 42	Lee Mazzilli	.15	.06	.01
☐ 43	Triple Threat: Pete Rose Larry Bowa Mike Schmidt	3.50	1.50	.35
☐ 44	J.R. Richard	.20	.08	.02
☐ 45	Lou Piniella	.30	.12	.03
☐ 46	Ken Landreaux	.15	.06	.01
☐ 47	Rollie Fingers	1.00	.40	.10
☐ 48	Joaquin Andujar	.20	.08	.02
☐ 49	Tom Seaver	3.50	1.50	.35
☐ 50	Bobby Grich	.20	.08	.02
☐ 51	Jon Matlack	.15	.06	.01
☐ 52	Jack Clark	.60	.25	.06
☐ 53	Jim Rice	.90	.40	.09
☐ 54	Rickey Henderson	7.50	3.25	.75
☐ 55	Roy Smalley	.15	.06	.01
☐ 56	Mike Flanagan	.20	.08	.02
☐ 57	Steve Rogers	.15	.06	.01
☐ 58	Carlton Fisk	1.50	.60	.15
☐ 59	Don Sutton	.75	.30	.07
☐ 60	Ken Griffey	.35	.15	.03
☐ 61	Burt Hooton	.15	.06	.01
☐ 62	Dusty Baker	.20	.08	.02
☐ 63	Vida Blue	.20	.08	.02
☐ 64	Al Oliver	.20	.08	.02
☐ 65	Jim Bibby	.15	.06	.01
☐ 66	Tony Perez	.75	.30	.07
☐ 67	Davey Lopes	.20	.08	.02
☐ 68	Bill Russell	.15	.06	.01
☐ 69	Larry Parrish	.15	.06	.01
☐ 70	Garry Maddox	.15	.06	.01
☐ 71	Phil Garner	.20	.08	.02
☐ 72	Graig Nettles	.40	.16	.04
☐ 73	Gary Carter	1.50	.60	.15
☐ 74	Pete Rose	4.50	2.00	.45
☐ 75	Greg Luzinski	.25	.10	.02
☐ 76	Ron Guidry	.50	.20	.05
☐ 77	Gorman Thomas	.20	.08	.02
☐ 78	Jose Cruz	.20	.08	.02
☐ 79	Bob Boone	.40	.16	.04
☐ 80	Bruce Sutter	.25	.10	.02
☐ 81	Chris Chambliss	.20	.08	.02
☐ 82	Paul Molitor	.75	.30	.07
☐ 83	Tug McGraw	.25	.10	.02
☐ 84	Ferguson Jenkins	1.25	.50	.12
☐ 85	Steve Carlton	2.50	1.00	.25
☐ 86	Miguel Dilone	.15	.06	.01
☐ 87	Reggie Smith	.25	.10	.02
☐ 88	Rick Cerone	.15	.06	.01
☐ 89	Alan Trammell	1.50	.60	.15
☐ 90	Doug DeCinces	.20	.08	.02
☐ 91	Sparky Lyle	.25	.10	.02
☐ 92	Warren Cromartie	.15	.06	.01
☐ 93	Rick Reuschel	.25	.10	.02
☐ 94	Larry Hisle	.15	.06	.01
☐ 95	Paul Splittorff	.15	.06	.01
☐ 96	Manny Trillo	.15	.06	.01
☐ 97	Frank White	.20	.08	.02
☐ 98	Fred Lynn	.50	.20	.05
☐ 99	Bob Horner	.35	.15	.03
☐ 100	Omar Moreno	.15	.06	.01
☐ 101	Dave Concepcion	.25	.10	.02
☐ 102	Larry Gura	.15	.06	.01
☐ 103	Ken Singleton	.20	.08	.02
☐ 104	Steve Stone	.15	.06	.01
☐ 105	Richie Zisk	.15	.06	.01
☐ 106	Willie Wilson	.25	.10	.02
☐ 107	Willie Randolph	.20	.08	.02
☐ 108	Nolan Ryan	9.00	4.00	.90
☐ 109	Joe Morgan	1.75	.70	.17
☐ 110	Bucky Dent	.40	.16	.04
☐ 111	Dave Kingman	.35	.15	.03
☐ 112	John Castino	.15	.06	.01
☐ 113	Joe Rudi	.20	.08	.02
☐ 114	Ed Farmer	.15	.06	.01
☐ 115	Reggie Jackson	3.50	1.50	.35
☐ 116	George Brett	3.50	1.50	.35
☐ 117	Eddie Murray	2.50	1.00	.25
☐ 118	Rich Gossage	.50	.20	.05
☐ 119	Dale Murphy	2.50	1.00	.25
☐ 120	Ted Simmons	.25	.10	.02
☐ 121	Tommy John	.50	.20	.05
☐ 122	Don Baylor	.40	.16	.04
☐ 123	Andre Dawson	2.50	1.00	.25
☐ 124	Jim Palmer	2.00	.80	.20
☐ 125	Garry Templeton	.20	.08	.02
☐ NNO	CL 1: Reggie Jackson	2.00	.80	.20
☐ NNO	CL 2: George Brett	2.00	.80	.20
☐ NNO	CL 3: Mike Schmidt	3.00	1.25	.30

1982 Fleer

The cards in this 660-card set measure 2 1/2" by 3 1/2". The 1982 Fleer set is again ordered by teams; in fact, the players within each team are listed in alphabetical order. The teams are ordered (by 1981 standings) as follows: Los Angeles (1-29), New York Yankees (30-56), Cincinnati (57-84), Oakland (85-

109), St. Louis (110-132), Milwaukee (133-156), Baltimore (157-182), Montreal (183-211), Houston (212-237), Philadelphia (238-262), Detroit (263-286), Boston (287-312), Texas (313-334), Chicago White Sox (335-358), Cleveland (359-382), San Francisco (383-403), Kansas City (404-427), Atlanta (428-449), California (450-474), Pittsburgh (475-501), Seattle (502-519), New York Mets (520-544), Minnesota (545-565), San Diego (566-585), Chicago Cubs (586-607), and Toronto (608-627). Cards numbered 628 through 646 are special cards highlighting some of the stars and leaders of the 1981 season. The last 14 cards in the set (647-660) are checklist cards. The backs feature player statistics and a full-color team logo in the upper right-hand corner of each card. The complete set price below does not include any of the more valuable variation cards listed. The key rookie cards in this set are George Bell, Cal Ripken Jr., Steve Sax, Lee Smith, and Dave Stewart.

	MINT	EXC	G-VG
COMPLETE SET (660)	80.00	36.00	12.00
COMMON PLAYER (1-660)	.05	.02	.00

		MINT	EXC	G-VG
☐ 1	Dusty Baker	.15	.05	.01
☐ 2	Robert Castillo	.05	.02	.00
☐ 3	Ron Cey	.10	.04	.01
☐ 4	Terry Forster	.10	.04	.01
☐ 5	Steve Garvey	.60	.25	.06
☐ 6	Dave Goltz	.05	.02	.00
☐ 7	Pedro Guerrero	.40	.16	.04
☐ 8	Burt Hooton	.05	.02	.00
☐ 9	Steve Howe	.05	.02	.00
☐ 10	Jay Johnstone	.10	.04	.01
☐ 11	Ken Landreaux	.05	.02	.00
☐ 12	Dave Lopes	.10	.04	.01
☐ 13	Mike Marshall (outfielder)	.35	.15	.03
☐ 14	Bobby Mitchell	.05	.02	.00
☐ 15	Rick Monday	.05	.02	.00
☐ 16	Tom Niedenfuer	.15	.06	.01
☐ 17	Ted Power	.15	.06	.01
☐ 18	Jerry Reuss	.05	.02	.00
☐ 19	Ron Roenicke	.05	.02	.00
☐ 20	Bill Russell	.10	.04	.01
☐ 21	Steve Sax	3.50	1.50	.35
☐ 22	Mike Scioscia	.35	.15	.03
☐ 23	Reggie Smith	.10	.04	.01
☐ 24	Dave Stewart	5.50	2.50	.55
☐ 25	Rick Sutcliffe	.15	.06	.01
☐ 26	Derrel Thomas	.05	.02	.00
☐ 27	Fernando Valenzuela	.40	.16	.04
☐ 28	Bob Welch	.35	.15	.03
☐ 29	Steve Yeager	.05	.02	.00
☐ 30	Bobby Brown	.05	.02	.00
☐ 31	Rick Cerone	.05	.02	.00
☐ 32	Ron Davis	.05	.02	.00
☐ 33	Bucky Dent	.10	.04	.01
☐ 34	Barry Foote	.05	.02	.00
☐ 35	George Frazier	.05	.02	.00
☐ 36	Oscar Gamble	.05	.02	.00
☐ 37	Rich Gossage	.20	.08	.02
☐ 38	Ron Guidry	.25	.10	.02
☐ 39	Reggie Jackson	1.75	.70	.17
☐ 40	Tommy John	.20	.08	.02
☐ 41	Rudy May	.05	.02	.00
☐ 42	Larry Milbourne	.05	.02	.00
☐ 43	Jerry Mumphrey	.05	.02	.00

		MINT	EXC	G-VG
☐ 44	Bobby Murcer	.10	.04	.01
☐ 45	Gene Nelson	.10	.04	.01
☐ 46	Graig Nettles	.15	.06	.01
☐ 47	Johnny Oates	.10	.04	.01
☐ 48	Lou Piniella	.10	.04	.01
☐ 49	Willie Randolph	.15	.06	.01
☐ 50	Rick Reuschel	.10	.04	.01
☐ 51	Dave Revering	.05	.02	.00
☐ 52	Dave Righetti	1.25	.50	.12
☐ 53	Aurelio Rodriguez	.05	.02	.00
☐ 54	Bob Watson	.05	.02	.00
☐ 55	Dennis Werth	.05	.02	.00
☐ 56	Dave Winfield	1.00	.40	.10
☐ 57	Johnny Bench	1.25	.50	.12
☐ 58	Bruce Berenyi	.05	.02	.00
☐ 59	Larry Biittner	.05	.02	.00
☐ 60	Scott Brown	.05	.02	.00
☐ 61	Dave Collins	.05	.02	.00
☐ 62	Geoff Combe	.05	.02	.00
☐ 63	Dave Concepcion	.15	.06	.01
☐ 64	Dan Driessen	.05	.02	.00
☐ 65	Joe Edelen	.05	.02	.00
☐ 66	George Foster	.15	.06	.01
☐ 67	Ken Griffey	.25	.10	.02
☐ 68	Paul Householder	.05	.02	.00
☐ 69	Tom Hume	.05	.02	.00
☐ 70	Junior Kennedy	.05	.02	.00
☐ 71	Ray Knight	.10	.04	.01
☐ 72	Mike LaCoss	.05	.02	.00
☐ 73	Rafael Landestoy	.05	.02	.00
☐ 74	Charlie Leibrandt	.10	.04	.01
☐ 75	Sam Mejias	.05	.02	.00
☐ 76	Paul Moskau	.05	.02	.00
☐ 77	Joe Nolan	.05	.02	.00
☐ 78	Mike O'Berry	.05	.02	.00
☐ 79	Ron Oester	.05	.02	.00
☐ 80	Frank Pastore	.05	.02	.00
☐ 81	Joe Price	.05	.02	.00
☐ 82	Tom Seaver	1.25	.50	.12
☐ 83	Mario Soto	.05	.02	.00
☐ 84	Mike Vail	.05	.02	.00
☐ 85	Tony Armas	.05	.02	.00
☐ 86	Shooty Babitt	.05	.02	.00
☐ 87	Dave Beard	.05	.02	.00
☐ 88	Rick Bosetti	.05	.02	.00
☐ 89	Keith Drumwright	.05	.02	.00
☐ 90	Wayne Gross	.05	.02	.00
☐ 91	Mike Heath	.05	.02	.00
☐ 92	Rickey Henderson	6.00	2.50	.60
☐ 93	Cliff Johnson	.05	.02	.00
☐ 94	Jeff Jones	.05	.02	.00
☐ 95	Matt Keough	.05	.02	.00
☐ 96	Brian Kingman	.05	.02	.00
☐ 97	Mickey Klutts	.05	.02	.00
☐ 98	Rick Langford	.05	.02	.00
☐ 99	Steve McCatty	.05	.02	.00
☐ 100	Dave McKay	.05	.02	.00
☐ 101	Dwayne Murphy	.05	.02	.00
☐ 102	Jeff Newman	.05	.02	.00
☐ 103	Mike Norris	.05	.02	.00
☐ 104	Bob Owchinko	.05	.02	.00
☐ 105	Mitchell Page	.05	.02	.00
☐ 106	Rob Picciolo	.05	.02	.00
☐ 107	Jim Spencer	.05	.02	.00
☐ 108	Fred Stanley	.05	.02	.00
☐ 109	Tom Underwood	.05	.02	.00
☐ 110	Joaquin Andujar	.10	.04	.01
☐ 111	Steve Braun	.05	.02	.00
☐ 112	Bob Forsch	.05	.02	.00
☐ 113	George Hendrick	.05	.02	.00
☐ 114	Keith Hernandez	.25	.10	.02
☐ 115	Tom Herr	.10	.04	.01
☐ 116	Dane Iorg	.05	.02	.00
☐ 117	Jim Kaat	.15	.06	.01
☐ 118	Tito Landrum	.05	.02	.00
☐ 119	Sixto Lezcano	.05	.02	.00
☐ 120	Mark Littell	.05	.02	.00
☐ 121	John Martin	.05	.02	.00
☐ 122	Silvio Martinez	.05	.02	.00
☐ 123	Ken Oberkfell	.05	.02	.00
☐ 124	Darrell Porter	.05	.02	.00
☐ 125	Mike Ramsey	.05	.02	.00
☐ 126	Orlando Sanchez	.05	.02	.00
☐ 127	Bob Shirley	.05	.02	.00
☐ 128	Lary Sorensen	.05	.02	.00
☐ 129	Bruce Sutter	.15	.06	.01
☐ 130	Bob Sykes	.05	.02	.00
☐ 131	Garry Templeton	.10	.04	.01
☐ 132	Gene Tenace	.10	.04	.01
☐ 133	Jerry Augustine	.05	.02	.00
☐ 134	Sal Bando	.10	.04	.01
☐ 135	Mark Brouhard	.05	.02	.00
☐ 136	Mike Caldwell	.05	.02	.00
☐ 137	Reggie Cleveland	.05	.02	.00

☐ 138	Cecil Cooper	.15	.06	.01
☐ 139	Jamie Easterly	.05	.02	.00
☐ 140	Marshall Edwards	.05	.02	.00
☐ 141	Rollie Fingers	.50	.20	.05
☐ 142	Jim Gantner	.05	.02	.00
☐ 143	Moose Haas	.05	.02	.00
☐ 144	Larry Hisle	.05	.02	.00
☐ 145	Roy Howell	.05	.02	.00
☐ 146	Rickey Keeton	.05	.02	.00
☐ 147	Randy Lerch	.05	.02	.00
☐ 148	Paul Molitor	.50	.20	.05
☐ 149	Don Money	.05	.02	.00
☐ 150	Charlie Moore	.05	.02	.00
☐ 151	Ben Oglivie	.05	.02	.00
☐ 152	Ted Simmons	.15	.06	.01
☐ 153	Jim Slaton	.05	.02	.00
☐ 154	Gorman Thomas	.10	.04	.01
☐ 155	Robin Yount	2.00	.80	.20
☐ 156	Pete Vuckovich	.05	.02	.00
☐ 157	Benny Ayala	.05	.02	.00
☐ 158	Mark Belanger	.10	.04	.01
☐ 159	Al Bumbry	.05	.02	.00
☐ 160	Terry Crowley	.05	.02	.00
☐ 161	Rich Dauer	.05	.02	.00
☐ 162	Doug DeCinces	.05	.02	.00
☐ 163	Rick Dempsey	.05	.02	.00
☐ 164	Jim Dwyer	.05	.02	.00
☐ 165	Mike Flanagan	.10	.04	.01
☐ 166	Dave Ford	.05	.02	.00
☐ 167	Dan Graham	.05	.02	.00
☐ 168	Wayne Krenchicki	.05	.02	.00
☐ 169	John Lowenstein	.05	.02	.00
☐ 170	Dennis Martinez	.15	.06	.01
☐ 171	Tippy Martinez	.05	.02	.00
☐ 172	Scott McGregor	.05	.02	.00
☐ 173	Jose Morales	.05	.02	.00
☐ 174	Eddie Murray	1.50	.60	.15
☐ 175	Jim Palmer	.90	.40	.09
☐ 176	Cal Ripken	48.00	20.00	5.00
☐ 177	Gary Roenicke	.05	.02	.00
☐ 178	Lenn Sakata	.05	.02	.00
☐ 179	Ken Singleton	.10	.04	.01
☐ 180	Sammy Stewart	.05	.02	.00
☐ 181	Tim Stoddard	.05	.02	.00
☐ 182	Steve Stone	.05	.02	.00
☐ 183	Stan Bahnsen	.05	.02	.00
☐ 184	Ray Burris	.05	.02	.00
☐ 185	Gary Carter	.50	.20	.05
☐ 186	Warren Cromartie	.05	.02	.00
☐ 187	Andre Dawson	1.25	.50	.12
☐ 188	Terry Francona	.05	.02	.00
☐ 189	Woodie Fryman	.05	.02	.00
☐ 190	Bill Gullickson	.10	.04	.01
☐ 191	Grant Jackson	.05	.02	.00
☐ 192	Wallace Johnson	.05	.02	.00
☐ 193	Charlie Lea	.05	.02	.00
☐ 194	Bill Lee	.05	.02	.00
☐ 195	Jerry Manuel	.05	.02	.00
☐ 196	Brad Mills	.05	.02	.00
☐ 197	John Milner	.05	.02	.00
☐ 198	Rowland Office	.05	.02	.00
☐ 199	David Palmer	.05	.02	.00
☐ 200	Larry Parrish	.05	.02	.00
☐ 201	Mike Phillips	.05	.02	.00
☐ 202	Tim Raines	2.00	.80	.20
☐ 203	Bobby Ramos	.05	.02	.00
☐ 204	Jeff Reardon	.75	.30	.07
☐ 205	Steve Rogers	.05	.02	.00
☐ 206	Scott Sanderson	.10	.04	.01
☐ 207	Rodney Scott UER (photo actually Tim Raines)	.20	.08	.02
☐ 208	Elias Sosa	.05	.02	.00
☐ 209	Chris Speier	.05	.02	.00
☐ 210	Tim Wallach	1.25	.50	.12
☐ 211	Jerry White	.05	.02	.00
☐ 212	Alan Ashby	.05	.02	.00
☐ 213	Cesar Cedeno	.10	.04	.01
☐ 214	Jose Cruz	.10	.04	.01
☐ 215	Kiko Garcia	.05	.02	.00
☐ 216	Phil Garner	.10	.04	.01
☐ 217	Danny Heep	.05	.02	.00
☐ 218	Art Howe	.10	.04	.01
☐ 219	Bob Knepper	.05	.02	.00
☐ 220	Frank LaCorte	.05	.02	.00
☐ 221	Joe Niekro	.10	.04	.01
☐ 222	Joe Pittman	.05	.02	.00
☐ 223	Terry Puhl	.05	.02	.00
☐ 224	Luis Pujols	.05	.02	.00
☐ 225	Craig Reynolds	.05	.02	.00
☐ 226	J.R. Richard	.10	.04	.01
☐ 227	Dave Roberts	.05	.02	.00
☐ 228	Vern Ruhle	.05	.02	.00
☐ 229	Nolan Ryan	5.75	2.50	.55
☐ 230	Joe Sambito	.05	.02	.00
☐ 231	Tony Scott	.05	.02	.00
☐ 232	Dave Smith	.10	.04	.01
☐ 233	Harry Spilman	.05	.02	.00
☐ 234	Don Sutton	.40	.16	.04
☐ 235	Dickie Thon	.10	.04	.01
☐ 236	Denny Walling	.05	.02	.00
☐ 237	Gary Woods	.05	.02	.00
☐ 238	Luis Aguayo	.05	.02	.00
☐ 239	Ramon Aviles	.05	.02	.00
☐ 240	Bob Boone	.10	.04	.01
☐ 241	Larry Bowa	.10	.04	.01
☐ 242	Warren Brusstar	.05	.02	.00
☐ 243	Steve Carlton	1.00	.40	.10
☐ 244	Larry Christenson	.05	.02	.00
☐ 245	Dick Davis	.05	.02	.00
☐ 246	Greg Gross	.05	.02	.00
☐ 247	Sparky Lyle	.10	.04	.01
☐ 248	Garry Maddox	.05	.02	.00
☐ 249	Gary Matthews	.05	.02	.00
☐ 250	Bake McBride	.05	.02	.00
☐ 251	Tug McGraw	.10	.04	.01
☐ 252	Keith Moreland	.05	.02	.00
☐ 253	Dickie Noles	.05	.02	.00
☐ 254	Mike Proly	.05	.02	.00
☐ 255	Ron Reed	.05	.02	.00
☐ 256	Pete Rose	1.50	.60	.15
☐ 257	Dick Ruthven	.05	.02	.00
☐ 258	Mike Schmidt	2.50	1.00	.25
☐ 259	Lonnie Smith	.25	.10	.02
☐ 260	Manny Trillo	.05	.02	.00
☐ 261	Del Unser	.05	.02	.00
☐ 262	George Vukovich	.05	.02	.00
☐ 263	Tom Brookens	.05	.02	.00
☐ 264	George Cappuzzello	.05	.02	.00
☐ 265	Marty Castillo	.05	.02	.00
☐ 266	Al Cowens	.05	.02	.00
☐ 267	Kirk Gibson	.75	.30	.07
☐ 268	Richie Hebner	.05	.02	.00
☐ 269	Ron Jackson	.05	.02	.00
☐ 270	Lynn Jones	.05	.02	.00
☐ 271	Steve Kemp	.05	.02	.00
☐ 272	Rick Leach	.05	.02	.00
☐ 273	Aurelio Lopez	.05	.02	.00
☐ 274	Jack Morris	.60	.25	.06
☐ 275	Kevin Saucier	.05	.02	.00
☐ 276	Lance Parrish	.30	.12	.03
☐ 277	Rick Peters	.05	.02	.00
☐ 278	Dan Petry	.05	.02	.00
☐ 279	Dave Rozema	.05	.02	.00
☐ 280	Stan Papi	.05	.02	.00
☐ 281	Dan Schatzeder	.05	.02	.00
☐ 282	Champ Summers	.05	.02	.00
☐ 283	Alan Trammell	.60	.25	.06
☐ 284	Lou Whitaker	.40	.16	.04
☐ 285	Milt Wilcox	.05	.02	.00
☐ 286	John Wockenfuss	.05	.02	.00
☐ 287	Gary Allenson	.05	.02	.00
☐ 288	Tom Burgmeier	.05	.02	.00
☐ 289	Bill Campbell	.05	.02	.00
☐ 290	Mark Clear	.05	.02	.00
☐ 291	Steve Crawford	.05	.02	.00
☐ 292	Dennis Eckersley	.50	.20	.05
☐ 293	Dwight Evans	.25	.10	.02
☐ 294	Rich Gedman	.20	.08	.02
☐ 295	Garry Hancock	.05	.02	.00
☐ 296	Glenn Hoffman	.05	.02	.00
☐ 297	Bruce Hurst	.60	.25	.06
☐ 298	Carney Lansford	.15	.06	.01
☐ 299	Rick Miller	.05	.02	.00
☐ 300	Reid Nichols	.05	.02	.00
☐ 301	Bob Ojeda	.50	.20	.05
☐ 302	Tony Perez	.30	.12	.03
☐ 303	Chuck Rainey	.05	.02	.00
☐ 304	Jerry Remy	.05	.02	.00
☐ 305	Jim Rice	.25	.10	.02
☐ 306	Joe Rudi	.10	.04	.01
☐ 307	Bob Stanley	.05	.02	.00
☐ 308	Dave Stapleton	.05	.02	.00
☐ 309	Frank Tanana	.10	.04	.01
☐ 310	Mike Torrez	.05	.02	.00
☐ 311	John Tudor	.15	.06	.01
☐ 312	Carl Yastrzemski	1.25	.50	.12
☐ 313	Buddy Bell	.10	.04	.01
☐ 314	Steve Comer	.05	.02	.00
☐ 315	Danny Darwin	.05	.02	.00
☐ 316	John Ellis	.05	.02	.00
☐ 317	John Grubb	.05	.02	.00
☐ 318	Rick Honeycutt	.05	.02	.00
☐ 319	Charlie Hough	.10	.04	.01
☐ 320	Ferguson Jenkins	.40	.16	.04
☐ 321	John Henry Johnson	.05	.02	.00
☐ 322	Jim Kern	.05	.02	.00
☐ 323	Jon Matlack	.05	.02	.00

#	Player			
☐ 324	Doc Medich	.05	.02	.00
☐ 325	Mario Mendoza	.05	.02	.00
☐ 326	Al Oliver	.10	.04	.01
☐ 327	Pat Putnam	.05	.02	.00
☐ 328	Mickey Rivers	.10	.04	.01
☐ 329	Leon Roberts	.05	.02	.00
☐ 330	Billy Sample	.05	.02	.00
☐ 331	Bill Stein	.05	.02	.00
☐ 332	Jim Sundberg	.05	.02	.00
☐ 333	Mark Wagner	.05	.02	.00
☐ 334	Bump Wills	.05	.02	.00
☐ 335	Bill Almon	.05	.02	.00
☐ 336	Harold Baines	.75	.30	.07
☐ 337	Ross Baumgarten	.05	.02	.00
☐ 338	Tony Bernazard	.05	.02	.00
☐ 339	Britt Burns	.05	.02	.00
☐ 340	Richard Dotson	.05	.02	.00
☐ 341	Jim Essian	.10	.04	.01
☐ 342	Ed Farmer	.05	.02	.00
☐ 343	Carlton Fisk	1.25	.50	.12
☐ 344	Kevin Hickey	.05	.02	.00
☐ 345	LaMarr Hoyt	.05	.02	.00
☐ 346	Lamar Johnson	.05	.02	.00
☐ 347	Jerry Koosman	.10	.04	.01
☐ 348	Rusty Kuntz	.05	.02	.00
☐ 349	Dennis Lamp	.05	.02	.00
☐ 350	Ron LeFlore	.05	.02	.00
☐ 351	Chet Lemon	.05	.02	.00
☐ 352	Greg Luzinski	.10	.04	.01
☐ 353	Bob Molinaro	.05	.02	.00
☐ 354	Jim Morrison	.05	.02	.00
☐ 355	Wayne Nordhagen	.05	.02	.00
☐ 356	Greg Pryor	.05	.02	.00
☐ 357	Mike Squires	.05	.02	.00
☐ 358	Steve Trout	.05	.02	.00
☐ 359	Alan Bannister	.05	.02	.00
☐ 360	Len Barker	.05	.02	.00
☐ 361	Bert Blyleven	.25	.10	.02
☐ 362	Joe Charboneau	.05	.02	.00
☐ 363	John Denny	.05	.02	.00
☐ 364	Bo Diaz	.05	.02	.00
☐ 365	Miguel Dilone	.05	.02	.00
☐ 366	Jerry Dybzinski	.05	.02	.00
☐ 367	Wayne Garland	.05	.02	.00
☐ 368	Mike Hargrove	.10	.04	.01
☐ 369	Toby Harrah	.05	.02	.00
☐ 370	Ron Hassey	.05	.02	.00
☐ 371	Von Hayes	.60	.25	.06
☐ 372	Pat Kelly	.05	.02	.00
☐ 373	Duane Kuiper	.05	.02	.00
☐ 374	Rick Manning	.05	.02	.00
☐ 375	Sid Monge	.05	.02	.00
☐ 376	Jorge Orta	.05	.02	.00
☐ 377	Dave Rosello	.05	.02	.00
☐ 378	Dan Spillner	.05	.02	.00
☐ 379	Mike Stanton	.05	.02	.00
☐ 380	Andre Thornton	.10	.04	.01
☐ 381	Tom Veryzer	.05	.02	.00
☐ 382	Rick Waits	.05	.02	.00
☐ 383	Doyle Alexander	.05	.02	.00
☐ 384	Vida Blue	.10	.04	.01
☐ 385	Fred Breining	.05	.02	.00
☐ 386	Enos Cabell	.05	.02	.00
☐ 387	Jack Clark	.25	.10	.02
☐ 388	Darrell Evans	.10	.04	.01
☐ 389	Tom Griffin	.05	.02	.00
☐ 390	Larry Herndon	.05	.02	.00
☐ 391	Al Holland	.05	.02	.00
☐ 392	Gary Lavelle	.05	.02	.00
☐ 393	Johnnie LeMaster	.05	.02	.00
☐ 394	Jerry Martin	.05	.02	.00
☐ 395	Milt May	.05	.02	.00
☐ 396	Greg Minton	.05	.02	.00
☐ 397	Joe Morgan	.60	.25	.06
☐ 398	Joe Pettini	.05	.02	.00
☐ 399	Allen Ripley	.05	.02	.00
☐ 400	Billy Smith	.05	.02	.00
☐ 401	Rennie Stennett	.05	.02	.00
☐ 402	Ed Whitson	.05	.02	.00
☐ 403	Jim Wohlford	.05	.02	.00
☐ 404	Willie Aikens	.05	.02	.00
☐ 405	George Brett	2.00	.80	.20
☐ 406	Ken Brett	.05	.02	.00
☐ 407	Dave Chalk	.05	.02	.00
☐ 408	Rich Gale	.05	.02	.00
☐ 409	Cesar Geronimo	.05	.02	.00
☐ 410	Larry Gura	.05	.02	.00
☐ 411	Clint Hurdle	.05	.02	.00
☐ 412	Mike Jones	.05	.02	.00
☐ 413	Dennis Leonard	.05	.02	.00
☐ 414	Renie Martin	.05	.02	.00
☐ 415	Lee May	.05	.02	.00
☐ 416	Hal McRae	.10	.04	.01
☐ 417	Darryl Motley	.05	.02	.00
☐ 418	Rance Mulliniks	.05	.02	.00
☐ 419	Amos Otis	.10	.04	.01
☐ 420	Ken Phelps	.15	.06	.01
☐ 421	Jamie Quirk	.05	.02	.00
☐ 422	Dan Quisenberry	.15	.06	.01
☐ 423	Paul Splittorff	.05	.02	.00
☐ 424	U.L. Washington	.05	.02	.00
☐ 425	John Wathan	.05	.02	.00
☐ 426	Frank White	.05	.02	.00
☐ 427	Willie Wilson	.15	.06	.01
☐ 428	Brian Asselstine	.05	.02	.00
☐ 429	Bruce Benedict	.05	.02	.00
☐ 430	Tommy Boggs	.05	.02	.00
☐ 431	Larry Bradford	.05	.02	.00
☐ 432	Rick Camp	.05	.02	.00
☐ 433	Chris Chambliss	.10	.04	.01
☐ 434	Gene Garber	.05	.02	.00
☐ 435	Preston Hanna	.05	.02	.00
☐ 436	Bob Horner	.10	.04	.01
☐ 437	Glenn Hubbard	.05	.02	.00
☐ 438A	Al Hrabosky ERR (height 5'1", All on reverse)	20.00	8.50	2.75
☐ 438B	Al Hrabosky ERR (height 5'1")	1.00	.40	.10
☐ 438C	Al Hrabosky (height 5'10")	.10	.04	.01
☐ 439	Rufino Linares	.05	.02	.00
☐ 440	Rick Mahler	.15	.06	.01
☐ 441	Ed Miller	.05	.02	.00
☐ 442	John Montefusco	.05	.02	.00
☐ 443	Dale Murphy	1.00	.40	.10
☐ 444	Phil Niekro	.40	.16	.04
☐ 445	Gaylord Perry	.40	.16	.04
☐ 446	Biff Pocoroba	.05	.02	.00
☐ 447	Rafael Ramirez	.05	.02	.00
☐ 448	Jerry Royster	.05	.02	.00
☐ 449	Claudell Washington	.05	.02	.00
☐ 450	Don Aase	.05	.02	.00
☐ 451	Don Baylor	.15	.06	.01
☐ 452	Juan Beniquez	.05	.02	.00
☐ 453	Rick Burleson	.05	.02	.00
☐ 454	Bert Campaneris	.10	.04	.01
☐ 455	Rod Carew	1.25	.50	.12
☐ 456	Bob Clark	.05	.02	.00
☐ 457	Brian Downing	.10	.04	.01
☐ 458	Dan Ford	.05	.02	.00
☐ 459	Ken Forsch	.05	.02	.00
☐ 460A	Dave Frost (5 mm space before ERA)	.30	.12	.03
☐ 460B	Dave Frost (1 mm space)	.10	.04	.01
☐ 461	Bobby Grich	.10	.04	.01
☐ 462	Larry Harlow	.05	.02	.00
☐ 463	John Harris	.05	.02	.00
☐ 464	Andy Hassler	.05	.02	.00
☐ 465	Butch Hobson	.10	.04	.01
☐ 466	Jesse Jefferson	.05	.02	.00
☐ 467	Bruce Kison	.05	.02	.00
☐ 468	Fred Lynn	.20	.08	.02
☐ 469	Angel Moreno	.05	.02	.00
☐ 470	Ed Ott	.05	.02	.00
☐ 471	Fred Patek	.05	.02	.00
☐ 472	Steve Renko	.05	.02	.00
☐ 473	Mike Witt	.25	.10	.02
☐ 474	Geoff Zahn	.05	.02	.00
☐ 475	Gary Alexander	.05	.02	.00
☐ 476	Dale Berra	.05	.02	.00
☐ 477	Kurt Bevacqua	.05	.02	.00
☐ 478	Jim Bibby	.05	.02	.00
☐ 479	John Candelaria	.05	.02	.00
☐ 480	Victor Cruz	.05	.02	.00
☐ 481	Mike Easler	.05	.02	.00
☐ 482	Tim Foli	.05	.02	.00
☐ 483	Lee Lacy	.05	.02	.00
☐ 484	Vance Law	.10	.04	.01
☐ 485	Bill Madlock	.10	.04	.01
☐ 486	Willie Montanez	.05	.02	.00
☐ 487	Omar Moreno	.05	.02	.00
☐ 488	Steve Nicosia	.05	.02	.00
☐ 489	Dave Parker	.50	.20	.05
☐ 490	Tony Pena	.35	.15	.03
☐ 491	Pascual Perez	.15	.06	.01
☐ 492	Johnny Ray	.20	.08	.02
☐ 493	Rick Rhoden	.05	.02	.00
☐ 494	Bill Robinson	.10	.04	.01
☐ 495	Don Robinson	.05	.02	.00
☐ 496	Enrique Romo	.05	.02	.00
☐ 497	Rod Scurry	.05	.02	.00
☐ 498	Eddie Solomon	.05	.02	.00
☐ 499	Willie Stargell	.50	.20	.05
☐ 500	Kent Tekulve	.10	.04	.01
☐ 501	Jason Thompson	.05	.02	.00
☐ 502	Glenn Abbott	.05	.02	.00

☐ 503	Jim Anderson	.05	.02	.00
☐ 504	Floyd Bannister	.05	.02	.00
☐ 505	Bruce Bochte	.05	.02	.00
☐ 506	Jeff Burroughs	.05	.02	.00
☐ 507	Bryan Clark	.05	.02	.00
☐ 508	Ken Clay	.05	.02	.00
☐ 509	Julio Cruz	.05	.02	.00
☐ 510	Dick Drago	.05	.02	.00
☐ 511	Gary Gray	.05	.02	.00
☐ 512	Dan Meyer	.05	.02	.00
☐ 513	Jerry Narron	.05	.02	.00
☐ 514	Tom Paciorek	.05	.02	.00
☐ 515	Casey Parsons	.05	.02	.00
☐ 516	Lenny Randle	.05	.02	.00
☐ 517	Shane Rawley	.05	.02	.00
☐ 518	Joe Simpson	.05	.02	.00
☐ 519	Richie Zisk	.05	.02	.00
☐ 520	Neil Allen	.05	.02	.00
☐ 521	Bob Bailor	.05	.02	.00
☐ 522	Hubie Brooks	.60	.25	.06
☐ 523	Mike Cubbage	.05	.02	.00
☐ 524	Pete Falcone	.05	.02	.00
☐ 525	Doug Flynn	.05	.02	.00
☐ 526	Tom Hausman	.05	.02	.00
☐ 527	Ron Hodges	.05	.02	.00
☐ 528	Randy Jones	.05	.02	.00
☐ 529	Mike Jorgensen	.05	.02	.00
☐ 530	Dave Kingman	.15	.06	.01
☐ 531	Ed Lynch	.05	.02	.00
☐ 532	Mike Marshall (screwball pitcher)	.10	.04	.01
☐ 533	Lee Mazzilli	.05	.02	.00
☐ 534	Dyar Miller	.05	.02	.00
☐ 535	Mike Scott	.25	.10	.02
☐ 536	Rusty Staub	.15	.06	.01
☐ 537	John Stearns	.05	.02	.00
☐ 538	Craig Swan	.05	.02	.00
☐ 539	Frank Taveras	.05	.02	.00
☐ 540	Alex Trevino	.05	.02	.00
☐ 541	Ellis Valentine	.05	.02	.00
☐ 542	Mookie Wilson	.15	.06	.01
☐ 543	Joel Youngblood	.05	.02	.00
☐ 544	Pat Zachry	.05	.02	.00
☐ 545	Glenn Adams	.05	.02	.00
☐ 546	Fernando Arroyo	.05	.02	.00
☐ 547	John Verhoeven	.05	.02	.00
☐ 548	Sal Butera	.05	.02	.00
☐ 549	John Castino	.05	.02	.00
☐ 550	Don Cooper	.05	.02	.00
☐ 551	Doug Corbett	.05	.02	.00
☐ 552	Dave Engle	.05	.02	.00
☐ 553	Roger Erickson	.05	.02	.00
☐ 554	Danny Goodwin	.05	.02	.00
☐ 555A	Darrell Jackson (black cap)	1.00	.40	.10
☐ 555B	Darrell Jackson (red cap with T)	.10	.04	.01
☐ 555C	Darrell Jackson (red cap, no emblem)	5.00	2.25	.50
☐ 556	Pete Mackanin	.05	.02	.00
☐ 557	Jack O'Connor	.05	.02	.00
☐ 558	Hosken Powell	.05	.02	.00
☐ 559	Pete Redfern	.05	.02	.00
☐ 560	Roy Smalley	.05	.02	.00
☐ 561	Chuck Baker UER (shortshop on front)	.05	.02	.00
☐ 562	Gary Ward	.05	.02	.00
☐ 563	Rob Wilfong	.05	.02	.00
☐ 564	Al Williams	.05	.02	.00
☐ 565	Butch Wynegar	.05	.02	.00
☐ 566	Randy Bass	.05	.02	.00
☐ 567	Juan Bonilla	.05	.02	.00
☐ 568	Danny Boone	.05	.02	.00
☐ 569	John Curtis	.05	.02	.00
☐ 570	Juan Eichelberger	.05	.02	.00
☐ 571	Barry Evans	.05	.02	.00
☐ 572	Tim Flannery	.05	.02	.00
☐ 573	Ruppert Jones	.05	.02	.00
☐ 574	Terry Kennedy	.05	.02	.00
☐ 575	Joe Lefebvre	.05	.02	.00
☐ 576A	John Littlefield ERR (left handed)	200.00	90.00	30.00
☐ 576B	John Littlefield COR (right handed)	.10	.04	.01
☐ 577	Gary Lucas	.05	.02	.00
☐ 578	Steve Mura	.05	.02	.00
☐ 579	Broderick Perkins	.05	.02	.00
☐ 580	Gene Richards	.05	.02	.00
☐ 581	Luis Salazar	.05	.02	.00
☐ 582	Ozzie Smith	1.50	.60	.15
☐ 583	John Urrea	.05	.02	.00
☐ 584	Chris Welsh	.05	.02	.00
☐ 585	Rick Wise	.05	.02	.00
☐ 586	Doug Bird	.05	.02	.00
☐ 587	Tim Blackwell	.05	.02	.00
☐ 588	Bobby Bonds	.10	.04	.01
☐ 589	Bill Buckner	.10	.04	.01
☐ 590	Bill Caudill	.05	.02	.00
☐ 591	Hector Cruz	.05	.02	.00
☐ 592	Jody Davis	.15	.06	.01
☐ 593	Ivan DeJesus	.05	.02	.00
☐ 594	Steve Dillard	.05	.02	.00
☐ 595	Leon Durham	.05	.02	.00
☐ 596	Rawly Eastwick	.05	.02	.00
☐ 597	Steve Henderson	.05	.02	.00
☐ 598	Mike Krukow	.05	.02	.00
☐ 599	Mike Lum	.05	.02	.00
☐ 600	Randy Martz	.05	.02	.00
☐ 601	Jerry Morales	.05	.02	.00
☐ 602	Ken Reitz	.05	.02	.00
☐ 603A	Lee Smith ERR (Cubs logo reversed)	3.25	1.35	.32
☐ 603B	Lee Smith COR	3.00	1.25	.30
☐ 604	Dick Tidrow	.05	.02	.00
☐ 605	Jim Tracy	.05	.02	.00
☐ 606	Mike Tyson	.05	.02	.00
☐ 607	Ty Waller	.05	.02	.00
☐ 608	Danny Ainge	.35	.15	.03
☐ 609	Jorge Bell	8.00	3.50	.80
☐ 610	Mark Bomback	.05	.02	.00
☐ 611	Barry Bonnell	.05	.02	.00
☐ 612	Jim Clancy	.05	.02	.00
☐ 613	Damaso Garcia	.05	.02	.00
☐ 614	Jerry Garvin	.05	.02	.00
☐ 615	Alfredo Griffin	.05	.02	.00
☐ 616	Garth Iorg	.05	.02	.00
☐ 617	Luis Leal	.05	.02	.00
☐ 618	Ken Macha	.05	.02	.00
☐ 619	John Mayberry	.10	.04	.01
☐ 620	Joey McLaughlin	.05	.02	.00
☐ 621	Lloyd Moseby	.10	.04	.01
☐ 622	Dave Stieb	.35	.15	.03
☐ 623	Jackson Todd	.05	.02	.00
☐ 624	Willie Upshaw	.05	.02	.00
☐ 625	Otto Velez	.05	.02	.00
☐ 626	Ernie Whitt	.05	.02	.00
☐ 627	Alvis Woods	.05	.02	.00
☐ 628	All Star Game Cleveland, Ohio	.05	.02	.00
☐ 629	All Star Infielders Frank White and Bucky Dent	.10	.04	.01
☐ 630	Big Red Machine Dan Driessen Dave Concepcion George Foster	.10	.04	.01
☐ 631	Bruce Sutter Top NL Relief Pitcher	.10	.04	.01
☐ 632	"Steve and Carlton" Steve Carlton and Carlton Fisk	.60	.25	.06
☐ 633	Carl Yastrzemski 3000th Game	.60	.25	.06
☐ 634	Dynamic Duo Johnny Bench and Tom Seaver	.90	.40	.09
☐ 635	West Meets East Fernando Valenzuela and Gary Carter	.20	.08	.02
☐ 636A	Fernando Valenzuela: NL SO King ("he" NL)	.35	.15	.03
☐ 636B	Fernando Valenzuela: NL SO King ("the" NL)	.15	.06	.01
☐ 637	Mike Schmidt Home Run King	1.00	.40	.10
☐ 638	NL All Stars Gary Carter and Dave Parker	.25	.10	.02
☐ 639	Perfect Game UER Len Barker and Bo Diaz (catcher actually Ron Hassey)	.10	.04	.01
☐ 640	Pete and Re-Pete Pete Rose and Son	1.75	.70	.17
☐ 641	Phillies Finest Lonnie Smith Mike Schmidt Steve Carlton	.60	.25	.06
☐ 642	Red Sox Reunion Fred Lynn and Dwight Evans	.10	.04	.01
☐ 643	Rickey Henderson Most Hits and Runs	2.50	1.00	.25
☐ 644	Rollie Fingers Most Saves AL	.25	.10	.02
☐ 645	Tom Seaver Most 1981 Wins	.75	.30	.07

			MINT	EXC	G-VG
☐ 646A	Yankee Powerhouse .... Reggie Jackson and Dave Winfield (comma on back after outfielder)		1.00	.40	.10
☐ 646B	Yankee Powerhouse .... Reggie Jackson and Dave Winfield (no comma)		.90	.40	.09
☐ 647	CL:Yankees/Dodgers		.15	.02	.00
☐ 648	CL:A's/Reds		.15	.02	.00
☐ 649	CL:Cards/Brewers		.15	.02	.00
☐ 650	CL:Expos/Orioles		.15	.02	.00
☐ 651	CL:Astros/Phillies		.15	.02	.00
☐ 652	CL:Tigers/Red Sox		.15	.02	.00
☐ 653	CL: Rangers/White Sox		.15	.02	.00
☐ 654	CL:Giants/Indians		.15	.02	.00
☐ 655	CL:Royals/Braves		.15	.02	.00
☐ 656	CL:Angels/Pirates		.15	.02	.00
☐ 657	CL:Mariners/Mets		.15	.02	.00
☐ 658	CL:Padres/Twins		.15	.02	.00
☐ 659	CL: Blue Jays/Cubs		.15	.02	.00
☐ 660	Specials Checklist		.15	.02	.00

1983 Fleer

Rod Carew — ANGELS - FIRST BASE

Rod Carew
FIRST BASE

The cards in this 660-card set measure 2 1/2" by 3 1/2". In 1983, for the third straight year, Fleer has produced a baseball series numbering 660 cards. Of these, 1-628 are player cards, 629-646 are special cards, and 647-660 are checklist cards. The player cards are again ordered alphabetically within team. The team order relates back to each team's on-field performance during the previous year, i.e., World Champion Cardinals (1-25), AL Champion Brewers (26-51), Baltimore (52-75), California (76-103), Kansas City (104-128), Atlanta (129-152), Philadelphia (153-176), Boston (177-200), Los Angeles (201-227), Chicago White Sox (228-251), San Francisco (252-276), Montreal (277-301), Pittsburgh (302-326), Detroit (327-351), San Diego (352-375), New York Yankees (376-399), Cleveland (400-423), Toronto (424-444), Houston (445-469), Seattle (470-489), Chicago Cubs (490-512), Oakland (513-535), New York Mets (536-561), Texas (562-583), Cincinnati (584-606), and Minnesota (607-628). The front of each card has a colorful team logo at bottom left and the player's name and position at lower right. The reverses are done in shades of brown on white. The cards are numbered on the back next to a small black and white photo of the player. The key rookie cards in this set are Wade Boggs, Tony Gwynn, Howard Johnson, Willie McGee, Ryne Sandberg, and Frank Viola.

	MINT	EXC	G-VG
COMPLETE SET (660)	120.00	55.00	18.00
COMMON PLAYER (1-660)	.05	.02	.00

☐ 1	Joaquin Andujar	.10	.04	.01
☐ 2	Doug Bair	.05	.02	.00
☐ 3	Steve Braun	.05	.02	.00
☐ 4	Glenn Brummer	.05	.02	.00
☐ 5	Bob Forsch	.05	.02	.00

☐ 6	David Green	.05	.02	.00
☐ 7	George Hendrick	.05	.02	.00
☐ 8	Keith Hernandez	.25	.10	.02
☐ 9	Tom Herr	.10	.04	.01
☐ 10	Danelorg	.05	.02	.00
☐ 11	Jim Kaat	.15	.06	.01
☐ 12	Jeff Lahti	.05	.02	.00
☐ 13	Tito Landrum	.05	.02	.00
☐ 14	Dave LaPoint	.10	.04	.01
☐ 15	Willie McGee	3.50	1.50	.35
☐ 16	Steve Mura	.05	.02	.00
☐ 17	Ken Oberkfell	.05	.02	.00
☐ 18	Darrell Porter	.05	.02	.00
☐ 19	Mike Ramsey	.05	.02	.00
☐ 20	Gene Roof	.05	.02	.00
☐ 21	Lonnie Smith	.15	.06	.01
☐ 22	Ozzie Smith	1.25	.50	.12
☐ 23	John Stuper	.05	.02	.00
☐ 24	Bruce Sutter	.15	.06	.01
☐ 25	Gene Tenace	.10	.04	.01
☐ 26	Jerry Augustine	.05	.02	.00
☐ 27	Dwight Bernard	.05	.02	.00
☐ 28	Mark Brouhard	.05	.02	.00
☐ 29	Mike Caldwell	.05	.02	.00
☐ 30	Cecil Cooper	.10	.04	.01
☐ 31	Jamie Easterly	.05	.02	.00
☐ 32	Marshall Edwards	.05	.02	.00
☐ 33	Rollie Fingers	.40	.16	.04
☐ 34	Jim Gantner	.05	.02	.00
☐ 35	Moose Haas	.05	.02	.00
☐ 36	Roy Howell	.05	.02	.00
☐ 37	Pete Ladd	.05	.02	.00
☐ 38	Bob McClure	.05	.02	.00
☐ 39	Doc Medich	.05	.02	.00
☐ 40	Paul Molitor	.40	.16	.04
☐ 41	Don Money	.05	.02	.00
☐ 42	Charlie Moore	.05	.02	.00
☐ 43	Ben Oglivie	.05	.02	.00
☐ 44	Ed Romero	.05	.02	.00
☐ 45	Ted Simmons	.10	.04	.01
☐ 46	Jim Slaton	.05	.02	.00
☐ 47	Don Sutton	.35	.15	.03
☐ 48	Gorman Thomas	.10	.04	.01
☐ 49	Pete Vuckovich	.05	.02	.00
☐ 50	Ned Yost	.05	.02	.00
☐ 51	Robin Yount	1.50	.60	.15
☐ 52	Benny Ayala	.05	.02	.00
☐ 53	Bob Bonner	.05	.02	.00
☐ 54	Al Bumbry	.05	.02	.00
☐ 55	Terry Crowley	.05	.02	.00
☐ 56	Storm Davis	.25	.10	.02
☐ 57	Rich Dauer	.05	.02	.00
☐ 58	Rick Dempsey UER .... (posing batting lefty)	.10	.04	.01
☐ 59	Jim Dwyer	.05	.02	.00
☐ 60	Mike Flanagan	.10	.04	.01
☐ 61	Dan Ford	.05	.02	.00
☐ 62	Glenn Gulliver	.05	.02	.00
☐ 63	John Lowenstein	.05	.02	.00
☐ 64	Dennis Martinez	.10	.04	.01
☐ 65	Tippy Martinez	.05	.02	.00
☐ 66	Scott McGregor	.05	.02	.00
☐ 67	Eddie Murray	1.25	.50	.12
☐ 68	Joe Nolan	.05	.02	.00
☐ 69	Jim Palmer	.75	.30	.07
☐ 70	Cal Ripken Jr.	12.50	5.50	1.65
☐ 71	Gary Roenicke	.05	.02	.00
☐ 72	Lenn Sakata	.05	.02	.00
☐ 73	Ken Singleton	.10	.04	.01
☐ 74	Sammy Stewart	.05	.02	.00
☐ 75	Tim Stoddard	.05	.02	.00
☐ 76	Don Aase	.05	.02	.00
☐ 77	Don Baylor	.10	.04	.01
☐ 78	Juan Beniquez	.05	.02	.00
☐ 79	Bob Boone	.10	.04	.01
☐ 80	Rick Burleson	.05	.02	.00
☐ 81	Rod Carew	1.00	.40	.10
☐ 82	Bobby Clark	.05	.02	.00
☐ 83	Doug Corbett	.05	.02	.00
☐ 84	John Curtis	.05	.02	.00
☐ 85	Doug DeCinces	.10	.04	.01
☐ 86	Brian Downing	.10	.04	.01
☐ 87	Joe Ferguson	.05	.02	.00
☐ 88	Tim Foli	.05	.02	.00
☐ 89	Ken Forsch	.05	.02	.00
☐ 90	Dave Goltz	.05	.02	.00
☐ 91	Bobby Grich	.10	.04	.01
☐ 92	Andy Hassler	.05	.02	.00
☐ 93	Reggie Jackson	1.25	.50	.12
☐ 94	Ron Jackson	.05	.02	.00
☐ 95	Tommy John	.15	.06	.01
☐ 96	Bruce Kison	.05	.02	.00
☐ 97	Fred Lynn	.20	.08	.02
☐ 98	Ed Ott	.05	.02	.00

☐ 99 Steve Renko	.05	.02	.00		
☐ 100 Luis Sanchez	.05	.02	.00		
☐ 101 Rob Wilfong	.05	.02	.00		
☐ 102 Mike Witt	.05	.02	.00		
☐ 103 Geoff Zahn	.05	.02	.00		
☐ 104 Willie Aikens	.05	.02	.00		
☐ 105 Mike Armstrong	.05	.02	.00		
☐ 106 Vida Blue	.10	.04	.01		
☐ 107 Bud Black	.40	.16	.04		
☐ 108 George Brett	1.50	.60	.15		
☐ 109 Bill Castro	.05	.02	.00		
☐ 110 Onix Concepcion	.05	.02	.00		
☐ 111 Dave Frost	.05	.02	.00		
☐ 112 Cesar Geronimo	.05	.02	.00		
☐ 113 Larry Gura	.05	.02	.00		
☐ 114 Steve Hammond	.05	.02	.00		
☐ 115 Don Hood	.05	.02	.00		
☐ 116 Dennis Leonard	.05	.02	.00		
☐ 117 Jerry Martin	.05	.02	.00		
☐ 118 Lee May	.05	.02	.00		
☐ 119 Hal McRae	.10	.04	.01		
☐ 120 Amos Otis	.10	.04	.01		
☐ 121 Greg Pryor	.05	.02	.00		
☐ 122 Dan Quisenberry	.10	.04	.01		
☐ 123 Don Slaught	.35	.15	.03		
☐ 124 Paul Splittorff	.05	.02	.00		
☐ 125 U.L. Washington	.05	.02	.00		
☐ 126 John Wathan	.05	.02	.00		
☐ 127 Frank White	.05	.02	.00		
☐ 128 Willie Wilson	.10	.04	.01		
☐ 129 Steve Bedrosian	.15	.06	.01		
☐ 130 Bruce Benedict	.05	.02	.00		
☐ 131 Tommy Boggs	.05	.02	.00		
☐ 132 Brett Butler	.75	.30	.07		
☐ 133 Rick Camp	.05	.02	.00		
☐ 134 Chris Chambliss	.10	.04	.01		
☐ 135 Ken Dayley	.05	.02	.00		
☐ 136 Gene Garber	.05	.02	.00		
☐ 137 Terry Harper	.05	.02	.00		
☐ 138 Bob Horner	.10	.04	.01		
☐ 139 Glenn Hubbard	.05	.02	.00		
☐ 140 Rufino Linares	.05	.02	.00		
☐ 141 Rick Mahler	.05	.02	.00		
☐ 142 Dale Murphy	.75	.30	.07		
☐ 143 Phil Niekro	.35	.15	.03		
☐ 144 Pascual Perez	.10	.04	.01		
☐ 145 Biff Pocoroba	.05	.02	.00		
☐ 146 Rafael Ramirez	.05	.02	.00		
☐ 147 Jerry Royster	.05	.02	.00		
☐ 148 Ken Smith	.05	.02	.00		
☐ 149 Bob Walk	.05	.02	.00		
☐ 150 Claudell Washington	.05	.02	.00		
☐ 151 Bob Watson	.05	.02	.00		
☐ 152 Larry Whisenton	.05	.02	.00		
☐ 153 Porfirio Altamirano	.05	.02	.00		
☐ 154 Marty Bystrom	.05	.02	.00		
☐ 155 Steve Carlton	1.00	.40	.10		
☐ 156 Larry Christenson	.05	.02	.00		
☐ 157 Ivan DeJesus	.05	.02	.00		
☐ 158 John Denny	.05	.02	.00		
☐ 159 Bob Dernier	.05	.02	.00		
☐ 160 Bo Diaz	.05	.02	.00		
☐ 161 Ed Farmer	.05	.02	.00		
☐ 162 Greg Gross	.05	.02	.00		
☐ 163 Mike Krukow	.05	.02	.00		
☐ 164 Garry Maddox	.05	.02	.00		
☐ 165 Gary Matthews	.05	.02	.00		
☐ 166 Tug McGraw	.10	.04	.01		
☐ 167 Bob Molinaro	.05	.02	.00		
☐ 168 Sid Monge	.05	.02	.00		
☐ 169 Ron Reed	.05	.02	.00		
☐ 170 Bill Robinson	.10	.04	.01		
☐ 171 Pete Rose	1.25	.50	.12		
☐ 172 Dick Ruthven	.05	.02	.00		
☐ 173 Mike Schmidt	2.00	.80	.20		
☐ 174 Manny Trillo	.05	.02	.00		
☐ 175 Ozzie Virgil	.05	.02	.00		
☐ 176 George Vukovich	.05	.02	.00		
☐ 177 Gary Allenson	.05	.02	.00		
☐ 178 Luis Aponte	.05	.02	.00		
☐ 179 Wade Boggs	24.00	10.50	3.50		
☐ 180 Tom Burgmeier	.05	.02	.00		
☐ 181 Mark Clear	.05	.02	.00		
☐ 182 Dennis Eckersley	.40	.16	.04		
☐ 183 Dwight Evans	.25	.10	.02		
☐ 184 Rich Gedman	.05	.02	.00		
☐ 185 Glenn Hoffman	.05	.02	.00		
☐ 186 Bruce Hurst	.15	.06	.01		
☐ 187 Carney Lansford	.10	.04	.01		
☐ 188 Rick Miller	.05	.02	.00		
☐ 189 Reid Nichols	.05	.02	.00		
☐ 190 Bob Ojeda	.10	.04	.01		
☐ 191 Tony Perez	.30	.12	.03		
☐ 192 Chuck Rainey	.05	.02	.00		
☐ 193 Jerry Remy	.05	.02	.00		
☐ 194 Jim Rice	.25	.10	.02		
☐ 195 Bob Stanley	.05	.02	.00		
☐ 196 Dave Stapleton	.05	.02	.00		
☐ 197 Mike Torrez	.05	.02	.00		
☐ 198 John Tudor	.10	.04	.01		
☐ 199 Julio Valdez	.05	.02	.00		
☐ 200 Carl Yastrzemski	1.00	.40	.10		
☐ 201 Dusty Baker	.10	.04	.01		
☐ 202 Joe Beckwith	.05	.02	.00		
☐ 203 Greg Brock	.10	.04	.01		
☐ 204 Ron Cey	.10	.04	.01		
☐ 205 Terry Forster	.05	.02	.00		
☐ 206 Steve Garvey	.50	.20	.05		
☐ 207 Pedro Guerrero	.35	.15	.03		
☐ 208 Burt Hooton	.05	.02	.00		
☐ 209 Steve Howe	.05	.02	.00		
☐ 210 Ken Landreaux	.05	.02	.00		
☐ 211 Mike Marshall	.10	.04	.01		
☐ 212 Candy Maldonado	.50	.20	.05		
☐ 213 Rick Monday	.05	.02	.00		
☐ 214 Tom Niedenfuer	.05	.02	.00		
☐ 215 Jorge Orta	.05	.02	.00		
☐ 216 Jerry Reuss	.05	.02	.00		
☐ 217 Ron Roenicke	.05	.02	.00		
☐ 218 Vicente Romo	.05	.02	.00		
☐ 219 Bill Russell	.10	.04	.01		
☐ 220 Steve Sax	.50	.20	.05		
☐ 221 Mike Scioscia	.10	.04	.01		
☐ 222 Dave Stewart	.75	.30	.07		
☐ 223 Derrel Thomas	.05	.02	.00		
☐ 224 Fernando Valenzuela	.25	.10	.02		
☐ 225 Bob Welch	.25	.10	.02		
☐ 226 Ricky Wright	.05	.02	.00		
☐ 227 Steve Yeager	.05	.02	.00		
☐ 228 Bill Almon	.05	.02	.00		
☐ 229 Harold Baines	.50	.20	.05		
☐ 230 Salome Barojas	.05	.02	.00		
☐ 231 Tony Bernazard	.05	.02	.00		
☐ 232 Britt Burns	.05	.02	.00		
☐ 233 Richard Dotson	.05	.02	.00		
☐ 234 Ernesto Escarrega	.05	.02	.00		
☐ 235 Carlton Fisk	1.00	.40	.10		
☐ 236 Jerry Hairston	.05	.02	.00		
☐ 237 Kevin Hickey	.05	.02	.00		
☐ 238 LaMarr Hoyt	.05	.02	.00		
☐ 239 Steve Kemp	.05	.02	.00		
☐ 240 Jim Kern	.05	.02	.00		
☐ 241 Ron Kittle	.40	.16	.04		
☐ 242 Jerry Koosman	.10	.04	.01		
☐ 243 Dennis Lamp	.05	.02	.00		
☐ 244 Rudy Law	.05	.02	.00		
☐ 245 Vance Law	.10	.04	.01		
☐ 246 Ron LeFlore	.05	.02	.00		
☐ 247 Greg Luzinski	.10	.04	.01		
☐ 248 Tom Paciorek	.05	.02	.00		
☐ 249 Aurelio Rodriguez	.05	.02	.00		
☐ 250 Mike Squires	.05	.02	.00		
☐ 251 Steve Trout	.05	.02	.00		
☐ 252 Jim Barr	.05	.02	.00		
☐ 253 Dave Bergman	.05	.02	.00		
☐ 254 Fred Breining	.05	.02	.00		
☐ 255 Bob Brenly	.05	.02	.00		
☐ 256 Jack Clark	.25	.10	.02		
☐ 257 Chili Davis	.60	.25	.06		
☐ 258 Darrell Evans	.10	.04	.01		
☐ 259 Alan Fowlkes	.05	.02	.00		
☐ 260 Rich Gale	.05	.02	.00		
☐ 261 Atlee Hammaker	.05	.02	.00		
☐ 262 Al Holland	.05	.02	.00		
☐ 263 Duane Kuiper	.05	.02	.00		
☐ 264 Bill Laskey	.05	.02	.00		
☐ 265 Gary Lavelle	.05	.02	.00		
☐ 266 Johnnie LeMaster	.05	.02	.00		
☐ 267 Renie Martin	.05	.02	.00		
☐ 268 Milt May	.05	.02	.00		
☐ 269 Greg Minton	.05	.02	.00		
☐ 270 Joe Morgan	.50	.20	.05		
☐ 271 Tom O'Malley	.05	.02	.00		
☐ 272 Reggie Smith	.10	.04	.01		
☐ 273 Guy Sularz	.05	.02	.00		
☐ 274 Champ Summers	.05	.02	.00		
☐ 275 Max Venable	.05	.02	.00		
☐ 276 Jim Wohlford	.05	.02	.00		
☐ 277 Ray Burris	.05	.02	.00		
☐ 278 Gary Carter	.40	.16	.04		
☐ 279 Warren Cromartie	.05	.02	.00		
☐ 280 Andre Dawson	1.25	.50	.12		
☐ 281 Terry Francona	.05	.02	.00		
☐ 282 Doug Flynn	.05	.02	.00		
☐ 283 Woodie Fryman	.05	.02	.00		
☐ 284 Bill Gullickson	.10	.04	.01		
☐ 285 Wallace Johnson	.05	.02	.00		
☐ 286 Charlie Lea	.05	.02	.00		

#	Name			
☐ 287	Randy Lerch	.05	.02	.00
☐ 288	Brad Mills	.05	.02	.00
☐ 289	Dan Norman	.05	.02	.00
☐ 290	Al Oliver	.10	.04	.01
☐ 291	David Palmer	.05	.02	.00
☐ 292	Tim Raines	.60	.25	.06
☐ 293	Jeff Reardon	.50	.20	.05
☐ 294	Steve Rogers	.05	.02	.00
☐ 295	Scott Sanderson	.10	.04	.01
☐ 296	Dan Schatzeder	.05	.02	.00
☐ 297	Bryn Smith	.15	.06	.01
☐ 298	Chris Speier	.05	.02	.00
☐ 299	Tim Wallach	.20	.08	.02
☐ 300	Jerry White	.05	.02	.00
☐ 301	Joel Youngblood	.05	.02	.00
☐ 302	Ross Baumgarten	.05	.02	.00
☐ 303	Dale Berra	.05	.02	.00
☐ 304	John Candelaria	.05	.02	.00
☐ 305	Dick Davis	.05	.02	.00
☐ 306	Mike Easler	.05	.02	.00
☐ 307	Richie Hebner	.05	.02	.00
☐ 308	Lee Lacy	.05	.02	.00
☐ 309	Bill Madlock	.10	.04	.01
☐ 310	Larry McWilliams	.05	.02	.00
☐ 311	John Milner	.05	.02	.00
☐ 312	Omar Moreno	.05	.02	.00
☐ 313	Jim Morrison	.05	.02	.00
☐ 314	Steve Nicosia	.05	.02	.00
☐ 315	Dav e Parker	.40	.16	.04
☐ 316	Tony Pena	.10	.04	.01
☐ 317	Johnny Ray	.05	.02	.00
☐ 318	Rick Rhoden	.05	.02	.00
☐ 319	Don Robinson	.05	.02	.00
☐ 320	Enrique Romo	.05	.02	.00
☐ 321	Manny Sarmiento	.05	.02	.00
☐ 322	Rod Scurry	.05	.02	.00
☐ 323	Jimmy Smith	.05	.02	.00
☐ 324	Willie Stargell	.50	.20	.05
☐ 325	Jason Thompson	.05	.02	.00
☐ 326	Kent Tekulve	.05	.02	.00
☐ 327A	Tom Brookens (Short .375" brown box shaded in on card back)	.05	.02	.00
☐ 327B	Tom Brookens (Longer 1.25" brown box shaded in on card back)	.05	.02	.00
☐ 328	Enos Cabell	.05	.02	.00
☐ 329	Kirk Gibson	.50	.20	.05
☐ 330	Larry Herndon	.05	.02	.00
☐ 331	Mike Ivie	.05	.02	.00
☐ 332	Howard Johnson	10.00	4.50	1.25
☐ 333	Lynn Jones	.05	.02	.00
☐ 334	Rick Leach	.05	.02	.00
☐ 335	Chet Lemon	.05	.02	.00
☐ 336	Jack Morris	.60	.25	.06
☐ 337	Lance Parrish	.25	.10	.02
☐ 338	Larry Pashnick	.05	.02	.00
☐ 339	Dan Petry	.05	.02	.00
☐ 340	Dave Rozema	.05	.02	.00
☐ 341	Dave Rucker	.05	.02	.00
☐ 342	Elias Sosa	.05	.02	.00
☐ 343	Dave Tobik	.05	.02	.00
☐ 344	Alan Trammell	.60	.25	.06
☐ 345	Jerry Turner	.05	.02	.00
☐ 346	Jerry Ujdur	.05	.02	.00
☐ 347	Pat Underwood	.05	.02	.00
☐ 348	Lou Whitaker	.35	.15	.03
☐ 349	Milt Wilcox	.05	.02	.00
☐ 350	Glenn Wilson	.10	.04	.01
☐ 351	John Wockenfuss	.05	.02	.00
☐ 352	Kurt Bevacqua	.05	.02	.00
☐ 353	Juan Bonilla	.05	.02	.00
☐ 354	Floyd Chiffer	.05	.02	.00
☐ 355	Luis DeLeon	.05	.02	.00
☐ 356	Dave Dravecky	.50	.20	.05
☐ 357	Dave Edwards	.05	.02	.00
☐ 358	Juan Eichelberger	.05	.02	.00
☐ 359	Tim Flannery	.05	.02	.00
☐ 360	Tony Gwynn	23.00	10.00	3.35
☐ 361	Ruppert Jones	.05	.02	.00
☐ 362	Terry Kennedy	.05	.02	.00
☐ 363	Joe Lefebvre	.05	.02	.00
☐ 364	Sixto Lezcano	.05	.02	.00
☐ 365	Tim Lollar	.05	.02	.00
☐ 366	Gary Lucas	.05	.02	.00
☐ 367	John Montefusco	.05	.02	.00
☐ 368	Broderick Perkins	.05	.02	.00
☐ 369	Joe Pittman	.05	.02	.00
☐ 370	Gene Richards	.05	.02	.00
☐ 371	Luis Salazar	.05	.02	.00
☐ 372	Eric Show	.15	.06	.01
☐ 373	Garry Templeton	.10	.04	.01
☐ 374	Chris Welsh	.05	.02	.00
☐ 375	Alan Wiggins	.05	.02	.00
☐ 376	Rick Cerone	.05	.02	.00
☐ 377	Dave Collins	.05	.02	.00
☐ 378	Roger Erickson	.05	.02	.00
☐ 379	George Frazier	.05	.02	.00
☐ 380	Oscar Gamble	.05	.02	.00
☐ 381	Goose Gossage	.15	.06	.01
☐ 382	Ken Griffey	.25	.10	.02
☐ 383	Ron Guidry	.25	.10	.02
☐ 384	Dave LaRoche	.05	.02	.00
☐ 385	Rudy May	.05	.02	.00
☐ 386	John Mayberry	.10	.04	.01
☐ 387	Lee Mazzilli	.05	.02	.00
☐ 388	Mike Morgan	.10	.04	.01
☐ 389	Jerry Mumphrey	.05	.02	.00
☐ 390	Bobby Murcer	.10	.04	.01
☐ 391	Graig Nettles	.10	.04	.01
☐ 392	Lou Piniella	.10	.04	.01
☐ 393	Willie Randolph	.10	.04	.01
☐ 394	Shane Rawley	.05	.02	.00
☐ 395	Dave Righetti	.25	.10	.02
☐ 396	Andre Robertson	.05	.02	.00
☐ 397	Roy Smalley	.05	.02	.00
☐ 398	Dave Winfield	.75	.30	.07
☐ 399	Butch Wynegar	.05	.02	.00
☐ 400	Chris Bando	.05	.02	.00
☐ 401	Alan Bannister	.05	.02	.00
☐ 402	Len Barker	.05	.02	.00
☐ 403	Tom Brennan	.05	.02	.00
☐ 404	Carmelo Castillo	.05	.02	.00
☐ 405	Miguel Dilone	.05	.02	.00
☐ 406	Jerry Dybzinski	.05	.02	.00
☐ 407	Mike Fischlin	.05	.02	.00
☐ 408	Ed Glynn UER (photo actually Bud Anderson)	.05	.02	.00
☐ 409	Mike Hargrove	.05	.02	.00
☐ 410	Toby Harrah	.05	.02	.00
☐ 411	Ron Hassey	.05	.02	.00
☐ 412	Von Hayes	.15	.06	.01
☐ 413	Rick Manning	.05	.02	.00
☐ 414	Bake McBride	.05	.02	.00
☐ 415	Larry Milbourne	.05	.02	.00
☐ 416	Bill Nahorodny	.05	.02	.00
☐ 417	Jack Perconte	.05	.02	.00
☐ 418	Lary Sorensen	.05	.02	.00
☐ 419	Dan Spillner	.05	.02	.00
☐ 420	Rick Sutcliffe	.15	.06	.01
☐ 421	Andre Thornton	.05	.02	.00
☐ 422	Rick Waits	.05	.02	.00
☐ 423	Eddie Whitson	.05	.02	.00
☐ 424	Jesse Barfield	.40	.16	.04
☐ 425	Barry Bonnell	.05	.02	.00
☐ 426	Jim Clancy	.05	.02	.00
☐ 427	Damaso Garcia	.05	.02	.00
☐ 428	Jerry Garvin	.05	.02	.00
☐ 429	Alfredo Griffin	.05	.02	.00
☐ 430	Garthlorg	.05	.02	.00
☐ 431	Roy Lee Jackson	.05	.02	.00
☐ 432	Luis Leal	.05	.02	.00
☐ 433	Buck Martinez	.05	.02	.00
☐ 434	Joey McLaughlin	.05	.02	.00
☐ 435	Lloyd Moseby	.10	.04	.01
☐ 436	Rance Mulliniks	.05	.02	.00
☐ 437	Dale Murray	.05	.02	.00
☐ 438	Wayne Nordhagen	.05	.02	.00
☐ 439	Geno Petralli	.10	.04	.01
☐ 440	Hosken Powell	.05	.02	.00
☐ 441	Dave Stieb	.25	.10	.02
☐ 442	Willie Upshaw	.05	.02	.00
☐ 443	Ernie Whitt	.05	.02	.00
☐ 444	Alvis Woods	.05	.02	.00
☐ 445	Alan Ashby	.05	.02	.00
☐ 446	Jose Cruz	.10	.04	.01
☐ 447	Kiko Garcia	.05	.02	.00
☐ 448	Phil Garner	.10	.04	.01
☐ 449	Danny Heep	.05	.02	.00
☐ 450	Art Howe	.10	.04	.01
☐ 451	Bob Knepper	.05	.02	.00
☐ 452	Alan Knicely	.05	.02	.00
☐ 453	Ray Knight	.10	.04	.01
☐ 454	Frank LaCorte	.05	.02	.00
☐ 455	Mik e LaCoss	.05	.02	.00
☐ 456	Randy Moffitt	.05	.02	.00
☐ 457	Joe Niekro	.10	.04	.01
☐ 458	Terry Puhl	.05	.02	.00
☐ 459	Luis Pujols	.05	.02	.00
☐ 460	Craig Reynolds	.05	.02	.00
☐ 461	Bert Roberge	.05	.02	.00
☐ 462	Vern Ruhle	.05	.02	.00
☐ 463	Nolan Ryan	5.25	2.25	.50
☐ 464	Joe Sambito	.05	.02	.00
☐ 465	Tony Scott	.05	.02	.00
☐ 466	Dave Smith	.05	.02	.00
☐ 467	Harry Spilman	.05	.02	.00

☐ 468	Dickie Thon	.10	.04	.01
☐ 469	Denny Walling	.05	.02	.00
☐ 470	Larry Andersen	.05	.02	.00
☐ 471	Floyd Bannister	.05	.02	.00
☐ 472	Jim Beattie	.05	.02	.00
☐ 473	Bruce Bochte	.05	.02	.00
☐ 474	Manny Castillo	.05	.02	.00
☐ 475	Bil l Caudill	.05	.02	.00
☐ 476	Bryan Clark	.05	.02	.00
☐ 477	Al Cowens	.05	.02	.00
☐ 478	Julio Cruz	.05	.02	.00
☐ 479	Todd Cruz	.05	.02	.00
☐ 480	Gary Gray	.05	.02	.00
☐ 481	Dave Henderson	1.25	.50	.12
☐ 482	Mike Moore	.90	.40	.09
☐ 483	Gaylord Perry	.35	.15	.03
☐ 484	Dave Revering	.05	.02	.00
☐ 485	Joe Simpson	.05	.02	.00
☐ 486	Mike Stanton	.05	.02	.00
☐ 487	Rick Sweet	.05	.02	.00
☐ 488	Ed VandeBerg	.05	.02	.00
☐ 489	Richie Zisk	.05	.02	.00
☐ 490	Doug Bird	.05	.02	.00
☐ 491	Larry Bowa	.10	.04	.01
☐ 492	Bill Buckner	.10	.04	.01
☐ 493	Bill Campbell	.05	.02	.00
☐ 494	Jody Davis	.05	.02	.00
☐ 495	Leon Durham	.05	.02	.00
☐ 496	Steve Henderson	.05	.02	.00
☐ 497	Willie Hernandez	.05	.02	.00
☐ 498	Ferguson Jenkins	.35	.15	.03
☐ 499	Jay Johnstone	.10	.04	.01
☐ 500	Junior Kennedy	.05	.02	.00
☐ 501	Randy Martz	.05	.02	.00
☐ 502	Jerry Morales	.05	.02	.00
☐ 503	Keith Moreland	.05	.02	.00
☐ 504	Dickie Noles	.05	.02	.00
☐ 505	Mike Proly	.05	.02	.00
☐ 506	Allen Ripley	.05	.02	.00
☐ 507	Ryne Sandberg UER	35.00	15.75	5.25
	(Should say High School in Spokane, Washington)			
☐ 508	Lee Smith	.60	.25	.06
☐ 509	Pat Tabler	.10	.04	.01
☐ 510	Dick Tidrow	.05	.02	.00
☐ 511	Bump Wills	.05	.02	.00
☐ 512	Gary Woods	.05	.02	.00
☐ 513	Tony Armas	.05	.02	.00
☐ 514	Dave Beard	.05	.02	.00
☐ 515	Jeff Burroughs	.05	.02	.00
☐ 516	John D'Acquisto	.05	.02	.00
☐ 517	Wayne Gross	.05	.02	.00
☐ 518	Mike Heath	.05	.02	.00
☐ 519	Rickey Henderson UER	5.00	2.25	.50
	(Brock record listed as 120 steals)			
☐ 520	Cliff Johnson	.05	.02	.00
☐ 521	Matt Keough	.05	.02	.00
☐ 522	Brian Kingman	.05	.02	.00
☐ 523	Rick Langford	.05	.02	.00
☐ 524	Dave Lopes	.10	.04	.01
☐ 525	Steve McCatty	.05	.02	.00
☐ 526	Dave McKay	.05	.02	.00
☐ 527	Dan Meyer	.05	.02	.00
☐ 528	Dwayne Murphy	.05	.02	.00
☐ 529	Jef f Newman	.05	.02	.00
☐ 530	Mike Norris	.05	.02	.00
☐ 531	Bob Owchinko	.05	.02	.00
☐ 532	Joe Rudi	.10	.04	.01
☐ 533	Jimmy Sexton	.05	.02	.00
☐ 534	Fred Stanley	.05	.02	.00
☐ 535	Tom Underwood	.05	.02	.00
☐ 536	Nei l Allen	.05	.02	.00
☐ 537	Wally Backman	.10	.04	.01
☐ 538	Bob Bailor	.05	.02	.00
☐ 539	Hubie Brooks	.25	.10	.02
☐ 540	Carlos Diaz	.05	.02	.00
☐ 541	Pete Falcone	.05	.02	.00
☐ 542	George Foster	.15	.06	.01
☐ 543	Ron Gardenhire	.05	.02	.00
☐ 544	Brian Giles	.05	.02	.00
☐ 545	Ron Hodges	.05	.02	.00
☐ 546	Randy Jones	.05	.02	.00
☐ 547	Mike Jorgensen	.05	.02	.00
☐ 548	Dave Kingman	.15	.06	.01
☐ 549	Ed Lynch	.05	.02	.00
☐ 550	Jesse Orosco	.05	.02	.00
☐ 551	Rick Ownbey	.05	.02	.00
☐ 552	Charlie Puleo	.05	.02	.00
☐ 553	Gary Rajsich	.05	.02	.00
☐ 554	Mike Scott	.20	.08	.02
☐ 555	Rusty Staub	.10	.04	.01
☐ 556	John Stearns	.05	.02	.00
☐ 557	Craig Swan	.05	.02	.00

☐ 558	Ellis Valentine	.05	.02	.00
☐ 559	Tom Veryzer	.05	.02	.00
☐ 560	Mookie Wilson	.10	.04	.01
☐ 561	Pat Zachry	.05	.02	.00
☐ 562	Buddy Bell	.10	.04	.01
☐ 563	John Butcher	.05	.02	.00
☐ 564	Steve Comer	.05	.02	.00
☐ 565	Danny Darwin	.05	.02	.00
☐ 566	Bucky Dent	.10	.04	.01
☐ 567	John Grubb	.05	.02	.00
☐ 568	Rick Honeycutt	.05	.02	.00
☐ 569	Dave Hostetler	.05	.02	.00
☐ 570	Charlie Hough	.05	.02	.00
☐ 571	Lamar Johnson	.05	.02	.00
☐ 572	Jon Matlack	.05	.02	.00
☐ 573	Paul Mirabella	.05	.02	.00
☐ 574	Larry Parrish	.05	.02	.00
☐ 575	Mike Richardt	.05	.02	.00
☐ 576	Mickey Rivers	.05	.02	.00
☐ 577	Billy Sample	.05	.02	.00
☐ 578	Dave Schmidt	.10	.04	.01
☐ 579	Bill Stein	.05	.02	.00
☐ 580	Jim Sundberg	.05	.02	.00
☐ 581	Frank Tanana	.10	.04	.01
☐ 582	Mark Wagner	.05	.02	.00
☐ 583	George Wright	.05	.02	.00
☐ 584	Johnny Bench	1.00	.40	.10
☐ 585	Bruce Berenyi	.05	.02	.00
☐ 586	Larry Biittner	.05	.02	.00
☐ 587	Cesar Cedeno	.10	.04	.01
☐ 588	Dave Concepcion	.10	.04	.01
☐ 589	Dan Driessen	.05	.02	.00
☐ 590	Greg Harris	.05	.02	.00
☐ 591	Ben Hayes	.05	.02	.00
☐ 592	Paul Householder	.05	.02	.00
☐ 593	Tom Hume	.05	.02	.00
☐ 594	Wayne Krenchicki	.05	.02	.00
☐ 595	Rafae l Landestoy	.05	.02	.00
☐ 596	Charlie Leibrandt	.10	.04	.01
☐ 597	Eddie Milner	.05	.02	.00
☐ 598	Ron Oester	.05	.02	.00
☐ 599	Frank Pastore	.05	.02	.00
☐ 600	Joe Price	.05	.02	.00
☐ 601	Tom Seaver	1.00	.40	.10
☐ 602	Bob Shirley	.05	.02	.00
☐ 603	Mario Soto	.05	.02	.00
☐ 604	Alex Trevino	.05	.02	.00
☐ 605	Mike Vail	.05	.02	.00
☐ 606	Duane Walker	.05	.02	.00
☐ 607	Tom Brunansky	.40	.16	.04
☐ 608	Bobby Castillo	.05	.02	.00
☐ 609	John Castino	.05	.02	.00
☐ 610	Ron Davis	.05	.02	.00
☐ 611	Lenny Faedo	.05	.02	.00
☐ 612	Terry Felton	.05	.02	.00
☐ 613	Gary Gaetti	1.00	.40	.10
☐ 614	Mickey Hatcher	.05	.02	.00
☐ 615	Brad Havens	.05	.02	.00
☐ 616	Kent Hrbek	1.00	.40	.10
☐ 617	Randy Johnson	.05	.02	.00
☐ 618	Tim Laudner	.05	.02	.00
☐ 619	Jeff Little	.05	.02	.00
☐ 620	Bobby Mitchell	.05	.02	.00
☐ 621	Jack O'Connor	.05	.02	.00
☐ 622	John Pacella	.05	.02	.00
☐ 623	Pete Redfern	.05	.02	.00
☐ 624	Jesus Vega	.05	.02	.00
☐ 625	Frank Viola	4.50	2.00	.45
☐ 626	Ron Washington	.05	.02	.00
☐ 627	Gary Ward	.05	.02	.00
☐ 628	Al Williams	.05	.02	.00
☐ 629	Red Sox All-Stars	.30	.12	.03
	Carl Yastrzemski Dennis Eckersley Mark Clear			
☐ 630	"300 Career Wins"	.10	.04	.01
	Gaylord Perry and Terry Bulling 5/6/82			
☐ 631	Pride of Venezuela	.10	.04	.01
	Dave Concepcion and Manny Trillo			
☐ 632	All-Sta r Infielders	.25	.10	.02
	Robin Yount and Buddy Bell			
☐ 633	Mr.Vet and Mr.Rookie	.25	.10	.02
	Dave Winfield and Kent Hrbek			
☐ 634	Fountain of Youth	.50	.20	.05
	Willie Stargell and Pete Rose			
☐ 635	Big Chiefs	.10	.04	.01
	Toby Harrah and Andre Thornton			
☐ 636	Smith Brothers	.30	.12	.03
	Ozzie and Lonnie			

☐ 637 Base Stealers' Threat	.10	.04	.01
Bo Diaz and			
Gary Carter			
☐ 638 All-Star Catchers	.20	.08	.02
Carlton Fisk and			
Gary Carter			
☐ 639 The Silver Shoe	2.00	.80	.20
Rickey Henderson			
☐ 640 Home Run Threats	.30	.12	.03
Ben Oglivie and			
Reggie Jackson			
☐ 641 Two Teams Same Day	.10	.04	.01
Joel Youngblood			
August 4, 1982			
☐ 642 Last Perfect Game	.10	.04	.01
Ron Hassey and			
Len Barker			
☐ 643 Black and Blue	.10	.04	.01
Vida Blue			
☐ 644 Black and Blue	.10	.04	.01
Bud Black			
☐ 645 Speed and Power	.40	.16	.04
Reggie Jackson			
☐ 646 Speed and Power	1.25	.50	.12
Rickey Henderson			
☐ 647 CL:Cards/Brewers	.15	.02	.00
☐ 648 CL:Orioles/Angels	.15	.02	.00
☐ 649 CL:Royals/Braves	.15	.02	.00
☐ 650 CL: Phillies/Red Sox	.15	.02	.00
☐ 651 CL: Dodgers/White Sox	.15	.02	.00
☐ 652 CL:Giants/Expos	.15	.02	.00
☐ 653 CL:Pirates/Tigers	.15	.02	.00
☐ 654 CL:Padres/Yankees	.15	.02	.00
☐ 655 CL: Indians/Blue Jays	.15	.02	.00
☐ 656 CL:Astros/Mariners	.15	.02	.00
☐ 657 CL:Cubs/A's	.15	.02	.00
☐ 658 CL:Mets/Rangers	.15	.02	.00
☐ 659 CL:Reds/Twins	.15	.02	.00
☐ 660 CL:Specials/Teams	.15	.02	.00

1984 Fleer

Tom Seaver
PITCHER

The cards in this 660-card set measure 2 1/2" by 3 1/2". The 1984 Fleer card set featured fronts with full-color team logos along with the player's name and position and the Fleer identification. The set features many imaginative photos, several multi-player cards, and many more action shots than the 1983 card set. The backs are quite similar to the 1983 backs except that blue rather than brown ink is used. The player cards are alphabetized within team and the teams are ordered by their 1983 season finish and won-lost record, e.g., Baltimore (1-23), Philadelphia (24-49), Chicago White Sox (50-73), Detroit (74-95), Los Angeles (96-118), New York Yankees (119-144), Toronto (145-169), Atlanta (170-193), Milwaukee (194-219), Houston (220-244), Pittsburgh (245-269), Montreal (270-293), San Diego (294-317), St. Louis (318-340), Kansas City (341-364), San Francisco (365-387), Boston (388-412), Texas (413-435), Oakland (436-461), Cincinnati (462-485), Chicago (486-507), California (508-532), Cleveland (533-555), Minnesota (556-579), New York Mets (580-603), and Seattle (604-625). Specials (626-646) and checklist cards (647-660)

make up the end of the set. The key rookie cards in this set are Tony Fernandez, Don Mattingly, Kevin McReynolds, Juan Samuel, Darryl Strawberry, and Andy Van Slyke.

	MINT	EXC	G-VG
COMPLETE SET (660)	225.00	100.00	33.00
COMMON PLAYER (1-660)	.09	.04	.01
☐ 1 Mike Boddicker	.25	.06	.01
☐ 2 Al Bumbry	.09	.04	.01
☐ 3 Todd Cruz	.09	.04	.01
☐ 4 Rich Dauer	.09	.04	.01
☐ 5 Storm Davis	.15	.06	.01
☐ 6 Rick Dempsey	.09	.04	.01
☐ 7 Jim Dwyer	.09	.04	.01
☐ 8 Mike Flanagan	.15	.06	.01
☐ 9 Dan Ford	.09	.04	.01
☐ 10 John Lowenstein	.09	.04	.01
☐ 11 Dennis Martinez	.15	.06	.01
☐ 12 Tippy Martinez	.09	.04	.01
☐ 13 Scott McGregor	.09	.04	.01
☐ 14 Eddie Murray	2.50	1.00	.25
☐ 15 Joe Nolan	.09	.04	.01
☐ 16 Jim Palmer	2.00	.80	.20
☐ 17 Cal Ripken	15.00	6.50	2.15
☐ 18 Gary Roenicke	.09	.04	.01
☐ 19 Lenn Sakata	.09	.04	.01
☐ 20 John Shelby	.25	.10	.02
☐ 21 Ken Singleton	.15	.06	.01
☐ 22 Sammy Stewart	.09	.04	.01
☐ 23 Tim Stoddard	.09	.04	.01
☐ 24 Marty Bystrom	.09	.04	.01
☐ 25 Steve Carlton	2.00	.80	.20
☐ 26 Ivan DeJesus	.09	.04	.01
☐ 27 John Denny	.09	.04	.01
☐ 28 Bob Dernier	.09	.04	.01
☐ 29 Bo Diaz	.09	.04	.01
☐ 30 Kiko Garcia	.09	.04	.01
☐ 31 Greg Gross	.09	.04	.01
☐ 32 Kevin Gross	.35	.15	.03
☐ 33 Von Hayes	.20	.08	.02
☐ 34 Willie Hernandez	.15	.06	.01
☐ 35 Al Holland	.09	.04	.01
☐ 36 Charles Hudson	.15	.06	.01
☐ 37 Joe Lefebvre	.09	.04	.01
☐ 38 Sixto Lezcano	.09	.04	.01
☐ 39 Garry Maddox	.09	.04	.01
☐ 40 Gary Matthews	.09	.04	.01
☐ 41 Len Matuszek	.09	.04	.01
☐ 42 Tug McGraw	.15	.06	.01
☐ 43 Joe Morgan	1.00	.40	.10
☐ 44 Tony Perez	.50	.20	.05
☐ 45 Ron Reed	.09	.04	.01
☐ 46 Pete Rose	2.00	.80	.20
☐ 47 Juan Samuel	4.50	2.00	.45
☐ 48 Mike Schmidt	8.00	3.50	.80
☐ 49 Ozzie Virgil	.09	.04	.01
☐ 50 Juan Agosto	.15	.06	.01
☐ 51 Harold Baines	.60	.25	.06
☐ 52 Floyd Bannister	.09	.04	.01
☐ 53 Salome Barojas	.09	.04	.01
☐ 54 Britt Burns	.09	.04	.01
☐ 55 Julio Cruz	.09	.04	.01
☐ 56 Richard Dotson	.09	.04	.01
☐ 57 Jerry Dybzinski	.09	.04	.01
☐ 58 Carlton Fisk	2.00	.80	.20
☐ 59 Scott Fletcher	.15	.06	.01
☐ 60 Jerry Hairston	.09	.04	.01
☐ 61 Kevin Hickey	.09	.04	.01
☐ 62 Marc Hill	.09	.04	.01
☐ 63 LaMarr Hoyt	.09	.04	.01
☐ 64 Ron Kittle	.15	.06	.01
☐ 65 Jerry Koosman	.15	.06	.01
☐ 66 Dennis Lamp	.09	.04	.01
☐ 67 Rudy Law	.09	.04	.01
☐ 68 Vance Law	.15	.06	.01
☐ 69 Greg Luzinski	.15	.06	.01
☐ 70 Tom Paciorek	.09	.04	.01
☐ 71 Mike Squires	.09	.04	.01
☐ 72 Dick Tidrow	.09	.04	.01
☐ 73 Greg Walker	.15	.06	.01
☐ 74 Glenn Abbott	.09	.04	.01
☐ 75 Howard Bailey	.09	.04	.01
☐ 76 Doug Bair	.09	.04	.01
☐ 77 Juan Berenguer	.09	.04	.01
☐ 78 Tom Brookens	.09	.04	.01
☐ 79 Enos Cabell	.09	.04	.01
☐ 80 Kirk Gibson	.75	.30	.07
☐ 81 John Grubb	.09	.04	.01
☐ 82 Larry Herndon	.09	.04	.01
☐ 83 Wayne Krenchicki	.09	.04	.01
☐ 84 Rick Leach	.09	.04	.01
☐ 85 Chet Lemon	.09	.04	.01

☐ 86	Aurelio Lopez	.09	.04	.01
☐ 87	Jack Morris	1.00	.40	.10
☐ 88	Lance Parrish	.40	.16	.04
☐ 89	Dan Petry	.09	.04	.01
☐ 90	Dave Rozema	.09	.04	.01
☐ 91	Alan Trammell	1.50	.60	.15
☐ 92	Lou Whitaker	.60	.25	.06
☐ 93	Milt Wilcox	.09	.04	.01
☐ 94	Glenn Wilson	.09	.04	.01
☐ 95	John Wockenfuss	.09	.04	.01
☐ 96	Dusty Baker	.15	.06	.01
☐ 97	Joe Beckwith	.09	.04	.01
☐ 98	Greg Brock	.15	.06	.01
☐ 99	Jack Fimple	.09	.04	.01
☐ 100	Pedro Guerrero	.40	.16	.04
☐ 101	Rick Honeycutt	.09	.04	.01
☐ 102	Burt Hooton	.09	.04	.01
☐ 103	Steve Howe	.09	.04	.01
☐ 104	Ken Landreaux	.09	.04	.01
☐ 105	Mike Marshall	.15	.06	.01
☐ 106	Rick Monday	.09	.04	.01
☐ 107	Jose Morales	.09	.04	.01
☐ 108	Tom Niedenfuer	.09	.04	.01
☐ 109	Alejandro Pena	.60	.25	.06
☐ 110	Jerry Reuss	.09	.04	.01
☐ 111	Bill Russell	.15	.06	.01
☐ 112	Steve Sax	.50	.20	.05
☐ 113	Mike Scioscia	.15	.06	.01
☐ 114	Derrel Thomas	.09	.04	.01
☐ 115	Fernando Valenzuela	.35	.15	.03
☐ 116	Bob Welch	.35	.15	.03
☐ 117	Steve Yeager	.09	.04	.01
☐ 118	Pat Zachry	.09	.04	.01
☐ 119	Don Baylor	.15	.06	.01
☐ 120	Bert Campaneris	.15	.06	.01
☐ 121	Rick Cerone	.09	.04	.01
☐ 122	Ray Fontenot	.09	.04	.01
☐ 123	George Frazier	.09	.04	.01
☐ 124	Oscar Gamble	.09	.04	.01
☐ 125	Goose Gossage	.25	.10	.02
☐ 126	Ken Griffey	.25	.10	.02
☐ 127	Ron Guidry	.35	.15	.03
☐ 128	Jay Howell	.20	.08	.02
☐ 129	Steve Kemp	.09	.04	.01
☐ 130	Matt Keough	.09	.04	.01
☐ 131	Don Mattingly	38.00	17.00	4.00
☐ 132	John Montefusco	.09	.04	.01
☐ 133	Omar Moreno	.09	.04	.01
☐ 134	Dale Murray	.09	.04	.01
☐ 135	Graig Nettles	.20	.08	.02
☐ 136	Lou Piniella	.15	.06	.01
☐ 137	Willie Randolph	.15	.06	.01
☐ 138	Shane Rawley	.09	.04	.01
☐ 139	Dave Righetti	.30	.12	.03
☐ 140	Andre Robertson	.09	.04	.01
☐ 141	Bob Shirley	.09	.04	.01
☐ 142	Roy Smalley	.09	.04	.01
☐ 143	Dave Winfield	1.75	.70	.17
☐ 144	Butch Wynegar	.09	.04	.01
☐ 145	Jim Acker	.15	.06	.01
☐ 146	Doyle Alexander	.09	.04	.01
☐ 147	Jesse Barfield	.25	.10	.02
☐ 148	Jorge Bell	2.00	.80	.20
☐ 149	Barry Bonnell	.09	.04	.01
☐ 150	Jim Clancy	.09	.04	.01
☐ 151	Dave Collins	.09	.04	.01
☐ 152	Tony Fernandez	4.00	1.75	.40
☐ 153	Damaso Garcia	.09	.04	.01
☐ 154	Dave Geisel	.09	.04	.01
☐ 155	Jim Gott	.20	.08	.02
☐ 156	Alfredo Griffin	.09	.04	.01
☐ 157	Garth Iorg	.09	.04	.01
☐ 158	Roy Lee Jackson	.09	.04	.01
☐ 159	Cliff Johnson	.09	.04	.01
☐ 160	Luis Leal	.09	.04	.01
☐ 161	Buck Martinez	.09	.04	.01
☐ 162	Joey McLaughlin	.09	.04	.01
☐ 163	Randy Moffitt	.09	.04	.01
☐ 164	Lloyd Moseby	.15	.06	.01
☐ 165	Rance Mulliniks	.09	.04	.01
☐ 166	Jorge Orta	.09	.04	.01
☐ 167	Dave Stieb	.35	.15	.03
☐ 168	Willie Upshaw	.09	.04	.01
☐ 169	Ernie Whitt	.09	.04	.01
☐ 170	Len Barker	.09	.04	.01
☐ 171	Steve Bedrosian	.15	.06	.01
☐ 172	Bruce Benedict	.09	.04	.01
☐ 173	Brett Butler	.45	.18	.04
☐ 174	Rick Camp	.09	.04	.01
☐ 175	Chris Chambliss	.15	.06	.01
☐ 176	Ken Dayley	.09	.04	.01
☐ 177	Pete Falcone	.09	.04	.01
☐ 178	Terry Forster	.15	.06	.01
☐ 179	Gene Garber	.09	.04	.01
☐ 180	Terry Harper	.09	.04	.01
☐ 181	Bob Horner	.15	.06	.01
☐ 182	Glenn Hubbard	.09	.04	.01
☐ 183	Randy Johnson	.09	.04	.01
☐ 184	Craig McMurtry	.09	.04	.01
☐ 185	Donnie Moore	.09	.04	.01
☐ 186	Dale Murphy	1.50	.60	.15
☐ 187	Phil Niekro	.60	.25	.06
☐ 188	Pascual Perez	.20	.08	.02
☐ 189	Biff Pocoroba	.09	.04	.01
☐ 190	Rafael Ramirez	.09	.04	.01
☐ 191	Jerry Royster	.09	.04	.01
☐ 192	Claudell Washington	.09	.04	.01
☐ 193	Bob Watson	.09	.04	.01
☐ 194	Jerry Augustine	.09	.04	.01
☐ 195	Mark Brouhard	.09	.04	.01
☐ 196	Mike Caldwell	.09	.04	.01
☐ 197	Tom Candiotti	.75	.30	.07
☐ 198	Cecil Cooper	.15	.06	.01
☐ 199	Rollie Fingers	.50	.20	.05
☐ 200	Jim Gantner	.09	.04	.01
☐ 201	Bob L. Gibson	.09	.04	.01
☐ 202	Moose Haas	.09	.04	.01
☐ 203	Roy Howell	.09	.04	.01
☐ 204	Pete Ladd	.09	.04	.01
☐ 205	Rick Manning	.09	.04	.01
☐ 206	Bob McClure	.09	.04	.01
☐ 207	Paul Molitor UER	.50	.20	.05
	('83 stats should say			
	.270 BA and 608 AB)			
☐ 208	Don Money	.09	.04	.01
☐ 209	Charlie Moore	.09	.04	.01
☐ 210	Ben Oglivie	.09	.04	.01
☐ 211	Chuck Porter	.09	.04	.01
☐ 212	Ed Romero	.09	.04	.01
☐ 213	Ted Simmons	.15	.06	.01
☐ 214	Jim Slaton	.09	.04	.01
☐ 215	Don Sutton	.60	.25	.06
☐ 216	Tom Tellmann	.09	.04	.01
☐ 217	Pete Vuckovich	.09	.04	.01
☐ 218	Ned Yost	.09	.04	.01
☐ 219	Robin Yount	3.25	1.35	.32
☐ 220	Alan Ashby	.09	.04	.01
☐ 221	Kevin Bass	.15	.06	.01
☐ 222	Jose Cruz	.15	.06	.01
☐ 223	Bill Dawley	.09	.04	.01
☐ 224	Frank DiPino	.09	.04	.01
☐ 225	Bill Doran	.60	.25	.06
☐ 226	Phil Garner	.15	.06	.01
☐ 227	Art Howe	.15	.06	.01
☐ 228	Bob Knepper	.09	.04	.01
☐ 229	Ray Knight	.15	.06	.01
☐ 230	Frank LaCorte	.09	.04	.01
☐ 231	Mike LaCoss	.09	.04	.01
☐ 232	Mike Madden	.09	.04	.01
☐ 233	Jerry Mumphrey	.09	.04	.01
☐ 234	Joe Niekro	.15	.06	.01
☐ 235	Terry Puhl	.09	.04	.01
☐ 236	Luis Pujols	.09	.04	.01
☐ 237	Craig Reynolds	.09	.04	.01
☐ 238	Vern Ruhle	.09	.04	.01
☐ 239	Nolan Ryan	11.00	5.00	1.35
☐ 240	Mike Scott	.25	.10	.02
☐ 241	Tony Scott	.09	.04	.01
☐ 242	Dave Smith	.09	.04	.01
☐ 243	Dickie Thon	.15	.06	.01
☐ 244	Denny Walling	.09	.04	.01
☐ 245	Dale Berra	.09	.04	.01
☐ 246	Jim Bibby	.09	.04	.01
☐ 247	John Candelaria	.09	.04	.01
☐ 248	Jose DeLeon	.35	.15	.03
☐ 249	Mike Easler	.09	.04	.01
☐ 250	Cecilio Guante	.09	.04	.01
☐ 251	Richie Hebner	.09	.04	.01
☐ 252	Lee Lacy	.09	.04	.01
☐ 253	Bill Madlock	.15	.06	.01
☐ 254	Milt May	.09	.04	.01
☐ 255	Lee Mazzilli	.09	.04	.01
☐ 256	Larry McWilliams	.09	.04	.01
☐ 257	Jim Morrison	.09	.04	.01
☐ 258	Dave Parker	.75	.30	.07
☐ 259	Tony Pena	.20	.08	.02
☐ 260	Johnny Ray	.09	.04	.01
☐ 261	Rick Rhoden	.09	.04	.01
☐ 262	Don Robinson	.09	.04	.01
☐ 263	Manny Sarmiento	.09	.04	.01
☐ 264	Rod Scurry	.09	.04	.01
☐ 265	Kent Tekulve	.09	.04	.01
☐ 266	Gene Tenace	.09	.04	.01
☐ 267	Jason Thompson	.09	.04	.01
☐ 268	Lee Tunnell	.09	.04	.01
☐ 269	Marvell Wynne	.15	.06	.01
☐ 270	Ray Burris	.09	.04	.01
☐ 271	Gary Carter	.75	.30	.07

☐ 272	Warren Cromartie	.09	.04	.01
☐ 273	Andre Dawson	2.50	1.00	.25
☐ 274	Doug Flynn	.09	.04	.01
☐ 275	Terry Francona	.09	.04	.01
☐ 276	Bill Gullickson	.15	.06	.01
☐ 277	Bob James	.09	.04	.01
☐ 278	Charlie Lea	.09	.04	.01
☐ 279	Bryan Little	.09	.04	.01
☐ 280	Al Oliver	.15	.06	.01
☐ 281	Tim Raines	.75	.30	.07
☐ 282	Bobby Ramos	.09	.04	.01
☐ 283	Jeff Reardon	.65	.25	.06
☐ 284	Steve Rogers	.09	.04	.01
☐ 285	Scott Sanderson	.15	.06	.01
☐ 286	Dan Schatzeder	.09	.04	.01
☐ 287	Bryn Smith	.15	.06	.01
☐ 288	Chris Speier	.09	.04	.01
☐ 289	Manny Trillo	.09	.04	.01
☐ 290	Mike Vail	.09	.04	.01
☐ 291	Tim Wallach	.25	.10	.02
☐ 292	Chris Welsh	.09	.04	.01
☐ 293	Jim Wohlford	.09	.04	.01
☐ 294	Kurt Bevacqua	.09	.04	.01
☐ 295	Juan Bonilla	.09	.04	.01
☐ 296	Bobby Brown	.09	.04	.01
☐ 297	Luis DeLeon	.09	.04	.01
☐ 298	Dave Dravecky	.20	.08	.02
☐ 299	Tim Flannery	.09	.04	.01
☐ 300	Steve Garvey	.80	.35	.08
☐ 301	Tony Gwynn	9.00	4.00	.90
☐ 302	Andy Hawkins	.35	.15	.03
☐ 303	Ruppert Jones	.09	.04	.01
☐ 304	Terry Kennedy	.09	.04	.01
☐ 305	Tim Lollar	.09	.04	.01
☐ 306	Gary Lucas	.09	.04	.01
☐ 307	Kevin McReynolds	5.50	2.50	.55
☐ 308	Sid Monge	.09	.04	.01
☐ 309	Mario Ramirez	.09	.04	.01
☐ 310	Gene Richards	.09	.04	.01
☐ 311	Luis Salazar	.09	.04	.01
☐ 312	Eric Show	.15	.06	.01
☐ 313	Elias Sosa	.09	.04	.01
☐ 314	Garry Templeton	.15	.06	.01
☐ 315	Mark Thurmond	.09	.04	.01
☐ 316	Ed Whitson	.09	.04	.01
☐ 317	Alan Wiggins	.09	.04	.01
☐ 318	Neil Allen	.09	.04	.01
☐ 319	Joaquin Andujar	.15	.06	.01
☐ 320	Steve Braun	.09	.04	.01
☐ 321	Glenn Brummer	.09	.04	.01
☐ 322	Bob Forsch	.09	.04	.01
☐ 323	David Green	.09	.04	.01
☐ 324	George Hendrick	.09	.04	.01
☐ 325	Tom Herr	.15	.06	.01
☐ 326	Dane Iorg	.09	.04	.01
☐ 327	Jeff Lahti	.09	.04	.01
☐ 328	Dave LaPoint	.09	.04	.01
☐ 329	Willie McGee	.90	.40	.09
☐ 330	Ken Oberkfell	.09	.04	.01
☐ 331	Darrell Porter	.09	.04	.01
☐ 332	Jamie Quirk	.09	.04	.01
☐ 333	Mike Ramsey	.09	.04	.01
☐ 334	Floyd Rayford	.09	.04	.01
☐ 335	Lonnie Smith	.25	.10	.02
☐ 336	Ozzie Smith	2.00	.80	.20
☐ 337	John Stuper	.09	.04	.01
☐ 338	Bruce Sutter	.20	.08	.02
☐ 339	Andy Van Slyke UER	4.50	2.00	.45
	(Batting and throwing both wrong on card back)			
☐ 340	Dave Von Ohlen	.09	.04	.01
☐ 341	Willie Aikens	.09	.04	.01
☐ 342	Mike Armstrong	.09	.04	.01
☐ 343	Bud Black	.15	.06	.01
☐ 344	George Brett	3.00	1.25	.30
☐ 345	Onix Concepcion	.09	.04	.01
☐ 346	Keith Creel	.09	.04	.01
☐ 347	Larry Gura	.09	.04	.01
☐ 348	Don Hood	.09	.04	.01
☐ 349	Dennis Leonard	.09	.04	.01
☐ 350	Hal McRae	.15	.06	.01
☐ 351	Amos Otis	.15	.06	.01
☐ 352	Gaylord Perry	.60	.25	.06
☐ 353	Greg Pryor	.09	.04	.01
☐ 354	Dan Quisenberry	.20	.08	.02
☐ 355	Steve Renko	.09	.04	.01
☐ 356	Leon Roberts	.09	.04	.01
☐ 357	Pat Sheridan	.15	.06	.01
☐ 358	Joe Simpson	.09	.04	.01
☐ 359	Don Slaught	.15	.06	.01
☐ 360	Paul Splittorff	.09	.04	.01
☐ 361	U.L. Washington	.09	.04	.01
☐ 362	John Wathan	.09	.04	.01
☐ 363	Frank White	.09	.04	.01

☐ 364	Willie Wilson	.15	.06	.01
☐ 365	Jim Barr	.09	.04	.01
☐ 366	Dave Bergman	.09	.04	.01
☐ 367	Fred Breining	.09	.04	.01
☐ 368	Bob Brenly	.09	.04	.01
☐ 369	Jack Clark	.30	.12	.03
☐ 370	Chili Davis	.40	.16	.04
☐ 371	Mark Davis	.20	.08	.02
☐ 372	Darrell Evans	.15	.06	.01
☐ 373	Atlee Hammaker	.09	.04	.01
☐ 374	Mike Krukow	.09	.04	.01
☐ 375	Duane Kuiper	.09	.04	.01
☐ 376	Bill Laskey	.09	.04	.01
☐ 377	Gary Lavelle	.09	.04	.01
☐ 378	Johnnie LeMaster	.09	.04	.01
☐ 379	Jeff Leonard	.09	.04	.01
☐ 380	Randy Lerch	.09	.04	.01
☐ 381	Renie Martin	.09	.04	.01
☐ 382	Andy McGaffigan	.09	.04	.01
☐ 383	Greg Minton	.09	.04	.01
☐ 384	Tom O'Malley	.09	.04	.01
☐ 385	Max Venable	.09	.04	.01
☐ 386	Brad Wellman	.09	.04	.01
☐ 387	Joel Youngblood	.09	.04	.01
☐ 388	Gary Allenson	.09	.04	.01
☐ 389	Luis Aponte	.09	.04	.01
☐ 390	Tony Armas	.09	.04	.01
☐ 391	Doug Bird	.09	.04	.01
☐ 392	Wade Boggs	10.00	4.50	1.25
☐ 393	Dennis Boyd	.35	.15	.03
☐ 394	Mike Brown UER	.09	.04	.01
	(Red Sox pitcher, shown with record of 31-104)			
☐ 395	Mark Clear	.09	.04	.01
☐ 396	Dennis Eckersley	.80	.35	.08
☐ 397	Dwight Evans	.35	.15	.03
☐ 398	Rich Gedman	.09	.04	.01
☐ 399	Glenn Hoffman	.09	.04	.01
☐ 400	Bruce Hurst	.20	.08	.02
☐ 401	John Henry Johnson	.09	.04	.01
☐ 402	Ed Jurak	.09	.04	.01
☐ 403	Rick Miller	.09	.04	.01
☐ 404	Jeff Newman	.09	.04	.01
☐ 405	Reid Nichols	.09	.04	.01
☐ 406	Bob Ojeda	.15	.06	.01
☐ 407	Jerry Remy	.09	.04	.01
☐ 408	Jim Rice	.25	.10	.02
☐ 409	Bob Stanley	.09	.04	.01
☐ 410	Dave Stapleton	.09	.04	.01
☐ 411	John Tudor	.20	.08	.02
☐ 412	Carl Yastrzemski	2.00	.80	.20
☐ 413	Buddy Bell	.15	.06	.01
☐ 414	Larry Biittner	.09	.04	.01
☐ 415	John Butcher	.09	.04	.01
☐ 416	Danny Darwin	.09	.04	.01
☐ 417	Bucky Dent	.15	.06	.01
☐ 418	Dave Hostetler	.09	.04	.01
☐ 419	Charlie Hough	.09	.04	.01
☐ 420	Bobby Johnson	.09	.04	.01
☐ 421	Odell Jones	.09	.04	.01
☐ 422	Jon Matlack	.09	.04	.01
☐ 423	Pete O'Brien	.60	.25	.06
☐ 424	Larry Parrish	.09	.04	.01
☐ 425	Mickey Rivers	.09	.04	.01
☐ 426	Billy Sample	.09	.04	.01
☐ 427	Dave Schmidt	.09	.04	.01
☐ 428	Mike Smithson	.09	.04	.01
☐ 429	Bill Stein	.09	.04	.01
☐ 430	Dave Stewart	1.00	.40	.10
☐ 431	Jim Sundberg	.09	.04	.01
☐ 432	Frank Tanana	.15	.06	.01
☐ 433	Dave Tobik	.09	.04	.01
☐ 434	Wayne Tolleson	.09	.04	.01
☐ 435	George Wright	.09	.04	.01
☐ 436	Bill Almon	.09	.04	.01
☐ 437	Keith Atherton	.09	.04	.01
☐ 438	Dave Beard	.09	.04	.01
☐ 439	Tom Burgmeier	.09	.04	.01
☐ 440	Jeff Burroughs	.09	.04	.01
☐ 441	Chris Codiroli	.09	.04	.01
☐ 442	Tim Conroy	.09	.04	.01
☐ 443	Mike Davis	.09	.04	.01
☐ 444	Wayne Gross	.09	.04	.01
☐ 445	Garry Hancock	.09	.04	.01
☐ 446	Mike Heath	.09	.04	.01
☐ 447	Rickey Henderson	10.00	4.50	1.25
☐ 448	Donnie Hill	.15	.06	.01
☐ 449	Bob Kearney	.09	.04	.01
☐ 450	Bill Krueger	.09	.04	.01
☐ 451	Rick Langford	.09	.04	.01
☐ 452	Carney Lansford	.15	.06	.01
☐ 453	Dave Lopes	.15	.06	.01
☐ 454	Steve McCatty	.09	.04	.01

#	Player			
☐ 455	Dan Meyer	.09	.04	.01
☐ 456	Dwayne Murphy	.09	.04	.01
☐ 457	Mike Norris	.09	.04	.01
☐ 458	Ricky Peters	.09	.04	.01
☐ 459	Tony Phillips	.75	.30	.07
☐ 460	Tom Underwood	.09	.04	.01
☐ 461	Mike Warren	.09	.04	.01
☐ 462	Johnny Bench	2.00	.80	.20
☐ 463	Bruce Berenyi	.09	.04	.01
☐ 464	Dann Bilardello	.09	.04	.01
☐ 465	Cesar Cedeno	.15	.06	.01
☐ 466	Dave Concepcion	.20	.08	.02
☐ 467	Dan Driessen	.09	.04	.01
☐ 468	Nick Esasky	.25	.10	.02
☐ 469	Rich Gale	.09	.04	.01
☐ 470	Ben Hayes	.09	.04	.01
☐ 471	Paul Householder	.09	.04	.01
☐ 472	Tom Hume	.09	.04	.01
☐ 473	Alan Knicely	.09	.04	.01
☐ 474	Eddie Milner	.09	.04	.01
☐ 475	Ron Oester	.09	.04	.01
☐ 476	Kelly Paris	.09	.04	.01
☐ 477	Frank Pastore	.09	.04	.01
☐ 478	Ted Power	.15	.06	.01
☐ 479	Joe Price	.09	.04	.01
☐ 480	Charlie Puleo	.09	.04	.01
☐ 481	Gary Redus	.40	.16	.04
☐ 482	Bill Scherrer	.09	.04	.01
☐ 483	Mario Soto	.09	.04	.01
☐ 484	Alex Trevino	.09	.04	.01
☐ 485	Duane Walker	.09	.04	.01
☐ 486	Larry Bowa	.15	.06	.01
☐ 487	Warren Brusstar	.09	.04	.01
☐ 488	Bill Buckner	.15	.06	.01
☐ 489	Bill Campbell	.09	.04	.01
☐ 490	Ron Cey	.15	.06	.01
☐ 491	Jody Davis	.09	.04	.01
☐ 492	Leon Durham	.09	.04	.01
☐ 493	Mel Hall	.65	.25	.06
☐ 494	Ferguson Jenkins	.60	.25	.06
☐ 495	Jay Johnstone	.15	.06	.01
☐ 496	Craig Lefferts	.40	.16	.04
☐ 497	Carmelo Martinez	.20	.08	.02
☐ 498	Jerry Morales	.09	.04	.01
☐ 499	Keith Moreland	.09	.04	.01
☐ 500	Dickie Noles	.09	.04	.01
☐ 501	Mike Proly	.09	.04	.01
☐ 502	Chuck Rainey	.09	.04	.01
☐ 503	Dick Ruthven	.09	.04	.01
☐ 504	Ryne Sandberg	18.00	7.50	2.50
☐ 505	Lee Smith	.65	.25	.06
☐ 506	Steve Trout	.09	.04	.01
☐ 507	Gary Woods	.09	.04	.01
☐ 508	Juan Beniquez	.09	.04	.01
☐ 509	Bob Boone	.15	.06	.01
☐ 510	Rick Burleson	.09	.04	.01
☐ 511	Rod Carew	2.00	.80	.20
☐ 512	Bobby Clark	.09	.04	.01
☐ 513	John Curtis	.09	.04	.01
☐ 514	Doug DeCinces	.15	.06	.01
☐ 515	Brian Downing	.15	.06	.01
☐ 516	Tim Foli	.09	.04	.01
☐ 517	Ken Forsch	.09	.04	.01
☐ 518	Bobby Grich	.15	.06	.01
☐ 519	Andy Hassler	.09	.04	.01
☐ 520	Reggie Jackson	2.50	1.00	.25
☐ 521	Ron Jackson	.09	.04	.01
☐ 522	Tommy John	.25	.10	.02
☐ 523	Bruce Kison	.09	.04	.01
☐ 524	Steve Lubratich	.09	.04	.01
☐ 525	Fred Lynn	.25	.10	.02
☐ 526	Gary Pettis	.30	.12	.03
☐ 527	Luis Sanchez	.09	.04	.01
☐ 528	Daryl Sconiers	.09	.04	.01
☐ 529	Ellis Valentine	.09	.04	.01
☐ 530	Rob Wilfong	.09	.04	.01
☐ 531	Mike Witt	.09	.04	.01
☐ 532	Geoff Zahn	.09	.04	.01
☐ 533	Bud Anderson	.09	.04	.01
☐ 534	Chris Bando	.09	.04	.01
☐ 535	Alan Bannister	.09	.04	.01
☐ 536	Bert Blyleven	.35	.15	.03
☐ 537	Tom Brennan	.09	.04	.01
☐ 538	Jamie Easterly	.09	.04	.01
☐ 539	Juan Eichelberger	.09	.04	.01
☐ 540	Jim Essian	.09	.04	.01
☐ 541	Mike Fischlin	.09	.04	.01
☐ 542	Julio Franco	4.00	1.75	.40
☐ 543	Mike Hargrove	.09	.04	.01
☐ 544	Toby Harrah	.09	.04	.01
☐ 545	Ron Hassey	.09	.04	.01
☐ 546	Neal Heaton	.25	.10	.02
☐ 547	Bake McBride	.09	.04	.01
☐ 548	Broderick Perkins	.09	.04	.01
☐ 549	Lary Sorensen	.09	.04	.01
☐ 550	Dan Spillner	.09	.04	.01
☐ 551	Rick Sutcliffe	.15	.06	.01
☐ 552	Pat Tabler	.15	.06	.01
☐ 553	Gorman Thomas	.15	.06	.01
☐ 554	Andre Thornton	.09	.04	.01
☐ 555	George Vukovich	.09	.04	.01
☐ 556	Darrell Brown	.09	.04	.01
☐ 557	Tom Brunansky	.25	.10	.02
☐ 558	Randy Bush	.20	.08	.02
☐ 559	Bobby Castillo	.09	.04	.01
☐ 560	John Castino	.09	.04	.01
☐ 561	Ron Davis	.09	.04	.01
☐ 562	Dave Engle	.09	.04	.01
☐ 563	Lenny Faedo	.09	.04	.01
☐ 564	Pete Filson	.09	.04	.01
☐ 565	Gary Gaetti	.30	.12	.03
☐ 566	Mickey Hatcher	.09	.04	.01
☐ 567	Kent Hrbek	.60	.25	.06
☐ 568	Rusty Kuntz	.09	.04	.01
☐ 569	Tim Laudner	.09	.04	.01
☐ 570	Rick Lysander	.09	.04	.01
☐ 571	Bobby Mitchell	.09	.04	.01
☐ 572	Ken Schrom	.09	.04	.01
☐ 573	Ray Smith	.09	.04	.01
☐ 574	Tim Teufel	.35	.15	.03
☐ 575	Frank Viola	1.50	.60	.15
☐ 576	Gary Ward	.09	.04	.01
☐ 577	Ron Washington	.09	.04	.01
☐ 578	Len Whitehouse	.09	.04	.01
☐ 579	Al Williams	.09	.04	.01
☐ 580	Bob Bailor	.09	.04	.01
☐ 581	Mark Bradley	.09	.04	.01
☐ 582	Hubie Brooks	.25	.10	.02
☐ 583	Carlos Diaz	.09	.04	.01
☐ 584	George Foster	.25	.10	.02
☐ 585	Brian Giles	.09	.04	.01
☐ 586	Danny Heep	.09	.04	.01
☐ 587	Keith Hernandez	.35	.15	.03
☐ 588	Ron Hodges	.09	.04	.01
☐ 589	Scott Holman	.09	.04	.01
☐ 590	Dave Kingman	.20	.08	.02
☐ 591	Ed Lynch	.09	.04	.01
☐ 592	Jose Oquendo	.30	.12	.03
☐ 593	Jesse Orosco	.09	.04	.01
☐ 594	Junior Ortiz	.15	.06	.01
☐ 595	Tom Seaver	3.50	1.50	.35
☐ 596	Doug Sisk	.09	.04	.01
☐ 597	Rusty Staub	.15	.06	.01
☐ 598	John Stearns	.09	.04	.01
☐ 599	Darryl Strawberry	40.00	18.00	6.00
☐ 600	Craig Swan	.09	.04	.01
☐ 601	Walt Terrell	.25	.10	.02
☐ 602	Mike Torrez	.09	.04	.01
☐ 603	Mookie Wilson	.15	.06	.01
☐ 604	Jamie Allen	.09	.04	.01
☐ 605	Jim Beattie	.09	.04	.01
☐ 606	Tony Bernazard	.09	.04	.01
☐ 607	Manny Castillo	.09	.04	.01
☐ 608	Bill Caudill	.09	.04	.01
☐ 609	Bryan Clark	.09	.04	.01
☐ 610	Al Cowens	.09	.04	.01
☐ 611	Dave Henderson	.75	.30	.07
☐ 612	Steve Henderson	.09	.04	.01
☐ 613	Orlando Mercado	.09	.04	.01
☐ 614	Mike Moore	.25	.10	.02
☐ 615	Ricky Nelson UER (Jamie Nelson's stats on back)	.15	.06	.01
☐ 616	Spike Owen	.35	.15	.03
☐ 617	Pat Putnam	.09	.04	.01
☐ 618	Ron Roenicke	.09	.04	.01
☐ 619	Mike Stanton	.09	.04	.01
☐ 620	Bob Stoddard	.09	.04	.01
☐ 621	Rick Sweet	.09	.04	.01
☐ 622	Roy Thomas	.09	.04	.01
☐ 623	Ed VandeBerg	.09	.04	.01
☐ 624	Matt Young	.15	.06	.01
☐ 625	Richie Zisk	.09	.04	.01
☐ 626	Fred Lynn 1982 AS Game RB	.15	.06	.01
☐ 627	Manny Trillo 1983 AS Game RB	.09	.04	.01
☐ 628	Steve Garvey NL Iron Man	.30	.12	.03
☐ 629	Rod Carew AL Batting Runner-Up	.50	.20	.05
☐ 630	Wade Boggs AL Batting Champion	1.00	.40	.10
☐ 631	Tim Raines: Letting Go of the Raines	.45	.18	.04
☐ 632	Al Oliver Double Trouble	.15	.06	.01
☐ 633	Steve Sax AS Second Base	.15	.06	.01

☐ 634	Dickie Thon AS Shortstop	.15	.06	.01
☐ 635	Ace Firemen Dan Quisenberry and Tippy Martinez	.15	.06	.01
☐ 636	Reds Reunited Joe Morgan Pete Rose Tony Perez	.60	.25	.06
☐ 637	Backstop Stars Lance Parrish Bob Boone	.15	.06	.01
☐ 638	Geo.Brett and G.Perry Pine Tar 7/24/83	.75	.30	.07
☐ 639	1983 No Hitters Dave Righetti Mike Warren Bob Forsch	.15	.06	.01
☐ 640	Bench and Yaz Retiring Superstars	2.50	1.00	.25
☐ 641	Gaylord Perry Going Out In Style	.30	.12	.03
☐ 642	Steve Carlton 300 Club and Strikeout Record	.50	.20	.05
☐ 643	Altobelli and Owens WS Managers	.09	.04	.01
☐ 644	Rick Dempsey World Series MVP	.09	.04	.01
☐ 645	Mike Boddicker WS Rookie Winner	.15	.06	.01
☐ 646	Scott McGregor WS Clincher	.09	.04	.01
☐ 647	CL: Orioles/Royals	.18	.02	.00
☐ 648	CL: Phillies/Giants	.18	.02	.00
☐ 649	CL: White Sox/Red Sox	.18	.02	.00
☐ 650	CL: Tigers/Rangers	.18	.02	.00
☐ 651	CL: Dodgers/A's	.18	.02	.00
☐ 652	CL: Yankees/Reds	.18	.02	.00
☐ 653	CL: Blue Jays/Cubs	.18	.02	.00
☐ 654	CL: Braves/Angels	.18	.02	.00
☐ 655	CL: Brewers/Indians	.18	.02	.00
☐ 656	CL: Astros/Twins	.18	.02	.00
☐ 657	CL: Pirates/Mets	.18	.02	.00
☐ 658	CL: Expos/Mariners	.18	.02	.00
☐ 659	CL: Padres/Specials	.18	.02	.00
☐ 660	CL: Cardinals/Teams	.18	.02	.00

1984 Fleer Update

The cards in this 132-card set measure 2 1/2" by 3 1/2". For the first time, the Fleer Gum Company issued a traded, extended, or update set. The purpose of the set was the same as the traded sets issued by Topps over the past four years, i.e., to portray players with their proper team for the current year and to portray rookies who were not in their regular issue. Like the Topps Traded sets of the past four years, the Fleer Update sets were distributed through hobby dealers only. The set was quite popular with collectors, and, apparently, the print run was relatively short, as the set was quickly in short supply and exhibited a rapid and dramatic price increase. The cards are numbered on the back with a U prefix; the order corresponds to the alphabetical order of the subjects' names. The key

(extended) rookie cards in this set are Roger Clemens, Alvin Davis, John Franco, Dwight Gooden, Jimmy Key, Mark Langston, Kirby Puckett, Jose Rijo, and Bret Saberhagen. Collectors are urged to be careful if purchasing single cards of Clemens, Darling, Gooden, Puckett, Rose, or Saberhagen as these specific cards have been illegally reprinted. These fakes are blurry when compared to the real thing.

		MINT	EXC	G-VG
COMPLETE SET (132)		625.00	250.00	75.00
COMMON PLAYER (1-132)		.30	.12	.03
☐ U1	Willie Aikens	.40	.16	.04
☐ U2	Luis Aponte	.30	.12	.03
☐ U3	Mark Bailey	.30	.12	.03
☐ U4	Bob Bailor	.30	.12	.03
☐ U5	Dusty Baker	.40	.16	.04
☐ U6	Steve Balboni	.40	.16	.04
☐ U7	Alan Bannister	.30	.12	.03
☐ U8	Marty Barrett	.60	.25	.06
☐ U9	Dave Beard	.30	.12	.03
☐ U10	Joe Beckwith	.30	.12	.03
☐ U11	Dave Bergman	.30	.12	.03
☐ U12	Tony Bernazard	.30	.12	.03
☐ U13	Bruce Bochte	.30	.12	.03
☐ U14	Barry Bonnell	.30	.12	.03
☐ U15	Phil Bradley	1.25	.50	.12
☐ U16	Fred Breining	.30	.12	.03
☐ U17	Mike Brown (Angels OF)	.30	.12	.03
☐ U18	Bill Buckner	.40	.16	.04
☐ U19	Ray Burris	.30	.12	.03
☐ U20	John Butcher	.30	.12	.03
☐ U21	Brett Butler	2.00	.80	.20
☐ U22	Enos Cabell	.30	.12	.03
☐ U23	Bill Campbell	.30	.12	.03
☐ U24	Bill Caudill	.30	.12	.03
☐ U25	Bobby Clark	.30	.12	.03
☐ U26	Bryan Clark	.30	.12	.03
☐ U27	Roger Clemens	250.00	110.00	37.50
☐ U28	Jaime Cocanower	.30	.12	.03
☐ U29	Ron Darling	6.00	2.50	.60
☐ U30	Alvin Davis	8.00	3.50	.80
☐ U31	Bob Dernier	.30	.12	.03
☐ U32	Carlos Diaz	.30	.12	.03
☐ U33	Mike Easler	.30	.12	.03
☐ U34	Dennis Eckersley	4.50	2.00	.45
☐ U35	Jim Essian	.40	.16	.04
☐ U36	Darrell Evans	.60	.25	.06
☐ U37	Mike Fitzgerald	.30	.12	.03
☐ U38	Tim Foli	.30	.12	.03
☐ U39	John Franco	9.00	4.00	.90
☐ U40	George Frazier	.30	.12	.03
☐ U41	Rich Gale	.30	.12	.03
☐ U42	Barbaro Garbey	.30	.12	.03
☐ U43	Dwight Gooden	120.00	55.00	18.00
☐ U44	Goose Gossage	1.00	.40	.10
☐ U45	Wayne Gross	.30	.12	.03
☐ U46	Mark Gubicza	4.00	1.75	.40
☐ U47	Jackie Gutierrez	.30	.12	.03
☐ U48	Toby Harrah	.40	.16	.04
☐ U49	Ron Hassey	.30	.12	.03
☐ U50	Richie Hebner	.30	.12	.03
☐ U51	Willie Hernandez	.40	.16	.04
☐ U52	Ed Hodge	.30	.12	.03
☐ U53	Ricky Horton	.40	.16	.04
☐ U54	Art Howe	.40	.16	.04
☐ U55	Dane Iorg	.30	.12	.03
☐ U56	Brook Jacoby	2.00	.80	.20
☐ U57	Dion James	.40	.16	.04
☐ U58	Mike Jeffcoat	.40	.16	.04
☐ U59	Ruppert Jones	.30	.12	.03
☐ U60	Bob Kearney	.30	.12	.03
☐ U61	Jimmy Key	10.00	4.50	1.25
☐ U62	Dave Kingman	.60	.25	.06
☐ U63	Brad Komminsk	.40	.16	.04
☐ U64	Jerry Koosman	.50	.20	.05
☐ U65	Wayne Krenchicki	.30	.12	.03
☐ U66	Rusty Kuntz	.30	.12	.03
☐ U67	Frank LaCorte	.30	.12	.03
☐ U68	Dennis Lamp	.30	.12	.03
☐ U69	Tito Landrum	.40	.16	.04
☐ U70	Mark Langston	22.00	9.50	3.15
☐ U71	Rick Leach	.30	.12	.03
☐ U72	Craig Lefferts	.60	.25	.06
☐ U73	Gary Lucas	.30	.12	.03
☐ U74	Jerry Martin	.30	.12	.03
☐ U75	Carmelo Martinez	.50	.20	.05
☐ U76	Mike Mason	.30	.12	.03
☐ U77	Gary Matthews	.40	.16	.04
☐ U78	Andy McGaffigan	.40	.16	.04
☐ U79	Joey McLaughlin	.30	.12	.03

☐ U80	Joe Morgan	5.00	2.25	.50
☐ U81	Darryl Motley	.30	.12	.03
☐ U82	Graig Nettles	.75	.30	.07
☐ U83	Phil Niekro	4.00	1.75	.40
☐ U84	Ken Oberkfell	.30	.12	.03
☐ U85	Al Oliver	.40	.16	.04
☐ U86	Jorge Orta	.30	.12	.03
☐ U87	Amos Otis	.40	.16	.04
☐ U88	Bob Owchinko	.30	.12	.03
☐ U89	Dave Parker	4.00	1.75	.40
☐ U90	Jack Perconte	.30	.12	.03
☐ U91	Tony Perez	4.50	2.00	.45
☐ U92	Gerald Perry	1.25	.50	.12
☐ U93	Kirby Puckett	225.00	100.00	33.00
☐ U94	Shane Rawley	.30	.12	.03
☐ U95	Floyd Rayford	.30	.12	.03
☐ U96	Ron Reed	.30	.12	.03
☐ U97	R.J. Reynolds	1.00	.40	.10
☐ U98	Gene Richards	.30	.12	.03
☐ U99	Jose Rijo	12.00	5.25	1.50
☐ U100	Jeff Robinson (Giants pitcher)	.40	.16	.04
☐ U101	Ron Romanick	.30	.12	.03
☐ U102	Pete Rose	17.00	7.25	2.50
☐ U103	Bret Saberhagen	45.00	20.00	5.00
☐ U104	Scott Sanderson	.60	.25	.06
☐ U105	Dick Schofield	1.00	.40	.10
☐ U106	Tom Seaver	21.00	9.00	3.00
☐ U107	Jim Slaton	.30	.12	.03
☐ U108	Mike Smithson	.30	.12	.03
☐ U109	Lary Sorensen	.30	.12	.03
☐ U110	Tim Stoddard	.30	.12	.03
☐ U111	Jeff Stone	.40	.16	.04
☐ U112	Champ Summers	.30	.12	.03
☐ U113	Jim Sundberg	.30	.12	.03
☐ U114	Rick Sutcliffe	.60	.25	.06
☐ U115	Craig Swan	.40	.16	.04
☐ U116	Derrel Thomas	.30	.12	.03
☐ U117	Gorman Thomas	.40	.16	.04
☐ U118	Alex Trevino	.30	.12	.03
☐ U119	Manny Trillo	.30	.12	.03
☐ U120	John Tudor	.50	.20	.05
☐ U121	Tom Underwood	.30	.12	.03
☐ U122	Mike Vail	.30	.12	.03
☐ U123	Tom Waddell	.30	.12	.03
☐ U124	Gary Ward	.30	.12	.03
☐ U125	Terry Whitfield	.30	.12	.03
☐ U126	Curtis Wilkerson	.30	.12	.03
☐ U127	Frank Williams	.30	.12	.03
☐ U128	Glenn Wilson	.30	.12	.03
☐ U129	John Wockenfuss	.30	.12	.03
☐ U130	Ned Yost	.30	.12	.03
☐ U131	Mike Young	.40	.16	.04
☐ U132	Checklist: 1-132	.30	.10	.02

1985 Fleer

The cards in this 660-card set measure 2 1/2" by 3 1/2". The 1985 Fleer set features fronts that contain the team logo along with the player's name and position. The borders enclosing the photo are color-coded to correspond to the player's team. In each case, the color is one of the standard colors of that team, e.g., orange for Baltimore, red for St. Louis, etc. The backs feature the same name, number, and statistics format that Fleer has been using over the past few years. The cards are ordered alphabetically within team. The teams are ordered based on their respective performance during the prior year, e.g., World Champion Detroit Tigers (1-25), NL Champion San Diego (26-48), Chicago Cubs (49-71), New York Mets (72-95), Toronto (96-119), New York Yankees (120-147), Boston (148-169), Baltimore (170-195), Kansas City (196-218), St. Louis (219-243), Philadelphia (244-269), Minnesota (270-292), California (293-317), Atlanta (318-342), Houston (343-365), Los Angeles (366-391), Montreal (392-413), Oakland (414-436), Cleveland (437-460), Pittsburgh (461-481), Seattle (482-505), Chicago White Sox (506-530), Cincinnati (531-554), Texas (555-575), Milwaukee (576-601), and San Francisco (602-625). Specials (626-643), Major League Prospects (644-653), and checklist cards (654-660) complete the set. The black and white photo on the reverse is included for the third straight year. This set is noted for containing the Rookie Cards of Roger Clemens, Alvin Davis, Eric Davis, Glenn Davis, Shawon Dunston, Dwight Gooden, Kelly Gruber, Orel Hershiser, Jimmy Key, Mark Langston, Terry Pendleton, Kirby Puckett, Jose Rijo, Bret Saberhagen, and Danny Tartabull.

		MINT	EXC	G-VG
COMPLETE SET (660)		180.00	80.00	27.00
COMMON PLAYER (1-660)		.07	.03	.01
☐ 1	Doug Bair	.12	.04	.01
☐ 2	Juan Berenguer	.07	.03	.01
☐ 3	Dave Bergman	.07	.03	.01
☐ 4	Tom Brookens	.07	.03	.01
☐ 5	Marty Castillo	.07	.03	.01
☐ 6	Darrell Evans	.12	.05	.01
☐ 7	Barbaro Garbey	.07	.03	.01
☐ 8	Kirk Gibson	.35	.15	.03
☐ 9	John Grubb	.07	.03	.01
☐ 10	Willie Hernandez	.10	.04	.01
☐ 11	Larry Herndon	.07	.03	.01
☐ 12	Howard Johnson	2.75	1.10	.27
☐ 13	Ruppert Jones	.07	.03	.01
☐ 14	Rusty Kuntz	.07	.03	.01
☐ 15	Chet Lemon	.07	.03	.01
☐ 16	Aurelio Lopez	.07	.03	.01
☐ 17	Sid Monge	.07	.03	.01
☐ 18	Jack Morris	.60	.25	.06
☐ 19	Lance Parrish	.25	.10	.02
☐ 20	Dan Petry	.07	.03	.01
☐ 21	Dave Rozema	.07	.03	.01
☐ 22	Bill Scherrer	.07	.03	.01
☐ 23	Alan Trammell	.60	.25	.06
☐ 24	Lou Whitaker	.40	.16	.04
☐ 25	Milt Wilcox	.07	.03	.01
☐ 26	Kurt Bevacqua	.07	.03	.01
☐ 27	Greg Booker	.07	.03	.01
☐ 28	Bobby Brown	.07	.03	.01
☐ 29	Luis DeLeon	.07	.03	.01
☐ 30	Dave Dravecky	.15	.06	.01
☐ 31	Tim Flannery	.07	.03	.01
☐ 32	Steve Garvey	.50	.20	.05
☐ 33	Goose Gossage	.15	.06	.01
☐ 34	Tony Gwynn	4.25	1.75	.42
☐ 35	Greg Harris	.07	.03	.01
☐ 36	Andy Hawkins	.10	.04	.01
☐ 37	Terry Kennedy	.07	.03	.01
☐ 38	Craig Lefferts	.10	.04	.01
☐ 39	Tim Lollar	.07	.03	.01
☐ 40	Carmelo Martinez	.07	.03	.01
☐ 41	Kevin McReynolds	.90	.40	.09
☐ 42	Graig Nettles	.12	.05	.01
☐ 43	Luis Salazar	.07	.03	.01
☐ 44	Eric Show	.07	.03	.01
☐ 45	Garry Templeton	.10	.04	.01
☐ 46	Mark Thurmond	.07	.03	.01
☐ 47	Ed Whitson	.07	.03	.01
☐ 48	Alan Wiggins	.07	.03	.01
☐ 49	Rich Bordi	.07	.03	.01
☐ 50	Larry Bowa	.10	.04	.01
☐ 51	Warren Brusstar	.07	.03	.01
☐ 52	Ron Cey	.10	.04	.01
☐ 53	Henry Cotto	.15	.06	.01
☐ 54	Jody Davis	.07	.03	.01
☐ 55	Bob Dernier	.07	.03	.01
☐ 56	Leon Durham	.07	.03	.01
☐ 57	Dennis Eckersley	.35	.15	.03
☐ 58	George Frazier	.07	.03	.01
☐ 59	Richie Hebner	.07	.03	.01
☐ 60	Dave Lopes	.10	.04	.01
☐ 61	Gary Matthews	.07	.03	.01
☐ 62	Keith Moreland	.07	.03	.01
☐ 63	Rick Reuschel	.12	.05	.01

#	Player			
☐ 64	Dick Ruthven	.07	.03	.01
☐ 65	Ryne Sandberg	6.50	2.75	.65
☐ 66	Scott Sanderson	.10	.04	.01
☐ 67	Lee Smith	.40	.16	.04
☐ 68	Tim Stoddard	.07	.03	.01
☐ 69	Rick Sutcliffe	.12	.05	.01
☐ 70	Steve Trout	.07	.03	.01
☐ 71	Gary Woods	.07	.03	.01
☐ 72	Wally Backman	.07	.03	.01
☐ 73	Bruce Berenyi	.07	.03	.01
☐ 74	Hubie Brooks UER	.15	.06	.01
	(Kelvin Chapman's			
	stats on card back)			
☐ 75	Kelvin Chapman	.07	.03	.01
☐ 76	Ron Darling	.35	.15	.03
☐ 77	Sid Fernandez	.50	.20	.05
☐ 78	Mike Fitzgerald	.07	.03	.01
☐ 79	George Foster	.15	.06	.01
☐ 80	Brent Gaff	.07	.03	.01
☐ 81	Ron Gardenhire	.07	.03	.01
☐ 82	Dwight Gooden	12.50	5.50	1.65
☐ 83	Tom Gorman	.07	.03	.01
☐ 84	Danny Heep	.07	.03	.01
☐ 85	Keith Hernandez	.25	.10	.02
☐ 86	Ray Knight	.10	.04	.01
☐ 87	Ed Lynch	.07	.03	.01
☐ 88	Jose Oquendo	.10	.04	.01
☐ 89	Jesse Orosco	.07	.03	.01
☐ 90	Rafael Santana	.12	.05	.01
☐ 91	Doug Sisk	.07	.03	.01
☐ 92	Rusty Staub	.12	.05	.01
☐ 93	Darryl Strawberry	12.50	5.50	1.65
☐ 94	Walt Terrell	.07	.03	.01
☐ 95	Mookie Wilson	.10	.04	.01
☐ 96	Jim Acker	.07	.03	.01
☐ 97	Willie Aikens	.07	.03	.01
☐ 98	Doyle Alexander	.07	.03	.01
☐ 99	Jesse Barfield	.17	.07	.01
☐ 100	George Bell	.90	.40	.09
☐ 101	Jim Clancy	.07	.03	.01
☐ 102	Dave Collins	.07	.03	.01
☐ 103	Tony Fernandez	.60	.25	.06
☐ 104	Damaso Garcia	.07	.03	.01
☐ 105	Jim Gott	.07	.03	.01
☐ 106	Alfredo Griffin	.07	.03	.01
☐ 107	Garth Iorg	.07	.03	.01
☐ 108	Roy Lee Jackson	.07	.03	.01
☐ 109	Cliff Johnson	.07	.03	.01
☐ 110	Jimmy Key	2.00	.80	.20
☐ 111	Dennis Lamp	.07	.03	.01
☐ 112	Rick Leach	.07	.03	.01
☐ 113	Luis Leal	.07	.03	.01
☐ 114	Buck Martinez	.07	.03	.01
☐ 115	Lloyd Moseby	.10	.04	.01
☐ 116	Rance Mulliniks	.07	.03	.01
☐ 117	Dave Stieb	.20	.08	.02
☐ 118	Willie Upshaw	.07	.03	.01
☐ 119	Ernie Whitt	.07	.03	.01
☐ 120	Mike Armstrong	.07	.03	.01
☐ 121	Don Baylor	.12	.05	.01
☐ 122	Marty Bystrom	.07	.03	.01
☐ 123	Rick Cerone	.07	.03	.01
☐ 124	Joe Cowley	.07	.03	.01
☐ 125	Brian Dayett	.07	.03	.01
☐ 126	Tim Foli	.07	.03	.01
☐ 127	Ray Fontenot	.07	.03	.01
☐ 128	Ken Griffey	.17	.07	.01
☐ 129	Ron Guidry	.20	.08	.02
☐ 130	Toby Harrah	.07	.03	.01
☐ 131	Jay Howell	.10	.04	.01
☐ 132	Steve Kemp	.07	.03	.01
☐ 133	Don Mattingly	10.00	4.50	1.25
☐ 134	Bobby Meacham	.07	.03	.01
☐ 135	John Montefusco	.07	.03	.01
☐ 136	Omar Moreno	.07	.03	.01
☐ 137	Dale Murray	.07	.03	.01
☐ 138	Phil Niekro	.30	.12	.03
☐ 139	Mike Pagliarulo	.60	.25	.06
☐ 140	Willie Randolph	.12	.05	.01
☐ 141	Dennis Rasmussen	.15	.06	.01
☐ 142	Dave Righetti	.15	.06	.01
☐ 143	Jose Rijo	2.50	1.00	.25
☐ 144	Andre Robertson	.07	.03	.01
☐ 145	Bob Shirley	.07	.03	.01
☐ 146	Dave Winfield	.80	.35	.08
☐ 147	Butch Wynegar	.07	.03	.01
☐ 148	Gary Allenson	.07	.03	.01
☐ 149	Tony Armas	.07	.03	.01
☐ 150	Marty Barrett	.10	.04	.01
☐ 151	Wade Boggs	5.00	2.25	.50
☐ 152	Dennis Boyd	.10	.04	.01
☐ 153	Bill Buckner	.10	.04	.01
☐ 154	Mark Clear	.07	.03	.01
☐ 155	Roger Clemens	37.50	16.00	4.00
☐ 156	Steve Crawford	.07	.03	.01
☐ 157	Mike Easler	.07	.03	.01
☐ 158	Dwight Evans	.20	.08	.02
☐ 159	Rich Gedman	.07	.03	.01
☐ 160	Jackie Gutierrez	.15	.06	.01
	(W.Boggs on deck)			
☐ 161	Bruce Hurst	.12	.05	.01
☐ 162	John Henry Johnson	.07	.03	.01
☐ 163	Rick Miller	.07	.03	.01
☐ 164	Reid Nichols	.07	.03	.01
☐ 165	Al Nipper	.07	.03	.01
☐ 166	Bob Ojeda	.10	.04	.01
☐ 167	Jerry Remy	.07	.03	.01
☐ 168	Jim Rice	.20	.08	.02
☐ 169	Bob Stanley	.07	.03	.01
☐ 170	Mike Boddicker	.07	.03	.01
☐ 171	Al Bumbry	.07	.03	.01
☐ 172	Todd Cruz	.07	.03	.01
☐ 173	Rich Dauer	.07	.03	.01
☐ 174	Storm Davis	.07	.03	.01
☐ 175	Rick Dempsey	.07	.03	.01
☐ 176	Jim Dwyer	.07	.03	.01
☐ 177	Mike Flanagan	.10	.04	.01
☐ 178	Dan Ford	.07	.03	.01
☐ 179	Wayne Gross	.07	.03	.01
☐ 180	John Lowenstein	.07	.03	.01
☐ 181	Dennis Martinez	.12	.05	.01
☐ 182	Tippy Martinez	.07	.03	.01
☐ 183	Scott McGregor	.07	.03	.01
☐ 184	Eddie Murray	1.25	.50	.12
☐ 185	Joe Nolan	.07	.03	.01
☐ 186	Floyd Rayford	.07	.03	.01
☐ 187	Cal Ripken	7.00	3.00	.70
☐ 188	Gary Roenicke	.07	.03	.01
☐ 189	Lenn Sakata	.07	.03	.01
☐ 190	John Shelby	.07	.03	.01
☐ 191	Ken Singleton	.10	.04	.01
☐ 192	Sammy Stewart	.07	.03	.01
☐ 193	Bill Swaggerty	.07	.03	.01
☐ 194	Tom Underwood	.07	.03	.01
☐ 195	Mike Young	.07	.03	.01
☐ 196	Steve Balboni	.07	.03	.01
☐ 197	Joe Beckwith	.07	.03	.01
☐ 198	Bud Black	.10	.04	.01
☐ 199	George Brett	1.50	.60	.15
☐ 200	Onix Concepcion	.07	.03	.01
☐ 201	Mark Gubicza	.75	.30	.07
☐ 202	Larry Gura	.07	.03	.01
☐ 203	Mark Huismann	.07	.03	.01
☐ 204	Dane Iorg	.07	.03	.01
☐ 205	Danny Jackson	.20	.08	.02
☐ 206	Charlie Leibrandt	.07	.03	.01
☐ 207	Hal McRae	.10	.04	.01
☐ 208	Darryl Motley	.07	.03	.01
☐ 209	Jorge Orta	.07	.03	.01
☐ 210	Greg Pryor	.07	.03	.01
☐ 211	Dan Quisenberry	.12	.05	.01
☐ 212	Bret Saberhagen	8.00	3.50	.80
☐ 213	Pat Sheridan	.07	.03	.01
☐ 214	Don Slaught	.07	.03	.01
☐ 215	U.L. Washington	.07	.03	.01
☐ 216	John Wathan	.07	.03	.01
☐ 217	Frank White	.07	.03	.01
☐ 218	Willie Wilson	.12	.05	.01
☐ 219	Neil Allen	.07	.03	.01
☐ 220	Joaquin Andujar	.10	.04	.01
☐ 221	Steve Braun	.07	.03	.01
☐ 222	Danny Cox	.07	.03	.01
☐ 223	Bob Forsch	.07	.03	.01
☐ 224	David Green	.07	.03	.01
☐ 225	George Hendrick	.07	.03	.01
☐ 226	Tom Herr	.10	.04	.01
☐ 227	Ricky Horton	.15	.06	.01
☐ 228	Art Howe	.10	.04	.01
☐ 229	Mike Jorgensen	.07	.03	.01
☐ 230	Kurt Kepshire	.07	.03	.01
☐ 231	Jeff Lahti	.07	.03	.01
☐ 232	Tito Landrum	.07	.03	.01
☐ 233	Dave LaPoint	.07	.03	.01
☐ 234	Willie McGee	.60	.25	.06
☐ 235	Tom Nieto	.07	.03	.01
☐ 236	Terry Pendleton	4.50	2.00	.45
☐ 237	Darrell Porter	.07	.03	.01
☐ 238	Dave Rucker	.07	.03	.01
☐ 239	Lonnie Smith	.15	.06	.01
☐ 240	Ozzie Smith	1.00	.40	.10
☐ 241	Bruce Sutter	.12	.05	.01
☐ 242	Andy Van Slyke UER	.90	.40	.09
	(Bats Right,			
	Throws Left)			
☐ 243	Dave Von Ohlen	.07	.03	.01
☐ 244	Larry Andersen	.07	.03	.01
☐ 245	Bill Campbell	.07	.03	.01
☐ 246	Steve Carlton	.90	.40	.09
☐ 247	Tim Corcoran	.07	.03	.01
☐ 248	Ivan DeJesus	.07	.03	.01

#	Player			
249	John Denny	.07	.03	.01
250	Bo Diaz	.07	.03	.01
251	Greg Gross	.07	.03	.01
252	Kevin Gross	.10	.04	.01
253	Von Hayes	.15	.06	.01
254	Al Holland	.07	.03	.01
255	Charles Hudson	.07	.03	.01
256	Jerry Koosman	.10	.04	.01
257	Joe Lefebvre	.07	.03	.01
258	Sixto Lezcano	.07	.03	.01
259	Garry Maddox	.07	.03	.01
260	Len Matuszek	.07	.03	.01
261	Tug McGraw	.12	.05	.01
262	Al Oliver	.10	.04	.01
263	Shane Rawley	.07	.03	.01
264	Juan Samuel	.50	.20	.05
265	Mike Schmidt	3.50	1.50	.35
266	Jeff Stone	.10	.04	.01
267	Ozzie Virgil	.07	.03	.01
268	Glenn Wilson	.07	.03	.01
269	John Wockenfuss	.07	.03	.01
270	Darrell Brown	.07	.03	.01
271	Tom Brunansky	.15	.06	.01
272	Randy Bush	.07	.03	.01
273	John Butcher	.07	.03	.01
274	Bobby Castillo	.07	.03	.01
275	Ron Davis	.07	.03	.01
276	Dave Engle	.07	.03	.01
277	Pete Filson	.07	.03	.01
278	Gary Gaetti	.15	.06	.01
279	Mickey Hatcher	.07	.03	.01
280	Ed Hodge	.07	.03	.01
281	Kent Hrbek	.35	.15	.03
282	Houston Jimenez	.07	.03	.01
283	Tim Laudner	.07	.03	.01
284	Rick Lysander	.07	.03	.01
285	Dave Meier	.07	.03	.01
286	Kirby Puckett	30.00	13.50	4.50
287	Pat Putnam	.07	.03	.01
288	Ken Schrom	.07	.03	.01
289	Mike Smithson	.07	.03	.01
290	Tim Teufel	.10	.04	.01
291	Frank Viola	.60	.25	.06
292	Ron Washington	.07	.03	.01
293	Don Aase	.07	.03	.01
294	Juan Beniquez	.07	.03	.01
295	Bob Boone	.12	.05	.01
296	Mike Brown	.07	.03	.01
	(Angels OF)			
297	Rod Carew	1.00	.40	.10
298	Doug Corbett	.07	.03	.01
299	Doug DeCinces	.10	.04	.01
300	Brian Downing	.10	.04	.01
301	Ken Forsch	.07	.03	.01
302	Bobby Grich	.10	.04	.01
303	Reggie Jackson	1.25	.50	.12
304	Tommy John	.17	.07	.01
305	Curt Kaufman	.07	.03	.01
306	Bruce Kison	.07	.03	.01
307	Fred Lynn	.17	.07	.01
308	Gary Pettis	.10	.04	.01
309	Ron Romanick	.07	.03	.01
310	Luis Sanchez	.07	.03	.01
311	Dick Schofield	.15	.06	.01
312	Daryl Sconiers	.07	.03	.01
313	Jim Slaton	.07	.03	.01
314	Derrel Thomas	.07	.03	.01
315	Rob Wilfong	.07	.03	.01
316	Mike Witt	.07	.03	.01
317	Geoff Zahn	.07	.03	.01
318	Len Barker	.07	.03	.01
319	Steve Bedrosian	.12	.05	.01
320	Bruce Benedict	.07	.03	.01
321	Rick Camp	.07	.03	.01
322	Chris Chambliss	.10	.04	.01
323	Jeff Dedmon	.07	.03	.01
324	Terry Forster	.07	.03	.01
325	Gene Garber	.07	.03	.01
326	Albert Hall	.07	.03	.01
327	Terry Harper	.07	.03	.01
328	Bob Horner	.10	.04	.01
329	Glenn Hubbard	.07	.03	.01
330	Randy Johnson	.07	.03	.01
331	Brad Komminsk	.07	.03	.01
332	Rick Mahler	.07	.03	.01
333	Craig McMurtry	.07	.03	.01
334	Donnie Moore	.07	.03	.01
335	Dale Murphy	.75	.30	.07
336	Ken Oberkfell	.07	.03	.01
337	Pascual Perez	.10	.04	.01
338	Gerald Perry	.15	.06	.01
339	Rafael Ramirez	.07	.03	.01
340	Jerry Royster	.07	.03	.01
341	Alex Trevino	.07	.03	.01
342	Claudell Washington	.07	.03	.01
343	Alan Ashby	.07	.03	.01
344	Mark Bailey	.07	.03	.01
345	Kevin Bass	.10	.04	.01
346	Enos Cabell	.07	.03	.01
347	Jose Cruz	.10	.04	.01
348	Bill Dawley	.07	.03	.01
349	Frank DiPino	.07	.03	.01
350	Bill Doran	.12	.05	.01
351	Phil Garner	.10	.04	.01
352	Bob Knepper	.07	.03	.01
353	Mike LaCoss	.07	.03	.01
354	Jerry Mumphrey	.07	.03	.01
355	Joe Niekro	.10	.04	.01
356	Terry Puhl	.07	.03	.01
357	Craig Reynolds	.07	.03	.01
358	Vern Ruhle	.07	.03	.01
359	Nolan Ryan	6.50	2.75	.65
360	Joe Sambito	.07	.03	.01
361	Mike Scott	.20	.08	.02
362	Dave Smith	.07	.03	.01
363	Julio Solano	.07	.03	.01
364	Dickie Thon	.07	.03	.01
365	Denny Walling	.07	.03	.01
366	Dave Anderson	.07	.03	.01
367	Bob Bailor	.07	.03	.01
368	Greg Brock	.07	.03	.01
369	Carlos Diaz	.07	.03	.01
370	Pedro Guerrero	.25	.10	.02
371	Orel Hershiser	5.00	2.25	.50
372	Rick Honeycutt	.07	.03	.01
373	Burt Hooton	.07	.03	.01
374	Ken Howell	.15	.06	.01
375	Ken Landreaux	.07	.03	.01
376	Candy Maldonado	.15	.06	.01
377	Mike Marshall	.10	.04	.01
378	Tom Niedenfuer	.07	.03	.01
379	Alejandro Pena	.07	.03	.01
380	Jerry Reuss	.07	.03	.01
381	R.J. Reynolds	.20	.08	.02
382	German Rivera	.07	.03	.01
383	Bill Russell	.07	.03	.01
384	Steve Sax	.35	.15	.03
385	Mike Scioscia	.10	.04	.01
386	Franklin Stubbs	.50	.20	.05
387	Fernando Valenzuela	.17	.07	.01
388	Bob Welch	.20	.08	.02
389	Terry Whitfield	.07	.03	.01
390	Steve Yeager	.07	.03	.01
391	Pat Zachry	.07	.03	.01
392	Fred Breining	.07	.03	.01
393	Gary Carter	.45	.18	.04
394	Andre Dawson	1.00	.40	.10
395	Miguel Dilone	.07	.03	.01
396	Dan Driessen	.07	.03	.01
397	Doug Flynn	.07	.03	.01
398	Terry Francona	.07	.03	.01
399	Bill Gullickson	.10	.04	.01
400	Bob James	.07	.03	.01
401	Charlie Lea	.07	.03	.01
402	Bryan Little	.07	.03	.01
403	Gary Lucas	.07	.03	.01
404	David Palmer	.07	.03	.01
405	Tim Raines	.40	.16	.04
406	Mike Ramsey	.07	.03	.01
407	Jeff Reardon	.40	.16	.04
408	Steve Rogers	.07	.03	.01
409	Dan Schatzeder	.07	.03	.01
410	Bryn Smith	.10	.04	.01
411	Mike Stenhouse	.07	.03	.01
412	Tim Wallach	.15	.06	.01
413	Jim Wohlford	.07	.03	.01
414	Bill Almon	.07	.03	.01
415	Keith Atherton	.07	.03	.01
416	Bruce Bochte	.07	.03	.01
417	Tom Burgmeier	.07	.03	.01
418	Ray Burris	.07	.03	.01
419	Bill Caudill	.07	.03	.01
420	Chris Codiroli	.07	.03	.01
421	Tim Conroy	.07	.03	.01
422	Mike Davis	.07	.03	.01
423	Jim Essian	.07	.03	.01
424	Mike Heath	.07	.03	.01
425	Rickey Henderson	5.00	2.25	.50
426	Donnie Hill	.07	.03	.01
427	Dave Kingman	.15	.06	.01
428	Bill Krueger	.07	.03	.01
429	Carney Lansford	.12	.05	.01
430	Steve McCatty	.07	.03	.01
431	Joe Morgan	.40	.16	.04
432	Dwayne Murphy	.07	.03	.01
433	Tony Phillips	.10	.04	.01
434	Lary Sorensen	.07	.03	.01
435	Mike Warren	.07	.03	.01
436	Curt Young	.15	.06	.01
437	Luis Aponte	.07	.03	.01

☐ 438	Chris Bando	.07	.03	.01
☐ 439	Tony Bernazard	.07	.03	.01
☐ 440	Bert Blyleven	.25	.10	.02
☐ 441	Brett Butler	.25	.10	.02
☐ 442	Ernie Camacho	.07	.03	.01
☐ 443	Joe Carter	6.50	2.75	.65
☐ 444	Carmelo Castillo	.07	.03	.01
☐ 445	Jamie Easterly	.07	.03	.01
☐ 446	Steve Farr	.35	.15	.03
☐ 447	Mike Fischlin	.07	.03	.01
☐ 448	Julio Franco	1.25	.50	.12
☐ 449	Mel Hall	.20	.08	.02
☐ 450	Mike Hargrove	.07	.03	.01
☐ 451	Neal Heaton	.10	.04	.01
☐ 452	Brook Jacoby	.17	.07	.01
☐ 453	Mike Jeffcoat	.07	.03	.01
☐ 454	Don Schulze	.10	.04	.01
☐ 455	Roy Smith	.07	.03	.01
☐ 456	Pat Tabler	.10	.04	.01
☐ 457	Andre Thornton	.10	.04	.01
☐ 458	George Vukovich	.07	.03	.01
☐ 459	Tom Waddell	.07	.03	.01
☐ 460	Jerry Willard	.07	.03	.01
☐ 461	Dale Berra	.07	.03	.01
☐ 462	John Candelaria	.07	.03	.01
☐ 463	Jose DeLeon	.07	.03	.01
☐ 464	Doug Frobel	.07	.03	.01
☐ 465	Cecilio Guante	.07	.03	.01
☐ 466	Brian Harper	.40	.16	.04
☐ 467	Lee Lacy	.07	.03	.01
☐ 468	Bill Madlock	.10	.04	.01
☐ 469	Lee Mazzilli	.07	.03	.01
☐ 470	Larry McWilliams	.07	.03	.01
☐ 471	Jim Morrison	.07	.03	.01
☐ 472	Tony Pena	.10	.04	.01
☐ 473	Johnny Ray	.07	.03	.01
☐ 474	Rick Rhoden	.07	.03	.01
☐ 475	Don Robinson	.07	.03	.01
☐ 476	Rod Scurry	.07	.03	.01
☐ 477	Kent Tekulve	.07	.03	.01
☐ 478	Jason Thompson	.07	.03	.01
☐ 479	John Tudor	.12	.05	.01
☐ 480	Lee Tunnell	.07	.03	.01
☐ 481	Marvell Wynne	.07	.03	.01
☐ 482	Salome Barojas	.07	.03	.01
☐ 483	Dave Beard	.07	.03	.01
☐ 484	Jim Beattie	.07	.03	.01
☐ 485	Barry Bonnell	.07	.03	.01
☐ 486	Phil Bradley	.35	.15	.03
☐ 487	Al Cowens	.07	.03	.01
☐ 488	Alvin Davis	1.50	.60	.15
☐ 489	Dave Henderson	.40	.16	.04
☐ 490	Steve Henderson	.07	.03	.01
☐ 491	Bob Kearney	.07	.03	.01
☐ 492	Mark Langston	4.50	2.00	.45
☐ 493	Larry Milbourne	.07	.03	.01
☐ 494	Paul Mirabella	.07	.03	.01
☐ 495	Mike Moore	.12	.05	.01
☐ 496	Edwin Nunez	.07	.03	.01
☐ 497	Spike Owen	.07	.03	.01
☐ 498	Jack Perconte	.07	.03	.01
☐ 499	Ken Phelps	.07	.03	.01
☐ 500	Jim Presley	.20	.08	.02
☐ 501	Mike Stanton	.07	.03	.01
☐ 502	Bob Stoddard	.07	.03	.01
☐ 503	Gorman Thomas	.10	.04	.01
☐ 504	Ed VandeBerg	.07	.03	.01
☐ 505	Matt Young	.07	.03	.01
☐ 506	Juan Agosto	.07	.03	.01
☐ 507	Harold Baines	.35	.15	.03
☐ 508	Floyd Bannister	.07	.03	.01
☐ 509	Britt Burns	.07	.03	.01
☐ 510	Julio Cruz	.07	.03	.01
☐ 511	Richard Dotson	.07	.03	.01
☐ 512	Jerry Dybzinski	.07	.03	.01
☐ 513	Carlton Fisk	1.00	.40	.10
☐ 514	Scott Fletcher	.07	.03	.01
☐ 515	Jerry Hairston	.07	.03	.01
☐ 516	Marc Hill	.07	.03	.01
☐ 517	LaMarr Hoyt	.07	.03	.01
☐ 518	Ron Kittle	.12	.05	.01
☐ 519	Rudy Law	.07	.03	.01
☐ 520	Vance Law	.07	.03	.01
☐ 521	Greg Luzinski	.12	.05	.01
☐ 522	Gene Nelson	.07	.03	.01
☐ 523	Tom Paciorek	.07	.03	.01
☐ 524	Ron Reed	.07	.03	.01
☐ 525	Bert Roberge	.07	.03	.01
☐ 526	Tom Seaver	1.00	.40	.10
☐ 527	Roy Smalley	.07	.03	.01
☐ 528	Dan Spillner	.07	.03	.01
☐ 529	Mike Squires	.07	.03	.01
☐ 530	Greg Walker	.07	.03	.01
☐ 531	Cesar Cedeno	.10	.04	.01
☐ 532	Dave Concepcion	.12	.05	.01
☐ 533	Eric Davis	13.50	6.00	1.85
☐ 534	Nick Esasky	.10	.04	.01
☐ 535	Tom Foley	.07	.03	.01
☐ 536	John Franco	1.50	.60	.15
☐ 537	Brad Gulden	.07	.03	.01
☐ 538	Tom Hume	.07	.03	.01
☐ 539	Wayne Krenchicki	.07	.03	.01
☐ 540	Andy McGaffigan	.07	.03	.01
☐ 541	Eddie Milner	.07	.03	.01
☐ 542	Ron Oester	.07	.03	.01
☐ 543	Bob Owchinko	.07	.03	.01
☐ 544	Dave Parker	.35	.15	.03
☐ 545	Frank Pastore	.07	.03	.01
☐ 546	Tony Perez	.20	.08	.02
☐ 547	Ted Power	.07	.03	.01
☐ 548	Joe Price	.07	.03	.01
☐ 549	Gary Redus	.10	.04	.01
☐ 550	Pete Rose	1.25	.50	.12
☐ 551	Jeff Russell	.20	.08	.02
☐ 552	Mario Soto	.07	.03	.01
☐ 553	Jay Tibbs	.07	.03	.01
☐ 554	Duane Walker	.07	.03	.01
☐ 555	Alan Bannister	.07	.03	.01
☐ 556	Buddy Bell	.10	.04	.01
☐ 557	Danny Darwin	.07	.03	.01
☐ 558	Charlie Hough	.07	.03	.01
☐ 559	Bobby Jones	.07	.03	.01
☐ 560	Odell Jones	.07	.03	.01
☐ 561	Jeff Kunkel	.07	.03	.01
☐ 562	Mike Mason	.07	.03	.01
☐ 563	Pete O'Brien	.10	.04	.01
☐ 564	Larry Parrish	.07	.03	.01
☐ 565	Mickey Rivers	.07	.03	.01
☐ 566	Billy Sample	.07	.03	.01
☐ 567	Dave Schmidt	.07	.03	.01
☐ 568	Donnie Scott	.07	.03	.01
☐ 569	Dave Stewart	.60	.25	.06
☐ 570	Frank Tanana	.10	.04	.01
☐ 571	Wayne Tolleson	.07	.03	.01
☐ 572	Gary Ward	.07	.03	.01
☐ 573	Curtis Wilkerson	.07	.03	.01
☐ 574	George Wright	.07	.03	.01
☐ 575	Ned Yost	.07	.03	.01
☐ 576	Mark Brouhard	.07	.03	.01
☐ 577	Mike Caldwell	.07	.03	.01
☐ 578	Bobby Clark	.07	.03	.01
☐ 579	Jaime Cocanower	.07	.03	.01
☐ 580	Cecil Cooper	.12	.05	.01
☐ 581	Rollie Fingers	.35	.15	.03
☐ 582	Jim Gantner	.07	.03	.01
☐ 583	Moose Haas	.07	.03	.01
☐ 584	Dion James	.07	.03	.01
☐ 585	Pete Ladd	.07	.03	.01
☐ 586	Rick Manning	.07	.03	.01
☐ 587	Bob McClure	.07	.03	.01
☐ 588	Paul Molitor	.35	.15	.03
☐ 589	Charlie Moore	.07	.03	.01
☐ 590	Ben Oglivie	.07	.03	.01
☐ 591	Chuck Porter	.07	.03	.01
☐ 592	Randy Ready	.15	.06	.01
☐ 593	Ed Romero	.07	.03	.01
☐ 594	Bill Schroeder	.07	.03	.01
☐ 595	Ray Searage	.07	.03	.01
☐ 596	Ted Simmons	.12	.05	.01
☐ 597	Jim Sundberg	.07	.03	.01
☐ 598	Don Sutton	.35	.15	.03
☐ 599	Tom Tellmann	.07	.03	.01
☐ 600	Rick Waits	.07	.03	.01
☐ 601	Robin Yount	1.50	.60	.15
☐ 602	Dusty Baker	.10	.04	.01
☐ 603	Bob Brenly	.07	.03	.01
☐ 604	Jack Clark	.25	.10	.02
☐ 605	Chili Davis	.20	.08	.02
☐ 606	Mark Davis	.12	.05	.01
☐ 607	Dan Gladden	.60	.25	.06
☐ 608	Atlee Hammaker	.07	.03	.01
☐ 609	Mike Krukow	.07	.03	.01
☐ 610	Duane Kuiper	.07	.03	.01
☐ 611	Bob Lacey	.07	.03	.01
☐ 612	Bill Laskey	.07	.03	.01
☐ 613	Gary Lavelle	.07	.03	.01
☐ 614	Johnnie LeMaster	.07	.03	.01
☐ 615	Jeff Leonard	.07	.03	.01
☐ 616	Randy Lerch	.07	.03	.01
☐ 617	Greg Minton	.07	.03	.01
☐ 618	Steve Nicosia	.07	.03	.01
☐ 619	Gene Richards	.07	.03	.01
☐ 620	Jeff Robinson	.15	.06	.01
	(Giants pitcher)			
☐ 621	Scot Thompson	.07	.03	.01
☐ 622	Manny Trillo	.07	.03	.01
☐ 623	Brad Wellman	.07	.03	.01
☐ 624	Frank Williams	.07	.03	.01
☐ 625	Joel Youngblood	.07	.03	.01
☐ 626	Cal Ripken IA	2.50	1.00	.25

☐	627	Mike Schmidt IA	1.00	.40	.10
☐	628	Giving The Signs	.10	.04	.01
		Sparky Anderson			
☐	629	AL Pitcher's Nightmare	.80	.35	.08
		Dave Winfield			
		Rickey Henderson			
☐	630	NL Pitcher's Nightmare	1.25	.50	.12
		Mike Schmidt			
		Ryne Sandberg			
☐	631	NL All-Stars	1.00	.40	.10
		Darryl Strawberry			
		Gary Carter			
		Steve Garvey			
		Ozzie Smith			
☐	632	A-S Winning Battery	.12	.05	.01
		Gary Carter			
		Charlie Lea			
☐	633	NL Pennant Clinchers	.15	.06	.01
		Steve Garvey			
		Goose Gossage			
☐	634	NL Rookie Phenoms	1.25	.50	.12
		Dwight Gooden			
		Juan Samuel			
☐	635	Toronto's Big Guns	.07	.03	.01
		Willie Upshaw			
☐	636	Toronto's Big Guns	.07	.03	.01
		Lloyd Moseby			
☐	637	HOLLAND: Al Holland	.07	.03	.01
☐	638	TUNNELL: Lee Tunnell	.07	.03	.01
☐	639	500th Homer	.40	.16	.04
		Reggie Jackson			
☐	640	4000th Hit	.45	.18	.04
		Pete Rose			
☐	641	Father and Son	1.75	.70	.17
		Cal Ripken Jr. and Sr.			
☐	642	Cubs: Division Champs	.07	.03	.01
☐	643	Two Perfect Games	.12	.05	.01
		and One No-Hitter:			
		Mike Witt			
		David Palmer			
		Jack Morris			
☐	644	Willie Lozado and	.10	.04	.01
		Vic Mata			
☐	645	Kelly Gruber and	9.50	4.25	1.00
		Randy O'Neal			
☐	646	Jose Roman and	.10	.04	.01
		Joel Skinner			
☐	647	Steve Kiefer and	7.00	3.00	.70
		Danny Tartabull			
☐	648	Rob Deer and	1.75	.70	.17
		Alejandro Sanchez			
☐	649	Billy Hatcher and	6.00	2.50	.60
		Shawon Dunston			
☐	650	Ron Robinson and	.60	.25	.06
		Mike Bielecki			
☐	651	Zane Smith and	1.25	.50	.12
		Paul Zuvella			
☐	652	Joe Hesketh and	9.00	4.00	.90
		Glenn Davis			
☐	653	John Russell and	.15	.06	.01
		Steve Jeltz			
☐	654	CL: Tigers/Padres	.15	.02	.00
		and Cubs/Mets			
☐	655	CL: Blue Jays/Yankees	.15	.02	.00
		and Red Sox/Orioles			
☐	656	CL: Royals/Cardinals	.15	.02	.00
		and Phillies/Twins			
☐	657	CL: Angels/Braves	.15	.02	.00
		and Astros/Dodgers			
☐	658	CL: Expos/A's	.15	.02	.00
		and Indians/Pirates			
☐	659	CL: Mariners/Wh.Sox	.15	.02	.00
		and Reds/Rangers			
☐	660	CL: Brewers/Giants	.15	.02	.00
		and Special Cards			

1985 Fleer Limited Edition

This 44-card set features standard size cards (2 1/2" by 3 1/2") which were distributed in a colorful box as a complete set. The back of the box gives a complete checklist of the cards in the set. The cards are ordered alphabetically by the player's name. Backs of the cards are yellow and white whereas the fronts show a picture of the player inside a red banner-type border.

	MINT	EXC	G-VG
COMPLETE SET (44)	5.00	2.25	.50
COMMON PLAYER (1-44)	.10	.04	.01

☐	1	Buddy Bell	.10	.04	.01
☐	2	Bert Blyleven	.15	.06	.01
☐	3	Wade Boggs	.90	.40	.09
☐	4	George Brett	.75	.30	.07
☐	5	Rod Carew	.60	.25	.06
☐	6	Steve Carlton	.50	.20	.05
☐	7	Alvin Davis	.15	.06	.01
☐	8	Andre Dawson	.35	.15	.03
☐	9	Steve Garvey	.30	.12	.03
☐	10	Goose Gossage	.15	.06	.01
☐	11	Tony Gwynn	.60	.25	.06
☐	12	Keith Hernandez	.15	.06	.01
☐	13	Kent Hrbek	.15	.06	.01
☐	14	Reggie Jackson	.75	.30	.07
☐	15	Dave Kingman	.10	.04	.01
☐	16	Ron Kittle	.10	.04	.01
☐	17	Mark Langston	.20	.08	.02
☐	18	Jeff Leonard	.10	.04	.01
☐	19	Bill Madlock	.10	.04	.01
☐	20	Don Mattingly	.75	.30	.07
☐	21	Jack Morris	.15	.06	.01
☐	22	Dale Murphy	.45	.18	.04
☐	23	Eddie Murray	.50	.20	.05
☐	24	Tony Pena	.10	.04	.01
☐	25	Dan Quisenberry	.10	.04	.01
☐	26	Tim Raines	.20	.08	.02
☐	27	Jim Rice	.20	.08	.02
☐	28	Cal Ripken	.90	.40	.09
☐	29	Pete Rose	.75	.30	.07
☐	30	Nolan Ryan	1.50	.60	.15
☐	31	Ryne Sandberg	1.00	.40	.10
☐	32	Steve Sax	.15	.06	.01
☐	33	Mike Schmidt	1.00	.40	.10
☐	34	Tom Seaver	.60	.25	.06
☐	35	Ozzie Smith	.30	.12	.03
☐	36	Mario Soto	.10	.04	.01
☐	37	Dave Stieb	.10	.04	.01
☐	38	Darryl Strawberry	.75	.30	.07
☐	39	Rick Sutcliffe	.10	.04	.01
☐	40	Alan Trammell	.25	.10	.02
☐	41	Willie Upshaw	.10	.04	.01
☐	42	Fernando Valenzuela	.20	.08	.02
☐	43	Dave Winfield	.30	.12	.03
☐	44	Robin Yount	.60	.25	.06

1985 Fleer Update

This 132-card set was issued late in the collecting year and features new players and players on new teams compared to the 1985 Fleer regular issue cards. Cards measure 2 1/2" by 3 1/2" and were distributed together as a complete set in a special box. The cards are numbered with a U prefix and are ordered alphabetically by the player's name. This set features the Extended Rookie Cards of Ivan Calderon, Vince Coleman, Ozzie Guillen, Teddy Higuera, and Mickey Tettleton.

	MINT	EXC	G-VG
COMPLETE SET (132)	30.00	13.50	4.50
COMMON PLAYER (1-132)	.10	.04	.01

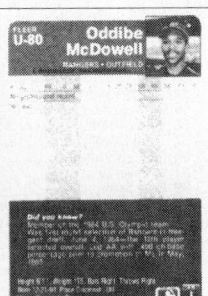

☐ U1	Don Aase	.20	.06	.01
☐ U2	Bill Almon	.10	.04	.01
☐ U3	Dusty Baker	.15	.06	.01
☐ U4	Dale Berra	.10	.04	.01
☐ U5	Karl Best	.10	.04	.01
☐ U6	Tim Birtsas	.15	.06	.01
☐ U7	Vida Blue	.15	.06	.01
☐ U8	Rich Bordi	.10	.04	.01
☐ U9	Daryl Boston	.35	.15	.03
☐ U10	Hubie Brooks	.30	.12	.03
☐ U11	Chris Brown	.15	.06	.01
☐ U12	Tom Browning	1.50	.60	.15
☐ U13	Al Bumbry	.10	.04	.01
☐ U14	Tim Burke	.40	.16	.04
☐ U15	Ray Burris	.10	.04	.01
☐ U16	Jeff Burroughs	.10	.04	.01
☐ U17	Ivan Calderon	3.00	1.25	.30
☐ U18	Jeff Calhoun	.10	.04	.01
☐ U19	Bill Campbell	.10	.04	.01
☐ U20	Don Carman	.20	.08	.02
☐ U21	Gary Carter	.80	.35	.08
☐ U22	Bobby Castillo	.10	.04	.01
☐ U23	Bill Caudill	.10	.04	.01
☐ U24	Rick Cerone	.10	.04	.01
☐ U25	Jack Clark	.40	.16	.04
☐ U26	Pat Clements	.15	.06	.01
☐ U27	Stewart Cliburn	.10	.04	.01
☐ U28	Vince Coleman	11.00	5.00	1.35
☐ U29	Dave Collins	.10	.04	.01
☐ U30	Fritz Connally	.10	.04	.01
☐ U31	Henry Cotto	.15	.06	.01
☐ U32	Danny Darwin	.10	.04	.01
☐ U33	Darren Daulton	.45	.18	.04
☐ U34	Jerry Davis	.10	.04	.01
☐ U35	Brian Dayett	.10	.04	.01
☐ U36	Ken Dixon	.10	.04	.01
☐ U37	Tommy Dunbar	.10	.04	.01
☐ U38	Mariano Duncan	.75	.30	.07
☐ U39	Bob Fallon	.10	.04	.01
☐ U40	Brian Fisher	.15	.06	.01
☐ U41	Mike Fitzgerald	.10	.04	.01
☐ U42	Ray Fontenot	.10	.04	.01
☐ U43	Greg Gagne	.35	.15	.03
☐ U44	Oscar Gamble	.15	.06	.01
☐ U45	Jim Gott	.15	.06	.01
☐ U46	David Green	.10	.04	.01
☐ U47	Alfredo Griffin	.15	.06	.01
☐ U48	Ozzie Guillen	2.00	.80	.20
☐ U49	Toby Harrah	.15	.06	.01
☐ U50	Ron Hassey	.15	.06	.01
☐ U51	Rickey Henderson	5.00	2.25	.50
☐ U52	Steve Henderson	.10	.04	.01
☐ U53	George Hendrick	.15	.06	.01
☐ U54	Teddy Higuera	.60	.25	.06
☐ U55	Al Holland	.10	.04	.01
☐ U56	Burt Hooton	.10	.04	.01
☐ U57	Jay Howell	.15	.06	.01
☐ U58	LaMarr Hoyt	.10	.04	.01
☐ U59	Tim Hulett	.15	.06	.01
☐ U60	Bob James	.10	.04	.01
☐ U61	Cliff Johnson	.10	.04	.01
☐ U62	Howard Johnson	2.75	1.10	.27
☐ U63	Ruppert Jones	.10	.04	.01
☐ U64	Steve Kemp	.10	.04	.01
☐ U65	Bruce Kison	.10	.04	.01
☐ U66	Mike LaCoss	.10	.04	.01
☐ U67	Lee Lacy	.10	.04	.01
☐ U68	Dave LaPoint	.10	.04	.01
☐ U69	Gary Lavelle	.10	.04	.01
☐ U70	Vance Law	.15	.06	.01
☐ U71	Manny Lee	.30	.12	.03
☐ U72	Sixto Lezcano	.10	.04	.01

☐ U73	Tim Lollar	.10	.04	.01
☐ U74	Urbano Lugo	.10	.04	.01
☐ U75	Fred Lynn	.25	.10	.02
☐ U76	Steve Lyons	.25	.10	.02
☐ U77	Mickey Mahler	.10	.04	.01
☐ U78	Ron Mathis	.10	.04	.01
☐ U79	Len Matuszek	.10	.04	.01
☐ U80	Oddibe McDowell UER (part of bio actually Roger's)	.25	.10	.02
☐ U81	Roger McDowell UER (part of bio actually Oddibe's)	.50	.20	.05
☐ U82	Donnie Moore	.10	.04	.01
☐ U83	Ron Musselman	.10	.04	.01
☐ U84	Al Oliver	.20	.08	.02
☐ U85	Joe Orsulak	.40	.16	.04
☐ U86	Dan Pasqua	.50	.20	.05
☐ U87	Chris Pittaro	.10	.04	.01
☐ U88	Rick Reuschel	.20	.08	.02
☐ U89	Earnie Riles	.20	.08	.02
☐ U90	Jerry Royster	.10	.04	.01
☐ U91	Dave Rozema	.10	.04	.01
☐ U92	Dave Rucker	.10	.04	.01
☐ U93	Vern Ruhle	.10	.04	.01
☐ U94	Mark Salas	.15	.06	.01
☐ U95	Luis Salazar	.10	.04	.01
☐ U96	Joe Sambito	.10	.04	.01
☐ U97	Billy Sample	.15	.06	.01
☐ U98	Alejandro Sanchez	.10	.04	.01
☐ U99	Calvin Schiraldi	.20	.08	.02
☐ U100	Rick Schu	.20	.08	.02
☐ U101	Larry Sheets	.25	.10	.02
☐ U102	Ron Shephard	.10	.04	.01
☐ U103	Nelson Simmons	.15	.06	.01
☐ U104	Don Slaught	.10	.04	.01
☐ U105	Roy Smalley	.10	.04	.01
☐ U106	Lonnie Smith	.25	.10	.02
☐ U107	Nate Snell	.10	.04	.01
☐ U108	Lary Sorensen	.10	.04	.01
☐ U109	Chris Speier	.10	.04	.01
☐ U110	Mike Stenhouse	.10	.04	.01
☐ U111	Tim Stoddard	.10	.04	.01
☐ U112	John Stuper	.10	.04	.01
☐ U113	Jim Sundberg	.10	.04	.01
☐ U114	Bruce Sutter	.25	.10	.02
☐ U115	Don Sutton	.50	.20	.05
☐ U116	Bruce Tanner	.10	.04	.01
☐ U117	Kent Tekulve	.15	.06	.01
☐ U118	Walt Terrell	.15	.06	.01
☐ U119	Mickey Tettleton	2.00	.80	.20
☐ U120	Rich Thompson	.10	.04	.01
☐ U121	Louis Thornton	.10	.04	.01
☐ U122	Alex Trevino	.10	.04	.01
☐ U123	John Tudor	.20	.08	.02
☐ U124	Jose Uribe	.25	.10	.02
☐ U125	Dave Valle	.15	.06	.01
☐ U126	Dave Von Ohlen	.10	.04	.01
☐ U127	Curt Wardle	.10	.04	.01
☐ U128	U.L. Washington	.10	.04	.01
☐ U129	Ed Whitson	.15	.06	.01
☐ U130	Herm Winningham	.15	.06	.01
☐ U131	Rich Yett	.10	.04	.01
☐ U132	Checklist U1-U132	.10	.01	.00

1986 Fleer

The cards in this 660-card set measure 2 1/2" by 3 1/2". The 1986 Fleer set features fronts that contain the team logo along with the player's name and position. The player cards are alphabetized within team and the teams are ordered by their 1985 season finish and won-lost record, e.g., Kansas City (1-25), St. Louis (26-49), Toronto (50-73), New York Mets (74-97), New York Yankees (98-122), Los Angeles (123-147), California (148-171), Cincinnati (172-196), Chicago White Sox (197-220), Detroit (221-243), Montreal (244-267), Baltimore (268-291), Houston (292-314), San Diego (315-338), Boston (339-360), Chicago Cubs (361-385), Minnesota (386-409), Oakland (410-432), Philadelphia (433-457), Seattle (458-481), Milwaukee (482-506), Atlanta (507-532), San Francisco (533-555), Texas (556-578), Cleveland (579-601), and Pittsburgh (602-625). Specials (626-643), Major League Prospects (644-653), and checklist cards (654-660) complete the set. The border enclosing the photo is dark blue. The backs feature the

FLEER 450
MIKE SCHMIDT
PHILLIES • FIRST BASE
Height 6'2", Weight 203, Bats Right, Throws Right
Born 9-27-49, Dayton, OH
Home Philadelphia, PA

MIKE SCHMIDT
FIRST BASE

same name, number, and statistics format that Fleer has been using over the past few years. The Dennis and Tippy Martinez cards were apparently switched in the set numbering, as their adjacent numbers (279 and 280) were reversed on the Orioles checklist card. The set includes the rookie cards of Jose Canseco, Vince Coleman, Kal Daniels, Len Dykstra, Cecil Fielder, and Benito Santiago.

	MINT	EXC	G-VG
COMPLETE SET (660)	135.00	60.00	12.50
COMMON PLAYER (1-660)	.06	.02	.00

		MINT	EXC	G-VG
☐ 1	Steve Balboni	.10	.03	.01
☐ 2	Joe Beckwith	.06	.02	.00
☐ 3	Buddy Biancalana	.06	.02	.00
☐ 4	Bud Black	.10	.04	.01
☐ 5	George Brett	.85	.35	.08
☐ 6	Onix Concepcion	.06	.02	.00
☐ 7	Steve Farr	.10	.04	.01
☐ 8	Mark Gubicza	.15	.06	.01
☐ 9	Dane Iorg	.06	.02	.00
☐ 10	Danny Jackson	.12	.05	.01
☐ 11	Lynn Jones	.06	.02	.00
☐ 12	Mike Jones	.06	.02	.00
☐ 13	Charlie Leibrandt	.06	.02	.00
☐ 14	Hal McRae	.10	.04	.01
☐ 15	Omar Moreno	.06	.02	.00
☐ 16	Darryl Motley	.06	.02	.00
☐ 17	Jorge Orta	.06	.02	.00
☐ 18	Dan Quisenberry	.12	.05	.01
☐ 19	Bret Saberhagen	1.00	.40	.10
☐ 20	Pat Sheridan	.06	.02	.00
☐ 21	Lonnie Smith	.12	.05	.01
☐ 22	Jim Sundberg	.06	.02	.00
☐ 23	John Wathan	.06	.02	.00
☐ 24	Frank White	.06	.02	.00
☐ 25	Willie Wilson	.10	.04	.01
☐ 26	Joaquin Andujar	.06	.02	.00
☐ 27	Steve Braun	.06	.02	.00
☐ 28	Bill Campbell	.06	.02	.00
☐ 29	Cesar Cedeno	.10	.04	.01
☐ 30	Jack Clark	.17	.07	.01
☐ 31	Vince Coleman	6.00	2.50	.60
☐ 32	Danny Cox	.06	.02	.00
☐ 33	Ken Dayley	.06	.02	.00
☐ 34	Ivan DeJesus	.06	.02	.00
☐ 35	Bob Forsch	.06	.02	.00
☐ 36	Brian Harper	.20	.08	.02
☐ 37	Tom Herr	.10	.04	.01
☐ 38	Ricky Horton	.06	.02	.00
☐ 39	Kurt Kepshire	.06	.02	.00
☐ 40	Jeff Lahti	.06	.02	.00
☐ 41	Tito Landrum	.06	.02	.00
☐ 42	Willie McGee	.25	.10	.02
☐ 43	Tom Nieto	.06	.02	.00
☐ 44	Terry Pendleton	.75	.30	.07
☐ 45	Darrell Porter	.06	.02	.00
☐ 46	Ozzie Smith	.75	.30	.07
☐ 47	John Tudor	.10	.04	.01
☐ 48	Andy Van Slyke	.35	.15	.03
☐ 49	Todd Worrell	.17	.07	.01
☐ 50	Jim Acker	.06	.02	.00
☐ 51	Doyle Alexander	.06	.02	.00
☐ 52	Jesse Barfield	.15	.06	.01
☐ 53	George Bell	.50	.20	.05
☐ 54	Jeff Burroughs	.06	.02	.00
☐ 55	Bill Caudill	.06	.02	.00
☐ 56	Jim Clancy	.06	.02	.00
☐ 57	Tony Fernandez	.20	.08	.02
☐ 58	Tom Filer	.06	.02	.00
☐ 59	Damaso Garcia	.06	.02	.00
☐ 60	Tom Henke	.40	.16	.04
☐ 61	Garth Iorg	.06	.02	.00
☐ 62	Cliff Johnson	.06	.02	.00
☐ 63	Jimmy Key	.30	.12	.03
☐ 64	Dennis Lamp	.06	.02	.00
☐ 65	Gary Lavelle	.06	.02	.00
☐ 66	Buck Martinez	.06	.02	.00
☐ 67	Lloyd Moseby	.10	.04	.01
☐ 68	Rance Mulliniks	.06	.02	.00
☐ 69	Al Oliver	.12	.05	.01
☐ 70	Dave Stieb	.15	.06	.01
☐ 71	Louis Thornton	.06	.02	.00
☐ 72	Willie Upshaw	.06	.02	.00
☐ 73	Ernie Whitt	.06	.02	.00
☐ 74	Rick Aguilera	.90	.40	.09
☐ 75	Wally Backman	.06	.02	.00
☐ 76	Gary Carter	.30	.12	.03
☐ 77	Ron Darling	.15	.06	.01
☐ 78	Len Dykstra	2.50	1.00	.25
☐ 79	Sid Fernandez	.17	.07	.01
☐ 80	George Foster	.12	.05	.01
☐ 81	Dwight Gooden	2.25	.90	.22
☐ 82	Tom Gorman	.06	.02	.00
☐ 83	Danny Heep	.06	.02	.00
☐ 84	Keith Hernandez	.17	.07	.01
☐ 85	Howard Johnson	.90	.40	.09
☐ 86	Ray Knight	.10	.04	.01
☐ 87	Terry Leach	.10	.04	.01
☐ 88	Ed Lynch	.06	.02	.00
☐ 89	Roger McDowell	.35	.15	.03
☐ 90	Jesse Orosco	.06	.02	.00
☐ 91	Tom Paciorek	.06	.02	.00
☐ 92	Ronn Reynolds	.06	.02	.00
☐ 93	Rafael Santana	.06	.02	.00
☐ 94	Doug Sisk	.06	.02	.00
☐ 95	Rusty Staub	.10	.04	.01
☐ 96	Darryl Strawberry	5.00	2.25	.50
☐ 97	Mookie Wilson	.10	.04	.01
☐ 98	Neil Allen	.06	.02	.00
☐ 99	Don Baylor	.10	.04	.01
☐ 100	Dale Berra	.06	.02	.00
☐ 101	Rich Bordi	.06	.02	.00
☐ 102	Marty Bystrom	.06	.02	.00
☐ 103	Joe Cowley	.06	.02	.00
☐ 104	Brian Fisher	.10	.04	.01
☐ 105	Ken Griffey	.15	.06	.01
☐ 106	Ron Guidry	.15	.06	.01
☐ 107	Ron Hassey	.06	.02	.00
☐ 108	Rickey Henderson UER (SB Record of 120, sic)	2.50	1.00	.25
☐ 109	Don Mattingly	4.00	1.75	.40
☐ 110	Bobby Meacham	.06	.02	.00
☐ 111	John Montefusco	.06	.02	.00
☐ 112	Phil Niekro	.25	.10	.02
☐ 113	Mike Pagliarulo	.10	.04	.01
☐ 114	Dan Pasqua	.17	.07	.01
☐ 115	Willie Randolph	.10	.04	.01
☐ 116	Dave Righetti	.12	.05	.01
☐ 117	Andre Robertson	.06	.02	.00
☐ 118	Billy Sample	.06	.02	.00
☐ 119	Bob Shirley	.06	.02	.00
☐ 120	Ed Whitson	.06	.02	.00
☐ 121	Dave Winfield	.65	.25	.06
☐ 122	Butch Wynegar	.06	.02	.00
☐ 123	Dave Anderson	.06	.02	.00
☐ 124	Bob Bailor	.06	.02	.00
☐ 125	Greg Brock	.06	.02	.00
☐ 126	Enos Cabell	.06	.02	.00
☐ 127	Bobby Castillo	.06	.02	.00
☐ 128	Carlos Diaz	.06	.02	.00
☐ 129	Mariano Duncan	.35	.15	.03
☐ 130	Pedro Guerrero	.20	.08	.02
☐ 131	Orel Hershiser	.75	.30	.07
☐ 132	Rick Honeycutt	.06	.02	.00
☐ 133	Ken Howell	.06	.02	.00
☐ 134	Ken Landreaux	.06	.02	.00
☐ 135	Bill Madlock	.10	.04	.01
☐ 136	Candy Maldonado	.10	.04	.01
☐ 137	Mike Marshall	.10	.04	.01
☐ 138	Len Matuszek	.06	.02	.00
☐ 139	Tom Niedenfuer	.06	.02	.00
☐ 140	Alejandro Pena	.12	.05	.01
☐ 141	Jerry Reuss	.06	.02	.00
☐ 142	Bill Russell	.10	.04	.01
☐ 143	Steve Sax	.25	.10	.02
☐ 144	Mike Scioscia	.10	.04	.01
☐ 145	Fernando Valenzuela	.12	.05	.01
☐ 146	Bob Welch	.12	.05	.01
☐ 147	Terry Whitfield	.06	.02	.00
☐ 148	Juan Beniquez	.06	.02	.00
☐ 149	Bob Boone	.12	.05	.01
☐ 150	John Candelaria	.06	.02	.00
☐ 151	Rod Carew	.75	.30	.07
☐ 152	Stewart Cliburn	.06	.02	.00

☐ 153	Doug DeCinces	.10	.04	.01
☐ 154	Brian Downing	.10	.04	.01
☐ 155	Ken Forsch	.06	.02	.00
☐ 156	Craig Gerber	.06	.02	.00
☐ 157	Bobby Grich	.10	.04	.01
☐ 158	George Hendrick	.06	.02	.00
☐ 159	Al Holland	.06	.02	.00
☐ 160	Reggie Jackson	1.00	.40	.10
☐ 161	Ruppert Jones	.06	.02	.00
☐ 162	Urbano Lugo	.06	.02	.00
☐ 163	Kirk McCaskill	.30	.12	.03
☐ 164	Donnie Moore	.06	.02	.00
☐ 165	Gary Pettis	.06	.02	.00
☐ 166	Ron Romanick	.06	.02	.00
☐ 167	Dick Schofield	.06	.02	.00
☐ 168	Daryl Sconiers	.06	.02	.00
☐ 169	Jim Slaton	.06	.02	.00
☐ 170	Don Sutton	.25	.10	.02
☐ 171	Mike Witt	.06	.02	.00
☐ 172	Buddy Bell	.10	.04	.01
☐ 173	Tom Browning	.35	.15	.03
☐ 174	Dave Concepcion	.12	.05	.01
☐ 175	Eric Davis	2.50	1.00	.25
☐ 176	Bo Diaz	.06	.02	.00
☐ 177	Nick Esasky	.10	.04	.01
☐ 178	John Franco	.15	.06	.01
☐ 179	Tom Hume	.06	.02	.00
☐ 180	Wayne Krenchicki	.06	.02	.00
☐ 181	Andy McGaffigan	.06	.02	.00
☐ 182	Eddie Milner	.06	.02	.00
☐ 183	Ron Oester	.06	.02	.00
☐ 184	Dave Parker	.25	.10	.02
☐ 185	Frank Pastore	.06	.02	.00
☐ 186	Tony Perez	.25	.10	.02
☐ 187	Ted Power	.06	.02	.00
☐ 188	Joe Price	.06	.02	.00
☐ 189	Gary Redus	.06	.02	.00
☐ 190	Ron Robinson	.06	.02	.00
☐ 191	Pete Rose	.75	.30	.07
☐ 192	Mario Soto	.06	.02	.00
☐ 193	John Stuper	.06	.02	.00
☐ 194	Jay Tibbs	.06	.02	.00
☐ 195	Dave Van Gorder	.06	.02	.00
☐ 196	Max Venable	.06	.02	.00
☐ 197	Juan Agosto	.06	.02	.00
☐ 198	Harold Baines	.25	.10	.02
☐ 199	Floyd Bannister	.06	.02	.00
☐ 200	Britt Burns	.06	.02	.00
☐ 201	Julio Cruz	.06	.02	.00
☐ 202	Joel Davis	.10	.04	.01
☐ 203	Richard Dotson	.06	.02	.00
☐ 204	Carlton Fisk	.75	.30	.07
☐ 205	Scott Fletcher	.06	.02	.00
☐ 206	Ozzie Guillen	1.00	.40	.10
☐ 207	Jerry Hairston	.06	.02	.00
☐ 208	Tim Hulett	.06	.02	.00
☐ 209	Bob James	.06	.02	.00
☐ 210	Ron Kittle	.10	.04	.01
☐ 211	Rudy Law	.06	.02	.00
☐ 212	Bryan Little	.06	.02	.00
☐ 213	Gene Nelson	.06	.02	.00
☐ 214	Reid Nichols	.06	.02	.00
☐ 215	Luis Salazar	.06	.02	.00
☐ 216	Tom Seaver	.90	.40	.09
☐ 217	Dan Spillner	.06	.02	.00
☐ 218	Bruce Tanner	.06	.02	.00
☐ 219	Greg Walker	.06	.02	.00
☐ 220	Dave Wehrmeister	.06	.02	.00
☐ 221	Juan Berenguer	.06	.02	.00
☐ 222	Dave Bergman	.06	.02	.00
☐ 223	Tom Brookens	.06	.02	.00
☐ 224	Darrell Evans	.10	.04	.01
☐ 225	Barbaro Garbey	.06	.02	.00
☐ 226	Kirk Gibson	.25	.10	.02
☐ 227	John Grubb	.06	.02	.00
☐ 228	Willie Hernandez	.06	.02	.00
☐ 229	Larry Herndon	.06	.02	.00
☐ 230	Chet Lemon	.06	.02	.00
☐ 231	Aurelio Lopez	.06	.02	.00
☐ 232	Jack Morris	.40	.16	.04
☐ 233	Randy O'Neal	.06	.02	.00
☐ 234	Lance Parrish	.17	.07	.01
☐ 235	Dan Petry	.06	.02	.00
☐ 236	Alejandro Sanchez	.06	.02	.00
☐ 237	Bill Scherrer	.06	.02	.00
☐ 238	Nelson Simmons	.06	.02	.00
☐ 239	Frank Tanana	.10	.04	.01
☐ 240	Walt Terrell	.06	.02	.00
☐ 241	Alan Trammell	.50	.20	.05
☐ 242	Lou Whitaker	.25	.10	.02
☐ 243	Milt Wilcox	.06	.02	.00
☐ 244	Hubie Brooks	.12	.05	.01
☐ 245	Tim Burke	.20	.08	.02
☐ 246	Andre Dawson	.75	.30	.07
☐ 247	Mike Fitzgerald	.06	.02	.00
☐ 248	Terry Francona	.06	.02	.00
☐ 249	Bill Gullickson	.10	.04	.01
☐ 250	Joe Hesketh	.12	.05	.01
☐ 251	Bill Laskey	.06	.02	.00
☐ 252	Vance Law	.06	.02	.00
☐ 253	Charlie Lea	.06	.02	.00
☐ 254	Gary Lucas	.06	.02	.00
☐ 255	David Palmer	.06	.02	.00
☐ 256	Tim Raines	.35	.15	.03
☐ 257	Jeff Reardon	.35	.15	.03
☐ 258	Bert Roberge	.06	.02	.00
☐ 259	Dan Schatzeder	.06	.02	.00
☐ 260	Bryn Smith	.06	.02	.00
☐ 261	Randy St.Claire	.06	.02	.00
☐ 262	Scot Thompson	.06	.02	.00
☐ 263	Tim Wallach	.12	.05	.01
☐ 264	U.L. Washington	.06	.02	.00
☐ 265	Mitch Webster	.17	.07	.01
☐ 266	Herm Winningham	.06	.02	.00
☐ 267	Floyd Youmans	.10	.04	.01
☐ 268	Don Aase	.06	.02	.00
☐ 269	Mike Boddicker	.06	.02	.00
☐ 270	Rich Dauer	.06	.02	.00
☐ 271	Storm Davis	.06	.02	.00
☐ 272	Rick Dempsey	.06	.02	.00
☐ 273	Ken Dixon	.06	.02	.00
☐ 274	Jim Dwyer	.06	.02	.00
☐ 275	Mike Flanagan	.10	.04	.01
☐ 276	Wayne Gross	.06	.02	.00
☐ 277	Lee Lacy	.06	.02	.00
☐ 278	Fred Lynn	.12	.05	.01
☐ 279	Tippy Martinez	.06	.02	.00
☐ 280	Dennis Martinez	.10	.04	.01
☐ 281	Scott McGregor	.06	.02	.00
☐ 282	Eddie Murray	.75	.30	.07
☐ 283	Floyd Rayford	.06	.02	.00
☐ 284	Cal Ripken	4.00	1.75	.40
☐ 285	Gary Roenicke	.06	.02	.00
☐ 286	Larry Sheets	.10	.04	.01
☐ 287	John Shelby	.06	.02	.00
☐ 288	Nate Snell	.06	.02	.00
☐ 289	Sammy Stewart	.06	.02	.00
☐ 290	Alan Wiggins	.06	.02	.00
☐ 291	Mike Young	.06	.02	.00
☐ 292	Alan Ashby	.06	.02	.00
☐ 293	Mark Bailey	.06	.02	.00
☐ 294	Kevin Bass	.06	.02	.00
☐ 295	Jeff Calhoun	.06	.02	.00
☐ 296	Jose Cruz	.10	.04	.01
☐ 297	Glenn Davis	1.50	.60	.15
☐ 298	Bill Dawley	.06	.02	.00
☐ 299	Frank DiPino	.06	.02	.00
☐ 300	Bill Doran	.10	.04	.01
☐ 301	Phil Garner	.10	.04	.01
☐ 302	Jeff Heathcock	.06	.02	.00
☐ 303	Charlie Kerfeld	.06	.02	.00
☐ 304	Bob Knepper	.06	.02	.00
☐ 305	Ron Mathis	.06	.02	.00
☐ 306	Jerry Mumphrey	.06	.02	.00
☐ 307	Jim Pankovits	.06	.02	.00
☐ 308	Terry Puhl	.06	.02	.00
☐ 309	Craig Reynolds	.06	.02	.00
☐ 310	Nolan Ryan	4.25	1.75	.42
☐ 311	Mike Scott	.15	.06	.01
☐ 312	Dave Smith	.06	.02	.00
☐ 313	Dickie Thon	.06	.02	.00
☐ 314	Denny Walling	.06	.02	.00
☐ 315	Kurt Bevacqua	.06	.02	.00
☐ 316	Al Bumbry	.06	.02	.00
☐ 317	Jerry Davis	.06	.02	.00
☐ 318	Luis DeLeon	.06	.02	.00
☐ 319	Dave Dravecky	.12	.05	.01
☐ 320	Tim Flannery	.06	.02	.00
☐ 321	Steve Garvey	.35	.15	.03
☐ 322	Goose Gossage	.15	.06	.01
☐ 323	Tony Gwynn	2.00	.80	.20
☐ 324	Andy Hawkins	.06	.02	.00
☐ 325	LaMarr Hoyt	.06	.02	.00
☐ 326	Roy Lee Jackson	.06	.02	.00
☐ 327	Terry Kennedy	.06	.02	.00
☐ 328	Craig Lefferts	.06	.02	.00
☐ 329	Carmelo Martinez	.06	.02	.00
☐ 330	Lance McCullers	.12	.05	.01
☐ 331	Kevin McReynolds	.35	.15	.03
☐ 332	Graig Nettles	.10	.04	.01
☐ 333	Jerry Royster	.06	.02	.00
☐ 334	Eric Show	.06	.02	.00
☐ 335	Tim Stoddard	.06	.02	.00
☐ 336	Garry Templeton	.10	.04	.01
☐ 337	Mark Thurmond	.06	.02	.00
☐ 338	Ed Wojna	.06	.02	.00
☐ 339	Tony Armas	.06	.02	.00
☐ 340	Marty Barrett	.06	.02	.00
☐ 341	Wade Boggs	2.50	1.00	.25
☐ 342	Dennis Boyd	.06	.02	.00

343	Bill Buckner	.10	.04	.01
344	Mark Clear	.06	.02	.00
345	Roger Clemens	8.50	3.75	.85
346	Steve Crawford	.06	.02	.00
347	Mike Easler	.06	.02	.00
348	Dwight Evans	.15	.06	.01
349	Rich Gedman	.06	.02	.00
350	Jackie Gutierrez	.06	.02	.00
351	Glenn Hoffman	.06	.02	.00
352	Bruce Hurst	.10	.04	.01
353	Bruce Kison	.06	.02	.00
354	Tim Lollar	.06	.02	.00
355	Steve Lyons	.06	.02	.00
356	Al Nipper	.06	.02	.00
357	Bob Ojeda	.10	.04	.01
358	Jim Rice	.15	.06	.01
359	Bob Stanley	.06	.02	.00
360	Mike Trujillo	.06	.02	.00
361	Thad Bosley	.06	.02	.00
362	Warren Brusstar	.06	.02	.00
363	Ron Cey	.10	.04	.01
364	Jody Davis	.06	.02	.00
365	Bob Dernier	.06	.02	.00
366	Shawon Dunston	.75	.30	.07
367	Leon Durham	.06	.02	.00
368	Dennis Eckersley	.30	.12	.03
369	Ray Fontenot	.06	.02	.00
370	George Frazier	.06	.02	.00
371	Billy Hatcher	.12	.05	.01
372	Dave Lopes	.10	.04	.01
373	Gary Matthews	.06	.02	.00
374	Ron Meredith	.06	.02	.00
375	Keith Moreland	.06	.02	.00
376	Reggie Patterson	.06	.02	.00
377	Dick Ruthven	.06	.02	.00
378	Ryne Sandberg	3.75	1.60	.37
379	Scott Sanderson	.10	.04	.01
380	Lee Smith	.35	.15	.03
381	Lary Sorensen	.06	.02	.00
382	Chris Speier	.06	.02	.00
383	Rick Sutcliffe	.12	.05	.01
384	Steve Trout	.06	.02	.00
385	Gary Woods	.06	.02	.00
386	Bert Blyleven	.15	.06	.01
387	Tom Brunansky	.10	.04	.01
388	Randy Bush	.06	.02	.00
389	John Butcher	.06	.02	.00
390	Ron Davis	.06	.02	.00
391	Dave Engle	.06	.02	.00
392	Frank Eufemia	.06	.02	.00
393	Pete Filson	.06	.02	.00
394	Gary Gaetti	.12	.05	.01
395	Greg Gagne	.10	.04	.01
396	Mickey Hatcher	.06	.02	.00
397	Kent Hrbek	.20	.08	.02
398	Tim Laudner	.06	.02	.00
399	Rick Lysander	.06	.02	.00
400	Dave Meier	.06	.02	.00
401	Kirby Puckett	7.00	3.00	.70
402	Mark Salas	.06	.02	.00
403	Ken Schrom	.06	.02	.00
404	Roy Smalley	.06	.02	.00
405	Mike Smithson	.06	.02	.00
406	Mike Stenhouse	.06	.02	.00
407	Tim Teufel	.10	.04	.01
408	Frank Viola	.35	.15	.03
409	Ron Washington	.06	.02	.00
410	Keith Atherton	.06	.02	.00
411	Dusty Baker	.10	.04	.01
412	Tim Birtsas	.10	.04	.01
413	Bruce Bochte	.06	.02	.00
414	Chris Codiroli	.06	.02	.00
415	Dave Collins	.06	.02	.00
416	Mike Davis	.06	.02	.00
417	Alfredo Griffin	.06	.02	.00
418	Mike Heath	.06	.02	.00
419	Steve Henderson	.06	.02	.00
420	Donnie Hill	.06	.02	.00
421	Jay Howell	.06	.02	.00
422	Tommy John	.17	.07	.01
423	Dave Kingman	.12	.05	.01
424	Bill Krueger	.06	.02	.00
425	Rick Langford	.06	.02	.00
426	Carney Lansford	.12	.05	.01
427	Steve McCatty	.06	.02	.00
428	Dwayne Murphy	.06	.02	.00
429	Steve Ontiveros	.06	.02	.00
430	Tony Phillips	.10	.04	.01
431	Jose Rijo	.35	.15	.03
432	Mickey Tettleton	1.25	.50	.12
433	Luis Aguayo	.06	.02	.00
434	Larry Andersen	.06	.02	.00
435	Steve Carlton	.65	.25	.06
436	Don Carman	.15	.06	.01
437	Tim Corcoran	.06	.02	.00
438	Darren Daulton	.30	.12	.03
439	John Denny	.06	.02	.00
440	Tom Foley	.06	.02	.00
441	Greg Gross	.06	.02	.00
442	Kevin Gross	.06	.02	.00
443	Von Hayes	.12	.05	.01
444	Charles Hudson	.06	.02	.00
445	Garry Maddox	.06	.02	.00
446	Shane Rawley	.06	.02	.00
447	Dave Rucker	.06	.02	.00
448	John Russell	.06	.02	.00
449	Juan Samuel	.25	.10	.02
450	Mike Schmidt	2.50	1.00	.25
451	Rick Schu	.06	.02	.00
452	Dave Shipanoff	.06	.02	.00
453	Dave Stewart	.35	.15	.03
454	Jeff Stone	.06	.02	.00
455	Kent Tekulve	.06	.02	.00
456	Ozzie Virgil	.06	.02	.00
457	Glenn Wilson	.06	.02	.00
458	Jim Beattie	.06	.02	.00
459	Karl Best	.06	.02	.00
460	Barry Bonnell	.06	.02	.00
461	Phil Bradley	.10	.04	.01
462	Ivan Calderon	2.00	.80	.20
463	Al Cowens	.06	.02	.00
464	Alvin Davis	.15	.06	.01
465	Dave Henderson	.35	.15	.03
466	Bob Kearney	.06	.02	.00
467	Mark Langston	.65	.25	.06
468	Bob Long	.06	.02	.00
469	Mike Moore	.10	.04	.01
470	Edwin Nunez	.06	.02	.00
471	Spike Owen	.06	.02	.00
472	Jack Perconte	.06	.02	.00
473	Jim Presley	.06	.02	.00
474	Donnie Scott	.06	.02	.00
475	Bill Swift	.12	.05	.01
476	Danny Tartabull	1.00	.40	.10
477	Gorman Thomas	.10	.04	.01
478	Roy Thomas	.06	.02	.00
479	Ed VandeBerg	.06	.02	.00
480	Frank Wills	.10	.04	.01
481	Matt Young	.06	.02	.00
482	Ray Burris	.06	.02	.00
483	Jaime Cocanower	.06	.02	.00
484	Cecil Cooper	.10	.04	.01
485	Danny Darwin	.06	.02	.00
486	Rollie Fingers	.25	.10	.02
487	Jim Gantner	.06	.02	.00
488	Bob L. Gibson	.06	.02	.00
489	Moose Haas	.06	.02	.00
490	Teddy Higuera	.45	.18	.04
491	Paul Householder	.06	.02	.00
492	Pete Ladd	.06	.02	.00
493	Rick Manning	.06	.02	.00
494	Bob McClure	.06	.02	.00
495	Paul Molitor	.25	.10	.02
496	Charlie Moore	.06	.02	.00
497	Ben Oglivie	.06	.02	.00
498	Randy Ready	.06	.02	.00
499	Earnie Riles	.15	.06	.01
500	Ed Romero	.06	.02	.00
501	Bill Schroeder	.06	.02	.00
502	Ray Searage	.06	.02	.00
503	Ted Simmons	.12	.05	.01
504	Pete Vuckovich	.06	.02	.00
505	Rick Waits	.06	.02	.00
506	Robin Yount	.80	.35	.08
507	Len Barker	.06	.02	.00
508	Steve Bedrosian	.10	.04	.01
509	Bruce Benedict	.06	.02	.00
510	Rick Camp	.06	.02	.00
511	Rick Cerone	.06	.02	.00
512	Chris Chambliss	.10	.04	.01
513	Jeff Dedmon	.06	.02	.00
514	Terry Forster	.06	.02	.00
515	Gene Garber	.06	.02	.00
516	Terry Harper	.06	.02	.00
517	Bob Horner	.10	.04	.01
518	Glenn Hubbard	.06	.02	.00
519	Joe Johnson	.10	.04	.01
520	Brad Komminsk	.06	.02	.00
521	Rick Mahler	.06	.02	.00
522	Dale Murphy	.50	.20	.05
523	Ken Oberkfell	.06	.02	.00
524	Pascual Perez	.10	.04	.01
525	Gerald Perry	.10	.04	.01
526	Rafael Ramirez	.06	.02	.00
527	Steve Shields	.06	.02	.00
528	Zane Smith	.35	.15	.03
529	Bruce Sutter	.12	.05	.01
530	Milt Thompson	.30	.12	.03
531	Claudell Washington	.06	.02	.00
532	Paul Zuvella	.06	.02	.00

□	#	Player			
□	533	Vida Blue	.10	.04	.01
□	534	Bob Brenly	.06	.02	.00
□	535	Chris Brown	.10	.04	.01
□	536	Chili Davis	.15	.06	.01
□	537	Mark Davis	.10	.04	.01
□	538	Rob Deer	.30	.12	.03
□	539	Dan Driessen	.06	.02	.00
□	540	Scott Garrelts	.12	.05	.01
□	541	Dan Gladden	.10	.04	.01
□	542	Jim Gott	.06	.02	.00
□	543	David Green	.06	.02	.00
□	544	Atlee Hammaker	.06	.02	.00
□	545	Mike Jeffcoat	.06	.02	.00
□	546	Mike Krukow	.06	.02	.00
□	547	Dave LaPoint	.06	.02	.00
□	548	Jeff Leonard	.06	.02	.00
□	549	Greg Minton	.06	.02	.00
□	550	Alex Trevino	.06	.02	.00
□	551	Manny Trillo	.06	.02	.00
□	552	Jose Uribe	.20	.08	.02
□	553	Brad Wellman	.06	.02	.00
□	554	Frank Williams	.06	.02	.00
□	555	Joel Youngblood	.06	.02	.00
□	556	Alan Bannister	.06	.02	.00
□	557	Glenn Brummer	.06	.02	.00
□	558	Steve Buechele	.65	.25	.06
□	559	Jose Guzman	.35	.15	.03
□	560	Toby Harrah	.06	.02	.00
□	561	Greg Harris	.06	.02	.00
□	562	Dwayne Henry	.15	.06	.01
□	563	Burt Hooton	.06	.02	.00
□	564	Charlie Hough	.06	.02	.00
□	565	Mike Mason	.06	.02	.00
□	566	Oddibe McDowell	.10	.04	.01
□	567	Dickie Noles	.06	.02	.00
□	568	Pete O'Brien	.06	.02	.00
□	569	Larry Parrish	.06	.02	.00
□	570	Dave Rozema	.06	.02	.00
□	571	Dave Schmidt	.06	.02	.00
□	572	Don Slaught	.06	.02	.00
□	573	Wayne Tolleson	.06	.02	.00
□	574	Duane Walker	.06	.02	.00
□	575	Gary Ward	.06	.02	.00
□	576	Chris Welsh	.06	.02	.00
□	577	Curtis Wilkerson	.06	.02	.00
□	578	George Wright	.06	.02	.00
□	579	Chris Bando	.06	.02	.00
□	580	Tony Bernazard	.06	.02	.00
□	581	Brett Butler	.17	.07	.01
□	582	Ernie Camacho	.06	.02	.00
□	583	Joe Carter	1.25	.50	.12
□	584	Carmen Castillo	.06	.02	.00
□	585	Jamie Easterly	.06	.02	.00
□	586	Julio Franco	.75	.30	.07
□	587	Mel Hall	.12	.05	.01
□	588	Mike Hargrove	.06	.02	.00
□	589	Neal Heaton	.06	.02	.00
□	590	Brook Jacoby	.10	.04	.01
□	591	Otis Nixon	.50	.20	.05
□	592	Jerry Reed	.06	.02	.00
□	593	Vern Ruhle	.06	.02	.00
□	594	Pat Tabler	.06	.02	.00
□	595	Rich Thompson	.06	.02	.00
□	596	Andre Thornton	.06	.02	.00
□	597	Dave Von Ohlen	.06	.02	.00
□	598	George Vukovich	.06	.02	.00
□	599	Tom Waddell	.06	.02	.00
□	600	Curt Wardle	.06	.02	.00
□	601	Jerry Willard	.06	.02	.00
□	602	Bill Almon	.06	.02	.00
□	603	Mike Bielecki	.10	.04	.01
□	604	Sid Bream	.10	.04	.01
□	605	Mike Brown OF	.06	.02	.00
□	606	Pat Clements	.06	.02	.00
□	607	Jose DeLeon	.06	.02	.00
□	608	Denny Gonzalez	.06	.02	.00
□	609	Cecilio Guante	.06	.02	.00
□	610	Steve Kemp	.06	.02	.00
□	611	Sammy Khalifa	.06	.02	.00
□	612	Lee Mazzilli	.06	.02	.00
□	613	Larry McWilliams	.06	.02	.00
□	614	Jim Morrison	.06	.02	.00
□	615	Joe Orsulak	.30	.12	.03
□	616	Tony Pena	.10	.04	.01
□	617	Johnny Ray	.06	.02	.00
□	618	Rick Reuschel	.10	.04	.01
□	619	R.J. Reynolds	.06	.02	.00
□	620	Rick Rhoden	.06	.02	.00
□	621	Don Robinson	.06	.02	.00
□	622	Jason Thompson	.06	.02	.00
□	623	Lee Tunnell	.06	.02	.00
□	624	Jim Winn	.06	.02	.00
□	625	Marvell Wynne	.06	.02	.00
□	626	Dwight Gooden IA	.60	.25	.06
□	627	Don Mattingly IA	1.25	.50	.12

□	#	Card			
□	628	4192 (Pete Rose)	.40	.16	.04
□	629	3000 Career Hits — Rod Carew	.40	.16	.04
□	630	300 Career Wins — Tom Seaver, Phil Niekro	.30	.12	.03
□	631	Ouch (Don Baylor)	.10	.04	.01
□	632	Instant Offense — Darryl Strawberry, Tim Raines	.60	.25	.06
□	633	Shortstops Supreme — Cal Ripken, Alan Trammell	.75	.30	.07
□	634	Boggs and "Hero" — Wade Boggs, George Brett	.90	.40	.09
□	635	Braves Dynamic Duo — Bob Horner, Dale Murphy	.15	.06	.01
□	636	Cardinal Ignitors — Willie McGee, Vince Coleman	.50	.20	.05
□	637	Terror on Basepaths — Vince Coleman	.60	.25	.06
□	638	Charlie Hustle / Dr.K — Pete Rose, Dwight Gooden	.75	.30	.07
□	639	1984 and 1985 AL Batting Champs — Wade Boggs, Don Mattingly	1.25	.50	.12
□	640	NL West Sluggers — Dale Murphy, Steve Garvey, Dave Parker	.30	.12	.03
□	641	Staff Aces — Fernando Valenzuela, Dwight Gooden	.30	.12	.03
□	642	Blue Jay Stoppers — Jimmy Key, Dave Stieb	.12	.05	.01
□	643	AL All-Star Backstops — Carlton Fisk, Rich Gedman	.12	.05	.01
□	644	Gene Walter and Benito Santiago	4.00	1.75	.40
□	645	Mike Woodard and Collin Ward	.10	.04	.01
□	646	Kal Daniels and Paul O'Neill	5.50	2.50	.55
□	647	Andres Galarraga and Fred Toliver	1.00	.40	.10
□	648	Bob Kipper and Curt Ford	.10	.04	.01
□	649	Jose Canseco and Eric Plunk	40.00	18.00	6.00
□	650	Mark McLemore and Gus Polidor	.10	.04	.01
□	651	Rob Woodward and Mickey Brantley	.15	.06	.01
□	652	Billy Jo Robidoux and Mark Funderburk	.10	.04	.01
□	653	Cecil Fielder and Cory Snyder	18.00	7.50	2.50
□	654	CL: Royals/Cardinals, Blue Jays/Mets	.15	.02	.00
□	655	CL: Yankees/Dodgers UER — Angels/Reds (168 Darly Sconiers)	.15	.02	.00
□	656	CL: White Sox/Tigers, Expos/Orioles (279 Dennis, 280 Tippy)	.15	.02	.00
□	657	CL: Astros/Padres, Red Sox/Cubs	.15	.02	.00
□	658	CL: Twins/A's, Phillies/Mariners	.15	.02	.00
□	659	CL: Brewers/Braves, Giants/Rangers	.15	.02	.00
□	660	CL: Indians/Pirates, Special Cards	.15	.02	.00

1986 Fleer Wax Box Cards

The cards in this eight-card set measure the standard 2 1/2" by 3 1/2" and were found on the bottom of the Fleer regular issue wax pack and cello pack boxes as four-card panel. Cards have essentially the same design as the 1986 Fleer regular issue set.

		MINT	EXC	G-VG
☐ 4	Gary Carter	1.00	.40	.10
	Catcher			
☐ 5	Cal Ripken	5.00	2.25	.50
	Shortstop			
☐ 6	Dave Parker	.75	.30	.07
	Outfield			
☐ 7	Rickey Henderson UER	5.00	2.25	.50
	Outfield			
	(Misspelled Ricky			
	on card back)			
☐ 8	Pedro Guerrero	.50	.20	.05
	Outfield			
☐ 9	Dan Quisenberry	.40	.16	.04
	Relief Pitcher			
☐ 10	Dwight Gooden	2.50	1.00	.25
	Right-Hand Pitcher			
☐ 11	Gorman Thomas	.40	.16	.04
	Designated Hitter			
☐ 12	John Tudor	.40	.16	.04
	Left-Hand Pitcher			

These eight cards (C1 to C8) are considered a separate set in their own right and are not typically included in a complete set of the regular issue 1986 Fleer cards. The value of the panel uncut is slightly greater, perhaps by 25 percent greater, than the value of the individual cards cut up carefully.

	MINT	EXC	G-VG
COMPLETE SET (8)	2.50	1.00	.25
COMMON PLAYERS	.10	.04	.01
☐ C1 Royals Logo	.10	.04	.01
☐ C2 George Brett	.75	.30	.07
☐ C3 Ozzie Guillen	.60	.25	.06
☐ C4 Dale Murphy	.60	.25	.06
☐ C5 Cardinals Logo	.10	.04	.01
☐ C6 Tom Browning	.20	.08	.02
☐ C7 Gary Carter	.25	.10	.02
☐ C8 Carlton Fisk	.45	.18	.04

1986 Fleer All-Star Inserts

Fleer selected a 12-card (Major League) All-Star team to be included as inserts in their 39 cent wax packs and 59 cent cello packs. However they were randomly inserted in such a way that not all wax packs contain the insert. Cards measure 2 1/2" by 3 1/2" and feature attractive red backgrounds (American Leaguers) and blue backgrounds (National Leaguers). The 12 selections cover each position, left and right-handed starting pitchers, a reliever, and a designated hitter.

		MINT	EXC	G-VG
COMPLETE SET (12)		20.00	8.50	2.75
COMMON PLAYER (1-12)		.40	.16	.04
☐ 1	Don Mattingly	5.00	2.25	.50
	First Base			
☐ 2	Tom Herr	.40	.16	.04
	Second Base			
☐ 3	George Brett	2.50	1.00	.25
	Third Base			

1986 Fleer Future HOF

These attractive cards were issued as inserts with the Fleer three-packs. They are the same size as the regular issue (2 1/2" by 3 1/2") and feature players that Fleer predicts will be "Future Hall of Famers." The card backs describe career highlights, records, and honors won by the player. The cards are numbered on the back; Pete Rose is given the honor of being card number 1.

		MINT	EXC	G-VG
COMPLETE SET (6)		9.00	4.00	.90
COMMON PLAYER (1-6)		1.25	.50	.12
☐ 1	Pete Rose	2.00	.80	.20
	Cincinnati Reds			
☐ 2	Steve Carlton	1.25	.50	.12
	Philadelphia Phillies			
☐ 3	Tom Seaver	2.25	.90	.22
	Chicago White Sox			
☐ 4	Rod Carew	1.50	.60	.15
	California Angels			
☐ 5	Nolan Ryan	4.00	1.75	.40
	Houston Astros			
☐ 6	Reggie Jackson	2.00	.80	.20
	California Angels			

1986 Fleer League Leaders

This 44-card set is also sometimes referred to as the Walgreen's set. Although the set was distributed through Walgreen's, there is no mention on the cards or box of that fact. The cards are easily recognizable by the fact that they contain the phrase "Fleer League Leaders" at the top of the obverse. Both sides of the cards are designed with a blue stripe on white pattern. The checklist for the set is given on the outside of the red, white, blue, and gold box in which the set was packaged. Cards are numbered on the back and measure the standard 2 1/2" by 3 1/2".

	MINT	EXC	G-VG
COMPLETE SET (44)	5.00	2.25	.50
COMMON PLAYER (1-44)	.10	.04	.01
☐ 1 Wade Boggs	.75	.30	.07
☐ 2 George Brett	.60	.25	.06
☐ 3 Jose Canseco	1.25	.50	.12
☐ 4 Rod Carew	.50	.20	.05
☐ 5 Gary Carter	.25	.10	.02
☐ 6 Jack Clark	.20	.08	.02
☐ 7 Vince Coleman	.40	.16	.04
☐ 8 Jose Cruz	.10	.04	.01
☐ 9 Alvin Davis	.15	.06	.01
☐ 10 Mariano Duncan	.10	.04	.01
☐ 11 Leon Durham	.10	.04	.01
☐ 12 Carlton Fisk	.40	.16	.04
☐ 13 Julio Franco	.25	.10	.02
☐ 14 Scott Garrelts	.10	.04	.01
☐ 15 Steve Garvey	.30	.12	.03
☐ 16 Dwight Gooden	.45	.18	.04
☐ 17 Ozzie Guillen	.20	.08	.02
☐ 18 Willie Hernandez	.10	.04	.01
☐ 19 Bob Horner	.15	.06	.01
☐ 20 Kent Hrbek	.20	.08	.02
☐ 21 Charlie Leibrandt	.10	.04	.01
☐ 22 Don Mattingly	.75	.30	.07
☐ 23 Oddibe McDowell	.10	.04	.01
☐ 24 Willie McGee	.20	.08	.02
☐ 25 Keith Moreland	.10	.04	.01
☐ 26 Lloyd Moseby	.10	.04	.01
☐ 27 Dale Murphy	.35	.15	.03
☐ 28 Phil Niekro	.20	.08	.02
☐ 29 Joe Orsulak	.10	.04	.01
☐ 30 Dave Parker	.25	.10	.02
☐ 31 Lance Parrish	.15	.06	.01
☐ 32 Kirby Puckett	.60	.25	.06
☐ 33 Tim Raines	.25	.10	.02
☐ 34 Earnie Riles	.10	.04	.01
☐ 35 Cal Ripken	.75	.30	.07
☐ 36 Pete Rose	.60	.25	.06
☐ 37 Bret Saberhagen	.35	.15	.03
☐ 38 Juan Samuel	.15	.06	.01
☐ 39 Ryne Sandberg	.75	.30	.07
☐ 40 Tom Seaver	.60	.25	.06
☐ 41 Lee Smith	.10	.04	.01
☐ 42 Ozzie Smith	.30	.12	.03
☐ 43 Dave Stieb	.15	.06	.01
☐ 44 Robin Yount	.45	.18	.04

1986 Fleer Limited Edition

The 44-card boxed set was produced by Fleer for McCrory's. The cards are standard size 2 1/2" by 3 1/2" and have green and yellow borders. Card backs are printed in red and black on white card stock. Cards are numbered on the back; the back of the original box gives a complete checklist of the players in the set. The set box also contains six logo stickers.

	MINT	EXC	G-VG
COMPLETE SET (44)	5.00	2.25	.50
COMMON PLAYER (1-44)	.10	.04	.01
☐ 1 Doyle Alexander	.10	.04	.01
☐ 2 Joaquin Andujar	.10	.04	.01
☐ 3 Harold Baines	.15	.06	.01
☐ 4 Wade Boggs	.75	.30	.07
☐ 5 Phil Bradley	.15	.06	.01
☐ 6 George Brett	.60	.25	.06
☐ 7 Hubie Brooks	.10	.04	.01
☐ 8 Chris Brown	.10	.04	.01
☐ 9 Tom Brunansky	.15	.06	.01
☐ 10 Gary Carter	.25	.10	.02
☐ 11 Vince Coleman	.40	.16	.04
☐ 12 Cecil Cooper	.15	.06	.01
☐ 13 Jose Cruz	.10	.04	.01
☐ 14 Mike Davis	.10	.04	.01
☐ 15 Carlton Fisk	.40	.16	.04
☐ 16 Julio Franco	.25	.10	.02
☐ 17 Damaso Garcia	.10	.04	.01
☐ 18 Rich Gedman	.10	.04	.01
☐ 19 Kirk Gibson	.30	.12	.03
☐ 20 Dwight Gooden	.45	.18	.04
☐ 21 Pedro Guerrero	.20	.08	.02
☐ 22 Tony Gwynn	.50	.20	.05
☐ 23 Rickey Henderson	.75	.30	.07
☐ 24 Orel Hershiser	.45	.18	.04
☐ 25 LaMarr Hoyt	.10	.04	.01
☐ 26 Reggie Jackson	.60	.25	.06
☐ 27 Don Mattingly	.75	.30	.07
☐ 28 Oddibe McDowell	.10	.04	.01
☐ 29 Willie McGee	.20	.08	.02
☐ 30 Paul Molitor	.20	.08	.02
☐ 31 Dale Murphy	.35	.15	.03
☐ 32 Eddie Murray	.40	.16	.04
☐ 33 Dave Parker	.25	.10	.02
☐ 34 Tony Pena	.10	.04	.01
☐ 35 Jeff Reardon	.25	.10	.02
☐ 36 Cal Ripken	.75	.30	.07
☐ 37 Pete Rose	.60	.25	.06
☐ 38 Bret Saberhagen	.35	.15	.03
☐ 39 Juan Samuel	.15	.06	.01
☐ 40 Ryne Sandberg	.75	.30	.07
☐ 41 Mike Schmidt	.75	.30	.07
☐ 42 Lee Smith	.20	.08	.02
☐ 43 Don Sutton	.20	.08	.02
☐ 44 Lou Whitaker	.20	.08	.02

1986 Fleer Mini

The Fleer "Classic Miniatures" set consists of 120 small cards with all new pictures of the players as compared to the 1986 Fleer regular issue. The cards are only 1 13/16" by 2 9/16", making them one of the smallest (in size) produced in recent memory. Card backs provide career year-by-year statistics. The complete set was distributed in a red, white, and silver box along with 18 logo stickers. The card numbering is done in team order as is the usual Fleer style.

	MINT	EXC	G-VG
COMPLETE SET (120)	15.00	6.50	2.15
COMMON PLAYER (1-120)	.05	.02	.00

☐ 1 George Brett	.50	.20	.05
☐ 2 Dan Quisenberry	.10	.04	.01
☐ 3 Bret Saberhagen	.35	.15	.03
☐ 4 Lonnie Smith	.10	.04	.01
☐ 5 Willie Wilson	.10	.04	.01
☐ 6 Jack Clark	.20	.08	.02
☐ 7 Vince Coleman	.40	.16	.04
☐ 8 Tom Herr	.05	.02	.00
☐ 9 Willie McGee	.15	.06	.01
☐ 10 Ozzie Smith	.25	.10	.02
☐ 11 John Tudor	.10	.04	.01
☐ 12 Jesse Barfield	.10	.04	.01
☐ 13 George Bell	.25	.10	.02
☐ 14 Tony Fernandez	.10	.04	.01
☐ 15 Damaso Garcia	.05	.02	.00
☐ 16 Dave Stieb	.15	.06	.01
☐ 17 Gary Carter	.20	.08	.02
☐ 18 Ron Darling	.10	.04	.01
☐ 19A Dwight Gooden (R on Mets logo)	1.50	.60	.15
☐ 19B Dwight Gooden (no R on Mets logo)	1.50	.60	.15
☐ 20 Keith Hernandez	.20	.08	.02
☐ 21 Darryl Strawberry	.75	.30	.07
☐ 22 Ron Guidry	.15	.06	.01
☐ 23 Rickey Henderson	1.00	.40	.10
☐ 24 Don Mattingly	.75	.30	.07
☐ 25 Dave Righetti	.10	.04	.01
☐ 26 Dave Winfield	.25	.10	.02
☐ 27 Mariano Duncan	.05	.02	.00
☐ 28 Pedro Guerrero	.15	.06	.01
☐ 29 Bill Madlock	.05	.02	.00
☐ 30 Mike Marshall	.10	.04	.01
☐ 31 Fernando Valenzuela	.15	.06	.01
☐ 32 Reggie Jackson	.45	.18	.04
☐ 33 Gary Pettis	.05	.02	.00
☐ 34 Ron Romanick	.05	.02	.00
☐ 35 Don Sutton	.15	.06	.01
☐ 36 Mike Witt	.05	.02	.00
☐ 37 Buddy Bell	.10	.04	.01
☐ 38 Tom Browning	.10	.04	.01
☐ 39 Dave Parker	.20	.08	.02
☐ 40 Pete Rose	.75	.30	.07
☐ 41 Mario Soto	.05	.02	.00
☐ 42 Harold Baines	.10	.04	.01
☐ 43 Carlton Fisk	.35	.15	.03
☐ 44 Ozzie Guillen	.15	.06	.01
☐ 45 Ron Kittle	.10	.04	.01
☐ 46 Tom Seaver	.45	.18	.04
☐ 47 Kirk Gibson	.25	.10	.02
☐ 48 Jack Morris	.20	.08	.02
☐ 49 Lance Parrish	.10	.04	.01
☐ 50 Alan Trammell	.20	.08	.02
☐ 51 Lou Whitaker	.15	.06	.01
☐ 52 Hubie Brooks	.10	.04	.01
☐ 53 Andre Dawson	.30	.12	.03
☐ 54 Tim Raines	.20	.08	.02
☐ 55 Bryn Smith	.05	.02	.00
☐ 56 Tim Wallach	.10	.04	.01
☐ 57 Mike Boddicker	.05	.02	.00
☐ 58 Eddie Murray	.40	.16	.04
☐ 59 Cal Ripken	.75	.30	.07
☐ 60 John Shelby	.05	.02	.00
☐ 61 Mike Young	.05	.02	.00
☐ 62 Jose Cruz	.05	.02	.00
☐ 63 Glenn Davis	.30	.12	.03
☐ 64 Phil Garner	.05	.02	.00
☐ 65 Nolan Ryan	1.50	.60	.15
☐ 66 Mike Scott	.10	.04	.01
☐ 67 Steve Garvey	.20	.08	.02
☐ 68 Goose Gossage	.15	.06	.01
☐ 69 Tony Gwynn	.40	.16	.04
☐ 70 Andy Hawkins	.05	.02	.00
☐ 71 Garry Templeton	.05	.02	.00
☐ 72 Wade Boggs	.90	.40	.09
☐ 73 Roger Clemens	1.00	.40	.10
☐ 74 Dwight Evans	.15	.06	.01
☐ 75 Rich Gedman	.05	.02	.00
☐ 76 Jim Rice	.20	.08	.02
☐ 77 Shawon Dunston	.25	.10	.02
☐ 78 Leon Durham	.05	.02	.00
☐ 79 Keith Moreland	.05	.02	.00
☐ 80 Ryne Sandberg	.90	.40	.09
☐ 81 Rick Sutcliffe	.10	.04	.01
☐ 82 Bert Blyleven	.15	.06	.01
☐ 83 Tom Brunansky	.10	.04	.01
☐ 84 Kent Hrbek	.15	.06	.01
☐ 85 Kirby Puckett	.60	.25	.06
☐ 86 Bruce Bochte	.05	.02	.00
☐ 87 Jose Canseco	3.00	1.25	.30
☐ 88 Mike Davis	.05	.02	.00
☐ 89 Jay Howell	.05	.02	.00
☐ 90 Dwayne Murphy	.05	.02	.00
☐ 91 Steve Carlton	.30	.12	.03

☐ 92 Von Hayes	.10	.04	.01
☐ 93 Juan Samuel	.10	.04	.01
☐ 94 Mike Schmidt	.75	.30	.07
☐ 95 Glenn Wilson	.05	.02	.00
☐ 96 Phil Bradley	.05	.02	.00
☐ 97 Alvin Davis	.10	.04	.01
☐ 98 Jim Presley	.05	.02	.00
☐ 99 Danny Tartabull	.40	.16	.04
☐ 100 Cecil Cooper	.10	.04	.01
☐ 101 Paul Molitor	.15	.06	.01
☐ 102 Ernie Riles	.05	.02	.00
☐ 103 Robin Yount	.50	.20	.05
☐ 104 Bob Horner	.10	.04	.01
☐ 105 Dale Murphy	.35	.15	.03
☐ 106 Bruce Sutter	.10	.04	.01
☐ 107 Claudell Washington	.05	.02	.00
☐ 108 Chris Brown	.05	.02	.00
☐ 109 Chili Davis	.10	.04	.01
☐ 110 Scott Garrelts	.05	.02	.00
☐ 111 Oddibe McDowell	.05	.02	.00
☐ 112 Pete O'Brien	.05	.02	.00
☐ 113 Gary Ward	.05	.02	.00
☐ 114 Brett Butler	.15	.06	.01
☐ 115 Julio Franco	.20	.08	.02
☐ 116 Brook Jacoby	.05	.02	.00
☐ 117 Mike Brown OF	.05	.02	.00
☐ 118 Joe Orsulak	.05	.02	.00
☐ 119 Tony Pena	.10	.04	.01
☐ 120 R.J. Reynolds	.05	.02	.00

1986 Fleer Sluggers/Pitchers

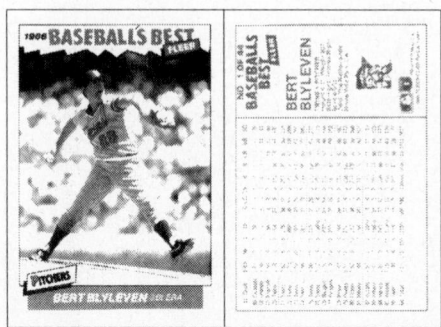

Fleer produced this 44-card boxed set although it was primarily distributed by Kress, McCrory, Newberry, T.G.Y., and other similar stores. The set features 22 sluggers and 22 pitchers and is subtitled "Baseball's Best". Cards are standard-size, 2 1/2" by 3 1/2", and were packaged in a red, white, blue, and yellow custom box along with six logo stickers. The set checklist is given on the back of the box.

	MINT	EXC	G-VG
COMPLETE SET (44)	7.50	3.25	.75
COMMON PLAYER (1-44)	.10	.04	.01
☐ 1 Bert Blyleven	.15	.06	.01
☐ 2 Wade Boggs	.75	.30	.07
☐ 3 George Brett	.50	.20	.05
☐ 4 Tom Browning	.10	.04	.01
☐ 5 Jose Canseco	2.00	.80	.20
☐ 6 Will Clark	2.00	.80	.20
☐ 7 Roger Clemens	.90	.40	.09
☐ 8 Alvin Davis	.15	.06	.01
☐ 9 Julio Franco	.20	.08	.02
☐ 10 Kirk Gibson	.25	.10	.02
☐ 11 Dwight Gooden	.45	.18	.04
☐ 12 Goose Gossage	.15	.06	.01
☐ 13 Pedro Guerrero	.20	.08	.02
☐ 14 Ron Guidry	.15	.06	.01
☐ 15 Tony Gwynn	.40	.16	.04
☐ 16 Orel Hershiser	.40	.16	.04
☐ 17 Kent Hrbek	.20	.08	.02
☐ 18 Reggie Jackson	.45	.18	.04
☐ 19 Wally Joyner	.90	.40	.09
☐ 20 Charlie Leibrandt	.10	.04	.01
☐ 21 Don Mattingly	.75	.30	.07

☐ 22	Willie McGee	.20	.08	.02
☐ 23	Jack Morris	.20	.08	.02
☐ 24	Dale Murphy	.35	.15	.03
☐ 25	Eddie Murray	.40	.16	.04
☐ 26	Jeff Reardon	.15	.06	.01
☐ 27	Rick Reuschel	.10	.04	.01
☐ 28	Cal Ripken	.75	.30	.07
☐ 29	Pete Rose	.60	.25	.06
☐ 30	Nolan Ryan	1.25	.50	.12
☐ 31	Bret Saberhagen	.35	.15	.03
☐ 32	Ryne Sandberg	.75	.30	.07
☐ 33	Mike Schmidt	.75	.30	.07
☐ 34	Tom Seaver	.60	.25	.06
☐ 35	Bryn Smith	.10	.04	.01
☐ 36	Mario Soto	.10	.04	.01
☐ 37	Dave Stieb	.15	.06	.01
☐ 38	Darryl Strawberry	.60	.25	.06
☐ 39	Rick Sutcliffe	.15	.06	.01
☐ 40	John Tudor	.15	.06	.01
☐ 41	Fernando Valenzuela	.20	.08	.02
☐ 42	Bobby Witt	.20	.08	.02
☐ 43	Mike Witt	.10	.04	.01
☐ 44	Robin Yount	.40	.16	.04

1986 Fleer Slug/Pitch Box Cards

The cards in this six-card set each measure the standard 2 1/2" by 3 1/2". Cards have essentially the same design as the 1986 Fleer Sluggers vs. Pitchers set of Baseball's Best. The cards were printed on the bottom of the counter display box which held 24 small boxed sets; hence theoretically these box cards are 1/24 as plentiful as the regular boxed set cards. These 6 cards, numbered M1 to M5 with one blank-back (unnumbered) card, are considered a separate set in their own right and are not typically included in a complete set of the 1986 Fleer Sluggers vs. Pitchers set of 44. The value of the panels uncut is slightly greater, perhaps by 25 percent greater, than the value of the individual cards cut up carefully.

		MINT	EXC	G-VG
COMPLETE SET		4.00	1.75	.40
COMMON PLAYERS		.10	.04	.01
☐ M1	Harold Baines	.25	.10	.02
☐ M2	Steve Carlton	1.00	.40	.10
☐ M3	Gary Carter	.60	.25	.06
☐ M4	Vince Coleman	1.25	.50	.12
☐ M5	Kirby Puckett	2.00	.80	.20
☐ xx	Team Logo	.10	.04	.01
	(unnumbered, blank back)			

1986 Fleer Sticker Cards

The stickers in this 132-sticker card set are standard card size, 2 1/2" by 3 1/2". The card photo on the front is surrounded by a yellow border and a cranberry frame. The backs are printed in

blue and black on white card stock. The backs contain year-by-year statistical information. They are numbered on the back in the upper left-hand corner.

		MINT	EXC	G-VG
COMPLETE SET (132)		30.00	13.50	4.50
COMMON PLAYER (1-132)		.05	.02	.00
☐ 1	Harold Baines	.15	.06	.01
☐ 2	Jesse Barfield	.10	.04	.01
☐ 3	Don Baylor	.10	.04	.01
☐ 4	Juan Beniquez	.05	.02	.00
☐ 5	Tim Birtsas	.05	.02	.00
☐ 6	Bert Blyleven	.15	.06	.01
☐ 7	Bruce Bochte	.05	.02	.00
☐ 8	Wade Boggs	1.00	.40	.10
☐ 9	Dennis Boyd	.10	.04	.01
☐ 10	Phil Bradley	.10	.04	.01
☐ 11	George Brett	.90	.40	.09
☐ 12	Hubie Brooks	.10	.04	.01
☐ 13	Chris Brown	.05	.02	.00
☐ 14	Tom Browning	.15	.06	.01
☐ 15	Tom Brunansky	.15	.06	.01
☐ 16	Bill Buckner	.10	.04	.01
☐ 17	Britt Burns	.05	.02	.00
☐ 18	Brett Butler	.15	.06	.01
☐ 19	Jose Canseco	3.50	1.50	.35
☐ 20	Rod Carew	.60	.25	.06
☐ 21	Steve Carlton	.40	.16	.04
☐ 22	Don Carman	.10	.04	.01
☐ 23	Gary Carter	.30	.12	.03
☐ 24	Jack Clark	.20	.08	.02
☐ 25	Vince Coleman	1.50	.60	.15
☐ 26	Cecil Cooper	.10	.04	.01
☐ 27	Jose Cruz	.05	.02	.00
☐ 28	Ron Darling	.15	.06	.01
☐ 29	Alvin Davis	.15	.06	.01
☐ 30	Jody Davis	.05	.02	.00
☐ 31	Mike Davis	.05	.02	.00
☐ 32	Andre Dawson	.35	.15	.03
☐ 33	Mariano Duncan	.10	.04	.01
☐ 34	Shawon Dunston	.25	.10	.02
☐ 35	Leon Durham	.05	.02	.00
☐ 36	Darrell Evans	.10	.04	.01
☐ 37	Tony Fernandez	.10	.04	.01
☐ 38	Carlton Fisk	.40	.16	.04
☐ 39	John Franco	.10	.04	.01
☐ 40	Julio Franco	.20	.08	.02
☐ 41	Damaso Garcia	.05	.02	.00
☐ 42	Scott Garrelts	.10	.04	.01
☐ 43	Steve Garvey	.40	.16	.04
☐ 44	Rich Gedman	.05	.02	.00
☐ 45	Kirk Gibson	.30	.12	.03
☐ 46	Dwight Gooden	.75	.30	.07
☐ 47	Pedro Guerrero	.20	.08	.02
☐ 48	Ron Guidry	.15	.06	.01
☐ 49	Ozzie Guillen	.30	.12	.03
☐ 50	Tony Gwynn	.60	.25	.06
☐ 51	Andy Hawkins	.05	.02	.00
☐ 52	Von Hayes	.10	.04	.01
☐ 53	Rickey Henderson	1.50	.60	.15
☐ 54	Tom Henke	.10	.04	.01
☐ 55	Keith Hernandez	.25	.10	.02
☐ 56	Willie Hernandez	.05	.02	.00
☐ 57	Tommy Herr	.05	.02	.00
☐ 58	Orel Hershiser	.50	.20	.05
☐ 59	Teddy Higuera	.35	.15	.03
☐ 60	Bob Horner	.10	.04	.01
☐ 61	Charlie Hough	.05	.02	.00
☐ 62	Jay Howell	.05	.02	.00
☐ 63	LaMarr Hoyt	.05	.02	.00

		MINT	EXC	G-VG
☐ 64	Kent Hrbek	.20	.08	.02
☐ 65	Reggie Jackson	.60	.25	.06
☐ 66	Bob James	.05	.02	.00
☐ 67	Dave Kingman	.10	.04	.01
☐ 68	Ron Kittle	.10	.04	.01
☐ 69	Charlie Leibrandt	.05	.02	.00
☐ 70	Fred Lynn	.15	.06	.01
☐ 71	Mike Marshall	.10	.04	.01
☐ 72	Don Mattingly	1.00	.40	.10
☐ 73	Oddibe McDowell	.05	.02	.00
☐ 74	Willie McGee	.15	.06	.01
☐ 75	Scott McGregor	.05	.02	.00
☐ 76	Paul Molitor	.20	.08	.02
☐ 77	Donnie Moore	.05	.02	.00
☐ 78	Keith Moreland	.05	.02	.00
☐ 79	Jack Morris	.20	.08	.02
☐ 80	Dale Murphy	.50	.20	.05
☐ 81	Eddie Murray	.60	.25	.06
☐ 82	Phil Niekro	.25	.10	.02
☐ 83	Joe Orsulak	.05	.02	.00
☐ 84	Dave Parker	.20	.08	.02
☐ 85	Lance Parrish	.15	.06	.01
☐ 86	Larry Parrish	.05	.02	.00
☐ 87	Tony Pena	.10	.04	.01
☐ 88	Gary Pettis	.05	.02	.00
☐ 89	Jim Presley	.05	.02	.00
☐ 90	Kirby Puckett	1.00	.40	.10
☐ 91	Dan Quisenberry	.10	.04	.01
☐ 92	Tim Raines	.20	.08	.02
☐ 93	Johnny Ray	.10	.04	.01
☐ 94	Jeff Reardon	.15	.06	.01
☐ 95	Rick Reuschel	.10	.04	.01
☐ 96	Jim Rice	.20	.08	.02
☐ 97	Dave Righetti	.15	.06	.01
☐ 98	Earnie Riles	.05	.02	.00
☐ 99	Cal Ripken	1.00	.40	.10
☐ 100	Ron Romanick	.05	.02	.00
☐ 101	Pete Rose	1.00	.40	.10
☐ 102	Nolan Ryan	2.00	.80	.20
☐ 103	Bret Saberhagen	.60	.25	.06
☐ 104	Mark Salas	.05	.02	.00
☐ 105	Juan Samuel	.15	.06	.01
☐ 106	Ryne Sandberg	1.00	.40	.10
☐ 107	Mike Schmidt	1.25	.50	.12
☐ 108	Mike Scott	.15	.06	.01
☐ 109	Tom Seaver	.50	.20	.05
☐ 110	Bryn Smith	.05	.02	.00
☐ 111	Dave Smith	.05	.02	.00
☐ 112	Lee Smith	.15	.06	.01
☐ 113	Ozzie Smith	.35	.15	.03
☐ 114	Mario Soto	.05	.02	.00
☐ 115	Dave Stieb	.15	.06	.01
☐ 116	Darryl Strawberry	1.00	.40	.10
☐ 117	Bruce Sutter	.10	.04	.01
☐ 118	Garry Templeton	.05	.02	.00
☐ 119	Gorman Thomas	.10	.04	.01
☐ 120	Andre Thornton	.05	.02	.00
☐ 121	Alan Trammell	.25	.10	.02
☐ 122	John Tudor	.15	.06	.01
☐ 123	Fernando Valenzuela	.20	.08	.02
☐ 124	Frank Viola	.25	.10	.02
☐ 125	Gary Ward	.05	.02	.00
☐ 126	Lou Whitaker	.15	.06	.01
☐ 127	Frank White	.05	.02	.00
☐ 128	Glenn Wilson	.05	.02	.00
☐ 129	Willie Wilson	.15	.06	.01
☐ 130	Dave Winfield	.35	.15	.03
☐ 131	Robin Yount	.60	.25	.06
☐ 132	Checklist Card	1.00	.40	.10
	Dwight Gooden			
	Dale Murphy			

1986 Fleer Sticker Wax Box

The bottoms of the Star Sticker wax boxes contained a set of four cards done in a similar format to the stickers; these cards (they are not stickers but truly cards) are numbered with the prefix S and are considered a separate set. Each individual card measures 2 1/2" by 3 1/2". The value of the panel uncut is slightly greater, perhaps by 25 percent greater, than the value of the individual cards cut up carefully.

		MINT	EXC	G-VG
COMPLETE SET (4)		2.50	1.00	.25
COMMON PLAYER (S1-S4)		.10	.04	.01

		MINT	EXC	G-VG
☐ S1	Team Logo (checklist back)	.10	.04	.01
☐ S2	Wade Boggs	1.50	.60	.15
☐ S3	Steve Garvey	.50	.20	.05
☐ S4	Dave Winfield	.50	.20	.05

1986 Fleer Update

This 132-card set was distributed by Fleer to dealers as a complete set in a custom box. In addition to the complete set of 132 cards, the box also contains 25 Team Logo Stickers. The card fronts look very similar to the 1986 Fleer regular issue. The cards are numbered (with a U prefix) alphabetically according to player's last name. Cards measure the standard size, 2 1/2" by 3 1/2". The key (extended) rookie cards in this set are Barry Bonds, Bobby Bonilla, Will Clark, Wally Joyner, Kevin Mitchell, and Ruben Sierra.

		MINT	EXC	G-VG
COMPLETE SET (132)		32.00	14.25	4.75
COMMON PLAYER (1-132)		.07	.03	.01
☐ U1	Mike Aldrete	.15	.06	.01
☐ U2	Andy Allanson	.10	.04	.01
☐ U3	Neil Allen	.07	.03	.01
☐ U4	Joaquin Andujar	.10	.04	.01
☐ U5	Paul Assenmacher	.12	.05	.01
☐ U6	Scott Bailes	.12	.05	.01
☐ U7	Jay Baller	.10	.04	.01
☐ U8	Scott Bankhead	.20	.08	.02
☐ U9	Bill Bathe	.10	.04	.01
☐ U10	Don Baylor	.12	.05	.01
☐ U11	Billy Beane	.10	.04	.01
☐ U12	Steve Bedrosian	.10	.04	.01
☐ U13	Juan Beniquez	.07	.03	.01
☐ U14	Barry Bonds	6.50	2.75	.65
☐ U15	Bobby Bonilla UER (wrong birthday)	6.00	2.50	.60
☐ U16	Rich Bordi	.07	.03	.01
☐ U17	Bill Campbell	.07	.03	.01
☐ U18	Tom Candiotti	.15	.06	.01

☐ U19	John Cangelosi	.10	.04	.01
☐ U20	Jose Canseco UER	10.00	4.50	1.25
	(headings on back			
	for a pitcher)			
☐ U21	Chuck Cary	.15	.06	.01
☐ U22	Juan Castillo	.07	.03	.01
☐ U23	Rick Cerone	.07	.03	.01
☐ U24	John Cerutti	.15	.06	.01
☐ U25	Will Clark	12.00	5.25	1.50
☐ U26	Mark Clear	.07	.03	.01
☐ U27	Darnell Coles	.07	.03	.01
☐ U28	Dave Collins	.07	.03	.01
☐ U29	Tim Conroy	.07	.03	.01
☐ U30	Ed Correa	.10	.04	.01
☐ U31	Joe Cowley	.07	.03	.01
☐ U32	Bill Dawley	.07	.03	.01
☐ U33	Rob Deer	.25	.10	.02
☐ U34	John Denny	.07	.03	.01
☐ U35	Jim Deshaies	.17	.07	.01
☐ U36	Doug Drabek	1.25	.50	.12
☐ U37	Mike Easler	.07	.03	.01
☐ U38	Mark Eichhorn	.15	.06	.01
☐ U39	Dave Engle	.07	.03	.01
☐ U40	Mike Fischlin	.07	.03	.01
☐ U41	Scott Fletcher	.07	.03	.01
☐ U42	Terry Forster	.10	.04	.01
☐ U43	Terry Francona	.07	.03	.01
☐ U44	Andres Galarraga	.40	.16	.04
☐ U45	Lee Guetterman	.15	.06	.01
☐ U46	Bill Gullickson	.12	.05	.01
☐ U47	Jackie Gutierrez	.07	.03	.01
☐ U48	Moose Haas	.07	.03	.01
☐ U49	Billy Hatcher	.15	.06	.01
☐ U50	Mike Heath	.07	.03	.01
☐ U51	Guy Hoffman	.07	.03	.01
☐ U52	Tom Hume	.07	.03	.01
☐ U53	Pete Incaviglia	.60	.25	.06
☐ U54	Dane Iorg	.07	.03	.01
☐ U55	Chris James	.35	.15	.03
☐ U56	Stan Javier	.20	.08	.02
☐ U57	Tommy John	.17	.07	.01
☐ U58	Tracy Jones	.12	.05	.01
☐ U59	Wally Joyner	2.50	1.00	.25
☐ U60	Wayne Krenchicki	.07	.03	.01
☐ U61	John Kruk	.60	.25	.06
☐ U62	Mike LaCoss	.07	.03	.01
☐ U63	Pete Ladd	.07	.03	.01
☐ U64	Dave LaPoint	.07	.03	.01
☐ U65	Mike LaValliere	.30	.12	.03
☐ U66	Rudy Law	.07	.03	.01
☐ U67	Dennis Leonard	.10	.04	.01
☐ U68	Steve Lombardozzi	.10	.04	.01
☐ U69	Aurelio Lopez	.07	.03	.01
☐ U70	Mickey Mahler	.07	.03	.01
☐ U71	Candy Maldonado	.15	.06	.01
☐ U72	Roger Mason	.10	.04	.01
☐ U73	Greg Mathews	.12	.05	.01
☐ U74	Andy McGaffigan	.07	.03	.01
☐ U75	Joel McKeon	.10	.04	.01
☐ U76	Kevin Mitchell	5.25	2.25	.50
☐ U77	Bill Mooneyham	.07	.03	.01
☐ U78	Omar Moreno	.07	.03	.01
☐ U79	Jerry Mumphrey	.07	.03	.01
☐ U80	Al Newman	.12	.05	.01
☐ U81	Phil Niekro	.30	.12	.03
☐ U82	Randy Niemann	.07	.03	.01
☐ U83	Juan Nieves	.12	.05	.01
☐ U84	Bob Ojeda	.10	.04	.01
☐ U85	Rick Ownbey	.07	.03	.01
☐ U86	Tom Paciorek	.07	.03	.01
☐ U87	David Palmer	.07	.03	.01
☐ U88	Jeff Parrett	.12	.05	.01
☐ U89	Pat Perry	.10	.04	.01
☐ U90	Dan Plesac	.17	.07	.01
☐ U91	Darrell Porter	.07	.03	.01
☐ U92	Luis Quinones	.12	.05	.01
☐ U93	Rey Quinones	.07	.03	.01
☐ U94	Gary Redus	.07	.03	.01
☐ U95	Jeff Reed	.07	.03	.01
☐ U96	Bip Roberts	.50	.20	.05
☐ U97	Billy Jo Robidoux	.07	.03	.01
☐ U98	Gary Roenicke	.07	.03	.01
☐ U99	Ron Roenicke	.07	.03	.01
☐ U100	Angel Salazar	.07	.03	.01
☐ U101	Joe Sambito	.07	.03	.01
☐ U102	Billy Sample	.07	.03	.01
☐ U103	Dave Schmidt	.07	.03	.01
☐ U104	Ken Schrom	.07	.03	.01
☐ U105	Ruben Sierra	9.00	4.00	.90
☐ U106	Ted Simmons	.20	.08	.02
☐ U107	Sammy Stewart	.07	.03	.01
☐ U108	Kurt Stillwell	.30	.12	.03
☐ U109	Dale Sveum	.12	.05	.01
☐ U110	Tim Teufel	.10	.04	.01
☐ U111	Bob Tewksbury	.10	.04	.01
☐ U112	Andres Thomas	.12	.05	.01
☐ U113	Jason Thompson	.07	.03	.01
☐ U114	Milt Thompson	.10	.04	.01
☐ U115	Robby Thompson	.40	.16	.04
☐ U116	Jay Tibbs	.07	.03	.01
☐ U117	Fred Toliver	.10	.04	.01
☐ U118	Wayne Tolleson	.07	.03	.01
☐ U119	Alex Trevino	.07	.03	.01
☐ U120	Manny Trillo	.07	.03	.01
☐ U121	Ed VandeBerg	.07	.03	.01
☐ U122	Ozzie Virgil	.07	.03	.01
☐ U123	Tony Walker	.10	.04	.01
☐ U124	Gene Walter	.07	.03	.01
☐ U125	Duane Ward	.35	.15	.03
☐ U126	Jerry Willard	.07	.03	.01
☐ U127	Mitch Williams	.40	.16	.04
☐ U128	Reggie Williams	.10	.04	.01
☐ U129	Bobby Witt	.50	.20	.05
☐ U130	Marvell Wynne	.07	.03	.01
☐ U131	Steve Yeager	.07	.03	.01
☐ U132	Checklist 1-132	.07	.01	.00

1987 Fleer

This 660-card set features a distinctive blue border, which fades to white on the card fronts. The backs are printed in blue, red, and pink on white card stock. The bottom of the card back shows an innovative graph of the player's ability, e.g., "He's got the stuff" for pitchers and "How he's hitting 'em," for hitters. Cards are numbered on the back and are again the standard 2 1/2" by 3 1/2". Cards are again organized numerically by teams, i.e., World Champion Mets (1-25), Boston Red Sox (26-48), Houston Astros (49-72), California Angels (73-95), New York Yankees (96-120), Texas Rangers (121-143), Detroit Tigers (144-168), Philadelphia Phillies (169-192), Cincinnati Reds (193-218), Toronto Blue Jays (219-240), Cleveland Indians (241-263), San Francisco Giants (264-288), St. Louis Cardinals (289-312), Montreal Expos (313-337), Milwaukee Brewers (338-361), Kansas City Royals (362-384), Oakland A's (385-410), San Diego Padres (411-435), Los Angeles Dodgers (436-460), Baltimore Orioles (461-483), Chicago White Sox (484-508), Atlanta Braves (509-532), Minnesota Twins (533-554), Chicago Cubs (555-578), Seattle Mariners (579-600), and Pittsburgh Pirates (601-624). The last 36 cards in the set consist of Specials (625-643), Rookie Pairs (644-653), and checklists (654-660). The key rookie cards in this set are Barry Bonds, Bobby Bonilla, Will Clark, Chuck Finley, Bo Jackson, Barry Larkin, Dave Magadan, Kevin Mitchell, Kevin Seitzer, and Ruben Sierra. Fleer also produced a "limited" edition version of this set with glossy coating and packaged in a "tin." However, this tin set was apparently not limited enough (estimated between 75,000 and 100,000 1987 tin sets produced by Fleer), since the price of the "tin" glossy cards is now the same as the regular set.

		MINT	EXC	G-VG
	COMPLETE SET (660)	100.00	45.00	15.00
	COMMON PLAYER (1-660)	.06	.02	.00
☐ 1	Rick Aguilera	.30	.08	.01
☐ 2	Richard Anderson	.06	.02	.00
☐ 3	Wally Backman	.06	.02	.00
☐ 4	Gary Carter	.30	.12	.03
☐ 5	Ron Darling	.15	.06	.01
☐ 6	Len Dykstra	.40	.16	.04
☐ 7	Kevin Elster	.25	.10	.02
☐ 8	Sid Fernandez	.15	.06	.01
☐ 9	Dwight Gooden	1.00	.40	.10
☐ 10	Ed Hearn	.06	.02	.00
☐ 11	Danny Heep	.06	.02	.00
☐ 12	Keith Hernandez	.20	.08	.02
☐ 13	Howard Johnson	.65	.25	.06
☐ 14	Ray Knight	.10	.04	.01
☐ 15	Lee Mazzilli	.06	.02	.00
☐ 16	Roger McDowell	.06	.02	.00
☐ 17	Kevin Mitchell	8.50	3.75	.85
☐ 18	Randy Niemann	.06	.02	.00
☐ 19	Bob Ojeda	.06	.02	.00
☐ 20	Jesse Orosco	.06	.02	.00
☐ 21	Rafael Santana	.06	.02	.00
☐ 22	Doug Sisk	.06	.02	.00
☐ 23	Darryl Strawberry	2.25	.90	.22
☐ 24	Tim Teufel	.06	.02	.00
☐ 25	Mookie Wilson	.10	.04	.01
☐ 26	Tony Armas	.06	.02	.00
☐ 27	Marty Barrett	.06	.02	.00
☐ 28	Don Baylor	.10	.04	.01
☐ 29	Wade Boggs	1.50	.60	.15
☐ 30	Oil Can Boyd	.06	.02	.00
☐ 31	Bill Buckner	.10	.04	.01
☐ 32	Roger Clemens	3.50	1.50	.35
☐ 33	Steve Crawford	.06	.02	.00
☐ 34	Dwight Evans	.20	.08	.02
☐ 35	Rich Gedman	.06	.02	.00
☐ 36	Dave Henderson	.25	.10	.02
☐ 37	Bruce Hurst	.12	.05	.01
☐ 38	Tim Lollar	.06	.02	.00
☐ 39	Al Nipper	.06	.02	.00
☐ 40	Spike Owen	.06	.02	.00
☐ 41	Jim Rice	.15	.06	.01
☐ 42	Ed Romero	.06	.02	.00
☐ 43	Joe Sambito	.06	.02	.00
☐ 44	Calvin Schiraldi	.06	.02	.00
☐ 45	Tom Seaver	.65	.25	.06
☐ 46	Jeff Sellers	.10	.04	.01
☐ 47	Bob Stanley	.06	.02	.00
☐ 48	Sammy Stewart	.06	.02	.00
☐ 49	Larry Andersen	.06	.02	.00
☐ 50	Alan Ashby	.06	.02	.00
☐ 51	Kevin Bass	.10	.04	.01
☐ 52	Jeff Calhoun	.06	.02	.00
☐ 53	Jose Cruz	.10	.04	.01
☐ 54	Danny Darwin	.06	.02	.00
☐ 55	Glenn Davis	.40	.16	.04
☐ 56	Jim Deshaies	.25	.10	.02
☐ 57	Bill Doran	.06	.02	.00
☐ 58	Phil Garner	.10	.04	.01
☐ 59	Billy Hatcher	.12	.05	.01
☐ 60	Charlie Kerfeld	.06	.02	.00
☐ 61	Bob Knepper	.06	.02	.00
☐ 62	Dave Lopes	.10	.04	.01
☐ 63	Aurelio Lopez	.06	.02	.00
☐ 64	Jim Pankovits	.06	.02	.00
☐ 65	Terry Puhl	.06	.02	.00
☐ 66	Craig Reynolds	.06	.02	.00
☐ 67	Nolan Ryan	3.00	1.25	.30
☐ 68	Mike Scott	.15	.06	.01
☐ 69	Dave Smith	.06	.02	.00
☐ 70	Dickie Thon	.06	.02	.00
☐ 71	Tony Walker	.06	.02	.00
☐ 72	Denny Walling	.06	.02	.00
☐ 73	Bob Boone	.12	.05	.01
☐ 74	Rick Burleson	.06	.02	.00
☐ 75	John Candelaria	.06	.02	.00
☐ 76	Doug Corbett	.06	.02	.00
☐ 77	Doug DeCinces	.10	.04	.01
☐ 78	Brian Downing	.10	.04	.01
☐ 79	Chuck Finley	4.00	1.75	.40
☐ 80	Terry Forster	.10	.04	.01
☐ 81	Bob Grich	.10	.04	.01
☐ 82	George Hendrick	.06	.02	.00
☐ 83	Jack Howell	.06	.02	.00
☐ 84	Reggie Jackson	.65	.25	.06
☐ 85	Ruppert Jones	.06	.02	.00
☐ 86	Wally Joyner	4.00	1.75	.40
☐ 87	Gary Lucas	.06	.02	.00
☐ 88	Kirk McCaskill	.06	.02	.00
☐ 89	Donnie Moore	.06	.02	.00
☐ 90	Gary Pettis	.06	.02	.00
☐ 91	Vern Ruhle	.06	.02	.00
☐ 92	Dick Schofield	.06	.02	.00
☐ 93	Don Sutton	.20	.08	.02
☐ 94	Rob Wilfong	.06	.02	.00
☐ 95	Mike Witt	.06	.02	.00
☐ 96	Doug Drabek	2.25	.90	.22
☐ 97	Mike Easler	.06	.02	.00
☐ 98	Mike Fischlin	.06	.02	.00
☐ 99	Brian Fisher	.06	.02	.00
☐ 100	Ron Guidry	.12	.05	.01
☐ 101	Rickey Henderson	2.00	.80	.20
☐ 102	Tommy John	.15	.06	.01
☐ 103	Ron Kittle	.10	.04	.01
☐ 104	Don Mattingly	2.00	.80	.20
☐ 105	Bobby Meacham	.06	.02	.00
☐ 106	Joe Niekro	.10	.04	.01
☐ 107	Mike Pagliarulo	.06	.02	.00
☐ 108	Dan Pasqua	.10	.04	.01
☐ 109	Willie Randolph	.10	.04	.01
☐ 110	Dennis Rasmussen	.06	.02	.00
☐ 111	Dave Righetti	.12	.05	.01
☐ 112	Gary Roenicke	.06	.02	.00
☐ 113	Rod Scurry	.06	.02	.00
☐ 114	Bob Shirley	.06	.02	.00
☐ 115	Joel Skinner	.06	.02	.00
☐ 116	Tim Stoddard	.06	.02	.00
☐ 117	Bob Tewksbury	.10	.04	.01
☐ 118	Wayne Tolleson	.06	.02	.00
☐ 119	Claudell Washington	.06	.02	.00
☐ 120	Dave Winfield	.50	.20	.05
☐ 121	Steve Buechele	.10	.04	.01
☐ 122	Ed Correa	.06	.02	.00
☐ 123	Scott Fletcher	.06	.02	.00
☐ 124	Jose Guzman	.10	.04	.01
☐ 125	Toby Harrah	.06	.02	.00
☐ 126	Greg Harris	.06	.02	.00
☐ 127	Charlie Hough	.06	.02	.00
☐ 128	Pete Incaviglia	.60	.25	.06
☐ 129	Mike Mason	.06	.02	.00
☐ 130	Oddibe McDowell	.10	.04	.01
☐ 131	Dale Mohorcic	.10	.04	.01
☐ 132	Pete O'Brien	.06	.02	.00
☐ 133	Tom Paciorek	.06	.02	.00
☐ 134	Larry Parrish	.06	.02	.00
☐ 135	Geno Petralli	.06	.02	.00
☐ 136	Darrell Porter	.06	.02	.00
☐ 137	Jeff Russell	.10	.04	.01
☐ 138	Ruben Sierra	15.00	6.50	2.15
☐ 139	Don Slaught	.06	.02	.00
☐ 140	Gary Ward	.06	.02	.00
☐ 141	Curtis Wilkerson	.06	.02	.00
☐ 142	Mitch Williams	.50	.20	.05
☐ 143	Bobby Witt	.90	.40	.09
☐ 144	Dave Bergman	.06	.02	.00
☐ 145	Tom Brookens	.06	.02	.00
☐ 146	Bill Campbell	.06	.02	.00
☐ 147	Chuck Cary	.12	.05	.01
☐ 148	Darnell Coles	.06	.02	.00
☐ 149	Dave Collins	.06	.02	.00
☐ 150	Darrell Evans	.12	.05	.01
☐ 151	Kirk Gibson	.25	.10	.02
☐ 152	John Grubb	.06	.02	.00
☐ 153	Willie Hernandez	.06	.02	.00
☐ 154	Larry Herndon	.06	.02	.00
☐ 155	Eric King	.20	.08	.02
☐ 156	Chet Lemon	.06	.02	.00
☐ 157	Dwight Lowry	.06	.02	.00
☐ 158	Jack Morris	.35	.15	.03
☐ 159	Randy O'Neal	.06	.02	.00
☐ 160	Lance Parrish	.12	.05	.01
☐ 161	Dan Petry	.06	.02	.00
☐ 162	Pat Sheridan	.06	.02	.00
☐ 163	Jim Slaton	.06	.02	.00
☐ 164	Frank Tanana	.10	.04	.01
☐ 165	Walt Terrell	.06	.02	.00
☐ 166	Mark Thurmond	.06	.02	.00
☐ 167	Alan Trammell	.40	.16	.04
☐ 168	Lou Whitaker	.20	.08	.02
☐ 169	Luis Aguayo	.06	.02	.00
☐ 170	Steve Bedrosian	.10	.04	.01
☐ 171	Don Carman	.06	.02	.00
☐ 172	Darren Daulton	.12	.05	.01
☐ 173	Greg Gross	.06	.02	.00
☐ 174	Kevin Gross	.06	.02	.00
☐ 175	Von Hayes	.12	.05	.01
☐ 176	Charles Hudson	.06	.02	.00
☐ 177	Tom Hume	.06	.02	.00
☐ 178	Steve Jeltz	.06	.02	.00
☐ 179	Mike Maddux	.12	.05	.01
☐ 180	Shane Rawley	.06	.02	.00
☐ 181	Gary Redus	.06	.02	.00
☐ 182	Ron Roenicke	.06	.02	.00
☐ 183	Bruce Ruffin	.10	.04	.01
☐ 184	John Russell	.06	.02	.00
☐ 185	Juan Samuel	.25	.10	.02
☐ 186	Dan Schatzeder	.06	.02	.00

☐	187	Mike Schmidt	1.50	.60	.15
☐	188	Rick Schu	.06	.02	.00
☐	189	Jeff Stone	.06	.02	.00
☐	190	Kent Tekulve	.06	.02	.00
☐	191	Milt Thompson	.10	.04	.01
☐	192	Glenn Wilson	.06	.02	.00
☐	193	Buddy Bell	.10	.04	.01
☐	194	Tom Browning	.12	.05	.01
☐	195	Sal Butera	.06	.02	.00
☐	196	Dave Concepcion	.12	.05	.01
☐	197	Kal Daniels	.35	.15	.03
☐	198	Eric Davis	1.00	.40	.10
☐	199	John Denny	.06	.02	.00
☐	200	Bo Diaz	.06	.02	.00
☐	201	Nick Esasky	.10	.04	.01
☐	202	John Franco	.10	.04	.01
☐	203	Bill Gullickson	.10	.04	.01
☐	204	Barry Larkin	6.00	2.50	.60
☐	205	Eddie Milner	.06	.02	.00
☐	206	Rob Murphy	.15	.06	.01
☐	207	Ron Oester	.06	.02	.00
☐	208	Dave Parker	.25	.10	.02
☐	209	Tony Perez	.20	.08	.02
☐	210	Ted Power	.06	.02	.00
☐	211	Joe Price	.06	.02	.00
☐	212	Ron Robinson	.06	.02	.00
☐	213	Pete Rose	.75	.30	.07
☐	214	Mario Soto	.06	.02	.00
☐	215	Kurt Stillwell	.35	.15	.03
☐	216	Max Venable	.06	.02	.00
☐	217	Chris Welsh	.06	.02	.00
☐	218	Carl Willis	.15	.06	.01
☐	219	Jesse Barfield	.15	.06	.01
☐	220	George Bell	.40	.16	.04
☐	221	Bill Caudill	.06	.02	.00
☐	222	John Cerutti	.15	.06	.01
☐	223	Jim Clancy	.06	.02	.00
☐	224	Mark Eichhorn	.15	.06	.01
☐	225	Tony Fernandez	.20	.08	.02
☐	226	Damaso Garcia	.06	.02	.00
☐	227	Kelly Gruber ERR (wrong birth year)	.75	.30	.07
☐	228	Tom Henke	.12	.05	.01
☐	229	Garth Iorg	.06	.02	.00
☐	230	Joe Johnson	.06	.02	.00
☐	231	Cliff Johnson	.06	.02	.00
☐	232	Jimmy Key	.15	.06	.01
☐	233	Dennis Lamp	.06	.02	.00
☐	234	Rick Leach	.06	.02	.00
☐	235	Buck Martinez	.06	.02	.00
☐	236	Lloyd Moseby	.06	.02	.00
☐	237	Rance Mulliniks	.06	.02	.00
☐	238	Dave Stieb	.15	.06	.01
☐	239	Willie Upshaw	.06	.02	.00
☐	240	Ernie Whitt	.06	.02	.00
☐	241	Andy Allanson	.06	.02	.00
☐	242	Scott Bailes	.10	.04	.01
☐	243	Chris Bando	.06	.02	.00
☐	244	Tony Bernazard	.06	.02	.00
☐	245	John Butcher	.06	.02	.00
☐	246	Brett Butler	.15	.06	.01
☐	247	Ernie Camacho	.06	.02	.00
☐	248	Tom Candiotti	.12	.05	.01
☐	249	Joe Carter	.75	.30	.07
☐	250	Carmen Castillo	.06	.02	.00
☐	251	Julio Franco	.60	.25	.06
☐	252	Mel Hall	.12	.05	.01
☐	253	Brook Jacoby	.10	.04	.01
☐	254	Phil Niekro	.20	.08	.02
☐	255	Otis Nixon	.17	.07	.01
☐	256	Dickie Noles	.06	.02	.00
☐	257	Bryan Oelkers	.06	.02	.00
☐	258	Ken Schrom	.06	.02	.00
☐	259	Don Schulze	.06	.02	.00
☐	260	Cory Snyder	.17	.07	.01
☐	261	Pat Tabler	.06	.02	.00
☐	262	Andre Thornton	.06	.02	.00
☐	263	Rich Yett	.06	.02	.00
☐	264	Mike Aldrete	.10	.04	.01
☐	265	Juan Berenguer	.06	.02	.00
☐	266	Vida Blue	.10	.04	.01
☐	267	Bob Brenly	.06	.02	.00
☐	268	Chris Brown	.06	.02	.00
☐	269	Will Clark	30.00	13.50	4.50
☐	270	Chili Davis	.12	.05	.01
☐	271	Mark Davis	.10	.04	.01
☐	272	Kelly Downs	.25	.10	.02
☐	273	Scott Garrelts	.10	.04	.01
☐	274	Dan Gladden	.06	.02	.00
☐	275	Mike Krukow	.06	.02	.00
☐	276	Randy Kutcher	.06	.02	.00
☐	277	Mike LaCoss	.06	.02	.00
☐	278	Jeff Leonard	.06	.02	.00
☐	279	Candy Maldonado	.10	.04	.01
☐	280	Roger Mason	.06	.02	.00
☐	281	Bob Melvin	.06	.02	.00
☐	282	Greg Minton	.06	.02	.00
☐	283	Jeff Robinson (Giants pitcher)	.10	.04	.01
☐	284	Harry Spilman	.06	.02	.00
☐	285	Robby Thompson	.40	.16	.04
☐	286	Jose Uribe	.06	.02	.00
☐	287	Frank Williams	.06	.02	.00
☐	288	Joel Youngblood	.06	.02	.00
☐	289	Jack Clark	.20	.08	.02
☐	290	Vince Coleman	.75	.30	.07
☐	291	Tim Conroy	.06	.02	.00
☐	292	Danny Cox	.06	.02	.00
☐	293	Ken Dayley	.06	.02	.00
☐	294	Curt Ford	.06	.02	.00
☐	295	Bob Forsch	.06	.02	.00
☐	296	Tom Herr	.10	.04	.01
☐	297	Ricky Horton	.06	.02	.00
☐	298	Clint Hurdle	.06	.02	.00
☐	299	Jeff Lahti	.06	.02	.00
☐	300	Steve Lake	.06	.02	.00
☐	301	Tito Landrum	.06	.02	.00
☐	302	Mike LaValliere	.35	.15	.03
☐	303	Greg Mathews	.10	.04	.01
☐	304	Willie McGee	.20	.08	.02
☐	305	Jose Oquendo	.06	.02	.00
☐	306	Terry Pendleton	.35	.15	.03
☐	307	Pat Perry	.06	.02	.00
☐	308	Ozzie Smith	.60	.25	.06
☐	309	Ray Soff	.06	.02	.00
☐	310	John Tudor	.12	.05	.01
☐	311	Andy Van Slyke ERR (Bats R, Throws L)	.30	.12	.03
☐	312	Todd Worrell	.12	.05	.01
☐	313	Dann Bilardello	.06	.02	.00
☐	314	Hubie Brooks	.12	.05	.01
☐	315	Tim Burke	.06	.02	.00
☐	316	Andre Dawson	.65	.25	.06
☐	317	Mike Fitzgerald	.06	.02	.00
☐	318	Tom Foley	.06	.02	.00
☐	319	Andres Galarraga	.15	.06	.01
☐	320	Joe Hesketh	.12	.05	.01
☐	321	Wallace Johnson	.06	.02	.00
☐	322	Wayne Krenchicki	.06	.02	.00
☐	323	Vance Law	.06	.02	.00
☐	324	Dennis Martinez	.12	.05	.01
☐	325	Bob McClure	.06	.02	.00
☐	326	Andy McGaffigan	.06	.02	.00
☐	327	Al Newman	.12	.05	.01
☐	328	Tim Raines	.35	.15	.03
☐	329	Jeff Reardon	.25	.10	.02
☐	330	Luis Rivera	.06	.02	.00
☐	331	Bob Sebra	.06	.02	.00
☐	332	Bryn Smith	.06	.02	.00
☐	333	Jay Tibbs	.06	.02	.00
☐	334	Tim Wallach	.12	.05	.01
☐	335	Mitch Webster	.06	.02	.00
☐	336	Jim Wohlford	.06	.02	.00
☐	337	Floyd Youmans	.06	.02	.00
☐	338	Chris Bosio	.40	.16	.04
☐	339	Glenn Braggs	.40	.16	.04
☐	340	Rick Cerone	.06	.02	.00
☐	341	Mark Clear	.06	.02	.00
☐	342	Bryan Clutterbuck	.06	.02	.00
☐	343	Cecil Cooper	.10	.04	.01
☐	344	Rob Deer	.15	.06	.01
☐	345	Jim Gantner	.06	.02	.00
☐	346	Ted Higuera	.12	.05	.01
☐	347	John Henry Johnson	.06	.02	.00
☐	348	Tim Leary	.15	.06	.01
☐	349	Rick Manning	.06	.02	.00
☐	350	Paul Molitor	.25	.10	.02
☐	351	Charlie Moore	.06	.02	.00
☐	352	Juan Nieves	.10	.04	.01
☐	353	Ben Oglivie	.06	.02	.00
☐	354	Dan Plesac	.20	.08	.02
☐	355	Ernest Riles	.06	.02	.00
☐	356	Billy Jo Robidoux	.06	.02	.00
☐	357	Bill Schroeder	.06	.02	.00
☐	358	Dale Sveum	.10	.04	.01
☐	359	Gorman Thomas	.10	.04	.01
☐	360	Bill Wegman	.12	.05	.01
☐	361	Robin Yount	.75	.30	.07
☐	362	Steve Balboni	.06	.02	.00
☐	363	Scott Bankhead	.15	.06	.01
☐	364	Buddy Biancalana	.06	.02	.00
☐	365	Bud Black	.06	.02	.00
☐	366	George Brett	.75	.30	.07
☐	367	Steve Farr	.10	.04	.01
☐	368	Mark Gubicza	.12	.05	.01
☐	369	Bo Jackson	20.00	8.50	2.75
☐	370	Danny Jackson	.10	.04	.01
☐	371	Mike Kingery	.10	.04	.01
☐	372	Rudy Law	.06	.02	.00
☐	373	Charlie Leibrandt	.06	.02	.00

374	Dennis Leonard	.06	.02	.00
375	Hal McRae	.10	.04	.01
376	Jorge Orta	.06	.02	.00
377	Jamie Quirk	.06	.02	.00
378	Dan Quisenberry	.12	.05	.01
379	Bret Saberhagen	.40	.16	.04
380	Angel Salazar	.06	.02	.00
381	Lonnie Smith	.12	.05	.01
382	Jim Sundberg	.06	.02	.00
383	Frank White	.06	.02	.00
384	Willie Wilson	.10	.04	.01
385	Joaquin Andujar	.06	.02	.00
386	Doug Bair	.06	.02	.00
387	Dusty Baker	.10	.04	.01
388	Bruce Bochte	.06	.02	.00
389	Jose Canseco	11.00	5.00	1.35
390	Chris Codiroli	.06	.02	.00
391	Mike Davis	.06	.02	.00
392	Alfredo Griffin	.06	.02	.00
393	Moose Haas	.06	.02	.00
394	Donnie Hill	.06	.02	.00
395	Jay Howell	.06	.02	.00
396	Dave Kingman	.12	.05	.01
397	Carney Lansford	.12	.05	.01
398	Dave Leiper	.06	.02	.00
399	Bill Mooneyham	.06	.02	.00
400	Dwayne Murphy	.06	.02	.00
401	Steve Ontiveros	.06	.02	.00
402	Tony Phillips	.06	.02	.00
403	Eric Plunk	.06	.02	.00
404	Jose Rijo	.25	.10	.02
405	Terry Steinbach	.75	.30	.07
406	Dave Stewart	.35	.15	.03
407	Mickey Tettleton	.20	.08	.02
408	Dave Von Ohlen	.06	.02	.00
409	Jerry Willard	.06	.02	.00
410	Curt Young	.06	.02	.00
411	Bruce Bochy	.06	.02	.00
412	Dave Dravecky	.12	.05	.01
413	Tim Flannery	.06	.02	.00
414	Steve Garvey	.40	.16	.04
415	Goose Gossage	.15	.06	.01
416	Tony Gwynn	1.25	.50	.12
417	Andy Hawkins	.06	.02	.00
418	LaMarr Hoyt	.06	.02	.00
419	Terry Kennedy	.06	.02	.00
420	John Kruk	.75	.30	.07
421	Dave LaPoint	.06	.02	.00
422	Craig Lefferts	.06	.02	.00
423	Carmelo Martinez	.06	.02	.00
424	Lance McCullers	.06	.02	.00
425	Kevin McReynolds	.25	.10	.02
426	Graig Nettles	.10	.04	.01
427	Bip Roberts	.65	.25	.06
428	Jerry Royster	.06	.02	.00
429	Benito Santiago	.60	.25	.06
430	Eric Show	.06	.02	.00
431	Bob Stoddard	.06	.02	.00
432	Garry Templeton	.10	.04	.01
433	Gene Walter	.06	.02	.00
434	Ed Whitson	.06	.02	.00
435	Marvell Wynne	.06	.02	.00
436	Dave Anderson	.06	.02	.00
437	Greg Brock	.06	.02	.00
438	Enos Cabell	.06	.02	.00
439	Mariano Duncan	.12	.05	.01
440	Pedro Guerrero	.20	.08	.02
441	Orel Hershiser	.35	.15	.03
442	Rick Honeycutt	.06	.02	.00
443	Ken Howell	.06	.02	.00
444	Ken Landreaux	.06	.02	.00
445	Bill Madlock	.10	.04	.01
446	Mike Marshall	.10	.04	.01
447	Len Matuszek	.06	.02	.00
448	Tom Niedenfuer	.06	.02	.00
449	Alejandro Pena	.12	.05	.01
450	Dennis Powell	.06	.02	.00
451	Jerry Reuss	.06	.02	.00
452	Bill Russell	.10	.04	.01
453	Steve Sax	.20	.08	.02
454	Mike Scioscia	.06	.02	.00
455	Franklin Stubbs	.06	.02	.00
456	Alex Trevino	.06	.02	.00
457	Fernando Valenzuela	.15	.06	.01
458	Ed VandeBerg	.06	.02	.00
459	Bob Welch	.15	.06	.01
460	Reggie Williams	.06	.02	.00
461	Don Aase	.06	.02	.00
462	Juan Beniquez	.06	.02	.00
463	Mike Boddicker	.06	.02	.00
464	Juan Bonilla	.06	.02	.00
465	Rich Bordi	.06	.02	.00
466	Storm Davis	.06	.02	.00
467	Rick Dempsey	.06	.02	.00
468	Ken Dixon	.06	.02	.00
469	Jim Dwyer	.06	.02	.00
470	Mike Flanagan	.10	.04	.01
471	Jackie Gutierrez	.06	.02	.00
472	Brad Havens	.06	.02	.00
473	Lee Lacy	.06	.02	.00
474	Fred Lynn	.12	.05	.01
475	Scott McGregor	.06	.02	.00
476	Eddie Murray	.60	.25	.06
477	Tom O'Malley	.06	.02	.00
478	Cal Ripken Jr.	2.50	1.00	.25
479	Larry Sheets	.06	.02	.00
480	John Shelby	.06	.02	.00
481	Nate Snell	.06	.02	.00
482	Jim Traber	.06	.02	.00
483	Mike Young	.06	.02	.00
484	Neil Allen	.06	.02	.00
485	Harold Baines	.25	.10	.02
486	Floyd Bannister	.06	.02	.00
487	Daryl Boston	.06	.02	.00
488	Ivan Calderon	.35	.15	.03
489	John Cangelosi	.06	.02	.00
490	Steve Carlton	.60	.25	.06
491	Joe Cowley	.06	.02	.00
492	Julio Cruz	.06	.02	.00
493	Bill Dawley	.06	.02	.00
494	Jose DeLeon	.06	.02	.00
495	Richard Dotson	.06	.02	.00
496	Carlton Fisk	.75	.30	.07
497	Ozzie Guillen	.20	.08	.02
498	Jerry Hairston	.06	.02	.00
499	Ron Hassey	.06	.02	.00
500	Tim Hulett	.06	.02	.00
501	Bob James	.06	.02	.00
502	Steve Lyons	.06	.02	.00
503	Joel McKeon	.06	.02	.00
504	Gene Nelson	.06	.02	.00
505	Dave Schmidt	.06	.02	.00
506	Ray Searage	.06	.02	.00
507	Bobby Thigpen	2.00	.80	.20
508	Greg Walker	.06	.02	.00
509	Jim Acker	.06	.02	.00
510	Doyle Alexander	.06	.02	.00
511	Paul Assenmacher	.06	.02	.00
512	Bruce Benedict	.06	.02	.00
513	Chris Chambliss	.10	.04	.01
514	Jeff Dedmon	.06	.02	.00
515	Gene Garber	.06	.02	.00
516	Ken Griffey	.15	.06	.01
517	Terry Harper	.06	.02	.00
518	Bob Horner	.12	.05	.01
519	Glenn Hubbard	.06	.02	.00
520	Rick Mahler	.06	.02	.00
521	Omar Moreno	.06	.02	.00
522	Dale Murphy	.50	.20	.05
523	Ken Oberkfell	.06	.02	.00
524	Ed Olwine	.06	.02	.00
525	David Palmer	.06	.02	.00
526	Rafael Ramirez	.06	.02	.00
527	Billy Sample	.06	.02	.00
528	Ted Simmons	.12	.05	.01
529	Zane Smith	.12	.05	.01
530	Bruce Sutter	.12	.05	.01
531	Andres Thomas	.15	.06	.01
532	Ozzie Virgil	.06	.02	.00
533	Allan Anderson	.25	.10	.02
534	Keith Atherton	.06	.02	.00
535	Billy Beane	.06	.02	.00
536	Bert Blyleven	.15	.06	.01
537	Tom Brunansky	.15	.06	.01
538	Randy Bush	.06	.02	.00
539	George Frazier	.06	.02	.00
540	Gary Gaetti	.15	.06	.01
541	Greg Gagne	.10	.04	.01
542	Mickey Hatcher	.06	.02	.00
543	Neal Heaton	.06	.02	.00
544	Kent Hrbek	.17	.07	.01
545	Roy Lee Jackson	.06	.02	.00
546	Tim Laudner	.06	.02	.00
547	Steve Lombardozzi	.06	.02	.00
548	Mark Portugal	.25	.10	.02
549	Kirby Puckett	3.25	1.35	.32
550	Jeff Reed	.06	.02	.00
551	Mark Salas	.06	.02	.00
552	Roy Smalley	.06	.02	.00
553	Mike Smithson	.06	.02	.00
554	Frank Viola	.30	.12	.03
555	Thad Bosley	.06	.02	.00
556	Ron Cey	.10	.04	.01
557	Jody Davis	.06	.02	.00
558	Ron Davis	.06	.02	.00
559	Bob Dernier	.06	.02	.00
560	Frank DiPino	.06	.02	.00
561	Shawon Dunston UER (wrong birth year listed on card back)	.30	.12	.03

□	#	Player	MINT	EXC	G-VG
□	562	Leon Durham	.06	.02	.00
□	563	Dennis Eckersley	.20	.08	.02
□	564	Terry Francona	.06	.02	.00
□	565	Dave Gumpert	.06	.02	.00
□	566	Guy Hoffman	.06	.02	.00
□	567	Ed Lynch	.06	.02	.00
□	568	Gary Matthews	.06	.02	.00
□	569	Keith Moreland	.06	.02	.00
□	570	Jamie Moyer	.10	.04	.01
□	571	Jerry Mumphrey	.06	.02	.00
□	572	Ryne Sandberg	2.25	.90	.22
□	573	Scott Sanderson	.10	.04	.01
□	574	Lee Smith	.25	.10	.02
□	575	Chris Speier	.06	.02	.00
□	576	Rick Sutcliffe	.10	.04	.01
□	577	Manny Trillo	.06	.02	.00
□	578	Steve Trout	.06	.02	.00
□	579	Karl Best	.06	.02	.00
□	580	Scott Bradley	.06	.02	.00
□	581	Phil Bradley	.06	.02	.00
□	582	Mickey Brantley	.06	.02	.00
□	583	Mike Brown (Mariners pitcher)	.06	.02	.00
□	584	Alvin Davis	.15	.06	.01
□	585	Lee Guetterman	.15	.06	.01
□	586	Mark Huismann	.06	.02	.00
□	587	Bob Kearney	.06	.02	.00
□	588	Pete Ladd	.06	.02	.00
□	589	Mark Langston	.35	.15	.03
□	590	Mike Moore	.10	.04	.01
□	591	Mike Morgan	.10	.04	.01
□	592	John Moses	.06	.02	.00
□	593	Ken Phelps	.06	.02	.00
□	594	Jim Presley	.06	.02	.00
□	595	Rey Quinones UER (Quinonez on front)	.06	.02	.00
□	596	Harold Reynolds	.20	.08	.02
□	597	Billy Swift	.10	.04	.01
□	598	Danny Tartabull	.45	.18	.04
□	599	Steve Yeager	.06	.02	.00
□	600	Matt Young	.06	.02	.00
□	601	Bill Almon	.06	.02	.00
□	602	Rafael Belliard	.40	.16	.04
□	603	Mike Bielecki	.10	.04	.01
□	604	Barry Bonds	11.00	5.00	1.35
□	605	Bobby Bonilla	10.00	4.50	1.25
□	606	Sid Bream	.06	.02	.00
□	607	Mike Brown (Pirates OF)	.06	.02	.00
□	608	Pat Clements	.06	.02	.00
□	609	Mike Diaz	.06	.02	.00
□	610	Cecilio Guante	.06	.02	.00
□	611	Barry Jones	.17	.07	.01
□	612	Bob Kipper	.06	.02	.00
□	613	Larry McWilliams	.06	.02	.00
□	614	Jim Morrison	.06	.02	.00
□	615	Joe Orsulak	.10	.04	.01
□	616	Junior Ortiz	.06	.02	.00
□	617	Tony Pena	.10	.04	.01
□	618	Johnny Ray	.06	.02	.00
□	619	Rick Reuschel	.10	.04	.01
□	620	R.J. Reynolds	.06	.02	.00
□	621	Rick Rhoden	.06	.02	.00
□	622	Don Robinson	.06	.02	.00
□	623	Bob Walk	.06	.02	.00
□	624	Jim Winn	.06	.02	.00
□	625	Youthful Power / Pete Incaviglia / Jose Canseco	.60	.25	.06
□	626	300 Game Winners / Don Sutton / Phil Niekro	.12	.05	.01
□	627	AL Firemen / Dave Righetti / Don Aase	.06	.02	.00
□	628	Rookie All-Stars / Wally Joyner / Jose Canseco	1.25	.50	.12
□	629	Magic Mets / Gary Carter / Sid Fernandez / Dwight Gooden / Keith Hernandez / Darryl Strawberry	.50	.20	.05
□	630	NL Best Righties / Mike Scott / Mike Krukow	.10	.04	.01
□	631	Sensational Southpaws / Fernando Valenzuela / John Franco	.10	.04	.01
□	632	Count'Em / Bob Horner	.06	.02	.00

□	#	Card	MINT	EXC	G-VG
□	633	AL Pitcher's Nightmare / Jose Canseco / Jim Rice / Kirby Puckett	.75	.30	.07
□	634	All-Star Battery / Gary Carter / Roger Clemens	.35	.15	.03
□	635	4000 Strikeouts / Steve Carlton	.25	.10	.02
□	636	Big Bats at First / Glenn Davis / Eddie Murray	.25	.10	.02
□	637	On Base / Wade Boggs / Keith Hernandez	.25	.10	.02
□	638	Sluggers Left Side / Don Mattingly / Darryl Strawberry	1.00	.40	.10
□	639	Former MVP's / Dave Parker / Ryne Sandberg	.25	.10	.02
□	640	Dr. K , Super K / Dwight Gooden / Roger Clemens	.75	.30	.07
□	641	AL West Stoppers / Mike Witt / Charlie Hough	.06	.02	.00
□	642	Doubles and Triples / Juan Samuel / Tim Raines	.12	.05	.01
□	643	Outfielders with Punch / Harold Baines / Jesse Barfield	.10	.04	.01
□	644	Dave Clark and / Greg Swindell	1.25	.50	.12
□	645	Ron Karkovice and / Russ Morman	.10	.04	.01
□	646	Devon White and / Willie Fraser	1.50	.60	.15
□	647	Mike Stanley and / Jerry Browne	.25	.10	.02
□	648	Dave Magadan and / Phil Lombardi	1.50	.60	.15
□	649	Jose Gonzalez and / Ralph Bryant	.12	.05	.01
□	650	Jimmy Jones and / Randy Asadoor	.18	.08	.01
□	651	Tracy Jones and / Marvin Freeman	.15	.06	.01
□	652	John Stefero and / Kevin Seitzer	.75	.30	.07
□	653	Rob Nelson and / Steve Fireovid	.12	.05	.01
□	654	CL: Mets/Red Sox / Astros/Angels	.10	.01	.00
□	655	CL: Yankees/Rangers / Tigers/Phillies	.10	.01	.00
□	656	CL: Reds/Blue Jays / Indians/Giants ERR (230/231 wrong)	.10	.01	.00
□	657	CL: Cardinals/Expos / Brewers/Royals	.10	.01	.00
□	658	CL: A's/Padres / Dodgers/Orioles	.10	.01	.00
□	659	CL: White Sox/Braves / Twins/Cubs	.10	.01	.00
□	660	CL: Mariners/Pirates / Special Cards / UER (580/581 wrong)	.10	.01	.00

1987 Fleer Wax Box Cards

The cards in this 16-card set measure the standard 2 1/2" by 3 1/2". Cards have essentially the same design as the 1987 Fleer regular issue set. The cards were printed on the bottoms of the regular issue wax pack boxes. These 16 cards (C1 to C16) are considered a separate set in their own right and are not typically included in a complete set of the regular issue 1987 Fleer cards. The value of the panel uncut is slightly greater, perhaps by 25 percent greater, than the value of the individual cards cut up carefully.

	MINT	EXC	G-VG
COMPLETE SET (16)	6.00	2.50	.60
COMMON CARDS (C1-C16)	.10	.04	.01

		MINT	EXC	G-VG
□ C1	Mets Logo	.10	.04	.01
□ C2	Jesse Barfield	.15	.06	.01
□ C3	George Brett	.60	.25	.06
□ C4	Dwight Gooden	.75	.30	.07
□ C5	Boston Logo	.10	.04	.01
□ C6	Keith Hernandez	.25	.10	.02
□ C7	Wally Joyner	1.25	.50	.12
□ C8	Dale Murphy	.60	.25	.06
□ C9	Astros Logo	.10	.04	.01
□ C10	Dave Parker	.30	.12	.03
□ C11	Kirby Puckett	.75	.30	.07
□ C12	Dave Righetti	.20	.08	.02
□ C13	Angels Logo	.10	.04	.01
□ C14	Ryne Sandberg	.90	.40	.09
□ C15	Mike Schmidt	.90	.40	.09
□ C16	Robin Yount	.60	.25	.06

1987 Fleer All-Star Inserts

This 12-card set was distributed as an insert in packs of the Fleer regular issue. The cards are 2 1/2" by 3 1/2" and designed with a color player photo superimposed on a gray or black background with yellow stars. The player's name, team, and position are printed in orange on black or gray at the bottom of the obverse. The card backs are done predominantly in gray, red, and black. Cards are numbered on the back in the upper right hand corner.

		MINT	EXC	G-VG
	COMPLETE SET (12)	17.00	7.25	2.50
	COMMON PLAYER (1-12)	.40	.16	.04
□ 1	Don Mattingly First Base	3.00	1.25	.30
□ 2	Gary Carter Catcher	1.00	.40	.10
□ 3	Tony Fernandez Shortstop	.60	.25	.06
□ 4	Steve Sax Second Base	.60	.25	.06
□ 5	Kirby Puckett Outfield	2.50	1.00	.25

		MINT	EXC	G-VG
□ 6	Mike Schmidt Third Base	3.00	1.25	.30
□ 7	Mike Easler Designated Hitter	.40	.16	.04
□ 8	Todd Worrell Relief Pitcher	.50	.20	.05
□ 9	George Bell Outfield	.60	.25	.06
□ 10	Fernando Valenzuela Left Hand Starter	.60	.25	.06
□ 11	Roger Clemens Right Hand Starter	3.50	1.50	.35
□ 12	Tim Raines Outfield	1.00	.40	.10

1987 Fleer Headliners

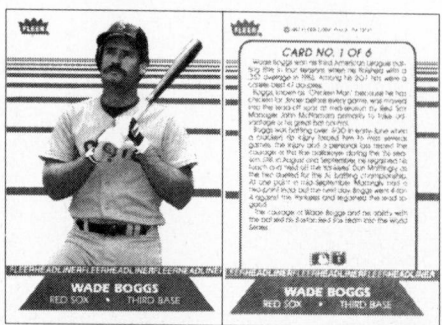

This six-card set was distributed as a special insert in rack packs as well as with three-pack wax pack rack packs. The obverse features the player photo against a beige background with irregular red stripes. Cards are 2 1/2" by 3 1/2". The cards are numbered on the back. The checklist below also lists each player's team affiliation.

		MINT	EXC	G-VG
	COMPLETE SET (6)	8.00	3.50	.80
	COMMON PLAYER (1-6)	.65	.25	.06
□ 1	Wade Boggs Boston Red Sox	2.00	.80	.20
□ 2	Jose Canseco Oakland Athletics	3.00	1.25	.30
□ 3	Dwight Gooden New York Mets	1.00	.40	.10
□ 4	Rickey Henderson New York Yankees	2.50	1.00	.25
□ 5	Keith Hernandez New York Mets	.65	.25	.06
□ 6	Jim Rice Boston Red Sox	.65	.25	.06

1987 Fleer Sticker Cards

These Star Stickers were distributed as a separate issue by Fleer with five star stickers and a logo sticker in each wax pack. The 132-card (sticker) set features 2 1/2" by 3 1/2" full-color fronts and even statistics on the sticker back, which is an indication that the Fleer Company understands that these stickers are rarely used as stickers but more like traditional cards. The card fronts are surrounded by a green border and the backs are printed in green and yellow on white card stock.

	MINT	EXC	G-VG
COMPLETE SET (132)	28.00	12.50	4.00
COMMON PLAYER (1-132)	.05	.02	.00

☐ 73	Bill Madlock	.05	.02	.00
☐ 74	Don Mattingly	1.25	.50	.12
☐ 75	Kirk McCaskill	.05	.02	.00
☐ 76	Lance McCullers	.05	.02	.00
☐ 77	Oddibe McDowell	.05	.02	.00
☐ 78	Paul Molitor	.20	.08	.02
☐ 79	Keith Moreland	.05	.02	.00
☐ 80	Jack Morris	.20	.08	.02
☐ 81	Jim Morrison	.05	.02	.00
☐ 82	Jerry Mumphrey	.05	.02	.00
☐ 83	Dale Murphy	.40	.16	.04
☐ 84	Eddie Murray	.50	.20	.05
☐ 85	Ben Oglivie	.05	.02	.00
☐ 86	Bob Ojeda	.10	.04	.01
☐ 87	Jesse Orosco	.05	.02	.00
☐ 88	Dave Parker	.20	.08	.02
☐ 89	Larry Parrish	.05	.02	.00
☐ 90	Tony Pena	.05	.02	.00
☐ 91	Jim Presley	.10	.04	.01
☐ 92	Kirby Puckett	1.25	.50	.12
☐ 93	Dan Quisenberry	.10	.04	.01
☐ 94	Tim Raines	.25	.10	.02
☐ 95	Dennis Rasmussen	.05	.02	.00
☐ 96	Shane Rawley	.05	.02	.00
☐ 97	Johnny Ray	.05	.02	.00
☐ 98	Jeff Reardon	.15	.06	.01
☐ 99	Jim Rice	.20	.08	.02
☐ 100	Dave Righetti	.15	.06	.01
☐ 101	Cal Ripken Jr.	1.25	.50	.12
☐ 102	Pete Rose	1.00	.40	.10
☐ 103	Nolan Ryan	2.00	.80	.20
☐ 104	Juan Samuel	.15	.06	.01
☐ 105	Ryne Sandberg	1.25	.50	.12
☐ 106	Steve Sax	.15	.06	.01
☐ 107	Mike Schmidt	1.25	.50	.12
☐ 108	Mike Scott	.15	.06	.01
☐ 109	Dave Smith	.05	.02	.00
☐ 110	Lee Smith	.15	.06	.01
☐ 111	Lonnie Smith	.10	.04	.01
☐ 112	Ozzie Smith	.35	.15	.03
☐ 113	Cory Snyder	.15	.06	.01
☐ 114	Darryl Strawberry	1.00	.40	.10
☐ 115	Don Sutton	.20	.08	.02
☐ 116	Kent Tekulve	.05	.02	.00
☐ 117	Andres Thomas	.05	.02	.00
☐ 118	Alan Trammell	.25	.10	.02
☐ 119	John Tudor	.15	.06	.01
☐ 120	Fernando Valenzuela	.20	.08	.02
☐ 121	Bob Welch	.20	.08	.02
☐ 122	Lou Whitaker	.15	.06	.01
☐ 123	Frank White	.10	.04	.01
☐ 124	Reggie Williams	.05	.02	.00
☐ 125	Willie Wilson	.10	.04	.01
☐ 126	Dave Winfield	.30	.12	.03
☐ 127	Mike Witt	.05	.02	.00
☐ 128	Todd Worrell	.10	.04	.01
☐ 129	Curt Young	.05	.02	.00
☐ 130	Robin Yount	.90	.40	.09
☐ 131	Checklist	2.00	.80	.20
	Jose Canseco			
	Don Mattingly			
☐ 132	Checklist	2.00	.80	.20
	Bo Jackson			
	Eric Davis			

☐ 1	Don Aase	.05	.02	.00
☐ 2	Harold Baines	.10	.04	.01
☐ 3	Floyd Bannister	.05	.02	.00
☐ 4	Jesse Barfield	.10	.04	.01
☐ 5	Marty Barrett	.05	.02	.00
☐ 6	Kevin Bass	.05	.02	.00
☐ 7	Don Baylor	.10	.04	.01
☐ 8	Steve Bedrosian	.10	.04	.01
☐ 9	George Bell	.25	.10	.02
☐ 10	Bert Blyleven	.15	.06	.01
☐ 11	Mike Boddicker	.10	.04	.01
☐ 12	Wade Boggs	1.25	.50	.12
☐ 13	Phil Bradley	.10	.04	.01
☐ 14	Sid Bream	.05	.02	.00
☐ 15	George Brett	.75	.30	.07
☐ 16	Hubie Brooks	.10	.04	.01
☐ 17	Tom Brunansky	.10	.04	.01
☐ 18	Tom Candiotti	.05	.02	.00
☐ 19	Jose Canseco	2.50	1.00	.25
☐ 20	Gary Carter	.35	.15	.03
☐ 21	Joe Carter	.35	.15	.03
☐ 22	Will Clark	2.50	1.00	.25
☐ 23	Mark Clear	.05	.02	.00
☐ 24	Roger Clemens	1.50	.60	.15
☐ 25	Vince Coleman	.40	.16	.04
☐ 26	Jose Cruz	.10	.04	.01
☐ 27	Ron Darling	.10	.04	.01
☐ 28	Alvin Davis	.10	.04	.01
☐ 29	Chili Davis	.15	.06	.01
☐ 30	Eric Davis	.90	.40	.09
☐ 31	Glenn Davis	.35	.15	.03
☐ 32	Mike Davis	.05	.02	.00
☐ 33	Andre Dawson	.35	.15	.03
☐ 34	Doug DeCinces	.05	.02	.00
☐ 35	Brian Downing	.05	.02	.00
☐ 36	Shawon Dunston	.25	.10	.02
☐ 37	Mark Eichhorn	.10	.04	.01
☐ 38	Dwight Evans	.20	.08	.02
☐ 39	Tony Fernandez	.15	.06	.01
☐ 40	Bob Forsch	.05	.02	.00
☐ 41	John Franco	.10	.04	.01
☐ 42	Julio Franco	.20	.08	.02
☐ 43	Gary Gaetti	.10	.04	.01
☐ 44	Gene Garber	.05	.02	.00
☐ 45	Scott Garrelts	.10	.04	.01
☐ 46	Steve Garvey	.40	.16	.04
☐ 47	Kirk Gibson	.30	.12	.03
☐ 48	Dwight Gooden	.75	.30	.07
☐ 49	Ken Griffey Sr.	.15	.06	.01
☐ 50	Ozzie Guillen	.20	.08	.02
☐ 51	Bill Gullickson	.05	.02	.00
☐ 52	Tony Gwynn	.60	.25	.06
☐ 53	Mel Hall	.15	.06	.01
☐ 54	Greg Harris	.05	.02	.00
☐ 55	Von Hayes	.10	.04	.01
☐ 56	Rickey Henderson	1.75	.70	.17
☐ 57	Tom Henke	.10	.04	.01
☐ 58	Keith Hernandez	.20	.08	.02
☐ 59	Willie Hernandez	.05	.02	.00
☐ 60	Ted Higuera	.10	.04	.01
☐ 61	Bob Horner	.10	.04	.01
☐ 62	Charlie Hough	.05	.02	.00
☐ 63	Jay Howell	.05	.02	.00
☐ 64	Kent Hrbek	.15	.06	.01
☐ 65	Bruce Hurst	.10	.04	.01
☐ 66	Pete Incaviglia	.20	.08	.02
☐ 67	Bob James	.05	.02	.00
☐ 68	Wally Joyner	1.00	.40	.10
☐ 69	Mike Krukow	.05	.02	.00
☐ 70	Mark Langston	.20	.08	.02
☐ 71	Carney Lansford	.15	.06	.01
☐ 72	Fred Lynn	.15	.06	.01

1987 Fleer Sticker Wax Box

The bottoms of the Star Sticker wax boxes contained two different sets of four cards done in a similar format to the stickers; these cards (they are not stickers but truly cards) are numbered with the prefix S and are considered a separate set. The value of the panels uncut is slightly greater, perhaps by 25 percent greater, than the value of the individual cards cut up carefully.

		MINT	EXC	G-VG
COMPLETE SET (8)		2.50	1.00	.25
COMMON PLAYER (S1-S8)		.10	.04	.01
☐ S1	Detroit Logo	.10	.04	.01
☐ S2	Wade Boggs	1.25	.50	.12
☐ S3	Bert Blyleven	.20	.08	.02
☐ S4	Jose Cruz	.15	.06	.01

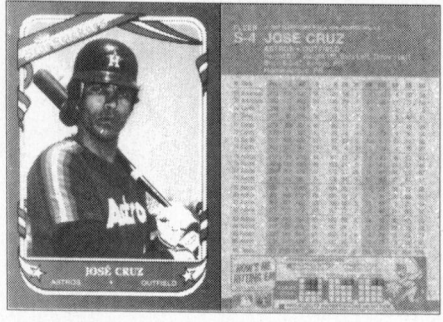

		MINT	EXC	G-VG
☐	S5 Glenn Davis	.30	.12	.03
☐	S6 Phillies Logo	.10	.04	.01
☐	S7 Bob Horner	.15	.06	.01
☐	S8 Don Mattingly	1.25	.50	.12

1987 Fleer Award Winners

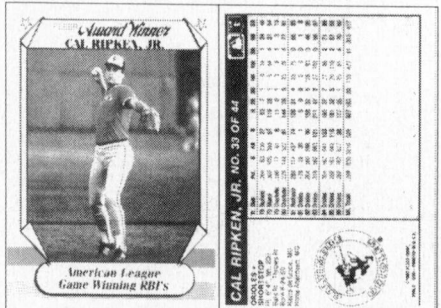

This small set of 44 cards was (mass)-produced for 7-Eleven stores by Fleer. The cards measure the standard 2 1/2" by 3 1/2" and feature full color fronts and yellow, white, and black backs. The card fronts are distinguished by their yellow frame around the player's full-color photo. The box for the cards describes the set as the "1987 Limited Edition Baseball's Award Winners." The checklist for the set is given on the back of the set box.

		MINT	EXC	G-VG
	COMPLETE SET (44)	4.00	1.75	.40
	COMMON PLAYER (1-44)	.10	.04	.01
☐	1 Marty Barrett	.10	.04	.01
☐	2 George Bell	.15	.06	.01
☐	3 Bert Blyleven	.15	.06	.01
☐	4 Bob Boone	.15	.06	.01
☐	5 John Candelaria	.10	.04	.01
☐	6 Jose Canseco	.90	.40	.09
☐	7 Gary Carter	.25	.10	.02
☐	8 Joe Carter	.15	.06	.01
☐	9 Roger Clemens	.90	.40	.09
☐	10 Cecil Cooper	.10	.04	.01
☐	11 Eric Davis	.50	.20	.05
☐	12 Tony Fernandez	.15	.06	.01
☐	13 Scott Fletcher	.10	.04	.01
☐	14 Bob Forsch	.10	.04	.01
☐	15 Dwight Gooden	.35	.15	.03
☐	16 Ron Guidry	.15	.06	.01
☐	17 Ozzie Guillen	.20	.08	.02
☐	18 Bill Gullickson	.15	.06	.01
☐	19 Tony Gwynn	.50	.20	.05
☐	20 Bob Knepper	.10	.04	.01
☐	21 Ray Knight	.15	.06	.01
☐	22 Mark Langston	.15	.06	.01

☐	23 Candy Maldonado	.10	.04	.01
☐	24 Don Mattingly	.75	.30	.07
☐	25 Roger McDowell	.10	.04	.01
☐	26 Dale Murphy	.35	.15	.03
☐	27 Dave Parker	.20	.08	.02
☐	28 Lance Parrish	.15	.06	.01
☐	29 Gary Pettis	.10	.04	.01
☐	30 Kirby Puckett	.60	.25	.06
☐	31 Johnny Ray	.10	.04	.01
☐	32 Dave Righetti	.15	.06	.01
☐	33 Cal Ripken	.75	.30	.07
☐	34 Bret Saberhagen	.20	.08	.02
☐	35 Ryne Sandberg	.75	.30	.07
☐	36 Mike Schmidt	.75	.30	.07
☐	37 Mike Scott	.20	.08	.02
☐	38 Ozzie Smith	.30	.12	.03
☐	39 Robby Thompson	.10	.04	.01
☐	40 Fernando Valenzuela	.15	.06	.01
☐	41 Mitch Webster UER	.10	.04	.01
	(Mike on front)			
☐	42 Frank White	.10	.04	.01
☐	43 Mike Witt	.10	.04	.01
☐	44 Todd Worrell	.15	.06	.01

1987 Fleer Exciting Stars

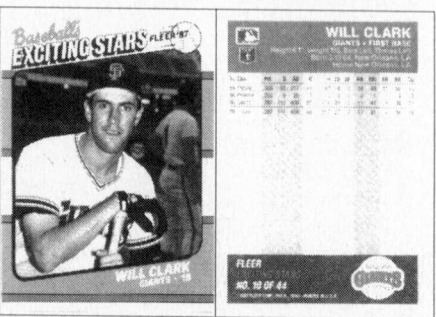

This small 44-card boxed set was produced by Fleer for distribution by the Cumberland Farm stores. The cards measure the standard 2 1/2" by 3 1/2" and feature full color fronts. The set is titled "Baseball's Exciting Stars." Each individual boxed set includes the 44 cards and 6 logo stickers. The checklist for the set is found on the back panel of the box.

		MINT	EXC	G-VG
	COMPLETE SET (44)	5.00	2.25	.50
	COMMON PLAYER (1-44)	.10	.04	.01
☐	1 Don Aase	.10	.04	.01
☐	2 Rick Aguilera	.15	.06	.01
☐	3 Jesse Barfield	.15	.06	.01
☐	4 Wade Boggs	.75	.30	.07
☐	5 Oil Can Boyd	.10	.04	.01
☐	6 Sid Bream	.10	.04	.01
☐	7 Jose Canseco	1.00	.40	.10
☐	8 Steve Carlton	.35	.15	.03
☐	9 Gary Carter	.25	.10	.02
☐	10 Will Clark	1.00	.40	.10
☐	11 Roger Clemens	.90	.40	.09
☐	12 Danny Cox	.10	.04	.01
☐	13 Alvin Davis	.10	.04	.01
☐	14 Eric Davis	.50	.20	.05
☐	15 Rob Deer	.15	.06	.01
☐	16 Brian Downing	.10	.04	.01
☐	17 Steve Garber	.10	.04	.01
☐	18 Steve Garvey	.30	.12	.03
☐	19 Dwight Gooden	.40	.16	.04
☐	20 Mark Gubicza	.15	.06	.01
☐	21 Mel Hall	.10	.04	.01
☐	22 Terry Harper	.10	.04	.01
☐	23 Von Hayes	.15	.06	.01
☐	24 Rickey Henderson	.75	.30	.07
☐	25 Tom Henke	.15	.06	.01
☐	26 Willie Hernandez	.10	.04	.01
☐	27 Ted Higuera	.15	.06	.01
☐	28 Rick Honeycutt	.10	.04	.01
☐	29 Kent Hrbek	.20	.08	.02

		MINT	EXC	G-VG
☐ 30	Wally Joyner	.45	.18	.04
☐ 31	Charlie Kerfeld	.10	.04	.01
☐ 32	Fred Lynn	.15	.06	.01
☐ 33	Don Mattingly	.75	.30	.07
☐ 34	Tim Raines	.25	.10	.02
☐ 35	Dennis Rasmussen	.10	.04	.01
☐ 36	Johnny Ray	.15	.06	.01
☐ 37	Jim Rice	.20	.08	.02
☐ 38	Pete Rose	.65	.25	.06
☐ 39	Lee Smith	.10	.04	.01
☐ 40	Cory Snyder	.20	.08	.02
☐ 41	Darryl Strawberry	.75	.30	.07
☐ 42	Kent Tekulve	.10	.04	.01
☐ 43	Willie Wilson	.15	.06	.01
☐ 44	Bobby Witt	.15	.06	.01

		MINT	EXC	G-VG
☐ 36	Ernest Riles	.10	.04	.01
☐ 37	Cal Ripken	.75	.30	.07
☐ 38	Ron Robinson	.10	.04	.01
☐ 39	Steve Sax	.15	.06	.01
☐ 40	Mike Schmidt	.75	.30	.07
☐ 41	John Tudor	.10	.04	.01
☐ 42	Fernando Valenzuela	.20	.08	.02
☐ 43	Mike Witt	.10	.04	.01
☐ 44	Curt Young	.10	.04	.01

1987 Fleer Game Winners

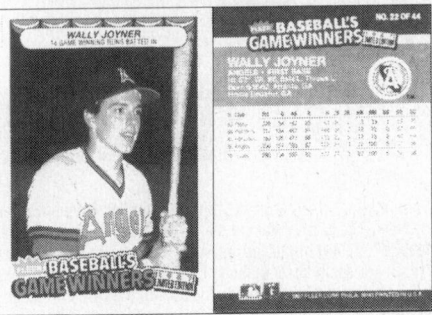

This small 44-card boxed set was produced by Fleer for distribution by several store chains, including Bi-Mart, Pay'n'Save, Mott's, M.E.Moses, and Winn's. The cards measure the standard 2 1/2" by 3 1/2" and feature full color fronts. The set is titled "Baseball's Game Winners." Each individual boxed set includes the 44 cards and 6 logo stickers. The checklist for the set is found on the back panel of the box.

		MINT	EXC	G-VG
COMPLETE SET (44)		4.00	1.75	.40
COMMON PLAYER (1-44)		.10	.04	.01
☐ 1	Harold Baines	.15	.06	.01
☐ 2	Don Baylor	.15	.06	.01
☐ 3	George Bell	.15	.06	.01
☐ 4	Tony Bernazard	.10	.04	.01
☐ 5	Wade Boggs	.75	.30	.07
☐ 6	George Brett	.45	.18	.04
☐ 7	Hubie Brooks	.15	.06	.01
☐ 8	Jose Canseco	1.00	.40	.10
☐ 9	Gary Carter	.25	.10	.02
☐ 10	Roger Clemens	.90	.40	.09
☐ 11	Eric Davis	.50	.20	.05
☐ 12	Glenn Davis	.25	.10	.02
☐ 13	Shawon Dunston	.25	.10	.02
☐ 14	Mark Eichhorn	.15	.06	.01
☐ 15	Gary Gaetti	.15	.06	.01
☐ 16	Steve Garvey	.30	.12	.03
☐ 17	Kirk Gibson	.30	.12	.03
☐ 18	Dwight Gooden	.35	.15	.03
☐ 19	Von Hayes	.15	.06	.01
☐ 20	Willie Hernandez	.10	.04	.01
☐ 21	Ted Higuera	.15	.06	.01
☐ 22	Wally Joyner	.45	.18	.04
☐ 23	Bob Knepper	.10	.04	.01
☐ 24	Mike Krukow	.10	.04	.01
☐ 25	Jeff Leonard	.10	.04	.01
☐ 26	Don Mattingly	.75	.30	.07
☐ 27	Kirk McCaskill	.10	.04	.01
☐ 28	Kevin McReynolds	.20	.08	.02
☐ 29	Jim Morrison	.10	.04	.01
☐ 30	Dale Murphy	.35	.15	.03
☐ 31	Pete O'Brien	.10	.04	.01
☐ 32	Bob Ojeda	.10	.04	.01
☐ 33	Larry Parrish	.10	.04	.01
☐ 34	Ken Phelps	.10	.04	.01
☐ 35	Dennis Rasmussen	.10	.04	.01

1987 Fleer Hottest Stars

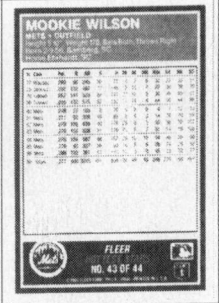

This 44-card boxed set was produced by Fleer for distribution by Revco stores all over the country. The cards measure the standard 2 1/2" by 3 1/2" and feature full color fronts and red, white, and black backs. The card fronts are easily distinguished by their solid red outside borders and and white and blue inner borders framing the player's picture. The box for the cards proclaims "1987 Limited Edition Baseball's Hottest Stars" and is styled in the same manner and color scheme as the cards themselves. The checklist for the set is given on the back of the set box.

		MINT	EXC	G-VG
COMPLETE SET (44)		5.00	2.25	.50
COMMON PLAYER (1-44)		.10	.04	.01
☐ 1	Joaquin Andujar	.10	.04	.01
☐ 2	Harold Baines	.15	.06	.01
☐ 3	Kevin Bass	.10	.04	.01
☐ 4	Don Baylor	.15	.06	.01
☐ 5	Barry Bonds	1.00	.40	.10
☐ 6	George Brett	.50	.20	.05
☐ 7	Tom Brunansky	.15	.06	.01
☐ 8	Brett Butler	.15	.06	.01
☐ 9	Jose Canseco	1.00	.40	.10
☐ 10	Roger Clemens	.90	.40	.09
☐ 11	Ron Darling	.20	.08	.02
☐ 12	Eric Davis	.50	.20	.05
☐ 13	Andre Dawson	.30	.12	.03
☐ 14	Doug DeCinces	.10	.04	.01
☐ 15	Leon Durham	.10	.04	.01
☐ 16	Mark Eichhorn	.15	.06	.01
☐ 17	Scott Garrelts	.15	.06	.01
☐ 18	Dwight Gooden	.45	.18	.04
☐ 19	Dave Henderson	.10	.04	.01
☐ 20	Rickey Henderson	.90	.40	.09
☐ 21	Keith Hernandez	.20	.08	.02
☐ 22	Ted Higuera	.15	.06	.01
☐ 23	Bob Horner	.15	.06	.01
☐ 24	Pete Incaviglia	.20	.08	.02
☐ 25	Wally Joyner	.45	.18	.04
☐ 26	Mark Langston	.20	.08	.02
☐ 27	Don Mattingly UER (Pirates logo on back)	.75	.30	.07
☐ 28	Dale Murphy	.35	.15	.03
☐ 29	Kirk McCaskill	.10	.04	.01
☐ 30	Willie McGee	.15	.06	.01
☐ 31	Dave Righetti	.15	.06	.01
☐ 32	Pete Rose	.65	.25	.06
☐ 33	Bruce Ruffin	.10	.04	.01
☐ 34	Steve Sax	.20	.08	.02

			MINT	EXC	G-VG
☐	35	Mike Schmidt	.75	.30	.07
☐	36	Larry Sheets	.10	.04	.01
☐	37	Eric Show	.10	.04	.01
☐	38	Dave Smith	.10	.04	.01
☐	39	Cory Snyder	.15	.06	.01
☐	40	Frank Tanana	.10	.04	.01
☐	41	Alan Trammell	.25	.10	.02
☐	42	Reggie Williams	.10	.04	.01
☐	43	Mookie Wilson	.10	.04	.01
☐	44	Todd Worrell	.15	.06	.01

			MINT	EXC	G-VG
☐	40	Mike Schmidt	.75	.30	.07
☐	41	Darryl Strawberry	.60	.25	.06
☐	42	Greg Walker	.15	.06	.01
☐	43	Bob Welch	.20	.08	.02
☐	44	Todd Worrell	.15	.06	.01

1987 Fleer League Leaders

This small set of 44 cards was produced for Walgreens by Fleer. The cards measure the standard 2 1/2" by 3 1/2" and feature full color fronts and red, white, and blue backs. The card fronts are easily distinguished by their light blue vertical stripes over a white background. The box for the cards proclaims a "Walgreens Exclusive" and is styled in the same manner and color scheme as the cards themselves. The checklist for the set is given on the back of the set box.

			MINT	EXC	G-VG
	COMPLETE SET (44)		5.00	2.25	.50
	COMMON PLAYER (1-44)		.10	.04	.01
☐	1	Jesse Barfield	.15	.06	.01
☐	2	Mike Boddicker	.10	.04	.01
☐	3	Wade Boggs	.75	.30	.07
☐	4	Phil Bradley	.15	.06	.01
☐	5	George Brett	.50	.20	.05
☐	6	Hubie Brooks	.15	.06	.01
☐	7	Chris Brown	.10	.04	.01
☐	8	Jose Canseco	1.00	.40	.10
☐	9	Joe Carter	.30	.12	.03
☐	10	Roger Clemens	.90	.40	.09
☐	11	Vince Coleman	.40	.16	.04
☐	12	Joe Cowley	.10	.04	.01
☐	13	Kal Daniels	.25	.10	.02
☐	14	Glenn Davis	.25	.10	.02
☐	15	Jody Davis	.10	.04	.01
☐	16	Darrell Evans	.15	.06	.01
☐	17	Dwight Evans	.20	.08	.02
☐	18	John Franco	.15	.06	.01
☐	19	Julio Franco	.25	.10	.02
☐	20	Dwight Gooden	.40	.16	.04
☐	21	Goose Gossage	.15	.06	.01
☐	22	Tom Herr	.10	.04	.01
☐	23	Ted Higuera	.15	.06	.01
☐	24	Bob Horner	.15	.06	.01
☐	25	Pete Incaviglia	.20	.08	.02
☐	26	Wally Joyner	.45	.18	.04
☐	27	Dave Kingman	.15	.06	.01
☐	28	Don Mattingly	.75	.30	.07
☐	29	Willie McGee	.20	.08	.02
☐	30	Donnie Moore	.10	.04	.01
☐	31	Keith Moreland	.10	.04	.01
☐	32	Eddie Murray	.35	.15	.03
☐	33	Mike Pagliarulo	.15	.06	.01
☐	34	Larry Parrish	.10	.04	.01
☐	35	Tony Pena	.10	.04	.01
☐	36	Kirby Puckett	.60	.25	.06
☐	37	Pete Rose	.65	.25	.06
☐	38	Juan Samuel	.20	.08	.02
☐	39	Ryne Sandberg	.75	.30	.07

1987 Fleer Baseball All-Stars

This small set of 44 cards was produced for Ben Franklin stores by Fleer. The cards measure the standard 2 1/2" by 3 1/2" and feature full color fronts and red, white, and blue backs. The card fronts are easily distinguished by their white vertical stripes over a bright red background. The box for the cards proclaims "Limited Edition Baseball All-Stars" and is styled in the same manner and color scheme as the cards themselves. The checklist for the set is given on the back of the set box.

			MINT	EXC	G-VG
	COMPLETE SET (44)		5.00	2.25	.50
	COMMON PLAYER (1-44)		.10	.04	.01
☐	1	Harold Baines	.15	.06	.01
☐	2	Jesse Barfield	.15	.06	.01
☐	3	Wade Boggs	.75	.30	.07
☐	4	Oil Can Boyd	.10	.04	.01
☐	5	Scott Bradley	.10	.04	.01
☐	6	Jose Canseco	1.00	.40	.10
☐	7	Gary Carter	.25	.10	.02
☐	8	Joe Carter	.30	.12	.03
☐	9	Mark Clear	.10	.04	.01
☐	10	Roger Clemens	.90	.40	.09
☐	11	Jose Cruz	.10	.04	.01
☐	12	Chili Davis	.10	.04	.01
☐	13	Jody Davis	.10	.04	.01
☐	14	Rob Deer	.15	.06	.01
☐	15	Brian Downing	.10	.04	.01
☐	16	Sid Fernandez	.15	.06	.01
☐	17	John Franco	.15	.06	.01
☐	18	Andres Galarraga	.25	.10	.02
☐	19	Dwight Gooden	.40	.16	.04
☐	20	Tony Gwynn	.50	.20	.05
☐	21	Charlie Hough	.10	.04	.01
☐	22	Bruce Hurst	.15	.06	.01
☐	23	Wally Joyner	.45	.18	.04
☐	24	Carney Lansford	.15	.06	.01
☐	25	Fred Lynn	.15	.06	.01
☐	26	Don Mattingly	.75	.30	.07
☐	27	Willie McGee	.20	.08	.02
☐	28	Jack Morris	.20	.08	.02
☐	29	Dale Murphy	.35	.15	.03
☐	30	Bob Ojeda	.10	.04	.01
☐	31	Tony Pena	.10	.04	.01
☐	32	Kirby Puckett	.60	.25	.06
☐	33	Dan Quisenberry	.15	.06	.01
☐	34	Tim Raines	.25	.10	.02
☐	35	Willie Randolph	.15	.06	.01
☐	36	Cal Ripken	.75	.30	.07
☐	37	Pete Rose	.60	.25	.06
☐	38	Nolan Ryan	1.25	.50	.12
☐	39	Juan Samuel	.15	.06	.01
☐	40	Mike Schmidt	.75	.30	.07
☐	41	Ozzie Smith	.30	.12	.03
☐	42	Andres Thomas	.10	.04	.01
☐	43	Fernando Valenzuela	.20	.08	.02
☐	44	Mike Witt	.10	.04	.01

1987 Fleer Limited Edition

This 44-card boxed set was (mass) produced by Fleer for distribution by McCrory's and is sometimes referred to as the McCrory's set. The numerical checklist on the back of the box shows that the set is numbered alphabetically. The cards measure 2 1/2" by 3 1/2".

	MINT	EXC	G-VG
COMPLETE SET (44)	4.00	1.75	.40
COMMON PLAYER (1-44)	.10	.04	.01
☐ 1 Floyd Bannister	.10	.04	.01
☐ 2 Marty Barrett	.10	.04	.01
☐ 3 Steve Bedrosian	.10	.04	.01
☐ 4 George Bell	.20	.08	.02
☐ 5 George Brett	.45	.18	.04
☐ 6 Jose Canseco	1.00	.40	.10
☐ 7 Joe Carter	.30	.12	.03
☐ 8 Will Clark	1.00	.40	.10
☐ 9 Roger Clemens	.75	.30	.07
☐ 10 Vince Coleman	.35	.15	.03
☐ 11 Glenn Davis	.20	.08	.02
☐ 12 Mike Davis	.10	.04	.01
☐ 13 Len Dykstra	.20	.08	.02
☐ 14 John Franco	.15	.06	.01
☐ 15 Julio Franco	.25	.10	.02
☐ 16 Steve Garvey	.30	.12	.03
☐ 17 Kirk Gibson	.30	.12	.03
☐ 18 Dwight Gooden	.45	.18	.04
☐ 19 Tony Gwynn	.50	.20	.05
☐ 20 Keith Hernandez	.15	.06	.01
☐ 21 Teddy Higuera	.10	.04	.01
☐ 22 Kent Hrbek	.15	.06	.01
☐ 23 Wally Joyner	.45	.18	.04
☐ 24 Mike Krukow	.10	.04	.01
☐ 25 Mike Marshall	.15	.06	.01
☐ 26 Don Mattingly	.75	.30	.07
☐ 27 Oddibe McDowell	.10	.04	.01
☐ 28 Jack Morris	.25	.10	.02
☐ 29 Lloyd Moseby	.10	.04	.01
☐ 30 Dale Murphy	.35	.15	.03
☐ 31 Eddie Murray	.40	.16	.04
☐ 32 Tony Pena	.10	.04	.01
☐ 33 Jim Presley	.10	.04	.01
☐ 34 Jeff Reardon	.20	.08	.02
☐ 35 Jim Rice	.20	.08	.02
☐ 36 Pete Rose	.60	.25	.06
☐ 37 Mike Schmidt	.75	.30	.07
☐ 38 Mike Scott	.15	.06	.01
☐ 39 Lee Smith	.15	.06	.01
☐ 40 Lonnie Smith	.10	.04	.01
☐ 41 Gary Ward	.10	.04	.01
☐ 42 Dave Winfield	.30	.12	.03
☐ 43 Todd Worrell	.15	.06	.01
☐ 44 Robin Yount	.50	.20	.05

1987 Fleer Limited Box Cards

The cards in this six-card set each measure the standard 2 1/2" by 3 1/2". Cards have essentially the same design as the 1987 Fleer Limited Edition cards which were distributed by McCrory's.

The cards were printed on the bottom of the counter display box which held 24 small boxed sets; hence theoretically these box cards are 1/24 as plentiful as the regular boxed set cards. These 6 cards, numbered C1 to C6, are considered a separate set in their own right and are not typically included in a complete set of the 1987 Fleer Limited Edition set of 44. The value of the panels uncut is slightly greater, perhaps by 25 percent greater, than the value of the individual cards cut up carefully.

	MINT	EXC	G-VG
COMPLETE SET (6)	1.50	.60	.15
COMMON PLAYERS (C1-C6)	.10	.04	.01
☐ C1 Ron Darling	.30	.12	.03
(box bottom card)			
☐ C2 Bill Buckner	.15	.06	.01
(box bottom card)			
☐ C3 John Candelaria	.15	.06	.01
(box bottom card)			
☐ C4 Jack Clark	.40	.16	.04
(box bottom card)			
☐ C5 Bret Saberhagen	1.00	.40	.10
(box bottom card)			
☐ C6 Team Logo	.10	.04	.01
(box bottom card; checklist back)			

1987 Fleer Mini

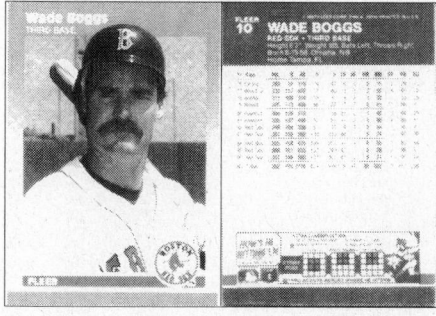

The 1987 Fleer "Classic Miniatures" set consists of 120 small cards with all new pictures of the players as compared to the 1987 Fleer regular issue. The cards are only 1 13/16" by 2 9/16", making them one of the smallest cards available. Card backs provide career year-by-year statistics. The complete set was distributed in a blue, red, white, and silver box along with 18 logo stickers. The card numbering is by alphabetical order.

	MINT	EXC	G-VG
COMPLETE SET (120)	8.00	3.50	.80
COMMON PLAYER (1-120)	.05	.02	.00

		MINT	EXC	G-VG
☐ 1	Don Aase	.05	.02	.00
☐ 2	Joaquin Andujar	.05	.02	.00
☐ 3	Harold Baines	.10	.04	.01
☐ 4	Jesse Barfield	.10	.04	.01
☐ 5	Kevin Bass	.05	.02	.00
☐ 6	Don Baylor	.10	.04	.01
☐ 7	George Bell	.15	.06	.01
☐ 8	Tony Bernazard	.05	.02	.00
☐ 9	Bert Blyleven	.10	.04	.01
☐ 10	Wade Boggs	.75	.30	.07
☐ 11	Phil Bradley	.10	.04	.01
☐ 12	Sid Bream	.05	.02	.00
☐ 13	George Brett	.50	.20	.05
☐ 14	Hubie Brooks	.05	.02	.00
☐ 15	Chris Brown	.05	.02	.00
☐ 16	Tom Candiotti	.10	.04	.01
☐ 17	Jose Canseco	1.00	.40	.10
☐ 18	Gary Carter	.20	.08	.02
☐ 19	Joe Carter	.25	.10	.02
☐ 20	Roger Clemens	.90	.40	.09
☐ 21	Vince Coleman	.25	.10	.02
☐ 22	Cecil Cooper	.10	.04	.01
☐ 23	Ron Darling	.10	.04	.01
☐ 24	Alvin Davis	.10	.04	.01
☐ 25	Chili Davis	.10	.04	.01
☐ 26	Eric Davis	.50	.20	.05
☐ 27	Glenn Davis	.20	.08	.02
☐ 28	Mike Davis	.05	.02	.00
☐ 29	Doug DeCinces	.05	.02	.00
☐ 30	Rob Deer	.10	.04	.01
☐ 31	Jim Deshaies	.05	.02	.00
☐ 32	Bo Diaz	.05	.02	.00
☐ 33	Richard Dotson	.05	.02	.00
☐ 34	Brian Downing	.05	.02	.00
☐ 35	Shawon Dunston	.15	.06	.01
☐ 36	Mark Eichhorn	.05	.02	.00
☐ 37	Dwight Evans	.10	.04	.01
☐ 38	Tony Fernandez	.10	.04	.01
☐ 39	Julio Franco	.20	.08	.02
☐ 40	Gary Gaetti	.10	.04	.01
☐ 41	Andres Galarraga	.20	.08	.02
☐ 42	Scott Garrelts	.05	.02	.00
☐ 43	Steve Garvey	.25	.10	.02
☐ 44	Kirk Gibson	.25	.10	.02
☐ 45	Dwight Gooden	.40	.16	.04
☐ 46	Ken Griffey Sr.	.10	.04	.01
☐ 47	Mark Gubicza	.10	.04	.01
☐ 48	Ozzie Guillen	.15	.06	.01
☐ 49	Bill Gullickson	.10	.04	.01
☐ 50	Tony Gwynn	.50	.20	.05
☐ 51	Von Hayes	.10	.04	.01
☐ 52	Rickey Henderson	.75	.30	.07
☐ 53	Keith Hernandez	.15	.06	.01
☐ 54	Willie Hernandez	.05	.02	.00
☐ 55	Ted Higuera	.10	.04	.01
☐ 56	Charlie Hough	.05	.02	.00
☐ 57	Kent Hrbek	.15	.06	.01
☐ 58	Pete Incaviglia	.15	.06	.01
☐ 59	Wally Joyner	.40	.16	.04
☐ 60	Bob Knepper	.05	.02	.00
☐ 61	Mike Krukow	.05	.02	.00
☐ 62	Mark Langston	.15	.06	.01
☐ 63	Carney Lansford	.10	.04	.01
☐ 64	Jim Lindeman	.05	.02	.00
☐ 65	Bill Madlock	.05	.02	.00
☐ 66	Don Mattingly	.75	.30	.07
☐ 67	Kirk McCaskill	.05	.02	.00
☐ 68	Lance McCullers	.05	.02	.00
☐ 69	Keith Moreland	.05	.02	.00
☐ 70	Jack Morris	.15	.06	.01
☐ 71	Jim Morrison	.05	.02	.00
☐ 72	Lloyd Moseby	.05	.02	.00
☐ 73	Jerry Mumphrey	.05	.02	.00
☐ 74	Dale Murphy	.35	.15	.03
☐ 75	Eddie Murray	.40	.16	.04
☐ 76	Pete O'Brien	.05	.02	.00
☐ 77	Bob Ojeda	.05	.02	.00
☐ 78	Jesse Orosco	.05	.02	.00
☐ 79	Dan Pasqua	.05	.02	.00
☐ 80	Dave Parker	.15	.06	.01
☐ 81	Larry Parrish	.05	.02	.00
☐ 82	Jim Presley	.05	.02	.00
☐ 83	Kirby Puckett	.60	.25	.06
☐ 84	Dan Quisenberry	.10	.04	.01
☐ 85	Tim Raines	.20	.08	.02
☐ 86	Dennis Rasmussen	.05	.02	.00
☐ 87	Johnny Ray	.05	.02	.00
☐ 88	Jeff Reardon	.15	.06	.01
☐ 89	Jim Rice	.20	.08	.02
☐ 90	Dave Righetti	.10	.04	.01
☐ 91	Earnest Riles	.05	.02	.00
☐ 92	Cal Ripken	.75	.30	.07
☐ 93	Ron Robinson	.05	.02	.00
☐ 94	Juan Samuel	.10	.04	.01
☐ 95	Ryne Sandberg	.75	.30	.07
☐ 96	Steve Sax	.15	.06	.01
☐ 97	Mike Schmidt	.75	.30	.07
☐ 98	Ken Schrom	.05	.02	.00
☐ 99	Mike Scott	.15	.06	.01
☐ 100	Ruben Sierra	.75	.30	.07
☐ 101	Lee Smith	.15	.06	.01
☐ 102	Ozzie Smith	.20	.08	.02
☐ 103	Cory Snyder	.10	.04	.01
☐ 104	Kent Tekulve	.05	.02	.00
☐ 105	Andres Thomas	.05	.02	.00
☐ 106	Robby Thompson	.05	.02	.00
☐ 107	Alan Trammell	.20	.08	.02
☐ 108	John Tudor	.10	.04	.01
☐ 109	Fernando Valenzuela	.15	.06	.01
☐ 110	Greg Walker	.05	.02	.00
☐ 111	Mitch Webster	.05	.02	.00
☐ 112	Lou Whitaker	.10	.04	.01
☐ 113	Frank White	.05	.02	.00
☐ 114	Reggie Williams	.05	.02	.00
☐ 115	Glenn Wilson	.05	.02	.00
☐ 116	Willie Wilson	.10	.04	.01
☐ 117	Dave Winfield	.30	.12	.03
☐ 118	Mike Witt	.05	.02	.00
☐ 119	Todd Worrell	.15	.06	.01
☐ 120	Floyd Youmans	.05	.02	.00

1987 Fleer Record Setters

This 44-card boxed set was produced by Fleer for distribution by Eckerd's Drug Stores and is sometimes referred to as the Eckerd's set. Six team logo stickers are included in the box with the complete set. The numerical checklist on the back of the box shows that the set is numbered alphabetically. The cards measure 2 1/2" by 3 1/2".

		MINT	EXC	G-VG
	COMPLETE SET (44)	5.00	2.25	.50
	COMMON PLAYER (1-44)	.10	.04	.01
☐ 1	George Brett	.45	.18	.04
☐ 2	Chris Brown	.10	.04	.01
☐ 3	Jose Canseco UER	1.00	.40	.10
	(3 of 444 on back)			
☐ 4	Roger Clemens	.90	.40	.09
☐ 5	Alvin Davis UER	.15	.06	.01
	(5 of 441 on back, upside down one)			
☐ 6	Shawon Dunston	.20	.08	.02
☐ 7	Tony Fernandez	.15	.06	.01
☐ 8	Carlton Fisk UER	.35	.15	.03
	(8 of 44' on back)			
☐ 9	Gary Gaetti UER	.15	.06	.01
	(9 of 444 on back)			
☐ 10	Gene Garber	.10	.04	.01
☐ 11	Rich Gedman	.10	.04	.01
☐ 12	Dwight Gooden	.45	.18	.04
☐ 13	Ozzie Guillen	.15	.06	.01
☐ 14	Bill Gullickson	.15	.06	.01
☐ 15	Billy Hatcher	.15	.06	.01
☐ 16	Orel Hershiser	.35	.15	.03
☐ 17	Wally Joyner	.45	.18	.04
☐ 18	Ray Knight	.15	.06	.01
☐ 19	Craig Lefferts	.10	.04	.01
☐ 20	Don Mattingly	.75	.30	.07

			MINT	EXC	G-VG
☐	21	Kevin Mitchell	.75	.30	.07
☐	22	Lloyd Moseby	.10	.04	.01
☐	23	Dale Murphy	.35	.15	.03
☐	24	Eddie Murray	.40	.16	.04
☐	25	Phil Niekro	.20	.08	.02
☐	26	Ben Oglivie	.10	.04	.01
☐	27	Jesse Orosco	.10	.04	.01
☐	28	Joe Orsulak	.10	.04	.01
☐	29	Larry Parrish	.10	.04	.01
☐	30	Tim Raines	.20	.08	.02
☐	31	Shane Rawley	.10	.04	.01
☐	32	Dave Righetti	.15	.06	.01
☐	33	Pete Rose	.60	.25	.06
☐	34	Steve Sax	.15	.06	.01
☐	35	Mike Schmidt	.75	.30	.07
☐	36	Mike Scott	.20	.08	.02
☐	37	Don Sutton	.20	.08	.02
☐	38	Alan Trammell	.20	.08	.02
☐	39	John Tudor	.10	.04	.01
☐	40	Gary Ward	.10	.04	.01
☐	41	Lou Whitaker	.15	.06	.01
☐	42	Willie Wilson	.15	.06	.01
☐	43	Todd Worrell	.15	.06	.01
☐	44	Floyd Youmans	.10	.04	.01

☐	25	Don Mattingly	.75	.30	.07
☐	26	Mark McGwire	.75	.30	.07
☐	27	Jack Morris	.15	.06	.01
☐	28	Dale Murphy	.35	.15	.03
☐	29	Dave Parker	.20	.08	.02
☐	30	Ken Phelps	.10	.04	.01
☐	31	Kirby Puckett	.50	.20	.05
☐	32	Tim Raines	.20	.08	.02
☐	33	Jeff Reardon	.15	.06	.01
☐	34	Dave Righetti	.15	.06	.01
☐	35	Cal Ripken	.75	.30	.07
☐	36	Bret Saberhagen	.35	.15	.03
☐	37	Mike Schmidt	.75	.30	.07
☐	38	Mike Scott	.15	.06	.01
☐	39	Kevin Seitzer	.30	.12	.03
☐	40	Darryl Strawberry	.75	.30	.07
☐	41	Rick Sutcliffe	.15	.06	.01
☐	42	Pat Tabler	.10	.04	.01
☐	43	Fernando Valenzuela	.20	.08	.02
☐	44	Mike Witt	.10	.04	.01

1987 Fleer Slug/Pitch Box Cards

1987 Fleer Sluggers/Pitchers

Fleer produced this 44-card boxed set although it was primarily distributed by McCrory, McLellan, Newberry, H.L. Green, T.G.Y., and other similar stores. The set features 28 sluggers and 16 pitchers and is subtitled "Baseball's Best". Cards are standard-size, 2 1/2" by 3 1/2", and were packaged in a red, white, blue, and yellow custom box along with six logo stickers. The set checklist is given on the back of the box. The checklist on the back of the set box misspells McGwire as McGuire.

			MINT	EXC	G-VG
	COMPLETE SET (44)		5.00	2.25	.50
	COMMON PLAYER (1-44)		.10	.04	.01
☐	1	Kevin Bass	.10	.04	.01
☐	2	Jesse Barfield	.15	.06	.01
☐	3	George Bell	.20	.08	.02
☐	4	Wade Boggs	.75	.30	.07
☐	5	Sid Bream	.10	.04	.01
☐	6	George Brett	.50	.20	.05
☐	7	Ivan Calderon	.15	.06	.01
☐	8	Jose Canseco	1.00	.40	.10
☐	9	Jack Clark	.20	.08	.02
☐	10	Roger Clemens	.90	.40	.09
☐	11	Eric Davis	.50	.20	.05
☐	12	Andre Dawson	.35	.15	.03
☐	13	Sid Fernandez	.15	.06	.01
☐	14	John Franco	.15	.06	.01
☐	15	Dwight Gooden	.35	.15	.03
☐	16	Pedro Guerrero	.20	.08	.02
☐	17	Tony Gwynn	.45	.18	.04
☐	18	Rickey Henderson	.75	.30	.07
☐	19	Tom Henke	.10	.04	.01
☐	20	Ted Higuera	.15	.06	.01
☐	21	Pete Incaviglia	.20	.08	.02
☐	22	Wally Joyner	.45	.18	.04
☐	23	Jeff Leonard	.10	.04	.01
☐	24	Joe Magrane	.15	.06	.01

The cards in this six-card set each measure the standard 2 1/2" by 3 1/2". Cards have essentially the same design as the 1987 Fleer Sluggers vs. Pitchers set of Baseball's Best. The cards were printed on the bottom of the counter display box which held 24 small boxed sets; hence theoretically these box cards are 1/24 as plentiful as the regular boxed set cards. These six cards, numbered M1 to M5 with one blank-back (unnumbered) card, are considered a separate set in their own right and are not typically included in a complete set of the 1987 Fleer Sluggers vs. Pitchers set of 44. The value of the panels uncut is slightly greater, perhaps by 25 percent greater, than the value of the individual cards cut up carefully.

			MINT	EXC	G-VG
	COMPLETE SET (6)		6.00	2.50	.60
	COMMON PLAYERS (M1-M5)		.10	.04	.01
☐	M1	Steve Bedrosian (box bottom card)	.15	.06	.01
☐	M2	Will Clark (box bottom card)	3.00	1.25	.30
☐	M3	Vince Coleman (box bottom card)	.50	.20	.05
☐	M4	Bo Jackson (box bottom card)	3.00	1.25	.30
☐	M5	Cory Snyder (box bottom card)	.25	.10	.02
☐	xx	Team Logo (box bottom card, unnumbered, blank back)	.10	.04	.01

1987 Fleer Update

This 132-card set was distributed by Fleer to dealers as a complete set in a custom box. In addition to the complete set of 132 cards, the box also contains 25 Team Logo stickers. The card fronts look very similar to the 1987 Fleer regular issue. The cards are numbered (with a U prefix) alphabetically according to player's last name. Cards measure the standard size, 2 1/2" by 3 1/2". Fleer misalphabetized Jim Winn in their set numbering by putting him ahead of the next four players listed. The key (extended) rookie cards in this set are Ellis Burks, Mike Greenwell, Fred McGriff, Mark McGwire and Matt Williams. Fleer also produced a "limited" edition version of this set with glossy coating and packaged in a "tin." However, this tin set was apparently not limited enough (estimated between 75,000 and 100,000 1987 Update tin sets produced by Fleer), since the price of the "tin" glossy cards is now the same as the regular set.

	MINT	EXC	G-VG
COMPLETE SET (132)	14.00	6.25	2.00
COMMON PLAYER (1-132)	.05	.02	.00

		MINT	EXC	G-VG
☐ U1	Scott Bankhead	.15	.05	.01
☐ U2	Eric Bell	.10	.04	.01
☐ U3	Juan Beniquez	.05	.02	.00
☐ U4	Juan Berenguer	.05	.02	.00
☐ U5	Mike Birkbeck	.10	.04	.01
☐ U6	Randy Bockus	.10	.04	.01
☐ U7	Rod Booker	.05	.02	.00
☐ U8	Thad Bosley	.05	.02	.00
☐ U9	Greg Brock	.05	.02	.00
☐ U10	Bob Brower	.05	.02	.00
☐ U11	Chris Brown	.05	.02	.00
☐ U12	Jerry Browne	.10	.04	.01
☐ U13	Ralph Bryant	.10	.04	.01
☐ U14	DeWayne Buice	.05	.02	.00
☐ U15	Ellis Burks	2.00	.80	.20
☐ U16	Casey Candaele	.10	.04	.01
☐ U17	Steve Carlton	.25	.10	.02
☐ U18	Juan Castillo	.05	.02	.00
☐ U19	Chuck Crim	.10	.04	.01
☐ U20	Mark Davidson	.10	.04	.01
☐ U21	Mark Davis	.10	.04	.01
☐ U22	Storm Davis	.05	.02	.00
☐ U23	Bill Dawley	.05	.02	.00
☐ U24	Andre Dawson	.40	.16	.04
☐ U25	Brian Dayett	.05	.02	.00
☐ U26	Rick Dempsey	.05	.02	.00
☐ U27	Ken Dowell	.05	.02	.00
☐ U28	Dave Dravecky	.15	.06	.01
☐ U29	Mike Dunne	.10	.04	.01
☐ U30	Dennis Eckersley	.20	.08	.02
☐ U31	Cecil Fielder	2.50	1.00	.25
☐ U32	Brian Fisher	.10	.04	.01
☐ U33	Willie Fraser	.10	.04	.01
☐ U34	Ken Gerhart	.05	.02	.00
☐ U35	Jim Gott	.10	.04	.01
☐ U36	Dan Gladden	.10	.04	.01
☐ U37	Mike Greenwell	2.25	.90	.22
☐ U38	Cecilio Guante	.05	.02	.00
☐ U39	Albert Hall	.05	.02	.00
☐ U40	Atlee Hammaker	.05	.02	.00
☐ U41	Mickey Hatcher	.05	.02	.00
☐ U42	Mike Heath	.05	.02	.00
☐ U43	Neal Heaton	.05	.02	.00
☐ U44	Mike Henneman	.30	.12	.03
☐ U45	Guy Hoffman	.10	.04	.01
☐ U46	Charles Hudson	.05	.02	.00
☐ U47	Chuck Jackson	.10	.04	.01
☐ U48	Mike Jackson	.20	.08	.02
☐ U49	Reggie Jackson	.40	.16	.04
☐ U50	Chris James	.15	.06	.01
☐ U51	Dion James	.10	.04	.01
☐ U52	Stan Javier	.10	.04	.01
☐ U53	Stan Jefferson	.10	.04	.01
☐ U54	Jimmy Jones	.10	.04	.01
☐ U55	Tracy Jones	.10	.04	.01
☐ U56	Terry Kennedy	.05	.02	.00
☐ U57	Mike Kingery	.10	.04	.01
☐ U58	Ray Knight	.10	.04	.01
☐ U59	Gene Larkin	.20	.08	.02
☐ U60	Mike LaValliere	.10	.04	.01
☐ U61	Jack Lazorko	.05	.02	.00
☐ U62	Terry Leach	.10	.04	.01
☐ U63	Rick Leach	.05	.02	.00
☐ U64	Craig Lefferts	.05	.02	.00
☐ U65	Jim Lindeman	.10	.04	.01
☐ U66	Bill Long	.10	.04	.01
☐ U67	Mike Loynd	.05	.02	.00
☐ U68	Greg Maddux	.90	.40	.09
☐ U69	Bill Madlock	.12	.05	.01
☐ U70	Dave Magadan	.30	.12	.03
☐ U71	Joe Magrane	.20	.08	.02
☐ U72	Fred Manrique	.10	.04	.01
☐ U73	Mike Mason	.05	.02	.00
☐ U74	Lloyd McClendon	.15	.06	.01
☐ U75	Fred McGriff	2.50	1.00	.25
☐ U76	Mark McGwire	2.00	.80	.20
☐ U77	Mark McLemore	.05	.02	.00
☐ U78	Kevin McReynolds	.15	.06	.01
☐ U79	Dave Meads	.05	.02	.00
☐ U80	Greg Minton	.05	.02	.00
☐ U81	John Mitchell	.10	.04	.01
☐ U82	Kevin Mitchell	1.50	.60	.15
☐ U83	John Morris	.10	.04	.01
☐ U84	Jeff Musselman	.10	.04	.01
☐ U85	Randy Myers	.20	.08	.02
☐ U86	Gene Nelson	.05	.02	.00
☐ U87	Joe Niekro	.10	.04	.01
☐ U88	Tom Nieto	.05	.02	.00
☐ U89	Reid Nichols	.05	.02	.00
☐ U90	Matt Nokes	.50	.20	.05
☐ U91	Dickie Noles	.05	.02	.00
☐ U92	Edwin Nunez	.05	.02	.00
☐ U93	Jose Nunez	.10	.04	.01
☐ U94	Paul O'Neill	.35	.15	.03
☐ U95	Jim Paciorek	.10	.04	.01
☐ U96	Lance Parrish	.12	.05	.01
☐ U97	Bill Pecota	.15	.06	.01
☐ U98	Tony Pena	.12	.05	.01
☐ U99	Luis Polonia	.50	.20	.05
☐ U100	Randy Ready	.12	.05	.01
☐ U101	Jeff Reardon	.17	.07	.01
☐ U102	Gary Redus	.05	.02	.00
☐ U103	Rick Rhoden	.05	.02	.00
☐ U104	Wally Ritchie	.10	.04	.01
☐ U105	Jeff Robinson UER (wrong Jeff's stats on back)	.12	.05	.01
☐ U106	Mark Salas	.05	.02	.00
☐ U107	Dave Schmidt	.10	.04	.01
☐ U108	Kevin Seitzer UER (wrong birth year)	.15	.06	.01
☐ U109	John Shelby	.05	.02	.00
☐ U110	John Smiley	.90	.40	.09
☐ U111	Lary Sorensen	.05	.02	.00
☐ U112	Chris Speier	.05	.02	.00
☐ U113	Randy St.Claire	.05	.02	.00
☐ U114	Jim Sundberg	.05	.02	.00
☐ U115	B.J. Surhoff	.20	.08	.02
☐ U116	Greg Swindell	.35	.15	.03
☐ U117	Danny Tartabull	.25	.10	.02
☐ U118	Dorn Taylor	.10	.04	.01
☐ U119	Lee Tunnell	.05	.02	.00
☐ U120	Ed VandeBerg	.05	.02	.00
☐ U121	Andy Van Slyke	.17	.07	.01
☐ U122	Gary Ward	.05	.02	.00
☐ U123	Devon White	.35	.15	.03
☐ U124	Alan Wiggins	.05	.02	.00
☐ U125	Bill Wilkinson	.05	.02	.00
☐ U126	Jim Winn	.05	.02	.00
☐ U127	Frank Williams	.05	.02	.00
☐ U128	Ken Williams	.10	.04	.01
☐ U129	Matt Williams	4.50	2.00	.45
☐ U130	Herm Winningham	.05	.02	.00
☐ U131	Matt Young	.05	.02	.00
☐ U132	Checklist Card	.05	.01	.00

1987 Fleer World Series

This 12-card set of 2 1/2" by 3 1/2" cards features highlights of the previous year's World Series between the Mets and the Red Sox. The sets were packaged as a complete set insert with the collated sets (of the 1987 Fleer regular issue) which were sold by Fleer directly to hobby card dealers; they were not available in the general retail candy store outlets.

	MINT	EXC	G-VG
COMPLETE SET (12)	4.00	1.75	.40
COMMON PLAYER (1-12)	.25	.10	.02
□ 1 Bruce Hurst Left Hand Finesse Beats Mets	.35	.15	.03
□ 2 Keith Hernandez and Wade Boggs	.60	.25	.06
□ 3 Roger Clemens HOR	1.25	.50	.12
□ 4 Clutch Hitting (Gary Carter)	.45	.18	.04
□ 5 Ron Darling Picks Up Slack	.35	.15	.03
□ 6 Marty Barrett .433 Series BA	.25	.10	.02
□ 7 Dwight Gooden	.60	.25	.06
□ 8 Strategy at Work (Mets Conference)	.25	.10	.02
□ 9 Dewey Evans (Congratulated by Rich Gedman)	.35	.15	.03
□ 10 One Strike From Boston Victory (Dave Henderson)	.35	.15	.03
□ 11 Series Home Run Duo (Ray Knight and Darryl Strawberry)	.60	.25	.06
□ 12 Ray Knight (Series MVP)	.35	.15	.03

1988 Fleer

This 660-card set features a distinctive white background with red and blue diagonal stripes across the card. The backs are printed in gray and red on white card stock. The bottom of the card back shows an innovative breakdown of the player's demonstrated ability with respect to day, night, home, and road games. Cards are numbered on the back and are again the standard 2 1/2" by 3 1/2". Cards are again organized numerically by teams, i.e., World Champion Twins (1-25), St. Louis Cardinals (26-50), Detroit Tigers (51-75), San Francisco Giants (76-101), Toronto Blue Jays (102-126), New York Mets (127-154), Milwaukee Brewers (155-178), Montreal Expos (179-201), New York Yankees (202-226), Cincinnati Reds (227-250), Kansas City Royals (251-274), Oakland A's (275-296), Philadelphia Phillies (297-320), Pittsburgh Pirates (321-342), Boston Red Sox (343-367), Seattle Mariners (368-390), Chicago White Sox (391-413), Chicago Cubs (414-436), Houston Astros

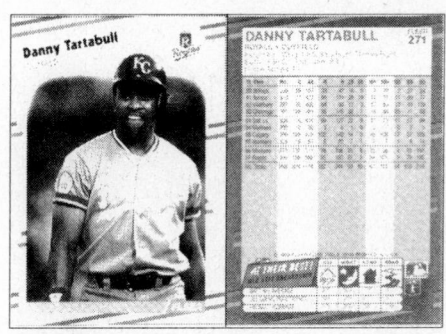

(437-460), Texas Rangers (461-483), California Angels (484-507), Los Angeles Dodgers (508-530), Atlanta Braves (531-552), Baltimore Orioles (553-575), San Diego Padres (576-599), and Cleveland Indians (600-621). The last 39 cards in the set consist of Specials (622-640), Rookie Pairs (641-653), and checklists (654-660). Cards 90 and 91 are incorrectly numbered on the checklist card number 654. The key rookie cards in this set are Ellis Burks, Ron Gant, Tom Glavine, Mark Grace, Gregg Jefferies, Roberto Kelly, Edgar Martinez, Jack McDowell, and Matt Williams. Fleer also produced a "limited" edition version of this set with glossy coating and packaged in a "tin." However, this tin set was apparently not limited enough (estimated between 40,000 and 60,000 1988 tin sets produced by Fleer), since the price of the "tin" glossy cards is now only double the price of the regular set.

	MINT	EXC	G-VG
COMPLETE SET (660)	36.00	16.00	3.25
COMMON PLAYER (1-660)	.04	.02	.00
□ 1 Keith Atherton	.07	.03	.01
□ 2 Don Baylor	.07	.03	.01
□ 3 Juan Berenguer	.04	.02	.00
□ 4 Bert Blyleven	.10	.04	.01
□ 5 Tom Brunansky	.07	.03	.01
□ 6 Randy Bush	.04	.02	.00
□ 7 Steve Carlton	.25	.10	.02
□ 8 Mark Davidson	.07	.03	.01
□ 9 George Frazier	.04	.02	.00
□ 10 Gary Gaetti	.07	.03	.01
□ 11 Greg Gagne	.04	.02	.00
□ 12 Dan Gladden	.04	.02	.00
□ 13 Kent Hrbek	.12	.05	.01
□ 14 Gene Larkin	.15	.06	.01
□ 15 Tim Laudner	.04	.02	.00
□ 16 Steve Lombardozzi	.04	.02	.00
□ 17 Al Newman	.04	.02	.00
□ 18 Joe Niekro	.07	.03	.01
□ 19 Kirby Puckett	.65	.25	.06
□ 20 Jeff Reardon	.15	.06	.01
□ 21A Dan Schatzeder ERR (misspelled Schatzader on card front)	.10	.04	.01
□ 21B Dan Schatzeder COR	.07	.03	.01
□ 22 Roy Smalley	.04	.02	.00
□ 23 Mike Smithson	.04	.02	.00
□ 24 Les Straker	.04	.02	.00
□ 25 Frank Viola	.12	.05	.01
□ 26 Jack Clark	.10	.04	.01
□ 27 Vince Coleman	.15	.06	.01
□ 28 Danny Cox	.04	.02	.00
□ 29 Bill Dawley	.04	.02	.00
□ 30 Ken Dayley	.04	.02	.00
□ 31 Doug DeCinces	.07	.03	.01
□ 32 Curt Ford	.04	.02	.00
□ 33 Bob Forsch	.04	.02	.00
□ 34 David Green	.04	.02	.00
□ 35 Tom Herr	.04	.02	.00
□ 36 Ricky Horton	.04	.02	.00
□ 37 Lance Johnson	.35	.15	.03
□ 38 Steve Lake	.04	.02	.00
□ 39 Jim Lindeman	.04	.02	.00
□ 40 Joe Magrane	.20	.08	.02
□ 41 Greg Mathews	.04	.02	.00
□ 42 Willie McGee	.10	.04	.01
□ 43 John Morris	.04	.02	.00
□ 44 Jose Oquendo	.04	.02	.00

☐ 45	Tony Pena	.07	.03	.01
☐ 46	Terry Pendleton	.20	.08	.02
☐ 47	Ozzie Smith	.30	.12	.03
☐ 48	John Tudor	.10	.04	.01
☐ 49	Lee Tunnell	.04	.02	.00
☐ 50	Todd Worrell	.07	.03	.01
☐ 51	Doyle Alexander	.04	.02	.00
☐ 52	Dave Bergman	.04	.02	.00
☐ 53	Tom Brookens	.04	.02	.00
☐ 54	Darrell Evans	.07	.03	.01
☐ 55	Kirk Gibson	.15	.06	.01
☐ 56	Mike Heath	.04	.02	.00
☐ 57	Mike Henneman	.30	.12	.03
☐ 58	Willie Hernandez	.04	.02	.00
☐ 59	Larry Herndon	.04	.02	.00
☐ 60	Eric King	.04	.02	.00
☐ 61	Chet Lemon	.04	.02	.00
☐ 62	Scott Lusader	.10	.04	.01
☐ 63	Bill Madlock	.07	.03	.01
☐ 64	Jack Morris	.17	.07	.01
☐ 65	Jim Morrison	.04	.02	.00
☐ 66	Matt Nokes	.60	.25	.06
☐ 67	Dan Petry	.04	.02	.00
☐ 68A	Jeff Robinson ERR	.30	.12	.03
	Detroit Tigers			
	(stats for other Jeff			
	Robinson on card back)			
☐ 68B	Jeff Robinson COR	.10	.04	.01
	Detroit Tigers			
☐ 69	Pat Sheridan	.04	.02	.00
☐ 70	Nate Snell	.04	.02	.00
☐ 71	Frank Tanana	.07	.03	.01
☐ 72	Walt Terrell	.04	.02	.00
☐ 73	Mark Thurmond	.04	.02	.00
☐ 74	Alan Trammell	.20	.08	.02
☐ 75	Lou Whitaker	.10	.04	.01
☐ 76	Mike Aldrete	.04	.02	.00
☐ 77	Bob Brenly	.04	.02	.00
☐ 78	Will Clark	3.00	1.25	.30
☐ 79	Chili Davis	.10	.04	.01
☐ 80	Kelly Downs	.07	.03	.01
☐ 81	Dave Dravecky	.10	.04	.01
☐ 82	Scott Garrelts	.04	.02	.00
☐ 83	Atlee Hammaker	.04	.02	.00
☐ 84	Dave Henderson	.15	.06	.01
☐ 85	Mike Krukow	.04	.02	.00
☐ 86	Mike LaCoss	.04	.02	.00
☐ 87	Craig Lefferts	.04	.02	.00
☐ 88	Jeff Leonard	.04	.02	.00
☐ 89	Candy Maldonado	.07	.03	.01
☐ 90	Eddie Milner	.04	.02	.00
☐ 91	Bob Melvin	.04	.02	.00
☐ 92	Kevin Mitchell	.75	.30	.07
☐ 93	Jon Perlman	.04	.02	.00
☐ 94	Rick Reuschel	.07	.03	.01
☐ 95	Don Robinson	.04	.02	.00
☐ 96	Chris Speier	.04	.02	.00
☐ 97	Harry Spilman	.04	.02	.00
☐ 98	Robby Thompson	.04	.02	.00
☐ 99	Jose Uribe	.04	.02	.00
☐ 100	Mark Wasinger	.07	.03	.01
☐ 101	Matt Williams	4.50	2.00	.45
☐ 102	Jesse Barfield	.10	.04	.01
☐ 103	George Bell	.17	.07	.01
☐ 104	Juan Beniquez	.04	.02	.00
☐ 105	John Cerutti	.04	.02	.00
☐ 106	Jim Clancy	.04	.02	.00
☐ 107	Rob Ducey	.12	.05	.01
☐ 108	Mark Eichhorn	.07	.03	.01
☐ 109	Tony Fernandez	.10	.04	.01
☐ 110	Cecil Fielder	.90	.40	.09
☐ 111	Kelly Gruber	.30	.12	.03
☐ 112	Tom Henke	.07	.03	.01
☐ 113A	Garth Iorg ERR	.20	.08	.02
	(misspelled Iorq			
	on card front)			
☐ 113B	Garth Iorg COR	.07	.03	.01
☐ 114	Jimmy Key	.10	.04	.01
☐ 115	Rick Leach	.04	.02	.00
☐ 116	Manny Lee	.04	.02	.00
☐ 117	Nelson Liriano	.10	.04	.01
☐ 118	Fred McGriff	1.50	.60	.15
☐ 119	Lloyd Moseby	.04	.02	.00
☐ 120	Rance Mulliniks	.04	.02	.00
☐ 121	Jeff Musselman	.04	.02	.00
☐ 122	Jose Nunez	.07	.03	.01
☐ 123	Dave Stieb	.10	.04	.01
☐ 124	Willie Upshaw	.04	.02	.00
☐ 125	Duane Ward	.10	.04	.01
☐ 126	Ernie Whitt	.04	.02	.00
☐ 127	Rick Aguilera	.07	.03	.01
☐ 128	Wally Backman	.04	.02	.00
☐ 129	Mark Carreon	.15	.06	.01
☐ 130	Gary Carter	.12	.05	.01
☐ 131	David Cone	.40	.16	.04
☐ 132	Ron Darling	.10	.04	.01
☐ 133	Len Dykstra	.12	.05	.01
☐ 134	Sid Fernandez	.10	.04	.01
☐ 135	Dwight Gooden	.25	.10	.02
☐ 136	Keith Hernandez	.10	.04	.01
☐ 137	Gregg Jefferies	2.75	1.10	.27
☐ 138	Howard Johnson	.35	.15	.03
☐ 139	Terry Leach	.04	.02	.00
☐ 140	Barry Lyons	.07	.03	.01
☐ 141	Dave Magadan	.10	.04	.01
☐ 142	Roger McDowell	.04	.02	.00
☐ 143	Kevin McReynolds	.12	.05	.01
☐ 144	Keith Miller	.20	.08	.02
	(New York Mets)			
☐ 145	John Mitchell	.07	.03	.01
☐ 146	Randy Myers	.10	.04	.01
☐ 147	Bob Ojeda	.04	.02	.00
☐ 148	Jesse Orosco	.04	.02	.00
☐ 149	Rafael Santana	.04	.02	.00
☐ 150	Doug Sisk	.04	.02	.00
☐ 151	Darryl Strawberry	.75	.30	.07
☐ 152	Tim Teufel	.04	.02	.00
☐ 153	Gene Walter	.04	.02	.00
☐ 154	Mookie Wilson	.04	.02	.00
☐ 155	Jay Aldrich	.04	.02	.00
☐ 156	Chris Bosio	.07	.03	.01
☐ 157	Glenn Braggs	.04	.02	.00
☐ 158	Greg Brock	.04	.02	.00
☐ 159	Juan Castillo	.04	.02	.00
☐ 160	Mark Clear	.04	.02	.00
☐ 161	Cecil Cooper	.07	.03	.01
☐ 162	Chuck Crim	.04	.02	.00
☐ 163	Rob Deer	.07	.03	.01
☐ 164	Mike Felder	.04	.02	.00
☐ 165	Jim Gantner	.04	.02	.00
☐ 166	Ted Higuera	.07	.03	.01
☐ 167	Steve Kiefer	.04	.02	.00
☐ 168	Rick Manning	.04	.02	.00
☐ 169	Paul Molitor	.15	.06	.01
☐ 170	Juan Nieves	.04	.02	.00
☐ 171	Dan Plesac	.04	.02	.00
☐ 172	Earnest Riles	.04	.02	.00
☐ 173	Bill Schroeder	.04	.02	.00
☐ 174	Steve Stanicek	.04	.02	.00
☐ 175	B.J. Surhoff	.10	.04	.01
☐ 176	Dale Sveum	.04	.02	.00
☐ 177	Bill Wegman	.07	.03	.01
☐ 178	Robin Yount	.35	.15	.03
☐ 179	Hubie Brooks	.07	.03	.01
☐ 180	Tim Burke	.04	.02	.00
☐ 181	Casey Candaele	.04	.02	.00
☐ 182	Mike Fitzgerald	.04	.02	.00
☐ 183	Tom Foley	.04	.02	.00
☐ 184	Andres Galarraga	.10	.04	.01
☐ 185	Neal Heaton	.04	.02	.00
☐ 186	Wallace Johnson	.04	.02	.00
☐ 187	Vance Law	.04	.02	.00
☐ 188	Dennis Martinez	.07	.03	.01
☐ 189	Bob McClure	.04	.02	.00
☐ 190	Andy McGaffigan	.04	.02	.00
☐ 191	Reid Nichols	.04	.02	.00
☐ 192	Pascual Perez	.04	.02	.00
☐ 193	Tim Raines	.15	.06	.01
☐ 194	Jeff Reed	.04	.02	.00
☐ 195	Bob Sebra	.04	.02	.00
☐ 196	Bryn Smith	.04	.02	.00
☐ 197	Randy St.Claire	.04	.02	.00
☐ 198	Tim Wallach	.07	.03	.01
☐ 199	Mitch Webster	.04	.02	.00
☐ 200	Herm Winningham	.04	.02	.00
☐ 201	Floyd Youmans	.04	.02	.00
☐ 202	Brad Arnsberg	.10	.04	.01
☐ 203	Rick Cerone	.04	.02	.00
☐ 204	Pat Clements	.04	.02	.00
☐ 205	Henry Cotto	.04	.02	.00
☐ 206	Mike Easler	.04	.02	.00
☐ 207	Ron Guidry	.10	.04	.01
☐ 208	Bill Gullickson	.07	.03	.01
☐ 209	Rickey Henderson	.60	.25	.06
☐ 210	Charles Hudson	.04	.02	.00
☐ 211	Tommy John	.10	.04	.01
☐ 212	Roberto Kelly	1.25	.50	.12
☐ 213	Ron Kittle	.07	.03	.01
☐ 214	Don Mattingly	.60	.25	.06
☐ 215	Bobby Meacham	.04	.02	.00
☐ 216	Mike Pagliarulo	.04	.02	.00
☐ 217	Dan Pasqua	.04	.02	.00
☐ 218	Willie Randolph	.07	.03	.01
☐ 219	Rick Rhoden	.04	.02	.00
☐ 220	Dave Righetti	.07	.03	.01
☐ 221	Jerry Royster	.04	.02	.00
☐ 222	Tim Stoddard	.04	.02	.00
☐ 223	Wayne Tolleson	.04	.02	.00

☐ 224	Gary Ward	.04	.02	.00
☐ 225	Claudell Washington	.04	.02	.00
☐ 226	Dave Winfield	.25	.10	.02
☐ 227	Buddy Bell	.07	.03	.01
☐ 228	Tom Browning	.07	.03	.01
☐ 229	Dave Concepcion	.07	.03	.01
☐ 230	Kal Daniels	.10	.04	.01
☐ 231	Eric Davis	.25	.10	.02
☐ 232	Bo Diaz	.04	.02	.00
☐ 233	Nick Esasky	.04	.02	.00
	(has a dollar sign before '87 SB totals)			
☐ 234	John Franco	.07	.03	.01
☐ 235	Guy Hoffman	.04	.02	.00
☐ 236	Tom Hume	.04	.02	.00
☐ 237	Tracy Jones	.04	.02	.00
☐ 238	Bill Landrum	.15	.06	.01
☐ 239	Barry Larkin	.60	.25	.06
☐ 240	Terry McGriff	.04	.02	.00
☐ 241	Rob Murphy	.04	.02	.00
☐ 242	Ron Oester	.04	.02	.00
☐ 243	Dave Parker	.15	.06	.01
☐ 244	Pat Perry	.04	.02	.00
☐ 245	Ted Power	.04	.02	.00
☐ 246	Dennis Rasmussen	.04	.02	.00
☐ 247	Ron Robinson	.04	.02	.00
☐ 248	Kurt Stillwell	.07	.03	.01
☐ 249	Jeff Treadway	.40	.16	.04
☐ 250	Frank Williams	.04	.02	.00
☐ 251	Steve Balboni	.04	.02	.00
☐ 252	Bud Black	.04	.02	.00
☐ 253	Thad Bosley	.04	.02	.00
☐ 254	George Brett	.35	.15	.03
☐ 255	John Davis	.07	.03	.01
☐ 256	Steve Farr	.04	.02	.00
☐ 257	Gene Garber	.04	.02	.00
☐ 258	Jerry Don Gleaton	.04	.02	.00
☐ 259	Mark Gubicza	.07	.03	.01
☐ 260	Bo Jackson	2.50	1.00	.25
☐ 261	Danny Jackson	.07	.03	.01
☐ 262	Ross Jones	.04	.02	.00
☐ 263	Charlie Leibrandt	.04	.02	.00
☐ 264	Bill Pecota	.10	.04	.01
☐ 265	Melido Perez	.30	.12	.03
☐ 266	Jamie Quirk	.04	.02	.00
☐ 267	Dan Quisenberry	.07	.03	.01
☐ 268	Bret Saberhagen	.20	.08	.02
☐ 269	Angel Salazar	.04	.02	.00
☐ 270	Kevin Seitzer UER	.10	.04	.01
	(wrong birth year)			
☐ 271	Danny Tartabull	.25	.10	.02
☐ 272	Gary Thurman	.12	.05	.01
☐ 273	Frank White	.04	.02	.00
☐ 274	Willie Wilson	.07	.03	.01
☐ 275	Tony Bernazard	.04	.02	.00
☐ 276	Jose Canseco	2.50	1.00	.25
☐ 277	Mike Davis	.04	.02	.00
☐ 278	Storm Davis	.04	.02	.00
☐ 279	Dennis Eckersley	.15	.06	.01
☐ 280	Alfredo Griffin	.04	.02	.00
☐ 281	Rick Honeycutt	.04	.02	.00
☐ 282	Jay Howell	.04	.02	.00
☐ 283	Reggie Jackson	.35	.15	.03
☐ 284	Dennis Lamp	.04	.02	.00
☐ 285	Carney Lansford	.07	.03	.01
☐ 286	Mark McGwire	1.25	.50	.12
☐ 287	Dwayne Murphy	.04	.02	.00
☐ 288	Gene Nelson	.04	.02	.00
☐ 289	Steve Ontiveros	.04	.02	.00
☐ 290	Tony Phillips	.04	.02	.00
☐ 291	Eric Plunk	.04	.02	.00
☐ 292	Luis Polonia	.50	.20	.05
☐ 293	Rick Rodriguez	.07	.03	.01
☐ 294	Terry Steinbach	.10	.04	.01
☐ 295	Dave Stewart	.12	.05	.01
☐ 296	Curt Young	.04	.02	.00
☐ 297	Luis Aguayo	.04	.02	.00
☐ 298	Steve Bedrosian	.07	.03	.01
☐ 299	Jeff Calhoun	.04	.02	.00
☐ 300	Don Carman	.04	.02	.00
☐ 301	Todd Frohwirth	.07	.03	.01
☐ 302	Greg Gross	.04	.02	.00
☐ 303	Kevin Gross	.04	.02	.00
☐ 304	Von Hayes	.10	.04	.01
☐ 305	Keith Hughes	.07	.03	.01
☐ 306	Mike Jackson	.20	.08	.02
☐ 307	Chris James	.10	.04	.01
☐ 308	Steve Jeltz	.04	.02	.00
☐ 309	Mike Maddux	.04	.02	.00
☐ 310	Lance Parrish	.10	.04	.01
☐ 311	Shane Rawley	.04	.02	.00
☐ 312	Wally Ritchie	.04	.02	.00
☐ 313	Bruce Ruffin	.04	.02	.00
☐ 314	Juan Samuel	.07	.03	.01
☐ 315	Mike Schmidt	.75	.30	.07
☐ 316	Rick Schu	.04	.02	.00
☐ 317	Jeff Stone	.04	.02	.00
☐ 318	Kent Tekulve	.04	.02	.00
☐ 319	Milt Thompson	.04	.02	.00
☐ 320	Glenn Wilson	.04	.02	.00
☐ 321	Rafael Belliard	.04	.02	.00
☐ 322	Barry Bonds	1.00	.40	.10
☐ 323	Bobby Bonilla UER	.90	.40	.09
	(wrong birth year)			
☐ 324	Sid Bream	.04	.02	.00
☐ 325	John Cangelosi	.04	.02	.00
☐ 326	Mike Diaz	.04	.02	.00
☐ 327	Doug Drabek	.20	.08	.02
☐ 328	Mike Dunne	.04	.02	.00
☐ 329	Brian Fisher	.04	.02	.00
☐ 330	Brett Gideon	.04	.02	.00
☐ 331	Terry Harper	.04	.02	.00
☐ 332	Bob Kipper	.04	.02	.00
☐ 333	Mike LaValliere	.04	.02	.00
☐ 334	Jose Lind	.40	.16	.04
☐ 335	Junior Ortiz	.04	.02	.00
☐ 336	Vicente Palacios	.15	.06	.01
☐ 337	Bob Patterson	.07	.03	.01
☐ 338	Al Pedrique	.04	.02	.00
☐ 339	R.J. Reynolds	.04	.02	.00
☐ 340	John Smiley	1.25	.50	.12
☐ 341	Andy Van Slyke UER	.17	.07	.01
	(wrong batting and throwing listed)			
☐ 342	Bob Walk	.04	.02	.00
☐ 343	Marty Barrett	.04	.02	.00
☐ 344	Todd Benzinger	.40	.16	.04
☐ 345	Wade Boggs	.50	.20	.05
☐ 346	Tom Bolton	.12	.05	.01
☐ 347	Oil Can Boyd	.04	.02	.00
☐ 348	Ellis Burks	2.00	.80	.20
☐ 349	Roger Clemens	1.00	.40	.10
☐ 350	Steve Crawford	.07	.03	.01
☐ 351	Dwight Evans	.10	.04	.01
☐ 352	Wes Gardner	.10	.04	.01
☐ 353	Rich Gedman	.04	.02	.00
☐ 354	Mike Greenwell	1.25	.50	.12
☐ 355	Sam Horn	.25	.10	.02
☐ 356	Bruce Hurst	.07	.03	.01
☐ 357	John Marzano	.07	.03	.01
☐ 358	Al Nipper	.04	.02	.00
☐ 359	Spike Owen	.04	.02	.00
☐ 360	Jody Reed	.75	.30	.07
☐ 361	Jim Rice	.10	.04	.01
☐ 362	Ed Romero	.04	.02	.00
☐ 363	Kevin Romine	.04	.02	.00
☐ 364	Joe Sambito	.04	.02	.00
☐ 365	Calvin Schiraldi	.04	.02	.00
☐ 366	Jeff Sellers	.04	.02	.00
☐ 367	Bob Stanley	.04	.02	.00
☐ 368	Scott Bankhead	.07	.03	.01
☐ 369	Phil Bradley	.04	.02	.00
☐ 370	Scott Bradley	.04	.02	.00
☐ 371	Mickey Brantley	.04	.02	.00
☐ 372	Mike Campbell	.07	.03	.01
☐ 373	Alvin Davis	.07	.03	.01
☐ 374	Lee Guetterman	.04	.02	.00
☐ 375	Dave Hengel	.07	.03	.01
☐ 376	Mike Kingery	.04	.02	.00
☐ 377	Mark Langston	.15	.06	.01
☐ 378	Edgar Martinez	1.25	.50	.12
☐ 379	Mike Moore	.07	.03	.01
☐ 380	Mike Morgan	.07	.03	.01
☐ 381	John Moses	.04	.02	.00
☐ 382	Donnell Nixon	.07	.03	.01
☐ 383	Edwin Nunez	.04	.02	.00
☐ 384	Ken Phelps	.04	.02	.00
☐ 385	Jim Presley	.04	.02	.00
☐ 386	Rey Quinones	.04	.02	.00
☐ 387	Jerry Reed	.04	.02	.00
☐ 388	Harold Reynolds	.07	.03	.01
☐ 389	Dave Valle	.04	.02	.00
☐ 390	Bill Wilkinson	.07	.03	.01
☐ 391	Harold Baines	.10	.04	.01
☐ 392	Floyd Bannister	.04	.02	.00
☐ 393	Daryl Boston	.04	.02	.00
☐ 394	Ivan Calderon	.10	.04	.01
☐ 395	Jose DeLeon	.04	.02	.00
☐ 396	Richard Dotson	.04	.02	.00
☐ 397	Carlton Fisk	.35	.15	.03
☐ 398	Ozzie Guillen	.10	.04	.01
☐ 399	Ron Hassey	.04	.02	.00
☐ 400	Donnie Hill	.04	.02	.00
☐ 401	Bob James	.04	.02	.00
☐ 402	Dave LaPoint	.04	.02	.00
☐ 403	Bill Lindsey	.04	.02	.00
☐ 404	Bill Long	.07	.03	.01
☐ 405	Steve Lyons	.04	.02	.00

☐ 406	Fred Manrique	.07	.03	.01
☐ 407	Jack McDowell	1.25	.50	.12
☐ 408	Gary Redus	.04	.02	.00
☐ 409	Ray Searage	.04	.02	.00
☐ 410	Bobby Thigpen	.15	.06	.01
☐ 411	Greg Walker	.04	.02	.00
☐ 412	Ken Williams	.07	.03	.01
☐ 413	Jim Winn	.04	.02	.00
☐ 414	Jody Davis	.04	.02	.00
☐ 415	Andre Dawson	.25	.10	.02
☐ 416	Brian Dayett	.04	.02	.00
☐ 417	Bob Dernier	.04	.02	.00
☐ 418	Frank DiPino	.04	.02	.00
☐ 419	Shawon Dunston	.12	.05	.01
☐ 420	Leon Durham	.04	.02	.00
☐ 421	Les Lancaster	.12	.05	.01
☐ 422	Ed Lynch	.04	.02	.00
☐ 423	Greg Maddux	.50	.20	.05
☐ 424	Dave Martinez	.15	.06	.01
☐ 425A	Keith Moreland ERR (photo actually Jody Davis)	2.00	.80	.20
☐ 425B	Keith Moreland COR (bat on shoulder)	.12	.05	.01
☐ 426	Jamie Moyer	.04	.02	.00
☐ 427	Jerry Mumphrey	.04	.02	.00
☐ 428	Paul Noce	.07	.03	.01
☐ 429	Rafael Palmeiro	1.50	.60	.15
☐ 430	Wade Rowdon	.04	.02	.00
☐ 431	Ryne Sandberg	1.00	.40	.10
☐ 432	Scott Sanderson	.07	.03	.01
☐ 433	Lee Smith	.15	.06	.01
☐ 434	Jim Sundberg	.04	.02	.00
☐ 435	Rick Sutcliffe	.07	.03	.01
☐ 436	Manny Trillo	.04	.02	.00
☐ 437	Juan Agosto	.04	.02	.00
☐ 438	Larry Andersen	.04	.02	.00
☐ 439	Alan Ashby	.04	.02	.00
☐ 440	Kevin Bass	.04	.02	.00
☐ 441	Ken Caminiti	.45	.18	.04
☐ 442	Rocky Childress	.04	.02	.00
☐ 443	Jose Cruz	.07	.03	.01
☐ 444	Danny Darwin	.04	.02	.00
☐ 445	Glenn Davis	.12	.05	.01
☐ 446	Jim Deshaies	.04	.02	.00
☐ 447	Bill Doran	.04	.02	.00
☐ 448	Ty Gainey	.04	.02	.00
☐ 449	Billy Hatcher	.07	.03	.01
☐ 450	Jeff Heathcock	.04	.02	.00
☐ 451	Bob Knepper	.04	.02	.00
☐ 452	Rob Mallicoat	.04	.02	.00
☐ 453	Dave Meads	.04	.02	.00
☐ 454	Craig Reynolds	.04	.02	.00
☐ 455	Nolan Ryan	1.50	.60	.15
☐ 456	Mike Scott	.10	.04	.01
☐ 457	Dave Smith	.04	.02	.00
☐ 458	Denny Walling	.04	.02	.00
☐ 459	Robbie Wine	.04	.02	.00
☐ 460	Gerald Young	.12	.05	.01
☐ 461	Bob Brower	.07	.03	.01
☐ 462A	Jerry Browne ERR (photo actually Bob Brower, white player)	2.00	.80	.20
☐ 462B	Jerry Browne COR (black player)	.12	.05	.01
☐ 463	Steve Buechele	.07	.03	.01
☐ 464	Edwin Correa	.04	.02	.00
☐ 465	Cecil Espy	.15	.06	.01
☐ 466	Scott Fletcher	.04	.02	.00
☐ 467	Jose Guzman	.07	.03	.01
☐ 468	Greg Harris	.04	.02	.00
☐ 469	Charlie Hough	.04	.02	.00
☐ 470	Pete Incaviglia	.10	.04	.01
☐ 471	Paul Kilgus	.07	.03	.01
☐ 472	Mike Loynd	.04	.02	.00
☐ 473	Oddibe McDowell	.04	.02	.00
☐ 474	Dale Mohorcic	.04	.02	.00
☐ 475	Pete O'Brien	.04	.02	.00
☐ 476	Larry Parrish	.04	.02	.00
☐ 477	Geno Petralli	.04	.02	.00
☐ 478	Jeff Russell	.04	.02	.00
☐ 479	Ruben Sierra	1.00	.40	.10
☐ 480	Mike Stanley	.04	.02	.00
☐ 481	Curtis Wilkerson	.04	.02	.00
☐ 482	Mitch Williams	.07	.03	.01
☐ 483	Bobby Witt	.10	.04	.01
☐ 484	Tony Armas	.04	.02	.00
☐ 485	Bob Boone	.07	.03	.01
☐ 486	Bill Buckner	.07	.03	.01
☐ 487	DeWayne Buice	.04	.02	.00
☐ 488	Brian Downing	.04	.02	.00
☐ 489	Chuck Finley	.30	.12	.03

☐ 490	Willie Fraser UER (wrong bio, stats for George Hendrick)	.04	.02	.00
☐ 491	Jack Howell	.04	.02	.00
☐ 492	Ruppert Jones	.04	.02	.00
☐ 493	Wally Joyner	.30	.12	.03
☐ 494	Jack Lazorko	.04	.02	.00
☐ 495	Gary Lucas	.04	.02	.00
☐ 496	Kirk McCaskill	.04	.02	.00
☐ 497	Mark McLemore	.04	.02	.00
☐ 498	Darrell Miller	.04	.02	.00
☐ 499	Greg Minton	.04	.02	.00
☐ 500	Donnie Moore	.04	.02	.00
☐ 501	Gus Polidor	.04	.02	.00
☐ 502	Johnny Ray	.04	.02	.00
☐ 503	Mark Ryal	.04	.02	.00
☐ 504	Dick Schofield	.04	.02	.00
☐ 505	Don Sutton	.15	.06	.01
☐ 506	Devon White	.15	.06	.01
☐ 507	Mike Witt	.04	.02	.00
☐ 508	Dave Anderson	.04	.02	.00
☐ 509	Tim Belcher	.20	.08	.02
☐ 510	Ralph Bryant	.04	.02	.00
☐ 511	Tim Crews	.07	.03	.01
☐ 512	Mike Devereaux	.30	.12	.03
☐ 513	Mariano Duncan	.07	.03	.01
☐ 514	Pedro Guerrero	.10	.04	.01
☐ 515	Jeff Hamilton	.07	.03	.01
☐ 516	Mickey Hatcher	.04	.02	.00
☐ 517	Brad Havens	.04	.02	.00
☐ 518	Orel Hershiser	.17	.07	.01
☐ 519	Shawn Hillegas	.10	.04	.01
☐ 520	Ken Howell	.04	.02	.00
☐ 521	Tim Leary	.10	.04	.01
☐ 522	Mike Marshall	.10	.04	.01
☐ 523	Steve Sax	.12	.05	.01
☐ 524	Mike Scioscia	.04	.02	.00
☐ 525	Mike Sharperson	.07	.03	.01
☐ 526	John Shelby	.04	.02	.00
☐ 527	Franklin Stubbs	.04	.02	.00
☐ 528	Fernando Valenzuela	.10	.04	.01
☐ 529	Bob Welch	.10	.04	.01
☐ 530	Matt Young	.04	.02	.00
☐ 531	Jim Acker	.04	.02	.00
☐ 532	Paul Assenmacher	.04	.02	.00
☐ 533	Jeff Blauser	.40	.16	.04
☐ 534	Joe Boever	.10	.04	.01
☐ 535	Martin Clary	.04	.02	.00
☐ 536	Kevin Coffman	.04	.02	.00
☐ 537	Jeff Dedmon	.04	.02	.00
☐ 538	Ron Gant	6.00	2.50	.60
☐ 539	Tom Glavine	3.50	1.50	.35
☐ 540	Ken Griffey	.10	.04	.01
☐ 541	Albert Hall	.04	.02	.00
☐ 542	Glenn Hubbard	.04	.02	.00
☐ 543	Dion James	.04	.02	.00
☐ 544	Dale Murphy	.25	.10	.02
☐ 545	Ken Oberkfell	.04	.02	.00
☐ 546	David Palmer	.04	.02	.00
☐ 547	Gerald Perry	.04	.02	.00
☐ 548	Charlie Puleo	.04	.02	.00
☐ 549	Ted Simmons	.07	.03	.01
☐ 550	Zane Smith	.07	.03	.01
☐ 551	Andres Thomas	.04	.02	.00
☐ 552	Ozzie Virgil	.04	.02	.00
☐ 553	Don Aase	.04	.02	.00
☐ 554	Jeff Ballard	.10	.04	.01
☐ 555	Eric Bell	.04	.02	.00
☐ 556	Mike Boddicker	.04	.02	.00
☐ 557	Ken Dixon	.04	.02	.00
☐ 558	Jim Dwyer	.04	.02	.00
☐ 559	Ken Gerhart	.04	.02	.00
☐ 560	Rene Gonzales	.07	.03	.01
☐ 561	Mike Griffin	.04	.02	.00
☐ 562	John Habyan UER (misspelled Hayban on both sides of card)	.07	.03	.01
☐ 563	Terry Kennedy	.04	.02	.00
☐ 564	Ray Knight	.07	.03	.01
☐ 565	Lee Lacy	.04	.02	.00
☐ 566	Fred Lynn	.10	.04	.01
☐ 567	Eddie Murray	.30	.12	.03
☐ 568	Tom Niedenfuer	.04	.02	.00
☐ 569	Bill Ripken	.20	.08	.02
☐ 570	Cal Ripken	1.00	.40	.10
☐ 571	Dave Schmidt	.04	.02	.00
☐ 572	Larry Sheets	.04	.02	.00
☐ 573	Pete Stanicek	.04	.02	.00
☐ 574	Mark Williamson	.10	.04	.01
☐ 575	Mike Young	.04	.02	.00
☐ 576	Shawn Abner	.07	.03	.01
☐ 577	Greg Booker	.04	.02	.00
☐ 578	Chris Brown	.04	.02	.00
☐ 579	Keith Comstock	.07	.03	.01

☐ 580	Joey Cora	.07	.03	.01
☐ 581	Mark Davis	.07	.03	.01
☐ 582	Tim Flannery (with surfboard)	.04	.02	.00
☐ 583	Goose Gossage	.10	.04	.01
☐ 584	Mark Grant	.04	.02	.00
☐ 585	Tony Gwynn	.45	.18	.04
☐ 586	Andy Hawkins	.04	.02	.00
☐ 587	Stan Jefferson	.07	.03	.01
☐ 588	Jimmy Jones	.07	.03	.01
☐ 589	John Kruk	.07	.03	.01
☐ 590	Shane Mack	.25	.10	.02
☐ 591	Carmelo Martinez	.04	.02	.00
☐ 592	Lance McCullers UER (6'11" tall)	.04	.02	.00
☐ 593	Eric Nolte	.07	.03	.01
☐ 594	Randy Ready	.04	.02	.00
☐ 595	Luis Salazar	.04	.02	.00
☐ 596	Benito Santiago	.20	.08	.02
☐ 597	Eric Show	.04	.02	.00
☐ 598	Garry Templeton	.07	.03	.01
☐ 599	Ed Whitson	.04	.02	.00
☐ 600	Scott Bailes	.04	.02	.00
☐ 601	Chris Bando	.04	.02	.00
☐ 602	Jay Bell	.75	.30	.07
☐ 603	Brett Butler	.12	.05	.01
☐ 604	Tom Candiotti	.07	.03	.01
☐ 605	Joe Carter	.35	.15	.03
☐ 606	Carmen Castillo	.04	.02	.00
☐ 607	Brian Dorsett	.07	.03	.01
☐ 608	John Farrell	.10	.04	.01
☐ 609	Julio Franco	.25	.10	.02
☐ 610	Mel Hall	.07	.03	.01
☐ 611	Tommy Hinzo	.04	.02	.00
☐ 612	Brook Jacoby	.04	.02	.00
☐ 613	Doug Jones	.25	.10	.02
☐ 614	Ken Schrom	.04	.02	.00
☐ 615	Cory Snyder	.10	.04	.01
☐ 616	Sammy Stewart	.04	.02	.00
☐ 617	Greg Swindell	.12	.05	.01
☐ 618	Pat Tabler	.04	.02	.00
☐ 619	Ed VandeBerg	.04	.02	.00
☐ 620	Eddie Williams	.07	.03	.01
☐ 621	Rich Yett	.04	.02	.00
☐ 622	Slugging Sophomores Wally Joyner Cory Snyder	.10	.04	.01
☐ 623	Dominican Dynamite George Bell Pedro Guerrero	.10	.04	.01
☐ 624	Oakland's Power Team Mark McGwire Jose Canseco	.50	.20	.05
☐ 625	Classic Relief Dave Righetti Dan Plesac	.07	.03	.01
☐ 626	All Star Righties Bret Saberhagen Mike Witt Jack Morris	.10	.04	.01
☐ 627	Game Closers John Franco Steve Bedrosian	.07	.03	.01
☐ 628	Masters/Double Play Ozzie Smith Ryne Sandberg	.35	.15	.03
☐ 629	Rookie Record Setter Mark McGwire	.25	.10	.02
☐ 630	Changing the Guard Mike Greenwell Ellis Burks Todd Benzinger	.20	.08	.02
☐ 631	NL Batting Champs Tony Gwynn Tim Raines	.15	.06	.01
☐ 632	Pitching Magic Mike Scott Orel Hershiser	.10	.04	.01
☐ 633	Big Bats at First Pat Tabler Mark McGwire	.12	.05	.01
☐ 634	Hitting King/Thief Tony Gwynn Vince Coleman	.20	.08	.02
☐ 635	Slugging Shortstops Tony Fernandez Cal Ripken Alan Trammell	.30	.12	.03
☐ 636	Tried/True Sluggers Mike Schmidt Gary Carter	.20	.08	.02
☐ 637	Crunch Time Darryl Strawberry Eric Davis	.25	.10	.02

☐ 638	AL All-Stars Matt Nokes Kirby Puckett	.15	.06	.01
☐ 639	NL All-Stars Keith Hernandez Dale Murphy	.10	.04	.01
☐ 640	The O's Brothers Billy Ripken Cal Ripken	.30	.12	.03
☐ 641	Mark Grace and Darrin Jackson	4.50	2.00	.45
☐ 642	Damon Berryhill and Jeff Montgomery	.35	.15	.03
☐ 643	Felix Fermin and Jesse Reid	.07	.03	.01
☐ 644	Greg Myers and Greg Tabor	.15	.06	.01
☐ 645	Joey Meyer and Jim Eppard	.10	.04	.01
☐ 646	Adam Peterson and Randy Velarde	.10	.04	.01
☐ 647	Peter Smith and Chris Gwynn	.25	.10	.02
☐ 648	Tom Newell and Greg Jelks	.07	.03	.01
☐ 649	Mario Diaz and Clay Parker	.12	.05	.01
☐ 650	Jack Savage and Todd Simmons	.07	.03	.01
☐ 651	John Burkett and Kirt Manwaring	.35	.15	.03
☐ 652	Dave Otto and Walt Weiss	.45	.18	.04
☐ 653	Jeff King and Randell Byers	.25	.10	.02
☐ 654	CL: Twins/Cards Tigers/Giants UER (90 Bob Melvin, 91 Eddie Milner)	.08	.01	.00
☐ 655	CL: Blue Jays/Mets Brewers/Expos UER (Mets listed before Blue Jays on card)	.08	.01	.00
☐ 656	CL: Yankees/Reds Royals/A's	.08	.01	.00
☐ 657	CL: Phillies/Pirates Red Sox/Mariners	.08	.01	.00
☐ 658	CL: White Sox/Cubs Astros/Rangers	.08	.01	.00
☐ 659	CL: Angels/Dodgers Braves/Orioles	.08	.01	.00
☐ 660	CL: Padres/Indians Rookies/Specials	.08	.01	.00

1988 Fleer Wax Box Cards

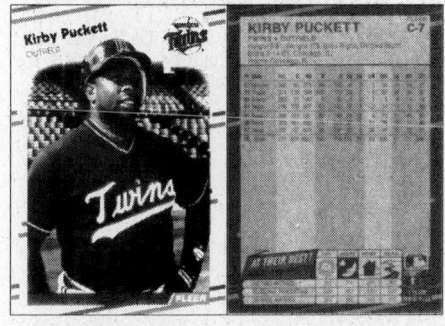

The cards in this 16-card set measure the standard 2 1/2" by 3 1/2". Cards have essentially the same design as the 1988 Fleer regular issue set. The cards were printed on the bottoms of the regular issue wax pack boxes. These 16 cards (C1 to C16) are considered a separate set in their own right and are not typically included in a complete set of the regular issue 1988 Fleer cards. The value of the panel uncut is slightly greater, perhaps by 25 percent greater, than the value of the individual cards cut up carefully.

	MINT	EXC	G-VG
COMPLETE SET (16)	5.00	2.25	.50
COMMON PLAYER (C1-C16)	.10	.04	.01
☐ C1 Cardinals Logo	.10	.04	.01
☐ C2 Dwight Evans	.20	.08	.02
☐ C3 Andres Galarraga	.25	.10	.02
☐ C4 Wally Joyner	.50	.20	.05
☐ C5 Twins Logo	.10	.04	.01
☐ C6 Dale Murphy	.40	.16	.04
☐ C7 Kirby Puckett	.75	.30	.07
☐ C8 Shane Rawley	.10	.04	.01
☐ C9 Giants Logo	.10	.04	.01
☐ C10 Ryne Sandberg	1.00	.40	.10
☐ C11 Mike Schmidt	1.00	.40	.10
☐ C12 Kevin Seitzer	.35	.15	.03
☐ C13 Tigers Logo	.10	.04	.01
☐ C14 Dave Stewart	.30	.12	.03
☐ C15 Tim Wallach	.15	.06	.01
☐ C16 Todd Worrell	.15	.06	.01

1988 Fleer All-Star Inserts

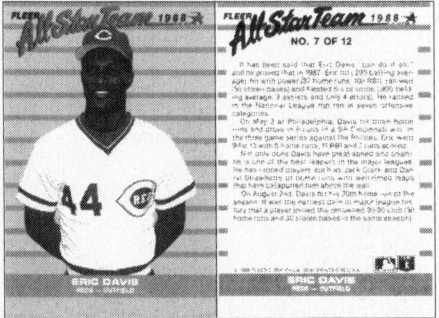

The cards in this 12-card set measure the standard 2 1/2" by 3 1/2". These cards were inserted (randomly) in wax and cello packs of the 1988 Fleer regular issue set. The cards show the player silhouetted against a light green background with dark green stripes. The player's name, team, and position are printed in yellow at the bottom of the obverse. The card backs are done predominantly in green, white, and black. Cards are numbered on the back. These 12 cards are considered a separate set in their own right and are not typically included in a complete set of the regular issue 1988 Fleer cards. The players are the "best" at each position, three pitchers, eight position players, and a designated hitter.

	MINT	EXC	G-VG
COMPLETE SET (12)	12.50	5.50	1.65
COMMON PLAYERS (1-12)	.35	.15	.03
☐ 1 Matt Nokes Catcher	.60	.25	.06
☐ 2 Tom Henke Relief Pitcher	.35	.15	.03
☐ 3 Ted Higuera Left Hand Pitcher	.45	.18	.04
☐ 4 Roger Clemens Right Hand Pitcher	4.00	1.75	.40
☐ 5 George Bell Outfielder	.75	.30	.07
☐ 6 Andre Dawson Outfielder	.90	.40	.09
☐ 7 Eric Davis Outfielder	2.00	.80	.20
☐ 8 Wade Boggs Third Baseman	2.50	1.00	.25
☐ 9 Alan Trammell Shortstop	.75	.30	.07
☐ 10 Juan Samuel Second Baseman	.45	.18	.04
☐ 11 Jack Clark First Baseman	.60	.25	.06
☐ 12 Paul Molitor Designated Hitter	.75	.30	.07

1988 Fleer Headliners

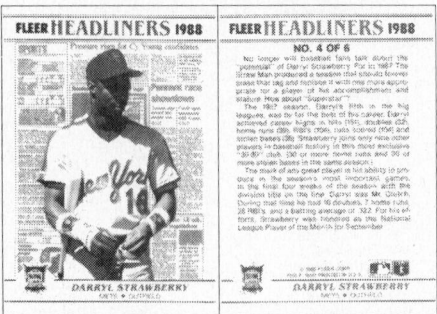

This six-card set was distributed as a special insert in rack packs. The obverse features the player photo superimposed on a gray newsprint background. Cards are 2 1/2" by 3 1/2". The cards are printed in red, black, and white on the back describing why that particular player made headlines the previous season. The cards are numbered on the back.

	MINT	EXC	G-VG
COMPLETE SET (6)	7.00	3.00	.70
COMMON PLAYER (1-6)	.75	.30	.07
☐ 1 Don Mattingly New York Yankees	1.50	.60	.15
☐ 2 Mark McGwire Oakland Athletics	1.50	.60	.15
☐ 3 Jack Morris Detroit Tigers	1.00	.40	.10
☐ 4 Darryl Strawberry New York Mets	1.50	.60	.15
☐ 5 Dwight Gooden New York Mets	1.00	.40	.10
☐ 6 Tim Raines Montreal Expos	.75	.30	.07

1988 Fleer Update

This 132-card set was distributed by Fleer to dealers as a complete set in a custom box. In addition to the complete set of 132 cards, the box also contains 25 Team Logo stickers. The card fronts look very similar to the 1988 Fleer regular issue. The cards are numbered (with a U prefix) alphabetically according to player's last name. Cards measure the standard size, 2 1/2" by 3 1/2". This was the first Fleer Update set to adopt the Fleer "alphabetical within team" numbering system. The key (extended) rookie cards in this set are Roberto Alomar, Craig Biggio, and Chris Sabo. Fleer also produced a "limited" edition version of this set with glossy coating and packaged in a "tin." However, this tin set was apparently not limited enough (estimated between 40,000 and 60,000 1988 Update tin sets produced by Fleer), since the price of the "tin" glossy cards is now only double the price of the regular set.

	MINT	EXC	G-VG
COMPLETE SET (132)	11.00	5.00	1.35
COMMON PLAYER (1-132)	.05	.02	.00

		MINT	EXC	G-VG
☐ U1	Jose Bautista	.10	.04	.01
☐ U2	Joe Orsulak	.10	.04	.01
☐ U3	Doug Sisk	.05	.02	.00
☐ U4	Craig Worthington	.10	.04	.01
☐ U5	Mike Boddicker	.10	.04	.01
☐ U6	Rick Cerone	.05	.02	.00
☐ U7	Larry Parrish	.05	.02	.00
☐ U8	Lee Smith	.12	.05	.01
☐ U9	Mike Smithson	.05	.02	.00
☐ U10	John Trautwein	.05	.02	.00
☐ U11	Sherman Corbett	.05	.02	.00
☐ U12	Chili Davis	.10	.04	.01
☐ U13	Jim Eppard	.05	.02	.00
☐ U14	Bryan Harvey	.60	.25	.06
☐ U15	John Davis	.05	.02	.00
☐ U16	Dave Gallagher	.10	.04	.01
☐ U17	Ricky Horton	.05	.02	.00
☐ U18	Dan Pasqua	.10	.04	.01
☐ U19	Melido Perez	.10	.04	.01
☐ U20	Jose Segura	.10	.04	.01
☐ U21	Andy Allanson	.05	.02	.00
☐ U22	Jon Perlman	.05	.02	.00
☐ U23	Domingo Ramos	.05	.02	.00
☐ U24	Rick Rodriguez	.05	.02	.00
☐ U25	Willie Upshaw	.05	.02	.00
☐ U26	Paul Gibson	.10	.04	.01
☐ U27	Don Heinkel	.05	.02	.00
☐ U28	Ray Knight	.10	.04	.01
☐ U29	Gary Pettis	.05	.02	.00
☐ U30	Luis Salazar	.05	.02	.00
☐ U31	Mike MacFarlane	.15	.06	.01
☐ U32	Jeff Montgomery	.15	.06	.01
☐ U33	Ted Power	.05	.02	.00
☐ U34	Israel Sanchez	.05	.02	.00
☐ U35	Kurt Stillwell	.10	.04	.01
☐ U36	Pat Tabler	.05	.02	.00
☐ U37	Don August	.10	.04	.01
☐ U38	Darryl Hamilton	.25	.10	.02
☐ U39	Jeff Leonard	.10	.04	.01
☐ U40	Joey Meyer	.10	.04	.01
☐ U41	Allan Anderson	.10	.04	.01
☐ U42	Brian Harper	.15	.06	.01
☐ U43	Tom Herr	.10	.04	.01
☐ U44	Charlie Lea	.05	.02	.00
☐ U45	John Moses	.05	.02	.00
	(listed as Hohn on			
	checklist card)			
☐ U46	John Candelaria	.05	.02	.00
☐ U47	Jack Clark	.10	.04	.01
☐ U48	Richard Dotson	.05	.02	.00
☐ U49	Al Leiter	.10	.04	.01
☐ U50	Rafael Santana	.05	.02	.00
☐ U51	Don Slaught	.05	.02	.00
☐ U52	Todd Burns	.10	.04	.01
☐ U53	Dave Henderson	.15	.06	.01
☐ U54	Doug Jennings	.10	.04	.01
☐ U55	Dave Parker	.15	.06	.01
☐ U56	Walt Weiss	.15	.06	.01
☐ U57	Bob Welch	.15	.06	.01
☐ U58	Henry Cotto	.05	.02	.00
☐ U59	Mario Diaz UER	.10	.04	.01
	(listed as Marion			
	on card front)			
☐ U60	Mike Jackson	.15	.06	.01
☐ U61	Bill Swift	.15	.06	.01
☐ U62	Jose Cecena	.10	.04	.01
☐ U63	Ray Hayward	.05	.02	.00
☐ U64	Jim Steels UER	.05	.02	.00
	(listed as Jim Steele			
	on card back)			
☐ U65	Pat Borders	.30	.12	.03
☐ U66	Sil Campusano	.12	.05	.01
☐ U67	Mike Flanagan	.10	.04	.01
☐ U68	Todd Stottlemyre	.75	.30	.07
☐ U69	David Wells	.20	.08	.02
☐ U70	Jose Alvarez	.10	.04	.01
☐ U71	Paul Runge	.05	.02	.00
☐ U72	Cesar Jimenez	.05	.02	.00
	(card was intended			
	for German Jiminez,			
	it's his photo)			
☐ U73	Pete Smith	.10	.04	.01

		MINT	EXC	G-VG
☐ U74	John Smoltz	2.50	1.00	.25
☐ U75	Damon Berryhill	.10	.04	.01
☐ U76	Goose Gossage	.12	.05	.01
☐ U77	Mark Grace	2.25	.90	.22
☐ U78	Darrin Jackson	.15	.06	.01
☐ U79	Vance Law	.05	.02	.00
☐ U80	Jeff Pico	.10	.04	.01
☐ U81	Gary Varsho	.15	.06	.01
☐ U82	Tim Birtsas	.10	.04	.01
☐ U83	Rob Dibble	1.00	.40	.10
☐ U84	Danny Jackson	.10	.04	.01
☐ U85	Paul O'Neill	.12	.05	.01
☐ U86	Jose Rijo	.20	.08	.02
☐ U87	Chris Sabo	2.00	.80	.20
☐ U88	John Fishel	.05	.02	.00
☐ U89	Craig Biggio	1.25	.50	.12
☐ U90	Terry Puhl	.05	.02	.00
☐ U91	Rafael Ramirez	.05	.02	.00
☐ U92	Louie Meadows	.05	.02	.00
☐ U93	Kirk Gibson	.12	.05	.01
☐ U94	Alfredo Griffin	.05	.02	.00
☐ U95	Jay Howell	.10	.04	.01
☐ U96	Jesse Orosco	.05	.02	.00
☐ U97	Alejandro Pena	.12	.05	.01
☐ U98	Tracy Woodson	.10	.04	.01
☐ U99	John Dopson	.10	.04	.01
☐ U100	Brian Holman	.35	.15	.03
☐ U101	Rex Hudler	.15	.06	.01
☐ U102	Jeff Parrett	.10	.04	.01
☐ U103	Nelson Santovenia	.12	.05	.01
☐ U104	Kevin Elster	.10	.04	.01
☐ U105	Jeff Innis	.10	.04	.01
☐ U106	Mackey Sasser	.15	.06	.01
☐ U107	Phil Bradley	.10	.04	.01
☐ U108	Danny Clay	.05	.02	.00
☐ U109	Greg Harris	.05	.02	.00
☐ U110	Ricky Jordan	.30	.12	.03
☐ U111	David Palmer	.05	.02	.00
☐ U112	Jim Gott	.05	.02	.00
☐ U113	Tommy Gregg UER	.10	.04	.01
	(photo actually			
	Randy Milligan)			
☐ U114	Barry Jones	.10	.04	.01
☐ U115	Randy Milligan	.35	.15	.03
☐ U116	Luis Alicea	.10	.04	.01
☐ U117	Tom Brunansky	.10	.04	.01
☐ U118	John Costello	.10	.04	.01
☐ U119	Jose DeLeon	.05	.02	.00
☐ U120	Bob Horner	.10	.04	.01
☐ U121	Scott Terry	.10	.04	.01
☐ U122	Roberto Alomar	3.50	1.50	.35
☐ U123	Dave Leiper	.05	.02	.00
☐ U124	Keith Moreland	.05	.02	.00
☐ U125	Mark Parent	.10	.04	.01
☐ U126	Dennis Rasmussen	.05	.02	.00
☐ U127	Randy Bockus	.05	.02	.00
☐ U128	Brett Butler	.12	.05	.01
☐ U129	Donell Nixon	.05	.02	.00
☐ U130	Earnest Riles	.05	.02	.00
☐ U131	Roger Samuels	.05	.02	.00
☐ U132	Checklist U1-U132	.05	.01	.00

1988 Fleer Award Winners

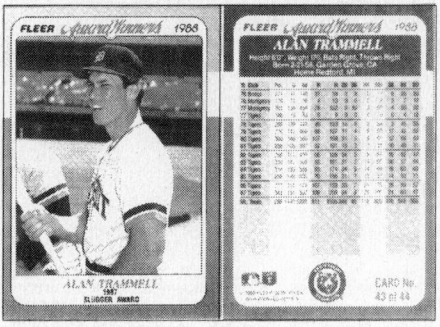

This small set of 44 cards was produced for 7-Eleven stores by Fleer. The cards measure the standard 2 1/2" by 3 1/2" and feature full color fronts and red, white, and blue backs. The card fronts are distinguished by the red, white, and blue frame around the player's full-color photo. The box for the cards describes the set as the "1988 Limited Edition Baseball Award Winners." The checklist for the set is given on the back of the set box.

		MINT	EXC	G-VG
	COMPLETE SET (44)	4.00	1.75	.40
	COMMON PLAYER (1-44)	.10	.04	.01
☐ 1	Steve Bedrosian	.10	.04	.01
☐ 2	George Bell	.20	.08	.02
☐ 3	Wade Boggs	.60	.25	.06
☐ 4	Jose Canseco	.90	.40	.09
☐ 5	Will Clark	.90	.40	.09
☐ 6	Roger Clemens	.75	.30	.07
☐ 7	Kal Daniels	.20	.08	.02
☐ 8	Eric Davis	.45	.18	.04
☐ 9	Andre Dawson	.25	.10	.02
☐ 10	Mike Dunne	.10	.04	.01
☐ 11	Dwight Evans	.15	.06	.01
☐ 12	Carlton Fisk	.30	.12	.03
☐ 13	Julio Franco	.20	.08	.02
☐ 14	Dwight Gooden	.30	.12	.03
☐ 15	Pedro Guerrero	.15	.06	.01
☐ 16	Tony Gwynn	.40	.16	.04
☐ 17	Orel Hershiser	.25	.10	.02
☐ 18	Tom Henke	.10	.04	.01
☐ 19	Ted Higuera	.15	.06	.01
☐ 20	Charlie Hough	.10	.04	.01
☐ 21	Wally Joyner	.25	.10	.02
☐ 22	Jimmy Key	.10	.04	.01
☐ 23	Don Mattingly	.75	.30	.07
☐ 24	Mark McGwire	.50	.20	.05
☐ 25	Paul Molitor	.15	.06	.01
☐ 26	Jack Morris	.20	.08	.02
☐ 27	Dale Murphy	.30	.12	.03
☐ 28	Terry Pendleton	.20	.08	.02
☐ 29	Kirby Puckett	.45	.18	.04
☐ 30	Tim Raines	.20	.08	.02
☐ 31	Jeff Reardon	.20	.08	.02
☐ 32	Harold Reynolds	.10	.04	.01
☐ 33	Dave Righetti	.15	.06	.01
☐ 34	Benito Santiago	.25	.10	.02
☐ 35	Mike Schmidt	.65	.25	.06
☐ 36	Mike Scott	.15	.06	.01
☐ 37	Kevin Seitzer	.15	.06	.01
☐ 38	Larry Sheets	.10	.04	.01
☐ 39	Ozzie Smith	.25	.10	.02
☐ 40	Darryl Strawberry	.60	.25	.06
☐ 41	Rick Sutcliffe	.10	.04	.01
☐ 42	Danny Tartabull	.30	.12	.03
☐ 43	Alan Trammell	.20	.08	.02
☐ 44	Tim Wallach	.15	.06	.01

1988 Fleer Baseball All-Stars

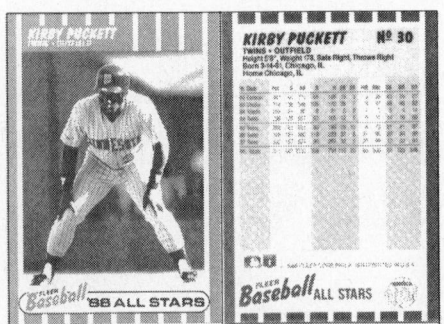

This small boxed set of 44 cards was produced exclusively for Ben Franklin Stores. The cards measure the standard 2 1/2" by 3 1/2" and feature full color fronts and white and blue backs. The card fronts are distinguished by the yellow and blue striped background behind the player's full-color photo. The box for the cards describes the set as the "1988 Fleer Baseball All-

Stars." The checklist for the set is given on the back of the set box.

		MINT	EXC	G-VG
	COMPLETE SET (44)	5.00	2.25	.50
	COMMON PLAYER (1-44)	.10	.04	.01
☐ 1	George Bell	.20	.08	.02
☐ 2	Wade Boggs	.65	.25	.06
☐ 3	Bobby Bonilla	.50	.20	.05
☐ 4	George Brett	.45	.18	.04
☐ 5	Jose Canseco	.90	.40	.09
☐ 6	Jack Clark	.20	.08	.02
☐ 7	Will Clark	.90	.40	.09
☐ 8	Roger Clemens	.75	.30	.07
☐ 9	Eric Davis	.50	.20	.05
☐ 10	Andre Dawson	.30	.12	.03
☐ 11	Julio Franco	.25	.10	.02
☐ 12	Dwight Gooden	.40	.16	.04
☐ 13	Tony Gwynn	.50	.20	.05
☐ 14	Orel Hershiser	.30	.12	.03
☐ 15	Teddy Higuera	.15	.06	.01
☐ 16	Charlie Hough	.10	.04	.01
☐ 17	Kent Hrbek	.20	.08	.02
☐ 18	Bruce Hurst	.15	.06	.01
☐ 19	Wally Joyner	.30	.12	.03
☐ 20	Mark Langston	.20	.08	.02
☐ 21	Dave LaPoint	.10	.04	.01
☐ 22	Candy Maldonado	.10	.04	.01
☐ 23	Don Mattingly	.75	.30	.07
☐ 24	Roger McDowell	.10	.04	.01
☐ 25	Mark McGwire	.60	.25	.06
☐ 26	Jack Morris	.20	.08	.02
☐ 27	Dale Murphy	.35	.15	.03
☐ 28	Eddie Murray	.40	.16	.04
☐ 29	Matt Nokes	.20	.08	.02
☐ 30	Kirby Puckett	.45	.18	.04
☐ 31	Tim Raines	.20	.08	.02
☐ 32	Willie Randolph	.15	.06	.01
☐ 33	Jeff Reardon	.20	.08	.02
☐ 34	Nolan Ryan	1.25	.50	.12
☐ 35	Juan Samuel	.15	.06	.01
☐ 36	Mike Schmidt	.75	.30	.07
☐ 37	Mike Scott	.15	.06	.01
☐ 38	Kevin Seitzer	.15	.06	.01
☐ 39	Ozzie Smith	.25	.10	.02
☐ 40	Darryl Strawberry	.60	.25	.06
☐ 41	Rick Sutcliffe	.15	.06	.01
☐ 42	Alan Trammell	.20	.08	.02
☐ 43	Tim Wallach	.15	.06	.01
☐ 44	Dave Winfield	.25	.10	.02

1988 Fleer Baseball MVP's

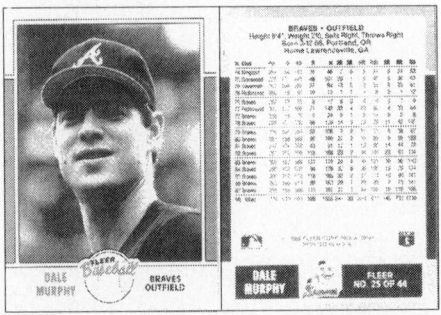

This small 44-card boxed set was produced by Fleer for distribution by the Toys'r'Us stores. The cards measure the standard 2 1/2" by 3 1/2" and feature full color fronts. The set is titled "Baseball MVP." Each individual boxed set includes the 44 cards and 6 logo stickers. The checklist for the set is found on the back panel of the box. The card fronts have a vanilla-yellow and blue border. The box refers to Toys'r'Us but there is no mention of Toys'r'Us anywhere on the cards themselves.

	MINT	EXC	G-VG
COMPLETE SET (44)	5.00	2.25	.50
COMMON PLAYER (1-44)	.10	.04	.01

		MINT	EXC	G-VG
☐ 1	George Bell	.20	.08	.02
☐ 2	Wade Boggs	.65	.25	.06
☐ 3	Jose Canseco	.90	.40	.09
☐ 4	Ivan Calderon	.15	.06	.01
☐ 5	Will Clark	.90	.40	.09
☐ 6	Roger Clemens	.75	.30	.07
☐ 7	Vince Coleman	.25	.10	.02
☐ 8	Eric Davis	.45	.18	.04
☐ 9	Andre Dawson	.30	.12	.03
☐ 10	Dave Dravecky	.15	.06	.01
☐ 11	Mike Dunne	.10	.04	.01
☐ 12	Dwight Evans	.15	.06	.01
☐ 13	Sid Fernandez	.15	.06	.01
☐ 14	Tony Fernandez	.15	.06	.01
☐ 15	Julio Franco	.20	.08	.02
☐ 16	Dwight Gooden	.35	.15	.03
☐ 17	Tony Gwynn	.45	.18	.04
☐ 18	Ted Higuera	.15	.06	.01
☐ 19	Charlie Hough	.10	.04	.01
☐ 20	Wally Joyner	.25	.10	.02
☐ 21	Mark Langston	.20	.08	.02
☐ 22	Don Mattingly	.75	.30	.07
☐ 23	Mark McGwire	.60	.25	.06
☐ 24	Jack Morris	.20	.08	.02
☐ 25	Dale Murphy	.35	.15	.03
☐ 26	Kirby Puckett	.50	.20	.05
☐ 27	Tim Raines	.20	.08	.02
☐ 28	Willie Randolph	.15	.06	.01
☐ 29	Ryne Sandberg	.75	.30	.07
☐ 30	Benito Santiago	.25	.10	.02
☐ 31	Mike Schmidt	.75	.30	.07
☐ 32	Mike Scott	.15	.06	.01
☐ 33	Kevin Seitzer	.15	.06	.01
☐ 34	Larry Sheets	.10	.04	.01
☐ 35	Ozzie Smith	.25	.10	.02
☐ 36	Dave Stewart	.20	.08	.02
☐ 37	Darryl Strawberry	.65	.25	.06
☐ 38	Rick Sutcliffe	.15	.06	.01
☐ 39	Alan Trammell	.20	.08	.02
☐ 40	Fernando Valenzuela	.20	.08	.02
☐ 41	Frank Viola	.20	.08	.02
☐ 42	Tim Wallach	.15	.06	.01
☐ 43	Dave Winfield	.25	.10	.02
☐ 44	Robin Yount	.50	.20	.05

☐ 3	George Bell	.20	.08	.02
☐ 4	Wade Boggs	.65	.25	.06
☐ 5	Mickey Brantley	.10	.04	.01
☐ 6	Sid Bream	.10	.04	.01
☐ 7	Jose Canseco	.90	.40	.09
☐ 8	Jack Clark	.20	.08	.02
☐ 9	Will Clark	.90	.40	.09
☐ 10	Roger Clemens	.75	.30	.07
☐ 11	Vince Coleman	.25	.10	.02
☐ 12	Eric Davis	.45	.18	.04
☐ 13	Andre Dawson	.30	.12	.03
☐ 14	Julio Franco	.20	.08	.02
☐ 15	Dwight Gooden	.45	.18	.04
☐ 16	Mike Greenwell	.50	.20	.05
☐ 17	Tony Gwynn	.50	.20	.05
☐ 18	Von Hayes	.15	.06	.01
☐ 19	Tom Henke	.10	.04	.01
☐ 20	Orel Hershiser	.30	.12	.03
☐ 21	Teddy Higuera	.15	.06	.01
☐ 22	Brook Jacoby	.15	.06	.01
☐ 23	Wally Joyner	.25	.10	.02
☐ 24	Jimmy Key	.15	.06	.01
☐ 25	Don Mattingly	.75	.30	.07
☐ 26	Mark McGwire	.60	.25	.06
☐ 27	Jack Morris	.20	.08	.02
☐ 28	Dale Murphy	.30	.12	.03
☐ 29	Matt Nokes	.20	.08	.02
☐ 30	Kirby Puckett	.45	.18	.04
☐ 31	Tim Raines	.20	.08	.02
☐ 32	Ryne Sandberg	.75	.30	.07
☐ 33	Benito Santiago	.25	.10	.02
☐ 34	Mike Schmidt	.75	.30	.07
☐ 35	Mike Scott	.15	.06	.01
☐ 36	Kevin Seitzer	.15	.06	.01
☐ 37	Larry Sheets	.10	.04	.01
☐ 38	Ruben Sierra	.75	.30	.07
☐ 39	Darryl Strawberry	.75	.30	.07
☐ 40	Rick Sutcliffe	.15	.06	.01
☐ 41	Danny Tartabull	.30	.12	.03
☐ 42	Alan Trammell	.20	.08	.02
☐ 43	Fernando Valenzuela	.15	.06	.01
☐ 44	Devon White	.20	.08	.02

1988 Fleer Hottest Stars

1988 Fleer Exciting Stars

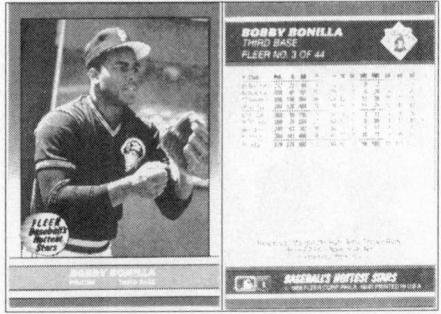

This small boxed set of 44 cards was produced exclusively for Cumberland Farm Stores. The cards measure the standard 2 1/2" by 3 1/2" and feature full color fronts and red, white, and blue backs. The card fronts are distinguished by the framing of the player's full-color photo with a blue border with a red and white bar stripe across the middle. The box for the cards describes the set as the "1988 Fleer Baseball's Exciting Stars." The checklist for the set is given on the back of the set box.

	MINT	EXC	G-VG
COMPLETE SET (44)	5.00	2.25	.50
COMMON PLAYER (1-44)	.10	.04	.01
☐ 1 Harold Baines	.15	.06	.01
☐ 2 Kevin Bass	.10	.04	.01

This 44-card boxed set was produced by Fleer for exclusive distribution by Revco Discount Drug stores all over the country. The cards measure the standard 2 1/2" by 3 1/2" and feature full color fronts and red, white, and blue backs. The card fronts are easily distinguished by the flaming baseball in the lower right corner which says "Fleer Baseball's Hottest Stars." The player's picture is framed in red fading from orange down to yellow. The box for the cards proclaims "1988 Limited Edition Baseball's Hottest Stars" and is styled in blue, red, and yellow. The checklist for the set is given on the back of the set box. The box refers to Revco but there is no mention of Revco anywhere on the cards themselves.

	MINT	EXC	G-VG
COMPLETE SET (44)	5.00	2.25	.50
COMMON PLAYER (1-44)	.10	.04	.01
☐ 1 George Bell	.20	.08	.02
☐ 2 Wade Boggs	.65	.25	.06

		MINT	EXC	G-VG
☐ 3	Bobby Bonilla	.50	.20	.05
☐ 4	George Brett	.45	.18	.04
☐ 5	Jose Canseco	.90	.40	.09
☐ 6	Will Clark	.90	.40	.09
☐ 7	Roger Clemens	.75	.30	.07
☐ 8	Eric Davis	.45	.18	.04
☐ 9	Andre Dawson	.30	.12	.03
☐ 10	Tony Fernandez	.15	.06	.01
☐ 11	Julio Franco	.20	.08	.02
☐ 12	Gary Gaetti	.15	.06	.01
☐ 13	Dwight Gooden	.35	.15	.03
☐ 14	Mike Greenwell	.50	.20	.05
☐ 15	Tony Gwynn	.50	.20	.05
☐ 16	Rickey Henderson	.75	.30	.07
☐ 17	Keith Hernandez	.20	.08	.02
☐ 18	Tom Herr	.10	.04	.01
☐ 19	Orel Hershiser	.30	.12	.03
☐ 20	Ted Higuera	.15	.06	.01
☐ 21	Wally Joyner	.30	.12	.03
☐ 22	Jimmy Key	.10	.04	.01
☐ 23	Mark Langston	.20	.08	.02
☐ 24	Don Mattingly	.75	.30	.07
☐ 25	Jack McDowell	.35	.15	.03
☐ 26	Mark McGwire	.60	.25	.06
☐ 27	Kevin Mitchell	.45	.18	.04
☐ 28	Jack Morris	.20	.08	.02
☐ 29	Dale Murphy	.35	.15	.03
☐ 30	Kirby Puckett	.45	.18	.04
☐ 31	Tim Raines	.20	.08	.02
☐ 32	Shane Rawley	.10	.04	.01
☐ 33	Benito Santiago	.25	.10	.02
☐ 34	Mike Schmidt	.75	.30	.07
☐ 35	Mike Scott	.15	.06	.01
☐ 36	Kevin Seitzer	.15	.06	.01
☐ 37	Larry Sheets	.10	.04	.01
☐ 38	Ruben Sierra	.60	.25	.06
☐ 39	Dave Smith	.10	.04	.01
☐ 40	Ozzie Smith	.30	.12	.03
☐ 41	Darryl Strawberry	.60	.25	.06
☐ 42	Rick Sutcliffe	.15	.06	.01
☐ 43	Pat Tabler	.10	.04	.01
☐ 44	Alan Trammell	.20	.08	.02

		MINT	EXC	G-VG
☐ 7	Vince Coleman	.30	.12	.03
☐ 8	Eric Davis	.45	.18	.04
☐ 9	Andre Dawson	.30	.12	.03
☐ 10	Bill Doran	.10	.04	.01
☐ 11	Dwight Evans	.15	.06	.01
☐ 12	Julio Franco	.20	.08	.02
☐ 13	Gary Gaetti	.15	.06	.01
☐ 14	Andres Galarraga	.20	.08	.02
☐ 15	Dwight Gooden	.40	.16	.04
☐ 16	Tony Gwynn	.45	.18	.04
☐ 17	Tom Henke	.10	.04	.01
☐ 18	Keith Hernandez	.20	.08	.02
☐ 19	Orel Hershiser	.30	.12	.03
☐ 20	Ted Higuera	.15	.06	.01
☐ 21	Kent Hrbek	.20	.08	.02
☐ 22	Wally Joyner	.25	.10	.02
☐ 23	Jimmy Key	.10	.04	.01
☐ 24	Mark Langston	.20	.08	.02
☐ 25	Don Mattingly	.75	.30	.07
☐ 26	Mark McGwire	.60	.25	.06
☐ 27	Paul Molitor	.20	.08	.02
☐ 28	Jack Morris	.20	.08	.02
☐ 29	Dale Murphy	.35	.15	.03
☐ 30	Kirby Puckett	.45	.18	.04
☐ 31	Tim Raines	.20	.08	.02
☐ 32	Rick Reuschel	.15	.06	.01
☐ 33	Bret Saberhagen	.30	.12	.03
☐ 34	Benito Santiago	.25	.10	.02
☐ 35	Mike Schmidt	.75	.30	.07
☐ 36	Mike Scott	.15	.06	.01
☐ 37	Kevin Seitzer	.15	.06	.01
☐ 38	Larry Sheets	.10	.04	.01
☐ 39	Ruben Sierra	.60	.25	.06
☐ 40	Darryl Strawberry	.60	.25	.06
☐ 41	Rick Sutcliffe	.15	.06	.01
☐ 42	Alan Trammell	.20	.08	.02
☐ 43	Andy Van Slyke	.15	.06	.01
☐ 44	Todd Worrell	.15	.06	.01

1988 Fleer League Leaders

This small boxed set of 44 cards was produced exclusively for Walgreen Drug Stores. The cards measure the standard 2 1/2" by 3 1/2" and feature full color fronts and pink, white, and blue backs. The card fronts are distinguished by the blue solid and striped background behind the player's full-color photo. The box for the cards describes the set as the "1988 Fleer Baseball's League Leaders." The checklist for the set is given on the back of the set box.

		MINT	EXC	G-VG
	COMPLETE SET (44)	5.00	2.25	.50
	COMMON PLAYER (1-44)	.10	.04	.01
☐ 1	George Bell	.20	.08	.02
☐ 2	Wade Boggs	.65	.25	.06
☐ 3	Ivan Calderon	.15	.06	.01
☐ 4	Jose Canseco	.90	.40	.09
☐ 5	Will Clark	.90	.40	.09
☐ 6	Roger Clemens	.75	.30	.07

1988 Fleer Mini

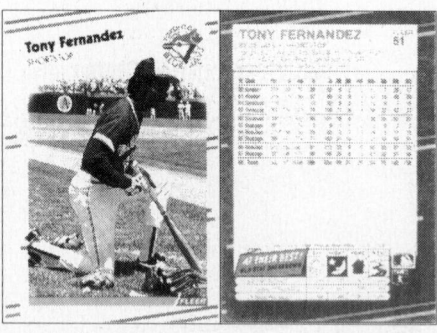

The 1988 Fleer "Classic Miniatures" set consists of 120 small cards with all new pictures of the players as compared to the 1988 Fleer regular issue. The cards are only 1 13/16" by 2 9/16", making them one of the smallest cards available. Card backs provide career year-by-year statistics. The complete set was distributed in a green, red, white, and silver box along with 18 logo stickers. The card numbering is by team order.

		MINT	EXC	G-VG
	COMPLETE SET (120)	11.00	5.00	1.35
	COMMON PLAYER (1-120)	.05	.02	.00
☐ 1	Eddie Murray	.30	.12	.03
☐ 2	Dave Schmidt	.05	.02	.00
☐ 3	Larry Sheets	.05	.02	.00
☐ 4	Wade Boggs	.75	.30	.07
☐ 5	Roger Clemens	.90	.40	.09
☐ 6	Dwight Evans	.10	.04	.01
☐ 7	Mike Greenwell	.45	.18	.04
☐ 8	Sam Horn	.10	.04	.01
☐ 9	Lee Smith	.10	.04	.01
☐ 10	Brian Downing	.05	.02	.00
☐ 11	Wally Joyner	.25	.10	.02
☐ 12	Devon White	.15	.06	.01

		MINT	EXC	G-VG
☐ 13	Mike Witt	.05	.02	.00
☐ 14	Ivan Calderon	.10	.04	.01
☐ 15	Ozzie Guillen	.15	.06	.01
☐ 16	Jack McDowell	.25	.10	.02
☐ 17	Kenny Williams	.05	.02	.00
☐ 18	Joe Carter	.20	.08	.02
☐ 19	Julio Franco	.15	.06	.01
☐ 20	Pat Tabler	.05	.02	.00
☐ 21	Doyle Alexander	.05	.02	.00
☐ 22	Jack Morris	.15	.06	.01
☐ 23	Matt Nokes	.15	.06	.01
☐ 24	Walt Terrell	.05	.02	.00
☐ 25	Alan Trammell	.20	.08	.02
☐ 26	Bret Saberhagen	.30	.12	.03
☐ 27	Kevin Seitzer	.15	.06	.01
☐ 28	Danny Tartabull	.30	.12	.03
☐ 29	Gary Thurman	.05	.02	.00
☐ 30	Ted Higuera	.10	.04	.01
☐ 31	Paul Molitor	.15	.06	.01
☐ 32	Dan Plesac	.05	.02	.00
☐ 33	Robin Yount	.45	.18	.04
☐ 34	Gary Gaetti	.10	.04	.01
☐ 35	Kent Hrbek	.15	.06	.01
☐ 36	Kirby Puckett	.45	.18	.04
☐ 37	Jeff Reardon	.15	.06	.01
☐ 38	Frank Viola	.15	.06	.01
☐ 39	Jack Clark	.15	.06	.01
☐ 40	Rickey Henderson	.75	.30	.07
☐ 41	Don Mattingly	.75	.30	.07
☐ 42	Willie Randolph	.10	.04	.01
☐ 43	Dave Righetti	.10	.04	.01
☐ 44	Dave Winfield	.30	.12	.03
☐ 45	Jose Canseco	.90	.40	.09
☐ 46	Mark McGwire	.60	.25	.06
☐ 47	Dave Parker	.20	.08	.02
☐ 48	Dave Stewart	.15	.06	.01
☐ 49	Walt Weiss	.30	.12	.03
☐ 50	Bob Welch	.10	.04	.01
☐ 51	Mickey Brantley	.05	.02	.00
☐ 52	Mark Langston	.15	.06	.01
☐ 53	Harold Reynolds	.05	.02	.00
☐ 54	Scott Fletcher	.05	.02	.00
☐ 55	Charlie Hough	.05	.02	.00
☐ 56	Pete Incaviglia	.15	.06	.01
☐ 57	Larry Parrish	.05	.02	.00
☐ 58	Ruben Sierra	.50	.20	.05
☐ 59	George Bell	.20	.08	.02
☐ 60	Mark Eichhorn	.05	.02	.00
☐ 61	Tony Fernandez	.10	.04	.01
☐ 62	Tom Henke	.05	.02	.00
☐ 63	Jimmy Key	.10	.04	.01
☐ 64	Dion James	.05	.02	.00
☐ 65	Dale Murphy	.30	.12	.03
☐ 66	Zane Smith	.10	.04	.01
☐ 67	Andre Dawson	.25	.10	.02
☐ 68	Mark Grace	1.00	.40	.10
☐ 69	Jerry Mumphrey	.05	.02	.00
☐ 70	Ryne Sandberg	.75	.30	.07
☐ 71	Rick Sutcliffe	.10	.04	.01
☐ 72	Kal Daniels	.15	.06	.01
☐ 73	Eric Davis	.50	.20	.05
☐ 74	John Franco	.05	.02	.00
☐ 75	Ron Robinson	.05	.02	.00
☐ 76	Jeff Treadway	.10	.04	.01
☐ 77	Kevin Bass	.05	.02	.00
☐ 78	Glenn Davis	.20	.08	.02
☐ 79	Nolan Ryan	1.25	.50	.12
☐ 80	Mike Scott	.10	.04	.01
☐ 81	Dave Smith	.05	.02	.00
☐ 82	Kirk Gibson	.20	.08	.02
☐ 83	Pedro Guerrero	.15	.06	.01
☐ 84	Orel Hershiser	.30	.12	.03
☐ 85	Steve Sax	.15	.06	.01
☐ 86	Fernando Valenzuela	.15	.06	.01
☐ 87	Tim Burke	.05	.02	.00
☐ 88	Andres Galarraga	.15	.06	.01
☐ 89	Neal Heaton	.05	.02	.00
☐ 90	Tim Raines	.20	.08	.02
☐ 91	Tim Wallach	.10	.04	.01
☐ 92	Dwight Gooden	.35	.15	.03
☐ 93	Keith Hernandez	.15	.06	.01
☐ 94	Gregg Jefferies	1.00	.40	.10
☐ 95	Howard Johnson	.20	.08	.02
☐ 96	Roger McDowell	.05	.02	.00
☐ 97	Darryl Strawberry	.50	.20	.05
☐ 98	Steve Bedrosian	.05	.02	.00
☐ 99	Von Hayes	.10	.04	.01
☐ 100	Shane Rawley	.05	.02	.00
☐ 101	Juan Samuel	.10	.04	.01
☐ 102	Mike Schmidt	.75	.30	.07
☐ 103	Bobby Bonilla	.45	.18	.04
☐ 104	Mike Dunne	.05	.02	.00
☐ 105	Andy Van Slyke	.15	.06	.01
☐ 106	Vince Coleman	.20	.08	.02
☐ 107	Bob Horner	.10	.04	.01
☐ 108	Willie McGee	.15	.06	.01
☐ 109	Ozzie Smith	.20	.08	.02
☐ 110	John Tudor	.10	.04	.01
☐ 111	Todd Worrell	.15	.06	.01
☐ 112	Tony Gwynn	.40	.16	.04
☐ 113	John Kruk	.10	.04	.01
☐ 114	Lance McCullers	.05	.02	.00
☐ 115	Benito Santiago	.25	.10	.02
☐ 116	Will Clark	.90	.40	.09
☐ 117	Jeff Leonard	.05	.02	.00
☐ 118	Candy Maldonado	.05	.02	.00
☐ 119	Kirt Manwaring	.05	.02	.00
☐ 120	Don Robinson	.05	.02	.00

1988 Fleer Record Setters

This small boxed set of 44 cards was produced exclusively for Eckerd's Drug Stores. The cards measure the standard 2 1/2" by 3 1/2" and feature full color fronts and red, white, and blue backs. The card fronts are distinguished by the red and blue frame around the player's full-color photo. The box for the cards describes the set as the "1988 Baseball Record Setters." The checklist for the set is given on the back of the set box.

		MINT	EXC	G-VG
COMPLETE SET (44)		5.00	2.25	.50
COMMON PLAYER (1-44)		.10	.04	.01
☐ 1	Jesse Barfield	.15	.06	.01
☐ 2	George Bell	.20	.08	.02
☐ 3	Wade Boggs	.60	.25	.06
☐ 4	Jose Canseco	.90	.40	.09
☐ 5	Jack Clark	.20	.08	.02
☐ 6	Will Clark	.90	.40	.09
☐ 7	Roger Clemens	.75	.30	.07
☐ 8	Alvin Davis	.15	.06	.01
☐ 9	Eric Davis	.45	.18	.04
☐ 10	Andre Dawson	.30	.12	.03
☐ 11	Mike Dunne	.10	.04	.01
☐ 12	John Franco	.10	.04	.01
☐ 13	Julio Franco	.20	.08	.02
☐ 14	Dwight Gooden	.40	.16	.04
☐ 15	Mark Gubicza	.15	.06	.01
	(listed as Gubiczo on box checklist)			
☐ 16	Ozzie Guillen	.15	.06	.01
☐ 17	Tony Gwynn	.45	.18	.04
☐ 18	Orel Hershiser	.30	.12	.03
☐ 19	Teddy Higuera	.15	.06	.01
☐ 20	Howard Johnson UER	.20	.08	.02
	(missing '87 stats on card back)			
☐ 21	Wally Joyner	.25	.10	.02
☐ 22	Jimmy Key	.15	.06	.01
☐ 23	Jeff Leonard	.10	.04	.01
☐ 24	Don Mattingly	.75	.30	.07
☐ 25	Mark McGwire	.60	.25	.06
☐ 26	Jack Morris	.20	.08	.02
☐ 27	Dale Murphy	.35	.15	.03
☐ 28	Larry Parrish	.10	.04	.01
☐ 29	Kirby Puckett	.50	.20	.05
☐ 30	Tim Raines	.20	.08	.02
☐ 31	Harold Reynolds	.10	.04	.01
☐ 32	Dave Righetti	.15	.06	.01
☐ 33	Cal Ripken	.75	.30	.07

			MINT	EXC	G-VG
☐ 34	Benito Santiago		.25	.10	.02
☐ 35	Mike Schmidt		.75	.30	.07
☐ 36	Mike Scott		.15	.06	.01
☐ 37	Kevin Seitzer		.15	.06	.01
☐ 38	Ozzie Smith		.25	.10	.02
☐ 39	Darryl Strawberry		.60	.25	.06
☐ 40	Rick Sutcliffe		.15	.06	.01
☐ 41	Alan Trammell		.20	.08	.02
☐ 42	Frank Viola		.20	.08	.02
☐ 43	Mitch Williams		.15	.06	.01
☐ 44	Todd Worrell		.15	.06	.01

	(misspelled Ripkin on card front)				
☐ 35	Chris Sabo		.60	.25	.06
☐ 36	Mike Schmidt		.75	.30	.07
☐ 37	Mike Scott		.15	.06	.01
☐ 38	Kevin Seitzer		.15	.06	.01
☐ 39	Dave Stewart		.20	.08	.02
☐ 40	Darryl Strawberry		.60	.25	.06
☐ 41	Greg Swindell		.15	.06	.01
☐ 42	Frank Tanana		.10	.04	.01
☐ 43	Dave Winfield		.25	.10	.02
☐ 44	Todd Worrell		.15	.06	.01

1988 Fleer Sluggers/Pitchers

Fleer produced this 44-card boxed set although it was primarily distributed by McCrory, McLellan, J.J Newberry, H.L.Green, T.G.Y., and other similar stores. The set is subtitled "Baseball's Best". Cards are standard-size, 2 1/2" by 3 1/2", and were packaged in a green custom box along with six logo stickers. The set checklist is given on the back of the box. The bottoms of the boxes which held the individual set boxes also contained a panel of six cards; these box bottom cards were numbered C1 through C6.

		MINT	EXC	G-VG
COMPLETE SET (44)		5.00	2.25	.50
COMMON PLAYER (1-44)		.10	.04	.01

			MINT	EXC	G-VG
☐ 1	George Bell		.20	.08	.02
☐ 2	Wade Boggs		.60	.25	.06
☐ 3	Bobby Bonilla		.45	.18	.04
☐ 4	Tom Brunansky		.15	.06	.01
☐ 5	Ellis Burks		.75	.30	.07
☐ 6	Jose Canseco		.90	.40	.09
☐ 7	Joe Carter		.25	.10	.02
☐ 8	Will Clark		.90	.40	.09
☐ 9	Roger Clemens		.75	.30	.07
☐ 10	Eric Davis		.45	.18	.04
☐ 11	Glenn Davis		.20	.08	.02
☐ 12	Andre Dawson		.30	.12	.03
☐ 13	Dennis Eckersley		.25	.10	.02
☐ 14	Andres Galarraga		.20	.08	.02
☐ 15	Dwight Gooden		.40	.16	.04
☐ 16	Pedro Guerrero		.20	.08	.02
☐ 17	Tony Gwynn		.45	.18	.04
☐ 18	Orel Hershiser		.30	.12	.03
☐ 19	Ted Higuera		.15	.06	.01
☐ 20	Pete Incaviglia		.15	.06	.01
☐ 21	Danny Jackson		.10	.04	.01
☐ 22	Doug Jennings		.15	.06	.01
☐ 23	Mark Langston		.20	.08	.02
☐ 24	Dave LaPoint		.10	.04	.01
☐ 25	Mike LaValliere		.10	.04	.01
☐ 26	Don Mattingly		.75	.30	.07
☐ 27	Mark McGwire		.60	.25	.06
☐ 28	Dale Murphy		.35	.15	.03
☐ 29	Ken Phelps		.10	.04	.01
☐ 30	Kirby Puckett		.45	.18	.04
☐ 31	Johnny Ray		.10	.04	.01
☐ 32	Jeff Reardon		.15	.06	.01
☐ 33	Dave Righetti		.15	.06	.01
☐ 34	Cal Ripken UER		.75	.30	.07

1988 Fleer Slug/Pitch Box Cards

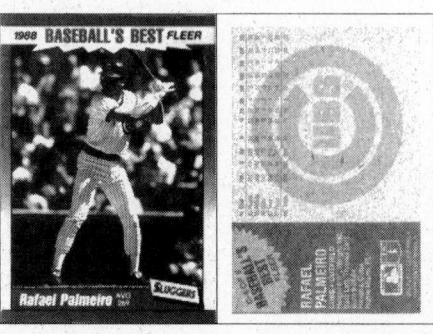

The cards in this six-card set each measure the standard 2 1/2" by 3 1/2". Cards have essentially the same design as the 1988 Fleer Sluggers vs. Pitchers set of Baseball's Best. The cards were printed on the bottom of the counter display box which held 24 small boxed sets; hence theoretically these box cards are 1/24 as plentiful as the regular boxed set cards. These six cards, numbered C1 to C6 are considered a separate set in their own right and are not typically included in a complete set of the 1988 Fleer Sluggers vs. Pitchers set of 44. The value of the panels uncut is slightly greater, perhaps by 25 percent greater, than the value of the individual cards cut up carefully.

		MINT	EXC	G-VG
COMPLETE SET (6)		3.00	1.25	.30
COMMON PLAYERS (C1-C6)		.10	.04	.01

		MINT	EXC	G-VG
☐ C1 Ron Darling (box bottom card)		.25	.10	.02
☐ C2 Rickey Henderson (box bottom card)		2.00	.80	.20
☐ C3 Carney Lansford (box bottom card)		.25	.10	.02
☐ C4 Rafael Palmeiro (box bottom card)		1.00	.40	.10
☐ C5 Frank Viola (box bottom card)		.40	.16	.04
☐ C6 Twins Logo (checklist back) (box bottom card)		.10	.04	.01

1988 Fleer Sticker Cards

These Star Stickers were distributed as a separate issue by Fleer, with five star stickers and a logo sticker in each wax pack. The 132-card (sticker) set features 2 1/2" by 3 1/2" full-color fronts and even statistics on the sticker back, which is an indication that the Fleer Company understands that these stickers are rarely used as stickers but more like traditional cards. The card fronts are surrounded by a silver-gray border and the backs are printed in red and black on white card stock.

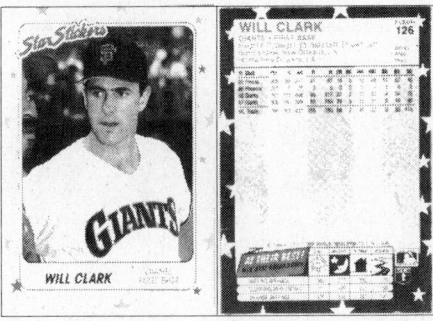

		MINT	EXC	G-VG
	COMPLETE SET (132)	21.00	9.00	3.00
	COMMON PLAYER (1-132)	.05	.02	.00
☐ 1	Mike Boddicker	.10	.04	.01
☐ 2	Eddie Murray	.30	.12	.03
☐ 3	Cal Ripken	1.00	.40	.10
☐ 4	Larry Sheets	.05	.02	.00
☐ 5	Wade Boggs	.90	.40	.09
☐ 6	Ellis Burks	.90	.40	.09
☐ 7	Roger Clemens	1.00	.40	.10
☐ 8	Dwight Evans	.15	.06	.01
☐ 9	Mike Greenwell	.60	.25	.06
☐ 10	Bruce Hurst	.10	.04	.01
☐ 11	Brian Downing	.05	.02	.00
☐ 12	Wally Joyner	.40	.16	.04
☐ 13	Mike Witt	.05	.02	.00
☐ 14	Ivan Calderon	.10	.04	.01
☐ 15	Jose DeLeon	.05	.02	.00
☐ 16	Ozzie Guillen	.15	.06	.01
☐ 17	Bobby Thigpen	.25	.10	.02
☐ 18	Joe Carter	.25	.10	.02
☐ 19	Julio Franco	.20	.08	.02
☐ 20	Brook Jacoby	.05	.02	.00
☐ 21	Cory Snyder	.15	.06	.01
☐ 22	Pat Tabler	.05	.02	.00
☐ 23	Doyle Alexander	.05	.02	.00
☐ 24	Kirk Gibson	.20	.08	.02
☐ 25	Mike Henneman	.10	.04	.01
☐ 26	Jack Morris	.20	.08	.02
☐ 27	Matt Nokes	.15	.06	.01
☐ 28	Walt Terrell	.05	.02	.00
☐ 29	Alan Trammell	.25	.10	.02
☐ 30	George Brett	.60	.25	.06
☐ 31	Charlie Leibrandt	.05	.02	.00
☐ 32	Bret Saberhagen	.35	.15	.03
☐ 33	Kevin Seitzer	.20	.08	.02
☐ 34	Danny Tartabull	.35	.15	.03
☐ 35	Frank White	.10	.04	.01
☐ 36	Rob Deer	.10	.04	.01
☐ 37	Ted Higuera	.10	.04	.01
☐ 38	Paul Molitor	.20	.08	.02
☐ 39	Dan Plesac	.10	.04	.01
☐ 40	Robin Yount	.50	.20	.05
☐ 41	Bert Blyleven	.15	.06	.01
☐ 42	Tom Brunansky	.10	.04	.01
☐ 43	Gary Gaetti	.10	.04	.01
☐ 44	Kent Hrbek	.15	.06	.01
☐ 45	Kirby Puckett	.75	.30	.07
☐ 46	Jeff Reardon	.15	.06	.01
☐ 47	Frank Viola	.15	.06	.01
☐ 48	Don Mattingly	1.00	.40	.10
☐ 49	Mike Pagliarulo	.05	.02	.00
☐ 50	Willie Randolph	.10	.04	.01
☐ 51	Rick Rhoden	.05	.02	.00
☐ 52	Dave Righetti	.10	.04	.01
☐ 53	Dave Winfield	.25	.10	.02
☐ 54	Jose Canseco	1.25	.50	.12
☐ 55	Carney Lansford	.15	.06	.01
☐ 56	Mark McGwire	.75	.30	.07
☐ 57	Dave Stewart	.20	.08	.02
☐ 58	Curt Young	.05	.02	.00
☐ 59	Alvin Davis	.10	.04	.01
☐ 60	Mark Langston	.15	.06	.01
☐ 61	Ken Phelps	.05	.02	.00
☐ 62	Harold Reynolds	.05	.02	.00
☐ 63	Scott Fletcher	.05	.02	.00
☐ 64	Charlie Hough	.05	.02	.00
☐ 65	Pete Incaviglia	.15	.06	.01
☐ 66	Oddibe McDowell	.05	.02	.00
☐ 67	Pete O'Brien	.05	.02	.00

☐ 68	Larry Parrish	.05	.02	.00
☐ 69	Ruben Sierra	.75	.30	.07
☐ 70	Jesse Barfield	.10	.04	.01
☐ 71	George Bell	.20	.08	.02
☐ 72	Tony Fernandez	.10	.04	.01
☐ 73	Tom Henke	.05	.02	.00
☐ 74	Jimmy Key	.10	.04	.01
☐ 75	Lloyd Moseby	.05	.02	.00
☐ 76	Dion James	.05	.02	.00
☐ 77	Dale Murphy	.40	.16	.04
☐ 78	Zane Smith	.05	.02	.00
☐ 79	Andre Dawson	.25	.10	.02
☐ 80	Ryne Sandberg	1.00	.40	.10
☐ 81	Rick Sutcliffe	.10	.04	.01
☐ 82	Kal Daniels	.15	.06	.01
☐ 83	Eric Davis	.75	.30	.07
☐ 84	John Franco	.05	.02	.00
☐ 85	Kevin Bass	.05	.02	.00
☐ 86	Glenn Davis	.15	.06	.01
☐ 87	Bill Doran	.05	.02	.00
☐ 88	Nolan Ryan	2.00	.80	.20
☐ 89	Mike Scott	.15	.06	.01
☐ 90	Dave Smith	.05	.02	.00
☐ 91	Pedro Guerrero	.15	.06	.01
☐ 92	Orel Hershiser	.35	.15	.03
☐ 93	Steve Sax	.15	.06	.01
☐ 94	Fernando Valenzuela	.15	.06	.01
☐ 95	Tim Burke	.05	.02	.00
☐ 96	Andres Galarraga	.20	.08	.02
☐ 97	Tim Raines	.20	.08	.02
☐ 98	Tim Wallach	.10	.04	.01
☐ 99	Mitch Webster	.05	.02	.00
☐ 100	Ron Darling	.10	.04	.01
☐ 101	Sid Fernandez	.10	.04	.01
☐ 102	Dwight Gooden	.40	.16	.04
☐ 103	Keith Hernandez	.15	.06	.01
☐ 104	Howard Johnson	.20	.08	.02
☐ 105	Roger McDowell	.05	.02	.00
☐ 106	Darryl Strawberry	.90	.40	.09
☐ 107	Steve Bedrosian	.05	.02	.00
☐ 108	Von Hayes	.10	.04	.01
☐ 109	Shane Rawley	.05	.02	.00
☐ 110	Juan Samuel	.15	.06	.01
☐ 111	Mike Schmidt	.90	.40	.09
☐ 112	Milt Thompson	.05	.02	.00
☐ 113	Sid Bream	.05	.02	.00
☐ 114	Bobby Bonilla	.50	.20	.05
☐ 115	Mike Dunne	.05	.02	.00
☐ 116	Andy Van Slyke	.15	.06	.01
☐ 117	Vince Coleman	.25	.10	.02
☐ 118	Willie McGee	.15	.06	.01
☐ 119	Terry Pendleton	.20	.08	.02
☐ 120	Ozzie Smith	.25	.10	.02
☐ 121	John Tudor	.10	.04	.01
☐ 122	Todd Worrell	.10	.04	.01
☐ 123	Tony Gwynn	.50	.20	.05
☐ 124	John Kruk	.10	.04	.01
☐ 125	Benito Santiago	.40	.16	.04
☐ 126	Will Clark	1.25	.50	.12
☐ 127	Dave Dravecky	.15	.06	.01
☐ 128	Jeff Leonard	.05	.02	.00
☐ 129	Candy Maldonado	.05	.02	.00
☐ 130	Rick Reuschel	.10	.04	.01
☐ 131	Don Robinson	.05	.02	.00
☐ 132	Checklist Card	.05	.02	.00

1988 Fleer Sticker Box Cards

The bottoms of the Star Sticker wax boxes contained two different sets of four cards done in a similar format to the stickers; these cards (they are not stickers but truly cards) are numbered with the prefix S and are considered a separate set. The value of the panels uncut is slightly greater, perhaps by 25 percent greater, than the value of the individual cards cut up carefully.

		MINT	EXC	G-VG
	COMPLETE SET (8)	4.00	1.75	.40
	COMMON PLAYER	.10	.04	.01
☐ S1	Don Baylor	.15	.06	.01
	(wax box card)			
☐ S2	Gary Carter	.50	.20	.05
	(wax box card)			
☐ S3	Ron Guidry	.25	.10	.02
	(wax box card)			

		MINT	EXC	G-VG
☐ S4	Rickey Henderson	2.00	.80	.20
	(wax box card)			
☐ S5	Kevin Mitchell	.75	.30	.07
	(wax box card)			
☐ S6	Mark McGwire and	1.50	.60	.15
	Eric Davis			
	(wax box card)			
☐ S7	Giants Logo	.10	.04	.01
	(wax box card)			
☐ S8	Detroit Logo	.10	.04	.01
	(wax box card)			

☐ 16	Teddy Higuera	.15	.06	.01
☐ 17	Kent Hrbek	.15	.06	.01
☐ 18	Wally Joyner	.25	.10	.02
☐ 19	Jimmy Key	.10	.04	.01
☐ 20	John Kruk	.10	.04	.01
☐ 21	Jeff Leonard	.10	.04	.01
☐ 22	Don Mattingly	.75	.30	.07
☐ 23	Mark McGwire	.60	.25	.06
☐ 24	Kevin McReynolds	.15	.06	.01
☐ 25	Dale Murphy	.30	.12	.03
☐ 26	Matt Nokes	.15	.06	.01
☐ 27	Terry Pendleton	.20	.08	.02
☐ 28	Kirby Puckett	.45	.18	.04
☐ 29	Tim Raines	.20	.08	.02
☐ 30	Rick Rhoden	.10	.04	.01
☐ 31	Cal Ripken	.75	.30	.07
☐ 32	Benito Santiago	.30	.12	.03
☐ 33	Mike Schmidt	.75	.30	.07
☐ 34	Mike Scott	.15	.06	.01
☐ 35	Kevin Seitzer	.15	.06	.01
☐ 36	Ruben Sierra	.50	.20	.05
☐ 37	Cory Snyder	.20	.08	.02
☐ 38	Darryl Strawberry	.60	.25	.06
☐ 39	Rick Sutcliffe	.10	.04	.01
☐ 40	Danny Tartabull	.30	.12	.03
☐ 41	Alan Trammell	.20	.08	.02
☐ 42	Kenny Williams	.10	.04	.01
☐ 43	Mike Witt	.10	.04	.01
☐ 44	Robin Yount	.40	.16	.04

1988 Fleer Superstars

Fleer produced this 44-card boxed set although it was primarily distributed by McCrory, McLellan, J.J Newberry, H.L.Green, T.G.Y., and other similar stores. The set is subtitled "Fleer Superstars." Cards are standard-size, 2 1/2" by 3 1/2", and were packaged in a red, white, blue, and yellow custom box along with six logo stickers. The set checklist is given on the back of the box. The bottoms of the boxes which held the individual set boxes also contained a panel of six cards; these box bottom cards were numbered C1 through C6.

	MINT	EXC	G-VG
COMPLETE SET (44)	4.00	1.75	.40
COMMON PLAYER (1-44)	.10	.04	.01

☐ 1	Steve Bedrosian	.10	.04	.01
☐ 2	George Bell	.20	.08	.02
☐ 3	Wade Boggs	.60	.25	.06
☐ 4	Barry Bonds	.60	.25	.06
☐ 5	Jose Canseco	.90	.40	.09
☐ 6	Joe Carter	.25	.10	.02
☐ 7	Jack Clark	.15	.06	.01
☐ 8	Will Clark	.90	.40	.09
☐ 9	Roger Clemens	.75	.30	.07
☐ 10	Alvin Davis	.10	.04	.01
☐ 11	Eric Davis	.45	.18	.04
☐ 12	Glenn Davis	.20	.08	.02
☐ 13	Andre Dawson	.30	.12	.03
☐ 14	Dwight Gooden	.35	.15	.03
☐ 15	Orel Hershiser	.30	.12	.03

1988 Fleer Superstars Box Cards

The cards in this six-card set each measure the standard 2 1/2" by 3 1/2". Cards have essentially the same design as the 1988 Fleer Superstars set. The cards were printed on the bottom of the counter display box which held 24 small boxed sets; hence theoretically these box cards are 1/24 as plentiful as the regular boxed set cards. These six cards, numbered C1 to C6 are considered a separate set in their own right and are not typically included in a complete set of the 1988 Fleer Superstars set of 44. The value of the panels uncut is slightly greater, perhaps by 25 percent greater, than the value of the individual cards cut up carefully.

	MINT	EXC	G-VG
COMPLETE SET (6)	3.50	1.50	.35
COMMON PLAYER (C1-C6)	.10	.04	.01

☐ C1	Pete Incaviglia	.30	.12	.03
	(box bottom card)			
☐ C2	Rickey Henderson	2.00	.80	.20
	(box bottom card)			
☐ C3	Tony Fernandez	.25	.10	.02
	(box bottom card)			
☐ C4	Shane Rawley	.10	.04	.01
	(box bottom card)			
☐ C5	Ryne Sandberg	1.50	.60	.15
	(box bottom card)			
☐ C6	Cardinals Logo	.10	.04	.01
	(checklist back)			
	(box bottom card)			

1988 Fleer Team Leaders

BOBBY THIGPEN
WHITE SOX • PITCHER

BOBBY THIGPEN
PITCHER

1988 Fleer World Series

"GRAND" HERO
IN GAME 1

"GRAND" HERO

NO. 1
OF 12

This 44-card boxed set was produced by Fleer for exclusive distribution by Kay Bee Toys and is sometimes referred to as the Fleer Kay Bee set. Six team logo stickers are included in the box with the complete set. The numerical checklist on the back of the box shows that the set is numbered alphabetically. The cards measure 2 1/2" by 3 1/2" and have a distinctive red border on the fronts. The Kay Bee logo is printed in the lower right corner of the obverse of each card.

		MINT	EXC	G-VG
COMPLETE SET (44)		5.00	2.25	.50
COMMON PLAYER (1-44)		.10	.04	.01
☐ 1	George Bell	.20	.08	.02
☐ 2	Wade Boggs	.60	.25	.06
☐ 3	Jose Canseco	.90	.40	.09
☐ 4	Will Clark	.90	.40	.09
☐ 5	Roger Clemens	.75	.30	.07
☐ 6	Eric Davis	.45	.18	.04
☐ 7	Andre Dawson	.30	.12	.03
☐ 8	Julio Franco	.20	.08	.02
☐ 9	Andres Galarraga	.20	.08	.02
☐ 10	Dwight Gooden	.40	.16	.04
☐ 11	Tony Gwynn	.45	.18	.04
☐ 12	Tom Henke	.10	.04	.01
☐ 13	Orel Hershiser	.30	.12	.03
☐ 14	Kent Hrbek	.15	.06	.01
☐ 15	Ted Higuera	.15	.06	.01
☐ 16	Wally Joyner	.25	.10	.02
☐ 17	Jimmy Key	.10	.04	.01
☐ 18	Mark Langston	.20	.08	.02
☐ 19	Don Mattingly	.75	.30	.07
☐ 20	Willie McGee	.20	.08	.02
☐ 21	Mark McGwire	.60	.25	.06
☐ 22	Paul Molitor	.20	.08	.02
☐ 23	Jack Morris	.20	.08	.02
☐ 24	Dale Murphy	.30	.12	.03
☐ 25	Larry Parrish	.10	.04	.01
☐ 26	Kirby Puckett	.50	.20	.05
☐ 27	Tim Raines	.20	.08	.02
☐ 28	Jeff Reardon	.20	.08	.02
☐ 29	Dave Righetti	.15	.06	.01
☐ 30	Cal Ripken	.75	.30	.07
☐ 31	Don Robinson	.10	.04	.01
☐ 32	Bret Saberhagen	.35	.15	.03
☐ 33	Juan Samuel	.15	.06	.01
☐ 34	Mike Schmidt	.75	.30	.07
☐ 35	Mike Scott	.15	.06	.01
☐ 36	Kevin Seitzer	.15	.06	.01
☐ 37	Dave Smith	.10	.04	.01
☐ 38	Ozzie Smith	.25	.10	.02
☐ 39	Zane Smith	.10	.04	.01
☐ 40	Darryl Strawberry	.75	.30	.07
☐ 41	Rick Sutcliffe	.15	.06	.01
☐ 42	Bobby Thigpen	.25	.10	.02
☐ 43	Alan Trammell	.25	.10	.02
☐ 44	Andy Van Slyke	.15	.06	.01

This 12-card set of 2 1/2" by 3 1/2" cards features highlights of the previous year's World Series between the Minnesota Twins and the St. Louis Cardinals. The sets were packaged as a complete set insert with the collated sets (of the 1988 Fleer regular issue) which were sold by Fleer directly to hobby card dealers; they were not available in the general retail candy store outlets.

		MINT	EXC	G-VG
COMPLETE SET (12)		4.00	1.75	.40
COMMON PLAYER (1-12)		.25	.10	.02
☐ 1	Dan Gladden	.25	.10	.02
	Grand Hero Game 1			
☐ 2	Randy Bush	.25	.10	.02
	Cardinals "Bush" Wacked			
☐ 3	John Tudor	.35	.15	.03
	Masterful Performance in Game 3			
☐ 4	Ozzie Smith	1.00	.40	.10
	The Wizard			
☐ 5	Todd Worrell and	.35	.15	.03
	Tony Pena Throw Smoke			
☐ 6	Vince Coleman	.50	.20	.05
	Cardinal Attack			
☐ 7	Tom Herr/Dan Driessen	.25	.10	.02
	Herr's Wallop			
☐ 8	Kirby Puckett	1.00	.40	.10
	Kirby's Bat Comes Alive			
☐ 9	Kent Hrbek	.50	.20	.05
	Hrbek's Slam Forces Game 7			
☐ 10	Tom Herr	.25	.10	.02
	Out at First			
☐ 11	Don Baylor	.25	.10	.02
	Game 7's Play At The Plate			
☐ 12	Frank Viola	.75	.30	.07
	Series MVP, 16 K's			

1989 Fleer

This 660-card set features a distinctive gray border background with white and yellow trim. The backs are printed in gray, black, and yellow on white card stock. The bottom of the card back shows an innovative breakdown of the player's demonstrated ability with respect to his performance before and after the All-Star break. Cards are numbered on the back and are again the standard 2 1/2" by 3 1/2". Cards are again organized numerically by teams and alphabetically within teams: Oakland A's (1-26), New York Mets (27-52), Los Angeles Dodgers (53-77), Boston Red Sox (78-101), Minnesota Twins (102-127), Detroit Tigers (128-151), Cincinnati Reds (152-175), Milwaukee Brewers

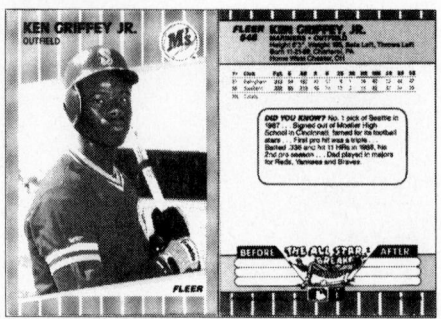

(176-200), Pittsburgh Pirates (201-224), Toronto Blue Jays (225-248), New York Yankees (249-274), Kansas City Royals (275-298), San Diego Padres (299-322), San Francisco Giants (323-347), Houston Astros (348-370), Montreal Expos (371-395), Cleveland Indians (396-417), Chicago Cubs (418-442), St. Louis Cardinals (443-466), California Angels (467-490), Chicago White Sox (491-513), Texas Rangers (514-537), Seattle Mariners (538-561), Philadelphia Phillies (562-584), Atlanta Braves (585-605), and Baltimore Orioles (606-627). However, pairs 148/149, 153/154, 272/273, 283/284, and 367/368 were apparently mis-alphabetized by Fleer. The last 33 cards in the set consist of Specials (628-639), Rookie Pairs (640-653), and checklists (654-660). Due to the early beginning of production of this set, it seems Fleer "presumed" that the A's would win the World Series, since they are listed as the first team in the numerical order; in fact, Fleer had the Mets over the underdog (but eventual World Champion) Dodgers as well. Approximately half of the California Angels players have white rather than yellow halos. Certain Oakland A's player cards have red instead of green lines for front photo borders. Checklist cards are available either with or without positions listed for each player. The key rookies in this set are Sandy Alomar Jr., Ken Griffey Jr., Felix Jose, Ramon Martinez, Hal Morris, and Gary Sheffield. Fleer also produced the last of their three-year run of "limited" edition glossy, tin sets. This tin set was limited, but only compared to the previous year, as collector and dealer interest in the tin sets was apparently waning. It has been estimated that approximately 30,000 1989 tin sets were produced by Fleer; as a result, the price of the "tin" glossy cards is now about double the price of the regular set cards.

		MINT	EXC	G-VG
COMPLETE SET (660)		24.00	10.50	3.50
COMMON PLAYER (1-660)		.04	.02	.00
☐ 1	Don Baylor	.10	.04	.01
☐ 2	Lance Blankenship	.07	.03	.01
☐ 3	Todd Burns UER	.07	.03	.01
	(Wrong birthdate; before/after All-Star stats missing)			
☐ 4	Greg Cadaret UER	.07	.03	.01
	(All-Star Break stats show 3 losses, should be 2)			
☐ 5	Jose Canseco	.65	.25	.06
☐ 6	Storm Davis	.04	.02	.00
☐ 7	Dennis Eckersley	.10	.04	.01
☐ 8	Mike Gallego	.04	.02	.00
☐ 9	Ron Hassey	.04	.02	.00
☐ 10	Dave Henderson	.10	.04	.01
☐ 11	Rick Honeycutt	.04	.02	.00
☐ 12	Glenn Hubbard	.04	.02	.00
☐ 13	Stan Javier	.04	.02	.00
☐ 14	Doug Jennings	.07	.03	.01
☐ 15	Felix Jose	.90	.40	.09
☐ 16	Carney Lansford	.07	.03	.01
☐ 17	Mark McGwire	.15	.06	.01
☐ 18	Gene Nelson	.04	.02	.00
☐ 19	Dave Parker	.10	.04	.01
☐ 20	Eric Plunk	.04	.02	.00
☐ 21	Luis Polonia	.07	.03	.01
☐ 22	Terry Steinbach	.07	.03	.01
☐ 23	Dave Stewart	.10	.04	.01
☐ 24	Walt Weiss	.07	.03	.01
☐ 25	Bob Welch	.07	.03	.01
☐ 26	Curt Young	.04	.02	.00
☐ 27	Rick Aguilera	.07	.03	.01
☐ 28	Wally Backman	.04	.02	.00
☐ 29	Mark Carreon UER	.07	.03	.01
	(after All-Star Break batting 7.14)			
☐ 30	Gary Carter	.07	.03	.01
☐ 31	David Cone	.10	.04	.01
☐ 32	Ron Darling	.07	.03	.01
☐ 33	Len Dykstra	.07	.03	.01
☐ 34	Kevin Elster	.04	.02	.00
☐ 35	Sid Fernandez	.07	.03	.01
☐ 36	Dwight Gooden	.15	.06	.01
☐ 37	Keith Hernandez	.10	.04	.01
☐ 38	Gregg Jefferies	.35	.15	.03
☐ 39	Howard Johnson	.15	.06	.01
☐ 40	Terry Leach	.04	.02	.00
☐ 41	Dave Magadan UER	.07	.03	.01
	(Bio says 15 doubles, should be 13)			
☐ 42	Bob McClure	.04	.02	.00
☐ 43	Roger McDowell UER	.04	.02	.00
	(Led Mets with 58, should be 62)			
☐ 44	Kevin McReynolds	.10	.04	.01
☐ 45	Keith Miller	.04	.02	.00
☐ 46	Randy Myers	.07	.03	.01
☐ 47	Bob Ojeda	.04	.02	.00
☐ 48	Mackey Sasser	.07	.03	.01
☐ 49	Darryl Strawberry	.35	.15	.03
☐ 50	Tim Teufel	.04	.02	.00
☐ 51	Dave West	.15	.06	.01
☐ 52	Mookie Wilson	.04	.02	.00
☐ 53	Dave Anderson	.04	.02	.00
☐ 54	Tim Belcher	.10	.04	.01
☐ 55	Mike Davis	.04	.02	.00
☐ 56	Mike Devereaux	.07	.03	.01
☐ 57	Kirk Gibson	.10	.04	.01
☐ 58	Alfredo Griffin	.04	.02	.00
☐ 59	Chris Gwynn	.07	.03	.01
☐ 60	Jeff Hamilton	.04	.02	.00
☐ 61A	Danny Heep	.40	.16	.04
	(Home: Lake Hills)			
☐ 61B	Danny Heep	.10	.04	.01
	(Home: San Antonio)			
☐ 62	Orel Hershiser	.10	.04	.01
☐ 63	Brian Holton	.04	.02	.00
☐ 64	Jay Howell	.04	.02	.00
☐ 65	Tim Leary	.07	.03	.01
☐ 66	Mike Marshall	.07	.03	.01
☐ 67	Ramon Martinez	2.00	.80	.20
☐ 68	Jesse Orosco	.04	.02	.00
☐ 69	Alejandro Pena	.07	.03	.01
☐ 70	Steve Sax	.10	.04	.01
☐ 71	Mike Scioscia	.04	.02	.00
☐ 72	Mike Sharperson	.04	.02	.00
☐ 73	John Shelby	.04	.02	.00
☐ 74	Franklin Stubbs	.04	.02	.00
☐ 75	John Tudor	.07	.03	.01
☐ 76	Fernando Valenzuela	.10	.04	.01
☐ 77	Tracy Woodson	.07	.03	.01
☐ 78	Marty Barrett	.04	.02	.00
☐ 79	Todd Benzinger	.04	.02	.00
☐ 80	Mike Boddicker UER	.04	.02	.00
	(Rochester in '76, should be '78)			
☐ 81	Wade Boggs	.25	.10	.02
☐ 82	Oil Can Boyd	.04	.02	.00
☐ 83	Ellis Burks	.17	.07	.01
☐ 84	Rick Cerone	.04	.02	.00
☐ 85	Roger Clemens	.40	.16	.04
☐ 86	Steve Curry	.07	.03	.01
☐ 87	Dwight Evans	.10	.04	.01
☐ 88	Wes Gardner	.04	.02	.00
☐ 89	Rich Gedman	.04	.02	.00
☐ 90	Mike Greenwell	.20	.08	.02
☐ 91	Bruce Hurst	.07	.03	.01
☐ 92	Dennis Lamp	.04	.02	.00
☐ 93	Spike Owen	.04	.02	.00
☐ 94	Larry Parrish UER	.04	.02	.00
	(before All-Star Break batting 1.90)			
☐ 95	Carlos Quintana	.30	.12	.03
☐ 96	Jody Reed	.07	.03	.01
☐ 97	Jim Rice	.10	.04	.01
☐ 98A	Kevin Romine ERR	.40	.16	.04
	(photo actually Randy Kutcher batting)			

☐ 98B Kevin Romine COR (arms folded)	.10	.04	.01
☐ 99 Lee Smith	.10	.04	.01
☐ 100 Mike Smithson	.04	.02	.00
☐ 101 Bob Stanley	.04	.02	.00
☐ 102 Allan Anderson	.04	.02	.00
☐ 103 Keith Atherton	.04	.02	.00
☐ 104 Juan Berenguer	.04	.02	.00
☐ 105 Bert Blyleven	.10	.04	.01
☐ 106 Eric Bullock UER (Bats/Throws Right, should be Left)	.07	.03	.01
☐ 107 Randy Bush	.04	.02	.00
☐ 108 John Christensen	.04	.02	.00
☐ 109 Mark Davidson	.04	.02	.00
☐ 110 Gary Gaetti	.07	.03	.01
☐ 111 Greg Gagne	.04	.02	.00
☐ 112 Dan Gladden	.04	.02	.00
☐ 113 German Gonzalez	.07	.03	.01
☐ 114 Brian Harper	.07	.03	.01
☐ 115 Tom Herr	.04	.02	.00
☐ 116 Kent Hrbek	.10	.04	.01
☐ 117 Gene Larkin	.07	.03	.01
☐ 118 Tim Laudner	.04	.02	.00
☐ 119 Charlie Lea	.04	.02	.00
☐ 120 Steve Lombardozzi	.04	.02	.00
☐ 121A John Moses (Home: Tempe)	.40	.16	.04
☐ 121B John Moses (Home: Phoenix)	.10	.04	.01
☐ 122 Al Newman	.04	.02	.00
☐ 123 Mark Portugal	.04	.02	.00
☐ 124 Kirby Puckett	.35	.15	.03
☐ 125 Jeff Reardon	.10	.04	.01
☐ 126 Fred Toliver	.04	.02	.00
☐ 127 Frank Viola	.10	.04	.01
☐ 128 Doyle Alexander	.04	.02	.00
☐ 129 Dave Bergman	.04	.02	.00
☐ 130A Tom Brookens ERR (Mike Heath back)	.75	.30	.07
☐ 130B Tom Brookens COR	.07	.03	.01
☐ 131 Paul Gibson	.10	.04	.01
☐ 132A Mike Heath ERR (Tom Brookens back)	.75	.30	.07
☐ 132B Mike Heath COR	.07	.03	.01
☐ 133 Don Heinkel	.04	.02	.00
☐ 134 Mike Henneman	.04	.02	.00
☐ 135 Guillermo Hernandez	.04	.02	.00
☐ 136 Eric King	.04	.02	.00
☐ 137 Chet Lemon	.04	.02	.00
☐ 138 Fred Lynn UER ('74, '75 stats missing)	.07	.03	.01
☐ 139 Jack Morris	.10	.04	.01
☐ 140 Matt Nokes	.10	.04	.01
☐ 141 Gary Pettis	.04	.02	.00
☐ 142 Ted Power	.04	.02	.00
☐ 143 Jeff M. Robinson	.04	.02	.00
☐ 144 Luis Salazar	.04	.02	.00
☐ 145 Steve Searcy	.07	.03	.01
☐ 146 Pat Sheridan	.04	.02	.00
☐ 147 Frank Tanana	.07	.03	.01
☐ 148 Alan Trammell	.15	.06	.01
☐ 149 Walt Terrell	.04	.02	.00
☐ 150 Jim Walewander	.07	.03	.01
☐ 151 Lou Whitaker	.07	.03	.01
☐ 152 Tim Birtsas	.04	.02	.00
☐ 153 Tom Browning	.07	.03	.01
☐ 154 Keith Brown	.07	.03	.01
☐ 155 Norm Charlton	.15	.06	.01
☐ 156 Dave Concepcion	.07	.03	.01
☐ 157 Kal Daniels	.07	.03	.01
☐ 158 Eric Davis	.15	.06	.01
☐ 159 Bo Diaz	.04	.02	.00
☐ 160 Rob Dibble	.35	.15	.03
☐ 161 Nick Esasky	.04	.02	.00
☐ 162 John Franco	.04	.02	.00
☐ 163 Danny Jackson	.07	.03	.01
☐ 164 Barry Larkin	.17	.07	.01
☐ 165 Rob Murphy	.04	.02	.00
☐ 166 Paul O'Neill	.10	.04	.01
☐ 167 Jeff Reed	.04	.02	.00
☐ 168 Jose Rijo	.10	.04	.01
☐ 169 Ron Robinson	.04	.02	.00
☐ 170 Chris Sabo	.75	.30	.07
☐ 171 Candy Sierra	.07	.03	.01
☐ 172 Van Snider	.07	.03	.01
☐ 173A Jeff Treadway (target registration mark above head on front in light blue)	10.00	4.50	1.25
☐ 173B Jeff Treadway (no target on front)	.07	.03	.01
☐ 174 Frank Williams (after All-Star Break stats are jumbled)	.04	.02	.00
☐ 175 Herm Winningham	.04	.02	.00
☐ 176 Jim Adduci	.04	.02	.00
☐ 177 Don August	.04	.02	.00
☐ 178 Mike Birkbeck	.04	.02	.00
☐ 179 Chris Bosio	.04	.02	.00
☐ 180 Glenn Braggs	.04	.02	.00
☐ 181 Greg Brock	.04	.02	.00
☐ 182 Mark Clear	.04	.02	.00
☐ 183 Chuck Crim	.04	.02	.00
☐ 184 Rob Deer	.07	.03	.01
☐ 185 Tom Filer	.04	.02	.00
☐ 186 Jim Gantner	.04	.02	.00
☐ 187 Darryl Hamilton	.15	.06	.01
☐ 188 Ted Higuera	.04	.02	.00
☐ 189 Odell Jones	.04	.02	.00
☐ 190 Jeffrey Leonard	.04	.02	.00
☐ 191 Joey Meyer	.04	.02	.00
☐ 192 Paul Mirabella	.04	.02	.00
☐ 193 Paul Molitor	.12	.05	.01
☐ 194 Charlie O'Brien	.07	.03	.01
☐ 195 Dan Plesac	.04	.02	.00
☐ 196 Gary Sheffield	.40	.16	.04
☐ 197 B.J. Surhoff	.07	.03	.01
☐ 198 Dale Sveum	.04	.02	.00
☐ 199 Bill Wegman	.04	.02	.00
☐ 200 Robin Yount	.20	.08	.02
☐ 201 Rafael Belliard	.04	.02	.00
☐ 202 Barry Bonds	.30	.12	.03
☐ 203 Bobby Bonilla	.25	.10	.02
☐ 204 Sid Bream	.04	.02	.00
☐ 205 Benny Distefano	.04	.02	.00
☐ 206 Doug Drabek	.10	.04	.01
☐ 207 Mike Dunne	.04	.02	.00
☐ 208 Felix Fermin	.04	.02	.00
☐ 209 Brian Fisher	.04	.02	.00
☐ 210 Jim Gott	.04	.02	.00
☐ 211 Bob Kipper	.04	.02	.00
☐ 212 Dave LaPoint	.04	.02	.00
☐ 213 Mike LaValliere	.04	.02	.00
☐ 214 Jose Lind	.04	.02	.00
☐ 215 Junior Ortiz	.04	.02	.00
☐ 216 Vicente Palacios	.07	.03	.01
☐ 217 Tom Prince	.04	.02	.00
☐ 218 Gary Redus	.04	.02	.00
☐ 219 R.J. Reynolds	.04	.02	.00
☐ 220 Jeff Robinson	.04	.02	.00
☐ 221 John Smiley	.07	.03	.01
☐ 222 Andy Van Slyke	.12	.05	.01
☐ 223 Bob Walk	.04	.02	.00
☐ 224 Glenn Wilson	.04	.02	.00
☐ 225 Jesse Barfield	.10	.04	.01
☐ 226 George Bell	.12	.05	.01
☐ 227 Pat Borders	.17	.07	.01
☐ 228 John Cerutti	.04	.02	.00
☐ 229 Jim Clancy	.04	.02	.00
☐ 230 Mark Eichhorn	.07	.03	.01
☐ 231 Tony Fernandez	.07	.03	.01
☐ 232 Cecil Fielder	.40	.16	.04
☐ 233 Mike Flanagan	.04	.02	.00
☐ 234 Kelly Gruber	.12	.05	.01
☐ 235 Tom Henke	.07	.03	.01
☐ 236 Jimmy Key	.07	.03	.01
☐ 237 Rick Leach	.04	.02	.00
☐ 238 Manny Lee UER (bio says regular shortstop, sic, Tony Fernandez)	.07	.03	.01
☐ 239 Nelson Liriano	.04	.02	.00
☐ 240 Fred McGriff	.20	.08	.02
☐ 241 Lloyd Moseby	.04	.02	.00
☐ 242 Rance Mulliniks	.04	.02	.00
☐ 243 Jeff Musselman	.04	.02	.00
☐ 244 Dave Stieb	.10	.04	.01
☐ 245 Todd Stottlemyre	.20	.08	.02
☐ 246 Duane Ward	.04	.02	.00
☐ 247 David Wells	.12	.05	.01
☐ 248 Ernie Whitt UER (HR total 21, should be 121)	.04	.02	.00
☐ 249 Luis Aguayo	.04	.02	.00
☐ 250A Neil Allen (Home: Sarasota, FL)	.75	.30	.07
☐ 250B Neil Allen (Home: Syosset, NY)	.10	.04	.01
☐ 251 John Candelaria	.04	.02	.00
☐ 252 Jack Clark	.07	.03	.01
☐ 253 Richard Dotson	.04	.02	.00
☐ 254 Rickey Henderson	.40	.16	.04
☐ 255 Tommy John	.10	.04	.01
☐ 256 Roberto Kelly	.17	.07	.01

#	Name			
☐ 257	Al Leiter	.04	.02	.00
☐ 258	Don Mattingly	.30	.12	.03
☐ 259	Dale Mohorcic	.04	.02	.00
☐ 260	Hal Morris	2.00	.80	.20
☐ 261	Scott Nielsen	.04	.02	.00
☐ 262	Mike Pagliarulo UER (wrong birthdate)	.04	.02	.00
☐ 263	Hipolito Pena	.07	.03	.01
☐ 264	Ken Phelps	.04	.02	.00
☐ 265	Willie Randolph	.07	.03	.01
☐ 266	Rick Rhoden	.04	.02	.00
☐ 267	Dave Righetti	.07	.03	.01
☐ 268	Rafael Santana	.04	.02	.00
☐ 269	Steve Shields	.04	.02	.00
☐ 270	Joel Skinner	.04	.02	.00
☐ 271	Don Slaught	.04	.02	.00
☐ 272	Claudell Washington	.04	.02	.00
☐ 273	Gary Ward	.04	.02	.00
☐ 274	Dave Winfield	.15	.06	.01
☐ 275	Luis Aquino	.04	.02	.00
☐ 276	Floyd Bannister	.04	.02	.00
☐ 277	George Brett	.20	.08	.02
☐ 278	Bill Buckner	.07	.03	.01
☐ 279	Nick Capra	.04	.02	.00
☐ 280	Jose DeJesus	.15	.06	.01
☐ 281	Steve Farr	.04	.02	.00
☐ 282	Jerry Don Gleaton	.04	.02	.00
☐ 283	Mark Gubicza	.07	.03	.01
☐ 284	Tom Gordon UER (16.2 innings in '88, should be 15.2)	.30	.12	.03
☐ 285	Bo Jackson	.60	.25	.06
☐ 286	Charlie Leibrandt	.04	.02	.00
☐ 287	Mike Macfarlane	.12	.05	.01
☐ 288	Jeff Montgomery	.07	.03	.01
☐ 289	Bill Pecota UER (photo actually Brad Wellman)	.07	.03	.01
☐ 290	Jamie Quirk	.04	.02	.00
☐ 291	Bret Saberhagen	.12	.05	.01
☐ 292	Kevin Seitzer	.07	.03	.01
☐ 293	Kurt Stillwell	.04	.02	.00
☐ 294	Pat Tabler	.04	.02	.00
☐ 295	Danny Tartabull	.12	.05	.01
☐ 296	Gary Thurman	.04	.02	.00
☐ 297	Frank White	.04	.02	.00
☐ 298	Willie Wilson	.07	.03	.01
☐ 299	Roberto Alomar	.75	.30	.07
☐ 300	Sandy Alomar Jr. UER (wrong birthdate, says 6/16/66, should say 6/18/66)	.60	.25	.06
☐ 301	Chris Brown	.04	.02	.00
☐ 302	Mike Brumley UER (133 hits in '88, should be 134)	.07	.03	.01
☐ 303	Mark Davis	.07	.03	.01
☐ 304	Mark Grant	.04	.02	.00
☐ 305	Tony Gwynn	.20	.08	.02
☐ 306	Greg W. Harris	.17	.07	.01
☐ 307	Andy Hawkins	.04	.02	.00
☐ 308	Jimmy Jones	.04	.02	.00
☐ 309	John Kruk	.04	.02	.00
☐ 310	Dave Leiper	.04	.02	.00
☐ 311	Carmelo Martinez	.04	.02	.00
☐ 312	Lance McCullers	.04	.02	.00
☐ 313	Keith Moreland	.04	.02	.00
☐ 314	Dennis Rasmussen	.04	.02	.00
☐ 315	Randy Ready UER (1214 games in '88, should be 114)	.04	.02	.00
☐ 316	Benito Santiago	.10	.04	.01
☐ 317	Eric Show	.04	.02	.00
☐ 318	Todd Simmons	.04	.02	.00
☐ 319	Garry Templeton	.07	.03	.01
☐ 320	Dickie Thon	.04	.02	.00
☐ 321	Ed Whitson	.04	.02	.00
☐ 322	Marvell Wynne	.04	.02	.00
☐ 323	Mike Aldrete	.04	.02	.00
☐ 324	Brett Butler	.10	.04	.01
☐ 325	Will Clark UER (three consecutive 100 RBI seasons)	.60	.25	.06
☐ 326	Kelly Downs UER ('88 stats missing)	.04	.02	.00
☐ 327	Dave Dravecky	.07	.03	.01
☐ 328	Scott Garrelts	.04	.02	.00
☐ 329	Atlee Hammaker	.04	.02	.00
☐ 330	Charlie Hayes	.12	.05	.01
☐ 331	Mike Krukow	.04	.02	.00
☐ 332	Craig Lefferts	.04	.02	.00
☐ 333	Candy Maldonado	.04	.02	.00
☐ 334	Kirt Manwaring UER (Bats Rights)	.04	.02	.00
☐ 335	Bob Melvin	.04	.02	.00
☐ 336	Kevin Mitchell	.20	.08	.02
☐ 337	Donell Nixon	.04	.02	.00
☐ 338	Tony Perezchica	.07	.03	.01
☐ 339	Joe Price	.04	.02	.00
☐ 340	Rick Reuschel	.07	.03	.01
☐ 341	Earnest Riles	.04	.02	.00
☐ 342	Don Robinson	.04	.02	.00
☐ 343	Chris Speier	.04	.02	.00
☐ 344	Robby Thompson UER (West Plam Beach)	.04	.02	.00
☐ 345	Jose Uribe	.04	.02	.00
☐ 346	Matt Williams	.30	.12	.03
☐ 347	Trevor Wilson	.15	.06	.01
☐ 348	Juan Agosto	.04	.02	.00
☐ 349	Larry Andersen	.04	.02	.00
☐ 350A	Alan Ashby ERR (Throws Rig)	3.00	1.25	.30
☐ 350B	Alan Ashby COR	.07	.03	.01
☐ 351	Kevin Bass	.04	.02	.00
☐ 352	Buddy Bell	.07	.03	.01
☐ 353	Craig Biggio	.60	.25	.06
☐ 354	Danny Darwin	.04	.02	.00
☐ 355	Glenn Davis	.10	.04	.01
☐ 356	Jim Deshaies	.04	.02	.00
☐ 357	Bill Doran	.04	.02	.00
☐ 358	John Fishel	.04	.02	.00
☐ 359	Billy Hatcher	.07	.03	.01
☐ 360	Bob Knepper	.04	.02	.00
☐ 361	Louie Meadows UER (bio says 10 EBH's and 6 SB's in '88, should be 3 and 4)	.07	.03	.01
☐ 362	Dave Meads	.04	.02	.00
☐ 363	Jim Pankovits	.04	.02	.00
☐ 364	Terry Puhl	.04	.02	.00
☐ 365	Rafael Ramirez	.04	.02	.00
☐ 366	Craig Reynolds	.04	.02	.00
☐ 367	Mike Scott (card number listed as 368 on Astros CL)	.10	.04	.01
☐ 368	Nolan Ryan (card number listed as 367 on Astros CL)	.75	.30	.07
☐ 369	Dave Smith	.04	.02	.00
☐ 370	Gerald Young	.04	.02	.00
☐ 371	Hubie Brooks	.07	.03	.01
☐ 372	Tim Burke	.04	.02	.00
☐ 373	John Dopson	.07	.03	.01
☐ 374	Mike Fitzgerald	.04	.02	.00
☐ 375	Tom Foley	.04	.02	.00
☐ 376	Andres Galarraga UER (Home: Caracus)	.07	.03	.01
☐ 377	Neal Heaton	.04	.02	.00
☐ 378	Joe Hesketh	.07	.03	.01
☐ 379	Brian Holman	.20	.08	.02
☐ 380	Rex Hudler	.07	.03	.01
☐ 381	Randy Johnson UER (innings for '85 and '86 shown as 27 and 120, should be 27.1 and 119.2)	.35	.15	.03
☐ 382	Wallace Johnson	.04	.02	.00
☐ 383	Tracy Jones	.04	.02	.00
☐ 384	Dave Martinez	.04	.02	.00
☐ 385	Dennis Martinez	.07	.03	.01
☐ 386	Andy McGaffigan	.04	.02	.00
☐ 387	Otis Nixon	.07	.03	.01
☐ 388	Johnny Paredes	.07	.03	.01
☐ 389	Jeff Parrett	.04	.02	.00
☐ 390	Pascual Perez	.04	.02	.00
☐ 391	Tim Raines	.12	.05	.01
☐ 392	Luis Rivera	.04	.02	.00
☐ 393	Nelson Santovenia	.10	.04	.01
☐ 394	Bryn Smith	.04	.02	.00
☐ 395	Tim Wallach	.07	.03	.01
☐ 396	Andy Allanson UER (1214 hits in '88, should be 114)	.04	.02	.00
☐ 397	Rod Allen	.07	.03	.01
☐ 398	Scott Bailes	.04	.02	.00
☐ 399	Tom Candiotti	.07	.03	.01
☐ 400	Joe Carter	.12	.05	.01
☐ 401	Carmen Castillo UER (after All-Star Break batting 2.50)	.04	.02	.00
☐ 402	Dave Clark UER (card front shows position as Rookie; after All-Star Break batting 3.14)	.07	.03	.01
☐ 403	John Farrell UER (typo in runs allowed in '88)	.04	.02	.00

☐ 404	Julio Franco	.12	.05	.01
☐ 405	Don Gordon	.04	.02	.00
☐ 406	Mel Hall	.07	.03	.01
☐ 407	Brad Havens	.04	.02	.00
☐ 408	Brook Jacoby	.04	.02	.00
☐ 409	Doug Jones	.04	.02	.00
☐ 410	Jeff Kaiser	.07	.03	.01
☐ 411	Luis Medina	.10	.04	.01
☐ 412	Cory Snyder	.07	.03	.01
☐ 413	Greg Swindell	.07	.03	.01
☐ 414	Ron Tingley UER	.07	.03	.01
	(hit HR in first ML			
	at-bat, should be			
	first AL at-bat)			
☐ 415	Willie Upshaw	.04	.02	.00
☐ 416	Ron Washington	.04	.02	.00
☐ 417	Rich Yett	.04	.02	.00
☐ 418	Damon Berryhill	.07	.03	.01
☐ 419	Mike Bielecki	.07	.03	.01
☐ 420	Doug Dascenzo	.10	.04	.01
☐ 421	Jody Davis UER	.04	.02	.00
	(Braves stats for			
	'88 missing)			
☐ 422	Andre Dawson	.15	.06	.01
☐ 423	Frank DiPino	.04	.02	.00
☐ 424	Shawon Dunston	.07	.03	.01
☐ 425	Goose Gossage	.07	.03	.01
☐ 426	Mark Grace UER	.40	.16	.04
	(Minor League stats			
	for '88 missing)			
☐ 427	Mike Harkey	.15	.06	.01
☐ 428	Darrin Jackson	.07	.03	.01
☐ 429	Les Lancaster	.04	.02	.00
☐ 430	Vance Law	.04	.02	.00
☐ 431	Greg Maddux	.10	.04	.01
☐ 432	Jamie Moyer	.04	.02	.00
☐ 433	Al Nipper	.04	.02	.00
☐ 434	Rafael Palmeiro UER	.20	.08	.02
	(170 hits in '88,			
	should be 178)			
☐ 435	Pat Perry	.04	.02	.00
☐ 436	Jeff Pico	.07	.03	.01
☐ 437	Ryne Sandberg	.40	.16	.04
☐ 438	Calvin Schiraldi	.04	.02	.00
☐ 439	Rick Sutcliffe	.07	.03	.01
☐ 440A	Manny Trillo ERR	3.00	1.25	.30
	(Throws Rig)			
☐ 440B	Manny Trillo COR	.07	.03	.01
☐ 441	Gary Varsho UER	.07	.03	.01
	(wrong birthdate;			
	.303 should be .302;			
	11/28 should be 9/19)			
☐ 442	Mitch Webster	.04	.02	.00
☐ 443	Luis Alicea	.07	.03	.01
☐ 444	Tom Brunansky	.07	.03	.01
☐ 445	Vince Coleman UER	.12	.05	.01
	(third straight with			
	83, should be fourth			
	straight with 81)			
☐ 446	John Costello	.04	.02	.00
☐ 447	Danny Cox	.04	.02	.00
☐ 448	Ken Dayley	.04	.02	.00
☐ 449	Jose DeLeon	.04	.02	.00
☐ 450	Curt Ford	.04	.02	.00
☐ 451	Pedro Guerrero	.07	.03	.01
☐ 452	Bob Horner	.07	.03	.01
☐ 453	Tim Jones	.07	.03	.01
☐ 454	Steve Lake	.04	.02	.00
☐ 455	Joe Magrane UER	.07	.03	.01
	(Des Moines, IO)			
☐ 456	Greg Mathews	.04	.02	.00
☐ 457	Willie McGee	.07	.03	.01
☐ 458	Larry McWilliams	.04	.02	.00
☐ 459	Jose Oquendo	.04	.02	.00
☐ 460	Tony Pena	.07	.03	.01
☐ 461	Terry Pendleton	.12	.05	.01
☐ 462	Steve Peters UER	.10	.04	.01
	(Lives in Harrah,			
	not Harah)			
☐ 463	Ozzie Smith	.17	.07	.01
☐ 464	Scott Terry	.04	.02	.00
☐ 465	Denny Walling	.04	.02	.00
☐ 466	Todd Worrell	.07	.03	.01
☐ 467	Tony Armas UER	.04	.02	.00
	(before All-Star Break			
	batting 2.39)			
☐ 468	Dante Bichette	.20	.08	.02
☐ 469	Bob Boone	.07	.03	.01
☐ 470	Terry Clark	.07	.03	.01
☐ 471	Stew Cliburn	.04	.02	.00
☐ 472	Mike Cook UER	.07	.03	.01
	(TM near Angels logo			
	missing from front)			
☐ 473	Sherman Corbett	.04	.02	.00

☐ 474	Chili Davis	.07	.03	.01
☐ 475	Brian Downing	.04	.02	.00
☐ 476	Jim Eppard	.04	.02	.00
☐ 477	Chuck Finley	.10	.04	.01
☐ 478	Willie Fraser	.04	.02	.00
☐ 479	Bryan Harvey UER	.30	.12	.03
	(ML record shows 0-0,			
	should be 7-5)			
☐ 480	Jack Howell	.04	.02	.00
☐ 481	Wally Joyner UER	.15	.06	.01
	(Yorba Linda, GA)			
☐ 482	Jack Lazorko	.04	.02	.00
☐ 483	Kirk McCaskill	.04	.02	.00
☐ 484	Mark McLemore	.04	.02	.00
☐ 485	Greg Minton	.04	.02	.00
☐ 486	Dan Petry	.04	.02	.00
☐ 487	Johnny Ray	.04	.02	.00
☐ 488	Dick Schofield	.04	.02	.00
☐ 489	Devon White	.07	.03	.01
☐ 490	Mike Witt	.04	.02	.00
☐ 491	Harold Baines	.07	.03	.01
☐ 492	Daryl Boston	.04	.02	.00
☐ 493	Ivan Calderon UER	.07	.03	.01
	('80 stats shifted)			
☐ 494	Mike Diaz	.04	.02	.00
☐ 495	Carlton Fisk	.17	.07	.01
☐ 496	Dave Gallagher	.10	.04	.01
☐ 497	Ozzie Guillen	.07	.03	.01
☐ 498	Shawn Hillegas	.04	.02	.00
☐ 499	Lance Johnson	.04	.02	.00
☐ 500	Barry Jones	.04	.02	.00
☐ 501	Bill Long	.04	.02	.00
☐ 502	Steve Lyons	.04	.02	.00
☐ 503	Fred Manrique	.04	.02	.00
☐ 504	Jack McDowell	.20	.08	.02
☐ 505	Donn Pall	.07	.03	.01
☐ 506	Kelly Paris	.04	.02	.00
☐ 507	Dan Pasqua	.04	.02	.00
☐ 508	Ken Patterson	.07	.03	.01
☐ 509	Melido Perez	.07	.03	.01
☐ 510	Jerry Reuss	.04	.02	.00
☐ 511	Mark Salas	.04	.02	.00
☐ 512	Bobby Thigpen UER	.10	.04	.01
	('86 ERA 4.69,			
	should be 4.68)			
☐ 513	Mike Woodard	.04	.02	.00
☐ 514	Bob Brower	.04	.02	.00
☐ 515	Steve Buechele	.04	.02	.00
☐ 516	Jose Cecena	.07	.03	.01
☐ 517	Cecil Espy	.07	.03	.01
☐ 518	Scott Fletcher	.04	.02	.00
☐ 519	Cecilio Guante	.04	.02	.00
	('87 Yankee stats			
	are off-centered)			
☐ 520	Jose Guzman	.04	.02	.00
☐ 521	Ray Hayward	.07	.03	.01
☐ 522	Charlie Hough	.04	.02	.00
☐ 523	Pete Incaviglia	.10	.04	.01
☐ 524	Mike Jeffcoat	.04	.02	.00
☐ 525	Paul Kilgus	.04	.02	.00
☐ 526	Chad Kreuter	.07	.03	.01
☐ 527	Jeff Kunkel	.04	.02	.00
☐ 528	Oddibe McDowell	.04	.02	.00
☐ 529	Pete O'Brien	.04	.02	.00
☐ 530	Geno Petralli	.04	.02	.00
☐ 531	Jeff Russell	.04	.02	.00
☐ 532	Ruben Sierra	.30	.12	.03
☐ 533	Mike Stanley	.04	.02	.00
☐ 534A	Ed VandeBerg ERR	3.00	1.25	.30
	(Throws Lef)			
☐ 534B	Ed VandeBerg COR	.07	.03	.01
☐ 535	Curtis Wilkerson ERR	.04	.02	.00
	(pitcher headings			
	at bottom)			
☐ 536	Mitch Williams	.04	.02	.00
☐ 537	Bobby Witt UER	.07	.03	.01
	('85 ERA .643,			
	should be 6.43)			
☐ 538	Steve Balboni	.04	.02	.00
☐ 539	Scott Bankhead	.07	.03	.01
☐ 540	Scott Bradley	.04	.02	.00
☐ 541	Mickey Brantley	.04	.02	.00
☐ 542	Jay Buhner	.17	.07	.01
☐ 543	Mike Campbell	.04	.02	.00
☐ 544	Darnell Coles	.04	.02	.00
☐ 545	Henry Cotto	.04	.02	.00
☐ 546	Alvin Davis	.07	.03	.01
☐ 547	Mario Diaz	.04	.02	.00
☐ 548	Ken Griffey Jr.	9.00	4.00	.90
☐ 549	Erik Hanson	.65	.25	.06
☐ 550	Mike Jackson UER	.04	.02	.00
	(Lifetime ERA 3.345,			
	should be 3.45)			
☐ 551	Mark Langston	.10	.04	.01

☐ 552 Edgar Martinez	.17	.07	.01
☐ 553 Bill McGuire	.04	.02	.00
☐ 554 Mike Moore	.07	.03	.01
☐ 555 Jim Presley	.04	.02	.00
☐ 556 Rey Quinones	.04	.02	.00
☐ 557 Jerry Reed	.04	.02	.00
☐ 558 Harold Reynolds	.07	.03	.01
☐ 559 Mike Schooler	.15	.06	.01
☐ 560 Bill Swift	.07	.03	.01
☐ 561 Dave Valle	.04	.02	.00
☐ 562 Steve Bedrosian	.07	.03	.01
☐ 563 Phil Bradley	.04	.02	.00
☐ 564 Don Carman	.04	.02	.00
☐ 565 Bob Dernier	.04	.02	.00
☐ 566 Marvin Freeman	.04	.02	.00
☐ 567 Todd Frohwirth	.04	.02	.00
☐ 568 Greg Gross	.04	.02	.00
☐ 569 Kevin Gross	.04	.02	.00
☐ 570 Greg Harris	.04	.02	.00
☐ 571 Von Hayes	.07	.03	.01
☐ 572 Chris James	.04	.02	.00
☐ 573 Steve Jeltz	.04	.02	.00
☐ 574 Ron Jones UER	.07	.03	.01
(Led IL in '88 with 85, should be 75)			
☐ 575 Ricky Jordan	.15	.06	.01
☐ 576 Mike Maddux	.04	.02	.00
☐ 577 David Palmer	.04	.02	.00
☐ 578 Lance Parrish	.07	.03	.01
☐ 579 Shane Rawley	.04	.02	.00
☐ 580 Bruce Ruffin	.04	.02	.00
☐ 581 Juan Samuel	.07	.03	.01
☐ 582 Mike Schmidt	.40	.16	.04
☐ 583 Kent Tekulve	.04	.02	.00
☐ 584 Milt Thompson UER	.04	.02	.00
(19 hits in '88, should be 109)			
☐ 585 Jose Alvarez	.07	.03	.01
☐ 586 Paul Assenmacher	.04	.02	.00
☐ 587 Bruce Benedict	.04	.02	.00
☐ 588 Jeff Blauser	.04	.02	.00
☐ 589 Terry Blocker	.07	.03	.01
☐ 590 Ron Gant	.50	.20	.05
☐ 591 Tom Glavine	.40	.16	.04
☐ 592 Tommy Gregg	.07	.03	.01
☐ 593 Albert Hall	.04	.02	.00
☐ 594 Dion James	.04	.02	.00
☐ 595 Rick Mahler	.04	.02	.00
☐ 596 Dale Murphy	.15	.06	.01
☐ 597 Gerald Perry	.04	.02	.00
☐ 598 Charlie Puleo	.04	.02	.00
☐ 599 Ted Simmons	.07	.03	.01
☐ 600 Pete Smith	.07	.03	.01
☐ 601 Zane Smith	.07	.03	.01
☐ 602 John Smoltz	.75	.30	.07
☐ 603 Bruce Sutter	.07	.03	.01
☐ 604 Andres Thomas	.04	.02	.00
☐ 605 Ozzie Virgil	.04	.02	.00
☐ 606 Brady Anderson	.07	.03	.01
☐ 607 Jeff Ballard	.04	.02	.00
☐ 608 Jose Bautista	.07	.03	.01
☐ 609 Ken Gerhart	.04	.02	.00
☐ 610 Terry Kennedy	.04	.02	.00
☐ 611 Eddie Murray	.15	.06	.01
☐ 612 Carl Nichols UER	.07	.03	.01
(before All-Star Break batting 1.88)			
☐ 613 Tom Niedenfuer	.04	.02	.00
☐ 614 Joe Orsulak	.04	.02	.00
☐ 615 Oswald Peraza UER	.10	.04	.01
(shown as Oswaldo)			
☐ 616A Bill Ripken ERR	9.00	4.00	.90
(Rick Face written on knob of bat)			
☐ 616B Bill Ripken	30.00	13.50	4.50
(bat knob whited out)			
☐ 616C Bill Ripken	9.00	4.00	.90
(words on bat knob scribbled out)			
☐ 616D Bill Ripken DP	.12	.05	.01
(black box covering bat knob)			
☐ 617 Cal Ripken	.50	.20	.05
☐ 618 Dave Schmidt	.04	.02	.00
☐ 619 Rick Schu	.04	.02	.00
☐ 620 Larry Sheets	.04	.02	.00
☐ 621 Doug Sisk	.04	.02	.00
☐ 622 Pete Stanicek	.04	.02	.00
☐ 623 Mickey Tettleton	.07	.03	.01
☐ 624 Jay Tibbs	.04	.02	.00
☐ 625 Jim Traber	.04	.02	.00
☐ 626 Mark Williamson	.04	.02	.00
☐ 627 Craig Worthington	.07	.03	.01
☐ 628 Speed/Power	.25	.10	.02
Jose Canseco			
☐ 629 Pitcher Perfect	.07	.03	.01
Tom Browning			
☐ 630 Like Father/Like Sons	.30	.12	.03
Roberto Alomar			
Sandy Alomar Jr.			
(names on card listed in wrong order) UER			
☐ 631 NL All Stars UER	.15	.06	.01
Will Clark			
Rafael Palmeiro			
(Gallaraga, sic; Clark 3 consecutive 100 RBI seasons; third with 102 RBI's)			
☐ 632 Homeruns - Coast	.25	.10	.02
to Coast UER			
Darryl Strawberry			
Will Clark (Homeruns should be two words)			
☐ 633 Hot Corners - Hot	.15	.06	.01
Hitters UER			
Wade Boggs			
Carney Lansford			
(Boggs hit .366 in '86, should be '88)			
☐ 634 Triple A's	.20	.08	.02
Jose Canseco			
Terry Steinbach			
Mark McGwire			
☐ 635 Dual Heat	.10	.04	.01
Mark Davis			
Dwight Gooden			
☐ 636 NL Pitching Power UER	.07	.03	.01
Danny Jackson			
David Cone			
(Hersheiser, sic)			
☐ 637 Cannon Arms UER	.15	.06	.01
Chris Sabo			
Bobby Bonilla			
(Bobby Bonds, sic)			
☐ 638 Double Trouble UER	.07	.03	.01
Andres Galarraga			
(misspelled Gallaraga on card back)			
Gerald Perry			
☐ 639 Power Center	.15	.06	.01
Kirby Puckett			
Eric Davis			
☐ 640 Steve Wilson and	.10	.04	.01
Cameron Drew			
☐ 641 Kevin Brown and	.50	.20	.05
Kevin Reimer			
☐ 642 Brad Pounders and	.25	.10	.02
Jerald Clark			
☐ 643 Mike Capel and	.12	.05	.01
Drew Hall			
☐ 644 Joe Girardi and	.12	.05	.01
Rolando Roomes			
☐ 645 Lenny Harris and	.20	.08	.02
Marty Brown			
☐ 646 Luis De Los Santos	.10	.04	.01
and Jim Campbell			
☐ 647 Randy Kramer and	.10	.04	.01
Miguel Garcia			
☐ 648 Torey Lovullo and	.10	.04	.01
Robert Palacios			
☐ 649 Jim Corsi and	.17	.07	.01
Bob Milacki			
☐ 650 Grady Hall and	.10	.04	.01
Mike Rochford			
☐ 651 Terry Taylor and	.10	.04	.01
Vance Lovelace			
☐ 652 Ken Hill and	.25	.10	.02
Dennis Cook			
☐ 653 Scott Service and	.10	.04	.01
Shane Turner			
☐ 654 CL: Oakland/Mets	.08	.01	.00
Dodgers/Red Sox			
(10 Hendersor; 68 Jess Orosco)			
☐ 655A CL: Twins/Tigers ERR	.08	.01	.00
Reds/Brewers			
(179 Boslo and Twins/Tigers positions listed)			
☐ 655B CL: Twins/Tigers COR	.08	.01	.00
Reds/Brewers			
(179 Boslo but Twins/Tigers positions not listed)			

		MINT	EXC	G-VG
☐ 656	CL: Pirates/Blue Jays .... Yankees/Royals (225 Jess Barfield)	.08	.01	.00
☐ 657	CL: Padres/Giants .... Astros/Expos (367/368 wrong)	.08	.01	.00
☐ 658	CL: Indians/Cubs .... Cardinals/Angels (449 Deleon)	.08	.01	.00
☐ 659	CL: White Sox/Rangers .... Mariners/Phillies	.08	.01	.00
☐ 660	CL: Braves/Orioles .... Specials/Checklists (632 hyphenated diff- erently and 650 Hall; 595 Rich Mahler; 619 Rich Schu)	.08	.01	.00

1989 Fleer Wax Box Cards

The cards in this 28-card set measure the standard 2 1/2" by 3 1/2". Cards have essentially the same design as the 1989 Fleer regular issue set. The cards were printed on the bottoms of the regular issue wax pack boxes. These 28 cards (C1 to C28) are considered a separate set in their own right and are not typically included in a complete set of the regular issue 1989 Fleer cards. The value of the panel uncut is slightly greater, perhaps by 25 percent greater, than the value of the individual cards cut up carefully. The wax box cards are further distinguished by the gray card stock used.

		MINT	EXC	G-VG
COMPLETE SET (28)		8.00	3.50	.80
COMMON PLAYER (C1-C28)		.10	.04	.01
☐ C1	Mets Logo	.10	.04	.01
☐ C2	Wade Boggs	.75	.30	.07
☐ C3	George Brett	.60	.25	.06
☐ C4	Jose Canseco UER .... ('88 strikeouts 121 and career strike- outs 49, should be 128 and 491)	1.25	.50	.12
☐ C5	A's Logo	.10	.04	.01
☐ C6	Will Clark	1.25	.50	.12
☐ C7	David Cone	.35	.15	.03
☐ C8	Andres Galarraga UER .... (career average .289 should be .269)	.25	.10	.02
☐ C9	Dodgers Logo	.10	.04	.01
☐ C10	Kirk Gibson	.25	.10	.02
☐ C11	Mike Greenwell	.50	.20	.05
☐ C12	Tony Gwynn	.60	.25	.06
☐ C13	Tigers Logo	.10	.04	.01
☐ C14	Orel Hershiser	.35	.15	.03
☐ C15	Danny Jackson	.15	.06	.01
☐ C16	Wally Joyner	.35	.15	.03
☐ C17	Red Sox Logo	.10	.04	.01
☐ C18	Yankees Logo	.10	.04	.01
☐ C19	Fred McGriff UER .... career BA of .289 should be .269)	.40	.16	.04
☐ C20	Kirby Puckett	.75	.30	.07
☐ C21	Chris Sabo	.50	.20	.05

		MINT	EXC	G-VG
☐ C22	Kevin Seitzer	.25	.10	.02
☐ C23	Pirates Logo	.10	.04	.01
☐ C24	Astros Logo	.10	.04	.01
☐ C25	Darryl Strawberry	.75	.30	.07
☐ C26	Alan Trammell	.30	.12	.03
☐ C27	Andy Van Slyke	.25	.10	.02
☐ C28	Frank Viola	.25	.10	.02

1989 Fleer All-Star Inserts

This twelve-card subset was randomly inserted in Fleer wax packs (15 regular cards) and Fleer value packs (36 regular cards). The players selected are the 1989 Fleer Major League All-Star team. One player has been selected for each position along with a DH and three pitchers. The cards are attractively designed and are standard size, 2 1/2" by 3 1/2". The cards are numbered on the backs and feature a distinctive green background on the card fronts.

		MINT	EXC	G-VG
COMPLETE SET (12)		12.00	5.25	1.50
COMMON PLAYER (1-12)		.35	.15	.03
☐ 1	Bobby Bonilla .... Third Baseman	1.25	.50	.12
☐ 2	Jose Canseco .... Outfielder	3.00	1.25	.30
☐ 3	Will Clark .... First Baseman	3.00	1.25	.30
☐ 4	Dennis Eckersley .... Relief Pitcher	.75	.30	.07
☐ 5	Julio Franco .... Second Baseman	.75	.30	.07
☐ 6	Mike Greenwell .... Outfielder	1.25	.50	.12
☐ 7	Orel Hershiser .... Righthand Pitcher	1.00	.40	.10
☐ 8	Paul Molitor .... Designated Hitter	.60	.25	.06
☐ 9	Mike Scioscia .... Catcher	.35	.15	.03
☐ 10	Darryl Strawberry .... Outfielder	1.50	.60	.15
☐ 11	Alan Trammell .... Shortstop	.75	.30	.07
☐ 12	Frank Viola .... Lefthand Pitcher	.60	.25	.06

1989 Fleer For The Record

This six-card subset was distributed randomly (as an insert) in Fleer rack packs. These cards are standard size, 2 1/2" by 3 1/2" and are quite attractive. The set is subtitled "For The Record" and commemorates record-breaking events for those players from the previous season. The cards are numbered on the backs. The card backs are printed in red, black, and gray on white card stock.

	MINT	EXC	G-VG
COMPLETE SET (6)	5.00	2.25	.50
COMMON PLAYER (1-6)	.60	.25	.06

		MINT	EXC	G-VG
☐ 1	Wade Boggs	1.25	.50	.12
	Boston Red Sox			
☐ 2	Roger Clemens	1.50	.60	.15
	Boston Red Sox			
☐ 3	Andres Galarraga	.60	.25	.06
	Montreal Expos			
☐ 4	Kirk Gibson	1.00	.40	.10
	Los Angeles Dodgers			
☐ 5	Greg Maddux	.60	.25	.06
	Chicago Cubs			
☐ 6	Don Mattingly UER	1.25	.50	.12
	New York Yankees			
	(won batting title			
	'83, should say '84)			

1989 Fleer Baseball All-Stars

The 1989 Fleer Baseball All-Stars set contains 44 standard-size (2 1/2" by 3 1/2") cards. The fronts are yellowish beige with salmon pinstripes; the vertically oriented backs are red, white and pink and feature career stats. The card numbering of this set is ordered alphabetically by player's name. The cards were distributed through Ben Franklin stores as a boxed set.

	MINT	EXC	G-VG
COMPLETE SET (44)	5.00	2.25	.50
COMMON PLAYER (1-44)	.10	.04	.01

☐ 1	Doyle Alexander	.10	.04	.01
☐ 2	George Bell	.15	.06	.01
☐ 3	Wade Boggs	.60	.25	.06
☐ 4	Bobby Bonilla	.40	.16	.04
☐ 5	Jose Canseco	.90	.40	.09
☐ 6	Will Clark	.90	.40	.09
☐ 7	Roger Clemens	.75	.30	.07
☐ 8	Vince Coleman	.25	.10	.02
☐ 9	David Cone	.20	.08	.02

☐ 10	Mark Davis	.10	.04	.01
☐ 11	Andre Dawson	.25	.10	.02
☐ 12	Dennis Eckersley	.20	.08	.02
☐ 13	Andres Galarraga	.20	.08	.02
☐ 14	Kirk Gibson	.20	.08	.02
☐ 15	Dwight Gooden	.40	.16	.04
☐ 16	Mike Greenwell	.40	.16	.04
☐ 17	Mark Gubicza	.15	.06	.01
☐ 18	Ozzie Guillen	.15	.06	.01
☐ 19	Tony Gwynn	.45	.18	.04
☐ 20	Rickey Henderson	.75	.30	.07
☐ 21	Orel Hershiser	.25	.10	.02
☐ 22	Danny Jackson	.10	.04	.01
☐ 23	Doug Jones	.10	.04	.01
☐ 24	Ricky Jordan	.15	.06	.01
☐ 25	Bob Knepper	.10	.04	.01
☐ 26	Barry Larkin	.20	.08	.02
☐ 27	Vance Law	.10	.04	.01
☐ 28	Don Mattingly	.75	.30	.07
☐ 29	Mark McGwire	.60	.25	.06
☐ 30	Paul Molitor	.20	.08	.02
☐ 31	Gerald Perry	.10	.04	.01
☐ 32	Kirby Puckett	.50	.20	.05
☐ 33	Johnny Ray	.10	.04	.01
☐ 34	Harold Reynolds	.10	.04	.01
☐ 35	Cal Ripken	.75	.30	.07
☐ 36	Don Robinson	.10	.04	.01
☐ 37	Ruben Sierra	.50	.20	.05
☐ 38	Dave Smith	.10	.04	.01
☐ 39	Darryl Strawberry	.60	.25	.06
☐ 40	Dave Stieb	.15	.06	.01
☐ 41	Alan Trammell	.20	.08	.02
☐ 42	Andy Van Slyke	.15	.06	.01
☐ 43	Frank Viola	.20	.08	.02
☐ 44	Dave Winfield	.25	.10	.02

1989 Fleer Baseball MVP's

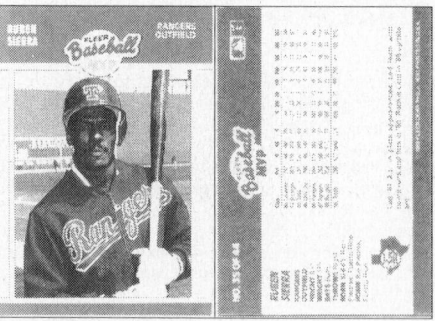

The 1989 Fleer Baseball MVP's set contains 44 standard-size (2 1/2" by 3 1/2") cards. The fronts and backs are green and yellow. The horizontally oriented backs feature career stats. The card numbering of this set is ordered alphabetically by player's name. The cards were distributed through Toys 'R' Us stores as a boxed set.

	MINT	EXC	G-VG
COMPLETE SET (44)	5.00	2.25	.50
COMMON PLAYER (1-44)	.10	.04	.01

☐ 1	Steve Bedrosian	.10	.04	.01
☐ 2	George Bell	.20	.08	.02
☐ 3	Wade Boggs	.60	.25	.06
☐ 4	George Brett	.40	.16	.04
☐ 5	Hubie Brooks	.15	.06	.01
☐ 6	Jose Canseco	.90	.40	.09
☐ 7	Will Clark	.90	.40	.09
☐ 8	Roger Clemens	.75	.30	.07
☐ 9	Eric Davis	.45	.18	.04
☐ 10	Glenn Davis	.20	.08	.02
☐ 11	Andre Dawson	.25	.10	.02
☐ 12	Andres Galarraga	.20	.08	.02
☐ 13	Kirk Gibson	.20	.08	.02
☐ 14	Dwight Gooden	.35	.15	.03
☐ 15	Mark Grace	.90	.40	.09
☐ 16	Mike Greenwell	.40	.16	.04

		MINT	EXC	G-VG
☐ 17	Tony Gwynn	.45	.18	.04
☐ 18	Bryan Harvey	.30	.12	.03
☐ 19	Orel Hershiser	.25	.10	.02
☐ 20	Ted Higuera	.15	.06	.01
☐ 21	Danny Jackson	.10	.04	.01
☐ 22	Mike Jackson	.10	.04	.01
☐ 23	Doug Jones	.10	.04	.01
☐ 24	Greg Maddux	.15	.06	.01
☐ 25	Mike Marshall	.10	.04	.01
☐ 26	Don Mattingly	.75	.30	.07
☐ 27	Fred McGriff	.30	.12	.03
☐ 28	Mark McGwire	.60	.25	.06
☐ 29	Kevin McReynolds	.15	.06	.01
☐ 30	Jack Morris	.20	.08	.02
☐ 31	Gerald Perry	.10	.04	.01
☐ 32	Kirby Puckett	.50	.20	.05
☐ 33	Chris Sabo	.45	.18	.04
☐ 34	Mike Scott	.15	.06	.01
☐ 35	Ruben Sierra	.50	.20	.05
☐ 36	Darryl Strawberry	.60	.25	.06
☐ 37	Danny Tartabull	.30	.12	.03
☐ 38	Bobby Thigpen	.20	.08	.02
☐ 39	Alan Trammell	.25	.10	.02
☐ 40	Andy Van Slyke	.15	.06	.01
☐ 41	Frank Viola	.20	.08	.02
☐ 42	Walt Weiss	.15	.06	.01
☐ 43	Dave Winfield	.25	.10	.02
☐ 44	Todd Worrell	.10	.04	.01

		MINT	EXC	G-VG
☐ 24	Orel Hershiser	.25	.10	.02
☐ 25	Danny Jackson	.10	.04	.01
☐ 26	Gregg Jefferies	.75	.30	.07
☐ 27	Ricky Jordan	.15	.06	.01
☐ 28	Wally Joyner	.20	.08	.02
☐ 29	Mark Langston	.15	.06	.01
☐ 30	Tim Leary	.10	.04	.01
☐ 31	Don Mattingly	.75	.30	.07
☐ 32	Mark McGwire	.60	.25	.06
☐ 33	Dale Murphy	.35	.15	.03
☐ 34	Kirby Puckett	.50	.20	.05
☐ 35	Chris Sabo	.45	.18	.04
☐ 36	Kevin Seitzer	.15	.06	.01
☐ 37	Ruben Sierra	.50	.20	.05
☐ 38	Ozzie Smith	.20	.08	.02
☐ 39	Dave Stewart	.15	.06	.01
☐ 40	Darryl Strawberry	.60	.25	.06
☐ 41	Alan Trammell	.25	.10	.02
☐ 42	Frank Viola	.20	.08	.02
☐ 43	Dave Winfield	.25	.10	.02
☐ 44	Robin Yount	.40	.16	.04

1989 Fleer Heroes of Baseball

Cal Ripken, Jr.

1989 Fleer Exciting Stars

The 1989 Fleer Exciting Stars set contains 44 standard-size (2 1/2" by 3 1/2") cards. The fronts have baby blue borders; the backs are pink and blue. The vertically oriented backs feature career stats. The card numbering of this set is ordered alphabetically by player's name. The cards were distributed as a boxed set.

The 1989 Fleer Heroes of Baseball set contains 44 standard-size (2 1/2" by 3 1/2") cards. The fronts and backs are red, white and blue. The vertically oriented backs feature career stats. The card numbering of this set is ordered alphabetically by player's name. The cards were distributed through Woolworth stores as a boxed set.

		MINT	EXC	G-VG
COMPLETE SET (44)		5.00	2.25	.50
COMMON PLAYER (1-44)		.10	.04	.01
☐ 1	Harold Baines	.15	.06	.01
☐ 2	Wade Boggs	.60	.25	.06
☐ 3	Jose Canseco	.90	.40	.09
☐ 4	Joe Carter	.25	.10	.02
☐ 5	Will Clark	.90	.40	.09
☐ 6	Roger Clemens	.75	.30	.07
☐ 7	Vince Coleman	.25	.10	.02
☐ 8	David Cone	.25	.10	.02
☐ 9	Eric Davis	.40	.16	.04
☐ 10	Glenn Davis	.20	.08	.02
☐ 11	Andre Dawson	.25	.10	.02
☐ 12	Dwight Evans	.15	.06	.01
☐ 13	Andres Galarraga	.20	.08	.02
☐ 14	Kirk Gibson	.20	.08	.02
☐ 15	Dwight Gooden	.35	.15	.03
☐ 16	Jim Gott	.10	.04	.01
☐ 17	Mark Grace	.75	.30	.07
☐ 18	Mike Greenwell	.40	.16	.04
☐ 19	Mark Gubicza	.15	.06	.01
☐ 20	Tony Gwynn	.45	.18	.04
☐ 21	Rickey Henderson	.75	.30	.07
☐ 22	Tom Henke	.10	.04	.01
☐ 23	Mike Henneman	.10	.04	.01

		MINT	EXC	G-VG
COMPLETE SET (44)		5.00	2.25	.50
COMMON PLAYER (1-44)		.10	.04	.01
☐ 1	George Bell	.20	.08	.02
☐ 2	Wade Boggs	.60	.25	.06
☐ 3	Barry Bonds	.60	.25	.06
☐ 4	Tom Brunansky	.15	.06	.01
☐ 5	Jose Canseco	.90	.40	.09
☐ 6	Joe Carter	.25	.10	.02
☐ 7	Will Clark	.90	.40	.09
☐ 8	Roger Clemens	.75	.30	.07
☐ 9	David Cone	.25	.10	.02
☐ 10	Eric Davis	.45	.18	.04
☐ 11	Glenn Davis	.20	.08	.02
☐ 12	Andre Dawson	.25	.10	.02
☐ 13	Dennis Eckersley	.20	.08	.02
☐ 14	John Franco	.10	.04	.01
☐ 15	Gary Gaetti	.15	.06	.01
☐ 16	Andres Galarraga	.20	.08	.02
☐ 17	Kirk Gibson	.20	.08	.02
☐ 18	Dwight Gooden	.35	.15	.03
☐ 19	Mike Greenwell	.40	.16	.04
☐ 20	Tony Gwynn	.45	.18	.04
☐ 21	Bryan Harvey	.25	.10	.02
☐ 22	Orel Hershiser	.25	.10	.02
☐ 23	Ted Higuera	.15	.06	.01
☐ 24	Danny Jackson	.10	.04	.01
☐ 25	Ricky Jordan	.15	.06	.01
☐ 26	Don Mattingly	.75	.30	.07
☐ 27	Fred McGriff	.30	.12	.03
☐ 28	Mark McGwire	.60	.25	.06
☐ 29	Kevin McReynolds	.15	.06	.01
☐ 30	Gerald Perry	.10	.04	.01

			MINT	EXC	G-VG
☐	31	Kirby Puckett	.50	.20	.05
☐	32	Johnny Ray	.10	.04	.01
☐	33	Harold Reynolds	.10	.04	.01
☐	34	Cal Ripken	.75	.30	.07
☐	35	Ryne Sandberg	.75	.30	.07
☐	36	Kevin Seitzer	.15	.06	.01
☐	37	Ruben Sierra	.50	.20	.05
☐	38	Darryl Strawberry	.60	.25	.06
☐	39	Bobby Thigpen	.20	.08	.02
☐	40	Alan Trammell	.25	.10	.02
☐	41	Andy Van Slyke	.15	.06	.01
☐	42	Frank Viola	.20	.08	.02
☐	43	Dave Winfield	.25	.10	.02
☐	44	Robin Yount	.40	.16	.04

			MINT	EXC	G-VG
☐	38	Greg Swindell	.15	.06	.01
☐	39	Bobby Thigpen	.20	.08	.02
☐	40	Alan Trammell	.25	.10	.02
☐	41	Andy Van Slyke	.15	.06	.01
☐	42	Frank Viola	.20	.08	.02
☐	43	Dave Winfield	.25	.10	.02
☐	44	Robin Yount	.40	.16	.04

1989 Fleer Superstars

The 1989 Fleer Superstars set contains 44 standard-size (2 1/2" by 3 1/2") cards. The fronts are red and beige; the horizontally oriented backs are yellow, and feature career stats. The card numbering of this set is ordered alphabetically by player's name. The cards were distributed as a boxed set. The back panel of the box contains the complete set checklist.

1989 Fleer League Leaders

Will Clark

The 1989 Fleer League Leaders set contains 44 standard-size (2 1/2" by 3 1/2") cards. The fronts are red and yellow; the horizontally oriented backs are light blue and red, and feature career stats. The card numbering of this set is ordered alphabetically by player's name. The cards were distributed through Woolworth stores as a boxed set.

			MINT	EXC	G-VG
	COMPLETE SET (44)		5.00	2.25	.50
	COMMON PLAYER (1-44)		.10	.04	.01
☐	1	Allan Anderson	.10	.04	.01
☐	2	Wade Boggs	.60	.25	.06
☐	3	Jose Canseco	.90	.40	.09
☐	4	Will Clark	.90	.40	.09
☐	5	Roger Clemens	.75	.30	.07
☐	6	Vince Coleman	.25	.10	.02
☐	7	David Cone	.20	.08	.02
☐	8	Kal Daniels	.15	.06	.01
☐	9	Chili Davis	.10	.04	.01
☐	10	Eric Davis	.45	.18	.04
☐	11	Glenn Davis	.20	.08	.02
☐	12	Andre Dawson	.25	.10	.02
☐	13	John Franco	.10	.04	.01
☐	14	Andres Galarraga	.20	.08	.02
☐	15	Kirk Gibson	.20	.08	.02
☐	16	Dwight Gooden	.35	.15	.03
☐	17	Mark Grace	.75	.30	.07
☐	18	Mike Greenwell	.35	.15	.03
☐	19	Tony Gwynn	.40	.16	.04
☐	20	Orel Hershiser	.20	.08	.02
☐	21	Pete Incaviglia	.15	.06	.01
☐	22	Danny Jackson	.10	.04	.01
☐	23	Gregg Jefferies	.75	.30	.07
☐	24	Joe Magrane	.15	.06	.01
☐	25	Don Mattingly	.75	.30	.07
☐	26	Fred McGriff	.30	.12	.03
☐	27	Mark McGwire	.60	.25	.06
☐	28	Dale Murphy	.35	.15	.03
☐	29	Dan Plesac	.10	.04	.01
☐	30	Kirby Puckett	.50	.20	.05
☐	31	Harold Reynolds	.10	.04	.01
☐	32	Cal Ripken	.75	.30	.07
☐	33	Jeff Robinson	.10	.04	.01
☐	34	Mike Scott	.15	.06	.01
☐	35	Ozzie Smith	.25	.10	.02
☐	36	Dave Stewart	.15	.06	.01
☐	37	Darryl Strawberry	.60	.25	.06

			MINT	EXC	G-VG
	COMPLETE SET (44)		5.00	2.25	.50
	COMMON PLAYER (1-44)		.10	.04	.01
☐	1	Roberto Alomar	.75	.30	.07
☐	2	Harold Baines	.15	.06	.01
☐	3	Tim Belcher	.15	.06	.01
☐	4	Wade Boggs	.60	.25	.06
☐	5	George Brett	.40	.16	.04
☐	6	Jose Canseco	.90	.40	.09
☐	7	Gary Carter	.20	.08	.02
☐	8	Will Clark	.90	.40	.09
☐	9	Roger Clemens	.75	.30	.07
☐	10	Kal Daniels UER (reverse negative photo on front)	.15	.06	.01
☐	11	Eric Davis	.45	.18	.04
☐	12	Andre Dawson	.25	.10	.02
☐	13	Tony Fernandez	.15	.06	.01
☐	14	Scott Fletcher	.10	.04	.01
☐	15	Andres Galarraga	.20	.08	.02
☐	16	Kirk Gibson	.20	.08	.02
☐	17	Dwight Gooden	.35	.15	.03
☐	18	Jim Gott	.10	.04	.01
☐	19	Mark Grace	.75	.30	.07
☐	20	Mike Greenwell	.35	.15	.03
☐	21	Tony Gwynn	.45	.18	.04
☐	22	Rickey Henderson	.75	.30	.07
☐	23	Orel Hershiser	.20	.08	.02
☐	24	Ted Higuera	.15	.06	.01
☐	25	Gregg Jefferies	.75	.30	.07
☐	26	Wally Joyner	.20	.08	.02
☐	27	Mark Langston	.15	.06	.01
☐	28	Greg Maddux	.15	.06	.01
☐	29	Don Mattingly	.75	.30	.07
☐	30	Fred McGriff	.30	.12	.03
☐	31	Mark McGwire	.60	.25	.06
☐	32	Dan Plesac	.10	.04	.01
☐	33	Kirby Puckett	.50	.20	.05
☐	34	Jeff Reardon	.10	.04	.01
☐	35	Chris Sabo	.45	.18	.04
☐	36	Mike Schmidt	.75	.30	.07
☐	37	Mike Scott	.15	.06	.01
☐	38	Cory Snyder	.15	.06	.01
☐	39	Darryl Strawberry	.60	.25	.06
☐	40	Alan Trammell	.25	.10	.02
☐	41	Frank Viola	.20	.08	.02
☐	42	Walt Weiss	.15	.06	.01
☐	43	Dave Winfield	.25	.10	.02

□ 44 Todd Worrell UER .... .10 .04 .01
   (statistical headings
   on back for hitter)

1989 Fleer World Series

This 12-card set of 2 1/2" by 3 1/2" cards features highlights of the previous year's World Series between the Dodgers and the Athletics. The sets were packaged as a complete set insert with the collated sets (of the 1989 Fleer regular issue) which were sold by Fleer directly to hobby card dealers; they were not available in the general retail candy store outlets.

	MINT	EXC	G-VG
COMPLETE SET (12)	3.00	1.25	.30
COMMON PLAYER (1-12)	.25	.10	.02
□ 1 Mickey Hatcher .... Dodgers' Secret Weapon	.25	.10	.02
□ 2 Tim Belcher .... Rookie Starts Series	.35	.15	.03
□ 3 Jose Canseco .... Canseco Slams L.A.	.90	.40	.09
□ 4 Mike Scioscia .... Dramatic Comeback	.25	.10	.02
□ 5 Kirk Gibson .... Gibson Steals The Show	.50	.20	.05
□ 6 Orel Hershiser .... Bulldog	.50	.20	.05
□ 7 Mike Marshall .... One Swing, Three RBI's	.25	.10	.02
□ 8 Mark McGwire .... Game-Winning Homer	.50	.20	.05
□ 9 Steve Sax UER .... Sax's Speed Wins Game 4 (actually stole 42 bases in '88)	.35	.15	.03
□ 10 Walt Weiss .... Series Caps Award-Winning Year	.25	.10	.02
□ 11 Orel Hershiser .... Series MVP Uses Shutout Magic	.50	.20	.05
□ 12 Dodger Blue .... World Champs	.25	.10	.02

1989 Fleer Update

The 1989 Fleer Update set contains 132 standard-size (2 1/2" by 3 1/2") cards. The fronts are gray with white pinstripes. The vertically-oriented backs show lifetime stats and performance "Before and After the All-Star Break." The set does not include a card of 1989 AL Rookie of the Year Gregg Olson, but contains the first major card of Greg Vaughn and special cards for Nolan Ryan's 5,000th strikeout and Mike Schmidt's retirement. Other

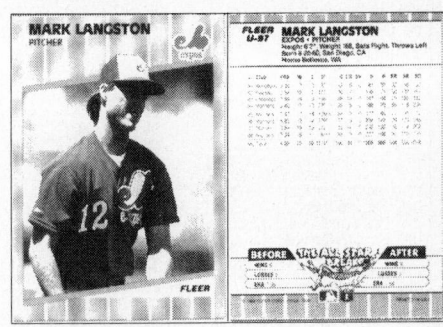

key rookies in this set are Joey (Albert) Belle, Junior Felix, Robin Ventura, Jerome Walton and Todd Zeile. Fleer did NOT produce a limited (tin) edition version of this set with glossy coating.

	MINT	EXC	G-VG
COMPLETE SET (132)	12.00	5.25	1.50
COMMON PLAYER (1-132)	.05	.02	.00
□ U1 Phil Bradley	.10	.03	.01
□ U2 Mike Devereaux	.10	.04	.01
□ U3 Steve Finley	.35	.15	.03
□ U4 Kevin Hickey	.05	.02	.00
□ U5 Brian Holton	.08	.03	.01
□ U6 Bob Milacki	.12	.05	.01
□ U7 Randy Milligan	.08	.03	.01
□ U8 John Dopson	.08	.03	.01
□ U9 Nick Esasky	.08	.03	.01
□ U10 Rob Murphy	.05	.02	.00
□ U11 Jim Abbott	1.25	.50	.12
□ U12 Bert Blyleven	.12	.05	.01
□ U13 Jeff Manto	.15	.06	.01
□ U14 Bob McClure	.05	.02	.00
□ U15 Lance Parrish	.12	.05	.01
□ U16 Lee Stevens	.65	.25	.06
□ U17 Claudell Washington	.05	.02	.00
□ U18 Mark Davis	.10	.04	.01
□ U19 Eric King	.08	.03	.01
□ U20 Ron Kittle	.08	.03	.01
□ U21 Matt Merullo	.10	.04	.01
□ U22 Steve Rosenberg	.08	.03	.01
□ U23 Robin Ventura	2.25	.90	.22
□ U24 Keith Atherton	.05	.02	.00
□ U25 Joey Belle	2.00	.80	.20
□ U26 Jerry Browne	.05	.02	.00
□ U27 Felix Fermin	.05	.02	.00
□ U28 Brad Komminsk	.05	.02	.00
□ U29 Pete O'Brien	.05	.02	.00
□ U30 Mike Brumley	.05	.02	.00
□ U31 Tracy Jones	.08	.03	.01
□ U32 Mike Schwabe	.08	.03	.01
□ U33 Gary Ward	.05	.02	.00
□ U34 Frank Williams	.05	.02	.00
□ U35 Kevin Appier	.50	.20	.05
□ U36 Bob Boone	.12	.05	.01
□ U37 Luis de los Santos	.10	.04	.01
□ U38 Jim Eisenreich	.10	.04	.01
□ U39 Jaime Navarro	.35	.15	.03
□ U40 Bill Spiers	.12	.05	.01
□ U41 Greg Vaughn	2.00	.80	.20
□ U42 Randy Veres	.08	.03	.01
□ U43 Wally Backman	.05	.02	.00
□ U44 Shane Rawley	.05	.02	.00
□ U45 Steve Balboni	.05	.02	.00
□ U46 Jesse Barfield	.10	.04	.01
□ U47 Alvaro Espinoza	.10	.04	.01
□ U48 Bob Geren	.08	.03	.01
□ U49 Mel Hall	.10	.04	.01
□ U50 Andy Hawkins	.05	.02	.00
□ U51 Hensley Meulens	.40	.16	.04
□ U52 Steve Sax	.12	.05	.01
□ U53 Deion Sanders	.60	.25	.06
□ U54 Rickey Henderson	.35	.15	.03
□ U55 Mike Moore	.12	.05	.01
□ U56 Tony Phillips	.08	.03	.01
□ U57 Greg Briley	.15	.06	.01
□ U58 Gene Harris	.10	.04	.01
□ U59 Randy Johnson	.12	.05	.01
□ U60 Jeffrey Leonard	.05	.02	.00
□ U61 Dennis Powell	.05	.02	.00
□ U62 Omar Vizquel	.08	.03	.01

☐ U63	Kevin Brown	.08	.03	.01
☐ U64	Julio Franco	.15	.06	.01
☐ U65	Jamie Moyer	.05	.02	.00
☐ U66	Rafael Palmeiro	.15	.06	.01
☐ U67	Nolan Ryan	1.50	.60	.15
☐ U68	Francisco Cabrera	.25	.10	.02
☐ U69	Junior Felix	.15	.06	.01
☐ U70	Al Leiter	.08	.03	.01
☐ U71	Alex Sanchez	.08	.03	.01
☐ U72	Geronimo Berroa	.05	.02	.00
☐ U73	Derek Lilliquist	.08	.03	.01
☐ U74	Lonnie Smith	.12	.05	.01
☐ U75	Jeff Treadway	.10	.04	.01
☐ U76	Paul Kilgus	.08	.03	.01
☐ U77	Lloyd McClendon	.08	.03	.01
☐ U78	Scott Sanderson	.08	.03	.01
☐ U79	Dwight Smith	.12	.05	.01
☐ U80	Jerome Walton	.40	.16	.04
☐ U81	Mitch Williams	.08	.03	.01
☐ U82	Steve Wilson	.08	.03	.01
☐ U83	Todd Benzinger	.08	.03	.01
☐ U84	Ken Griffey Sr.	.15	.06	.01
☐ U85	Rick Mahler	.05	.02	.00
☐ U86	Rolando Roomes	.08	.03	.01
☐ U87	Scott Scudder	.20	.08	.02
☐ U88	Jim Clancy	.05	.02	.00
☐ U89	Rick Rhoden	.05	.02	.00
☐ U90	Dan Schatzeder	.05	.02	.00
☐ U91	Mike Morgan	.08	.03	.01
☐ U92	Eddie Murray	.12	.05	.01
☐ U93	Willie Randolph	.10	.04	.01
☐ U94	Ray Searage	.05	.02	.00
☐ U95	Mike Aldrete	.05	.02	.00
☐ U96	Kevin Gross	.08	.03	.01
☐ U97	Mark Langston	.10	.04	.01
☐ U98	Spike Owen	.05	.02	.00
☐ U99	Zane Smith	.10	.04	.01
☐ U100	Don Aase	.05	.02	.00
☐ U101	Barry Lyons	.05	.02	.00
☐ U102	Juan Samuel	.10	.04	.01
☐ U103	Wally Whitehurst	.10	.04	.01
☐ U104	Dennis Cook	.08	.03	.01
☐ U105	Len Dykstra	.10	.04	.01
☐ U106	Charlie Hayes	.08	.03	.01
☐ U107	Tommy Herr	.08	.03	.01
☐ U108	Ken Howell	.08	.03	.01
☐ U109	John Kruk	.08	.03	.01
☐ U110	Roger McDowell	.08	.03	.01
☐ U111	Terry Mulholland	.10	.04	.01
☐ U112	Jeff Parrett	.05	.02	.00
☐ U113	Neal Heaton	.05	.02	.00
☐ U114	Jeff King	.10	.04	.01
☐ U115	Randy Kramer	.08	.03	.01
☐ U116	Bill Landrum	.08	.03	.01
☐ U117	Cris Carpenter	.08	.03	.01
☐ U118	Frank DiPino	.05	.02	.00
☐ U119	Ken Hill	.10	.04	.01
☐ U120	Dan Quisenberry	.10	.04	.01
☐ U121	Milt Thompson	.08	.03	.01
☐ U122	Todd Zeile	1.50	.60	.15
☐ U123	Jack Clark	.10	.04	.01
☐ U124	Bruce Hurst	.08	.03	.01
☐ U125	Mark Parent	.08	.03	.01
☐ U126	Bip Roberts	.12	.05	.01
☐ U127	Jeff Brantley UER	.20	.08	.02
	(photo actually			
	Joe Kmak)			
☐ U128	Terry Kennedy	.05	.02	.00
☐ U129	Mike LaCoss	.05	.02	.00
☐ U130	Greg Litton	.10	.04	.01
☐ U131	Mike Schmidt	.90	.40	.09
☐ U132	Checklist 1-132	.05	.01	.00

1990 Fleer

The 1990 Fleer set contains 660 standard-size (2 1/2" by 3 1/2")
cards. The outer front borders are white; the inner, ribbon-like
borders are different depending on the team. The vertically-
oriented backs are white, red, pink, and navy. The set is again
ordered numerically by teams, followed by combination cards,
rookie prospect pairs, and checklists. Just as with the 1989 set,
Fleer incorrectly anticipated the outcome of the 1989 Playoffs
according to the team ordering. The A's, listed first, did win the
World Series, but their opponents were the Giants, not the
Cubs. The complete team ordering is as follows: Oakland A's

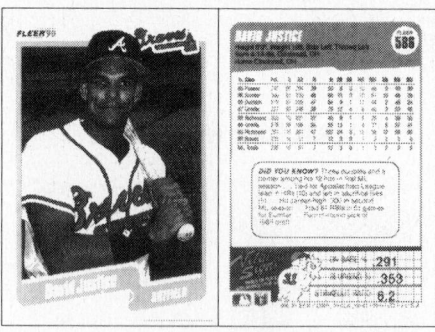

(1-24), Chicago Cubs (25-49), San Francisco Giants (50-75),
Toronto Blue Jays (76-99), Kansas City Royals (100-124),
California Angels (125-148), San Diego Padres (149-171),
Baltimore Orioles (172-195), New York Mets (196-219), Houston
Astros (220-241), St. Louis Cardinals (242-265), Boston Red
Sox (266-289), Texas Rangers (290-315), Milwaukee Brewers
(316-340), Montreal Expos (341-364), Minnesota Twins (365-
388), Los Angeles Dodgers (389-411), Cincinnati Reds (412-
435), New York Yankees (436-458), Pittsburgh Pirates (459-
482), Cleveland Indians (483-504), Seattle Mariners (505-
528), Chicago White Sox (529-551), Philadelphia Phillies (552-
573), Atlanta Braves (574-598), and Detroit Tigers (599-620).
The key rookie cards in this set are Alex Cole, Delino DeShields,
Juan Gonzalez, Marquis Grissom, Dave Justice, Kevin Maas,
and Ben McDonald. The following five cards have minor printing
differences, 6, 162, 260, 469, and 550; these differences are so
minor that collectors have deemed them not significant enough
to effect a price differential. Fleer also produced a separate set
for Canada. The Canadian set only differs from the regular set
in that it shows copyright "FLEER LTD./LTEE PTD. IN CANADA"
on the card backs. Although these Canadian cards were
undoubtedly produced in much lesser quantities compared to
the U.S. issue, the fact that the versions are so similar has kept
the demand (and the price differential) for the Canadian cards
down.

		MINT	EXC	G-VG
COMPLETE SET (660)		18.00	7.50	2.50
COMMON PLAYER (1-660)		.03	.01	.00
☐ 1	Lance Blankenship	.06	.02	.00
☐ 2	Todd Burns	.03	.01	.00
☐ 3	Jose Canseco	.40	.16	.04
☐ 4	Jim Corsi	.03	.01	.00
☐ 5	Storm Davis	.03	.01	.00
☐ 6	Dennis Eckersley	.08	.03	.01
☐ 7	Mike Gallego	.03	.01	.00
☐ 8	Ron Hassey	.03	.01	.00
☐ 9	Dave Henderson	.08	.03	.01
☐ 10	Rickey Henderson	.25	.10	.02
☐ 11	Rick Honeycutt	.03	.01	.00
☐ 12	Stan Javier	.03	.01	.00
☐ 13	Felix Jose	.20	.08	.02
☐ 14	Carney Lansford	.06	.02	.00
☐ 15	Mark McGwire	.15	.06	.01
☐ 16	Mike Moore	.06	.02	.00
☐ 17	Gene Nelson	.03	.01	.00
☐ 18	Dave Parker	.08	.03	.01
☐ 19	Tony Phillips	.03	.01	.00
☐ 20	Terry Steinbach	.06	.02	.00
☐ 21	Dave Stewart	.08	.03	.01
☐ 22	Walt Weiss	.06	.02	.00
☐ 23	Bob Welch	.08	.03	.01
☐ 24	Curt Young	.03	.01	.00
☐ 25	Paul Assenmacher	.03	.01	.00
☐ 26	Damon Berryhill	.03	.01	.00
☐ 27	Mike Bielecki	.03	.01	.00
☐ 28	Kevin Blankenship	.03	.01	.00
☐ 29	Andre Dawson	.10	.04	.01
☐ 30	Shawon Dunston	.08	.03	.01
☐ 31	Joe Girardi	.03	.01	.00
☐ 32	Mark Grace	.12	.05	.01
☐ 33	Mike Harkey	.06	.02	.00

☐ 34 Paul Kilgus	.03	.01	.00
☐ 35 Les Lancaster	.03	.01	.00
☐ 36 Vance Law	.03	.01	.00
☐ 37 Greg Maddux	.06	.02	.00
☐ 38 Lloyd McClendon	.03	.01	.00
☐ 39 Jeff Pico	.03	.01	.00
☐ 40 Ryne Sandberg	.30	.12	.03
☐ 41 Scott Sanderson	.03	.01	.00
☐ 42 Dwight Smith	.06	.02	.00
☐ 43 Rick Sutcliffe	.06	.02	.00
☐ 44 Jerome Walton	.08	.03	.01
☐ 45 Mitch Webster	.03	.01	.00
☐ 46 Curt Wilkerson	.03	.01	.00
☐ 47 Dean Wilkins	.10	.04	.01
☐ 48 Mitch Williams	.03	.01	.00
☐ 49 Steve Wilson	.03	.01	.00
☐ 50 Steve Bedrosian	.03	.01	.00
☐ 51 Mike Benjamin	.10	.04	.01
☐ 52 Jeff Brantley	.08	.03	.01
☐ 53 Brett Butler	.08	.03	.01
☐ 54 Will Clark UER	.30	.12	.03
("Did You Know" says first in runs, should say tied for first)			
☐ 55 Kelly Downs	.03	.01	.00
☐ 56 Scott Garrelts	.03	.01	.00
☐ 57 Atlee Hammaker	.03	.01	.00
☐ 58 Terry Kennedy	.03	.01	.00
☐ 59 Mike LaCoss	.03	.01	.00
☐ 60 Craig Lefferts	.03	.01	.00
☐ 61 Greg Litton	.03	.01	.00
☐ 62 Candy Maldonado	.03	.01	.00
☐ 63 Kirt Manwaring UER	.03	.01	.00
(no '88 Phoenix stats as noted in box)			
☐ 64 Randy McCament	.08	.03	.01
☐ 65 Kevin Mitchell	.10	.04	.01
☐ 66 Donell Nixon	.03	.01	.00
☐ 67 Ken Oberkfell	.03	.01	.00
☐ 68 Rick Reuschel	.06	.02	.00
☐ 69 Ernest Riles	.03	.01	.00
☐ 70 Don Robinson	.03	.01	.00
☐ 71 Pat Sheridan	.03	.01	.00
☐ 72 Chris Speier	.03	.01	.00
☐ 73 Robby Thompson	.03	.01	.00
☐ 74 Jose Uribe	.03	.01	.00
☐ 75 Matt Williams	.15	.06	.01
☐ 76 George Bell	.08	.03	.01
☐ 77 Pat Borders	.03	.01	.00
☐ 78 John Cerutti	.03	.01	.00
☐ 79 Junior Felix	.06	.02	.00
☐ 80 Tony Fernandez	.06	.02	.00
☐ 81 Mike Flanagan	.03	.01	.00
☐ 82 Mauro Gozzo	.08	.03	.01
☐ 83 Kelly Gruber	.08	.03	.01
☐ 84 Tom Henke	.06	.02	.00
☐ 85 Jimmy Key	.06	.02	.00
☐ 86 Manny Lee	.03	.01	.00
☐ 87 Nelson Liriano UER	.03	.01	.00
(should say "led the IL" instead of "led the TL")			
☐ 88 Lee Mazzilli	.03	.01	.00
☐ 89 Fred McGriff	.10	.04	.01
☐ 90 Lloyd Moseby	.03	.01	.00
☐ 91 Rance Mulliniks	.03	.01	.00
☐ 92 Alex Sanchez	.06	.02	.00
☐ 93 Dave Stieb	.08	.03	.01
☐ 94 Todd Stottlemyre	.08	.03	.01
☐ 95 Duane Ward UER	.06	.02	.00
(double line of '87 Syracuse stats)			
☐ 96 David Wells	.06	.02	.00
☐ 97 Ernie Whitt	.03	.01	.00
☐ 98 Frank Wills	.03	.01	.00
☐ 99 Mookie Wilson	.03	.01	.00
☐ 100 Kevin Appier	.15	.06	.01
☐ 101 Luis Aquino	.03	.01	.00
☐ 102 Bob Boone	.06	.02	.00
☐ 103 George Brett	.12	.05	.01
☐ 104 Jose DeJesus	.03	.01	.00
☐ 105 Luis De Los Santos	.03	.01	.00
☐ 106 Jim Eisenreich	.03	.01	.00
☐ 107 Steve Farr	.03	.01	.00
☐ 108 Tom Gordon	.06	.02	.00
☐ 109 Mark Gubicza	.06	.02	.00
☐ 110 Bo Jackson	.40	.16	.04
☐ 111 Terry Leach	.03	.01	.00
☐ 112 Charlie Leibrandt	.03	.01	.00
☐ 113 Rick Luecken	.08	.03	.01
☐ 114 Mike Macfarlane	.03	.01	.00
☐ 115 Jeff Montgomery	.03	.01	.00
☐ 116 Bret Saberhagen	.08	.03	.01
☐ 117 Kevin Seitzer	.06	.02	.00
☐ 118 Kurt Stillwell	.03	.01	.00
☐ 119 Pat Tabler	.03	.01	.00
☐ 120 Danny Tartabull	.08	.03	.01
☐ 121 Gary Thurman	.03	.01	.00
☐ 122 Frank White	.03	.01	.00
☐ 123 Willie Wilson	.06	.02	.00
☐ 124 Matt Winters	.10	.04	.01
☐ 125 Jim Abbott	.17	.07	.01
☐ 126 Tony Armas	.03	.01	.00
☐ 127 Dante Bichette	.06	.02	.00
☐ 128 Bert Blyleven	.08	.03	.01
☐ 129 Chili Davis	.06	.02	.00
☐ 130 Brian Downing	.03	.01	.00
☐ 131 Mike Fetters	.08	.03	.01
☐ 132 Chuck Finley	.08	.03	.01
☐ 133 Willie Fraser	.03	.01	.00
☐ 134 Bryan Harvey	.06	.02	.00
☐ 135 Jack Howell	.03	.01	.00
☐ 136 Wally Joyner	.08	.03	.01
☐ 137 Jeff Manto	.08	.03	.01
☐ 138 Kirk McCaskill	.03	.01	.00
☐ 139 Bob McClure	.03	.01	.00
☐ 140 Greg Minton	.03	.01	.00
☐ 141 Lance Parrish	.08	.03	.01
☐ 142 Dan Petry	.03	.01	.00
☐ 143 Johnny Ray	.03	.01	.00
☐ 144 Dick Schofield	.03	.01	.00
☐ 145 Lee Stevens	.15	.06	.01
☐ 146 Claudell Washington	.03	.01	.00
☐ 147 Devon White	.06	.02	.00
☐ 148 Mike Witt	.03	.01	.00
☐ 149 Roberto Alomar	.15	.06	.01
☐ 150 Sandy Alomar Jr.	.10	.04	.01
☐ 151 Andy Benes	.15	.06	.01
☐ 152 Jack Clark	.08	.03	.01
☐ 153 Pat Clements	.03	.01	.00
☐ 154 Joey Cora	.03	.01	.00
☐ 155 Mark Davis	.06	.02	.00
☐ 156 Mark Grant	.03	.01	.00
☐ 157 Tony Gwynn	.15	.06	.01
☐ 158 Greg W. Harris	.03	.01	.00
☐ 159 Bruce Hurst	.06	.02	.00
☐ 160 Darrin Jackson	.06	.02	.00
☐ 161 Chris James	.06	.02	.00
☐ 162 Carmelo Martinez	.03	.01	.00
☐ 163 Mike Pagliarulo	.03	.01	.00
☐ 164 Mark Parent	.03	.01	.00
☐ 165 Dennis Rasmussen	.03	.01	.00
☐ 166 Bip Roberts	.03	.01	.00
☐ 167 Benito Santiago	.08	.03	.01
☐ 168 Calvin Schiraldi	.03	.01	.00
☐ 169 Eric Show	.03	.01	.00
☐ 170 Garry Templeton	.03	.01	.00
☐ 171 Ed Whitson	.03	.01	.00
☐ 172 Brady Anderson	.03	.01	.00
☐ 173 Jeff Ballard	.03	.01	.00
☐ 174 Phil Bradley	.03	.01	.00
☐ 175 Mike Devereaux	.03	.01	.00
☐ 176 Steve Finley	.10	.04	.01
☐ 177 Pete Harnisch	.06	.02	.00
☐ 178 Kevin Hickey	.03	.01	.00
☐ 179 Brian Holton	.03	.01	.00
☐ 180 Ben McDonald	.75	.30	.07
☐ 181 Bob Melvin	.03	.01	.00
☐ 182 Bob Milacki	.03	.01	.00
☐ 183 Randy Milligan UER	.06	.02	.00
(double line of '87 stats)			
☐ 184 Gregg Olson	.15	.06	.01
☐ 185 Joe Orsulak	.03	.01	.00
☐ 186 Bill Ripken	.03	.01	.00
☐ 187 Cal Ripken	.30	.12	.03
☐ 188 Dave Schmidt	.03	.01	.00
☐ 189 Larry Sheets	.03	.01	.00
☐ 190 Mickey Tettleton	.06	.02	.00
☐ 191 Mark Thurmond	.03	.01	.00
☐ 192 Jay Tibbs	.03	.01	.00
☐ 193 Jim Traber	.03	.01	.00
☐ 194 Mark Williamson	.03	.01	.00
☐ 195 Craig Worthington	.03	.01	.00
☐ 196 Don Aase	.03	.01	.00
☐ 197 Blaine Beatty	.08	.03	.01
☐ 198 Mark Carreon	.03	.01	.00
☐ 199 Gary Carter	.08	.03	.01
☐ 200 David Cone	.06	.02	.00
☐ 201 Ron Darling	.06	.02	.00
☐ 202 Kevin Elster	.03	.01	.00
☐ 203 Sid Fernandez	.06	.02	.00
☐ 204 Dwight Gooden	.10	.04	.01
☐ 205 Keith Hernandez	.06	.02	.00
☐ 206 Jeff Innis	.08	.03	.01
☐ 207 Gregg Jefferies	.10	.04	.01
☐ 208 Howard Johnson	.08	.03	.01
☐ 209 Barry Lyons UER	.03	.01	.00
(double line of '87 stats)			

#	Player			
☐ 210	Dave Magadan	.06	.02	.00
☐ 211	Kevin McReynolds	.08	.03	.01
☐ 212	Jeff Musselman	.03	.01	.00
☐ 213	Randy Myers	.03	.01	.00
☐ 214	Bob Ojeda	.03	.01	.00
☐ 215	Juan Samuel	.06	.02	.00
☐ 216	Mackey Sasser	.03	.01	.00
☐ 217	Darryl Strawberry	.25	.10	.02
☐ 218	Tim Teufel	.03	.01	.00
☐ 219	Frank Viola	.08	.03	.01
☐ 220	Juan Agosto	.03	.01	.00
☐ 221	Larry Andersen	.03	.01	.00
☐ 222	Eric Anthony	.17	.07	.01
☐ 223	Kevin Bass	.03	.01	.00
☐ 224	Craig Biggio	.08	.03	.01
☐ 225	Ken Caminiti	.03	.01	.00
☐ 226	Jim Clancy	.03	.01	.00
☐ 227	Danny Darwin	.03	.01	.00
☐ 228	Glenn Davis	.08	.03	.01
☐ 229	Jim Deshaies	.03	.01	.00
☐ 230	Bill Doran	.03	.01	.00
☐ 231	Bob Forsch	.03	.01	.00
☐ 232	Brian Meyer	.06	.02	.00
☐ 233	Terry Puhl	.03	.01	.00
☐ 234	Rafael Ramirez	.03	.01	.00
☐ 235	Rick Rhoden	.03	.01	.00
☐ 236	Dan Schatzeder	.03	.01	.00
☐ 237	Mike Scott	.08	.03	.01
☐ 238	Dave Smith	.03	.01	.00
☐ 239	Alex Trevino	.03	.01	.00
☐ 240	Glenn Wilson	.03	.01	.00
☐ 241	Gerald Young	.03	.01	.00
☐ 242	Tom Brunansky	.06	.02	.00
☐ 243	Cris Carpenter	.03	.01	.00
☐ 244	Alex Cole	.30	.12	.03
☐ 245	Vince Coleman	.08	.03	.01
☐ 246	John Costello	.03	.01	.00
☐ 247	Ken Dayley	.03	.01	.00
☐ 248	Jose DeLeon	.03	.01	.00
☐ 249	Frank DiPino	.03	.01	.00
☐ 250	Pedro Guerrero	.08	.03	.01
☐ 251	Ken Hill	.03	.01	.00
☐ 252	Joe Magrane	.03	.01	.00
☐ 253	Willie McGee UER	.08	.03	.01
	(no decimal point before 353)			
☐ 254	John Morris	.03	.01	.00
☐ 255	Jose Oquendo	.03	.01	.00
☐ 256	Tony Pena	.06	.02	.00
☐ 257	Terry Pendleton	.08	.03	.01
☐ 258	Ted Power	.03	.01	.00
☐ 259	Dan Quisenberry	.06	.02	.00
☐ 260	Ozzie Smith	.10	.04	.01
☐ 261	Scott Terry	.03	.01	.00
☐ 262	Milt Thompson	.03	.01	.00
☐ 263	Denny Walling	.03	.01	.00
☐ 264	Todd Worrell	.06	.02	.00
☐ 265	Todd Zeile	.40	.16	.04
☐ 266	Marty Barrett	.03	.01	.00
☐ 267	Mike Boddicker	.03	.01	.00
☐ 268	Wade Boggs	.15	.06	.01
☐ 269	Ellis Burks	.08	.03	.01
☐ 270	Rick Cerone	.03	.01	.00
☐ 271	Roger Clemens	.30	.12	.03
☐ 272	John Dopson	.03	.01	.00
☐ 273	Nick Esasky	.03	.01	.00
☐ 274	Dwight Evans	.06	.02	.00
☐ 275	Wes Gardner	.03	.01	.00
☐ 276	Rich Gedman	.03	.01	.00
☐ 277	Mike Greenwell	.12	.05	.01
☐ 278	Danny Heep	.03	.01	.00
☐ 279	Eric Hetzel	.03	.01	.00
☐ 280	Dennis Lamp	.03	.01	.00
☐ 281	Rob Murphy UER	.03	.01	.00
	('89 stats say Reds, should say Red Sox)			
☐ 282	Joe Price	.03	.01	.00
☐ 283	Carlos Quintana	.08	.03	.01
☐ 284	Jody Reed	.06	.02	.00
☐ 285	Luis Rivera	.03	.01	.00
☐ 286	Kevin Romine	.03	.01	.00
☐ 287	Lee Smith	.06	.02	.00
☐ 288	Mike Smithson	.03	.01	.00
☐ 289	Bob Stanley	.03	.01	.00
☐ 290	Harold Baines	.08	.03	.01
☐ 291	Kevin Brown	.03	.01	.00
☐ 292	Steve Buechele	.03	.01	.00
☐ 293	Scott Coolbaugh	.10	.04	.01
☐ 294	Jack Daugherty	.08	.03	.01
☐ 295	Cecil Espy	.03	.01	.00
☐ 296	Julio Franco	.10	.04	.01
☐ 297	Juan Gonzalez	2.00	.80	.20
☐ 298	Cecilio Guante	.03	.01	.00
☐ 299	Drew Hall	.03	.01	.00
☐ 300	Charlie Hough	.03	.01	.00
☐ 301	Pete Incaviglia	.06	.02	.00
☐ 302	Mike Jeffcoat	.03	.01	.00
☐ 303	Chad Kreuter	.03	.01	.00
☐ 304	Jeff Kunkel	.03	.01	.00
☐ 305	Rick Leach	.03	.01	.00
☐ 306	Fred Manrique	.03	.01	.00
☐ 307	Jamie Moyer	.03	.01	.00
☐ 308	Rafael Palmeiro	.12	.05	.01
☐ 309	Geno Petralli	.03	.01	.00
☐ 310	Kevin Reimer	.03	.01	.00
☐ 311	Kenny Rogers	.06	.02	.00
☐ 312	Jeff Russell	.03	.01	.00
☐ 313	Nolan Ryan	.50	.20	.05
☐ 314	Ruben Sierra	.17	.07	.01
☐ 315	Bobby Witt	.06	.02	.00
☐ 316	Chris Bosio	.03	.01	.00
☐ 317	Glenn Braggs UER	.03	.01	.00
	(stats say 111 K's, but bio says 117 K's)			
☐ 318	Greg Brock	.03	.01	.00
☐ 319	Chuck Crim	.03	.01	.00
☐ 320	Rob Deer	.06	.02	.00
☐ 321	Mike Felder	.03	.01	.00
☐ 322	Tom Filer	.03	.01	.00
☐ 323	Tony Fossas	.06	.02	.00
☐ 324	Jim Gantner	.03	.01	.00
☐ 325	Darryl Hamilton	.06	.02	.00
☐ 326	Teddy Higuera	.03	.01	.00
☐ 327	Mark Knudson	.03	.01	.00
☐ 328	Bill Krueger UER	.03	.01	.00
	('86 stats missing)			
☐ 329	Tim McIntosh	.12	.05	.01
☐ 330	Paul Molitor	.08	.03	.01
☐ 331	Jaime Navarro	.06	.02	.00
☐ 332	Charlie O'Brien	.03	.01	.00
☐ 333	Jeff Peterek	.08	.03	.01
☐ 334	Dan Plesac	.03	.01	.00
☐ 335	Jerry Reuss	.03	.01	.00
☐ 336	Gary Sheffield UER	.08	.03	.01
	(bio says played for 3 teams in '87, but stats say in '88)			
☐ 337	Bill Spiers	.06	.02	.00
☐ 338	B.J. Surhoff	.06	.02	.00
☐ 339	Greg Vaughn	.50	.20	.05
☐ 340	Robin Yount	.12	.05	.01
☐ 341	Hubie Brooks	.06	.02	.00
☐ 342	Tim Burke	.03	.01	.00
☐ 343	Mike Fitzgerald	.03	.01	.00
☐ 344	Tom Foley	.03	.01	.00
☐ 345	Andres Galarraga	.06	.02	.00
☐ 346	Damaso Garcia	.03	.01	.00
☐ 347	Marquis Grissom	.40	.16	.04
☐ 348	Kevin Gross	.03	.01	.00
☐ 349	Joe Hesketh	.03	.01	.00
☐ 350	Jeff Huson	.08	.03	.01
☐ 351	Wallace Johnson	.03	.01	.00
☐ 352	Mark Langston	.08	.03	.01
☐ 353A	Dave Martinez	3.00	1.25	.30
	(yellow on front)			
☐ 353B	Dave Martinez	.06	.02	.00
	(red on front)			
☐ 354	Dennis Martinez UER	.06	.02	.00
	('87 ERA is 616, should be 6.16)			
☐ 355	Andy McGaffigan	.03	.01	.00
☐ 356	Otis Nixon	.06	.02	.00
☐ 357	Spike Owen	.03	.01	.00
☐ 358	Pascual Perez	.03	.01	.00
☐ 359	Tim Raines	.08	.03	.01
☐ 360	Nelson Santovenia	.03	.01	.00
☐ 361	Bryn Smith	.03	.01	.00
☐ 362	Zane Smith	.06	.02	.00
☐ 363	Larry Walker	.25	.10	.02
☐ 364	Tim Wallach	.06	.02	.00
☐ 365	Rick Aguilera	.06	.02	.00
☐ 366	Allan Anderson	.03	.01	.00
☐ 367	Wally Backman	.03	.01	.00
☐ 368	Doug Baker	.03	.01	.00
☐ 369	Juan Berenguer	.03	.01	.00
☐ 370	Randy Bush	.03	.01	.00
☐ 371	Carmen Castillo	.03	.01	.00
☐ 372	Mike Dyer	.08	.03	.01
☐ 373	Gary Gaetti	.06	.02	.00
☐ 374	Greg Gagne	.03	.01	.00
☐ 375	Dan Gladden	.03	.01	.00
☐ 376	German Gonzalez UER	.03	.01	.00
	(bio says 31 saves in '88, but stats say 30)			
☐ 377	Brian Harper	.03	.01	.00
☐ 378	Kent Hrbek	.08	.03	.01
☐ 379	Gene Larkin	.03	.01	.00
☐ 380	Tim Laudner UER	.03	.01	.00
	(no decimal point before '85 BA of 238)			

	No.	Player			
☐	381	John Moses	.03	.01	.00
☐	382	Al Newman	.03	.01	.00
☐	383	Kirby Puckett	.20	.08	.02
☐	384	Shane Rawley	.03	.01	.00
☐	385	Jeff Reardon	.06	.02	.00
☐	386	Roy Smith	.03	.01	.00
☐	387	Gary Wayne	.08	.03	.01
☐	388	Dave West	.03	.01	.00
☐	389	Tim Belcher	.06	.02	.00
☐	390	Tim Crews UER	.03	.01	.00
		(stats say 163 IP for '83, but bio says 136)			
☐	391	Mike Davis	.03	.01	.00
☐	392	Rick Dempsey	.03	.01	.00
☐	393	Kirk Gibson	.08	.03	.01
☐	394	Jose Gonzalez	.03	.01	.00
☐	395	Alfredo Griffin	.03	.01	.00
☐	396	Jeff Hamilton	.03	.01	.00
☐	397	Lenny Harris	.03	.01	.00
☐	398	Mickey Hatcher	.03	.01	.00
☐	399	Orel Hershiser	.08	.03	.01
☐	400	Jay Howell	.03	.01	.00
☐	401	Mike Marshall	.06	.02	.00
☐	402	Ramon Martinez	.25	.10	.02
☐	403	Mike Morgan	.06	.02	.00
☐	404	Eddie Murray	.10	.04	.01
☐	405	Alejandro Pena	.06	.02	.00
☐	406	Willie Randolph	.06	.02	.00
☐	407	Mike Scioscia	.03	.01	.00
☐	408	Ray Searage	.03	.01	.00
☐	409	Fernando Valenzuela	.08	.03	.01
☐	410	Jose Vizcaino	.12	.05	.01
☐	411	John Wetteland	.08	.03	.01
☐	412	Jack Armstrong	.08	.03	.01
☐	413	Todd Benzinger UER	.03	.01	.00
		(bio says .323 at Pawtucket, but stats say .321)			
☐	414	Tim Birtsas	.03	.01	.00
☐	415	Tom Browning	.06	.02	.00
☐	416	Norm Charlton	.03	.01	.00
☐	417	Eric Davis	.10	.04	.01
☐	418	Rob Dibble	.06	.02	.00
☐	419	John Franco	.03	.01	.00
☐	420	Ken Griffey Sr.	.06	.02	.00
☐	421	Chris Hammond	.25	.10	.02
		(no 1989 used for "Did Not Play" stat, actually did play for Nashville in 1989)			
☐	422	Danny Jackson	.03	.01	.00
☐	423	Barry Larkin	.12	.05	.01
☐	424	Tim Leary	.06	.02	.00
☐	425	Rick Mahler	.03	.01	.00
☐	426	Joe Oliver	.06	.02	.00
☐	427	Paul O'Neill	.06	.02	.00
☐	428	Luis Quinones UER	.03	.01	.00
		('86-'88 stats are omitted from card but included in totals)			
☐	429	Jeff Reed	.03	.01	.00
☐	430	Jose Rijo	.08	.03	.01
☐	431	Ron Robinson	.03	.01	.00
☐	432	Rolando Roomes	.03	.01	.00
☐	433	Chris Sabo	.10	.04	.01
☐	434	Scott Scudder	.06	.02	.00
☐	435	Herm Winningham	.03	.01	.00
☐	436	Steve Balboni	.03	.01	.00
☐	437	Jesse Barfield	.06	.02	.00
☐	438	Mike Blowers	.10	.04	.01
☐	439	Tom Brookens	.03	.01	.00
☐	440	Greg Cadaret	.03	.01	.00
☐	441	Alvaro Espinoza UER	.03	.01	.00
		(career games say 218, should be 219)			
☐	442	Bob Geren	.03	.01	.00
☐	443	Lee Guetterman	.03	.01	.00
☐	444	Mel Hall	.06	.02	.00
☐	445	Andy Hawkins	.03	.01	.00
☐	446	Roberto Kelly	.08	.03	.01
☐	447	Don Mattingly	.20	.08	.02
☐	448	Lance McCullers	.03	.01	.00
☐	449	Hensley Meulens	.12	.05	.01
☐	450	Dale Mohorcic	.03	.01	.00
☐	451	Clay Parker	.03	.01	.00
☐	452	Eric Plunk	.03	.01	.00
☐	453	Dave Righetti	.06	.02	.00
☐	454	Deion Sanders	.15	.06	.01
☐	455	Steve Sax	.06	.02	.00
☐	456	Don Slaught	.03	.01	.00
☐	457	Walt Terrell	.03	.01	.00
☐	458	Dave Winfield	.10	.04	.01
☐	459	Jay Bell	.03	.01	.00
☐	460	Rafael Belliard	.03	.01	.00
☐	461	Barry Bonds	.17	.07	.01
☐	462	Bobby Bonilla	.15	.06	.01
☐	463	Sid Bream	.03	.01	.00
☐	464	Benny Distefano	.03	.01	.00
☐	465	Doug Drabek	.06	.02	.00
☐	466	Jim Gott	.03	.01	.00
☐	467	Billy Hatcher UER	.06	.02	.00
		(.1 hits for Cubs in 1984)			
☐	468	Neal Heaton	.03	.01	.00
☐	469	Jeff King	.06	.02	.00
☐	470	Bob Kipper	.03	.01	.00
☐	471	Randy Kramer	.03	.01	.00
☐	472	Bill Landrum	.03	.01	.00
☐	473	Mike LaValliere	.03	.01	.00
☐	474	Jose Lind	.03	.01	.00
☐	475	Junior Ortiz	.03	.01	.00
☐	476	Gary Redus	.03	.01	.00
☐	477	Rick Reed	.08	.03	.01
☐	478	R.J. Reynolds	.03	.01	.00
☐	479	Jeff Robinson	.03	.01	.00
☐	480	John Smiley	.06	.02	.00
☐	481	Andy Van Slyke	.08	.03	.01
☐	482	Bob Walk	.03	.01	.00
☐	483	Andy Allanson	.03	.01	.00
☐	484	Scott Bailes	.03	.01	.00
☐	485	Joey Belle UER	.50	.20	.05
		(has Jay Bell "Did You Know")			
☐	486	Bud Black	.03	.01	.00
☐	487	Jerry Browne	.03	.01	.00
☐	488	Tom Candiotti	.06	.02	.00
☐	489	Joe Carter	.10	.04	.01
☐	490	Dave Clark	.03	.01	.00
		(no '84 stats)			
☐	491	John Farrell	.03	.01	.00
☐	492	Felix Fermin	.03	.01	.00
☐	493	Brook Jacoby	.03	.01	.00
☐	494	Dion James	.03	.01	.00
☐	495	Doug Jones	.03	.01	.00
☐	496	Brad Komminsk	.03	.01	.00
☐	497	Rod Nichols	.03	.01	.00
☐	498	Pete O'Brien	.03	.01	.00
☐	499	Steve Olin	.08	.03	.01
☐	500	Jesse Orosco	.03	.01	.00
☐	501	Joel Skinner	.03	.01	.00
☐	502	Cory Snyder	.06	.02	.00
☐	503	Greg Swindell	.06	.02	.00
☐	504	Rich Yett	.03	.01	.00
☐	505	Scott Bankhead	.06	.02	.00
☐	506	Scott Bradley	.03	.01	.00
☐	507	Greg Briley UER	.06	.02	.00
		(28 SB's in bio, but 27 in stats)			
☐	508	Jay Buhner	.08	.03	.01
☐	509	Darnell Coles	.03	.01	.00
☐	510	Keith Comstock	.03	.01	.00
☐	511	Henry Cotto	.03	.01	.00
☐	512	Alvin Davis	.06	.02	.00
☐	513	Ken Griffey Jr.	1.50	.60	.15
☐	514	Erik Hanson	.08	.03	.01
☐	515	Gene Harris	.06	.02	.00
☐	516	Brian Holman	.06	.02	.00
☐	517	Mike Jackson	.03	.01	.00
☐	518	Randy Johnson	.06	.02	.00
☐	519	Jeffrey Leonard	.03	.01	.00
☐	520	Edgar Martinez	.10	.04	.01
☐	521	Dennis Powell	.03	.01	.00
☐	522	Jim Presley	.03	.01	.00
☐	523	Jerry Reed	.03	.01	.00
☐	524	Harold Reynolds	.06	.02	.00
☐	525	Mike Schooler	.06	.02	.00
☐	526	Bill Swift	.03	.01	.00
☐	527	Dave Valle	.03	.01	.00
☐	528	Omar Vizquel	.03	.01	.00
☐	529	Ivan Calderon	.06	.02	.00
☐	530	Carlton Fisk UER	.12	.05	.01
		(Bellow Falls, should be Bellows Falls)			
☐	531	Scott Fletcher	.03	.01	.00
☐	532	Dave Gallagher	.03	.01	.00
☐	533	Ozzie Guillen	.06	.02	.00
☐	534	Greg Hibbard	.15	.06	.01
☐	535	Shawn Hillegas	.03	.01	.00
☐	536	Lance Johnson	.03	.01	.00
☐	537	Eric King	.03	.01	.00
☐	538	Ron Kittle	.06	.02	.00
☐	539	Steve Lyons	.03	.01	.00
☐	540	Carlos Martinez	.06	.02	.00
☐	541	Tom McCarthy	.08	.03	.01
☐	542	Matt Merullo	.06	.02	.00
		(had 5 ML runs scored entering '90, not 6)			

☐ 543	Donn Pall UER .... (stats say pro career began in '85, bio says '88)	.03	.01	.00
☐ 544	Dan Pasqua	.03	.01	.00
☐ 545	Ken Patterson	.03	.01	.00
☐ 546	Melido Perez	.03	.01	.00
☐ 547	Steve Rosenberg	.06	.02	.00
☐ 548	Sammy Sosa	.25	.10	.02
☐ 549	Bobby Thigpen	.06	.02	.00
☐ 550	Robin Ventura	.50	.20	.05
☐ 551	Greg Walker	.03	.01	.00
☐ 552	Don Carman	.03	.01	.00
☐ 553	Pat Combs .... (6 walks for Phillies in '89 in stats, brief bio says 4)	.06	.02	.00
☐ 554	Dennis Cook	.03	.01	.00
☐ 555	Darren Daulton	.03	.01	.00
☐ 556	Len Dykstra	.06	.02	.00
☐ 557	Curt Ford	.03	.01	.00
☐ 558	Charlie Hayes	.03	.01	.00
☐ 559	Von Hayes	.06	.02	.00
☐ 560	Tommy Herr	.03	.01	.00
☐ 561	Ken Howell	.03	.01	.00
☐ 562	Steve Jeltz	.03	.01	.00
☐ 563	Ron Jones	.03	.01	.00
☐ 564	Ricky Jordan UER .... (duplicate line of statistics on back)	.06	.02	.00
☐ 565	John Kruk	.03	.01	.00
☐ 566	Steve Lake	.03	.01	.00
☐ 567	Roger McDowell	.03	.01	.00
☐ 568	Terry Mulholland UER .... ("Did You Know" re- fers to Dave Magadan)	.06	.02	.00
☐ 569	Dwayne Murphy	.03	.01	.00
☐ 570	Jeff Parrett	.03	.01	.00
☐ 571	Randy Ready	.03	.01	.00
☐ 572	Bruce Ruffin	.03	.01	.00
☐ 573	Dickie Thon	.03	.01	.00
☐ 574	Jose Alvarez UER .... ('78 and '79 stats are reversed)	.03	.01	.00
☐ 575	Geronimo Berroa	.03	.01	.00
☐ 576	Jeff Blauser	.03	.01	.00
☐ 577	Joe Boever	.03	.01	.00
☐ 578	Marty Clary UER .... (no comma between city and state)	.03	.01	.00
☐ 579	Jody Davis	.03	.01	.00
☐ 580	Mark Eichhorn	.03	.01	.00
☐ 581	Darrell Evans	.06	.02	.00
☐ 582	Ron Gant	.25	.10	.02
☐ 583	Tom Glavine	.20	.08	.02
☐ 584	Tommy Greene	.30	.12	.03
☐ 585	Tommy Gregg	.03	.01	.00
☐ 586	Dave Justice UER .... (Actually had 16 2B in Sumter in '86)	2.50	1.00	.25
☐ 587	Mark Lemke	.10	.04	.01
☐ 588	Derek Lilliquist	.03	.01	.00
☐ 589	Oddibe McDowell	.03	.01	.00
☐ 590	Kent Mercker ERA .... (bio says 2.75 ERA, stats say 2.68 ERA)	.15	.06	.01
☐ 591	Dale Murphy	.10	.04	.01
☐ 592	Gerald Perry	.03	.01	.00
☐ 593	Lonnie Smith	.06	.02	.00
☐ 594	Pete Smith	.03	.01	.00
☐ 595	John Smoltz	.15	.06	.01
☐ 596	Mike Stanton UER .... (no comma between city and state)	.08	.03	.01
☐ 597	Andres Thomas	.03	.01	.00
☐ 598	Jeff Treadway	.03	.01	.00
☐ 599	Doyle Alexander	.03	.01	.00
☐ 600	Dave Bergman	.03	.01	.00
☐ 601	Brian Dubois	.10	.04	.01
☐ 602	Paul Gibson	.03	.01	.00
☐ 603	Mike Heath	.03	.01	.00
☐ 604	Mike Henneman	.03	.01	.00
☐ 605	Guillermo Hernandez	.03	.01	.00
☐ 606	Shawn Holman	.08	.03	.01
☐ 607	Tracy Jones	.03	.01	.00
☐ 608	Chet Lemon	.03	.01	.00
☐ 609	Fred Lynn	.06	.02	.00
☐ 610	Jack Morris	.08	.03	.01
☐ 611	Matt Nokes	.03	.01	.00
☐ 612	Gary Pettis	.03	.01	.00
☐ 613	Kevin Ritz	.10	.04	.01
☐ 614	Jeff Robinson .... ('88 stats are not in line)	.03	.01	.00
☐ 615	Steve Searcy	.03	.01	.00
☐ 616	Frank Tanana	.06	.02	.00
☐ 617	Alan Trammell	.08	.03	.01
☐ 618	Gary Ward	.03	.01	.00
☐ 619	Lou Whitaker	.06	.02	.00
☐ 620	Frank Williams	.03	.01	.00
☐ 621A	George Brett '80 .... ERR (had 10 .390 hitting seasons)	2.00	.80	.20
☐ 621A	George Brett '80 COR	.08	.03	.01
☐ 622	Fern.Valenzuela '81	.06	.02	.00
☐ 623	Dale Murphy '82	.08	.03	.01
☐ 624A	Cal Ripken '83 ERR .... (misspelled Ripkin on card back)	3.00	1.25	.30
☐ 624B	Cal Ripken '83 COR	.12	.05	.01
☐ 625	Ryne Sandberg '84	.12	.05	.01
☐ 626	Don Mattingly '85	.12	.05	.01
☐ 627	Roger Clemens '86	.12	.05	.01
☐ 628	George Bell '87	.08	.03	.01
☐ 629	Jose Canseco '88 UER .... (Reggie won MVP in '83, should say '73)	.20	.08	.02
☐ 630A	Will Clark '89 ERR .... (32 total bases on card back)	2.00	.80	.20
☐ 630B	Will Clark '89 COR .... (321 total bases; technically still an error, listing only 24 runs)	.15	.06	.01
☐ 631	Game Savers .... Mark Davis Mitch Williams	.06	.02	.00
☐ 632	Boston Igniters .... Wade Boggs Mike Greenwell	.12	.05	.01
☐ 633	Starter and Stopper .... Mark Gubicza Jeff Russell	.06	.02	.00
☐ 634	League's Best .... Shortstops Tony Fernandez Cal Ripken	.15	.06	.01
☐ 635	Human Dynamos .... Kirby Puckett Bo Jackson	.20	.08	.02
☐ 636	300 Strikeout Club .... Nolan Ryan Mike Scott	.20	.08	.02
☐ 637	The Dynamic Duo .... Will Clark Kevin Mitchell	.15	.06	.01
☐ 638	AL All-Stars .... Don Mattingly Mark McGwire	.15	.06	.01
☐ 639	NL East Rivals .... Howard Johnson Ryne Sandberg	.12	.05	.01
☐ 640	Rudy Seanez .... Colin Charland	.17	.07	.01
☐ 641	George Canale .... Kevin Maas UER (Canale listed as INF on front, 1B on back)	1.25	.50	.12
☐ 642	Kelly Mann .... Dave Hansen	.25	.10	.02
☐ 643	Greg Smith .... Stu Tate	.10	.04	.01
☐ 644	Tom Drees .... Dann Howitt	.12	.05	.01
☐ 645	Mike Roesler .... Derrick May	.15	.06	.01
☐ 646	Scott Hemond .... Mark Gardner	.20	.08	.02
☐ 647	John Orton .... Scott Leius	.20	.08	.02
☐ 648	Rich Monteleone .... Dana Williams	.10	.04	.01
☐ 649	Mike Huff .... Steve Frey	.15	.06	.01
☐ 650	Chuck McElroy .... Moises Alou	.17	.07	.01
☐ 651	Bobby Rose .... Mike Hartley	.15	.06	.01
☐ 652	Matt Kinzer .... Wayne Edwards	.10	.04	.01
☐ 653	Delino DeShields .... Jason Grimsley	.45	.18	.04
☐ 654	CL: A's/Cubs .... Giants/Blue Jays	.06	.01	.00
☐ 655	CL: Royals/Angels .... Padres/Orioles	.06	.01	.00

		MINT	EXC	G-VG
☐ 656	CL: Mets/Astros .... Cards/Red Sox	.06	.01	.00
☐ 657	CL: Rangers/Brewers .... Expos/Twins	.06	.01	.00
☐ 658	CL: Dodgers/Reds .... Yankees/Pirates	.06	.01	.00
☐ 659	CL: Indians/Mariners .... White Sox/Phillies	.06	.01	.00
☐ 660A	CL: Braves/Tigers .... Specials/Checklists (Checklist-660 in small-er print on card front)	.06	.01	.00
☐ 660B	CL: Braves/Tigers .... Specials/Checklists (Checklist-660 in nor-mal print on card front)	.06	.01	.00

1990 Fleer Wax Box Cards

The 1990 Fleer wax box cards comprise seven different box bottoms with four cards each, for a total of 28 standard-size (2 1/2" by 3 1/2") cards. The outer front borders are white; the inner, ribbon-like borders are different depending on the team. The vertically-oriented backs are gray. The cards are numbered with a C prefix.

		MINT	EXC	G-VG
	COMPLETE SET (28)	9.00	4.00	.90
	COMMON PLAYER (C1-C28)	.10	.04	.01
☐ C1	Giants Logo	.10	.04	.01
☐ C2	Tim Belcher	.15	.06	.01
☐ C3	Roger Clemens	1.00	.40	.10
☐ C4	Eric Davis	.60	.25	.06
☐ C5	Glenn Davis	.30	.12	.03
☐ C6	Cubs Logo	.10	.04	.01
☐ C7	John Franco	.15	.06	.01
☐ C8	Mike Greenwell	.50	.20	.05
☐ C9	A's Logo	.10	.04	.01
☐ C10	Ken Griffey Jr.	2.00	.80	.20
☐ C11	Pedro Guerrero	.15	.06	.01
☐ C12	Tony Gwynn	.60	.25	.06
☐ C13	Blue Jays Logo	.10	.04	.01
☐ C14	Orel Hershiser	.30	.12	.03
☐ C15	Bo Jackson	1.50	.60	.15
☐ C16	Howard Johnson	.30	.12	.03
☐ C17	Mets Logo	.10	.04	.01
☐ C18	Cardinals Logo	.10	.04	.01
☐ C19	Don Mattingly	1.00	.40	.10
☐ C20	Mark McGwire	.75	.30	.07
☐ C21	Kevin Mitchell	.50	.20	.05
☐ C22	Kirby Puckett	.60	.25	.06
☐ C23	Royals Logo	.10	.04	.01
☐ C24	Orioles Logo	.10	.04	.01
☐ C25	Ruben Sierra	.75	.30	.07
☐ C26	Dave Stewart	.20	.08	.02
☐ C27	Jerome Walton	.60	.25	.06
☐ C28	Robin Yount	.50	.20	.05

1990 Fleer All-Star Inserts

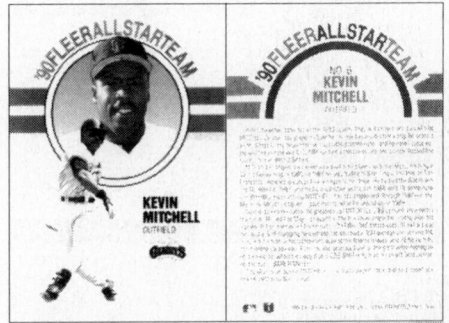

The 1990 Fleer All-Star insert set includes 12 standard-size (2 1/2" by 3 1/2") cards. The fronts are white with a light gray screen and bright red stripes. The vertically-oriented backs are red, pink and white. The player selection for the set is Fleer's opinion of the best Major Leaguer at each position. Cards were individually distributed as an insert in 33-card cellos and random wax packs.

		MINT	EXC	G-VG
	COMPLETE SET (12)	9.00	4.00	.90
	COMMON PLAYER (1-12)	.35	.15	.03
☐ 1	Harold Baines .... Designated Hitter	.45	.18	.04
☐ 2	Will Clark .... First Base	2.00	.80	.20
☐ 3	Mark Davis .... Relief Pitcher	.45	.18	.04
☐ 4	Howard Johnson UER .... Third Base (in middle of 5th line, the is misspelled th)	.60	.25	.06
☐ 5	Joe Magrane .... Left Handed Pitcher	.35	.15	.03
☐ 6	Kevin Mitchell .... Outfielder	1.00	.40	.10
☐ 7	Kirby Puckett .... Outfielder	1.25	.50	.12
☐ 8	Cal Ripken .... Shortstop	1.50	.60	.15
☐ 9	Ryne Sandberg .... Second Base	1.50	.60	.15
☐ 10	Mike Scott .... Right Handed Pitcher	.45	.18	.04
☐ 11	Ruben Sierra .... Outfielder	1.25	.50	.12
☐ 12	Mickey Tettleton .... Catcher	.35	.15	.03

1990 Fleer League Standouts

This six-card subset was distributed randomly (as an insert) in Fleer's 45-card rack packs. These cards are standard size, 2 1/2" by 3 1/2" and are quite attractive. The set is subtitled "Standouts" and commemorates outstanding events for those players from the previous season. The cards are numbered on the backs. The card backs are printed on white card stock.

		MINT	EXC	G-VG
	COMPLETE SET (6)	4.50	2.00	.45
	COMMON PLAYER (1-6)	.60	.25	.06
☐ 1	Barry Larkin .... Cincinnati Reds	.60	.25	.06
☐ 2	Don Mattingly .... New York Yankees	1.00	.40	.10

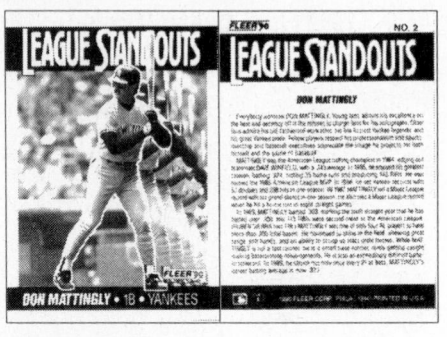

☐ 3 Darryl Strawberry	1.00	.40	.10
New York Mets			
☐ 4 Jose Canseco	1.25	.50	.12
Oakland A's			
☐ 5 Wade Boggs	1.00	.40	.10
Boston Red Sox			
☐ 6 Mark Grace	.90	.40	.09
Chicago Cubs			

1990 Fleer Soaring Stars

The 1990 Fleer Soaring Stars set was issued by Fleer in their jumbo cello packs. This 12-card, standard-size (2 1/2" by 3 1/2") set featured 12 of the most popular young players entering the 1990 season. The set gives the visual impression of rockets exploding in the air to honor these young players.

	MINT	EXC	G-VG
COMPLETE SET (12)	10.00	4.50	1.25
COMMON PLAYER (1-12)	.35	.15	.03
☐ 1 Todd Zeile	.75	.30	.07
☐ 2 Mike Stanton	.35	.15	.03
☐ 3 Larry Walker	.75	.30	.07
☐ 4 Robin Ventura	1.50	.60	.15
☐ 5 Scott Coolbaugh	.35	.15	.03
☐ 6 Ken Griffey Jr.	4.50	2.00	.45
☐ 7 Tom Gordon	.60	.25	.06
☐ 8 Jerome Walton	.75	.30	.07
☐ 9 Junior Felix	.60	.25	.06
☐ 10 Jim Abbott	1.50	.60	.15
☐ 11 Ricky Jordan	.45	.18	.04
☐ 12 Dwight Smith	.45	.18	.04

1990 Fleer Award Winners

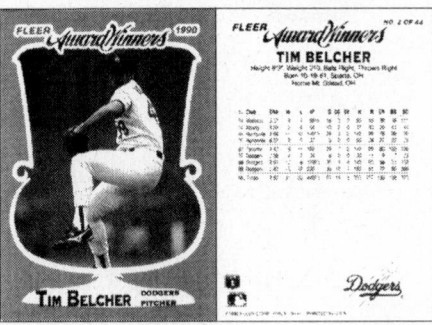

The 1990 Fleer Award Winners set was printed by Fleers for Hills stores (as well as for some 7/Eleven's) and released early in the summer of 1990. An unattractive design of a face inside solid blue borders with the players photo within the face caricature. This 44-card, standard-size (2 1/2" by 3 1/2") set is numbered in alphabetical order. Card number 10 is listed on the box checklist as being Ron Darling, but Darling is not in the set. Consequently the numbers on the box checklist between 10 and 37 are off by one. Darryl Strawberry (38) is not listed on the box, but is included in the set. The box also includes six peel-off team logo stickers. The original suggested retail price for the set at Hills was 2.49.

	MINT	EXC	G-VG
COMPLETE SET (44)	4.00	1.75	.40
COMMON PLAYER (1-44)	.10	.04	.01
☐ 1 Jeff Ballard	.10	.04	.01
☐ 2 Tim Belcher	.15	.06	.01
☐ 3 Bert Blyleven	.15	.06	.01
☐ 4 Wade Boggs	.50	.20	.05
☐ 5 Bob Boone	.15	.06	.01
☐ 6 Jose Canseco	.90	.40	.09
☐ 7 Will Clark	.90	.40	.09
☐ 8 Jack Clark	.15	.06	.01
☐ 9 Vince Coleman	.20	.08	.02
☐ 10 Eric Davis	.35	.15	.03
☐ 11 Jose DeLeon	.10	.04	.01
☐ 12 Tony Fernandez	.15	.06	.01
☐ 13 Carlton Fisk	.25	.10	.02
☐ 14 Scott Garrelts	.10	.04	.01
☐ 15 Tom Gordon	.20	.08	.02
☐ 16 Ken Griffey Jr.	1.25	.50	.12
☐ 17 Von Hayes	.15	.06	.01
☐ 18 Rickey Henderson	.75	.30	.07
☐ 19 Bo Jackson	1.00	.40	.10
☐ 20 Howard Johnson	.15	.06	.01
☐ 21 Don Mattingly	.75	.30	.07
☐ 22 Fred McGriff	.25	.10	.02
☐ 23 Kevin Mitchell	.30	.12	.03
☐ 24 Gregg Olson	.20	.08	.02
☐ 25 Gary Pettis	.10	.04	.01
☐ 26 Kirby Puckett	.40	.16	.04
☐ 27 Harold Reynolds	.10	.04	.01
☐ 28 Jeff Russell	.10	.04	.01
☐ 29 Nolan Ryan	1.00	.40	.10
☐ 30 Bret Saberhagen	.25	.10	.02
☐ 31 Ryne Sandberg	.75	.30	.07
☐ 32 Benito Santiago	.20	.08	.02
☐ 33 Mike Scott	.15	.06	.01
☐ 34 Ruben Sierra	.40	.16	.04
☐ 35 Lonnie Smith	.10	.04	.01
☐ 36 Ozzie Smith	.25	.10	.02
☐ 37 Dave Stewart	.15	.06	.01
☐ 38 Darryl Strawberry	.50	.20	.05
☐ 39 Greg Swindell	.15	.06	.01
☐ 40 Andy Van Slyke	.15	.06	.01
☐ 41 Tim Wallach	.15	.06	.01
☐ 42 Jerome Walton	.25	.10	.02
☐ 43 Mitch Williams	.10	.04	.01
☐ 44 Robin Yount	.35	.15	.03

1990 Fleer Baseball All-Stars

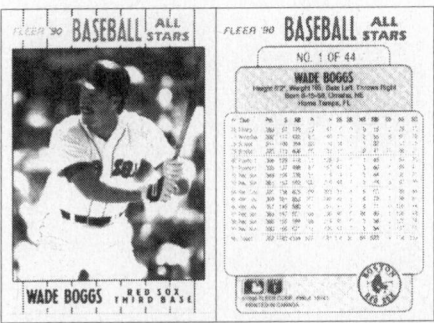

1990 Fleer Baseball MVP's

The 1990 Fleer Baseball All-Stars Set was produced by Fleer for the Ben Franklin chain and released early in the summer of 1990. This standard-size (2 1/2" by 3 1/2"), 44-card set features some of the best of today's players in alphabetical order. The design of the cards has vertical stripes on the front of the card. The set's custom box gives the set checklist on the back panel. The box also includes six peel-off team logo stickers each with a trivia quiz on back.

The 1990 Fleer Baseball MVP's were produced by Fleer exclusively for the Toys'R'Us chain and released early in the summer of 1990. This set has a multi-colored border, is standard size, 2 1/2" by 3 1/2", and has 44 players arranged in alphabetical order. The set's custom box gives the set checklist on the back panel. The box also includes six peel-off team logo stickers.

	MINT	EXC	G-VG
COMPLETE SET (44)	4.00	1.75	.40
COMMON PLAYER (1-44)	.10	.04	.01
☐ 1 Wade Boggs	.50	.20	.05
☐ 2 Bobby Bonilla	.30	.12	.03
☐ 3 Tim Burke	.10	.04	.01
☐ 4 Jose Canseco	.90	.40	.09
☐ 5 Will Clark	.90	.40	.09
☐ 6 Eric Davis	.35	.15	.03
☐ 7 Glenn Davis	.20	.08	.02
☐ 8 Julio Franco	.20	.08	.02
☐ 9 Tony Fernandez	.15	.06	.01
☐ 10 Gary Gaetti	.15	.06	.01
☐ 11 Scott Garrelts	.10	.04	.01
☐ 12 Mark Grace	.35	.15	.03
☐ 13 Mike Greenwell	.35	.15	.03
☐ 14 Ken Griffey Jr.	1.25	.50	.12
☐ 15 Mark Gubicza	.10	.04	.01
☐ 16 Pedro Guerrero	.15	.06	.01
☐ 17 Von Hayes	.15	.06	.01
☐ 18 Orel Hershiser	.20	.08	.02
☐ 19 Bruce Hurst	.10	.04	.01
☐ 20 Bo Jackson	1.00	.40	.10
☐ 21 Howard Johnson	.20	.08	.02
☐ 22 Doug Jones	.10	.04	.01
☐ 23 Barry Larkin	.20	.08	.02
☐ 24 Don Mattingly	.75	.30	.07
☐ 25 Mark McGwire	.50	.20	.05
☐ 26 Kevin McReynolds	.15	.06	.01
☐ 27 Kevin Mitchell	.25	.10	.02
☐ 28 Dan Plesac	.10	.04	.01
☐ 29 Kirby Puckett	.35	.15	.03
☐ 30 Cal Ripken	.75	.30	.07
☐ 31 Bret Saberhagen	.25	.10	.02
☐ 32 Ryne Sandberg	.75	.30	.07
☐ 33 Steve Sax	.15	.06	.01
☐ 34 Ruben Sierra	.35	.15	.03
☐ 35 Ozzie Smith	.25	.10	.02
☐ 36 John Smoltz	.15	.06	.01
☐ 37 Daryl Strawberry	.50	.20	.05
☐ 38 Terry Steinbach	.15	.06	.01
☐ 39 Dave Stewart	.15	.06	.01
☐ 40 Bobby Thigpen	.20	.08	.02
☐ 41 Alan Trammell	.20	.08	.02
☐ 42 Devon White	.15	.06	.01
☐ 43 Mitch Williams	.10	.04	.01
☐ 44 Robin Yount	.35	.15	.03

	MINT	EXC	G-VG
COMPLETE SET (44)	4.00	1.75	.40
COMMON PLAYER (1-44)	.10	.04	.01
☐ 1 George Bell	.20	.08	.02
☐ 2 Bert Blyleven	.15	.06	.01
☐ 3 Wade Boggs	.50	.20	.05
☐ 4 Bobby Bonilla	.35	.15	.03
☐ 5 George Brett	.40	.16	.04
☐ 6 Jose Canseco	.90	.40	.09
☐ 7 Will Clark	.90	.40	.09
☐ 8 Roger Clemens	.75	.30	.07
☐ 9 Eric Davis	.35	.15	.03
☐ 10 Glenn Davis	.20	.08	.02
☐ 11 Tony Fernandez	.15	.06	.01
☐ 12 Dwight Gooden	.30	.12	.03
☐ 13 Mike Greenwell	.30	.12	.03
☐ 14 Ken Griffey Jr.	1.25	.50	.12
☐ 15 Pedro Guerrero	.15	.06	.01
☐ 16 Tony Gwynn	.35	.15	.03
☐ 17 Rickey Henderson	.75	.30	.07
☐ 18 Tom Herr	.10	.04	.01
☐ 19 Orel Hershiser	.20	.08	.02
☐ 20 Kent Hrbek	.15	.06	.01
☐ 21 Bo Jackson	1.00	.40	.10
☐ 22 Howard Johnson	.20	.08	.02
☐ 23 Don Mattingly	.75	.30	.07
☐ 24 Fred McGriff	.30	.12	.03
☐ 25 Mark McGwire	.50	.20	.05
☐ 26 Kevin Mitchell	.35	.15	.03
☐ 27 Paul Molitor	.20	.08	.02
☐ 28 Dale Murphy	.30	.12	.03
☐ 29 Kirby Puckett	.35	.15	.03
☐ 30 Tim Raines	.20	.08	.02
☐ 31 Cal Ripken	.75	.30	.07
☐ 32 Bret Saberhagen	.25	.10	.02
☐ 33 Ryne Sandberg	.75	.30	.07
☐ 34 Ruben Sierra	.30	.12	.03
☐ 35 Dwight Smith	.15	.06	.01
☐ 36 Ozzie Smith	.25	.10	.02
☐ 37 Darryl Strawberry	.50	.20	.05
☐ 38 Dave Stewart	.15	.06	.01
☐ 39 Greg Swindell	.15	.06	.01
☐ 40 Bobby Thigpen	.20	.08	.02
☐ 41 Alan Trammell	.20	.08	.02
☐ 42 Jerome Walton	.20	.08	.02
☐ 43 Mitch Williams	.10	.04	.01
☐ 44 Robin Yount	.35	.15	.03

1990 Fleer League Leaders

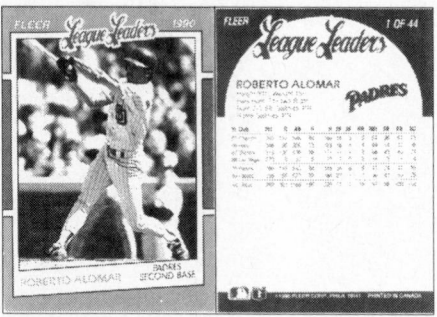

1990 Fleer World Series

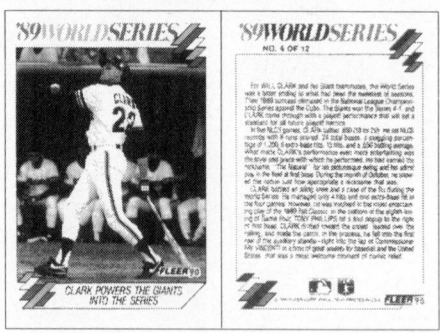

The 1990 Fleer League Leader set was issued by Fleer for Walgreen stores. This set design features solid blue borders with the players photo inset within the middle of the card. This 44-card, standard-size (2 1/2" by 3 1/2") set is numbered in alphabetical order. The set's custom box gives the set checklist on the back panel. The box also includes six peel-off team logo stickers. The original suggested retail price for the set at Walgreen's was 2.49.

	MINT	EXC	G-VG
COMPLETE SET (44)	4.00	1.75	.40
COMMON PLAYER (1-44)	.10	.04	.01
☐ 1 Roberto Alomar	.60	.25	.06
☐ 2 Tim Belcher	.15	.06	.01
☐ 3 George Bell	.15	.06	.01
☐ 4 Wade Boggs	.50	.20	.05
☐ 5 Jose Canseco	.90	.40	.09
☐ 6 Will Clark	.90	.40	.09
☐ 7 David Cone	.25	.10	.02
☐ 8 Eric Davis	.35	.15	.03
☐ 9 Glenn Davis	.20	.08	.02
☐ 10 Nick Esasky	.10	.04	.01
☐ 11 Dennis Eckersley	.15	.06	.01
☐ 12 Mark Grace	.45	.18	.04
☐ 13 Mike Greenwell	.30	.12	.03
☐ 14 Ken Griffey Jr.	1.25	.50	.12
☐ 15 Mark Gubicza	.10	.04	.01
☐ 16 Pedro Guerrero	.15	.06	.01
☐ 17 Tony Gwynn	.35	.15	.03
☐ 18 Rickey Henderson	.75	.30	.07
☐ 19 Bo Jackson	1.00	.40	.10
☐ 20 Doug Jones	.10	.04	.01
☐ 21 Ricky Jordan	.15	.06	.01
☐ 22 Barry Larkin	.20	.08	.02
☐ 23 Don Mattingly	.75	.30	.07
☐ 24 Fred McGriff	.30	.12	.03
☐ 25 Mark McGwire	.50	.20	.05
☐ 26 Kevin Mitchell	.30	.12	.03
☐ 27 Jack Morris	.15	.06	.01
☐ 28 Gregg Olson	.20	.08	.02
☐ 29 Dan Plesac	.10	.04	.01
☐ 30 Kirby Puckett	.30	.12	.03
☐ 31 Nolan Ryan	1.00	.40	.10
☐ 32 Bret Saberhagen	.25	.10	.02
☐ 33 Ryne Sandberg	.75	.30	.07
☐ 34 Steve Sax	.15	.06	.01
☐ 35 Mike Scott	.15	.06	.01
☐ 36 Ruben Sierra	.30	.12	.03
☐ 37 Lonnie Smith	.10	.04	.01
☐ 38 Darryl Strawberry	.45	.18	.04
☐ 39 Bobby Thigpen	.20	.08	.02
☐ 40 Andy Van Slyke	.15	.06	.01
☐ 41 Tim Wallach	.15	.06	.01
☐ 42 Jerome Walton UER (photo actually Eric Yelding)	.20	.08	.02
☐ 43 Devon White	.15	.06	.01
☐ 44 Robin Yount	.35	.15	.03

This 12-card standard size, 2 1/2" by 3 1/2" set was issued as an insert in with the Fleer factory sets, celebrating the 1989 World Series. This set marked the fourth year that Fleer issued a special World Series set in their factory (or vend) set. The design of these cards are different from the regular Fleer issue as the photo is framed by a white border with red and blue World Series cards and the player description in black.

	MINT	EXC	G-VG
COMPLETE SET (12)	3.00	1.25	.30
COMMON PLAYER (1-12)	.25	.10	.02
☐ 1 Mike Moore The final piece of the puzzle	.25	.10	.02
☐ 2 Kevin Mitchell N.L. MVP	.50	.20	.05
☐ 3 Terry Steinbach Game Two's Crushing Blow	.25	.10	.02
☐ 4 Will Clark Clark Powers Giants into the Series	.75	.30	.07
☐ 5 Jose Canseco Canseco Crushed World Series Slump	.75	.30	.07
☐ 6 Walt Weiss Great Leather in the field	.25	.10	.02
☐ 7 Terry Steinbach Game One and A's Break Out on Top	.25	.10	.02
☐ 8 Dave Stewart Oakland's MVP	.35	.15	.03
☐ 9 Dave Parker Parker's Bat Produces Power	.35	.15	.03
☐ 10 Dave Parker, Jose Canseco, and Will Clark: World Series Record Book Game 3	.50	.20	.05
☐ 11 Rickey Henderson Henderson Swipes Championship Series Records	.75	.30	.07
☐ 12 Oakland A's Celebrate Oakland A's: Baseball's Best in 89	.25	.10	.02

1990 Fleer Update

The 1990 Fleer Update set contains 132 standard-size (2 1/2" by 3 1/2") cards. This set marked the seventh consecutive year Fleer issued an end of season Update set. The set was issued exclusively as a boxed set through hobby dealers. The set is checklisted alphabetically by team for each league and then alphabetically within each team. The fronts are styled the same as the 1990 Fleer regular issue set. The backs are numbered

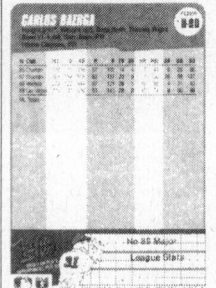

with the prefix U for Update. The key rookies in this set are Alex Fernandez, Travis Fryman, Jose Offerman, John Olerud, Frank Thomas, and Mark Whiten.

		MINT	EXC	G-VG
COMPLETE SET (132)		10.00	4.50	1.25
COMMON PLAYER (1-132)		.05	.02	.00

☐ U1	Steve Avery	1.25	.30	.06
☐ U2	Francisco Cabrera	.10	.04	.01
☐ U3	Nick Esasky	.05	.02	.00
☐ U4	Jim Kremers	.10	.04	.01
☐ U5	Greg Olson	.20	.08	.02
☐ U6	Jim Presley	.05	.02	.00
☐ U7	Shawn Boskie	.12	.05	.01
☐ U8	Joe Kraemer	.10	.04	.01
☐ U9	Luis Salazar	.05	.02	.00
☐ U10	Hector Villanueve	.12	.05	.01
☐ U11	Glenn Braggs	.08	.03	.01
☐ U12	Mariano Duncan	.08	.03	.01
☐ U13	Billy Hatcher	.08	.03	.01
☐ U14	Tim Layana	.10	.04	.01
☐ U15	Hal Morris	.35	.15	.03
☐ U16	Javier Ortiz	.12	.05	.01
☐ U17	Dave Rohde	.10	.04	.01
☐ U18	Eric Yelding	.10	.04	.01
☐ U19	Hubie Brooks	.10	.04	.01
☐ U20	Kal Daniels	.08	.03	.01
☐ U21	Dave Hansen	.20	.08	.02
☐ U22	Mike Hartley	.10	.04	.01
☐ U23	Stan Javier	.05	.02	.00
☐ U24	Jose Offerman	.25	.10	.02
☐ U25	Juan Samuel	.10	.04	.01
☐ U26	Dennis Boyd	.05	.02	.00
☐ U27	Delino DeShields	.35	.15	.03
☐ U28	Steve Frey	.08	.03	.01
☐ U29	Mark Gardner	.10	.04	.01
☐ U30	Chris Nabholz	.20	.08	.02
☐ U31	Bill Sampen	.12	.05	.01
☐ U32	Dave Schmidt	.05	.02	.00
☐ U33	Daryl Boston	.08	.03	.01
☐ U34	Chuck Carr	.10	.04	.01
☐ U35	John Franco	.08	.03	.01
☐ U36	Todd Hundley	.30	.12	.03
☐ U37	Julio Machado	.05	.02	.00
☐ U38	Alejandro Pena	.08	.03	.01
☐ U39	Darren Reed	.12	.05	.01
☐ U40	Kelvin Torve	.05	.02	.00
☐ U41	Darrel Akerfelds	.05	.02	.00
☐ U42	Jose DeJesus	.10	.04	.01
☐ U43	Dave Hollins	.35	.15	.03
	(misspelled Dane			
	on card back)			
☐ U44	Carmelo Martinez	.05	.02	.00
☐ U45	Brad Moore	.10	.04	.01
☐ U46	Dale Murphy	.12	.05	.01
☐ U47	Wally Backman	.05	.02	.00
☐ U48	Stan Belinda	.12	.05	.01
☐ U49	Bob Patterson	.05	.02	.00
☐ U50	Ted Power	.05	.02	.00
☐ U51	Don Slaught	.05	.02	.00
☐ U52	Geronimo Pena	.12	.05	.01
☐ U53	Lee Smith	.12	.05	.01
☐ U54	John Tudor	.10	.04	.01
☐ U55	Joe Carter	.15	.06	.01
☐ U56	Tom Howard	.12	.05	.01
☐ U57	Craig Lefferts	.05	.02	.00
☐ U58	Rafael Valdez	.10	.04	.01
☐ U59	Dave Anderson	.05	.02	.00
☐ U60	Kevin Bass	.05	.02	.00

☐ U61	John Burkett	.15	.06	.01
☐ U62	Gary Carter	.10	.04	.01
☐ U63	Rick Parker	.08	.03	.01
☐ U64	Trevor Wilson	.08	.03	.01
☐ U65	Chris Hoiles	.20	.08	.02
☐ U66	Tim Hulett	.05	.02	.00
☐ U67	Dave Johnson	.10	.04	.01
☐ U68	Curt Schilling	.08	.03	.01
☐ U69	David Segui	.15	.06	.01
☐ U70	Tom Brunansky	.08	.03	.01
☐ U71	Greg Harris	.05	.02	.00
☐ U72	Dana Kiecker	.10	.04	.01
☐ U73	Tim Naehring	.25	.10	.02
☐ U74	Tony Pena	.08	.03	.01
☐ U75	Jeff Reardon	.10	.04	.01
☐ U76	Jerry Reed	.05	.02	.00
☐ U77	Mark Eichhorn	.08	.03	.01
☐ U78	Mark Langston	.10	.04	.01
☐ U79	John Orton	.08	.03	.01
☐ U80	Luis Polonia	.08	.03	.01
☐ U81	Dave Winfield	.12	.05	.01
☐ U82	Cliff Young	.12	.05	.01
☐ U83	Wayne Edwards	.08	.03	.01
☐ U84	Alex Fernandez	.75	.30	.07
☐ U85	Craig Grebeck	.10	.04	.01
☐ U86	Scott Radinsky	.12	.05	.01
☐ U87	Frank Thomas	5.50	2.50	.55
☐ U88	Beau Allred	.12	.05	.01
☐ U89	Sandy Alomar Jr.	.10	.04	.01
☐ U90	Carlos Baerga	.35	.15	.03
☐ U91	Kevin Bearse	.10	.04	.01
☐ U92	Chris James	.08	.03	.01
☐ U93	Candy Maldonado	.08	.03	.01
☐ U94	Jeff Manto	.08	.03	.01
☐ U95	Cecil Fielder	.35	.15	.03
☐ U96	Travis Fryman	1.25	.50	.12
☐ U97	Lloyd Moseby	.05	.02	.00
☐ U98	Edwin Nunez	.05	.02	.00
☐ U99	Tony Phillips	.05	.02	.00
☐ U100	Larry Sheets	.05	.02	.00
☐ U101	Mark Davis	.08	.03	.01
☐ U102	Storm Davis	.05	.02	.00
☐ U103	Gerald Perry	.05	.02	.00
☐ U104	Terry Shumpert	.12	.05	.01
☐ U105	Edgar Diaz	.10	.04	.01
☐ U106	Dave Parker	.10	.04	.01
☐ U107	Tim Drummond	.10	.04	.01
☐ U108	Junior Ortiz	.05	.02	.00
☐ U109	Park Pittman	.10	.04	.01
☐ U110	Kevin Tapani	.30	.12	.03
☐ U111	Oscar Azocar	.12	.05	.01
☐ U112	Jim Leyritz	.10	.04	.01
☐ U113	Kevin Maas	1.25	.50	.12
☐ U114	Alan Mills	.12	.05	.01
☐ U115	Matt Nokes	.10	.04	.01
☐ U116	Pascual Perez	.08	.03	.01
☐ U117	Ozzie Canseco	.10	.04	.01
☐ U118	Scott Sanderson	.08	.03	.01
☐ U119	Tino Martinez	.50	.20	.05
☐ U120	Jeff Schneider	.10	.04	.01
☐ U121	Matt Young	.05	.02	.00
☐ U122	Brian Bohanon	.10	.04	.01
☐ U123	Jeff Huson	.08	.03	.01
☐ U124	Ramon Manon	.10	.04	.01
☐ U125	Gary Mielke UER	.08	.03	.01
	(shown as Blue			
	Jay on front)			
☐ U126	Willie Blair	.10	.04	.01
☐ U127	Glenallen Hill	.08	.03	.01
☐ U128	John Olerud	1.00	.40	.10
☐ U129	Luis Sojo	.12	.05	.01
☐ U130	Mark Whiten	.60	.25	.06
☐ U131	Nolan Ryan	.65	.25	.06
☐ U132	Checklist Card	.05	.01	.00

1991 Fleer

The 1991 Fleer set consists of 720 cards which measure the now standard size of 2 1/2" by 3 1/2". This set marks Fleer's eleventh consecutive year of issuing sets of current players. This set does not have what has been a Fleer tradition in recent years, the two-player rookie cards and there are less two-player special cards than in prior years. Apparently this was an attempt by Fleer to increase the number of single player cards in the set. The design features solid yellow borders with the information in black indicating name, position, and team. The backs feature beautiful full-color photos along with the career statistics and a biography for those players where there is room. The set is again ordered numerically by teams, followed by combination cards, rookie prospect pairs, and checklists. Again Fleer incorrectly anticipated the outcome of the 1990 Playoffs according to the team ordering. The A's, listed first, did not win the World Series and their opponents (and Series winners) were the Reds, not the Pirates. The complete team ordering is as follows: Oakland A's (1-28), Pittsburgh Pirates (29-54), Cincinnati Reds (55-82), Boston Red Sox (83-113), Chicago White Sox (114-139), New York Mets (140-166), Toronto Blue Jays (167-192), Los Angeles Dodgers (193-223), Montreal Expos (224-251), San Francisco Giants (252-277), Texas Rangers (278-304), California Angels (305-330), Detroit Tigers (331-357), Cleveland Indians (358-385), Philadelphia Phillies (386-412), Chicago Cubs (413-441), Seattle Mariners (442-465), Baltimore Orioles (466-496), Houston Astros (497-522), San Diego Padres (523-548), Kansas City Royals (549-575), Milwaukee Brewers (576-601), Minnesota Twins (602-627), St. Louis Cardinals (628-654), New York Yankees (655-680), and Atlanta Braves (681-708). A number of the cards in the set can be found with photos cropped (very slightly) differently as Fleer used two separate printers in their attempt to maximize production. The key rookie cards in this set are Wes Chamberlain, Luis Gonzalez, Brian McRae, and Phil Plantier.

		MINT	EXC	G-VG
COMPLETE SET (720)		18.00	7.50	2.50
COMMON PLAYER (1-720)		.03	.01	.00
☐ 1	Troy Afenir	.10	.03	.01
☐ 2	Harold Baines	.06	.02	.00
☐ 3	Lance Blankenship	.03	.01	.00
☐ 4	Todd Burns	.03	.01	.00
☐ 5	Jose Canseco	.25	.10	.02
☐ 6	Dennis Eckersley	.08	.03	.01
☐ 7	Mike Gallego	.03	.01	.00
☐ 8	Ron Hassey	.03	.01	.00
☐ 9	Dave Henderson	.06	.02	.00
☐ 10	Rickey Henderson	.20	.08	.02
☐ 11	Rick Honeycutt	.03	.01	.00
☐ 12	Doug Jennings	.03	.01	.00
☐ 13	Joe Klink	.06	.02	.00
☐ 14	Carney Lansford	.06	.02	.00
☐ 15	Darren Lewis	.20	.08	.02
☐ 16	Willie McGee UER	.06	.02	.00
	(Height 6'11")			
☐ 17	Mark McGwire UER	.10	.04	.01
	(183 extra base			
	hits in 1987)			
☐ 18	Mike Moore	.06	.02	.00
☐ 19	Gene Nelson	.03	.01	.00
☐ 20	Dave Otto	.03	.01	.00
☐ 21	Jamie Quirk	.03	.01	.00
☐ 22	Willie Randolph	.03	.01	.00
☐ 23	Scott Sanderson	.03	.01	.00
☐ 24	Terry Steinbach	.03	.01	.00
☐ 25	Dave Stewart	.08	.03	.01
☐ 26	Walt Weiss	.06	.02	.00
☐ 27	Bob Welch	.06	.02	.00
☐ 28	Curt Young	.03	.01	.00
☐ 29	Wally Backman	.03	.01	.00

☐ 30	Stan Belinda UER	.03	.01	.00
	(Born in Huntington,			
	should be State College)			
☐ 31	Jay Bell	.03	.01	.00
☐ 32	Rafael Belliard	.03	.01	.00
☐ 33	Barry Bonds	.12	.05	.01
☐ 34	Bobby Bonilla	.10	.04	.01
☐ 35	Sid Bream	.03	.01	.00
☐ 36	Doug Drabek	.06	.02	.00
☐ 37	Carlos Garcia	.08	.03	.01
☐ 38	Neal Heaton	.03	.01	.00
☐ 39	Jeff King	.06	.02	.00
☐ 40	Bob Kipper	.03	.01	.00
☐ 41	Bill Landrum	.03	.01	.00
☐ 42	Mike LaValliere	.03	.01	.00
☐ 43	Jose Lind	.03	.01	.00
☐ 44	Carmelo Martinez	.03	.01	.00
☐ 45	Bob Patterson	.03	.01	.00
☐ 46	Ted Power	.03	.01	.00
☐ 47	Gary Redus	.03	.01	.00
☐ 48	R.J. Reynolds	.03	.01	.00
☐ 49	Don Slaught	.03	.01	.00
☐ 50	John Smiley	.06	.02	.00
☐ 51	Zane Smith	.06	.02	.00
☐ 52	Randy Tomlin	.17	.07	.01
☐ 53	Andy Van Slyke	.08	.03	.01
☐ 54	Bob Walk	.03	.01	.00
☐ 55	Jack Armstrong	.06	.02	.00
☐ 56	Todd Benzinger	.03	.01	.00
☐ 57	Glenn Braggs	.03	.01	.00
☐ 58	Keith Brown	.03	.01	.00
☐ 59	Tom Browning	.06	.02	.00
☐ 60	Norm Charlton	.03	.01	.00
☐ 61	Eric Davis	.10	.04	.01
☐ 62	Rob Dibble	.06	.02	.00
☐ 63	Bill Doran	.03	.01	.00
☐ 64	Mariano Duncan	.03	.01	.00
☐ 65	Chris Hammond	.06	.02	.00
☐ 66	Billy Hatcher	.03	.01	.00
☐ 67	Danny Jackson	.03	.01	.00
☐ 68	Barry Larkin	.08	.03	.01
☐ 69	Tim Layana	.03	.01	.00
	(Black line over made			
	in first text line)			
☐ 70	Terry Lee	.08	.03	.01
☐ 71	Rick Mahler	.03	.01	.00
☐ 72	Hal Morris	.10	.04	.01
☐ 73	Randy Myers	.03	.01	.00
☐ 74	Ron Oester	.03	.01	.00
☐ 75	Joe Oliver	.03	.01	.00
☐ 76	Paul O'Neill	.06	.02	.00
☐ 77	Luis Quinones	.03	.01	.00
☐ 78	Jeff Reed	.03	.01	.00
☐ 79	Jose Rijo	.06	.02	.00
☐ 80	Chris Sabo	.08	.03	.01
☐ 81	Scott Scudder	.06	.02	.00
☐ 82	Herm Winningham	.03	.01	.00
☐ 83	Larry Andersen	.03	.01	.00
☐ 84	Marty Barrett	.03	.01	.00
☐ 85	Mike Boddicker	.03	.01	.00
☐ 86	Wade Boggs	.12	.05	.01
☐ 87	Tom Bolton	.03	.01	.00
☐ 88	Tom Brunansky	.06	.02	.00
☐ 89	Ellis Burks	.08	.03	.01
☐ 90	Roger Clemens	.15	.06	.01
☐ 91	Scott Cooper	.17	.07	.01
☐ 92	John Dopson	.03	.01	.00
☐ 93	Dwight Evans	.06	.02	.00
☐ 94	Wes Gardner	.03	.01	.00
☐ 95	Jeff Gray	.08	.03	.01
☐ 96	Mike Greenwell	.10	.04	.01
☐ 97	Greg Harris	.03	.01	.00
☐ 98	Daryl Irvine	.08	.03	.01
☐ 99	Dana Kiecker	.03	.01	.00
☐ 100	Randy Kutcher	.03	.01	.00
☐ 101	Dennis Lamp	.03	.01	.00
☐ 102	Mike Marshall	.06	.02	.00
☐ 103	John Marzano	.03	.01	.00
☐ 104	Rob Murphy	.03	.01	.00
☐ 105	Tim Naehring	.10	.04	.01
☐ 106	Tony Pena	.06	.02	.00
☐ 107	Phil Plantier	1.25	.50	.12
☐ 108	Carlos Quintana	.06	.02	.00
☐ 109	Jeff Reardon	.06	.02	.00
☐ 110	Jerry Reed	.03	.01	.00
☐ 111	Jody Reed	.06	.02	.00
☐ 112	Luis Rivera UER	.03	.01	.00
	(Born 1/3/84)			
☐ 113	Kevin Romine	.03	.01	.00
☐ 114	Phil Bradley	.06	.02	.00
☐ 115	Ivan Calderon	.06	.02	.00
☐ 116	Wayne Edwards	.03	.01	.00
☐ 117	Alex Fernandez	.20	.08	.02
☐ 118	Carlton Fisk	.10	.04	.01

☐ 119	Scott Fletcher	.03	.01	.00
☐ 120	Craig Grebeck	.03	.01	.00
☐ 121	Ozzie Guillen	.06	.02	.00
☐ 122	Greg Hibbard	.03	.01	.00
☐ 123	Lance Johnson UER	.03	.01	.00
	(Born Cincinnati, should			
	be Lincoln Heights)			
☐ 124	Barry Jones	.03	.01	.00
☐ 125	Ron Karkovice	.03	.01	.00
☐ 126	Eric King	.03	.01	.00
☐ 127	Steve Lyons	.03	.01	.00
☐ 128	Carlos Martinez	.03	.01	.00
☐ 129	Jack McDowell UER	.08	.03	.01
	(Stanford misspelled			
	as Standford on back)			
☐ 130	Donn Pall	.03	.01	.00
	(No dots over any			
	i's in text)			
☐ 131	Dan Pasqua	.03	.01	.00
☐ 132	Ken Patterson	.03	.01	.00
☐ 133	Melido Perez	.03	.01	.00
☐ 134	Adam Peterson	.03	.01	.00
☐ 135	Scott Radinsky	.06	.02	.00
☐ 136	Sammy Sosa	.08	.03	.01
☐ 137	Bobby Thigpen	.06	.02	.00
☐ 138	Frank Thomas	1.25	.50	.12
☐ 139	Robin Ventura	.20	.08	.02
☐ 140	Daryl Boston	.03	.01	.00
☐ 141	Chuck Carr	.03	.01	.00
☐ 142	Mark Carreon	.03	.01	.00
☐ 143	David Cone	.06	.02	.00
☐ 144	Ron Darling	.06	.02	.00
☐ 145	Kevin Elster	.03	.01	.00
☐ 146	Sid Fernandez	.06	.02	.00
☐ 147	John Franco	.03	.01	.00
☐ 148	Dwight Gooden	.10	.04	.01
☐ 149	Tom Herr	.03	.01	.00
☐ 150	Todd Hundley	.10	.04	.01
☐ 151	Gregg Jefferies	.08	.03	.01
☐ 152	Howard Johnson	.08	.03	.01
☐ 153	Dave Magadan	.06	.02	.00
☐ 154	Kevin McReynolds	.06	.02	.00
☐ 155	Keith Miller UER	.03	.01	.00
	(Text says Rochester in			
	'87, stats say Tide-			
	water, mixed up with			
	other Keith Miller)			
☐ 156	Bob Ojeda	.03	.01	.00
☐ 157	Tom O'Malley	.03	.01	.00
☐ 158	Alejandro Pena	.06	.02	.00
☐ 159	Darren Reed	.03	.01	.00
☐ 160	Mackey Sasser	.03	.01	.00
☐ 161	Darryl Strawberry	.15	.06	.01
☐ 162	Tim Teufel	.03	.01	.00
☐ 163	Kelvin Torve	.03	.01	.00
☐ 164	Julio Valera	.08	.03	.01
☐ 165	Frank Viola	.08	.03	.01
☐ 166	Wally Whitehurst	.03	.01	.00
☐ 167	Jim Acker	.03	.01	.00
☐ 168	Derek Bell	.35	.15	.03
☐ 169	George Bell	.08	.03	.01
☐ 170	Willie Blair	.03	.01	.00
☐ 171	Pat Borders	.03	.01	.00
☐ 172	John Cerutti	.03	.01	.00
☐ 173	Junior Felix	.06	.02	.00
☐ 174	Tony Fernandez	.06	.02	.00
☐ 175	Kelly Gruber UER	.08	.03	.01
	(Born in Houston,			
	should be Bellaire)			
☐ 176	Tom Henke	.06	.02	.00
☐ 177	Glenallen Hill	.06	.02	.00
☐ 178	Jimmy Key	.06	.02	.00
☐ 179	Manny Lee	.03	.01	.00
☐ 180	Fred McGriff	.08	.03	.01
☐ 181	Rance Mulliniks	.03	.01	.00
☐ 182	Greg Myers	.03	.01	.00
☐ 183	John Olerud	.12	.05	.01
☐ 184	Luis Sojo	.06	.02	.00
☐ 185	Dave Stieb	.06	.02	.00
☐ 186	Todd Stottlemyre	.06	.02	.00
☐ 187	Duane Ward	.03	.01	.00
☐ 188	David Wells	.03	.01	.00
☐ 189	Mark Whiten	.17	.07	.01
☐ 190	Ken Williams	.03	.01	.00
☐ 191	Frank Wills	.03	.01	.00
☐ 192	Mookie Wilson	.03	.01	.00
☐ 193	Don Aase	.03	.01	.00
☐ 194	Tim Belcher UER	.06	.02	
	(Born Sparta, Ohio,			
	should say Mt. Gilead)			
☐ 195	Hubie Brooks	.06	.02	.00
☐ 196	Dennis Cook	.03	.01	.00
☐ 197	Tim Crews	.03	.01	.00
☐ 198	Kal Daniels	.06	.02	.00
☐ 199	Kirk Gibson	.08	.03	.01
☐ 200	Jim Gott	.03	.01	.00
☐ 201	Alfredo Griffin	.03	.01	.00
☐ 202	Chris Gwynn	.03	.01	.00
☐ 203	Dave Hansen	.06	.02	.00
☐ 204	Lenny Harris	.03	.01	.00
☐ 205	Mike Hartley	.03	.01	.00
☐ 206	Mickey Hatcher	.03	.01	.00
☐ 207	Carlos Hernandez	.08	.03	.01
☐ 208	Orel Hershiser	.08	.03	.01
☐ 209	Jay Howell UER	.03	.01	.00
	(No 1982 Yankee stats)			
☐ 210	Mike Huff	.06	.02	.00
☐ 211	Stan Javier	.03	.01	.00
☐ 212	Ramon Martinez	.10	.04	.01
☐ 213	Mike Morgan	.03	.01	.00
☐ 214	Eddie Murray	.10	.04	.01
☐ 215	Jim Neidlinger	.10	.04	.01
☐ 216	Jose Offerman	.10	.04	.01
☐ 217	Jim Poole	.10	.04	.01
☐ 218	Juan Samuel	.06	.02	.00
☐ 219	Mike Scioscia	.03	.01	.00
☐ 220	Ray Searage	.03	.01	.00
☐ 221	Mike Sharperson	.03	.01	.00
☐ 222	Fernando Valenzuela	.06	.02	.00
☐ 223	Jose Vizcaino	.03	.01	.00
☐ 224	Mike Aldrete	.03	.01	.00
☐ 225	Scott Anderson	.08	.03	.01
☐ 226	Dennis Boyd	.03	.01	.00
☐ 227	Tim Burke	.03	.01	.00
☐ 228	Delino DeShields	.10	.04	.01
☐ 229	Mike Fitzgerald	.03	.01	.00
☐ 230	Tom Foley	.03	.01	.00
☐ 231	Steve Frey	.03	.01	.00
☐ 232	Andres Galarraga	.06	.02	.00
☐ 233	Mark Gardner	.06	.02	.00
☐ 234	Marquis Grissom	.10	.04	.01
☐ 235	Kevin Gross	.03	.01	.00
	(No date given for			
	first Expos win)			
☐ 236	Drew Hall	.03	.01	.00
☐ 237	Dave Martinez	.03	.01	.00
☐ 238	Dennis Martinez	.06	.02	.00
☐ 239	Dale Mohorcic	.03	.01	.00
☐ 240	Chris Nabholz	.06	.02	.00
☐ 241	Otis Nixon	.06	.02	.00
☐ 242	Junior Noboa	.03	.01	.00
☐ 243	Spike Owen	.03	.01	.00
☐ 244	Tim Raines	.08	.03	.01
☐ 245	Mel Rojas UER	.06	.02	.00
	(Stats show 3.60 ERA,			
	bio says 3.19 ERA)			
☐ 246	Scott Ruskin	.08	.03	.01
☐ 247	Bill Sampen	.03	.01	.00
☐ 248	Nelson Santovenia	.03	.01	.00
☐ 249	Dave Schmidt	.03	.01	.00
☐ 250	Larry Walker	.08	.03	.01
☐ 251	Tim Wallach	.06	.02	.00
☐ 252	Dave Anderson	.03	.01	.00
☐ 253	Kevin Bass	.03	.01	.00
☐ 254	Steve Bedrosian	.03	.01	.00
☐ 255	Jeff Brantley	.03	.01	.00
☐ 256	John Burkett	.03	.01	.00
☐ 257	Brett Butler	.06	.02	.00
☐ 258	Gary Carter	.08	.03	.01
☐ 259	Will Clark	.20	.08	.02
☐ 260	Steve Decker	.25	.10	.02
☐ 261	Kelly Downs	.03	.01	.00
☐ 262	Scott Garrelts	.03	.01	.00
☐ 263	Terry Kennedy	.03	.01	.00
☐ 264	Mike LaCoss	.03	.01	.00
☐ 265	Mark Leonard	.12	.05	.01
☐ 266	Greg Litton	.03	.01	.00
☐ 267	Kevin Mitchell	.10	.04	.01
☐ 268	Randy O'Neal	.03	.01	.00
☐ 269	Rick Parker	.03	.01	.00
☐ 270	Rick Reuschel	.06	.02	.00
☐ 271	Ernest Riles	.03	.01	.00
☐ 272	Don Robinson	.03	.01	.00
☐ 273	Robby Thompson	.03	.01	.00
☐ 274	Mark Thurmond	.03	.01	.00
☐ 275	Jose Uribe	.03	.01	.00
☐ 276	Matt Williams	.10	.04	.01
☐ 277	Trevor Wilson	.03	.01	.00
☐ 278	Gerald Alexander	.10	.04	.01
☐ 279	Brad Arnsberg	.03	.01	.00
☐ 280	Kevin Belcher	.10	.04	.01
☐ 281	Joe Bitker	.08	.03	.01
☐ 282	Kevin Brown	.03	.01	.00
☐ 283	Steve Buechele	.03	.01	.00
☐ 284	Jack Daugherty	.03	.01	.00
☐ 285	Julio Franco	.08	.03	.01
☐ 286	Juan Gonzalez	.30	.12	.03
☐ 287	Bill Haselman	.08	.03	.01

☐ 288	Charlie Hough	.03	.01	.00
☐ 289	Jeff Huson	.03	.01	.00
☐ 290	Pete Incaviglia	.06	.02	.00
☐ 291	Mike Jeffcoat	.03	.01	.00
☐ 292	Jeff Kunkel	.03	.01	.00
☐ 293	Gary Mielke	.03	.01	.00
☐ 294	Jamie Moyer	.03	.01	.00
☐ 295	Rafael Palmeiro	.10	.04	.01
☐ 296	Geno Petralli	.03	.01	.00
☐ 297	Gary Pettis	.03	.01	.00
☐ 298	Kevin Reimer	.08	.03	.01
☐ 299	Kenny Rogers	.03	.01	.00
☐ 300	Jeff Russell	.03	.01	.00
☐ 301	John Russell	.03	.01	.00
☐ 302	Nolan Ryan	.35	.15	.03
☐ 303	Ruben Sierra	.12	.05	.01
☐ 304	Bobby Witt	.06	.02	.00
☐ 305	Jim Abbott	.10	.04	.01
☐ 306	Kent Anderson	.03	.01	.00
☐ 307	Dante Bichette	.03	.01	.00
☐ 308	Bert Blyleven	.06	.02	.00
☐ 309	Chili Davis	.06	.02	.00
☐ 310	Brian Downing	.03	.01	.00
☐ 311	Mark Eichhorn	.03	.01	.00
☐ 312	Mike Fetters	.03	.01	.00
☐ 313	Chuck Finley	.06	.02	.00
☐ 314	Willie Fraser	.03	.01	.00
☐ 315	Bryan Harvey	.06	.02	.00
☐ 316	Donnie Hill	.03	.01	.00
☐ 317	Wally Joyner	.08	.03	.01
☐ 318	Mark Langston	.06	.02	.00
☐ 319	Kirk McCaskill	.03	.01	.00
☐ 320	John Orton	.03	.01	.00
☐ 321	Lance Parrish	.06	.02	.00
☐ 322	Luis Polonia UER (1984 Madfison, should be Madison)	.03	.01	.00
☐ 323	Johnny Ray	.03	.01	.00
☐ 324	Bobby Rose	.03	.01	.00
☐ 325	Dick Schofield	.03	.01	.00
☐ 326	Rick Schu	.03	.01	.00
☐ 327	Lee Stevens	.08	.03	.01
☐ 328	Devon White	.06	.02	.00
☐ 329	Dave Winfield	.10	.04	.01
☐ 330	Cliff Young	.03	.01	.00
☐ 331	Dave Bergman	.03	.01	.00
☐ 332	Phil Clark	.15	.06	.01
☐ 333	Darnell Coles	.03	.01	.00
☐ 334	Milt Cuyler	.15	.06	.01
☐ 335	Cecil Fielder	.15	.06	.01
☐ 336	Travis Fryman	.40	.16	.04
☐ 337	Paul Gibson	.03	.01	.00
☐ 338	Jerry Don Gleaton	.03	.01	.00
☐ 339	Mike Heath	.03	.01	.00
☐ 340	Mike Henneman	.03	.01	.00
☐ 341	Chet Lemon	.03	.01	.00
☐ 342	Lance McCullers	.03	.01	.00
☐ 343	Jack Morris	.08	.03	.01
☐ 344	Lloyd Moseby	.03	.01	.00
☐ 345	Edwin Nunez	.03	.01	.00
☐ 346	Clay Parker	.03	.01	.00
☐ 347	Dan Petry	.03	.01	.00
☐ 348	Tony Phillips	.03	.01	.00
☐ 349	Jeff Robinson	.03	.01	.00
☐ 350	Mark Salas	.03	.01	.00
☐ 351	Mike Schwabe	.03	.01	.00
☐ 352	Larry Sheets	.03	.01	.00
☐ 353	John Shelby	.03	.01	.00
☐ 354	Frank Tanana	.06	.02	.00
☐ 355	Alan Trammell	.08	.03	.01
☐ 356	Gary Ward	.03	.01	.00
☐ 357	Lou Whitaker	.06	.02	.00
☐ 358	Beau Allred	.06	.02	.00
☐ 359	Sandy Alomar Jr.	.08	.03	.01
☐ 360	Carlos Baerga	.10	.04	.01
☐ 361	Kevin Bearse	.03	.01	.00
☐ 362	Tom Brookens	.03	.01	.00
☐ 363	Jerry Browne UER (No dot over i in first text line)	.03	.01	.00
☐ 364	Tom Candiotti	.06	.02	.00
☐ 365	Alex Cole	.08	.03	.01
☐ 366	John Farrell UER (Born in Neptune, should be Monmouth)	.03	.01	.00
☐ 367	Felix Fermin	.03	.01	.00
☐ 368	Keith Hernandez	.06	.02	.00
☐ 369	Brook Jacoby	.03	.01	.00
☐ 370	Chris James	.03	.01	.00
☐ 371	Dion James	.03	.01	.00
☐ 372	Doug Jones	.03	.01	.00
☐ 373	Candy Maldonado	.03	.01	.00
☐ 374	Steve Olin	.03	.01	.00
☐ 375	Jesse Orosco	.03	.01	.00

☐ 376	Rudy Seanez	.06	.02	.00
☐ 377	Joel Skinner	.03	.01	.00
☐ 378	Cory Snyder	.06	.02	.00
☐ 379	Greg Swindell	.06	.02	.00
☐ 380	Sergio Valdez	.06	.02	.00
☐ 381	Mike Walker	.03	.01	.00
☐ 382	Colby Ward	.08	.03	.01
☐ 383	Turner Ward	.12	.05	.01
☐ 384	Mitch Webster	.03	.01	.00
☐ 385	Kevin Wickander	.03	.01	.00
☐ 386	Darrel Akerfelds	.03	.01	.00
☐ 387	Joe Boever	.03	.01	.00
☐ 388	Rod Booker	.03	.01	.00
☐ 389	Sil Campusano	.03	.01	.00
☐ 390	Don Carman	.03	.01	.00
☐ 391	Wes Chamberlain	.45	.18	.04
☐ 392	Pat Combs	.03	.01	.00
☐ 393	Darren Daulton	.03	.01	.00
☐ 394	Jose DeJesus	.03	.01	.00
☐ 395	Len Dykstra	.06	.02	.00
☐ 396	Jason Grimsley	.03	.01	.00
☐ 397	Charlie Hayes	.03	.01	.00
☐ 398	Von Hayes	.06	.02	.00
☐ 399	David Hollins UER (Atl-bats, should say at-bats)	.08	.03	.01
☐ 400	Ken Howell	.03	.01	.00
☐ 401	Ricky Jordan	.06	.02	.00
☐ 402	John Kruk	.03	.01	.00
☐ 403	Steve Lake	.03	.01	.00
☐ 404	Chuck Malone	.06	.02	.00
☐ 405	Roger McDowell UER (Says Phillies is saves, should say in)	.03	.01	.00
☐ 406	Chuck McElroy	.03	.01	.00
☐ 407	Mickey Morandini	.10	.04	.01
☐ 408	Terry Mulholland	.03	.01	.00
☐ 409	Dale Murphy	.10	.04	.01
☐ 410A	Randy Ready ERR (No Brewers stats listed for 1983)	.06	.02	.00
☐ 410B	Randy Ready COR	.06	.02	.00
☐ 411	Bruce Ruffin	.03	.01	.00
☐ 412	Dickie Thon	.03	.01	.00
☐ 413	Paul Assenmacher	.03	.01	.00
☐ 414	Damon Berryhill	.03	.01	.00
☐ 415	Mike Bielecki	.03	.01	.00
☐ 416	Shawn Boskie	.03	.01	.00
☐ 417	Dave Clark	.03	.01	.00
☐ 418	Doug Dascenzo	.03	.01	.00
☐ 419A	Andre Dawson ERR (No stats for 1976)	.12	.05	.01
☐ 419B	Andre Dawson COR	.12	.05	.01
☐ 420	Shawon Dunston	.06	.02	.00
☐ 421	Joe Girardi	.03	.01	.00
☐ 422	Mark Grace	.08	.03	.01
☐ 423	Mike Harkey	.06	.02	.00
☐ 424	Les Lancaster	.03	.01	.00
☐ 425	Bill Long	.03	.01	.00
☐ 426	Greg Maddux	.06	.02	.00
☐ 427	Derrick May	.08	.03	.01
☐ 428	Jeff Pico	.03	.01	.00
☐ 429	Domingo Ramos	.03	.01	.00
☐ 430	Luis Salazar	.03	.01	.00
☐ 431	Ryne Sandberg	.20	.08	.02
☐ 432	Dwight Smith	.06	.02	.00
☐ 433	Greg Smith	.03	.01	.00
☐ 434	Rick Sutcliffe	.06	.02	.00
☐ 435	Gary Varsho	.03	.01	.00
☐ 436	Hector Villanueva	.06	.02	.00
☐ 437	Jerome Walton	.08	.03	.01
☐ 438	Curtis Wilkerson	.03	.01	.00
☐ 439	Mitch Williams	.03	.01	.00
☐ 440	Steve Wilson	.03	.01	.00
☐ 441	Marvell Wynne	.03	.01	.00
☐ 442	Scott Bankhead	.03	.01	.00
☐ 443	Scott Bradley	.03	.01	.00
☐ 444	Greg Briley	.03	.01	.00
☐ 445	Mike Brumley UER (Text 40 SB's in 1988, stats say 41)	.03	.01	.00
☐ 446	Jay Buhner	.06	.02	.00
☐ 447	Dave Burba	.10	.04	.01
☐ 448	Henry Cotto	.03	.01	.00
☐ 449	Alvin Davis	.06	.02	.00
☐ 450A	Ken Griffey Jr. (Bat .300)	.75	.30	.07
☐ 450B	Ken Griffey Jr. (Bat around .300)	.75	.30	.07
☐ 451	Erik Hanson	.06	.02	.00
☐ 452	Gene Harris UER (63 career runs, should be 73)	.03	.01	.00
☐ 453	Brian Holman	.03	.01	.00

#	Player			
☐ 454	Mike Jackson	.03	.01	.00
☐ 455	Randy Johnson	.06	.02	.00
☐ 456	Jeffrey Leonard	.03	.01	.00
☐ 457	Edgar Martinez	.06	.02	.00
☐ 458	Tino Martinez	.15	.06	.01
☐ 459	Pete O'Brien UER	.03	.01	.00
	(1987 BA .266, should be .286)			
☐ 460	Harold Reynolds	.06	.02	.00
☐ 461	Mike Schooler	.03	.01	.00
☐ 462	Bill Swift	.03	.01	.00
☐ 463	David Valle	.03	.01	.00
☐ 464	Omar Vizquel	.03	.01	.00
☐ 465	Matt Young	.03	.01	.00
☐ 466	Brady Anderson	.03	.01	.00
☐ 467	Jeff Ballard UER	.03	.01	.00
	(Missing top of right parenthesis after Saberhagen in last text line)			
☐ 468	Juan Bell	.06	.02	.00
☐ 469A	Mike Devereaux	.06	.02	.00
	(First line of text ends with six)			
☐ 469B	Mike Devereaux	.06	.02	.00
	(First line of text ends with runs)			
☐ 470	Steve Finley	.06	.02	.00
☐ 471	Dave Gallagher	.03	.01	.00
☐ 472	Leo Gomez	.25	.10	.02
☐ 473	Rene Gonzales	.03	.01	.00
☐ 474	Pete Harnisch	.06	.02	.00
☐ 475	Kevin Hickey	.03	.01	.00
☐ 476	Chris Hoiles	.08	.03	.01
☐ 477	Sam Horn	.06	.02	.00
☐ 478	Tim Hulett	.03	.01	.00
	(Photo shows National Leaguer sliding into second base)			
☐ 479	Dave Johnson	.03	.01	.00
☐ 480	Ron Kittle UER	.06	.02	.00
	(Edmonton misspelled as Edmundton)			
☐ 481	Ben McDonald	.10	.04	.01
☐ 482	Bob Melvin	.03	.01	.00
☐ 483	Bob Milacki	.03	.01	.00
☐ 484	Randy Milligan	.06	.02	.00
☐ 485	John Mitchell	.03	.01	.00
☐ 486	Gregg Olson	.08	.03	.01
☐ 487	Joe Orsulak	.03	.01	.00
☐ 488	Joe Price	.03	.01	.00
☐ 489	Bill Ripken	.03	.01	.00
☐ 490	Cal Ripken	.20	.08	.02
☐ 491	Curt Schilling	.03	.01	.00
☐ 492	David Segui	.08	.03	.01
☐ 493	Anthony Telford	.08	.03	.01
☐ 494	Mickey Tettleton	.06	.02	.00
☐ 495	Mark Williamson	.03	.01	.00
☐ 496	Craig Worthington	.03	.01	.00
☐ 497	Juan Agosto	.03	.01	.00
☐ 498	Eric Anthony	.08	.03	.01
☐ 499	Craig Biggio	.06	.02	.00
☐ 500	Ken Caminiti UER	.03	.01	.00
	(Born 4/4, should be 4/21)			
☐ 501	Casey Candaele	.03	.01	.00
☐ 502	Andujar Cedeno	.35	.15	.03
☐ 503	Danny Darwin	.03	.01	.00
☐ 504	Mark Davidson	.03	.01	.00
☐ 505	Glenn Davis	.08	.03	.01
☐ 506	Jim Deshaies	.03	.01	.00
☐ 507	Luis Gonzalez	.40	.16	.04
☐ 508	Bill Gullickson	.06	.02	.00
☐ 509	Xavier Hernandez	.06	.02	.00
☐ 510	Brian Meyer	.03	.01	.00
☐ 511	Ken Oberkfell	.03	.01	.00
☐ 512	Mark Portugal	.03	.01	.00
☐ 513	Rafael Ramirez	.03	.01	.00
☐ 514	Karl Rhodes	.06	.02	.00
☐ 515	Mike Scott	.06	.02	.00
☐ 516	Mike Simms	.12	.05	.01
☐ 517	Dave Smith	.03	.01	.00
☐ 518	Franklin Stubbs	.03	.01	.00
☐ 519	Glenn Wilson	.03	.01	.00
☐ 520	Eric Yelding UER	.03	.01	.00
	(Text has 63 steals, stats have 64, which is correct)			
☐ 521	Gerald Young	.03	.01	.00
☐ 522	Shawn Abner	.03	.01	.00
☐ 523	Roberto Alomar	.10	.04	.01
☐ 524	Andy Benes	.08	.03	.01
☐ 525	Joe Carter	.08	.03	.01
☐ 526	Jack Clark	.06	.02	.00
☐ 527	Joey Cora	.03	.01	.00
☐ 528	Paul Faries	.08	.03	.01
☐ 529	Tony Gwynn	.12	.05	.01
☐ 530	Atlee Hammaker	.03	.01	.00
☐ 531	Greg Harris	.03	.01	.00
☐ 532	Thomas Howard	.03	.01	.00
☐ 533	Bruce Hurst	.06	.02	.00
☐ 534	Craig Lefferts	.03	.01	.00
☐ 535	Derek Lilliquist	.03	.01	.00
☐ 536	Fred Lynn	.06	.02	.00
☐ 537	Mike Pagliarulo	.03	.01	.00
☐ 538	Mark Parent	.03	.01	.00
☐ 539	Dennis Rasmussen	.03	.01	.00
☐ 540	Bip Roberts	.03	.01	.00
☐ 541	Richard Rodriguez	.03	.01	.00
☐ 542	Benito Santiago	.06	.02	.00
☐ 543	Calvin Schiraldi	.03	.01	.00
☐ 544	Eric Show	.03	.01	.00
☐ 545	Phil Stephenson	.03	.01	.00
☐ 546	Garry Templeton UER	.03	.01	.00
	(Born 3/24/57, should be 3/24/56)			
☐ 547	Ed Whitson	.03	.01	.00
☐ 548	Eddie Williams	.03	.01	.00
☐ 549	Kevin Appier	.06	.02	.00
☐ 550	Luis Aquino	.03	.01	.00
☐ 551	Bob Boone	.06	.02	.00
☐ 552	George Brett	.10	.04	.01
☐ 553	Jeff Conine	.15	.06	.01
☐ 554	Steve Crawford	.03	.01	.00
☐ 555	Mark Davis	.03	.01	.00
☐ 556	Storm Davis	.03	.01	.00
☐ 557	Jim Eisenreich	.03	.01	.00
☐ 558	Steve Farr	.03	.01	.00
☐ 559	Tom Gordon	.06	.02	.00
☐ 560	Mark Gubicza	.06	.02	.00
☐ 561	Bo Jackson	.25	.10	.02
☐ 562	Mike Macfarlane	.03	.01	.00
☐ 563	Brian McRae	.45	.18	.04
☐ 564	Jeff Montgomery	.03	.01	.00
☐ 565	Bill Pecota	.03	.01	.00
☐ 566	Gerald Perry	.03	.01	.00
☐ 567	Bret Saberhagen	.08	.03	.01
☐ 568	Jeff Schulz	.10	.04	.01
☐ 569	Kevin Seitzer	.06	.02	.00
☐ 570	Terry Shumpert	.03	.01	.00
☐ 571	Kurt Stillwell	.03	.01	.00
☐ 572	Danny Tartabull	.08	.03	.01
☐ 573	Gary Thurman	.03	.01	.00
☐ 574	Frank White	.03	.01	.00
☐ 575	Willie Wilson	.06	.02	.00
☐ 576	Chris Bosio	.03	.01	.00
☐ 577	Greg Brock	.03	.01	.00
☐ 578	George Canale	.03	.01	.00
☐ 579	Chuck Crim	.03	.01	.00
☐ 580	Rob Deer	.06	.02	.00
☐ 581	Edgar Diaz	.06	.02	.00
☐ 582	Tom Edens	.08	.03	.01
☐ 583	Mike Felder	.03	.01	.00
☐ 584	Jim Gantner	.03	.01	.00
☐ 585	Darryl Hamilton	.03	.01	.00
☐ 586	Ted Higuera	.03	.01	.00
☐ 587	Mark Knudson	.03	.01	.00
☐ 588	Bill Krueger	.03	.01	.00
☐ 589	Tim McIntosh	.06	.02	.00
☐ 590	Paul Mirabella	.03	.01	.00
☐ 591	Paul Molitor	.08	.03	.01
☐ 592	Jaime Navarro	.03	.01	.00
☐ 593	Dave Parker	.08	.03	.01
☐ 594	Dan Plesac	.03	.01	.00
☐ 595	Ron Robinson	.03	.01	.00
☐ 596	Gary Sheffield	.08	.03	.01
☐ 597	Bill Spiers	.03	.01	.00
☐ 598	B.J. Surhoff	.03	.01	.00
☐ 599	Greg Vaughn	.10	.04	.01
☐ 600	Randy Veres	.03	.01	.00
☐ 601	Robin Yount	.10	.04	.01
☐ 602	Rick Aguilera	.03	.01	.00
☐ 603	Allan Anderson	.03	.01	.00
☐ 604	Juan Berenguer	.03	.01	.00
☐ 605	Randy Bush	.03	.01	.00
☐ 606	Carmen Castillo	.03	.01	.00
☐ 607	Tim Drummond	.03	.01	.00
☐ 608	Scott Erickson	.75	.30	.07
☐ 609	Gary Gaetti	.06	.02	.00
☐ 610	Greg Gagne	.03	.01	.00
☐ 611	Dan Gladden	.03	.01	.00
☐ 612	Mark Guthrie	.06	.02	.00
☐ 613	Brian Harper	.06	.02	.00
☐ 614	Kent Hrbek	.06	.02	.00
☐ 615	Gene Larkin	.03	.01	.00
☐ 616	Terry Leach	.03	.01	.00
☐ 617	Nelson Liriano	.03	.01	.00
☐ 618	Shane Mack	.06	.02	.00

☐	619	John Moses	.03	.01	.00
☐	620	Pedro Munoz	.17	.07	.01
☐	621	Al Newman	.03	.01	.00
☐	622	Junior Ortiz	.03	.01	.00
☐	623	Kirby Puckett	.12	.05	.01
☐	624	Roy Smith	.03	.01	.00
☐	625	Kevin Tapani	.08	.03	.01
☐	626	Gary Wayne	.03	.01	.00
☐	627	David West	.03	.01	.00
☐	628	Cris Carpenter	.03	.01	.00
☐	629	Vince Coleman	.08	.03	.01
☐	630	Ken Dayley	.03	.01	.00
☐	631	Jose DeLeon	.03	.01	.00
☐	632	Frank DiPino	.03	.01	.00
☐	633	Bernard Gilkey	.15	.06	.01
☐	634	Pedro Guerrero	.06	.02	.00
☐	635	Ken Hill	.03	.01	.00
☐	636	Felix Jose	.08	.03	.01
☐	637	Ray Lankford	.35	.15	.03
☐	638	Joe Magrane	.03	.01	.00
☐	639	Tom Niedenfuer	.03	.01	.00
☐	640	Jose Oquendo	.03	.01	.00
☐	641	Tom Pagnozzi	.03	.01	.00
☐	642	Terry Pendleton	.08	.03	.01
☐	643	Mike Perez	.08	.03	.01
☐	644	Bryn Smith	.03	.01	.00
☐	645	Lee Smith	.06	.02	.00
☐	646	Ozzie Smith	.10	.04	.01
☐	647	Scott Terry	.03	.01	.00
☐	648	Bob Tewksbury	.03	.01	.00
☐	649	Milt Thompson	.03	.01	.00
☐	650	John Tudor	.06	.02	.00
☐	651	Denny Walling	.03	.01	.00
☐	652	Craig Wilson	.10	.04	.01
☐	653	Todd Worrell	.06	.02	.00
☐	654	Todd Zeile	.10	.04	.01
☐	655	Oscar Azocar	.06	.02	.00
☐	656	Steve Balboni UER (Born 1/5/57, should be 1/16)	.03	.01	.00
☐	657	Jesse Barfield	.06	.02	.00
☐	658	Greg Cadaret	.03	.01	.00
☐	659	Chuck Cary	.03	.01	.00
☐	660	Rick Cerone	.03	.01	.00
☐	661	David Eiland	.03	.01	.00
☐	662	Alvaro Espinoza	.03	.01	.00
☐	663	Bob Geren	.03	.01	.00
☐	664	Lee Guetterman	.03	.01	.00
☐	665	Mel Hall	.03	.01	.00
☐	666	Andy Hawkins	.03	.01	.00
☐	667	Jimmy Jones	.03	.01	.00
☐	668	Roberto Kelly	.08	.03	.01
☐	669	Dave LaPoint UER (No '81 Brewers stats, totals also are wrong)	.03	.01	.00
☐	670	Tim Leary	.06	.02	.00
☐	671	Jim Leyritz	.06	.02	.00
☐	672	Kevin Maas	.15	.06	.01
☐	673	Don Mattingly	.12	.05	.01
☐	674	Matt Nokes	.06	.02	.00
☐	675	Pascual Perez	.03	.01	.00
☐	676	Eric Plunk	.03	.01	.00
☐	677	Dave Righetti	.06	.02	.00
☐	678	Jeff Robinson	.03	.01	.00
☐	679	Steve Sax	.06	.02	.00
☐	680	Mike Witt	.03	.01	.00
☐	681	Steve Avery UER (Born in New Jersey, should say Michigan)	.35	.15	.03
☐	682	Mike Bell	.12	.05	.01
☐	683	Jeff Blauser	.03	.01	.00
☐	684	Francisco Cabrera UER (Born 10/16, should say 10/10)	.06	.02	.00
☐	685	Tony Castillo	.03	.01	.00
☐	686	Marty Clary UER (Shown pitching righty, but bio has left)	.03	.01	.00
☐	687	Nick Esasky	.03	.01	.00
☐	688	Ron Gant	.12	.05	.01
☐	689	Tom Glavine	.12	.05	.01
☐	690	Mark Grant	.03	.01	.00
☐	691	Tommy Gregg	.03	.01	.00
☐	692	Dwayne Henry	.03	.01	.00
☐	693	Dave Justice	.50	.20	.05
☐	694	Jimmy Kremers	.03	.01	.00
☐	695	Charlie Leibrandt	.03	.01	.00
☐	696	Mark Lemke	.06	.02	.00
☐	697	Oddibe McDowell	.06	.02	.00
☐	698	Greg Olson	.06	.02	.00
☐	699	Jeff Parrett	.03	.01	.00
☐	700	Jim Presley	.03	.01	.00
☐	701	Victor Rosario	.08	.03	.01
☐	702	Lonnie Smith	.06	.02	.00

☐	703	Pete Smith	.03	.01	.00
☐	704	John Smoltz	.08	.03	.01
☐	705	Mike Stanton	.03	.01	.00
☐	706	Andres Thomas	.03	.01	.00
☐	707	Jeff Treadway	.03	.01	.00
☐	708	Jim Vatcher	.08	.03	.01
☐	709	Home Run Kings Ryne Sandberg Cecil Fielder	.15	.06	.01
☐	710	2nd Generation Stars Barry Bonds Ken Griffey Jr.	.25	.10	.02
☐	711	NLCS Team Leaders Bobby Bonilla Barry Larkin	.08	.03	.01
☐	712	Top Game Savers Bobby Thigpen John Franco	.06	.02	.00
☐	713	Chicago's 100 Club Andre Dawson Ryne Sandberg UER (Ryno misspelled Rhino)	.10	.04	.01
☐	714	CL:A's/Pirates Reds/Red Sox	.06	.01	.00
☐	715	CL:White Sox/Mets Blue Jays/Dodgers	.06	.01	.00
☐	716	CL:Expos/Giants Rangers/Angels	.06	.01	.00
☐	717	CL:Tigers/Indians Phillies/Cubs	.06	.01	.00
☐	718	CL:Mariners/Orioles Astros/Padres	.06	.01	.00
☐	719	CL:Royals/Brewers Twins/Cardinals	.06	.01	.00
☐	720	CL:Yankees/Braves Superstars/Specials	.06	.01	.00

1991 Fleer Wax Box Cards

These cards were issued on the bottom of 1991 Fleer wax boxes. This set celebrated the spate of no-hitters in 1990 and were printed on three different boxes. These standard size cards, 2 1/2" by 3 1/2", come four to a box, three about the no-hitters and one team logo card on each box. The cards are blank backed and are numbered on the front in a subtle way. They are ordered below as they are numbered, which is by chronological order of their no-hitters. Only the player cards are listed below since there was a different team logo card on each box.

			MINT	EXC	G-VG
	COMPLETE SET (9)		2.00	.80	.20
	COMMON PLAYER (1-9)		.10	.04	.01
☐	1	Mark Langston and Mike Witt	.10	.04	.01
☐	2	Randy Johnson	.25	.10	.02
☐	3	Nolan Ryan	1.00	.40	.10
☐	4	Dave Stewart	.25	.10	.02
☐	5	Fernando Valenzuela	.25	.10	.02
☐	6	Andy Hawkins	.10	.04	.01
☐	7	Melido Perez	.10	.04	.01
☐	8	Terry Mulholland	.10	.04	.01
☐	9	Dave Stieb	.20	.08	.02

1991 Fleer All-Star Inserts

For the sixth consecutive year Fleer issued an All-Star insert set. This year the cards were only available in Fleer cello packs. This 10-card set measures the standard size of 2 1/2" by 3 1/2" and is reminiscent of the 1971 Topps Greatest Moments set with the two pictures on the front with a photo on the back as well.

		MINT	EXC	G-VG
COMPLETE SET (10)		20.00	8.50	2.75
COMMON PLAYER (1-10)		.75	.30	.07
☐ 1	Ryne Sandberg	2.75	1.10	.27
☐ 2	Barry Larkin	1.25	.50	.12
☐ 3	Matt Williams	1.50	.60	.15
☐ 4	Cecil Fielder	2.00	.80	.20
☐ 5	Barry Bonds	1.75	.70	.17
☐ 6	Rickey Henderson	2.25	.90	.22
☐ 7	Ken Griffey Jr.	6.00	2.50	.60
☐ 8	Jose Canseco	3.00	1.25	.30
☐ 9	Benito Santiago	.75	.30	.07
☐ 10	Roger Clemens	2.25	.90	.22

1991 Fleer Pro-Visions

This 12-card subset is in the standard size of 2 1/2" by 3 1/2" and features drawings by talented artist Terry Smith on the front of the card with a description on the back explaining why the card is painted in that way. These cards were only available in Fleer wax and Rak packs. The formal description of this set is the 1991 Fleer Pro-Visions TM Sports Art Cards. The cards have distinctive black borders.

		MINT	EXC	G-VG
COMPLETE SET (12)		4.50	2.00	.45
COMMON PLAYER (1-12)		.30	.12	.03
☐ 1	Kirby Puckett UER (.326 average, should be .328)	.35	.15	.03

☐ 2	Will Clark UER (On tenth line, pennant misspelled pennent)	.60	.25	.06
☐ 3	Ruben Sierra UER (No apostrophe in hasn't)	.35	.15	.03
☐ 4	Mark McGwire UER (Fisk won ROY in '72, not '82)	.30	.12	.03
☐ 5	Bo Jackson (Bio says 6', others have him at 6'1")	.90	.40	.09
☐ 6	Jose Canseco UER (Bio 6'3", 230, text has 6'4", 240)	.90	.40	.09
☐ 7	Dwight Gooden UER (2.80 ERA in Lynchburg, should be 2.50)	.30	.12	.03
☐ 8	Mike Greenwell UER (.328 BA and 87 RBI, should be .325 and 95)	.30	.12	.03
☐ 9	Roger Clemens	.40	.16	.04
☐ 10	Eric Davis	.30	.12	.03
☐ 11	Don Mattingly	.40	.16	.04
☐ 12	Darryl Strawberry	.40	.16	.04

1991 Fleer Pro-Visions Factory

This four-card set was inserted only into factory sets. The standard-size (2 1/2" by 3 1/2") cards feature on the fronts colorful player portraits by artist Terry Smith. The pictures are bordered in white, with the player's name immediately below in red lettering. The backs of each card have different colors as well as biography and career highlights. The cards are numbered on the back.

		MINT	EXC	G-VG
COMPLETE SET (4)		3.00	1.25	.30
COMMON PLAYER (1F-4F)		.40	.16	.04
☐ 1F	Barry Bonds Pittsburgh Pirates	.90	.40	.09
☐ 2F	Rickey Henderson Oakland Athletics	1.25	.50	.12
☐ 3F	Ryne Sandberg Chicago Cubs	1.25	.50	.12
☐ 4F	Dave Stewart Oakland Athletics	.40	.16	.04

1991 Fleer Update

The 1991 Fleer Update set contains 132 cards measuring the standard size (2 1/2" by 3 1/2"). The glossy color action photos on the fronts are placed on a yellow card face and accentuated by black lines above and below. The backs have a head shot (circular format), biography, and complete Major League statistics. The cards are checklisted below alphabetically within and according to teams for each league as follows: Baltimore Orioles (1-3), Boston Red Sox (4-7), California Angels (8-10), Chicago White Sox (11-15), Cleveland Indians (16-21), Detroit Tigers (22-24), Kansas City Royals (25-28), Milwaukee Brewers (29-35), Minnesota Twins (36-41), New York Yankees (42-49), Oakland Athletics (50-51), Seattle Mariners (52-57), Texas Rangers (58-62), Toronto Blue Jays (63-69), Atlanta Braves (70-76), Chicago Cubs (77-83), Cincinnati Reds (84-86), Houston Astros (87-90), Los Angeles Dodgers (91-96), Montreal Expos (97-99), New York Mets (100-104), Philadelphia Phillies (105-110), Pittsburgh Pirates (111-115), St. Louis Cardinals (116-119), San Diego Padres (120-127), and San Francisco Giants (128-131). The key rookie cards in this set are Jeff Bagwell and Ivan Rodriguez.

	MINT	EXC	G-VG
COMPLETE SET (132)	10.00	4.50	1.25
COMMON PLAYER (U1-U132)	.05	.02	.00
☐ U1 Glenn Davis	.10	.04	.01
☐ U2 Dwight Evans	.08	.03	.01
☐ U3 Jose Mesa	.08	.03	.01
☐ U4 Jack Clark	.08	.03	.01
☐ U5 Danny Darwin	.05	.02	.00
☐ U6 Steve Lyons	.05	.02	.00
☐ U7 Mo Vaughn	.60	.25	.06
☐ U8 Floyd Bannister	.05	.02	.00
☐ U9 Gary Gaetti	.08	.03	.01
☐ U10 Dave Parker	.10	.04	.01
☐ U11 Joey Cora	.05	.02	.00
☐ U12 Charlie Hough	.05	.02	.00
☐ U13 Matt Merullo	.08	.03	.01
☐ U14 Warren Newson	.20	.08	.02
☐ U15 Tim Raines	.08	.03	.01
☐ U16 Albert Belle	.17	.07	.01
☐ U17 Glenallen Hill	.08	.03	.01
☐ U18 Shawn Hillegas	.05	.02	.00
☐ U19 Mark Lewis	.20	.08	.02
☐ U20 Charles Nagy	.10	.04	.01
☐ U21 Mark Whiten	.20	.08	.02
☐ U22 John Cerutti	.05	.02	.00
☐ U23 Rob Deer	.08	.03	.01
☐ U24 Mickey Tettleton	.08	.03	.01
☐ U25 Warren Cromartie	.05	.02	.00
☐ U26 Kirk Gibson	.08	.03	.01
☐ U27 David Howard	.12	.05	.01
☐ U28 Brent Mayne	.10	.04	.01
☐ U29 Dante Bichette	.05	.02	.00
☐ U30 Mark Lee	.10	.04	.01
☐ U31 Julio Machado	.05	.02	.00
☐ U32 Edwin Nunez	.05	.02	.00
☐ U33 Willie Randolph	.08	.03	.01
☐ U34 Franklin Stubbs	.05	.02	.00
☐ U35 Bill Wegman	.05	.02	.00
☐ U36 Chili Davis	.08	.03	.01
☐ U37 Chuck Knoblauch	.40	.16	.04
☐ U38 Scott Leius	.12	.05	.01
☐ U39 Jack Morris	.10	.04	.01
☐ U40 Mike Pagliarulo	.05	.02	.00
☐ U41 Lenny Webster	.12	.05	.01
☐ U42 John Habyan	.05	.02	.00
☐ U43 Steve Howe	.05	.02	.00
☐ U44 Jeff Johnson	.17	.07	.01
☐ U45 Scott Kamieniecki	.17	.07	.01
☐ U46 Pat Kelly	.25	.10	.02
☐ U47 Hensley Meulens	.08	.03	.01
☐ U48 Wade Taylor	.17	.07	.01

☐ U49 Bernie Williams	.25	.10	.02
☐ U50 Kirk Dressendorfer	.20	.08	.02
☐ U51 Ernest Riles	.05	.02	.00
☐ U52 Rich DeLucia	.12	.05	.01
☐ U53 Tracy Jones	.05	.02	.00
☐ U54 Bill Krueger	.05	.02	.00
☐ U55 Alonzo Powell	.12	.05	.01
☐ U56 Jeff Schaefer	.05	.02	.00
☐ U57 Russ Swan	.08	.03	.01
☐ U58 John Barfield	.08	.03	.01
☐ U59 Rich Gossage	.08	.03	.01
☐ U60 Jose Guzman	.08	.03	.01
☐ U61 Dean Palmer	.35	.15	.03
☐ U62 Ivan Rodriguez	2.00	.80	.20
☐ U63 Roberto Alomar	.12	.05	.01
☐ U64 Tom Candiotti	.08	.03	.01
☐ U65 Joe Carter	.10	.04	.01
☐ U66 Ed Sprague	.12	.05	.01
☐ U67 Pat Tabler	.05	.02	.00
☐ U68 Mike Timlin	.12	.05	.01
☐ U69 Devon White	.08	.03	.01
☐ U70 Rafael Belliard	.05	.02	.00
☐ U71 Juan Berenguer	.05	.02	.00
☐ U72 Sid Bream	.05	.02	.00
☐ U73 Marvin Freeman	.05	.02	.00
☐ U74 Kent Mercker	.08	.03	.01
☐ U75 Otis Nixon	.08	.03	.01
☐ U76 Terry Pendleton	.10	.04	.01
☐ U77 George Bell	.10	.04	.01
☐ U78 Danny Jackson	.08	.03	.01
☐ U79 Chuck McElroy	.08	.03	.01
☐ U80 Gary Scott	.25	.10	.02
☐ U81 Heathcliff Slocumb	.10	.04	.01
☐ U82 Dave Smith	.05	.02	.00
☐ U83 Rick Wilkins	.17	.07	.01
☐ U84 Freddie Benavides	.12	.05	.01
☐ U85 Ted Power	.05	.02	.00
☐ U86 Mo Sanford	.20	.08	.02
☐ U87 Jeff Bagwell	3.00	1.25	.30
☐ U88 Steve Finley	.08	.03	.01
☐ U89 Pete Harnisch	.08	.03	.01
☐ U90 Darryl Kile	.12	.05	.01
☐ U91 Brett Butler	.08	.03	.01
☐ U92 John Candelaria	.05	.02	.00
☐ U93 Gary Carter	.08	.03	.01
☐ U94 Kevin Gross	.05	.02	.00
☐ U95 Bob Ojeda	.05	.02	.00
☐ U96 Darryl Strawberry	.20	.08	.02
☐ U97 Ivan Calderon	.08	.03	.01
☐ U98 Ron Hassey	.05	.02	.00
☐ U99 Gilberto Reyes	.05	.02	.00
☐ U100 Hubie Brooks	.08	.03	.01
☐ U101 Rick Cerone	.05	.02	.00
☐ U102 Vince Coleman	.10	.04	.01
☐ U103 Jeff Innis	.05	.02	.00
☐ U104 Pete Schourek	.12	.05	.01
☐ U105 Andy Ashby	.12	.05	.01
☐ U106 Wally Backman	.05	.02	.00
☐ U107 Darrin Fletcher	.10	.04	.01
☐ U108 Tommy Greene	.08	.03	.01
☐ U109 John Morris	.05	.02	.00
☐ U110 Mitch Williams	.08	.03	.01
☐ U111 Lloyd McClendon	.05	.02	.00
☐ U112 Orlando Merced	.35	.15	.03
☐ U113 Vicente Palacios	.05	.02	.00
☐ U114 Gary Varsho	.05	.02	.00
☐ U115 John Wehner	.25	.10	.02
☐ U116 Rex Hudler	.08	.03	.01
☐ U117 Tim Jones	.05	.02	.00
☐ U118 Geronimo Pena	.05	.02	.00
☐ U119 Gerald Perry	.05	.02	.00
☐ U120 Larry Andersen	.05	.02	.00
☐ U121 Jerald Clark	.05	.02	.00
☐ U122 Scott Coolbaugh	.05	.02	.00
☐ U123 Tony Fernandez	.08	.03	.01
☐ U124 Darrin Jackson	.08	.03	.01
☐ U125 Fred McGriff	.10	.04	.01
☐ U126 Jose Mota	.17	.07	.01
☐ U127 Tim Teufel	.05	.02	.00
☐ U128 Bud Black	.05	.02	.00
☐ U129 Mike Felder	.05	.02	.00
☐ U130 Willie McGee	.08	.03	.01
☐ U131 Dave Righetti	.08	.03	.01
☐ U132 Checklist Card	.05	.01	.00

1991 Fleer World Series

This eight-card set captures highlights from the 1990 World Series between the Cincinnati Reds and the Oakland Athletics. The set was only available as an insert with the 1991 Fleer factory sets. The standard-size (2 1/2" by 3 1/2") cards have on the fronts color action photos, bordered in blue on a white card face. The words "World Series '90" appears in red and blue lettering above the pictures. The backs have a similar design, only with a summary of an aspect of the Series on a yellow background. The cards are numbered on the back.

	MINT	EXC	G-VG
COMPLETE SET (8)	3.00	1.25	.30
COMMON PLAYER (1-8)	.25	.10	.02
☐ 1 Eric Davis	.50	.20	.05
☐ 2 Billy Hatcher	.35	.15	.03
☐ 3 Jose Canseco	.75	.30	.07
☐ 4 Rickey Henderson	.75	.30	.07
☐ 5 Chris Sabo	.50	.20	.05
☐ 6 Dave Stewart	.35	.15	.03
☐ 7 Jose Rijo	.35	.15	.03
☐ 8 Reds Celebrate	.25	.10	.02

1991 Fleer Ultra

This 400-card standard size (2 1/2" by 3 1/2") set marked Fleer's first entry into the high-end premium card market. The set was released in wax packs and features the best players in the majors along with a good mix of young prospects. The cards feature full color action photography on the fronts and three full-color photos on the backs along with 1990 and career statistics. Fleer claimed in their original press release that there would only be 15 percent of Elite issued as there was of the regular issue. Fleer also issued the sets in their now traditional alphabetical order as well as the teams in alphabetical order.

The card numbering is as follows, Atlanta Braves (1-13), Baltimore Orioles (14-26), Boston Red Sox (27-42), California Angels (43-54), Chicago Cubs (55-71), Chicago White Sox (72-86), Cincinnati Reds (87-103), Cleveland Indians (104-119), Detroit Tigers (120-130), Houston Astros (131-142), Kansas City Royals (143-158), Los Angeles Dodgers (159-171), Milwaukee Brewers (172-184), Minnesota Twins (185-196), Montreal Expos (197-210), New York Mets (211-227), New York Yankees (228-242), Oakland Athletics (243-257), Philadelphia Phillies (258-272), Pittsburgh Pirates (273-287), St. Louis Cardinals (288-299), San Diego Padres (300-313), San Francisco Giants (314-331), Seattle Mariners (332-345), Texas Rangers (346-357), Toronto Blue Jays (358-372), Major League Prospects (373-390), Elite Performance (391-396), and Checklists (397-400). The key rookie cards in this set are Wes Chamberlain, Brian McRae, and Phil Plantier.

	MINT	EXC	G-VG
COMPLETE SET (400)	40.00	18.00	6.00
COMMON PLAYER (1-400)	.06	.02	.00
☐ 1 Steve Avery	2.00	.50	.10
☐ 2 Jeff Blauser	.06	.02	.00
☐ 3 Francisco Cabrera	.06	.02	.00
☐ 4 Ron Gant	.30	.12	.03
☐ 5 Tom Glavine	.20	.08	.02
☐ 6 Tommy Gregg	.06	.02	.00
☐ 7 Dave Justice	2.50	1.00	.25
☐ 8 Oddibe McDowell	.06	.02	.00
☐ 9 Greg Olson	.10	.04	.01
☐ 10 Terry Pendleton	.15	.06	.01
☐ 11 Lonnie Smith	.10	.04	.01
☐ 12 John Smoltz	.15	.06	.01
☐ 13 Jeff Treadway	.06	.02	.00
☐ 14 Glenn Davis	.10	.04	.01
☐ 15 Mike Devereaux	.06	.02	.00
☐ 16 Leo Gomez	.50	.20	.05
☐ 17 Chris Hoiles	.10	.04	.01
☐ 18 Dave Johnson	.06	.02	.00
☐ 19 Ben McDonald	.20	.08	.02
☐ 20 Randy Milligan	.10	.04	.01
☐ 21 Gregg Olson	.10	.04	.01
☐ 22 Joe Orsulak	.06	.02	.00
☐ 23 Bill Ripken	.06	.02	.00
☐ 24 Cal Ripken	.75	.30	.07
☐ 25 David Segui	.12	.05	.01
☐ 26 Craig Worthington	.06	.02	.00
☐ 27 Wade Boggs	.25	.10	.02
☐ 28 Tom Bolton	.06	.02	.00
☐ 29 Tom Brunansky	.10	.04	.01
☐ 30 Ellis Burks	.12	.05	.01
☐ 31 Roger Clemens	.50	.20	.05
☐ 32 Mike Greenwell	.15	.06	.01
☐ 33 Greg Harris	.06	.02	.00
☐ 34 Daryl Irvine	.12	.05	.01
☐ 35 Mike Marshall UER	.10	.04	.01
(1990 in stats is			
shown as 990)			
☐ 36 Tim Naehring	.15	.06	.01
☐ 37 Tony Pena	.10	.04	.01
☐ 38 Phil Plantier	4.50	2.00	.45
☐ 39 Carlos Quintana	.10	.04	.01
☐ 40 Jeff Reardon	.12	.05	.01
☐ 41 Jody Reed	.10	.04	.01
☐ 42 Luis Rivera	.06	.02	.00
☐ 43 Jim Abbott	.20	.08	.02
☐ 44 Chuck Finley	.12	.05	.01
☐ 45 Bryan Harvey	.10	.04	.01
☐ 46 Donnie Hill	.06	.02	.00
☐ 47 Jack Howell	.06	.02	.00
☐ 48 Wally Joyner	.12	.05	.01
☐ 49 Mark Langston	.10	.04	.01
☐ 50 Kirk McCaskill	.06	.02	.00
☐ 51 Lance Parrish	.10	.04	.01
☐ 52 Dick Schofield	.06	.02	.00
☐ 53 Lee Stevens	.25	.10	.02
☐ 54 Dave Winfield	.17	.07	.01
☐ 55 George Bell	.12	.05	.01
☐ 56 Damon Berryhill	.06	.02	.00
☐ 57 Mike Bielecki	.06	.02	.00
☐ 58 Andre Dawson	.20	.08	.02
☐ 59 Shawon Dunston	.10	.04	.01
☐ 60 Joe Girardi UER	.06	.02	.00
(Bats right, LH hitter			
shown is Doug Dascenzo)			
☐ 61 Mark Grace	.15	.06	.01
☐ 62 Mike Harkey	.10	.04	.01
☐ 63 Les Lancaster	.06	.02	.00
☐ 64 Greg Maddux	.10	.04	.01

□	65	Derrick May	.12	.05	.01
□	66	Ryne Sandberg	.60	.25	.06
□	67	Luis Salazar	.06	.02	.00
□	68	Dwight Smith	.10	.04	.01
□	69	Hector Villanueva	.10	.04	.01
□	70	Jerome Walton	.10	.04	.01
□	71	Mitch Williams	.06	.02	.00
□	72	Carlton Fisk	.25	.10	.02
□	73	Scott Fletcher	.06	.02	.00
□	74	Ozzie Guillen	.10	.04	.01
□	75	Greg Hibbard	.06	.02	.00
□	76	Lance Johnson	.06	.02	.00
□	77	Steve Lyons	.06	.02	.00
□	78	Jack McDowell	.12	.05	.01
□	79	Dan Pasqua	.06	.02	.00
□	80	Melido Perez	.06	.02	.00
□	81	Tim Raines	.10	.04	.01
□	82	Sammy Sosa	.10	.04	.01
□	83	Cory Snyder	.10	.04	.01
□	84	Bobby Thigpen	.10	.04	.01
□	85	Frank Thomas	6.00	2.50	.60
		(Card says he is			
		an outfielder)			
□	86	Robin Ventura	.60	.25	.06
□	87	Todd Benzinger	.06	.02	.00
□	88	Glenn Braggs	.06	.02	.00
□	89	Tom Browning UER	.10	.04	.01
		(Front photo actually			
		Norm Charlton)			
□	90	Norm Charlton	.06	.02	.00
□	91	Eric Davis	.17	.07	.01
□	92	Rob Dibble	.10	.04	.01
□	93	Bill Doran	.06	.02	.00
□	94	Mariano Duncan UER	.06	.02	.00
		(Right back photo			
		is Billy Hatcher)			
□	95	Billy Hatcher	.10	.04	.01
□	96	Barry Larkin	.15	.06	.01
□	97	Randy Myers	.06	.02	.00
□	98	Hal Morris	.17	.07	.01
□	99	Joe Oliver	.06	.02	.00
□	100	Paul O'Neill	.10	.04	.01
□	101	Jeff Reed	.06	.02	.00
		(See also 104)			
□	102	Jose Rijo	.10	.04	.01
□	103	Chris Sabo	.12	.05	.01
		(See also 106)			
□	104	Beau Allred UER	.15	.06	.01
		(Card number is 101)			
□	105	Sandy Alomar Jr.	.12	.05	.01
□	106	Carlos Baerga UER	.25	.10	.02
		(Card number is 103)			
□	107	Albert Belle	.50	.20	.05
□	108	Jerry Browne	.06	.02	.00
□	109	Tom Candiotti	.10	.04	.01
□	110	Alex Cole	.10	.04	.01
□	111	John Farrell	.06	.02	.00
		(See also 114)			
□	112	Felix Fermin	.06	.02	.00
□	113	Brook Jacoby	.06	.02	.00
□	114	Chris James UER	.06	.02	.00
		(Card number is 111)			
□	115	Doug Jones	.06	.02	.00
□	116	Steve Olin	.06	.02	.00
		(See also 119)			
□	117	Greg Swindell	.10	.04	.01
□	118	Turner Ward	.25	.10	.02
□	119	Mitch Webster UER	.06	.02	.00
		(Card number is 116)			
□	120	Dave Bergman	.06	.02	.00
□	121	Cecil Fielder	.40	.16	.04
□	122	Travis Fryman	1.75	.70	.17
□	123	Mike Henneman	.06	.02	.00
□	124	Lloyd Moseby	.06	.02	.00
□	125	Dan Petry	.06	.02	.00
□	126	Tony Phillips	.06	.02	.00
□	127	Mark Salas	.06	.02	.00
□	128	Frank Tanana	.10	.04	.01
□	129	Alan Trammell	.15	.06	.01
□	130	Lou Whitaker	.12	.05	.01
□	131	Eric Anthony	.10	.04	.01
□	132	Craig Biggio	.10	.04	.01
□	133	Ken Caminiti	.06	.02	.00
□	134	Casey Candaele	.06	.02	.00
□	135	Andujar Cedeno	1.00	.40	.10
□	136	Mark Davidson	.06	.02	.00
□	137	Jim Deshaies	.06	.02	.00
□	138	Mark Portugal	.06	.02	.00
□	139	Rafael Ramirez	.06	.02	.00
□	140	Mike Scott	.10	.04	.01
□	141	Eric Yelding	.06	.02	.00
□	142	Gerald Young	.06	.02	.00
□	143	Kevin Appier	.10	.04	.01
□	144	George Brett	.20	.08	.02
□	145	Jeff Conine	.20	.08	.02
□	146	Jim Eisenreich	.06	.02	.00
□	147	Tom Gordon	.10	.04	.01
□	148	Mark Gubicza	.10	.04	.01
□	149	Bo Jackson	.60	.25	.06
□	150	Brent Mayne	.20	.08	.02
□	151	Mike Macfarlane	.06	.02	.00
□	152	Brian McRae	1.25	.50	.12
□	153	Jeff Montgomery	.06	.02	.00
□	154	Bret Saberhagen	.12	.05	.01
□	155	Kevin Seitzer	.10	.04	.01
□	156	Terry Shumpert	.06	.02	.00
□	157	Kurt Stillwell	.06	.02	.00
□	158	Danny Tartabull	.12	.05	.01
□	159	Tim Belcher	.10	.04	.01
□	160	Kal Daniels	.10	.04	.01
□	161	Alfredo Griffin	.06	.02	.00
□	162	Lenny Harris	.06	.02	.00
□	163	Jay Howell	.06	.02	.00
□	164	Ramon Martinez	.30	.12	.03
□	165	Mike Morgan	.10	.04	.01
□	166	Eddie Murray	.20	.08	.02
□	167	Jose Offerman	.12	.05	.01
□	168	Juan Samuel	.10	.04	.01
□	169	Mike Scioscia	.06	.02	.00
□	170	Mike Sharperson	.06	.02	.00
□	171	Darryl Strawberry	.40	.16	.04
□	172	Greg Brock	.06	.02	.00
□	173	Chuck Crim	.06	.02	.00
□	174	Jim Gantner	.06	.02	.00
□	175	Ted Higuera	.06	.02	.00
□	176	Mark Knudson	.06	.02	.00
□	177	Tim McIntosh	.06	.02	.00
□	178	Paul Molitor	.12	.05	.01
□	179	Dan Plesac	.06	.02	.00
□	180	Gary Sheffield	.10	.04	.01
□	181	Bill Spiers	.06	.02	.00
□	182	B.J. Surhoff	.06	.02	.00
□	183	Greg Vaughn	.20	.08	.02
□	184	Robin Yount	.25	.10	.02
□	185	Rick Aguilera	.10	.04	.01
□	186	Greg Gagne	.06	.02	.00
□	187	Dan Gladden	.06	.02	.00
□	188	Brian Harper	.10	.04	.01
□	189	Kent Hrbek	.12	.05	.01
□	190	Gene Larkin	.06	.02	.00
□	191	Shane Mack	.10	.04	.01
□	192	Pedro Munoz	.60	.25	.06
□	193	Al Newman	.06	.02	.00
□	194	Junior Ortiz	.06	.02	.00
□	195	Kirby Puckett	.25	.10	.02
□	196	Kevin Tapani	.12	.05	.01
□	197	Dennis Boyd	.06	.02	.00
□	198	Tim Burke	.06	.02	.00
□	199	Ivan Calderon	.10	.04	.01
□	200	Delino DeShields	.15	.06	.01
□	201	Mike Fitzgerald	.06	.02	.00
□	202	Steve Frey	.10	.04	.01
□	203	Andres Galarraga	.10	.04	.01
□	204	Marquis Grissom	.15	.06	.01
□	205	Dave Martinez	.06	.02	.00
□	206	Dennis Martinez	.10	.04	.01
□	207	Junior Noboa	.06	.02	.00
□	208	Spike Owen	.06	.02	.00
□	209	Scott Ruskin	.10	.04	.01
□	210	Tim Wallach	.10	.04	.01
□	211	Daryl Boston	.06	.02	.00
□	212	Vince Coleman	.12	.05	.01
□	213	David Cone	.10	.04	.01
□	214	Ron Darling	.10	.04	.01
□	215	Kevin Elster	.06	.02	.00
□	216	Sid Fernandez	.10	.04	.01
□	217	John Franco	.06	.02	.00
□	218	Dwight Gooden	.18	.08	.01
□	219	Tom Herr	.06	.02	.00
□	220	Todd Hundley	.10	.04	.01
□	221	Gregg Jefferies	.12	.05	.01
□	222	Howard Johnson	.15	.06	.01
□	223	Dave Magadan	.10	.04	.01
□	224	Kevin McReynolds	.10	.04	.01
□	225	Keith Miller	.06	.02	.00
□	226	Mackey Sasser	.06	.02	.00
□	227	Frank Viola	.10	.04	.01
□	228	Jesse Barfield	.10	.04	.01
□	229	Greg Cadaret	.06	.02	.00
□	230	Alvaro Espinoza	.06	.02	.00
□	231	Bob Geren	.06	.02	.00
□	232	Lee Guetterman	.06	.02	.00
□	233	Mel Hall	.06	.02	.00
□	234	Andy Hawkins UER	.06	.02	.00
		(Back center photo			
		is not him)			
□	235	Roberto Kelly	.10	.04	.01
□	236	Tim Leary	.10	.04	.01

#	Player			
☐ 237	Jim Leyritz	.06	.02	.00
☐ 238	Kevin Maas	.30	.12	.03
☐ 239	Don Mattingly	.30	.12	.03
☐ 240	Hensley Meulens	.12	.05	.01
☐ 241	Eric Plunk	.06	.02	.00
☐ 242	Steve Sax	.10	.04	.01
☐ 243	Todd Burns	.06	.02	.00
☐ 244	Jose Canseco	.75	.30	.07
☐ 245	Dennis Eckersley	.10	.04	.01
☐ 246	Mike Gallego	.06	.02	.00
☐ 247	Dave Henderson	.10	.04	.01
☐ 248	Rickey Henderson	.40	.16	.04
☐ 249	Rick Honeycutt	.06	.02	.00
☐ 250	Carney Lansford	.10	.04	.01
☐ 251	Mark McGwire	.15	.06	.01
☐ 252	Mike Moore	.10	.04	.01
☐ 253	Terry Steinbach	.06	.02	.00
☐ 254	Dave Stewart	.10	.04	.01
☐ 255	Walt Weiss	.10	.04	.01
☐ 256	Bob Welch	.10	.04	.01
☐ 257	Curt Young	.06	.02	.00
☐ 258	Wes Chamberlain	1.25	.50	.12
☐ 259	Pat Combs	.06	.02	.00
☐ 260	Darren Daulton	.06	.02	.00
☐ 261	Jose DeJesus	.06	.02	.00
☐ 262	Len Dykstra	.10	.04	.01
☐ 263	Charlie Hayes	.06	.02	.00
☐ 264	Von Hayes	.10	.04	.01
☐ 265	Ken Howell	.06	.02	.00
☐ 266	John Kruk	.06	.02	.00
☐ 267	Roger McDowell	.06	.02	.00
☐ 268	Mickey Morandini	.15	.06	.01
☐ 269	Terry Mulholland	.10	.04	.01
☐ 270	Dale Murphy	.15	.06	.01
☐ 271	Randy Ready	.06	.02	.00
☐ 272	Dickie Thon	.06	.02	.00
☐ 273	Stan Belinda	.06	.02	.00
☐ 274	Jay Bell	.06	.02	.00
☐ 275	Barry Bonds	.30	.12	.03
☐ 276	Bobby Bonilla	.20	.08	.02
☐ 277	Doug Drabek	.10	.04	.01
☐ 278	Carlos Garcia	.20	.08	.02
☐ 279	Neal Heaton	.06	.02	.00
☐ 280	Jeff King	.10	.04	.01
☐ 281	Bill Landrum	.06	.02	.00
☐ 282	Mike LaValliere	.06	.02	.00
☐ 283	Jose Lind	.06	.02	.00
☐ 284	Orlando Merced	.90	.40	.09
☐ 285	Gary Redus	.06	.02	.00
☐ 286	Don Slaught	.06	.02	.00
☐ 287	Andy Van Slyke	.10	.04	.01
☐ 288	Jose DeLeon	.06	.02	.00
☐ 289	Pedro Guerrero	.10	.04	.01
☐ 290	Ray Lankford	.60	.25	.06
☐ 291	Joe Magrane	.06	.02	.00
☐ 292	Jose Oquendo	.06	.02	.00
☐ 293	Tom Pagnozzi	.06	.02	.00
☐ 294	Bryn Smith	.06	.02	.00
☐ 295	Lee Smith	.10	.04	.01
☐ 296	Ozzie Smith UER	.25	.10	.02
	(Born 12-26, 54,			
	should have hyphen)			
☐ 297	Milt Thompson	.06	.02	.00
☐ 298	Craig Wilson	.15	.06	.01
☐ 299	Todd Zeile	.20	.08	.02
☐ 300	Shawn Abner	.06	.02	.00
☐ 301	Andy Benes	.15	.06	.01
☐ 302	Paul Faries	.12	.05	.01
☐ 303	Tony Gwynn	.25	.10	.02
☐ 304	Greg W. Harris	.06	.02	.00
☐ 305	Thomas Howard	.06	.02	.00
☐ 306	Bruce Hurst	.10	.04	.01
☐ 307	Craig Lefferts	.06	.02	.00
☐ 308	Fred McGriff	.15	.06	.01
☐ 309	Dennis Rasmussen	.06	.02	.00
☐ 310	Bip Roberts	.06	.02	.00
☐ 311	Benito Santiago	.10	.04	.01
☐ 312	Garry Templeton	.06	.02	.00
☐ 313	Ed Whitson	.06	.02	.00
☐ 314	Dave Anderson	.06	.02	.00
☐ 315	Kevin Bass	.06	.02	.00
☐ 316	Jeff Brantley	.06	.02	.00
☐ 317	John Burkett	.06	.02	.00
☐ 318	Will Clark	.60	.25	.06
☐ 319	Steve Decker	.40	.16	.04
☐ 320	Scott Garrelts	.06	.02	.00
☐ 321	Terry Kennedy	.06	.02	.00
☐ 322	Mark Leonard	.20	.08	.02
☐ 323	Darren Lewis	.60	.25	.06
☐ 324	Greg Litton	.06	.02	.00
☐ 325	Willie McGee	.10	.04	.01
☐ 326	Kevin Mitchell	.15	.06	.01
☐ 327	Don Robinson	.06	.02	.00
☐ 328	Andres Santana	.30	.12	.03

#	Player			
☐ 329	Robby Thompson	.06	.02	.00
☐ 330	Jose Uribe	.06	.02	.00
☐ 331	Matt Williams	.17	.07	.01
☐ 332	Scott Bradley	.06	.02	.00
☐ 333	Henry Cotto	.06	.02	.00
☐ 334	Alvin Davis	.10	.04	.01
☐ 335	Ken Griffey Sr.	.10	.04	.01
☐ 336	Ken Griffey Jr.	3.00	1.25	.30
☐ 337	Erik Hanson	.10	.04	.01
☐ 338	Brian Holman	.10	.04	.01
☐ 339	Randy Johnson	.10	.04	.01
☐ 340	Edgar Martinez UER	.10	.04	.01
	(Listed as playing SS)			
☐ 341	Tino Martinez	.30	.12	.03
☐ 342	Pete O'Brien	.06	.02	.00
☐ 343	Harold Reynolds	.10	.04	.01
☐ 344	Dave Valle	.06	.02	.00
☐ 345	Omar Vizquel	.06	.02	.00
☐ 346	Brad Arnsberg	.06	.02	.00
☐ 347	Kevin Brown	.06	.02	.00
☐ 348	Julio Franco	.12	.05	.01
☐ 349	Jeff Huson	.06	.02	.00
☐ 350	Rafael Palmeiro	.17	.07	.01
☐ 351	Geno Petralli	.06	.02	.00
☐ 352	Gary Pettis	.06	.02	.00
☐ 353	Kenny Rogers	.06	.02	.00
☐ 354	Jeff Russell	.06	.02	.00
☐ 355	Nolan Ryan	1.25	.50	.12
☐ 356	Ruben Sierra	.30	.12	.03
☐ 357	Bobby Witt	.10	.04	.01
☐ 358	Roberto Alomar	.25	.10	.02
☐ 359	Pat Borders	.06	.02	.00
☐ 360	Joe Carter UER	.15	.06	.01
	(Reverse negative			
	on back photo)			
☐ 361	Kelly Gruber	.10	.04	.01
☐ 362	Tom Henke	.10	.04	.01
☐ 363	Glenallen Hill	.10	.04	.01
☐ 364	Jimmy Key	.10	.04	.01
☐ 365	Manny Lee	.06	.02	.00
☐ 366	Rance Mulliniks	.06	.02	.00
☐ 367	John Olerud UER	.25	.10	.02
	(Throwing left on card;			
	back has throws right)			
☐ 368	Dave Stieb	.10	.04	.01
☐ 369	Duane Ward	.06	.02	.00
☐ 370	David Wells	.06	.02	.00
☐ 371	Mark Whiten	.30	.12	.03
☐ 372	Mookie Wilson	.06	.02	.00
☐ 373	Willie Banks MLP	.40	.16	.04
☐ 374	Steve Carter MLP	.10	.04	.01
☐ 375	Scott Chiamparino MLP	.12	.05	.01
☐ 376	Steve Chitren MLP	.12	.05	.01
☐ 377	Darrin Fletcher MLP	.15	.06	.01
☐ 378	Rich Garces MLP	.15	.06	.01
☐ 379	Reggie Jefferson MLP	.75	.30	.07
☐ 380	Eric Karros MLP	.90	.40	.09
☐ 381	Pat Kelly MLP	.60	.25	.06
☐ 382	Chuck Knoblauch MLP	2.00	.80	.20
☐ 383	Denny Neagle MLP	.75	.30	.07
☐ 384	Dan Opperman MLP	.25	.10	.02
☐ 385	John Ramos MLP	.35	.15	.03
☐ 386	Henry Rodriguez MLP	.30	.12	.03
☐ 387	Maurice Vaughn MLP	1.50	.60	.15
☐ 388	Gerald Williams MLP	.60	.25	.06
☐ 389	Mike York MLP	.20	.08	.02
☐ 390	Eddie Zosky MLP	.25	.10	.02
☐ 391	Barry Bonds EP	.20	.08	.02
☐ 392	Cecil Fielder EP	.20	.08	.02
☐ 393	Rickey Henderson EP	.30	.12	.03
☐ 394	Dave Justice EP	.75	.30	.07
☐ 395	Nolan Ryan EP	.40	.16	.04
☐ 396	Bobby Thigpen EP	.10	.04	.01
☐ 397	Checklist Card	.10	.04	.01
	Gregg Jefferies			
☐ 398	Checklist Card	.10	.04	.01
	Von Hayes			
☐ 399	Checklist Card	.10	.04	.01
	Terry Kennedy			
☐ 400	Checklist Card	.15	.06	.01
	Nolan Ryan			

1991 Fleer Ultra Gold

This ten-card set presents ¯leer's 1991 Ultra Team. The cards measure the standard size (2 1/2" by 3 1/2"). On a gold background that fades as one moves toward the bottom of the card, the front design has a color head shot, with two cut-out action shots below. Player information is given in a dark blue strip at the bottom of the card face. In blue print on white background with gold borders, the back highlights the player's outstanding achievements. The cards are numbered on the back.

	MINT	EXC	G-VG
COMPLETE SET (10)	14.00	6.25	2.00
COMMON PLAYER (1-10)	.50	.20	.05

		MINT	EXC	G-VG
☐ 1	Barry Bonds	1.25	.50	.12
☐ 2	Will Clark	1.75	.70	.17
☐ 3	Doug Drabek	.50	.20	.05
☐ 4	Ken Griffey Jr.	4.00	1.75	.40
☐ 5	Rickey Henderson	1.50	.60	.15
☐ 6	Bo Jackson	2.00	.80	.20
☐ 7	Ramon Martinez	1.00	.40	.10
☐ 8	Kirby Puckett UER	1.25	.50	.12
	(Boggs won 1988 batting title, so Puckett didn't win consecutive titles)			
☐ 9	Chris Sabo	.60	.25	.06
☐ 10	Ryne Sandberg UER	1.75	.70	.17
	(Johnson and Hornsby didn't hit 40 homers in 1990, Fielder did hit 51 in '90)			

1991 Fleer Ultra Update

The 1991 Fleer Ultra Baseball Update set contains 120 cards and 20 team logo stickers. The set includes the year's hottest rookies and important veteran players traded after the original Ultra series was produced. The cards measure the standard size (2 1/2" by 3 1/2"). The front has a color action shot, while the back has a portrait photo and two full-figure action shots. The cards are numbered and checklisted below alphabetically within and according to teams for each league as follow:

Baltimore Orioles (1-4), Boston Red Sox (5-7), California Angels (8-12), Chicago White Sox (13-18), Cleveland Indians (19-21), Detroit Tigers (22-24), Kansas City Royals (25-29), Milwaukee Brewers (30-33), Minnesota Twins (34-39), New York Yankees (40-44), Oakland Athletics (45-48), Seattle Mariners (49-53), Texas Rangers (54-58), Toronto Blue Jays (59-64), Atlanta Braves (65-69), Chicago Cubs (70-75), Cincinnati Reds (76-78), Houston Astros (79-84), Los Angeles Dodgers (85-89), Montreal Expos (90-93), New York Mets (94-97), Philadelphia Phillies (98-101), Pittsburgh Pirates (102-104), St. Louis Cardinals (105-109), San Diego Padres (110-114), and San Francisco Giants (115-119). The key rookie cards in this set are Jeff Bagwell and Ivan Rodriguez.

		MINT	EXC	G-VG
COMPLETE SET (120)		22.00	9.50	3.15
COMMON PLAYER (1-120)		.07	.03	.01

		MINT	EXC	G-VG
☐ 1	Dwight Evans	.10	.04	.01
☐ 2	Chito Martinez	1.25	.50	.12
☐ 3	Bob Melvin	.07	.03	.01
☐ 4	Mike Mussina	.75	.30	.07
☐ 5	Jack Clark	.12	.05	.01
☐ 6	Dana Kiecker	.07	.03	.01
☐ 7	Steve Lyons	.07	.03	.01
☐ 8	Gary Gaetti	.10	.04	.01
☐ 9	Dave Gallagher	.07	.03	.01
☐ 10	Dave Parker	.12	.05	.01
☐ 11	Luis Polonia	.10	.04	.01
☐ 12	Luis Sojo	.10	.04	.01
☐ 13	Wilson Alvarez	.17	.07	.01
☐ 14	Alex Fernandez	.40	.16	.04
☐ 15	Craig Grebeck	.07	.03	.01
☐ 16	Ron Karkovice	.07	.03	.01
☐ 17	Warren Newson	.30	.12	.03
☐ 18	Scott Radinsky	.10	.04	.01
☐ 19	Glenallen Hill	.10	.04	.01
☐ 20	Charles Nagy	.15	.06	.01
☐ 21	Mark Whiten	.30	.12	.03
☐ 22	Milt Cuyler	.30	.12	.03
☐ 23	Paul Gibson	.07	.03	.01
☐ 24	Mickey Tettleton	.10	.04	.01
☐ 25	Todd Benzinger	.07	.03	.01
☐ 26	Storm Davis	.07	.03	.01
☐ 27	Kirk Gibson	.12	.05	.01
☐ 28	Bill Pecota	.07	.03	.01
☐ 29	Gary Thurman	.07	.03	.01
☐ 30	Darryl Hamilton	.10	.04	.01
☐ 31	Jaime Navarro	.07	.03	.01
☐ 32	Willie Randolph	.10	.04	.01
☐ 33	Bill Wegman	.07	.03	.01
☐ 34	Randy Bush	.07	.03	.01
☐ 35	Chili Davis	.10	.04	.01
☐ 36	Scott Erickson	2.00	.80	.20
☐ 37	Chuck Knoblauch	1.00	.40	.10
☐ 38	Scott Leius	.12	.05	.01
☐ 39	Jack Morris	.15	.06	.01
☐ 40	John Habyan	.07	.03	.01
☐ 41	Pat Kelly	.50	.20	.05
☐ 42	Matt Nokes	.10	.04	.01
☐ 43	Scott Sanderson	.10	.04	.01
☐ 44	Bernie Williams	1.00	.40	.10
☐ 45	Harold Baines	.12	.05	.01
☐ 46	Brook Jacoby	.07	.03	.01
☐ 47	Earnest Riles	.07	.03	.01
☐ 48	Willie Wilson	.10	.04	.01
☐ 49	Jay Buhner	.12	.05	.01
☐ 50	Rich DeLucia	.25	.10	.02
☐ 51	Mike Jackson	.07	.03	.01
☐ 52	Bill Krueger	.07	.03	.01
☐ 53	Bill Swift	.10	.04	.01
☐ 54	Brian Downing	.10	.04	.01
☐ 55	Juan Gonzalez	2.50	1.00	.25
☐ 56	Dean Palmer	.75	.30	.07
☐ 57	Kevin Reimer	.15	.06	.01
☐ 58	Ivan Rodriguez	4.00	1.75	.40
☐ 59	Tom Candiotti	.10	.04	.01
☐ 60	Juan Guzman	1.25	.50	.12
☐ 61	Bob MacDonald	.17	.07	.01
☐ 62	Greg Myers	.07	.03	.01
☐ 63	Ed Sprague	.20	.08	.02
☐ 64	Devon White	.10	.04	.01
☐ 65	Rafael Belliard	.07	.03	.01
☐ 66	Juan Berenguer	.07	.03	.01
☐ 67	Brian Hunter	1.50	.60	.15
☐ 68	Kent Mercker	.10	.04	.01
☐ 69	Otis Nixon	.10	.04	.01
☐ 70	Danny Jackson	.10	.04	.01
☐ 71	Chuck McElroy	.10	.04	.01
☐ 72	Gary Scott	.45	.18	.04

☐ 73	Heathcliff Slocumb	.15	.06	.01
☐ 74	Chico Walker	.10	.04	.01
☐ 75	Rick Wilkins	.35	.15	.03
☐ 76	Chris Hammond	.15	.06	.01
☐ 77	Luis Quinones	.07	.03	.01
☐ 78	Herm Winningham	.07	.03	.01
☐ 79	Jeff Bagwell	5.00	2.25	.50
☐ 80	Jim Corsi	.07	.03	.01
☐ 81	Steve Finley	.12	.05	.01
☐ 82	Luis Gonzalez	1.50	.60	.15
☐ 83	Pete Harnisch	.10	.04	.01
☐ 84	Darryl Kile	.25	.10	.02
☐ 85	Brett Butler	.12	.05	.01
☐ 86	Gary Carter	.12	.05	.01
☐ 87	Tim Crews	.07	.03	.01
☐ 88	Orel Hershiser	.12	.05	.01
☐ 89	Bob Ojeda	.07	.03	.01
☐ 90	Bret Barberie	.50	.20	.05
☐ 91	Barry Jones	.07	.03	.01
☐ 92	Gilberto Reyes	.07	.03	.01
☐ 93	Larry Walker	.15	.06	.01
☐ 94	Hubie Brooks	.10	.04	.01
☐ 95	Tim Burke	.07	.03	.01
☐ 96	Rick Cerone	.07	.03	.01
☐ 97	Jeff Innis	.07	.03	.01
☐ 98	Wally Backman	.07	.03	.01
☐ 99	Tommy Greene	.12	.05	.01
☐ 100	Ricky Jordan	.10	.04	.01
☐ 101	Mitch Williams	.10	.04	.01
☐ 102	John Smiley	.12	.05	.01
☐ 103	Randy Tomlin	.50	.20	.05
☐ 104	Gary Varsho	.07	.03	.01
☐ 105	Cris Carpenter	.07	.03	.01
☐ 106	Ken Hill	.10	.04	.01
☐ 107	Felix Jose	.20	.08	.02
☐ 108	Omar Olivares	.25	.10	.02
☐ 109	Gerald Perry	.07	.03	.01
☐ 110	Jerald Clark	.10	.04	.01
☐ 111	Tony Fernandez	.10	.04	.01
☐ 112	Darrin Jackson	.10	.04	.01
☐ 113	Mike Maddux	.10	.04	.01
☐ 114	Tim Teufel	.10	.04	.01
☐ 115	Bud Black	.07	.03	.01
☐ 116	Kelly Downs	.07	.03	.01
☐ 117	Mike Felder	.07	.03	.01
☐ 118	Willie McGee	.12	.05	.01
☐ 119	Trevor Wilson	.07	.03	.01
☐ 120	Checklist Card	.07	.01	.00

1992 Fleer

The 1992 Fleer set contains 720 cards measuring the standard size (2 1/2" by 3 1/2"). The card fronts shade from metallic pale green to white as one moves down the face. The team logo and player's name appear to the right of the picture, running the length of the card. The top portion of the backs has a different color player photo and biography, while the bottom portion includes statistics and player profile. The cards are checklisted below alphabetically within and according to teams for each league as follows: Baltimore Orioles (1-31), Boston Red Sox (32-49), California Angels (50-73), Chicago White Sox (74-101), Cleveland Indians (102-126), Detroit Tigers (127-149), Kansas City Royals (150-172), Milwaukee Brewers (173-194),

Minnesota Twins (195-220), New York Yankees (221-247), Oakland Athletics (248-272), Seattle Mariners (273-296), Texas Rangers (297-321), Toronto Blue Jays (322-348), Atlanta Braves (349-374), Chicago Cubs (375-397), Cincinnati Reds (398-423), Houston Astros (424-446), Los Angeles Dodgers (447-471), Montreal Expos (472-494), New York Mets (495-520), Philadelphia Phillies (521-547), Pittsburgh Pirates (548-573), St. Louis Cardinals (574-596), San Diego Padres (597-624), and San Francisco Giants (625-651). Topical subsets feature Major League Prospects (652-680), Record Setters (681-687), League Leaders (688-697), Super Star Specials (698-707), Pro Visions (708-713), and Checklists (714-720).

		MINT	EXC	G-VG
COMPLETE SET (720)		36.00	16.25	5.50
COMMON PLAYER (1-720)		.04	.02	.00
☐ 1	Brady Anderson	.04	.02	.00
☐ 2	Jose Bautista	.04	.02	.00
☐ 3	Juan Bell	.04	.02	.00
☐ 4	Glenn Davis	.07	.03	.01
☐ 5	Mike Devereaux	.04	.02	.00
☐ 6	Dwight Evans	.07	.03	.01
☐ 7	Mike Flanagan	.07	.03	.01
☐ 8	Leo Gomez	.15	.06	.01
☐ 9	Chris Hoiles	.07	.03	.01
☐ 10	Sam Horn	.04	.02	.00
☐ 11	Tim Hulett	.04	.02	.00
☐ 12	Dave Johnson	.04	.02	.00
☐ 13	Chito Martinez	.30	.12	.03
☐ 14	Ben McDonald	.10	.04	.01
☐ 15	Bob Melvin	.04	.02	.00
☐ 16	Luis Mercedes	.20	.08	.02
☐ 17	Jose Mesa	.04	.02	.00
☐ 18	Bob Milacki	.04	.02	.00
☐ 19	Randy Milligan	.07	.03	.01
☐ 20	Mike Mussina	.20	.08	.02
☐ 21	Gregg Olson	.07	.03	.01
☐ 22	Joe Orsulak	.04	.02	.00
☐ 23	Jim Poole	.07	.03	.01
☐ 24	Arthur Rhodes	.25	.10	.02
☐ 25	Billy Ripken	.04	.02	.00
☐ 26	Cal Ripken	.40	.16	.04
☐ 27	David Segui	.07	.03	.01
☐ 28	Roy Smith	.04	.02	.00
☐ 29	Anthony Telford	.04	.02	.00
☐ 30	Mark Williamson	.04	.02	.00
☐ 31	Craig Worthington	.04	.02	.00
☐ 32	Wade Boggs	.20	.08	.02
☐ 33	Tom Bolton	.04	.02	.00
☐ 34	Tom Brunansky	.07	.03	.01
☐ 35	Ellis Burks	.07	.03	.01
☐ 36	Jack Clark	.07	.03	.01
☐ 37	Roger Clemens	.25	.10	.02
☐ 38	Danny Darwin	.04	.02	.00
☐ 39	Mike Greenwell	.12	.05	.01
☐ 40	Joe Hesketh	.04	.02	.00
☐ 41	Daryl Irvine	.04	.02	.00
☐ 42	Dennis Lamp	.04	.02	.00
☐ 43	Tony Pena	.07	.03	.01
☐ 44	Phil Plantier	.75	.30	.07
☐ 45	Carlos Quintana	.07	.03	.01
☐ 46	Jeff Reardon	.07	.03	.01
☐ 47	Jody Reed	.07	.03	.01
☐ 48	Luis Rivera	.04	.02	.00
☐ 49	Mo Vaughn	.35	.15	.03
☐ 50	Jim Abbott	.12	.05	.01
☐ 51	Kyle Abbott	.15	.06	.01
☐ 52	Ruben Amaro Jr.	.10	.04	.01
☐ 53	Scott Bailes	.04	.02	.00
☐ 54	Chris Beasley	.15	.06	.01
☐ 55	Mark Eichhorn	.04	.02	.00
☐ 56	Mike Fetters	.04	.02	.00
☐ 57	Chuck Finley	.07	.03	.01
☐ 58	Gary Gaetti	.07	.03	.01
☐ 59	Dave Gallagher	.04	.02	.00
☐ 60	Donnie Hill	.04	.02	.00
☐ 61	Bryan Harvey	.07	.03	.01
☐ 62	Wally Joyner	.07	.03	.01
☐ 63	Mark Langston	.07	.03	.01
☐ 64	Kirk McCaskill	.04	.02	.00
☐ 65	John Orton	.04	.02	.00
☐ 66	Lance Parrish	.07	.03	.01
☐ 67	Luis Polonia	.07	.03	.01
☐ 68	Bobby Rose	.04	.02	.00
☐ 69	Dick Schofield	.04	.02	.00
☐ 70	Luis Sojo	.04	.02	.00
☐ 71	Lee Stevens	.07	.03	.01
☐ 72	Dave Winfield	.12	.05	.01
☐ 73	Cliff Young	.04	.02	.00

#	Name				#	Name			
74	Wilson Alvarez	.12	.05	.01	166	Harvey Pulliam	.20	.08	.02
75	Esteban Beltre	.15	.06	.01	167	Bret Saberhagen	.10	.04	.01
76	Joey Cora	.04	.02	.00	168	Kevin Seitzer	.07	.03	.01
77	Brian Drahman	.07	.03	.01	169	Terry Shumpert	.04	.02	.00
78	Alex Fernandez	.12	.05	.01	170	Kurt Stillwell	.04	.02	.00
79	Carlton Fisk	.12	.05	.01	171	Danny Tartabull	.10	.04	.01
80	Scott Fletcher	.04	.02	.00	172	Gary Thurman	.04	.02	.00
81	Craig Grebeck	.04	.02	.00	173	Dante Bichette	.04	.02	.00
82	Ozzie Guillen	.07	.03	.01	174	Kevin Brown	.07	.03	.01
83	Greg Hibbard	.04	.02	.00	175	Chuck Crim	.04	.02	.00
84	Charlie Hough	.04	.02	.00	176	Jim Gantner	.04	.02	.00
85	Mike Huff	.04	.02	.00	177	Darryl Hamilton	.04	.02	.00
86	Bo Jackson	.35	.15	.03	178	Ted Higuera	.04	.02	.00
87	Lance Johnson	.04	.02	.00	179	Darren Holmes	.07	.03	.01
88	Ron Karkovice	.04	.02	.00	180	Mark Lee	.07	.03	.01
89	Jack McDowell	.07	.03	.01	181	Julio Machado	.04	.02	.00
90	Matt Merullo	.04	.02	.00	182	Paul Molitor	.07	.03	.01
91	Warren Newson	.07	.03	.01	183	Jaime Navarro	.04	.02	.00
92	Donn Pall UER (Called Dunn on card back)				184	Edwin Nunez	.04	.02	.00
					185	Dan Plesac	.04	.02	.00
					186	Willie Randolph	.04	.02	.00
93	Dan Pasqua	.04	.02	.00	187	Ron Robinson	.04	.02	.00
94	Ken Patterson	.04	.02	.00	188	Gary Sheffield	.07	.03	.01
95	Melido Perez	.04	.02	.00	189	Bill Spiers	.04	.02	.00
96	Scott Radinsky	.04	.02	.00	190	B.J. Surhoff	.07	.03	.01
97	Tim Raines	.07	.03	.01	191	Dale Sveum	.04	.02	.00
98	Sammy Sosa	.07	.03	.01	192	Greg Vaughn	.07	.03	.01
99	Bobby Thigpen	.07	.03	.01	193	Bill Wegman	.04	.02	.00
100	Frank Thomas	1.25	.50	.12	194	Robin Yount	.15	.06	.01
101	Robin Ventura	.25	.10	.02	195	Rick Aguilera	.04	.02	.00
102	Mike Aldrete	.04	.02	.00	196	Allan Anderson	.04	.02	.00
103	Sandy Alomar Jr.	.07	.03	.01	197	Steve Bedrosian	.04	.02	.00
104	Carlos Baerga	.12	.05	.01	198	Randy Bush	.04	.02	.00
105	Albert Belle	.15	.06	.01	199	Larry Casian	.07	.03	.01
106	Willie Blair	.04	.02	.00	200	Chili Davis	.07	.03	.01
107	Jerry Browne	.04	.02	.00	201	Scott Erickson	.45	.18	.04
108	Alex Cole	.07	.03	.01	202	Greg Gagne	.04	.02	.00
109	Felix Fermin	.04	.02	.00	203	Dan Gladden	.04	.02	.00
110	Glenallen Hill	.07	.03	.01	204	Brian Harper	.04	.02	.00
111	Shawn Hillegas	.04	.02	.00	205	Kent Hrbek	.07	.03	.01
112	Chris James	.04	.02	.00	206	Chuck Knoblauch	.35	.15	.03
113	Reggie Jefferson	.20	.08	.02	207	Gene Larkin	.04	.02	.00
114	Doug Jones	.04	.02	.00	208	Terry Leach	.04	.02	.00
115	Eric King	.04	.02	.00	209	Scott Leius	.07	.03	.01
116	Mark Lewis	.15	.06	.01	210	Shane Mack	.07	.03	.01
117	Carlos Martinez	.04	.02	.00	211	Jack Morris	.07	.03	.01
118	Charles Nagy	.07	.03	.01	212	Pedro Munoz	.15	.06	.01
119	Rod Nichols	.04	.02	.00	213	Denny Neagle	.25	.10	.02
120	Steve Olin	.04	.02	.00	214	Al Newman	.04	.02	.00
121	Jesse Orosco	.04	.02	.00	215	Junior Ortiz	.04	.02	.00
122	Rudy Seanez	.04	.02	.00	216	Mike Pagliarulo	.04	.02	.00
123	Joel Skinner	.04	.02	.00	217	Kirby Puckett	.20	.08	.02
124	Greg Swindell	.07	.03	.01	218	Paul Sorrento	.04	.02	.00
125	Jim Thome	.60	.25	.06	219	Kevin Tapani	.07	.03	.01
126	Mark Whiten	.15	.06	.01	220	Lenny Webster	.07	.03	.01
127	Scott Aldred	.04	.02	.00	221	Jesse Barfield	.07	.03	.01
128	Andy Allanson	.04	.02	.00	222	Greg Cadaret	.04	.02	.00
129	John Cerutti	.04	.02	.00	223	Dave Eiland	.04	.02	.00
130	Milt Cuyler	.07	.03	.01	224	Alvaro Espinoza	.04	.02	.00
131	Mike Dalton	.15	.06	.01	225	Steve Farr	.04	.02	.00
132	Rob Deer	.04	.02	.00	226	Bob Geren	.04	.02	.00
133	Cecil Fielder	.25	.10	.02	227	Lee Guetterman	.04	.02	.00
134	Travis Fryman	.30	.12	.03	228	John Habyan	.04	.02	.00
135	Dan Gakeler	.07	.03	.01	229	Mel Hall	.07	.03	.01
136	Paul Gibson	.04	.02	.00	230	Steve Howe	.04	.02	.00
137	Bill Gullickson	.04	.02	.00	231	Mike Humphreys	.07	.03	.01
138	Mike Henneman	.04	.02	.00	232	Scott Kamieniecki	.07	.03	.01
139	Pete Incaviglia	.07	.03	.01	233	Pat Kelly	.15	.06	.01
140	Mark Leiter	.07	.03	.01	234	Roberto Kelly	.07	.03	.01
141	Scott Livingstone	.18	.08	.01	235	Tim Leary	.07	.03	.01
142	Lloyd Moseby	.04	.02	.00	236	Kevin Maas	.18	.08	.01
143	Tony Phillips	.04	.02	.00	237	Don Mattingly	.20	.08	.02
144	Mark Salas	.04	.02	.00	238	Hensley Meulens	.07	.03	.01
145	Frank Tanana	.07	.03	.01	239	Matt Nokes	.07	.03	.01
146	Walt Terrell	.04	.02	.00	240	Pascual Perez	.04	.02	.00
147	Mickey Tettleton	.07	.03	.01	241	Eric Plunk	.04	.02	.00
148	Alan Trammell	.07	.03	.01	242	John Ramos	.18	.08	.01
149	Lou Whitaker	.07	.03	.01	243	Scott Sanderson	.04	.02	.00
150	Kevin Appier	.07	.03	.01	244	Steve Sax	.07	.03	.01
151	Luis Aquino	.04	.02	.00	245	Wade Taylor	.07	.03	.01
152	Todd Benzinger	.04	.02	.00	246	Randy Velarde	.04	.02	.00
153	Mike Boddicker	.04	.02	.00	247	Bernie Williams	.25	.10	.02
154	George Brett	.15	.06	.01	248	Troy Afenir	.04	.02	.00
155	Storm Davis	.04	.02	.00	249	Harold Baines	.07	.03	.01
156	Jim Eisenreich	.04	.02	.00	250	Lance Blankenship	.04	.02	.00
157	Kirk Gibson	.07	.03	.01	251	Mike Bordick	.07	.03	.01
158	Tom Gordon	.07	.03	.01	252	Jose Canseco	.35	.15	.03
159	Mark Gubicza	.07	.03	.01	253	Steve Chitren	.04	.02	.00
160	David Howard	.07	.03	.01	254	Ron Darling	.04	.02	.00
161	Mike Macfarlane	.04	.02	.00	255	Dennis Eckersley	.07	.03	.01
162	Brent Mayne	.07	.03	.01	256	Mike Gallego	.04	.02	.00
163	Brian McRae	.18	.08	.01	257	Dave Henderson	.07	.03	.01
164	Jeff Montgomery	.04	.02	.00	258	Rickey Henderson	.30	.12	.03
165	Bill Pecota	.04	.02	.00	259	Rick Honeycutt	.04	.02	.00

#	Player			
☐ 260	Brook Jacoby	.04	.02	.00
☐ 261	Carney Lansford	.07	.03	.01
☐ 262	Mark McGwire	.12	.05	.01
☐ 263	Mike Moore	.07	.03	.01
☐ 264	Gene Nelson	.04	.02	.00
☐ 265	Jamie Quirk	.04	.02	.00
☐ 266	Joe Slusarski	.07	.03	.01
☐ 267	Terry Steinbach	.07	.03	.01
☐ 268	Dave Stewart	.07	.03	.01
☐ 269	Todd Van Poppel	.75	.30	.07
☐ 270	Walt Weiss	.07	.03	.01
☐ 271	Bob Welch	.07	.03	.01
☐ 272	Curt Young	.04	.02	.00
☐ 273	Scott Bradley	.04	.02	.00
☐ 274	Greg Briley	.04	.02	.00
☐ 275	Jay Buhner	.07	.03	.01
☐ 276	Henry Cotto	.04	.02	.00
☐ 277	Alvin Davis	.07	.03	.01
☐ 278	Rich DeLucia	.04	.02	.00
☐ 279	Ken Griffey Jr.	.75	.30	.07
☐ 280	Erik Hanson	.07	.03	.01
☐ 281	Brian Holman	.04	.02	.00
☐ 282	Mike Jackson	.04	.02	.00
☐ 283	Randy Johnson	.07	.03	.01
☐ 284	Tracy Jones	.04	.02	.00
☐ 285	Bill Krueger	.04	.02	.00
☐ 286	Edgar Martinez	.07	.03	.01
☐ 287	Tino Martinez	.15	.06	.01
☐ 288	Rob Murphy	.04	.02	.00
☐ 289	Pete O'Brien	.04	.02	.00
☐ 290	Alonzo Powell	.07	.03	.01
☐ 291	Harold Reynolds	.04	.02	.00
☐ 292	Mike Schooler	.04	.02	.00
☐ 293	Russ Swan	.04	.02	.00
☐ 294	Bill Swift	.04	.02	.00
☐ 295	Dave Valle	.04	.02	.00
☐ 296	Omar Vizquel	.04	.02	.00
☐ 297	Gerald Alexander	.04	.02	.00
☐ 298	Brad Arnsberg	.04	.02	.00
☐ 299	Kevin Brown	.07	.03	.01
☐ 300	Jack Daugherty	.04	.02	.00
☐ 301	Mario Diaz	.04	.02	.00
☐ 302	Brian Downing	.04	.02	.00
☐ 303	Julio Franco	.07	.03	.01
☐ 304	Juan Gonzalez	.35	.15	.03
☐ 305	Rich Gossage	.07	.03	.01
☐ 306	Jose Guzman	.04	.02	.00
☐ 307	Jose Hernandez	.18	.08	.01
☐ 308	Jeff Huson	.04	.02	.00
☐ 309	Mike Jeffcoat	.04	.02	.00
☐ 310	Terry Mathews	.10	.04	.01
☐ 311	Rafael Palmeiro	.12	.05	.01
☐ 312	Dean Palmer	.25	.10	.02
☐ 313	Geno Petralli	.04	.02	.00
☐ 314	Gary Pettis	.04	.02	.00
☐ 315	Kevin Reimer	.07	.03	.01
☐ 316	Ivan Rodriguez	.90	.40	.09
☐ 317	Kenny Rogers	.04	.02	.00
☐ 318	Wayne Rosenthal	.12	.05	.01
☐ 319	Jeff Russell	.04	.02	.00
☐ 320	Nolan Ryan	.50	.20	.05
☐ 321	Ruben Sierra	.20	.08	.02
☐ 322	Jim Acker	.04	.02	.00
☐ 323	Roberto Alomar	.12	.05	.01
☐ 324	Derek Bell	.35	.15	.03
☐ 325	Pat Borders	.04	.02	.00
☐ 326	Tom Candiotti	.07	.03	.01
☐ 327	Joe Carter	.10	.04	.01
☐ 328	Rob Ducey	.04	.02	.00
☐ 329	Kelly Gruber	.07	.03	.01
☐ 330	Juan Guzman	.65	.25	.06
☐ 331	Tom Henke	.04	.02	.00
☐ 332	Jimmy Key	.07	.03	.01
☐ 333	Manny Lee	.04	.02	.00
☐ 334	Al Leiter	.04	.02	.00
☐ 335	Bob MacDonald	.07	.03	.01
☐ 336	Candy Maldonado	.04	.02	.00
☐ 337	Rance Mulliniks	.04	.02	.00
☐ 338	Greg Myers	.04	.02	.00
☐ 339	John Olerud	.15	.06	.01
☐ 340	Ed Sprague	.10	.04	.01
☐ 341	Dave Stieb	.07	.03	.01
☐ 342	Todd Stottlemyre	.07	.03	.01
☐ 343	Mike Timlin	.07	.03	.01
☐ 344	Duane Ward	.04	.02	.00
☐ 345	David Wells	.04	.02	.00
☐ 346	Devon White	.07	.03	.01
☐ 347	Mookie Wilson	.07	.03	.01
☐ 348	Eddie Zosky	.12	.05	.01
☐ 349	Steve Avery	.30	.12	.03
☐ 350	Mike Bell	.07	.03	.01
☐ 351	Rafael Belliard	.04	.02	.00
☐ 352	Juan Berenguer	.04	.02	.00
☐ 353	Jeff Blauser	.04	.02	.00
☐ 354	Sid Bream	.04	.02	.00
☐ 355	Francisco Cabrera	.04	.02	.00
☐ 356	Marvin Freeman	.04	.02	.00
☐ 357	Ron Gant	.15	.06	.01
☐ 358	Tom Glavine	.10	.04	.01
☐ 359	Brian Hunter	.60	.25	.06
☐ 360	Dave Justice	.60	.25	.06
☐ 361	Charlie Leibrandt	.04	.02	.00
☐ 362	Mark Lemke	.04	.02	.00
☐ 363	Kent Mercker	.04	.02	.00
☐ 364	Keith Mitchell	.25	.10	.02
☐ 365	Greg Olson	.04	.02	.00
☐ 366	Terry Pendleton	.07	.03	.01
☐ 367	Armando Reynoso	.12	.05	.01
☐ 368	Deion Sanders	.10	.04	.01
☐ 369	Lonnie Smith	.07	.03	.01
☐ 370	Pete Smith	.04	.02	.00
☐ 371	John Smoltz	.10	.04	.01
☐ 372	Mike Stanton	.04	.02	.00
☐ 373	Jeff Treadway	.04	.02	.00
☐ 374	Mark Wohlers	.30	.12	.03
☐ 375	Paul Assenmacher	.04	.02	.00
☐ 376	George Bell	.07	.03	.01
☐ 377	Shawn Boskie	.04	.02	.00
☐ 378	Frank Castillo	.04	.02	.00
☐ 379	Andre Dawson	.12	.05	.01
☐ 380	Shawon Dunston	.07	.03	.01
☐ 381	Mark Grace	.10	.04	.01
☐ 382	Mike Harkey	.04	.02	.00
☐ 383	Danny Jackson	.04	.02	.00
☐ 384	Les Lancaster	.04	.02	.00
☐ 385	Cedric Landrum	.10	.04	.01
☐ 386	Greg Maddux	.07	.03	.01
☐ 387	Derrick May	.07	.03	.01
☐ 388	Chuck McElroy	.04	.02	.00
☐ 389	Ryne Sandberg	.35	.15	.03
☐ 390	Heathcliff Slocumb	.04	.02	.00
☐ 391	Dave Smith	.04	.02	.00
☐ 392	Dwight Smith	.07	.03	.01
☐ 393	Rick Sutcliffe	.07	.03	.01
☐ 394	Hector Villanueva	.07	.03	.01
☐ 395	Chico Walker	.04	.02	.00
☐ 396	Jerome Walton	.07	.03	.01
☐ 397	Rick Wilkins	.10	.04	.01
☐ 398	Jack Armstrong	.07	.03	.01
☐ 399	Freddie Benavides	.04	.02	.00
☐ 400	Glenn Braggs	.04	.02	.00
☐ 401	Tom Browning	.07	.03	.01
☐ 402	Norm Charlton	.04	.02	.00
☐ 403	Eric Davis	.12	.05	.01
☐ 404	Rob Dibble	.07	.03	.01
☐ 405	Bill Doran	.04	.02	.00
☐ 406	Mariano Duncan	.04	.02	.00
☐ 407	Kip Gross	.15	.06	.01
☐ 408	Chris Hammond	.07	.03	.01
☐ 409	Billy Hatcher	.04	.02	.00
☐ 410	Chris Jones	.07	.03	.01
☐ 411	Barry Larkin	.12	.05	.01
☐ 412	Hal Morris	.10	.04	.01
☐ 413	Randy Myers	.04	.02	.00
☐ 414	Joe Oliver	.04	.02	.00
☐ 415	Paul O'Neill	.07	.03	.01
☐ 416	Ted Power	.04	.02	.00
☐ 417	Luis Quinones	.04	.02	.00
☐ 418	Jeff Reed	.04	.02	.00
☐ 419	Jose Rijo	.07	.03	.01
☐ 420	Chris Sabo	.07	.03	.01
☐ 421	Reggie Sanders	.25	.10	.02
☐ 422	Scott Scudder	.04	.02	.00
☐ 423	Glenn Sutko	.07	.03	.01
☐ 424	Eric Anthony	.07	.03	.01
☐ 425	Jeff Bagwell	1.25	.50	.12
☐ 426	Craig Biggio	.07	.03	.01
☐ 427	Ken Caminiti	.04	.02	.00
☐ 428	Casey Candaele	.04	.02	.00
☐ 429	Mike Capel	.04	.02	.00
☐ 430	Andujar Cedeno	.20	.08	.02
☐ 431	Jim Corsi	.04	.02	.00
☐ 432	Mark Davidson	.04	.02	.00
☐ 433	Steve Finley	.07	.03	.01
☐ 434	Luis Gonzalez	.20	.08	.02
☐ 435	Pete Harnisch	.07	.03	.01
☐ 436	Dwayne Henry	.04	.02	.00
☐ 437	Xavier Hernandez	.04	.02	.00
☐ 438	Jimmy Jones	.04	.02	.00
☐ 439	Darryl Kile	.10	.04	.01
☐ 440	Rob Mallicoat	.04	.02	.00
☐ 441	Andy Mota	.10	.04	.01
☐ 442	Al Osuna	.04	.02	.00
☐ 443	Mark Portugal	.04	.02	.00
☐ 444	Scott Servais	.07	.03	.01
☐ 445	Mike Simms	.07	.03	.01
☐ 446	Gerald Young	.04	.02	.00
☐ 447	Tim Belcher	.07	.03	.01

☐ 448 Brett Butler	.07	.03	.01
☐ 449 John Candelaria	.04	.02	.00
☐ 450 Gary Carter	.07	.03	.01
☐ 451 Dennis Cook	.04	.02	.00
☐ 452 Tim Crews	.04	.02	.00
☐ 453 Kal Daniels	.07	.03	.01
☐ 454 Jim Gott	.04	.02	.00
☐ 455 Alfredo Griffin	.04	.02	.00
☐ 456 Kevin Gross	.04	.02	.00
☐ 457 Chris Gwynn	.04	.02	.00
☐ 458 Lenny Harris	.04	.02	.00
☐ 459 Orel Hershiser	.07	.03	.01
☐ 460 Jay Howell	.04	.02	.00
☐ 461 Stan Javier	.04	.02	.00
☐ 462 Eric Karros	.25	.10	.02
☐ 463 Ramon Martinez	.15	.06	.01
☐ 464 Roger McDowell	.04	.02	.00
☐ 465 Mike Morgan	.07	.03	.01
☐ 466 Eddie Murray	.12	.05	.01
☐ 467 Jose Offerman	.07	.03	.01
☐ 468 Bob Ojeda	.04	.02	.00
☐ 469 Juan Samuel	.07	.03	.01
☐ 470 Mike Scioscia	.04	.02	.00
☐ 471 Darryl Strawberry	.25	.10	.02
☐ 472 Bret Barberie	.15	.06	.01
☐ 473 Brian Barnes	.04	.02	.00
☐ 474 Eric Bullock	.04	.02	.00
☐ 475 Ivan Calderon	.07	.03	.01
☐ 476 Delino DeShields	.07	.03	.01
☐ 477 Jeff Fassero	.07	.03	.01
☐ 478 Mike Fitzgerald	.04	.02	.00
☐ 479 Steve Frey	.04	.02	.00
☐ 480 Andres Galarraga	.07	.03	.01
☐ 481 Mark Gardner	.04	.02	.00
☐ 482 Marquis Grissom	.07	.03	.01
☐ 483 Chris Haney	.10	.04	.01
☐ 484 Barry Jones	.04	.02	.00
☐ 485 Dave Martinez	.04	.02	.00
☐ 486 Dennis Martinez	.07	.03	.01
☐ 487 Chris Nabholz	.04	.02	.00
☐ 488 Spike Owen	.04	.02	.00
☐ 489 Gilberto Reyes	.04	.02	.00
☐ 490 Mel Rojas	.07	.03	.01
☐ 491 Scott Ruskin	.04	.02	.00
☐ 492 Bill Sampen	.04	.02	.00
☐ 493 Larry Walker	.07	.03	.01
☐ 494 Tim Wallach	.07	.03	.01
☐ 495 Daryl Boston	.04	.02	.00
☐ 496 Hubie Brooks	.07	.03	.01
☐ 497 Tim Burke	.04	.02	.00
☐ 498 Mark Carreon	.04	.02	.00
☐ 499 Tony Castillo	.04	.02	.00
☐ 500 Vince Coleman	.07	.03	.01
☐ 501 David Cone	.07	.03	.01
☐ 502 Kevin Elster	.04	.02	.00
☐ 503 Sid Fernandez	.07	.03	.01
☐ 504 John Franco	.04	.02	.00
☐ 505 Dwight Gooden	.12	.05	.01
☐ 506 Todd Hundley	.10	.04	.01
☐ 507 Jeff Innis	.04	.02	.00
☐ 508 Gregg Jefferies	.10	.04	.01
☐ 509 Howard Johnson	.10	.04	.01
☐ 510 Dave Magadan	.07	.03	.01
☐ 511 Terry McDaniel	.12	.05	.01
☐ 512 Kevin McReynolds	.07	.03	.01
☐ 513 Keith Miller	.04	.02	.00
☐ 514 Charlie O'Brien	.04	.02	.00
☐ 515 Mackey Sasser	.04	.02	.00
☐ 516 Pete Schourek	.07	.03	.01
☐ 517 Julio Valera	.04	.02	.00
☐ 518 Frank Viola	.07	.03	.01
☐ 519 Wally Whitehurst	.04	.02	.00
☐ 520 Anthony Young	.17	.07	.01
☐ 521 Andy Ashby	.15	.06	.01
☐ 522 Kim Batiste	.12	.05	.01
☐ 523 Joe Boever	.04	.02	.00
☐ 524 Wes Chamberlain	.25	.10	.02
☐ 525 Pat Combs	.04	.02	.00
☐ 526 Danny Cox	.04	.02	.00
☐ 527 Darren Daulton	.04	.02	.00
☐ 528 Jose DeJesus	.04	.02	.00
☐ 529 Len Dykstra	.07	.03	.01
☐ 530 Darrin Fletcher	.04	.02	.00
☐ 531 Tommy Greene	.07	.03	.01
☐ 532 Jason Grimsley	.04	.02	.00
☐ 533 Charlie Hayes	.04	.02	.00
☐ 534 Von Hayes	.07	.03	.01
☐ 535 Dave Hollins	.04	.02	.00
☐ 536 Ricky Jordan	.07	.03	.01
☐ 537 John Kruk	.04	.02	.00
☐ 538 Jim Lindeman	.04	.02	.00
☐ 539 Mickey Morandini	.07	.03	.01
☐ 540 Terry Mulholland	.04	.02	.00
☐ 541 Dale Murphy	.10	.04	.01

☐ 542 Randy Ready	.04	.02	.00
☐ 543 Wally Ritchie	.04	.02	.00
☐ 544 Bruce Ruffin	.04	.02	.00
☐ 545 Steve Searcy	.04	.02	.00
☐ 546 Dickie Thon	.04	.02	.00
☐ 547 Mitch Williams	.04	.02	.00
☐ 548 Stan Belinda	.04	.02	.00
☐ 549 Jay Bell	.04	.02	.00
☐ 550 Barry Bonds	.18	.08	.01
☐ 551 Bobby Bonilla	.15	.06	.01
☐ 552 Steve Buechele	.07	.03	.01
☐ 553 Doug Drabek	.07	.03	.01
☐ 554 Neal Heaton	.04	.02	.00
☐ 555 Jeff King	.04	.02	.00
☐ 556 Bob Kipper	.04	.02	.00
☐ 557 Bill Landrum	.04	.02	.00
☐ 558 Mike LaValliere	.04	.02	.00
☐ 559 Jose Lind	.04	.02	.00
☐ 560 Lloyd McClendon	.04	.02	.00
☐ 561 Orlando Merced	.18	.08	.01
☐ 562 Bob Patterson	.04	.02	.00
☐ 563 Joe Redfield	.20	.08	.02
☐ 564 Gary Redus	.04	.02	.00
☐ 565 Rosario Rodriguez	.07	.03	.01
☐ 566 Don Slaught	.04	.02	.00
☐ 567 John Smiley	.07	.03	.01
☐ 568 Zane Smith	.04	.02	.00
☐ 569 Randy Tomlin	.07	.03	.01
☐ 570 Andy Van Slyke	.07	.03	.01
☐ 571 Gary Varsho	.04	.02	.00
☐ 572 Bob Walk	.04	.02	.00
☐ 573 John Wehner	.20	.08	.02
☐ 574 Juan Agosto	.04	.02	.00
☐ 575 Cris Carpenter	.04	.02	.00
☐ 576 Jose DeLeon	.04	.02	.00
☐ 577 Rich Gedman	.04	.02	.00
☐ 578 Bernard Gilkey	.12	.05	.01
☐ 579 Pedro Guerrero	.07	.03	.01
☐ 580 Ken Hill	.04	.02	.00
☐ 581 Rex Hudler	.04	.02	.00
☐ 582 Felix Jose	.10	.04	.01
☐ 583 Ray Lankford	.15	.06	.01
☐ 584 Omar Olivares	.07	.03	.01
☐ 585 Jose Oquendo	.04	.02	.00
☐ 586 Tom Pagnozzi	.04	.02	.00
☐ 587 Geronimo Pena	.04	.02	.00
☐ 588 Mike Perez	.04	.02	.00
☐ 589 Gerald Perry	.04	.02	.00
☐ 590 Bryn Smith	.04	.02	.00
☐ 591 Lee Smith	.07	.03	.01
☐ 592 Ozzie Smith	.12	.05	.01
☐ 593 Scott Terry	.04	.02	.00
☐ 594 Bob Tewksbury	.04	.02	.00
☐ 595 Milt Thompson	.04	.02	.00
☐ 596 Todd Zeile	.12	.05	.01
☐ 597 Larry Andersen	.04	.02	.00
☐ 598 Oscar Azocar	.04	.02	.00
☐ 599 Andy Benes	.07	.03	.01
☐ 600 Ricky Bones	.07	.03	.01
☐ 601 Jerald Clark	.04	.02	.00
☐ 602 Pat Clements	.04	.02	.00
☐ 603 Paul Faries	.04	.02	.00
☐ 604 Tony Fernandez	.07	.03	.01
☐ 605 Tony Gwynn	.20	.08	.02
☐ 606 Greg Harris	.04	.02	.00
☐ 607 Thomas Howard	.04	.02	.00
☐ 608 Bruce Hurst	.07	.03	.01
☐ 609 Darrin Jackson	.04	.02	.00
☐ 610 Tom Lampkin	.04	.02	.00
☐ 611 Craig Lefferts	.04	.02	.00
☐ 612 Jim Lewis	.12	.05	.01
☐ 613 Mike Maddux	.04	.02	.00
☐ 614 Fred McGriff	.12	.05	.01
☐ 615 Jose Melendez	.07	.03	.01
☐ 616 Jose Mota	.10	.04	.01
☐ 617 Dennis Rasmussen	.04	.02	.00
☐ 618 Bip Roberts	.04	.02	.00
☐ 619 Rich Rodriguez	.04	.02	.00
☐ 620 Benito Santiago	.07	.03	.01
☐ 621 Craig Shipley	.12	.05	.01
☐ 622 Tim Teufel	.04	.02	.00
☐ 623 Kevin Ward	.15	.06	.01
☐ 624 Ed Whitson	.04	.02	.00
☐ 625 Dave Anderson	.04	.02	.00
☐ 626 Kevin Bass	.04	.02	.00
☐ 627 Rod Beck	.12	.05	.01
☐ 628 Bud Black	.04	.02	.00
☐ 629 Jeff Brantley	.04	.02	.00
☐ 630 John Burkett	.04	.02	.00
☐ 631 Will Clark	.30	.12	.03
☐ 632 Royce Clayton	.25	.10	.02
☐ 633 Steve Decker	.15	.06	.01
☐ 634 Kelly Downs	.04	.02	.00
☐ 635 Mike Felder	.04	.02	.00

☐ 636	Scott Garrelts	.25	.10	.02
☐ 637	Eric Gunderson	.04	.02	.00
☐ 638	Bryan Hickerson	.17	.07	.01
☐ 639	Darren Lewis	.15	.06	.01
☐ 640	Greg Litton	.04	.02	.00
☐ 641	Kirt Manwaring	.04	.02	.00
☐ 642	Paul McClellan	.07	.03	.01
☐ 643	Willie McGee	.07	.03	.01
☐ 644	Kevin Mitchell	.10	.04	.01
☐ 645	Francisco Oliveras	.04	.02	.00
☐ 646	Mike Remlinger	.04	.02	.00
☐ 647	Dave Righetti	.07	.03	.01
☐ 648	Robby Thompson	.04	.02	.00
☐ 649	Jose Uribe	.04	.02	.00
☐ 650	Matt Williams	.12	.05	.01
☐ 651	Trevor Wilson	.04	.02	.00
☐ 652	Tom Goodwin	.18	.08	.01
☐ 653	Terry Bross	.04	.02	.00
☐ 654	Mike Christopher	.12	.05	.01
☐ 655	Kenny Lofton	.25	.10	.02
☐ 656	Chris Cron	.15	.06	.01
☐ 657	Willie Banks	.15	.06	.01
☐ 658	Pat Rice	.18	.08	.01
☐ 659	Rob Maurer	.35	.15	.03
☐ 660	Don Harris	.10	.04	.01
☐ 661	Henry Rodriguez	.07	.03	.01
☐ 662	Cliff Brantley	.20	.08	.02
☐ 663	Mike Linskey	.04	.02	.00
☐ 664	Gary Disarcina	.04	.02	.00
☐ 665	Gil Heredia	.12	.05	.01
☐ 666	Vinny Castilla	.12	.05	.01
☐ 667	Paul Abbott	.04	.02	.00
☐ 668	Monty Fariss	.10	.04	.01
☐ 669	Jarvis Brown	.15	.06	.01
☐ 670	Wayne Kirby	.15	.06	.01
☐ 671	Scott Brosius	.15	.06	.01
☐ 672	Bob Hamelin	.07	.03	.01
☐ 673	Joel Johnston	.15	.06	.01
☐ 674	Tim Spehr	.10	.04	.01
☐ 675	Jeff Gardner	.12	.05	.01
☐ 676	Rico Rossy	.15	.06	.01
☐ 677	Roberto Hernandez	.18	.08	.01
☐ 678	Ted Wood	.30	.12	.03
☐ 679	Cal Eldred	.10	.04	.01
☐ 680	Sean Berry	.07	.03	.01
☐ 681	Rickey Henderson RS	.15	.06	.01
☐ 682	Nolan Ryan RS	.30	.12	.03
☐ 683	Dennis Martinez RS	.07	.03	.01
☐ 684	Wilson Alvarez RS	.07	.03	.01
☐ 685	Joe Carter RS	.07	.03	.01
☐ 686	Dave Winfield RS	.10	.04	.01
☐ 687	David Cone RS	.07	.03	.01
☐ 688	Jose Canseco LL	.20	.08	.02
☐ 689	Howard Johnson LL	.07	.03	.01
☐ 690	Julio Franco LL	.07	.03	.01
☐ 691	Terry Pendleton LL	.07	.03	.01
☐ 692	Cecil Fielder LL	.12	.05	.01
☐ 693	Scott Erickson LL	.20	.08	.02
☐ 694	Tom Glavine LL	.07	.03	.01
☐ 695	Dennis Martinez LL	.07	.03	.01
☐ 696	Bryan Harvey LL	.07	.03	.01
☐ 697	Lee Smith LL	.07	.03	.01
☐ 698	Super Siblings Roberto Alomar Sandy Alomar Jr.	.10	.04	.01
☐ 699	The Indispensables Bobby Bonilla Will Clark	.18	.08	.01
☐ 700	Teamwork Mark Wohlers Kent Mercker Alejandro Pena	.12	.05	.01
☐ 701	Tiger Tandems Stacy Jones Bo Jackson Gregg Olson Frank Thomas	.30	.12	.03
☐ 702	The Ignitors Paul Molitor Brett Butler	.07	.03	.01
☐ 703	Indispensables II Cal Ripken Joe Carter	.15	.06	.01
☐ 704	Power Packs Barry Larkin Kirby Puckett	.12	.05	.01
☐ 705	Today and Tomorrow Mo Vaughn Cecil Fielder	.18	.08	.01
☐ 706	Teenage Sensations Ramon Martinez Ozzie Guillen	.10	.04	.01

☐ 707	Designated Hitters Harold Baines Wade Boggs	.10	.04	.01
☐ 708	Robin Yount PV	.10	.04	.01
☐ 709	Ken Griffey Jr. PV	.40	.16	.04
☐ 710	Nolan Ryan PV	.30	.12	.03
☐ 711	Cal Ripken PV	.20	.08	.02
☐ 712	Frank Thomas PV	.60	.25	.06
☐ 713	Dave Justice PV	.30	.12	.03
☐ 714	Checklist Card	.07	.03	.01
☐ 715	Checklist Card	.07	.03	.01
☐ 716	Checklist Card	.07	.03	.01
☐ 717	Checklist Card	.07	.03	.01
☐ 718	Checklist Card	.07	.03	.01
☐ 719	Checklist Card	.07	.03	.01
☐ 720	Checklist Card	.07	.03	.01

1992 Fleer Clemens Inserts

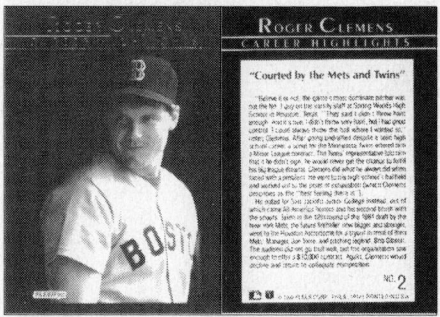

The 12-card Roger Clemens "Career Highlights" series was randomly inserted in 1992 Fleer wax packs. Some signed cards were inserted and one could be won by entering a drawing. Moreover, a three-card Clemens subset was available through a special mail-in offer. The cards measure the standard size (2 1/2" by 3 1/2"). The glossy color photos on the fronts are bordered in black and accented with gold stripes and lettering on the top of the card. On a pale yellow background with black borders, the back has player profile and career highlights. The cards are numbered on the back.

	MINT	EXC	G-VG
COMPLETE SET (12)	22.00	9.00	2.00
COMMON PLAYER (1-12)	2.00	.80	.22
☐ 1 Quiet Storm	2.00	.80	.22
☐ 2 Courted By Mets and Twins	2.00	.80	.22
☐ 3 The Show	2.00	.80	.22
☐ 4 Rocket Launched	2.00	.80	.22
☐ 5 Time Of Trial	2.00	.80	.22
☐ 6 Break Through	2.00	.80	.22
☐ 7 Play It Again Roger	2.00	.80	.22
☐ 8 Business As Usual	2.00	.80	.22
☐ 9 Heeee's Back	2.00	.80	.22
☐ 10 Blood, Sweat, and Tears	2.00	.80	.22
☐ 11 Prime Of Life	2.00	.80	.22
☐ 12 Man For Every Season	2.00	.80	.22

1992 Fleer All-Star Inserts

The 24-card All-Stars series was randomly inserted in 1992 Fleer wax packs (fin-sealed single packs). The cards measure the standard size (2 1/2" by 3 1/2"). The glossy color photos on the fronts are bordered in black and accented above and below with gold stripes and lettering. A diamond with a color head shot of the player is superimposed at the lower right corner of the picture. On a white background with black borders, the back has career highlights. The cards are numbered on the back.

	MINT	EXC	G-VG
COMPLETE SET (24)	40.00	18.00	3.50
COMMON PLAYER (1-24)	.60	.25	.06
☐ 1 Felix Jose	.90	.40	.09
☐ 2 Tony Gwynn	2.00	.80	.25
☐ 3 Barry Bonds	2.00	.80	.25
☐ 4 Bobby Bonilla	2.00	.80	.25
☐ 5 Mike LaValliere	.60	.25	.06
☐ 6 Tom Glavine	.90	.40	.09
☐ 7 Ramon Martinez	1.25	.55	.15
☐ 8 Lee Smith	.60	.25	.07
☐ 9 Mickey Tettleton	.60	.25	.07
☐ 10 Scott Erickson	2.50	1.00	.30
☐ 11 Frank Thomas	9.00	4.00	.90
☐ 12 Danny Tartabull	1.00	.45	.12
☐ 13 Will Clark	3.50	1.50	.45
☐ 14 Ryne Sandberg	3.50	1.50	.45
☐ 15 Terry Pendleton	.90	.40	.10
☐ 16 Barry Larkin	1.00	.45	.10
☐ 17 Rafael Palmeiro	1.00	.45	.10
☐ 18 Julio Franco	.90	.40	.10
☐ 19 Robin Ventura	2.50	1.00	.30
☐ 20 Cal Ripken	4.00	1.75	.35
☐ 21 Joe Carter	1.00	.45	.10
☐ 22 Kirby Puckett	2.50	1.00	.30
☐ 23 Ken Griffey Jr.	5.25	2.25	.55
☐ 24 Jose Canseco	4.00	1.75	.40

1992 Fleer Rookie Sensations

The 20-card Fleer Rookie Sensations series was randomly inserted in 1992 Fleer 35-card cello packs. The cards measure the standard size (2 1/2" by 3 1/2"). The glossy color photos on the fronts have a white border on a royal blue card face. The words "Rookie Sensations" appear above the picture in gold foil lettering, while the player's name appears on a gold foil plaque beneath the picture. On a light blue background with royal blue

borders, the backs have career summary. The cards are numbered on the back.

	MINT	EXC	G-VG
COMPLETE SET (20)	100.00	40.00	8.00
COMMON PLAYER (1-20)	2.00	.80	.20
☐ 1 Frank Thomas	25.00	10.00	2.50
☐ 2 Todd Van Poppel	7.00	3.00	.70
☐ 3 Orlando Merced	3.00	1.20	.30
☐ 4 Jeff Bagwell	12.50	5.50	1.25
☐ 5 Jeff Fassero	2.00	.80	.20
☐ 6 Wes Chamberlain	4.00	1.75	.40
☐ 7 Tito Martinez	3.00	1.20	.30
☐ 8 Ray Lankford	4.00	1.75	.40
☐ 9 Phil Plantier	12.50	5.50	1.25
☐ 10 Darren Lewis	2.50	1.00	.25
☐ 11 Milt Cuyler	2.50	1.00	.25
☐ 12 Mike Timlin	2.00	.80	.20
☐ 13 Brian McRae	3.50	1.50	.35
☐ 14 Scott Leuis	2.00	.80	.20
☐ 15 Rich DeLucia	2.00	.80	.20
☐ 16 Juan Guzman	3.50	1.50	.35
☐ 17 Steve Chitren	2.00	.80	.20
☐ 18 Mark Wohlers	3.50	1.50	.35
☐ 19 Chuck Knoblauch	5.50	2.50	.55
☐ 20 Ivan Rodriguez	8.00	3.50	.80

1992 Fleer Team Leaders

The 20-card Fleer Team Leaders series was randomly inserted in 1992 Fleer 42-card rack packs. The cards measure the standard size (2 1/2" by 3 1/2"). The glossy color photos on the fronts are bordered in white and green. Two gold foil stripes below the picture intersect a diamond-shaped "Team Leaders" emblem. On a pale green background with green borders, the backs have career summary. The cards are numbered on the back.

	MINT	EXC	G-VG
COMPLETE SET (20)	20.00	8.50	2.75
COMMON PLAYER (1-20)	.75	.30	.07
☐ 1 Don Mattingly	2.00	.80	.20
☐ 2 Howard Johnson	1.00	.40	.10
☐ 3 Chris Sabo	.90	.40	.09
☐ 4 Carlton Fisk	1.00	.40	.10
☐ 5 Kirby Puckett	2.00	.80	.20
☐ 6 Cecil Fielder	1.50	.60	.15
☐ 7 Tony Gwynn	1.50	.60	.15
☐ 8 Will Clark	2.50	1.00	.25
☐ 9 Bobby Bonilla	1.00	.40	.10
☐ 10 Len Dykstra	.75	.30	.07
☐ 11 Tom Glavine	.75	.30	.07
☐ 12 Rafael Palmeiro	.90	.40	.09
☐ 13 Wade Boggs	1.50	.60	.15
☐ 14 Joe Carter	.90	.40	.09
☐ 15 Ken Griffey Jr.	4.00	1.75	.40
☐ 16 Darryl Strawberry	2.50	1.00	.25
☐ 17 Cal Ripken	2.50	1.00	.25
☐ 18 Danny Tartabull	.75	.30	.07
☐ 19 Jose Canseco	2.50	1.00	.25
☐ 20 Andre Dawson	1.00	.40	.10

1916 Fleischmann Bread

This 103-card set was produced by Fleischmann Breads in 1916. These unnumbered cards are arranged here for convenience in alphabetical order; cards with tabs intact are worth 50 percent more than the prices listed below. The catalog designation for this set is D381. The cards measure approximately 2 3/4" by 5 1/2" (with tab) or 2 3/4" by 4 13/16" (without tab). There is also a similar set issued by Ferguson Bread which is harder to find and is distinguished by having the photo caption written on only one line rather than two as with the Fleischmann cards.

	EX-MT	VG-E	GOOD
COMPLETE SET (103)	5000.00	2250.00	500.00
COMMON PLAYER (1-103)	35.00	15.75	5.25

		EX-MT	VG-E	GOOD
☐ 1	Charles B. Adams	35.00	15.75	5.25
☐ 2	Grover Alexander	100.00	45.00	15.00
☐ 3	Walt E. Alexander	35.00	15.75	5.25
☐ 4	Frank Allen	35.00	15.75	5.25
☐ 5	Fred Anderson	35.00	15.75	5.25
☐ 6	Dave Bancroft	70.00	32.00	10.50
☐ 7	Jack Barry	35.00	15.75	5.25
☐ 8	Beals Becker	35.00	15.75	5.25
☐ 9	Eddie Burns	35.00	15.75	5.25
☐ 10	Geo. J. Burns	35.00	15.75	5.25
☐ 11	Bobby Byrne	35.00	15.75	5.25
☐ 12	Ray B. Caldwell	35.00	15.75	5.25
☐ 13	James J. Callahan	35.00	15.75	5.25
☐ 14	William Carrigan	35.00	15.75	5.25
☐ 15	Larry Cheney	35.00	15.75	5.25
☐ 16	Tom Clarke	35.00	15.75	5.25
☐ 17	Ty Cobb	1000.00	400.00	100.00
☐ 18	Ray W. Collins	35.00	15.75	5.25
☐ 19	Jack Coombs	45.00	20.00	6.75
☐ 20	A. Wilbur Cooper	35.00	15.75	5.25
☐ 21	George Cutshaw	35.00	15.75	5.25
☐ 22	Jake Daubert	40.00	18.00	6.00
☐ 23	Wm.G. Dell	35.00	15.75	5.25
☐ 24	Wm.E. Donovan	35.00	15.75	5.25
☐ 25	Larry Doyle	35.00	15.75	5.25
☐ 26	R.J. Egan	35.00	15.75	5.25
☐ 27	Johnny Evers	80.00	36.00	12.00
☐ 28	Ray Fisher	35.00	15.75	5.25
☐ 29	Harry Gardner (sic)	35.00	15.75	5.25
☐ 30	Joe Gedeon	35.00	15.75	5.25
☐ 31	Larry Gilbert	35.00	15.75	5.25
☐ 32	Frank Gilhooley	35.00	15.75	5.25
☐ 33	Henry M. Gowdy	40.00	18.00	6.00
☐ 34	Sylvanus Gregg	35.00	15.75	5.25
☐ 35	Tom Griffith	35.00	15.75	5.25
☐ 36	Heinie Groh	40.00	18.00	6.00
☐ 37	Robert Harmon	35.00	15.75	5.25
☐ 38	Roy A. Hartzell	35.00	15.75	5.25
☐ 39	Claude Hendriksen	35.00	15.75	5.25
☐ 40	Olaf Hendriksen	35.00	15.75	5.25
☐ 41	Chas.Buck Herzog	35.00	15.75	5.25
☐ 42	Hugh High	35.00	15.75	5.25
☐ 43	Dick Hoblitzell	35.00	15.75	5.25
☐ 44	Herb H. Hunter	35.00	15.75	5.25
☐ 45	Harold Janvrin	35.00	15.75	5.25
☐ 46	Hugh Jennings	70.00	32.00	10.50
☐ 47	John Johnston	35.00	15.75	5.25
☐ 48	Erving Kantlehner	35.00	15.75	5.25
☐ 49	Bennie Kauff	35.00	15.75	5.25
☐ 50	Ray H. Keating	35.00	15.75	5.25
☐ 51	Wade Killefer	35.00	15.75	5.25
☐ 52	Elmer Knetzer	35.00	15.75	5.25
☐ 53	Brad W. Kocher	35.00	15.75	5.25
☐ 54	Ed Konetchy	35.00	15.75	5.25
☐ 55	Fred Lauderus (sic)	35.00	15.75	5.25
☐ 56	H.B. Leonard	40.00	18.00	6.00
☐ 57	Duffy Lewis	35.00	15.75	5.25
☐ 58	E.H.(Slim) Love	35.00	15.75	5.25
☐ 59	Albert L. Mamaux	35.00	15.75	5.25
☐ 60	Walter Maranville	70.00	32.00	10.50
☐ 61	Rube Marquard	70.00	32.00	10.50
☐ 62	Christy Mathewson	250.00	110.00	37.50
☐ 63	Wm.B. McKechnie	70.00	32.00	10.50
☐ 64	Chief Meyer (sic)	35.00	15.75	5.25
☐ 65	Otto Miller	35.00	15.75	5.25
☐ 66	Fred Mollwitz	35.00	15.75	5.25
☐ 67	Herbie Moran	35.00	15.75	5.25
☐ 68	Mike Mowrey	35.00	15.75	5.25
☐ 69	Dan Murphy	35.00	15.75	5.25
☐ 70	Art N. Nehf	35.00	15.75	5.25
☐ 71	Rube Oldring	35.00	15.75	5.25
☐ 72	Oliver O'Mara	35.00	15.75	5.25
☐ 73	Dode Paskert	35.00	15.75	5.25
☐ 74	D.C.Pat Ragan	35.00	15.75	5.25
☐ 75	Wm.A. Rariden	35.00	15.75	5.25
☐ 76	Davis Robertson	35.00	15.75	5.25
☐ 77	Wm. Rodgers	35.00	15.75	5.25
☐ 78	Edw.F.Rousch (sic)	80.00	36.00	12.00
☐ 79	Nap Rucker	35.00	15.75	5.25
☐ 80	Dick Rudolph	35.00	15.75	5.25
☐ 81	Walter Schang	40.00	18.00	6.00
☐ 82	A.J.(Rube) Schauer	35.00	15.75	5.25
☐ 83	Pete Schneider	35.00	15.75	5.25
☐ 84	Ferd M. Schupp	35.00	15.75	5.25
☐ 85	Ernie Shore	40.00	18.00	6.00
☐ 86	Red Smith	35.00	15.75	5.25
☐ 87	Fred Snodgrass	40.00	18.00	6.00
☐ 88	Tris Speaker	125.00	57.50	18.75
☐ 89	George T.Stallings	35.00	15.75	5.25
☐ 90	Chas.D. Stengel	165.00	75.00	22.50
☐ 91	R. Stroud	35.00	15.75	5.25
☐ 92	Amos Strunk	35.00	15.75	5.25
☐ 93	Charles D. Thomas	35.00	15.75	5.25
☐ 94	Fred Toney	35.00	15.75	5.25
☐ 95	Walter Tragresser	35.00	15.75	5.25
☐ 96	Chas. Tresreau	35.00	15.75	5.25
☐ 97	Honus Wagner	250.00	110.00	37.50
☐ 98	Carl Weilman	35.00	15.75	5.25
☐ 99	Zack Wheat	70.00	32.00	10.50
☐ 100	George Whitted	35.00	15.75	5.25
☐ 101	Arthur Wilson	35.00	15.75	5.25
☐ 102	Ivy Wingo	35.00	15.75	5.25
☐ 103	Joe Wood	60.00	27.00	9.00

1987 French Bray Orioles

16 SCOTT McGREGOR, P
Compliments of
FRENCH/BRAY, INC.

The 1987 French Bray set contains 30 cards (featuring members of the Baltimore Orioles) measuring 2 1/4 by 3 inches. The fronts have facial photos with white and orange borders; the horizontally-oriented backs are white and feature career stats. The cards were given away in perforated sheet form on Photo Card Day at the Orioles home game on July 26, 1987. A large team photo was also included as one of the three panels in this perforated card set. The cards are unnumbered except for uniform number.

	MINT	EXC	G-VG
COMPLETE SET (30)	12.50	5.50	1.65
COMMON PLAYER	.35	.15	.03
☐ 2 Alan Wiggins	.35	.15	.03
☐ 3 Bill Ripken	.60	.25	.06
☐ 6 Floyd Rayford	.35	.15	.03
☐ 7 Cal Ripken Sr. MG	.60	.25	.06
☐ 8 Cal Ripken	3.00	1.25	.30
☐ 9 Jim Dwyer	.35	.15	.03
☐ 10 Terry Crowley CO	.35	.15	.03
☐ 15 Terry Kennedy	.35	.15	.03
☐ 16 Scott McGregor	.45	.18	.04
☐ 18 Larry Sheets	.45	.18	.04
☐ 19 Fred Lynn	.60	.25	.06
☐ 20 Frank Robinson CO	1.25	.50	.12
☐ 24 Dave Schmidt	.45	.18	.04
☐ 25 Ray Knight	.45	.18	.04
☐ 27 Lee Lacy	.35	.15	.03
☐ 31 Mark Wiley CO	.35	.15	.03
☐ 32 Mark Williamson	.35	.15	.03
☐ 33 Eddie Murray	1.25	.50	.12
☐ 38 Ken Gerhart	.35	.15	.03
☐ 39 Ken Dixon	.35	.15	.03
☐ 40 Jimmy Williams CO	.35	.15	.03
☐ 42 Mike Griffin	.35	.15	.03
☐ 43 Mike Young	.35	.15	.03
☐ 44 Elrod Hendricks CO	.35	.15	.03
☐ 45 Eric Bell	.35	.15	.03
☐ 46 Mike Flanagan	.45	.18	.04
☐ 49 Tom Niedenfuer	.35	.15	.03
☐ 52 Mike Boddicker	.45	.18	.04
☐ 54 John Habyan	.35	.15	.03
☐ 57 Tony Arnold	.35	.15	.03

1988 French Bray Orioles

20 FRANK ROBINSON, Manager
Compliments of
FRENCH/BRAY, INC.

This set was distributed as a perforated set of 30 full-color cards attached to a large team photo on July 31, 1988, the Baltimore Orioles' Photo Card Day. The cards measure approximately 2 1/4" by 3 1/16". Card backs are simply done in black and white with statistics but no narrative or any personal information. Cards are unnumbered except for uniform number. Card front have a thin orange inner border and have the French Bray (Printing and Graphic Communication) logo in the lower right corner.

	MINT	EXC	G-VG
COMPLETE SET (30)	10.00	4.50	1.25
COMMON PLAYER	.35	.15	.03
☐ 2 Don Buford CO	.35	.15	.03
☐ 6 Joe Orsulak	.45	.18	.04
☐ 7 Bill Ripken	.45	.18	.04
☐ 8 Cal Ripken	2.50	1.00	.25
☐ 9 Jim Dwyer	.35	.15	.03
☐ 10 Terry Crowley CO	.35	.15	.03
☐ 12 Mike Morgan	.45	.18	.04
☐ 14 Mickey Tettleton	.60	.25	.06
☐ 15 Terry Kennedy	.35	.15	.03
☐ 17 Pete Stanicek	.35	.15	.03
☐ 18 Larry Sheets	.45	.18	.04
☐ 19 Fred Lynn	.60	.25	.06
☐ 20 Frank Robinson MG	1.00	.40	.10

	MINT	EXC	G-VG
☐ 23 Ozzie Peraza	.45	.18	.04
☐ 24 Dave Schmidt	.45	.18	.04
☐ 25 Rick Schu	.35	.15	.03
☐ 28 Jim Traber	.35	.15	.03
☐ 31 Herm Starrette CO	.35	.15	.03
☐ 33 Eddie Murray	1.00	.40	.10
☐ 34 Jeff Ballard	.45	.18	.04
☐ 38 Ken Gerhart	.35	.15	.03
☐ 40 Minnie Mendoza CO	.35	.15	.03
☐ 41 Don Aase	.35	.15	.03
☐ 44 Elrod Hendricks CO	.35	.15	.03
☐ 47 John Hart CO	.35	.15	.03
☐ 48 Jose Bautista	.35	.15	.03
☐ 49 Tom Niedenfuer	.35	.15	.03
☐ 52 Mike Boddicker	.45	.18	.04
☐ 53 Jay Tibbs	.35	.15	.03
☐ 88 Rene Gonzales	.35	.15	.03

1989 French Bray/WWF Orioles

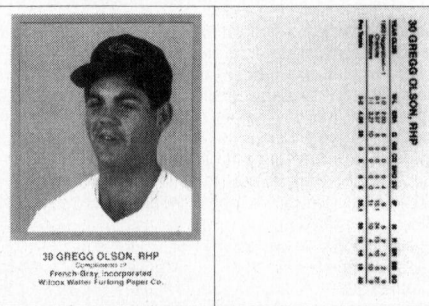

30 GREGG OLSON, RHP
Compliments of
French Bray, Incorporated
Wilcox Walter Furlong Paper Co.

The 1989 French Bray/WWF Orioles set contains 31 cards measuring 2 1/4" by 3". The fronts have facial photos with orange and white borders; the backs are white and feature career stats. The set was given away at a Baltimore home game on May 12, 1989. The cards are numbered by the players' uniform numbers.

	MINT	EXC	G-VG
COMPLETE SET (32)	10.00	4.50	1.25
COMMON PLAYER	.35	.15	.03
☐ 3 Bill Ripken	.45	.18	.04
☐ 6 Joe Orsulak	.45	.18	.04
☐ 7 Cal Ripken Sr. CO	.45	.18	.04
☐ 8 Cal Ripken	2.00	.80	.20
☐ 9 Brady Anderson	.45	.18	.04
☐ 10 Steve Finley	.60	.25	.06
☐ 11 Craig Worthington	.45	.18	.04
☐ 12 Mike Devereaux	.45	.18	.04
☐ 14 Mickey Tettleton	.60	.25	.06
☐ 15 Randy Milligan	.75	.30	.07
☐ 16 Phil Bradley	.45	.18	.04
☐ 18 Bob Milacki	.60	.25	.06
☐ 19 Larry Sheets	.45	.18	.04
☐ 20 Frank Robinson MG	1.00	.40	.10
☐ 21 Mark Thurmond	.35	.15	.03
☐ 23 Kevin Hickey	.35	.15	.03
☐ 24 Dave Schmidt	.45	.18	.04
☐ 28 Jim Traber	.35	.15	.03
☐ 29 Jeff Ballard	.45	.18	.04
☐ 30 Gregg Olson	1.25	.50	.12
☐ 31 Al Jackson CO	.35	.15	.03
☐ 32 Mark Williamson	.35	.15	.03
☐ 36 Bob Melvin	.35	.15	.03
☐ 37 Brian Holton	.35	.15	.03
☐ 40 Tom McCraw CO	.35	.15	.03
☐ 42 Pete Harnisch	.45	.18	.04
☐ 43 Francisco Melendez	.45	.18	.04
☐ 44 Elrod Hendricks CO	.35	.15	.03
☐ 46 Johnny Oates CO	.45	.18	.04
☐ 48 Jose Bautista	.35	.15	.03
☐ 88 Rene Gonzales	.35	.15	.03
☐ xx Sponsor ad	.35	.15	.03

1928 Fro Joy

The cards in this six-card set measure approximately 2 1/16" by 4". The Fro Joy set of 1928 was designed to exploit the advertising potential of the mighty Babe Ruth. Six black and white cards explained specific baseball techniques while the reverse advertising extolled the virtues of Fro Joy ice cream and ice cream cones. Unfortunately this small set has been illegally reprinted (several times) and many of these virtually-worthless fakes have been introduced into the hobby. The easiest fakes to spot are those cards (or uncut sheets) that are slightly oversized and blue tinted; however some of the other fakes are more cleverly faithful to the original. Be very careful before purchasing Fro-Joys; obtain a qualified opinion on authenticity from an experienced dealer (preferably one who is unrelated to the dealer trying to sell you his cards). You might also show the cards (before you commit to purchase them) to an experienced printer who can advise you on the true age of the paper stock. More than one dealer has been quoted as saying that 99 percent of the Fro Joys he sees are fakes.

	EX-MT	VG-E	GOOD
COMPLETE SET (6)	600.00	270.00	90.00
COMMON PLAYER (1-6)	100.00	45.00	15.00
☐ 1 George Herman (Babe) Ruth	150.00	67.50	22.50
☐ 2 Look Out, Mr. Pitcher	100.00	45.00	15.00
☐ 3 Bang; The Babe Lines one out	100.00	45.00	15.00
☐ 4 When the Babe Comes Out	100.00	45.00	15.00
☐ 5 Babe Ruth's Grip	100.00	45.00	15.00
☐ 6 Ruth is a Crack Fielder	100.00	45.00	15.00

1991 Front Row Draft Picks

This 50-card premier edition set includes 27 of the top 40 eligible players from the 1991 Baseball Draft. The cards measure the standard size (2 1/2" by 3 1/2"), and only 240,000 sets were produced. Each set contains a numbered card registering the set and one card from a limited Draft Pick subset as a bonus card. In exchange for returning the bonus card, the collector received card number 50 (Benji Gil), a mini-update set (51-54; sent to the first 120,000 respondents), and one card from a five-card Frankie Rodriguez subset. The photos on both sides of the card are highlighted with an ultra violet finish. The obverse has

glossy color player photos bordered in gray, with the player's name in black lettering below the picture. The words "Front Row" appear in a baseball in the upper right corner, while the words "'91 Draft Pick" appear in a diamond in the lower left corner. The reverse has a color photo of the player in little league, biography, statistics, and career achievements. The cards are numbered on the back.

	MINT	EXC	G-VG
COMPLETE SET (50)	9.00	4.00	.90
COMMON PLAYER (1-50)	.08	.03	.01
COMMON PLAYER (51-54)	.10	.04	.01
☐ 1 Frankie Rodriguez	1.50	.60	.15
☐ 2 Aaron Sele	.25	.10	.02
☐ 3 Chad Schoenvogel	.08	.03	.01
☐ 4 Scott Ruffcorn	.25	.10	.02
☐ 5 Dan Cholowsky UER	.15	.06	.01
☐ 6 Gene Schall	.08	.03	.01
☐ 7 Trever Miller	.20	.08	.02
☐ 8 Chris Durkin	.20	.08	.02
☐ 9 Mike Neill	.08	.03	.01
☐ 10 Kevin Stocker	.10	.04	.01
☐ 11 Bobby Jones	.25	.10	.02
☐ 12 Jon Farrell	.25	.10	.02
☐ 13 Ronnie Allen	.08	.03	.01
☐ 14 Mike Rossiter	.15	.06	.01
☐ 15 Scott Hatteberg	.20	.08	.02
☐ 16 Rodney Pedraza	.08	.03	.01
☐ 17 Mike Durant	.20	.08	.02
☐ 18 Ryan Long	.08	.03	.01
☐ 19 Greg Anthony	.15	.06	.01
☐ 20 Jon Barnes	.08	.03	.01
☐ 21 Brian Barber	.15	.06	.01
☐ 22 Brent Gates	.30	.12	.03
☐ 23 Calvin Reese	.20	.08	.02
☐ 24 Terry Horn	.15	.06	.01
☐ 25 Scott Stahoviak	.25	.10	.02
☐ 26 Jason Pruitt	.15	.06	.01
☐ 27 Shawn Curran	.08	.03	.01
☐ 28 Jimmy Lewis	.08	.03	.01
☐ 29 Alex Ochoa	.10	.04	.01
☐ 30 Joe DeBerry	.08	.03	.01
☐ 31 Justin Thompson	.08	.03	.01
☐ 32 Jimmy Gonzalez	.15	.06	.01
☐ 33 Eddie Ramos	.08	.03	.01
☐ 34 Tyler Green	.50	.20	.05
☐ 35 Toby Rumfield	.15	.06	.01
☐ 36 Dave Doornenweerd	.10	.04	.01
☐ 37 Jeff Hostetler	.08	.03	.01
☐ 38 Shawn Livsey	.20	.08	.02
☐ 39 Mike Groppuso	.15	.06	.01
☐ 40 Steve Whitaker	.15	.06	.01
☐ 41 Tom McKinnon	.15	.06	.01
☐ 42 Buck McNabb	.08	.03	.01
☐ 43 Al Shirley	.75	.30	.07
☐ 44 Allen Watson	.18	.08	.01
☐ 45 Bill Bliss	.08	.03	.01
☐ 46 Todd Hallandsworth	.08	.03	.01
☐ 47 Manny Ramirez	.90	.40	.09
☐ 48 J.J. Johnson	.15	.06	.01
☐ 49 Cliff Floyd	.40	.16	.04
☐ 50 Bonus Card	1.00	.40	.10
☐ 50B Benji Gil	.50	.20	.05
☐ 51 Herb Perry	.10	.04	.01
☐ 52 Tarrik Brock	.25	.10	.02
☐ 53 Trevor Mallory	.10	.04	.01
☐ 54 Chris Pritchett	.15	.06	.01

		MINT	EXC	G-VG
☐ FR1	Frankie Rodriguez Pitching (just after release)	.90	.40	.09
☐ FR2	Frankie Rodriguez Pitching (ball in hand behind body)	.90	.40	.09
☐ FR3	Frankie Rodriguez Batting (middle of swing)	.90	.40	.09
☐ FR4	Frankie Rodriguez Pitching (just after release)	.90	.40	.09
☐ FR5	Frankie Rodriguez Batting (bat cocked above shoulder)	.90	.40	.09

1983 Gardner's Brewers

The cards in this 22-card set measure 2 1/2" by 3 1/2". The 1983 Gardner's Brewers set features Milwaukee Brewer players and manager Harvey Kuenn. Topps printed the set for the Madison (Wisconsin) bakery, hence, the backs are identical to the 1983 Topps backs except for the card number. The fronts of the cards, however, feature all new photos and include the Gardner's logo and the Brewers' logo. Many of the cards are grease laden, as they were issued with packages of bread and hamburger and hot-dog buns. The card numbering for this set is essentially in alphabetical order by player's name (after the manager is listed first).

		MINT	EXC	G-VG
	COMPLETE SET (22)	27.00	12.00	4.00
	COMMON PLAYER (1-22)	.60	.25	.06
☐ 1	Harvey Kuenn MG	1.00	.40	.10
☐ 2	Dwight Bernard	.60	.25	.06
☐ 3	Mark Brouhard	.60	.25	.06
☐ 4	Mike Caldwell	.75	.30	.07
☐ 5	Cecil Cooper	1.50	.60	.15
☐ 6	Marshall Edwards	.60	.25	.06
☐ 7	Rollie Fingers	6.00	2.50	.60
☐ 8	Jim Gantner	.75	.30	.07
☐ 9	Moose Haas	.75	.30	.07
☐ 10	Bob McClure	.60	.25	.06
☐ 11	Paul Molitor	5.00	2.25	.50
☐ 12	Don Money	.75	.30	.07
☐ 13	Charlie Moore	.75	.30	.07
☐ 14	Ben Oglivie	.90	.40	.09
☐ 15	Ed Romero	.60	.25	.06
☐ 16	Ted Simmons	1.50	.60	.15
☐ 17	Jim Slaton	.75	.30	.07
☐ 18	Don Sutton	3.00	1.25	.30
☐ 19	Gorman Thomas	1.00	.40	.10
☐ 20	Pete Vuckovich	.75	.30	.07
☐ 21	Ned Yost	.60	.25	.06
☐ 22	Robin Yount	9.00	4.00	.90

1984 Gardner's Brewers

The cards in this 22-card set measure 2 1/2" by 3 1/2". For the second year in a row, the Gardner Bakery Company issued a set of cards available in packages of Gardner Bakery products. The set was manufactured by Topps, and the backs of the cards are identical to the Topps cards of this year except for the numbers. The Gardner logo appears on the fronts of the cards with the player's name, position abbreviation, the name Brewers, and the words 1984 Series II. The card numbering for this set is essentially in alphabetical order by player's name (after the manager is listed first).

		MINT	EXC	G-VG
	COMPLETE SET (22)	10.00	4.50	1.25
	COMMON PLAYER (1-22)	.35	.15	.03
☐ 1	Rene Lachemann MG	.45	.18	.04
☐ 2	Mark Brouhard	.35	.15	.03
☐ 3	Mike Caldwell	.45	.18	.04
☐ 4	Bobby Clark	.35	.15	.03
☐ 5	Cecil Cooper	.75	.30	.07
☐ 6	Rollie Fingers	2.50	1.00	.25
☐ 7	Jim Gantner	.60	.25	.06
☐ 8	Moose Haas	.45	.18	.04
☐ 9	Roy Howell	.35	.15	.03
☐ 10	Pete Ladd	.35	.15	.03
☐ 11	Rick Manning	.35	.15	.03
☐ 12	Bob McClure	.35	.15	.03
☐ 13	Paul Molitor	2.00	.80	.20
☐ 14	Charlie Moore	.45	.18	.04
☐ 15	Ben Oglivie	.60	.25	.06
☐ 16	Ed Romero	.35	.15	.03
☐ 17	Ted Simmons	1.00	.40	.10
☐ 18	Jim Sundberg	.45	.18	.04
☐ 19	Don Sutton	1.75	.70	.17
☐ 20	Tom Tellman	.35	.15	.03
☐ 21	Pete Vuckovich	.60	.25	.06
☐ 22	Robin Yount	4.00	1.75	.40

1985 Gardner's Brewers

The cards in this 22-card set measure 2 1/2" by 3 1/2". For the third year in a row, the Gardner Bakery Company issued a set of cards available in packages of Gardner Bakery products. The set was manufactured by Topps, and the backs of the cards are identical to the Topps cards of this year except for the card numbers and copyright information. The Gardner logo appears on the fronts of the cards with the player's name, position abbreviation, and the name Brewers. The card numbering for this set is essentially in alphabetical order.

		MINT	EXC	G-VG
	COMPLETE SET (22)	10.00	4.50	1.25
	COMMON PLAYER (1-22)	.35	.15	.03
☐ 1	George Bamberger MG	.45	.18	.04
☐ 2	Mark Brouhard	.35	.15	.03

		MINT	EXC	G-VG
☐ 3	Bobby Clark	.35	.15	.03
☐ 4	Jaime Cocanower	.35	.15	.03
☐ 5	Cecil Cooper	.75	.30	.07
☐ 6	Rollie Fingers	2.50	1.00	.25
☐ 7	Jim Gantner	.45	.18	.04
☐ 8	Moose Haas	.45	.18	.04
☐ 9	Dion James	.35	.15	.03
☐ 10	Pete Ladd	.35	.15	.03
☐ 11	Rick Manning	.35	.15	.03
☐ 12	Bob McClure	.35	.15	.03
☐ 13	Paul Molitor	2.00	.80	.20
☐ 14	Charlie Moore	.45	.18	.04
☐ 15	Ben Oglivie	.60	.25	.06
☐ 16	Chuck Porter	.35	.15	.03
☐ 17	Ed Romero	.35	.15	.03
☐ 18	Bill Schroeder	.45	.18	.04
☐ 19	Ted Simmons	1.00	.40	.10
☐ 20	Tom Tellman	.35	.15	.03
☐ 21	Pete Vuckovich	.60	.25	.06
☐ 22	Robin Yount	4.00	1.75	.40

1989 Gardner's Brewers

The 1989 Gardner's Brewers set contains 15 standard-size (2 1/2" by 3 1/2") cards. The fronts feature airbrushed mugshots with sky blue backgrounds and white borders. The backs are white and feature career stats. One card was distributed in each specially marked Gardner's bakery product. Cards were issued during the middle of the season. For some reason Riles is included in the set even though he had been traded by the Brewers during the 1988 season.

		MINT	EXC	G-VG
	COMPLETE SET (15)	6.00	2.50	.60
	COMMON PLAYER (1-15)	.25	.10	.02
☐ 1	Paul Molitor	1.25	.50	.12
☐ 2	Robin Yount	2.50	1.00	.25
☐ 3	Jim Gantner	.35	.15	.03
☐ 4	Rob Deer	.50	.20	.05
☐ 5	B.J. Surhoff	.50	.20	.05
☐ 6	Dale Sveum	.25	.10	.02

☐ 7	Ted Higuera	.50	.20	.05
☐ 8	Dan Plesac	.35	.15	.03
☐ 9	Bill Wegman	.35	.15	.03
☐ 10	Juan Nieves	.25	.10	.02
☐ 11	Greg Brock	.25	.10	.02
☐ 12	Glenn Braggs	.35	.15	.03
☐ 13	Joey Meyer	.25	.10	.02
☐ 14	Earnest Riles	.25	.10	.02
☐ 15	Don August	.25	.10	.02

1987 Gatorade Indians

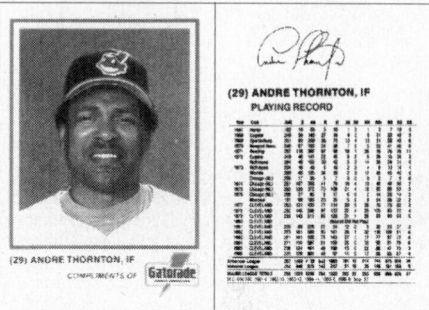

Gatorade sponsored this perforated set of 30 full-color cards of the Cleveland Indians. The cards measure 2 1/8" by 3" (or 3 1/8") and feature the Gatorade logo prominently on the fronts of the cards. The cards were distributed as a tri-folded sheet (each part approximately 9 5/8" by 11 3/16") on April 25th at the stadium during the game against the Yankees. The large team photo is approximately 11 3/16" by 9 5/8". Card backs for the individual players contain year-by-year stats for that player. The cards are referenced and listed below by uniform number.

		MINT	EXC	G-VG
	COMPLETE SET (30)	10.00	4.50	1.25
	COMMON PLAYER	.25	.10	.02
☐ 2	Brett Butler	.60	.25	.06
☐ 4	Tony Bernazard	.35	.15	.03
☐ 6	Andy Allanson	.35	.15	.03
☐ 7	Pat Corrales MG	.25	.10	.02
☐ 8	Carmen Castillo	.25	.10	.02
☐ 10	Pat Tabler	.35	.15	.03
☐ 11	Jamie Easterly	.25	.10	.02
☐ 12	Dave Clark	.35	.15	.03
☐ 13	Ernie Camacho	.25	.10	.02
☐ 14	Julio Franco	.90	.40	.09
☐ 17	Junior Noboa	.35	.15	.03
☐ 18	Ken Schrom	.25	.10	.02
☐ 20	Otis Nixon	.60	.25	.06
☐ 21	Greg Swindell	.90	.40	.09
☐ 22	Frank Wills	.25	.10	.02
☐ 23	Chris Bando	.25	.10	.02
☐ 24	Rick Dempsey	.25	.10	.02
☐ 26	Brook Jacoby	.50	.20	.05
☐ 27	Mel Hall	.60	.25	.06
☐ 28	Cory Snyder	.60	.25	.06
☐ 29	Andre Thornton	.35	.15	.03
☐ 30	Joe Carter	1.25	.50	.12
☐ 35	Phil Niekro	1.00	.40	.10
☐ 36	Ed VandeBerg	.25	.10	.02
☐ 42	Rich Yett	.25	.10	.02
☐ 43	Scott Bailes	.25	.10	.02
☐ 46	Doug Jones	.50	.20	.05
☐ 49	Tom Candiotti	.35	.15	.03
☐ 54	Tom Waddell	.25	.10	.02
☐ xx	Indians MG/Coaches	.35	.15	.03
	Bobby Bonds 25			
	Johnny Goryl 45			
	Pat Corrales MG 7			
	Doc Edwards 32			
	Jack Aker 1			
☐ xx	Team Photo	1.25	.50	.12
	(large size)			

1988 Gatorade Indians

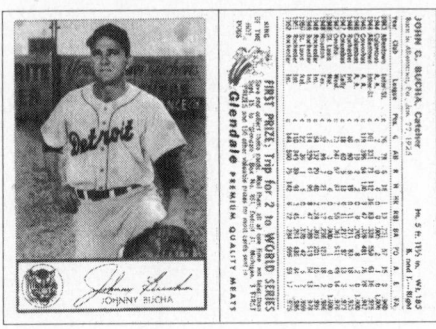

This set was distributed as 30 perforated player cards attached to a large team photo of the Cleveland Indians. The cards measure approximately 2 1/4" by 3". Card backs are oriented either horizontally or vertically. Card backs are printed in red, blue, and black on white card stock. Card backs contain a facsimile autograph of the player. Cards are not arranged on the sheet in any order. The cards are unnumbered except for uniform number, which is given on the front and back of each card. The cards are referenced and listed below by uniform number. The Gatorade logo is on the front of every card in the lower right corner.

		MINT	EXC	G-VG
COMPLETE SET (30)		9.00	4.00	.90
COMMON PLAYER		.25	.10	.02
☐ 2	Tom Spencer CO	.25	.10	.02
☐ 6	Andy Allanson	.25	.10	.02
☐ 7	Luis Isaac CO	.25	.10	.02
☐ 8	Carmen Castillo	.25	.10	.02
☐ 9	Charlie Manuel CO	.25	.10	.02
☐ 10	Pat Tabler	.35	.15	.03
☐ 11	Doug Jones	.35	.15	.03
☐ 14	Julio Franco	.60	.25	.06
☐ 15	Ron Washington	.25	.10	.02
☐ 16	Jay Bell	.60	.25	.06
☐ 17	Bill Laskey	.25	.10	.02
☐ 20	Willie Upshaw	.25	.10	.02
☐ 21	Greg Swindell	.60	.25	.06
☐ 23	Chris Bando	.25	.10	.02
☐ 25	Dave Clark	.35	.15	.03
☐ 26	Brook Jacoby	.35	.15	.03
☐ 27	Mel Hall	.50	.20	.05
☐ 28	Cory Snyder	.50	.20	.05
☐ 30	Joe Carter	.90	.40	.09
☐ 31	Dan Schatzeder	.25	.10	.02
☐ 32	Doc Edwards MG	.25	.10	.02
☐ 33	Ron Kittle	.35	.15	.03
☐ 35	Mark Wiley CO	.25	.10	.02
☐ 42	Rich Yett	.25	.10	.02
☐ 43	Scott Bailes	.35	.15	.03
☐ 45	John Goryl CO	.25	.10	.02
☐ 47	Jeff Kaiser	.25	.10	.02
☐ 49	Tom Candiotti	.35	.15	.03
☐ 50	Jeff Dedmon	.25	.10	.02
☐ 52	John Farrell	.35	.15	.03
☐ xx	Team Photo	1.25	.50	.12
	(large size)			

1953 Glendale

The cards in this 28-card set measure 2 5/8" by 3 3/4". The 1953 Glendale Meats set of full-color, unnumbered cards features Detroit Tiger ballplayers exclusively and was distributed one per package of Glendale Meats in the Detroit area. The back contains the complete major and minor league record through the 1952 season. The scarcer cards of the set command higher prices, with the Houtteman card being the most difficult to find. There is an album associated with the set (which also is quite scarce now). The catalog designation for this scarce regional set is F151. Since the cards are unnumbered, they are ordered below alphabetically.

		NRMT	VG-E	GOOD
COMPLETE SET (28)		6500.00	2800.00	650.00
COMMON PLAYER (1-28)		150.00	67.50	22.50
☐ 1	Matt Batts	150.00	67.50	22.50
☐ 2	Johnny Bucha	150.00	67.50	22.50
☐ 3	Frank Carswell	150.00	67.50	22.50
☐ 4	Jim Delsing	150.00	67.50	22.50
☐ 5	Walt Dropo	175.00	80.00	27.00
☐ 6	Hal Erickson	150.00	67.50	22.50
☐ 7	Paul Foytack	150.00	67.50	22.50
☐ 8	Owen Friend	150.00	67.50	22.50
☐ 9	Ned Garver	150.00	67.50	22.50
☐ 10	Joe Ginsberg	375.00	165.00	55.00
☐ 11	Ted Gray	150.00	67.50	22.50
☐ 12	Fred Hatfield	150.00	67.50	22.50
☐ 13	Ray Herbert	150.00	67.50	22.50
☐ 14	Bill Hitchcock	150.00	67.50	22.50
☐ 15	Bill Hoeft	250.00	110.00	37.50
☐ 16	Art Houtteman	2250.00	900.00	225.00
☐ 17	Milt Jordan	175.00	80.00	27.00
☐ 18	Harvey Kuenn	500.00	225.00	75.00
☐ 19	Don Lund	150.00	67.50	22.50
☐ 20	Dave Madison	150.00	67.50	22.50
☐ 21	Dick Marlowe	150.00	67.50	22.50
☐ 22	Pat Mullin	150.00	67.50	22.50
☐ 23	Bob Nieman	150.00	67.50	22.50
☐ 24	Johnny Pesky	175.00	80.00	27.00
☐ 25	Jerry Priddy	150.00	67.50	22.50
☐ 26	Steve Souchock	150.00	67.50	22.50
☐ 27	Russ Sullivan	150.00	67.50	22.50
☐ 28	Bill Wight	175.00	80.00	27.00

1961 Golden Press

The cards in this 33-card set measure 2 1/2" by 3 1/2". The 1961 Golden Press set of full color cards features members of Baseball's Hall of Fame. The cards came in a booklet with perforations for punching the cards out of the book. The catalog designation is W524. The price for the full book intact is 50 percent higher than the complete set price listed.

		NRMT	VG-E	GOOD
COMPLETE SET (33)		80.00	36.00	12.00
COMMON PLAYER (1-33)		1.00	.40	.10
☐ 1	Mel Ott	2.50	1.00	.25
☐ 2	Grover C. Alexander	2.00	.80	.20
☐ 3	Babe Ruth	25.00	11.00	3.50
☐ 4	Hank Greenberg	2.00	.80	.20
☐ 5	Bill Terry	1.25	.50	.12
☐ 6	Carl Hubbell	1.25	.50	.12
☐ 7	Rogers Hornsby	3.00	1.25	.30
☐ 8	Dizzy Dean	6.00	2.50	.60
☐ 9	Joe DiMaggio	20.00	8.50	2.75
☐ 10	Charlie Gehringer	1.25	.50	.12
☐ 11	Gabby Hartnett	1.00	.40	.10

		EX-MT	VG-E	GOOD
	COMPLETE SET (239)	42500.	17500.	4500.
	COMMON PLAYER (1-40)	90.00	40.00	13.50
	COMMON PLAYER (41-44)	60.00	27.00	9.00
	COMMON PLAYER (45-52)	90.00	40.00	13.50
	COMMON PLAYER (53-240)	60.00	27.00	9.00
☐ 1	Benny Bengough	1250.00	75.00	15.00
☐ 2	Dazzy Vance	180.00	80.00	27.00
☐ 3	Hugh Critz	90.00	40.00	13.50
☐ 4	Heine Schuble	90.00	40.00	13.50
☐ 5	Babe Herman	120.00	55.00	18.00
☐ 6	Jimmy Dykes	120.00	55.00	18.00
☐ 7	Ted Lyons	180.00	80.00	27.00
☐ 8	Roy Johnson	90.00	40.00	13.50
☐ 9	Dave Harris	90.00	40.00	13.50
☐ 10	Glenn Myatt	90.00	40.00	13.50
☐ 11	Billy Rogell	90.00	40.00	13.50
☐ 12	George Pipgras	90.00	40.00	13.50
☐ 13	Lafayette Thompson	90.00	40.00	13.50
☐ 14	Henry Johnson	90.00	40.00	13.50
☐ 15	Victor Sorrell	90.00	40.00	13.50
☐ 16	George Blaeholder	90.00	40.00	13.50
☐ 17	Watson Clark	90.00	40.00	13.50
☐ 18	Muddy Ruel	90.00	40.00	13.50
☐ 19	Bill Dickey	375.00	165.00	55.00
☐ 20	Bill Terry THROW	275.00	120.00	40.00
☐ 21	Phil Collins	90.00	40.00	13.50
☐ 22	Pie Traynor	225.00	100.00	33.00
☐ 23	Kiki Cuyler	180.00	80.00	27.00
☐ 24	Horace Ford	90.00	40.00	13.50
☐ 25	Paul Waner	180.00	80.00	27.00
☐ 26	Chalmer Cissell	90.00	40.00	13.50
☐ 27	George Connally	90.00	40.00	13.50
☐ 28	Dick Bartell	90.00	40.00	13.50
☐ 29	Jimmy Foxx	450.00	200.00	67.50
☐ 30	Frank Hogan	90.00	40.00	13.50
☐ 31	Tony Lazzeri	300.00	135.00	45.00
☐ 32	Bud Clancy	90.00	40.00	13.50
☐ 33	Ralph Kress	90.00	40.00	13.50
☐ 34	Bob O'Farrell	90.00	40.00	13.50
☐ 35	Al Simmons	300.00	135.00	45.00
☐ 36	Tommy Thevenow	90.00	40.00	13.50
☐ 37	Jimmy Wilson	90.00	40.00	13.50
☐ 38	Fred Brickell	90.00	40.00	13.50
☐ 39	Mark Koenig	90.00	40.00	13.50
☐ 40	Taylor Douthit	90.00	40.00	13.50
☐ 41	Gus Mancuso	60.00	27.00	9.00
☐ 42	Eddie Collins	120.00	55.00	18.00
☐ 43	Lew Fonseca	60.00	27.00	9.00
☐ 44	Jim Bottomley	120.00	55.00	18.00
☐ 45	Larry Benton	90.00	40.00	13.50
☐ 46	Ethan Allen	90.00	40.00	13.50
☐ 47	Heinie Manush BAT	180.00	80.00	27.00
☐ 48	Marty McManus	90.00	40.00	13.50
☐ 49	Frank Frisch	275.00	120.00	40.00
☐ 50	Ed Brandt	90.00	40.00	13.50
☐ 51	Charlie Grimm	120.00	55.00	18.00
☐ 52	Andy Cohen	90.00	40.00	13.50
☐ 53	Babe Ruth	4500.00	1800.00	450.00
☐ 54	Ray Kremer	60.00	27.00	9.00
☐ 55	Pat Malone	60.00	27.00	9.00
☐ 56	Red Ruffing	150.00	67.50	22.50
☐ 57	Earl Clark	60.00	27.00	9.00
☐ 58	Lefty O'Doul	75.00	34.00	11.25
☐ 59	Bing Miller	60.00	27.00	9.00
☐ 60	Waite Hoyt	120.00	55.00	18.00
☐ 61	Max Bishop	60.00	27.00	9.00
☐ 62	Pepper Martin	90.00	40.00	13.50
☐ 63	Joe Cronin BAT	150.00	67.50	22.50
☐ 64	Burleigh Grimes	120.00	55.00	18.00
☐ 65	Milt Gaston	60.00	27.00	9.00
☐ 66	George Grantham	60.00	27.00	9.00
☐ 67	Guy Bush	60.00	27.00	9.00
☐ 68	Horace Lisenbee	60.00	27.00	9.00
☐ 69	Randy Moore	60.00	27.00	9.00
☐ 70	Floyd (Pete) Scott	60.00	27.00	9.00
☐ 71	Robert J. Burke	60.00	27.00	9.00
☐ 72	Owen Carroll	60.00	27.00	9.00
☐ 73	Jess Haines	120.00	55.00	18.00
☐ 74	Eppa Rixey	120.00	55.00	18.00
☐ 75	Willie Kamm	60.00	27.00	9.00
☐ 76	Mickey Cochrane	180.00	80.00	27.00
☐ 77	Adam Comorosky	60.00	27.00	9.00
☐ 78	Jack Quinn	60.00	27.00	9.00
☐ 79	Red Faber	120.00	55.00	18.00
☐ 80	Clyde Manion	60.00	27.00	9.00
☐ 81	Sam Jones	60.00	27.00	9.00
☐ 82	Dibrell Williams	60.00	27.00	9.00
☐ 83	Pete Jablonowski	60.00	27.00	9.00
☐ 84	Glenn Spencer	60.00	27.00	9.00
☐ 85	Heine Sand	60.00	27.00	9.00
☐ 86	Phil Todt	60.00	27.00	9.00
☐ 87	Frank O'Rourke	60.00	27.00	9.00

☐ 12	Mickey Cochrane	1.00	.40	.10
☐ 13	George Sisler	1.00	.40	.10
☐ 14	Joe Cronin	1.00	.40	.10
☐ 15	Pie Traynor	1.00	.40	.10
☐ 16	Lou Gehrig	20.00	8.50	2.75
☐ 17	Lefty Grove	2.50	1.00	.25
☐ 18	Chief Bender	1.00	.40	.10
☐ 19	Frankie Frisch	1.00	.40	.10
☐ 20	Al Simmons	1.00	.40	.10
☐ 21	Home Run Baker	1.00	.40	.10
☐ 22	Jimmy Foxx	3.00	1.25	.30
☐ 23	John McGraw	1.25	.50	.12
☐ 24	Christy Mathewson	5.00	2.25	.50
☐ 25	Ty Cobb	20.00	8.50	2.75
☐ 26	Dazzy Vance	1.00	.40	.10
☐ 27	Bill Dickey	2.00	.80	.20
☐ 28	Eddie Collins	1.00	.40	.10
☐ 29	Walter Johnson	5.00	2.25	.50
☐ 30	Tris Speaker	3.00	1.25	.30
☐ 31	Nap Lajoie	3.00	1.25	.30
☐ 32	Honus Wagner	5.00	2.25	.50
☐ 33	Cy Young	4.00	1.75	.40

1933 Goudey

The cards in this 240-card set measure 2 3/8" by 2 7/8". The 1933 Goudey set, designated R319 by the ACC, was that company's first baseball issue. The four Babe Ruth and two Lou Gehrig cards in the set are extremely popular with collectors. Card number 106, Napoleon Lajoie, was not printed in 1933, and was circulated to a limited number of collectors in 1934 upon request (it was printed along with the 1934 Goudey cards). An album was offered to house the 1933 set. Several minor leaguers are depicted. Card number 1 (Bengough) is very rarely found in mint condition; in fact, as a general rule all the first series cards are more difficult to find in Mint condition. Players with more than one card are also sometimes differentiated below by their pose: BAT (Batting), FIELD (Fielding), PIT (Pitching), THROW (Throwing). One of the Babe Ruth cards was double printed (DP) apparently in place of the Lajoie and hence is easier to obtain than the others. Due to the scarcity of the Lajoie card, the set is considered complete at 239 cards and is priced as such below.

	#	Name			
☐	88	Russell Rollings	60.00	27.00	9.00
☐	89	Tris Speaker	350.00	160.00	52.50
☐	90	Jess Petty	60.00	27.00	9.00
☐	91	Tom Zachary	60.00	27.00	9.00
☐	92	Lou Gehrig	2500.00	1000.00	250.00
☐	93	John Welch	60.00	27.00	9.00
☐	94	Bill Walker	60.00	27.00	9.00
☐	95	Alvin Crowder	60.00	27.00	9.00
☐	96	Willis Hudlin	60.00	27.00	9.00
☐	97	Joe Morrissey	60.00	27.00	9.00
☐	98	Walter Berger	75.00	34.00	11.25
☐	99	Tony Cuccinello	75.00	34.00	11.25
☐	100	George Uhle	60.00	27.00	9.00
☐	101	Richard Coffman	60.00	27.00	9.00
☐	102	Travis Jackson	120.00	55.00	18.00
☐	103	Earl Combs	120.00	55.00	18.00
☐	104	Fred Marberry	60.00	27.00	9.00
☐	105	Bernie Friberg	60.00	27.00	9.00
☐	106	Napoleon Lajoie (not issued until 1934)	25000.	9000.00	3000.00
☐	107	Heinie Manush	120.00	55.00	18.00
☐	108	Joe Kuhel	60.00	27.00	9.00
☐	109	Joe Cronin	150.00	67.50	22.50
☐	110	Goose Goslin	120.00	55.00	18.00
☐	111	Monte Weaver	60.00	27.00	9.00
☐	112	Fred Schulte	60.00	27.00	9.00
☐	113	Oswald Bluege	60.00	27.00	9.00
☐	114	Luke Sewell	75.00	34.00	11.25
☐	115	Cliff Heathcote	60.00	27.00	9.00
☐	116	Eddie Morgan	60.00	27.00	9.00
☐	117	Rabbit Maranville	120.00	55.00	18.00
☐	118	Val Picinich	60.00	27.00	9.00
☐	119	Rogers Hornsby FIELD	350.00	160.00	52.50
☐	120	Carl Reynolds	60.00	27.00	9.00
☐	121	Walter Stewart	60.00	27.00	9.00
☐	122	Alvin Crowder	60.00	27.00	9.00
☐	123	Jack Russell	60.00	27.00	9.00
☐	124	Earl Whitehill	60.00	27.00	9.00
☐	125	Bill Terry	225.00	100.00	33.00
☐	126	Joe Moore	60.00	27.00	9.00
☐	127	Mel Ott	250.00	110.00	37.50
☐	128	Chuck Klein	180.00	80.00	27.00
☐	129	Hal Schumacher PIT	60.00	27.00	9.00
☐	130	Fred Fitzsimmons	60.00	27.00	9.00
☐	131	Fred Frankhouse	60.00	27.00	9.00
☐	132	Jim Elliott	60.00	27.00	9.00
☐	133	Fred Lindstrom	120.00	55.00	18.00
☐	134	Sam Rice	120.00	55.00	18.00
☐	135	Woody English	60.00	27.00	9.00
☐	136	Flint Rhem	60.00	27.00	9.00
☐	137	Fred (Red) Lucas	60.00	27.00	9.00
☐	138	Herb Pennock	120.00	55.00	18.00
☐	139	Ben Cantwell	60.00	27.00	9.00
☐	140	Bump Hadley	60.00	27.00	9.00
☐	141	Ray Benge	60.00	27.00	9.00
☐	142	Paul Richards	75.00	34.00	11.25
☐	143	Glenn Wright	60.00	27.00	9.00
☐	144	Babe Ruth BAT DP	3500.00	1400.00	350.00
☐	145	George Walberg	60.00	27.00	9.00
☐	146	Walter Stewart PIT	60.00	27.00	9.00
☐	147	Leo Durocher	150.00	67.50	22.50
☐	148	Eddie Farrell	60.00	27.00	9.00
☐	149	Babe Ruth	4500.00	1800.00	450.00
☐	150	Ray Kolp	60.00	27.00	9.00
☐	151	Jake Flowers	60.00	27.00	9.00
☐	152	Zack Taylor	60.00	27.00	9.00
☐	153	Buddy Myer	60.00	27.00	9.00
☐	154	Jimmy Foxx	350.00	160.00	52.50
☐	155	Joe Judge	60.00	27.00	9.00
☐	156	Danny MacFayden	60.00	27.00	9.00
☐	157	Sam Byrd	60.00	27.00	9.00
☐	158	Moe Berg	150.00	67.50	22.50
☐	159	Oswald Bluege	60.00	27.00	9.00
☐	160	Lou Gehrig	2500.00	1000.00	250.00
☐	161	Al Spohrer	60.00	27.00	9.00
☐	162	Leo Mangum	60.00	27.00	9.00
☐	163	Luke Sewell	75.00	34.00	11.25
☐	164	Lloyd Waner	120.00	55.00	18.00
☐	165	Joe Sewell	120.00	55.00	18.00
☐	166	Sam West	60.00	27.00	9.00
☐	167	Jack Russell	60.00	27.00	9.00
☐	168	Goose Goslin	120.00	55.00	18.00
☐	169	Al Thomas	60.00	27.00	9.00
☐	170	Harry McCurdy	60.00	27.00	9.00
☐	171	Charlie Jamieson	60.00	27.00	9.00
☐	172	Billy Hargrave	60.00	27.00	9.00
☐	173	Roscoe Holm	60.00	27.00	9.00
☐	174	Warren(Curly) Ogden	60.00	27.00	9.00
☐	175	Dan Howley	60.00	27.00	9.00
☐	176	John Ogden	60.00	27.00	9.00
☐	177	Walter French	60.00	27.00	9.00
☐	178	Jackie Warner	60.00	27.00	9.00
☐	179	Fred Leach	60.00	27.00	9.00
☐	180	Eddie Moore	60.00	27.00	9.00
☐	181	Babe Ruth	4500.00	1800.00	450.00
☐	182	Andy High	60.00	27.00	9.00
☐	183	George Walberg	60.00	27.00	9.00
☐	184	Charley Berry	60.00	27.00	9.00
☐	185	Bob Smith	60.00	27.00	9.00
☐	186	John Schulte	60.00	27.00	9.00
☐	187	Heinie Manush	120.00	55.00	18.00
☐	188	Rogers Hornsby	350.00	160.00	52.50
☐	189	Joe Cronin	150.00	67.50	22.50
☐	190	Fred Schulte	60.00	27.00	9.00
☐	191	Ben Chapman	75.00	34.00	11.25
☐	192	Walter Brown	60.00	27.00	9.00
☐	193	Lynford Lary	60.00	27.00	9.00
☐	194	Earl Averill	120.00	55.00	18.00
☐	195	Evar Swanson	60.00	27.00	9.00
☐	196	Leroy Mahaffey	60.00	27.00	9.00
☐	197	Rick Ferrell	120.00	55.00	18.00
☐	198	Jack Burns	60.00	27.00	9.00
☐	199	Tom Bridges	75.00	34.00	11.25
☐	200	Bill Hallahan	60.00	27.00	9.00
☐	201	Ernie Orsatti	60.00	27.00	9.00
☐	202	Gabby Hartnett	120.00	55.00	18.00
☐	203	Lon Warneke	75.00	34.00	11.25
☐	204	Riggs Stephenson	75.00	34.00	11.25
☐	205	Heinie Meine	60.00	27.00	9.00
☐	206	Gus Suhr	60.00	27.00	9.00
☐	207	Mel Ott BAT	275.00	120.00	40.00
☐	208	Bernie James	60.00	27.00	9.00
☐	209	Adolfo Luque	60.00	27.00	9.00
☐	210	Virgil Davis	60.00	27.00	9.00
☐	211	Hack Wilson	250.00	110.00	37.50
☐	212	Billy Urbanski	60.00	27.00	9.00
☐	213	Earl Adams	60.00	27.00	9.00
☐	214	John Kerr	60.00	27.00	9.00
☐	215	Russ Van Atta	60.00	27.00	9.00
☐	216	Lefty Gomez	350.00	160.00	52.50
☐	217	Frank Crosetti	120.00	55.00	18.00
☐	218	Wes Ferrell	75.00	34.00	11.25
☐	219	Mule Haas	60.00	27.00	9.00
☐	220	Lefty Grove	425.00	190.00	63.00
☐	221	Dale Alexander	60.00	27.00	9.00
☐	222	Charley Gehringer	250.00	110.00	37.50
☐	223	Dizzy Dean	750.00	325.00	110.00
☐	224	Frank Demaree	60.00	27.00	9.00
☐	225	Bill Jurges	60.00	27.00	9.00
☐	226	Charley Root	60.00	27.00	9.00
☐	227	Billy Herman	120.00	55.00	18.00
☐	228	Tony Piet	60.00	27.00	9.00
☐	229	Floyd(Arky) Vaughan	120.00	55.00	18.00
☐	230	Carl Hubbell PIT	200.00	90.00	30.00
☐	231	Joe Moore FIELD	60.00	27.00	9.00
☐	232	Lefty O'Doul	75.00	34.00	11.25
☐	233	Johnny Vergez	60.00	27.00	9.00
☐	234	Carl Hubbell	200.00	90.00	30.00
☐	235	Fred Fitzsimmons	75.00	34.00	11.25
☐	236	George Davis	60.00	27.00	9.00
☐	237	Gus Mancuso	60.00	27.00	9.00
☐	238	Hugh Critz	60.00	27.00	9.00
☐	239	Leroy Parmelee	60.00	27.00	9.00
☐	240	Hal Schumacher	120.00	55.00	18.00

1934 Goudey

The cards in this 96-card set measure 2 3/8" by 2 7/8". The 1934 Goudey set of color cards carries the catalog number R320. Cards 1-48 are considered to be the easiest to find (although card number 1, Foxx, is very scarce in mint condition) while 73-96 are much more difficult to find. Cards of this 1934 Goudey series are slightly less abundant than cards of the 1933 Goudey set. Of the 96 cards, 84 contain a "Lou Gehrig Says" line on the front in a blue design, while 12 of the high series contain a "Chuck Klein Says" line in a red design. These Chuck Klein cards are indicated in the checklist below by CK and are in fact the 12 National Leaguers in the high series.

		EX-MT	VG-E	GOOD
COMPLETE SET (96)		18000.00	7500.00	1800.00
COMMON PLAYER (1-48)		60.00	27.00	9.00
COMMON PLAYER (49-72)		80.00	36.00	12.00
COMMON PLAYER (73-96)		250.00	110.00	37.50
☐ 1	Jimmy Foxx	750.00	125.00	25.00
☐ 2	Mickey Cochrane	180.00	80.00	27.00
☐ 3	Charlie Grimm	75.00	34.00	11.25
☐ 4	Woody English	60.00	27.00	9.00
☐ 5	Ed Brandt	60.00	27.00	9.00
☐ 6	Dizzy Dean	600.00	270.00	90.00
☐ 7	Leo Durocher	120.00	55.00	18.00
☐ 8	Tony Piet	60.00	27.00	9.00
☐ 9	Ben Chapman	75.00	34.00	11.25
☐ 10	Chuck Klein	120.00	55.00	18.00
☐ 11	Paul Waner	120.00	55.00	18.00
☐ 12	Carl Hubbell	180.00	80.00	27.00
☐ 13	Frank Frisch	180.00	80.00	27.00
☐ 14	Willie Kamm	60.00	27.00	9.00
☐ 15	Alvin Crowder	60.00	27.00	9.00
☐ 16	Joe Kuhel	60.00	27.00	9.00
☐ 17	Hugh Critz	60.00	27.00	9.00
☐ 18	Heinie Manush	120.00	55.00	18.00
☐ 19	Lefty Grove	275.00	120.00	40.00
☐ 20	Frank Hogan	60.00	27.00	9.00
☐ 21	Bill Terry	180.00	80.00	27.00
☐ 22	Arky Vaughan	120.00	55.00	18.00
☐ 23	Charlie Gehringer	180.00	80.00	27.00
☐ 24	Ray Benge	60.00	27.00	9.00
☐ 25	Roger Cramer	75.00	34.00	11.25
☐ 26	Gerald Walker	60.00	27.00	9.00
☐ 27	Luke Appling	120.00	55.00	18.00
☐ 28	Ed Coleman	60.00	27.00	9.00
☐ 29	Larry French	60.00	27.00	9.00
☐ 30	Julius Solters	60.00	27.00	9.00
☐ 31	Buck Jordan	60.00	27.00	9.00
☐ 32	Blondy Ryan	60.00	27.00	9.00
☐ 33	Frank Hurst	60.00	27.00	9.00
☐ 34	Chick Hafey	120.00	55.00	18.00
☐ 35	Ernie Lombardi	120.00	55.00	18.00
☐ 36	Walter Betts	60.00	27.00	9.00
☐ 37	Lou Gehrig	2750.00	1100.00	275.00
☐ 38	Oral Hildebrand	60.00	27.00	9.00
☐ 39	Fred Walker	60.00	27.00	9.00
☐ 40	John Stone	60.00	27.00	9.00
☐ 41	George Earnshaw	60.00	27.00	9.00
☐ 42	John Allen	60.00	27.00	9.00
☐ 43	Dick Porter	60.00	27.00	9.00
☐ 44	Tom Bridges	75.00	34.00	11.25
☐ 45	Oscar Melillo	60.00	27.00	9.00
☐ 46	Joe Stripp	60.00	27.00	9.00
☐ 47	John Frederick	60.00	27.00	9.00
☐ 48	Tex Carleton	60.00	27.00	9.00
☐ 49	Sam Leslie	80.00	36.00	12.00
☐ 50	Walter Beck	80.00	36.00	12.00
☐ 51	Rip Collins	80.00	36.00	12.00
☐ 52	Herman Bell	80.00	36.00	12.00
☐ 53	George Watkins	80.00	36.00	12.00
☐ 54	Wesley Schulmerich	80.00	36.00	12.00
☐ 55	Ed Holley	80.00	36.00	12.00
☐ 56	Mark Koenig	80.00	36.00	12.00
☐ 57	Bill Swift	80.00	36.00	12.00
☐ 58	Earl Grace	80.00	36.00	12.00
☐ 59	Joe Mowry	80.00	36.00	12.00
☐ 60	Lynn Nelson	80.00	36.00	12.00
☐ 61	Lou Gehrig	3000.00	1200.00	300.00
☐ 62	Hank Greenberg	350.00	160.00	52.50
☐ 63	Minter Hayes	80.00	36.00	12.00
☐ 64	Frank Grube	80.00	36.00	12.00
☐ 65	Cliff Bolton	80.00	36.00	12.00
☐ 66	Mel Harder	120.00	55.00	18.00
☐ 67	Bob Weiland	80.00	36.00	12.00
☐ 68	Bob Johnson	120.00	55.00	18.00
☐ 69	John Marcum	80.00	36.00	12.00
☐ 70	Pete Fox	80.00	36.00	12.00
☐ 71	Lyle Tinning	80.00	36.00	12.00
☐ 72	Arndt Jorgens	80.00	36.00	12.00
☐ 73	Ed Wells	250.00	110.00	37.50
☐ 74	Bob Boken	250.00	110.00	37.50
☐ 75	Bill Werber	250.00	110.00	37.50
☐ 76	Hal Trosky	275.00	120.00	40.00
☐ 77	Joe Vosmik	250.00	110.00	37.50
☐ 78	Pinky Higgins	275.00	120.00	40.00
☐ 79	Ed Durham	250.00	110.00	37.50
☐ 80	Marty McManus CK	250.00	110.00	37.50
☐ 81	Bob Brown CK	250.00	110.00	37.50
☐ 82	Bill Hallahan CK	250.00	110.00	37.50
☐ 83	Jim Mooney CK	250.00	110.00	37.50
☐ 84	Paul Derringer CK	300.00	135.00	45.00
☐ 85	Adam Comorosky CK	250.00	110.00	37.50
☐ 86	Lloyd Johnson CK	250.00	110.00	37.50
☐ 87	George Darrow CK	250.00	110.00	37.50
☐ 88	Homer Peel CK	250.00	110.00	37.50
☐ 89	Linus Frey CK	250.00	110.00	37.50
☐ 90	Ki-Ki Cuyler CK	500.00	225.00	75.00
☐ 91	Dolph Camilli CK	275.00	120.00	40.00
☐ 92	Steve Larkin	250.00	110.00	37.50
☐ 93	Fred Ostermueller	250.00	110.00	37.50
☐ 94	Red Rolfe	275.00	120.00	40.00
☐ 95	Myril Hoag	250.00	110.00	37.50
☐ 96	James DeShong	350.00	160.00	52.50

1935 Goudey Puzzle

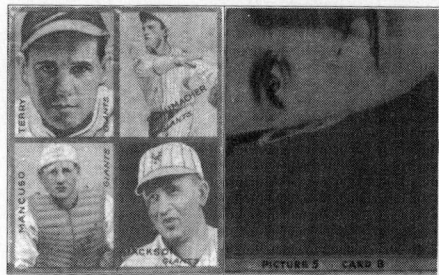

The cards in this 36-card set (the number of different front pictures) measure 2 3/8" by 2 7/8". The 1935 Goudey set is sometimes called the Goudey Puzzle Set, the Goudey 4-in-1's, or R321 (ACC). There are 36 different card fronts but 114 different front/back combinations. The card number in the checklist refers to the back puzzle number, as the backs can be arranged to form a puzzle picturing a player or team. To avoid the confusion caused by two different fronts having the same back number, the rarer cards have been arbitrarily given a "1" prefix. The scarcer puzzle cards are hence all listed at the numerical end of the list below, i.e. rare puzzle 1 is listed as number 11, rare puzzle 2 is listed as 12, etc. The BLUE in the checklist refers to a card with a blue border, as most cards have a red border. The set price below includes all the cards listed. The following is the list of the puzzle back pictures: 1) Detroit Tigers; 2) Chuck Klein; 3) Frankie Frisch; 4) Mickey Cochrane; 5) Joe Cronin; 6) Jimmy Foxx; 7) Al Simmons; 8) Cleveland Indians; and 9) Washington Senators.

		EX-MT	VG-E	GOOD
COMPLETE SET (114)		16500.00	7500.00	1650.00
COMMON CARDS (1-9)		60.00	27.00	9.00
COMMON CARDS (11-17)		100.00	45.00	15.00
☐ 1A	F.Frisch/Dizzy Dean Orsatti/Carleton	165.00	75.00	22.50
☐ 1B	Mahaffey/Jimmie Foxx Williams/Higgins	120.00	55.00	18.00
☐ 1C	Heinie Manush/Lary Weaver/Hadley	75.00	34.00	11.25
☐ 1D	Cochrane/C.Gehringer Bridges/Rogell	120.00	55.00	18.00
☐ 1E	Paul Waner/Bush W.Hoyt/Lloyd Waner	120.00	55.00	18.00
☐ 1F	B.Grimes/Chuck Klein K.Cuyler/English	120.00	55.00	18.00
☐ 1G	Leslie/Frey Joe Stripp/Clark	60.00	27.00	9.00
☐ 1H	Piet/Comorosky Bottomley/Adams	75.00	34.00	11.25
☐ 1I	Earnshaw/Dykes Luke Sewell/Appling	75.00	34.00	11.25
☐ 1J	Babe Ruth/McManus Brandt/Maranville	1000.00	400.00	100.00
☐ 1K	Bill Terry/Schumacher	120.00	55.00	18.00

Card			
Mancuso/T.Jackson			
☐ 1L Kamm/Hildebrand	75.00	34.00	11.25
Averill/Trosky			
☐ 2A F.Frisch/Dizzy Dean	165.00	75.00	22.50
Orsatti/Carleton			
☐ 2B Mahaffey/Jimmie Foxx	120.00	55.00	18.00
Williams/Higgins			
☐ 2C Heinie Manush/Lary	75.00	34.00	11.25
Weaver/Hadley			
☐ 2D Cochrane/C.Gehringer	120.00	55.00	18.00
Bridges/Rogell			
☐ 2E Kamm/Hildebrand	75.00	34.00	11.25
Earl Averill/Trosky			
☐ 2F Earnshaw/Dykes	75.00	34.00	11.25
Luke Sewell/Appling			
☐ 3A Babe Ruth/McManus	1000.00	400.00	100.00
Brandt/Maranville			
☐ 3B Bill Terry/Schumacher	120.00	55.00	18.00
Mancuso/T.Jackson			
☐ 3C Paul Waner/Bush	120.00	55.00	18.00
W.Hoyt/Lloyd Waner			
☐ 3D B.Grimes/Chuck Klein	120.00	55.00	18.00
K.Cuyler/English			
☐ 3E Leslie/Frey	60.00	27.00	9.00
Joe Stripp/Clark			
☐ 3F Piet/Comorosky	75.00	34.00	11.25
Jim Bottomley/Adams			
☐ 4A Critz/D.Bartell BLUE	100.00	45.00	15.00
Mel Ott/Mancuso			
☐ 4B Pie Traynor/Lucas BLUE	75.00	34.00	11.25
Tom Thevenow/Wright			
☐ 4C Berry/Burke BLUE	75.00	34.00	11.25
Kress/Dazzy Vance			
☐ 4D R.Ruffing/Malone BLUE	165.00	75.00	22.50
Lazzeri/Bill Dickey			
☐ 4E Moore/Hogan BLUE	60.00	27.00	9.00
Frankhouse/Brandt			
☐ 4F Martin/O'Farrell BLUE	60.00	27.00	9.00
Byrd/MacFayden			
☐ 5A Ruel/Al Simmons	120.00	55.00	18.00
Kamm/M.Cochrane			
☐ 5B Willis Hudlin/Myatt	75.00	34.00	11.25
Comorosky/Bottomley			
☐ 5C Paul Waner/Bush	120.00	55.00	18.00
W.Hoyt/Lloyd Waner			
☐ 5D West/Oscar Melillo	60.00	27.00	9.00
Blaeholder/Coffman			
☐ 5E Leslie/Frey	60.00	27.00	9.00
Joe Stripp/Clark			
☐ 5F Schuble/Marberry	75.00	34.00	11.25
Goose Goslin/Crowder			
☐ 6A Ruel/Al Simmons	120.00	55.00	18.00
Kamm/M.Cochrane			
☐ 6B Willis Hudlin/Myatt	75.00	34.00	11.25
Comorosky/Bottomley			
☐ 6C Wilson/Allen	60.00	27.00	9.00
Jonnard/Brickell			
☐ 6D West/Oscar Melillo	60.00	27.00	9.00
Blaeholder/Coffman			
☐ 6E Joe Cronin/Reynolds	75.00	34.00	11.25
Bishop/Cissell			
☐ 6F Schuble/Marberry	75.00	34.00	11.25
Goose Goslin/Crowder			
☐ 7A Critz/Bartell BLUE	100.00	45.00	15.00
Mel Ott/Mancuso			
☐ 7B Pie Traynor/Lucas BLUE	75.00	34.00	11.25
Tom Thevenow/Wright			
☐ 7C Berry/Burke BLUE	75.00	34.00	11.25
Kress/Dazzy Vance			
☐ 7D R.Ruffing/Malone BLUE	165.00	75.00	22.50
Lazzeri/Bill Dickey			
☐ 7E Moore/Hogan BLUE	60.00	27.00	9.00
Frankhouse/Brandt			
☐ 7F Martin/O'Farrell BLUE	60.00	27.00	9.00
Byrd/MacFayden			
☐ 8A M.Koenig/Fitzsimmons	60.00	27.00	9.00
Benge/Zachary			
☐ 8B Hayes/Ted Lyons	75.00	34.00	11.25
Haas/Zeke Bonura			
☐ 8C Burns/Rollie Hemsley	60.00	27.00	9.00
Grube/Weiland			
☐ 8D Campbell/Meyers	60.00	27.00	9.00
Goodman/Kampouris			
☐ 8E DeShong/Allen	60.00	27.00	9.00
Red Rolfe/Walker			
☐ 8F P.Fox/Hank Greenberg	100.00	45.00	15.00
Walker/Rowe			
☐ 8G Werber/Rick Ferrell	75.00	34.00	11.25
W.Ferrell/Ostermueller			
☐ 8H Joe Kuhel/Whitehill	60.00	27.00	9.00
Meyer/Stone			
☐ 8I J.Vosmik/Knickerbocker	60.00	27.00	9.00
Mel Harder/Stewart			
☐ 8J Johnson/Coleman	60.00	27.00	9.00
Marcum/Cramer			
☐ 8K Herman/Suhr	60.00	27.00	9.00
Padden/Blanton			
☐ 8L Spohrer/Rhem	60.00	27.00	9.00
Cantwell/Benton			
☐ 8M M.Koenig/Fitzsimmons	60.00	27.00	9.00
Benge/Zachary			
☐ 9B Hayes/Ted Lyons	75.00	34.00	11.25
Haas/Zeke Bonura			
☐ 9C Burns/Rollie Hemsley	60.00	27.00	9.00
Grube/Weiland			
☐ 9D Campbell/Meyers	60.00	27.00	9.00
Goodman/Kampouris			
☐ 9E DeShong/Allen	60.00	27.00	9.00
Red Rolfe/Walker			
☐ 9F P.Fox/Hank Greenberg	100.00	45.00	15.00
Walker/Rowe			
☐ 9G Werber/Rick Ferrell	75.00	34.00	11.25
W.Ferrell/Ostermueller			
☐ 9H Joe Kuhel/Whitehill	60.00	27.00	9.00
Meyer/Stone			
☐ 9I J.Vosmik/Knickerbocker	60.00	27.00	9.00
Mel Harder/Stewart			
☐ 9J Johnson/Coleman	60.00	27.00	9.00
Marcum/Cramer			
☐ 9K Herman/Suhr	60.00	27.00	9.00
Padden/Blanton			
☐ 9L Spohrer/Rhem	60.00	27.00	9.00
Cantwell/Benton			
☐ 11E Wilson/Allen	100.00	45.00	15.00
Jonnard/Brickell			
☐ 11F West/Melillo	100.00	45.00	15.00
Blaeholder/Coffman			
☐ 11G Joe Cronin/Reynolds	150.00	67.50	22.50
Bishop/Cissel			
☐ 11H Schuble/Marberry	125.00	57.50	18.75
Goose Goslin/Crowder			
☐ 11J Ruel/Al Simmons	180.00	80.00	27.00
Kamm/M.Cochrane			
☐ 11K Hudlin/Myatt	125.00	57.50	18.75
Comorosky/Bottomley			
☐ 12A Critz/Bartell BLUE	150.00	67.50	22.50
Mel Ott/Mancuso			
☐ 12B P.Traynor/Lucas BLUE	125.00	57.50	18.75
Thevenow/Wright			
☐ 12C Berry/Burke BLUE	125.00	57.50	18.75
Kress/D.Vance			
☐ 12D Ruffing/Malone BLUE	250.00	110.00	37.50
Lazzeri/Bill Dickey			
☐ 12E Moore/Hogan BLUE	100.00	45.00	15.00
Frankhouse/Brandt			
☐ 12F Martin/O'Farrell BLUE	100.00	45.00	15.00
Byrd/MacFayden			
☐ 13A Ruel/Al Simmons	180.00	80.00	27.00
Kamm/M.Cochrane			
☐ 13B Hudlin/Myatt	125.00	57.50	18.75
Comorosky/Bottomley			
☐ 13C Wilson/Allen	100.00	45.00	15.00
Jonnard/Brickell			
☐ 13D West/Oscar Melillo	100.00	45.00	15.00
Blaeholder/Coffman			
☐ 13E Joe Cronin/Reynolds	125.00	57.50	18.75
Bishop/Cissell			
☐ 13F Schuble/Marberry	125.00	57.50	18.75
Goose Goslin/Crowder			
☐ 14A Babe Ruth/McManus	2000.00	800.00	200.00
Brandt/Maranville			
☐ 14B Bill Terry/Schumacher	160.00	72.00	24.00
Mancuso/T.Jackson			
☐ 14C Paul Waner/Bush	160.00	72.00	24.00
W.Hoyt/Lloyd Waner			
☐ 14D B.Grimes/Chuck Klein	160.00	72.00	24.00
K.Cuyler/English			
☐ 14E Leslie/Frey	100.00	45.00	15.00
Joe Stripp/Clark			
☐ 14F Piet/Comorosky	125.00	57.50	18.75
Jim Bottomley/Adams			
☐ 15A Babe Ruth/McManus	2000.00	800.00	200.00
Brandt/Maranville			
☐ 15B Bill Terry/Schumacher	160.00	72.00	24.00
Mancuso/T.Jackson			
☐ 15C Wilson/Allen	100.00	45.00	15.00
Jonnard/Brickell			
☐ 15D B.Grimes/Chuck Klein	160.00	72.00	24.00
K.Cuyler/English			
☐ 15E Joe Cronin/Reynolds	125.00	57.50	18.75
Bishop/Cissell			
☐ 15F Piet/Comorosky	125.00	57.50	18.75
Jim Bottomley/Adams			
☐ 16A F.Frisch/Dizzy Dean	250.00	110.00	37.50
E.Orsatti/Carleton			
☐ 16B Mahaffey/Jimmie Foxx	160.00	72.00	24.00
Williams/Higgins			
☐ 16C Heinie Manush/Lary	125.00	57.50	18.75
Weaver/Hadley			

		EX-MT	VG-E	GOOD
☐ 16D	Cochrane/C.Gehringer .... Tom Bridges/Rogell	180.00	80.00	27.00
☐ 16E	Kamm/Hildebrand .... Earl Averill/Trosky	125.00	57.50	18.75
☐ 16F	G.Earnshaw/Dykes .... Luke Sewell/Appling	125.00	57.50	18.75
☐ 17A	F.Frisch/Dizzy Dean .... E.Orsatti/Carleton	250.00	110.00	37.50
☐ 17B	Mahaffey/Jimmie Foxx .... Williams/Higgins	160.00	72.00	24.00
☐ 17C	Heinie Manush/Lary .... Weaver/Hadley	125.00	57.50	18.75
☐ 17D	Cochrane/C.Gehringer .... Tom Bridges/Rogell	180.00	80.00	27.00
☐ 17E	Kamm/Hildebrand .... Earl Averill/Trosky	125.00	57.50	18.75
☐ 17F	G.Earnshaw/Dykes .... Luke Sewell/Appling	125.00	57.50	18.75

1936 Goudey B/W

THREE BAGGER

What a smash down 1st base line!—Too fast for the 1st sacker to even get near it.

The cards in this 25-card black and white set measure 2 3/8" by 2 7/8". In contrast to the color artwork of its previous sets, the 1936 Goudey set contained a simple black and white player photograph. A facsimile autograph appeared within the picture area. Each card was issued with a number of different "game situation" backs, and there may be as many as 200 different front/back combinations. The catalog designation for this set is R322.

		EX-MT	VG-E	GOOD
COMPLETE SET (25)		1700.00	750.00	175.00
COMMON PLAYER (1-25)		40.00	18.00	6.00
☐ 1	Wally Berger	45.00	20.00	6.75
☐ 2	Zeke Bonura	40.00	18.00	6.00
☐ 3	Stan Bordagaray	40.00	18.00	6.00
☐ 4	Bill Brubaker	40.00	18.00	6.00
☐ 5	Dolph Camilli	40.00	18.00	6.00
☐ 6	Clyde Castleman	40.00	18.00	6.00
☐ 7	Mickey Cochrane	160.00	72.00	24.00
☐ 8	Joe Coscarart	40.00	18.00	6.00
☐ 9	Frank Crosetti	75.00	34.00	11.25
☐ 10	Kiki Cuyler	90.00	40.00	13.50
☐ 11	Paul Derringer	50.00	22.50	7.50
☐ 12	Jimmy Dykes	45.00	20.00	6.75
☐ 13	Rick Ferrell	90.00	40.00	13.50
☐ 14	Lefty Gomez	175.00	80.00	27.00
☐ 15	Hank Greenberg	225.00	100.00	33.00
☐ 16	Bucky Harris	80.00	36.00	12.00
☐ 17	Rollie Hemsley	40.00	18.00	6.00
☐ 18	Pinky Higgins	40.00	18.00	6.00
☐ 19	Oral Hildebrand	40.00	18.00	6.00
☐ 20	Chuck Klein	100.00	45.00	15.00
☐ 21	Pepper Martin	60.00	27.00	9.00
☐ 22	Bobo Newsom	45.00	20.00	6.75
☐ 23	Joe Vosmik	40.00	18.00	6.00
☐ 24	Paul Waner	90.00	40.00	13.50
☐ 25	Bill Werber	40.00	18.00	6.00

1938 Goudey Heads Up

The cards in this 48-card set measure 2 3/8" by 2 7/8". The 1938 Goudey set is commonly referred to as the Heads-Up set, or R323 (ACC). These very popular but difficult to obtain cards came in two series of the same 24 players. The first series, numbers 241-264, is distinguished from the second series, numbers 265-288, in that the second contains etched cartoons and comments surrounding the player picture. Although the set starts with number 241, it is not a continuation of the 1933 Goudey set, but a separate set in its own right.

		EX-MT	VG-E	GOOD
COMPLETE SET (48)		17000.00	7500.00	1650.00
COMMON PLAYER (241-264)		100.00	45.00	15.00
COMMON PLAYER (265-288)		125.00	57.50	18.75
☐ 241	Charlie Gehringer	350.00	160.00	52.50
☐ 242	Pete Fox	100.00	45.00	15.00
☐ 243	Joe Kuhel	100.00	45.00	15.00
☐ 244	Frank Demaree	100.00	45.00	15.00
☐ 245	Frank Pytlak	100.00	45.00	15.00
☐ 246	Ernie Lombardi	200.00	90.00	30.00
☐ 247	Joe Vosmik	100.00	45.00	15.00
☐ 248	Dick Bartell	100.00	45.00	15.00
☐ 249	Jimmie Foxx	450.00	200.00	67.50
☐ 250	Joe DiMaggio	3750.00	1500.00	375.00
☐ 251	Bump Hadley	100.00	45.00	15.00
☐ 252	Zeke Bonura	100.00	45.00	15.00
☐ 253	Hank Greenberg	400.00	180.00	60.00
☐ 254	Van Lingle Mungo	100.00	45.00	15.00
☐ 255	Moose Solters	100.00	45.00	15.00
☐ 256	Vernon Kennedy	100.00	45.00	15.00
☐ 257	Al Lopez	200.00	90.00	30.00
☐ 258	Bobby Doerr	350.00	160.00	52.50
☐ 259	Billy Werber	100.00	45.00	15.00
☐ 260	Rudy York	100.00	45.00	15.00
☐ 261	Rip Radcliff	100.00	45.00	15.00
☐ 262	Joe Medwick	300.00	135.00	45.00
☐ 263	Marvin Owen	100.00	45.00	15.00
☐ 264	Bob Feller	700.00	315.00	105.00
☐ 265	Charlie Gehringer	425.00	190.00	63.00
☐ 266	Pete Fox	125.00	57.50	18.75
☐ 267	Joe Kuhel	125.00	57.50	18.75
☐ 268	Frank Demaree	125.00	57.50	18.75
☐ 269	Frank Pytlak	125.00	57.50	18.75
☐ 270	Ernie Lombardi	250.00	110.00	37.50
☐ 271	Joe Vosmik	125.00	57.50	18.75
☐ 272	Dick Bartell	125.00	57.50	18.75
☐ 273	Jimmie Foxx	550.00	240.00	80.00
☐ 274	Joe DiMaggio	4500.00	1800.00	450.00
☐ 275	Bump Hadley	125.00	57.50	18.75
☐ 276	Zeke Bonura	125.00	57.50	18.75
☐ 277	Hank Greenberg	500.00	225.00	75.00
☐ 278	Van Lingle Mungo	125.00	57.50	18.75
☐ 279	Moose Solters	125.00	57.50	18.75
☐ 280	Vernon Kennedy	125.00	57.50	18.75
☐ 281	Al Lopez	250.00	110.00	37.50
☐ 282	Bobby Doerr	450.00	200.00	67.50
☐ 283	Billy Werber	125.00	57.50	18.75
☐ 284	Rudy York	125.00	57.50	18.75
☐ 285	Rip Radcliff	125.00	57.50	18.75
☐ 286	Joe Medwick	375.00	165.00	55.00
☐ 287	Marvin Owen	125.00	57.50	18.75
☐ 288	Bob Feller	850.00	375.00	125.00

1981 Granny Goose

Matthew Lon Keough
27 Pitcher
Height: 6'2"
Weight: 175
Bats: Right
Throws: Right

Matt proved to be a durable pitcher in 1980, completing 20 games which was 3rd best in the league. He had a 2.92 ERA, which was 4th in the American League.

© 1981 East West Promotions, Inc.

MATT KEOUGH
27 PITCHER

This set is the hardest to obtain of the three years Granny Goose issued cards of the Oakland A's. The Revering card was supposedly destroyed by the printer soon after he was traded away and hence is in shorter supply than the other 14 cards in the set. Wayne Gross is also supposedly available in lesser quantity compared to the other players. Cards are standard size (2 1/2" by 3 1/2") and were issued in bags of potato chips. Cards are numbered on the front and back by the player's uniform number.

	MINT	EXC	G-VG
COMPLETE SET (15)	90.00	40.00	13.50
COMMON PLAYER	1.50	.60	.15
☐ 1 Billy Martin MG	9.00	4.00	.90
☐ 2 Mike Heath	1.50	.60	.15
☐ 5 Jeff Newman	1.50	.60	.15
☐ 6 Mitchell Page	1.50	.60	.15
☐ 8 Rob Picciolo	1.50	.60	.15
☐ 10 Wayne Gross	6.00	2.50	.60
☐ 13 Dave Revering SP	35.00	15.75	5.25
☐ 17 Mike Norris	1.50	.60	.15
☐ 20 Tony Armas	2.00	.80	.20
☐ 21 Dwayne Murphy	2.00	.80	.20
☐ 22 Rick Langford	2.00	.80	.20
☐ 27 Matt Keough	1.50	.60	.15
☐ 35 Rickey Henderson	40.00	18.00	6.00
☐ 39 Dave McKay	1.50	.60	.15
☐ 54 Steve McCatty	1.50	.60	.15

1982 Granny Goose

Billy Martin
1 Manager

Billy was named winner of the 1981 AP, UPI and Sporting News Manager of the Year Award for his performance in 1981. Billy has won 963 games, losing only 768, a .556 percentage, trailing only Weaver, Anderson and Lasorda among active managers.

© 1982 Granny Goose Foods, Inc.

The cards in this 15-card set measure 2 1/2" by 3 1/2". Granny Goose Foods, Inc., a California based company, repeated its successful promotional idea of 1981 by issuing a new set of Oakland A's baseball cards for 1982. Each color player picture is surrounded by white borders and has trim and lettering done in Oakland's green and yellow colors. The cards are, in a sense, numbered according to the uniform number of the player; the card numbering below is according to alphabetical order by name. The card backs carry vital statistics done in black print on a white background. The cards were distributed in packages of potato chips and were also handed out on Fan Appreciation Day at the stadium. Although Picciolo was traded, his card was not withdrawn (as was Revering in 1981) and, therefore, its value is no greater than other cards in the set.

	MINT	EXC	G-VG
COMPLETE SET (15)	21.00	9.00	3.00
COMMON PLAYER (1-15)	.60	.25	.06
☐ 1 Tony Armas	.75	.30	.07
☐ 2 Wayne Gross	.60	.25	.06
☐ 3 Mike Heath	.60	.25	.06
☐ 4 Rickey Henderson	13.50	6.00	1.85
☐ 5 Cliff Johnson	.75	.30	.07
☐ 6 Matt Keough	.60	.25	.06
☐ 7 Rick Langford	.75	.30	.07
☐ 8 Davey Lopes	.90	.40	.09
☐ 9 Billy Martin MG	3.00	1.25	.30
☐ 10 Steve McCatty	.60	.25	.06
☐ 11 Dwayne Murphy	.75	.30	.07
☐ 12 Jeff Newman	.60	.25	.06
☐ 13 Mike Norris	.75	.30	.07
☐ 14 Rob Picciolo	.60	.25	.06
☐ 15 Fred Stanley	.60	.25	.06

1983 Granny Goose

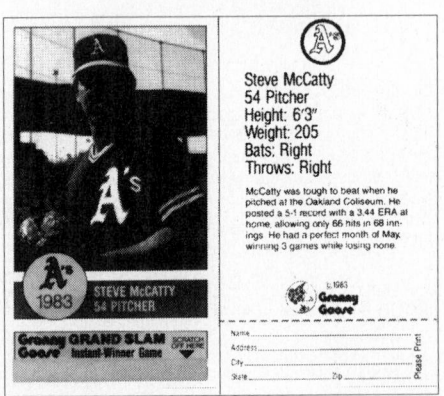

Steve McCatty
54 Pitcher
Height: 6'3"
Weight: 205
Bats: Right
Throws: Right

McCatty was tough to beat when he pitched at the Oakland Coliseum. He posted a 5-1 record with a 3.44 ERA all home, allowing only 66 hits in 68 innings. He had a perfect month of May, winning 3 games while losing none.

© 1983

Granny Goose

1983
STEVE McCATTY
54 PITCHER

Granny Goose GRAND SLAM Instant Winner Game   SCRATCH OFF HERE

Name
Address
City
State   Zip

Please Print

The cards in this 15-card set measure 2 1/2" by 4 1/4". The 1983 Granny Goose Potato Chips set again features Oakland A's players. The cards that were issued in bags of potato chips have a tear off coupon on the bottom with a scratch off section featuring prizes. In addition to their release in bags of potato chips, the Granny Goose cards were also given away to fans attending the Oakland game of July 3, 1983. These give away cards did not contain the coupon on the bottom. Prices listed below are for cards without the detachable tabs that came on the bottom of the cards; cards with tabs intact are valued 50 percent higher than the prices below. The card numbering below is according to uniform number.

	MINT	EXC	G-VG
COMPLETE SET (15)	15.00	6.50	2.15
COMMON PLAYER	.60	.25	.06
☐ 2 Mike Heath	.60	.25	.06
☐ 4 Carney Lansford	2.00	.80	.20
☐ 10 Wayne Gross	.60	.25	.06
☐ 14 Steve Boros MG	.60	.25	.06
☐ 15 Davey Lopes	.90	.40	.09
☐ 16 Mike Davis	.75	.30	.07

☐	17	Mike Norris	.75	.30	.07
☐	21	Dwayne Murphy	.75	.30	.07
☐	22	Rick Langford	.75	.30	.07
☐	27	Matt Keough	.60	.25	.06
☐	31	Tom Underwood	.60	.25	.06
☐	33	Dave Beard	.60	.25	.06
☐	35	Rickey Henderson	9.00	4.00	.90
☐	39	Tom Burgmeier	.60	.25	.06
☐	54	Steve McCatty	.60	.25	.06

1974 Greyhound Heroes of the Base Paths

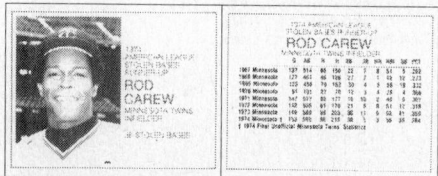

Beginning in 1965, the Greyhound Award for Stolen Bases was given to the champions in each league and the second-place finishers. The 1974 Heroes of the Base Paths pamphlet unfolds to reveal five 4" by 9" panels. The first panel is the title page and features on the back a picture of Maury Wills holding the trophy. The second and third panels have on the fronts the history of the award and major league statistics pertaining to stolen bases, while the backs have an essay on the art of base stealing. Finally, the fourth and fifth panels display six player cards; after perforation, the cards measure approximately 4" by 3". Cards 1-4 feature the AL and NL winners, and the runner-ups for each league, in that order. The player cards display a black and white head shot of the player on the left half, with player information and number of stolen bases on the right half. The backs have statistics. Both sides of the cards are framed by thin brown border stripes. Cards 5-6 display black and white player photos of past winners in the AL and NL respectively. The cards are unnumbered.

		NRMT	VG-E	GOOD
COMPLETE SET (6)		10.00	4.50	1.25
COMMON PLAYER (1-6)		1.25	.50	.12
☐ 1	Bill North	1.25	.50	.12
☐ 2	Lou Brock	3.50	1.50	.35
☐ 3	Rod Carew	3.50	1.50	.35
☐ 4	Davey Lopes	1.25	.50	.12
☐ 5	American League	1.25	.50	.12
	Dagoberto Campaneris			
	Tommy Harper			
	Amos Otis			
	Dave Nelson			
	Billy North			
	Don Buford			
	Fred Patek			
	Rod Carew			
☐ 6	National League	1.50	.60	.15
	Lou Brock			
	Maury Wills			
	Bobby Tolan			
	Joe Morgan			
	Sonny Jackson			
	Jose Cardenal			
	Davey Lopes			

1975 Greyhound Heroes of the Base Paths

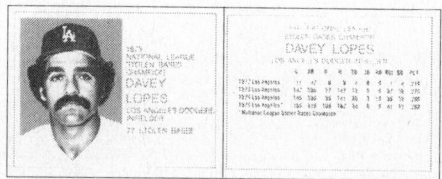

The Greyhound Award for Stolen Bases was given to the champions in each league and the second-place finishers. The 1975 Heroes of the Base Paths pamphlet unfolds to reveal five 4" by 9" panels. The first panel is the title page and features on the back a picture of Maury Wills holding the trophy. The second and third panels have on the fronts the history of the award and major league statistics pertaining to stolen bases, while the backs have an essay on the art of base stealing. Finally, the fourth and fifth panels display six player cards; after perforation, the cards measure 4" by 3". Cards 1-4 feature the AL and NL winners, and the runner-ups for each league, in that order. The player cards display a black and white head shot of the player on the left half, with player information and number of stolen bases on the right half. The backs have statistics. Both sides of the cards are framed by thin powder blue border stripes. Cards 5-6 display black and white player photos of Billy North and Davey Lopes. The cards are unnumbered.

		NRMT	VG-E	GOOD
COMPLETE SET (6)		7.00	3.00	.70
COMMON PLAYER (1-6)		1.00	.40	.10
☐ 1	Mickey Rivers	1.00	.40	.10
☐ 2	Davey Lopes	1.00	.40	.10
☐ 3	Claudell Washington	1.00	.40	.10
☐ 4	Joe Morgan	3.50	1.50	.35
☐ 5	Billy North	1.00	.40	.10
☐ 6	Davey Lopes	1.00	.40	.10

1976 Greyhound Heroes of the Base Paths

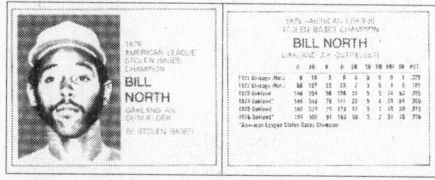

The Greyhound Award for Stolen Bases was given to the champions in each league and the second-place finishers. The 1976 Heroes of the Base Paths pamphlet unfolds to reveal five 4" by 9" panels. The first panel is the title page and features on the back a picture of Maury Wills holding the trophy. The second and third panels have on the fronts the history of the award and major league statistics pertaining to stolen bases, while the backs have an essay on the art of base stealing. Finally, the fourth and fifth panels display six player cards; after perforation, the cards measure approximately 4" by 3". Cards 1-4 feature the AL and NL winners, and the runner-ups for each league, in that order. The player cards display a black and white head shot of the player on the left half, with player information and number of stolen bases on the right half. The backs have statistics. Both sides of the cards are framed by thin powder reddish-brown stripes. Cards 5-6 display black and white player photos of Billy North and Davey Lopes. The cards are unnumbered.

	NRMT	VG-E	GOOD
COMPLETE SET (6)	7.00	3.00	.70
COMMON PLAYER (1-6)	1.00	.40	.10

		NRMT	VG-E	GOOD
☐ 1	Bill North	1.00	.40	.10
☐ 2	Davey Lopes	1.00	.40	.10
☐ 3	Ron LeFlore	1.00	.40	.10
☐ 4	Joe Morgan	3.50	1.50	.35
☐ 5	Billy North	1.00	.40	.10
☐ 6	Davey Lopes	1.00	.40	.10

1991 Griffey Gazette

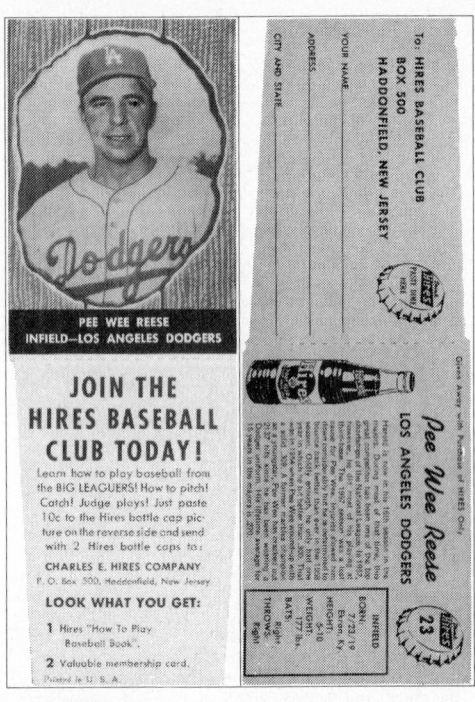

These standard-size (2 1/2" by 3 1/2") cards were issued in honor of Ken Griffey Jr. The high gloss color photos on the fronts have gold borders. The horizontally oriented backs have dark blue print on a light blue background and captions to the front pictures. The cards are numbered on the back.

	MINT	EXC	G-VG
COMPLETE SET (4)	6.00	2.50	.60
COMMON PLAYER (1-4)	2.00	.80	.20

		MINT	EXC	G-VG
☐ 1	Crowd Pleaser	2.00	.80	.20
☐ 2	Holdin' On	2.00	.80	.20
☐ 3	A 24ct. Gold Moment	2.00	.80	.20
☐ 4	Next of Ken	2.00	.80	.20
	Ken Griffey Sr.			
	Ken Griffey Jr.			

1958 Hires

The cards in this 66-card set measure approximately 2 5/16" by 3 1/2" or 2 5/16" by 7" with tabs. The 1958 Hires Root Beer set of numbered, colored cards was issued with detachable coupons as inserts with Hires Root Beer cartons. Cards with the coupon still intact are worth double the prices listed below. The card front picture is surrounded by a wood grain effect which makes it look like the player is seen through a knot hole. The numbering of this set is rather strange in that it begins with 10 and skips 69.

	NRMT	VG-E	GOOD
COMPLETE SET (66)	1350.00	600.00	125.00
COMMON PLAYER (10-76)	10.00	4.50	1.25

		NRMT	VG-E	GOOD
☐ 10	Richie Ashburn	35.00	15.75	5.25
☐ 11	Chico Carrasquel	10.00	4.50	1.25
☐ 12	Dave Philley	10.00	4.50	1.25
☐ 13	Don Newcombe	17.50	7.50	2.25
☐ 14	Wally Post	10.00	4.50	1.25
☐ 15	Rip Repulski	10.00	4.50	1.25
☐ 16	Chico Fernandez	10.00	4.50	1.25
☐ 17	Larry Doby	15.00	6.50	2.15
☐ 18	Hector Brown	10.00	4.50	1.25
☐ 19	Danny O'Connell	10.00	4.50	1.25
☐ 20	Granny Hamner	10.00	4.50	1.25
☐ 21	Dick Groat	13.50	6.00	1.85
☐ 22	Ray Narleski	10.00	4.50	1.25
☐ 23	Pee Wee Reese	60.00	27.00	9.00
☐ 24	Bob Friend	12.00	5.25	1.50
☐ 25	Willie Mays	225.00	100.00	33.00
☐ 26	Bob Nieman	10.00	4.50	1.25
☐ 27	Frank Thomas	10.00	4.50	1.25
☐ 28	Curt Simmons	12.00	5.25	1.50
☐ 29	Stan Lopata	10.00	4.50	1.25
☐ 30	Bob Skinner	10.00	4.50	1.25
☐ 31	Ron Kline	10.00	4.50	1.25
☐ 32	Willie Miranda	10.00	4.50	1.25
☐ 33	Bobby Avila	10.00	4.50	1.25
☐ 34	Clem Labine	12.00	5.25	1.50
☐ 35	Ray Jablonski	10.00	4.50	1.25
☐ 36	Bill Mazeroski	17.50	7.50	2.25
☐ 37	Billy Gardner	10.00	4.50	1.25
☐ 38	Pete Runnels	12.00	5.25	1.50
☐ 39	Jack Sanford	10.00	4.50	1.25
☐ 40	Dave Sisler	10.00	4.50	1.25
☐ 41	Don Zimmer	15.00	6.50	2.15
☐ 42	Johnny Podres	15.00	6.50	2.15
☐ 43	Dick Farrell	10.00	4.50	1.25
☐ 44	Hank Aaron	225.00	100.00	33.00
☐ 45	Bill Virdon	15.00	6.50	2.15
☐ 46	Bobby Thomson	15.00	6.50	2.15
☐ 47	Willard Nixon	10.00	4.50	1.25
☐ 48	Billy Loes	10.00	4.50	1.25
☐ 49	Hank Sauer	12.00	5.25	1.50
☐ 50	Johnny Antonelli	12.00	5.25	1.50
☐ 51	Daryl Spencer	10.00	4.50	1.25
☐ 52	Ken Lehman	10.00	4.50	1.25
☐ 53	Sammy White	10.00	4.50	1.25
☐ 54	Charley Neal	12.00	5.25	1.50
☐ 55	Don Drysdale	50.00	22.50	7.50
☐ 56	Jackie Jensen	17.50	7.50	2.25
☐ 57	Ray Katt	10.00	4.50	1.25
☐ 58	Frank Sullivan	10.00	4.50	1.25

			NRMT	VG-E	GOOD
☐	59	Roy Face	13.50	6.00	1.85
☐	60	Willie Jones	10.00	4.50	1.25
☐	61	Duke Snider	110.00	50.00	16.50
☐	62	Whitey Lockman	10.00	4.50	1.25
☐	63	Gino Cimoli	10.00	4.50	1.25
☐	64	Marv Grissom	10.00	4.50	1.25
☐	65	Gene Baker	10.00	4.50	1.25
☐	66	George Zuverink	10.00	4.50	1.25
☐	67	Ted Kluszewski	20.00	8.50	2.75
☐	68	Jim Busby	10.00	4.50	1.25
☐	69	Not Issued	00.00	.00	.00
☐	70	Curt Barclay	10.00	4.50	1.25
☐	71	Hank Foiles	10.00	4.50	1.25
☐	72	Gene Stephens	10.00	4.50	1.25
☐	73	Al Worthington	10.00	4.50	1.25
☐	74	Al Walker	10.00	4.50	1.25
☐	75	Bob Boyd	10.00	4.50	1.25
☐	76	Al Pilarcik	10.00	4.50	1.25

1958 Hires Test

The cards in this eight-card test set measure approximately 2 5/16" by 3 1/2" or 2 5/16" by 7" with tabs. The 1958 Hires Root Beer test set features unnumbered, color cards. The card front photos are shown on a yellow or orange back ground instead of the wood grain background used in the Hires regular set. The cards contain a detachable coupon just as the regular Hires issue does. Cards were test marketed on a very limited basis in a few cities. Cards with the coupon still intact are especially tough to find and are worth triple the prices in the checklist below. The checklist below is ordered alphabetically.

			NRMT	VG-E	GOOD
		COMPLETE SET (8)	1250.00	500.00	120.00
		COMMON PLAYER (1-8)	120.00	55.00	18.00
☐	1	Johnny Antonelli	150.00	67.50	22.50
☐	2	Jim Busby	120.00	55.00	18.00
☐	3	Chico Fernandez	120.00	55.00	18.00
☐	4	Bob Friend	150.00	67.50	22.50
☐	5	Vern Law	150.00	67.50	22.50
☐	6	Stan Lopata	120.00	55.00	18.00
☐	7	Willie Mays	500.00	225.00	75.00
☐	8	Al Pilarcik	120.00	55.00	18.00

1959 Home Run Derby

This 20-card set was produced in 1959 by American Motors to publicize a TV program. The cards are black and white and blank backed. The cards measure approximately 3 1/8" by 5 1/4". The cards are unnumbered and are ordered alphabetically below for convenience. During 1988, the 19 player cards in this set were publicly reprinted.

ED MATHEWS
MILWAUKEE BRAVES

			NRMT	VG-E	GOOD
		COMPLETE SET (20)	2750.00	1200.00	275.00
		COMMON PLAYER (1-20)	45.00	20.00	6.75
☐	1	Hank Aaron	350.00	160.00	52.50
☐	2	Bob Allison	45.00	20.00	6.75
☐	3	Ernie Banks	150.00	67.50	22.50
☐	4	Ken Boyer	65.00	29.00	9.75
☐	5	Bob Cerv	45.00	20.00	6.75
☐	6	Rocky Colavito	90.00	40.00	13.50
☐	7	Gil Hodges	100.00	45.00	15.00
☐	8	Jackie Jensen	65.00	29.00	9.75
☐	9	Al Kaline	165.00	75.00	22.50
☐	10	Harmon Killebrew	135.00	60.00	20.00
☐	11	Jim Lemon	45.00	20.00	6.75
☐	12	Mickey Mantle	900.00	400.00	135.00
☐	13	Ed Mathews	135.00	60.00	20.00
☐	14	Willie Mays	350.00	160.00	52.50
☐	15	Wally Post	45.00	20.00	6.75
☐	16	Frank Robinson	135.00	60.00	20.00
☐	17	Mark Scott (TV show host)	45.00	20.00	6.75
☐	18	Duke Snider	200.00	90.00	30.00
☐	19	Dick Stuart	45.00	20.00	6.75
☐	20	Gus Triandos	45.00	20.00	6.75

1990 Homers Cookies Pirates

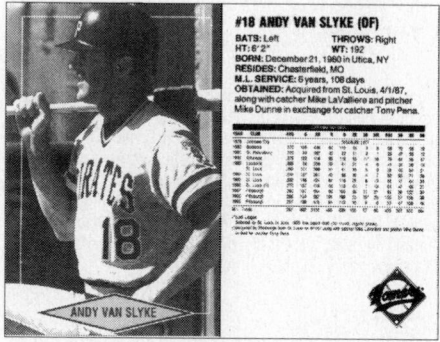

The 1990 Homers Cookies Pittsburgh Pirates set is an attractive 31-card set measuring approximately 4" by 6", used as a giveaway at a Pirates home game. It has been reported that 25,000 of these sets were produced. Four Homers Baseball trivia question cards were also included with the complete set. The fronts are full-color action photos with the backs containing complete statistical information. The set has been checklisted alphabetically below.

	MINT	EXC	G-VG
COMPLETE SET (31)	12.50	5.50	1.65
COMMON PLAYER (1-31)	.35	.15	.03

		MINT	EXC	G-VG
☐	1 Wally Backman	.35	.15	.03
☐	2 Doug Bair	.35	.15	.03
☐	3 Rafael Belliard	.35	.15	.03
☐	4 Jay Bell	.60	.25	.06
☐	5 Barry Bonds	2.00	.80	.20
☐	6 Bobby Bonilla	1.50	.60	.15
☐	7 Sid Bream	.35	.15	.03
☐	8 John Cangelosi	.35	.15	.03
☐	9 Rich Donnelly CO	.35	.15	.03
☐	10 Doug Drabek	.75	.30	.07
☐	11 Billy Hatcher	.45	.18	.04
☐	12 Neal Heaton	.35	.15	.03
☐	13 Jeff King	.60	.25	.06
☐	14 Bob Kipper	.35	.15	.03
☐	15 Randy Kramer	.35	.15	.03
☐	16 Gene Lamont CO	.35	.15	.03
☐	17 Bill Landrum	.35	.15	.03
☐	18 Mike LaValliere	.35	.15	.03
☐	19 Jim Leyland MG	.45	.18	.04
☐	20 Jose Lind	.45	.18	.04
☐	21 Milt May	.35	.15	.03
☐	22 Ray Miller CO	.35	.15	.03
☐	23 Ted Power	.35	.15	.03
☐	24 Gary Redus	.35	.15	.03
☐	25 R.J. Reynolds	.35	.15	.03
☐	26 Tommy Sandt CO	.35	.15	.03
☐	27 Don Slaught	.35	.15	.03
☐	28 Walt Terrell	.35	.15	.03
☐	29 Andy Van Slyke	.75	.30	.07
☐	30 John Smiley	.75	.30	.07
☐	31 Bob Walk	.35	.15	.03

1991 Homers Classics

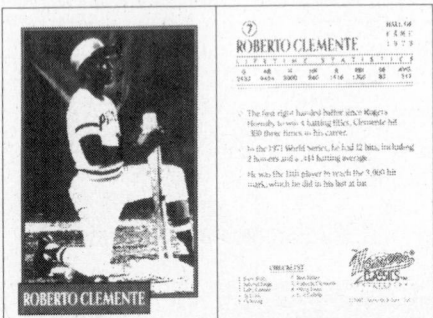

This nine-card set was sponsored by Legend Food Products in honor of Hall of Famers in baseball history. One free card was randomly inserted in each box of Homers Baseball Cookies. The standard-size (2 1/2" by 3 1/2") cards have vintage sepia-toned player photos, with bronze borders on a white card face. The player's name appears in a bronze stripe overlaying the bottom edge of the picture. In black print on white, the back presents lifetime statistics, career highlights, and a checklist for the set. The cards are numbered on the back.

	MINT	EXC	G-VG
COMPLETE SET (9)	7.50	3.25	.75
COMMON PLAYER (1-9)	1.00	.40	.10

		MINT	EXC	G-VG
☐	1 Babe Ruth	2.50	1.00	.25
☐	2 Satchel Paige	1.00	.40	.10
☐	3 Lefty Gomez	1.00	.40	.10
☐	4 Ty Cobb	1.50	.60	.15
☐	5 Cy Young	1.00	.40	.10
☐	6 Bob Feller	1.00	.40	.10
☐	7 Roberto Clemente	1.50	.60	.15
☐	8 Dizzy Dean	1.50	.60	.15
☐	9 Lou Gehrig	1.50	.60	.15

1947 Homogenized Bond

The cards in this 48-card set measure 2 1/4" by 3 1/2". The 1947 W571/D305 Homogenized Bread are sets of unnumbered cards containing 44 baseball players and four boxers. The W571 set exists in two styles. Style one is identical to the D305 set except for the back printing while style two has perforated edges and movie stars depicted on the backs. The second style of W571 cards contains only 13 cards. The four boxers in the checklist below are indicated by BOX. The checklist below is ordered alphabetically. There are 24 cards in the set which were definitely produced in greater supply. These 24 (marked by DP below) are quite a bit more common than the other 24 cards in the set.

	NRMT	VG-E	GOOD
COMPLETE SET	700.00	315.00	105.00
COMMON PLAYER (1-48)	10.00	4.50	1.25
COMMON BOXER	5.00	2.25	.50
COMMON DP BASEBALL	2.00	.80	.20
COMMON DP BOXER	1.50	.60	.15

		NRMT	VG-E	GOOD
☐	1 Rex Barney	10.00	4.50	1.25
☐	2 Larry(Yogi) Berra	100.00	45.00	15.00
☐	3 Ewell Blackwell DP	2.00	.80	.20
☐	4 Lou Boudreau DP	5.00	2.25	.50
☐	5 Ralph Branca	11.00	5.00	1.35
☐	6 Harry Brecheen DP	2.00	.80	.20
☐	7 Primo Carnera BOX DP	1.50	.60	.15
☐	8 Marcel Cerdan BOX	5.00	2.25	.50
☐	9 Dom DiMaggio	12.50	5.50	1.65
☐	10 Joe DiMaggio	165.00	75.00	22.50
☐	11 Bobby Doerr DP	5.00	2.25	.50
☐	12 Bruce Edwards	10.00	4.50	1.25
☐	13 Bob Elliott DP	2.00	.80	.20
☐	14 Del Ennis DP	2.00	.80	.20
☐	15 Bob Feller DP	10.00	4.50	1.25
☐	16 Carl Furillo	15.00	6.50	2.15
☐	17 Joe Gordon DP	2.00	.80	.20
☐	18 Sid Gordon	10.00	4.50	1.25
☐	19 Joe Hatten	10.00	4.50	1.25
☐	20 Gil Hodges	50.00	22.50	7.50
☐	21 Tommy Holmes DP	2.00	.80	.20
☐	22 Larry Jansen	10.00	4.50	1.25
☐	23 Sheldon Jones	10.00	4.50	1.25
☐	24 Edwin Joost	10.00	4.50	1.25
☐	25 Charlie Keller	12.50	5.50	1.65
☐	26 Ken Keltner DP	2.00	.80	.20
☐	27 Buddy Kerr	10.00	4.50	1.25
☐	28 Ralph Kiner DP	7.50	3.25	.75
☐	29 Jake LaMotta BOX	12.50	5.50	1.65
☐	30 John Lindell	10.00	4.50	1.25
☐	31 Whitey Lockman	10.00	4.50	1.25
☐	32 Joe Louis BOX DP	6.00	2.50	.60
☐	33 Willard Marshall	10.00	4.50	1.25
☐	34 Johnny Mize DP	7.50	3.25	.75
☐	35 Stan Musial DP	36.00	16.25	5.50
☐	36 Andy Pafko DP	2.00	.80	.20
☐	37 Johnny Pesky DP	2.00	.80	.20
☐	38 Pee Wee Reese	50.00	22.50	7.50
☐	39 Phil Rizzuto DP	10.00	4.50	1.25

			NRMT	VG-E	GOOD
☐	40	Aaron Robinson DP	2.00	.80	.20
☐	41	Jackie Robinson DP	45.00	20.00	6.75
☐	42	John Sain DP	4.00	1.75	.40
☐	43	Enos Slaughter DP	7.50	3.25	.75
☐	44	Vern Stephens DP	2.00	.80	.20
☐	45	George Tebbetts DP	10.00	4.50	1.25
☐	46	Bobby Thomson	12.50	5.50	1.65
☐	47	Johnny VanderMeer	12.50	5.50	1.65
☐	48	Ted Williams DP	45.00	20.00	6.75

1975 Hostess

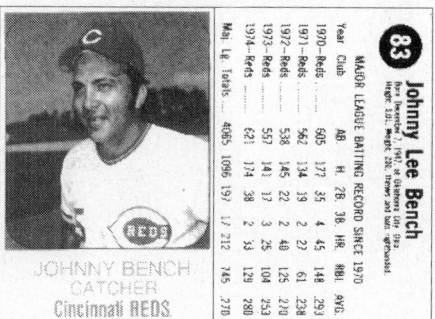

The cards in this 150-card set measure 2 1/4" by 3 1/4" individually or 3 1/4" by 7 1/4" as panels of three. The 1975 Hostess set was issued in panels of three cards each on the backs of family-size packages of Hostess cakes. Card number 125, Bill Madlock, was listed correctly as an infielder and incorrectly as a pitcher. Number 11, Burt Hooton, and number 89, Doug Rader, are spelled two different ways. Some panels are more difficult to find than others as they were issued only on the backs of less popular Hostess products. These scarcer panels are shown with asterisks in the checklist. Although complete panel prices are not explicitly listed, they would generally have a value 25 percent greater than the sum of the values of the individual players on that panel. One of the more interesting cards in the set is that of Robin Yount; Hostess issued one of the few Yount cards available in 1975, his rookie year for cards.

		NRMT	VG-E	GOOD
COMPLETE INDIV.SET		225.00	100.00	33.00
COMMON PLAYER (1-150)		.60	.25	.06

			NRMT	VG-E	GOOD
☐	1	Bob Tolan	.60	.25	.06
☐	2	Cookie Rojas	.60	.25	.06
☐	3	Darrell Evans	.90	.40	.09
☐	4	Sal Bando	.75	.30	.07
☐	5	Joe Morgan	4.50	2.00	.45
☐	6	Mickey Lolich	.90	.40	.09
☐	7	Don Sutton	3.00	1.25	.30
☐	8	Bill Melton	.60	.25	.06
☐	9	Tim Foli	.60	.25	.06
☐	10	Joe Lahoud	.60	.25	.06
☐	11A	Bert Hooten (sic)	1.25	.50	.12
☐	11B	Burt Hooton	1.25	.50	.12
☐	12	Paul Blair	.75	.30	.07
☐	13	Jim Barr	.60	.25	.06
☐	14	Toby Harrah	.75	.30	.07
☐	15	John Milner	.60	.25	.06
☐	16	Ken Holtzman	.75	.30	.07
☐	17	Cesar Cedeno	.75	.30	.07
☐	18	Dwight Evans	1.75	.70	.17
☐	19	Willie McCovey	3.25	1.35	.32
☐	20	Tony Oliva	1.00	.40	.10
☐	21	Manny Sanguillen	.75	.30	.07
☐	22	Mickey Rivers	.75	.30	.07
☐	23	Lou Brock	4.00	1.75	.40
☐	24	Graig Nettles UER (Craig on front)	1.50	.60	.15
☐	25	Jim Wynn	.75	.30	.07
☐	26	George Scott	.75	.30	.07

			NRMT	VG-E	GOOD
☐	27	Greg Luzinski	.90	.40	.09
☐	28	Bert Campaneris	.75	.30	.07
☐	29	Pete Rose	10.00	4.50	1.25
☐	30	Buddy Bell	.90	.40	.09
☐	31	Gary Matthews	.75	.30	.07
☐	32	Freddie Patek	.60	.25	.06
☐	33	Mike Lum	.60	.25	.06
☐	34	Ellie Rodriguez	.60	.25	.06
☐	35	Milt May UER (photo actually Lee May)	.75	.30	.07
☐	36	Willie Horton	.75	.30	.07
☐	37	Dave Winfield	8.00	3.50	.80
☐	38	Tom Grieve	.75	.30	.07
☐	39	Barry Foote	.60	.25	.06
☐	40	Joe Rudi	.75	.30	.07
☐	41	Bake McBride	.60	.25	.06
☐	42	Mike Cuellar	.75	.30	.07
☐	43	Garry Maddox	.75	.30	.07
☐	44	Carlos May	.60	.25	.06
☐	45	Bud Harrelson	.75	.30	.07
☐	46	Dave Chalk	.60	.25	.06
☐	47	Dave Concepcion	.90	.40	.09
☐	48	Carl Yastrzemski	8.00	3.50	.80
☐	49	Steve Garvey	4.50	2.00	.45
☐	50	Amos Otis	.75	.30	.07
☐	51	Rick Reuschel	.75	.30	.07
☐	52	Rollie Fingers	3.00	1.25	.30
☐	53	Bob Watson	.75	.30	.07
☐	54	John Ellis	.60	.25	.06
☐	55	Bob Bailey	.60	.25	.06
☐	56	Rod Carew	6.00	2.50	.60
☐	57	Rich Hebner	.60	.25	.06
☐	58	Nolan Ryan	18.00	7.50	2.50
☐	59	Reggie Smith	.75	.30	.07
☐	60	Joe Coleman	.60	.25	.06
☐	61	Ron Cey	.75	.30	.07
☐	62	Darrell Porter	.60	.25	.06
☐	63	Steve Carlton	5.00	2.25	.50
☐	64	Gene Tenace	.75	.30	.07
☐	65	Jose Cardenal	.60	.25	.06
☐	66	Bill Lee	.75	.30	.07
☐	67	Dave Lopes	.75	.30	.07
☐	68	Wilbur Wood	.75	.30	.07
☐	69	Steve Renko	.60	.25	.06
☐	70	Joe Torre	1.00	.40	.10
☐	71	Ted Sizemore	.60	.25	.06
☐	72	Bobby Grich	.75	.30	.07
☐	73	Chris Speier	.60	.25	.06
☐	74	Bert Blyleven	1.00	.40	.10
☐	75	Tom Seaver	7.50	3.25	.75
☐	76	Nate Colbert	.60	.25	.06
☐	77	Don Kessinger	.75	.30	.07
☐	78	George Medich	.60	.25	.06
☐	79	Andy Messersmith *	.75	.30	.07
☐	80	Robin Yount *	30.00	13.50	4.50
☐	81	Al Oliver *	.90	.40	.09
☐	82	Bill Singer *	.75	.30	.07
☐	83	Johnny Bench *	8.00	3.50	.80
☐	84	Gaylord Perry *	4.00	1.75	.40
☐	85	Dave Kingman *	1.00	.40	.10
☐	86	Ed Herrmann *	.75	.30	.07
☐	87	Ralph Garr *	.75	.30	.07
☐	88	Reggie Jackson *	9.00	4.00	.90
☐	89A	Doug Radar ERR * (sic, Rader)	1.25	.50	.12
☐	89B	Doug Radar COR *	5.00	2.25	.50
☐	90	Elliott Maddox *	.75	.30	.07
☐	91	Bill Russell *	.90	.40	.09
☐	92	John Mayberry *	.90	.40	.09
☐	93	Dave Cash *	.75	.30	.07
☐	94	Jeff Burroughs *	.90	.40	.09
☐	95	Ted Simmons *	1.50	.60	.15
☐	96	Joe Decker *	.75	.30	.07
☐	97	Bill Buckner *	1.00	.40	.10
☐	98	Bobby Darwin *	.75	.30	.07
☐	99	Phil Niekro *	3.50	1.50	.35
☐	100	Jim Sundberg	.90	.40	.09
☐	101	Greg Gross	.60	.25	.06
☐	102	Luis Tiant	.90	.40	.09
☐	103	Glenn Beckert	.60	.25	.06
☐	104	Hal McRae	1.00	.40	.10
☐	105	Mike Jorgensen	.60	.25	.06
☐	106	Mike Hargrove	.90	.40	.09
☐	107	Don Gullett	.75	.30	.07
☐	108	Tito Fuentes	.60	.25	.06
☐	109	John Grubb	.60	.25	.06
☐	110	Jim Kaat	1.25	.50	.12
☐	111	Felix Millan	.60	.25	.06
☐	112	Don Money	.60	.25	.06
☐	113	Rick Monday	.75	.30	.07
☐	114	Dick Bosman	.60	.25	.06
☐	115	Roger Metzger	.60	.25	.06
☐	116	Fergie Jenkins	3.50	1.50	.35

☐ 117	Dusty Baker	.75	.30	.07
☐ 118	Billy Champion *	.75	.30	.07
☐ 119	Bob Gibson *	4.00	1.75	.40
☐ 120	Bill Freehan *	.90	.40	.09
☐ 121	Cesar Geronimo	.60	.25	.06
☐ 122	Jorge Orta	.60	.25	.06
☐ 123	Cleon Jones	.60	.25	.06
☐ 124	Steve Busby	.75	.30	.07
☐ 125A	Bill Madlock ERR (pitcher)	1.50	.60	.15
☐ 125B	Bill Madlock COR (infielder)	1.50	.60	.15
☐ 126	Jim Palmer	4.00	1.75	.40
☐ 127	Tony Perez	2.00	.80	.20
☐ 128	Larry Hisle	.75	.30	.07
☐ 129	Rusty Staub	.90	.40	.09
☐ 130	Hank Aaron *	10.00	4.50	1.25
☐ 131	Rennie Stennett *	.75	.30	.07
☐ 132	Rico Petrocelli *	.75	.30	.07
☐ 133	Mike Schmidt	10.00	4.50	1.25
☐ 134	Sparky Lyle	.90	.40	.09
☐ 135	Willie Stargell	4.00	1.75	.40
☐ 136	Ken Henderson	.60	.25	.06
☐ 137	Willie Montanez	.60	.25	.06
☐ 138	Thurman Munson	6.00	2.50	.60
☐ 139	Richie Zisk	.75	.30	.07
☐ 140	George Hendrick	.75	.30	.07
☐ 141	Bobby Murcer	1.00	.40	.10
☐ 142	Lee May	.75	.30	.07
☐ 143	Carlton Fisk	3.50	1.50	.35
☐ 144	Brooks Robinson	4.00	1.75	.40
☐ 145	Bobby Bonds	1.00	.40	.10
☐ 146	Gary Sutherland	.60	.25	.06
☐ 147	Oscar Gamble	.75	.30	.07
☐ 148	Jim Hunter	3.00	1.25	.30
☐ 149	Tug McGraw	1.00	.40	.10
☐ 150	Dave McNally	.75	.30	.07

☐ 13	Jim Barr	1.00	.40	.10
☐ 14	Toby Harrah	1.00	.40	.10
☐ 15	John Milner	1.00	.40	.10
☐ 16	Ken Holtzman	1.00	.40	.10
☐ 17	Cesar Cedeno	1.25	.50	.12
☐ 18	Dwight Evans	1.75	.70	.17
☐ 19	Willie McCovey	3.25	1.35	.32
☐ 20	Tony Oliva	1.50	.60	.15
☐ 21	Manny Sanguillen	1.00	.40	.10
☐ 22	Mickey Rivers	1.00	.40	.10
☐ 23	Lou Brock	4.00	1.75	.40
☐ 24	Graig Nettles UER (Craig on front)	1.50	.60	.15
☐ 25	Jim Wynn	1.00	.40	.10
☐ 26	George Scott	1.00	.40	.10
☐ 27	Greg Luzinski	1.25	.50	.12
☐ 28	Bert Campaneris	1.00	.40	.10
☐ 29	Pete Rose	10.00	4.50	1.25
☐ 30	Buddy Bell	1.25	.50	.12
☐ 31	Gary Matthews	1.00	.40	.10
☐ 32	Freddie Patek	1.00	.40	.10
☐ 33	Mike Lum	1.00	.40	.10
☐ 34	Ellie Rodriguez	1.00	.40	.10
☐ 35	Milt May UER (Lee May picture)	1.00	.40	.10
☐ 36	Willie Horton	1.25	.50	.12
☐ 40	Joe Rudi	1.25	.50	.12
☐ 43	Garry Maddox	1.00	.40	.10
☐ 46	Dave Chalk	1.00	.40	.10
☐ 49	Steve Garvey	4.50	2.00	.45
☐ 52	Rollie Fingers	3.00	1.25	.30
☐ 58	Nolan Ryan	18.00	7.50	2.50
☐ 61	Ron Cey	1.25	.50	.10
☐ 64	Gene Tenace	1.00	.40	.10
☐ 65	Jose Cardenal	1.00	.40	.10
☐ 67	Dave Lopes	1.25	.50	.12
☐ 68	Wilbur Wood	1.00	.40	.10
☐ 73	Chris Speier	1.00	.40	.10
☐ 77	Don Kessinger	1.25	.50	.12
☐ 79	Andy Messersmith	1.00	.40	.10
☐ 80	Robin Yount	30.00	13.50	4.50
☐ 82	Bill Singer	1.00	.40	.10
☐ 103	Glenn Beckert	1.00	.40	.10
☐ 110	Jim Kaat	1.50	.60	.15
☐ 112	Don Money	1.00	.40	.10
☐ 113	Rick Monday	1.00	.40	.10
☐ 122	Jorge Orta	1.00	.40	.10
☐ 125	Bill Madlock	1.50	.60	.15
☐ 130	Hank Aaron	10.00	4.50	1.25
☐ 136	Ken Henderson	1.00	.40	.10

1975 Hostess Twinkie

The cards in this 60-card set measure 2 1/4" by 3 1/4". The 1975 Hostess Twinkie set was issued on a limited basis in the far western part of the country. The set contains the same numbers as the regular set to number 36; however, the set is skip numbered after number 36. The cards were issued as the backs for 25-cent Twinkies packs. The fronts are indistinguishable from the regular Hostess cards; however the card backs are different in that the Twinkie cards have a thick black bar in the middle of the reverse. One of the more interesting cards in the set is that of Robin Yount; Hostess issued one of the few Yount cards available in 1975, his rookie year for cards.

	NRMT	VG-E	GOOD
COMPLETE SET (60)	110.00	50.00	16.50
COMMON PLAYER	1.00	.40	.10

☐ 1	Bob Tolan	1.00	.40	.10
☐ 2	Cookie Rojas	1.00	.40	.10
☐ 3	Darrell Evans	1.25	.50	.12
☐ 4	Sal Bando	1.25	.50	.12
☐ 5	Joe Morgan	4.50	2.00	.45
☐ 6	Mickey Lolich	1.25	.50	.12
☐ 7	Don Sutton	3.00	1.25	.30
☐ 8	Bill Melton	1.00	.40	.10
☐ 9	Tim Foli	1.00	.40	.10
☐ 10	Joe Lahoud	1.00	.40	.10
☐ 11	Bert Hooten (sic)	1.25	.50	.12
☐ 12	Paul Blair	1.00	.40	.10

1976 Hostess

The cards in this 150-card set measure 2 1/4" by 3 1/4" individually or 3 1/4" by 7 1/4" as panels of three. The 1976 Hostess set contains full-color, numbered cards issued in panels of three cards each on family-size packages of Hostess cakes. Scarcer panels (those only found on less popular Hostess products) are listed in the checklist below with asterisks. Complete panels of three have a value 25 percent more than the sum of the individual cards on the panel. Nine additional numbers (151-159) were apparently planned but never actually issued. These exist as proof cards and are quite scarce, e.g., 151 Ferguson Jenkins, 152 Mike Cuellar, 153 Tom Murphy, 154 Al Cowens, 155 Barry Foote, 156 Steve Carlton, 157 Richie Zisk, 158 Ken Holtzman, and 159 Cliff Johnson. One of the more interesting cards in the set is that of Dennis Eckersley; Hostess issued one of the few Eckersley cards available in 1976, his rookie year for cards.

	NRMT	VG-E	GOOD
COMPLETE INDIV.SET(150)	225.00	100.00	33.00
COMMON PLAYER (1-150)	.60	.25	.06
☐ 1 Fred Lynn	1.25	.50	.12
☐ 2 Joe Morgan	4.00	1.75	.40
☐ 3 Phil Niekro	3.25	1.35	.32
☐ 4 Gaylord Perry	3.25	1.35	.32
☐ 5 Bob Watson	.75	.30	.07
☐ 6 Bill Freehan	.90	.40	.09
☐ 7 Lou Brock	3.75	1.60	.37
☐ 8 Al Fitzmorris	.60	.25	.06
☐ 9 Rennie Stennett	.60	.25	.06
☐ 10 Tony Oliva	1.25	.50	.12
☐ 11 Robin Yount	12.50	5.50	1.65
☐ 12 Rick Manning	.60	.25	.06
☐ 13 Bobby Grich	.75	.30	.07
☐ 14 Terry Forster	.75	.30	.07
☐ 15 Dave Kingman	.90	.40	.09
☐ 16 Thurman Munson	6.00	2.50	.60
☐ 17 Rick Reuschel	.75	.30	.07
☐ 18 Bobby Bonds	1.00	.40	.10
☐ 19 Steve Garvey	4.00	1.75	.40
☐ 20 Vida Blue	.75	.30	.07
☐ 21 Dave Rader	.60	.25	.06
☐ 22 Johnny Bench	6.00	2.50	.60
☐ 23 Luis Tiant	.90	.40	.09
☐ 24 Darrell Evans	.75	.30	.07
☐ 25 Larry Dierker	.60	.25	.06
☐ 26 Willie Horton	.75	.30	.07
☐ 27 John Ellis	.60	.25	.06
☐ 28 Al Cowens	.60	.25	.06
☐ 29 Jerry Reuss	.60	.25	.06
☐ 30 Reggie Smith	.75	.30	.07
☐ 31 Bobby Darwin *	.75	.30	.07
☐ 32 Fritz Peterson *	.75	.30	.07
☐ 33 Rod Carew *	6.00	2.50	.60
☐ 34 Carlos May *	.75	.30	.07
☐ 35 Tom Seaver *	8.00	3.50	.80
☐ 36 Brooks Robinson *	5.00	2.25	.50
☐ 37 Jose Cardenal	.60	.25	.06
☐ 38 Ron Blomberg	.60	.25	.06
☐ 39 Leroy Stanton	.60	.25	.06
☐ 40 Dave Cash	.60	.25	.06
☐ 41 John Montefusco	.75	.30	.07
☐ 42 Bob Tolan	.60	.25	.06
☐ 43 Carl Morton	.60	.25	.06
☐ 44 Rick Burleson	.75	.30	.07
☐ 45 Don Gullett	.75	.30	.07
☐ 46 Vern Ruhle	.60	.25	.06
☐ 47 Cesar Cedeno	.75	.30	.07
☐ 48 Toby Harrah	.75	.30	.07
☐ 49 Willie Stargell	3.75	1.60	.37
☐ 50 Al Hrabosky	.75	.30	.07
☐ 51 Amos Otis	.75	.30	.07
☐ 52 Bud Harrelson	.75	.30	.07
☐ 53 Jim Hughes	.60	.25	.06
☐ 54 George Scott	.75	.30	.07
☐ 55 Mike Vail *	.75	.30	.07
☐ 56 Jim Palmer *	5.00	2.25	.50
☐ 57 Jorge Orta *	.75	.30	.07
☐ 58 Chris Chambliss *	1.00	.40	.10
☐ 59 Dave Chalk *	.75	.30	.07
☐ 60 Ray Burris *	.75	.30	.07
☐ 61 Bert Campaneris *	.90	.40	.09
☐ 62 Gary Carter *	7.50	3.25	.75
☐ 63 Ron Cey *	.90	.40	.09
☐ 64 Carlton Fisk *	3.50	1.50	.35
☐ 65 Marty Perez *	.75	.30	.07
☐ 66 Pete Rose *	10.00	4.50	1.25
☐ 67 Roger Metzger *	.75	.30	.07
☐ 68 Jim Sundberg *	.75	.30	.07
☐ 69 Ron LeFlore *	.90	.40	.09
☐ 70 Ted Sizemore *	.75	.30	.07
☐ 71 Steve Busby *	.90	.40	.09
☐ 72 Manny Sanguillen *	.90	.40	.09
☐ 73 Larry Hisle *	.75	.30	.07
☐ 74 Pete Broberg *	.75	.30	.07
☐ 75 Boog Powell *	1.00	.40	.10
☐ 76 Ken Singleton *	.90	.40	.09
☐ 77 Rich Gossage *	1.50	.60	.15
☐ 78 Jerry Grote *	.75	.30	.07
☐ 79 Nolan Ryan *	18.00	7.50	2.50
☐ 80 Rick Monday *	.90	.40	.09
☐ 81 Graig Nettles *	1.25	.50	.12
☐ 82 Chris Speier *	.60	.25	.06
☐ 83 Dave Winfield *	6.00	2.50	.60
☐ 84 Mike Schmidt *	9.00	4.00	.90
☐ 85 Buzz Capra *	.60	.25	.06
☐ 86 Tony Perez	1.50	.60	.15
☐ 87 Dwight Evans	1.25	.50	.12
☐ 88 Mike Hargrove	.75	.30	.07
☐ 89 Joe Coleman	.60	.25	.06
☐ 90 Greg Gross	.60	.25	.06
☐ 91 John Mayberry	.75	.30	.07
☐ 92 John Candelaria	.75	.30	.07
☐ 93 Bake McBride	.60	.25	.06
☐ 94 Hank Aaron	8.00	3.50	.80
☐ 95 Buddy Bell	.75	.30	.07
☐ 96 Steve Braun	.60	.25	.06
☐ 97 Jon Matlack	.75	.30	.07
☐ 98 Lee May	.75	.30	.07
☐ 99 Wilbur Wood	.75	.30	.07
☐ 100 Bill Madlock	.90	.40	.09
☐ 101 Frank Tanana	.75	.30	.07
☐ 102 Mickey Rivers	.60	.25	.06
☐ 103 Mike Ivie	.60	.25	.06
☐ 104 Rollie Fingers	3.00	1.25	.30
☐ 105 Dave Lopes	.75	.30	.07
☐ 106 George Foster	1.25	.50	.12
☐ 107 Denny Doyle	.60	.25	.06
☐ 108 Earl Williams	.60	.25	.06
☐ 109 Tom Veryzer	.60	.25	.06
☐ 110 J.R. Richard	.75	.30	.07
☐ 111 Jeff Burroughs	.75	.30	.07
☐ 112 Al Oliver	.90	.40	.09
☐ 113 Ted Simmons	1.00	.40	.10
☐ 114 George Brett	12.50	5.50	1.65
☐ 115 Frank Duffy	.60	.25	.06
☐ 116 Bert Blyleven	1.00	.40	.10
☐ 117 Darrell Porter	.75	.30	.07
☐ 118 Don Baylor	1.00	.40	.10
☐ 119 Bucky Dent	.90	.40	.09
☐ 120 Felix Millan	.60	.25	.06
☐ 121 Mike Cuellar	.75	.30	.07
☐ 122 Gene Tenace	.75	.30	.07
☐ 123 Bobby Murcer	.90	.40	.09
☐ 124 Willie McCovey	3.00	1.25	.30
☐ 125 Greg Luzinski	.90	.40	.09
☐ 126 Larry Parrish	.75	.30	.07
☐ 127 Jim Rice	3.50	1.50	.35
☐ 128 Dave Concepcion	.90	.40	.09
☐ 129 Jim Wynn	.75	.30	.07
☐ 130 Tom Grieve	.75	.30	.07
☐ 131 Mike Cosgrove	.60	.25	.06
☐ 132 Dan Meyer	.60	.25	.06
☐ 133 Dave Parker	3.00	1.25	.30
☐ 134 Don Kessinger	.90	.40	.09
☐ 135 Hal McRae	.90	.40	.09
☐ 136 Don Money	.60	.25	.06
☐ 137 Dennis Eckersley	7.50	3.25	.75
☐ 138 Fergie Jenkins	3.50	1.50	.35
☐ 139 Mike Torrez	.75	.30	.07
☐ 140 Jerry Morales	.60	.25	.06
☐ 141 Jim Hunter	3.00	1.25	.30
☐ 142 Gary Matthews	.75	.30	.07
☐ 143 Randy Jones	.75	.30	.07
☐ 144 Mike Jorgensen	.60	.25	.06
☐ 145 Larry Bowa	.90	.40	.09
☐ 146 Reggie Jackson	7.00	3.00	.70
☐ 147 Steve Yeager	.60	.25	.06
☐ 148 Dave May	.60	.25	.06
☐ 149 Carl Yastrzemski	7.00	3.00	.70
☐ 150 Cesar Geronimo	.60	.25	.06

1976 Hostess Twinkie

The cards in this 60-card set measure 2 1/4" by 3 1/4". The 1976 Hostess Twinkies set contains the first 60 cards of the 1976 Hostess set. These cards were issued as backs on 25-cent Twinkie packages as in the 1975 Twinkies set. The fronts are indistinguishable from the regular Hostess cards; however the card backs are different in that the Twinkie cards have a thick black bar in the middle of the reverse.

	NRMT	VG-E	GOOD
COMPLETE SET (60)	110.00	50.00	16.50
COMMON PLAYER (1-60)	1.00	.40	.10
☐ 1 Fred Lynn	1.25	.50	.12

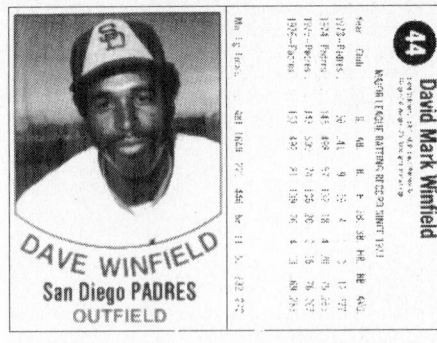

☐ 2	Joe Morgan	4.00	1.75	.40
☐ 3	Phil Niekro	3.25	1.35	.32
☐ 4	Gaylord Perry	3.25	1.35	.32
☐ 5	Bob Watson	1.00	.40	.10
☐ 6	Bill Freehan	1.25	.50	.12
☐ 7	Lou Brock	3.75	1.60	.37
☐ 8	Al Fitzmorris	1.00	.40	.10
☐ 9	Rennie Stennett	1.00	.40	.10
☐ 10	Tony Oliva	1.50	.60	.15
☐ 11	Robin Yount	12.50	5.50	1.65
☐ 12	Rick Manning	1.00	.40	.10
☐ 13	Bobby Grich	1.25	.50	.12
☐ 14	Terry Forster	1.00	.40	.10
☐ 15	Dave Kingman	1.25	.50	.12
☐ 16	Thurman Munson	6.00	2.50	.60
☐ 17	Rick Reuschel	1.25	.50	.12
☐ 18	Bobby Bonds	1.25	.50	.12
☐ 19	Steve Garvey	4.00	1.75	.40
☐ 20	Vida Blue	1.25	.50	.12
☐ 21	Dave Rader	1.00	.40	.10
☐ 22	Johnny Bench	6.00	2.50	.60
☐ 23	Luis Tiant	1.25	.50	.12
☐ 24	Darrell Evans	1.25	.50	.12
☐ 25	Larry Dierker	1.00	.40	.10
☐ 26	Willie Horton	1.25	.50	.12
☐ 27	John Ellis	1.00	.40	.10
☐ 28	Al Cowens	1.00	.40	.10
☐ 29	Jerry Reuss	1.00	.40	.10
☐ 30	Reggie Smith	1.25	.50	.12
☐ 31	Bobby Darwin	1.00	.40	.10
☐ 32	Fritz Peterson	1.00	.40	.10
☐ 33	Rod Carew	6.00	2.50	.60
☐ 34	Carlos May	1.00	.40	.10
☐ 35	Tom Seaver	8.00	3.50	.80
☐ 36	Brooks Robinson	5.00	2.25	.50
☐ 37	Jose Cardenal	1.00	.40	.10
☐ 38	Ron Blomberg	1.00	.40	.10
☐ 39	Leroy Stanton	1.00	.40	.10
☐ 40	Dave Cash	1.00	.40	.10
☐ 41	John Montefusco	1.00	.40	.10
☐ 42	Bob Tolan	1.00	.40	.10
☐ 43	Carl Morton	1.00	.40	.10
☐ 44	Rick Burleson	1.25	.50	.12
☐ 45	Don Gullett	1.00	.40	.10
☐ 46	Vern Ruhle	1.00	.40	.10
☐ 47	Cesar Cedeno	1.25	.50	.12
☐ 48	Toby Harrah	1.00	.40	.10
☐ 49	Willie Stargell	3.75	1.60	.37
☐ 50	Al Hrabosky	1.00	.40	.10
☐ 51	Amos Otis	1.25	.50	.12
☐ 52	Bud Harrelson	1.25	.50	.12
☐ 53	Jim Hughes	1.00	.40	.10
☐ 54	George Scott	1.00	.40	.10
☐ 55	Mike Vail	1.00	.40	.10
☐ 56	Jim Palmer	5.00	2.25	.50
☐ 57	Jorge Orta	1.00	.40	.10
☐ 58	Chris Chambliss	1.25	.50	.12
☐ 59	Dave Chalk	1.00	.40	.10
☐ 60	Ray Burris	1.00	.40	.10

1977 Hostess

The cards in this 150-card set measure 2 1/4" by 3 1/4" individually or 3 1/4" by 7 1/4" as panels of three. The 1977 Hostess set contains full-color, numbered cards issued in panels of three cards each with Hostess family-size cake products. Scarcer panels are listed in the checklist below with

asterisks. Although complete panel prices are not explicitly listed below, they would generally have a value 25 percent greater than the sum of the individual players on the panel. There were 10 additional cards proofed, but not produced or distributed; they are 151 Ed Kranepool, 152 Ross Grimsley, 153 Ken Brett, 154 Rowland Office, 155 Rick Wise, 156 Paul Splittorff, 157 Gerald Augustine, 158 Ken Forsch, 159 Jerry Reuss (Reuss is also number 119 in the set), and 160 Nelson Briles. There is also a complete variation set that was available one card per Twinkie package. Common cards in this Twinkie set are worth double the prices listed below, although the stars are only worth about 20 percent more. The Twinkie cards are distinguished by the thick printing bar or band printed on the card backs just below the statistics.

		NRMT	VG-E	GOOD
COMPLETE IND.SET (150)		225.00	100.00	33.00
COMMON PLAYER (1-150)		.60	.25	.06
☐ 1	Jim Palmer	4.00	1.75	.40
☐ 2	Joe Morgan	4.00	1.75	.40
☐ 3	Reggie Jackson	7.00	3.00	.70
☐ 4	Carl Yastrzemski	7.00	3.00	.70
☐ 5	Thurman Munson	5.00	2.25	.50
☐ 6	Johnny Bench	6.00	2.50	.60
☐ 7	Tom Seaver	7.00	3.00	.70
☐ 8	Pete Rose	9.00	4.00	.90
☐ 9	Rod Carew	5.50	2.50	.55
☐ 10	Luis Tiant	.90	.40	.09
☐ 11	Phil Garner	.75	.30	.07
☐ 12	Sixto Lezcano	.60	.25	.06
☐ 13	Mike Torrez	.60	.25	.06
☐ 14	Dave Lopes	.75	.30	.07
☐ 15	Doug DeCinces	.75	.30	.07
☐ 16	Jim Spencer	.60	.25	.06
☐ 17	Hal McRae	.90	.40	.09
☐ 18	Mike Hargrove	.75	.30	.07
☐ 19	Willie Montanez *	.75	.30	.07
☐ 20	Roger Metzger *	.75	.30	.07
☐ 21	Dwight Evans *	1.50	.60	.15
☐ 22	Steve Rogers *	.75	.30	.07
☐ 23	Jim Rice *	3.50	1.50	.35
☐ 24	Pete Falcone *	.75	.30	.07
☐ 25	Greg Luzinski *	1.00	.40	.10
☐ 26	Randy Jones *	.90	.40	.09
☐ 27	Willie Stargell *	4.00	1.75	.40
☐ 28	John Hiller *	.90	.40	.09
☐ 29	Bobby Murcer *	.90	.40	.09
☐ 30	Rick Monday *	.90	.40	.09
☐ 31	John Montefusco *	.75	.30	.07
☐ 32	Lou Brock *	4.00	1.75	.40
☐ 33	Bill North *	.75	.30	.07
☐ 34	Robin Yount *	10.00	4.50	1.25
☐ 35	Steve Garvey *	5.00	2.25	.50
☐ 36	George Brett *	10.00	4.50	1.25
☐ 37	Toby Harrah *	.90	.40	.09
☐ 38	Jerry Royster *	.75	.30	.07
☐ 39	Bob Watson *	.90	.40	.09
☐ 40	George Foster	1.00	.40	.10
☐ 41	Gary Carter	3.75	1.60	.37
☐ 42	John Denny	.75	.30	.07
☐ 43	Mike Schmidt	8.00	3.50	.80
☐ 44	Dave Winfield	5.00	2.25	.50
☐ 45	Al Oliver	.90	.40	.09
☐ 46	Mark Fidrych	1.00	.40	.10
☐ 47	Larry Herndon	.60	.25	.06
☐ 48	Dave Goltz	.60	.25	.06

☐ 49 Jerry Morales	.60	.25	.06
☐ 50 Ron LeFlore	.75	.30	.07
☐ 51 Fred Lynn	1.25	.50	.12
☐ 52 Vida Blue	.75	.30	.07
☐ 53 Rick Manning	.60	.25	.06
☐ 54 Bill Buckner	.90	.40	.09
☐ 55 Lee May	.75	.30	.07
☐ 56 John Mayberry	.75	.30	.07
☐ 57 Darrell Chaney	.60	.25	.06
☐ 58 Cesar Cedeno	.75	.30	.07
☐ 59 Ken Griffey	1.25	.50	.12
☐ 60 Dave Kingman	.90	.40	.09
☐ 61 Ted Simmons	1.25	.50	.12
☐ 62 Larry Bowa	.75	.30	.07
☐ 63 Frank Tanana	.75	.30	.07
☐ 64 Jason Thompson	.75	.30	.07
☐ 65 Ken Brett	.60	.25	.06
☐ 66 Roy Smalley	.75	.30	.07
☐ 67 Ray Burris	.60	.25	.06
☐ 68 Rick Burleson	.75	.30	.07
☐ 69 Buddy Bell	.90	.40	.09
☐ 70 Don Sutton	2.50	1.00	.25
☐ 71 Mark Belanger	.75	.30	.07
☐ 72 Dennis Leonard	.75	.30	.07
☐ 73 Gaylord Perry	3.00	1.25	.30
☐ 74 Dick Ruthven	.60	.25	.06
☐ 75 Jose Cruz	.75	.30	.07
☐ 76 Cesar Geronimo	.60	.25	.06
☐ 77 Jerry Koosman	.90	.40	.09
☐ 78 Garry Templeton	.75	.30	.07
☐ 79 Jim Hunter	3.00	1.25	.30
☐ 80 John Candelaria	.75	.30	.07
☐ 81 Nolan Ryan	18.00	7.50	2.50
☐ 82 Rusty Staub	.90	.40	.09
☐ 83 Jim Barr	.60	.25	.06
☐ 84 Butch Wynegar	.60	.25	.06
☐ 85 Jose Cardenal	.60	.25	.06
☐ 86 Claudell Washington	.75	.30	.07
☐ 87 Bill Travers	.60	.25	.06
☐ 88 Rick Waits	.60	.25	.06
☐ 89 Ron Cey	.90	.40	.09
☐ 90 Al Bumbry	.60	.25	.06
☐ 91 Bucky Dent	.90	.40	.09
☐ 92 Amos Otis	.75	.30	.07
☐ 93 Tom Grieve	.60	.25	.06
☐ 94 Enos Cabell	.60	.25	.06
☐ 95 Dave Concepcion	.90	.40	.09
☐ 96 Felix Millan	.60	.25	.06
☐ 97 Bake McBride	.60	.25	.06
☐ 98 Chris Chambliss	.75	.30	.07
☐ 99 Butch Metzger	.60	.25	.06
☐ 100 Rennie Stennett	.60	.25	.06
☐ 101 Dave Roberts	.60	.25	.06
☐ 102 Lyman Bostock	.75	.30	.07
☐ 103 Rick Reuschel	.75	.30	.07
☐ 104 Carlton Fisk	3.00	1.25	.30
☐ 105 Jim Slaton	.60	.25	.06
☐ 106 Dennis Eckersley	2.50	1.00	.25
☐ 107 Ken Singleton	.75	.30	.07
☐ 108 Ralph Garr	.75	.30	.07
☐ 109 Freddie Patek *	.75	.30	.07
☐ 110 Jim Sundberg *	.75	.30	.07
☐ 111 Phil Niekro *	3.00	1.25	.30
☐ 112 J.R. Richard *	.75	.30	.07
☐ 113 Gary Nolan *	.75	.30	.07
☐ 114 Jon Matlack *	.75	.30	.07
☐ 115 Keith Hernandez *	4.00	1.75	.40
☐ 116 Graig Nettles *	1.00	.40	.10
☐ 117 Steve Carlton *	5.00	2.25	.50
☐ 118 Bill Madlock *	1.25	.50	.12
☐ 119 Jerry Reuss *	.75	.30	.07
☐ 120 Aurelio Rodriguez *	.75	.30	.07
☐ 121 Dan Ford *	.75	.30	.07
☐ 122 Ray Fosse *	.75	.30	.07
☐ 123 George Hendrick *	.75	.30	.07
☐ 124 Alan Ashby	.60	.25	.06
☐ 125 Joe Lis	.60	.25	.06
☐ 126 Sal Bando	.75	.30	.07
☐ 127 Richie Zisk	.75	.30	.07
☐ 128 Rich Gossage	1.00	.40	.10
☐ 129 Don Baylor	.90	.40	.09
☐ 130 Dave McKay	.60	.25	.06
☐ 131 Bob Grich	.75	.30	.07
☐ 132 Dave Pagan	.60	.25	.06
☐ 133 Dave Cash	.60	.25	.06
☐ 134 Steve Braun	.60	.25	.06
☐ 135 Dan Meyer	.60	.25	.06
☐ 136 Bill Stein	.60	.25	.06
☐ 137 Rollie Fingers	3.00	1.25	.30
☐ 138 Brian Downing	.75	.30	.07
☐ 139 Bill Singer	.60	.25	.06
☐ 140 Doyle Alexander	.75	.30	.07
☐ 141 Gene Tenace	.75	.30	.07
☐ 142 Gary Matthews	.75	.30	.07

☐ 143 Don Gullett	.75	.30	.07
☐ 144 Wayne Garland	.60	.25	.06
☐ 145 Pete Broberg	.60	.25	.06
☐ 146 Joe Rudi	.75	.30	.07
☐ 147 Glenn Abbott	.60	.25	.06
☐ 148 George Scott	.75	.30	.07
☐ 149 Bert Campaneris	.75	.30	.07
☐ 150 Andy Messersmith	.75	.30	.07

1978 Hostess

The cards in this 150-card set measure 2 1/4" by 3 1/4" individually or 3 1/4" by 7 1/4" as panels of three. The 1978 Hostess set contains full-color, numbered cards issued in panels of three cards each on family packages of Hostess cake products. Scarcer panels are listed in the checklist with asterisks. The 1978 Hostess panels are considered by some collectors to be somewhat more difficult to obtain than Hostess panels of other years. Although complete panel prices are not explicitly listed below, they would generally have a value 25 percent greater than the sum of the individual players on the panel. There is additional interest in Eddie Murray number 31, since this card corresponds to his "rookie" year in cards.

	NRMT	VG-E	GOOD
COMPLETE IND.SET (150)	225.00	100.00	33.00
COMMON PLAYER (1-150)	.60	.25	.06
☐ 1 Butch Hobson	1.00	.40	.10
☐ 2 George Foster	1.25	.50	.12
☐ 3 Bob Forsch	.75	.30	.07
☐ 4 Tony Perez	1.50	.60	.15
☐ 5 Bruce Sutter	1.25	.50	.12
☐ 6 Hal McRae	.90	.40	.09
☐ 7 Tommy John	1.50	.60	.15
☐ 8 Greg Luzinski	.90	.40	.09
☐ 9 Enos Cabell	.60	.25	.06
☐ 10 Doug DeCinces	.75	.30	.07
☐ 11 Willie Stargell	3.25	1.35	.32
☐ 12 Ed Halicki	.60	.25	.06
☐ 13 Larry Hisle	.60	.25	.06
☐ 14 Jim Slaton	.60	.25	.06
☐ 15 Buddy Bell	.75	.30	.07
☐ 16 Earl Williams	.60	.25	.06
☐ 17 Glenn Abbott	.60	.25	.06
☐ 18 Dan Ford	.60	.25	.06
☐ 19 Gary Matthews	.75	.30	.07
☐ 20 Eric Soderholm	.60	.25	.06
☐ 21 Bump Wills	.60	.25	.06
☐ 22 Keith Hernandez	2.50	1.00	.25
☐ 23 Dave Cash	.60	.25	.06
☐ 24 George Scott	.75	.30	.07
☐ 25 Ron Guidry	2.00	.80	.20
☐ 26 Dave Kingman	.90	.40	.09
☐ 27 George Brett	8.50	3.75	.85
☐ 28 Bob Watson *	.75	.30	.07
☐ 29 Bob Boone *	1.25	.50	.12
☐ 30 Reggie Smith *	.90	.40	.09
☐ 31 Eddie Murray *	21.00	9.00	3.00
☐ 32 Gary Lavelle *	.75	.30	.07
☐ 33 Rennie Stennett *	.75	.30	.07
☐ 34 Duane Kuiper *	.75	.30	.07

☐ 35 Sixto Lezcano *	.75	.30	.07
☐ 36 Dave Rozema *	.75	.30	.07
☐ 37 Butch Wynegar *	.75	.30	.07
☐ 38 Mitchell Page *	.75	.30	.07
☐ 39 Bill Stein *	.75	.30	.07
☐ 40 Elliott Maddox	.60	.25	.06
☐ 41 Mike Hargrove	.75	.30	.07
☐ 42 Bobby Bonds	1.00	.40	.10
☐ 43 Garry Templeton	.75	.30	.07
☐ 44 Johnny Bench	5.50	2.50	.55
☐ 45 Jim Rice	3.00	1.25	.30
☐ 46 Bill Buckner	.90	.40	.09
☐ 47 Reggie Jackson	6.00	2.50	.60
☐ 48 Freddie Patek	.60	.25	.06
☐ 49 Steve Carlton	3.75	1.60	.37
☐ 50 Cesar Cedeno	.75	.30	.07
☐ 51 Steve Yeager	.60	.25	.06
☐ 52 Phil Garner	.75	.30	.07
☐ 53 Lee May	.75	.30	.07
☐ 54 Darrell Evans	.75	.30	.07
☐ 55 Steve Kemp	.60	.25	.06
☐ 56 Dusty Baker	.75	.30	.07
☐ 57 Ray Fosse	.60	.25	.06
☐ 58 Manny Sanguillen	.75	.30	.07
☐ 59 Tom Johnson	.60	.25	.06
☐ 60 Lee Stanton	.60	.25	.06
☐ 61 Jeff Burroughs	.60	.25	.06
☐ 62 Bobby Grich	.75	.30	.07
☐ 63 Dave Winfield	4.50	2.00	.45
☐ 64 Dan Driessen	.75	.30	.07
☐ 65 Ted Simmons	1.00	.40	.10
☐ 66 Jerry Remy	.60	.25	.06
☐ 67 Al Cowens	.75	.30	.07
☐ 68 Sparky Lyle	.90	.40	.09
☐ 69 Manny Trillo	.75	.30	.07
☐ 70 Don Sutton	2.50	1.00	.25
☐ 71 Larry Bowa	.90	.40	.09
☐ 72 Jose Cruz	.75	.30	.07
☐ 73 Willie McCovey	3.00	1.25	.30
☐ 74 Bert Blyleven	1.00	.40	.10
☐ 75 Ken Singleton	.75	.30	.07
☐ 76 Bill North	.60	.25	.06
☐ 77 Jason Thompson	.60	.25	.06
☐ 78 Dennis Eckersley	2.00	.80	.20
☐ 79 Jim Sundberg	.75	.30	.07
☐ 80 Jerry Koosman	.90	.40	.09
☐ 81 Bruce Bochte	.60	.25	.06
☐ 82 George Hendrick	.60	.25	.06
☐ 83 Nolan Ryan	18.00	7.50	2.50
☐ 84 Roy Howell	.60	.25	.06
☐ 85 Roger Metzger	.60	.25	.06
☐ 86 Doc Medich	.60	.25	.06
☐ 87 Joe Morgan	3.50	1.50	.35
☐ 88 Dennis Leonard	.75	.30	.07
☐ 89 Willie Randolph	.90	.40	.09
☐ 90 Bobby Murcer	.90	.40	.09
☐ 91 Rick Manning	.60	.25	.06
☐ 92 J.R. Richard	.75	.30	.07
☐ 93 Ron Cey	.75	.30	.07
☐ 94 Sal Bando	.75	.30	.07
☐ 95 Ron LeFlore	.75	.30	.07
☐ 96 Dave Goltz	.60	.25	.06
☐ 97 Dan Meyer	.60	.25	.06
☐ 98 Chris Chambliss	.75	.30	.07
☐ 99 Biff Pocoroba	.60	.25	.06
☐ 100 Oscar Gamble	.75	.30	.07
☐ 101 Frank Tanana	.75	.30	.07
☐ 102 Len Randle	.60	.25	.06
☐ 103 Tommy Hutton	.60	.25	.06
☐ 104 John Candelaria	.75	.30	.07
☐ 105 Jorge Orta	.60	.25	.06
☐ 106 Ken Reitz	.60	.25	.06
☐ 107 Bill Campbell	.60	.25	.06
☐ 108 Dave Concepcion	.90	.40	.09
☐ 109 Joe Ferguson	.60	.25	.06
☐ 110 Mickey Rivers	.75	.30	.07
☐ 111 Paul Splittorff	.75	.30	.07
☐ 112 Dave Lopes	.75	.30	.07
☐ 113 Mike Schmidt	8.50	3.75	.85
☐ 114 Joe Rudi	.75	.30	.07
☐ 115 Milt May	.60	.25	.06
☐ 116 Jim Palmer	3.75	1.60	.37
☐ 117 Bill Madlock	1.00	.40	.10
☐ 118 Roy Smalley	.75	.30	.07
☐ 119 Cecil Cooper	1.25	.50	.12
☐ 120 Rick Langford	.75	.30	.07
☐ 121 Ruppert Jones	.75	.30	.07
☐ 122 Phil Niekro	2.00	.80	.20
☐ 123 Toby Harrah	.75	.30	.07
☐ 124 Chet Lemon	.75	.30	.07
☐ 125 Gene Tenace	.75	.30	.07
☐ 126 Steve Henderson	.60	.25	.06
☐ 127 Mike Torrez	.60	.25	.06
☐ 128 Pete Rose	9.00	4.00	.90

☐ 129 John Denny	.75	.30	.07
☐ 130 Darrell Porter	.75	.30	.07
☐ 131 Rick Reuschel	.75	.30	.07
☐ 132 Graig Nettles	.90	.40	.09
☐ 133 Garry Maddox	.60	.25	.06
☐ 134 Mike Flanagan	.75	.30	.07
☐ 135 Dave Parker	2.50	1.00	.25
☐ 136 Terry Whitfield	.60	.25	.06
☐ 137 Wayne Garland	.60	.25	.06
☐ 138 Robin Yount	8.50	3.75	.85
☐ 139 Gaylord Perry	2.50	1.00	.25
☐ 140 Rod Carew	5.00	2.25	.50
☐ 141 Wayne Gross	.60	.25	.06
☐ 142 Barry Bonnell	.60	.25	.06
☐ 143 Willie Montanez	.60	.25	.06
☐ 144 Rollie Fingers	2.75	1.10	.27
☐ 145 Lyman Bostock	.75	.30	.07
☐ 146 Gary Carter	3.75	1.60	.37
☐ 147 Ron Blomberg	.60	.25	.06
☐ 148 Bob Bailor	.60	.25	.06
☐ 149 Tom Seaver	6.50	2.75	.65
☐ 150 Thurman Munson	5.00	2.25	.50

1979 Hostess

The cards in this 150-card set measure approximately 2 1/4" by 3 1/4" individually or 3 1/4" by 7 1/4" as panels of three. The 1979 Hostess set contains full color, numbered cards issued in panels of three cards each on the backs of family sized Hostess cake products. Scarcer panels are listed in the checklist below with asterisks. Although complete panel prices are not explicitly listed below they would generally have a value 25 percent greater than the sum of the individual players on the panel. There is additional interest in Ozzie Smith number 102 since this card corresponds to his rookie year in cards.

	NRMT	VG-E	GOOD
COMPLETE INDIV. SET	225.00	100.00	33.00
COMMON PLAYER (1-150)	.60	.25	.06
☐ 1 John Denny	.75	.30	.07
☐ 2 Jim Rice	3.00	1.25	.30
☐ 3 Doug Bair	.60	.25	.06
☐ 4 Darrell Porter	.60	.25	.06
☐ 5 Ross Grimsley	.60	.25	.06
☐ 6 Bobby Murcer	.90	.40	.09
☐ 7 Lee Mazzilli	.60	.25	.06
☐ 8 Steve Garvey	3.75	1.60	.37
☐ 9 Mike Schmidt	8.00	3.50	.80
☐ 10 Terry Whitfield	.60	.25	.06
☐ 11 Jim Palmer	3.50	1.50	.35
☐ 12 Omar Moreno	.60	.25	.06
☐ 13 Duane Kuiper	.60	.25	.06
☐ 14 Mike Caldwell	.60	.25	.06
☐ 15 Steve Kemp	.60	.25	.06
☐ 16 Dave Goltz	.60	.25	.06
☐ 17 Mitchell Page	.60	.25	.06
☐ 18 Bill Stein	.60	.25	.06
☐ 19 Gene Tenace	.75	.30	.07
☐ 20 Jeff Burroughs	.60	.25	.06
☐ 21 Francisco Barrios	.60	.25	.06
☐ 22 Mike Torrez	.60	.25	.06
☐ 23 Ken Reitz	.60	.25	.06
☐ 24 Gary Carter	3.25	1.35	.32

		MINT	EXC	G-VG
☐ 25	Al Hrabosky	.75	.30	.07
☐ 26	Thurman Munson	4.50	2.00	.45
☐ 27	Bill Buckner	.90	.40	.09
☐ 28	Ron Cey *	.90	.40	.09
☐ 29	J.R. Richard *	.75	.30	.07
☐ 30	Greg Luzinski *	1.00	.40	.10
☐ 31	Ed Ott *	.75	.30	.07
☐ 32	Dennis Martinez *	1.25	.50	.12
☐ 33	Darrell Evans *	.90	.40	.09
☐ 34	Ron LeFlore	.75	.30	.07
☐ 35	Rick Waits	.60	.25	.06
☐ 36	Cecil Cooper	1.00	.40	.10
☐ 37	Leon Roberts	.60	.25	.06
☐ 38	Rod Carew	5.00	2.25	.50
☐ 39	John Henry Johnson	.60	.25	.06
☐ 40	Chet Lemon	.75	.30	.07
☐ 41	Craig Swan	.60	.25	.06
☐ 42	Gary Matthews	.75	.30	.07
☐ 43	Lamar Johnson	.60	.25	.06
☐ 44	Ted Simmons	1.00	.40	.10
☐ 45	Ken Griffey	1.25	.50	.12
☐ 46	Fred Patek	.60	.25	.06
☐ 47	Frank Tanana	.75	.30	.07
☐ 48	Goose Gossage	1.25	.50	.12
☐ 49	Burt Hooton	.60	.25	.06
☐ 50	Ellis Valentine	.60	.25	.06
☐ 51	Ken Forsch	.60	.25	.06
☐ 52	Bob Knepper	.60	.25	.06
☐ 53	Dave Parker	2.50	1.00	.25
☐ 54	Doug DeCinces	.75	.30	.07
☐ 55	Robin Yount	7.00	3.00	.70
☐ 56	Rusty Staub	.90	.40	.09
☐ 57	Gary Alexander	.60	.25	.06
☐ 58	Julio Cruz	.60	.25	.06
☐ 59	Matt Keough	.60	.25	.06
☐ 60	Roy Smalley	.60	.25	.06
☐ 61	Joe Morgan	3.25	1.35	.32
☐ 62	Phil Niekro	2.25	.90	.22
☐ 63	Don Baylor	.90	.40	.09
☐ 64	Dwight Evans	1.25	.50	.12
☐ 65	Tom Seaver	6.00	2.50	.60
☐ 66	George Hendrick	.60	.25	.06
☐ 67	Rick Reuschel	.75	.30	.07
☐ 68	George Brett	7.00	3.00	.70
☐ 69	Lou Piniella	1.00	.40	.10
☐ 70	Enos Cabell	.60	.25	.06
☐ 71	Steve Carlton	3.75	1.60	.37
☐ 72	Reggie Smith	.75	.30	.07
☐ 73	Rick Dempsey *	.75	.30	.07
☐ 74	Vida Blue *	.90	.40	.09
☐ 75	Phil Garner *	.75	.30	.07
☐ 76	Rick Manning *	.75	.30	.07
☐ 77	Mark Fidrych *	1.00	.40	.10
☐ 78	Mario Guerrero *	.75	.30	.07
☐ 79	Bob Stinson *	.75	.30	.07
☐ 80	Al Oliver *	1.00	.40	.10
☐ 81	Doug Flynn *	.75	.30	.07
☐ 82	John Mayberry	.75	.30	.07
☐ 83	Gaylord Perry	2.25	.90	.22
☐ 84	Joe Rudi	.75	.30	.07
☐ 85	Dave Concepcion	.90	.40	.09
☐ 86	John Candelaria	.75	.30	.07
☐ 87	Pete Vuckovich	.75	.30	.07
☐ 88	Ivan DeJesus	.60	.25	.06
☐ 89	Ron Guidry	1.75	.70	.17
☐ 90	Hal McRae	.90	.40	.09
☐ 91	Cesar Cedeno	.75	.30	.07
☐ 92	Don Sutton	2.25	.90	.22
☐ 93	Andre Thornton	.75	.30	.07
☐ 94	Roger Erickson	.60	.25	.06
☐ 95	Larry Hisle	.75	.30	.07
☐ 96	Jason Thompson	.60	.25	.06
☐ 97	Jim Sundberg	.75	.30	.07
☐ 98	Bob Horner	1.50	.60	.15
☐ 99	Ruppert Jones	.60	.25	.06
☐ 100	Willie Montanez	.60	.25	.06
☐ 101	Nolan Ryan	18.00	7.50	2.50
☐ 102	Ozzie Smith	21.00	9.00	3.00
☐ 103	Eric Soderholm	.60	.25	.06
☐ 104	Willie Stargell	3.00	1.25	.30
☐ 105A	Bob Bailor ERR	.75	.30	.07
	(reverse negative)			
☐ 105B	Bob Bailor COR	1.50	.60	.15
☐ 106	Carlton Fisk	3.00	1.25	.30
☐ 107	George Foster	1.25	.50	.12
☐ 108	Keith Hernandez	2.50	1.00	.25
☐ 109	Dennis Leonard	.75	.30	.07
☐ 110	Graig Nettles	.90	.40	.09
☐ 111	Jose Cruz	.75	.30	.07
☐ 112	Bobby Grich	.75	.30	.07
☐ 113	Bob Boone	1.00	.40	.10
☐ 114	Dave Lopes	.75	.30	.07
☐ 115	Eddie Murray	9.00	4.00	.90
☐ 116	Jack Clark	2.50	1.00	.25
☐ 117	Lou Whitaker	2.00	.80	.20
☐ 118	Miguel Dilone	.60	.25	.06
☐ 119	Sal Bando	.75	.30	.07
☐ 120	Reggie Jackson	6.00	2.50	.60
☐ 121	Dale Murphy	9.00	4.00	.90
☐ 122	Jon Matlack	.75	.30	.07
☐ 123	Bruce Bochte	.60	.25	.06
☐ 124	John Stearns	.60	.25	.06
☐ 125	Dave Winfield	4.00	1.75	.40
☐ 126	Jorge Orta	.60	.25	.06
☐ 127	Garry Templeton	.75	.30	.07
☐ 128	Johnny Bench	4.00	1.75	.40
☐ 129	Butch Hobson	.75	.30	.07
☐ 130	Bruce Sutter	1.25	.50	.12
☐ 131	Bucky Dent	.90	.40	.09
☐ 132	Amos Otis	.75	.30	.07
☐ 133	Bert Blyleven	1.00	.40	.10
☐ 134	Larry Bowa	.90	.40	.09
☐ 135	Ken Singleton	.75	.30	.07
☐ 136	Sixto Lezcano	.60	.25	.06
☐ 137	Roy Howell	.60	.25	.06
☐ 138	Bill Madlock	.90	.40	.10
☐ 139	Dave Revering	.60	.25	.06
☐ 140	Richie Zisk	.75	.30	.07
☐ 141	Butch Wynegar	.60	.25	.06
☐ 142	Alan Ashby	.60	.25	.06
☐ 143	Sparky Lyle	.90	.40	.09
☐ 144	Pete Rose	9.00	4.00	.90
☐ 145	Dennis Eckersley	1.50	.60	.15
☐ 146	Dave Kingman	.90	.40	.09
☐ 147	Buddy Bell	.75	.30	.07
☐ 148	Mike Hargrove	.75	.30	.07
☐ 149	Jerry Koosman	.75	.30	.07
☐ 150	Toby Harrah	.75	.30	.07

1985 Hostess Braves

The cards in this 22-card set measure 2 1/2" by 3 1/2" and feature players of the Atlanta Braves. Cards were produced by Topps for Hostess (Continental Baking Co.) and are quite attractive. The card backs are similar in design to the 1985 Topps regular issue; however all photos are different from those that Topps used as these were apparently taken during Spring Training. Cards were available in boxes of Hostess products in packs of four (three players and a contest card).

		MINT	EXC	G-VG
COMPLETE SET (22)		8.00	3.50	.80
COMMON PLAYER (1-22)		.30	.12	.03
☐ 1	Eddie Haas MG	.30	.12	.03
☐ 2	Len Barker	.30	.12	.03
☐ 3	Steve Bedrosian	.60	.25	.06
☐ 4	Bruce Benedict	.30	.12	.03
☐ 5	Rick Camp	.30	.12	.03
☐ 6	Rick Cerone	.30	.12	.03
☐ 7	Chris Chambliss	.50	.20	.05
☐ 8	Terry Forster	.40	.16	.04
☐ 9	Gene Garber	.30	.12	.03
☐ 10	Albert Hall	.30	.12	.03
☐ 11	Bob Horner	.75	.30	.07
☐ 12	Glenn Hubbard	.30	.12	.03
☐ 13	Brad Komminsk	.40	.16	.04
☐ 14	Rick Mahler	.30	.12	.03

		NRMT	VG-E	GOOD
☐ 15	Craig McMurtry	.30	.12	.03
☐ 16	Dale Murphy	4.00	1.75	.40
☐ 17	Ken Oberkfell	.30	.12	.03
☐ 18	Pascual Perez	.50	.20	.05
☐ 19	Gerald Perry	.40	.16	.04
☐ 20	Rafael Ramirez	.30	.12	.03
☐ 21	Bruce Sutter	.75	.30	.07
☐ 22	Claudell Washington	.40	.16	.04

1963 IDL Pirates

This 25-card set measures approximately 4" by 5" and is blank backed. The fronts have black and white photos on the top of the card along with the IDL Drug Store logo in the lower left corner of the card and the players name printed in block letters underneath the picture. The only card which has any designation as to position is the manager card of Danny Murtaugh. These cards are unnumbered and feature members of the Pittsburgh Pirates. The catalog designation for the set is H801-13 although it is infrequently referenced. The Stargell card is one of his few cards from 1963, his rookie year for cards.

		NRMT	VG-E	GOOD
	COMPLETE SET (25)	75.00	34.00	11.25
	COMMON PLAYER (1-25)	2.00	.80	.20
☐ 1	Bob Bailey	2.00	.80	.20
☐ 2	Smoky Burgess	2.50	1.00	.25
☐ 3	Don Cardwell	2.00	.80	.20
☐ 4	Roberto Clemente	30.00	13.50	4.50
☐ 5	Donn Clendenon	2.50	1.00	.25
☐ 6	Roy Face	3.00	1.25	.30
☐ 7	Earl Francis	2.00	.80	.20
☐ 8	Bob Friend	2.50	1.00	.25
☐ 9	Joe Gibbon	2.00	.80	.20
☐ 10	Julio Gotay	2.00	.80	.20
☐ 11	Harvey Haddix	2.50	1.00	.25
☐ 12	Bill Mazeroski	6.00	2.50	.60
☐ 13	Al McBean	2.00	.80	.20
☐ 14	Danny Murtaugh MG	2.00	.80	.20
☐ 15	Sam Narron CO	2.00	.80	.20
☐ 16	Ron Northey CO	2.00	.80	.20
☐ 17	Frank Oceak CO	2.00	.80	.20
☐ 18	Jim Pagliaroni	2.00	.80	.20
☐ 19	Ted Savage	2.00	.80	.20
☐ 20	Dick Schofield	2.00	.80	.20
☐ 21	Willie Stargell	25.00	11.00	3.50
☐ 22	Tom Sturdivant	2.00	.80	.20
☐ 23	Virgil(Fire) Trucks CO	2.00	.80	.20
☐ 24	Bob Veale	2.50	1.00	.25
☐ 25	Bill Virdon	3.00	1.25	.30

1991 Jimmy Dean Signature

Michael Schechter Associates (MSA) produced this 25-card set on behalf of Jimmy Dean Sausage. These standard-size (2 1/2" by 3 1/2") cards feature an obverse with a color player photo, enframed by yellow and red borders. Since these player photos were not expressly licensed by Major League Baseball, the team logos have been airbrushed out. In a red and white panel with yellow borders, the back has biographical information, complete major (and minor where appropriate) league statistics, and the player's facsimile autograph. The cards are numbered on the back.

		MINT	EXC	G-VG
	COMPLETE SET (25)	15.00	6.50	2.15
	COMMON PLAYER (1-25)	.40	.16	.04
☐ 1	Will Clark	1.00	.40	.10
☐ 2	Ken Griffey Jr.	2.00	.80	.20
☐ 3	Dale Murphy	.50	.20	.05
☐ 4	Barry Bonds	.60	.25	.06
☐ 5	Darryl Strawberry	.75	.30	.07
☐ 6	Ryne Sandberg	1.00	.40	.10
☐ 7	Gary Sheffield	.40	.16	.04
☐ 8	Sandy Alomar Jr.	.40	.16	.04
☐ 9	Frank Thomas	2.00	.80	.20
☐ 10	Barry Larkin	.50	.20	.05
☐ 11	Kirby Puckett	.75	.30	.07
☐ 12	George Brett	.60	.25	.06
☐ 13	Kevin Mitchell	.50	.20	.05
☐ 14	Dave Justice	1.00	.40	.10
☐ 15	Cal Ripken	1.00	.40	.10
☐ 16	Craig Biggio	.40	.16	.04
☐ 17	Rickey Henderson	1.00	.40	.10
☐ 18	Roger Clemens	1.00	.40	.10
☐ 19	Jose Canseco	1.00	.40	.10
☐ 20	Ozzie Smith	.50	.20	.05
☐ 21	Cecil Fielder	.75	.30	.07
☐ 22	Dave Winfield	.50	.20	.05
☐ 23	Kevin Maas	.50	.20	.05
☐ 24	Nolan Ryan	2.00	.80	.20
☐ 25	Dwight Gooden	.50	.20	.05

1973 Johnny Pro Orioles

1974 Johnny Pro Phillies

This 25-card set measures approximately 4 1/4" by 7 1/4" and features members of the 1973 Baltimore Orioles. The cards were designed to be pushed-out in a style similar to the 1964 Topps Stand Ups. The sides of the cards have a small advertisement for Johnny Pro Enterprises and even gives a phone number where they could have been reached. Oddly, the Orlando Pena card was not available in a die-cut version. The cards have the player's photo against a distinctive solid green background. The cards are blank backed. There are several variations within the set; the complete set price below does not include the any of the variation cards. The set is checklisted in order by uniform number. According to informed sources, there were 15,000 sets produced.

This 11-card set measures approximately 3 3/4" by 7 1/8" and features members of the 1974 Philadelphia Phillies. The most significant player in this series is an early card of Mike Schmidt. The cards are designed to be pushed out and have the players photo against a solid white background. The backs are blank and marked the second straight year that Johnny Pro issued cards of a major league team. The set is checklisted by uniform number. According to informed sources, there were less than 15,000 sets produced.

	NRMT	VG-E	GOOD
COMPLETE SET (11)	135.00	55.00	20.00
COMMON PLAYER	4.00	1.75	.40
☐ 8 Bob Boone C	12.00	5.25	1.50
☐ 10 Larry Bowa IF	6.00	2.50	.60
☐ 16 Dave Cash IF	4.00	1.75	.40
☐ 19 Greg Luzinski OF	8.00	3.50	.80
☐ 20 Mike Schmidt IF	100.00	45.00	15.00
☐ 22 Mike Anderson OF	4.00	1.75	.40
☐ 24 Bill Robinson OF	6.00	2.50	.60
☐ 27 Willie Montanez IF	4.00	1.75	.40
☐ 32 Steve Carlton P	24.00	10.50	3.50
☐ 37 Ron Schueler P	4.00	1.75	.40
☐ 41 Jim Lonborg P	6.00	2.50	.60

	NRMT	VG-E	GOOD
COMPLETE SET (25)	150.00	67.50	22.50
COMMON PLAYER	4.00	1.75	.40
☐ 1 Al Bumbry OF	4.00	1.75	.40
☐ 2 Rich Coggins OF	4.00	1.75	.40
☐ 3A Bobby Grich 2B	8.00	3.50	.80
(fielding)			
☐ 3B Bobby Grich 2B	12.00	5.25	1.50
(batting)			
☐ 4 Earl Weaver MG	8.00	3.50	.80
☐ 5A Brooks Robinson 3B	20.00	8.50	2.75
(fielding)			
☐ 5B Brooks Robinson 3B	30.00	13.50	4.50
(batting)			
☐ 6 Paul Blair OF	6.00	2.50	.60
☐ 7 Mark Belanger SS	6.00	2.50	.60
☐ 8 Andy Etchebarren C	4.00	1.75	.40
☐ 10 Elrod Hendricks C	4.00	1.75	.40
☐ 11 Terry Crowley OF	4.00	1.75	.40
☐ 12 Tommy Davis OF	6.00	2.50	.60
☐ 13 Doyle Alexander P	6.00	2.50	.60
☐ 14 Merv Rettenmund OF	4.00	1.75	.40
☐ 15 Frank Baker IF	4.00	1.75	.40
☐ 19 Dave McNally P	6.00	2.50	.60
☐ 21 Larry Brown IF	4.00	1.75	.40
☐ 22A Jim Palmer P	20.00	8.50	2.75
☐ 22B Jim Palmer P	30.00	13.50	4.50
(pitching)			
☐ 23 Grant Jackson P	4.00	1.75	.40
☐ 25 Don Baylor OF	8.00	3.50	.80
☐ 26 John(Boog) Powell 1B	10.00	4.50	1.25
☐ 27 Orlando Pena P	12.00	5.25	1.50
(NOT die-cut)			
☐ 32 Earl Williams C	4.00	1.75	.40
☐ 34 Bob Reynolds P	4.00	1.75	.40
☐ 35 Mike Cuellar P	6.00	2.50	.60
☐ 39 Eddie Watt P	4.00	1.75	.40

1953 Johnston Cookies

The cards in this 25-card set measure 2 9/16" by 3 5/8". The 1953 Johnston's Cookies set of numbered cards features Milwaukee Braves players only. This set is the most plentiful of the three Johnston's Cookies sets and no known scarcities exist. The catalog designation for this set is D356-1.

	NRMT	VG-E	GOOD
COMPLETE SET (25)	250.00	110.00	37.50
COMMON PLAYER (1-25)	9.00	4.00	.90

		NRMT	VG-E	GOOD
☐ 1	Charlie Grimm MG	10.00	4.50	1.25
☐ 2	John Antonelli	10.00	4.50	1.25
☐ 3	Vern Bickford	9.00	4.00	.90
☐ 4	Bob Buhl	9.00	4.00	.90
☐ 5	Lew Burdette	13.50	6.00	1.85
☐ 6	Dave Cole	9.00	4.00	.90
☐ 7	Ernie Johnson	10.00	4.50	1.25
☐ 8	Dave Jolly	9.00	4.00	.90
☐ 9	Don Liddle	9.00	4.00	.90
☐ 10	Warren Spahn	60.00	27.00	9.00
☐ 11	Max Surkont	9.00	4.00	.90
☐ 12	Jim Wilson	9.00	4.00	.90
☐ 13	Sibbi Sisti	9.00	4.00	.90
☐ 14	Walker Cooper	9.00	4.00	.90
☐ 15	Del Crandall	12.00	5.25	1.50
☐ 16	Ebba St.Claire	9.00	4.00	.90
☐ 17	Joe Adcock	13.50	6.00	1.85
☐ 18	George Crowe	9.00	4.00	.90
☐ 19	Jack Dittmer	9.00	4.00	.90
☐ 20	Johnny Logan	10.00	4.50	1.25
☐ 21	Ed Mathews	60.00	27.00	9.00
☐ 22	Bill Bruton	10.00	4.50	1.25
☐ 23	Sid Gordon	9.00	4.00	.90
☐ 24	Andy Pafko	10.00	4.50	1.25
☐ 25	Jim Pendleton	9.00	4.00	.90

☐ 10	Bob Buhl	12.00	5.25	1.50
☐ 11	Phil Paine	12.00	5.25	1.50
☐ 12	Ben Johnson	12.00	5.25	1.50
☐ 13	Sibbi Sisti	12.00	5.25	1.50
☐ 15	Charles Gorin	12.00	5.25	1.50
☐ 16	Chet Nichols	12.00	5.25	1.50
☐ 17	Dave Jolly	12.00	5.25	1.50
☐ 19	Jim Wilson	12.00	5.25	1.50
☐ 20	Ray Crone	12.00	5.25	1.50
☐ 21	Warren Spahn	75.00	34.00	11.25
☐ 22	Gene Conley	12.00	5.25	1.50
☐ 23	Johnny Logan	15.00	6.50	2.15
☐ 24	Charlie White	12.00	5.25	1.50
☐ 27	George Metkovich	12.00	5.25	1.50
☐ 28	Johnny Cooney CO	12.00	5.25	1.50
☐ 29	Paul Burris	12.00	5.25	1.50
☐ 31	Bucky Walters CO	15.00	6.50	2.15
☐ 32	Ernie Johnson	15.00	6.50	2.15
☐ 33	Lou Burdette	25.00	11.00	3.50
☐ 34	Bob Thomson	250.00	110.00	37.50
☐ 35	Bob Keely	12.00	5.25	1.50
☐ 38	Bill Bruton	15.00	6.50	2.15
☐ 40	Charlie Grimm MG	15.00	6.50	2.15
☐ 41	Eddie Mathews	75.00	34.00	11.25
☐ 42	Sam Calderone	12.00	5.25	1.50
☐ 47	Joey Jay	12.00	5.25	1.50
☐ 48	Andy Pafko	12.00	5.25	1.50
☐ 49	Dr. Charles Lacks (unnumbered)	12.00	5.25	1.50
☐ 50	Joseph F. Taylor (unnumbered)	12.00	5.25	1.50

1954 Johnston Cookies

The cards in this 35-card set measure 2" by 3 7/8". The 1954 Johnston's Cookies set of color cards of Milwaukee Braves are numbered according to the player's uniform number, except for the non-players, Lacks and Taylor, who are found at the end of the set. The Bobby Thomson card was withdrawn early in the year after his injury and is scarce. The catalog number for this set is D356-2. The Hank Aaron card shows him with uniform number 5, rather than the more familiar 44, that he switched to shortly thereafter.

	NRMT	VG-E	GOOD
COMPLETE SET (35)	1250.00	500.00	125.00
COMMON PLAYER (1-50)	12.00	5.25	1.50

		NRMT	VG-E	GOOD
☐ 1	Del Crandall	15.00	6.50	2.15
☐ 3	Jim Pendleton	12.00	5.25	1.50
☐ 4	Danny O'Connell	12.00	5.25	1.50
☐ 5	Hank Aaron	600.00	270.00	90.00
☐ 6	Jack Dittmer	12.00	5.25	1.50
☐ 9	Joe Adcock	15.00	6.50	2.15

1955 Johnston Cookies

The cards in this 35-card set measure approximately 2 3/4" by 4". This set of Milwaukee Braves issued in 1955 by Johnston Cookies are numbered by the uniform number of the player depicted, except for non-players Lacks, Lewis and Taylor. The cards were issued in strips of six which accounts for the rouletted edges found on single cards. They are larger in size than the two previous sets but are printed on thinner cardboard. Each player in the checklist has been marked to show on which panel or strip he appeared (Pafko appears twice). A complete panel of six cards is worth 25 percent more than the sum of the individual players. The catalog designation for this set is D356-3.

	NRMT	VG-E	GOOD
COMPLETE SET (35)	1100.00	500.00	125.00
COMMON PLAYER (1-51)	20.00	8.50	2.75

		NRMT	VG-E	GOOD
☐ 1	Del Crandall P1	22.50	9.75	3.25
☐ 3	Jim Pendleton P3	20.00	8.50	2.75
☐ 4	Danny O'Connell P1	20.00	8.50	2.75
☐ 6	Jack Dittmer P6	20.00	8.50	2.75
☐ 9	Joe Adcock P2	25.00	11.00	3.50
☐ 10	Bob Buhl P6	20.00	8.50	2.75
☐ 11	Phil Paine P5	20.00	8.50	2.75
☐ 12	Ray Crone P5	20.00	8.50	2.75
☐ 15	Charlie Gorin P1	20.00	8.50	2.75
☐ 16	Dave Jolly P4	20.00	8.50	2.75
☐ 17	Chet Nichols P2	20.00	8.50	2.75
☐ 18	Chuck Tanner P5	25.00	11.00	3.50

			NRMT	VG-E	GOOD
☐	19	Jim Wilson P6	20.00	8.50	2.75
☐	20	Dave Koslo P4	20.00	8.50	2.75
☐	21	Warren Spahn P3	90.00	40.00	13.50
☐	22	Gene Conley P3	20.00	8.50	2.75
☐	23	Johnny Logan P4	22.50	9.75	3.25
☐	24	Charlie White P2	20.00	8.50	2.75
☐	28	Johnny Cooney P4 CO	20.00	8.50	2.75
☐	30	Roy Smalley P3	20.00	8.50	2.75
☐	31	Bucky Walters P6 CO	22.50	9.75	3.25
☐	32	Ernie Johnson P5	22.50	9.75	3.25
☐	33	Lew Burdette P1	35.00	15.75	5.25
☐	34	Bobby Thomson P6	27.00	12.00	4.00
☐	35	Bob Keely P1	20.00	8.50	2.75
☐	38	Bill Bruton P4	22.50	9.75	3.25
☐	39	George Crowe P3	20.00	8.50	2.75
☐	40	Charlie Grimm MG P6	22.50	9.75	3.25
☐	41	Eddie Mathews P5	90.00	40.00	13.50
☐	44	Hank Aaron P1	350.00	160.00	52.50
☐	47	Joey Jay P2	20.00	8.50	2.75
☐	48	Andy Pafko P2 P4	20.00	8.50	2.75
☐	49	Dr. Charles Leaks P2 (unnumbered)	20.00	8.50	2.75
☐	50	Duffy Lewis P5 (unnumbered)	20.00	8.50	2.75
☐	51	Joe Taylor P3 (unnumbered)	20.00	8.50	2.75

1956 Kahn's

Compliments of Kahn's Wieners
"THE WIENER THE WORLD AWAITED"

The cards in this 15-card set measure 3 1/4" by 4". The 1956 Kahn's set was the first set to be issued with Kahn's meat products. The cards are blank backed. The set is distinguished by the old style, short sleeve shirts on the players and the existence of backgounds (Kahn's cards of later years utilize a blank background). Cards which have the tab still intact are worth approximately 50 percent more than cards without the tab. Cincinnati Redlegs players only are featured. The cards are listed and numbered below in alphabetical order by the subject's name.

			NRMT	VG-E	GOOD
	COMPLETE SET (15)		1650.00	700.00	175.00
	COMMON PLAYER (1-15)		80.00	36.00	12.00
☐	1	Ed Bailey	80.00	36.00	12.00
☐	2	Gus Bell	90.00	40.00	13.50
☐	3	Joe Black	90.00	40.00	13.50
☐	4	Smoky Burgess	90.00	40.00	13.50
☐	5	Art Fowler	80.00	36.00	12.00
☐	6	Herschel Freeman	80.00	36.00	12.00
☐	7	Ray Jablonski	80.00	36.00	12.00
☐	8	John Klippstein	80.00	36.00	12.00
☐	9	Ted Kluszewski	165.00	75.00	22.50
☐	10	Brooks Lawrence	80.00	36.00	12.00
☐	11	Roy McMillan	80.00	36.00	12.00
☐	12	Joe Nuxhall	90.00	40.00	13.50
☐	13	Wally Post	80.00	36.00	12.00
☐	14	Frank Robinson	500.00	225.00	75.00
☐	15	Johnny Temple	90.00	40.00	13.50

1955 Kahn's

Compliments of Kahn's Wieners
"THE WIENER THE WORLD AWAITED"

The cards in this 6-card set measure 3 1/4" by 4". The 1955 Kahn's Wieners set received very limited distribution. The cards were supposedly given away at an amusement park. The set portrays the players in street clothes rather than in uniform and hence are sometimes referred to as "street clothes" Kahn's. All Kahn's sets from 1955 through 1963 are black and white and contain a 1/2" tab. Cards with the tab still intact are worth approximately 50 percent more than cards without the tab. Cards feature a facsimile autograph of the player on the front. Cards are blank-backed. Cincinnati Redlegs players only are featured.

			NRMT	VG-E	GOOD
	COMPLETE SET (6)		3000.00	1200.00	300.00
	COMMON PLAYER (1-6)		450.00	200.00	67.50
☐	1	Gus Bell (street clothes)	750.00	325.00	110.00
☐	2	Ted Kluszewski (street clothes)	750.00	325.00	110.00
☐	3	Roy McMillan (street clothes)	450.00	200.00	67.50
☐	4	Joe Nuxhall (street clothes)	500.00	225.00	75.00
☐	5	Wally Post (street clothes)	450.00	200.00	67.50
☐	6	Johnny Temple (street clothes)	450.00	200.00	67.50

1957 Kahn's

The cards in this 29-card set measure 3 1/4" by 4". The 1957 Kahn's Wieners set contains black and white, blank backed, unnumbered cards. The set features the Cincinnati Redlegs and Pittsburgh Pirates only. The cards feature a light background. Each card features a facsimile autograph of the player on the front. The Groat card exists with a "Richard Groat" autograph and also exists with the printed name "Dick Groat" on the card. The catalog designation is F155-3. The cards are listed and numbered below in alphabetical order by the subject's name.

			NRMT	VG-E	GOOD
	COMPLETE SET (29)		2750.00	1200.00	300.00
	COMMON PLAYER (1-29)		60.00	27.00	9.00
☐	1	Tom Acker	60.00	27.00	9.00
☐	2	Ed Bailey	60.00	27.00	9.00
☐	3	Gus Bell	75.00	34.00	11.25
☐	4	Smoky Burgess	75.00	34.00	11.25

		NRMT	VG-E	GOOD
☐ 5	Robert Clemente	750.00	325.00	110.00
☐ 6	George Crowe	60.00	27.00	9.00
☐ 7	Elroy Face	90.00	40.00	13.50
☐ 8	Herschel Freeman	60.00	27.00	9.00
☐ 9	Bob Friend	75.00	34.00	11.25
☐ 10	Dick Groat	90.00	40.00	13.50
☐ 11	Richard Groat	175.00	80.00	27.00
☐ 12	Don Gross	60.00	27.00	9.00
☐ 13	Warren Hacker	60.00	27.00	9.00
☐ 14	Don Hoak	60.00	27.00	9.00
☐ 15	Hal Jeffcoat	60.00	27.00	9.00
☐ 16	Ron Kline	60.00	27.00	9.00
☐ 17	John Klippstein	60.00	27.00	9.00
☐ 18	Ted Kluszewski	135.00	60.00	20.00
☐ 19	Brooks Lawrence	60.00	27.00	9.00
☐ 20	Dale Long	75.00	34.00	11.25
☐ 21	Bill Mazeroski	135.00	60.00	20.00
☐ 22	Roy McMillan	60.00	27.00	9.00
☐ 23	Joe Nuxhall	75.00	34.00	11.25
☐ 24	Wally Post	60.00	27.00	9.00
☐ 25	Frank Robinson	250.00	110.00	37.50
☐ 26	John Temple	75.00	34.00	11.25
☐ 27	Frank Thomas	75.00	34.00	11.25
☐ 28	Bob Thurman	60.00	27.00	9.00
☐ 29	Lee Walls	60.00	27.00	9.00

1958 Kahn's

The cards in this 29-card set measure 3 1/4" by 4". The 1958 Kahn's Wieners set of unnumbered, black and white cards features Cincinnati Redlegs, Philadelphia Phillies, and Pittsburgh Pirates. The backs present a story for each player entitled "My Greatest Thrill in Baseball". A method of distinguishing 1958 Kahn's from 1959 Kahn's is that the word Wieners is found on the front of the 1958 but not on the front of the 1959 cards. Cards of Wally Post, Charlie Rabe, and Frank Thomas are somewhat more difficult to find and are marked with an asterisk in the checklist below. The cards are listed and numbered below in alphabetical order by the subject's name.

		NRMT	VG-E	GOOD
COMPLETE SET (29)		3000.00	1250.00	325.00
COMMON PLAYER (1-29)		50.00	22.50	7.50
☐ 1	Ed Bailey	50.00	22.50	7.50
☐ 2	Gene Baker	50.00	22.50	7.50

☐ 3	Gus Bell	60.00	27.00	9.00
☐ 4	Smoky Burgess	60.00	27.00	9.00
☐ 5	Roberto Clemente	550.00	240.00	80.00
☐ 6	George Crowe	50.00	22.50	7.50
☐ 7	Elroy Face	75.00	34.00	11.25
☐ 8	Hank Foiles	50.00	22.50	7.50
☐ 9	Dee Fondy	50.00	22.50	7.50
☐ 10	Bob Friend	60.00	27.00	9.00
☐ 11	Dick Groat	75.00	34.00	11.25
☐ 12	Harvey Haddix	60.00	27.00	9.00
☐ 13	Don Hoak	50.00	22.50	7.50
☐ 14	Hal Jeffcoat	50.00	22.50	7.50
☐ 15	Ron Kline	50.00	22.50	7.50
☐ 16	Ted Kluszewski	110.00	50.00	16.50
☐ 17	Vernon Law	60.00	27.00	9.00
☐ 18	Brooks Lawrence	50.00	22.50	7.50
☐ 19	Bill Mazeroski	90.00	40.00	13.50
☐ 20	Roy McMillan	50.00	22.50	7.50
☐ 21	Joe Nuxhall	60.00	27.00	9.00
☐ 22	Wally Post *	300.00	135.00	45.00
☐ 23	John Powers	50.00	22.50	7.50
☐ 24	Bob Purkey	50.00	22.50	7.50
☐ 25	Charlie Rabe *	300.00	135.00	45.00
☐ 26	Frank Robinson	225.00	100.00	33.00
☐ 27	Bob Skinner	50.00	22.50	7.50
☐ 28	Johnny Temple	60.00	27.00	9.00
☐ 29	Frank Thomas *	300.00	135.00	45.00

1959 Kahn's

The cards in this 38-card set measure 3 1/4" by 4". The 1959 Kahn's set features members of the Cincinnati Reds, Cleveland Indians, and Pittsburgh Pirates. The backs feature stories entitled "The Toughest Play I have to Make," or "The Toughest Batter I Have To Face." The Brodowski card is very scarce while Haddix, Held and McLish are considered quite difficult to obtain; these scarcities are the asterisked cards in the checklist below. The cards are listed and numbered below in alphabetical order by the subject's name.

		NRMT	VG-E	GOOD
COMPLETE SET (38)		4000.00	1800.00	400.00
COMMON PLAYER (1-38)		50.00	22.50	7.50
☐ 1	Ed Bailey	50.00	22.50	7.50
☐ 2	Gary Bell	50.00	22.50	7.50
☐ 3	Gus Bell	60.00	27.00	9.00
☐ 4	Dick Brodowski *	500.00	225.00	75.00
☐ 5	Smoky Burgess	60.00	27.00	9.00
☐ 6	Roberto Clemente	500.00	225.00	75.00
☐ 7	Rocky Colavito	110.00	50.00	16.50
☐ 8	Elroy Face	75.00	34.00	11.25
☐ 9	Bob Friend	60.00	27.00	9.00
☐ 10	Joe Gordon MG	60.00	27.00	9.00
☐ 11	Jim Grant	50.00	22.50	7.50
☐ 12	Dick Groat	75.00	34.00	11.25
☐ 13	Harvey Haddix * (blank back)	350.00	160.00	52.50
☐ 14	Woodie Held *	350.00	160.00	52.50
☐ 15	Don Hoak	50.00	22.50	7.50
☐ 16	Ron Kline	50.00	22.50	7.50
☐ 17	Ted Kluszewski	100.00	45.00	15.00
☐ 18	Vernon Law	60.00	27.00	9.00
☐ 19	Jerry Lynch	50.00	22.50	7.50
☐ 20	Billy Martin	125.00	57.50	18.75

		NRMT	VG-E	GOOD
☐ 21	Bill Mazeroski	90.00	40.00	13.50
☐ 22	Cal McLish *	350.00	160.00	52.50
☐ 23	Roy McMillan	50.00	22.50	7.50
☐ 24	Minnie Minoso	90.00	40.00	13.50
☐ 25	Russ Nixon	60.00	27.00	9.00
☐ 26	Joe Nuxhall	60.00	27.00	9.00
☐ 27	Jim Perry	75.00	34.00	11.25
☐ 28	Vada Pinson	75.00	34.00	11.25
☐ 29	Vic Power	50.00	22.50	7.50
☐ 30	Bob Purkey	50.00	22.50	7.50
☐ 31	Frank Robinson	200.00	90.00	30.00
☐ 32	Herb Score	75.00	34.00	11.25
☐ 33	Bob Skinner	50.00	22.50	7.50
☐ 34	George Strickland	50.00	22.50	7.50
☐ 35	Dick Stuart	60.00	27.00	9.00
☐ 36	Johnny Temple	50.00	22.50	7.50
☐ 37	Frank Thomas	60.00	27.00	9.00
☐ 38	George Witt	50.00	22.50	7.50

		NRMT	VG-E	GOOD
☐ 29	Russ Nixon	30.00	13.50	4.50
☐ 30	Joe Nuxhall	30.00	13.50	4.50
☐ 31	Jim O'Toole	25.00	11.00	3.50
☐ 32	Jim Perry	30.00	13.50	4.50
☐ 33	Vada Pinson	35.00	15.75	5.25
☐ 34	Vic Power	25.00	11.00	3.50
☐ 35	Bob Purkey	25.00	11.00	3.50
☐ 36	Frank Robinson	150.00	67.50	22.50
☐ 37	Herb Score	35.00	15.75	5.25
☐ 38	Bob Skinner	25.00	11.00	3.50
☐ 39	Dick Stuart	30.00	13.50	4.50
☐ 40	Johnny Temple	30.00	13.50	4.50
☐ 41	Frank Thomas	30.00	13.50	4.50
☐ 42	Lee Walls	25.00	11.00	3.50

1961 Kahn's

1960 Kahn's

The cards in this 42-card set measure 3 1/4" by 4". The 1960 Kahn's set features players of the Chicago Cubs, Chicago White Sox, Cincinnati Redlegs, Cleveland Indians, Pittsburgh Pirates, and St. Louis Cardinals. The backs give vital player information and records through the 1959 season. Kline appears with either St. Louis or Pittsburgh. The Harvey Kuenn card (asterisked below) appears with a blank back, and is scarce. The cards are listed and numbered below in alphabetical order by the subject's name.

		NRMT	VG-E	GOOD
COMPLETE SET (43)		1800.00	800.00	200.00
COMMON PLAYER (1-42)		25.00	11.00	3.50
☐ 1	Ed Bailey	25.00	11.00	3.50
☐ 2	Gary Bell	25.00	11.00	3.50
☐ 3	Gus Bell	30.00	13.50	4.50
☐ 4	Smoky Burgess	30.00	13.50	4.50
☐ 5	Gino Cimoli	25.00	11.00	3.50
☐ 6	Roberto Clemente	350.00	160.00	52.50
☐ 7	Roy Face	35.00	15.75	5.25
☐ 8	Tito Francona	25.00	11.00	3.50
☐ 9	Bob Friend	30.00	13.50	4.50
☐ 10	Jim Grant	25.00	11.00	3.50
☐ 11	Dick Groat	35.00	15.75	5.25
☐ 12	Harvey Haddix	30.00	13.50	4.50
☐ 13	Woodie Held	25.00	11.00	3.50
☐ 14	Bill Henry	25.00	11.00	3.50
☐ 15	Don Hoak	25.00	11.00	3.50
☐ 16	Jay Hook	25.00	11.00	3.50
☐ 17	Eddie Kasko	25.00	11.00	3.50
☐ 18A	Ron Kline (Pittsburgh)	45.00	20.00	6.75
☐ 18B	Ron Kline (St. Louis)	45.00	20.00	6.75
☐ 19	Ted Kluszewski	55.00	25.00	8.25
☐ 20	Harvey Kuenn (blank back)	300.00	135.00	45.00
☐ 21	Vernon Law	30.00	13.50	4.50
☐ 22	Brooks Lawrence	25.00	11.00	3.50
☐ 23	Jerry Lynch	25.00	11.00	3.50
☐ 24	Billy Martin	60.00	27.00	9.00
☐ 25	Bill Mazeroski	40.00	18.00	6.00
☐ 26	Cal McLish	25.00	11.00	3.50
☐ 27	Roy McMillan	25.00	11.00	3.50
☐ 28	Don Newcombe	35.00	15.75	5.25

The cards in this 43-card set measure approximately 3 1/4" by 4". The 1961 Kahn's Wieners set of black and white, unnumbered cards features members of the Cincinnati Reds, Cleveland Indians, and Pittsburgh Pirates. This year was the first year Kahn's made complete sets available to the public; hence they are more available, especially in the better condition grades, than the Kahn's of the previous years. The backs give vital player information and year by year career statistics through 1960. The catalog designation is F155-7. The cards are listed and numbered below in alphabetical order by the subject's name.

		NRMT	VG-E	GOOD
COMPLETE SET (43)		800.00	350.00	120.00
COMMON PLAYER (1-43)		12.50	5.50	1.65
☐ 1	John Antonelli	14.00	6.25	2.00
☐ 2	Ed Bailey	12.50	5.50	1.65
☐ 3	Gary Bell	12.50	5.50	1.65
☐ 4	Gus Bell	14.00	6.25	2.00
☐ 5	Jim Brosnan	12.50	5.50	1.65
☐ 6	Smoky Burgess	16.00	6.75	2.25
☐ 7	Gino Cimoli	12.50	5.50	1.65
☐ 8	Roberto Clemente	250.00	110.00	37.50
☐ 9	Gordie Coleman	12.50	5.50	1.65
☐ 10	Jimmy Dykes MG	14.00	6.25	2.00
☐ 11	Roy Face	16.00	6.75	2.25
☐ 12	Tito Francona	12.50	5.50	1.65
☐ 13	Gene Freese	12.50	5.50	1.65
☐ 14	Bob Friend	14.00	6.25	2.00
☐ 15	Jim Grant	12.50	5.50	1.65
☐ 16	Dick Groat	18.00	7.50	2.50
☐ 17	Harvey Haddix	14.00	6.25	2.00
☐ 18	Woodie Held	12.50	5.50	1.65
☐ 19	Don Hoak	12.50	5.50	1.65
☐ 20	Jay Hook	12.50	5.50	1.65
☐ 21	Joey Jay	12.50	5.50	1.65
☐ 22	Eddie Kasko	12.50	5.50	1.65
☐ 23	Willie Kirkland	12.50	5.50	1.65
☐ 24	Vernon Law	14.00	6.25	2.00
☐ 25	Jerry Lynch	12.50	5.50	1.65
☐ 26	Jim Maloney	16.00	6.75	2.25
☐ 27	Bill Mazeroski	20.00	8.50	2.75
☐ 28	Wilmer Mizell	12.50	5.50	1.65
☐ 29	Rocky Nelson	12.50	5.50	1.65
☐ 30	Jim O'Toole	12.50	5.50	1.65
☐ 31	Jim Perry	16.00	6.75	2.25
☐ 32	Bubba Phillips	12.50	5.50	1.65
☐ 33	Vada Pinson	18.00	7.50	2.50

		NRMT	VG-E	GOOD
☐ 34	Wally Post	12.50	5.50	1.65
☐ 35	Vic Power	12.50	5.50	1.65
☐ 36	Bob Purkey	12.50	5.50	1.65
☐ 37	Frank Robinson	100.00	45.00	15.00
☐ 38	John Romano	12.50	5.50	1.65
☐ 39	Dick Schofield	12.50	5.50	1.65
☐ 40	Bob Skinner	12.50	5.50	1.65
☐ 41	Hal Smith	12.50	5.50	1.65
☐ 42	Dick Stuart	16.00	6.75	2.25
☐ 43	Johnny Temple	12.50	5.50	1.65

1962 Kahn's

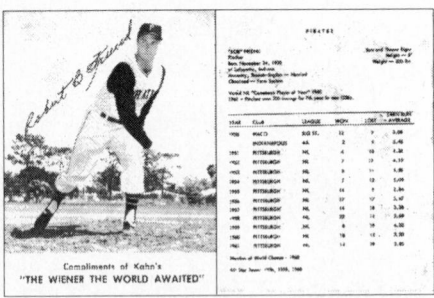

Compliments of Kahn's
"THE WIENER THE WORLD AWAITED"

The cards in this 38-card set measure approximately 3 1/4" by 4". The 1962 Kahn's Wieners set of black and white, unnumbered cards features Cincinnati, Cleveland, Minnesota, and Pittsburgh players. Card numbers 1 Bell, 33 Power, and 34 Purkey exist in two different forms; these variations are listed in the checklist below. The backs of the cards contain career information. The catalog designation is F155-8. The set price below includes the set with all variation cards. The cards are listed and numbered below in alphabetical order by the subject's name.

		NRMT	VG-E	GOOD
COMPLETE SET (41)		1100.00	500.00	125.00
COMMON PLAYER (1-38)		11.00	5.00	1.35
☐ 1A	Gary Bell	100.00	45.00	15.00
	(with fat man)			
☐ 1B	Gary Bell	35.00	15.75	5.25
	(no fat man)			
☐ 2	Jim Brosnan	11.00	5.00	1.35
☐ 3	Smoky Burgess	12.50	5.50	1.65
☐ 4	Chico Cardenas	11.00	5.00	1.35
☐ 5	Roberto Clemente	200.00	90.00	30.00
☐ 6	Ty Cline	11.00	5.00	1.35
☐ 7	Gordon Coleman	11.00	5.00	1.35
☐ 8	Dick Donovan	11.00	5.00	1.35
☐ 9	John Edwards	11.00	5.00	1.35
☐ 10	Tito Francona	11.00	5.00	1.35
☐ 11	Gene Freese	11.00	5.00	1.35
☐ 12	Bob Friend	12.50	5.50	1.65
☐ 13	Joe Gibbon	100.00	45.00	15.00
☐ 14	Jim Grant	11.00	5.00	1.35
☐ 15	Dick Groat	15.00	6.50	2.15
☐ 16	Harvey Haddix	12.50	5.50	1.65
☐ 17	Woodie Held	11.00	5.00	1.35
☐ 18	Bill Henry	11.00	5.00	1.35
☐ 19	Don Hoak	11.00	5.00	1.35
☐ 20	Ken Hunt	11.00	5.00	1.35
☐ 21	Joey Jay	11.00	5.00	1.35
☐ 22	Eddie Kasko	11.00	5.00	1.35
☐ 23	Willie Kirkland	11.00	5.00	1.35
☐ 24	Barry Latman	11.00	5.00	1.35
☐ 25	Jerry Lynch	11.00	5.00	1.35
☐ 26	Jim Maloney	12.50	5.50	1.65
☐ 27	Bill Mazeroski	16.00	6.75	2.25
☐ 28	Jim O'Toole	11.00	5.00	1.35
☐ 29	Jim Perry	12.50	5.50	1.65
☐ 30	Bubba Phillips	11.00	5.00	1.35
☐ 31	Vada Pinson	15.00	6.50	2.15
☐ 32	Wally Post	11.00	5.00	1.35
☐ 33A	Vic Power (Indians)	35.00	15.75	5.25
☐ 33B	Vic Power (Twins)	100.00	45.00	15.00
☐ 34A	Bob Purkey	35.00	15.75	5.25
	(with autograph)			
☐ 34B	Bob Purkey	100.00	45.00	15.00
	(no autograph)			
☐ 35	Frank Robinson	85.00	38.00	12.75
☐ 36	John Romano	11.00	5.00	1.35
☐ 37	Dick Stuart	12.50	5.50	1.65
☐ 38	Bill Virdon	15.00	6.50	2.15

1962 Kahn's Atlanta

Compliments of Kahn's
"THE WIENER THE WORLD AWAITED"

The cards in this 24-card set measure 3 1/4" by 4". The 1962 Kahn's Wieners Atlanta set features unnumbered, black and white cards of the Atlanta Crackers of the International League. The backs contain player statistical information as well as instructions on how to obtain free tickets. The catalog designation is F155-9. The cards are listed and numbered below in alphabetical order by the subject's name.

		NRMT	VG-E	GOOD
COMPLETE SET (24)		375.00	165.00	55.00
COMMON PLAYER (1-24)		12.50	5.50	1.65
☐ 1	Jim Beauchamp	15.00	6.50	2.15
☐ 2	Gerry Buchek	12.50	5.50	1.65
☐ 3	Bob Burda	12.50	5.50	1.65
☐ 4	Dick Dietz	15.00	6.50	2.15
☐ 5	Bob Duliba	12.50	5.50	1.65
☐ 6	Harry Fanok	12.50	5.50	1.65
☐ 7	Phil Gagliano	15.00	6.50	2.15
☐ 8	John Glenn	12.50	5.50	1.65
☐ 9	Leroy Gregory	12.50	5.50	1.65
☐ 10	Dick Hughes	12.50	5.50	1.65
☐ 11	Johnny Kucks	15.00	6.50	2.15
☐ 12	Johnny Lewis	12.50	5.50	1.65
☐ 13	Tim McCarver	75.00	34.00	11.25
☐ 14	Bob Milliken	12.50	5.50	1.65
☐ 15	Joe M. Morgan	20.00	8.50	2.75
☐ 16	Ron Plaza	12.50	5.50	1.65
☐ 17	Bob Sadowski	12.50	5.50	1.65
☐ 18	Jim Saul	12.50	5.50	1.65
☐ 19	Willard Schmidt	12.50	5.50	1.65
☐ 20	Joe Schultz MG	12.50	5.50	1.65
☐ 21	Mike Shannon	30.00	13.50	4.50
☐ 22	Paul Toth	12.50	5.50	1.65
☐ 23	Lou Vickery	12.50	5.50	1.65
☐ 24	Fred Whitfield	15.00	6.50	2.15

1963 Kahn's

The cards in this 30-card set measure 3 1/4" by 4". The 1963 Kahn's Wieners set of black and white, unnumbered cards features players from Cincinnati, Cleveland, St. Louis, Pittsburgh and the New York Yankees. The cards feature a white border around the picture of the players. The backs contain career information. The catalog designation is F155-10. The cards are listed and numbered below in alphabetical order by the subject's name.

	NRMT	VG-E	GOOD
COMPLETE SET (30)	600.00	270.00	90.00
COMMON PLAYER (1-30)	11.00	5.00	1.35

		NRMT	VG-E	GOOD
☐ 1	Bob Bailey	11.00	5.00	1.35
☐ 2	Don Blasingame	11.00	5.00	1.35
☐ 3	Clete Boyer	13.50	6.00	1.85
☐ 4	Smoky Burgess	11.00	5.00	1.35
☐ 5	Chico Cardenas	11.00	5.00	1.35
☐ 6	Roberto Clemente	200.00	90.00	30.00
☐ 7	Donn Clendenon	12.00	5.25	1.50
☐ 8	Gordon Coleman	11.00	5.00	1.35
☐ 9	John Edwards	11.00	5.00	1.35
☐ 10	Gene Freese	11.00	5.00	1.35
☐ 11	Bob Friend	12.00	5.25	1.50
☐ 12	Joe Gibbon	11.00	5.00	1.35
☐ 13	Dick Groat	15.00	6.50	2.15
☐ 14	Harvey Haddix	12.00	5.25	1.50
☐ 15	Elston Howard	18.00	7.50	2.50
☐ 16	Joey Jay	11.00	5.00	1.35
☐ 17	Eddie Kasko	11.00	5.00	1.35
☐ 18	Tony Kubek	25.00	11.00	3.50
☐ 19	Jerry Lynch	11.00	5.00	1.35
☐ 20	Jim Maloney	12.00	5.25	1.50
☐ 21	Bill Mazeroski	16.00	6.75	2.25
☐ 22	Joe Nuxhall	12.00	5.25	1.50
☐ 23	Jim O'Toole	11.00	5.00	1.35
☐ 24	Vada Pinson	15.00	6.50	2.15
☐ 25	Bob Purkey	11.00	5.00	1.35
☐ 26	Bobby Richardson	25.00	11.00	3.50
☐ 27	Frank Robinson	85.00	38.00	12.75
☐ 28	Bill Stafford	11.00	5.00	1.35
☐ 29	Ralph Terry	12.00	5.25	1.50
☐ 30	Bill Virdon	12.00	5.25	1.50

1964 Kahn's

The cards in this 31-card set measure 3" by 3 1/2". The 1964 Kahn's set marks the beginning of the full color cards and the elimination of the tabs which existed on previous Kahn's cards. The set of unnumbered cards contains player information through the 1963 season on the backs. The set features Cincinnati, Cleveland and Pittsburgh players. The cards are listed and numbered below in alphabetical order by the subject's name.

	NRMT	VG-E	GOOD
COMPLETE SET (31)	850.00	375.00	125.00
COMMON PLAYER (1-31)	11.00	5.00	1.35

☐ 1 Max Alvis	11.00	5.00	1.35
☐ 2 Bob Bailey	11.00	5.00	1.35
☐ 3 Chico Cardenas	11.00	5.00	1.35
☐ 4 Roberto Clemente	200.00	90.00	30.00
☐ 5 Donn Clendenon	12.00	5.25	1.50
☐ 6 Vic Davalillo	11.00	5.00	1.35
☐ 7 Dick Donovan	11.00	5.00	1.35
☐ 8 John Edwards	11.00	5.00	1.35
☐ 9 Bob Friend	12.00	5.25	1.50
☐ 10 Jim Grant	11.00	5.00	1.35
☐ 11 Tommy Harper	12.00	5.25	1.50
☐ 12 Woodie Held	11.00	5.00	1.35
☐ 13 Joey Jay	11.00	5.00	1.35
☐ 14 Jack Kralick	11.00	5.00	1.35
☐ 15 Jerry Lynch	11.00	5.00	1.35
☐ 16 Jim Maloney	12.00	5.25	1.50
☐ 17 Bill Mazeroski	16.00	6.75	2.25
☐ 18 Alvin McBean	11.00	5.00	1.35
☐ 19 Joe Nuxhall	12.00	5.25	1.50
☐ 20 Jim Pagliaroni	11.00	5.00	1.35
☐ 21 Vada Pinson	15.00	6.50	2.15
☐ 22 Bob Purkey	11.00	5.00	1.35
☐ 23 Pedro Ramos	11.00	5.00	1.35
☐ 24 Frank Robinson	85.00	38.00	12.75
☐ 25 John Romano	11.00	5.00	1.35
☐ 26 Pete Rose	350.00	160.00	52.50
☐ 27 John Tsitouris	11.00	5.00	1.35
☐ 28 Bob Veale	12.00	5.25	1.50
☐ 29 Bill Virdon	12.00	5.25	1.50
☐ 30 Leon Wagner	11.00	5.00	1.35
☐ 31 Fred Whitfield	11.00	5.00	1.35

1965 Kahn's

The cards in this 45-card set measure 3" by 3 1/2". The 1965 Kahn's set contains full color, unnumbered cards. The set features Cincinnati, Cleveland, Pittsburgh, and Milwaukee players. Backs contain statistical information through the 1964 season. The cards are listed and numbered below in alphabetical order by the subject's name.

	NRMT	VG-E	GOOD
COMPLETE SET (45)	1000.00	400.00	100.00
COMMON PLAYER (1-45)	11.00	5.00	1.35

☐ 1 Henry Aaron	150.00	67.50	22.50
☐ 2 Max Alvis	11.00	5.00	1.35
☐ 3 Joe Azcue	11.00	5.00	1.35
☐ 4 Bob Bailey	11.00	5.00	1.35
☐ 5 Frank Bolling	11.00	5.00	1.35
☐ 6 Chico Cardenas	11.00	5.00	1.35
☐ 7 Rico Carty	15.00	6.50	2.15
☐ 8 Donn Clendenon	12.00	5.25	1.50
☐ 9 Tony Cloninger	11.00	5.00	1.35
☐ 10 Gordon Coleman	11.00	5.00	1.35
☐ 11 Vic Davalillo	11.00	5.00	1.35
☐ 12 John Edwards	11.00	5.00	1.35
☐ 13 Sammy Ellis	11.00	5.00	1.35
☐ 14 Bob Friend	12.00	5.25	1.50
☐ 15 Tommy Harper	12.00	5.25	1.50
☐ 16 Chuck Hinton	11.00	5.00	1.35
☐ 17 Dick Howser	15.00	6.50	2.15
☐ 18 Joey Jay	11.00	5.00	1.35
☐ 19 Deron Johnson	11.00	5.00	1.35
☐ 20 Jack Kralick	11.00	5.00	1.35
☐ 21 Denver LeMaster	11.00	5.00	1.35
☐ 22 Jerry Lynch	11.00	5.00	1.35
☐ 23 Jim Maloney	12.00	5.25	1.50

			NRMT	VG-E	GOOD
☐ 24	Lee Maye		11.00	5.00	1.35
☐ 25	Bill Mazeroski		16.00	6.75	2.25
☐ 26	Alvin McBean		11.00	5.00	1.35
☐ 27	Bill McCool		11.00	5.00	1.35
☐ 28	Sam McDowell		13.50	6.00	1.85
☐ 29	Don McMahon		11.00	5.00	1.35
☐ 30	Denis Menke		11.00	5.00	1.35
☐ 31	Joe Nuxhall		12.00	5.25	1.50
☐ 32	Gene Oliver		11.00	5.00	1.35
☐ 33	Jim O'Toole		11.00	5.00	1.35
☐ 34	Jim Pagliaroni		11.00	5.00	1.35
☐ 35	Vada Pinson		15.00	6.50	2.15
☐ 36	Frank Robinson		85.00	38.00	12.75
☐ 37	Pete Rose		225.00	100.00	33.00
☐ 38	Willie Stargell		100.00	45.00	15.00
☐ 39	Ralph Terry		12.00	5.25	1.50
☐ 40	Luis Tiant		15.00	6.50	2.15
☐ 41	Joe Torre		18.00	7.50	2.50
☐ 42	John Tsitouris		11.00	5.00	1.35
☐ 43	Bob Veale		12.00	5.25	1.50
☐ 44	Bill Virdon		12.00	5.25	1.50
☐ 45	Leon Wagner		11.00	5.00	1.35

1966 Kahn's

The cards in this 32-card set measure 2 13/16" by 4". 1966 Kahn's full color, unnumbered set features players from Atlanta, Cincinnati, Cleveland, and Pittsburgh. The set is identified by yellow and white vertical stripes and the name Kahn's written in red across a red rose at the top. The cards contain a 1 5/16" ad in the form of a (tab). Cards with the ad (tab) are worth twice as much as cards without the ad, i.e., double the prices below. The cards are listed and numbered below in alphabetical order by the subject's name.

		NRMT	VG-E	GOOD
	COMPLETE SET (32)	600.00	270.00	90.00
	COMMON PLAYER (1-32)	9.00	4.00	.90
☐ 1	Henry Aaron (portrait, no windbreaker under jersey)	100.00	45.00	15.00
☐ 2	Felipe Alou: Braves (full pose, batting screen in background)	10.00	4.50	1.25
☐ 3	Max Alvis: Indians (kneeling, full pose, with bat, no patch on jersey)	9.00	4.00	.90
☐ 4	Bob Bailey	9.00	4.00	.90
☐ 5	Wade Blasingame	9.00	4.00	.90
☐ 6	Frank Bolling	9.00	4.00	.90
☐ 7	Chico Cardenas: Reds (fielding, feet at base)	9.00	4.00	.90
☐ 8	Roberto Clemente	100.00	45.00	15.00
☐ 9	Tony Cloninger: Braves (pitching, foulpole in background)	9.00	4.00	.90

		NRMT	VG-E	GOOD
☐ 10	Vic Davalillo	9.00	4.00	.90
☐ 11	John Edwards: Reds (catching)	9.00	4.00	.90
☐ 12	Sam Ellis: Reds (white hat)	9.00	4.00	.90
☐ 13	Pedro Gonzalez	9.00	4.00	.90
☐ 14	Tommy Harper: Reds (arm cocked)	9.00	4.00	.90
☐ 15	Deron Johnson: Reds (batting with batting cage in background)	9.00	4.00	.90
☐ 16	Mack Jones	9.00	4.00	.90
☐ 17	Denver Lemaster	9.00	4.00	.90
☐ 18	Jim Maloney: Reds (pitching, white hat)	10.00	4.50	1.25
☐ 19	Bill Mazeroski: Pirates (throwing)	12.00	5.25	1.50
☐ 20	Bill McCool: Reds (white hat)	9.00	4.00	.90
☐ 21	Sam McDowell: Indians (kneeling)	10.00	4.50	1.25
☐ 22	Denis Menke: Braves (white windbreaker under jersey)	9.00	4.00	.90
☐ 23	Joe Nuxhall	10.00	4.50	1.25
☐ 24	Jim Pagliaroni: Pirates (catching)	9.00	4.00	.90
☐ 25	Milt Pappas	10.00	4.50	1.25
☐ 26	Vada Pinson: Reds (fielding, ball on ground)	12.00	5.25	1.50
☐ 27	Pete Rose: Reds (with glove)	125.00	57.50	18.75
☐ 28	Sonny Siebert: Indians (pitching, signature at feet)	9.00	4.00	.90
☐ 29	Willie Stargell: Pirates (batting, clouds in sky)	40.00	18.00	6.00
☐ 30	Joe Torre: Braves (catching with hand on mask)	12.00	5.25	1.50
☐ 31	Bob Veale: Pirates (hands at knee with glasses)	9.00	4.00	.90
☐ 32	Fred Whitfield	9.00	4.00	.90

1967 Kahn's

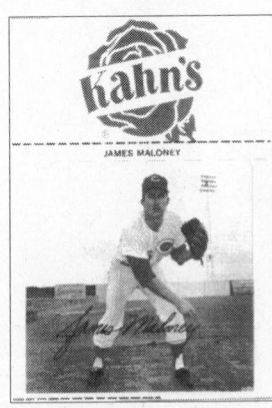

The cards in this 41-player set measure 2 13/16" by 4". The 1967 Kahn's set of full color, unnumbered cards is almost identical in style to the 1966 issue. Different meat products had different background colors (yellow and white stripes, red and white stripes, etc.). The set features players from Atlanta, Cincinnati, Cleveland, New York Mets and Pittsburgh. Cards with the ads (see 1966 set) are worth twice as much as cards without the ad, i.e., double the prices below. The complete set price below includes all variations. The cards are listed and numbered below in alphabetical order by the subject's name.

	NRMT	VG-E	GOOD
COMPLETE SET (51)	800.00	350.00	120.00
COMMON PLAYER (1-41)	9.00	4.00	.90
☐ 1A Henry Aaron: Braves (swinging pose, batting glove, ball, and hat on ground)	100.00	45.00	15.00
☐ 1B Henry Aaron: Braves (swinging pose, batting glove, ball, and hat on ground; Cut Along Dotted Lines printed on lower tab)	125.00	57.50	18.75
☐ 2 Gene Alley: Pirates (portrait)	9.00	4.00	.90
☐ 3 Felipe Alou: Braves (full pose, bat on shoulder)	10.00	4.50	1.25
☐ 4A Matty Alou: Pirates (portrait with bat, "Matio Rojas Alou"; yellow stripes)	10.00	4.50	1.25
☐ 4B Matty Alou: Pirates (portrait with bat, "Matio Rojas Alou"; red stripes)	12.00	5.25	1.50
☐ 5 Max Alvis: Indians (fielding, hands on knees)	9.00	4.00	.90
☐ 6A Ken Boyer (batting righthanded; autograph at waist)	12.00	5.25	1.50
☐ 6B Ken Boyer (batting righthanded; autograph at shoulders; Cut Along Dotted Lines printed on lower tab)	16.00	6.75	2.25
☐ 7 Chico Cardenas: Reds (fielding, hand on knee)	9.00	4.00	.90
☐ 8 Rico Carty	12.00	5.25	1.50
☐ 9 Tony Cloninger: Braves (pitching, no foul- pole in background)	9.00	4.00	.90
☐ 10 Tommy Davis	10.00	4.50	1.25
☐ 11 John Edwards: Reds (kneeling with bat)	9.00	4.00	.90
☐ 12A Sam Ellis: Reds (all red hat)	9.00	4.00	.90
☐ 12B Sam Ellis: Reds (all red hat) Cut Along Dotted Lines printed on lower tab)	10.00	4.50	1.25
☐ 13 Jack Fisher	9.00	4.00	.90
☐ 14 Steve Hargan: Indians (pitching, no clouds, blue sky)	9.00	4.00	.90
☐ 15 Tommy Harper: Reds (fielding, glove on ground)	10.00	4.50	1.25
☐ 16A Tommy Helms (batting righthanded; top of bat visible)	10.00	4.50	1.25
☐ 16B Tommy Helms (batting righthanded; bat chopped above hat; Cut Along Dotted Lines printed on lower tab)	12.00	5.25	1.50
☐ 17 Deron Johnson: Reds (batting, blue sky)	9.00	4.00	.90
☐ 18 Ken Johnson	9.00	4.00	.90
☐ 19 Cleon Jones	9.00	4.00	.90
☐ 20A Ed Kranepool (ready for throw; yellow stripes)	10.00	4.50	1.25
☐ 20B Ed Kranepool (ready for throw; red stripes)	12.00	5.25	1.50
☐ 21A Jim Maloney: Reds (pitching, red hat, follow thru delivery; yellow stripes)	10.00	4.50	1.25
☐ 21B Jim Maloney: Reds (pitching, red hat, follow thru delivery; red stripes)	12.00	5.25	1.50
☐ 22 Lee May: Reds (hands on knee)	10.00	4.50	1.25
☐ 23A Bill Mazeroski:	12.00	5.25	1.50

	NRMT	VG-E	GOOD
Pirates (portrait; autograph below waist)			
☐ 23B Bill Mazeroski: Pirates (portrait; autograph above waist; Cut Along Dotted Lines printed on lower tab)	16.00	6.75	2.25
☐ 24 Bill McCool: Reds (red hat, left hand out)	9.00	4.00	.90
☐ 25 Sam McDowell: Indians (pitching, left hand under glove)	10.00	4.50	1.25
☐ 26 Denis Menke: Braves (blue sleeves)	9.00	4.00	.90
☐ 27 Jim Pagliaroni: Pirates (catching, no chest protector)	9.00	4.00	.90
☐ 28 Don Pavletich	9.00	4.00	.90
☐ 29 Tony Perez: Reds (throwing)	25.00	11.00	3.50
☐ 30 Vada Pinson: Reds (ready to throw)	12.00	5.25	1.50
☐ 31 Dennis Ribant	9.00	4.00	.90
☐ 32 Pete Rose: Reds (batting)	125.00	57.50	18.75
☐ 33 Art Shamsky: Reds	9.00	4.00	.90
☐ 34 Bob Shaw	9.00	4.00	.90
☐ 35 Sonny Siebert: Indians (pitching, signature at knees)	9.00	4.00	.90
☐ 36 Willie Stargell: Pirates (batting, no clouds)	40.00	18.00	6.00
☐ 37A Joe Torre: Braves (catching, mask on ground)	12.00	5.25	1.50
☐ 37B Joe Torre: Braves (catching, mask on ground; Cut Along Dotted Lines printed on lower tab)	16.00	6.75	2.25
☐ 38 Bob Veale: Pirates (portrait, hands not shown)	9.00	4.00	.90
☐ 39 Leon Wagner: Indians (fielding)	9.00	4.00	.90
☐ 40A Fred Whitfield (batting lefthanded)	9.00	4.00	.90
☐ 40B Fred Whitfield (batting lefthanded; Cut Along Dotted Lines printed on lower tab)	10.00	4.50	1.25
☐ 41 Woody Woodward	10.00	4.50	1.25

1968 Kahn's

The cards in this 50-card set contain two different sizes. The smaller of the two sizes, which contains 12 cards, is 2 13/16" by 3 1/4" with the ad tab and 2 13/16" by 1 7/8" without the ad tab. The larger size, which contains 38 cards, measures 2 13/

16" by 3 7/8" with the ad tab and 2 13/16" by 2 11/16" without the ad tab. The 1968 Kahn's set of full color, blank backed, unnumbered cards features players from Atlanta, Chicago Cubs, Chicago White Sox, Cincinnati, Cleveland, Detroit, New York Mets, and Pittsburgh. In the set of 12, listed with the letter A in the checklist, Maloney exists with either yellow or yellow and green stripes at the top of the card. The large set of 38, listed with a letter B in the checklist, contains five cards which exist in two variations. The variations in this large set have either yellow or red stripes at the top of the cards, with Maloney being an exception. Maloney has either a yellow stripe or a Blue Mountain ad at the top. Cards with the ad tabs (see other Kahn's sets) are worth twice as much as cards without the ad, i.e., double the prices below. The cards are listed and numbered below in alphabetical order (within each subset) by the subject's name.

		NRMT	VG-E	GOOD
	COMPLETE SET (50)	1000.00	400.00	100.00
	COMMON PLAYER	9.00	4.00	.90
☐ A1	Hank Aaron	100.00	45.00	15.00
☐ A2	Gene Alley	9.00	4.00	.90
☐ A3	Max Alvis	9.00	4.00	.90
☐ A4	Clete Boyer	10.00	4.50	1.25
☐ A5	Chico Cardenas	9.00	4.00	.90
☐ A6	Bill Freehan	12.00	5.25	1.50
☐ A7	Jim Maloney (2)	10.00	4.50	1.25
☐ A8	Lee May	9.00	4.00	.90
☐ A9	Bill Mazeroski	12.00	5.25	1.50
☐ A10	Vada Pinson	12.00	5.25	1.50
☐ A11	Joe Torre	12.00	5.25	1.50
☐ A12	Bob Veale	9.00	4.00	.90
☐ B1	Hank Aaron: Braves (full pose, batting bat cocked)	100.00	45.00	15.00
☐ B2	Tommy Agee	9.00	4.00	.90
☐ B3	Gene Alley: Pirates (fielding, full pose)	9.00	4.00	.90
☐ B4	Felipe Alou (full pose, batting, swinging, player in background)	10.00	4.50	1.25
☐ B5	Matty Alou: Pirates (portrait with bat, "Matio Alou" (2)	10.00	4.50	1.25
☐ B6	Max Alvis (fielding, glove on ground)	9.00	4.00	.90
☐ B7	Gerry Arrigo: Reds (pitching, follow thru delivery)	9.00	4.00	.90
☐ B8	John Bench	350.00	160.00	52.50
☐ B9	Clete Boyer	10.00	4.50	1.25
☐ B10	Larry Brown	9.00	4.00	.90
☐ B11	Leo Cardenas: Reds (leaping in the air)	9.00	4.00	.90
☐ B12	Bill Freehan	12.00	5.25	1.50
☐ B13	Steve Hargan: Indians (pitching, clouds in background)	9.00	4.00	.90
☐ B14	Joel Horlen: White Sox (portrait)	9.00	4.00	.90
☐ B15	Tony Horton: Indians (portrait, signed Anthony)	9.00	4.00	.90
☐ B16	Willie Horton	10.00	4.50	1.25
☐ B17	Ferguson Jenkins	40.00	18.00	6.00
☐ B18	Deron Johnson: Braves	9.00	4.00	.90
☐ B19	Mack Jones: Reds	9.00	4.00	.90
☐ B20	Bob Lee	9.00	4.00	.90
☐ B21	Jim Maloney: Reds (red hat, pitching hands up) (2)	10.00	4.50	1.25
☐ B22	Lee May: Reds (batting)	10.00	4.50	1.25
☐ B23	Bill Mazeroski: Pirates (fielding, hands in front of body)	12.00	5.25	1.50
☐ B24	Dick McAuliffe	10.00	4.50	1.25
☐ B25	Bill McCool (red hat, left hand down)	9.00	4.00	.90
☐ B26	Sam McDowell: Indians (pitching, left hand over glove (2)	10.00	4.50	1.25
☐ B27	Tony Perez (fielding ball in glove (2)	25.00	11.00	3.50

		NRMT	VG-E	GOOD
☐ B28	Gary Peters: White Sox (portrait)	9.00	4.00	.90
☐ B29	Vada Pinson: Reds (batting)	12.00	5.25	1.50
☐ B30	Chico Ruiz	9.00	4.00	.90
☐ B31	Ron Santo: Cubs (batting, follow thru (2)	15.00	6.50	2.15
☐ B32	Art Shamsky: Mets	9.00	4.00	.90
☐ B33	Luis Tiant: Indians (hands over head)	12.00	5.25	1.50
☐ B34	Joe Torre: Braves (batting)	12.00	5.25	1.50
☐ B35	Bob Veale: Pirates (hands chest high)	9.00	4.00	.90
☐ B36	Leon Wagner: Indians (batting)	9.00	4.00	.90
☐ B37	Billy Williams: Cubs (bat behind back)	35.00	15.75	5.25
☐ B38	Earl Wilson	9.00	4.00	.90

1969 Kahn's

The cards in this 25-card set contain two different sizes. The three small cards (see 1968 description) measure 2 13/16" by 3 1/4" and the 22 large cards (see 1968 description) measure 2 13/16" by 3 15/16". The 1969 Kahn's Wieners set of full color, unnumbered cards features players from Atlanta, Chicago Cubs, Chicago White Sox, Cincinnati, Cleveland, Pittsburgh, and St. Louis. The small cards have the letter A in the checklist while the large cards have the letter B in the checklist. Four of the larger cards exist in two variations (red or yellow color stripes at the top of the card). These variations are identified in the checklist below. Cards with the ad tabs (see other Kahn's sets) are worth twice as much as cards without the ad, i.e., double the prices below. The cards are listed and numbered below in alphabetical order (within each subset) by the subject's name.

		NRMT	VG-E	GOOD
	COMPLETE SET (25)	450.00	200.00	67.50
	COMMON PLAYER	9.00	4.00	.90
☐ A1	Hank Aaron (portrait)	100.00	45.00	15.00
☐ A2	Jim Maloney (pitching, hands at side)	10.00	4.50	1.25
☐ A3	Tony Perez (glove on)	25.00	11.00	3.50
☐ B1	Hank Aaron	100.00	45.00	15.00
☐ B2	Matty Alou (batting)	10.00	4.50	1.25
☐ B3	Max Alvis ('69 patch)	9.00	4.00	.90
☐ B4	Gerry Arrigo (leg up)	9.00	4.00	.90

☐	B5	Steve Blass	10.00	4.50	1.25
☐	B6	Clay Carroll	9.00	4.00	.90
☐	B7	Tony Cloninger: Reds	9.00	4.00	.90
☐	B8	George Culver	9.00	4.00	.90
☐	B9	Joel Horlen (pitching)	9.00	4.00	.90
☐	B10	Tony Horton (batting)	9.00	4.00	.90
☐	B11	Alex Johnson	9.00	4.00	.90
☐	B12	Jim Maloney	10.00	4.50	1.25
☐	B13	Lee May (foot on bag) (2)	10.00	4.50	1.25
☐	B14	Bill Mazeroski (hands on knees) (2)	12.00	5.25	1.50
☐	B15	Sam McDowell (leg up) (2)	10.00	4.50	1.25
☐	B16	Tony Perez	25.00	11.00	3.50
☐	B17	Gary Peters (pitching)	9.00	4.00	.90
☐	B18	Ron Santo (emblem) (2)	13.50	6.00	1.85
☐	B19	Luis Tiant (glove at knee)	12.00	5.25	1.50
☐	B20	Joe Torre: Cardinals	12.00	5.25	1.50
☐	B21	Bob Veale (hands at knees, no glasses)	9.00	4.00	.90
☐	B22	Billy Williams (bat behind head)	35.00	15.75	5.25

1987 Kahn's Reds

This 30-card set was issued to the first 20,000 fans at the August 2nd game between the Reds and the San Francisco Giants at Riverfront Stadium by Kahn's Wieners. Cards are standard size, 2 1/2" by 3 1/2". The cards are unnumbered except for uniform number and feature full-color photos bordered in red and white on the front. The Kahn's logo is printed in red in the corner of the reverse.

		MINT	EXC	G-VG
COMPLETE SET (30)		22.50	9.75	3.25
COMMON PLAYER		.50	.20	.05
☐ 6	Bo Diaz	.50	.20	.05
☐ 10	Terry Francona	.50	.20	.05
☐ 11	Kurt Stillwell	.75	.30	.07
☐ 12	Nick Esasky	.75	.30	.07
☐ 13	Dave Concepcion	1.00	.40	.10
☐ 15	Barry Larkin	5.00	2.25	.50
☐ 16	Ron Oester	.50	.20	.05
☐ 21	Paul O'Neill	1.50	.60	.15
☐ 23	Lloyd McClendon	.50	.20	.05
☐ 25	Buddy Bell	.75	.30	.07
☐ 28	Kal Daniels	2.50	1.00	.25
☐ 29	Tracy Jones	.60	.25	.06
☐ 30	Guy Hoffman	.50	.20	.05
☐ 31	John Franco	1.00	.40	.10
☐ 32	Tom Browning	1.25	.50	.12
☐ 33	Ron Robinson	.75	.30	.07
☐ 34	Bill Gullickson	.60	.25	.06
☐ 35	Pat Pacillo	.60	.25	.06
☐ 39	Dave Parker	1.50	.60	.15
☐ 43	Bill Landrum	.50	.20	.05
☐ 44	Eric Davis	5.00	2.25	.50
☐ 46	Rob Murphy	.60	.25	.06
☐ 47	Frank Williams	.50	.20	.05

☐	48	Ted Power	.50	.20	.05
☐	xx	Pete Rose MG	1.50	.60	.15
☐	xx	Coaches Card	.50	.20	.05
		Scott Breeden			
		Billy DeMars			
		Tommy Helms			
		Bruce Kimm			
		Jim Lett			
		Tony Perez			
☐	xx	Ad Card	.50	.20	.05
		Save 25 cents on Corn Dogs			
☐	xx	Ad Card	.50	.20	.05
		Save 30 cents on Smokeys			

1988 Kahn's Mets

These 32-card sets were issued to the first 48,000 fans at the June 30th game between the Mets and the Houston Astros at Shea Stadium. The set includes 30 players, a team card, and a discount coupon card (to be redeemed at the grocery store). Cards are standard size, 2 1/2" by 3 1/2". The cards are unnumbered except for uniform number and feature full-color photos bordered in blue and orange on the front. The Kahn's logo is printed in red in the corner of the reverse.

		MINT	EXC	G-VG
COMPLETE SET (32)		16.00	6.75	2.25
COMMON PLAYER		.45	.18	.04
☐ 1	Mookie Wilson	.60	.25	.06
☐ 2	Mackey Sasser	.60	.25	.06
☐ 3	Bud Harrelson CO	.60	.25	.06
☐ 4	Len Dykstra	.75	.30	.07
☐ 5	Davey Johnson MG	.60	.25	.06
☐ 6	Wally Backman	.45	.18	.04
☐ 8	Gary Carter	.90	.40	.09
☐ 11	Tim Teufel	.60	.25	.06
☐ 12	Ron Darling	.60	.25	.06
☐ 13	Lee Mazzilli	.45	.18	.04
☐ 15	Rick Aguilera	.60	.25	.06
☐ 16	Dwight Gooden	1.25	.50	.12
☐ 17	Keith Hernandez	.75	.30	.07
☐ 18	Darryl Strawberry	2.00	.80	.20
☐ 19	Bob Ojeda	.60	.25	.06
☐ 20	Howard Johnson	1.00	.40	.10
☐ 21	Kevin Elster	.45	.18	.04
☐ 22	Kevin McReynolds	.90	.40	.09
☐ 26	Terry Leach	.45	.18	.04
☐ 28	Bill Robinson CO	.60	.25	.06
☐ 29	Dave Magadan	.60	.25	.06
☐ 30	Mel Stottlemyre CO	.60	.25	.06
☐ 31	Gene Walter	.45	.18	.04
☐ 33	Barry Lyons	.45	.18	.04
☐ 34	Sam Perlozzo CO	.45	.18	.04
☐ 42	Roger McDowell	.60	.25	.06
☐ 44	David Cone	1.25	.50	.12
☐ 48	Randy Myers	.60	.25	.06
☐ 50	Sid Fernandez	.60	.25	.06
☐ 52	Greg Pavlick CO	.45	.18	.04
☐ x	Team Photo Card (unnumbered)	.45	.18	.04
☐ x	Discount Coupon (unnumbered)	.45	.18	.04

1988 Kahn's Reds

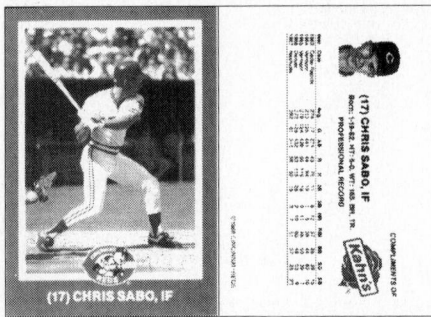

These 26-card sets were issued to fans at the August 14th game between the Reds and the Atlanta Braves at Riverfront Stadium. Cards are standard size, 2 1/2" by 3 1/2". The cards are unnumbered except for uniform number and feature full-color photos bordered in red and white on the front. The Kahn's logo is printed in red in the corner of the reverse. The cards are numbered below by uniform number which is listed parenthetically on the front of the cards.

	MINT	EXC	G-VG
COMPLETE SET (26)	15.00	6.50	2.15
COMMON PLAYER	.45	.18	.04
☐ 6 Bo Diaz	.45	.18	.04
☐ 8 Terry McGriff	.45	.18	.04
☐ 9 Eddie Milner	.45	.18	.04
☐ 10 Leon Durham	.45	.18	.04
☐ 11 Barry Larkin	1.50	.60	.15
☐ 12 Nick Esasky	.60	.25	.06
☐ 13 Dave Concepcion	.75	.30	.07
☐ 14 Pete Rose MG	1.00	.40	.10
☐ 15 Jeff Treadway	.60	.25	.06
☐ 17 Chris Sabo	3.00	1.25	.30
☐ 20 Danny Jackson	.60	.25	.06
☐ 21 Paul O'Neill	.90	.40	.09
☐ 22 Dave Collins	.45	.18	.04
☐ 27 Jose Rijo	1.00	.40	.10
☐ 28 Kal Daniels	1.00	.40	.10
☐ 29 Tracy Jones	.45	.18	.04
☐ 30 Lloyd McClendon	.45	.18	.04
☐ 31 John Franco	.60	.25	.06
☐ 32 Tom Browning	.75	.30	.07
☐ 33 Ron Robinson	.60	.25	.06
☐ 40 Jack Armstrong	.75	.30	.07
☐ 44 Eric Davis	1.50	.60	.15
☐ 46 Rob Murphy	.60	.25	.06
☐ 47 Frank Williams	.45	.18	.04
☐ 48 Tim Birtsas	.45	.18	.04
☐ xx Reds Coaches	.60	.25	.06

Lee May CO
Tony Perez CO
Bruce Kimm CO
Tommy Helms CO
Jim Lett CO
Scott Breeden CO

1989 Kahn's Cooperstown

The 1989 Kahn's Cooperstown set contains 11 standard-size (2 1/2 by 3 1/2 inch) cards. This set is sometimes referenced as Hillshire Farms or Kahn's Cooperstown Collection. All players included in the set are members (for the most part they are recent inductees) of the Hall of Fame. The pictures are actually paintings and are surrounded by gold borders. The fronts resemble plaques and also have facsimile autographs. The cards were available from the company via a send-in offer. A set of cards was available in return for three proofs of purchase

(and 1.00 postage and handling) from Hillshire Farms. The last card in the set is actually a coupon card for Kahn's products; this card is not even considered part of the set by some collectors. A related promotion offered two coin cards (coins laminated on cards) featuring Johnny Bench and Carl Yastrzemski. These coin cards are approximately 5 1/2" by 3 3/4" and are blank backed.

	MINT	EXC	G-VG
COMPLETE SET (12)	7.00	3.00	.70
COMMON PLAYER (1-11)	.50	.20	.05
☐ 1 Cool Papa Bell	.50	.20	.05
☐ 2 Johnny Bench	1.00	.40	.10
☐ 3 Lou Brock	.75	.30	.07
☐ 4 Whitey Ford	.75	.30	.07
☐ 5 Bob Gibson	.75	.30	.07
☐ 6 Billy Herman	.50	.20	.05
☐ 7 Harmon Killebrew	.75	.30	.07
☐ 8 Eddie Mathews	1.00	.40	.10
☐ 9 Brooks Robinson	1.00	.40	.10
☐ 10 Willie Stargell	1.00	.40	.10
☐ 11 Carl Yastrzemski	1.25	.50	.12
☐ 12 Coupon Card	.50	.20	.05

1989 Kahn's Mets

The 1989 Kahn's Mets set contains 36 (32 original and 4 update) standard-size (2 1/2" by 3 1/2") cards. The fronts have color photos with Mets' colored borders (blue, orange and white). The horizontally-oriented backs have career stats. The cards were available from Kahn's by sending three UPC symbols from Kahn's products and a coupon appearing in certain local newspapers. There was also a small late-season update set of Kahn's Mets showing new Mets players arriving in mid-season trades, e.g., Jeff Innis, Keith Miller, Jeff Musselman, and Frank Viola. This "Update" subset was distributed at a different Mets Baseball Card Night game than the main set. The main set is referenced below by uniform number. The update cards are given the prefix U in the checklist below.

	MINT	EXC	G-VG
COMPLETE SET (32)	10.00	4.50	1.25
COMPLETE UPDATE SET (4)	3.00	1.25	.30
COMMON PLAYER	.30	.12	.03
COMMON UPDATE PLAYER	.60	.25	.06
☐ 1 Mookie Wilson	.40	.16	.04
☐ 2 Mackey Sasser	.40	.16	.04
☐ 3 Bud Harrelson CO	.40	.16	.04
☐ 5 Davey Johnson MG	.40	.16	.04
☐ 7 Juan Samuel	.50	.20	.05
☐ 8 Gary Carter	.75	.30	.07
☐ 9 Gregg Jefferies	1.00	.40	.10
☐ 11 Tim Teufel	.30	.12	.03
☐ 12 Ron Darling	.40	.16	.04
☐ 13 Lee Mazzilli	.30	.12	.03
☐ 16 Dwight Gooden	.90	.40	.09
☐ 17 Keith Hernandez	.50	.20	.05
☐ 18 Darryl Strawberry	1.25	.50	.12
☐ 19 Bob Ojeda	.40	.16	.04
☐ 20 Howard Johnson	.90	.40	.09
☐ 21 Kevin Elster	.40	.16	.04
☐ 22 Kevin McReynolds	.50	.20	.05
☐ 28 Bill Robinson CO	.40	.16	.04
☐ 29 Dave Magadan	.50	.20	.05
☐ 30 Mel Stottlemyre CO	.40	.16	.04
☐ 32 Mark Carreon	.40	.16	.04
☐ 33 Barry Lyons	.30	.12	.03
☐ 34 Sam Perlozzo CO	.30	.12	.03
☐ 38 Rick Aguilera	.30	.12	.03
☐ 44 David Cone	.75	.30	.07
☐ 46 Dave West	.40	.16	.04
☐ 48 Randy Myers	.40	.16	.04
☐ 49 Don Aase	.30	.12	.03
☐ 50 Sid Fernandez	.50	.20	.05
☐ 52 Greg Pavlick CO	.30	.12	.03
☐ xx Mets Team Photo	.40	.16	.04
☐ xx Sponsors Card	.30	.12	.03
☐ U1 Jeff Innis	.60	.25	.06
☐ U2 Keith Miller	.75	.30	.07
☐ U3 Jeff Musselman	.60	.25	.06
☐ U4 Frank Viola	1.50	.60	.15

☐ 27 Jose Rijo	.90	.40	.09
☐ 28 Kal Daniels	.75	.30	.07
☐ 29 Herm Winningham	.35	.15	.03
☐ 30 Ken Griffey Sr.	.75	.30	.07
☐ 31 John Franco	.50	.20	.05
☐ 32 Tom Browning	.60	.25	.06
☐ 33 Ron Robinson	.50	.20	.05
☐ 34 Jeff Reed	.35	.15	.03
☐ 36 Rolando Roomes	.50	.20	.05
☐ 37 Norm Charlton	.50	.20	.05
☐ 42 Rick Mahler	.35	.15	.03
☐ 43 Kent Tekulve	.35	.15	.03
☐ 44 Eric Davis	1.50	.60	.15
☐ 48 Tim Birtsas	.35	.15	.03
☐ 49 Rob Dibble	.75	.30	.07
☐ xx Coaches Card	.50	.20	.05
☐ xx Sponsors Card	.35	.15	.03
☐ xx Sponsors Card	.35	.15	.03

1990 Kahn's Mets

The 1990 Kahn's Met Set was given away as a New York Mets stadium promotion. This standard-size (2 1/2" by 3 1/2") set is skip-numbered by uniform number within the set and features 34 cards and two Kahn's coupon cards. Three players, Thornton, Magadan, and Mercado are wearing different uniform numbers than listed on the front of their cards. In addition to the Shea Stadium promotion, the complete set was also available in specially marked three-packs of Kahn's Wieners.

	MINT	EXC	G-VG
COMPLETE SET (34)	8.00	3.50	.80
COMMON PLAYER	.25	.10	.02
☐ 1 Lou Thornton	.25	.10	.02
☐ 2 Mackey Sasser	.35	.15	.03
☐ 3 Bud Harrelson CO	.35	.15	.03
☐ 4 Mike Cubbage	.25	.10	.02
☐ 5 Davey Johnson MG	.35	.15	.03
☐ 6 Mike Marshall	.35	.15	.03
☐ 9 Gregg Jefferies	.75	.30	.07
☐ 10 Dave Magadan	.50	.20	.05
☐ 11 Tim Teufel	.25	.10	.02
☐ 13 Jeff Musselman	.25	.10	.02
☐ 15 Ron Darling	.35	.15	.03
☐ 16 Dwight Gooden	.75	.30	.07
☐ 18 Darryl Strawberry	1.00	.40	.10
☐ 19 Bob Ojeda	.35	.15	.03
☐ 20 Howard Johnson	.75	.30	.07
☐ 21 Kevin Elster	.25	.10	.02
☐ 22 Kevin McReynolds	.50	.20	.05
☐ 25 Keith Miller	.35	.15	.03
☐ 26 Alejandro Pena	.35	.15	.03
☐ 27 Tom O'Malley	.25	.10	.02
☐ 29 Frank Viola	.50	.20	.05
☐ 30 Mel Stottlemyre CO	.35	.15	.03
☐ 31 John Franco	.35	.15	.03
☐ 32 Doc Edwards CO	.25	.10	.02
☐ 33 Barry Lyons	.25	.10	.02
☐ 35 Orlando Mercado	.25	.10	.02
☐ 40 Jeff Innis	.25	.10	.02
☐ 44 David Cone	.50	.20	.05
☐ 45 Mark Carreon	.35	.15	.03
☐ 47 Wally Whitehurst	.35	.15	.03

1989 Kahn's Reds

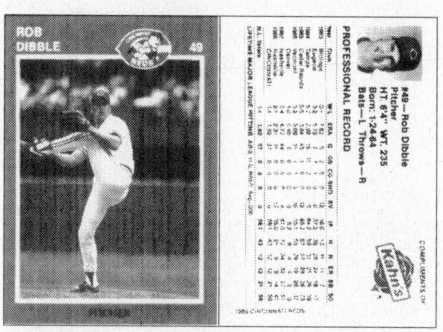

The 1989 Kahn's Reds set contains 28 standard-size (2 1/2" by 3 1/2") cards; each card features a member of the Cincinnati Reds. The fronts have color photos with red borders. The horizontally-oriented backs have career stats. The card numbering below is according to uniform number.

	MINT	EXC	G-VG
COMPLETE SET (28)	12.50	5.50	1.65
COMMON PLAYER	.35	.15	.03
☐ 6 Bo Diaz	.35	.15	.03
☐ 7 Lenny Harris	.50	.20	.05
☐ 11 Barry Larkin	1.25	.50	.12
☐ 12 Joel Youngblood	.35	.15	.03
☐ 14 Pete Rose MG	1.00	.40	.10
☐ 16 Ron Oester	.35	.15	.03
☐ 17 Chris Sabo	1.00	.40	.10
☐ 20 Danny Jackson	.50	.20	.05
☐ 21 Paul O'Neill	.75	.30	.07
☐ 25 Todd Benzinger	.50	.20	.05

		MINT	EXC	G-VG
☐ 48	Julio Machado	.35	.15	.03
☐ 50	Sid Fernandez	.35	.15	.03
☐ 52	Greg Pavlick CO	.25	.10	.02
☐ xx	Team Photo	.35	.15	.03

1990 Kahn's Reds

This 27-card, standard size, 2 1/2" by 3 1/2", set was issued by Kahn's Meats. This set which continued a more than 30-year tradition of Kahn's issuing Cincinnati Reds cards had the player's photos framed by red and white borders. The front have full-color photos while the back have a small black and white photo in the upper left hand corner and complete career statistics on the back of the card. The set is checklisted alphabetically since the cards are unnumbered except for uniform number. The number next to the player represents his uniform number.

		MINT	EXC	G-VG
COMPLETE SET (27)		11.00	5.00	1.35
COMMON PLAYER (1-27)		.40	.16	.04
☐ 1	Jack Armstrong 40	.60	.25	.06
☐ 2	Todd Benzinger 25	.50	.20	.05
☐ 3	Tim Birtsas 48	.40	.16	.04
☐ 4	Glenn Braggs 15	.50	.20	.05
☐ 5	Tom Browning 32	.60	.25	.06
☐ 6	Norm Charlton 37	.50	.20	.05
☐ 7	Eric Davis 44	2.00	.80	.20
☐ 8	Rob Dibble 49	.75	.30	.07
☐ 9	Mariano Duncan 7	.50	.20	.05
☐ 10	Ken Griffey 30	.75	.30	.07
☐ 11	Billy Hatcher 22	.60	.25	.06
☐ 12	Barry Larkin 11	1.00	.40	.10
☐ 13	Danny Jackson 20	.50	.20	.05
☐ 14	Tim Layana 43	.50	.20	.05
☐ 15	Rick Mahler 42	.40	.16	.04
☐ 16	Hal Morris 23	1.25	.50	.12
☐ 17	Randy Myers 28	.60	.25	.06
☐ 18	Ron Oester 16	.40	.16	.04
☐ 19	Joe Oliver 9	.60	.25	.06
☐ 20	Paul O'Neill 21	.60	.25	.06
☐ 21	Lou Piniella MG 41	.60	.25	.06
☐ 22	Luis Quinones 10	.40	.16	.04
☐ 23	Jeff Reed 34	.40	.16	.04
☐ 24	Jose Rijo 27	.75	.30	.07
☐ 25	Chris Sabo 17	1.00	.40	.10
☐ 26	Herm Winningham 29	.40	.16	.04
☐ 27	Red Coaches	.50	.20	.05
	Jackie Moore			
	Tony Perez			
	Sam Perlozzo			
	Larry Rothschild			
	Stan Williams			

1991 Kahn's Mets

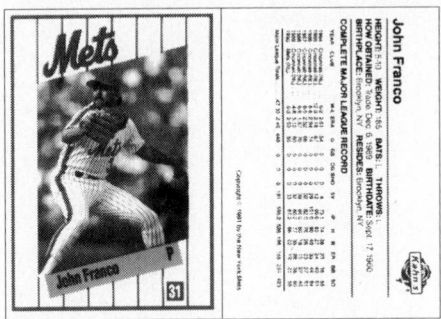

The 1991 Kahn's Met set contains 33 cards measuring the standard size (2 1/2" by 3 1/2"). The set is skip-numbered on the card fronts by uniform number and includes two Kahn's coupon cards. The front features color action player photos, on a white and blue pinstripe pattern. The player's name is given in an orange stripe below the picture. In a horizontal format the back presents biographical information, major league statistics, and minor league statistics where appropriate. A complete set was given away to each fan attending the Mets game at Shea Stadium on June 17, 1991.

		MINT	EXC	G-VG
COMPLETE SET (33)		8.00	3.50	.80
COMMON PLAYER		.25	.10	.02
☐ 1	Vince Coleman	.75	.30	.07
☐ 2	Mackey Sasser	.35	.15	.03
☐ 3	Bud Harrelson MG	.35	.15	.03
☐ 4	Mike Cubbage CO	.25	.10	.02
☐ 5	Charlie O'Brien	.25	.10	.02
☐ 7	Hubie Brooks	.35	.15	.03
☐ 8	Daryl Boston	.35	.15	.03
☐ 9	Gregg Jefferies	.75	.30	.07
☐ 10	Dave Magadan	.35	.15	.03
☐ 11	Tim Teufel	.25	.10	.02
☐ 13	Rick Cerone	.25	.10	.02
☐ 15	Ron Darling	.35	.15	.03
☐ 16	Dwight Gooden	.75	.30	.07
☐ 17	David Cone	.50	.20	.05
☐ 20	Howard Johnson	.75	.30	.07
☐ 21	Kevin Elster	.25	.10	.02
☐ 22	Kevin McReynolds	.50	.20	.05
☐ 25	Keith Miller	.35	.15	.03
☐ 26	Alejandro Pena	.35	.15	.03
☐ 28	Tom Herr	.25	.10	.02
☐ 29	Frank Viola	.50	.20	.05
☐ 30	Mel Stottlemyre CO	.35	.15	.03
☐ 31	John Franco	.35	.15	.03
☐ 32	Doc Edwards CO	.25	.10	.02
☐ 40	Jeff Innis	.25	.10	.02
☐ 43	Doug Simons	.25	.10	.02
☐ 45	Mark Carreon	.25	.10	.02
☐ 47	Wally Whitehurst	.25	.10	.02
☐ 48	Pete Schourek	.25	.10	.02
☐ 50	Sid Fernandez	.35	.15	.03
☐ 51	Tom Spencer CO	.25	.10	.02
☐ 52	Greg Pavlick CO	.25	.10	.02
☐ xx	1991 New York Mets	.35	.15	.03
	Team photo			

1991 Kahn's Reds

The 1991 Kahn's Reds set contains 28 cards measuring the standard size (2 1/2" by 3 1/2"). The set is skip-numbered by uniform number and includes two Kahn's coupon cards. The front features color action player photos which are mounted diagonally on the card face. Red pinstripe borders frame the picture above and below. The front lettering is printed in red and black on a white background. In a horizontal format the back is printed in red and black, and presents complete statistical information. The Kahn's logo in the lower right corner rounds out the back.

	MINT	EXC	G-VG
COMPLETE SET (28)	8.00	3.50	.80
COMMON PLAYER	.25	.10	.02
☐ 00 Schottzie	.25	.10	.02
Mascot			
☐ 7 Mariano Duncan	.35	.15	.03
☐ 9 Joe Oliver	.35	.15	.03
☐ 10 Luis Quinones	.25	.10	.02
☐ 11 Barry Larkin	.75	.30	.07
☐ 15 Glenn Braggs	.35	.15	.03
☐ 17 Chris Sabo	.60	.25	.06
☐ 19 Bill Doran	.35	.15	.03
☐ 21 Paul O'Neill	.35	.15	.03
☐ 22 Billy Hatcher	.35	.15	.03
☐ 23 Hal Morris	.75	.30	.07
☐ 25 Todd Benzinger	.35	.15	.03
☐ 27 Jose Rijo	.50	.20	.05
☐ 28 Randy Myers	.35	.15	.03
☐ 29 Herm Winningham	.25	.10	.02
☐ 32 Tom Browning	.35	.15	.03
☐ 34 Jeff Reed	.25	.10	.02
☐ 36 Don Carman	.25	.10	.02
☐ 37 Norm Charlton	.25	.10	.02
☐ 40 Jack Armstrong	.35	.15	.03
☐ 41 Lou Piniella MG	.35	.15	.03
☐ 44 Eric Davis	1.00	.40	.10
☐ 45 Chris Hammond	.50	.20	.05
☐ 47 Scott Scudder	.35	.15	.03
☐ 48 Ted Power	.25	.10	.02
☐ 49 Rob Dibble	.50	.20	.05
☐ 57 Freddie Benavides	.25	.10	.02
☐ xx Coaches Card	.35	.15	.03
Jackie Moore			
Tony Perez			
Sam Perlozzo			
Larry Rothschild			
Stan Williams			

1983 Kaline Story

This 72-card set was issued in 1983 to celebrate Al Kaline's thirtieth year of association with the Detroit Tigers. The set was issued in its own orange box and most of the cards in the series have orange borders. There are some cards which have black borders and those cards are the cards in the set which feature color photos. The set is basically in chronological order and covers events crucial to Kaline's career and the backs of the cards give further details about the picture on the front. The set was produced by Homeplate Sports Cards.

	MINT	EXC	G-VG
COMPLETE SET (73)	12.50	5.50	1.65
COMMON PLAYER (1-72)	.20	.08	.02
☐ 1A Autographed Title Card	1.50	.60	.15

(color)			
☐ 1B I'd play for nothing	.40	.16	.04
(color)			
☐ 2 Sandlot Days	.20	.08	.02
☐ 3 Prep MVP	.20	.08	.02
☐ 4 Learning the Ropes	.20	.08	.02
☐ 5 Working for a Living	.20	.08	.02
☐ 6 Pleasing a Young Fan	.20	.08	.02
☐ 7 The Newlyweds	.20	.08	.02
Al and Louise Kaline			
☐ 8 Al and Pat Mullin	.20	.08	.02
☐ 9 How Al Does It, 1	.20	.08	.02
☐ 10 How Al Does It, 2	.20	.08	.02
☐ 11 Silver Bat 1955	.30	.12	.03
☐ 12 Al and George Stark	.20	.08	.02
☐ 13 Al watching Gordie Howe	.75	.30	.07
(Howe taking batting practice)			
☐ 14 Kaline and Mantle	.75	.30	.07
☐ 15 1958 Group Photo	.20	.08	.02
(Jim Hegan, Billy Martin, Ray Boone, Harvey Kuenn, Jim Bunning, Al Kaline)			
☐ 16 All All-Stars	.60	.25	.06
Billy Martin, Al Kaline, Harvey Kuenn, Mickey Mantle, Whitey Ford (color)			
☐ 17 Crossing the Plate	.20	.08	.02
☐ 18 1959 All-Star Game	.20	.08	.02
(Bill Skowron and Al Kaline)			
☐ 19 1960 Tigers Stars	.40	.16	.04
(Norm Cash, Rocky Colavito, Al Kaline)			
☐ 20 Kaline Slides Under Fox	.40	.16	.04
(Al Kaline and Nellie Fox)			
☐ 21 1961 Gold Glove	.30	.12	.03
☐ 22 1962 Tigers	.30	.12	.03
Al Kaline, Jim Campbell GM, Norm Cash			
☐ 23 Costly Catch	.20	.08	.02
☐ 24 Japanese Tour 1962	.20	.08	.02
(Jim Bunning, Al Kaline, Norm Cash, and others)			
☐ 25 Perfect Form	.20	.08	.02
☐ 26 Receiving Awards	.30	.12	.03
(Ernie Harwell ANN, Al Kaline, George Kell ANN)			
☐ 27 Life Isn't Always Easy	.20	.08	.02
☐ 28 Family Game 1964	.20	.08	.02
(Al, Michael, and Mark Kaline)			
☐ 29 Al and Charlie Dressen	.20	.08	.02
☐ 30 George Kell and Al	.40	.16	.04
☐ 31 Al and Hal Newhouser	.30	.12	.03
☐ 32 The Kaline Family	.20	.08	.02
(Michael, Louise, Al, and Mark Kaline)			
☐ 33 Receiving Gold Glove	.40	.16	.04
(Al Kaline, Charlie Gehringer, and Bill Freehan)			
☐ 34 Rapping a Hit, 1967	.40	.16	.04
(color)			
☐ 35 Veteran Rivals	.75	.30	.07
(Mickey Mantle and Al)			

☐ 36	Al Homers vs. Boston	.20	.08	.02
☐ 37	1968 World Series Homer	.20	.08	.02
☐ 38	Premier Fielder	.20	.08	.02
☐ 39	1969 All-Time Tigers	.20	.08	.02
	(Hank Greenberg, Hal			
	Newhouser, Billy			
	Rogell, Al Kaline,			
	John Fetzer OWN,			
	Dennis McLain, George			
	Kell, Charlie Gehringer)			
☐ 40	Part of the Game	.20	.08	.02
☐ 41	Family Portrait	.40	.16	.04
	(color)			
☐ 42	Spring Training Tribute	.20	.08	.02
☐ 43	Billy Martin and Al	.20	.08	.02
☐ 44	First 100,000 Tiger	.20	.08	.02
	(with John Fetzer OWN			
	and Jim Campbell GM)			
☐ 45	On Deck, 1972	.30	.12	.03
	(color)			
☐ 46	A Close Call	.20	.08	.02
☐ 47	On Deck in Baltimore	.20	.08	.02
☐ 48	Hit Number 3,000	.30	.12	.03
☐ 49	April 17, 1955, ...	.20	.08	.02
	Three Homers			
☐ 50	All-Star Game Record	.20	.08	.02
☐ 51	1968 World Series	.40	.16	.04
	(Al Kaline and			
	Orlando Cepeda)			
☐ 52	1968 World Series	.30	.12	.03
	Celebration			
	(Al Kaline, John			
	Hiller, Jim Northrup)			
☐ 53	Al Kaline Day	.50	.20	.05
☐ 54	3,000 Hit Day	.20	.08	.02
	(Al Kaline, Father			
	and Mother, Lee			
	McPhail PRES, Jim			
	Campbell GM)			
☐ 55	September 29, 1974, ...	.20	.08	.02
	Thank You			
☐ 56	Silver Salute	.20	.08	.02
☐ 57	Al and George Kell	.40	.16	.04
	(color)			
☐ 58	Voices of the Tigers	.30	.12	.03
	Al and George Kell			
☐ 59	Tiger Record Setter	.30	.12	.03
	(color)			
☐ 60	Al's Last All-Star Team	.30	.12	.03
	(color)			
☐ 61	Pat Mullin and Al	.20	.08	.02
☐ 62	Al and Mickey Lolich	.50	.20	.05
	(color)			
☐ 63	Hall of Fame Plaque	.20	.08	.02
☐ 64	Al and Bowie Kuhn	.40	.16	.04
	(color)			
☐ 65	Al and Parents	.30	.12	.03
	(color)			
☐ 66	Kaline Family at Hall	.30	.12	.03
	(color)			
☐ 67	The Man and the Boy	.50	.20	.05
	(Stan Musial and Al)			
☐ 68	Two Kids	.50	.20	.05
	(Ted Williams and Al)			
☐ 69	Master Glovemen	.50	.20	.05
	(Al and Brooks			
	Robinson) (color)			
☐ 70	Coach and Pupil	.20	.08	.02
	(Al and Pat Underwood)			
☐ 71	Al at Batting Cage	.20	.08	.02
☐ 72	A Tiger Forever	.50	.20	.05
	(color)			

1986 Kay-Bee

This 33-card, standard-sized (2 1/2" by 3 1/2") set was produced by Topps, although manufactured in Northern Ireland. This boxed set retailed in Kay-Bee stores for 1.99; the checklist was listed on the back of the box. The set is subtitled "Young Superstars of Baseball" and does indeed feature many young players. The cards are numbered on the back; the set card numbering is alphabetical by player's name.

		MINT	EXC	G-VG
COMPLETE SET (33)		5.00	2.25	.50
COMMON PLAYER (1-33)		.10	.04	.01
☐ 1	Rick Aguilera	.15	.06	.01
☐ 2	Chris Brown	.10	.04	.01
☐ 3	Tom Browning	.15	.06	.01
☐ 4	Tom Brunansky	.15	.06	.01
☐ 5	Vince Coleman	.30	.12	.03
☐ 6	Ron Darling	.15	.06	.01
☐ 7	Alvin Davis	.15	.06	.01
☐ 8	Mariano Duncan	.15	.06	.01
☐ 9	Shawon Dunston	.25	.10	.02
☐ 10	Sid Fernandez	.15	.06	.01
☐ 11	Tony Fernandez	.20	.08	.02
☐ 12	Brian Fisher	.10	.04	.01
☐ 13	John Franco	.15	.06	.01
☐ 14	Julio Franco	.30	.12	.03
☐ 15	Dwight Gooden	.75	.30	.07
☐ 16	Ozzie Guillen	.25	.10	.02
☐ 17	Tony Gwynn	.75	.30	.07
☐ 18	Jimmy Key	.15	.06	.01
☐ 19	Don Mattingly	.75	.30	.07
☐ 20	Oddibe McDowell	.10	.04	.01
☐ 21	Roger McDowell	.10	.04	.01
☐ 22	Dan Pasqua	.10	.04	.01
☐ 23	Terry Pendleton	.20	.08	.02
☐ 24	Jim Presley	.10	.04	.01
☐ 25	Kirby Puckett	.75	.30	.07
☐ 26	Earnie Riles	.10	.04	.01
☐ 27	Bret Saberhagen	.35	.15	.03
☐ 28	Mark Salas	.10	.04	.01
☐ 29	Juan Samuel	.15	.06	.01
☐ 30	Jeff Stone	.10	.04	.01
☐ 31	Darryl Strawberry	.75	.30	.07
☐ 32	Andy Van Slyke	.20	.08	.02
☐ 33	Frank Viola	.20	.08	.02

1987 Kay-Bee

This small 33-card boxed set was produced by Topps for Kay-Bee Toy Stores. The set is subtitled "Super Stars of Baseball" and measures the standard 2 1/2" by 3 1/2" with full-color fronts. The card backs are printed in blue and black on white card stock. The checklist for the set is printed on the back panel of the yellow box. The set card numbering is alphabetical by player's name.

	MINT	EXC	G-VG
COMPLETE SET (33)	5.00	2.25	.50
COMMON PLAYER (1-33)	.10	.04	.01

		MINT	EXC	G-VG
☐ 1	Harold Baines	.15	.06	.01
☐ 2	Jesse Barfield	.15	.06	.01
☐ 3	Don Baylor	.10	.04	.01
☐ 4	Wade Boggs	.60	.25	.06
☐ 5	George Brett	.45	.18	.04
☐ 6	Hubie Brooks	.15	.06	.01
☐ 7	Jose Canseco	.90	.40	.09
☐ 8	Gary Carter	.20	.08	.02
☐ 9	Joe Carter	.25	.10	.02
☐ 10	Roger Clemens	.75	.30	.07
☐ 11	Vince Coleman	.25	.10	.02
☐ 12	Glenn Davis	.20	.08	.02
☐ 13	Dwight Gooden	.40	.16	.04
☐ 14	Pedro Guerrero	.20	.08	.02
☐ 15	Tony Gwynn	.50	.20	.05
☐ 16	Rickey Henderson	.75	.30	.07
☐ 17	Keith Hernandez	.20	.08	.02
☐ 18	Wally Joyner	.35	.15	.03
☐ 19	Don Mattingly	.75	.30	.07
☐ 20	Jack Morris	.25	.10	.02
☐ 21	Dale Murphy	.35	.15	.03
☐ 22	Eddie Murray	.40	.16	.04
☐ 23	Dave Parker	.25	.10	.02
☐ 24	Kirby Puckett	.60	.25	.06
☐ 25	Tim Raines	.20	.08	.02
☐ 26	Jim Rice	.20	.08	.02
☐ 27	Dave Righetti	.15	.06	.01
☐ 28	Ryne Sandberg	.75	.30	.07
☐ 29	Mike Schmidt	.75	.30	.07
☐ 30	Mike Scott	.15	.06	.01
☐ 31	Darryl Strawberry	.60	.25	.06
☐ 32	Fernando Valenzuela	.20	.08	.02
☐ 33	Dave Winfield	.30	.12	.03

1988 Kay-Bee

This small 33-card boxed set was produced by Topps for Kay-Bee Toy Stores. The set is subtitled "Superstars of Baseball" and measures the standard 2 1/2" by 3 1/2" with full-color fronts. The card backs are printed in blue and green on white card stock. The checklist for the set is printed on the back panel of the box. These cards are numbered on the back. The set card numbering is alphabetical by player's name.

	MINT	EXC	G-VG
COMPLETE SET (33)	4.00	1.75	.40
COMMON PLAYER (1-33)	.10	.04	.01

		MINT	EXC	G-VG
☐ 1	George Bell	.20	.08	.02
☐ 2	Wade Boggs	.50	.20	.05
☐ 3	Jose Canseco	.75	.30	.07
☐ 4	Joe Carter	.25	.10	.02
☐ 5	Jack Clark	.20	.08	.02
☐ 6	Alvin Davis	.15	.06	.01
☐ 7	Eric Davis	.40	.16	.04
☐ 8	Andre Dawson	.25	.10	.02

		MINT	EXC	G-VG
☐ 9	Darrell Evans	.10	.04	.01
☐ 10	Dwight Evans	.15	.06	.01
☐ 11	Gary Gaetti	.15	.06	.01
☐ 12	Pedro Guerrero	.15	.06	.01
☐ 13	Tony Gwynn	.45	.18	.04
☐ 14	Howard Johnson	.25	.10	.02
☐ 15	Wally Joyner	.25	.10	.02
☐ 16	Don Mattingly	.75	.30	.07
☐ 17	Willie McGee	.20	.08	.02
☐ 18	Mark McGwire	.60	.25	.06
☐ 19	Paul Molitor	.20	.08	.02
☐ 20	Dale Murphy	.30	.12	.03
☐ 21	Dave Parker	.20	.08	.02
☐ 22	Lance Parrish	.15	.06	.01
☐ 23	Kirby Puckett	.50	.20	.05
☐ 24	Tim Raines	.20	.08	.02
☐ 25	Cal Ripken	.75	.30	.07
☐ 26	Juan Samuel	.15	.06	.01
☐ 27	Mike Schmidt	.60	.25	.06
☐ 28	Ruben Sierra	.50	.20	.05
☐ 29	Darryl Strawberry	.60	.25	.06
☐ 30	Danny Tartabull	.30	.12	.03
☐ 31	Alan Trammell	.20	.08	.02
☐ 32	Tim Wallach	.15	.06	.01
☐ 33	Dave Winfield	.25	.10	.02

1989 Kay-Bee

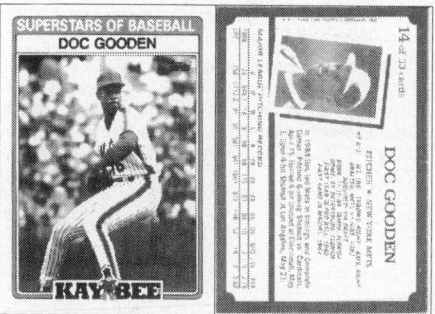

The 1989 Kay-Bee set contains 33 standard-size (2 1/2" by 3 1/2") glossy cards. The fronts have magenta and yellow borders. The horizontally oriented backs are brown and yellow. The cards were distributed as boxed sets through Kay-Bee toy stores. The set card numbering is alphabetical by player's name.

	MINT	EXC	G-VG
COMPLETE SET (33)	4.00	1.75	.40
COMMON PLAYER (1-33)	.15	.06	.01

		MINT	EXC	G-VG
☐ 1	Wade Boggs	.50	.20	.05
☐ 2	George Brett	.35	.15	.03
☐ 3	Jose Canseco	.90	.40	.09
☐ 4	Gary Carter	.20	.08	.02
☐ 5	Jack Clark	.20	.08	.02
☐ 6	Will Clark	.90	.40	.09
☐ 7	Roger Clemens	.75	.30	.07
☐ 8	Eric Davis	.35	.15	.03
☐ 9	Andre Dawson	.25	.10	.02
☐ 10	Dwight Evans	.15	.06	.01
☐ 11	Carlton Fisk	.30	.12	.03
☐ 12	Andres Galarraga	.20	.08	.02
☐ 13	Kirk Gibson	.20	.08	.02
☐ 14	Dwight Gooden	.35	.15	.03
☐ 15	Mike Greenwell	.30	.12	.03
☐ 16	Pedro Guerrero	.15	.06	.01
☐ 17	Tony Gwynn	.45	.18	.04
☐ 18	Rickey Henderson	.75	.30	.07
☐ 19	Orel Hershiser	.25	.10	.02
☐ 20	Don Mattingly	.60	.25	.06
☐ 21	Mark McGwire	.50	.20	.05
☐ 22	Dale Murphy	.30	.12	.03
☐ 23	Eddie Murray	.35	.15	.03
☐ 24	Kirby Puckett	.45	.18	.04
☐ 25	Tim Raines	.20	.08	.02
☐ 26	Ryne Sandberg	.60	.25	.06
☐ 27	Mike Schmidt	.60	.25	.06

		MINT	EXC	G-VG
☐ 28	Ozzie Smith	.20	.08	.02
☐ 29	Darryl Strawberry	.50	.20	.05
☐ 30	Alan Trammell	.20	.08	.02
☐ 31	Frank Viola	.15	.06	.01
☐ 32	Dave Winfield	.20	.08	.02
☐ 33	Robin Yount	.45	.18	.04

1990 Kay-Bee

The 1990 Kay-Bee Kings of Baseball set is a standard-size (2 1/2" by 3 1/2"), 33-card set sequenced alphabetically that Topps produced for the Kay-Bee toy store chain. A solid red border inside a purple white striped box is the major design feature of this set. The set card numbering is alphabetical by player's name.

		MINT	EXC	G-VG
COMPLETE SET (33)		4.00	1.75	.40
COMMON PLAYER (1-33)		.10	.04	.01
☐ 1	Doyle Alexander	.10	.04	.01
☐ 2	Bert Blyleven	.15	.06	.01
☐ 3	Wade Boggs	.50	.20	.05
☐ 4	George Brett	.35	.15	.03
☐ 5	John Candelaria	.10	.04	.01
☐ 6	Gary Carter	.20	.08	.02
☐ 7	Vince Coleman	.20	.08	.02
☐ 8	Andre Dawson	.25	.10	.02
☐ 9	Dennis Eckersley	.15	.06	.01
☐ 10	Darrell Evans	.10	.04	.01
☐ 11	Dwight Evans	.15	.06	.01
☐ 12	Carlton Fisk	.25	.10	.02
☐ 13	Ken Griffey Sr.	.15	.06	.01
☐ 14	Tony Gwynn	.35	.15	.03
☐ 15	Rickey Henderson	.60	.25	.06
☐ 16	Keith Hernandez	.15	.06	.01
☐ 17	Charlie Hough	.10	.04	.01
☐ 18	Don Mattingly	.60	.25	.06
☐ 19	Jack Morris	.15	.06	.01
☐ 20	Dale Murphy	.30	.12	.03
☐ 21	Eddie Murray	.35	.15	.03
☐ 22	Dave Parker	.20	.08	.02
☐ 23	Kirby Puckett	.30	.12	.03
☐ 24	Tim Raines	.20	.08	.02
☐ 25	Rick Reuschel	.10	.04	.01
☐ 26	Jerry Reuss	.10	.04	.01
☐ 27	Jim Rice	.20	.08	.02
☐ 28	Nolan Ryan	.90	.40	.09
☐ 29	Ozzie Smith	.25	.10	.02
☐ 30	Frank Tanana	.10	.04	.01
☐ 31	Willie Wilson	.15	.06	.01
☐ 32	Dave Winfield	.20	.08	.02
☐ 33	Robin Yount	.30	.12	.03

1968 KDKA Pirates

This 23-card set measures approximately 2 3/8" by 4" and was issued by radio and television station KDKA to promote the

Pittsburgh Pirates, whom they were covering at the time. The fronts have the players' photo on the top 2/3 of the card and a facsimile autograph, the players name and position and uniform number on the lower left hand corner and an ad for KDKA on the lower right corner of the card. The back has an advertisement for both KDKA radio and television. The set is checklisted below by uniform number.

		NRMT	VG-E	GOOD
COMPLETE SET (23)		75.00	34.00	11.25
COMMON PLAYER		2.00	.80	.20
☐ 7	Larry Shepard MG	2.00	.80	.20
☐ 8	Willie Stargell	18.00	7.50	2.50
☐ 9	Bill Mazeroski	6.00	2.50	.60
☐ 10	Gary Kolb	2.00	.80	.20
☐ 11	Jose Pagan	2.00	.80	.20
☐ 12	Jerry May	2.00	.80	.20
☐ 14	Jim Bunning	6.00	2.50	.60
☐ 15	Manny Mota	3.00	1.25	.30
☐ 17	Donn Clendenon	2.50	1.00	.25
☐ 18	Matty Alou	2.50	1.00	.25
☐ 21	Bob Clemente	30.00	13.50	4.50
☐ 22	Gene Alley	2.50	1.00	.25
☐ 25	Tommy Sisk	2.00	.80	.20
☐ 26	Roy Face	3.00	1.25	.30
☐ 27	Ron Kline	2.00	.80	.20
☐ 28	Steve Blass	2.50	1.00	.25
☐ 29	Juan Pizzaro	2.00	.80	.20
☐ 30	Maury Wills	6.00	2.50	.60
☐ 34	Al McBean	2.00	.80	.20
☐ 35	Manny Sanguillen	2.50	1.00	.25
☐ 38	Bob Moose	2.50	1.00	.25
☐ 39	Bob Veale	2.50	1.00	.25
☐ 40	Dave Wickersham	2.00	.80	.20

1970 Kellogg's

The cards in this 75-card set measure 2 1/4" by 3 1/2". The 1970 Kellogg's set was Kellogg's first venture into the baseball card producing field. The design incorporates a brilliant color photo of the player set against an indistinct background, which is then covered with a layer of plastic to simulate a 3-D look. Some veteran card dealers consider cards 16-30 to be in shorter supply than the other cards in the set.

		NRMT	VG-E	GOOD
COMPLETE SET (75)		175.00	80.00	27.00
COMMON PLAYER (1-15)		1.00	.40	.10
COMMON PLAYER (16-30)		1.00	.40	.10
COMMON PLAYER (31-75)		1.00	.40	.10
☐ 1	Ed Kranepool	1.00	.40	.10
☐ 2	Pete Rose	18.00	7.50	2.50
☐ 3	Cleon Jones	1.00	.40	.10
☐ 4	Willie McCovey	6.00	2.50	.60
☐ 5	Mel Stottlemyre	1.50	.60	.15
☐ 6	Frank Howard	1.50	.60	.15
☐ 7	Tom Seaver	15.00	6.50	2.15

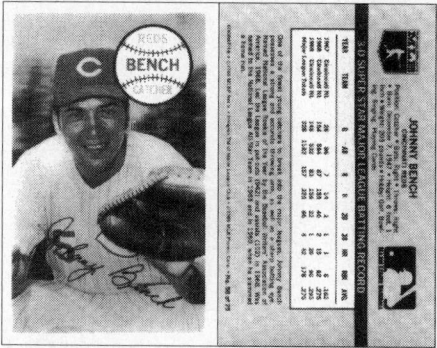

☐ 73 Denny McLain	1.50	.60	.15
☐ 74 Tommy Harper	1.00	.40	.10
☐ 75 Don Mincher	1.00	.40	.10

1971 Kellogg's

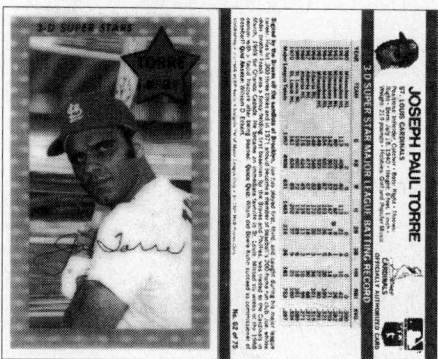

The cards in this 75-card set measure 2 1/4" by 3 1/2". The 1971 set of 3-D cards marketed by the Kellogg Company is the scarcest of all that company's issues. It was distributed as single cards, one in each package of cereal, without the usual complete set mail-in offer. In addition, card dealers were unable to obtain this set in quantity, as they have in other years. All the cards are available with and without the year 1970 before XOGRAPH on the back in the lower left corner; the version without carries a slight premium for most numbers. Prices listed below are for the more common variety with the year 1970.

	NRMT	VG-E	GOOD
COMPLETE SET (75)	850.00	375.00	125.00
COMMON PLAYER (1-75)	6.50	2.75	.65

☐ 1 Wayne Simpson		6.50	2.75	.65
☐ 2 Tom Seaver		35.00	15.75	5.25
☐ 3 Jim Perry		7.50	3.25	.75
☐ 4 Bob Robertson		6.50	2.75	.65
☐ 5 Roberto Clemente		35.00	15.75	5.25
☐ 6 Gaylord Perry		21.00	9.00	3.00
☐ 7 Felipe Alou		7.50	3.25	.75
☐ 8 Denis Menke		6.50	2.75	.65
☐ 9A Don Kessinger (no 1970 date)		8.50	3.75	.85
☐ 9B Don Kessinger ERR (dated, 1970 hits 167, avg. .265)		8.50	3.75	.85
☐ 9C Don Kessinger COR (dated, 1970 hits 168, avg. .266)		8.50	3.75	.85
☐ 10 Willie Mays		40.00	18.00	6.00
☐ 11 Jim Hickman		6.50	2.75	.65
☐ 12 Tony Oliva		10.00	4.50	1.25
☐ 13 Manny Sanguillen		7.50	3.25	.75
☐ 14 Frank Howard		8.50	3.75	.85
☐ 15 Frank Robinson		24.00	10.50	3.50
☐ 16 Willie Davis		8.50	3.75	.85
☐ 17 Lou Brock		24.00	10.50	3.50
☐ 18 Cesar Tovar		6.50	2.75	.65
☐ 19 Luis Aparicio		16.00	6.75	2.25
☐ 20 Boog Powell		10.00	4.50	1.25
☐ 21 Dick Selma		6.50	2.75	.65
☐ 22 Danny Walton		6.50	2.75	.65
☐ 23 Carl Morton		6.50	2.75	.65
☐ 24 Sonny Siebert		6.50	2.75	.65
☐ 25 Jim Merritt		6.50	2.75	.65
☐ 26 Jose Cardenal		6.50	2.75	.65
☐ 27 Don Mincher		6.50	2.75	.65
☐ 28A Clyde Wright (no 1970 date, team logo is Angels crest)		10.00	4.50	1.25

☐ 8 Don Sutton	3.50	1.50	.35
☐ 9 Jim Wynn	1.50	.60	.15
☐ 10 Jim Maloney	1.50	.60	.15
☐ 11 Tommie Agee	1.00	.40	.10
☐ 12 Willie Mays	15.00	6.50	2.15
☐ 13 Juan Marichal	5.00	2.25	.50
☐ 14 Dave McNally	1.50	.60	.15
☐ 15 Frank Robinson	5.00	2.25	.50
☐ 16 Carlos May	1.00	.40	.10
☐ 17 Bill Singer	1.00	.40	.10
☐ 18 Rick Reichardt	1.00	.40	.10
☐ 19 Boog Powell	1.50	.60	.15
☐ 20 Gaylord Perry	5.00	2.25	.50
☐ 21 Brooks Robinson	6.50	2.75	.65
☐ 22 Luis Aparicio	4.00	1.75	.40
☐ 23 Joel Horlen	1.00	.40	.10
☐ 24 Mike Epstein	1.00	.40	.10
☐ 25 Tom Haller	1.00	.40	.10
☐ 26 Willie Crawford	1.00	.40	.10
☐ 27 Roberto Clemente	15.00	6.50	2.15
☐ 28 Matty Alou	1.00	.40	.10
☐ 29 Willie Stargell	6.00	2.50	.60
☐ 30 Tim Cullen	1.00	.40	.10
☐ 31 Randy Hundley	1.00	.40	.10
☐ 32 Reggie Jackson	18.00	7.50	2.50
☐ 33 Rich Allen	1.00	.40	.10
☐ 34 Tim McCarver	1.50	.60	.15
☐ 35 Ray Culp	1.00	.40	.10
☐ 36 Jim Fregosi	1.50	.60	.15
☐ 37 Billy Williams	4.00	1.75	.40
☐ 38 Johnny Odom	1.00	.40	.10
☐ 39 Bert Campaneris	1.50	.60	.15
☐ 40 Ernie Banks	7.50	3.25	.75
☐ 41 Chris Short	1.00	.40	.10
☐ 42 Ron Santo	1.50	.60	.15
☐ 43 Glenn Beckert	1.00	.40	.10
☐ 44 Lou Brock	5.00	2.25	.50
☐ 45 Larry Hisle	1.00	.40	.10
☐ 46 Reggie Smith	1.50	.60	.15
☐ 47 Rod Carew	7.50	3.25	.75
☐ 48 Curt Flood	1.50	.60	.15
☐ 49 Jim Lonborg	1.50	.60	.15
☐ 50 Sam McDowell	1.50	.60	.15
☐ 51 Sal Bando	1.50	.60	.15
☐ 52 Al Kaline	7.50	3.25	.75
☐ 53 Gary Nolan	1.00	.40	.10
☐ 54 Rico Petrocelli	1.00	.40	.10
☐ 55 Ollie Brown	1.00	.40	.10
☐ 56 Luis Tiant	1.50	.60	.15
☐ 57 Bill Freehan	1.50	.60	.15
☐ 58 Johnny Bench	15.00	6.50	2.15
☐ 59 Joe Pepitone	1.50	.60	.15
☐ 60 Bobby Murcer	1.50	.60	.15
☐ 61 Harmon Killebrew	5.00	2.25	.50
☐ 62 Don Wilson	1.00	.40	.10
☐ 63 Tony Oliva	2.00	.80	.20
☐ 64 Jim Perry	1.50	.60	.15
☐ 65 Mickey Lolich	1.50	.60	.15
☐ 66 Jose Laboy	1.00	.40	.10
☐ 67 Dean Chance	1.00	.40	.10
☐ 68 Ken Harrelson	1.50	.60	.15
☐ 69 Willie Horton	1.00	.40	.10
☐ 70 Wally Bunker	1.00	.40	.10
☐ 71A Bob Gibson ERR (1959 innings pitched is blank)	6.00	2.50	.60
☐ 71B Bob Gibson COR (1959 innings is 76)	6.00	2.50	.60
☐ 72 Joe Morgan	5.00	2.25	.50

☐ 28B	Clyde Wright .... (no 1970 date, team logo is California outline with Angels written inside)	10.00	4.50	1.25
☐ 28C	Clyde Wright .... (dated 1970, team logo is California state outline)	7.50	3.25	.75
☐ 29	Les Cain	6.50	2.75	.65
☐ 30	Danny Cater	6.50	2.75	.65
☐ 31	Don Sutton	18.00	7.50	2.50
☐ 32	Chuck Dobson	6.50	2.75	.65
☐ 33	Willie McCovey	24.00	10.50	3.50
☐ 34	Mike Epstein	6.50	2.75	.65
☐ 35	Paul Blair	6.50	2.75	.65
☐ 36A	Gary Nolan .... (no 1970 date)	7.50	3.25	.75
☐ 36B	Gary Nolan .... (dated 1970, 1970 BB 95, SO 177)	7.50	3.25	.75
☐ 36C	Gary Nolan .... (dated 1970, 1970 BB 96, SO 181)	7.50	3.25	.75
☐ 37	Sam McDowell	7.50	3.25	.75
☐ 38	Amos Otis	7.50	3.25	.75
☐ 39	Ray Fosse	6.50	2.75	.65
☐ 40	Mel Stottlemyre	8.50	3.75	.85
☐ 41	Clarence Gaston	8.50	3.75	.85
☐ 42	Dick Dietz	6.50	2.75	.65
☐ 43	Roy White	7.50	3.25	.75
☐ 44	Al Kaline	30.00	13.50	4.50
☐ 45	Carlos May	6.50	2.75	.65
☐ 46	Tommie Agee	6.50	2.75	.65
☐ 47	Tommy Harper	6.50	2.75	.65
☐ 48	Larry Dierker	6.50	2.75	.65
☐ 49	Mike Cuellar	6.50	2.75	.65
☐ 50	Ernie Banks	30.00	13.50	4.50
☐ 51	Bob Gibson	24.00	10.50	3.50
☐ 52	Reggie Smith	7.50	3.25	.75
☐ 53	Matty Alou	7.50	3.25	.75
☐ 54A	Alex Johnson .... (no 1970 date, team logo is Angels crest)	10.00	4.50	1.25
☐ 54B	Alex Johnson .... (no 1970 date, team logo is California state outline)	10.00	4.50	1.25
☐ 54C	Alex Johnson .... (dated 1970, team logo is California state outline)	7.50	3.25	.75
☐ 55	Harmon Killebrew	24.00	10.50	3.50
☐ 56	Bill Grabarkewitz	6.50	2.75	.65
☐ 57	Richie Allen	11.00	5.00	1.35
☐ 58	Tony Perez	15.00	6.50	2.15
☐ 59	Dave McNally	7.50	3.25	.75
☐ 60	Jim Palmer	30.00	13.50	4.50
☐ 61	Billy Williams	21.00	9.00	3.00
☐ 62	Joe Torre	11.00	5.00	1.35
☐ 63	Jim Northrup	7.50	3.25	.75
☐ 64A	Jim Fregosi .... (no 1970 date, team logo is Angels crest)	10.00	4.50	1.25
☐ 64B	Jim Fregosi .... (no 1970 date, team logo is California state outline	10.00	4.50	1.25
☐ 64C	Jim Fregosi .... (dated1970, 1970 Hits 166, avg. .276)	8.50	3.75	.85
☐ 64D	Jim Fregosi .... (dated1970, 1970 Hits 167, avg. .278)	8.50	3.75	.85
☐ 65	Pete Rose	60.00	27.00	9.00
☐ 66A	Bud Harrelson .... (no 1970 date)	8.50	3.75	.85
☐ 66B	Bud Harrelson ERR .... (dated 1970, 1970 RBI 43)	8.50	3.75	.85
☐ 66C	Bud Harrelson COR .... (dated 1970, 1970 RBI 42)	8.50	3.75	.85
☐ 67	Tony Taylor	6.50	2.75	.65
☐ 68	Willie Stargell	24.00	10.50	3.50
☐ 69	Tony Horton	7.50	3.25	.75
☐ 70A	Claude Osteen ERR .... (no 1970 date, card number missing)	10.00	4.50	1.25
☐ 70B	Claude Osteen COR .... (no 1970 date, card number present)	10.00	4.50	1.25
☐ 70C	Claude Osteen COR .... (dated 1970)	7.50	3.25	.75

☐ 71	Glenn Beckert	6.50	2.75	.65
☐ 72	Nate Colbert	6.50	2.75	.65
☐ 73A	Rick Monday .... (no 1970 date)	8.50	3.75	.85
☐ 73B	Rick Monday ERR .... (dated 1970, 1970 AB 377, avg. .289)	8.50	3.75	.85
☐ 73C	Rick Monday COR .... (dated 1970, 1970 AB 376, avg. .290)	8.50	3.75	.85
☐ 74	Tommy John	12.50	5.50	1.65
☐ 75	Chris Short	6.50	2.75	.65

1972 Kellogg's

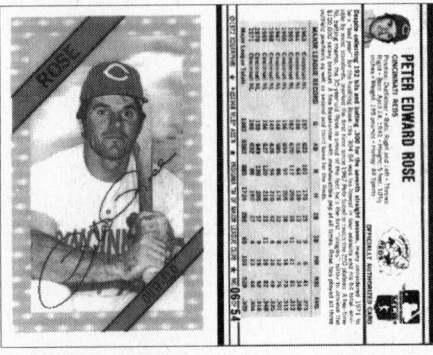

The cards in this 54-card set measure 2 1/8" by 3 1/4". The dimensions of the cards in the 1972 Kellogg's set were reduced in comparison to those of the 1971 series. In addition, the length of the set was set at 54 cards rather than the 75 of the previous year. The cards of this Kellogg's set are characterized by the diagonal bands found on the obverse.

		NRMT	VG-E	GOOD
COMPLETE SET (54)		75.00	34.00	11.25
COMMON PLAYER (1-54)		.65	.25	.06
☐ 1A	Tom Seaver ERR .... (1970 ERA 2.85)	10.00	4.50	1.25
☐ 1B	Tom Seaver COR .... (1970 ERA 2.81)	20.00	8.50	2.75
☐ 2	Amos Otis	.75	.30	.07
☐ 3A	Willie Davis ERR .... (lifetime runs 842)	1.50	.60	.15
☐ 3B	Willie Davis COR .... (lifetime runs 841)	.75	.30	.07
☐ 4	Wilbur Wood	.65	.25	.06
☐ 5	Bill Parsons	.65	.25	.06
☐ 6	Pete Rose	15.00	6.50	2.15
☐ 7A	Willie McCovey ERR .... (lifetime HR 360)	3.50	1.50	.35
☐ 7B	Willie McCovey COR .... (lifetime HR 370)	7.00	3.00	.70
☐ 8	Ferguson Jenkins	3.00	1.25	.30
☐ 9A	Vida Blue ERR .... (lifetime ERA 2.35)	1.50	.60	.15
☐ 9B	Vida Blue COR .... (lifetime ERA 2.31)	.75	.30	.07
☐ 10	Joe Torre	1.00	.40	.10
☐ 11	Merv Rettenmund	.65	.25	.06
☐ 12	Bill Melton	.65	.25	.06
☐ 13A	Jim Palmer ERR .... (lifetime games 170)	4.50	2.00	.45
☐ 13B	Jim Palmer COR .... (lifetime games 168)	9.00	4.00	.90
☐ 14	Doug Rader	.75	.30	.07
☐ 15A	Dave Roberts ERR .... ("NL" missing in bio)	.65	.25	.06
☐ 15B	Dave Roberts COR .... ("NL" in bio, line 2)	1.25	.50	.12
☐ 16	Bobby Murcer	.75	.30	.07
☐ 17	Wes Parker	.75	.30	.07
☐ 18A	Joe Coleman ERR	1.25	.50	.12

(lifetime BB 294)

☐	18B	Joe Coleman COR	.65	.25	.06
		(lifetime BB 393)			
☐	19	Manny Sanguillen	.75	.30	.07
☐	20	Reggie Jackson	12.00	5.25	1.50
☐	21	Ralph Garr	.65	.25	.06
☐	22	Jim Hunter	2.50	1.00	.25
☐	23	Rick Wise	.65	.25	.06
☐	24	Glenn Beckert	.65	.25	.06
☐	25	Tony Oliva	1.50	.60	.15
☐	26A	Bob Gibson ERR	8.00	3.50	.80
		(lifetime SO 2577)			
☐	26B	Bob Gibson COR	4.00	1.75	.40
		(lifetime SO 2578)			
☐	27A	Mike Cuellar ERR	1.25	.50	.12
		(1971 ERA 3.80)			
☐	27B	Mike Cuellar COR	.65	.25	.06
		(1971 ERA 3.08)			
☐	28	Chris Speier	.65	.25	.06
☐	29A	Dave McNally ERR	1.50	.60	.15
		(lifetime ERA 3.18)			
☐	29B	Dave McNally COR	.75	.30	.07
		(lifetime ERA 3.15)			
☐	30	Leo Cardenas	.65	.25	.06
☐	31A	Bill Freehan ERR	.75	.30	.07
		(lifetime runs 497)			
☐	31B	Bill Freehan COR	1.50	.60	.15
		(lifetime runs 500)			
☐	32A	Bud Harrelson ERR	1.50	.60	.15
		(lifetime hits 634)			
☐	32B	Bud Harrelson COR	.75	.30	.07
		(lifetime hits 624)			
☐	33A	Sam McDowell ERR	.75	.30	.07
		(bio line 3 has			
		"less than 200")			
☐	33B	Sam McDowell COR	1.50	.60	.15
		(bio line 3 has			
		"less than 225")			
☐	34A	Claude Osteen ERR	.65	.25	.06
		(1971 ERA 3.25)			
☐	34B	Claude Osteen COR	1.25	.50	.12
		(1971 ERA 3.51)			
☐	35	Reggie Smith	.75	.30	.07
☐	36	Sonny Siebert	.65	.25	.06
☐	37	Lee May	.75	.30	.07
☐	38	Mickey Lolich	1.00	.40	.10
☐	39A	Cookie Rojas ERR	1.25	.50	.12
		(lifetime 2B 149)			
☐	39B	Cookie Rojas COR	.65	.25	.06
		(lifetime 2B 150)			
☐	40A	Dick Drago ERR	1.25	.50	.12
		(bio line 3			
		has Poyals)			
☐	40B	Dick Drago COR	.65	.25	.06
		(bio line 3			
		has Royals)			
☐	41	Nate Colbert	.65	.25	.06
☐	42	Andy Messersmith	.75	.30	.07
☐	43A	Dave Johnson ERR	2.00	.80	.20
		(lifetime AB 3110,			
		avg. .262)			
☐	43B	Dave Johnson COR	1.00	.40	.10
		(lifetime AB 3113,			
		avg. .264)			
☐	44	Steve Blass	.75	.30	.07
☐	45	Bob Robertson	.65	.25	.06
☐	46A	Billy Williams ERR	3.50	1.50	.35
		(bio has "missed			
		only one game")			
☐	46B	Billy Williams COR	7.00	3.00	.70
		(bio has that line			
		eliminated)			
☐	47	Juan Marichal	3.50	1.50	.35
☐	48	Lou Brock	4.00	1.75	.40
☐	49	Roberto Clemente	10.00	4.50	1.25
☐	50	Mel Stottlemyre	.75	.30	.07
☐	51	Don Wilson	.65	.25	.06
☐	52A	Sal Bando ERR	.75	.30	.07
		(lifetime RBI 355)			
☐	52B	Sal Bando COR	1.50	.60	.15
		(lifetime RBI 356)			
☐	53A	Willie Stargell ERR	8.00	3.50	.80
		(lifetime 2B 197)			
☐	53B	Willie Stargell COR	4.00	1.75	.40
		(lifetime 2B 196)			
☐	54A	Willie Mays ERR	20.00	8.50	2.75
		(lifetime RBI 1855)			
☐	54B	Willie Mays COR	10.00	4.50	1.25
		(lifetime RBI 1856)			

1972 Kellogg's ATG

The cards in this 15-card set measure 2 1/4" by 3 1/2". The 1972 All-Time Greats 3-D set was issued with Kellogg's Danish Go Rounds. The set contains two different cards of Babe Ruth. The set is a reissue of a 1970 set issued by Rold Gold Pretzels to commemorate baseball's first 100 years. The Rold Gold cards are copyrighted 1970 on the reverse and are valued at approximately double the prices listed below.

			NRMT	VG-E	GOOD
	COMPLETE SET (15)		20.00	8.50	2.75
	COMMON PLAYER (1-15)		.65	.25	.06
☐	1	Walter Johnson	1.50	.60	.15
☐	2	Rogers Hornsby	1.00	.40	.10
☐	3	John McGraw	.65	.25	.06
☐	4	Mickey Cochrane	.75	.30	.07
☐	5	George Sisler	.75	.30	.07
☐	6	Babe Ruth	5.00	2.25	.50
☐	7	Lefty Grove	1.00	.40	.10
☐	8	Pie Traynor	.65	.25	.06
☐	9	Honus Wagner	1.50	.60	.15
☐	10	Eddie Collins	.65	.25	.06
☐	11	Tris Speaker	.90	.40	.09
☐	12	Cy Young	1.50	.60	.15
☐	13	Lou Gehrig	3.00	1.25	.30
☐	14	Babe Ruth	5.00	2.25	.50
☐	15	Ty Cobb	3.00	1.25	.30

1973 Kellogg's 2D

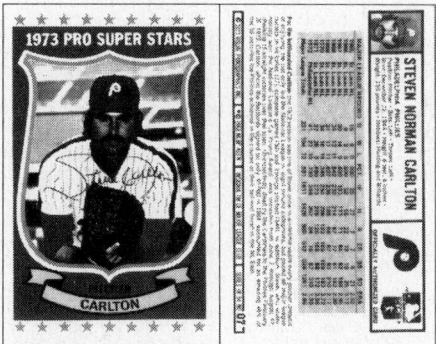

The cards in this 54-card set measure 2 1/4" by 3 1/2". The 1973 Kellogg's set is the only non-3D set produced by the Kellogg Company. Apparently Kellogg's decided to have the cards produced through Visual Panographics rather than by Xograph, as in the other years. The complete set could be obtained from the company through a box-top redemption procedure. The card size is slightly larger than the previous year.

		NRMT	VG-E	GOOD
	COMPLETE SET (54)	75.00	34.00	11.25
	COMMON PLAYER (1-54)	.65	.25	.06
☐ 1	Amos Otis	.75	.30	.07
☐ 2	Ellie Rodriguez	.65	.25	.06
☐ 3	Mickey Lolich	1.00	.40	.10
☐ 4	Tony Oliva	1.25	.50	.12
☐ 5	Don Sutton	2.50	1.00	.25
☐ 6	Pete Rose	15.00	6.50	2.15
☐ 7	Steve Carlton	5.00	2.25	.50
☐ 8	Bobby Bonds	1.00	.40	.10
☐ 9	Wilbur Wood	.65	.25	.06
☐ 10	Billy Williams	3.00	1.25	.30
☐ 11	Steve Blass	.75	.30	.07
☐ 12	Jon Matlack	.75	.30	.07
☐ 13	Cesar Cedeno	.75	.30	.07
☐ 14	Bob Gibson	3.00	1.25	.30
☐ 15	Sparky Lyle	1.00	.40	.10
☐ 16	Nolan Ryan	20.00	8.50	2.75
☐ 17	Jim Palmer	4.50	2.00	.45
☐ 18	Ray Fosse	.65	.25	.06
☐ 19	Bobby Murcer	.90	.40	.09
☐ 20	Jim Hunter	2.50	1.00	.25
☐ 21	Tom McCraw	.65	.25	.06
☐ 22	Reggie Jackson	9.00	4.00	.90
☐ 23	Bill Stoneman	.65	.25	.06
☐ 24	Lou Piniella	1.00	.40	.10
☐ 25	Willie Stargell	3.50	1.50	.35
☐ 26	Dick Allen	1.00	.40	.10
☐ 27	Carlton Fisk	6.00	2.50	.60
☐ 28	Ferguson Jenkins	3.00	1.25	.30
☐ 29	Phil Niekro	2.50	1.00	.25
☐ 30	Gary Nolan	.65	.25	.06
☐ 31	Joe Torre	1.00	.40	.10
☐ 32	Bobby Tolan	.65	.25	.06
☐ 33	Nate Colbert	.65	.25	.06
☐ 34	Joe Morgan	3.50	1.50	.35
☐ 35	Bert Blyleven	1.00	.40	.10
☐ 36	Joe Rudi	.75	.30	.07
☐ 37	Ralph Garr	.65	.25	.06
☐ 38	Gaylord Perry	2.50	1.00	.25
☐ 39	Bobby Grich	.75	.30	.07
☐ 40	Lou Brock	3.00	1.25	.30
☐ 41	Pete Broberg	.65	.25	.06
☐ 42	Manny Sanguillen	.75	.30	.07
☐ 43	Willie Davis	.75	.30	.07
☐ 44	Dave Kingman	.90	.40	.09
☐ 45	Carlos May	.65	.25	.06
☐ 46	Tom Seaver	7.50	3.25	.75
☐ 47	Mike Cuellar	.65	.25	.06
☐ 48	Joe Coleman	.65	.25	.06
☐ 49	Claude Osteen	.65	.25	.06
☐ 50	Steve Kline	.65	.25	.06
☐ 51	Rod Carew	5.50	2.50	.55
☐ 52	Al Kaline	5.50	2.50	.55
☐ 53	Larry Dierker	.65	.25	.06
☐ 54	Ron Santo	1.00	.40	.10

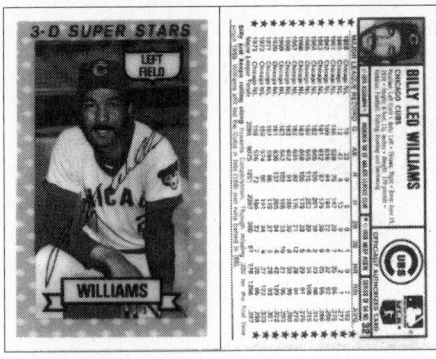

1974 Kellogg's

The cards in this 54-card set measure 2 1/8" by 3 1/4". In 1974 the Kellogg's set returned to its 3-D format; it also returned to the smaller-size card. Complete sets could be obtained from the company through a box-top offer. The cards are numbered on the back.

		NRMT	VG-E	GOOD
	COMPLETE SET (54)	65.00	29.00	9.75
	COMMON PLAYER (1-54)	.50	.20	.05
☐ 1	Bob Gibson	3.25	1.35	.32
☐ 2	Rick Monday	.60	.25	.06
☐ 3	Joe Coleman	.50	.20	.05
☐ 4	Bert Campaneris	.60	.25	.06
☐ 5	Carlton Fisk	3.00	1.25	.30
☐ 6	Jim Palmer	3.25	1.35	.32
☐ 7A	Ron Santo ERR	5.00	2.25	.50
	Chicago Cubs			
☐ 7B	Ron Santo COR	.75	.30	.07
	Chicago White Sox			
☐ 8	Nolan Ryan	18.00	7.50	2.50

		NRMT	VG-E	GOOD
☐ 9	Greg Luzinski	.75	.30	.07
☐ 10	Buddy Bell	.60	.25	.06
☐ 11	Bob Watson	.60	.25	.06
☐ 12	Bill Singer	.50	.20	.05
☐ 13	Dave May	.50	.20	.05
☐ 14	Jim Brewer	.50	.20	.05
☐ 15	Manny Sanguillen	.50	.20	.05
☐ 16	Jeff Burroughs	.50	.20	.05
☐ 17	Amos Otis	.60	.25	.06
☐ 18	Ed Goodson	.50	.20	.05
☐ 19	Nate Colbert	.50	.20	.05
☐ 20	Reggie Jackson	9.00	4.00	.90
☐ 21	Ted Simmons	.90	.40	.09
☐ 22	Bobby Murcer	.75	.30	.07
☐ 23	Willie Horton	.60	.25	.06
☐ 24	Orlando Cepeda	1.00	.40	.10
☐ 25	Ron Hunt	.50	.20	.05
☐ 26	Wayne Twitchell	.50	.20	.05
☐ 27	Ron Fairly	.50	.20	.05
☐ 28	Johnny Bench	6.50	2.75	.65
☐ 29	John Mayberry	.60	.25	.06
☐ 30	Rod Carew	5.50	2.50	.55
☐ 31	Ken Holtzman	.60	.25	.06
☐ 32	Billy Williams	2.25	.90	.22
☐ 33	Dick Allen	.90	.40	.09
☐ 34A	Wilbur Wood ERR	3.00	1.25	.30
	(1973 K 198)			
☐ 34B	Wilbur Wood COR	.50	.20	.05
	(1973 K 199)			
☐ 35	Danny Thompson	.50	.20	.05
☐ 36	Joe Morgan	3.00	1.25	.30
☐ 37	Willie Stargell	3.00	1.25	.30
☐ 38	Pete Rose	12.00	5.25	1.50
☐ 39	Bobby Bonds	.75	.30	.07
☐ 40	Chris Speier	.50	.20	.05
☐ 41	Sparky Lyle	.90	.40	.09
☐ 42	Cookie Rojas	.50	.20	.05
☐ 43	Tommy Davis	.60	.25	.06
☐ 44	Jim Hunter	2.25	.90	.22
☐ 45	Willie Davis	.75	.30	.07
☐ 46	Bert Blyleven	.90	.40	.09
☐ 47	Pat Kelly	.50	.20	.05
☐ 48	Ken Singleton	.60	.25	.06
☐ 49	Manny Mota	.60	.25	.06
☐ 50	Dave Johnson	.75	.30	.07
☐ 51	Sal Bando	.60	.25	.06
☐ 52	Tom Seaver	6.50	2.75	.65
☐ 53	Felix Millan	.50	.20	.05
☐ 54	Ron Blomberg	.50	.20	.05

1975 Kellogg's

The cards in this 57-card set measure 2 1/8" by 3 1/4". The 1975 Kellogg's 3-D set could be obtained card by card in cereal boxes or as a set from a box-top offer from the company. Card number 44, Jim Hunter, exists with the A's emblem or the Yankees emblem on the back of the card.

	NRMT	VG-E	GOOD
COMPLETE SET (57)	165.00	70.00	20.00
COMMON PLAYER (1-57)	.75	.30	.07

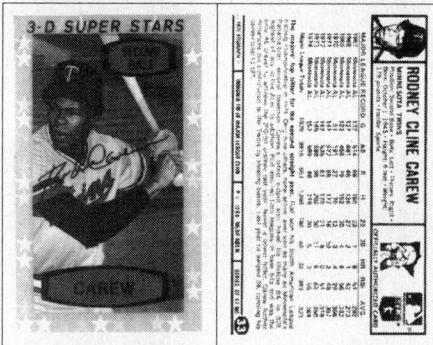

☐ 1 Roy White	.75	.30	.07
☐ 2 Ross Grimsley	.75	.30	.07
☐ 3 Reggie Smith	1.00	.40	.10
☐ 4A Bob Grich ERR	1.00	.40	.10
(bio last line begins "1973 work")			
☐ 4B Bob Grich COR	2.00	.80	.20
(bio last line begins "because his fielding")			
☐ 5 Greg Gross	.75	.30	.07
☐ 6 Bob Watson	.90	.40	.09
☐ 7 Johnny Bench	11.00	5.00	1.35
☐ 8 Jeff Burroughs	.75	.30	.07
☐ 9 Elliott Maddox	.75	.30	.07
☐ 10 Jon Matlack	.75	.30	.07
☐ 11 Pete Rose	18.00	7.50	2.50
☐ 12 Lee Stanton	.75	.30	.07
☐ 13 Bake McBride	.75	.30	.07
☐ 14 Jorge Orta	.75	.30	.07
☐ 15 Al Oliver	1.00	.40	.10
☐ 16 John Briggs	.75	.30	.07
☐ 17 Steve Garvey	6.50	2.75	.65
☐ 18 Brooks Robinson	5.50	2.50	.55
☐ 19 John Hiller	.75	.30	.07
☐ 20 Lynn McGlothen	.75	.30	.07
☐ 21 Cleon Jones	.75	.30	.07
☐ 22 Fergie Jenkins	3.50	1.50	.35
☐ 23 Bill North	.75	.30	.07
☐ 24 Steve Busby	.90	.40	.09
☐ 25 Richie Zisk	.90	.40	.09
☐ 26 Nolan Ryan	22.50	9.75	3.25
☐ 27 Joe Morgan	4.00	1.75	.40
☐ 28 Joe Rudi	.90	.40	.09
☐ 29 Jose Cardenal	.75	.30	.07
☐ 30 Andy Messersmith	.75	.30	.07
☐ 31 Willie Montanez	.75	.30	.07
☐ 32 Bill Buckner	1.00	.40	.10
☐ 33 Rod Carew	6.50	2.75	.65
☐ 34 Lou Piniella	1.25	.50	.12
☐ 35 Ralph Garr	.75	.30	.07
☐ 36 Mike Marshall	.90	.40	.09
☐ 37 Garry Maddox	.75	.30	.07
☐ 38 Dwight Evans	1.50	.60	.15
☐ 39 Lou Brock	5.50	2.50	.55
☐ 40 Ken Singleton	.90	.40	.09
☐ 41 Steve Braun	.75	.30	.07
☐ 42 Rich Allen	1.00	.40	.10
☐ 43 John Grubb	.75	.30	.07
☐ 44A Jim Hunter	4.00	1.75	.40
(Oakland A's team logo on back)			
☐ 44B Jim Hunter	10.00	4.50	1.25
(New York Yankees team logo on back)			
☐ 45 Gaylord Perry	3.00	1.25	.30
☐ 46 George Hendrick	.90	.40	.09
☐ 47 Sparky Lyle	.90	.40	.09
☐ 48 Dave Cash	.75	.30	.07
☐ 49 Luis Tiant	1.00	.40	.10
☐ 50 Cesar Geronimo	.75	.30	.07
☐ 51 Carl Yastrzemski	15.00	6.50	2.15
☐ 52 Ken Brett	.75	.30	.07
☐ 53 Hal McRae	1.00	.40	.10
☐ 54 Reggie Jackson	16.00	6.75	2.25
☐ 55 Rollie Fingers	4.00	1.75	.40
☐ 56 Mike Schmidt	16.00	6.75	2.25
☐ 57 Richie Hebner	.75	.30	.07

1976 Kellogg's

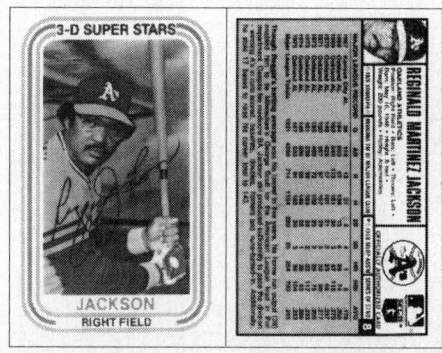

The cards in this 57-card set measure 2 1/8" by 3 1/4". The 1976 Kellogg's 3-D set could be obtained card by card in cereal boxes or as a set from the company for box-tops. Card number 6, that of Clay Carroll, exists with both a Reds or White Sox emblem on the back. Cards 1-3 (marked in the checklist below with SP) were apparently printed apart from the other 54 and are in shorter supply.

	NRMT	VG-E	GOOD
COMPLETE SET	90.00	40.00	13.50
COMMON PLAYER (1-3) SP	9.00	4.00	.90
COMMON PLAYER (4-57)	.45	.18	.04
☐ 1 Steve Hargan SP	9.00	4.00	.90
☐ 2 Claudell Washington SP	9.00	4.00	.90
☐ 3 Don Gullett SP	9.00	4.00	.90
☐ 4 Randy Jones	.60	.25	.06
☐ 5 Jim Hunter	2.25	.90	.22
☐ 6A Clay Carroll	1.00	.40	.10
(Team logo Chicago White Sox on back)			
☐ 6B Clay Carroll	1.00	.40	.10
(Team logo Cincinnati Reds on back)			
☐ 7 Joe Rudi	.60	.25	.06
☐ 8 Reggie Jackson	7.00	3.00	.70
☐ 9 Felix Millan	.45	.18	.04
☐ 10 Jim Rice	3.00	1.25	.30
☐ 11 Bert Blyleven	.75	.30	.07
☐ 12 Ken Singleton	.60	.25	.06
☐ 13 Don Sutton	1.75	.70	.17
☐ 14 Joe Morgan	3.50	1.50	.35
☐ 15 Dave Parker	2.25	.90	.22
☐ 16 Dave Cash	.45	.18	.04
☐ 17 Ron LeFlore	.45	.18	.04
☐ 18 Greg Luzinski	1.00	.40	.10
☐ 19 Dennis Eckersley	4.00	1.75	.40
☐ 20 Bill Madlock	.75	.30	.07
☐ 21 George Scott	.45	.18	.04
☐ 22 Willie Stargell	2.75	1.10	.27
☐ 23 Al Hrabosky	.60	.25	.06
☐ 24 Carl Yastrzemski	7.00	3.00	.70
☐ 25A Jim Kaat	1.25	.50	.12
(team logo Philadelphia Phillies on back)			
☐ 25B Jim Kaat	1.25	.50	.12
(team logo Chicago White Sox on back)			
☐ 26 Marty Perez	.45	.18	.04
☐ 27 Bob Watson	.60	.25	.06
☐ 28 Eric Soderholm	.45	.18	.04
☐ 29 Bill Lee	.60	.25	.06
☐ 30A Frank Tanana ERR	.75	.30	.07
(1975 ERA 2.63)			
☐ 30B Frank Tanana COR	.75	.30	.07
(1975 ERA 2.62)			
☐ 31 Fred Lynn	1.50	.60	.15
☐ 32A Tom Seaver ERR	7.50	3.25	.75
(1967 Pct. 552 with no decimal point)			
☐ 32B Tom Seaver COR	7.50	3.25	.75
(1967 Pct. .552)			
☐ 33 Steve Busby	.60	.25	.06

			NRMT	VG-E	GOOD
☐	34	Gary Carter	3.75	1.60	.37
☐	35	Rick Wise	.60	.25	.06
☐	36	Johnny Bench	5.50	2.50	.55
☐	37	Jim Palmer	3.00	1.25	.30
☐	38	Bobby Murcer	.75	.30	.07
☐	39	Von Joshua	.45	.18	.04
☐	40	Lou Brock	3.25	1.35	.32
☐	41A	Mickey Rivers (missing line in bio about Yankees)	.75	.30	.07
☐	41B	Mickey Rivers (bio has "Yankees obtained ...")	.75	.30	.07
☐	42	Manny Sanguillen	.60	.25	.06
☐	43	Jerry Reuss	.45	.18	.04
☐	44	Ken Griffey	.90	.40	.09
☐	45A	Jorge Orta ERR (lifetime AB 1615)	.60	.25	.06
☐	45B	Jorge Orta COR (lifetime AB 1616)	.60	.25	.06
☐	46	John Mayberry	.60	.25	.06
☐	47A	Vida Blue (bio "struck out more batters")	.75	.30	.07
☐	47B	Vida Blue (bio "pitched more innings")	.75	.30	.07
☐	48	Rod Carew	4.50	2.00	.45
☐	49A	Jon Matlack ERR (1975 ER 87)	.75	.30	.07
☐	49B	Jon Matlack COR (1975 ER 86)	.75	.30	.07
☐	50	Boog Powell	.75	.30	.07
☐	51A	Mike Hargrove ERR (lifetime AB 935)	.75	.30	.07
☐	51B	Mike Hargrove COR (lifetime AB 934)	.75	.30	.07
☐	52A	Paul Lindblad ERR (1975 ERA 2.43)	.60	.25	.06
☐	52B	Paul Lindblad COR (1975 ERA 2.72)	.60	.25	.06
☐	53	Thurman Munson	4.50	2.00	.45
☐	54	Steve Garvey	3.50	1.50	.35
☐	55	Pete Rose	12.00	5.25	1.50
☐	56A	Greg Gross ERR (lifetime games 334)	.60	.25	.06
☐	56B	Greg Gross COR (lifetime games 302)	.60	.25	.06
☐	57	Ted Simmons	.90	.40	.09

1977 Kellogg's

The cards in this 57-card set measure 2 1/8" by 3 1/4". The 1977 Kellogg's series of 3-D baseball player cards could be obtained card by card from cereal boxes or by sending in box-tops and money. Each player's picture appears in miniature form on the reverse, an idea begun in 1971 and replaced in subsequent years by the use of a picture of the Kellogg's mascot.

		NRMT	VG-E	GOOD
COMPLETE SET (57)		60.00	27.00	9.00
COMMON PLAYER (1-57)		.40	.16	.04

			NRMT	VG-E	GOOD
☐	1	George Foster	1.00	.40	.10
☐	2	Bert Campaneris	.50	.20	.05
☐	3	Fergie Jenkins	2.25	.90	.22
☐	4	Dock Ellis	.40	.16	.04
☐	5	John Montefusco	.40	.16	.04
☐	6	George Brett	8.00	3.50	.80
☐	7	John Candelaria	.50	.20	.05
☐	8	Fred Norman	.40	.16	.04
☐	9	Bill Travers	.40	.16	.04
☐	10	Hal McRae	.60	.25	.06
☐	11	Doug Rau	.40	.16	.04
☐	12	Greg Luzinski	.60	.25	.06
☐	13	Ralph Garr	.50	.20	.05
☐	14	Steve Garvey	3.50	1.50	.35
☐	15	Rick Manning	.40	.16	.04
☐	16A	Lyman Bostock ERR (Dock Ellis photo on back)	2.00	.80	.20
☐	16B	Lyman Bostock COR	.50	.20	.05
☐	17	Randy Jones	.40	.16	.04
☐	18	Ron Cey	.60	.25	.06
☐	19	Dave Parker	1.50	.60	.15
☐	20	Pete Rose	9.00	4.00	.90
☐	21A	Wayne Garland (no trade to Cleveland is mentioned)	.50	.20	.05
☐	21B	Wayne Garland (trade mentioned, bio ends "now flip for Cleveland)	1.50	.60	.15
☐	22	Bill North	.40	.16	.04
☐	23	Thurman Munson	3.50	1.50	.35
☐	24	Tom Poquette	.40	.16	.04
☐	25	Ron LeFlore	.50	.20	.05
☐	26	Mark Fidrych	.90	.40	.09
☐	27	Sixto Lezcano	.40	.16	.04
☐	28	Dave Winfield	3.50	1.50	.35
☐	29	Jerry Koosman	.60	.25	.06
☐	30	Mike Hargrove	.50	.20	.05
☐	31	Willie Montanez	.40	.16	.04
☐	32	Don Stanhouse	.40	.16	.04
☐	33	Jay Johnstone	.50	.20	.05
☐	34	Bake McBride	.40	.16	.04
☐	35	Dave Kingman	.75	.30	.07
☐	36	Fred Patek	.40	.16	.04
☐	37	Garry Maddox	.40	.16	.04
☐	38A	Ken Reitz (no trade mentioned)	.50	.20	.05
☐	38B	Ken Reitz (trade mentioned)	1.50	.60	.15
☐	39	Bobby Grich	.50	.20	.05
☐	40	Cesar Geronimo	.40	.16	.04
☐	41	Jim Lonborg	.50	.20	.05
☐	42	Ed Figueroa	.40	.16	.04
☐	43	Bill Madlock	.75	.30	.07
☐	44	Jerry Remy	.40	.16	.04
☐	45	Frank Tanana	.50	.20	.05
☐	46	Al Oliver	.75	.30	.07
☐	47	Charlie Hough	.50	.20	.05
☐	48	Lou Piniella	.90	.40	.09
☐	49	Ken Griffey	.90	.40	.09
☐	50	Jose Cruz	.50	.20	.05
☐	51	Rollie Fingers	2.50	1.00	.25
☐	52	Chris Chambliss	.50	.20	.05
☐	53	Rod Carew	4.50	2.00	.45
☐	54	Andy Messersmith	.50	.20	.05
☐	55	Mickey Rivers	.50	.20	.05
☐	56	Butch Wynegar	.40	.16	.04
☐	57	Steve Carlton	4.25	1.75	.42

1978 Kellogg's

The cards in this 57-card set measure 2 1/8" by 3 1/4". This 1978 3-D Kellogg's series marks the first year in which Tony the Tiger appears on the reverse of each card next to the team and MLB logos. Once again the set could be obtained as individually wrapped cards in cereal boxes or as a set via a mail-in offer.

		NRMT	VG-E	GOOD
COMPLETE SET (57)		60.00	27.00	9.00
COMMON PLAYER (1-57)		.40	.16	.04

			NRMT	VG-E	GOOD
☐	1	Steve Carlton	4.00	1.75	.40
☐	2	Bucky Dent	.60	.25	.06
☐	3	Mike Schmidt	7.00	3.00	.70
☐	4	Ken Griffey	.75	.30	.07
☐	5	Al Cowens	.40	.16	.04

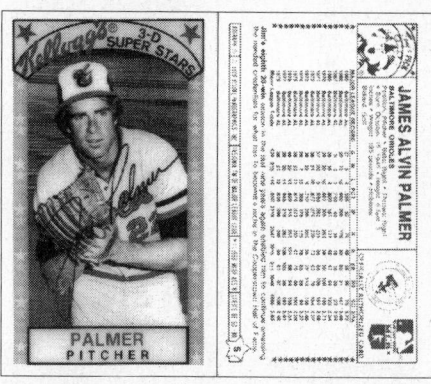

		NRMT	VG-E	GOOD
☐ 6	George Brett	7.00	3.00	.70
☐ 7	Lou Brock	2.50	1.00	.25
☐ 8	Rich Gossage	.90	.40	.09
☐ 9	Tom Johnson	.40	.16	.04
☐ 10	George Foster	.90	.40	.09
☐ 11	Dave Winfield	3.50	1.50	.35
☐ 12	Dan Meyer	.40	.16	.04
☐ 13	Chris Chambliss	.50	.20	.05
☐ 14	Paul Dade	.40	.16	.04
☐ 15	Jeff Burroughs	.40	.16	.04
☐ 16	Jose Cruz	.50	.20	.05
☐ 17	Mickey Rivers	.50	.20	.05
☐ 18	John Candelaria	.50	.20	.05
☐ 19	Ellis Valentine	.40	.16	.04
☐ 20	Hal McRae	.60	.25	.06
☐ 21	Dave Rozema	.40	.16	.04
☐ 22	Lenny Randle	.40	.16	.04
☐ 23	Willie McCovey	2.25	.90	.22
☐ 24	Ron Cey	.60	.25	.06
☐ 25	Eddie Murray	20.00	8.50	2.75
☐ 26	Larry Bowa	.60	.25	.06
☐ 27	Tom Seaver	6.00	2.50	.60
☐ 28	Garry Maddox	.50	.20	.05
☐ 29	Rod Carew	4.50	2.00	.45
☐ 30	Thurman Munson	4.50	2.00	.45
☐ 31	Garry Templeton	.50	.20	.05
☐ 32	Eric Soderholm	.40	.16	.04
☐ 33	Greg Luzinski	.60	.25	.06
☐ 34	Reggie Smith	.50	.20	.05
☐ 35	Dave Goltz	.40	.16	.04
☐ 36	Tommy John	.75	.30	.07
☐ 37	Ralph Garr	.40	.16	.04
☐ 38	Alan Bannister	.40	.16	.04
☐ 39	Bob Bailor	.40	.16	.04
☐ 40	Reggie Jackson	6.00	2.50	.60
☐ 41	Cecil Cooper	.60	.25	.06
☐ 42	Burt Hooton	.40	.16	.04
☐ 43	Sparky Lyle	.50	.20	.05
☐ 44	Steve Ontiveros	.40	.16	.04
☐ 45	Rick Reuschel	.60	.25	.06
☐ 46	Lyman Bostock	.50	.20	.05
☐ 47	Mitchell Page	.40	.16	.04
☐ 48	Bruce Sutter	.75	.30	.07
☐ 49	Jim Rice	2.00	.80	.20
☐ 50	Ken Forsch	.40	.16	.04
☐ 51	Nolan Ryan	11.00	5.00	1.35
☐ 52	Dave Parker	1.75	.70	.17
☐ 53	Bert Blyleven	.60	.25	.06
☐ 54	Frank Tanana	.50	.20	.05
☐ 55	Ken Singleton	.50	.20	.05
☐ 56	Mike Hargrove	.50	.20	.05
☐ 57	Don Sutton	1.50	.60	.15

1979 Kellogg's

The cards in this 60-card set measure approximately 1 15/16" by 3 1/4". The 1979 edition of Kellogg's 3-D baseball cards have a 3/16" reduced width from the previous year; a nicely designed curved panel above the picture gives this set a distinctive appearance. The set contains the largest number of cards issued in a Kellogg's set since the 1971 series. Three different press runs produced numerous variations in this set. The first

two printings were included in cereal boxes, while the third printing was for the complete set mail-in offer. Forty-seven cards have three variations, while thirteen cards (4, 6, 9, 15, 19, 20, 30, 33, 41, 43, 45, 51, and 54) are unchanged from the second and third printings. The three printings may be distinguished by the placement of the registered symbol by Tony the Tiger and by team logos. In the third printing, four cards (16, 18, 22, 44) show the "P" team logo (no registered symbol), and card numbers 56 and 57 omit the registered symbol by Tony.

		NRMT	VG-E	GOOD
	COMPLETE SET (60)	36.00	16.25	5.50
	COMMON PLAYER (1-60)	.25	.10	.02
☐ 1	Bruce Sutter	.50	.20	.05
☐ 2	Ted Simmons	.50	.20	.05
☐ 3	Ross Grimsley	.25	.10	.02
☐ 4	Wayne Nordhagen	.25	.10	.02
☐ 5	Jim Palmer	2.50	1.00	.25
☐ 6	John Henry Johnson	.25	.10	.02
☐ 7	Jason Thompson	.25	.10	.02
☐ 8	Pat Zachry	.25	.10	.02
☐ 9	Dennis Eckersley	1.25	.50	.12
☐ 10	Paul Splittorff	.25	.10	.02
☐ 11	Ron Guidry	1.25	.50	.12
☐ 12	Jeff Burroughs	.25	.10	.02
☐ 13	Rod Carew	3.00	1.25	.30
☐ 14A	Buddy Bell	1.50	.60	.15
	(no trade mentioned)			
☐ 14B	Buddy Bell	.35	.15	.03
	(traded to Rangers)			
☐ 15	Jim Rice	1.75	.70	.17
☐ 16	Garry Maddox	.25	.10	.02
☐ 17	Willie McCovey	1.75	.70	.17
☐ 18	Steve Carlton	2.50	1.00	.25
☐ 19	J.R. Richard	.35	.15	.03
☐ 20	Paul Molitor	1.50	.60	.15
☐ 21	Dave Parker	1.50	.60	.15
☐ 22	Pete Rose	7.00	3.00	.70
☐ 23	Vida Blue	.35	.15	.03
☐ 24	Richie Zisk	.25	.10	.02
☐ 25	Darrell Porter	.25	.10	.02
☐ 26	Dan Driessen	.25	.10	.02
☐ 27	Geoff Zahn	.25	.10	.02
☐ 28	Phil Niekro	1.25	.50	.12
☐ 29	Tom Seaver	4.50	2.00	.45
☐ 30	Fred Lynn	.75	.30	.07
☐ 31	Bill Bonham	.25	.10	.02
☐ 32	George Foster	.60	.25	.06
☐ 33	Terry Puhl	.25	.10	.02
☐ 34	John Candelaria	.35	.15	.03
☐ 35	Bob Knepper	.25	.10	.02
☐ 36	Fred Patek	.25	.10	.02
☐ 37	Chris Chambliss	.35	.15	.03
☐ 38	Bob Forsch	.25	.10	.02
☐ 39	Ken Griffey	.50	.20	.05
☐ 40	Jack Clark	1.50	.60	.15
☐ 41	Dwight Evans	1.00	.40	.10
☐ 42	Lee Mazzilli	.25	.10	.02
☐ 43	Mario Guerrero	.25	.10	.02
☐ 44	Larry Bowa	.35	.15	.03
☐ 45	Carl Yastrzemski	5.00	2.25	.50
☐ 46	Reggie Jackson	5.50	2.50	.55
☐ 47	Rick Reuschel	.50	.20	.05

			MINT	EXC	G-VG
☐ 48	Mike Flanagan		.35	.15	.03
☐ 49	Gaylord Perry		2.25	.90	.22
☐ 50	George Brett		5.00	2.25	.50
☐ 51	Craig Reynolds		.25	.10	.02
☐ 52	Dave Lopes		.35	.15	.03
☐ 53	Bill Almon		.25	.10	.02
☐ 54	Roy Howell		.25	.10	.02
☐ 55	Frank Tanana		.35	.15	.03
☐ 56	Doug Rau		.25	.10	.02
☐ 57	Rick Monday		.35	.15	.03
☐ 58	Jon Matlack		.25	.10	.02
☐ 59	Ron Jackson		.25	.10	.02
☐ 60	Jim Sundberg		.25	.10	.02

1980 Kellogg's

The cards in this 60-card set measure 1 7/8" by 3 1/4". The 1980 Kellogg's 3-D set is quite similar to, but smaller (narrower) than, the other recent Kellogg's issues. Sets could be obtained card by card from cereal boxes or as a set from a box-top offer from the company.

			MINT	EXC	G-VG
COMPLETE SET (60)			30.00	13.50	4.50
COMMON PLAYER (1-60)			.25	.10	.02
☐ 1	Ross Grimsley		.25	.10	.02
☐ 2	Mike Schmidt		5.00	2.25	.50
☐ 3	Mike Flanagan		.35	.15	.03
☐ 4	Ron Guidry		.75	.30	.07
☐ 5	Bert Blyleven		.60	.25	.06
☐ 6	Dave Kingman		.50	.20	.05
☐ 7	Jeff Newman		.25	.10	.02
☐ 8	Steve Rogers		.25	.10	.02
☐ 9	George Brett		4.50	2.00	.45
☐ 10	Bruce Sutter		.60	.25	.06
☐ 11	Gorman Thomas		.35	.15	.03
☐ 12	Darrell Porter		.25	.10	.02
☐ 13	Roy Smalley		.25	.10	.02
☐ 14	Steve Carlton		2.50	1.00	.25
☐ 15	Jim Palmer		2.50	1.00	.25
☐ 16	Bob Bailor		.25	.10	.02
☐ 17	Jason Thompson		.25	.10	.02
☐ 18	Graig Nettles		.35	.15	.03
☐ 19	Ron Cey		.35	.15	.03
☐ 20	Nolan Ryan		8.00	3.50	.80
☐ 21	Ellis Valentine		.25	.10	.02
☐ 22	Larry Hisle		.25	.10	.02
☐ 23	Dave Parker		1.25	.50	.12
☐ 24	Eddie Murray		4.00	1.75	.40
☐ 25	Willie Stargell		1.75	.70	.17
☐ 26	Reggie Jackson		4.00	1.75	.40
☐ 27	Carl Yastrzemski		3.50	1.50	.35
☐ 28	Andre Thornton		.25	.10	.02
☐ 29	Dave Lopes		.35	.15	.03
☐ 30	Ken Singleton		.35	.15	.03
☐ 31	Steve Garvey		2.00	.80	.20
☐ 32	Dave Winfield		2.50	1.00	.25
☐ 33	Steve Kemp		.35	.15	.03
☐ 34	Claudell Washington		.35	.15	.03
☐ 35	Pete Rose		6.00	2.50	.60

☐ 36	Cesar Cedeno		.35	.15	.03
☐ 37	John Stearns		.25	.10	.02
☐ 38	Lee Mazzilli		.25	.10	.02
☐ 39	Larry Bowa		.35	.15	.03
☐ 40	Fred Lynn		.60	.25	.06
☐ 41	Carlton Fisk		1.75	.70	.17
☐ 42	Vida Blue		.35	.15	.03
☐ 43	Keith Hernandez		1.25	.50	.12
☐ 44	Jim Rice		1.50	.60	.15
☐ 45	Ted Simmons		.60	.25	.06
☐ 46	Chet Lemon		.35	.15	.03
☐ 47	Ferguson Jenkins		2.00	.80	.20
☐ 48	Gary Matthews		.35	.15	.03
☐ 49	Tom Seaver		4.00	1.75	.40
☐ 50	George Foster		.60	.25	.06
☐ 51	Phil Niekro		1.25	.50	.12
☐ 52	Johnny Bench		3.00	1.25	.30
☐ 53	Buddy Bell		.45	.18	.04
☐ 54	Lance Parrish		1.00	.40	.10
☐ 55	Joaquin Andujar		.35	.15	.03
☐ 56	Don Baylor		.35	.15	.03
☐ 57	Jack Clark		.90	.40	.09
☐ 58	J.R. Richard		.35	.15	.03
☐ 59	Bruce Bochte		.25	.10	.02
☐ 60	Rod Carew		3.25	1.35	.32

1981 Kellogg's

The cards in this 66-card set measure 2 1/2" by 3 1/2". The 1981 Kellogg's set witnessed an increase in both the size of the card and the size of the set. For the first time, cards were not packed in cereal sizes but available only by mail-in procedure. The offer for the card set was advertised on boxes of Kellogg's Corn Flakes. The cards were printed on a different stock than in previous years, presumably to prevent the cracking problem which has plagued all Kellogg's 3-D issues. At the end of the promotion, the remainder of the sets not distributed (to cereal-eaters), were "sold" into the organized hobby, thus creating a situation where the set is relatively plentiful compared to other years of Kellogg's.

			MINT	EXC	G-VG
COMPLETE SET (66)			12.50	5.50	1.65
COMMON PLAYER (1-66)			.10	.04	.01
☐ 1	George Foster		.20	.08	.02
☐ 2	Jim Palmer		.60	.25	.06
☐ 3	Reggie Jackson		1.50	.60	.15
☐ 4	Al Oliver		.10	.04	.01
☐ 5	Mike Schmidt		1.50	.60	.15
☐ 6	Nolan Ryan		2.50	1.00	.25
☐ 7	Bucky Dent		.15	.06	.01
☐ 8	George Brett		1.50	.60	.15
☐ 9	Jim Rice		.30	.12	.03
☐ 10	Steve Garvey		.50	.20	.05
☐ 11	Willie Stargell		.50	.20	.05
☐ 12	Phil Niekro		.35	.15	.03
☐ 13	Dave Parker		.35	.15	.03
☐ 14	Cesar Cedeno		.10	.04	.01
☐ 15	Don Baylor		.15	.06	.01
☐ 16	J.R. Richard		.10	.04	.01
☐ 17	Tony Perez		.30	.12	.03
☐ 18	Eddie Murray		1.25	.50	.12

		MINT	EXC	G-VG
☐ 19	Chet Lemon	.10	.04	.01
☐ 20	Ben Oglivie	.10	.04	.01
☐ 21	Dave Winfield	.75	.30	.07
☐ 22	Joe Morgan	.60	.25	.06
☐ 23	Vida Blue	.10	.04	.01
☐ 24	Willie Wilson	.15	.06	.01
☐ 25	Steve Henderson	.10	.04	.01
☐ 26	Rod Carew	1.00	.40	.10
☐ 27	Garry Templeton	.10	.04	.01
☐ 28	Dave Concepcion	.15	.06	.01
☐ 29	Dave Lopes	.10	.04	.01
☐ 30	Ken Landreaux	.10	.04	.01
☐ 31	Keith Hernandez	.30	.12	.03
☐ 32	Cecil Cooper	.15	.06	.01
☐ 33	Rickey Henderson	1.75	.70	.17
☐ 34	Frank White	.10	.04	.01
☐ 35	George Hendrick	.10	.04	.01
☐ 36	Reggie Smith	.15	.06	.01
☐ 37	Tug McGraw	.15	.06	.01
☐ 38	Tom Seaver	1.25	.50	.12
☐ 39	Ken Singleton	.10	.04	.01
☐ 40	Fred Lynn	.15	.06	.01
☐ 41	Rich Gossage	.15	.06	.01
☐ 42	Terry Puhl	.10	.04	.01
☐ 43	Larry Bowa	.15	.06	.01
☐ 44	Phil Garner	.10	.04	.01
☐ 45	Ron Guidry	.20	.08	.02
☐ 46	Lee Mazzilli	.10	.04	.01
☐ 47	Dave Kingman	.15	.06	.01
☐ 48	Carl Yastrzemski	1.00	.40	.10
☐ 49	Rick Burleson	.10	.04	.01
☐ 50	Steve Carlton	.75	.30	.07
☐ 51	Alan Trammell	.35	.15	.03
☐ 52	Tommy John	.15	.06	.01
☐ 53	Paul Molitor	.30	.12	.03
☐ 54	Joe Charboneale	.10	.04	.01
☐ 55	Rick Langford	.10	.04	.01
☐ 56	Bruce Sutter	.10	.04	.01
☐ 57	Robin Yount	1.25	.50	.12
☐ 58	Steve Stone	.10	.04	.01
☐ 59	Larry Gura	.10	.04	.01
☐ 60	Mike Flanagan	.15	.06	.01
☐ 61	Bob Horner	.15	.06	.01
☐ 62	Bruce Bochte	.10	.04	.01
☐ 63	Pete Rose	1.00	.40	.10
☐ 64	Buddy Bell	.10	.04	.01
☐ 65	Johnny Bench	.90	.40	.09
☐ 66	Mike Hargrove	.10	.04	.01

1982 Kellogg's

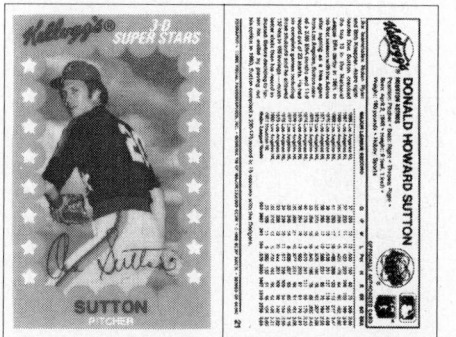

The cards in this 64-card set measure 2 1/8" by 3 1/4". The 1982 version of 3-D cards prepared for the Kellogg Company by Visual Panographics, Inc., is not only smaller in physical dimensions from the 1981 series (which was standard card size at 2 1/2" by 3 1/2") but is also two cards shorter in length (64 in '82 and 66 in '81). In addition, while retaining the policy of not inserting single cards into cereal packages and offering the sets through box-top mail-ins only, the Kellogg Company accepted box tops from four types of cereals, as opposed to only one type the previous year. Each card features a color 3-D ballplayer picture with a vertical line of white stars on each side set upon

a blue background. The player's name and the word Kellogg's are printed in red on the obverse, and the card number is found on the bottom right of the reverse. Every card in the set has a statistical procedural error that was never corrected. All seasonal averages were added up and then divided by the number of seasons played.

		MINT	EXC	G-VG
COMPLETE SET (64)		18.00	7.50	2.50
COMMON PLAYER (1-64)		.15	.06	.01
☐ 1	Richie Zisk	.15	.06	.01
☐ 2	Bill Buckner	.25	.10	.02
☐ 3	George Brett	1.50	.60	.15
☐ 4	Rickey Henderson	2.00	.80	.20
☐ 5	Jack Morris	.30	.12	.03
☐ 6	Ozzie Smith	.75	.30	.07
☐ 7	Rollie Fingers	.50	.20	.05
☐ 8	Tom Seaver	1.25	.50	.12
☐ 9	Fernando Valuenzuela	.40	.16	.04
☐ 10	Hubie Brooks	.15	.06	.01
☐ 11	Nolan Ryan	2.00	.80	.20
☐ 12	Dave Winfield	.50	.20	.05
☐ 13	Bob Horner	.20	.08	.02
☐ 14	Reggie Jackson	1.25	.50	.12
☐ 15	Burt Hooton	.15	.06	.01
☐ 16	Mike Schmidt	1.25	.50	.12
☐ 17	Bruce Sutter	.20	.08	.02
☐ 18	Pete Rose	1.00	.40	.10
☐ 19	Dave Kingman	.20	.08	.02
☐ 20	Neil Allen	.15	.06	.01
☐ 21	Don Sutton	.35	.15	.03
☐ 22	Dave Concepcion	.20	.08	.02
☐ 23	Keith Hernandez	.25	.10	.02
☐ 24	Gary Carter	.35	.15	.03
☐ 25	Carlton Fisk	.50	.20	.05
☐ 26	Ron Guidry	.20	.08	.02
☐ 27	Steve Carlton	.60	.25	.06
☐ 28	Robin Yount	1.25	.50	.12
☐ 29	John Castino	.15	.06	.01
☐ 30	Johnny Bench	.90	.40	.09
☐ 31	Bob Knepper	.15	.06	.01
☐ 32	Rich Gossage	.20	.08	.02
☐ 33	Buddy Bell	.15	.06	.01
☐ 34	Art Howe	.15	.06	.01
☐ 35	Tony Armas	.15	.06	.01
☐ 36	Phil Niekro	.30	.12	.03
☐ 37	Len Barker	.15	.06	.01
☐ 38	Bob Grich	.15	.06	.01
☐ 39	Steve Kemp	.15	.06	.01
☐ 40	Kirk Gibson	.40	.16	.04
☐ 41	Carney Lansford	.25	.10	.02
☐ 42	Jim Palmer	.60	.25	.06
☐ 43	Carl Yastrzemski	1.00	.40	.10
☐ 44	Rick Burleson	.15	.06	.01
☐ 45	Dwight Evans	.20	.08	.02
☐ 46	Ron Cey	.20	.08	.02
☐ 47	Steve Garvey	.45	.18	.04
☐ 48	Dave Parker	.30	.12	.03
☐ 49	Mike Easler	.15	.06	.01
☐ 50	Dusty Baker	.15	.06	.01
☐ 51	Rod Carew	1.00	.40	.10
☐ 52	Chris Chambliss	.20	.08	.02
☐ 53	Tim Raines	.40	.16	.04
☐ 54	Chet Lemon	.15	.06	.01
☐ 55	Bill Madlock	.20	.08	.02
☐ 56	George Foster	.25	.10	.02
☐ 57	Dwayne Murphy	.15	.06	.01
☐ 58	Ken Singleton	.20	.08	.02
☐ 59	Mike Norris	.15	.06	.01
☐ 60	Cecil Cooper	.20	.08	.02
☐ 61	Al Oliver	.20	.08	.02
☐ 62	Willie Wilson	.20	.08	.02
☐ 63	Vida Blue	.20	.08	.02
☐ 64	Eddie Murray	1.00	.40	.10

1983 Kellogg's

The cards in this 60-card set measure 1 7/8" by 3 1/4". For the 14th year in a row, the Kellogg Company issued a card set of Major League players. The set of 3-D cards contains the photo, player's autograph, Kellogg's logo, and name and position of the player on the front of the card. The backs feature the player's team logo, career statistics, player biography, and a narrative

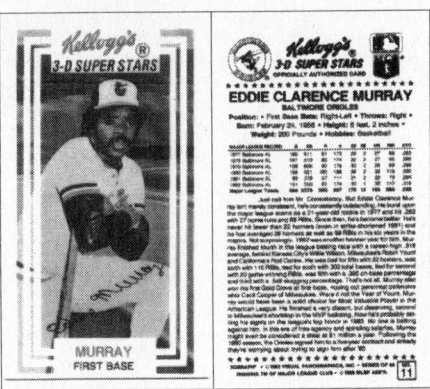

			MINT	EXC	G-VG
			1.50	.60	.15
☐ 58	Mike Schmidt				
☐ 59	Bill Buckner		.20	.08	.02
☐ 60	Bob Grich		.20	.08	.02

1991 Kellogg's Stand Ups

on the player's career. Every card in the set has a statistical procedural error that was never corrected. All seasonal averages were added up and then divided by the number of seasons played.

	MINT	EXC	G-VG
COMPLETE SET (60)	18.00	7.50	2.50
COMMON PLAYER (1-60)	.15	.06	.01
☐ 1 Rod Carew	1.00	.40	.10
☐ 2 Rollie Fingers	.75	.30	.07
☐ 3 Reggie Jackson	1.25	.50	.12
☐ 4 George Brett	1.25	.50	.12
☐ 5 Hal McRae	.20	.08	.02
☐ 6 Pete Rose	1.00	.40	.10
☐ 7 Fernando Valenzuela	.30	.12	.03
☐ 8 Rickey Henderson	1.50	.60	.15
☐ 9 Carl Yastrzemski	1.00	.40	.10
☐ 10 Rich Gossage	.15	.06	.01
☐ 11 Eddie Murray	1.00	.40	.10
☐ 12 Buddy Bell	.20	.08	.02
☐ 13 Jim Rice	.30	.12	.03
☐ 14 Robin Yount	1.00	.40	.10
☐ 15 Dave Winfield	.45	.18	.04
☐ 16 Harold Baines	.20	.08	.02
☐ 17 Garry Templeton	.15	.06	.01
☐ 18 Bill Madlock	.20	.08	.02
☐ 19 Pete Vuckovich	.15	.06	.01
☐ 20 Pedro Guerrero	.25	.10	.02
☐ 21 Ozzie Smith	.60	.25	.06
☐ 22 George Foster	.25	.10	.02
☐ 23 Willie Wilson	.20	.08	.02
☐ 24 Johnny Ray	.15	.06	.01
☐ 25 George Hendrick	.15	.06	.01
☐ 26 Andre Thornton	.15	.06	.01
☐ 27 Leon Durham	.15	.06	.01
☐ 28 Cecil Cooper	.20	.08	.02
☐ 29 Don Baylor	.25	.10	.02
☐ 30 Lonnie Smith	.20	.08	.02
☐ 31 Nolan Ryan	2.00	.80	.20
☐ 32 Dan Quisenberry	.20	.08	.02
☐ 33 Len Barker	.15	.06	.01
☐ 34 Neil Allen	.15	.06	.01
☐ 35 Jack Morris	.30	.12	.03
☐ 36 Dave Stieb	.25	.10	.02
☐ 37 Bruce Sutter	.25	.10	.02
☐ 38 Jim Sundberg	.15	.06	.01
☐ 39 Jim Palmer	.75	.30	.07
☐ 40 Lance Parrish	.25	.10	.02
☐ 41 Floyd Bannister	.15	.06	.01
☐ 42 Larry Gura	.15	.06	.01
☐ 43 Britt Burns	.15	.06	.01
☐ 44 Toby Harrah	.15	.06	.01
☐ 45 Steve Carlton	.75	.30	.07
☐ 46 Greg Minton	.15	.06	.01
☐ 47 Gorman Thomas	.15	.06	.01
☐ 48 Jack Clark	.25	.10	.02
☐ 49 Keith Hernandez	.25	.10	.02
☐ 50 Greg Luzinski	.20	.08	.02
☐ 51 Fred Lynn	.25	.10	.02
☐ 52 Dale Murphy	.75	.30	.07
☐ 53 Kent Hrbek	.30	.12	.03
☐ 54 Bob Horner	.20	.08	.02
☐ 55 Gary Carter	.35	.15	.03
☐ 56 Carlton Fisk	.50	.20	.05
☐ 57 Dave Concepcion	.20	.08	.02

This set was sponsored by Kellogg's in honor of six retired baseball stars as part of a promotion entitled "Baseball Greats." Six different stars are featured on the backs of (specially marked 7 oz. and 12 oz.) Kellogg's Corn Flakes boxes. Since there were two different size boxes, there are two sizes of each card, the larger is approximately 9 1/4" by 6" coming from the 12 oz. box. The color action portraits can be cut out and stood up for display, and career highlights appear to the right of the stand up. The boxes are unnumbered and checklisted below in alphabetical order. All six of these players were also included in the 15-card Kellogg's 3D Baseball Greats set. The complete set price below includes only the six small package cards.

	MINT	EXC	G-VG
COMPLETE SET (6)	10.00	4.50	1.25
COMMON PLAYER (1-6)	2.00	.80	.20
☐ 1A Hank Aaron (Small size)	3.00	1.25	.30
☐ 1B Hank Aaron (Large size)	3.00	1.25	.30
☐ 2A Ernie Banks (Small size)	2.00	.80	.20
☐ 2B Ernie Banks (Large size)	2.00	.80	.20
☐ 3A Yogi Berra (Small size)	2.00	.80	.20
☐ 3B Yogi Berra (Large size)	2.00	.80	.20
☐ 4A Lou Brock (Small size)	2.00	.80	.20
☐ 4B Lou Brock (Large size)	2.00	.80	.20
☐ 5A Steve Carlton (Small size)	2.00	.80	.20
☐ 5B Steve Carlton (Large size)	2.00	.80	.20
☐ 6A Bob Gibson (Small size)	2.00	.80	.20
☐ 6B Bob Gibson (Large size)	2.00	.80	.20

1991 Kellogg's 3D

Sportflics/Optigraphics produced this 15-card set for Kellogg's, and the cards measure approximately 2 1/2" by 3 5/16". The fronts have a three-dimensional image that alternates between a posed or action color shot and a head and shoulders close-up. The card face is aqua blue, with white stripes (that turn pink) and white borders. In red and dark blue print, the horizontally oriented backs have a facial drawing of the player on the left half, and career summary on the right half. The cards are numbered on the back. The cards were inserted in specially marked boxes (18 oz. and 24 oz. only) of Kellogg's Corn Flakes. In addition, the complete set and a blue display rack were available through a mail-in offer for 4.95 and two UPC symbols.

	MINT	EXC	G-VG
COMPLETE SET (15)	7.50	3.25	.75
COMMON PLAYER (1-15)	.50	.20	.05

		MINT	EXC	G-VG
☐ 1	Gaylord Perry	.60	.25	.06
☐ 2	Hank Aaron	1.00	.40	.10
☐ 3	Willie Mays	1.00	.40	.10
☐ 4	Ernie Banks	.75	.30	.07
☐ 5	Bob Gibson	.60	.25	.06
☐ 6	Harmon Killebrew	.60	.25	.06
☐ 7	Rollie Fingers	.60	.25	.06
☐ 8	Steve Carlton	.75	.30	.07
☐ 9	Billy Williams	.60	.25	.06
☐ 10	Lou Brock	.75	.30	.07
☐ 11	Yogi Berra	.75	.30	.07
☐ 12	Warren Spahn	.75	.30	.07
☐ 13	Boog Powell	.50	.20	.05
☐ 14	Don Baylor	.50	.20	.05
☐ 15	Ralph Kiner	.75	.30	.07

1982 K-Mart

The cards in this 44-card set measure 2 1/2" by 3 1/2". This set was produced by Topps for K Mart's 20th Anniversary Celebration. The set features Topps cards of National and American League MVP's from 1962 through 1981. The backs highlight individual MVP winning performances. The dual National League MVP winners of 1979 and special cards commemorating the accomplishments of Drysdale (scoreless consecutive innings pitched streak), Aaron (home run record), and Rose (National League most hits lifetime record) round out the set. The 1975 Fred Lynn card is an original construction from the multi-player "Rookie Outfielders" card of Lynn of

1975. The Maury Wills card number 2, similarly, was created after the fact as Maury was not originally included in the 1962 Topps set. Topps had solved the same problem in essentially the same way

	MINT	EXC	G-VG
COMPLETE SET (44)	1.25	.50	.12
COMMON PLAYER (1-44)	.02	.01	.00

		MINT	EXC	G-VG
☐ 1	Mickey Mantle: 62AL	.25	.10	.02
☐ 2	Maury Wills: 62NL	.02	.01	.00
☐ 3	Elston Howard: 63AL	.02	.01	.00
☐ 4	Sandy Koufax: 63NL	.07	.03	.01
☐ 5	Brooks Robinson: 64AL	.05	.02	.00
☐ 6	Ken Boyer: 64NL	.02	.01	.00
☐ 7	Zoilo Versalles: 65AL	.02	.01	.00
☐ 8	Willie Mays: 65NL	.10	.04	.01
☐ 9	Frank Robinson: 66AL	.04	.02	.00
☐ 10	Bob Clemente: 66NL	.08	.03	.01
☐ 11	Carl Yastrzemski: 67AL	.10	.04	.01
☐ 12	Orlando Cepeda: 67NL	.02	.01	.00
☐ 13	Denny McLain: 68AL	.02	.01	.00
☐ 14	Bob Gibson: 68NL	.04	.02	.00
☐ 15	Harmon Killebrew: 69AL	.03	.01	.00
☐ 16	Willie McCovey: 69NL	.04	.02	.00
☐ 17	Boog Powell: 70AL	.02	.01	.00
☐ 18	Johnny Bench: 70NL	.07	.03	.01
☐ 19	Vida Blue: 71AL	.02	.01	.00
☐ 20	Joe Torre: 71NL	.02	.01	.00
☐ 21	Rich Allen: 72AL	.02	.01	.00
☐ 22	Johnny Bench: 72NL	.07	.03	.01
☐ 23	Reggie Jackson: 73AL	.08	.03	.01
☐ 24	Pete Rose: 73NL	.08	.03	.01
☐ 25	Jeff Burroughs: 74AL	.02	.01	.00
☐ 26	Steve Garvey: 74NL	.04	.02	.00
☐ 27	Fred Lynn: 75AL	.02	.01	.00
☐ 28	Joe Morgan: 75NL	.03	.01	.00
☐ 29	Thurman Munson: 76AL	.05	.02	.00
☐ 30	Joe Morgan: 76NL	.03	.01	.00
☐ 31	Rod Carew: 77AL	.05	.02	.00
☐ 32	George Foster: 77NL	.02	.01	.00
☐ 33	Jim Rice: 78AL	.02	.01	.00
☐ 34	Dave Parker: 78NL	.02	.01	.00
☐ 35	Don Baylor: 79AL	.02	.01	.00
☐ 36	Keith Hernandez: 79NL	.02	.01	.00
☐ 37	Willie Stargell: 79NL	.04	.02	.00
☐ 38	George Brett: 80AL	.07	.03	.01
☐ 39	Mike Schmidt: 80NL	.08	.03	.01
☐ 40	Rollie Fingers: 81AL	.03	.01	.00
☐ 41	Mike Schmidt: 81NL	.08	.03	.01
☐ 42	'68 HL: Don Drysdale .... (scoreless innings)	.03	.01	.00
☐ 43	'74 HL: Hank Aaron .... (home run record)	.10	.04	.01
☐ 44	'81 HL: Pete Rose .... (NL most hits)	.10	.04	.01

1987 K-Mart

Topps produced this 33-card boxed set for K-Mart. The set celebrates K-Mart's 25th anniversary and is subtitled, "Stars of the Decades." Card fronts feature a color photo of the player oriented diagonally. Cards measure 2 1/2" by 3 1/2" and are numbered on the back. Card backs provide statistics for the player's best decade.

	MINT	EXC	G-VG
COMPLETE SET (33)	4.00	1.75	.40
COMMON PLAYER (1-33)	.10	.04	.01
☐ 1 Hank Aaron	.40	.16	.04
☐ 2 Roberto Clemente	.35	.15	.03
☐ 3 Bob Gibson	.15	.06	.01
☐ 4 Harmon Killebrew	.15	.06	.01
☐ 5 Mickey Mantle	1.00	.40	.10
☐ 6 Juan Marichal	.15	.06	.01
☐ 7 Roger Maris	.30	.12	.03
☐ 8 Willie Mays	.40	.16	.04
☐ 9 Brooks Robinson	.20	.08	.02
☐ 10 Frank Robinson	.15	.06	.01
☐ 11 Carl Yastrzemski	.30	.12	.03
☐ 12 Johnny Bench	.25	.10	.02
☐ 13 Lou Brock	.20	.08	.02
☐ 14 Rod Carew	.25	.10	.02
☐ 15 Steve Carlton	.25	.10	.02
☐ 16 Reggie Jackson	.35	.15	.03
☐ 17 Jim Palmer	.25	.10	.02
☐ 18 Jim Rice	.10	.04	.01
☐ 19 Pete Rose	.50	.20	.05
☐ 20 Nolan Ryan	1.00	.40	.10
☐ 21 Tom Seaver	.45	.18	.04
☐ 22 Willie Stargell	.15	.06	.01
☐ 23 Wade Boggs	.40	.16	.04
☐ 24 George Brett	.35	.15	.03
☐ 25 Gary Carter	.15	.06	.01
☐ 26 Dwight Gooden	.30	.12	.03
☐ 27 Rickey Henderson	.50	.20	.05
☐ 28 Don Mattingly	.50	.20	.05
☐ 29 Dale Murphy	.25	.10	.02
☐ 30 Eddie Murray	.30	.12	.03
☐ 31 Mike Schmidt	.50	.20	.05
☐ 32 Darryl Strawberry	.40	.16	.04
☐ 33 Fernando Valenzuela	.15	.06	.01

☐ 12 Tony Gywnn	.40	.16	.04
☐ 13 Rickey Henderson	.75	.30	.07
☐ 14 Keith Hernandez	.20	.08	.02
☐ 15 Don Mattingly	.60	.25	.06
☐ 16 Mark McGwire	.50	.20	.05
☐ 17 Paul Molitor	.15	.06	.01
☐ 18 Dale Murphy	.30	.12	.03
☐ 19 Tim Raines	.20	.08	.02
☐ 20 Dave Righetti	.15	.06	.01
☐ 21 Cal Ripken	.75	.30	.07
☐ 22 Pete Rose	.60	.25	.06
☐ 23 Nolan Ryan	1.00	.40	.10
☐ 24 Benito Santiago	.25	.10	.02
☐ 25 Mike Schmidt	.75	.30	.07
☐ 26 Mike Scott	.15	.06	.01
☐ 27 Kevin Seitzer	.15	.06	.01
☐ 28 Ozzie Smith	.25	.10	.02
☐ 29 Darryl Strawberry	.50	.20	.05
☐ 30 Rick Sutcliffe	.10	.04	.01
☐ 31 Fernando Valenzuela	.15	.06	.01
☐ 32 Todd Worrell	.10	.04	.01
☐ 33 Robin Yount	.45	.18	.04

1989 K-Mart Career Batting Leaders

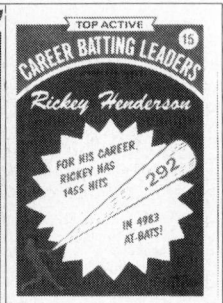

The 1989 K-Mart Career Batting Leaders set contains 22 standard-size (2 1/2 by 3 1/2 inch) glossy cards. The fronts are bright red. The set depicts the 22 veterans with the highest lifetime batting averages. The cards were distributed one per Topps blister pack. These blister packs were sold exclusively through K-Mart stores. The cards in the set were numbered by K-Mart essentially in order of highest active career batting average entering the 1989 season.

	MINT	EXC	G-VG
COMPLETE SET (22)	9.00	4.00	.90
COMMON PLAYER (1-22)	.30	.12	.03
☐ 1 Wade Boggs	.90	.40	.09
☐ 2 Tony Gwynn	.90	.40	.09
☐ 3 Don Mattingly	.90	.40	.09
☐ 4 Kirby Puckett	.75	.30	.07
☐ 5 George Brett	.75	.30	.07
☐ 6 Pedro Guerrero	.40	.16	.04
☐ 7 Tim Raines	.40	.16	.04
☐ 8 Keith Hernandez	.40	.16	.04
☐ 9 Jim Rice	.40	.16	.04
☐ 10 Paul Molitor	.40	.16	.04
☐ 11 Eddie Murray	.60	.25	.06
☐ 12 Willie McGee	.30	.12	.03
☐ 13 Dave Parker	.40	.16	.04
☐ 14 Julio Franco	.40	.16	.04
☐ 15 Rickey Henderson	1.00	.40	.10
☐ 16 Kent Hrbek	.40	.16	.04
☐ 17 Willie Wilson	.30	.12	.03
☐ 18 Johnny Ray	.30	.12	.03
☐ 19 Pat Tabler	.30	.12	.03
☐ 20 Carney Lansford	.30	.12	.03
☐ 21 Robin Yount	.75	.30	.07
☐ 22 Alan Trammell	.40	.16	.04

1988 K-Mart Moments

Topps produced this 33-card boxed set exclusively for K-Mart. The set is subtitled, "Memorable Moments." Card fronts feature a color photo of the player with the K-Mart logo in lower right corner. Cards measure 2 1/2 by 3 1/2 and are numbered on the back. Card backs provide details for that player's "memorable moment." The set is packaged in a bright yellow and green box with a checklist on the back panel of the box. The cards in the set were numbered by K-Mart essentially in alphabetical order.

	MINT	EXC	G-VG
COMPLETE SET (33)	4.00	1.75	.40
COMMON PLAYER (1-33)	.10	.04	.01
☐ 1 George Bell	.15	.06	.01
☐ 2 Wade Boggs	.50	.20	.05
☐ 3 George Brett	.40	.16	.04
☐ 4 Jose Canseco	.90	.40	.09
☐ 5 Jack Clark	.15	.06	.01
☐ 6 Will Clark	.90	.40	.09
☐ 7 Roger Clemens	.75	.30	.07
☐ 8 Vince Coleman	.25	.10	.02
☐ 9 Andre Dawson	.25	.10	.02
☐ 10 Dwight Gooden	.30	.12	.03
☐ 11 Pedro Guerrero	.15	.06	.01

1989 K-Mart Dream Team

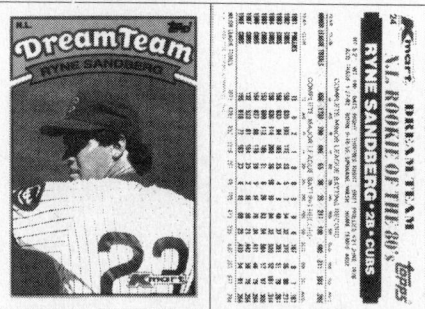

The 1989 K-Mart Dream Team set contains 33 standard-size (2 1/2" by 3 1/2") glossy cards. The fronts are blue. The cards were distributed as a boxed set through K-Mart stores. The set features 11 major league rookies of 1988 plus 11 "American League Rookies of the '80s" and 11 "National League Rookies of the '80s". The complete subject list for the set is provided on the back panel of the custom box.

	MINT	EXC	G-VG
COMPLETE SET (33)	3.50	1.50	.35
COMMON PLAYER (1-33)	.10	.04	.01
☐ 1 Mark Grace	.50	.20	.05
☐ 2 Ron Gant	.60	.25	.06
☐ 3 Chris Sabo	.50	.20	.05
☐ 4 Walt Weiss	.15	.06	.01
☐ 5 Jay Buhner	.25	.10	.02
☐ 6 Cecil Espy	.10	.04	.01
☐ 7 Dave Gallagher	.10	.04	.01
☐ 8 Damon Berryhill	.10	.04	.01
☐ 9 Tim Belcher	.15	.06	.01
☐ 10 Paul Gibson	.10	.04	.01
☐ 11 Gregg Jefferies	.60	.25	.06
☐ 12 Don Mattingly	.60	.25	.06
☐ 13 Harold Reynolds	.10	.04	.01
☐ 14 Wade Boggs	.50	.20	.05
☐ 15 Cal Ripken	.60	.25	.06
☐ 16 Kirby Puckett	.45	.18	.04
☐ 17 George Bell	.20	.08	.02
☐ 18 Jose Canseco	.75	.30	.07
☐ 19 Terry Steinbach	.15	.06	.01
☐ 20 Roger Clemens	.75	.30	.07
☐ 21 Mark Langston	.15	.06	.01
☐ 22 Harold Baines	.15	.06	.01
☐ 23 Will Clark	.75	.30	.07
☐ 24 Ryne Sandberg	.75	.30	.07
☐ 25 Tim Wallach	.15	.06	.01
☐ 26 Shawon Dunston	.15	.06	.01
☐ 27 Tim Raines	.20	.08	.02
☐ 28 Darryl Strawberry	.50	.20	.05
☐ 29 Tony Gwynn	.40	.16	.04
☐ 30 Tony Pena	.10	.04	.01
☐ 31 Dwight Gooden	.25	.10	.02
☐ 32 Fernando Valenzuela	.20	.08	.02
☐ 33 Pedro Guerrero	.15	.06	.01

1990 K-Mart Career Batting Leaders

The 1990 K-Mart Career Batting Leaders set contains 22 standard-size (2 1/2 by 3 1/2 inch) cards. The front borders are emerald green, and the backs are white, blue and evergreen. This set, like the 1989 set of the same name, depicts the 22 major leaguers with the highest lifetime batting averages (minimum 765 games). The card numbers correspond to the player's rank in terms of career batting average. Many of the photos are the same as those from the 1989 set. The cards were distributed one per special Topps blister pack available only at

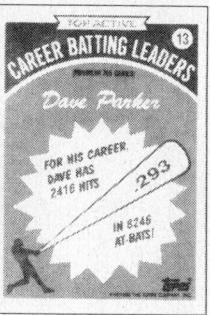

K-Mart stores and were produced by Topps. The K-Mart logo does not appear anywhere on the cards themselves, although there is a Topps logo on the front and back of each card.

	MINT	EXC	G-VG
COMPLETE SET (22)	7.50	3.25	.75
COMMON PLAYER (1-22)	.25	.10	.02
☐ 1 Wade Boggs	.75	.30	.07
☐ 2 Tony Gwynn	.75	.30	.07
☐ 3 Kirby Puckett	.60	.25	.06
☐ 4 Don Mattingly	.75	.30	.07
☐ 5 George Brett	.60	.25	.06
☐ 6 Pedro Guerrero	.35	.15	.03
☐ 7 Tim Raines	.35	.15	.03
☐ 8 Paul Molitor	.35	.15	.03
☐ 9 Jim Rice	.35	.15	.03
☐ 10 Keith Hernandez	.35	.15	.03
☐ 11 Julio Franco	.30	.12	.03
☐ 12 Carney Lansford	.25	.10	.02
☐ 13 Dave Parker	.35	.15	.03
☐ 14 Willie McGee	.30	.12	.03
☐ 15 Robin Yount	.60	.25	.06
☐ 16 Tony Fernandez	.25	.10	.02
☐ 17 Eddie Murray	.40	.16	.04
☐ 18 Johnny Ray	.25	.10	.02
☐ 19 Lonnie Smith	.25	.10	.02
☐ 20 Phil Bradley	.25	.10	.02
☐ 21 Rickey Henderson	.90	.40	.09
☐ 22 Kent Hrbek	.30	.12	.03

1990 K-Mart Superstars

The 1990 K-Mart Superstars set is a 33-card, standard-size (2 1/2" by 3 1/2") set issued for the K-Mart chain by the Topps Company. This set was issued with a piece of gum in the custom set box.

	MINT	EXC	G-VG
COMPLETE SET (33)	3.50	1.50	.35
COMMON PLAYER (1-33)	.10	.04	.01

☐ 1	Will Clark	.60	.25	.06
☐ 2	Ryne Sandberg	.60	.25	.06
☐ 3	Howard Johnson	.20	.08	.02
☐ 4	Ozzie Smith	.20	.08	.02
☐ 5	Tony Gwynn	.40	.16	.04
☐ 6	Kevin Mitchell	.30	.12	.03
☐ 7	Jerome Walton	.15	.06	.01
☐ 8	Craig Biggio	.15	.06	.01
☐ 9	Mike Scott	.15	.06	.01
☐ 10	Dwight Gooden	.25	.10	.02
☐ 11	Sid Fernandez	.15	.06	.01
☐ 12	Joe Magrane	.10	.04	.01
☐ 13	Jay Howell	.10	.04	.01
☐ 14	Mark Davis	.10	.04	.01
☐ 15	Pedro Guerrero	.15	.06	.01
☐ 16	Glenn Davis	.15	.06	.01
☐ 17	Don Mattingly	.60	.25	.06
☐ 18	Julio Franco	.20	.08	.02
☐ 19	Wade Boggs	.50	.20	.05
☐ 20	Cal Ripken	.60	.25	.06
☐ 21	Jose Canseco	.60	.25	.06
☐ 22	Kirby Puckett	.45	.18	.04
☐ 23	Rickey Henderson	.75	.30	.07
☐ 24	Mickey Tettleton	.10	.04	.01
☐ 25	Nolan Ryan	.90	.40	.09
☐ 26	Bret Saberhagen	.20	.08	.02
☐ 27	Jeff Ballard	.10	.04	.01
☐ 28	Chuck Finley	.15	.06	.01
☐ 29	Dennis Eckersley	.15	.06	.01
☐ 30	Dan Plesac	.10	.04	.01
☐ 31	Fred McGriff	.20	.08	.02
☐ 32	Mark McGwire	.45	.18	.04
☐ 33	Tony LaRussa MG and Roger Craig MG	.10	.04	.01

1988 Kodak White Sox

This five-card, approximately 8" by 11 1/2" set was issued by Kodak including members of the 1988 Chicago White Sox. The cards are borderless and say "1988 Kodak Collectible Series" on top with the player's photo dominating the middle of the photo. Underneath the photo is a facsimile autograph and on the bottom left of the photo is an advertisement for Kodak and the bottom right of the card the White Sox logo is featured. The backs are blank.

	MINT	EXC	G-VG
COMPLETE SET (5)	8.00	3.50	.80
COMMON PLAYER (1-5)	1.25	.50	.12
☐ 1 Ozzie Guillen	2.00	.80	.20
☐ 2 Carlton Fisk	3.50	1.50	.35
☐ 3 Rick Horton	1.25	.50	.12
☐ 4 Ivan Calderon	1.75	.70	.17
☐ 5 Harold Baines	2.00	.80	.20

1989 Kodak White Sox

For the second consecutive year Kodak in conjunction with the Chicago White Sox issued a set about the White Sox. The 1989 set was marked by a color photo of the active star dominating the upper right half of the card and the bottom half of the card was another famous player at the same position that the current star played. This six-card, approximately 8" by 11 1/2", set was given away at various games at Comiskey Park.

	MINT	EXC	G-VG
COMPLETE SET (6)	8.00	3.50	.80
COMMON PLAYER (1-6)	1.50	.60	.15
☐ 1 Greg Walker / Dick Allen / Ted Kluszewski	1.50	.60	.15
☐ 2 Steve Lyons / Eddie Collins / Nellie Fox	1.50	.60	.15
☐ 3 Carlton Fisk / Sherm Lollar / Ray Schalk	3.00	1.25	.30
☐ 4 Harold Baines / Minnie Minoso / Jim Landis	1.50	.60	.15
☐ 5 Bobby Thigpen / Gerry Staley / Hoyt Wilhelm	1.50	.60	.15
☐ 6 Ozzie Guillen / Luke Appling / Luis Aparicio	2.00	.80	.20

1990 Kodak White Sox

In 1990 Kodak again in conjunction with the Chicago White Sox issued a beautiful six-card set about some key members of the 1990 White Sox. This was slightly reduced in size (from the previous two years) to be approximately 7" by 11" and featured a full-color picture with an advertisement for Kodak on the lower left corner of the front of the card and the White Sox logo in the lower right hand corner. The cards were again borderless and blank-backed.

	MINT	EXC	G-VG
COMPLETE SET (6)	7.00	3.00	.70
COMMON PLAYER (1-6)	1.00	.40	.10
☐ 1 Carlton Fisk	2.50	1.00	.25
☐ 2 Melido Perez	1.25	.50	.12
☐ 3 Ozzie Guillen	1.50	.60	.15

1990 Kodak Collectible Series #2

Melido Perez
Pitcher

☐	23	Robin Ventura	1.00	.40	.10
☐	25	Sammy Sosa	.50	.20	.05
☐	27	Greg Hibbard	.40	.16	.04
☐	28	Cory Snyder	.40	.16	.04
☐	29	Jack McDowell	.60	.25	.06
☐	30	Tim Raines	.50	.20	.05
☐	31	Scott Radinsky	.40	.16	.04
☐	32	Alex Fernandez	.60	.25	.06
☐	33	Melido Perez	.40	.16	.04
☐	34	Ken Patterson	.30	.12	.03
☐	35	Frank Thomas	4.00	1.75	.40
☐	37	Bobby Thigpen	.50	.20	.05
☐	44	Dan Pasqua	.40	.16	.04
☐	45	Wayne Edwards	.30	.12	.03
☐	49	Charlie Hough	.30	.12	.03
☐	50	Brian Drahman	.30	.12	.03
☐	72	Carlton Fisk	1.00	.40	.10
☐	xx	No. 1 Draft Choices	1.50	.60	.15
		Jack McDowell			
		Robin Ventura			
		Alex Fernandez			
		Frank Thomas			
☐	xx	1991 Co-Captains	.50	.20	.05
		Carlton Fisk and			
		Ozzie Guillen			
☐	xx	1991 Coaching Staff	.40	.16	.04
		Walt Hriniak			
		Sammy Ellis			
		Terry Bevington			
		Barry Foote			
		Joe Nossek			
		John Stephenson			
		Dave LaRoche			

☐	4	Ron Kittle	1.25	.50	.12
☐	5	Scott Fletcher	1.00	.40	.10
☐	6	Comiskey Park	1.00	.40	.10

1991 Kodak White Sox

This 28-card set was sponsored by Kodak and measures 2 5/8" by 3 1/2". The front design depicts borderless glossy color action player photos. A Comiskey Park insignia is superimposed at the upper left corner of the picture. The player's name appears in black lettering in a silver stripe toward the card bottom, with a black oversized (uniform) number in the lower left corner. In a horizontal format, the backs are printed in black on white with gray borders, and provide 1990 statistics and highlights. The cards are skip-numbered by uniform number and checklisted below accordingly, with the unnumbered cards listed at the end.

			MINT	EXC	G-VG
	COMPLETE SET (28)		12.50	5.50	1.65
	COMMON PLAYER		.30	.12	.03
☐	1	Lance Johnson	.40	.16	.04
☐	5	Matt Merullo	.40	.16	.04
☐	7	Scott Fletcher	.30	.12	.03
☐	8	Bo Jackson	2.50	1.00	.25
☐	10	Jeff Torborg MG	.40	.16	.04
☐	13	Ozzie Guillen	.50	.20	.05
☐	14	Craig Grebeck	.40	.16	.04
☐	20	Ron Karkovice	.30	.12	.03
☐	21	Joey Cora	.30	.12	.03
☐	22	Donn Pall	.30	.12	.03

1960 Lake to Lake

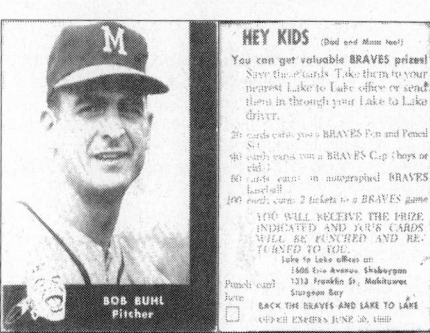

BOB BUHL
Pitcher

The cards in this 28-card set measure 2 1/2" by 3 1/4". The 1960 Lake to Lake set of unnumbered, blue tinted cards features Milwaukee Braves players only. For some reason, this set of Braves does not include Eddie Mathews. The cards were issued on milk cartons by Lake to Lake Dairy. Most cards have staple holes in the upper right corner. The backs are in red and give details and prizes associated with the card promotion. Cards with staple holes can be considered very good to excellent at best. The catalog designation for this set is F102-1.

			NRMT	VG-E	GOOD
	COMPLETE SET (28)		1200.00	500.00	120.00
	COMMON PLAYER (1-28)		16.00	6.75	2.25
☐	1	Hank Aaron	350.00	160.00	52.50
☐	2	Joe Adcock	22.50	9.75	3.25
☐	3	Ray Boone	135.00	60.00	20.00
☐	4	Bill Bruton	250.00	110.00	37.50
☐	5	Bob Buhl	16.00	6.75	2.25
☐	6	Lew Burdette	25.00	11.00	3.50
☐	7	Chuck Cottier	16.00	6.75	2.25
☐	8	Wes Covington	16.00	6.75	2.25
☐	9	Del Crandall	20.00	8.50	2.75
☐	10	Chuck Dressen MG	16.00	6.75	2.25
☐	11	Bob Giggie	16.00	6.75	2.25
☐	12	Joey Jay	16.00	6.75	2.25
☐	13	Johnny Logan	20.00	8.50	2.75

		NRMT	VG-E	GOOD
☐ 14	Felix Mantilla	16.00	6.75	2.25
☐ 15	Lee Maye	16.00	6.75	2.25
☐ 16	Don McMahon	16.00	6.75	2.25
☐ 17	George Myatt CO	16.00	6.75	2.25
☐ 18	Andy Pafko CO	16.00	6.75	2.25
☐ 19	Juan Pizarro	16.00	6.75	2.25
☐ 20	Mel Roach	16.00	6.75	2.25
☐ 21	Bob Rush	16.00	6.75	2.25
☐ 22	Bob Scheffing CO	16.00	6.75	2.25
☐ 23	Red Schoendienst	50.00	22.50	7.50
☐ 24	Warren Spahn	75.00	34.00	11.25
☐ 25	Al Spangler	16.00	6.75	2.25
☐ 26	Frank Torre	16.00	6.75	2.25
☐ 27	Carlton Willey	16.00	6.75	2.25
☐ 28	Whit Wyatt CO	16.00	6.75	2.25

1968 Laughlin World Series

This set of 64 cards was apparently a limited test issue by sports artist R.G. Laughlin for the World Series set concept that was mass marketed by Fleer two and three years later. The cards are slightly oversized, 2 3/4" by 3 1/2" and are black and white on the front and red and white on the back. All the years are represented except for 1904 when no World Series was played. In the list below, the winning series team is listed first.

		NRMT	VG-E	GOOD
COMPLETE SET (64)		75.00	34.00	11.25
COMMON PLAYER (1-64)		1.25	.50	.12
☐ 1	1903 Red Sox/Pirates	1.25	.50	.12
☐ 2	1905 Giants/A's (Christy Mathewson)	1.50	.60	.15
☐ 3	1906 White Sox/Cubs	1.25	.50	.12
☐ 4	1907 Cubs/Tigers	1.25	.50	.12
☐ 5	1908 Cubs/Tigers (Tinker/Evers/Chance)	1.50	.60	.15
☐ 6	1909 Pirates/Tigers (Wagner/Cobb)	2.50	1.00	.25
☐ 7	1910 A's/Cubs	1.25	.50	.12
☐ 8	1911 A's/Giants (John McGraw)	1.50	.60	.15
☐ 9	1912 Red Sox/Giants	1.25	.50	.12
☐ 10	1913 A's/Giants	1.25	.50	.12
☐ 11	1914 Braves/A's	1.25	.50	.12
☐ 12	1915 Red Sox/Phillies (Babe Ruth)	3.00	1.25	.30
☐ 13	1916 Red Sox/Dodgers (Babe Ruth)	3.00	1.25	.30
☐ 14	1917 White Sox/Giants	1.25	.50	.12
☐ 15	1918 Red Sox/Cubs	1.25	.50	.12
☐ 16	1919 Reds/White Sox	1.25	.50	.12
☐ 17	1920 Indians/Dodgers	1.25	.50	.12
☐ 18	1921 Giants/Yankees (Waite Hoyt)	1.25	.50	.12
☐ 19	1922 Giants/Yankees (Frisch/Groh)	1.25	.50	.12
☐ 20	1923 Yankees/Giants (Babe Ruth)	3.00	1.25	.30
☐ 21	1924 Senators/Giants	1.25	.50	.12
☐ 22	1925 Pirates/Senators (Walter Johnson)	2.00	.80	.20
☐ 23	1926 Cardinals/Yankees (Alexander/Lazzeri)	1.50	.60	.15
☐ 24	1927 Yankees/Pirates	1.25	.50	.12
☐ 25	1928 Yankees/Cardinals (Ruth/Gehrig)	3.00	1.25	.30
☐ 26	1929 A's/Cubs	1.25	.50	.12
☐ 27	1930 A's/Cardinals	1.25	.50	.12
☐ 28	1931 Cardinals/A's (Pepper Martin)	1.25	.50	.12
☐ 29	1932 Yankees/Cubs (Babe Ruth)	3.00	1.25	.30
☐ 30	1933 Giants/Senators (Mel Ott)	1.50	.60	.15
☐ 31	1934 Cardinals/Tigers (Dizzy/Paul Dean)	1.50	.60	.15
☐ 32	1935 Tigers/Cubs	1.25	.50	.12
☐ 33	1936 Yankees/Giants	1.25	.50	.12
☐ 34	1937 Yankees/Giants (Carl Hubbell)	1.50	.60	.15
☐ 35	1938 Yankees/Cubs	1.25	.50	.12
☐ 36	1939 Yankees/Reds (Joe DiMaggio)	2.50	1.00	.25
☐ 37	1940 Reds/Tigers	1.25	.50	.12
☐ 38	1941 Yankees/Dodgers (Mickey Owen)	1.25	.50	.12
☐ 39	1942 Cardinals/Yankees	1.25	.50	.12
☐ 40	1943 Yankees/Cardinals (Joe McCarthy)	1.25	.50	.12
☐ 41	1944 Cardinals/Browns	1.25	.50	.12
☐ 42	1945 Tigers/Cubs (Hank Greenberg)	1.50	.60	.15
☐ 43	1946 Cardinals/Red Sox (Enos Slaughter)	1.50	.60	.15
☐ 44	1947 Yankees/Dodgers (Al Gionfriddo)	1.25	.50	.12
☐ 45	1948 Indians/Braves (Bob Feller)	1.50	.60	.15
☐ 46	1949 Yankees/Dodgers (Reynolds/Roe)	1.25	.50	.12
☐ 47	1950 Yankees/Phillies	1.25	.50	.12
☐ 48	1951 Yankees/Giants	1.25	.50	.12
☐ 49	1952 Yankees/Dodgers (Mize/Snider)	1.50	.60	.15
☐ 50	1953 Yankees/Dodgers (Casey Stengel)	1.50	.60	.15
☐ 51	1954 Giants/Indians (Dusty Rhodes)	1.25	.50	.12
☐ 52	1955 Dodgers/Yankees (Johnny Podres)	1.25	.50	.12
☐ 53	1956 Yankees/Dodgers (Don Larsen)	1.50	.60	.15
☐ 54	1957 Braves/Yankees (Lew Burdette)	1.25	.50	.12
☐ 55	1958 Yankees/Braves (Hank Bauer)	1.25	.50	.12
☐ 56	1959 Dodgers/Wh.Sox (Larry Sherry)	1.25	.50	.12
☐ 57	1960 Pirates/Yankees	1.25	.50	.12
☐ 58	1961 Yankees/Reds (Whitey Ford)	1.50	.60	.15
☐ 59	1962 Yankees/Giants	1.25	.50	.12
☐ 60	1963 Dodgers/Yankees (Sandy Koufax)	1.50	.60	.15
☐ 61	1964 Cardinals/Yankees (Mickey Mantle)	2.50	1.00	.25
☐ 62	1965 Dodgers/Twins	1.25	.50	.12
☐ 63	1966 Orioles/Dodgers	1.25	.50	.12
☐ 64	1967 Cardinals/Red Sox (Bob Gibson)	1.50	.60	.15

1972 Laughlin Great Feats

This set of 51 cards is printed on white card stock. Sports artist R.G. Laughlin 1972 is copyrighted only on the unnumbered title card but not on each card. The obverses are line drawings in black and white inside a red border. The cards measure approximately 2 9/16" by 3 9/16". The set features "Great Feats" from baseball's past. The cards are blank backed and hence are numbered and captioned on the front. There is a variation set with a blue border and colored in flesh tones in the players pictured; this variation is a little more attractive and hence is valued a little higher. The blue-bordered variation set has larger type in the captions; in fact, the type has been reset and there are some minor wording differences. The blue-bordered set is also 1/16" wider.

	NRMT	VG-E	GOOD
COMPLETE SET (51)	20.00	8.50	2.75
COMMON PLAYER (1-51)	.35	.15	.03

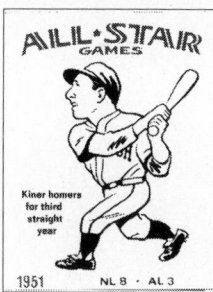

☐ 1	Joe DiMaggio	2.00	.80	.20
☐ 2	Walter Johnson	1.00	.40	.10
☐ 3	Rudy York	.35	.15	.03
☐ 4	Sandy Koufax	1.00	.40	.10
☐ 5	George Sisler	.45	.18	.04
☐ 6	Iron Man McGinnity	.35	.15	.03
☐ 7	Johnny VanderMeer	.35	.15	.03
☐ 8	Lou Gehrig	1.25	.50	.12
☐ 9	Max Carey	.35	.15	.03
☐ 10	Ed Delahanty	.35	.15	.03
☐ 11	Pinky Higgins	.35	.15	.03
☐ 12	Jack Chesbro	.35	.15	.03
☐ 13	Jim Bottomley	.35	.15	.03
☐ 14	Rube Marquard	.35	.15	.03
☐ 15	Rogers Hornsby	.60	.25	.06
☐ 16	Lefty Grove	.45	.18	.04
☐ 17	Johnny Mize	.60	.25	.06
☐ 18	Lefty Gomez	.45	.18	.04
☐ 19	Jimmie Foxx	.60	.25	.06
☐ 20	Casey Stengel	.75	.30	.07
☐ 21	Dazzy Vance	.35	.15	.03
☐ 22	Jerry Lynch	.35	.15	.03
☐ 23	Hughie Jennings	.35	.15	.03
☐ 24	Stan Musial	.75	.30	.07
☐ 25	Christy Mathewson	.75	.30	.07
☐ 26	Elroy Face	.35	.15	.03
☐ 27	Hack Wilson	.45	.18	.04
☐ 28	Smoky Burgess	.35	.15	.03
☐ 29	Cy Young	.60	.25	.06
☐ 30	Wilbert Robinson	.35	.15	.03
☐ 31	Wee Willie Keeler	.35	.15	.03
☐ 32	Babe Ruth	2.00	.80	.20
☐ 33	Mickey Mantle	2.00	.80	.20
☐ 34	Hub Leonard	.35	.15	.03
☐ 35	Ty Cobb	1.25	.50	.12
☐ 36	Carl Hubbell	.35	.15	.03
☐ 37	Joe Oeschger and Leon Cadore	.35	.15	.03
☐ 38	Don Drysdale	.50	.20	.05
☐ 39	Fred Toney and Hippo Vaughn	.35	.15	.03
☐ 40	Joe Sewell	.35	.15	.03
☐ 41	Grover C. Alexander	.45	.18	.04
☐ 42	Joe Adcock	.35	.15	.03
☐ 43	Eddie Collins	.35	.15	.03
☐ 44	Bob Feller	.60	.25	.06
☐ 45	Don Larsen	.35	.15	.03
☐ 46	Dave Philley	.35	.15	.03
☐ 47	Bill Fischer	.35	.15	.03
☐ 48	Dale Long	.35	.15	.03
☐ 49	Bill Wambsganss	.35	.15	.03
☐ 50	Roger Maris	.60	.25	.06
☐ x	Title Card	.35	.15	.03

1974 Laughlin All-Star Games

This set of 40 cards is printed on white card stock. Sports artist R.G. Laughlin 1974 is copyrighted at the bottom of the reverse of each card. The obverses are line drawings primarily in red, light blue, black, and white inside a white border. The cards measure approximately 2 11/16" by 3 3/8". The set features memorable moments from each year's All-Star Game(s). The cards are numbered on the back according to the last two digits of the year and captioned on the front. The backs are printed in blue on white stock. There is no card number 45 in the set as there was no All-Star Game played in 1945 because of World War II.

		NRMT	VG-E	GOOD
COMPLETE SET (40)		30.00	13.50	4.50
COMMON PLAYER (33-73)		.50	.20	.05
☐ 33	Babe's Homer	3.00	1.25	.30
☐ 34	Hubbell Fans Five	.75	.30	.07
☐ 35	Foxx Smashes Homer	.75	.30	.07
☐ 36	Ol' Diz Fogs 'Em	.90	.40	.09
☐ 37	Four Hits for Ducky	.60	.25	.06
☐ 38	No-Hit Vandy	.50	.20	.05
☐ 39	DiMaggio Homers	2.00	.80	.20
☐ 40	West's 3-Run Shot	.50	.20	.05
☐ 41	Vaughan Busts Two	.60	.25	.06
☐ 42	York's 2-Run Smash	.50	.20	.05
☐ 43	Doerr 3-Run Blast	.60	.25	.06
☐ 44	Cavarretta Reaches	.50	.20	.05
☐ 46	Field Day for Ted	1.50	.60	.15
☐ 47	Big Cat Plants One	.90	.40	.09
☐ 48	Raschi Pitches	.60	.25	.06
☐ 49	Jackie Scores	1.25	.50	.12
☐ 50	Schoendienst Breaks	.75	.30	.07
☐ 51	Kiner Homers	.75	.30	.07
☐ 52	Sauer's Shot	.50	.20	.05
☐ 53	Slaughter Hustles	.75	.30	.07
☐ 54	Rosen Hits	.50	.20	.05
☐ 55	Stan the Man's Homer	1.00	.40	.10
☐ 56	Ken Boyer Super	.50	.20	.05
☐ 57	Kaline Hits	.90	.40	.09
☐ 58	Only Nellie Gets Two	.60	.25	.06
☐ 59	F.Robbie Perfect	.75	.30	.07
☐ 60	Willie 3-for-4	1.25	.50	.12
☐ 61	Bunning Hitless	.60	.25	.06
☐ 62	Roberto Perfect	1.25	.50	.12
☐ 63	Monster Strikeouts	.50	.20	.05
☐ 64	Callison's Homer	.50	.20	.05
☐ 65	Stargell Big Day	.75	.30	.07
☐ 66	Brooks Hits	.90	.40	.09
☐ 67	Fergie Fans Six	.75	.30	.07
☐ 68	Tom Terrific	1.25	.50	.12
☐ 69	Stretch Belts Two	.75	.30	.07
☐ 70	Yaz Four Hits	.90	.40	.09
☐ 71	Reggie Unloads	1.25	.50	.12
☐ 72	Henry Hammers	1.25	.50	.12
☐ 73	Bonds Perfect	.60	.25	.06

1974 Laughlin Old Time Black Stars

This set of 36 cards is printed on flat (non-glossy) white card stock. Sports artist R.G. Laughlin's work is evident but there are no copyright notices or any mention of him anywhere on any of the cards in this set. The obverses are line drawings in tan and brown. The cards measure approximately 2 5/8" by 3 1/2". The set features outstanding black players form the past. The cards are numbered on the back. The backs are printed in brown on white stock.

		NRMT	VG-E	GOOD
COMPLETE SET (36)		30.00	13.50	4.50
COMMON PLAYER (1-36)		.75	.30	.07
☐ 1	Smokey Joe Williams	1.25	.50	.12
☐ 2	Rap Dixon	.75	.30	.07

			NRMT	VG-E	GOOD
☐	4	Anchor Man	.25	.10	.02
☐	5	Mascot	.25	.10	.02
☐	6	Annie Oakley	.25	.10	.02
☐	7	Taxi Squad	.25	.10	.02
☐	8	Dukes	.25	.10	.02
☐	9	Rookie	.25	.10	.02
☐	10	Jinx	.25	.10	.02
☐	11	Dark Horse	.25	.10	.02
☐	12	Hat Trick	.25	.10	.02
☐	13	Bell Wether	.25	.10	.02
☐	14	Love	.25	.10	.02
☐	15	Red Dog	.25	.10	.02
☐	16	Barnstorm	.25	.10	.02
☐	17	Bull's Eye	.25	.10	.02
☐	18	Rabbit Punch	.25	.10	.02
☐	19	The Upper Hand	.25	.10	.02
☐	20	Handi Cap	.25	.10	.02
☐	21	Marathon	.25	.10	.02
☐	22	Southpaw	.25	.10	.02
☐	23	Boner	.25	.10	.02
☐	24	Gridiron	.25	.10	.02
☐	25	Fan	.25	.10	.02
☐	26	Moxie	.25	.10	.02
☐	27	Birdie	.25	.10	.02
☐	28	Sulky	.25	.10	.02
☐	29	Dribble	.25	.10	.02
☐	30	Donnybrook	.25	.10	.02
☐	31	The Real McCoy	.25	.10	.02
☐	32	Even Stephen	.25	.10	.02
☐	33	Chinese Homer	.25	.10	.02
☐	34	English	.25	.10	.02
☐	35	Garrison Finish	.25	.10	.02
☐	36	Foot in the Bucket	.25	.10	.02
☐	37	Steeple Chase	.25	.10	.02
☐	38	Long Shot	.25	.10	.02
☐	39	Nip and Tuck	.25	.10	.02
☐	40	Battery	.25	.10	.02
☐	xx	Title Card	.25	.10	.02
		(unnumbered)			

			NRMT	VG-E	GOOD
☐	3	Oliver Marcelle	.75	.30	.07
☐	4	Bingo DeMoss	.90	.40	.09
☐	5	Willie Foster	.90	.40	.09
☐	6	John Beckwith	.75	.30	.07
☐	7	Floyd(Jelly) Gardner	.75	.30	.07
☐	8	Josh Gibson	2.50	1.00	.25
☐	9	Jose Mendez	.75	.30	.07
☐	10	Pete Hill	.75	.30	.07
☐	11	Buck Leonard	1.25	.50	.12
☐	12	Jud Wilson	.75	.30	.07
☐	13	Willie Wells	1.00	.40	.10
☐	14	Jimmie Lyons	.75	.30	.07
☐	15	Satchel Paige	2.50	1.00	.25
☐	16	Louis Santop	.75	.30	.07
☐	17	Frank Grant	.75	.30	.07
☐	18	Christobel Torrienti	.90	.40	.09
☐	19	Bullet Rogon	.75	.30	.07
☐	20	Dave Malarcher	.90	.40	.09
☐	21	Spot Poles	.75	.30	.07
☐	22	Home Run Johnson	.90	.40	.09
☐	23	Charlie Grant	.75	.30	.07
☐	24	Cool Papa Bell	1.25	.50	.12
☐	25	Cannonball Dick Redding	.75	.30	.07
☐	26	Ray Dandridge	1.25	.50	.12
☐	27	Biz Mackey	1.00	.40	.10
☐	28	Fats Jenkins	.75	.30	.07
☐	29	Martin Dihigo	1.25	.50	.12
☐	30	Mule Suttles	.75	.30	.07
☐	31	Bill Monroe	.75	.30	.07
☐	32	Dan McClellan	.75	.30	.07
☐	33	John Henry Lloyd	1.25	.50	.12
☐	34	Oscar Charleston	1.25	.50	.12
☐	35	Andrew(Rube) Foster	1.25	.50	.12
☐	36	William(Judy) Johnson	1.25	.50	.12

1974 Laughlin Sportslang

This set of 41 cards is printed on white card stock. Sports artist R.G. Laughlin 1974 is copyrighted at the bottom of every reverse. The obverses are drawings in red and blue on a white enamel card stock. The cards measure approximately 2 3/4" by 3 3/8". The set actually features the slang of several sports, not just baseball. The cards are numbered on the back and captioned on the front. The card back also provides an explanation of the slang term pictured on the card front.

		NRMT	VG-E	GOOD
COMPLETE SET (41)		8.00	3.50	.80
COMMON PLAYER (1-41)		.25	.10	.02
☐ 1	Bull Pen	.25	.10	.02
☐ 2	Charley Horse	.25	.10	.02
☐ 3	Derby	.25	.10	.02

1975 Laughlin Batty Baseball

This set of 25 cards is printed on white card stock. Sports artist R.G. Laughlin 1975 is copyrighted on the title card. The obverses are line drawings primarily in orange, black, and white. The cards measure approximately 2 9/16" by 3 7/16". The set features a card for each team with a depiction of a fractured nickname for the team. The cards are numbered on the front. The backs are blank, but on white stock.

		NRMT	VG-E	GOOD
COMPLETE SET (25)		5.00	2.25	.50
COMMON PLAYER (1-24)		.25	.10	.02
☐ 1	Oakland Daze	.25	.10	.02
☐ 2	Boston Wet Sox	.25	.10	.02
☐ 3	Cincinnati Dreads	.25	.10	.02
☐ 4	Chicago Wide Sox	.25	.10	.02
☐ 5	Milwaukee Boozers	.25	.10	.02
☐ 6	Philadelphia Fillies	.25	.10	.02
☐ 7	Cleveland Engines	.25	.10	.02
☐ 8	New York Mitts	.25	.10	.02
☐ 9	Texas Ranchers	.25	.10	.02
☐ 10	San Francisco Gents	.25	.10	.02
☐ 11	Houston Disastros	.25	.10	.02
☐ 12	Chicago Clubs	.25	.10	.02

		NRMT	VG-E	GOOD
☐ 13	Minnesota Wins	.25	.10	.02
☐ 14	St. Louis Gardeners	.25	.10	.02
☐ 15	New York Yankers	.25	.10	.02
☐ 16	California Angles	.25	.10	.02
☐ 17	Pittsburgh Irates	.25	.10	.02
☐ 18	Los Angeles Smoggers	.25	.10	.02
☐ 19	Baltimore Oreos	.25	.10	.02
☐ 20	Montreal Expose	.25	.10	.02
☐ 21	San Diego Parties	.25	.10	.02
☐ 22	Detroit Taggers	.25	.10	.02
☐ 23	Kansas City Broils	.25	.10	.02
☐ 24	Atlanta Briefs	.25	.10	.02
☐ xx	Title Card	.25	.10	.02
	(unnumbered)			

1976 Laughlin Diamond Jubilee

This set of 32 cards is printed on flat (non-glossy) white card stock. Sports artist R.Laughlin 1976 is copyrighted at the bottom of the reverse of each card. The obverses are line drawings primarily in red, blue, black, and white inside a red border. The cards measure approximately 2 13/16" by 3 15/16". The set features memorable moments voted by the media and fans in each major league city. The cards are numbered on the back and captioned on the front. The backs are printed in dark blue on white stock.

		NRMT	VG-E	GOOD
	COMPLETE SET (32)	30.00	13.50	4.50
	COMMON PLAYER (1-32)	.65	.25	.06
☐ 1	Nolan Ryan	4.50	2.00	.45
☐ 2	Ernie Banks	1.00	.40	.10
☐ 3	Mickey Lolich	.65	.25	.06
☐ 4	Sandy Koufax	1.50	.60	.15
☐ 5	Frank Robinson	1.00	.40	.10
☐ 6	Bill Mazeroski	.65	.25	.06
☐ 7	Jim Hunter	.80	.35	.08
☐ 8	Hank Aaron	1.50	.60	.15
☐ 9	Carl Yastrzemski	1.50	.60	.15
☐ 10	Jim Bunning	.80	.35	.08
☐ 11	Brooks Robinson	1.00	.40	.10
☐ 12	John VanderMeer	.65	.25	.06
☐ 13	Harmon Killebrew	.90	.40	.09
☐ 14	Lou Brock	1.00	.40	.10
☐ 15	Steve Busby	.65	.25	.06
☐ 16	Nate Colbert	.65	.25	.06
☐ 17	Don Larsen	.80	.35	.08
☐ 18	Willie Mays	1.50	.60	.15
☐ 19	David Clyde	.65	.25	.06
☐ 20	Mack Jones	.65	.25	.06
☐ 21	Mike Hegan	.65	.25	.06
☐ 22	Jerry Koosman	.80	.35	.08
☐ 23	Early Wynn	.90	.40	.09
☐ 24	Nellie Fox	.80	.35	.08
☐ 25	Joe DiMaggio	2.00	.80	.20
☐ 26	Jackie Robinson	1.50	.60	.15
☐ 27	Ted Williams	1.50	.60	.15
☐ 28	Lou Gehrig	2.00	.80	.20
☐ 29	Bobby Thomson	.80	.35	.08
☐ 30	Roger Maris	.90	.40	.09
☐ 31	Harvey Haddix	.65	.25	.06
☐ 32	Babe Ruth	3.00	1.25	.30

1976 Laughlin Indianapolis Clowns

This 42-card set was issued to commemorate the Indianapolis Clowns, a black team that began touring in 1929 and played many games for charity. The cards measure 2 5/8" by 4 1/4". The front design has black , white player photos, inside a white frame against a light blue card face. The team name is printed in red and white above the picture. In red courier-style print on white, the backs present extended captions. The cards are numbered on the front.

		NRMT	VG-E	GOOD
	COMPLETE SET (42)	25.00	11.00	3.50
	COMMON PLAYER (1-40)	.60	.25	.06
☐ 1	Ed Hamman	1.00	.40	.10
	Ed the Clown			
☐ 2	Dero Austin	.60	.25	.06
☐ 3	James Williams	.60	.25	.06
	Nickname Natureboy			
☐ 4	Sam Brison	.60	.25	.06
	Nickname Birmingham			
☐ 5	Richard King	.60	.25	.06
	Nickname King Tut			
☐ 6	Syd Pollock	.60	.25	.06
	Founder			
☐ 7	Nataniel(Lefty) Small	.60	.25	.06
☐ 8	Grant Greene	.60	.25	.06
	Nickname Double Duty			
☐ 9	Nancy Miller	.75	.30	.07
	Lady umpire			
☐ 10	Billy Vaughn	.60	.25	.06
☐ 11	Sam Brison	.60	.25	.06
	Putout for Sam			
☐ 12	Ed Hamman	.60	.25	.06
☐ 13	Dero Austin	.60	.25	.06
	Home delivery			
☐ 14	Steve(Nub) Anderson	.60	.25	.06
☐ 15	Joe Cherry	.60	.25	.06
☐ 16	Reece(Goose) Tatum	2.00	.80	.20
☐ 17	James Williams	.60	.25	.06
	Natureboy			
☐ 18	Byron Purnell	.60	.25	.06
☐ 19	Bat boy	.60	.25	.06
☐ 20	Spec BeBop	.60	.25	.06
☐ 21	Satchel Paige	2.00	.80	.20
☐ 22	Prince Jo Henry	.60	.25	.06
☐ 23	Ed Hamman	.60	.25	.06
	Syd Pollock			
☐ 24	Paul Casanova	1.00	.40	.10
☐ 25	Steve(Nub) Anderson	.60	.25	.06
	Nub singles			
☐ 26	Comiskey Park	.60	.25	.06
☐ 27	Toni Stone	.60	.25	.06
	Second basewoman			
☐ 28	Dero Austin	.60	.25	.06
	Small target			
☐ 29	Sam Brison and	.60	.25	.06
	Natureboy Williams			
	Calling Dr. Kildare			
☐ 30	Oscar Charleston	1.25	.50	.12
☐ 31	Richard King	.60	.25	.06
	King Tut			
☐ 32	Ed Hamman	.60	.25	.06
	Joe Cherry			
	Hal King			
	Ed and prospects			
☐ 33	In style	.60	.25	.06
	Team bus			

		NRMT	VG-E	GOOD
☐	34 Hank Aaron	2.50	1.00	.25
☐	35 The Great Yogi	2.00	.80	.20
☐	36 W.H.(Chauff) Wilson	.60	.25	.06
☐	37 Sam Brison	.60	.25	.06
	Sonny Jackson			
	Doin' their thing			
☐	38 Billy Vaughn	.60	.25	.06
	The hard way			
☐	39 James Williams	.60	.25	.06
	1B the easy way			
☐	40 Ed Hamman	1.25	.50	.12
	Casey Stengel			
	Casey and Ed			
☐	xx Title Card	.60	.25	.06
☐	xx Baseball Laff Book	.60	.25	.06

☐	33 Quincy Troupe	.60	.25	.06
☐	34 Hilton Smith	.60	.25	.06
☐	35 Jim Crutchfield	.60	.25	.06
☐	36 Ted Radcliffe	.75	.30	.07

1980 Laughlin Famous Feats

This set of 40 cards is printed on white card stock. Sports artist R.G. Laughlin 1980 is copyrighted at the bottom of every obverse. The obverses are line drawings primarily in many colors. The cards measure approximately 2 1/2" by 3 1/2". The set is subtitled as the "Second Series" of Famous Feats. The cards are numbered on the front. The backs are blank, but on white stock.

1978 Laughlin Long Ago Black Stars

This set of 36 cards is printed on flat (non-glossy) white card stock. Sports artist R.G. Laughlin's work is evident and the reverse of each card indicates copyright by R.G. Laughlin 1978. The obverses are line drawings in light and dark green. The cards measure approximately 2 5/8" by 3 1/2". The set features outstanding black players form the past. The cards are numbered on the back. The backs are printed in black on white stock. This is not a reissue of the similar Laughlin set from 1974 Old Time Black Stars but is actually in effect a second series with all new players.

		NRMT	VG-E	GOOD
	COMPLETE SET (36)	20.00	8.50	2.75
	COMMON PLAYER (1-36)	.60	.25	.06
☐	1 Ted Trent	.75	.30	.07
☐	2 Larry Brown	.60	.25	.06
☐	3 Newt Allen	.75	.30	.07
☐	4 Norman Stearns	.60	.25	.06
☐	5 Leon Day	1.00	.40	.10
☐	6 Dick Lundy	.60	.25	.06
☐	7 Bruce Petway	.75	.30	.07
☐	8 Bill Drake	.60	.25	.06
☐	9 Chaney White	.60	.25	.06
☐	10 Webster McDonald	.60	.25	.06
☐	11 Tommy Butts	.60	.25	.06
☐	12 Ben Taylor	.60	.25	.06
☐	13 James (Joe) Greene	.60	.25	.06
☐	14 Dick Seay	.60	.25	.06
☐	15 Sammy Hughes	.60	.25	.06
☐	16 Ted Page	.90	.40	.09
☐	17 Willie Cornelius	.60	.25	.06
☐	18 Pat Patterson	.60	.25	.06
☐	19 Frank Wickware	.60	.25	.06
☐	20 Albert Haywood	.60	.25	.06
☐	21 Bill Holland	.60	.25	.06
☐	22 Sol White	.60	.25	.06
☐	23 Chet Brewer	.90	.40	.09
☐	24 Crush Holloway	.60	.25	.06
☐	25 George Johnson	.60	.25	.06
☐	26 George Scales	.60	.25	.06
☐	27 Dave Brown	.60	.25	.06
☐	28 John Donaldson	.60	.25	.06
☐	29 William Johnson	.75	.30	.07
☐	30 Bill Yancey	.60	.25	.06
☐	31 Sam Bankhead	.75	.30	.07
☐	32 Leroy Matlock	.60	.25	.06

		MINT	EXC	G-VG
	COMPLETE SET (40)	10.00	4.50	1.25
	COMMON PLAYER (1-40)	.20	.08	.02
☐	1 Honus Wagner	.50	.20	.05
☐	2 Herb Pennock	.20	.08	.02
☐	3 Al Simmons	.20	.08	.02
☐	4 Hack Wilson	.25	.10	.02
☐	5 Dizzy Dean	.35	.15	.03
☐	6 Chuck Klein	.20	.08	.02
☐	7 Nellie Fox	.20	.08	.02
☐	8 Lefty Grove	.30	.12	.03
☐	9 George Sisler	.20	.08	.02
☐	10 Lou Gehrig	.75	.30	.07
☐	11 Rube Waddell	.20	.08	.02
☐	12 Max Carey	.20	.08	.02
☐	13 Thurman Munson	.35	.15	.03
☐	14 Mel Ott	.35	.15	.03
☐	15 Doc White	.20	.08	.02
☐	16 Babe Ruth	1.00	.40	.10
☐	17 Schoolboy Rowe	.20	.08	.02
☐	18 Jackie Robinson	.50	.20	.05
☐	19 Joe Medwick	.20	.08	.02
☐	20 Casey Stengel	.35	.15	.03
☐	21 Roberto Clemente	.35	.15	.03
☐	22 Christy Mathewson	.35	.15	.03
☐	23 Jimmie Foxx	.30	.12	.03
☐	24 Joe Jackson	.90	.40	.09
☐	25 Walter Johnson	.35	.15	.03
☐	26 Tony Lazzeri	.25	.10	.02
☐	27 Hugh Casey	.20	.08	.02
☐	28 Ty Cobb	.75	.30	.07
☐	29 Stuffy McInnis	.20	.08	.02
☐	30 Cy Young	.35	.15	.03
☐	31 Lefty O'Doul	.20	.08	.02
☐	32 Eddie Collins	.20	.08	.02
☐	33 Joe McCarthy	.20	.08	.02
☐	34 Ed Walsh	.20	.08	.02
☐	35 George Burns	.20	.08	.02
☐	36 Walt Dropo	.20	.08	.02
☐	37 Connie Mack	.30	.12	.03
☐	38 Babe Adams	.20	.08	.02
☐	39 Rogers Hornsby	.35	.15	.03
☐	40 Grover C. Alexander	.30	.12	.03

1980 Laughlin 300/400/500

This square (approximately 3 1/4" square) set of 30 players features members of the 300/400/500 club, namely, 300 pitching wins, batting .400 or better, or hitting 500 homers since 1900. Cards are blank backed but are numbered on the front. The cards feature the artwork of R.G. Laughlin for the player's body connected to an out of proportion head shot stock photo. This creates an effect faintly reminiscent of the Goudey Heads Up cards.

		NRMT	VG-E	GOOD
COMPLETE SET (30)		15.00	6.50	2.15
COMMON PLAYER (1-30)		.50	.20	.05
☐ 1	Title Card	.50	.20	.05
☐ 2	Babe Ruth	1.50	.60	.15
☐ 3	Walter Johnson	.75	.30	.07
☐ 4	Ty Cobb	1.00	.40	.10
☐ 5	Christy Mathewson	.75	.30	.07
☐ 6	Ted Williams	1.00	.40	.10
☐ 7	Bill Terry	.60	.25	.06
☐ 8	Grover C. Alexander	.60	.25	.06
☐ 9	Napoleon Lajoie	.60	.25	.06
☐ 10	Willie Mays	1.00	.40	.10
☐ 11	Cy Young	.75	.30	.07
☐ 12	Mel Ott	.75	.30	.07
☐ 13	Joe Jackson	1.25	.50	.12
☐ 14	Harmon Killebrew	.60	.25	.06
☐ 15	Warren Spahn	.60	.25	.06
☐ 16	Hank Aaron	1.00	.40	.10
☐ 17	Rogers Hornsby	.60	.25	.06
☐ 18	Mickey Mantle	1.50	.60	.15
☐ 19	Lefty Grove	.60	.25	.06
☐ 20	Ted Williams	1.00	.40	.10
☐ 21	Jimmie Foxx	.60	.25	.06
☐ 22	Eddie Plank	.50	.20	.05
☐ 23	Frank Robinson	.60	.25	.06
☐ 24	George Sisler	.50	.20	.05
☐ 25	Eddie Mathews	.60	.25	.06
☐ 26	Early Wynn	.50	.20	.05
☐ 27	Ernie Banks	.75	.30	.07
☐ 28	Harry Heilmann	.50	.20	.05
☐ 29	Lou Gehrig	1.00	.40	.10
☐ 30	Willie McCovey	.60	.25	.06

1948-49 Leaf

The cards in this 98-card set measure 2 3/8" by 2 7/8". The 1948-49 Leaf set was the first post-war baseball series issued in color. This effort was not entirely successful due to a lack of refinement which resulted in many color variations and cards out of register. In addition, the set was skip numbered from 1-168, with 49 of the 98 cards printed in limited quantities (marked with an asterisk in the checklist). Cards 102 and 136 have variations, and cards are sometimes found with overprinted or incorrect backs. The notable rookie cards in this set include Stan Musial, Satchel Paige, and Jackie Robinson.

		NRMT	VG-E	GOOD
COMPLETE SET (98)		28000.00	12500.00	3300.00
COMMON NUMBERS		25.00	11.00	3.50
COMMON * NUMBERS		350.00	160.00	52.50
☐ 1	Joe DiMaggio	2000.00	750.00	150.00
☐ 3	Babe Ruth	2200.00	900.00	180.00
☐ 4	Stan Musial	750.00	325.00	110.00
☐ 5	Virgil Trucks *	400.00	180.00	60.00
☐ 8	Satchel Paige *	2100.00	900.00	180.00
☐ 10	Dizzy Trout	25.00	11.00	3.50
☐ 11	Phil Rizzuto	190.00	85.00	28.50
☐ 13	Cass Michaels *	350.00	160.00	52.50
☐ 14	Billy Johnson	25.00	11.00	3.50
☐ 17	Frank Overmire	25.00	11.00	3.50
☐ 19	Johnny Wyrostek *	350.00	160.00	52.50
☐ 20	Hank Sauer *	400.00	180.00	60.00
☐ 22	Al Evans	25.00	11.00	3.50
☐ 26	Sam Chapman	25.00	11.00	3.50
☐ 27	Mickey Harris	25.00	11.00	3.50
☐ 28	Jim Hegan	28.00	12.50	4.00
☐ 29	Elmer Valo	25.00	11.00	3.50
☐ 30	Billy Goodman *	350.00	160.00	52.50
☐ 31	Lou Brissie	25.00	11.00	3.50
☐ 32	Warren Spahn	275.00	120.00	40.00
☐ 33	Peanuts Lowrey *	350.00	160.00	52.50
☐ 36	Al Zarilla *	350.00	160.00	52.50
☐ 38	Ted Kluszewski	85.00	38.00	12.75
☐ 39	Ewell Blackwell	55.00	25.00	8.25
☐ 42	Kent Peterson	25.00	11.00	3.50
☐ 43	Ed Stevens *	350.00	160.00	52.50
☐ 45	Ken Keltner *	350.00	160.00	52.50
☐ 46	Johnny Mize	110.00	50.00	16.50
☐ 47	George Vico	25.00	11.00	3.50
☐ 48	Johnny Schmitz *	350.00	160.00	52.50
☐ 49	Del Ennis	38.00	16.00	4.00
☐ 50	Dick Wakefield	25.00	11.00	3.50
☐ 51	Al Dark *	450.00	200.00	67.50
☐ 53	Johnny VanderMeer	45.00	20.00	6.75
☐ 54	Bobby Adams *	350.00	160.00	52.50
☐ 55	Tommy Henrich *	450.00	200.00	67.50
☐ 56	Larry Jansen	28.00	12.50	4.00
☐ 57	Bob McCall	25.00	11.00	3.50
☐ 59	Luke Appling	90.00	40.00	13.50
☐ 61	Jake Early	25.00	11.00	3.50
☐ 62	Eddie Joost *	350.00	160.00	52.50
☐ 63	Barney McCosky *	350.00	160.00	52.50
☐ 65	Robert Elliott (misspelled Elliot on card front)	35.00	15.75	5.25
☐ 66	Orval Grove *	350.00	160.00	52.50
☐ 68	Eddie Miller *	350.00	160.00	52.50
☐ 70	Honus Wagner	280.00	115.00	35.00
☐ 72	Hank Edwards	25.00	11.00	3.50
☐ 73	Pat Seerey	25.00	11.00	3.50
☐ 75	Dom DiMaggio *	550.00	240.00	80.00
☐ 76	Ted Williams	650.00	300.00	100.00
☐ 77	Roy Smalley	25.00	11.00	3.50
☐ 78	Hoot Evers *	350.00	160.00	52.50
☐ 79	Jackie Robinson	700.00	315.00	105.00
☐ 81	Whitey Kurowski *	350.00	160.00	52.50
☐ 82	Johnny Lindell	25.00	11.00	3.50
☐ 83	Bobby Doerr	125.00	57.50	18.75
☐ 84	Sid Hudson	25.00	11.00	3.50
☐ 85	Dave Philley *	350.00	160.00	52.50
☐ 86	Ralph Weigel	25.00	11.00	3.50
☐ 88	Frank Gustine *	350.00	160.00	52.50
☐ 91	Ralph Kiner	185.00	80.00	25.00
☐ 93	Bob Feller *	1450.00	650.00	125.00
☐ 95	George Stirnweiss	30.00	13.50	4.50
☐ 97	Marty Marion	50.00	22.50	7.50
☐ 98	Hal Newhouser *	550.00	240.00	80.00
☐ 102A	Gene Hermansk (sic)	300.00	135.00	45.00
☐ 102B	Gene Hermanski	25.00	11.00	3.50
☐ 104	Eddie Stewart *	350.00	160.00	52.50

☐ 106	Lou Boudreau	110.00	50.00	16.50
☐ 108	Matt Batts *	350.00	160.00	52.50
☐ 111	Jerry Priddy	25.00	11.00	3.50
☐ 113	Dutch Leonard *	400.00	180.00	60.00
☐ 117	Joe Gordon	36.00	16.25	5.50
☐ 120	George Kell *	650.00	300.00	100.00
☐ 121	Johnny Pesky *	400.00	180.00	60.00
☐ 123	Cliff Fannin *	350.00	160.00	52.50
☐ 125	Andy Pafko *	28.00	12.50	4.00
☐ 127	Enos Slaughter *	750.00	325.00	110.00
☐ 128	Buddy Rosar	25.00	11.00	3.50
☐ 129	Kirby Higbe *	350.00	160.00	52.50
☐ 131	Sid Gordon *	350.00	160.00	52.50
☐ 133	Tommy Holmes *	400.00	180.00	60.00
☐ 136A	Cliff Aberson (full sleeve)	25.00	11.00	3.50
☐ 136B	Cliff Aberson (short sleeve)	300.00	135.00	45.00
☐ 137	Harry Walker *	400.00	180.00	60.00
☐ 138	Larry Doby *	550.00	240.00	80.00
☐ 139	Johnny Hopp *	28.00	12.50	4.00
☐ 142	Danny Murtaugh *	400.00	180.00	60.00
☐ 143	Dick Sisler *	400.00	180.00	60.00
☐ 144	Bob Dillinger *	350.00	160.00	52.50
☐ 146	Pete Reiser *	450.00	200.00	67.50
☐ 149	Hank Majeski *	350.00	160.00	52.50
☐ 153	Floyd Baker *	350.00	160.00	52.50
☐ 158	Harry Brecheen *	400.00	180.00	60.00
☐ 159	Mizell Platt	25.00	11.00	3.50
☐ 160	Bob Scheffing *	350.00	160.00	52.50
☐ 161	Vern Stephens *	400.00	180.00	60.00
☐ 163	Fred Hutchinson *	450.00	200.00	67.50
☐ 165	Dale Mitchell *	400.00	180.00	60.00
☐ 168	Phil Cavarretta *	450.00	200.00	67.50

1960 Leaf

DUKE SNIDER
OUTFIELDER—LOS ANGELES DODGERS

The cards in this 144-card set measure 2 1/2" by 3 1/2". The 1960 Leaf set was issued in a regular gum package style but with a marble instead of gum. The series was a joint production by Sports Novelties, Inc., and Leaf, two Chicago-based companies. Cards 73-144 are more difficult to find than the lower numbers. Photo variations exist (probably proof cards) for the seven cards listed with an asterisk and there is a well-known error card, number 25 showing Brooks Lawrence (in a Reds uniform) with Jim Grant's name on front, and Grant's biography and record on back. The corrected version with Grant's photo is the more difficult variety. The only notable rookie card in this set is Dallas Green. The complete set price below includes both versions of Jim Grant.

	NRMT	VG-E	GOOD
COMPLETE SET (145)	1200.00	500.00	125.00
COMMON PLAYER (1-72)	2.25	.90	.22
COMMON PLAYER (73-144)	13.50	6.00	1.85

☐ 1	Luis Aparicio *	20.00	7.50	1.50
☐ 2	Woody Held	2.25	.90	.22
☐ 3	Frank Lary	3.00	1.25	.30
☐ 4	Camilo Pascual	3.00	1.25	.30
☐ 5	Pancho Herrera	2.25	.90	.22
☐ 6	Felipe Alou	4.00	1.75	.40
☐ 7	Benjamin Daniels	2.25	.90	.22

☐ 8	Roger Craig	4.50	2.00	.45
☐ 9	Eddie Kasko	2.25	.90	.22
☐ 10	Bob Grim	3.00	1.25	.30
☐ 11	Jim Busby	2.25	.90	.22
☐ 12	Ken Boyer	5.50	2.50	.55
☐ 13	Bob Boyd	2.25	.90	.22
☐ 14	Sam Jones	2.25	.90	.22
☐ 15	Larry Jackson	2.25	.90	.22
☐ 16	Elroy Face	4.00	1.75	.40
☐ 17	Walt Moryn *	2.25	.90	.22
☐ 18	Jim Gilliam	4.50	2.00	.45
☐ 19	Don Newcombe	4.00	1.75	.40
☐ 20	Glen Hobbie	2.25	.90	.22
☐ 21	Pedro Ramos	2.25	.90	.22
☐ 22	Ryne Duren *	4.00	1.75	.40
☐ 23	Joey Jay *	2.25	.90	.22
☐ 24	Lou Berberet	2.25	.90	.22
☐ 25A	Jim Grant ERR (photo actually Brooks Lawrence)	12.50	5.50	1.65
☐ 25B	Jim Grant COR	18.00	7.50	2.50
☐ 26	Tom Borland	2.25	.90	.22
☐ 27	Brooks Robinson	28.00	12.50	4.00
☐ 28	Jerry Adair	2.25	.90	.22
☐ 29	Ron Jackson	2.25	.90	.22
☐ 30	George Strickland	2.25	.90	.22
☐ 31	Rocky Bridges	2.25	.90	.22
☐ 32	Bill Tuttle	2.25	.90	.22
☐ 33	Ken Hunt	2.25	.90	.22
☐ 34	Hal Griggs	2.25	.90	.22
☐ 35	Jim Coates *	2.25	.90	.22
☐ 36	Brooks Lawrence	2.25	.90	.22
☐ 37	Duke Snider	36.00	16.25	5.50
☐ 38	Al Spangler	2.25	.90	.22
☐ 39	Jim Owens	2.25	.90	.22
☐ 40	Bill Virdon	3.50	1.50	.35
☐ 41	Ernie Broglio	3.00	1.25	.30
☐ 42	Andre Rodgers	2.25	.90	.22
☐ 43	Julio Becquer	2.25	.90	.22
☐ 44	Tony Taylor	3.00	1.25	.30
☐ 45	Jerry Lynch	2.25	.90	.22
☐ 46	Cletis Boyer	3.50	1.50	.35
☐ 47	Jerry Lumpe	2.25	.90	.22
☐ 48	Charlie Maxwell	3.00	1.25	.30
☐ 49	Jim Perry	4.00	1.75	.40
☐ 50	Danny McDevitt	2.25	.90	.22
☐ 51	Juan Pizarro	2.25	.90	.22
☐ 52	Dallas Green	6.00	2.50	.60
☐ 53	Bob Friend	3.00	1.25	.30
☐ 54	Jack Sanford	3.00	1.25	.30
☐ 55	Jim Rivera	2.25	.90	.22
☐ 56	Ted Wills	2.25	.90	.22
☐ 57	Milt Pappas	3.00	1.25	.30
☐ 58	Hal Smith *	2.25	.90	.22
☐ 59	Bobby Avila	2.25	.90	.22
☐ 60	Clem Labine	3.00	1.25	.30
☐ 61	Norman Rehm *	2.25	.90	.22
☐ 62	John Gabler	2.25	.90	.22
☐ 63	John Tsitouris	2.25	.90	.22
☐ 64	Dave Sisler	2.25	.90	.22
☐ 65	Vic Power	2.25	.90	.22
☐ 66	Earl Battey	2.25	.90	.22
☐ 67	Bob Purkey	2.25	.90	.22
☐ 68	Moe Drabowsky	2.25	.90	.22
☐ 69	Hoyt Wilhelm	15.00	6.50	2.15
☐ 70	Humberto Robinson	2.25	.90	.22
☐ 71	Whitey Herzog	5.00	2.25	.50
☐ 72	Dick Donovan *	2.25	.90	.22
☐ 73	Gordon Jones	13.50	6.00	1.85
☐ 74	Joe Hicks	13.50	6.00	1.85
☐ 75	Ray Culp	15.00	6.50	2.15
☐ 76	Dick Drott	13.50	6.00	1.85
☐ 77	Bob Duliba	13.50	6.00	1.85
☐ 78	Art Ditmar	13.50	6.00	1.85
☐ 79	Steve Korcheck	13.50	6.00	1.85
☐ 80	Henry Mason	13.50	6.00	1.85
☐ 81	Harry Simpson	13.50	6.00	1.85
☐ 82	Gene Green	13.50	6.00	1.85
☐ 83	Bob Shaw	13.50	6.00	1.85
☐ 84	Howard Reed	13.50	6.00	1.85
☐ 85	Dick Stigman	13.50	6.00	1.85
☐ 86	Rip Repulski	13.50	6.00	1.85
☐ 87	Seth Morehead	13.50	6.00	1.85
☐ 88	Camilo Carreon	13.50	6.00	1.85
☐ 89	John Blanchard	15.00	6.50	2.15
☐ 90	Billy Hoeft	13.50	6.00	1.85
☐ 91	Fred Hopke	13.50	6.00	1.85
☐ 92	Joe Martin	13.50	6.00	1.85
☐ 93	Wally Shannon	13.50	6.00	1.85
☐ 94	Two Hal Smith's Hal R. Smith Hal W. Smith	17.00	7.25	2.50
☐ 95	Al Schroll	13.50	6.00	1.85
☐ 96	John Kucks	13.50	6.00	1.85

☐ 97	Tom Morgan	13.50	6.00	1.85
☐ 98	Willie Jones	13.50	6.00	1.85
☐ 99	Marshall Renfroe	13.50	6.00	1.85
☐ 100	Willie Tasby	13.50	6.00	1.85
☐ 101	Irv Noren	13.50	6.00	1.85
☐ 102	Russ Snyder	13.50	6.00	1.85
☐ 103	Bob Turley	15.00	6.50	2.15
☐ 104	Jim Woods	13.50	6.00	1.85
☐ 105	Ronnie Kline	13.50	6.00	1.85
☐ 106	Steve Bilko	13.50	6.00	1.85
☐ 107	Elmer Valo	13.50	6.00	1.85
☐ 108	Tom McAvoy	13.50	6.00	1.85
☐ 109	Stan Williams	15.00	6.50	2.15
☐ 110	Earl Averill Jr.	13.50	6.00	1.85
☐ 111	Lee Walls	13.50	6.00	1.85
☐ 112	Paul Richards MG	15.00	6.50	2.15
☐ 113	Ed Sadowski	13.50	6.00	1.85
☐ 114	Stover McIlwain	13.50	6.00	1.85
☐ 115	Chuck Tanner	15.00	6.50	2.15
	(photo actually			
	Ken Kuhn)			
☐ 116	Lou Klimchock	13.50	6.00	1.85
☐ 117	Neil Chrisley	13.50	6.00	1.85
☐ 118	John Callison	15.00	6.50	2.15
☐ 119	Hal Smith	13.50	6.00	1.85
☐ 120	Carl Sawatski	13.50	6.00	1.85
☐ 121	Frank Leja	13.50	6.00	1.85
☐ 122	Earl Torgeson	13.50	6.00	1.85
☐ 123	Art Schult	13.50	6.00	1.85
☐ 124	Jim Brosnan	15.00	6.50	2.15
☐ 125	George Anderson	35.00	15.75	5.25
☐ 126	Joe Pignatano	13.50	6.00	1.85
☐ 127	Rocky Nelson	13.50	6.00	1.85
☐ 128	Orlando Cepeda	45.00	20.00	6.75
☐ 129	Daryl Spencer	13.50	6.00	1.85
☐ 130	Ralph Lumenti	13.50	6.00	1.85
☐ 131	Sam Taylor	13.50	6.00	1.85
☐ 132	Harry Brecheen CO	15.00	6.50	2.15
☐ 133	Johnny Groth	13.50	6.00	1.85
☐ 134	Wayne Terwilliger	13.50	6.00	1.85
☐ 135	Kent Hadley	13.50	6.00	1.85
☐ 136	Faye Throneberry	13.50	6.00	1.85
☐ 137	Jack Meyer	13.50	6.00	1.85
☐ 138	Chuck Cottier	13.50	6.00	1.85
☐ 139	Joe DeMaestri	13.50	6.00	1.85
☐ 140	Gene Freese	13.50	6.00	1.85
☐ 141	Curt Flood	22.00	9.50	3.15
☐ 142	Gino Cimoli	13.50	6.00	1.85
☐ 143	Clay Dalrymple	13.50	6.00	1.85
☐ 144	Jim Bunning	50.00	17.50	3.50

1987 Leaf Special Olympics

This set is also known as the Candy City team as that is the logo which appears on the front of the card. This set was issued for the proceeds of the set to go to the Special Olympics. The set was in the style of the 1983 Donruss Hall of Fame Heroes set and the only additions were generic cards about various sports. The cards are standard size, 2 1/2" by 3 1/2".

	MINT	VG-E	F-G
COMPLETE SET (18)	4.00	1.75	.40
COMMON PLAYER (H1-H12)	.20	.08	.02
COMMON PLAYER (S1-S6)	.10	.04	.01

☐ H1	Mickey Mantle	1.00	.40	.10
☐ H2	Yogi Berra	.40	.16	.04
☐ H3	Roy Campanella	.40	.16	.04
☐ H4	Stan Musial	.40	.16	.04
☐ H5	Ted Williams	.40	.16	.04
☐ H6	Duke Snider	.30	.12	.03
☐ H7	Hank Aaron	.40	.16	.04
☐ H8	Pee Wee Reese	.30	.12	.03
☐ H9	Brooks Robinson	.30	.12	.03
☐ H10	Al Kaline	.30	.12	.03
☐ H11	Willie McCovey	.30	.12	.03
☐ H12	Cool Papa Bell	.20	.08	.02
☐ S1	Basketball	.20	.08	.02
☐ S2	Softball	.10	.04	.01
☐ S3	Track And Field	.10	.04	.01
☐ S4	Soccer	.20	.08	.02
☐ S5	Gymnastics	.10	.04	.01
☐ S6	VII International	.10	.04	.01
	Summer Games			

1990 Leaf Preview

The 1990 Leaf Preview set contains standard-size (2 1/2" by 3 1/2") cards which were mailed to dealers to announce the 1990 version of Donruss' second major set of the year marketed as an upscale alternative under their Leaf name. This 12-card set was presented in the same style as the other Leaf cards were done in except that "Special Preview" was imprinted in white on the back. The cards were released in two series of 264 and the first series was not released until mid-season.

	MINT	EXC	G-VG
COMPLETE SET (12)	500.00	225.00	75.00
COMMON PLAYER (1-12)	30.00	13.50	4.50

☐ 1	Steve Sax	30.00	13.50	4.50
☐ 2	Joe Carter	50.00	22.50	7.50
☐ 3	Dennis Eckersley	40.00	18.00	6.00
☐ 4	Ken Griffey Jr.	150.00	67.50	22.50
☐ 5	Barry Larkin	50.00	22.50	7.50
☐ 6	Mark Langston	40.00	18.00	6.00
☐ 7	Eric Anthony	40.00	18.00	6.00
☐ 8	Robin Ventura	75.00	34.00	11.25
☐ 9	Greg Vaughn	60.00	27.00	9.00
☐ 10	Bobby Bonilla	75.00	34.00	11.25
☐ 11	Gary Gaetti	30.00	13.50	4.50
☐ 12	Ozzie Smith	75.00	34.00	11.25

1990 Leaf I

The 1990 Leaf set was another major, premium set introduced by Donruss in 1990. This set, which was produced on high quality paper stock, was issued in two separate series of 264 cards each. The cards are in the standard size of 2 1/2" by 3 1/2" and have full-color photos on both the front and the back of the cards. The first card of the set includes a brief history of the

Leaf company and the checklists feature player photos in a style very reminiscent to the Topps checklists of the late 1960s. The card style is very similar to Upper Deck, but the Leaf sets were only distributed through hobby channels. The key rookie cards in this series are Delino DeShields, Marquis Grissom, Ben McDonald, John Olerud, Sammy Sosa, and Todd Zeile.

		MINT	EXC	G-VG
COMPLETE SET (264)		120.00	55.00	18.00
COMMON PLAYER (1-264)		.20	.08	.02

		MINT	EXC	G-VG
☐ 1	Introductory Card	.20	.08	.02
☐ 2	Mike Henneman	.20	.08	.02
☐ 3	Steve Bedrosian	.20	.08	.02
☐ 4	Mike Scott	.25	.10	.02
☐ 5	Allan Anderson	.20	.08	.02
☐ 6	Rick Sutcliffe	.25	.10	.02
☐ 7	Gregg Olson	.75	.30	.07
☐ 8	Kevin Elster	.20	.08	.02
☐ 9	Pete O'Brien	.20	.08	.02
☐ 10	Carlton Fisk	1.00	.40	.10
☐ 11	Joe Magrane	.20	.08	.02
☐ 12	Roger Clemens	2.25	.90	.22
☐ 13	Tom Glavine	1.25	.50	.12
☐ 14	Tom Gordon	.25	.10	.02
☐ 15	Todd Benzinger	.20	.08	.02
☐ 16	Hubie Brooks	.20	.08	.02
☐ 17	Roberto Kelly	.30	.12	.03
☐ 18	Barry Larkin	.60	.25	.06
☐ 19	Mike Boddicker	.20	.08	.02
☐ 20	Roger McDowell	.20	.08	.02
☐ 21	Nolan Ryan	7.00	3.00	.70
☐ 22	John Farrell	.20	.08	.02
☐ 23	Bruce Hurst	.20	.08	.02
☐ 24	Wally Joyner	.40	.16	.04
☐ 25	Greg Maddux	.25	.10	.02
☐ 26	Chris Bosio	.20	.08	.02
☐ 27	John Cerutti	.20	.08	.02
☐ 28	Tim Burke	.20	.08	.02
☐ 29	Dennis Eckersley	.35	.15	.03
☐ 30	Glenn Davis	.30	.12	.03
☐ 31	Jim Abbott	1.75	.70	.17
☐ 32	Mike LaValliere	.20	.08	.02
☐ 33	Andres Thomas	.20	.08	.02
☐ 34	Lou Whitaker	.25	.10	.02
☐ 35	Alvin Davis	.25	.10	.02
☐ 36	Melido Perez	.20	.08	.02
☐ 37	Craig Biggio	.75	.30	.07
☐ 38	Rick Aguilera	.25	.10	.02
☐ 39	Pete Harnisch	.45	.18	.04
☐ 40	David Cone	.35	.15	.03
☐ 41	Scott Garrelts	.20	.08	.02
☐ 42	Jay Howell	.20	.08	.02
☐ 43	Eric King	.20	.08	.02
☐ 44	Pedro Guerrero	.30	.12	.03
☐ 45	Mike Bielecki	.20	.08	.02
☐ 46	Bob Boone	.25	.10	.02
☐ 47	Kevin Brown	.25	.10	.02
☐ 48	Jerry Browne	.20	.08	.02
☐ 49	Mike Scioscia	.20	.08	.02
☐ 50	Chuck Cary	.20	.08	.02
☐ 51	Wade Boggs	1.50	.60	.15
☐ 52	Von Hayes	.25	.10	.02
☐ 53	Tony Fernandez	.25	.10	.02
☐ 54	Dennis Martinez	.25	.10	.02
☐ 55	Tom Candiotti	.25	.10	.02
☐ 56	Andy Benes	1.50	.60	.15
☐ 57	Rob Dibble	.25	.10	.02
☐ 58	Chuck Crim	.20	.08	.02
☐ 59	John Smoltz	1.50	.60	.15

		MINT	EXC	G-VG
☐ 60	Mike Heath	.20	.08	.02
☐ 61	Kevin Gross	.20	.08	.02
☐ 62	Mark McGwire	.75	.30	.07
☐ 63	Bert Blyleven	.25	.10	.02
☐ 64	Bob Walk	.20	.08	.02
☐ 65	Mickey Tettleton	.25	.10	.02
☐ 66	Sid Fernandez	.25	.10	.02
☐ 67	Terry Kennedy	.20	.08	.02
☐ 68	Fernando Valenzuela	.25	.10	.02
☐ 69	Don Mattingly	1.50	.60	.15
☐ 70	Paul O'Neill	.25	.10	.02
☐ 71	Robin Yount	1.00	.40	.10
☐ 72	Bret Saberhagen	.40	.16	.04
☐ 73	Geno Petralli	.20	.08	.02
☐ 74	Brook Jacoby	.20	.08	.02
☐ 75	Roberto Alomar	1.50	.60	.15
☐ 76	Devon White	.25	.10	.02
☐ 77	Jose Lind	.20	.08	.02
☐ 78	Pat Combs	.20	.08	.02
☐ 79	Dave Stieb	.25	.10	.02
☐ 80	Tim Wallach	.25	.10	.02
☐ 81	Dave Stewart	.35	.15	.03
☐ 82	Eric Anthony	.60	.25	.06
☐ 83	Randy Bush	.20	.08	.02
☐ 84	Checklist Card	.35	.15	.03
	(Rickey Henderson)			
☐ 85	Jaime Navarro	.30	.12	.03
☐ 86	Tommy Gregg	.20	.08	.02
☐ 87	Frank Tanana	.25	.10	.02
☐ 88	Omar Vizquel	.20	.08	.02
☐ 89	Ivan Calderon	.25	.10	.02
☐ 90	Vince Coleman	.35	.15	.03
☐ 91	Barry Bonds	1.25	.50	.12
☐ 92	Randy Milligan	.25	.10	.02
☐ 93	Frank Viola	.30	.12	.03
☐ 94	Matt Williams	.75	.30	.07
☐ 95	Alfredo Griffin	.20	.08	.02
☐ 96	Steve Sax	.25	.10	.02
☐ 97	Gary Gaetti	.25	.10	.02
☐ 98	Ryne Sandberg	3.00	1.25	.30
☐ 99	Danny Tartabull	.40	.16	.04
☐ 100	Rafael Palmeiro	.75	.30	.07
☐ 101	Jesse Orosco	.20	.08	.02
☐ 102	Garry Templeton	.20	.08	.02
☐ 103	Frank DiPino	.20	.08	.02
☐ 104	Tony Pena	.25	.10	.02
☐ 105	Dickie Thon	.20	.08	.02
☐ 106	Kelly Gruber	.30	.12	.03
☐ 107	Marquis Grissom	3.00	1.25	.30
☐ 108	Jose Canseco	3.75	1.60	.37
☐ 109	Mike Blowers	.30	.12	.03
☐ 110	Tom Browning	.20	.08	.02
☐ 111	Greg Vaughn	4.25	1.75	.42
☐ 112	Oddibe McDowell	.20	.08	.02
☐ 113	Gary Ward	.20	.08	.02
☐ 114	Jay Buhner	.30	.12	.03
☐ 115	Eric Show	.20	.08	.02
☐ 116	Bryan Harvey	.25	.10	.02
☐ 117	Andy Van Slyke	.35	.15	.03
☐ 118	Jeff Ballard	.20	.08	.02
☐ 119	Barry Lyons	.20	.08	.02
☐ 120	Kevin Mitchell	.75	.30	.07
☐ 121	Mike Gallego	.20	.08	.02
☐ 122	Dave Smith	.20	.08	.02
☐ 123	Kirby Puckett	1.75	.70	.17
☐ 124	Jerome Walton	.35	.15	.03
☐ 125	Bo Jackson	3.75	1.60	.37
☐ 126	Harold Baines	.25	.10	.02
☐ 127	Scott Bankhead	.20	.08	.02
☐ 128	Ozzie Guillen	.25	.10	.02
☐ 129	Jose Oquendo UER	.20	.08	.02
	(League misspelled as Legue)			
☐ 130	John Dopson	.20	.08	.02
☐ 131	Charlie Hayes	.25	.10	.02
☐ 132	Fred McGriff	.75	.30	.07
☐ 133	Chet Lemon	.20	.08	.02
☐ 134	Gary Carter	.30	.12	.03
☐ 135	Rafael Ramirez	.20	.08	.02
☐ 136	Shane Mack	.25	.10	.02
☐ 137	Mark Grace UER	.60	.25	.06
	(Card back has OB:L, should be B:L)			
☐ 138	Phil Bradley	.20	.08	.02
☐ 139	Dwight Gooden	.60	.25	.06
☐ 140	Harold Reynolds	.25	.10	.02
☐ 141	Scott Fletcher	.20	.08	.02
☐ 142	Ozzie Smith	.75	.30	.07
☐ 143	Mike Greenwell	.65	.25	.06
☐ 144	Pete Smith	.20	.08	.02
☐ 145	Mark Gubicza	.25	.10	.02
☐ 146	Chris Sabo	.60	.25	.06
☐ 147	Ramon Martinez	5.00	2.25	.50
☐ 148	Tim Leary	.25	.10	.02
☐ 149	Randy Myers	.20	.08	.02

☐ 150	Jody Reed	.25	.10	.02
☐ 151	Bruce Ruffin	.20	.08	.02
☐ 152	Jeff Russell	.20	.08	.02
☐ 153	Doug Jones	.20	.08	.02
☐ 154	Tony Gwynn	1.25	.50	.12
☐ 155	Mark Langston	.35	.15	.03
☐ 156	Mitch Williams	.20	.08	.02
☐ 157	Gary Sheffield	.35	.15	.03
☐ 158	Tom Henke	.25	.10	.02
☐ 159	Oil Can Boyd	.20	.08	.02
☐ 160	Rickey Henderson	2.50	1.00	.25
☐ 161	Bill Doran	.20	.08	.02
☐ 162	Chuck Finley	.40	.16	.04
☐ 163	Jeff King	.25	.10	.02
☐ 164	Nick Esasky	.20	.08	.02
☐ 165	Cecil Fielder	2.25	.90	.22
☐ 166	Dave Valle	.20	.08	.02
☐ 167	Robin Ventura	8.50	3.75	.85
☐ 168	Jim Deshaies	.20	.08	.02
☐ 169	Juan Berenguer	.20	.08	.02
☐ 170	Craig Worthington	.20	.08	.02
☐ 171	Gregg Jeffries	.45	.18	.04
☐ 172	Will Clark	3.00	1.25	.30
☐ 173	Kirk Gibson	.30	.12	.03
☐ 174	Checklist Card	.25	.10	.02
	(Carlton Fisk)			
☐ 175	Bobby Thigpen	.25	.10	.02
☐ 176	John Tudor	.25	.10	.02
☐ 177	Andre Dawson	.65	.25	.06
☐ 178	George Brett	1.00	.40	.10
☐ 179	Steve Buechele	.20	.08	.02
☐ 180	Joey Belle	6.00	2.50	.60
☐ 181	Eddie Murray	.65	.25	.06
☐ 182	Bob Geren	.25	.10	.02
☐ 183	Rob Murphy	.20	.08	.02
☐ 184	Tom Herr	.25	.10	.02
☐ 185	George Bell	.50	.20	.05
☐ 186	Spike Owen	.20	.08	.02
☐ 187	Cory Snyder	.25	.10	.02
☐ 188	Fred Lynn	.25	.10	.02
☐ 189	Eric Davis	.60	.25	.06
☐ 190	Dave Parker	.30	.12	.03
☐ 191	Jeff Blauser	.20	.08	.02
☐ 192	Matt Nokes	.25	.10	.02
☐ 193	Delino DeShields	3.00	1.25	.30
☐ 194	Scott Sanderson	.20	.08	.02
☐ 195	Lance Parrish	.25	.10	.02
☐ 196	Bobby Bonilla	1.00	.40	.10
☐ 197	Cal Ripken	3.25	1.35	.32
☐ 198	Kevin McReynolds	.30	.12	.03
☐ 199	Robby Thompson	.20	.08	.02
☐ 200	Tim Belcher	.25	.10	.02
☐ 201	Jesse Barfield	.25	.10	.02
☐ 202	Mariano Duncan	.20	.08	.02
☐ 203	Bill Spiers	.25	.10	.02
☐ 204	Frank White	.25	.10	.02
☐ 205	Julio Franco	.40	.16	.04
☐ 206	Greg Swindell	.25	.10	.02
☐ 207	Benito Santiago	.30	.12	.03
☐ 208	Johnny Ray	.20	.08	.02
☐ 209	Gary Redus	.20	.08	.02
☐ 210	Jeff Parrett	.20	.08	.02
☐ 211	Jimmy Key	.25	.10	.02
☐ 212	Tim Raines	.35	.15	.03
☐ 213	Carney Lansford	.25	.10	.02
☐ 214	Gerald Young	.20	.08	.02
☐ 215	Gene Larkin	.20	.08	.02
☐ 216	Dan Plesac	.20	.08	.02
☐ 217	Lonnie Smith	.25	.10	.02
☐ 218	Alan Trammell	.45	.18	.04
☐ 219	Jeffrey Leonard	.20	.08	.02
☐ 220	Sammy Sosa	1.50	.60	.15
☐ 221	Todd Zeile	2.00	.80	.20
☐ 222	Bill Landrum	.20	.08	.02
☐ 223	Mike Devereaux	.20	.08	.02
☐ 224	Mike Marshall	.25	.10	.02
☐ 225	Jose Uribe	.20	.08	.02
☐ 226	Juan Samuel	.25	.10	.02
☐ 227	Mel Hall	.25	.10	.02
☐ 228	Kent Hrbek	.25	.10	.02
☐ 229	Shawon Dunston	.25	.10	.02
☐ 230	Kevin Seitzer	.25	.10	.02
☐ 231	Pete Incaviglia	.25	.10	.02
☐ 232	Sandy Alomar Jr.	.60	.25	.06
☐ 233	Bip Roberts	.25	.10	.02
☐ 234	Scott Terry	.20	.08	.02
☐ 235	Dwight Evans	.25	.10	.02
☐ 236	Ricky Jordan	.25	.10	.02
☐ 237	John Olerud	5.00	2.25	.50
☐ 238	Zane Smith	.25	.10	.02
☐ 239	Walt Weiss	.25	.10	.02
☐ 240	Alvaro Espinoza	.20	.08	.02
☐ 241	Billy Hatcher	.20	.08	.02
☐ 242	Paul Molitor	.35	.15	.03
☐ 243	Dale Murphy	.50	.20	.05

☐ 244	Dave Bergman	.20	.08	.02
☐ 245	Ken Griffey Jr.	22.00	9.50	3.15
☐ 246	Ed Whitson	.20	.08	.02
☐ 247	Kirk McCaskill	.20	.08	.02
☐ 248	Jay Bell	.20	.08	.02
☐ 249	Ben McDonald	4.00	1.75	.40
☐ 250	Darryl Strawberry	1.75	.70	.17
☐ 251	Brett Butler	.25	.10	.02
☐ 252	Terry Steinbach	.25	.10	.02
☐ 253	Ken Caminiti	.20	.08	.02
☐ 254	Dan Gladden	.20	.08	.02
☐ 255	Dwight Smith	.25	.10	.02
☐ 256	Kurt Stillwell	.20	.08	.02
☐ 257	Ruben Sierra	1.75	.70	.17
☐ 258	Mike Schooler	.25	.10	.02
☐ 259	Lance Johnson	.20	.08	.02
☐ 260	Terry Pendleton	.40	.16	.04
☐ 261	Ellis Burks	.45	.18	.04
☐ 262	Len Dykstra	.25	.10	.02
☐ 263	Mookie Wilson	.20	.08	.02
☐ 264	Checklist Card	.60	.25	.06
	(Nolan Ryan) UER			
	(No TM after Ranger			
	logo)			

1990 Leaf II

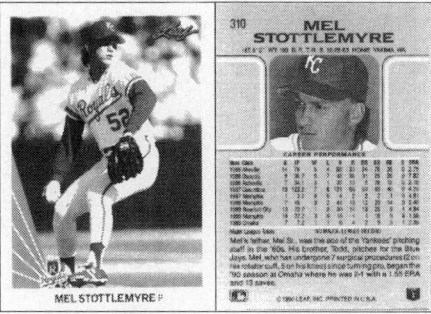

MEL STOTTLEMYRE P

This 264-card, standard size, 2 1/2" by 3 1/2" set was issued approximately six weeks after the release of the first series. The cards, which were in the same style as series one, were issued as more expensive Donruss cards and were not available in factory sets. The key rookies in the set are Carlos Baerga, Dave Justice, Kevin Maas, Jose Offerman, Kevin Tapani, Frank Thomas, and Mark Whiten.

		MINT	EXC	G-VG
COMPLETE SET (264)		160.00	72.00	24.00
COMMON PLAYER (265-528)		.20	.08	.02
☐ 265	No Hit King	2.00	.80	.20
	(Nolan Ryan)			
☐ 266	Brian DuBois	.30	.12	.03
☐ 267	Don Robinson	.20	.08	.02
☐ 268	Glenn Wilson	.20	.08	.02
☐ 269	Kevin Tapani	3.00	1.25	.30
☐ 270	Marvell Wynne	.20	.08	.02
☐ 271	Billy Ripken	.20	.08	.02
☐ 272	Howard Johnson	.50	.20	.05
☐ 273	Brian Holman	.25	.10	.02
☐ 274	Dan Pasqua	.20	.08	.02
☐ 275	Ken Dayley	.20	.08	.02
☐ 276	Jeff Reardon	.25	.10	.02
☐ 277	Jim Presley	.20	.08	.02
☐ 278	Jim Eisenreich	.20	.08	.02
☐ 279	Danny Jackson	.25	.10	.02
☐ 280	Orel Hershiser	.35	.15	.03
☐ 281	Andy Hawkins	.20	.08	.02
☐ 282	Jose Rijo	.25	.10	.02
☐ 283	Luis Rivera	.20	.08	.02
☐ 284	John Kruk	.25	.10	.02
☐ 285	Jeff Huson	.25	.10	.02
☐ 286	Joel Skinner	.20	.08	.02
☐ 287	Jack Clark	.30	.12	.03
☐ 288	Chili Davis	.25	.10	.02
☐ 289	Joe Girardi	.25	.10	.02

#	Player			
☐ 290	B.J. Surhoff	.25	.10	.02
☐ 291	Luis Sojo	.35	.15	.03
☐ 292	Tom Foley	.20	.08	.02
☐ 293	Mike Moore	.25	.10	.02
☐ 294	Ken Oberkfell	.20	.08	.02
☐ 295	Luis Polonia	.25	.10	.02
☐ 296	Doug Drabek	.25	.10	.02
☐ 297	Dave Justice	36.00	16.25	5.50
☐ 298	Paul Gibson	.20	.08	.02
☐ 299	Edgar Martinez	.50	.20	.05
☐ 300	Frank Thomas UER	65.00	29.00	9.75
	(No B in front			
	of birthdate)			
☐ 301	Eric Yelding	.25	.10	.02
☐ 302	Greg Gagne	.20	.08	.02
☐ 303	Brad Komminsk	.20	.08	.02
☐ 304	Ron Darling	.25	.10	.02
☐ 305	Kevin Bass	.20	.08	.02
☐ 306	Jeff Hamilton	.20	.08	.02
☐ 307	Ron Karkovice	.20	.08	.02
☐ 308	Milt Thompson UER	.25	.10	.02
	(Ray Lankford pictured			
	on card back)			
☐ 309	Mike Harkey	.25	.10	.02
☐ 310	Mel Stottlemyre Jr.	.20	.08	.02
☐ 311	Kenny Rogers	.25	.10	.02
☐ 312	Mitch Webster	.20	.08	.02
☐ 313	Kal Daniels	.25	.10	.02
☐ 314	Matt Nokes	.25	.10	.02
☐ 315	Dennis Lamp	.20	.08	.02
☐ 316	Ken Howell	.20	.08	.02
☐ 317	Glenallen Hill	.25	.10	.02
☐ 318	Dave Martinez	.20	.08	.02
☐ 319	Chris James	.20	.08	.02
☐ 320	Mike Pagliarulo	.20	.08	.02
☐ 321	Hal Morris	4.00	1.75	.40
☐ 322	Rob Deer	.25	.10	.02
☐ 323	Greg Olson	.65	.25	.06
☐ 324	Tony Phillips	.20	.08	.02
☐ 325	Larry Walker	1.00	.40	.10
☐ 326	Ron Hassey	.20	.08	.02
☐ 327	Jack Howell	.20	.08	.02
☐ 328	John Smiley	.25	.10	.02
☐ 329	Steve Finley	.50	.20	.05
☐ 330	Dave Magadan	.25	.10	.02
☐ 331	Greg Litton	.25	.10	.02
☐ 332	Mickey Hatcher	.20	.08	.02
☐ 333	Lee Guetterman	.20	.08	.02
☐ 334	Norm Charlton	.25	.10	.02
☐ 335	Edgar Diaz	.25	.10	.02
☐ 336	Willie Wilson	.25	.10	.02
☐ 337	Bobby Witt	.25	.10	.02
☐ 338	Candy Maldonado	.25	.10	.02
☐ 339	Craig Lefferts	.20	.08	.02
☐ 340	Dante Bichette	.35	.15	.03
☐ 341	Wally Backman	.20	.08	.02
☐ 342	Dennis Cook	.20	.08	.02
☐ 343	Pat Borders	.25	.10	.02
☐ 344	Wallace Johnson	.20	.08	.02
☐ 345	Willie Randolph	.20	.08	.02
☐ 346	Danny Darwin	.20	.08	.02
☐ 347	Al Newman	.20	.08	.02
☐ 348	Mark Knudson	.20	.08	.02
☐ 349	Joe Boever	.20	.08	.02
☐ 350	Larry Sheets	.20	.08	.02
☐ 351	Mike Jackson	.20	.08	.02
☐ 352	Wayne Edwards	.30	.12	.03
☐ 353	Bernard Gilkey	1.50	.60	.15
☐ 354	Don Slaught	.20	.08	.02
☐ 355	Joe Orsulak	.20	.08	.02
☐ 356	John Franco	.20	.08	.02
☐ 357	Jeff Brantley	.25	.10	.02
☐ 358	Mike Morgan	.25	.10	.02
☐ 359	Deion Sanders	1.00	.40	.10
☐ 360	Terry Leach	.20	.08	.02
☐ 361	Les Lancaster	.20	.08	.02
☐ 362	Storm Davis	.20	.08	.02
☐ 363	Scott Coolbaugh	.30	.12	.03
☐ 364	Checklist Card	.25	.10	.02
	(Ozzie Smith)			
☐ 365	Cecilio Guante	.20	.08	.02
☐ 366	Joey Cora	.20	.08	.02
☐ 367	Willie McGee	.30	.12	.03
☐ 368	Jerry Reed	.20	.08	.02
☐ 369	Darren Daulton	.20	.08	.02
☐ 370	Manny Lee	.20	.08	.02
☐ 371	Mark Gardner	.45	.18	.04
☐ 372	Rick Honeycutt	.20	.08	.02
☐ 373	Steve Balboni	.20	.08	.02
☐ 374	Jack Armstrong	.25	.10	.02
☐ 375	Charlie O'Brien	.20	.08	.02
☐ 376	Ron Gant	1.50	.60	.15
☐ 377	Lloyd Moseby	.20	.08	.02
☐ 378	Gene Harris	.25	.10	.02
☐ 379	Joe Carter	.65	.25	.06
☐ 380	Scott Bailes	.20	.08	.02
☐ 381	R.J. Reynolds	.20	.08	.02
☐ 382	Bob Melvin	.20	.08	.02
☐ 383	Tim Teufel	.20	.08	.02
☐ 384	John Burkett	.35	.15	.03
☐ 385	Felix Jose	3.50	1.50	.35
☐ 386	Larry Andersen	.20	.08	.02
☐ 387	David West	.25	.10	.02
☐ 388	Luis Salazar	.20	.08	.02
☐ 389	Mike MacFurlane	.25	.10	.02
☐ 390	Charlie Hough	.20	.08	.02
☐ 391	Greg Briley	.25	.10	.02
☐ 392	Donn Pall	.20	.08	.02
☐ 393	Bryn Smith	.20	.08	.02
☐ 394	Carlos Quintana	.45	.18	.04
☐ 395	Steve Lake	.20	.08	.02
☐ 396	Mark Whiten	3.00	1.25	.30
☐ 397	Edwin Nunez	.20	.08	.02
☐ 398	Rick Parker	.25	.10	.02
☐ 399	Mark Portugal	.20	.08	.02
☐ 400	Roy Smith	.20	.08	.02
☐ 401	Hector Villanueva	.30	.12	.03
☐ 402	Bob Milacki	.25	.10	.02
☐ 403	Alejandro Pena	.25	.10	.02
☐ 404	Scott Bradley	.20	.08	.02
☐ 405	Ron Kittle	.25	.10	.02
☐ 406	Bob Tewksbury	.20	.08	.02
☐ 407	Wes Gardner	.20	.08	.02
☐ 408	Ernie Whitt	.20	.08	.02
☐ 409	Terry Shumpert	.35	.15	.03
☐ 410	Tim Layana	.30	.12	.03
☐ 411	Chris Gwynn	.25	.10	.02
☐ 412	Jeff Robinson	.20	.08	.02
☐ 413	Scott Scudder	.35	.15	.03
☐ 414	Kevin Romine	.20	.08	.02
☐ 415	Jose DeJesus	.25	.10	.02
☐ 416	Mike Jeffcoat	.20	.08	.02
☐ 417	Rudy Seanez	.45	.18	.04
☐ 418	Mike Dunne	.20	.08	.02
☐ 419	Dick Schofield	.20	.08	.02
☐ 420	Steve Wilson	.25	.10	.02
☐ 421	Bill Krueger	.20	.08	.02
☐ 422	Junior Felix	.25	.10	.02
☐ 423	Drew Hall	.20	.08	.02
☐ 424	Curt Young	.20	.08	.02
☐ 425	Franklin Stubbs	.20	.08	.02
☐ 426	Dave Winfield	.65	.25	.06
☐ 427	Rick Reed	.25	.10	.02
☐ 428	Charlie Leibrandt	.20	.08	.02
☐ 429	Jeff Robinson	.20	.08	.02
☐ 430	Erik Hanson	.65	.25	.06
☐ 431	Barry Jones	.20	.08	.02
☐ 432	Alex Trevino	.20	.08	.02
☐ 433	John Moses	.20	.08	.02
☐ 434	Dave Johnson	.25	.10	.02
☐ 435	Mackey Sasser	.25	.10	.02
☐ 436	Rick Leach	.20	.08	.02
☐ 437	Lenny Harris	.25	.10	.02
☐ 438	Carlos Martinez	.25	.10	.02
☐ 439	Rex Hudler	.20	.08	.02
☐ 440	Domingo Ramos	.20	.08	.02
☐ 441	Gerald Perry	.20	.08	.02
☐ 442	Jeff Russell	.20	.08	.02
☐ 443	Carlos Baerga	2.50	1.00	.25
☐ 444	Checklist Card	.40	.16	.04
	(Will Clark)			
☐ 445	Stan Javier	.20	.08	.02
☐ 446	Kevin Maas	7.50	3.25	.75
☐ 447	Tom Brunansky	.25	.10	.02
☐ 448	Carmelo Martinez	.20	.08	.02
☐ 449	Willie Blair	.25	.10	.02
☐ 450	Andres Galarraga	.25	.10	.02
☐ 451	Bud Black	.20	.08	.02
☐ 452	Greg Harris	.35	.15	.03
☐ 453	Joe Oliver	.25	.10	.02
☐ 454	Greg Brock	.20	.08	.02
☐ 455	Jeff Treadway	.25	.10	.02
☐ 456	Lance McCullers	.20	.08	.02
☐ 457	Dave Schmidt	.20	.08	.02
☐ 458	Todd Burns	.20	.08	.02
☐ 459	Max Venable	.20	.08	.02
☐ 460	Neal Heaton	.20	.08	.02
☐ 461	Mark Williamson	.20	.08	.02
☐ 462	Keith Miller	.20	.08	.02
☐ 463	Mike LaCoss	.20	.08	.02
☐ 464	Jose Offerman	1.25	.50	.12
☐ 465	Jim Leyritz	.25	.10	.02
☐ 466	Glenn Braggs	.20	.08	.02
☐ 467	Ron Robinson	.20	.08	.02
☐ 468	Mark Davis	.25	.10	.02
☐ 469	Gary Pettis	.20	.08	.02
☐ 470	Keith Hernandez	.25	.10	.02
☐ 471	Dennis Rasmussen	.20	.08	.02

☐ 472	Mark Eichhorn	.25	.10	.02
☐ 473	Ted Power	.20	.08	.02
☐ 474	Terry Mulholland	.25	.10	.02
☐ 475	Todd Stottlemyre	.35	.15	.03
☐ 476	Jerry Goff	.25	.10	.02
☐ 477	Gene Nelson	.20	.08	.02
☐ 478	Rich Gedman	.20	.08	.02
☐ 479	Brian Harper	.25	.10	.02
☐ 480	Mike Felder	.20	.08	.02
☐ 481	Steve Avery	18.00	7.50	2.50
☐ 482	Jack Morris	.40	.16	.04
☐ 483	Randy Johnson	.75	.30	.07
☐ 484	Scott Radinsky	.40	.16	.04
☐ 485	Jose DeLeon	.20	.08	.02
☐ 486	Stan Belinda	.35	.15	.03
☐ 487	Brian Holton	.20	.08	.02
☐ 488	Mark Carreon	.20	.08	.02
☐ 489	Trevor Wilson	.30	.12	.03
☐ 490	Mike Sharperson	.20	.08	.02
☐ 491	Alan Mills	.35	.15	.03
☐ 492	John Candelaria	.20	.08	.02
☐ 493	Paul Assenmacher	.20	.08	.02
☐ 494	Steve Crawford	.20	.08	.02
☐ 495	Brad Arnsberg	.20	.08	.02
☐ 496	Sergio Valdez	.25	.10	.02
☐ 497	Mark Parent	.20	.08	.02
☐ 498	Tom Pagnozzi	.20	.08	.02
☐ 499	Greg Harris	.20	.08	.02
☐ 500	Randy Ready	.20	.08	.02
☐ 501	Duane Ward	.25	.10	.02
☐ 502	Nelson Santovenia	.20	.08	.02
☐ 503	Joe Klink	.35	.15	.03
☐ 504	Eric Plunk	.20	.08	.02
☐ 505	Jeff Reed	.20	.08	.02
☐ 506	Ted Higuera	.25	.10	.02
☐ 507	Joe Hesketh	.20	.08	.02
☐ 508	Dan Petry	.20	.08	.02
☐ 509	Matt Young	.20	.08	.02
☐ 510	Jerald Clark	.25	.10	.02
☐ 511	John Orton	.25	.10	.02
☐ 512	Scott Ruskin	.35	.15	.03
☐ 513	Chris Hoiles	.60	.25	.06
☐ 514	Daryl Boston	.20	.08	.02
☐ 515	Francisco Oliveras	.25	.10	.02
☐ 516	Ozzie Canseco	.30	.12	.03
☐ 517	Xavier Hernandez	.25	.10	.02
☐ 518	Fred Manrique	.20	.08	.02
☐ 519	Shawn Boskie	.35	.15	.03
☐ 520	Jeff Montgomery	.25	.10	.02
☐ 521	Jack Daugherty	.20	.08	.02
☐ 522	Keith Comstock	.20	.08	.02
☐ 523	Greg Hibbard	.60	.25	.06
☐ 524	Lee Smith	.25	.10	.02
☐ 525	Dana Kiecker	.25	.10	.02
☐ 526	Darrel Akerfelds	.20	.08	.02
☐ 527	Greg Myers	.20	.08	.02
☐ 528	Checklist Card	.40	.16	.04
	(Ryne Sandberg)			

1991 Leaf Preview

The 1991 Leaf Preview set consists of 26 cards measuring the standard size (2 1/2" by 3 1/2"). The front design has color action player photos, with white and silver borders. Black photo mounts are drawn in at the corners of the pictures, just as one would find in an old-fashioned photo album. The back has a color head shot and biography in the top portion on a black background. A red stripe cuts across the card, and career statistics are given below it on a silver background. The words "1991 Preview Card" appear in white block lettering beneath the statistics. The cards are numbered on the back.

		MINT	EXC	G-VG
COMPLETE SET (26)		150.00	67.50	22.50
COMMON PLAYER (1-26)		4.00	1.75	.40
☐ 1	Dave Justice	12.50	5.50	1.65
☐ 2	Ryne Sandberg	10.00	4.50	1.25
☐ 3	Barry Larkin	6.00	2.50	.60
☐ 4	Craig Biggio	4.00	1.75	.40
☐ 5	Ramon Martinez	6.00	2.50	.60
☐ 6	Tim Wallach	4.00	1.75	.40
☐ 7	Dwight Gooden	6.00	2.50	.60
☐ 8	Len Dykstra	4.00	1.75	.40
☐ 9	Barry Bonds	7.00	3.00	.70
☐ 10	Ray Lankford	6.00	2.50	.60
☐ 11	Tony Gwynn	7.00	3.00	.70
☐ 12	Will Clark	10.00	4.50	1.25
☐ 13	Leo Gomez	6.00	2.50	.60
☐ 14	Wade Boggs	8.00	3.50	.80
☐ 15	Chuck Finley UER	4.00	1.75	.40
	(Position on card back is First Base)			
☐ 16	Carlton Fisk	6.00	2.50	.60
☐ 17	Sandy Alomar Jr.	5.00	2.25	.50
☐ 18	Cecil Fielder	7.00	3.00	.70
☐ 19	Bo Jackson	12.50	5.50	1.65
☐ 20	Paul Molitor	6.00	2.50	.60
☐ 21	Kirby Puckett	7.00	3.00	.70
☐ 22	Don Mattingly	9.00	4.00	.90
☐ 23	Rickey Henderson	10.00	4.50	1.25
☐ 24	Tino Martinez	5.00	2.25	.50
☐ 25	Nolan Ryan	16.00	6.75	2.25
☐ 26	Dave Stieb	4.00	1.75	.40

1991 Leaf I

This 264-card standard size 2 1/2" by 3 1/2" set marks the second year Donruss has produced a premium set using the Leaf name. This set features a photo of the player which is surrounded by black and white borders. The whole card is framed in gray borders. The Leaf logo is in the upper right corner of the card. The back of the card features a gray, red and black back with white lettering on the black background and black lettering on the gray and red backgrounds. The backs of the cards also features biographical and statistical information along with a write-up when room is provided. The set was issued using the Donruss dealer distribution network with very little Leaf product being released in other fashions. The key rookie cards in this series are Wes Chamberlain and Brian McRae.

	MINT	EXC	G-VG
COMPLETE SET (264)	35.00	15.75	5.25
COMMON PLAYER (1-264)	.08	.03	.01

☐ 1	The Leaf Card	.12	.05	.01
☐ 2	Kurt Stillwell	.08	.03	.01
☐ 3	Bobby Witt	.12	.05	.01
☐ 4	Tony Phillips	.08	.03	.01
☐ 5	Scott Garrelts	.08	.03	.01
☐ 6	Greg Swindell	.12	.05	.01
☐ 7	Billy Ripken	.08	.03	.01
☐ 8	Dave Martinez	.08	.03	.01
☐ 9	Kelly Gruber	.15	.06	.01
☐ 10	Juan Samuel	.12	.05	.01
☐ 11	Brian Holman	.08	.03	.01
☐ 12	Craig Biggio	.17	.07	.01
☐ 13	Lonnie Smith	.12	.05	.01
☐ 14	Ron Robinson	.08	.03	.01
☐ 15	Mike LaValliere	.08	.03	.01
☐ 16	Mark Davis	.08	.03	.01
☐ 17	Jack Daugherty	.08	.03	.01
☐ 18	Mike Henneman	.08	.03	.01
☐ 19	Mike Greenwell	.25	.10	.02
☐ 20	Dave Magadan	.12	.05	.01
☐ 21	Mark Williamson	.08	.03	.01
☐ 22	Marquis Grissom	.25	.10	.02
☐ 23	Pat Borders	.08	.03	.01
☐ 24	Mike Scioscia	.08	.03	.01
☐ 25	Shawon Dunston	.15	.06	.01
☐ 26	Randy Bush	.08	.03	.01
☐ 27	John Smoltz	.25	.10	.02
☐ 28	Chuck Crim	.08	.03	.01
☐ 29	Don Slaught	.08	.03	.01
☐ 30	Mike Macfarlane	.08	.03	.01
☐ 31	Wally Joyner	.20	.08	.02
☐ 32	Pat Combs	.12	.05	.01
☐ 33	Tony Pena	.12	.05	.01
☐ 34	Howard Johnson	.25	.10	.02
☐ 35	Leo Gomez	.75	.30	.07
☐ 36	Spike Owen	.08	.03	.01
☐ 37	Eric Davis	.30	.12	.03
☐ 38	Roberto Kelly	.15	.06	.01
☐ 39	Jerome Walton	.15	.06	.01
☐ 40	Shane Mack	.12	.05	.01
☐ 41	Kent Mercker	.12	.05	.01
☐ 42	B.J. Surhoff	.08	.03	.01
☐ 43	Jerry Browne	.08	.03	.01
☐ 44	Lee Smith	.12	.05	.01
☐ 45	Chuck Finley	.15	.06	.01
☐ 46	Terry Mulholland	.12	.05	.01
☐ 47	Tom Bolton	.08	.03	.01
☐ 48	Tom Herr	.08	.03	.01
☐ 49	Jim Deshaies	.08	.03	.01
☐ 50	Walt Weiss	.12	.05	.01
☐ 51	Hal Morris	.30	.12	.03
☐ 52	Lee Guetterman	.08	.03	.01
☐ 53	Paul Assenmacher	.08	.03	.01
☐ 54	Brian Harper	.12	.05	.01
☐ 55	Paul Gibson	.08	.03	.01
☐ 56	John Burkett	.08	.03	.01
☐ 57	Doug Jones	.08	.03	.01
☐ 58	Jose Oquendo	.08	.03	.01
☐ 59	Dick Schofield	.08	.03	.01
☐ 60	Dickie Thon	.08	.03	.01
☐ 61	Ramon Martinez	.60	.25	.06
☐ 62	Jay Buhner	.15	.06	.01
☐ 63	Mark Portugal	.08	.03	.01
☐ 64	Bob Welch	.12	.05	.01
☐ 65	Chris Sabo	.17	.07	.01
☐ 66	Chuck Cary	.08	.03	.01
☐ 67	Mark Langston	.15	.06	.01
☐ 68	Joe Boever	.08	.03	.01
☐ 69	Jody Reed	.12	.05	.01
☐ 70	Alejandro Pena	.12	.05	.01
☐ 71	Jeff King	.12	.05	.01
☐ 72	Tom Pagnozzi	.08	.03	.01
☐ 73	Joe Oliver	.08	.03	.01
☐ 74	Mike Witt	.08	.03	.01
☐ 75	Hector Villanueva	.12	.05	.01
☐ 76	Dan Gladden	.08	.03	.01
☐ 77	Dave Justice	4.00	1.75	.40
☐ 78	Mike Gallego	.08	.03	.01
☐ 79	Tom Candiotti	.12	.05	.01
☐ 80	Ozzie Smith	.35	.15	.03
☐ 81	Luis Polonia	.12	.05	.01
☐ 82	Randy Ready	.08	.03	.01
☐ 83	Greg Harris	.08	.03	.01
☐ 84	Checklist Card	.25	.10	.02
	Dave Justice			
☐ 85	Kevin Mitchell	.30	.12	.03
☐ 86	Mark McLemore	.08	.03	.01
☐ 87	Terry Steinbach	.08	.03	.01
☐ 88	Tom Browning	.12	.05	.01
☐ 89	Matt Nokes	.12	.05	.01
☐ 90	Mike Harkey	.12	.05	.01
☐ 91	Omar Vizquel	.08	.03	.01
☐ 92	Dave Bergman	.08	.03	.01
☐ 93	Matt Williams	.30	.12	.03

☐ 94	Steve Olin	.08	.03	.01
☐ 95	Craig Wilson	.20	.08	.02
☐ 96	Dave Stieb	.12	.05	.01
☐ 97	Ruben Sierra	.50	.20	.05
☐ 98	Jay Howell	.08	.03	.01
☐ 99	Scott Bradley	.08	.03	.01
☐ 100	Eric Yelding	.08	.03	.01
☐ 101	Rickey Henderson	.75	.30	.07
☐ 102	Jeff Reed	.08	.03	.01
☐ 103	Jimmy Key	.12	.05	.01
☐ 104	Terry Shumpert	.12	.05	.01
☐ 105	Kenny Rogers	.08	.03	.01
☐ 106	Cecil Fielder	.75	.30	.07
☐ 107	Robby Thompson	.08	.03	.01
☐ 108	Alex Cole	.15	.06	.01
☐ 109	Randy Milligan	.12	.05	.01
☐ 110	Andres Galarraga	.12	.05	.01
☐ 111	Bill Spiers	.08	.03	.01
☐ 112	Kal Daniels	.15	.06	.01
☐ 113	Henry Cotto	.08	.03	.01
☐ 114	Casey Candaele	.08	.03	.01
☐ 115	Jeff Blauser	.08	.03	.01
☐ 116	Robin Yount	.35	.15	.03
☐ 117	Ben McDonald	.35	.15	.03
☐ 118	Bret Saberhagen	.15	.06	.01
☐ 119	Juan Gonzalez	4.00	1.75	.40
☐ 120	Lou Whitaker	.15	.06	.01
☐ 121	Ellis Burks	.17	.07	.01
☐ 122	Charlie O'Brien	.08	.03	.01
☐ 123	John Smiley	.12	.05	.01
☐ 124	Tim Burke	.08	.03	.01
☐ 125	John Olerud	.40	.16	.04
☐ 126	Eddie Murray	.30	.12	.03
☐ 127	Greg Maddux	.12	.05	.01
☐ 128	Kevin Tapani	.20	.08	.02
☐ 129	Ron Gant	.40	.16	.04
☐ 130	Jay Bell	.08	.03	.01
☐ 131	Chris Hoiles	.17	.07	.01
☐ 132	Tom Gordon	.12	.05	.01
☐ 133	Kevin Seitzer	.12	.05	.01
☐ 134	Jeff Huson	.08	.03	.01
☐ 135	Jerry Don Gleaton	.08	.03	.01
☐ 136	Jeff Brantley	.08	.03	.01
☐ 137	Felix Fermin	.08	.03	.01
☐ 138	Mike Devereaux	.08	.03	.01
☐ 139	Delino DeShields	.25	.10	.02
☐ 140	David Wells	.08	.03	.01
☐ 141	Tim Crews	.08	.03	.01
☐ 142	Erik Hanson	.12	.05	.01
☐ 143	Mark Davidson	.08	.03	.01
☐ 144	Tommy Gregg	.08	.03	.01
☐ 145	Jim Gantner	.08	.03	.01
☐ 146	Jose Lind	.08	.03	.01
☐ 147	Danny Tartabull	.15	.06	.01
☐ 148	Geno Petralli	.08	.03	.01
☐ 149	Travis Fryman	2.25	.90	.22
☐ 150	Tim Naehring	.15	.06	.01
☐ 151	Kevin McReynolds	.15	.06	.01
☐ 152	Joe Orsulak	.08	.03	.01
☐ 153	Steve Frey	.15	.06	.01
☐ 154	Duane Ward	.08	.03	.01
☐ 155	Stan Javier	.08	.03	.01
☐ 156	Damon Berryhill	.08	.03	.01
☐ 157	Gene Larkin	.08	.03	.01
☐ 158	Greg Olson	.12	.05	.01
☐ 159	Mark Knudson	.08	.03	.01
☐ 160	Carmelo Martinez	.08	.03	.01
☐ 161	Storm Davis	.08	.03	.01
☐ 162	Jim Abbott	.30	.12	.03
☐ 163	Len Dykstra	.15	.06	.01
☐ 164	Tom Brunansky	.12	.05	.01
☐ 165	Dwight Gooden	.30	.12	.03
☐ 166	Jose Mesa	.08	.03	.01
☐ 167	Oil Can Boyd	.08	.03	.01
☐ 168	Barry Larkin	.30	.12	.03
☐ 169	Scott Sanderson	.12	.05	.01
☐ 170	Mark Grace	.20	.08	.02
☐ 171	Mark Guthrie	.15	.06	.01
☐ 172	Tom Glavine	.30	.12	.03
☐ 173	Gary Sheffield	.15	.06	.01
☐ 174	Checklist Card	.15	.06	.01
	Roger Clemens			
☐ 175	Chris James	.08	.03	.01
☐ 176	Milt Thompson	.08	.03	.01
☐ 177	Donnie Hill	.08	.03	.01
☐ 178	Wes Chamberlain	2.00	.80	.20
☐ 179	John Marzano	.08	.03	.01
☐ 180	Frank Viola	.15	.06	.01
☐ 181	Eric Anthony	.15	.06	.01
☐ 182	Jose Canseco	1.25	.50	.12
☐ 183	Scott Scudder	.12	.05	.01
☐ 184	Dave Eiland	.08	.03	.01
☐ 185	Luis Salazar	.08	.03	.01
☐ 186	Pedro Munoz	.75	.30	.07

		MINT	EXC	G-VG
☐ 187	Steve Searcy	.08	.03	.01
☐ 188	Don Robinson	.08	.03	.01
☐ 189	Sandy Alomar Jr.	.15	.06	.01
☐ 190	Jose DeLeon	.08	.03	.01
☐ 191	John Orton	.08	.03	.01
☐ 192	Darren Daulton	.12	.05	.01
☐ 193	Mike Morgan	.12	.05	.01
☐ 194	Greg Briley	.08	.03	.01
☐ 195	Karl Rhodes	.12	.05	.01
☐ 196	Harold Baines	.12	.05	.01
☐ 197	Bill Doran	.08	.03	.01
☐ 198	Alvaro Espinoza	.08	.03	.01
☐ 199	Kirk McCaskill	.08	.03	.01
☐ 200	Jose DeJesus	.08	.03	.01
☐ 201	Jack Clark	.12	.05	.01
☐ 202	Daryl Boston	.08	.03	.01
☐ 203	Randy Tomlin	.60	.25	.06
☐ 204	Pedro Guerrero	.12	.05	.01
☐ 205	Billy Hatcher	.12	.05	.01
☐ 206	Tim Leary	.12	.05	.01
☐ 207	Ryne Sandberg	1.00	.40	.10
☐ 208	Kirby Puckett	.50	.20	.05
☐ 209	Charlie Leibrandt	.08	.03	.01
☐ 210	Rick Honeycutt	.08	.03	.01
☐ 211	Joel Skinner	.08	.03	.01
☐ 212	Rex Hudler	.08	.03	.01
☐ 213	Bryan Harvey	.12	.05	.01
☐ 214	Charlie Hayes	.08	.03	.01
☐ 215	Matt Young	.08	.03	.01
☐ 216	Terry Kennedy	.08	.03	.01
☐ 217	Carl Nichols	.08	.03	.01
☐ 218	Mike Moore	.12	.05	.01
☐ 219	Paul O'Neill	.12	.05	.01
☐ 220	Steve Sax	.12	.05	.01
☐ 221	Shawn Boskie	.12	.05	.01
☐ 222	Rich DeLucia	.30	.12	.03
☐ 223	Lloyd Moseby	.08	.03	.01
☐ 224	Mike Kingery	.08	.03	.01
☐ 225	Carlos Baerga	.30	.12	.03
☐ 226	Bryn Smith	.08	.03	.01
☐ 227	Todd Stottlemyre	.12	.05	.01
☐ 228	Julio Franco	.20	.08	.02
☐ 229	Jim Gott	.08	.03	.01
☐ 230	Mike Schooler	.08	.03	.01
☐ 231	Steve Finley	.12	.05	.01
☐ 232	Dave Henderson	.15	.06	.01
☐ 233	Luis Quinones	.08	.03	.01
☐ 234	Mark Whiten	.35	.15	.03
☐ 235	Brian McRae	2.00	.80	.20
☐ 236	Rich Gossage	.12	.05	.01
☐ 237	Rob Deer	.12	.05	.01
☐ 238	Will Clark	1.00	.40	.10
☐ 239	Albert Belle	.60	.25	.06
☐ 240	Bob Melvin	.08	.03	.01
☐ 241	Larry Walker	.12	.05	.01
☐ 242	Dante Bichette	.08	.03	.01
☐ 243	Orel Hershiser	.15	.06	.01
☐ 244	Pete O'Brien	.08	.03	.01
☐ 245	Pete Harnisch	.12	.05	.01
☐ 246	Jeff Treadway	.08	.03	.01
☐ 247	Julio Machado	.08	.03	.01
☐ 248	Dave Johnson	.08	.03	.01
☐ 249	Kirk Gibson	.15	.06	.01
☐ 250	Kevin Brown	.08	.03	.01
☐ 251	Milt Cuyler	.40	.16	.04
☐ 252	Jeff Reardon	.15	.06	.01
☐ 253	David Cone	.12	.05	.01
☐ 254	Gary Redus	.08	.03	.01
☐ 255	Junior Noboa	.08	.03	.01
☐ 256	Greg Myers	.08	.03	.01
☐ 257	Dennis Cook	.08	.03	.01
☐ 258	Joe Girardi	.08	.03	.01
☐ 259	Allan Anderson	.08	.03	.01
☐ 260	Paul Marak	.15	.06	.01
☐ 261	Barry Bonds	.50	.20	.05
☐ 262	Juan Bell	.12	.05	.01
☐ 263	Russ Morman	.08	.03	.01
☐ 264	Checklist Card	.15	.06	.01
	George Brett			

1991 Leaf II

The second series of the 1991 Leaf set contains 264 cards, measuring the standard size (2 1/2" by 3 1/2"). As with the first series, the glossy color player photos on the fronts are bordered in black and white, with a gray outer border framing the whole card. On a silver, red, and black background, the backs feature

a color head shot, biography, and career performance statistics, with a career highlights when space allows. The cards are numbered on the back. The key rookie cards in this series are Orlando Merced and Denny Neagle.

		MINT	EXC	G-VG
COMPLETE SET (264)		40.00	18.00	6.00
COMMON PLAYER (265-528)		.08	.03	.01
☐ 265	Jerald Clark	.12	.05	.01
☐ 266	Dwight Evans	.12	.05	.01
☐ 267	Roberto Alomar	.40	.16	.04
☐ 268	Danny Jackson	.08	.03	.01
☐ 269	Brian Downing	.08	.03	.01
☐ 270	John Cerutti	.08	.03	.01
☐ 271	Robin Ventura	1.25	.50	.12
☐ 272	Gerald Perry	.08	.03	.01
☐ 273	Wade Boggs	.50	.20	.05
☐ 274	Dennis Martinez	.12	.05	.01
☐ 275	Andy Benes	.20	.08	.02
☐ 276	Tony Fossas	.08	.03	.01
☐ 277	Franklin Stubbs	.08	.03	.01
☐ 278	John Kruk	.08	.03	.01
☐ 279	Kevin Gross	.08	.03	.01
☐ 280	Von Hayes	.12	.05	.01
☐ 281	Frank Thomas	8.00	3.50	.80
☐ 282	Rob Dibble	.15	.06	.01
☐ 283	Mel Hall	.12	.05	.01
☐ 284	Rick Mahler	.08	.03	.01
☐ 285	Dennis Eckersley	.15	.06	.01
☐ 286	Bernard Gilkey	.25	.10	.02
☐ 287	Dan Plesac	.08	.03	.01
☐ 288	Jason Grimsley	.15	.06	.01
☐ 289	Mark Lewis	.75	.30	.07
☐ 290	Tony Gwynn	.50	.20	.05
☐ 291	Jeff Russell	.08	.03	.01
☐ 292	Curt Schilling	.08	.03	.01
☐ 293	Pascual Perez	.08	.03	.01
☐ 294	Jack Morris	.15	.06	.01
☐ 295	Hubie Brooks	.12	.05	.01
☐ 296	Alex Fernandez	.60	.25	.06
☐ 297	Harold Reynolds	.12	.05	.01
☐ 298	Craig Worthington	.08	.03	.01
☐ 299	Willie Wilson	.12	.05	.01
☐ 300	Mike Maddux	.08	.03	.01
☐ 301	Dave Righetti	.12	.05	.01
☐ 302	Paul Molitor	.15	.06	.01
☐ 303	Gary Gaetti	.12	.05	.01
☐ 304	Terry Pendleton	.20	.08	.02
☐ 305	Kevin Elster	.08	.03	.01
☐ 306	Scott Fletcher	.08	.03	.01
☐ 307	Jeff Robinson	.08	.03	.01
☐ 308	Jesse Barfield	.12	.05	.01
☐ 309	Mike LaCoss	.08	.03	.01
☐ 310	Andy Van Slyke	.15	.06	.01
☐ 311	Glenallen Hill	.12	.05	.01
☐ 312	Bud Black	.08	.03	.01
☐ 313	Kent Hrbek	.15	.06	.01
☐ 314	Tim Teufel	.08	.03	.01
☐ 315	Tony Fernandez	.12	.05	.01
☐ 316	Beau Allred	.17	.07	.01
☐ 317	Curtis Wilkerson	.08	.03	.01
☐ 318	Bill Sampen	.12	.05	.01
☐ 319	Randy Johnson	.12	.05	.01
☐ 320	Mike Heath	.08	.03	.01
☐ 321	Sammy Sosa	.15	.06	.01
☐ 322	Mickey Tettleton	.12	.05	.01
☐ 323	Jose Vizcaino	.15	.06	.01
☐ 324	John Candelaria	.08	.03	.01

	#	Name			
☐	325	Dave Howard	.20	.08	.02
☐	326	Jose Rijo	.12	.05	.01
☐	327	Todd Zeile	.30	.12	.03
☐	328	Gene Nelson	.08	.03	.01
☐	329	Dwayne Henry	.08	.03	.01
☐	330	Mike Boddicker	.08	.03	.01
☐	331	Ozzie Guillen	.12	.05	.01
☐	332	Sam Horn	.12	.05	.01
☐	333	Wally Whitehurst	.08	.03	.01
☐	334	Dave Parker	.15	.06	.01
☐	335	George Brett	.35	.15	.03
☐	336	Bobby Thigpen	.12	.05	.01
☐	337	Ed Whitson	.08	.03	.01
☐	338	Ivan Calderon	.12	.05	.01
☐	339	Mike Pagliarulo	.08	.03	.01
☐	340	Jack McDowell	.17	.07	.01
☐	341	Dana Kiecker	.08	.03	.01
☐	342	Fred McGriff	.25	.10	.02
☐	343	Mark Lee	.20	.08	.02
☐	344	Alfredo Griffin	.08	.03	.01
☐	345	Scott Bankhead	.08	.03	.01
☐	346	Darrin Jackson	.12	.05	.01
☐	347	Rafael Palmeiro	.25	.10	.02
☐	348	Steve Farr	.08	.03	.01
☐	349	Hensley Meulens	.17	.07	.01
☐	350	Danny Cox	.08	.03	.01
☐	351	Alan Trammell	.20	.08	.02
☐	352	Edwin Nunez	.08	.03	.01
☐	353	Joe Carter	.25	.10	.02
☐	354	Eric Show	.08	.03	.01
☐	355	Vance Law	.08	.03	.01
☐	356	Jeff Gray	.15	.06	.01
☐	357	Bobby Bonilla	.40	.16	.04
☐	358	Ernest Riles	.08	.03	.01
☐	359	Ron Hassey	.08	.03	.01
☐	360	Willie McGee	.15	.06	.01
☐	361	Mackey Sasser	.08	.03	.01
☐	362	Glenn Braggs	.08	.03	.01
☐	363	Mario Diaz	.08	.03	.01
☐	364	Checklist Card Barry Bonds	.12	.05	.01
☐	365	Kevin Bass	.08	.03	.01
☐	366	Pete Incaviglia	.12	.05	.01
☐	367	Luis Sojo UER (1989 stats interspersed with 1990's)	.12	.05	.01
☐	368	Lance Parrish	.12	.05	.01
☐	369	Mark Leonard	.30	.12	.03
☐	370	Heathcliff Slocumb	.17	.07	.01
☐	371	Jimmy Jones	.08	.03	.01
☐	372	Ken Griffey Jr.	5.00	2.25	.50
☐	373	Chris Hammond	.15	.06	.01
☐	374	Chili Davis	.12	.05	.01
☐	375	Joey Cora	.08	.03	.01
☐	376	Ken Hill	.08	.03	.01
☐	377	Darryl Strawberry	.75	.30	.07
☐	378	Ron Darling	.12	.05	.01
☐	379	Sid Bream	.08	.03	.01
☐	380	Bill Swift	.08	.03	.01
☐	381	Shawn Abner	.08	.03	.01
☐	382	Eric King	.08	.03	.01
☐	383	Mickey Morandini	.17	.07	.01
☐	384	Carlton Fisk	.35	.15	.03
☐	385	Steve Lake	.08	.03	.01
☐	386	Mike Jeffcoat	.08	.03	.01
☐	387	Darren Holmes	.17	.07	.01
☐	388	Tim Wallach	.12	.05	.01
☐	389	George Bell	.20	.08	.02
☐	390	Craig Lefferts	.08	.03	.01
☐	391	Ernie Whitt	.08	.03	.01
☐	392	Felix Jose	.30	.12	.03
☐	393	Kevin Maas	.60	.25	.06
☐	394	Devon White	.12	.05	.01
☐	395	Otis Nixon	.12	.05	.01
☐	396	Chuck Knoblauch	2.50	1.00	.25
☐	397	Scott Coolbaugh	.08	.03	.01
☐	398	Glenn Davis	.15	.06	.01
☐	399	Manny Lee	.08	.03	.01
☐	400	Andre Dawson	.25	.10	.02
☐	401	Scott Chiamparino	.15	.06	.01
☐	402	Bill Gullickson	.12	.05	.01
☐	403	Lance Johnson	.08	.03	.01
☐	404	Juan Agosto	.08	.03	.01
☐	405	Danny Darwin	.08	.03	.01
☐	406	Barry Jones	.08	.03	.01
☐	407	Larry Andersen	.08	.03	.01
☐	408	Luis Rivera	.08	.03	.01
☐	409	Jaime Navarro	.08	.03	.01
☐	410	Roger McDowell	.08	.03	.01
☐	411	Brett Butler	.12	.05	.01
☐	412	Dale Murphy	.17	.07	.01
☐	413	Tim Raines UER (Listed as hitting .500 in 1980, should be .050)	.15	.06	.01
☐	414	Norm Charlton	.08	.03	.01
☐	415	Greg Cadaret	.08	.03	.01
☐	416	Chris Nabholz	.15	.06	.01
☐	417	Dave Stewart	.15	.06	.01
☐	418	Rich Gedman	.08	.03	.01
☐	419	Willie Randolph	.12	.05	.01
☐	420	Mitch Williams	.12	.05	.01
☐	421	Brook Jacoby	.08	.03	.01
☐	422	Greg Harris	.08	.03	.01
☐	423	Nolan Ryan	2.50	1.00	.25
☐	424	Dave Rohde	.15	.06	.01
☐	425	Don Mattingly	.50	.20	.05
☐	426	Greg Gagne	.08	.03	.01
☐	427	Vince Coleman	.15	.06	.01
☐	428	Dan Pasqua	.08	.03	.01
☐	429	Alvin Davis	.12	.05	.01
☐	430	Cal Ripken	1.25	.50	.12
☐	431	Jamie Quirk	.08	.03	.01
☐	432	Benito Santiago	.15	.06	.01
☐	433	Jose Uribe	.08	.03	.01
☐	434	Candy Maldonado	.08	.03	.01
☐	435	Junior Felix	.12	.05	.01
☐	436	Deion Sanders	.20	.08	.02
☐	437	John Franco	.08	.03	.01
☐	438	Greg Hibbard	.08	.03	.01
☐	439	Floyd Bannister	.08	.03	.01
☐	440	Steve Howe	.08	.03	.01
☐	441	Steve Decker	.50	.20	.05
☐	442	Vicente Palacios	.08	.03	.01
☐	443	Pat Tabler	.08	.03	.01
☐	444	Checklist Card Darryl Strawberry	.12	.05	.01
☐	445	Mike Felder	.08	.03	.01
☐	446	Al Newman	.08	.03	.01
☐	447	Chris Donnels	.60	.25	.06
☐	448	Rich Rodriguez	.15	.06	.01
☐	449	Turner Ward	.30	.12	.03
☐	450	Bob Walk	.08	.03	.01
☐	451	Gilberto Reyes	.08	.03	.01
☐	452	Mike Jackson	.08	.03	.01
☐	453	Rafael Belliard	.08	.03	.01
☐	454	Wayne Edwards	.08	.03	.01
☐	455	Andy Allanson	.08	.03	.01
☐	456	Dave Smith	.08	.03	.01
☐	457	Gary Carter	.15	.06	.01
☐	458	Warren Cromartie	.08	.03	.01
☐	459	Jack Armstrong	.12	.05	.01
☐	460	Bob Tewksbury	.08	.03	.01
☐	461	Joe Klink	.08	.03	.01
☐	462	Xavier Hernandez	.08	.03	.01
☐	463	Scott Radinsky	.12	.05	.01
☐	464	Jeff Robinson	.08	.03	.01
☐	465	Gregg Jefferies	.20	.08	.02
☐	466	Denny Neagle	.90	.40	.09
☐	467	Carmelo Martinez	.08	.03	.01
☐	468	Donn Pall	.08	.03	.01
☐	469	Bruce Hurst	.12	.05	.01
☐	470	Eric Bullock	.08	.03	.01
☐	471	Rick Aguilera	.12	.05	.01
☐	472	Charlie Hough	.08	.03	.01
☐	473	Carlos Quintana	.12	.05	.01
☐	474	Marty Barrett	.08	.03	.01
☐	475	Kevin Brown	.08	.03	.01
☐	476	Bobby Ojeda	.08	.03	.01
☐	477	Edgar Martinez	.12	.05	.01
☐	478	Bip Roberts	.08	.03	.01
☐	479	Mike Flanagan	.12	.05	.01
☐	480	John Habyan	.08	.03	.01
☐	481	Larry Casian	.17	.07	.01
☐	482	Wally Backman	.08	.03	.01
☐	483	Doug Dascenzo	.08	.03	.01
☐	484	Rick Dempsey	.08	.03	.01
☐	485	Ed Sprague	.25	.10	.02
☐	486	Steve Chitren	.15	.06	.01
☐	487	Mark McGwire	.25	.10	.02
☐	488	Roger Clemens	.75	.30	.07
☐	489	Orlando Merced	1.50	.60	.15
☐	490	Rene Gonzales	.08	.03	.01
☐	491	Mike Stanton	.08	.03	.01
☐	492	Al Osuna	.30	.12	.03
☐	493	Rick Cerone	.08	.03	.01
☐	494	Mariano Duncan	.08	.03	.01
☐	495	Zane Smith	.12	.05	.01
☐	496	John Morris	.08	.03	.01
☐	497	Frank Tanana	.12	.05	.01
☐	498	Junior Ortiz	.08	.03	.01
☐	499	Dave Winfield	.30	.12	.03
☐	500	Gary Varsho	.08	.03	.01
☐	501	Chico Walker	.08	.03	.01
☐	502	Ken Caminiti	.08	.03	.01
☐	503	Ken Griffey Sr.	.12	.05	.01
☐	504	Randy Myers	.08	.03	.01
☐	505	Steve Bedrosian	.12	.05	.01
☐	506	Cory Snyder	.12	.05	.01

		MINT	EXC	G-VG
☐ 507	Cris Carpenter	.08	.03	.01
☐ 508	Tim Belcher	.12	.05	.01
☐ 509	Jeff Hamilton	.08	.03	.01
☐ 510	Steve Avery	2.50	1.00	.25
☐ 511	Dave Valle	.08	.03	.01
☐ 512	Tom Lampkin	.08	.03	.01
☐ 513	Shawn Hillegas	.08	.03	.01
☐ 514	Reggie Jefferson	1.25	.50	.12
☐ 515	Ron Karkovice	.08	.03	.01
☐ 516	Doug Drabek	.12	.05	.01
☐ 517	Tom Henke	.12	.05	.01
☐ 518	Chris Bosio	.08	.03	.01
☐ 519	Gregg Olson	.15	.06	.01
☐ 520	Bob Scanlan	.17	.07	.01
☐ 521	Alonzo Powell	.17	.07	.01
☐ 522	Jeff Ballard	.08	.03	.01
☐ 523	Ray Lankford	1.25	.50	.12
☐ 524	Tommy Greene	.15	.06	.01
☐ 525	Mike Timlin	.25	.10	.02
☐ 526	Juan Berenguer	.08	.03	.01
☐ 527	Scott Erickson	4.00	1.75	.40
☐ 528	Checklist Card	.12	.05	.01
	Sandy Alomar Jr.			

		MINT	EXC	G-VG
☐ BC19	Roger Salkeld	5.00	2.25	.50
☐ BC20	Andujar Cedeno	5.00	2.25	.50
☐ BC21	Ryan Klesko UER	14.00	6.25	2.00
	(1990 Sumter BA .289; should be .368)			
☐ BC22	Mike Huff	1.50	.60	.15
☐ BC23	Anthony Young	2.25	.90	.22
☐ BC24	Eddie Zosky	3.00	1.25	.30
☐ BC25	Nolan Ryan UER	7.50	3.25	.75
	No Hitter 7 (Word other repeated in 7th line)			
☐ BC26	Rickey Henderson	5.00	2.25	.50
	Record Steal			

1991 Leaf Gold Rookies

This 26-card standard size (2 1/2" by 3 1/2") set was issued by Leaf as an adjunct (inserted in packs) to their 1991 Leaf regular issue. The set features some of the most popular prospects active in baseball. This set marks the first time Leaf Inc. and/or Donruss had produced a card utilizing any of the first 24 young players. The first twelve cards were issued as random inserts in with the first series of 1991 Leaf foil packs. The rest are issued as random inserts in with the second series. The earliest Leaf Gold Rookie cards issued with the first series can sometimes be found with erroneous regular numbered backs 265 through 276 instead of the correct BC1 through BC12. These numbered variations are very tough to find and are valued at ten times the values listed below.

		MINT	EXC	G-VG
COMPLETE SET (26)		100.00	45.00	15.00
COMMON PLAYER (1-12)		1.50	.60	.15
COMMON PLAYER (13-26)		1.50	.60	.15
☐ BC1	Scott Leius	2.25	.90	.22
☐ BC2	Luis Gonzalez	5.00	2.25	.50
☐ BC3	Wilfredo Cordero	3.50	1.50	.35
☐ BC4	Gary Scott	3.00	1.25	.30
☐ BC5	Willie Banks	3.00	1.25	.30
☐ BC6	Arthur Rhodes	3.00	1.25	.30
☐ BC7	Mo Vaughn	7.00	3.00	.70
☐ BC8	Henry Rodriguez	2.00	.80	.20
☐ BC9	Todd Van Poppel	9.00	4.00	.90
☐ BC10	Reggie Sanders	5.00	2.25	.50
☐ BC11	Rico Brogna	4.00	1.75	.40
☐ BC12	Mike Mussina	5.00	2.25	.50
☐ BC13	Kirk Dressendorfer	3.00	1.25	.30
☐ BC14	Jeff Bagwell	14.00	6.25	2.00
☐ BC15	Pete Schourek	2.50	1.00	.25
☐ BC16	Wade Taylor	2.25	.90	.22
☐ BC17	Pat Kelly	3.50	1.50	.35
☐ BC18	Tim Costo	3.00	1.25	.30

1991 Leaf Studio Preview

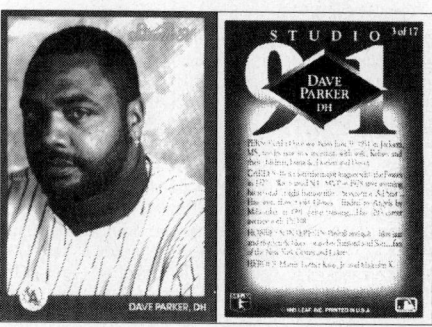

This 18-card preview set was inserted in 1991 (specially marked) Donruss retail factory sets. The standard-size (2 1/2" by 3 1/2") cards are exactly the same style as those in the Studio series, with black and white player photos bordered in mauve and player information on the backs. The cards are numbered on the back.

		MINT	EXC	G-VG
COMPLETE SET (18)		60.00	27.00	9.00
COMMON PLAYER (1-17)		3.00	1.25	.30
☐ 1	Juan Bell	3.00	1.25	.30
☐ 2	Roger Clemens	8.00	3.50	.80
☐ 3	Dave Parker	4.00	1.75	.40
☐ 4	Tim Raines	4.00	1.75	.40
☐ 5	Kevin Seitzer	3.00	1.25	.30
☐ 6	Ted Higuera	3.00	1.25	.30
☐ 7	Bernie Williams	6.00	2.50	.60
☐ 8	Harold Baines	4.00	1.75	.40
☐ 9	Gary Pettis	3.00	1.25	.30
☐ 10	Dave Justice	9.00	4.00	.90
☐ 11	Eric Davis	6.00	2.50	.60
☐ 12	Andujar Cedeno	5.00	2.25	.50
☐ 13	Tom Foley	3.00	1.25	.30
☐ 14	Dwight Gooden	5.00	2.25	.50
☐ 15	Doug Drabek	4.00	1.75	.40
☐ 16	Steve Decker	5.00	2.25	.50
☐ 17	Joe Torre MG	4.00	1.75	.40
☐ xx	Title card	3.00	1.25	.30

1991 Leaf Studio

The 1991 Leaf Studio set contains 264 cards and a puzzle of recently inducted Hall of Famer Rod Carew. The Carew puzzle was issued on twenty-one 2 1/2" by 3 1/2" cards, with 3 puzzle pieces per card, for a total of 63 pieces. The player cards measure the standard-size (2 1/2" by 3 1/2"), and the fronts feature posed black and white head-and-shoulders player photos with mauve borders. The team logo, player's name, and position appear along the bottom of the card face. The backs are printed

TERRY PENDLETON, 3B

in black and white and have four categories of information: personal, career, hobbies and interests, and heroes. The cards are numbered on the back. The cards are checklisted below alphabetically within and according to teams for each league as follows: Baltimore Orioles (1-10), Boston Red Sox (11-20), California Angels (21-30), Chicago White Sox (31-40), Cleveland Indians (41-50), Detroit Tigers (51-60), Kansas City Royals (61-70), Milwaukee Brewers (71-80), Minnesota Twins (81-90), New York Yankees (91-100), Oakland Athletics (101-110), Seattle Mariners (111-120), Texas Rangers (121-130), Toronto Blue Jays (131-140), Atlanta Braves (141-150), Chicago Cubs (151-160), Cincinnati Reds (161-170), Houston Astros (171-180), Los Angeles Dodgers (181-190), Montreal Expos (191-200), New York Mets (201-210), Philadelphia Phillies (211-220), Pittsburgh Pirates (221-230), St. Louis Cardinals (231-240), San Diego Padres (241-250), and San Francisco Giants (251-260). The key rookie cards in the set are Jeff Bagwell, Wes Chamberlain, Phil Plantier, and Todd Van Poppel. Among the other notable cards are Frank Thomas and Dave Justice.

	MINT	EXC	G-VG
COMPLETE SET (264)	45.00	20.00	6.75
COMMON PLAYER (1-263)	.08	.03	.01
☐ 1 Glenn Davis	.15	.06	.01
☐ 2 Dwight Evans	.12	.05	.01
☐ 3 Leo Gomez	.75	.30	.07
☐ 4 Chris Hoiles	.20	.08	.02
☐ 5 Sam Horn	.12	.05	.01
☐ 6 Ben McDonald	.35	.15	.03
☐ 7 Randy Milligan	.12	.05	.01
☐ 8 Gregg Olson	.15	.06	.01
☐ 9 Cal Ripken	1.25	.50	.12
☐ 10 David Segui	.15	.06	.01
☐ 11 Wade Boggs	.50	.20	.05
☐ 12 Ellis Burks	.20	.08	.02
☐ 13 Jack Clark	.15	.06	.01
☐ 14 Roger Clemens	.75	.30	.07
☐ 15 Mike Greenwell	.30	.12	.03
☐ 16 Tim Naehring	.15	.06	.01
☐ 17 Tony Pena	.12	.05	.01
☐ 18 Phil Plantier	6.00	2.50	.60
☐ 19 Jeff Reardon	.15	.06	.01
☐ 20 Mo Vaughn	2.00	.80	.20
☐ 21 Jimmy Reese CO	.08	.03	.01
☐ 22 Jim Abbott	.30	.12	.03
☐ 23 Bert Blyleven	.15	.06	.01
☐ 24 Chuck Finley	.17	.07	.01
☐ 25 Gary Gaetti	.12	.05	.01
☐ 26 Wally Joyner	.20	.08	.02
☐ 27 Mark Langston	.15	.06	.01
☐ 28 Kirk McCaskill	.08	.03	.01
☐ 29 Lance Parrish	.12	.05	.01
☐ 30 Dave Winfield	.30	.12	.03
☐ 31 Alex Fernandez	.45	.18	.04
☐ 32 Carlton Fisk	.35	.15	.03
☐ 33 Scott Fletcher	.08	.03	.01
☐ 34 Greg Hibbard	.08	.03	.01
☐ 35 Charlie Hough	.08	.03	.01
☐ 36 Jack McDowell	.17	.07	.01
☐ 37 Tim Raines	.15	.06	.01
☐ 38 Sammy Sosa	.15	.06	.01
☐ 39 Bobby Thigpen	.12	.05	.01
☐ 40 Frank Thomas	7.50	3.25	.75
☐ 41 Sandy Alomar Jr.	.15	.06	.01
☐ 42 John Farrell	.08	.03	.01
☐ 43 Glenallen Hill	.08	.03	.01
☐ 44 Brook Jacoby	.08	.03	.01
☐ 45 Chris James	.08	.03	.01
☐ 46 Doug Jones	.08	.03	.01
☐ 47 Eric King	.08	.03	.01
☐ 48 Mark Lewis	.60	.25	.06
☐ 49 Greg Swindell UER	.12	.05	.01
(Photo actually Turner Ward)			
☐ 50 Mark Whiten	.35	.15	.03
☐ 51 Milt Cuyler	.35	.15	.03
☐ 52 Rob Deer	.12	.05	.01
☐ 53 Cecil Fielder	.75	.30	.07
☐ 54 Travis Fryman	2.25	.90	.22
☐ 55 Bill Gullickson	.12	.05	.01
☐ 56 Lloyd Moseby	.08	.03	.01
☐ 57 Frank Tanana	.12	.05	.01
☐ 58 Mickey Tettleton	.12	.05	.01
☐ 59 Alan Trammell	.17	.07	.01
☐ 60 Lou Whitaker	.12	.05	.01
☐ 61 Mike Boddicker	.08	.03	.01
☐ 62 George Brett	.35	.15	.03
☐ 63 Jeff Conine	.25	.10	.02
☐ 64 Warren Cromartie	.08	.03	.01
☐ 65 Storm Davis	.08	.03	.01
☐ 66 Kirk Gibson	.15	.06	.01
☐ 67 Mark Gubicza	.12	.05	.01
☐ 68 Brian McRae	2.00	.80	.20
☐ 69 Bret Saberhagen	.17	.07	.01
☐ 70 Kurt Stillwell	.08	.03	.01
☐ 71 Tim McIntosh	.08	.03	.01
☐ 72 Candy Maldonado	.08	.03	.01
☐ 73 Paul Molitor	.15	.06	.01
☐ 74 Willie Randolph	.08	.03	.01
☐ 75 Ron Robinson	.08	.03	.01
☐ 76 Gary Sheffield	.15	.06	.01
☐ 77 Franklin Stubbs	.08	.03	.01
☐ 78 B.J. Surhoff	.08	.03	.01
☐ 79 Greg Vaughn	.35	.15	.03
☐ 80 Robin Yount	.40	.16	.04
☐ 81 Rick Aguilera	.12	.05	.01
☐ 82 Steve Bedrosian	.08	.03	.01
☐ 83 Scott Erickson	3.00	1.25	.30
☐ 84 Greg Gagne	.08	.03	.01
☐ 85 Dan Gladden	.08	.03	.01
☐ 86 Brian Harper	.12	.05	.01
☐ 87 Kent Hrbek	.15	.06	.01
☐ 88 Shane Mack	.12	.05	.01
☐ 89 Jack Morris	.17	.07	.01
☐ 90 Kirby Puckett	.50	.20	.05
☐ 91 Jesse Barfield	.12	.05	.01
☐ 92 Steve Farr	.08	.03	.01
☐ 93 Steve Howe	.08	.03	.01
☐ 94 Roberto Kelly	.15	.06	.01
☐ 95 Tim Leary	.12	.05	.01
☐ 96 Kevin Maas	.60	.25	.06
☐ 97 Don Mattingly	.50	.20	.05
☐ 98 Hensley Meulens	.15	.06	.01
☐ 99 Scott Sanderson	.08	.03	.01
☐ 100 Steve Sax	.12	.05	.01
☐ 101 Jose Canseco	1.25	.50	.12
☐ 102 Dennis Eckersley	.15	.06	.01
☐ 103 Dave Henderson	.15	.06	.01
☐ 104 Rickey Henderson	.75	.30	.07
☐ 105 Rick Honeycutt	.08	.03	.01
☐ 106 Mark McGwire	.25	.10	.02
☐ 107 Dave Stewart	.15	.06	.01
☐ 108 Eric Show	.08	.03	.01
☐ 109 Todd Van Poppel	4.00	1.75	.40
☐ 110 Bob Welch	.12	.05	.01
☐ 111 Alvin Davis	.12	.05	.01
☐ 112 Ken Griffey Jr.	5.00	2.25	.50
☐ 113 Ken Griffey Sr.	.15	.06	.01
☐ 114 Erik Hanson	.15	.06	.01
☐ 115 Brian Holman	.12	.05	.01
☐ 116 Randy Johnson	.12	.05	.01
☐ 117 Edgar Martinez	.15	.06	.01
☐ 118 Tino Martinez	.35	.15	.03
☐ 119 Harold Reynolds	.12	.05	.01
☐ 120 David Valle	.08	.03	.01
☐ 121 Kevin Belcher	.20	.08	.02
☐ 122 Scott Chiamparino	.15	.06	.01
☐ 123 Julio Franco	.20	.08	.02
☐ 124 Juan Gonzalez	4.00	1.75	.40
☐ 125 Rich Gossage	.12	.05	.01
☐ 126 Jeff Kunkel	.08	.03	.01
☐ 127 Rafael Palmeiro	.25	.10	.02
☐ 128 Nolan Ryan	2.50	1.00	.25
☐ 129 Ruben Sierra	.50	.20	.05
☐ 130 Bobby Witt	.12	.05	.01
☐ 131 Roberto Alomar	.40	.16	.04
☐ 132 Tom Candiotti	.12	.05	.01
☐ 133 Joe Carter	.30	.12	.03
☐ 134 Ken Dayley	.08	.03	.01
☐ 135 Kelly Gruber	.15	.06	.01
☐ 136 John Olerud	.35	.15	.03

□	#	Player			
□	137	Dave Stieb	.12	.05	.01
□	138	Turner Ward	.30	.12	.03
□	139	Devon White	.12	.05	.01
□	140	Mookie Wilson	.08	.03	.01
□	141	Steve Avery	2.50	1.00	.25
□	142	Sid Bream	.08	.03	.01
□	143	Nick Esasky	.08	.03	.01
□	144	Ron Gant	.35	.15	.03
□	145	Tom Glavine	.30	.12	.03
□	146	David Justice	4.00	1.75	.40
□	147	Kelly Mann	.08	.03	.01
□	148	Terry Pendleton	.17	.07	.01
□	149	John Smoltz	.20	.08	.02
□	150	Jeff Treadway	.08	.03	.01
□	151	George Bell	.20	.08	.02
□	152	Shawn Boskie	.12	.05	.01
□	153	Andre Dawson	.30	.12	.03
□	154	Lance Dickson	.50	.20	.05
□	155	Shawon Dunston	.15	.06	.01
□	156	Joe Girardi	.12	.05	.01
□	157	Mark Grace	.25	.10	.02
□	158	Ryne Sandberg	1.00	.40	.10
□	159	Gary Scott	.50	.20	.05
□	160	Dave Smith	.08	.03	.01
□	161	Tom Browning	.12	.05	.01
□	162	Eric Davis	.30	.12	.03
□	163	Rob Dibble	.15	.06	.01
□	164	Mariano Duncan	.08	.03	.01
□	165	Chris Hammond	.15	.06	.01
□	166	Billy Hatcher	.12	.05	.01
□	167	Barry Larkin	.30	.12	.03
□	168	Hal Morris	.30	.12	.03
□	169	Paul O'Neill	.12	.05	.01
□	170	Chris Sabo	.15	.06	.01
□	171	Eric Anthony	.15	.06	.01
□	172	Jeff Bagwell	6.00	2.50	.60
□	173	Craig Biggio	.20	.08	.02
□	174	Ken Caminiti	.08	.03	.01
□	175	Jim Deshaies	.08	.03	.01
□	176	Steve Finley	.12	.05	.01
□	177	Pete Harnisch	.12	.05	.01
□	178	Darryl Kile	.25	.10	.02
□	179	Curt Schilling	.08	.03	.01
□	180	Mike Scott	.12	.05	.01
□	181	Brett Butler	.12	.05	.01
□	182	Gary Carter	.15	.06	.01
□	183	Orel Hershiser	.15	.06	.01
□	184	Ramon Martinez	.60	.25	.06
□	185	Eddie Murray	.30	.12	.03
□	186	Jose Offerman	.15	.06	.01
□	187	Bob Ojeda	.08	.03	.01
□	188	Juan Samuel	.12	.05	.01
□	189	Mike Scioscia	.08	.03	.01
□	190	Darryl Strawberry	.75	.30	.07
□	191	Moises Alou	.15	.06	.01
□	192	Brian Barnes	.25	.10	.02
□	193	Oil Can Boyd	.08	.03	.01
□	194	Ivan Calderon	.12	.05	.01
□	195	Delino DeShields	.25	.10	.02
□	196	Mike Fitzgerald	.08	.03	.01
□	197	Andres Galarraga	.12	.05	.01
□	198	Marquis Grissom	.25	.10	.02
□	199	Bill Sampen	.15	.06	.01
□	200	Tim Wallach	.12	.05	.01
□	201	Daryl Boston	.08	.03	.01
□	202	Vince Coleman	.15	.06	.01
□	203	John Franco	.08	.03	.01
□	204	Dwight Gooden	.30	.12	.03
□	205	Tom Herr	.08	.03	.01
□	206	Gregg Jefferies	.20	.08	.02
□	207	Howard Johnson	.25	.10	.02
□	208	Dave Magadan UER (Born 1862, should be 1962)	.12	.05	.01
□	209	Kevin McReynolds	.15	.06	.01
□	210	Frank Viola	.15	.06	.01
□	211	Wes Chamberlain	2.00	.80	.20
□	212	Darren Daulton	.08	.03	.01
□	213	Lenny Dykstra	.12	.05	.01
□	214	Charlie Hayes	.08	.03	.01
□	215	Ricky Jordan	.12	.05	.01
□	216	Steve Lake (Pictured with parrot on his shoulder)	.08	.03	.01
□	217	Roger McDowell	.08	.03	.01
□	218	Mickey Morandini	.20	.08	.02
□	219	Terry Mulholland	.12	.05	.01
□	220	Dale Murphy	.20	.08	.02
□	221	Jay Bell	.08	.03	.01
□	222	Barry Bonds	.50	.20	.05
□	223	Bobby Bonilla	.40	.16	.04
□	224	Doug Drabek	.15	.06	.01
□	225	Bill Landrum	.08	.03	.01
□	226	Mike LaValliere	.08	.03	.01
□	227	Jose Lind	.08	.03	.01
□	228	Don Slaught	.08	.03	.01
□	229	John Smiley	.12	.05	.01
□	230	Andy Van Slyke	.15	.06	.01
□	231	Bernard Gilkey	.25	.10	.02
□	232	Pedro Guerrero	.15	.06	.01
□	233	Rex Hudler	.08	.03	.01
□	234	Ray Lankford	.90	.40	.09
□	235	Joe Magrane	.08	.03	.01
□	236	Jose Oquendo	.08	.03	.01
□	237	Lee Smith	.12	.05	.01
□	238	Ozzie Smith	.35	.15	.03
□	239	Milt Thompson	.08	.03	.01
□	240	Todd Zeile	.30	.12	.03
□	241	Larry Andersen	.08	.03	.01
□	242	Andy Benes	.20	.08	.02
□	243	Paul Faries	.15	.06	.01
□	244	Tony Fernandez	.12	.05	.01
□	245	Tony Gwynn	.50	.20	.05
□	246	Atlee Hammaker	.08	.03	.01
□	247	Fred McGriff	.25	.10	.02
□	248	Bip Roberts	.08	.03	.01
□	249	Bentio Santiago	.15	.06	.01
□	250	Ed Whitson	.08	.03	.01
□	251	Dave Anderson	.08	.03	.01
□	252	Mike Benjamin	.08	.03	.01
□	253	John Burkett UER (Front photo actually Trevor Wilson)	.12	.05	.01
□	254	Will Clark	1.00	.40	.10
□	255	Scott Garrelts	.08	.03	.01
□	256	Willie McGee	.15	.06	.01
□	257	Kevin Mitchell	.30	.12	.03
□	258	Dave Righetti	.12	.05	.01
□	259	Matt Williams	.30	.12	.03
□	260	Black and Decker Bud Black Steve Decker	.17	.07	.01
□	261	Checklist Card 1-88 Sparky Anderson MG	.12	.02	.00
□	262	Checklist Card 89-176 Tom Lasorda MG	.12	.02	.00
□	263	Checklist Card 177-263 Tony LaRussa MG	.12	.02	.00
□	xx	Title Card (unnumbered)	.12	.05	.01

1989 Lennox HSE Astros

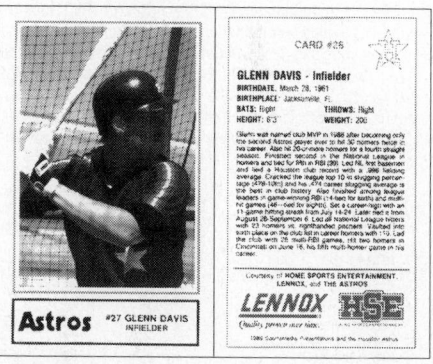

The 1989 Lennox HSE Astros set contains 26 cards measuring approximately 2 5/8" by 4 1/8". The fronts have color photos with burnt orange and white borders; the backs feature biographical information and career highlights. The set looks very much like the Police Astros sets of the previous years but is not since it was not sponsored by any Police Department and does not have a safety tip anywhere on the card.

		MINT	EXC	G-VG
COMPLETE SET (26)		7.00	3.00	.70
COMMON PLAYER (1-26)		.25	.10	.02
□ 1	Billy Hatcher	.35	.15	.03
□ 2	Greg Gross	.25	.10	.02
□ 3	Rick Rhoden	.25	.10	.02
□ 4	Mike Scott	.60	.25	.06

		MINT	EXC	G-VG
☐ 5	Kevin Bass	.35	.15	.03
☐ 6	Alex Trevino	.25	.10	.02
☐ 7	Jim Clancy	.25	.10	.02
☐ 8	Bill Doran	.35	.15	.03
☐ 9	Dan Schatzeder	.25	.10	.02
☐ 10	Bob Knepper	.25	.10	.02
☐ 11	Jim Deshaies	.35	.15	.03
☐ 12	Eric Yelding	.35	.15	.03
☐ 13	Danny Darwin	.25	.10	.02
☐ 14	Astros Coaches	.35	.15	.03
☐ 15	Craig Reynolds	.25	.10	.02
☐ 16	Rafael Ramirez	.25	.10	.02
☐ 17	Juan Agosto	.25	.10	.02
☐ 18	Larry Andersen	.25	.10	.02
☐ 19	Dave Smith	.35	.15	.03
☐ 20	Gerald Young	.35	.15	.03
☐ 21	Ken Caminiti	.35	.15	.03
☐ 22	Terry Puhl	.35	.15	.03
☐ 23	Bob Forsch	.35	.15	.03
☐ 24	Craig Biggio	.75	.30	.07
☐ 25	Art Howe MG	.35	.15	.03
☐ 26	Glenn Davis	.75	.30	.07

1990 Lennox HSE Astros

This 28-card, approximately 3 1/2" by 5", set (of 1990 Houston Astros) was issued in conjunction with HSE Cable Network and Lennox Heating and Air Conditioning as indicated on both the front and back of the cards. The front of the cards have full color portraits of the player while the back gives brief information about the player. The set has been checklisted below in alphabetical order with the player's uniform number noted next to his name.

		MINT	EXC	G-VG
COMPLETE SET (28)		11.00	5.00	1.35
COMMON PLAYER (1-28)		.40	.16	.04
☐ 1	Juan Agosto 49	.40	.16	.04
☐ 2	Larry Andersen 47	.40	.16	.04
☐ 3	Eric Anthony 23	.75	.30	.07
☐ 4	Craig Biggio 7	1.00	.40	.10
☐ 5	Ken Caminiti 11	.60	.25	.06
☐ 6	Casey Candaele 1	.40	.16	.04
☐ 7	Jose Cano 39	.40	.16	.04
☐ 8	Jim Clancy 38	.40	.16	.04
☐ 9	Danny Darwin 44	.40	.16	.04
☐ 10	Mark Davidson 22	.40	.16	.04
☐ 11	Glenn Davis 27	1.00	.40	.10
☐ 12	Jim Deshaies 43	.40	.16	.04
☐ 13	Bill Doran 19	.50	.20	.05
☐ 14	Bill Gullickson 36	.60	.25	.06
☐ 15	Xavier Hernandez 31	.40	.16	.04
☐ 16	Art Howe MG 18	.50	.20	.05
☐ 17	Mark Portugal 51	.50	.20	.05
☐ 18	Terry Puhl 21	.50	.20	.05
☐ 19	Rafael Ramirez 16	.40	.16	.04
☐ 20	David Rohde 6	.50	.20	.05
☐ 21	Dan Schatzeder 20	.40	.16	.04
☐ 22	Mike Scott 33	.75	.30	.07
☐ 23	Dave Smith 45	.50	.20	.05
☐ 24	Franklin Stubbs 24	.50	.20	.05
☐ 25	Alex Trevino 9	.40	.16	.04
☐ 26	Glenn Wilson 12	.40	.16	.04
☐ 27	Eric Yelding 15	.50	.20	.05
☐ 28	Gerald Young 13	.40	.16	.04

1991 Line Drive Ryne Sandberg

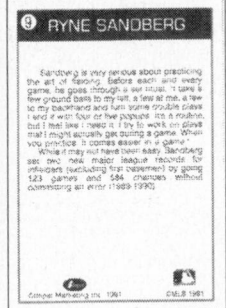

This 20-card set was sold as part of a boxed Ryne Sandberg Baseball Card Kit that included a personalized collector's album, the Ryne Sandberg Story, and a free mail-in offer to receive an 8" by 10" color photo of a top baseball star. The standard-size (2 1/2" by 3 1/2") cards feature color action photos, with blue borders on the left half of the card and red on the right half, on a white card face. In blue and red lettering, the player's name appears above the picture. In dark blue lettering and red borders, the back presents assorted information on Sandberg. The cards are numbered on the back.

		MINT	EXC	G-VG
COMPLETE SET (20)		10.00	4.50	1.25
COMMON PLAYER (1-20)		.75	.30	.07
☐ 1	Ryne Sandberg (Catching pop up)	.75	.30	.07
☐ 2	Ryne Sandberg (Running to 1st, Dodger in background)	.75	.30	.07
☐ 3	Ryne Sandberg (Ready to release bat)	.75	.30	.07
☐ 4	Ryne Sandberg (Glove on ground, Waiting for ball)	.75	.30	.07
☐ 5	Ryne Sandberg (Follow through, Hands crossed, Blue uniform)	.75	.30	.07
☐ 6	Ryne Sandberg (Blue uniform, Glove at waist)	.75	.30	.07
☐ 7	Ryne Sandberg (Bat just below waist)	.75	.30	.07
☐ 8	Ryne Sandberg (Posed ready to swing)	.75	.30	.07
☐ 9	Ryne Sandberg (Portrait shot with moustache)	.75	.30	.07
☐ 10	Ryne Sandberg (Transferring ball from glove to hand)	.75	.30	.07
☐ 11	Ryne Sandberg (Dropping bat running to first)	.75	.30	.07
☐ 12	Ryne Sandberg (Running the bases)	.75	.30	.07
☐ 13	Ryne Sandberg (Following through, end of swing, White uniform)	.75	.30	.07
☐ 14	Ryne Sandberg (Following through, end of swing, Blue uniform)	.75	.30	.07
☐ 15	Ryne Sandberg (Leading off base)	.75	.30	.07
☐ 16	Ryne Sandberg (Bat behind body)	.75	.30	.07
☐ 17	Ryne Sandberg (Throwing)	.75	.30	.07
☐ 18	Ryne Sandberg (Follow through, hands crossed, white uniform)	.75	.30	.07
☐ 19	Ryne Sandberg	.75	.30	.07

(Glove at waist,
White uniform)

			MINT	EXC	G-VG
☐	20	Ryne Sandberg	.75	.30	.07

(Beginning of swing)

☐	46	Casey Stengel	.25	.10	.02
☐	47	Satchel Paige	.35	.15	.03
☐	48	Ty Cobb	.50	.20	.05
☐	49	Mickey Cochrane	.15	.06	.01
☐	50	Dizzy Dean	.35	.15	.03

1991 Line Drive

 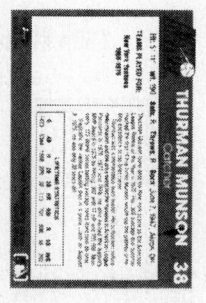

This 50-card set features notable retired players and managers. The cards measure the standard size (2 1/2" by 3 1/2"). The fronts of card numbers 1-42 have color player photos, with blue borders on a white card face. Card numbers 43-50 are similar in design but have sepia-toned photos. The backs of all cards are horizontally oriented and feature biography, career highlights, and lifetime statistics, all inside a red border. The cards are numbered on the back.

			MINT	EXC	G-VG
		COMPLETE SET (50)	8.00	3.50	.80
		COMMON PLAYER (1-50)	.10	.04	.01
☐	1	Don Drysdale	.40	.16	.04
☐	2	Joe Torre	.20	.08	.02
☐	3	Bob Gibson	.40	.16	.04
☐	4	Bobby Richardson	.20	.08	.02
☐	5	Ron Santo	.20	.08	.02
☐	6	Eric Soderholm	.10	.04	.01
☐	7	Yogi Berra	.50	.20	.05
☐	8	Steve Garvey	.40	.16	.04
☐	9	Steve Carlton	.50	.20	.05
☐	10	Toby Harrah	.10	.04	.01
☐	11	Luis Tiant	.15	.06	.01
☐	12	Earl Weaver MG	.15	.06	.01
☐	13	Bill Mazeroski	.15	.06	.01
☐	14	Don Baylor	.15	.06	.01
☐	15	Lew Burdette	.10	.04	.01
☐	16	Jim Lonborg	.10	.04	.01
☐	17	Jerry Grote	.10	.04	.01
☐	18	Ernie Banks	.40	.16	.04
☐	19	Doug DeCinces	.10	.04	.01
☐	20	Jimmy Piersall	.15	.06	.01
☐	21	Ken Holtzman	.10	.04	.01
☐	22	Manny Mota	.10	.04	.01
☐	23	Alvin Dark	.10	.04	.01
☐	24	Lou Brock	.40	.16	.04
☐	25	Ralph Houk	.10	.04	.01
☐	26	Graig Nettles	.15	.06	.01
☐	27	Bill White	.15	.06	.01
☐	28	Billy Williams	.30	.12	.03
☐	29	Willie Horton	.15	.06	.01
☐	30	Tommie Agee	.10	.04	.01
☐	31	Rico Petrocelli	.10	.04	.01
☐	32	Julio Cruz	.10	.04	.01
☐	33	Robin Roberts	.30	.12	.03
☐	34	Dave Johnson	.10	.04	.01
☐	35	Wilbur Wood	.10	.04	.01
☐	36	Cesar Cedeno	.15	.06	.01
☐	37	George Foster	.15	.06	.01
☐	38	Thurman Munson	.40	.16	.04
☐	39	Roberto Clemente	.50	.20	.05
☐	40	Eddie Mathews	.40	.16	.04
☐	41	Harmon Killebrew	.30	.12	.03
☐	42	Monte Irvin	.25	.10	.02
☐	43	Bob Feller	.30	.12	.03
☐	44	Jimmie Foxx	.20	.08	.02
☐	45	Walter Johnson	.25	.10	.02

1990 Little Sun Writers

This 24-card set honors some of the more influential writers in baseball history, i.e., "major league writers." Cards measure the standard, 2 1/2" by 3 1/2", and have yellow and green borders surrounding black and white photos of the writers pictured. The writer's name is given in black lettering below the picture. The backs have brief biographies of the writers along with "Did you know" features usually about writers not in the set. The cards are numbered on the back in the upper left corner.

			MINT	EXC	G-VG
		COMPLETE SET (24)	5.00	2.25	.50
		COMMON PLAYER (1-24)	.25	.10	.02
☐	1	Checklist Card	.25	.10	.02
☐	2	Henry Chadwick	.35	.15	.03
☐	3	Jacob C. Morse	.25	.10	.02
☐	4	Francis C. Richter	.25	.10	.02
☐	5	Grantland Rice	.35	.15	.03
☐	6	Lee Allen	.25	.10	.02
☐	7	Joe Reichler	.25	.10	.02
☐	8	Red Smith	.35	.15	.03
☐	9	Dick Young	.35	.15	.03
☐	10	Jim Brosnan	.35	.15	.03
☐	11	Charles Einstein	.45	.18	.04
☐	12	Lawrence Ritter	.35	.15	.03
☐	13	Roger Kahn	.35	.15	.03
☐	14	Robert Creamer	.35	.15	.03
☐	15	W.P. Kinsella	.35	.15	.03
☐	16	Harold Seymour	.25	.10	.02
☐	17	Ron Shelton	.25	.10	.02
☐	18	Tom Clark	.25	.10	.02
☐	19	Mark Harris	.25	.10	.02
☐	20	John Holway	.25	.10	.02
☐	21	Peter Golenbock	.35	.15	.03
☐	22	Jim Bouton	.60	.25	.06
☐	23	John Thorn	.35	.15	.03
☐	24	Mike Shannon	.25	.10	.02

(Not the ex-Cardinal player)

1960 MacGregor Staff

This 25-card set represents members of the MacGregor Sporting Goods Advisory Staff. Since the cards are unnumbered they ordered below in alphabetical order. The cards are blank backed and measure approximately 3 3/4" by 5". The photos are in black and white. The catalog designation for the set is H825-1. Cards have a facsimile autograph in white lettering on the front.

	NRMT	VG-E	GOOD
COMPLETE SET (25)	525.00	225.00	75.00
COMMON PLAYER (1-25)	10.00	4.50	1.25
□ 1 Hank Aaron	125.00	57.50	18.75
□ 2 Richie Ashburn	20.00	8.50	2.75
□ 3 Gus Bell	10.00	4.50	1.25
□ 4 Lou Berberet	10.00	4.50	1.25
□ 5 Jerry Casale	10.00	4.50	1.25
□ 6 Del Crandall	10.00	4.50	1.25
□ 7 Art Ditmar	10.00	4.50	1.25
□ 8 Gene Freese	10.00	4.50	1.25
□ 9 James Gilliam	13.50	6.00	1.85
□ 10 Ted Kluszewski	18.00	7.50	2.50
□ 11 Jim Landis	10.00	4.50	1.25
□ 12 Al Lopez	13.50	6.00	1.85
□ 13 Willie Mays	125.00	57.50	18.75
□ 14 Bill Mazeroski	13.50	6.00	1.85
□ 15 Mike McCormick	10.00	4.50	1.25
□ 16 Gil McDougald	13.50	6.00	1.85
□ 17 Russ Nixon	10.00	4.50	1.25
□ 18 Bill Rigney	10.00	4.50	1.25
□ 19 Robin Roberts	22.50	9.75	3.25
□ 20 Frank Robinson	40.00	18.00	6.00
□ 21 John Roseboro	10.00	4.50	1.25
□ 22 Red Schoendienst	22.50	9.75	3.25
□ 23 Bill Skowron	13.50	6.00	1.85
□ 24 Daryl Spencer	10.00	4.50	1.25
□ 25 Johnny Temple	10.00	4.50	1.25

1965 MacGregor Staff

This 10-card set represents members of the MacGregor Sporting Goods Advisory Staff. Since the cards are unnumbered they ordered below in alphabetical order. The cards are blank backed and measure approximately 3 9/16" by 5 1/8". The photos are in black and white. The catalog designation for the set is H825-2.

	NRMT	VG-E	GOOD
COMPLETE SET (10)	250.00	110.00	37.50
COMMON PLAYER (1-10)	8.00	3.50	.80

□ 1 Roberto Clemente	100.00	45.00	15.00
□ 2 Al Downing	8.00	3.50	.80
□ 3 Johnny Edwards	8.00	3.50	.80
□ 4 Ron Hansen	8.00	3.50	.80
□ 5 Deron Johnson	8.00	3.50	.80
□ 6 Willie Mays	110.00	50.00	16.50
□ 7 Tony Oliva	16.00	6.75	2.25
□ 8 Claude Osteen	8.00	3.50	.80
□ 9 Bobby Richardson	16.00	6.75	2.25
□ 10 Zoilo Versalles	8.00	3.50	.80

1989 Marathon Tigers

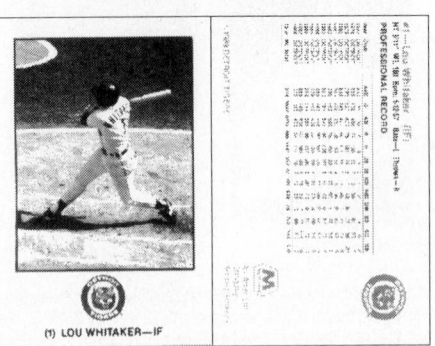

(1) LOU WHITAKER—IF

The 1989 Marathon Tigers set features 28 cards measuring 2 3/4" by 4 1/2". The set features color photos surrounded by blue borders and a white background. The Tigers logo is featured prominently under the photo and then the players uniform number name and position is underneath the Tiger logo. The horizontally oriented backs show career stats. The set was given away at the July 15, 1989 Tigers home game against the Seattle Mariners. The cards are numbered by the players' uniform numbers.

	MINT	EXC	G-VG
COMPLETE SET (28)	8.00	3.50	.80
COMMON PLAYER	.25	.10	.02
□ 1 Lou Whitaker	.60	.25	.06
□ 3 Alan Trammell	.90	.40	.09
□ 8 Mike Heath	.25	.10	.02
□ 9 Fred Lynn	.45	.18	.04
□ 10 Keith Moreland	.25	.10	.02
□ 11 Sparky Anderson MG	.45	.18	.04
□ 12 Mike Brumley	.25	.10	.02
□ 14 Dave Bergman	.25	.10	.02
□ 15 Pat Sheridan	.25	.10	.02
□ 17 Al Pedrique	.25	.10	.02
□ 18 Ramon Pena	.25	.10	.02
□ 19 Doyle Alexander	.35	.15	.03
□ 21 Guillermo Hernandez	.35	.15	.03
□ 23 Torey Lovullo	.25	.10	.02
□ 24 Gary Pettis	.25	.10	.02
□ 25 Ken Williams	.25	.10	.02
□ 26 Frank Tanana	.35	.15	.03
□ 27 Charles Hudson	.25	.10	.02
□ 32 Gary Ward	.25	.10	.02
□ 33 Matt Nokes	.45	.18	.04
□ 34 Chet Lemon	.35	.15	.03
□ 35 Rick Schu	.25	.10	.02
□ 36 Frank Williams	.25	.10	.02
□ 39 Mike Henneman	.35	.15	.03
□ 44 Jeff Robinson	.35	.15	.03
□ 47 Jack Morris	.90	.40	.09
□ 48 Paul Gibson	.35	.15	.03
□ xx Tiger Coaches	.35	.15	.03
Billy Consolo			
Alex Grammas			
Billy Muffet			
Vada Pinson			
Dick Tracewski			

1970 McDonald's Brewers

This 31-card set features cards measuring approximately 2 15/16" by 4 3/8" and was issued during the Brewers' first year in Milwaukee after moving from Seattle. The cards are drawings of the members of the 1970 Milwaukee Brewers and underneath the drawings there is information about the players. These cards are still often found in uncut sheet form and hence have no extra value in that form. The backs are blank. The set is checklisted alphabetically with the number of the sheet being listed next to the players name. There were six different sheets of six cards each although only one sheet contained six players; the other sheets depicted five players and a Brewers' logo.

		NRMT	VG-E	GOOD
COMPLETE SET (31)		6.50	2.75	.65
COMMON PLAYER (1-31)		.25	.10	.02
☐ 1	Max Alvis 6	.25	.10	.02
☐ 2	Bob Bolin 1	.25	.10	.02
☐ 3	Gene Brabender 3	.25	.10	.02
☐ 4	Dave Bristol 5	.35	.15	.03
☐ 5	Wayne Comer 2	.25	.10	.02
☐ 6	Cal Ermer 3	.25	.10	.02
☐ 7	John Gelner 4	.25	.10	.02
☐ 8	Greg Goossen 5	.25	.10	.02
☐ 9	Tommy Harper 5	.35	.15	.03
☐ 10	Mike Hegan 3	.35	.15	.03
☐ 11	Mike Hershberger 3	.25	.10	.02
☐ 12	Steve Hovley 2	.25	.10	.02
☐ 13	John Kennedy 2	.25	.10	.02
☐ 14	Lew Krausse 4	.25	.10	.02
☐ 15	Ted Kubiak 1	.25	.10	.02
☐ 16	George Lauzerique 6	.25	.10	.02
☐ 17	Bob Locker 5	.25	.10	.02
☐ 18	Roy McMillan 4	.35	.15	.03
☐ 19	Jerry McNertney 4	.25	.10	.02
☐ 20	Bob Meyer 2	.25	.10	.02
☐ 21	Jackie Moore 6	.35	.15	.03
☐ 22	John Morris 1	.25	.10	.02
☐ 23	John O'Donoghue 1	.25	.10	.02
☐ 24	Marty Pattin 6	.25	.10	.02
☐ 25	Rich Rollins 4	.35	.15	.03
☐ 26	Phil Roof 5	.25	.10	.02
☐ 27	Ted Savage 1	.25	.10	.02
☐ 28	Russ Snyder 6	.25	.10	.02
☐ 29	Wes Stock 2	.35	.15	.03
☐ 30	Sandy Valdespino 2	.25	.10	.02
☐ 31	Danny Walton 3	.25	.10	.02

1984 Mets Fan Club

The cards in this eight-player set measure 2 1/2" by 3 1/2". The sheets were produced by Topps for the New York Mets and feature only Mets. The full sheet measures 7 1/2" by 10 1/2".

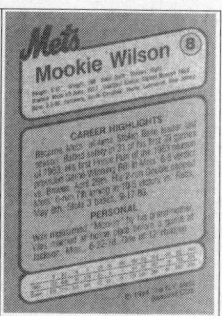

Cards are together on the sheet but are perforated for those collectors who want to separate the individual player cards. The middle (ninth) card is a Mets Fan club membership card which details various promotional days at Shea Stadium on the back. The cards are numbered on the back and printed in orange and blue.

		MINT	EXC	G-VG
COMPLETE SET (8)		12.00	5.25	1.50
COMMON PLAYER		.50	.20	.05
☐ 1	Dave Johnson MG	.60	.25	.06
☐ 2	Ron Darling	1.50	.60	.15
☐ 3	George Foster	1.00	.40	.10
☐ 4	Keith Hernandez	1.50	.60	.15
☐ 5	Jesse Orosco	.50	.20	.05
☐ 6	Rusty Staub	1.00	.40	.10
☐ 7	Darryl Strawberry	9.00	4.00	.90
☐ 8	Mookie Wilson	.75	.30	.07
☐ x	Membership Card	.50	.20	.05

1985 Mets Fan Club

The cards in this eight-player set measure 2 1/2" by 3 1/2". The sheets were produced by Topps for the New York Mets and feature only Mets players. The full sheet measures approximately 7 1/2" by 10 1/2". Cards are together on the sheet but are perforated for those collectors who want to separate the individual player cards. The middle (ninth) card is a Mets Fan club membership card. The set was available as a membership premium for joining the Junior Mets Fan Club for 4.00. The cards are listed below in alphabetical order for convenience.

		MINT	EXC	G-VG
COMPLETE SET (8)		18.00	7.50	2.50
COMMON PLAYER		.50	.20	.05
☐ 1	Wally Backman	.50	.20	.05
☐ 2	Bruce Berenyi	.50	.20	.05
☐ 3	Gary Carter	1.50	.60	.15

		MINT	EXC	G-VG
☐ 4	George Foster	1.00	.40	.10
☐ 5	Dwight Gooden	10.00	4.50	1.25
☐ 6	Keith Hernandez	1.50	.60	.15
☐ 7	Doug Sisk	.50	.20	.05
☐ 8	Darryl Strawberry	6.00	2.50	.60
☐ x	Membership Card	.50	.20	.05

1986 Mets Fan Club

 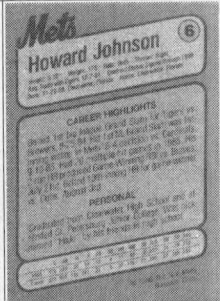

The cards in this eight-player set measure 2 1/2" by 3 1/2". The sheets were produced by Topps for the New York Mets and feature only Mets. The full sheet measures approximately 7 1/2" by 10 1/2". Cards are together on the sheet but are perforated for those collectors who want to separate the individual player cards. The middle (ninth) card is a Mets Fan club membership card. The set was available as a membership premium for joining the Junior Mets Fan Club for 5.00. The cards are listed below in alphabetical order for convenience.

		MINT	EXC	G-VG
COMPLETE SET (8)		14.00	6.25	2.00
COMMON PLAYER		.50	.20	.05
☐ 1	Wally Backman	.50	.20	.05
☐ 2	Gary Carter	1.50	.60	.15
☐ 3	Ron Darling	1.00	.40	.10
☐ 4	Dwight Gooden	5.00	2.25	.50
☐ 5	Keith Hernandez	1.50	.60	.15
☐ 6	Howard Johnson	1.50	.60	.15
☐ 7	Roger McDowell	.75	.30	.07
☐ 8	Darryl Strawberry	5.00	2.25	.50
☐ x	Membership Card	.50	.20	.05

1987 Mets Fan Club

The cards in this eight-player set measure 2 1/2" by 3 1/2". The sheets were produced by Topps for the New York Mets and feature only Mets. The full sheet measures approximately 7 1/2" by 10 1/2". Cards are together on the sheet but are perforated for those collectors who want to separate the individual player cards. The cards have an outer orange border. The set was available as a membership premium for joining the Junior Mets Fan Club for 6.00. The set and club were also sponsored by Farmland Dairies Milk. The cards are unnumbered on the back although they do contain the player's uniform number on the front.

		MINT	EXC	G-VG
COMPLETE SET (9)		9.00	4.00	.90
COMMON PLAYER		.50	.20	.05
☐ 1	Gary Carter 8	1.50	.60	.15
☐ 2	Ron Darling 12	1.00	.40	.10
☐ 3	Lenny Dykstra 4	1.25	.50	.12
☐ 4	Roger McDowell 42	.60	.25	.06

		MINT	EXC	G-VG
☐ 5	Kevin McReynolds 22	2.00	.80	.20
☐ 6	Bob Ojeda 19	.75	.30	.07
☐ 7	Darryl Strawberry 18	5.00	2.25	.50
☐ 8	Mookie Wilson 1	.60	.25	.06
☐ 9	Mets Team Card	.50	.20	.05
	(1986 World Champs)			

1988 Mets Fan Club

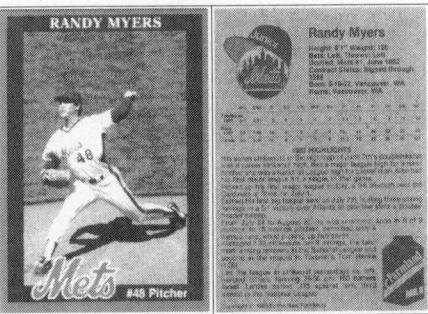

The cards in this nine-player set measure 2 1/2" by 3 1/2". The sheets were produced by Topps for the New York Mets and feature only Mets. The full sheet measures 7 1/2" by 10 1/2". Cards are together on the sheet but are perforated for those collectors who want to separate the individual player cards. The cards have an outer orange border and an inner dark blue border. The set was available as a membership premium for joining the Junior Mets Fan Club for 6.00. The set and club were also sponsored by Farmland Dairies Milk. The cards are unnumbered on the back although they do contain the player's uniform number on the front.

		MINT	EXC	G-VG
COMPLETE SET (9)		6.00	2.50	.60
COMMON PLAYER		.40	.16	.04
☐ 8	Gary Carter	.90	.40	.09
☐ 16	Dwight Gooden	1.00	.40	.10
☐ 17	Keith Hernandez	.75	.30	.07
☐ 18	Darryl Strawberry	2.00	.80	.20
☐ 20	Howard Johnson	1.00	.40	.10
☐ 21	Kevin Elster	.50	.20	.05
☐ 42	Roger McDowell	.40	.16	.04
☐ 48	Randy Myers	.50	.20	.05
☐ 50	Sid Fernandez	.60	.25	.06

1989 Mets Fan Club

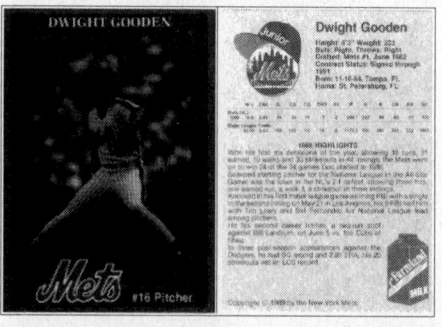

This set was produced by Topps for the Mets Fan Club as a sheet of nine cards each featuring a member of the New York Mets. The individual cards are standard size, 2 1/2" by 3 1/2"; however the set is typically traded as a sheet rather than as individual cards.

	MINT	EXC	G-VG
COMPLETE SET (9)	6.00	2.50	.60
COMMON PLAYER	.40	.16	.04
☐ 8 Gary Carter	.90	.40	.09
☐ 9 Gregg Jefferies	1.25	.50	.12
☐ 16 Dwight Gooden	1.00	.40	.10
☐ 18 Darryl Strawberry	1.50	.60	.15
☐ 22 Kevin McReynolds	.75	.30	.07
☐ 25 Keith Miller	.50	.20	.05
☐ 42 Roger McDowell	.40	.16	.04
☐ 44 David Cone	1.00	.40	.10
☐ xx Mets Team Card	.50	.20	.05
Eastern Div. Champs			

1990 Mets Fan Club

The 1990 Mets Fan Club Tropicana set was issued by the New York Mets fan club in association with the Tropicana Juice Company. For the seventh year, the Mets issued a perforated card sheet in conjunction with their fan clubs. This nine-card, standard-size (2 1/2" by 3 1/2") set is skip-numbered and arranged by uniform numbers.

	MINT	EXC	G-VG
COMPLETE SET (9)	6.00	2.50	.60
COMMON PLAYER	.40	.16	.04
☐ 9 Gregg Jefferies	.90	.40	.09
☐ 16 Dwight Gooden	.90	.40	.09
☐ 18 Darryl Strawberry	1.00	.40	.10

☐ 20 Howard Johnson	.90	.40	.09
☐ 21 Kevin Elster	.40	.16	.04
☐ 25 Keith Miller	.50	.20	.05
☐ 29 Frank Viola	.75	.30	.07
☐ 44 David Cone	.75	.30	.07
☐ 50 Sid Fernandez	.50	.20	.05

1984 Milton Bradley

The cards in this 30-card set measure 2 1/2" by 3 1/2". This set of full color cards was produced by Topps for the Milton Bradley Co. The set was included in a board game entitled Championship Baseball. The fronts feature portraits of the players and the name, Championship Baseball, by Milton Bradley. The backs feature the Topps logo, statistics for the past year (pitchers' cards have career statistics), and dice rolls which are part of the board game. Pitcher cards have no dice roll charts. There are 15 players from each league. These unnumbered cards are listed below in alphabetical order. The cap logos and uniforms have been air-brushed to remove all team references.

	MINT	EXC	G-VG
COMPLETE SET (30)	11.00	5.00	1.35
COMMON PLAYER (1-30)	.15	.06	.01
☐ 1 Wade Boggs	1.00	.40	.10
☐ 2 George Brett	.90	.40	.09
☐ 3 Rod Carew	.75	.30	.07
☐ 4 Steve Carlton	.60	.25	.06
☐ 5 Gary Carter	.35	.15	.03
☐ 6 Dave Concepcion	.20	.08	.02
☐ 7 Cecil Cooper	.15	.06	.01
☐ 8 Andre Dawson	.50	.20	.05
☐ 9 Carlton Fisk	.50	.20	.05
☐ 10 Steve Garvey	.40	.16	.04
☐ 11 Pedro Guerrero	.25	.10	.02
☐ 12 Ron Guidry	.25	.10	.02
☐ 13 Rickey Henderson	1.00	.40	.10
☐ 14 Reggie Jackson	.90	.40	.09
☐ 15 Ron Kittle	.15	.06	.01
☐ 16 Bill Madlock	.15	.06	.01
☐ 17 Dale Murphy	.60	.25	.06
☐ 18 Al Oliver	.15	.06	.01
☐ 19 Darrell Porter	.15	.06	.01
☐ 20 Cal Ripken	1.00	.40	.10
☐ 21 Pete Rose	1.00	.40	.10
☐ 22 Steve Sax	.25	.10	.02
☐ 23 Mike Schmidt	1.00	.40	.10
☐ 24 Ted Simmons	.20	.08	.02
☐ 25 Ozzie Smith	.50	.20	.05
☐ 26 Dave Stieb	.20	.08	.02
☐ 27 Fernando Valenzuela	.20	.08	.02
☐ 28 Lou Whitaker	.25	.10	.02
☐ 29 Dave Winfield	.35	.15	.03
☐ 30 Robin Yount	.90	.40	.09

1987 MnM's Star Lineup

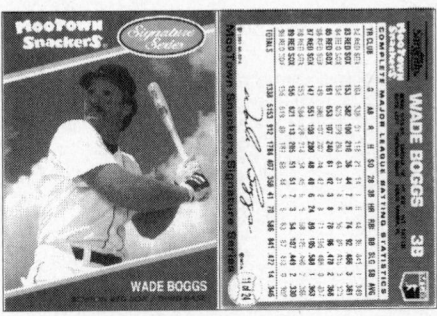

The Mars Candy Company is the sponsor of this 24-card set of cards. The cards were printed in perforated pairs. The pairs measure 5" by 3 1/2" whereas the individual cards measure the standard 2 1/2" by 3 1/2". The players are shown without team logos. The cards were designed and produced by MSA, Mike Schechter Associates. The cards are numbered on the front and back. The backs show statistics for every year since 1980 even if the player was not even playing during those earlier years. The values below are for individual players; panels intact would be valued at 25 percent more than the sum of the two individual players.

	MINT	EXC	G-VG
COMPLETE SET (24)	9.00	4.00	.90
COMMON PLAYER (1-24)	.30	.12	.03
☐ 1 Wally Joyner	.75	.30	.07
☐ 2 Tony Pena	.30	.12	.03
☐ 3 Mike Schmidt	1.00	.40	.10
☐ 4 Ryne Sandberg	1.25	.50	.12
☐ 5 Wade Boggs	1.00	.40	.10
☐ 6 Jack Morris	.60	.25	.06
☐ 7 Roger Clemens	1.25	.50	.12
☐ 8 Harold Baines	.40	.16	.04
☐ 9 Dale Murphy	.75	.30	.07
☐ 10 Jose Canseco	1.25	.50	.12
☐ 11 Don Mattingly	1.25	.50	.12
☐ 12 Gary Carter	.60	.25	.06
☐ 13 Cal Ripken	1.25	.50	.12
☐ 14 George Brett	.90	.40	.09
☐ 15 Kirby Puckett	.90	.40	.09
☐ 16 Joe Carter	.50	.20	.05
☐ 17 Mike Witt	.30	.12	.03
☐ 18 Mike Scott	.35	.15	.03
☐ 19 Fernando Valenzuela	.35	.15	.03
☐ 20 Steve Garvey	.60	.25	.06
☐ 21 Steve Sax	.40	.16	.04
☐ 22 Nolan Ryan	1.75	.70	.17
☐ 23 Tony Gwynn	.90	.40	.09
☐ 24 Ozzie Smith	.60	.25	.06

1991 MooTown Snackers

This 24-card standard size (2 1/2" by 3 1/2") set was sponsored by MooTown Snackers. One player card and an attached mail-in certificate (with checklist on back) were included in five-ounce packages of MooTown Snackers cheese snacks. The complete set could be purchased through the mail by sending in the mail-in certificate, three MooTown Snackers UPC codes, and 5.95. The front features a high gloss color action player photo, which is mounted diagonally on the card face. White and yellow stripes border the picture above and below. At the card top appears the company logo on a red triangle, while the words "Signature Series" appears in an aqua blue oval in the upper right corner. The player's name appears in the red triangle

below the picture. The backs present statistical information in red, white, and black. On the bottom of the card a facsimile autograph and a card number round out the back.

	MINT	EXC	G-VG
COMPLETE SET (24)	13.50	5.50	1.50
COMMON PLAYER (1-24)	.30	.12	.03
☐ 1 Jose Canseco	1.00	.40	.10
☐ 2 Kirby Puckett	.75	.30	.07
☐ 3 Barry Bonds	.60	.25	.06
☐ 4 Ken Griffey Jr.	2.00	.80	.20
☐ 5 Ryne Sandberg	1.00	.40	.10
☐ 6 Tony Gwynn	.75	.30	.07
☐ 7 Kal Daniels	.30	.12	.03
☐ 8 Ozzie Smith	.50	.20	.05
☐ 9 Dave Justice	1.25	.50	.12
☐ 10 Sandy Alomar Jr.	.40	.16	.04
☐ 11 Wade Boggs	.90	.40	.09
☐ 12 Ozzie Guillen	.30	.12	.03
☐ 13 Dave Magadan	.30	.12	.03
☐ 14 Cal Ripken	1.00	.40	.10
☐ 15 Don Mattingly	.90	.40	.09
☐ 16 Ruben Sierra	.75	.30	.07
☐ 17 Robin Yount	.75	.30	.07
☐ 18 Len Dykstra	.30	.12	.03
☐ 19 George Brett	.75	.30	.07
☐ 20 Lance Parrish	.30	.12	.03
☐ 21 Chris Sabo	.40	.16	.04
☐ 22 Craig Biggio	.40	.16	.04
☐ 23 Kevin Mitchell	.60	.25	.06
☐ 24 Cecil Fielder	.75	.30	.07

1959 Morrell

The cards in this 12-card set measure 2 1/2" by 3 1/2". The 1959 Morrell Meats set of full color, unnumbered cards features Los Angeles Dodger players only. The photos used are the same as those selected for the Dodger team issue postcards in 1959.

The Morrell Meats logo is on the backs of the cards. The Clem Labine card actually features a picture of Stan Williams and the Norm Larker card actually features a picture of Joe Pignatano as indicated in the checklist below. The catalog designation is F172-1.

	NRMT	VG-E	GOOD
COMPLETE SET (12)	1350.00	600.00	135.00
COMMON PLAYER (1-12)	70.00	32.00	10.50
☐ 1 Don Drysdale	150.00	67.50	22.50
☐ 2 Carl Furillo	90.00	40.00	13.50
☐ 3 Jim Gilliam	90.00	40.00	13.50
☐ 4 Gil Hodges	150.00	67.50	22.50
☐ 5 Sandy Koufax	300.00	135.00	45.00
☐ 6 Clem Labine UER (photo actually Stan Williams)	70.00	32.00	10.50
☐ 7 Norm Larker UER (photo actually Joe Pignatano)	70.00	32.00	10.50
☐ 8 Charlie Neal	70.00	32.00	10.50
☐ 9 Johnny Podres	90.00	40.00	13.50
☐ 10 John Roseboro	70.00	32.00	10.50
☐ 11 Duke Snider	300.00	135.00	45.00
☐ 12 Don Zimmer	90.00	40.00	13.50

1960 Morrell

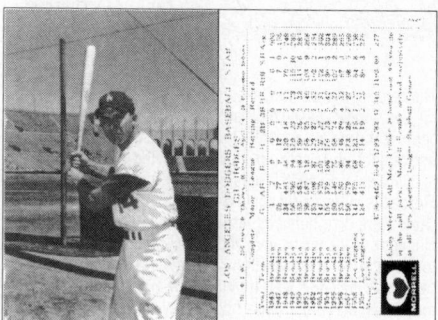

The cards in this 12-card set measure 2 1/2" by 3 1/2". The 1960 Morrell Meats set of full color, unnumbered cards is similar in format to the 1959 Morrell set but can be distinguished from the 1959 set by a red heart which appears in the Morrell logo on the back. The photos used are the same as those selected for the Dodger team issue postcards in 1960. The Furillo, Hodges, and Snider cards received limited distribution and are hence more scarce. The catalog designation is F172-2. The cards were printed in Japan.

	NRMT	VG-E	GOOD
COMPLETE SET (12)	900.00	400.00	135.00
COMMON PLAYER (1-12)	22.00	9.50	3.15
☐ 1 Walt Alston MG	45.00	20.00	6.75
☐ 2 Roger Craig	33.00	15.00	5.00
☐ 3 Don Drysdale	60.00	27.00	9.00
☐ 4 Carl Furillo SP	100.00	45.00	15.00
☐ 5 Gil Hodges SP	150.00	67.50	22.50
☐ 6 Sandy Koufax	150.00	67.50	22.50
☐ 7 Wally Moon	22.00	9.50	3.15
☐ 8 Charlie Neal	22.00	9.50	3.15
☐ 9 Johnny Podres	27.00	12.00	4.00
☐ 10 John Roseboro	22.00	9.50	3.15
☐ 11 Larry Sherry	22.00	9.50	3.15
☐ 12 Duke Snider SP	300.00	135.00	45.00

1961 Morrell

The cards in this 6-card set measure 2 1/2" by 3 1/2". The 1961 Morrell Meats set of full color, unnumbered cards features Los Angeles Dodger players only and contains statistical information on the backs of the cards in brown print. The catalog designation is F172-3.

	NRMT	VG-E	GOOD
COMPLETE SET (6)	250.00	110.00	37.50
COMMON PLAYER (1-6)	18.00	7.50	2.50
☐ 1 Tommy Davis	22.00	9.50	3.15
☐ 2 Don Drysdale	55.00	25.00	8.25
☐ 3 Frank Howard	27.00	12.00	4.00
☐ 4 Sandy Koufax	135.00	60.00	20.00
☐ 5 Norm Larker	18.00	7.50	2.50
☐ 6 Maury Wills	40.00	18.00	6.00

1983 Mother's Giants

The cards in this 20-card set measure 2 1/2" by 3 1/2". For the first time in 30 years, Mother's Cookies issued a baseball card set. The full color set, produced by hobbyist Barry Colla, features San Francisco Giants players only. Fifteen cards were issued at the Astros vs. Giants game of August 7, 1983. Five of the cards were redeemable by sending in a coupon. The five additional cards received from redemption of the coupon were not guaranteed to be the five needed to complete the set. The fronts feature the player's photo, his name, and the Giants' logo, while the backs feature player biographies and the Mother's Cookies logo. The backs also contain a space in which to obtain the player's autograph.

		MINT	EXC	G-VG
	COMPLETE SET (20)	18.00	7.50	2.50
	COMMON PLAYER (1-20)	.60	.25	.06
☐ 1	Frank Robinson MG	3.00	1.25	.30
☐ 2	Jack Clark	2.50	1.00	.25
☐ 3	Chili Davis	2.00	.80	.20
☐ 4	Johnnie LeMaster	.60	.25	.06
☐ 5	Greg Minton	.75	.30	.07
☐ 6	Bob Brenly	.60	.25	.06
☐ 7	Fred Breining	.60	.25	.06
☐ 8	Jeff Leonard	.90	.40	.09
☐ 9	Darrell Evans	1.25	.50	.12
☐ 10	Tom O'Malley	.60	.25	.06
☐ 11	Duane Kuiper	.60	.25	.06
☐ 12	Mike Krukow	.75	.30	.07
☐ 13	Atlee Hammaker	.75	.30	.07
☐ 14	Gary Lavelle	.60	.25	.06
☐ 15	Bill Laskey	.60	.25	.06
☐ 16	Max Venable	.60	.25	.06
☐ 17	Joel Youngblood	.60	.25	.06
☐ 18	Dave Bergman	.60	.25	.06
☐ 19	Mike Vail	.60	.25	.06
☐ 20	Andy McGaffigan	.60	.25	.06

☐ 19	Jim Essian	.50	.20	.05
☐ 20	Mike Warren	.40	.16	.04
☐ 21	Davey Lopes	.50	.20	.05
☐ 22	Ray Burris	.50	.20	.05
☐ 23	Tony Phillips	.60	.25	.06
☐ 24	Tim Conroy	.40	.16	.04
☐ 25	Jeff Bettendorf	.40	.16	.04
☐ 26	Keith Atherton	.40	.16	.04
☐ 27	A's Coaches	.40	.16	.04
☐ 28	A's Checklist	.50	.20	.05

1984 Mother's Astros

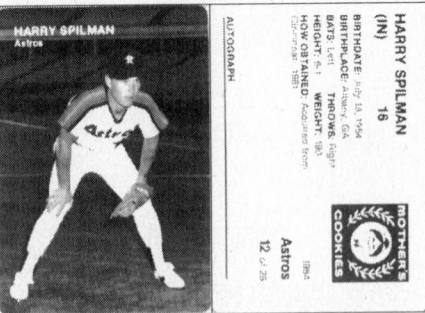

The cards in this 28-card set measure 2 1/2" by 3 1/2". In 1984, the Los Angeles based Mother's Cookies Co. issued five sets of cards featuring players from major league teams. The Houston Astros set features current players depicted by photos. Similar to their 1952 and 1953 issues, the cards have rounded corners. The backs of the cards contain the Mother's Cookies logo. The cards were distributed in partial sets to fans at the respective stadiums of the teams involved. Whereas 20 cards were given to each patron, a redemption card, redeemable for eight more cards was included. Unfortunately, the eight cards received by redeeming the coupon were not necessarily the eight needed to complete a set. Hobbyist Barry Colla was involved in the production of these sets.

		MINT	EXC	G-VG
	COMPLETE SET (28)	15.00	6.50	2.15
	COMMON PLAYER (1-28)	.35	.15	.03
☐ 1	Nolan Ryan	7.50	3.25	.75
☐ 2	Joe Niekro	.75	.30	.07
☐ 3	Alan Ashby	.45	.18	.04
☐ 4	Bill Doran	.90	.40	.09
☐ 5	Phil Garner	.60	.25	.06
☐ 6	Ray Knight	.60	.25	.06
☐ 7	Dickie Thon	.60	.25	.06
☐ 8	Jose Cruz	.60	.25	.06
☐ 9	Jerry Mumphrey	.35	.15	.03
☐ 10	Terry Puhl	.45	.18	.04
☐ 11	Enos Cabell	.35	.15	.03
☐ 12	Harry Spilman	.35	.15	.03
☐ 13	Dave Smith	.60	.25	.06
☐ 14	Mike Scott	1.25	.50	.12
☐ 15	Bob Lillis MG	.35	.15	.03
☐ 16	Bob Knepper	.35	.15	.03
☐ 17	Frank DiPino	.35	.15	.03
☐ 18	Tom Wieghaus	.35	.15	.03
☐ 19	Denny Walling	.35	.15	.03
☐ 20	Tony Scott	.35	.15	.03
☐ 21	Alan Bannister	.35	.15	.03
☐ 22	Bill Dawley	.35	.15	.03
☐ 23	Vern Ruhle	.35	.15	.03
☐ 24	Mike LaCoss	.35	.15	.03
☐ 25	Mike Madden	.35	.15	.03
☐ 26	Craig Reynolds	.45	.18	.04
☐ 27	Astros' Coaches	.35	.15	.03
☐ 28	Astros' Checklist	.35	.15	.03

1984 Mother's A's

The cards in this 28-card set measure 2 1/2" by 3 1/2". In 1984, the Los Angeles based Mother's Cookies Co. issued five sets of cards featuring players from major league teams. The Oakland A's set features current players depicted by photos. Similar to their 1952 and 1953 issues, the cards have rounded corners. The backs of the cards contain the Mother's Cookies logo. The cards were distributed in partial sets to fans at the respective stadiums of the teams involved. Whereas 20 cards were given to each patron, a redemption card, redeemable for eight more cards was included. Unfortunately, the eight cards received by redeeming the coupon were not necessarily the eight needed to complete a set. Hobbyist Barry Colla was involved in the production of these sets.

		MINT	EXC	G-VG
	COMPLETE SET (28)	17.00	7.25	2.50
	COMMON PLAYER (1-28)	.40	.16	.04
☐ 1	Steve Boros MG	.40	.16	.04
☐ 2	Rickey Henderson	6.75	3.00	.90
☐ 3	Joe Morgan	2.25	.90	.22
☐ 4	Dwayne Murphy	.60	.25	.06
☐ 5	Mike Davis	.50	.20	.05
☐ 6	Bruce Bochte	.40	.16	.04
☐ 7	Carney Lansford	.90	.40	.09
☐ 8	Steve McCatty	.40	.16	.04
☐ 9	Mike Heath	.40	.16	.04
☐ 10	Chris Codiroli	.40	.16	.04
☐ 11	Bill Almon	.40	.16	.04
☐ 12	Bill Caudill	.50	.20	.05
☐ 13	Donnie Hill	.40	.16	.04
☐ 14	Lary Sorensen	.40	.16	.04
☐ 15	Dave Kingman	.80	.35	.08
☐ 16	Garry Hancock	.40	.16	.04
☐ 17	Jeff Burroughs	.50	.20	.05
☐ 18	Tom Burgmeier	.40	.16	.04

1984 Mother's Giants

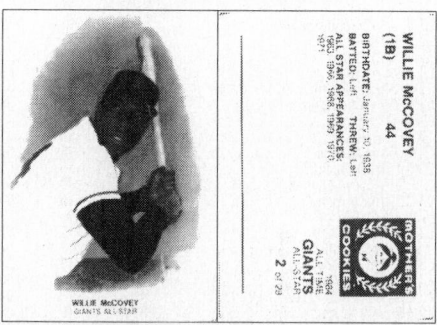

The cards in this 28-card set measure 2 1/2" by 3 1/2". In 1984, the Los Angeles based Mother's Cookies Co. issued five sets of cards featuring players from major league teams. The San Francisco Giants set features previous Giant All-Star selections depicted by drawings. Similar to their 1952 and 1953 issues, the cards have rounded corners. The backs of the cards contain the Mother's Cookies logo. The cards were distributed in partial sets to fans at the respective stadiums of the teams involved. Whereas 20 cards were given to each patron, a redemption card, redeemable for eight more cards was included. Unfortunately, the eight cards received by redeeming the coupon were not necessarily the eight needed to complete a set. Hobbyist Barry Colla was involved in the production of these sets.

		MINT	EXC	G-VG
	COMPLETE SET (28)	16.00	6.75	2.25
	COMMON PLAYER (1-28)	.40	.16	.04
☐	1 Willie Mays	4.00	1.75	.40
☐	2 Willie McCovey	2.50	1.00	.25
☐	3 Juan Marichal	2.00	.80	.20
☐	4 Gaylord Perry	2.00	.80	.20
☐	5 Tom Haller	.40	.16	.04
☐	6 Jim Davenport	.40	.16	.04
☐	7 Jack Clark	1.25	.50	.12
☐	8 Greg Minton	.40	.16	.04
☐	9 Atlee Hammaker	.40	.16	.04
☐	10 Gary Lavelle	.40	.16	.04
☐	11 Orlando Cepeda	1.00	.40	.10
☐	12 Bobby Bonds	.80	.35	.08
☐	13 John Antonelli	.40	.16	.04
☐	14 Bob Schmidt (photo actually Wes Westrum)	.40	.16	.04
☐	15 Sam Jones	.40	.16	.04
☐	16 Mike McCormick	.40	.16	.04
☐	17 Ed Bailey	.40	.16	.04
☐	18 Stu Miller	.40	.16	.04
☐	19 Felipe Alou	.60	.25	.06
☐	20 Jim Ray Hart	.40	.16	.04
☐	21 Dick Dietz	.40	.16	.04
☐	22 Chris Speier	.40	.16	.04
☐	23 Bobby Murcer	.60	.25	.06
☐	24 John Montefusco	.40	.16	.04
☐	25 Vida Blue	.50	.20	.05
☐	26 Ed Whitson	.50	.20	.05
☐	27 Darrell Evans	.75	.30	.07
☐	28 Checklist Card	.40	.16	.04

1984 Mother's Mariners

The cards in this 28-card set measure 2 1/2" by 3 1/2". In 1984, The Los Angeles-based Mother's Cookies Co. issued five sets of cards featuring players from major league teams. The Seattle Mariners set features current players depicted by photos. Similar to their 1952 and 1953 issues, the cards have rounded

corners. The backs of the cards contain the Mother's Cookies logo. The cards were distributed in partial sets to fans at the respective stadiums of the teams involved. Whereas 20 cards were given to each patron, a redemption card, redeemable for eight more cards was included. Unfortunately, the eight cards received by redeeming the coupon were not necessarily the eight needed to complete a set. Hobbyist Barry Colla was involved in the production of these sets.

		MINT	EXC	G-VG
	COMPLETE SET (28)	15.00	6.50	2.15
	COMMON PLAYER (1-28)	.40	.16	.04
☐	1 Del Crandall MG	.50	.20	.05
☐	2 Barry Bonnell	.40	.16	.04
☐	3 Dave Henderson	.90	.40	.09
☐	4 Bob Kearney	.40	.16	.04
☐	5 Mike Moore	1.00	.40	.10
☐	6 Spike Owen	.50	.20	.05
☐	7 Gorman Thomas	.60	.25	.06
☐	8 Ed VandeBerg	.40	.16	.04
☐	9 Matt Young	.40	.16	.04
☐	10 Larry Milbourne	.40	.16	.04
☐	11 Dave Beard	.40	.16	.04
☐	12 Jim Beattie	.40	.16	.04
☐	13 Mark Langston	3.50	1.50	.35
☐	14 Orlando Mercado	.40	.16	.04
☐	15 Jack Perconte	.40	.16	.04
☐	16 Pat Putnam	.40	.16	.04
☐	17 Paul Mirabella	.40	.16	.04
☐	18 Domingo Ramos	.40	.16	.04
☐	19 Al Cowens	.40	.16	.04
☐	20 Mike Stanton	.40	.16	.04
☐	21 Steve Henderson	.40	.16	.04
☐	22 Bob Stoddard	.40	.16	.04
☐	23 Alvin Davis	2.00	.80	.20
☐	24 Phil Bradley	.90	.40	.09
☐	25 Roy Thomas	.40	.16	.04
☐	26 Darnell Coles	.50	.20	.05
☐	27 Mariners' Coaches	.40	.16	.04
☐	28 Mariners' Checklist	.40	.16	.04

1984 Mother's Padres

The cards in this 28-card set measure 2 1/2" by 3 1/2". In 1984, the Los Angeles based Mother's Cookies Co. issued five sets of cards featuring players from major league teams. The San Diego Padres set features current players depicted by photos. Similar to their 1952 and 1953 issues, the cards have rounded corners. The backs of the cards contain the Mother's Cookies logo. The cards were distributed in partial sets to fans at the respective stadiums of the teams involved. Whereas 20 cards were given to each patron, a redemption card, redeemable for eight more cards was included. Unfortunately, the eight cards received by redeeming the coupon were not necessarily the eight needed to complete a set. Hobbyist Barry Colla was involved in the production of these sets.

	MINT	EXC	G-VG
COMPLETE SET (28)	20.00	8.50	2.75
COMMON PLAYER (1-28)	.50	.20	.05
☐ 1 Dick Williams MG	.60	.25	.06
☐ 2 Rich Gossage	1.00	.40	.10
☐ 3 Tim Lollar	.50	.20	.05
☐ 4 Eric Show	.75	.30	.07
☐ 5 Terry Kennedy	.60	.25	.06
☐ 6 Kurt Bevacqua	.50	.20	.05
☐ 7 Steve Garvey	2.00	.80	.20
☐ 8 Garry Templeton	.60	.25	.06
☐ 9 Tony Gwynn	5.00	2.25	.50
☐ 10 Alan Wiggins	.50	.20	.05
☐ 11 Dave Dravecky	1.25	.50	.12
☐ 12 Tim Flannery	.50	.20	.05
☐ 13 Kevin McReynolds	3.50	1.50	.35
☐ 14 Bobby Brown	.50	.20	.05
☐ 15 Ed Whitson	.75	.30	.07
☐ 16 Doug Gwosdz	.50	.20	.05
☐ 17 Luis DeLeon	.50	.20	.05
☐ 18 Andy Hawkins	.75	.30	.07
☐ 19 Craig Lefferts	.60	.25	.06
☐ 20 Carmelo Martinez	.60	.25	.06
☐ 21 Sid Monge	.50	.20	.05
☐ 22 Graig Nettles	.75	.30	.07
☐ 23 Mario Ramirez	.50	.20	.05
☐ 24 Luis Salazar	.60	.25	.06
☐ 25 Champ Summers	.50	.20	.05
☐ 26 Mark Thurmond	.50	.20	.05
☐ 27 Padres' Coaches	.50	.20	.05
☐ 28 Padres' Checklist	.50	.20	.05

1985 Mother's A's

The cards in this 28-card set measure 2 1/2" by 3 1/2". In 1985, the Los Angeles based Mother's Cookies Co. again issued five sets of cards featuring players from major league teams. The Oakland A's set features current players depicted by photos on cards with rounded corners. The backs of the cards contain the Mother's Cookies logo. Cards were passed out at the stadium on July 6.

	MINT	EXC	G-VG
COMPLETE SET (28)	12.00	5.25	1.50
COMMON PLAYER (1-28)	.35	.15	.03
☐ 1 Jackie Moore MG	.35	.15	.03
☐ 2 Dave Kingman	.75	.30	.07
☐ 3 Don Sutton	1.25	.50	.12
☐ 4 Mike Heath	.35	.15	.03
☐ 5 Alfredo Griffin	.45	.18	.04
☐ 6 Dwayne Murphy	.45	.18	.04
☐ 7 Mike Davis	.45	.18	.04
☐ 8 Carney Lansford	.75	.30	.07
☐ 9 Chris Codiroli	.35	.15	.03
☐ 10 Bruce Bochte	.35	.15	.03
☐ 11 Mickey Tettleton	.90	.40	.09
☐ 12 Donnie Hill	.35	.15	.03
☐ 13 Rob Picciolo	.35	.15	.03
☐ 14 Dave Collins	.35	.15	.03
☐ 15 Dusty Baker	.45	.18	.04
☐ 16 Tim Conroy	.35	.15	.03
☐ 17 Keith Atherton	.35	.15	.03
☐ 18 Jay Howell	.45	.18	.04
☐ 19 Mike Warren	.35	.15	.03
☐ 20 Steve McCatty	.35	.15	.03
☐ 21 Bill Krueger	.35	.15	.03
☐ 22 Curt Young	.45	.18	.04
☐ 23 Dan Meyer	.35	.15	.03
☐ 24 Mike Gallego	.45	.18	.04
☐ 25 Jeff Kaiser	.35	.15	.03
☐ 26 Steve Henderson	.35	.15	.03
☐ 27 A's Coaches	.35	.15	.03
☐ 28 A's Checklist	.35	.15	.03

1985 Mother's Astros

The cards in this 28-card set measure 2 1/2" by 3 1/2". In 1985, the Los Angeles-based Mother's Cookies Co. again issued five sets of cards featuring players from major league teams. The Houston Astros set features current players depicted by photos on cards with rounded corners. The backs of the cards contain the Mother's Cookies logo. Cards were passed out at the stadium on July 13. The checklist card features the Astros logo on the obverse.

	MINT	EXC	G-VG
COMPLETE SET (28)	14.00	6.25	2.00
COMMON PLAYER (1-28)	.35	.15	.03
☐ 1 Bob Lillis MG	.35	.15	.03
☐ 2 Nolan Ryan	6.00	2.50	.60
☐ 3 Phil Garner	.45	.18	.04
☐ 4 Jose Cruz	.60	.25	.06
☐ 5 Denny Walling	.35	.15	.03
☐ 6 Joe Niekro	.75	.30	.07
☐ 7 Terry Puhl	.45	.18	.04
☐ 8 Bill Doran	.60	.25	.06
☐ 9 Dickie Thon	.45	.18	.04
☐ 10 Enos Cabell	.35	.15	.03
☐ 11 Frank DiPino	.35	.15	.03
☐ 12 Julio Solano	.35	.15	.03
☐ 13 Alan Ashby	.45	.18	.04
☐ 14 Craig Reynolds	.35	.15	.03
☐ 15 Jerry Mumphrey	.35	.15	.03
☐ 16 Bill Dawley	.35	.15	.03
☐ 17 Mark Bailey	.35	.15	.03

		MINT	EXC	G-VG
☐ 18	Mike Scott	1.00	.40	.10
☐ 19	Harry Spilman	.35	.15	.03
☐ 20	Bob Knepper	.35	.15	.03
☐ 21	Dave Smith	.45	.18	.04
☐ 22	Kevin Bass	.45	.18	.04
☐ 23	Tim Tolman	.35	.15	.03
☐ 24	Jeff Calhoun	.35	.15	.03
☐ 25	Jim Pankovits	.35	.15	.03
☐ 26	Ron Mathis	.35	.15	.03
☐ 27	Astros' Coaches	.35	.15	.03
☐ 28	Astros' Checklist	.35	.15	.03

1985 Mother's Giants

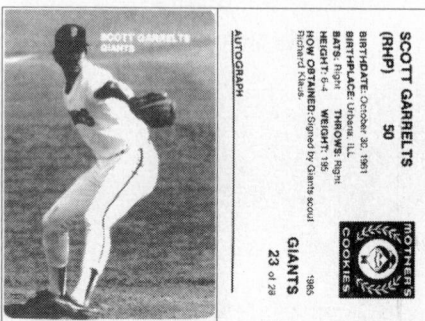

The cards in this 28-card set measure 2 1/2" by 3 1/2". In 1985, the Los Angeles based Mother's Cookies Co. again issued five sets of cards featuring players from major league teams. The San Francisco Giants set features current players depicted by photos on cards with rounded corners. The backs of the cards contain the Mother's Cookies logo. Cards were passed out at the stadium on June 30.

		MINT	EXC	G-VG
COMPLETE SET (28)		11.00	5.00	1.35
COMMON PLAYER (1-28)		.35	.15	.03
☐ 1	Jim Davenport MG	.35	.15	.03
☐ 2	Chili Davis	.90	.40	.09
☐ 3	Dan Gladden	.75	.30	.07
☐ 4	Jeff Leonard	.45	.18	.04
☐ 5	Manny Trillo	.35	.15	.03
☐ 6	Atlee Hammaker	.45	.18	.04
☐ 7	Bob Brenly	.35	.15	.03
☐ 8	Greg Minton	.35	.15	.03
☐ 9	Bill Laskey	.35	.15	.03
☐ 10	Vida Blue	.50	.20	.05
☐ 11	Mike Krukow	.45	.18	.04
☐ 12	Frank Williams	.35	.15	.03
☐ 13	Jose Uribe	.50	.20	.05
☐ 14	Johnnie LeMaster	.35	.15	.03
☐ 15	Scot Thompson	.35	.15	.03
☐ 16	Dave LaPoint	.35	.15	.03
☐ 17	David Green	.35	.15	.03
☐ 18	Chris Brown	.35	.15	.03
☐ 19	Joel Youngblood	.35	.15	.03
☐ 20	Mark Davis	.90	.40	.09
☐ 21	Jim Gott	.50	.20	.05
☐ 22	Doug Gwosdz	.35	.15	.03
☐ 23	Scott Garrelts	.75	.30	.07
☐ 24	Gary Rajsich	.35	.15	.03
☐ 25	Rob Deer	.90	.40	.09
☐ 26	Brad Wellman	.35	.15	.03
☐ 27	Giants' Coaches	.35	.15	.03
☐ 28	Giants' Checklist	.35	.15	.03

1985 Mother's Mariners

The cards in this 28-card set measure 2 1/2" by 3 1/2". In 1985, the Los Angeles based Mother's Cookies Co. again issued five

sets of cards featuring players from major league teams. The Seattle Mariners set features current players depicted by photos on cards with rounded corners. The backs of the cards contain the Mother's Cookies logo. Cards were passed out at the stadium on August 10.

		MINT	EXC	G-VG
COMPLETE SET (28)		12.50	5.50	1.65
COMMON PLAYER (1-28)		.35	.15	.03
☐ 1	Chuck Cottier MG	.35	.15	.03
☐ 2	Alvin Davis	1.00	.40	.10
☐ 3	Mark Langston	1.75	.70	.17
☐ 4	Dave Henderson	.75	.30	.07
☐ 5	Ed VandeBerg	.35	.15	.03
☐ 6	Al Cowens	.35	.15	.03
☐ 7	Spike Owen	.35	.15	.03
☐ 8	Mike Moore	.75	.30	.07
☐ 9	Gorman Thomas	.50	.20	.05
☐ 10	Barry Bonnell	.35	.15	.03
☐ 11	Jack Perconte	.35	.15	.03
☐ 12	Domingo Ramos	.35	.15	.03
☐ 13	Bob Kearney	.35	.15	.03
☐ 14	Matt Young	.35	.15	.03
☐ 15	Jim Beattie	.35	.15	.03
☐ 16	Mike Stanton	.35	.15	.03
☐ 17	David Valle	.35	.15	.03
☐ 18	Ken Phelps	.45	.18	.04
☐ 19	Salome Barojas	.35	.15	.03
☐ 20	Jim Presley	.60	.25	.06
☐ 21	Phil Bradley	.75	.30	.07
☐ 22	Dave Geisel	.35	.15	.03
☐ 23	Harold Reynolds	.90	.40	.09
☐ 24	Ed Nunez	.45	.18	.04
☐ 25	Mike Morgan	.75	.30	.07
☐ 26	Ivan Calderon	1.00	.40	.10
☐ 27	Mariners Coaches	.35	.15	.03
☐ 28	Checklist Card	.35	.15	.03

1985 Mother's Padres

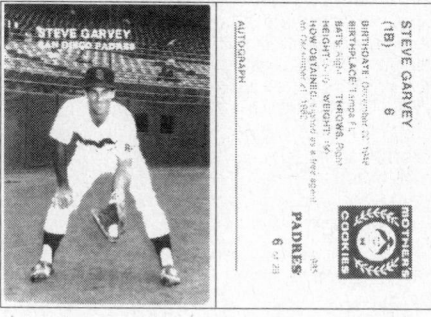

The cards in this 28-card set measure 2 1/2" by 3 1/2". In 1985, the Los Angeles based Mother's Cookies Co. again issued five sets of cards featuring players from major league teams. The

San Diego Padres set features current players depicted by photos on cards with rounded corners. The backs of the cards contain the Mother's Cookies logo. Cards were passed out at the stadium on August 11.

	MINT	EXC	G-VG
COMPLETE SET (28)	12.50	5.50	1.65
COMMON PLAYER (1-28)	.35	.15	.03
☐ 1 Dick Williams MG	.35	.15	.03
☐ 2 Tony Gwynn	3.00	1.25	.30
☐ 3 Kevin McReynolds	1.50	.60	.15
☐ 4 Graig Nettles	.75	.30	.07
☐ 5 Rich Gossage	.90	.40	.09
☐ 6 Steve Garvey	1.50	.60	.15
☐ 7 Garry Templeton	.50	.20	.05
☐ 8 Dave Dravecky	.75	.30	.07
☐ 9 Eric Show	.50	.20	.05
☐ 10 Terry Kennedy	.35	.15	.03
☐ 11 Luis DeLeon	.35	.15	.03
☐ 12 Bruce Bochy	.35	.15	.03
☐ 13 Andy Hawkins	.50	.20	.05
☐ 14 Kurt Bevacqua	.35	.15	.03
☐ 15 Craig Lefferts	.50	.20	.05
☐ 16 Mario Ramirez	.35	.15	.03
☐ 17 LaMarr Hoyt	.35	.15	.03
☐ 18 Jerry Royster	.35	.15	.03
☐ 19 Tim Stoddard	.35	.15	.03
☐ 20 Tim Flannery	.35	.15	.03
☐ 21 Mark Thurmond	.35	.15	.03
☐ 22 Greg Booker	.35	.15	.03
☐ 23 Bobby Brown	.35	.15	.03
☐ 24 Carmelo Martinez	.50	.20	.05
☐ 25 Al Bumbry	.35	.15	.03
☐ 26 Jerry Davis	.35	.15	.03
☐ 27 Padres' Coaches	.35	.15	.03
☐ 28 Padres' Checklist	.35	.15	.03

☐ 14 Rick Langford	.50	.20	.05
☐ 15 Chris Codiroli	.40	.16	.04
☐ 16 Moose Haas	.40	.16	.04
☐ 17 Keith Atherton	.40	.16	.04
☐ 18 Jay Howell	.50	.20	.05
☐ 19 Tony Phillips	.50	.20	.05
☐ 20 Steve Henderson	.40	.16	.04
☐ 21 Bill Krueger	.40	.16	.04
☐ 22 Steve Ontiveros	.40	.16	.04
☐ 23 Bill Bathe	.40	.16	.04
☐ 24 Ricky Peters	.40	.16	.04
☐ 25 Tim Birtsas	.40	.16	.04
☐ 26 A's Trainers and Equipment Managers	.40	.16	.04
☐ 27 A's Coaches	.40	.16	.04
☐ 28 Checklist Card	.40	.16	.04

1986 Mother's Astros

This set consists of 28 full-color, rounded-corner cards each measuring 2 1/2" by 3 1/2". Starter sets (only 20 cards but also including a certificate for eight more cards) were given out at the ballpark and collectors were encouraged to trade to fill in the rest of their set. Cards were originally given out at the Astrodome on July 10th. Since the 1986 All-Star Game was held in Houston, the set features Astro All-Stars since 1962 as painted by artist Richard Wallich.

	MINT	EXC	G-VG
COMPLETE SET (28)	11.00	5.00	1.35
COMMON PLAYER (1-28)	.35	.15	.03
☐ 1 Dick Farrell	.35	.15	.03
☐ 2 Hal Woodeshick	.35	.15	.03
☐ 3 Joe Morgan	1.50	.60	.15
☐ 4 Claude Raymond	.35	.15	.03
☐ 5 Mike Cuellar	.50	.20	.05
☐ 6 Rusty Staub	.75	.30	.07
☐ 7 Jimmy Wynn	.60	.25	.06
☐ 8 Larry Dierker	.50	.20	.05
☐ 9 Denis Menke	.35	.15	.03
☐ 10 Don Wilson	.35	.15	.03
☐ 11 Cesar Cedeno	.60	.25	.06
☐ 12 Lee May	.50	.20	.05
☐ 13 Bob Watson	.50	.20	.05
☐ 14 Ken Forsch	.35	.15	.03
☐ 15 Joaquin Andujar	.50	.20	.05
☐ 16 Terry Puhl	.50	.20	.05
☐ 17 Joe Niekro	.60	.25	.06
☐ 18 Craig Reynolds	.35	.15	.03
☐ 19 Joe Sambito	.35	.15	.03
☐ 20 Jose Cruz	.60	.25	.06
☐ 21 J.R. Richard	.50	.20	.05
☐ 22 Bob Knepper	.35	.15	.03
☐ 23 Nolan Ryan	5.00	2.25	.50
☐ 24 Ray Knight	.50	.20	.05
☐ 25 Bill Dawley	.35	.15	.03
☐ 26 Dickie Thon	.45	.18	.04
☐ 27 Jerry Mumphrey	.35	.15	.03
☐ 28 Checklist Card	.35	.15	.03

1986 Mother's A's

This set consists of 28 full-color, rounded-corner cards each measuring 2 1/2" by 3 1/2". Starter sets (only 20 cards but also including a certificate for eight more cards) were given out at the ballpark and collectors were encouraged to trade to fill in the rest of their set. The cards were originally given away on July 20th at Oakland Coliseum.

	MINT	EXC	G-VG
COMPLETE SET (28)	30.00	13.50	4.50
COMMON PLAYER (1-28)	.40	.16	.04
☐ 1 Jackie Moore MG	.40	.16	.04
☐ 2 Dave Kingman	.75	.30	.07
☐ 3 Dusty Baker	.60	.25	.06
☐ 4 Joaquin Andujar	.50	.20	.05
☐ 5 Alfredo Griffin	.50	.20	.05
☐ 6 Dwayne Murphy	.50	.20	.05
☐ 7 Mike Davis	.50	.20	.05
☐ 8 Carney Lansford	.75	.30	.07
☐ 9 Jose Canseco	20.00	8.50	2.75
☐ 10 Bruce Bochte	.40	.16	.04
☐ 11 Mickey Tettleton	.60	.25	.06
☐ 12 Donnie Hill	.40	.16	.04
☐ 13 Jose Rijo	1.50	.60	.15

1986 Mother's Giants

This set consists of 28 full-color, rounded-corner cards each measuring 2 1/2" by 3 1/2". Starter sets (only 20 cards but also including a certificate for eight more cards) were given out at the ballpark and collectors were encouraged to trade to fill in the rest of their set. Cards were originally given out at Candlestick Park on July 13th.

	MINT	EXC	G-VG
COMPLETE SET (28)	25.00	11.00	3.50
COMMON PLAYER (1-28)	.40	.16	.04
□ 1 Roger Craig MG	.60	.25	.06
□ 2 Chili Davis	.75	.30	.07
□ 3 Dan Gladden	.50	.20	.05
□ 4 Jeff Leonard	.50	.20	.05
□ 5 Bob Brenly	.40	.16	.04
□ 6 Atlee Hammaker	.50	.20	.05
□ 7 Will Clark	18.00	7.50	2.50
□ 8 Greg Minton	.40	.16	.04
□ 9 Candy Maldonado	.60	.25	.06
□ 10 Vida Blue	.50	.20	.05
□ 11 Mike Krukow	.50	.20	.05
□ 12 Bob Melvin	.40	.16	.04
□ 13 Jose Uribe	.50	.20	.05
□ 14 Dan Driessen	.40	.16	.04
□ 15 Jeff Robinson	.50	.20	.05
□ 16 Robby Thompson	.60	.25	.06
□ 17 Mike LaCoss	.40	.16	.04
□ 18 Chris Brown	.40	.16	.04
□ 19 Scott Garrelts	.50	.20	.05
□ 20 Mark Davis	.60	.25	.06
□ 21 Jim Gott	.50	.20	.05
□ 22 Brad Wellman	.40	.16	.04
□ 23 Roger Mason	.40	.16	.04
□ 24 Bill Laskey	.40	.16	.04
□ 25 Brad Gulden	.40	.16	.04
□ 26 Joel Youngblood	.40	.16	.04
□ 27 Juan Berenguer	.40	.16	.04
□ 28 Checklist Card	.40	.16	.04

1986 Mother's Mariners

This set consists of 28 full-color, rounded-corner cards each measuring 2 1/2" by 3 1/2". Starter sets (only 20 cards but also including a certificate for eight more cards) were given out at the ballpark and collectors were encouraged to trade to fill in the rest of their set. Cards were originally given out on July 27th at the Seattle Kingdome.

	MINT	EXC	G-VG
COMPLETE SET (28)	12.00	5.25	1.50
COMMON PLAYER (1-28)	.35	.15	.03
□ 1 Dick Williams MG	.45	.18	.04
□ 2 Alvin Davis	.75	.30	.07
□ 3 Mark Langston	1.25	.50	.12
□ 4 Dave Henderson	.75	.30	.07
□ 5 Steve Yeager	.45	.18	.04
□ 6 Al Cowens	.35	.15	.03
□ 7 Jim Presley	.45	.18	.04
□ 8 Phil Bradley	.60	.25	.06
□ 9 Gorman Thomas	.45	.18	.04
□ 10 Barry Bonnell	.35	.15	.03
□ 11 Milt Wilcox	.35	.15	.03
□ 12 Domingo Ramos	.35	.15	.03
□ 13 Paul Mirabella	.35	.15	.03
□ 14 Matt Young	.45	.18	.04
□ 15 Ivan Calderon	.75	.30	.07
□ 16 Bill Swift	.60	.25	.06
□ 17 Pete Ladd	.35	.15	.03
□ 18 Ken Phelps	.45	.18	.04
□ 19 Karl Best	.35	.15	.03
□ 20 Spike Owen	.45	.18	.04
□ 21 Mike Moore	.60	.25	.06
□ 22 Danny Tartabull	2.50	1.00	.25
□ 23 Bob Kearney	.35	.15	.03
□ 24 Edwin Nunez	.35	.15	.03
□ 25 Mike Morgan	.60	.25	.06
□ 26 Roy Thomas	.35	.15	.03
□ 27 Jim Beattie	.35	.15	.03
□ 28 Checklist Card	.35	.15	.03

1987 Mother's A's

This set consists of 28 full-color, rounded-corner cards each measuring 2 1/2" by 3 1/2". Starter sets (only 20 cards but also including a certificate for eight more cards) were given out at the ballpark and collectors were encouraged to trade to fill in the rest of their set. The cards were originally given away on July 5th at Oakland Coliseum during a game against the Boston Red Sox. This set is actually an All-Time All-Star set including every A's All-Star player since 1968 (when the franchise moved to Oakland). The vintage photos (each shot during the year of All-Star appearance) were taken from the collection of Doug McWilliams. The set is sequenced by what year the player made the All-Star team. The sets were supposedly given out free to the first 25,000 paid admissions at the game.

		MINT	EXC	G-VG
COMPLETE SET (28)		20.00	8.50	2.75
COMMON PLAYER (1-28)		.40	.16	.04
☐ 1	Bert Campaneris	.50	.20	.05
☐ 2	Rick Monday	.50	.20	.05
☐ 3	John Odom	.40	.16	.04
☐ 4	Sal Bando	.50	.20	.05
☐ 5	Reggie Jackson	2.50	1.00	.25
☐ 6	Jim Hunter	1.25	.50	.12
☐ 7	Vida Blue	.60	.25	.06
☐ 8	Dave Duncan	.40	.16	.04
☐ 9	Joe Rudi	.50	.20	.05
☐ 10	Rollie Fingers	1.50	.60	.15
☐ 11	Ken Holtzman	.40	.16	.04
☐ 12	Dick Williams MG	.40	.16	.04
☐ 13	Alvin Dark MG	.40	.16	.04
☐ 14	Gene Tenace	.50	.20	.05
☐ 15	Claudell Washington	.40	.16	.04
☐ 16	Phil Garner	.50	.20	.05
☐ 17	Wayne Gross	.40	.16	.04
☐ 18	Matt Keough	.40	.16	.04
☐ 19	Jeff Newman	.40	.16	.04
☐ 20	Rickey Henderson	4.00	1.75	.40
☐ 21	Tony Armas	.50	.20	.05
☐ 22	Mike Norris	.40	.16	.04
☐ 23	Billy Martin MG	1.00	.40	.10
☐ 24	Bill Caudill	.40	.16	.04
☐ 25	Jay Howell	.50	.20	.05
☐ 26	Jose Canseco	5.00	2.25	.50
☐ 27	Jose and Reggie (Canseco and Jackson)	3.50	1.50	.35
☐ 28	Checklist Card	.40	.16	.04

1987 Mother's Astros

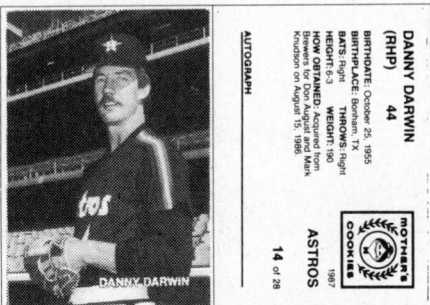

This set consists of 28 full-color, rounded-corner cards each measuring 2 1/2" by 3 1/2". Starter sets (only 20 cards but also including a certificate for eight more cards) were given out at the ballpark and collectors were encouraged to trade to fill in the rest of their set. Cards were originally given out at the Astrodome on July 17th during a game against the Phillies. Photos were taken by Barry Colla. The sets were supposedly given out free to the first 25,000 paid admissions at the game.

		MINT	EXC	G-VG
COMPLETE SET (28)		12.00	5.25	1.50
COMMON PLAYER (1-28)		.35	.15	.03
☐ 1	Hal Lanier MG	.45	.18	.04
☐ 2	Mike Scott	.90	.40	.09
☐ 3	Jose Cruz	.60	.25	.06
☐ 4	Bill Doran	.60	.25	.06
☐ 5	Bob Knepper	.35	.15	.03
☐ 6	Phil Garner	.50	.20	.05
☐ 7	Terry Puhl	.50	.20	.05
☐ 8	Nolan Ryan	5.00	2.25	.50
☐ 9	Kevin Bass	.45	.18	.04
☐ 10	Glenn Davis	1.00	.40	.10
☐ 11	Alan Ashby	.35	.15	.03
☐ 12	Charlie Kerfeld	.35	.15	.03
☐ 13	Denny Walling	.35	.15	.03
☐ 14	Danny Darwin	.35	.15	.03
☐ 15	Mark Bailey	.35	.15	.03
☐ 16	Davey Lopes	.50	.20	.05

		MINT	EXC	G-VG
☐ 17	Dave Meads	.35	.15	.03
☐ 18	Aurelio Lopez	.35	.15	.03
☐ 19	Craig Reynolds	.35	.15	.03
☐ 20	Dave Smith	.45	.18	.04
☐ 21	Larry Andersen	.35	.15	.03
☐ 22	Jim Pankovits	.35	.15	.03
☐ 23	Jim Deshaies	.45	.18	.04
☐ 24	Bert Pena	.35	.15	.03
☐ 25	Dickie Thon	.45	.18	.04
☐ 26	Billy Hatcher	.60	.25	.06
☐ 27	Astros' Coaches	.35	.15	.03
☐ 28	Checklist Card	.35	.15	.03

1987 Mother's Dodgers

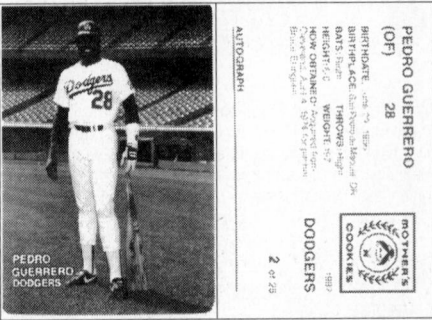

This set consists of 28 full-color, rounded-corner cards each measuring 2 1/2" by 3 1/2". Starter sets (only 20 cards but also including a certificate for eight more cards) were given out at the ballpark and collectors were encouraged to trade to fill in the rest of their set. Cards were originally given out at Dodger Stadium on August 9th. Photos were taken by Barry Colla. The sets were supposedly given out free to all game attendees 14 years of age and under.

		MINT	EXC	G-VG
COMPLETE SET (28)		12.00	5.25	1.50
COMMON PLAYER (1-28)		.35	.15	.03
☐ 1	Tom Lasorda MG	.75	.30	.07
☐ 2	Pedro Guerrero	1.00	.40	.10
☐ 3	Steve Sax	.75	.30	.07
☐ 4	Fernando Valenzuela	.90	.40	.09
☐ 5	Mike Marshall	.50	.20	.05
☐ 6	Orel Hershiser	1.75	.70	.17
☐ 7	Mariano Duncan	.50	.20	.05
☐ 8	Bill Madlock	.50	.20	.05
☐ 9	Bob Welch	.90	.40	.09
☐ 10	Mike Scioscia	.45	.18	.04
☐ 11	Mike Ramsey	.45	.18	.04
☐ 12	Matt Young	.35	.15	.03
☐ 13	Franklin Stubbs	.45	.18	.04
☐ 14	Tom Niedenfuer	.35	.15	.03
☐ 15	Reggie Williams	.35	.15	.03
☐ 16	Rick Honeycutt	.45	.18	.04
☐ 17	Dave Anderson	.35	.15	.03
☐ 18	Alejandro Pena	.60	.25	.06
☐ 19	Ken Howell	.35	.15	.03
☐ 20	Len Matuszek	.35	.15	.03
☐ 21	Tim Leary	.60	.25	.06
☐ 22	Tracy Woodson	.45	.18	.04
☐ 23	Alex Trevino	.35	.15	.03
☐ 24	Ken Landreaux	.35	.15	.03
☐ 25	Mickey Hatcher	.35	.15	.03
☐ 26	Brian Holton	.35	.15	.03
☐ 27	Dodgers' Coaches	.35	.15	.03
☐ 28	Checklist Card	.35	.15	.03

1987 Mother's Giants

This set consists of 28 full-color, rounded-corner cards each measuring 2 1/2" by 3 1/2". Starter sets (only 20 cards but also including a certificate for eight more cards) were given out at the ballpark and collectors were encouraged to trade to fill in the rest of their set. Cards were originally given out at Candlestick Park on June 27th during a game against the Astros. Photos were taken by Dennis Desprois. The sets were supposedly given out free to the first 25,000 paid admissions at the game.

	MINT	EXC	G-VG
COMPLETE SET (28)	17.50	7.00	2.00
COMMON PLAYER (1-28)	.40	.16	.04

		MINT	EXC	G-VG
☐ 1	Roger Craig MG	.60	.25	.06
☐ 2	Will Clark	5.00	2.25	.50
☐ 3	Chili Davis	.60	.25	.06
☐ 4	Bob Brenly	.40	.16	.04
☐ 5	Chris Brown	.40	.16	.04
☐ 6	Mike Krukow	.40	.16	.04
☐ 7	Candy Maldonado	.60	.25	.06
☐ 8	Jeffrey Leonard	.50	.20	.05
☐ 9	Greg Minton	.40	.16	.04
☐ 10	Robby Thompson	.50	.20	.05
☐ 11	Scott Garrelts	.50	.20	.05
☐ 12	Bob Melvin	.40	.16	.04
☐ 13	Jose Uribe	.50	.20	.05
☐ 14	Mark Davis	.60	.25	.06
☐ 15	Eddie Milner	.40	.16	.04
☐ 16	Harry Spilman	.40	.16	.04
☐ 17	Kelly Downs	.60	.25	.06
☐ 18	Chris Speier	.40	.16	.04
☐ 19	Jim Gott	.50	.20	.05
☐ 20	Joel Youngblood	.40	.16	.04
☐ 21	Mike LaCoss	.40	.16	.04
☐ 22	Matt Williams	4.00	1.75	.40
☐ 23	Roger Mason	.40	.16	.04
☐ 24	Mike Aldrete	.40	.16	.04
☐ 25	Jeff Robinson	.50	.20	.05
☐ 26	Mark Grant	.40	.16	.04
☐ 27	Giants' Coaches	.40	.16	.04
☐ 28	Checklist Card	.40	.16	.04

1987 Mother's Mariners

This set consists of 28 full-color, rounded-corner cards each measuring 2 1/2" by 3 1/2". Starter sets (only 20 cards but also including a certificate for eight more cards) were given out at the ballpark and collectors were encouraged to trade to fill in the rest of their set. Cards were originally given out on August 9th at the Seattle Kingdome. Photos were taken by Barry Colla. The sets were supposedly given out free to the first 20,000 paid admissions at the game.

	MINT	EXC	G-VG
COMPLETE SET (28)	11.00	5.00	1.35
COMMON PLAYER (1-28)	.40	.16	.04

		MINT	EXC	G-VG
☐ 1	Dick Williams MG	.50	.20	.05
☐ 2	Alvin Davis	.75	.30	.07
☐ 3	Mike Moore	.60	.25	.06
☐ 4	Jim Presley	.50	.20	.05
☐ 5	Mark Langston	1.00	.40	.10
☐ 6	Phil Bradley	.50	.20	.05
☐ 7	Ken Phelps	.50	.20	.05
☐ 8	Mike Morgan	.60	.25	.06
☐ 9	David Valle	.40	.16	.04
☐ 10	Harold Reynolds	.75	.30	.07
☐ 11	Edwin Nunez	.40	.16	.04
☐ 12	Bob Kearney	.40	.16	.04
☐ 13	Scott Bankhead	.50	.20	.05
☐ 14	Scott Bradley	.40	.16	.04
☐ 15	Mickey Brantley	.50	.20	.05
☐ 16	Mark Huismann	.40	.16	.04
☐ 17	Mike Kingery	.40	.16	.04
☐ 18	John Moses	.40	.16	.04
☐ 19	Donell Nixon	.40	.16	.04
☐ 20	Rey Quinones	.40	.16	.04
☐ 21	Domingo Ramos	.40	.16	.04
☐ 22	Jerry Reed	.40	.16	.04
☐ 23	Rich Renteria	.50	.20	.05
☐ 24	Rich Monteleone	.40	.16	.04
☐ 25	Mike Trujillo	.40	.16	.04
☐ 26	Bill Wilkinson	.40	.16	.04
☐ 27	John Christensen	.40	.16	.04
☐ 28	Checklist Card	.40	.16	.04

1987 Mother's McGwire

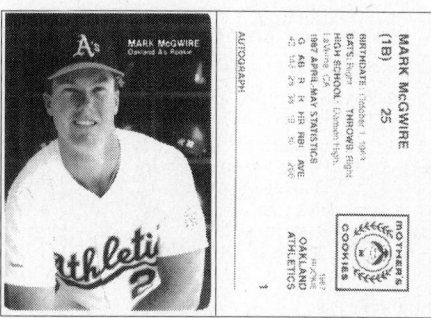

This set consists of 4 full-color, rounded-corner cards each measuring 2 1/2" by 3 1/2" and showing a different pose of A's slugging rookie Mark McGwire. Cards were originally given out at the national Card Collectors Convention in San Francisco. Later they were available through a mail-in offer involving collectors sending in two proofs-of-purchase from any Mother's Cookies products to get one free card. Photos were taken by Doug McWilliams. The cards are numbered on the back.

	MINT	EXC	G-VG
COMPLETE SET (4)	16.00	6.75	2.25
COMMON PLAYER (1-4)	4.00	1.75	.40

		MINT	EXC	G-VG
☐ 1	Mark McGwire .... (Close-up shot, head and shoulders)	4.00	1.75	.40
☐ 2	Mark McGwire .... (Waist up, holding bat)	4.50	2.00	.45
☐ 3	Mark McGwire .... (Batting stance, ready to swing)	4.50	2.00	.45
☐ 4	Mark McGwire .... (Home run swing, follow through)	5.00	2.25	.50

1987 Mother's Rangers

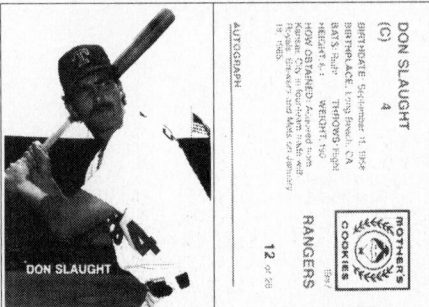

This set consists of 28 full-color, rounded-corner cards each measuring 2 1/2" by 3 1/2". Starter sets (only 20 cards but also including a certificate for eight more cards) were given out at the ballpark and collectors were encouraged to trade to fill in the rest of their set. Cards were originally given out on July 17th during the game against the Yankees. Photos were taken by Barry Colla. The sets were supposedly given out free to the first 25,000 paid admissions at the game.

		MINT	EXC	G-VG
	COMPLETE SET (28)	12.00	5.25	1.50
	COMMON PLAYER (1-28)	.40	.16	.04
☐ 1	Bobby Valentine MG	.50	.20	.05
☐ 2	Pete Incaviglia	.75	.30	.07
☐ 3	Charlie Hough	.50	.20	.05
☐ 4	Oddibe McDowell	.50	.20	.05
☐ 5	Larry Parrish	.40	.16	.04
☐ 6	Scott Fletcher	.40	.16	.04
☐ 7	Steve Buechele	.60	.25	.06
☐ 8	Tom Paciorek	.40	.16	.04
☐ 9	Pete O'Brien	.50	.20	.05
☐ 10	Darrell Porter	.40	.16	.04
☐ 11	Greg Harris	.40	.16	.04
☐ 12	Don Slaught	.40	.16	.04
☐ 13	Ruben Sierra	5.00	2.25	.50
☐ 14	Curtis Wilkerson	.40	.16	.04
☐ 15	Dale Mohorcic	.40	.16	.04
☐ 16	Ron Meredith	.40	.16	.04
☐ 17	Mitch Williams	.60	.25	.06
☐ 18	Bob Brower	.40	.16	.04
☐ 19	Edwin Correa	.40	.16	.04
☐ 20	Geno Petralli	.40	.16	.04
☐ 21	Mike Loynd	.40	.16	.04
☐ 22	Jerry Browne	.50	.20	.05
☐ 23	Jose Guzman	.60	.25	.06
☐ 24	Jeff Kunkel	.50	.20	.05
☐ 25	Bobby Witt	1.00	.40	.10
☐ 26	Jeff Russell	.60	.25	.06
☐ 27	Ranger's Trainers	.40	.16	.04
☐ 28	Checklist Card	.40	.16	.04

1988 Mother's A's

This set consists of 28 full-color, rounded-corner cards each measuring 2 1/2" by 3 1/2". Starter sets (only 20 cards but also including a certificate for eight more cards) were given out at the ballpark and collectors were encouraged to trade to fill in the rest of their set. The cards were originally given away on July 23rd at Oakland Coliseum during a game. Short sets (20 cards plus certificate) were supposedly given out free to the first 35,000 paid admissions at the game.

		MINT	EXC	G-VG
	COMPLETE SET (28)	17.00	7.25	2.50
	COMMON PLAYER (1-28)	.40	.16	.04
☐ 1	Tony LaRussa MG	.60	.25	.06
☐ 2	Mark McGwire	2.00	.80	.20
☐ 3	Dave Stewart	1.00	.40	.10
☐ 4	Terry Steinbach	.75	.30	.07
☐ 5	Dave Parker	.75	.30	.07
☐ 6	Carney Lansford	.75	.30	.07
☐ 7	Jose Canseco	3.50	1.50	.35
☐ 8	Don Baylor	.50	.20	.05
☐ 9	Bob Welch	.75	.30	.07
☐ 10	Dennis Eckersley	1.25	.50	.12
☐ 11	Walt Weiss	1.25	.50	.12
☐ 12	Tony Phillips	.50	.20	.05
☐ 13	Steve Ontiveros	.40	.16	.04
☐ 14	Dave Henderson	.75	.30	.07
☐ 15	Stan Javier	.50	.20	.05
☐ 16	Ron Hassey	.40	.16	.04
☐ 17	Curt Young	.40	.16	.04
☐ 18	Glenn Hubbard	.40	.16	.04
☐ 19	Storm Davis	.60	.25	.06
☐ 20	Eric Plunk	.40	.16	.04
☐ 21	Matt Young	.40	.16	.04
☐ 22	Mike Gallego	.50	.20	.05
☐ 23	Rick Honeycutt	.40	.16	.04
☐ 24	Doug Jennings	.50	.20	.05
☐ 25	Gene Nelson	.40	.16	.04
☐ 26	Greg Cadaret	.40	.16	.04
☐ 27	Athletics Coaches	.40	.16	.04
☐ 28	Checklist Card	.40	.16	.04

1988 Mother's Astros

This set consists of 28 full-color, rounded-corner cards each measuring 2 1/2" by 3 1/2". Starter sets (only 20 cards but also including a certificate for eight more cards) were given out at the ballpark and collectors were encouraged to trade to fill in the rest of their set. Cards were originally given out at the Astrodome on August 26th during a game. The sets were supposedly given out free to the first 25,000 paid admissions at the game.

		MINT	EXC	G-VG
	COMPLETE SET (28)	11.00	5.00	1.35
	COMMON PLAYER (1-28)	.40	.16	.04
☐ 1	Hal Lanier MG	.40	.16	.04
☐ 2	Mike Scott	.90	.40	.09

		MINT	EXC	G-VG
☐ 3	Gerald Young	.50	.20	.05
☐ 4	Bill Doran	.50	.20	.05
☐ 5	Bob Knepper	.40	.16	.04
☐ 6	Billy Hatcher	.50	.20	.05
☐ 7	Terry Puhl	.50	.20	.05
☐ 8	Nolan Ryan	4.00	1.75	.40
☐ 9	Kevin Bass	.50	.20	.05
☐ 10	Glenn Davis	1.00	.40	.10
☐ 11	Alan Ashby	.40	.16	.04
☐ 12	Steve Henderson	.40	.16	.04
☐ 13	Denny Walling	.40	.16	.04
☐ 14	Danny Darwin	.40	.16	.04
☐ 15	Mark Bailey	.40	.16	.04
☐ 16	Ernie Camacho	.40	.16	.04
☐ 17	Rafael Ramirez	.40	.16	.04
☐ 18	Jeff Heathcock	.40	.16	.04
☐ 19	Craig Reynolds	.40	.16	.04
☐ 20	Dave Smith	.50	.20	.05
☐ 21	Larry Andersen	.40	.16	.04
☐ 22	Jim Pankovits	.40	.16	.04
☐ 23	Jim Deshaies	.40	.16	.04
☐ 24	Juan Agosto	.40	.16	.04
☐ 25	Chuck Jackson	.40	.16	.04
☐ 26	Joaquin Andujar	.50	.20	.05
☐ 27	Astros' Coaches	.40	.16	.04
☐ 28	Checklist Card	.40	.16	.04

1988 Mother's Will Clark

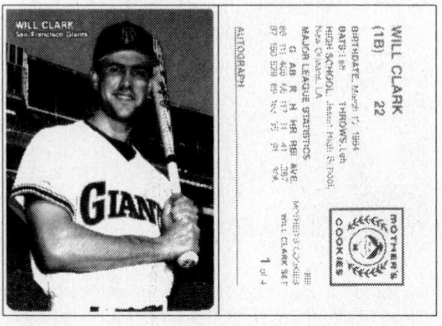

This regional set consists of 4 full-color, rounded-corner cards each measuring 2 1/2" by 3 1/2" and showing a different pose of Giants' slugging first baseman Will Clark. Cards were originally found in 18 oz. packages of "Big Bags" of Mother's Cookies at stores in the Northern California area in February and March of 1988. The cards are numbered on the back. Card backs are done in red and purple on white card stock.

		MINT	EXC	G-VG
	COMPLETE SET (4)	16.00	6.75	2.25
	COMMON PLAYER (1-4)	4.00	1.75	.40
☐ 1	Will Clark (Batting Pose, Waist Up)	4.50	2.00	.45
☐ 2	Will Clark (Kneeling In On Deck Circle)	4.00	1.75	.40
☐ 3	Will Clark (Follow Through Swing)	4.00	1.75	.40
☐ 4	Will Clark (Starting Toward First Base)	4.50	2.00	.45

1988 Mother's Dodgers

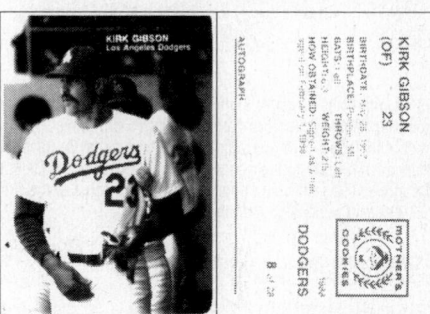

This set consists of 28 full-color, rounded-corner cards each measuring 2 1/2" by 3 1/2". Starter sets (only 20 cards but also including a certificate for eight more cards) were given out at the ballpark and collectors were encouraged to trade to fill in the rest of their set. Cards were originally given out at Dodger Stadium on July 31st. Photos were taken by Barry Colla. The sets were supposedly given out free to the first 25,000 game attendees 14 years of age and under.

		MINT	EXC	G-VG
	COMPLETE SET (28)	12.50	5.50	1.65
	COMMON PLAYER (1-28)	.40	.16	.04
☐ 1	Tom Lasorda MG	.60	.25	.06
☐ 2	Pedro Guerrero	.80	.35	.08
☐ 3	Steve Sax	.80	.35	.08
☐ 4	Fernando Valenzuela	.80	.35	.08
☐ 5	Mike Marshall	.50	.20	.05
☐ 6	Orel Hershiser	1.25	.50	.12
☐ 7	Alfredo Griffin	.40	.16	.04
☐ 8	Kirk Gibson	1.00	.40	.10
☐ 9	Don Sutton	.80	.35	.08
☐ 10	Mike Scioscia	.50	.20	.05
☐ 11	Franklin Stubbs	.50	.20	.05
☐ 12	Mike Davis	.40	.16	.04
☐ 13	Jesse Orosco	.40	.16	.04
☐ 14	John Shelby	.40	.16	.04
☐ 15	Rick Dempsey	.40	.16	.04
☐ 16	Jay Howell	.50	.20	.05
☐ 17	Dave Anderson	.40	.16	.04
☐ 18	Alejandro Pena	.60	.25	.06
☐ 19	Jeff Hamilton	.40	.16	.04
☐ 20	Danny Heep	.40	.16	.04
☐ 21	Tim Leary	.60	.25	.06
☐ 22	Brad Havens	.40	.16	.04
☐ 23	Tim Belcher	.75	.30	.07
☐ 24	Ken Howell	.40	.16	.04
☐ 25	Mickey Hatcher	.40	.16	.04
☐ 26	Brian Holton	.40	.16	.04
☐ 27	Mike Devereaux	.50	.20	.05
☐ 28	Checklist Card	.40	.16	.04

1988 Mother's Giants

This set consists of 28 full-color, rounded-corner cards each measuring 2 1/2" by 3 1/2". Starter sets (only 20 cards but also

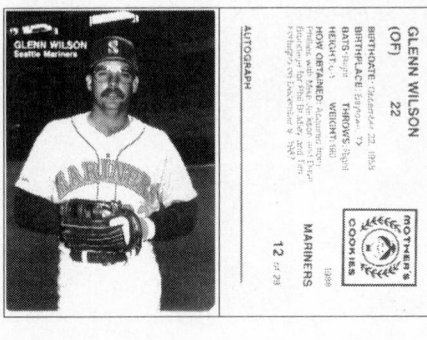

including a certificate for eight more cards) were given out at the ballpark and collectors were encouraged to trade to fill in the rest of their set. Cards were originally given out at Candlestick Park on July 30th during a game. Photos were taken by Dennis Desprois. The sets were supposedly given out free to the first 35,000 paid admissions at the game.

	MINT	EXC	G-VG
COMPLETE SET (28)	12.00	5.25	1.50
COMMON PLAYER (1-28)	.35	.15	.03

		MINT	EXC	G-VG
☐ 1	Roger Craig MG	.50	.20	.05
☐ 2	Will Clark	3.50	1.50	.35
☐ 3	Kevin Mitchell	1.25	.50	.12
☐ 4	Bob Brenly	.35	.15	.03
☐ 5	Mike Aldrete	.35	.15	.03
☐ 6	Mike Krukow	.35	.15	.03
☐ 7	Candy Maldonado	.50	.20	.05
☐ 8	Jeffrey Leonard	.45	.18	.04
☐ 9	Dave Dravecky	.60	.25	.06
☐ 10	Robby Thompson	.60	.25	.06
☐ 11	Scott Garrelts	.50	.20	.05
☐ 12	Bob Melvin	.35	.15	.03
☐ 13	Jose Uribe	.45	.18	.04
☐ 14	Brett Butler	.75	.30	.07
☐ 15	Rick Reuschel	.45	.18	.04
☐ 16	Harry Spilman	.35	.15	.03
☐ 17	Kelly Downs	.50	.20	.05
☐ 18	Chris Speier	.35	.15	.03
☐ 19	Atlee Hammaker	.35	.15	.03
☐ 20	Joel Youngblood	.35	.15	.03
☐ 21	Mike LaCoss	.35	.15	.03
☐ 22	Don Robinson	.35	.15	.03
☐ 23	Mark Wasinger	.45	.18	.04
☐ 24	Craig Lefferts	.50	.20	.05
☐ 25	Phil Garner	.50	.20	.05
☐ 26	Joe Price	.35	.15	.03
☐ 27	Giants' Coaches	.35	.15	.03
☐ 28	Checklist Card	.35	.15	.03

1988 Mother's Mariners

This set consists of 28 full-color, rounded-corner cards each measuring 2 1/2" by 3 1/2". Starter sets (only 20 cards but also including a certificate for eight more cards) were given out at the ballpark and collectors were encouraged to trade to fill in the rest of their set. Cards were originally given out on August 14th at the Seattle Kingdome. Photos were taken by Barry Colla. The sets were supposedly given out free to the first 20,000 paid admissions at the game.

	MINT	EXC	G-VG
COMPLETE SET (28)	10.00	4.50	1.25
COMMON PLAYER (1-28)	.40	.16	.04

		MINT	EXC	G-VG
☐ 1	Dick Williams MG	.40	.16	.04
☐ 2	Alvin Davis	.75	.30	.07
☐ 3	Mike Moore	.60	.25	.06
☐ 4	Jim Presley	.50	.20	.05
☐ 5	Mark Langston	.90	.40	.09
☐ 6	Henry Cotto	.40	.16	.04
☐ 7	Ken Phelps	.40	.16	.04
☐ 8	Steve Trout	.40	.16	.04
☐ 9	David Valle	.40	.16	.04
☐ 10	Harold Reynolds	.60	.25	.06
☐ 11	Edwin Nunez	.40	.16	.04
☐ 12	Glenn Wilson	.40	.16	.04
☐ 13	Scott Bankhead	.50	.20	.05
☐ 14	Scott Bradley	.40	.16	.04
☐ 15	Mickey Brantley	.40	.16	.04
☐ 16	Bruce Fields	.40	.16	.04
☐ 17	Mike Kingery	.40	.16	.04
☐ 18	Mike Campbell	.40	.16	.04
☐ 19	Mike Jackson	.60	.25	.06
☐ 20	Rey Quinones	.40	.16	.04
☐ 21	Mario Diaz	.40	.16	.04
☐ 22	Jerry Reed	.40	.16	.04
☐ 23	Rich Renteria	.40	.16	.04
☐ 24	Julio Solano	.40	.16	.04
☐ 25	Bill Swift	.50	.20	.05
☐ 26	Bill Wilkinson	.40	.16	.04
☐ 27	Mariners Coaches	.40	.16	.04
☐ 28	Checklist Card	.40	.16	.04

1988 Mother's McGwire

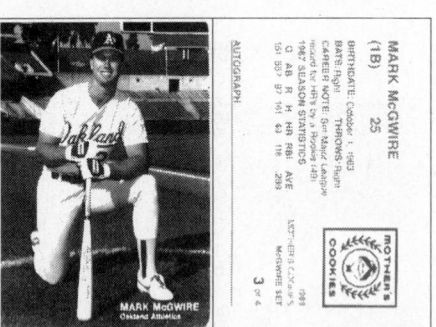

This regional set consists of 4 full-color, rounded-corner cards each measuring 2 1/2" by 3 1/2" and showing a different pose of Athletics' slugging first baseman Mark McGwire. Cards were originally found in 18 oz. packages of "Big Bags" of Mother's Cookies at stores in the Northern California area in February and March of 1988. The cards are numbered on the back. Card backs are done in red and purple on white card stock.

	MINT	EXC	G-VG
COMPLETE SET (4)	13.50	6.00	1.85
COMMON PLAYER (1-4)	4.00	1.75	.40

		MINT	EXC	G-VG
☐ 1	Mark McGwire (Holding Big Bat)	4.00	1.75	.40
☐ 2	Mark McGwire (Fielding at First Base)	4.00	1.75	.40

☐ 3	Mark McGwire .... (Kneeling In On Deck Circle)	4.00	1.75	.40
☐ 4	Mark McGwire .... (Batting Pose, Waist Up)	4.00	1.75	.40

1988 Mother's Rangers

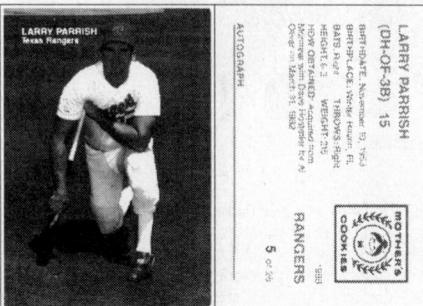

This set consists of 28 full-color, rounded-corner cards each measuring 2 1/2" by 3 1/2". Starter sets (only 20 cards but also including a certificate for eight more cards) were given out at the ballpark and collectors were encouraged to trade to fill in the rest of their set. Cards were originally given out on August 7th. Photos were taken by Barry Colla. The sets were supposedly given out free to the first 25,000 paid admissions at the game.

		MINT	EXC	G-VG
	COMPLETE SET (28)	10.00	4.50	1.25
	COMMON PLAYER (1-28)	.35	.15	.03
☐ 1	Bobby Valentine MG	.50	.20	.05
☐ 2	Pete Incaviglia	.60	.25	.06
☐ 3	Charlie Hough	.45	.18	.04
☐ 4	Oddibe McDowell	.45	.18	.04
☐ 5	Larry Parrish	.35	.15	.03
☐ 6	Scott Fletcher	.35	.15	.03
☐ 7	Steve Buechele	.45	.18	.04
☐ 8	Steve Kemp	.35	.15	.03
☐ 9	Pete O'Brien	.45	.18	.04
☐ 10	Ruben Sierra	1.50	.60	.15
☐ 11	Mike Stanley	.35	.15	.03
☐ 12	Jose Cecena	.35	.15	.03
☐ 13	Cecil Espy	.35	.15	.03
☐ 14	Curtis Wilkerson	.35	.15	.03
☐ 15	Dale Mohorcic	.35	.15	.03
☐ 16	Ray Hayward	.35	.15	.03
☐ 17	Mitch Williams	.50	.20	.05
☐ 18	Bob Brower	.35	.15	.03
☐ 19	Paul Kilgus	.35	.15	.03
☐ 20	Geno Petralli	.35	.15	.03
☐ 21	James Steels	.35	.15	.03
☐ 22	Jerry Browne	.45	.18	.04
☐ 23	Jose Guzman	.45	.18	.04
☐ 24	DeWayne Vaughn	.35	.15	.03
☐ 25	Bobby Witt	.60	.25	.06
☐ 26	Jeff Russell	.50	.20	.05
☐ 27	Rangers Coaches	.35	.15	.03
☐ 28	Checklist Card	.35	.15	.03

1989 Mother's A's

The 1989 Mother's Cookies Oakland A's set contains 28 standard-size (2 1/2" by 3 1/2") cards with rounded corners. The fronts have borderless color photos, and the horizontally-oriented backs have biographical information. Starter sets containing 20 of these cards were given away at an A's home game during the 1989 season.

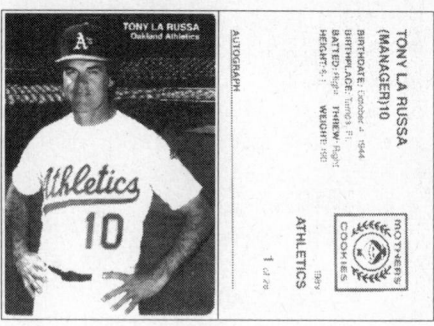

		MINT	EXC	G-VG
	COMPLETE SET (28)	15.00	6.50	2.15
	COMMON PLAYER (1-28)	.40	.16	.04
☐ 1	Tony LaRussa MG	.60	.25	.06
☐ 2	Mark McGwire	1.25	.50	.12
☐ 3	Terry Steinbach	.60	.25	.06
☐ 4	Dave Parker	.75	.30	.07
☐ 5	Carney Lansford	.75	.30	.07
☐ 6	Dave Stewart	.75	.30	.07
☐ 7	Jose Canseco	2.50	1.00	.25
☐ 8	Walt Weiss	.60	.25	.06
☐ 9	Bob Welch	.75	.30	.07
☐ 10	Dennis Eckersley	.90	.40	.09
☐ 11	Tony Phillips	.50	.20	.05
☐ 12	Mike Moore	.60	.25	.06
☐ 13	Dave Henderson	.60	.25	.06
☐ 14	Curt Young	.40	.16	.04
☐ 15	Ron Hassey	.40	.16	.04
☐ 16	Eric Plunk	.40	.16	.04
☐ 17	Luis Polonia	.60	.25	.06
☐ 18	Storm Davis	.50	.20	.05
☐ 19	Glenn Hubbard	.40	.16	.04
☐ 20	Greg Cadaret	.50	.20	.05
☐ 21	Stan Javier	.50	.20	.05
☐ 22	Felix Jose	1.00	.40	.10
☐ 23	Mike Gallego	.50	.20	.05
☐ 24	Todd Burns	.50	.20	.05
☐ 25	Rick Honeycutt	.40	.16	.04
☐ 26	Gene Nelson	.40	.16	.04
☐ 27	A's Coaches	.40	.16	.04
☐ 28	Checklist Card	.40	.16	.04

1989 Mother's A's ROY's

The 1989 Mother's A's ROY's set contains four standard-size (2 1/2" by 3 1/2") cards with rounded corners. The fronts have borderless color photos, and the horizontally-oriented backs have biographical information. One card was included in each specially marked box of Mother's Cookies. On the first three cards in the set Rookie of the Year (and year) is mentioned under the player's name.

	MINT	EXC	G-VG
COMPLETE SET (4)	12.00	5.25	1.50
COMMON PLAYER (1-4) ...	2.50	1.00	.25
☐ 1 Jose Canseco	5.00	2.25	.50
1986 ROY			
☐ 2 Mark McGwire	3.75	1.60	.37
1987 ROY			
☐ 3 Walt Weiss	2.50	1.00	.25
1988 ROY			
☐ 4 Walt Weiss,	3.75	1.60	.37
Mark McGwire,			
and Jose Canseco			

1989 Mother's Astros

The 1989 Mother's Cookies Houston Astros set contains 28 standard-size (2 1/2" by 3 1/2") cards with rounded corners. The fronts have borderless color photos, and the horizontally-oriented backs have biographical information. Starter sets containing 20 of these cards were given away at an Astros home game during the 1989 season.

	MINT	EXC	G-VG
COMPLETE SET (28)	10.00	4.50	1.25
COMMON PLAYER (1-28) ...	.40	.16	.04
☐ 1 Art Howe MG	.50	.20	.05
☐ 2 Mike Scott	.75	.30	.07
☐ 3 Gerald Young	.50	.20	.05
☐ 4 Bill Doran	.50	.20	.05
☐ 5 Billy Hatcher	.50	.20	.05
☐ 6 Terry Puhl	.50	.20	.05
☐ 7 Bob Knepper	.40	.16	.04
☐ 8 Kevin Bass	.50	.20	.05
☐ 9 Glenn Davis	1.00	.40	.10
☐ 10 Alan Ashby	.40	.16	.04
☐ 11 Bob Forsch	.40	.16	.04
☐ 12 Greg Gross	.40	.16	.04
☐ 13 Danny Darwin	.40	.16	.04
☐ 14 Craig Biggio	1.00	.40	.10
☐ 15 Jim Clancy	.40	.16	.04
☐ 16 Rafael Ramirez	.40	.16	.04
☐ 17 Alex Trevino	.40	.16	.04
☐ 18 Craig Reynolds	.40	.16	.04
☐ 19 Dave Smith	.50	.20	.05
☐ 20 Larry Andersen	.40	.16	.04
☐ 21 Eric Yelding	.50	.20	.05
☐ 22 Jim Deshaies	.40	.16	.04
☐ 23 Juan Agosto	.40	.16	.04
☐ 24 Rick Rhoden	.40	.16	.04
☐ 25 Ken Caminiti	.50	.20	.05
☐ 26 Dave Meads	.40	.16	.04
☐ 27 Astros Coaches	.40	.16	.04
☐ 28 Checklist Card	.40	.16	.04

1989 Mother's Canseco

The 1989 Mother's Jose Canseco set contains four standard-size (2 1/2" by 3 1/2") cards with rounded corners. The fronts have borderless color photos, and the horizontally-oriented backs have biographical information. One card was included in each specially marked box of Mother's Cookies. Since all four cards picture Jose Canseco, the pose is identified parenthetically in the checklist below in order to distinguish the card fronts.

	MINT	EXC	G-VG
COMPLETE SET (4)	12.00	5.25	1.50
COMMON PLAYER (1-4)	3.50	1.50	.35
☐ 1 Jose Canseco	3.50	1.50	.35
(Holding ball			
in hand)			
☐ 2 Jose Canseco	3.50	1.50	.35
(On one knee			
with bat)			
☐ 3 Jose Canseco	3.50	1.50	.35
(Swinging at pitch)			
☐ 4 Jose Canseco	3.50	1.50	.35
(Running toward			
second)			

1989 Mother's Will Clark

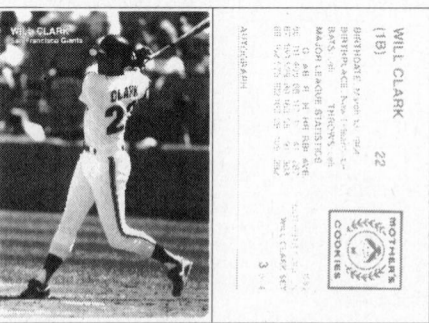

The 1989 Mother's Cookies Will Clark set contains four standard-size (2 1/2" by 3 1/2") cards with rounded corners. The fronts have borderless color photos, and the horizontally-oriented backs have biographical information. One card was included in each specially marked box of Mother's Cookies. Since all four cards picture Will Clark, the pose is identified parenthetically in the checklist below in order to distinguish the card fronts.

	MINT	EXC	G-VG
COMPLETE SET (4)	12.00	5.25	1.50
COMMON PLAYER (1-4)	3.50	1.50	.35

			MINT	EXC	G-VG
☐	1	Will Clark	3.50	1.50	.35
		(Ball in glove)			
☐	2	Will Clark	3.50	1.50	.35
		(Batting stance posed)			
☐	3	Will Clark	3.50	1.50	.35
		(Swing follow through)			
☐	4	Will Clark	3.50	1.50	.35
		(Starting toward first after hit, still holding bat)			

1989 Mother's Dodgers

The 1989 Mother's Los Angeles Dodgers set contains 28 standard-size (2 1/2" by 3 1/2") cards with rounded corners. The fronts have borderless color photos, and the horizontally-oriented backs have biographical information. Starter sets containing 20 of these cards were given away at a Dodgers home game during the 1989 season.

			MINT	EXC	G-VG
		COMPLETE SET (28)	10.00	4.50	1.25
		COMMON PLAYER (1-28)	.40	.16	.04
☐	1	Tom Lasorda MG	.60	.25	.06
☐	2	Eddie Murray	1.00	.40	.10
☐	3	Mike Scioscia	.50	.20	.05
☐	4	Fernando Valenzuela	.75	.30	.07
☐	5	Mike Marshall	.50	.20	.05
☐	6	Orel Hershiser	1.00	.40	.10
☐	7	Alfredo Griffin	.40	.16	.04
☐	8	Kirk Gibson	.75	.30	.07
☐	9	John Tudor	.50	.20	.05
☐	10	Willie Randolph	.50	.20	.05
☐	11	Franklin Stubbs	.50	.20	.05
☐	12	Mike Davis	.40	.16	.04
☐	13	Mike Morgan	.60	.25	.06
☐	14	John Shelby	.40	.16	.04
☐	15	Rick Dempsey	.40	.16	.04
☐	16	Jay Howell	.50	.20	.05
☐	17	Dave Anderson	.40	.16	.04
☐	18	Alejandro Pena	.50	.20	.05
☐	19	Jeff Hamilton	.40	.16	.04
☐	20	Ricky Horton	.40	.16	.04
☐	21	Tim Leary	.50	.20	.05
☐	22	Ray Searage	.40	.16	.04
☐	23	Tim Belcher	.75	.30	.07
☐	24	Tim Crews	.40	.16	.04
☐	25	Mickey Hatcher	.40	.16	.04
☐	26	Mariano Duncan	.50	.20	.05
☐	27	Dodgers Coaches	.40	.16	.04
☐	28	Checklist Card	.40	.16	.04

1989 Mother's Giants

The 1989 Mother's Cookies San Francisco Giants set contains 28 standard-size (2 1/2" by 3 1/2") cards with rounded corners.

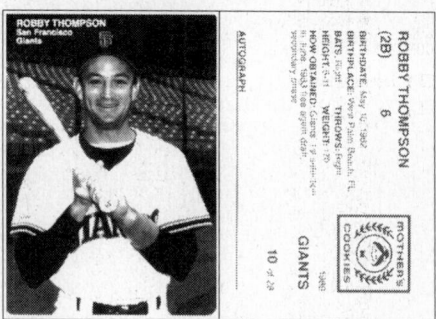

The fronts have borderless color photos, and the horizontally-oriented backs have biographical information. Starter sets containing 20 of these cards were given away at a Giants home game during the 1989 season.

			MINT	EXC	G-VG
		COMPLETE SET (28)	13.50	6.00	1.85
		COMMON PLAYER (1-28)	.40	.16	.04
☐	1	Roger Craig MG	.50	.20	.05
☐	2	Will Clark	2.50	1.00	.25
☐	3	Kevin Mitchell	1.00	.40	.10
☐	4	Kelly Downs	.60	.25	.06
☐	5	Brett Butler	.75	.30	.07
☐	6	Mike Krukow	.40	.16	.04
☐	7	Candy Maldonado	.50	.20	.05
☐	8	Terry Kennedy	.40	.16	.04
☐	9	Dave Dravecky	.60	.25	.06
☐	10	Robby Thompson	.60	.25	.06
☐	11	Scott Garrelts	.50	.20	.05
☐	12	Matt Williams	1.25	.50	.12
☐	13	Jose Uribe	.40	.16	.04
☐	14	Tracy Jones	.40	.16	.04
☐	15	Rick Reuschel	.50	.20	.05
☐	16	Ernest Riles	.40	.16	.04
☐	17	Jeff Brantley	.50	.20	.05
☐	18	Chris Speier	.40	.16	.04
☐	19	Atlee Hammaker	.40	.16	.04
☐	20	Ed Jurak	.40	.16	.04
☐	21	Mike LaCoss	.40	.16	.04
☐	22	Don Robinson	.40	.16	.04
☐	23	Kirt Manwaring	.40	.16	.04
☐	24	Craig Lefferts	.50	.20	.05
☐	25	Donell Nixon	.40	.16	.04
☐	26	Joe Price	.40	.16	.04
☐	27	Rich Gossage	.60	.25	.06
☐	28	Checklist Card	.40	.16	.04

1989 Mother's Griffey Jr.

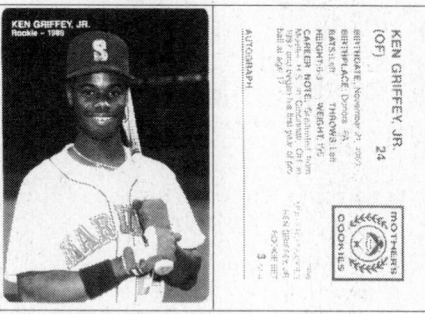

The 1989 Mother's Cookies Ken Griffey Jr. set contains four standard-size (2 1/2" by 3 1/2") cards with rounded corners. The fronts have borderless color photos, and the horizontally-oriented backs have biographical information. One card was included in each specially marked box of Mother's Cookies. Since all four cards picture Ken Griffey Jr., the pose is identified parenthetically in the checklist below in order to distinguish the card fronts. Each card back provides a different aspect or background on Ken and his career. The photos were shot by noted sports photographer Barry Colla.

	MINT	EXC	G-VG
COMPLETE SET (4)	16.00	6.75	2.25
COMMON PLAYER (1-4)	4.50	2.00	.45
☐ 1 Ken Griffey Jr.	4.50	2.00	.45
(Arms folded)			
☐ 2 Ken Griffey Jr.	4.50	2.00	.45
(Baseball in hand)			
☐ 3 Ken Griffey Jr.	4.50	2.00	.45
(Looking straight ahead with bat)			
☐ 4 Ken Griffey Jr.	4.50	2.00	.45
(Looking over shoulder with bat)			

1989 Mother's Mariners

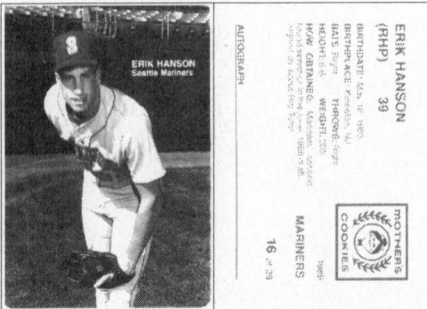

The 1989 Mother's Cookies Seattle Mariners set contains 28 standard-size (2 1/2" by 3 1/2") cards with rounded corners. The fronts have borderless color photos, and the horizontally-oriented backs have biographical information. Starter sets containing 20 of these cards were given away at a Mariners home game during the 1989 season.

	MINT	EXC	G-VG
COMPLETE SET (28)	15.00	6.50	2.15
COMMON PLAYER (1-28)	.35	.15	.03
☐ 1 Jim Lefebvre MG	.35	.15	.03
☐ 2 Alvin Davis	.60	.25	.06
☐ 3 Ken Griffey Jr.	7.50	3.25	.75
☐ 4 Jim Presley	.45	.18	.04
☐ 5 Mark Langston	.75	.30	.07
☐ 6 Henry Cotto	.35	.15	.03
☐ 7 Mickey Brantley	.35	.15	.03
☐ 8 Jeffrey Leonard	.45	.18	.04
☐ 9 Dave Valle	.35	.15	.03
☐ 10 Harold Reynolds	.60	.25	.06
☐ 11 Edgar Martinez	1.00	.40	.10
☐ 12 Tom Niedenfuer	.35	.15	.03
☐ 13 Scott Bankhead	.50	.20	.05
☐ 14 Scott Bradley	.35	.15	.03
☐ 15 Omar Vizquel	.45	.18	.04
☐ 16 Erik Hanson	1.00	.40	.10
☐ 17 Bill Swift	.60	.25	.06
☐ 18 Mike Campbell	.35	.15	.03
☐ 19 Mike Jackson	.45	.18	.04
☐ 20 Rich Renteria	.35	.15	.03
☐ 21 Mario Diaz	.35	.15	.03
☐ 22 Jerry Reed	.35	.15	.03
☐ 23 Darnell Coles	.35	.15	.03
☐ 24 Steve Trout	.35	.15	.03
☐ 25 Mike Schooler	.60	.25	.06
☐ 26 Julio Solano	.35	.15	.03
☐ 27 Mariners Coaches	.35	.15	.03
☐ 28 Checklist Card	.35	.15	.03

1989 Mother's McGwire

The 1989 Mother's Cookies Mark McGwire set contains four standard-size (2 1/2" by 3 1/2") cards with rounded corners. The fronts have borderless color photos, and the horizontally-oriented backs have biographical information. One card was included in each specially marked box of Mother's Cookies. Since all four cards picture Mark McGwire, the pose is identified parenthetically in the checklist below in order to distinguish the card fronts.

	MINT	EXC	G-VG
COMPLETE SET (4)	10.00	4.50	1.25
COMMON PLAYER (1-4)	3.00	1.25	.30
☐ 1 Mark McGwire	3.00	1.25	.30
(Bat on shoulder)			
☐ 2 Mark McGwire	3.00	1.25	.30
(Batting stance)			
☐ 3 Mark McGwire	3.00	1.25	.30
(Holding bat in front)			
☐ 4 Mark McGwire	3.00	1.25	.30
(Batting, follow through)			

1989 Mother's Rangers

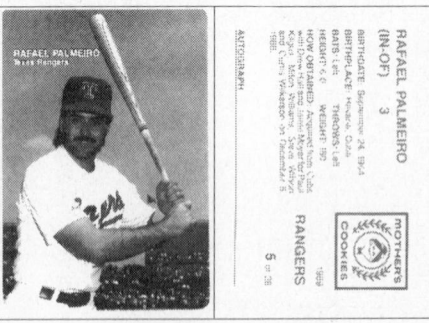

The 1989 Mother's Cookies Texas Rangers set contains 28 standard-size (2 1/2" by 3 1/2") cards with rounded corners. The fronts have borderless color photos, and the horizontally-oriented backs have biographical information. Starter sets containing 20 of these cards were given away at a Rangers home game during the 1989 season.

	MINT	EXC	G-VG
COMPLETE SET (28)	11.00	5.00	1.35
COMMON PLAYER (1-28)	.35	.15	.03

		MINT	EXC	G-VG
☐ 1	Bobby Valentine MG	.50	.20	.05
☐ 2	Nolan Ryan	3.50	1.50	.35
☐ 3	Julio Franco	1.00	.40	.10
☐ 4	Charlie Hough	.50	.20	.05
☐ 5	Rafael Palmeiro	1.50	.60	.15
☐ 6	Jeff Russell	.50	.20	.05
☐ 7	Ruben Sierra	1.50	.60	.15
☐ 8	Steve Buechele	.45	.18	.04
☐ 9	Buddy Bell	.50	.20	.05
☐ 10	Pete Incaviglia	.50	.20	.05
☐ 11	Geno Petralli	.35	.15	.03
☐ 12	Cecil Espy	.35	.15	.03
☐ 13	Scott Fletcher	.35	.15	.03
☐ 14	Bobby Witt	.60	.25	.06
☐ 15	Brad Arnsberg	.45	.18	.04
☐ 16	Rick Leach	.35	.15	.03
☐ 17	Jamie Moyer	.35	.15	.03
☐ 18	Kevin Brown	.60	.25	.06
☐ 19	Jeff Kunkel	.35	.15	.03
☐ 20	Craig McMurtry	.35	.15	.03
☐ 21	Kenny Rogers	.50	.20	.05
☐ 22	Mike Stanley	.35	.15	.03
☐ 23	Cecilio Guante	.35	.15	.03
☐ 24	Jim Sundberg	.35	.15	.03
☐ 25	Jose Guzman	.45	.18	.04
☐ 26	Jeff Stone	.35	.15	.03
☐ 27	Rangers Coaches	.35	.15	.03
☐ 28	Checklist Card	.35	.15	.03

		MINT	EXC	G-VG
☐ 15	Danny Darwin	.35	.15	.03
☐ 16	Ken Oberkfell	.35	.15	.03
☐ 17	Dave Smith	.45	.18	.04
☐ 18	Dan Schatzeder	.35	.15	.03
☐ 19	Rafael Ramirez	.35	.15	.03
☐ 20	Larry Andersen	.35	.15	.03
☐ 21	Alex Trevino	.35	.15	.03
☐ 22	Glenn Wilson	.35	.15	.03
☐ 23	Jim Clancy	.35	.15	.03
☐ 24	Eric Yelding	.45	.18	.04
☐ 25	Casey Candaele	.35	.15	.03
☐ 26	Juan Agosto	.35	.15	.03
☐ 27	Coaches Card	.35	.15	.03
	Billy Bowman			
	Bob Cluck			
	Phil Garner			
	Matt Galante			
	Ed Napoleon			
	Rudy Jaramillo			
☐ 28	Personnel Card	.35	.15	.03
	Dave Labossiere TR			
	Dennis Liborio EQ.MG			
	Doc Ewell TR			

1990 Mother's Astros

This standard-size, 2 1/2" by 3 1/2", 28-card set features members of the 1990 Houston Astros. This set features the traditional rounded corners and has biographical information about each player on the back. These Astros cards were given away on July 15th to the first 25,000 fans at the Astrodome. They were distributed in 20 card random packets at the game and eight more at the redemption booths. However, both groups of cards were random and there was no guarantee of getting a complete set in the cards. The promotional idea was that the only way one could finish the set was to trade for them. The certificates of redemption for eight were redeemable at the major card show at the AstroArena on August 24-26, 1990.

		MINT	EXC	G-VG
COMPLETE SET (28)		10.00	4.50	1.25
COMMON PLAYER (1-28)		.35	.15	.03
☐ 1	Art Howe MG	.45	.18	.04
☐ 2	Glenn Davis	1.00	.40	.10
☐ 3	Eric Anthony	.60	.25	.06
☐ 4	Mike Scott	.60	.25	.06
☐ 5	Craig Biggio	.60	.25	.06
☐ 6	Ken Caminiti	.45	.18	.04
☐ 7	Bill Doran	.45	.18	.04
☐ 8	Gerald Young	.45	.18	.04
☐ 9	Terry Puhl	.35	.15	.03
☐ 10	Mark Portugal	.35	.15	.03
☐ 11	Mark Davidson	.35	.15	.03
☐ 12	Jim Deshaies	.35	.15	.03
☐ 13	Bill Gullickson	.45	.18	.04
☐ 14	Franklin Stubbs	.45	.18	.04

1990 Mother's Athletics

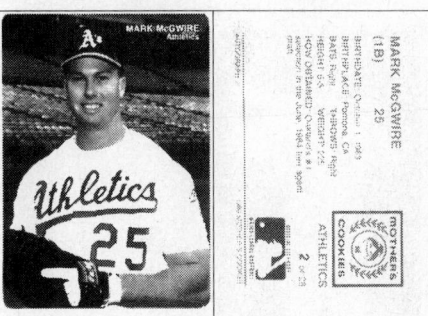

1990 Mother's Cookies Oakland Athletics set contains 28 cards measuring standard size, 2 1/2" by 3 1/2", with rounded corners. The envelope containing the cards honors the 1989 World Championship Oakland Athletics. The A's cards were released at the July 22nd game to the first 35,000 fans to walk through the gates. They were distributed in 20-card random packets at the game and eight more at the redemption booths. However, both groups of cards were random and there was no guarantee of getting a complete set in the cards. The promotional idea was that the only way one could finish the set was to trade for them. The redemption certificates were to be used at the Labor Day San Francisco card show. In addition to this the Mother's Giants cards were also redeemable at that show.

		MINT	EXC	G-VG
COMPLETE SET (28)		12.50	5.50	1.65
COMMON PLAYER (1-28)		.35	.15	.03
☐ 1	Tony LaRussa MG	.50	.20	.05
☐ 2	Mark McGwire	1.00	.40	.10
☐ 3	Terry Steinbach	.50	.20	.05
☐ 4	Rickey Henderson	2.00	.80	.20
☐ 5	Dave Stewart	.75	.30	.07
☐ 6	Jose Canseco	2.00	.80	.20
☐ 7	Dennis Eckersley	.75	.30	.07
☐ 8	Carney Lansford	.60	.25	.06
☐ 9	Mike Moore	.60	.25	.06
☐ 10	Walt Weiss	.60	.25	.06
☐ 11	Scott Sanderson	.50	.20	.05
☐ 12	Ron Hassey	.35	.15	.03
☐ 13	Rick Honeycutt	.35	.15	.03
☐ 14	Ken Phelps	.35	.15	.03
☐ 15	Jamie Quirk	.35	.15	.03
☐ 16	Bob Welch	.60	.25	.06
☐ 17	Felix Jose	.75	.30	.07
☐ 18	Dave Henderson	.60	.25	.06
☐ 19	Mike Norris	.35	.15	.03

☐ 20	Todd Burns	.35	.15	.03
☐ 21	Lance Blankenship	.35	.15	.03
☐ 22	Gene Nelson	.35	.15	.03
☐ 23	Stan Javier	.45	.18	.04
☐ 24	Curt Young	.35	.15	.03
☐ 25	Mike Gallego	.45	.18	.04
☐ 26	Joe Klink	.35	.15	.03
☐ 27	A's Coaches	.35	.15	.03
	Rene Lachemann			
	Dave Duncan			
	Merv Rettenmund			
	Tommie Reynolds			
	Art Kusnyer			
	Dave McKay			
☐ 28	Checklist Card	.35		
	A's Personnel			
	Larry Davis, TR			
	Steve Vuchinch,			
	Visiting Club Mgr.			
	Frank Cienscyk,			
	Equipment Mgr.			
	Barry Weinberg, TR			

1990 Mother's Canseco

This is a standard Mother's Cookies set with four cards each measuring 2 1/2" by 3 1/2" with rounded corners issued to capitalize on Jose Canseco's popularity. This four-card set features Canseco in various batting poses.

	MINT	EXC	G-VG
COMPLETE SET (4)	12.00	5.25	1.50
COMMON PLAYER (1-4)	3.50	1.50	.35
☐ 1 Jose Canseco	3.50	1.50	.35
(Sitting with bat over shoulders)			
☐ 2 Jose Canseco	3.50	1.50	.35
(Standing with bat behind shoulders)			
☐ 3 Jose Canseco	3.50	1.50	.35
(Batting Pose)			
☐ 4 Jose Canseco	3.50	1.50	.35
(Sitting on dugout steps)			

1990 Mother's Will Clark

This is a standard Mother's Cookies set with four cards each measuring 2 1/2" by 3 1/2" with rounded corners issued to capitalize on Will Clark's popularity. This four-card set features Clark in various poses as indicated in the checklist below.

	MINT	EXC	G-VG
COMPLETE SET (4)	12.00	5.25	1.50
COMMON PLAYER (1-4)	3.50	1.50	.35

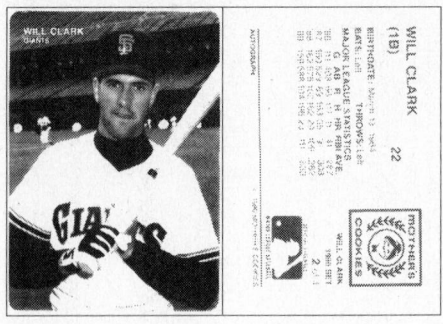

		MINT	EXC	G-VG
☐ 1	Will Clark	3.50	1.50	.35
	(Batting pose looking over right shoulder)			
☐ 2	Will Clark	3.50	1.50	.35
	(Holding bat on left shoulder)			
☐ 3	Will Clark	3.50	1.50	.35
	(Holding bat ready to swing)			
☐ 4	Will Clark	3.50	1.50	.35
	(Standing with bat behind shoulders)			

1990 Mother's Dodgers

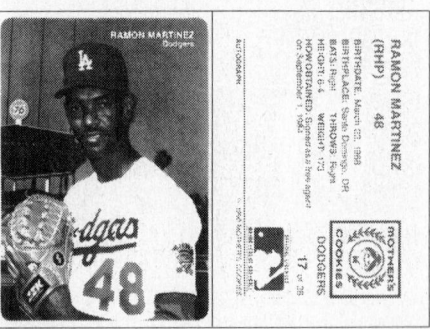

The 1990 Mother's Cookies Los Angeles Dodgers set contains 28 cards (2 1/2" by 3 1/2") issued with rounded corners and beautiful full color fronts with biographical information on the back. These Dodgers cards were given away at Chavez Ravine to all fans fourteen and under at the August 19th game. They were distributed in 20-card random packets at the game and eight more at the redemption booths. However, both groups of cards were random and there was no guarantee of getting a complete set in the cards. The promotional idea was that the only way one could finish the set was to trade for them. The redemption for eight more cards was done at the 22nd Annual Labor Day card show at the Anaheim Convention Center.

		MINT	EXC	G-VG
COMPLETE SET (28)		10.00	4.50	1.25
COMMON PLAYER (1-28)		.35	.15	.03
☐ 1	Tom Lasorda MG	.50	.20	.05
☐ 2	Fernando Valenzuela	.60	.25	.06
☐ 3	Kal Daniels	.60	.25	.06
☐ 4	Mike Scioscia	.35	.15	.03
☐ 5	Eddie Murray	.80	.35	.08
☐ 6	Mickey Hatcher	.35	.15	.03
☐ 7	Juan Samuel	.50	.20	.05
☐ 8	Alfredo Griffin	.35	.15	.03
☐ 9	Tim Belcher	.60	.25	.06

			MINT	EXC	G-VG
☐	10	Hubie Brooks	.50	.20	.05
☐	11	Jose Gonzalez	.45	.18	.04
☐	12	Orel Hershiser	.90	.40	.09
☐	13	Kirk Gibson	.75	.30	.07
☐	14	Chris Gwynn	.50	.20	.05
☐	15	Jay Howell	.50	.20	.05
☐	16	Rick Dempsey	.35	.15	.03
☐	17	Ramon Martinez	1.50	.60	.15
☐	18	Lenny Harris	.50	.20	.05
☐	19	John Wetteland	.60	.25	.06
☐	20	Mike Sharperson	.35	.15	.03
☐	21	Mike Morgan	.45	.18	.04
☐	22	Ray Searage	.35	.15	.03
☐	23	Jeff Hamilton	.35	.15	.03
☐	24	Jim Gott	.35	.15	.03
☐	25	John Shelby	.35	.15	.03
☐	26	Tim Crews	.35	.15	.03
☐	27	Don Aase	.35	.15	.03
☐	28	Dodger Coaches	.35	.15	.03
		Joe Ferguson			
		Ron Perranoski			
		Mark Cresse			
		Ben Hines			
		Joe Amalfitano			
		Bill Russell			
		Manny Mota			

			MINT	EXC	G-VG
☐	17	Jose Uribe	.35	.15	.03
☐	18	Greg Litton	.45	.18	.04
☐	19	Dave Anderson	.35	.15	.03
☐	20	Don Robinson	.35	.15	.03
☐	21	Giants Coaches	.35	.15	.03
		Dusty Baker			
		Bob Lillis			
		Bill Fahey			
		Norm Sherry			
		Wendall Kim			
☐	22	Bill Bathe	.35	.15	.03
☐	23	Randy O'Neal	.35	.15	.03
☐	24	Kevin Bass	.45	.18	.04
☐	25	Jeff Brantley	.45	.18	.04
☐	26	John Burkett	.75	.30	.07
☐	27	Ernie Camacho	.35	.15	.03
☐	28	Checklist Card	.35	.15	.03

1990 Mother's Mariners

1990 Mother's Cookies Seattle Mariners set contains 28 cards in standard size (2 1/2" by 3 1/2") with the traditional Mother's Cookies rounded corners. The cards have full-color fronts and biographical information with no stats on the back. These Mariners cards were released for the August 5th game and given to the first 25,000 people who passed through the gates. They were distributed in 20-card random packets at the game and eight more at the redemption booths. However, both groups of cards were random and there was no guarantee of getting a complete set in the cards. The promotional idea was that the only way one could finish the set was to trade for them. The redemption for eight more cards were available at the Kingdome Card Show on August 12, 1990.

1990 Mother's Giants

The 1990 Mother's Cookies San Francisco Giants set features cards with rounded corners measuring 2 1/2" by 3 1/2". The cards have full-color fronts and biographical information with no stats on the back. The Giants cards were given away at the July 29th game to the first 25,000 children 14 and under. They were distributed in 20-card random packets at the game and eight more at the redemption booths. However, both groups of cards were random and there was no guarantee of getting a complete set in the cards. The promotional idea was that the only way one could finish the set was to trade for them. The redemption certificates were to be used at the Labor Day San Francisco card show. In addition to this the Mother's A's cards were also redeemable at that show.

			MINT	EXC	G-VG
COMPLETE SET (28)			11.00	5.00	1.35
COMMON PLAYER (1-28)			.35	.15	.03
☐	1	Roger Craig MG	.50	.20	.05
☐	2	Will Clark	2.00	.80	.20
☐	3	Gary Carter	.75	.30	.07
☐	4	Kelly Downs	.50	.20	.05
☐	5	Kevin Mitchell	1.00	.40	.10
☐	6	Steve Bedrosian	.45	.18	.04
☐	7	Brett Butler	.60	.25	.06
☐	8	Rick Reuschel	.45	.18	.04
☐	9	Matt Williams	1.25	.50	.12
☐	10	Robby Thompson	.50	.20	.05
☐	11	Mike LaCoss	.35	.15	.03
☐	12	Terry Kennedy	.35	.15	.03
☐	13	Atlee Hammaker	.35	.15	.03
☐	14	Rick Leach	.35	.15	.03
☐	15	Ernest Riles	.35	.15	.03
☐	16	Scott Garrelts	.45	.18	.04

			MINT	EXC	G-VG
COMPLETE SET (28)			11.00	5.00	1.35
COMMON PLAYER (1-28)			.35	.15	.03
☐	1	Jim Lefebvre MG	.45	.18	.04
☐	2	Alvin Davis	.60	.25	.06
☐	3	Ken Griffey Jr.	4.50	2.00	.45
☐	4	Jeffrey Leonard	.45	.18	.04
☐	5	David Valle	.35	.15	.03
☐	6	Harold Reynolds	.60	.25	.06
☐	7	Jay Buhner	.75	.30	.07
☐	8	Erik Hanson	.75	.30	.07
☐	9	Henry Cotto	.35	.15	.03
☐	10	Edgar Martinez	.75	.30	.07
☐	11	Bill Swift	.60	.25	.06
☐	12	Omar Vizquel	.45	.18	.04
☐	13	Randy Johnson	.60	.25	.06
☐	14	Greg Briley	.45	.18	.04
☐	15	Gene Harris	.45	.18	.04
☐	16	Matt Young	.35	.15	.03
☐	17	Pete O'Brien	.45	.18	.04
☐	18	Brent Knackert	.45	.18	.04
☐	19	Mike Jackson	.45	.18	.04
☐	20	Brian Holman	.60	.25	.06
☐	21	Mike Schooler	.60	.25	.06
☐	22	Darnell Coles	.35	.15	.03
☐	23	Keith Comstock	.35	.15	.03
☐	24	Scott Bankhead	.45	.18	.04
☐	25	Scott Bradley	.35	.15	.03

		MINT	EXC	G-VG
☐ 26	Mike Brumley	.35	.15	.03
☐ 27	Mariners Coaches	.35	.15	.03
	Rusty Kuntz			
	Gene Clines			
	Bill Plummer			
	Mike Paul			
	Bob Didier			
☐ 28	Checklist Card	.35	.15	.03
	Mariners Personnel			
	Henry Genzale EQ.MG			
	Tom Newberg ATR			
	Rick Griffin TR			

1990 Mother's McGwire

This is a standard Mother's Cookies set with four cards each measuring 2 1/2" by 3 1/2" with rounded corners issued to capitalize on Mark McGwire's popularity. This four-card set features McGwire in various poses as indicated in the checklist below.

		MINT	EXC	G-VG
COMPLETE SET (4)		10.00	4.50	1.25
COMMON PLAYER (1-4)		3.00	1.25	.30
☐ 1	Mark McGwire	3.00	1.25	.30
	(Standing with bat on right shoulder)			
☐ 2	Mark McGwire	3.00	1.25	.30
	(Standing in dugout with bat in front)			
☐ 3	Mark McGwire	3.00	1.25	.30
	(Fielding pose)			
☐ 4	Mark McGwire	3.00	1.25	.30
	(Sitting on dugout steps)			

1990 Mother's Rangers

This 28-card, standard-size, 2 1/2" by 3 1/2", set features members of the 1990 Texas Rangers. The set has beautiful full-color photos on the front along with biographical information on the back. The set also features the now traditional Mother's Cookies rounded corners. The Rangers cards were distributed on July 22nd to the first 25,000 game attendees in Arlington. They were distributed in 20-card random packets at the game and eight more at the redemption booths. However, both groups of cards were random and there was no guarantee of getting a complete set in the cards. The promotional idea was that the only way one could finish the set was to trade for them. The certificates to redeem the cards for eigth more cards were able to be redeemed at the 17th annual Dallas Card Convention on August 18-19, 1990.

		MINT	EXC	G-VG
COMPLETE SET (28)		11.00	5.00	1.35
COMMON PLAYER (1-28)		.35	.15	.03
☐ 1	Bobby Valentine MG	.45	.18	.04
☐ 2	Nolan Ryan	3.00	1.25	.30
☐ 3	Ruben Sierra	1.25	.50	.12
☐ 4	Pete Incaviglia	.50	.20	.05
☐ 5	Charlie Hough	.45	.18	.04
☐ 6	Harold Baines	.50	.20	.05
☐ 7	Gino Petralli	.35	.15	.03
☐ 8	Jeff Russell	.45	.18	.04
☐ 9	Rafael Palmiero	.90	.40	.09
☐ 10	Julio Franco	.75	.30	.07
☐ 11	Jack Daugherty	.35	.15	.03
☐ 12	Gary Pettis	.35	.15	.03
☐ 13	Brian Bohanon	.45	.18	.04
☐ 14	Steve Buechele	.45	.18	.04
☐ 15	Bobby Witt	.60	.25	.06
☐ 16	Thad Bosley	.35	.15	.03
☐ 17	Gary Mielke	.35	.15	.03
☐ 18	Jeff Kunkel	.35	.15	.03
☐ 19	Mike Jeffcoat	.35	.15	.03
☐ 20	Mike Stanley	.35	.15	.03
☐ 21	Kevin Brown	.50	.20	.05
☐ 22	Kenny Rogers	.35	.15	.03
☐ 23	Jeff Huson	.35	.15	.03
☐ 24	Jamie Moyer	.35	.15	.03
☐ 25	Cecil Espy	.35	.15	.03
☐ 26	John Russell	.35	.15	.03
☐ 27	Coaches Card	.35	.15	.03
	Dave Oliver			
	Davey Lopes			
	Tom Robson			
	Tom House			
	Toby Harrah			
☐ 28	Trainers Card	.35	.15	.03
	Bill Zeigler TR			
	Joe Macko EQ.MG.			

Marty Stajduhar,
Strength and Cond.

Danny Wheat ATR

1990 Mother's Ryan

This is a typical Mother's Cookies set with four cards each measuring the standard size of 2 1/2" by 3 1/2" with rounded corners honoring Ryan's more than 5,000 strikeouts over his career. This four-card set features Ryan in various pitching poses. The second card in the set is considered tougher to find than the other three in the set.

		MINT	EXC	G-VG
COMPLETE SET (4)		16.00	6.75	2.25
COMMON PLAYER (1-4)		3.50	1.50	.35
☐ 1	Nolan Ryan	3.50	1.50	.35
	(Holding ball)			
☐ 2	Nolan Ryan	7.50	3.25	.75
	(Dugout pose)			

		MINT	EXC	G-VG
☐ 3	Nolan Ryan (Holding ball behind waist)	3.50	1.50	.35
☐ 4	Nolan Ryan (Holding ball with 5,000 K's)	3.50	1.50	.35

1990 Mother's Matt Williams

This is a standard Mother's Cookies set with four cards each measuring 2 1/2" by 3 1/2" with rounded corners issued to capitalize on Matt Williams' popularity. This four-card set features Williams in various poses as indicated in the checklist below.

		MINT	EXC	G-VG
COMPLETE SET (4)		12.00	5.25	1.50
COMMON PLAYER (1-4)		3.50	1.50	.35
☐ 1	Matt Williams (Standing with bat on right shoulder)	3.50	1.50	.35
☐ 2	Matt Williams (Smiling batting pose)	3.50	1.50	.35
☐ 3	Matt Williams (Posing with glove)	3.50	1.50	.35
☐ 4	Matt Williams (Fielding pose with glove between legs)	3.50	1.50	.35

1991 Mother's Astros

The 1991 Mother's Cookies Houston Astros set contains 28 cards with rounded corners measuring the standard size (2 1/2" by 3 1/2"). The front design has borderless glossy color player photos from the waist up. The horizontally oriented backs are printed in red and purple, present biographical information, and have blank slots for player autographs. The cards are numbered on the back.

		MINT	EXC	G-VG
COMPLETE SET (28)		11.00	5.00	1.35
COMMON PLAYER (1-28)		.35	.15	.03
☐ 1	Art Howe MG	.45	.18	.04
☐ 2	Steve Finley	.60	.25	.06
☐ 3	Pete Harnisch	.45	.18	.04
☐ 4	Mike Scott	.60	.25	.06
☐ 5	Craig Biggio	.75	.30	.07
☐ 6	Ken Caminiti	.45	.18	.04
☐ 7	Eric Yelding	.35	.15	.03
☐ 8	Jeff Bagwell	2.50	1.00	.25
☐ 9	Jim Deshaies	.35	.15	.03
☐ 10	Mark Portugal	.35	.15	.03
☐ 11	Mark Davidson	.35	.15	.03
☐ 12	Jimmy Jones	.35	.15	.03
☐ 13	Luis Gonzalez	1.25	.50	.12
☐ 14	Karl Rhodes	.45	.18	.04
☐ 15	Curt Schilling	.35	.15	.03
☐ 16	Ken Oberkfell	.35	.15	.03
☐ 17	Mark McLemore	.35	.15	.03
☐ 18	Dave Rohde	.45	.18	.04
☐ 19	Rafael Ramirez	.35	.15	.03
☐ 20	Al Osuna	.45	.18	.04
☐ 21	Jim Corsi	.35	.15	.03
☐ 22	Carl Nichols	.35	.15	.03
☐ 23	Jim Clancy	.35	.15	.03
☐ 24	Dwayne Henry	.45	.18	.04
☐ 25	Casey Candaele	.35	.15	.03
☐ 26	Xavier Hernandez	.35	.15	.03
☐ 27	Darryl Kile	.45	.18	.04
☐ 28	Checklist Card Phil Garner CO Bob Cluck CO Ed Ott CO Matt Galante CO Rudy Jaramillo CO	.45	.18	.04

1991 Mother's Athletics

The 1991 Mother's Cookies Oakland Athletics set contains 28 cards with rounded corners measuring the standard size (2 1/2" by 3 1/2"). The set includes an additional card advertising a trading card collectors album. The front design has borderless glossy color player photos from the waist up. The horizontally oriented backs are printed in red and purple, present biographical information, and have blank slots for player autographs. The cards are numbered on the back.

		MINT	EXC	G-VG
COMPLETE SET (28)		12.00	5.25	1.50
COMMON PLAYER (1-28)		.35	.15	.03
☐ 1	Tony LaRussa MG	.45	.18	.04
☐ 2	Mark McGwire	1.00	.40	.10
☐ 3	Terry Steinbach	.45	.18	.04
☐ 4	Rickey Henderson	1.75	.70	.17
☐ 5	Dave Stewart	.60	.25	.06
☐ 6	Jose Canseco	2.00	.80	.20
☐ 7	Dennis Eckersley	.60	.25	.06

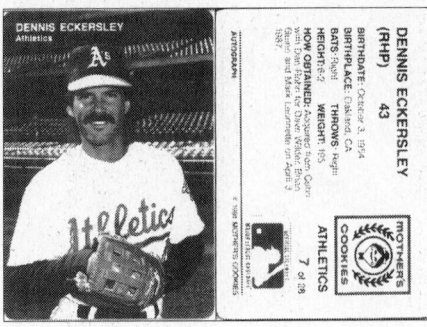

		MINT	EXC	G-VG
☐ 8	Carney Lansford	.45	.18	.04
☐ 9	Bob Welch	.45	.18	.04
☐ 10	Walt Weiss	.45	.18	.04
☐ 11	Mike Moore	.45	.18	.04
☐ 12	Vance Law	.35	.15	.03
☐ 13	Rick Honeycutt	.35	.15	.03
☐ 14	Harold Baines	.45	.18	.04
☐ 15	Jamie Quirk	.35	.15	.03
☐ 16	Ernest Riles	.35	.15	.03
☐ 17	Willie Wilson	.45	.18	.04
☐ 18	Dave Henderson	.45	.18	.04
☐ 19	Kirk Dressendorfer	.60	.25	.06
☐ 20	Todd Burns	.35	.15	.03
☐ 21	Lance Blankenship	.35	.15	.03
☐ 22	Gene Nelson	.35	.15	.03
☐ 23	Eric Show	.35	.15	.03
☐ 24	Curt Young	.35	.15	.03
☐ 25	Mike Gallego	.35	.15	.03
☐ 26	Joe Klink	.35	.15	.03
☐ 27	Steve Chitren	.35	.15	.03
☐ 28	Checklist Card	.45	.18	.04

Tommie Reynolds CO
Art Kusnyer CO
Reggie Jackson CO
Rick Burleson CO
Rene Lachemann CO
Dave Duncan CO
Dave McKay CO

1991 Mother's Dodgers

The 1991 Mother's Cookies Los Angeles Dodgers set contains 28 cards with rounded corners measuring the standard size (2 1/2" by 3 1/2"). The front design has borderless glossy color player photos. The horizontally oriented backs are printed in red and purple, present biographical information, and have blank slots for player autographs. The cards are numbered on the back.

	MINT	EXC	G-VG
COMPLETE SET (28)	10.00	4.50	1.25
COMMON PLAYER (1-28)	.35	.15	.03

		MINT	EXC	G-VG
☐ 1	Tom Lasorda MG	.45	.18	.04
☐ 2	Darryl Strawberry	1.25	.50	.12
☐ 3	Kal Daniels	.60	.25	.06
☐ 4	Mike Scioscia	.45	.18	.04
☐ 5	Eddie Murray	.75	.30	.07
☐ 6	Brett Butler	.45	.18	.04
☐ 7	Juan Samuel	.45	.18	.04
☐ 8	Alfredo Griffin	.35	.15	.03
☐ 9	Tim Belcher	.45	.18	.04
☐ 10	Ramon Martinez	.75	.30	.07
☐ 11	Jose Gonzalez	.35	.15	.03
☐ 12	Orel Hershiser	.75	.30	.07
☐ 13	Bob Ojeda	.45	.18	.04
☐ 14	Chris Gwynn	.35	.15	.03
☐ 15	Jay Howell	.45	.18	.04
☐ 16	Gary Carter	.60	.25	.06
☐ 17	Kevin Gross	.35	.15	.03
☐ 18	Lenny Harris	.45	.18	.04
☐ 19	Mike Hartley	.45	.18	.04
☐ 20	Mike Sharperson	.35	.15	.03
☐ 21	Mike Morgan	.45	.18	.04
☐ 22	John Candelaria	.35	.15	.03
☐ 23	Jeff Hamilton	.35	.15	.03
☐ 24	Jim Gott	.35	.15	.03
☐ 25	Barry Lyons	.35	.15	.03
☐ 26	Tim Crews	.35	.15	.03
☐ 27	Stan Javier	.35	.15	.03
☐ 28	Checklist Card	.35	.15	.03

Joe Ferguson CO
Ben Hines CO
Mark Cresse CO
Joe Amalfitano CO
Ron Perranoski CO
Manny Mota CO
Bill Russell CO

1991 Mother's Giants

The 1991 Mother's Cookies San Francisco Giants set contains 28 cards with rounded corners measuring the standard size (2 1/2" by 3 1/2"). The set includes an additional card advertising a trading card collectors album. The front design has borderless glossy color player photos from the waist up. The horizontally oriented backs are printed in red and purple, present biographical information, and have blank slots for player autographs. The cards are numbered on the back.

	MINT	EXC	G-VG
COMPLETE SET (28)	10.00	4.50	1.25
COMMON PLAYER (1-28)	.35	.15	.03

		MINT	EXC	G-VG
☐ 1	Roger Craig MG	.45	.18	.04
☐ 2	Will Clark	2.00	.80	.20
☐ 3	Steve Decker	.60	.25	.06
☐ 4	Kelly Downs	.35	.15	.03
☐ 5	Kevin Mitchell	.75	.30	.07
☐ 6	Willie McGee	.45	.18	.04
☐ 7	Bud Black	.35	.15	.03
☐ 8	Dave Righetti	.45	.18	.04
☐ 9	Matt Williams	.75	.30	.07
☐ 10	Robby Thompson	.45	.18	.04
☐ 11	Mike LaCoss	.35	.15	.03
☐ 12	Terry Kennedy	.35	.15	.03
☐ 13	Mark Leonard	.45	.18	.04

		MINT	EXC	G-VG
☐ 14	Rick Reuschel	.35	.15	.03
☐ 15	Mike Felder	.35	.15	.03
☐ 16	Scott Garrelts	.35	.15	.03
☐ 17	Jose Uribe	.35	.15	.03
☐ 18	Greg Litton	.35	.15	.03
☐ 19	Dave Anderson	.35	.15	.03
☐ 20	Don Robinson	.35	.15	.03
☐ 21	Mike Kingery	.35	.15	.03
☐ 22	Trevor Wilson	.35	.15	.03
☐ 23	Kirt Manwaring	.35	.15	.03
☐ 24	Kevin Bass	.35	.15	.03
☐ 25	Jeff Brantley	.35	.15	.03
☐ 26	John Burkett	.45	.18	.04
☐ 27	Giant's Coaches	.45	.18	.04
	Dusty Baker			
	Bill Fahey			
	Wendell Kim			
	Bob Lillis			
	Norm Sherry			
☐ 28	Checklist Card	.35	.15	.03
	Mark Letendre TR			
	Greg Lynn TR			

1991 Mother's Griffeys

The 1991 Mother's Cookies Father and Son set contains 4 cards with rounded corners measuring the standard size (2 1/2" by 3 1/2"). The front design has borderless glossy color player photos. The horizontally oriented backs are printed in red and purple, and present biographical information as well as career notes. A blank slot for the player's autograph appears at the bottom of each card. The cards are numbered on the back.

		MINT	EXC	G-VG
	COMPLETE SET (4)	6.00	2.50	.60
	COMMON PLAYER (1-4)	1.00	.40	.10
☐ 1	Ken Griffey Jr. (Holding bat)	3.00	1.25	.30
☐ 2	Ken Griffey Sr. (Holding glove)	1.00	.40	.10
☐ 3	Ken Griffey Sr. and Ken Griffey Jr. (Pose with gloves)	2.00	.80	.20
☐ 4	Ken Griffey Sr. and Ken Griffey Jr. (Looking over shoulder)	2.00	.80	.20

1991 Mother's Rangers

The 1991 Mother's Cookies Texas Rangers set contains 28 cards with rounded corners measuring the standard size (2 1/2" by 3 1/2"). The front design has borderless glossy color player photos, with the locker room as the background. The horizontally oriented backs are printed in red and purple,

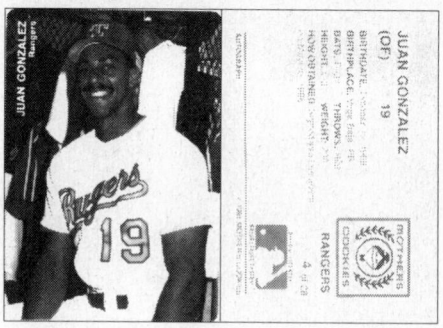

present biographical information, and have blank slots for player autographs. The cards are numbered on the back.

		MINT	EXC	G-VG
	COMPLETE SET (28)	11.00	5.00	1.35
	COMMON PLAYER (1-28)	.35	.15	.03
☐ 1	Bobby Valentine MG	.45	.18	.04
☐ 2	Nolan Ryan	3.00	1.25	.30
☐ 3	Ruben Sierra	1.25	.50	.12
☐ 4	Juan Gonzalez	1.25	.50	.12
☐ 5	Steve Buechele	.45	.18	.04
☐ 6	Bobby Witt	.45	.18	.04
☐ 7	Geno Petralli	.35	.15	.03
☐ 8	Jeff Russell	.45	.18	.04
☐ 9	Rafael Palmeiro	.90	.40	.09
☐ 10	Julio Franco	.75	.30	.07
☐ 11	Jack Daugherty	.35	.15	.03
☐ 12	Gary Pettis	.35	.15	.03
☐ 13	John Barfield	.35	.15	.03
☐ 14	Scott Chiamparino	.45	.18	.04
☐ 15	Kevin Reimer	.45	.18	.04
☐ 16	Rich Gossage	.60	.25	.06
☐ 17	Brian Downing	.45	.18	.04
☐ 18	Denny Walling	.35	.15	.03
☐ 19	Mike Jeffcoat	.35	.15	.03
☐ 20	Mike Stanley	.35	.15	.03
☐ 21	Kevin Brown	.45	.18	.04
☐ 22	Kenny Rogers	.45	.18	.04
☐ 23	Jeff Huson	.35	.15	.03
☐ 24	Mario Diaz	.35	.15	.03
☐ 25	Brad Arnsberg	.45	.18	.04
☐ 26	John Russell	.35	.15	.03
☐ 27	Gerald Alexander	.45	.18	.04
☐ 28	Checklist Card	.45	.18	.04
	Tom Robson CO			
	Toby Harrah CO			
	Orlando Gomez CO			
	Tom House CO			
	Dave Oliver CO			
	Davey Lopes CO			

1991 Mother's Nolan Ryan

This four-card set was sponsored by Mother's Cookies in honor of Nolan Ryan, baseball's latest 300-game winner. One card was packaged in each box of Mother's Cookies 18-ounce family size bags of five different flavored cookies (Chocolate Chip, Cookie Parade, Oatmeal Raisin, Fudge'N Chips, and Costadas). Also collectors could purchase an uncut strip of the four cards for 7.95 with four proof-of-purchase seals, and a protective sleeve for 1.00. The standard-size (2 1/2" by 3 1/2") cards have on the fronts full-bleed color posed photos with rounded corners. In red and purple print, the horizontally oriented backs have biographical information, career notes, statistics, and space for an autograph. The cards are numbered on the back.

	MINT	EXC	G-VG
COMPLETE SET (4)	6.00	2.50	.60
COMMON PLAYER (1-4)	2.00	.80	.20

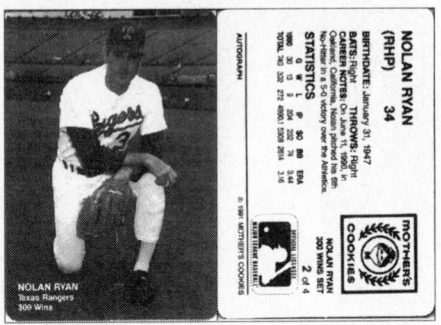

☐ 1 Nolan Ryan (Front pose Hand in glove)	2.00	.80	.20
☐ 2 Nolan Ryan (Kneeling on one knee)	2.00	.80	.20
☐ 3 Nolan Ryan (Side pose)	2.00	.80	.20
☐ 4 Nolan Ryan (Front pose, Ball in hand)	2.00	.80	.20

1976 Motorola Old Timers

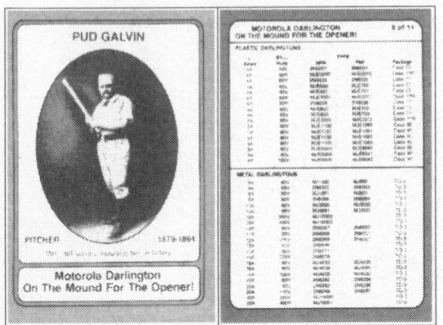

This 11-card, standard size, 2 1/2" by 3 1/2", set was issued by Motorola in 1976 and honored some of Baseball's all-time greats. The front of the cards were about the player while the backs of the cards talked in technical terms about Motorola products. The cards are also made on a thin (paper-like) card stock and are very flimsy.

	MINT	EXC	G-VG
COMPLETE SET (11)	20.00	8.50	2.75
COMMON PLAYER (1-11)	1.00	.40	.10
☐ 1 Honus Wagner	4.00	1.75	.40
☐ 2 Nap Lajoie	3.00	1.25	.30
☐ 3 Ty Cobb	5.00	2.25	.50
☐ 4 William Wambsganss	1.00	.40	.10
☐ 5 Three Fingers Brown	2.00	.80	.20
☐ 6 Ray Schalk	2.00	.80	.20
☐ 7 Frank Frisch	2.00	.80	.20
☐ 8 Pud Galvin	2.00	.80	.20
☐ 9 Babe Ruth	7.50	3.25	.75
☐ 10 Grover C. Alexander	2.50	1.00	.25
☐ 11 Frank L. Chance	2.00	.80	.20

1989 MSA Cereal Superstars

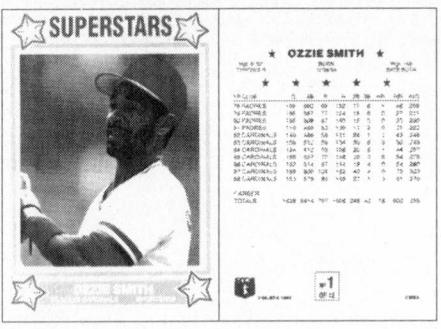

This 12-card, standard size, 2 1/2" by 3 1/2", set was issued by MSA (Michael Schechter Associates) and celebrated 12 of the leading players in the game as of 1989. The sets have an attractive design of stars in each of the front corners with the word Superstars on the top of the card and players name, team, and position underneath the full color photo of the player. Like most of the MSA sets there are no team logos used. The vertically-oriented backs show career statistics. Supposedly two cards were included in each specially-marked Ralston Purina cereal box.

	MINT	EXC	G-VG
COMPLETE SET (12)	7.50	3.25	.75
COMMON PLAYER (1-12)	.50	.20	.05
☐ 1 Ozzie Smith	.65	.25	.06
☐ 2 Andre Dawson	.65	.25	.06
☐ 3 Darryl Strawberry	.80	.35	.08
☐ 4 Mike Schmidt	1.00	.40	.10
☐ 5 Orel Hershiser	.50	.20	.05
☐ 6 Tim Raines	.50	.20	.05
☐ 7 Roger Clemens	1.00	.40	.10
☐ 8 Kirby Puckett	.80	.35	.08
☐ 9 George Brett	.80	.35	.08
☐ 10 Alan Trammell	.50	.20	.05
☐ 11 Don Mattingly	.80	.35	.08
☐ 12 Jose Canseco	1.00	.40	.10

1990 MSA AGFA

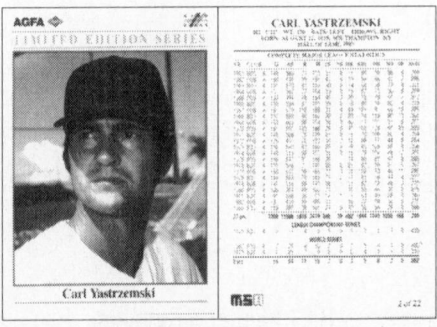

This 22-card set was issued by MSA (Michael Schechter Associates) for AGFA. The cards measure the standard size (2 1/2" by 3 1/2"). The fronts display color head and shoulders shots, with a thin red border on a white card face. In turquoise lettering, the words "Limited Edition Series" appear above the pictures; the player's name is given below the pictures. In black on white, the backs present complete year by year major league statistics. The cards are numbered on the back. The promotion supposedly consisted of a three-card pack of these cards given away with any purchase of a three-pack of AGFA film.

	MINT	EXC	G-VG
COMPLETE SET (22)	17.50	7.50	2.00
COMMON PLAYER (1-22)	.40	.16	.04

		MINT	EXC	G-VG
☐ 1	Willie Mays	1.50	.60	.15
☐ 2	Carl Yastrzemski	1.25	.50	.12
☐ 3	Harmon Killebrew	.75	.30	.07
☐ 4	Joe Torre	.40	.16	.04
☐ 5	Al Kaline	.90	.40	.09
☐ 6	Hank Aaron	1.50	.60	.15
☐ 7	Rod Carew	1.25	.50	.12
☐ 8	Roberto Clemente	1.25	.50	.12
☐ 9	Luis Aparicio	.60	.25	.06
☐ 10	Roger Maris	.90	.40	.09
☐ 11	Joe Morgan	.75	.30	.07
☐ 12	Maury Wills	.40	.16	.04
☐ 13	Brooks Robinson	.90	.40	.09
☐ 14	Tom Seaver	1.50	.60	.15
☐ 15	Steve Carlton	.90	.40	.09
☐ 16	Whitey Ford	.90	.40	.09
☐ 17	Jim Palmer	.90	.40	.09
☐ 18	Rollie Fingers	.90	.40	.09
☐ 19	Bruce Sutter	.40	.16	.04
☐ 20	Willie McCovey	.90	.40	.09
☐ 21	Mike Schmidt	1.25	.50	.12
☐ 22	Yogi Berra	1.00	.40	.10

1990 MSA Soda Superstars

This 24-card, standard size, 2 1/2" by 3 1/2", set was issued by MSA (Michael Schechter Associates) for 7/11, Squirt, and Dr. Pepper, and other carbonated beverages (but there are no markings on the cards whatsoever to indicate who sponsored the set other than MSA). These cards were distributed and issued inside 12-packs of sodas. The 12-packs included a checklist on one panel, and the cards themselves were glued on the inside of the pack so that it was difficult to remove a card without damaging it. The fronts feature a red-white and blue design framing the players photos while the back has major league career statistics and a sentence of career highlights. The back also has a fascimile autograph of the player on the back. Like many of the sets sponsored by MSA there are no team logos on the cards as they have been airbrushed away.

	MINT	EXC	G-VG
COMPLETE SET (24)	32.00	14.25	4.75
COMMON PLAYER (1-24)	.65	.25	.06

		MINT	EXC	G-VG
☐ 1	George Brett	1.00	.40	.10
☐ 2	Mark McGwire	1.00	.40	.10
☐ 3	Wade Boggs	1.25	.50	.12
☐ 4	Cal Ripken	1.25	.50	.12
☐ 5	Rickey Henderson	2.00	.80	.20
☐ 6	Dwight Gooden	1.00	.40	.10
☐ 7	Bo Jackson	3.00	1.25	.30

☐ 8	Roger Clemens	1.75	.70	.17
☐ 9	Orel Hershiser	.80	.35	.08
☐ 10	Ozzie Smith	.80	.35	.08
☐ 11	Don Mattingly	1.25	.50	.12
☐ 12	Kirby Puckett	1.25	.50	.12
☐ 13	Robin Yount	1.00	.40	.10
☐ 14	Tony Gwynn	1.25	.50	.12
☐ 15	Jose Canseco	2.00	.80	.20
☐ 16	Nolan Ryan	3.50	1.50	.35
☐ 17	Ken Griffey Jr.	5.00	2.25	.50
☐ 18	Will Clark	2.00	.80	.20
☐ 19	Ryne Sandberg	2.00	.80	.20
☐ 20	Kent Hrbek	.65	.25	.06
☐ 21	Carlton Fisk	1.00	.40	.10
☐ 22	Paul Molitor	.65	.25	.06
☐ 23	Dave Winfield	.80	.35	.08
☐ 24	Andre Dawson	.80	.35	.08

1916 M101-4 Sporting News

The cards in this 200-card set measure approximately 1 5/8" by 3". Issued in 1916 as a premium offer, the M101-4 set features black and white photos of current ballplayers. Each card is numbered and the reverse carries Sporting News advertising. The fronts are the same as D329, H801-9 and the unclassified Famous and Barr set. Most of the players in this also appear in the M101-5 set. Those cards which are asterisked in the checklist below are those cards which do not appear in the companion M101-5 set issued the year before.

	EX-MT	VG-E	GOOD
COMPLETE SET (200)	16500.00	7250.00	1750.00
COMMON PLAYER (1-200)	35.00	15.75	5.25

		EX-MT	VG-E	GOOD
☐ 1	Babe Adams	35.00	15.75	5.25
☐ 2	Sam Agnew	35.00	15.75	5.25
☐ 3	Eddie Ainsmith	35.00	15.75	5.25
☐ 4	Grover Alexander	100.00	45.00	15.00
☐ 5	Leon Ames	35.00	15.75	5.25
☐ 6	Jimmy Archer	35.00	15.75	5.25
☐ 7	Jimmy Austin	35.00	15.75	5.25
☐ 8	H.D. Baird *	40.00	18.00	6.00
☐ 9	Frank Baker	80.00	36.00	12.00
☐ 10	Dave Bancroft	70.00	32.00	10.50
☐ 11	Jack Barry	35.00	15.75	5.25
☐ 12	Zinn Beck	35.00	15.75	5.25
☐ 13	Chief Bender *	90.00	40.00	13.50
☐ 14	Joe Benz	35.00	15.75	5.25
☐ 15	Bob Bescher	35.00	15.75	5.25
☐ 16	Al Betzel	35.00	15.75	5.25
☐ 17	Mordecai Brown	70.00	32.00	10.50
☐ 18	Eddie Burns	35.00	15.75	5.25
☐ 19	George Burns *	40.00	18.00	6.00
☐ 20	George J. Burns	35.00	15.75	5.25
☐ 21	Joe Bush	35.00	15.75	5.25
☐ 22	Donie Bush *	40.00	18.00	6.00

#	Name			
☐ 23	Art Butler	35.00	15.75	5.25
☐ 24	Bobbie Byrne	35.00	15.75	5.25
☐ 25	Forrest Cady *	40.00	18.00	6.00
☐ 26	Jim Callahan	35.00	15.75	5.25
☐ 27	Ray Caldwell	35.00	15.75	5.25
☐ 28	Max Carey	70.00	32.00	10.50
☐ 29	George Chalmers	35.00	15.75	5.25
☐ 30	Ray Chapman	50.00	22.50	7.50
☐ 31	Larry Cheney	35.00	15.75	5.25
☐ 32	Ed Cicotte	50.00	22.50	7.50
☐ 33	Tommy Clarke	35.00	15.75	5.25
☐ 34	Eddie Collins	80.00	36.00	12.00
☐ 35	Shano Collins	35.00	15.75	5.25
☐ 36	Charles Comiskey	80.00	36.00	12.00
☐ 37	Joe Connolly	35.00	15.75	5.25
☐ 38	Ty Cobb *	1800.00	800.00	200.00
☐ 39	Harry Coveleskie	35.00	15.75	5.25
☐ 40	Gabby Cravath	40.00	18.00	6.00
☐ 41	Sam Crawford	70.00	32.00	10.50
☐ 42	Jean Dale	35.00	15.75	5.25
☐ 43	Jake Daubert	40.00	18.00	6.00
☐ 44	Charles Deal	35.00	15.75	5.25
☐ 45	Frank Demaree	35.00	15.75	5.25
☐ 46	Josh Devore *	40.00	18.00	6.00
☐ 47	William Doak	35.00	15.75	5.25
☐ 48	Bill Donovan	35.00	15.75	5.25
☐ 49	Red Dooin	35.00	15.75	5.25
☐ 50	Mike Doolan	35.00	15.75	5.25
☐ 51	Larry Doyle	35.00	15.75	5.25
☐ 52	Jean Dubuc	35.00	15.75	5.25
☐ 53	Oscar J. Dugey	35.00	15.75	5.25
☐ 54	John Evers	70.00	32.00	10.50
☐ 55	Red Faber	70.00	32.00	10.50
☐ 56	Happy Felsch	50.00	22.50	7.50
☐ 57	Bill Fischer	35.00	15.75	5.25
☐ 58	Ray Fisher	35.00	15.75	5.25
☐ 59	Max Flack	35.00	15.75	5.25
☐ 60	Art Fletcher	35.00	15.75	5.25
☐ 61	Eddie Foster	35.00	15.75	5.25
☐ 62	Jacques Fournier	35.00	15.75	5.25
☐ 63	Del Gainer	35.00	15.75	5.25
☐ 64	Chick Gandil *	70.00	32.00	10.50
☐ 65	Larry Gardner	35.00	15.75	5.25
☐ 66	Joe Gedeon	35.00	15.75	5.25
☐ 67	Gus Getz	35.00	15.75	5.25
☐ 68	George Gibson	35.00	15.75	5.25
☐ 69	Wilbur Good	35.00	15.75	5.25
☐ 70	Hank Gowdy	35.00	15.75	5.25
☐ 71	Jack Graney	35.00	15.75	5.25
☐ 72	Clark Griffith *	100.00	45.00	15.00
☐ 73	Tommy Griffith	35.00	15.75	5.25
☐ 74	Heine Groh	40.00	18.00	6.00
☐ 75	Earl Hamilton	35.00	15.75	5.25
☐ 76	Bob Harmon	35.00	15.75	5.25
☐ 77	Roy Hartzell	35.00	15.75	5.25
☐ 78	Claude Hendrix	35.00	15.75	5.25
☐ 79	Olaf Henriksen	35.00	15.75	5.25
☐ 80	John Henry	35.00	15.75	5.25
☐ 81	Buck Herzog	35.00	15.75	5.25
☐ 82	Hugh High	35.00	15.75	5.25
☐ 83	Dick Hoblitzell	35.00	15.75	5.25
☐ 84	Harry Hooper	70.00	32.00	10.50
☐ 85	Ivan Howard	35.00	15.75	5.25
☐ 86	Miller Huggins	70.00	32.00	10.50
☐ 87	Joe Jackson	2250.00	900.00	225.00
☐ 88	William James	35.00	15.75	5.25
☐ 89	Harold Janvrin	35.00	15.75	5.25
☐ 90	Hughie Jennings	70.00	32.00	10.50
☐ 91	Walter Johnson	500.00	225.00	75.00
☐ 92	Fielder Jones	35.00	15.75	5.25
☐ 93	Joe Judge *	40.00	18.00	6.00
☐ 94	Benny Kauff	35.00	15.75	5.25
☐ 95	Bill Killifer	35.00	15.75	5.25
☐ 96	Ed Konetchy	35.00	15.75	5.25
☐ 97	Nap Lajoie	225.00	100.00	33.00
☐ 98	Jack Lapp	35.00	15.75	5.25
☐ 99	John Lavan	35.00	15.75	5.25
☐ 100	Jimmy Lavender	35.00	15.75	5.25
☐ 101	Nemo Leibold	35.00	15.75	5.25
☐ 102	Hub Leonard	35.00	15.75	5.25
☐ 103	Duffy Lewis	35.00	15.75	5.25
☐ 104	Hans Lobert	35.00	15.75	5.25
☐ 105	Tom Long	35.00	15.75	5.25
☐ 106	Fred Luderus	35.00	15.75	5.25
☐ 107	Connie Mack	175.00	80.00	27.00
☐ 108	Lee Magee	35.00	15.75	5.25
☐ 109	Sherry Magee *	40.00	18.00	6.00
☐ 110	Al Mamaux	35.00	15.75	5.25
☐ 111	Leslie Mann	35.00	15.75	5.25
☐ 112	Rabbit Maranville	70.00	32.00	10.50
☐ 113	Rube Marquard	70.00	32.00	10.50
☐ 114	J.E. Mayer	35.00	15.75	5.25
☐ 115	George McBride	35.00	15.75	5.25
☐ 116	John McGraw	100.00	45.00	15.00
☐ 117	Jack McInnis	40.00	18.00	6.00
☐ 118	Fred Merkle	40.00	18.00	6.00
☐ 119	Chief Meyers	35.00	15.75	5.25
☐ 120	Clyde Milan	35.00	15.75	5.25
☐ 121	John Miller *	40.00	18.00	6.00
☐ 122	Otto Miller	35.00	15.75	5.25
☐ 123	Willie Mitchell	35.00	15.75	5.25
☐ 124	Fred Mollwitz	35.00	15.75	5.25
☐ 125	Pat Moran	35.00	15.75	5.25
☐ 126	Ray Morgan	35.00	15.75	5.25
☐ 127	George Moriarty	35.00	15.75	5.25
☐ 128	Guy Morton	35.00	15.75	5.25
☐ 129	Mike Mowrey *	40.00	18.00	6.00
☐ 130	Eddie Murphy	35.00	15.75	5.25
☐ 131	Hy Myers	35.00	15.75	5.25
☐ 132	Bert Niehoff	35.00	15.75	5.25
☐ 133	Rube Oldring	35.00	15.75	5.25
☐ 134	Oliver O'Mara	35.00	15.75	5.25
☐ 135	Steve O'Neill	35.00	15.75	5.25
☐ 136	Dode Paskert	35.00	15.75	5.25
☐ 137	Roger Peckinpaugh	35.00	15.75	5.25
☐ 138	Walter Pipp	35.00	20.00	6.75
☐ 139	Del Pratt	35.00	15.75	5.25
☐ 140	Pat Ragan *	40.00	18.00	6.00
☐ 141	Bill Rariden	35.00	15.75	5.25
☐ 142	Eppa Rixey	70.00	32.00	10.50
☐ 143	Davey Robertson	35.00	15.75	5.25
☐ 144	Wilbert Robinson	100.00	45.00	15.00
☐ 145	Bob Roth	35.00	15.75	5.25
☐ 146	Eddie Roush	80.00	36.00	12.00
☐ 147	Clarence Rowland	35.00	15.75	5.25
☐ 148	Nap Rucker	35.00	15.75	5.25
☐ 149	Dick Rudolph	35.00	15.75	5.25
☐ 150	Reb Russell	35.00	15.75	5.25
☐ 151	Babe Ruth	4250.00	1800.00	425.00
☐ 152	Vic Saier	35.00	15.75	5.25
☐ 153	Slim Sallee	35.00	15.75	5.25
☐ 154	Ray Schalk	70.00	32.00	10.50
☐ 155	Wally Schang	35.00	15.75	5.25
☐ 156	Frank Schulte	35.00	15.75	5.25
☐ 157	Everett Scott	40.00	18.00	6.00
☐ 158	Jim Scott	35.00	15.75	5.25
☐ 159	Tom Seaton	35.00	15.75	5.25
☐ 160	Howard Shanks	35.00	15.75	5.25
☐ 161	Bob Shawkey	40.00	18.00	6.00
☐ 162	Ernie Shore	40.00	18.00	6.00
☐ 163	Bert Shotton	35.00	15.75	5.25
☐ 164	George Sisler	100.00	45.00	15.00
☐ 165	J.C. Smith	35.00	15.75	5.25
☐ 166	Fred Snodgrass	35.00	15.75	5.25
☐ 167	George Stallings	35.00	15.75	5.25
☐ 168	Oscar Stanage	35.00	15.75	5.25
☐ 169	Charles Stengel	500.00	225.00	75.00
☐ 170	Milton Stock	35.00	15.75	5.25
☐ 171	Amos Strunk	35.00	15.75	5.25
☐ 172	Billy Sullivan	40.00	18.00	6.00
☐ 173	Jeff Tesreau	35.00	15.75	5.25
☐ 174	Joe Tinker	70.00	32.00	10.50
☐ 175	Fred Toney	35.00	15.75	5.25
☐ 176	Terry Turner	35.00	15.75	5.25
☐ 177	George Tyler *	40.00	18.00	6.00
☐ 178	Jim Vaughn	35.00	15.75	5.25
☐ 179	Bobby Veach	35.00	15.75	5.25
☐ 180	James Viox	35.00	15.75	5.25
☐ 181	Oscar Vitt	35.00	15.75	5.25
☐ 182	Honus Wagner	500.00	225.00	75.00
☐ 183	Clarence Walker	35.00	15.75	5.25
☐ 184	Ed Walsh	70.00	32.00	10.50
☐ 185	Bill Wambsganss *	40.00	18.00	6.00
☐ 186	Buck Weaver	50.00	22.50	7.50
☐ 187	Carl Weilman	35.00	15.75	5.25
☐ 188	Zack Wheat	70.00	32.00	10.50
☐ 189	George Whitted	35.00	15.75	5.25
☐ 190	Fred Williams	35.00	15.75	5.25
☐ 191	Arthur Wilson	35.00	15.75	5.25
☐ 192	J.O. Wilson	35.00	15.75	5.25
☐ 193	Ivy Wingo	35.00	15.75	5.25
☐ 194	Meldon Wolfgang	35.00	15.75	5.25
☐ 195	Joe Wood	50.00	22.50	7.50
☐ 196	Steve Yerkes	35.00	15.75	5.25
☐ 197	Pep Young * (Detroit Tigers)	40.00	18.00	6.00
☐ 198	Rollie Zeider	35.00	15.75	5.25
☐ 199	Heine Zimmerman	35.00	15.75	5.25
☐ 200	Dutch Zwilling	35.00	15.75	5.25

1915 M101-5 Sporting News

EVERETT SCOTT
S. S.—Boston Red Sox
160

The cards in this 200-card set measure 1 5/8 by 3". The 1915 M101-5 series of black and white, numbered baseball cards is very similar in style to M101-4. The set was offered as a marketing promotion by C.C. Spink and Son, publishers of The Sporting News ("The Baseball Paper of the World"). Most of the players in this also appear in the M101-4 set. Those cards which are asterisked in the checklist below are those cards which do not appear in the companion M101-4 set issued the next year.

	EX-MT	VG-E	GOOD
COMPLETE SET (200)	20000.00	8000.00	2000.00
COMMON PLAYER (1-200)	40.00	18.00	6.00

		EX-MT	VG-E	GOOD
☐ 1	Babe Adams	40.00	18.00	6.00
☐ 2	Sam Agnew	40.00	18.00	6.00
☐ 3	Ed Ainsmith	40.00	18.00	6.00
☐ 4	Grover Alexander	120.00	55.00	18.00
☐ 5	Leon Ames	40.00	18.00	6.00
☐ 6	Jimmy Archer	40.00	18.00	6.00
☐ 7	Jimmy Austin	40.00	18.00	6.00
☐ 8	Frank Baker	90.00	40.00	13.50
☐ 9	Dave Bancroft	80.00	36.00	12.00
☐ 10	Jack Barry	40.00	18.00	6.00
☐ 11	Zinn Beck	40.00	18.00	6.00
☐ 12	Luke Boone *	45.00	20.00	6.75
☐ 13	Joe Benz	40.00	18.00	6.00
☐ 14	Bob Bescher	40.00	18.00	6.00
☐ 15	Al Betzel	40.00	18.00	6.00
☐ 16	Roger Bresnahan *	90.00	40.00	13.50
☐ 17	Eddie Burns	40.00	18.00	6.00
☐ 18	G.J. Burns	40.00	18.00	6.00
☐ 19	Joe Bush	40.00	18.00	6.00
☐ 20	Owen Bush *	45.00	20.00	6.75
☐ 21	Art Butler	40.00	18.00	6.00
☐ 22	Bobby Byrne	40.00	18.00	6.00
☐ 23	Mordecai Brown	80.00	36.00	12.00
☐ 24	Jimmy Callahan	40.00	18.00	6.00
☐ 25	Ray Caldwell	40.00	18.00	6.00
☐ 26	Max Carey	80.00	36.00	12.00
☐ 27	George Chalmers	40.00	18.00	6.00
☐ 28	Frank Chance *	120.00	55.00	18.00
☐ 29	Ray Chapman	60.00	27.00	9.00
☐ 30	Larry Cheney	40.00	18.00	6.00
☐ 31	Ed Cicotte	60.00	27.00	9.00
☐ 32	Tommy Clarke	40.00	18.00	6.00
☐ 33	Eddie Collins	90.00	40.00	13.50
☐ 34	Shano Collins	40.00	18.00	6.00
☐ 35	Charles Comiskey	90.00	40.00	13.50
☐ 36	Joe Connolly	40.00	18.00	6.00
☐ 37	L. Cook *	45.00	20.00	6.75
☐ 38	Jack Coombs *	90.00	40.00	13.50
☐ 39	Dan Costello *	45.00	20.00	6.75
☐ 40	Harry Coveleskie	40.00	18.00	6.00
☐ 41	Gavvy Cravath	45.00	20.00	6.75
☐ 42	Sam Crawford	80.00	36.00	12.00
☐ 43	Jean Dale	40.00	18.00	6.00
☐ 44	Jake Daubert	45.00	20.00	6.75
☐ 45	G.A. Davis Jr. *	45.00	20.00	6.75
☐ 46	Charles Deal	40.00	18.00	6.00
☐ 47	Frank Demaree	40.00	18.00	6.00
☐ 48	Bill Doak	40.00	18.00	6.00
☐ 49	Bill Donovan	40.00	18.00	6.00
☐ 50	Red Dooin	40.00	18.00	6.00
☐ 51	Mike Doolan	40.00	18.00	6.00
☐ 52	Larry Doyle	40.00	18.00	6.00
☐ 53	Jean Dubuc	40.00	18.00	6.00
☐ 54	Oscar Dugey	40.00	18.00	6.00
☐ 55	John Evers	80.00	36.00	12.00
☐ 56	Red Faber	80.00	36.00	12.00
☐ 57	Happy Felsch	60.00	27.00	9.00
☐ 58	Bill Fischer	40.00	18.00	6.00
☐ 59	Ray Fisher	40.00	18.00	6.00
☐ 60	Max Flack	40.00	18.00	6.00
☐ 61	Art Fletcher	40.00	18.00	6.00
☐ 62	Eddie Foster	40.00	18.00	6.00
☐ 63	Jacques Fournier	40.00	18.00	6.00
☐ 64	Del Gainer	40.00	18.00	6.00
☐ 65	Larry Gardner	40.00	18.00	6.00
☐ 66	Joe Gedeon	40.00	18.00	6.00
☐ 67	Gus Getz	40.00	18.00	6.00
☐ 68	George Gibson	40.00	18.00	6.00
☐ 69	Wilbur Good	40.00	18.00	6.00
☐ 70	Hank Gowdy	40.00	18.00	6.00
☐ 71	Jack Graney	40.00	18.00	6.00
☐ 72	Tommy Griffith	40.00	18.00	6.00
☐ 73	Heine Groh	45.00	20.00	6.75
☐ 74	Earl Hamilton	40.00	18.00	6.00
☐ 75	Bob Harmon	40.00	18.00	6.00
☐ 76	Roy Hartzell	40.00	18.00	6.00
☐ 77	Claude Hendrix	40.00	18.00	6.00
☐ 78	Olaf Henriksen	40.00	18.00	6.00
☐ 79	John Henry	40.00	18.00	6.00
☐ 80	Buck Herzog	40.00	18.00	6.00
☐ 81	Hugh High	40.00	18.00	6.00
☐ 82	Dick Hoblitzell	40.00	18.00	6.00
☐ 83	Harry Hooper	80.00	36.00	12.00
☐ 84	Ivan Howard	40.00	18.00	6.00
☐ 85	Miller Huggins	80.00	36.00	12.00
☐ 86	Joe Jackson	2750.00	1100.00	275.00
☐ 87	William James	40.00	18.00	6.00
☐ 88	Harold Janvrin	40.00	18.00	6.00
☐ 89	Hughie Jennings	80.00	36.00	12.00
☐ 90	Walter Johnson	600.00	270.00	90.00
☐ 91	Fielder Jones	40.00	18.00	6.00
☐ 92	Benny Kauff	40.00	18.00	6.00
☐ 93	Bill Killefer	40.00	18.00	6.00
☐ 94	Ed Konetchy	40.00	18.00	6.00
☐ 95	Napoleon Lajoie	250.00	110.00	37.50
☐ 96	Jack Lapp	40.00	18.00	6.00
☐ 97	John Lavan	40.00	18.00	6.00
☐ 98	Jimmy Lavender	40.00	18.00	6.00
☐ 99	Nemo Leibold	40.00	18.00	6.00
☐ 100	Hub Leonard	40.00	18.00	6.00
☐ 101	Duffy Lewis	40.00	18.00	6.00
☐ 102	Hans Lobert	40.00	18.00	6.00
☐ 103	Tom Long	40.00	18.00	6.00
☐ 104	Fred Luderus	40.00	18.00	6.00
☐ 105	Connie Mack	200.00	90.00	30.00
☐ 106	Lee Magee	40.00	18.00	6.00
☐ 107	Al Mamaux	40.00	18.00	6.00
☐ 108	Leslie Mann	40.00	18.00	6.00
☐ 109	Rabbit Maranville	80.00	36.00	12.00
☐ 110	Rube Marquard	80.00	36.00	12.00
☐ 111	Armando Marsans *	45.00	20.00	6.75
☐ 112	J.E. Mayer	40.00	18.00	6.00
☐ 113	George McBride	40.00	18.00	6.00
☐ 114	John McGraw	120.00	55.00	18.00
☐ 115	Jack McInnis	45.00	20.00	6.75
☐ 116	Fred Merkle	45.00	20.00	6.75
☐ 117	Chief Meyers	40.00	18.00	6.00
☐ 118	Clyde Milan	40.00	18.00	6.00
☐ 119	Otto Miller	40.00	18.00	6.00
☐ 120	Willie Mitchell	40.00	18.00	6.00
☐ 121	Fred Mollwitz	40.00	18.00	6.00
☐ 122	J.H. Moran *	45.00	20.00	6.75
☐ 123	Pat Moran	40.00	18.00	6.00
☐ 124	Ray Morgan	40.00	18.00	6.00
☐ 125	George Moriarty	40.00	18.00	6.00
☐ 126	Guy Morton	40.00	18.00	6.00
☐ 127	Eddie Murphy	40.00	18.00	6.00
☐ 128	Jack Murray *	45.00	20.00	6.75
☐ 129	Hy Myers	40.00	18.00	6.00
☐ 130	Bert Niehoff	40.00	18.00	6.00
☐ 131	Les Nunamaker *	45.00	20.00	6.75
☐ 132	Rube Oldring	40.00	18.00	6.00
☐ 133	Oliver O'Mara	40.00	18.00	6.00
☐ 134	Steve O'Neill	40.00	18.00	6.00
☐ 135	Dode Paskert	40.00	18.00	6.00
☐ 136	Roger Peckinpaugh	40.00	18.00	6.00
☐ 137	E.J. Pfeffer *	45.00	20.00	6.75
☐ 138	George Pierce *	45.00	20.00	6.75
☐ 139	Walter Pipp	50.00	22.50	7.50
☐ 140	Del Pratt	40.00	18.00	6.00

		EX-MT	VG-E	GOOD
☐ 141	Bill Rariden	40.00	18.00	6.00
☐ 142	Eppa Rixey	80.00	36.00	12.00
☐ 143	Davey Robertson	40.00	18.00	6.00
☐ 144	Wilbert Robinson	120.00	55.00	18.00
☐ 145	Bob Roth	40.00	18.00	6.00
☐ 146	Eddie Roush	90.00	40.00	13.50
☐ 147	Clarence Rowland	40.00	18.00	6.00
☐ 148	Nap Rucker	40.00	18.00	6.00
☐ 149	Dick Rudolph	40.00	18.00	6.00
☐ 150	Reb Russell	40.00	18.00	6.00
☐ 151	Babe Ruth	6000.00	2250.00	550.00
☐ 152	Vic Saier	40.00	18.00	6.00
☐ 153	Slim Sallee	40.00	18.00	6.00
☐ 154	Germany Schaefer *	45.00	20.00	6.75
☐ 155	Ray Schalk	80.00	36.00	12.00
☐ 156	Wally Schang	40.00	18.00	6.00
☐ 157	Chas. Schmidt *	45.00	20.00	6.75
☐ 158	Frank Schulte	40.00	18.00	6.00
☐ 159	Jim Scott	40.00	18.00	6.00
☐ 160	Everett Scott	45.00	20.00	6.75
☐ 161	Tom Seaton	40.00	18.00	6.00
☐ 162	Howard Shanks	40.00	18.00	6.00
☐ 163	Bob Shawkey	45.00	20.00	6.75
☐ 164	Ernie Shore	45.00	20.00	6.75
☐ 165	Bert Shotton	40.00	18.00	6.00
☐ 166	George Sisler	120.00	55.00	18.00
☐ 167	J.C. Smith	40.00	18.00	6.00
☐ 168	Fred Snodgrass	40.00	18.00	6.00
☐ 169	George Stallings	40.00	18.00	6.00
☐ 170	Oscar Stanage	40.00	18.00	6.00
☐ 171	Charles Stengel	600.00	270.00	90.00
☐ 172	Milton Stock	40.00	18.00	6.00
☐ 173	Amos Strunk	40.00	18.00	6.00
☐ 174	Billy Sullivan	45.00	20.00	6.75
☐ 175	Jeff Tesreau	40.00	18.00	6.00
☐ 176	Jim Thorpe *	2500.00	1000.00	250.00
☐ 177	Joe Tinker	80.00	36.00	12.00
☐ 178	Fred Toney	40.00	18.00	6.00
☐ 179	Terry Turner	40.00	18.00	6.00
☐ 180	Jim Vaughn	40.00	18.00	6.00
☐ 181	Bobby Veach	40.00	18.00	6.00
☐ 182	James Viox	40.00	18.00	6.00
☐ 183	Oscar Vitt	40.00	18.00	6.00
☐ 184	Honus Wagner	600.00	270.00	90.00
☐ 185	Clarence Walker	40.00	18.00	6.00
☐ 186	Zack Wheat	80.00	36.00	12.00
☐ 187	Ed Walsh	80.00	36.00	12.00
☐ 188	Buck Weaver	60.00	27.00	9.00
☐ 189	Carl Weilman	40.00	18.00	6.00
☐ 190	George Whitted	40.00	18.00	6.00
☐ 191	Fred Williams	40.00	18.00	6.00
☐ 192	Arthur Wilson	40.00	18.00	6.00
☐ 193	J.O. Wilson	40.00	18.00	6.00
☐ 194	Ivy Wingo	40.00	18.00	6.00
☐ 195	Meldon Wolfgang	40.00	18.00	6.00
☐ 196	Joe Wood	60.00	27.00	9.00
☐ 197	Steve Yerkes	40.00	18.00	6.00
☐ 198	Rollie Zeider	40.00	18.00	6.00
☐ 199	Heinie Zimmerman	40.00	18.00	6.00
☐ 200	Dutch Zwilling	40.00	18.00	6.00

1911 M116 Sporting Life

The cards in this 288-card set measure 1 1/2" by 2 5/8". The Sporting Life set was offered as a premium to the publication's subscribers in 1911. Each of the 24 series of 12 cards came in an envelope printed with a list of the players within. Cards marked with an asterisk are also found with a special blue background and are worth double the listed price. McConnell

appears with both Boston AL (common) and Chicago White Sox (scarce); McQuillan appears with Phillies (common) and Cincinnati (scarce). Cards are numbered in the checklist below alphabetically within team. Teams are ordered alphabetically within league: Boston AL (1-19), Chicago AL (20-36), Cleveland (37-52), Detroit (53-73), New York AL (74-84), Philadelphia AL (85-105), St. Louis AL (106-120), Washington (121-134), Boston NL (135-147), Brooklyn (148-164), Chicago NL (165-185), Cincinnati (186-203), New York NL (204-223), Philadelphia NL (224-242), Pittsburgh (243-261), and St. Louis (262-279). Cards 280-288 feature minor leaguers and are somewhat more difficult to find since most are from the tougher higher series

		EX-MT	VG-E	GOOD
COMPLETE SET (290)		24000.00	9500.00	2500.00
COMMON MAJOR (1-279)		45.00	20.00	6.75
COMMON MINOR (280-288)		60.00	27.00	9.00
COMMON S21-S24		100.00	45.00	15.00

		EX-MT	VG-E	GOOD
☐ 1	Frank Arellanes	45.00	20.00	6.75
☐ 2	Bill Carrigan	45.00	20.00	6.75
☐ 3	Ed Cicotte	65.00	29.00	9.75
☐ 4	Ray Collins S24	100.00	45.00	15.00
☐ 5	Pat Donahue	45.00	20.00	6.75
☐ 6	Donovan S21	100.00	45.00	15.00
☐ 7	Arthur Engle	45.00	20.00	6.75
☐ 8	Larry Gardner S24	100.00	45.00	15.00
☐ 9	Charles Hall	45.00	20.00	6.75
☐ 10	Harry Hooper S23	250.00	110.00	37.50
☐ 11	Edwin Karger	45.00	20.00	6.75
☐ 12	Harry Lord *	45.00	20.00	6.75
☐ 13	Thomas Madden S24	100.00	45.00	15.00
☐ 14A	Amy McConnell (Boston AL)	45.00	20.00	6.75
☐ 14B	Amy McConnell (Chicago AL)	1500.00	600.00	150.00
☐ 15	Tris Speaker S23	450.00	200.00	67.50
☐ 16	Jake Stahl	50.00	22.50	7.50
☐ 17	John Thoney	45.00	20.00	6.75
☐ 18	Heine Wagner	50.00	22.50	7.50
☐ 19	Joe Wood S23	175.00	80.00	27.00
☐ 20	Lena Blackburn UER (sic, Blackburne)	45.00	20.00	6.75
☐ 21	James J. Block S21	100.00	45.00	15.00
☐ 22	Patsy Dougherty	45.00	20.00	6.75
☐ 23	Hugh Duffy	125.00	57.50	18.75
☐ 24	Ed Hahn	45.00	20.00	6.75
☐ 25	Paul Meloan S24	100.00	45.00	15.00
☐ 26	Fred Parent	45.00	20.00	6.75
☐ 27	Frederick Payne S21	100.00	45.00	15.00
☐ 28	William Purtell	45.00	20.00	6.75
☐ 29	James Scott S23	100.00	45.00	15.00
☐ 30	Frank Smith	45.00	20.00	6.75
☐ 31	Billy Sullivan	45.00	20.00	6.75
☐ 32	Lee Tannehill	45.00	20.00	6.75
☐ 33	Ed Walsh	100.00	45.00	15.00
☐ 34	Guy (Doc) White	45.00	20.00	6.75
☐ 35	Irv Young	45.00	20.00	6.75
☐ 36	Dutch Zwilling S24	100.00	45.00	15.00
☐ 37	Harry Bemis	45.00	20.00	6.75
☐ 38	Charles Berger	45.00	20.00	6.75
☐ 39	Joseph Birmingham	45.00	20.00	6.75
☐ 40	Hugh Bradley	45.00	20.00	6.75
☐ 41	Nig Clarke	45.00	20.00	6.75
☐ 42	Cy Falkenberg	45.00	20.00	6.75
☐ 43	Elmer Flick	125.00	57.50	18.75
☐ 44	Addie Joss	150.00	67.50	22.50
☐ 45	Napoleon Lajoie *	225.00	100.00	33.00
☐ 46	Frederick Linke S20	100.00	45.00	15.00
☐ 47	B. Lord	45.00	20.00	6.75
☐ 48	Deacon McGuire	45.00	20.00	6.75
☐ 49	Harry Niles	45.00	20.00	6.75
☐ 50	George Stovall	45.00	20.00	6.75
☐ 51	Terry Turner	45.00	20.00	6.75
☐ 52	Cy Young	225.00	100.00	33.00
☐ 53	Heine Beckendorf	45.00	20.00	6.75
☐ 54	Donie Bush	45.00	20.00	6.75
☐ 55	Ty Cobb *	2000.00	800.00	200.00
☐ 56	Sam Crawford *	125.00	57.50	18.75
☐ 57	Jim Delehanty	50.00	22.50	7.50
☐ 58	Bill Donovan	45.00	20.00	6.75
☐ 59	Hugh Jennings *	100.00	45.00	15.00
☐ 60	Davy Jones	45.00	20.00	6.75
☐ 61	Tom Jones	45.00	20.00	6.75
☐ 62	Chick Lathers S21	100.00	45.00	15.00
☐ 63	Matty McIntyre	45.00	20.00	6.75
☐ 64	George Moriarty	45.00	20.00	6.75
☐ 65	George Mullin	45.00	20.00	6.75
☐ 66	Charley O'Leary	45.00	20.00	6.75
☐ 67	Hub Pernoll S23	100.00	45.00	15.00
☐ 68	Boss Schmidt	45.00	20.00	6.75

☐ 69	Oscar Stanage	45.00	20.00	6.75
☐ 70	Stroud S21	100.00	45.00	15.00
☐ 71	Ed Summers	45.00	20.00	6.75
☐ 72	Ed Willett	45.00	20.00	6.75
☐ 73	Ralph Works	45.00	20.00	6.75
☐ 74	Jimmy Austin S19	100.00	45.00	15.00
☐ 75	Hal Chase *	75.00	34.00	11.25
☐ 76	Birdie Cree	45.00	20.00	6.75
☐ 77	Lou Criger	45.00	20.00	6.75
☐ 78	Russ Ford S23	100.00	45.00	15.00
☐ 79	Earle Gardner S23	100.00	45.00	15.00
☐ 80	John Knight S19	100.00	45.00	15.00
☐ 81	Frank LaPorte	45.00	20.00	6.75
☐ 82	George Stallings MG	45.00	20.00	6.75
☐ 83	Jeff Sweeney S19	100.00	45.00	15.00
☐ 84	Harry Wolter	45.00	20.00	6.75
☐ 85	Atkins S24	100.00	45.00	15.00
☐ 86	Frank Baker	125.00	57.50	18.75
☐ 87	Jack Barry	45.00	20.00	6.75
☐ 88	Chief Bender *	100.00	45.00	15.00
☐ 89	Eddie Collins *	125.00	57.50	18.75
☐ 90	Jack Coombs *	60.00	27.00	9.00
☐ 91	Harry Davis *	45.00	20.00	6.75
☐ 92	Jimmy Dygert	45.00	20.00	6.75
☐ 93	Topsy Hartsel	45.00	20.00	6.75
☐ 94	Heinie Heitmuller	45.00	20.00	6.75
☐ 95	Harry Krause	45.00	20.00	6.75
☐ 96	Jack Lapp S24	100.00	45.00	15.00
☐ 97	Paddy Livingstone	45.00	20.00	6.75
☐ 98	Connie Mack	175.00	80.00	27.00
☐ 99	Stuffy McInnes S24	100.00	45.00	15.00
☐ 100	Cy Morgan	45.00	20.00	6.75
☐ 101	Danny Murphy	45.00	20.00	6.75
☐ 102	Rube Oldring	45.00	20.00	6.75
☐ 103	Eddie Plank	175.00	80.00	27.00
☐ 104	Amos Strunk S24	100.00	45.00	15.00
☐ 105	Ira Thomas *	45.00	20.00	6.75
☐ 106	Bill Bailey	45.00	20.00	6.75
☐ 107	Dode Criss S19	100.00	45.00	15.00
☐ 108	Bert Graham	45.00	20.00	6.75
☐ 109	Roy Hartzell	45.00	20.00	6.75
☐ 110	Danny Hoffman	45.00	20.00	6.75
☐ 111	Harry Howell	45.00	20.00	6.75
☐ 112	Joe Lake S19	100.00	45.00	15.00
☐ 113	Jack O'Conner	45.00	20.00	6.75
☐ 114	Barney Pelty	45.00	20.00	6.75
☐ 115	Jack Powell	45.00	20.00	6.75
☐ 116	Al Schweitzer	45.00	20.00	6.75
☐ 117	Jim Stephens	45.00	20.00	6.75
☐ 118	George Stone	45.00	20.00	6.75
☐ 119	Rube Waddell	125.00	57.50	18.75
☐ 120	Bobby Wallace	90.00	40.00	13.50
☐ 121	Wid Conroy	45.00	20.00	6.75
☐ 122	Kid Elberfeld	45.00	20.00	6.75
☐ 123	Eddie Foster	45.00	20.00	6.75
☐ 124	Doc Gessler	45.00	20.00	6.75
☐ 125	Walter Johnson	500.00	225.00	75.00
☐ 126	Red Killifer S22	100.00	45.00	15.00
☐ 127	Jimmy McAleer MG	45.00	20.00	6.75
☐ 128	George McBride S21	100.00	45.00	15.00
☐ 129	Clyde Milan	45.00	20.00	6.75
☐ 130	Miller S23	100.00	45.00	15.00
☐ 131	Doc Reisling	45.00	20.00	6.75
☐ 132	Germany Schaefer	45.00	20.00	6.75
☐ 133	Gabby Street	45.00	20.00	6.75
☐ 134	Bob Unglaub	45.00	20.00	6.75
☐ 135	Fred Beck	45.00	20.00	6.75
☐ 136	Buster Brown	45.00	20.00	6.75
☐ 137	Cliff Curtis S23	100.00	45.00	15.00
☐ 138	George Ferguson	45.00	20.00	6.75
☐ 139	Samuel Frock S20	100.00	45.00	15.00
☐ 140	Peaches Graham	45.00	20.00	6.75
☐ 141	Buck Herzog	45.00	20.00	6.75
☐ 142	Fred Lake	45.00	20.00	6.75
☐ 143	Bayard Sharpe S23	100.00	45.00	15.00
☐ 144	David Shean S20	100.00	45.00	15.00
☐ 145	Charlie Smith S22	100.00	45.00	15.00
☐ 146	Harry Smith	45.00	20.00	6.75
☐ 147	Bill Sweeney	45.00	20.00	6.75
☐ 148	Cy Barger	45.00	20.00	6.75
☐ 149	George Bell	45.00	20.00	6.75
☐ 150	Bill Bergen	45.00	20.00	6.75
☐ 151	Al Burch	45.00	20.00	6.75
☐ 152	Bill Dahlen	50.00	22.50	7.50
☐ 153	William Davidson S21	100.00	45.00	15.00
☐ 154	Frank Dessau S21	100.00	45.00	15.00
☐ 155	Tex Erwin S20	100.00	45.00	15.00
☐ 156	John Hummel	45.00	20.00	6.75
☐ 157	George Hunter	45.00	20.00	6.75
☐ 158	Tim Jordan *	45.00	20.00	6.75
☐ 159	Ed Lennox	45.00	20.00	6.75
☐ 160	Pryor McElveen	45.00	20.00	6.75
☐ 161	Tommy McMillan	45.00	20.00	6.75
☐ 162	Nap Rucker	45.00	20.00	6.75
☐ 163	Doc Scanlon UER	45.00	20.00	6.75
	(sic, Scanlan)			
☐ 164	Kaiser Wilhelm	45.00	20.00	6.75
☐ 165	Jimmy Archer S22	100.00	45.00	15.00
☐ 166	Ginger Beaumont	45.00	20.00	6.75
☐ 167	Mordecai Brown *	125.00	57.50	18.75
☐ 168	Frank Chance *	150.00	67.50	22.50
☐ 169	Johnny Evers	125.00	57.50	18.75
☐ 170	Solly Hofman	45.00	20.00	6.75
☐ 171	John Kane	45.00	20.00	6.75
☐ 172	Johnny Kling	45.00	20.00	6.75
☐ 173	Rube Kroh	45.00	20.00	6.75
☐ 174	Harry McIntire	45.00	20.00	6.75
☐ 175	Tom Needham	45.00	20.00	6.75
☐ 176	Orvie Overall	45.00	20.00	6.75
☐ 177	Big Jeff Pfeffer S23	100.00	45.00	15.00
☐ 178	Pfiester	45.00	20.00	6.75
☐ 179	Ed Reulbach	50.00	22.50	7.50
☐ 180	Lew Richie	45.00	20.00	6.75
☐ 181	Frank Schulte	45.00	20.00	6.75
☐ 182	Jimmy Sheckard	45.00	20.00	6.75
☐ 183	Harry Steinfeldt	50.00	22.50	7.50
☐ 184	Joe Tinker	125.00	57.50	18.75
☐ 185	Heinie Zimmerman S19	100.00	45.00	15.00
☐ 186	Fred Beebe	45.00	20.00	6.75
☐ 187	Bob Bescher	45.00	20.00	6.75
☐ 188	Chappy Charles	45.00	20.00	6.75
☐ 189	Tommy Clarke S20	100.00	45.00	15.00
☐ 190	Tom Downey	45.00	20.00	6.75
☐ 191	Jim Doyle	45.00	20.00	6.75
☐ 192	Dick Eagan UER	45.00	20.00	6.75
	(sic, Egan)			
☐ 193	Art Fromme	45.00	20.00	6.75
☐ 194	Harry Gaspar S19	100.00	45.00	15.00
☐ 195	Clark Griffith	100.00	45.00	15.00
☐ 196	Doc Hoblitzel	45.00	20.00	6.75
☐ 197	Hans Lobert	45.00	20.00	6.75
☐ 198	Larry McLean	45.00	20.00	6.75
☐ 199	Mike Mitchell	45.00	20.00	6.75
☐ 200	Art Phelan S23	100.00	45.00	15.00
☐ 201	Jack Rowan	45.00	20.00	6.75
☐ 202	Bob Space UER	45.00	20.00	6.75
	(sic, Spade)			
☐ 203	George Suggs	45.00	20.00	6.75
☐ 204	Red Ames S22	100.00	45.00	15.00
☐ 205	Al Bridwell	45.00	20.00	6.75
☐ 206	Doc Crandall	45.00	20.00	6.75
☐ 207	Art Devlin	45.00	20.00	6.75
☐ 208	Josh Devore S19	100.00	45.00	15.00
☐ 209	Larry Doyle *	45.00	20.00	6.75
☐ 210	Art Fletcher S22	100.00	45.00	15.00
☐ 211	Christy Mathewson	500.00	225.00	75.00
☐ 212	John McGraw	175.00	80.00	27.00
☐ 213	Fred Merkle	50.00	22.50	7.50
☐ 214	Red Murray	45.00	20.00	6.75
☐ 215	Chief Myers S23	100.00	45.00	15.00
	(UER (sic, Meyers)			
☐ 216	Bugs Raymond	45.00	20.00	6.75
☐ 217	Admiral Schlei	45.00	20.00	6.75
☐ 218	Cy Seymour	45.00	20.00	6.75
☐ 219	Tillie Shafer S19	100.00	45.00	15.00
☐ 220	Fred Snodgrass	45.00	20.00	6.75
☐ 221	Fred Tenney *	45.00	20.00	6.75
☐ 222	Art Wilson S23	100.00	45.00	15.00
☐ 223	Hooks Wiltse	45.00	20.00	6.75
☐ 224	Johnny Bates	45.00	20.00	6.75
☐ 225	Kitty Bransfeld	45.00	20.00	6.75
☐ 226	Red Dooin *	45.00	20.00	6.75
☐ 227	Mickey Doolan	45.00	20.00	6.75
☐ 228	Bob Ewing	45.00	20.00	6.75
☐ 229	Bill Foxen	45.00	20.00	6.75
☐ 230	Eddie Grant	45.00	20.00	6.75
☐ 231	Fred Jacklitsch	45.00	20.00	6.75
☐ 232	Otto Knabe	45.00	20.00	6.75
☐ 233	Sherry Magee	45.00	20.00	6.75
☐ 234A	Geo.McQuillan *	45.00	20.00	6.75
	(Philadelphia NL)			
☐ 234B	Geo.McQuillan	1500.00	600.00	150.00
	(Cincinnati NL)			
☐ 235	Earl Moore	45.00	20.00	6.75
☐ 236	Pat Moran	45.00	20.00	6.75
☐ 237	Lew Moren	45.00	20.00	6.75
☐ 238	Dode Paskert S19	100.00	45.00	15.00
☐ 239	Lou Schettler S20	100.00	45.00	15.00
☐ 240	Tully Sparks	45.00	20.00	6.75
☐ 241	John Titus S23	100.00	45.00	15.00
☐ 242A	Jimmy Walsh S20	150.00	67.50	22.50
	dark background			
☐ 242B	Jimmy Walsh S22	150.00	67.50	22.50
	white background			
☐ 243	Ed Abbaticchio	45.00	20.00	6.75
☐ 244	Babe Adams	45.00	20.00	6.75
☐ 245	Bobby Byrne	45.00	20.00	6.75
☐ 246	Howie Camnitz	45.00	20.00	6.75

☐ 247	Vin Campbell S21	100.00	45.00	15.00
☐ 248	Fred Clarke	125.00	57.50	18.75
☐ 249	John Flynn S20	100.00	45.00	15.00
☐ 250	George Gibson *	45.00	20.00	6.75
☐ 251	Ham Hyatt	45.00	20.00	6.75
☐ 252	Fred Leach *	45.00	20.00	6.75
☐ 253	Sam Leever	45.00	20.00	6.75
☐ 254	Lefty Leifield	45.00	20.00	6.75
☐ 255	Nick Maddox	45.00	20.00	6.75
☐ 256	Dots Miller	45.00	20.00	6.75
☐ 257	Paddy O'Conner	45.00	20.00	6.75
☐ 258	Deacon Phillipe	50.00	22.50	7.50
☐ 259	Mike Simon S21	100.00	45.00	15.00
☐ 260	Hans Wagner *	500.00	225.00	75.00
☐ 261	Chief Wilson	45.00	20.00	6.75
☐ 262	Les Bachman UER	45.00	20.00	6.75
	(sic, Backman)			
☐ 263	Jack Bliss S21	100.00	45.00	15.00
☐ 264	Roger Bresnahan	100.00	45.00	15.00
☐ 265	Frank Corridon	45.00	20.00	6.75
☐ 266	Ray Demmitt S22	100.00	45.00	15.00
☐ 267	Rube Ellis	45.00	20.00	6.75
☐ 268	Steve Evans S23	100.00	45.00	15.00
☐ 269	Bob Harmon S20	100.00	45.00	15.00
☐ 270	Miller Huggins	100.00	45.00	15.00
☐ 271	Rudy Hulswitt	45.00	20.00	6.75
☐ 272	Ed Konetchy	45.00	20.00	6.75
☐ 273	Johnny Lush	45.00	20.00	6.75
☐ 274	Al Mattern	45.00	20.00	6.75
☐ 275	Mike Mowery S21	100.00	45.00	15.00
☐ 276	Rebel Oakes S24	100.00	45.00	15.00
☐ 277	Ed Phelps	45.00	20.00	6.75
☐ 278	Slim Sallee	45.00	20.00	6.75
☐ 279	Vic Willis	60.00	27.00	9.00
☐ 280	Coveleskie:	150.00	67.50	22.50
	Louisville S22			
☐ 281	Foster: Rochester	100.00	45.00	15.00
	S19			
☐ 282	Frill: Jersey	100.00	45.00	15.00
	City S20			
☐ 283	Hughes: Rochester	100.00	45.00	15.00
	S23			
☐ 284	Krueger: Sacramento	100.00	45.00	15.00
	S20			
☐ 285	Mitchell: Rochester	100.00	`45.00	15.00
	S19			
☐ 286	O'Hara: Toronto	60.00	27.00	9.00
☐ 287	Perring: Columbus	100.00	45.00	15.00
	S20			
☐ 288	Ray: Western League	100.00	45.00	15.00
	S24			

N28 Allen and Ginter

This 50-card set of The World's Champions was marketed by Allen and Ginter in 1887. The cards feature color lithographs of champion athletes from seven categories of sport, with baseball, rowing and boxing each having 10 individuals portrayed. Cards numbered 1 to 10 depict baseball players and cards numbered 11 to 20 depict popular boxers of the era. This set is called the first series although no such title appears on the cards. All 50 cards are checklisted on the reverse, and they are unnumbered. An album (ACC: A16) and an advertising banner (ACC: G20) were also issued in conjunction with this set.

		EX-MT	VG-E	GOOD
	COMPLETE SET (50)	9000.00	3750.00	1000.00
	COMMON BASEBALL (1-10)	325.00	150.00	50.00
	COMMON BOXERS (11-20)	100.00	45.00	15.00
	COMMON OTHERS (21-50)	30.00	13.50	4.50
☐ 1	Cap Anson	1600.00	700.00	175.00
☐ 2	Charlie Bennett	325.00	150.00	32.50
☐ 3	Bob Caruthers	375.00	165.00	37.50
☐ 4	John Clarkson	750.00	350.00	75.00
☐ 5	Charles Comiskey	750.00	350.00	75.00
☐ 6	Capt.Jack Glasscock	375.00	165.00	55.00
☐ 7	Timothy Keefe	750.00	325.00	110.00
☐ 8	Mike Kelly	1050.00	450.00	120.00
☐ 9	Joseph Mulvey	325.00	150.00	50.00
☐ 10	John M. Ward	750.00	325.00	110.00
☐ 11	Jimmy Carney	100.00	45.00	15.00
☐ 12	Jimmy Carroll	100.00	45.00	15.00
☐ 13	Jack Dempsey	150.00	67.50	22.50
☐ 14	Jake Kilrain	120.00	55.00	18.00
☐ 15	Joe Lannon	100.00	45.00	15.00
☐ 16	Jack McAuliffe	100.00	45.00	15.00
☐ 17	Charlie Mitchell	120.00	55.00	18.00
☐ 18	Jem Smith	100.00	45.00	15.00
☐ 19	John L. Sullivan	200.00	90.00	30.00
☐ 20	Ike Weir	100.00	45.00	15.00
☐ 21	Wm. Beach	30.00	13.50	4.50
☐ 22	Geo. Bubear	30.00	13.50	4.50
☐ 23	Jacob Gaudaur	30.00	13.50	4.50
☐ 24	Albert Hamm	30.00	13.50	4.50
☐ 25	Ed. Hanlan	30.00	13.50	4.50
☐ 26	Geo. H. Hosmer	30.00	13.50	4.50
☐ 27	John McKay	30.00	13.50	4.50
☐ 28	Wallace Ross	30.00	13.50	4.50
☐ 29	John Teemer	30.00	13.50	4.50
☐ 30	E.A. Trickett	30.00	13.50	4.50
☐ 31	Joe Acton	30.00	13.50	4.50
☐ 32	Theo. Bauer	30.00	13.50	4.50
☐ 33	Young Bibby	50.00	22.50	7.50
	(Geo. Mehling)			
☐ 34	J.F. McLaughlin	30.00	13.50	4.50
☐ 35	John McMahon	30.00	13.50	4.50
☐ 36	Wm. Muldoon	50.00	22.50	7.50
☐ 37	Matsada Sorakichi	30.00	13.50	4.50
☐ 38	Capt. A.H. Bogardus	30.00	13.50	4.50
☐ 39	Dr. W.F. Carver	30.00	13.50	4.50
☐ 40	Hon. W.F. Cody	125.00	57.50	18.75
	(Buffalo Bill)			
☐ 41	Miss Annie Oakley	90.00	40.00	13.50
☐ 42	Yank Adams	30.00	13.50	4.50
☐ 43	Maurice Daly	30.00	13.50	4.50
☐ 44	Jos. Dion	30.00	13.50	4.50
☐ 45	J. Schaefer	30.00	13.50	4.50
☐ 46	Wm. Sexton	30.00	13.50	4.50
☐ 47	Geo. F. Slosson	30.00	13.50	4.50
☐ 48	M. Vignaux	30.00	13.50	4.50
☐ 49	Albert Frey	30.00	13.50	4.50
☐ 50	J.L. Malone	30.00	13.50	4.50

N29 Allen and Ginter

The second series of The World's Champions was probably issued in 1888. Like the first series, the cards are backlisted and unnumbered. However, there are 17 distinct categories of sports represented in this set, with only six baseball players portrayed (as opposed to 10 in the first series). Each card has a color lithograph of the individual set against a white background. An album (ACC: A17) and an advertising banner (ACC: G21) were issued in conjunction with the set. The numbering below is alphabetical within sport, e.g., baseball players (1-6), boxers (7-14), and other sports (15-50).

		EX-MT	VG-E	GOOD
COMPLETE SET (50)		10000.00	4000.00	950.00
COMMON BASEBALL (1-6)		900.00	400.00	135.00
COMMON BOXERS (7-14)		300.00	135.00	45.00
COMMON OTHERS (15-50)		75.00	34.00	11.25
☐ 1	Wm. Ewing	1800.00	750.00	225.00
☐ 2	Jas. H. Fogarty	900.00	400.00	135.00
☐ 3	Charles H. Getzin	900.00	400.00	135.00
☐ 4	Geo. F. Miller	900.00	400.00	135.00
☐ 5	John Morrell	900.00	400.00	135.00
☐ 6	James Ryan	900.00	400.00	135.00
☐ 7	Patsey Duffy	300.00	135.00	45.00
☐ 8	Billy Edwards	300.00	135.00	45.00
☐ 9	Jack Havlin	300.00	135.00	45.00
☐ 10	Patsey Kerrigan	300.00	135.00	45.00
☐ 11	Geo. La Blance	300.00	135.00	45.00
☐ 12	Jack McGee	300.00	135.00	45.00
☐ 13	Frank Murphy	300.00	135.00	45.00
☐ 14	Johnny Murphy	300.00	135.00	45.00
☐ 15	Capt. J.C. Daly	75.00	34.00	11.25
☐ 16	M.W. Ford	75.00	34.00	11.25
☐ 17	Duncan C. Ross	75.00	34.00	11.25
☐ 18	W.E. Crist	75.00	34.00	11.25
☐ 19	H.G. Crocken	75.00	34.00	11.25
☐ 20	Willie Harradon	75.00	34.00	11.25
☐ 21	F.F. Ives	75.00	34.00	11.25
☐ 22	Wm. A. Rowe	75.00	34.00	11.25
☐ 23	Percy Stone	75.00	34.00	11.25
☐ 24	Ralph Temple	75.00	34.00	11.25
☐ 25	Fred Wood	75.00	34.00	11.25
☐ 26	Dr. James Dwight	90.00	40.00	13.50
☐ 27	Thomas Pettit	75.00	34.00	11.25
☐ 28	R.D. Sears	90.00	40.00	13.50
☐ 29	H.W. Slocum Jr.	75.00	34.00	11.25
☐ 30	Theobaud Bauer	75.00	34.00	11.25
☐ 31	Edwin Bibby	75.00	34.00	11.25
☐ 32	Hugh McCormack	75.00	34.00	11.25
☐ 33	Axel Paulsen	75.00	34.00	11.25
☐ 34	T. Ray	75.00	34.00	11.25
☐ 35	C.W.V. Clarke	75.00	34.00	11.25
☐ 36	E.D. Lange	75.00	34.00	11.25
☐ 37	E.C. Carter	75.00	34.00	11.25
☐ 38	Wm. Cummings	75.00	34.00	11.25
☐ 39	W.G. George	75.00	34.00	11.25
☐ 40	L.E. Myers	75.00	34.00	11.25
☐ 41	James Albert	75.00	34.00	11.25
☐ 42	Patrick Fitzgerald	75.00	34.00	11.25
☐ 43	W.B. Page	75.00	34.00	11.25
☐ 44	C.A.J. Queckberner	75.00	34.00	11.25
☐ 45	W.J.M. Barry	75.00	34.00	11.25
☐ 46	Wm. G. East	75.00	34.00	11.25
☐ 47	Wm. O'Connor	75.00	34.00	11.25
☐ 48	Gus Hill	75.00	34.00	11.25
☐ 49	Capt. Paul Boyton	75.00	34.00	11.25
☐ 50	Capt. Matthew Webb	75.00	34.00	11.25

N43 Allen and Ginter

The primary designs of this 50-card set are identical to those of N29, but these are placed on a much larger card with extraneous background detail. The set was produced in 1888 by Allen and Ginter as inserts for a larger tobacco package than those in which sets N28 and N29 were marketed. Cards of this set, which is backlisted, are considered to be much scarcer than their counterparts in N29.

		EX-MT	VG-E	GOOD
COMPLETE SET (50)		13500.00	6000.00	1350.00
COMMON BASEBALL (1-6)		1200.00	500.00	150.00
COMMON BOXERS (7-14)		400.00	180.00	60.00
COMMON OTHERS (15-50)		100.00	45.00	15.00
☐ 1	William Ewing	2250.00	900.00	225.50
☐ 2	Jas. J. Fogarty	1200.00	500.00	150.00
☐ 3	Charles Getzein	1200.00	500.00	150.00

☐ 4	Geo. F. Miller	1200.00	500.00	150.00
☐ 5	John Morrell	1200.00	500.00	150.00
☐ 6	James Ryan	1200.00	500.00	150.00
☐ 7	Patsey Duffy	400.00	180.00	60.00
☐ 8	Billy Edwards	400.00	180.00	60.00
☐ 9	Jack Havlin	400.00	180.00	60.00
☐ 10	Patsey Kerrigan	400.00	180.00	60.00
☐ 11	George LaBlanche	400.00	180.00	60.00
☐ 12	Jack McGee	400.00	180.00	60.00
☐ 13	Frank Murphy	400.00	180.00	60.00
☐ 14	Johnny Murphy	400.00	180.00	60.00
☐ 15	James Albert	100.00	45.00	15.00
☐ 16	W.J.M. Barry	100.00	45.00	15.00
☐ 17	Theobaud Bauer	100.00	45.00	15.00
☐ 18	Edwin Bibby	100.00	45.00	15.00
☐ 19	Capt. Paul Boyton	100.00	45.00	15.00
☐ 20	E.C. Carter	100.00	45.00	15.00
☐ 21	C.W.V. Clarke	100.00	45.00	15.00
☐ 22	W.E. Crist	100.00	45.00	15.00
☐ 23	H.G. Crocker	100.00	45.00	15.00
☐ 24	Wm. Cummings	100.00	45.00	15.00
☐ 25	Capt. J.C. Daly	100.00	45.00	15.00
☐ 26	Dr. James Dwight	120.00	55.00	18.00
☐ 27	Wm. G. East	100.00	45.00	15.00
☐ 28	Patrick Fitzgerald	100.00	45.00	15.00
☐ 29	M.W. Ford	100.00	45.00	15.00
☐ 30	W.G. George	100.00	45.00	15.00
☐ 31	Willie Harradon	100.00	45.00	15.00
☐ 32	Gus Hill	100.00	45.00	15.00
☐ 33	F.F. Ives	100.00	45.00	15.00
☐ 34	E.D. Lange	100.00	45.00	15.00
☐ 35	Hugh McCormack	100.00	45.00	15.00
☐ 36	L.E. Myers	100.00	45.00	15.00
☐ 37	Wm. O'Connor	100.00	45.00	15.00
☐ 38	W.B. Page	100.00	45.00	15.00
☐ 39	Axel. Paulsen	100.00	45.00	15.00
☐ 40	Thomas Pettitt	100.00	45.00	15.00
☐ 41	C.A.J. Queckberner	100.00	45.00	15.00
☐ 42	T. Ray	100.00	45.00	15.00
☐ 43	Duncan C. Ross	100.00	45.00	15.00
☐ 44	Wm. A. Rowe	100.00	45.00	15.00
☐ 45	R.D. Sears	120.00	55.00	18.00

		EX-MT	VG-E	GOOD
☐ 46	H.W. Slocum Jr.	100.00	45.00	15.00
☐ 47	Percy Stone	100.00	45.00	15.00
☐ 48	Ralph Temple	100.00	45.00	15.00
☐ 49	Capt. Matthew Webb	100.00	45.00	15.00
☐ 50	Fred Wood	100.00	45.00	15.00

N162 Goodwin

This 50-card set issued by Goodwin was one of the major competitors to the N28 and N29 sets marketed by Allen and Ginter. It contains individuals representing 18 sports, with eight baseball players pictured. Each color card is backlisted and bears advertising for "Old Judge" and "Gypsy Queen" cigarettes on the front. The set was released to the public in 1888 and an album (ACC: A36) is associated with it as a premium issue.

		EX-MT	VG-E	GOOD
	COMPLETE SET (50)	11000.00	4500.00	1100.00
	COMMON BASEBALL (1-8)	600.00	270.00	90.00
	COMMON BOXER	200.00	90.00	30.00
	COMMON OTHERS	50.00	22.50	7.50
☐ 1	Andrews: Phila.	600.00	270.00	90.00
☐ 2	Anson: Chicago	2500.00	1000.00	350.00
☐ 3	Brouthers: Detroit	1050.00	450.00	110.00
☐ 4	Caruthers: Brooklyn	650.00	300.00	100.00
☐ 5	Dunlap: Detroit	600.00	270.00	90.00
☐ 6	Glasscock: Indianapolis	650.00	300.00	100.00
☐ 7	Keefe: New York	1050.00	450.00	110.00
☐ 8	Kelly: Boston	1500.00	650.00	160.00
☐ 9	Acton (Wrestler)	75.00	34.00	11.25
☐ 10	Albert (Pedestrian)	50.00	22.50	7.50
☐ 11	Beach (Oarsman)	50.00	22.50	7.50
☐ 12	Beecher (Football)	750.00	325.00	110.00
☐ 13	Beeckman (Lawn Tennis)	75.00	34.00	11.25
☐ 14	Bogardus (Marksman)	50.00	22.50	7.50
☐ 15	Buffalo Bill (Wild West Hunter)	200.00	90.00	30.00
☐ 16	Daly (Billiards)	50.00	22.50	7.50
☐ 17	Dempsey (Pugilist)	300.00	135.00	45.00
☐ 18	D'oro (Pool)	50.00	22.50	7.50
☐ 19	Dwight (Lawn Tennis)	75.00	34.00	11.25
☐ 20	Fitzgerald (Pedestrian)	50.00	22.50	7.50
☐ 21	Garrison (Jockey)	50.00	22.50	7.50
☐ 22	Gaudaur (Oarsman)	50.00	22.50	7.50
☐ 23	Hanlan (Oarsman)	50.00	22.50	7.50
☐ 24	Kilrain (Pugilist)	250.00	110.00	37.50
☐ 25	MacKenzie (Chess)	50.00	22.50	7.50
☐ 26	McLaughlin (Jockey)	50.00	22.50	7.50
☐ 27	Mitchell (Pugilist)	250.00	110.00	37.50
☐ 28	Muldoon (Wrestler)	75.00	34.00	11.25
☐ 29	Murphy (Jockey)	50.00	22.50	7.50
☐ 30	Myers (Runner)	50.00	22.50	7.50
☐ 31	Page (High Jumper)	50.00	22.50	7.50
☐ 32	Prince (Bicyclist)	50.00	22.50	7.50
☐ 33	Ross (Broadswordsman)	50.00	22.50	7.50
☐ 34	Rowe (Bicyclist)	50.00	22.50	7.50
☐ 35	Rowell (Pedestrian)	50.00	22.50	7.50
☐ 36	Schaefer (Billiards)	50.00	22.50	7.50
☐ 37	Sears (Lawn Tennis)	75.00	34.00	11.25
☐ 38	Sexton (Billiards)	50.00	22.50	7.50
☐ 39	Slosson (Billiards)	50.00	22.50	7.50
☐ 40	Smith (Pugilist)	200.00	90.00	30.00
☐ 41	Steinitz (Chess)	50.00	22.50	7.50
☐ 42	Stevens (Bicyclist)	50.00	22.50	7.50
☐ 43	Sullivan (Pugilist)	350.00	160.00	52.50
☐ 44	Taylor (Lawn Tennis)	60.00	27.00	9.00
☐ 45	Teemer (Oarsman)	50.00	22.50	7.50
☐ 46	Vignaux (Billiards)	50.00	22.50	7.50
☐ 47	Voss (Strongest Man in the World)	50.00	22.50	7.50
☐ 48	Wood (Bicyclist)	50.00	22.50	7.50
☐ 49	Wood (Jockey)	50.00	22.50	7.50
☐ 50	Zukertort (Chess)	60.00	27.00	9.00

N172 Old Judge

The Goodwin Company's baseball series depicts hundreds of ballplayers from more than 40 major and minor league teams as well as boxers and wrestlers. The cards (approximately 1 1/2" by 2 1/2") are actually photographs from the Hall studio in New York which were pasted onto thick cardboard. The pictures are sepia in color with either a white or pink cast, and the cards are blank backed. They are found either numbered or unnumbered, with or without a copyright date, and with hand printed or machine printed names. All known cards have the name "Goodwin Co., New York" at the base. The cards were marketed during the period 1887-1890 in packs of "Old Judge" and "Gypsy Queen" cigarettes (cards marked with the latter brand are worth double the values listed below). They have been listed alphabetically and assigned numbers in the checklist below for simplicity's sake; the various poses known for some players also have not been listed for the same reason. Some of the players are pictured in horizontal (HOR) poses. In all, more than 2300 different Goodwin cards are known to collectors, with more being discovered every year. Cards from the "Spotted Tie" sub-series are denoted in the checklist below by SPOT.

	EX-MT	VG-E	GOOD
COMPLETE SET	110000.	46000.	11000.
COMMON PLAYER	110.00	50.00	16.50
COMMON PLAYER (DOUBLE)	150.00	67.50	22.50
COMMON BROWNS CHAMP	250.00	110.00	37.50
COMMON PLAYER (PCL)	1200.00	500.00	120.00
COMMON SPOTTED TIE	350.00	160.00	52.50
1 Gus Albert: Cleveland-Milwaukee	110.00	50.00	16.50
2 Charles Alcott: St. Louis Whites-Mansfield	110.00	50.00	16.50
3 Alexander: Des Moines	110.00	50.00	16.50
4 Myron Allen: K.C.	110.00	50.00	16.50
5 Bob Allen: Pitts.-Phila. N.L.	110.00	50.00	16.50
6 Uncle Bill Alvord: Toledo-Des Moines	110.00	50.00	16.50
7 Varney Anderson: St.Paul	110.00	50.00	16.50
8 Ed Andrews: Phila.	110.00	50.00	16.50
9 Andrews and Hoover: Philadelphia	150.00	67.50	22.50
10 Wally Andrews: Omaha	110.00	50.00	16.50
11 Bill Annis: Omaha-Worchester	110.00	50.00	16.50
12A Cap Anson: Chicago (in uniform)	12000.00	5000.00	1200.00
12B Cap Anson: Chicago (not in uniform)	1800.00	800.00	180.00
13 Old Hoss Ardner: Kansas City-St. Joe	110.00	50.00	16.50
14 Tug Arundel: Indianapolis-Whites	110.00	50.00	16.50
15 Bakley: Jersey-Cleve.	110.00	50.00	16.50
16 Clarence Baldwin: Cincinnati	110.00	50.00	16.50
17 Mark(Fido) Baldwin: Chicago-Columbus	110.00	50.00	16.50
18 Lady Baldwin: Detroit	110.00	50.00	16.50
19 James Banning: Wash.	110.00	50.00	16.50
20 Samuel Barkley: Pittsburgh-K.C.	110.00	50.00	16.50
21 John Barnes: Mgr. St. Paul	110.00	50.00	16.50
22 Bald Billy Barnie: Mgr. Baltimore	150.00	67.50	22.50
23 Charles Bassett: Indianapolis-N.Y.	110.00	50.00	16.50
24 Charles Bastian: Phila.-Chicago	110.00	50.00	16.50
25 Bastian and Shriver: Philadelphia	150.00	67.50	22.50
26 Ollie Beard: Cinc.	110.00	50.00	16.50
27 Ebenezer Beatin: Cleve.	110.00	50.00	16.50
28 Jake Beckley: "Eagle Eye" Whites-Pittsburgh	500.00	225.00	75.00
29 Stephen Behel SPOT	450.00	200.00	67.50
30 Charles Bennett: Detroit-Boston	110.00	50.00	16.50
31 Louis Bierbauer: A's	110.00	50.00	16.50
32 Bierbauer and Gamble Athletics	150.00	67.50	22.50
33 Bill Bishop: Pittsburgh-Syracuse	110.00	50.00	16.50
34 William Blair: A's-Hamiltons	110.00	50.00	16.50
35 Ned Bligh: Columbus	110.00	50.00	16.50
36 Bogart: Indianapolis	110.00	50.00	16.50
37 Boyce: Washington	110.00	50.00	16.50
38 Jake Boyd: Maroons	150.00	67.50	22.50
39 Honest John Boyle: St. Louis-Chicago	110.00	50.00	16.50
40 Handsome Henry Boyle Indianapolis-N.Y.	110.00	50.00	16.50
41 Nick Bradley: K.C.- Worchester	110.00	50.00	16.50
42 George(Grin) Bradley Sioux City	110.00	50.00	16.50
43 Stephen Brady SPOT	450.00	200.00	67.50
44 Breckinridge: Sacramento PCL	1200.00	500.00	120.00
45 Jim Brennan: Kansas City- A's	110.00	50.00	16.50
46 Timothy Brosnan: Minn.-Sioux City	110.00	50.00	16.50
47 Cal Broughton: Detroit-Boston	110.00	50.00	16.50
48 Big Dan Brouthers: Detroit-Boston	450.00	200.00	67.50
49 Thomas Brown: Pittsburgh-Boston	110.00	50.00	16.50
50 Brown: California-N.Y.	110.00	50.00	16.50
51 Pete Browning: "Gladiator" Louisville	250.00	110.00	37.50
52 Charles Brynan: Chicago-Des Moines	110.00	50.00	16.50
53 Al Buckenberger: Mgr. Columbus	110.00	50.00	16.50
54 Dick Buckley: Indianapolis-N.Y.	110.00	50.00	16.50
55 Charles Buffington: Philadelphia	110.00	50.00	16.50
56 Ernest Burch: Brooklyn-Whites	110.00	50.00	16.50
57 Bill Burdick: Omaha-Indianapolis	110.00	50.00	16.50
58 Black Jack Burdock: Boston-Brooklyn	110.00	50.00	16.50
59 Robert Burks: Sioux City	110.00	50.00	16.50
60 George Burnham "Watch" Mgr. Indianapolis	150.00	67.50	22.50
61 Burns: Omaha	110.00	50.00	16.50
62 Jimmy Burns: K.C.	110.00	50.00	16.50
63 Tommy (Oyster) Burns Baltimore-Brooklyn	110.00	50.00	16.50
64 Thomas E. Burns: Chicago	110.00	50.00	16.50
65A Doc Bushong: Brook.	110.00	50.00	16.50
65B Doc Bushong: Browns Champ	250.00	110.00	37.50
66 Patsy Cahill: Ind.	110.00	50.00	16.50
67 Count Campau: Kansas City-Detroit	110.00	50.00	16.50
68 Jimmy Canavan: Omaha	110.00	50.00	16.50
69 Bart Cantz: Whites-Baltimore	110.00	50.00	16.50
70 Handsome Jack Carney Washington	110.00	50.00	16.50
71 Hick Carpenter: Cincinnati	110.00	50.00	16.50
72 Cliff Carroll: Wash.	110.00	50.00	16.50
73 Scrappy Carroll: St.Paul-Chicago	110.00	50.00	16.50
74 Frederick Carroll: Pitts.	110.00	50.00	16.50
75 Jumbo Cartwright: Kansas City-St. Joe	110.00	50.00	16.50
76A Bob Caruthers: "Parisian" Brooklyn	150.00	67.50	22.50
76B Bob Caruthers: "Parisian" Browns Champs	300.00	135.00	45.00
77 Daniel Casey: Phila.	110.00	50.00	16.50
78 Icebox Chamberlain: St. Louis	110.00	50.00	16.50
79 Cupid Childs: Phila.-Syracuse	110.00	50.00	16.50
80 Bob Clark: Washington	110.00	50.00	16.50
81 Owen Clark: Washington	110.00	50.00	16.50
82 Clarke and Hughes: Brooklyn HOR	150.00	67.50	22.50
83 William(Dad) Clarke: Chicago-Omaha	110.00	50.00	16.50
84 John Clarkson: Chicago-Boston	450.00	200.00	67.50
85 Jack Clements: Philadelphia	110.00	50.00	16.50
86 Elmer Cleveland: Omaha-New York	110.00	50.00	16.50
87 Monk Cline: K.C.-Sioux City	110.00	50.00	16.50
88 Cody: Des Moines	110.00	50.00	16.50
89 John Coleman: Pittsburgh - A's	110.00	50.00	16.50
90 Bill Collins: New York-Newark	110.00	50.00	16.50
91 Hub Collins: Louisville-Brooklyn	110.00	50.00	16.50
92A Charles Comiskey: Browns Champs	800.00	350.00	120.00
92B Commy Comiskey: Minn.-Chicago	500.00	225.00	75.00
93 Pete Connell: Des Moines	110.00	50.00	16.50

No.	Name / Team			
94A	Roger Connor: All-Star	500.00	225.00	75.00
94B	Roger Connor: New York	500.00	225.00	75.00
95	Richard Conway: Boston-Worchester	110.00	50.00	16.50
96	Peter Conway: Det.-Pitts.-Ind.	110.00	50.00	16.50
97	James Conway: K.C.	110.00	50.00	16.50
98	Paul Cook: Louisville	110.00	50.00	16.50
99	Jimmy Cooney: Omaha-Chicago	110.00	50.00	16.50
100	Larry Corcoran: Indianapolis-London	110.00	50.00	16.50
101	Pop Corkhill: Cincinnnati-Brooklyn	110.00	50.00	16.50
102	Roscoe Coughlin: Maroons-Chicago	150.00	67.50	22.50
103	Cannon Ball Crane: New York	110.00	50.00	16.50
104	Samuel Crane: Wash.	110.00	50.00	16.50
105	Jack Crogan: Maroons	150.00	67.50	22.50
106	John Crooks: Whites-Omaha	110.00	50.00	16.50
107	Lave Cross: Louisville-A's-Phila.	110.00	50.00	16.50
108	Bill Crossley: Milw.	110.00	50.00	16.50
109A	Joe Crotty SPOT	400.00	180.00	60.00
109B	Joe Crotty: Sioux City	110.00	50.00	16.50
110	Billy Crowell: Cleveland-St. Joe	110.00	50.00	16.50
111	Jim Cudworth: St. Louis-Worchester	110.00	50.00	16.50
112	Bert Cunningham: Baltimore-Phila.	110.00	50.00	16.50
113	Tacks Curtis: St. Joe	110.00	50.00	16.50
114A	Ed Cushman SPOT	450.00	200.00	67.50
114B	Ed Cushman: Toledo	110.00	50.00	16.50
115	Tony Cusick: Mil.	110.00	50.00	16.50
116	Dailey: Oakland PCL	1200.00	500.00	120.00
117	Edward Dailey: Phil.-Wash.-Columbus	110.00	50.00	16.50
118	Bill Daley: Boston	110.00	50.00	16.50
119	Con Daley: Boston-Indianapolis	110.00	50.00	16.50
120	Abner Dalrymple: Pittsburgh-Denver	110.00	50.00	16.50
121	Tom Daly: Chicago-Wash.-Cleve.	110.00	50.00	16.50
122	James Daly: Minn.	110.00	50.00	16.50
123	Law Daniels: K.C.	110.00	50.00	16.50
124	Dell Darling: Chicago	110.00	50.00	16.50
125	Wm. Darnbrough: Denver	110.00	50.00	16.50
126	D. Davin: Milwaukee	110.00	50.00	16.50
127	Jumbo Davis: K.C.	110.00	50.00	16.50
128	Pat Dealey: Wash.	110.00	50.00	16.50
129	Thomas Deasley: New York-Washington	110.00	50.00	16.50
130	Edward Decker: Phil.	110.00	50.00	16.50
131	Big Ed Delahanty: Philadelphia	900.00	400.00	135.00
132	Jeremiah Denny: Indianapolis-New York	110.00	50.00	16.50
133	James Devlin: St.L.	110.00	50.00	16.50
134	Thomas Dolan: Whites-St. Louis-Denver	110.00	50.00	16.50
135	Jack Donahue: San Francisco PCL	1200.00	500.00	120.00
136A	James Donahue SPOT	400.00	180.00	60.00
136B	James Donahue: K.C.	110.00	50.00	16.50
137	James Donnelly: Washington	110.00	50.00	16.50
138	Dooley: Oakland PCL	1200.00	500.00	120.00
139	J. Doran: Omaha	110.00	50.00	16.50
140	Michael Dorgan: N.Y.	110.00	50.00	16.50
141	Doyle: San Fran. PCL	1200.00	500.00	120.00
142	Homerun Duffe: St.L.	110.00	50.00	16.50
143	Hugh Duffy: Chicago	500.00	225.00	75.00
144	Dan Dugdale: Maroons-Minneapolis	150.00	67.50	22.50
145	Dugrahm: Maroons	150.00	67.50	22.50
146	Duck Duke: Minn.	110.00	50.00	16.50
147	Sure Shot Dunlap: Pittsburgh	110.00	50.00	16.50
148	J. Dunn: Maroons	150.00	67.50	22.50
149	Jesse(Cyclone)Duryea St. Paul-Cinc.	110.00	50.00	16.50
150	John Dwyer: Chicago-Maroons	150.00	67.50	22.50
151	Billy Earle: Cincinnati-St.Paul	110.00	50.00	16.50
152	Buck Ebright: Wash.	110.00	50.00	16.50
153	Red Ehret: Louisville	110.00	50.00	16.50
154	R. Emmerke: Des Moines	110.00	50.00	16.50
155	Dude Esterbrook: Louisville-Ind.-New York-All Star	110.00	50.00	16.50
156	Henry Esterday: K.C.-Columbus	110.00	50.00	16.50
157	Long John Ewing: Louisville-N.Y.	110.00	50.00	16.50
158	Buck Ewing: New York	450.00	200.00	67.50
159	Ewing and Mascot: New York	350.00	160.00	52.50
160	Jay Faatz: Cleveland	110.00	50.00	16.50
161	Clinkgers Fagan: Kansas City-Denver	110.00	50.00	16.50
162	William Farmer: Pittsburgh-St. Paul	110.00	50.00	16.50
163	Sidney Farrar: Philadelphia	110.00	50.00	16.50
164	John(Moose)Farrell: Wash.-Baltimore	110.00	50.00	16.50
165	Charles(Duke)Farrell Chicago	110.00	50.00	16.50
166	Frank Fennelly: Cincinnati-A's	110.00	50.00	16.50
167	Chas. Ferguson: Phila.	110.00	50.00	16.50
168	Colonel Ferson: Washington	110.00	50.00	16.50
169	Wallace Fessenden: Umpire National	150.00	67.50	22.50
170	Jocko Fields: Pitts.	110.00	50.00	16.50
171	Fischer: Maroons	150.00	67.50	22.50
172	Thomas Flanigan: Cleve.-Sioux City	110.00	50.00	16.50
173	Silver Flint: Chicago	110.00	50.00	16.50
174	Thomas Flood: St. Joe	110.00	50.00	16.50
175	Flynn: Omaha	900.00	400.00	135.00
176	James Fogarty: Philadelphia	110.00	50.00	16.50
177	Frank(Monkey)Foreman Baltimore-Cinc.	110.00	50.00	16.50
178	Thomas Forster: Milwaukee-Hartford	110.00	50.00	16.50
179A	Elmer E. Foster SPOT	400.00	180.00	60.00
179B	Elmer Foster: New York-Chicago	110.00	50.00	16.50
180	F.W. Foster SPOT T.W. Forster (sic)	450.00	200.00	67.50
181A	Scissors Foutz: Browns Champ	250.00	110.00	37.50
181B	Scissors Foutz: Brooklyn	110.00	50.00	16.50
182	Julie Freeman: St.L.-Milwaukee	110.00	50.00	16.50
183	Will Fry: St. Joe	110.00	50.00	16.50
184	Fudger: Oakland PCL	1200.00	500.00	120.00
185	William Fuller: Milwaukee	110.00	50.00	16.50
186	Shorty Fuller: St.Louis	110.00	50.00	16.50
187	Christopher Fullmer: Baltimore	110.00	50.00	16.50
188	Fullmer and Tucker: Baltimore HOR	150.00	67.50	22.50
189	Honest John Gaffney: Mgr. Washington	150.00	67.50	22.50
190	Pud Galvin: Pitts.	500.00	225.00	75.00
191	Robert Gamble: A's	110.00	50.00	16.50
192	Charles Ganzel: Detroit-Boston	110.00	50.00	16.50
193	Frank (Gid) Gardner: Phila.-Washington	110.00	50.00	16.50
194	Gardner and Murray: Washington HOR	150.00	67.50	22.50
195	Ed Gastfield: Omaha	110.00	50.00	16.50
196	Hank Gastreich: Columbus	110.00	50.00	16.50
197	Emil Geiss: Chicago	110.00	50.00	16.50
198	Frenchy Genins: Sioux City	110.00	50.00	16.50
199	William George: N.Y.	110.00	50.00	16.50

□	#	Name			
□	200	Move Up Joe Gerhardt .... All Star-Jersey City	110.00	50.00	16.50
□	201	Pretzels Getzein: .... Detroit-Ind.	110.00	50.00	16.50
□	202	Lee Gibson: A's	110.00	50.00	16.50
□	203	Robert Gilks: Cleve.	110.00	50.00	16.50
□	204	Pete Gillespie: N.Y.	110.00	50.00	16.50
□	205	Barney Gilligan .... Washington-Detroit	110.00	50.00	16.50
□	206	Frank Gilmore: Wash.	110.00	50.00	16.50
□	207	Pebbly Jack Glasscock .... Indianapolis-N.Y.	150.00	67.50	22.50
□	208	Kid Gleason: Phila.	110.00	50.00	16.50
□	209A	Brother Bill Gleason .... A's-Louisville	110.00	50.00	16.50
□	209B	William Bill Gleason .... Browns Champs	250.00	110.00	37.50
□	210	Mouse Glenn: .... Sioux City	110.00	50.00	16.50
□	211	Walt Goldsby: Balt.	110.00	50.00	16.50
□	212	Michael Goodfellow: .... Cleveland-Detroit	110.00	50.00	16.50
□	213	George Gore .... (Pianolegs) New York	110.00	50.00	16.50
□	214	Frank Graves: Minn.	110.00	50.00	16.50
□	215	William Greenwood: .... Baltimore-Columbus	110.00	50.00	16.50
□	216	Michael Greer: .... Cleveland-Brooklyn	110.00	50.00	16.50
□	217	Mike Griffin: .... Baltimore-Phila NL	110.00	50.00	16.50
□	218	Clark Griffith: .... Milwaukee	550.00	240.00	80.00
□	219	Henry Gruber: Cleve.	110.00	50.00	16.50
□	220	Addison Gumbert: .... Chicago-Boston	110.00	50.00	16.50
□	221	Thomas Gunning: .... Philadelphia-A's	110.00	50.00	16.50
□	222	Joseph Gunson: K.C.	110.00	50.00	16.50
□	223	George Haddock: .... Washington	110.00	50.00	16.50
□	224	William Hafner: K.C.	110.00	50.00	16.50
□	225	Willie Hahm: .... Chicago Mascot Philadelphia	110.00	50.00	16.50
□	226	William Hallman: .... Philadelphia	110.00	50.00	16.50
□	227	Charlie Hallstrom: .... Minn.	110.00	50.00	16.50
□	228	Billy Hamilton: .... Kansas City-Phila.	550.00	240.00	80.00
□	229	Hamm and Williamson:	150.00	67.50	22.50
□	230A	Frank Hankinson: .... SPOT	400.00	180.00	60.00
□	230B	Frank Hankinson: .... Kansas City	110.00	50.00	16.50
□	231	Ned Hanlon: .... Det.-Boston-Pitts.	150.00	67.50	22.50
□	232	William Hanrahan: .... Maroons-Minn.	150.00	67.50	22.50
□	233	Hapeman: .... Sacramento PCL	1200.00	500.00	120.00
□	234	Pa Harkins: .... Brooklyn-Baltimore	110.00	50.00	16.50
□	235	William Hart: .... Cinc.-Des Moines	110.00	50.00	16.50
□	236	Wm. Hasamdear: K.C.	110.00	50.00	16.50
□	237	Colonel Hatfield: .... New York	110.00	50.00	16.50
□	238	Egyptian Healey: .... Wash.-Indianapolis	110.00	50.00	16.50
□	239	J.C. Healy: .... Omaha-Denver	110.00	50.00	16.50
□	240	Guy Hecker: .... Louisville	110.00	50.00	16.50
□	241	Tony Hellman: .... Sioux City	110.00	50.00	16.50
□	242	Hardie Henderson: .... Brook.-Pitts.-Balt.	110.00	50.00	16.50
□	243	Henderson and Greer: .... Brooklyn	150.00	67.50	22.50
□	244	Moxie Hengle: .... Maroons-Minneapolis	150.00	67.50	22.50
□	245	John Henry: Phila.	110.00	50.00	16.50
□	246	Edward Herr: .... Whites-Milwaukee	110.00	50.00	16.50
□	247	Hunkey Hines: Whites	110.00	50.00	16.50
□	248	Paul Hines: .... Wash.-Indianapolis	110.00	50.00	16.50
□	249	Texas Wonder Hoffman: .... Denver	110.00	50.00	16.50
□	250	Eddie Hogan: Cleve.	110.00	50.00	16.50
□	251A	William Holbert .... SPOT	350.00	160.00	52.50
□	251B	William Holbert: .... Brooklyn-Mets- Jersey City	110.00	50.00	16.50
□	252	James(Bugs) Holliday: .... Des Moines-Cinc.	110.00	50.00	16.50
□	253	Charles Hoover: .... Maroons-Chi.-K.C.	150.00	67.50	22.50
□	254	Buster Hoover: .... Phila.-Toronto	110.00	50.00	16.50
□	255	Jack Horner: .... Milwaukee-New Haven	110.00	50.00	16.50
□	256	Horner and Warner: .... Milwaukee	150.00	67.50	22.50
□	257	Michael Horning: .... Boston-Balt.-N.Y.	110.00	50.00	16.50
□	258	Pete Hotaling: .... Cleveland	110.00	50.00	16.50
□	259	William Howes: .... Minn.-St. Paul	110.00	50.00	16.50
□	260	Dummy Hoy: .... Washington	300.00	135.00	45.00
□	261A	Nat Hudson: .... Browns Champ	250.00	110.00	37.50
□	261B	Nat Hudson: .... St. Louis	110.00	50.00	16.50
□	262	Mickey Hughes: Brk.	110.00	50.00	16.50
□	263	Hungler: Sioux City	110.00	50.00	16.50
□	264	Wild Bill Hutchinson: .... Chicago	110.00	50.00	16.50
□	265	John Irwin: .... Wash.-Wilkes Barre	110.00	50.00	16.50
□	266	Cutrate Irwin: .... Phila.-Boston-Wash.	110.00	50.00	16.50
□	267	A.C. Jantzen: Minn.	110.00	50.00	16.50
□	268	Frederick Jevne: .... Minn.-St. Paul	110.00	50.00	16.50
□	269	John Johnson: .... K.C.-Columbus	110.00	50.00	16.50
□	270	Richard Johnston: .... Boston	110.00	50.00	16.50
□	271	Jordan: Minneapolis	110.00	50.00	16.50
□	272	Heinie Kappell: .... Columbus-Cincinnati	110.00	50.00	16.50
□	273	Keas: Milwaukee	110.00	50.00	16.50
□	274	Sir Timothy Keefe: .... New York	450.00	200.00	67.50
□	275	Keefe and Richardson .... Stealing 2nd Base New York HOR	350.00	160.00	52.50
□	276	George Keefe: Wash.	110.00	50.00	16.50
□	277	James Keenan: Cinc.	110.00	50.00	16.50
□	278	Mike (King) Kelly .... "10,000" Chic-Boston	900.00	400.00	135.00
□	279	Honest John Kelly: .... Mgr. Louisville	150.00	67.50	22.50
□	280	Kelly: (Umpire) .... Western Association	150.00	67.50	22.50
□	281	Charles Kelly: .... Philadelphia	110.00	50.00	16.50
□	282	Kelly and Powell: .... Umpire and Manager Sioux City	150.00	67.50	22.50
□	283A	Rudolph Kemmler: .... Browns Champ	250.00	110.00	37.50
□	283B	Rudolph Kemmler: .... St. Paul	110.00	50.00	16.50
□	284	Theodore Kennedy: .... Des Moines-Omaha	150.00	67.50	22.50
□	285	J.J. Kenyon: .... Whites-Des Moines	110.00	50.00	16.50
□	286	John Kerins: .... Louisville	110.00	50.00	16.50
□	287	Matthew Kilroy: .... Baltimore-Boston	110.00	50.00	16.50
□	288	Charles King: .... St.L.-Chi.	110.00	50.00	16.50
□	289	Aug. Kloff: .... Minn.-St.Joe	110.00	50.00	16.50
□	290	William Klusman: .... Milwaukee-Denver	110.00	50.00	16.50
□	291	Phillip Knell: .... St. Joe-Phila.	110.00	50.00	16.50
□	292	Fred Knouf: .... St. Louis	110.00	50.00	16.50
□	293	Charles Kremmeyer: .... Sacramento PCL	1200.00	500.00	120.00
□	294	William Krieg: .... Wash.-St. Joe-Minn.	110.00	50.00	16.50
□	295	Krieg and Kloff: .... Minneapolis	150.00	67.50	22.50
□	296	Gus Krock: Chicago	110.00	50.00	16.50
□	297	Willie Kuehne: .... Pittsburgh	110.00	50.00	16.50

☐ 298	Frederick Lange: .... Maroons	150.00	67.50	22.50
☐ 299	Ted Larkin: A's	110.00	50.00	16.50
☐ 300A	Arlie Latham: .... Browns Champ	250.00	110.00	37.50
☐ 300B	Arlie Latham: .... St. Louis-Chicago	150.00	67.50	22.50
☐ 301	John Lauer: .... Pittsburgh	110.00	50.00	16.50
☐ 302	Lawless: Columbus	110.00	50.00	16.50
☐ 303	John Leighton: Omaha	110.00	50.00	16.50
☐ 304	Levy: San Fran. PCL	1200.00	500.00	120.00
☐ 305	Tom Loftus MG: .... Whites-Cleveland	110.00	50.00	16.50
☐ 306	Lohbeck: Cleveland	110.00	50.00	16.50
☐ 307	Herman(Germany)Long ...... Maroons-K.C.	200.00	90.00	30.00
☐ 308	Danny Long: Oak. PCL	1200.00	500.00	120.00
☐ 309	Tom Lovett: .... Omaha-Brooklyn	110.00	50.00	16.50
☐ 310	Bobby (Link) Lowe: .... Milwaukee	200.00	90.00	30.00
☐ 311A	Jack Lynch SPOT	450.00	200.00	67.50
☐ 311B	John Lynch: .... All Stars	110.00	50.00	16.50
☐ 312	Dennis Lyons: A's	110.00	50.00	16.50
☐ 313	Harry Lyons: St. L.	110.00	50.00	16.50
☐ 314	Connie Mack: Wash.	1500.00	600.00	150.00
☐ 315	Joe (Reddie) Mack: .... Louisville	110.00	50.00	16.50
☐ 316	James (Little Mack) .... Macullar: Des Moines-Milwaukee	110.00	50.00	16.50
☐ 317	Kid Madden: Boston	110.00	50.00	16.50
☐ 318	Daniel Mahoney: .... St. Joe	110.00	50.00	16.50
☐ 319	Willard(Grasshopper) .... Maines: St. Paul	110.00	50.00	16.50
☐ 320	Fred Mann: .... St.Louis-Hartford	110.00	50.00	16.50
☐ 321	Jimmy Manning: K.C.	110.00	50.00	16.50
☐ 322	Charles(Lefty) Marr: .... Col.-Cinc.	110.00	50.00	16.50
☐ 323	Mascot (Willie .... Breslin): New York	125.00	57.50	18.75
☐ 324	Samuel Maskery: .... Milwaukee-Des Moines	110.00	50.00	16.50
☐ 325	Bobby Mathews: A's	110.00	50.00	16.50
☐ 326	Michael Mattimore: .... New York-A's	110.00	50.00	16.50
☐ 327	Albert Maul: Pitts.	110.00	50.00	16.50
☐ 328A	Albert Mays SPOT	350.00	160.00	52.50
☐ 328B	Albert Mays: .... Columbus	110.00	50.00	16.50
☐ 329	James McAleer: .... Cleveland	110.00	50.00	16.50
☐ 330	Thomas McCarthy: .... Phila.-St. Louis	450.00	200.00	67.50
☐ 331	John McCarthy: K.C.	110.00	50.00	16.50
☐ 332	James McCauley: .... Maroons-Phila.	150.00	67.50	22.50
☐ 333	William McClellan: .... Brooklyn-Denver	110.00	50.00	16.50
☐ 334	John McCormack: .... Whites	110.00	50.00	16.50
☐ 335	Big Jim McCormick: .... Chicago-Pittsburgh	110.00	50.00	16.50
☐ 336	McCreachery: .... Mgr. Indianapolis	150.00	67.50	22.50
☐ 337	Thomas McCullum: .... Minneapolis	110.00	50.00	16.50
☐ 338	James(Chippy)McGarr: .... St. Louis-K.C.	110.00	50.00	16.50
☐ 339	Jack McGeachy: Ind.	110.00	50.00	16.50
☐ 340	John McGlone: .... Cleveland-Detroit	110.00	50.00	16.50
☐ 341	James(Deacon)McGuire ...... Phila.-Toronto	110.00	50.00	16.50
☐ 342	Bill (Gunner) .... McGunnigle: Mgr. Brooklyn	150.00	67.50	22.50
☐ 343	Ed McKean: Cleveland	110.00	50.00	16.50
☐ 344	Alex McKinnon: .... Pittsburgh	110.00	50.00	16.50
☐ 345	Thomas McLaughlin .... SPOT	400.00	180.00	60.00
☐ 346	John (Bid) McPhee: .... Cincinnati	150.00	67.50	22.50
☐ 347	James McQuaid: .... Denver	110.00	50.00	16.50
☐ 348	John McQuaid: .... Umpire Amer. Assoc.	150.00	67.50	22.50
☐ 349	Jame McTamany: .... Brook.-Col.-K.C.	110.00	50.00	16.50
☐ 350	George McVey: .... Mil.-Denver-St. Joe	110.00	50.00	16.50
☐ 351	Meegan: San Fran. .... PCL	1200.00	500.00	120.00
☐ 352	John Messitt: Omaha	110.00	50.00	16.50
☐ 353	George(Doggie)Miller .... Pittsburgh	110.00	50.00	16.50
☐ 354	Joseph Miller: .... Omaha-Minneapolis	110.00	50.00	16.50
☐ 355	Jocko Milligan: .... St. Louis-Phila.	110.00	50.00	16.50
☐ 356	E.L. Mills: .... Milwaukee	110.00	50.00	16.50
☐ 357	Minnehan: .... Minneapolis	110.00	50.00	16.50
☐ 358	Samuel Moffet: Ind.	110.00	50.00	16.50
☐ 359	Honest Morrill: .... Boston-Washington	110.00	50.00	16.50
☐ 360	Ed Morris .... (Cannonball): Pittsburgh	110.00	50.00	16.50
☐ 361	Morrisey: St. Paul	110.00	50.00	16.50
☐ 362	Tony(Count) Mullane: .... Cincinnati	150.00	67.50	22.50
☐ 363	Joseph Mulvey: .... Philadelphia	110.00	50.00	16.50
☐ 364	P.L. Murphy: .... St. Paul	110.00	50.00	16.50
☐ 365	P.J. Murphy: .... New York	110.00	50.00	16.50
☐ 366	Miah Murray: Wash.	110.00	50.00	16.50
☐ 367	James (Truthful) .... Mutrie: Mgr. N.Y.	110.00	50.00	16.50
☐ 368	George Myers: .... Indianapolis-Phila.	110.00	50.00	16.50
☐ 369	Al (Cod) Myers: .... Washington	110.00	50.00	16.50
☐ 370	Thomas Nagle: .... Omaha-Chi.	110.00	50.00	16.50
☐ 371	Billy Nash: Boston	110.00	50.00	16.50
☐ 372	Jack(Candy) Nelson: .... SPOT	400.00	180.00	60.00
☐ 373	Kid Nichols: Omaha	650.00	300.00	100.00
☐ 374	Samuel Nichols: .... Pittsburgh	110.00	50.00	16.50
☐ 375	J.W. Nicholson: .... Maroons-Minn.	150.00	67.50	22.50
☐ 376	Tom Nicholson .... (Parson): Whites-Cleveland	110.00	50.00	16.50
☐ 377A	Nicholls Nicol .... Browns Champ	250.00	110.00	37.50
☐ 377B	Hugh Nicol: Cinc.	110.00	50.00	16.50
☐ 378	Nicol and Reilly .... Cincinnati	150.00	67.50	22.50
☐ 379	Frederick Nyce .... Whites-Burlington	110.00	50.00	16.50
☐ 380	Doc Oberlander .... Cleveland-Syracuse	110.00	50.00	16.50
☐ 381	Jack O'Brien .... Brooklyn-Baltimore	110.00	50.00	16.50
☐ 382	William O'Brien: .... Washington	110.00	50.00	16.50
☐ 383	O'Brien and Irwin:	150.00	67.50	22.50
☐ 384	Darby O'Brien: .... Brooklyn	110.00	50.00	16.50
☐ 385	John O'Brien: Cleve.	110.00	50.00	16.50
☐ 386	P.J. O'Connell: .... Omaha-Des Moines	110.00	50.00	16.50
☐ 387	John O'Connor: .... Cincinnati-Columbus	110.00	50.00	16.50
☐ 388	Hank O'Day: .... Washington-New York	110.00	50.00	16.50
☐ 389A	James O'Neil: .... St. Louis-Chicago	110.00	50.00	16.50
☐ 389B	James O'Neil: .... Browns Champs	250.00	110.00	37.50
☐ 390	O'Neill: Oakland .... PCL	1200.00	500.00	120.00
☐ 391	Orator O'Rourke: .... New York	500.00	225.00	75.00
☐ 392	Thomas O'Rourke: .... Boston-Jersey City	110.00	50.00	16.50
☐ 393A	David Orr SPOT .... Brooklyn-Columbus	350.00	160.00	52.50
☐ 393B	David Orr: .... All Star-Brooklyn-Columbus	110.00	50.00	16.50
☐ 394	Parsons: Minneapolis	110.00	50.00	16.50
☐ 395	Owen Patton: .... Minn.-Des Moines	110.00	50.00	16.50
☐ 396	James Peeples: .... Brooklyn-Columbus	110.00	50.00	16.50
☐ 397	Peeples and Henderson ...... Brooklyn	150.00	67.50	22.50

☐ 398	Hip Perrier: .... San Francisco PCL	1200.00	500.00	120.00
☐ 399	Patrick Pettee: Milwaukee-London	110.00	50.00	16.50
☐ 400	Pettee and Lowe: .... Milwaukee	150.00	67.50	22.50
☐ 401	Bob Pettit: Chicago	110.00	50.00	16.50
☐ 402	Dandelion Pfeffer: .... Chi.	110.00	50.00	16.50
☐ 403	Dick Phelan: .... Des Moines	110.00	50.00	16.50
☐ 404	William Phillips: .... Brooklyn-Kansas City	110.00	50.00	16.50
☐ 405	Horace Phillips: .... Pittsburgh	110.00	50.00	16.50
☐ 406	John Pickett: .... St. Paul-K.C.-Phila.	110.00	50.00	16.50
☐ 407	George Pinkney: .... Brooklyn	110.00	50.00	16.50
☐ 408	Thomas Poorman: .... A's-Milwaukee	110.00	50.00	16.50
☐ 409	Henry Porter: .... Brooklyn-Kansas City	110.00	50.00	16.50
☐ 410	James Powell: .... Sioux City	110.00	50.00	16.50
☐ 411	Tom Powers: .... San Francisco PCL	1200.00	500.00	120.00
☐ 412	Bill Blondie Purcell: .... Baltimore-A's	110.00	50.00	16.50
☐ 413	Thomas Quinn: .... Baltimore	110.00	50.00	16.50
☐ 414	Joseph Quinn: .... Des Moines-Boston	110.00	50.00	16.50
☐ 415A	Old Hoss Radbourne: .... Boston (portrait)	750.00	325.00	110.00
☐ 415B	Old Hoss Radbourne: .... Boston (non-portrait)	500.00	225.00	75.00
☐ 416	Shorty Radford: .... Brooklyn-Cleveland	110.00	50.00	16.50
☐ 417	Tom Ramsey: .... Louisville	110.00	50.00	16.50
☐ 418	Rehse: Minneapolis	110.00	50.00	16.50
☐ 419	Long John Reilly: .... Cincinnati	110.00	50.00	16.50
☐ 420	Charles Reilly: .... (Princeton) St.Paul	110.00	50.00	16.50
☐ 421	Charles Reynolds: .... Kansas City	110.00	50.00	16.50
☐ 422	Hardie Richardson .... Detroit-Boston	110.00	50.00	16.50
☐ 423	Danny Richardson: .... New York	110.00	50.00	16.50
☐ 424	Frank Ringo: .... St. Paul	110.00	50.00	16.50
☐ 425	Charles Ripslager .... SPOT	400.00	180.00	60.00
☐ 426	John Roach: New York	110.00	50.00	16.50
☐ 427	Wilbert Robinson .... (Uncle Robbie): A's	550.00	240.00	80.00
☐ 428	M.C. Robinson: Minn.	110.00	50.00	16.50
☐ 429A	Yank Robinson: .... St. Louis	110.00	50.00	16.50
☐ 429B	Wm.(Yank) Robinson: ...... Browns Champs	250.00	110.00	37.50
☐ 430	George Rooks: .... Maroons-Detroit	150.00	67.50	22.50
☐ 431	James(Chief) Roseman .... SPOT	400.00	180.00	60.00
☐ 432	Davis Rowe: .... Mgr. K.C.-Denver	110.00	50.00	16.50
☐ 433	Jack Rowe: Detroit- .... Pittsburgh	110.00	50.00	16.50
☐ 434	Amos (Hoosier .... Thunderbolt) Rusie: Ind.-New York	750.00	325.00	110.00
☐ 435	James Ryan: Chicago	110.00	50.00	16.50
☐ 436	Henry Sage: .... Des Moines-Toledo	110.00	50.00	16.50
☐ 437	Sage and Van Dyke: .... Des Moines-Toledo	150.00	67.50	22.50
☐ 438	Frank Salee .... Omaha-Boston	110.00	50.00	16.50
☐ 439	Sanders: Omaha	110.00	50.00	16.50
☐ 440	Al (Ben) Sanders: .... Philadelphia	110.00	50.00	16.50
☐ 441	Frank Scheibeck: .... Detroit	110.00	50.00	16.50
☐ 442	Albert Schellhase: .... St. Joseph	110.00	50.00	16.50
☐ 443	William Schenkle: .... Milwaukee	110.00	50.00	16.50
☐ 444	Bill Schildknecht: .... Des Moines-Milwaukee	110.00	50.00	16.50
☐ 445	Gus (Pink Whiskers) .... Schmelz Mgr. Cincinnati	110.00	50.00	16.50
☐ 446	R. F. Schoch: Wash.	110.00	50.00	16.50
☐ 447	Lewis Schoeneck .... (Jumbo): Maroons-Indianapolis	150.00	67.50	22.50
☐ 448	Pop Schriver: Phila.	110.00	50.00	16.50
☐ 449	John Seery: Ind.	110.00	50.00	16.50
☐ 450	William Serad .... Cincinnnati-Toronto	110.00	50.00	16.50
☐ 451	Edward Seward: A's	110.00	50.00	16.50
☐ 452	George(Orator)Shafer .... Des Moines	110.00	50.00	16.50
☐ 453	Frank Shafer: .... St. Paul	110.00	50.00	16.50
☐ 454	Daniel Shannon: .... Omaha-L'ville-Phila.	110.00	50.00	16.50
☐ 455	William Sharsig: .... Mgr. Athletics	150.00	67.50	22.50
☐ 456	Samuel Shaw: .... Baltimore-Newark	110.00	50.00	16.50
☐ 457	John Shaw: .... Minneapolis	110.00	50.00	16.50
☐ 458	William Shindle: .... Baltimore-Phila.	110.00	50.00	16.50
☐ 459	George Shock: Wash.	110.00	50.00	16.50
☐ 460	Otto Shomberg: Ind.	110.00	50.00	16.50
☐ 461	Lev Shreve: Ind.	110.00	50.00	16.50
☐ 462	Ed (Baldy) Silch: .... Brooklyn-Denver	110.00	50.00	16.50
☐ 463	Michael Slattery: .... New York	110.00	50.00	16.50
☐ 464	Sam(Skyrocket)Smith: .... Louisville	110.00	50.00	16.50
☐ 465A	John (Phenomenal) .... Smith (portrait)	750.00	325.00	110.00
☐ 465B	John (Phenomenal) .... Smith: Balt.-A's (non-portrait)	110.00	50.00	16.50
☐ 466	Elmer Smith: .... Cincinnati	110.00	50.00	16.50
☐ 467	Fred(Sam) Smith: .... Des Moines	110.00	50.00	16.50
☐ 468	George Smith .... (Germany) Brooklyn	110.00	50.00	16.50
☐ 469	Pop Smith: .... Pitt.-Bos.-Phila.	110.00	50.00	16.50
☐ 470	Nick Smith: St. Joe	110.00	50.00	16.50
☐ 471	Pop Snyder: Cleve.	110.00	50.00	16.50
☐ 472	P.T. Somers: .... St. Louis	110.00	50.00	16.50
☐ 473	Joe Sommer: Balt.	110.00	50.00	16.50
☐ 474	Pete Sommers: .... Chicago-New York	110.00	50.00	16.50
☐ 475	William Sowders: .... Boston-Pittsburgh	110.00	50.00	16.50
☐ 476	John Sowders: .... St. Paul-Kansas City	110.00	50.00	16.50
☐ 477	Charles Sprague: .... Maroons-Chi.-Cleve.	150.00	67.50	22.50
☐ 478	Edward Sproat: .... Whites	110.00	50.00	16.50
☐ 479	Harry Staley: .... Whites-Pittsburgh	110.00	50.00	16.50
☐ 480	Daniel Stearns: .... Des Moines-K.C.	110.00	50.00	16.50
☐ 481	Billy (Cannonball) .... Stemmyer: Boston-Cleveland	110.00	50.00	16.50
☐ 482	Stengel: Columbus	110.00	50.00	16.50
☐ 483	B.F. Stephens: Milw.	110.00	50.00	16.50
☐ 484	John C. Sterling: .... Minneapolis	110.00	50.00	16.50
☐ 485	Stockwell: S.F. PCL	1200.00	500.00	120.00
☐ 486	Harry Stovey: .... A's-Boston	250.00	110.00	37.50
☐ 487	C. Scott Stratton: .... Louisville	110.00	50.00	16.50
☐ 488	Joseph Straus: .... Omaha-Milwaukee	110.00	50.00	16.50
☐ 489	John (Cub) Stricker: .... Cleveland	110.00	50.00	16.50
☐ 490	J.O. Struck: Milw.	110.00	50.00	16.50
☐ 491	Marty Sullivan: .... Chicago-Ind.	110.00	50.00	16.50
☐ 492	Michael Sullivan: .... A's	110.00	50.00	16.50
☐ 493	Billy Sunday: .... Chicago-Pittsburgh	500.00	225.00	75.00
☐ 494	Sy Sutcliffe: Cleve.	110.00	50.00	16.50
☐ 495	Ezra Sutton: .... Boston-Milwaukee	110.00	50.00	16.50

☐ 496	Ed Cyrus Swartwood: .... Brook.-D.Moines-Ham.	110.00	50.00	16.50
☐ 497	Parke Swartzel: K.C.	110.00	50.00	16.50
☐ 498	Peter Sweeney: Wash.	110.00	50.00	16.50
☐ 499	Sylvester: Sacra. .... PCL	1200.00	500.00	120.00
☐ 500	Ed (Dimples) Tate: .... Boston-Baltimore	110.00	50.00	16.50
☐ 501	Patsy Tebeau: .... Chi.-Cleve.-Minn.	110.00	50.00	16.50
☐ 502	John Tener: Chicago	150.00	67.50	22.50
☐ 503	Bill (Adonis) Terry: .... Brooklyn	110.00	50.00	16.50
☐ 504	Big Sam Thompson: .... Detroit-Philadelphia	450.00	200.00	67.50
☐ 505	Silent Mike Tiernan: .... New York	110.00	50.00	16.50
☐ 506	Ledell Titcomb: N.Y.	110.00	50.00	16.50
☐ 507	Phillip Tomney: .... Louisville	110.00	50.00	16.50
☐ 508	Stephen Toole: .... Brooklyn-K.C.-Rochester	110.00	50.00	16.50
☐ 509	George Townsend: A's	110.00	50.00	16.50
☐ 510	William Traffley: .... Des Moines	110.00	50.00	16.50
☐ 511	George Treadway: .... St. Paul-Denver	110.00	50.00	16.50
☐ 512	Samuel Trott: .... Baltimore-Newark	110.00	50.00	16.50
☐ 513	Trott and Burns: .... Baltimore HOR	150.00	67.50	22.50
☐ 514	Tom(Foghorn) Tucker: .... Baltimore	110.00	50.00	16.50
☐ 515	William Tuckerman: .... St. Paul	110.00	50.00	16.50
☐ 516	Turner: Minneapolis	110.00	50.00	16.50
☐ 517	Lawrence Twitchell: .... Detroit-Cleveland	110.00	50.00	16.50
☐ 518	James Tyng: Phila.	110.00	50.00	16.50
☐ 519	William Van Dyke: .... Des Moines-Toledo	110.00	50.00	16.50
☐ 520	George Rip VanHaltren .... Chicago	110.00	50.00	16.50
☐ 521	Harry Vaughn: .... (Farmer) Louisville-New York	110.00	50.00	16.50
☐ 522	Peek-a-Boo Veach: .... St. Paul	300.00	135.00	45.00
☐ 523	Veach: Sacra. PCL	1200.00	500.00	120.00
☐ 524	Leon Viau: .... Cincinnati	110.00	50.00	16.50
☐ 525	William Vinton: .... Minneapolis	110.00	50.00	16.50
☐ 526	Joseph Visner: .... Brooklyn	110.00	50.00	16.50
☐ 527	Christian VonDer Ahe .... Owner Browns Champs	350.00	160.00	52.50
☐ 528	Joseph Walsh: Omaha	110.00	50.00	16.50
☐ 529	John (Monte) Ward: .... New York	450.00	200.00	67.50
☐ 530	E.H. Warner: .... Milwaukee	300.00	135.00	45.00
☐ 531	William Watkins: .... Mgr. Detroit-Kansas City	150.00	67.50	22.50
☐ 532	Bill Weaver: .... (Farmer) Louisville	110.00	50.00	16.50
☐ 533	Charles Weber: .... Sioux City	110.00	50.00	16.50
☐ 534	George Weidman .... (Stump): Detroit-New York	110.00	50.00	16.50
☐ 535	William Weidner: .... Columbus	110.00	50.00	16.50
☐ 536A	Curtis Welch: .... Browns Champ	250.00	110.00	37.50
☐ 536B	Curtis Welch: A's	110.00	50.00	16.50
☐ 537	Welch and Gleason: .... Athletics	150.00	67.50	22.50
☐ 538	Smilin'Mickey Welch: .... All Star-New York	500.00	225.00	75.00
☐ 539	Jake Wells: K.C.	110.00	50.00	16.50
☐ 540	Frank Wells: .... Des Moines-Mil.	150.00	67.50	22.50
☐ 541	Joseph Werrick: .... Louisville-St. Paul	110.00	50.00	16.50
☐ 542	Milton(Buck) West: .... Minneapolis	110.00	50.00	16.50
☐ 543	Gus (Cannonball) .... Weyhing: A's	110.00	50.00	16.50

☐ 544	John Weyhing: .... Athletics-Columbus	110.00	50.00	16.50
☐ 545	Bobby Wheelock: .... Boston-Detroit	110.00	50.00	16.50
☐ 546	Whitacre: A's	110.00	50.00	16.50
☐ 547	Pat Whitaker: Balt.	110.00	50.00	16.50
☐ 548	Deacon White: .... Detroit-Pittsburgh	110.00	50.00	16.50
☐ 549	William White: .... Louisville	110.00	50.00	16.50
☐ 550	Jim (Grasshopper) .... Whitney: Wash.-Indianapolis	110.00	50.00	16.50
☐ 551	Arthur Whitney: .... Pittsburgh-New York	110.00	50.00	16.50
☐ 552	G. Whitney: .... St. Joseph	110.00	50.00	16.50
☐ 553	James Williams: .... Mgr. Cleveland	150.00	67.50	22.50
☐ 554	Ned Williamson: Chi.	150.00	67.50	22.50
☐ 555	Williamson and .... Mascot	150.00	67.50	22.50
☐ 556	C.H. Willis: Omaha	110.00	50.00	16.50
☐ 557	Walt Wilmot: .... Washington-Chicago	110.00	50.00	16.50
☐ 558	George Winkleman: .... Minneapolis-Hartford	110.00	50.00	16.50
☐ 559	Samuel Wise: .... Boston-Washington	110.00	50.00	16.50
☐ 560	William Wolf .... (Chicken) Louisville	110.00	50.00	16.50
☐ 561	George (Dandy) Wood: .... Philadelphia	110.00	50.00	16.50
☐ 562	Peter Wood: Phila.	110.00	50.00	16.50
☐ 563	Harry Wright: .... Mgr. Philadelphia	1350.00	600.00	135.00
☐ 564	Charles Zimmer .... (Chief) Cleveland	110.00	50.00	16.50
☐ 565	Frank Zinn: .... Athletics	110.00	50.00	16.50

N184 Kimball's

This set of 50 color pictures of contemporary athletes was Kimball's answer to the sets produced by Allen , Ginter (N28 and N29) and Goodwin (N162). Issued in 1888, the cards are backlisted but are not numbered. The cards are listed below in alphabetical order without regard to sport. There are four baseball players in the set. An album (ACC: A42) was offered as a premium in exchange for coupons found in the tobacco packages. The baseball players are noted in the checklist below by BB after their name.

	EX-MT	VG-E	GOOD
COMPLETE SET (50)	5000.00	2000.00	500.00
COMMON BASEBALL	600.00	270.00	90.00
COMMON BOXER	200.00	90.00	30.00
COMMON OTHERS	50.00	22.50	7.50

☐ 1	Wm. Beach	50.00	22.50	7.50
☐ 2	Marve Beardsley	50.00	22.50	7.50
☐ 3	Chas. P. Blatt	50.00	22.50	7.50

☐	4	Blondin	50.00	22.50	7.50
☐	5	Paul Boynton	50.00	22.50	7.50
☐	6	E.A.(Ernie) Burch BB	600.00	270.00	90.00
☐	7	Patsy Cardiff	50.00	22.50	7.50
☐	8	Phillip Casey	50.00	22.50	7.50
☐	9	J.C. Cockburn	50.00	22.50	7.50
☐	10	Dell Darling BB	600.00	270.00	90.00
☐	11	Jack Dempsey BOX	300.00	135.00	45.00
☐	12	Della Ferrell	50.00	22.50	7.50
☐	13	Clarence Freeman	50.00	22.50	7.50
☐	14	Louis George	50.00	22.50	7.50
☐	15	W.G. George	50.00	22.50	7.50
☐	16	George W. Hamilton	50.00	22.50	7.50
☐	17	Edward Hanlan	50.00	22.50	7.50
☐	18	C.H. Heins	50.00	22.50	7.50
☐	19	Hardie Henderson BB	600.00	270.00	90.00
☐	20	Thomas H. Hume	50.00	22.50	7.50
☐	21	J.H. Jordon	50.00	22.50	7.50
☐	22	Johnny Kane	50.00	22.50	7.50
☐	23	James McLaughlin	50.00	22.50	7.50
☐	24	John McPherson	50.00	22.50	7.50
☐	25	Joseph Morsler	50.00	22.50	7.50
☐	26	William Muldoon	75.00	34.00	11.25
☐	27	S. Muller	50.00	22.50	7.50
☐	28	Isaac Murphy	50.00	22.50	7.50
☐	29	John Murphy	50.00	22.50	7.50
☐	30	L.E. Myers	50.00	22.50	7.50
☐	31	Annie Oakley	125.00	57.50	18.75
☐	32	Daniel O'Leary	50.00	22.50	7.50
☐	33	James O'Neil BB	700.00	315.00	105.00
☐	34	Wm. Byrd Page	50.00	22.50	7.50
☐	35	Axel Paulsen	50.00	22.50	7.50
☐	36	Master Ray Perry	50.00	22.50	7.50
☐	37	Duncan C. Ross	50.00	22.50	7.50
☐	38	W.A. Rowe	50.00	22.50	7.50
☐	39	Jacob Schaefer	50.00	22.50	7.50
☐	40	M. Schloss	50.00	22.50	7.50
☐	41	Jem Smith	50.00	22.50	7.50
☐	42	Lillian Smith	50.00	22.50	7.50
☐	43	Hattie Stewart	50.00	22.50	7.50
☐	44	John L. Sullivan BOX	350.00	160.00	52.50
☐	45	Arthur Wallace	50.00	22.50	7.50
☐	46	Tommy Warren BOX	200.00	90.00	30.00
☐	47	Ada Webb	50.00	22.50	7.50
☐	48	John Wessels	50.00	22.50	7.50
☐	49	Clarence Whistler	50.00	22.50	7.50
☐	50	Charles Wood	50.00	22.50	7.50

N284 Buchner

The baseball players found in this Buchner set are a part of a larger group of cards portraying policemen, jockeys and actors, all of which were issued with the tobacco brand "Gold Coin." The set is comprised of three major groupings or types. In the first type, nine players from eight teams, plus three Brooklyn players, are all portrayed in identical poses according to position. In the second type, St. Louis has 14 players depicted in poses which are not repeated. The last group contains 53 additional cards which vary according to pose, team change, spelling, etc. These third type cards are indicated in the checklist below by an asterisk. In all, there are 116 individuals portrayed on 142 cards. The existence of an additional player in the set, McClellan of Brooklyn, has never been verified. The set was issued circa 1887. The cards are numbered below in alphabetical order

within team with teams themselves listed in alphabetical order: Baltimore (1-4), Boston (5-13), Brooklyn (14-17), Chicago (18-26), Detroit (27-35), Indianapolis (36-47), LaCrosse (48-51), Milwaukee (52-55), New York Mets (56-63), New York (64-73), Philadelphia (74-83), Pittsburgh (84-92), St. Louis (93-106), and Washington (107-117).

	EX-MT	VG-E	GOOD
COMPLETE SET (152)	15000.00	6000.00	1500.00
COMMON PLAYERS	75.00	34.00	11.25
COMMON ST. LOUIS	100.00	45.00	15.00
COMMON PLAYERS *	100.00	45.00	15.00

			EX-MT	VG-E	GOOD
☐	1	Burns: Baltimore *	100.00	45.00	15.00
☐	2	Fulmer: Baltimore *	100.00	45.00	15.00
☐	3	Kilroy: Baltimore *	100.00	45.00	15.00
☐	4	Purcell: Baltimore *	100.00	45.00	15.00
☐	5	John Burdock: Boston	75.00	34.00	11.25
☐	6	Bill Daley: Boston	75.00	34.00	11.25
☐	7	Joe Hornung: Boston	75.00	34.00	11.25
☐	8	Johnston: Boston	75.00	34.00	11.25
☐	9A	King Kelly: Boston (right field)	225.00	100.00	33.00
☐	9B	King Kelly: Boston (catcher) *	325.00	150.00	50.00
☐	10A	Morrill: Boston (both hands out-stretched face high)	75.00	34.00	11.25
☐	10B	Morrill: Boston * (hands clasped near chin)	100.00	45.00	15.00
☐	11A	Hoss Radbourne: Boston	175.00	80.00	27.00
☐	11B	Hoss Radbourne: Boston * (hands together above waist)	275.00	120.00	40.00
☐	12	Sutton: Boston	75.00	34.00	11.25
☐	13	Wise: Boston	75.00	34.00	11.25
☐	14	McClellan: Brooklyn (never confirmed)	00.00	00.00	0.00
☐	15	Peoples: Brooklyn	75.00	34.00	11.25
☐	16	Phillips: Brooklyn	75.00	34.00	11.25
☐	17	Porter: Brooklyn	75.00	34.00	11.25
☐	18A	Adrian Anson: Chicago (both hands out-stretched face high)	400.00	180.00	60.00
☐	18B	Adrian Anson: Chicago * (left hand on hip, right hand down)	600.00	270.00	90.00
☐	19	Burns: Chicago	75.00	34.00	11.25
☐	20A	John Clarkson: Chicago	175.00	80.00	27.00
☐	20B	John Clarkson: Chicago * (right arm extended, left arm near side)	275.00	120.00	40.00
☐	21	Silver Flint: Chicago	75.00	34.00	11.25
☐	22	Pfeffer: Chicago	75.00	34.00	11.25
☐	23	Ryan: Chicago	75.00	34.00	11.25
☐	24	Billy Sullivan: Chicago	90.00	40.00	13.50
☐	25	Billy Sunday: Chicago	200.00	90.00	30.00
☐	26A	Williamson: Chicago (shortstop)	75.00	34.00	11.25
☐	26B	Williamson: Chicago (second base) *	100.00	45.00	15.00
☐	27	Bennett: Detroit	75.00	34.00	11.25
☐	28A	Dan Brouthers: Detroit (fielding)	175.00	80.00	27.00
☐	28B	Dan Brouthers: Detroit * (batting)	275.00	120.00	40.00
☐	29	Dunlap: Detroit	75.00	34.00	11.25
☐	30	Getzein: Detroit	75.00	34.00	11.25
☐	31	Hanlon: Detroit	75.00	34.00	11.25
☐	32	Manning: Detoit	75.00	34.00	11.25
☐	33A	Richardson: Detroit (hands together in front of chest)	75.00	34.00	11.25
☐	33B	Richardson: Detroit * (right hand holding ball above head)	100.00	45.00	15.00
☐	34A	Sam Thompson: Detroit (looking up with hands at waist)	175.00	80.00	27.00

☐ 34B Sam Thompson: .... Detroit * (hands chest high)	275.00	120.00	40.00
☐ 35 White: Detroit	75.00	34.00	11.25
☐ 36 Arundel: .... Indianapolis	75.00	34.00	11.25
☐ 37 Bassett: .... Indianapolis	75.00	34.00	11.25
☐ 38 Boyle: .... Indianapolis *	75.00	34.00	11.25
☐ 39 Cahill: .... Indianapolis *	100.00	45.00	15.00
☐ 40A Denny: .... Indianapolis (hands on knees, legs bent)	75.00	34.00	11.25
☐ 40B Denny: .... Indianapolis * (hands on knees, legs not bent)	100.00	45.00	15.00
☐ 41A Jack Glasscock: .... Indianapolis (crouching, catch- ing a grounder)	100.00	45.00	15.00
☐ 41B Jack Glasscock: .... Indianapolis * (hands on knees)	125.00	57.50	18.75
☐ 42 Healy: Indianapolis	75.00	34.00	11.25
☐ 43 Meyers: .... Indianapolis *	100.00	45.00	15.00
☐ 44 McGeachy: .... Indianapolis	75.00	34.00	11.25
☐ 45 Polhemus: .... Indianapolis	75.00	34.00	11.25
☐ 46A Seery: .... Indianapolis (hands together in front of chest)	75.00	34.00	11.25
☐ 46B Seery: .... Indianapolis * (hands outstretched head high)	100.00	45.00	15.00
☐ 47 Shomberg: .... Indianapolis	75.00	34.00	11.25
☐ 48 Corbett: LaCrosse *	100.00	45.00	15.00
☐ 49 Crowley: LaCrosse *	100.00	45.00	15.00
☐ 50 Kennedy: LaCrosse *	100.00	45.00	15.00
☐ 51 Rooks: Lacrosse *	100.00	45.00	15.00
☐ 52 Forster: Milwaukee *	100.00	45.00	15.00
☐ 53 Hart: Milwaukee *	100.00	45.00	15.00
☐ 54 Morrissy: .... Milwaukee *	100.00	45.00	15.00
☐ 55 Strauss: Milwaukee *	100.00	45.00	15.00
☐ 56 Cushmann: NY Mets *	100.00	45.00	15.00
☐ 57 Jim Donohue: .... NY Mets *	100.00	45.00	15.00
☐ 58 Esterbrooke (sic): .... NY Mets *	100.00	45.00	15.00
☐ 59 Joe Gerhardt: .... NY Mets *	100.00	45.00	15.00
☐ 60 Frank Hankinson: .... NY Mets *	100.00	45.00	15.00
☐ 61 Jack Nelson: .... NY Mets *	100.00	45.00	15.00
☐ 62 Dave Orr: NY Mets *	100.00	45.00	15.00
☐ 63 James Rosemann: .... NY Mets *	100.00	45.00	15.00
☐ 64A Roger Connor: .... New York (both hands out- stretched face high)	175.00	80.00	27.00
☐ 64B Roger Connor: .... New York * (hands outstretched, palms up)	275.00	120.00	40.00
☐ 65 Deasley: New York *	100.00	45.00	15.00
☐ 66A Mike Dorgan: .... New York (fielding)	75.00	34.00	11.25
☐ 66B Mike Dorgan: .... New York (batting) *	100.00	45.00	15.00
☐ 67A Buck Ewing: .... New York (ball in left hand, right arm out shoulder high)	175.00	80.00	27.00
☐ 67B Buck Ewing: .... New York * (appears ready to clap)	275.00	120.00	40.00
☐ 68A Pete Gillespie: .... New York (fielding)	75.00	34.00	11.25
☐ 68B Pete Gillespie: .... New York (batting) *	100.00	45.00	15.00
☐ 69 George Gore: .... New York	75.00	34.00	11.25

☐ 70A Tim Keefe: .... New York	175.00	80.00	27.00
☐ 70B Tim Keefe: .... New York * (ball just released from right hand)	275.00	120.00	40.00
☐ 71A Jim O'Rourke: .... New York (hands cupped in front, thigh high)	175.00	80.00	27.00
☐ 71B Jim O'Rourke: .... New York * (hands on knees, looking right)	275.00	120.00	40.00
☐ 72A Danny Richardson: .... New York (third base)	75.00	34.00	11.25
☐ 72B Danny Richardson: .... New York (second base) *	100.00	45.00	15.00
☐ 73A John M. Ward: .... New York (crouching, catch- ing a grounder)	175.00	80.00	27.00
☐ 73B John M. Ward: .... New York * (hands by left knee)	275.00	120.00	40.00
☐ 73C John M. Ward: .... New York * (hands on knees)	275.00	120.00	40.00
☐ 74A Andrews: .... Philadelphia (hands together in front of neck)	75.00	34.00	11.25
☐ 74B Andrews: .... Philadelphia * (catching, hands waist high)	100.00	45.00	15.00
☐ 75 Bastian: .... Philadelphia	75.00	34.00	11.25
☐ 76 Dan Casey: .... Philadelphia *	100.00	45.00	15.00
☐ 77 Clements: .... Philadelphia	75.00	34.00	11.25
☐ 78 Sid Farrar: .... Philadelphia	75.00	34.00	11.25
☐ 79 Ferguson: .... Philadelphia	75.00	34.00	11.25
☐ 80 Fogerty: .... Philadelphia	75.00	34.00	11.25
☐ 81 Irwin: Philadelphia	75.00	34.00	11.25
☐ 82A Mulvey: .... Philadelphia (hands on knees)	75.00	34.00	11.25
☐ 82B Mulvey: .... Philadelphia * (hands together above head)	100.00	45.00	15.00
☐ 83A Pete Wood: Phila- delphia (fielding)	75.00	34.00	11.25
☐ 83B Pete Wood: Phila- delphia HOR (Stealing a Base) *	100.00	45.00	15.00
☐ 84 Barkley: Pittsburgh	75.00	34.00	11.25
☐ 85 Beecher: Pittsburgh	75.00	34.00	11.25
☐ 86 Brown: Pittsburgh	75.00	34.00	11.25
☐ 87 Carroll: Pittsburgh	75.00	34.00	11.25
☐ 88 Coleman: Pittsburgh	75.00	34.00	11.25
☐ 89 McCormick: Pittsburgh	75.00	34.00	11.25
☐ 90 Miller: Pittsburgh	75.00	34.00	11.25
☐ 91 Smith: Pittsburgh	75.00	34.00	11.25
☐ 92 Whitney: Pittsburgh	75.00	34.00	11.25
☐ 93 Barkley: St. Louis	100.00	45.00	15.00
☐ 94 Bushong: St. Louis	100.00	45.00	15.00
☐ 95 Bob Carruthers .... (sic): St. Louis	125.00	57.50	18.75
☐ 96 Charles Comiskey: .... St. Louis	325.00	150.00	50.00
☐ 97 Dave Foutz: .... St. Louis	100.00	45.00	15.00
☐ 98 William Gleason: .... St. Louis	100.00	45.00	15.00
☐ 99 Arlie Latham: .... St. Louis	100.00	45.00	15.00
☐ 100 McGinnis: St. Louis	100.00	45.00	15.00
☐ 101 Hugh Nicol: .... St. Louis	100.00	45.00	15.00
☐ 102 James O'Neil: .... St. Louis	100.00	45.00	15.00
☐ 103 Robinson: St. Louis	100.00	45.00	15.00
☐ 104 Sullivan: St. Louis	100.00	45.00	15.00
☐ 105 Chris Von Der Ahe: .... St. Louis (actually a photo, rather than drawing)	300.00	135.00	45.00

			EX-MT	VG-E	GOOD
☐	106	Curt Welch: .... St. Louis	100.00	45.00	15.00
☐	107	Carroll: Washington	75.00	34.00	11.25
☐	108	Craig: Washington *	100.00	45.00	15.00
☐	109	Crane: Washington *	100.00	45.00	15.00
☐	110	Dailey: Washington	75.00	34.00	11.25
☐	111	Donnelly: Washington	75.00	34.00	11.25
☐	112A	Farrell: .... Washington (ball in left hand, right arm out shoulder high)	75.00	34.00	11.25
☐	112B	Farrell: .... Washington * (ball in hands near right knee)	100.00	45.00	15.00
☐	113	Gilligan: Washington	75.00	34.00	11.25
☐	114A	Hines: Washington .... (fielding)	75.00	34.00	11.25
☐	114B	Hines: Washington .... (batting) *	100.00	45.00	15.00
☐	115	Myers: Washington	75.00	34.00	11.25
☐	116	O'Brien: Washington	75.00	34.00	11.25
☐	117	Whitney: Washington	75.00	34.00	11.25

N300 Mayo

The Mayo Tobacco Works of Richmond, Va., issued this set of 48 ballplayers about 1895. The cards contain sepia portraits although some pictures appear to be black and white. There are 40 different individuals known in the set; cards 1 to 28 appear in uniform, while the last twelve (29-40) appear in street clothes. Eight of the former also appear with variations in uniform. The player's name appears within the picture area and a "Mayo's Cut Plug" ad is printed in a panel at the base of the card.

			EX-MT	VG-E	GOOD
		COMPLETE SET (48)	20000.00	8000.00	2500.00
		COMMON PLAYERS (1-28)	300.00	135.00	45.00
		COMMON PLAYERS (29-40)	300.00	135.00	45.00
☐	1	Cap Anson: Chicago	1800.00	750.00	200.00
☐	2	Bannon RF: Boston	300.00	135.00	45.00
☐	3A	Dan Brouthers 1B: .... Baltimore	650.00	300.00	100.00
☐	3B	Dan Brouthers 1B: .... Louisville	800.00	350.00	120.00
☐	4	John Clarkson P: .... St. Louis	650.00	300.00	100.00
☐	5	T.W. Corcoran SS: .... Brooklyn	300.00	135.00	45.00
☐	6	Cross 2B: .... Philadelphia	300.00	135.00	45.00
☐	7	Hugh Duffy CF: .... Boston	650.00	300.00	100.00
☐	8A	Buck Ewing RF: .... Cincinnati	700.00	315.00	105.00
☐	8B	Buck Ewing RF: .... Cleveland	700.00	315.00	105.00
☐	9	Dave Foutz 1B: .... Brooklyn	300.00	135.00	45.00
☐	10	Ganzel C: Boston	300.00	135.00	45.00
☐	11A	Glasscock SS: .... Pittsburgh	325.00	150.00	50.00
☐	11B	Glasscock SS: .... Louisville	325.00	150.00	50.00
☐	12	Griffin CF: .... Brooklyn	300.00	135.00	45.00

			EX-MT	VG-E	GOOD
☐	13A	Haddock P: .... Philadelphia	300.00	135.00	45.00
☐	13B	Haddock P: no team	300.00	135.00	45.00
☐	14	Joyce CF: Brooklyn	300.00	135.00	45.00
☐	15	Wm. Kennedy P: .... Brooklyn	300.00	135.00	45.00
☐	16A	Tom F. Kinslow C: .... Pitts.	300.00	135.00	45.00
☐	16B	Tom F. Kinslow C: .... no team	300.00	135.00	45.00
☐	17	Arlie Latham 3B: .... Cincinnati	300.00	135.00	45.00
☐	18	Long SS: Boston	325.00	150.00	50.00
☐	19	Lovett P: Boston	300.00	135.00	45.00
☐	20	Lowe 2B: Boston	325.00	150.00	50.00
☐	21	McCarthy LF: Boston	650.00	300.00	100.00
☐	22	Murphy SS: New York	300.00	135.00	45.00
☐	23	Billy Nash 3B: Boston	300.00	135.00	45.00
☐	24	Nicols P: Boston	650.00	300.00	100.00
☐	25A	Pfeffer 2B: .... Louisville	300.00	135.00	45.00
☐	25B	Pfeffer (retired)	300.00	135.00	45.00
☐	26A	Amos Rusie P: .... New York	950.00	425.00	140.00
☐	26B	Amos Russie (sic) P: .... New York	700.00	315.00	105.00
☐	27	Tucker 1B: Boston	300.00	135.00	45.00
☐	28A	John Ward 2B: .... New York	650.00	300.00	100.00
☐	28B	John Ward (retired)	800.00	350.00	120.00
☐	29	Chas. S. Abbey CF: .... Washington	300.00	135.00	45.00
☐	30	E.W. Cartwright FB: .... Washington	300.00	135.00	45.00
☐	31	W. F. Dahlen SS: .... Chicago	325.00	150.00	50.00
☐	32	T.P. Daly 2B: .... Brooklyn	300.00	135.00	45.00
☐	33	E.J. Delehanty LF: .... Phila.	950.00	425.00	140.00
☐	34	W.W. Hallman 2B: .... Phila.	300.00	135.00	45.00
☐	35	W.R. Hamilton CF: .... Phila.	650.00	300.00	100.00
☐	36	W. Robinson C: .... Baltimore	650.00	300.00	100.00
☐	37	James Ryan RF: .... Chicago	300.00	135.00	45.00
☐	38	Wm. Shindle 3B: .... Brooklyn	300.00	135.00	45.00
☐	39	Geo. J. Smith SS: .... Cinc.	300.00	135.00	45.00
☐	40	Otis H. Stockdale P: .... Washington	300.00	135.00	45.00

1986 National Photo Royals

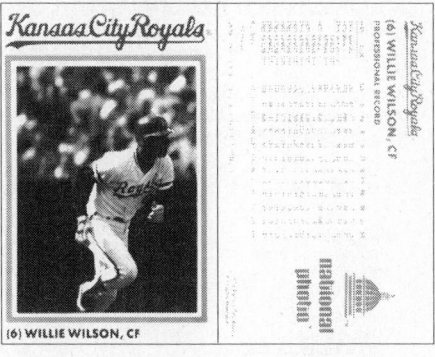

(6) WILLIE WILSON, CF

The set contains 24 cards which are numbered only by uniform number except for the checklist card and discount card, which entitles the bearer to a 40 percent discount at National Photo. Cards measure 2 7/8" by 4 1/4". Cards were distributed at the stadium on August 14th. The set was supposedly later available for 3.00 directly from the Royals.

	MINT	EXC	G-VG
COMPLETE SET (24)	11.00	5.00	1.35
COMMON PLAYER	.35	.15	.03
☐ 1 Buddy Biancalana	.35	.15	.03
☐ 3 Jorge Orta	.35	.15	.03
☐ 4 Greg Pryor	.35	.15	.03
☐ 5 George Brett	3.00	1.25	.30
☐ 6 Willie Wilson	.75	.30	.07
☐ 8 Jim Sundberg	.35	.15	.03
☐ 10 Dick Howser MG	.60	.25	.06
☐ 11 Hal McRae	.75	.30	.07
☐ 20 Frank White	.60	.25	.06
☐ 21 Lonnie Smith	.75	.30	.07
☐ 22 Dennis Leonard	.50	.20	.05
☐ 23 Mark Gubicza	1.00	.40	.10
☐ 24 Darryl Motley	.35	.15	.03
☐ 25 Danny Jackson	.60	.25	.06
☐ 26 Steve Farr	.45	.18	.04
☐ 29 Dan Quisenberry	.60	.25	.06
☐ 31 Bret Saberhagen	1.50	.60	.15
☐ 35 Lynn Jones	.35	.15	.03
☐ 37 Charlie Leibrandt	.50	.20	.05
☐ 38 Mark Huismann	.35	.15	.03
☐ 40 Bud Black	.50	.20	.05
☐ 45 Steve Balboni	.50	.20	.05
☐ xx Discount card	.35	.15	.03
(unnumbered)			
☐ xx Checklist card	.35	.15	.03
(unnumbered)			

1986 Negro League Fritsch

This 119-card set of Negro League stars was issued in the standard size of 2 1/2" by 3 1/2". The set features black and white photos framed by the title "Negro League Baseball Stars" in red above the player's name and the player's name in red below the photo. Each card back features a brief biography of the player pictured on the front of the card. The set was produced by long time Wisconsin card hobbyist Larry Fritsch and featured most of the great players of the old Negro Leagues.

	MINT	VG-E	F-G
COMPLETE SET (119)	11.00	5.00	1.35
COMMON PLAYER (1-119)	.10	.04	.01
☐ 1 Buck Leonard	.50	.20	.05
☐ 2 Ted Page	.30	.12	.03
☐ 3 Cool Papa Bell	.50	.20	.05
☐ 4 Charleston/Gibson/ Page/Johnson	.50	.20	.05
☐ 5 Judy Johnson	.50	.20	.05
☐ 6 Monte Irvin	.50	.20	.05
☐ 7 Ray Dandridge	.50	.20	.05
☐ 8 Oscar Charleston	.50	.20	.05
☐ 9 Josh Gibson	.75	.30	.07
☐ 10 Satchel Paige	.75	.30	.07
☐ 11 Jackie Robinson	.75	.30	.07
☐ 12 Lorenzo Piper Davis	.20	.08	.02
☐ 13 Josh Johnson	.10	.04	.01
☐ 14 Lou Dials	.40	.16	.04
☐ 15 Andy Porter	.10	.04	.01
☐ 16 John Henry Lloyd	.50	.20	.05
☐ 17 Andy Watts	.10	.04	.01

☐ 18 Rube Foster	.50	.20	.05
☐ 19 Martin Dihigo	.50	.20	.05
☐ 20 Lou Dials	.40	.16	.04
☐ 21 Satchel Paige	.75	.30	.07
☐ 22 Crush Holloway	.10	.04	.01
☐ 23 Josh Gibson	.75	.30	.07
☐ 24 Oscar Charleston	.50	.20	.05
☐ 25 Jackie Robinson	.75	.30	.07
☐ 26 Larry Brown	.10	.04	.01
☐ 27 Hilton Smith	.10	.04	.01
☐ 28 Moses F. Walker	.10	.04	.01
☐ 29 Jimmie Crutchfield	.10	.04	.01
☐ 30 Josh Gibson	.75	.30	.07
☐ 31 Josh Gibson	.75	.30	.07
☐ 32 Bullet Rogan	.20	.08	.02
☐ 33 Clint Thomas	.10	.04	.01
☐ 34 Rats Henderson	.10	.04	.01
☐ 35 Pat Scantlebury	.10	.04	.01
☐ 36 Sydney Sy Morton	.10	.04	.01
☐ 37 Larry Kimbrough	.10	.04	.01
☐ 38 Sam Jethroe	.20	.08	.02
☐ 39 Normal (Tweed) Webb	.10	.04	.01
☐ 40 Mahlon Duckett	.10	.04	.01
☐ 41 Andy Anderson	.10	.04	.01
☐ 42 Buster Haywood	.10	.04	.01
☐ 43 Bob Trice	.10	.04	.01
☐ 44 Buster Clarkson	.10	.04	.01
☐ 45 Buck O'Neil	.10	.04	.01
☐ 46 Jim Zapp	.10	.04	.01
☐ 47 Lorenzo Piper Davis	.10	.04	.01
☐ 48 Ed Steel	.10	.04	.01
☐ 49 Bob Boyd	.10	.04	.01
☐ 50 Marlin Carter	.10	.04	.01
☐ 51 George Giles	.10	.04	.01
☐ 52 Bill Byrd	.10	.04	.01
☐ 53 Art Pennington	.10	.04	.01
☐ 54 Max Manning	.10	.04	.01
☐ 55 Ronald Teasley	.10	.04	.01
☐ 56 Ziggy Marcell	.10	.04	.01
☐ 57 Bill Cash	.10	.04	.01
☐ 58 Joe Scott	.10	.04	.01
☐ 59 Joe Fillmore	.10	.04	.01
☐ 60 Bob Thurman	.10	.04	.01
☐ 61 Larry Kimbrough	.10	.04	.01
☐ 62 Verdell Mathis	.10	.04	.01
☐ 63 Josh Johnson	.20	.08	.02
☐ 64 Ted Radcliffe	.20	.08	.02
☐ 65 William Bobby Robinson	.15	.06	.01
☐ 66 Bingo DeMoss	.20	.08	.02
☐ 67 John Beckwith	.10	.04	.01
☐ 68 Bill Jackman	.10	.04	.01
☐ 69 Bill Drake	.10	.04	.01
☐ 70 Charlie Grant	.10	.04	.01
☐ 71 Willie Wells	.20	.08	.02
☐ 72 Jose Fernandez	.10	.04	.01
☐ 73 Isidro Fabri	.10	.04	.01
☐ 74 Frank Austin	.10	.04	.01
☐ 75 Dick Lundy	.10	.04	.01
☐ 76 Junior Gilliam	.30	.12	.03
☐ 77 John Donaldson	.10	.04	.01
☐ 78 Rap Dixon	.10	.04	.01
☐ 79 Slim Jones	.10	.04	.01
☐ 80 Sam Jones	.15	.06	.01
☐ 81 Dave Hoskins	.10	.04	.01
☐ 82 Jerry Benjamin	.10	.04	.01
☐ 83 Luke Easter	.20	.08	.02
☐ 84 Ramon Herrera	.10	.04	.01
☐ 85 Matthew Carlisle	.10	.04	.01
☐ 86 Smokey Joe Williams	.30	.12	.03
☐ 87 Marvin Williams	.10	.04	.01
☐ 88 William Yancey	.10	.04	.01
☐ 89 Monte Irvin	.50	.20	.05
☐ 90 Cool Papa Bell	.50	.20	.05
☐ 91 Biz Mackey	.40	.16	.04
☐ 92 Harry Simpson	.20	.08	.02
☐ 93 Lazerio Salazar	.10	.04	.01
☐ 94 Bill Perkins	.10	.04	.01
☐ 95 Johnny Davis	.10	.04	.01
☐ 96 Jelly Jackson	.20	.08	.02
☐ 97 Sam Bankhead	.10	.04	.01
☐ 98 Hank Thompson	.20	.08	.02
☐ 99 William Bell	.10	.04	.01
☐ 100 Cliff Bell	.10	.04	.01
☐ 101 Dave Barnhill	.10	.04	.01
☐ 102 Dan Bankhead	.10	.04	.01
☐ 103 Pepper Bassett	.10	.04	.01
☐ 104 Newt Allen	.15	.06	.01
☐ 105 George Jefferson	.10	.04	.01
☐ 106 Pat Paterson	.10	.04	.01
☐ 107 Goose Tatum	.35	.15	.03
☐ 108 Dave Malarcher	.20	.08	.02
☐ 109 Home Run Johnson	.20	.08	.02
☐ 110 Bill Monroe	.10	.04	.01
☐ 111 Sammy Hughes	.10	.04	.01

		MINT	EXC	G-VG
☐ 112	Dick Redding	.20	.08	.02
☐ 113	Fats Jenkins	.10	.04	.01
☐ 114	Jimmie Lyons	.10	.04	.01
☐ 115	Mule Suttles	.10	.04	.01
☐ 116	Ted Trent	.10	.04	.01
☐ 117	George Sweatt	.10	.04	.01
☐ 118	Frank Duncan	.10	.04	.01
☐ 119	Checklist Card	.10	.04	.01

1988 Negro League Duquesne

This 20-card set was sponsored by the Pittsburgh Pirates with the assistance of Rob Ruck of Chatham College and Duquesne Light Company. The set celebrates Negro League Baseball by depicting major black stars who played or were involved in the negro leagues in the Pittsburgh area. The set was given away at the Pittsburgh Pirates' home game on September 10, 1988. The set was issued in a sheet with five rows of four cards each; after perforation, the cards measure the standard size (2 1/2" by 3 1/2"). The fronts have sepia-toned player photos, with thin black borders on a white card face. A mustard-colored banner above the pictures reads "Negro League Stars." Also a mustard-colored baseball field logo appears in the lower right corner of the card face. The backs are printed in black on white and have biography as well as career summary. The Pirates' logo appears in the lower right corner, and the cards are numbered on the back.

		MINT	EXC	G-VG
	COMPLETE SET (20)	16.00	6.75	2.25
	COMMON PLAYER (1-20)	.75	.30	.07
☐ 1	Andrew(Rube) Foster	1.50	.60	.15
☐ 2	1913 Homestead Grays	.75	.30	.07
☐ 3	Cum Posey	.75	.30	.07
☐ 4	1926 Pittsburgh Crawfords	.75	.30	.07
☐ 5	Gus Greenlee, Owner	.75	.30	.07
☐ 6	John Henry(Pop) Lloyd	1.50	.60	.15
☐ 7	Oscar Charleston	1.50	.60	.15
☐ 8	Smokey Joe Williams	1.00	.40	.10
☐ 9	William(Judy) Johnson	1.50	.60	.15
☐ 10	Martin Dihigo	1.50	.60	.15
☐ 11	LeRoy(Satchel) Paige	2.00	.80	.20
☐ 12	Josh Gibson	2.00	.80	.20
☐ 13	Sam Streeter	.75	.30	.07
☐ 14	James(Cool Papa) Bell	1.50	.60	.15
☐ 15	Ted Page	1.00	.40	.10
☐ 16	Walter(Buck) Leonard	1.50	.60	.15
☐ 17	Ray(Hooks) Dandridge	1.50	.60	.15
☐ 18	Willis Moody and Ralph(Lefty) Mellix	.75	.30	.07
☐ 19	Harold Tinker	.75	.30	.07
☐ 20	Monte Irvin	1.50	.60	.15

1990 Negro League Stars

The exclusion of black and Latino players from Major League Baseball from 1889 to 1947 resulted in these same players forming their own teams and leagues, and this 36-card set pays tribute to these men. These standard size (2 1/2" by 3 1/2") cards feature beautiful water color portraits of the players, painted by Mark Chiarello. The left side of the picture has a white border, while the bottom has a black border. The intersection of the two borders in the lower left corner is red in color. The player's name appears in the bottom black border. The backs are printed in black on white and summarize the player's career. The cards are numbered on the back.

		MINT	EXC	G-VG
	COMPLETE SET (36)	10.00	4.50	1.25
	COMMON PLAYER (1-36)	.30	.12	.03
☐ 1	Title Card	.30	.12	.03
☐ 2	Josh Gibson	1.00	.40	.10
☐ 3	Cannonball Redding	.40	.16	.04
☐ 4	Biz Mackey	.50	.20	.05
☐ 5	Pop Lloyd	.75	.30	.07
☐ 6	Bingo Demoss	.50	.20	.05
☐ 7	Willard Brown	.30	.12	.03
☐ 8	John Donaldson	.30	.12	.03
☐ 9	Monte Irvin	.75	.30	.07
☐ 10	Ben Taylor	.30	.12	.03
☐ 11	Willie Wells	.50	.20	.05
☐ 12	Dave Brown	.30	.12	.03
☐ 13	Leon Day	.60	.25	.06
☐ 14	Ray Dandridge	.75	.30	.07
☐ 15	Turkey Stearnes	.30	.12	.03
☐ 16	Rube Foster	.75	.30	.07
☐ 17	Oliver Marcelle	.30	.12	.03
☐ 18	Judy Johnson	.75	.30	.07
☐ 19	Christobel Torrienti	.50	.20	.05
☐ 20	Satchel Paige	1.00	.40	.10
☐ 21	Mule Suttles	.40	.16	.04
☐ 22	John Beckwith	.30	.12	.03
☐ 23	Martin Dihigo	.75	.30	.07
☐ 24	Willie Foster	.30	.12	.03
☐ 25	Dick Lundy	.30	.12	.03
☐ 26	Buck Leonard	.75	.30	.07
☐ 27	Smokey Joe Williams	.40	.16	.04
☐ 28	Cool Papa Bell	.75	.30	.07
☐ 29	Bullet Rogan	.40	.16	.04
☐ 30	Newt Allen	.40	.16	.04
☐ 31	Bruce Petway	.40	.16	.04
☐ 32	Jose Mendez	.30	.12	.03
☐ 33	Louis Santop	.30	.12	.03
☐ 34	Jud Wilson	.30	.12	.03
☐ 35	Sammy T. Hughes	.30	.12	.03
☐ 36	Oscar Charleston	.75	.30	.07

1991 Negro League Ron Lewis

This 26-card boxed set was produced by the Negro League Baseball Players Association and noted sports artist Ron Lewis and was subtitled Living Legends. Production quantities were limited to 10,000 sets, and each card of the set bears a unique serial number on the back. Also 200 uncut sheets were printed. The cards were issued in the postcard format and measure approximately 3 1/2" by 5 1/4". The front design features a full color painting of the player by Ron Lewis. The paintings are bordered in white, and the player's name appears at the bottom of the front. The backs have brief biographical information and the card number in the upper left corner.

	MINT	EXC	G-VG
COMPLETE SET (30)	25.00	11.00	3.50
COMMON PLAYER (1-30)	1.00	.40	.10
☐ 1 George Giles	1.00	.40	.10
☐ 2 Bill Cash	1.00	.40	.10
☐ 3 Bob Harvey	1.00	.40	.10
☐ 4 Lyman Bostock Sr.	1.25	.50	.12
☐ 5 Ray Dandridge	2.00	.80	.20
☐ 6 Leon Day	1.50	.60	.15
☐ 7 Lefty Mathis	1.00	.40	.10
☐ 8 Jimmie Crutchfield	1.25	.50	.12
☐ 9 Clyde McNeal	1.00	.40	.10
☐ 10 Bill Wright	1.00	.40	.10
☐ 11 Mahlon Duckett	1.00	.40	.10
☐ 12 Bobby Robinson	1.25	.50	.12
☐ 13 Max Manning	1.00	.40	.10
☐ 14 Armando Vazquez	1.00	.40	.10
☐ 15 Jehosie Heard	1.00	.40	.10
☐ 16 Quincy Trouppe	1.00	.40	.10
☐ 17 Wilmer Fields	1.00	.40	.10
☐ 18 Lonnie Blair	1.00	.40	.10
☐ 19 Garnett Blair	1.00	.40	.10
☐ 20 Monte Irvin	2.50	1.00	.25
☐ 21 Willie Mays	5.00	2.25	.50
☐ 22 Buck Leonard	2.00	.80	.20
☐ 23 Frank Evans	1.00	.40	.10
☐ 24 Josh Gibson Jr.	1.50	.60	.15
☐ 25 Ted Radcliffe	1.25	.50	.12
☐ 26 Josh Johnson	1.00	.40	.10
☐ 27 Gene Benson	1.00	.40	.10
☐ 28 Lester Lockett	1.25	.50	.12
☐ 29 Bubba Hyde	1.00	.40	.10
☐ 30 Rufus Lewis	1.00	.40	.10

1984 Nestle Dream Team

The cards in this 22-card set measure 2 1/2" by 3 1/2". In conjunction with Topps, the Nestle Company issued this set entitled the Dream Team. The fronts have the Nestle trademark in the upper frameline, and the backs are identical to the Topps cards of this year except for the number and the Nestle's logo. Cards 1-11 feature stars of the American League while cards 12-22 show National League stars. Each league's "Dream Team" consists of eight position players and three pitchers. The cards were included with the Nestle chocolate bars as a pack of four (three player cards and a checklist header card. This set should not be confused with the Nestle 792-card (same player-number correspondence as 1984 Topps 792) set.

	MINT	EXC	G-VG
COMPLETE SET (22)	22.50	9.75	3.25
COMMON PLAYER (1-22)	.60	.25	.06
☐ 1 Eddie Murray	2.00	.80	.20
☐ 2 Lou Whitaker	.75	.30	.07
☐ 3 George Brett	2.50	1.00	.25
☐ 4 Cal Ripken	3.00	1.25	.30
☐ 5 Jim Rice	.90	.40	.09
☐ 6 Dave Winfield	1.50	.60	.15
☐ 7 Lloyd Moseby	.60	.25	.06
☐ 8 Lance Parrish	.75	.30	.07
☐ 9 LaMarr Hoyt	.60	.25	.06
☐ 10 Ron Guidry	.75	.30	.07
☐ 11 Dan Quisenberry	.75	.30	.07
☐ 12 Steve Garvey	1.25	.50	.12
☐ 13 Johnny Ray	.60	.25	.06
☐ 14 Mike Schmidt	3.50	1.50	.35
☐ 15 Ozzie Smith	1.50	.60	.15
☐ 16 Andre Dawson	1.50	.60	.15
☐ 17 Tim Raines	.90	.40	.09
☐ 18 Dale Murphy	2.00	.80	.20
☐ 19 Tony Pena	.60	.25	.06
☐ 20 John Denny	.60	.25	.06
☐ 21 Steve Carlton	1.50	.60	.15
☐ 22 Al Holland	.60	.25	.06
☐ xx Checklist card (unnumbered)	.60	.25	.06

1984 Nestle 792

The cards in this 792-card set measure 2 1/2" by 3 1/2" and are extremely similar to the 1984 Topps regular issue (except for the Nestle logo instead of Topps logo on the front). In conjunction with Topps, the Nestle Company issued this set as six sheets available as a premium. The set was (as detailed on the back of the checklist card for the Nestle Dream Team cards) originally available from the Nestle Company in full sheets of 132 cards, 24" by 48", for 4.95 plus five Nestle candy wrappers per sheet. The backs are virtually identical to the Topps cards of this year, i.e., same player-number correspondence. These sheets have been cut up into individual cards and are available from a few dealers around the country. This is one of the few instances in this hobby where the complete uncut sheet is worth considerably less than the sum of the individual cards due to the expense required in having the sheet cut professionally (and precisely) into individual cards. Supposedly less than 5000 sets were printed. Since the checklist is exactly the same as that of the 1984 Topps, these Nestle cards are generally priced as a multiple of the corresponding Topps card. The list below shows only the two most expensive cards in the set. Cards not listed below are priced at four times the corresponding 1984 Topps price. Beware also on this set to look for fakes and forgeries. Cards billed as Nestle proofs in black and white are fakes. There are even a few counterfeits in color; the two cards listed below are the cards most likely to be reprinted illegally as they are the most valuable in the set.

	MINT	EXC	G-VG
COMPLETE CUT SET (792)	375.00	165.00	55.00
COMMON PLAYER (1-792)	.25	.10	.02
☐ 8 Don Mattingly	90.00	40.00	13.50
☐ 182 Darryl Strawberry	90.00	40.00	13.50

1987 Nestle Dream Team

This 33-card set is, in a sense, three sets: Golden Era (1-11 gold), AL Modern Era (12-22 red), and NL Modern Era (23-33 blue). Cards are 2 1/2" by 3 1/2" and have color coded borders by era. The first 11 card photos are in black and white. The Nestle set was apparently not licensed by Major League Baseball and hence the team logos are not shown in the photos. Six-packs of certain Nestle candy bars contained three cards; cards were also available through a send-in offer.

	MINT	EXC	G-VG
COMPLETE SET (33)	8.00	3.50	.80
COMMON PLAYER (1-33)	.15	.06	.01
☐ 1 Lou Gehrig	.75	.30	.07
☐ 2 Rogers Hornsby	.25	.10	.02
☐ 3 Pie Traynor	.15	.06	.01
☐ 4 Honus Wagner	.40	.16	.04
☐ 5 Babe Ruth	1.00	.40	.10
☐ 6 Tris Speaker	.25	.10	.02
☐ 7 Ty Cobb	.75	.30	.07
☐ 8 Mickey Cochrane	.25	.10	.02
☐ 9 Walter Johnson	.40	.16	.04
☐ 10 Carl Hubbell	.25	.10	.02
☐ 11 Jimmy Foxx	.30	.12	.03
☐ 12 Rod Carew	.35	.15	.03
☐ 13 Nellie Fox	.15	.06	.01
☐ 14 Brooks Robinson	.25	.10	.02
☐ 15 Luis Aparicio	.15	.06	.01
☐ 16 Frank Robinson	.25	.10	.02
☐ 17 Mickey Mantle	1.00	.40	.10
☐ 18 Ted Williams	.60	.25	.06
☐ 19 Yogi Berra	.40	.16	.04
☐ 20 Bob Feller	.35	.15	.03
☐ 21 Whitey Ford	.30	.12	.03

		MINT	EXC	G-VG
☐ 22	Harmon Killebrew	.25	.10	.02
☐ 23	Stan Musial	.40	.16	.04
☐ 24	Jackie Robinson	.50	.20	.05
☐ 25	Eddie Mathews	.25	.10	.02
☐ 26	Ernie Banks	.25	.10	.02
☐ 27	Roberto Clemente	.45	.18	.04
☐ 28	Willie Mays	.50	.20	.05
☐ 29	Hank Aaron	.50	.20	.05
☐ 30	Johnny Bench	.35	.15	.03
☐ 31	Bob Gibson	.25	.10	.02
☐ 32	Warren Spahn	.25	.10	.02
☐ 33	Duke Snider	.35	.15	.03
☐ xx	Checklist card (unnumbered)	.50	.20	.05

1988 Nestle

This 44-card set was produced for Nestle by Mike Schechter Associates and was printed in Canada. Cards are 2 1/2" by 3 1/2" and have yellow borders. The Nestle set was apparently not licensed by Major League Baseball and hence the team logos are not shown in the photos. The cards are numbered on the back. The backs are printed in red and blue on white card stock.

		MINT	EXC	G-VG
COMPLETE SET (44)		20.00	8.50	2.75
COMMON PLAYER (1-44)		.35	.15	.03
☐ 1	Roger Clemens	2.00	.80	.20
☐ 2	Dale Murphy	.90	.40	.09
☐ 3	Eric Davis	.90	.40	.09
☐ 4	Gary Gaetti	.35	.15	.03
☐ 5	Ozzie Smith	.75	.30	.07
☐ 6	Mike Schmidt	1.50	.60	.15
☐ 7	Ozzie Guillen	.45	.18	.04
☐ 8	John Franco	.35	.15	.03
☐ 9	Andre Dawson	.75	.30	.07
☐ 10	Mark McGwire	.90	.40	.09
☐ 11	Bret Saberhagen	.75	.30	.07
☐ 12	Benito Santiago	.60	.25	.06
☐ 13	Jose Uribe	.35	.15	.03
☐ 14	Will Clark	2.00	.80	.20
☐ 15	Don Mattingly	1.25	.50	.12
☐ 16	Juan Samuel	.35	.15	.03
☐ 17	Jack Clark	.50	.20	.05
☐ 18	Darryl Strawberry	1.50	.60	.15
☐ 19	Bill Doran	.35	.15	.03
☐ 20	Pete Incaviglia	.50	.20	.05
☐ 21	Dwight Gooden	.90	.40	.09
☐ 22	Willie Randolph	.35	.15	.03
☐ 23	Tim Wallach	.35	.15	.03
☐ 24	Pedro Guerrero	.50	.20	.05
☐ 25	Steve Bedrosian	.35	.15	.03
☐ 26	Gary Carter	.60	.25	.06
☐ 27	Jeff Reardon	.45	.18	.04
☐ 28	Dave Righetti	.45	.18	.04
☐ 29	Frank White	.35	.15	.03
☐ 30	Buddy Bell	.35	.15	.03
☐ 31	Tim Raines	.60	.25	.06
☐ 32	Wade Boggs	1.50	.60	.15
☐ 33	Dave Winfield	.75	.30	.07
☐ 34	George Bell	.60	.25	.06
☐ 35	Alan Trammell	.60	.25	.06
☐ 36	Joe Carter	.60	.25	.06
☐ 37	Jose Canseco	2.00	.80	.20
☐ 38	Carlton Fisk	1.00	.40	.10

		NRMT	VG-E	GOOD
☐ 39	Kirby Puckett	1.25	.50	.12
☐ 40	Tony Gwynn	1.00	.40	.10
☐ 41	Matt Nokes	.35	.15	.03
☐ 42	Keith Hernandez	.50	.20	.05
☐ 43	Nolan Ryan	2.50	1.00	.25
☐ 44	Wally Joyner	.75	.30	.07

1954 N.Y. Journal American

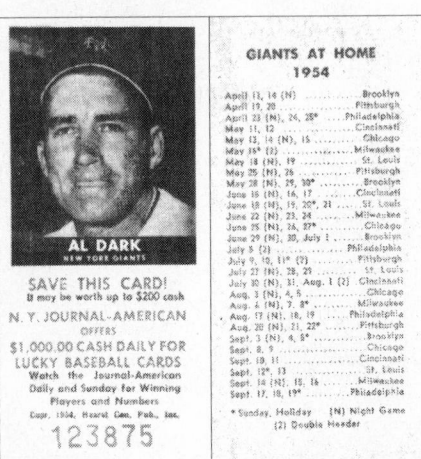

The cards in this 59-card set measure 2" by 4". The 1954 New York Journal American set contains black and white, unnumbered cards issued in conjunction with the newspaper. News stands were given boxes of cards to be distributed with purchases and each card had a serial number for redemption in the contest. The set spotlights New York teams only and carries game schedules on the reverse. The cards have been assigned numbers in the listing below alphabetically within team so that Brooklyn Dodgers are 1-19, New York Giants are 20-39, and New York Yankees are 40-59. There is speculation that a 20th Dodger card may exist. The catalog designation for this set is M127.

		NRMT	VG-E	GOOD
COMPLETE SET (59)		1800.00	800.00	180.00
COMMON PLAYER (1-59)		11.00	5.00	1.35
☐ 1	Joe Black	12.50	5.50	1.65
☐ 2	Roy Campanella	110.00	50.00	16.50
☐ 3	Billy Cox	11.00	5.00	1.35
☐ 4	Carl Erskine	15.00	6.50	2.15
☐ 5	Carl Furillo	18.00	7.50	2.50
☐ 6	Junior Gilliam	16.50	7.00	2.35
☐ 7	Gil Hodges	45.00	20.00	6.75
☐ 8	Jim Hughes	11.00	5.00	1.35
☐ 9	Clem Labine	12.50	5.50	1.65
☐ 10	Billy Loes	11.00	5.00	1.35
☐ 11	Russ Meyer	11.00	5.00	1.35
☐ 12	Don Newcombe	18.00	7.50	2.50
☐ 13	Ervin Palica	11.00	5.00	1.35
☐ 14	Pee Wee Reese	60.00	27.00	9.00
☐ 15	Jackie Robinson	135.00	60.00	20.00
☐ 16	Preacher Roe	18.00	7.50	2.50
☐ 17	George Shuba	11.00	5.00	1.35
☐ 18	Duke Snider	110.00	50.00	16.50
☐ 19	Dick Williams	15.00	6.50	2.15
☐ 20	Johnny Antonelli	12.50	5.50	1.65
☐ 21	Alvin Dark	15.00	6.50	2.15
☐ 22	Marv Grissom	11.00	5.00	1.35
☐ 23	Ruben Gomez	11.00	5.00	1.35
☐ 24	Jim Hearn	11.00	5.00	1.35
☐ 25	Bobby Hofman	11.00	5.00	1.35
☐ 26	Monte Irvin	35.00	15.75	5.25
☐ 27	Larry Jansen	11.00	5.00	1.35
☐ 28	Ray Katt	11.00	5.00	1.35

		NRMT	VG-E	GOOD
☐ 29	Don Liddle	11.00	5.00	1.35
☐ 30	Whitey Lockman	11.00	5.00	1.35
☐ 31	Sal Maglie	16.50	7.00	2.35
☐ 32	Willie Mays	225.00	100.00	33.00
☐ 33	Don Mueller	12.50	5.50	1.65
☐ 34	Dusty Rhodes	12.50	5.50	1.65
☐ 35	Hank Thompson	12.50	5.50	1.65
☐ 36	Wes Westrum	11.00	5.00	1.35
☐ 37	Hoyt Wilhelm	40.00	18.00	6.00
☐ 38	Davey Williams	11.00	5.00	1.35
☐ 39	Al Worthington	11.00	5.00	1.35
☐ 40	Hank Bauer	16.50	7.00	2.35
☐ 41	Yogi Berra	110.00	50.00	16.50
☐ 42	Harry Byrd	11.00	5.00	1.35
☐ 43	Andy Carey	11.00	5.00	1.35
☐ 44	Jerry Coleman	11.00	5.00	1.35
☐ 45	Joe Collins	11.00	5.00	1.35
☐ 46	Whitey Ford	60.00	27.00	9.00
☐ 47	Steve Kraly	11.00	5.00	1.35
☐ 48	Bob Kuzava	11.00	5.00	1.35
☐ 49	Frank Leja	11.00	5.00	1.35
☐ 50	Ed Lopat	18.00	7.50	2.50
☐ 51	Mickey Mantle	450.00	200.00	67.50
☐ 52	Gil McDougald	16.50	7.00	2.35
☐ 53	Bill Miller	11.00	5.00	1.35
☐ 54	Tom Morgan	11.00	5.00	1.35
☐ 55	Irv Noren	11.00	5.00	1.35
☐ 56	Allie Reynolds	18.00	7.50	2.50
☐ 57	Phil Rizzuto	45.00	20.00	6.75
☐ 58	Eddie Robinson	11.00	5.00	1.35
☐ 59	Gene Woodling	12.50	5.50	1.65

1989 J.J. Nissen

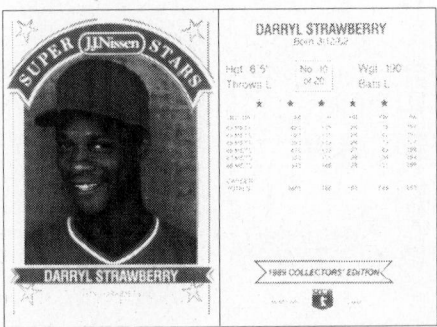

The 1989 J.J. Nissen set contains 20 standard-size (2 1/2" by 3 1/2") cards. The fronts have airbrushed facial photos with white and yellow borders and orange trim. The backs are white and feature career stats. The complete set price below does not include the error version of Mark Grace.

		MINT	EXC	G-VG
COMPLETE SET (20)		11.00	5.00	1.35
COMMON PLAYER (1-20)		.35	.15	.03
☐ 1	Wally Joyner	.60	.25	.06
☐ 2	Wade Boggs	.90	.40	.09
☐ 3	Ellis Burks	.75	.30	.07
☐ 4	Don Mattingly	.90	.40	.09
☐ 5	Jose Canseco	1.00	.40	.10
☐ 6	Mike Greenwell	.50	.20	.05
☐ 7	Eric Davis	.50	.20	.05
☐ 8	Kirby Puckett	.60	.25	.06
☐ 9	Kevin Seitzer	.35	.15	.03
☐ 10	Darryl Strawberry	.90	.40	.09
☐ 11	Gregg Jefferies	.75	.30	.07
☐ 12A	Mark Grace ERR (photo actually Vance Law)	12.00	5.25	1.50
☐ 12B	Mark Grace COR	1.00	.40	.10
☐ 13	Matt Nokes	.35	.15	.03
☐ 14	Mark McGwire	.60	.25	.06
☐ 15	Bobby Bonilla	.60	.25	.06
☐ 16	Roger Clemens	1.00	.40	.10
☐ 17	Frank Viola	.50	.20	.05
☐ 18	Orel Hershiser	.50	.20	.05
☐ 19	David Cone	.50	.20	.05
☐ 20	Ted Williams	1.00	.40	.10

1960 Nu-Card Hi-Lites

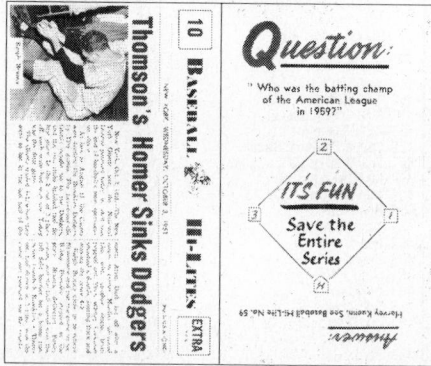

The cards in this 72-card set measure 3 1/4" by 5 3/8". In 1960, the Nu-Card Company introduced its Baseball Hi-Lites set of newspaper style cards. Each card singled out an individual baseball achievement with a picture and story. The reverses contain a baseball quiz. Cards 1-18 are more valuable if found printed totally in black on the front; these are copy-righted CVC as opposed to the NCI designation found on the red and black printed fronts.

	NRMT	VG-E	GOOD
COMPLETE SET (72)	250.00	110.00	37.50
COMMON PLAYER (1-72)	2.50	1.00	.25
☐ 1 Babe Hits 3 Homers In A Series Game	12.00	5.25	1.50
☐ 2 Podres Pitching Wins Series	2.50	1.00	.25
☐ 3 Bevans Pitches No Hitter, Almost	2.50	1.00	.25
☐ 4 Box Score Devised By Reporter	2.50	1.00	.25
☐ 5 VanderMeer Pitches Two No Hitters	2.50	1.00	.25
☐ 6 Indians Take Bums	2.50	1.00	.25
☐ 7 DiMag Comes Thru	12.00	5.25	1.50
☐ 8 Mathewson Pitches Three WS Shutouts	3.00	1.25	.30
☐ 9 Haddix Pitches 12 Perfect Innings	2.50	1.00	.25
☐ 10 Thomson's Homer Sinks Dodgers	3.00	1.25	.30
☐ 11 Hubbell Strikes Out Five A.L. Stars	2.50	1.00	.25
☐ 12 Pickoff Ends Series	2.50	1.00	.25
☐ 13 Cards Take Series From Yanks	2.50	1.00	.25
☐ 14 Dizzy And Daffy Dean Win Series	3.00	1.25	.30
☐ 15 Owen Drops 3rd Strike	2.50	1.00	.25
☐ 16 Ruth Calls Shot	12.00	5.25	1.50
☐ 17 Merkle Pulls Boner	2.50	1.00	.25
☐ 18 Larsen Hurls Perfect World Series Game	3.00	1.25	.30
☐ 19 Bean Ball Ends Career of Mickey Cochrane	2.50	1.00	.25
☐ 20 Banks Belts 47 Homers Earns MVP	4.00	1.75	.40
☐ 21 Stan Musial Hits Five Homers In One Day	6.00	2.50	.60
☐ 22 Mickey Mantle Hits Longest Homer	15.00	6.50	2.15
☐ 23 Sievers Captures Home Run Title	2.50	1.00	.25
☐ 24 Gehrig 2130 Consecutive Game Record Ends	7.50	3.25	.75
☐ 25 Red Schoendienst Key Player Braves Pennant	3.00	1.25	.30
☐ 26 Midget Pinch-Hits For St. Louis	3.00	1.25	.30
☐ 27 Willie Mays Makes Greatest Catch	7.50	3.25	.75
☐ 28 Homer by Yogi Berra Puts Yanks In 1st	5.00	2.25	.50
☐ 29 Campy NL MVP	5.00	2.25	.50
☐ 30 Bob Turley Hurls Yankees To WS Champions	2.50	1.00	.25
☐ 31 Dodgers Take Series From Sox in Six	2.50	1.00	.25
☐ 32 Furillo Hero as Dodgers Beat Chicago in 3rd WS Game	2.50	1.00	.25
☐ 33 Adcock Gets 4 Homers And A Double	2.50	1.00	.25
☐ 34 Dickey Chosen All- Star Catcher	2.50	1.00	.25
☐ 35 Burdette Beats Yanks In Three WS Games	2.50	1.00	.25
☐ 36 Umpires Clear White Sox Bench	2.50	1.00	.25
☐ 37 Reese Honored As Greatest Dodger SS	3.50	1.50	.35
☐ 38 Joe DiMaggio Hits In 56 Straight	12.00	5.25	1.50
☐ 39 Ted Williams Hits .406 For Season	7.50	3.25	.75
☐ 40 Walter Johnson Pitches 56 Straight	3.00	1.25	.30
☐ 41 Hodges Hits 4 Home Runs In Nite Game	3.00	1.25	.30
☐ 42 Greenberg Returns to Tigers From Army	3.00	1.25	.30
☐ 43 Ty Cobb Named Best Player Of All Time	9.00	4.00	.90
☐ 44 Robin Roberts Wins 28 Games	3.00	1.25	.30
☐ 45 Rizzuto's Two Runs Save 1st Place	3.00	1.25	.30
☐ 46 Tigers Beat Out Senators For Pennant	2.50	1.00	.25
☐ 47 Babe Ruth Hits 60th Home Run	12.00	5.25	1.50
☐ 48 Cy Young Honored	3.00	1.25	.30
☐ 49 Killebrew Starts Spring Training	4.00	1.75	.40
☐ 50 Mantle Hits Longest Homer at Stadium	15.00	6.50	2.15
☐ 51 Braves Take Pennant	2.50	1.00	.25
☐ 52 Ted Williams Hero Of All-Star Game	7.50	3.25	.75
☐ 53 Robinson Saves Dodgers For Play-off Series	6.00	2.50	.60
☐ 54 Snodgrass Muffs Fly	2.50	1.00	.25
☐ 55 Snider Belts 2 Homers Ties Homer Record	4.00	1.75	.40
☐ 56 Giants Win 26 Straight	2.50	1.00	.25
☐ 57 Ted Kluszewski Stars In 1st Series Win	3.00	1.25	.30
☐ 58 Ott Walks 5 Times In Single Game	3.00	1.25	.30
☐ 59 Harvey Kuenn Takes A.L. Batting Title	2.50	1.00	.25
☐ 60 Bob Feller Hurls 3rd No-Hitter of Career	4.00	1.75	.40
☐ 61 Yanks Champs Again	2.50	1.00	.25
☐ 62 Aaron's Bat Beats Yankees In Series	7.50	3.25	.75
☐ 63 Warren Spahn Beats Yanks in W.S.	4.00	1.75	.40
☐ 64 Ump's Wrong Call Helps Dodgers Beat Yanks	2.50	1.00	.25
☐ 65 Kaline Hits 3 Homers Two In Same Inning	4.00	1.75	.40
☐ 66 Bob Allison Named AL Rookie of the Year	2.50	1.00	.25
☐ 67 McCovey Blasts Way Into Giant Lineup	4.00	1.75	.40
☐ 68 Colavito Hits Four Homers in One Game	3.50	1.50	.35
☐ 69 Erskine Sets Strike Out Record in World Series	2.50	1.00	.25
☐ 70 Sal Maglie Pitches No-Hit Game	2.50	1.00	.25
☐ 71 Early Wynn Victory Crushes Yanks	3.00	1.25	.30
☐ 72 Nellie Fox AL MVP	3.00	1.25	.30

1961 Nu-Card Scoops

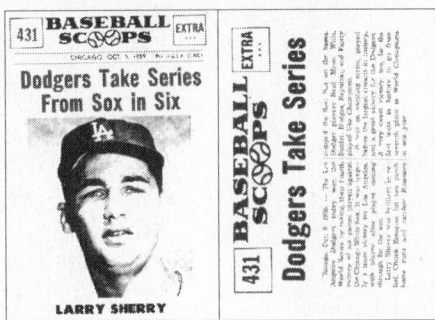

The cards in this 80-card set measure 2 1/2" by 3 1/2". This series depicts great moments in the history of individual ballplayers. Each card is designed as a miniature newspaper front-page, complete with data and picture. Both the number (401-480) and title are printed in red on the obverse, and the story is found on the back. An album was issued to hold the set. The set has been illegally reprinted, which has served to suppress the demand for the originals as well as the reprints.

	NRMT	VG-E	GOOD
COMPLETE SET (80)	125.00	57.50	18.75
COMMON PLAYER (401-480)	.75	.30	.07
☐ 401 Jim Gentile	.75	.30	.07
☐ 402 Warren Spahn (No-hitter)	3.00	1.25	.30
☐ 403 Bill Mazeroski	1.00	.40	.10
☐ 404 Willie Mays: (three triples)	6.00	2.50	.60
☐ 405 Woodie Held	.75	.30	.07
☐ 406 Vern Law	1.00	.40	.10
☐ 407 Pete Runnels	.75	.30	.07
☐ 408 Lew Burdette (No-hitter)	1.00	.40	.10
☐ 409 Dick Stuart	.75	.30	.07
☐ 410 Don Cardwell	.75	.30	.07
☐ 411 Camilo Pascual	.75	.30	.07
☐ 412 Ed Mathews	3.00	1.25	.30
☐ 413 Dick Groat	1.00	.40	.10
☐ 414 Gene Autry	2.50	1.00	.25
☐ 415 Bobby Richardson	1.50	.60	.15
☐ 416 Roger Maris	6.00	2.50	.60
☐ 417 Fred Merkle	.75	.30	.07
☐ 418 Don Larsen	1.00	.40	.10
☐ 419 Mickey Cochrane	1.00	.40	.10
☐ 420 Ernie Banks	3.00	1.25	.30
☐ 421 Stan Musial	5.00	2.25	.50
☐ 422 Mickey Mantle (longest homer)	12.00	5.25	1.50
☐ 423 Roy Sievers	.75	.30	.07
☐ 424 Lou Gehrig	6.00	2.50	.60
☐ 425 Red Schoendienst	2.00	.80	.20
☐ 426 Eddie Gaedel	1.50	.60	.15
☐ 427 Willie Mays (greatest catch)	6.00	2.50	.60
☐ 428 Jackie Robinson	5.00	2.25	.50
☐ 429 Roy Campanella	5.00	2.25	.50
☐ 430 Bob Turley	.75	.30	.07
☐ 431 Larry Sherry	.75	.30	.07
☐ 432 Carl Furillo	1.00	.40	.10
☐ 433 Joe Adcock	.75	.30	.07
☐ 434 Bill Dickey	1.00	.40	.10
☐ 435 Burdette 3 wins	.75	.30	.07
☐ 436 Umpire Clears Bench	.75	.30	.07
☐ 437 Pee Wee Reese	3.00	1.25	.30
☐ 438 Joe DiMaggio (56 Game Hit Streak)	9.00	4.00	.90
☐ 439 Ted Williams Hits .406	6.00	2.50	.60
☐ 440 Walter Johnson	3.00	1.25	.30
☐ 441 Gil Hodges	2.00	.80	.20
☐ 442 Hank Greenberg	2.00	.80	.20
☐ 443 Ty Cobb	7.50	3.25	.75
☐ 444 Robin Roberts	2.50	1.00	.25
☐ 445 Phil Rizzuto	2.00	.80	.20

☐ 446 Hal Newhouser	1.00	.40	.10
☐ 447 Babe Ruth 60th Homer	10.00	4.50	1.25
☐ 448 Cy Young	3.00	1.25	.30
☐ 449 Harmon Killebrew	3.00	1.25	.30
☐ 450 Mickey Mantle (longest homer)	10.00	4.50	1.25
☐ 451 Braves Take Pennant	.75	.30	.07
☐ 452 Ted Williams (All-Star Hero)	6.00	2.50	.60
☐ 453 Yogi Berra	5.00	2.25	.50
☐ 454 Fred Snodgrass	.75	.30	.07
☐ 455 Ruth 3 Homers	10.00	4.50	1.25
☐ 456 Giants 26 Game Streak	.75	.30	.07
☐ 457 Ted Kluszewski	1.25	.50	.12
☐ 458 Mel Ott	1.50	.60	.15
☐ 459 Harvey Kuenn	1.00	.40	.10
☐ 460 Bob Feller	3.50	1.50	.35
☐ 461 Casey Stengel	2.50	1.00	.25
☐ 462 Hank Aaron	6.00	2.50	.60
☐ 463 Spahn Beats Yanks	2.00	.80	.20
☐ 464 Ump's Wrong Call	.75	.30	.07
☐ 465 Al Kaline	3.50	1.50	.35
☐ 466 Bob Allison	.75	.30	.07
☐ 467 Joe DiMaggio (Four Homers)	9.00	4.00	.90
☐ 468 Rocky Colavito	1.25	.50	.12
☐ 469 Carl Erskine	1.00	.40	.10
☐ 470 Sal Maglie	1.00	.40	.10
☐ 471 Early Wynn	2.00	.80	.20
☐ 472 Nellie Fox	1.50	.60	.15
☐ 473 Marty Marion	1.00	.40	.10
☐ 474 Johnny Podres	.75	.30	.07
☐ 475 Mickey Owen	.75	.30	.07
☐ 476 Dean Brothers (Dizzy and Daffy)	2.50	1.00	.25
☐ 477 Christy Mathewson	2.50	1.00	.25
☐ 478 Harvey Haddix	.75	.30	.07
☐ 479 Carl Hubbell	1.00	.40	.10
☐ 480 Bobby Thomson	1.00	.40	.10

1952 Num Num

The cards in this 20-card set measure approximately 3 1/2" by 4 1/2". The 1952 Num Num Potato Chips issue features black and white, numbered cards of the Cleveland Indians. Cards came with and without coupons (tabs). The cards were issued without coupons directly by the Cleveland baseball club. When the complete set was obtained the tabs were cut off and exchanged for an autographed baseball. Card Number 16, Kennedy, is rather scarce. Cards with the tabs still intact are worth approximately 25 percent more than the values listed below. The catalog designation for this set is F337-2.

	NRMT	VG-E	GOOD
COMPLETE SET (20)	1000.00	400.00	100.00
COMMON PLAYER (1-20)	25.00	11.00	3.50
☐ 1 Lou Brissie	25.00	11.00	3.50
☐ 2 Jim Hegan	25.00	11.00	3.50
☐ 3 Birdie Tebbetts	25.00	11.00	3.50
☐ 4 Bob Lemon	65.00	29.00	9.75

		MINT	EXC	G-VG
☐ 5	Bob Feller	110.00	50.00	16.50
☐ 6	Early Wynn	65.00	29.00	9.75
☐ 7	Mike Garcia	30.00	13.50	4.50
☐ 8	Steve Gromek	25.00	11.00	3.50
☐ 9	Bob Chakales	25.00	11.00	3.50
☐ 10	Al Rosen	45.00	20.00	6.75
☐ 11	Dick Rozek	25.00	11.00	3.50
☐ 12	Luke Easter	25.00	11.00	3.50
☐ 13	Ray Boone	25.00	11.00	3.50
☐ 14	Bobby Avila	25.00	11.00	3.50
☐ 15	Dale Mitchell	25.00	11.00	3.50
☐ 16	Bob Kennedy	400.00	180.00	60.00
☐ 17	Harry Simpson	25.00	11.00	3.50
☐ 18	Larry Doby	45.00	20.00	6.75
☐ 19	Sam Jones	25.00	11.00	3.50
☐ 20	Al Lopez MG	65.00	29.00	9.75

1986 Oh Henry Indians

This 30-card set features Cleveland Indians and was distributed at the stadium to fans in attendance on Baseball Card Day. The cards were printed in one folded sheet which was perforated for easy separation into individual cards. The cards have white borders with a blue frame around each photo. The card backs include detailed career year-by-year statistics. The individual cards measure 2 1/4" by 3 1/8" and have full-color fronts.

		MINT	EXC	G-VG
	COMPLETE SET (30)	15.00	6.50	2.15
	COMMON PLAYER	.45	.18	.04
☐ 2	Brett Butler	.90	.40	.09
☐ 4	Tony Bernazard	.60	.25	.06
☐ 6	Andy Allanson	.45	.18	.04
☐ 7	Pat Corrales MG	.45	.18	.04
☐ 8	Carmen Castillo	.45	.18	.04
☐ 10	Pat Tabler	.60	.25	.06
☐ 13	Ernie Camacho	.45	.18	.04
☐ 14	Julio Franco	2.00	.80	.20
☐ 15	Dan Rohn	.45	.18	.04
☐ 18	Ken Schrom	.45	.18	.04
☐ 20	Otis Nixon	.75	.30	.07
☐ 22	Fran Mullins	.45	.18	.04
☐ 23	Chris Bando	.45	.18	.04
☐ 24	Ed Williams	.45	.18	.04
☐ 26	Brook Jacoby	.75	.30	.07
☐ 27	Mel Hall	.75	.30	.07
☐ 29	Andre Thornton	.75	.30	.07
☐ 30	Joe Carter	2.00	.80	.20
☐ 35	Phil Niekro	1.50	.60	.15
☐ 36	Jamie Easterly	.35	.15	.03
☐ 37	Don Schulze	.35	.15	.03
☐ 42	Rick Yett	.35	.15	.03
☐ 43	Scott Bailes	.35	.15	.03
☐ 44	Neal Heaton	.35	.15	.03
☐ 46	Jim Kern	.35	.15	.03
☐ 48	Dickie Noles	.35	.15	.03
☐ 49	Tom Candiotti	.60	.25	.06
☐ 53	Reggie Ritter	.35	.15	.03
☐ 54	Tom Waddell	.35	.15	.03
☐ xx	Coaching Staff	.35	.15	.03
	Jack Aker			
	Bobby Bonds			
	Doc Edwards			
	John Goryl			

1991 O-Pee-Chee Premier

The 1991 O-Pee-Chee Premier set contains 132 standard-size (2 1/2" by 3 1/2") cards. The fronts feature color action player photos on a white card face. All the pictures are bordered in gold above, while the color of the border stripes on the other three sides varies from card to card. The player's name, team name, and position (the last item in English and French) appear below the picture. In a horizontal format, the backs have a color head shot and the team logo in a circular format. Biography and statistics (1990 and career) are presented on an orange and yellow striped background. The cards are arranged in alphabetical order and numbered on the back. Small packs of these cards were given out at the Fan Fest to commemorate the 1991 All-Star Game in Canada. The key rookie cards in this set are Lance Dickson, Kirk Dressendorfer, and Gary Scott.

		MINT	EXC	G-VG
	COMPLETE SET (132)	45.00	20.00	6.75
	COMMON PLAYER (1-132)	.08	.03	.01
☐ 1	Roberto Alomar	.50	.20	.05
☐ 2	Sandy Alomar Jr.	.20	.08	.02
☐ 3	Moises Alou	.12	.05	.01
☐ 4	Brian Barnes	.30	.12	.03
☐ 5	Steve Bedrosian	.08	.03	.01
☐ 6	George Bell	.30	.12	.03
☐ 7	Juan Bell	.12	.05	.01
☐ 8	Albert Belle	.90	.40	.09
☐ 9	Bud Black	.08	.03	.01
☐ 10	Mike Boddicker	.08	.03	.01
☐ 11	Wade Boggs	.75	.30	.07
☐ 12	Barry Bonds	.75	.30	.07
☐ 13	Denis Boucher	.30	.12	.03
☐ 14	George Brett	.50	.20	.05
☐ 15	Hubie Brooks	.12	.05	.01
☐ 16	Brett Butler	.12	.05	.01
☐ 17	Ivan Calderon	.12	.05	.01
☐ 18	Jose Canseco	2.00	.80	.20
☐ 19	Gary Carter	.17	.07	.01
☐ 20	Joe Carter	.35	.15	.03
☐ 21	Jack Clark	.17	.07	.01
☐ 22	Will Clark	1.50	.60	.15
☐ 23	Roger Clemens	1.25	.50	.12
☐ 24	Alex Cole	.17	.07	.01
☐ 25	Vince Coleman	.17	.07	.01
☐ 26	Jeff Conine	.30	.12	.03
☐ 27	Milt Cuyler	.50	.20	.05
☐ 28	Danny Darwin	.08	.03	.01
☐ 29	Eric Davis	.35	.15	.03
☐ 30	Glenn Davis	.17	.07	.01
☐ 31	Andre Dawson	.35	.15	.03
☐ 32	Ken Dayley	.08	.03	.01
☐ 33	Steve Decker	.60	.25	.06
☐ 34	Delino DeShields	.35	.15	.03
☐ 35	Lance Dickson	.50	.20	.05
☐ 36	Kirk Dressendorfer	.60	.25	.06
☐ 37	Shawon Dunston	.15	.06	.01
☐ 38	Dennis Eckersley	.17	.07	.01
☐ 39	Dwight Evans	.12	.05	.01
☐ 40	Howard Farmer	.15	.06	.01
☐ 41	Junior Felix	.12	.05	.01
☐ 42	Alex Fernandez	.50	.20	.05
☐ 43	Tony Fernandez	.12	.05	.01
☐ 44	Cecil Fielder	1.25	.50	.12

☐ 45	Carlton Fisk	.50	.20	.05
☐ 46	Willie Fraser	.08	.03	.01
☐ 47	Gary Gaetti	.12	.05	.01
☐ 48	Andres Galarraga	.12	.05	.01
☐ 49	Ron Gant	.50	.20	.05
☐ 50	Kirk Gibson	.15	.06	.01
☐ 51	Bernard Gilkey	.30	.12	.03
☐ 52	Leo Gomez	.90	.40	.09
☐ 53	Rene Gonzalez	.08	.03	.01
☐ 54	Juan Gonzalez	5.00	2.25	.50
☐ 55	Dwight Gooden	.35	.15	.03
☐ 56	Ken Griffey Jr.	7.00	3.00	.70
☐ 57	Kelly Gruber	.15	.06	.01
☐ 58	Pedro Guerrero	.15	.06	.01
☐ 59	Tony Gwynn	.75	.30	.07
☐ 60	Chris Hammond	.20	.08	.02
☐ 61	Ron Hassey	.08	.03	.01
☐ 62	Rickey Henderson	1.25	.50	.12
☐ 63	Tom Henke	.12	.05	.01
☐ 64	Orel Hershiser	.20	.08	.02
☐ 65	Chris Hoiles	.20	.08	.02
☐ 66	Todd Hundley	.30	.12	.03
☐ 67	Pete Incaviglia	.12	.05	.01
☐ 68	Danny Jackson	.12	.05	.01
☐ 69	Barry Jones	.08	.03	.01
☐ 70	Dave Justice	6.00	2.50	.60
☐ 71	Jimmy Key	.12	.05	.01
☐ 72	Ray Lankford	1.00	.40	.10
☐ 73	Darren Lewis	.75	.30	.07
☐ 74	Kevin Maas	.75	.30	.07
☐ 75	Denny Martinez	.12	.05	.01
☐ 76	Tino Martinez	.50	.20	.05
☐ 77	Don Mattingly	.75	.30	.07
☐ 78	Willie McGee	.17	.07	.01
☐ 79	Fred McGriff	.35	.15	.03
☐ 80	Hensley Meulens	.20	.08	.02
☐ 81	Kevin Mitchell	.35	.15	.03
☐ 82	Paul Molitor	.20	.08	.02
☐ 83	Mickey Morandini	.30	.12	.03
☐ 84	Jack Morris	.20	.08	.02
☐ 85	Dale Murphy	.30	.12	.03
☐ 86	Eddie Murray	.35	.15	.03
☐ 87	Chris Nabholz	.17	.07	.01
☐ 88	Tim Naehring	.20	.08	.02
☐ 89	Otis Nixon	.12	.05	.01
☐ 90	Jose Offerman	.20	.08	.02
☐ 91	Bob Ojeda	.08	.03	.01
☐ 92	John Olerud	.60	.25	.06
☐ 93	Gregg Olson	.15	.06	.01
☐ 94	Dave Parker	.15	.06	.01
☐ 95	Terry Pendleton	.20	.08	.02
☐ 96	Kirby Puckett	.75	.30	.07
☐ 97	Tim Raines	.20	.08	.02
☐ 98	Jeff Reardon	.15	.06	.01
☐ 99	Dave Righetti	.12	.05	.01
☐ 100	Cal Ripken	2.00	.80	.20
☐ 101	Mel Rojas	.08	.03	.01
☐ 102	Nolan Ryan	6.00	2.50	.60
☐ 103	Ryne Sandberg	1.50	.60	.15
☐ 104	Scott Sanderson	.12	.05	.01
☐ 105	Benny Santiago	.15	.06	.01
☐ 106	Pete Schourek	.30	.12	.03
☐ 107	Gary Scott	.60	.25	.06
☐ 108	Terry Shumpert	.08	.03	.01
☐ 109	Ruben Sierra	.75	.30	.07
☐ 110	Doug Simons	.25	.10	.02
☐ 111	Dave Smith	.08	.03	.01
☐ 112	Ozzie Smith	.40	.16	.04
☐ 113	Cory Snyder	.12	.05	.01
☐ 114	Luis Sojo	.12	.05	.01
☐ 115	Dave Stewart	.15	.06	.01
☐ 116	Dave Stieb	.12	.05	.01
☐ 117	Darryl Strawberry	1.25	.50	.12
☐ 118	Pat Tabler	.08	.03	.01
☐ 119	Wade Taylor	.30	.12	.03
☐ 120	Bobby Thigpen	.12	.05	.01
☐ 121	Frank Thomas	15.00	6.50	2.15
☐ 122	Mike Timlin	.30	.12	.03
☐ 123	Alan Trammell	.30	.12	.03
☐ 124	Mo Vaughn	2.00	.80	.20
☐ 125	Tim Wallach	.12	.05	.01
☐ 126	Devon White	.12	.05	.01
☐ 127	Mark Whiten	.60	.25	.06
☐ 128	Bernie Williams	1.50	.60	.15
☐ 129	Willie Wilson	.12	.05	.01
☐ 130	Dave Winfield	.30	.12	.03
☐ 131	Robin Yount	.50	.20	.05
☐ 132	Checklist Card	.08	.01	.00

1980-83 Pacific Legends

ROY CAMPANELLA

This 124-card set is actually four 30-card subsets plus a four-card wax box bottom panel. The set was distributed by series over several years beginning in 1980 with the first 30 cards. The set was produced by Pacific Trading Cards and is frequently referred to as Cramer Legends, for the founder of Pacific Trading cards, Mike Cramer. Cards are standard size, 2 1/2" by 3 1/2" and are golden-toned. Even though the wax box cards are numbered from 121-124 and called "series 5," the set is considered complete without them.

		MINT	EXC	G-VG
	COMPLETE SET (120)	15.00	6.50	2.15
	COMMON PLAYER (1-120)	.10	.04	.01
	COMMON PLAYER (121-124)	.30	.12	.03
☐ 1	Babe Ruth	1.50	.60	.15
☐ 2	Heinie Manush	.10	.04	.01
☐ 3	Rabbit Maranville	.10	.04	.01
☐ 4	Earl Averill	.10	.04	.01
☐ 5	Joe DiMaggio	1.00	.40	.10
☐ 6	Mickey Mantle	1.25	.50	.12
☐ 7	Hank Aaron	.60	.25	.06
☐ 8	Stan Musial	.40	.16	.04
☐ 9	Bill Terry	.10	.04	.01
☐ 10	Sandy Koufax	.40	.16	.04
☐ 11	Ernie Lombardi	.10	.04	.01
☐ 12	Dizzy Dean	.30	.12	.03
☐ 13	Lou Gehrig	.75	.30	.07
☐ 14	Walter Alston	.10	.04	.01
☐ 15	Jackie Robinson	.40	.16	.04
☐ 16	Jimmie Foxx	.20	.08	.02
☐ 17	Billy Southworth	.10	.04	.01
☐ 18	Honus Wagner	.35	.15	.03
☐ 19	Duke Snider	.30	.12	.03
☐ 20	Rogers Hornsby UER	.25	.10	.02
	(At bat total of 1873 is incorrect)			
☐ 21	Paul Waner	.10	.04	.01
☐ 22	Luke Appling	.10	.04	.01
☐ 23	Billy Herman	.10	.04	.01
☐ 24	Lloyd Waner	.10	.04	.01
☐ 25	Fred Hutchinson	.10	.04	.01
☐ 26	Eddie Collins	.10	.04	.01
☐ 27	Lefty Grove	.20	.08	.02
☐ 28	Chuck Connors	.20	.08	.02
☐ 29	Lefty O'Doul	.10	.04	.01
☐ 30	Hank Greenberg	.25	.10	.02
☐ 31	Ty Cobb	.75	.30	.07
☐ 32	Enos Slaughter	.15	.06	.01
☐ 33	Ernie Banks	.30	.12	.03
☐ 34	Christy Mathewson	.25	.10	.02
☐ 35	Mel Ott	.15	.06	.01
☐ 36	Pie Traynor	.10	.04	.01
☐ 37	Clark Griffith	.10	.04	.01
☐ 38	Mickey Cochrane	.10	.04	.01
☐ 39	Joe Cronin	.10	.04	.01
☐ 40	Leo Durocher	.15	.06	.01
☐ 41	Home Run Baker	.10	.04	.01
☐ 42	Joe Tinker	.10	.04	.01
☐ 43	John McGraw	.10	.04	.01
☐ 44	Bill Dickey	.15	.06	.01
☐ 45	Walter Johnson	.25	.10	.02
☐ 46	Frankie Frisch	.10	.04	.01
☐ 47	Casey Stengel	.25	.10	.02
☐ 48	Willie Mays	.60	.25	.06

☐ 49	Johnny Mize	.15	.06	.01
☐ 50	Roberto Clemente	.35	.15	.03
☐ 51	Burleigh Grimes	.10	.04	.01
☐ 52	Pee Wee Reese	.25	.10	.02
☐ 53	Bob Feller	.25	.10	.02
☐ 54	Brooks Robinson	.25	.10	.02
☐ 55	Sam Crawford	.10	.04	.01
☐ 56	Robin Roberts	.15	.06	.01
☐ 57	Warren Spahn	.25	.10	.02
☐ 58	Joe McCarthy	.10	.04	.01
☐ 59	Jocko Conlan	.10	.04	.01
☐ 60	Satchel Paige	.35	.15	.03
☐ 61	Ted Williams	.50	.20	.05
☐ 62	George Kelly	.10	.04	.01
☐ 63	Gil Hodges	.10	.04	.01
☐ 64	Jim Bottomley	.10	.04	.01
☐ 65	Al Kaline	.25	.10	.02
☐ 66	Harvey Kuenn	.10	.04	.01
☐ 67	Yogi Berra	.35	.15	.03
☐ 68	Nellie Fox	.10	.04	.01
☐ 69	Harmon Killebrew	.20	.08	.02
☐ 70	Edd Roush	.10	.04	.01
☐ 71	Mordecai Brown	.10	.04	.01
☐ 72	Gabby Hartnett	.10	.04	.01
☐ 73	Early Wynn	.15	.06	.01
☐ 74	Nap Lajoie	.10	.04	.01
☐ 75	Charlie Grimm	.10	.04	.01
☐ 76	Joe Garagiola	.25	.10	.02
☐ 77	Ted Lyons	.10	.04	.01
☐ 78	Mickey Vernon	.10	.04	.01
☐ 79	Lou Boudreau	.10	.04	.01
☐ 80	Al Dark	.10	.04	.01
☐ 81	Ralph Kiner	.20	.08	.02
☐ 82	Phil Rizzuto	.20	.08	.02
☐ 83	Stan Hack	.10	.04	.01
☐ 84	Frank Chance	.10	.04	.01
☐ 85	Ray Schalk	.10	.04	.01
☐ 86	Bill McKechnie	.10	.04	.01
☐ 87	Travis Jackson	.10	.04	.01
☐ 88	Pete Reiser	.10	.04	.01
☐ 89	Carl Hubbell	.15	.06	.01
☐ 90	Roy Campanella	.30	.12	.03
☐ 91	Cy Young	.20	.08	.02
☐ 92	Kiki Cuyler	.10	.04	.01
☐ 93	Chief Bender	.10	.04	.01
☐ 94	Richie Ashburn	.20	.08	.02
☐ 95	Riggs Stephenson	.10	.04	.01
☐ 96	Minnie Minoso	.10	.04	.01
☐ 97	Hack Wilson	.10	.04	.01
☐ 98	Al Lopez	.10	.04	.01
☐ 99	Willie Keeler	.10	.04	.01
☐ 100	Fred Lindstrom	.10	.04	.01
☐ 101	Roger Maris	.25	.10	.02
☐ 102	Roger Bresnahan	.10	.04	.01
☐ 103	Monty Stratton	.15	.06	.01
☐ 104	Goose Goslin	.10	.04	.01
☐ 105	Earl Combs	.10	.04	.01
☐ 106	Pepper Martin	.10	.04	.01
☐ 107	Joe Jackson	.60	.25	.06
☐ 108	George Sisler	.10	.04	.01
☐ 109	Red Ruffing	.10	.04	.01
☐ 110	Johnny Vander Meer	.10	.04	.01
☐ 111	Herb Pennock	.10	.04	.01
☐ 112	Chuck Klein	.10	.04	.01
☐ 113	Paul Derringer	.10	.04	.01
☐ 114	Addie Joss	.10	.04	.01
☐ 115	Bobby Thomson	.10	.04	.01
☐ 116	Chick Hafey	.10	.04	.01
☐ 117	Lefty Gomez	.15	.06	.01
☐ 118	George Kell	.10	.04	.01
☐ 119	Al Simmons	.10	.04	.01
☐ 120	Bob Lemon	.10	.04	.01
☐ 121	Hoyt Wilhelm (wax box card)	.35	.15	.03
☐ 122	Arky Vaughan (wax box card)	.30	.12	.03
☐ 123	Frank Robinson (wax box card)	.50	.20	.05
☐ 124	Grover Alexander (wax box card)	.35	.15	.03

1988 Pacific Eight Men Out

This set was produced by Mike Cramer's Pacific Trading Cards of Edmonds, Washington. The set was released in conjunction with the popular movie of the same name, which told the story of the "fix" of the 1919 World Series between the Cincinnati

Reds and the Chicago "Black" Sox. The cards are standard size, 2 1/2" by 3 1/2" and have a raspberry-colored border on the card fronts as well as raspberry-colored print on the white card stock backs. The cards were available either as wax packs or as collated sets. Generally the cards relating to the movie (showing actors) are in full-color whereas the vintage photography showing the actual players involved is in a sepia tone.

		MINT	EXC	G-VG
	COMPLETE SET (110)	8.00	3.50	.80
	COMMON PLAYER (1-110)	.10	.04	.01
☐ 1	We're Going To See The Sox	.10	.04	.01
☐ 2	White Sox Win The Pennant	.10	.04	.01
☐ 3	The Series	.10	.04	.01
☐ 4	1919 Chicago White Sox	.10	.04	.01
☐ 5	The Black Sox Scandal	.10	.04	.01
☐ 6	Eddie Cicotte 29-7 in 1919	.15	.06	.01
☐ 7	"Buck's Their Favorite"	.10	.04	.01
☐ 8	Eddie Collins	.20	.08	.02
☐ 9	Michael Rooker as Chick Gandil	.10	.04	.01
☐ 10	Charlie Sheen as Hap Felsch	.30	.12	.03
☐ 11	James Read as Lefty Williams	.10	.04	.01
☐ 12	John Cusak as Buck Weaver	.10	.04	.01
☐ 13	D.B. Sweeney as Joe Jackson	.15	.06	.01
☐ 14	David Strathairn as Eddie Cicotte	.10	.04	.01
☐ 15	Perry Lang as Fred McMullin	.10	.04	.01
☐ 16	Don Harvey as Swede Risberg	.10	.04	.01
☐ 17	The Gambler Burns And Maharg	.10	.04	.01
☐ 18	"Sleepy"Bill Burns	.10	.04	.01
☐ 19	The Key is Cicotte	.10	.04	.01
☐ 20	C'mon Betsy	.10	.04	.01
☐ 21	The Fix	.10	.04	.01
☐ 22	Chick Approaches Cicotte	.10	.04	.01
☐ 23	Kid Gleason	.10	.04	.01
☐ 24	Charles Comiskey Owner	.10	.04	.01
☐ 25	Chick Gandil 1st Baseman	.15	.06	.01
☐ 26	Swede Risberg	.10	.04	.01
☐ 27	Sport Sullivan	.10	.04	.01
☐ 28	Abe Attell And Arnold Rothstein	.10	.04	.01
☐ 29	Hugh Fullerton Sportswriter	.10	.04	.01
☐ 30	Ring Lardner Sportswriter	.10	.04	.01
☐ 31	"Shoeless"Joe His Batting Eye	.20	.08	.02
☐ 32	"Shoeless"Joe	.25	.10	.02
☐ 33	Buck Can't Sleep	.10	.04	.01
☐ 34	George"Buck" Weaver	.10	.04	.01
☐ 35	Hugh and Ring Confront Kid	.10	.04	.01

☐ 36 Joe Doesn't Want To Play	.10	.04	.01
☐ 37 "Shoeless" Joe Jackson	.25	.10	.02
☐ 38 "Sore Arm, Cicotte," "Old Man Cicotte"	.10	.04	.01
☐ 39 The Fix Is On	.10	.04	.01
☐ 40 Buck Plays To Win	.10	.04	.01
☐ 41 Hap Makes A Great Catch	.10	.04	.01
☐ 42 Hugh and Ring Suspect	.10	.04	.01
☐ 43 Ray Gets Things Going	.10	.04	.01
☐ 44 Lefty Loses Game Two	.10	.04	.01
☐ 45 Lefty Crosses Up Catcher Ray Schalk	.10	.04	.01
☐ 46 Chick's RBI Wins Game Three	.10	.04	.01
☐ 47 Dickie Kerr Wins Game Three	.10	.04	.01
☐ 48 Chick Leaves Buck At Third	.10	.04	.01
☐ 49 Williams Loses Game Five	.10	.04	.01
☐ 50 Ray Schalk	.10	.04	.01
☐ 51 Schalk Blocks The Plate	.10	.04	.01
☐ 52 Schalk Is Thrown Out	.10	.04	.01
☐ 53 Chicago Stickball Game	.10	.04	.01
☐ 54 I'm Forever Blowing Ball Games	.10	.04	.01
☐ 55 Felsch Scores Jackson	.20	.08	.02
☐ 56 Kerr Wins Game Six	.10	.04	.01
☐ 57 Where's The Money	.10	.04	.01
☐ 58 Cicotte Wins Game Seven	.10	.04	.01
☐ 59 Kid Watches Eddie	.10	.04	.01
☐ 60 Lefty Is Threatened	.10	.04	.01
☐ 61 James, Get Your Arm Ready, Fast	.10	.04	.01
☐ 62 Shoeless Joe's Home Run	.20	.08	.02
☐ 63 Buck Played His Best	.10	.04	.01
☐ 64 Hugh Exposes The Fix	.10	.04	.01
☐ 65 "Sign The Petition"	.10	.04	.01
☐ 66 Baseball Owners Hire A Commissioner	.10	.04	.01
☐ 67 Judge Kenesaw Mountain Landis	.10	.04	.01
☐ 68 Grand Jury Summoned	.10	.04	.01
☐ 69 "Say It Ain't So, Joe"	.15	.06	.01
☐ 70 The Swede's A Hard Guy	.10	.04	.01
☐ 71 Buck Loves The Game	.10	.04	.01
☐ 72 The Trial	.10	.04	.01
☐ 73 Kid Gleason Takes The Stand	.10	.04	.01
☐ 74 The Verdict	.10	.04	.01
☐ 75 Eight Men Out	.10	.04	.01
☐ 76 Oscar"Happy" Felsch	.20	.08	.02
☐ 77 Who's Joe Jackson	.20	.08	.02
☐ 78 Ban Johnson	.10	.04	.01
☐ 79 Judge Landis	.10	.04	.01
☐ 80 Charles Comiskey	.10	.04	.01
☐ 81 Heinie Groh	.10	.04	.01
☐ 82 Slim Sallee	.10	.04	.01
☐ 83 Dutch Ruether	.10	.04	.01
☐ 84 Edd Roush	.25	.10	.02
☐ 85 Morrie Rath	.10	.04	.01
☐ 86 Bill Rariden	.10	.04	.01
☐ 87 Jimmy Ring	.10	.04	.01
☐ 88 Greasy Neale	.15	.06	.01
☐ 89 Pat Moran	.10	.04	.01
☐ 90 Adolfo Luque	.10	.04	.01
☐ 91 Larry Kopf	.10	.04	.01
☐ 92 Ray Fisher	.10	.04	.01
☐ 93 Hod Eller	.10	.04	.01
☐ 94 Pat Duncan	.10	.04	.01
☐ 95 Jake Daubert	.10	.04	.01
☐ 96 Red Faber	.20	.08	.02
☐ 97 Dickie Kerr	.10	.04	.01
☐ 98 Shano Collins	.10	.04	.01
☐ 99 Eddie Collins	.20	.08	.02
☐ 100 Ray Schalk	.20	.08	.02
☐ 101 Nemo Leibold	.10	.04	.01
☐ 102 Kid Gleason	.10	.04	.01
☐ 103 Swede Risberg	.15	.06	.01
☐ 104 Eddie Cicotte	.15	.06	.01
☐ 105 Fred McMullin	.10	.04	.01
☐ 106 Chick Gandil	.15	.06	.01
☐ 107 Buck Weaver	.15	.06	.01
☐ 108 Lefty Williams	.15	.06	.01
☐ 109 Happy Felsch	.15	.06	.01
☐ 110 Joe Jackson	.50	.20	.05

1988 Pacific Legends I

This attractive set of 110 full-color cards was produced by Mike Cramer's Pacific Trading Cards of Edmonds, Washington. The cards are silver bordered and are standard size, 2 1/2" by 3 1/2". Card backs are printed in yellow, black, and gray on white card stock. The cards were available either as wax packs or as collated sets. The players pictured in the set had retired many years before, but most are still well remembered. The statistics on the card backs give the player's career and "best season" statistics. The set was licensed by Major League Baseball Players Alumni.

	MINT	EXC	G-VG
COMPLETE SET (110)	11.00	5.00	1.35
COMMON PLAYER (1-110)	.05	.02	.00
☐ 1 Hank Aaron	.75	.30	.07
☐ 2 Red Schoendienst	.25	.10	.02
☐ 3 Brooks Robinson	.35	.15	.03
☐ 4 Luke Appling	.20	.08	.02
☐ 5 Gene Woodling	.05	.02	.00
☐ 6 Stan Musial	.60	.25	.06
☐ 7 Mickey Mantle	1.00	.40	.10
☐ 8 Richie Ashburn	.20	.08	.02
☐ 9 Ralph Kiner	.25	.10	.02
☐ 10 Phil Rizzuto	.20	.08	.02
☐ 11 Harvey Haddix	.05	.02	.00
☐ 12 Ken Boyer	.10	.04	.01
☐ 13 Clete Boyer	.05	.02	.00
☐ 14 Ken Harrelson	.10	.04	.01
☐ 15 Robin Roberts	.20	.08	.02
☐ 16 Catfish Hunter	.20	.08	.02
☐ 17 Frank Howard	.10	.04	.01
☐ 18 Jim Perry	.05	.02	.00
☐ 19A Elston Howard ERR (reversed negative)	.15	.06	.01
☐ 19B Elston Howard COR	.15	.06	.01
☐ 20 Jim Bouton	.10	.04	.01
☐ 21 Pee Wee Reese	.25	.10	.02
☐ 22A Mel Stottlemyre ERR (spelled Stottlemyer on card front)	.15	.06	.01
☐ 22B Mel Stottlemyre COR	.15	.06	.01
☐ 23 Hank Sauer	.05	.02	.00
☐ 24 Willie Mays	.75	.30	.07
☐ 25 Tom Tresh	.10	.04	.01
☐ 26 Roy Sievers	.05	.02	.00
☐ 27 Leo Durocher	.20	.08	.02
☐ 28 Al Dark	.05	.02	.00
☐ 29 Tony Kubek	.15	.06	.01
☐ 30 Johnny VanderMeer	.10	.04	.01
☐ 31 Joe Adcock	.05	.02	.00
☐ 32 Bob Lemon	.15	.06	.01
☐ 33 Don Newcombe	.10	.04	.01
☐ 34 Thurman Munson	.30	.12	.03
☐ 35 Earl Battey	.05	.02	.00
☐ 36 Ernie Banks	.35	.15	.03
☐ 37 Matty Alou	.05	.02	.00
☐ 38 Dave McNally	.05	.02	.00
☐ 39 Mickey Lolich	.10	.04	.01
☐ 40 Jackie Robinson	.50	.20	.05
☐ 41 Allie Reynolds	.10	.04	.01
☐ 42A Don Larsen ERR (misspelled Larson on card front)	.15	.06	.01
☐ 42B Don Larsen COR	.15	.06	.01

☐ 43	Fergie Jenkins	.30	.12	.03
☐ 44	Jim Gilliam	.10	.04	.01
☐ 45	Bobby Thomson	.10	.04	.01
☐ 46	Sparky Anderson	.10	.04	.01
☐ 47	Roy Campanella	.35	.15	.03
☐ 48	Marv Throneberry	.10	.04	.01
☐ 49	Bill Virdon	.05	.02	.00
☐ 50	Ted Williams	.50	.20	.05
☐ 51	Minnie Minoso	.15	.06	.01
☐ 52	Bob Turley	.05	.02	.00
☐ 53	Yogi Berra	.35	.15	.03
☐ 54	Juan Marichal	.20	.08	.02
☐ 55	Duke Snider	.35	.15	.03
☐ 56	Harvey Kuenn	.10	.04	.01
☐ 57	Nellie Fox	.15	.06	.01
☐ 58	Felipe Alou	.05	.02	.00
☐ 59	Tony Oliva	.10	.04	.01
☐ 60	Bill Mazeroski	.10	.04	.01
☐ 61	Bobby Shantz	.05	.02	.00
☐ 62	Mark Fidrych	.10	.04	.01
☐ 63	Johnny Mize	.20	.08	.02
☐ 64	Ralph Terry	.10	.04	.01
☐ 65	Gus Bell	.05	.02	.00
☐ 66	Jerry Koosman	.10	.04	.01
☐ 67	Mike McCormick	.05	.02	.00
☐ 68	Lou Burdette	.10	.04	.01
☐ 69	George Kell	.20	.08	.02
☐ 70	Vic Raschi	.10	.04	.01
☐ 71	Chuck Connors	.20	.08	.02
☐ 72	Ted Kluszewski	.20	.08	.02
☐ 73	Bobby Doerr	.20	.08	.02
☐ 74	Bobby Richardson	.15	.06	.01
☐ 75	Carl Erskine	.10	.04	.01
☐ 76	Hoyt Wilhelm	.20	.08	.02
☐ 77	Bob Purkey	.05	.02	.00
☐ 78	Bob Friend	.05	.02	.00
☐ 79	Monte Irvin	.20	.08	.02
☐ 80A	Jim Lonborg ERR	.15	.06	.01
	(misspelled Longborg on card front)			
☐ 80B	Jim Lonborg COR	.15	.06	.01
☐ 81	Wally Moon	.05	.02	.00
☐ 82	Moose Skowron	.10	.04	.01
☐ 83	Tommy Davis	.10	.04	.01
☐ 84	Enos Slaughter	.20	.08	.02
☐ 85	Sal Maglie UER	.10	.04	.01
	(1945-1917 on back)			
☐ 86	Harmon Killebrew	.20	.08	.02
☐ 87	Gil Hodges	.20	.08	.02
☐ 88	Jim Kaat	.10	.04	.01
☐ 89	Roger Maris	.40	.16	.04
☐ 90	Billy Williams	.20	.08	.02
☐ 91	Luis Aparicio	.20	.08	.02
☐ 92	Jim Bunning	.15	.06	.01
☐ 93	Bill Freehan	.10	.04	.01
☐ 94	Orlando Cepeda	.15	.06	.01
☐ 95	Early Wynn	.20	.08	.02
☐ 96	Tug McGraw	.10	.04	.01
☐ 97	Ron Santo	.10	.04	.01
☐ 98	Del Crandall	.05	.02	.00
☐ 99	Sal Bando	.05	.02	.00
☐ 100	Joe DiMaggio	.75	.30	.07
☐ 101	Bob Feller	.35	.15	.03
☐ 102	Larry Doby	.10	.04	.01
☐ 103	Rollie Fingers	.30	.12	.03
☐ 104	Al Kaline	.30	.12	.03
☐ 105	Johnny Podres	.10	.04	.01
☐ 106	Lou Boudreau	.20	.08	.02
☐ 107	Zoilo Versalles	.05	.02	.00
☐ 108	Dick Groat	.10	.04	.01
☐ 109	Warren Spahn	.30	.12	.03
☐ 110	Johnny Bench	.40	.16	.04

1989 Pacific Legends II

The 1989 Pacific Legends Series II set contains 110 standard-size (2 1/2" by 3 1/2") cards. The fronts have vintage color photos with silver borders. The backs are gray and feature career highlights and lifetime statistics. The cards were distributed as sets and in ten-card wax packs.

	MINT	EXC	G-VG
COMPLETE SET (110)	11.00	5.00	1.35
COMMON PLAYER (111-220)	.05	.02	.00

☐ 111	Reggie Jackson	.75	.30	.07
☐ 112	Rich Reese	.05	.02	.00

☐ 113	Frankie Frisch	.10	.04	.01
☐ 114	Ed Kranepool	.05	.02	.00
☐ 115	Al Hrabosky	.05	.02	.00
☐ 116	Eddie Mathews	.25	.10	.02
☐ 117	Ty Cobb	.60	.25	.06
☐ 118	Jim Davenport	.05	.02	.00
☐ 119	Buddy Lewis	.05	.02	.00
☐ 120	Virgil Trucks	.05	.02	.00
☐ 121	Del Ennis	.05	.02	.00
☐ 122	Dick Radatz	.05	.02	.00
☐ 123	Andy Pafko	.05	.02	.00
☐ 124	Wilbur Wood	.05	.02	.00
☐ 125	Joe Sewell	.10	.04	.01
☐ 126	Herb Score	.05	.02	.00
☐ 127	Paul Waner	.10	.04	.01
☐ 128	Lloyd Waner	.10	.04	.01
☐ 129	Brooks Robinson	.30	.12	.03
☐ 130	Bo Belinsky	.05	.02	.00
☐ 131	Phil Cavarretta	.05	.02	.00
☐ 132	Claude Osteen	.05	.02	.00
☐ 133	Tito Francona	.05	.02	.00
☐ 134	Billy Pierce	.05	.02	.00
☐ 135	Roberto Clemente	.40	.16	.04
☐ 136	Spud Chandler	.05	.02	.00
☐ 137	Enos Slaughter	.20	.08	.02
☐ 138	Ken Holtzman	.05	.02	.00
☐ 139	John Hopp	.05	.02	.00
☐ 140	Tony LaRussa	.10	.04	.01
☐ 141	Ryne Duren	.05	.02	.00
☐ 142	Glenn Beckert UER	.05	.02	.00
	(Misspelled Glen on card front)			
☐ 143	Ken Keltner	.05	.02	.00
☐ 144	Hank Bauer	.05	.02	.00
☐ 145	Roger Craig	.10	.04	.01
☐ 146	Frank Baker	.10	.04	.01
☐ 147	Jim O'Toole	.05	.02	.00
☐ 148	Rogers Hornsby	.20	.08	.02
☐ 149	Jose Cardenal	.05	.02	.00
☐ 150	Bobby Doerr	.15	.06	.01
☐ 151	Mickey Cochrane	.15	.06	.01
☐ 152	Gaylord Perry	.25	.10	.02
☐ 153	Frank Thomas	.05	.02	.00
☐ 154	Ted Williams	.50	.20	.05
☐ 155	Sam McDowell	.05	.02	.00
☐ 156	Bob Feller	.35	.15	.03
☐ 157	Bert Campaneris	.05	.02	.00
☐ 158	Thornton Lee UER	.05	.02	.00
	(misspelled Thorton on card front)			
☐ 159	Gary Peters	.05	.02	.00
☐ 160	Joe Medwick	.15	.06	.01
☐ 161	Joe Nuxhall	.05	.02	.00
☐ 162	Joe Schultz	.05	.02	.00
☐ 163	Harmon Killebrew	.25	.10	.02
☐ 164	Bucky Walters	.05	.02	.00
☐ 165	Bob Allison	.05	.02	.00
☐ 166	Lou Boudreau	.15	.06	.01
☐ 167	Joe Cronin	.15	.06	.01
☐ 168	Mike Torrez	.05	.02	.00
☐ 169	Rich Rollins	.05	.02	.00
☐ 170	Tony Cuccinello	.05	.02	.00
☐ 171	Hoyt Wilhelm	.20	.08	.02
☐ 172	Ernie Harwell	.10	.04	.01
	(announcer)			
☐ 173	George Foster	.10	.04	.01
☐ 174	Lou Gehrig	.60	.25	.06
☐ 175	Dave Kingman	.10	.04	.01
☐ 176	Babe Ruth	.90	.40	.09
☐ 177	Joe Black	.05	.02	.00
☐ 178	Roy Face	.05	.02	.00
☐ 179	Earl Weaver	.10	.04	.01
☐ 180	Johnny Mize	.20	.08	.02

		MINT	EXC	G-VG
☐ 181	Roger Cramer	.05	.02	.00
☐ 182	Jim Piersall	.05	.02	.00
☐ 183	Ned Garver	.05	.02	.00
☐ 184	Billy Williams	.15	.06	.01
☐ 185	Lefty Grove	.15	.06	.01
☐ 186	Jim Grant	.05	.02	.00
☐ 187	Elmer Valo	.05	.02	.00
☐ 188	Ewell Blackwell	.05	.02	.00
☐ 189	Mel Ott	.15	.06	.01
☐ 190	Harry Walker	.05	.02	.00
☐ 191	Bill Campbell	.05	.02	.00
☐ 192	Walter Johnson	.20	.08	.02
☐ 193	Catfish Hunter	.20	.08	.02
☐ 194	Charlie Keller	.05	.02	.00
☐ 195	Hank Greenberg	.20	.08	.02
☐ 196	Bobby Murcer	.10	.04	.01
☐ 197	Al Lopez	.15	.06	.01
☐ 198	Vida Blue	.05	.02	.00
☐ 199	Shag Crawford UMP	.05	.02	.00
☐ 200	Arky Vaughan	.15	.06	.01
☐ 201	Smoky Burgess	.05	.02	.00
☐ 202	Rip Sewell	.05	.02	.00
☐ 203	Earl Averill	.10	.04	.01
☐ 204	Milt Pappas	.05	.02	.00
☐ 205	Mel Harder	.05	.02	.00
☐ 206	Sam Jethroe	.05	.02	.00
☐ 207	Randy Hundley	.05	.02	.00
☐ 208	Jesse Haines	.05	.02	.00
☐ 209	Jack Brickhouse (announcer)	.05	.02	.00
☐ 210	Whitey Ford	.25	.10	.02
☐ 211	Honus Wagner	.35	.15	.03
☐ 212	Phil Niekro	.15	.06	.01
☐ 213	Gary Bell	.05	.02	.00
☐ 214	Jon Matlack	.05	.02	.00
☐ 215	Moe Drabowsky	.05	.02	.00
☐ 216	Edd Roush	.15	.06	.01
☐ 217	Joel Horlen	.05	.02	.00
☐ 218	Casey Stengel	.20	.08	.02
☐ 219	Burt Hooton	.05	.02	.00
☐ 220	Joe Jackson	.60	.25	.06

1989-90 Pacific Senior League

The 1989-90 Pacific Trading Cards Senior League set contains 220 standard-size (2 1/2" by 3 1/2") cards. The fronts feature color photos with silver borders and player names and positions at the bottom. The horizontally-oriented backs are red, white, and blue, and show vital statistics and career highlights. The cards were distributed as a boxed set with 15 card-sized logo stickers/puzzle pieces as well as in wax packs. There are several In Action cards in the set, designated by IA in the checklist below. The Nettles card was corrected very late according to the set's producer.

	MINT	EXC	G-VG
COMPLETE SET (220)	11.00	5.00	1.35
COMMON PLAYER (1-220)	.05	.02	.00

☐ 1	Bobby Tolan	.15	.06	.01
☐ 2	Sergio Ferrer	.05	.02	.00
☐ 3	David Rajsich	.05	.02	.00
☐ 4	Ron LeFlore	.15	.06	.01
☐ 5	Steve Henderson	.05	.02	.00

☐ 6	Jerry Martin	.05	.02	.00
☐ 7	Gary Rajsich	.05	.02	.00
☐ 8	Elias Sosa	.05	.02	.00
☐ 9	Jon Matlack	.10	.04	.01
☐ 10	Steve Kemp	.10	.04	.01
☐ 11	Lenny Randle	.05	.02	.00
☐ 12	Roy Howell	.05	.02	.00
☐ 13	Milt Wilcox	.05	.02	.00
☐ 14	Alan Bannister	.05	.02	.00
☐ 15	Dock Ellis	.05	.02	.00
☐ 16	Mike Williams	.05	.02	.00
☐ 17	Luis Gomez	.05	.02	.00
☐ 18	Joe Sambito	.05	.02	.00
☐ 19	Bake McBride	.05	.02	.00
☐ 20	Pat Zachry UER (Photo actually Dick Bosman)	.05	.02	.00
☐ 21	Dwight Lowry	.05	.02	.00
☐ 22	Ozzie Virgil Sr.	.05	.02	.00
☐ 23	Randy Lerch	.05	.02	.00
☐ 24	Butch Benton	.05	.02	.00
☐ 25	Tom Zimmer UER (No bio information)	.05	.02	.00
☐ 26	Al Holland UER (Photo actually Nardi Contreras)	.15	.06	.01
☐ 27	Sammy Stewart	.05	.02	.00
☐ 28	Bill Lee	.10	.04	.01
☐ 29	Ferguson Jenkins	1.50	.60	.15
☐ 30	Leon Roberts	.05	.02	.00
☐ 31	Rick Wise	.10	.04	.01
☐ 32	Butch Hobson	.15	.06	.01
☐ 33	Pete LaCock	.05	.02	.00
☐ 34	Bill Campbell	.05	.02	.00
☐ 35	Doug Simunic	.05	.02	.00
☐ 36	Mario Guerrero	.05	.02	.00
☐ 37	Jim Willoughby	.05	.02	.00
☐ 38	Joe Pittman	.05	.02	.00
☐ 39	Mark Bomback	.05	.02	.00
☐ 40	Tommy McMillian	.05	.02	.00
☐ 41	Gary Allanson	.05	.02	.00
☐ 42	Cecil Cooper	.15	.06	.01
☐ 43	John LaRosa	.05	.02	.00
☐ 44	Darrell Brandon	.05	.02	.00
☐ 45	Bernie Carbo	.05	.02	.00
☐ 46	Mike Cuellar	.15	.06	.01
☐ 47	Al Bumbry	.05	.02	.00
☐ 48	Gene Richards	.05	.02	.00
☐ 49	Pedro Borbon	.05	.02	.00
☐ 50	Julio Solo	.05	.02	.00
☐ 51	Ed Nottle	.05	.02	.00
☐ 52	Jim Bibby	.05	.02	.00
☐ 53	Doug Griffin	.05	.02	.00
☐ 54	Ed Clements	.05	.02	.00
☐ 55	Dalton Jones	.05	.02	.00
☐ 56	Earl Weaver MG	.50	.20	.05
☐ 57	Jesus De La Rosa	.05	.02	.00
☐ 58	Paul Casanova	.05	.02	.00
☐ 59	Frank Riccelli	.05	.02	.00
☐ 60	Rafael Landestoy UER (Misspelled Raphael on card back)	.05	.02	.00
☐ 61	George Hendrick	.10	.04	.01
☐ 62	Cesar Cedeno	.15	.06	.01
☐ 63	Bert Campaneris	.15	.06	.01
☐ 64	Derrell Thomas	.05	.02	.00
☐ 65	Bobby Ramos	.05	.02	.00
☐ 66	Grant Jackson	.05	.02	.00
☐ 67	Steve Whitaker	.05	.02	.00
☐ 68	Pedro Ramos	.05	.02	.00
☐ 69	Joe Hicks UER (No height or weight information)	.05	.02	.00
☐ 70	Taylor Duncan	.05	.02	.00
☐ 71	Tom Shopay	.05	.02	.00
☐ 72	Ken Clay	.05	.02	.00
☐ 73	Mike Kekich	.05	.02	.00
☐ 74	Ed Halicki	.05	.02	.00
☐ 75	Ed Figueroa	.10	.04	.01
☐ 76	Paul Blair	.10	.04	.01
☐ 77	Luis Tiant	.25	.10	.02
☐ 78	Stan Bahnsen	.05	.02	.00
☐ 79	Rennie Stennett	.05	.02	.00
☐ 80	Bobby Molinaro	.05	.02	.00
☐ 81	Jim Gideon	.05	.02	.00
☐ 82	Orlando Gonzalez	.05	.02	.00
☐ 83	Amos Otis	.20	.08	.02
☐ 84	Dennis Leonard	.10	.04	.01
☐ 85	Pat Putman	.05	.02	.00
☐ 86	Rick Manning	.05	.02	.00
☐ 87	Pat Dobson	.10	.04	.01
☐ 88	Marty Castillo	.05	.02	.00
☐ 89	Steve McCatty	.05	.02	.00
☐ 90	Doug Bird	.05	.02	.00

☐ 91	Rick Waits	.05	.02	.00
☐ 92	Ron Jackson	.05	.02	.00
☐ 93	Tim Hosley	.05	.02	.00
☐ 94	Steve Luebber	.05	.02	.00
☐ 95	Rich Gale	.05	.02	.00
☐ 96	Champ Summers	.05	.02	.00
☐ 97	Dave LaRoche	.05	.02	.00
☐ 98	Bobby Jones	.05	.02	.00
☐ 99	Kim Allen	.05	.02	.00
☐ 100	Wayne Garland	.05	.02	.00
☐ 101	Tom Spencer	.05	.02	.00
☐ 102	Dan Driessen	.10	.04	.01
☐ 103	Ron Pruitt	.05	.02	.00
☐ 104	Tim Ireland	.05	.02	.00
☐ 105	Dan Driessen IA	.10	.04	.01
☐ 106	Pepe Frias UER	.05	.02	.00
	(misspelled Pepi on card front)			
☐ 107	Eric Rasmussen	.05	.02	.00
☐ 108	Don Hood	.05	.02	.00
☐ 109	Joe Coleman UER	.05	.02	.00
	(photo actually Tony Torchia)			
☐ 110	Jim Slaton	.05	.02	.00
☐ 111	Clint Hurdie	.05	.02	.00
☐ 112	Larry Milbourne	.05	.02	.00
☐ 113	Al Holland	.05	.02	.00
☐ 114	George Foster	.15	.06	.01
☐ 115	Graig Nettles	.15	.06	.01
☐ 116	Oscar Gamble	.10	.04	.01
☐ 117	Ross Grimsley	.10	.04	.01
☐ 118	Bill Travers	.05	.02	.00
☐ 119	Jose Beniquez	.10	.04	.01
☐ 120	Jerry Grote IA	.05	.02	.00
☐ 121	John D'Acquisto	.05	.02	.00
☐ 122	Tom Murphy	.05	.02	.00
☐ 123	Walt Williams UER	.10	.04	.01
	(Listed as pitcher)			
☐ 124	Roy Thomas	.05	.02	.00
☐ 125	Jerry Grote	.05	.02	.00
☐ 126A	Jim Nettles ERR	.50	.20	.05
	(Writing on bat knob)			
☐ 126B	Jim Nettles COR	5.00	2.25	.50
☐ 127	Randy Niemann	.05	.02	.00
☐ 128	Bobby Bonds	.50	.20	.05
☐ 129	Ed Glynn	.05	.02	.00
☐ 130	Ed Hicks	.05	.02	.00
☐ 131	Ivan Murrell	.05	.02	.00
☐ 132	Graig Nettles	.30	.12	.03
☐ 133	Hal McRae	.20	.08	.02
☐ 134	Pat Kelly	.10	.04	.01
☐ 135	Sammy Stewart	.05	.02	.00
☐ 136	Bruce Kison	.10	.04	.01
☐ 137	Jim Morrison	.05	.02	.00
☐ 138	Omar Moreno	.05	.02	.00
☐ 139	Tom Brown	.05	.02	.00
☐ 140	Steve Dillard	.05	.02	.00
☐ 141	Gary Alexander	.05	.02	.00
☐ 142	Al Oliver	.25	.10	.02
☐ 143	Rick Lysander	.05	.02	.00
☐ 144	Tippy Martinez	.10	.04	.01
☐ 145	Al Cowens	.10	.04	.01
☐ 146	Gene Clines	.05	.02	.00
☐ 147	Willie Aikens	.10	.04	.01
☐ 148	Tommy Moore	.05	.02	.00
☐ 149	Clete Boyer	.10	.04	.01
☐ 150	Stan Cliburn	.05	.02	.00
☐ 151	Ken Kravec	.05	.02	.00
☐ 152	Garth Iorg	.05	.02	.00
☐ 153	Rick Peterson	.05	.02	.00
☐ 154	Wayne Nordhagen	.05	.02	.00
	(misspelled Nordgahen on card back)			
☐ 155	Danny Meyer	.05	.02	.00
☐ 156	Wayne Garrett	.05	.02	.00
☐ 157	Wayne Krenchicki	.05	.02	.00
☐ 158	Graig Nettles	.30	.12	.03
☐ 159	Earl Stephenson	.05	.02	.00
☐ 160	Carl Taylor	.05	.02	.00
☐ 161	Rollie Fingers	1.25	.50	.12
☐ 162	Toby Harrah	.10	.04	.01
☐ 163	Mickey Rivers	.10	.04	.01
☐ 164	Dave Kingman	.15	.06	.01
☐ 165	Paul Mirabella	.05	.02	.00
☐ 166	Dick Williams MG	.10	.04	.01
☐ 167	Luis Pujols	.05	.02	.00
☐ 168	Tito Landrum	.10	.04	.01
☐ 169	Tom Underwood	.05	.02	.00
☐ 170	Mark Wagner	.05	.02	.00
☐ 171	Odell Jones	.05	.02	.00
☐ 172	Doug Capilla	.05	.02	.00
☐ 173	Allie Rondon	.05	.02	.00
☐ 174	Lowell Palmer	.05	.02	.00

☐ 175	Juan Eichelberger	.05	.02	.00
☐ 176	Wes Clements	.05	.02	.00
☐ 177	Rodney Scott	.05	.02	.00
☐ 178	Ron Washington	.10	.04	.01
☐ 179	Al Hrabosky	.10	.04	.01
☐ 180	Sid Monge	.05	.02	.00
☐ 181	Randy Johnson	.05	.02	.00
☐ 182	Tim Stoddard	.05	.02	.00
☐ 183	Dick Williams MG	.10	.04	.01
☐ 184	Lee Lacy	.10	.04	.01
☐ 185	Jerry White	.05	.02	.00
☐ 186	Dave Kingman	.15	.06	.01
☐ 187	Checklist 1-110	.05	.02	.00
☐ 188	Jose Cruz	.15	.06	.01
☐ 189	Jamie Easterly	.05	.02	.00
☐ 190	Ike Blessit	.05	.02	.00
☐ 191	Johnny Grubb	.05	.02	.00
☐ 192	Dave Cash	.05	.02	.00
☐ 193	Doug Corbett	.05	.02	.00
☐ 194	Bruce Bochy	.05	.02	.00
☐ 195	Mark Corey	.05	.02	.00
☐ 196	Gil Rondon	.05	.02	.00
☐ 197	Jerry Martin	.05	.02	.00
☐ 198	Gerry Pirtle	.05	.02	.00
☐ 199	Gates Brown	.10	.04	.01
☐ 200	Bob Galasso	.05	.02	.00
☐ 201	Bake McBride	.10	.04	.01
☐ 202	Wayne Granger	.05	.02	.00
☐ 203	Larry Milbourne	.05	.02	.00
☐ 204	Tom Paciorek	.10	.04	.01
☐ 205	U.L. Washington	.05	.02	.00
☐ 206	Larvell Blanks	.05	.02	.00
☐ 207	Bob Shirley	.05	.02	.00
☐ 208	Pete Falcone	.05	.02	.00
☐ 209	Sal Butera	.05	.02	.00
☐ 210	Roy Branch	.05	.02	.00
☐ 211	Dyar Miller	.05	.02	.00
☐ 212	Paul Siebert	.05	.02	.00
☐ 213	Ken Reitz	.05	.02	.00
☐ 214	Bill Madlock	.20	.08	.02
☐ 215	Vida Blue	.15	.06	.01
☐ 216	Dave Hilton	.05	.02	.00
☐ 217	Ramos and Bren	.05	.02	.00
☐ 218	Checklist 111-220	.05	.02	.00
☐ 219	Dobson and Weaver	.20	.08	.02
☐ 220	Curt Flood COMM	.25	.10	.02

1990 Pacific Legends

The 1990 Pacific Legends set was a 110-card set issued by Pacific Trading Cards. The set numbering is basically arranged in two alphabetical sequences. This is a standard size (2 1/2" by 3 1/2") set which was available as factory set as well as in wax packs. The set does include some active players, Willie Wilson and Jesse Barfield, the last two players in the set.

		MINT	EXC	G-VG
COMPLETE SET (110)		9.00	4.00	.90
COMMON PLAYER (1-110)		.05	.02	.00
☐ 1	Hank Aaron	.60	.25	.06
☐ 2	Tommie Agee	.05	.02	.00
☐ 3	Luke Appling	.20	.08	.02
☐ 4	Sal Bando	.05	.02	.00
☐ 5	Ernie Banks	.35	.15	.03

☐ 6	Don Baylor	.10	.04	.01
☐ 7	Yogi Berra	.40	.16	.04
☐ 8	Vida Blue	.05	.02	.00
☐ 9	Lou Boudreau	.15	.06	.01
☐ 10	Clete Boyer	.05	.02	.00
☐ 11	George Bamberger	.05	.02	.00
☐ 12	Lou Brock	.25	.10	.02
☐ 13	Ralph Branca	.05	.02	.00
☐ 14	Carl Erskine	.05	.02	.00
☐ 15	Bert Campaneris	.05	.02	.00
☐ 16	Steve Carlton	.25	.10	.02
☐ 17	Rod Carew	.40	.16	.04
☐ 18	Rocky Colavito	.15	.06	.01
☐ 19	Frankie Crosetti	.10	.04	.01
☐ 20	Larry Doby	.10	.04	.01
☐ 21	Bobby Doerr	.15	.06	.01
☐ 22	Walt Dropo	.05	.02	.00
☐ 23	Rick Ferrell	.10	.04	.01
☐ 24	Joe Garagiola	.20	.08	.02
☐ 25	Ralph Garr	.05	.02	.00
☐ 26	Dick Groat	.05	.02	.00
☐ 27	Steve Garvey	.20	.08	.02
☐ 28	Bob Gibson	.25	.10	.02
☐ 29	Don Drysdale	.20	.08	.02
☐ 30	Billy Herman	.15	.06	.01
☐ 31	Bobby Grich	.05	.02	.00
☐ 32	Monte Irvin	.15	.06	.01
☐ 33	Dave Johnson	.05	.02	.00
☐ 34	Don Kessinger	.05	.02	.00
☐ 35	Harmon Killebrew	.20	.08	.02
☐ 36	Ralph Kiner	.20	.08	.02
☐ 37	Vern Law	.05	.02	.00
☐ 38	Ed Lopat	.10	.04	.01
☐ 39	Bill Mazeroski	.10	.04	.01
☐ 40	Rick Monday	.05	.02	.00
☐ 41	Manny Mota	.05	.02	.00
☐ 42	Don Newcombe	.10	.04	.01
☐ 43	Gaylord Perry	.20	.08	.02
☐ 44	Jim Piersall	.10	.04	.01
☐ 45	Johnny Podres	.10	.04	.01
☐ 46	Boog Powell	.10	.04	.01
☐ 47	Robin Roberts	.20	.08	.02
☐ 48	Ron Santo	.10	.04	.01
☐ 49	Herb Score	.10	.04	.01
☐ 50	Enos Slaughter	.20	.08	.02
☐ 51	Warren Spahn	.25	.10	.02
☐ 52	Rusty Staub	.10	.04	.01
☐ 53	Frank Torre	.05	.02	.00
☐ 54	Bob Horner	.05	.02	.00
☐ 55	Lee May	.05	.02	.00
☐ 56	Bill White	.10	.04	.01
☐ 57	Hoyt Wilhelm	.15	.06	.01
☐ 58	Billy Williams	.20	.08	.02
☐ 59	Ted Williams	.40	.16	.04
☐ 60	Tom Seaver	.50	.20	.05
☐ 61	Carl Yastrzemski	.50	.20	.05
☐ 62	Marv Throneberry	.05	.02	.00
☐ 63	Steve Stone	.05	.02	.00
☐ 64	Rico Petrocelli	.05	.02	.00
☐ 65	Orlando Cepeda	.15	.06	.01
☐ 66	Eddie Mathews	.20	.08	.02
☐ 67	Joe Sewell	.10	.04	.01
☐ 68	Catfish Hunter	.20	.08	.02
☐ 69	Alvin Dark	.10	.04	.01
☐ 70	Richie Ashburn	.15	.06	.01
☐ 71	Dusty Baker	.05	.02	.00
☐ 72	George Foster	.10	.04	.01
☐ 73	Eddie Yost	.05	.02	.00
☐ 74	Buddy Bell	.05	.02	.00
☐ 75	Manny Sanguillen	.05	.02	.00
☐ 76	Jim Bunning	.10	.04	.01
☐ 77	Smoky Burgess	.05	.02	.00
☐ 78	Al Rosen	.10	.04	.01
☐ 79	Gene Conley	.05	.02	.00
☐ 80	Dave Dravecky	.05	.02	.00
☐ 81	Charlie Gehringer	.15	.06	.01
☐ 82	Billy Pierce	.05	.02	.00
☐ 83	Willie Horton	.05	.02	.00
☐ 84	Ron Hunt	.05	.02	.00
☐ 85	Bob Feller	.25	.10	.02
☐ 86	George Kell	.15	.06	.01
☐ 87	Dave Kingman	.10	.04	.01
☐ 88	Jerry Koosman	.10	.04	.01
☐ 89	Clem Labine	.05	.02	.00
☐ 90	Tony LaRussa	.10	.04	.01
☐ 91	Dennis Leonard	.05	.02	.00
☐ 92	Dale Long	.05	.02	.00
☐ 93	Sparky Lyle	.10	.04	.01
☐ 94	Gil McDougald	.10	.04	.01
☐ 95	Don Mossi	.05	.02	.00
☐ 96	Phil Niekro	.25	.10	.02
☐ 97	Tom Paciorek	.05	.02	.00
☐ 98	Mel Parnell	.05	.02	.00
☐ 99	Lou Piniella	.15	.06	.01

☐ 100	Bobby Richardson	.15	.06	.01
☐ 101	Phil Rizzuto	.25	.10	.02
☐ 102	Brooks Robinson	.25	.10	.02
☐ 103	Pete Runnels	.05	.02	.00
☐ 104	Diego Segui	.05	.02	.00
☐ 105	Bobby Shantz	.05	.02	.00
☐ 106	Bobby Thomson	.15	.06	.01
☐ 107	Joe Torre	.25	.10	.02
☐ 108	Earl Weaver MG	.20	.08	.02
☐ 109	Willie Wilson	.10	.04	.01
☐ 110	Jesse Barfield	.15	.06	.01

1991 Pacific Nolan Ryan Texas Express

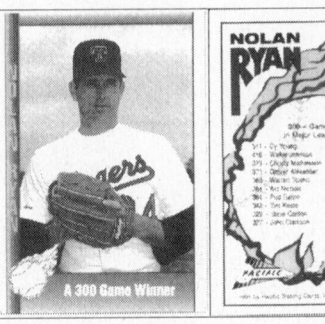

This 110-card set measures the standard 2 1/2" by 3 1/2" and traces the career of Nolan Ryan from the start of his career into the 1991 season as well as his personal life with his family on his ranch in Alvin, Texas. This set features glossy full-color photos on the front and either biographical information or an action shot of Ryan on the back which is framed by a fireball. The backs are printed in purple and red on a white background. Inside a flaming baseball design, one finds biography, career highlights, player quote, or an extended caption to the front picture. The cards are numbered on the back. This set was issued by Pacific Trading cards and was the first set featuring an individual baseball player to be sold in wax packs since the 1959 Fleer Ted Williams issue. The cards were available in 12-card foil packs and factory sets.

		MINT	EXC	G-VG
	COMPLETE SET (110)	10.00	4.50	1.25
	COMMON PLAYER (1-110)	.10	.04	.01
☐ 1	Future Hall of Famer	.20	.08	.02
☐ 2	From Little League to the Major Leagues	.10	.04	.01
☐ 3	A Dream Come True	.10	.04	.01
☐ 4	Signed by the Mets	.10	.04	.01
☐ 5	Fireball Pitcher	.10	.04	.01
☐ 6	New York Mets Rookie Pitcher	.10	.04	.01
☐ 7	First Major League Win	.10	.04	.01
☐ 8	Early in 1969	.10	.04	.01
☐ 9	Tensions of a Pennant Race	.10	.04	.01
☐ 10	Mets Clinch NL East	.10	.04	.01
☐ 11	Keep the Ball Down	.10	.04	.01
☐ 12	Playoff Victory for Ryan	.10	.04	.01
☐ 13	World Series Victory	.10	.04	.01
☐ 14	The Amazin' Mets	.10	.04	.01
☐ 15	Nolan Sets Met Record for Strikeouts	.10	.04	.01
☐ 16	One of the Worst Trades in Baseball	.10	.04	.01
☐ 17	Slow Start with Mets	.10	.04	.01
☐ 18	Pitcher New York Mets	.10	.04	.01
☐ 19	Traded to the Angels	.10	.04	.01
☐ 20	Meeting New Friends	.10	.04	.01
☐ 21	Throwing Fast Balls	.10	.04	.01

		MINT	EXC	G-VG

□ 22 Move the Ball Around .... .10 .04 .01
□ 23 Nolan Heat .... .10 .04 .01
□ 24 No-Hitter Number 1 .... .10 .04 .01
□ 25 Looking Back on .... .10 .04 .01
    Number 1
□ 26 No-Hitter Number 2 .... .10 .04 .01
□ 27 Single Season .... .10 .04 .01
    Strikeout Record
□ 28 21 Wins in 1973 .... .10 .04 .01
□ 29 Fastest Pitch Ever .... .15 .06 .01
    Thrown Clocked
    at 100.9 MPH
□ 30 No-Hitter Number 3 .... .10 .04 .01
□ 31 No-Hitter Number 4 .... .10 .04 .01
□ 32 Ryan and Tanana .... .15 .06 .01
□ 33 Learning Change-Up .... .10 .04 .01
□ 34 Pitcher California .... .10 .04 .01
    Angels
□ 35 Nolan Joins Astros .... .10 .04 .01
□ 36 Starting Pitcher .... .15 .06 .01
    Nolan Ryan
□ 37 Taking Batting .... .10 .04 .01
    Practice
□ 38 The Game's Greatest .... .10 .04 .01
    Power Pitcher
□ 39 3000 Career Strikeout .... .10 .04 .01
□ 40 A Ryan Home Run .... .15 .06 .01
□ 41 The Fast Ball Grip .... .10 .04 .01
□ 42 Record 5th No-Hitter .... .10 .04 .01
□ 43 No-Hitter Number 5 .... .10 .04 .01
□ 44 A Dream Fulfilled .... .10 .04 .01
□ 45 Nolan passes Walter .... .15 .06 .01
    Johnson
□ 46 Strikeout 4000 .... .10 .04 .01
□ 47 Astros win Western .... .10 .04 .01
    Division Title
□ 48 Pitcher Houston .... .10 .04 .01
    Astros
□ 49 Milestone Strikeouts .... .10 .04 .01
□ 50 Post Season .... .10 .04 .01
    Participant
□ 51 Hurling for Houston .... .10 .04 .01
□ 52 135 NL Wins .... .10 .04 .01
□ 53 Through with Chew .... .10 .04 .01
□ 54 Signed by Rangers .... .10 .04 .01
    1989
□ 55 Pleasant Change .... .10 .04 .01
    for Nolan
□ 56 Real Special Moment .... .10 .04 .01
□ 57 Nolan Enters 1989 .... .10 .04 .01
    All-Star Game
□ 58 Pitching in 1989 .... .10 .04 .01
    All-Star Game
□ 59 5000 Strikeouts; .... .10 .04 .01
    A Standing Ovation
□ 60 Great Moments in 1989 .... .10 .04 .01
□ 61 Nolan with Dan Smith, ... .15 .06 .01
    Rangers First
    Draft Pick
□ 62 Ranger Club Record, ... .10 .04 .01
    16 Strikeouts
□ 63 Last Pitch No-Hitter .... .10 .04 .01
    Number 6
□ 64 Sweet Number 6 .... .10 .04 .01
□ 65 Oldest To Throw .... .10 .04 .01
    No-Hitter
□ 66 Another Ryan Win .... .10 .04 .01
□ 67 20th Pitcher to Win .... .10 .04 .01
    300, Acknowledging
    the Fans
□ 68 300 Game Win Battery, ... .10 .04 .01
    Arnsberg/Ryan/Petralli
□ 69 A 300 Game Winner .... .10 .04 .01
□ 70 Perfect Mechanics .... .10 .04 .01
□ 71 22 Seasons with 100 .... .10 .04 .01
    or more Strikeouts
□ 72 11th Strikeout Title .... .10 .04 .01
□ 73 232 Strikeouts, 1990 .... .10 .04 .01
□ 74 The 1990 Season .... .10 .04 .01
□ 75 Pitcher Texas Rangers .... .15 .06 .01
□ 76 1991, Nolan's 25th .... .10 .04 .01
    Season
□ 77 Throwing Spirals .... .15 .06 .01
□ 78 Running the Steps .... .10 .04 .01
□ 79 Hard Work and .... .10 .04 .01
    Conditioning
□ 80 The Rigid Workout .... .10 .04 .01
□ 81 Ryan's Routine .... .10 .04 .01
□ 82 Ryan's Routine .... .10 .04 .01
    Between Starts
□ 83 Running in Outfield .... .10 .04 .01
    Before the Big Game
□ 84 B.P. in Texas .... .10 .04 .01

□ 85 18 Career Low-Hitters .... .10 .04 .01
□ 86 My Job is to Give My .... .10 .04 .01
    Team a Chance to Win
□ 87 The Spring Workout .... .10 .04 .01
□ 88 Power versus Power .... .10 .04 .01
□ 89 Awesome Power .... .10 .04 .01
□ 90 Blazing Speed .... .10 .04 .01
□ 91 The Pick Off .... .10 .04 .01
□ 92 Nolan's a Real Gamer .... .75 .30 .07
    (Bloody lip and
    blood all over jersey)
□ 93 Ranger Battery Mates .... .10 .04 .01
□ 94 The Glare .... .10 .04 .01
□ 95 The High Leg Kick .... .10 .04 .01
□ 96 Day Off from Pitcher .... .10 .04 .01
□ 97 A New Ball for Nolan .... .10 .04 .01
□ 98 Going to Rosin Bag .... .10 .04 .01
□ 99 Time for Relief .... .10 .04 .01
□ 100 A Lone Star Legend .... .10 .04 .01
□ 101 Fans' Favorite .... .10 .04 .01
□ 102 Watching Nolan Pitch .... .10 .04 .01
□ 103 Our Family of Five .... .10 .04 .01
□ 104 Texas Beefmaster .... .10 .04 .01
□ 105 Gentleman Rancher .... .10 .04 .01
□ 106 Texas Cowboy Life .... .10 .04 .01
□ 107 The Ryan Family .... .10 .04 .01
□ 108 Participating in .... .10 .04 .01
    Cutting Horse Contest
□ 109 Nolan Interviews .... .10 .04 .01
□ 110 Lynn Nolan Ryan .... .20 .08 .02

1991 Pacific Nolan Ryan 7th No-Hitter

This seven-card set was produced by Pacific Trading Cards Inc. to capture various moments of Nolan Ryan's 7th no-hitter. These cards were produced in the following numbers: 1,000 of each card in gold foil and 10,000 of each card in silver foil. The cards measure the standard size (2 1/2" by 3 1/2") and they were randomly inserted in foil packs only. The fronts feature glossy color photos, with silver or gold borders on the sides and faded red borders above and below the picture. In addition, the player's name is written vertically in a multi-colored stripe on the left side of the picture. A flaming baseball in the lower left corner completes the card face. The backs are printed in purple and red on a white background. Inside a flaming baseball design, one finds an extended caption to the front picture. The cards are numbered on the back. Supposedly as many as half of the cards were destroyed and never released. The prices below refer to the silver versions; the gold versions would be valued at quadruple the prices below.

	MINT	EXC	G-VG
COMPLETE SET (7)	150.00	67.50	22.50
COMMON PLAYER (1-7)	25.00	11.00	3.50
□ 1 Last Pitch 7th	25.00	11.00	3.50
No-Hitter			
□ 2 No-Hitter Number 7	25.00	11.00	3.50
□ 3 Number 7 Was	25.00	11.00	3.50
The Best			

☐ 4	Time to Celebrate	25.00	11.00	3.50
☐ 5	Congratulations from .... Ranger Fans	25.00	11.00	3.50
☐ 6	Catcher Mike Stanley .... and Nolan hold the No-Hitter Ball UER (Back reads Bryan, should read Ryan)	25.00	11.00	3.50
☐ 7	All in a Day's Work	25.00	11.00	3.50

1991 Pacific Nolan Ryan Silver Inserts

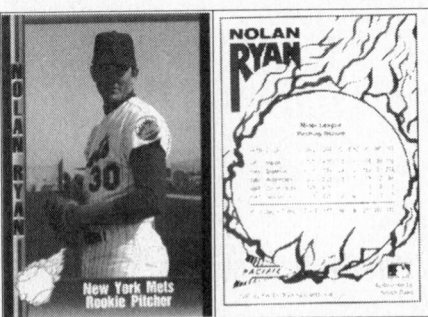

These eight standard-size (2 1/2" by 3 1/2") cards were inserts in 1991 Pacific Nolan Ryan Texas Express wax packs. As with the regular issue, the fronts display glossy color photos that are bordered in silver foil and either purple/red or red/orange border stripes. Inside a flaming baseball design, the back presents either a player photo, statistics, or career highlights. The cards are unnumbered and checklisted below in chronological order. Besides the silver cards, they were also issued on a much more limited basis in gold. The gold versions are valued at quadruple the prices listed below.

		MINT	EXC	G-VG
	COMPLETE SET (8)	150.00	67.50	22.50
	COMMON PLAYER (1-8)	25.00	11.00	3.50
☐ 1	New York Mets Rookie .... Pitcher	25.00	11.00	3.50
☐ 2	No-Hitter 1	25.00	11.00	3.50
☐ 3	No-Hitter 2	25.00	11.00	3.50
☐ 4	No-Hitter 3	25.00	11.00	3.50
☐ 5	No-Hitter 4	25.00	11.00	3.50
☐ 6	No-Hitter 5	25.00	11.00	3.50
☐ 7	Sweet 6	25.00	11.00	3.50
☐ 8	1991: Nolan's 25th .... Season	25.00	11.00	3.50

1991 Pacific Senior League

Pacific Trading Cards released this 160-card set just after the Senior League suspended operations. The standard size (2 1/2" by 3 1/2") cards were sold in wax packs and as complete sets. The fronts have glossy color player photos, with white borders and the team name written vertically in a stripe running down the left side of the picture. The backs are mint-colored and feature career highlights. Apparently there are two different versions of cards for the following players: Jim Rice, Rollie Fingers, Vida Blue, Dave Cash, Dan Norman, Ron LeFlore, Cesar Cedeno, Rafael Landestoy, and Dan Driessen. The cards are numbered on the back.

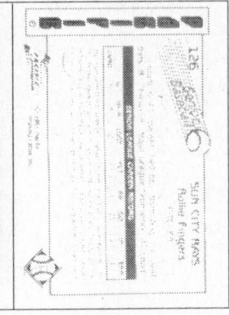

		MINT	EXC	G-VG
	COMPLETE SET (160)	10.00	4.00	1.00
	COMMON PLAYER (1-160)	.05	.02	.00
☐ 1	Dan Driessen	.10	.04	.01
☐ 2	Marty Castillo	.05	.02	.00
☐ 3	Jerry White	.05	.02	.00
☐ 4	Bud Anderson	.05	.02	.00
☐ 5	Ron Jackson	.05	.02	.00
☐ 6	Fred Stanley	.10	.04	.01
☐ 7	Steve Luebber	.05	.02	.00
☐ 8	Jerry Terrell	.05	.02	.00
☐ 9	Pat Dobson	.10	.04	.01
☐ 10	Ken Kravec	.05	.02	.00
☐ 11	Gil Rondon	.05	.02	.00
☐ 12	Dyar Miller	.05	.02	.00
☐ 13	Bobby Molinaro	.05	.02	.00
☐ 14	Jerry Martin	.05	.02	.00
☐ 15	Rick Waits	.10	.04	.01
☐ 16	Steve McCatty	.10	.04	.01
☐ 17	Roger Slagle	.05	.02	.00
☐ 18	Mike Ramsey	.10	.04	.01
☐ 19	Rich Gale	.10	.04	.01
☐ 20	Larry Harlow	.05	.02	.00
☐ 21	Dan Rohn	.05	.02	.00
☐ 22	Don Cooper	.05	.02	.00
☐ 23	Marv Foley	.05	.02	.00
☐ 24	Rafael Landestoy	.05	.02	.00
☐ 25	Eddie Milner	.05	.02	.00
☐ 26	Amos Otis	.10	.04	.01
☐ 27	Odell Jones	.05	.02	.00
☐ 28	Tippy Martinez	.10	.04	.01
☐ 29	Stu Cliburn	.05	.02	.00
☐ 30	Stan Cliburn	.05	.02	.00
☐ 31	Tony Cloninger	.05	.02	.00
☐ 32	Jeff Jones	.05	.02	.00
☐ 33	Ken Reitz	.05	.02	.00
☐ 34	Dave Sax	.05	.02	.00
☐ 35	Orlando Gonzalez	.05	.02	.00
☐ 36	Jose Cruz	.10	.04	.01
☐ 37	Mickey Mahler	.05	.02	.00
☐ 38	Derek Botelho	.05	.02	.00
☐ 39	Rick Lysander	.05	.02	.00
☐ 40	Cesar Cedeno	.15	.06	.01
☐ 41	Garth Iorg	.05	.02	.00
☐ 42	Wayne Krenchicki	.05	.02	.00
☐ 43	Clete Boyer MG	.10	.04	.01
☐ 44	Dan Boone	.10	.04	.01
☐ 45	George Vukovich	.05	.02	.00
☐ 46	Omar Moreno	.05	.02	.00
☐ 47	Ron Washington	.10	.04	.01
☐ 48	Ron Washington .... Most Valuable Player	.10	.04	.01
☐ 49	Rick Peterson	.05	.02	.00
☐ 50	Tack Wilson	.10	.04	.01
☐ 51	Stan and Stu Cliburn	.10	.04	.01
☐ 52	Rick Lysander .... Player of the Year	.10	.04	.01
☐ 53	Cedeno and LaCock	.10	.04	.01
☐ 54	Marshall and Boyer	.10	.04	.01
☐ 55	Doug Simunic	.05	.02	.00
☐ 56	Pat Kelly	.05	.02	.00
☐ 57	Roy Branch	.05	.02	.00
☐ 58	Dave Cash	.10	.04	.01
☐ 59	Bobby Jones	.05	.02	.00
☐ 60	Hector Cruz	.05	.02	.00
☐ 61	Reggie Cleveland	.05	.02	.00
☐ 62	Gary Lance	.05	.02	.00
☐ 63	Ron LeFlore	.10	.04	.01
☐ 64	Dan Norman	.05	.02	.00
☐ 65	Renie Martin	.05	.02	.00
☐ 66	Pete Mackanin	.05	.02	.00

☐ 66	Pete Mackanin	.05	.02	.00
☐ 67	Frank Riccelli	.05	.02	.00
☐ 68	Alfie Rondon	.05	.02	.00
☐ 69	Rodney Scott	.05	.02	.00
☐ 70	Jim Tracy	.05	.02	.00
☐ 71	Ed Dennis	.05	.02	.00
☐ 72	Rick Lindell	.05	.02	.00
☐ 73	Stu Pepper	.05	.02	.00
☐ 74	Jeff Youngbauer	.05	.02	.00
☐ 75	Russ Foster	.05	.02	.00
☐ 76	Jeff Capriati	.05	.02	.00
☐ 77	Art DeFreites	.05	.02	.00
☐ 78	Alfie Rondon	.05	.02	.00
☐ 79	Reggie Cleveland IA	.05	.02	.00
☐ 80	Dave Cash	.10	.04	.01
☐ 81	Vida Blue	.15	.06	.01
☐ 82	Ed Glynn	.05	.02	.00
☐ 83	Bob Owchinko	.05	.02	.00
☐ 84	Bill Fleming	.05	.02	.00
☐ 85	Ron and Gary Roenicke	.10	.04	.01
☐ 86	Tom Thompson	.05	.02	.00
☐ 87	Derrell Thomas	.05	.02	.00
☐ 88	Jim Willoughby	.05	.02	.00
☐ 89	Jim Pankovits	.05	.02	.00
☐ 90	Jack Cooley	.05	.02	.00
☐ 91	Lenn Sakata	.05	.02	.00
☐ 92	Mike Brocki	.05	.02	.00
☐ 93	Chuck Fick	.05	.02	.00
☐ 94	Tom Benedict	.05	.02	.00
☐ 95	Anthony Davis	.10	.04	.01
☐ 96	Cardell Camper	.05	.02	.00
☐ 97	Leon Roberts	.05	.02	.00
☐ 98	Roger Erickson	.05	.02	.00
☐ 99	Kim Allen	.05	.02	.00
☐ 100	Dave Skaggs	.05	.02	.00
☐ 101	Joe Decker	.05	.02	.00
☐ 102	U.L. Washington	.05	.02	.00
☐ 103	Don Fletcher	.05	.02	.00
☐ 104	Gary Roenicke	.10	.04	.01
☐ 105	Rich Dauer	.10	.04	.01
☐ 106	Ron Roenicke	.10	.04	.01
☐ 107	Mike Norris	.10	.04	.01
☐ 108	Ferguson Jenkins	.75	.30	.07
☐ 109	Ronn Reynolds	.05	.02	.00
☐ 110	Pete Falcone	.05	.02	.00
☐ 111	Gary Allenson	.05	.02	.00
☐ 112	Mark Wagner	.05	.02	.00
☐ 113	Jack Lazorko	.05	.02	.00
☐ 114	Bob Galasso	.05	.02	.00
☐ 115	Ron Davis	.05	.02	.00
☐ 116	Lenny Randle	.05	.02	.00
☐ 117	Ricky Peters	.05	.02	.00
☐ 118	Jim Dwyer	.05	.02	.00
☐ 119	Juan Eichelberger	.05	.02	.00
☐ 120	Pete LaCock	.10	.04	.01
☐ 121	Tony Scott	.10	.04	.01
☐ 122	Rick Lancellotti	.05	.02	.00
☐ 123	Barry Bonnell	.10	.04	.01
☐ 124	Dave Hilton	.05	.02	.00
☐ 125	Bill Campbell	.10	.04	.01
☐ 126	Rollie Fingers	.75	.30	.07
☐ 127	Jim Marshall	.05	.02	.00
☐ 128	Razor Shines	.05	.02	.00
☐ 129	Guy Sularz	.05	.02	.00
☐ 130	Roy Thomas	.05	.02	.00
☐ 131	Joel Youngblood	.05	.02	.00
☐ 132	Ernie Camacho	.10	.04	.01
☐ 133	Hilton, Marshall, and Stanley	.05	.02	.00
☐ 134	Ken Landreaux	.10	.04	.01
☐ 135	Dave Rozema	.05	.02	.00
☐ 136	Tom Zimmer	.05	.02	.00
☐ 137	Elias Sosa	.05	.02	.00
☐ 138	Ossie Virgil Sr. MG	.05	.02	.00
☐ 139	Al Holland	.05	.02	.00
☐ 140	Milt Wilcox	.10	.04	.01
☐ 141	Jerry Reed	.05	.02	.00
☐ 142	Chris Welch	.05	.02	.00
☐ 143	Luis Gomez	.05	.02	.00
☐ 144	Steve Henderson	.05	.02	.00
☐ 145	Butch Benton	.05	.02	.00
☐ 146	Bill Lee	.10	.04	.01
☐ 147	Todd Cruz	.05	.02	.00
☐ 148	Jim Rice	.25	.10	.02
☐ 149	Tito Landrum	.10	.04	.01
☐ 150	Ozzie Virgil Jr.	.10	.04	.01
☐ 151	Joe Pittman	.05	.02	.00
☐ 152	Bobby Tolan	.10	.04	.01
☐ 153	Len Barker	.10	.04	.01
☐ 154	Dave Rajsich	.05	.02	.00
☐ 155	Glenn Gulliver	.05	.02	.00
☐ 156	Gary Rajsich	.05	.02	.00
☐ 157	Joe Sambito	.10	.04	.01
☐ 158	Frank Vito	.05	.02	.00
☐ 159	Ozzie Virgil Jr./Sr.	.10	.04	.01
☐ 160	Dave and Gary Rajsich	.10	.04	.01

1991 Pacific Gas and Electric Giants

These cards were issued on six-card sheets; after perforation they measure approximately 2 1/2" by 3 1/2". One sheet was inserted in each of the first five 1991 San Francisco Giants Magazines, which were published by Woodford. The front design has color action player photos, with gray borders on a white card face. Toward the bottom of the picture are the words "San Francisco Giants," two bats, and a red banner with player information. The horizontally oriented backs are printed in black on white and include biography, Major League statistics, and various PGE (Pacific Gas and Electric) advertisements. The cards are numbered on the back in the upper right corner.

		MINT	EXC	G-VG
COMPLETE SET (30)		10.00	4.50	1.25
COMMON PLAYER (1-30)		.30	.12	.03
☐ 1	Kevin Mitchell	.75	.30	.07
☐ 2	Robby Thompson	.40	.16	.04
☐ 3	John Burkett	.40	.16	.04
☐ 4	Kelly Downs	.30	.12	.03
☐ 5	Terry Kennedy	.30	.12	.03
☐ 6	Roger Craig MG	.40	.16	.04
☐ 7	Jeff Brantley	.40	.16	.04
☐ 8	Greg Litton	.30	.12	.03
☐ 9	Trevor Wilson	.40	.16	.04
☐ 10	Kevin Bass	.30	.12	.03
☐ 11	Matt Williams	.75	.30	.07
☐ 12	Jose Uribe	.30	.12	.03
☐ 13	Steve Decker	.60	.25	.06
☐ 14	Will Clark	1.50	.60	.15
☐ 15	Dave Righetti	.40	.16	.04
☐ 16	Mike Kingery	.30	.12	.03
☐ 17	Mike LaCoss	.30	.12	.03
☐ 18	Dave Anderson	.30	.12	.03
☐ 19	Bud Black	.40	.16	.04
☐ 20	Mike Benjamin	.30	.12	.03
☐ 21	Don Robinson	.30	.12	.03
☐ 22	Mark Leonard	.40	.16	.04
☐ 23	Willie McGee	.50	.20	.05
☐ 24	Francisco Oliveras	.30	.12	.03
☐ 25	Kirt Manwaring	.30	.12	.03
☐ 26	Rick Parker	.30	.12	.03
☐ 27	Mike Remlinger	.30	.12	.03
☐ 28	Mike Felder	.30	.12	.03
☐ 29	Scott Garrelts	.40	.16	.04
☐ 30	Tony Perezchica	.30	.12	.03

1958 Packard Bell

This seven-card set included members of the Los Angeles Dodgers and San Francisco Giants and was issued in both teams' first year on the West Coast. This black and white, unnumbered set features cards measuring approximately 3 3/8" by 5 3/8". The backs are advertisements for Packard Bell (a television and radio manufacturer) along with a schedule for either the Giants or Dodgers. There were four Giants printed and three Dodgers. The catalog designation for this set is H805-5.

	NRMT	VG-E	GOOD
COMPLETE SET (7)	450.00	200.00	67.50
COMMON CARD (1-7)	40.00	18.00	6.00
☐ 1 Walt Alston MG	75.00	34.00	11.25
Los Angeles Dodgers			
☐ 2 Johnny Antonelli	40.00	18.00	6.00
San Francisco Giants			
☐ 3 Jim Gilliam	50.00	22.50	7.50
Los Angeles Dodgers			
☐ 4 Gil Hodges	100.00	45.00	15.00
Los Angeles Dodgers			
☐ 5 Willie Mays	200.00	90.00	30.00
San Francisco Giants			
☐ 6 Bill Rigney MG	40.00	18.00	6.00
San Francisco Giants			
☐ 7 Hank Sauer	40.00	18.00	6.00
San Francisco Giants			

1977 Padres Schedule Cards

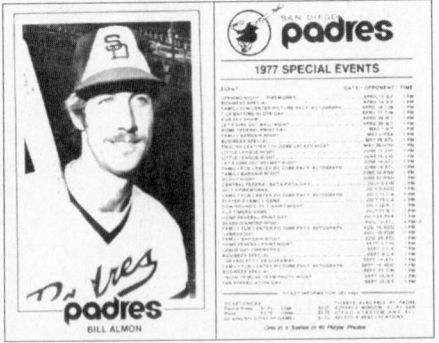

This 40-card set was issued in 1977 and was about members of the 1977 San Diego Padres. The cards measure approximately 2 1/4" by 3 3/8" and had black and white photos on the front of the cards with a schedule of the 1977 Padres special events on the back. The set is checklisted alphabetically in the list below.

	NRMT	VG-E	GOOD
COMPLETE SET (40)	13.50	6.00	1.85
COMMON PLAYER (1-40)	.35	.15	.03

☐ 1 Bill Almon	.35	.15	.03
☐ 2 Joe Amalfitano CO	.35	.15	.03
☐ 3 Vic Bernal	.35	.15	.03
☐ 4 Buzzie Bavasi GM	.45	.18	.04
☐ 5 Mike Champion	.35	.15	.03
☐ 6 Champion And Almon	.45	.18	.04
☐ 7 Roger Craig CO	.45	.18	.04
☐ 8 John D'Acquisto	.35	.15	.03
☐ 9 Bob Davis	.35	.15	.03
☐ 10 Rollie Fingers	1.50	.60	.15
☐ 11 Dave Freisleben	.35	.15	.03
☐ 12 Tom Griffin	.35	.15	.03
☐ 13 George Hendrick	.45	.18	.04
☐ 14 Enzo Hernandez	.35	.15	.03
☐ 15 Mike Ivie	.35	.15	.03
☐ 16 Randy Jones	.45	.18	.04
Following Through			
☐ 17 Randy Jones	.45	.18	.04
Holding Cy Young Award			
☐ 18 John McNamara MG	.45	.18	.04
☐ 19 Luis Melendez	.35	.15	.03
☐ 20 Butch Metzger	.35	.15	.03
☐ 21 Bob Owchinko	.35	.15	.03
☐ 22 Doug Rader	.45	.18	.04
☐ 23 Gene Richards	.35	.15	.03
☐ 24 Dave Roberts	.35	.15	.03
☐ 25 Merv Rettenmund	.35	.15	.03
☐ 26 Rick Sawyer	.35	.15	.03
☐ 27 Bob Shirley	.35	.15	.03
☐ 28 Bob Skinner CO	.35	.15	.03
☐ 29 Dan Spillner	.35	.15	.03
☐ 30 Brent Strom	.35	.15	.03
☐ 31 Gary Sutherland	.35	.15	.03
☐ 32 Gene Tenace	.45	.18	.04
☐ 33 Dave Tomlin	.35	.15	.03
☐ 34 Jerry Turner	.35	.15	.03
☐ 35 Bobby Valentine	.45	.18	.04
☐ 36 Dave Wehrmeister	.35	.15	.03
☐ 37 Whitey Wietelmann CO	.35	.15	.03
☐ 38 Don Williams CO	.35	.15	.03
☐ 39 Dave Winfield	2.50	1.00	.25
(Bat on shoulders)			
☐ 40 Dave Winfield	2.50	1.00	.25
(Bat at Waist)			

1978 Padres Family Fun

This 39-card set features members of the 1978 San Diego Padres. These large cards measure approximately 3 1/2" by 5 1/2" and are framed in a style similar to the 1962 Topps set with wood-grain borders. The cards have full color photos on the front of the card along with the Padres logo and Family Fun Centers underneath the photo in circles and the name of the player on the bottom of the card. The backs of the card asked each person what their greatest thrill in Baseball was. This set is especially noteworthy for having one of the earliest Ozzie Smith cards printed. The set is checklisted alphabetically in the list below.

	MINT	EXC	G-VG
COMPLETE SET (39)	18.00	7.50	2.50
COMMON PLAYER (1-39)	.35	.15	.03

☐ 1	Bill Almon	.35	.15	.03
☐ 2	Tucker Ashford	.35	.15	.03
☐ 3	Chuck Baker	.35	.15	.03
☐ 4	Dave Campbell (announcer)	.35	.15	.03
☐ 5	Mike Champion	.35	.15	.03
☐ 6	Jerry Coleman (announcer)	.45	.18	.04
☐ 7	Roger Craig MG	.60	.25	.06
☐ 8	John D'Acquisto	.35	.15	.03
☐ 9	Bob Davis	.35	.15	.03
☐ 10	Chuck Estrada CO	.45	.18	.04
☐ 11	Rollie Fingers	1.50	.60	.15
☐ 12	Dave Freisleben	.35	.15	.03
☐ 13	Oscar Gamble	.45	.18	.04
☐ 14	Fernando Gonzalez	.35	.15	.03
☐ 15	Billy Herman CO	.60	.25	.06
☐ 16	Randy Jones	.45	.18	.04
☐ 17	Ray Kroc (Owner)	.60	.25	.06
☐ 18	Mark Lee	.35	.15	.03
☐ 19	Mickey Lolich	.60	.25	.06
☐ 20	Bob Owchinko	.35	.15	.03
☐ 21	Broderick Perkins	.35	.15	.03
☐ 22	Gaylord Perry	1.50	.60	.15
☐ 23	Eric Rasmussen	.35	.15	.03
☐ 24	Don Reynolds	.35	.15	.03
☐ 25	Gene Richards	.35	.15	.03
☐ 26	Dave Roberts	.35	.15	.03
☐ 27	Phil Roof CO	.35	.15	.03
☐ 28	Bob Shirley	.35	.15	.03
☐ 29	Ozzie Smith	9.00	4.00	.90
☐ 30	Dan Spillner	.35	.15	.03
☐ 31	Rick Sweet	.35	.15	.03
☐ 32	Gene Tenace	.45	.18	.04
☐ 33	Derrel Thomas	.35	.15	.03
☐ 34	Jerry Turner	.35	.15	.03
☐ 35	Dave Wehrmeister	.35	.15	.03
☐ 36	Whitey Wietelmann CO	.35	.15	.03
☐ 37	Don Williams CO	.35	.15	.03
☐ 38	Dave Winfield	2.50	1.00	.25
☐ 39	1978 All-Star Game	.35	.15	.03

☐ 4	Willie McCovey (McCovey hits 16th career grand slam)	1.00	.40	.10
☐ 5	John Kruk	.50	.20	.05
☐ 6	Jack Clark	.60	.25	.06
☐ 7	Eric Show	.40	.16	.04
☐ 8	Rollie Fingers (Fingers wins NL Saves title for second time)	1.00	.40	.10
☐ 9	The Alomars Sandy Alomar Sr. Sandy Alomar Jr. Roberto Alomar	1.00	.40	.10
☐ 10	Carmelo Martinez	.30	.12	.03
☐ 11	Benito Santiago	1.00	.40	.10
☐ 12	Nate Colbert (Colbert 5 HR's, 13 RBI's in Doubleheader)	.30	.12	.03
☐ 13	Mark Davis	.40	.16	.04
☐ 14	Roberto Alomar	1.50	.60	.15
☐ 15	Tim Flannery	.30	.12	.03
☐ 16	Randy Jones (Jones wins Cy Young Award)	.40	.16	.04
☐ 17	Dennis Rasmussen	.40	.16	.04
☐ 18	Greg W. Harris	.50	.20	.05
☐ 19	Garry Templeton	.40	.16	.04
☐ 20	Steve Garvey (Garvey's HR ties NLCS)	.60	.25	.06
☐ 21	Bruce Hurst	.50	.20	.05
☐ 22	Ed Whitson	.40	.16	.04
☐ 23	Chris James	.40	.16	.04
☐ 24	Gaylord Perry (Perry Wins Cy Young Award in Both Leagues)	1.00	.40	.10

1990 Padres Magazine/Unocal

1989 Padres Magazine

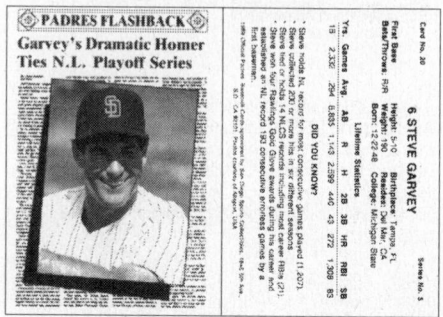

These 2 1/2" by 3 1/2" cards came as an insert in issues of "Padres" magazine sold in San Diego. These cards were sponsored by San Diego Sports Collectibles, a major hobby dealer. The cards feature beautiful full-color photos on the front and interesting did-you-know facts on the back along with one line of career statistics. The cards of retired Padres feature an highlight of their career in San Diego. The suggested retail price of each of the six different Padres magazines was 1.50.

	MINT	EXC	G-VG
COMPLETE SET (24)	12.50	5.50	1.65
COMMON PLAYER (1-24)	.30	.12	.03
☐ 1 Jack McKeon MG	.30	.12	.03
☐ 2 Sandy Alomar Jr.	1.00	.40	.10
☐ 3 Tony Gwynn	2.50	1.00	.25

This 24-card set was sponsored by Unocal 76 and was available in the San Diego Padres' game programs for 17.50. The cards were divided into six series, and each series was issued on a 5" by 9" sheet of four cards with a sponsor's coupon. After perforation, the cards measure the standard size (2 1/2" by 3 1/2"). Some players appear in more than one series. The front features a color action player photo with white borders. The player's name is given in a tan stripe below the picture, with the Unocal 76 logo to the right of the name. The backs are printed in black on white and have biography, statistics, and career highlights. The cards are numbered on the back. Coupons from the magazine were to be turned into Unocal for 25 Jack McKeon, 26 Bip Roberts, and 27 Joe Carter.

	MINT	EXC	G-VG
COMPLETE SET (27)	16.00	6.75	2.25
COMMON PLAYER (1-24)	.30	.12	.03
COMMON PLAYER (25-27)	.75	.30	.07

		MINT	EXC	G-VG
☐ 1	Tony Gwynn	2.00	.80	.20
☐ 2	Benito Santiago	1.00	.40	.10
☐ 3	Mike Pagliarulo	.40	.16	.04
☐ 4	Dennis Rasmussen	.30	.12	.03
☐ 5	Eric Show	.40	.16	.04
☐ 6	Darrin Jackson	.50	.20	.05
☐ 7	Mark Parent	.30	.12	.03
☐ 8	Padres Announcers	.30	.12	.03
	Jerry Coleman			
	Rick Monday			
☐ 9	Andy Benes	1.00	.40	.10
☐ 10	Roberto Alomar	1.00	.40	.10
☐ 11	Craig Lefferts	.40	.16	.04
☐ 12	Ed Whitson	.40	.16	.04
☐ 13	Calvin Schiraldi	.30	.12	.03
☐ 14	Garry Templeton	.40	.16	.04
☐ 15	Tony Gwynn	2.00	.80	.20
☐ 16	Padres Announcers	.30	.12	.03
	Bob Chandler and			
	Ted Leitner			
☐ 17	Fred Lynn	.40	.16	.04
☐ 18	Jack Clark	.50	.20	.05
☐ 19	Mike Dunne	.30	.12	.03
☐ 20	Mark Grant	.30	.12	.03
☐ 21	Benito Santiago	1.00	.40	.10
☐ 22	The Coaches	.40	.16	.04
	Sandy Alomar Sr.			
	Pat Dobson			
	Amos Otis			
	Greg Riddoch			
	Denny Sommers			
☐ 23	Bruce Hurst	.50	.20	.05
☐ 24	Greg W. Harris	.50	.20	.05
☐ 25	Jack McKeon MG	.75	.30	.07
☐ 26	Bip Roberts	1.25	.50	.12
☐ 27	Joe Carter	2.50	1.00	.25

		MINT	EXC	G-VG
☐ 2	Dennis Rasmussen	.40	.16	.04
☐ 3	Thomas Howard	.40	.16	.04
☐ 4	Tom Lampkin	.30	.12	.03
☐ 5	Bruce Hurst	.50	.20	.05
☐ 6	Darrin Jackson	.40	.16	.04
☐ 7	Jerald Clark	.40	.16	.04
☐ 8	Shawn Abner	.30	.12	.03
☐ 9	Bip Roberts	.50	.20	.05
☐ 10	Marty Barrett	.30	.12	.03
☐ 11	Jim Vatcher	.30	.12	.03
☐ 12	Greg Gross CO	.30	.12	.03
☐ 13	Greg W. Harris	.40	.16	.04
☐ 14	Ed Whitson	.40	.16	.04
☐ 15	Jerald Clark	.40	.16	.04
☐ 16	Rich Rodriguez	.40	.16	.04
☐ 17	Larry Andersen	.30	.12	.03
☐ 18	Andy Benes	.75	.30	.07
☐ 19	Bruce Hurst	.50	.20	.05
☐ 20	Paul Faries	.40	.16	.04
☐ 21	Craig Lefferts	.40	.16	.04
☐ 22	Tony Gwynn	2.00	.80	.20
☐ 23	Jim Presley	.30	.12	.03
☐ 24	Fred McGriff	1.25	.50	.12

1988 Pepsi Tigers

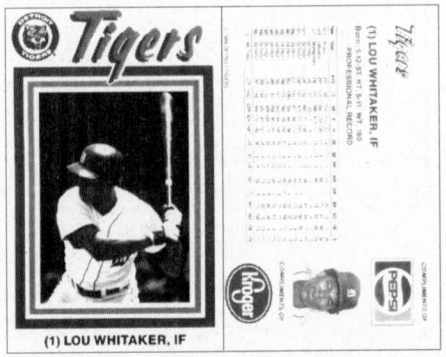

This set of 25 cards features members of the Detroit Tigers and was sponsored by Pepsi Cola and Kroger. The cards are in full color on the fronts and measure approximately 2 7/8" by 4 1/4". The card backs contain complete Major and Minor League season-by-season statistics. The cards are unnumbered so they are listed below by uniform number, which is given on the card.

		MINT	EXC	G-VG
COMPLETE SET (25)		10.00	4.50	1.25
COMMON PLAYER		.35	.15	.03
☐ 1	Lou Whitaker	.75	.30	.07
☐ 2	Alan Trammell	1.00	.40	.10
☐ 8	Mike Heath	.35	.15	.03
☐ 11	Sparky Anderson MG	.45	.18	.04
☐ 12	Luis Salazar	.35	.15	.03
☐ 14	Dave Bergman	.35	.15	.03
☐ 15	Pat Sheridan	.35	.15	.03
☐ 16	Tom Brookens	.35	.15	.03
☐ 19	Doyle Alexander	.45	.18	.04
☐ 21	Guillermo Hernandez	.45	.18	.04
☐ 22	Ray Knight	.45	.18	.04
☐ 24	Gary Pettis	.45	.18	.04
☐ 25	Eric King	.45	.18	.04
☐ 26	Frank Tanana	.45	.18	.04
☐ 31	Larry Herndon	.35	.15	.03
☐ 32	Jim Walewander	.35	.15	.03
☐ 33	Matt Nokes	.60	.25	.06
☐ 34	Chet Lemon	.45	.18	.04
☐ 35	Walt Terrell	.45	.18	.04
☐ 39	Mike Henneman	.45	.18	.04
☐ 41	Darrell Evans	.60	.25	.06
☐ 44	Jeff M. Robinson	.45	.18	.04
☐ 47	Jack Morris	.90	.40	.09
☐ 48	Paul Gibson	.45	.18	.04

1991 Padres Magazine/Rally's

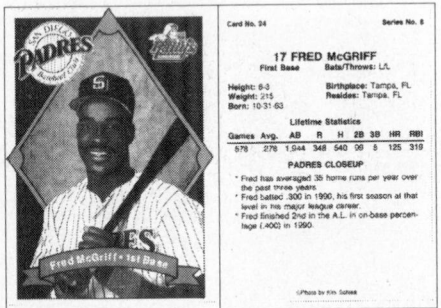

This 24-card set was sponsored by Rally's Hamburgers. The cards were divided into six series, and each series was issued on a 5" by 9" sheet of four cards with a sponsor's coupon. After perforation, the cards measure the standard size (2 1/2" by 3 1/2"). The front features a color pose shot (from the waist up) of the player, inside a tan baseball diamond framework. Outside the diamond the card background is dark blue, with white borders. The player's name is given in an orange banner at the bottom of the card. Team and sponsor logos in the upper corners round out the front. The backs are printed in black on white and have biography, statistics, and career highlights. The cards are numbered on the back. Some players appear in more than one series. Moreover, there are reportedly variations involving Schiraldi, Gardner, and Presley, who were released during the season.

		MINT	EXC	G-VG
COMPLETE SET (24)		10.00	4.50	1.25
COMMON PLAYER (1-24)		.30	.12	.03
☐ 1	Greg Riddoch MG	.30	.12	.03

	MINT	EXC	G-VG

☐ xx Tigers Coaches ....
     Billy Consolo
     Alex Grammas
     Billy Muffett
     Vada Pinson
     Dick Tracewski
	.35	.15	.03

1989 Pepsi McGwire

This set includes 12 cards each depicting Mark McGwire. The cards are standard size, 2 1/2" by 3 1/2" and are printed on rather thin card stock. The cards have a distinctive blue outer border. The cards are numbered on the back in the lower right corner. The Pepsi logo is shown on the front and back of each card. All the pictures used in the set are posed showing McGwire in a generic uniform with a Pepsi patch on his upper arm and his number 25 on his chest; in each case his cap or batting helmet is in the Oakland colors but without their logo. The card backs all contain exactly the same statistical and biographical information, only the card number is different. Supposedly cards were distributed inside specially marked 12-packs of Pepsi in the Northern California area.

	MINT	EXC	G-VG
COMPLETE SET (12)	25.00	11.00	3.50
COMMON PLAYER (1-12)	2.50	1.00	.25

☐ 1 Mark McGwire ....
     (batting stance with
     left foot lifted)
	2.50	1.00	.25

☐ 2 Mark McGwire ....
     (fielding position
     at first base)
	2.50	1.00	.25

☐ 3 Mark McGwire ....
     (reaching out with
     glove for ball)
	2.50	1.00	.25

☐ 4 Mark McGwire ....
     (batting stance
     in empty stadium)
	2.50	1.00	.25

☐ 5 Mark McGwire ....
     (on one knee
     with bat)
	2.50	1.00	.25

☐ 6 Mark McGwire ....
     (stretching for
     ball at first base)
	2.50	1.00	.25

☐ 7 Mark McGwire ....
     (smiling with bat
     on shoulder
     facing camera)
	2.50	1.00	.25

☐ 8 Mark McGwire ....
     (holding bat in
     green windbreaker)
	2.50	1.00	.25

☐ 9 Mark McGwire ....
     (Rawlings bat on
     left shoulder)
	2.50	1.00	.25

☐ 10 Mark McGwire ....
     (holding bat parallel
     to ground in
     green windbreaker)
	2.50	1.00	.25

☐ 11 Mark McGwire ....
     (holding bat parallel
     to ground in uniform,
     toothy smile)
	2.50	1.00	.25

☐ 12 Mark McGwire ....
     (serious looking
     follow through)
	2.50	1.00	.25

1990 Pepsi Jose Canseco

This 10-card, standard-size set of 2 1/2" by 3 1/2" cards was issued in conjunction with Pepsi-Cola. These blue-bordered cards do not have the team logos. This set is very similar in style to the Pepsi McGwire set issued the year before. All the pictures used in the set are posed showing Canseco in a generic uniform with a Pepsi patch.

	MINT	EXC	G-VG
COMPLETE SET (10)	20.00	8.50	2.75
COMMON PLAYER (1-10)	2.25	.90	.22

☐ 1 Jose Canseco ....
     (Follow Through
     Waist)
	2.25	.90	.22

☐ 2 Jose Canseco ....
     (Follow Through
     Shoulder)
	2.25	.90	.22

☐ 3 Jose Canseco .... (Catching Ball)	2.25	.90	.22
☐ 4 Jose Canseco .... (Batting Pose)	2.25	.90	.22
☐ 5 Jose Canseco .... (Glove Over Chest)	2.25	.90	.22

☐ 6 Jose Canseco ....
     (Action Follow
     Through)
	2.25	.90	.22

☐ 7 Jose Canseco ....
     (Sitting on
     Dugout Steps)
	2.25	.90	.22

☐ 8 Jose Canseco .... (Waiting for Pitch)	2.25	.90	.22

☐ 9 Jose Canseco ....
     (Portrait/Bat
     at Waist)
	2.25	.90	.22

☐ 10 Jose Canseco .... (Portrait)	2.25	.90	.22

1990 Pepsi Red Sox

The 1990 Pepsi Boston Red Sox set is a 20-card standard-size set, 2 1/2" by 3 1/2", which is checklisted alphabetically below. This set was apparently prepared very early in the 1990 season as Bill Buckner and Lee Smith are still members of the Red Sox in this set. The top of the front of the card have Boston Red Sox printed while the bottom of the card has the players name surrounded by the Pepsi and the Diet Pepsi logo. The backs of the cards have the Score feel to them except the Pepsi and Diet Pepsi logos are again featured prominently on the back of the cards. The cards were supposedly available as a store promotion with one card per specially marked 12-pack of Pepsi. The cards

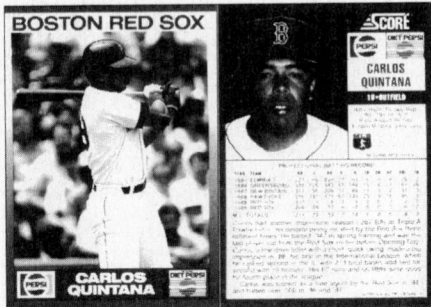

were difficult to remove from the boxes, thus making perfect mint cards worth an extra premium.

	MINT	EXC	G-VG
COMPLETE SET (20)	35.00	15.75	5.25
COMMON PLAYER (1-20)	1.25	.50	.12
☐ 1 Marty Barrett	1.25	.50	.12
☐ 2 Mike Boddicker	1.50	.60	.15
☐ 3 Wade Boggs	7.50	3.25	.75
☐ 4 Bill Buckner	1.50	.60	.15
☐ 5 Ellis Burks	3.50	1.50	.35
☐ 6 Roger Clemens	12.00	5.25	1.50
☐ 7 John Dopson	1.25	.50	.12
☐ 8 Dwight Evans	2.50	1.00	.25
☐ 9 Wes Gardner	1.25	.50	.12
☐ 10 Rich Gedman	1.25	.50	.12
☐ 11 Mike Greenwell	4.50	2.00	.45
☐ 12 Dennis Lamp	1.25	.50	.12
☐ 13 Rob Murphy	1.25	.50	.12
☐ 14 Tony Pena	1.50	.60	.15
☐ 15 Carlos Quintana	2.00	.80	.20
☐ 16 Jeff Reardon	2.50	1.00	.25
☐ 17 Jody Reed	1.75	.70	.17
☐ 18 Luis Rivera	1.25	.50	.12
☐ 19 Kevin Romine	1.25	.50	.12
☐ 20 Lee Smith	2.00	.80	.20

1991 Pepsi Ken Griffey Jr.

This eight-card set was sponsored by Pepsi-Cola, and the its company logo appears on the front and back of each card. The cards measure the standard size (2 1/2" by 3 1/2"). The color player photos are bordered in red, white, and purple, with Ken Griffey, Jr. in red block lettering below each picture. The backs are either horizontally or vertically oriented and present biographical as well as statistical information in black print on a white background. The cards are numbered on the back.

	MINT	EXC	G-VG
COMPLETE SET (8)	12.00	5.25	1.50
COMMON PLAYER (1-8)	.75	.30	.07

	MINT	EXC	G-VG
☐ 1 Ken Griffey Jr.	2.25	.90	.22
Swinging the bat			
☐ 2 Ken Griffey Jr.	2.25	.90	.22
Throwing from the outfield			
☐ 3 Ken Griffey Jr.	2.25	.90	.22
Catching ball at wall			
☐ 4 Ken Griffey Jr.	2.25	.90	.22
Posing with bat on shoulder			
☐ 5 Ken Griffey Jr.	2.25	.90	.22
Posing with Dad seated			
☐ 6 Ken Griffey Jr.	2.25	.90	.22
Standing beside Dad			
☐ 7 Ken Griffey Sr.	.75	.30	.07
At bat			
☐ 8 Ken Griffey Sr.	.75	.30	.07
Catching fly ball			

1991 Pepsi Rickey Henderson

These standard-size (2 1/2" by 3 1/2") cards were sponsored by Pepsi and feature Rickey Henderson. The front design has a color player photo, enframed by red borders on blue and white pinstripe background. The white pinstripes become farther and farther apart as one moves toward the right side of the card. An icon of a baseball and baserunner in the lower right corner rounds out the card face. In a horizontal format, the backs have the same career performance statistics but differing career highlights. The cards are numbered on the back.

	MINT	EXC	G-VG
COMPLETE SET (10)	12.50	5.50	1.65
COMMON PLAYER (1-10)	1.50	.60	.15
☐ 1 Rickey Henderson	1.50	.60	.15
(Follow through, left side)			
☐ 2 Rickey Henderson	1.50	.60	.15
(Running bases)			
☐ 3 Rickey Henderson	1.50	.60	.15
(Stretching hamstring)			
☐ 4 Rickey Henderson	1.50	.60	.15
(Ready to run)			
☐ 5 Rickey Henderson	1.50	.60	.15
(Bat on shoulder)			
☐ 6 Rickey Henderson	1.50	.60	.15
(Follow through, Right side)			
☐ 7 Rickey Henderson	1.50	.60	.15
(Squatting with bat)			
☐ 8 Rickey Henderson	1.50	.60	.15
(After throw)			
☐ 9 Rickey Henderson	1.50	.60	.15
(Leading off base)			
☐ 10 Rickey Henderson	1.50	.60	.15
(Warming up with bat)			

1991 Pepsi Red Sox

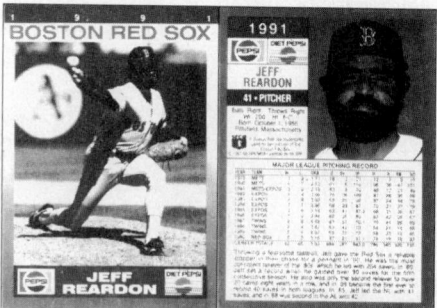

This 20-card set was sponsored by Pepsi and officially licensed by Mike Schechter Associates on behalf of the MLBPA. The 1991 edition consists of 100,000 sets that were available from July 1 through August 10, 1991 in the New England area, with one card per specially marked pack of Pepsi and Diet Pepsi. The promotion also includes a sweepstakes offering a grand prize trip for four to Red Sox Spring training camp. The standard-size (2 1/2" by 3 1/2") cards have color action player photos with a red, white, and blue front design. Two Pepsi logos adorn the card face below the picture. The backs are bordered in red and have a color head shot, biography, professional batting record, and career summary. The cards are unnumbered and checklisted below in alphabetical order.

	MINT	EXC	G-VG
COMPLETE SET (20)	20.00	8.50	2.75
COMMON PLAYER (1-20)	.60	.25	.06
☐ 1 Tom Bolton	.60	.25	.06
☐ 2 Tom Brunansky	.75	.30	.07
☐ 3 Ellis Burks	1.50	.60	.15
☐ 4 Jack Clark	1.00	.40	.10
☐ 5 Roger Clemens	4.00	1.75	.40
☐ 6 Danny Darwin	.60	.25	.06
☐ 7 Jeff Gray	.75	.30	.07
☐ 8 Mike Greenwell	1.50	.60	.15
☐ 9 Greg A. Harris	.60	.25	.06
☐ 10 Dana Kiecker	.60	.25	.06
☐ 11 Dennis Lamp	.60	.25	.06
☐ 12 John Marzano	.60	.25	.06
☐ 13 Tim Naehring	.75	.30	.07
☐ 14 Tony Pena	.75	.30	.07
☐ 15 Phil Plantier	6.00	2.50	.60
☐ 16 Carlos Quintana	1.00	.40	.10
☐ 17 Jeff Reardon	1.00	.40	.10
☐ 18 Jody Reed	.90	.40	.09
☐ 19 Luis Rivera	.60	.25	.06
☐ 20 Matt Young	.60	.25	.06

1991 Pepsi Reds

This 20-card set was produced by MSA (Michael Schechter Associates) for Pepsi-Cola of Ohio, and Pepsi logos adorn the upper corners of the card face. The cards measure the standard size (2 1/2" by 3 1/2") and were placed inside of 24-soda packs of Pepsi, Diet Pepsi, Caffeine-Free Pepsi, Caffeine Free Diet-Pepsi, Mountain Dew, and Diet Mountain Dew. The fronts display color player photos bordered in white and red and with the team logos airbrushed away. The horizontally oriented backs are trimmed in navy blue and present biography, statistics, and the player's autograph. The cards are unnumbered and checklisted below in alphabetical order.

	MINT	EXC	G-VG
COMPLETE SET (20)	12.00	5.25	1.50
COMMON PLAYER (1-20)	.50	.20	.05
☐ 1 Jack Armstrong	.60	.25	.06
☐ 2 Todd Benzinger	.50	.20	.05
☐ 3 Glenn Braggs	.50	.20	.05
☐ 4 Tom Browning	.60	.25	.06
☐ 5 Norm Charlton	.50	.20	.05
☐ 6 Eric Davis	1.50	.60	.15
☐ 7 Rob Dibble	.75	.30	.07
☐ 8 Bill Doran	.60	.25	.06
☐ 9 Mariano Duncan	.60	.25	.06
☐ 10 Billy Hatcher	.60	.25	.06
☐ 11 Barry Larkin	1.50	.60	.15
☐ 12 Hal Morris	1.25	.50	.12
☐ 13 Randy Myers	.60	.25	.06
☐ 14 Joe Oliver	.60	.25	.06
☐ 15 Paul O'Neill	.75	.30	.07
☐ 16 Lou Piniella MG	.75	.30	.07
☐ 17 Jeff Reed	.50	.20	.05
☐ 18 Jose Rijo	.75	.30	.07
☐ 19 Chris Sabo	1.25	.50	.12
☐ 20 Herm Winningham	.50	.20	.05

1991 Pepsi Superstar

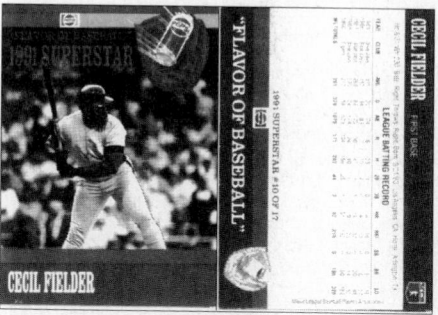

This 17-card set was sponsored by Pepsi-Cola of Florida as part of the "Flavor of Baseball" promotion. The promotion featured a chance to win one of 104 rare, older cards, including one 1952 Mickey Mantle rookie card. The Superstar cards were glued inside specially-marked 12 packs of Pepsi-Cola products in Orlando, Tampa, and Miami. It is difficult to remove the cards without creasing them; supposedly area supervisors for Pepsi each received a few sets. The cards measure the standard size (2 1/2" by 3 1/2"). The fronts have color action player photos, with a baseball glove "catching" a can of Pepsi superimposed at the upper right corner of the picture. The player photo has two top (purple and red/blue) and two bottom (red and purple) color stripes serving as borders but none on its sides. In a horizontal format, the backs have blue and red stripes, and present Major League statistics as well as biography. The cards are numbered on the back.

	MINT	EXC	G-VG
COMPLETE SET (17)	60.00	27.00	9.00
COMMON PLAYER (1-17)	1.50	.60	.15
☐ 1 Dwight Gooden	4.00	1.75	.40
☐ 2 Andre Dawson	4.00	1.75	.40
☐ 3 Ryne Sandberg	7.50	3.25	.75
☐ 4 Dave Stieb	1.50	.60	.15
☐ 5 Jose Rijo	1.50	.60	.15
☐ 6 Roger Clemens	7.50	3.25	.75
☐ 7 Barry Bonds	5.00	2.25	.50
☐ 8 Cal Ripken	7.50	3.25	.75
☐ 9 Dave Justice	7.50	3.25	.75
☐ 10 Cecil Fielder	5.00	2.25	.50
☐ 11 Don Mattingly	5.00	2.25	.50
☐ 12 Ozzie Smith	4.00	1.75	.40
☐ 13 Kirby Puckett	4.00	1.75	.40
☐ 14 Rafael Palmiero	3.00	1.25	.30
☐ 15 Bobby Bonilla	4.00	1.75	.40
☐ 16 Len Dykstra	1.50	.60	.15
☐ 17 Jose Canseco	7.50	3.25	.75

1981 Perma-Graphic Credit Card

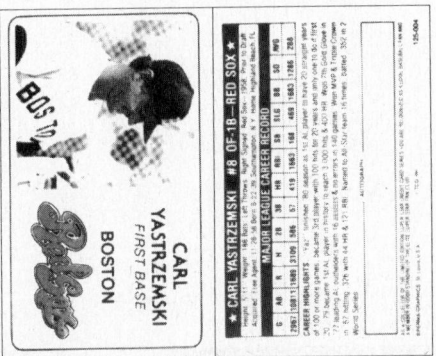

Perma-Graphic began their three-year foray into card manufacturing with this 32-card set of "credit cards" each measuring 2 1/8" by 3 3/8". The set featured 32 of the leading players of 1981. This set's design is split on the front between a full-color photo of the player and an identification of said player while the back has one line of career statistics and lines of career highlights. These sets (made of plastic) were issued with the cooperation of Topps Chewing Gum. This first set of Perma-Graphic cards seems to have been produced in greater quantities than the other five Perma-Graphic sets.

	MINT	EXC	G-VG
COMPLETE SET (32)	32.00	14.25	4.75
COMMON PLAYER (1-32)	.75	.30	.07
☐ 1 Johnny Bench	2.00	.80	.20
☐ 2 Mike Schmidt	3.00	1.25	.30
☐ 3 George Brett	2.00	.80	.20
☐ 4 Carl Yastrzemski	2.00	.80	.20
☐ 5 Pete Rose	3.00	1.25	.30
☐ 6 Bob Horner	.75	.30	.07
☐ 7 Reggie Jackson	2.50	1.00	.25
☐ 8 Keith Hernandez	1.00	.40	.10
☐ 9 George Foster	.75	.30	.07
☐ 10 Garry Templeton	.75	.30	.07
☐ 11 Tom Seaver	2.50	1.00	.25
☐ 12 Steve Garvey	1.50	.60	.15
☐ 13 Dave Parker	1.50	.60	.15
☐ 14 Willie Stargell	1.75	.70	.17
☐ 15 Cecil Cooper	.75	.30	.07
☐ 16 Steve Carlton	2.00	.80	.20
☐ 17 Ted Simmons	1.00	.40	.10
☐ 18 Dave Kingman	1.00	.40	.10
☐ 19 Rickey Henderson	3.00	1.25	.30

	MINT	EXC	G-VG
☐ 20 Fred Lynn	1.00	.40	.10
☐ 21 Dave Winfield	2.50	1.00	.25
☐ 22 Rod Carew	2.00	.80	.20
☐ 23 Jim Rice	1.25	.50	.12
☐ 24 Bruce Sutter	.75	.30	.07
☐ 25 Cesar Cedeno	.75	.30	.07
☐ 26 Nolan Ryan	4.00	1.75	.40
☐ 27 Dusty Baker	.75	.30	.07
☐ 28 Jim Palmer	1.75	.70	.17
☐ 29 Gorman Thomas	.75	.30	.07
☐ 30 Ben Oglivie	.75	.30	.07
☐ 31 Willie Wilson	1.00	.40	.10
☐ 32 Gary Carter	1.25	.50	.12

1981 Perma-Graphic All-Stars

This set commemorates the starters of the 1981 All-Star game. This 18-card set measure 2 1/8" by 3 3/8" and has rounded corners. Because of the players strike of 1981 plenty of time was available to prepare the player's biography with appropriate notes. The set is framed on the front in red for the National League and Blue for the American league.

	MINT	EXC	G-VG
COMPLETE SET (18)	30.00	13.50	4.50
COMMON PLAYER (1-18)	1.00	.40	.10
☐ 1 Gary Carter	1.50	.60	.15
☐ 2 Dave Concepcion	1.25	.50	.12
☐ 3 Andre Dawson	1.75	.70	.17
☐ 4 George Foster	1.00	.40	.10
☐ 5 Davey Lopes	1.00	.40	.10
☐ 6 Dave Parker	1.50	.60	.15
☐ 7 Pete Rose	4.00	1.75	.40
☐ 8 Mike Schmidt	4.00	1.75	.40
☐ 9 Fernando Valenzuela	1.50	.60	.15
☐ 10 George Brett	3.00	1.25	.30
☐ 11 Rod Carew	2.50	1.00	.25
☐ 12 Bucky Dent	1.00	.40	.10
☐ 13 Carlton Fisk	2.50	1.00	.25
☐ 14 Reggie Jackson	3.00	1.25	.30
☐ 15 Jack Morris	1.75	.70	.17
☐ 16 Willie Randolph	1.00	.40	.10
☐ 17 Ken Singleton	1.00	.40	.10
☐ 18 Dave Winfield	2.50	1.00	.25

1982 Perma-Graphic Credit Cards

For the second year Perma-Graphics, in association with Topps produced a high-quality set on plastic honoring the leading players in baseball of 1982. The players photo is on the front middle of the card and is framed by a brown border with many innovative designs. This 24-card set features plastic cards each measuring approximately 2 1/8" by 3 3/8". On the card back there is one line of career statistics along with career highlights.

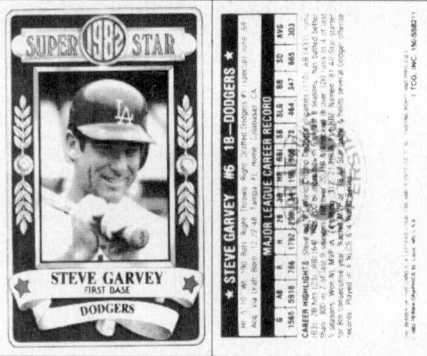

For the second time Perma-Graphic issued a special set commemorating the starters of the 1982 All-Star game. This 18-card set measures 2 1/8" by 3 3/8" and features a colorful design framing the players photo on the front The back again feature one line of complete All-Star game statistics including the 1982 game and career highlites. Perma-Graphics also issued the set in a limited "gold" edition, i.e., with a gold tint to the cards. The gold edition cards are valued at double the prices listed below.

	MINT	EXC	G-VG
COMPLETE SET (18)	30.00	13.50	4.50
COMMON PLAYER (1-18)	1.00	.40	.10
☐ 1 Dennis Eckersley	1.50	.60	.15
☐ 2 Cecil Cooper	1.00	.40	.10
☐ 3 Carlton Fisk	2.00	.80	.20
☐ 4 Robin Yount	2.50	1.00	.25
☐ 5 Bobby Grich	1.00	.40	.10
☐ 6 Rickey Henderson	3.50	1.50	.35
☐ 7 Reggie Jackson	2.50	1.00	.25
☐ 8 Fred Lynn	1.25	.50	.12
☐ 9 George Brett	2.50	1.00	.25
☐ 10 Gary Carter	1.50	.60	.15
☐ 11 Dave Concepcion	1.00	.40	.10
☐ 12 Andre Dawson	2.00	.80	.20
☐ 13 Tim Raines	1.50	.60	.15
☐ 14 Dale Murphy	2.00	.80	.20
☐ 15 Steve Rogers	1.00	.40	.10
☐ 16 Pete Rose	3.00	1.25	.30
☐ 17 Mike Schmidt	3.00	1.25	.30
☐ 18 Manny Trillo	1.00	.40	.10

1983 Perma-Graphic Credit Cards

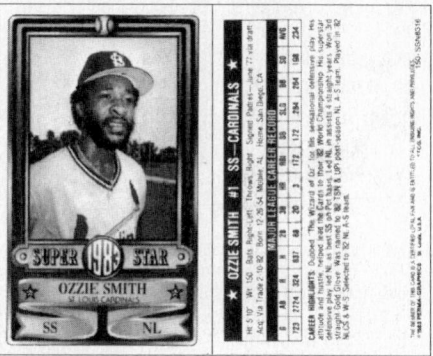

This set was the third straight year Perma-Graphic, with approval from Topps issued their high-quality plastic set. This 36-card set which measures 2 1/8" by 3 3/8" have the players photos framed by colorful backgrounds. The backs again feature one line of career statistics and several informative lines of career highlights. Perma-Graphics also issued the set in a limited "gold" edition, i.e., with a gold tint to the cards. The gold edition cards are valued at double the prices listed below.

	MINT	EXC	G-VG
COMPLETE SET (36)	50.00	22.50	7.50
COMMON PLAYER (1-36)	1.25	.50	.12
☐ 1 Bill Buckner	1.25	.50	.12
☐ 2 Steve Carlton	2.50	1.00	.25
☐ 3 Gary Carter	1.75	.70	.17
☐ 4 Andre Dawson	2.00	.80	.20
☐ 5 Pedro Guerrero	1.50	.60	.15
☐ 6 George Hendrick	1.25	.50	.12
☐ 7 Keith Hernandez	1.50	.60	.15
☐ 8 Bill Madlock	1.25	.50	.12
☐ 9 Dale Murphy	2.00	.80	.20
☐ 10 Al Oliver	1.25	.50	.12
☐ 11 Dave Parker	1.75	.70	.17

Perma-Graphics also issued the set in a limited "gold" edition, i.e., with a gold tint to the cards. The gold edition cards are valued at double the prices listed below. Again in 1982 Perma-Graphic issued these sets in conjuction and with the approval of Topps Chewing Gum.

	MINT	EXC	G-VG
COMPLETE SET (24)	40.00	18.00	6.00
COMMON PLAYER (1-24)	1.00	.40	.10
☐ 1 Johnny Bench	2.50	1.00	.25
☐ 2 Tom Seaver	3.00	1.25	.30
☐ 3 Mike Schmidt	3.00	1.25	.30
☐ 4 Gary Carter	1.50	.60	.15
☐ 5 Willie Stargell	1.75	.70	.17
☐ 6 Tim Raines	1.25	.50	.12
☐ 7 Bill Madlock	1.00	.40	.10
☐ 8 Keith Hernandez	1.25	.50	.12
☐ 9 Pete Rose	3.00	1.25	.30
☐ 10 Steve Carlton	2.00	.80	.20
☐ 11 Steve Garvey	2.00	.80	.20
☐ 12 Fernando Valenzuela	1.25	.50	.12
☐ 13 Carl Yastrzemski	3.00	1.25	.30
☐ 14 Dave Winfield	2.50	1.00	.25
☐ 15 Carney Lansford	1.00	.40	.10
☐ 16 Rollie Fingers	2.50	1.00	.25
☐ 17 Tony Armas	1.00	.40	.10
☐ 18 Cecil Cooper	1.00	.40	.10
☐ 19 George Brett	3.00	1.25	.30
☐ 20 Reggie Jackson	3.00	1.25	.30
☐ 21 Rod Carew	2.50	1.00	.25
☐ 22 Eddie Murray	3.00	1.25	.30
☐ 23 Rickey Henderson	3.50	1.50	.35
☐ 24 Kirk Gibson	1.50	.60	.15

1982 Perma-Graphic All-Stars

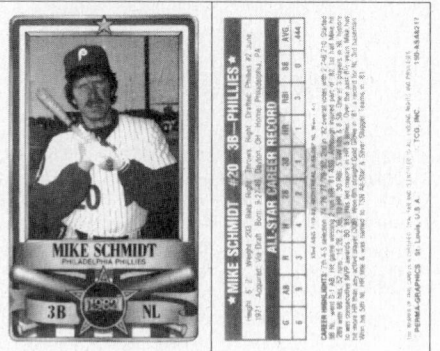

			MINT	EXC	G-VG
☐	12	Darrell Porter	1.25	.50	.12
☐	13	Pete Rose	3.00	1.25	.30
☐	14	Mike Schmidt	3.00	1.25	.30
☐	15	Lonnie Smith	1.25	.50	.12
☐	16	Ozzie Smith	2.00	.80	.20
☐	17	Bruce Sutter	1.25	.50	.12
☐	18	Fernando Valenzuela	1.50	.60	.15
☐	19	George Brett	3.00	1.25	.30
☐	20	Rod Carew	2.50	1.00	.25
☐	21	Cecil Cooper	1.25	.50	.12
☐	22	Doug DeCinces	1.25	.50	.12
☐	23	Rollie Fingers	2.50	1.00	.25
☐	24	Damaso Garcia	1.25	.50	.12
☐	25	Toby Harrah	1.25	.50	.12
☐	26	Rickey Henderson	3.50	1.50	.35
☐	27	Reggie Jackson	3.00	1.25	.30
☐	28	Hal McRae	1.25	.50	.12
☐	29	Eddie Murray	2.50	1.00	.25
☐	30	Lance Parrish	1.50	.60	.15
☐	31	Jim Rice	1.50	.60	.15
☐	32	Gorman Thomas	1.25	.50	.12
☐	33	Willie Wilson	1.25	.50	.12
☐	34	Dave Winfield	2.50	1.00	.25
☐	35	Carl Yastrzemski	3.00	1.25	.30
☐	36	Robin Yount	2.50	1.00	.25

1983 Perma-Graphic All-Stars

The 1983 All-Star Set was the third set Perma-Graphics issued commemorating the starters of the All-Star game. Again, Perma-Graphics used the Topps photos and issued their sets on plastics. This 18-card set features cards each measuring approximately 2 1/8" by 3 3/8". Perma-Graphics also issued the set in a limited "gold" edition, i.e., with a gold tint to the cards. The gold edition cards are valued at double the prices listed below.

			MINT	EXC	G-VG
	COMPLETE SET (18)		30.00	13.50	4.50
	COMMON PLAYER (1-18)		1.25	.50	.12
☐	1	George Brett	2.50	1.00	.25
☐	2	Rod Carew	2.50	1.00	.25
☐	3	Fred Lynn	1.50	.60	.15
☐	4	Jim Rice	1.50	.60	.15
☐	5	Ted Simmons	1.50	.60	.15
☐	6	Dave Stieb	1.50	.60	.15
☐	7	Dave Winfield	2.50	1.00	.25
☐	8	Manny Trillo	1.25	.50	.12
☐	9	Robin Yount	2.50	1.00	.25
☐	10	Gary Carter	1.75	.70	.17
☐	11	Andre Dawson	2.00	.80	.20
☐	12	Dale Murphy	2.00	.80	.20
☐	13	Al Oliver	1.25	.50	.12
☐	14	Tim Raines	1.75	.70	.17
☐	15	Steve Sax	1.50	.60	.15
☐	16	Mike Schmidt	3.50	1.50	.35
☐	17	Ozzie Smith	2.00	.80	.20
☐	18	Mario Soto	1.25	.50	.12

1991 Petro-Canada Standups

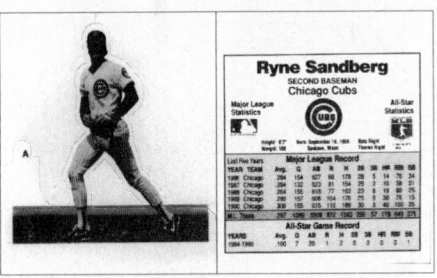

These 3-D action collector cards consist of three cardboard sheets measuring approximately 2 7/8" by 3 13/16" and joined at one end. The front cover has blue and red stripe borders and features either an American or National league logo inside a baseball diamond. The inside cover has a color photo of the crowd at the game. The middle sheet consists of a 3-D standup of the player. The inside of the last sheet has biographical information, career regular season statistics, and All-Star game statistics. The back has career highlights in a sky blue box and "Play the All Star Quiz" questions and answers. The set was first released in Toronto at the All-Star Game in conjunction with the All-Star Fanfest. The cards are numbered on the front.

			MINT	EXC	G-VG
	COMPLETE SET (26)		50.00	22.50	7.50
	COMMON PLAYER (1-26)		1.25	.50	.12
☐	1	Cal Ripken	5.00	2.25	.50
☐	2	Greg Olson	1.25	.50	.12
☐	3	Roger Clemens	5.00	2.25	.50
☐	4	Ryne Sandberg	5.00	2.25	.50
☐	5	Dave Winfield	2.50	1.00	.25
☐	6	Eric Davis	2.50	1.00	.25
☐	7	Carlton Fisk	2.50	1.00	.25
☐	8	Mike Scott	1.25	.50	.12
☐	9	Sandy Alomar Jr.	1.75	.70	.17
☐	10	Tim Wallach	1.25	.50	.12
☐	11	Cecil Fielder	3.00	1.25	.30
☐	12	Dwight Gooden	2.50	1.00	.25
☐	13	George Brett	2.50	1.00	.25
☐	14	Dale Murphy	2.50	1.00	.25
☐	15	Paul Molitor	1.75	.70	.17
☐	16	Barry Bonds	2.50	1.00	.25
☐	17	Kirby Puckett	3.00	1.25	.30
☐	18	Ozzie Smith	2.50	1.00	.25
☐	19	Don Mattingly	3.00	1.25	.30
☐	20	Will Clark	5.00	2.25	.50
☐	21	Rickey Henderson	5.00	2.25	.50
☐	22	Orel Hershiser	1.75	.70	.17
☐	23	Ken Griffey Jr.	9.00	4.00	.90
☐	24	Tony Gwynn	3.00	1.25	.30
☐	25	Nolan Ryan	9.00	4.00	.90
☐	26	Kelly Gruber	1.25	.50	.12

1964 Philadelphia Bulletin

This 27-player set was produced by the Philadelphia Bulletin, a newspaper. The catalog designation for this set is M130-5. These large, approximately 8" by 10", photo cards are unnumbered and blank backed.

			NRMT	VG-E	GOOD
	COMPLETE SET (27)		150.00	67.50	22.50
	COMMON PLAYER (1-27)		5.00	2.25	.50
☐	1	Rich Allen	12.50	5.50	1.65
☐	2	Ruben Amaro	5.00	2.25	.50
☐	3	Jack Baldschun	5.00	2.25	.50
☐	4	Dennis Bennett	5.00	2.25	.50
☐	5	John Boozer	5.00	2.25	.50

		MINT	VG-E	F-G
☐ 6	Johnny Briggs	5.00	2.25	.50
☐ 7	Jim Bunning (2)	12.50	5.50	1.65
☐ 8	Johnny Callison	6.00	2.50	.60
☐ 9	Danny Cater	5.00	2.25	.50
☐ 10	Wes Covington	6.00	2.50	.60
☐ 11	Ray Culp	5.00	2.25	.50
☐ 12	Clay Dalrymple	5.00	2.25	.50
☐ 13	Tony Gonzales	6.00	2.50	.60
☐ 14	John Herrnstein	5.00	2.25	.50
☐ 15	Alex Johnson	6.00	2.50	.60
☐ 16	Art Mahaffey	5.00	2.25	.50
☐ 17	Gene Mauch MG	7.50	3.25	.75
☐ 18	Vic Power	6.00	2.50	.60
☐ 19	Ed Roebuck	5.00	2.25	.50
☐ 20	Cookie Rojas	6.00	2.50	.60
☐ 21	Bobby Shantz	6.00	2.50	.60
☐ 22	Chris Short	6.00	2.50	.60
☐ 23	Tony Taylor	6.00	2.50	.60
☐ 24	Frank Thomas	6.00	2.50	.60
☐ 25	Gus Triandos	6.00	2.50	.60
☐ 26	Bobby Wine	6.00	2.50	.60
☐ 27	Rick Wise	6.00	2.50	.60

1984 Phillies Tastykake

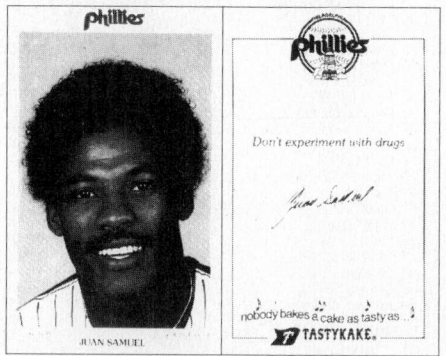

This set features the Philadelphia Phillies and was sponsored by Tastykake. The card fronts feature a colorful picture of the player or subject inside a white border. The cards measure approximately 3 1/2" by 5 1/4". The set was distributed to fans attending a specific game. There were four additional cards which were put out late in the year updating new players (after the first 40 had been out for some time). The update cards are numbered 41-44 after the first group. The card backs contain a brief message (tip) from the player with his facsimile autograph. The cards are unnumbered but the title card gives a numbering system essentially by position; that system is used below for the first 40 cards.

	MINT	VG-E	F-G
COMPLETE SET (44)	12.00	5.25	1.50
COMMON PLAYER (1-40)	.25	.10	.02

		MINT	VG-E	F-G
COMMON PLAYER (41-44)		.50	.20	.05
☐ 1	Logo Card/Checklist	.25	.10	.02
☐ 2	Team Photo	.25	.10	.02
☐ 3	Phillie Phanatic	.25	.10	.02
☐ 4	Veterans Stadium	.25	.10	.02
☐ 5	Steve Carlton Hall of Fame	1.25	.50	.12
☐ 6	Mike Schmidt Hall of Fame	1.75	.70	.17
☐ 7	Phillies Broadcasters	.25	.10	.02
☐ 8	Paul Owens MG	.25	.10	.02
☐ 9	Dave Bristol CO	.25	.10	.02
☐ 10	John Felske CO	.25	.10	.02
☐ 11	Deron Johnson CO	.25	.10	.02
☐ 12	Claude Osteen CO	.25	.10	.02
☐ 13	Mike Ryan CO	.25	.10	.02
☐ 14	Larry Andersen	.35	.15	.03
☐ 15	Marty Bystrom	.25	.10	.02
☐ 16	Bill Campbell	.25	.10	.02
☐ 17	Steve Carlton	1.25	.50	.12
☐ 18	John Denny	.35	.15	.03
☐ 19	Tony Ghelfi	.25	.10	.02
☐ 20	Kevin Gross	.35	.15	.03
☐ 21	Al Holland	.25	.10	.02
☐ 22	Charles Hudson	.25	.10	.02
☐ 23	Jerry Koosman	.35	.15	.03
☐ 24	Tug McGraw	.45	.18	.04
☐ 25	Bo Diaz	.25	.10	.02
☐ 26	Ozzie Virgil	.25	.10	.02
☐ 27	John Wockenfuss	.25	.10	.02
☐ 28	Luis Aguayo	.25	.10	.02
☐ 29	Ivan DeJesus	.25	.10	.02
☐ 30	Kiko Garcia	.25	.10	.02
☐ 31	Len Matuszek	.25	.10	.02
☐ 32	Juan Samuel	.75	.30	.07
☐ 33	Mike Schmidt	1.75	.70	.17
☐ 34	Tim Corcoran	.25	.10	.02
☐ 35	Greg Gross	.25	.10	.02
☐ 36	Von Hayes	.60	.25	.06
☐ 37	Joe Lefebvre	.25	.10	.02
☐ 38	Sixto Lezcano	.25	.10	.02
☐ 39	Garry Maddox	.35	.15	.03
☐ 40	Glenn Wilson	.25	.10	.02
☐ 41	Don Carman	.50	.20	.05
☐ 42	John Russell	.50	.20	.05
☐ 43	Jeff Stone	.50	.20	.05
☐ 44	Dave Wehrmeister	.50	.20	.05

1985 Phillies Tastykake

The 1985 Tastykake Philadelphia Phillies set consists of 47 cards, each measuring approximately 3 1/2" by 5 1/4". They feature a color photo of the player framed against white borders. The group shots of the various parts of the teams were posed after the other cards were issued so there are stylistic differences between the group shots and the individual shots. The backs feature brief biographies of the players.

	MINT	VG-E	F-G
COMPLETE SET (47)	11.00	5.00	1.35
COMMON PLAYER (1-47)	.25	.10	.02

☐ 1 Checklist Card	.25	.10	.02
☐ 2 John Felske MG	.25	.10	.02
☐ 3 Dave Bristol CO	.25	.10	.02
☐ 4 Lee Elia CO	.25	.10	.02
☐ 5 Claude Osteen CO	.25	.10	.02
☐ 6 Mike Ryan CO	.25	.10	.02
☐ 7 Del Unser CO	.25	.10	.02
☐ 8 John Felske MG and	.25	.10	.02
Del Unser CO			
Dave Bristol CO			
Lee Elia CO			
Mike Ryan CO			
Hank King CO			
Claude Osteen CO			
☐ 9 Pitching Staff	.25	.10	.02
Zachry, Andersen,			
Hudson, Rawley,			
Denny, Carlton,			
Gross, Holland,			
Koosman, Carman,			
Bill Campbell			
☐ 10 Catchers	.25	.10	.02
Darren Daulton,			
Bo Diaz,			
Ozzie Virgil			
☐ 11 Infielders	.35	.15	.03
Schmidt, Jeltz,			
Ivan DeJesus, Samuel,			
Aguayo, Russell			
☐ 12 Outfielders	.25	.10	.02
Corcoran, Gross,			
Hayes, Lefebvre,			
Stone, Wilson			
☐ 13 Larry Andersen	.35	.15	.03
☐ 14 Steve Carlton	1.25	.50	.12
☐ 15 Don Carman	.25	.10	.02
☐ 16 John Denny	.35	.15	.03
☐ 17 Tony Ghelfi	.25	.10	.02
☐ 18 Kevin Gross	.35	.15	.03
☐ 19 Al Holland	.25	.10	.02
☐ 20 Charles Hudson	.25	.10	.02
☐ 21 Jerry Koosman	.35	.15	.03
☐ 22 Shane Rawley	.25	.10	.02
☐ 23 Pat Zachry	.25	.10	.02
☐ 24 Darren Daulton	.60	.25	.06
☐ 25 Bo Diaz	.25	.10	.02
☐ 26 Ozzie Virgil	.25	.10	.02
☐ 27 John Wockenfuss	.25	.10	.02
☐ 28 Luis Aguayo	.25	.10	.02
☐ 29 Kiko Garcia	.25	.10	.02
☐ 30 Steve Jeltz	.25	.10	.02
☐ 31 John Russell	.25	.10	.02
☐ 32 Juan Samuel	.50	.20	.05
☐ 33 Mike Schmidt	1.75	.70	.17
☐ 34 Tim Corcoran	.25	.10	.02
☐ 35 Greg Gross	.25	.10	.02
☐ 36 Von Hayes	.50	.20	.05
☐ 37 Joe Lefebvre	.25	.10	.02
☐ 38 Garry Maddox	.35	.15	.03
☐ 39 Jeff Stone	.25	.10	.02
☐ 40 Glenn Wilson	.25	.10	.02
☐ 41 Ramon Caraballo	.25	.10	.02
and Mike Diaz			
☐ 42 Mike Maddux	.25	.10	.02
and Rodger Cole			
☐ 43 Rick Schu and	.35	.15	.03
Chris James			
☐ 44 Francisco Melendez	.25	.10	.02
and Ken Jackson			
☐ 45 Randy Salava and	.25	.10	.02
Rocky Childress			
☐ 46 Rich Surhoff and	.25	.10	.02
Ralph Citarella			
☐ 47 Team Photo	.25	.10	.02

1986 Phillies Tastykake

The 1986 Tastykake Philadelphia Phillies set consists of 47 cards, which measure approximately 3 1/2" by 5 1/4". This set features members of the 1986 Philadelphia Phillies. The front of the cards features a full-color photo of the player against white borders while the back has brief biographies. The set has been checklisted for reference below in order by uniform number.

Steve has played pro baseball for 22 years, beginning in 1964 ... Has pitched in 20 major league seasons, the last 13 with the Phillies and is one of the greatest pitchers in baseball history ... Was acquired in a trade with St. Louis in 1972 ... Ranks 11th all-time with 314 wins, second to Nolan Ryan in strikeouts, eighth in games started, 10th in innings pitched and 14th in ERA ... Four-time Cy Young Award Winner (1972, 1977, 1980 and 1982) ... Selected to 10 All-Star games.
Born December 22, 1944 in Miami, Florida Resides in Chesterfield, Missouri with his wife Bev and sons Steve and Scott
Hobbies: collecting wine and crossword puzzles

#32   STEVE CARLTON   LHP

TASTYKAKE.

	MINT	VG-E	F-G
COMPLETE SET (47)	11.00	5.00	1.35
COMMON PLAYER	.25	.10	.02
☐ 2 Jim Davenport CO	.35	.15	.03
☐ 3 Claude Osteen CO	.25	.10	.02
☐ 4 Lee Elia CO	.25	.10	.02
☐ 5 Mike Ryan CO	.25	.10	.02
☐ 6 John Russell	.25	.10	.02
☐ 7 John Felske MG	.25	.10	.02
☐ 8 Juan Samuel	.50	.20	.05
☐ 9 Von Hayes	.50	.20	.05
☐ 10 Darren Daulton	.50	.20	.05
☐ 11 Tom Foley	.25	.10	.02
☐ 12 Glenn Wilson	.25	.10	.02
☐ 14 Jeff Stone	.25	.10	.02
☐ 15 Rick Schu	.25	.10	.02
☐ 16 Luis Aguayo	.25	.10	.02
☐ 20 Mike Schmidt	1.75	.70	.17
☐ 21 Greg Gross	.25	.10	.02
☐ 22 Gary Redus	.35	.15	.03
☐ 23 Joe Lefebvre	.25	.10	.02
☐ 24 Milt Thompson	.35	.15	.03
☐ 25 Del Unser CO	.25	.10	.02
☐ 26 Chris James	.50	.20	.05
☐ 27 Kent Tekulve	.35	.15	.03
☐ 28 Shane Rawley	.25	.10	.02
☐ 29 Ronn Reynolds	.25	.10	.02
☐ 30 Steve Jeltz	.25	.10	.02
☐ 31 Garry Maddox	.35	.15	.03
☐ 32 Steve Carlton	1.25	.50	.12
☐ 33 David Shipanoff	.25	.10	.02
☐ 35 Randy Lerch	.25	.10	.02
☐ 36 Robin Roberts	.75	.30	.07
☐ 39 Dave Rucker	.25	.10	.02
☐ 40 Steve Bedrosian	.35	.15	.03
☐ 41 Tom Hume	.25	.10	.02
☐ 42 Don Carman	.25	.10	.02
☐ 43 Fred Toliver	.25	.10	.02
☐ 46 Kevin Gross	.35	.15	.03
☐ 47 Larry Andersen	.35	.15	.03
☐ 48 Dave Stewart	1.00	.40	.10
☐ 49 Charles Hudson	.25	.10	.02
☐ 50 Rocky Childress	.25	.10	.02
☐ xx Future Phillies	.25	.10	.02
Ramon Caraballo			
Joe Cipolloni			
☐ xx Future Phillies	.25	.10	.02
Arturo Gonzalez			
Mike Maddux			
☐ xx Future Phillies	.50	.20	.05
Francisco Melendez			
Ricky Jordan			
☐ xx Future Phillies	.25	.10	.02
Kevin Ward			
Randy Day			
☐ xx Night to Remember	.25	.10	.02
26-7, June 11, 1985			
☐ xx Pennant Winning Team	.25	.10	.02
1915 Phillies			
☐ xx Pennant Winning Team	.25	.10	.02
1950 Phillies			
☐ xx Pennant Winning Team	.25	.10	.02
1980 Phillies			
☐ xx Pennant Winning Team	.25	.10	.02
1983 Phillies			

1987 Phillies Tastykake

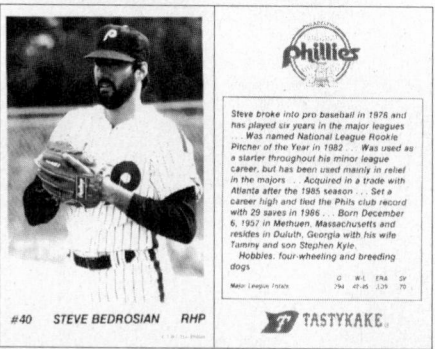

#40 STEVE BEDROSIAN RHP

The 1987 Tastykake Philadelphia Phillies set consists of 47 cards which measure approximately 3 1/2" by 5 1/4". The sets again feature full-color photos against a solid white background. There were two number 39s in this set as the Phillies changed personnel during the season, Joe Cowley and Bob Scanlon. For convenience uniform numbers are used below as a basis for numbering and checklisting this set.

		MINT	VG-E	F-G
COMPLETE SET (47)		11.00	5.00	1.35
COMMON PLAYER		.25	.10	.02
☐ 6	John Russell	.25	.10	.02
☐ 7	John Felske MG	.25	.10	.02
☐ 8	Juan Samuel	.50	.20	.05
☐ 9	Von Hayes	.50	.20	.05
☐ 10	Darren Daulton	.50	.20	.05
☐ 11	Greg Legg	.25	.10	.02
☐ 12	Glenn Wilson	.25	.10	.02
☐ 13	Lance Parrish	.60	.25	.06
☐ 14	Jeff Stone	.25	.10	.02
☐ 15	Rick Schu	.25	.10	.02
☐ 16	Luis Aguayo	.25	.10	.02
☐ 17	Ron Roenicke	.25	.10	.02
☐ 18	Chris James	.50	.20	.05
☐ 20	Mike Schmidt	1.75	.70	.17
☐ 21	Greg Gross	.25	.10	.02
☐ 23	Joe Cipolloni	.25	.10	.02
☐ 24	Milt Thompson	.35	.15	.03
☐ 27	Kent Tekulve	.35	.15	.03
☐ 28	Shane Rawley	.25	.10	.02
☐ 29	Ronn Reynolds	.25	.10	.02
☐ 30	Steve Jeltz	.25	.10	.02
☐ 33	Mike Jackson	.50	.20	.05
☐ 34	Mike Easler	.25	.10	.02
☐ 35	Dan Schatzeder	.25	.10	.02
☐ 37	Ken Howell	.35	.15	.03
☐ 38	Jim Olander	.25	.10	.02
☐ 39A	Joe Cowley	.25	.10	.02
☐ 39B	Bob Scanlan	.35	.15	.03
☐ 40	Steve Bedrosian	.35	.15	.03
☐ 41	Tom Hume	.25	.10	.02
☐ 42	Don Carman	.25	.10	.02
☐ 43	Freddie Toliver	.25	.10	.02
☐ 44	Mike Maddux	.25	.10	.02
☐ 45	Greg Jelks	.25	.10	.02
☐ 46	Kevin Gross	.35	.15	.03
☐ 47	Bruce Ruffin	.25	.10	.02
☐ 48	Marvin Freeman	.25	.10	.02
☐ 49	Len Watts	.25	.10	.02
☐ 50	Tom Newell	.35	.15	.03
☐ 51	Ken Jackson	.25	.10	.02
☐ 52	Todd Frohwirth	.25	.10	.02
☐ 58	Doug Bair	.25	.10	.02
☐ xx	Phillie Phanatic (team mascot)	.25	.10	.02
☐ xx	Team Photo	.25	.10	.02
☐ xx	Shawn Barton and Rick Lundblade	.25	.10	.02
☐ xx	Jeff Kaye and Darren Loy	.25	.10	.02

☐ xx	Coaches Card	.25	.10	.02
	Claude Osteen CO			
	Del Unser CO			
	Jim Davenport CO			
	Mike Ryan CO			
	Lee Elia CO			

1988 Phillies Tastykake

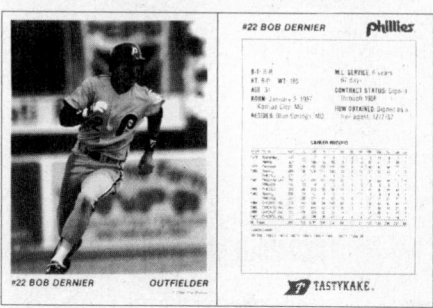

#22 BOB DERNIER OUTFIELDER

The 1988 Tastykake Philadelphia Phillies set is a 30-card set measuring approximately 4 7/8" by 6 1/4". This set is listed below alphabetically by player. The cards have a full-color photo front and complete player history on the back. There was also a nine-card update set issued later in the year which included a Ricky Jordan card; the update cards are numbered as 31-39 and are blank backed.

		MINT	EXC	G-VG
COMPLETE SET (39)		10.00	4.50	1.25
COMMON PLAYER (1-30)		.25	.10	.02
COMMON PLAYER (31-39)		.25	.10	.02
☐ 1	Luis Aguayo	.25	.10	.02
☐ 2	Bill Almon	.25	.10	.02
☐ 3	Steve Bedrosian	.35	.15	.03
☐ 4	Phil Bradley	.35	.15	.03
☐ 5	Jeff Calhoun	.25	.10	.02
☐ 6	Don Carman	.25	.10	.02
☐ 7	Darren Daulton	.45	.18	.04
☐ 8	Bob Dernier	.25	.10	.02
☐ 9A	Lee Elia MG (Vertical format)	.25	.10	.02
☐ 9B	Lee Elia MG (Horizontal format)	.25	.10	.02
☐ 10	Todd Frohwirth	.25	.10	.02
☐ 11	Greg Gross	.25	.10	.02
☐ 12	Kevin Gross	.35	.15	.03
☐ 13	Von Hayes	.45	.18	.04
☐ 14	Chris James	.35	.15	.03
☐ 15	Steve Jeltz	.25	.10	.02
☐ 16	Mike Maddux	.25	.10	.02
☐ 17	Dave Palmer	.35	.15	.03
☐ 18	Lance Parrish	.45	.18	.04
☐ 19	Shane Rawley	.25	.10	.02
☐ 20	Wally Ritchie	.25	.10	.02
☐ 21	Bruce Ruffin	.25	.10	.02
☐ 22	Juan Samuel	.45	.18	.04
☐ 23	Mike Schmidt	1.50	.60	.15
☐ 24	Kent Tekulve	.35	.15	.03
☐ 25	Milt Thompson	.35	.15	.03
☐ 26	Mike Young	.25	.10	.02
☐ 27	Phillies Prospects	.25	.10	.02
	Tom Barrett			
	Brad Brink			
	Steve DeAngelis			
	Ron Jones			
	Keith Miller			
	Brad Moore			
	Howard Nichols			
	Shane Turner			

		MINT	EXC	G-VG
☐ 28	Team Card	.25	.10	.02
☐ 29	Phillies Coaches	.25	.10	.02
	Claude Osteen			
	Del Unser			
	John Vuckovich			
	Dave Bristol			
	Tony Taylor			
	Mike Ryan			
☐ 30	Phillie Phanatic	.25	.10	.02
	(Mascot)			
☐ 31	Larry Bowa CO	.35	.15	.03
☐ 32	Lee Elia CO	.25	.10	.02
☐ 33	Jackie Gutierrez	.25	.10	.02
☐ 34	Greg A. Harris	.35	.15	.03
☐ 35	Ricky Jordan	.35	.15	.03
☐ 36	Keith Miller	.35	.15	.03
☐ 37	John Russell	.25	.10	.02
☐ 38	John Vuckovich CO	.25	.10	.02
☐ 39	Phillies Announcers	.35	.15	.03
	Garry Maddox			
	Richie Ashburn			
	Chris Wheeler			
	Harry Kalas			
	Andy Musser			

		MINT	EXC	G-VG
☐ 18	Nick Levya MG	.25	.10	.02
☐ 19	Mike Maddux	.25	.10	.02
☐ 20	Alex Madrid	.25	.10	.02
☐ 21	Larry McWilliams	.25	.10	.02
☐ 22	Denis Menke CO	.25	.10	.02
☐ 23	Dwayne Murphy	.25	.10	.02
☐ 24	Tom Nieto	.25	.10	.02
☐ 25	Randy O'Neal	.25	.10	.02
☐ 26	Steve Ontiveros	.25	.10	.02
☐ 27	Jeff Parrett	.25	.10	.02
☐ 28	Bruce Ruffin	.25	.10	.02
☐ 29	Mike Ryal	.25	.10	.02
☐ 30	Mike Ryan CO	.25	.10	.02
☐ 31	Juan Samuel	.45	.18	.04
☐ 32	Mike Schmidt	1.50	.60	.15
☐ 33	Tony Taylor CO	.25	.10	.02
☐ 34	Dickie Thon	.35	.15	.03
☐ 35	John Vuckovich CO	.25	.10	.02
☐ 36	Floyd Youmans	.25	.10	.02
☐ 37	Jim Adduci	.35	.15	.03
☐ 38	Eric Bullock	.35	.15	.03
☐ 39	Dennis Cook	.45	.18	.04
☐ 40	Len Dykstra	.75	.30	.07
☐ 41	Charlie Hayes	.60	.25	.06
☐ 42	John Kruk	.45	.18	.04
☐ 43	Roger McDowell	.45	.18	.04
☐ 44	Terry Mulholland	.60	.25	.06
☐ 45	Randy Ready	.35	.15	.03

1989 Phillies Tastykake

1990 Phillies Tastycake

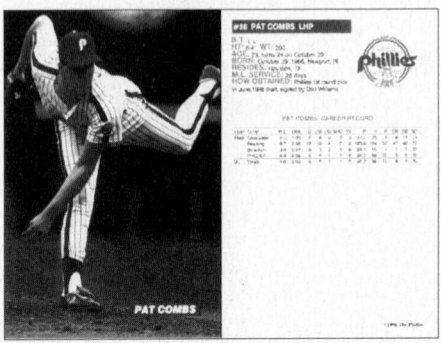

This set was a 36-card set of Philadelphia Phillies measuring approximately 4 1/8" by 6" featuring full-color fronts with complete biographical information and career stats on the back. The set is checklisted alphabetically in the list below. The set was a give away to fans attending the Phillies Tastykake Photocard Night on May 13, 1989 and was later available from a mail-away offer. There was also a nine-player extended set issued later during the 1989 season; the extended players are numbered below in alphabetical order, numbers 37-45. Chris James' card lists him as uniform number 26, but his number is 18 as 26 was Ron Jones' number.

		MINT	EXC	G-VG
COMPLETE SET (45)		12.00	5.25	1.50
COMMON PLAYER (1-36)		.25	.10	.02
COMMON PLAYER (37-45)		.35	.15	.03
☐ 1	Steve Bedrosian	.35	.15	.03
☐ 2	Larry Bowa CO	.35	.15	.03
☐ 3	Don Carman	.25	.10	.02
☐ 4	Darren Daulton	.45	.18	.04
☐ 5	Bob Dernier	.25	.10	.02
☐ 6	Curt Ford	.25	.10	.02
☐ 7	Todd Frohwirth	.25	.10	.02
☐ 8	Greg A. Harris	.35	.15	.03
☐ 9	Von Hayes	.45	.18	.04
☐ 10	Tom Herr	.35	.15	.03
☐ 11	Ken Howell	.35	.15	.03
☐ 12	Chris James UER	.35	.15	
	(wrong uniform number on card)			
☐ 13	Steve Jeltz	.25	.10	.02
☐ 14	Ron Jones	.35	.15	.03
☐ 15	Ricky Jordan	.35	.15	.03
☐ 16	Darold Knowles CO	.25	.10	.02
☐ 17	Steve Lake	.25	.10	.02

The 1990 Tastykake Philadelphia Phillies set is a 36-card set measuring approximately 4 1/8" by 6" which features players, coaches and manager, four players who have had their uniform numbers retired, broadcasters, and even the Phillies Mascot. The set is checklisted alphabetically, with complete biography and complete stats on the back.

		MINT	EXC	G-VG
COMPLETE SET (36)		9.00	4.00	.90
COMMON PLAYER (1-36)		.25	.10	.02
☐ 1	Darrel Akerfelds	.25	.10	.02
☐ 2	Rod Booker	.25	.10	.02
☐ 3	Sil Campusano	.35	.15	.03
☐ 4	Don Carman	.25	.10	.02
☐ 5	Pat Combs	.35	.15	.03
☐ 6	Dennis Cook	.35	.15	.03
☐ 7	Darren Daulton	.35	.15	.03
☐ 8	Len Dykstra	.60	.25	.06
☐ 9	Curt Ford	.25	.10	.02
☐ 10	Jason Grimsley	.25	.10	.02
☐ 11	Charlie Hayes	.35	.15	.03
☐ 12	Von Hayes	.45	.18	.04
☐ 13	Tommy Herr	.35	.15	.03
☐ 14	Dave Hollins	.45	.18	.04
☐ 15	Ken Howell	.35	.15	.03
☐ 16	Ron Jones	.35	.15	.03
☐ 17	Ricky Jordan	.35	.15	.03
☐ 18	John Kruk	.35	.15	.03
☐ 19	Steve Lake	.25	.10	.02
☐ 20	Nick Levya MG	.25	.10	.02
☐ 21	Carmelo Martinez	.25	.10	.02
☐ 22	Roger McDowell	.35	.15	.03

		MINT	EXC	G-VG
☐ 23	Chuck McElroy	.25	.10	.02
☐ 24	Terry Mulholland	.35	.15	.03
☐ 25	Jeff Parrett	.25	.10	.02
☐ 26	Randy Ready	.25	.10	.02
☐ 27	Bruce Ruffin	.25	.10	.02
☐ 28	Dickie Thon	.35	.15	.03
☐ 29	Richie Ashburn	.50	.20	.05
☐ 30	Steve Carlton	1.00	.40	.10
☐ 31	Robin Roberts	.75	.30	.07
☐ 32	Mike Schmidt	1.50	.60	.15
☐ 33	Phillie Phanatic (Mascot)	.25	.10	.02
☐ 34	Phillie Coaches Denis Menke Mike Ryan John Vuckovich Hal Lanier Darold Knowles Larry Bowa	.25	.10	.02
☐ 35	Phillies Broadcasters Chris Wheeler Andy Musser Harry Kalas Richie Ashburn	.25	.10	.02
☐ 36	Phillies Broadcasters Mike Schmidt Jim Barniak Garry Maddox	.35	.15	.03

☐ 22	John Kruk	.35	.15	.03
☐ 23	Steve Lake	.25	.10	.02
☐ 24	Hal Lanier CO	.25	.10	.02
☐ 25	Tim Mauser	.35	.15	.03
☐ 26	Roger McDowell	.25	.10	.02
☐ 27	Denis Menke CO	.25	.10	.02
☐ 28	Mickey Morandini	.35	.15	.03
☐ 29	John Morris	.25	.10	.02
☐ 30	Terry Mulholland	.35	.15	.03
☐ 31	Dale Murphy	.75	.30	.07
☐ 32	Johnny Podres CO	.35	.15	.03
☐ 33	Randy Ready	.25	.10	.02
☐ 34	Dickie Thon	.35	.15	.03
☐ 35	John Vukovich CO	.25	.10	.02

1991 Phillies Medford

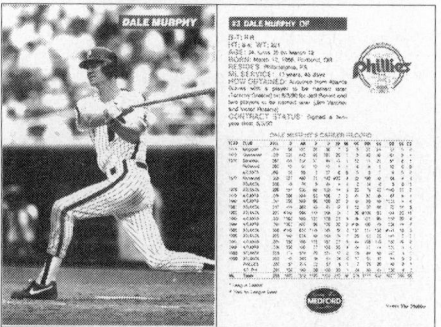

This 35-card set was sponsored by Medford (rather than by Tastykake as in past years), and its company logo is found on the bottom of the reverse. The oversized cards measure 4 1/8" by 6" and feature borderless glossy color action player photos on the obverse. The player's name is given in a red bar at either the top or bottom of the picture. The backs are printed in red and black on white and present biographical as well as statistical information. The cards are unnumbered and checklisted below in alphabetical order.

		MINT	EXC	G-VG
	COMPLETE SET (35)	9.00	4.00	.90
	COMMON PLAYER (1-35)	.25	.10	.02
☐ 1	Darrel Akerfelds	.25	.10	.02
☐ 2	Andy Ashby	.35	.15	.03
☐ 3	Wally Backman	.25	.10	.02
☐ 4	Joe Boever	.25	.10	.02
☐ 5	Rod Booker	.25	.10	.02
☐ 6	Larry Bowa CO	.35	.15	.03
☐ 7	Sil Campusano	.25	.10	.02
☐ 8	Wes Chamberlain	.75	.30	.07
☐ 9	Pat Combs	.35	.15	.03
☐ 10	Danny Cox	.25	.10	.02
☐ 11	Darren Daulton	.35	.15	.03
☐ 12	Jose DeJesus	.25	.10	.02
☐ 13	Len Dykstra	.50	.20	.05
☐ 14	Darrin Fletcher	.25	.10	.02
☐ 15	Tommy Greene	.50	.20	.05
☐ 16	Jason Grimsley	.35	.15	.03
☐ 17	Charlie Hayes	.35	.15	.03
☐ 18	Von Hayes	.35	.15	.03
☐ 19	Dave Hollins	.35	.15	.03
☐ 20	Ken Howell	.25	.10	.02
☐ 21	Ricky Jordan	.35	.15	.03

1939 Playball

The cards in this 161-card set measure 2 1/2" by 3 1/8". Gum Incorporated introduced a brief (war-shortened) but innovative era of baseball card production with its set of 1939. The combination of actual player photos (black and white), large card size, and extensive biography proved extremely popular. Player names are found either entirely capitalized or with initial caps only, and a "sample card" overprint is not uncommon. Card number 126 was never issued, and cards 116-162 were produced in lesser quantities than 1-115. The catalog designation for this set is R334.

		EX-MT	VG-E	GOOD
	COMPLETE SET	12500.00	5500.00	1250.00
	COMMON PLAYER (1-115)	15.00	6.50	2.15
	COMMON PLAYER (116-162)	135.00	60.00	20.00
☐ 1	Jake Powell	75.00	10.00	2.00
☐ 2	Lee Grissom	15.00	6.50	2.15
☐ 3	Red Ruffing	85.00	38.00	12.75
☐ 4	Eldon Auker	15.00	6.50	2.15
☐ 5	Luke Sewell	20.00	8.50	2.75
☐ 6	Leo Durocher	60.00	27.00	9.00
☐ 7	Bobby Doerr	85.00	38.00	12.75
☐ 8	Henry Pippen	15.00	6.50	2.15
☐ 9	James Tobin	15.00	6.50	2.15
☐ 10	James DeShong	15.00	6.50	2.15
☐ 11	Johnny Rizzo	15.00	6.50	2.15
☐ 12	Hershel Martin	15.00	6.50	2.15
☐ 13	Luke Hamlin	15.00	6.50	2.15
☐ 14	Jim Tabor	15.00	6.50	2.15
☐ 15	Paul Derringer	25.00	11.00	3.50
☐ 16	John Peacock	15.00	6.50	2.15
☐ 17	Emerson Dickman	15.00	6.50	2.15
☐ 18	Harry Danning	15.00	6.50	2.15
☐ 19	Paul Dean	25.00	11.00	3.50
☐ 20	Joe Heving	15.00	6.50	2.15
☐ 21	Dutch Leonard	20.00	8.50	2.75
☐ 22	Bucky Walters	20.00	8.50	2.75
☐ 23	Burgess Whitehead	15.00	6.50	2.15
☐ 24	Richard Coffman	15.00	6.50	2.15
☐ 25	George Selkirk	25.00	11.00	3.50
☐ 26	Joe DiMaggio	2000.00	800.00	200.00
☐ 27	Fred Ostermueller	15.00	6.50	2.15
☐ 28	Sylvester Johnson	15.00	6.50	2.15
☐ 29	John(Jack) Wilson	15.00	6.50	2.15
☐ 30	Bill Dickey	150.00	67.50	22.50
☐ 31	Sam West	15.00	6.50	2.15
☐ 32	Bob Seeds	15.00	6.50	2.15
☐ 33	Del Young	15.00	6.50	2.15

☐ 34	Frank Demaree	15.00	6.50	2.15
☐ 35	Bill Jurges	15.00	6.50	2.15
☐ 36	Frank McCormick	20.00	8.50	2.75
☐ 37	Virgil Davis	15.00	6.50	2.15
☐ 38	Billy Myers	15.00	6.50	2.15
☐ 39	Rick Ferrell	65.00	29.00	9.75
☐ 40	James Bagby Jr.	15.00	6.50	2.15
☐ 41	Lon Warneke	15.00	6.50	2.15
☐ 42	Arndt Jorgens	15.00	6.50	2.15
☐ 43	Melo Almada	15.00	6.50	2.15
☐ 44	Don Heffner	15.00	6.50	2.15
☐ 45	Merrill May	15.00	6.50	2.15
☐ 46	Morris Arnovich	15.00	6.50	2.15
☐ 47	Buddy Lewis	15.00	6.50	2.15
☐ 48	Lefty Gomez	125.00	57.50	18.75
☐ 49	Eddie Miller	15.00	6.50	2.15
☐ 50	Charlie Gehringer	125.00	57.50	18.75
☐ 51	Mel Ott	150.00	67.50	22.50
☐ 52	Tommy Henrich	30.00	13.50	4.50
☐ 53	Carl Hubbell	125.00	57.50	18.75
☐ 54	Harry Gumpert	15.00	6.50	2.15
☐ 55	Arky Vaughan	65.00	29.00	9.75
☐ 56	Hank Greenberg	150.00	67.50	22.50
☐ 57	Buddy Hassett	15.00	6.50	2.15
☐ 58	Lou Chiozza	15.00	6.50	2.15
☐ 59	Ken Chase	15.00	6.50	2.15
☐ 60	Schoolboy Rowe	20.00	8.50	2.75
☐ 61	Tony Cuccinello	15.00	6.50	2.15
☐ 62	Tom Carey	15.00	6.50	2.15
☐ 63	Emmett Mueller	15.00	6.50	2.15
☐ 64	Wally Moses	20.00	8.50	2.75
☐ 65	Harry Craft	15.00	6.50	2.15
☐ 66	Jimmy Ripple	15.00	6.50	2.15
☐ 67	Ed Joost	15.00	6.50	2.15
☐ 68	Fred Sington	15.00	6.50	2.15
☐ 69	Elbie Fletcher	15.00	6.50	2.15
☐ 70	Fred Frankhouse	15.00	6.50	2.15
☐ 71	Monte Pearson	15.00	6.50	2.15
☐ 72	Debs Garms	15.00	6.50	2.15
☐ 73	Hal Schumacher	15.00	6.50	2.15
☐ 74	Cookie Lavagetto	15.00	6.50	2.15
☐ 75	Stan Bordagaray	15.00	6.50	2.15
☐ 76	Goody Rosen	15.00	6.50	2.15
☐ 77	Lew Riggs	15.00	6.50	2.15
☐ 78	Julius Solters	15.00	6.50	2.15
☐ 79	Jo Jo Moore	15.00	6.50	2.15
☐ 80	Pete Fox	15.00	6.50	2.15
☐ 81	Babe Dahlgren	15.00	6.50	2.15
☐ 82	Chuck Klein	125.00	57.50	18.75
☐ 83	Gus Suhr	15.00	6.50	2.15
☐ 84	Skeeter Newsom	15.00	6.50	2.15
☐ 85	Johnny Cooney	15.00	6.50	2.15
☐ 86	Dolph Camilli	15.00	6.50	2.15
☐ 87	Milburn Shoffner	15.00	6.50	2.15
☐ 88	Charlie Keller	25.00	11.00	3.50
☐ 89	Lloyd Waner	70.00	32.00	10.50
☐ 90	Robert Klinger	15.00	6.50	2.15
☐ 91	John Knott	15.00	6.50	2.15
☐ 92	Ted Williams	2000.00	800.00	200.00
☐ 93	Charles Gelbert	15.00	6.50	2.15
☐ 94	Heinie Manush	65.00	29.00	9.75
☐ 95	Whit Wyatt	15.00	6.50	2.15
☐ 96	Babe Phelps	15.00	6.50	2.15
☐ 97	Bob Johnson	20.00	8.50	2.75
☐ 98	Pinky Whitney	15.00	6.50	2.15
☐ 99	Wally Berger	20.00	8.50	2.75
☐ 100	Charles Myer	15.00	6.50	2.15
☐ 101	Roger Cramer	20.00	8.50	2.75
☐ 102	Lem Young	15.00	6.50	2.15
☐ 103	Moe Berg	35.00	15.75	5.25
☐ 104	Tom Bridges	20.00	8.50	2.75
☐ 105	Rabbit McNair	15.00	6.50	2.15
☐ 106	Dolly Stark	20.00	8.50	2.75
☐ 107	Joe Vosmik	15.00	6.50	2.15
☐ 108	Frank Hayes	15.00	6.50	2.15
☐ 109	Myril Hoag	15.00	6.50	2.15
☐ 110	Fred Fitzsimmons	15.00	6.50	2.15
☐ 111	Van Lingle Mungo	20.00	8.50	2.75
☐ 112	Paul Waner	75.00	34.00	11.25
☐ 113	Al Schacht	20.00	8.50	2.75
☐ 114	Cecil Travis	15.00	6.50	2.15
☐ 115	Ralph Kress	15.00	6.50	2.15
☐ 116	Gene Desautels	135.00	60.00	20.00
☐ 117	Wayne Ambler	135.00	60.00	20.00
☐ 118	Lynn Nelson	135.00	60.00	20.00
☐ 119	Will Hershberger	135.00	60.00	20.00
☐ 120	Rabbit Warstler	135.00	60.00	20.00
☐ 121	Bill Posedel	135.00	60.00	20.00
☐ 122	George McQuinn	135.00	60.00	20.00
☐ 123	Ray T. Davis	135.00	60.00	20.00
☐ 124	Walter Brown	135.00	60.00	20.00
☐ 125	Cliff Melton	135.00	60.00	20.00
☐ 126	Not issued	000.00	00.00	00.00
☐ 127	Gil Brack	135.00	60.00	20.00
☐ 128	Joe Bowman	135.00	60.00	20.00

☐ 129	Bill Swift	135.00	60.00	20.00
☐ 130	Bill Brubaker	135.00	60.00	20.00
☐ 131	Mort Cooper	165.00	75.00	22.50
☐ 132	Jim Brown	135.00	60.00	20.00
☐ 133	Lynn Myers	135.00	60.00	20.00
☐ 134	Tot Presnell	135.00	60.00	20.00
☐ 135	Mickey Owen	165.00	75.00	22.50
☐ 136	Roy Bell	135.00	60.00	20.00
☐ 137	Pete Appleton	135.00	60.00	20.00
☐ 138	George Case	165.00	75.00	22.50
☐ 139	Vito Tamulis	135.00	60.00	20.00
☐ 140	Ray Hayworth	135.00	60.00	20.00
☐ 141	Pete Coscarart	135.00	60.00	20.00
☐ 142	Ira Hutchinson	135.00	60.00	20.00
☐ 143	Earl Averill	375.00	165.00	55.00
☐ 144	Zeke Bonura	135.00	60.00	20.00
☐ 145	Hugh Mulcahy	135.00	60.00	20.00
☐ 146	Tom Sunkel	135.00	60.00	20.00
☐ 147	George Coffman	135.00	60.00	20.00
☐ 148	Bill Trotter	135.00	60.00	20.00
☐ 149	Max West	135.00	60.00	20.00
☐ 150	James Walkup	135.00	60.00	20.00
☐ 151	Hugh Casey	165.00	75.00	22.50
☐ 152	Roy Weatherly	135.00	60.00	20.00
☐ 153	Paul Trout	165.00	75.00	22.50
☐ 154	Johnny Hudson	135.00	60.00	20.00
☐ 155	Jimmy Outlaw	135.00	60.00	20.00
☐ 156	Ray Berres	135.00	60.00	20.00
☐ 157	Don Padgett	135.00	60.00	20.00
☐ 158	Bud Thomas	135.00	60.00	20.00
☐ 159	Red Evans	135.00	60.00	20.00
☐ 160	Gene Moore	135.00	60.00	20.00
☐ 161	Lonnie Frey	135.00	60.00	20.00
☐ 162	Whitey Moore	165.00	75.00	22.50

1940 Playball

The cards in this 240-card series measure 2 1/2" by 3 1/8". Gum Inc. improved upon its 1939 design by enclosing the 1940 black and white player photo with a frame line and printing the player's name in a panel below the picture (often using a nickname). The set included many Hall of Famers and Old Timers. Cards 181-240 are scarcer than cards 1-180. The backs contain an extensive biography and a dated copyright line. The catalog number for this set is R335.

	EX-MT	VG-E	GOOD
COMPLETE SET (240)	18000.00	8000.00	1800.00
COMMON PLAYER (1-120)	16.00	6.75	2.25
COMMON PLAYER (121-180)	18.00	7.50	2.50
COMMON PLAYER (181-240)	75.00	34.00	11.25

☐ 1	Joe DiMaggio	2500.00	625.00	125.00
☐ 2	Art Jorgens	16.00	6.75	2.25
☐ 3	Babe Dahlgren	20.00	8.50	2.75
☐ 4	Tommy Henrich	30.00	13.50	4.50
☐ 5	Monte Pearson	20.00	8.50	2.75
☐ 6	Lefty Gomez	175.00	80.00	27.00
☐ 7	Bill Dickey	200.00	90.00	30.00
☐ 8	George Selkirk	25.00	11.00	3.50
☐ 9	Charlie Keller	30.00	13.50	4.50
☐ 10	Red Ruffing	90.00	40.00	13.50
☐ 11	Jake Powell	16.00	6.75	2.25
☐ 12	Johnny Schulte	16.00	6.75	2.25
☐ 13	Jack Knott	16.00	6.75	2.25
☐ 14	Rabbit McNair	16.00	6.75	2.25

	#	Name			
☐	15	George Case	20.00	8.50	2.75
☐	16	Cecil Travis	16.00	6.75	2.25
☐	17	Buddy Myer	16.00	6.75	2.25
☐	18	Charlie Gelbert	16.00	6.75	2.25
☐	19	Ken Chase	16.00	6.75	2.25
☐	20	Buddy Lewis	16.00	6.75	2.25
☐	21	Rick Ferrell	70.00	32.00	10.50
☐	22	Sammy West	16.00	6.75	2.25
☐	23	Dutch Leonard	20.00	8.50	2.75
☐	24	Frank Hayes	16.00	6.75	2.25
☐	25	Bob Johnson	20.00	8.50	2.75
☐	26	Wally Moses	20.00	8.50	2.75
☐	27	Ted Williams	1500.00	600.00	150.00
☐	28	Gene Desautels	16.00	6.75	2.25
☐	29	Doc Cramer	20.00	8.50	2.75
☐	30	Moe Berg	35.00	15.75	5.25
☐	31	Jack Wilson	16.00	6.75	2.25
☐	32	Jim Bagby	16.00	6.75	2.25
☐	33	Fritz Ostermueller	16.00	6.75	2.25
☐	34	John Peacock	16.00	6.75	2.25
☐	35	Joe Heving	16.00	6.75	2.25
☐	36	Jim Tabor	16.00	6.75	2.25
☐	37	Emerson Dickman	16.00	6.75	2.25
☐	38	Bobby Doerr	80.00	36.00	12.00
☐	39	Tom Carey	16.00	6.75	2.25
☐	40	Hank Greenberg	200.00	90.00	30.00
☐	41	Charley Gehringer	150.00	67.50	22.50
☐	42	Bud Thomas	16.00	6.75	2.25
☐	43	Pete Fox	16.00	6.75	2.25
☐	44	Dizzy Trout	20.00	8.50	2.75
☐	45	Red Kress	16.00	6.75	2.25
☐	46	Earl Averill	90.00	40.00	13.50
☐	47	Oscar Vitt	16.00	6.75	2.25
☐	48	Luke Sewell	20.00	8.50	2.75
☐	49	Stormy Weatherly	16.00	6.75	2.25
☐	50	Hal Trosky	20.00	8.50	2.75
☐	51	Don Heffner	16.00	6.75	2.25
☐	52	Myril Hoag	16.00	6.75	2.25
☐	53	Mac McQuinn	16.00	6.75	2.25
☐	54	Bill Trotter	16.00	6.75	2.25
☐	55	Slick Coffman	16.00	6.75	2.25
☐	56	Eddie Miller	16.00	6.75	2.25
☐	57	Max West	16.00	6.75	2.25
☐	58	Bill Posedel	16.00	6.75	2.25
☐	59	Rabbit Warstler	16.00	6.75	2.25
☐	60	John Cooney	16.00	6.75	2.25
☐	61	Tony Cuccinello	16.00	6.75	2.25
☐	62	Buddy Hassett	16.00	6.75	2.25
☐	63	Pete Coscarart	16.00	6.75	2.25
☐	64	Van Lingle Mungo	20.00	8.50	2.75
☐	65	Fitz Fitzsimmons	16.00	6.75	2.25
☐	66	Babe Phelps	16.00	6.75	2.25
☐	67	Whit Wyatt	20.00	8.50	2.75
☐	68	Dolph Camilli	16.00	6.75	2.25
☐	69	Cookie Lavagetto	16.00	6.75	2.25
☐	70	Hot Potato Hamlin	16.00	6.75	2.25
☐	71	Mel Almada	16.00	6.75	2.25
☐	72	Chuck Dressen	20.00	8.50	2.75
☐	73	Bucky Walters	20.00	8.50	2.75
☐	74	Duke Derringer	25.00	11.00	3.50
☐	75	Buck McCormick	20.00	8.50	2.75
☐	76	Lonny Frey	16.00	6.75	2.25
☐	77	Bill Hershberger	16.00	6.75	2.25
☐	78	Lew Riggs	16.00	6.75	2.25
☐	79	Harry Wildfire Craft	16.00	6.75	2.25
☐	80	Billy Myers	16.00	6.75	2.25
☐	81	Wally Berger	20.00	8.50	2.75
☐	82	Hank Gowdy	16.00	6.75	2.25
☐	83	Cliff Melton	16.00	6.75	2.25
☐	84	Jo Jo Moore	16.00	6.75	2.25
☐	85	Hal Schumacher	16.00	6.75	2.25
☐	86	Harry Gumbert	16.00	6.75	2.25
☐	87	Carl Hubbell	150.00	67.50	22.50
☐	88	Mel Ott	180.00	80.00	27.00
☐	89	Bill Jurges	16.00	6.75	2.25
☐	90	Frank Demaree	16.00	6.75	2.25
☐	91	Suitcase Seeds	16.00	6.75	2.25
☐	92	Whitey Whitehead	16.00	6.75	2.25
☐	93	Harry Danning	16.00	6.75	2.25
☐	94	Gus Suhr	16.00	6.75	2.25
☐	95	Mul Mulcahy	16.00	6.75	2.25
☐	96	Heinie Mueller	16.00	6.75	2.25
☐	97	Morry Arnovich	16.00	6.75	2.25
☐	98	Pinky May	16.00	6.75	2.25
☐	99	Syl Johnson	16.00	6.75	2.25
☐	100	Hersh Martin	16.00	6.75	2.25
☐	101	Del Young	16.00	6.75	2.25
☐	102	Chuck Klein	125.00	57.50	18.75
☐	103	Elbie Fletcher	16.00	6.75	2.25
☐	104	Big Poison Waner	90.00	40.00	13.50
☐	105	Little Poison Waner	90.00	40.00	13.50
☐	106	Pep Young	16.00	6.75	2.25
☐	107	Arky Vaughan	75.00	34.00	11.25
☐	108	Johnny Rizzo	16.00	6.75	2.25
☐	109	Don Padgett	16.00	6.75	2.25
☐	110	Tom Sunkel	16.00	6.75	2.25
☐	111	Mickey Owen	20.00	8.50	2.75
☐	112	Jimmy Brown	16.00	6.75	2.25
☐	113	Mort Cooper	20.00	8.50	2.75
☐	114	Lon Warneke	16.00	6.75	2.25
☐	115	Mike Gonzales	16.00	6.75	2.25
☐	116	Al Schacht	20.00	8.50	2.75
☐	117	Dolly Stark	20.00	8.50	2.75
☐	118	Schoolboy Hoyt	90.00	40.00	13.50
☐	119	Ol Pete Alexander	175.00	80.00	27.00
☐	120	Walter Johnson	250.00	110.00	37.50
☐	121	Atley Donald	18.00	7.50	2.50
☐	122	Sandy Sundra	18.00	7.50	2.50
☐	123	Hildy Hildebrand	18.00	7.50	2.50
☐	124	Colonel Earle Combs	125.00	57.50	18.75
☐	125	Art Fletcher	18.00	7.50	2.50
☐	126	Jake Solters	18.00	7.50	2.50
☐	127	Muddy Ruel	18.00	7.50	2.50
☐	128	Pete Appleton	18.00	7.50	2.50
☐	129	Bucky Harris	70.00	32.00	10.50
☐	130	Deerfoot Milan	18.00	7.50	2.50
☐	131	Zeke Bonura	18.00	7.50	2.50
☐	132	Connie Mack	175.00	80.00	27.00
☐	133	Jimmie Foxx	250.00	110.00	37.50
☐	134	Joe Cronin	150.00	67.50	22.50
☐	135	Line Drive Nelson	18.00	7.50	2.50
☐	136	Cotton Pippen	18.00	7.50	2.50
☐	137	Bing Miller	18.00	7.50	2.50
☐	138	Beau Bell	18.00	7.50	2.50
☐	139	Elden Auker	18.00	7.50	2.50
☐	140	Dick Coffman	18.00	7.50	2.50
☐	141	Casey Stengel	225.00	100.00	33.00
☐	142	Highpockets Kelly	90.00	40.00	13.50
☐	143	Gene Moore	18.00	7.50	2.50
☐	144	Joe Vosmik	18.00	7.50	2.50
☐	145	Vito Tamulis	18.00	7.50	2.50
☐	146	Tot Pressnell	18.00	7.50	2.50
☐	147	Johnny Hudson	18.00	7.50	2.50
☐	148	Hugh Casey	18.00	7.50	2.50
☐	149	Pinky Shoffner	18.00	7.50	2.50
☐	150	Whitey Moore	18.00	7.50	2.50
☐	151	Edwin Joost	18.00	7.50	2.50
☐	152	Jimmy Wilson	18.00	7.50	2.50
☐	153	Bill McKechnie	80.00	36.00	12.00
☐	154	Jumbo Brown	18.00	7.50	2.50
☐	155	Ray Hayworth	18.00	7.50	2.50
☐	156	Daffy Dean	30.00	13.50	4.50
☐	157	Lou Chiozza	18.00	7.50	2.50
☐	158	Travis Jackson	90.00	40.00	13.50
☐	159	Pancho Snyder	18.00	7.50	2.50
☐	160	Hans Lobert	18.00	7.50	2.50
☐	161	Debs Garms	18.00	7.50	2.50
☐	162	Joe Bowman	18.00	7.50	2.50
☐	163	Spud Davis	18.00	7.50	2.50
☐	164	Ray Berres	18.00	7.50	2.50
☐	165	Bob Klinger	18.00	7.50	2.50
☐	166	Bill Brubaker	18.00	7.50	2.50
☐	167	Frankie Frisch	125.00	57.50	18.75
☐	168	Honus Wagner	300.00	135.00	45.00
☐	169	Gabby Street	18.00	7.50	2.50
☐	170	Tris Speaker	250.00	110.00	37.50
☐	171	Harry Heilmann	125.00	57.50	18.75
☐	172	Chief Bender	90.00	40.00	13.50
☐	173	Larry Lajoie	250.00	110.00	37.50
☐	174	Johnny Evers	90.00	40.00	13.50
☐	175	Christy Mathewson	300.00	135.00	45.00
☐	176	Heinie Manush	90.00	40.00	13.50
☐	177	Homerun Baker	125.00	57.50	18.75
☐	178	Max Carey	90.00	40.00	13.50
☐	179	George Sisler	125.00	57.50	18.75
☐	180	Mickey Cochrane	180.00	80.00	27.00
☐	181	Spud Chandler	100.00	45.00	15.00
☐	182	Knick Knickerbocker	75.00	34.00	11.25
☐	183	Marvin Breuer	75.00	34.00	11.25
☐	184	Mule Haas	75.00	34.00	11.25
☐	185	Joe Kuhel	75.00	34.00	11.25
☐	186	Taft Wright	75.00	34.00	11.25
☐	187	Jimmy Dykes	90.00	40.00	13.50
☐	188	Joe Krakauskas	75.00	34.00	11.25
☐	189	Jim Bloodworth	75.00	34.00	11.25
☐	190	Charley Berry	75.00	34.00	11.25
☐	191	John Babich	75.00	34.00	11.25
☐	192	Dick Siebert	75.00	34.00	11.25
☐	193	Chubby Dean	75.00	34.00	11.25
☐	194	Sam Chapman	75.00	34.00	11.25
☐	195	Dee Miles	75.00	34.00	11.25
☐	196	Nonny Nonnenkamp	75.00	34.00	11.25
☐	197	Lou Finney	75.00	34.00	11.25
☐	198	Denny Galehouse	75.00	34.00	11.25
☐	199	Pinky Higgins	75.00	34.00	11.25
☐	200	Soup Campbell	75.00	34.00	11.25
☐	201	Barney McCosky	75.00	34.00	11.25
☐	202	Al Milnar	75.00	34.00	11.25
☐	203	Bad News Hale	75.00	34.00	11.25
☐	204	Harry Eisenstat	75.00	34.00	11.25

		EX-MT	VG-E	GOOD
☐ 205	Rollie Hemsley	75.00	34.00	11.25
☐ 206	Chet Laabs	75.00	34.00	11.25
☐ 207	Gus Mancuso	75.00	34.00	11.25
☐ 208	Lee Gamble	75.00	34.00	11.25
☐ 209	Hy Vandenberg	75.00	34.00	11.25
☐ 210	Bill Lohrman	75.00	34.00	11.25
☐ 211	Pop Joiner	75.00	34.00	11.25
☐ 212	Babe Young	75.00	34.00	11.25
☐ 213	John Rucker	75.00	34.00	11.25
☐ 214	Ken O'Dea	75.00	34.00	11.25
☐ 215	Johnnie McCarthy	75.00	34.00	11.25
☐ 216	Joe Marty	75.00	34.00	11.25
☐ 217	Walter Beck	75.00	34.00	11.25
☐ 218	Wally Millies	75.00	34.00	11.25
☐ 219	Russ Bauers	75.00	34.00	11.25
☐ 220	Mace Brown	75.00	34.00	11.25
☐ 221	Lee Handley	75.00	34.00	11.25
☐ 222	Max Butcher	75.00	34.00	11.25
☐ 223	Hugh Jennings	150.00	67.50	22.50
☐ 224	Pie Traynor	175.00	80.00	27.00
☐ 225	Shoeless Joe Jackson	2000.00	800.00	200.00
☐ 226	Harry Hooper	150.00	67.50	22.50
☐ 227	Pop Haines	150.00	67.50	22.50
☐ 228	Charley Grimm	90.00	40.00	13.50
☐ 229	Buck Herzog	75.00	34.00	11.25
☐ 230	Red Faber	150.00	67.50	22.50
☐ 231	Dolf Luque	75.00	34.00	11.25
☐ 232	Goose Goslin	150.00	67.50	22.50
☐ 233	Moose Earnshaw	75.00	34.00	11.25
☐ 234	Frank(Husk) Chance	175.00	80.00	27.00
☐ 235	John J. McGraw	200.00	90.00	30.00
☐ 236	Jim Bottomley	150.00	67.50	22.50
☐ 237	Wee Willie Keeler	225.00	100.00	33.00
☐ 238	Tony Lazzeri	175.00	80.00	27.00
☐ 239	George Uhle	75.00	34.00	11.25
☐ 240	Bill Atwood	100.00	45.00	15.00

1941 Playball

HARRY "GUNBOAT" GUMBERT

26. HARRY EDWARD GUMBERT

The cards in this 72-card set measure 2 1/2" by 3 1/8". Many of the cards in the 1941 Play Ball series are simply color versions of pictures appearing in the 1940 set. This was the only color baseball card set produced by Gum, Inc., and it carries the catalog designation R336. Card numbers 49-72 are slightly more difficult to obtain as they were not issued until 1942. In 1942, numbers 1-48 were also reissued but without the copyright date. The cards were also printed on paper without a cardboard backing; these are generally encountered in sheets or strips.

		EX-MT	VG-E	GOOD
COMPLETE SET		10000.00	4000.00	1000.00
COMMON PLAYER (1-48)		45.00	20.00	6.75
COMMON PLAYER (49-72)		75.00	34.00	11.25
☐ 1	Eddie Miller	135.00	30.00	6.00
☐ 2	Max West	45.00	20.00	6.75
☐ 3	Bucky Walters	55.00	25.00	8.25
☐ 4	Paul Derringer	55.00	25.00	8.25
☐ 5	Buck McCormick	55.00	25.00	8.25
☐ 6	Carl Hubbell	200.00	90.00	30.00
☐ 7	Harry Danning	45.00	20.00	6.75
☐ 8	Mel Ott	250.00	110.00	37.50
☐ 9	Pinky May	45.00	20.00	6.75
☐ 10	Arky Vaughan	100.00	45.00	15.00
☐ 11	Debs Garms	45.00	20.00	6.75
☐ 12	Jimmy Brown	45.00	20.00	6.75
☐ 13	Jimmy Foxx	375.00	165.00	55.00

		EX-MT	VG-E	GOOD
☐ 14	Ted Williams	1500.00	600.00	150.00
☐ 15	Joe Cronin	125.00	57.50	18.75
☐ 16	Hal Trosky	55.00	25.00	8.25
☐ 17	Roy Weatherly	45.00	20.00	6.75
☐ 18	Hank Greenberg	250.00	110.00	37.50
☐ 19	Charlie Gehringer	200.00	90.00	30.00
☐ 20	Red Ruffing	125.00	57.50	18.75
☐ 21	Charlie Keller	75.00	34.00	11.25
☐ 22	Indian Bob Johnson	60.00	27.00	9.00
☐ 23	George McQuinn	45.00	20.00	6.75
☐ 24	Dutch Leonard	55.00	25.00	8.25
☐ 25	Gene Moore	45.00	20.00	6.75
☐ 26	Harry Gumpert	45.00	20.00	6.75
☐ 27	Babe Young	45.00	20.00	6.75
☐ 28	Joe Marty	45.00	20.00	6.75
☐ 29	Jack Wilson	45.00	20.00	6.75
☐ 30	Lou Finney	45.00	20.00	6.75
☐ 31	Joe Kuhel	45.00	20.00	6.75
☐ 32	Taft Wright	45.00	20.00	6.75
☐ 33	Al Milnar	45.00	20.00	6.75
☐ 34	Rollie Hemsley	45.00	20.00	6.75
☐ 35	Pinky Higgins	45.00	20.00	6.75
☐ 36	Barney McCosky	45.00	20.00	6.75
☐ 37	Bruce Campbell	45.00	20.00	6.75
☐ 38	Atley Donald	45.00	20.00	6.75
☐ 39	Tom Henrich	75.00	34.00	11.25
☐ 40	John Babich	45.00	20.00	6.75
☐ 41	Frank Blimp Hayes	45.00	20.00	6.75
☐ 42	Wally Moses	55.00	25.00	8.25
☐ 43	Al Brancato	45.00	20.00	6.75
☐ 44	Sam Chapman	45.00	20.00	6.75
☐ 45	Eldon Auker	45.00	20.00	6.75
☐ 46	Sid Hudson	45.00	20.00	6.75
☐ 47	Buddy Lewis	45.00	20.00	6.75
☐ 48	Cecil Travis	45.00	20.00	6.75
☐ 49	Babe Dahlgren	90.00	40.00	13.50
☐ 50	Johnny Cooney	75.00	34.00	11.25
☐ 51	Dolph Camilli	90.00	40.00	13.50
☐ 52	Kirby Higbe	75.00	34.00	11.25
☐ 53	Luke Hamlin	75.00	34.00	11.25
☐ 54	Pee Wee Reese	750.00	325.00	110.00
☐ 55	Whit Wyatt	90.00	40.00	13.50
☐ 56	Johnny VanderMeer	125.00	57.50	18.75
☐ 57	Moe Arnovich	75.00	34.00	11.25
☐ 58	Frank Demaree	75.00	34.00	11.25
☐ 59	Bill Jurges	75.00	34.00	11.25
☐ 60	Chuck Klein	200.00	90.00	30.00
☐ 61	Vince DiMaggio	250.00	110.00	37.50
☐ 62	Elbie Fletcher	75.00	34.00	11.25
☐ 63	Dom DiMaggio	250.00	110.00	37.50
☐ 64	Bobby Doerr	175.00	80.00	27.00
☐ 65	Tommy Bridges	90.00	40.00	13.50
☐ 66	Harland Clift	75.00	34.00	11.25
☐ 67	Walt Judnich	75.00	34.00	11.25
☐ 68	John Knott	75.00	34.00	11.25
☐ 69	George Case	90.00	40.00	13.50
☐ 70	Bill Dickey	500.00	225.00	75.00
☐ 71	Joe DiMaggio	2250.00	900.00	225.00
☐ 72	Lefty Gomez	450.00	125.00	25.00

1985 Polaroid Indians

Polaroid
JCPenney

BRETT
BUTLER
Outfielder

BRETT BUTLER

This 32-card set features cards (each measuring 2 13/16" by 4 1/8") of the Cleveland Indians. The cards are unnumbered except for uniform number, as they are listed below. The set was also sponsored by J.C. Penney and was distributed at the stadium to fans in attendance on Baseball Card Day.

		MINT	EXC	G-VG
COMPLETE SET (32)		21.00	9.00	3.00
COMMON PLAYER		.50	.20	.05
☐ 2	Brett Butler	1.25	.50	.12
☐ 4	Tony Bernazard	.60	.25	.06
☐ 8	Carmen Castillo	.50	.20	.05
☐ 10	Pat Tabler	.60	.25	.06
☐ 12	Benny Ayala	.50	.20	.05
☐ 13	Ernie Camacho	.50	.20	.05
☐ 14	Julio Franco	2.50	1.00	.25
☐ 16	Jerry Willard	.60	.25	.06
☐ 18	Pat Corrales MG	.60	.25	.06
☐ 20	Otis Nixon	1.00	.40	.10
☐ 21	Mike Hargrove	.90	.40	.09
☐ 22	Mike Fischlin	.50	.20	.05
☐ 23	Chris Bando	.50	.20	.05
☐ 24	George Vukovich	.50	.20	.05
☐ 26	Brook Jacoby	.75	.30	.07
☐ 27	Mel Hall	.90	.40	.09
☐ 28	Bert Blyleven	1.25	.50	.12
☐ 29	Andre Thornton	.90	.40	.09
☐ 30	Joe Carter	2.50	1.00	.25
☐ 32	Rick Behenna	.50	.20	.05
☐ 33	Roy Smith	.50	.20	.05
☐ 35	Jerry Reed	.50	.20	.05
☐ 36	Jamie Easterly	.50	.20	.05
☐ 38	Dave Von Ohlen	.50	.20	.05
☐ 41	Rich Thompson	.50	.20	.05
☐ 43	Bryan Clark	.50	.20	.05
☐ 44	Neal Heaton	.60	.25	.06
☐ 48	Vern Ruhle	.50	.20	.05
☐ 49	Jeff Barkley	.50	.20	.05
☐ 50	Ramon Romero	.50	.20	.05
☐ 54	Tom Waddell	.50	.20	.05
☐ xx	Coaching Staff	.50	.20	.05
	Bobby Bonds			
	John Goryl			
	Don McMahon			
	Ed Napolean			
	Dennis Sommers			

1979 Police Giants

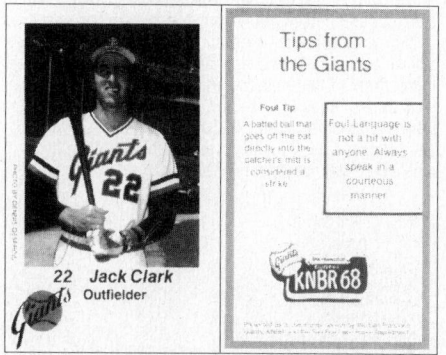

22 Jack Clark
Outfielder

The cards in this 30-card set measure 2 5/8" by 4 1/8". The 1979 Police Giants set features cards numbered by the player's uniform number. This full color set features the player's photo, the Giants' logo, and the player's name, number and position on the front of the cards. A facsimile autograph in an attractive blue ink is also contained on the front. The backs, printed in orange and black, feature Tips from the Giants, the Giants' and sponsoring radio station, KNBR, logos and a line listing the Giants, KNBR, and the San Francisco Police Department as sponsors of the set. The 15 cards which are shown with an asterisk below were available only from the Police. The other 15 cards were given away at the ballpark on June 17, 1979. These cards look very similar to the Giants police set issued in 1980,

the following year. Both sets credit Dennis Desprois photographically on each card but this (1979) set seems to have a fuzzier focus on the pictures. The sets can be distinguished on the front since this set's cards have a number sign before the player's uniform number on the front. Also on the card backs the KNBR logo is usually left justified for the cards in the 1979 set whereas the 1980 set has the KNBR logo centered on the card back.

		NRMT	VG-E	GOOD
COMPLETE SET (30)		18.00	7.50	2.50
COMMON PLAYER		.50	.20	.05
☐ 1	Dave Bristol MG	.50	.20	.05
☐ 2	Marc Hill	.50	.20	.05
☐ 3	Mike Sadek *	.60	.25	.06
☐ 5	Tom Haller	.50	.20	.05
☐ 6	Joe Altobelli CO *	.60	.25	.06
☐ 8	Larry Shepard CO *	.60	.25	.06
☐ 9	Heity Cruz	.50	.20	.05
☐ 10	Johnnie LeMaster	.50	.20	.05
☐ 12	Jim Davenport CO	.60	.25	.06
☐ 14	Vida Blue	.75	.30	.07
☐ 15	Mike Ivie	.50	.20	.05
☐ 16	Roger Metzger	.50	.20	.05
☐ 17	Randy Moffitt	.50	.20	.05
☐ 18	Bill Madlock	.75	.30	.07
☐ 21	Rob Andrews *	.60	.25	.06
☐ 22	Jack Clark *	3.00	1.25	.30
☐ 25	Dave Roberts	.50	.20	.05
☐ 26	John Montefusco	.60	.25	.06
☐ 28	Ed Halicki *	.60	.25	.06
☐ 30	John Tamargo	.50	.20	.05
☐ 31	Larry Herndon	.50	.20	.05
☐ 36	Bill North *	.60	.25	.06
☐ 39	Bob Knepper *	.75	.30	.07
☐ 40	John Curtis *	.60	.25	.06
☐ 41	Darrell Evans *	1.25	.50	.12
☐ 43	Tom Griffin *	.60	.25	.06
☐ 44	Willie McCovey *	3.50	1.50	.35
☐ 45	Terry Whitfield *	.60	.25	.06
☐ 46	Gary Lavelle *	.60	.25	.06
☐ 49	Max Venable *	.60	.25	.06

1980 Police Dodgers

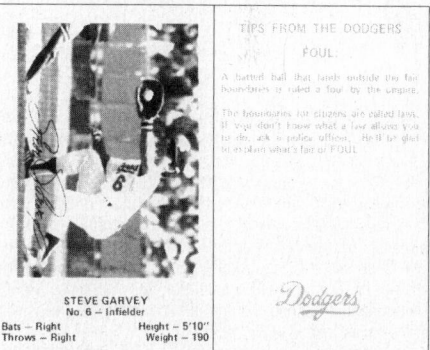

STEVE GARVEY
No. 6 – Infielder
Bats – Right   Height – 5'10"
Throws – Right   Weight – 190

The cards in this 30-card set measure 2 13/16" by 4 1/8". The full color 1980 Police Los Angeles Dodgers set features the player's name, uniform number, position, and biographical data on the fronts in addition to the photo. The backs feature Tips from the Dodgers, the LAPD logo, and the Dodgers' logo. The cards are listed below according to uniform number.

		MINT	EXC	G-VG
COMPLETE SET (30)		11.00	5.00	1.35
COMMON PLAYER		.35	.15	.03
☐ 5	Johnny Oates	.45	.18	.04
☐ 6	Steve Garvey	1.25	.50	.12
☐ 7	Steve Yeager	.35	.15	.03

		MINT	EXC	G-VG
☐ 8	Reggie Smith	.60	.25	.06
☐ 9	Gary Thomasson	.35	.15	.03
☐ 10	Ron Cey	.60	.25	.06
☐ 12	Dusty Baker	.60	.25	.06
☐ 13	Joe Ferguson	.35	.15	.03
☐ 15	Davey Lopes	.60	.25	.06
☐ 16	Rick Monday	.45	.18	.04
☐ 18	Bill Russell	.60	.25	.06
☐ 20	Don Sutton	1.00	.40	.10
☐ 21	Jay Johnstone	.60	.25	.06
☐ 23	Teddy Martinez	.35	.15	.03
☐ 27	Joe Beckwith	.35	.15	.03
☐ 28	Pedro Guerrero	1.25	.50	.12
☐ 29	Don Stanhouse	.35	.15	.03
☐ 30	Derrel Thomas	.35	.15	.03
☐ 31	Doug Rau	.35	.15	.03
☐ 34	Ken Brett	.35	.15	.03
☐ 35	Bob Welch	1.00	.40	.10
☐ 37	Robert Castillo	.35	.15	.03
☐ 38	Dave Goltz	.35	.15	.03
☐ 41	Jerry Reuss	.45	.18	.04
☐ 43	Rick Sutcliffe	.75	.30	.07
☐ 44	Mickey Hatcher	.35	.15	.03
☐ 46	Burt Hooton	.35	.15	.03
☐ 49	Charlie Hough	.45	.18	.04
☐ xx	Team Card (unnumbered)	.45	.18	.04

		MINT	EXC	G-VG
☐ 20	Joe Strain	.35	.15	.03
☐ 22	Jack Clark	2.00	.80	.20
☐ 26	John Montefusco	.45	.18	.04
☐ 28	Ed Halicki	.35	.15	.03
☐ 31	Larry Herndon	.35	.15	.03
☐ 32	Ed Whitson	.60	.25	.06
☐ 36	Bill North	.35	.15	.03
☐ 38	Greg Minton	.35	.15	.03
☐ 39	Bob Knepper	.45	.18	.04
☐ 41	Darrell Evans	1.00	.40	.10
☐ 42	John Van Ornum	.35	.15	.03
☐ 43	Tom Griffin	.35	.15	.03
☐ 44	Willie McCovey	2.50	1.00	.25
☐ 45	Terry Whitfield	.35	.15	.03
☐ 46	Gary Lavelle	.35	.15	.03
☐ 47	Don McMahon CO	.35	.15	.03

1981 Police Braves

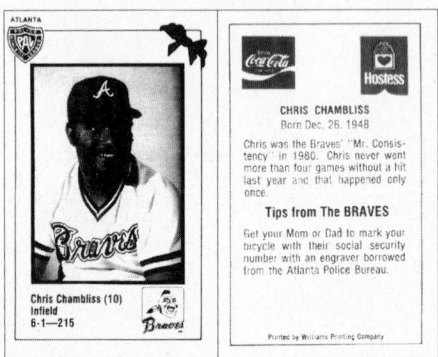

CHRIS CHAMBLISS
Born Dec. 26, 1948

Chris was the Braves' "Mr. Consistency" in 1980. Chris never went more than four games without a hit last year and that happened only once.

Tips from The BRAVES

Get your Mom or Dad to mark your bicycle with their social security number with an engraver borrowed from the Atlanta Police Bureau.

Chris Chambliss (10)
Infield
6-1—215

Printed by Williams Printing Company

1980 Police Giants

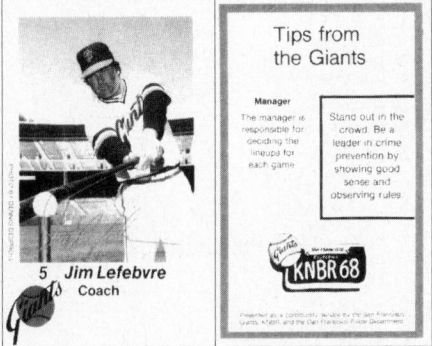

Tips from the Giants

Manager
The manager is responsible for deciding the lineup for each game

Stand out in the crowd. Be a leader in crime prevention by showing good sense and observing rules.

5   Jim Lefebvre
Coach

Presented as a contribution to the San Francisco Giants, KNBR, and the San Francisco Police Department.

The cards in this 31-card set measure 2 5/8" by 4 1/8". The 1980 Police San Francisco Giants set features cards numbered by the player's uniform number. This full color set features the player's photo, the Giants' logo, and the player's name, number and position on the front of the cards. A facsimile autograph in an attractive blue ink is also contained on the front. The backs, printed in orange and black, feature Tips from the Giants, the Giants' and sponsoring radio station, KNBR, logos and a line listing the Giants, KNBR, and the San Francisco Police Department as sponsors of the set. The sets were given away at the ballpark on May 31, 1980.

		MINT	EXC	G-VG
	COMPLETE SET (31)	12.00	5.25	1.50
	COMMON PLAYER	.35	.15	.03
☐ 1	Dave Bristol MG	.35	.15	.03
☐ 2	Marc Hill	.35	.15	.03
☐ 3	Mike Sadek	.35	.15	.03
☐ 5	Jim Lefebvre CO	.45	.18	.04
☐ 6	Rennie Stennett	.35	.15	.03
☐ 7	Milt May	.35	.15	.03
☐ 8	Vern Benson CO	.35	.15	.03
☐ 9	Jim Wohlford	.35	.15	.03
☐ 10	Johnnie LeMaster	.35	.15	.03
☐ 12	Jim Davenport CO	.45	.18	.04
☐ 14	Vida Blue	.60	.25	.06
☐ 15	Mike Ivie	.35	.15	.03
☐ 16	Roger Metzger	.35	.15	.03
☐ 17	Randy Moffitt	.35	.15	.03
☐ 19	Al Holland	.35	.15	.03

The cards in this 27-card set measure 2 5/8" by 4 1/8". This first Atlanta Police set features full color cards sponsored by the Braves, the Atlanta Police Department, Coca-Cola and Hostess. The cards are numbered by uniform number, which is contained on the front along with an Atlanta Police Athletic League logo, a black and white Braves logo, and a green bow in the upper right corner of the frameline. The backs feature brief player biographies, logos of Coke and Hostess, and Tips from the Braves. It is reported that 33,000 of these sets were printed. The Terry Harper card is supposed to be slightly more difficult to obtain than other cards in the set.

		MINT	EXC	G-VG
	COMPLETE SET (27)	11.00	5.00	1.35
	COMMON PLAYER	.35	.15	.03
☐ 1	Jerry Royster	.35	.15	.03
☐ 3	Dale Murphy	3.00	1.25	.30
☐ 4	Biff Pocoroba	.35	.15	.03
☐ 5	Bob Horner	.75	.30	.07
☐ 6	Bobby Cox MG	.35	.15	.03
☐ 9	Luis Gomez	.35	.15	.03
☐ 10	Chris Chambliss	.60	.25	.06
☐ 15	Bill Nahorodny	.35	.15	.03
☐ 16	Rafael Ramirez	.45	.18	.04
☐ 17	Glenn Hubbard	.35	.15	.03
☐ 18	Claudell Washington	.45	.18	.04
☐ 19	Terry Harper SP	.75	.30	.07
☐ 20	Bruce Benedict	.35	.15	.03
☐ 24	John Montefusco	.45	.18	.04
☐ 25	Rufino Linares	.35	.15	.03
☐ 26	Gene Garber	.45	.18	.04
☐ 30	Brian Asselstine	.35	.15	.03
☐ 34	Larry Bradford	.35	.15	.03
☐ 35	Phil Niekro	1.75	.70	.17
☐ 37	Rick Camp	.35	.15	.03
☐ 39	Al Hrabosky	.45	.18	.04
☐ 40	Tommy Boggs	.35	.15	.03
☐ 42	Rick Mahler	.45	.18	.04
☐ 44	Hank Aaron CO	2.50	1.00	.25
☐ 45	Ed Miller	.35	.15	.03
☐ 46	Gaylord Perry	1.75	.70	.17
☐ 49	Preston Hanna	.35	.15	.03

1981 Police Dodgers

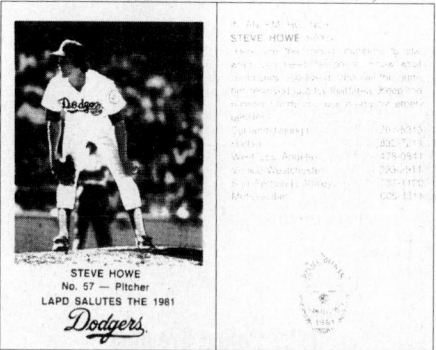

STEVE HOWE
No. 57 — Pitcher
LAPD SALUTES THE 1981
Dodgers

The cards in this 32-card set measure 2 13/16" by 4 1/8". The full color set of 1981 Los Angeles Dodgers features the player's name, number, position and a line stating that the LAPD salutes the 1981 Dodgers, in addition to the player's photo. The backs feature the LAPD logo and short narratives, attributable to the player on the front of the card, revealing police associated tips. The cards of Ken Landreaux and Dave Stewart are reported to be more difficult to obtain than other cards in this set due to the fact that they are replacements for Stanhouse (released 4/17/81) and Hatcher (traded for Landreaux 3/30/81). The complete set price below refers to all 32 cards, i.e., including the variations.

		MINT	EXC	G-VG
COMPLETE SET (32)		12.00	5.25	1.50
COMMON PLAYER		.35	.15	.03
☐ 2	Tom Lasorda MG	.60	.25	.06
☐ 3	Rudy Law	.35	.15	.03
☐ 6	Steve Garvey	1.25	.50	.12
☐ 7	Steve Yeager	.35	.15	.03
☐ 8	Reggie Smith	.60	.25	.06
☐ 10	Ron Cey	.60	.25	.06
☐ 12	Dusty Baker	.60	.25	.06
☐ 13	Joe Ferguson	.35	.15	.03
☐ 14	Mike Scioscia	.45	.18	.04
☐ 15	Davey Lopes	.60	.25	.06
☐ 16	Rick Monday	.45	.18	.04
☐ 18	Bill Russell	.60	.25	.06
☐ 21	Jay Johnstone	.60	.25	.06
☐ 26	Don Stanhouse	.45	.18	.04
☐ 27	Joe Beckwith	.35	.15	.03
☐ 28	Pedro Guerrero	1.00	.40	.10
☐ 30	Derrel Thomas	.35	.15	.03
☐ 34	Fernando Valenzuela	2.00	.80	.20
☐ 35	Bob Welch	.75	.30	.07
☐ 36	Pepe Frias	.35	.15	.03
☐ 37	Robert Castillo	.35	.15	.03
☐ 38	Dave Goltz	.35	.15	.03
☐ 41	Jerry Reuss	.45	.18	.04
☐ 43	Rick Sutcliffe	.75	.30	.07
☐ 44A	Mickey Hatcher	.45	.18	.04
☐ 44B	Ken Landreaux	1.25	.50	.12
☐ 46	Burt Hooton	.35	.15	.03
☐ 48	Dave Stewart	2.50	1.00	.25
☐ 51	Terry Forster	.45	.18	.04
☐ 57	Steve Howe	.35	.15	.03
☐ xx	Team Photo (Checklist) (unnumbered)	.45	.18	.04
☐ xx	Coaching Staff (unnumbered)	.35	.15	.03

    Monty Basgall
    Tom Lasorda MG
    Danny Ozark
    Ron Perranoski
    Manny Mota
    Mark Creese

1981 Police Mariners

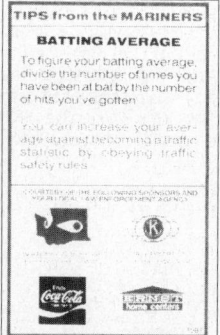

JULIO CRUZ Second Base
Seattle Mariners

The cards in this 16-card set measure 2 5/8" by 4 1/8". The full color Seattle Mariners Police set of this year was sponsored by the Washington State Crime Prevention Association, the Kiwanis Club, Coca-Cola and Ernst Home Centers. The fronts feature the player's name, his position, and the Seattle Mariners name in addition to the player's photo. The backs, in red and blue, feature Tips from the Mariners and the logos of the four sponsors of the set. The cards are numbered in the lower left corners of the backs.

		MINT	EXC	G-VG
COMPLETE SET (16)		5.50	2.50	.55
COMMON PLAYER (1-16)		.35	.15	.03
☐ 1	Jeff Burroughs	.50	.20	.05
☐ 2	Floyd Bannister	.50	.20	.05
☐ 3	Glenn Abbott	.35	.15	.03
☐ 4	Jim Anderson	.35	.15	.03
☐ 5	Danny Meyer	.35	.15	.03
☐ 6	Julio Cruz	.50	.20	.05
☐ 7	Dave Edler	.35	.15	.03
☐ 8	Kenny Clay	.35	.15	.03
☐ 9	Lenny Randle	.35	.15	.03
☐ 10	Mike Parrott	.35	.15	.03
☐ 11	Tom Paciorek	.50	.20	.05
☐ 12	Jerry Narron	.35	.15	.03
☐ 13	Richie Zisk	.50	.20	.05
☐ 14	Maury Wills MG	.75	.30	.07
☐ 15	Joe Simpson	.35	.15	.03
☐ 16	Shane Rawley	.50	.20	.05

1981 Police Royals

FRANK WHITE

2nd Base
5'-11"
170 lbs.

The cards in this 10-card set measure 2 1/2" by 4 1/8". The 1981 Police Kansas City Royals set features full color cards of Royals players. The fronts feature the player's name, position, height and weight, and the Royals' logo in addition to the photo and facsimile autograph of the player. The backs feature player statistics, Tips from the Royals, and identification of the sponsoring organizations. This set can be distinguished from the 1983 Police Royals set by the statistics on the backs of these 1981 cards, whereas the 1983 cards only show a biographical paragraph in tyhe same space.

	MINT	EXC	G-VG
COMPLETE SET (10)	30.00	13.50	4.50
COMMON PLAYER (1-10)	2.00	.80	.20
☐ 1 Willie Aikens	2.00	.80	.20
☐ 2 George Brett	18.00	7.50	2.50
☐ 3 Rich Gale	2.00	.80	.20
☐ 4 Clint Hurdle	2.00	.80	.20
☐ 5 Dennis Leonard	2.50	1.00	.25
☐ 6 Hal McRae	3.00	1.25	.30
☐ 7 Amos Otis	2.50	1.00	.25
☐ 8 U.L. Washington	2.00	.80	.20
☐ 9 Frank White	3.50	1.50	.35
☐ 10 Willie Wilson	3.50	1.50	.35

1982 Police Braves

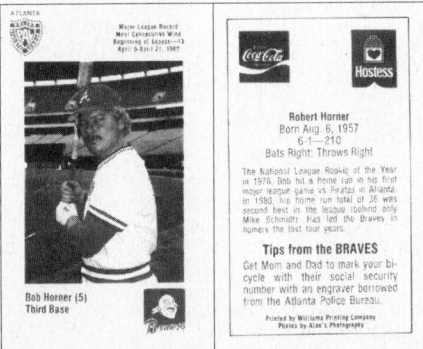

Bob Horner (5)
Third Base

The cards in this 30-card set measure 2 5/8" by 4 1/8". The Atlanta Police Department followed up on their successful 1981 safety set by publishing a new Braves set for 1982. Featured in excellent color photos are manager Joe Torre, 24 players, and 5 coaches. The cards are numbered, by uniform number, on the front only, while the backs contain a short biography of the individual and a Tips from the Braves section. The logos for the Atlanta PAL and the Braves appear on the front; those of Coca-Cola and Hostess are found on the back. A line commemorating Atlanta's record-shattering, season-beginning win streak is located in the upper right corner on every card obverse. The player list on the reverse of the Torre card is a roster list and not a checklist for the set. There were 8,000 sets reportedly printed. The Bob Watson card is supposedly more difficult to obtain than others in this set.

	MINT	EXC	G-VG
COMPLETE SET (30)	18.00	7.50	2.50
COMMON PLAYER	.50	.20	.05
☐ 1 Jerry Royster	.50	.20	.05
☐ 3 Dale Murphy	5.00	2.25	.50
☐ 4 Biff Pocoroba	.50	.20	.05
☐ 5 Bob Horner	.90	.40	.09
☐ 6 Randy Johnson	.50	.20	.05
☐ 8 Bob Watson	1.50	.60	.15
☐ 9 Joe Torre MG	1.00	.40	.10
☐ 10 Chris Chambliss	.75	.30	.07
☐ 15 Claudell Washington	.60	.25	.06
☐ 16 Rafael Ramirez	.50	.20	.05

☐ 17 Glenn Hubbard	.50	.20	.05
☐ 20 Bruce Benedict	.50	.20	.05
☐ 22 Brett Butler	1.25	.50	.12
☐ 23 Tommy Aaron CO	.60	.25	.06
☐ 25 Rufino Linares	.50	.20	.05
☐ 26 Gene Garber	.50	.20	.05
☐ 27 Larry McWilliams	.50	.20	.05
☐ 28 Larry Whisenton	.50	.20	.05
☐ 32 Steve Bedrosian	.90	.40	.09
☐ 35 Phil Niekro	2.50	1.00	.25
☐ 37 Rick Camp	.50	.20	.05
☐ 38 Joe Cowley	.50	.20	.05
☐ 39 Al Hrabosky	.60	.25	.06
☐ 42 Rick Mahler	.50	.20	.05
☐ 43 Bob Walk	.75	.30	.07
☐ 45 Bob Gibson CO	1.50	.60	.15
☐ 49 Preston Hanna	.50	.20	.05
☐ 52 Joe Pignatano CO	.50	.20	.05
☐ 53 Dal Maxvill CO	.50	.20	.05
☐ 54 Rube Walker CO	.50	.20	.05

1982 Police Brewers

PAUL MOLITOR
No. 4 — Third Base
New Berlin Police Department
Salutes The 1982
Milwaukee Brewers

The cards in this 30-card set measure 2 13/16" by 4 1/8". This set of Milwaukee Brewers baseball cards is noted for its excellent color photographs set upon a simple white background. The set was initially distributed at the stadium on May 5th, but was also handed out by several local police departments, and credit lines for the Wisconsin State Fair Park Police (no shield design on reverse), Milwaukee, Brookfield, and Wauwatosa PD's have already been found. The reverses feature advice concerning safety measures, social situations, and crime prevention (Romero card in both Spanish and English). The team card carries a checklist which lists the Brewer's coaches separately although they all appear on a single card; VP/GM Harry Dalton is not mentioned on this list but is included in the set. The prices below are for the basic set without regard to the Police Department listed on the backs. Cards from the more obscure corners and small towns of Wisconsin (where fewer cards were produced) will be valued higher.

	MINT	EXC	G-VG
COMPLETE SET (30)	14.00	6.25	2.00
COMMON PLAYER	.40	.16	.04
☐ 4 Paul Molitor	1.50	.60	.15
☐ 5 Ned Yost	.40	.16	.04
☐ 7 Don Money	.40	.16	.04
☐ 9 Larry Hisle	.50	.20	.05
☐ 10 Bob McClure	.40	.16	.04
☐ 11 Ed Romero	.40	.16	.04
☐ 13 Roy Howell	.40	.16	.04
☐ 15 Cecil Cooper	.75	.30	.07
☐ 17 Jim Gantner	.60	.25	.06
☐ 19 Robin Yount	3.00	1.25	.30
☐ 20 Gorman Thomas	.60	.25	.06
☐ 22 Charlie Moore	.40	.16	.04
☐ 23 Ted Simmons	.75	.30	.07
☐ 24 Ben Oglivie	.50	.20	.05

		MINT	EXC	G-VG
☐ 26	Kevin Bass	.50	.20	.05
☐ 28	Jamie Easterly	.40	.16	.04
☐ 29	Mark Brouhard	.40	.16	.04
☐ 30	Moose Haas	.40	.16	.04
☐ 34	Rollie Fingers	1.50	.60	.15
☐ 35	Randy Lerch	.40	.16	.04
☐ 41	Jim Slaton	.40	.16	.04
☐ 45	Doug Jones	.75	.30	.07
☐ 46	Jerry Augustine	.40	.16	.04
☐ 47	Dwight Bernard	.40	.16	.04
☐ 48	Mike Caldwell	.50	.20	.05
☐ 50	Pete Vuckovich	.50	.20	.05
☐ xx	Team Card	.50	.20	.05
	(unnumbered)			
☐ xx	Harry Dalton GM	.40	.16	.04
	(unnumbered)			
☐ xx	Buck Rodgers MG	.50	.20	.05
	(unnumbered)			
☐ xx	Brewer Coaches	.40	.16	.04
	(unnumbered)			
	Ron Hansen			
	Bob Rodgers MG			
	Harry Warner			
	Larry Haney			
	Cal McLish			

1982 Police Dodgers

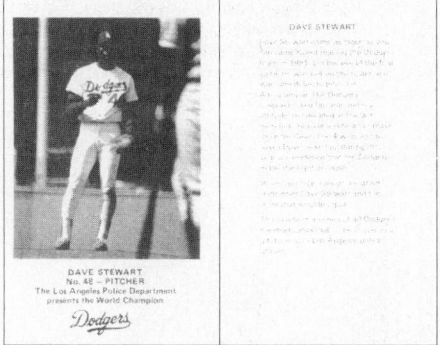

DAVE STEWART
No. 48 – PITCHER
The Los Angeles Police Department
presents the World Champion
Dodgers

The cards in this 30-card set measure 2 13/16" by 4 1/8". The 1982 Los Angeles Dodgers police set depicts the players and events of the 1981 season. There is a World Series trophy card, three cards commemorating the Division, League, and World Series wins, one manager card, and 25 player cards. The obverses have brilliant color photos set on white, and the player cards are numbered according to the uniform number of the individual. The reverses contain biographical material, information about stadium events, and a safety feature emphasizing "the team that wouldn't quit."

		MINT	EXC	G-VG
	COMPLETE SET (30)	9.00	4.00	.90
	COMMON PLAYER	.25	.10	.02
☐ 2	Tom Lasorda MG	.45	.18	.04
☐ 6	Steve Garvey	1.00	.40	.10
☐ 7	Steve Yeager	.25	.10	.02
☐ 8	Mark Belanger	.35	.15	.03
☐ 10	Ron Cey	.45	.18	.04
☐ 12	Dusty Baker	.35	.15	.03
☐ 14	Mike Scioscia	.35	.15	.03
☐ 16	Rick Monday	.35	.15	.03
☐ 18	Bill Russell	.35	.15	.03
☐ 21	Jay Johnstone	.35	.15	.03
☐ 26	Alejandro Pena	.45	.18	.04
☐ 28	Pedro Guerrero	1.00	.40	.10
☐ 30	Derrel Thomas	.25	.10	.02
☐ 31	Jorge Orta	.25	.10	.02
☐ 34	Fernando Valenzuela	1.00	.40	.10
☐ 35	Bob Welch	.60	.25	.06
☐ 38	Dave Goltz	.25	.10	.02
☐ 40	Ron Roenicke	.25	.10	.02
☐ 41	Jerry Reuss	.25	.10	.02
☐ 44	Ken Landreaux	.25	.10	.02
☐ 46	Burt Hooton	.25	.10	.02

		MINT	EXC	G-VG
☐ 48	Dave Stewart	.75	.30	.07
☐ 49	Tom Niedenfuer	.25	.10	.02
☐ 51	Terry Forster	.35	.15	.03
☐ 52	Steve Sax	1.00	.40	.10
☐ 57	Steve Howe	.25	.10	.02
☐ xx	World Series Trophy	.25	.10	.02
	(checklist back)			
	(unnumbered)			
☐ xx	World Series	.25	.10	.02
	Commemorative			
	(unnumbered)			
☐ xx	NL Champions	.25	.10	.02
	(unnumbered)			
☐ xx	Division Champs	.25	.10	.02
	(unnumbered)			

1983 Police Braves

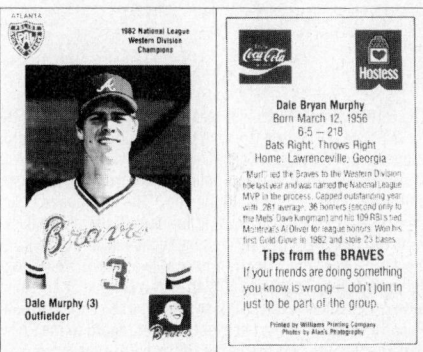

The cards in this 30-card set measure 2 5/8" by 4 1/8". For the third year in a row, the Atlanta Braves, in cooperation with the Atlanta Police Department, Coca-Cola, and Hostess, issued a full color safety set. The set features Joe Torre, five coaches, and 24 of the Atlanta Braves. Numbered only by uniform number, the statement that the Braves were the 1982 National League Western Division Champions is included on the fronts along with the Braves and Police Athletic biographies, a short narrative on the player, Tips from the Braves, and the Coke and Hostess logos.

		MINT	EXC	G-VG
	COMPLETE SET (30)	12.50	5.50	1.65
	COMMON PLAYER	.35	.15	.03
☐ 1	Jerry Royster	.35	.15	.03
☐ 3	Dale Murphy	3.50	1.50	.35
☐ 4	Biff Pocoroba	.35	.15	.03
☐ 5	Bob Horner	.90	.40	.09
☐ 6	Randy Johnson	.35	.15	.03
☐ 8	Bob Watson	.50	.20	.05
☐ 9	Joe Torre MG	.75	.30	.07
☐ 10	Chris Chambliss	.50	.20	.05
☐ 11	Ken Smith	.35	.15	.03
☐ 15	Claudell Washington	.50	.20	.05
☐ 16	Rafael Ramirez	.35	.15	.03
☐ 17	Glenn Hubbard	.35	.15	.03
☐ 19	Terry Harper	.35	.15	.03
☐ 20	Bruce Benedict	.35	.15	.03
☐ 22	Brett Butler	.90	.40	.09
☐ 24	Larry Owen	.35	.15	.03
☐ 26	Gene Garber	.35	.15	.03
☐ 27	Pascual Perez	.60	.25	.06
☐ 29	Craig McMurtry	.35	.15	.03
☐ 32	Steve Bedrosian	.60	.25	.06
☐ 33	Pete Falcone	.35	.15	.03
☐ 35	Phil Niekro	1.50	.60	.15
☐ 36	Sonny Jackson CO	.35	.15	.03
☐ 37	Rick Camp	.35	.15	.03
☐ 45	Bob Gibson CO	1.50	.60	.15
☐ 49	Rick Behenna	.35	.15	.03
☐ 51	Terry Forster	.50	.20	.05
☐ 52	Joe Pignatano CO	.35	.15	.03
☐ 53	Dal Maxvill CO	.35	.15	.03
☐ 54	Rube Walker CO	.35	.15	.03

1983 Police Brewers

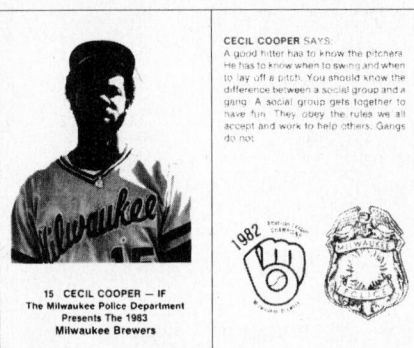

The cards in this 30-card set measure 2 13/16" by 4 1/8". The 1983 Police Milwaukee Brewers set contains full color cards issued by the Milwaukee Police Department in conjunction with the Brewers. The cards are numbered on the fronts by the player uniform number and contain the line, "The Milwaukee Police Department Presents the 1983 Milwaukee Braves." The backs contain a brief narrative attributable to the player on the front, the Milwaukee Police logo, and a Milwaukee Brewers logo stating that they were the 1982 American League Champions. In all, 28 variations of these Police sets have been found to date. Prices below are for the basic set without regard to the Police Department listed on the backs of the cards; cards from the more obscure corners and small towns of Wisconsin (whose cards were produced in lesser quantities) will be valued higher.

		MINT	EXC	G-VG
COMPLETE SET (30)		9.00	4.00	.90
COMMON PLAYER		.25	.10	.02
☐ 4	Paul Molitor	1.00	.40	.10
☐ 5	Ned Yost	.25	.10	.02
☐ 7	Don Money	.35	.15	.03
☐ 8	Rob Picciolo	.25	.10	.02
☐ 10	Bob McClure	.25	.10	.02
☐ 11	Ed Romero	.25	.10	.02
☐ 12	Larry Haney CO	.25	.10	.02
☐ 13	Roy Howell	.25	.10	.02
☐ 15	Cecil Cooper	.50	.20	.05
☐ 16	Marshall Edwards	.25	.10	.02
☐ 17	Jim Gantner	.35	.15	.03
☐ 18	Ron Hansen CO	.25	.10	.02
☐ 19	Robin Yount	2.00	.80	.20
☐ 20	Gorman Thomas	.50	.20	.05
☐ 21	Don Sutton	1.00	.40	.10
☐ 22	Charlie Moore	.25	.10	.02
☐ 23	Ted Simmons	.60	.25	.06
☐ 24	Ben Oglivie	.35	.15	.03
☐ 26	Bob Skube	.25	.10	.02
☐ 27	Pete Ladd	.25	.10	.02
☐ 28	Jamie Easterly	.25	.10	.02
☐ 30	Moose Haas	.35	.15	.03
☐ 32	Harvey Kuenn MG	.50	.20	.05
☐ 34	Rollie Fingers	1.25	.50	.12
☐ 40	Bob L. Gibson	.25	.10	.02
☐ 41	Jim Slaton	.25	.10	.02
☐ 42	Tom Tellmann	.25	.10	.02
☐ 45	Pat Dobson CO	.35	.15	.03
☐ 46	Jerry Augustine	.25	.10	.02
☐ 48	Mike Caldwell	.35	.15	.03
☐ 50	Pete Vuckovich	.35	.15	.03
☐ xx	Dave Garcia CO	.25	.10	.02
☐ xx	Team Photo	.35	.15	.03
	(Checklist back)			
	(unnumbered)			

1983 Police Dodgers

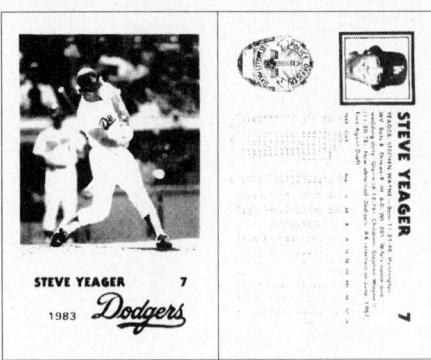

The cards in this 30-card set measure 2 13/16" by 4 1/8". The full color Police Los Angeles Dodgers set of 1983 features the player's name and uniform number on the front along with the Dodger's logo, the year, and the player's photo. The backs feature a small insert portrait picture of the player, player biographies, and career statistics. The logo of the Los Angeles Police Department, the sponsor of the set, is found on the backs of the cards.

		MINT	EXC	G-VG
COMPLETE SET (30)		8.00	3.50	.80
COMMON PLAYER		.25	.10	.02
☐ 2	Tom Lasorda MG	.45	.18	.04
☐ 3	Steve Sax	.75	.30	.07
☐ 5	Mike Marshall	.45	.18	.04
☐ 7	Steve Yeager	.35	.15	.03
☐ 12	Dusty Baker	.35	.15	.03
☐ 14	Mike Scioscia	.35	.15	.03
☐ 16	Rick Monday	.35	.15	.03
☐ 17	Greg Brock	.25	.10	.02
☐ 18	Bill Russell	.35	.15	.03
☐ 20	Candy Maldonado	.35	.15	.03
☐ 21	Ricky Wright	.25	.10	.02
☐ 22	Mark Bradley	.25	.10	.02
☐ 23	Dave Sax	.25	.10	.02
☐ 26	Alejandro Pena	.35	.15	.03
☐ 27	Joe Beckwith	.25	.10	.02
☐ 28	Pedro Guerrero	.75	.30	.07
☐ 30	Derrel Thomas	.25	.10	.02
☐ 34	Fernando Valenzuela	.75	.30	.07
☐ 35	Bob Welch	.60	.25	.06
☐ 38	Pat Zachry	.25	.10	.02
☐ 40	Ron Roenicke	.25	.10	.02
☐ 41	Jerry Reuss	.25	.10	.02
☐ 43	Jose Morales	.25	.10	.02
☐ 44	Ken Landreaux	.25	.10	.02
☐ 46	Burt Hooton	.25	.10	.02
☐ 47	Larry White	.25	.10	.02
☐ 48	Dave Stewart	.75	.30	.07
☐ 49	Tom Niedenfuer	.25	.10	.02
☐ 57	Steve Howe	.25	.10	.02
☐ xx	Coaching Staff	.25	.10	.02
	(unnumbered)			

1983 Police Royals

The cards in this 10-card set measure 2 1/2" by 4 1/8". The 1983 Police Kansas City Royals set features full color cards of Royals players. The fronts feature the player's name, height and weight, and the Royals' logo in addition to the player's photo and a facsimile autograph. The backs feature Kids and Cops Facts about the players, Tips from the Royals, and identification of the sponsors of the set. The cards are unnumbered. This set can be distinguished from the 1981 Police Royals set by the

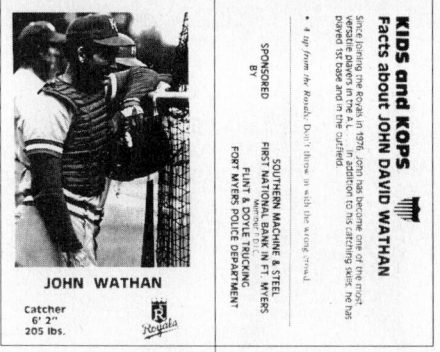

JOHN WATHAN

Catcher
6' 2"
205 lbs.

KIDS and KOPS
Facts about JOHN DAVID WATHAN

SPONSORED BY

SOUTHERN MACHINE & STEEL
FIRST NATIONAL BANK IN FT. MYERS
FLINT & DOYLE TRUCKING
FORT MYERS POLICE DEPARTMENT

• 4 up from the Royals: Don't throw in with the wrong crowd.

Since joining the Royals in 1976, John has become one of the most versatile players in addition to his catching skills, he has played first base and in the outfield.

absence of statistics on the backs of these 1983 cards, since these 1983 cards only show a brief biographical paragraph.

	MINT	EXC	G-VG
COMPLETE SET (10)	28.00	12.50	4.00
COMMON PLAYER (1-10)	1.75	.70	.17

		MINT	EXC	G-VG
☐	1 Willie Aikens	1.75	.70	.17
☐	2 George Brett	16.00	6.75	2.25
☐	3 Dennis Leonard	2.25	.90	.22
☐	4 Hal McRae	3.00	1.25	.30
☐	5 Amos Otis	2.25	.90	.22
☐	6 Dan Quisenberry	3.00	1.25	.30
☐	7 U.L. Washington	1.75	.70	.17
☐	8 John Wathan	2.25	.90	.22
☐	9 Frank White	3.00	1.25	.30
☐	10 Willie Wilson	3.00	1.25	.30

1984 Police Braves

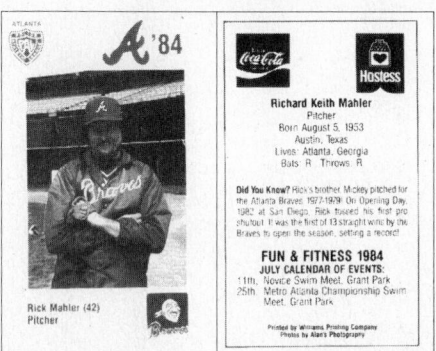

ATLANTA

A '84

Richard Keith Mahler
Pitcher
Born August 5, 1953
Austin, Texas
Lives: Atlanta, Georgia
Bats: R Throws: R

Did You Know? Rick's brother Mickey pitched for the Atlanta Braves 1977-1979. On Opening Day, 1982 at San Diego, Rick tossed his first pro shutout. It was the first of 13 straight wins by the Braves to open the season, setting a record.

FUN & FITNESS 1984
JULY CALENDAR OF EVENTS:
11th. Novice Swim Meet, Grant Park
25th. Metro Atlanta Championship Swim Meet, Grant Park

Rick Mahler (42)
Pitcher

Printed by Williams Printing Company
Photos by Alan's Photography

The cards in this 30-card set measure 2 5/8" by 4 1/8". For the fourth straight year, the Atlanta Police Department issued a full color set of Atlanta Braves. The cards were given out two per week by Atlanta police officers. In addition to the police department, the set was sponsored by Coke and Hostess. The backs of the cards of Perez and Ramirez are in Spanish. The Joe Torre card contains the checklist.

	MINT	EXC	G-VG
COMPLETE SET (30)	12.00	5.25	1.50
COMMON PLAYER	.30	.12	.03

		MINT	EXC	G-VG
☐	1 Jerry Royster	.30	.12	.03
☐	3 Dale Murphy	3.00	1.25	.30
☐	5 Bob Horner	.75	.30	.07
☐	6 Randy Johnson	.30	.12	.03
☐	8 Bob Watson	.40	.16	.04
☐	9 Joe Torre MG	.60	.25	.06
	(checklist back)			

		MINT	EXC	G-VG
☐	10 Chris Chambliss	.50	.20	.05
☐	11 Mike Jorgensen	.30	.12	.03
☐	15 Claudell Washington	.40	.16	.04
☐	16 Rafael Ramirez	.30	.12	.03
☐	17 Glenn Hubbard	.30	.12	.03
☐	19 Terry Harper	.30	.12	.03
☐	20 Bruce Benedict	.30	.12	.03
☐	25 Alex Trevino	.30	.12	.03
☐	26 Gene Garber	.30	.12	.03
☐	27 Pascual Perez	.50	.20	.05
☐	28 Gerald Perry	.50	.20	.05
☐	29 Craig McMurtry	.30	.12	.03
☐	31 Donnie Moore	.30	.12	.03
☐	32 Steve Bedrosian	.50	.20	.05
☐	33 Pete Falcone	.30	.12	.03
☐	37 Rick Camp	.30	.12	.03
☐	39 Len Barker	.40	.16	.04
☐	42 Rick Mahler	.30	.12	.03
☐	45 Bob Gibson CO	1.00	.40	.10
☐	51 Terry Forster	.40	.16	.04
☐	52 Joe Pignatano CO	.30	.12	.03
☐	53 Dal Maxvill CO	.30	.12	.03
☐	54 Rube Walker CO	.30	.12	.03
☐	55 Luke Appling CO	.60	.25	.06

1984 Police Brewers

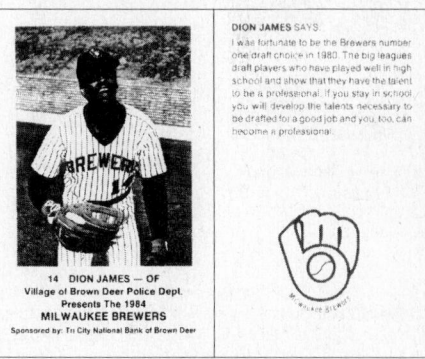

DION JAMES SAYS:
I was fortunate to be the Brewers number one draft choice in 1980. The big leagues draft players who have played well in high school and show that they have the talent to be a professional. If you stay in school, you will develop the talents necessary to be drafted for a good job and you, too, can become a professional.

14 DION JAMES — OF
Village of Brown Deer Police Dept.
Presents The 1984
MILWAUKEE BREWERS
Sponsored by: Tri City National Bank of Brown Deer

The cards in this 30-card set measure 2 13/16" by 4 1/8". Again this year, the police departments in and around Milwaukee issued sets of the Milwaukee Brewers. Although each set contained the same players and numbers, the individual police departments placed their own name on the fronts of cards to show that they were the particular jurisdiction issuing the set. The backs contain the Brewers logo, a safety tip, and in some cases, a badge of the jurisdiction. To date, 59 variations of this set have been found. Prices below are for the basic set without regard to the Police Department issuing the cards; cards from the more obscure corners and small towns of Wisconsin will be valued higher. Cards are numbered by uniform number.

	MINT	EXC	G-VG
COMPLETE SET (30)	7.00	3.00	.70
COMMON PLAYER	.20	.08	.02

		MINT	EXC	G-VG
☐	2 Randy Ready	.25	.10	.02
☐	4 Paul Molitor	.75	.30	.07
☐	8 Jim Sundberg	.25	.10	.02
☐	9 Rene Lachemann MG	.25	.10	.02
☐	10 Bob McClure	.20	.08	.02
☐	11 Ed Romero	.20	.08	.02
☐	13 Roy Howell	.20	.08	.02
☐	14 Dion James	.25	.10	.02
☐	15 Cecil Cooper	.45	.18	.04
☐	17 Jim Gantner	.30	.12	.03
☐	19 Robin Yount	1.75	.70	.17
☐	20 Don Sutton	.75	.30	.07
☐	21 Bill Schroeder	.25	.10	.02
☐	22 Charlie Moore	.20	.08	.02
☐	23 Ted Simmons	.60	.25	.06
☐	24 Ben Oglivie	.35	.15	.03
☐	25 Bob Clark	.20	.08	.02

			MINT	EXC	G-VG
☐	27	Pete Ladd	.20	.08	.02
☐	28	Rick Manning	.20	.08	.02
☐	29	Mark Brouhard	.20	.08	.02
☐	30	Moose Haas	.25	.10	.02
☐	34	Rollie Fingers	.90	.40	.09
☐	42	Tom Tellmann	.20	.08	.02
☐	43	Chuck Porter	.20	.08	.02
☐	46	Jerry Augustine	.20	.08	.02
☐	47	Jaime Cocanower	.20	.08	.02
☐	48	Mike Caldwell	.25	.10	.02
☐	50	Pete Vuckovich	.30	.12	.03
☐	xx	Coaches Card (unnumbered)	.25	.10	.02
☐	xx	Team Photo (Checklist back) (unnumbered)	.25	.10	.02

1984 Police Dodgers

The cards in this 30-card set measure 2 13/16" by 4 1/8". For the fifth straight year, the Los Angeles Police Department sponsored a set of Dodger baseball cards. The set is numbered by player uniform number, which is featured on both the fronts and backs of the cards. The Dodgers' logo appears on the front, and the LAPD logo is superimposed on the backs of the cards. The backs are printed in Dodger blue ink and contain a small photo of the player on the front. Player biographical data and "Dare to Say No" antidrug information are featured on the back.

			MINT	EXC	G-VG
	COMPLETE SET (30)		8.00	3.50	.80
	COMMON PLAYER		.20	.08	.02
☐	2	Tom Lasorda MG	.40	.16	.04
☐	3	Steve Sax	.75	.30	.07
☐	5	Mike Marshall	.40	.16	.04
☐	7	Steve Yeager	.30	.12	.03
☐	9	Greg Brock	.20	.08	.02
☐	10	Dave Anderson	.20	.08	.02
☐	14	Mike Scioscia	.30	.12	.03
☐	16	Rick Monday	.25	.10	.02
☐	17	Rafael Landestoy	.20	.08	.02
☐	18	Bill Russell	.30	.12	.03
☐	20	Candy Maldonado	.30	.12	.03
☐	21	Bob Bailor	.20	.08	.02
☐	25	German Rivera	.20	.08	.02
☐	26	Alejandro Pena	.30	.12	.03
☐	27	Carlos Diaz	.20	.08	.02
☐	28	Pedro Guerrero	.75	.30	.07
☐	31	Jack Fimple	.20	.08	.02
☐	34	Fernando Valenzuela	.75	.30	.07
☐	35	Bob Welch	.60	.25	.06
☐	38	Pat Zachry	.20	.08	.02
☐	40	Rick Honeycutt	.20	.08	.02
☐	41	Jerry Reuss	.20	.08	.02
☐	43	Jose Morales	.20	.08	.02
☐	44	Ken Landreaux	.20	.08	.02
☐	45	Terry Whitfield	.20	.08	.02
☐	46	Burt Hooton	.20	.08	.02
☐	49	Tom Niedenfuer	.25	.10	.02
☐	55	Orel Hershiser	3.00	1.25	.30

			MINT	EXC	G-VG
☐	56	Richard Rodas	.20	.08	.02
☐	xx	Coaching Staff (unnumbered)	.20	.08	.02

1985 Police Braves

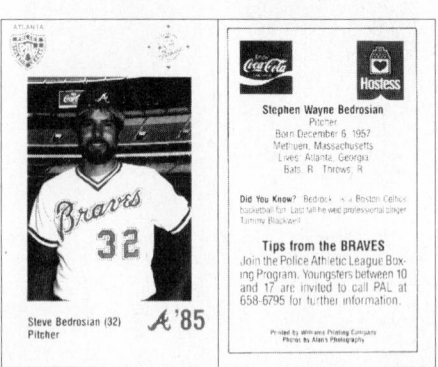

The cards in this 30-card set measure 2 5/8" by 4 1/8". For the fifth straight year, the Atlanta Police Department issued a full color set of Atlanta Braves. The set was also sponsored by Coca Cola and Hostess. In the upper right of the obverse is a logo commemorating the 20th anniversary of the Braves in Atlanta. Cards are numbered by uniform number. Cards feature a safety tip on the back. Each card except for Manager Haas has an interesting "Did You Know" fact about the player.

			MINT	EXC	G-VG
	COMPLETE SET (30)		11.00	5.00	1.35
	COMMON PLAYER		.30	.12	.03
☐	2	Albert Hall	.40	.16	.04
☐	3	Dale Murphy	3.00	1.25	.30
☐	5	Rick Cerone	.30	.12	.03
☐	7	Bobby Wine CO	.30	.12	.03
☐	10	Chris Chambliss	.50	.20	.05
☐	11	Bob Horner	.75	.30	.07
☐	12	Paul Runge	.30	.12	.03
☐	15	Claudell Washington	.40	.16	.04
☐	16	Rafael Ramirez	.30	.12	.03
☐	17	Glenn Hubbard	.30	.12	.03
☐	18	Paul Zuvella	.30	.12	.03
☐	19	Terry Harper	.30	.12	.03
☐	20	Bruce Benedict	.30	.12	.03
☐	22	Eddie Haas MG	.30	.12	.03
☐	24	Ken Oberkfell	.30	.12	.03
☐	26	Gene Garber	.30	.12	.03
☐	27	Pascual Perez	.50	.20	.05
☐	28	Gerald Perry	.40	.16	.04
☐	29	Craig McMurtry	.30	.12	.03
☐	32	Steve Bedrosian	.50	.20	.05
☐	33	Johnny Sain CO	.60	.25	.06
☐	34	Zane Smith	.60	.25	.06
☐	36	Brad Komminsk	.40	.16	.04
☐	37	Rick Camp	.30	.12	.03
☐	39	Len Barker	.40	.16	.04
☐	40	Bruce Sutter	.60	.25	.06
☐	42	Rick Mahler	.30	.12	.03
☐	51	Terry Forster	.40	.16	.04
☐	52	Leo Mazzone CO	.30	.12	.03
☐	53	Bobby Dews CO	.30	.12	.03

1985 Police Brewers

The cards in this 30-card set measure 2 3/4" by 4 1/8". Again this year, the police departments in and around Milwaukee issued sets of the Milwaukee Brewers. The backs contain the Brewers

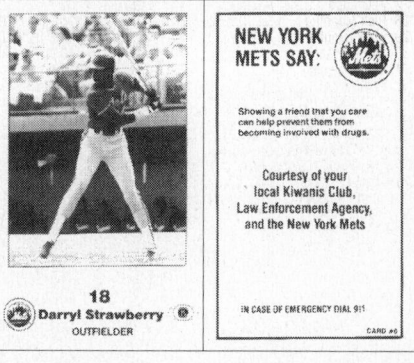

logo, a safety tip, and in some cases, a badge of the jurisdiction. Prices below are for the basic set without regard to the Police Department issuing the cards; cards from the more obscure corners and small towns of Wisconsin (smaller production) will be valued higher. Cards are numbered by uniform number.

	MINT	EXC	G-VG
COMPLETE SET (30)	7.00	3.00	.70
COMMON PLAYER	.20	.08	.02
☐ 2 Randy Ready	.25	.10	.02
☐ 4 Paul Molitor	.75	.30	.07
☐ 5 Doug Loman	.25	.10	.02
☐ 7 Paul Householder	.20	.08	.02
☐ 10 Bob McClure	.20	.08	.02
☐ 11 Ed Romero	.20	.08	.02
☐ 14 Dion James	.25	.10	.02
☐ 15 Cecil Cooper	.45	.18	.04
☐ 17 Jim Gantner	.30	.12	.03
☐ 18 Danny Darwin	.25	.10	.02
☐ 19 Robin Yount	1.75	.70	.17
☐ 21 Bill Schroeder	.25	.10	.02
☐ 22 Charlie Moore	.20	.08	.02
☐ 23 Ted Simmons	.50	.20	.05
☐ 24 Ben Oglivie	.35	.15	.03
☐ 26 Brian Giles	.25	.10	.02
☐ 27 Pete Ladd	.20	.08	.02
☐ 28 Rick Manning	.20	.08	.02
☐ 29 Mark Brouhard	.20	.08	.02
☐ 30 Moose Haas	.25	.10	.02
☐ 31 George Bamberger MG	.25	.10	.02
☐ 34 Rollie Fingers	.90	.40	.09
☐ 40 Bob L. Gibson	.20	.08	.02
☐ 41 Ray Searage	.20	.08	.02
☐ 47 Jaime Cocanower	.20	.08	.02
☐ 48 Ray Burris	.20	.08	.02
☐ 49 Ted Higuera	.60	.25	.06
☐ 50 Pete Vuckovich	.30	.12	.03
☐ xx Team Roster (unnumbered)	.20	.08	.02
☐ xx Coaches Card (unnumbered)	.20	.08	.02
☐ xx Newspaper Carrier (unnumbered)	.20	.08	.02

1985 Police Mets/Yankees

This 12-card set was supposedly issued courtesy of the Kiwanis Club, a local law enforcement agency, and the New York Mets and New York Yankees. The cards measure approximately 2 9/16" by 4 1/16". The fronts feature color player photos with white borders. Beneath the photo, player information appears between the team logo and the Kiwanis International logo. The backs have anti-drug messages introduced by the words "New York Mets Say" or "New York Yankees Say." The cards are numbered on the back and are indicated below by a prefix for Mets or Yankees.

	MINT	EXC	G-VG
COMPLETE SET (12)	10.00	4.50	1.25
COMMON PLAYER (M1-M6)	.50	.20	.05
COMMON PLAYER (Y1-Y6)	.50	.20	.05
☐ M1 George Foster and Bill Robinson CO	.90	.40	.09
☐ M2 Davey Johnson MG and Gary Carter	.90	.40	.09
☐ M3 Dwight Gooden	2.50	1.00	.25
☐ M4 Mookie Wilson	.50	.20	.05
☐ M5 Keith Hernandez	.75	.30	.07
☐ M6 Darryl Strawberry	2.50	1.00	.25
☐ Y1 Willie Randolph	.50	.20	.05
☐ Y2 Phil Niekro	1.00	.40	.10
☐ Y3 Ron Guidry	.75	.30	.07
☐ Y4 Dave Winfield	1.50	.60	.15
☐ Y5 Dave Righetti	.75	.30	.07
☐ Y6 Billy Martin MG	.75	.30	.07

1986 Police Astros

This 26-card safety set was also sponsored by Kool-Aid. The backs contain a biographical paragraph above a "Tip from the Dugout". The front features a full-color photo of the player, his name, and uniform number. The cards are numbered on the back and measure 2 5/8" by 4 1/8". The backs are printed in orange and blue on white card stock. Sets were distributed at the Astrodome on June 14th as well as given away throughout the summer by the Houston Police.

	MINT	EXC	G-VG
COMPLETE SET (26)	8.00	3.50	.80
COMMON PLAYER (1-26)	.20	.08	.02
☐ 1 Jim Pankovits	.20	.08	.02
☐ 2 Nolan Ryan	3.50	1.50	.35
☐ 3 Mike Scott	.60	.25	.06

		MINT	EXC	G-VG
☐ 4	Kevin Bass	.30	.12	.03
☐ 5	Bill Doran	.30	.12	.03
☐ 6	Hal Lanier MG	.25	.10	.02
☐ 7	Denny Walling	.20	.08	.02
☐ 8	Alan Ashby	.20	.08	.02
☐ 9	Phil Garner	.30	.12	.03
☐ 10	Charlie Kerfeld	.20	.08	.02
☐ 11	Dave Smith	.30	.12	.03
☐ 12	Jose Cruz	.40	.16	.04
☐ 13	Craig Reynolds	.20	.08	.02
☐ 14	Mark Bailey	.20	.08	.02
☐ 15	Bob Knepper	.20	.08	.02
☐ 16	Julio Solano	.20	.08	.02
☐ 17	Dickie Thon	.30	.12	.03
☐ 18	Mike Madden	.20	.08	.02
☐ 19	Jeff Calhoun	.20	.08	.02
☐ 20	Tony Walker	.20	.08	.02
☐ 21	Terry Puhl	.30	.12	.03
☐ 22	Glenn Davis	1.25	.50	.12
☐ 23	Billy Hatcher	.35	.15	.03
☐ 24	Jim Deshaies	.25	.10	.02
☐ 25	Frank DiPino	.20	.08	.02
☐ 26	Coaching Staff	.20	.08	.02

1986 Police Braves

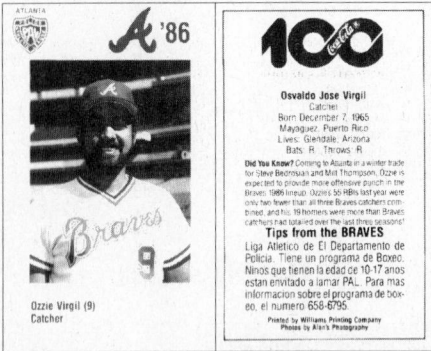

Ozzie Virgil (9)
Catcher

This 30-card safety set was also sponsored by Coca-Cola. The backs contain the usual biographical info and safety tip. The front features a full-color photo of the player, his name, and uniform number. The cards measure 2 5/8" by 4 1/8". Cards were freely distributed throughout the summer by the Police Departments in the Atlanta area. Cards are numbered below by uniform number.

		MINT	EXC	G-VG
COMPLETE SET (30)		10.00	4.50	1.25
COMMON PLAYER		.30	.12	.03
☐ 2	Russ Nixon CO	.30	.12	.03
☐ 3	Dale Murphy	2.50	1.00	.25
☐ 4	Bob Skinner CO	.40	.16	.04
☐ 5	Billy Sample	.40	.16	.04
☐ 7	Chuck Tanner MG	.40	.16	.04
☐ 8	Willie Stargell CO	1.00	.40	.10
☐ 9	Ozzie Virgil	.30	.12	.03
☐ 10	Chris Chambliss	.50	.20	.05
☐ 11	Bob Horner	.60	.25	.06
☐ 14	Andres Thomas	.40	.16	.04
☐ 15	Claudell Washington	.40	.16	.04
☐ 16	Rafael Ramirez	.30	.12	.03
☐ 17	Glenn Hubbard	.30	.12	.03
☐ 18	Omar Moreno	.30	.12	.03
☐ 19	Terry Harper	.30	.12	.03
☐ 20	Bruce Benedict	.30	.12	.03
☐ 23	Ted Simmons	.50	.20	.05
☐ 24	Ken Oberkfell	.30	.12	.03
☐ 26	Gene Garber	.30	.12	.03
☐ 29	Craig McMurtry	.30	.12	.03
☐ 30	Paul Assenmacher	.30	.12	.03
☐ 33	Johnny Sain CO	.50	.20	.05
☐ 34	Zane Smith	.50	.20	.05
☐ 38	Joe Johnson	.30	.12	.03
☐ 40	Bruce Sutter	.60	.25	.06

☐ 42	Rick Mahler	.40	.16	.04
☐ 46	David Palmer	.40	.16	.04
☐ 48	Duane Ward	.50	.20	.05
☐ 49	Jeff Dedmon	.30	.12	.03
☐ 52	Al Monchak CO	.30	.12	.03

1986 Police Brewers

Rick Cerone says:

Every kid that plays baseball dreams of playing in the big leagues someday, but only a few make it. They begin learning the game at an early age and develop their skills at each level they play in, little league, high school, college, and the minor leagues.

Your education is very important. If you want a big league job, stay in school, work hard at it, and learn. You'll end up succeeding and your family and friends will be proud of you.

11 Rick Cerone C
The Eagle and Palmyra Police Dept and Eagle & Palmyra Lions Clubs present the 1986
Milwaukee Brewers

Listen to WTMJ Radio in Milwaukee or your local Brewers network station to learn who will be the 2 players featured on next weeks baseball cards.

This 32-card safety set was also sponsored by WTMJ Radio and Kinney Shoes. The backs contain the usual biographical info and safety tip. The front features a full-color photo of the player, his name, position, and uniform number. The cards measure 2 5/8" by 4 1/8". Cards were freely distributed throughout the summer by the Police Departments in the Milwaukee area. Cards are numbered below by uniform number.

		MINT	EXC	G-VG
COMPLETE SET (32)		6.50	2.75	.65
COMMON PLAYER		.20	.08	.02
☐ 1	Ernest Riles	.25	.10	.02
☐ 2	Randy Ready	.20	.08	.02
☐ 3	Juan Castillo	.20	.08	.02
☐ 4	Paul Molitor	.65	.25	.06
☐ 7	Paul Householder	.20	.08	.02
☐ 8	Andy Etchebarren CO	.20	.08	.02
☐ 10	Bob McClure	.20	.08	.02
☐ 11	Rick Cerone	.20	.08	.02
☐ 12	Larry Haney CO	.20	.08	.02
☐ 13	Billy Jo Robidoux	.25	.10	.02
☐ 15	Cecil Cooper	.35	.15	.03
☐ 16	Mike Felder	.25	.10	.02
☐ 17	Jim Gantner	.25	.10	.02
☐ 18	Danny Darwin	.25	.10	.02
☐ 19	Robin Yount	1.50	.60	.15
☐ 20	Juan Nieves	.25	.10	.02
☐ 21	Bill Schroeder	.25	.10	.02
☐ 22	Charlie Moore	.20	.08	.02
☐ 24	Ben Oglivie	.30	.12	.03
☐ 25	Mark Clear	.20	.08	.02
☐ 28	Rick Manning	.20	.08	.02
☐ 31	George Bamberger MG	.20	.08	.02
☐ 33	Frank Howard CO	.25	.10	.02
☐ 35	Tony Muser CO	.20	.08	.02
☐ 37	Dan Plesac	.25	.10	.02
☐ 38	Herm Starrette CO	.20	.08	.02
☐ 39	Tim Leary	.35	.15	.03
☐ 42	Tom Trebelhorn CO	.25	.10	.02
☐ 45	Rob Deer	.45	.18	.04
☐ 46	Bill Wegman	.30	.12	.03
☐ 47	Jaime Cocanower	.20	.08	.02
☐ 49	Teddy Higuera	.50	.20	.05

1986 Police Dodgers

This 30-card set features full-color cards each measuring 2 13/16" by 4 1/8". The cards are unnumbered except for uniform

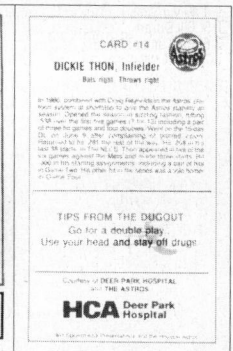

numbers. The backs give a safety tip as well as a short capsule
biography. The sets were given away at Dodger Stadium on
May 18th.

	MINT	EXC	G-VG
COMPLETE SET (30)	6.50	2.75	.65
COMMON PLAYER	.20	.08	.02
2 Tom Lasorda MG	.40	.16	.04
3 Steve Sax	.60	.25	.06
5 Mike Marshall	.40	.16	.04
9 Greg Brock	.20	.08	.02
10 Dave Anderson	.20	.08	.02
12 Bill Madlock	.30	.12	.03
14 Mike Scioscia	.30	.12	.03
17 Len Matuszek	.20	.08	.02
18 Bill Russell	.30	.12	.03
22 Franklin Stubbs	.30	.12	.03
23 Enos Cabell	.20	.08	.02
25 Mariano Duncan	.30	.12	.03
26 Alejandro Pena	.30	.12	.03
27 Carlos Diaz	.20	.08	.02
28 Pedro Guerrero	.75	.30	.07
29 Alex Trevino	.20	.08	.02
31 Ed VandeBerg	.20	.08	.02
34 Fernando Valenzuela	.75	.30	.07
35 Bob Welch	.50	.20	.05
40 Rick Honeycutt	.20	.08	.02
41 Jerry Reuss	.25	.10	.02
43 Ken Howell	.20	.08	.02
44 Ken Landreaux	.20	.08	.02
45 Terry Whitfield	.20	.08	.02
48 Dennis Powell	.20	.08	.02
49 Tom Niedenfuer	.20	.08	.02
51 Reggie Williams	.20	.08	.02
55 Orel Hershiser	1.00	.40	.10
xx Coaching Staff	.20	.08	.02
(unnumbered)			
Don McMahon			
Mark Cresse			
Ben Hines			
Ron Perranoski			
Monty Basgall			
Manny Mota			
Joe Amalfitano			
xx Team Photo	.20	.08	.02
(unnumbered)			
(checklist back)			

1987 Police Astros

This 26-card safety set was sponsored by the Astros, Deer Park
Hospital, and Sportsmedia Presentations. The backs contain a
biographical paragraph above a "Tip from the Dugout". The
front features a full-color photo of the player, his name,
position, and uniform number. The cards are numbered on the
back and measure 2 5/8" by 4 1/8". The first twelve cards were
distributed at the Astrodome on July 14th and the rest were
given away later in the summer by the Deer Park Hospital.

	MINT	EXC	G-VG
COMPLETE SET (26)	7.00	3.00	.70
COMMON PLAYER (1-26)	.20	.08	.02
1 Larry Andersen	.25	.10	.02
2 Mark Bailey	.20	.08	.02
3 Jose Cruz	.35	.15	.03
4 Danny Darwin	.25	.10	.02
5 Bill Doran	.35	.15	.03
6 Billy Hatcher	.35	.15	.03
7 Hal Lanier MG	.25	.10	.02
8 Davey Lopes	.30	.12	.03
9 Dave Meads	.20	.08	.02
10 Craig Reynolds	.25	.10	.02
11 Mike Scott	.60	.25	.06
12 Denny Walling	.20	.08	.02
13 Aurelio Lopez	.20	.08	.02
14 Dickie Thon	.25	.10	.02
15 Terry Puhl	.25	.10	.02
16 Nolan Ryan	3.00	1.25	.30
17 Dave Smith	.30	.12	.03
18 Julio Solano	.20	.08	.02
19 Jim Deshaies	.25	.10	.02
20 Bob Knepper	.20	.08	.02
21 Alan Ashby	.20	.08	.02
22 Kevin Bass	.25	.10	.02
23 Glenn Davis	.75	.30	.07
24 Phil Garner	.30	.12	.03
25 Jim Pankovits	.20	.08	.02
26 Coaching Staff	.20	.08	.02

1987 Police Brewers

This 30-card safety set was also sponsored by WTMJ Radio
and Kinney Shoes. The backs contain the usual biographical
info and safety tip. The front features a full-color photo of the
player, his name, position, and uniform number. The cards
measure 2 5/8" by 4 1/8". Cards were freely distributed throughout
the summer by the Police Departments in the Milwaukee area

and throughout other parts of Wisconsin. Cards are numbered below by uniform number.

	MINT	EXC	G-VG
COMPLETE SET (30)	6.00	2.50	.60
COMMON PLAYER	.20	.08	.02
☐ 1 Ernest Riles	.25	.10	.02
☐ 2 Edgar Diaz	.25	.10	.02
☐ 3 Juan Castillo	.20	.08	.02
☐ 4 Paul Molitor	.75	.30	.07
☐ 5 B.J. Surhoff	.50	.20	.05
☐ 7 Dale Sveum	.25	.10	.02
☐ 9 Greg Brock	.25	.10	.02
☐ 13 Billy Jo Robidoux	.20	.08	.02
☐ 14 Jim Paciorek	.20	.08	.02
☐ 15 Cecil Cooper	.35	.15	.03
☐ 16 Mike Felder	.20	.08	.02
☐ 17 Jim Gantner	.30	.12	.03
☐ 19 Robin Yount	1.50	.60	.15
☐ 20 Juan Nieves	.25	.10	.02
☐ 21 Bill Schroeder	.25	.10	.02
☐ 25 Mark Clear	.20	.08	.02
☐ 26 Glenn Braggs	.30	.12	.03
☐ 28 Rick Manning	.20	.08	.02
☐ 29 Chris Bosio	.35	.15	.03
☐ 32 Chuck Crim	.20	.08	.02
☐ 34 Mark Ciardi	.20	.08	.02
☐ 37 Dan Plesac	.25	.10	.02
☐ 38 John Henry Johnson	.20	.08	.02
☐ 40 Mike Birkbeck	.25	.10	.02
☐ 42 Tom Trebelhorn MG	.25	.10	.02
☐ 45 Rob Deer	.35	.15	.03
☐ 46 Bill Wegman	.30	.12	.03
☐ 49 Teddy Higuera	.40	.16	.04
☐ xx Coaching Staff	.20	.08	.02
☐ xx Brewers Team	.20	.08	.02
(Checklist on back)			

1987 Police Dodgers

PEDRO GUERRERO   28

This 30-card set features full-color cards each measuring 2 13/16" by 4 1/8". The cards are unnumbered except for uniform numbers. The backs give a safety tip as well as a short capsule biography. Cards were given away at Dodger Stadium on April 24th and later during the summer by LAPD officers at a rate of two cards per week.

	MINT	EXC	G-VG
COMPLETE SET (30)	6.00	2.50	.60
COMMON PLAYER (1-30)	.20	.08	.02
☐ 1 Tom Lasorda MG 2	.40	.16	.04
☐ 2 Steve Sax 3	.60	.25	.06
☐ 3 Mike Marshall 5	.30	.12	.03
☐ 4 Dave Anderson 10	.20	.08	.02
☐ 5 Bill Madlock 12	.30	.12	.03
☐ 6 Mike Scioscia 14	.30	.12	.03
☐ 7 Gilberto Reyes 15	.30	.12	.03
☐ 8 Len Matuszek 17	.20	.08	.02
☐ 9 Reggie Williams 21	.20	.08	.02
☐ 10 Franklin Stubbs 22	.30	.12	.03

	MINT	EXC	G-VG
☐ 11 Tim Leary 23	.35	.15	.03
☐ 12 Mariano Duncan 25	.30	.12	.03
☐ 13 Alejandro Pena 26	.30	.12	.03
☐ 14 Pedro Guerrero 28	.75	.30	.07
☐ 15 Alex Trevino 29	.20	.08	.02
☐ 16 Jeff Hamilton 33	.25	.10	.02
☐ 17 Fernando Valenzuela 34	.60	.25	.06
☐ 18 Bob Welch 35	.50	.20	.05
☐ 19 Matt Young 36	.25	.10	.02
☐ 20 Rick Honeycutt 40	.20	.08	.02
☐ 21 Jerry Reuss 41	.20	.08	.02
☐ 22 Ken Howell 43	.20	.08	.02
☐ 23 Ken Landreaux 44	.20	.08	.02
☐ 24 Ralph Bryant 46	.20	.08	.02
☐ 25 Jose Gonzalez 47	.20	.08	.02
☐ 26 Tom Niedenfuer 49	.20	.08	.02
☐ 27 Brian Holton 51	.20	.08	.02
☐ 28 Orel Hershiser 55	.90	.40	.09
☐ 29 Coaching Staff	.20	.08	.02
☐ 30 Dodgers Stadium	.20	.08	.02
(25th Anniversary)			

1988 Police Astros

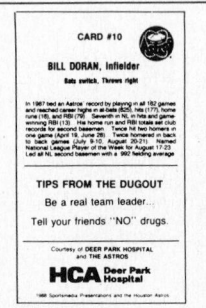

This 26-card safety set was sponsored by the Astros, Deer Park Hospital, and Sportsmedia Presentations. The backs contain a biographical paragraph above "Tips from the Dugout". The front features a full-color photo of the player, his name, position, and uniform number. The cards are numbered on the back and measure 2 5/8" by 4 1/8". The sets were supposedly distributed to the first 15,000 youngsters attending the New York Mets game against the Astros at the Astrodome on July 9th.

	MINT	EXC	G-VG
COMPLETE SET (26)	7.00	3.00	.70
COMMON PLAYER (1-26)	.25	.10	.02
☐ 1 Juan Agosto	.25	.10	.02
☐ 2 Larry Andersen	.25	.10	.02
☐ 3 Joaquin Andujar	.35	.15	.03
☐ 4 Alan Ashby	.25	.10	.02
☐ 5 Mark Bailey	.25	.10	.02
☐ 6 Kevin Bass	.35	.15	.03
☐ 7 Danny Darwin	.30	.12	.03
☐ 8 Glenn Davis	.75	.30	.07
☐ 9 Jim Deshaies	.30	.12	.03
☐ 10 Bill Doran	.35	.15	.03
☐ 11 Billy Hatcher	.35	.15	.03
☐ 12 Jeff Heathcock	.25	.10	.02
☐ 13 Steve Henderson	.25	.10	.02
☐ 14 Chuck Jackson	.25	.10	.02
☐ 15 Bob Knepper	.25	.10	.02
☐ 16 Jim Pankovits	.25	.10	.02
☐ 17 Terry Puhl	.35	.15	.03
☐ 18 Rafael Ramirez	.25	.10	.02
☐ 19 Craig Reynolds	.30	.12	.03
☐ 20 Nolan Ryan	3.00	1.25	.30
☐ 21 Mike Scott	.75	.30	.07
☐ 22 Dave Smith	.35	.15	.03
☐ 23 Denny Walling	.25	.10	.02
☐ 24 Gerald Young	.35	.15	.03
☐ 25 Hal Lanier MG	.25	.10	.02
☐ 26 Coaching Staff	.25	.10	.02

1988 Police Brewers

Rob Deer says:

"Do you take safety for granted? Please don't. Baseball catchers play it safe by wearing special equipment to protect themselves from injury and hitters wear batting helmets. Baseball parks have a screen to protect fans from foul balls.

Kids should practice safety every day at school and when playing. Streets, construction sites, and vacant buildings are dangerous and unsafe. Don't play there. Use your park, school yard, or gymnasium and play it safe."

45   **Rob Deer**   OF
The Waukesha County Deputy Sheriff's Assoc.
25th Anniv. National Police Week (May 17-24)
and First Wisconsin Bank — Waukesha
present the 1988
Milwaukee Brewers

Listen to **WTMJ Radio** in Milwaukee or your local Brewers network station to learn who will be the 2 players featured on next week's baseball cards.

This 30-card safety set was also sponsored by WTMJ Radio and Stadia Athletic Shoes. The backs contain the usual biographical info and safety tip. The front features a full-color photo of the player, his name, position, and uniform number. The cards measure approximately 2 7/8" by 4 1/8". Cards were freely distributed throughout the summer by the Police Departments in the Milwaukee area and throughout other parts of Wisconsin. Cards are numbered below by uniform number.

	MINT	EXC	G-VG
COMPLETE SET (30)	6.00	2.50	.60
COMMON PLAYER	.20	.08	.02
☐ 1 Ernest Riles	.20	.08	.02
☐ 3 Juan Castillo	.20	.08	.02
☐ 4 Paul Molitor	.65	.25	.06
☐ 5 B.J. Surhoff	.35	.15	.03
☐ 7 Dale Sveum	.25	.10	.02
☐ 9 Greg Brock	.20	.08	.02
☐ 11 Charlie O'Brien	.20	.08	.02
☐ 14 Jim Adduci	.25	.10	.02
☐ 16 Mike Felder	.25	.10	.02
☐ 17 Jim Gantner	.30	.12	.03
☐ 19 Robin Yount	1.50	.60	.15
☐ 20 Juan Nieves	.25	.10	.02
☐ 21 Bill Schroeder	.25	.10	.02
☐ 23 Joey Meyer	.25	.10	.02
☐ 25 Mark Clear	.20	.08	.02
☐ 26 Glenn Braggs	.30	.12	.03
☐ 28 Odell Jones	.20	.08	.02
☐ 29 Chris Bosio	.35	.15	.03
☐ 30 Steve Kiefer	.20	.08	.02
☐ 32 Chuck Crim	.20	.08	.02
☐ 33 Jay Aldrich	.20	.08	.02
☐ 37 Dan Plesac	.25	.10	.02
☐ 40 Mike Birkbeck	.25	.10	.02
☐ 42 Tom Trebelhorn MG	.25	.10	.02
☐ 43 Dave Stapleton	.20	.08	.02
☐ 45 Rob Deer	.35	.15	.03
☐ 46 Bill Wegman	.30	.12	.03
☐ 49 Ted Higuera	.40	.16	.04
☐ x Team Photo HOR	.20	.08	.02
(unnumbered)			
☐ x Manager and	.20	.08	.02
Coaches HOR			
(unnumbered)			

1988 Police Dodgers

This 30-card set features full-color cards each measuring approximately 2 13/16" by 4 1/8". The cards are unnumbered except for uniform numbers. The backs give a safety tip as well as a short capsule biography. Cards were given during the summer by LAPD officers. The set is very similar to the 1987 set, the 1988 set is distinguished by the fact that it does not have the 25th anniversary (of Dodger Stadium) logo on the card front.

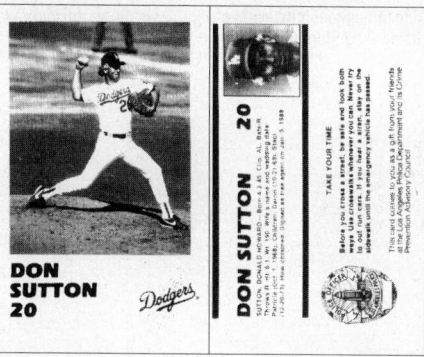

DON SUTTON 20

SUTTON, DONALD HOWARD - Born 4.2.45, Clio, AL. Bats R. Throws R. Ht 6-1, Wt 190. Wife's name and wedding date. Resides in . Don Sutton was obtained and signed as a free agent on Jan 6, 1989.

TAKE YOUR TIME

Before you cross a street, be alert and look both ways. Like crosswalks whenever you can. Never try to beat a car. If you must cross, stay out of the sidewalk until the emergency vehicle has passed.

This card comes to you as a gift from your friends at the Los Angeles Police Department and is the Crime Prevention Advisory Council.

	MINT	EXC	G-VG
COMPLETE SET (30)	6.00	2.50	.60
COMMON PLAYER	.20	.08	.02
☐ 2 Tom Lasorda MG	.40	.16	.04
☐ 3 Steve Sax	.50	.20	.05
☐ 5 Mike Marshall	.30	.12	.03
☐ 7 Alfredo Griffin	.25	.10	.02
☐ 9 Mickey Hatcher	.20	.08	.02
☐ 10 Dave Anderson	.20	.08	.02
☐ 12 Danny Heep	.25	.10	.02
☐ 14 Mike Scioscia	.25	.10	.02
☐ 20 Don Sutton	.60	.25	.06
☐ 21 Tito Landrum and	.20	.08	.02
17 Len Matuszak			
☐ 22 Franklin Stubbs	.30	.12	.03
☐ 23 Kirk Gibson	.75	.30	.07
☐ 25 Mariano Duncan	.30	.12	.03
☐ 26 Alejandro Pena	.30	.12	.03
☐ 27 Mike Sharperson and	.20	.08	.02
52 Tim Crews			
☐ 28 Pedro Guerrero	.50	.20	.05
☐ 29 Alex Trevino	.20	.08	.02
☐ 31 John Shelby	.20	.08	.02
☐ 33 Jeff Hamilton	.25	.10	.02
☐ 34 Fernando Valenzuela	.50	.20	.05
☐ 37 Mike Davis	.20	.08	.02
☐ 41 Brad Havens	.20	.08	.02
☐ 43 Ken Howell	.25	.10	.02
☐ 47 Jesse Orosco	.20	.08	.02
☐ 49 Tim Belcher and	.35	.15	.03
57 Shawn Hillegas			
☐ 50 Jay Howell	.30	.12	.03
☐ 51 Brian Holton	.20	.08	.02
☐ 54 Tim Leary	.35	.15	.03
☐ 55 Orel Hershiser	.90	.40	.09
☐ x Tom Lasorda MG	.30	.12	.03
and Coaches			
(unnumbered)			

1988 Police Tigers

Protective headgear is worn by every player who steps up to bat.

Don't be caught without your protective gear while riding in an automobile. **WEAR YOUR SAFETY BELT.**

SPARKY ANDERSON   MGR.
B: R T: R HT: 5'9" WT: 168 BURN: 2-22-34

This set was sponsored by the Michigan State Police and the Detroit Tigers organization. There are 14 blue-bordered cards in the set; each card measures approximately 2 1/2" by 3 1/2". The cards are completely unnumbered as there is not even any reference to uniform numbers on the cards; the cards are listed below in alphabetical order.

	MINT	EXC	G-VG
COMPLETE SET (14)	35.00	15.75	5.25
COMMON PLAYER (1-14)	1.50	.60	.15
☐ 1 Doyle Alexander	2.00	.80	.20
☐ 2 Sparky Anderson MG	3.50	1.50	.35
☐ 3 Dave Bergman	1.50	.60	.15
☐ 4 Tom Brookens	1.50	.60	.15
☐ 5 Darrell Evans	2.50	1.00	.25
☐ 6 Larry Herndon	1.50	.60	.15
☐ 7 Chet Lemon	2.00	.80	.20
☐ 8 Jack Morris	5.00	2.25	.50
☐ 9 Matt Nokes	3.50	1.50	.35
☐ 10 Jeff M. Robinson	3.00	1.25	.30
☐ 11 Frank Tanana	2.00	.80	.20
☐ 12 Walt Terrell	1.50	.60	.15
☐ 13 Alan Trammell	7.00	3.00	.70
☐ 14 Lou Whitaker	4.50	2.00	.45

1989 Police Brewers

The 1989 Police Milwaukee Brewers set contains 30 cards measuring approximately 2 3/4" by 4 1/4". The fronts have color photos with white borders; the backs feature safety tips. The unnumbered cards were given away by various local Wisconsin police departments. The cards are numbered below by uniform number.

	MINT	EXC	G-VG
COMPLETE SET (30)	6.00	2.50	.60
COMMON PLAYER	.20	.08	.02
☐ 1 Gary Sheffield	.75	.30	.07
☐ 4 Paul Molitor	.60	.25	.06
☐ 5 B.J. Surhoff	.30	.12	.03
☐ 6 Bill Spiers	.30	.12	.03
☐ 7 Dale Sveum	.20	.08	.02
☐ 9 Greg Brock	.20	.08	.02
☐ 14 Gus Polidor	.20	.08	.02
☐ 16 Mike Felder	.20	.08	.02
☐ 17 Jim Gantner	.25	.10	.02
☐ 19 Robin Yount	1.25	.50	.12
☐ 20 Juan Nieves	.25	.10	.02
☐ 22 Charlie O'Brien	.20	.08	.02
☐ 23 Joey Meyer	.25	.10	.02
☐ 25 Dave Engle	.20	.08	.02
☐ 26 Glenn Braggs	.25	.10	.02
☐ 27 Paul Mirabella	.20	.08	.02
☐ 29 Chris Bosio	.30	.12	.03
☐ 30 Terry Francona	.20	.08	.02
☐ 32 Chuck Crim	.20	.08	.02
☐ 37 Dan Plesac	.25	.10	.02
☐ 38 Don August	.25	.10	.02
☐ 40 Mike Birkbeck	.20	.08	.02
☐ 41 Mark Knudson	.20	.08	.02
☐ 42 Tom Trebelhorn MG	.25	.10	.02

	MINT	EXC	G-VG
☐ 45 Rob Deer	.30	.12	.03
☐ 46 Bill Wegman	.30	.12	.03
☐ 48 Bryan Clutterbuck	.20	.08	.02
☐ 49 Teddy Higuera	.30	.12	.03
☐ xx Team Card	.20	.08	.02
(checklist on back)			
☐ xx Coaches Card	.20	.08	.02

1989 Police Dodgers

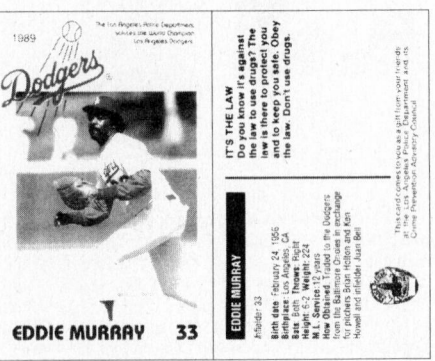

The 1989 Police Los Angeles Dodgers set contains 30 cards measuring approximately 2 5/8" by 4 1/4". The fronts have color photos with white borders; the backs feature safety tips and biographical information. The unnumbered cards were given away by various Los Angeles-area police departments. The cards were also issued as an uncut, perforated sheet to children (age 14 and under) at Dodger Stadium on Baseball Card Night, May 5, 1989.

	MINT	EXC	G-VG
COMPLETE SET (30)	6.00	2.50	.60
COMMON PLAYER	.20	.08	.02
☐ 1 Dodger Coaches	.20	.08	.02
☐ 2 Tom Lasorda MG	.30	.12	.03
☐ 3 Jeff Hamilton	.20	.08	.02
☐ 4 Mike Marshall	.30	.12	.03
☐ 5 Alfredo Griffin	.25	.10	.02
☐ 6 Mickey Hatcher	.20	.08	.02
☐ 7 Dave Anderson	.20	.08	.02
☐ 8 Willie Randolph	.30	.12	.03
☐ 9 Mike Scioscia	.30	.12	.03
☐ 10 Rick Dempsey	.20	.08	.02
☐ 11 Mike Davis	.20	.08	.02
☐ 12 Tracy Woodson	.25	.10	.02
☐ 13 Franklin Stubbs	.25	.10	.02
☐ 14 Kirk Gibson	.50	.20	.05
☐ 15 Mariano Duncan	.25	.10	.02
☐ 16 Alejandro Pena	.30	.12	.03
☐ 17 Mike Sharperson	.20	.08	.02
☐ 18 Ricky Horton	.25	.10	.02
☐ 19 John Tudor	.30	.12	.03
☐ 20 John Shelby	.20	.08	.02
☐ 21 Eddie Murray	.60	.25	.06
☐ 22 Fernando Valenzuela	.50	.20	.05
☐ 23 Mike Morgan	.30	.12	.03
☐ 24 Ramon Martinez	.90	.40	.09
☐ 25 Tim Belcher	.35	.15	.03
☐ 26 Jay Howell	.25	.10	.02
☐ 27 Tim Crews	.20	.08	.02
☐ 28 Tim Leary	.30	.12	.03
☐ 29 Orel Hershiser	.60	.25	.06
☐ 30 Ray Searage	.20	.08	.02

1989 Police Tigers

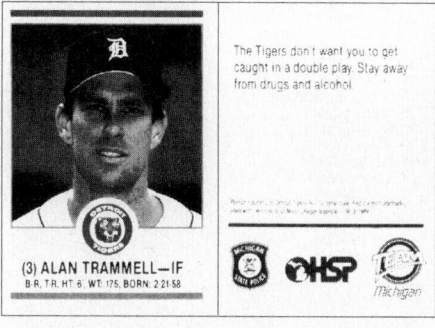

The Tigers don't want you to get caught in a double play. Stay away from drugs and alcohol.

(3) ALAN TRAMMELL—IF
B-R, T-R, HT 6, WT 175, BORN 2-21-58

The 1989 Police Detroit Tigers set contains 14 standard-size (2 1/2" by 3 1/2") cards. The fronts have color photos with blue and orange borders; the backs feature safety tips. These unnumbered cards were given away by the Michigan state police. The cards are numbered below according to uniform number.

		MINT	EXC	G-VG
COMPLETE SET (14)		12.00	5.25	1.50
COMMON PLAYER		.60	.25	.06
☐ 1	Lou Whitaker	1.25	.50	.12
☐ 3	Alan Trammell	2.50	1.00	.25
☐ 9	Fred Lynn	.90	.40	.09
☐ 14	Dave Bergman	.60	.25	.06
☐ 15	Pat Sheridan	.60	.25	.06
☐ 19	Doyle Alexander	.75	.30	.07
☐ 21	Guillermo Hernandez	.75	.30	.07
☐ 26	Frank Tanana	.75	.30	.07
☐ 33	Matt Nokes	.90	.40	.09
☐ 34	Chet Lemon	.75	.30	.07
☐ 39	Mike Henneman	.75	.30	.07
☐ 44	Jeff M. Robinson	.75	.30	.07
☐ 47	Jack Morris	1.50	.60	.15
☐ xx	Sparky Anderson MG	1.00	.40	.10

1990 Police Brewers

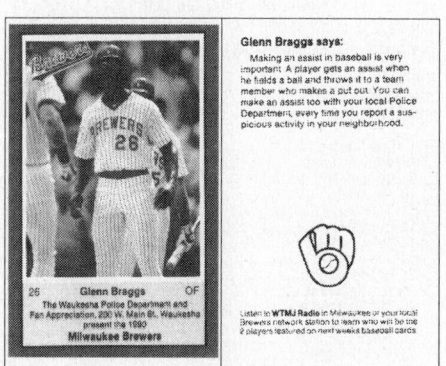

Glenn Braggs says:

Making an assist in baseball is very important. A player gets an assist when he fields a ball and throws it to a team member who makes a put out. You can make an assist too with your local Police Department, every time you report a suspicious activity in your neighborhood.

26   Glenn Braggs   OF
The Waukesha Police Department and Fan Appreciation, 200 W. Main St., Waukesha present the 1990
Milwaukee Brewers

Listen to WTMJ Radio in Milwaukee or your local Brewers network station to learn who will be the 2 players featured on next weeks baseball cards

This 30-card police set was issued in conjunction with the Fan Appreciation store of Waukesha, Wisconsin and the Waukesha Police department. This set measures approximately 2 13/16" by 4 1/8" and is checklisted by uniform number. The front of the card is a full-color photo surrounded by a blue border while the back has anti-crime tips.

		MINT	EXC	G-VG
COMPLETE SET (30)		6.00	2.50	.60
COMMON PLAYER		.20	.08	.02
☐ 2	Edgar Diaz	.25	.10	.02
☐ 4	Paul Molitor	.60	.25	.06
☐ 7	Dale Sveum	.20	.08	.02
☐ 11	Gary Sheffield	.40	.16	.04
☐ 14	Gus Polidor	.20	.08	.02
☐ 16	Mike Felder	.20	.08	.02
☐ 17	Jim Gantner	.30	.12	.03
☐ 19	Robin Yount	.90	.40	.09
☐ 20	Juan Nieves	.25	.10	.02
☐ 22	Charlie O'Brien	.20	.08	.02
☐ 23	Greg Vaughn	.60	.25	.06
☐ 24	Darryl Hamilton	.35	.15	.03
☐ 26	Glenn Braggs	.25	.10	.02
☐ 27	Paul Mirabella	.20	.08	.02
☐ 28	Tom Filer	.20	.08	.02
☐ 29	Chris Bosio	.30	.12	.03
☐ 30	Terry Francona	.20	.08	.02
☐ 31	Jaime Navarro	.25	.10	.02
☐ 32	Chuck Crim	.20	.08	.02
☐ 34	Billy Bates	.25	.10	.02
☐ 36	Tony Fossas	.20	.08	.02
☐ 37	Dan Plesac	.25	.10	.02
☐ 38	Don August	.25	.10	.02
☐ 39	Dave Parker	.60	.25	.06
☐ 40	Mike Birkbeck	.20	.08	.02
☐ 41	Mark Knudson	.25	.10	.02
☐ 42	Tom Trebelhorn MG	.25	.10	.02
☐ 45	Rob Deer	.35	.15	.03
☐ 46	Bill Wegman	.30	.12	.03
☐ 47	Bill Krueger	.20	.08	.02
☐ 49	Teddy Higuera	.30	.12	.03
☐ xx	Coaches	.20	.08	.02

Larry Haney 12
Don Baylor 25
Ray Burris 50
Andy Etchebarren 8
Duffy Dyer 10

1990 Police Dodgers

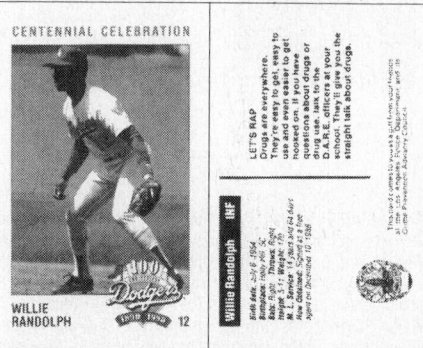

CENTENNIAL CELEBRATION

WILLIE RANDOLPH   12

LET'S RAP
Drugs are everywhere. They're easy to get, easy to use and even easier to get hooked on. If you have questions about drugs or drug use, talk to the D.A.R.E. officers at your school. They'll give you the straight talk about drugs.

This 26-card set measures approximately 2 13/16" by 4 1/8" and was distributed by both the Los Angeles Police Department and at a pre-season Dodger-Angel exhibition game. This set also commemorated the 100th anniversary of the Dodgers existence. The front has a full-color photo of the player on the front while the back has a brief profile of the player with an anti-crime message. This set is checklisted below by uniform number.

		MINT	EXC	G-VG
COMPLETE SET (26)		5.00	2.25	.50
COMMON PLAYER		.20	.08	.02
☐ 1	Tommy Lasorda MG	.30	.12	.03
☐ 3	Jeff Hamilton	.20	.08	.02
☐ 7	Alfredo Griffin	.20	.08	.02
☐ 8	Mickey Hatcher	.20	.08	.02
☐ 10	Juan Samuel	.30	.12	.03
☐ 12	Willie Randolph	.30	.12	.03
☐ 14	Mike Scioscia	.30	.12	.03
☐ 15	Chris Gwynn	.30	.12	.03

			MINT	EXC	G-VG
☐	17	Rick Dempsey	.20	.08	.02
☐	21	Hubie Brooks	.30	.12	.03
☐	22	Franklin Stubbs	.30	.12	.03
☐	23	Kirk Gibson	.50	.20	.05
☐	27	Mike Sharperson	.20	.08	.02
☐	28	Kal Daniels	.40	.16	.04
☐	29	Lenny Harris	.30	.12	.03
☐	31	John Shelby	.20	.08	.02
☐	33	Eddie Murray	.60	.25	.06
☐	34	Fernando Valenzuela	.50	.20	.05
☐	35	Jim Gott	.20	.08	.02
☐	36	Mike Morgan	.30	.12	.03
☐	38	Jose Gonzalez	.20	.08	.02
☐	39	Jim Neidlinger	.30	.12	.03
☐	46	Mike Hartley	.30	.12	.03
☐	49	Tim Belcher	.35	.15	.03
☐	50	Jay Howell	.25	.10	.02
☐	52	Tim Crews	.20	.08	.02
☐	55	Orel Hershiser	.50	.20	.05
☐	57	John Wetteland	.35	.15	.03
☐	59	Ray Searage	.20	.08	.02
☐	xx	Coaches Card	.20	.08	.02

Ben Hines
Ron Perranowski
Mark Cresse
Manny Mota
Tommy Lasorda MG
Joe Amalfitano
Joe Ferguson
Bill Russell

			MINT	EXC	G-VG
☐	17	Edwin Nunez	.20	.08	.02
☐	18	Dan Plesac	.20	.08	.02
☐	19	Willie Randolph	.30	.12	.03
☐	20	Ron Robinson	.30	.12	.03
☐	20	Gary Sheffield	.40	.16	.04
☐	21	Bill Spiers	.30	.12	.03
☐	22	Franklin Stubbs	.30	.12	.03
☐	23	B.J. Surhoff	.30	.12	.03
☐	24	Dale Sveum	.20	.08	.02
☐	25	Tom Trebelhorn MG	.20	.08	.02
☐	26	Greg Vaughn	.50	.20	.05
☐	27	Bill Wegman	.30	.12	.03
☐	28	Robin Yount	.90	.40	.09
☐	xx	Coaches Card	.20	.08	.02

Don Baylor
Ray Burris
Duffy Dyer
Andy Etchebarren
Larry Haney
Fred Stanley

1991 Police Cardinals

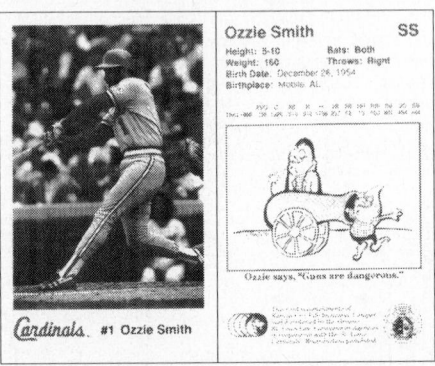

Cardinals #1 Ozzie Smith

1991 Police Brewers

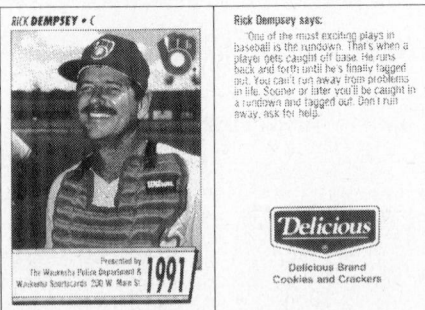

Presented by
The Waukesha Police Department &
Waukesha Sportscards 200 W. Main St.
1991

Delicious Brand
Cookies and Crackers

This 30-card set was sponsored by the Waukesha Police Department, Waukesha Sportscards, and Delicious Brand Cookies and Crackers. These sponsors are mentioned at the bottom of both sides of the card. The cards measure the standard size (2 1/2" by 3 1/2"). The fronts feature mostly color action player photos with light gray borders. The team logo is superimposed at the upper right corner. The backs have black print on a white background and feature public service tips by the players. The cards are numbered on the back.

This 24-card police set was sponsored by the Kansas City Life Insurance Company and distributed by Greater St. Louis Law Enforcement Agencies. The cards measure 2 5/8" by 4 1/8" and feature on the fronts a mix of posed and action color player photos with white borders. The team name, uniform number, and player's name appear in the white border below the pictures. In red print on white, the backs have biography, statistics, a safety cartoon with caption, and sponsor's logo. The cards are checklisted below by uniform number.

	MINT	EXC	G-VG
COMPLETE SET (30)	6.00	2.50	.60
COMMON PLAYER (1-30)	.20	.08	.02

			MINT	EXC	G-VG
☐	1	Don August	.20	.08	.02
☐	2	Dante Bichette	.30	.12	.03
☐	3	Chris Bosio	.30	.12	.03
☐	4	Greg Brock	.20	.08	.02
☐	5	Kevin M. Brown	.30	.12	.03
☐	6	Chuck Crim	.20	.08	.02
☐	7	Rick Dempsey	.20	.08	.02
☐	8	Jim Gantner	.30	.12	.03
☐	9	Darryl Hamilton	.30	.12	.03
☐	10	Teddy Higuera	.30	.12	.03
☐	11	Mark Lee	.30	.12	.03
☐	12	Mark Knudson	.20	.08	.02
☐	13	Julio Machado	.20	.08	.02
☐	14	Candy Maldonado	.30	.12	.03
☐	15	Paul Molitor	.60	.25	.06
☐	16	Jaime Navarro	.30	.12	.03

	MINT	EXC	G-VG
COMPLETE SET (24)	12.50	5.25	1.50
COMMON PLAYER	.50	.20	.05

			MINT	EXC	G-VG
☐	1	Ozzie Smith	1.00	.40	.10
☐	7	Geronimo Pena	.60	.25	.06
☐	9	Joe Torre MG	.75	.30	.07
☐	10	Rex Hudler	.60	.25	.06
☐	11	Jose Oquendo	.50	.20	.05
☐	12	Craig Wilson	.50	.20	.05
☐	16	Ray Lankford	1.00	.40	.10
☐	19	Tom Pagnozzi	.50	.20	.05
☐	21	Gerald Perry	.50	.20	.05
☐	23	Bernard Gilkey	.75	.30	.07
☐	25	Milt Thompson	.50	.20	.05
☐	27	Todd Zeile	1.00	.40	.10
☐	28	Pedro Guerrero	.90	.40	.09
☐	29	Rich Gedman	.50	.20	.05
☐	34	Felix Jose	1.00	.40	.10
☐	35	Frank DiPino	.50	.20	.05
☐	36	Bryn Smith	.60	.25	.06
☐	37	Scott Terry	.50	.20	.05
☐	38	Todd Worrell	.60	.25	.06
☐	39	Bob Tewksbury	.50	.20	.05
☐	43	Ken Hill	.60	.25	.06
☐	47	Lee Smith	.75	.30	.07
☐	48	Jose DeLeon	.50	.20	.05
☐	49	Juan Agosto	.50	.20	.05

1991 Police Dodgers

1991 Police Royals

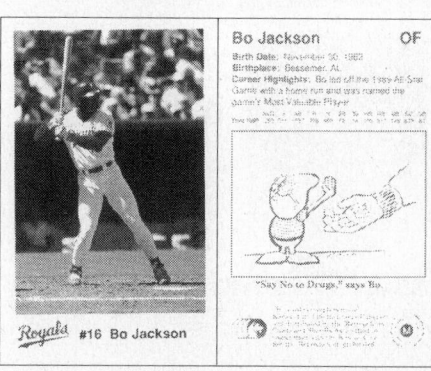

This 30-card set was sponsored by the Los Angeles Police Department and its Crime Prevention Advisory Council. The cards measure approximately 2 13/16" by 4 1/8". The fronts feature color action player photos with the top corners rounded off and white borders on all sides. A black line divides the horizontally oriented back into two halves. While the left half presents biographical information, the right half has an anti-drug or alcohol message. The cards are skip-numbered by uniform number on the fronts.

	MINT	EXC	G-VG
COMPLETE SET (30)	5.00	2.25	.50
COMMON PLAYER	.20	.08	.02
☐ 3 Jeff Hamilton	.20	.08	.02
☐ 5 Stan Javier	.20	.08	.02
☐ 7 Alfredo Griffin	.20	.08	.02
☐ 10 Juan Samuel	.30	.12	.03
☐ 12 Gary Carter	.40	.16	.04
☐ 14 Mike Scioscia	.30	.12	.03
☐ 15 Chris Gwynn	.30	.12	.03
☐ 17 Bob Ojeda	.30	.12	.03
☐ 22 Brett Butler	.40	.16	.04
☐ 25 Dennis Cook	.20	.08	.02
☐ 27 Mike Sharperson	.20	.08	.02
☐ 28 Kal Daniels	.40	.16	.04
☐ 29 Lenny Harris	.30	.12	.03
☐ 30 Jose Offerman	.40	.16	.04
☐ 31 Jim Neidlinger	.30	.12	.03
☐ 33 Eddie Murray	.50	.20	.05
☐ 35 Jim Gott	.30	.12	.03
☐ 36 Mike Morgan	.30	.12	.03
☐ 38 Jose Gonzalez	.20	.08	.02
☐ 40 Barry Lyons	.20	.08	.02
☐ 44 Darryl Strawberry	.90	.40	.09
☐ 45 Kevin Gross	.20	.08	.02
☐ 46 Mike Hartley	.20	.08	.02
☐ 48 Ramon Martinez	.50	.20	.05
☐ 49 Tim Belcher	.30	.12	.03
☐ 50 Jay Howell	.30	.12	.03
☐ 52 Tim Crews	.20	.08	.02
☐ 54 John Candelaria	.20	.08	.02
☐ 55 Orel Hershiser	.50	.20	.05
☐ xx Coaches Card	.20	.08	.02
Ben Hines			
Ron Perranoski			
Mark Cresse			
Manny Mota			
Tommy Lasorda MG			
Joe Amalfitano			
Joe Ferguson			
Bill Russell			

This 27-card set was distributed by the Metropolitan Chiefs and Sheriffs Association. The cards measure 2 5/8" by 4 1/8". The front design has glossy color action photos with white borders. The player's number and name appear below the picture. In blue print, the backs present biography, statistics, and a cartoon with a public service announcement by the player. The cards are unnumbered and checklisted below in alphabetical order, with the coaches' cards listed at the end. Supposedly many of the Bo Jackson cards were burned after Bo was cut from the team.

	MINT	EXC	G-VG
COMPLETE SET (27)	18.00	7.50	2.50
COMMON PLAYER (1-27)	.25	.10	.02
☐ 1 Kevin Appier	.50	.20	.05
☐ 2 Luis Aquino	.25	.10	.02
☐ 3 Mike Boddicker	.35	.15	.03
☐ 4 George Brett	.90	.40	.09
☐ 5 Steve Crawford	.25	.10	.02
☐ 6 Mark Davis	.35	.15	.03
☐ 7 Storm Davis	.35	.15	.03
☐ 8 Jim Eisenreich	.35	.15	.03
☐ 9 Kirk Gibson	.50	.20	.05
☐ 10 Tom Gordon	.50	.20	.05
☐ 11 Mark Gubicza	.35	.15	.03
☐ 12 Bo Jackson SP	9.00	4.00	.90
☐ 13 Mike Macfarlane	.35	.15	.03
☐ 14 Andy McGaffigan	.25	.10	.02
☐ 15 Brian McRae	.60	.25	.06
☐ 16 Jeff Montgomery	.35	.15	.03
☐ 17 Bill Pecota	.35	.15	.03
☐ 18 Bret Saberhagen	.90	.40	.09
☐ 19 Kevin Seitzer	.35	.15	.03
☐ 20 Terry Shumpert	.35	.15	.03
☐ 21 Kurt Stillwell	.35	.15	.03
☐ 22 Danny Tartabull	.90	.40	.09
☐ 23 Gary Thurman	.25	.10	.02
☐ 24 John Wathan MG	.25	.10	.02
☐ 25 Coaches	.25	.10	.02
Pat Dodson			
Adrian Garrett			
☐ 26 Coaches	.25	.10	.02
Glenn Ezell			
Lynn Jones			
Bob Schaefer			
☐ 27 Checklist Card	.25	.10	.02

1961 Post Cereal

BASEBALL STAR CARD No.**167**

★ ★ ★ ★ ★ ★ ★

Duke Snider

LOS ANGELES DODGERS — OUTFIELDER
Ht.—6'1"; Wt.—207; Bats—Left; Throws—Right
Born—Sept. 19, 1926; Home—Fallbrook, Calif.
Only two batters in National League history (Mel Ott and Stan Musial) have hit more homers than Duke Snider. He is the only player to hit 4 home runs in two different World Series. Duke was selected for the All Star Team 1950-51-53-54-55-56

MAJOR LEAGUE BATTING RECORD								
	Games	At Bat	Runs	Hits	2 B	3 B	HR	RBI	Avg.
1960	101	235	38	57	13	5	14	36	.243
LIFE	1,758	6,249	1,136	1,882	324	76	368	1,185	.301

The cards in this 200-card set measure 2 1/2" by 3 1/2". The 1961 Post set was this company's first major set. The cards were available on thick cardbox stock, singly or in various panel sizes from cereal boxes (BOX), or in team sheets, printed on thinner cardboard stock, directly from the Post Cereal Company (COM). Many variations exist and are noted in the checklist below. There are many cards which were produced in lesser quantities; the prices below reflect the relative scarcity of each of these cards. Cards 10, 23, 70, 73, 94, 113, 135, 163, and 183 are examples of cards printed in limited quantities and hence commanding premium prices. The cards are numbered essentially in team groups, i.e., New York Yankees (1-18), Chicago White Sox (19-34), Detroit (35-46), Boston (47-56), Cleveland (57-67), Baltimore (68-80), Kansas City (81-90), Minnesota (91-100), Milwaukee (101-114), Philadelphia (115-124), Pittsburgh (125-140), San Francisco (141-155), Los Angeles Dodgers (156-170), St. Louis (171-180), Cincinnati (181-190), and Chicago Cubs (191-200). The catalog number is F278-33. The complete set prices refers to a set, with all variations (357). There was also an album produced by Post to hold the cards.

	NRMT	VG-E	GOOD
COMPLETE SET (357)	2750.00	1100.00	275.00
COMMON PLAYER (1-200)	3.00	1.25	.30

		NRMT	VG-E	GOOD
☐ 1A	Yogi Berra COM	25.00	11.00	3.50
☐ 1B	Yogi Berra BOX	25.00	11.00	3.50
☐ 2A	Elston Howard COM	4.00	1.75	.40
☐ 2B	Elston Howard BOX	4.00	1.75	.40
☐ 3A	Bill Skowron COM	4.00	1.75	.40
☐ 3B	Bill Skowron BOX	3.00	1.25	.30
☐ 4A	Mickey Mantle COM	120.00	55.00	18.00
☐ 4B	Mickey Mantle BOX	120.00	55.00	18.00
☐ 5	Bob Turley COM only	20.00	8.50	2.75
☐ 6A	Whitey Ford COM	9.00	4.00	.90
☐ 6B	Whitey Ford BOX	9.00	4.00	.90
☐ 7A	Roger Maris COM	27.00	12.00	4.00
☐ 7B	Roger Maris BOX	27.00	12.00	4.00
☐ 8A	B.Richardson COM	4.00	1.75	.40
☐ 8B	B.Richardson BOX	3.00	1.25	.30
☐ 9A	Tony Kubek COM	4.00	1.75	.40
☐ 9B	Tony Kubek BOX	3.00	1.25	.30
☐ 10	G.McDougald BOX only	40.00	18.00	6.00
☐ 11	Cletis Boyer BOX only	3.00	1.25	.30
☐ 12A	Hector Lopes COM	3.00	1.25	.30
☐ 12B	Hector Lopes BOX	3.00	1.25	.30
☐ 13	Bob Cerv BOX only	3.00	1.25	.30
☐ 14	Ryne Duren BOX only	3.00	1.25	.30
☐ 15	Bobby Shantz BOX only	3.00	1.25	.30
☐ 16	Art Ditmar BOX only	3.00	1.25	.30
☐ 17	Jim Coates BOX only	3.00	1.25	.30
☐ 18	J.Blanchard BOX only	3.00	1.25	.30
☐ 19A	Luis Aparicio COM	7.50	3.25	.75
☐ 19B	Luis Aparicio BOX	6.00	2.50	.60
☐ 20A	Nelson Fox COM	6.00	2.50	.60
☐ 20B	Nelson Fox BOX	5.00	2.25	.50
☐ 21A	Bill Pierce COM	4.00	1.75	.40
☐ 21B	Bill Pierce BOX	6.00	2.50	.60

		NRMT	VG-E	GOOD
☐ 22A	Early Wynn COM	10.00	4.50	1.25
☐ 22B	Early Wynn BOX	12.00	5.25	1.50
☐ 23	Bob Shaw BOX only	100.00	45.00	15.00
☐ 24A	Al Smith COM	3.00	1.25	.30
☐ 24B	Al Smith BOX	3.00	1.25	.30
☐ 25A	Minnie Minoso COM	4.00	1.75	.40
☐ 25B	Minnie Minoso BOX	3.00	1.25	.30
☐ 26A	Roy Sievers COM	3.00	1.25	.30
☐ 26B	Roy Sievers BOX	3.00	1.25	.30
☐ 27A	Jim Landis COM	3.00	1.25	.30
☐ 27B	Jim Landis BOX	3.00	1.25	.30
☐ 28A	Sherm Lollar COM	3.00	1.25	.30
☐ 28B	Sherm Lollar BOX	3.00	1.25	.30
☐ 29	Gerry Staley BOX only	3.00	1.25	.30
☐ 30A	Gene Freese COM (Reds)	9.00	4.00	.90
☐ 30B	Gene Freese BOX (White Sox)	3.00	1.25	.30
☐ 31	Ted Kluszewski BOX only	4.00	1.75	.40
☐ 32	Turk Lown BOX only	3.00	1.25	.30
☐ 33A	Jim Rivera COM	3.00	1.25	.30
☐ 33B	Jim Rivera BOX	3.00	1.25	.30
☐ 34	F.Baumann BOX only	3.00	1.25	.30
☐ 35A	Al Kaline COM	18.00	7.50	2.50
☐ 35B	Al Kaline BOX	18.00	7.50	2.50
☐ 36A	Rocky Colavito COM	7.50	3.25	.75
☐ 36B	Rocky Colavito BOX	5.00	2.25	.50
☐ 37A	C.Maxwell COM	3.00	1.25	.30
☐ 37B	C.Maxwell BOX	3.00	1.25	.30
☐ 38A	Frank Lary COM	3.00	1.25	.30
☐ 38B	Frank Lary BOX	3.00	1.25	.30
☐ 39A	Jim Bunning COM	5.00	2.25	.50
☐ 39B	Jim Bunning BOX	4.00	1.75	.40
☐ 40A	Norm Cash COM	3.00	1.25	.30
☐ 40B	Norm Cash BOX	3.00	1.25	.30
☐ 41A	Frank Bolling COM (Braves, "Charlie Gehringer" in bio)	5.00	2.25	.50
☐ 41B	Frank Bolling BOX (Tigers, "Charlie Derringer" in bio)	7.50	3.25	.75
☐ 42A	Don Mossi COM	3.00	1.25	.30
☐ 42B	Don Mossi BOX	3.00	1.25	.30
☐ 43A	Lou Berberet COM	3.00	1.25	.30
☐ 43B	Lou Berberet BOX	3.00	1.25	.30
☐ 44	Dave Sisler BOX only	3.00	1.25	.30
☐ 45	Ed Yost BOX only	3.00	1.25	.30
☐ 46	Pete Burnside BOX only	3.00	1.25	.30
☐ 47A	Pete Runnels COM	3.00	1.25	.30
☐ 47B	Pete Runnels BOX	4.00	1.75	.40
☐ 48A	Frank Malzone COM	3.00	1.25	.30
☐ 48B	Frank Malzone BOX	3.00	1.25	.30
☐ 49A	Vic Wertz COM	5.00	2.25	.50
☐ 49B	Vic Wertz BOX	5.00	2.25	.50
☐ 50A	Tom Brewer COM	3.00	1.25	.30
☐ 50B	Tom Brewer BOX	3.00	1.25	.30
☐ 51A	Willie Tasby COM (Sold to Wash.)	6.00	2.50	.60
☐ 51B	Willie Tasby BOX (no sale mention)	3.00	1.25	.30
☐ 52A	Russ Nixon COM	3.00	1.25	.30
☐ 52B	Russ Nixon BOX	3.00	1.25	.30
☐ 53A	Don Buddin COM	3.00	1.25	.30
☐ 53B	Don Buddin BOX	3.00	1.25	.30
☐ 54A	B.Monbouquette COM	3.00	1.25	.30
☐ 54B	B.Monbouquette BOX	3.00	1.25	.30
☐ 55A	Frank Sullivan COM (Phillies)	9.00	4.00	.90
☐ 55B	Frank Sullivan BOX (Red Sox)	3.00	1.25	.30
☐ 56A	H.Sullivan COM	3.00	1.25	.30
☐ 56B	H.Sullivan BOX	3.00	1.25	.30
☐ 57A	Harvey Kuenn COM (Giants)	6.00	2.50	.60
☐ 57B	Harvey Kuenn BOX (Indians)	4.00	1.75	.40
☐ 58A	Gary Bell COM	4.00	1.75	.40
☐ 58B	Gary Bell BOX	5.00	2.25	.50
☐ 59A	Jim Perry COM	3.00	1.25	.30
☐ 59B	Jim Perry BOX	3.00	1.25	.30
☐ 60A	Jim Grant COM	3.00	1.25	.30
☐ 60B	Jim Grant BOX	4.00	1.75	.40
☐ 61A	Johnny Temple COM	3.00	1.25	.30
☐ 61B	Johnny Temple BOX	3.00	1.25	.30
☐ 62A	Paul Foytack COM	3.00	1.25	.30
☐ 62B	Paul Foytack BOX	3.00	1.25	.30
☐ 63A	Vic Power COM	3.00	1.25	.30
☐ 63B	Vic Power BOX	3.00	1.25	.30
☐ 64A	Tito Francona COM	3.00	1.25	.30
☐ 64B	Tito Francona BOX	3.00	1.25	.30

☐ 65A Ken Aspromonte COM	7.50	3.25	.75
(Sold to L.A.)			
☐ 65B Ken Aspromonte BOX	7.50	3.25	.75
(no sale mention)			
☐ 66 Bob Wilson BOX only	3.00	1.25	.30
☐ 67A John Romano COM	3.00	1.25	.30
☐ 67B John Romano BOX	3.00	1.25	.30
☐ 68A Jim Gentile COM	4.00	1.75	.40
☐ 68B Jim Gentile BOX	3.00	1.25	.30
☐ 69A Gus Triandos COM	3.00	1.25	.30
☐ 69B Gus Triandos BOX	4.00	1.75	.40
☐ 70 G.Woodling BOX only	35.00	15.75	5.25
☐ 71A Milt Pappas COM	4.00	1.75	.40
☐ 71B Milt Pappas BOX	4.00	1.75	.40
☐ 72A Ron Hansen COM	3.00	1.25	.30
☐ 72B Ron Hansen BOX	3.00	1.25	.30
☐ 73 Chuck Estrada	100.00	45.00	15.00
COM only			
☐ 74A Steve Barber COM	3.00	1.25	.30
☐ 74B Steve Barber BOX	3.00	1.25	.30
☐ 75A B.Robinson COM	25.00	11.00	3.50
☐ 75B B.Robinson BOX	20.00	8.50	2.75
☐ 76A Jackie Brandt COM	3.00	1.25	.30
☐ 76B Jackie Brandt BOX	3.00	1.25	.30
☐ 77A Marv Breeding COM	3.00	1.25	.30
☐ 77B Marv Breeding BOX	3.00	1.25	.30
☐ 78 Hal Brown BOX only	3.00	1.25	.30
☐ 79 Billy Klaus BOX only	3.00	1.25	.30
☐ 80A Hoyt Wilhelm COM	9.00	4.00	.90
☐ 80B Hoyt Wilhelm BOX	6.00	2.50	.60
☐ 81A Jerry Lumpe COM	5.00	2.25	.50
☐ 81B Jerry Lumpe BOX	5.00	2.25	.50
☐ 82A Norm Siebern COM	3.00	1.25	.30
☐ 82B Norm Siebern BOX	3.00	1.25	.30
☐ 83A Bud Daley COM	4.00	1.75	.40
☐ 83B Bud Daley BOX	3.00	1.25	.30
☐ 84A Bill Tuttle COM	3.00	1.25	.30
☐ 84B Bill Tuttle BOX	3.00	1.25	.30
☐ 85A M.Throneberry COM	3.00	1.25	.30
☐ 85B M.Throneberry BOX	3.00	1.25	.30
☐ 86A Dick Williams COM	3.00	1.25	.30
☐ 86B Dick Williams BOX	3.00	1.25	.30
☐ 87A Ray Herbert COM	3.00	1.25	.30
☐ 87B Ray Herbert BOX	3.00	1.25	.30
☐ 88A Whitey Herzog COM	4.00	1.75	.40
☐ 88B Whitey Herzog BOX	3.00	1.25	.30
☐ 89A Ken Hamlin COM	18.00	7.50	2.50
(Sold to L.A.)			
☐ 89B Ken Hamlin BOX	3.00	1.25	.30
(no sale mention)			
☐ 90A Hank Bauer COM	4.00	1.75	.40
☐ 90B Hank Bauer BOX	3.00	1.25	.30
☐ 91A Bob Allison COM	5.00	2.25	.50
(Minnesota)			
☐ 91B Bob Allison BOX	5.00	2.25	.50
(Minneapolis)			
☐ 92A Harmon Killebrew	35.00	15.75	5.25
(Minnesota) COM			
☐ 92B Harmon Killebrew	25.00	11.00	3.50
(Minneapolis) BOX			
☐ 93A Jim Lemon COM	20.00	8.50	2.75
(Minnesota)			
☐ 93B Jim Lemon BOX	60.00	27.00	9.00
(Minneapolis)			
☐ 94A Chuck Stobbs	165.00	75.00	22.00
(Minnesota)			
COM only			
☐ 95A Reno Bertoia COM	5.00	2.25	.50
(Minnesota)			
☐ 95B Reno Bertoia BOX	3.00	1.25	.30
(Minneapolis)			
☐ 96A Billy Gardner COM	5.00	2.25	.50
(Minnesota)			
☐ 96B Billy Gardner BOX	3.00	1.25	.30
(Minneapolis)			
☐ 97A Earl Battey COM	5.00	2.25	.50
(Minnesota)			
☐ 97B Earl Battey BOX	3.00	1.25	.30
(Minneapolis)			
☐ 98A Pedro Ramos COM	5.00	2.25	.50
(Minnesota)			
☐ 98B Pedro Ramos BOX	3.00	1.25	.30
(Minneapolis)			
☐ 99A Camilo Pascual COM	5.00	2.25	.50
(Minnesota)			
☐ 99B Camilo Pascual BOX	3.00	1.25	.30
(Minneapolis)			
☐ 100A Billy Consolo COM	5.00	2.25	.50
(Minnesota)			
☐ 100B Billy Consolo BOX	3.00	1.25	.30
(Minneapolis)			
☐ 101A Warren Spahn COM	25.00	11.00	3.50
☐ 101B Warren Spahn BOX	20.00	8.50	2.75
☐ 102A Lew Burdette COM	4.00	1.75	.40
☐ 102B Lew Burdette BOX	3.00	1.25	.30
☐ 103A Bob Buhl COM	3.00	1.25	.30
☐ 103B Bob Buhl BOX	3.00	1.25	.30
☐ 104A Joe Adcock COM	4.00	1.75	.40
☐ 104B Joe Adcock BOX	4.00	1.75	.40
☐ 105A John Logan COM	4.00	1.75	.40
☐ 105B John Logan BOX	4.00	1.75	.40
☐ 106 Ed Mathews COM only	30.00	13.50	4.50
☐ 107A Hank Aaron COM	30.00	13.50	4.50
☐ 107B Hank Aaron BOX	25.00	11.00	3.50
☐ 108A Wes Covington COM	3.00	1.25	.30
☐ 108B Wes Covington BOX	3.00	1.25	.30
☐ 109A Bill Bruton COM	6.00	2.50	.60
(Tigers)			
☐ 109B Bill Bruton BOX	6.00	2.50	.60
(Braves)			
☐ 110A Del Crandall COM	4.00	1.75	.40
☐ 110B Del Crandall BOX	4.00	1.75	.40
☐ 111 Red Schoendienst	4.00	1.75	.40
BOX only			
☐ 112 Juan Pizarro	3.00	1.25	.30
BOX only			
☐ 113 Chuck Cottier	15.00	6.50	2.15
BOX only			
☐ 114 Al Spangler BOX only	3.00	1.25	.30
☐ 115A Dick Farrell COM	5.00	2.25	.50
☐ 115B Dick Farrell BOX	5.00	2.25	.50
☐ 116A Jim Owens COM	5.00	2.25	.50
☐ 116B Jim Owens BOX	5.00	2.25	.50
☐ 117A Robin Roberts COM	9.00	4.00	.90
☐ 117B Robin Roberts BOX	6.00	2.50	.60
☐ 118A Tony Taylor COM	3.00	1.25	.30
☐ 118B Tony Taylor BOX	3.00	1.25	.30
☐ 119A Lee Walls COM	3.00	1.25	.30
☐ 119B Lee Walls BOX	3.00	1.25	.30
☐ 120A Tony Curry COM	3.00	1.25	.30
☐ 120B Tony Curry BOX	3.00	1.25	.30
☐ 121A Pancho Herrera COM	3.00	1.25	.30
☐ 121B Pancho Herrera BOX	3.00	1.25	.30
☐ 122A Ken Walters COM	3.00	1.25	.30
☐ 122B Ken Walters BOX	3.00	1.25	.30
☐ 123A John Callison COM	3.00	1.25	.30
☐ 123B John Callison BOX	3.00	1.25	.30
☐ 124A Gene Conley COM	9.00	4.00	.90
(Red Sox)			
☐ 124B Gene Conley BOX	3.00	1.25	.30
(Phillies)			
☐ 125A Bob Friend COM	4.00	1.75	.40
☐ 125B Bob Friend BOX	4.00	1.75	.40
☐ 126A Vernon Law COM	4.00	1.75	.40
☐ 126B Vernon Law BOX	4.00	1.75	.40
☐ 127A Dick Stuart COM	3.00	1.25	.30
☐ 127B Dick Stuart BOX	3.00	1.25	.30
☐ 128A Bill Mazeroski COM	4.00	1.75	.40
☐ 128B Bill Mazeroski BOX	3.00	1.25	.30
☐ 129A Dick Groat COM	4.00	1.75	.40
☐ 129B Dick Groat BOX	3.00	1.25	.30
☐ 130A Don Hoak COM	3.00	1.25	.30
☐ 130B Don Hoak BOX	3.00	1.25	.30
☐ 131A Bob Skinner COM	3.00	1.25	.30
☐ 131B Bob Skinner BOX	3.00	1.25	.30
☐ 132A Bob Clemente COM	35.00	15.75	5.25
☐ 132B Bob Clemente BOX	30.00	13.50	4.50
☐ 133 Roy Face BOX only	4.00	1.75	.40
☐ 134 H.Haddix BOX only	3.00	1.25	.30
☐ 135 Bill Virdon BOX only	40.00	18.00	6.00
☐ 136A Gino Cimoli COM	3.00	1.25	.30
☐ 136B Gino Cimoli BOX	3.00	1.25	.30
☐ 137 Rocky Nelson	3.00	1.25	.30
BOX only			
☐ 138A Smoky Burgess COM	4.00	1.75	.40
☐ 138B Smoky Burgess BOX	3.00	1.25	.30
☐ 139 Hal Smith BOX only	3.00	1.25	.30
☐ 140 Wilmer Mizell	3.00	1.25	.30
BOX only			
☐ 141A M.McCormick COM	3.00	1.25	.30
☐ 141B M.McCormick BOX	3.00	1.25	.30
☐ 142A John Antonelli COM	5.00	2.25	.50
(Cleveland)			
☐ 142B John Antonelli BOX	4.00	1.75	.40
(San Francisco)			
☐ 143A Sam Jones COM	4.00	1.75	.40
☐ 143B Sam Jones BOX	5.00	2.25	.50
☐ 144A Orlando Cepeda COM	7.50	3.25	.75
☐ 144B Orlando Cepeda BOX	6.00	2.50	.60
☐ 145A Willie Mays COM	35.00	15.75	5.25
☐ 145B Willie Mays BOX	25.00	11.00	3.50
☐ 146A Willie Kirkland	5.00	2.25	.50
(Cleve.) COM			
☐ 146B Willie Kirkland	4.00	1.75	.40
(San Fran.) BOX			
☐ 147A Willie McCovey COM	12.50	5.50	1.65
☐ 147B Willie McCovey BOX	7.50	3.25	.75
☐ 148A Don Blasingame COM	3.00	1.25	.30

			NRMT	VG-E	GOOD
☐	148B	Don Blasingame BOX	3.00	1.25	.30
☐	149A	Jim Davenport COM	4.00	1.75	.40
☐	149B	Jim Davenport BOX	3.00	1.25	.30
☐	150A	Hobie Landrith COM	3.00	1.25	.30
☐	150B	Hobie Landrith BOX	3.00	1.25	.30
☐	151	Bob Schmidt BOX only	3.00	1.25	.30
☐	152A	Ed Bressoud COM	3.00	1.25	.30
☐	152B	Ed Bressoud BOX	3.00	1.25	.30
☐	153A	Andre Rodgers	18.00	7.50	2.50
		(no trade mention)			
		BOX only			
☐	153B	Andre Rodgers	4.00	1.75	.40
		(Traded to Milw.)			
		BOX only			
☐	154	Jack Sanford	3.00	1.25	.30
		BOX only			
☐	155	Billy O'Dell	3.00	1.25	.30
		BOX only			
☐	156A	Norm Larker COM	3.00	1.25	.30
☐	156B	Norm Larker BOX	3.00	1.25	.30
☐	157A	Charlie Neal COM	3.00	1.25	.30
☐	157B	Charlie Neal BOX	3.00	1.25	.30
☐	158A	Jim Gilliam COM	5.00	2.25	.50
☐	158B	Jim Gilliam BOX	4.00	1.75	.40
☐	159A	Wally Moon COM	4.00	1.75	.40
☐	159B	Wally Moon BOX	3.00	1.25	.30
☐	160A	Don Drysdale COM	12.50	5.50	1.65
☐	160B	Don Drysdale BOX	9.00	4.00	.90
☐	161A	Larry Sherry COM	4.00	1.75	.40
☐	161B	Larry Sherry BOX	3.00	1.25	.30
☐	162	Stan Williams	6.00	2.50	.60
		BOX only			
☐	163	Mel Roach BOX only	75.00	34.00	11.25
☐	164A	Maury Wills COM	6.00	2.50	.60
☐	164B	Maury Wills BOX	4.00	1.75	.40
☐	165	Tommy Davis BOX only	3.00	1.25	.30
☐	166A	John Roseboro COM	3.00	1.25	.30
☐	166B	John Roseboro BOX	3.00	1.25	.30
☐	167A	Duke Snider COM	12.50	5.50	1.65
☐	167B	Duke Snider BOX	6.00	2.50	.60
☐	168A	Gil Hodges COM	10.00	4.50	1.25
☐	168B	Gil Hodges BOX	6.00	2.50	.60
☐	169	John Podres BOX only	3.00	1.25	.30
☐	170	Ed Roebuck BOX only	3.00	1.25	.30
☐	171A	Ken Boyer COM	9.00	4.00	.90
☐	171B	Ken Boyer BOX	7.00	3.00	.70
☐	172A	J.Cunningham COM	3.00	1.25	.30
☐	172B	J.Cunningham BOX	3.00	1.25	.30
☐	173A	Daryl Spencer COM	3.00	1.25	.30
☐	173B	Daryl Spencer BOX	3.00	1.25	.30
☐	174A	Larry Jackson COM	3.00	1.25	.30
☐	174B	Larry Jackson BOX	3.00	1.25	.30
☐	175A	Lindy McDaniel COM	3.00	1.25	.30
☐	175B	Lindy McDaniel BOX	3.00	1.25	.30
☐	176A	Bill White COM	4.00	1.75	.40
☐	176B	Bill White BOX	3.00	1.25	.30
☐	177A	Alex Grammas COM	3.00	1.25	.30
☐	177B	Alex Grammas BOX	3.00	1.25	.30
☐	178A	Curt Flood COM	4.00	1.75	.40
☐	178B	Curt Flood BOX	3.00	1.25	.30
☐	179A	Ernie Broglio COM	3.00	1.25	.30
☐	179B	Ernie Broglio BOX	3.00	1.25	.30
☐	180A	Hal Smith COM	3.00	1.25	.30
☐	180B	Hal Smith BOX	3.00	1.25	.30
☐	181A	Vada Pinson COM	4.00	1.75	.40
☐	181B	Vada Pinson BOX	3.00	1.25	.30
☐	182A	Frank Robinson COM	35.00	15.75	5.25
☐	182B	Frank Robinson BOX	30.00	13.50	4.50
☐	183	Roy McMillan	90.00	40.00	13.50
		BOX only			
☐	184A	Bob Purkey COM	3.00	1.25	.30
☐	184B	Bob Purkey BOX	3.00	1.25	.30
☐	185A	Ed Kasko COM	3.00	1.25	.30
☐	185B	Ed Kasko BOX	3.00	1.25	.30
☐	186A	Gus Bell COM	3.00	1.25	.30
☐	186B	Gus Bell BOX	3.00	1.25	.30
☐	187A	Jerry Lynch COM	3.00	1.25	.30
☐	187B	Jerry Lynch BOX	3.00	1.25	.30
☐	188A	Ed Bailey COM	3.00	1.25	.30
☐	188B	Ed Bailey BOX	3.00	1.25	.30
☐	189A	Jim O'Toole COM	3.00	1.25	.30
☐	189B	Jim O'Toole BOX	3.00	1.25	.30
☐	190A	Billy Martin COM	9.00	4.00	.90
		(Sold to Milw.)			
☐	190B	Billy Martin BOX	4.00	1.75	.40
		(no sale mention)			
☐	191A	Ernie Banks COM	25.00	11.00	3.50
☐	191B	Ernie Banks BOX	20.00	8.50	2.75
☐	192A	Richie Ashburn COM	5.00	2.25	.50
☐	192B	Richie Ashburn BOX	4.00	1.75	.40
☐	193A	Frank Thomas COM	15.00	6.50	2.15
☐	193B	Frank Thomas BOX	35.00	15.75	5.25
☐	194A	Don Cardwell COM	3.00	1.25	.30
☐	194B	Don Cardwell BOX	3.00	1.25	.30

			NRMT	VG-E	GOOD
☐	195A	George Altman COM	3.00	1.25	.30
☐	195B	George Altman BOX	3.00	1.25	.30
☐	196A	Ron Santo COM	4.00	1.75	.40
☐	196B	Ron Santo BOX	3.00	1.25	.30
☐	197A	Glen Hobbie COM	3.00	1.25	.30
☐	197B	Glen Hobbie BOX	3.00	1.25	.30
☐	198A	Sam Taylor COM	3.00	1.25	.30
☐	198B	Sam Taylor BOX	3.00	1.25	.30
☐	199A	Jerry Kindall COM	3.00	1.25	.30
☐	199B	Jerry Kindall BOX	3.00	1.25	.30
☐	200A	Don Elston COM	3.00	1.25	.30
☐	200B	Don Elston BOX	3.00	1.25	.30

1962 Post Cereal

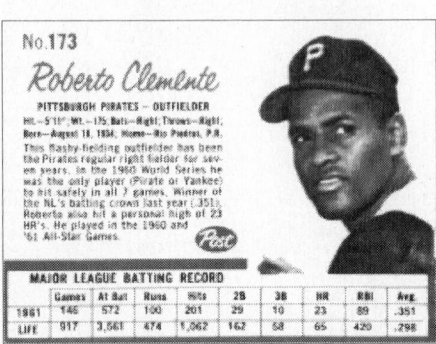

The cards in this 200-card series measure 2 1/2" by 3 1/2". The 1962 Post set is the easiest of the Post sets to complete. The cards are grouped numerically by team, for example, New York Yankees (1-13), Detroit (14-26), Baltimore (27-36), Cleveland (37-45), Chicago White Sox (46-55), Boston (56-64), Washington (65-73), Los Angeles Angels (74-82), Minnesota (83-91), Kansas City (92-100), Los Angeles Dodgers (101-115), Cincinnati (116-130), San Francisco (131-144), Milwaukee (145-157), St. Louis (158-168), Pittsburgh (169-181), Chicago Cubs (182-191), and Philadelphia (192-200). Cards 5B and 6B were printed on thin stock in a two card panel and distributed in a magazine promotion. The scarce cards are 55, 92, 101, 116, 121, and 140. The checklist for this set is the same as that of 1962 Jello and 1962 Post Canadian, but those sets are considered separate issues. The catalog number for this set is F278-37.

			NRMT	VG-E	GOOD
	COMPLETE SET (208)		1800.00	800.00	180.00
	COMMON PLAYER (1-200)		2.25	.90	.22
☐	1	Bill Skowron	3.00	1.25	.30
☐	2	Bobby Richardson	3.00	1.25	.30
☐	3	Cletis Boyer	2.25	.90	.22
☐	4	Tony Kubek	3.00	1.25	.30
☐	5A	Mickey Mantle	90.00	40.00	13.50
☐	5B	Mickey Mantle AD	90.00	40.00	13.50
☐	6A	Roger Maris	25.00	11.00	3.50
☐	6B	Roger Maris AD	25.00	11.00	3.50
☐	7	Yogi Berra	20.00	8.50	2.75
☐	8	Elston Howard	3.00	1.25	.30
☐	9	Whitey Ford	9.00	4.00	.90
☐	10	Ralph Terry	2.25	.90	.22
☐	11	John Blanchard	2.25	.90	.22
☐	12	Luis Arroyo	2.25	.90	.22
☐	13	Bill Stafford	2.25	.90	.22
☐	14A	Norm Cash ERR	15.00	6.50	2.15
		(Throws: right)			
☐	14B	Norm Cash COR	2.25	.90	.22
		(Throws: left)			
☐	15	Jake Wood	2.25	.90	.22
☐	16	Steve Boros	2.25	.90	.22
☐	17	Chico Fernandez	2.25	.90	.22
☐	18	Bill Bruton	2.25	.90	.22
☐	19	Rocky Colavito	3.50	1.50	.35
☐	20	Al Kaline	15.00	6.50	2.15
☐	21	Dick Brown	2.25	.90	.22
☐	22	Frank Lary	2.25	.90	.22

☐ 23	Don Mossi	2.25	.90	.22
☐ 24	Phil Regan	2.25	.90	.22
☐ 25	Charley Maxwell	2.25	.90	.22
☐ 26	Jim Bunning	4.00	1.75	.40
☐ 27A	Jim Gentile	3.00	1.25	.30
	Home: Baltimore			
☐ 27B	Jim Gentile	15.00	6.50	2.15
	Home: San Lorenzo			
☐ 28	Marv Breeding	2.25	.90	.22
☐ 29	Brooks Robinson	15.00	6.50	2.15
☐ 30A	Ron Hansen	3.00	1.25	.30
	(At-Bats)			
☐ 30B	Ron Hansen	3.00	1.25	.30
	(At Bats)			
☐ 31	Jackie Brandt	2.25	.90	.22
☐ 32	Dick Williams	2.25	.90	.22
☐ 33	Gus Triandos	2.25	.90	.22
☐ 34	Milt Pappas	2.25	.90	.22
☐ 35	Hoyt Wilhelm	8.00	3.50	.80
☐ 36	Chuck Estrada	7.00	3.00	.70
☐ 37	Vic Power	2.25	.90	.22
☐ 38	Johnny Temple	2.25	.90	.22
☐ 39	Bubba Phillips	2.25	.90	.22
☐ 40	Tito Francona	2.25	.90	.22
☐ 41	Willie Kirkland	2.25	.90	.22
☐ 42	John Romano	2.25	.90	.22
☐ 43	Jim Perry	2.25	.90	.22
☐ 44	Woodie Held	2.25	.90	.22
☐ 45	Chuck Essegian	2.25	.90	.22
☐ 46	Roy Sievers	2.25	.90	.22
☐ 47	Nellie Fox	3.50	1.50	.35
☐ 48	Al Smith	2.25	.90	.22
☐ 49	Luis Aparicio	4.00	1.75	.40
☐ 50	Jim Landis	2.25	.90	.22
☐ 51	Minnie Minoso	3.00	1.25	.30
☐ 52	Andy Carey	2.25	.90	.22
☐ 53	Sherman Lollar	2.25	.90	.22
☐ 54	Bill Pierce	3.00	1.25	.30
☐ 55	Early Wynn	30.00	13.50	4.50
☐ 56	Chuck Schilling	2.25	.90	.22
☐ 57	Pete Runnels	2.25	.90	.22
☐ 58	Frank Malzone	2.25	.90	.22
☐ 59	Don Buddin	2.25	.90	.22
☐ 60	Gary Geiger	2.25	.90	.22
☐ 61	Carl Yastrzemski	40.00	18.00	6.00
☐ 62	Jackie Jensen	2.25	.90	.22
☐ 63	Jim Pagliaroni	2.25	.90	.22
☐ 64	Don Schwall	2.25	.90	.22
☐ 65	Dale Long	2.25	.90	.22
☐ 66	Chuck Cottier	2.25	.90	.22
☐ 67	Billy Klaus	2.25	.90	.22
☐ 68	Coot Veal	2.25	.90	.22
☐ 69	Marty Keough	35.00	15.75	5.25
☐ 70	Willie Tasby	2.25	.90	.22
☐ 71	Gene Woodling	2.25	.90	.22
☐ 72	Gene Green	2.25	.90	.22
☐ 73	Dick Donovan	2.25	.90	.22
☐ 74	Steve Bilko	2.25	.90	.22
☐ 75	Rocky Bridges	2.25	.90	.22
☐ 76	Eddie Yost	2.25	.90	.22
☐ 77	Leon Wagner	2.25	.90	.22
☐ 78	Albie Pearson	2.25	.90	.22
☐ 79	Ken Hunt	2.25	.90	.22
☐ 80	Earl Averill Jr.	2.25	.90	.22
☐ 81	Ryne Duren	2.25	.90	.22
☐ 82	Ted Kluszewski	3.00	1.25	.30
☐ 83	Bob Allison	30.00	13.50	4.50
☐ 84	Billy Martin	3.50	1.50	.35
☐ 85	Harmon Killebrew	9.00	4.00	.90
☐ 86	Zoilo Versalles	2.25	.90	.22
☐ 87	Lenny Green	2.25	.90	.22
☐ 88	Bill Tuttle	2.25	.90	.22
☐ 89	Jim Lemon	2.25	.90	.22
☐ 90	Earl Battey	2.25	.90	.22
☐ 91	Camilo Pascual	2.25	.90	.22
☐ 92	Norm Sieburn	65.00	29.00	9.75
☐ 93	Jerry Lumpe	2.25	.90	.22
☐ 94	Dick Howser	3.00	1.25	.30
☐ 95A	Gene Stephens	3.00	1.25	.30
	Born: Jan. 5			
☐ 95B	Gene Stephens	15.00	6.50	2.15
	Born: Jan. 20			
☐ 96	Leo Posada	2.25	.90	.22
☐ 97	Joe Pignatano	2.25	.90	.22
☐ 98	Jim Archer	2.25	.90	.22
☐ 99	Haywood Sullivan	2.25	.90	.22
☐ 100	Art Ditmar	2.25	.90	.22
☐ 101	Gil Hodges	90.00	40.00	13.50
☐ 102	Charlie Neal	2.25	.90	.22
☐ 103	Daryl Spencer	25.00	11.00	3.50
☐ 104	Maury Wills	5.00	2.25	.50
☐ 105	Tommy Davis	3.00	1.25	.30
☐ 106	Willie Davis	3.00	1.25	.30
☐ 107	John Roseboro	2.25	.90	.22
☐ 108	John Podres	3.00	1.25	.30
☐ 109A	Sandy Koufax	30.00	13.50	4.50
☐ 109B	Sandy Koufax	65.00	29.00	9.75
	(with blue lines)			
☐ 110	Don Drysdale	9.00	4.00	.90
☐ 111	Larry Sherry	3.50	1.50	.35
☐ 112	Jim Gilliam	3.00	1.25	.30
☐ 113	Norm Larker	35.00	15.75	5.25
☐ 114	Duke Snider	8.00	3.50	.80
☐ 115	Stan Williams	2.25	.90	.22
☐ 116	Gordy Coleman	90.00	40.00	13.50
☐ 117	Don Blasingame	2.25	.90	.22
☐ 118	Gene Freese	2.25	.90	.22
☐ 119	Ed Kasko	2.25	.90	.22
☐ 120	Gus Bell	2.25	.90	.22
☐ 121	Vada Pinson	3.00	1.25	.30
☐ 122	Frank Robinson	30.00	13.50	4.50
☐ 123	Bob Purkey	2.25	.90	.22
☐ 124A	Joey Jay	3.00	1.25	.30
☐ 124B	Joey Jay	15.00	6.50	2.15
	(with blue lines)			
☐ 125	Jim Brosnan	30.00	13.50	4.50
☐ 126	Jim O'Toole	2.25	.90	.22
☐ 127	Jerry Lynch	60.00	27.00	9.00
☐ 128	Wally Post	2.25	.90	.22
☐ 129	Ken Hunt	2.25	.90	.22
☐ 130	Jerry Zimmerman	2.25	.90	.22
☐ 131	Willie McCovey	90.00	40.00	13.50
☐ 132	Jose Pagan	2.25	.90	.22
☐ 133	Felipe Alou	2.25	.90	.22
☐ 134	Jim Davenport	2.25	.90	.22
☐ 135	Harvey Kuenn	3.00	1.25	.30
☐ 136	Orlando Cepeda	4.50	2.00	.45
☐ 137	Ed Bailey	2.25	.90	.22
☐ 138	Sam Jones	2.25	.90	.22
☐ 139	Mike McCormick	2.25	.90	.22
☐ 140	Juan Marichal	100.00	45.00	15.00
☐ 141	Jack Sanford	2.25	.90	.22
☐ 142	Willie Mays	35.00	15.75	5.25
☐ 143	Stu Miller	7.50	3.25	.75
☐ 144	Joe Amalfitano	18.00	7.50	2.50
☐ 145A	Joe Adcock	3.00	1.25	.30
☐ 145B	Joe Adock (sic) ERR	60.00	27.00	9.00
☐ 146	Frank Bolling	2.25	.90	.22
☐ 147	Ed Mathews	12.00	5.25	1.50
☐ 148	Roy McMillan	2.25	.90	.22
☐ 149	Hank Aaron	35.00	15.75	5.25
☐ 150	Gino Cimoli	2.25	.90	.22
☐ 151	Frank Thomas	2.25	.90	.22
☐ 152	Joe Torre	3.00	1.25	.30
☐ 153	Lew Burdette	3.00	1.25	.30
☐ 154	Bob Buhl	2.25	.90	.22
☐ 155	Carlton Willey	2.25	.90	.22
☐ 156	Lee Maye	2.25	.90	.22
☐ 157	Al Spangler	2.25	.90	.22
☐ 158	Bill White	45.00	20.00	6.75
☐ 159	Ken Boyer	3.50	1.50	.35
☐ 160	Joe Cunningham	2.25	.90	.22
☐ 161	Carl Warwick	2.25	.90	.22
☐ 162	Carl Sawatski	2.25	.90	.22
☐ 163	Lindy McDaniel	2.25	.90	.22
☐ 164	Ernie Broglio	2.25	.90	.22
☐ 165	Larry Jackson	2.25	.90	.22
☐ 166	Curt Flood	3.00	1.25	.30
☐ 167	Curt Simmons	2.25	.90	.22
☐ 168	Alex Grammas	2.25	.90	.22
☐ 169	Dick Stuart	2.25	.90	.22
☐ 170	Bill Mazeroski UER	3.00	1.25	.30
	(Card reads 1959, should read 1960)			
☐ 171	Don Hoak	2.25	.90	.22
☐ 172	Dick Groat	3.00	1.25	.30
☐ 173A	Roberto Clemente	25.00	11.00	3.50
☐ 173B	Roberto Clemente	65.00	29.00	9.75
	(with blue lines)			
☐ 174	Bob Skinner	2.25	.90	.22
☐ 175	Bill Virdon	2.25	.90	.22
☐ 176	Smoky Burgess	2.25	.90	.22
☐ 177	Elroy Face	3.00	1.25	.30
☐ 178	Bob Friend	2.25	.90	.22
☐ 179	Vernon Law	2.25	.90	.22
☐ 180	Harvey Haddix	2.25	.90	.22
☐ 181	Hal Smith	2.25	.90	.22
☐ 182	Ed Bouchee	2.25	.90	.22
☐ 183	Don Zimmer	2.25	.90	.22
☐ 184	Ron Santo	3.00	1.25	.30
☐ 185	Andre Rodgers	2.25	.90	.22
☐ 186	Richie Ashburn	4.00	1.75	.40
☐ 187	George Altman	2.25	.90	.22
☐ 188	Ernie Banks	15.00	6.50	2.15
☐ 189	Sam Taylor	4.50	2.00	.45
☐ 190	Don Elston	2.25	.90	.22
☐ 191	Jerry Kindall	2.25	.90	.22
☐ 192	Pancho Herrera	2.25	.90	.22

		NRMT	VG-E	GOOD
☐ 193	Tony Taylor	2.25	.90	.22
☐ 194	Ruben Amaro	2.25	.90	.22
☐ 195	Don Demeter	2.25	.90	.22
☐ 196	Bobby Gene Smith	2.25	.90	.22
☐ 197	Clay Dalrymple	2.25	.90	.22
☐ 198	Robin Roberts	7.00	3.00	.70
☐ 199	Art Mahaffey	2.25	.90	.22
☐ 200	John Buzhardt	2.25	.90	.22

1963 Post Cereal

The cards in this 200-card set measure 2 1/2" by 3 1/2". The players are grouped by team with American Leaguers comprising 1-100 and National Leaguers 101-200. The ordering of teams is as follows: Minnesota (1-11), New York Yankees, Los Angeles Angels (24-34), Chicago White Sox (35-45), Detroit (46-56), Baltimore (57-66), Cleveland (67-76), Boston (77-84), Kansas City (85-92), Washington (93-100), San Francisco (101-112), Los Angeles Dodgers (113-124), Cincinnati (125-136), Pittsburgh (137-147), Milwaukee (148-157), St. Louis (158-168), Chicago Cubs (169-176), Philadelphia (177-184), Houston (185-192), and New York Mets (193-200). In contrast to the 1962 issue, the 1963 Post baseball card series is very difficult to complete. There are many card scarcities reflected in the price list below. Cards of the Post set are easily confused with those of the 1963 Jello set, which are 1/4" narrower (a difference which is often eliminated by bad cutting). The catalog designation is F278-38. There was also an album produced by Post to hold the cards.

		NRMT	VG-E	GOOD
COMPLETE SET (205)		4200.00	1800.00	425.00
COMMON PLAYER (1-200)		3.00	1.25	.30
☐ 1	Vic Power	3.00	1.25	.30
☐ 2	Bernie Allen	3.00	1.25	.30
☐ 3	Zoilo Versalles	3.00	1.25	.30
☐ 4	Rich Rollins	3.00	1.25	.30
☐ 5	Harmon Killebrew	18.00	7.50	2.50
☐ 6	Lenny Green	45.00	20.00	6.75
☐ 7	Bob Allison	3.00	1.25	.30
☐ 8	Earl Battey	3.00	1.25	.30
☐ 9	Camilo Pascual	3.00	1.25	.30
☐ 10	Jim Kaat	4.00	1.75	.40
☐ 11	Jack Kralick	3.00	1.25	.30
☐ 12	Bill Skowron	3.50	1.50	.35
☐ 13	Bobby Richardson	4.00	1.75	.40
☐ 14	Cletis Boyer	3.00	1.25	.30
☐ 15	Mickey Mantle	300.00	135.00	45.00
☐ 16	Roger Maris	165.00	70.00	22.00
☐ 17	Yogi Berra	18.00	7.50	2.50
☐ 18	Elston Howard	3.50	1.50	.35
☐ 19	Whitey Ford	12.50	5.50	1.65
☐ 20	Ralph Terry	3.00	1.25	.30
☐ 21	Jim Blanchard	3.00	1.25	.30
☐ 22	Bill Stafford	3.00	1.25	.30
☐ 23	Tom Tresh	3.00	1.25	.30
☐ 24	Steve Bilko	3.00	1.25	.30
☐ 25	Bill Moran	3.00	1.25	.30
☐ 26A	Joe Koppe (BA: .277)	3.00	1.25	.30
☐ 26B	Joe Koppe (BA: .227)	15.00	6.50	2.15

		NRMT	VG-E	GOOD
☐ 27	Felix Torres	3.00	1.25	.30
☐ 28A	Leon Wagner (BA: .278)	3.00	1.25	.30
☐ 28B	Leon Wagner (BA: .272)	15.00	6.50	2.15
☐ 29	Albie Pearson	3.00	1.25	.30
☐ 30	Lee Thomas UER (Photo actually George Thomas)	90.00	40.00	13.50
☐ 31	Bob Rodgers	3.00	1.25	.30
☐ 32	Dean Chance	3.00	1.25	.30
☐ 33	Ken McBride	3.00	1.25	.30
☐ 34	George Thomas UER (Photo actually Lee Thomas)	3.00	1.25	.30
☐ 35	Joe Cunningham	3.00	1.25	.30
☐ 36	Nelson Fox	4.00	1.75	.40
☐ 37	Luis Aparicio	6.00	2.50	.60
☐ 38	Al Smith	40.00	18.00	6.00
☐ 39	Floyd Robinson	110.00	50.00	16.50
☐ 40	Jim Landis	3.00	1.25	.30
☐ 41	Charlie Maxwell	3.00	1.25	.30
☐ 42	Sherman Lollar	3.00	1.25	.30
☐ 43	Early Wynn	7.50	3.25	.75
☐ 44	Juan Pizarro	3.00	1.25	.30
☐ 45	Ray Herbert	3.00	1.25	.30
☐ 46	Norm Cash	3.00	1.25	.30
☐ 47	Steve Boros	3.00	1.25	.30
☐ 48	Dick McAuliffe	25.00	11.00	3.50
☐ 49	Bill Bruton	3.50	1.50	.35
☐ 50	Rocky Colavito	5.00	2.25	.50
☐ 51	Al Kaline	21.00	9.00	3.00
☐ 52	Dick Brown	3.00	1.25	.30
☐ 53	Jim Bunning	165.00	70.00	22.00
☐ 54	Hank Aguirre	3.00	1.25	.30
☐ 55	Frank Lary	3.00	1.25	.30
☐ 56	Don Mossi	3.00	1.25	.30
☐ 57	Jim Gentile	3.00	1.25	.30
☐ 58	Jackie Brandt	3.00	1.25	.30
☐ 59	Brooks Robinson	24.00	10.50	3.50
☐ 60	Ron Hansen	3.50	1.50	.35
☐ 61	Jerry Adair	200.00	90.00	30.00
☐ 62	John (Boog) Powell	4.00	1.75	.40
☐ 63	Russ Snyder	3.00	1.25	.30
☐ 64	Steve Barber	3.00	1.25	.30
☐ 65	Milt Pappas	3.00	1.25	.30
☐ 66	Robin Roberts	7.50	3.25	.75
☐ 67	Tito Francona	3.00	1.25	.30
☐ 68	Jerry Kindall	3.00	1.25	.30
☐ 69	Woody Held	3.00	1.25	.30
☐ 70	Bubba Phillips	14.00	6.25	2.00
☐ 71	Chuck Essegian	3.00	1.25	.30
☐ 72	Willie Kirkland	3.00	1.25	.30
☐ 73	Al Luplow	3.00	1.25	.30
☐ 74	Ty Cline	3.00	1.25	.30
☐ 75	Dick Donovan	3.00	1.25	.30
☐ 76	John Romano	3.00	1.25	.30
☐ 77	Pete Runnels	3.00	1.25	.30
☐ 78	Ed Bressoud	3.00	1.25	.30
☐ 79	Frank Malzone	3.00	1.25	.30
☐ 80	Carl Yastrzemski	325.00	150.00	50.00
☐ 81	Gary Geiger	3.00	1.25	.30
☐ 82	Lou Clinton	3.00	1.25	.30
☐ 83	Earl Wilson	3.00	1.25	.30
☐ 84	Bill Monbouquette	3.00	1.25	.30
☐ 85	Norm Siebeinn	3.00	1.25	.30
☐ 86	Jerry Lumpe	120.00	55.00	18.00
☐ 87	Manny Jimenez	120.00	55.00	18.00
☐ 88	Gino Cimoli	3.00	1.25	.30
☐ 89	Ed Charles	3.00	1.25	.30
☐ 90	Ed Rakow	3.00	1.25	.30
☐ 91	Bob Del Greco	3.00	1.25	.30
☐ 92	Haywood Sullivan	3.00	1.25	.30
☐ 93	Chuck Hinton	3.00	1.25	.30
☐ 94	Ken Retzer	3.00	1.25	.30
☐ 95	Harry Bright	3.00	1.25	.30
☐ 96	Bob Johnson	3.00	1.25	.30
☐ 97	Dave Stenhouse	14.00	6.25	2.00
☐ 98	Chuck Cottier	24.00	10.50	3.50
☐ 99	Tom Cheney	3.00	1.25	.30
☐ 100	Claude Osteen	14.00	6.25	2.00
☐ 101	Orlando Cepeda	5.00	2.25	.50
☐ 102	Chuck Hiller	3.00	1.25	.30
☐ 103	Jose Pagan	3.00	1.25	.30
☐ 104	Jim Davenport	3.00	1.25	.30
☐ 105	Harvey Kuenn	3.50	1.50	.35
☐ 106	Willie Mays	45.00	20.00	6.75
☐ 107	Felipe Alou	3.00	1.25	.30
☐ 108	Tom Haller	120.00	55.00	18.00
☐ 109	Juan Marichal	7.00	3.00	.70
☐ 110	Jack Sanford	3.00	1.25	.30
☐ 111	Bill O'Dell	3.00	1.25	.30
☐ 112	Willie McCovey	9.00	4.00	.90
☐ 113	Lee Walls	3.00	1.25	.30

☐ 114	Jim Gilliam	3.50	1.50	.35
☐ 115	Maury Wills	4.00	1.75	.40
☐ 116	Ron Fairly	3.00	1.25	.30
☐ 117	Tommy Davis	3.00	1.25	.30
☐ 118	Duke Snider	10.00	4.50	1.25
☐ 119	Willie Davis	200.00	90.00	30.00
☐ 120	John Roseboro	3.00	1.25	.30
☐ 121	Sandy Koufax	30.00	13.50	4.50
☐ 122	Stan Williams	3.00	1.25	.30
☐ 123	Don Drysdale	8.00	3.50	.80
☐ 124	Daryl Spencer	3.00	1.25	.30
☐ 125	Gordy Coleman	3.00	1.25	.30
☐ 126	Don Blasingame	3.00	1.25	.30
☐ 127	Leo Cardenas	3.00	1.25	.30
☐ 128	Eddie Kasko	200.00	90.00	30.00
☐ 129	Jerry Lynch	15.00	6.50	2.15
☐ 130	Vada Pinson	3.50	1.50	.35
☐ 131A	Frank Robinson (no stripes)	20.00	8.50	2.75
☐ 131B	Frank Robinson (stripes on hat)	50.00	22.50	7.50
☐ 132	John Edwards	3.00	1.25	.30
☐ 133	Joey Jay	3.00	1.25	.30
☐ 134	Bob Purkey	3.00	1.25	.30
☐ 135	Marty Keough	30.00	13.50	4.50
☐ 136	Jim O'Toole	3.00	1.25	.30
☐ 137	Dick Stuart	3.00	1.25	.30
☐ 138	Bill Mazeroski	4.00	1.75	.40
☐ 139	Dick Groat	3.50	1.50	.35
☐ 140	Don Hoak	35.00	15.75	5.25
☐ 141	Bob Skinner	18.00	7.50	2.50
☐ 142	Bill Virdon	3.50	1.50	.35
☐ 143	Roberto Clemente	30.00	13.50	4.50
☐ 144	Smoky Burgess	3.00	1.25	.30
☐ 145	Bob Friend	3.00	1.25	.30
☐ 146	Al McBean	3.00	1.25	.30
☐ 147	Elroy Face	3.50	1.50	.35
☐ 148	Joe Adcock	3.50	1.50	.35
☐ 149	Frank Bolling	3.00	1.25	.30
☐ 150	Roy McMillan	3.00	1.25	.30
☐ 151	Eddie Mathews	18.00	7.50	2.50
☐ 152	Hank Aaron	135.00	60.00	20.00
☐ 153	Del Crandall	35.00	15.75	5.25
☐ 154A	Bob Shaw COR	3.00	1.25	.30
☐ 154B	Bob Shaw ERR (two "in 1959" in same sentence)	15.00	6.50	2.15
☐ 155	Lew Burdette	3.50	1.50	.35
☐ 156	Joe Torre	4.00	1.75	.40
☐ 157	Tony Cloninger	3.00	1.25	.30
☐ 158A	Bill White (Ht. 6'0")	4.00	1.75	.40
☐ 158B	Bill White (Ht. 6';)	4.00	1.75	.40
☐ 159	Julian Javier	3.00	1.25	.30
☐ 160	Ken Boyer	4.00	1.75	.40
☐ 161	Julio Gotay	3.00	1.25	.30
☐ 162	Curt Flood	135.00	60.00	20.00
☐ 163	Charlie James	4.00	1.75	.40
☐ 164	Gene Oliver	3.00	1.25	.30
☐ 165	Ernie Broglio	3.00	1.25	.30
☐ 166	Bob Gibson	8.00	3.50	.80
☐ 167A	Lindy McDaniel (no asterisk)	6.00	2.50	.60
☐ 167B	Lindy McDaniel (asterisk traded line)	6.00	2.50	.60
☐ 168	Ray Washburn	3.00	1.25	.30
☐ 169	Ernie Banks	15.00	6.50	2.15
☐ 170	Ron Santo	4.00	1.75	.40
☐ 171	George Altman	3.00	1.25	.30
☐ 172	Billy Williams	165.00	70.00	22.00
☐ 173	Andre Rodgers	15.00	6.50	2.15
☐ 174	Ken Hubbs	30.00	13.50	4.50
☐ 175	Don Landrum	3.00	1.25	.30
☐ 176	Dick Bertell	18.00	7.50	2.50
☐ 177	Roy Sievers	3.00	1.25	.30
☐ 178	Tony Taylor	3.00	1.25	.30
☐ 179	John Callison	3.00	1.25	.30
☐ 180	Don Demeter	3.00	1.25	.30
☐ 181	Tony Gonzalez	14.00	6.25	2.00
☐ 182	Wes Covington	24.00	10.50	3.50
☐ 183	Art Mahaffey	3.00	1.25	.30
☐ 184	Clay Dalrymple	3.00	1.25	.30
☐ 185	Al Spangler	3.50	1.50	.35
☐ 186	Roman Mejias	3.00	1.25	.30
☐ 187	Bob Aspromonte	375.00	165.00	55.00
☐ 188	Norm Larker	35.00	15.75	5.25
☐ 189	Johnny Temple	3.00	1.25	.30
☐ 190	Carl Warwick	3.00	1.25	.30
☐ 191	Bob Lillis	3.00	1.25	.30
☐ 192	Dick Farrell	3.00	1.25	.30
☐ 193	Gil Hodges	8.00	3.50	.80
☐ 194	Marv Throneberry	3.00	1.25	.30
☐ 195	Charlie Neal	9.00	4.00	.90
☐ 196	Frank Thomas	200.00	90.00	30.00
☐ 197	Richie Ashburn	25.00	11.00	3.50
☐ 198	Felix Mantilla	3.00	1.25	.30
☐ 199	Rod Kanehl	18.00	7.50	2.50
☐ 200	Roger Craig	3.50	1.50	.35

1990 Post

The 1990 Post Cereal set is a 30-card, standard-size (2 1/2" by 3 1/2") set issued with the assistance of Mike Schechter Associates. The sets do not have either team logos or other uniform identification on them. There is also a facsimile autograph on the back of the cards. The cards were inserted randomly as a cello pack (with three cards) inside specially marked boxes on Post cereals. The cards feature red, white, and blue fronts with the words, "First Collector Series". Card backs feature a facsimile autograph. The relatively high cost of the set is due to the fact that the cards were not available as a complete set as a part of any mail-in offer from the company.

		MINT	EXC	G-VG
COMPLETE SET (30)		18.00	7.50	2.50
COMMON PLAYER (1-30)		.50	.20	.05
☐ 1	Don Mattingly	1.50	.60	.15
☐ 2	Roger Clemens	1.50	.60	.15
☐ 3	Kirby Puckett	1.00	.40	.10
☐ 4	George Brett	1.00	.40	.10
☐ 5	Tony Gwynn	1.00	.40	.10
☐ 6	Ozzie Smith	.75	.30	.07
☐ 7	Will Clark	1.50	.60	.15
☐ 8	Orel Hershiser	.75	.30	.07
☐ 9	Ryne Sandberg	1.50	.60	.15
☐ 10	Darryl Strawberry	1.25	.50	.12
☐ 11	Nolan Ryan	2.00	.80	.20
☐ 12	Mark McGwire	1.00	.40	.10
☐ 13	Jim Abbott	1.00	.40	.10
☐ 14	Bo Jackson	2.00	.80	.20
☐ 15	Kevin Mitchell	.75	.30	.07
☐ 16	Jose Canseco	1.50	.60	.15
☐ 17	Wade Boggs	1.00	.40	.10
☐ 18	Dale Murphy	.75	.30	.07
☐ 19	Mark Grace	.75	.30	.07
☐ 20	Mike Scott	.50	.20	.05
☐ 21	Cal Ripken	1.50	.60	.15
☐ 22	Pedro Guerrero	.50	.20	.05
☐ 23	Ken Griffey Jr.	3.00	1.25	.30
☐ 24	Eric Davis	.75	.30	.07
☐ 25	Rickey Henderson	1.50	.60	.15
☐ 26	Robin Yount	1.00	.40	.10
☐ 27	Von Hayes	.50	.20	.05
☐ 28	Alan Trammell	.60	.25	.06
☐ 29	Dwight Gooden	.75	.30	.07
☐ 30	Joe Carter	.75	.30	.07

1991 Post

1991 Post Canada

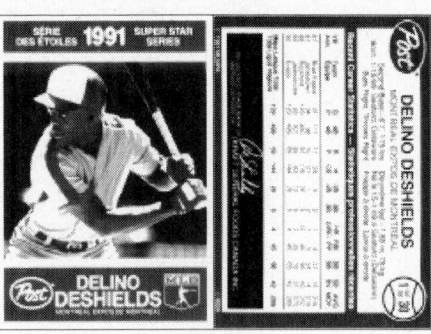

This 30-card set, which measures the standard 2 1/2" by 3 1/2", was released early in 1991 by Post Cereal in conjunction with Michael Schechter Associates (MSA). The players pictured are some of the star players of baseball entering the 1991 season. The design of the set features the Post logo in the upper left hand corner, the MLB logo in the upper right hand corner, and the players name and team underneath the portrait shot of the player pictured on the card. The cards were inserted three-at-a-time in boxes of the following cereals: Post Honeycomb, Super Golden Crisp, Cocoa Pebbles, Fruity Pebbles, Alpha-Bits, and Marshmallow Alpha-Bits. The fronts feature either posed or action color player photos, with blue and yellow borders. The words "1991 Collector Series" appear in a white stripe at the card top. Some cards (numbers 1, 6, 25, and 30) have a banner at the top that reads "Rookie Star". The player's name is given in a white stripe below the picture. The horizontally oriented backs are printed in aqua and dark blue on white and present complete Major League statistical information and a facsimile autograph on the bottom of the card. The cards are numbered on the back.

	MINT	EXC	G-VG
COMPLETE SET (30)	12.00	5.25	1.50
COMMON PLAYER (1-30)	.30	.12	.03
☐ 1 Dave Justice	1.50	.60	.15
☐ 2 Mark McGwire	.75	.30	.07
☐ 3 Will Clark	1.00	.40	.10
☐ 4 Jose Canseco	1.00	.40	.10
☐ 5 Vince Coleman	.50	.20	.05
☐ 6 Sandy Alomar Jr.	.40	.16	.04
☐ 7 Darryl Strawberry	1.00	.40	.10
☐ 8 Len Dykstra	.30	.12	.03
☐ 9 Gregg Jefferies	.50	.20	.05
☐ 10 Tony Gwynn	.75	.30	.07
☐ 11 Ken Griffey Jr.	2.00	.80	.20
☐ 12 Roger Clemens	1.00	.40	.10
☐ 13 Chris Sabo	.40	.16	.04
☐ 14 Bobby Bonilla	.60	.25	.06
☐ 15 Gary Sheffield	.40	.16	.04
☐ 16 Ryne Sandberg	1.00	.40	.10
☐ 17 Nolan Ryan	1.50	.60	.15
☐ 18 Barry Larkin	.40	.16	.04
☐ 19 Cal Ripken	1.00	.40	.10
☐ 20 Jim Abbott	.75	.30	.07
☐ 21 Barry Bonds	.60	.25	.06
☐ 22 Mark Grace	.50	.20	.05
☐ 23 Cecil Fielder	.60	.25	.06
☐ 24 Kevin Mitchell	.50	.20	.05
☐ 25 Todd Zeile	.50	.20	.05
☐ 26 George Brett	.60	.25	.06
☐ 27 Rickey Henderson	1.00	.40	.10
☐ 28 Kirby Puckett	.75	.30	.07
☐ 29 Don Mattingly	.75	.30	.07
☐ 30 Kevin Maas	.50	.20	.05

This 30-card Super Stars set was sponsored by Post and features 14 National League and 16 American League players. One card was inserted in specially-marked boxes of Post Alpha-Bits, Sugar Crisp, and Honeycomb sold in Canada. The cards measure the standard size (2 1/2" by 3 1/2") and are bilingual (French and English) on both sides. While all the cards feature color player photos (action or posed) on the fronts, the NL cards (1-14) are accentuated with red stripes while the AL cards (15-30) have royal blue stripes. In a horizontal format, the backs have biography, recent career statistics, and a facsimile autograph. The cards are numbered on the back.

	MINT	EXC	G-VG
COMPLETE SET (30)	50.00	22.50	7.50
COMMON PLAYER (1-30)	1.00	.40	.10
☐ 1 Delino DeShields	1.50	.60	.15
☐ 2 Tim Wallach	1.00	.40	.10
☐ 3 Andres Galarraga	1.00	.40	.10
☐ 4 Dave Magadan	1.00	.40	.10
☐ 5 Barry Bonds	2.50	1.00	.25
☐ 6 Len Dykstra	1.00	.40	.10
☐ 7 Andre Dawson	2.50	1.00	.25
☐ 8 Ozzie Smith	2.00	.80	.20
☐ 9 Will Clark	3.50	1.50	.35
☐ 10 Chris Sabo	1.50	.60	.15
☐ 11 Eddie Murray	2.50	1.00	.25
☐ 12 Dave Justice	5.00	2.25	.50
☐ 13 Benito Santiago	1.50	.60	.15
☐ 14 Glenn Davis	1.50	.60	.15
☐ 15 Kelly Gruber	1.50	.60	.15
☐ 16 Dave Stieb	1.00	.40	.10
☐ 17 John Olerud	2.00	.80	.20
☐ 18 Roger Clemens	3.50	1.50	.35
☐ 19 Cecil Fielder	2.50	1.00	.25
☐ 20 Kevin Maas	2.00	.80	.20
☐ 21 Robin Yount	2.00	.80	.20
☐ 22 Cal Ripken	3.50	1.50	.35
☐ 23 Sandy Alomar Jr.	2.00	.80	.20
☐ 24 Rickey Henderson	3.50	1.50	.35
☐ 25 Bobby Thigpen	1.50	.60	.15
☐ 26 Ken Griffey Jr.	6.00	2.50	.60
☐ 27 Nolan Ryan	6.00	2.50	.60
☐ 28 Dave Winfield	2.50	1.00	.25
☐ 29 George Brett	2.50	1.00	.25
☐ 30 Kirby Puckett	2.50	1.00	.25

1986 Quaker Granola

This set of 33 cards was available in packages of Quaker Oats Chewy Granola, three player cards plus a complete set offer card in each package. The set was also available through a mail-in offer where anyone sending in four UPC seals from Chewy Granola (before 12/31/86) would receive a complete set. The cards were produced by Topps for Quaker Oats and are 2 1/2" by 3 1/2". Card backs are printed in red and blue on gray card stock. The cards are numbered on the front and the back.

		MINT	EXC	G-VG
COMPLETE SET (33)		7.50	3.25	.75
COMMON PLAYER (1-33)		.20	.08	.02
☐ 1	Willie McGee	.25	.10	.02
☐ 2	Dwight Gooden	.50	.20	.05
☐ 3	Vince Coleman	.35	.15	.03
☐ 4	Gary Carter	.30	.12	.03
☐ 5	Jack Clark	.25	.10	.02
☐ 6	Steve Garvey	.35	.15	.03
☐ 7	Tony Gwynn	.60	.25	.06
☐ 8	Dale Murphy	.40	.16	.04
☐ 9	Dave Parker	.25	.10	.02
☐ 10	Tim Raines	.25	.10	.02
☐ 11	Pete Rose	.65	.25	.06
☐ 12	Nolan Ryan	1.25	.50	.12
☐ 13	Ryne Sandberg	.75	.30	.07
☐ 14	Mike Schmidt	.75	.30	.07
☐ 15	Ozzie Smith	.40	.16	.04
☐ 16	Darryl Strawberry	.60	.25	.06
☐ 17	Fernando Valenzuela	.25	.10	.02
☐ 18	Don Mattingly	.60	.25	.06
☐ 19	Bret Saberhagen	.35	.15	.03
☐ 20	Ozzie Guillen	.20	.08	.02
☐ 21	Bert Blyleven	.20	.08	.02
☐ 22	Wade Boggs	.65	.25	.06
☐ 23	George Brett	.65	.25	.06
☐ 24	Darrell Evans	.20	.08	.02
☐ 25	Rickey Henderson	1.00	.40	.10
☐ 26	Reggie Jackson	.65	.25	.06
☐ 27	Eddie Murray	.50	.20	.05
☐ 28	Phil Niekro	.30	.12	.03
☐ 29	Dan Quisenberry	.20	.08	.02
☐ 30	Jim Rice	.25	.10	.02
☐ 31	Cal Ripken	.75	.30	.07
☐ 32	Tom Seaver	.60	.25	.06
☐ 33	Dave Winfield	.35	.15	.03
☐ 34	Offer Card for the complete set (unnumbered)	.03	.01	.00

1984 Ralston Purina

The cards in this 33-card set measure 2 1/2" by 3 1/2". In 1984 the Ralston Purina Company issued what it has entitled "The First Annual Collectors Edition of Baseball Cards." The cards feature portrait photos of the players rather than batting action shots. The Topps logo appears along with the Ralston logo on the front of the card. The backs are completely different from the Topps cards of this year; in fact, they contain neither a Topps logo nor a Topps copyright. Large quantities of these cards were obtained by card dealers for direct distribution into the organized hobby, hence the relatively low price of the set.

		MINT	EXC	G-VG
COMPLETE SET (33)		4.00	1.75	.40
COMMON PLAYER (1-33)		.10	.04	.01
☐ 1	Eddie Murray	.35	.15	.03
☐ 2	Ozzie Smith	.25	.10	.02
☐ 3	Ted Simmons	.10	.04	.01
☐ 4	Pete Rose	.50	.20	.05
☐ 5	Greg Luzinski	.10	.04	.01

☐ 6	Andre Dawson	.30	.12	.03
☐ 7	Dave Winfield	.25	.10	.02
☐ 8	Tom Seaver	.40	.16	.04
☐ 9	Jim Rice	.15	.06	.01
☐ 10	Fernando Valenzuela	.15	.06	.01
☐ 11	Wade Boggs	.40	.16	.04
☐ 12	Dale Murphy	.30	.12	.03
☐ 13	George Brett	.40	.16	.04
☐ 14	Nolan Ryan	.75	.30	.07
☐ 15	Rickey Henderson	.60	.25	.06
☐ 16	Steve Carlton	.25	.10	.02
☐ 17	Rod Carew	.30	.12	.03
☐ 18	Steve Garvey	.25	.10	.02
☐ 19	Reggie Jackson	.45	.18	.04
☐ 20	Dave Concepcion	.15	.06	.01
☐ 21	Robin Yount	.35	.15	.03
☐ 22	Mike Schmidt	.60	.25	.06
☐ 23	Jim Palmer	.25	.10	.02
☐ 24	Bruce Sutter	.10	.04	.01
☐ 25	Dan Quisenberry	.10	.04	.01
☐ 26	Bill Madlock	.10	.04	.01
☐ 27	Cecil Cooper	.10	.04	.01
☐ 28	Gary Carter	.15	.06	.01
☐ 29	Fred Lynn	.10	.04	.01
☐ 30	Pedro Guerrero	.15	.06	.01
☐ 31	Ron Guidry	.10	.04	.01
☐ 32	Keith Hernandez	.15	.06	.01
☐ 33	Carlton Fisk	.30	.12	.03

1987 Ralston Purina

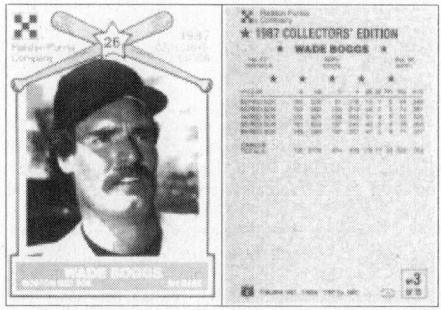

The Ralston Purina Company issued a set of 15 cards picturing players without their respective team logos. The cards measure approximately 2 1/2" by 3 3/8" and are in full-color on the front. The cards are numbered on the back in the lower right hand corner; the player's uniform number is prominently displayed on the front. The cards were distributed as inserts inside packages of certain flavors of Ralston Purina's breakfast cereals. Three cards and a contest card were packaged in cellophane and inserted within the cereal box. The set was also available as an uncut sheet through a mail-in offer. Since the uncut sheets are relatively common, the value of the sheet is essentially the same as the value of the sum of the individual cards. In fact there were two uncut sheets issued, one had "Honey Graham Chex" printed at the top and the other had "Cookie Crisp" printed at the top. Also cards were issued with and without the words "1987 Collectors Edition" printed in blue on the front. Supposedly 100,000 of the uncut sheets were given away free via instant win certificates inserted in with the cereal or collectors could send in two non-winning contest cards plus 1.00 for each uncut sheet.

	MINT	EXC	G-VG
COMPLETE SET (15)	10.00	4.50	1.25
COMMON PLAYER (1-15)	.50	.20	.05
☐ 1 Nolan Ryan	2.50	1.00	.25
☐ 2 Steve Garvey	.60	.25	.06
☐ 3 Wade Boggs	1.25	.50	.12
☐ 4 Dave Winfield	.75	.30	.07
☐ 5 Don Mattingly	1.25	.50	.12
☐ 6 Don Sutton	.60	.25	.06
☐ 7 Dave Parker	.50	.20	.05
☐ 8 Eddie Murray	1.00	.40	.10
☐ 9 Gary Carter	.75	.30	.07
☐ 10 Roger Clemens	1.50	.60	.15
☐ 11 Fernando Valenzuela	.60	.25	.06
☐ 12 Cal Ripken	1.25	.50	.12
☐ 13 Ozzie Smith	.75	.30	.07
☐ 14 Mike Schmidt	1.25	.50	.12
☐ 15 Ryne Sandberg	1.25	.50	.12

1983 Rangers Affiliated Food

The cards in this 28-card set measure 2 3/8" by 3 1/2". The Affiliated Food Stores chain of Arlington, Texas, produced this set of Texas Rangers late during the 1983 baseball season. Complete sets were given to children 13 and under at the September 3, 1983, Rangers game. The cards are numbered by uniform number and feature the player's name, card number, and the words "1983 Rangers" on the bottom front. The backs contain biographical data, career totals, a small black and white insert picture of the player, and the Affiliated Food Stores' logo. The coaches card is unnumbered.

	MINT	EXC	G-VG
COMPLETE SET (28)	7.00	3.00	.70
COMMON PLAYER	.25	.10	.02
☐ 1 Bill Stein	.25	.10	.02
☐ 2 Mike Richardt	.25	.10	.02
☐ 3 Wayne Tolleson	.25	.10	.02
☐ 5 Billy Sample	.35	.15	.03
☐ 6 Bobby Jones	.25	.10	.02
☐ 7 Bucky Dent	.50	.20	.05
☐ 8 Bobby Johnson	.25	.10	.02
☐ 9 Pete O'Brien	.60	.25	.06
☐ 10 Jim Sundberg	.35	.15	.03
☐ 11 Doug Rader MG	.35	.15	.03
☐ 12 Dave Hostetler	.25	.10	.02

	MINT	EXC	G-VG
☐ 14 Larry Biittner	.25	.10	.02
☐ 15 Larry Parrish	.35	.15	.03
☐ 17 Mickey Rivers	.35	.15	.03
☐ 21 Odell Jones	.25	.10	.02
☐ 24 Dave Schmidt	.35	.15	.03
☐ 25 Buddy Bell	.50	.20	.05
☐ 26 George Wright	.25	.10	.02
☐ 28 Frank Tanana	.35	.15	.03
☐ 29 John Butcher	.25	.10	.02
☐ 32 Jon Matlack	.35	.15	.03
☐ 40 Rick Honeycutt	.25	.10	.02
☐ 41 Dave Tobik	.25	.10	.02
☐ 44 Danny Darwin	.35	.15	.03
☐ 46 Jim Anderson	.25	.10	.02
☐ 48 Mike Smithson	.25	.10	.02
☐ 49 Charlie Hough	.35	.15	.03
☐ xx Rangers Coaches: (unnumbered)	.25	.10	.02

Wayne Terwilliger 42
Merv Rettenmund 22
Dick Such 52
Glenn Ezell 18
Rich Donnelly 37

1984 Rangers Jarvis Press

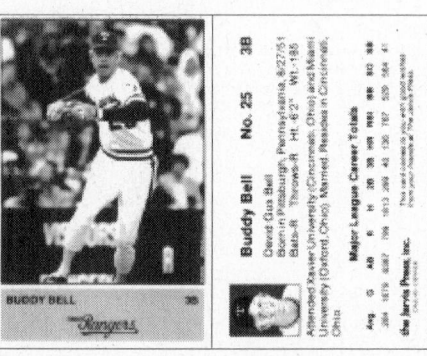

The cards in this 30-card set measure 2 1/2" by 3 1/2". The Jarvis Press of Dallas issued this full-color regional set of Texas Rangers. Cards are numbered on the front by the players uniform number. The cards were issued on an uncut sheet. Twenty-seven player cards, a manager card, a trainer card (unnumbered) and a coaches card (unnumbered) comprise this set. The backs are black and white and contain biographical information, statistics, and an additional photo of the player.

	MINT	EXC	G-VG
COMPLETE SET (30)	7.00	3.00	.70
COMMON PLAYER	.25	.10	.02
☐ 1 Bill Stein	.25	.10	.02
☐ 2 Alan Bannister	.25	.10	.02
☐ 3 Wayne Tolleson	.25	.10	.02
☐ 5 Billy Sample	.35	.15	.03
☐ 6 Bobby Jones	.25	.10	.02
☐ 7 Ned Yost	.25	.10	.02
☐ 9 Pete O'Brien	.35	.15	.03
☐ 11 Doug Rader MG	.35	.15	.03
☐ 13 Tommy Dunbar	.25	.10	.02
☐ 14 Jim Anderson	.25	.10	.02
☐ 15 Larry Parrish	.35	.15	.03
☐ 16 Mike Mason	.25	.10	.02
☐ 17 Mickey Rivers	.35	.15	.03
☐ 19 Curtis Wilkerson	.25	.10	.02
☐ 20 Jeff Kunkel	.35	.15	.03
☐ 21 Odell Jones	.25	.10	.02
☐ 24 Dave Schmidt	.35	.15	.03
☐ 25 Buddy Bell	.50	.20	.05
☐ 26 George Wright	.25	.10	.02
☐ 28 Frank Tanana	.35	.15	.03
☐ 30 Marv Foley	.25	.10	.02
☐ 31 Dave Stewart	.90	.40	.09
☐ 32 Gary Ward	.25	.10	.02
☐ 36 Dickie Noles	.25	.10	.02

			MINT	EXC	G-VG
☐	43	Donnie Scott	.25	.10	.02
☐	44	Danny Darwin	.35	.15	.03
☐	49	Charlie Hough	.35	.15	.03
☐	53	Joey McLaughlin	.25	.10	.02
☐	xx	Bill Ziegler	.25	.10	.02
		(Trainer)			
		(unnumbered)			
☐	xx	Rangers Coaches:	.25	.10	.02
		(unnumbered)			
		Merv Rettenmund 22			
		Rich Donnelly 37			
		Glenn Ezell 18			
		Dick Such 52			
		Wayne Terwilliger 42			

Glenn Ezell 18
Tom House 35
Wayne Terwilliger 42

1986 Rangers Performance

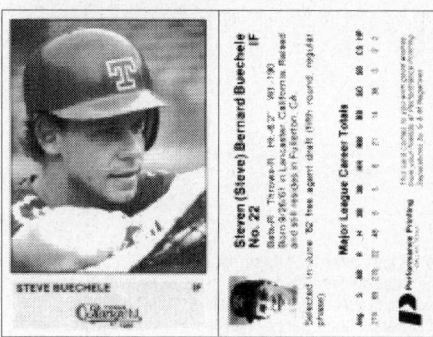

STEVE BUECHELE

Performance Printing of Dallas produced a 28-card set of Texas Rangers which were given out at the stadium on August 23rd. Cards measure 2 3/8" by 3 1/2" and are in full color. The cards are unnumbered except for uniform number which is given on the card back. Card backs feature black printing on white card stock with a small picture of the player's head in the upper left corner. The set seems to be more desirable than the previous Ranger sets due to the Rangers' 1986 success which was directly related to their outstanding rookie crop.

1985 Rangers Performance

CHARLIE HOUGH

The cards in this 28-card set measure 2 3/8" by 3 1/2". Performance Printing sponsored this full-color regional set of Texas Rangers. Cards are numbered on the back by the players uniform number. The cards were also issued on an uncut sheet. Twenty-five player cards, a manager card, a trainer card (unnumbered) and a coaches card (unnumbered) comprise this set. The backs are black and white and contain biographical information, statistics, and an additional photo of the player.

			MINT	EXC	G-VG
	COMPLETE SET (28)		7.00	3.00	.70
	COMMON PLAYER		.25	.10	.02
☐	0	Oddibe McDowell	.35	.15	.03
☐	1	Bill Stein	.25	.10	.02
☐	2	Bobby Valentine MG	.35	.15	.03
☐	3	Wayne Tolleson	.25	.10	.02
☐	4	Don Slaught	.25	.10	.02
☐	5	Alan Bannister	.25	.10	.02
☐	6	Bobby Jones	.25	.10	.02
☐	7	Glenn Brummer	.25	.10	.02
☐	8	Luis Pujols	.25	.10	.02
☐	9	Pete O'Brien	.35	.15	.03
☐	11	Toby Harrah	.35	.15	.03
☐	13	Tommy Dunbar	.25	.10	.02
☐	15	Larry Parrish	.35	.15	.03
☐	16	Mike Mason	.25	.10	.02
☐	19	Curtis Wilkerson	.25	.10	.02
☐	24	Dave Schmidt	.35	.15	.03
☐	25	Buddy Bell	.50	.20	.05
☐	27	Greg A. Harris	.35	.15	.03
☐	30	Dave Rozema	.25	.10	.02
☐	32	Gary Ward	.25	.10	.02
☐	36	Dickie Noles	.25	.10	.02
☐	41	Chris Welsh	.25	.10	.02
☐	44	Cliff Johnson	.25	.10	.02
☐	46	Burt Hooton	.25	.10	.02
☐	48	Dave Stewart	.75	.30	.07
☐	49	Charlie Hough	.35	.15	.03
☐	xx	Trainers:Bill Ziegler	.25	.10	.02
		Danny Wheat			
		(unnumbered)			
☐	xx	Rangers Coaches:	.25	.10	.02
		(unnumbered)			
		Art Howe 10			
		Rich Donnelly 37			

			MINT	EXC	G-VG
	COMPLETE SET (28)		10.00	4.50	1.25
	COMMON PLAYER		.20	.08	.02
☐	0	Oddibe McDowell	.30	.12	.03
☐	1	Scott Fletcher	.30	.12	.03
☐	2	Bobby Valentine MG	.30	.12	.03
☐	3	Ruben Sierra	4.00	1.75	.40
☐	4	Don Slaught	.20	.08	.02
☐	9	Pete O'Brien	.30	.12	.03
☐	11	Toby Harrah	.30	.12	.03
☐	12	Geno Petralli	.20	.08	.02
☐	15	Larry Parrish	.30	.12	.03
☐	16	Mike Mason	.20	.08	.02
☐	17	Darrell Porter	.20	.08	.02
☐	18	Edwin Correa	.30	.12	.03
☐	19	Curtis Wilkerson	.20	.08	.02
☐	22	Steve Buechele	.40	.16	.04
☐	23	Jose Guzman	.40	.16	.04
☐	24	Ricky Wright	.20	.08	.02
☐	27	Greg A. Harris	.20	.08	.02
☐	28	Mitch Williams	.50	.20	.05
☐	29	Pete Incaviglia	.75	.30	.07
☐	32	Gary Ward	.20	.08	.02
☐	34	Dale Mohorcic	.20	.08	.02
☐	40	Jeff Russell	.30	.12	.03
☐	44	Tom Paciorek	.20	.08	.02
☐	46	Mike Loynd	.30	.12	.03
☐	48	Bobby Witt	.75	.30	.07
☐	49	Charlie Hough	.30	.12	.03
☐	xx	Coaching Staff:	.20	.08	.02
		(unnumbered)			
		Art Howe 10			
		Joe Ferguson 13			
		Tim Foli 14			
		Tom Robson 31			
		Tom House 35			
☐	xx	Trainers:	.20	.08	.02
		(unnumbered)			
		Bill Zeigler			
		Danny Wheat			

1954 Red Heart

The cards in this 33-card set measure 2 5/8" by 3 3/4". The 1954 Red Heart baseball series was marketed by Red Heart dog food, which, incidentally, was a subsidiary of Morrell Meats. The set consists of three series of eleven unnumbered cards each of which could be ordered from the company via an offer (two can labels plus ten cents for each series) on the can label. Each series has a specific color background (red, green or blue) behind the color player photo. Cards with red backgrounds are considered scarcer and are marked with an asterisk in the checklist (which has been alphabetized and numbered for reference). The catalog designation is F156.

	NRMT	VG-E	GOOD
COMPLETE SET (33)	2200.00	900.00	225.00
COMMON PLAYER (1-33)	30.00	13.50	4.50
COMMON * (RED) PLAYER	35.00	15.75	5.25
☐ 1 Richie Ashburn *	65.00	29.00	9.75
☐ 2 Frank Baumholtz *	35.00	15.75	5.25
☐ 3 Gus Bell	30.00	13.50	4.50
☐ 4 Billy Cox	30.00	13.50	4.50
☐ 5 Alvin Dark	35.00	15.75	5.25
☐ 6 Carl Erskine *	45.00	20.00	6.75
☐ 7 Ferris Fain	30.00	13.50	4.50
☐ 8 Dee Fondy	30.00	13.50	4.50
☐ 9 Nelson Fox	50.00	22.50	7.50
☐ 10 Jim Gilliam	35.00	15.75	5.25
☐ 11 Jim Hegan *	35.00	15.75	5.25
☐ 12 George Kell	60.00	27.00	9.00
☐ 13 Ralph Kiner *	85.00	38.00	12.75
☐ 14 Ted Kluszewski *	65.00	29.00	9.75
☐ 15 Harvey Kuenn	35.00	15.75	5.25
☐ 16 Bob Lemon *	75.00	34.00	11.25
☐ 17 Sherman Lollar	30.00	13.50	4.50
☐ 18 Mickey Mantle	500.00	225.00	75.00
☐ 19 Billy Martin	65.00	29.00	9.75
☐ 20 Gil McDougald *	45.00	20.00	6.75
☐ 21 Roy McMillan	30.00	13.50	4.50
☐ 22 Minnie Minoso	35.00	15.75	5.25
☐ 23 Stan Musial *	350.00	160.00	52.50
☐ 24 Billy Pierce	35.00	15.75	5.25
☐ 25 Al Rosen *	45.00	20.00	6.75
☐ 26 Hank Sauer	30.00	13.50	4.50
☐ 27 Red Schoendienst *	75.00	34.00	11.25
☐ 28 Enos Slaughter	70.00	32.00	10.50
☐ 29 Duke Snider	125.00	57.50	18.75
☐ 30 Warren Spahn	65.00	29.00	9.75
☐ 31 Sammy White	30.00	13.50	4.50
☐ 32 Eddie Yost	30.00	13.50	4.50
☐ 33 Gus Zernial	30.00	13.50	4.50

from each league. Cards that have the tab (coupon) attached are generally worth two and a half times the price of cards with the tab removed. Card numbers are located on the tabs. The prices listed below refer to cards without tabs.

	NRMT	VG-E	GOOD
COMPLETE SET (52)	850.00	375.00	125.00
COMMON PLAYER	8.00	3.50	.80
☐ AL1 Casey Stengel MG	24.00	10.50	3.50
☐ AL2 Roberto Avila	8.00	3.50	.80
☐ AL3 Yogi Berra	40.00	18.00	6.00
☐ AL4 Gil Coan	8.00	3.50	.80
☐ AL5 Dom DiMaggio	11.00	5.00	1.35
☐ AL6 Larry Doby	9.00	4.00	.90
☐ AL7 Ferris Fain	8.00	3.50	.80
☐ AL8 Bob Feller	32.00	14.25	4.75
☐ AL9 Nelson Fox	14.00	6.25	2.00
☐ AL10 Johnny Groth	8.00	3.50	.80
☐ AL11 Jim Hegan	8.00	3.50	.80
☐ AL12 Eddie Joost	8.00	3.50	.80
☐ AL13 George Kell	18.00	7.50	2.50
☐ AL14 Gil McDougald	11.00	5.00	1.35
☐ AL15 Minnie Minoso	11.00	5.00	1.35
☐ AL16 Billy Pierce	9.00	4.00	.90
☐ AL17 Bob Porterfield	8.00	3.50	.80
☐ AL18 Eddie Robinson	8.00	3.50	.80
☐ AL19 Saul Rogovin	8.00	3.50	.80
☐ AL20 Bobby Shantz	8.00	3.50	.80
☐ AL21 Vern Stephens	8.00	3.50	.80
☐ AL22 Vic Wertz	8.00	3.50	.80
☐ AL23 Ted Williams	120.00	55.00	18.00
☐ AL24 Early Wynn	18.00	7.50	2.50
☐ AL25 Eddie Yost	8.00	3.50	.80
☐ AL26 Gus Zernial	8.00	3.50	.80
☐ NL1 Leo Durocher MG	18.00	7.50	2.50
☐ NL2 Richie Ashburn	16.00	6.75	2.25
☐ NL3 Ewell Blackwell	8.00	3.50	.80
☐ NL4 Cliff Chambers	8.00	3.50	.80
☐ NL5 Murray Dickson	8.00	3.50	.80
☐ NL6 Sid Gordon	8.00	3.50	.80
☐ NL7 Granny Hamner	8.00	3.50	.80
☐ NL8 Jim Hearn	8.00	3.50	.80
☐ NL9 Monte Irvin	16.00	6.75	2.25
☐ NL10 Larry Jansen	8.00	3.50	.80
☐ NL11 Willie Jones	8.00	3.50	.80
☐ NL12 Ralph Kiner	24.00	10.50	3.50
☐ NL13 Whitey Lockman	8.00	3.50	.80
☐ NL14 Sal Maglie	11.00	5.00	1.35
☐ NL15 Willie Mays	90.00	40.00	13.50
☐ NL16 Stan Musial	90.00	40.00	13.50
☐ NL17 Pee Wee Reese	32.00	14.25	4.75
☐ NL18 Robin Roberts	22.00	9.50	3.15
☐ NL19 Al Schoendienst	18.00	7.50	2.50
☐ NL20 Enos Slaughter	22.00	9.50	3.15
☐ NL21 Duke Snider	55.00	25.00	8.25
☐ NL22 Warren Spahn	25.00	11.00	3.50
☐ NL23 Ed Stanky	9.00	4.00	.90
☐ NL24 Bobby Thomson	11.00	5.00	1.35
☐ NL25 Earl Torgeson	8.00	3.50	.80
☐ NL26 Wes Westrum	8.00	3.50	.80

1952 Red Man

The cards in this 52-card set measure 3 1/2" by 4" (or 3 1/2" by 3 5/8" without the tab). This Red Man issue was the first nationally available tobacco issue since the T cards of the teens early in this century. This 52-card set contains 26 top players

1953 Red Man

The cards in this 52-card set measure 3 1/2" by 4" (or 3 1/2" by 3 5/8" without the tab). The 1953 Red Man set contains 26 National League stars and 26 American League stars. Card

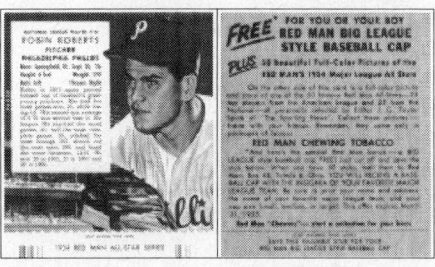

numbers are located both on the write-up of the player and on the tab. Cards that have the tab (coupon) attached are generally worth two and a half times the price of cards with the tab removed. The prices listed below refer to cards without tabs.

	NRMT	VG-E	GOOD
COMPLETE SET (52)	750.00	325.00	110.00
COMMON PLAYER	8.00	3.50	.80
□ AL1 Casey Stengel MG	24.00	10.50	3.50
□ AL2 Hank Bauer	11.00	5.00	1.35
□ AL3 Yogi Berra	40.00	18.00	6.00
□ AL4 Walt Dropo	8.00	3.50	.80
□ AL5 Nelson Fox	14.00	6.25	2.00
□ AL6 Jackie Jensen	11.00	5.00	1.35
□ AL7 Eddie Joost	8.00	3.50	.80
□ AL8 George Kell	18.00	7.50	2.50
□ AL9 Dale Mitchell	8.00	3.50	.80
□ AL10 Phil Rizzuto	18.00	7.50	2.50
□ AL11 Eddie Robinson	8.00	3.50	.80
□ AL12 Gene Woodling	9.00	4.00	.90
□ AL13 Gus Zernial	8.00	3.50	.80
□ AL14 Early Wynn	18.00	7.50	2.50
□ AL15 Joe Dobson	8.00	3.50	.80
□ AL16 Billy Pierce	9.00	4.00	.90
□ AL17 Bob Lemon	18.00	7.50	2.50
□ AL18 Johnny Mize	21.00	9.00	3.00
□ AL19 Bob Porterfield	8.00	3.50	.80
□ AL20 Bobby Shantz	8.00	3.50	.80
□ AL21 Mickey Vernon	9.00	4.00	.90
□ AL22 Dom DiMaggio	11.00	5.00	1.35
□ AL23 Gil McDougald	11.00	5.00	1.35
□ AL24 Al Rosen	11.00	5.00	1.35
□ AL25 Mel Parnell	8.00	3.50	.80
□ AL26 Bobby Avila	8.00	3.50	.80
□ NL1 Charlie Dressen MG	8.00	3.50	.80
□ NL2 Bobby Adams	8.00	3.50	.80
□ NL3 Richie Ashburn	16.00	6.75	2.25
□ NL4 Joe Black	9.00	4.00	.90
□ NL5 Roy Campanella	55.00	25.00	8.25
□ NL6 Ted Kluszewski	14.00	6.25	2.00
□ NL7 Whitey Lockman	8.00	3.50	.80
□ NL8 Sal Maglie	11.00	5.00	1.35
□ NL9 Andy Pafko	8.00	3.50	.80
□ NL10 Pee Wee Reese	32.00	14.25	4.75
□ NL11 Robin Roberts	22.00	9.50	3.15
□ NL12 Al Schoendienst	18.00	7.50	2.50
□ NL13 Enos Slaughter	22.00	9.50	3.15
□ NL14 Duke Snider	55.00	25.00	8.25
□ NL15 Ralph Kiner	22.00	9.50	3.15
□ NL16 Hank Sauer	8.00	3.50	.80
□ NL17 Del Ennis	8.00	3.50	.80
□ NL18 Granny Hamner	8.00	3.50	.80
□ NL19 Warren Spahn	25.00	11.00	3.50
□ NL20 Wes Westrum	8.00	3.50	.80
□ NL21 Hoyt Wilhelm	18.00	7.50	2.50
□ NL22 Murray Dickson	8.00	3.50	.80
□ NL23 Warren Hacker	8.00	3.50	.80
□ NL24 Gerry Staley	8.00	3.50	.80
□ NL25 Bobby Thomson	11.00	5.00	1.35
□ NL26 Stan Musial	90.00	40.00	13.50

1954 Red Man

The cards in this 50-card set measure 3 1/2" by 4" (or 3 1/2" by 3 5/8" without the tab). The 1954 Red Man set witnessed a reduction to 25 players from each league. George Kell, Sam

Mele, and Dave Philley are known to exist with two different teams. Card number 19 of the National League exists as Enos Slaughter and as Gus Bell. Card numbers are on the write-ups of the players. Cards that have the tab (coupon) attached are generally worth two and a half times the price of cards with the tab removed. The prices listed below refer to cards without tabs. The complete set price below refers to all 54 cards including the four variations.

	NRMT	VG-E	GOOD
COMPLETE SET (54)	950.00	425.00	140.00
COMMON PLAYERS	8.00	3.50	.80
□ AL1 Bobby Avila	8.00	3.50	.80
□ AL2 Jim Busby	8.00	3.50	.80
□ AL3 Nelson Fox	14.00	6.25	2.00
□ AL4A George Kell (Boston)	25.00	11.00	3.50
□ AL4B George Kell (Chicago)	60.00	27.00	9.00
□ AL5 Sherman Lollar	8.00	3.50	.80
□ AL6A Sam Mele (Baltimore)	11.00	5.00	1.35
□ AL6B Sam Mele (Chicago)	35.00	15.75	5.25
□ AL7 Minnie Minoso	11.00	5.00	1.35
□ AL8 Mel Parnell	8.00	3.50	.80
□ AL9A Dave Philley (Cleveland)	11.00	5.00	1.35
□ AL9B Dave Philley (Philadelphia)	35.00	15.75	5.25
□ AL10 Billy Pierce	9.00	4.00	.90
□ AL11 Jim Piersall	11.00	5.00	1.35
□ AL12 Al Rosen	11.00	5.00	1.35
□ AL13 Mickey Vernon	9.00	4.00	.90
□ AL14 Sammy White	8.00	3.50	.80
□ AL15 Gene Woodling	9.00	4.00	.90
□ AL16 Whitey Ford	32.00	14.25	4.75
□ AL17 Phil Rizzuto	22.00	9.50	3.15
□ AL18 Bob Porterfield	8.00	3.50	.80
□ AL19 Chico Carrasquel	8.00	3.50	.80
□ AL20 Yogi Berra	40.00	18.00	6.00
□ AL21 Bob Lemon	18.00	7.50	2.50
□ AL22 Ferris Fain	8.00	3.50	.80
□ AL23 Hank Bauer	11.00	5.00	1.35
□ AL24 Jim Delsing	8.00	3.50	.80
□ AL25 Gil McDougald	11.00	5.00	1.35
□ NL1 Richie Ashburn	16.00	6.75	2.25
□ NL2 Billy Cox	8.00	3.50	.80
□ NL3 Bob Crandall	8.00	3.50	.80
□ NL4 Carl Erskine	10.00	4.50	1.25
□ NL5 Monte Irvin	16.00	6.75	2.25
□ NL6 Ted Kluszewski	14.00	6.25	2.00
□ NL7 Don Mueller	8.00	3.50	.80
□ NL8 Andy Pafko	8.00	3.50	.80
□ NL9 Del Rice	8.00	3.50	.80
□ NL10 Al Schoendienst	18.00	7.50	2.50
□ NL11 Warren Spahn	25.00	11.00	3.50
□ NL12 Curt Simmons	8.00	3.50	.80
□ NL13 Roy Campanella	55.00	25.00	8.25
□ NL14 Jim Gilliam	11.00	5.00	1.35
□ NL15 Pee Wee Reese	32.00	14.25	4.75
□ NL16 Duke Snider	55.00	25.00	8.25
□ NL17 Rip Repulski	8.00	3.50	.80
□ NL18 Robin Roberts	22.00	9.50	3.15
□ NL19A Enos Slaughter	65.00	29.00	9.75
□ NL19B Gus Bell	30.00	13.50	4.50
□ NL20 Johnny Logan	8.00	3.50	.80
□ NL21 John Antonelli	8.00	3.50	.80
□ NL22 Gil Hodges	24.00	10.50	3.50
□ NL23 Eddie Mathews	25.00	11.00	3.50
□ NL24 Lew Burdette	10.00	4.50	1.25
□ NL25 Willie Mays	90.00	40.00	13.50

1955 Red Man

The cards in this 50-card set measure 3 1/2" by 4" (or 3 1/2" by 3 5/8" without the tab). The 1955 Red Man set contains 25 players from each league. Card numbers are on the write-ups of the players. Cards that have the tab (coupon) attached are generally worth two and a half times the price of cards with the tab removed. The prices listed below refer to cards without tabs.

	NRMT	VG-E	GOOD
COMPLETE SET (50)	700.00	315.00	105.00
COMMON PLAYER	8.00	3.50	.80
☐ AL1 Ray Boone	8.00	3.50	.80
☐ AL2 Jim Busby	8.00	3.50	.80
☐ AL3 Whitey Ford	32.00	14.25	4.75
☐ AL4 Nelson Fox	14.00	6.25	2.00
☐ AL5 Bob Grim	8.00	3.50	.80
☐ AL6 Jack Harshman	8.00	3.50	.80
☐ AL7 Jim Hegan	8.00	3.50	.80
☐ AL8 Bob Lemon	18.00	7.50	2.50
☐ AL9 Irv Noren	8.00	3.50	.80
☐ AL10 Bob Porterfield	8.00	3.50	.80
☐ AL11 Al Rosen	11.00	5.00	1.35
☐ AL12 Mickey Vernon	8.00	3.50	.80
☐ AL13 Vic Wertz	8.00	3.50	.80
☐ AL14 Early Wynn	18.00	7.50	2.50
☐ AL15 Bobby Avila	8.00	3.50	.80
☐ AL16 Yogi Berra	40.00	18.00	6.00
☐ AL17 Joe Coleman	8.00	3.50	.80
☐ AL18 Larry Doby	9.00	4.00	.90
☐ AL19 Jackie Jensen	8.00	3.50	.80
☐ AL20 Pete Runnels	8.00	3.50	.80
☐ AL21 Jim Piersall	11.00	5.00	1.35
☐ AL22 Hank Bauer	11.00	5.00	1.35
☐ AL23 Chico Carrasquel	8.00	3.50	.80
☐ AL24 Minnie Minoso	11.00	5.00	1.35
☐ AL25 Sandy Consuegra	8.00	3.50	.80
☐ NL1 Richie Ashburn	16.00	6.75	2.25
☐ NL2 Del Crandall	8.00	3.50	.80
☐ NL3 Gil Hodges	24.00	10.50	3.50
☐ NL4 Brooks Lawrence	8.00	3.50	.80
☐ NL5 Johnny Logan	8.00	3.50	.80
☐ NL6 Sal Maglie	9.00	4.00	.90
☐ NL7 Willie Mays	90.00	40.00	13.50
☐ NL8 Don Mueller	8.00	3.50	.80
☐ NL9 Bill Sarni	8.00	3.50	.80
☐ NL10 Warren Spahn	25.00	11.00	3.50
☐ NL11 Hank Thompson	8.00	3.50	.80
☐ NL12 Hoyt Wilhelm	18.00	7.50	2.50
☐ NL13 John Antonelli	8.00	3.50	.80
☐ NL14 Carl Erskine	9.00	4.00	.90
☐ NL15 Granny Hamner	8.00	3.50	.80
☐ NL16 Ted Kluszewski	14.00	6.25	2.00
☐ NL17 Pee Wee Reese	32.00	14.25	4.75
☐ NL18 Al Schoendienst	18.00	7.50	2.50
☐ NL19 Duke Snider	55.00	25.00	8.25
☐ NL20 Frank Thomas	8.00	3.50	.80
☐ NL21 Ray Jablonski	8.00	3.50	.80
☐ NL22 Dusty Rhodes	8.00	3.50	.80
☐ NL23 Gus Bell	8.00	3.50	.80
☐ NL24 Curt Simmons	8.00	3.50	.80
☐ NL25 Marv Grissom	8.00	3.50	.80

1955 Rodeo Meats

The cards in this 47-card set measure 2 1/2" by 3 1/2". The 1955 Rodeo Meats set contains unnumbered, color cards of the first Kansas City A's team. There are many background color variations noted in the checklist, and the card reverses carry a scrapbook offer. The Grimes and Kryhoski cards listed in the scrapbook album were apparently never issued. The catalog number for this set is F152-1. The cards have been arranged in alphabetical order and assigned numbers for reference.

	NRMT	VG-E	GOOD
COMPLETE SET (47)	5000.00	2000.00	500.00
COMMON PLAYER (1-47)	80.00	36.00	12.00
☐ 1 Joe Astroth	80.00	36.00	12.00
☐ 2 Harold Bevan	100.00	45.00	15.00
☐ 3 Charles Bishop	100.00	45.00	15.00
☐ 4 Don Bollweg	100.00	45.00	15.00
☐ 5 Lou Boudreau MG	250.00	110.00	37.50
☐ 6 Cloyd Boyer (salmon)	80.00	36.00	12.00
☐ 7 Cloyd Boyer (light blue)	125.00	57.50	18.75
☐ 8 Ed Burtschy	150.00	67.50	22.50
☐ 9 Art Ceccarelli	100.00	45.00	15.00
☐ 10 Joe DeMaestri (yellow)	80.00	36.00	12.00
☐ 11 Joe DeMaestri (green)	80.00	36.00	12.00
☐ 12 Art Ditmar	80.00	36.00	12.00
☐ 13 John Dixon	100.00	45.00	15.00
☐ 14 Jim Finigan	80.00	36.00	12.00
☐ 15 Marion Fricano	100.00	45.00	15.00
☐ 16 Tom Gorman	80.00	36.00	12.00
☐ 17 John Gray	100.00	45.00	15.00
☐ 18 Ray Herbert	80.00	36.00	12.00
☐ 19 Forest Jacobs	150.00	67.50	22.50
☐ 20 Alex Kellner	80.00	36.00	12.00
☐ 21 Harry Kraft CO	80.00	36.00	12.00
☐ 22 Jack Littrell	80.00	36.00	12.00
☐ 23 Hector Lopez	80.00	36.00	12.00
☐ 24 Oscar Melillo CO	80.00	36.00	12.00
☐ 25 Arnold Portocarrero (purple)	125.00	57.50	18.75
☐ 26 Arnold Portocarrero (gray)	80.00	36.00	12.00
☐ 27 Vic Power (yellow)	80.00	36.00	12.00
☐ 28 Vic Power (pink)	125.00	57.50	18.75
☐ 29 Vic Raschi	125.00	57.50	18.75
☐ 30 Bill Renna (lavender)	80.00	36.00	12.00
☐ 31 Bill Renna (dark pink)	125.00	57.50	18.75
☐ 32 Al Robertson	100.00	45.00	15.00
☐ 33 Johnny Sain	175.00	80.00	27.00
☐ 35 Bobby Schantz ERR (misspelling)	250.00	110.00	37.50
☐ 34 Bobby Shantz COR	150.00	67.50	22.50
☐ 36 Wilmer Shantz (orange)	80.00	36.00	12.00
☐ 37 Wilmer Shantz (lavender)	80.00	36.00	12.00
☐ 38 Harry Simpson	80.00	36.00	12.00
☐ 39 Enos Slaughter	300.00	135.00	45.00
☐ 40 Lou Sleater	80.00	36.00	12.00

		NRMT	VG-E	GOOD
☐ 41	George Susce	100.00	45.00	15.00
☐ 42	Bob Trice	100.00	45.00	15.00
☐ 43	Elmer Valo (yellow)	125.00	57.50	18.75
☐ 44	Elmer Valo (green sky)	80.00	36.00	12.00
☐ 45	Bill Wilson (yellow)	125.00	57.50	18.75
☐ 46	Bill Wilson (lavender sky)	80.00	36.00	12.00
☐ 47	Gus Zernial	80.00	36.00	12.00

1956 Rodeo Meats

Art Ditmar

The cards in this 12-card set measure 2 1/2" by 3 1/2". The unnumbered, color cards of the 1956 Rodeo baseball series are easily distinguished from their 1955 counterparts by the absence of the scrapbook offer on the reverse. They were available only in packages of Rodeo All-Meat Wieners. The catalog designation for this set is F152-2, and the cards have been assigned numbers in alphabetical order in the checklist below.

		NRMT	VG-E	GOOD
COMPLETE SET (12)		1350.00	600.00	135.00
COMMON PLAYER (1-12)		80.00	36.00	12.00
☐ 1	Joe Astroth	80.00	36.00	12.00
☐ 2	Lou Boudreau MG	250.00	110.00	37.50
☐ 3	Joe DeMaestri	80.00	36.00	12.00
☐ 4	Art Ditmar	80.00	36.00	12.00
☐ 5	Jim Finigan	80.00	36.00	12.00
☐ 6	Hector Lopez	80.00	36.00	12.00
☐ 7	Vic Power	80.00	36.00	12.00
☐ 8	Bobby Shantz	125.00	57.50	18.75
☐ 9	Harry Simpson	80.00	36.00	12.00
☐ 10	Enos Slaughter	300.00	135.00	45.00
☐ 11	Elmer Valo	80.00	36.00	12.00
☐ 12	Gus Zernial	80.00	36.00	12.00

1958 S.F. Call-Bulletin

The cards in this 25-card set measure 2" by 4". The 1958 San Francisco Call-Bulletin set of unnumbered cards features black print on orange paper. These cards were given away as inserts in the San Francisco Call-Bulletin newspaper. The backs of the cards list the Giants home schedule and a radio station ad. The cards are entitled "Giant Payoff" and feature San Francisco Giant players only. The bottom part of the card (tab) could be detached as a ticket stub; hence, cards with the tab intact are worth approximately double the prices listed below. The catalog designation for this set is M126. The Tom Bowers card was issued in very short supply; also Bressoud, Jablonski, and Kirkland are tougher to find than the others. All of these tougher cards are asterisked in the checklist below.

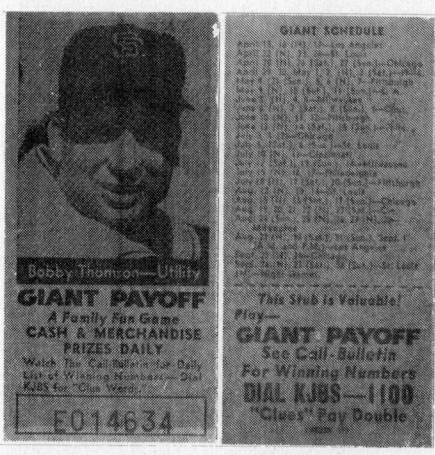

		NRMT	VG-E	GOOD
COMPLETE SET (25)		1250.00	500.00	125.00
COMMON PLAYER (1-25)		7.50	3.25	.75
☐ 1	John Antonelli	9.00	4.00	.90
☐ 2	Curt Barclay	7.50	3.25	.75
☐ 3	Tom Bowers *	600.00	270.00	90.00
☐ 4	Ed Bressoud *	125.00	57.50	18.75
☐ 5	Orlando Cepeda	60.00	27.00	9.00
☐ 6	Ray Crone	7.50	3.25	.75
☐ 7	Jim Davenport	9.00	4.00	.90
☐ 8	Paul Giel	25.00	11.00	3.50
☐ 9	Ruben Gomez	7.50	3.25	.75
☐ 10	Marv Grissom	7.50	3.25	.75
☐ 11	Ray Jablonski *	125.00	57.50	18.75
☐ 12	Willie Kirkland *	150.00	67.50	22.50
☐ 13	Whitey Lockman	7.50	3.25	.75
☐ 14	Willie Mays	200.00	90.00	30.00
☐ 15	Mike McCormick	10.00	4.50	1.25
☐ 16	Stu Miller	9.00	4.00	.90
☐ 17	Ray Monzant	7.50	3.25	.75
☐ 18	Danny O'Connell	7.50	3.25	.75
☐ 19	Bill Rigney MG	9.00	4.00	.90
☐ 20	Hank Sauer	9.00	4.00	.90
☐ 21	Bob Schmidt	7.50	3.25	.75
☐ 22	Daryl Spencer	7.50	3.25	.75
☐ 23	Valmy Thomas	7.50	3.25	.75
☐ 24	Bobby Thomson	25.00	11.00	3.50
☐ 25	Al Worthington	7.50	3.25	.75

1991 S.F. Examiner Athletics

The fifteen 6" by 9" giant-sized cards in this set were issued on yellow cardboard sheets measuring 8 1/2" by 11" and designed for storage in a three-ring binder. The card fronts are green and have color player photos enframed by thin yellow border stripes. The team name appears in a green banner at the top, while the words "Examiner's Finest" appear in a yellow stripe at the bottom of the card. The back has a black and white head shot, biography, career summary, and complete Major League statistics. The cards are unnumbered and checklisted below in alphabetical order.

		MINT	EXC	G-VG
COMPLETE SET (15)		24.00	10.50	3.50
COMMON PLAYER (1-15)		1.00	.40	.10
☐ 1	Harold Baines	1.50	.60	.15
☐ 2	Jose Canseco	5.00	2.25	.50
☐ 3	Dennis Eckersley	2.00	.80	.20
☐ 4	Mike Gallego	1.00	.40	.10
☐ 5	Dave Henderson	1.50	.60	.15
☐ 6	Rickey Henderson	4.00	1.75	.40
☐ 7	Rick Honeycutt	1.00	.40	.10
☐ 8	Mark McGwire	3.00	1.25	.30

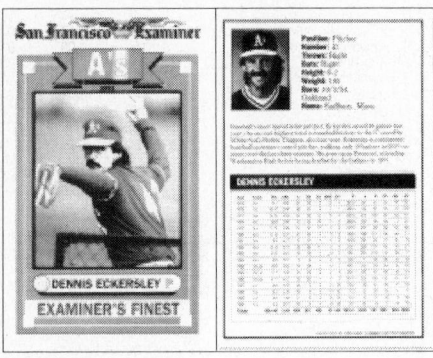

		MINT	EXC	G-VG
☐ 9	Mike Moore	1.50	.60	.15
☐ 10	Gene Nelson	1.00	.40	.10
☐ 11	Eric Show	1.00	.40	.10
☐ 12	Terry Steinbach	1.50	.60	.15
☐ 13	Dave Stewart	2.00	.80	.20
☐ 14	Walt Weiss	1.50	.60	.15
☐ 15	Bob Welch	1.50	.60	.15

1991 S.F. Examiner Giants

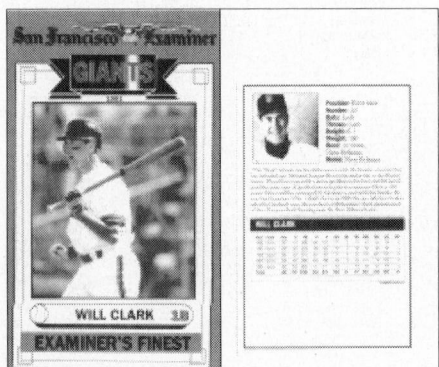

The sixteen 6" by 9" giant-sized cards in this set were issued on orange cardboard sheets measuring 8 1/2" by 11" and designed for storage in a three-ring binder. The cards fronts are light gray and have color player photos enframed by thin orange border stripes. The team name appears in a black banner at the top, while the words "Examiner's Finest" appear in an orange stripe at the bottom of the card. The back has a black and white head shot, biography, career summary, and complete Major League statistics. The cards are unnumbered and checklisted below in alphabetical order.

		MINT	EXC	G-VG
COMPLETE SET (16)		21.00	9.00	3.00
COMMON PLAYER (1-16)		1.00	.40	.10
☐ 1	Kevin Bass	1.00	.40	.10
☐ 2	Mike Benjamin	1.00	.40	.10
☐ 3	Bud Black	1.00	.40	.10
☐ 4	Jeff Brantley	1.50	.60	.15
☐ 5	John Burkett	1.50	.60	.15
☐ 6	Will Clark	5.00	2.25	.50
☐ 7	Steve Decker	2.00	.80	.20
☐ 8	Scott Garrelts	1.50	.60	.15
☐ 9	Mike LaCoss	1.00	.40	.10
☐ 10	Willie McGee	1.50	.60	.15
☐ 11	Kevin Mitchell	3.00	1.25	.30

☐ 12	Dave Righetti	1.50	.60	.15
☐ 13	Don Robinson	1.00	.40	.10
☐ 14	Robby Thompson	1.50	.60	.15
☐ 15	Jose Uribe	1.00	.40	.10
☐ 16	Matt Williams	3.00	1.25	.30

1987-88 Score Test Samples

Late in 1987 near the end of the season, Score prepared some samples to show prospective dealers and buyers of the new Score cards what they would look like. These sample cards are distinguished by the fact that there is a row of zeroes for the 1987 season statistics since the season was not over when these sample cards were being printed. The cards are standard size, 2 1/2" by 3 1/2" and are virtually indistinguishable from the regular 1988 Score cards of the same players except for border color variations in a few instances.

		MINT	EXC	G-VG
COMPLETE SET (6)		30.00	13.50	4.50
COMMON PLAYER		5.00	2.25	.50
☐ 30	Mark Langston	7.50	3.25	.75
☐ 48	Tony Pena	6.00	2.50	.60
☐ 71	Keith Moreland	5.00	2.25	.50
☐ 72	Barry Larkin	12.00	5.25	1.50
☐ 121	Dennis Boyd	5.00	2.25	.50
☐ 145	Denny Walling	5.00	2.25	.50

1988 Score

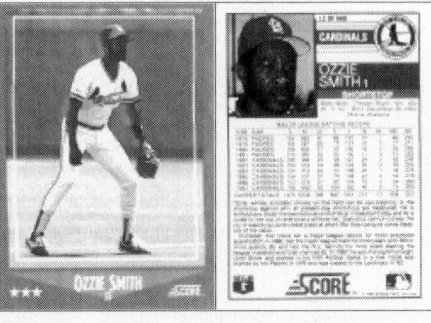

This 660-card set was distributed by Major League Marketing. Cards measure 2 1/2" by 3 1/2" and feature six distinctive border colors on the front. Highlights (652-660) and Rookie Prospects (623-647) are included in the set. Reggie Jackson's career is honored with a 5-card subset on cards 500-504. Card number 501, showing Reggie as a member of the Baltimore Orioles, is one of the few opportunities collectors have to visually remember (on a regular card) Reggie's one-year stay with the Orioles. The set is distinguished by the fact that each card back shows a full-color picture of the player. The key rookie cards in this set are Ellis Burks, Ron Gant, Tom Glavine, Gregg Jefferies, Roberto Kelly and Matt Williams. The company also produced a very limited "glossy" set, that is valued at eight times the value of the regular (non-glossy) set. Although exact production quantities of this glossy set are not known, it is generally accepted that the number of Score glossy sets produced in 1988 was much smaller (estimated only 10 percent to 15 percent as many) than the number of Topps Tiffany or Fleer Tin sets.

	MINT	EXC	G-VG
COMPLETE SET (660)	20.00	8.50	2.75
COMMON PLAYER (1-660)	.03	.01	.00

		MINT	EXC	G-VG
☐	1 Don Mattingly	.30	.10	.02
☐	2 Wade Boggs	.30	.12	.03
☐	3 Tim Raines	.10	.04	.01
☐	4 Andre Dawson	.15	.06	.01
☐	5 Mark McGwire	.40	.16	.04
☐	6 Kevin Seitzer	.08	.03	.01
☐	7 Wally Joyner	.15	.06	.01
☐	8 Jesse Barfield	.08	.03	.01
☐	9 Pedro Guerrero	.08	.03	.01
☐	10 Eric Davis	.15	.06	.01
☐	11 George Brett	.20	.08	.02
☐	12 Ozzie Smith	.17	.07	.01
☐	13 Rickey Henderson	.30	.12	.03
☐	14 Jim Rice	.08	.03	.01
☐	15 Matt Nokes	.25	.10	.02
☐	16 Mike Schmidt	.35	.15	.03
☐	17 Dave Parker	.10	.04	.01
☐	18 Eddie Murray	.15	.06	.01
☐	19 Andres Galarraga	.08	.03	.01
☐	20 Tony Fernandez	.08	.03	.01
☐	21 Kevin McReynolds	.10	.04	.01
☐	22 B.J. Surhoff	.08	.03	.01
☐	23 Pat Tabler	.03	.01	.00
☐	24 Kirby Puckett	.30	.12	.03
☐	25 Benny Santiago	.12	.05	.01
☐	26 Ryne Sandberg	.40	.16	.04
☐	27 Kelly Downs (Will Clark in background, out of focus)	.08	.03	.01
☐	28 Jose Cruz	.06	.02	.00
☐	29 Pete O'Brien	.03	.01	.00
☐	30 Mark Langston	.08	.03	.01
☐	31 Lee Smith	.10	.04	.01
☐	32 Juan Samuel	.08	.03	.01
☐	33 Kevin Bass	.03	.01	.00
☐	34 R.J. Reynolds	.03	.01	.00
☐	35 Steve Sax	.10	.04	.01
☐	36 John Kruk	.06	.02	.00
☐	37 Alan Trammell	.15	.06	.01
☐	38 Chris Bosio	.06	.02	.00
☐	39 Brook Jacoby	.03	.01	.00
☐	40 Willie McGee UER (Excited misspelled as excitd)	.08	.03	.01
☐	41 Dave Magadan	.08	.03	.01
☐	42 Fred Lynn	.08	.03	.01
☐	43 Kent Hrbek	.10	.04	.01
☐	44 Brian Downing	.06	.02	.00
☐	45 Jose Canseco	.75	.30	.07
☐	46 Jim Presley	.03	.01	.00
☐	47 Mike Stanley	.03	.01	.00
☐	48 Tony Pena	.06	.02	.00
☐	49 David Cone	.20	.08	.02
☐	50 Rick Sutcliffe	.06	.02	.00
☐	51 Doug Drabek	.12	.05	.01
☐	52 Bill Doran	.03	.01	.00
☐	53 Mike Scioscia	.03	.01	.00
☐	54 Candy Maldonado	.06	.02	.00
☐	55 Dave Winfield	.15	.06	.01
☐	56 Lou Whitaker	.10	.04	.01
☐	57 Tom Henke	.06	.02	.00
☐	58 Ken Gerhart	.03	.01	.00
☐	59 Glenn Braggs	.03	.01	.00
☐	60 Julio Franco	.15	.06	.01
☐	61 Charlie Leibrandt	.03	.01	.00
☐	62 Gary Gaetti	.08	.03	.01
☐	63 Bob Boone	.08	.03	.01
☐	64 Luis Polonia	.25	.10	.02
☐	65 Dwight Evans	.08	.03	.01
☐	66 Phil Bradley	.03	.01	.00
☐	67 Mike Boddicker	.03	.01	.00
☐	68 Vince Coleman	.10	.04	.01
☐	69 Howard Johnson	.15	.06	.01
☐	70 Tim Wallach	.08	.03	.01
☐	71 Keith Moreland	.03	.01	.00
☐	72 Barry Larkin	.20	.08	.02
☐	73 Alan Ashby	.03	.01	.00
☐	74 Rick Rhoden	.03	.01	.00
☐	75 Darrell Evans	.06	.02	.00
☐	76 Dave Stieb	.08	.03	.01
☐	77 Dan Plesac	.03	.01	.00
☐	78 Will Clark UER (Born 3/17/64, should be 3/13/64)	.75	.30	.07
☐	79 Frank White	.03	.01	.00
☐	80 Joe Carter	.20	.08	.02
☐	81 Mike Witt	.03	.01	.00
☐	82 Terry Steinbach	.08	.03	.01
☐	83 Alvin Davis	.06	.02	.00
☐	84 Tommy Herr (Will Clark shown sliding into second)	.08	.03	.01
☐	85 Vance Law	.03	.01	.00
☐	86 Kal Daniels	.08	.03	.01
☐	87 Rick Honeycutt UER (wrong years for stats on back)	.03	.01	.00
☐	88 Alfredo Griffin	.03	.01	.00
☐	89 Bret Saberhagen	.12	.05	.01
☐	90 Bert Blyleven	.08	.03	.01
☐	91 Jeff Reardon	.10	.04	.01
☐	92 Cory Snyder	.08	.03	.01
☐	93A Greg Walker ERR (93 of 66)	4.00	1.75	.40
☐	93B Greg Walker COR (93 of 660)	.06	.02	.00
☐	94 Joe Magrane	.12	.05	.01
☐	95 Rob Deer	.06	.02	.00
☐	96 Ray Knight	.06	.02	.00
☐	97 Casey Candaele	.03	.01	.00
☐	98 John Cerutti	.03	.01	.00
☐	99 Buddy Bell	.06	.02	.00
☐	100 Jack Clark	.08	.03	.01
☐	101 Eric Bell	.03	.01	.00
☐	102 Willie Wilson	.08	.03	.01
☐	103 Dave Schmidt	.03	.01	.00
☐	104 Dennis Eckersley UER (Complete games stats are wrong)	.10	.04	.01
☐	105 Don Sutton	.10	.04	.01
☐	106 Danny Tartabull	.15	.06	.01
☐	107 Fred McGriff	.60	.25	.06
☐	108 Les Straker	.03	.01	.00
☐	109 Lloyd Moseby	.03	.01	.00
☐	110 Roger Clemens	.35	.15	.03
☐	111 Glenn Hubbard	.03	.01	.00
☐	112 Ken Williams	.06	.02	.00
☐	113 Ruben Sierra	.35	.15	.03
☐	114 Stan Jefferson	.06	.02	.00
☐	115 Milt Thompson	.03	.01	.00
☐	116 Bobby Bonilla	.30	.12	.03
☐	117 Wayne Tolleson	.03	.01	.00
☐	118 Matt Williams	1.50	.60	.15
☐	119 Chet Lemon	.03	.01	.00
☐	120 Dale Sveum	.03	.01	.00
☐	121 Dennis Boyd	.03	.01	.00
☐	122 Brett Butler	.08	.03	.01
☐	123 Terry Kennedy	.03	.01	.00
☐	124 Jack Howell	.03	.01	.00
☐	125 Curt Young	.03	.01	.00
☐	126A Dave Valle ERR (misspelled Dale on card front)	.12	.05	.01
☐	126B Dave Valle COR	.06	.02	.00
☐	127 Curt Wilkerson	.03	.01	.00
☐	128 Tim Teufel	.03	.01	.00
☐	129 Ozzie Virgil	.03	.01	.00
☐	130 Brian Fisher	.03	.01	.00
☐	131 Lance Parrish	.08	.03	.01
☐	132 Tom Browning	.06	.02	.00
☐	133A Larry Andersen ERR (misspelled Anderson on card front)	.12	.05	.01
☐	133B Larry Andersen COR	.06	.02	.00
☐	134A Bob Brenly ERR (misspelled Brenley on card front)	.12	.05	.01
☐	134B Bob Brenly COR	.06	.02	.00
☐	135 Mike Marshall	.06	.02	.00
☐	136 Gerald Perry	.03	.01	.00
☐	137 Bobby Meacham	.03	.01	.00
☐	138 Larry Herndon	.03	.01	.00
☐	139 Fred Manrique	.06	.02	.00
☐	140 Charlie Hough	.03	.01	.00

☐ 141 Ron Darling	.08	.03	.01
☐ 142 Herm Winningham	.03	.01	.00
☐ 143 Mike Diaz	.03	.01	.00
☐ 144 Mike Jackson	.10	.04	.01
☐ 145 Denny Walling	.03	.01	.00
☐ 146 Robby Thompson	.03	.01	.00
☐ 147 Franklin Stubbs	.03	.01	.00
☐ 148 Albert Hall	.03	.01	.00
☐ 149 Bobby Witt	.08	.03	.01
☐ 150 Lance McCullers	.03	.01	.00
☐ 151 Scott Bradley	.03	.01	.00
☐ 152 Mark McLemore	.03	.01	.00
☐ 153 Tim Laudner	.03	.01	.00
☐ 154 Greg Swindell	.08	.03	.01
☐ 155 Marty Barrett	.03	.01	.00
☐ 156 Mike Heath	.03	.01	.00
☐ 157 Gary Ward	.03	.01	.00
☐ 158A Lee Mazzilli ERR	.12	.05	.01
(misspelled Mazilli			
on card front)			
☐ 158B Lee Mazzilli COR	.06	.02	.00
☐ 159 Tom Foley	.03	.01	.00
☐ 160 Robin Yount	.20	.08	.02
☐ 161 Steve Bedrosian	.06	.02	.00
☐ 162 Bob Walk	.03	.01	.00
☐ 163 Nick Esasky	.03	.01	.00
☐ 164 Ken Caminiti	.20	.08	.02
☐ 165 Jose Uribe	.03	.01	.00
☐ 166 Dave Anderson	.03	.01	.00
☐ 167 Ed Whitson	.03	.01	.00
☐ 168 Ernie Whitt	.03	.01	.00
☐ 169 Cecil Cooper	.06	.02	.00
☐ 170 Mike Pagliarulo	.03	.01	.00
☐ 171 Pat Sheridan	.03	.01	.00
☐ 172 Chris Bando	.03	.01	.00
☐ 173 Lee Lacy	.03	.01	.00
☐ 174 Steve Lombardozzi	.03	.01	.00
☐ 175 Mike Greenwell	.40	.16	.04
☐ 176 Greg Minton	.03	.01	.00
☐ 177 Moose Haas	.03	.01	.00
☐ 178 Mike Kingery	.03	.01	.00
☐ 179 Greg A. Harris	.03	.01	.00
☐ 180 Bo Jackson	.60	.25	.06
☐ 181 Carmelo Martinez	.03	.01	.00
☐ 182 Alex Trevino	.03	.01	.00
☐ 183 Ron Oester	.03	.01	.00
☐ 184 Danny Darwin	.03	.01	.00
☐ 185 Mike Krukow	.03	.01	.00
☐ 186 Rafael Palmeiro	.50	.20	.05
☐ 187 Tim Burke	.03	.01	.00
☐ 188 Roger McDowell	.03	.01	.00
☐ 189 Garry Templeton	.06	.02	.00
☐ 190 Terry Pendleton	.12	.05	.01
☐ 191 Larry Parrish	.03	.01	.00
☐ 192 Rey Quinones	.03	.01	.00
☐ 193 Joaquin Andujar	.03	.01	.00
☐ 194 Tom Brunansky	.06	.02	.00
☐ 195 Donnie Moore	.03	.01	.00
☐ 196 Dan Pasqua	.06	.02	.00
☐ 197 Jim Gantner	.03	.01	.00
☐ 198 Mark Eichhorn	.06	.02	.00
☐ 199 John Grubb	.03	.01	.00
☐ 200 Bill Ripken	.12	.05	.01
☐ 201 Sam Horn	.15	.06	.01
☐ 202 Todd Worrell	.08	.03	.01
☐ 203 Terry Leach	.03	.01	.00
☐ 204 Garth Iorg	.03	.01	.00
☐ 205 Brian Dayett	.03	.01	.00
☐ 206 Bo Diaz	.03	.01	.00
☐ 207 Craig Reynolds	.03	.01	.00
☐ 208 Brian Holton	.06	.02	.00
☐ 209 Marvell Wynne UER	.06	.02	.00
(misspelled Marvelle			
on card front)			
☐ 210 Dave Concepcion	.08	.03	.01
☐ 211 Mike Davis	.03	.01	.00
☐ 212 Devon White	.10	.04	.01
☐ 213 Mickey Brantley	.03	.01	.00
☐ 214 Greg Gagne	.03	.01	.00
☐ 215 Oddibe McDowell	.03	.01	.00
☐ 216 Jimmy Key	.06	.02	.00
☐ 217 Dave Bergman	.03	.01	.00
☐ 218 Calvin Schiraldi	.03	.01	.00
☐ 219 Larry Sheets	.03	.01	.00
☐ 220 Mike Easler	.03	.01	.00
☐ 221 Kurt Stillwell	.06	.02	.00
☐ 222 Chuck Jackson	.06	.02	.00
☐ 223 Dave Martinez	.08	.03	.01
☐ 224 Tim Leary	.08	.03	.01
☐ 225 Steve Garvey	.15	.06	.01
☐ 226 Greg Mathews	.03	.01	.00
☐ 227 Doug Sisk	.03	.01	.00
☐ 228 Dave Henderson	.08	.03	.01
☐ 229 Jimmy Dwyer	.03	.01	.00

☐ 230 Larry Owen	.03	.01	.00
☐ 231 Andre Thornton	.03	.01	.00
☐ 232 Mark Salas	.03	.01	.00
☐ 233 Tom Brookens	.03	.01	.00
☐ 234 Greg Brock	.03	.01	.00
☐ 235 Rance Mulliniks	.03	.01	.00
☐ 236 Bob Brower	.03	.01	.00
☐ 237 Joe Niekro	.06	.02	.00
☐ 238 Scott Bankhead	.06	.02	.00
☐ 239 Doug DeCinces	.03	.01	.00
☐ 240 Tommy John	.08	.03	.01
☐ 241 Rich Gedman	.03	.01	.00
☐ 242 Ted Power	.03	.01	.00
☐ 243 Dave Meads	.03	.01	.00
☐ 244 Jim Sundberg	.03	.01	.00
☐ 245 Ken Oberkfell	.03	.01	.00
☐ 246 Jimmy Jones	.06	.02	.00
☐ 247 Ken Landreaux	.03	.01	.00
☐ 248 Jose Oquendo	.03	.01	.00
☐ 249 John Mitchell	.06	.02	.00
☐ 250 Don Baylor	.08	.03	.01
☐ 251 Scott Fletcher	.03	.01	.00
☐ 252 Al Newman	.03	.01	.00
☐ 253 Carney Lansford	.08	.03	.01
☐ 254 Johnny Ray	.03	.01	.00
☐ 255 Gary Pettis	.03	.01	.00
☐ 256 Ken Phelps	.03	.01	.00
☐ 257 Rick Leach	.03	.01	.00
☐ 258 Tim Stoddard	.03	.01	.00
☐ 259 Ed Romero	.03	.01	.00
☐ 260 Sid Bream	.03	.01	.00
☐ 261A Tom Niedenfuer ERR	.12	.05	.01
(misspelled Neidenfuer			
on card front)			
☐ 261B Tom Niedenfuer COR	.06	.02	.00
☐ 262 Rick Dempsey	.03	.01	.00
☐ 263 Lonnie Smith	.08	.03	.01
☐ 264 Bob Forsch	.03	.01	.00
☐ 265 Barry Bonds	.35	.15	.03
☐ 266 Willie Randolph	.06	.02	.00
☐ 267 Mike Ramsey	.06	.02	.00
☐ 268 Don Slaught	.03	.01	.00
☐ 269 Mickey Tettleton	.08	.03	.01
☐ 270 Jerry Reuss	.03	.01	.00
☐ 271 Marc Sullivan	.03	.01	.00
☐ 272 Jim Morrison	.03	.01	.00
☐ 273 Steve Balboni	.03	.01	.00
☐ 274 Dick Schofield	.03	.01	.00
☐ 275 John Tudor	.08	.03	.01
☐ 276 Gene Larkin	.12	.05	.01
☐ 277 Harold Reynolds	.06	.02	.00
☐ 278 Jerry Browne	.03	.01	.00
☐ 279 Willie Upshaw	.03	.01	.00
☐ 280 Ted Higuera	.06	.02	.00
☐ 281 Terry McGriff	.03	.01	.00
☐ 282 Terry Puhl	.03	.01	.00
☐ 283 Mark Wasinger	.06	.02	.00
☐ 284 Luis Salazar	.03	.01	.00
☐ 285 Ted Simmons	.08	.03	.01
☐ 286 John Shelby	.03	.01	.00
☐ 287 John Smiley	.45	.18	.04
☐ 288 Curt Ford	.03	.01	.00
☐ 289 Steve Crawford	.03	.01	.00
☐ 290 Dan Quisenberry	.08	.03	.01
☐ 291 Alan Wiggins	.03	.01	.00
☐ 292 Randy Bush	.03	.01	.00
☐ 293 John Candelaria	.03	.01	.00
☐ 294 Tony Phillips	.03	.01	.00
☐ 295 Mike Morgan	.06	.02	.00
☐ 296 Bill Wegman	.03	.01	.00
☐ 297A Terry Francona ERR	.12	.05	.01
(misspelled Franconia			
on card front)			
☐ 297B Terry Francona COR	.06	.02	.00
☐ 298 Mickey Hatcher	.03	.01	.00
☐ 299 Andres Thomas	.03	.01	.00
☐ 300 Bob Stanley	.03	.01	.00
☐ 301 Al Pedrique	.03	.01	.00
☐ 302 Jim Lindeman	.03	.01	.00
☐ 303 Wally Backman	.03	.01	.00
☐ 304 Paul O'Neill	.12	.05	.01
☐ 305 Hubie Brooks	.08	.03	.01
☐ 306 Steve Buechele	.06	.02	.00
☐ 307 Bobby Thigpen	.10	.04	.01
☐ 308 George Hendrick	.03	.01	.00
☐ 309 John Moses	.03	.01	.00
☐ 310 Ron Guidry	.08	.03	.01
☐ 311 Bill Schroeder	.03	.01	.00
☐ 312 Jose Nunez	.06	.02	.00
☐ 313 Bud Black	.03	.01	.00
☐ 314 Joe Sambito	.03	.01	.00
☐ 315 Scott McGregor	.03	.01	.00
☐ 316 Rafael Santana	.03	.01	.00
☐ 317 Frank Williams	.03	.01	.00

#	Name			
☐ 318	Mike Fitzgerald	.03	.01	.00
☐ 319	Rick Mahler	.03	.01	.00
☐ 320	Jim Gott	.03	.01	.00
☐ 321	Mariano Duncan	.03	.01	.00
☐ 322	Jose Guzman	.06	.02	.00
☐ 323	Lee Guetterman	.03	.01	.00
☐ 324	Dan Gladden	.03	.01	.00
☐ 325	Gary Carter	.08	.03	.01
☐ 326	Tracy Jones	.03	.01	.00
☐ 327	Floyd Youmans	.03	.01	.00
☐ 328	Bill Dawley	.03	.01	.00
☐ 329	Paul Noce	.06	.02	.00
☐ 330	Angel Salazar	.03	.01	.00
☐ 331	Goose Gossage	.08	.03	.01
☐ 332	George Frazier	.03	.01	.00
☐ 333	Ruppert Jones	.03	.01	.00
☐ 334	Billy Jo Robidoux	.03	.01	.00
☐ 335	Mike Scott	.08	.03	.01
☐ 336	Randy Myers	.06	.02	.00
☐ 337	Bob Sebra	.03	.01	.00
☐ 338	Eric Show	.03	.01	.00
☐ 339	Mitch Williams	.06	.02	.00
☐ 340	Paul Molitor	.10	.04	.01
☐ 341	Gus Polidor	.03	.01	.00
☐ 342	Steve Trout	.03	.01	.00
☐ 343	Jerry Don Gleaton	.03	.01	.00
☐ 344	Bob Knepper	.03	.01	.00
☐ 345	Mitch Webster	.03	.01	.00
☐ 346	John Morris	.03	.01	.00
☐ 347	Andy Hawkins	.03	.01	.00
☐ 348	Dave Leiper	.03	.01	.00
☐ 349	Ernest Riles	.03	.01	.00
☐ 350	Dwight Gooden	.15	.06	.01
☐ 351	Dave Righetti	.06	.02	.00
☐ 352	Pat Dodson	.06	.02	.00
☐ 353	John Habyan	.03	.01	.00
☐ 354	Jim Deshaies	.03	.01	.00
☐ 355	Butch Wynegar	.03	.01	.00
☐ 356	Bryn Smith	.03	.01	.00
☐ 357	Matt Young	.03	.01	.00
☐ 358	Tom Pagnozzi	.12	.05	.01
☐ 359	Floyd Rayford	.03	.01	.00
☐ 360	Darryl Strawberry	.35	.15	.03
☐ 361	Sal Butera	.03	.01	.00
☐ 362	Domingo Ramos	.03	.01	.00
☐ 363	Chris Brown	.03	.01	.00
☐ 364	Jose Gonzalez	.06	.02	.00
☐ 365	Dave Smith	.03	.01	.00
☐ 366	Andy McGaffigan	.03	.01	.00
☐ 367	Stan Javier	.03	.01	.00
☐ 368	Henry Cotto	.03	.01	.00
☐ 369	Mike Birkbeck	.03	.01	.00
☐ 370	Len Dykstra	.08	.03	.01
☐ 371	Dave Collins	.03	.01	.00
☐ 372	Spike Owen	.03	.01	.00
☐ 373	Geno Petralli	.03	.01	.00
☐ 374	Ron Karkovice	.03	.01	.00
☐ 375	Shane Rawley	.03	.01	.00
☐ 376	DeWayne Buice	.03	.01	.00
☐ 377	Bill Pecota	.08	.03	.01
☐ 378	Leon Durham	.03	.01	.00
☐ 379	Ed Olwine	.03	.01	.00
☐ 380	Bruce Hurst	.06	.02	.00
☐ 381	Bob McClure	.03	.01	.00
☐ 382	Mark Thurmond	.03	.01	.00
☐ 383	Buddy Biancalana	.03	.01	.00
☐ 384	Tim Conroy	.03	.01	.00
☐ 385	Tony Gwynn	.25	.10	.02
☐ 386	Greg Gross	.03	.01	.00
☐ 387	Barry Lyons	.08	.03	.01
☐ 388	Mike Felder	.06	.02	.00
☐ 389	Pat Clements	.03	.01	.00
☐ 390	Ken Griffey	.10	.04	.01
☐ 391	Mark Davis	.06	.02	.00
☐ 392	Jose Rijo	.10	.04	.01
☐ 393	Mike Young	.03	.01	.00
☐ 394	Willie Fraser	.03	.01	.00
☐ 395	Dion James	.03	.01	.00
☐ 396	Steve Shields	.03	.01	.00
☐ 397	Randy St.Claire	.03	.01	.00
☐ 398	Danny Jackson	.06	.02	.00
☐ 399	Cecil Fielder	.35	.15	.03
☐ 400	Keith Hernandez	.08	.03	.01
☐ 401	Don Carman	.03	.01	.00
☐ 402	Chuck Crim	.03	.01	.00
☐ 403	Rob Woodward	.03	.01	.00
☐ 404	Junior Ortiz	.03	.01	.00
☐ 405	Glenn Wilson	.03	.01	.00
☐ 406	Ken Howell	.03	.01	.00
☐ 407	Jeff Kunkel	.03	.01	.00
☐ 408	Jeff Reed	.03	.01	.00
☐ 409	Chris James	.08	.03	.01
☐ 410	Zane Smith	.08	.03	.01
☐ 411	Ken Dixon	.03	.01	.00
☐ 412	Ricky Horton	.03	.01	.00
☐ 413	Frank DiPino	.03	.01	.00
☐ 414	Shane Mack	.15	.06	.01
☐ 415	Danny Cox	.03	.01	.00
☐ 416	Andy Van Slyke	.10	.04	.01
☐ 417	Danny Heep	.03	.01	.00
☐ 418	John Cangelosi	.03	.01	.00
☐ 419A	John Christensen ERR (Christiansen on card front)	.12	.05	.01
☐ 419B	John Christensen COR	.06	.02	.00
☐ 420	Joey Cora	.06	.02	.00
☐ 421	Mike LaValliere	.03	.01	.00
☐ 422	Kelly Gruber	.15	.06	.01
☐ 423	Bruce Benedict	.03	.01	.00
☐ 424	Len Matuszek	.03	.01	.00
☐ 425	Kent Tekulve	.03	.01	.00
☐ 426	Rafael Ramirez	.03	.01	.00
☐ 427	Mike Flanagan	.06	.02	.00
☐ 428	Mike Gallego	.03	.01	.00
☐ 429	Juan Castillo	.03	.01	.00
☐ 430	Neal Heaton	.03	.01	.00
☐ 431	Phil Garner	.03	.01	.00
☐ 432	Mike Dunne	.03	.01	.00
☐ 433	Wallace Johnson	.03	.01	.00
☐ 434	Jack O'Connor	.03	.01	.00
☐ 435	Steve Jeltz	.03	.01	.00
☐ 436	Donnell Nixon	.06	.02	.00
☐ 437	Jack Lazorko	.03	.01	.00
☐ 438	Keith Comstock	.03	.01	.00
☐ 439	Jeff D. Robinson (Pirates pitcher)	.03	.01	.00
☐ 440	Graig Nettles	.08	.03	.01
☐ 441	Mel Hall	.06	.02	.00
☐ 442	Gerald Young	.08	.03	.01
☐ 443	Gary Redus	.03	.01	.00
☐ 444	Charlie Moore	.03	.01	.00
☐ 445	Bill Madlock	.06	.02	.00
☐ 446	Mark Clear	.03	.01	.00
☐ 447	Greg Booker	.03	.01	.00
☐ 448	Rick Schu	.03	.01	.00
☐ 449	Ron Kittle	.06	.02	.00
☐ 450	Dale Murphy	.15	.06	.01
☐ 451	Bob Dernier	.03	.01	.00
☐ 452	Dale Mohorcic	.03	.01	.00
☐ 453	Rafael Belliard	.03	.01	.00
☐ 454	Charlie Puleo	.03	.01	.00
☐ 455	Dwayne Murphy	.03	.01	.00
☐ 456	Jim Eisenreich	.03	.01	.00
☐ 457	David Palmer	.03	.01	.00
☐ 458	Dave Stewart	.08	.03	.01
☐ 459	Pascual Perez	.03	.01	.00
☐ 460	Glenn Davis	.10	.04	.01
☐ 461	Dan Petry	.03	.01	.00
☐ 462	Jim Winn	.03	.01	.00
☐ 463	Darrell Miller	.03	.01	.00
☐ 464	Mike Moore	.06	.02	.00
☐ 465	Mike LaCoss	.03	.01	.00
☐ 466	Steve Farr	.03	.01	.00
☐ 467	Jerry Mumphrey	.03	.01	.00
☐ 468	Kevin Gross	.03	.01	.00
☐ 469	Bruce Bochy	.03	.01	.00
☐ 470	Orel Hershiser	.10	.04	.01
☐ 471	Eric King	.03	.01	.00
☐ 472	Ellis Burks	.60	.25	.06
☐ 473	Darren Daulton	.03	.01	.00
☐ 474	Mookie Wilson	.03	.01	.00
☐ 475	Frank Viola	.08	.03	.01
☐ 476	Ron Robinson	.03	.01	.00
☐ 477	Bob Melvin	.03	.01	.00
☐ 478	Jeff Musselman	.03	.01	.00
☐ 479	Charlie Kerfeld	.03	.01	.00
☐ 480	Richard Dotson	.03	.01	.00
☐ 481	Kevin Mitchell	.25	.10	.02
☐ 482	Gary Roenicke	.03	.01	.00
☐ 483	Tim Flannery	.03	.01	.00
☐ 484	Rich Yett	.03	.01	.00
☐ 485	Pete Incaviglia	.08	.03	.01
☐ 486	Rick Cerone	.03	.01	.00
☐ 487	Tony Armas	.03	.01	.00
☐ 488	Jerry Reed	.03	.01	.00
☐ 489	Dave Lopes	.06	.02	.00
☐ 490	Frank Tanana	.06	.02	.00
☐ 491	Mike Loynd	.03	.01	.00
☐ 492	Bruce Ruffin	.03	.01	.00
☐ 493	Chris Speier	.03	.01	.00
☐ 494	Tom Hume	.03	.01	.00
☐ 495	Jesse Orosco	.03	.01	.00
☐ 496	Robbie Wine UER (misspelled Robby on card front)	.03	.01	.00
☐ 497	Jeff Montgomery	.20	.08	.02
☐ 498	Jeff Dedmon	.03	.01	.00
☐ 499	Luis Aguayo	.03	.01	.00

☐ 500	Reggie Jackson (Oakland A's)	.20	.08	.02
☐ 501	Reggie Jackson (Baltimore Orioles)	.25	.10	.02
☐ 502	Reggie Jackson (New York Yankees)	.20	.08	.02
☐ 503	Reggie Jackson (California Angels)	.20	.08	.02
☐ 504	Reggie Jackson (Oakland A's)	.20	.08	.02
☐ 505	Billy Hatcher	.06	.02	.00
☐ 506	Ed Lynch	.03	.01	.00
☐ 507	Willie Hernandez	.03	.01	.00
☐ 508	Jose DeLeon	.03	.01	.00
☐ 509	Joel Youngblood	.03	.01	.00
☐ 510	Bob Welch	.08	.03	.01
☐ 511	Steve Ontiveros	.03	.01	.00
☐ 512	Randy Ready	.03	.01	.00
☐ 513	Juan Nieves	.03	.01	.00
☐ 514	Jeff Russell	.03	.01	.00
☐ 515	Von Hayes	.08	.03	.01
☐ 516	Mark Gubicza	.06	.02	.00
☐ 517	Ken Dayley	.03	.01	.00
☐ 518	Don Aase	.03	.01	.00
☐ 519	Rick Reuschel	.06	.02	.00
☐ 520	Mike Henneman	.15	.06	.01
☐ 521	Rick Aguilera	.06	.02	.00
☐ 522	Jay Howell	.03	.01	.00
☐ 523	Ed Correa	.03	.01	.00
☐ 524	Manny Trillo	.03	.01	.00
☐ 525	Kirk Gibson	.08	.03	.01
☐ 526	Wally Ritchie	.03	.01	.00
☐ 527	Al Nipper	.03	.01	.00
☐ 528	Atlee Hammaker	.03	.01	.00
☐ 529	Shawon Dunston	.10	.04	.01
☐ 530	Jim Clancy	.03	.01	.00
☐ 531	Tom Paciorek	.03	.01	.00
☐ 532	Joel Skinner	.03	.01	.00
☐ 533	Scott Garrelts	.03	.01	.00
☐ 534	Tom O'Malley	.03	.01	.00
☐ 535	John Franco	.06	.02	.00
☐ 536	Paul Kilgus	.06	.02	.00
☐ 537	Darrell Porter	.03	.01	.00
☐ 538	Walt Terrell	.03	.01	.00
☐ 539	Bill Long	.06	.02	.00
☐ 540	George Bell	.12	.05	.01
☐ 541	Jeff Sellers	.03	.01	.00
☐ 542	Joe Boever	.08	.03	.01
☐ 543	Steve Howe	.03	.01	.00
☐ 544	Scott Sanderson	.06	.02	.00
☐ 545	Jack Morris	.12	.05	.01
☐ 546	Todd Benzinger	.20	.08	.02
☐ 547	Steve Henderson	.03	.01	.00
☐ 548	Eddie Milner	.03	.01	.00
☐ 549	Jeff M. Robinson (Tigers pitcher)	.08	.03	.01
☐ 550	Cal Ripken	.40	.16	.04
☐ 551	Jody Davis	.03	.01	.00
☐ 552	Kirk McCaskill	.03	.01	.00
☐ 553	Craig Lefferts	.03	.01	.00
☐ 554	Darnell Coles	.03	.01	.00
☐ 555	Phil Niekro	.15	.06	.01
☐ 556	Mike Aldrete	.03	.01	.00
☐ 557	Pat Perry	.03	.01	.00
☐ 558	Juan Agosto	.03	.01	.00
☐ 559	Rob Murphy	.03	.01	.00
☐ 560	Dennis Rasmussen	.03	.01	.00
☐ 561	Manny Lee	.03	.01	.00
☐ 562	Jeff Blauser	.17	.07	.01
☐ 563	Bob Ojeda	.03	.01	.00
☐ 564	Dave Dravecky	.08	.03	.01
☐ 565	Gene Garber	.03	.01	.00
☐ 566	Ron Roenicke	.03	.01	.00
☐ 567	Tommy Hinzo	.03	.01	.00
☐ 568	Eric Nolte	.03	.01	.00
☐ 569	Ed Hearn	.03	.01	.00
☐ 570	Mark Davidson	.03	.01	.00
☐ 571	Jim Walewander	.06	.02	.00
☐ 572	Donnie Hill	.03	.01	.00
☐ 573	Jamie Moyer	.03	.01	.00
☐ 574	Ken Schrom	.03	.01	.00
☐ 575	Nolan Ryan	.45	.18	.04
☐ 576	Jim Acker	.03	.01	.00
☐ 577	Jamie Quirk	.03	.01	.00
☐ 578	Jay Aldrich	.03	.01	.00
☐ 579	Claudell Washington	.03	.01	.00
☐ 580	Jeff Leonard	.03	.01	.00
☐ 581	Carmen Castillo	.03	.01	.00
☐ 582	Daryl Boston	.03	.01	.00
☐ 583	Jeff DeWillis	.03	.01	.00
☐ 584	John Marzano	.03	.01	.00
☐ 585	Bill Gullickson	.06	.02	.00
☐ 586	Andy Allanson	.03	.01	.00
☐ 587	Lee Tunnell UER (1987 stat line reads .4.84 ERA)	.03	.01	.00
☐ 588	Gene Nelson	.03	.01	.00
☐ 589	Dave LaPoint	.03	.01	.00
☐ 590	Harold Baines	.08	.03	.01
☐ 591	Bill Buckner	.06	.02	.00
☐ 592	Carlton Fisk	.20	.08	.02
☐ 593	Rick Manning	.03	.01	.00
☐ 594	Doug Jones	.12	.05	.01
☐ 595	Tom Candiotti	.06	.02	.00
☐ 596	Steve Lake	.03	.01	.00
☐ 597	Jose Lind	.20	.08	.02
☐ 598	Ross Jones	.03	.01	.00
☐ 599	Gary Matthews	.03	.01	.00
☐ 600	Fernando Valenzuela	.08	.03	.01
☐ 601	Dennis Martinez	.06	.02	.00
☐ 602	Les Lancaster	.08	.03	.01
☐ 603	Ozzie Guillen	.08	.03	.01
☐ 604	Tony Bernazard	.03	.01	.00
☐ 605	Chili Davis	.08	.03	.01
☐ 606	Roy Smalley	.03	.01	.00
☐ 607	Ivan Calderon	.08	.03	.01
☐ 608	Jay Tibbs	.03	.01	.00
☐ 609	Guy Hoffman	.03	.01	.00
☐ 610	Doyle Alexander	.03	.01	.00
☐ 611	Mike Bielecki	.03	.01	.00
☐ 612	Shawn Hillegas	.08	.03	.01
☐ 613	Keith Atherton	.03	.01	.00
☐ 614	Eric Plunk	.03	.01	.00
☐ 615	Sid Fernandez	.08	.03	.01
☐ 616	Dennis Lamp	.03	.01	.00
☐ 617	Dave Engle	.03	.01	.00
☐ 618	Harry Spilman	.03	.01	.00
☐ 619	Don Robinson	.03	.01	.00
☐ 620	John Farrell	.08	.03	.01
☐ 621	Nelson Liriano	.08	.03	.01
☐ 622	Floyd Bannister	.03	.01	.00
☐ 623	Randy Milligan	.35	.15	.03
☐ 624	Kevin Elster	.06	.02	.00
☐ 625	Jody Reed	.30	.12	.03
☐ 626	Shawn Abner	.06	.02	.00
☐ 627	Kurt Manwaring	.08	.03	.01
☐ 628	Pete Stanicek	.06	.02	.00
☐ 629	Rob Ducey	.10	.04	.01
☐ 630	Steve Kiefer	.03	.01	.00
☐ 631	Gary Thurman	.10	.04	.01
☐ 632	Darrel Akerfelds	.08	.03	.01
☐ 633	Dave Clark	.06	.02	.00
☐ 634	Roberto Kelly	.60	.25	.06
☐ 635	Keith Hughes	.06	.02	.00
☐ 636	John Davis	.06	.02	.00
☐ 637	Mike Devereaux	.15	.06	.01
☐ 638	Tom Glavine	1.00	.40	.10
☐ 639	Keith Miller (New York Mets)	.12	.05	.01
☐ 640	Chris Gwynn UER (wrong batting and throwing on back)	.15	.06	.01
☐ 641	Tim Crews	.06	.02	.00
☐ 642	Mackey Sasser	.15	.06	.01
☐ 643	Vicente Palacios	.10	.04	.01
☐ 644	Kevin Romine	.03	.01	.00
☐ 645	Gregg Jefferies	1.00	.40	.10
☐ 646	Jeff Treadway	.20	.08	.02
☐ 647	Ron Gant	2.50	1.00	.25
☐ 648	Mark McGwire and Matt Nokes (Rookie Sluggers)	.08	.03	.01
☐ 649	Eric Davis and Tim Raines (Speed and Power)	.08	.03	.01
☐ 650	Don Mattingly and Jack Clark	.10	.04	.01
☐ 651	Tony Fernandez, Alan Trammell, and Cal Ripken	.20	.08	.02
☐ 652	Vince Coleman HL 100 Stolen Bases	.08	.03	.01
☐ 653	Kirby Puckett HL 10 Hits in a Row	.15	.06	.01
☐ 654	Benito Santiago HL Hitting Streak	.08	.03	.01
☐ 655	Juan Nieves HL No Hitter	.06	.02	.00
☐ 656	Steve Bedrosian HL Saves Record	.06	.02	.00
☐ 657	Mike Schmidt HL 500 Homers	.20	.08	.02
☐ 658	Don Mattingly HL Home Run Streak	.12	.05	.01
☐ 659	Mark McGwire HL Rookie HR Record	.10	.04	.01
☐ 660	Paul Molitor Hitting Streak	.08	.03	.01

1988 Score Box Bottoms

There are six different wax box bottom panels each featuring three players and a trivia (related to a particular stadium for a given year) question. The players and trivia question cards are individually numbered. The trivia are numbered below with the prefix T in order to avoid confusion. The trivia cards are very unpopular with collectors since they do not picture any players. When panels of four are cut into individuals, the cards are standard size, 2/1/2" by 3 1/2". The card backs of the players feature the respective League logos most prominently.

		MINT	EXC	G-VG
COMPLETE SET (24)		7.00	3.00	.70
COMMON PLAYER (1-18)		.10	.04	.01
COMMON TRIVIA (T1-T6)		.05	.02	.00
☐ 1	Terry Kennedy	.10	.04	.01
☐ 2	Don Mattingly	.75	.30	.07
☐ 3	Willie Randolph	.15	.06	.01
☐ 4	Wade Boggs	.75	.30	.07
☐ 5	Cal Ripken	.75	.30	.07
☐ 6	George Bell	.25	.10	.02
☐ 7	Rickey Henderson	.75	.30	.07
☐ 8	Dave Winfield	.35	.15	.03
☐ 9	Bret Saberhagen	.35	.15	.03
☐ 10	Gary Carter	.25	.10	.02
☐ 11	Jack Clark	.20	.08	.02
☐ 12	Ryne Sandberg	.75	.30	.07
☐ 13	Mike Schmidt	.75	.30	.07
☐ 14	Ozzie Smith	.35	.15	.03
☐ 15	Eric Davis	.40	.16	.04
☐ 16	Andre Dawson	.35	.15	.03
☐ 17	Darryl Strawberry	.75	.30	.07
☐ 18	Mike Scott	.15	.06	.01
☐ T1	Fenway Park '60 Ted (Williams) Hits To The End	.10	.04	.01
☐ T2	Comiskey Park '83 Grand Slam (Fred Lynn) Breaks Jinx	.05	.02	.00
☐ T3	Anaheim Stadium '87 Old Rookie Record Falls (Mark McGwire)	.10	.04	.01
☐ T4	Wrigley Field '38 Gabby (Hartnett) Gets Pennant Homer	.05	.02	.00
☐ T5	Comiskey Park '50 Red (Schoendienst) Rips Winning HR	.05	.02	.00
☐ T6	County Stadium '87 Rookie (John Farrell) Stops Hit Streak (Paul Molitor)	.05	.02	.00

1988 Score Young Superstars I

This attractive high-gloss 40-card set of "Young Superstars" was distributed in a small blue box which had the checklist of the set on a side panel of the box. The cards were also distributed as an insert, one per rak pak. These attractive cards

are in full color on the front and also have a full-color small portrait on the card back. The cards are standard size, 2 1/2" by 3 1/2". The cards in this series are distinguishable from the cards in Series II by the fact that this series has a blue and green border on the card front instead of the (Series II) blue and pink border.

		MINT	EXC	G-VG
COMPLETE SET (40)		9.00	4.00	.90
COMMON PLAYER (1-40)		.20	.08	.02
☐ 1	Mark McGwire	.75	.30	.07
☐ 2	Benito Santiago	.50	.20	.05
☐ 3	Sam Horn	.25	.10	.02
☐ 4	Chris Bosio	.30	.12	.03
☐ 5	Matt Nokes	.35	.15	.03
☐ 6	Ken Williams	.20	.08	.02
☐ 7	Dion James	.20	.08	.02
☐ 8	B.J. Surhoff	.30	.12	.03
☐ 9	Joe Magrane	.25	.10	.02
☐ 10	Kevin Seitzer	.30	.12	.03
☐ 11	Stanley Jefferson	.20	.08	.02
☐ 12	Devon White	.35	.15	.03
☐ 13	Nelson Liriano	.20	.08	.02
☐ 14	Chris James	.25	.10	.02
☐ 15	Mike Henneman	.25	.10	.02
☐ 16	Terry Steinbach	.25	.10	.02
☐ 17	John Kruk	.30	.12	.03
☐ 18	Matt Williams	1.00	.40	.10
☐ 19	Kelly Downs	.25	.10	.02
☐ 20	Bill Ripken	.20	.08	.02
☐ 21	Ozzie Guillen	.25	.10	.02
☐ 22	Luis Polonia	.30	.12	.03
☐ 23	Dave Magadan	.35	.15	.03
☐ 24	Mike Greenwell	.60	.25	.06
☐ 25	Will Clark	1.00	.40	.10
☐ 26	Mike Dunne	.20	.08	.02
☐ 27	Wally Joyner	.40	.16	.04
☐ 28	Robby Thompson	.25	.10	.02
☐ 29	Ken Caminiti	.20	.08	.02
☐ 30	Jose Canseco	1.00	.40	.10
☐ 31	Todd Benzinger	.25	.10	.02
☐ 32	Pete Incaviglia	.30	.12	.03
☐ 33	John Farrell	.25	.10	.02
☐ 34	Casey Candaele	.20	.08	.02
☐ 35	Mike Aldrete	.20	.08	.02
☐ 36	Ruben Sierra	.75	.30	.07
☐ 37	Ellis Burks	.75	.30	.07
☐ 38	Tracy Jones	.20	.08	.02
☐ 39	Kal Daniels	.35	.15	.03
☐ 40	Cory Snyder	.25	.10	.02

1988 Score Young Superstars II

This attractive high-gloss 40-card set of "Young Superstars" was distributed in a small purple box which had the checklist of the set on a side panel of the box. The cards were not distributed as an insert with rak paks as the first series was, but were only available as a complete set from hobby dealers or through a mail-in offer direct from the company. These attractive cards are in full color on the front and also have a full-color small portrait on the card back. The cards are standard size, 2 1/2" by

3 1/2". The cards in this series are distinguishable from the cards in Series I by the fact that this series has a blue and pink border on the card front instead of the (Series I) blue and green border.

	MINT	EXC	G-VG
COMPLETE SET (40)	7.50	3.25	.75
COMMON PLAYER (1-40)	.20	.08	.02

		MINT	EXC	G-VG
☐ 1	Don Mattingly	.75	.30	.07
☐ 2	Glenn Braggs	.25	.10	.02
☐ 3	Dwight Gooden	.50	.20	.05
☐ 4	Jose Lind	.25	.10	.02
☐ 5	Danny Tartabull	.50	.20	.05
☐ 6	Tony Fernandez	.25	.10	.02
☐ 7	Julio Franco	.35	.15	.03
☐ 8	Andres Galarraga	.30	.12	.03
☐ 9	Bobby Bonilla	.60	.25	.06
☐ 10	Eric Davis	.60	.25	.06
☐ 11	Gerald Young	.20	.08	.02
☐ 12	Barry Bonds	.60	.25	.06
☐ 13	Jerry Browne	.20	.08	.02
☐ 14	Jeff Blauser	.20	.08	.02
☐ 15	Mickey Brantley	.20	.08	.02
☐ 16	Floyd Youmans	.20	.08	.02
☐ 17	Bret Saberhagen	.35	.15	.03
☐ 18	Shawon Dunston	.30	.12	.03
☐ 19	Len Dykstra	.30	.12	.03
☐ 20	Darryl Strawberry	.75	.30	.07
☐ 21	Rick Aguilera	.25	.10	.02
☐ 22	Ivan Calderon	.30	.12	.03
☐ 23	Roger Clemens	.75	.30	.07
☐ 24	Vince Coleman	.35	.15	.03
☐ 25	Gary Thurman	.20	.08	.02
☐ 26	Jeff Treadway	.20	.08	.02
☐ 27	Oddibe McDowell	.20	.08	.02
☐ 28	Fred McGriff	.50	.20	.05
☐ 29	Mark McLemore	.20	.08	.02
☐ 30	Jeff Musselman	.20	.08	.02
☐ 31	Matt Williams	1.00	.40	.10
☐ 32	Dan Plesac	.20	.08	.02
☐ 33	Juan Nieves	.20	.08	.02
☐ 34	Barry Larkin	.40	.16	.04
☐ 35	Greg Mathews	.20	.08	.02
☐ 36	Shane Mack	.30	.12	.03
☐ 37	Scott Bankhead	.20	.08	.02
☐ 38	Eric Bell	.20	.08	.02
☐ 39	Greg Swindell	.30	.12	.03
☐ 40	Kevin Elster	.20	.08	.02

1988 Score Traded

This 110-card set featured traded players (1-65) and rookies (66-110) for the 1988 season. The cards are distinguishable from the regular Score set by the orange borders and by the fact that the numbering on the back has a T suffix. The cards are standard size, 2 1/2" by 3 1/2", and were distributed by Score as a collated set in a special collector box along with some trivia cards. Score also produced a limited "glossy" Traded set, that is valued at one and a half times the value of the regular (non-glossy) set. It should be noted that the set itself (non-glossy) set

is now considered somewhat scarce. Apparently Score's first attempt at a Rookie/Traded set was produced very conservatively, resulting in a set which is now recognized as being much tougher to find than the other Rookie/Traded sets from the other major companies of that year. The key (extended) rookie cards in this set are Roberto Alomar, Craig Biggio, Rob Dibble, Mark Grace, Jack McDowell, Chris Sabo, and Walt Weiss.

	MINT	EXC	G-VG
COMPLETE SET (110)	60.00	27.00	9.00
COMMON PLAYER (1-65)	.12	.05	.01
COMMON PLAYER (66-110)	.12	.05	.01

		MINT	EXC	G-VG
☐ 1T	Jack Clark	.30	.10	.02
☐ 2T	Danny Jackson	.20	.08	.02
☐ 3T	Brett Butler	.30	.12	.03
☐ 4T	Kurt Stillwell	.20	.08	.02
☐ 5T	Tom Brunansky	.20	.08	.02
☐ 6T	Dennis Lamp	.12	.05	.01
☐ 7T	Jose DeLeon	.12	.05	.01
☐ 8T	Tom Herr	.12	.05	.01
☐ 9T	Keith Moreland	.12	.05	.01
☐ 10T	Kirk Gibson	.30	.12	.03
☐ 11T	Bud Black	.20	.08	.02
☐ 12T	Rafael Ramirez	.12	.05	.01
☐ 13T	Luis Salazar	.12	.05	.01
☐ 14T	Goose Gossage	.30	.12	.03
☐ 15T	Bob Welch	.30	.12	.03
☐ 16T	Vance Law	.12	.05	.01
☐ 17T	Ray Knight	.20	.08	.02
☐ 18T	Dan Quisenberry	.20	.08	.02
☐ 19T	Don Slaught	.12	.05	.01
☐ 20T	Lee Smith	.40	.16	.04
☐ 21T	Rick Cerone	.12	.05	.01
☐ 22T	Pat Tabler	.12	.05	.01
☐ 23T	Larry McWilliams	.12	.05	.01
☐ 24T	Ricky Horton	.12	.05	.01
☐ 25T	Graig Nettles	.20	.08	.02
☐ 26T	Dan Petry	.12	.05	.01
☐ 27T	Jose Rijo	.30	.12	.03
☐ 28T	Chili Davis	.30	.12	.03
☐ 29T	Dickie Thon	.20	.08	.02
☐ 30T	Mackey Sasser	.50	.20	.05
☐ 31T	Mickey Tettleton	.30	.12	.03
☐ 32T	Rick Dempsey	.12	.05	.01
☐ 33T	Ron Hassey	.12	.05	.01
☐ 34T	Phil Bradley	.12	.05	.01
☐ 35T	Jay Howell	.12	.05	.01
☐ 36T	Bill Buckner	.20	.08	.02
☐ 37T	Alfredo Griffin	.12	.05	.01
☐ 38T	Gary Pettis	.12	.05	.01
☐ 39T	Calvin Schiraldi	.12	.05	.01
☐ 40T	John Candelaria	.12	.05	.01
☐ 41T	Joe Orsulak	.12	.05	.01
☐ 42T	Willie Upshaw	.12	.05	.01
☐ 43T	Herm Winningham	.12	.05	.01
☐ 44T	Ron Kittle	.20	.08	.02
☐ 45T	Bob Dernier	.12	.05	.01
☐ 46T	Steve Balboni	.12	.05	.01
☐ 47T	Steve Shields	.12	.05	.01
☐ 48T	Henry Cotto	.12	.05	.01
☐ 49T	Dave Henderson	.40	.16	.04
☐ 50T	Dave Parker	.40	.16	.04
☐ 51T	Mike Young	.12	.05	.01
☐ 52T	Mark Salas	.12	.05	.01
☐ 53T	Mike Davis	.12	.05	.01
☐ 54T	Rafael Santana	.12	.05	.01
☐ 55T	Don Baylor	.20	.08	.02
☐ 56T	Dan Pasqua	.20	.08	.02

		MINT	EXC	G-VG
☐ 57T	Ernest Riles	.12	.05	.01
☐ 58T	Glenn Hubbard	.12	.05	.01
☐ 59T	Mike Smithson	.12	.05	.01
☐ 60T	Richard Dotson	.12	.05	.01
☐ 61T	Jerry Reuss	.12	.05	.01
☐ 62T	Mike Jackson	.20	.08	.02
☐ 63T	Floyd Bannister	.12	.05	.01
☐ 64T	Jesse Orosco	.12	.05	.01
☐ 65T	Larry Parrish	.12	.05	.01
☐ 66T	Jeff Bittiger	.20	.08	.02
☐ 67T	Ray Hayward	.12	.05	.01
☐ 68T	Ricky Jordan	1.00	.40	.10
☐ 69T	Tommy Gregg	.25	.10	.02
☐ 70T	Brady Anderson	.30	.12	.03
☐ 71T	Jeff Montgomery	.25	.10	.02
☐ 72T	Darryl Hamilton	.75	.30	.07
☐ 73T	Cecil Espy	.30	.12	.03
☐ 74T	Greg Briley	.60	.25	.06
☐ 75T	Joey Meyer	.20	.08	.02
☐ 76T	Mike Macfarlane	.40	.16	.04
☐ 77T	Oswald Peraza	.20	.08	.02
☐ 78T	Jack Armstrong	.60	.25	.06
☐ 79T	Don Heinkel	.12	.05	.01
☐ 80T	Mark Grace	15.00	6.50	2.15
☐ 81T	Steve Curry	.20	.08	.02
☐ 82T	Damon Berryhill	.25	.10	.02
☐ 83T	Steve Ellsworth	.20	.08	.02
☐ 84T	Pete Smith	.25	.10	.02
☐ 85T	Jack McDowell	5.00	2.25	.50
☐ 86T	Rob Dibble	4.00	1.75	.40
☐ 87T	Bryan Harvey	2.00	.80	.20
☐ 88T	John Dopson	.25	.10	.02
☐ 89T	Dave Gallagher	.25	.10	.02
☐ 90T	Todd Stottlemyre	3.00	1.25	.30
☐ 91T	Mike Schooler	.60	.25	.06
☐ 92T	Don Gordon	.12	.05	.01
☐ 93T	Sil Campusano	.25	.10	.02
☐ 94T	Jeff Pico	.20	.08	.02
☐ 95T	Jay Buhner	3.00	1.25	.30
☐ 96T	Nelson Santovenia	.25	.10	.02
☐ 97T	Al Leiter	.20	.08	.02
☐ 98T	Luis Alicea	.20	.08	.02
☐ 99T	Pat Borders	.90	.40	.09
☐ 100T	Chris Sabo	8.00	3.50	.80
☐ 101T	Tim Belcher	.50	.20	.05
☐ 102T	Walt Weiss	1.00	.40	.10
☐ 103T	Craig Biggio	4.50	2.00	.45
☐ 104T	Don August	.20	.08	.02
☐ 105T	Roberto Alomar	20.00	8.50	2.75
☐ 106T	Todd Burns	.25	.10	.02
☐ 107T	John Costello	.20	.08	.02
☐ 108T	Melido Perez	.60	.25	.06
☐ 109T	Darrin Jackson	.60	.25	.06
☐ 110T	Orestes Destrade	.30	.10	.02

1989 Score

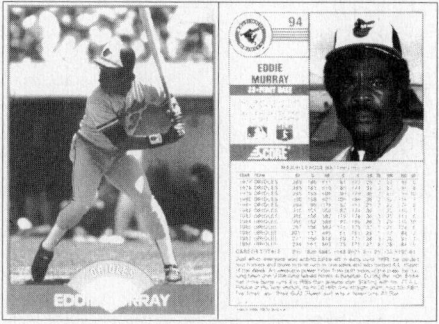

This 660-card set was distributed by Major League Marketing. Cards measure 2 1/2" by 3 1/2" and feature six distinctive inner border (inside a white outer border) colors on the front. Highlights (652-660) and Rookie Prospects (621-651) are included in the set. The set is distinguished by the fact that each card back shows a full-color picture (portrait) of the player. Score "missed" many of the mid-season and later trades; there are numerous examples of inconsistency with regard to the treatment of these players. Study as examples of this inconsistency of handling of late trades, cards numbered 49, 71, 77, 83, 106, 126, 139, 145, 173, 177, 242, 348, 384, 420, 439, 488, 494, and 525. The key rookie cards in this set are Sandy Alomar Jr., Felix Jose, Ramon Martinez, Gary Sheffield, and John Smoltz.

		MINT	EXC	G-VG
	COMPLETE SET (660)	18.00	7.50	2.50
	COMMON PLAYER (1-660)	.03	.01	.00
☐ 1	Jose Canseco	.50	.25	.05
☐ 2	Andre Dawson	.12	.05	.01
☐ 3	Mark McGwire UER	.12	.05	.01
	(bio says 116 RBI's,			
	should be 118)			
☐ 4	Benito Santiago	.08	.03	.01
☐ 5	Rick Reuschel	.06	.02	.00
☐ 6	Fred McGriff	.15	.06	.01
☐ 7	Kal Daniels	.08	.03	.01
☐ 8	Gary Gaetti	.06	.02	.00
☐ 9	Ellis Burks	.15	.06	.01
☐ 10	Darryl Strawberry	.30	.12	.03
☐ 11	Julio Franco	.10	.04	.01
☐ 12	Lloyd Moseby	.03	.01	.00
☐ 13	Jeff Pico	.06	.02	.00
☐ 14	Johnny Ray	.03	.01	.00
☐ 15	Cal Ripken	.35	.15	.03
☐ 16	Dick Schofield	.03	.01	.00
☐ 17	Mel Hall	.06	.02	.00
☐ 18	Bill Ripken	.03	.01	.00
☐ 19	Brook Jacoby	.03	.01	.00
☐ 20	Kirby Puckett	.30	.12	.03
☐ 21	Bill Doran	.03	.01	.00
☐ 22	Pete O'Brien	.03	.01	.00
☐ 23	Matt Nokes	.06	.02	.00
☐ 24	Brian Fisher	.03	.01	.00
☐ 25	Jack Clark	.08	.03	.01
☐ 26	Gary Pettis	.03	.01	.00
☐ 27	Dave Valle	.03	.01	.00
☐ 28	Willie Wilson	.06	.02	.00
☐ 29	Curt Young	.03	.01	.00
☐ 30	Dale Murphy	.12	.05	.01
☐ 31	Barry Larkin	.15	.06	.01
☐ 32	Dave Stewart	.08	.03	.01
☐ 33	Mike LaValliere	.03	.01	.00
☐ 34	Glenn Hubbard	.03	.01	.00
☐ 35	Ryne Sandberg	.35	.15	.03
☐ 36	Tony Pena	.06	.02	.00
☐ 37	Greg Walker	.06	.02	.00
☐ 38	Von Hayes	.06	.02	.00
☐ 39	Kevin Mitchell	.15	.06	.01
☐ 40	Tim Raines	.10	.04	.01
☐ 41	Keith Hernandez	.08	.03	.01
☐ 42	Keith Moreland	.03	.01	.00
☐ 43	Ruben Sierra	.25	.10	.02
☐ 44	Chet Lemon	.03	.01	.00
☐ 45	Willie Randolph	.06	.02	.00
☐ 46	Andy Allanson	.03	.01	.00
☐ 47	Candy Maldonado	.06	.02	.00
☐ 48	Sid Bream	.03	.01	.00
☐ 49	Denny Walling	.03	.01	.00
☐ 50	Dave Winfield	.12	.05	.01
☐ 51	Alvin Davis	.06	.02	.00
☐ 52	Cory Snyder	.06	.02	.00
☐ 53	Hubie Brooks	.06	.02	.00
☐ 54	Chili Davis	.06	.02	.00
☐ 55	Kevin Seitzer	.06	.02	.00
☐ 56	Jose Uribe	.03	.01	.00
☐ 57	Tony Fernandez	.06	.02	.00
☐ 58	Tim Teufel	.03	.01	.00
☐ 59	Oddibe McDowell	.03	.01	.00
☐ 60	Les Lancaster	.03	.01	.00
☐ 61	Billy Hatcher	.06	.02	.00
☐ 62	Dan Gladden	.03	.01	.00
☐ 63	Marty Barrett	.03	.01	.00
☐ 64	Nick Esasky	.03	.01	.00
☐ 65	Wally Joyner	.12	.05	.01
☐ 66	Mike Greenwell	.15	.06	.01
☐ 67	Ken Williams	.03	.01	.00
☐ 68	Bob Horner	.06	.02	.00
☐ 69	Steve Sax	.08	.03	.01
☐ 70	Rickey Henderson	.35	.15	.03
☐ 71	Mitch Webster	.03	.01	.00
☐ 72	Rob Deer	.06	.02	.00
☐ 73	Jim Presley	.03	.01	.00
☐ 74	Albert Hall	.03	.01	.00
☐ 75A	George Brett ERR	.60	.25	.06
	(at age 33)			
☐ 75B	George Brett COR	.15	.06	.01
	(at age 35)			
☐ 76	Brian Downing	.03	.01	.00

☐ 77 Dave Martinez	.03	.01	.00		
☐ 78 Scott Fletcher	.03	.01	.00		
☐ 79 Phil Bradley	.03	.01	.00		
☐ 80 Ozzie Smith	.12	.05	.01		
☐ 81 Larry Sheets	.03	.01	.00		
☐ 82 Mike Aldrete	.03	.01	.00		
☐ 83 Darnell Coles	.03	.01	.00		
☐ 84 Len Dykstra	.08	.03	.01		
☐ 85 Jim Rice	.08	.03	.01		
☐ 86 Jeff Treadway	.03	.01	.00		
☐ 87 Jose Lind	.03	.01	.00		
☐ 88 Willie McGee	.08	.03	.01		
☐ 89 Mickey Brantley	.03	.01	.00		
☐ 90 Tony Gwynn	.17	.07	.01		
☐ 91 R.J. Reynolds	.03	.01	.00		
☐ 92 Milt Thompson	.03	.01	.00		
☐ 93 Kevin McReynolds	.08	.03	.01		
☐ 94 Eddie Murray UER	.12	.05	.01		
('86 batting .205, should be .305)					
☐ 95 Lance Parrish	.08	.03	.01		
☐ 96 Ron Kittle	.06	.02	.00		
☐ 97 Gerald Young	.03	.01	.00		
☐ 98 Ernie Whitt	.03	.01	.00		
☐ 99 Jeff Reed	.03	.01	.00		
☐ 100 Don Mattingly	.20	.08	.02		
☐ 101 Gerald Perry	.03	.01	.00		
☐ 102 Vance Law	.03	.01	.00		
☐ 103 John Shelby	.03	.01	.00		
☐ 104 Chris Sabo	.60	.25	.06		
☐ 105 Danny Tartabull	.10	.04	.01		
☐ 106 Glenn Wilson	.03	.01	.00		
☐ 107 Mark Davidson	.03	.01	.00		
☐ 108 Dave Parker	.08	.03	.01		
☐ 109 Eric Davis	.10	.04	.01		
☐ 110 Alan Trammell	.12	.05	.01		
☐ 111 Ozzie Virgil	.03	.01	.00		
☐ 112 Frank Tanana	.06	.02	.00		
☐ 113 Rafael Ramirez	.03	.01	.00		
☐ 114 Dennis Martinez	.06	.02	.00		
☐ 115 Jose DeLeon	.03	.01	.00		
☐ 116 Bob Ojeda	.03	.01	.00		
☐ 117 Doug Drabek	.08	.03	.01		
☐ 118 Andy Hawkins	.03	.01	.00		
☐ 119 Greg Maddux	.08	.03	.01		
☐ 120 Cecil Fielder UER	.30	.12	.03		
(photo on back reversed)					
☐ 121 Mike Scioscia	.03	.01	.00		
☐ 122 Dan Petry	.03	.01	.00		
☐ 123 Terry Kennedy	.03	.01	.00		
☐ 124 Kelly Downs	.03	.01	.00		
☐ 125 Greg Gross UER	.03	.01	.00		
(Gregg on back)					
☐ 126 Fred Lynn	.08	.03	.01		
☐ 127 Barry Bonds	.25	.10	.02		
☐ 128 Harold Baines	.08	.03	.01		
☐ 129 Doyle Alexander	.03	.01	.00		
☐ 130 Kevin Elster	.03	.01	.00		
☐ 131 Mike Heath	.03	.01	.00		
☐ 132 Teddy Higuera	.03	.01	.00		
☐ 133 Charlie Leibrandt	.03	.01	.00		
☐ 134 Tim Laudner	.03	.01	.00		
☐ 135A Ray Knight ERR	.65	.25	.06		
(reverse negative)					
☐ 135B Ray Knight COR	.10	.04	.01		
☐ 136 Howard Johnson	.12	.05	.01		
☐ 137 Terry Pendleton	.10	.04	.01		
☐ 138 Andy McGaffigan	.03	.01	.00		
☐ 139 Ken Oberkfell	.03	.01	.00		
☐ 140 Butch Wynegar	.03	.01	.00		
☐ 141 Rob Murphy	.03	.01	.00		
☐ 142 Rich Renteria	.06	.02	.00		
☐ 143 Jose Guzman	.03	.01	.00		
☐ 144 Andres Galarraga	.06	.02	.00		
☐ 145 Ricky Horton	.03	.01	.00		
☐ 146 Frank DiPino	.03	.01	.00		
☐ 147 Glenn Braggs	.03	.01	.00		
☐ 148 John Kruk	.03	.01	.00		
☐ 149 Mike Schmidt	.35	.15	.03		
☐ 150 Lee Smith	.08	.03	.01		
☐ 151 Robin Yount	.15	.06	.01		
☐ 152 Mark Eichhorn	.06	.02	.00		
☐ 153 DeWayne Buice	.03	.01	.00		
☐ 154 B.J. Surhoff	.06	.02	.00		
☐ 155 Vince Coleman	.10	.04	.01		
☐ 156 Tony Phillips	.03	.01	.00		
☐ 157 Willie Fraser	.03	.01	.00		
☐ 158 Lance McCullers	.03	.01	.00		
☐ 159 Greg Gagne	.03	.01	.00		
☐ 160 Jesse Barfield	.08	.03	.01		
☐ 161 Mark Langston	.08	.03	.01		
☐ 162 Kurt Stillwell	.03	.01	.00		
☐ 163 Dion James	.03	.01	.00		

☐ 164 Glenn Davis	.08	.03	.01
☐ 165 Walt Weiss	.08	.03	.01
☐ 166 Dave Concepcion	.06	.02	.00
☐ 167 Alfredo Griffin	.03	.01	.00
☐ 168 Don Heinkel	.03	.01	.00
☐ 169 Luis Rivera	.03	.01	.00
☐ 170 Shane Rawley	.03	.01	.00
☐ 171 Darrell Evans	.06	.02	.00
☐ 172 Robby Thompson	.03	.01	.00
☐ 173 Jody Davis	.03	.01	.00
☐ 174 Andy Van Slyke	.08	.03	.01
☐ 175 Wade Boggs UER	.20	.08	.02
(bio says .364, should be .356)			
☐ 176 Garry Templeton	.06	.02	.00
('85 stats off-centered)			
☐ 177 Gary Redus	.03	.01	.00
☐ 178 Craig Lefferts	.03	.01	.00
☐ 179 Carney Lansford	.06	.02	.00
☐ 180 Ron Darling	.06	.02	.00
☐ 181 Kirk McCaskill	.03	.01	.00
☐ 182 Tony Armas	.03	.01	.00
☐ 183 Steve Farr	.03	.01	.00
☐ 184 Tom Brunansky	.06	.02	.00
☐ 185 Bryan Harvey UER	.25	.10	.02
('87 games 47, should be 3)			
☐ 186 Mike Marshall	.06	.02	.00
☐ 187 Bo Diaz	.03	.01	.00
☐ 188 Willie Upshaw	.03	.01	.00
☐ 189 Mike Pagliarulo	.03	.01	.00
☐ 190 Mike Krukow	.03	.01	.00
☐ 191 Tommy Herr	.03	.01	.00
☐ 192 Jim Pankovits	.03	.01	.00
☐ 193 Dwight Evans	.06	.02	.00
☐ 194 Kelly Gruber	.10	.04	.01
☐ 195 Bobby Bonilla	.20	.08	.02
☐ 196 Wallace Johnson	.03	.01	.00
☐ 197 Dave Stieb	.08	.03	.01
☐ 198 Pat Borders	.15	.06	.01
☐ 199 Rafael Palmeiro	.15	.06	.01
☐ 200 Dwight Gooden	.12	.05	.01
☐ 201 Pete Incaviglia	.06	.02	.00
☐ 202 Chris James	.03	.01	.00
☐ 203 Marvell Wynne	.03	.01	.00
☐ 204 Pat Sheridan	.03	.01	.00
☐ 205 Don Baylor	.06	.02	.00
☐ 206 Paul O'Neill	.08	.03	.01
☐ 207 Pete Smith	.06	.02	.00
☐ 208 Mark McLemore	.03	.01	.00
☐ 209 Henry Cotto	.03	.01	.00
☐ 210 Kirk Gibson	.08	.03	.01
☐ 211 Claudell Washington	.03	.01	.00
☐ 212 Randy Bush	.03	.01	.00
☐ 213 Joe Carter	.12	.05	.01
☐ 214 Bill Buckner	.06	.02	.00
☐ 215 Bert Blyleven UER	.08	.03	.01
(wrong birth year)			
☐ 216 Brett Butler	.08	.03	.01
☐ 217 Lee Mazzilli	.03	.01	.00
☐ 218 Spike Owen	.03	.01	.00
☐ 219 Bill Swift	.03	.01	.00
☐ 220 Tim Wallach	.06	.02	.00
☐ 221 David Cone	.08	.03	.01
☐ 222 Don Carman	.03	.01	.00
☐ 223 Rich Gossage	.08	.03	.01
☐ 224 Bob Walk	.03	.01	.00
☐ 225 Dave Righetti	.06	.02	.00
☐ 226 Kevin Bass	.03	.01	.00
☐ 227 Kevin Gross	.03	.01	.00
☐ 228 Tim Burke	.03	.01	.00
☐ 229 Rick Mahler	.03	.01	.00
☐ 230 Lou Whitaker UER	.08	.03	.01
(252 games in '85, should be 152)			
☐ 231 Luis Alicea	.03	.01	.00
☐ 232 Roberto Alomar	.60	.25	.06
☐ 233 Bob Boone	.06	.02	.00
☐ 234 Dickie Thon	.03	.01	.00
☐ 235 Shawon Dunston	.08	.03	.01
☐ 236 Pete Stanicek	.03	.01	.00
☐ 237 Craig Biggio	.35	.15	.03
(inconsistent design, portrait on front)			
☐ 238 Dennis Boyd	.03	.01	.00
☐ 239 Tom Candiotti	.06	.02	.00
☐ 240 Gary Carter	.08	.03	.01
☐ 241 Mike Stanley	.03	.01	.00
☐ 242 Ken Phelps	.03	.01	.00
☐ 243 Chris Bosio	.03	.01	.00
☐ 244 Les Straker	.03	.01	.00
☐ 245 Dave Smith	.03	.01	.00
☐ 246 John Candelaria	.03	.01	.00

#	Player			
247	Joe Orsulak	.03	.01	.00
248	Storm Davis	.03	.01	.00
249	Floyd Bannister UER (ML Batting Record)	.03	.01	.00
250	Jack Morris	.10	.04	.01
251	Bret Saberhagen	.10	.04	.01
252	Tom Niedenfuer	.03	.01	.00
253	Neal Heaton	.03	.01	.00
254	Eric Show	.03	.01	.00
255	Juan Samuel	.06	.02	.00
256	Dale Sveum	.03	.01	.00
257	Jim Gott	.03	.01	.00
258	Scott Garrelts	.03	.01	.00
259	Larry McWilliams	.03	.01	.00
260	Steve Bedrosian	.06	.02	.00
261	Jack Howell	.03	.01	.00
262	Jay Tibbs	.03	.01	.00
263	Jamie Moyer	.03	.01	.00
264	Doug Sisk	.03	.01	.00
265	Todd Worrell	.06	.02	.00
266	John Farrell	.03	.01	.00
267	Dave Collins	.03	.01	.00
268	Sid Fernandez	.06	.02	.00
269	Tom Brookens	.03	.01	.00
270	Shane Mack	.08	.03	.01
271	Paul Kilgus	.03	.01	.00
272	Chuck Crim	.03	.01	.00
273	Bob Knepper	.03	.01	.00
274	Mike Moore	.06	.02	.00
275	Guillermo Hernandez	.03	.01	.00
276	Dennis Eckersley	.08	.03	.01
277	Graig Nettles	.06	.02	.00
278	Rich Dotson	.03	.01	.00
279	Larry Herndon	.03	.01	.00
280	Gene Larkin	.03	.01	.00
281	Roger McDowell	.03	.01	.00
282	Greg Swindell	.06	.02	.00
283	Juan Agosto	.03	.01	.00
284	Jeff M. Robinson	.03	.01	.00
	Detroit Tigers			
285	Mike Dunne	.03	.01	.00
286	Greg Mathews	.03	.01	.00
287	Kent Tekulve	.03	.01	.00
288	Jerry Mumphrey	.03	.01	.00
289	Jack McDowell	.17	.07	.01
290	Frank Viola	.08	.03	.01
291	Mark Gubicza	.06	.02	.00
292	Dave Schmidt	.03	.01	.00
293	Mike Henneman	.03	.01	.00
294	Jimmy Jones	.03	.01	.00
295	Charlie Hough	.03	.01	.00
296	Rafael Santana	.03	.01	.00
297	Chris Speier	.03	.01	.00
298	Mike Witt	.03	.01	.00
299	Pascual Perez	.03	.01	.00
300	Nolan Ryan	.50	.20	.05
301	Mitch Williams	.03	.01	.00
302	Mookie Wilson	.03	.01	.00
303	Mackey Sasser	.06	.02	.00
304	John Cerutti	.03	.01	.00
305	Jeff Reardon	.08	.03	.01
306	Randy Myers UER (6 hits in '87, should be 61)	.03	.01	.00
307	Greg Brock	.03	.01	.00
308	Bob Welch	.08	.03	.01
309	Jeff D. Robinson	.03	.01	.00
	Pittsburgh Pirates			
310	Harold Reynolds	.06	.02	.00
311	Jim Walewander	.03	.01	.00
312	Dave Magadan	.06	.02	.00
313	Jim Gantner	.03	.01	.00
314	Walt Terrell	.03	.01	.00
315	Wally Backman	.03	.01	.00
316	Luis Salazar	.03	.01	.00
317	Rick Rhoden	.03	.01	.00
318	Tom Henke	.06	.02	.00
319	Mike Macfarlane	.10	.04	.01
320	Dan Plesac	.03	.01	.00
321	Calvin Schiraldi	.03	.01	.00
322	Stan Javier	.03	.01	.00
323	Devon White	.06	.02	.00
324	Scott Bradley	.03	.01	.00
325	Bruce Hurst	.06	.02	.00
326	Manny Lee	.03	.01	.00
327	Rick Aguilera	.06	.02	.00
328	Bruce Ruffin	.03	.01	.00
329	Ed Whitson	.03	.01	.00
330	Bo Jackson	.50	.20	.05
331	Ivan Calderon	.06	.02	.00
332	Mickey Hatcher	.03	.01	.00
333	Barry Jones	.03	.01	.00
334	Ron Hassey	.03	.01	.00
335	Bill Wegman	.03	.01	.00
336	Damon Berryhill	.06	.02	.00
337	Steve Ontiveros	.03	.01	.00
338	Dan Pasqua	.03	.01	.00
339	Bill Pecota	.03	.01	.00
340	Greg Cadaret	.03	.01	.00
341	Scott Bankhead	.06	.02	.00
342	Ron Guidry	.08	.03	.01
343	Danny Heep	.03	.01	.00
344	Bob Brower	.03	.01	.00
345	Rich Gedman	.03	.01	.00
346	Nelson Santovenia	.08	.03	.01
347	George Bell	.10	.04	.01
348	Ted Power	.03	.01	.00
349	Mark Grant	.03	.01	.00
350A	Roger Clemens ERR (778 career wins)	4.00	1.75	.40
350B	Roger Clemens COR (78 career wins)	.35	.15	.03
351	Bill Long	.03	.01	.00
352	Jay Bell	.10	.04	.01
353	Steve Balboni	.03	.01	.00
354	Bob Kipper	.03	.01	.00
355	Steve Jeltz	.03	.01	.00
356	Jesse Orosco	.03	.01	.00
357	Bob Dernier	.03	.01	.00
358	Mickey Tettleton	.06	.02	.00
359	Duane Ward	.06	.02	.00
360	Darrin Jackson	.10	.04	.01
361	Rey Quinones	.03	.01	.00
362	Mark Grace	.30	.12	.03
363	Steve Lake	.03	.01	.00
364	Pat Perry	.03	.01	.00
365	Terry Steinbach	.06	.02	.00
366	Alan Ashby	.03	.01	.00
367	Jeff Montgomery	.06	.02	.00
368	Steve Buechele	.03	.01	.00
369	Chris Brown	.03	.01	.00
370	Orel Hershiser	.08	.03	.01
371	Todd Benzinger	.03	.01	.00
372	Ron Gant	.45	.18	.04
373	Paul Assenmacher	.03	.01	.00
374	Joey Meyer	.03	.01	.00
375	Neil Allen	.03	.01	.00
376	Mike Davis	.03	.01	.00
377	Jeff Parrett	.03	.01	.00
378	Jay Howell	.03	.01	.00
379	Rafael Belliard	.03	.01	.00
380	Luis Polonia UER (2 triples in '87, should be 10)	.08	.03	.01
381	Keith Atherton	.03	.01	.00
382	Kent Hrbek	.08	.03	.01
383	Bob Stanley	.03	.01	.00
384	Dave LaPoint	.03	.01	.00
385	Rance Mulliniks	.03	.01	.00
386	Melido Perez	.08	.03	.01
387	Doug Jones	.03	.01	.00
388	Steve Lyons	.03	.01	.00
389	Alejandro Pena	.06	.02	.00
390	Frank White	.03	.01	.00
391	Pat Tabler	.03	.01	.00
392	Eric Plunk	.03	.01	.00
393	Mike Maddux	.03	.01	.00
394	Allan Anderson	.03	.01	.00
395	Bob Brenly	.03	.01	.00
396	Rick Cerone	.03	.01	.00
397	Scott Terry	.03	.01	.00
398	Mike Jackson	.03	.01	.00
399	Bobby Thigpen UER (bio says 37 saves in '88, should be 34)	.08	.03	.01
400	Don Sutton	.10	.04	.01
401	Cecil Espy	.03	.01	.00
402	Junior Ortiz	.03	.01	.00
403	Mike Smithson	.03	.01	.00
404	Bud Black	.03	.01	.00
405	Tom Foley	.03	.01	.00
406	Andres Thomas	.03	.01	.00
407	Rick Sutcliffe	.06	.02	.00
408	Brian Harper	.06	.02	.00
409	John Smiley	.06	.02	.00
410	Juan Nieves	.03	.01	.00
411	Shawn Abner	.03	.01	.00
412	Wes Gardner	.03	.01	.00
413	Darren Daulton	.06	.02	.00
414	Juan Berenguer	.03	.01	.00
415	Charles Hudson	.03	.01	.00
416	Rick Honeycutt	.03	.01	.00
417	Greg Booker	.03	.01	.00
418	Tim Belcher	.10	.04	.01
419	Don August	.03	.01	.00
420	Dale Mohorcic	.03	.01	.00
421	Steve Lombardozzi	.03	.01	.00
422	Atlee Hammaker	.03	.01	.00

☐ 423 Jerry Don Gleaton	.03	.01	.00
☐ 424 Scott Bailes	.03	.01	.00
☐ 425 Bruce Sutter	.08	.03	.01
☐ 426 Randy Ready	.03	.01	.00
☐ 427 Jerry Reed	.03	.01	.00
☐ 428 Bryn Smith	.03	.01	.00
☐ 429 Tim Leary	.06	.02	.00
☐ 430 Mark Clear	.03	.01	.00
☐ 431 Terry Leach	.03	.01	.00
☐ 432 John Moses	.03	.01	.00
☐ 433 Ozzie Guillen	.06	.02	.00
☐ 434 Gene Nelson	.03	.01	.00
☐ 435 Gary Ward	.03	.01	.00
☐ 436 Luis Aguayo	.03	.01	.00
☐ 437 Fernando Valenzuela	.08	.03	.01
☐ 438 Jeff Russell UER	.03	.01	.00
(Saves total does not add up correctly)			
☐ 439 Cecilio Guante	.03	.01	.00
☐ 440 Don Robinson	.03	.01	.00
☐ 441 Rick Anderson	.03	.01	.00
☐ 442 Tom Glavine	.35	.15	.03
☐ 443 Daryl Boston	.03	.01	.00
☐ 444 Joe Price	.03	.01	.00
☐ 445 Stewart Cliburn	.03	.01	.00
☐ 446 Manny Trillo	.03	.01	.00
☐ 447 Joel Skinner	.03	.01	.00
☐ 448 Charlie Puleo	.03	.01	.00
☐ 449 Carlton Fisk	.15	.06	.01
☐ 450 Will Clark	.40	.16	.04
☐ 451 Otis Nixon	.06	.02	.00
☐ 452 Rick Schu	.03	.01	.00
☐ 453 Todd Stottlemyre UER	.15	.06	.01
(ML Batting Record)			
☐ 454 Tim Birtsas	.03	.01	.00
☐ 455 Dave Gallagher	.08	.03	.01
☐ 456 Barry Lyons	.03	.01	.00
☐ 457 Fred Manrique	.03	.01	.00
☐ 458 Ernest Riles	.03	.01	.00
☐ 459 Doug Jennings	.06	.02	.00
☐ 460 Joe Magrane	.06	.02	.00
☐ 461 Jamie Quirk	.03	.01	.00
☐ 462 Jack Armstrong	.10	.04	.01
☐ 463 Bobby Witt	.06	.02	.00
☐ 464 Keith Miller	.06	.02	.00
New York Mets			
☐ 465 Todd Burns	.08	.03	.01
☐ 466 John Dopson	.08	.03	.01
☐ 467 Rich Yett	.03	.01	.00
☐ 468 Craig Reynolds	.03	.01	.00
☐ 469 Dave Bergman	.03	.01	.00
☐ 470 Rex Hudler	.06	.02	.00
☐ 471 Eric King	.03	.01	.00
☐ 472 Joaquin Andujar	.03	.01	.00
☐ 473 Sil Campusano	.08	.03	.01
☐ 474 Terry Mulholland	.06	.02	.00
☐ 475 Mike Flanagan	.03	.01	.00
☐ 476 Greg A. Harris	.03	.01	.00
Philadelphia Phillies			
☐ 477 Tommy John	.08	.03	.01
☐ 478 Dave Anderson	.03	.01	.00
☐ 479 Fred Toliver	.03	.01	.00
☐ 480 Jimmy Key	.06	.02	.00
☐ 481 Donell Nixon	.03	.01	.00
☐ 482 Mark Portugal	.03	.01	.00
☐ 483 Tom Pagnozzi	.03	.01	.00
☐ 484 Jeff Kunkel	.03	.01	.00
☐ 485 Frank Williams	.03	.01	.00
☐ 486 Jody Reed	.08	.03	.01
☐ 487 Roberto Kelly	.12	.05	.01
☐ 488 Shawn Hillegas UER	.03	.01	.00
(165 innings in '87, should be 165.2)			
☐ 489 Jerry Reuss	.03	.01	.00
☐ 490 Mark Davis	.06	.02	.00
☐ 491 Jeff Sellers	.03	.01	.00
☐ 492 Zane Smith	.06	.02	.00
☐ 493 Al Newman	.03	.01	.00
☐ 494 Mike Young	.03	.01	.00
☐ 495 Larry Parrish	.03	.01	.00
☐ 496 Herm Winningham	.03	.01	.00
☐ 497 Carmen Castillo	.03	.01	.00
☐ 498 Joe Hesketh	.06	.02	.00
☐ 499 Darrell Miller	.03	.01	.00
☐ 500 Mike LaCoss	.03	.01	.00
☐ 501 Charlie Lea	.03	.01	.00
☐ 502 Bruce Benedict	.03	.01	.00
☐ 503 Chuck Finley	.08	.03	.01
☐ 504 Brad Wellman	.03	.01	.00
☐ 505 Tim Crews	.03	.01	.00
☐ 506 Ken Gerhart	.03	.01	.00
☐ 507 Brian Holton UER	.06	.02	.00
(born 1/25/65 Denver, should be 11/29/59			

in McKeesport)			
☐ 508 Dennis Lamp	.03	.01	.00
☐ 509 Bobby Meacham UER	.06	.02	.00
('84 games 099)			
☐ 510 Tracy Jones	.03	.01	.00
☐ 511 Mike Fitzgerald	.03	.01	.00
Montreal Expos			
☐ 512 Jeff Bittiger	.06	.02	.00
☐ 513 Tim Flannery	.03	.01	.00
☐ 514 Ray Hayward	.03	.01	.00
☐ 515 Dave Leiper	.03	.01	.00
☐ 516 Rod Scurry	.03	.01	.00
☐ 517 Carmelo Martinez	.03	.01	.00
☐ 518 Curtis Wilkerson	.03	.01	.00
☐ 519 Stan Jefferson	.03	.01	.00
☐ 520 Dan Quisenberry	.08	.03	.01
☐ 521 Lloyd McClendon	.03	.01	.00
☐ 522 Steve Trout	.03	.01	.00
☐ 523 Larry Andersen	.03	.01	.00
☐ 524 Don Aase	.03	.01	.00
☐ 525 Bob Forsch	.03	.01	.00
☐ 526 Geno Petralli	.03	.01	.00
☐ 527 Angel Salazar	.03	.01	.00
☐ 528 Mike Schooler	.12	.05	.01
☐ 529 Jose Oquendo	.03	.01	.00
☐ 530 Jay Buhner	.15	.06	.01
☐ 531 Tom Bolton	.08	.03	.01
☐ 532 Al Nipper	.03	.01	.00
☐ 533 Dave Henderson	.08	.03	.01
☐ 534 John Costello	.03	.01	.00
☐ 535 Donnie Moore	.03	.01	.00
☐ 536 Mike Laga	.03	.01	.00
☐ 537 Mike Gallego	.03	.01	.00
☐ 538 Jim Clancy	.03	.01	.00
☐ 539 Joel Youngblood	.03	.01	.00
☐ 540 Rick Leach	.03	.01	.00
☐ 541 Kevin Romine	.03	.01	.00
☐ 542 Mark Salas	.03	.01	.00
☐ 543 Greg Minton	.03	.01	.00
☐ 544 Dave Palmer	.03	.01	.00
☐ 545 Dwayne Murphy UER	.03	.01	.00
(game-sinning)			
☐ 546 Jim Deshaies	.03	.01	.00
☐ 547 Don Gordon	.03	.01	.00
☐ 548 Ricky Jordan	.12	.05	.01
☐ 549 Mike Boddicker	.03	.01	.00
☐ 550 Mike Scott	.08	.03	.01
☐ 551 Jeff Ballard	.03	.01	.00
☐ 552A Jose Rijo ERR	.65	.25	.06
(uniform listed as 27 on back)			
☐ 552B Jose Rijo COR	.15	.06	.01
(uniform listed as 24 on back)			
☐ 553 Danny Darwin	.03	.01	.00
☐ 554 Tom Browning	.06	.02	.00
☐ 555 Danny Jackson	.06	.02	.00
☐ 556 Rick Dempsey	.03	.01	.00
☐ 557 Jeffrey Leonard	.03	.01	.00
☐ 558 Jeff Musselman	.03	.01	.00
☐ 559 Ron Robinson	.03	.01	.00
☐ 560 John Tudor	.06	.02	.00
☐ 561 Don Slaught UER	.03	.01	.00
(237 games in 1987)			
☐ 562 Dennis Rasmussen	.03	.01	.00
☐ 563 Brady Anderson	.08	.03	.01
☐ 564 Pedro Guerrero	.08	.03	.01
☐ 565 Paul Molitor	.10	.04	.01
☐ 566 Terry Clark	.06	.02	.00
☐ 567 Terry Puhl	.03	.01	.00
☐ 568 Mike Campbell	.03	.01	.00
☐ 569 Paul Mirabella	.03	.01	.00
☐ 570 Jeff Hamilton	.03	.01	.00
☐ 571 Oswald Peraza	.06	.02	.00
☐ 572 Bob McClure	.03	.01	.00
☐ 573 Jose Bautista	.06	.02	.00
☐ 574 Alex Trevino	.03	.01	.00
☐ 575 John Franco	.03	.01	.00
☐ 576 Mark Parent	.08	.03	.01
☐ 577 Nelson Liriano	.03	.01	.00
☐ 578 Steve Shields	.03	.01	.00
☐ 579 Odell Jones	.03	.01	.00
☐ 580 Al Leiter	.03	.01	.00
☐ 581 Dave Stapleton	.06	.02	.00
☐ 582 World Series '88	.08	.03	.01
Orel Hershiser			
Jose Canseco			
Kirk Gibson			
Dave Stewart			
☐ 583 Donnie Hill	.03	.01	.00
☐ 584 Chuck Jackson	.03	.01	.00
☐ 585 Rene Gonzales	.03	.01	.00
☐ 586 Tracy Woodson	.03	.01	.00
☐ 587 Jim Adduci	.03	.01	.00

☐ 588	Mario Soto	.03	.01	.00
☐ 589	Jeff Blauser	.03	.01	.00
☐ 590	Jim Traber	.03	.01	.00
☐ 591	Jon Perlman	.03	.01	.00
☐ 592	Mark Williamson	.06	.02	.00
☐ 593	Dave Meads	.03	.01	.00
☐ 594	Jim Eisenreich	.03	.01	.00
☐ 595A	Paul Gibson P1	1.00	.40	.10
☐ 595B	Paul Gibson P2	.10	.04	.01
	(airbrushed leg on			
	player in background)			
☐ 596	Mike Birkbeck	.03	.01	.00
☐ 597	Terry Francona	.03	.01	.00
☐ 598	Paul Zuvella	.03	.01	.00
☐ 599	Franklin Stubbs	.03	.01	.00
☐ 600	Gregg Jefferies	.30	.12	.03
☐ 601	John Cangelosi	.03	.01	.00
☐ 602	Mike Sharperson	.03	.01	.00
☐ 603	Mike Diaz	.03	.01	.00
☐ 604	Gary Varsho	.08	.03	.01
☐ 605	Terry Blocker	.06	.02	.00
☐ 606	Charlie O'Brien	.06	.02	.00
☐ 607	Jim Eppard	.03	.01	.00
☐ 608	John Davis	.03	.01	.00
☐ 609	Ken Griffey Sr.	.08	.03	.01
☐ 610	Buddy Bell	.06	.02	.00
☐ 611	Ted Simmons UER	.08	.03	.01
	('78 stats Cardinal)			
☐ 612	Matt Williams	.20	.08	.02
☐ 613	Danny Cox	.03	.01	.00
☐ 614	Al Pedrique	.03	.01	.00
☐ 615	Ron Oester	.03	.01	.00
☐ 616	John Smoltz	.50	.20	.05
☐ 617	Bob Melvin	.03	.01	.00
☐ 618	Rob Dibble	.25	.10	.02
☐ 619	Kirt Manwaring	.03	.01	.00
☐ 620	Felix Fermin	.03	.01	.00
☐ 621	Doug Dascenzo	.08	.03	.01
☐ 622	Bill Brennan	.06	.02	.00
☐ 623	Carlos Quintana	.25	.10	.02
☐ 624	Mike Harkey UER	.12	.05	.01
	(13 and 31 walks			
	in '88, should			
	be 35 and 33)			
☐ 625	Gary Sheffield	.30	.12	.03
☐ 626	Tom Prince	.03	.01	.00
☐ 627	Steve Searcy	.08	.03	.01
☐ 628	Charlie Hayes	.12	.05	.01
	(listed as outfielder)			
☐ 629	Felix Jose UER	.75	.30	.07
	(Modesto misspelled			
	as Modasta)			
☐ 630	Sandy Alomar Jr.	.40	.16	.04
	(inconsistent design,			
	portrait on front)			
☐ 631	Derek Lilliquist	.08	.03	.01
☐ 632	Geronimo Berroa	.06	.02	.00
☐ 633	Luis Medina	.10	.04	.01
☐ 634	Tom Gordon UER	.20	.08	.02
	(height 6'0")			
☐ 635	Ramon Martinez	1.25	.50	.12
☐ 636	Craig Worthington	.08	.03	.01
☐ 637	Edgar Martinez	.20	.08	.02
☐ 638	Chad Kreuter	.08	.03	.01
☐ 639	Ron Jones	.08	.03	.01
☐ 640	Van Snider	.08	.03	.01
☐ 641	Lance Blankenship	.08	.03	.01
☐ 642	Dwight Smith UER	.12	.05	.01
	(10 HR's in '87,			
	should be 18)			
☐ 643	Cameron Drew	.03	.01	.00
☐ 644	Jerald Clark	.17	.07	.01
☐ 645	Randy Johnson	.35	.15	.03
☐ 646	Norm Charlton	.12	.05	.01
☐ 647	Todd Frohwirth UER	.06	.02	.00
	(southpaw on back)			
☐ 648	Luis De Los Santos	.06	.02	.00
☐ 649	Tim Jones	.03	.01	.00
☐ 650	Dave West UER	.10	.04	.01
	(ML hits 3,			
	should be 6)			
☐ 651	Bob Milacki	.15	.06	.01
☐ 652	Wrigley Field HL	.03	.01	.00
	(Let There Be Lights)			
☐ 653	Orel Hershiser HL	.08	.03	.01
	(The Streak)			
☐ 654A	Wade Boggs HL ERR	4.00	1.75	.40
	(Wade Whacks 'Em)			
	("seaason" on back)			
☐ 654B	Wade Boggs HL COR	.12	.05	.01
	(Wade Whacks 'Em)			
☐ 655	Jose Canseco HL	.20	.08	.02
	(One of a Kind)			
☐ 656	Doug Jones HL	.03	.01	.00

	(Doug Sets Saves)			
☐ 657	Rickey Henderson HL	.17	.07	.01
	(Rickey Rocks 'Em)			
☐ 658	Tom Browning HL	.06	.02	.00
	(Tom Perfect Pitches)			
☐ 659	Mike Greenwell HL	.08	.03	.01
	(Greenwell Gamers)			
☐ 660	Boston Red Sox HL	.06	.02	.00
	(Joe Morgan MG,			
	Sox Sock 'Em)			

1989 Score Hottest 100 Rookies

This set was distributed by Publications International in January 1989 through many retail stores and chains; the card set was packaged along with a colorful 48-page book for a suggested retail price of 12.95. Supposedly 225,000 sets were produced. The cards measure the standard 2 1/2" by 3 1/2" and show full color on both sides of the card. The cards were produced by Score as indicated on the card backs. The set is subtitled "Rising Star" on the reverse. The first six cards (1-6) of a 12-card set of Score's trivia cards, subtitled "Rookies to Remember" is included along with each set. The cards are numbered on the back. This set is distinguished by the sharp blue borders and the player's first initial inside a yellow triangle in the lower left corner of the obverse.

	MINT	EXC	G-VG
COMPLETE SET (100)	12.00	5.25	1.50
COMMON PLAYER (1-100)	.05	.02	.00

☐ 1	Gregg Jefferies	.75	.30	.07
☐ 2	Vicente Palacios	.10	.04	.01
☐ 3	Cameron Drew	.05	.02	.00
☐ 4	Doug Dascenzo	.10	.04	.01
☐ 5	Luis Medina	.10	.04	.01
☐ 6	Craig Worthington	.10	.04	.01
☐ 7	Rob Ducey	.10	.04	.01
☐ 8	Hal Morris	.75	.30	.07
☐ 9	Bill Brennan	.05	.02	.00
☐ 10	Gary Sheffield	.50	.20	.05
☐ 11	Mike Devereaux	.10	.04	.01
☐ 12	Hensley Meulens	.40	.16	.04
☐ 13	Carlos Quintana	.30	.12	.03
☐ 14	Todd Frohwirth	.05	.02	.00
☐ 15	Scott Lusader	.05	.02	.00
☐ 16	Mark Carreon	.10	.04	.01
☐ 17	Torey Lovullo	.05	.02	.00
☐ 18	Randy Velarde	.05	.02	.00
☐ 19	Billy Bean	.05	.02	.00
☐ 20	Lance Blankenship	.05	.02	.00
☐ 21	Chris Gwynn	.10	.04	.01
☐ 22	Felix Jose	.50	.20	.05
☐ 23	Derek Lilliquist	.05	.02	.00
☐ 24	Gary Thurman	.10	.04	.01
☐ 25	Ron Jones	.10	.04	.01
☐ 26	Dave Justice	1.50	.60	.15
☐ 27	Johnny Paredes	.05	.02	.00
☐ 28	Tim Jones	.05	.02	.00
☐ 29	Jose Gonzales	.05	.02	.00
☐ 30	Geronimo Berroa	.05	.02	.00

		MINT	EXC	G-VG
☐ 31	Trevor Wilson	.10	.04	.01
☐ 32	Morris Madden	.05	.02	.00
☐ 33	Lance Johnson	.10	.04	.01
☐ 34	Marvin Freeman	.05	.02	.00
☐ 35	Jose Cecena	.05	.02	.00
☐ 36	Jim Corsi	.05	.02	.00
☐ 37	Rolando Roomes	.05	.02	.00
☐ 38	Scott Medvin	.05	.02	.00
☐ 39	Charlie Hayes	.15	.06	.01
☐ 40	Edgar Martinez	.40	.16	.04
☐ 41	Van Snider	.05	.02	.00
☐ 42	John Fishel	.05	.02	.00
☐ 43	Bruce Fields	.05	.02	.00
☐ 44	Darryl Hamilton	.10	.04	.01
☐ 45	Tom Prince	.05	.02	.00
☐ 46	Kirt Manwaring	.05	.02	.00
☐ 47	Steve Searcy	.05	.02	.00
☐ 48	Mike Harkey	.30	.12	.03
☐ 49	German Gonzalez	.05	.02	.00
☐ 50	Tony Perezchica	.05	.02	.00
☐ 51	Chad Kreuter	.05	.02	.00
☐ 52	Luis De los Santos	.10	.04	.01
☐ 53	Steve Curry	.05	.02	.00
☐ 54	Greg Briley	.15	.06	.01
☐ 55	Ramon Martinez	.90	.40	.09
☐ 56	Ron Tingley	.05	.02	.00
☐ 57	Randy Kramer	.05	.02	.00
☐ 58	Alex Madrid	.05	.02	.00
☐ 59	Kevin Reimer	.15	.06	.01
☐ 60	Dave Otto	.10	.04	.01
☐ 61	Ken Patterson	.05	.02	.00
☐ 62	Keith Miller	.10	.04	.01
☐ 63	Randy Johnson	.25	.10	.02
☐ 64	Dwight Smith	.20	.08	.02
☐ 65	Eric Yelding	.10	.04	.01
☐ 66	Bob Geren	.10	.04	.01
☐ 67	Shane Turner	.10	.04	.01
☐ 68	Tom Gordon	.30	.12	.03
☐ 69	Jeff Huson	.10	.04	.01
☐ 70	Marty Brown	.10	.04	.01
☐ 71	Nelson Santovenia	.10	.04	.01
☐ 72	Roberto Alomar	.75	.30	.07
☐ 73	Mike Schooler	.20	.08	.02
☐ 74	Pete Smith	.10	.04	.01
☐ 75	John Costello	.10	.04	.01
☐ 76	Chris Sabo	.50	.20	.05
☐ 77	Damon Berryhill	.10	.04	.01
☐ 78	Mark Grace	.75	.30	.07
☐ 79	Melido Perez	.15	.06	.01
☐ 80	Al Leiter	.10	.04	.01
☐ 81	Todd Stottlemyre	.15	.06	.01
☐ 82	Mackey Sasser	.10	.04	.01
☐ 83	Don August	.10	.04	.01
☐ 84	Jeff Treadway	.10	.04	.01
☐ 85	Jody Reed	.15	.06	.01
☐ 86	Mike Campbell	.10	.04	.01
☐ 87	Ron Gant	1.00	.40	.10
☐ 88	Ricky Jordan	.15	.06	.01
☐ 89	Terry Clark	.05	.02	.00
☐ 90	Roberto Kelly	.40	.16	.04
☐ 91	Pat Borders	.15	.06	.01
☐ 92	Bryan Harvey	.25	.10	.02
☐ 93	Joey Meyer	.05	.02	.00
☐ 94	Tim Belcher	.15	.06	.01
☐ 95	Walt Weiss	.25	.10	.02
☐ 96	Dave Gallagher	.10	.04	.01
☐ 97	Mike Macfarlane	.10	.04	.01
☐ 98	Craig Biggio	.35	.15	.03
☐ 99	Jack Armstrong	.20	.08	.02
☐ 100	Todd Burns	.10	.04	.01

1989 Score Hottest 100 Stars

This set was distributed by Publications International in January 1989 through many retail stores and chains; the card set was packaged along with a colorful 48-page book for a suggested retail price of 12.95. Supposedly 225,000 sets were produced. The cards measure the standard 2 1/2" by 3 1/2" and show full color on both sides of the card. The cards were produced by Score as indicated on the card backs. The set is subtitled "Superstar" on the reverse. The last six cards (7-12) of a 12-card set of Score's trivia cards, subtitled "Rookies to Remember" is included along with each set. The cards are numbered on the back. This set is distinguished by the sharp red borders and the player's first initial inside a yellow triangle in the upper left corner of the obverse.

		MINT	EXC	G-VG
COMPLETE SET (100)		12.00	5.25	1.50
COMMON PLAYER (1-100)		.05	.02	.00
☐ 1	Jose Canseco	1.00	.40	.10
☐ 2	David Cone	.20	.08	.02
☐ 3	Dave Winfield	.30	.12	.03
☐ 4	George Brett	.30	.12	.03
☐ 5	Frank Viola	.15	.06	.01
☐ 6	Cory Snyder	.10	.04	.01
☐ 7	Alan Trammell	.20	.08	.02
☐ 8	Dwight Evans	.10	.04	.01
☐ 9	Tim Leary	.05	.02	.00
☐ 10	Don Mattingly	.75	.30	.07
☐ 11	Kirby Puckett	.75	.30	.07
☐ 12	Carney Lansford	.15	.06	.01
☐ 13	Dennis Martinez	.10	.04	.01
☐ 14	Kent Hrbek	.15	.06	.01
☐ 15	Dwight Gooden	.30	.12	.03
☐ 16	Dennis Eckersley	.20	.08	.02
☐ 17	Kevin Seitzer	.10	.04	.01
☐ 18	Lee Smith	.15	.06	.01
☐ 19	Danny Tartabull	.30	.12	.03
☐ 20	Gerald Perry	.05	.02	.00
☐ 21	Gary Gaetti	.10	.04	.01
☐ 22	Rick Reuschel	.05	.02	.00
☐ 23	Keith Hernandez	.10	.04	.01
☐ 24	Jeff Reardon	.15	.06	.01
☐ 25	Mark McGwire	.60	.25	.06
☐ 26	Juan Samuel	.10	.04	.01
☐ 27	Jack Clark	.10	.04	.01
☐ 28	Robin Yount	.35	.15	.03
☐ 29	Steve Bedrosian	.05	.02	.00
☐ 30	Kirk Gibson	.15	.06	.01
☐ 31	Barry Bonds	.60	.25	.06
☐ 32	Dan Plesac	.05	.02	.00
☐ 33	Steve Sax	.10	.04	.01
☐ 34	Jeff M. Robinson	.05	.02	.00
☐ 35	Orel Hershiser	.20	.08	.02
☐ 36	Julio Franco	.20	.08	.02
☐ 37	Dave Righetti	.10	.04	.01
☐ 38	Bob Knepper	.05	.02	.00
☐ 39	Carlton Fisk	.30	.12	.03
☐ 40	Tony Gwynn	.50	.20	.05
☐ 41	Doug Jones	.05	.02	.00
☐ 42	Bobby Bonilla	.50	.20	.05
☐ 43	Ellis Burks	.30	.12	.03
☐ 44	Pedro Guerrero	.15	.06	.01
☐ 45	Rickey Henderson	.75	.30	.07
☐ 46	Glenn Davis	.20	.08	.02
☐ 47	Benny Santiago	.20	.08	.02
☐ 48	Greg Maddux	.10	.04	.01
☐ 49	Teddy Higuera	.10	.04	.01
☐ 50	Darryl Strawberry	.75	.30	.07
☐ 51	Ozzie Guillen	.10	.04	.01
☐ 52	Barry Larkin	.25	.10	.02
☐ 53	Tony Fernandez	.10	.04	.01
☐ 54	Ryne Sandberg	.75	.30	.07
☐ 55	Joe Carter	.25	.10	.02
☐ 56	Rafael Palmeiro	.25	.10	.02
☐ 57	Paul Molitor	.15	.06	.01
☐ 58	Eric Davis	.45	.18	.04
☐ 59	Mike Henneman	.05	.02	.00
☐ 60	Mike Scott	.10	.04	.01
☐ 61	Tom Browning	.10	.04	.01
☐ 62	Mark Davis	.05	.02	.00
☐ 63	Tom Henke	.05	.02	.00
☐ 64	Nolan Ryan	1.25	.50	.12
☐ 65	Fred McGriff	.50	.20	.05
☐ 66	Dale Murphy	.35	.15	.03
☐ 67	Mark Langston	.10	.04	.01

		MINT	EXC	G-VG
☐ 68	Bobby Thigpen	.15	.06	.01
☐ 69	Mark Gubicza	.10	.04	.01
☐ 70	Mike Greenwell	.35	.15	.03
☐ 71	Ron Darling	.10	.04	.01
☐ 72	Gerald Young	.10	.04	.01
☐ 73	Wally Joyner	.20	.08	.02
☐ 74	Andres Galarraga	.15	.06	.01
☐ 75	Danny Jackson	.10	.04	.01
☐ 76	Mike Schmidt	.75	.30	.07
☐ 77	Cal Ripken	.75	.30	.07
☐ 78	Alvin Davis	.10	.04	.01
☐ 79	Bruce Hurst	.10	.04	.01
☐ 80	Andre Dawson	.30	.12	.03
☐ 81	Bob Boone	.10	.04	.01
☐ 82	Harold Reynolds	.10	.04	.01
☐ 83	Eddie Murray	.35	.15	.03
☐ 84	Robby Thompson	.05	.02	.00
☐ 85	Will Clark	1.00	.40	.10
☐ 86	Vince Coleman	.20	.08	.02
☐ 87	Doug Drabek	.20	.08	.02
☐ 88	Ozzie Smith	.30	.12	.03
☐ 89	Bob Welch	.15	.06	.01
☐ 90	Roger Clemens	.75	.30	.07
☐ 91	George Bell	.20	.08	.02
☐ 92	Andy Van Slyke	.15	.06	.01
☐ 93	Willie McGee	.15	.06	.01
☐ 94	Todd Worrell	.10	.04	.01
☐ 95	Tim Raines	.20	.08	.02
☐ 96	Kevin McReynolds	.20	.08	.02
☐ 97	John Franco	.10	.04	.01
☐ 98	Jim Gott	.05	.02	.00
☐ 99	Johnny Ray	.05	.02	.00
☐ 100	Wade Boggs	.60	.25	.06

		MINT	EXC	G-VG
☐ 20	Walt Weiss	.25	.10	.02
☐ 21	Doug Drabek	.25	.10	.02
☐ 22	Kirt Manwaring	.15	.06	.01
☐ 23	Keith Miller	.20	.08	.02
☐ 24	Damon Berryhill	.20	.08	.02
☐ 25	Gary Sheffield	.45	.18	.04
☐ 26	Brady Anderson	.15	.06	.01
☐ 27	Mitch Williams	.20	.08	.02
☐ 28	Roberto Alomar	.60	.25	.06
☐ 29	Bobby Thigpen	.25	.10	.02
☐ 30	Bryan Harvey UER	.25	.10	.02
	(47 games in '87)			
☐ 31	Jose Rijo	.25	.10	.02
☐ 32	Dave West	.20	.08	.02
☐ 33	Joey Meyer	.15	.06	.01
☐ 34	Allan Anderson	.15	.06	.01
☐ 35	Rafael Palmeiro	.35	.15	.03
☐ 36	Tim Belcher UER	.25	.10	.02
	(Back reads 1937, should read 1987)			
☐ 37	John Smiley	.20	.08	.02
☐ 38	Mackey Sasser	.20	.08	.02
☐ 39	Greg Maddux	.25	.10	.02
☐ 40	Ramon Martinez	.60	.25	.06
☐ 41	Randy Myers	.20	.08	.02
☐ 42	Scott Bankhead	.15	.06	.01

1989 Score Young Superstars I

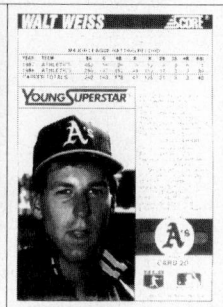

The 1989 Score Young Superstars set I contains 42 standard-size (2 1/2" by 3 1/2") cards. The fronts are pink, white and blue. The vertically-oriented backs have color facial shots, 1988 and career stats, and biographical information. One card was included in each 1989 Score rack pack, and the cards were also distributed as a boxed set with five Magic Motion trivia cards.

		MINT	EXC	G-VG
COMPLETE SET (42)		7.50	3.25	.75
COMMON PLAYER (1-42)		.15	.06	.01
☐ 1	Gregg Jefferies	.60	.25	.06
☐ 2	Jody Reed	.20	.08	.02
☐ 3	Mark Grace	.60	.25	.06
☐ 4	Dave Gallagher	.20	.08	.02
☐ 5	Bo Jackson	1.00	.40	.10
☐ 6	Jay Buhner	.35	.15	.03
☐ 7	Melido Perez	.20	.08	.02
☐ 8	Bobby Witt	.20	.08	.02
☐ 9	David Cone	.25	.10	.02
☐ 10	Chris Sabo	.35	.15	.03
☐ 11	Pat Borders	.25	.10	.02
☐ 12	Mark Grant	.15	.06	.01
☐ 13	Mike Macfarlane	.15	.06	.01
☐ 14	Mike Jackson	.20	.08	.02
☐ 15	Ricky Jordan	.20	.08	.02
☐ 16	Ron Gant	.75	.30	.07
☐ 17	Al Leiter	.15	.06	.01
☐ 18	Jeff Parrett	.15	.06	.01
☐ 19	Pete Smith	.15	.06	.01

1989 Score Young Superstars II

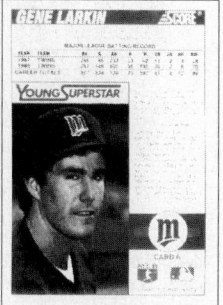

The 1989 Score Young Superstars II set contains 42 standard-size (2 1/2" by 3 1/2") cards. The fronts are orange, white and purple. The vertically-oriented backs have color facial shots, 1988 and career stats, and biographical information. The cards were distributed as a boxed set with five Magic Motion trivia cards.

		MINT	EXC	G-VG
COMPLETE SET (42)		6.00	2.50	.60
COMMON PLAYER (1-42)		.15	.06	.01
☐ 1	Sandy Alomar Jr.	.50	.20	.05
☐ 2	Tom Gordon	.35	.15	.03
☐ 3	Ron Jones	.15	.06	.01
☐ 4	Todd Burns	.15	.06	.01
☐ 5	Paul O'Neill	.25	.10	.02
☐ 6	Gene Larkin	.20	.08	.02
☐ 7	Eric King	.15	.06	.01
☐ 8	Jeff M. Robinson	.15	.06	.01
☐ 9	Bill Wegman	.20	.08	.02
☐ 10	Cecil Espy	.15	.06	.01
☐ 11	Jose Guzman	.20	.08	.02
☐ 12	Kelly Gruber	.30	.12	.03
☐ 13	Duane Ward	.20	.08	.02
☐ 14	Mark Gubicza	.20	.08	.02
☐ 15	Norm Charlton	.25	.10	.02
☐ 16	Jose Oquendo	.15	.06	.01
☐ 17	Geronimo Berroa	.15	.06	.01
☐ 18	Ken Griffey Jr.	2.00	.80	.20
☐ 19	Lance McCullers	.15	.06	.01
☐ 20	Todd Stottlemyre	.25	.10	.02
☐ 21	Craig Worthington	.20	.08	.02
☐ 22	Mike Devereaux	.20	.08	.02
☐ 23	Tom Glavine	.50	.20	.05
☐ 24	Dale Sveum	.15	.06	.01
☐ 25	Roberto Kelly	.45	.18	.04
☐ 26	Luis Medina	.20	.08	.02

			MINT	EXC	G-VG
☐	27	Steve Searcy	.15	.06	.01
☐	28	Don August	.15	.06	.01
☐	29	Shawn Hillegas	.15	.06	.01
☐	30	Mike Campbell	.15	.06	.01
☐	31	Mike Harkey	.30	.12	.03
☐	32	Randy Johnson	.30	.12	.03
☐	33	Craig Biggio	.35	.15	.03
☐	34	Mike Schooler	.20	.08	.02
☐	35	Andres Thomas	.15	.06	.01
☐	36	Jerome Walton	.35	.15	.03
☐	37	Cris Carpenter	.20	.08	.02
☐	38	Kevin Mitchell	.50	.20	.05
☐	39	Eddie Williams	.15	.06	.01
☐	40	Chad Kreuter	.15	.06	.01
☐	41	Danny Jackson	.20	.08	.02
☐	42	Kurt Stillwell	.20	.08	.02

1989 Score Scoremasters

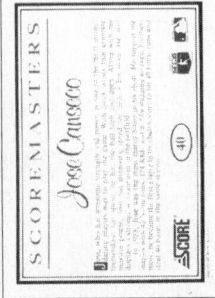

The 1989 Score Scoremasters set contains 42 standard-size (2 1/2" by 3 1/2") cards. The fronts are "pure" with attractively-drawn action portraits. The backs feature write-ups of the players' careers. The cards were distributed as a boxed set.

			MINT	EXC	G-VG
	COMPLETE SET (42)		9.00	4.00	.90
	COMMON PLAYER (1-42)		.20	.08	.02
☐	1	Bo Jackson	1.00	.40	.10
☐	2	Jerome Walton	.40	.16	.04
☐	3	Cal Ripken	.75	.30	.07
☐	4	Mike Scott	.20	.08	.02
☐	5	Nolan Ryan	1.00	.40	.10
☐	6	Don Mattingly	.60	.25	.06
☐	7	Tom Gordon	.30	.12	.03
☐	8	Jack Morris	.40	.16	.04
☐	9	Carlton Fisk	.50	.20	.05
☐	10	Will Clark	.90	.40	.09
☐	11	George Brett	.50	.20	.05
☐	12	Kevin Mitchell	.50	.20	.05
☐	13	Mark Langston	.25	.10	.02
☐	14	Dave Stewart	.25	.10	.02
☐	15	Dale Murphy	.40	.16	.04
☐	16	Gary Gaetti	.20	.08	.02
☐	17	Wade Boggs	.75	.30	.07
☐	18	Eric Davis	.50	.20	.05
☐	19	Kirby Puckett	.75	.30	.07
☐	20	Roger Clemens	.90	.40	.09
☐	21	Orel Hershiser	.30	.12	.03
☐	22	Mark Grace	.75	.30	.07
☐	23	Ryne Sandberg	.75	.30	.07
☐	24	Barry Larkin	.35	.15	.03
☐	25	Ellis Burks	.40	.16	.04
☐	26	Dwight Gooden	.35	.15	.03
☐	27	Ozzie Smith	.30	.12	.03
☐	28	Andre Dawson	.30	.12	.03
☐	29	Julio Franco	.25	.10	.02
☐	30	Ken Griffey Jr.	1.50	.60	.15
☐	31	Ruben Sierra	.60	.25	.06
☐	32	Mark McGwire	.60	.25	.06
☐	33	Andres Galarraga	.25	.10	.02
☐	34	Joe Carter	.30	.12	.03
☐	35	Vince Coleman	.30	.12	.03
☐	36	Mike Greenwell	.35	.15	.03
☐	37	Tony Gwynn	.60	.25	.06
☐	38	Andy Van Slyke	.20	.08	.02

			MINT	EXC	G-VG
☐	39	Gregg Jefferies	.60	.25	.06
☐	40	Jose Canseco	.90	.40	.09
☐	41	Dave Winfield	.35	.15	.03
☐	42	Darryl Strawberry	.60	.25	.06

1989 Score Nat West Yankees

The 1989 Score National Westminster Bank New York Yankees set features 33 standard-size (2 1/2" by 3 1/2") cards. The fronts and backs are navy; the backs have color mug shots, 1988 and career stats. The set was given away at a 1989 Yankees' home game.

			MINT	EXC	G-VG
	COMPLETE SET (33)		18.00	7.50	2.50
	COMMON PLAYER (1-33)		.35	.15	.03
☐	1	Don Mattingly	2.50	1.00	.25
☐	2	Steve Sax	.75	.30	.07
☐	3	Alvaro Espinoza	.35	.15	.03
☐	4	Luis Polonia	.60	.25	.06
☐	5	Jesse Barfield	.45	.18	.04
☐	6	Dave Righetti	.45	.18	.04
☐	7	Dave Winfield	1.25	.50	.12
☐	8	John Candelaria	.35	.15	.03
☐	9	Wayne Tolleson	.35	.15	.03
☐	10	Ken Phelps	.35	.15	.03
☐	11	Rafael Santana	.35	.15	.03
☐	12	Don Slaught	.35	.15	.03
☐	13	Mike Pagliarulo	.45	.18	.04
☐	14	Lance McCullers	.35	.15	.03
☐	15	Dave LaPoint	.35	.15	.03
☐	16	Dale Mohorcic	.35	.15	.03
☐	17	Steve Balboni	.35	.15	.03
☐	18	Roberto Kelly	.75	.30	.07
☐	19	Andy Hawkins	.45	.18	.04
☐	20	Mel Hall	.45	.18	.04
☐	21	Tom Brookens	.35	.15	.03
☐	22	Deion Sanders	1.25	.50	.12
☐	23	Richard Dotson	.35	.15	.03
☐	24	Lee Guetterman	.35	.15	.03
☐	25	Bob Geren	.35	.15	.03
☐	26	Jimmy Jones	.35	.15	.03
☐	27	Chuck Cary	.35	.15	.03
☐	28	Ron Guidry	.60	.25	.06
☐	29	Hal Morris	1.25	.50	.12
☐	30	Clay Parker	.35	.15	.03
☐	31	Dallas Green MG	.45	.18	.04
☐	32	Thurman Munson (memorial)	3.00	1.25	.30
☐	33	Yankees Team Card	.75	.30	.07

1989 Score Traded

The 1989 Score Traded set contains 110 standard-size (2 1/2" by 3 1/2") cards. The fronts have coral green borders with pink diamonds at the bottom. The vertically-oriented backs have color facial shots, career stats, and biographical information.

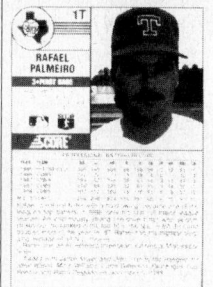

Cards 1-80 feature traded players; cards 81-110 feature 1989 rookies. The set was distributed in a blue box with 10 Magic Motion trivia cards. The key rookie cards in this set are Jim Abbott, Joey (Albert) Belle, Junior Felix, Ken Griffey Jr., and Jerome Walton.

	MINT	EXC	G-VG
COMPLETE SET (110)	12.00	5.25	1.50
COMMON PLAYER (1-80)	.05	.02	.00
COMMON PLAYER (81-110)	.05	.02	.00

☐ 1T	Rafael Palmeiro	.15	.05	.01
☐ 2T	Nolan Ryan	1.50	.60	.15
☐ 3T	Jack Clark	.10	.04	.01
☐ 4T	Dave LaPoint	.05	.02	.00
☐ 5T	Mike Moore	.08	.03	.01
☐ 6T	Pete O'Brien	.05	.02	.00
☐ 7T	Jeffrey Leonard	.05	.02	.00
☐ 8T	Rob Murphy	.05	.02	.00
☐ 9T	Tom Herr	.05	.02	.00
☐ 10T	Claudell Washington	.05	.02	.00
☐ 11T	Mike Pagliarulo	.05	.02	.00
☐ 12T	Steve Lake	.05	.02	.00
☐ 13T	Spike Owen	.05	.02	.00
☐ 14T	Andy Hawkins	.05	.02	.00
☐ 15T	Todd Benzinger	.05	.02	.00
☐ 16T	Mookie Wilson	.08	.03	.01
☐ 17T	Bert Blyleven	.10	.04	.01
☐ 18T	Jeff Treadway	.08	.03	.01
☐ 19T	Bruce Hurst	.10	.04	.01
☐ 20T	Steve Sax	.10	.04	.01
☐ 21T	Juan Samuel	.10	.04	.01
☐ 22T	Jesse Barfield	.10	.04	.01
☐ 23T	Carmen Castillo	.05	.02	.00
☐ 24T	Terry Leach	.05	.02	.00
☐ 25T	Mark Langston	.10	.04	.01
☐ 26T	Eric King	.08	.03	.01
☐ 27T	Steve Balboni	.05	.02	.00
☐ 28T	Len Dykstra	.10	.04	.01
☐ 29T	Keith Moreland	.05	.02	.00
☐ 30T	Terry Kennedy	.05	.02	.00
☐ 31T	Eddie Murray	.12	.05	.01
☐ 32T	Mitch Williams	.10	.04	.01
☐ 33T	Jeff Parrett	.05	.02	.00
☐ 34T	Wally Backman	.05	.02	.00
☐ 35T	Julio Franco	.12	.05	.01
☐ 36T	Lance Parrish	.10	.04	.01
☐ 37T	Nick Esasky	.05	.02	.00
☐ 38T	Luis Polonia	.08	.03	.01
☐ 39T	Kevin Gross	.05	.02	.00
☐ 40T	John Dopson	.05	.02	.00
☐ 41T	Willie Randolph	.08	.03	.01
☐ 42T	Jim Clancy	.05	.02	.00
☐ 43T	Tracy Jones	.05	.02	.00
☐ 44T	Phil Bradley	.05	.02	.00
☐ 45T	Milt Thompson	.05	.02	.00
☐ 46T	Chris James	.08	.03	.01
☐ 47T	Scott Fletcher	.05	.02	.00
☐ 48T	Kal Daniels	.10	.04	.01
☐ 49T	Steve Bedrosian	.08	.03	.01
☐ 50T	Rickey Henderson	.35	.15	.03
☐ 51T	Dion James	.05	.02	.00
☐ 52T	Tim Leary	.08	.03	.01
☐ 53T	Roger McDowell	.05	.02	.00
☐ 54T	Mel Hall	.08	.03	.01
☐ 55T	Dickie Thon	.08	.03	.01
☐ 56T	Zane Smith	.08	.03	.01
☐ 57T	Danny Heep	.05	.02	.00
☐ 58T	Bob McClure	.05	.02	.00
☐ 59T	Brian Holton	.05	.02	.00
☐ 60T	Randy Ready	.05	.02	.00

☐ 61T	Bob Melvin	.05	.02	.00
☐ 62T	Harold Baines	.10	.04	.01
☐ 63T	Lance McCullers	.05	.02	.00
☐ 64T	Jody Davis	.05	.02	.00
☐ 65T	Darrell Evans	.08	.03	.01
☐ 66T	Joel Youngblood	.05	.02	.00
☐ 67T	Frank Viola	.10	.04	.01
☐ 68T	Mike Aldrete	.05	.02	.00
☐ 69T	Greg Cadaret	.08	.03	.01
☐ 70T	John Kruk	.10	.04	.01
☐ 71T	Pat Sheridan	.05	.02	.00
☐ 72T	Oddibe McDowell	.05	.02	.00
☐ 73T	Tom Brookens	.05	.02	.00
☐ 74T	Bob Boone	.10	.04	.01
☐ 75T	Walt Terrell	.05	.02	.00
☐ 76T	Joel Skinner	.05	.02	.00
☐ 77T	Randy Johnson	.12	.05	.01
☐ 78T	Felix Fermin	.05	.02	.00
☐ 79T	Rick Mahler	.05	.02	.00
☐ 80T	Richard Dotson	.05	.02	.00
☐ 81T	Cris Carpenter	.10	.04	.01
☐ 82T	Bill Spiers	.12	.05	.01
☐ 83T	Junior Felix	.15	.06	.01
☐ 84T	Joe Girardi	.10	.04	.01
☐ 85T	Jerome Walton	.40	.16	.04
☐ 86T	Greg Litton	.10	.04	.01
☐ 87T	Greg W.Harris	.15	.06	.01
☐ 88T	Jim Abbott	1.25	.50	.12
☐ 89T	Kevin Brown	.10	.04	.01
☐ 90T	John Wetteland	.15	.06	.01
☐ 91T	Gary Wayne	.10	.04	.01
☐ 92T	Rich Monteleone	.10	.04	.01
☐ 93T	Bob Geren	.10	.04	.01
☐ 94T	Clay Parker	.08	.03	.01
☐ 95T	Steve Finley	.35	.15	.03
☐ 96T	Gregg Olson	.60	.25	.06
☐ 97T	Ken Patterson	.08	.03	.01
☐ 98T	Ken Hill	.25	.10	.02
☐ 99T	Scott Scudder	.20	.08	.02
☐ 100T	Ken Griffey Jr.	6.00	2.50	.60
☐ 101T	Jeff Brantley	.20	.08	.02
☐ 102T	Donn Pall	.08	.03	.01
☐ 103T	Carlos Martinez	.15	.06	.01
☐ 104T	Joe Oliver	.20	.08	.02
☐ 105T	Omar Vizquel	.08	.03	.01
☐ 106T	Joey Belle	2.00	.80	.20
☐ 107T	Kenny Rogers	.10	.04	.01
☐ 108T	Mark Carreon	.10	.04	.01
☐ 109T	Rolando Roomes	.08	.03	.01
☐ 110T	Pete Harnisch	.25	.10	.02

1990 Score

The 1990 Score set contains 704 standard-size (2 1/2" by 3 1/2") cards. The front borders are red, blue, green or white. The vertically-oriented backs are white with borders that match the fronts, and feature color mugshots. Cards numbered 661-682 contain the first round draft picks subset noted as DC for "draft choice" in the checklist below. Cards numbered 683-695 contain the "Dream Team" subset noted by DT in the checklist below. The key rookie cards in this set are Juan Gonzalez, Dave Justice, Chuck Knoblauch, Kevin Maas, Ben McDonald, John Olerud, and Frank Thomas.

		MINT	EXC	G-VG
	COMPLETE SET (704)	20.00	8.50	2.75
	COMMON PLAYER (1-704)	.03	.01	.00
☐ 1	Don Mattingly	.20	.08	.02
☐ 2	Cal Ripken	.30	.12	.03
☐ 3	Dwight Evans	.06	.02	.00
☐ 4	Barry Bonds	.17	.07	.01
☐ 5	Kevin McReynolds	.08	.03	.01
☐ 6	Ozzie Guillen	.06	.02	.00
☐ 7	Terry Kennedy	.03	.01	.00
☐ 8	Bryan Harvey	.06	.02	.00
☐ 9	Alan Trammell	.08	.03	.01
☐ 10	Cory Snyder	.06	.02	.00
☐ 11	Jody Reed	.06	.02	.00
☐ 12	Roberto Alomar	.15	.06	.01
☐ 13	Pedro Guerrero	.08	.03	.01
☐ 14	Gary Redus	.03	.01	.00
☐ 15	Marty Barrett	.03	.01	.00
☐ 16	Ricky Jordan	.06	.02	.00
☐ 17	Joe Magrane	.03	.01	.00
☐ 18	Sid Fernandez	.06	.02	.00
☐ 19	Richard Dotson	.03	.01	.00
☐ 20	Jack Clark	.08	.03	.01
☐ 21	Bob Walk	.03	.01	.00
☐ 22	Ron Karkovice	.03	.01	.00
☐ 23	Lenny Harris	.06	.02	.00
☐ 24	Phil Bradley	.03	.01	.00
☐ 25	Andres Galarraga	.06	.02	.00
☐ 26	Brian Downing	.03	.01	.00
☐ 27	Dave Martinez	.03	.01	.00
☐ 28	Eric King	.03	.01	.00
☐ 29	Barry Lyons	.03	.01	.00
☐ 30	Dave Schmidt	.03	.01	.00
☐ 31	Mike Boddicker	.03	.01	.00
☐ 32	Tom Foley	.03	.01	.00
☐ 33	Brady Anderson	.03	.01	.00
☐ 34	Jim Presley	.03	.01	.00
☐ 35	Lance Parrish	.06	.02	.00
☐ 36	Von Hayes	.06	.02	.00
☐ 37	Lee Smith	.06	.02	.00
☐ 38	Herm Winningham	.03	.01	.00
☐ 39	Alejandro Pena	.06	.02	.00
☐ 40	Mike Scott	.06	.02	.00
☐ 41	Joe Orsulak	.03	.01	.00
☐ 42	Rafael Ramirez	.03	.01	.00
☐ 43	Gerald Young	.03	.01	.00
☐ 44	Dick Schofield	.03	.01	.00
☐ 45	Dave Smith	.03	.01	.00
☐ 46	Dave Magadan	.06	.02	.00
☐ 47	Dennis Martinez	.03	.01	.00
☐ 48	Greg Minton	.03	.01	.00
☐ 49	Milt Thompson	.03	.01	.00
☐ 50	Orel Hershiser	.08	.03	.01
☐ 51	Bip Roberts	.03	.01	.00
☐ 52	Jerry Browne	.03	.01	.00
☐ 53	Bob Ojeda	.03	.01	.00
☐ 54	Fernando Valenzuela	.08	.03	.01
☐ 55	Matt Nokes	.06	.02	.00
☐ 56	Brook Jacoby	.03	.01	.00
☐ 57	Frank Tanana	.03	.01	.00
☐ 58	Scott Fletcher	.03	.01	.00
☐ 59	Ron Oester	.03	.01	.00
☐ 60	Bob Boone	.06	.02	.00
☐ 61	Dan Gladden	.03	.01	.00
☐ 62	Darnell Coles	.03	.01	.00
☐ 63	Gregg Olson	.12	.05	.01
☐ 64	Todd Burns	.03	.01	.00
☐ 65	Todd Benzinger	.03	.01	.00
☐ 66	Dale Murphy	.10	.04	.01
☐ 67	Mike Flanagan	.03	.01	.00
☐ 68	Jose Oquendo	.03	.01	.00
☐ 69	Cecil Espy	.03	.01	.00
☐ 70	Chris Sabo	.10	.04	.01
☐ 71	Shane Rawley	.03	.01	.00
☐ 72	Tom Brunansky	.06	.02	.00
☐ 73	Vance Law	.03	.01	.00
☐ 74	B.J. Surhoff	.06	.02	.00
☐ 75	Lou Whitaker	.06	.02	.00
☐ 76	Ken Caminiti UER (Euclid, Ohio should be Hanford, California)	.03	.01	.00
☐ 77	Nelson Liriano	.03	.01	.00
☐ 78	Tommy Gregg	.03	.01	.00
☐ 79	Don Slaught	.03	.01	.00
☐ 80	Eddie Murray	.10	.04	.01
☐ 81	Joe Boever	.03	.01	.00
☐ 82	Charlie Leibrandt	.03	.01	.00
☐ 83	Jose Lind	.03	.01	.00
☐ 84	Tony Phillips	.03	.01	.00
☐ 85	Mitch Webster	.03	.01	.00
☐ 86	Dan Plesac	.03	.01	.00
☐ 87	Rick Mahler	.03	.01	.00
☐ 88	Steve Lyons	.03	.01	.00
☐ 89	Tony Fernandez	.06	.02	.00
☐ 90	Ryne Sandberg	.30	.12	.03
☐ 91	Nick Esasky	.03	.01	.00
☐ 92	Luis Salazar	.03	.01	.00
☐ 93	Pete Incaviglia	.06	.02	.00
☐ 94	Ivan Calderon	.06	.02	.00
☐ 95	Jeff Treadway	.03	.01	.00
☐ 96	Kurt Stillwell	.03	.01	.00
☐ 97	Gary Sheffield	.08	.03	.01
☐ 98	Jeffrey Leonard	.03	.01	.00
☐ 99	Andres Thomas	.03	.01	.00
☐ 100	Roberto Kelly	.08	.03	.01
☐ 101	Alvaro Espinoza	.03	.01	.00
☐ 102	Greg Gagne	.03	.01	.00
☐ 103	John Farrell	.03	.01	.00
☐ 104	Willie Wilson	.06	.02	.00
☐ 105	Glenn Braggs	.03	.01	.00
☐ 106	Chet Lemon	.03	.01	.00
☐ 107A	Jamie Moyer ERR (scintilating)	.06	.02	.00
☐ 107B	Jamie Moyer COR (scintillating)	.25	.10	.02
☐ 108	Chuck Crim	.03	.01	.00
☐ 109	Dave Valle	.03	.01	.00
☐ 110	Walt Weiss	.06	.02	.00
☐ 111	Larry Sheets	.03	.01	.00
☐ 112	Don Robinson	.03	.01	.00
☐ 113	Danny Heep	.03	.01	.00
☐ 114	Carmelo Martinez	.03	.01	.00
☐ 115	Dave Gallagher	.03	.01	.00
☐ 116	Mike LaValliere	.03	.01	.00
☐ 117	Bob McClure	.03	.01	.00
☐ 118	Rene Gonzales	.03	.01	.00
☐ 119	Mark Parent	.03	.01	.00
☐ 120	Wally Joyner	.08	.03	.01
☐ 121	Mark Gubicza	.06	.02	.00
☐ 122	Tony Pena	.06	.02	.00
☐ 123	Carmen Castillo	.03	.01	.00
☐ 124	Howard Johnson	.08	.03	.01
☐ 125	Steve Sax	.06	.02	.00
☐ 126	Tim Belcher	.06	.02	.00
☐ 127	Tim Burke	.03	.01	.00
☐ 128	Al Newman	.03	.01	.00
☐ 129	Dennis Rasmussen	.03	.01	.00
☐ 130	Doug Jones	.03	.01	.00
☐ 131	Fred Lynn	.06	.02	.00
☐ 132	Jeff Hamilton	.03	.01	.00
☐ 133	German Gonzalez	.03	.01	.00
☐ 134	John Morris	.03	.01	.00
☐ 135	Dave Parker	.08	.03	.01
☐ 136	Gary Pettis	.03	.01	.00
☐ 137	Dennis Boyd	.03	.01	.00
☐ 138	Candy Maldonado	.03	.01	.00
☐ 139	Rick Cerone	.03	.01	.00
☐ 140	George Brett	.12	.05	.01
☐ 141	Dave Clark	.03	.01	.00
☐ 142	Dickie Thon	.03	.01	.00
☐ 143	Junior Ortiz	.03	.01	.00
☐ 144	Don August	.03	.01	.00
☐ 145	Gary Gaetti	.06	.02	.00
☐ 146	Kirt Manwaring	.03	.01	.00
☐ 147	Jeff Reed	.03	.01	.00
☐ 148	Jose Alvarez	.03	.01	.00
☐ 149	Mike Schooler	.03	.01	.00
☐ 150	Mark Grace	.12	.05	.01
☐ 151	Geronimo Berroa	.03	.01	.00
☐ 152	Barry Jones	.03	.01	.00
☐ 153	Geno Petralli	.03	.01	.00
☐ 154	Jim Deshaies	.03	.01	.00
☐ 155	Barry Larkin	.12	.05	.01
☐ 156	Alfredo Griffin	.03	.01	.00
☐ 157	Tom Henke	.06	.02	.00
☐ 158	Mike Jeffcoat	.03	.01	.00
☐ 159	Bob Welch	.06	.02	.00
☐ 160	Julio Franco	.08	.03	.01
☐ 161	Henry Cotto	.03	.01	.00
☐ 162	Terry Steinbach	.06	.02	.00
☐ 163	Damon Berryhill	.03	.01	.00
☐ 164	Tim Crews	.03	.01	.00
☐ 165	Tom Browning	.06	.02	.00
☐ 166	Fred Manrique	.03	.01	.00
☐ 167	Harold Reynolds	.06	.02	.00
☐ 168A	Ron Hassey ERR (27 on back)	.06	.02	.00
☐ 168B	Ron Hassey COR (24 on back)	1.25	.50	.12
☐ 169	Shawon Dunston	.08	.03	.01
☐ 170	Bobby Bonilla	.15	.06	.01
☐ 171	Tommy Herr	.03	.01	.00
☐ 172	Mike Heath	.03	.01	.00
☐ 173	Rich Gedman	.03	.01	.00
☐ 174	Bill Ripken	.03	.01	.00
☐ 175	Pete O'Brien	.03	.01	.00
☐ 176A	Lloyd McClendon ERR (uniform number on back listed as 1)	.75	.30	.07

☐ 176B Lloyd McClendon COR (uniform number on back listed as 10)	.06	.02	.00
☐ 177 Brian Holton	.03	.01	.00
☐ 178 Jeff Blauser	.03	.01	.00
☐ 179 Jim Eisenreich	.03	.01	.00
☐ 180 Bert Blyleven	.06	.02	.00
☐ 181 Rob Murphy	.03	.01	.00
☐ 182 Bill Doran	.03	.01	.00
☐ 183 Curt Ford	.03	.01	.00
☐ 184 Mike Henneman	.03	.01	.00
☐ 185 Eric Davis	.10	.04	.01
☐ 186 Lance McCullers	.03	.01	.00
☐ 187 Steve Davis	.08	.03	.01
☐ 188 Bill Wegman	.03	.01	.00
☐ 189 Brian Harper	.06	.02	.00
☐ 190 Mike Moore	.06	.02	.00
☐ 191 Dale Mohorcic	.03	.01	.00
☐ 192 Tim Wallach	.06	.02	.00
☐ 193 Keith Hernandez	.06	.02	.00
☐ 194 Dave Righetti	.06	.02	.00
☐ 195A Bret Saberhagen ERR (joke)	.08	.03	.01
☐ 195B Bret Saberhagen COR (joker)	.30	.12	.03
☐ 196 Paul Kilgus	.03	.01	.00
☐ 197 Bud Black	.03	.01	.00
☐ 198 Juan Samuel	.06	.02	.00
☐ 199 Kevin Seitzer	.06	.02	.00
☐ 200 Darryl Strawberry	.25	.10	.02
☐ 201 Dave Stieb	.06	.02	.00
☐ 202 Charlie Hough	.03	.01	.00
☐ 203 Jack Morris	.08	.03	.01
☐ 204 Rance Mulliniks	.03	.01	.00
☐ 205 Alvin Davis	.06	.02	.00
☐ 206 Jack Howell	.03	.01	.00
☐ 207 Ken Patterson	.03	.01	.00
☐ 208 Terry Pendleton	.08	.03	.01
☐ 209 Craig Lefferts	.03	.01	.00
☐ 210 Kevin Brown UER (First mention of '89 Rangers should be '88)	.03	.01	.00
☐ 211 Dan Petry	.03	.01	.00
☐ 212 Dave Leiper	.03	.01	.00
☐ 213 Daryl Boston	.03	.01	.00
☐ 214 Kevin Hickey	.03	.01	.00
☐ 215 Mike Krukow	.03	.01	.00
☐ 216 Terry Francona	.03	.01	.00
☐ 217 Kirk McCaskill	.03	.01	.00
☐ 218 Scott Bailes	.03	.01	.00
☐ 219 Bob Forsch	.03	.01	.00
☐ 220A Mike Aldrete ERR (25 on back)	.06	.02	.00
☐ 220B Mike Aldrete COR (24 on back)	.25	.10	.02
☐ 221 Steve Buechele	.03	.01	.00
☐ 222 Jesse Barfield	.06	.02	.00
☐ 223 Juan Berenguer	.03	.01	.00
☐ 224 Andy McGaffigan	.03	.01	.00
☐ 225 Pete Smith	.03	.01	.00
☐ 226 Mike Witt	.03	.01	.00
☐ 227 Jay Howell	.03	.01	.00
☐ 228 Scott Bradley	.03	.01	.00
☐ 229 Jerome Walton	.08	.03	.01
☐ 230 Greg Swindell	.06	.02	.00
☐ 231 Atlee Hammaker	.03	.01	.00
☐ 232A Mike Devereaux ERR (RF on front)	.06	.02	.00
☐ 232B Mike Devereaux COR (CF on front)	1.25	.50	.12
☐ 233 Ken Hill	.08	.03	.01
☐ 234 Craig Worthington	.03	.01	.00
☐ 235 Scott Terry	.03	.01	.00
☐ 236 Brett Butler	.06	.02	.00
☐ 237 Doyle Alexander	.03	.01	.00
☐ 238 Dave Anderson	.03	.01	.00
☐ 239 Bob Milacki	.03	.01	.00
☐ 240 Dwight Smith	.06	.02	.00
☐ 241 Otis Nixon	.03	.01	.00
☐ 242 Pat Tabler	.03	.01	.00
☐ 243 Derek Lilliquist	.03	.01	.00
☐ 244 Danny Tartabull	.08	.03	.01
☐ 245 Wade Boggs	.15	.06	.01
☐ 246 Scott Garrelts (should say Relief Pitcher on front)	.03	.01	.00
☐ 247 Spike Owen	.03	.01	.00
☐ 248 Norm Charlton	.03	.01	.00
☐ 249 Gerald Perry	.03	.01	.00
☐ 250 Nolan Ryan	.50	.20	.05
☐ 251 Kevin Gross	.03	.01	.00
☐ 252 Randy Milligan	.06	.02	.00
☐ 253 Mike LaCoss	.03	.01	.00
☐ 254 Dave Bergman	.03	.01	.00
☐ 255 Tony Gwynn	.15	.06	.01
☐ 256 Felix Fermin	.03	.01	.00
☐ 257 Greg W. Harris	.06	.02	.00
☐ 258 Junior Felix	.06	.02	.00
☐ 259 Mark Davis	.06	.02	.00
☐ 260 Vince Coleman	.08	.03	.01
☐ 261 Paul Gibson	.03	.01	.00
☐ 262 Mitch Williams	.03	.01	.00
☐ 263 Jeff Russell	.03	.01	.00
☐ 264 Omar Vizquel	.03	.01	.00
☐ 265 Andre Dawson	.10	.04	.01
☐ 266 Storm Davis	.03	.01	.00
☐ 267 Guillermo Hernandez	.03	.01	.00
☐ 268 Mike Felder	.03	.01	.00
☐ 269 Tom Candiotti	.06	.02	.00
☐ 270 Bruce Hurst	.06	.02	.00
☐ 271 Fred McGriff	.10	.04	.01
☐ 272 Glenn Davis	.08	.03	.01
☐ 273 John Franco	.03	.01	.00
☐ 274 Rich Yett	.03	.01	.00
☐ 275 Craig Biggio	.08	.03	.01
☐ 276 Gene Larkin	.03	.01	.00
☐ 277 Rob Dibble	.08	.03	.01
☐ 278 Randy Bush	.03	.01	.00
☐ 279 Kevin Bass	.03	.01	.00
☐ 280A Bo Jackson ERR (Watham)	.40	.16	.04
☐ 280B Bo Jackson COR (Wathan)	.75	.30	.07
☐ 281 Wally Backman	.03	.01	.00
☐ 282 Larry Andersen	.03	.01	.00
☐ 283 Chris Bosio	.03	.01	.00
☐ 284 Juan Agosto	.03	.01	.00
☐ 285 Ozzie Smith	.12	.05	.01
☐ 286 George Bell	.08	.03	.01
☐ 287 Rex Hudler	.03	.01	.00
☐ 288 Pat Borders	.03	.01	.00
☐ 289 Danny Jackson	.03	.01	.00
☐ 290 Carlton Fisk	.12	.05	.01
☐ 291 Tracy Jones	.03	.01	.00
☐ 292 Allan Anderson	.03	.01	.00
☐ 293 Johnny Ray	.03	.01	.00
☐ 294 Lee Guetterman	.03	.01	.00
☐ 295 Paul O'Neill	.06	.02	.00
☐ 296 Carney Lansford	.06	.02	.00
☐ 297 Tom Brookens	.03	.01	.00
☐ 298 Claudell Washington	.03	.01	.00
☐ 299 Hubie Brooks	.03	.01	.00
☐ 300 Will Clark	.30	.12	.03
☐ 301 Kenny Rogers	.06	.02	.00
☐ 302 Darrell Evans	.06	.02	.00
☐ 303 Greg Briley	.06	.02	.00
☐ 304 Donn Pall	.03	.01	.00
☐ 305 Teddy Higuera	.03	.01	.00
☐ 306 Dan Pasqua	.03	.01	.00
☐ 307 Dave Winfield	.10	.04	.01
☐ 308 Dennis Powell	.03	.01	.00
☐ 309 Jose DeLeon	.03	.01	.00
☐ 310 Roger Clemens UER (dominate, should say dominant)	.30	.12	.03
☐ 311 Melido Perez	.03	.01	.00
☐ 312 Devon White	.06	.02	.00
☐ 313 Dwight Gooden	.10	.04	.01
☐ 314 Carlos Martinez	.03	.01	.00
☐ 315 Dennis Eckersley	.08	.03	.01
☐ 316 Clay Parker UER (Height 6'11")	.03	.01	.00
☐ 317 Rick Honeycutt	.03	.01	.00
☐ 318 Tim Laudner	.03	.01	.00
☐ 319 Joe Carter	.10	.04	.01
☐ 320 Robin Yount	.12	.05	.01
☐ 321 Felix Jose	.20	.08	.02
☐ 322 Mickey Tettleton	.06	.02	.00
☐ 323 Mike Gallego	.03	.01	.00
☐ 324 Edgar Martinez	.08	.03	.01
☐ 325 Dave Henderson	.06	.02	.00
☐ 326 Chili Davis	.06	.02	.00
☐ 327 Steve Balboni	.03	.01	.00
☐ 328 Jody Davis	.03	.01	.00
☐ 329 Shawn Hillegas	.03	.01	.00
☐ 330 Jim Abbott	.17	.07	.01
☐ 331 John Dopson	.03	.01	.00
☐ 332 Mark Williamson	.03	.01	.00
☐ 333 Jeff D. Robinson	.03	.01	.00
☐ 334 John Smiley	.06	.02	.00
☐ 335 Bobby Thigpen	.06	.02	.00
☐ 336 Garry Templeton	.03	.01	.00
☐ 337 Marvell Wynne	.03	.01	.00
☐ 338A Ken Griffey Sr. ERR (uniform number on back listed as 25)	.10	.04	.01
☐ 338B Ken Griffey Sr. COR (uniform number on back listed as 30)	1.75	.70	.17
☐ 339 Steve Finley	.10	.04	.01

☐ 340 Ellis Burks	.10	.04	.01
☐ 341 Frank Williams	.03	.01	.00
☐ 342 Mike Morgan	.03	.01	.00
☐ 343 Kevin Mitchell	.10	.04	.01
☐ 344 Joel Youngblood	.03	.01	.00
☐ 345 Mike Greenwell	.12	.05	.01
☐ 346 Glenn Wilson	.03	.01	.00
☐ 347 John Costello	.03	.01	.00
☐ 348 Wes Gardner	.03	.01	.00
☐ 349 Jeff Ballard	.03	.01	.00
☐ 350 Mark Thurmond UER (ERA is 192, should be 1.92)	.03	.01	.00
☐ 351 Randy Myers	.03	.01	.00
☐ 352 Shawn Abner	.03	.01	.00
☐ 353 Jesse Orosco	.03	.01	.00
☐ 354 Greg Walker	.03	.01	.00
☐ 355 Pete Harnisch	.06	.02	.00
☐ 356 Steve Farr	.03	.01	.00
☐ 357 Dave LaPoint	.03	.01	.00
☐ 358 Willie Fraser	.03	.01	.00
☐ 359 Mickey Hatcher	.03	.01	.00
☐ 360 Rickey Henderson	.25	.10	.02
☐ 361 Mike Fitzgerald	.03	.01	.00
☐ 362 Bill Schroeder	.03	.01	.00
☐ 363 Mark Carreon	.03	.01	.00
☐ 364 Ron Jones	.03	.01	.00
☐ 365 Jeff Montgomery	.03	.01	.00
☐ 366 Bill Krueger	.03	.01	.00
☐ 367 John Cangelosi	.03	.01	.00
☐ 368 Jose Gonzalez	.03	.01	.00
☐ 369 Greg Hibbard	.15	.06	.01
☐ 370 John Smoltz	.15	.06	.01
☐ 371 Jeff Brantley	.08	.03	.01
☐ 372 Frank White	.03	.01	.00
☐ 373 Ed Whitson	.03	.01	.00
☐ 374 Willie McGee	.08	.03	.01
☐ 375 Jose Canseco	.40	.16	.04
☐ 376 Randy Ready	.03	.01	.00
☐ 377 Don Aase	.03	.01	.00
☐ 378 Tony Armas	.03	.01	.00
☐ 379 Steve Bedrosian	.03	.01	.00
☐ 380 Chuck Finley	.06	.02	.00
☐ 381 Kent Hrbek	.08	.03	.01
☐ 382 Jim Gantner	.03	.01	.00
☐ 383 Mel Hall	.06	.02	.00
☐ 384 Mike Marshall	.06	.02	.00
☐ 385 Mark McGwire	.15	.06	.01
☐ 386 Wayne Tolleson	.03	.01	.00
☐ 387 Brian Holman	.08	.03	.01
☐ 388 John Wetteland	.06	.02	.00
☐ 389 Darren Daulton	.03	.01	.00
☐ 390 Rob Deer	.06	.02	.00
☐ 391 John Moses	.03	.01	.00
☐ 392 Todd Worrell	.06	.02	.00
☐ 393 Chuck Cary	.03	.01	.00
☐ 394 Stan Javier	.03	.01	.00
☐ 395 Willie Randolph	.06	.02	.00
☐ 396 Bill Buckner	.06	.02	.00
☐ 397 Robby Thompson	.03	.01	.00
☐ 398 Mike Scioscia	.03	.01	.00
☐ 399 Lonnie Smith	.06	.02	.00
☐ 400 Kirby Puckett	.20	.08	.02
☐ 401 Mark Langston	.08	.03	.01
☐ 402 Danny Darwin	.03	.01	.00
☐ 403 Greg Maddux	.06	.02	.00
☐ 404 Lloyd Moseby	.03	.01	.00
☐ 405 Rafael Palmeiro	.12	.05	.01
☐ 406 Chad Kreuter	.03	.01	.00
☐ 407 Jimmy Key	.06	.02	.00
☐ 408 Tim Birtsas	.03	.01	.00
☐ 409 Tim Raines	.08	.03	.01
☐ 410 Dave Stewart	.08	.03	.01
☐ 411 Eric Yelding	.06	.02	.00
☐ 412 Kent Anderson	.06	.02	.00
☐ 413 Les Lancaster	.03	.01	.00
☐ 414 Rick Dempsey	.03	.01	.00
☐ 415 Randy Johnson	.06	.02	.00
☐ 416 Gary Carter	.08	.03	.01
☐ 417 Rolando Roomes	.03	.01	.00
☐ 418 Dan Schatzeder	.03	.01	.00
☐ 419 Bryn Smith	.03	.01	.00
☐ 420 Ruben Sierra	.17	.07	.01
☐ 421 Steve Jeltz	.03	.01	.00
☐ 422 Ken Oberkfell	.03	.01	.00
☐ 423 Sid Bream	.03	.01	.00
☐ 424 Jim Clancy	.03	.01	.00
☐ 425 Kelly Gruber	.10	.04	.01
☐ 426 Rick Leach	.03	.01	.00
☐ 427 Len Dykstra	.08	.03	.01
☐ 428 Jeff Pico	.03	.01	.00
☐ 429 John Cerutti	.03	.01	.00
☐ 430 David Cone	.08	.03	.01
☐ 431 Jeff Kunkel	.03	.01	.00
☐ 432 Luis Aquino	.03	.01	.00
☐ 433 Ernie Whitt	.03	.01	.00
☐ 434 Bo Diaz	.03	.01	.00
☐ 435 Steve Lake	.03	.01	.00
☐ 436 Pat Perry	.03	.01	.00
☐ 437 Mike Davis	.03	.01	.00
☐ 438 Cecilio Guante	.03	.01	.00
☐ 439 Duane Ward	.03	.01	.00
☐ 440 Andy Van Slyke	.08	.03	.01
☐ 441 Gene Nelson	.03	.01	.00
☐ 442 Luis Polonia	.03	.01	.00
☐ 443 Kevin Elster	.03	.01	.00
☐ 444 Keith Moreland	.03	.01	.00
☐ 445 Roger McDowell	.03	.01	.00
☐ 446 Ron Darling	.06	.02	.00
☐ 447 Ernest Riles	.03	.01	.00
☐ 448 Mookie Wilson	.03	.01	.00
☐ 449A Billy Spiers ERR (no birth year)	.75	.30	.07
☐ 449B Billy Spiers COR (born in 1966)	.06	.02	.00
☐ 450 Rick Sutcliffe	.06	.02	.00
☐ 451 Nelson Santovenia	.03	.01	.00
☐ 452 Andy Allanson	.03	.01	.00
☐ 453 Bob Melvin	.03	.01	.00
☐ 454 Benito Santiago	.08	.03	.01
☐ 455 Jose Uribe	.03	.01	.00
☐ 456 Bill Landrum	.03	.01	.00
☐ 457 Bobby Witt	.06	.02	.00
☐ 458 Kevin Romine	.03	.01	.00
☐ 459 Lee Mazzilli	.03	.01	.00
☐ 460 Paul Molitor	.08	.03	.01
☐ 461 Ramon Martinez	.25	.10	.02
☐ 462 Frank DiPino	.03	.01	.00
☐ 463 Walt Terrell	.03	.01	.00
☐ 464 Bob Geren	.03	.01	.00
☐ 465 Rick Reuschel	.06	.02	.00
☐ 466 Mark Grant	.03	.01	.00
☐ 467 John Kruk	.03	.01	.00
☐ 468 Gregg Jefferies	.10	.04	.01
☐ 469 R.J. Reynolds	.03	.01	.00
☐ 470 Harold Baines	.08	.03	.01
☐ 471 Dennis Lamp	.03	.01	.00
☐ 472 Tom Gordon	.08	.03	.01
☐ 473 Terry Puhl	.03	.01	.00
☐ 474 Curt Wilkerson	.03	.01	.00
☐ 475 Dan Quisenberry	.06	.02	.00
☐ 476 Oddibe McDowell	.03	.01	.00
☐ 477 Zane Smith UER (Career ERA .393)	.06	.02	.00
☐ 478 Franklin Stubbs	.03	.01	.00
☐ 479 Wallace Johnson	.03	.01	.00
☐ 480 Jay Tibbs	.03	.01	.00
☐ 481 Tom Glavine	.20	.08	.02
☐ 482 Manny Lee	.03	.01	.00
☐ 483 Joe Hesketh UER (says Rookiess on back, should say Rookies)	.06	.02	.00
☐ 484 Mike Bielecki	.03	.01	.00
☐ 485 Greg Brock	.03	.01	.00
☐ 486 Pascual Perez	.03	.01	.00
☐ 487 Kirk Gibson	.08	.03	.01
☐ 488 Scott Sanderson	.03	.01	.00
☐ 489 Domingo Ramos	.03	.01	.00
☐ 490 Kal Daniels	.06	.02	.00
☐ 491A David Wells ERR (reverse negative photo on card back)	1.75	.70	.17
☐ 491B David Wells COR	.08	.03	.01
☐ 492 Jerry Reed	.03	.01	.00
☐ 493 Eric Show	.03	.01	.00
☐ 494 Mike Pagliarulo	.03	.01	.00
☐ 495 Ron Robinson	.03	.01	.00
☐ 496 Brad Komminsk	.03	.01	.00
☐ 497 Greg Litton	.03	.01	.00
☐ 498 Chris James	.03	.01	.00
☐ 499 Luis Quinones	.03	.01	.00
☐ 500 Frank Viola	.08	.03	.01
☐ 501 Tim Teufel UER (Twins '85, the s is lower case, should be upper case)	.03	.01	.00
☐ 502 Terry Leach	.03	.01	.00
☐ 503 Matt Williams	.15	.06	.01
☐ 504 Tim Leary	.06	.02	.00
☐ 505 Doug Drabek	.06	.02	.00
☐ 506 Mariano Duncan	.03	.01	.00
☐ 507 Charlie Hayes	.03	.01	.00
☐ 508 Joey Belle	.50	.20	.05
☐ 509 Pat Sheridan	.03	.01	.00
☐ 510 Mackey Sasser	.03	.01	.00
☐ 511 Jose Rijo	.06	.02	.00
☐ 512 Mike Smithson	.03	.01	.00
☐ 513 Gary Ward	.03	.01	.00

#	Name			
514	Dion James	.03	.01	.00
515	Jim Gott	.03	.01	.00
516	Drew Hall	.03	.01	.00
517	Doug Bair	.03	.01	.00
518	Scott Scudder	.08	.03	.01
519	Rick Aguilera	.06	.02	.00
520	Rafael Belliard	.03	.01	.00
521	Jay Buhner	.08	.03	.01
522	Jeff Reardon	.06	.02	.00
523	Steve Rosenberg	.06	.02	.00
524	Randy Velarde	.03	.01	.00
525	Jeff Musselman	.03	.01	.00
526	Bill Long	.03	.01	.00
527	Gary Wayne	.06	.02	.00
528	Dave Johnson (P)	.08	.03	.01
529	Ron Kittle	.06	.02	.00
530	Erik Hanson UER (5th line on back says seson, should say season)	.10	.04	.01
531	Steve Wilson	.03	.01	.00
532	Joey Meyer	.03	.01	.00
533	Curt Young	.03	.01	.00
534	Kelly Downs	.03	.01	.00
535	Joe Girardi	.03	.01	.00
536	Lance Blankenship	.03	.01	.00
537	Greg Mathews	.03	.01	.00
538	Donell Nixon	.03	.01	.00
539	Mark Knudson	.03	.01	.00
540	Jeff Wetherby	.08	.03	.01
541	Darrin Jackson	.06	.02	.00
542	Terry Mulholland	.06	.02	.00
543	Eric Hetzel	.03	.01	.00
544	Rick Reed	.08	.03	.01
545	Dennis Cook	.06	.02	.00
546	Mike Jackson	.03	.01	.00
547	Brian Fisher	.03	.01	.00
548	Gene Harris	.06	.02	.00
549	Jeff King	.06	.02	.00
550	Dave Dravecky	.06	.02	.00
551	Randy Kutcher	.03	.01	.00
552	Mark Portugal	.03	.01	.00
553	Jim Corsi	.03	.01	.00
554	Todd Stottlemyre	.08	.03	.01
555	Scott Bankhead	.06	.02	.00
556	Ken Dayley	.03	.01	.00
557	Rick Wrona	.06	.02	.00
558	Sammy Sosa	.25	.10	.02
559	Keith Miller	.03	.01	.00
560	Ken Griffey Jr.	1.50	.60	.15
561A	Ryne Sandberg HL ERR (position on front listed as 3B)	9.00	4.00	.90
561B	Ryne Sandberg HL COR	.15	.06	.01
562	Billy Hatcher	.03	.01	.00
563	Jay Bell	.03	.01	.00
564	Jack Daugherty	.06	.02	.00
565	Rich Monteleone	.03	.01	.00
566	Bo Jackson AS-MVP	.25	.10	.02
567	Tony Fossas	.06	.02	.00
568	Roy Smith	.03	.01	.00
569	Jaime Navarro	.06	.02	.00
570	Lance Johnson	.03	.01	.00
571	Mike Dyer	.08	.03	.01
572	Kevin Ritz	.08	.03	.01
573	Dave West	.03	.01	.00
574	Gary Mielke	.08	.03	.01
575	Scott Lusader	.03	.01	.00
576	Joe Oliver	.06	.02	.00
577	Sandy Alomar Jr.	.10	.04	.01
578	Andy Benes UER (extra comma between day and year)	.17	.07	.01
579	Tim Jones	.03	.01	.00
580	Randy McCament	.08	.03	.01
581	Curt Schilling	.03	.01	.00
582	John Orton	.08	.03	.01
583A	Milt Cuyler ERR (998 games)	1.50	.60	.15
583B	Milt Cuyler COR (98 games)	.50	.20	.05
584	Eric Anthony	.17	.07	.01
585	Greg Vaughn	.50	.20	.05
586	Deion Sanders	.20	.08	.02
587	Jose DeJesus	.03	.01	.00
588	Chip Hale	.08	.03	.01
589	John Olerud	1.00	.40	.10
590	Steve Olin	.10	.04	.01
591	Marquis Grissom	.45	.18	.04
592	Moises Alou	.12	.05	.01
593	Mark Lemke	.06	.02	.00
594	Dean Palmer	.75	.30	.07
595	Robin Ventura	.75	.30	.07
596	Tino Martinez	.50	.20	.05
597	Mike Huff	.12	.05	.01
598	Scott Hemond	.12	.05	.01
599	Wally Whitehurst	.06	.02	.00
600	Todd Zeile	.35	.15	.03
601	Glenallen Hill	.06	.02	.00
602	Hal Morris	.35	.15	.03
603	Juan Bell	.06	.02	.00
604	Bobby Rose	.10	.04	.01
605	Matt Merullo	.08	.03	.01
606	Kevin Maas	1.25	.50	.12
607	Randy Nosek	.08	.03	.01
608A	Billy Bates (Text mentions 12 triples in tenth line)	.10	.04	.01
608B	Billy Bates (Text has no mention of triples)	.10	.04	.01
609	Mike Stanton	.10	.04	.01
610	Mauro Gozzo	.10	.04	.01
611	Charles Nagy	.20	.08	.02
612	Scott Coolbaugh	.10	.04	.01
613	Jose Vizcaino	.10	.04	.01
614	Greg Smith	.10	.04	.01
615	Jeff Huson	.08	.03	.01
616	Mickey Weston	.08	.03	.01
617	John Pawlowski	.06	.02	.00
618A	Joe Skalski ERR (27 on back)	.06	.02	.00
618B	Joe Skalski COR (67 on back)	1.25	.50	.12
619	Bernie Williams	.60	.25	.06
620	Shawn Holman	.10	.04	.01
621	Gary Eave	.08	.03	.01
622	Darrin Fletcher UER (Elmherst, should be Elmhurst)	.15	.06	.01
623	Pat Combs	.06	.02	.00
624	Mike Blowers	.10	.04	.01
625	Kevin Appier	.20	.08	.02
626	Pat Austin	.08	.03	.01
627	Kelly Mann	.08	.03	.01
628	Matt Kinzer	.08	.03	.01
629	Chris Hammond	.30	.12	.03
630	Dean Wilkins	.10	.04	.01
631	Larry Walker UER (Uniform number 55 on front and 33 on back)	.25	.10	.02
632	Blaine Beatty	.10	.04	.01
633A	Tommy Barrett ERR (29 on back)	.08	.03	.01
633B	Tommy Barrett COR (14 on back)	3.50	1.50	.35
634	Stan Belinda	.12	.05	.01
635	Mike (Tex) Smith	.08	.03	.01
636	Hensley Meulens	.12	.05	.01
637	Juan Gonzalez	2.00	.80	.20
638	Lenny Webster	.12	.05	.01
639	Mark Gardner	.17	.07	.01
640	Tommy Greene	.25	.10	.02
641	Mike Hartley	.15	.06	.01
642	Phil Stephenson	.06	.02	.00
643	Kevin Mmahat	.10	.04	.01
644	Ed Whited	.10	.04	.01
645	Delino DeShields	.45	.18	.04
646	Kevin Blankenship	.03	.01	.00
647	Paul Sorrento	.10	.04	.01
648	Mike Roesler	.10	.04	.01
649	Jason Grimsley	.08	.03	.01
650	Dave Justice	2.50	1.00	.25
651	Scott Cooper	.45	.18	.04
652	Dave Eiland	.06	.02	.00
653	Mike Munoz	.08	.03	.01
654	Jeff Fischer	.08	.03	.01
655	Terry Jorgenson	.08	.03	.01
656	George Canale	.10	.04	.01
657	Brian Dubois	.10	.04	.01
658	Carlos Quintana	.06	.02	.00
659	Luis De Los Santos	.03	.01	.00
660	Jerald Clark	.03	.01	.00
661	Donald Harris DC	.12	.05	.01
662	Paul Coleman DC	.17	.07	.01
663	Frank Thomas DC	6.00	2.50	.60
664	Brent Mayne DC	.20	.08	.02
665	Eddie Zosky DC	.35	.15	.03
666	Steve Hosey DC	.17	.07	.01
667	Scott Bryant DC	.17	.07	.01
668	Tom Goodwin DC	.35	.15	.03
669	Cal Eldred DC	.12	.05	.01
670	Earl Cunningham DC	.15	.06	.01
671	Alan Zinter DC	.10	.04	.01
672	Chuck Knoblauch DC	2.00	.80	.20
673	Kyle Abbott DC	.35	.15	.03
674	Roger Salkeld DC	.75	.30	.07
675	Maurice Vaughn DC	1.50	.60	.15

		MINT	EXC	G-VG
☐ 676	Keith (Kiki) Jones DC	.20	.08	.02
☐ 677	Tyler Houston DC	.12	.05	.01
☐ 678	Jeff Jackson DC	.10	.04	.01
☐ 679	Greg Gohr DC	.20	.08	.02
☐ 680	Ben McDonald DC	.75	.30	.07
☐ 681	Greg Blosser DC	.25	.10	.02
☐ 682	Willie Green DC UER (Name misspelled on card, should be Greene)	.15	.06	.01
☐ 683	Wade Boggs DT UER (Text says 215 hits in '89, should be 205)	.10	.04	.01
☐ 684	Will Clark DT	.15	.06	.01
☐ 685	Tony Gwynn DT UER (Text reads batting instead of batting)	.08	.03	.01
☐ 686	Rickey Henderson DT	.15	.06	.01
☐ 687	Bo Jackson DT	.25	.10	.02
☐ 688	Mark Langston DT	.06	.02	.00
☐ 689	Barry Larkin DT	.08	.03	.01
☐ 690	Kirby Puckett DT	.10	.04	.01
☐ 691	Ryne Sandberg DT	.15	.06	.01
☐ 692	Mike Scott DT	.06	.02	.00
☐ 693A	Terry Steinbach DT ERR (cathers)	.06	.02	.00
☐ 693B	Terry Steinbach DT COR (catchers)	.25	.10	.02
☐ 694	Bobby Thigpen DT	.06	.02	.00
☐ 695	Mitch Williams DT	.06	.02	.00
☐ 696	Nolan Ryan HL	.25	.10	.02
☐ 697	Bo Jackson FB/BB	3.50	1.50	.35
☐ 698	Rickey Henderson ALCS-MVP	.12	.05	.01
☐ 699	Will Clark NLCS-MVP	.12	.05	.01
☐ 700	WS Games 1/2	.06	.02	.00
☐ 701	Candlestick	.08	.03	.01
☐ 702	WS Game 3	.06	.02	.00
☐ 703	WS Wrap-up	.06	.02	.00
☐ 704	Wade Boggs HL	.10	.04	.01

1990 Score Dream Team Rookies

The 1990 Score Dream Team Rookies Insert contains ten standard-size (2 1/2" by 3 1/2") cards. The ten cards represent one player for each position and Bart Giamatti. The sets were inserted in the Score factory collated sets hobby dealers received early in 1990, but not the retail sets issued later in 1990. Card B1 is a special commemorative card of the late Commissioner A. Bartlett Giamatti.

		MINT	EXC	G-VG
COMPLETE SET (10)		10.00	4.50	1.25
COMMON PLAYER (B1-B10)		.25	.10	.02
☐ B1	A.Bartlett Giamatti (late Commissioner)	1.00	.40	.10
☐ B2	Pat Combs	.35	.15	.03
☐ B3	Todd Zeile	2.00	.80	.20
☐ B4	Luis de los Santos	.25	.10	.02
☐ B5	Mark Lemke	.60	.25	.06
☐ B6	Robin Ventura	5.00	2.25	.50
☐ B7	Jeff Huson	.25	.10	.02
☐ B8	Greg Vaughn	3.50	1.50	.35
☐ B9	Marquis Grissom	2.25	.90	.22
☐ B10	Eric Anthony	.60	.25	.06

1990 Score Commemorative Nolan Ryan

This 2 1/2" by 3 1/2" card was issued by Optigraphics (producer of Score and Sportflics) to commemorate the 11th National Sports Card Collectors Convention held in Arlington, Texas in July of 1990. This card featured a Score front similar to the Ryan 1990 Score highlight card except for the 11th National Convention Logo on the bottom right of the card. On the other side a Ryan Sportflics card was printed that stated (reflected) either Sportflics or 1990 National Sports Collectors Convention on the bottom of the card This issue was limited to a printing of 600 cards with Ryan himself destroying the presses.

	MINT	EXC	G-VG
☐ xx Nolan Ryan (no number on back; card back is actually another front in Sportflics style)	750.00	325.00	110.00

1990 Score Young Superstars I

1990 Score Young Superstars I are glossy full color cards featuring 42 of the most popular young players. The first series was issued with Score rak packs while the second series was available only via a mailaway from the Company. The set contains standard-size (2 1/2" by 3 1/2") cards.

		MINT	EXC	G-VG
COMPLETE SET (42)		6.00	2.50	.60
COMMON PLAYER (1-42)		.15	.06	.01
☐ 1	Bo Jackson	1.00	.40	.10
☐ 2	Dwight Smith	.20	.08	.02
☐ 3	Joey Belle	.60	.25	.06
☐ 4	Gregg Olson	.25	.10	.02
☐ 5	Jim Abbott	.60	.25	.06
☐ 6	Felix Fermin	.15	.06	.01
☐ 7	Brian Holman	.20	.08	.02
☐ 8	Clay Parker	.15	.06	.01

		MINT	EXC	G-VG
☐ 9	Junior Felix	.20	.08	.02
☐ 10	Joe Oliver	.15	.06	.01
☐ 11	Steve Finley	.25	.10	.02
☐ 12	Greg Briley	.20	.08	.02
☐ 13	Greg Vaughn	.50	.20	.05
☐ 14	Bill Spiers	.20	.08	.02
☐ 15	Eric Yelding	.20	.08	.02
☐ 16	Jose Gonzalez	.15	.06	.01
☐ 17	Mark Carreon	.15	.06	.01
☐ 18	Greg W. Harris	.20	.08	.02
☐ 19	Felix Jose	.50	.20	.05
☐ 20	Bob Milacki	.15	.06	.01
☐ 21	Kenny Rogers	.15	.06	.01
☐ 22	Rolando Roomes	.15	.06	.01
☐ 23	Bip Roberts	.20	.08	.02
☐ 24	Jeff Brantley	.15	.06	.01
☐ 25	Jeff Ballard	.20	.08	.02
☐ 26	John Dopson	.15	.06	.01
☐ 27	Ken Patterson	.15	.06	.01
☐ 28	Omar Vizquel	.15	.06	.01
☐ 29	Kevin Brown	.20	.08	.02
☐ 30	Derek Lilliquist	.15	.06	.01
☐ 31	David Wells	.20	.08	.02
☐ 32	Ken Hill	.20	.08	.02
☐ 33	Greg Litton	.15	.06	.01
☐ 34	Rob Ducey	.20	.08	.02
☐ 35	Carlos Martinez	.20	.08	.02
☐ 36	John Smoltz	.45	.18	.04
☐ 37	Lenny Harris	.20	.08	.02
☐ 38	Charlie Hayes	.25	.10	.02
☐ 39	Tommy Gregg	.15	.06	.01
☐ 40	John Wetteland	.25	.10	.02
☐ 41	Jeff Huson	.15	.06	.01
☐ 42	Eric Anthony	.25	.10	.02

		MINT	EXC	G-VG
☐ 20	Greg Hibbard	.20	.08	.02
☐ 21	Stan Javier	.15	.06	.01
☐ 22	Mark Lemke	.20	.08	.02
☐ 23	Steve Olin	.15	.06	.01
☐ 24	Tommy Greene	.25	.10	.02
☐ 25	Sammy Sosa	.30	.12	.03
☐ 26	Gary Wayne	.15	.06	.01
☐ 27	Deion Sanders	.35	.15	.03
☐ 28	Steve Wilson	.15	.06	.01
☐ 29	Joe Girardi	.20	.08	.02
☐ 30	John Orton	.20	.08	.02
☐ 31	Kevin Tapani	.35	.15	.03
☐ 32	Carlos Baerga	.40	.16	.04
☐ 33	Glenallen Hill	.25	.10	.02
☐ 34	Mike Blowers	.20	.08	.02
☐ 35	Dave Hollins	.25	.10	.02
☐ 36	Lance Blankenship	.15	.06	.01
☐ 37	Hal Morris	.40	.16	.04
☐ 38	Lance Johnson	.20	.08	.02
☐ 39	Chris Gwynn	.20	.08	.02
☐ 40	Doug Dascenzo	.15	.06	.01
☐ 41	Jerald Clark	.20	.08	.02
☐ 42	Carlos Quintana	.30	.12	.03

1990 Score McDonald's

This 25-card set was produced by Score for McDonald's restaurants; included with the set were 15 World Series Trivia cards. The player cards were given away four to a pack and free with the purchase of fries and a drink, at only 11 McDonald's in the United States (in Idaho and Eastern Oregon during a special promotion which lasted approximately three weeks. The cards measure the standard size (2 1/2" by 3 1/2"). The front has color action player photos, with white and yellow borders on a purple card face that fades as one moves toward the middle of the card. The upper left corner of the picture is cut off to allow space for the McDonald's logo; the player's name and team logo at the bottom round out the card face. The backs have color mugshots, biography, statistics, and career summary. The cards are numbered on the back.

1990 Score Young Superstars II

1990 Score Young Superstars II are glossy full color cards featuring 42 of the most popular young players. Whereas the first series was issued with Score rack packs, this second series was available only via a mailaway from the Company. The set contains standard-size (2 1/2" by 3 1/2") cards.

		MINT	EXC	G-VG
COMPLETE SET (42)		6.00	2.50	.60
COMMON PLAYER (1-42)		.15	.06	.01
☐ 1	Todd Zeile	.40	.16	.04
☐ 2	Ben McDonald	.40	.16	.04
☐ 3	Delino DeShields	.40	.16	.04
☐ 4	Pat Combs	.20	.08	.02
☐ 5	John Olerud	.60	.25	.06
☐ 6	Marquis Grissom	.35	.15	.03
☐ 7	Mike Stanton	.20	.08	.02
☐ 8	Robin Ventura	.75	.30	.07
☐ 9	Larry Walker	.30	.12	.03
☐ 10	Dante Bichette	.20	.08	.02
☐ 11	Jack Armstrong	.20	.08	.02
☐ 12	Jay Bell	.25	.10	.02
☐ 13	Andy Benes	.40	.16	.04
☐ 14	Joey Cora	.20	.08	.02
☐ 15	Rob Dibble	.35	.15	.03
☐ 16	Jeff King	.20	.08	.02
☐ 17	Jeff Hamilton	.20	.08	.02
☐ 18	Erik Hanson	.30	.12	.03
☐ 19	Pete Harnisch	.25	.10	.02

		MINT	EXC	G-VG
COMPLETE SET (25)		125.00	57.50	18.75
COMMON PLAYER (1-25)		3.00	1.25	.30
☐ 1	Will Clark	15.00	6.50	2.15
☐ 2	Sandy Alomar Jr.	6.00	2.50	.60
☐ 3	Julio Franco	5.00	2.25	.50
☐ 4	Carlton Fisk	7.50	3.25	.75
☐ 5	Rickey Henderson	15.00	6.50	2.15
☐ 6	Matt Williams	6.00	2.50	.60
☐ 7	John Franco	3.00	1.25	.30
☐ 8	Ryne Sandberg	12.00	5.25	1.50
☐ 9	Kelly Gruber	3.00	1.25	.30
☐ 10	Andre Dawson	6.00	2.50	.60
☐ 11	Barry Bonds	7.50	3.25	.75
☐ 12	Gary Sheffield	4.00	1.75	.40
☐ 13	Ramon Martinez	7.50	3.25	.75
☐ 14	Len Dykstra	4.00	1.75	.40
☐ 15	Benito Santiago	5.00	2.25	.50
☐ 16	Cecil Fielder	9.00	4.00	.90
☐ 17	John Olerud	7.50	3.25	.75
☐ 18	Roger Clemens	12.00	5.25	1.50
☐ 19	George Brett	7.50	3.25	.75

☐ 20	George Bell	5.00	2.25	.50
☐ 21	Ozzie Guillen	3.00	1.25	.30
☐ 22	Steve Sax	3.00	1.25	.30
☐ 23	Dave Stewart	3.00	1.25	.30
☐ 24	Ozzie Smith	5.00	2.25	.50
☐ 25	Robin Yount	7.50	3.25	.75

1990 Score Nat West Yankees

1990 Score National Westminster Bank Yankees is a 32-card, standard-size (2 1/2" by 3 1/2") set featuring members of the 1990 New York Yankees. This set also has a special Billy Martin memorial card which honored the late Yankee manager who died in a truck accident on 12/25/89.

		MINT	EXC	G-VG
COMPLETE SET (32)		13.50	6.00	1.85
COMMON PLAYER (1-32)		.35	.15	.03
☐ 1	Stump Merrill MG	.45	.18	.04
☐ 2	Don Mattingly	1.50	.60	.15
☐ 3	Steve Sax	.60	.25	.06
☐ 4	Alvaro Espinoza	.35	.15	.03
☐ 5	Jesse Barfield	.60	.25	.06
☐ 6	Roberto Kelly	.90	.40	.09
☐ 7	Mel Hall	.45	.18	.04
☐ 8	Claudell Washington	.45	.18	.04
☐ 9	Bob Geren	.45	.18	.04
☐ 10	Jim Leyritz	.35	.15	.03
☐ 11	Pascual Perez	.45	.18	.04
☐ 12	Dave LaPoint	.35	.15	.03
☐ 13	Tim Leary	.45	.18	.04
☐ 14	Mike Witt	.35	.15	.03
☐ 15	Chuck Cary	.35	.15	.03
☐ 16	Dave Righetti	.45	.18	.04
☐ 17	Lee Guetterman	.35	.15	.03
☐ 18	Andy Hawkins	.35	.15	.03
☐ 19	Greg Cadaret	.35	.15	.03
☐ 20	Eric Plunk	.35	.15	.03
☐ 21	Jimmy Jones	.35	.15	.03
☐ 22	Deion Sanders	.90	.40	.09
☐ 23	Jeff D. Robinson	.35	.15	.03
☐ 24	Matt Nokes	.60	.25	.06
☐ 25	Steve Balboni	.35	.15	.03
☐ 26	Wayne Tolleson	.35	.15	.03
☐ 27	Randy Velarde	.35	.15	.03
☐ 28	Rick Cerone	.35	.15	.03
☐ 29	Alan Mills	.45	.18	.04
☐ 30	Billy Martin (memorial)	.75	.30	.07
☐ 31	Stadium Card	.35	.15	.03
☐ 32	All-Time Yankee Record	.35	.15	.03

1990 Score 100 Rising Stars

The 1990 Score Rising Stars set contains 100 standard size (2 1/2" by 3 1/2") cards. The fronts are green, blue and white. The vertically-oriented backs feature a large color facial shot and

career highlights. The cards were distributed as a set in a blister pack, which also included a full color booklet with more information about each player.

		MINT	EXC	G-VG
COMPLETE SET (100)		12.00	5.25	1.50
COMMON PLAYER (1-100)		.05	.02	.00
☐ 1	Tom Gordon	.20	.08	.02
☐ 2	Jerome Walton	.25	.10	.02
☐ 3	Ken Griffey Jr.	1.00	.40	.10
☐ 4	Dwight Smith	.15	.06	.01
☐ 5	Jim Abbott	.60	.25	.06
☐ 6	Todd Zeile	.40	.16	.04
☐ 7	Donn Pall	.05	.02	.00
☐ 8	Rick Reed	.05	.02	.00
☐ 9	Joey Belle	.50	.20	.05
☐ 10	Gregg Jefferies	.30	.12	.03
☐ 11	Kevin Ritz	.10	.04	.01
☐ 12	Charlie Hayes	.10	.04	.01
☐ 13	Kevin Appier	.20	.08	.02
☐ 14	Jeff Huson	.05	.02	.00
☐ 15	Gary Wayne	.10	.04	.01
☐ 16	Eric Yelding	.05	.02	.00
☐ 17	Clay Parker	.05	.02	.00
☐ 18	Junior Felix	.15	.06	.01
☐ 19	Derek Lilliquist	.05	.02	.00
☐ 20	Gary Sheffield	.25	.10	.02
☐ 21	Craig Worthington	.10	.04	.01
☐ 22	Jeff Brantley	.10	.04	.01
☐ 23	Eric Hetzel	.05	.02	.00
☐ 24	Greg W.Harris	.10	.04	.01
☐ 25	John Wetteland	.15	.06	.01
☐ 26	Joe Oliver	.10	.04	.01
☐ 27	Kevin Maas	.75	.30	.07
☐ 28	Kevin Brown	.10	.04	.01
☐ 29	Mike Stanton	.10	.04	.01
☐ 30	Greg Vaughn	.35	.15	.03
☐ 31	Ron Jones	.10	.04	.01
☐ 32	Gregg Olson	.25	.10	.02
☐ 33	Joe Girardi	.10	.04	.01
☐ 34	Ken Hill	.10	.04	.01
☐ 35	Sammy Sosa	.30	.12	.03
☐ 36	Geronimo Berroa	.05	.02	.00
☐ 37	Omar Vizquel	.05	.02	.00
☐ 38	Dean Palmer	.40	.16	.04
☐ 39	John Olerud	.75	.30	.07
☐ 40	Deion Sanders	.40	.16	.04
☐ 41	Randy Kramer	.05	.02	.00
☐ 42	Scott Lusader	.05	.02	.00
☐ 43	Dave Johnson (P)	.05	.02	.00
☐ 44	Jeff Wetherby	.10	.04	.01
☐ 45	Eric Anthony	.25	.10	.02
☐ 46	Kenny Rogers	.05	.02	.00
☐ 47	Matt Winters	.10	.04	.01
☐ 48	Mauro Gozzo	.10	.04	.01
☐ 49	Carlos Quintana	.15	.06	.01
☐ 50	Bob Geren	.05	.02	.00
☐ 51	Chad Kreuter	.05	.02	.00
☐ 52	Randy Johnson	.15	.06	.01
☐ 53	Hensley Meulens	.25	.10	.02
☐ 54	Gene Harris	.10	.04	.01
☐ 55	Bill Spiers	.10	.04	.01
☐ 56	Kelly Mann	.10	.04	.01
☐ 57	Tom McCarthy	.10	.04	.01
☐ 58	Steve Finley	.15	.06	.01
☐ 59	Ramon Martinez	.50	.20	.05
☐ 60	Greg Briley	.10	.04	.01
☐ 61	Jack Daugherty	.05	.02	.00
☐ 62	Tim Jones	.05	.02	.00
☐ 63	Doug Strange	.10	.04	.01
☐ 64	John Orton	.10	.04	.01

		MINT	EXC	G-VG
☐ 65	Scott Scudder	.15	.06	.01
☐ 66	Mark Gardner	.10	.04	.01
☐ 67	Mark Carreon	.05	.02	.00
☐ 68	Bob Milacki	.10	.04	.01
☐ 69	Andy Benes	.45	.18	.04
☐ 70	Carlos Martinez	.10	.04	.01
☐ 71	Jeff King	.10	.04	.01
☐ 72	Brad Arnsberg	.10	.04	.01
☐ 73	Rick Wrona	.10	.04	.01
☐ 74	Cris Carpenter	.10	.04	.01
☐ 75	Dennis Cook	.10	.04	.01
☐ 76	Pete Harnisch	.15	.06	.01
☐ 77	Greg Hibbard	.10	.04	.01
☐ 78	Ed Whited	.10	.04	.01
☐ 79	Scott Coolbaugh	.10	.04	.01
☐ 80	Billy Bates	.10	.04	.01
☐ 81	German Gonzalez	.05	.02	.00
☐ 82	Lance Blankenship	.05	.02	.00
☐ 83	Lenny Harris	.15	.06	.01
☐ 84	Milt Cuyler	.35	.15	.03
☐ 85	Erik Hanson	.25	.10	.02
☐ 86	Kent Anderson	.05	.02	.00
☐ 87	Hal Morris	.50	.20	.05
☐ 88	Mike Brumley	.05	.02	.00
☐ 89	Ken Patterson	.10	.04	.01
☐ 90	Mike Devereaux	.10	.04	.01
☐ 91	Greg Litton	.05	.02	.00
☐ 92	Rolando Roomes	.05	.02	.00
☐ 93	Ben McDonald	.50	.20	.05
☐ 94	Curt Schilling	.05	.02	.00
☐ 95	Jose DeJesus	.10	.04	.01
☐ 96	Robin Ventura	.75	.30	.07
☐ 97	Steve Searcy	.05	.02	.00
☐ 98	Chip Hale	.05	.02	.00
☐ 99	Marquis Grissom	.35	.15	.03
☐ 100	Luis de los Santos	.10	.04	.01

1990 Score 100 Superstars

The 1990 Score Superstars set contains 100 standard size (2 1/2" by 3 1/2") cards. The fronts are red, white, blue and purple. The vertically-oriented backs feature a large color facial shot and career highlights. The cards were distributed as a set in a blister pack, which also included a full color booklet with more information about each player.

		MINT	EXC	G-VG
	COMPLETE SET (100)	12.00	5.25	1.50
	COMMON PLAYER (1-100)	.05	.02	.00
☐ 1	Kirby Puckett	.45	.18	.04
☐ 2	Steve Sax	.15	.06	.01
☐ 3	Tony Gwynn	.50	.20	.05
☐ 4	Willie Randolph	.10	.04	.01
☐ 5	Jose Canseco	.90	.40	.09
☐ 6	Ozzie Smith	.25	.10	.02
☐ 7	Rick Reuschel	.10	.04	.01
☐ 8	Bill Doran	.05	.02	.00
☐ 9	Mickey Tettleton	.15	.06	.01
☐ 10	Don Mattingly	.60	.25	.06
☐ 11	Greg Swindell	.15	.06	.01
☐ 12	Bert Blyleven	.10	.04	.01
☐ 13	Dave Stewart	.15	.06	.01
☐ 14	Andres Galarraga	.10	.04	.01
☐ 15	Darryl Strawberry	.60	.25	.06

		MINT	EXC	G-VG
☐ 16	Ellis Burks	.30	.12	.03
☐ 17	Paul O'Neill	.15	.06	.01
☐ 18	Bruce Hurst	.10	.04	.01
☐ 19	Dave Smith	.05	.02	.00
☐ 20	Carney Lansford	.10	.04	.01
☐ 21	Robby Thompson	.05	.02	.00
☐ 22	Gary Gaetti	.10	.04	.01
☐ 23	Jeff Russell	.05	.02	.00
☐ 24	Chuck Finley	.15	.06	.01
☐ 25	Mark McGwire	.50	.20	.05
☐ 26	Alvin Davis	.05	.02	.00
☐ 27	George Bell	.15	.06	.01
☐ 28	Cory Snyder	.10	.04	.01
☐ 29	Keith Hernandez	.10	.04	.01
☐ 30	Will Clark	.90	.40	.09
☐ 31	Steve Bedrosian	.05	.02	.00
☐ 32	Ryne Sandberg	.75	.30	.07
☐ 33	Tom Browning	.10	.04	.01
☐ 34	Tim Burke	.05	.02	.00
☐ 35	John Smoltz	.25	.10	.02
☐ 36	Phil Bradley	.05	.02	.00
☐ 37	Bobby Bonilla	.40	.16	.04
☐ 38	Kirk McCaskill	.05	.02	.00
☐ 39	Dave Righetti	.10	.04	.01
☐ 40	Bo Jackson	1.00	.40	.10
☐ 41	Alan Trammell	.15	.06	.01
☐ 42	Mike Moore UER	.05	.02	.00
	(Uniform number is 21, not 23 as on front)			
☐ 43	Harold Reynolds	.10	.04	.01
☐ 44	Nolan Ryan	1.00	.40	.10
☐ 45	Fred McGriff	.35	.15	.03
☐ 46	Brian Downing	.05	.02	.00
☐ 47	Brett Butler	.10	.04	.01
☐ 48	Mike Scioscia	.05	.02	.00
☐ 49	John Franco	.05	.02	.00
☐ 50	Kevin Mitchell	.40	.16	.04
☐ 51	Mark Davis	.05	.02	.00
☐ 52	Glenn Davis	.15	.06	.01
☐ 53	Barry Bonds	.45	.18	.04
☐ 54	Dwight Evans	.15	.06	.01
☐ 55	Terry Steinbach	.10	.04	.01
☐ 56	Dave Gallagher	.05	.02	.00
☐ 57	Roberto Kelly	.30	.12	.03
☐ 58	Rafael Palmeiro	.25	.10	.02
☐ 59	Joe Carter	.25	.10	.02
☐ 60	Mark Grace	.60	.25	.06
☐ 61	Pedro Guerrero	.10	.04	.01
☐ 62	Von Hayes	.10	.04	.01
☐ 63	Benito Santiago	.20	.08	.02
☐ 64	Dale Murphy	.40	.16	.04
☐ 65	John Smiley	.05	.02	.00
☐ 66	Cal Ripken	.75	.30	.07
☐ 67	Mike Greenwell	.25	.10	.02
☐ 68	Devon White	.10	.04	.01
☐ 69	Ed Whitson	.05	.02	.00
☐ 70	Carlton Fisk	.30	.12	.03
☐ 71	Lou Whitaker	.10	.04	.01
☐ 72	Danny Tartabull	.25	.10	.02
☐ 73	Vince Coleman	.20	.08	.02
☐ 74	Andre Dawson	.30	.12	.03
☐ 75	Tim Raines	.20	.08	.02
☐ 76	George Brett	.35	.15	.03
☐ 77	Tom Herr	.05	.02	.00
☐ 78	Andy Van Slyke	.10	.04	.01
☐ 79	Roger Clemens	.90	.40	.09
☐ 80	Wade Boggs	.60	.25	.06
☐ 81	Wally Joyner	.25	.10	.02
☐ 82	Lonnie Smith	.10	.04	.01
☐ 83	Howard Johnson	.20	.08	.02
☐ 84	Julio Franco	.20	.08	.02
☐ 85	Ruben Sierra	.50	.20	.05
☐ 86	Dan Plesac	.05	.02	.00
☐ 87	Bobby Thigpen	.15	.06	.01
☐ 88	Kevin Seitzer	.10	.04	.01
☐ 89	Dave Stieb	.15	.06	.01
☐ 90	Rickey Henderson	.75	.30	.07
☐ 91	Jeffrey Leonard	.05	.02	.00
☐ 92	Robin Yount	.40	.16	.04
☐ 93	Mitch Williams	.10	.04	.01
☐ 94	Orel Hershiser	.20	.08	.02
☐ 95	Eric Davis	.40	.16	.04
☐ 96	Mark Langston	.10	.04	.01
☐ 97	Mike Scott	.10	.04	.01
☐ 98	Paul Molitor	.10	.04	.01
☐ 99	Dwight Gooden	.25	.10	.02
☐ 100	Kevin Bass	.10	.04	.01

1990 Score Traded

The 1990 Score Rookie/Traded set marks the fourth consecutive year Score has issued an end of the year set to mark trades and give rookies early cards. This now-standard set consists of 110 cards; cards measure the standard size of 2 1/2" by 3 1/2". The first 66 cards are traded players while the last 44 cards are rookie cards. Included in the rookie part of the set are cross-athletes Eric Lindros (hockey) and D.J. Dozier (football). The key baseball player rookie cards in the set are Derek Bell and Ray Lankford.

	MINT	EXC	G-VG
COMPLETE SET (110)	20.00	8.50	2.75
COMMON PLAYER (1-66)	.06	.02	.00
COMMON PLAYER (67-110)	.10	.04	.01

		MINT	EXC	G-VG
☐ 1T	Dave Winfield	.15	.06	.01
☐ 2T	Kevin Bass	.06	.02	.00
☐ 3T	Nick Esasky	.06	.02	.00
☐ 4T	Mitch Webster	.06	.02	.00
☐ 5T	Pascual Perez	.06	.02	.00
☐ 6T	Gary Pettis	.06	.02	.00
☐ 7T	Tony Pena	.10	.04	.01
☐ 8T	Candy Maldonado	.10	.04	.01
☐ 9T	Cecil Fielder	.35	.15	.03
☐ 10T	Carmelo Martinez	.06	.02	.00
☐ 11T	Mark Langston	.10	.04	.01
☐ 12T	Dave Parker	.10	.04	.01
☐ 13T	Don Slaught	.06	.02	.00
☐ 14T	Tony Phillips	.06	.02	.00
☐ 15T	John Franco	.10	.04	.01
☐ 16T	Randy Myers	.10	.04	.01
☐ 17T	Jeff Reardon	.12	.05	.01
☐ 18T	Sandy Alomar Jr.	.15	.06	.01
☐ 19T	Joe Carter	.12	.05	.01
☐ 20T	Fred Lynn	.10	.04	.01
☐ 21T	Storm Davis	.06	.02	.00
☐ 22T	Craig Lefferts	.06	.02	.00
☐ 23T	Pete O'Brien	.06	.02	.00
☐ 24T	Dennis Boyd	.06	.02	.00
☐ 25T	Lloyd Moseby	.06	.02	.00
☐ 26T	Mark Davis	.10	.04	.01
☐ 27T	Tim Leary	.10	.04	.01
☐ 28T	Gerald Perry	.06	.02	.00
☐ 29T	Don Aase	.06	.02	.00
☐ 30T	Ernie Whitt	.06	.02	.00
☐ 31T	Dale Murphy	.12	.05	.01
☐ 32T	Alejandro Pena	.10	.04	.01
☐ 33T	Juan Samuel	.10	.04	.01
☐ 34T	Hubie Brooks	.10	.04	.01
☐ 35T	Gary Carter	.12	.05	.01
☐ 36T	Jim Presley	.06	.02	.00
☐ 37T	Wally Backman	.06	.02	.00
☐ 38T	Matt Nokes	.10	.04	.01
☐ 39T	Dan Petry	.06	.02	.00
☐ 40T	Franklin Stubbs	.06	.02	.00
☐ 41T	Jeff Huson	.10	.04	.01
☐ 42T	Billy Hatcher	.10	.04	.01
☐ 43T	Terry Leach	.06	.02	.00
☐ 44T	Phil Bradley	.06	.02	.00
☐ 45T	Claudell Washington	.06	.02	.00
☐ 46T	Luis Polonia	.06	.02	.00
☐ 47T	Daryl Boston	.06	.02	.00
☐ 48T	Lee Smith	.10	.04	.01
☐ 49T	Tom Brunansky	.10	.04	.01
☐ 50T	Mike Witt	.06	.02	.00
☐ 51T	Willie Randolph	.10	.04	.01
☐ 52T	Stan Javier	.06	.02	.00
☐ 53T	Brad Komminsk	.06	.02	.00
☐ 54T	John Candelaria	.06	.02	.00
☐ 55T	Bryn Smith	.06	.02	.00
☐ 56T	Glenn Braggs	.06	.02	.00
☐ 57T	Keith Hernandez	.12	.05	.01
☐ 58T	Ken Oberkfell	.06	.02	.00
☐ 59T	Steve Jeltz	.06	.02	.00
☐ 60T	Chris James	.10	.04	.01
☐ 61T	Scott Sanderson	.10	.04	.01
☐ 62T	Bill Long	.06	.02	.00
☐ 63T	Rick Cerone	.06	.02	.00
☐ 64T	Scott Bailes	.06	.02	.00
☐ 65T	Larry Sheets	.06	.02	.00
☐ 66T	Junior Ortiz	.06	.02	.00
☐ 67T	Francisco Cabrera	.12	.05	.01
☐ 68T	Gary DiSarcina	.12	.05	.01
☐ 69T	Greg Olson	.20	.08	.02
☐ 70T	Beau Allred	.12	.05	.01
☐ 71T	Oscar Azocar	.12	.05	.01
☐ 72T	Kent Mercker	.17	.07	.01
☐ 73T	John Burkett	.15	.06	.01
☐ 74T	Carlos Baerga	.60	.25	.06
☐ 75T	Dave Hollins	.40	.16	.04
☐ 76T	Todd Hundley	.50	.20	.05
☐ 77T	Rick Parker	.10	.04	.01
☐ 78T	Steve Cummings	.10	.04	.01
☐ 79T	Bill Sampen	.12	.05	.01
☐ 80T	Jerry Kutzler	.10	.04	.01
☐ 81T	Derek Bell	2.50	1.00	.25
☐ 82T	Kevin Tapani	.60	.25	.06
☐ 83T	Jim Leyritz	.10	.04	.01
☐ 84T	Ray Lankford	1.50	.60	.15
☐ 85T	Wayne Edwards	.10	.04	.01
☐ 86T	Frank Thomas	9.00	4.00	.90
☐ 87T	Tim Naehring	.25	.10	.02
☐ 88T	Willie Blair	.10	.04	.01
☐ 89T	Alan Mills	.12	.05	.01
☐ 90T	Scott Radinsky	.12	.05	.01
☐ 91T	Howard Farmer	.12	.05	.01
☐ 92T	Julio Machado	.10	.04	.01
☐ 93T	Rafael Valdez	.10	.04	.01
☐ 94T	Shawn Boskie	.12	.05	.01
☐ 95T	David Segui	.17	.07	.01
☐ 96T	Chris Hoiles	.20	.08	.02
☐ 97T	D.J. Dozier	.40	.16	.04
☐ 98T	Hector Villanueva	.12	.05	.01
☐ 99T	Eric Gunderson	.17	.07	.01
☐ 100T	Eric Lindros	6.50	2.75	.65
☐ 101T	Dave Otto	.10	.04	.01
☐ 102T	Dana Kiecker	.10	.04	.01
☐ 103T	Tim Drummond	.10	.04	.01
☐ 104T	Mickey Pina	.10	.04	.01
☐ 105T	Craig Grebeck	.10	.04	.01
☐ 106T	Bernard Gilkey	.50	.20	.05
☐ 107T	Tim Layana	.10	.04	.01
☐ 108T	Scott Chiamparino	.15	.06	.01
☐ 109T	Steve Avery	3.00	1.25	.30
☐ 110T	Terry Shumpert	.12	.05	.01

1991 Score

The 1991 Score set contains 893 cards. The cards feature a solid color border framing the full-color photo of the cards. The cards measure the standard card size of 2 1/2" by 3 1/2" and also feature Score trademark full-color photos on the back. The backs also include a brief biography on each player. This set marks the fourth consecutive year that Score has issued a major set but the first time Score issued the set in two series. Score also reused their successful Dream Team concept by using non-baseball photos of Today's stars. Series one contains 441 cards and ends with the Annie Leibowitz photo of Jose Canseco used in American Express ads. This first series also includes 49 Rookie prospects, 12 First Round Draft Picks and five each of the Master Blaster, K-Man, and Rifleman subsets. The All-Star sets in the first series are all American Leaguers (which are all caricatures). The key rookie cards in the first series are Jeromy Burnitz, Wes Chamberlain, Brian McRae, Marc Newfield, Phil Plantier, and Todd Van Poppel. There are a number of pitchers whose card backs show Innings Pitched totals which do not equal the added year-by-year total; the following card numbers were affected, 4, 24, 29, 30, 51, 81, 109, 111, 118, 141, 150, 156, 177, 204, 218, 232, 235, 255, 287, 289, 311, and 328. The second series was issued approximately three months after the release of Series One and included many of the special cards Score is noted for, e.g., the continuation of the Dream Team set begun in Series One, All-Star Cartoons featuring National Leaguers, a continuation of the 1990 first round draft picks, and 61 rookie prospects.

	MINT	EXC	G-VG
COMPLETE SET (893)	22.50	9.75	3.25
COMMON PLAYER (1-441)	.03	.01	.00
COMMON PLAYER (442-893)	.03	.01	.00

		MINT	EXC	G-VG
☐ 1	Jose Canseco	.25	.10	.02
☐ 2	Ken Griffey Jr.	.75	.30	.07
☐ 3	Ryne Sandberg	.20	.08	.02
☐ 4	Nolan Ryan	.35	.15	.03
☐ 5	Bo Jackson	.25	.10	.02
☐ 6	Bret Saberhagen UER (In bio, missed misspelled as mised)	.08	.03	.01
☐ 7	Will Clark	.20	.08	.02
☐ 8	Ellis Burks	.08	.03	.01
☐ 9	Joe Carter	.10	.04	.01
☐ 10	Rickey Henderson	.20	.08	.02
☐ 11	Ozzie Guillen	.06	.02	.00
☐ 12	Wade Boggs	.12	.05	.01
☐ 13	Jerome Walton	.08	.03	.01
☐ 14	John Franco	.03	.01	.00
☐ 15	Ricky Jordan UER (League misspelled as legue)	.06	.02	.00
☐ 16	Wally Backman	.03	.01	.00
☐ 17	Rob Dibble	.06	.02	.00
☐ 18	Glenn Braggs	.03	.01	.00
☐ 19	Cory Snyder	.06	.02	.00
☐ 20	Kal Daniels	.06	.02	.00
☐ 21	Mark Langston	.06	.02	.00
☐ 22	Kevin Gross	.03	.01	.00
☐ 23	Don Mattingly UER (First line, ' is missing from Yankee)	.12	.05	.01
☐ 24	Dave Righetti	.06	.02	.00
☐ 25	Roberto Alomar	.12	.05	.01
☐ 26	Robby Thompson	.03	.01	.00
☐ 27	Jack McDowell	.06	.02	.00
☐ 28	Bip Roberts UER (Bio reads playd)	.03	.01	.00
☐ 29	Jay Howell	.03	.01	.00
☐ 30	Dave Stieb UER (17 wins in bio, 18 in stats)	.06	.02	.00
☐ 31	Johnny Ray	.03	.01	.00
☐ 32	Steve Sax	.06	.02	.00
☐ 33	Terry Mulholland	.03	.01	.00
☐ 34	Lee Guetterman	.03	.01	.00
☐ 35	Tim Raines	.08	.03	.01
☐ 36	Scott Fletcher	.03	.01	.00
☐ 37	Lance Parrish	.06	.02	.00
☐ 38	Tony Phillips UER (Born 4/15, should be 4/25)	.03	.01	.00
☐ 39	Todd Stottlemyre	.06	.02	.00
☐ 40	Alan Trammell	.08	.03	.01
☐ 41	Todd Burns	.03	.01	.00
☐ 42	Mookie Wilson	.03	.01	.00
☐ 43	Chris Bosio	.03	.01	.00
☐ 44	Jeffrey Leonard	.03	.01	.00
☐ 45	Doug Jones	.03	.01	.00
☐ 46	Mike Scott UER (in first line, dominate should read dominating)	.06	.02	.00
☐ 47	Andy Hawkins	.03	.01	.00
☐ 48	Harold Reynolds	.06	.02	.00
☐ 49	Paul Molitor	.08	.03	.01
☐ 50	John Farrell	.03	.01	.00
☐ 51	Danny Darwin	.03	.01	.00
☐ 52	Jeff Blauser	.03	.01	.00
☐ 53	John Tudor UER (41 wins in '81)	.06	.02	.00
☐ 54	Milt Thompson	.03	.01	.00
☐ 55	Dave Justice	.50	.20	.05
☐ 56	Greg Olson	.06	.02	.00
☐ 57	Willie Blair	.03	.01	.00
☐ 58	Rick Parker	.03	.01	.00
☐ 59	Shawn Boskie	.03	.01	.00
☐ 60	Kevin Tapani	.06	.02	.00
☐ 61	Dave Hollins	.08	.03	.01
☐ 62	Scott Radinsky	.06	.02	.00
☐ 63	Francisco Cabrera	.03	.01	.00
☐ 64	Tim Layana	.03	.01	.00
☐ 65	Jim Leyritz	.03	.01	.00
☐ 66	Wayne Edwards	.03	.01	.00
☐ 67	Lee Stevens	.08	.03	.01
☐ 68	Bill Sampen UER (Fourth line, long is spelled along)	.03	.01	.00
☐ 69	Craig Grebeck UER (Born in Cerritos, not Johnstown)	.03	.01	.00
☐ 70	John Burkett	.03	.01	.00
☐ 71	Hector Villanueva	.06	.02	.00
☐ 72	Oscar Azocar	.03	.01	.00
☐ 73	Alan Mills	.03	.01	.00
☐ 74	Carlos Baerga	.10	.04	.01
☐ 75	Charles Nagy	.10	.04	.01
☐ 76	Tim Drummond	.03	.01	.00
☐ 77	Dana Kiecker	.03	.01	.00
☐ 78	Tom Edens	.08	.03	.01
☐ 79	Kent Mercker	.06	.02	.00
☐ 80	Steve Avery	.30	.12	.03
☐ 81	Lee Smith	.06	.02	.00
☐ 82	Dave Martinez	.03	.01	.00
☐ 83	Dave Winfield	.10	.04	.01
☐ 84	Bill Spiers	.03	.01	.00
☐ 85	Dan Pasqua	.03	.01	.00
☐ 86	Randy Milligan	.06	.02	.00
☐ 87	Tracy Jones	.03	.01	.00
☐ 88	Greg Myers	.03	.01	.00
☐ 89	Keith Hernandez	.06	.02	.00
☐ 90	Todd Benzinger	.03	.01	.00
☐ 91	Mike Jackson	.03	.01	.00
☐ 92	Mike Stanley	.03	.01	.00
☐ 93	Candy Maldonado	.03	.01	.00
☐ 94	John Kruk UER (No decimal point before 1990 BA)	.03	.01	.00
☐ 95	Cal Ripken UER (Genius spelled genuis)	.20	.08	.02
☐ 96	Willie Fraser	.03	.01	.00
☐ 97	Mike Felder	.03	.01	.00
☐ 98	Bill Landrum	.03	.01	.00
☐ 99	Chuck Crim	.03	.01	.00
☐ 100	Chuck Finley	.06	.02	.00
☐ 101	Kirk Manwaring	.03	.01	.00
☐ 102	Jaime Navarro	.03	.01	.00
☐ 103	Dickie Thon	.03	.01	.00
☐ 104	Brian Downing	.03	.01	.00
☐ 105	Jim Abbott	.10	.04	.01
☐ 106	Tom Brookens	.03	.01	.00
☐ 107	Darryl Hamilton UER (Bio info is for Jeff Hamilton)	.03	.01	.00
☐ 108	Bryan Harvey	.06	.02	.00
☐ 109	Greg A. Harris UER (Shown pitching lefty, bio says righty)	.03	.01	.00
☐ 110	Greg Swindell	.06	.02	.00
☐ 111	Juan Berenguer	.03	.01	.00
☐ 112	Mike Heath	.03	.01	.00
☐ 113	Scott Bradley	.03	.01	.00
☐ 114	Jack Morris	.08	.03	.01
☐ 115	Barry Jones	.03	.01	.00
☐ 116	Kevin Romine	.03	.01	.00
☐ 117	Garry Templeton	.03	.01	.00
☐ 118	Scott Sanderson	.03	.01	.00
☐ 119	Roberto Kelly	.08	.03	.01
☐ 120	George Brett	.10	.04	.01
☐ 121	Oddibe McDowell	.03	.01	.00
☐ 122	Jim Acker	.03	.01	.00
☐ 123	Bill Swift UER (Born 12/27/61, should be 10/27)	.03	.01	.00
☐ 124	Eric King	.03	.01	.00
☐ 125	Jay Buhner	.06	.02	.00

☐ 126	Matt Young	.03	.01	.00
☐ 127	Alvaro Espinoza	.03	.01	.00
☐ 128	Greg Hibbard	.03	.01	.00
☐ 129	Jeff M. Robinson	.03	.01	.00
☐ 130	Mike Greenwell	.10	.04	.01
☐ 131	Dion James	.03	.01	.00
☐ 132	Donn Pall UER	.03	.01	.00
	(1988 ERA in stats 0.00)			
☐ 133	Lloyd Moseby	.03	.01	.00
☐ 134	Randy Velarde	.03	.01	.00
☐ 135	Allan Anderson	.03	.01	.00
☐ 136	Mark Davis	.03	.01	.00
☐ 137	Eric Davis	.10	.04	.01
☐ 138	Phil Stephenson	.03	.01	.00
☐ 139	Felix Fermin	.03	.01	.00
☐ 140	Pedro Guerrero	.06	.02	.00
☐ 141	Charlie Hough	.03	.01	.00
☐ 142	Mike Henneman	.03	.01	.00
☐ 143	Jeff Montgomery	.03	.01	.00
☐ 144	Lenny Harris	.03	.01	.00
☐ 145	Bruce Hurst	.06	.02	.00
☐ 146	Eric Anthony	.08	.03	.01
☐ 147	Paul Assenmacher	.03	.01	.00
☐ 148	Jesse Barfield	.06	.02	.00
☐ 149	Carlos Quintana	.06	.02	.00
☐ 150	Dave Stewart	.08	.03	.01
☐ 151	Roy Smith	.03	.01	.00
☐ 152	Paul Gibson	.03	.01	.00
☐ 153	Mickey Hatcher	.03	.01	.00
☐ 154	Jim Eisenreich	.03	.01	.00
☐ 155	Kenny Rogers	.03	.01	.00
☐ 156	Dave Schmidt	.03	.01	.00
☐ 157	Lance Johnson	.03	.01	.00
☐ 158	Dave West	.03	.01	.00
☐ 159	Steve Balboni	.03	.01	.00
☐ 160	Jeff Brantley	.03	.01	.00
☐ 161	Craig Biggio	.06	.02	.00
☐ 162	Brook Jacoby	.03	.01	.00
☐ 163	Dan Gladden	.03	.01	.00
☐ 164	Jeff Reardon UER	.06	.02	.00
	(Total IP shown as 943.2, should be 943.1)			
☐ 165	Mark Carreon	.03	.01	.00
☐ 166	Mel Hall	.03	.01	.00
☐ 167	Gary Mielke	.03	.01	.00
☐ 168	Cecil Fielder	.15	.06	.01
☐ 169	Darrin Jackson	.03	.01	.00
☐ 170	Rick Aguilera	.03	.01	.00
☐ 171	Walt Weiss	.06	.02	.00
☐ 172	Steve Farr	.03	.01	.00
☐ 173	Jody Reed	.06	.02	.00
☐ 174	Mike Jeffcoat	.03	.01	.00
☐ 175	Mark Grace	.08	.03	.01
☐ 176	Larry Sheets	.03	.01	.00
☐ 177	Bill Gullickson	.06	.02	.00
☐ 178	Chris Gwynn	.03	.01	.00
☐ 179	Melido Perez	.03	.01	.00
☐ 180	Sid Fernandez UER	.06	.02	.00
	(779 runs in 1990)			
☐ 181	Tim Burke	.03	.01	.00
☐ 182	Gary Pettis	.03	.01	.00
☐ 183	Rob Murphy	.03	.01	.00
☐ 184	Craig Lefferts	.03	.01	.00
☐ 185	Howard Johnson	.08	.03	.01
☐ 186	Ken Caminiti	.03	.01	.00
☐ 187	Tim Belcher	.06	.02	.00
☐ 188	Greg Cadaret	.03	.01	.00
☐ 189	Matt Williams	.10	.04	.01
☐ 190	Dave Magadan	.06	.02	.00
☐ 191	Geno Petralli	.03	.01	.00
☐ 192	Jeff D. Robinson	.03	.01	.00
☐ 193	Jim Deshaies	.03	.01	.00
☐ 194	Willie Randolph	.03	.01	.00
☐ 195	George Bell	.08	.03	.01
☐ 196	Hubie Brooks	.06	.02	.00
☐ 197	Tom Gordon	.06	.02	.00
☐ 198	Mike Fitzgerald	.03	.01	.00
☐ 199	Mike Pagliarulo	.03	.01	.00
☐ 200	Kirby Puckett	.12	.05	.01
☐ 201	Shawon Dunston	.06	.02	.00
☐ 202	Dennis Boyd	.03	.01	.00
☐ 203	Junior Felix UER	.06	.02	.00
	(Text has him in NL)			
☐ 204	Alejandro Pena	.06	.02	.00
☐ 205	Pete Smith	.03	.01	.00
☐ 206	Tom Glavine UER	.12	.05	.01
	(Lefty spelled leftie)			
☐ 207	Luis Salazar	.03	.01	.00
☐ 208	John Smoltz	.10	.04	.01
☐ 209	Doug Dascenzo	.03	.01	.00
☐ 210	Tim Wallach	.06	.02	.00
☐ 211	Greg Gagne	.03	.01	.00
☐ 212	Mark Gubicza	.03	.01	.00
☐ 213	Mark Parent	.03	.01	.00
☐ 214	Ken Oberkfell	.03	.01	.00
☐ 215	Gary Carter	.08	.03	.01
☐ 216	Rafael Palmeiro	.10	.04	.01
☐ 217	Tom Niedenfuer	.03	.01	.00
☐ 218	Dave LaPoint	.03	.01	.00
☐ 219	Jeff Treadway	.03	.01	.00
☐ 220	Mitch Williams UER	.03	.01	.00
	('89 ERA shown as 2.76, should be 2.64)			
☐ 221	Jose DeLeon	.03	.01	.00
☐ 222	Mike LaValliere	.03	.01	.00
☐ 223	Darrel Akerfelds	.03	.01	.00
☐ 224A	Kent Anderson ERR	.03	.01	.00
	(first line, flachy should read flashy)			
☐ 224B	Kent Anderson COR			
	(corrected in factory sets)			
☐ 225	Dwight Evans	.06	.02	.00
☐ 226	Gary Redus	.03	.01	.00
☐ 227	Paul O'Neill	.06	.02	.00
☐ 228	Marty Barrett	.03	.01	.00
☐ 229	Tom Browning	.06	.02	.00
☐ 230	Terry Pendleton	.03	.01	.00
☐ 231	Jack Armstrong	.06	.02	.00
☐ 232	Mike Boddicker	.03	.01	.00
☐ 233	Neal Heaton	.03	.01	.00
☐ 234	Marquis Grissom	.10	.04	.01
☐ 235	Bert Blyleven	.06	.02	.00
☐ 236	Curt Young	.03	.01	.00
☐ 237	Don Carman	.03	.01	.00
☐ 238	Charlie Hayes	.03	.01	.00
☐ 239	Mark Knudson	.03	.01	.00
☐ 240	Todd Zeile	.10	.04	.01
☐ 241	Larry Walker UER	.06	.02	.00
	(Maple River, should be Maple Ridge)			
☐ 242	Jerald Clark	.03	.01	.00
☐ 243	Jeff Ballard	.03	.01	.00
☐ 244	Jeff King	.03	.01	.00
☐ 245	Tom Brunansky	.06	.02	.00
☐ 246	Darren Daulton	.03	.01	.00
☐ 247	Scott Terry	.03	.01	.00
☐ 248	Rob Deer	.06	.02	.00
☐ 249	Brady Anderson UER	.03	.01	.00
	(1990 Hagerstown 1 hit, should say 13 hits)			
☐ 250	Len Dykstra	.06	.02	.00
☐ 251	Greg W. Harris	.03	.01	.00
☐ 252	Mike Hartley	.03	.01	.00
☐ 253	Joey Cora	.03	.01	.00
☐ 254	Ivan Calderon	.06	.02	.00
☐ 255	Ted Power	.03	.01	.00
☐ 256	Sammy Sosa	.08	.03	.01
☐ 257	Steve Buechele	.03	.01	.00
☐ 258	Mike Devereaux UER	.03	.01	.00
	(No comma between city and state)			
☐ 259	Brad Komminsk UER	.03	.01	.00
	(Last text line, Ba should be BA)			
☐ 260	Teddy Higuera	.03	.01	.00
☐ 261	Shawn Abner	.03	.01	.00
☐ 262	Dave Valle	.03	.01	.00
☐ 263	Jeff Huson	.03	.01	.00
☐ 264	Edgar Martinez	.06	.02	.00
☐ 265	Carlton Fisk	.10	.04	.01
☐ 266	Steve Finley	.06	.02	.00
☐ 267	John Wetteland	.06	.02	.00
☐ 268	Kevin Appier	.06	.02	.00
☐ 269	Steve Lyons	.03	.01	.00
☐ 270	Mickey Tettleton	.06	.02	.00
☐ 271	Luis Rivera	.03	.01	.00
☐ 272	Steve Jeltz	.03	.01	.00
☐ 273	R.J. Reynolds	.03	.01	.00
☐ 274	Carlos Martinez	.03	.01	.00
☐ 275	Dan Plesac	.03	.01	.00
☐ 276	Mike Morgan UER	.03	.01	.00
	(Total IP shown as 1149.1, should be 1149)			
☐ 277	Jeff Russell	.03	.01	.00
☐ 278	Pete Incaviglia	.06	.02	.00
☐ 279	Kevin Seitzer UER	.06	.02	.00
	(Bio has 200 hits twice and .300 four times, should be once and three times)			
☐ 280	Bobby Thigpen	.06	.02	.00
☐ 281	Stan Javier UER	.03	.01	.00
	(Born 1/9, should say 9/1)			
☐ 282	Henry Cotto	.03	.01	.00
☐ 283	Gary Wayne	.03	.01	.00
☐ 284	Shane Mack	.06	.02	.00

☐ 285	Brian Holman	.06	.02	.00
☐ 286	Gerald Perry	.03	.01	.00
☐ 287	Steve Crawford	.03	.01	.00
☐ 288	Nelson Liriano	.03	.01	.00
☐ 289	Don Aase	.03	.01	.00
☐ 290	Randy Johnson	.06	.02	.00
☐ 291	Harold Baines	.06	.02	.00
☐ 292	Kent Hrbek	.06	.02	.00
☐ 293A	Les Lancaster ERR	.06	.02	.00
	(No comma between			
	Dallas and Texas)			
☐ 293B	Les Lancaster COR	.06	.02	.00
	(corrected in			
	factory sets)			
☐ 294	Jeff Musselman	.03	.01	.00
☐ 295	Kurt Stillwell	.03	.01	.00
☐ 296	Stan Belinda	.03	.01	.00
☐ 297	Lou Whitaker	.06	.02	.00
☐ 298	Glenn Wilson	.03	.01	.00
☐ 299	Omar Vizquel UER	.03	.01	.00
	(Born 5/15, should be			
	4/24, there is a decimal			
	before GP total for '90)			
☐ 300	Ramon Martinez	.10	.04	.01
☐ 301	Dwight Smith	.03	.01	.00
☐ 302	Tim Crews	.03	.01	.00
☐ 303	Lance Blankenship	.03	.01	.00
☐ 304	Sid Bream	.03	.01	.00
☐ 305	Rafael Ramirez	.03	.01	.00
☐ 306	Steve Wilson	.03	.01	.00
☐ 307	Mackey Sasser	.03	.01	.00
☐ 308	Franklin Stubbs	.03	.01	.00
☐ 309	Jack Daugherty UER	.03	.01	.00
	(Born 6/3/60,			
	should say July)			
☐ 310	Eddie Murray	.10	.04	.01
☐ 311	Bob Welch	.06	.02	.00
☐ 312	Brian Harper	.06	.02	.00
☐ 313	Lance McCullers	.03	.01	.00
☐ 314	Dave Smith	.03	.01	.00
☐ 315	Bobby Bonilla	.10	.04	.01
☐ 316	Jerry Don Gleaton	.03	.01	.00
☐ 317	Greg Maddux	.06	.02	.00
☐ 318	Keith Miller	.03	.01	.00
☐ 319	Mark Portugal	.03	.01	.00
☐ 320	Robin Ventura	.20	.08	.02
☐ 321	Bob Ojeda	.03	.01	.00
☐ 322	Mike Harkey	.06	.02	.00
☐ 323	Jay Bell	.03	.01	.00
☐ 324	Mark McGwire	.10	.04	.01
☐ 325	Gary Gaetti	.06	.02	.00
☐ 326	Jeff Pico	.03	.01	.00
☐ 327	Kevin McReynolds	.06	.02	.00
☐ 328	Frank Tanana	.06	.02	.00
☐ 329	Eric Yelding UER	.03	.01	.00
	(Listed as 6'3",			
	should be 5'11")			
☐ 330	Barry Bonds	.12	.05	.01
☐ 331	Brian McRae RP UER	.45	.18	.04
	(No comma between			
	city and state)			
☐ 332	Pedro Munoz RP	.17	.07	.01
☐ 333	Daryl Irvine RP	.08	.03	.01
☐ 334	Chris Hoiles RP	.08	.03	.01
☐ 335	Thomas Howard RP	.10	.04	.01
☐ 336	Jeff Schulz RP	.10	.04	.01
☐ 337	Jeff Manto RP	.06	.02	.00
☐ 338	Beau Allred RP	.06	.02	.00
☐ 339	Mike Bordick RP	.10	.04	.01
☐ 340	Todd Hundley RP	.10	.04	.01
☐ 341	Jim Vatcher RP UER	.08	.03	.01
	(Height 6'9",			
	should be 5'9")			
☐ 342	Luis Sojo RP	.08	.03	.01
☐ 343	Jose Offerman RP UER	.10	.04	.01
	(Born 1969, should			
	say 1968)			
☐ 344	Pete Coachman RP	.12	.05	.01
☐ 345	Mike Benjamin RP	.08	.03	.01
☐ 346	Ozzie Canseco RP	.08	.03	.01
☐ 347	Tim McIntosh RP	.08	.03	.01
☐ 348	Phil Plantier RP	1.25	.50	.12
☐ 349	Terry Shumpert RP	.03	.01	.00
☐ 350	Darren Lewis RP	.20	.08	.02
☐ 351	David Walsh RP	.10	.04	.01
☐ 352A	Scott Chiamparino RP	.10	.04	.01
	ERR (Bats left,			
	should be right)			
☐ 352B	Scott Chiamparino RP	.10	.04	.01
	COR (corrected in			
	factory sets)			
☐ 353	Julio Valera RP	.08	.03	.01
	UER (Progressed mis-			
	spelled as progessed)			

☐ 354	Anthony Telford RP	.08	.03	.01
☐ 355	Kevin Wickander RP	.03	.01	.00
☐ 356	Tim Naehring RP	.10	.04	.01
☐ 357	Jim Poole RP	.10	.04	.01
☐ 358	Mark Whiten RP UER	.20	.08	.02
	(Shown hitting lefty,			
	bio says righty)			
☐ 359	Terry Wells RP	.08	.03	.01
☐ 360	Rafael Valdez RP	.06	.02	.00
☐ 361	Mel Stottlemyre Jr. RP	.03	.01	.00
☐ 362	David Segui RP	.08	.03	.01
☐ 363	Paul Abbott RP	.10	.04	.01
☐ 364	Steve Howard RP	.08	.03	.01
☐ 365	Karl Rhodes RP	.08	.03	.01
☐ 366	Rafael Novoa RP	.08	.03	.01
☐ 367	Joe Grahe RP	.08	.03	.01
☐ 368	Darren Reed RP	.08	.03	.01
☐ 369	Jeff McKnight RP	.08	.03	.01
☐ 370	Scott Leius RP	.10	.04	.01
☐ 371	Mark Dewey RP	.10	.04	.01
☐ 372	Mark Lee RP UER	.10	.04	.01
	(Shown hitting lefty,			
	bio says righty, born			
	in Dakota, should			
	say North Dakota)			
☐ 373	Rosario Rodriguez RP	.10	.04	.01
	(Shown hitting lefty,			
	bio says righty) UER			
☐ 374	Chuck McElroy RP	.08	.03	.01
☐ 375	Mike Bell RP	.10	.04	.01
☐ 376	Mickey Morandini RP	.10	.04	.01
☐ 377	Bill Haselman RP	.08	.03	.01
☐ 378	Dave Pavlas RP	.08	.03	.01
☐ 379	Derrick May RP	.08	.03	.01
☐ 380	Jeromy Burnitz FDP	.75	.30	.07
☐ 381	Donald Peters FDP	.15	.06	.01
☐ 382	Alex Fernandez FDP	.20	.08	.02
☐ 383	Michael Mussina FDP	.35	.15	.03
☐ 384	Daniel Smith FDP	.12	.05	.01
☐ 385	Lance Dickson FDP	.17	.07	.01
☐ 386	Carl Everett FDP	.25	.10	.02
☐ 387	Thomas Nevers FDP	.15	.06	.01
☐ 388	Adam Hyzdu FDP	.15	.06	.01
☐ 389	Todd Van Poppel FDP	1.25	.50	.12
☐ 390	Rondell White FDP	.40	.16	.04
☐ 391	Marc Newfield FDP	1.00	.40	.10
☐ 392	Julio Franco AS	.06	.02	.00
☐ 393	Wade Boggs AS	.08	.03	.01
☐ 394	Ozzie Guillen AS	.06	.02	.00
☐ 395	Cecil Fielder AS	.10	.04	.01
☐ 396	Ken Griffey Jr. AS	.30	.12	.03
☐ 397	Rickey Henderson AS	.12	.05	.01
☐ 398	Jose Canseco AS	.15	.06	.01
☐ 399	Roger Clemens AS	.10	.04	.01
☐ 400	Sandy Alomar Jr. AS	.08	.03	.01
☐ 401	Bobby Thigpen AS	.06	.02	.00
☐ 402	Bobby Bonilla MB	.08	.03	.01
☐ 403	Eric Davis MB	.08	.03	.01
☐ 404	Fred McGriff MB	.08	.03	.01
☐ 405	Glenn Davis MB	.06	.02	.00
☐ 406	Kevin Mitchell MB	.08	.03	.01
☐ 407	Rob Dibble KM	.06	.02	.00
☐ 408	Ramon Martinez KM	.08	.03	.01
☐ 409	David Cone KM	.06	.02	.00
☐ 410	Bobby Witt KM	.06	.02	.00
☐ 411	Mark Langston KM	.06	.02	.00
☐ 412	Bo Jackson RIF	.15	.06	.01
☐ 413	Shawon Dunston RIF	.06	.02	.00
	UER (In the baseball,			
	should say in baseball)			
☐ 414	Jesse Barfield RIF	.06	.02	.00
☐ 415	Ken Caminiti RIF	.03	.01	.00
☐ 416	Benito Santiago RIF	.06	.02	.00
☐ 417	Nolan Ryan RIF	.20	.08	.02
☐ 418	Bobby Thigpen HL UER	.06	.02	.00
	(Back refers to Hal			
	McRae Jr., should			
	say Brian McRae)			
☐ 419	Ramon Martinez HL	.08	.03	.01
☐ 420	Bo Jackson HL	.15	.06	.01
☐ 421	Carlton Fisk HL	.08	.03	.01
☐ 422	Jimmy Key	.06	.02	.00
☐ 423	Junior Noboa	.03	.01	.00
☐ 424	Al Newman	.03	.01	.00
☐ 425	Pat Borders	.03	.01	.00
☐ 426	Von Hayes	.06	.02	.00
☐ 427	Tim Teufel	.03	.01	.00
☐ 428	Eric Plunk UER	.03	.01	.00
	(Text says Eric's had,			
	no apostrophe needed)			
☐ 429	John Moses	.03	.01	.00
☐ 430	Mike Witt	.03	.01	.00
☐ 431	Otis Nixon	.06	.02	.00
☐ 432	Tony Fernandez	.06	.02	.00

#	Player			
☐ 433	Rance Mulliniks	.03	.01	.00
☐ 434	Dan Petry	.03	.01	.00
☐ 435	Bob Geren	.03	.01	.00
☐ 436	Steve Frey	.06	.02	.00
☐ 437	Jamie Moyer	.03	.01	.00
☐ 438	Junior Ortiz	.03	.01	.00
☐ 439	Tom O'Malley	.03	.01	.00
☐ 440	Pat Combs	.03	.01	.00
☐ 441	Jose Canseco DT	2.25	.90	.22
☐ 442	Alfredo Griffin	.03	.01	.00
☐ 443	Andres Galarraga	.06	.02	.00
☐ 444	Bryn Smith	.03	.01	.00
☐ 445	Andre Dawson	.10	.04	.01
☐ 446	Juan Samuel	.06	.02	.00
☐ 447	Mike Aldrete	.03	.01	.00
☐ 448	Ron Gant	.12	.05	.01
☐ 449	Fernando Valenzuela	.06	.02	.00
☐ 450	Vince Coleman	.08	.03	.01
	(Should say topped majors in steals four times, not three times)			
☐ 451	Kevin Mitchell	.10	.04	.01
☐ 452	Spike Owen	.03	.01	.00
☐ 453	Mike Bielecki	.03	.01	.00
☐ 454	Dennis Martinez	.06	.02	.00
☐ 455	Brett Butler	.06	.02	.00
☐ 456	Ron Darling	.06	.02	.00
☐ 457	Dennis Rasmussen	.03	.01	.00
☐ 458	Ken Howell	.03	.01	.00
☐ 459	Steve Bedrosian	.03	.01	.00
☐ 460	Frank Viola	.08	.03	.01
☐ 461	Jose Lind	.03	.01	.00
☐ 462	Chris Sabo	.08	.03	.01
☐ 463	Dante Bichette	.03	.01	.00
☐ 464	Rick Mahler	.03	.01	.00
☐ 465	John Smiley	.03	.01	.00
☐ 466	Devon White	.06	.02	.00
☐ 467	John Orton	.03	.01	.00
☐ 468	Mike Stanton	.03	.01	.00
☐ 469	Billy Hatcher	.03	.01	.00
☐ 470	Wally Joyner	.08	.03	.01
☐ 471	Gene Larkin	.03	.01	.00
☐ 472	Doug Drabek	.06	.02	.00
☐ 473	Gary Sheffield	.08	.03	.01
☐ 474	David Wells	.03	.01	.00
☐ 475	Andy Van Slyke	.08	.03	.01
☐ 476	Mike Gallego	.03	.01	.00
☐ 477	B.J. Surhoff	.03	.01	.00
☐ 478	Gene Nelson	.03	.01	.00
☐ 479	Mariano Duncan	.03	.01	.00
☐ 480	Fred McGriff	.08	.03	.01
☐ 481	Jerry Browne	.03	.01	.00
☐ 482	Alvin Davis	.06	.02	.00
☐ 483	Bill Wegman	.03	.01	.00
☐ 484	Dave Parker	.08	.03	.01
☐ 485	Dennis Eckersley	.06	.02	.00
☐ 486	Erik Hanson UER	.06	.02	.00
	(Basketball misspelled as baseketball)			
☐ 487	Bill Ripken	.03	.01	.00
☐ 488	Tom Candiotti	.06	.02	.00
☐ 489	Mike Schooler	.03	.01	.00
☐ 490	Gregg Olson	.06	.02	.00
☐ 491	Chris James	.03	.01	.00
☐ 492	Pete Harnisch	.06	.02	.00
☐ 493	Julio Franco	.08	.03	.01
☐ 494	Greg Briley	.03	.01	.00
☐ 495	Ruben Sierra	.12	.05	.01
☐ 496	Steve Olin	.03	.01	.00
☐ 497	Mike Fetters	.03	.01	.00
☐ 498	Mark Williams	.08	.03	.01
☐ 499	Bob Tewksbury	.03	.01	.00
☐ 500	Tony Gwynn	.12	.05	.01
☐ 501	Randy Myers	.03	.01	.00
☐ 502	Keith Comstock	.03	.01	.00
☐ 503	Craig Worthington UER	.03	.01	.00
	(DeCinces misspelled DiCinces on back)			
☐ 504	Mark Eichhorn UER	.03	.01	.00
	(Stats incomplete, doesn't have '89 Braves stint)			
☐ 505	Barry Larkin	.08	.03	.01
☐ 506	Dave Johnson	.03	.01	.00
☐ 507	Bobby Witt	.06	.02	.00
☐ 508	Joe Orsulak	.03	.01	.00
☐ 509	Pete O'Brien	.03	.01	.00
☐ 510	Brad Arnsberg	.03	.01	.00
☐ 511	Storm Davis	.03	.01	.00
☐ 512	Bob Milacki	.03	.01	.00
☐ 513	Bill Pecota	.03	.01	.00
☐ 514	Glenallen Hill	.03	.01	.00
☐ 515	Danny Tartabull	.08	.03	.01
☐ 516	Mike Moore	.03	.01	.00
☐ 517	Ron Robinson UER	.03	.01	.00
	(577 K's in 1990)			
☐ 518	Mark Gardner	.03	.01	.00
☐ 519	Rick Wrona	.03	.01	.00
☐ 520	Mike Scioscia	.03	.01	.00
☐ 521	Frank Wills	.03	.01	.00
☐ 522	Greg Brock	.03	.01	.00
☐ 523	Jack Clark	.06	.02	.00
☐ 524	Bruce Ruffin	.03	.01	.00
☐ 525	Robin Yount	.10	.04	.01
☐ 526	Tom Foley	.03	.01	.00
☐ 527	Pat Perry	.03	.01	.00
☐ 528	Greg Vaughn	.10	.04	.01
☐ 529	Wally Whitehurst	.03	.01	.00
☐ 530	Norm Charlton	.03	.01	.00
☐ 531	Marvell Wynne	.03	.01	.00
☐ 532	Jim Gantner	.03	.01	.00
☐ 533	Greg Litton	.03	.01	.00
☐ 534	Manny Lee	.03	.01	.00
☐ 535	Scott Bailes	.03	.01	.00
☐ 536	Charlie Leibrandt	.03	.01	.00
☐ 537	Roger McDowell	.03	.01	.00
☐ 538	Andy Benes	.08	.03	.01
☐ 539	Rick Honeycutt	.03	.01	.00
☐ 540	Dwight Gooden	.10	.04	.01
☐ 541	Scott Garrelts	.03	.01	.00
☐ 542	Dave Clark	.03	.01	.00
☐ 543	Lonnie Smith	.06	.02	.00
☐ 544	Rick Reuschel	.06	.02	.00
☐ 545	Delino DeShields UER	.10	.04	.01
	(Rockford misspelled as Rock Ford in '88)			
☐ 546	Mike Sharperson	.03	.01	.00
☐ 547	Mike Kingery	.03	.01	.00
☐ 548	Terry Kennedy	.03	.01	.00
☐ 549	David Cone	.08	.03	.01
☐ 550	Orel Hershiser	.08	.03	.01
☐ 551	Matt Nokes	.06	.02	.00
☐ 552	Eddie Williams	.03	.01	.00
☐ 553	Frank DiPino	.03	.01	.00
☐ 554	Fred Lynn	.06	.02	.00
☐ 555	Alex Cole	.08	.03	.01
☐ 556	Terry Leach	.03	.01	.00
☐ 557	Chet Lemon	.03	.01	.00
☐ 558	Paul Mirabella	.03	.01	.00
☐ 559	Bill Long	.03	.01	.00
☐ 560	Phil Bradley	.03	.01	.00
☐ 561	Duane Ward	.03	.01	.00
☐ 562	Dave Bergman	.03	.01	.00
☐ 563	Eric Show	.03	.01	.00
☐ 564	Xavier Hernandez	.06	.02	.00
☐ 565	Jeff Parrett	.03	.01	.00
☐ 566	Chuck Cary	.03	.01	.00
☐ 567	Ken Hill	.03	.01	.00
☐ 568	Bob Welch Hand	.06	.02	.00
	(Complement should be compliment) UER			
☐ 569	John Mitchell	.03	.01	.00
☐ 570	Travis Fryman	.45	.18	.04
☐ 571	Derek Lilliquist	.03	.01	.00
☐ 572	Steve Lake	.03	.01	.00
☐ 573	John Barfield	.08	.03	.01
☐ 574	Randy Bush	.03	.01	.00
☐ 575	Joe Magrane	.03	.01	.00
☐ 576	Eddie Diaz	.08	.03	.01
☐ 577	Casey Candaele	.03	.01	.00
☐ 578	Jesse Orosco	.03	.01	.00
☐ 579	Tom Henke	.06	.02	.00
☐ 580	Rick Cerone UER	.03	.01	.00
	(Actually his third go-round with Yankees)			
☐ 581	Drew Hall	.03	.01	.00
☐ 582	Tony Castillo	.06	.02	.00
☐ 583	Jimmy Jones	.03	.01	.00
☐ 584	Rick Reed	.03	.01	.00
☐ 585	Joe Girardi	.03	.01	.00
☐ 586	Jeff Gray	.08	.03	.01
☐ 587	Luis Polonia	.03	.01	.00
☐ 588	Joe Klink	.06	.02	.00
☐ 589	Rex Hudler	.03	.01	.00
☐ 590	Kirk McCaskill	.03	.01	.00
☐ 591	Juan Agosto	.03	.01	.00
☐ 592	Wes Gardner	.03	.01	.00
☐ 593	Rich Rodriguez	.08	.03	.01
☐ 594	Mitch Webster	.03	.01	.00
☐ 595	Kelly Gruber	.06	.02	.00
☐ 596	Dale Mohorcic	.03	.01	.00
☐ 597	Willie McGee	.06	.02	.00
☐ 598	Bill Krueger	.03	.01	.00
☐ 599	Bob Walk UER	.03	.01	.00
	(Cards says he's 33, but actually he's 34)			
☐ 600	Kevin Maas	.15	.06	.01
☐ 601	Danny Jackson	.03	.01	.00

#	Player			
☐ 602	Craig McMurtry UER (Anonymously misspelled anonimously)	.03	.01	.00
☐ 603	Curtis Wilkerson	.03	.01	.00
☐ 604	Adam Peterson	.03	.01	.00
☐ 605	Sam Horn	.03	.01	.00
☐ 606	Tommy Gregg	.03	.01	.00
☐ 607	Ken Dayley	.03	.01	.00
☐ 608	Carmelo Castillo	.03	.01	.00
☐ 609	John Shelby	.03	.01	.00
☐ 610	Don Slaught	.03	.01	.00
☐ 611	Calvin Schiraldi	.03	.01	.00
☐ 612	Dennis Lamp	.03	.01	.00
☐ 613	Andres Thomas	.03	.01	.00
☐ 614	Jose Gonzalez	.03	.01	.00
☐ 615	Randy Ready	.03	.01	.00
☐ 616	Kevin Bass	.03	.01	.00
☐ 617	Mike Marshall	.06	.02	.00
☐ 618	Daryl Boston	.03	.01	.00
☐ 619	Andy McGaffigan	.03	.01	.00
☐ 620	Joe Oliver	.03	.01	.00
☐ 621	Jim Gott	.03	.01	.00
☐ 622	Jose Oquendo	.03	.01	.00
☐ 623	Jose DeJesus	.03	.01	.00
☐ 624	Mike Brumley	.03	.01	.00
☐ 625	John Olerud	.12	.05	.01
☐ 626	Ernest Riles	.03	.01	.00
☐ 627	Gene Harris	.03	.01	.00
☐ 628	Jose Uribe	.03	.01	.00
☐ 629	Darnell Coles	.03	.01	.00
☐ 630	Carney Lansford	.06	.02	.00
☐ 631	Tim Leary	.03	.01	.00
☐ 632	Tim Hulett	.03	.01	.00
☐ 633	Kevin Elster	.03	.01	.00
☐ 634	Tony Fossas	.03	.01	.00
☐ 635	Francisco Oliveras	.03	.01	.00
☐ 636	Bob Patterson	.03	.01	.00
☐ 637	Gary Ward	.03	.01	.00
☐ 638	Rene Gonzales	.03	.01	.00
☐ 639	Don Robinson	.03	.01	.00
☐ 640	Darryl Strawberry	.15	.06	.01
☐ 641	Dave Anderson	.03	.01	.00
☐ 642	Scott Scudder	.03	.01	.00
☐ 643	Reggie Harris UER (Hepatitis misspelled as hepititis)	.08	.03	.01
☐ 644	Dave Henderson	.06	.02	.00
☐ 645	Ben McDonald	.10	.04	.01
☐ 646	Bob Kipper	.03	.01	.00
☐ 647	Hal Morris UER (It's should be its)	.10	.04	.01
☐ 648	Tim Birtsas	.03	.01	.00
☐ 649	Steve Searcy	.03	.01	.00
☐ 650	Dale Murphy	.10	.04	.01
☐ 651	Ron Oester	.03	.01	.00
☐ 652	Mike LaCoss	.03	.01	.00
☐ 653	Ron Jones	.03	.01	.00
☐ 654	Kelly Downs	.03	.01	.00
☐ 655	Roger Clemens	.15	.06	.01
☐ 656	Herm Winningham	.03	.01	.00
☐ 657	Trevor Wilson	.03	.01	.00
☐ 658	Jose Rijo	.06	.02	.00
☐ 659	Dann Bilardello UER (Bio has 13 games, 1 hit, and 32 AB, stats show 19, 2, and 37)	.03	.01	.00
☐ 660	Gregg Jefferies	.08	.03	.01
☐ 661	Doug Drabek AS UER (Through is misspelled though)	.06	.02	.00
☐ 662	Randy Myers AS	.03	.01	.00
☐ 663	Benny Santiago AS	.06	.02	.00
☐ 664	Will Clark AS	.12	.05	.01
☐ 665	Ryne Sandberg AS	.12	.05	.01
☐ 666	Barry Larkin AS UER (Line 13, coolly misspelled cooly)	.08	.03	.01
☐ 667	Matt Williams AS	.08	.03	.01
☐ 668	Barry Bonds AS	.08	.03	.01
☐ 669	Eric Davis AS	.08	.03	.01
☐ 670	Bobby Bonilla AS	.08	.03	.01
☐ 671	Chipper Jones FDP	.30	.12	.03
☐ 672	Eric Christopherson FDP	.12	.05	.01
☐ 673	Robbie Beckett FDP	.12	.05	.01
☐ 674	Shane Andrews FDP	.20	.08	.02
☐ 675	Steve Karsay FDP	.25	.10	.02
☐ 676	Aaron Holbert FDP	.15	.06	.01
☐ 677	Donovan Osborne FDP	.15	.06	.01
☐ 678	Todd Ritchie FDP	.15	.06	.01
☐ 679	Ron Walden FDP	.15	.06	.01
☐ 680	Tim Costo FDP	.25	.10	.02
☐ 681	Dan Wilson FDP	.20	.08	.02
☐ 682	Kurt Miller FDP	.17	.07	.01
☐ 683	Mike Lieberthal FDP	.12	.05	.01
☐ 684	Roger Clemens KM	.10	.04	.01
☐ 685	Doc Gooden KM	.08	.03	.01
☐ 686	Nolan Ryan KM	.20	.08	.02
☐ 687	Frank Viola KM	.06	.02	.00
☐ 688	Erik Hanson KM	.06	.02	.00
☐ 689	Matt Williams MB	.08	.03	.01
☐ 690	Jose Canseco MB UER (Mammoth misspelled as monmouth)	.15	.06	.01
☐ 691	Darryl Strawberry MB	.10	.04	.01
☐ 692	Bo Jackson MB	.15	.06	.01
☐ 693	Cecil Fielder MB	.10	.04	.01
☐ 694	Sandy Alomar Jr. RF	.08	.03	.01
☐ 695	Cory Snyder RF	.06	.02	.00
☐ 696	Eric Davis RF	.08	.03	.01
☐ 697	Ken Griffey Jr. RF	.30	.12	.03
☐ 698	Andy Van Slyke RF UER (Line 2, outfielders does not need)	.06	.02	.00
☐ 699	Langston/Witt NH Mark Langston Mike Witt	.06	.02	.00
☐ 700	Randy Johnson NH	.06	.02	.00
☐ 701	Nolan Ryan NH	.30	.12	.03
☐ 702	Dave Stewart NH	.06	.02	.00
☐ 703	Fernando Valenzuela NH	.06	.02	.00
☐ 704	Andy Hawkins NH	.03	.01	.00
☐ 705	Melido Perez NH	.03	.01	.00
☐ 706	Terry Mulholland NH	.03	.01	.00
☐ 707	Dave Stieb NH	.06	.02	.00
☐ 708	Brian Barnes RP	.12	.05	.01
☐ 709	Bernard Gilkey RP	.15	.06	.01
☐ 710	Steve Decker RP	.25	.10	.02
☐ 711	Paul Faries RP	.08	.03	.01
☐ 712	Paul Marak RP	.08	.03	.01
☐ 713	Wes Chamberlain RP	.45	.18	.04
☐ 714	Kevin Belcher RP	.10	.04	.01
☐ 715	Dan Boone RP UER (IP adds up to 101, but card has 101.2)	.03	.01	.00
☐ 716	Steve Adkins RP	.10	.04	.01
☐ 717	Geronimo Pena RP	.08	.03	.01
☐ 718	Howard Farmer RP	.03	.01	.00
☐ 719	Mark Leonard RP	.12	.05	.01
☐ 720	Tom Lampkin RP	.03	.01	.00
☐ 721	Mike Gardiner RP	.15	.06	.01
☐ 722	Jeff Conine RP	.15	.06	.01
☐ 723	Efrain Valdez RP	.08	.03	.01
☐ 724	Chuck Malone RP	.06	.02	.00
☐ 725	Leo Gomez RP	.25	.10	.02
☐ 726	Paul McClellan RP	.15	.06	.01
☐ 727	Mark Leiter RP	.12	.05	.01
☐ 728	Rich DeLucia RP UER (Line 2, all told is written alltold)	.12	.05	.01
☐ 729	Mel Rojas RP	.08	.03	.01
☐ 730	Hector Wagner RP	.10	.04	.01
☐ 731	Ray Lankford RP	.25	.10	.02
☐ 732	Turner Ward RP	.15	.06	.01
☐ 733	Gerald Alexander RP	.10	.04	.01
☐ 734	Scott Anderson RP	.08	.03	.01
☐ 735	Tony Perezchica RP	.06	.02	.00
☐ 736	Jimmy Kremers RP	.06	.02	.00
☐ 737	American Flag (Pray for Peace)	.30	.12	.03
☐ 738	Mike York RP	.10	.04	.01
☐ 739	Mike Rochford RP	.06	.02	.00
☐ 740	Scott Aldred RP	.08	.03	.01
☐ 741	Rico Brogna RP	.25	.10	.02
☐ 742	Dave Burba RP	.08	.03	.01
☐ 743	Ray Stephens RP	.10	.04	.01
☐ 744	Eric Gunderson RP	.06	.02	.00
☐ 745	Troy Afenir RP	.08	.03	.01
☐ 746	Jeff Shaw RP	.08	.03	.01
☐ 747	Orlando Merced RP	.35	.15	.03
☐ 748	Omar Olivares RP UER (Line 9, league is misspelled legaue)	.10	.04	.01
☐ 749	Jerry Kutzler RP	.03	.01	.00
☐ 750	Mo Vaughn RP UER (44 SB's in 1990)	.30	.12	.03
☐ 751	Matt Stark RP	.12	.05	.01
☐ 752	Randy Hennis RP	.08	.03	.01
☐ 753	Andujar Cedeno RP	.35	.15	.03
☐ 754	Kelvin Torve RP	.06	.02	.00
☐ 755	Joe Kraemer RP	.06	.02	.00
☐ 756	Phil Clark RP	.15	.06	.01
☐ 757	Ed Vosberg RP	.08	.03	.01
☐ 758	Mike Perez RP	.08	.03	.01
☐ 759	Scott Lewis RP	.10	.04	.01
☐ 760	Steve Chitren RP	.08	.03	.01
☐ 761	Ray Young RP	.10	.04	.01

☐ 762	Andres Santana RP	.15	.06	.01
☐ 763	Rodney McCray RP	.10	.04	.01
☐ 764	Sean Berry RP UER	.12	.05	.01
	(Name misspelled			
	Barry on card front)			
☐ 765	Brent Mayne RP	.06	.02	.00
☐ 766	Mike Simms RP	.12	.05	.01
☐ 767	Glenn Sutko RP	.10	.04	.01
☐ 768	Gary DiSarcina RP	.03	.01	.00
☐ 769	George Brett HL	.08	.03	.01
☐ 770	Cecil Fielder HL	.10	.04	.01
☐ 771	Jim Presley	.03	.01	.00
☐ 772	John Dopson	.03	.01	.00
☐ 773	Bo Jackson Breaker	.25	.10	.02
☐ 774	Brent Knackert UER	.06	.02	.00
	(Born in 1954, shown			
	throwing righty, but			
	bio says lefty)			
☐ 775	Bill Doran UER	.03	.01	.00
	(Reds in NL East)			
☐ 776	Dick Schofield	.03	.01	.00
☐ 777	Nelson Santovenia	.03	.01	.00
☐ 778	Mark Guthrie	.06	.02	.00
☐ 779	Mark Lemke	.03	.01	.00
☐ 780	Terry Steinbach	.03	.01	.00
☐ 781	Tom Bolton	.03	.01	.00
☐ 782	Randy Tomlin	.17	.07	.01
☐ 783	Jeff Kunkel	.03	.01	.00
☐ 784	Felix Jose	.10	.04	.01
☐ 785	Rick Sutcliffe	.06	.02	.00
☐ 786	John Cerutti	.03	.01	.00
☐ 787	Jose Vizcaino UER	.03	.01	.00
	(Offerman not Opperman)			
☐ 788	Curt Schilling	.03	.01	.00
☐ 789	Ed Whitson	.03	.01	.00
☐ 790	Tony Pena	.06	.02	.00
☐ 791	John Candelaria	.03	.01	.00
☐ 792	Carmelo Martinez	.03	.01	.00
☐ 793	Sandy Alomar Jr. UER	.08	.03	.01
	(Indian's should			
	say Indians')			
☐ 794	Jim Neidlinger	.10	.04	.01
☐ 795	Barry Larkin WS	.08	.03	.01
	and Chris Sabo			
☐ 796	Paul Sorrento	.03	.01	.00
☐ 797	Tom Pagnozzi	.03	.01	.00
☐ 798	Tino Martinez	.15	.06	.01
☐ 799	Scott Ruskin UER	.08	.03	.01
	(Text says first three			
	seasons but lists			
	averages for four)			
☐ 800	Kirk Gibson	.06	.02	.00
☐ 801	Walt Terrell	.03	.01	.00
☐ 802	John Russell	.03	.01	.00
☐ 803	Chili Davis	.06	.02	.00
☐ 804	Chris Nabholz	.08	.03	.01
☐ 805	Juan Gonzalez	.30	.12	.03
☐ 806	Ron Hassey	.03	.01	.00
☐ 807	Todd Worrell	.03	.01	.00
☐ 808	Tommy Greene	.03	.01	.00
☐ 809	Joel Skinner UER	.03	.01	.00
	(Joel, not Bob, was			
	drafted in 1979)			
☐ 810	Benito Santiago	.06	.02	.00
☐ 811	Pat Tabler UER	.03	.01	.00
	(Line 3, always			
	misspelled alway)			
☐ 812	Scott Erickson UER	.75	.30	.07
	(Record spelled rcord)			
☐ 813	Moises Alou	.08	.03	.01
☐ 814	Dale Sveum	.03	.01	.00
☐ 815	Ryne Sandberg MANYR	.25	.10	.02
☐ 816	Rick Dempsey	.03	.01	.00
☐ 817	Scott Bankhead	.03	.01	.00
☐ 818	Jason Grimsley	.03	.01	.00
☐ 819	Doug Jennings	.03	.01	.00
☐ 820	Tom Herr	.03	.01	.00
☐ 821	Rob Ducey	.03	.01	.00
☐ 822	Luis Quinones	.03	.01	.00
☐ 823	Greg Minton	.03	.01	.00
☐ 824	Mark Grant	.03	.01	.00
☐ 825	Ozzie Smith UER	.10	.04	.01
	(Shortstop misspelled			
	shortsop)			
☐ 826	Dave Eiland	.03	.01	.00
☐ 827	Danny Heep	.03	.01	.00
☐ 828	Hensley Meulens	.08	.03	.01
☐ 829	Charlie O'Brien	.03	.01	.00
☐ 830	Glenn Davis	.06	.02	.00
☐ 831	John Marzano UER	.03	.01	.00
	(International mis-			
	spelled Internaional)			
☐ 832	Steve Ontiveros	.03	.01	.00
☐ 833	Ron Karkovice	.03	.01	.00

☐ 834	Jerry Goff	.06	.02	.00
☐ 835	Ken Griffey Sr.	.06	.02	.00
☐ 836	Kevin Reimer	.08	.03	.01
☐ 837	Randy Kutcher UER	.03	.01	.00
	(Infectious mis-			
	spelled infectous)			
☐ 838	Mike Blowers	.03	.01	.00
☐ 839	Mike Macfarlane	.03	.01	.00
☐ 840	Frank Thomas UER	1.25	.50	.12
	(1989 Sarasota stats,			
	15 games but 188 AB)			
☐ 841	The Griffeys	1.25	.50	.12
	Ken Griffey Jr.			
	Ken Griffey Sr.			
☐ 842	Jack Howell	.03	.01	.00
☐ 843	Goose Gozzo	.03	.01	.00
☐ 844	Gerald Young	.03	.01	.00
☐ 845	Zane Smith	.06	.02	.00
☐ 846	Kevin Brown	.03	.01	.00
☐ 847	Sil Campusano	.03	.01	.00
☐ 848	Larry Andersen	.03	.01	.00
☐ 849	Cal Ripken FRAN	.15	.06	.01
☐ 850	Roger Clemens FRAN	.12	.05	.01
☐ 851	Sandy Alomar Jr. FRAN	.08	.03	.01
☐ 852	Alan Trammell FRAN	.08	.03	.01
☐ 853	George Brett FRAN	.08	.03	.01
☐ 854	Robin Yount FRAN	.08	.03	.01
☐ 855	Kirby Puckett FRAN	.10	.04	.01
☐ 856	Don Mattingly FRAN	.12	.05	.01
☐ 857	Rickey Henderson FRAN	.20	.08	.02
☐ 858	Ken Griffey Jr. FRAN	.60	.25	.06
☐ 859	Ruben Sierra FRAN	.12	.05	.01
☐ 860	John Olerud FRAN	.10	.04	.01
☐ 861	Dave Justice FRAN	.50	.20	.05
☐ 862	Ryne Sandberg FRAN	.25	.10	.02
☐ 863	Eric Davis FRAN	.08	.03	.01
☐ 864	Darryl Strawberry FRAN	.12	.05	.01
☐ 865	Tim Wallach FRAN	.06	.02	.00
☐ 866	Doc Gooden FRAN	.08	.03	.01
☐ 867	Len Dykstra FRAN	.06	.02	.00
☐ 868	Barry Bonds FRAN	.08	.03	.01
☐ 869	Todd Zeile FRAN UER	.10	.04	.01
	(Powerful misspelled			
	as poweful)			
☐ 870	Benito Santiago FRAN	.06	.02	.00
☐ 871	Will Clark FRAN	.20	.08	.02
☐ 872	Craig Biggio FRAN	.06	.02	.00
☐ 873	Wally Joyner FRAN	.08	.03	.01
☐ 874	Frank Thomas FRAN	.90	.40	.09
☐ 875	Rickey Henderson MVP	.12	.05	.01
☐ 876	Barry Bonds MVP	.08	.03	.01
☐ 877	Bob Welch CY	.06	.02	.00
☐ 878	Doug Drabek CY	.06	.02	.00
☐ 879	Sandy Alomar Jr ROY	.08	.03	.01
☐ 880	Dave Justice ROY	.30	.12	.03
☐ 881	Damon Berryhill	.03	.01	.00
☐ 882	Frank Viola DT	.12	.05	.01
☐ 883	Dave Stewart DT	.15	.06	.01
☐ 884	Doug Jones DT	.06	.02	.00
☐ 885	Randy Myers DT	.06	.02	.00
☐ 886	Will Clark DT	.40	.16	.04
☐ 887	Roberto Alomar DT	.20	.08	.02
☐ 888	Barry Larkin DT	.15	.06	.01
☐ 889	Wade Boggs DT	.30	.12	.03
☐ 890	Rickey Henderson DT	.90	.40	.09
☐ 891	Kirby Puckett DT	.30	.12	.03
☐ 892	Ken Griffey Jr DT	1.50	.60	.15
☐ 893	Benny Santiago DT	.15	.06	.01

1991 Score Cooperstown

These standard-size (2 1/2" by 3 1/2") cards were available only as a set contained in factory sets, and their design is not like that of the regular Score issue. On a white card face, the fronts feature portraits of the players in an oval-shaped format. The words "Cooperstown Card" and a thin yellow stripe traverse the top of the card, while another yellow stripe and the player's name appears at the bottom. On a pale yellow background with green borders, the backs summarize the player's accomplishments. The cards are numbered on the back.

	MINT	VG-E	F-G
COMPLETE SET (1-7)	10.00	4.50	1.25
COMMON PLAYER (B1-B7)	.75	.30	.07

☐ B1	Wade Boggs	1.50	.60	.15
☐ B2	Barry Larkin	.75	.30	.07
☐ B3	Ken Griffey Jr.	4.00	1.75	.40
☐ B4	Rickey Henderson	2.00	.80	.20
☐ B5	George Brett	1.25	.50	.12
☐ B6	Will Clark	2.00	.80	.20
☐ B7	Nolan Ryan	3.00	1.25	.30

1991 Score Mickey Mantle Promo

This seven-card set measures the standard 2 1/2" by 3 1/2" and features Mickey Mantle at various points in his career. This set was released to dealers and media members on Score's mailing list and was individually numbered on the back. This numbered dealer/media set was limited to 5,000 sets produced. The cards were sent in seven-card packs in the Yankees colors. The fronts are full-color glossy shots of Mantle while the backs are in a horizontal format with a full-color photo and some narrative information. The pictures have red and white borders, with the caption appearing in a blue stripe below the photo. The card number and the set serial number appear on the back.These were essentially the same cards Score used in their second series promotion.

	MINT	EXC	G-VG
COMPLETE SET (7)	400.00	180.00	60.00
COMMON PLAYER (1-7)	75.00	35.00	11.25
☐ 1 The Rookie	75.00	35.00	11.25
(with Billy Martin)			
☐ 2 Triple Crown	75.00	35.00	11.25
☐ 3 World Series	75.00	35.00	11.25
☐ 4 Going, Going, Gone	75.00	35.00	11.25
☐ 5 Speed and Grace	75.00	35.00	11.25
☐ 6 A True Yankee	75.00	35.00	11.25
☐ 7 Twilight	75.00	35.00	11.25
☐ x Autographed Card	700.00	300.00	80.00

1991 Score Hot Rookies

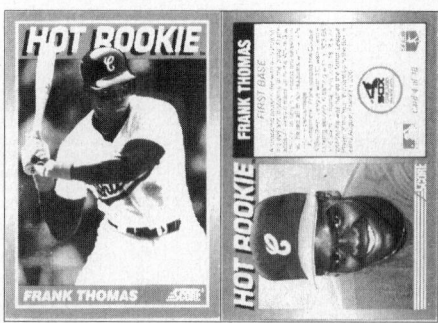

This ten-card set measures the standard size (2 1/2" by 3 1/2"), and one of these cards was inserted in the 1991 Score blister (100-card) packs. The front features a color action player photo, with white borders and the words "Hot Rookie" in yellow above the picture. The card background shades from orange to yellow to orange as one moves down the card face. In a horizontal format, the left half of the back has a color head shot, while the right half has career summary. The cards are numbered on the back.

	MINT	EXC	G-VG
COMPLETE SET (10)	15.00	6.50	2.15
COMMON PLAYER (1-10)	.75	.30	.07
☐ 1 Dave Justice	4.00	1.75	.40
☐ 2 Kevin Maas	1.50	.60	.15
☐ 3 Hal Morris	1.25	.50	.12
☐ 4 Frank Thomas	6.50	2.75	.65
☐ 5 Jeff Conine	.75	.30	.07
☐ 6 Sandy Alomar Jr.	1.00	.40	.10
☐ 7 Ray Lankford	1.50	.60	.15
☐ 8 Steve Decker	1.00	.40	.10
☐ 9 Juan Gonzalez	4.00	1.75	.40
☐ 10 Jose Offerman	1.25	.50	.12

1991 Score Rookies 40

This 40-card set measuring the standard size (2 1/2" by 3 1/2") was distributed with five magic motion trivia cards. The fronts feature high glossy color action player photos, on a blue card face with meandering green lines. The picture has a yellow border on its right side, and red and yellow borders below. The words "1991 Rookie" appear to the left of the picture running the length of the card. The team logo in the lower right corner rounds out the card face. On a yellow background, the backs have a color head shot, biography, and career highlights. The cards are numbered on the back.

	MINT	EXC	G-VG
COMPLETE SET (40)	7.00	3.00	.70
COMMON PLAYER (1-40)	.15	.06	.01

		MINT	EXC	G-VG
☐ 1	Mel Rojas	.20	.08	.02
☐ 2	Ray Lankford	.90	.40	.09
☐ 3	Scott Aldred	.20	.08	.02
☐ 4	Turner Ward	.25	.10	.02
☐ 5	Omar Olivares	.20	.08	.02
☐ 6	Mo Vaughn	.90	.40	.09
☐ 7	Phil Clark	.20	.08	.02
☐ 8	Brent Mayne	.20	.08	.02
☐ 9	Scott Lewis	.20	.08	.02
☐ 10	Brian Barnes	.25	.10	.02
☐ 11	Bernard Gilkey	.35	.15	.03
☐ 12	Steve Decker	.45	.18	.04
☐ 13	Paul Marak	.15	.06	.01
☐ 14	Wes Chamberlain	.60	.25	.06
☐ 15	Kevin Belcher	.25	.10	.02
☐ 16	Steve Adkins	.15	.06	.01
☐ 17	Geronimo Pena	.15	.06	.01
☐ 18	Mark Leonard	.15	.06	.01
☐ 19	Jeff Conine	.20	.08	.02
☐ 20	Leo Gomez	.50	.20	.05
☐ 21	Chuck Malone	.15	.06	.01
☐ 22	Beau Allred	.20	.08	.02
☐ 23	Todd Hundley	.30	.12	.03
☐ 24	Lance Dickson	.25	.10	.02
☐ 25	Mike Benjamin	.15	.06	.01
☐ 26	Jose Offerman	.30	.12	.03
☐ 27	Terry Shumpert	.15	.06	.01
☐ 28	Darren Lewis	.35	.15	.03
☐ 29	Scott Chiamparino	.20	.08	.02
☐ 30	Tim Naehring	.25	.10	.02
☐ 31	David Segui	.25	.10	.02
☐ 32	Karl Rhodes	.15	.06	.01
☐ 33	Mickey Morandini	.25	.10	.02
☐ 34	Chuck McElroy	.15	.06	.01
☐ 35	Tim McIntosh	.25	.10	.02
☐ 36	Derrick May	.25	.10	.02
☐ 37	Rich DeLucia	.20	.08	.02
☐ 38	Tino Martinez	.40	.16	.04
☐ 39	Hensley Meulens	.30	.12	.03
☐ 40	Andujar Cedeno	.60	.25	.06

1991 Score All-Star Fanfest

This ten-card set was issued with a 3-D 1946 World Series trivia card. The cards measure the standard size (2 1/2" by 3 1/2") and feature on the fronts color action player photos, with red borders above and below the pictures. The card face is lime green with miniature yellow baseballs and blue player icons, and it can be seen at the top and bottom of the card front. The backs have a similar pattern on a white background and present biographical information as well as career highlights. The cards are numbered on the back.

	MINT	EXC	G-VG
COMPLETE SET (10)	18.00	7.50	2.50
COMMON PLAYER (1-10)	1.00	.40	.10

		MINT	EXC	G-VG
☐ 1	Ray Lankford	3.00	1.25	.30
☐ 2	Steve Decker	2.00	.80	.20
☐ 3	Gary Scott	2.00	.80	.20
☐ 4	Hensley Meulens	2.00	.80	.20
☐ 5	Tim Naehring	1.25	.50	.12
☐ 6	Mark Whiten	2.00	.80	.20
☐ 7	Ed Sprague	1.25	.50	.12
☐ 8	Charles Nagy	1.50	.60	.15
☐ 9	Terry Shumpert	1.00	.40	.10
☐ 10	Chuck Knoblauch	5.00	2.25	.50

1991 Score Toronto Blue Jays

The 1991 Score Toronto Blue Jays set contains 40 player cards plus five magic motion trivia cards. The standard-size (2 1/2" by 3 1/2") cards feature on the fronts glossy color action photos with white borders. The bottom corners of the pictures are cut off by aqua-shaped triangles. The player's name and position appear in an aqua stripe above the picture. The producer's name and the team logo at the bottom round out the card face. The backs have a color head shot of the player, biography, Major League statistics, and a player profile. The cards are numbered on the back.

	MINT	EXC	G-VG
COMPLETE SET (40)	15.00	6.50	2.15
COMMON PLAYER (1-40)	.30	.12	.03

		MINT	EXC	G-VG
☐ 1	Joe Carter	1.00	.40	.10
☐ 2	Tom Henke	.40	.16	.04
☐ 3	Jimmy Key	.50	.20	.05
☐ 4	Al Leiter	.30	.12	.03
☐ 5	Dave Stieb	.50	.20	.05
☐ 6	Todd Stottlemyre	.50	.20	.05
☐ 7	Mike Timlin	.40	.16	.04
☐ 8	Duane Ward	.40	.16	.04
☐ 9	David Wells	.40	.16	.04
☐ 10	Frank Wills	.30	.12	.03
☐ 11	Pat Borders	.40	.16	.04
☐ 12	Greg Myers	.30	.12	.03
☐ 13	Roberto Alomar	1.00	.40	.10
☐ 14	Rene Gonzales	.30	.12	.03
☐ 15	Kelly Gruber	.50	.20	.05
☐ 16	Manny Lee	.30	.12	.03
☐ 17	Rance Mulliniks	.30	.12	.03
☐ 18	John Olerud	.75	.30	.07
☐ 19	Pat Tabler	.30	.12	.03
☐ 20	Derek Bell	1.00	.40	.10
☐ 21	Jim Acker	.30	.12	.03
☐ 22	Rob Ducey	.40	.16	.04
☐ 23	Devon White	.50	.20	.05
☐ 24	Mookie Wilson	.40	.16	.04
☐ 25	Juan Guzman	.75	.30	.07
☐ 26	Ed Sprague	.40	.16	.04
☐ 27	Ken Dayley	.30	.12	.03
☐ 28	Tom Candiotti	.40	.16	.04
☐ 29	Candy Maldonado	.40	.16	.04
☐ 30	Eddie Zosky	.40	.16	.04
☐ 31	Steve Karsay	.50	.20	.05
☐ 32	Bob MacDonald	.40	.16	.04
☐ 33	Ray Giannelli	.40	.16	.04
☐ 34	Jerry Schunk	.40	.16	.04
☐ 35	Dave Weathers	.50	.20	.05
☐ 36	Cito Gaston MG	.40	.16	.04

		MINT	EXC	G-VG
☐ 37	Joe Carter AS	.75	.30	.07
☐ 38	Jimmy Key AS	.40	.16	.04
☐ 39	Roberto Alomar AS	.75	.30	.07
☐ 40	1991 All-Star Game	.30	.12	.03

1991 Score Nolan Ryan Life and Times

This four-card standard-size (2 1/2" by 3 1/2") set was issued by Score to commemorate four significant milestones in Nolan Ryan's illustrious career. They are part of "The Life and Times of Nolan Ryan," a special collector set that consists of four volumes along with the cards packaged in a folder. The color action photos on the fronts are full-bleed, except on the left side, where blue and red border stripes run the length of the card. The horizontally oriented backs feature a different color player photo on the left half. The right half is accented with blue and red stripes and has career highlights on a pale yellow background. The cards are numbered on the back.

	MINT	EXC	G-VG
COMPLETE SET (4)	20.00	8.50	2.75
COMMON PLAYER (1-4)	6.00	2.50	.60
☐ 1 Nolan Ryan (5,000th Career Strikeout)	6.00	2.50	.60
☐ 2 Nolan Ryan (6th Career No-Hitter)	6.00	2.50	.60
☐ 3 Nolan Ryan (300th Career Victory)	6.00	2.50	.60
☐ 4 Nolan Ryan (7th Career No-Hitter)	6.00	2.50	.60

1991 Score Rookie/Traded

The 1991 Score Rookie and Traded set contains 110 standard-size (2 1/2" by 3 1/2") player cards and 10 "World Series II" magic motion trivia cards. The front design features glossy color action photos, with white and purple borders on a mauve card face. The player's name, team, and position are given above the pictures. In a horizontal format, the left portion of the back has a color head shot and biography, while the right portion has statistics and player profile on a pale yellow background. The cards are numbered on the back. Cards 1-80 feature traded players, while cards 81-110 focus on rookies.

	MINT	EXC	G-VG
COMPLETE SET (110)	10.00	4.50	1.25
COMMON PLAYER (1T-80T)	.05	.02	.00
COMMON PLAYER (81T-110T)	.10	.04	.01
☐ 1T Bo Jackson	1.00	.40	.10
☐ 2T Mike Flanagan	.08	.03	.01
☐ 3T Pete Incaviglia	.08	.03	.01
☐ 4T Jack Clark	.10	.04	.01

		MINT	EXC	G-VG
☐ 5T	Hubie Brooks	.08	.03	.01
☐ 6T	Ivan Calderon	.08	.03	.01
☐ 7T	Glenn Davis	.10	.04	.01
☐ 8T	Wally Backman	.05	.02	.00
☐ 9T	Dave Smith	.05	.02	.00
☐ 10T	Tim Raines	.10	.04	.01
☐ 11T	Joe Carter	.10	.04	.01
☐ 12T	Sid Bream	.05	.02	.00
☐ 13T	George Bell	.10	.04	.01
☐ 14T	Steve Bedrosian	.08	.03	.01
☐ 15T	Willie Wilson	.08	.03	.01
☐ 16T	Darryl Strawberry	.20	.08	.02
☐ 17T	Danny Jackson	.05	.02	.00
☐ 18T	Kirk Gibson	.10	.04	.01
☐ 19T	Willie McGee	.08	.03	.01
☐ 20T	Junior Felix	.05	.02	.00
☐ 21T	Steve Farr	.05	.02	.00
☐ 22T	Pat Tabler	.05	.02	.00
☐ 23T	Brett Butler	.08	.03	.01
☐ 24T	Danny Darwin	.05	.02	.00
☐ 25T	Mickey Tettleton	.08	.03	.01
☐ 26T	Gary Carter	.10	.04	.01
☐ 27T	Mitch Williams	.08	.03	.01
☐ 28T	Candy Maldonado	.05	.02	.00
☐ 29T	Otis Nixon	.08	.03	.01
☐ 30T	Brian Downing	.05	.02	.00
☐ 31T	Tom Candiotti	.08	.03	.01
☐ 32T	John Candelaria	.05	.02	.00
☐ 33T	Rob Murphy	.05	.02	.00
☐ 34T	Deion Sanders	.12	.05	.01
☐ 35T	Willie Randolph	.08	.03	.01
☐ 36T	Pete Harnisch	.08	.03	.01
☐ 37T	Dante Bichette	.05	.02	.00
☐ 38T	Garry Templeton	.05	.02	.00
☐ 39T	Gary Gaetti	.08	.03	.01
☐ 40T	John Cerutti	.05	.02	.00
☐ 41T	Rick Cerone	.05	.02	.00
☐ 42T	Mike Pagliarulo	.05	.02	.00
☐ 43T	Ron Hassey	.05	.02	.00
☐ 44T	Roberto Alomar	.12	.05	.01
☐ 45T	Mike Boddicker	.05	.02	.00
☐ 46T	Bud Black	.05	.02	.00
☐ 47T	Rob Deer	.08	.03	.01
☐ 48T	Devon White	.08	.03	.01
☐ 49T	Luis Sojo	.05	.02	.00
☐ 50T	Terry Pendleton	.10	.04	.01
☐ 51T	Kevin Gross	.05	.02	.00
☐ 52T	Mike Huff	.05	.02	.00
☐ 53T	Dave Righetti	.08	.03	.01
☐ 54T	Matt Young	.05	.02	.00
☐ 55T	Earnest Riles	.05	.02	.00
☐ 56T	Bill Gullickson	.08	.03	.01
☐ 57T	Vince Coleman	.10	.04	.01
☐ 58T	Fred McGriff	.12	.05	.01
☐ 59T	Franklin Stubbs	.05	.02	.00
☐ 60T	Eric King	.05	.02	.00
☐ 61T	Cory Snyder	.08	.03	.01
☐ 62T	Dwight Evans	.08	.03	.01
☐ 63T	Gerald Perry	.05	.02	.00
☐ 64T	Eric Show	.05	.02	.00
☐ 65T	Shawn Hillegas	.05	.02	.00
☐ 66T	Tony Fernandez	.08	.03	.01
☐ 67T	Tim Teufel	.05	.02	.00
☐ 68T	Mitch Webster	.05	.02	.00
☐ 69T	Mike Heath	.05	.02	.00
☐ 70T	Chili Davis	.08	.03	.01
☐ 71T	Larry Andersen	.05	.02	.00
☐ 72T	Gary Varsho	.05	.02	.00
☐ 73T	Juan Berenguer	.05	.02	.00
☐ 74T	Jack Morris	.10	.04	.01
☐ 75T	Barry Jones	.05	.02	.00
☐ 76T	Rafael Belliard	.05	.02	.00

☐ 77T	Steve Buechele	.05	.02	.00
☐ 78T	Scott Sanderson	.05	.02	.00
☐ 79T	Bob Ojeda	.05	.02	.00
☐ 80T	Curt Schilling	.05	.02	.00
☐ 81T	Brian Drahman	.10	.04	.01
☐ 82T	Ivan Rodriguez	2.00	.80	.20
☐ 83T	David Howard	.12	.05	.01
☐ 84T	Heathcliff Slocumb	.12	.05	.01
☐ 85T	Mike Timlin	.12	.05	.01
☐ 86T	Darryl Kile	.12	.05	.01
☐ 87T	Pete Schourek	.12	.05	.01
☐ 88T	Bruce Walton	.12	.05	.01
☐ 89T	Al Osuna	.15	.06	.01
☐ 90T	Gary Scott	.25	.10	.02
☐ 91T	Doug Simons	.12	.05	.01
☐ 92T	Chris Jones	.15	.06	.01
☐ 93T	Chuck Knoblauch	.40	.16	.04
☐ 94T	Dana Allison	.15	.06	.01
☐ 95T	Erik Pappas	.12	.05	.01
☐ 96T	Jeff Bagwell	3.00	1.25	.30
☐ 97T	Kirk Dressendorfer	.25	.10	.02
☐ 98T	Freddie Benavides	.12	.05	.01
☐ 99T	Luis Gonzalez	.45	.18	.04
☐ 100T	Wade Taylor	.17	.07	.01
☐ 101T	Ed Sprague	.12	.05	.01
☐ 102T	Bob Scanlan	.12	.05	.01
☐ 103T	Rick Wilkins	.17	.07	.01
☐ 104T	Chris Donnels	.25	.10	.02
☐ 105T	Joe Slusarski	.12	.05	.01
☐ 106T	Mark Lewis	.20	.08	.02
☐ 107T	Pat Kelly	.30	.12	.03
☐ 108T	John Briscoe	.15	.06	.01
☐ 109T	Luis Lopez	.20	.08	.02
☐ 110T	Jeff Johnson	.20	.08	.02

1991 Score 100 Rising Stars

TODD HUNDLEY
CATCHER

The 1991 Score 100 Rising Stars sets were issued by Score with or without special books which goes with the cards. The cards, which feature 100 of the most popular rising stars, are the standard size 2 1/2" by 3 1/2". The fronts of the cards are beautiful full-color photos surrounded by blue and green borders while the backs have a full color photo on the back and give a brief biography of the player. The sets (with the special book with brief biography on the players) are marketed for retail purposes at a suggested price of 12.95.

		MINT	VG-E	F-G
COMPLETE SET (100)		12.00	5.25	1.50
COMMON PLAYER (1-100)		.05	.02	.00

☐ 1	Sandy Alomar Jr.	.25	.10	.02
☐ 2	Tom Edens	.10	.04	.01
☐ 3	Terry Shumpert	.10	.04	.01
☐ 4	Shawn Boskie	.10	.04	.01
☐ 5	Steve Avery	.75	.30	.07
☐ 6	Deion Sanders	.35	.15	.03
☐ 7	John Burkett	.10	.04	.01
☐ 8	Stan Belinda	.10	.04	.01
☐ 9	Thomas Howard	.10	.04	.01
☐ 10	Wayne Edwards	.10	.04	.01
☐ 11	Rick Parker	.05	.02	.00
☐ 12	Randy Veres	.10	.04	.01
☐ 13	Alex Cole	.25	.10	.02

☐ 14	Scott Chiamparino	.10	.04	.01
☐ 15	Greg Olson	.10	.04	.01
☐ 16	Jose DeJesus	.10	.04	.01
☐ 17	Mike Blowers	.10	.04	.01
☐ 18	Jeff Huson	.05	.02	.00
☐ 19	Willie Blair	.05	.02	.00
☐ 20	Howard Farmer	.10	.04	.01
☐ 21	Larry Walker	.15	.06	.01
☐ 22	Scott Hemond	.15	.06	.01
☐ 23	Mel Stottlemyre Jr.	.05	.02	.00
☐ 24	Mark Whiten	.35	.15	.03
☐ 25	Jeff Schulz	.10	.04	.01
☐ 26	Gary DiSarcina	.05	.02	.00
☐ 27	George Canale	.10	.04	.01
☐ 28	Dean Palmer	.35	.15	.03
☐ 29	Jim Leyritz	.05	.02	.00
☐ 30	Carlos Baerga	.35	.15	.03
☐ 31	Rafael Valdez	.10	.04	.01
☐ 32	Derek Bell	.75	.30	.07
☐ 33	Francisco Cabrera	.15	.06	.01
☐ 34	Chris Hoiles	.15	.06	.01
☐ 35	Craig Grebeck	.10	.04	.01
☐ 36	Scott Coolbaugh	.10	.04	.01
☐ 37	Kevin Wickander	.10	.04	.01
☐ 38	Marquis Grissom	.25	.10	.02
☐ 39	Chip Hale	.05	.02	.00
☐ 40	Kevin Maas	.50	.20	.05
☐ 41	Juan Gonzalez	.75	.30	.07
☐ 42	Eric Anthony	.20	.08	.02
☐ 43	Luis Sojo	.10	.04	.01
☐ 44	Paul Sorrento	.10	.04	.01
☐ 45	Dave Justice	.75	.30	.07
☐ 46	Oscar Azocar	.10	.04	.01
☐ 47	Charles Nagy	.15	.06	.01
☐ 48	Robin Ventura	.50	.20	.05
☐ 49	Reggie Harris	.15	.06	.01
☐ 50	Ben McDonald	.30	.12	.03
☐ 51	Hector Villanueva	.20	.08	.02
☐ 52	Kevin Tapani	.20	.08	.02
☐ 53	Brian Bohanon	.15	.06	.01
☐ 54	Tim Layana	.10	.04	.01
☐ 55	Delino DeShields	.30	.12	.03
☐ 56	Beau Allred	.10	.04	.01
☐ 57	Eric Gunderson	.10	.04	.01
☐ 58	Kent Mercker	.10	.04	.01
☐ 59	Juan Bell	.10	.04	.01
☐ 60	Glenallen Hill	.10	.04	.01
☐ 61	David Segui	.20	.08	.02
☐ 62	Alan Mills	.10	.04	.01
☐ 63	Mike Harkey	.15	.06	.01
☐ 64	Bill Sampen	.10	.04	.01
☐ 65	Greg Vaughn	.30	.12	.03
☐ 66	Alex Fernandez	.30	.12	.03
☐ 67	Mike Hartley	.10	.04	.01
☐ 68	Travis Fryman	.60	.25	.06
☐ 69	Dave Rohde	.10	.04	.01
☐ 70	Tom Lampkin	.05	.02	.00
☐ 71	Mark Gardner	.10	.04	.01
☐ 72	Pat Combs	.10	.04	.01
☐ 73	Kevin Appier	.15	.06	.01
☐ 74	Mike Fetters	.10	.04	.01
☐ 75	Greg Myers	.10	.04	.01
☐ 76	Steve Searcy	.05	.02	.00
☐ 77	Tim Naehring	.15	.06	.01
☐ 78	Frank Thomas	1.50	.60	.15
☐ 79	Todd Hundley	.20	.08	.02
☐ 80	Ed Vosberg	.05	.02	.00
☐ 81	Todd Zeile	.25	.10	.02
☐ 82	Lee Stevens	.25	.10	.02
☐ 83	Scott Radinsky	.10	.04	.01
☐ 84	Hensley Meulens	.20	.08	.02
☐ 85	Brian DuBois	.10	.04	.01
☐ 86	Steve Olin	.10	.04	.01
☐ 87	Julio Machado	.05	.02	.00
☐ 88	Jose Vizcaino	.05	.02	.00
☐ 89	Mark Lemke	.15	.06	.01
☐ 90	Felix Jose	.40	.16	.04
☐ 91	Wally Whitehurst	.10	.04	.01
☐ 92	Dana Kiecker	.10	.04	.01
☐ 93	Mike Munoz	.15	.06	.01
☐ 94	Adam Peterson	.10	.04	.01
☐ 95	Tim Drummond	.10	.04	.01
☐ 96	Dave Hollins	.20	.08	.02
☐ 97	Craig Wilson	.15	.06	.01
☐ 98	Hal Morris	.35	.15	.03
☐ 99	Jose Offerman	.25	.10	.02
☐ 100	John Olerud	.30	.12	.03

1991 Score 100 Superstars

The 1991 Score 100 Superstars sets were issued by Score with or without special books which goes with the cards. The cards, which feature 100 of the most popular superstars, are the standard size 2 1/2" by 3 1/2". The fronts of the cards feature beautiful full-color photos surrounded by red, white and blue borders while the backs are surrounded by red and blue borders and feature a full-color photo on the back along with a brief biography. The sets (with the special book with brief biography on the players) are marketed for retail purposes at a suggested price of 12.95.

		MINT	VG-E	F-G
COMPLETE SET (1-100)		12.00	5.25	1.50
COMMON PLAYER (1-100)		.05	.02	.00
☐ 1	Jose Canseco	.90	.40	.09
☐ 2	Bo Jackson	1.00	.40	.10
☐ 3	Wade Boggs	.50	.20	.05
☐ 4	Will Clark	.90	.40	.09
☐ 5	Ken Griffey Jr.	1.25	.50	.12
☐ 6	Doug Drabek	.15	.06	.01
☐ 7	Kirby Puckett	.40	.16	.04
☐ 8	Joe Orsulak	.05	.02	.00
☐ 9	Eric Davis	.30	.12	.03
☐ 10	Rickey Henderson	.90	.40	.09
☐ 11	Len Dykstra	.10	.04	.01
☐ 12	Ruben Sierra	.35	.15	.03
☐ 13	Paul Molitor	.10	.04	.01
☐ 14	Ron Gant	.50	.20	.05
☐ 15	Ozzie Guillen	.10	.04	.01
☐ 16	Ramon Martinez	.35	.15	.03
☐ 17	Edgar Martinez	.15	.06	.01
☐ 18	Ozzie Smith	.20	.08	.02
☐ 19	Charlie Hayes	.10	.04	.01
☐ 20	Barry Larkin	.20	.08	.02
☐ 21	Cal Ripken	.90	.40	.09
☐ 22	Andy Van Slyke	.10	.04	.01
☐ 23	Don Mattingly	.60	.25	.06
☐ 24	Dave Stewart	.10	.04	.01
☐ 25	Nolan Ryan	1.00	.40	.10
☐ 26	Barry Bonds	.45	.18	.04
☐ 27	Gregg Olson	.20	.08	.02
☐ 28	Chris Sabo	.25	.10	.02
☐ 29	John Franco	.10	.04	.01
☐ 30	Gary Sheffield	.20	.08	.02
☐ 31	Jeff Treadway	.05	.02	.00
☐ 32	Tom Browning	.05	.02	.00
☐ 33	Jose Lind	.05	.02	.00
☐ 34	Dave Magadan	.10	.04	.01
☐ 35	Dale Murphy	.30	.12	.03
☐ 36	Tom Candiotti	.10	.04	.01
☐ 37	Willie McGee	.15	.06	.01
☐ 38	Robin Yount	.30	.12	.03
☐ 39	Mark McGwire	.40	.16	.04
☐ 40	George Bell	.15	.06	.01
☐ 41	Carlton Fisk	.30	.12	.03
☐ 42	Bobby Bonilla	.30	.12	.03
☐ 43	Randy Milligan	.10	.04	.01
☐ 44	Dave Parker	.15	.06	.01
☐ 45	Shawon Dunston	.15	.06	.01
☐ 46	Brian Harper	.10	.04	.01
☐ 47	John Tudor	.05	.02	.00
☐ 48	Ellis Burks	.30	.12	.03
☐ 49	Bob Welch	.10	.04	.01
☐ 50	Roger Clemens	.90	.40	.09
☐ 51	Mike Henneman	.05	.02	.00
☐ 52	Eddie Murray	.30	.12	.03
☐ 53	Kal Daniels	.10	.04	.01
☐ 54	Doug Jones	.05	.02	.00
☐ 55	Craig Biggio	.20	.08	.02
☐ 56	Rafael Palmeiro	.20	.08	.02
☐ 57	Wally Joyner	.20	.08	.02
☐ 58	Tim Wallach	.10	.04	.01
☐ 59	Bret Saberhagen	.20	.08	.02
☐ 60	Ryne Sandberg	.90	.40	.09
☐ 61	Benito Santiago	.15	.06	.01
☐ 62	Darryl Strawberry	.60	.25	.06
☐ 63	Alan Trammell	.20	.08	.02
☐ 64	Kelly Gruber	.15	.06	.01
☐ 65	Dwight Gooden	.30	.12	.03
☐ 66	Dave Winfield	.25	.10	.02
☐ 67	Rick Aguilera	.05	.02	.00
☐ 68	Dave Righetti	.10	.04	.01
☐ 69	Jim Abbott	.35	.15	.03
☐ 70	Frank Viola	.15	.06	.01
☐ 71	Fred McGriff	.25	.10	.02
☐ 72	Steve Sax	.10	.04	.01
☐ 73	Dennis Eckersley	.15	.06	.01
☐ 74	Cory Snyder	.10	.04	.01
☐ 75	Mackey Sasser	.10	.04	.01
☐ 76	Candy Maldonado	.10	.04	.01
☐ 77	Matt Williams	.30	.12	.03
☐ 78	Kent Hrbek	.10	.04	.01
☐ 79	Randy Myers	.05	.02	.00
☐ 80	Gregg Jefferies	.25	.10	.02
☐ 81	Joe Carter	.20	.08	.02
☐ 82	Mike Greenwell	.30	.12	.03
☐ 83	Jack Armstong	.10	.04	.01
☐ 84	Julio Franco	.20	.08	.02
☐ 85	George Brett	.30	.12	.03
☐ 86	Howard Johnson	.20	.08	.02
☐ 87	Andre Dawson	.25	.10	.02
☐ 88	Cecil Fielder	.50	.20	.05
☐ 89	Tim Raines	.15	.06	.01
☐ 90	Chuck Finley	.15	.06	.01
☐ 91	Mark Grace	.40	.16	.04
☐ 92	Brook Jacoby	.10	.04	.01
☐ 93	Dave Stieb	.15	.06	.01
☐ 94	Tony Gwynn	.40	.16	.04
☐ 95	Bobby Thigpen	.10	.04	.01
☐ 96	Roberto Kelly	.25	.10	.02
☐ 97	Kevin Seitzer	.10	.04	.01
☐ 98	Kevin Mitchell	.30	.12	.03
☐ 99	Dwight Evans	.10	.04	.01
☐ 100	Roberto Alomar	.40	.16	.04

1992 Score Preview

The 1992 Score Preview set contains six cards, each measuring standard size, 2 1/2" by 3 1/2", done in the same style as the 1992 Score baseball cards. Supposedly the Sandberg and Mack cards are tougher as they were only available at the St. Louis card show that Score attended in November 1991.

		MINT	EXC	G-VG
COMPLETE SET (6)		35.00	15.75	5.25
COMMON PLAYER (1-6)		5.00	2.25	.50
☐ 1	Ken Griffey Jr.	10.00	4.50	1.25
☐ 2	Dave Justice	7.50	3.25	.75
☐ 3	Robin Ventura	5.00	2.25	.50

		MINT	EXC	G-VG
☐ 4	Steve Avery	5.00	2.25	.50
☐ 5	Ryne Sandberg	10.00	4.50	1.25
☐ 6	Shane Mack	7.50	3.25	.75

1992 Score I

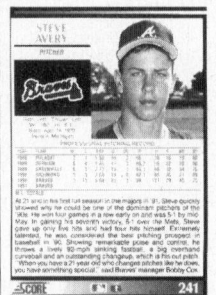

The 1992 Score I set contains 442 cards measuring the standard size (2 1/2" by 3 1/2"). The glossy color action photos on the fronts are bordered above and below by stripes of the same color, and a thicker, different color stripe runs the length of the card to one side of the picture. The backs have a color close-up shot in the upper right corner, with biography, complete career statistics, and player profile printed on a yellow background. Hall of Famer Joe DiMaggio is remembered in a five-card subset. He autographed 2,500 cards; 2,495 of these were randomly inserted in Series I packs, while the other five were given away through a mail-in sweepstakes. Another 150,000 unsigned DiMaggio cards were inserted in Series I Count Goods packs only. Score later extended its DiMaggio promotion to Series I blister packs; one hundred signed and twelve thousand unsigned cards were randomly inserted in these packs. Also a special "World Series II" trivia card was inserted into each pack. These cards highlight crucial games and heroes from past Octobers. Topical subsets included in the set focus on Rookie Prospects (395-424), No-Hit Club (425-428), Highlights (429-430), AL All-Stars (431-440; with color montages displaying Chris Greco's player caricatures), and Dream Team (441-442). The cards are numbered on the back.

		MINT	EXC	G-VG
	COMPLETE SET (442)	13.50	6.00	1.85
	COMMON PLAYER (1-442)	.03	.01	.00
☐ 1	Ken Griffey Jr.	.50	.20	.05
☐ 2	Nolan Ryan	.30	.12	.03
☐ 3	Will Clark	.20	.08	.02
☐ 4	Dave Justice	.30	.12	.03
☐ 5	Dave Henderson	.06	.02	.00
☐ 6	Bret Saberhagen	.08	.03	.01
☐ 7	Fred McGriff	.08	.03	.01
☐ 8	Erik Hanson	.06	.02	.00
☐ 9	Darryl Strawberry	.15	.06	.01
☐ 10	Dwight Gooden	.08	.03	.01
☐ 11	Juan Gonzalez	.25	.10	.02
☐ 12	Mark Langston	.06	.02	.00
☐ 13	Lonnie Smith	.03	.01	.00
☐ 14	Jeff Montgomery	.03	.01	.00
☐ 15	Roberto Alomar	.08	.03	.01
☐ 16	Delino DeShields	.06	.02	.00
☐ 17	Steve Bedrosian	.03	.01	.00
☐ 18	Terry Pendleton	.06	.02	.00
☐ 19	Mark Carreon	.03	.01	.00
☐ 20	Mark McGwire	.10	.04	.01
☐ 21	Roger Clemens	.15	.06	.01
☐ 22	Chuck Crim	.03	.01	.00
☐ 23	Don Mattingly	.12	.05	.01
☐ 24	Dickie Thon	.03	.01	.00
☐ 25	Ron Gant	.10	.04	.01
☐ 26	Milt Cuyler	.08	.03	.01
☐ 27	Mike Macfarlane	.03	.01	.00
☐ 28	Dan Gladden	.03	.01	.00
☐ 29	Melido Perez	.03	.01	.00
☐ 30	Willie Randolph	.03	.01	.00
☐ 31	Albert Belle	.12	.05	.01
☐ 32	Dave Winfield	.10	.04	.01
☐ 33	Jimmy Jones	.03	.01	.00
☐ 34	Kevin Gross	.03	.01	.00
☐ 35	Andres Galarraga	.06	.02	.00
☐ 36	Mike Devereaux	.03	.01	.00
☐ 37	Chris Bosio	.03	.01	.00
☐ 38	Mike LaValliere	.03	.01	.00
☐ 39	Gary Gaetti	.06	.02	.00
☐ 40	Felix Jose	.08	.03	.01
☐ 41	Alvaro Espinoza	.03	.01	.00
☐ 42	Rick Aguilera	.03	.01	.00
☐ 43	Mike Gallego	.03	.01	.00
☐ 44	Eric Davis	.10	.04	.01
☐ 45	George Bell	.08	.03	.01
☐ 46	Tom Brunansky	.06	.02	.00
☐ 47	Steve Farr	.03	.01	.00
☐ 48	Duane Ward	.03	.01	.00
☐ 49	David Wells	.03	.01	.00
☐ 50	Cecil Fielder	.15	.06	.01
☐ 51	Walt Weiss	.06	.02	.00
☐ 52	Todd Zeile	.10	.04	.01
☐ 53	Doug Jones	.03	.01	.00
☐ 54	Bob Walk	.03	.01	.00
☐ 55	Rafael Palmeiro	.08	.03	.01
☐ 56	Rob Deer	.03	.01	.00
☐ 57	Paul O'Neill	.06	.02	.00
☐ 58	Jeff Reardon	.06	.02	.00
☐ 59	Randy Ready	.03	.01	.00
☐ 60	Scott Erickson	.17	.07	.01
☐ 61	Paul Molitor	.08	.03	.01
☐ 62	Jack McDowell	.08	.03	.01
☐ 63	Jim Acker	.03	.01	.00
☐ 64	Jay Buhner	.06	.02	.00
☐ 65	Travis Fryman	.15	.06	.01
☐ 66	Marquis Grissom	.08	.03	.01
☐ 67	Mike Harkey	.06	.02	.00
☐ 68	Luis Polonia	.06	.02	.00
☐ 69	Ken Caminiti	.03	.01	.00
☐ 70	Chris Sabo	.08	.03	.01
☐ 71	Gregg Olson	.06	.02	.00
☐ 72	Carlton Fisk	.10	.04	.01
☐ 73	Juan Samuel	.06	.02	.00
☐ 74	Todd Stottlemyre	.06	.02	.00
☐ 75	Andre Dawson	.10	.04	.01
☐ 76	Alvin Davis	.06	.02	.00
☐ 77	Bill Doran	.03	.01	.00
☐ 78	B.J. Surhoff	.06	.02	.00
☐ 79	Kirk McCaskill	.03	.01	.00
☐ 80	Dale Murphy	.10	.04	.01
☐ 81	Jose DeLeon	.03	.01	.00
☐ 82	Alex Fernandez	.10	.04	.01
☐ 83	Ivan Calderon	.06	.02	.00
☐ 84	Brent Mayne	.06	.02	.00
☐ 85	Jody Reed	.06	.02	.00
☐ 86	Randy Tomlin	.08	.03	.01
☐ 87	Randy Milligan	.06	.02	.00
☐ 88	Pascual Perez	.03	.01	.00
☐ 89	Hensley Meulens	.06	.02	.00
☐ 90	Joe Carter	.08	.03	.01
☐ 91	Mike Moore	.06	.02	.00
☐ 92	Ozzie Guillen	.06	.02	.00
☐ 93	Shawn Hillegas	.03	.01	.00
☐ 94	Chili Davis	.06	.02	.00
☐ 95	Vince Coleman	.08	.03	.01
☐ 96	Jimmy Key	.06	.02	.00
☐ 97	Billy Ripken	.03	.01	.00
☐ 98	Dave Smith	.03	.01	.00
☐ 99	Tom Bolton	.03	.01	.00
☐ 100	Barry Larkin	.08	.03	.01
☐ 101	Kenny Rogers	.03	.01	.00
☐ 102	Mike Boddicker	.03	.01	.00
☐ 103	Kevin Elster	.03	.01	.00
☐ 104	Ken Hill	.03	.01	.00
☐ 105	Charlie Leibrandt	.03	.01	.00
☐ 106	Pat Combs	.03	.01	.00
☐ 107	Hubie Brooks	.06	.02	.00
☐ 108	Julio Franco	.08	.03	.01
☐ 109	Vicente Palacios	.03	.01	.00
☐ 110	Kal Daniels	.06	.02	.00
☐ 111	Bruce Hurst	.06	.02	.00
☐ 112	Willie McGee	.06	.02	.00
☐ 113	Ted Power	.03	.01	.00
☐ 114	Milt Thompson	.03	.01	.00
☐ 115	Doug Drabek	.06	.02	.00
☐ 116	Rafael Belliard	.03	.01	.00
☐ 117	Scott Garrelts	.03	.01	.00
☐ 118	Terry Mulholland	.03	.01	.00
☐ 119	Jay Howell	.03	.01	.00
☐ 120	Danny Jackson	.03	.01	.00
☐ 121	Scott Ruskin	.03	.01	.00

#	Name			
☐ 122	Robin Ventura	.15	.06	.01
☐ 123	Bip Roberts	.03	.01	.00
☐ 124	Jeff Russell	.03	.01	.00
☐ 125	Hal Morris	.08	.03	.01
☐ 126	Teddy Higuera	.03	.01	.00
☐ 127	Luis Sojo	.03	.01	.00
☐ 128	Carlos Baerga	.08	.03	.01
☐ 129	Jeff Ballard	.03	.01	.00
☐ 130	Tom Gordon	.06	.02	.00
☐ 131	Sid Bream	.03	.01	.00
☐ 132	Rance Mulliniks	.03	.01	.00
☐ 133	Andy Benes	.08	.03	.01
☐ 134	Mickey Tettleton	.06	.02	.00
☐ 135	Rich DeLucia	.03	.01	.00
☐ 136	Tom Pagnozzi	.03	.01	.00
☐ 137	Harold Baines	.06	.02	.00
☐ 138	Danny Darwin	.03	.01	.00
☐ 139	Kevin Bass	.03	.01	.00
☐ 140	Chris Nabholz	.03	.01	.00
☐ 141	Pete O'Brien	.03	.01	.00
☐ 142	Jeff Treadway	.03	.01	.00
☐ 143	Mickey Morandini	.06	.02	.00
☐ 144	Eric King	.03	.01	.00
☐ 145	Danny Tartabull	.08	.03	.01
☐ 146	Lance Johnson	.03	.01	.00
☐ 147	Casey Candaele	.03	.01	.00
☐ 148	Felix Fermin	.03	.01	.00
☐ 149	Rich Rodriguez	.06	.02	.00
☐ 150	Dwight Evans	.06	.02	.00
☐ 151	Joe Klink	.03	.01	.00
☐ 152	Kevin Reimer	.06	.02	.00
☐ 153	Orlando Merced	.12	.05	.01
☐ 154	Mel Hall	.06	.02	.00
☐ 155	Randy Myers	.03	.01	.00
☐ 156	Greg Harris	.03	.01	.00
☐ 157	Jeff Brantley	.03	.01	.00
☐ 158	Jim Eisenreich	.03	.01	.00
☐ 159	Luis Rivera	.03	.01	.00
☐ 160	Cris Carpenter	.03	.01	.00
☐ 161	Bruce Ruffin	.03	.01	.00
☐ 162	Omar Vizquel	.03	.01	.00
☐ 163	Gerald Alexander	.03	.01	.00
☐ 164	Mark Guthrie	.03	.01	.00
☐ 165	Scott Lewis	.08	.03	.01
☐ 166	Bill Sampen	.03	.01	.00
☐ 167	Dave Anderson	.03	.01	.00
☐ 168	Kevin McReynolds	.06	.02	.00
☐ 169	Jose Vizcaino	.03	.01	.00
☐ 170	Bob Geren	.03	.01	.00
☐ 171	Mike Morgan	.06	.02	.00
☐ 172	Jim Gott	.03	.01	.00
☐ 173	Mike Pagliarulo	.03	.01	.00
☐ 174	Mike Jeffcoat	.03	.01	.00
☐ 175	Craig Lefferts	.03	.01	.00
☐ 176	Steve Finley	.06	.02	.00
☐ 177	Wally Backman	.03	.01	.00
☐ 178	Kent Mercker	.03	.01	.00
☐ 179	John Cerutti	.03	.01	.00
☐ 180	Jay Bell	.03	.01	.00
☐ 181	Dale Sveum	.03	.01	.00
☐ 182	Greg Gagne	.03	.01	.00
☐ 183	Donnie Hill	.03	.01	.00
☐ 184	Rex Hudler	.03	.01	.00
☐ 185	Pat Kelly	.10	.04	.01
☐ 186	Jeff Robinson	.03	.01	.00
☐ 187	Jeff Gray	.03	.01	.00
☐ 188	Jerry Willard	.03	.01	.00
☐ 189	Carlos Quintana	.06	.02	.00
☐ 190	Dennis Eckersley	.06	.02	.00
☐ 191	Kelly Downs	.03	.01	.00
☐ 192	Gregg Jefferies	.08	.03	.01
☐ 193	Darrin Fletcher	.03	.01	.00
☐ 194	Mike Jackson	.03	.01	.00
☐ 195	Eddie Murray	.10	.04	.01
☐ 196	Bill Landrum	.03	.01	.00
☐ 197	Eric Yelding	.03	.01	.00
☐ 198	Devon White	.06	.02	.00
☐ 199	Larry Walker	.06	.02	.00
☐ 200	Ryne Sandberg	.18	.08	.01
☐ 201	Dave Magadan	.06	.02	.00
☐ 202	Steve Chitren	.03	.01	.00
☐ 203	Scott Fletcher	.03	.01	.00
☐ 204	Dwayne Henry	.03	.01	.00
☐ 205	Scott Coolbaugh	.03	.01	.00
☐ 206	Tracy Jones	.03	.01	.00
☐ 207	Von Hayes	.06	.02	.00
☐ 208	Bob Melvin	.03	.01	.00
☐ 209	Scott Scudder	.03	.01	.00
☐ 210	Luis Gonzalez	.12	.05	.01
☐ 211	Scott Sanderson	.03	.01	.00
☐ 212	Chris Donnels	.12	.05	.01
☐ 213	Heathcliff Slocumb	.03	.01	.00
☐ 214	Mike Timlin	.06	.02	.00
☐ 215	Brian Harper	.03	.01	.00
☐ 216	Juan Berenguer	.03	.01	.00
☐ 217	Mike Henneman	.03	.01	.00
☐ 218	Bill Spiers	.03	.01	.00
☐ 219	Scott Terry	.03	.01	.00
☐ 220	Frank Viola	.06	.02	.00
☐ 221	Mark Eichhorn	.03	.01	.00
☐ 222	Ernest Riles	.03	.01	.00
☐ 223	Ray Lankford	.10	.04	.01
☐ 224	Pete Harnisch	.06	.02	.00
☐ 225	Bobby Bonilla	.10	.04	.01
☐ 226	Mike Scioscia	.03	.01	.00
☐ 227	Joel Skinner	.03	.01	.00
☐ 228	Brian Holman	.03	.01	.00
☐ 229	Gilberto Reyes	.03	.01	.00
☐ 230	Matt Williams	.10	.04	.01
☐ 231	Jaime Navarro	.03	.01	.00
☐ 232	Jose Rijo	.06	.02	.00
☐ 233	Atlee Hammaker	.03	.01	.00
☐ 234	Tim Teufel	.03	.01	.00
☐ 235	John Kruk	.06	.02	.00
☐ 236	Kurt Stillwell	.03	.01	.00
☐ 237	Dan Pasqua	.03	.01	.00
☐ 238	Tim Crews	.03	.01	.00
☐ 239	Dave Gallagher	.03	.01	.00
☐ 240	Leo Gomez	.10	.04	.01
☐ 241	Steve Avery	.20	.08	.02
☐ 242	Bill Gullickson	.03	.01	.00
☐ 243	Mark Portugal	.03	.01	.00
☐ 244	Lee Guetterman	.03	.01	.00
☐ 245	Benito Santiago	.08	.03	.01
☐ 246	Jim Gantner	.03	.01	.00
☐ 247	Robby Thompson	.03	.01	.00
☐ 248	Terry Shumpert	.03	.01	.00
☐ 249	Mike Bell	.06	.02	.00
☐ 250	Harold Reynolds	.03	.01	.00
☐ 251	Mike Felder	.03	.01	.00
☐ 252	Bill Pecota	.03	.01	.00
☐ 253	Bill Krueger	.03	.01	.00
☐ 254	Alfredo Griffin	.03	.01	.00
☐ 255	Lou Whitaker	.06	.02	.00
☐ 256	Roy Smith	.03	.01	.00
☐ 257	Jerald Clark	.03	.01	.00
☐ 258	Sammy Sosa	.06	.02	.00
☐ 259	Tim Naehring	.06	.02	.00
☐ 260	Dave Righetti	.06	.02	.00
☐ 261	Paul Gibson	.03	.01	.00
☐ 262	Chris James	.03	.01	.00
☐ 263	Larry Andersen	.03	.01	.00
☐ 264	Storm Davis	.03	.01	.00
☐ 265	Jose Lind	.03	.01	.00
☐ 266	Greg Hibbard	.03	.01	.00
☐ 267	Norm Charlton	.03	.01	.00
☐ 268	Paul Kilgus	.03	.01	.00
☐ 269	Greg Maddux	.06	.02	.00
☐ 270	Ellis Burks	.08	.03	.01
☐ 271	Frank Tanana	.06	.02	.00
☐ 272	Gene Larkin	.03	.01	.00
☐ 273	Ron Hassey	.03	.01	.00
☐ 274	Jeff Robinson	.03	.01	.00
☐ 275	Steve Howe	.03	.01	.00
☐ 276	Daryl Boston	.03	.01	.00
☐ 277	Mark Lee	.06	.02	.00
☐ 278	Jose Segura	.06	.02	.00
☐ 279	Lance Blankenship	.03	.01	.00
☐ 280	Don Slaught	.03	.01	.00
☐ 281	Russ Swan	.03	.01	.00
☐ 282	Bob Tewksbury	.03	.01	.00
☐ 283	Geno Petralli	.03	.01	.00
☐ 284	Shane Mack	.06	.02	.00
☐ 285	Bob Scanlan	.06	.02	.00
☐ 286	Tim Leary	.06	.02	.00
☐ 287	John Smoltz	.08	.03	.01
☐ 288	Pat Borders	.03	.01	.00
☐ 289	Mark Davidson	.03	.01	.00
☐ 290	Sam Horn	.03	.01	.00
☐ 291	Lenny Harris	.03	.01	.00
☐ 292	Franklin Stubbs	.03	.01	.00
☐ 293	Thomas Howard	.03	.01	.00
☐ 294	Steve Lyons	.03	.01	.00
☐ 295	Francisco Oliveras	.03	.01	.00
☐ 296	Terry Leach	.03	.01	.00
☐ 297	Barry Jones	.03	.01	.00
☐ 298	Lance Parrish	.06	.02	.00
☐ 299	Wally Whitehurst	.03	.01	.00
☐ 300	Bob Welch	.06	.02	.00
☐ 301	Charlie Hayes	.03	.01	.00
☐ 302	Charlie Hough	.03	.01	.00
☐ 303	Gary Redus	.03	.01	.00
☐ 304	Scott Bradley	.03	.01	.00
☐ 305	Jose Oquendo	.03	.01	.00
☐ 306	Pete Incaviglia	.06	.02	.00
☐ 307	Marvin Freeman	.03	.01	.00
☐ 308	Gary Pettis	.03	.01	.00
☐ 309	Joe Slusarski	.06	.02	.00

☐ 310	Kevin Seitzer	.06	.02	.00
☐ 311	Jeff Reed	.03	.01	.00
☐ 312	Pat Tabler	.03	.01	.00
☐ 313	Mike Maddux	.03	.01	.00
☐ 314	Bob Milacki	.03	.01	.00
☐ 315	Eric Anthony	.06	.02	.00
☐ 316	Dante Bichette	.03	.01	.00
☐ 317	Steve Decker	.10	.04	.01
☐ 318	Jack Clark	.06	.02	.00
☐ 319	Doug Dascenzo	.03	.01	.00
☐ 320	Scott Leius	.06	.02	.00
☐ 321	Jim Lindeman	.03	.01	.00
☐ 322	Bryan Harvey	.06	.02	.00
☐ 323	Spike Owen	.03	.01	.00
☐ 324	Roberto Kelly	.08	.03	.01
☐ 325	Stan Belinda	.03	.01	.00
☐ 326	Joey Cora	.03	.01	.00
☐ 327	Jeff Innis	.03	.01	.00
☐ 328	Willie Wilson	.06	.02	.00
☐ 329	Juan Agosto	.03	.01	.00
☐ 330	Charles Nagy	.06	.02	.00
☐ 331	Scott Bailes	.03	.01	.00
☐ 332	Pete Schourek	.06	.02	.00
☐ 333	Mike Flanagan	.06	.02	.00
☐ 334	Omar Olivares	.06	.02	.00
☐ 335	Dennis Lamp	.03	.01	.00
☐ 336	Tommy Greene	.06	.02	.00
☐ 337	Randy Velarde	.03	.01	.00
☐ 338	Tom Lampkin	.03	.01	.00
☐ 339	John Russell	.03	.01	.00
☐ 340	Bob Kipper	.03	.01	.00
☐ 341	Todd Burns	.03	.01	.00
☐ 342	Ron Jones	.03	.01	.00
☐ 343	Dave Valle	.03	.01	.00
☐ 344	Mike Heath	.03	.01	.00
☐ 345	John Olerud	.10	.04	.01
☐ 346	Gerald Young	.03	.01	.00
☐ 347	Ken Patterson	.03	.01	.00
☐ 348	Les Lancaster	.03	.01	.00
☐ 349	Steve Crawford	.03	.01	.00
☐ 350	John Candelaria	.03	.01	.00
☐ 351	Mike Aldrete	.03	.01	.00
☐ 352	Mariano Duncan	.03	.01	.00
☐ 353	Julio Machado	.03	.01	.00
☐ 354	Ken Williams	.03	.01	.00
☐ 355	Walt Terrell	.03	.01	.00
☐ 356	Mitch Williams	.03	.01	.00
☐ 357	Al Newman	.03	.01	.00
☐ 358	Bud Black	.03	.01	.00
☐ 359	Joe Hesketh	.03	.01	.00
☐ 360	Paul Assenmacher	.03	.01	.00
☐ 361	Bo Jackson	.25	.10	.02
☐ 362	Jeff Blauser	.03	.01	.00
☐ 363	Mike Brumley	.03	.01	.00
☐ 364	Jim Deshaies	.03	.01	.00
☐ 365	Brady Anderson	.03	.01	.00
☐ 366	Chuck McElroy	.03	.01	.00
☐ 367	Matt Merullo	.03	.01	.00
☐ 368	Tim Belcher	.06	.02	.00
☐ 369	Luis Aquino	.03	.01	.00
☐ 370	Joe Oliver	.03	.01	.00
☐ 371	Greg Swindell	.06	.02	.00
☐ 372	Lee Stevens	.06	.02	.00
☐ 373	Mark Knudson	.03	.01	.00
☐ 374	Bill Wegman	.03	.01	.00
☐ 375	Jerry Don Gleaton	.03	.01	.00
☐ 376	Pedro Guerrero	.06	.02	.00
☐ 377	Randy Bush	.03	.01	.00
☐ 378	Greg Harris	.03	.01	.00
☐ 379	Eric Plunk	.03	.01	.00
☐ 380	Jose DeJesus	.03	.01	.00
☐ 381	Bobby Witt	.06	.02	.00
☐ 382	Curtis Wilkerson	.03	.01	.00
☐ 383	Gene Nelson	.03	.01	.00
☐ 384	Wes Chamberlain	.12	.05	.01
☐ 385	Tom Henke	.03	.01	.00
☐ 386	Mark Lemke	.03	.01	.00
☐ 387	Greg Briley	.03	.01	.00
☐ 388	Rafael Ramirez	.03	.01	.00
☐ 389	Tony Fossas	.03	.01	.00
☐ 390	Henry Cotto	.03	.01	.00
☐ 391	Tim Hulett	.03	.01	.00
☐ 392	Dean Palmer	.17	.07	.01
☐ 393	Glenn Braggs	.03	.01	.00
☐ 394	Mark Salas	.03	.01	.00
☐ 395	Rusty Meacham	.08	.03	.01
☐ 396	Andy Ashby	.08	.03	.01
☐ 397	Jose Melendez	.08	.03	.01
☐ 398	Warren Newson	.08	.03	.01
☐ 399	Frank Castillo	.08	.03	.01
☐ 400	Chito Martinez	.25	.10	.02
☐ 401	Bernie Williams	.12	.05	.01
☐ 402	Derek Bell	.15	.06	.01
☐ 403	Javier Ortiz	.06	.02	.00

☐ 404	Tim Sherrill	.06	.02	.00
☐ 405	Rob MacDonald	.06	.02	.00
☐ 406	Phil Plantier	.30	.12	.03
☐ 407	Troy Afenir	.03	.01	.00
☐ 408	Gino Minutelli	.08	.03	.01
☐ 409	Reggie Jefferson	.15	.06	.01
☐ 410	Mike Remlinger	.03	.01	.00
☐ 411	Carlos Rodriguez	.06	.02	.00
☐ 412	Joe Redfield	.15	.06	.01
☐ 413	Alonzo Powell	.06	.02	.00
☐ 414	Scott Livingstone UER (Travis Fryman, not Woody, should be referenced on back)	.10	.04	.01
☐ 415	Scott Kamieniecki	.06	.02	.00
☐ 416	Tim Spehr	.08	.03	.01
☐ 417	Brian Hunter	.35	.15	.03
☐ 418	Ced Landrum	.08	.03	.01
☐ 419	Bret Barberie	.15	.06	.01
☐ 420	Kevin Morton	.06	.02	.00
☐ 421	Doug Henry	.12	.05	.01
☐ 422	Doug Piatt	.08	.03	.01
☐ 423	Pat Rice	.12	.05	.01
☐ 424	Juan Guzman	.17	.07	.01
☐ 425	Nolan Ryan NH	.18	.08	.01
☐ 426	Tommy Greene NH	.06	.02	.00
☐ 427	Bob Milacki and Mike Flanagan NH (Mark Williamson and Gregg Olson)	.06	.02	.00
☐ 428	Wilson Alvarez NH	.06	.02	.00
☐ 429	Otis Nixon HL	.06	.02	.00
☐ 430	Rickey Henderson HL	.12	.05	.01
☐ 431	Cecil Fielder AS	.10	.04	.01
☐ 432	Julio Franco AS	.06	.02	.00
☐ 433	Cal Ripken AS	.12	.05	.01
☐ 434	Wade Boggs AS	.10	.04	.01
☐ 435	Joe Carter AS	.08	.03	.01
☐ 436	Ken Griffey Jr. AS	.20	.08	.02
☐ 437	Ruben Sierra AS	.10	.04	.01
☐ 438	Scott Erickson AS	.10	.04	.01
☐ 439	Tom Henke AS	.03	.01	.00
☐ 440	Terry Steinbach AS	.03	.01	.00
☐ 441	Rickey Henderson DT	.20	.08	.02
☐ 442	Ryne Sandberg DT	.25	.10	.02

1992 Score II

The 1992 Score II set marks the second year that Score has released their set in two different series. Series II contains 451 standard size (2 1/2" by 3 1/2") cards. Topical subsets, some of which are continuations from the first series, focus on Rookies (736-772, 814-877), NL All-Stars (773-782), Highlights (783, 795-797), No-Hit Club (784-787), Draft Picks (799-810), Memorabilia (878-882), and Dream Team (883-893). The cards are numbered on the back.

	MINT	EXC	G-VG
COMPLETE SET (451)	13.50	6.00	1.85
COMMON PLAYER (443-893)	.03	.01	.00

☐ 443	Otis Nixon	.06	.02	.00
☐ 444	Scott Radinsky	.03	.01	.00
☐ 445	Mark Grace	.08	.03	.01

No.	Name			
☐ 446	Tony Pena	.06	.02	.00
☐ 447	Billy Hatcher	.03	.01	.00
☐ 448	Glenallen Hill	.06	.02	.00
☐ 449	Chris Gwynn	.03	.01	.00
☐ 450	Tom Glavine	.08	.03	.01
☐ 451	John Habyan	.03	.01	.00
☐ 452	Al Osuna	.03	.01	.00
☐ 453	Tony Phillips	.03	.01	.00
☐ 454	Greg Cadaret	.03	.01	.00
☐ 455	Rob Dibble	.06	.02	.00
☐ 456	Rick Honeycutt	.03	.01	.00
☐ 457	Jerome Walton	.06	.02	.00
☐ 458	Mookie Wilson	.03	.01	.00
☐ 459	Mark Gubicza	.03	.01	.00
☐ 460	Craig Biggio	.06	.02	.00
☐ 461	Dave Cochrane	.03	.01	.00
☐ 462	Keith Miller	.03	.01	.00
☐ 463	Alex Cole	.06	.02	.00
☐ 464	Pete Smith	.03	.01	.00
☐ 465	Brett Butler	.06	.02	.00
☐ 466	Jeff Huson	.03	.01	.00
☐ 467	Steve Lake	.03	.01	.00
☐ 468	Lloyd Moseby	.03	.01	.00
☐ 469	Tim McIntosh	.03	.01	.00
☐ 470	Dennis Martinez	.06	.02	.00
☐ 471	Greg Myers	.03	.01	.00
☐ 472	Mackey Sasser	.03	.01	.00
☐ 473	Junior Ortiz	.03	.01	.00
☐ 474	Greg Olson	.03	.01	.00
☐ 475	Steve Sax	.06	.02	.00
☐ 476	Ricky Jordan	.03	.01	.00
☐ 477	Max Venable	.03	.01	.00
☐ 478	Brian McRae	.12	.05	.01
☐ 479	Doug Simons	.03	.01	.00
☐ 480	Rickey Henderson	.18	.08	.01
☐ 481	Gary Varsho	.03	.01	.00
☐ 482	Carl Willis	.03	.01	.00
☐ 483	Rick Wilkins	.08	.03	.01
☐ 484	Donn Pall	.03	.01	.00
☐ 485	Edgar Martinez	.06	.02	.00
☐ 486	Tom Foley	.03	.01	.00
☐ 487	Mark Williamson	.03	.01	.00
☐ 488	Jack Armstrong	.06	.02	.00
☐ 489	Gary Carter	.08	.03	.01
☐ 490	Ruben Sierra	.12	.05	.01
☐ 491	Gerald Perry	.03	.01	.00
☐ 492	Rob Murphy	.03	.01	.00
☐ 493	Zane Smith	.03	.01	.00
☐ 494	Darryl Kile	.08	.03	.01
☐ 495	Kelly Gruber	.06	.02	.00
☐ 496	Jerry Browne	.03	.01	.00
☐ 497	Darryl Hamilton	.03	.01	.00
☐ 498	Mike Stanton	.03	.01	.00
☐ 499	Mark Leonard	.03	.01	.00
☐ 500	Jose Canseco	.20	.08	.02
☐ 501	Dave Martinez	.03	.01	.00
☐ 502	Jose Guzman	.03	.01	.00
☐ 503	Terry Kennedy	.03	.01	.00
☐ 504	Ed Sprague	.08	.03	.01
☐ 505	Frank Thomas	.75	.30	.07
☐ 506	Darren Daulton	.06	.02	.00
☐ 507	Kevin Tapani	.06	.02	.00
☐ 508	Luis Salazar	.03	.01	.00
☐ 509	Paul Faries	.03	.01	.00
☐ 510	Sandy Alomar Jr.	.08	.03	.01
☐ 511	Jeff King	.03	.01	.00
☐ 512	Gary Thurman	.03	.01	.00
☐ 513	Chris Hammond	.06	.02	.00
☐ 514	Pedro Munoz	.10	.04	.01
☐ 515	Alan Trammell	.08	.03	.01
☐ 516	Geronimo Pena	.03	.01	.00
☐ 517	Rodney McCray	.03	.01	.00
☐ 518	Manny Lee	.03	.01	.00
☐ 519	Junior Felix	.06	.02	.00
☐ 520	Kirk Gibson	.06	.02	.00
☐ 521	Darrin Jackson	.03	.01	.00
☐ 522	John Burkett	.03	.01	.00
☐ 523	Jeff Johnson	.06	.02	.00
☐ 524	Jim Corsi	.03	.01	.00
☐ 525	Robin Yount	.10	.04	.01
☐ 526	Jamie Quirk	.03	.01	.00
☐ 527	Bob Ojeda	.03	.01	.00
☐ 528	Mark Lewis	.12	.05	.01
☐ 529	Bryn Smith	.03	.01	.00
☐ 530	Kent Hrbek	.06	.02	.00
☐ 531	Dennis Boyd	.03	.01	.00
☐ 532	Ron Karkovice	.03	.01	.00
☐ 533	Don August	.03	.01	.00
☐ 534	Todd Frohwirth	.03	.01	.00
☐ 535	Wally Joyner	.08	.03	.01
☐ 536	Dennis Rasmussen	.03	.01	.00
☐ 537	Andy Allanson	.03	.01	.00
☐ 538	Goose Gossage	.06	.02	.00
☐ 539	John Marzano	.03	.01	.00
☐ 540	Cal Ripken	.20	.08	.02
☐ 541	Bill Swift	.03	.01	.00
☐ 542	Kevin Appier	.03	.01	.00
☐ 543	Dave Bergman	.03	.01	.00
☐ 544	Bernard Gilkey	.10	.04	.01
☐ 545	Mike Greenwell	.10	.04	.01
☐ 546	Jose Uribe	.03	.01	.00
☐ 547	Jesse Orosco	.03	.01	.00
☐ 548	Bob Patterson	.03	.01	.00
☐ 549	Mike Stanley	.03	.01	.00
☐ 550	Howard Johnson	.08	.03	.01
☐ 551	Joe Orsulak	.03	.01	.00
☐ 552	Dick Schofield	.03	.01	.00
☐ 553	Dave Hollins	.06	.02	.00
☐ 554	David Segui	.06	.02	.00
☐ 555	Barry Bonds	.12	.05	.01
☐ 556	Mo Vaughn	.25	.10	.02
☐ 557	Craig Wilson	.08	.03	.01
☐ 558	Bobby Rose	.03	.01	.00
☐ 559	Rod Nichols	.03	.01	.00
☐ 560	Len Dykstra	.06	.02	.00
☐ 561	Craig Grebeck	.03	.01	.00
☐ 562	Darren Lewis	.10	.04	.01
☐ 563	Todd Benzinger	.03	.01	.00
☐ 564	Ed Whitson	.03	.01	.00
☐ 565	Jesse Barfield	.06	.02	.00
☐ 566	Lloyd McClendon	.03	.01	.00
☐ 567	Dan Plesac	.03	.01	.00
☐ 568	Danny Cox	.03	.01	.00
☐ 569	Skeeter Barnes	.03	.01	.00
☐ 570	Bobby Thigpen	.06	.02	.00
☐ 571	Deion Sanders	.08	.03	.01
☐ 572	Chuck Knoblauch	.20	.08	.02
☐ 573	Matt Nokes	.06	.02	.00
☐ 574	Herm Winningham	.03	.01	.00
☐ 575	Tom Candiotti	.06	.02	.00
☐ 576	Jeff Bagwell	.75	.30	.07
☐ 577	Brook Jacoby	.03	.01	.00
☐ 578	Chico Walker	.03	.01	.00
☐ 579	Brian Downing	.03	.01	.00
☐ 580	Dave Stewart	.06	.02	.00
☐ 581	Francisco Cabrera	.03	.01	.00
☐ 582	Rene Gonzales	.03	.01	.00
☐ 583	Stan Javier	.03	.01	.00
☐ 584	Randy Johnson	.06	.02	.00
☐ 585	Chuck Finley	.06	.02	.00
☐ 586	Mark Gardner	.03	.01	.00
☐ 587	Mark Whiten	.10	.04	.01
☐ 588	Garry Templeton	.03	.01	.00
☐ 589	Gary Sheffield	.08	.03	.01
☐ 590	Ozzie Smith	.10	.04	.01
☐ 591	Candy Maldonado	.03	.01	.00
☐ 592	Mike Sharperson	.03	.01	.00
☐ 593	Carlos Martinez	.03	.01	.00
☐ 594	Scott Bankhead	.03	.01	.00
☐ 595	Tim Wallach	.06	.02	.00
☐ 596	Tino Martinez	.10	.04	.01
☐ 597	Roger McDowell	.03	.01	.00
☐ 598	Cory Snyder	.06	.02	.00
☐ 599	Andujar Cedeno	.15	.06	.01
☐ 600	Kirby Puckett	.12	.05	.01
☐ 601	Rick Parker	.03	.01	.00
☐ 602	Todd Hundley	.08	.03	.01
☐ 603	Greg Litton	.03	.01	.00
☐ 604	Dave Johnson	.03	.01	.00
☐ 605	John Franco	.03	.01	.00
☐ 606	Mike Fetters	.03	.01	.00
☐ 607	Luis Alicea	.03	.01	.00
☐ 608	Trevor Wilson	.03	.01	.00
☐ 609	Rob Ducey	.03	.01	.00
☐ 610	Ramon Martinez	.10	.04	.01
☐ 611	Dave Burba	.03	.01	.00
☐ 612	Dwight Smith	.06	.02	.00
☐ 613	Kevin Maas	.12	.05	.01
☐ 614	John Costello	.03	.01	.00
☐ 615	Glenn Davis	.06	.02	.00
☐ 616	Shawn Abner	.03	.01	.00
☐ 617	Scott Hemond	.06	.02	.00
☐ 618	Tom Prince	.03	.01	.00
☐ 619	Wally Ritchie	.03	.01	.00
☐ 620	Jim Abbott	.10	.04	.01
☐ 621	Charlie O'Brien	.03	.01	.00
☐ 622	Jack Daugherty	.03	.01	.00
☐ 623	Tommy Gregg	.03	.01	.00
☐ 624	Jeff Shaw	.03	.01	.00
☐ 625	Tony Gwynn	.12	.05	.01
☐ 626	Mark Leiter	.06	.02	.00
☐ 627	Jim Clancy	.03	.01	.00
☐ 628	Tim Layana	.03	.01	.00
☐ 629	Jeff Schaefer	.03	.01	.00
☐ 630	Lee Smith	.06	.02	.00
☐ 631	Wade Taylor	.06	.02	.00
☐ 632	Mike Simms	.06	.02	.00
☐ 633	Terry Steinbach	.06	.02	.00

☐ 634	Shawon Dunston	.06	.02	.00
☐ 635	Tim Raines	.08	.03	.01
☐ 636	Kirt Manwaring	.03	.01	.00
☐ 637	Warren Cromartie	.03	.01	.00
☐ 638	Luis Quinones	.03	.01	.00
☐ 639	Greg Vaughn	.08	.03	.01
☐ 640	Kevin Mitchell	.10	.04	.01
☐ 641	Chris Hoiles	.06	.02	.00
☐ 642	Tom Browning	.06	.02	.00
☐ 643	Mitch Webster	.03	.01	.00
☐ 644	Steve Olin	.03	.01	.00
☐ 645	Tony Fernandez	.06	.02	.00
☐ 646	Juan Bell	.03	.01	.00
☐ 647	Joe Boever	.03	.01	.00
☐ 648	Carney Lansford	.06	.02	.00
☐ 649	Mike Benjamin	.03	.01	.00
☐ 650	George Brett	.10	.04	.01
☐ 651	Tim Burke	.03	.01	.00
☐ 652	Jack Morris	.06	.02	.00
☐ 653	Orel Hershiser	.06	.02	.00
☐ 654	Mike Schooler	.03	.01	.00
☐ 655	Andy Van Slyke	.06	.02	.00
☐ 656	Dave Stieb	.06	.02	.00
☐ 657	Dave Clark	.03	.01	.00
☐ 658	Ben McDonald	.08	.03	.01
☐ 659	John Smiley	.06	.02	.00
☐ 660	Wade Boggs	.12	.05	.01
☐ 661	Eric Bullock	.03	.01	.00
☐ 662	Eric Show	.03	.01	.00
☐ 663	Lenny Webster	.06	.02	.00
☐ 664	Mike Huff	.03	.01	.00
☐ 665	Rick Sutcliffe	.06	.02	.00
☐ 666	Jeff Manto	.03	.01	.00
☐ 667	Mike Fitzgerald	.03	.01	.00
☐ 668	Matt Young	.03	.01	.00
☐ 669	Dave West	.03	.01	.00
☐ 670	Mike Hartley	.03	.01	.00
☐ 671	Curt Schilling	.03	.01	.00
☐ 672	Brian Bohanon	.03	.01	.00
☐ 673	Cecil Espy	.03	.01	.00
☐ 674	Joe Grahe	.03	.01	.00
☐ 675	Sid Fernandez	.06	.02	.00
☐ 676	Edwin Nunez	.03	.01	.00
☐ 677	Hector Villanueva	.06	.02	.00
☐ 678	Sean Berry	.08	.03	.01
☐ 679	Dave Eiland	.03	.01	.00
☐ 680	Dave Cone	.08	.03	.01
☐ 681	Mike Bordick	.06	.02	.00
☐ 682	Tony Castillo	.03	.01	.00
☐ 683	John Barfield	.03	.01	.00
☐ 684	Jeff Hamilton	.03	.01	.00
☐ 685	Ken Dayley	.03	.01	.00
☐ 686	Carmelo Martinez	.03	.01	.00
☐ 687	Mike Capel	.03	.01	.00
☐ 688	Scott Chiamparino	.03	.01	.00
☐ 689	Rich Gedman	.03	.01	.00
☐ 690	Rich Monteleone	.03	.01	.00
☐ 691	Alejandro Pena	.03	.01	.00
☐ 692	Oscar Azocar	.03	.01	.00
☐ 693	Jim Poole	.06	.02	.00
☐ 694	Mike Gardiner	.06	.02	.00
☐ 695	Steve Buechele	.03	.01	.00
☐ 696	Rudy Seanez	.03	.01	.00
☐ 697	Paul Abbott	.03	.01	.00
☐ 698	Steve Searcy	.03	.01	.00
☐ 699	Jose Offerman	.06	.02	.00
☐ 700	Ivan Rodriguez	.60	.25	.06
☐ 701	Joe Girardi	.03	.01	.00
☐ 702	Tony Perezchica	.03	.01	.00
☐ 703	Paul McClellan	.06	.02	.00
☐ 704	David Howard	.06	.02	.00
☐ 705	Dan Petry	.03	.01	.00
☐ 706	Jack Howell	.03	.01	.00
☐ 707	Jose Mesa	.03	.01	.00
☐ 708	Randy St. Claire	.03	.01	.00
☐ 709	Kevin Brown	.06	.02	.00
☐ 710	Ron Darling	.03	.01	.00
☐ 711	Jason Grimsley	.03	.01	.00
☐ 712	John Orton	.03	.01	.00
☐ 713	Shawn Boskie	.03	.01	.00
☐ 714	Pat Clements	.03	.01	.00
☐ 715	Brian Barnes	.03	.01	.00
☐ 716	Luis Lopez	.08	.03	.01
☐ 717	Bob McClure	.03	.01	.00
☐ 718	Mark Davis	.03	.01	.00
☐ 719	Dann Bilardello	.03	.01	.00
☐ 720	Tom Edens	.03	.01	.00
☐ 721	Willie Fraser	.03	.01	.00
☐ 722	Curt Young	.03	.01	.00
☐ 723	Neal Heaton	.03	.01	.00
☐ 724	Craig Worthington	.03	.01	.00
☐ 725	Mel Rojas	.06	.02	.00
☐ 726	Daryl Irvine	.03	.01	.00
☐ 727	Roger Mason	.03	.01	.00

☐ 728	Kirk Dressendorfer	.08	.03	.01
☐ 729	Scott Aldred	.03	.01	.00
☐ 730	Willie Blair	.03	.01	.00
☐ 731	Allan Anderson	.03	.01	.00
☐ 732	Dana Kiecker	.03	.01	.00
☐ 733	Jose S...	.03	.01	.00
☐ 734	Brian Drahman	.06	.02	.00
☐ 735	Brad Komminsk	.03	.01	.00
☐ 736	Arthur Rhodes	.15	.06	.01
☐ 737	Terry Mathews	.10	.04	.01
☐ 738	Jeff Fassero	.06	.02	.00
☐ 739	Mike Magnante	.12	.05	.01
☐ 740	Kip Gross	.12	.05	.01
☐ 741	Jim Hunter	.10	.04	.01
☐ 742	Jose Mota	.08	.03	.01
☐ 743	Joe Bitker	.03	.01	.00
☐ 744	Tim Mauser	.10	.04	.01
☐ 745	Ramon Garcia	.06	.02	.00
☐ 746	Rod Beck	.12	.05	.01
☐ 747	Jim Austin	.10	.04	.01
☐ 748	Keith Mitchell	.15	.06	.01
☐ 749	Wayne Rosenthal	.10	.04	.01
☐ 750	Bryan Hickerson	.12	.05	.01
☐ 751	Bruce Egloff	.08	.03	.01
☐ 752	John Wehner	.12	.05	.01
☐ 753	Darren Holmes	.08	.03	.01
☐ 754	Dave Hansen	.06	.02	.00
☐ 755	Mike Mussina	.12	.05	.01
☐ 756	Anthony Young	.12	.05	.01
☐ 757	Ron Tingley	.03	.01	.00
☐ 758	Ricky Bones	.06	.02	.00
☐ 759	Mark Wohlers	.20	.08	.02
☐ 760	Wilson Alvarez	.08	.03	.01
☐ 761	Harvey Pulliam	.12	.05	.01
☐ 762	Ryan Bowen	.08	.03	.01
☐ 763	Terry Bross	.03	.01	.00
☐ 764	Joel Johnston	.08	.03	.01
☐ 765	Terry McDaniel	.12	.05	.01
☐ 766	Esteban Beltre	.10	.04	.01
☐ 767	Rob Maurer	.20	.08	.02
☐ 768	Ted Wood	.20	.08	.02
☐ 769	Mo Sanford	.15	.06	.01
☐ 770	Jeff Carter	.06	.02	.00
☐ 771	Gil Heredia	.12	.05	.01
☐ 772	Monty Fariss	.08	.03	.01
☐ 773	Will Clark AS	.12	.05	.01
☐ 774	Ryne Sandberg AS	.12	.05	.01
☐ 775	Barry Larkin AS	.08	.03	.01
☐ 776	Howard Johnson AS	.08	.03	.01
☐ 777	Barry Bonds AS	.10	.04	.01
☐ 778	Brett Butler AS	.06	.02	.00
☐ 779	Tony Gwynn AS	.10	.04	.01
☐ 780	Ramon Martinez AS	.08	.03	.01
☐ 781	Lee Smith AS	.06	.02	.00
☐ 782	Mike Scioscia AS	.03	.01	.00
☐ 783	Dennis Martinez HL	.06	.02	.00
☐ 784	Dennis Martinez	.06	.02	.00
	No-Hit Club			
☐ 785	Mark Gardner	.03	.01	.00
	No-Hit Club			
☐ 786	Bret Saberhagen	.08	.03	.01
	No-Hit Club			
☐ 787	Kent Mercker	.06	.02	.00
	Mark Wohlers			
	Alejandro Pena			
	No-Hit Club			
☐ 788	Cal Ripken MVP	.12	.05	.01
☐ 789	Terry Pendleton MVP	.06	.02	.00
☐ 790	Roger Clemens CY	.10	.04	.01
☐ 791	Tom Glavine CY	.08	.03	.01
☐ 792	Chuck Knoblauch ROY	.15	.06	.01
☐ 793	Jeff Bagwell ROY	.40	.16	.04
☐ 794	Cal Ripken	.12	.05	.01
	Man of the Year			
☐ 795	David Cone HL	.08	.03	.01
☐ 796	Kirby Puckett HL	.10	.04	.01
☐ 797	Steve Avery HL	.12	.05	.01
☐ 798	Jack Morris HL	.08	.03	.01
☐ 799	Allen Watson Draft	.20	.08	.02
☐ 800	Manny Ramirez Draft	.40	.16	.04
☐ 801	Cliff Floyd Draft	.25	.10	.02
☐ 802	Al Shirley Draft	.30	.12	.03
☐ 803	Brian Barber Draft	.12	.05	.01
☐ 804	Jon Farrell Draft	.20	.08	.02
☐ 805	Brent Gates Draft	.12	.05	.01
☐ 806	Scott Ruffcorn Draft	.20	.08	.02
☐ 807	Tyrone Hill Draft	.25	.10	.02
☐ 808	Benji Gil Draft	.30	.12	.03
☐ 809	Aaron Sele Draft	.20	.08	.02
☐ 810	Tyler Green Draft	.40	.16	.04
☐ 811	Chris Jones	.03	.01	.00
☐ 812	Steve Wilson	.03	.01	.00
☐ 813	Cliff Young	.06	.02	.00
☐ 814	Don Wakamatsu	.10	.04	.01

☐	815 Mike Humphreys	.08	.03	.01
☐	816 Scott Servais	.08	.03	.01
☐	817 Rico Rossy	.10	.04	.01
☐	818 John Ramos	.12	.05	.01
☐	819 Rob Mallicoat	.03	.01	.00
☐	820 Milt Hill	.12	.05	.01
☐	821 Carlos Garcia	.06	.02	.00
☐	822 Stan Royer	.06	.02	.00
☐	823 Jeff Plympton	.12	.05	.01
☐	824 Braulio Castillo	.25	.10	.02
☐	825 David Haas	.06	.02	.00
☐	826 Luis Mercedes	.15	.06	.01
☐	827 Eric Karros	.20	.08	.02
☐	828 Shawn Hare	.12	.05	.01
☐	829 Reggie Sanders	.15	.06	.01
☐	830 Tom Goodwin	.12	.05	.01
☐	831 Dan Gakeler	.08	.03	.01
☐	832 Stacy Jones	.10	.04	.01
☐	833 Kim Batiste	.08	.03	.01
☐	834 Cal Eldred	.08	.03	.01
☐	835 Chris George	.10	.04	.01
☐	836 Wayne Housie	.12	.05	.01
☐	837 Mike Ignasiak	.12	.05	.01
☐	838 Josias Manzanillo	.12	.05	.01
☐	839 Jim Olander	.12	.05	.01
☐	840 Gary Cooper	.12	.05	.01
☐	841 Royce Clayton	.15	.06	.01
☐	842 Hector Fajardo	.20	.08	.02
☐	843 Blaine Beatty	.03	.01	.00
☐	844 Jorge Pedre	.12	.05	.01
☐	845 Kenny Lofton	.20	.08	.02
☐	846 Scott Brosius	.10	.04	.01
☐	847 Chris Cron	.12	.05	.01
☐	848 Denis Boucher	.06	.02	.00
☐	849 Kyle Abbott	.10	.04	.01
☐	850 Robert Zupcic	.18	.08	.01
☐	851 Rheal Cormier	.15	.06	.01
☐	852 Jim Lewis	.10	.04	.01
☐	853 Anthony Telford	.03	.01	.00
☐	854 Cliff Brantley	.12	.05	.01
☐	855 Kevin Campbell	.12	.05	.01
☐	856 Craig Shipley	.10	.04	.01
☐	857 Chuck Carr	.03	.01	.00
☐	858 Tony Eusebio	.12	.05	.01
☐	859 Jim Thome	.30	.12	.03
☐	860 Vinny Castilla	.10	.04	.01
☐	861 Dann Howitt	.03	.01	.00
☐	862 Kevin Ward	.10	.04	.01
☐	863 Steve Wapnick	.06	.02	.00
☐	864 Rod Brewer	.06	.02	.00
☐	865 Todd Van Poppel	.45	.18	.04
☐	866 Jose Hernandez	.10	.04	.01
☐	867 Amalio Carreno	.10	.04	.01
☐	868 Calvin Jones	.10	.04	.01
☐	869 Jeff Gardner	.10	.04	.01
☐	870 Jarvis Brown	.12	.05	.01
☐	871 Eddie Taubensee	.15	.06	.01
☐	872 Andy Mota	.08	.03	.01
☐	873 Chris Haney	.06	.02	.00
☐	874 Roberto Hernandez	.12	.05	.01
☐	875 Laddie Renfroe	.10	.04	.01
☐	876 Scott Cooper	.10	.04	.01
☐	877 Armando Reynoso	.10	.04	.01
☐	878 Ty Cobb (Memorabilia)	.25	.10	.02
☐	879 Babe Ruth (Memorabilia)	.35	.15	.03
☐	880 Honus Wagner (Memorabilia)	.15	.06	.01
☐	881 Lou Gehrig (Memorabilia)	.25	.10	.02
☐	882 Satchel Paige (Memorabilia)	.15	.06	.01
☐	883 Will Clark DT	.25	.10	.02
☐	884 Cal Ripken DT	.40	.16	.04
☐	885 Wade Boggs DT	.20	.08	.02
☐	886 Tony Gwynn DT	.20	.08	.02
☐	887 Kirby Puckett DT	.20	.08	.02
☐	888 Craig Biggio DT	.08	.03	.01
☐	889 Scott Erickson DT	.35	.15	.03
☐	890 Tom Glavine DT	.15	.06	.01
☐	891 Rob Dibble DT	.08	.03	.01
☐	892 Mitch Williams DT	.06	.02	.00
☐	893 Frank Thomas DT	1.00	.40	.10

1992 Score Joe DiMaggio

This five-card standard-size (2 1/2" by 3 1/2") set was issued in honor of one of baseball's all-time greats, Joe DiMaggio. Supposedly 30,000 of each card were produced. On a white card face, the fronts have vintage photos that have been colorized by red, white, and blue border stripes. The player's name appears in an orange bar and the card title in a white banner beneath the picture. The backs feature a different colorized player photo and career highlights (on gray), framed between a red top stripe and a navy blue bottom stripe. The cards are numbered on the back.

	MINT	EXC	G-VG
COMPLETE SET (5)	225.00	100.00	33.00
COMMON PLAYER (1-5)	50.00	22.50	7.50
☐ 1 Joe DiMaggio The Rookie	50.00	22.50	7.50
☐ 2 Joe DiMaggio The Minors	60.00	27.00	9.00
☐ 3 Joe DiMaggio The MVP	50.00	22.50	7.50
☐ 4 Joe DiMaggio The Streak	50.00	22.50	7.50
☐ 5 Joe DiMaggio The Legend	50.00	22.50	7.50
☐ x Autographed Card	500.00	225.00	75.00

1992 Score 100 Rising Stars

The 1992 Score Rising Stars set contains 100 player cards and six "Magic Motion" trivia cards. The cards measure the standard size (2 1/2" by 3 1/2"). The fronts display color action player photos on a card face that shades from green to yellow and back to green. The words "Rising Star" appear above the picture, with the player's name in a blue stripe at the card bottom. The horizontally oriented backs have a color head shot on the left half, with player profile and team logo on the right half. The cards are numbered on the back.

	MINT	EXC	G-VG
COMPLETE SET (100)	10.00	4.50	1.25
COMMON PLAYER (1-100)	.05	.02	.00
☐ 1 Milt Cuyler	.10	.04	.01
☐ 2 David Howard	.05	.02	.00
☐ 3 Brian Hunter	.25	.10	.02
☐ 4 Darryl Kile	.10	.04	.01
☐ 5 Pat Kelly	.15	.06	.01
☐ 6 Luis Gonzalez	.20	.08	.02
☐ 7 Mike Benjamin	.05	.02	.00
☐ 8 Eric Anthony	.10	.04	.01
☐ 9 Moises Alou	.10	.04	.01
☐ 10 Darren Lewis	.15	.06	.01
☐ 11 Chuck Knoblauch	.30	.12	.03
☐ 12 Geronimo Pena	.05	.02	.00
☐ 13 Jeff Plympton	.10	.04	.01
☐ 14 Bret Barberie	.15	.06	.01
☐ 15 Chris Haney	.10	.04	.01
☐ 16 Rick Wilkins	.10	.04	.01
☐ 17 Julio Valera	.05	.02	.00
☐ 18 Joe Slusarski	.10	.04	.01
☐ 19 Jose Melendez	.10	.04	.01
☐ 20 Pete Schourek	.10	.04	.01
☐ 21 Jeff Conine	.15	.06	.01
☐ 22 Paul Faries	.05	.02	.00
☐ 23 Scott Kamieniecki	.10	.04	.01
☐ 24 Bernard Gilkey	.15	.06	.01
☐ 25 Wes Chamberlain	.25	.10	.02
☐ 26 Charles Nagy	.10	.04	.01
☐ 27 Juan Guzman	.25	.10	.02
☐ 28 Heath Slocumb	.05	.02	.00
☐ 29 Eddie Taubensee	.15	.06	.01
☐ 30 Cedric Landrum	.10	.04	.01
☐ 31 Jose Offerman	.15	.06	.01
☐ 32 Andres Santana	.15	.06	.01
☐ 33 David Segui	.10	.04	.01
☐ 34 Bernie Williams	.25	.10	.02
☐ 35 Jeff Bagwell	.75	.30	.07
☐ 36 Kevin Morton	.10	.04	.01
☐ 37 Kirk Dressendorfer	.15	.06	.01
☐ 38 Mike Fetters	.05	.02	.00
☐ 39 Darren Holmes	.10	.04	.01
☐ 40 Jeff Johnson	.10	.04	.01
☐ 41 Scott Aldred	.10	.04	.01
☐ 42 Kevin Ward	.15	.06	.01
☐ 43 Ray Lankford	.20	.08	.02
☐ 44 Terry Shumpert	.05	.02	.00
☐ 45 Wade Taylor	.10	.04	.01
☐ 46 Rob MacDonald	.10	.04	.01
☐ 47 Jose Mota	.10	.04	.01
☐ 48 Reggie Harris	.05	.02	.00
☐ 49 Mike Remlinger	.05	.02	.00
☐ 50 Mark Lewis	.15	.06	.01
☐ 51 Tino Martinez	.15	.06	.01
☐ 52 Ed Sprague	.10	.04	.01
☐ 53 Freddie Benavides	.05	.02	.00
☐ 54 Rich DeLucia	.05	.02	.00
☐ 55 Brian Drahman	.10	.04	.01
☐ 56 Steve Decker	.20	.08	.02
☐ 57 Scott Livingstone	.20	.08	.02
☐ 58 Mike Timlin	.15	.06	.01
☐ 59 Bob Scanlan	.10	.04	.01
☐ 60 Dean Palmer	.25	.10	.02
☐ 61 Frank Castillo	.10	.04	.01
☐ 62 Mark Leonard	.10	.04	.01
☐ 63 Chuck McElroy	.10	.04	.01
☐ 64 Derek Bell	.25	.10	.02
☐ 65 Andujar Cedeno	.20	.08	.02
☐ 66 Leo Gomez	.25	.10	.02
☐ 67 Rusty Meacham	.10	.04	.01
☐ 68 Dann Howitt	.10	.04	.01
☐ 69 Chris Jones	.05	.02	.00
☐ 70 Dave Cochrane	.10	.04	.01
☐ 71 Carlos Martinez	.05	.02	.00
☐ 72 Hensley Meulens	.10	.04	.01
☐ 73 Rich Reed	.05	.02	.00
☐ 74 Pedro Munoz	.20	.08	.02
☐ 75 Orlando Merced	.20	.08	.02
☐ 76 Chito Martinez	.30	.12	.03
☐ 77 Ivan Rodriguez	.60	.25	.06
☐ 78 Brian Barnes	.10	.04	.01
☐ 79 Chris Donnels	.15	.06	.01
☐ 80 Todd Hundley	.15	.06	.01
☐ 81 Gary Scott	.20	.08	.02
☐ 82 John Wehner	.20	.08	.02
☐ 83 Al Osuna	.10	.04	.01
☐ 84 Luis Lopez	.15	.06	.01
☐ 85 Brent Mayne	.10	.04	.01

	MINT	EXC	G-VG
☐ 86 Phil Plantier	.75	.30	.07
☐ 87 Joe Bitker	.05	.02	.00
☐ 88 Scott Cooper	.15	.06	.01
☐ 89 Chris Hammond	.15	.06	.01
☐ 90 Tim Sherrill	.10	.04	.01
☐ 91 Doug Simons	.10	.04	.01
☐ 92 Kip Gross	.10	.04	.01
☐ 93 Tim McIntosh	.10	.04	.01
☐ 94 Larry Casian	.10	.04	.01
☐ 95 Mike Dalton	.15	.06	.01
☐ 96 Lance Dickson	.15	.06	.01
☐ 97 Joe Grahe	.10	.04	.01
☐ 98 Glenn Sutko	.10	.04	.01
☐ 99 Gerald Alexander	.10	.04	.01
☐ 100 Mo Vaughn	.35	.15	.03

1992 Score 100 Superstars

The 1992 Score Superstars set contains 100 player cards and six "Magic Motion" trivia cards. The cards measure the standard size (2 1/2" by 3 1/2"). The fronts display color action player photos on a card face that shades from reddish-orange to yellow and back to reddish-orange again. The words "Superstar" appear above the pictures, with the player's name in a purple stripe at the card bottom. The horizontally oriented backs have a color head shot on the left half, with player profile and team logo on the right half. The cards are numbered on the back.

	MINT	EXC	G-VG
COMPLETE SET (100)	9.00	4.00	.90
COMMON PLAYER (1-100)	.05	.02	.00
☐ 1 Ken Griffey Jr.	.75	.30	.07
☐ 2 Scott Erickson	.25	.10	.02
☐ 3 John Smiley	.10	.04	.01
☐ 4 Rick Aguilera	.05	.02	.00
☐ 5 Jeff Reardon	.10	.04	.01
☐ 6 Chuck Finley	.10	.04	.01
☐ 7 Kirby Puckett	.20	.08	.02
☐ 8 Paul Molitor	.10	.04	.01
☐ 9 Dave Winfield	.15	.06	.01
☐ 10 Mike Greenwell	.15	.06	.01
☐ 11 Bret Saberhagen	.10	.04	.01
☐ 12 Pete Harnisch	.05	.02	.00
☐ 13 Ozzie Guillen	.05	.02	.00
☐ 14 Hal Morris	.15	.06	.01
☐ 15 Tom Glavine	.15	.06	.01
☐ 16 David Cone	.10	.04	.01
☐ 17 Edgar Martinez	.10	.04	.01
☐ 18 Willie McGee	.10	.04	.01
☐ 19 Jim Abbott	.15	.06	.01
☐ 20 Mark Grace	.15	.06	.01
☐ 21 George Brett	.20	.08	.02
☐ 22 Jack McDowell	.10	.04	.01
☐ 23 Don Mattingly	.20	.08	.02
☐ 24 Will Clark	.30	.12	.03
☐ 25 Dwight Gooden	.15	.06	.01
☐ 26 Barry Bonds	.20	.08	.02
☐ 27 Rafael Palmeiro	.15	.06	.01
☐ 28 Lee Smith	.10	.04	.01
☐ 29 Wally Joyner	.10	.04	.01
☐ 30 Wade Boggs	.20	.08	.02
☐ 31 Tom Henke	.05	.02	.00
☐ 32 Mark Langston	.10	.04	.01

			MINT	EXC	G-VG
☐	33	Robin Ventura	.25	.10	.02
☐	34	Steve Avery	.25	.10	.02
☐	35	Joe Carter	.15	.06	.01
☐	36	Benito Santiago	.10	.04	.01
☐	37	Dave Stieb	.10	.04	.01
☐	38	Julio Franco	.15	.06	.01
☐	39	Albert Belle	.20	.08	.02
☐	40	Dale Murphy	.15	.06	.01
☐	41	Rob Dibble	.10	.04	.01
☐	42	Dave Justice	.40	.16	.04
☐	43	Jose Rijo	.10	.04	.01
☐	44	Eric Davis	.20	.08	.02
☐	45	Terry Pendleton	.15	.06	.01
☐	46	Kevin Maas	.20	.08	.02
☐	47	Ozzie Smith	.15	.06	.01
☐	48	Andre Dawson	.20	.08	.02
☐	49	Sandy Alomar Jr.	.15	.06	.01
☐	50	Nolan Ryan	.75	.30	.07
☐	51	Frank Thomas	.75	.30	.07
☐	52	Craig Biggio	.10	.04	.01
☐	53	Doug Drabek	.10	.04	.01
☐	54	Bobby Thigpen	.10	.04	.01
☐	55	Darryl Strawberry	.30	.12	.03
☐	56	Dennis Eckersley	.10	.04	.01
☐	57	John Franco	.05	.02	.00
☐	58	Paul O'Neill	.10	.04	.01
☐	59	Scott Sanderson	.05	.02	.00
☐	60	Dave Stewart	.10	.04	.01
☐	61	Ivan Calderon	.10	.04	.01
☐	62	Frank Viola	.10	.04	.01
☐	63	Mark McGwire	.20	.08	.02
☐	64	Kelly Gruber	.10	.04	.01
☐	65	Fred McGriff	.15	.06	.01
☐	66	Cecil Fielder	.25	.10	.02
☐	67	Jose Canseco	.30	.12	.03
☐	68	Howard Johnson	.15	.06	.01
☐	69	Juan Gonzalez	.35	.15	.03
☐	70	Tim Wallach	.10	.04	.01
☐	71	John Olerud	.15	.06	.01
☐	72	Carlton Fisk	.20	.08	.02
☐	73	Otis Nixon	.10	.04	.01
☐	74	Roger Clemens	.35	.15	.03
☐	75	Ramon Martinez	.20	.08	.02
☐	76	Ron Gant	.20	.08	.02
☐	77	Barry Larkin	.20	.08	.02
☐	78	Eddie Murray	.20	.08	.02
☐	79	Vince Coleman	.15	.06	.01
☐	80	Bobby Bonilla	.15	.06	.01
☐	81	Tony Gwynn	.20	.08	.02
☐	82	Roberto Alomar	.15	.06	.01
☐	83	Ellis Burks	.15	.06	.01
☐	84	Robin Yount	.20	.08	.02
☐	85	Ryne Sandberg	.30	.12	.03
☐	86	Len Dykstra	.10	.04	.01
☐	87	Ruben Sierra	.25	.10	.02
☐	88	George Bell	.15	.06	.01
☐	89	Cal Ripken	.40	.16	.04
☐	90	Danny Tartabull	.15	.06	.01
☐	91	Gregg Olson	.10	.04	.01
☐	92	Dave Henderson	.10	.04	.01
☐	93	Kevin Mitchell	.20	.08	.02
☐	94	Ben McDonald	.15	.06	.01
☐	95	Matt Williams	.15	.06	.01
☐	96	Roberto Kelly	.15	.06	.01
☐	97	Dennis Martinez	.05	.02	.00
☐	98	Kent Hrbek	.10	.04	.01
☐	99	Felix Jose	.15	.06	.01
☐	100	Rickey Henderson	.35	.15	.03

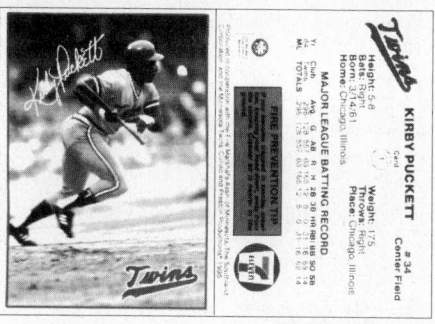

☐	3	Mickey Hatcher	.30	.12	.03
☐	4	Kent Hrbek	1.00	.40	.10
☐	5	John Butcher	.30	.12	.03
☐	6	Roy Smalley	.30	.12	.03
☐	7	Tom Brunansky	.50	.20	.05
☐	8	Ron Davis	.30	.12	.03
☐	9	Gary Gaetti	.75	.30	.07
☐	10	Tim Teufel	.40	.16	.04
☐	11	Mike Smithson	.30	.12	.03
☐	12	Tim Laudner	.30	.12	.03
☐	xx	Checklist Card	.30	.12	.03

1991 SilverStar Holograms

These hologram cards measure the standard size (2 1/2" by 3 1/2") and were issued to commemorate outstanding achievements of the players. The backs of the hologram cards are brightly colored and have statistics as well as a player profile. Each card also comes with a 2 1/16" by 5 3/8" blank-backed ticket. The tickets have a color player photo, serial number, and a description of the achievement honored. The Henderson hologram honors him as the all-time stolen base leader; the Ryan hologram celebrates his 7th no-hitter; and the Justice hologram commemorates his two-run homer against the Reds on October 1 that led to a 7-6 Braves' victory in the NL West pennant race. The cards are unnumbered and checklisted below chronologically by release dates.

1985 7-Eleven Twins

This 13-card set of Minnesota Twins was produced and distributed by the Twins in conjunction with the 7-Eleven stores and the Fire Marshall's Association. The cards measure approximately 2 1/2" by 3 1/2" and are in full color. Supposedly 20,000 sets of cards were distributed during the promotion which began on June 2nd and lasted throughout the month of July. The card backs have some statistics and a fire safety tip. The set features an early Kirby Puckett card.

	MINT	EXC	G-VG
COMPLETE SET (13)	9.00	4.00	.90
COMMON PLAYER (1-13)	.30	.12	.03
☐ 1 Kirby Puckett	4.50	2.00	.45
☐ 2 Frank Viola	1.00	.40	.10

	MINT	EXC	G-VG
COMPLETE SET (4)	20.00	8.50	2.75
COMMON PLAYER (1-4)	6.00	2.50	.60
☐ 1 Rickey Henderson	6.00	2.50	.60
☐ 2 Nolan Ryan	6.00	2.50	.60
☐ 3 Dave Justice	6.00	2.50	.60
☐ 4 Cal Ripken	6.00	2.50	.60

1984 Smokey Angels

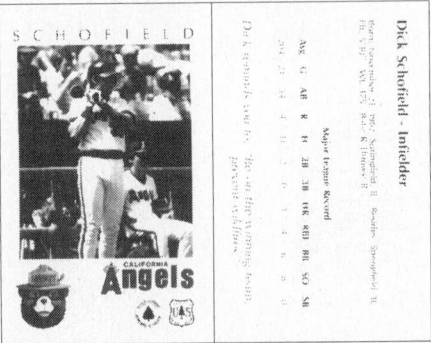

The cards in this 32-card set measure 2 1/2" by 3 3/4" and feature the California Angels in full color. Sets were given out to persons 15 and under attending the June 16th game against the Indians. Unlike the Padres set of this year, Smokey the Bear is not featured on these cards. The player's photo, the Angels' logo, and the Smokey the Bear logo appear on the front, in addition to the California Department of Forestry and the U.S. Forest Service logos. The abbreviated backs contain short biographical data, career statistics, and an anti-wildfire hint from the player on the front. Since the cards are unnumbered, they are ordered and numbered below alphabetically by the player's name.

	MINT	EXC	G-VG
COMPLETE SET (32)	9.00	4.00	.90
COMMON PLAYER (1-32)	.25	.10	.02
☐ 1 Don Aase	.25	.10	.02
☐ 2 Juan Beniquez	.25	.10	.02
☐ 3 Bob Boone	.50	.20	.05
☐ 4 Rick Burleson	.35	.15	.03
☐ 5 Rod Carew	1.50	.60	.15
☐ 6 John Curtis	.25	.10	.02
☐ 7 Doug DeCinces	.35	.15	.03
☐ 8 Brian Downing	.35	.15	.03
☐ 9 Ken Forsch	.25	.10	.02
☐ 10 Bobby Grich	.35	.15	.03
☐ 11 Reggie Jackson	1.75	.70	.17
☐ 12 Ron Jackson	.25	.10	.02
☐ 13 Tommy John	.60	.25	.06
☐ 14 Curt Kaufman	.25	.10	.02
☐ 15 Bruce Kison	.25	.10	.02
☐ 16 Frank LaCorte	.25	.10	.02
☐ 17 Logo Card	.25	.10	.02
(Forestry Dept.)			
☐ 18 Fred Lynn	.35	.15	.03
☐ 19 John McNamara MG	.35	.15	.03
☐ 20 Jerry Narron	.25	.10	.02
☐ 21 Gary Pettis	.35	.15	.03
☐ 22 Rob Picciolo	.25	.10	.02
☐ 23 Ron Romanick	.25	.10	.02
☐ 24 Luis Sanchez	.25	.10	.02
☐ 25 Dick Schofield	.35	.15	.03
☐ 26 Daryl Sconiers	.25	.10	.02
☐ 27 Jim Slaton	.25	.10	.02
☐ 28 Smokey the Bear	.25	.10	.02
☐ 29 Ellis Valentine	.25	.10	.02
☐ 30 Rob Wilfong	.25	.10	.02
☐ 31 Mike Witt	.35	.15	.03
☐ 32 Geoff Zahn	.25	.10	.02

1984 Smokey Dodgers

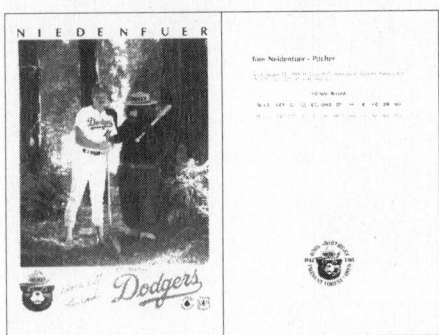

This four-card set was not widely distributed and has not proven to be very popular with collectors. Cards were supposedly distributed by fire agencies in Southern California at fairs, mall displays, and special events. Cards are approximately 5" by 7" and feature a color picture of Smokey the Bear with a Dodger. The cards were printed on relatively thin card stock; printing on the back is black on white.

	MINT	EXC	G-VG
COMPLETE SET (4)	15.00	6.50	2.15
COMMON PLAYER (1-4)	2.50	1.00	.25
☐ 1 Ken Landreaux	3.50	1.50	.35
with Smokey			
☐ 2 Tom Niedenfuer	3.50	1.50	.35
with Smokey			
☐ 3 Steve Sax	8.50	3.75	.85
with Smokey			
☐ 4 Smokey the Bear	2.50	1.00	.25
(batting pose)			

1984 Smokey Padres

The cards in this 29-card set measure 2 1/2" by 3 3/4". This unnumbered, full color set features the Fire Prevention Bear and a Padres player, coach, manager, or associate on each card. The set was given out at the ballpark at the May 14th game against the Expos. Logos of the California Department of Forestry and the U.S. Forest Service appear in conjunction with a Smokey the Bear logo on the obverse. The set commemorates the 40th birthday of Smokey the Bear. The backs contain short biographical data, statistics and a fire prevention hint from the player pictured on the front.

	MINT	EXC	G-VG
COMPLETE SET (29)	11.00	5.00	1.35
COMMON PLAYER (1-29)	.30	.12	.03
☐ 1 Kurt Bevacqua	.30	.12	.03
☐ 3 Dave Campbell (Broadcast Team)	.30	.12	.03
☐ 4 The Chicken (Mascot)	.60	.25	.06
☐ 5 Jerry Coleman (Broadcast Team)	.30	.12	.03
☐ 6 Luis DeLeon	.30	.12	.03
☐ 7 Dave Dravecky	.90	.40	.09
☐ 8 Harry Dunlop CO	.30	.12	.03
☐ 9 Tim Flannery	.30	.12	.03
☐ 10 Steve Garvey	1.25	.50	.12
☐ 11 Doug Gwosdz	.30	.12	.03
☐ 12 Tony Gwynn	2.00	.80	.20
☐ 13 Harold (Doug) Harvey (ex-UMP)	.40	.16	.04
☐ 14 Terry Kennedy	.30	.12	.03
☐ 15 Jack Krol CO	.30	.12	.03
☐ 16 Tim Lollar	.30	.12	.03
☐ 17 Jack McKeon (VP for Baseball Operations)	.50	.20	.05
☐ 18 Kevin McReynolds	1.75	.70	.17
☐ 19 Sid Monge	.30	.12	.03
☐ 20 Luis Salazar	.30	.12	.03
☐ 21 Norm Sherry CO	.30	.12	.03
☐ 22 Eric Show	.40	.16	.04
☐ 23 Smokey the Bear	.30	.12	.03
☐ 24 Garry Templeton	.40	.16	.04
☐ 25 Mark Thurmond	.30	.12	.03
☐ 26 Ozzie Virgil CO	.30	.12	.03
☐ 27 Ed Whitson	.40	.16	.04
☐ 28 Alan Wiggins	.30	.12	.03
☐ 29 Dick Williams MG	.40	.16	.04

1985 Smokey Angels

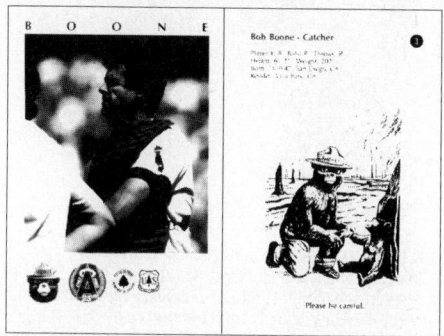

The cards in this 24-card set measure 4 1/4 by 6" and feature the California Angels in full color. The player's photo, the Angels' logo, and the Smokey the Bear logo appear on the front, in addition to the California Department of Forestry and the U.S. Forest Service logos. The abbreviated backs contain short biographical data and an anti-wildfire hint.

	MINT	EXC	G-VG
COMPLETE SET (24)	7.00	3.00	.70
COMMON PLAYER (1-24)	.25	.10	.02
☐ 1 Mike Witt	.35	.15	.03
☐ 2 Reggie Jackson	1.25	.50	.12
☐ 3 Bob Boone	.60	.25	.06
☐ 4 Mike Brown	.25	.10	.02
☐ 5 Rod Carew	1.00	.40	.10
☐ 6 Doug DeCinces	.35	.15	.03
☐ 7 Brian Downing	.35	.15	.03
☐ 8 Ken Forsch	.25	.10	.02
☐ 9 Gary Pettis	.35	.15	.03
☐ 10 Jerry Narron	.25	.10	.02

	MINT	EXC	G-VG
☐ 11 Ron Romanick	.25	.10	.02
☐ 12 Bobby Grich	.35	.15	.03
☐ 13 Dick Schofield	.35	.15	.03
☐ 14 Juan Beniquez	.25	.10	.02
☐ 15 Geoff Zahn	.25	.10	.02
☐ 16 Luis Sanchez	.25	.10	.02
☐ 17 Jim Slaton	.25	.10	.02
☐ 18 Doug Corbett	.25	.10	.02
☐ 19 Ruppert Jones	.25	.10	.02
☐ 20 Rob Wilfong	.25	.10	.02
☐ 21 Donnie Moore	.25	.10	.02
☐ 22 Pat Clements	.25	.10	.02
☐ 23 Tommy John	.60	.25	.06
☐ 24 Gene Mauch MG	.25	.10	.02

1986 Smokey Angels

The Forestry Service (in conjunction with the California Angels) produced this large, attractive 24-card set. The cards feature Smokey the Bear pictured in the upper right corner of the card. The card backs give a fire safety tip. The set was given out free at Anaheim Stadium on August 9th. The cards measure 4 1/4" by 6" and are subtitled "Wildfire Prevention" on the front.

	MINT	EXC	G-VG
COMPLETE SET (24)	8.00	3.50	.80
COMMON PLAYER (1-24)	.25	.10	.02
☐ 1 Mike Witt	.35	.15	.03
☐ 2 Reggie Jackson	1.25	.50	.12
☐ 3 Bob Boone	.60	.25	.06
☐ 4 Don Sutton	.75	.30	.07
☐ 5 Kirk McCaskill	.50	.20	.05
☐ 6 Doug DeCinces	.35	.15	.03
☐ 7 Brian Downing	.35	.15	.03
☐ 8 Doug Corbett	.25	.10	.02
☐ 9 Gary Pettis	.35	.15	.03
☐ 10 Jerry Narron	.25	.10	.02
☐ 11 Ron Romanick	.25	.10	.02
☐ 12 Bobby Grich	.35	.15	.03
☐ 13 Dick Schofield	.35	.15	.03
☐ 14 George Hendrick	.35	.15	.03
☐ 15 Rick Burleson	.35	.15	.03
☐ 16 John Candelaria	.35	.15	.03
☐ 17 Jim Slaton	.25	.10	.02
☐ 18 Darrell Miller	.35	.15	.03
☐ 19 Ruppert Jones	.25	.10	.02
☐ 20 Rob Wilfong	.25	.10	.02
☐ 21 Donnie Moore	.25	.10	.02
☐ 22 Wally Joyner	2.00	.80	.20
☐ 23 Terry Forster	.25	.10	.02
☐ 24 Gene Mauch MG	.25	.10	.02

1987 Smokey A's Colorgrams

These cards are actually pages of a booklet featuring members of the Oakland A's and Smokey's fire safety tips. The booklet

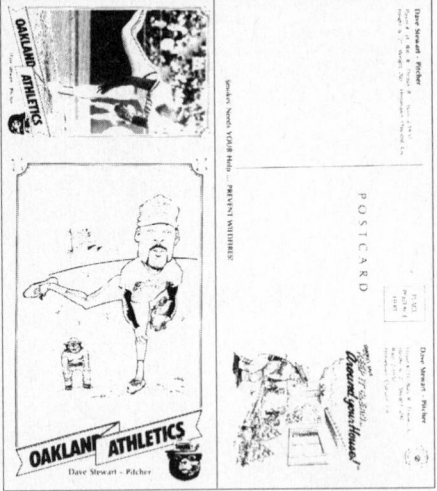

Smokey the Bear pictured on every card with the player. The card backs give a fire safety tip. The cards measure approximately 4" by 6" and are subtitled "National Smokey Bear Day 1987" on the front. The cards were printed on an uncut (but perforated) sheet that measured 18" by 24".

	MINT	EXC	G-VG
COMPLETE SET (16)	7.00	3.00	.70
COMMON PLAYER (1-16)	.30	.12	.03
☐ 1 Jose Canseco	2.00	.80	.2
☐ 2 Dennis Oil Can Boyd	.30	.12	.0
☐ 3 John Candelaria	.30	.12	.03
☐ 4 Harold Baines	.40	.16	.04
☐ 5 Joe Carter	.75	.30	.07
☐ 6 Jack Morris	.60	.25	.06
☐ 7 Buddy Biancalana	.30	.12	.03
☐ 8 Kirby Puckett	1.25	.50	.12
☐ 9 Mike Pagliarulo	.40	.16	.04
☐ 10 Larry Sheets	.30	.12	.03
☐ 11 Mike Moore	.40	.16	.04
☐ 12 Charlie Hough	.30	.12	.03
☐ 13 National Smokey .... Bear Day 1987	.30	.12	.03
☐ 14 Tom Henke	.40	.16	.04
☐ 15 Jim Gantner	.30	.12	.03
☐ 16 American League .... Smokey Bear Day 1987	.30	.12	.03

has 12 pages each containing a black and white photo card (approximately 2 1/2" by 3 3/4") and a black and white player caricature (oversized head) postcard (approximately 3 3/4" by 5 5/8"). The cards are unnumbered but they have biographical information and a fire-prevention cartoon on the back of the card.

	MINT	EXC	G-VG
COMPLETE SET (12)	12.00	5.25	1.50
COMMON PLAYER (1-12)	.60	.25	.06
☐ 1 Joaquin Andujar	.75	.30	.07
☐ 2 Jose Canseco	4.50	2.00	.45
☐ 3 Mike Davis	.60	.25	.06
☐ 4 Alfredo Griffin	.60	.25	.06
☐ 5 Moose Haas	.60	.25	.06
☐ 6 Jay Howell	.90	.40	.09
☐ 7 Reggie Jackson	2.00	.80	.20
☐ 8 Carney Lansford	1.00	.40	.10
☐ 9 Dwayne Murphy	.75	.30	.07
☐ 10 Tony Phillips	.75	.30	.07
☐ 11 Dave Stewart	1.25	.50	.12
☐ 12 Curt Young	.60	.25	.06

1987 Smokey American League

The U.S. Forestry Service (in conjunction with Major League Baseball) produced this large, attractive 14-player card set to commemorate the 43rd birthday of Smokey. The cards feature

1987 Smokey Angels

The U.S. Forestry Service (in conjunction with the California Angels) produced this large, attractive 24-card set to commemorate the 43rd birthday of Smokey. The cards feature Smokey the Bear pictured at the bottom of every card. The card backs give a cartoon fire safety tip. The cards measure 4" by 6" and are subtitled "Wildfire Prevention" on the front.

	MINT	EXC	G-VG
COMPLETE SET (24)	8.00	3.50	.80
COMMON PLAYER (1-24)	.30	.12	.03
☐ 1 John Candelaria	.40	.16	.04
☐ 2 Don Sutton	.75	.30	.07
☐ 3 Mike Witt	.40	.16	.04
☐ 4 Gary Lucas	.30	.12	.03
☐ 5 Kirk McCaskill	.40	.16	.04
☐ 6 Chuck Finley	.75	.30	.07
☐ 7 Willie Fraser	.30	.12	.03
☐ 8 Donnie Moore	.30	.12	.03
☐ 9 Urbano Lugo	.30	.12	.03
☐ 10 Butch Wynegar	.30	.12	.03
☐ 11 Darrell Miller	.30	.12	.03
☐ 12 Wally Joyner	1.00	.40	.10
☐ 13 Mark McLemore	.30	.12	.03
☐ 14 Mark Ryal	.30	.12	.03
☐ 15 Dick Schofield	.40	.16	.04
☐ 16 Jack Howell	.40	.16	.04
☐ 17 Doug DeCinces	.40	.16	.04
☐ 18 Gus Polidor	.30	.12	.03
☐ 19 Brian Downing	.40	.16	.04
☐ 20 Gary Pettis	.40	.16	.04

		MINT	EXC	G-VG
☐ 21	Ruppert Jones	.30	.12	.03
☐ 22	George Hendrick	.40	.16	.04
☐ 23	Devon White	.90	.40	.09
☐ 24	Checklist Card	.30	.12	.03

1987 Smokey Braves

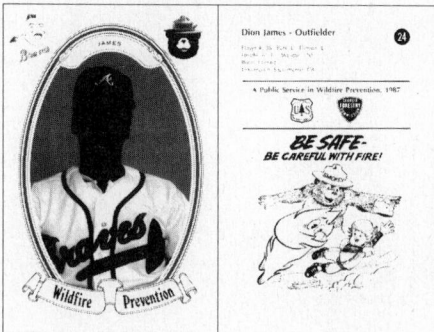

The U.S. Forestry Service (in conjunction with the Atlanta Braves) produced this large, attractive 27-card set to commemorate the 43rd birthday of Smokey. The cards feature Smokey the Bear pictured in the top right corner of every card. The card backs give a cartoon fire safety tip. The cards measure 4" by 6" and are subtitled "Wildfire Prevention" on the front. Distribution of the cards was gradual at the stadium throughout the summer. These large cards are numbered on the back.

		MINT	EXC	G-VG
COMPLETE SET (27)		20.00	8.50	2.75
COMMON PLAYER (1-26)		.60	.25	.06
☐ 1	Zane Smith	.90	.40	.09
☐ 2	Charlie Puleo	.60	.25	.06
☐ 3	Randy O'Neal	.60	.25	.06
☐ 4	David Palmer	.75	.30	.07
☐ 5	Rick Mahler	.75	.30	.07
☐ 6	Ed Olwine	.60	.25	.06
☐ 7	Jeff Dedmon	.60	.25	.06
☐ 8	Paul Assenmacher	.60	.25	.06
☐ 9	Gene Garber	.60	.25	.06
☐ 10	Jim Acker	.60	.25	.06
☐ 11	Bruce Benedict	.60	.25	.06
☐ 12	Ozzie Virgil	.60	.25	.06
☐ 13	Ted Simmons	1.25	.50	.12
☐ 14	Dale Murphy	3.00	1.25	.30
☐ 15	Graig Nettles	1.00	.40	.10
☐ 16	Ken Oberkfell	.60	.25	.06
☐ 17	Gerald Perry	.75	.30	.07
☐ 18	Rafael Ramirez	.60	.25	.06
☐ 19	Ken Griffey	1.00	.40	.10
☐ 20	Andres Thomas	.75	.30	.07
☐ 21	Glenn Hubbard	.60	.25	.06
☐ 22	Damaso Garcia	.60	.25	.06
☐ 23	Gary Roenicke	.60	.25	.06
☐ 24	Dion James	.60	.25	.06
☐ 25	Albert Hall	.60	.25	.06
☐ 26	Chuck Tanner MG	.60	.25	.06
☐ xx	Smokey/Checklist (unnumbered)	.60	.25	.06

1987 Smokey Cardinals

The U.S. Forestry Service (in conjunction with the St. Louis Cardinals) produced this large, attractive 25-card set to commemorate the 43rd birthday of Smokey. The cards feature Smokey the Bear pictured in the top right corner of every card. The card backs give a cartoon fire safety tip. The cards measure

4" by 6" and are subtitled "Wildfire Prevention" on the front. Sets were supposedly available from the Cardinals team for 3.50 postpaid. Also a limited number of 8 1/2" by 12" full-color team photos were available from the team to those who sent in a large SASE. The large team photo is not considered part of the complete set.

		MINT	EXC	G-VG
COMPLETE SET (25)		14.00	6.25	2.00
COMMON PLAYER (1-25)		.45	.18	.04
☐ 1	Ray Soff	.45	.18	.04
☐ 2	Todd Worrell	.65	.25	.06
☐ 3	John Tudor	.65	.25	.06
☐ 4	Pat Perry	.45	.18	.04
☐ 5	Rick Horton	.45	.18	.04
☐ 6	Danny Cox	.65	.25	.06
☐ 7	Bob Forsch	.45	.18	.04
☐ 8	Greg Mathews	.45	.18	.04
☐ 9	Bill Dawley	.45	.18	.04
☐ 10	Steve Lake	.45	.18	.04
☐ 11	Tony Pena	.65	.25	.06
☐ 12	Tom Pagnozzi	.45	.18	.04
☐ 13	Jack Clark	.90	.40	.09
☐ 14	Jim Lindeman	.45	.18	.04
☐ 15	Mike Laga	.45	.18	.04
☐ 16	Terry Pendleton	.90	.40	.09
☐ 17	Ozzie Smith	1.50	.60	.15
☐ 18	Jose Oquendo	.65	.25	.06
☐ 19	Tom Lawless	.45	.18	.04
☐ 20	Tom Herr	.65	.25	.06
☐ 21	Curt Ford	.45	.18	.04
☐ 22	Willie McGee	.90	.40	.09
☐ 23	Tito Landrum	.45	.18	.04
☐ 24	Vince Coleman	1.25	.50	.12
☐ 25	Whitey Herzog MG	.65	.25	.06
☐ xx	Team Photo (large)	2.00	.80	.20

1987 Smokey Dodger All-Stars

This 40-card set was issued by the U.S. Forestry Service to commemorate the Los Angeles Dodgers selected for the All-Star game over the past 25 years. The cards measure 2 1/2" by 3 3/4" and have full-color fronts. The card fronts are distinguished by their thick silver borders and the bats, balls, and stadium design layout. The 25th anniversary logo for Dodger Stadium is in the lower right corner of each card.

		MINT	EXC	G-VG
COMPLETE SET (40)		13.50	6.00	1.85
COMMON PLAYER (1-40)		.30	.12	.03
☐ 1	Walt Alston MG	.60	.25	.06
☐ 2	Dusty Baker	.40	.16	.04
☐ 3	Jim Brewer	.30	.12	.03
☐ 4	Ron Cey	.50	.20	.05
☐ 5	Tommy Davis	.40	.16	.04
☐ 6	Willie Davis	.40	.16	.04
☐ 7	Don Drysdale	.90	.40	.09
☐ 8	Steve Garvey	.90	.40	.09
☐ 9	Bill Grabarkewitz	.30	.12	.03

Smokey the Bear pictured on every card with the player. The card backs give a fire safety tip. The cards measure 4" by 6" and are subtitled "National Smokey Bear Day 1987" on the front. The set price below does not include the more difficult variation cards.

		MINT	EXC	G-VG
COMPLETE SET (15)		7.00	3.00	.70
COMMON PLAYER (1-15)		.25	.10	.02
☐ 1	Steve Sax	.50	.20	.05
☐ 2A	Dale Murphy (holding bat)	2.00	.80	.20
☐ 2B	Dale Murphy (no bat, arm around Smokey)	12.50	5.50	1.65
☐ 3A	Jody Davis (kneeling with Smokey)	.50	.20	.05
☐ 3B	Jody Davis (standing, shaking Smokey's hand)	7.50	3.25	.75
☐ 4	Bill Gullickson	.35	.15	.03
☐ 5	Mike Scott	.50	.20	.05
☐ 6	Roger McDowell	.35	.15	.03
☐ 7	Steve Bedrosian	.35	.15	.03
☐ 8	Johnny Ray	.25	.10	.02
☐ 9	Ozzie Smith	.75	.30	.07
☐ 10	Steve Garvey	.75	.30	.07
☐ 11	National Smokey Bear Day	.25	.10	.02
☐ 12	Mike Krukow	.25	.10	.02
☐ 13	Smokey the Bear	.25	.10	.02
☐ 14	Mike Fitzgerald	.25	.10	.02
☐ 15	National League Logo	.25	.10	.02

☐ 10	Pedro Guerrero	.60	.25	.06
☐ 11	Tom Haller	.30	.12	.03
☐ 12	Orel Hershiser	.60	.25	.06
☐ 13	Burt Hooton	.30	.12	.03
☐ 14	Steve Howe	.30	.12	.03
☐ 15	Tommy John	.50	.20	.05
☐ 16	Sandy Koufax	1.25	.50	.12
☐ 17	Tom Lasorda MG	.50	.20	.05
☐ 18	Jim Lefebvre	.40	.16	.04
☐ 19	Davey Lopes	.40	.16	.04
☐ 20	Mike Marshall (pitcher)	.40	.16	.04
☐ 21	Mike Marshall (outfielder)	.40	.16	.04
☐ 22	Andy Messersmith	.30	.12	.03
☐ 23	Rick Monday	.30	.12	.03
☐ 24	Manny Mota	.40	.16	.04
☐ 25	Claude Osteen	.30	.12	.03
☐ 26	Johnny Podres	.40	.16	.04
☐ 27	Phil Regan	.30	.12	.03
☐ 28	Jerry Reuss	.30	.12	.03
☐ 29	Rick Rhoden	.30	.12	.03
☐ 30	John Roseboro	.30	.12	.03
☐ 31	Bill Russell	.40	.16	.04
☐ 32	Steve Sax	.50	.20	.05
☐ 33	Bill Singer	.30	.12	.03
☐ 34	Reggie Smith	.40	.16	.04
☐ 35	Don Sutton	.80	.35	.08
☐ 36	Fernando Valenzuela	.50	.20	.05
☐ 37	Bob Welch	.40	.16	.04
☐ 38	Maury Wills	.50	.20	.05
☐ 39	Jim Wynn	.40	.16	.04
☐ 40	Checklist Card	.30	.12	.03

1987 Smokey National League

The U.S. Forestry Service (in conjunction with Major League Baseball) produced this large, attractive 14 player card set to commemorate the 43rd birthday of Smokey. The cards feature

1987 Smokey Rangers

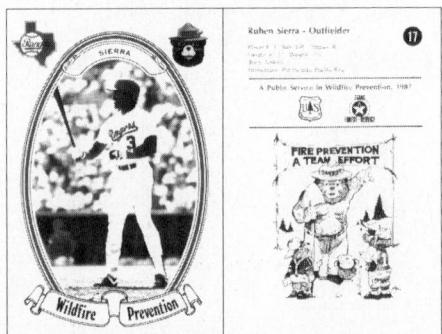

The U.S. Forestry Service (in conjunction with the Texas Rangers) produced this large, attractive 32-card set. The cards feature Smokey the Bear pictured in the upper-right corner of every player's card. The card backs give a cartoon fire safety tip. The cards measure approximately 4 1/4" by 6" and are subtitled "Wildfire Prevention" on the front. These large cards are numbered on the back. Cards 4 Mike Mason and 14 Tom Paciorek were withdrawn and were never formally released as part of the set and hence are quite scarce.

		MINT	EXC	G-VG
COMPLETE SET (32)		80.00	36.00	12.00
COMMON PLAYER (1-32)		.35	.15	.03
☐ 1	Charlie Hough	.60	.25	.06
☐ 2	Greg A. Harris	.35	.15	.03
☐ 3	Jose Guzman	.50	.20	.05
☐ 4	Mike Mason SP	35.00	15.75	5.25
☐ 5	Dale Mohorcic	.35	.15	.03
☐ 6	Bobby Witt	1.00	.40	.10
☐ 7	Mitch Williams	.75	.30	.07
☐ 8	Geno Petralli	.35	.15	.03
☐ 9	Don Slaught	.35	.15	.03

			MINT	EXC	G-VG
☐	10	Darrell Porter	.35	.15	.03
☐	11	Steve Buechele	.60	.25	.06
☐	12	Pete O'Brien	.50	.20	.05
☐	13	Scott Fletcher	.35	.15	.03
☐	14	Tom Paciorek SP	35.00	15.75	5.25
☐	15	Pete Incaviglia	.90	.40	.09
☐	16	Oddibe McDowell	.50	.20	.05
☐	17	Ruben Sierra	4.00	1.75	.40
☐	18	Larry Parrish	.50	.20	.05
☐	19	Bobby Valentine MG	.50	.20	.05
☐	20	Tom House CO	.35	.15	.03
☐	21	Tom Robson CO	.35	.15	.03
☐	22	Edwin Correa	.35	.15	.03
☐	23	Mike Stanley	.35	.15	.03
☐	24	Joe Ferguson CO	.35	.15	.03
☐	25	Art Howe CO	.50	.20	.05
☐	26	Bob Brower	.35	.15	.03
☐	27	Mike Loynd	.35	.15	.03
☐	28	Curtis Wilkerson	.35	.15	.03
☐	29	Tim Foli CO	.35	.15	.03
☐	30	Dave Oliver CO	.35	.15	.03
☐	31	Jerry Browne	.50	.20	.05
☐	32	Jeff Russell	.60	.25	.06

1988 Smokey Cardinals

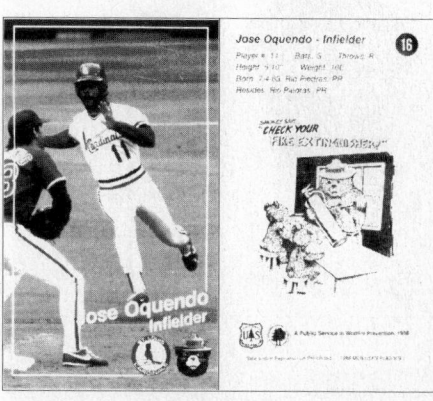

The U.S. Forestry Service (in conjunction with the St. Louis Cardinals) produced this attractive 25-card set. The cards feature Smokey the Bear pictured in the lower right corner of every card. The card backs give a cartoon fire safety tip. The cards measure approximately 3" by 5" and are in full color. The cards are numbered on the backs. The sets were distributed on July 19th during the Cardinals' game against the Los Angeles Dodgers to fans 15 years of age and under.

			MINT	EXC	G-VG
		COMPLETE SET (25)	12.50	5.50	1.65
		COMMON PLAYER (1-25)	.40	.16	.04
☐	1	Whitey Herzog MG	.60	.25	.06
☐	2	Danny Cox	.50	.20	.05
☐	3	Ken Dayley	.40	.16	.04
☐	4	Jose DeLeon	.50	.20	.05
☐	5	Bob Forsch	.40	.16	.04
☐	6	Joe Magrane	.60	.25	.06
☐	7	Greg Mathews	.40	.16	.04
☐	8	Scott Terry	.40	.16	.04
☐	9	John Tudor	.50	.20	.05
☐	10	Todd Worrell	.50	.20	.05
☐	11	Steve Lake	.40	.16	.04
☐	12	Tom Pagnozzi	.40	.16	.04
☐	13	Tony Pena	.50	.20	.05
☐	14	Bob Horner	.50	.20	.05
☐	15	Tom Lawless	.40	.16	.04
☐	16	Jose Oquendo	.50	.20	.05
☐	17	Terry Pendleton	.90	.40	.09
☐	18	Ozzie Smith	1.25	.50	.12
☐	19	Vince Coleman	1.25	.50	.12
☐	20	Curt Ford	.40	.16	.04
☐	21	Willie McGee	.75	.30	.07
☐	22	Larry McWilliams	.40	.16	.04
☐	23	Steve Peters	.50	.20	.05
☐	24	Luis Alicea	.40	.16	.04
☐	25	Tom Brunansky	.60	.25	.06

1988 Smokey Angels

The U.S. Forestry Service (in conjunction with the California Angels) produced this attractive 25-card set. The cards feature Smokey the Bear pictured at the bottom of every card. The card backs give a cartoon fire safety tip. The cards measure approximately 2 1/2" by 3 1/2" and are in full color. The cards are numbered on the back. They were distributed during promotions on August 28, September 4, and September 18.

			MINT	EXC	G-VG
		COMPLETE SET (25)	10.00	4.50	1.25
		COMMON PLAYER (1-24)	.35	.15	.03
☐	1	Cookie Rojas MG	.35	.15	.03
☐	2	Johnny Ray	.50	.20	.05
☐	3	Jack Howell	.50	.20	.05
☐	4	Mike Witt	.35	.15	.03
☐	5	Tony Armas	.50	.20	.05
☐	6	Gus Polidor	.35	.15	.03
☐	7	DeWayne Buice	.35	.15	.03
☐	8	Dan Petry	.50	.20	.05
☐	9	Bob Boone	.75	.30	.07
☐	10	Chili Davis	.75	.30	.07
☐	11	Greg Minton	.35	.15	.03
☐	12	Kirk McCaskill	.50	.20	.05
☐	13	Devon White	.75	.30	.07
☐	14	Willie Fraser	.35	.15	.03
☐	15	Chuck Finley	.75	.30	.07
☐	16	Dick Schofield	.50	.20	.05
☐	17	Wally Joyner	1.00	.40	.10
☐	18	Brian Downing	.50	.20	.05
☐	19	Stewart Cliburn	.35	.15	.03
☐	20	Donnie Moore	.35	.15	.03
☐	21	Bryan Harvey	.75	.30	.07
☐	22	Mark McLemore	.35	.15	.03
☐	23	Butch Wynegar	.35	.15	.03
☐	24	George Hendrick	.50	.20	.05
☐	xx	Checklist/Logo Card	.35	.15	.03

1988 Smokey Dodgers

This 32-card set was issued by the U.S. Forestry Service as a perforated sheet that could be separated into individual cards. The set commemorates Los Angeles Dodgers who hold various team and league records, i.e., "L.A. Dodgers Record-Breakers." The cards measure approximately 2 1/2" by 4" and have full-color fronts. The card fronts are distinguished by their thick light blue borders and the bats, balls, and stadium design layout. The sheets of cards were distributed at the Dodgers' Smokey Bear Day game on September 9th.

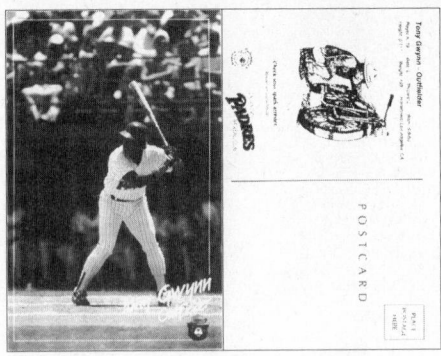

	MINT	EXC	G-VG
COMPLETE SET (32)	12.00	5.25	1.50
COMMON PLAYER (1-32)	.35	.15	.03

		MINT	EXC	G-VG
☐	1 Walter Alston MG	.60	.25	.06
☐	2 John Roseboro	.35	.15	.03
☐	3 Frank Howard	.45	.18	.04
☐	4 Sandy Koufax	.90	.40	.09
☐	5 Manny Mota	.45	.18	.04
☐	6 Sandy Koufax, ...	.45	.18	.04
	Jerry Reuss, and			
	Bill Singer			
☐	7 Maury Wills	.60	.25	.06
☐	8 Tommy Davis	.45	.18	.04
☐	9 Phil Regan	.35	.15	.03
☐	10 Wes Parker	.45	.18	.04
☐	11 Don Drysdale	.75	.30	.07
☐	12 Willie Davis	.45	.18	.04
☐	13 Bill Russell	.45	.18	.04
☐	14 Jim Brewer	.35	.15	.03
☐	15 Steve Garvey, ...	.45	.18	.04
	Davey Lopes,			
	Bill Russell, and			
	Ron Cey			
☐	16 Mike Marshall	.45	.18	.04
☐	17 Steve Garvey	.75	.30	.07
☐	18 Davey Lopes	.45	.18	.04
☐	19 Burt Hooton	.35	.15	.03
☐	20 Jim Wynn	.45	.18	.04
☐	21 Dusty Baker, ...	.45	.18	.04
	Ron Cey,			
	Steve Garvey, and			
	Reggie Smith			
☐	22 Dusty Baker	.45	.18	.04
☐	23 Tommy Lasorda MG	.60	.25	.06
☐	24 Fernando Valenzuela	.60	.25	.06
☐	25 Steve Sax	.60	.25	.06
☐	26 Dodger Stadium	.35	.15	.03
☐	27 Ron Cey	.45	.18	.04
☐	28 Pedro Guerrero	.60	.25	.06
☐	29 Mike Marshall	.45	.18	.04
☐	30 Don Sutton	.75	.30	.07
☐	xx Checklist Card	.35	.15	.03
	(unnumbered)			
☐	xx Smokey Bear	.35	.15	.03
	(unnumbered)			

1988 Smokey Padres

The cards in this 31-card set measure approximately 3 3/4" by 5 3/4". This unnumbered, full color set features the Fire Prevention Bear, Smokey, and a Padres player, coach, manager, or associate on each card. The set was given out at Jack Murphy Stadium to fans under the age of 14 during the Smokey Bear Day game promotion. The logo of the California Department of Forestry appears on the reverse in conjunction with a Smokey the Bear logo on the obverse. The backs contain short biographical data and a fire prevention hint from Smokey. The set is numbered below in alphabetical order. The card backs are actually postcards that can be addressed and mailed. Cards of

Larry Bowa and Candy Sierra were printed but were not officially released since they were no longer members of the Padres by the time the cards were to be distributed.

		MINT	EXC	G-VG
COMPLETE SET (31)		24.00	10.50	3.50
COMMON PLAYER (1-31)		.60	.25	.06

		MINT	EXC	G-VG
☐	1 Shawn Abner	.75	.30	.07
☐	2 Roberto Alomar	4.50	2.00	.45
☐	3 Sandy Alomar CO	.75	.30	.07
☐	4 Greg Booker	.60	.25	.06
☐	5 Chris Brown	.60	.25	.06
☐	6 Mark Davis	.90	.40	.09
☐	7 Pat Dobson CO	.75	.30	.07
☐	8 Tim Flannery	.60	.25	.06
☐	9 Mark Grant	.60	.25	.06
☐	10 Tony Gwynn	3.50	1.50	.35
☐	11 Andy Hawkins	.60	.25	.06
☐	12 Stan Jefferson	.60	.25	.06
☐	13 Jimmy Jones	.75	.30	.07
☐	14 John Kruk	.90	.40	.09
☐	15 Dave Leiper	.60	.25	.06
☐	16 Shane Mack	1.25	.50	.12
☐	17 Carmelo Martinez	.75	.30	.07
☐	18 Lance McCullers	.60	.25	.06
☐	19 Keith Moreland	.60	.25	.06
☐	20 Eric Nolte	.60	.25	.06
☐	21 Amos Otis CO	.75	.30	.07
☐	22 Mark Parent	.60	.25	.06
☐	23 Randy Ready	.75	.30	.07
☐	24 Greg Riddoch CO	.75	.30	.07
☐	25 Benito Santiago	2.50	1.00	.25
☐	26 Eric Show	.75	.30	.07
☐	27 Denny Sommers CO	.60	.25	.06
☐	28 Garry Templeton	.75	.30	.07
☐	29 Dickie Thon	.75	.30	.07
☐	30 Ed Whitson	.75	.30	.07
☐	31 Marvell Wynne	.60	.25	.06

1988 Smokey Rangers

The cards in this 21-card set measure approximately 3 1/2" by 5". This numbered, full color set features the Fire Prevention Bear, Smokey, and a Rangers player (or manager) on each card. The set was given out at Arlington Stadium to fans during the Smokey Bear Day game promotion on August 7th. The logos of the Texas Forest Service and the U.S. Forestry Service appear on the reverse in conjunction with a Smokey the Bear logo on the obverse. The backs contain short biographical data and a fire prevention hint from Smokey.

		MINT	EXC	G-VG
COMPLETE SET (21)		12.50	5.50	1.65
COMMON PLAYER (1-21)		.60	.25	.06

		MINT	EXC	G-VG
☐	1 Tom O'Malley	.60	.25	.06
☐	2 Pete O'Brien	.75	.30	.07
☐	3 Geno Petralli	.60	.25	.06
☐	4 Pete Incaviglia	.90	.40	.09

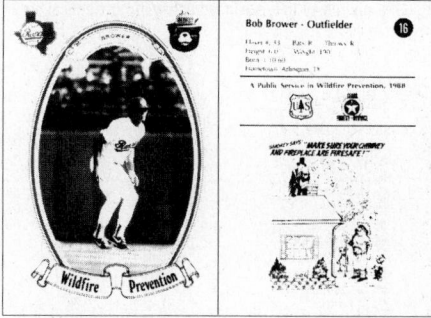

		MINT	EXC	G-VG
☐ 8	Floyd Bannister	.40	.16	.04
☐ 9	Bud Black	.50	.20	.05
☐ 10	Steve Farr	.50	.20	.05
☐ 11	Gene Garber	.40	.16	.04
☐ 12	Mark Gubicza	.75	.30	.07
☐ 13	Charlie Liebrandt	.50	.20	.05
☐ 14	Ted Power	.40	.16	.04
☐ 15	Dan Quisenberry	.60	.25	.06
☐ 16	Bret Saberhagen	1.25	.50	.12
☐ 17	Mike Macfarlane	.50	.20	.05
☐ 18	Scotti Madison	.40	.16	.04
☐ 19	Jamie Quirk	.40	.16	.04
☐ 20	George Brett	1.25	.50	.12
☐ 21	Kevin Seitzer	.60	.25	.06
☐ 22	Bill Pecota	.50	.20	.05
☐ 23	Kurt Stillwell	.50	.20	.05
☐ 24	Brad Wellman	.40	.16	.04
☐ 25	Frank White	.50	.20	.05
☐ 26	Jim Eisenreich	.50	.20	.05
☐ 27	Smokey Bear	.40	.16	.04
☐ xx	Checklist Card	.40	.16	.04

1988 Smokey Twins Colorgrams

These cards are actually pages of a booklet featuring members of the Minnesota Twins and Smokey's fire safety tips. The booklet has 12 pages each containing a black and white photo card (approximately 2 1/2" by 3 3/4") and a black and white player caricature (oversized head) postcard (approximately 3 3/4" by 5 5/8"). The cards are unnumbered but they have biographical information and a fire-prevention cartoon on the back of the card.

		MINT	EXC	G-VG
COMPLETE SET (12)		12.50	5.50	1.65
COMMON PLAYER (1-12)		.65	.25	.06
☐ 1	Frank Viola	1.50	.60	.15
☐ 2	Gary Gaetti	1.00	.40	.10
☐ 3	Kent Hrbek	1.25	.50	.12
☐ 4	Jeff Reardon	1.50	.60	.15
☐ 5	Gene Larkin	.90	.40	.09
☐ 6	Bert Blyleven	1.25	.50	.12
☐ 7	Tim Laudner	.65	.25	.06
☐ 8	Greg Gagne	.90	.40	.09
☐ 9	Randy Bush	.65	.25	.06
☐ 10	Dan Gladden	.65	.25	.06
☐ 11	Al Newman	.65	.25	.06
☐ 12	Kirby Puckett	3.50	1.50	.35

		MINT	EXC	G-VG
☐ 5	Oddibe McDowell	.75	.30	.07
☐ 6	Dale Mohorcic	.60	.25	.06
☐ 7	Bobby Witt	.90	.40	.09
☐ 8	Bobby Valentine MG	.75	.30	.07
☐ 9	Ruben Sierra	2.50	1.00	.25
☐ 10	Scott Fletcher	.60	.25	.06
☐ 11	Mike Stanley	.60	.25	.06
☐ 12	Steve Buechele	.75	.30	.07
☐ 13	Charlie Hough	.75	.30	.07
☐ 14	Larry Parrish	.75	.30	.07
☐ 15	Jerry Browne	.75	.30	.07
☐ 16	Bob Brower	.60	.25	.06
☐ 17	Jeff Russell	.75	.30	.07
☐ 18	Edwin Correa	.60	.25	.06
☐ 19	Mitch Williams	.75	.30	.07
☐ 20	Jose Guzman	.75	.30	.07
☐ 21	Curtis Wilkerson	.60	.25	.06

1988 Smokey Royals

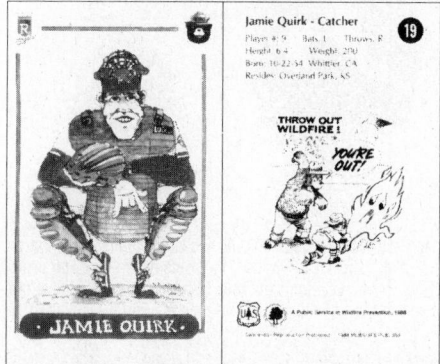

This set of 28 cards features caricatures of the Kansas City Royals players. The cards are nunmbered on the back except for the unnumbered title/checklist card. The card set was distributed as a giveaway item at the stadium on August 14th to kids age 14 and under. The cards are approximately 3" by 5" and are in full color on the card fronts. The Smokey logo is in the upper right corner of every obverse.

		MINT	EXC	G-VG
COMPLETE SET (28)		12.50	5.50	1.65
COMMON PLAYER (1-27)		.40	.16	.04
☐ 1	John Wathan MG	.50	.20	.05
☐ 2	Royals Coaches	.40	.16	.04
☐ 3	Willie Wilson	.60	.25	.06
☐ 4	Danny Tartabull	1.25	.50	.12
☐ 5	Bo Jackson	2.50	1.00	.25
☐ 6	Gary Thurman	.50	.20	.05
☐ 7	Jerry Don Gleaton	.40	.16	.04

1989 Smokey Angels All-Stars

 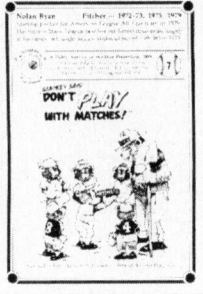

The 1989 Smokey Angels All-Stars set contains 20 standard-size (2 1/2 by 3 1/2 inch) cards. The fronts have red and white borders. The backs are blue and red and feature career highlights. This set, which depicts current and former Angels who appeared in the All-Star game, was given away at the June 25, 1989 Angels home game.

	MINT	EXC	G-VG
COMPLETE SET (20)	7.00	3.00	.70
COMMON PLAYER (1-20)	.25	.10	.02
☐ 1 Bill Rigney	.25	.10	.02
☐ 2 Dean Chance	.35	.15	.03
☐ 3 Jim Fregosi	.35	.15	.03
☐ 4 Bobby Knoop	.25	.10	.02
☐ 5 Don Mincher	.25	.10	.02
☐ 6 Clyde Wright	.25	.10	.02
☐ 7 Nolan Ryan	2.00	.80	.20
☐ 8 Frank Robinson	.75	.30	.07
☐ 9 Frank Tanana	.35	.15	.03
☐ 10 Rod Carew	1.00	.40	.10
☐ 11 Bobby Grich	.35	.15	.03
☐ 12 Brian Downing	.35	.15	.03
☐ 13 Don Baylor	.35	.15	.03
☐ 14 Fred Lynn	.35	.15	.03
☐ 15 Reggie Jackson	1.00	.40	.10
☐ 16 Doug DeCinces	.35	.15	.03
☐ 17 Bob Boone	.50	.20	.05
☐ 18 Wally Joyner	.75	.30	.07
☐ 19 Mike Witt	.35	.15	.03
☐ 20 Johnny Ray	.25	.10	.02

1989 Smokey Cardinals

 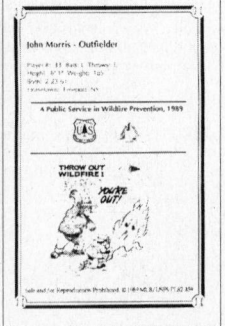

The 1989 Smokey Cardinals set contains 24 cards measuring 4" by 6". The fronts have color photos with white and red borders. The backs feature biographical information. The cards

are unnumbered so they are listed below in alphabetical order for reference.

	MINT	EXC	G-VG
COMPLETE SET (24)	10.00	4.50	1.25
COMMON PLAYER (1-24)	.35	.15	.03
☐ 1 Tom Brunansky	.60	.25	.06
☐ 2 Vince Coleman	.90	.40	.09
☐ 3 John Costello	.45	.18	.04
☐ 4 Ken Dayley	.35	.15	.03
☐ 5 Jose DeLeon	.45	.18	.04
☐ 6 Frank DiPino	.35	.15	.03
☐ 7 Pedro Guerrero	.90	.40	.09
☐ 8 Whitey Herzog MG	.60	.25	.06
☐ 9 Ken Hill	.45	.18	.04
☐ 10 Tim Jones	.35	.15	.03
☐ 11 Jim Lindeman	.35	.15	.03
☐ 12 Joe Magrane	.45	.18	.04
☐ 13 Willie McGee	.75	.30	.07
☐ 14 John Morris	.35	.15	.03
☐ 15 Jose Oquendo	.45	.18	.04
☐ 16 Tom Pagnozzi	.35	.15	.03
☐ 17 Tony Pena	.45	.18	.04
☐ 18 Terry Pendleton	.90	.40	.09
☐ 19 Dan Quisenberry	.60	.25	.06
☐ 20 Ozzie Smith	.90	.40	.09
☐ 21 Scott Terry	.35	.15	.03
☐ 22 Milt Thompson	.35	.15	.03
☐ 23 Denny Walling	.35	.15	.03
☐ 24 Todd Worrell	.45	.18	.04

1989 Smokey Colt .45s

The 1989 Smokey Houston Colt .45s set contains 29 standard-size (2 1/2" by 3 1/2") cards. The fronts have black and white photos with white and light blue borders. This set depicts old Houston Colt .45s' players from their inaugural 1962 season.

	MINT	EXC	G-VG
COMPLETE SET (29)	6.00	2.50	.60
COMMON PLAYER (1-29)	.25	.10	.02
☐ 1 Bob Bruce	.25	.10	.02
☐ 2 Al Cicotte	.25	.10	.02
☐ 3 Dave Giusti	.35	.15	.03
☐ 4 Jim Golden	.25	.10	.02
☐ 5 Ken Johnson	.25	.10	.02
☐ 6 Tom Borland	.25	.10	.02
☐ 7 Bobby Shantz	.35	.15	.03
☐ 8 Dick Farrell	.35	.15	.03
☐ 9 Jim Umbricht	.25	.10	.02
☐ 10 Hal Woodeshick	.25	.10	.02
☐ 11 Merritt Ranew	.25	.10	.02
☐ 12 Hal Smith	.25	.10	.02
☐ 13 Jim Campbell	.25	.10	.02
☐ 14 Norm Larker	.25	.10	.02
☐ 15 Joe Amalfitano	.25	.10	.02
☐ 16 Bob Aspromonte	.25	.10	.02
☐ 17 Bob Lillis	.35	.15	.03
☐ 18 Dick Gernert	.25	.10	.02
☐ 19 Don Buddin	.25	.10	.02
☐ 20 Pidge Browne	.25	.10	.02
☐ 21 Von McDaniel	.25	.10	.02
☐ 22 Don Taussig	.25	.10	.02

☐ 23	Al Spangler	.35	.15	.03
☐ 24	Al Heist	.25	.10	.02
☐ 25	Jim Pendleton	.25	.10	.02
☐ 26	Johnny Weekly	.25	.10	.02
☐ 27	Harry Craft MG	.25	.10	.02
☐ 28	Colt Coaches	.25	.10	.02
☐ 29	1962 Houston Colt 45s	.25	.10	.02

1989 Smokey Dodger Greats

The 1989 Smokey Dodger Greats set contains 104 standard-size (2 1/2" by 3 1/2") cards. The fronts and backs have white and blue borders. The backs are vertically-oriented and feature career totals and fire prevention cartoons. The set depicts notable Dodgers of all eras, and was distributed in perforated sheet format.

	MINT	EXC	G-VG
COMPLETE SET (104)	16.00	6.75	2.25
COMMON PLAYER (1-104)	.10	.04	.01

☐ 1	Walter Alston	.30	.12	.03
☐ 2	David Bancroft	.25	.10	.02
☐ 3	Dan Brouthers	.25	.10	.02
☐ 4	Roy Campanella	.50	.20	.05
☐ 5	Max Carey	.25	.10	.02
☐ 6	Hazen"KiKi" Cuyler	.25	.10	.02
☐ 7	Don Drysdale	.35	.15	.03
☐ 8	Burleigh Grimes	.25	.10	.02
☐ 9	Billy Herman	.25	.10	.02
☐ 10	Waite Hoyt	.25	.10	.02
☐ 11	Hughie Jennings	.25	.10	.02
☐ 12	Willie Keeler	.25	.10	.02
☐ 13	Joseph Kelley	.25	.10	.02
☐ 14	George Kelly	.25	.10	.02
☐ 15	Sandy Koufax	.50	.20	.05
☐ 16	Henry"Heinie" Manush	.25	.10	.02
☐ 17	Juan Marichal	.35	.15	.03
☐ 18	Rabbit Maranville	.25	.10	.02
☐ 19	Rube Marquard	.25	.10	.02
☐ 20	Thomas McCarthy	.25	.10	.02
☐ 21	Joseph McGinnity	.25	.10	.02
☐ 22	Joe Medwick	.25	.10	.02
☐ 23	Pee Wee Reese	.35	.15	.03
☐ 24	Frank Robinson	.35	.15	.03
☐ 25	Jackie Robinson	.75	.30	.07
☐ 26	George"Babe" Ruth	.75	.30	.07
☐ 27	Duke Snider	.50	.20	.05
☐ 28	Casey Stengel	.50	.20	.05
☐ 29	Dazzy Vance	.25	.10	.02
☐ 30	Arky Vaughan	.25	.10	.02
☐ 31	Mike Scioscia	.10	.04	.01
☐ 32	Lloyd Waner	.25	.10	.02
☐ 33	John"Monte" Ward	.25	.10	.02
☐ 34	Zack Wheat	.25	.10	.02
☐ 35	Hoyt Wilhelm	.25	.10	.02
☐ 36	Hack Wilson	.25	.10	.02
☐ 37	Tony Cuccinello	.10	.04	.01
☐ 38	Al Lopez	.25	.10	.02
☐ 39	Leo Durocher	.25	.10	.02
☐ 40	Cookie Lavagetto	.10	.04	.01
☐ 41	Babe Phelps	.10	.04	.01
☐ 42	Dolph Camilli	.10	.04	.01
☐ 43	Whitlow Wyatt	.10	.04	.01
☐ 44	Mickey Owen	.10	.04	.01

☐ 45	Van Mungo	.10	.04	.01
☐ 46	Pete Coscarart	.10	.04	.01
☐ 47	Pete Reiser	.15	.06	.01
☐ 48	Augie Galan	.10	.04	.01
☐ 49	Dixie Walker	.10	.04	.01
☐ 50	Kirby Higbe	.10	.04	.01
☐ 51	Ralph Branca	.20	.08	.02
☐ 52	Bruce Edwards	.10	.04	.01
☐ 53	Eddie Stanky	.10	.04	.01
☐ 54	Gil Hodges	.25	.10	.02
☐ 55	Don Newcombe	.20	.08	.02
☐ 56	Preacher Roe	.20	.08	.02
☐ 57	Willie Randolph	.10	.04	.01
☐ 58	Carl Furillo	.20	.08	.02
☐ 59	Charlie Dressen	.10	.04	.01
☐ 60	Carl Erskine	.20	.08	.02
☐ 61	Clem Labine	.10	.04	.01
☐ 62	Gino Cimoli	.10	.04	.01
☐ 63	Johnny Podres	.20	.08	.02
☐ 64	Johnny Roseboro	.10	.04	.01
☐ 65	Wally Moon	.10	.04	.01
☐ 66	Charlie Neal	.10	.04	.01
☐ 67	Norm Larker	.10	.04	.01
☐ 68	Stan Williams	.10	.04	.01
☐ 69	Maury Wills	.20	.08	.02
☐ 70	Tommy Davis	.20	.08	.02
☐ 71	Jim Lefebvre	.15	.06	.01
☐ 72	Phil Regan	.10	.04	.01
☐ 73	Claude Osteen	.10	.04	.01
☐ 74	Tom Haller	.10	.04	.01
☐ 75	Bill Singer	.10	.04	.01
☐ 76	Bill Grabarkewitz	.10	.04	.01
☐ 77	Willie Davis	.10	.04	.01
☐ 78	Don Sutton	.25	.10	.02
☐ 79	Jim Brewer	.10	.04	.01
☐ 80	Manny Mota	.15	.06	.01
☐ 81	Bill Russell	.15	.06	.01
☐ 82	Ron Cey	.15	.06	.01
☐ 83	Steve Garvey	.30	.12	.03
☐ 84	Mike G. Marshall	.10	.04	.01
☐ 85	Andy Messersmith	.10	.04	.01
☐ 86	Jimmy Wynn	.15	.06	.01
☐ 87	Rick Rhoden	.10	.04	.01
☐ 88	Reggie Smith	.15	.06	.01
☐ 89	Jay Howell	.15	.06	.01
☐ 90	Rick Monday	.10	.04	.01
☐ 91	Tommy John	.20	.08	.02
☐ 92	Bob Welch	.20	.08	.02
☐ 93	Dusty Baker	.15	.06	.01
☐ 94	Pedro Guerrero	.20	.08	.02
☐ 95	Burt Hooton	.10	.04	.01
☐ 96	Davey Lopes	.15	.06	.01
☐ 97	Fernando Valenzuela	.20	.08	.02
☐ 98	Steve Howe	.10	.04	.01
☐ 99	Steve Sax	.20	.08	.02
☐ 100	Orel Hershiser	.25	.10	.02
☐ 101	Mike A. Marshall	.20	.08	.02
☐ 102	Ernie Lombardi	.25	.10	.02
☐ 103	Fred Lindstrom	.25	.10	.02
☐ 104	Wilbert Robinson	.25	.10	.02

1989 Smokey Rangers

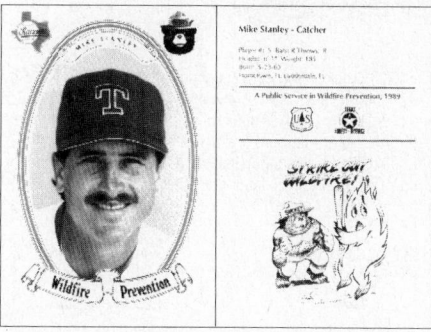

The 1989 Smokey Rangers set features 34 unnumbered cards measuring approximately 4 1/4" by 6". The fronts feature mugshot photos with white borders. The backs feature biographical information and fire prevention tips. The set was given away at a 1989 Rangers' home game.

	MINT	EXC	G-VG
COMPLETE SET (34)	17.50	7.00	2.00
COMMON PLAYER (1-34)	.45	.18	.04
☐ 1 Darrel Akerfelds	.45	.18	.04
☐ 2 Brad Arnsberg	.60	.25	.06
☐ 3 Buddy Bell	.75	.30	.07
☐ 4 Kevin Brown	.75	.30	.07
☐ 5 Steve Buechele	.60	.25	.06
☐ 6 Dick Egan CO	.45	.18	.04
☐ 7 Cecil Espy	.45	.18	.04
☐ 8 Scott Fletcher	.45	.18	.04
☐ 9 Julio Franco	1.00	.40	.10
☐ 10 Cecilio Guante	.45	.18	.04
☐ 11 Jose Guzman	.60	.25	.06
☐ 12 Drew Hall	.45	.18	.04
☐ 13 Toby Harrah CO	.60	.25	.06
☐ 14 Charlie Hough	.60	.25	.06
☐ 15 Tom House CO	.45	.18	.04
☐ 16 Pete Incaviglia	.75	.30	.07
☐ 17 Chad Kreuter	.45	.18	.04
☐ 18 Jeff Kunkel	.45	.18	.04
☐ 19 Rick Leach	.45	.18	.04
☐ 20 Davey Lopes	.60	.25	.06
☐ 21 Craig McMurtry	.45	.18	.04
☐ 22 Jamie Moyer	.45	.18	.04
☐ 23 Dave Oliver CO	.45	.18	.04
☐ 24 Rafael Palmeiro	1.00	.40	.10
☐ 25 Geno Petralli	.45	.18	.04
☐ 26 Tom Robson CO	.45	.18	.04
☐ 27 Kenny Rogers	.60	.25	.06
☐ 28 Jeff Russell	.60	.25	.06
☐ 29 Nolan Ryan	3.50	1.50	.35
☐ 30 Ruben Sierra	3.00	1.25	.30
☐ 31 Mike Stanley	.45	.18	.04
☐ 32 Jim Sundberg	.60	.25	.06
☐ 33 Bobby Valentine MG	.60	.25	.06
☐ 34 Bobby Witt	.75	.30	.07

1990 Smokey Angels

The 1990 Smokey Angels set contains standard-size (2 1/2" by 3 1/2") cards which were produced by the U.S. Forest Service and Bureau of Land Management in conjunction with the California Department of Forestry. The first 18 cards in the set are alphabetically arranged. Bailes and McClure were apparently added to the checklist later than these 18, after they were acquired by the Angels.

	MINT	EXC	G-VG
COMPLETE SET (20)	7.00	3.00	.70
COMMON PLAYER (1-20)	.30	.12	.03
☐ 1 Jim Abbott	1.25	.50	.12
☐ 2 Bert Blyleven	.50	.20	.05
☐ 3 Chili Davis	.50	.20	.05
☐ 4 Brian Downing	.40	.16	.04
☐ 5 Chuck Finley	.60	.25	.06
☐ 6 Willie Fraser	.30	.12	.03
☐ 7 Bryan Harvey	.50	.20	.05
☐ 8 Jack Howell	.40	.16	.04

	MINT	EXC	G-VG
☐ 9 Wally Joyner	.75	.30	.07
☐ 10 Mark Langston	.50	.20	.05
☐ 11 Kirk McCaskill	.40	.16	.04
☐ 12 Mark McLemore	.30	.12	.03
☐ 13 Lance Parrish	.50	.20	.05
☐ 14 Johnny Ray	.40	.16	.04
☐ 15 Dick Schofield	.40	.16	.04
☐ 16 Mike Witt	.30	.12	.03
☐ 17 Claudell Washington	.40	.16	.04
☐ 18 Devon White	.50	.20	.05
☐ 19 Scott Bailes	.30	.12	.03
☐ 20 Bob McClure	.30	.12	.03

1990 Smokey Cardinals

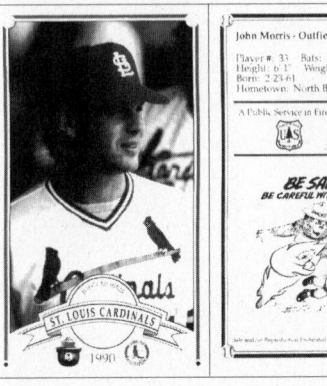

This 27-card, approximately 3" by 5", set was issued about the 1990 St. Louis Cardinals in conjuction with the US Forest Service which was using the popular character Smokey the Bear. The set has full color action photos of the Cardinals on the front of the card while the back of the card has fire safety tips on the bottom of the card. The set has been checklisted alphabetically for reference. The cards are unnumbered; not even uniform numbers are displayed prominently.

	MINT	EXC	G-VG
COMPLETE SET (27)	12.50	5.50	1.65
COMMON PLAYER (1-27)	.45	.18	.04
☐ 1 Vince Coleman	.90	.40	.09
☐ 2 Dave Collins	.45	.18	.04
☐ 3 Danny Cox	.45	.18	.04
☐ 4 Ken Dayley	.45	.18	.04
☐ 5 Frank DiPino	.45	.18	.04
☐ 6 Jose DeLeon	.45	.18	.04
☐ 7 Pedro Guerrero	.75	.30	.07
☐ 8 Whitey Herzog MG	.60	.25	.06
☐ 9 Rick Horton	.45	.18	.04
☐ 10 Rex Hudler	.60	.25	.06
☐ 11 Tim Jones	.45	.18	.04
☐ 12 Joe Magrane	.60	.25	.06
☐ 13 Greg Mathews	.45	.18	.04
☐ 14 Willie McGee	.75	.30	.07
☐ 15 John Morris	.45	.18	.04
☐ 16 Tom Niedenfuer	.45	.18	.04
☐ 17 Jose Oquendo	.45	.18	.04
☐ 18 Tom Pagnozzi	.45	.18	.04
☐ 19 Terry Pendleton	.90	.40	.09
☐ 20 Bryn Smith	.60	.25	.06
☐ 21 Lee Smith	.75	.30	.07
☐ 22 Ozzie Smith	.90	.40	.09
☐ 23 Scott Terry	.45	.18	.04
☐ 24 Milt Thompson	.45	.18	.04
☐ 25 John Tudor	.60	.25	.06
☐ 26 Denny Walling	.45	.18	.04
☐ 27 Todd Zeile	.90	.40	.09

1990 Smokey Southern Cal

This 12-card set was sponsored by the USDA Forest Service in conjunction with other federal agencies. The standard-size cards (2 1/2" by 3 1/2") have on their fronts black and white photos of outstanding players (except for legendary coach Rod Dedeaux) from past USC baseball teams who went on to play in the major Leagues. The team name and player information appears in maroon stripes above and below the picture. A yellow stripe on the bottom and left side of the picture serve as a shadow border. School and Smokey logos superimposed on the picture round out the card face. In black lettering on white, each back has career summary and a fire prevention cartoon starring Smokey. The cards are unnumbered and checklisted below in alphabetical order, with the player's number after the name.

	MINT	EXC	G-VG
COMPLETE SET (12)	10.00	4.50	1.25
COMMON PLAYER (1-12)	.50	.20	.05
☐ 1 Don Buford	.60	.25	.06
☐ 2 Steve Busby	.60	.25	.06
☐ 3 Rich Dauer	.50	.20	.05
☐ 4 Rod Dedeaux CO	.60	.25	.06
☐ 5 Ron Fairly	.60	.25	.06
☐ 6 Steve Kemp	.50	.20	.05
☐ 7 Dave Kingman	.75	.30	.07
☐ 8 Bill Lee	.60	.25	.06
☐ 9 Fred Lynn	.75	.30	.07
☐ 10 Mark McGwire	2.00	.80	.20
☐ 11 Tom Seaver	4.00	1.75	.40
☐ 12 Roy Smalley	.50	.20	.05

1991 Smokey Angels

This 20-card set was sponsored by the USDA Forest Service and USDI Bureau of Land Management in cooperation with the California Department of Forestry. The standard size (2 1/2" by 3 1/2") cards have on their fronts color action player photos with gray borders. Also a dark blue stripe borders the picture above and below. The player's name appears in the white stripe at the card bottom, sandwiched between the team logo and Smokey icon. The player's position is given in a red vertical stripe in the lower left corner. The backs are printed in blue and red on white, and present biography as well as a fire prevention cartoon starring Smokey. The cards are numbered in the upper right corner on the back.

	MINT	EXC	G-VG
COMPLETE SET (20)	6.00	2.50	.60
COMMON PLAYER (1-20)	.30	.12	.03
☐ 1 Luis Polonia	.50	.20	.05
☐ 2 Junior Felix	.40	.16	.04
☐ 3 Dave Winfield	.75	.30	.07
☐ 4 Dave Parker	.60	.25	.06
☐ 5 Lance Parrish	.50	.20	.05
☐ 6 Wally Joyner	.75	.30	.07
☐ 7 Jim Abbott	.60	.25	.06
☐ 8 Mark Langston	.50	.20	.05
☐ 9 Chuck Finley	.50	.20	.05
☐ 10 Kirk McCaskill	.40	.16	.04
☐ 11 Jack Howell	.30	.12	.03
☐ 12 Donnie Hill	.30	.12	.03
☐ 13 Gary Gaetti	.40	.16	.04
☐ 14 Dick Schofield	.40	.16	.04
☐ 15 Luis Sojo	.40	.16	.04
☐ 16 Mark Eichorn	.40	.16	.04
☐ 17 Bryan Harvey	.50	.20	.05
☐ 18 Jeff D. Robinson	.30	.12	.03
☐ 19 Scott Lewis	.40	.16	.04
☐ 20 John Orton	.30	.12	.03

1989 Socko Orel Hershiser

The 1989 Socko Orel Hershiser set contains seven unnumbered standard-size (2 1/2" by 3 1/2") cards. The fronts are blue, green and yellow, and feature full color photos of Hershiser with the Dodger logos airbrushed out. The backs are white and include "Tips from Orel." The cards were distributed as a promotional set through Socko beverages.

	MINT	EXC	G-VG
COMPLETE SET (7)	13.50	6.00	1.85
COMMON PLAYER (1-7)	2.50	1.00	.25
☐ 1 Orel Hershiser The Kick	2.50	1.00	.25
☐ 2 Orel Hershiser The Follow-Through	2.50	1.00	.25
☐ 3 Orel Hershiser The Release	2.50	1.00	.25
☐ 4 Orel Hershiser Backing Up The Catcher	2.50	1.00	.25
☐ 5 Orel Hershiser Barehanding the Ball	2.50	1.00	.25

			NRMT	VG-E	GOOD
☐	6	Orel Hershiser The Grip	2.50	1.00	.25
☐	7	Orel Hershiser Pitching from the Stretch	2.50	1.00	.25

1957 Sohio Indians

The 1957 Sohio Cleveland Indians set consists of 18 perforated photos, approximately 5" by 7", in black and white with facsimile autographs on the front which were designed to be pasted into a special photo album issued by SOHIO (Standard Oil of Ohio). The set features one of the earliest Roger Maris cards which even predates his 1958 Topps rookie card. In addition, the Rocky Colavito card is popular as well as 1957 was Rocky's rookie year for cards.

			NRMT	VG-E	GOOD
	COMPLETE SET (18)		225.00	100.00	33.00
	COMMON PLAYER (1-18)		5.00	2.25	.50
☐	1	Bob Avila	6.00	2.50	.60
☐	2	Jim Busby	5.00	2.25	.50
☐	3	Chico Carrasquel	5.00	2.25	.50
☐	4	Rocky Colavito	30.00	13.50	4.50
☐	5	Mike Garcia	6.00	2.50	.60
☐	6	Jim Hegan	6.00	2.50	.60
☐	7	Bob Lemon	16.00	6.75	2.25
☐	8	Roger Maris	125.00	57.50	18.75
☐	9	Don Mossi	6.00	2.50	.60
☐	10	Ray Narleski	5.00	2.25	.50
☐	11	Russ Nixon	6.00	2.50	.60
☐	12	Herb Score	8.00	3.50	.80
☐	13	Al Smith	5.00	2.25	.50
☐	14	George Strickland	5.00	2.25	.50
☐	15	Bob Usher	5.00	2.25	.50
☐	16	Vic Wertz	6.00	2.50	.60
☐	17	Gene Woodling	6.00	2.50	.60
☐	18	Early Wynn	16.00	6.75	2.25

1957 Sohio Reds

The 1957 Sohio Cincinnati Reds set consists of 18 perforated photos, approximately 5" by 7", in black and white with facsimile autographs on the front which were designed to be pasted into a special photo album issued by SOHIO (Standard Oil of Ohio). The set features an early Frank Robinson card.

			NRMT	VG-E	GOOD
	COMPLETE SET (18)		175.00	80.00	27.00
	COMMON PLAYER (1-18)		5.00	2.25	.50
☐	1	Ed Bailey	5.00	2.25	.50
☐	2	Gus Bell	6.00	2.50	.60
☐	3	Rocky Bridges	5.00	2.25	.50
☐	4	Smoky Burgess	6.00	2.50	.60
☐	5	Hersh Freeman	5.00	2.25	.50

			NRMT	VG-E	GOOD
☐	6	Alex Grammas	5.00	2.25	.50
☐	7	Don Gross	5.00	2.25	.50
☐	8	Warren Hacker	5.00	2.25	.50
☐	9	Don Hoak	5.00	2.25	.50
☐	10	Hal Jeffcoat	5.00	2.25	.50
☐	11	Johnny Klippstein	5.00	2.25	.50
☐	12	Ted Kluszewski	20.00	8.50	2.75
☐	13	Brooks Lawrence	5.00	2.25	.50
☐	14	Roy McMillan	5.00	2.25	.50
☐	15	Joe Nuxhall	6.00	2.50	.60
☐	16	Wally Post	6.00	2.50	.60
☐	17	Frank Robinson	90.00	40.00	13.50
☐	18	John Temple	6.00	2.50	.60

1953-54 Spic and Span 3x5

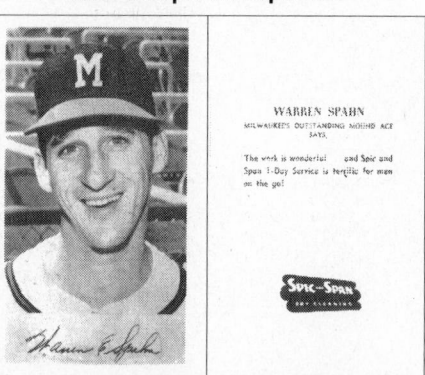

This 27-card set features only members of the Milwaukee Braves. The cards are black and white and approximately 3 1/4" by 5 1/2". Some of the photos in the set are posed against blank backgrounds, but most are posed against seats and a chain link fence, hence the set is sometimes referred to as the "chain link fence" set. There is a facsimile autograph at the bottom of the card. The set was probably issued in 1953 and 1954 since Hank Aaron is not included in the set and Don Liddle, Ebba St.Claire, and Johnny Antonelli were traded from the Braves on February 1, 1954 for Bobby Thomson (who is also in the set). Cards can be found either blank back or with player's name, comment, and logo in blue on the back

			NRMT	VG-E	GOOD
	COMPLETE SET (27)		900.00	400.00	135.00
	COMMON PLAYER (1-27)		27.00	12.00	4.00
☐	1	Joe Adcock	36.00	16.25	5.50
☐	2	Johnny Antonelli	32.00	14.25	4.75
☐	3	Vern Bickford	27.00	12.00	4.00
☐	4	Bill Bruton	32.00	14.25	4.75
☐	5	Bob Buhl	32.00	14.25	4.75
☐	6	Lew Burdette	36.00	16.25	5.50
☐	7	Dick Cole	27.00	12.00	4.00
☐	8	Walker Cooper	27.00	12.00	4.00

			NRMT	VG-E	GOOD
☐	9	Del Crandall	32.00	14.25	4.75
☐	10	George Crowe	27.00	12.00	4.00
☐	11	Jack Dittmer	27.00	12.00	4.00
☐	12	Sid Gordon	27.00	12.00	4.00
☐	13	Ernie Johnson	32.00	14.25	4.75
☐	14	Dave Jolly	27.00	12.00	4.00
☐	15	Don Liddle	27.00	12.00	4.00
☐	16	John Logan	32.00	14.25	4.75
☐	17	Ed Mathews	125.00	57.50	18.75
☐	18	Danny O'Connell	27.00	12.00	4.00
☐	19	Andy Pafko	27.00	12.00	4.00
☐	20	Jim Pendleton	27.00	12.00	4.00
☐	21	Ebba St.Claire	27.00	12.00	4.00
☐	22	Warren Spahn	125.00	57.50	18.75
☐	23	Max Surkont	27.00	12.00	4.00
☐	24	Bob Thomson	36.00	16.25	5.50
☐	25	Bob Thorpe	27.00	12.00	4.00
☐	26	Roberto Vargas	27.00	12.00	4.00
☐	27	Jim Wilson	27.00	12.00	4.00

1953-56 Spic and Span 7x10

This 13-card set features only members of the Milwaukee Braves. The set was issued beginning in 1953 but may have been issued for several years as they seem to be the most common of all the Spic and Span issues. In addition, Danny O'Connell and Bobby Thomson were not on the '53 Braves team. The front of each card shows the logo, "Spic and Span Dry Cleaners ... the Choice of Your Favorite Braves." There is a thick white border around the cards with facsimile autograph in black in the bottom border. The cards have blank backs and are approximately 7" by 10".

			NRMT	VG-E	GOOD
	COMPLETE SET (13)		150.00	67.50	22.50
	COMMON PLAYER (1-13)		7.50	3.25	.75
☐	1	Joe Adcock	15.00	6.50	2.15
☐	2	William H. Bruton	9.00	4.00	.90
☐	3	Robert Buhl	9.00	4.00	.90
☐	4	Lew Burdette	15.00	6.50	2.15
☐	5	Del Crandall	10.00	4.50	1.25
☐	6	Jack Dittmer	7.50	3.25	.75
☐	7	Johnny Logan	9.00	4.00	.90
☐	8	Edwin L.Mathews, Jr.	40.00	18.00	6.00
☐	9	Chet Nichols	7.50	3.25	.75
☐	10	Danny O'Connell	7.50	3.25	.75
☐	11	Andy Pafko	7.50	3.25	.75
☐	12	Warren Spahn	40.00	18.00	6.00
☐	13	Bob Thomson	15.00	6.50	2.15

1954 Spic and Span Postcards

This black and white set features only members of the Milwaukee Braves. The cards have postcard backs and measure approximately 3 11/16" by 6". The postcards were issued beginning in 1954. There is a facsimile autograph on the front in black or white ink. The set apparently was also issued with white borders in a 5" by 7" size. The catalog designation for this set is PC756. The front of each card shows the logo, "Spic and Span Dry Cleaners ... the Choice of Your Favorite Braves."

			NRMT	VG-E	GOOD
	COMPLETE SET (18)		500.00	225.00	75.00
	COMMON PLAYER (1-18)		15.00	6.50	2.15
☐	1	Henry Aaron	175.00	80.00	27.00
☐	2	Joe Adcock	24.00	10.50	3.50
☐	3	Billy Bruton	18.00	7.50	2.50
☐	4	Bob Buhl	18.00	7.50	2.50
☐	5	Lew Burdette	24.00	10.50	3.50
☐	6	Gene Conley	15.00	6.50	2.15
☐	7	Del Crandall	18.00	7.50	2.50
☐	8	Ray Crone	15.00	6.50	2.15
☐	9	Jack Dittmer	15.00	6.50	2.15
☐	10	Ernie Johnson	18.00	7.50	2.50
☐	11	Dave Jolly	15.00	6.50	2.15
☐	12	Johnny Logan	18.00	7.50	2.50
☐	13	Edwin L. Mathews, Jr.	75.00	34.00	11.25
☐	14	Chet Nichols	15.00	6.50	2.15
☐	15	Danny O'Connell	15.00	6.50	2.15
☐	16	Andy Pafko	15.00	6.50	2.15
☐	17	Warren Spahn	75.00	34.00	11.25
☐	18	Bob Thomson	24.00	10.50	3.50

1955 Spic and Span Die-Cut

This 18-card, die-cut, set features only members of the Milwaukee Braves. Each player measures differently according to the pose but they are, on average, approximately 8" by 8". The cards could be folded together to stand up. Each card contains a logo in the middle at the bottom and a copyright notice, "1955 Spic and Span Cleaners" in the lower right corner.

	NRMT	VG-E	GOOD
COMPLETE SET (18)	3500.00	1400.00	350.00
COMMON PLAYER (1-18)	120.00	55.00	18.00
☐ 1 Hank Aaron	900.00	400.00	135.00
☐ 2 Joe Adcock	180.00	80.00	27.00
☐ 3 William H. Bruton	150.00	67.50	22.50
☐ 4 Robert Buhl	150.00	67.50	22.50
☐ 5 Lew Burdette	180.00	80.00	27.00
☐ 6 Gene Conley	120.00	55.00	18.00
☐ 7 Del Crandall	150.00	67.50	22.50
☐ 8 Jack Dittmer	120.00	55.00	18.00
☐ 9 Ernie Johnson	150.00	67.50	22.50
☐ 10 Dave Jolly	120.00	55.00	18.00
☐ 11 Johnny Logan	150.00	67.50	22.50
☐ 12 Edwin L. Mathews	375.00	165.00	55.00
☐ 13 Chet Nichols	120.00	55.00	18.00
☐ 14 Danny O'Connell	120.00	55.00	18.00
☐ 15 Andy Pafko	120.00	55.00	18.00
☐ 16 Warren E. Spahn	375.00	165.00	55.00
☐ 17 Bob Thomson	180.00	80.00	27.00
☐ 18 Jim Wilson	120.00	55.00	18.00

1957 Spic and Span 4x5

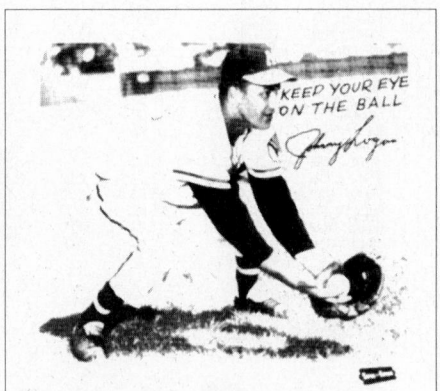

This set contains 20 black and white photos each with a blue-printed message such as "Stay in There and Pitch" and blue facsimile autograph The set features only members of the Milwaukee Braves. Red Schoendienst was traded to the Braves on June 15, 1957 in exchange for Danny O'Connell, Ray Crone, and Bobby Thomson. Wes Covington, Felix Mantilla, and Bob Trowbridge are also listed as shorter-printed (SP) cards as they were apparently mid-season call-ups. The cards are approximately 4 5/16" by 5" with a thick white border and are blank backed. Spic and Span appears in blue in the white border in the lower right corner of the card.

	NRMT	VG-E	GOOD
COMPLETE SET (20)	450.00	200.00	67.50
COMMON PLAYER (1-20)	10.00	4.50	1.25
COMMON PLAYER SP	25.00	11.00	3.50
☐ 1 Henry Aaron	135.00	60.00	20.00
☐ 2 Joe Adcock	16.00	6.75	2.25
☐ 3 Billy Bruton	12.00	5.25	1.50
☐ 4 Bob Buhl	12.00	5.25	1.50
☐ 5 Lew Burdette	16.00	6.75	2.25
☐ 6 Gene Conley	10.00	4.50	1.25
☐ 7 Wes Covington SP	25.00	11.00	3.50
☐ 8 Del Crandall	12.00	5.25	1.50
☐ 9 Ray Crone	10.00	4.50	1.25
☐ 9 Fred Haney MG	10.00	4.50	1.25
☐ 10 Ernie Johnson	12.00	5.25	1.50
☐ 11 Johnny Logan	12.00	5.25	1.50

☐ 12 Felix Mantilla SP	25.00	11.00	3.50
☐ 12 Ed Mathews	60.00	27.00	9.00
☐ 13 Danny O'Connell	10.00	4.50	1.25
☐ 14 Andy Pafko	10.00	4.50	1.25
☐ 15 Red Schoendienst SP	60.00	27.00	9.00
☐ 15 Warren Spahn	60.00	27.00	9.00
☐ 16 Bob Thomson	16.00	6.75	2.25
☐ 16 Bob Trowbridge SP	25.00	11.00	3.50

1960 Spic and Span

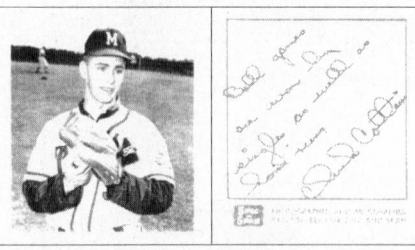

This 26-card set features only members of the Milwaukee Braves. These small cards each measure approximately 2 13/16" by 3 1/16". The cards have a thin white border around a black and white photo with no other writing or words on the front. The card backs have the Spic and Span logo at the bottom along with "Photographed and Autographed Exclusively for Spic and Span". A message and facsimile autograph from the player is presented inside a square box all in blue on the card back.

	NRMT	VG-E	GOOD
COMPLETE SET (27)	550.00	240.00	80.00
COMMON PLAYER (1-26)	10.00	4.50	1.25
☐ 1 Henry Aaron	135.00	60.00	20.00
☐ 2 Joe Adcock	16.00	6.75	2.25
☐ 3 Billy Bruton	12.00	5.25	1.50
☐ 4 Bob Buhl	12.00	5.25	1.50
☐ 5 Lew Burdette	16.00	6.75	2.25
☐ 6 Chuck Cottier	10.00	4.50	1.25
☐ 7A Del Crandall ERR (reversed negative)	60.00	27.00	9.00
☐ 7B Del Crandall COR	16.00	6.75	2.25
☐ 8 Charlie Dressen MG	12.00	5.25	1.50
☐ 9 Joey Jay	10.00	4.50	1.25
☐ 10 Johnny Logan	12.00	5.25	1.50
☐ 11 Felix Mantilla	10.00	4.50	1.25
☐ 12 Ed Mathews	60.00	27.00	9.00
☐ 13 Lee Maye	10.00	4.50	1.25
☐ 14 Don McMahon	10.00	4.50	1.25
☐ 15 George Myatt CO	10.00	4.50	1.25
☐ 16 Andy Pafko	10.00	4.50	1.25
☐ 17 Juan Pizarro	10.00	4.50	1.25
☐ 18 Mel Roach	10.00	4.50	1.25
☐ 19 Bob Rush	10.00	4.50	1.25
☐ 20 Bob Scheffing CO	10.00	4.50	1.25
☐ 21 Red Schoendienst	40.00	18.00	6.00
☐ 22 Warren Spahn	60.00	27.00	9.00
☐ 23 Al Spangler	10.00	4.50	1.25
☐ 24 Frank Torre	12.00	5.25	1.50
☐ 25 Carl Willey	10.00	4.50	1.25
☐ 26 Whit Wyatt CO	12.00	5.25	1.50

1985-86 Sportflics Prototypes

The 1985-86 Sportflics Proof set contains four standard-size (2 1/2" by 3 1/2") unnumbered cards, one mini (1 5/16" by 1 5/16") Joe DiMaggio card, and one trivia card (1 3/4" by 2"). The standard-size cards resemble regular 1986 Sportflics cards, but have different photos and stats only through 1984. One of the Winfield cards has a bio only; unfortunately the biographical statements on the back are incorrect in several instances. The DiMaggio card has black and white photos on the front, and career totals on the back. The trivia card is the same as those distributed with 1986 Sportflics, except it shows the major league baseball logo on the front. These test cards were apparently produced in limited quantity to show Major League Baseball and the Major League Baseball Players Association what Sportflics was proposing in order to be a new licensee for producing cards. These cards are very difficult to find. These cards are considerably rarer than the Sportflics Test cards which were given out after the Sportflics license had been granted.

	MINT	EXC	G-VG
COMPLETE SET (5)	125.00	57.50	18.75
COMMON PLAYER (1-5)	12.00	5.25	1.50
☐ 1 Joe DiMaggio (small size)	35.00	15.75	5.25
☐ 2 Mike Schmidt (stats on back)	45.00	20.00	6.75
☐ 3 Bruce Sutter (stats on back)	12.00	5.25	1.50
☐ 4 Dave Winfield (biographical back)	20.00	8.50	2.75
☐ 5 Dave Winfield (stats on back)	30.00	13.50	4.50

1985-86 Sportflics Test

This three-card pack was a test, distributed freely by salesmen to potential buyers to show them what the new Sportflics product would look like. The set is sometimes referred to as the Vendor Sample Kit. Some of these packs even found their way to the retail counters. They are not rare although they are obviously much less common than the regular issue of Sportflics. The cards show statistics only up through 1984. The copyright date on the card backs shows 1986. The cards are standard size, 2 1/2" by 3 1/2".

	MINT	EXC	G-VG
COMPLETE SET (3)	22.50	9.75	3.25
COMMON PLAYER	6.00	2.50	.60
☐ 1 RBI Sluggers Mike Schmidt Dale Murphy Jim Rice	6.00	2.50	.60

		MINT	EXC	G-VG
☐ 43	Pete Rose (pictured with batting helmet; Pete is number 50 in regular 1986 set)	12.00	5.25	1.50
☐ 45	Tom Seaver (Tom is number 25 in regular 1986 set)	12.00	5.25	1.50

1986 Sportflics

This 200-card set was marketed with 133 small trivia cards. This inaugural set for Sportflics was initially fairly well received by the public. Sportflics was distributed by Major League Marketing; the company is also affiliated with Wrigley and Amurol. The set features 139 single player "magic motion" cards (which can be tilted to show three different pictures of the same player), 50 "Tri-Stars" (which show three different players), 10 "Big Six" cards (which show six players who share similar achievements), and one World Champs card featuring 12 members of the victorious Kansas City Royals. All cards measure 2 1/2" by 3 1/2". Some of the cards also have (limited production and rarely seen) proof versions with some player selection differences; a proof version of number 178 includes Jim Wilson instead of Mark Funderburk. Also a proof of number 179 with Karl Best, Mark Funderburk, Andres Galarraga, Dwayne Henry, Pete Incaviglia, and Todd Worrell was produced.

	MINT	EXC	G-VG
COMPLETE SET (200)	40.00	18.00	6.00
COMMON PLAYER (1-200)	.12	.05	.01
☐ 1 George Brett	1.25	.50	.12
☐ 2 Don Mattingly	2.50	1.00	.25
☐ 3 Wade Boggs	2.50	1.00	.25
☐ 4 Eddie Murray	1.00	.40	.10
☐ 5 Dale Murphy	.75	.30	.07
☐ 6 Rickey Henderson	2.50	1.00	.25
☐ 7 Harold Baines	.25	.10	.02
☐ 8 Cal Ripken	2.50	1.00	.25

#	Player			
9	Orel Hershiser	.75	.30	.07
10	Bret Saberhagen	.75	.30	.07
11	Tim Raines	.40	.16	.04
12	Fernando Valenzuela	.30	.12	.03
13	Tony Gwynn	1.25	.50	.12
14	Pedro Guerrero	.25	.10	.02
15	Keith Hernandez	.25	.10	.02
16	Earnie Riles	.15	.06	.01
17	Jim Rice	.30	.12	.03
18	Ron Guidry	.25	.10	.02
19	Willie McGee	.25	.10	.02
20	Ryne Sandberg	2.50	1.00	.25
21	Kirk Gibson	.30	.12	.03
22	Ozzie Guillen	.50	.20	.05
23	Dave Parker	.25	.10	.02
24	Vince Coleman	2.00	.80	.20
25	Tom Seaver	1.00	.40	.10
26	Brett Butler	.30	.12	.03
27	Steve Carlton	.50	.20	.05
28	Gary Carter	.40	.16	.04
29	Cecil Cooper	.20	.08	.02
30	Jose Cruz	.15	.06	.01
31	Alvin Davis	.20	.08	.02
32	Dwight Evans	.25	.10	.02
33	Julio Franco	.50	.20	.05
34	Damaso Garcia	.12	.05	.01
35	Steve Garvey	.50	.20	.05
36	Kent Hrbek	.25	.10	.02
37	Reggie Jackson	1.25	.50	.12
38	Fred Lynn	.20	.08	.02
39	Paul Molitor	.15	.06	.01
40	Jim Presley	.15	.06	.01
41	Dave Righetti	.20	.08	.02
42A	Robin Yount ERR	7.50	3.25	.75
	New York Yankees			
42B	Robin Yount COR	1.25	.50	.12
	Milwaukee Brewers			
43	Nolan Ryan	4.00	1.75	.40
44	Mike Schmidt	2.00	.80	.20
45	Lee Smith	.15	.06	.01
46	Rick Sutcliffe	.15	.06	.01
47	Bruce Sutter	.15	.06	.01
48	Lou Whitaker	.20	.08	.02
49	Dave Winfield	.50	.20	.05
50	Pete Rose	1.25	.50	.12
51	NL MVP's	.75	.30	.07
	Ryne Sandberg			
	Steve Garvey			
	Pete Rose			
52	Slugging Stars	.40	.16	.04
	George Brett			
	Harold Baines			
	Jim Rice			
53	No-Hitters	.20	.08	.02
	Phil Niekro			
	Jerry Reuss			
	Mike Witt			
54	Big Hitters	1.25	.50	.12
	Don Mattingly			
	Cal Ripken			
	Robin Yount			
55	Bullpen Aces	.20	.08	.02
	Dan Quisenberry			
	Goose Gossage			
	Lee Smith			
56	Rookies of The Year	1.00	.40	.10
	Darryl Strawberry			
	Steve Sax			
	Pete Rose			
57	AL MVP's	.60	.25	.06
	Cal Ripken			
	Don Baylor			
	Reggie Jackson			
58	Repeat Batting Champs	.75	.30	.07
	Dave Parker			
	Bill Madlock			
	Pete Rose			
59	Cy Young Winners	.15	.06	.01
	LaMarr Hoyt			
	Mike Flanagan			
	Ron Guidry			
60	Double Award Winners	.35	.15	.03
	Fernando Valenzuela			
	Rick Sutcliffe			
	Tom Seaver			
61	Home Run Champs	.65	.25	.06
	Reggie Jackson			
	Jim Rice			
	Tony Armas			
62	NL MVP's	.75	.30	.07
	Keith Hernandez			
	Dale Murphy			
	Mike Schmidt			
63	AL MVP's	.60	.25	.06
	Robin Yount			
	George Brett			
	Fred Lynn			
64	Comeback Players	.15	.06	.01
	Bert Blyleven			
	Jerry Koosman			
	John Denny			
65	Cy Young Relievers	.25	.10	.02
	Willie Hernandez			
	Rollie Fingers			
	Bruce Sutter			
66	Rookies of The Year	.20	.08	.02
	Bob Horner			
	Andre Dawson			
	Gary Matthews			
67	Rookies of The Year	.50	.20	.05
	Ron Kittle			
	Carlton Fisk			
	Tom Seaver			
68	Home Run Champs	.35	.15	.03
	Mike Schmidt			
	George Foster			
	Dave Kingman			
69	Double Award Winners	1.25	.50	.12
	Cal Ripken			
	Rod Carew			
	Pete Rose			
70	Cy Young Winners	.50	.20	.05
	Rick Sutcliffe			
	Steve Carlton			
	Tom Seaver			
71	Top Sluggers	.50	.20	.05
	Reggie Jackson			
	Fred Lynn			
	Robin Yount			
72	Rookies of The Year	.25	.10	.02
	Dave Righetti			
	Fernando Valenzuela			
	Rick Sutcliffe			
73	Rookies of The Year	.75	.30	.07
	Fred Lynn			
	Eddie Murray			
	Cal Ripken			
74	Rookies of The Year	.25	.10	.02
	Alvin Davis			
	Lou Whitaker			
	Rod Carew			
75	Batting Champs	1.00	.40	.10
	Don Mattingly			
	Wade Boggs			
	Carney Lansford			
76	Jesse Barfield	.20	.08	.02
77	Phil Bradley	.15	.06	.01
78	Chris Brown	.12	.05	.01
79	Tom Browning	.20	.08	.02
80	Tom Brunansky	.20	.08	.02
81	Bill Buckner	.15	.06	.01
82	Chili Davis	.20	.08	.02
83	Mike Davis	.12	.05	.01
84	Rich Gedman	.12	.05	.01
85	Willie Hernandez	.15	.06	.01
86	Ron Kittle	.20	.08	.02
87	Lee Lacy	.12	.05	.01
88	Bill Madlock	.20	.08	.02
89	Mike Marshall	.20	.08	.02
90	Keith Moreland	.12	.05	.01
91	Graig Nettles	.20	.08	.02
92	Lance Parrish	.30	.12	.03
93	Kirby Puckett	3.00	1.25	.30
94	Juan Samuel	.25	.10	.02
95	Steve Sax	.30	.12	.03
96	Dave Stieb	.25	.10	.02
97	Darryl Strawberry	2.00	.80	.20
98	Willie Upshaw	.12	.05	.01
99	Frank Viola	.50	.20	.05
100	Dwight Gooden	1.50	.60	.15
101	Joaquin Andujar	.12	.05	.01
102	George Bell	.40	.16	.04
103	Bert Blyleven	.25	.10	.02
104	Mike Boddicker	.15	.06	.01
105	Britt Burns	.12	.05	.01
106	Rod Carew	.75	.30	.07
107	Jack Clark	.25	.10	.02
108	Danny Cox	.15	.06	.01
109	Ron Darling	.20	.08	.02
110	Andre Dawson	.60	.25	.06
111	Leon Durham	.12	.05	.01
112	Tony Fernandez	.20	.08	.02
113	Tommy Herr	.12	.05	.01
114	Teddy Higuera	.25	.10	.02
115	Bob Horner	.15	.06	.01
116	Dave Kingman	.20	.08	.02
117	Jack Morris	.40	.16	.04
118	Dan Quisenberry	.20	.08	.02

☐ 119 Jeff Reardon	.30	.12	.03
☐ 120 Bryn Smith	.12	.05	.01
☐ 121 Ozzie Smith	.75	.30	.07
☐ 122 John Tudor	.15	.06	.01
☐ 123 Tim Wallach	.15	.06	.01
☐ 124 Willie Wilson	.15	.06	.01
☐ 125 Carlton Fisk	.75	.30	.07
☐ 126 RBI Sluggers	.20	.08	.02
Gary Carter			
Al Oliver			
George Foster			
☐ 127 Run Scorers	.45	.18	.04
Tim Raines			
Ryne Sandberg			
Keith Hernandez			
☐ 128 Run Scorers	.50	.20	.05
Paul Molitor			
Cal Ripken			
Willie Wilson			
☐ 129 No-Hitters	.15	.06	.01
John Candelaria			
Dennis Eckersley			
Bob Forsch			
☐ 130 World Series MVP's	.60	.25	.06
Pete Rose			
Ron Cey			
Rollie Fingers			
☐ 131 All-Star Game MVP's	.15	.06	.01
Dave Concepcion			
George Foster			
Bill Madlock			
☐ 132 Cy Young Winners	.15	.06	.01
John Denny			
Fernando Valenzuela			
Vida Blue			
☐ 133 Comeback Players	.12	.05	.01
Rich Dotson			
Joaquin Andujar			
Doyle Alexander			
☐ 134 Big Winners	.40	.16	.04
Rick Sutcliffe			
Tom Seaver			
John Denny			
☐ 135 Veteran Pitchers	.75	.30	.07
Tom Seaver			
Phil Niekro			
Don Sutton			
☐ 136 Rookies of The Year	.75	.30	.07
Dwight Gooden			
Vince Coleman			
Alfredo Griffin			
☐ 137 All-Star Game MVP's	.40	.16	.04
Gary Carter			
Fred Lynn			
Steve Garvey			
☐ 138 Veteran Hitters	.60	.25	.06
Tony Perez			
Rusty Staub			
Pete Rose			
☐ 139 Power Hitters	.50	.20	.05
Mike Schmidt			
Jim Rice			
George Foster			
☐ 140 Batting Champs	.30	.12	.03
Tony Gwynn			
Al Oliver			
Bill Buckner			
☐ 141 No-Hitters	1.25	.50	.12
Nolan Ryan			
Jack Morris			
Dave Righetti			
☐ 142 No-Hitters	.35	.15	.03
Tom Seaver			
Bert Blyleven			
Vida Blue			
☐ 143 Strikeout Kings	1.50	.60	.15
Nolan Ryan			
Fernando Valenzuela			
Dwight Gooden			
☐ 144 Base Stealers	.20	.08	.02
Tim Raines			
Willie Wilson			
Davey Lopes			
☐ 145 RBI Sluggers	.25	.10	.02
Tony Armas			
Cecil Cooper			
Eddie Murray			
☐ 146 AL MVP's	.60	.25	.06
Rod Carew			
Jim Rice			
Rollie Fingers			
☐ 147 World Series MVP's	.40	.16	.04
Alan Trammell			
Rick Dempsey			
Reggie Jackson			
☐ 148 World Series MVP's	.40	.16	.04
Darrell Porter			
Pedro Guerrero			
Mike Schmidt			
☐ 149 ERA Leaders	.15	.06	.01
Mike Boddicker			
Rick Sutcliffe			
Ron Guidry			
☐ 150 Comeback Players	.35	.15	.03
Reggie Jackson			
Dave Kingman			
Fred Lynn			
☐ 151 Buddy Bell	.15	.06	.01
☐ 152 Dennis Boyd	.15	.06	.01
☐ 153 Dave Concepcion	.20	.08	.02
☐ 154 Brian Downing	.12	.05	.01
☐ 155 Shawon Dunston	.60	.25	.06
☐ 156 John Franco	.25	.10	.02
☐ 157 Scott Garrelts	.20	.08	.02
☐ 158 Bob James	.12	.05	.01
☐ 159 Charlie Leibrandt	.15	.06	.01
☐ 160 Oddibe McDowell	.15	.06	.01
☐ 161 Roger McDowell	.15	.06	.01
☐ 162 Mike Moore	.20	.08	.02
☐ 163 Phil Niekro	.30	.12	.03
☐ 164 Al Oliver	.15	.06	.01
☐ 165 Tony Pena	.20	.08	.02
☐ 166 Ted Power	.12	.05	.01
☐ 167 Mike Scioscia	.15	.06	.01
☐ 168 Mario Soto	.12	.05	.01
☐ 169 Bob Stanley	.12	.05	.01
☐ 170 Garry Templeton	.15	.06	.01
☐ 171 Andre Thornton	.12	.05	.01
☐ 172 Alan Trammell	.50	.20	.05
☐ 173 Doug DeCinces	.15	.06	.01
☐ 174 Greg Walker	.12	.05	.01
☐ 175 Don Sutton	.35	.15	.03
☐ 176 1985 Award Winners	1.00	.40	.10
Ozzie Guillen			
Bret Saberhagen			
Don Mattingly			
Vince Coleman			
Dwight Gooden			
Willie McGee			
☐ 177 1985 Hot Rookies	.25	.10	.02
Stew Cliburn			
Brian Fisher UER			
(Photo actually			
Mike Pagliarulo)			
Joe Hesketh			
Joe Orsulak			
Mark Salas			
Larry Sheets			
☐ 178 1986 Rookies To Watch	9.00	4.00	.90
Jose Canseco			
Mark Funderburk			
Mike Greenwell			
Steve Lombardozzi UER			
(Photo actually			
Mark Salas)			
Billy Joe Robidoux			
Danny Tartabull			
☐ 179 1985 Gold Glovers	.75	.30	.07
George Brett			
Ron Guidry			
Keith Hernandez			
Don Mattingly			
Willie McGee			
Dale Murphy			
☐ 180 Active Lifetime .300	.75	.30	.07
Wade Boggs			
George Brett			
Rod Carew			
Cecil Cooper			
Don Mattingly			
Willie Wilson			
☐ 181 Active Lifetime .300	.60	.25	.06
Tony Gwynn			
Bill Madlock			
Pedro Guerrero			
Dave Parker			
Pete Rose			
Keith Hernandez			
☐ 182 1985 Milestones	.75	.30	.07
Rod Carew			
Phil Niekro			
Pete Rose			
Nolan Ryan			
Tom Seaver			
Matt Tallman (fan)			

		MINT	EXC	G-VG
☐ 183	1985 Triple Crown	.75	.30	.07
	Wade Boggs			
	Darrell Evans			
	Don Mattingly			
	Willie McGee			
	Dale Murphy			
	Dave Parker			
☐ 184	1985 Highlights	.75	.30	.07
	Wade Boggs			
	Dwight Gooden			
	Rickey Henderson			
	Don Mattingly			
	Willie McGee			
	John Tudor			
☐ 185	1985 20 Game Winners	.75	.30	.07
	Dwight Gooden			
	Ron Guidry			
	John Tudor			
	Joaquin Andujar			
	Bret Saberhagen			
	Tom Browning			
☐ 186	World Series Champs	.30	.12	.03
	L. Smith, Dane Iorg			
	W. Wilson, Leibrandt			
	G. Brett, Saberhagen			
	Motley, Quisenberry			
	D. Jackson, Sundberg			
	S. Balboni, F. White			
☐ 187	Hubie Brooks	.20	.08	.02
☐ 188	Glenn Davis	1.00	.40	.10
☐ 189	Darrell Evans	.20	.08	.02
☐ 190	Rich Gossage	.25	.10	.02
☐ 191	Andy Hawkins	.12	.05	.01
☐ 192	Jay Howell	.12	.05	.01
☐ 193	LaMarr Hoyt	.12	.05	.01
☐ 194	Davey Lopes	.12	.05	.01
☐ 195	Mike Scott	.25	.10	.02
☐ 196	Ted Simmons	.20	.08	.02
☐ 197	Gary Ward	.12	.05	.01
☐ 198	Bob Welch	.25	.10	.02
☐ 199	Mike Young	.12	.05	.01
☐ 200	Buddy Biancalana	.12	.05	.01

1986 Sportflics Decade Greats

This set of 75 three-phase "animated" cards was produced by Sportflics and manufactured by Opti-Graphics of Arlington, Texas. Cards are standard size, 2 1/2" by 3 1/2", and feature both sepia (players of the '30s and '40s) and full color cards. The concept of the set was that the best players at each position for each decade (from the '30s to the '80s) were chosen. The bios were written by Les Woodcock. Also included with the set in the specially designed collector box are 51 trivia cards with historical questions about the six decades of All-Star games.

	MINT	EXC	G-VG
COMPLETE SET (75)	15.00	6.50	2.15
COMMON PLAYER (1-75)	.15	.06	.01

		MINT	EXC	G-VG
☐ 1	Babe Ruth	3.00	1.25	.30
☐ 2	Jimmie Foxx	.35	.15	.03
☐ 3	Lefty Grove	.35	.15	.03
☐ 4	Hank Greenberg	.35	.15	.03
☐ 5	Al Simmons	.25	.10	.02
☐ 6	Carl Hubbell	.25	.10	.02
☐ 7	Joe Cronin	.25	.10	.02

		MINT	EXC	G-VG
☐ 8	Mel Ott	.35	.15	.03
☐ 9	Lefty Gomez	.35	.15	.03
☐ 10	Lou Gehrig	1.00	.40	.10
	(Best '30s Player)			
☐ 11	Pie Traynor	.25	.10	.02
☐ 12	Charlie Gehringer	.25	.10	.02
☐ 13	Best '30s Catchers	.25	.10	.02
	Bill Dickey			
	Mickey Cochrane			
	Gabby Hartnett			
☐ 14	Best '30s Pitchers	.25	.10	.02
	Dizzy Dean			
	Red Ruffing			
	Paul Derringer			
☐ 15	Best '30s Outfielders	.15	.06	.01
	Paul Waner			
	Joe Medwick			
	Earl Averill			
☐ 16	Bob Feller	.75	.30	.07
☐ 17	Lou Boudreau	.25	.10	.02
☐ 18	Enos Slaughter	.35	.15	.03
☐ 19	Hal Newhouser	.15	.06	.01
☐ 20	Joe DiMaggio	1.50	.60	.15
☐ 21	Pee Wee Reese	.50	.20	.05
☐ 22	Phil Rizzuto	.35	.15	.03
☐ 23	Ernie Lombardi	.15	.06	.01
☐ 24	Best '40s Infielders	.25	.10	.02
	Johnny Mize			
	Joe Gordon			
	George Kell			
☐ 25	Ted Williams	1.00	.40	.10
	(Best '40s Player)			
☐ 26	Mickey Mantle	3.00	1.25	.30
☐ 27	Warren Spahn	.35	.15	.03
☐ 28	Jackie Robinson	.75	.30	.07
☐ 29	Ernie Banks	.35	.15	.03
☐ 30	Stan Musial	.75	.30	.07
	(Best '50s Player)			
☐ 31	Yogi Berra	.75	.30	.07
☐ 32	Duke Snider	.75	.30	.07
☐ 33	Roy Campanella	.75	.30	.07
☐ 34	Eddie Mathews	.35	.15	.03
☐ 35	Ralph Kiner	.25	.10	.02
☐ 36	Early Wynn	.25	.10	.02
☐ 37	Double Play Duo	.25	.10	.02
	Nellie Fox			
	Luis Aparicio			
☐ 38	Best '50s First Base	.15	.06	.01
	Gil Hodges			
	Ted Kluszewski			
	Mickey Vernon			
☐ 39	Best '50s Pitchers	.15	.06	.01
	Bob Lemon			
	Don Newcombe			
	Robin Roberts			
☐ 40	Henry Aaron	1.00	.40	.10
☐ 41	Frank Robinson	.35	.15	.03
☐ 42	Bob Gibson	.35	.15	.03
☐ 43	Roberto Clemente	.90	.40	.09
☐ 44	Whitey Ford	.50	.20	.05
☐ 45	Brooks Robinson	.60	.25	.06
☐ 46	Juan Marichal	.25	.10	.02
☐ 47	Carl Yastrzemski	.90	.40	.09
☐ 48	Best '60s First Base	.25	.10	.02
	Willie McCovey			
	Harmon Killebrew			
	Orlando Cepeda			
☐ 49	Best '60s Catchers	.15	.06	.01
	Joe Torre			
	Elston Howard			
	Bill Freehan			
☐ 50	Willie Mays	1.00	.40	.10
	(Best '50s Player)			
☐ 51	Best '60s Outfielders	.25	.10	.02
	Al Kaline			
	Tony Oliva			
	Billy Williams			
☐ 52	Tom Seaver	1.25	.50	.12
☐ 53	Reggie Jackson	1.00	.40	.10
☐ 54	Steve Carlton	.75	.30	.07
☐ 55	Mike Schmidt	1.25	.50	.12
☐ 56	Joe Morgan	.50	.20	.05
☐ 57	Jim Rice	.25	.10	.02
☐ 58	Jim Palmer	.50	.20	.05
☐ 59	Lou Brock	.35	.15	.03
☐ 60	Pete Rose	1.25	.50	.12
	(Best '70s Player)			
☐ 61	Steve Garvey	.50	.20	.05
☐ 62	Best '70s Catchers	.50	.20	.05
	Thurman Munson			
	Carlton Fisk			
	Ted Simmons			

			MINT	EXC	G-VG
☐	63	Best '70s Pitchers	.60	.25	.06
		Vida Blue			
		Catfish Hunter			
		Nolan Ryan			
☐	64	George Brett	1.00	.40	.10
☐	65	Don Mattingly	1.25	.50	.12
☐	66	Fernando Valenzuela	.25	.10	.02
☐	67	Dale Murphy	.75	.30	.07
☐	68	Wade Boggs	1.00	.40	.10
☐	69	Rickey Henderson	1.50	.60	.15
☐	70	Eddie Murray	.75	.30	.07
		(Best '80s Player)			
☐	71	Ron Guidry	.15	.06	.01
☐	72	Best '80s Catchers	.25	.10	.02
		Gary Carter			
		Lance Parrish			
		Tony Pena			
☐	73	Best '80s Infielders	.30	.12	.03
		Cal Ripken			
		Lou Whitaker			
		Robin Yount			
☐	74	Best '80s Outfielders	.25	.10	.02
		Pedro Guerrero			
		Tim Raines			
		Dave Winfield			
☐	75	Dwight Gooden	.60	.25	.06

1986 Sportflics Rookies

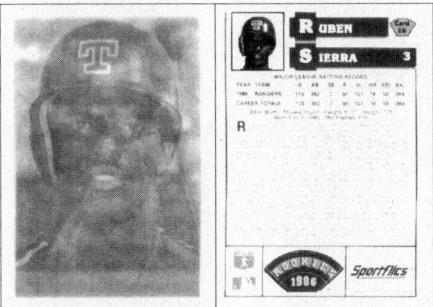

This set of 50 three-phase "animated" cards features top rookies of 1986 as well as a few outstanding rookies from the past. These "Magic Motion" cards are standard size, 2 1/2" by 3 1/2", and feature a distinctive light blue border on the front of the card. Cards were distributed in a light blue box, which also contained 34 trivia cards, each measuring 1 3/4" by 2". There are 47 single player cards along with two Tri-Stars and one Big Six.

			MINT	EXC	G-VG
		COMPLETE SET (50)	18.00	7.50	2.50
		COMMON PLAYER (1-50)	.12	.05	.01
☐	1	John Kruk	.30	.12	.03
☐	2	Edwin Correa	.12	.05	.01
☐	3	Pete Incaviglia	.50	.20	.05
☐	4	Dale Sveum	.12	.05	.01
☐	5	Juan Nieves	.12	.05	.01
☐	6	Will Clark	6.00	2.50	.60
☐	7	Wally Joyner	1.75	.70	.17
☐	8	Lance McCullers	.15	.06	.01
☐	9	Scott Bailes	.15	.06	.01
☐	10	Dan Plesac	.15	.06	.01
☐	11	Jose Canseco	6.00	2.50	.60
☐	12	Bobby Witt	.40	.16	.04
☐	13	Barry Bonds	3.50	1.50	.35
☐	14	Andres Thomas	.12	.05	.01
☐	15	Jim Deshaies	.15	.06	.01
☐	16	Ruben Sierra	4.00	1.75	.40
☐	17	Steve Lombardozzi	.12	.05	.01
☐	18	Cory Snyder	.15	.06	.01
☐	19	Reggie Williams	.12	.05	.01
☐	20	Mitch Williams	.20	.08	.02
☐	21	Glenn Braggs	.20	.08	.02
☐	22	Danny Tartabull	1.25	.50	.12
☐	23	Charlie Kerfeld	.12	.05	.01
☐	24	Paul Assenmacher	.12	.05	.01

			MINT	EXC	G-VG
☐	25	Robby Thompson	.25	.10	.02
☐	26	Bobby Bonilla	3.00	1.25	.30
☐	27	Andres Galarraga	.40	.16	.04
☐	28	Billy Jo Robidoux	.12	.05	.01
☐	29	Bruce Ruffin	.12	.05	.01
☐	30	Greg Swindell	.40	.16	.04
☐	31	John Cangelosi	.12	.05	.01
☐	32	Jim Traber	.12	.05	.01
☐	33	Russ Morman	.12	.05	.01
☐	34	Barry Larkin	2.25	.90	.22
☐	35	Todd Worrell	.30	.12	.03
☐	36	John Cerutti	.12	.05	.01
☐	37	Mike Kingery	.12	.05	.01
☐	38	Mark Eichhorn	.12	.05	.01
☐	39	Scott Bankhead	.20	.08	.02
☐	40	Bo Jackson	6.00	2.50	.60
☐	41	Greg Mathews	.12	.05	.01
☐	42	Eric King	.15	.06	.01
☐	43	Kal Daniels	.60	.25	.06
☐	44	Calvin Schiraldi	.12	.05	.01
☐	45	Mickey Brantley	.15	.06	.01
☐	46	Tri-Stars	.50	.20	.05
		Willie Mays			
		Pete Rose			
		Fred Lynn			
☐	47	Tri-Stars	.60	.25	.06
		Tom Seaver			
		Fern. Valenzuela			
		Dwight Gooden			
☐	48	Big Six	.60	.25	.06
		Eddie Murray, Lou			
		Whitaker, Dave Righetti,			
		Steve Sax, Cal Ripken,			
		Darryl Strawberry			
☐	49	Kevin Mitchell	2.50	1.00	.25
☐	50	Mike Diaz	.15	.06	.01

1987 Sportflics

This 200-card set was produced by Sportflics and again features three sequence action pictures on each card. Cards measure 2 1/2" by 3 1/2" and are in full color. Also included with the cards were 136 small team logo and trivia cards. There are 165 individual players, 20 Tri-Stars (the top three players in each league at each position), and 15 other miscellaneous multi-player cards. The cards feature a red border on the front. A full-color face shot of the player is printed on the back of the card. Cards are numbered on the back in the upper right corner. The cards in the factory-collated sets are copyrighted 1986, while the cards in the wax packs are copyrighted 1987 or show no copyright year on the back. Cards from wax packs with 1987 copyright are 1-35, 41-75, 81-115, 121-155, and 161-195; the rest of the numbers (when taken from wax packs) are found without a copyright year.

			MINT	EXC	G-VG
		COMPLETE SET (200)	35.00	15.75	5.25
		COMMON PLAYER (1-200)	.12	.05	.01
☐	1	Don Mattingly	1.50	.60	.15
☐	2	Wade Boggs	1.00	.40	.10
☐	3	Dale Murphy	.50	.20	.05
☐	4	Rickey Henderson	1.50	.60	.15
☐	5	George Brett	.75	.30	.07

☐ 6	Eddie Murray	.75	.30	.07
☐ 7	Kirby Puckett	1.25	.50	.12
☐ 8	Ryne Sandberg	1.50	.60	.15
☐ 9	Cal Ripken	1.50	.60	.15
☐ 10	Roger Clemens	1.50	.60	.15
☐ 11	Ted Higuera	.15	.06	.01
☐ 12	Steve Sax	.20	.08	.02
☐ 13	Chris Brown	.12	.05	.01
☐ 14	Jesse Barfield	.15	.06	.01
☐ 15	Kent Hrbek	.20	.08	.02
☐ 16	Robin Yount	.60	.25	.06
☐ 17	Glenn Davis	.40	.16	.04
☐ 18	Hubie Brooks	.15	.06	.01
☐ 19	Mike Scott	.15	.06	.01
☐ 20	Darryl Strawberry	1.25	.50	.12
☐ 21	Alvin Davis	.20	.08	.02
☐ 22	Eric Davis	.75	.30	.07
☐ 23	Danny Tartabull	.75	.30	.07
☐ 24A	Cory Snyder ERR '86 (photo on front is Pat Tabler)	4.00	1.75	.40
☐ 24B	Cory Snyder ERR '87 (photos on front and back are Pat Tabler)	2.00	.80	.20
☐ 24C	Cory Snyder COR '86	2.00	.80	.20
☐ 25	Pete Rose	1.00	.40	.10
☐ 26	Wally Joyner	1.00	.40	.10
☐ 27	Pedro Guerrero	.25	.10	.02
☐ 28	Tom Seaver	.75	.30	.07
☐ 29	Bob Knepper	.15	.06	.01
☐ 30	Mike Schmidt	1.00	.40	.10
☐ 31	Tony Gwynn	.90	.40	.09
☐ 32	Don Slaught	.12	.05	.01
☐ 33	Todd Worrell	.15	.06	.01
☐ 34	Tim Raines	.20	.08	.02
☐ 35	Dave Parker	.25	.10	.02
☐ 36	Bob Ojeda	.15	.06	.01
☐ 37	Pete Incaviglia	.40	.16	.04
☐ 38	Bruce Hurst	.20	.08	.02
☐ 39	Bobby Witt	.30	.12	.03
☐ 40	Steve Garvey	.40	.16	.04
☐ 41	Dave Winfield	.50	.20	.05
☐ 42	Jose Cruz	.15	.06	.01
☐ 43	Orel Hershiser	.35	.15	.03
☐ 44	Reggie Jackson	.75	.30	.07
☐ 45	Chili Davis	.15	.06	.01
☐ 46	Robby Thompson	.15	.06	.01
☐ 47	Dennis Boyd	.12	.05	.01
☐ 48	Kirk Gibson	.25	.10	.02
☐ 49	Fred Lynn	.15	.06	.01
☐ 50	Gary Carter	.30	.12	.03
☐ 51	George Bell	.30	.12	.03
☐ 52	Pete O'Brien	.12	.05	.01
☐ 53	Ron Darling	.15	.06	.01
☐ 54	Paul Molitor	.20	.08	.02
☐ 55	Mike Pagliarulo	.12	.05	.01
☐ 56	Mike Boddicker	.12	.05	.01
☐ 57	Dave Righetti	.20	.08	.02
☐ 58	Len Dykstra	.35	.15	.03
☐ 59	Mike Witt	.12	.05	.01
☐ 60	Tony Bernazard	.12	.05	.01
☐ 61	John Kruk	.20	.08	.02
☐ 62	Mike Krukow	.12	.05	.01
☐ 63	Sid Fernandez	.15	.06	.01
☐ 64	Gary Gaetti	.15	.06	.01
☐ 65	Vince Coleman	.60	.25	.06
☐ 66	Pat Tabler	.12	.05	.01
☐ 67	Mike Scioscia	.12	.05	.01
☐ 68	Scott Garrelts	.12	.05	.01
☐ 69	Brett Butler	.20	.08	.02
☐ 70	Bill Buckner	.15	.06	.01
☐ 71A	Dennis Rasmussen ERR '86 copyright (photo on back is John Montefusco)	1.00	.40	.10
☐ 71B	Dennis Rasmussen COR '87 copyright (photo with mustache)	.50	.20	.05
☐ 72	Tim Wallach	.15	.06	.01
☐ 73	Bob Horner	.15	.06	.01
☐ 74	Willie McGee	.20	.08	.02
☐ 75	Tri-Stars Don Mattingly Wally Joyner Eddie Murray	1.25	.50	.12
☐ 76A	Jesse Orosco COR '86 copyright	.35	.15	.03
☐ 76B	Jesse Orosco ERR '87 copyright (number on back is 96)	.15	.06	.01
☐ 77	Tri-Stars Todd Worrell Jeff Reardon Lee Smith	.20	.08	.02

☐ 78	Candy Maldonado	.15	.06	.01
☐ 79	Tri-Stars Ozzie Smith Hubie Brooks Shawon Dunston	.25	.10	.02
☐ 80	Tri-Stars George Bell Jose Canseco Jim Rice	.90	.40	.09
☐ 81	Bert Blyleven	.20	.08	.02
☐ 82	Mike Marshall	.15	.06	.01
☐ 83	Ron Guidry	.20	.08	.02
☐ 84	Julio Franco	.30	.12	.03
☐ 85	Willie Wilson	.20	.08	.02
☐ 86	Lee Lacy	.12	.05	.01
☐ 87	Jack Morris	.30	.12	.03
☐ 88	Ray Knight	.20	.08	.02
☐ 89	Phil Bradley	.15	.06	.01
☐ 90	Jose Canseco	2.00	.80	.20
☐ 91	Gary Ward	.12	.05	.01
☐ 92	Mike Easler	.12	.05	.01
☐ 93	Tony Pena	.15	.06	.01
☐ 94	Dave Smith	.12	.05	.01
☐ 95	Will Clark	2.00	.80	.20
☐ 96	Lloyd Moseby (See also 76B)	.15	.06	.01
☐ 97	Jim Rice	.20	.08	.02
☐ 98	Shawon Dunston	.25	.10	.02
☐ 99	Don Sutton	.25	.10	.02
☐ 100	Dwight Gooden	.75	.30	.07
☐ 101	Lance Parrish	.20	.08	.02
☐ 102	Mark Langston	.15	.06	.01
☐ 103	Floyd Youmans	.12	.05	.01
☐ 104	Lee Smith	.20	.08	.02
☐ 105	Willie Hernandez	.15	.06	.01
☐ 106	Doug DeCinces	.15	.06	.01
☐ 107	Ken Schrom	.12	.05	.01
☐ 108	Don Carman	.12	.05	.01
☐ 109	Brook Jacoby	.15	.06	.01
☐ 110	Steve Bedrosian	.15	.06	.01
☐ 111	Tri-Stars Roger Clemens Jack Morris Ted Higuera	.60	.25	.06
☐ 112	Tri-Stars Marty Barrett Tony Bernazard Lou Whitaker	.15	.06	.01
☐ 113	Tri-Stars Cal Ripken Scott Fletcher Tony Fernandez	.30	.12	.03
☐ 114	Tri-Stars Wade Boggs George Brett Gary Gaetti	.75	.30	.07
☐ 115	Tri-Stars Mike Schmidt Chris Brown Tim Wallach	.50	.20	.05
☐ 116	Tri-Stars Ryne Sandberg Johnny Ray Bill Doran	.35	.15	.03
☐ 117	Tri-Stars Dave Parker Tony Gwynn Kevin Bass	.25	.10	.02
☐ 118	Big Six Rookies Ty Gainey Terry Steinbach Dave Clark Pat Dodson Phil Lombardi Benito Santiago	1.00	.40	.10
☐ 119	Hi-Lite Tri-Stars Dave Righetti Fernando Valenzuela Mike Scott	.20	.08	.02
☐ 120	Tri-Stars Fernando Valenzuela Mike Scott Dwight Gooden	.50	.20	.05
☐ 121	Johnny Ray	.12	.05	.01
☐ 122	Keith Moreland	.12	.05	.01
☐ 123	Juan Samuel	.20	.08	.02
☐ 124	Wally Backman	.12	.05	.01
☐ 125	Nolan Ryan	2.50	1.00	.25
☐ 126	GregA. Harris	.12	.05	.01
☐ 127	Kirk McCaskill	.12	.05	.01
☐ 128	Dwight Evans	.20	.08	.02
☐ 129	Rick Rhoden	.12	.05	.01
☐ 130	Bill Madlock	.12	.05	.01
☐ 131	Oddibe McDowell	.15	.06	.01

☐ 132	Darrell Evans	.20	.08	.02
☐ 133	Keith Hernandez	.20	.08	.02
☐ 134	Tom Brunansky	.15	.06	.01
☐ 135	Kevin McReynolds	.25	.10	.02
☐ 136	Scott Fletcher	.12	.05	.01
☐ 137	Lou Whitaker	.20	.08	.02
☐ 138	Carney Lansford	.15	.06	.01
☐ 139	Andre Dawson	.50	.20	.05
☐ 140	Carlton Fisk	.50	.20	.05
☐ 141	Buddy Bell	.15	.06	.01
☐ 142	Ozzie Smith	.40	.16	.04
☐ 143	Dan Pasqua	.20	.08	.02
☐ 144	Kevin Mitchell	.90	.40	.09
☐ 145	Bret Saberhagen	.30	.12	.03
☐ 146	Charlie Kerfeld	.12	.05	.01
☐ 147	Phil Niekro	.25	.10	.02
☐ 148	John Candelaria	.12	.05	.01
☐ 149	Rich Gedman	.12	.05	.01
☐ 150	Fernando Valenzuela	.20	.08	.02
☐ 151	Tri-Stars	.15	.06	.01
	Gary Carter			
	Mike Scioscia			
	Tony Pena			
☐ 152	Tri-Stars	.30	.12	.03
	Tim Raines			
	Jose Cruz			
	Vince Coleman			
☐ 153	Tri-Stars	.20	.08	.02
	Jesse Barfield			
	Harold Baines			
	Dave Winfield			
☐ 154	Tri-Stars	.15	.06	.01
	Lance Parrish			
	Don Slaught			
	Rich Gedman			
☐ 155	Tri-Stars	.60	.25	.06
	Dale Murphy			
	Kevin McReynolds			
	Eric Davis			
☐ 156	Hi-Lite Tri-Stars	.45	.18	.04
	Don Sutton			
	Mike Schmidt			
	Jim Deshaies			
☐ 157	Speedburners	.40	.16	.04
	Rickey Henderson			
	John Cangelosi			
	Gary Pettis			
☐ 158	Big Six Rookies	1.25	.50	.12
	Randy Asadoor			
	Casey Candaele			
	Kevin Seitzer			
	Rafael Palmeiro			
	Tim Pyznarski			
	Dave Cochrane			
☐ 159	Big Six	1.50	.60	.15
	Don Mattingly			
	Rickey Henderson			
	Roger Clemens			
	Dale Murphy			
	Eddie Murray			
	Dwight Gooden			
☐ 160	Roger McDowell	.15	.06	.01
☐ 161	Brian Downing	.12	.05	.01
☐ 162	Bill Doran	.15	.06	.01
☐ 163	Don Baylor	.15	.06	.01
☐ 164A	Alfredo Griffin ERR	.25	.10	.02
	(no uniform number			
	on card back) '87			
☐ 164B	Alfredo Griffin	.25	.10	.02
	COR '86			
☐ 165	Don Aase	.12	.05	.01
☐ 166	Glenn Wilson	.12	.05	.01
☐ 167	Dan Quisenberry	.20	.08	.02
☐ 168	Frank White	.15	.06	.01
☐ 169	Cecil Cooper	.15	.06	.01
☐ 170	Jody Davis	.12	.05	.01
☐ 171	Harold Baines	.25	.10	.02
☐ 172	Rob Deer	.20	.08	.02
☐ 173	John Tudor	.15	.06	.01
☐ 174	Larry Parrish	.15	.06	.01
☐ 175	Kevin Bass	.15	.06	.01
☐ 176	Joe Carter	.50	.20	.05
☐ 177	Mitch Webster	.12	.05	.01
☐ 178	Dave Kingman	.15	.06	.01
☐ 179	Jim Presley	.12	.05	.01
☐ 180	Mel Hall	.20	.08	.02
☐ 181	Shane Rawley	.12	.05	.01
☐ 182	Marty Barrett	.12	.05	.01
☐ 183	Damaso Garcia	.12	.05	.01
☐ 184	Bobby Grich	.15	.06	.01
☐ 185	Leon Durham	.12	.05	.01
☐ 186	Ozzie Guillen	.25	.10	.02
☐ 187	Tony Fernandez	.20	.08	.02
☐ 188	Alan Trammell	.30	.12	.03

☐ 189	Jim Clancy	.12	.05	.01
☐ 190	Bo Jackson	2.50	1.00	.25
☐ 191	Bob Forsch	.12	.05	.01
☐ 192	John Franco	.20	.08	.02
☐ 193	Von Hayes	.20	.08	.02
☐ 194	Tri-Stars	.15	.06	.01
	Don Aase			
	Dave Righetti			
	Mark Eichhorn			
☐ 195	Tri-Stars	.60	.25	.06
	Keith Hernandez			
	Will Clark			
	Glenn Davis			
☐ 196	Hi-Lite Tri-Stars	.45	.18	.04
	Roger Clemens			
	Joe Cowley			
	Bob Horner			
☐ 197	Big Six	.75	.30	.07
	George Brett			
	Hubie Brooks			
	Tony Gwynn			
	Ryne Sandberg			
	Tim Raines			
	Wade Boggs			
☐ 198	Tri-Stars	.60	.25	.06
	Kirby Puckett			
	Rickey Henderson			
	Fred Lynn			
☐ 199	Speedburners	.60	.25	.06
	Tim Raines			
	Vince Coleman			
	Eric Davis			
☐ 200	Steve Carlton	.35	.15	.03

1987 Sportflics Dealer Panels

These "Magic Motion" card panels of four were issued only to dealers who were ordering other Sportflics product in quantity. If cut into individual cards, the interior white borders will be slightly narrower than the regular issue Sportflics since the panels of four measure a shade under 4 7/8" by 6 7/8". The cards have a 1986 copyright on the back same as the factory collated sets. Other than the slight difference in size, these cards are essentially styled the same as the regular issue of 1987 Sportflics. This set of sixteen top players was accompanied by the inclusion of four smaller panels of four team logo/team fact cards. The 16 small team cards correspond directly to the 16 players in the sets. The checklist below prices the panels and gives the card number for each player, which is the same as the player's card number in the Sportflics regular set.

	MINT	EXC	G-VG
COMPLETE SET (4)	10.00	4.50	1.25
COMMON PANEL (1-4)	3.00	1.25	.30
☐ 1 Don Mattingly 1	4.50	2.00	.45
Roger Clemens 10			
Mike Schmidt 30			
Tim Raines 34			

		MINT	EXC	G-VG
☐ 2	Wade Boggs 2 .... Eddie Murray 6 Wally Joyner 26 Fern.Valenzuela 150	3.50	1.50	.35
☐ 3	Dale Murphy 3 .... Tony Gwynn 31 Jim Rice 97 Keith Hernandez 133	3.00	1.25	.30
☐ 4	Rickey Henderson 4 .... George Brett 5 Cal Ripken 9 Dwight Gooden 100	4.50	2.00	.45

1987 Sportflics Team Preview

This 26-card set features a card for each Major League team. Each card shows 12 different players on that team via four "Magic Motion" trios. The cards are numbered on the backs. The narrative on the back gives Outlook, Newcomers to Watch, and Summary for each team. The list of players appearing on the front is given at the bottom of the reverse of each card. Cards are standard size, 2 1/2" by 3 1/2". The was distributed as a complete set in its own box along with 26 team logo trivia cards measuring 1 3/4" by 2".

		MINT	EXC	G-VG
COMPLETE SET (26)		5.00	2.25	.50
COMMON PLAYER (1-26)		.30	.12	.03
☐ 1	Texas Rangers	.30	.12	.03
☐ 2	New York Mets	.40	.16	.04
☐ 3	Cleveland Indians	.30	.12	.03
☐ 4	Cincinnati Reds	.40	.16	.04
☐ 5	Toronto Blue Jays	.30	.12	.03
☐ 6	Philadelphia Phillies	.30	.12	.03
☐ 7	New York Yankees	.40	.16	.04
☐ 8	Houston Astros	.30	.12	.03
☐ 9	Boston Red Sox	.40	.16	.04
☐ 10	San Francisco Giants	.30	.12	.03
☐ 11	California Angels	.30	.12	.03
☐ 12	St. Louis Cardinals	.40	.16	.04
☐ 13	Kansas City Royals	.40	.16	.04
☐ 14	Los Angeles Dodgers	.40	.16	.04
☐ 15	Detroit Tigers	.40	.16	.04
☐ 16	San Diego Padres	.30	.12	.03
☐ 17	Minnesota Twins	.40	.16	.04
☐ 18	Pittsburgh Pirates	.30	.12	.03
☐ 19	Milwaukee Brewers	.30	.12	.03
☐ 20	Montreal Expos	.30	.12	.03
☐ 21	Baltimore Orioles	.40	.16	.04
☐ 22	Chicago Cubs	.30	.12	.03
☐ 23	Oakland Athletics	.40	.16	.04
☐ 24	Atlanta Braves	.30	.12	.03
☐ 25	Seattle Mariners	.30	.12	.03
☐ 26	Chicago White Sox	.30	.12	.03

1987 Sportflics Rookie Packs

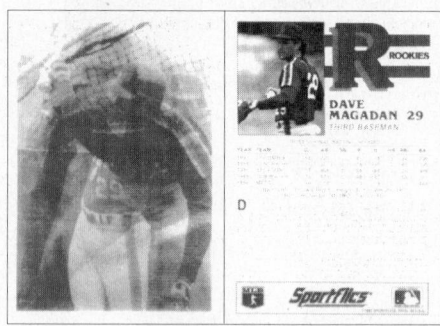

This two pack-set consists of 10 "rookie" players and 2 trivia cards. Each of the two different packs had half the set and the outside of the wrapper told which cards were inside. The cards are all 2 1/2" by 3 1/2". The set includes the first major league baseball cards ever of Alonzo Powell, John Smiley, and Brick Smith. Dealers received one rookie pack with every Team Preview set they ordered. The card backs also feature a full-color small photo of the player.

		MINT	EXC	G-VG
COMPLETE SET (10)		7.00	3.00	.70
COMMON PLAYER (1-10)		.40	.16	.04
☐ 1	Terry Steinbach .... (pack two)	1.00	.40	.10
☐ 2	Rafael Palmeiro .... (pack one)	2.00	.80	.20
☐ 3	Dave Magadan .... (pack two)	1.00	.40	.10
☐ 4	Marvin Freeman .... (pack two)	.40	.16	.04
☐ 5	Brick Smith .... (pack two)	.40	.16	.04
☐ 6	B.J. Surhoff .... (pack two)	.75	.30	.07
☐ 7	John Smiley .... (pack one)	1.00	.40	.10
☐ 8	Alonzo Powell .... (pack one)	.40	.16	.04
☐ 9	Benito Santiago .... (pack one)	2.00	.80	.20
☐ 10	Devon White .... (pack one)	1.25	.50	.12

1987 Sportflics Rookies I

These "Magic Motion" cards were issued as a series of 25 cards packaged in its own complete set box, along with 17 trivia cards. Cards are 2 1/2" by 3 1/2." The three front photos show the player in two action poses and one portrait pose. The card backs also provide a full-color photo (1 3/8" by 2 1/4") of the player as well as the usual statistics and biographical notes. The front photos are framed by a wide, round-cornered, red border and have the player's name and uniform number at the bottom. The cards in the set are numbered essentially in alphabetical order by player's name.

	MINT	EXC	G-VG
COMPLETE SET (25)	8.00	3.50	.80
COMMON PLAYER (1-25)	.12	.05	.01

		MINT	EXC	G-VG
☐	1 Eric Bell	.12	.05	.01
☐	2 Chris Bosio	.20	.08	.02
☐	3 Bob Brower	.12	.05	.01
☐	4 Jerry Browne	.20	.08	.02
☐	5 Ellis Burks	1.25	.50	.12
☐	6 Casey Candaele	.12	.05	.01
☐	7 Ken Gerhart	.12	.05	.01
☐	8 Mike Greenwell	1.25	.50	.12
☐	9 Stan Jefferson	.20	.08	.02
☐	10 Dave Magadan	.35	.15	.03
☐	11 Joe Magrane	.30	.12	.03
☐	12 Fred McGriff	1.25	.50	.12
☐	13 Mark McGwire	1.50	.60	.15
☐	14 Mark McLemore	.12	.05	.01
☐	15 Jeff Musselman	.12	.05	.01
☐	16 Matt Nokes	.30	.12	.03
☐	17 Paul O'Neill	.30	.12	.03
☐	18 Luis Polonia	.25	.10	.02
☐	19 Benito Santiago	.75	.30	.07
☐	20 Kevin Seitzer	.40	.16	.04
☐	21 John Smiley	.40	.16	.04
☐	22 Terry Steinbach	.35	.15	.03
☐	23 B.J. Surhoff	.25	.10	.02
☐	24 Devon White	.30	.12	.03
☐	25 Matt Williams	2.50	1.00	.25

1987 Sportflics Rookies II

These "Magic Motion" cards were issued as a series of 25 cards packaged in its own complete set box along with 17 trivia cards. Cards are 2 1/2" by 3 1/2." In this second set the card numbering begins with number 26. The three front photos show the player in two action poses and one portrait pose. The card backs also provide a full-color photo (1 3/8" by 2 1/4") of the player as well as the usual statistics and biographical notes. The front photos are framed by a wide, round-cornered, red border and have the player's name and uniform number at the bottom.

	MINT	EXC	G-VG
COMPLETE SET (25)	4.00	1.75	.40
COMMON PLAYER (26-50)	.12	.05	.01

		MINT	EXC	G-VG
☐	26 DeWayne Buice	.12	.05	.01
☐	27 Willie Fraser	.12	.05	.01
☐	28 Billy Ripken	.20	.08	.02
☐	29 Mike Henneman	.25	.10	.02
☐	30 Shawn Hillegas	.12	.05	.01
☐	31 Shane Mack	.35	.15	.03
☐	32 Rafael Palmeiro	1.25	.50	.12

		MINT	EXC	G-VG
☐	33 Mike Jackson	.20	.08	.02
☐	34 Gene Larkin	.20	.08	.02
☐	35 Jimmy Jones	.15	.06	.01
☐	36 Gerald Young	.20	.08	.02
☐	37 Ken Caminiti	.20	.08	.02
☐	38 Sam Horn	.20	.08	.02
☐	39 David Cone	.90	.40	.09
☐	40 Mike Dunne	.12	.05	.01
☐	41 Ken Williams	.20	.08	.02
☐	42 John Morris	.12	.05	.01
☐	43 Jim Lindeman	.12	.05	.01
☐	44 Mike Stanley	.12	.05	.01
☐	45 Les Straker	.12	.05	.01
☐	46 Jeff M. Robinson	.20	.08	.02
☐	47 Todd Benzinger	.25	.10	.02
☐	48 Jeff Blauser	.20	.08	.02
☐	49 John Marzano	.15	.06	.01
☐	50 Keith Miller	.25	.10	.02

1988 Sportflics

This 225-card set was produced by Sportflics and again features three sequence action pictures on each card. Cards measure 2 1/2" by 3 1/2" and are in full color. There are 219 individual players, 3 Highlights trios, and 3 Rookie Prospect trio cards. The cards feature a red border on the front. A full-color action picture of the player is printed on the back of the card. Cards are numbered on the back in the lower right corner.

	MINT	EXC	G-VG
COMPLETE SET (225)	40.00	18.00	6.00
COMMON PLAYER (1-225)	.12	.05	.01

		MINT	EXC	G-VG
☐	1 Don Mattingly	1.00	.40	.10
☐	2 Tim Raines	.20	.08	.02
☐	3 Andre Dawson	.35	.15	.03
☐	4 George Bell	.20	.08	.02
☐	5 Joe Carter	.35	.15	.03
☐	6 Matt Nokes	.25	.10	.02
☐	7 Dave Winfield	.35	.15	.03
☐	8 Kirby Puckett	.90	.40	.09
☐	9 Will Clark	1.50	.60	.15
☐	10 Eric Davis	.75	.30	.07
☐	11 Rickey Henderson	1.50	.60	.15
☐	12 Ryne Sandberg	1.25	.50	.12
☐	13 Jesse Barfield UER (misspelled Jessie on card back)	.25	.10	.02
☐	14 Ozzie Guillen	.20	.08	.02
☐	15 Bret Saberhagen	.30	.12	.03
☐	16 Tony Gwynn	.75	.30	.07
☐	17 Kevin Seitzer	.25	.10	.02
☐	18 Jack Clark	.15	.06	.01
☐	19 Danny Tartabull	.50	.20	.05
☐	20 Ted Higuera	.15	.06	.01
☐	21 Charlie Leibrandt UER (misspelled Liebrandt on card front)	.15	.06	.01
☐	22 Benito Santiago	.50	.20	.05
☐	23 Fred Lynn	.20	.08	.02
☐	24 Robby Thompson	.15	.06	.01
☐	25 Alan Trammell	.30	.12	.03
☐	26 Tony Fernandez	.20	.08	.02
☐	27 Rick Sutcliffe	.15	.06	.01
☐	28 Gary Carter	.30	.12	.03

☐ 29 Cory Snyder	.15	.06	.01	☐ 122 Tommy John	.25	.10	.02
☐ 30 Lou Whitaker	.20	.08	.02	☐ 123 Bill Madlock	.12	.05	.01
☐ 31 Keith Hernandez	.20	.08	.02	☐ 124 Ken Caminiti	.20	.08	.02
☐ 32 Mike Witt	.12	.05	.01	☐ 125 Gary Ward	.12	.05	.01
☐ 33 Harold Baines	.20	.08	.02	☐ 126 Candy Maldonado	.15	.06	.01
☐ 34 Robin Yount	.60	.25	.06	☐ 127 Harold Reynolds	.15	.06	.01
☐ 35 Mike Schmidt	1.00	.40	.10	☐ 128 Joe Magrane	.20	.08	.02
☐ 36 Dion James	.12	.05	.01	☐ 129 Mike Henneman	.20	.08	.02
☐ 37 Tom Candiotti	.15	.06	.01	☐ 130 Jim Gantner	.12	.05	.01
☐ 38 Tracy Jones	.15	.06	.01	☐ 131 Bobby Bonilla	.50	.20	.05
☐ 39 Nolan Ryan	2.00	.80	.20	☐ 132 John Farrell	.20	.08	.02
☐ 40 Fernando Valenzuela	.20	.08	.02	☐ 133 Frank Tanana	.15	.06	.01
☐ 41 Vance Law	.12	.05	.01	☐ 134 Zane Smith	.15	.06	.01
☐ 42 Roger McDowell	.12	.05	.01	☐ 135 Dave Righetti	.15	.06	.01
☐ 43 Carlton Fisk	.40	.16	.04	☐ 136 Rick Reuschel	.15	.06	.01
☐ 44 Scott Garrelts	.15	.06	.01	☐ 137 Dwight Evans	.20	.08	.02
☐ 45 Lee Guetterman	.12	.05	.01	☐ 138 Howard Johnson	.35	.15	.03
☐ 46 Mark Langston	.20	.08	.02	☐ 139 Terry Leach	.12	.05	.01
☐ 47 Willie Randolph	.15	.06	.01	☐ 140 Casey Candaele	.12	.05	.01
☐ 48 Bill Doran	.15	.06	.01	☐ 141 Tom Herr	.12	.05	.01
☐ 49 Larry Parrish	.12	.05	.01	☐ 142 Tony Pena	.15	.06	.01
☐ 50 Wade Boggs	.90	.40	.09	☐ 143 Lance Parrish	.25	.10	.02
☐ 51 Shane Rawley	.12	.05	.01	☐ 144 Ellis Burks	.90	.40	.09
☐ 52 Alvin Davis	.15	.06	.01	☐ 145 Pete O'Brien	.12	.05	.01
☐ 53 Jeff Reardon	.25	.10	.02	☐ 146 Mike Boddicker	.15	.06	.01
☐ 54 Jim Presley	.12	.05	.01	☐ 147 Buddy Bell	.15	.06	.01
☐ 55 Kevin Bass	.12	.05	.01	☐ 148 Bo Jackson	2.00	.80	.20
☐ 56 Kevin McReynolds	.20	.08	.02	☐ 149 Frank White	.15	.06	.01
☐ 57 B.J. Surhoff	.20	.08	.02	☐ 150 George Brett	.50	.20	.05
☐ 58 Julio Franco	.25	.10	.02	☐ 151 Tim Wallach	.15	.06	.01
☐ 59 Eddie Murray	.45	.18	.04	☐ 152 Cal Ripken	1.25	.50	.12
☐ 60 Jody Davis	.12	.05	.01	☐ 153 Brett Butler	.15	.06	.01
☐ 61 Todd Worrell	.15	.06	.01	☐ 154 Gary Gaetti	.15	.06	.01
☐ 62 Von Hayes	.20	.08	.02	☐ 155 Darryl Strawberry	.90	.40	.09
☐ 63 Billy Hatcher	.15	.06	.01	☐ 156 Alredo Griffin	.12	.05	.01
☐ 64 John Kruk	.20	.08	.02	☐ 157 Marty Barrett	.12	.05	.01
☐ 65 Tom Henke	.15	.06	.01	☐ 158 Jim Rice	.20	.08	.02
☐ 66 Mike Scott	.20	.08	.02	☐ 159 Terry Pendleton	.30	.12	.03
☐ 67 Vince Coleman	.25	.10	.02	☐ 160 Orel Hershiser	.30	.12	.03
☐ 68 Ozzie Smith	.30	.12	.03	☐ 161 Larry Sheets	.12	.05	.01
☐ 69 Ken Williams	.12	.05	.01	☐ 162 Dave Stewart UER	.35	.15	.03
☐ 70 Steve Bedrosian	.12	.05	.01	(Braves logo)			
☐ 71 Luis Polonia	.25	.10	.02	☐ 163 Shawon Dunston	.25	.10	.02
☐ 72 Brook Jacoby	.15	.06	.01	☐ 164 Keith Moreland	.12	.05	.01
☐ 73 Ron Darling	.15	.06	.01	☐ 165 Ken Oberkfell	.12	.05	.01
☐ 74 Lloyd Moseby	.12	.05	.01	☐ 166 Ivan Calderon	.25	.10	.02
☐ 75 Wally Joyner	.35	.15	.03	☐ 167 Bob Welch	.25	.10	.02
☐ 76 Dan Quisenberry	.15	.06	.01	☐ 168 Fred McGriff	.60	.25	.06
☐ 77 Scott Fletcher	.12	.05	.01	☐ 169 Pete Incaviglia	.20	.08	.02
☐ 78 Kirk McCaskill	.12	.05	.01	☐ 170 Dale Murphy	.35	.15	.03
☐ 79 Paul Molitor	.25	.10	.02	☐ 171 Mike Dunne	.12	.05	.01
☐ 80 Mike Aldrete	.12	.05	.01	☐ 172 Chili Davis	.20	.08	.02
☐ 81 Neal Heaton	.12	.05	.01	☐ 173 Milt Thompson	.12	.05	.01
☐ 82 Jeffrey Leonard	.12	.05	.01	☐ 174 Terry Steinbach	.15	.06	.01
☐ 83 Dave Magadan	.25	.10	.02	☐ 175 Oddibe McDowell	.12	.05	.01
☐ 84 Danny Cox	.12	.05	.01	☐ 176 Jack Morris	.25	.10	.02
☐ 85 Lance McCullers	.12	.05	.01	☐ 177 Sid Fernandez	.15	.06	.01
☐ 86 Jay Howell	.12	.05	.01	☐ 178 Ken Griffey	.20	.08	.02
☐ 87 Charlie Hough	.12	.05	.01	☐ 179 Lee Smith	.20	.08	.02
☐ 88 Gene Garber	.12	.05	.01	☐ 180 Highlights 1987	.50	.20	.05
☐ 89 Jesse Orosco	.12	.05	.01	Kirby Puckett			
☐ 90 Don Robinson	.12	.05	.01	Juan Nieves			
☐ 91 Willie McGee	.20	.08	.02	Mike Schmidt			
☐ 92 Bert Blyleven	.15	.06	.01	☐ 181 Brian Downing	.12	.05	.01
☐ 93 Phil Bradley	.15	.06	.01	☐ 182 Andres Galarraga	.20	.08	.02
☐ 94 Terry Kennedy	.12	.05	.01	☐ 183 Rob Deer	.20	.08	.02
☐ 95 Kent Hrbek	.20	.08	.02	☐ 184 Greg Brock	.12	.05	.01
☐ 96 Juan Samuel	.15	.06	.01	☐ 185 Doug DeCinces	.12	.05	.01
☐ 97 Pedro Guerrero	.15	.06	.01	☐ 186 Johnny Ray	.12	.05	.01
☐ 98 Sid Bream	.12	.05	.01	☐ 187 Hubie Brooks	.15	.06	.01
☐ 99 Devon White	.25	.10	.02	☐ 188 Darrell Evans	.12	.05	.01
☐ 100 Mark McGwire	.75	.30	.07	☐ 189 Mel Hall	.15	.06	.01
☐ 101 Dave Parker	.20	.08	.02	☐ 190 Jim Deshaies	.12	.05	.01
☐ 102 Glenn Davis	.25	.10	.02	☐ 191 Dan Plesac	.12	.05	.01
☐ 103 Greg Walker	.12	.05	.01	☐ 192 Willie Wilson	.15	.06	.01
☐ 104 Rick Rhoden	.12	.05	.01	☐ 193 Mike LaValliere	.12	.05	.01
☐ 105 Mitch Webster	.12	.05	.01	☐ 194 Tom Brunansky	.15	.06	.01
☐ 106 Len Dykstra	.25	.10	.02	☐ 195 John Franco	.15	.06	.01
☐ 107 Gene Larkin	.12	.05	.01	☐ 196 Frank Viola	.25	.10	.02
☐ 108 Floyd Youmans	.12	.05	.01	☐ 197 Bruce Hurst	.20	.08	.02
☐ 109 Andy Van Slyke	.20	.08	.02	☐ 198 John Tudor	.15	.06	.01
☐ 110 Mike Scioscia	.12	.05	.01	☐ 199 Bob Forsch	.12	.05	.01
☐ 111 Kirk Gibson	.25	.10	.02	☐ 200 Dwight Gooden	.50	.20	.05
☐ 112 Kal Daniels	.20	.08	.02	☐ 201 Jose Canseco	1.50	.60	.15
☐ 113 Ruben Sierra	1.00	.40	.10	☐ 202 Carney Lansford	.15	.06	.01
☐ 114 Sam Horn	.20	.08	.02	☐ 203 Kelly Downs	.12	.05	.01
☐ 115 Ray Knight	.20	.08	.02	☐ 204 Glenn Wilson	.12	.05	.01
☐ 116 Jimmy Key	.15	.06	.01	☐ 205 Pat Tabler	.12	.05	.01
☐ 117 Bo Diaz	.12	.05	.01	☐ 206 Mike Davis	.12	.05	.01
☐ 118 Mike Greenwell	.90	.40	.09	☐ 207 Roger Clemens	1.25	.50	.12
☐ 119 Barry Bonds	.75	.30	.07	☐ 208 Dave Smith	.12	.05	.01
☐ 120 Reggie Jackson UER	.75	.30	.07	☐ 209 Curt Young	.12	.05	.01
(463 lifetime homers)				☐ 210 Mark Eichhorn	.15	.06	.01
☐ 121 Mike Pagliarulo	.12	.05	.01	☐ 211 Juan Nieves	.12	.05	.01

		MINT	EXC	G-VG
☐ 212	Bob Boone	.20	.08	.02
☐ 213	Don Sutton	.20	.08	.02
☐ 214	Willie Upshaw	.12	.05	.01
☐ 215	Jim Clancy	.12	.05	.01
☐ 216	Bill Ripken	.20	.08	.02
☐ 217	Ozzie Virgil	.12	.05	.01
☐ 218	Dave Concepcion	.20	.08	.02
☐ 219	Alan Ashby	.12	.05	.01
☐ 220	Mike Marshall	.15	.06	.01
☐ 221	Highlights 1987 Mark McGwire Paul Molitor Vince Coleman	.50	.20	.05
☐ 222	Highlights 1987 Benito Santiago Steve Bedrosian Don Mattingly	.75	.30	.07
☐ 223	Rookie Prospects Shawn Abner Jay Buhner Gary Thurman	.30	.12	.03
☐ 224	Rookie Prospects Tim Crews Vincente Palacios John Davis	.15	.06	.01
☐ 225	Rookie Prospects Jody Reed Jeff Treadway Keith Miller	.40	.16	.04

1988 Sportflics Gamewinners

This 25-card set of "Gamewinners" was distributed in a green and yellow box along with 17 trivia cards by Weiser Card Company of New Jersey. The 25 players selected for the set show a strong New York preference. The set was ostensibly produced for use as a youth organizational fund raiser. The cards are the standard size, 2 1/2" by 3 1/2" and are done in the typical Sportflics' Magic Motion (three picture) style. The cards are numbered on the back.

		MINT	EXC	G-VG
COMPLETE SET (25)		9.00	4.00	.90
COMMON PLAYER (1-25)		.20	.08	.02
☐ 1	Don Mattingly	.90	.40	.09
☐ 2	Mark McGwire	.60	.25	.06
☐ 3	Wade Boggs	.75	.30	.07
☐ 4	Will Clark	.90	.40	.09
☐ 5	Eric Davis	.60	.25	.06
☐ 6	Willie Randolph	.20	.08	.02
☐ 7	Dave Winfield	.50	.20	.05
☐ 8	Rickey Henderson	.90	.40	.09
☐ 9	Dwight Gooden	.40	.16	.04
☐ 10	Benito Santiago	.40	.16	.04
☐ 11	Keith Hernandez	.30	.12	.03
☐ 12	Juan Samuel	.25	.10	.02
☐ 13	Kevin Seitzer	.25	.10	.02
☐ 14	Gary Carter	.40	.16	.04
☐ 15	Darryl Strawberry	.90	.40	.09
☐ 16	Rick Rhoden	.20	.08	.02
☐ 17	Howard Johnson	.45	.18	.04
☐ 18	Matt Nokes	.25	.10	.02
☐ 19	Dave Righetti	.25	.10	.02
☐ 20	Roger Clemens	.90	.40	.09

		MINT	EXC	G-VG
☐ 21	Mike Schmidt	.90	.40	.09
☐ 22	Kevin McReynolds	.25	.10	.02
☐ 23	Mike Pagliarulo	.20	.08	.02
☐ 24	Kevin Elster	.20	.08	.02
☐ 25	Jack Clark	.30	.12	.03

1989 Sportflics

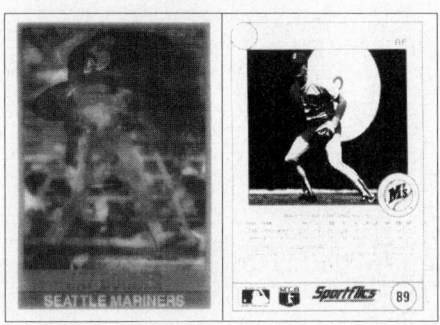

This 225-card set was produced by Sportflics (distributed by Major League Marketing) and again features three sequence action pictures on each card. Cards measure 2 1/2" by 3 1/2" and are in full color. There are 220 individual players, 2 Highlights trios, and 3 Rookie Prospect trio cards. The cards feature a white border on the front with red and blue inner trim colors. A full-color action picture of the player is printed on the back of the card. Cards are numbered on the back in the lower right corner.

		MINT	EXC	G-VG
COMPLETE SET (225)		40.00	18.00	6.00
COMMON PLAYER (1-225)		.12	.05	.01
☐ 1	Jose Canseco	1.50	.60	.15
☐ 2	Wally Joyner	.50	.20	.05
☐ 3	Roger Clemens	1.00	.40	.10
☐ 4	Greg Swindell	.25	.10	.02
☐ 5	Jack Morris	.25	.10	.02
☐ 6	Mickey Brantley	.12	.05	.01
☐ 7	Jim Presley	.12	.05	.01
☐ 8	Pete O'Brien	.12	.05	.01
☐ 9	Jesse Barfield	.15	.06	.01
☐ 10	Frank Viola	.20	.08	.02
☐ 11	Kevin Bass	.12	.05	.01
☐ 12	Glenn Wilson	.12	.05	.01
☐ 13	Chris Sabo	.30	.12	.03
☐ 14	Fred McGriff	.35	.15	.03
☐ 15	Mark Grace	.90	.40	.09
☐ 16	Devon White	.20	.08	.02
☐ 17	Juan Samuel	.15	.06	.01
☐ 18	Lou Whitaker UER (Card back says Bats: Right and Throws: Left)	.20	.08	.02
☐ 19	Greg Walker	.12	.05	.01
☐ 20	Roberto Alomar	1.00	.40	.10
☐ 21	Mike Schmidt	.75	.30	.07
☐ 22	Benito Santiago	.30	.12	.03
☐ 23	Dave Stewart	.20	.08	.02
☐ 24	Dave Winfield	.35	.15	.03
☐ 25	George Bell	.25	.10	.02
☐ 26	Jack Clark	.15	.06	.01
☐ 27	Doug Drabek	.25	.10	.02
☐ 28	Ron Gant	.90	.40	.09
☐ 29	Glenn Braggs	.15	.06	.01
☐ 30	Rafael Palmeiro	.30	.12	.03
☐ 31	Brett Butler	.20	.08	.02
☐ 32	Ron Darling	.15	.06	.01
☐ 33	Alvin Davis	.15	.06	.01
☐ 34	Bob Walk	.12	.05	.01
☐ 35	Dave Stieb	.20	.08	.02
☐ 36	Orel Hershiser	.25	.10	.02
☐ 37	John Farrell	.15	.06	.01
☐ 38	Doug Jones	.15	.06	.01
☐ 39	Kelly Downs	.15	.06	.01
☐ 40	Bob Boone	.15	.06	.01

No.	Player			
☐ 41	Gary Sheffield UER (7 career triples, should be 0)	.75	.30	.07
☐ 42	Doug Dascenzo	.15	.06	.01
☐ 43	Chad Kreuter	.12	.05	.01
☐ 44	Ricky Jordan	.20	.08	.02
☐ 45	Dave West	.15	.06	.01
☐ 46	Danny Tartabull	.40	.16	.04
☐ 47	Teddy Higuera	.15	.06	.01
☐ 48	Gary Gaetti	.15	.06	.01
☐ 49	Dave Parker	.20	.08	.02
☐ 50	Don Mattingly	.75	.30	.07
☐ 51	David Cone	.25	.10	.02
☐ 52	Kal Daniels	.15	.06	.01
☐ 53	Carney Lansford	.15	.06	.01
☐ 54	Mike Marshall	.15	.06	.01
☐ 55	Kevin Seitzer	.15	.06	.01
☐ 56	Mike Henneman	.15	.06	.01
☐ 57	Bill Doran	.15	.06	.01
☐ 58	Steve Sax	.15	.06	.01
☐ 59	Lance Parrish	.15	.06	.01
☐ 60	Keith Hernandez	.20	.08	.02
☐ 61	Jose Uribe	.12	.05	.01
☐ 62	Jose Lind	.12	.05	.01
☐ 63	Steve Bedrosian	.12	.05	.01
☐ 64	George Brett UER (Text says .380 in 1980, should be .390)	.35	.15	.03
☐ 65	Kirk Gibson	.20	.08	.02
☐ 66	Cal Ripken	.90	.40	.09
☐ 67	Mitch Webster	.12	.05	.01
☐ 68	Fred Lynn	.15	.06	.01
☐ 69	Eric Davis	.35	.15	.03
☐ 70	Bo Jackson	1.50	.60	.15
☐ 71	Kevin Elster	.12	.05	.01
☐ 72	Rick Reuschel	.15	.06	.01
☐ 73	Tim Burke	.12	.05	.01
☐ 74	Mark Davis	.12	.05	.01
☐ 75	Claudell Washington	.12	.05	.01
☐ 76	Lance McCullers	.12	.05	.01
☐ 77	Mike Moore	.15	.06	.01
☐ 78	Robby Thompson	.15	.06	.01
☐ 79	Roger McDowell	.12	.05	.01
☐ 80	Danny Jackson	.15	.06	.01
☐ 81	Tim Leary	.15	.06	.01
☐ 82	Bobby Witt	.15	.06	.01
☐ 83	Jim Gott	.12	.05	.01
☐ 84	Andy Hawkins	.12	.05	.01
☐ 85	Ozzie Guillen	.20	.08	.02
☐ 86	John Tudor	.15	.06	.01
☐ 87	Todd Burns	.15	.06	.01
☐ 88	Dave Gallagher	.12	.05	.01
☐ 89	Jay Buhner	.25	.10	.02
☐ 90	Gregg Jefferies	.75	.30	.07
☐ 91	Bob Welch	.20	.08	.02
☐ 92	Charlie Hough	.12	.05	.01
☐ 93	Tony Fernandez	.15	.06	.01
☐ 94	Ozzie Virgil	.12	.05	.01
☐ 95	Andre Dawson	.30	.12	.03
☐ 96	Hubie Brooks	.15	.06	.01
☐ 97	Kevin McReynolds	.15	.06	.01
☐ 98	Mike LaValliere	.12	.05	.01
☐ 99	Terry Pendleton	.35	.15	.03
☐ 100	Wade Boggs	.60	.25	.06
☐ 101	Dennis Eckersley	.20	.08	.02
☐ 102	Mark Gubicza	.15	.06	.01
☐ 103	Frank Tanana	.15	.06	.01
☐ 104	Joe Carter	.35	.15	.03
☐ 105	Ozzie Smith	.30	.12	.03
☐ 106	Dennis Martinez	.15	.06	.01
☐ 107	Jeff Treadway	.15	.06	.01
☐ 108	Greg Maddux	.20	.08	.02
☐ 109	Bret Saberhagen	.30	.12	.03
☐ 110	Dale Murphy	.40	.16	.04
☐ 111	Rob Deer	.15	.06	.01
☐ 112	Pete Incaviglia	.15	.06	.01
☐ 113	Vince Coleman	.20	.08	.02
☐ 114	Tim Wallach	.15	.06	.01
☐ 115	Nolan Ryan	2.00	.80	.20
☐ 116	Walt Weiss	.20	.08	.02
☐ 117	Brian Downing	.12	.05	.01
☐ 118	Melido Perez	.15	.06	.01
☐ 119	Terry Steinbach	.15	.06	.01
☐ 120	Mike Scott	.15	.06	.01
☐ 121	Tim Belcher	.15	.06	.01
☐ 122	Mike Boddicker	.12	.05	.01
☐ 123	Len Dykstra	.20	.08	.02
☐ 124	Fernando Valenzuela	.15	.06	.01
☐ 125	Gerald Young	.12	.05	.01
☐ 126	Tom Henke	.15	.06	.01
☐ 127	Dave Henderson	.15	.06	.01
☐ 128	Dan Plesac	.12	.05	.01
☐ 129	Chili Davis	.15	.06	.01
☐ 130	Bryan Harvey	.25	.10	.02
☐ 131	Don August	.12	.05	.01
☐ 132	Mike Harkey	.30	.12	.03
☐ 133	Luis Polonia	.20	.08	.02
☐ 134	Craig Worthington	.15	.06	.01
☐ 135	Joey Meyer	.12	.05	.01
☐ 136	Barry Larkin	.30	.12	.03
☐ 137	Glenn Davis	.25	.10	.02
☐ 138	Mike Scioscia	.12	.05	.01
☐ 139	Andres Galarraga	.15	.06	.01
☐ 140	Dwight Gooden	.30	.12	.03
☐ 141	Keith Moreland	.12	.05	.01
☐ 142	Kevin Mitchell	.50	.20	.05
☐ 143	Mike Greenwell	.35	.15	.03
☐ 144	Mel Hall	.15	.06	.01
☐ 145	Rickey Henderson	.75	.30	.07
☐ 146	Barry Bonds	.50	.20	.05
☐ 147	Eddie Murray	.35	.15	.03
☐ 148	Lee Smith	.20	.08	.02
☐ 149	Julio Franco	.25	.10	.02
☐ 150	Tim Raines	.15	.06	.01
☐ 151	Mitch Williams	.15	.06	.01
☐ 152	Tim Laudner	.12	.05	.01
☐ 153	Mike Pagliarulo	.12	.05	.01
☐ 154	Floyd Bannister	.12	.05	.01
☐ 155	Gary Carter	.20	.08	.02
☐ 156	Kirby Puckett	.75	.30	.07
☐ 157	Harold Baines	.15	.06	.01
☐ 158	Dave Righetti	.15	.06	.01
☐ 159	Mark Langston	.15	.06	.01
☐ 160	Tony Gwynn	.50	.20	.05
☐ 161	Tom Brunansky	.15	.06	.01
☐ 162	Vance Law	.12	.05	.01
☐ 163	Kelly Gruber	.25	.10	.02
☐ 164	Gerald Perry	.12	.05	.01
☐ 165	Harold Reynolds	.12	.05	.01
☐ 166	Andy Van Slyke	.15	.06	.01
☐ 167	Jimmy Key	.12	.05	.01
☐ 168	Jeff Reardon	.25	.10	.02
☐ 169	Milt Thompson	.12	.05	.01
☐ 170	Will Clark	1.25	.50	.12
☐ 171	Chet Lemon	.12	.05	.01
☐ 172	Pat Tabler	.12	.05	.01
☐ 173	Jim Rice	.20	.08	.02
☐ 174	Billy Hatcher	.15	.06	.01
☐ 175	Bruce Hurst	.15	.06	.01
☐ 176	John Franco	.15	.06	.01
☐ 177	Van Snider	.12	.05	.01
☐ 178	Ron Jones	.12	.05	.01
☐ 179	Jerald Clark	.15	.06	.01
☐ 180	Tom Browning	.15	.06	.01
☐ 181	Von Hayes	.15	.06	.01
☐ 182	Bobby Bonilla	.40	.16	.04
☐ 183	Todd Worrell	.15	.06	.01
☐ 184	John Kruk	.15	.06	.01
☐ 185	Scott Fletcher	.12	.05	.01
☐ 186	Willie Wilson	.15	.06	.01
☐ 187	Jody Davis	.12	.05	.01
☐ 188	Kent Hrbek	.15	.06	.01
☐ 189	Ruben Sierra	.50	.20	.05
☐ 190	Shawon Dunston	.20	.08	.02
☐ 191	Ellis Burks	.35	.15	.03
☐ 192	Brook Jacoby	.15	.06	.01
☐ 193	Jeff M. Robinson (Detroit Tigers)	.12	.05	.01
☐ 194	Rich Dotson	.12	.05	.01
☐ 195	Johnny Ray	.12	.05	.01
☐ 196	Cory Snyder	.15	.06	.01
☐ 197	Mike Witt	.12	.05	.01
☐ 198	Marty Barrett	.12	.05	.01
☐ 199	Robin Yount	.40	.16	.04
☐ 200	Mark McGwire	.50	.20	.05
☐ 201	Ryne Sandberg	.75	.30	.07
☐ 202	John Candelaria	.12	.05	.01
☐ 203	Matt Nokes	.15	.06	.01
☐ 204	Dwight Evans	.20	.08	.02
☐ 205	Darryl Strawberry	.75	.30	.07
☐ 206	Willie McGee	.20	.08	.02
☐ 207	Bobby Thigpen	.20	.08	.02
☐ 208	B.J. Surhoff	.15	.06	.01
☐ 209	Paul Molitor	.20	.08	.02
☐ 210	Jody Reed	.15	.06	.01
☐ 211	Doyle Alexander	.12	.05	.01
☐ 212	Dennis Rasmussen	.12	.05	.01
☐ 213	Kevin Gross	.12	.05	.01
☐ 214	Kirk McCaskill	.12	.05	.01
☐ 215	Alan Trammell	.25	.10	.02
☐ 216	Damon Berryhill	.15	.06	.01
☐ 217	Rick Sutcliffe	.15	.06	.01
☐ 218	Don Slaught	.12	.05	.01
☐ 219	Carlton Fisk	.35	.15	.03
☐ 220	Allan Anderson	.15	.06	.01
☐ 221	Jose Canseco	.90	.40	.09
	Wade Boggs			
	Mike Greenwell			

		MINT	EXC	G-VG
☐ 222	Orel Hershiser	.30	.12	.03
	Dennis Eckersley			
	Tom Browning			
☐ 223	Gary Sheffield	1.50	.60	.15
	Gregg Jefferies			
	Sandy Alomar Jr.			
☐ 224	Bob Milacki	.75	.30	.07
	Randy Johnson			
	Ramon Martinez			
☐ 225	Cameron Drew	.15	.06	.01
	Geronimo Berroa			
	Ron Jones			

1990 Sportflics

The 1990 Sportflics set contains 225 standard-size (2 1/2" by 3 1/2") cards. On the fronts, the black, white, orange, and yellow borders surround two photos, which can each be seen depending on the angle. The set is considered an improvement over the previous years' versions by many collectors due to the increased clarity of the fronts, caused by having two images rather than three. The backs are dominated by large color photos.

		MINT	EXC	G-VG
	COMPLETE SET (225)	40.00	18.00	6.00
	COMMON PLAYER (1-225)	.12	.05	.01
☐ 1	Kevin Mitchell	.35	.15	.03
☐ 2	Wade Boggs	.45	.18	.04
☐ 3	Cory Snyder	.15	.06	.01
☐ 4	Paul O'Neill	.15	.06	.01
☐ 5	Will Clark	.90	.40	.09
☐ 6	Tony Fernandez	.15	.06	.01
☐ 7	Ken Griffey Jr.	2.50	1.00	.25
☐ 8	Nolan Ryan	2.00	.80	.20
☐ 9	Rafael Palmeiro	.25	.10	.02
☐ 10	Jesse Barfield	.15	.06	.01
☐ 11	Kirby Puckett	.45	.18	.04
☐ 12	Steve Sax	.15	.06	.01
☐ 13	Fred McGriff	.30	.12	.03
☐ 14	Gregg Jefferies	.35	.15	.03
☐ 15	Mark Grace	.35	.15	.03
☐ 16	Ozzie Smith	.25	.10	.02
☐ 17	George Bell	.20	.08	.02
☐ 18	Robin Yount	.30	.12	.03
☐ 19	Glenn Davis	.15	.06	.01
☐ 20	Jeffrey Leonard	.12	.05	.01
☐ 21	Chili Davis	.15	.06	.01
☐ 22	Craig Biggio	.25	.10	.02
☐ 23	Jose Canseco	.90	.40	.09
☐ 24	Derek Lilliquist	.12	.05	.01
☐ 25	Chris Bosio	.15	.06	.01
☐ 26	Dave Stieb	.15	.06	.01
☐ 27	Bobby Thigpen	.15	.06	.01
☐ 28	Jack Clark	.15	.06	.01
☐ 29	Kevin Ritz	.15	.06	.01
☐ 30	Tom Gordon	.20	.08	.02
☐ 31	Bryan Harvey	.20	.08	.02
☐ 32	Jim Deshaies	.12	.05	.01
☐ 33	Terry Steinbach	.15	.06	.01
☐ 34	Tom Glavine	.35	.15	.03
☐ 35	Bob Welch	.20	.08	.02
☐ 36	Charlie Hayes	.15	.06	.01
☐ 37	Jeff Reardon	.20	.08	.02
☐ 38	Joe Orsulak	.12	.05	.01
☐ 39	Scott Garrelts	.15	.06	.01
☐ 40	Bob Boone	.15	.06	.01
☐ 41	Scott Bankhead	.15	.06	.01
☐ 42	Tom Henke	.15	.06	.01
☐ 43	Greg Briley	.15	.06	.01
☐ 44	Teddy Higuera	.15	.06	.01
☐ 45	Pat Borders	.15	.06	.01
☐ 46	Kevin Seitzer	.15	.06	.01
☐ 47	Bruce Hurst	.15	.06	.01
☐ 48	Ozzie Guillen	.15	.06	.01
☐ 49	Wally Joyner	.25	.10	.02
☐ 50	Mike Greenwell	.25	.10	.02
☐ 51	Gary Gaetti	.15	.06	.01
☐ 52	Gary Sheffield UER	.30	.12	.03
	(Uniform listed as			
	21, should be 1)			
☐ 53	Dennis Martinez	.15	.06	.01
☐ 54	Ryne Sandberg	.75	.30	.07
☐ 55	Mike Scott	.15	.06	.01
☐ 56	Todd Benzinger	.12	.05	.01
☐ 57	Kelly Gruber	.20	.08	.02
☐ 58	Jose Lind	.12	.05	.01
☐ 59	Allan Anderson	.12	.05	.01
☐ 60	Robby Thompson	.12	.05	.01
☐ 61	John Smoltz	.25	.10	.02
☐ 62	Mark Davis	.12	.05	.01
☐ 63	Tom Herr	.12	.05	.01
☐ 64	Randy Johnson	.15	.06	.01
☐ 65	Lonnie Smith	.15	.06	.01
☐ 66	Pedro Guerrero	.15	.06	.01
☐ 67	Jerome Walton	.35	.15	.03
☐ 68	Ramon Martinez	.75	.30	.07
☐ 69	Tim Raines	.15	.06	.01
☐ 70	Matt Williams	.35	.15	.03
☐ 71	Joe Oliver	.20	.08	.02
☐ 72	Nick Esasky	.15	.06	.01
☐ 73	Kevin Brown	.15	.06	.01
☐ 74	Walt Weiss	.15	.06	.01
☐ 75	Roger McDowell	.12	.05	.01
☐ 76	Jose DeLeon	.12	.05	.01
☐ 77	Brian Downing	.12	.05	.01
☐ 78	Jay Howell	.12	.05	.01
☐ 79	Jose Uribe	.12	.05	.01
☐ 80	Ellis Burks	.25	.10	.02
☐ 81	Sammy Sosa	.40	.16	.04
☐ 82	Johnny Ray	.12	.05	.01
☐ 83	Danny Darwin	.12	.05	.01
☐ 84	Carney Lansford	.15	.06	.01
☐ 85	Jose Oquendo	.12	.05	.01
☐ 86	John Cerutti	.12	.05	.01
☐ 87	Dave Winfield	.25	.10	.02
☐ 88	Dave Righetti	.15	.06	.01
☐ 89	Danny Jackson	.12	.05	.01
☐ 90	Andy Benes	.45	.18	.04
☐ 91	Tom Browning	.15	.06	.01
☐ 92	Pete O'Brien	.12	.05	.01
☐ 93	Roberto Alomar	.40	.16	.04
☐ 94	Bret Saberhagen	.25	.10	.02
☐ 95	Phil Bradley	.15	.06	.01
☐ 96	Doug Jones	.15	.06	.01
☐ 97	Eric Davis	.25	.10	.02
☐ 98	Tony Gwynn	.40	.16	.04
☐ 99	Jim Abbott	.75	.30	.07
☐ 100	Cal Ripken	.75	.30	.07
☐ 101	Andy Van Slyke	.15	.06	.01
☐ 102	Dan Plesac	.12	.05	.01
☐ 103	Lou Whitaker	.15	.06	.01
☐ 104	Steve Bedrosian	.12	.05	.01
☐ 105	Dave Gallagher	.15	.06	.01
☐ 106	Keith Hernandez	.15	.06	.01
☐ 107	Duane Ward	.12	.05	.01
☐ 108	Andre Dawson	.25	.10	.02
☐ 109	Howard Johnson	.20	.08	.02
☐ 110	Mark Langston	.20	.08	.02
☐ 111	Jerry Browne	.12	.05	.01
☐ 112	Alvin Davis	.15	.06	.01
☐ 113	Sid Fernandez	.15	.06	.01
☐ 114	Mike Devereaux	.12	.05	.01
☐ 115	Benito Santiago	.20	.08	.02
☐ 116	Bip Roberts	.15	.06	.01
☐ 117	Craig Worthington	.15	.06	.01
☐ 118	Kevin Elster	.12	.05	.01
☐ 119	Harold Reynolds	.12	.05	.01
☐ 120	Joe Carter	.30	.12	.03
☐ 121	Brian Harper	.15	.06	.01
☐ 122	Frank Viola	.20	.08	.02
☐ 123	Jeff Ballard	.12	.05	.01
☐ 124	John Kruk	.15	.06	.01
☐ 125	Harold Baines	.15	.06	.01
☐ 126	Tom Candiotti	.12	.05	.01
☐ 127	Kevin McReynolds	.15	.06	.01
☐ 128	Mookie Wilson	.15	.06	.01
☐ 129	Danny Tartabull	.25	.10	.02
☐ 130	Craig Lefferts	.12	.05	.01
☐ 131	Jose DeJesus	.12	.05	.01

☐	132	John Orton	.20	.08	.02
☐	133	Curt Schilling	.12	.05	.01
☐	134	Marquis Grissom	.45	.18	.04
☐	135	Greg Vaughn	.75	.30	.07
☐	136	Brett Butler	.15	.06	.01
☐	137	Rob Deer	.15	.06	.01
☐	138	John Franco	.15	.06	.01
☐	139	Keith Moreland	.12	.05	.01
☐	140	Dave Smith	.12	.05	.01
☐	141	Mark McGwire	.35	.15	.03
☐	142	Vince Coleman	.20	.08	.02
☐	143	Barry Bonds	.40	.16	.04
☐	144	Mike Henneman	.15	.06	.01
☐	145	Dwight Gooden	.30	.12	.03
☐	146	Darryl Strawberry	.40	.16	.04
☐	147	Von Hayes	.15	.06	.01
☐	148	Andres Galarraga	.15	.06	.01
☐	149	Roger Clemens	.75	.30	.07
☐	150	Don Mattingly	.60	.25	.06
☐	151	Joe Magrane	.15	.06	.01
☐	152	Dwight Smith	.15	.06	.01
☐	153	Ricky Jordan	.15	.06	.01
☐	154	Alan Trammell	.25	.10	.02
☐	155	Brook Jacoby	.15	.06	.01
☐	156	Len Dykstra	.15	.06	.01
☐	157	Mike LaValliere	.12	.05	.01
☐	158	Julio Franco	.25	.10	.02
☐	159	Joey Belle	.50	.20	.05
☐	160	Barry Larkin	.25	.10	.02
☐	161	Rick Reuschel	.15	.06	.01
☐	162	Nelson Santovenia	.12	.05	.01
☐	163	Mike Scioscia	.12	.05	.01
☐	164	Damon Berryhill	.12	.05	.01
☐	165	Todd Worrell	.15	.06	.01
☐	166	Jim Eisenreich	.12	.05	.01
☐	167	Ivan Calderon	.15	.06	.01
☐	168	Mauro Gozzo	.15	.06	.01
☐	169	Kirk McCaskill	.12	.05	.01
☐	170	Dennis Eckersley	.20	.08	.02
☐	171	Mickey Tettleton	.20	.08	.02
☐	172	Chuck Finley	.20	.08	.02
☐	173	Dave Magadan	.15	.06	.01
☐	174	Terry Pendleton	.25	.10	.02
☐	175	Willie Randolph	.15	.06	.01
☐	176	Jeff Huson	.15	.06	.01
☐	177	Todd Zeile	.75	.30	.07
☐	178	Steve Olin	.15	.06	.01
☐	179	Eric Anthony	.40	.16	.04
☐	180	Scott Coolbaugh	.15	.06	.01
☐	181	Rick Sutcliffe	.15	.06	.01
☐	182	Tim Wallach	.15	.06	.01
☐	183	Paul Molitor	.20	.08	.02
☐	184	Roberto Kelly	.25	.10	.02
☐	185	Mike Moore	.15	.06	.01
☐	186	Junior Felix	.25	.10	.02
☐	187	Mike Schooler	.15	.06	.01
☐	188	Ruben Sierra	.40	.16	.04
☐	189	Dale Murphy	.25	.10	.02
☐	190	Dan Gladden	.12	.05	.01
☐	191	John Smiley	.20	.08	.02
☐	192	Jeff Russell	.15	.06	.01
☐	193	Bert Blyleven	.15	.06	.01
☐	194	Dave Stewart	.15	.06	.01
☐	195	Bobby Bonilla	.35	.15	.03
☐	196	Mitch Williams	.15	.06	.01
☐	197	Orel Hershiser	.20	.08	.02
☐	198	Kevin Bass	.12	.05	.01
☐	199	Tim Burke	.12	.05	.01
☐	200	Bo Jackson	1.25	.50	.12
☐	201	David Cone	.15	.06	.01
☐	202	Gary Pettis	.12	.05	.01
☐	203	Kent Hrbek	.15	.06	.01
☐	204	Carlton Fisk	.30	.12	.03
☐	205	Bob Geren	.15	.06	.01
☐	206	Bill Spiers	.15	.06	.01
☐	207	Oddibe McDowell	.12	.05	.01
☐	208	Rickey Henderson	.90	.40	.09
☐	209	Ken Caminiti	.15	.06	.01
☐	210	Devon White	.20	.08	.02
☐	211	Greg Maddux	.15	.06	.01
☐	212	Ed Whitson	.12	.05	.01
☐	213	Carlos Martinez	.15	.06	.01
☐	214	George Brett	.40	.16	.04
☐	215	Gregg Olson	.35	.15	.03
☐	216	Kenny Rogers	.15	.06	.01
☐	217	Dwight Evans	.15	.06	.01
☐	218	Pat Tabler	.12	.05	.01
☐	219	Jeff Treadway	.12	.05	.01
☐	220	Scott Fletcher	.12	.05	.01
☐	221	Deion Sanders	.50	.20	.05
☐	222	Robin Ventura	.60	.25	.06
☐	223	Chip Hale	.15	.06	.01
☐	224	Tommy Greene	.35	.15	.03
☐	225	Dean Palmer	.45	.18	.04

1981 Squirt

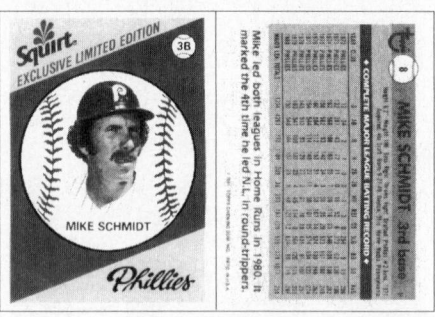

The cards in this 22-panel set consist of 33 different individual cards, each measuring 2 1/2" by 3 1/2" while the panels measure 2 1/2" by 10 1/2" as the 1981 Squirt cards were issued individually as well as in two card panels. Cards numbered 1-11 appear twice, whereas cards 12-33 appear only once in the 22-panel set. The pattern for pairings was 1/12 and 1/23, 2/13 and 2/24, 3/14 and 3/25, and so forth on up to 11/22 and 11/33. Two card panels have a value equal to the sum of the individual cards on the panel. Supposedly panels 4/15, 4/26, 5/27, and 6/28 are more difficult to find than the other panels and are marked as SP in the checklist below.

	MINT	EXC	G-VG
COMPLETE PANEL SET	20.00	8.50	2.75
COMPLETE IND. SET	11.00	5.00	1.35
COMMON PANEL	.40	.16	.04
COMMON PLAYER (1-11) DP	.25	.10	.02
COMMON PLAYER (12-33)	.25	.10	.02

☐	1	George Brett DP	.60	.25	.06
☐	2	George Foster DP	.25	.10	.02
☐	3	Ben Oglivie DP	.25	.10	.02
☐	4	Steve Garvey DP	.75	.30	.07
☐	5	Reggie Jackson DP	.90	.40	.09
☐	6	Bill Buckner DP	.25	.10	.02
☐	7	Jim Rice DP	.30	.12	.03
☐	8	Mike Schmidt DP	.90	.40	.09
☐	9	Rod Carew DP	.75	.30	.07
☐	10	Dave Parker DP	.30	.12	.03
☐	11	Pete Rose DP	.90	.40	.09
☐	12	Garry Templeton	.25	.10	.02
☐	13	Rick Burleson	.25	.10	.02
☐	14	Dave Kingman	.25	.10	.02
☐	15	Eddie Murray SP	4.00	1.75	.40
☐	16	Don Sutton	.60	.25	.06
☐	17	Dusty Baker	.25	.10	.02
☐	18	Jack Clark	.50	.20	.05
☐	19	Dave Winfield	1.25	.50	.12
☐	20	Johnny Bench	1.25	.50	.12
☐	21	Lee Mazzilli	.25	.10	.02
☐	22	Al Oliver	.25	.10	.02
☐	23	Jerry Mumphrey	.25	.10	.02
☐	24	Tony Armas	.25	.10	.02
☐	25	Fred Lynn	.30	.12	.03
☐	26	Ron LeFlore SP	1.00	.40	.10
☐	27	Steve Kemp SP	1.00	.40	.10
☐	28	Rickey Henderson SP	8.00	3.50	.80
☐	29	John Castino	.25	.10	.02
☐	30	Cecil Cooper	.25	.10	.02
☐	31	Bruce Bochte	.25	.10	.02
☐	32	Joe Charboneau	.25	.10	.02
☐	33	Chet Lemon	.25	.10	.02

1982 Squirt

The cards in this 22-card set measure 2 1/2" by 3 1/2". Although the 1982 "Exclusive Limited Edition" was prepared for Squirt by Topps, the format and pictures are completely different from the regular Topps cards of this year. Each color picture is obliquely cut and the word Squirt is printed in red in the top left corner. The cards are numbered 1 through 22 and the reverses are yellow and black on white. The cards were issued on four types of panels: (1) yellow attachment card at top with picture card in center and scratch-off game at bottom; (2) yellow attachment card at top with scratch-off game in center and picture card at bottom; (3) white attachment card at top with "Collect all 22" panel in center and picture card at bottom; (4) two card panel with attachment card at top. The two card panels have parallel cards; that is, numbers 1 and 12 together, numbers 2 and 13 together, etc. Two card panels have a value equal to the sum of the individual cards on the panel. The two types (1 and 2) with the scratch-off games are more slightly difficult to obtain than the other two types and hence command prices double those below.

	MINT	EXC	G-VG
COMPLETE SET (22)	8.00	3.50	.80
COMMON PLAYER (1-22)	.25	.10	.02
☐ 1 Cecil Cooper	.25	.10	.02
☐ 2 Jerry Remy	.25	.10	.02
☐ 3 George Brett	.90	.40	.09
☐ 4 Alan Trammell	.45	.18	.04
☐ 5 Reggie Jackson	.90	.40	.09
☐ 6 Kirk Gibson	.45	.18	.04
☐ 7 Dave Winfield	.60	.25	.06
☐ 8 Carlton Fisk	.60	.25	.06
☐ 9 Ron Guidry	.35	.15	.03
☐ 10 Dennis Leonard	.25	.10	.02
☐ 11 Rollie Fingers	.60	.25	.06
☐ 12 Pete Rose	1.00	.40	.10
☐ 13 Phil Garner	.25	.10	.02
☐ 14 Mike Schmidt	1.00	.40	.10
☐ 15 Dave Concepcion	.25	.10	.02
☐ 16 George Hendrick	.25	.10	.02
☐ 17 Andre Dawson	.60	.25	.06
☐ 18 George Foster	.35	.15	.03
☐ 19 Gary Carter	.45	.18	.04
☐ 20 Fernando Valenzuela	.35	.15	.03
☐ 21 Tom Seaver	1.00	.40	.10
☐ 22 Bruce Sutter	.35	.15	.03

1976 SSPC

The cards in this 630-card set measure 2 1/2" by 3 1/2". The 1976 "Pure Card" set issued by TCMA derives its name from the lack of borders, logos, signatures, etc., which often clutter up the picture areas of some baseball sets. It differs from other sets produced by this company in that it cannot be re-issued due to an agreement entered into by the manufacturer. Thus, while not technically a legitimate issue, it is significant because it cannot be reprinted, unlike other collector issues. There are no scarcities known. The cards are numbered in team groups, i.e., Atlanta (1-21), Cincinnati (22-46), Houston (47-65), Los Angeles (66-91), San Francisco (92-113), San Diego (114-133), Chicago White Sox (134-158), Kansas City (159-195), California (186-204), Minnesota (205-225), Milwaukee (226-251), Texas (252-273), St. Louis (274-300), Chicago Cubs (301-321), Montreal (322-351), Detroit (352-373), Baltimore (374-401), Boston (402-424), New York Yankees (425-455), Philadelphia (456-477), Oakland (478-503), Cleveland (504-532), New York Mets (533-560), and Pittsburgh (561-586). The rest of the numbers are filled in with checklists (589-595), miscellaneous players, and a heavy dose of coaches. There are a few instances in the set where the team identified on the back is different from the team shown on the front due to trades made after the completion of the 1975 season.

	NRMT	VG-E	GOOD
COMPLETE SET (630)	100.00	45.00	15.00
COMMON PLAYER (1-630)	.12	.05	.01
☐ 1 Buzz Capra	.12	.05	.01
☐ 2 Tom House	.20	.08	.02
☐ 3 Max Leon	.12	.05	.01
☐ 4 Carl Morton	.12	.05	.01
☐ 5 Phil Niekro	2.00	.80	.20
☐ 6 Mike Thompson	.12	.05	.01
☐ 7 Elias Sosa	.12	.05	.01
☐ 8 Larvell Blanks	.12	.05	.01
☐ 9 Darrell Evans	.35	.15	.03
☐ 10 Rod Gilbreath	.12	.05	.01
☐ 11 Mike Lum	.12	.05	.01
☐ 12 Craig Robinson	.12	.05	.01
☐ 13 Earl Williams	.12	.05	.01
☐ 14 Vic Correll	.12	.05	.01
☐ 15 Biff Pocoroba	.12	.05	.01
☐ 16 Dusty Baker	.20	.08	.02
☐ 17 Ralph Garr	.20	.08	.02
☐ 18 Cito Gaston	.30	.12	.03
☐ 19 Dave May	.12	.05	.01
☐ 20 Rowland Office	.12	.05	.01
☐ 21 Bob Beall	.12	.05	.01
☐ 22 Sparky Anderson MG	.50	.20	.05
☐ 23 Jack Billingham	.12	.05	.01
☐ 24 Pedro Borbon	.12	.05	.01
☐ 25 Clay Carroll	.12	.05	.01
☐ 26 Pat Darcy	.12	.05	.01
☐ 27 Don Gullett	.20	.08	.02
☐ 28 Clay Kirby	.12	.05	.01
☐ 29 Gary Nolan	.12	.05	.01
☐ 30 Fred Norman	.12	.05	.01
☐ 31 Johnny Bench	7.00	3.00	.70
☐ 32 Bill Plummer	.12	.05	.01
☐ 33 Darrel Chaney	.12	.05	.01
☐ 34 Dave Concepcion	.30	.12	.03
☐ 35 Terry Crowley	.12	.05	.01
☐ 36 Dan Driessen	.20	.08	.02
☐ 37 Doug Flynn	.12	.05	.01
☐ 38 Joe Morgan	4.50	2.00	.45
☐ 39 Tony Perez	1.50	.60	.15
☐ 40 Ken Griffey	.50	.20	.05
☐ 41 Pete Rose	10.00	4.50	1.25
☐ 42 Ed Armbrister	.12	.05	.01
☐ 43 John Vukovich	.12	.05	.01
☐ 44 George Foster	1.00	.40	.10
☐ 45 Cesar Geronimo	.12	.05	.01
☐ 46 Merv Rettenmund	.12	.05	.01
☐ 47 Jim Crawford	.12	.05	.01
☐ 48 Ken Forsch	.12	.05	.01
☐ 49 Doug Konieczny	.12	.05	.01
☐ 50 Joe Niekro	.30	.12	.03
☐ 51 Cliff Johnson	.12	.05	.01
☐ 52 Skip Jutze	.12	.05	.01
☐ 53 Milt May	.12	.05	.01
☐ 54 Rob Andrews	.12	.05	.01
☐ 55 Ken Boswell	.12	.05	.01

#	Player			
☐ 56	Tommy Helms	.20	.08	.02
☐ 57	Roger Metzger	.12	.05	.01
☐ 58	Larry Milbourne	.12	.05	.01
☐ 59	Doug Rader	.20	.08	.02
☐ 60	Bob Watson	.20	.08	.02
☐ 61	Enos Cabell	.12	.05	.01
☐ 62	Jose Cruz	.30	.12	.03
☐ 63	Cesar Cedeno	.20	.08	.02
☐ 64	Greg Gross	.12	.05	.01
☐ 65	Wilbur Howard	.12	.05	.01
☐ 66	Al Downing	.12	.05	.01
☐ 67	Burt Hooton	.12	.05	.01
☐ 68	Charlie Hough	.20	.08	.02
☐ 69	Tommy John	.75	.30	.07
☐ 70	Andy Messersmith	.20	.08	.02
☐ 71	Doug Rau	.12	.05	.01
☐ 72	Rick Rhoden	.20	.08	.02
☐ 73	Don Sutton	1.25	.50	.12
☐ 74	Rick Auerbach	.12	.05	.01
☐ 75	Ron Cey	.40	.16	.04
☐ 76	Ivan DeJesus	.12	.05	.01
☐ 77	Steve Garvey	4.00	1.75	.40
☐ 78	Lee Lacy	.12	.05	.01
☐ 79	Dave Lopes	.20	.08	.02
☐ 80	Ken McMullen	.12	.05	.01
☐ 81	Joe Ferguson	.12	.05	.01
☐ 82	Paul Powell	.12	.05	.01
☐ 83	Steve Yeager	.12	.05	.01
☐ 84	Willie Crawford	.12	.05	.01
☐ 85	Henry Cruz	.12	.05	.01
☐ 86	Charlie Manuel	.12	.05	.01
☐ 87	Manny Mota	.20	.08	.02
☐ 88	Tom Paciorek	.12	.05	.01
☐ 89	Jim Wynn	.20	.08	.02
☐ 90	Walt Alston MG	.75	.30	.07
☐ 91	Bill Buckner	.40	.16	.04
☐ 92	Jim Barr	.12	.05	.01
☐ 93	Mike Caldwell	.20	.08	.02
☐ 94	John D'Acquisto	.12	.05	.01
☐ 95	Dave Heaverlo	.12	.05	.01
☐ 96	Gary Lavelle	.12	.05	.01
☐ 97	John Montefusco	.20	.08	.02
☐ 98	Charlie Williams	.12	.05	.01
☐ 99	Chris Arnold	.12	.05	.01
☐ 100	Marc Hill	.12	.05	.01
☐ 101	Dave Rader	.12	.05	.01
☐ 102	Bruce Miller	.12	.05	.01
☐ 103	Willie Montanez	.12	.05	.01
☐ 104	Steve Ontiveros	.12	.05	.01
☐ 105	Chris Speier	.12	.05	.01
☐ 106	Derrel Thomas	.12	.05	.01
☐ 107	Gary Thomasson	.12	.05	.01
☐ 108	Glenn Adams	.12	.05	.01
☐ 109	Von Joshua	.12	.05	.01
☐ 110	Gary Matthews	.20	.08	.02
☐ 111	Bobby Murcer	.40	.16	.04
☐ 112	Horace Speed	.12	.05	.01
☐ 113	Wes Westrum MG	.12	.05	.01
☐ 114	Rich Folkers	.12	.05	.01
☐ 115	Alan Foster	.12	.05	.01
☐ 116	Dave Freisleben	.12	.05	.01
☐ 117	Dan Frisella	.12	.05	.01
☐ 118	Randy Jones	.20	.08	.02
☐ 119	Dan Spillner	.12	.05	.01
☐ 120	Larry Hardy	.12	.05	.01
☐ 121	Randy Hundley	.12	.05	.01
☐ 122	Fred Kendall	.12	.05	.01
☐ 123	John McNamara MG	.20	.08	.02
☐ 124	Tito Fuentes	.12	.05	.01
☐ 125	Enzo Hernandez	.12	.05	.01
☐ 126	Steve Huntz	.12	.05	.01
☐ 127	Mike Ivie	.12	.05	.01
☐ 128	Hector Torres	.12	.05	.01
☐ 129	Ted Kubiak	.12	.05	.01
☐ 130	John Grubb	.12	.05	.01
☐ 131	John Scott	.12	.05	.01
☐ 132	Bob Tolan	.12	.05	.01
☐ 133	Dave Winfield	6.00	2.50	.60
☐ 134	Bill Gogolewski	.12	.05	.01
☐ 135	Dan Osborn	.12	.05	.01
☐ 136	Jim Kaat	.60	.25	.06
☐ 137	Claude Osteen	.20	.08	.02
☐ 138	Cecil Upshaw	.12	.05	.01
☐ 139	Wilbur Wood	.20	.08	.02
☐ 140	Lloyd Allen	.12	.05	.01
☐ 141	Brian Downing	.25	.10	.02
☐ 142	Jim Essian	.20	.08	.02
☐ 143	Bucky Dent	.40	.16	.04
☐ 144	Jorge Orta	.12	.05	.01
☐ 145	Lee Richard	.12	.05	.01
☐ 146	Bill Stein	.12	.05	.01
☐ 147	Ken Henderson	.12	.05	.01
☐ 148	Carlos May	.12	.05	.01
☐ 149	Nyls Nyman	.12	.05	.01
☐ 150	Bob Coluccio	.12	.05	.01
☐ 151	Chuck Tanner MG	.20	.08	.02
☐ 152	Pat Kelly	.12	.05	.01
☐ 153	Jerry Hairston	.12	.05	.01
☐ 154	Pete Varney	.12	.05	.01
☐ 155	Bill Melton	.12	.05	.01
☐ 156	Rich Gossage	1.00	.40	.10
☐ 157	Terry Forster	.20	.08	.02
☐ 158	Rich Hinton	.12	.05	.01
☐ 159	Nelson Briles	.12	.05	.01
☐ 160	Al Fitzmorris	.12	.05	.01
☐ 161	Steve Mingori	.12	.05	.01
☐ 162	Marty Pattin	.12	.05	.01
☐ 163	Paul Splittorff	.20	.08	.02
☐ 164	Dennis Leonard	.20	.08	.02
☐ 165	Buck Martinez	.12	.05	.01
☐ 166	Bob Stinson	.12	.05	.01
☐ 167	George Brett	15.00	6.50	2.15
☐ 168	Harmon Killebrew	3.00	1.25	.30
☐ 169	John Mayberry	.20	.08	.02
☐ 170	Fred Patek	.12	.05	.01
☐ 171	Cookie Rojas	.12	.05	.01
☐ 172	Rodney Scott	.12	.05	.01
☐ 173	Tony Solaita	.12	.05	.01
☐ 174	Frank White	.25	.10	.02
☐ 175	Al Cowens	.20	.08	.02
☐ 176	Hal McRae	.35	.15	.03
☐ 177	Amos Otis	.25	.10	.02
☐ 178	Vada Pinson	.35	.15	.03
☐ 179	Jim Wohlford	.12	.05	.01
☐ 180	Doug Bird	.12	.05	.01
☐ 181	Mark Littell	.12	.05	.01
☐ 182	Bob McClure	.12	.05	.01
☐ 183	Steve Busby	.20	.08	.02
☐ 184	Fran Healy	.12	.05	.01
☐ 185	Whitey Herzog MG	.30	.12	.03
☐ 186	Andy Hassler	.12	.05	.01
☐ 187	Nolan Ryan	20.00	8.50	2.75
☐ 188	Bill Singer	.12	.05	.01
☐ 189	Frank Tanana	.20	.08	.02
☐ 190	Ed Figueroa	.12	.05	.01
☐ 191	Dave Collins	.20	.08	.02
☐ 192	Dick Williams MG	.20	.08	.02
☐ 193	Ellie Rodriguez	.12	.05	.01
☐ 194	Dave Chalk	.12	.05	.01
☐ 195	Winston Llenas	.12	.05	.01
☐ 196	Rudy Meoli	.12	.05	.01
☐ 197	Orlando Ramirez	.12	.05	.01
☐ 198	Jerry Remy	.12	.05	.01
☐ 199	Billy Smith	.12	.05	.01
☐ 200	Bruce Bochte	.12	.05	.01
☐ 201	Joe Lahoud	.12	.05	.01
☐ 202	Morris Nettles	.12	.05	.01
☐ 203	Mickey Rivers	.20	.08	.02
☐ 204	Leroy Stanton	.12	.05	.01
☐ 205	Vic Albury	.12	.05	.01
☐ 206	Tom Burgmeier	.12	.05	.01
☐ 207	Bill Butler	.12	.05	.01
☐ 208	Bill Campbell	.12	.05	.01
☐ 209	Ray Corbin	.12	.05	.01
☐ 210	Joe Decker	.12	.05	.01
☐ 211	Jim Hughes	.12	.05	.01
☐ 212	Ed Bane UER (photo actually Mike Pazik)	.12	.05	.01
☐ 213	Glenn Borgmann	.12	.05	.01
☐ 214	Rod Carew	7.00	3.00	.70
☐ 215	Steve Brye	.12	.05	.01
☐ 216	Dan Ford	.12	.05	.01
☐ 217	Tony Oliva	.90	.40	.09
☐ 218	Dave Goltz	.12	.05	.01
☐ 219	Bert Blyleven	.75	.30	.07
☐ 220	Larry Hisle	.12	.05	.01
☐ 221	Steve Braun	.12	.05	.01
☐ 222	Jerry Terrell	.12	.05	.01
☐ 223	Eric Soderholm	.12	.05	.01
☐ 224	Phil Roof	.12	.05	.01
☐ 225	Danny Thompson	.12	.05	.01
☐ 226	Jim Colborn	.12	.05	.01
☐ 227	Tom Murphy	.12	.05	.01
☐ 228	Ed Rodriquez	.12	.05	.01
☐ 229	Jim Slaton	.12	.05	.01
☐ 230	Ed Sprague	.12	.05	.01
☐ 231	Charlie Moore	.12	.05	.01
☐ 232	Darrell Porter	.12	.05	.01
☐ 233	Kurt Bevacqua	.12	.05	.01
☐ 234	Pedro Garcia	.12	.05	.01
☐ 235	Mike Hegan	.12	.05	.01
☐ 236	Don Money	.12	.05	.01
☐ 237	George Scott	.20	.08	.02
☐ 238	Robin Yount	15.00	6.50	2.15
☐ 239	Hank Aaron	9.00	4.00	.90
☐ 240	Rob Ellis	.12	.05	.01
☐ 241	Sixto Lezcano	.12	.05	.01

#	Name			
☐ 242	Bob Mitchell	.12	.05	.01
☐ 243	Gorman Thomas	.25	.10	.02
☐ 244	Bill Travers	.12	.05	.01
☐ 245	Pete Broberg	.12	.05	.01
☐ 246	Bill Sharp	.12	.05	.01
☐ 247	Bobby Darwin	.12	.05	.01
☐ 248	Rick Austin UER	.12	.05	.01
	(photo actually			
	Larry Anderson)			
☐ 249	Larry Anderson UER	.12	.05	.01
	(photo actually			
	Rick Austin)			
☐ 250	Tom Bianco	.12	.05	.01
☐ 251	Lafayette Currence	.12	.05	.01
☐ 252	Steve Foucault	.12	.05	.01
☐ 253	Bill Hands	.12	.05	.01
☐ 254	Steve Hargan	.12	.05	.01
☐ 255	Fergie Jenkins	4.00	1.75	.40
☐ 256	Bob Sheldon	.12	.05	.01
☐ 257	Jim Umbarger	.12	.05	.01
☐ 258	Clyde Wright	.12	.05	.01
☐ 259	Bill Fahey	.12	.05	.01
☐ 260	Jim Sundberg	.20	.08	.02
☐ 261	Leo Cardenas	.12	.05	.01
☐ 262	Jim Fregosi	.25	.10	.02
☐ 263	Mike Hargrove	.20	.08	.02
☐ 264	Toby Harrah	.20	.08	.02
☐ 265	Roy Howell	.12	.05	.01
☐ 266	Lenny Randle	.12	.05	.01
☐ 267	Roy Smalley	.20	.08	.02
☐ 268	Jim Spencer	.12	.05	.01
☐ 269	Jeff Burroughs	.20	.08	.02
☐ 270	Tom Grieve	.20	.08	.02
☐ 271	Joe Lovitto	.12	.05	.01
☐ 272	Frank Lucchesi MG	.12	.05	.01
☐ 273	Dave Nelson	.12	.05	.01
☐ 274	Ted Simmons	.90	.40	.09
☐ 275	Lou Brock	4.00	1.75	.40
☐ 276	Ron Fairly	.12	.05	.01
☐ 277	Bake McBride	.12	.05	.01
☐ 278	Reggie Smith	.30	.12	.03
☐ 279	Willie Davis	.20	.08	.02
☐ 280	Ken Reitz	.12	.05	.01
☐ 281	Buddy Bradford	.12	.05	.01
☐ 282	Luis Melendez	.12	.05	.01
☐ 283	Mike Tyson	.12	.05	.01
☐ 284	Ted Sizemore	.12	.05	.01
☐ 285	Mario Guerrero	.12	.05	.01
☐ 286	Larry Lintz	.12	.05	.01
☐ 287	Ken Rudolph	.12	.05	.01
☐ 288	Dick Billings	.12	.05	.01
☐ 289	Jerry Mumphrey	.12	.05	.01
☐ 290	Mike Wallace	.12	.05	.01
☐ 291	Al Hrabosky	.20	.08	.02
☐ 292	Ken Reynolds	.12	.05	.01
☐ 293	Mike Garman	.12	.05	.01
☐ 294	Bob Forsch	.20	.08	.02
☐ 295	John Denny	.20	.08	.02
☐ 296	Harry Rasmussen	.12	.05	.01
☐ 297	Lynn McGlothen	.12	.05	.01
☐ 298	Mike Barlow	.12	.05	.01
☐ 299	Greg Terlecky	.12	.05	.01
☐ 300	Red Schoendienst MG	.75	.30	.07
☐ 301	Rick Reuschel	.40	.16	.04
☐ 302	Steve Stone	.20	.08	.02
☐ 303	Bill Bonham	.12	.05	.01
☐ 304	Oscar Zamora	.12	.05	.01
☐ 305	Ken Frailing	.12	.05	.01
☐ 306	Milt Wilcox	.12	.05	.01
☐ 307	Darold Knowles	.12	.05	.01
☐ 308	Jim Marshall MG	.12	.05	.01
☐ 309	Bill Madlock	.75	.30	.07
☐ 310	Jose Cardenal	.12	.05	.01
☐ 311	Rick Monday	.20	.08	.02
☐ 312	Jerry Morales	.12	.05	.01
☐ 313	Tim Hosley	.12	.05	.01
☐ 314	Gene Hiser	.12	.05	.01
☐ 315	Don Kessinger	.20	.08	.02
☐ 316	Manny Trillo	.12	.05	.01
☐ 317	Pete LaCock	.12	.05	.01
☐ 318	George Mitterwald	.12	.05	.01
☐ 319	Steve Swisher	.12	.05	.01
☐ 320	Rob Sperring	.12	.05	.01
☐ 321	Vic Harris	.12	.05	.01
☐ 322	Ron Dunn	.12	.05	.01
☐ 323	Jose Morales	.12	.05	.01
☐ 324	Pete Mackanin	.12	.05	.01
☐ 325	Jim Cox	.12	.05	.01
☐ 326	Larry Parrish	.35	.15	.03
☐ 327	Mike Jorgensen	.12	.05	.01
☐ 328	Tim Foli	.12	.05	.01
☐ 329	Hal Breeden	.12	.05	.01
☐ 330	Nate Colbert	.12	.05	.01
☐ 331	Pepe Frias	.12	.05	.01
☐ 332	Pat Scanlon	.12	.05	.01
☐ 333	Bob Bailey	.12	.05	.01
☐ 334	Gary Carter	4.50	2.00	.45
☐ 335	Pepe Mangual	.12	.05	.01
☐ 336	Larry Biittner	.12	.05	.01
☐ 337	Jim Lyttle	.12	.05	.01
☐ 338	Gary Roenicke	.12	.05	.01
☐ 339	Tony Scott	.12	.05	.01
☐ 340	Jerry White	.12	.05	.01
☐ 341	Jim Dwyer	.12	.05	.01
☐ 342	Ellis Valentine	.12	.05	.01
☐ 343	Fred Scherman	.12	.05	.01
☐ 344	Dennis Blair	.12	.05	.01
☐ 345	Woodie Fryman	.12	.05	.01
☐ 346	Chuck Taylor	.12	.05	.01
☐ 347	Dan Warthen	.12	.05	.01
☐ 348	Dan Carrithers	.12	.05	.01
☐ 349	Steve Rogers	.20	.08	.02
☐ 350	Dale Murray	.12	.05	.01
☐ 351	Duke Snider CO	3.00	1.25	.30
☐ 352	Ralph Houk MG	.20	.08	.02
☐ 353	John Hiller	.20	.08	.02
☐ 354	Mickey Lolich	.40	.16	.04
☐ 355	Dave Lemancyzk	.12	.05	.01
☐ 356	Lerrin LaGrow	.12	.05	.01
☐ 357	Fred Arroyo	.12	.05	.01
☐ 358	Joe Coleman	.12	.05	.01
☐ 359	Ben Oglivie	.20	.08	.02
☐ 360	Willie Horton	.20	.08	.02
☐ 361	John Knox	.12	.05	.01
☐ 362	Leon Roberts	.12	.05	.01
☐ 363	Ron LeFlore	.20	.08	.02
☐ 364	Gary Sutherland	.12	.05	.01
☐ 365	Dan Meyer	.12	.05	.01
☐ 366	Aurelio Rodriguez	.12	.05	.01
☐ 367	Tom Veryzer	.12	.05	.01
☐ 368	Jack Pierce	.12	.05	.01
☐ 369	Gene Michael	.20	.08	.02
☐ 370	Billy Baldwin	.12	.05	.01
☐ 371	Gates Brown	.20	.08	.02
☐ 372	Mickey Stanley	.20	.08	.02
☐ 373	Terry Humphrey	.12	.05	.01
☐ 374	Doyle Alexander	.25	.10	.02
☐ 375	Mike Cuellar	.20	.08	.02
☐ 376	Wayne Garland	.12	.05	.01
☐ 377	Ross Grimsley	.12	.05	.01
☐ 378	Grant Jackson	.12	.05	.01
☐ 379	Dyar Miller	.12	.05	.01
☐ 380	Jim Palmer	5.00	2.25	.50
☐ 381	Mike Torrez	.12	.05	.01
☐ 382	Mike Willis	.12	.05	.01
☐ 383	Dave Duncan	.20	.08	.02
☐ 384	Ellie Hendricks	.12	.05	.01
☐ 385	Jim Hutto	.12	.05	.01
☐ 386	Bob Bailor	.12	.05	.01
☐ 387	Doug DeCinces	.30	.12	.03
☐ 388	Bob Grich	.25	.10	.02
☐ 389	Lee May	.25	.10	.02
☐ 390	Tony Muser	.12	.05	.01
☐ 391	Tim Nordbrook	.12	.05	.01
☐ 392	Brooks Robinson	5.00	2.25	.50
☐ 393	Royle Stillman	.12	.05	.01
☐ 394	Don Baylor	.40	.16	.04
☐ 395	Paul Blair	.20	.08	.02
☐ 396	Al Bumbry	.12	.05	.01
☐ 397	Larry Harlow	.12	.05	.01
☐ 398	Tommy Davis	.20	.08	.02
☐ 399	Jim Northrup	.20	.08	.02
☐ 400	Ken Singleton	.25	.10	.02
☐ 401	Tom Shopay	.12	.05	.01
☐ 402	Fred Lynn	1.00	.40	.10
☐ 403	Carlton Fisk	4.00	1.75	.40
☐ 404	Cecil Cooper	.50	.20	.05
☐ 405	Jim Rice	3.00	1.25	.30
☐ 406	Juan Beniquez	.20	.08	.02
☐ 407	Denny Doyle	.12	.05	.01
☐ 408	Dwight Evans	1.00	.40	.10
☐ 409	Carl Yastrzemski	8.00	3.50	.80
☐ 410	Rick Burleson	.20	.08	.02
☐ 411	Bernie Carbo	.12	.05	.01
☐ 412	Doug Griffin	.12	.05	.01
☐ 413	Rico Petrocelli	.20	.08	.02
☐ 414	Bob Montgomery	.12	.05	.01
☐ 415	Tim Blackwell	.12	.05	.01
☐ 416	Rick Miller	.12	.05	.01
☐ 417	Darrell Johnson MG	.12	.05	.01
☐ 418	Jim Burton	.12	.05	.01
☐ 419	Jim Willoughby	.12	.05	.01
☐ 420	Rogelio Moret	.12	.05	.01
☐ 421	Bill Lee	.20	.08	.02
☐ 422	Dick Drago	.12	.05	.01
☐ 423	Diego Segui	.12	.05	.01
☐ 424	Luis Tiant	.35	.15	.03
☐ 425	Jim Hunter	3.50	1.50	.35

☐ 426	Rick Sawyer	.12	.05	.01
☐ 427	Rudy May	.12	.05	.01
☐ 428	Dick Tidrow	.12	.05	.01
☐ 429	Sparky Lyle	.50	.20	.05
☐ 430	Doc Medich	.12	.05	.01
☐ 431	Pat Dobson	.20	.08	.02
☐ 432	Dave Pagan	.12	.05	.01
☐ 433	Thurman Munson	4.50	2.00	.45
☐ 434	Chris Chambliss	.30	.12	.03
☐ 435	Roy White	.20	.08	.02
☐ 436	Walt Williams	.12	.05	.01
☐ 437	Graig Nettles	.75	.30	.07
☐ 438	Rick Dempsey	.20	.08	.02
☐ 439	Bobby Bonds	.50	.20	.05
☐ 440	Ed Herrmann	.12	.05	.01
☐ 441	Sandy Alomar	.12	.05	.01
☐ 442	Fred Stanley	.12	.05	.01
☐ 443	Terry Whitfield	.12	.05	.01
☐ 444	Rich Bladt	.12	.05	.01
☐ 445	Lou Piniella	.50	.20	.05
☐ 446	Rich Coggins	.12	.05	.01
☐ 447	Ed Brinkman	.12	.05	.01
☐ 448	Jim Mason	.12	.05	.01
☐ 449	Larry Murray	.12	.05	.01
☐ 450	Ron Blomberg	.12	.05	.01
☐ 451	Elliott Maddox	.12	.05	.01
☐ 452	Kerry Dineen	.12	.05	.01
☐ 453	Billy Martin MG	1.00	.40	.10
☐ 454	Dave Bergman	.12	.05	.01
☐ 455	Otto Velez	.12	.05	.01
☐ 456	Joe Hoerner	.12	.05	.01
☐ 457	Tug McGraw	.40	.16	.04
☐ 458	Gene Garber	.20	.08	.02
☐ 459	Steve Carlton	4.50	2.00	.45
☐ 460	Larry Christenson	.12	.05	.01
☐ 461	Tom Underwood	.12	.05	.01
☐ 462	Jim Lonborg	.20	.08	.02
☐ 463	Jay Johnstone	.20	.08	.02
☐ 464	Larry Bowa	.35	.15	.03
☐ 465	Dave Cash	.12	.05	.01
☐ 466	Ollie Brown	.12	.05	.01
☐ 467	Greg Luzinski	.30	.12	.03
☐ 468	Johnny Oates	.12	.05	.01
☐ 469	Mike Anderson	.12	.05	.01
☐ 470	Mike Schmidt	15.00	6.50	2.15
☐ 471	Bob Boone	.60	.25	.06
☐ 472	Tom Hutton	.12	.05	.01
☐ 473	Rich Allen	.50	.20	.05
☐ 474	Tony Taylor	.12	.05	.01
☐ 475	Jerry Martin	.12	.05	.01
☐ 476	Danny Ozark MG	.12	.05	.01
☐ 477	Dick Ruthven	.12	.05	.01
☐ 478	Jim Todd	.12	.05	.01
☐ 479	Paul Lindblad	.12	.05	.01
☐ 480	Rollie Fingers	3.50	1.50	.35
☐ 481	Vida Blue	.30	.12	.03
☐ 482	Ken Holtzman	.20	.08	.02
☐ 483	Dick Bosman	.12	.05	.01
☐ 484	Sonny Siebert	.12	.05	.01
☐ 485	Glenn Abbott	.12	.05	.01
☐ 486	Stan Bahnsen	.12	.05	.01
☐ 487	Mike Norris	.20	.08	.02
☐ 488	Alvin Dark MG	.12	.05	.01
☐ 489	Claudell Washington	.20	.08	.02
☐ 490	Joe Rudi	.20	.08	.02
☐ 491	Bill North	.12	.05	.01
☐ 492	Bert Campaneris	.20	.08	.02
☐ 493	Gene Tenace	.20	.08	.02
☐ 494	Reggie Jackson	10.00	4.50	1.25
☐ 495	Phil Garner	.20	.08	.02
☐ 496	Billy Williams	3.00	1.25	.30
☐ 497	Sal Bando	.20	.08	.02
☐ 498	Jim Holt	.12	.05	.01
☐ 499	Ted Martinez	.12	.05	.01
☐ 500	Ray Fosse	.12	.05	.01
☐ 501	Matt Alexander	.12	.05	.01
☐ 502	Larry Haney	.12	.05	.01
☐ 503	Angel Mangual	.12	.05	.01
☐ 504	Fred Beene	.12	.05	.01
☐ 505	Tom Buskey	.12	.05	.01
☐ 506	Dennis Eckersley	10.00	4.50	1.25
☐ 507	Roric Harrison	.12	.05	.01
☐ 508	Don Hood	.12	.05	.01
☐ 509	Jim Kern	.12	.05	.01
☐ 510	Dave LaRoche	.12	.05	.01
☐ 511	Fritz Peterson	.12	.05	.01
☐ 512	Jim Strickland	.12	.05	.01
☐ 513	Rick Waits	.12	.05	.01
☐ 514	Alan Ashby	.12	.05	.01
☐ 515	John Ellis	.12	.05	.01
☐ 516	Rick Cerone	.12	.05	.01
☐ 517	Buddy Bell	.40	.16	.04
☐ 518	Jack Brohamer	.12	.05	.01
☐ 519	Rico Carty	.20	.08	.02
☐ 520	Ed Crosby	.12	.05	.01
☐ 521	Frank Duffy	.12	.05	.01
☐ 522	Duane Kuiper UER (photo actually Rick Manning)	.12	.05	.01
☐ 523	Joe Lis	.12	.05	.01
☐ 524	Boog Powell	.60	.25	.06
☐ 525	Frank Robinson	4.00	1.75	.40
☐ 526	Oscar Gamble	.20	.08	.02
☐ 527	George Hendrick	.20	.08	.02
☐ 528	John Lowenstein	.12	.05	.01
☐ 529	Rick Manning UER (photo actually Duane Kuiper)	.12	.05	.01
☐ 530	Tommy Smith	.12	.05	.01
☐ 531	Charlie Spikes	.12	.05	.01
☐ 532	Steve Kline	.12	.05	.01
☐ 533	Ed Kranepool	.20	.08	.02
☐ 534	Mike Vail	.12	.05	.01
☐ 535	Del Unser	.12	.05	.01
☐ 536	Felix Millan	.12	.05	.01
☐ 537	Rusty Staub	.35	.15	.03
☐ 538	Jesus Alou	.12	.05	.01
☐ 539	Wayne Garrett	.12	.05	.01
☐ 540	Mike Phillips	.12	.05	.01
☐ 541	Joe Torre	.60	.25	.06
☐ 542	Dave Kingman	.75	.30	.07
☐ 543	Gene Clines	.12	.05	.01
☐ 544	Jack Heidemann	.12	.05	.01
☐ 545	Bud Harrelson	.20	.08	.02
☐ 546	John Stearns	.20	.08	.02
☐ 547	John Milner	.20	.08	.02
☐ 548	Bob Apodaca	.12	.05	.01
☐ 549	Skip Lockwood	.12	.05	.01
☐ 550	Ken Sanders	.12	.05	.01
☐ 551	Tom Seaver	9.00	4.00	.90
☐ 552	Rick Baldwin	.12	.05	.01
☐ 553	Hank Webb	.12	.05	.01
☐ 554	Jon Matlack	.20	.08	.02
☐ 555	Randy Tate	.12	.05	.01
☐ 556	Tom Hall	.12	.05	.01
☐ 557	George Stone	.12	.05	.01
☐ 558	Craig Swan	.20	.08	.02
☐ 559	Jerry Cram	.12	.05	.01
☐ 560	Roy Staiger	.12	.05	.01
☐ 561	Kent Tekulve	.20	.08	.02
☐ 562	Jerry Reuss	.20	.08	.02
☐ 563	John Candelaria	.25	.10	.02
☐ 564	Larry Demery	.12	.05	.01
☐ 565	Dave Giusti	.20	.08	.02
☐ 566	Jim Rooker	.12	.05	.01
☐ 567	Ramon Hernandez	.12	.05	.01
☐ 568	Bruce Kison	.12	.05	.01
☐ 569	Ken Brett	.12	.05	.01
☐ 570	Bob Moose	.20	.08	.02
☐ 571	Manny Sanguillen	.20	.08	.02
☐ 572	Dave Parker	3.00	1.25	.30
☐ 573	Willie Stargell	4.00	1.75	.40
☐ 574	Richie Zisk	.20	.08	.02
☐ 575	Rennie Stennett	.12	.05	.01
☐ 576	Al Oliver	.75	.30	.07
☐ 577	Bill Robinson	.30	.12	.03
☐ 578	Bob Robertson	.12	.05	.01
☐ 579	Rich Hebner	.12	.05	.01
☐ 580	Ed Kirkpatrick	.12	.05	.01
☐ 581	Duffy Dyer	.12	.05	.01
☐ 582	Craig Reynolds	.12	.05	.01
☐ 583	Frank Taveras	.12	.05	.01
☐ 584	Willie Randolph	1.25	.50	.12
☐ 585	Art Howe	.25	.10	.02
☐ 586	Danny Murtaugh MG	.12	.05	.01
☐ 587	Rick McKinney	.12	.05	.01
☐ 588	Ed Goodson	.12	.05	.01
☐ 589	Checklist 1 George Brett Al Cowens	1.25	.50	.12
☐ 590	Checklist 2 Keith Hernandez Lou Brock	1.25	.50	.12
☐ 591	Checklist 3 Jerry Koosman Duke Snider	.75	.30	.07
☐ 592	Checklist 4 Maury Wills John Knox	.25	.10	.02
☐ 593A	Checklist 5 ERR Jim Hunter Nolan Ryan (Noland on front)	100.00	45.00	15.00
☐ 593B	Checklist 5 COR Jim Hunter Nolan Ryan	6.00	2.50	.60

			NRMT	VG-E	GOOD
☐ 594	Checklist 6		.30	.12	.03
	Ralph Branca				
	Carl Erskine				
	Pee Wee Reese				
☐ 595	Checklist 7		.75	.30	.07
	Willie Mays				
	Herb Score				
☐ 596	Larry Cox		.12	.05	.01
☐ 597	Gene Mauch MG		.20	.08	.02
☐ 598	Whitey Wietelmann CO		.12	.05	.01
☐ 599	Wayne Simpson		.12	.05	.01
☐ 600	Mel Thomason		.12	.05	.01
☐ 601	Ike Hampton		.12	.05	.01
☐ 602	Ken Crosby		.12	.05	.01
☐ 603	Ralph Rowe		.12	.05	.01
☐ 604	Jim Tyrone		.12	.05	.01
☐ 605	Mick Kelleher		.12	.05	.01
☐ 606	Mario Mendoza		.12	.05	.01
☐ 607	Mike Rogodzinski		.12	.05	.01
☐ 608	Bob Gallagher		.12	.05	.01
☐ 609	Jerry Koosman		.25	.10	.02
☐ 610	Joe Frazier MG		.12	.05	.01
☐ 611	Karl Kuehl MG		.12	.05	.01
☐ 612	Frank LaCorte		.12	.05	.01
☐ 613	Ray Bare		.12	.05	.01
☐ 614	Billy Muffett CO		.12	.05	.01
☐ 615	Bill Laxton		.12	.05	.01
☐ 616	Willie Mays CO		7.00	3.00	.70
☐ 617	Phil Cavarretta CO		.20	.08	.02
☐ 618	Ted Kluszewski CO		.40	.16	.04
☐ 619	Elston Howard CO		.35	.15	.03
☐ 620	Alex Grammas CO		.12	.05	.01
☐ 621	Mickey Vernon CO		.20	.08	.02
☐ 622	Dick Sisler CO		.12	.05	.01
☐ 623	Harvey Haddix CO		.20	.08	.02
☐ 624	Bobby Winkles CO		.12	.05	.01
☐ 625	John Pesky CO		.12	.05	.01
☐ 626	Jim Davenport CO		.20	.08	.02
☐ 627	Dave Tomlin		.12	.05	.01
☐ 628	Roger Craig CO		.35	.15	.03
☐ 629	Joe Amalfitano CO		.12	.05	.01
☐ 630	Jim Reese CO		.20	.08	.02

1953 Stahl Meyer

The cards in this nine-card set measure approximately 3 1/4" by 4 1/2". The 1953 Stahl Meyer set of full color, unnumbered cards includes three players from each of the three New York teams. The cards have white borders. The Lockman card is the most plentiful of any card in the set. Some batting and fielding statistics and short biography are included on the back. The cards are ordered in the checklist below by alphabetical order without regard to team affiliation.

		NRMT	VG-E	GOOD
COMPLETE SET		4250.00	1800.00	400.00
COMMON PLAYER (1-9)		125.00	57.50	18.75
☐ 1	Hank Bauer	150.00	67.50	22.50
☐ 2	Roy Campanella	600.00	270.00	90.00
☐ 3	Gil Hodges	300.00	135.00	45.00
☐ 4	Monte Irvin	200.00	90.00	30.00
☐ 5	Whitey Lockman	125.00	57.50	18.75
☐ 6	Mickey Mantle	2250.00	900.00	225.00

			NRMT	VG-E	GOOD
☐ 7	Phil Rizzuto		300.00	135.00	45.00
☐ 8	Duke Snider		600.00	270.00	90.00
☐ 9	Bobby Thomson		150.00	67.50	22.50

1954 Stahl Meyer

The cards in this 12-card set measure approximately 3 1/4" by 4 1/2". The 1954 Stahl Meyer set of full color, unnumbered cards includes four players from each of the three New York teams. The cards have yellow borders and the backs, oriented horizontally, include an ad for a baseball kit and the player's statistics. No player biography is included on the back. The cards are ordered in the checklist below by alphabetical order without regard to team affiliation.

		NRMT	VG-E	GOOD
COMPLETE SET		6750.00	2700.00	675.00
COMMON PLAYER (1-12)		175.00	80.00	27.00
☐ 1	Hank Bauer	200.00	90.00	30.00
☐ 2	Carl Erskine	200.00	90.00	30.00
☐ 3	Gil Hodges	325.00	150.00	50.00
☐ 4	Monte Irvin	275.00	120.00	40.00
☐ 5	Whitey Lockman	175.00	80.00	27.00
☐ 6	Mickey Mantle	3000.00	1200.00	300.00
☐ 7	Willie Mays	1500.00	600.00	150.00
☐ 8	Gil McDougald	200.00	90.00	30.00
☐ 9	Don Mueller	175.00	80.00	27.00
☐ 10	Don Newcombe	200.00	90.00	30.00
☐ 11	Phil Rizzuto	325.00	150.00	50.00
☐ 12	Duke Snider	650.00	300.00	100.00

1955 Stahl Meyer

The cards in this 12 card set measure approximately 3 1/4" by 4 1/2". The 1955 Stahl Meyer set of full color, unnumbered cards contains four players each from the three New York teams. As in the 1954 set, the cards have yellow borders; however, the back of the cards contain a sketch of Mickey Mantle with an ad for a baseball cap or a pennant. The cards are ordered in the checklist below by alphabetical order without regard to team affiliation.

	NRMT	VG-E	GOOD
COMPLETE SET	5500.00	2200.00	550.00
COMMON PLAYER (1-12)	175.00	80.00	27.00
☐ 1 Hank Bauer	200.00	90.00	30.00
☐ 2 Carl Erskine	200.00	90.00	30.00
☐ 3 Gil Hodges	325.00	150.00	50.00
☐ 4 Monte Irvin	275.00	120.00	40.00
☐ 5 Whitey Lockman	175.00	80.00	27.00
☐ 6 Mickey Mantle	3000.00	1200.00	300.00
☐ 7 Gil McDougald	200.00	90.00	30.00
☐ 8 Don Mueller	175.00	80.00	27.00
☐ 9 Don Newcombe	200.00	90.00	30.00
☐ 10 Dusty Rhodes	175.00	80.00	27.00
☐ 11 Phil Rizzuto	325.00	150.00	50.00
☐ 12 Duke Snider	650.00	300.00	100.00

☐ 20 Chris Sabo	.30	.12	.03
☐ 21 Darryl Strawberry	.50	.20	.05
☐ 22 Wade Boggs	.50	.20	.05
☐ 23 Tim Raines	.25	.10	.02
☐ 24 Alan Trammell	.30	.12	.03
☐ 25 Chris Sabo	.30	.12	.03
☐ 26 Nolan Ryan	.75	.30	.07
☐ 27 Mark McGwire	.45	.18	.04
☐ 28 Don Mattingly	.60	.25	.06
☐ 29 Tony Gwynn	.45	.18	.04
☐ 30 Glenn Davis	.25	.10	.02
☐ 31 Bobby Bonilla	.40	.16	.04
☐ 32 Gregg Jefferies	.40	.16	.04
☐ 33 Ruben Sierra	.45	.18	.04
☐ 34 John Smoltz	.30	.12	.03
☐ 35 Don Mattingly	.60	.25	.06
☐ 36 Bret Saberhagen	.30	.12	.03
☐ 37 Darryl Strawberry	.50	.20	.05
☐ 38 Eric Davis	.35	.15	.03
☐ 39 Tim Raines	.25	.10	.02
☐ 40 Mark Grace	.40	.16	.04

1990 Starline Long John Silver

The 1990 Starline Long John Silver set was issued over an eight-week promotion, five cards at a time within a cello pack. The set was initially available only through the Long John Silver seafood fast-food chain with one pack being given to each customer who ordered a meal with a 32-ounce Coke. However after the promotion was over, leftover sets found their way into the organized card-collecting hobby. This 40-card, standard-size (2 1/2" by 3 1/2") set was featured the best of today's players. There are several cards for some of the players in the set. After the promotion at Long John Silver had been completed, there were reportedly more than 100,000 sets left over that were released into the organized hobby.

	MINT	EXC	G-VG
COMPLETE SET (40)	11.00	5.00	1.35
COMMON PLAYER (1-40)	.25	.10	.02
☐ 1 Don Mattingly	.60	.25	.06
☐ 2 Mark Grace	.40	.16	.04
☐ 3 Eric Davis	.35	.15	.03
☐ 4 Tony Gwynn	.45	.18	.04
☐ 5 Bobby Bonilla	.40	.16	.04
☐ 6 Wade Boggs	.50	.20	.05
☐ 7 Frank Viola	.25	.10	.02
☐ 8 Ruben Sierra	.45	.18	.04
☐ 9 Mark McGwire	.40	.16	.04
☐ 10 Alan Trammell	.30	.12	.03
☐ 11 Mark McGwire	.40	.16	.04
☐ 12 Gregg Jefferies	.40	.16	.04
☐ 13 Nolan Ryan	.75	.30	.07
☐ 14 John Smoltz	.30	.12	.03
☐ 15 Glenn Davis	.25	.10	.02
☐ 16 Mark Grace	.40	.16	.04
☐ 17 Wade Boggs	.50	.20	.05
☐ 18 Frank Viola	.25	.10	.02
☐ 19 Bret Saberhagen	.30	.12	.03

1962 Sugardale

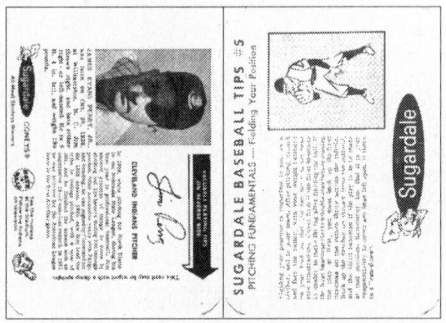

The cards in this 22-card set measure 3 3/4" by 5 1/8". The 1962 Sugardale Meats set of black and white, numbered and lettered cards features the Cleveland Indians and the Pittsburgh Pirates. The Indians are numbered while the Pirates are lettered. The backs, in red print, give player tips. The Bob Nieman card was just recently discovered and is quite scarce. The catalog designation is F174-1.

	NRMT	VG-E	GOOD
COMPLETE SET (22)	2000.00	800.00	200.00
COMMON PLAYER (1-19)	50.00	22.50	7.50
COMMON PLAYER (A-D)	75.00	34.00	11.25
☐ 1 Barry Latman	50.00	22.50	7.50
☐ 2 Gary Bell	50.00	22.50	7.50
☐ 3 Dick Donovan	50.00	22.50	7.50
☐ 4 Frank Funk	50.00	22.50	7.50
☐ 5 Jim Perry	75.00	34.00	11.25
☐ 6 Not issued	00.00	00.00	0.00
☐ 7 John Romano	50.00	22.50	7.50
☐ 8 Ty Cline	50.00	22.50	7.50
☐ 9 Tito Francona	50.00	22.50	7.50
☐ 10 Bob Nieman	250.00	110.00	37.50
☐ 11 Willie Kirkland	50.00	22.50	7.50
☐ 12 Woody Held	50.00	22.50	7.50
☐ 13 Jerry Kindall	50.00	22.50	7.50
☐ 14 Bubba Phillips	50.00	22.50	7.50
☐ 15 Mel Harder CO	60.00	27.00	9.00
☐ 16 Salty Parker CO	50.00	22.50	7.50
☐ 17 Ray Katt CO	50.00	22.50	7.50
☐ 18 Mel McGaha MG	50.00	22.50	7.50
☐ 19 Pedro Ramos	50.00	22.50	7.50
☐ A Dick Groat	90.00	40.00	13.50
☐ B Robert Clemente	900.00	400.00	135.00
☐ C Don Hoak	75.00	34.00	11.25
☐ D Dick Stuart	90.00	40.00	13.50

1963 Sugardale

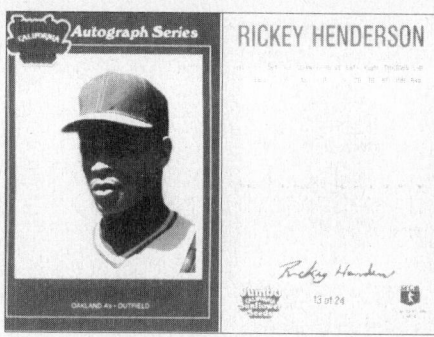

The cards in this 31-card set measure 3 3/4" by 5 1/8". The 1963 Sugardale Meats set of 31 black and white, numbered cards features the Cleveland Indians and Pittsburgh Pirates. The backs are printed in red and give player tips. The 1963 Sugardale set can be distinguished from the 1962 Sugardale set by examining the biographies on the card for mention of the 1962 season. The Perry and Skinner cards were withdrawn after June trades and are difficult to obtain.

		NRMT	VG-E	GOOD
COMPLETE SET (31)		1800.00	725.00	180.00
COMMON PLAYER (1-33)		50.00	22.50	7.50
COMMON PLAYER (34-38)		75.00	34.00	11.25
☐ 1	Barry Latman	50.00	22.50	7.50
☐ 2	Gary Bell	50.00	22.50	7.50
☐ 3	Dick Donovan	50.00	22.50	7.50
☐ 4	Joe Adcock	75.00	34.00	11.25
☐ 5	Jim Perry	175.00	80.00	27.00
☐ 6	Not issued	00.00	00.00	0.00
☐ 7	John Romano	50.00	22.50	7.50
☐ 8	Mike de la Hoz	50.00	22.50	7.50
☐ 9	Tito Francona	50.00	22.50	7.50
☐ 10	Gene Green	50.00	22.50	7.50
☐ 11	Willie Kirkland	50.00	22.50	7.50
☐ 12	Woody Held	50.00	22.50	7.50
☐ 13	Jerry Kindall	50.00	22.50	7.50
☐ 14	Max Alvis	50.00	22.50	7.50
☐ 15	Mel Harder	60.00	27.00	9.00
☐ 16	George Strickland	50.00	22.50	7.50
☐ 17	Elmer Valo	50.00	22.50	7.50
☐ 18	Birdie Tebbetts	50.00	22.50	7.50
☐ 19	Pedro Ramos	50.00	22.50	7.50
☐ 20	Al Luplow	50.00	22.50	7.50
☐ 21	Not issued	00.00	00.00	0.00
☐ 22	Not issued	00.00	00.00	0.00
☐ 23	Jim Grant	60.00	27.00	9.00
☐ 24	Victor Davalillo	50.00	22.50	7.50
☐ 25	Jerry Walker	50.00	22.50	7.50
☐ 26	Sam McDowell	75.00	34.00	11.25
☐ 27	Fred Whitfield	50.00	22.50	7.50
☐ 28	Jack Kralick	50.00	22.50	7.50
☐ 29	Not issued	00.00	00.00	0.00
☐ 30	Not issued	00.00	00.00	0.00
☐ 31	Not issued	00.00	00.00	0.00
☐ 32	Not issued	00.00	00.00	0.00
☐ 33	Bob Allen	50.00	22.50	7.50
☐ 34	Don Cardwell	75.00	34.00	11.25
☐ 35	Bob Skinner	250.00	110.00	37.50
☐ 36	Don Schwall	75.00	34.00	11.25
☐ 37	Jim Pagliaroni	75.00	34.00	11.25
☐ 38	Dick Schofield	75.00	34.00	11.25

1990 Sunflower Seeds

This 24-card, standard-size, 2 1/2" by 3 1/2" set is an attractive set which frames the players photo by solid blue borders. In the upper left hand of the card the description, Jumbo California Sunflower Seeds, was placed and underneath the photo is the player's name in red and the team name in very small printing

in white. The back of the card features the complete major league record of the player and a short write up as well. This set was issued by Stagi and Scriven Farms Inc. with the cooperation of Michael Schechter Associates (MSA) and features some of the big-name stars in baseball at the time of printing of the set. The set was an attempt by the company to promote sunflower seeds as an alternative to chewing tobacco in the dugout. Three cards were available as an insert in each specially marked bag of Jumbo California Sunflower Seeds.

		MINT	EXC	G-VG
COMPLETE SET (24)		18.00	7.50	2.50
COMMON PLAYER (1-24)		.50	.20	.05
☐ 1	Kevin Mitchell	.75	.30	.07
☐ 2	Ken Griffey Jr.	3.00	1.25	.30
☐ 3	Howard Johnson	.60	.25	.06
☐ 4	Bo Jackson	1.75	.70	.17
☐ 5	Kirby Puckett	1.00	.40	.10
☐ 6	Robin Yount	.75	.30	.07
☐ 7	Dave Stieb	.50	.20	.05
☐ 8	Don Mattingly	1.00	.40	.10
☐ 9	Barry Bonds	1.00	.40	.10
☐ 10	Pedro Guerrero	.50	.20	.05
☐ 11	Tony Gwynn	1.00	.40	.10
☐ 12	Von Hayes	.50	.20	.05
☐ 13	Rickey Henderson	1.75	.70	.17
☐ 14	Tim Raines	.60	.25	.06
☐ 15	Alan Trammell	.75	.30	.07
☐ 16	Dave Stewart	.50	.20	.05
☐ 17	Will Clark	1.75	.70	.17
☐ 18	Roger Clemens	1.50	.60	.15
☐ 19	Wally Joyner	.75	.30	.07
☐ 20	Ryne Sandberg	1.75	.70	.17
☐ 21	Eric Davis	.90	.40	.09
☐ 22	Mike Scott	.50	.20	.05
☐ 23	Cal Ripken	1.50	.60	.15
☐ 24	Eddie Murray	1.00	.40	.10

1991 Sunflower Seeds

This 24-card standard size (2 1/2" by 3 1/2") set was sponsored by Jumbo California Sunflower Seeds. The posed color player photos are framed by white and yellow borders on a red background. The company logo and the words "Autograph Series II" appear above the photo, with the player's name, team, and position given below the picture. A facsimile autograph is inscribed across the picture. The backs are printed in red on white and present Major League statistics and career highlights. The cards are numbered on the back. The set was again issued by Stagi and Scriven Farms Inc. with the cooperation of Michael Schechter Associates (MSA). The set was another attempt by the company to promote sunflower seeds as an alternative to chewing tobacco in the dugout. Two cards were available as an insert in each specially marked bag of Jumbo California Sunflower Seeds.

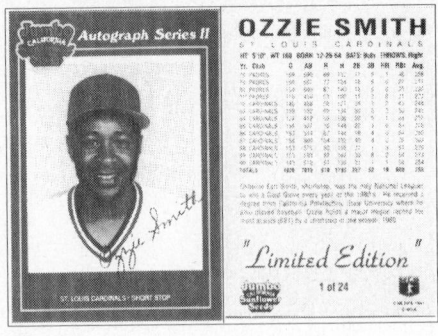

	MINT	EXC	G-VG
COMPLETE SET (24)	15.00	6.50	2.15
COMMON PLAYER (1-24)	.40	.16	.04

		MINT	EXC	G-VG
☐	1 Ozzie Smith	.60	.25	.06
☐	2 Wade Boggs	1.00	.40	.10
☐	3 Bobby Bonilla	.75	.30	.07
☐	4 George Brett	.75	.30	.07
☐	5 Kal Daniels	.40	.16	.04
☐	6 Glenn Davis	.50	.20	.05
☐	7 Chuck Finley	.40	.16	.04
☐	8 Cecil Fielder	1.00	.40	.10
☐	9 Len Dykstra	.40	.16	.04
☐	10 Dwight Gooden	.60	.25	.06
☐	11 Ken Griffey Jr.	2.50	1.00	.25
☐	12 Kelly Gruber	.40	.16	.04
☐	13 Kent Hrbek	.40	.16	.04
☐	14 Andre Dawson	.75	.30	.07
☐	15 Dave Justice	1.25	.50	.12
☐	16 Barry Larkin	.60	.25	.06
☐	17 Ben McDonald	.75	.30	.07
☐	18 Mark McGwire	.75	.30	.07
☐	19 Roberto Alomar	.75	.30	.07
☐	20 Nolan Ryan	2.00	.80	.20
☐	21 Sandy Alomar Jr.	.50	.20	.05
☐	22 Bobby Thigpen	.40	.16	.04
☐	23 Tim Wallach	.40	.16	.04
☐	24 Matt Williams	.60	.25	.06

☐	2 Amazing Record: Reiser's Debut With Dodgers	20.00	8.50	2.75
☐	3 Dramatic Debut: Jackie Robinson ROY	150.00	67.50	22.50
☐	4 Greatest Pitcher of Them All: W.Johnson	60.00	27.00	9.00
☐	5 Three Strikes Not Out: Lost Third Strike Changes Tide of 1941 World Series	20.00	8.50	2.75
☐	6 Home Run Wins Series: Bill Dickey's Last Home Run	30.00	13.50	4.50
☐	7 Never Say Die Pitcher: Schumacher Pitching	20.00	8.50	2.75
☐	8 Five Strikeouts: Nationals Lose All Star Game (Hubbell)	30.00	13.50	4.50
☐	9 Greatest Catch: Al Gionfriddo's Catch	30.00	13.50	4.50
☐	10 No Hits No Runs: VanderMeer Comes Back	30.00	13.50	4.50
☐	11 Bases Loaded: Alexander The Great	45.00	20.00	6.75
☐	12 Most Dramatic Homer: Babe Ruth Points	165.00	75.00	22.50
☐	13 Winning Run: Bridges' Pitching and Goslin's Single Wins 1935 World Series	20.00	8.50	2.75
☐	14 Great Slugging: Lou Gehrig's Four Homers	110.00	50.00	16.50
☐	15 Four Men To Stop Him: DiMaggio's Bat Streak	50.00	22.50	7.50
☐	16 Three Run Homer in Ninth: Williams' Homer	165.00	75.00	22.50
☐	17 Football Block: Lindell's Football Block Paves Way For Yank's Series Victory	20.00	8.50	2.75
☐	18 Home Run To Fame: Reese's Grand Slam	50.00	22.50	7.50
☐	19 Strikeout Record: Feller Whiffs Five	50.00	22.50	7.50
☐	20 Rifle Arm: Furillo	45.00	20.00	6.75

1948 Swell Sport Thrills

The cards in this 20-card set measure approximately 2 7/16" by 3". The 1948 Swell Gum Sports Thrills set of black and white, numbered cards highlights events from baseball history. The cards have picture framed borders with the title "Sports Thrills Highlights in the World of Sport" on the front. The backs of the cards give the story of the event pictured on the front. Cards numbered 9, 11, 16, and 20 are more difficult to obtain than the other cards in this set. The catalog designation is R448.

	NRMT	VG-E	GOOD
COMPLETE SET (20)	1000.00	400.00	100.00
COMMON PLAYER (1-20)	20.00	8.50	2.75

☐	1 Greatest Single Inning Athletics' 10 Run Rally	20.00	8.50	2.75

1989 Swell Baseball Greats

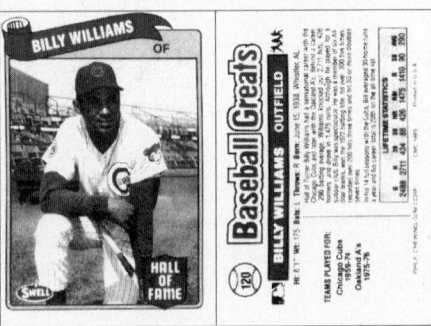

The 1989 Swell Baseball Greats set contains 135 standard-size (2 1/2" by 3 1/2") cards. The fronts have vintage color photos with beige, red and white borders. The horizontally-oriented backs are white and scarlet, and feature career highlights and lifetime stats. The set was produced by Philadelphia Chewing Gum Corporation.

	MINT	EXC	G-VG
COMPLETE SET (135)	10.00	4.50	1.25
COMMON PLAYER (1-135)	.05	.02	.00

☐	1 Babe Ruth	1.00	.40	.10
☐	2 Ty Cobb	.65	.25	.06

☐	3	Walter Johnson	.35	.15	.03
☐	4	Honus Wagner	.35	.15	.03
☐	5	Cy Young	.25	.10	.02
☐	6	Joe Adcock	.05	.02	.00
☐	7	Jim Bunning	.10	.04	.01
☐	8	Orlando Cepeda	.10	.04	.01
☐	9	Harvey Kuenn	.05	.02	.00
☐	10	Jim Hunter	.20	.08	.02
☐	11	Johnny VanderMeer	.10	.04	.01
☐	12	Tony Oliva	.10	.04	.01
☐	13	Harvey Haddix UER (reverse negative)	.10	.04	.01
☐	14	Dick McAuliffe	.05	.02	.00
☐	15	Lefty Grove	.20	.08	.02
☐	16	Bo Belinsky	.05	.02	.00
☐	17	Claude Osteen	.05	.02	.00
☐	18	Doc Medich	.05	.02	.00
☐	19	Del Ennis	.05	.02	.00
☐	20	Rogers Hornsby	.25	.10	.02
☐	21	Bob Buhl	.05	.02	.00
☐	22	Phil Niekro	.20	.08	.02
☐	23	Don Zimmer	.10	.04	.01
☐	24	Greg Luzinski	.05	.02	.00
☐	25	Lou Gehrig	.65	.25	.06
☐	26	Ken Singleton	.10	.04	.01
☐	27	Bob Allison	.05	.02	.00
☐	28	Ed Kranepool	.05	.02	.00
☐	29	Manny Sanguillen	.05	.02	.00
☐	30	Luke Appling	.20	.08	.02
☐	31	Ralph Terry	.05	.02	.00
☐	32	Smoky Burgess	.05	.02	.00
☐	33	Gil Hodges	.20	.08	.02
☐	34	Harry Walker	.05	.02	.00
☐	35	Edd Roush	.15	.06	.01
☐	36	Ron Santo	.10	.04	.01
☐	37	Jim Perry	.05	.02	.00
☐	38	Jose Morales	.05	.02	.00
☐	39	Stan Bahnsen	.05	.02	.00
☐	40	Al Kaline	.35	.15	.03
☐	41	Mel Harder	.05	.02	.00
☐	42	Ralph Houk	.05	.02	.00
☐	43	Jack Billingham	.05	.02	.00
☐	44	Carl Erskine	.10	.04	.01
☐	45	Hoyt Wilhelm	.20	.08	.02
☐	46	Dick Radatz	.05	.02	.00
☐	47	Roy Sievers	.05	.02	.00
☐	48	Jim Lonborg	.05	.02	.00
☐	49	Bobby Richardson	.10	.04	.01
☐	50	Whitey Ford	.30	.12	.03
☐	51	Roy Face	.10	.04	.01
☐	52	Tom Tresh	.05	.02	.00
☐	53	Joe Nuxhall	.05	.02	.00
☐	54	Mickey Vernon	.05	.02	.00
☐	55	Johnny Mize	.20	.08	.02
☐	56	Scott McGregor	.05	.02	.00
☐	57	Billy Pierce	.10	.04	.01
☐	58	Dave Giusti	.05	.02	.00
☐	59	Minnie Minoso	.10	.04	.01
☐	60	Early Wynn	.15	.06	.01
☐	61	Jose Cardenal	.05	.02	.00
☐	62	Sam Jethroe	.05	.02	.00
☐	63	Sal Bando	.05	.02	.00
☐	64	Elrod Hendricks	.05	.02	.00
☐	65	Enos Slaughter	.20	.08	.02
☐	66	Jim Bouton	.05	.02	.00
☐	67	Bill Mazeroski	.10	.04	.01
☐	68	Tony Kubek	.10	.04	.01
☐	69	Joe Black	.05	.02	.00
☐	70	Harmon Killebrew	.25	.10	.02
☐	71	Sam McDowell	.05	.02	.00
☐	72	Bucky Dent	.10	.04	.01
☐	73	Virgil Trucks	.05	.02	.00
☐	74	Andy Pafko	.05	.02	.00
☐	75	Bob Feller	.35	.15	.03
☐	76	Tito Francona	.05	.02	.00
☐	77	Al Dark	.05	.02	.00
☐	78	Larry Dierker	.05	.02	.00
☐	79	Nellie Briles	.05	.02	.00
☐	80	Lou Boudreau	.20	.08	.02
☐	81	Wally Moon	.05	.02	.00
☐	82	Hank Bauer	.05	.02	.00
☐	83	Jim Piersall	.05	.02	.00
☐	84	Jim Grant	.05	.02	.00
☐	85	Richie Ashburn	.15	.06	.01
☐	86	Bob Friend	.05	.02	.00
☐	87	Ken Keltner	.05	.02	.00
☐	88	Jim Kaat	.10	.04	.01
☐	89	Dean Chance	.05	.02	.00
☐	90	Al Lopez	.15	.06	.01
☐	91	Dick Groat	.10	.04	.01
☐	92	Johnny Blanchard	.05	.02	.00
☐	93	Chuck Hinton	.05	.02	.00
☐	94	Clete Boyer	.05	.02	.00
☐	95	Steve Carlton	.30	.12	.03
☐	96	Tug McGraw	.10	.04	.01
☐	97	Mickey Lolich	.10	.04	.01
☐	98	Earl Weaver	.10	.04	.01
☐	99	Sal Maglie	.10	.04	.01
☐	100	Ted Williams	.65	.25	.06
☐	101	Allie Reynolds UER (photo actually Marius Russo)	.20	.08	.02
☐	102	Gene Woodling UER (photo actually Irv Noren)	.20	.08	.02
☐	103	Moe Drabowsky	.05	.02	.00
☐	104	Mickey Stanley	.05	.02	.00
☐	105	Jim Palmer	.30	.12	.03
☐	106	Bill Freehan	.10	.04	.01
☐	107	Bob Robertson	.05	.02	.00
☐	108	Walt Dropo	.05	.02	.00
☐	109	Jerry Koosman	.10	.04	.01
☐	110	Bobby Doerr	.20	.08	.02
☐	111	Phil Rizzuto	.25	.10	.02
☐	112	Don Kessinger	.10	.04	.01
☐	113	Milt Pappas	.10	.04	.01
☐	114	Herb Score	.10	.04	.01
☐	115	Larry Doby	.10	.04	.01
☐	116	Glenn Beckert	.05	.02	.00
☐	117	Andre Thornton	.05	.02	.00
☐	118	Gary Matthews	.05	.02	.00
☐	119	Bill Virdon	.10	.04	.01
☐	120	Billy Williams	.20	.08	.02
☐	121	Johnny Sain	.10	.04	.01
☐	122	Don Newcombe	.10	.04	.01
☐	123	Rico Petrocelli	.05	.02	.00
☐	124	Dick Bosman	.05	.02	.00
☐	125	Roberto Clemente	.40	.16	.04
☐	126	Rocky Colavito	.15	.06	.01
☐	127	Wilbur Wood	.05	.02	.00
☐	128	Duke Sims	.05	.02	.00
☐	129	Ken Holtzman	.05	.02	.00
☐	130	Casey Stengel	.20	.08	.02
☐	131	Bobby Shantz	.10	.04	.01
☐	132	Del Crandall	.10	.04	.01
☐	133	Bobby Thomson	.10	.04	.01
☐	134	Brooks Robinson	.35	.15	.03
☐	135	Checklist Card	.05	.02	.00

1990 Swell Baseball Greats

The 1990 Swell Baseball Greats set is a standard-size (2 1/2" by 3 1/2"), 135-card set. The words Baseball Greats is boldly proclaimed on the top of the card. This set was issued by Swell in both complete set form and in 10-card wax packs.

		MINT	EXC	G-VG
COMPLETE SET (135)		10.00	4.50	1.25
COMMON PLAYER (1-135)		.05	.02	.00
☐ 1	Tom Seaver	.60	.25	.06
☐ 2	Hank Aaron	.50	.20	.05
☐ 3	Mickey Cochrane	.15	.06	.01
☐ 4	Rod Carew	.45	.18	.04
☐ 5	Carl Yastrzemski	.45	.18	.04
☐ 6	Dizzy Dean	.25	.10	.02
☐ 7	Sal Bando	.05	.02	.00
☐ 8	Whitey Ford	.25	.10	.02
☐ 9	Bill White	.10	.04	.01
☐ 10	Babe Ruth	1.00	.40	.10

☐ 11	Robin Roberts	.20	.08	.02
☐ 12	Warren Spahn	.25	.10	.02
☐ 13	Billy Williams	.20	.08	.02
☐ 14	Joe Garagiola	.20	.08	.02
☐ 15	Ty Cobb	.65	.25	.06
☐ 16	Boog Powell	.10	.04	.01
☐ 17	Tom Tresh	.05	.02	.00
☐ 18	Luke Appling	.20	.08	.02
☐ 19	Tommie Agee	.05	.02	.00
☐ 20	Roberto Clemente	.50	.20	.05
☐ 21	Bobby Thomson	.10	.04	.01
☐ 22	Charlie Keller	.10	.04	.01
☐ 23	George Bamberger	.05	.02	.00
☐ 24	Eddie Lopat	.10	.04	.01
☐ 25	Lou Gehrig	.65	.25	.06
☐ 26	Manny Mota	.05	.02	.00
☐ 27	Steve Stone	.05	.02	.00
☐ 28	Orlando Cepeda	.15	.06	.01
☐ 29	Al Bumbry	.05	.02	.00
☐ 30	Grover Alexander	.15	.06	.01
☐ 31	Lou Boudreau	.15	.06	.01
☐ 32	Herb Score	.10	.04	.01
☐ 33	Harry Walker	.05	.02	.00
☐ 34	Deron Johnson	.05	.02	.00
☐ 35	Edd Roush	.10	.04	.01
☐ 36	Carl Erskine	.10	.04	.01
☐ 37	Ken Forsch	.05	.02	.00
☐ 38	Sal Maglie	.10	.04	.01
☐ 39	Al Rosen	.10	.04	.01
☐ 40	Casey Stengel	.20	.08	.02
☐ 41	Cesar Cedeno	.05	.02	.00
☐ 42	Roy White	.05	.02	.00
☐ 43	Larry Doby	.10	.04	.01
☐ 44	Rod Kanehl	.05	.02	.00
☐ 45	Tris Speaker	.20	.08	.02
☐ 46	Ralph Garr	.05	.02	.00
☐ 47	Andre Thornton	.05	.02	.00
☐ 48	Frankie Crosetti	.10	.04	.01
☐ 49	Dick Groat	.10	.04	.01
☐ 50	Honus Wagner	.30	.12	.03
☐ 51	Rogers Hornsby	.25	.10	.02
☐ 52	Ken Brett	.05	.02	.00
☐ 53	Lenny Randle	.05	.02	.00
☐ 54	Enos Slaughter	.20	.08	.02
☐ 55	Mel Ott	.20	.08	.02
☐ 56	Rico Petrocelli	.05	.02	.00
☐ 57	Walt Dropo	.05	.02	.00
☐ 58	Bob Grich	.05	.02	.00
☐ 59	Billy Herman	.10	.04	.01
☐ 60	Bob Feller	.30	.12	.03
☐ 61	Davey Johnson	.10	.04	.01
☐ 62	Don Drysdale	.25	.10	.02
☐ 63	Lary Sorensen	.05	.02	.00
☐ 64	Ron Santo	.10	.04	.01
☐ 65	Eddie Mathews	.25	.10	.02
☐ 66	Gaylord Perry	.20	.08	.02
☐ 67	Lee May	.05	.02	.00
☐ 68	Johnnie LeMaster	.05	.02	.00
☐ 69	Don Kessinger	.10	.04	.01
☐ 70	Lefty Grove	.20	.08	.02
☐ 71	Lou Brock	.25	.10	.02
☐ 72	Don Cardwell	.05	.02	.00
☐ 73	Harvey Haddix	.05	.02	.00
☐ 74	Frank Torre	.05	.02	.00
☐ 75	Walter Johnson	.30	.12	.03
☐ 76	Don Newcombe	.10	.04	.01
☐ 77	Marv Throneberry	.05	.02	.00
☐ 78	Jim Northrup	.05	.02	.00
☐ 79	Fritz Peterson	.05	.02	.00
☐ 80	Ralph Kiner	.20	.08	.02
☐ 81	Mickey Lolich	.10	.04	.01
☐ 82	Donn Clendenon	.05	.02	.00
☐ 83	Pete Vuckovich	.05	.02	.00
☐ 84	Lefty Gomez	.20	.08	.02
☐ 85	Monte Irvin	.15	.06	.01
☐ 86	Rick Ferrell	.10	.04	.01
☐ 87	Tommy Hutton	.05	.02	.00
☐ 88	Julio Cruz	.05	.02	.00
☐ 89	Vida Blue	.10	.04	.01
☐ 90	Johnny Mize	.20	.08	.02
☐ 91	Rusty Staub	.10	.04	.01
☐ 92	Jimmy Piersall	.10	.04	.01
☐ 93	Bill Mazeroski	.10	.04	.01
☐ 94	Lee Lacy	.05	.02	.00
☐ 95	Ernie Banks	.30	.12	.03
☐ 96	Bobby Doerr	.20	.08	.02
☐ 97	George Foster	.10	.04	.01
☐ 98	Eric Soderholm	.05	.02	.00
☐ 99	Johnny Vander Meer	.10	.04	.01
☐ 100	Cy Young	.25	.10	.02
☐ 101	Jimmie Foxx	.30	.12	.03
☐ 102	Clete Boyer	.10	.04	.01
☐ 103	Steve Garvey	.25	.10	.02
☐ 104	Johnny Podres	.10	.04	.01

☐ 105	Yogi Berra	.40	.16	.04
☐ 106	Bill Monbouquette	.05	.02	.00
☐ 107	Milt Pappas	.05	.02	.00
☐ 108	Dave LaRoche	.05	.02	.00
☐ 109	Elliott Maddox	.05	.02	.00
☐ 110	Steve Carlton	.30	.12	.03
☐ 111	Bud Harrelson	.10	.04	.01
☐ 112	Mark Littell	.05	.02	.00
☐ 113	Frank Thomas	.05	.02	.00
☐ 114	Bill Robinson	.10	.04	.01
☐ 115	Satchel Paige	.30	.12	.03
☐ 116	John Denny	.05	.02	.00
☐ 117	Clyde King	.05	.02	.00
☐ 118	Billy Sample	.05	.02	.00
☐ 119	Rocky Colavito	.15	.06	.01
☐ 120	Bob Gibson	.30	.12	.03
☐ 121	Bert Campaneris	.05	.02	.00
☐ 122	Mark Fidrych	.10	.04	.01
☐ 123	Ed Charles	.05	.02	.00
☐ 124	Jim Lonborg	.10	.04	.01
☐ 125	Ted Williams	.60	.25	.06
☐ 126	Manny Sanguillen	.10	.04	.01
☐ 127	Matt Keough	.05	.02	.00
☐ 128	Vern Ruhle	.05	.02	.00
☐ 129	Bob Skinner	.05	.02	.00
☐ 130	Joe Torre	.15	.06	.01
☐ 131	Ralph Houk	.05	.02	.00
☐ 132	Gil Hodges	.25	.10	.02
☐ 133	Ralph Branca	.10	.04	.01
☐ 134	Christy Mathewson	.30	.12	.03
☐ 135	Checklist Card	.05	.02	.00

1991 Swell Baseball Greats

This set marks the third year Philadelphia Chewing Gum (using the Swell trade name) issued a set honoring famous and other important retired players. The front of the cards feature yellow and red borders framing the full-color photo of the player(where full color was available) The cards were issued with cooperation from Impel Marketing. This 150-card set measures the now-standard size of 2 1/2" by 3 1/2" and is sequenced in several alphabetical orders.

	MINT	EXC	G-VG
COMPLETE SET (150)	10.00	4.50	1.25
COMMON PLAYER (1-150)	.05	.02	.00

☐ 1	Tommie Agee	.05	.02	.00
☐ 2	Matty Alou	.05	.02	.00
☐ 3	Luke Appling	.20	.08	.02
☐ 4	Richie Ashburn	.15	.06	.01
☐ 5	Ernie Banks	.30	.12	.03
☐ 6	Don Baylor	.10	.04	.01
☐ 7	Buddy Bell	.10	.04	.01
☐ 8	Yogi Berra	.40	.16	.04
☐ 9	Joe Black	.10	.04	.01
☐ 10	Vida Blue	.10	.04	.01
☐ 11	Bobby Bonds	.10	.04	.01
☐ 12	Lou Boudreau	.15	.06	.01
☐ 13	Lou Brock	.25	.10	.02
☐ 14	Ralph Branca	.10	.04	.01
☐ 15	Bobby Brown	.10	.04	.01
☐ 16	Lou Burdette	.10	.04	.01
☐ 17	Steve Carlton	.30	.12	.03
☐ 18	Rico Carty	.10	.04	.01
☐ 19	Jerry Coleman	.10	.04	.01

□	20	Frankie Crosetti	.10	.04	.01
□	21	Julio Cruz	.05	.02	.00
□	22	Alvin Dark	.05	.02	.00
□	23	Doug DeCinces	.05	.02	.00
□	24	Larry Doby	.10	.04	.01
□	25	Bobby Doerr	.20	.08	.02
□	26	Don Drysdale	.20	.08	.02
□	27	Carl Erskine	.10	.04	.01
□	28	Elroy Face	.10	.04	.01
□	29	Rick Ferrell	.10	.04	.01
□	30	Rollie Fingers	.25	.10	.02
□	31	Joe Garagiola	.20	.08	.02
□	32	Steve Garvey	.30	.12	.03
□	33	Bob Gibson	.20	.08	.02
□	34	Mudcat Grant	.05	.02	.00
□	35	Dick Groat	.10	.04	.01
□	36	Jerry Grote	.05	.02	.00
□	37	Toby Harrah	.05	.02	.00
□	38	Bud Harrelson	.05	.02	.00
□	39	Billy Herman	.15	.06	.01
□	40	Ken Holtzman	.05	.02	.00
□	41	Willie Horton	.05	.02	.00
□	42	Ralph Houk	.05	.02	.00
□	43	Al Hrabosky	.05	.02	.00
□	44	Monte Irvin	.20	.08	.02
□	45	Fergie Jenkins	.25	.10	.02
□	46	Davey Johnson	.05	.02	.00
□	47	George Kell	.15	.06	.01
□	48	Charlie Keller	.10	.04	.01
□	49	Harmon Killebrew	.25	.10	.02
□	50	Ralph Kiner	.25	.10	.02
□	51	Clyde King	.05	.02	.00
□	52	Dave Kingman	.10	.04	.01
□	53	Al Kaline	.35	.15	.03
□	54	Clem Labine	.10	.04	.01
□	55	Vern Law	.10	.04	.01
□	56	Mickey Lolich	.10	.04	.01
□	57	Jim Lonborg	.10	.04	.01
□	58	Eddie Lopat	.10	.04	.01
□	59	Sal Maglie	.10	.04	.01
□	60	Bill Mazeroski	.10	.04	.01
□	61	Johnny VanderMeer	.10	.04	.01
□	62	Johnny Mize	.20	.08	.02
□	63	Manny Mota	.05	.02	.00
□	64	Wally Moon	.05	.02	.00
□	65	Rick Monday	.05	.02	.00
□	66	Tom Tresh	.10	.04	.01
□	67	Graig Nettles	.10	.04	.01
□	68	Don Newcombe	.10	.04	.01
□	69	Milt Pappas	.05	.02	.00
□	70	Gaylord Perry	.25	.10	.02
□	71	Rico Petrocelli	.05	.02	.00
□	72	Jimmy Piersall	.10	.04	.01
□	73	Johnny Podres	.10	.04	.01
□	74	Boog Powell	.10	.04	.01
□	75	Bobby Richardson	.10	.04	.01
□	76	Vern Ruhle	.05	.02	.00
□	77	Robin Roberts	.20	.08	.02
□	78	Al Rosen	.10	.04	.01
□	79	Billy Sample	.10	.04	.01
□	80	Manny Sanguillen	.10	.04	.01
□	81	Ron Santo	.10	.04	.01
□	82	Herb Score	.10	.04	.01
□	83	Bobby Shantz	.10	.04	.01
□	84	Enos Slaughter	.20	.08	.02
□	85	Eric Soderholm	.05	.02	.00
□	86	Warren Spahn	.25	.10	.02
□	87	Rusty Staub	.10	.04	.01
□	88	Bobby Thomson	.10	.04	.01
□	89	Marv Throneberry	.05	.02	.00
□	90	Luis Tiant	.10	.04	.01
□	91	Frank Torre	.05	.02	.00
□	92	Joe Torre	.15	.06	.01
□	93	Bill Virdon	.10	.04	.01
□	94	Harry Walker	.05	.02	.00
□	95	Earl Weaver	.10	.04	.01
□	96	Bill White	.10	.04	.01
□	97	Roy White	.05	.02	.00
□	98	Billy Williams	.20	.08	.02
□	99	Dick Williams	.05	.02	.00
□	100	Ted Williams	.60	.25	.06
□	101	Gene Woodling	.10	.04	.01
□	102	Hank Aaron	.60	.25	.06
□	103	Rod Carew	.45	.18	.04
□	104	Cesar Cedeno	.10	.04	.01
□	105	Orlando Cepeda	.15	.06	.01
□	106	Willie Mays	.60	.25	.06
□	107	Tom Seaver	.60	.25	.06
□	108	Carl Yastrzemski	.45	.18	.04
□	109	Clete Boyer	.10	.04	.01
□	110	Bert Campaneris	.05	.02	.00
□	111	Walt Dropo	.05	.02	.00
□	112	George Foster	.10	.04	.01
□	113	Phil Garner	.10	.04	.01

□	114	Harvey Kuenn	.10	.04	.01
□	115	Don Kessinger	.10	.04	.01
□	116	Rocky Colavito	.15	.06	.01
□	117	Bobby Murcer	.10	.04	.01
□	118	Mel Painell	.05	.02	.00
□	119	Ken Reitz	.05	.02	.00
□	120	Earl Wilson	.05	.02	.00
□	121	Wilbur Wood	.05	.02	.00
□	122	Ed Yost	.05	.02	.00
□	123	Jim Bouton	.10	.04	.01
□	124	Babe Ruth	1.00	.40	.10
□	125	Lou Gehrig	.65	.25	.06
□	126	Honus Wagner	.25	.10	.02
□	127	Ty Cobb	.65	.25	.06
□	128	Grover C. Alexander	.20	.08	.02
□	129	Lefty Gomez	.20	.08	.02
□	130	Walter Johnson	.30	.12	.03
□	131	Gil Hodges	.20	.08	.02
□	132	Roberto Clemente	.45	.18	.04
□	133	Satchel Paige	.30	.12	.03
□	134	Edd Roush	.15	.06	.01
□	135	Cy Young	.25	.10	.02
□	136	Casey Stengel	.25	.10	.02
□	137	Rogers Hornsby	.25	.10	.02
□	138	Dizzy Dean	.35	.15	.03
□	139	Lefty Grove	.20	.08	.02
□	140	Tris Speaker	.20	.08	.02
□	141	Christy Mathewson	.30	.12	.03
□	142	Mickey Cochrane	.15	.06	.01
□	143	Jimmie Foxx	.30	.12	.03
□	144	Mel Ott	.25	.10	.02
□	145	Bob Feller	.30	.12	.03
□	146	Brooks Robinson	.25	.10	.02
□	147	Eddie Mathews	.25	.10	.02
□	148	Pie Traynor	.15	.06	.01
□	149	Thurman Munson	.25	.10	.02
□	150	Checklist Card	.05	.02	.00

1957 Swifts Franks

The cards in this 18-card set measure 3 1/2" by 4". These full color, numbered cards issued in 1957 by the Swift Company are die-cut. Each card consists of several pieces which can be punched out and assembled to form a stand-up model of the player. The cards and a game board were available directly from the company. The company-direct set consisted of three panels each containing six cards; sets found in this "uncut" state carry a value 25 percent higher than the values listed below. The catalog designation for this set is F162.

		NRMT	VG-E	GOOD
COMPLETE SET (18)		2000.00	800.00	200.00
COMMON PLAYER (1-18)		60.00	27.00	9.00
□ 1	John Podres	75.00	34.00	11.25
□ 2	Gus Triandos	60.00	27.00	9.00
□ 3	Dale Long	60.00	27.00	9.00
□ 4	Billy Pierce	75.00	34.00	11.25
□ 5	Ed Bailey	60.00	27.00	9.00
□ 6	Vic Wertz	60.00	27.00	9.00
□ 7	Nelson Fox	120.00	55.00	18.00
□ 8	Ken Boyer	100.00	45.00	15.00

		MINT	EXC	G-VG
☐ 9	Gil McDougald	90.00	40.00	13.50
☐ 10	Junior Gilliam	90.00	40.00	13.50
☐ 11	Eddie Yost	60.00	27.00	9.00
☐ 12	Johnny Logan	60.00	27.00	9.00
☐ 13	Hank Aaron	600.00	270.00	90.00
☐ 14	Bill Tuttle	60.00	27.00	9.00
☐ 15	Jackie Jensen	90.00	40.00	13.50
☐ 16	Frank Robinson	200.00	90.00	30.00
☐ 17	Richie Ashburn	135.00	60.00	20.00
☐ 18	Rocky Colavito	120.00	55.00	18.00

1990 Target Dodgers

The 1990 Target Dodgers is one of the largest sets ever made. This over-1,000 card set features cards each measuring approximately 2" by 3" individually and was issued in large perforated sheets of 15 cards. Players in the set played at one time or another for one of the Dodgers franchises. As such many of the players in the set are older and relatively unknown to today's younger collectors. The set was apparently intended to be arranged in alphabetical order. There were several numbers not used (408, 458, 463, 792, 902, 907, 969, 996, 1031, 1054, 1061, and 1098) as well as a few instances of duplicated numbers.

		MINT	EXC	G-VG
COMPLETE SET (1106)		100.00	45.00	15.00
COMMON PLAYER		.10	.04	.01
☐ 1	Bert Abbey	.10	.04	.01
☐ 2	Cal Abrams	.10	.04	.01
☐ 3	Hank Aguirre	.10	.04	.01
☐ 4	Eddie Ainsmith	.10	.04	.01
☐ 5	Ed Albosta	.10	.04	.01
☐ 6	Luis Alcaraz	.10	.04	.01
☐ 7	Doyle Alexander	.10	.04	.01
☐ 8	Dick Allen	.20	.08	.02
☐ 9	Frank Allen	.10	.04	.01
☐ 10	Johnny Allen	.10	.04	.01
☐ 11	Mel Almada	.10	.04	.01
☐ 12	Walter Alston	.35	.15	.03
☐ 13	Ed Amelung	.10	.04	.01
☐ 14	Sandy Amoros	.15	.06	.01
☐ 15	Dave Anderson	.10	.04	.01
☐ 16	Ferrell Anderson	.10	.04	.01
☐ 17	John Anderson	.10	.04	.01
☐ 18	Stan Andrews	.10	.04	.01
☐ 19	Bill Antonello	.10	.04	.01
☐ 20	Jimmy Archer	.10	.04	.01
☐ 21	Bob Aspromonte	.10	.04	.01
☐ 22	Rick Auerbach	.10	.04	.01
☐ 23	Charlie Babb	.10	.04	.01
☐ 24	Johnny Babich	.10	.04	.01
☐ 25	Bob Bailey	.10	.04	.01
☐ 26	Bob Bailor	.10	.04	.01
☐ 27	Dusty Baker	.20	.08	.02
☐ 28	Tom Baker	.10	.04	.01
☐ 29	Dave Bancroft	.25	.10	.02
☐ 30	Dan Bankhead	.10	.04	.01
☐ 31	Jack Banta	.10	.04	.01
☐ 32	Jim Barbieri	.10	.04	.01
☐ 33	Red Barkley	.10	.04	.01
☐ 34	Jesse Barnes	.10	.04	.01
☐ 35	Rex Barney	.10	.04	.01
☐ 36	Billy Barnie	.10	.04	.01
☐ 37	Bob Barrett	.10	.04	.01
☐ 38	Jim Baxes	.10	.04	.01
☐ 39	Billy Bean	.10	.04	.01
☐ 40	BoomBoom Beck	.10	.04	.01
☐ 41	Joe Beckwith	.10	.04	.01
☐ 42	Hank Behrman	.10	.04	.01
☐ 43	Mark Belanger	.20	.08	.02
☐ 44	Wayne Belardi	.10	.04	.01
☐ 45	Tim Belcher	.20	.08	.02
☐ 46	George Bell	.10	.04	.01
☐ 47	Ray Benge	.10	.04	.01
☐ 48	Moe Berg	.20	.08	.02
☐ 49	Bill Bergen	.10	.04	.01
☐ 50	Ray Belles	.10	.04	.01
☐ 51	Don Bessent	.10	.04	.01
☐ 52	Steve Bilko	.10	.04	.01
☐ 53	Jack Billingham	.10	.04	.01
☐ 54	Babe Birrer	.10	.04	.01
☐ 55	Del Bissonette	.10	.04	.01
☐ 56	Joe Black	.20	.08	.02
☐ 57	Lu Blue	.10	.04	.01
☐ 58	George Boehler	.10	.04	.01
☐ 59	Sammy Bohne	.10	.04	.01
☐ 60	John Bolling	.10	.04	.01
☐ 61	Ike Boone	.10	.04	.01
☐ 62	Frenchy Bordagaray	.10	.04	.01
☐ 63	Ken Boyer	.20	.08	.02
☐ 64	Buzz Boyle	.10	.04	.01
☐ 65	Mark Bradley	.10	.04	.01
☐ 66	Bobby Bragan	.10	.04	.01
☐ 67	Ralph Branca	.20	.08	.02
☐ 68	Ed Brandt	.10	.04	.01
☐ 69	Sid Bream	.10	.04	.01
☐ 70	Marv Breeding	.10	.04	.01
☐ 71	Tom Brennan	.10	.04	.01
☐ 72	William Brennan	.10	.04	.01
☐ 73	Rube Bressler	.10	.04	.01
☐ 74	Ken Brett	.10	.04	.01
☐ 75	Jim Brewer	.10	.04	.01
☐ 76	Tony Brewer	.10	.04	.01
☐ 77	Rocky Bridges	.10	.04	.01
☐ 78	Greg Brock	.10	.04	.01
☐ 79	Dan Brouthers	.30	.12	.03
☐ 80	Eddie Brown	.10	.04	.01
☐ 81	Elmer Brown	.10	.04	.01
☐ 82	Lindsay Brown	.10	.04	.01
☐ 83	Lloyd Brown	.10	.04	.01
☐ 84	Mace Brown	.10	.04	.01
☐ 85	Tommy Brown	.10	.04	.01
☐ 86	Pete Browning	.20	.08	.02
☐ 87	Ralph Bryant	.10	.04	.01
☐ 88	Jim Bucher	.10	.04	.01
☐ 89	Bill Buckner	.20	.08	.02
☐ 90	Jim Bunning	.30	.12	.03
☐ 91	Jack Burdock	.10	.04	.01
☐ 92	Glenn Burke	.10	.04	.01
☐ 93	Buster Burrell	.10	.04	.01
☐ 94	Larry Burright	.10	.04	.01
☐ 95	Doc Bushong	.10	.04	.01
☐ 96	Max Butcher	.10	.04	.01
☐ 97	Johnny Butler	.10	.04	.01
☐ 98	Enos Cabell	.10	.04	.01
☐ 99	Leon Cadore	.10	.04	.01
☐ 100	Bruce Caldwell	.10	.04	.01
☐ 101	Dick Calmus	.10	.04	.01
☐ 102	Dolf Camilli	.10	.04	.01
☐ 103	Doug Camilli	.10	.04	.01
☐ 104	Roy Campanella	.60	.25	.06
☐ 105	Al Campanis	.25	.10	.02
☐ 106	Jim Campanis	.10	.04	.01
☐ 107A	Leo Callahan	.10	.04	.01
☐ 107B	Gilly Campbell	.10	.04	.01
☐ 108	Jimmy Canavan	.10	.04	.01
☐ 109	Chris Cannizzaro	.10	.04	.01
☐ 110	Guy Cantrell	.10	.04	.01
☐ 111	Ben Cantwell	.10	.04	.01
☐ 112	Andy Carey	.10	.04	.01
☐ 113	Max Carey	.30	.12	.03
☐ 114	Tex Carleton	.10	.04	.01
☐ 115	Ownie Carroll	.10	.04	.01
☐ 116	Bob Caruthers	.15	.06	.01
☐ 117	Doc Casey	.10	.04	.01
☐ 118	Hugh Casey	.10	.04	.01
☐ 119	Bobby Castillo	.10	.04	.01
☐ 120	Cesar Cedeno	.15	.06	.01
☐ 121	Ron Cey	.20	.08	.02
☐ 122	Ed Chandler	.10	.04	.01
☐ 123	Ben Chapman	.15	.06	.01
☐ 124	Larry Cheney	.10	.04	.01
☐ 125	Bob Chipman	.10	.04	.01
☐ 126	Chuck Churn	.10	.04	.01
☐ 127	Gino Cimoli	.10	.04	.01
☐ 128	Moose Clabaugh	.10	.04	.01

No.	Player				No.	Player			
129	Bud Clancy	.10	.04	.01	224	Cecil Espy	.10	.04	.01
130	Bob Clark	.10	.04	.01	225	Chuck Essegian	.15	.06	.01
131	Watty Clark	.10	.04	.01	226	Dude Esterbrook	.10	.04	.01
132	Alta Cohen	.10	.04	.01	227	Red Evans	.10	.04	.01
133	Rocky Colavito	.30	.12	.03	228	Bunny Fabrique	.10	.04	.01
134	Jackie Collum	.10	.04	.01	229	Jim Fairey	.10	.04	.01
135	Chuck Connors	.35	.15	.03	230	Ron Fairly	.20	.08	.02
136	Jack Coombs	.25	.10	.02	231	George Fallon	.10	.04	.01
137	Johnny Cooney	.10	.04	.01	232	Turk Farrell	.10	.04	.01
138	Tommy Corcoran	.10	.04	.01	233	Duke Farrel	.10	.04	.01
139	Pop Corkhill	.10	.04	.01	234	Jim Faulkner	.10	.04	.01
140	John Corriden	.10	.04	.01	235	Alex Ferguson	.10	.04	.01
141	Pete Coscarart	.10	.04	.01	236	Joe Ferguson	.15	.06	.01
142	Wes Covington	.10	.04	.01	237	Chico Fernandez	.10	.04	.01
143	Billy Cox	.20	.08	.02	238	Sid Fernandez	.20	.08	.02
144	Roger Craig	.20	.08	.02	239	Al Ferrara	.10	.04	.01
146	Willie Crawford	.10	.04	.01	240	Wes Ferrell	.20	.08	.02
147	Tim Crews	.10	.04	.01	241	Lou Fette	.10	.04	.01
148	John Cronin	.10	.04	.01	242	Chick Fewster	.10	.04	.01
149	Lave Cross	.10	.04	.01	243	Jack Fimple	.10	.04	.01
150	Bill Crouch	.10	.04	.01	244	Neal Mickey Finn	.10	.04	.01
151	Don Crow	.10	.04	.01	245	Bob Fisher	.10	.04	.01
152	Henry Cruz	.10	.04	.01	246	Freddie Fitzsimmons	.10	.04	.01
153	Tony Cuccinello	.10	.04	.01	247	Tim Flood	.10	.04	.01
154	Roy Cullenbine	.10	.04	.01	248	Jake Flowers	.10	.04	.01
155	George Culver	.10	.04	.01	249	Hod Ford	.10	.04	.01
156	Nick Cullop	.10	.04	.01	250	Terry Forster	.20	.08	.02
157	George Cutshaw	.10	.04	.01	251	Alan Foster	.10	.04	.01
158	Kiki Cuyler	.30	.12	.03	252	Jack Fournier	.10	.04	.01
159	Bill Dahlen	.20	.08	.02	253	Dave Foutz	.10	.04	.01
160	Babe Dahlgren	.10	.04	.01	254	Art Fowler	.10	.04	.01
161	Jack Dalton	.10	.04	.01	255	Fred Frankhouse	.10	.04	.01
162	Tom Daly	.10	.04	.01	256	Herman Franks	.10	.04	.01
163	Cliff Dapper	.10	.04	.01	257	Johnny Frederick	.10	.04	.01
164	Bob Darnell	.10	.04	.01	258	Larry French	.10	.04	.01
165	Bobby Darwin	.10	.04	.01	259	Lonny Frey	.10	.04	.01
166	Jake Daubert	.20	.08	.02	260	Pepe Frias	.10	.04	.01
167	Vic Davalillo	.10	.04	.01	261	Charlie Fuchs	.10	.04	.01
168	Curt Davis	.10	.04	.01	262	Carl Furillo	.20	.08	.02
169	Mike Davis	.10	.04	.01	263	Len Gabrielson	.10	.04	.01
170	Ron Davis	.10	.04	.01	264	Augie Galan	.10	.04	.01
171	Tommy Davis	.20	.08	.02	265	Joe Gallagher	.10	.04	.01
172	Willie Davis	.20	.08	.02	266	Phil Gallivan	.10	.04	.01
173	Pea Ridge Day	.10	.04	.01	267	Balvino Galvez	.10	.04	.01
174	Tommy Dean	.10	.04	.01	268	Mike Garman	.10	.04	.01
175	Hank DeBerry	.10	.04	.01	269	Phil Garner	.15	.06	.01
176	Art Decatur	.10	.04	.01	270	Steve Garvey	.35	.15	.03
177	Raoul Dedeaux	.10	.04	.01	271	Ned Garvin	.10	.04	.01
178	Ivan DeJesus	.10	.04	.01	272	Hank Gastright	.10	.04	.01
179	Don Demeter	.10	.04	.01	273	Sid Gautreaux	.10	.04	.01
180	Gene DeMontreville	.10	.04	.01	274	Jim Gentile	.15	.06	.01
181	Rick Dempsey	.10	.04	.01	275	Greek George	.10	.04	.01
182	Eddie Dent	.10	.04	.01	276	Ben Geraghty	.10	.04	.01
183	Mike Devereaux	.10	.04	.01	277	Gus Getz	.10	.04	.01
184	Carlos Diaz	.10	.04	.01	278	Bob Giallombardo	.10	.04	.01
185	Dick Dietz	.10	.04	.01	279	Kirk Gibson	.35	.15	.03
186	Pop Dillon	.10	.04	.01	280	Charlie Gilbert	.10	.04	.01
187	Bill Doak	.10	.04	.01	281	Jim Gilliam	.20	.08	.02
188	John Dobbs	.10	.04	.01	282	Al Gionfriddo	.10	.04	.01
189	George Dockins	.10	.04	.01	283	Tony Giuliani	.10	.04	.01
190	Cozy Dolan	.10	.04	.01	284	Al Glossop	.10	.04	.01
191	Patsy Donovan	.10	.04	.01	285	John Gochnaur	.10	.04	.01
192	Wild Bill Donovan	.10	.04	.01	286	Jim Golden	.10	.04	.01
193	Mickey Doolan	.10	.04	.01	287	Dave Goltz	.10	.04	.01
194	Jack Doscher	.10	.04	.01	288	Jose Gonzales	.10	.04	.01
195	Phil Douglas	.10	.04	.01	289	Johnny Gooch	.10	.04	.01
196	Snooks Dowd	.10	.04	.01	290	Ed Goodson	.10	.04	.01
197	Al Downing	.10	.04	.01	291	Billy Grabarkewitz	.10	.04	.01
198	Red Downs	.10	.04	.01	292	Jack Graham	.10	.04	.01
199	Jack Doyle	.10	.04	.01	293	Mudcat Grant	.10	.04	.01
200	Solly Drake	.10	.04	.01	294	Dick Gray	.10	.04	.01
201	Tom Drake	.10	.04	.01	295	Kent Greenfield	.10	.04	.01
202	Chuck Dressen	.20	.08	.02	296	Hal Gregg	.10	.04	.01
203	Don Drysdale	.35	.15	.03	297	Alfredo Griffin	.10	.04	.01
204	Clise Dudley	.10	.04	.01	298	Mike Griffin	.10	.04	.01
205	Mariano Duncan	.20	.08	.02	299	Derrell Griffith	.10	.04	.01
206	Jack Dunn	.10	.04	.01	300	Tommy Griffith	.10	.04	.01
207	Bull Durham	.10	.04	.01	301	Burleigh Grimes	.30	.12	.03
208	Leo Durocher	.35	.15	.03	302	Lee Grissom	.10	.04	.01
209	Billy Earle	.10	.04	.01	303	Jerry Grote	.10	.04	.01
210	George Earnshaw	.10	.04	.01	304	Pedro Guerrero	.30	.12	.03
211	Ox Eckhardt	.10	.04	.01	305	Brad Gulden	.10	.04	.01
212	Bruce Edwards	.10	.04	.01	306	Ad Gumbert	.10	.04	.01
213	Hank Edwards	.10	.04	.01	307	Chris Gwynn	.20	.08	.02
214	Dick W. Egan	.10	.04	.01	308	Bert Haas	.10	.04	.01
215	Harry Eisenstat	.10	.04	.01	309	John Hale	.10	.04	.01
216	Kid Elberfeld	.10	.04	.01	310	Tom Haller	.10	.04	.01
217	Jumbo Elliot	.10	.04	.01	311	Bill Hallman	.10	.04	.01
218	Don Elston	.10	.04	.01	312	Jeff Hamilton	.10	.04	.01
219	Gil English	.10	.04	.01	313	Luke Hamlin	.10	.04	.01
220	Johnny Enzmann	.10	.04	.01	314	Ned Hanlon	.15	.06	.01
221	Al Epperly	.10	.04	.01	315	Gerald Hannahs	.10	.04	.01
222	Carl Erskine	.20	.08	.02	316	Charlie Hargreaves	.10	.04	.01
223	Tex Erwin	.10	.04	.01	317	Tim Harkiness	.10	.04	.01

#	Name			
☐ 318	Harry Harper	.10	.04	.01
☐ 319	Joe Harris	.10	.04	.01
☐ 320	Lenny Harris	.20	.08	.02
☐ 321	Bill F. Hart	.10	.04	.01
☐ 322	Buddy Hassett	.10	.04	.01
☐ 323	Mickey Hatcher	.10	.04	.01
☐ 324	Joe Hatten	.10	.04	.01
☐ 325	Phil Haugstad	.10	.04	.01
☐ 326	Brad Havens	.10	.04	.01
☐ 327	Ray Hayworth	.10	.04	.01
☐ 328	Ed Head	.10	.04	.01
☐ 329	Danny Heep	.10	.04	.01
☐ 330	Fred Heimach	.10	.04	.01
☐ 331	Harvey Hendrick	.10	.04	.01
☐ 332	Weldon Henley	.10	.04	.01
☐ 333	Butch Henline	.10	.04	.01
☐ 334	Dutch Henry	.10	.04	.01
☐ 335	Roy Henshaw	.10	.04	.01
☐ 336	Babe Herman	.20	.08	.02
☐ 337	Billy Herman	.30	.12	.03
☐ 338	Gene Hermanski	.10	.04	.01
☐ 339	Enzo Hernandez	.10	.04	.01
☐ 340	Art Herring	.10	.04	.01
☐ 341	Orel Hershiser	.35	.15	.03
☐ 342	Dave J. Hickman	.10	.04	.01
☐ 343	Jim Hickman	.10	.04	.01
☐ 344	Kirby Higbe	.10	.04	.01
☐ 345	Andy High	.10	.04	.01
☐ 346	George Hildebrand	.10	.04	.01
☐ 347	Hunkey Hines	.10	.04	.01
☐ 348	Don Hoak	.10	.04	.01
☐ 349	Oris Hockett	.10	.04	.01
☐ 350	Gil Hodges	.35	.15	.03
☐ 351	Glenn Hoffman	.10	.04	.01
☐ 352	Al Hollingsworth	.10	.04	.01
☐ 353	Tommy Holmes	.20	.08	.02
☐ 354	Brian Holton	.10	.04	.01
☐ 355	Rick Honeycutt	.10	.04	.01
☐ 356	Burt Hooton	.15	.06	.01
☐ 357	Gail Hopkins	.10	.04	.01
☐ 358	Johnny Hopp	.15	.06	.01
☐ 359	Charlie Hough	.20	.08	.02
☐ 360	Frank Howard	.25	.10	.02
☐ 361	Steve Howe	.10	.04	.01
☐ 362	Dixie Howell	.10	.04	.01
☐ 363	Harry Howell	.10	.04	.01
☐ 364	Jay Howell	.20	.08	.02
☐ 365	Ken Howell	.20	.08	.02
☐ 366	Waite Hoyt	.30	.12	.03
☐ 367	Johnny Hudson	.10	.04	.01
☐ 368	Jim J. Hughes	.10	.04	.01
☐ 369	Jim R. Hughes	.10	.04	.01
☐ 370	Mickey Hughes	.10	.04	.01
☐ 371	John Hummel	.10	.04	.01
☐ 372	Ron Hunt	.10	.04	.01
☐ 373	Willard Hunter	.10	.04	.01
☐ 374	Ira Hutchinson	.10	.04	.01
☐ 375	Tom Hutton	.10	.04	.01
☐ 376	Charlie Irwin	.10	.04	.01
☐ 377	Fred Jacklitsch	.10	.04	.01
☐ 378	Randy Jackson	.10	.04	.01
☐ 379	Merwin Jacobson	.10	.04	.01
☐ 380	Cleo James	.10	.04	.01
☐ 381	Hal Janvrin	.10	.04	.01
☐ 382	Roy Jarvis	.10	.04	.01
☐ 383	George Jeffcoat	.10	.04	.01
☐ 384	Jack Jenkins	.10	.04	.01
☐ 385	Hughie Jennings	.30	.12	.03
☐ 386	Tommy John	.25	.10	.02
☐ 387	Lou Johnson	.10	.04	.01
☐ 388	Fred Ivy Johnston	.10	.04	.01
☐ 389	Jimmy Johnston	.10	.04	.01
☐ 390	Jay Johnstone	.20	.08	.02
☐ 391	Fielder Jones	.10	.04	.01
☐ 392	Oscar Jones	.10	.04	.01
☐ 393	Tim Jordan	.10	.04	.01
☐ 394	Spider Jorgensen	.10	.04	.01
☐ 395	Von Joshua	.10	.04	.01
☐ 396	Bill Joyce	.10	.04	.01
☐ 397	Joe Judge	.10	.04	.01
☐ 398	Alex Kampouris	.10	.04	.01
☐ 399	Willie Keeler	.35	.15	.03
☐ 400	Mike Kekich	.10	.04	.01
☐ 401	John Kelleher	.10	.04	.01
☐ 402	Frank Kellert	.10	.04	.01
☐ 403	Joe Kelley	.35	.15	.03
☐ 404	George Kelly	.30	.12	.03
☐ 405	Bob Kennedy	.10	.04	.01
☐ 406	Brickyard Kennedy	.10	.04	.01
☐ 407	John Kennedy	.10	.04	.01
☐ 408	Not issued	.00	.00	.00
☐ 409	Newt Kimball	.10	.04	.01
☐ 410	Clyde King	.10	.04	.01
☐ 411	Enos Kirkpatrick	.10	.04	.01
☐ 412	Frank Kitson	.10	.04	.01
☐ 413	Johnny Klippstein	.10	.04	.01
☐ 414	Elmer Klumpp	.10	.04	.01
☐ 415	Len Koenecke	.10	.04	.01
☐ 416	Ed Konetchy	.10	.04	.01
☐ 417	Andy Kosco	.10	.04	.01
☐ 418	Sandy Koufax	.60	.25	.06
☐ 419	Ernie Koy	.10	.04	.01
☐ 420	Charlie Kress	.10	.04	.01
☐ 421	Bill Krueger	.10	.04	.01
☐ 422	Ernie Krueger	.10	.04	.01
☐ 423	Clem Labine	.15	.06	.01
☐ 424	Candy LaChance	.10	.04	.01
☐ 425	Lee Lacy	.10	.04	.01
☐ 426	Lerrin LaGrow	.10	.04	.01
☐ 427	Bill Lamar	.10	.04	.01
☐ 428	Wayne LaMaster	.10	.04	.01
☐ 429	Ray Lamb	.10	.04	.01
☐ 430	Rafael Landestoy	.10	.04	.01
☐ 431	Ken Landreaux	.15	.06	.01
☐ 432	Tito Landrum	.15	.06	.01
☐ 433	Norm Larker	.15	.06	.01
☐ 434	Lyn Lary	.10	.04	.01
☐ 435	Tom Lasorda	.35	.15	.03
☐ 436	Cookie Lavagetto	.15	.06	.01
☐ 437	Rudy Law	.10	.04	.01
☐ 438	Tony Lazzeri	.30	.12	.03
☐ 439	Tim Leary	.20	.08	.02
☐ 440	Bob Lee	.10	.04	.01
☐ 441	Hal Lee	.10	.04	.01
☐ 442	Leron Lee	.10	.04	.01
☐ 443	Jim Lefebvre	.20	.08	.02
☐ 444	Ken Lehman	.10	.04	.01
☐ 445	Don LeJohn	.10	.04	.01
☐ 446	Steve Lembo	.10	.04	.01
☐ 447	Ed Lennox	.10	.04	.01
☐ 448	Dutch Leonard	.20	.08	.02
☐ 449	Jeffery Leonard	.15	.06	.01
☐ 451	Dennis Lewallyn	.10	.04	.01
☐ 452	Bob Lillis	.10	.04	.01.
☐ 453	Jim Lindsey	.10	.04	.01
☐ 454	Fred Lindstrom	.30	.12	.03
☐ 455	Billy Loes	.15	.06	.01
☐ 456	Bob Logan	.10	.04	.01
☐ 457	Bill Lohrman	.10	.04	.01
☐ 458	Not issued	.00	.00	.00
☐ 459	Vic Lombardi	.10	.04	.01
☐ 460	Davey Lopes	.20	.08	.02
☐ 461	Al Lopez	.30	.12	.03
☐ 462	Ray Lucas	.10	.04	.01
☐ 463	Not issued	.00	.00	.00
☐ 464	Harry Lumley	.10	.04	.01
☐ 465	Don Lund	.10	.04	.01
☐ 466	Dolf Luque	.10	.04	.01
☐ 467	Jim Lyttle	.10	.04	.01
☐ 468	Max Macon	.10	.04	.01
☐ 469	Bill Madlock	.20	.08	.02
☐ 470	Lee Magee	.10	.04	.01
☐ 471	Sal Maglie	.25	.10	.02
☐ 472	George Magoon	.10	.04	.01
☐ 473	Duster Mails	.10	.04	.01
☐ 474	Candy Maldonado	.20	.08	.02
☐ 475	Tony Malinosky	.10	.04	.01
☐ 476	Lew Malone	.10	.04	.01
☐ 477	Al Mamaux	.10	.04	.01
☐ 478	Gus Mancuso	.10	.04	.01
☐ 479	Charlie Manuel	.10	.04	.01
☐ 480	Heinie Manush	.30	.12	.03
☐ 481	Rabbit Maranville	.30	.12	.03
☐ 482	Juan Marichal	.40	.16	.04
☐ 483	Rube Marquard	.30	.12	.03
☐ 484	Bill Marriott	.10	.04	.01
☐ 485	Buck Marrow	.10	.04	.01
☐ 486	Mike A. Marshall	.20	.08	.02
☐ 487	Mike G. Marshall	.20	.08	.02
☐ 488	Morrie Martin	.10	.04	.01
☐ 489	Ramon Martinez	.60	.25	.06
☐ 490	Teddy Martinez	.10	.04	.01
☐ 491	Earl Mattingly	.10	.04	.01
☐ 492	Len Matuszek	.10	.04	.01
☐ 493	Gene Mauch	.20	.08	.02
☐ 494	Al Maul	.10	.04	.01
☐ 495	Carmen Mauro	.10	.04	.01
☐ 496	Alvin McBean	.10	.04	.01
☐ 497	Bill McCarren	.10	.04	.01
☐ 498	Jack McCarthy	.10	.04	.01
☐ 499	Tommy McCarthy	.10	.04	.01
☐ 500	Lew McCarty	.10	.04	.01
☐ 501	Mike J. McCormick	.10	.04	.01
☐ 502	Judge McCreedie	.10	.04	.01
☐ 503	Tom McCreery	.10	.04	.01
☐ 504	Danny McDevitt	.10	.04	.01
☐ 505	Chappie McFarland	.10	.04	.01
☐ 506	Joe McGinnity	.35	.15	.03

#	Player				#	Player			
☐ 507	Bob McGraw	.10	.04	.01	☐ 601	Don Padgett	.10	.04	.01
☐ 508	Deacon McGuire	.10	.04	.01	☐ 602	Andy Pafko	.15	.06	.01
☐ 509	Bill McGunnigle	.10	.04	.01	☐ 603	Erv Palica	.10	.04	.01
☐ 510	Harry McIntyre	.10	.04	.01	☐ 604	Ed Palmquist	.10	.04	.01
☐ 511	Cal McLish	.10	.04	.01	☐ 605	Wes Parker	.20	.08	.02
☐ 512	Ken McMullen	.10	.04	.01	☐ 606	Jay Partridge	.10	.04	.01
☐ 513	Dough McWeeny	.10	.04	.01	☐ 607	Camilio Pascual	.20	.08	.02
☐ 514	Joe Medwick	.30	.12	.03	☐ 608	Kevin Pasley	.10	.04	.01
☐ 515	Rube Melton	.10	.04	.01	☐ 609	Dave Patterson	.10	.04	.01
☐ 516	Fred Merkle	.20	.08	.02	☐ 610	Harley Payne	.10	.04	.01
☐ 517	Orland Mercado	.10	.04	.01	☐ 611	Johnny Peacock	.10	.04	.01
☐ 518	Andy Messersmith	.20	.08	.02	☐ 612	Hal Peck	.10	.04	.01
☐ 519	Irish Meusel	.15	.06	.01	☐ 613	Stu Pederson	.10	.04	.01
☐ 520	Benny Meyer	.10	.04	.01	☐ 614	Alejandro Pena	.25	.10	.02
☐ 521	Russ Meyer	.10	.04	.01	☐ 615	Jose Pena	.10	.04	.01
☐ 522	Chief Meyers	.10	.04	.01	☐ 616	Jack Perconte	.10	.04	.01
☐ 523	Gene Michael	.20	.08	.02	☐ 617	Charlie Perkins	.10	.04	.01
☐ 524	Pete Mikkelsen	.10	.04	.01	☐ 618	Ron Perranoski	.20	.08	.02
☐ 525	Eddie Miksis	.10	.04	.01	☐ 619	Jim Peterson	.10	.04	.01
☐ 526	Johnny Miljus	.10	.04	.01	☐ 620	Jesse Petty	.10	.04	.01
☐ 527	Bob Miller	.10	.04	.01	☐ 621	Jeff Pfeffer	.10	.04	.01
☐ 528	Larry Miller	.10	.04	.01	☐ 622	Babe Phelps	.10	.04	.01
☐ 529	Otto Miller	.10	.04	.01	☐ 623	Val Picinich	.10	.04	.01
☐ 530	Ralph Miller	.10	.04	.01	☐ 624	Joe Pignatano	.10	.04	.01
☐ 531	Walt Miller	.10	.04	.01	☐ 625	George Pinckney	.10	.04	.01
☐ 532	Wally Millies	.10	.04	.01	☐ 626	Ed Pipgras	.10	.04	.01
☐ 533	Bob Milliken	.10	.04	.01	☐ 627	Bud Podbielan	.10	.04	.01
☐ 534	Buster Mills	.10	.04	.01	☐ 628	Johnny Podres	.20	.08	.02
☐ 535	Paul Minner	.10	.04	.01	☐ 629	Boots Poffenberger	.10	.04	.01
☐ 536	Bobby Mitchell	.10	.04	.01	☐ 630	Nick Polly	.10	.04	.01
☐ 537	Clarence Mitchell	.10	.04	.01	☐ 631	Paul Popovich	.10	.04	.01
☐ 538	Dale Mitchell	.15	.06	.01	☐ 632	Bill Posedel	.10	.04	.01
☐ 539	Fred Mitchell	.10	.04	.01	☐ 633	Boog Powell	.20	.08	.02
☐ 540	Johnny Mitchell	.10	.04	.01	☐ 634	Dennis Powell	.10	.04	.01
☐ 541	Joe Moeller	.10	.04	.01	☐ 635	Paul Ray Powell	.10	.04	.01
☐ 542	Rick Monday	.15	.06	.01	☐ 636	Ted Power	.10	.04	.01
☐ 543	Wally Moon	.15	.06	.01	☐ 637	Tot Pressnell	.10	.04	.01
☐ 544	Cy Moore	.10	.04	.01	☐ 638	John Purdin	.10	.04	.01
☐ 545	Dee Moore	.10	.04	.01	☐ 639	Jack Quinn	.10	.04	.01
☐ 546	Eddie Moore	.10	.04	.01	☐ 640	Marv Rackley	.10	.04	.01
☐ 547	Gene Moore	.10	.04	.01	☐ 641	Jack Radtke	.10	.04	.01
☐ 548	Randy Moore	.10	.04	.01	☐ 642	Pat Ragan	.10	.04	.01
☐ 549	Ray Moore	.10	.04	.01	☐ 643	Ed Rakow	.10	.04	.01
☐ 550	Jose Morales	.10	.04	.01	☐ 644	Bob Ramazzotti	.10	.04	.01
☐ 551	Bobby Morgan	.10	.04	.01	☐ 645	Willie Ramsdell	.10	.04	.01
☐ 552	Eddie Morgan	.10	.04	.01	☐ 646	Mike James Ramsey	.10	.04	.01
☐ 553	Mike Morgan	.15	.06	.01	☐ 647	Mike Jeffery Ramsey	.10	.04	.01
☐ 554	Johnny Morrison	.10	.04	.01	☐ 648	Willie Randolph	.20	.08	.02
☐ 555	Walt Moryn	.10	.04	.01	☐ 649	Doug Rau	.10	.04	.01
☐ 556	Ray Moss	.10	.04	.01	☐ 650	Lance Rautzhan	.10	.04	.01
☐ 557	Manny Mota	.20	.08	.02	☐ 651	Howie Reed	.10	.04	.01
☐ 558	Joe Mulvey	.10	.04	.01	☐ 652	Pee Wee Reese	.45	.18	.04
☐ 559	Van Lingle Mungo	.15	.06	.01	☐ 653	Phil Regan	.20	.08	.02
☐ 560	Les Munns	.10	.04	.01	☐ 654	Bill Reidy	.10	.04	.01
☐ 561	Mike Munoz	.20	.08	.02	☐ 655	Bobby Reis	.10	.04	.01
☐ 562	Simmy Murch	.10	.04	.01	☐ 656	Pete Reiser	.20	.08	.02
☐ 563	Eddie Murray	.45	.18	.04	☐ 657	Rip Repulski	.10	.04	.01
☐ 564	Hy Myers	.10	.04	.01	☐ 658	Ed Reulbach	.20	.08	.02
☐ 565	Sam Nahem	.10	.04	.01	☐ 659	Jerry Reuss	.15	.06	.01
☐ 566	Earl Naylor	.10	.04	.01	☐ 660	R.J. Reynolds	.15	.06	.01
☐ 567	Charlie Neal	.15	.06	.01	☐ 661	Billy Rhiel	.10	.04	.01
☐ 568	Ron Negray	.10	.04	.01	☐ 662	Rick Rhoden	.15	.06	.01
☐ 569	Bernie Neis	.10	.04	.01	☐ 663	Paul Richards	.20	.08	.02
☐ 570	Rocky Nelson	.10	.04	.01	☐ 664	Danny Richardson	.10	.04	.01
☐ 571	Dick Nen	.10	.04	.01	☐ 665	Pete Richert	.10	.04	.01
☐ 572	Don Newcombe	.25	.10	.02	☐ 666	Harry Riconda	.10	.04	.01
☐ 573	Bobo Newsom	.20	.08	.02	☐ 667	Joe Riggert	.10	.04	.01
☐ 574	Doc Newton	.10	.04	.01	☐ 668	Lew Riggs	.10	.04	.01
☐ 575	Tom Niedenfuer	.10	.04	.01	☐ 669	Jimmy Ripple	.10	.04	.01
☐ 576	Otho Nitcholas	.10	.04	.01	☐ 670	Lou Ritter	.10	.04	.01
☐ 577	Al Nixon	.10	.04	.01	☐ 671	German Rivera	.10	.04	.01
☐ 578	Jerry Nops	.10	.04	.01	☐ 672	Johnny Rizzo	.10	.04	.01
☐ 579	Irv Noren	.10	.04	.01	☐ 673	Jim Roberts	.10	.04	.01
☐ 580	Fred Norman	.10	.04	.01	☐ 674	Earl Robinson	.10	.04	.01
☐ 581	Bill North	.10	.04	.01	☐ 675	Frank Robinson	.45	.18	.04
☐ 582	Johnny Oates	.15	.06	.01	☐ 676	Jackie Robinson	.60	.25	.06
☐ 583	Bob O'Brien	.10	.04	.01	☐ 677A	Wilbert Robinson	.35	.15	.03
☐ 584	John O'Brien	.10	.04	.01	☐ 678B	Sergio Robles	.10	.04	.01
☐ 585	Lefty O'Doul	.20	.08	.02	☐ 678	Rich Rodas	.10	.04	.01
☐ 586	Joe Oeschger	.10	.04	.01	☐ 679	Ellie Rodriguez	.10	.04	.01
☐ 587	Al Oliver	.20	.08	.02	☐ 680	Preacher Roe	.20	.08	.02
☐ 588	Nate Oliver	.10	.04	.01	☐ 681	Ed Roebuck	.10	.04	.01
☐ 589	Luis Olmo	.10	.04	.01	☐ 682	Ron Roenicke	.10	.04	.01
☐ 590	Ivy Olson	.10	.04	.01	☐ 683	Oscar Roettger	.10	.04	.01
☐ 591	Mickey O'Neil	.10	.04	.01	☐ 684	Lee Rogers	.10	.04	.01
☐ 592	Joe Orengo	.10	.04	.01	☐ 685	Packy Rogers	.10	.04	.01
☐ 593	Jesse Orosco	.10	.04	.01	☐ 686	Stan Rojek	.10	.04	.01
☐ 594	Frank O'Rourke	.10	.04	.01	☐ 687	Vicente Romo	.10	.04	.01
☐ 595	Jorge Orta	.10	.04	.01	☐ 688	Johnny Roseboro	.15	.06	.01
☐ 596	Phil Ortega	.10	.04	.01	☐ 689	Goody Rosen	.10	.04	.01
☐ 597	Claude Osteen	.20	.08	.02	☐ 690	Don Ross	.10	.04	.01
☐ 598	Fritz Ostermueller	.10	.04	.01	☐ 691	Ken Rowe	.10	.04	.01
☐ 599	Mickey Owen	.20	.08	.02	☐ 692	Schoolboy Rowe	.20	.08	.02
☐ 600	Tom Paciorek	.10	.04	.01	☐ 693	Luther Roy	.10	.04	.01

☐ 694	Jerry Royster	.10	.04	.01
☐ 695	Nap Rucker	.10	.04	.01
☐ 696	Dutch Ruether	.10	.04	.01
☐ 697	Bill Russell	.20	.08	.02
☐ 698	Jim Russell	.10	.04	.01
☐ 699	John Russell UER	.10	.04	.01
	(photo actually			
	current catcher			
	John Russell)			
☐ 700	Johnny Rutherford	.10	.04	.01
☐ 701	John Ryan	.10	.04	.01
☐ 702	Rosy Ryan	.10	.04	.01
☐ 703	Mike Sandlock	.10	.04	.01
☐ 704	Ted Savage	.10	.04	.01
☐ 705	Dave Sax	.10	.04	.01
☐ 706	Steve Sax	.20	.08	.02
☐ 707	Bill Sayles	.10	.04	.01
☐ 708	Bill Schardt	.10	.04	.01
☐ 709	Johnny Schmitz	.10	.04	.01
☐ 710	Dick Schofield	.15	.06	.01
☐ 711	Howie Schultz	.10	.04	.01
☐ 712	Ferdie Schupp	.10	.04	.01
☐ 713	Mike Scioscia	.20	.08	.02
☐ 714	Dick Scott	.10	.04	.01
☐ 715	Tom Seats	.10	.04	.01
☐ 716	Jimmy Sebring	.10	.04	.01
☐ 717	Larry See	.10	.04	.01
☐ 718	Dave Sells	.10	.04	.01
☐ 719	Greg Shanahan	.10	.04	.01
☐ 720	Mike Sharperson	.10	.04	.01
☐ 721	Joe Shaute	.10	.04	.01
☐ 722	Merv Shea	.10	.04	.01
☐ 723	Jimmy Sheckhard	.10	.04	.01
☐ 724	Jack Sheehan	.10	.04	.01
☐ 725	John Shelby	.10	.04	.01
☐ 726	Vince Sherlock	.10	.04	.01
☐ 727	Larry Sherry	.20	.08	.02
☐ 728	Norm Sherry	.15	.06	.01
☐ 729	Bill Shindle	.10	.04	.01
☐ 730	Craig Shipley	.15	.06	.01
☐ 731	Bart Shirley	.10	.04	.01
☐ 732	Steve Shirley	.10	.04	.01
☐ 733	Burt Shotton	.15	.06	.01
☐ 734	George Shuba	.15	.06	.01
☐ 735	Dick Siebert	.10	.04	.01
☐ 736	Joe Simpson	.10	.04	.01
☐ 737	Duke Sims	.10	.04	.01
☐ 738	Bill Singer	.15	.06	.01
☐ 739	Fred Sington	.10	.04	.01
☐ 740	Ted Sizemore	.15	.06	.01
☐ 741	Frank Skaff	.10	.04	.01
☐ 742	Bill Skowron	.20	.08	.02
☐ 743	Gordon Slade	.10	.04	.01
☐ 744	Dwain Lefty Sloat	.10	.04	.01
☐ 745	Charley Smith	.10	.04	.01
☐ 746	Dick Smith	.10	.04	.01
☐ 747	George Smith	.10	.04	.01
☐ 748	Germany Smith	.10	.04	.01
☐ 749	Jack Smith	.10	.04	.01
☐ 750	Reggie Smith	.20	.08	.02
☐ 751	Sherry Smith	.10	.04	.01
☐ 752	Harry Smythe	.10	.04	.01
☐ 753	Duke Snider	.60	.25	.06
☐ 754	Eddie Solomon	.10	.04	.01
☐ 755	Elias Sosa	.10	.04	.01
☐ 756	Daryl Spencer	.10	.04	.01
☐ 757	Roy Spencer	.10	.04	.01
☐ 758	Karl Spooner	.10	.04	.01
☐ 759	Eddie Stack	.10	.04	.01
☐ 760	Tuck Stainback	.10	.04	.01
☐ 761	George Stallings	.10	.04	.01
☐ 762	Jerry Standaert	.10	.04	.01
☐ 763	Don Stanhouse	.15	.06	.01
☐ 764	Eddie Stanky	.20	.08	.02
☐ 765	Dolly Stark	.20	.08	.02
☐ 766	Jigger Statz	.10	.04	.01
☐ 767	Casey Stengel	.40	.16	.04
☐ 768	Jerry Stephenson	.10	.04	.01
☐ 769	Ed Stevens	.10	.04	.01
☐ 770	Dave Stewart	.30	.12	.03
☐ 771	Stuffy Stewart	.10	.04	.01
☐ 772	Bob Stinson	.10	.04	.01
☐ 773	Milt Stock	.10	.04	.01
☐ 774	Harry Stovey	.20	.08	.02
☐ 775	Mike Strahler	.10	.04	.01
☐ 776	Sammy Strang	.10	.04	.01
☐ 777	Elmer Stricklett	.10	.04	.01
☐ 778	Joe Stripp	.10	.04	.01
☐ 779	Dick Stuart	.20	.08	.02
☐ 780	Franklin Stubbs	.20	.08	.02
☐ 781	Bill Sudakis	.10	.04	.01
☐ 782	Clyde Sukeforth	.10	.04	.01
☐ 783	Billy Sullivan	.20	.08	.02
☐ 784	Tom Sunkel	.10	.04	.01
☐ 785	Rick Sutcliffe	.20	.08	.02
☐ 786	Don Sutton	.30	.12	.03
☐ 787	Bill Swift	.10	.04	.01
☐ 788	Vito Tamulis	.10	.04	.01
☐ 789	Danny Taylor	.10	.04	.01
☐ 790	Harry Taylor	.10	.04	.01
☐ 791	Zack Taylor	.10	.04	.01
☐ 792	Not issued	.00	.00	.00
☐ 793	Chuck Templeton	.10	.04	.01
☐ 794	Wayne Terwilliger	.10	.04	.01
☐ 795	Derrell Thomas	.10	.04	.01
☐ 796	Fay Thomas	.10	.04	.01
☐ 797	Gary Thomasson	.10	.04	.01
☐ 798	Don Thompson	.10	.04	.01
☐ 799	Fresco Thompson	.15	.06	.01
☐ 800	Tim Thompson	.10	.04	.01
☐ 801	Hank Thormahlen	.10	.04	.01
☐ 802	Sloppy Thurston	.10	.04	.01
☐ 803	Cotton Tierney	.10	.04	.01
☐ 804	Al Todd	.10	.04	.01
☐ 805	Bert Tooley	.10	.04	.01
☐ 806	Jeff Torborg	.20	.08	.02
☐ 807	Dick Tracewski	.10	.04	.01
☐ 808	Nick Tremark	.10	.04	.01
☐ 809	Alex Trevino	.10	.04	.01
☐ 810	Tommy Tucker	.10	.04	.01
☐ 811	John Tudor	.20	.08	.02
☐ 812	Mike Vail	.10	.04	.01
☐ 813	Rene Valdes	.10	.04	.01
☐ 814	Bobby Valentine	.25	.10	.02
☐ 815	Fernando Valenzuela	.30	.12	.03
☐ 816	Elmer Valo	.10	.04	.01
☐ 817	Dazzy Vance	.30	.12	.03
☐ 818	Sandy Vance	.10	.04	.01
☐ 819	Chris Van Cuyk	.10	.04	.01
☐ 820	Ed VandeBerg	.10	.04	.01
☐ 821	Arky Vaughan	.30	.12	.03
☐ 822	Zoilo Versalles	.20	.08	.02
☐ 823	Joe Vosmik	.10	.04	.01
☐ 824	Ben Wade	.10	.04	.01
☐ 825	Dixie Walker	.10	.04	.01
☐ 826	Rube Walker	.10	.04	.01
☐ 827	Stan Wall	.10	.04	.01
☐ 828	Lee Walls	.10	.04	.01
☐ 829	Danny Walton	.10	.04	.01
☐ 830	Lloyd Waner	.30	.12	.03
☐ 831	Paul Waner	.30	.12	.03
☐ 832	Chuck Ward	.10	.04	.01
☐ 833	John Monte Ward	.30	.12	.03
☐ 834	Preston Ward	.10	.04	.01
☐ 835	Jack Warner	.10	.04	.01
☐ 836	Tommy Warren	.10	.04	.01
☐ 837	Carl Warwick	.10	.04	.01
☐ 838	Jimmy Wasdell	.10	.04	.01
☐ 839	Ron Washington	.10	.04	.01
☐ 840	George Watkins	.10	.04	.01
☐ 841	Hank Webb	.10	.04	.01
☐ 842	Les Webber	.10	.04	.01
☐ 843	Gary Weiss	.10	.04	.01
☐ 844	Bob Welch	.30	.12	.03
☐ 845	Brad Wellman	.10	.04	.01
☐ 846	John Werhas	.15	.06	.01
☐ 847	Max West	.10	.04	.01
☐ 848	Gus Weyhing	.10	.04	.01
☐ 849	Mack Wheat	.10	.04	.01
☐ 850	Zack Wheat	.30	.12	.03
☐ 851	Ed Wheeler	.10	.04	.01
☐ 852	Larry White	.10	.04	.01
☐ 853	Myron White	.10	.04	.01
☐ 854	Terry Whitfield	.10	.04	.01
☐ 855	Dick Whitman	.10	.04	.01
☐ 856	Possum Whitted	.10	.04	.01
☐ 857	Kemp Wicker	.10	.04	.01
☐ 858	Hoyt Wilhelm	.35	.15	.03
☐ 859	Kaiser Wilhelm	.10	.04	.01
☐ 860	Nick Willhite	.10	.04	.01
☐ 861	Dick Williams	.15	.06	.01
☐ 862	Reggie Williams	.10	.04	.01
☐ 863	Stan Williams	.15	.06	.01
☐ 864	Woody Williams	.10	.04	.01
☐ 865	Maury Wills	.30	.12	.03
☐ 866	Hack Wilson	.30	.12	.03
☐ 867	Robert Wilson	.10	.04	.01
☐ 868	Gordon Windhorn	.10	.04	.01
☐ 869	Jim Winford	.10	.04	.01
☐ 870	Lave Winham	.10	.04	.01
☐ 871	Tom Winsett	.10	.04	.01
☐ 872	Hank Winston	.10	.04	.01
☐ 873	Whitney Witt	.10	.04	.01
☐ 874	Pete Wojey	.10	.04	.01
☐ 875	Tracy Woodson	.10	.04	.01
☐ 876	Clarence Wright	.10	.04	.01
☐ 877	Glenn Wright	.10	.04	.01
☐ 878	Ricky Wright	.10	.04	.01

☐ 879 Whit Wyatt	.15	.06	.01			
☐ 880 Jimmy Wynn	.15	.06	.01			
☐ 881 Joe Yeager	.10	.04	.01			
☐ 882 Steve Yeager	.15	.06	.01			
☐ 883 Matt Young	.10	.04	.01			
☐ 884 Tom Zachary	.10	.04	.01			
☐ 885 Pat Zachry	.15	.06	.01			
☐ 886 Geoff Zahn	.10	.04	.01			
☐ 887 Don Zimmer	.20	.08	.02			
☐ 888 Morrie Aderholt	.10	.04	.01			
☐ 889 Raleigh Aitchison	.10	.04	.01			
☐ 890 Whitey Alperman	.10	.04	.01			
☐ 891 Orlando Alvarez	.10	.04	.01			
☐ 892 Pat Ankeman	.10	.04	.01			
☐ 893 Ed Appleton	.10	.04	.01			
☐ 894 Doug Baird	.10	.04	.01			
☐ 895 Lady Baldwin	.10	.04	.01			
☐ 896 Win Ballou	.10	.04	.01			
☐ 897 Bob Barr	.10	.04	.01			
☐ 898 Boyd Bartley	.10	.04	.01			
☐ 899 Eddie Basinski	.10	.04	.01			
☐ 900 Erve Beck	.10	.04	.01			
☐ 901 Ralph Birkofer	.10	.04	.01			
☐ 902 Not issued	.00	.00	.00			
☐ 903 Joe Bradshaw	.10	.04	.01			
☐ 904 Bruce Brubaker	.10	.04	.01			
☐ 905 Oyster Burns	.10	.04	.01			
☐ 906 John Butler	.10	.04	.01			
☐ 907 Not issued	.00	.00	.00			
☐ 908 Kid Carsey	.10	.04	.01			
☐ 909 Pete Cassidy	.10	.04	.01			
☐ 910 Tom Catterson	.10	.04	.01			
☐ 911 Glenn Chapman	.10	.04	.01			
☐ 912 Paul Chervinko	.10	.04	.01			
☐ 913 George Cisar	.10	.04	.01			
☐ 914 Wally Clement	.10	.04	.01			
☐ 915 Bill Collins	.10	.04	.01			
☐ 916 Chuck Corgan	.10	.04	.01			
☐ 917 Dick Cox	.10	.04	.01			
☐ 918 George Crable	.10	.04	.01			
☐ 919 Sam Crane	.10	.04	.01			
☐ 920 Cliff Curtis	.10	.04	.01			
☐ 921 Fats Dantonio	.10	.04	.01			
☐ 922 Con Daily	.10	.04	.01			
☐ 923 Jud Daley	.10	.04	.01			
☐ 924 Jake Daniel	.10	.04	.01			
☐ 925 Kal Daniels	.20	.08	.02			
☐ 926 Dan Daub	.10	.04	.01			
☐ 927 Lindsay Deal	.10	.04	.01			
☐ 928 Artie Dede	.10	.04	.01			
☐ 929 Pat Deisel	.10	.04	.01			
☐ 930 Bert Delmas	.10	.04	.01			
☐ 931 Rube Dessau	.10	.04	.01			
☐ 932 Leo Dickerman	.10	.04	.01			
☐ 933 John Douglas	.10	.04	.01			
☐ 934 Red Downey	.10	.04	.01			
☐ 935 Carl Doyle	.10	.04	.01			
☐ 936 John Duffie	.10	.04	.01			
☐ 937 Dick Durning	.10	.04	.01			
☐ 938 Red Durrett	.10	.04	.01			
☐ 939 Mal Eason	.10	.04	.01			
☐ 940 Charlie Ebbetts	.15	.06	.01			
☐ 941 Rube Ehardt	.10	.04	.01			
☐ 942 Rowdy Elliot	.10	.04	.01			
☐ 943 Bones Ely	.10	.04	.01			
☐ 944 Woody English	.10	.04	.01			
☐ 945 Roy Evans	.10	.04	.01			
☐ 946 Gus Felix	.10	.04	.01			
☐ 947 Bill Fischer	.10	.04	.01			
☐ 948 Jeff Fischer	.10	.04	.01			
☐ 949 Chauncey Fisher	.10	.04	.01			
☐ 950 Tom Fitzsimmons	.10	.04	.01			
☐ 951 Darrin Fletcher	.15	.06	.01			
☐ 952 Wes Flowers	.10	.04	.01			
☐ 953 Howard Freigau	.10	.04	.01			
☐ 954 Nig Fuller	.10	.04	.01			
☐ 955 John Gaddy	.10	.04	.01			
☐ 956 Welcome Gaston	.10	.04	.01			
☐ 957 Frank Gatins	.10	.04	.01			
☐ 958 Pete Gilbert	.10	.04	.01			
☐ 959 Wally Gilbert	.10	.04	.01			
☐ 960 Carden Gillenwater	.10	.04	.01			
☐ 961 Roy Gleason	.10	.04	.01			
☐ 962 Harvey Green	.10	.04	.01			
☐ 963 Nelson Greene	.10	.04	.01			
☐ 964 John Grim	.10	.04	.01			
☐ 965 Dan Griner	.10	.04	.01			
☐ 967 Bill Hall	.10	.04	.01			
☐ 968 Johnny Hall	.10	.04	.01			
☐ 969 Not issued	.00	.00	.00			
☐ 970 Pat Hanifin	.10	.04	.01			
☐ 971 Bill Harris	.10	.04	.01			
☐ 972 Bill W. Hart	.10	.04	.01			
☐ 973 Chris Hartje	.10	.04	.01			
☐ 974 Mike Hartley	.15	.06	.01
☐ 975 Gil Hatfield	.10	.04	.01
☐ 976 Chris Haughey	.10	.04	.01
☐ 977 Hugh Hearne	.10	.04	.01
☐ 978 Mike Hechinger	.10	.04	.01
☐ 979 Jake Hehl	.10	.04	.01
☐ 980 Bob Higgins	.10	.04	.01
☐ 981 Still Bill Hill	.10	.04	.01
☐ 982 Shawn Hillegas	.15	.06	.01
☐ 983 Wally Hood	.10	.04	.01
☐ 984 Lefty Hopper	.10	.04	.01
☐ 985 Ricky Horton	.10	.04	.01
☐ 986 Ed Householder	.10	.04	.01
☐ 987 Bill Hubbell	.10	.04	.01
☐ 988 Al Humphrey	.10	.04	.01
☐ 989 Bernie Hungling	.10	.04	.01
☐ 990 George Hunter	.10	.04	.01
☐ 991 Pat Hurley	.10	.04	.01
☐ 992 Joe Hutcheson	.10	.04	.01
☐ 993 Roy Hutson	.10	.04	.01
☐ 994 Bert Inks	.10	.04	.01
☐ 995 Dutch Jordan	.10	.04	.01
☐ 996 Not issued	.00	.00	.00
☐ 997 Frank Kane	.10	.04	.01
☐ 998 Chet Kehn	.10	.04	.01
☐ 999 Maury Kent	.10	.04	.01
☐ 1000 Tom Kinslow	.10	.04	.01
☐ 1001 Fred Kipp	.10	.04	.01
☐ 1002 Joe Klugman	.10	.04	.01
☐ 1003 Elmer Knetzer	.10	.04	.01
☐ 1004 Barney Koch	.10	.04	.01
☐ 1005 Jim Korwan	.10	.04	.01
☐ 1006 Joe Koukalik	.10	.04	.01
☐ 1007 Lou Koupal	.10	.04	.01
☐ 1008 Joe Kustus	.10	.04	.01
☐ 1009 Frank Lamanske	.10	.04	.01
☐ 1010 Tacks Latimer	.10	.04	.01
☐ 1011 Bill Leard	.10	.04	.01
☐ 1012 Phil Lewis	.10	.04	.01
☐ 1013 Mickey Livingston	.10	.04	.01
☐ 1014 Dick Loftus	.10	.04	.01
☐ 1015 Charlie Loudenslager	.10	.04	.01
☐ 1016 Tom Lovett	.10	.04	.01
☐ 1017 Charlie Malay	.10	.04	.01
☐ 1018 Mal Mallette	.10	.04	.01
☐ 1019 Ralph Mauriello	.10	.04	.01
☐ 1020 Bill McCabe	.10	.04	.01
☐ 1021 Gene McCann	.10	.04	.01
☐ 1022 Mike W. McCormick	.10	.04	.01
☐ 1023 Terry McDermott	.10	.04	.01
☐ 1024 John McDougal	.10	.04	.01
☐ 1025 Pryor McElveen	.10	.04	.01
☐ 1026 Dan McGann	.10	.04	.01
☐ 1027 Pat McGlothin	.10	.04	.01
☐ 1028 Doc McJames	.10	.04	.01
☐ 1029 Kit McKenna	.10	.04	.01
☐ 1030 Sadie McMahon	.10	.04	.01
☐ 1031 Not issued	.00	.00	.00
☐ 1032 Tommy McMillan	.10	.04	.01
☐ 1033 Glenn Mickens	.10	.04	.01
☐ 1034 Don Miles	.10	.04	.01
☐ 1035 Hack Miller	.10	.04	.01
☐ 1036 John Miller	.10	.04	.01
☐ 1037 Lemmie Miller	.10	.04	.01
☐ 1038 George Mohart	.10	.04	.01
☐ 1039 Gary Moore	.10	.04	.01
☐ 1040 Herbie Moran	.10	.04	.01
☐ 1041 Earl Mossor	.10	.04	.01
☐ 1042 Glen Moulder	.10	.04	.01
☐ 1043 Billy Mullen	.10	.04	.01
☐ 1045 Curly Onis	.10	.04	.01
☐ 1046 Tiny Osborne	.10	.04	.01
☐ 1047 Jim Pastorius	.10	.04	.01
☐ 1048 Art Parks	.10	.04	.01
☐ 1049 Chink Outen	.10	.04	.01
☐ 1050 Jimmy Pattison	.10	.04	.01
☐ 1051 Norman Plitt	.10	.04	.01
☐ 1052 Doc Reisling	.10	.04	.01
☐ 1053 Gilberto Reyes	.15	.06	.01
☐ 1054 Not issued	.00	.04	.00
☐ 1055 Lou Rochelli	.10	.04	.01
☐ 1056 Jim Romano	.10	.04	.01
☐ 1057 Max Rosenfeld	.10	.04	.01
☐ 1058 Andy Rush	.10	.04	.01
☐ 1059 Jack Ryan	.10	.04	.01
☐ 1060 Jack Savage	.15	.06	.01
☐ 1061 Not issued	.00	.00	.00
☐ 1062 Ray Schmandt	.10	.04	.01
☐ 1063 Henry Schmidt	.10	.04	.01
☐ 1064 Charlie Schmutz	.10	.04	.01
☐ 1065 Joe Schultz	.10	.04	.01
☐ 1066 Ray Searage	.10	.04	.01
☐ 1067 Elmer Sexauer	.10	.04	.01
☐ 1068 George Sharrott	.10	.04	.01

☐ 1069	Tommy Sheehan	.10	.04	.01
☐ 1071	George Shoch	.10	.04	.01
☐ 1072	Broadway Aleck Smith	.10	.04	.01
☐ 1073	Hap Smith	.10	.04	.01
☐ 1074	Red Smith	.10	.04	.01
☐ 1075	Tony Smith	.10	.04	.01
☐ 1076	Gene Snyder	.10	.04	.01
☐ 1077	Denny Sothern	.10	.04	.01
☐ 1078	Bill Steele	.10	.04	.01
☐ 1080	Farmer Steelman	.10	.04	.01
☐ 1081	Dutch Stryker	.10	.04	.01
☐ 1082	Tommy Tatum	.10	.04	.01
☐ 1084	Adonis Terry	.10	.04	.01
☐ 1085	Ray Thomas	.10	.04	.01
☐ 1086	George Treadway	.10	.04	.01
☐ 1087	Overton Tremper	.10	.04	.01
☐ 1088	Ty Tyson	.10	.04	.01
☐ 1089	Rube Vickers	.10	.04	.01
☐ 1090	Jose Vizcaino	.10	.04	.01
☐ 1091	Bull Wagner	.10	.04	.01
☐ 1092	Butts Wagner	.10	.04	.01
☐ 1093	Rube Ward	.10	.04	.01
☐ 1094	John Wetteland	.20	.08	.02
☐ 1095	Eddie Wilson	.10	.04	.01
☐ 1096	Tex Wilson	.10	.04	.01
☐ 1097	Zeke Wrigley	.10	.04	.01
☐ 1098	Not issued	.00	.00	.00
☐ 1099	Rube Yarrison	.10	.04	.01
☐ 1100	Earl Yingling	.10	.04	.01
☐ 1101	Chink Zachary	.10	.04	.01
☐ 1102	Lefty Davis	.10	.04	.01
☐ 1103	Bob Hall	.10	.04	.01
☐ 1104	Darby O'Brien	.10	.04	.01
☐ 1105	Larry LeJeune	.10	.04	.01
☐ 1144	Hub Northen	.10	.04	.01

1986 Texas Gold Reds

(36) MARIO SOTO P

Texas Gold Ice Cream is the sponsor of this 28-card set of Cincinnati Reds. The cards are 2 1/2" by 3 1/2" and feature player photos in full color with a red and white border on the front of the card. The set was distributed to fans attending the Reds game at Riverfront Stadium on September 19th. The card backs contain the player's career statistics, uniform number, name, position, and the Texas Gold logo.

		MINT	EXC	G-VG
	COMPLETE SET (28)	32.00	14.25	4.75
	COMMON PLAYER	.60	.25	.06
☐ 6	Bo Diaz	.60	.25	.06
☐ 9	Max Venable	.60	.25	.06
☐ 11	Kurt Stillwell	.75	.30	.07
☐ 12	Nick Esasky	.75	.30	.07
☐ 13	Dave Concepcion	1.00	.40	.10
☐ 14A	Pete Rose INF	3.00	1.25	.30
☐ 14B	Pete Rose MG	3.00	1.25	.30
☐ 14C	Pete Rose (commemorative)	3.00	1.25	.30
☐ 16	Ron Oester	.60	.25	.06
☐ 20	Eddie Milner	.60	.25	.06
☐ 22	Sal Butera	.60	.25	.06
☐ 24	Tony Perez	1.50	.60	.15
☐ 25	Buddy Bell	.75	.30	.07
☐ 28	Kal Daniels	2.50	1.00	.25

☐ 29	Tracy Jones	.75	.30	.07
☐ 31	John Franco	1.00	.40	.10
☐ 32	Tom Browning	1.00	.40	.10
☐ 33	Ron Robinson	.75	.30	.07
☐ 34	Bill Gullickson	.75	.30	.07
☐ 36	Mario Soto	.75	.30	.07
☐ 39	Dave Parker	1.25	.50	.12
☐ 40	John Denny	.75	.30	.07
☐ 44	Eric Davis	7.50	3.25	.75
☐ 45	Chris Welsh	.60	.25	.06
☐ 48	Ted Power	.60	.25	.06
☐ 49	Joe Price	.60	.25	.06
☐ xx	Reds Coaches	.60	.25	.06
	George Scherger			
	Bruce Kimm			
	Billy DeMars			
	Tommy Helms			
	Scott Breeden			
	Jim Lett			
☐ xx	Preferred Customer Card (Discount Coupon)	.60	.25	.06

1971 Ticketron Dodgers

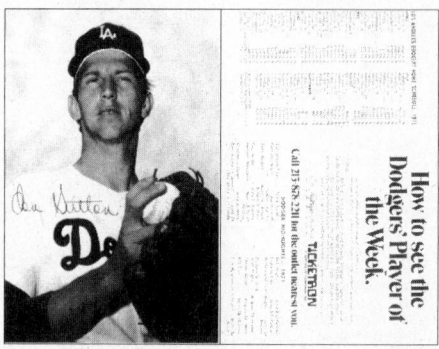

The 1971 Ticketron Los Angeles Dodgers set is a 20-card set with cards measuring approximately 4" by 6". This set has a 1971 Garvey rookie year card as well as 18 other players including Richie Allen in his only year as a Dodger. The fronts are beautiful full-color photos which also have a facsimile autograph on the front and are borderless while the backs contain an advertisement for Ticketron, the 1971 Dodger home schedule and a list of promotional events scheduled for 1971.

		NRMT	VG-E	GOOD
	COMPLETE SET (20)	100.00	45.00	15.00
	COMMON PLAYER (1-20)	3.00	1.25	.30
☐ 1	Richie Allen	6.00	2.50	.60
☐ 2	Walter Alston MG	7.50	3.25	.75
☐ 3	Jim Brewer	3.00	1.25	.30
☐ 4	Willie Crawford	3.00	1.25	.30
☐ 5	Willie Davis	4.00	1.75	.40
☐ 6	Steve Garvey	35.00	15.75	5.25
☐ 7	Bill Grabarkewitz	3.00	1.25	.30
☐ 8	Jim Lefebvre	4.00	1.75	.40
☐ 9	Pete Mikkelsen	3.00	1.25	.30
☐ 10	Joe Moeller	3.00	1.25	.30
☐ 11	Manny Mota	4.00	1.75	.40
☐ 12	Claude Osteen	4.00	1.75	.40
☐ 13	Wes Parker	4.00	1.75	.40
☐ 14	Bill Russell	4.00	1.75	.40
☐ 15	Duke Sims	3.00	1.25	.30
☐ 16	Bill Singer	3.00	1.25	.30
☐ 17	Bill Sudakis	3.00	1.25	.30
☐ 18	Don Sutton	7.50	3.25	.75
☐ 19	Maury Wills	6.00	2.50	.60
☐ 20	Vic Scully and Jerry Doggett (announcers)	4.00	1.75	.40

1971 Ticketron Giants

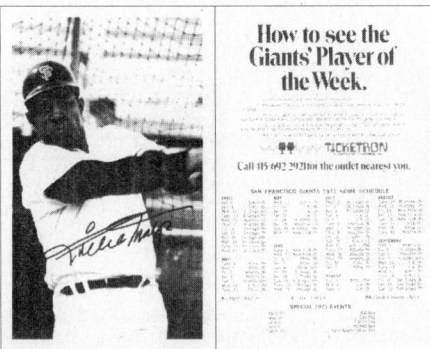

The 1971 Ticketron San Francisco Giants set is a 10-card set featuring members of the division-winning 1971 San Francisco Giants. The set measures approximately 3 7/8" by 6" and features an attractive full-color photo framed by white borders on the front along with a facsimile autograph. The back contains an ad for Ticketron as well as the 1971 Giants home schedule.

	NRMT	VG-E	GOOD
COMPLETE SET (10)	80.00	36.00	12.00
COMMON PLAYER (1-10)	3.00	1.25	.30
☐ 1 Bobby Bonds	6.00	2.50	.60
☐ 2 Dick Dietz	3.00	1.25	.30
☐ 3 Charles Fox MG	3.00	1.25	.30
☐ 4 Tito Fuentes	3.00	1.25	.30
☐ 5 Ken Henderson	3.00	1.25	.30
☐ 6 Juan Marichal	12.00	5.25	1.50
☐ 7 Willie Mays	36.00	16.25	5.50
☐ 8 Willie McCovey	16.00	6.75	2.25
☐ 9 Don McMahon	3.00	1.25	.30
☐ 10 Gaylord Perry	12.00	5.25	1.50

1947 Tip Top

The cards in this 163-card set measure approximately 2 1/4" by 3". The 1947 Tip Top Bread issue contains unnumbered cards with black and white player photos. The set is of interest to baseball historians in that it contains cards of many players not appearing in any other card sets. The cards were issued locally for the eleven following teams: Red Sox (1-15), White Sox (16-30), Tigers (31-45), Yankees (46-60), Browns (61-75), Braves (76-90), Dodgers (91-104), Cubs (105-119), Giants (120-135), Pirates (136-149), and Cardinals (150-164). Players of

the Red Sox, Tigers, White Sox, Braves, and the Cubs are scarcer than those of the other teams; players from these tougher teams are marked by SP below to indicate their scarcity. The catalog designation is D323.

	NRMT	VG-E	GOOD
COMPLETE SET (163)	10500.00	4500.00	1250.00
COMMON PLAYER (1-164)	25.00	11.00	3.50
COMMON SP PLAYER	85.00	38.00	12.75
☐ 1 Leon Culberson SP	85.00	38.00	12.75
☐ 2 Dom DiMaggio SP	150.00	67.50	22.50
☐ 3 Joe Dobson SP	85.00	38.00	12.75
☐ 4 Bob Doerr SP	250.00	110.00	37.50
☐ 5 Dave(Boo) Ferris SP	85.00	38.00	12.75
☐ 6 Mickey Harris SP	85.00	38.00	12.75
☐ 7 Frank Hayes SP	85.00	38.00	12.75
☐ 8 Cecil Hughson SP	85.00	38.00	12.75
☐ 9 Earl Johnson SP	85.00	38.00	12.75
☐ 10 Roy Partee SP	85.00	38.00	12.75
☐ 11 Johnny Pesky SP	100.00	45.00	15.00
☐ 12 Rip Russell SP	85.00	38.00	12.75
☐ 13 Hal Wagner SP	85.00	38.00	12.75
☐ 14 Rudy York SP	110.00	50.00	16.50
☐ 15 Bill Zuber SP	85.00	38.00	12.75
☐ 16 Floyd Baker SP	85.00	38.00	12.75
☐ 17 Earl Caldwell SP	85.00	38.00	12.75
☐ 18 Lloyd Christopher SP	85.00	38.00	12.75
☐ 19 George Dickey SP	85.00	38.00	12.75
☐ 20 Ralph Hodgin SP	85.00	38.00	12.75
☐ 21 Bob Kennedy SP	85.00	38.00	12.75
☐ 22 Joe Kuhel SP	85.00	38.00	12.75
☐ 23 Thornton Lee SP	85.00	38.00	12.75
☐ 24 Ed Lopat SP	150.00	67.50	22.50
☐ 25 Cass Michaels SP	85.00	38.00	12.75
☐ 26 John Rigney SP	85.00	38.00	12.75
☐ 27 Mike Tresh SP	85.00	38.00	12.75
☐ 28 Thurman Tucker SP	85.00	38.00	12.75
☐ 29 Jack Wallasca SP	85.00	38.00	12.75
☐ 30 Taft Wright SP	85.00	38.00	12.75
☐ 31 Walter(Hoot)Evers SP	85.00	38.00	12.75
☐ 32 John Gorsica SP	85.00	38.00	12.75
☐ 33 Fred Hutchinson SP	110.00	50.00	16.50
☐ 34 George Kell SP	400.00	180.00	60.00
☐ 35 Eddie Lake SP	85.00	38.00	12.75
☐ 36 Ed Mayo SP	85.00	38.00	12.75
☐ 37 Arthur Mills SP	85.00	38.00	12.75
☐ 38 Pat Mullin SP	85.00	38.00	12.75
☐ 39 James Outlaw SP	85.00	38.00	12.75
☐ 40 Frank Overmire SP	85.00	38.00	12.75
☐ 41 Bob Swift SP	85.00	38.00	12.75
☐ 42 Birdie Tebbetts SP	85.00	38.00	12.75
☐ 43 Paul(Diz) Trout SP	100.00	45.00	15.00
☐ 44 Virgil Trucks SP	100.00	45.00	15.00
☐ 45 Dick Wakefield SP	85.00	38.00	12.75
☐ 46 Larry Berra	400.00	180.00	60.00
☐ 47 Floyd(Bill) Bevans	25.00	11.00	3.50
☐ 48 Bobby Brown	45.00	20.00	6.75
☐ 49 Thomas Byrne	25.00	11.00	3.50
☐ 50 Frank Crosetti	40.00	18.00	6.00
☐ 51 Tom Henrich	40.00	18.00	6.00
☐ 52 Charlie Keller	35.00	15.75	5.25
☐ 53 Johnny Lindell	25.00	11.00	3.50
☐ 54 Joe Page	25.00	11.00	3.50
☐ 55 Mel Queen	25.00	11.00	3.50
☐ 56 Allie Reynolds	45.00	20.00	6.75
☐ 57 Phil Rizzuto	135.00	60.00	20.00
☐ 58 Aaron Robinson	25.00	11.00	3.50
☐ 59 George Stirnweiss	25.00	11.00	3.50
☐ 60 Charles Wensloff	25.00	11.00	3.50
☐ 61 John Berardino	25.00	11.00	3.50
☐ 62 Clifford Fannin	25.00	11.00	3.50
☐ 63 Dennis Galehouse	25.00	11.00	3.50
☐ 64 Jeff Heath	25.00	11.00	3.50
☐ 65 Walter Judnich	25.00	11.00	3.50
☐ 66 Jack Kramer	25.00	11.00	3.50
☐ 67 Paul Lehner	25.00	11.00	3.50
☐ 68 Lester Moss	25.00	11.00	3.50
☐ 69 Bob Muncrief	25.00	11.00	3.50
☐ 70 Nelson Potter	25.00	11.00	3.50
☐ 71 Fred Sanford	25.00	11.00	3.50
☐ 72 Joe Schultz	25.00	11.00	3.50
☐ 73 Vern Stephens	35.00	15.75	5.25
☐ 74 Jerry Witte	25.00	11.00	3.50
☐ 75 Al Zarilla	25.00	11.00	3.50
☐ 76 Charles Barrett SP	85.00	38.00	12.75
☐ 77 Hank Camelli SP	85.00	38.00	12.75
☐ 78 Dick Culler SP	85.00	38.00	12.75
☐ 79 Nanny Fernandez SP	85.00	38.00	12.75
☐ 80 Si Johnson SP	85.00	38.00	12.75
☐ 81 Danny Litwhiler SP	85.00	38.00	12.75
☐ 82 Phil Masi SP	85.00	38.00	12.75
☐ 83 Carvel Rowell SP	85.00	38.00	12.75

			MINT	EXC	G-VG
☐	84	Connie Ryan SP	85.00	38.00	12.75
☐	85	John Sain SP	150.00	67.50	22.50
☐	86	Ray Sanders SP	85.00	38.00	12.75
☐	87	Sibby Sisti SP	85.00	38.00	12.75
☐	88	Billy Southworth SP	85.00	38.00	12.75
☐	89	Warren Spahn SP	500.00	225.00	75.00
☐	90	Ed Wright SP	85.00	38.00	12.75
☐	91	Bob Bragan	25.00	11.00	3.50
☐	92	Ralph Branca	35.00	15.75	5.25
☐	93	Hugh Casey	25.00	11.00	3.50
☐	94	Bruce Edwards	25.00	11.00	3.50
☐	95	Hal Gregg	25.00	11.00	3.50
☐	96	Joe Hatten	25.00	11.00	3.50
☐	97	Gene Hermanski	25.00	11.00	3.50
☐	98	John Jorgensen	25.00	11.00	3.50
☐	99	Harry Lavagetto	25.00	11.00	3.50
☐	100	Vic Lombardi	25.00	11.00	3.50
☐	101	Frank Melton	25.00	11.00	3.50
☐	102	Ed Miksis	25.00	11.00	3.50
☐	103	Marv Rackley	25.00	11.00	3.50
☐	104	Ed Stevens	25.00	11.00	3.50
☐	105	Phil Cavarretta SP	135.00	60.00	20.00
☐	106	Bob Chipman SP	85.00	38.00	12.75
☐	107	Stanley Hack SP	100.00	45.00	15.00
☐	108	Don Johnson SP	85.00	38.00	12.75
☐	109	Emil Kush SP	85.00	38.00	12.75
☐	110	Bill Lee SP	100.00	45.00	15.00
☐	111	Mickey Livingston SP	85.00	38.00	12.75
☐	112	Harry Lowrey SP	85.00	38.00	12.75
☐	113	Clyde McCullough SP	85.00	38.00	12.75
☐	114	Andy Pafko SP	100.00	45.00	15.00
☐	115	Marv Rickert SP	85.00	38.00	12.75
☐	116	John Schmitz SP	85.00	38.00	12.75
☐	117	Bobby Sturgeon SP	85.00	38.00	12.75
☐	118	Ed Waitkus SP	85.00	38.00	12.75
☐	119	Henry Wyse SP	85.00	38.00	12.75
☐	120	Bill Ayers	25.00	11.00	3.50
☐	121	Robert Blattner	25.00	11.00	3.50
☐	122	Mike Budnick	25.00	11.00	3.50
☐	123	Sid Gordon	25.00	11.00	3.50
☐	124	Clinton Hartung	25.00	11.00	3.50
☐	125	Monte Kennedy	25.00	11.00	3.50
☐	126	Dave Koslo	25.00	11.00	3.50
☐	127	Carroll Lockman	25.00	11.00	3.50
☐	128	Jack Lohrke	25.00	11.00	3.50
☐	129	Ernie Lombardi	80.00	36.00	12.00
☐	130	Willard Marshall	25.00	11.00	3.50
☐	131	John Mize	100.00	45.00	15.00
☐	132	Eugene Thompson (does not exist)	00.00	00.00	0.00
☐	133	Ken Trinkle	25.00	11.00	3.50
☐	134	Bill Voiselle	25.00	11.00	3.50
☐	135	Mickey Witek	25.00	11.00	3.50
☐	136	Eddie Basinski	25.00	11.00	3.50
☐	137	Ernie Bonham	25.00	11.00	3.50
☐	138	Billy Cox	35.00	15.75	5.25
☐	139	Elbie Fletcher	25.00	11.00	3.50
☐	140	Frank Gustine	25.00	11.00	3.50
☐	141	Kirby Higbe	25.00	11.00	3.50
☐	142	Leroy Jarvis	25.00	11.00	3.50
☐	143	Ralph Kiner	100.00	45.00	15.00
☐	144	Fred Ostermueller	25.00	11.00	3.50
☐	145	Preacher Roe	45.00	20.00	6.75
☐	146	Jim Russell	25.00	11.00	3.50
☐	147	Rip Sewell	25.00	11.00	3.50
☐	148	Nick Strincevich	25.00	11.00	3.50
☐	149	Honus Wagner	125.00	57.50	18.75
☐	150	Alpha Brazle	25.00	11.00	3.50
☐	151	Ken Burkhart	25.00	11.00	3.50
☐	152	Bernard Creger	25.00	11.00	3.50
☐	153	Joffre Cross	25.00	11.00	3.50
☐	154	Charles E. Diering	25.00	11.00	3.50
☐	155	Ervin Dusak	25.00	11.00	3.50
☐	156	Joe Garagiola	100.00	45.00	15.00
☐	157	Tony Kaufmann	25.00	11.00	3.50
☐	158	George Kurowski	25.00	11.00	3.50
☐	159	Marty Marion	50.00	22.50	7.50
☐	160	George Munger	25.00	11.00	3.50
☐	161	Del Rice	25.00	11.00	3.50
☐	162	Dick Sisler	25.00	11.00	3.50
☐	163	Enos Slaughter	100.00	45.00	15.00
☐	164	Ted Wilks	25.00	11.00	3.50

1988 T/M Umpires

This set of 64 cards was distributed as a small boxed set featuring Major League umpires exclusively. The box itself is blank, white, and silver. The set was produced by T and M

Sports under licenses from Major League Baseball and the Major League Umpires Association. The cards are in color and are standard size, 2 1/2" by 3 1/2". Card backs are printed in black on light blue. All the cards are black bordered, but the American Leaguers have a red thin inner border, whereas the National Leaguers have a green thin inner border. A short biographical sketch is given on the back for each umpire. The cards are numbered on the back; the number on the front of each card refers to the umpire's uniform number.

			MINT	EXC	G-VG
	COMPLETE SET (64)		12.00	5.25	1.50
	COMMON PLAYER (1-64)		.25	.10	.02
☐	1	Doug Harvey	.50	.20	.05
☐	2	Lee Weyer	.25	.10	.02
☐	3	Billy Williams	.25	.10	.02
☐	4	John Kibler	.25	.10	.02
☐	5	Bob Engel	.35	.15	.03
☐	6	Harry Wendelstedt	.35	.15	.03
☐	7	Larry Barnett	.25	.10	.02
☐	8	Don Denkinger	.35	.15	.03
☐	9	Dave Phillips	.35	.15	.03
☐	10	Larry McCoy	.25	.10	.02
☐	11	Bruce Froemming	.35	.15	.03
☐	12	John McSherry	.35	.15	.03
☐	13	Jim Evans	.25	.10	.02
☐	14	Frank Pulli	.25	.10	.02
☐	15	Joe Brinkman	.25	.10	.02
☐	16	Terry Tata	.25	.10	.02
☐	17	Paul Runge	.25	.10	.02
☐	18	Dutch Rennert	.25	.10	.02
☐	19	Nick Bremigan	.25	.10	.02
☐	20	Jim McKean	.25	.10	.02
☐	21	Terry Cooney	.25	.10	.02
☐	22	Rich Garcia	.35	.15	.03
☐	23	Dale Ford	.25	.10	.02
☐	24	Al Clark	.25	.10	.02
☐	25	Greg Kose	.25	.10	.02
☐	26	Jim Quick	.25	.10	.02
☐	27	Ed Montague	.25	.10	.02
☐	28	Jerry Crawford	.25	.10	.02
☐	29	Steve Palermo	.60	.25	.06
☐	30	Durwood Merrill	.25	.10	.02
☐	31	Ken Kaiser	.35	.15	.03
☐	32	Vic Voltaggio	.25	.10	.02
☐	33	Mike Reilly	.25	.10	.02
☐	34	Eric Gregg	.45	.18	.04
☐	35	Ted Hendry	.25	.10	.02
☐	36	Joe West	.25	.10	.02
☐	37	Dave Pallone	.35	.15	.03
☐	38	Fred Brocklander	.25	.10	.02
☐	39	John Shulock	.25	.10	.02
☐	40	Derryl Cousins	.25	.10	.02
☐	41	Charlie Williams	.25	.10	.02
☐	42	Rocky Roe	.25	.10	.02
☐	43	Randy Marsh	.25	.10	.02
☐	44	Bob Davidson	.25	.10	.05
☐	45	Drew Coble	.25	.10	.02
☐	46	Tim McClelland	.25	.10	.02
☐	47	Dan Morrison	.25	.10	.02
☐	48	Rick Reed	.25	.10	.02
☐	49	Steve Rippley	.25	.10	.02
☐	50	John Hirshbeck	.25	.10	.02
☐	51	Mark Johnson	.25	.10	.02
☐	52	Gerry Davis	.25	.10	.02
☐	53	Dana DeMuth	.25	.10	.02
☐	54	Larry Young	.25	.10	.02
☐	55	Tim Welke	.25	.10	.02

		MINT	EXC	G-VG
☐ 56	Greg Bonin	.25	.10	.02
☐ 57	Tom Hallion	.25	.10	.02
☐ 58	Dale Scott	.25	.10	.02
☐ 59	Tim Tschida	.25	.10	.02
☐ 60	Dick Stello	.25	.10	.02
☐ 61	All-Star Game	.25	.10	.02
☐ 62	World Series	.25	.10	.02
☐ 63	Jocko Conlan	.60	.25	.06
☐ 64	Checklist Card	.25	.10	.02

1989 T/M Umpires

The 1989 Umpires set contains 63 standard-size (2 1/2 by 3 1/2 inch) cards. The fronts have borderless color photos with AL or NL logos. The backs are grey and include biographical information. The cards were distributed as a boxed set along with a custom album.

		MINT	EXC	G-VG
COMPLETE SET (63)		10.00	4.50	1.25
COMMON PLAYER (1-63)		.25	.10	.02
☐ 1	Doug Harvey	.50	.20	.05
☐ 2	John Kibler	.25	.10	.02
☐ 3	Bob Engel	.35	.15	.03
☐ 4	Harry Wendelstedt	.35	.15	.03
☐ 5	Larry Barnett	.25	.10	.02
☐ 6	Don Denkinger	.35	.15	.03
☐ 7	Dave Phillips	.35	.15	.03
☐ 8	Larry McCoy	.25	.10	.02
☐ 9	Bruce Froemming	.35	.15	.03
☐ 10	John McSherry	.35	.15	.03
☐ 11	Jim Evans	.25	.10	.02
☐ 12	Frank Pulli	.25	.10	.02
☐ 13	Joe Brinkman	.25	.10	.02
☐ 14	Terry Tata	.25	.10	.02
☐ 15	Nick Bremigan	.25	.10	.02
☐ 16	Jim McKean	.25	.10	.02
☐ 17	Paul Runge	.25	.10	.02
☐ 18	Dutch Rennert	.25	.10	.02
☐ 19	Terry Cooney	.25	.10	.02
☐ 20	Rich Garcia	.35	.15	.03
☐ 21	Dale Ford	.25	.10	.02
☐ 22	Al Clark	.25	.10	.02
☐ 23	Greg Kosc	.25	.10	.02
☐ 24	Jim Quick	.25	.10	.02
☐ 25	Eddie Montague	.25	.10	.02
☐ 26	Jerry Crawford	.25	.10	.02
☐ 27	Steve Palermo	.60	.25	.06
☐ 28	Durwood Merrill	.25	.10	.02
☐ 29	Ken Kaiser	.35	.15	.03
☐ 30	Vic Voltaggio	.25	.10	.02
☐ 31	Mike Reilly	.25	.10	.02
☐ 32	Eric Gregg	.45	.18	.04
☐ 33	Ted Hendry	.25	.10	.02
☐ 34	Joe West	.25	.10	.02
☐ 35	Dave Pallone	.35	.15	.03
☐ 36	Fred Brocklander	.25	.10	.02
☐ 37	John Shulock	.25	.10	.02
☐ 38	Derryl Cousins	.25	.10	.02
☐ 39	Charlie Williams	.25	.10	.02
☐ 40	Rocky Roe	.25	.10	.02
☐ 41	Randy Marsh	.25	.10	.02
☐ 42	Bob Davidson	.25	.10	.02
☐ 43	Drew Coble	.25	.10	.02
☐ 44	Tim McClelland	.25	.10	.02

		MINT	EXC	G-VG
☐ 45	Dan Morrison	.25	.10	.02
☐ 46	Rick Reed	.25	.10	.02
☐ 47	Steve Rippley	.25	.10	.02
☐ 48	John Hirschbeck	.25	.10	.02
☐ 49	Mark Johnson	.25	.10	.02
☐ 50	Gerry Davis	.25	.10	.02
☐ 51	Dana DeMuth	.25	.10	.02
☐ 52	Larry Young	.25	.10	.02
☐ 53	Tim Welke	.25	.10	.02
☐ 54	Greg Bonin	.25	.10	.02
☐ 55	Tom Hallion	.25	.10	.02
☐ 56	Dale Scott	.25	.10	.02
☐ 57	Tim Tschida	.25	.10	.02
☐ 58	Gary Darling	.25	.10	.02
☐ 59	Mark Hirschbeck	.25	.10	.02
☐ 60	All Star	.25	.10	.02
☐ 61	World Series	.25	.10	.02
☐ 62	Lee Weyer	.25	.10	.02
☐ 63	Connolly/Klem	.50	.20	.05

1989-90 T/M Senior League

The 1989-90 T/M Senior League set contains 120 standard-size (2 1/2" by 3 1/2") cards depicting members of the new Senior League. The fronts are borderless, with full color photos and black bands at the bottom with player names and positions. The vertically-oriented backs are gray and red, and show career major league totals and highlights. The cards were distributed as a boxed set with a checklist card and eight card-sized puzzle pieces.

		MINT	EXC	G-VG
COMPLETE SET (120)		9.00	4.00	.90
COMMON PLAYER (1-120)		.10	.04	.01
☐ 1	Curt Flood (commissioner)	.30	.12	.03
☐ 2	Willie Aikens	.20	.08	.02
☐ 3	Gary Allenson	.10	.04	.01
☐ 4	Stan Bahnsen	.10	.04	.01
☐ 5	Alan Bannister	.10	.04	.01
☐ 6	Juan Beniquez	.15	.06	.01
☐ 7	Jim Bibby	.15	.06	.01
☐ 8	Paul Blair	.20	.08	.02
☐ 9	Vida Blue	.20	.08	.02
☐ 10	Bobby Bonds	.35	.15	.03
☐ 11	Pedro Borbon	.10	.04	.01
☐ 12	Clete Boyer	.20	.08	.02
☐ 13	Gates Brown	.20	.08	.02
☐ 14	Al Bumbry	.10	.04	.01
☐ 15	Sal Butera	.10	.04	.01
☐ 16	Bert Campaneris	.20	.08	.02
☐ 17	Bill Campbell	.10	.04	.01
☐ 18	Bernie Carbo	.10	.04	.01
☐ 19	Dave Cash	.10	.04	.01
☐ 20	Cesar Cedeno	.20	.08	.02
☐ 21	Gene Clines	.10	.04	.01
☐ 22	Dave Collins	.20	.08	.02
☐ 23	Cecil Cooper	.20	.08	.02
☐ 24	Doug Corbett	.10	.04	.01
☐ 25	Al Cowens	.20	.08	.02
☐ 26	Jose Cruz	.20	.08	.02
☐ 27	Mike Cuellar	.20	.08	.02
☐ 28	Pat Dobson	.20	.08	.02

☐ 29	Dick Drago	.10	.04	.01
☐ 30	Dan Driessen	.20	.08	.02
☐ 31	Jamie Easterly	.10	.04	.01
☐ 32	Juan Eichelberger	.10	.04	.01
☐ 33	Dock Ellis	.10	.04	.01
☐ 34	Ed Figueroa	.10	.04	.01
☐ 35	Rollie Fingers	.90	.40	.09
☐ 36	George Foster	.30	.12	.03
☐ 37	Oscar Gamble	.20	.08	.02
☐ 38	Wayne Garland	.10	.04	.01
☐ 39	Wayne Garrett	.10	.04	.01
☐ 40	Ross Grimsley	.10	.04	.01
☐ 41	Jerry Grote	.10	.04	.01
☐ 42	Johnny Grubb	.10	.04	.01
☐ 43	Mario Guerrero	.10	.04	.01
☐ 44	Toby Harrah	.20	.08	.02
☐ 45	Steve Henderson	.10	.04	.01
☐ 46	George Hendrick	.20	.08	.02
☐ 47	Butch Hobson	.20	.08	.02
☐ 48	Roy Howell	.10	.04	.01
☐ 49	Al Hrabosky	.20	.08	.02
☐ 50	Clint Hurdle	.15	.06	.01
☐ 51	Garth Iorg	.10	.04	.01
☐ 52	Tim Ireland	.10	.04	.01
☐ 53	Grant Jackson	.10	.04	.01
☐ 54	Ron Jackson	.10	.04	.01
☐ 55	Ferguson Jenkins	.90	.40	.09
☐ 56	Odell Jones	.10	.04	.01
☐ 57	Mike Kekich	.10	.04	.01
☐ 58	Steve Kemp	.20	.08	.02
☐ 59	Dave Kingman	.30	.12	.03
☐ 60	Bruce Kison	.10	.04	.01
☐ 61	Lee Lacy	.10	.04	.01
☐ 62	Rafael Landestoy	.10	.04	.01
☐ 63	Ken Landreaux	.20	.08	.02
☐ 64	Tito Landrum	.10	.04	.01
☐ 65	Dave LaRoche	.10	.04	.01
☐ 66	Bill Lee	.20	.08	.02
☐ 67	Ron LeFlore	.20	.08	.02
☐ 68	Dennis Leonard	.20	.08	.02
☐ 69	Bill Madlock	.30	.12	.03
☐ 70	Mickey Mahler	.10	.04	.01
☐ 71	Rich Manning	.10	.04	.01
☐ 72	Tippy Martinez	.10	.04	.01
☐ 73	Jon Matlack	.20	.08	.02
☐ 74	Bake McBride	.15	.06	.01
☐ 75	Steve McCatty	.10	.04	.01
☐ 76	Hal McRae	.25	.10	.02
☐ 77	Dan Meyer	.10	.04	.01
☐ 78	Felix Millan	.10	.04	.01
☐ 79	Paul Mirabella	.10	.04	.01
☐ 80	Omar Moreno	.10	.04	.01
☐ 81	Jim Morrison	.10	.04	.01
☐ 82	Graig Nettles	.30	.12	.03
☐ 83	Al Oliver	.30	.12	.03
☐ 84	Amos Otis	.20	.08	.02
☐ 85	Tom Paciorek	.10	.04	.01
☐ 86	Lowell Palmer	.10	.04	.01
☐ 87	Pat Putnam	.10	.04	.01
☐ 88	Lenny Randle	.10	.04	.01
☐ 89	Ken Reitz	.10	.04	.01
☐ 90	Gene Richards	.10	.04	.01
☐ 91	Mickey Rivers	.20	.08	.02
☐ 92	Leon Roberts	.10	.04	.01
☐ 93	Joe Sambito	.10	.04	.01
☐ 94	Rodney Scott	.10	.04	.01
☐ 95	Bob Shirley	.10	.04	.01
☐ 96	Jim Slaton	.10	.04	.01
☐ 97	Elias Sosa	.10	.04	.01
☐ 98	Fred Stanley	.10	.04	.01
☐ 99	Bill Stein	.10	.04	.01
☐ 100	Rennie Stennett	.10	.04	.01
☐ 101	Sammy Stewart	.10	.04	.01
☐ 102	Tim Stoddard	.10	.04	.01
☐ 103	Champ Summers	.10	.04	.01
☐ 104	Derrel Thomas	.10	.04	.01
☐ 105	Luis Tiant	.30	.12	.03
☐ 106	Bobby Tolan	.20	.08	.02
☐ 107	Bill Travers	.10	.04	.01
☐ 108	Tom Underwood	.10	.04	.01
☐ 109	Rick Waits	.10	.04	.01
☐ 110	Ron Washington	.10	.04	.01
☐ 111	U.L. Washington	.10	.04	.01
☐ 112	Earl Weaver MG	.30	.12	.03
☐ 113	Jerry White	.10	.04	.01
☐ 114	Milt Wilcox	.10	.04	.01
☐ 115	Dick Williams MG	.20	.08	.02
☐ 116	Walt Williams	.15	.06	.01
☐ 117	Rick Wise	.15	.06	.01
☐ 118	Favorite Suns Luis Tiant Cesar Cedeno	.20	.08	.02
☐ 119	Home Run Legends George Foster Bobby Bonds	.35	.15	.03

☐ 120	Sunshine Skippers Earl Weaver Dick Williams	.15	.06	.01
☐ 121	Checklist 1-120 (unnumbered)	.10	.04	.01

1990 T/M Umpires

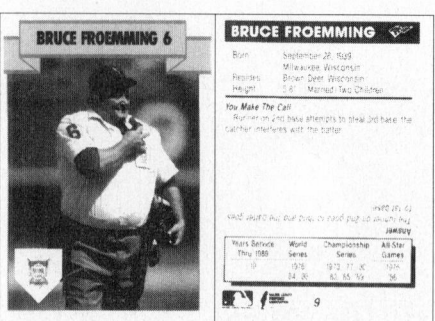

The 1990 T/M Umpires set is a standard-size (2 1/2" by 3 1/2") set which features a picture of each umpire on the front of the card with a baseball rules question on the back of the card. The set was issued as a boxed set as well as in packs.

	MINT	EXC	G-VG
COMPLETE SET (70)	10.00	4.50	1.25
COMMON PLAYER (1-70)	.20	.08	.02

☐ 1	Doug Harvey	.40	.16	.04
☐ 2	John Kibler	.20	.08	.02
☐ 3	Bob Engel	.30	.12	.03
☐ 4	Harry Wendelstedt	.30	.12	.03
☐ 5	Larry Barnett	.20	.08	.02
☐ 6	Don Denkinger	.30	.12	.03
☐ 7	Dave Phillips	.30	.12	.03
☐ 8	Larry McCoy	.20	.08	.02
☐ 9	Bruce Froemming	.30	.12	.03
☐ 10	John McSherry	.20	.08	.02
☐ 11	Jim Evans	.20	.08	.02
☐ 12	Frank Pulli	.20	.08	.02
☐ 13	Joe Brinkman	.20	.08	.02
☐ 14	Terry Tata	.20	.08	.02
☐ 15	Jim McKean	.20	.08	.02
☐ 16	Dutch Rennert	.20	.08	.02
☐ 17	Paul Runge	.20	.08	.02
☐ 18	Terry Cooney	.20	.08	.02
☐ 19	Rich Garcia	.30	.12	.03
☐ 20	Dale Ford	.20	.08	.02
☐ 21	Al Clark	.20	.08	.02
☐ 22	Greg Kosc	.20	.08	.02
☐ 23	Jim Quick	.20	.08	.02
☐ 24	Eddie Montague	.20	.08	.02
☐ 25	Jerry Crawford	.20	.08	.02
☐ 26	Steve Palermo	.50	.20	.05
☐ 27	Durwood Merrill	.20	.08	.02
☐ 28	Ken Kaiser	.30	.12	.03
☐ 29	Vic Voltaggio	.20	.08	.02
☐ 30	Mike Reilly	.20	.08	.02
☐ 31	Eric Gregg	.40	.16	.04
☐ 32	Ted Hendry	.20	.08	.02
☐ 33	Joe West	.20	.08	.02
☐ 34	Fred Brocklander	.20	.08	.02
☐ 35	John Shulock	.20	.08	.02
☐ 36	Derryl Cousins	.20	.08	.02
☐ 37	Charlie Williams	.20	.08	.02
☐ 38	Rocky Roe	.20	.08	.02
☐ 39	Randy Marsh	.20	.08	.02
☐ 40	Bob Davidson	.20	.08	.02
☐ 41	Drew Coble	.20	.08	.02
☐ 42	Tim McClelland	.20	.08	.02
☐ 43	Dan Morrison	.20	.08	.02
☐ 44	Rick Reed	.20	.08	.02
☐ 45	Steve Ripley	.20	.08	.02
☐ 46	John Hirschbeck	.20	.08	.02
☐ 47	Mark Johnson	.20	.08	.02
☐ 48	Gerry Davis	.20	.08	.02
☐ 49	Dana DeMuth	.20	.08	.02

				NRMT	VG-E	GOOD
☐	50	Larry Young		.20	.08	.02
☐	51	Tim Welke		.20	.08	.02
☐	52	Greg Bonin		.20	.08	.02
☐	53	Tom Hallion		.20	.08	.02
☐	54	Dale Scott		.20	.08	.02
☐	55	Tim Tschida		.20	.08	.02
☐	56	Gary Darling		.20	.08	.02
☐	57	Mark Hirschbeck		.20	.08	.02
☐	58	Jerry Layne		.20	.08	.02
☐	59	Jim Joyce		.20	.08	.02
☐	60	Bill Hohn		.20	.08	.02
☐	61	All-Star Game		.20	.08	.02
☐	62	World Series		.20	.08	.02
☐	63	Nick Bremigan		.20	.08	.02
☐	64	The Runges		.30	.12	.03
☐	65	A.Bartlett Giamatti (memorial)		.50	.20	.05
☐	66	Puzzle Piece 1		.20	.08	.02
☐	67	Puzzle Piece 2		.20	.08	.02
☐	68	Puzzle Piece 3		.20	.08	.02
☐	69	Puzzle Piece 4		.20	.08	.02
☐	70	Checklist Card		.20	.08	.02
☐	71	Al Barlick		1.00	.40	.10

				NRMT	VG-E	GOOD
☐	26	Chico Carrasquel		35.00	15.75	5.25
☐	27	Andy Pafko		37.50	16.50	5.50
☐	28	Harry Brecheen		37.50	16.50	5.50
☐	29	Granville Hamner		35.00	15.75	5.25
☐	30	Enos Slaughter		130.00	60.00	20.00
☐	31	Lou Brissie		35.00	15.75	5.25
☐	32	Bob Elliott		37.50	16.50	5.50
☐	33	Don Lenhardt		35.00	15.75	5.25
☐	34	Earl Torgeson		35.00	15.75	5.25
☐	35	Tommy Byrne		37.50	16.50	5.50
☐	36	Cliff Fannin		35.00	15.75	5.25
☐	37	Bobby Doerr		110.00	50.00	16.50
☐	38	Irv Noren		37.50	16.50	5.50
☐	39	Ed Lopat		45.00	20.00	6.75
☐	40	Vic Wertz		40.00	18.00	6.00
☐	41	Johnny Schmitz		35.00	15.75	5.25
☐	42	Bruce Edwards		35.00	15.75	5.25
☐	43	Willie Jones		35.00	15.75	5.25
☐	44	Johnny Wyrostek		35.00	15.75	5.25
☐	45	Billy Pierce		45.00	20.00	6.75
☐	46	Gerry Priddy		35.00	15.75	5.25
☐	47	Herman Wehmeier		35.00	15.75	5.25
☐	48	Billy Cox		40.00	18.00	6.00
☐	49	Hank Sauer		37.50	16.50	5.50
☐	50	Johnny Mize		140.00	63.00	21.00
☐	51	Eddie Waitkus		35.00	15.75	5.25
☐	52	Sam Chapman		50.00	20.00	4.00

1951 Topps Blue Backs

The cards in this 52-card set measure 2" by 2 5/8". The 1951 Topps series of blue backed baseball cards could be used to play a baseball game by shuffling the cards and drawing them from a pile. These cards were marketed with a piece of caramel candy, which often melted or was squashed in such a way as to damage the card and wrapper (despite the fact that a paper shield was inserted between candy and card). Blue Backs are more difficult to obtain than the similarly styled Red Backs. The set is denoted on the cards as "Set B" and the Red Back set is correspondingly Set A. Appropriately leading off the set is Eddie Yost. The only notable rookie card in the set is Billy Pierce.

				NRMT	VG-E	GOOD
	COMPLETE SET (52)			2100.00	900.00	200.00
	COMMON PLAYER (1-52)			35.00	15.75	5.25
☐	1	Eddie Yost		50.00	20.00	4.00
☐	2	Hank Majeski		35.00	15.75	5.25
☐	3	Richie Ashburn		165.00	75.00	22.50
☐	4	Del Ennis		40.00	18.00	6.00
☐	5	Johnny Pesky		40.00	18.00	6.00
☐	6	Red Schoendienst		120.00	55.00	18.00
☐	7	Gerry Staley		35.00	15.75	5.25
☐	8	Dick Sisler		35.00	15.75	5.25
☐	9	Johnny Sain		45.00	20.00	6.75
☐	10	Joe Page		40.00	18.00	6.00
☐	11	Johnny Groth		35.00	15.75	5.25
☐	12	Sam Jethroe		35.00	15.75	5.25
☐	13	Mickey Vernon		40.00	18.00	6.00
☐	14	Red Munger		35.00	15.75	5.25
☐	15	Eddie Joost		35.00	15.75	5.25
☐	16	Murry Dickson		35.00	15.75	5.25
☐	17	Roy Smalley		35.00	15.75	5.25
☐	18	Ned Garver		35.00	15.75	5.25
☐	19	Phil Masi		35.00	15.75	5.25
☐	20	Ralph Branca		45.00	20.00	6.75
☐	21	Billy Johnson		37.50	16.50	5.50
☐	22	Bob Kuzava		35.00	15.75	5.25
☐	23	Dizzy Trout		35.00	15.75	5.25
☐	24	Sherman Lollar		37.50	16.50	5.50
☐	25	Sam Mele		35.00	15.75	5.25

1951 Topps Red Backs

The cards in this 52-card set measure 2" by 2 5/8". The 1951 Topps Red Back set is identical in style to the Blue Back set of the same year. The cards have rounded corners and were designed to be used as a baseball game. Zernial, number 36, is listed with either the White Sox or Athletics, and Holmes, number 52, with either the Braves or Hartford. The set is denoted on the cards as "Set A" and the Blue Back set is correspondingly Set B. The only notable rookie card in the set is Monte Irvin.

				NRMT	VG-E	GOOD
	COMPLETE SET (54)			750.00	325.00	110.00
	COMMON PLAYER (1-52)			7.00	3.00	.70
☐	1	Yogi Berra		125.00	40.00	8.00
☐	2	Sid Gordon		7.00	3.00	.70
☐	3	Ferris Fain		8.00	3.50	.80
☐	4	Vern Stephens		8.00	3.50	.80
☐	5	Phil Rizzuto		33.00	15.00	5.00
☐	6	Allie Reynolds		11.00	5.00	1.35
☐	7	Howie Pollet		7.00	3.00	.70
☐	8	Early Wynn		20.00	8.50	2.75
☐	9	Roy Sievers		8.00	3.50	.80
☐	10	Mel Parnell		8.00	3.50	.80
☐	11	Gene Hermanski		7.00	3.00	.70
☐	12	Jim Hegan		8.00	3.50	.80
☐	13	Dale Mitchell		8.00	3.50	.80
☐	14	Wayne Terwilliger		7.00	3.00	.70
☐	15	Ralph Kiner		30.00	13.50	4.50
☐	16	Preacher Roe		9.00	4.00	.90
☐	17	Dave (Gus) Bell		9.00	4.00	.90
☐	18	Gerry Coleman		9.00	4.00	.90
☐	19	Dick Kokos		7.00	3.00	.70
☐	20	Dom DiMaggio		12.00	5.25	1.50
☐	21	Larry Jansen		8.00	3.50	.80
☐	22	Bob Feller		45.00	20.00	6.75
☐	23	Ray Boone		9.00	4.00	.90

		NRMT	VG-E	GOOD
☐ 24	Hank Bauer	13.00	5.75	1.75
☐ 25	Cliff Chambers	7.00	3.00	.70
☐ 26	Luke Easter	8.00	3.50	.80
☐ 27	Wally Westlake	7.00	3.00	.70
☐ 28	Elmer Valo	7.00	3.00	.70
☐ 29	Bob Kennedy	8.00	3.50	.80
☐ 30	Warren Spahn	45.00	20.00	6.75
☐ 31	Gil Hodges	33.00	15.00	5.00
☐ 32	Henry Thompson	8.00	3.50	.80
☐ 33	William Werle	7.00	3.00	.70
☐ 34	Grady Hatton	7.00	3.00	.70
☐ 35	Al Rosen	13.00	5.75	1.75
☐ 36A	Gus Zernial (Chicago)	33.00	15.00	5.00
☐ 36B	Gus Zernial (Philadelphia)	20.00	8.50	2.75
☐ 37	Wes Westrum	8.00	3.50	.80
☐ 38	Duke Snider	80.00	36.00	12.00
☐ 39	Ted Kluszewski	16.00	6.75	2.25
☐ 40	Mike Garcia	8.00	3.50	.80
☐ 41	Whitey Lockman	8.00	3.50	.80
☐ 42	Ray Scarborough	7.00	3.00	.70
☐ 43	Maurice McDermott	7.00	3.00	.70
☐ 44	Sid Hudson	7.00	3.00	.70
☐ 45	Andy Seminick	7.00	3.00	.70
☐ 46	Billy Goodman	8.00	3.50	.80
☐ 47	Tommy Glaviano	7.00	3.00	.70
☐ 48	Eddie Stanky	9.00	4.00	.90
☐ 49	Al Zarilla	7.00	3.00	.70
☐ 50	Monte Irvin	45.00	20.00	6.75
☐ 51	Eddie Robinson	7.00	3.00	.70
☐ 52A	Tommy Holmes (Boston)	33.00	15.00	5.00
☐ 52B	Tommy Holmes (Hartford)	20.00	8.50	2.75

		NRMT	VG-E	GOOD
☐ 1	Boston Red Sox	350.00	160.00	52.50
☐ 2	Brooklyn Dodgers	250.00	110.00	37.50
☐ 3	Chicago White Sox	200.00	90.00	30.00
☐ 4	Cincinnati Reds	175.00	80.00	27.00
☐ 5	New York Giants	200.00	90.00	30.00
☐ 6	Philadelphia Athletics	175.00	80.00	27.00
☐ 7	Philadelphia Phillies	175.00	80.00	27.00
☐ 8	St. Louis Cardinals	325.00	150.00	50.00
☐ 9	Washington Senators	175.00	80.00	27.00

1951 Topps Connie Mack

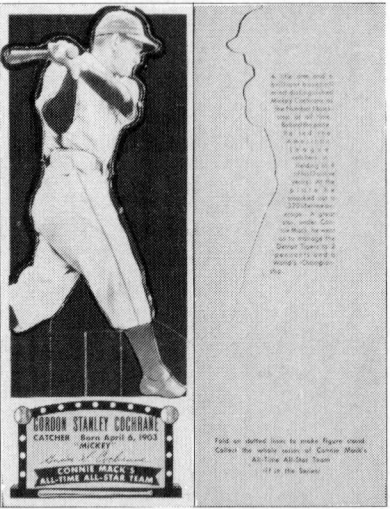

The cards in this 11-card set measure approximately 2 1/16" by 5 1/4". The series of die-cut cards which comprise the set entitled Connie Mack All-Stars was one of Topps' most distinctive and fragile card designs. Printed on thin cardboard, these elegant cards were protected in the wrapper by panels of accompanying Red Backs, but once removed were easily damaged (after all, they were intended to be folded and used as toy figures). Cards without tops have a value less than one-half of that listed below. The cards are unnumbered and are listed below in alphabetical order.

		NRMT	VG-E	GOOD
COMPLETE SET (11)		6250.00	2500.00	625.00
COMMON PLAYER (1-11)		150.00	67.50	22.50
☐ 1	Grover C. Alexander	400.00	180.00	60.00
☐ 2	Mickey Cochrane	300.00	135.00	45.00
☐ 3	Ed Collins	150.00	67.50	22.50
☐ 4	Jimmy Collins	150.00	67.50	22.50
☐ 5	Lou Gehrig	1800.00	750.00	175.00
☐ 6	Walter Johnson	600.00	270.00	90.00
☐ 7	Connie Mack	300.00	135.00	45.00
☐ 8	Christy Mathewson	300.00	135.00	45.00
☐ 9	Babe Ruth	2400.00	900.00	250.00
☐ 10	Tris Speaker	150.00	67.50	22.50
☐ 11	Honus Wagner	300.00	135.00	45.00

1951 Topps Teams

The cards in this nine-card set measure approximately 2 1/16" by 5 1/4". These unnumbered team cards issued by Topps in 1951 carry black and white photographs framed by a yellow border. They are found with or without "1950" printed in the name panel before the team name (no difference in value for either variety). These cards were issued in the same 5 cent wrapper as the Connie Mack and Current All Stars. They have been assigned reference numbers in the checklist alphabetically by team city and name.

	NRMT	VG-E	GOOD
COMPLETE SET (9)	1850.00	800.00	200.00
COMMON TEAM (1-9)	175.00	80.00	27.00

1951 Topps Current AS

The cards in this 11-card set measure approximately 2 1/16" by 5 1/4". The 1951 Topps Current All-Star series is probably the rarest of all legitimate, nationally issued, post war baseball to 80 were issued with red or black backs, both of which are less plentiful than card numbers 81 to 250. In fact, the first series is considered the most difficult with respect to finding perfect condition cards. Card number 48 (Joe Page) and number 49 (Johnny Sain) can be found with each other's write-up on their back. Card numbers 251 to 310 are somewhat scarce and numbers 311 to 407 are quite scarce. Cards 281-300 were single printed compared to the other cards in the next to last series. Cards 311-313 were double printed on the last high number printing sheet. The key card in the set is obviously Mickey Mantle, number 311, Mickey's first of many Topps cards. Although rarely seen, there exist salesman sample panels of three cards containing the fronts of regular cards with ad information on the back. Two such panels seen are Bob Mahoney/Robin Roberts/Sid Hudson and Wally Westlake/Dizzy Trout/Irv Noren. The key rookies in this set are Billy Martin, Eddie Mathews, and Hoyt Wilhelm.

		NRMT	VG-E	GOOD
COMPLETE SET (407)		60000.	22500.	7500.
COMMON PLAYER (1-80)		55.00	25.00	8.25
COMMON PLAYER (81-250)		27.00	12.00	4.00
COMMON PLAYER (251-280)		45.00	20.00	6.75
COMMON PLAYER (281-300)		55.00	25.00	8.25
COMMON PLAYER (301-310)		45.00	20.00	6.75
COMMON PLAYER (311-407)		175.00	80.00	27.00
☐ 1	Andy Pafko	1250.00	125.00	30.00
☐ 2	Pete Runnels	65.00	29.00	9.75
☐ 3	Hank Thompson	60.00	27.00	9.00
☐ 4	Don Lenhardt	55.00	25.00	8.25
☐ 5	Larry Jansen	60.00	27.00	9.00
☐ 6	Grady Hatton	55.00	25.00	8.25
☐ 7	Wayne Terwilliger	55.00	25.00	8.25
☐ 8	Fred Marsh	55.00	25.00	8.25
☐ 9	Robert Hogue	55.00	25.00	8.25
☐ 10	Al Rosen	90.00	40.00	13.50
☐ 11	Phil Rizzuto	180.00	80.00	27.00
☐ 12	Monty Basgall	55.00	25.00	8.25
☐ 13	Johnny Wyrostek	55.00	25.00	8.25
☐ 14	Bob Elliott	60.00	27.00	9.00
☐ 15	Johnny Pesky	65.00	29.00	9.75
☐ 16	Gene Hermanski	55.00	25.00	8.25
☐ 17	Jim Hegan	60.00	27.00	9.00
☐ 18	Merrill Combs	55.00	25.00	8.25
☐ 19	Johnny Bucha	55.00	25.00	8.25
☐ 20	Billy Loes	110.00	50.00	16.50
☐ 21	Ferris Fain	60.00	27.00	9.00
☐ 22	Dom DiMaggio	95.00	42.00	10.00
☐ 23	Billy Goodman	60.00	27.00	9.00
☐ 24	Luke Easter	60.00	27.00	9.00
☐ 25	Johnny Groth	55.00	25.00	8.25
☐ 26	Monte Irvin	110.00	50.00	16.50
☐ 27	Sam Jethroe	55.00	25.00	8.25
☐ 28	Jerry Priddy	55.00	25.00	8.25
☐ 29	Ted Kluszewski	100.00	45.00	15.00
☐ 30	Mel Parnell	60.00	27.00	9.00
☐ 31	Gus Zernial	65.00	29.00	9.75
☐ 32	Eddie Robinson	55.00	25.00	8.25
☐ 33	Warren Spahn	250.00	110.00	37.50
☐ 34	Elmer Valo	55.00	25.00	8.25
☐ 35	Hank Sauer	65.00	29.00	9.75
☐ 36	Gil Hodges	175.00	80.00	27.00
☐ 37	Duke Snider	300.00	135.00	45.00
☐ 38	Wally Westlake	55.00	25.00	8.25
☐ 39	Dizzy Trout	55.00	25.00	8.25
☐ 40	Irv Noren	55.00	25.00	8.25
☐ 41	Bob Wellman	55.00	25.00	8.25
☐ 42	Lou Kretlow	55.00	25.00	8.25
☐ 43	Ray Scarborough	55.00	25.00	8.25
☐ 44	Con Dempsey	55.00	25.00	8.25
☐ 45	Eddie Joost	55.00	25.00	8.25
☐ 46	Gordon Goldsberry	55.00	25.00	8.25
☐ 47	Willie Jones	55.00	25.00	8.25
☐ 48A	Joe Page COR	75.00	34.00	11.25
☐ 48B	Joe Page ERR (bio for Sain)	325.00	150.00	50.00
☐ 49A	Johnny Sain COR	100.00	45.00	15.00
☐ 49B	Johnny Sain ERR (bio for Page)	325.00	150.00	50.00
☐ 50	Marv Rickert	55.00	25.00	8.25
☐ 51	Jim Russell	55.00	25.00	8.25
☐ 52	Don Mueller	60.00	27.00	9.00
☐ 53	Chris Van Cuyk	55.00	25.00	8.25
☐ 54	Leo Kiely	55.00	25.00	8.25
☐ 55	Ray Boone	60.00	27.00	9.00
☐ 56	Tommy Glaviano	55.00	25.00	8.25
☐ 57	Ed Lopat	100.00	45.00	15.00

issues. The set price listed below does not include the prices for the cards of Konstanty, Roberts and Stanky, which likely never were released to the public in gum packs. These three cards (SP in the checklist below) were probably obtained directly from the company and exist in extremely limited numbers. As with the Connie Mack set, cards without the die-cut background are worth half of the value listed below. The cards are unnumbered and are listed below in alphabetical order.

		NRMT	VG-E	GOOD
COMPLETE SET (8)		4500.00	1800.00	450.00
COMMON PLAYER (1-11)		250.00	110.00	37.50
☐ 1	Yogi Berra	1500.00	225.00	75.00
☐ 2	Larry Doby	250.00	110.00	37.50
☐ 3	Walt Dropo	250.00	110.00	37.50
☐ 4	Hoot Evers	250.00	110.00	37.50
☐ 5	George Kell	600.00	270.00	90.00
☐ 6	Ralph Kiner	750.00	325.00	110.00
☐ 7	Jim Konstanty SP	12500.00	5500.00	1500.00
☐ 8	Bob Lemon	600.00	270.00	90.00
☐ 9	Phil Rizzuto	600.00	270.00	90.00
☐ 10	Robin Roberts SP	15000.00	6000.00	1600.00
☐ 11	Eddie Stanky SP	12500.00	5500.00	1500.00

1952 Topps

The cards in this 407-card set measure 2 5/8" by 3 3/4". The 1952 Topps set is Topps' first truly major set. Card numbers 1

No.	Player			
☐ 58	Bob Mahoney	55.00	25.00	8.25
☐ 59	Robin Roberts	140.00	63.00	21.00
☐ 60	Sid Hudson	55.00	25.00	8.25
☐ 61	Tookie Gilbert	55.00	25.00	8.25
☐ 62	Chuck Stobbs	55.00	25.00	8.25
☐ 63	Howie Pollet	55.00	25.00	8.25
☐ 64	Roy Sievers	60.00	27.00	9.00
☐ 65	Enos Slaughter	140.00	63.00	21.00
☐ 66	Preacher Roe	100.00	45.00	15.00
☐ 67	Allie Reynolds	100.00	45.00	15.00
☐ 68	Cliff Chambers	55.00	25.00	8.25
☐ 69	Virgil Stallcup	55.00	25.00	8.25
☐ 70	Al Zarilla	55.00	25.00	8.25
☐ 71	Tom Upton	55.00	25.00	8.25
☐ 72	Karl Olson	55.00	25.00	8.25
☐ 73	Bill Werle	55.00	25.00	8.25
☐ 74	Andy Hansen	55.00	25.00	8.25
☐ 75	Wes Westrum	55.00	25.00	8.25
☐ 76	Eddie Stanky	60.00	27.00	9.00
☐ 77	Bob Kennedy	55.00	25.00	8.25
☐ 78	Ellis Kinder	55.00	25.00	8.25
☐ 79	Gerry Staley	55.00	25.00	8.25
☐ 80	Herman Wehmeier	55.00	25.00	8.25
☐ 81	Vernon Law	32.00	14.25	4.75
☐ 82	Duane Pillette	27.00	12.00	4.00
☐ 83	Billy Johnson	30.00	13.50	4.50
☐ 84	Vern Stephens	32.00	14.25	4.75
☐ 85	Bob Kuzava	27.00	12.00	4.00
☐ 86	Ted Gray	27.00	12.00	4.00
☐ 87	Dale Coogan	27.00	12.00	4.00
☐ 88	Bob Feller	160.00	72.00	24.00
☐ 89	Johnny Lipon	27.00	12.00	4.00
☐ 90	Mickey Grasso	27.00	12.00	4.00
☐ 91	Red Schoendienst	80.00	36.00	12.00
☐ 92	Dale Mitchell	30.00	13.50	4.50
☐ 93	Al Sima	27.00	12.00	4.00
☐ 94	Sam Mele	27.00	12.00	4.00
☐ 95	Ken Holcombe	27.00	12.00	4.00
☐ 96	Willard Marshall	27.00	12.00	4.00
☐ 97	Earl Torgeson	27.00	12.00	4.00
☐ 98	Billy Pierce	32.00	14.25	4.75
☐ 99	Gene Woodling	60.00	27.00	9.00
☐ 100	Del Rice	27.00	12.00	4.00
☐ 101	Max Lanier	27.00	12.00	4.00
☐ 102	Bill Kennedy	27.00	12.00	4.00
☐ 103	Cliff Mapes	27.00	12.00	4.00
☐ 104	Don Kolloway	27.00	12.00	4.00
☐ 105	Johnny Pramesa	27.00	12.00	4.00
☐ 106	Mickey Vernon	30.00	13.50	4.50
☐ 107	Connie Ryan	27.00	12.00	4.00
☐ 108	Jim Konstanty	30.00	13.50	4.50
☐ 109	Ted Wilks	27.00	12.00	4.00
☐ 110	Dutch Leonard	30.00	13.50	4.50
☐ 111	Peanuts Lowrey	27.00	12.00	4.00
☐ 112	Hank Majeski	27.00	12.00	4.00
☐ 113	Dick Sisler	27.00	12.00	4.00
☐ 114	Willard Ramsdell	27.00	12.00	4.00
☐ 115	Red Munger	27.00	12.00	4.00
☐ 116	Carl Scheib	27.00	12.00	4.00
☐ 117	Sherm Lollar	30.00	13.50	4.50
☐ 118	Ken Raffensberger	27.00	12.00	4.00
☐ 119	Mickey McDermott	27.00	12.00	4.00
☐ 120	Bob Chakales	27.00	12.00	4.00
☐ 121	Gus Niarhos	27.00	12.00	4.00
☐ 122	Jackie Jensen	70.00	32.00	10.50
☐ 123	Eddie Yost	27.00	12.00	4.00
☐ 124	Monte Kennedy	27.00	12.00	4.00
☐ 125	Bill Rigney	27.00	12.00	4.00
☐ 126	Fred Hutchinson	30.00	13.50	4.50
☐ 127	Paul Minner	27.00	12.00	4.00
☐ 128	Don Bollweg	27.00	12.00	4.00
☐ 129	Johnny Mize	80.00	36.00	12.00
☐ 130	Sheldon Jones	27.00	12.00	4.00
☐ 131	Morrie Martin	27.00	12.00	4.00
☐ 132	Clyde Kluttz	27.00	12.00	4.00
☐ 133	Al Widmar	27.00	12.00	4.00
☐ 134	Joe Tipton	27.00	12.00	4.00
☐ 135	Dixie Howell	27.00	12.00	4.00
☐ 136	Johnny Schmitz	27.00	12.00	4.00
☐ 137	Roy McMillan	30.00	13.50	4.50
☐ 138	Bill MacDonald	27.00	12.00	4.00
☐ 139	Ken Wood	27.00	12.00	4.00
☐ 140	Johnny Antonelli	32.00	14.25	4.75
☐ 141	Clint Hartung	27.00	12.00	4.00
☐ 142	Harry Perkowski	27.00	12.00	4.00
☐ 143	Les Moss	27.00	12.00	4.00
☐ 144	Ed Blake	27.00	12.00	4.00
☐ 145	Joe Haynes	27.00	12.00	4.00
☐ 146	Frank House	27.00	12.00	4.00
☐ 147	Bob Young	27.00	12.00	4.00
☐ 148	Johnny Klippstein	27.00	12.00	4.00
☐ 149	Dick Kryhoski	27.00	12.00	4.00
☐ 150	Ted Beard	27.00	12.00	4.00
☐ 151	Wally Post	30.00	13.50	4.50
☐ 152	Al Evans	27.00	12.00	4.00
☐ 153	Bob Rush	27.00	12.00	4.00
☐ 154	Joe Muir	27.00	12.00	4.00
☐ 155	Frank Overmire	27.00	12.00	4.00
☐ 156	Frank Hiller	27.00	12.00	4.00
☐ 157	Bob Usher	27.00	12.00	4.00
☐ 158	Eddie Waitkus	27.00	12.00	4.00
☐ 159	Saul Rogovin	27.00	12.00	4.00
☐ 160	Owen Friend	27.00	12.00	4.00
☐ 161	Bud Byerly	27.00	12.00	4.00
☐ 162	Del Crandall	30.00	13.50	4.50
☐ 163	Stan Rojek	27.00	12.00	4.00
☐ 164	Walt Dubiel	27.00	12.00	4.00
☐ 165	Eddie Kazak	27.00	12.00	4.00
☐ 166	Paul LaPalme	27.00	12.00	4.00
☐ 167	Bill Howerton	27.00	12.00	4.00
☐ 168	Charlie Silvera	32.00	14.25	4.75
☐ 169	Howie Judson	27.00	12.00	4.00
☐ 170	Gus Bell	32.00	14.25	4.75
☐ 171	Ed Erautt	27.00	12.00	4.00
☐ 172	Eddie Miksis	27.00	12.00	4.00
☐ 173	Roy Smalley	27.00	12.00	4.00
☐ 174	Clarence Marshall	27.00	12.00	4.00
☐ 175	Billy Martin	350.00	160.00	52.50
☐ 176	Hank Edwards	27.00	12.00	4.00
☐ 177	Bill Wight	27.00	12.00	4.00
☐ 178	Cass Michaels	27.00	12.00	4.00
☐ 179	Frank Smith	27.00	12.00	4.00
☐ 180	Charley Maxwell	30.00	13.50	4.50
☐ 181	Bob Swift	27.00	12.00	4.00
☐ 182	Billy Hitchcock	27.00	12.00	4.00
☐ 183	Erv Dusak	27.00	12.00	4.00
☐ 184	Bob Ramazzotti	27.00	12.00	4.00
☐ 185	Bill Nicholson	27.00	12.00	4.00
☐ 186	Walt Masterson	27.00	12.00	4.00
☐ 187	Bob Miller	27.00	12.00	4.00
☐ 188	Clarence Podbielan	27.00	12.00	4.00
☐ 189	Pete Reiser	35.00	15.75	5.25
☐ 190	Don Johnson	27.00	12.00	4.00
☐ 191	Yogi Berra	400.00	180.00	60.00
☐ 192	Myron Ginsberg	27.00	12.00	4.00
☐ 193	Harry Simpson	27.00	12.00	4.00
☐ 194	Joe Hatton	27.00	12.00	4.00
☐ 195	Minnie Minoso	120.00	55.00	18.00
☐ 196	Solly Hemus	27.00	12.00	4.00
☐ 197	George Strickland	27.00	12.00	4.00
☐ 198	Phil Haugstad	27.00	12.00	4.00
☐ 199	George Zuverink	27.00	12.00	4.00
☐ 200	Ralph Houk	65.00	29.00	9.75
☐ 201	Alex Kellner	27.00	12.00	4.00
☐ 202	Joe Collins	35.00	15.75	5.25
☐ 203	Curt Simmons	30.00	13.50	4.50
☐ 204	Ron Northey	27.00	12.00	4.00
☐ 205	Clyde King	27.00	12.00	4.00
☐ 206	Joe Ostrowski	27.00	12.00	4.00
☐ 207	Mickey Harris	27.00	12.00	4.00
☐ 208	Marlin Stuart	27.00	12.00	4.00
☐ 209	Howie Fox	27.00	12.00	4.00
☐ 210	Dick Fowler	27.00	12.00	4.00
☐ 211	Ray Coleman	27.00	12.00	4.00
☐ 212	Ned Garver	27.00	12.00	4.00
☐ 213	Nippy Jones	27.00	12.00	4.00
☐ 214	Johnny Hopp	30.00	13.50	4.50
☐ 215	Hank Bauer	48.00	22.00	5.50
☐ 216	Richie Ashburn	100.00	45.00	15.00
☐ 217	Snuffy Stirnweiss	32.00	14.25	4.75
☐ 218	Clyde McCullough	27.00	12.00	4.00
☐ 219	Bobby Shantz	35.00	15.75	5.25
☐ 220	Joe Presko	27.00	12.00	4.00
☐ 221	Granny Hamner	27.00	12.00	4.00
☐ 222	Hoot Evers	27.00	12.00	4.00
☐ 223	Del Ennis	32.00	14.25	4.75
☐ 224	Bruce Edwards	27.00	12.00	4.00
☐ 225	Frank Baumholtz	27.00	12.00	4.00
☐ 226	Dave Philley	27.00	12.00	4.00
☐ 227	Joe Garagiola	135.00	60.00	20.00
☐ 228	Al Brazle	27.00	12.00	4.00
☐ 229	Gene Bearden	30.00	13.50	4.50
☐ 230	Matt Batts	27.00	12.00	4.00
☐ 231	Sam Zoldak	27.00	12.00	4.00
☐ 232	Billy Cox	30.00	13.50	4.50
☐ 233	Bob Friend	32.00	14.25	4.75
☐ 234	Steve Souchock	27.00	12.00	4.00
☐ 235	Walt Dropo	30.00	13.50	4.50
☐ 236	Ed Fitzgerald	27.00	12.00	4.00
☐ 237	Jerry Coleman	32.00	14.25	4.75
☐ 238	Art Houtteman	27.00	12.00	4.00
☐ 239	Rocky Bridges	27.00	12.00	4.00
☐ 240	Jack Phillips	27.00	12.00	4.00
☐ 241	Tommy Byrne	27.00	12.00	4.00
☐ 242	Tom Poholsky	27.00	12.00	4.00
☐ 243	Larry Doby	40.00	18.00	6.00
☐ 244	Vic Wertz	30.00	13.50	4.50
☐ 245	Sherry Robertson	27.00	12.00	4.00
☐ 246	George Kell	75.00	34.00	11.25
☐ 247	Randy Gumpert	27.00	12.00	4.00

	#	Player			
☐	248	Frank Shea	27.00	12.00	4.00
☐	249	Bobby Adams	27.00	12.00	4.00
☐	250	Carl Erskine	65.00	29.00	9.75
☐	251	Chico Carrasquel	45.00	20.00	6.75
☐	252	Vern Bickford	45.00	20.00	6.75
☐	253	Johnny Berardino	55.00	25.00	8.25
☐	254	Joe Dobson	45.00	20.00	6.75
☐	255	Clyde Vollmer	45.00	20.00	6.75
☐	256	Pete Suder	45.00	20.00	6.75
☐	257	Bobby Avila	50.00	22.50	7.50
☐	258	Steve Gromek	45.00	20.00	6.75
☐	259	Bob Addis	45.00	20.00	6.75
☐	260	Pete Castiglione	45.00	20.00	6.75
☐	261	Willie Mays	1750.00	700.00	175.00
☐	262	Virgil Trucks	50.00	22.50	7.50
☐	263	Harry Brecheen	50.00	22.50	7.50
☐	264	Roy Hartsfield	45.00	20.00	6.75
☐	265	Chuck Diering	45.00	20.00	6.75
☐	266	Murry Dickson	45.00	20.00	6.75
☐	267	Sid Gordon	45.00	20.00	6.75
☐	268	Bob Lemon	175.00	80.00	27.00
☐	269	Willard Nixon	45.00	20.00	6.75
☐	270	Lou Brissie	45.00	20.00	6.75
☐	271	Jim Delsing	45.00	20.00	6.75
☐	272	Mike Garcia	50.00	22.50	7.50
☐	273	Erv Palica	45.00	20.00	6.75
☐	274	Ralph Branca	80.00	36.00	12.00
☐	275	Pat Mullin	45.00	20.00	6.75
☐	276	Jim Wilson	45.00	20.00	6.75
☐	277	Early Wynn	175.00	80.00	27.00
☐	278	Allie Clark	45.00	20.00	6.75
☐	279	Eddie Stewart	45.00	20.00	6.75
☐	280	Cloyd Boyer	50.00	22.50	7.50
☐	281	Tommy Brown SP	55.00	25.00	8.25
☐	282	Birdie Tebbetts SP	60.00	27.00	9.00
☐	283	Phil Masi SP	55.00	25.00	8.25
☐	284	Hank Arft SP	55.00	25.00	8.25
☐	285	Cliff Fannin SP	55.00	25.00	8.25
☐	286	Joe DeMaestri SP	55.00	25.00	8.25
☐	287	Steve Bilko SP	55.00	25.00	8.25
☐	288	Chet Nichols SP	55.00	25.00	8.25
☐	289	Tommy Holmes SP	65.00	29.00	9.75
☐	290	Joe Astroth SP	55.00	25.00	8.25
☐	291	Gil Coan SP	55.00	25.00	8.25
☐	292	Floyd Baker SP	55.00	25.00	8.25
☐	293	Sibby Sisti SP	55.00	25.00	8.25
☐	294	Walker Cooper SP	55.00	25.00	8.25
☐	295	Phil Cavarretta SP	65.00	29.00	9.75
☐	296	Red Rolfe SP	65.00	29.00	9.75
☐	297	Andy Seminick SP	55.00	25.00	8.25
☐	298	Bob Ross SP	55.00	25.00	8.25
☐	299	Ray Murray SP	55.00	25.00	8.25
☐	300	Barney McCosky SP	55.00	25.00	8.25
☐	301	Bob Porterfield	45.00	20.00	6.75
☐	302	Max Surkont	45.00	20.00	6.75
☐	303	Harry Dorish	45.00	20.00	6.75
☐	304	Sam Dente	45.00	20.00	6.75
☐	305	Paul Richards	50.00	22.50	7.50
☐	306	Lou Sleater	45.00	20.00	6.75
☐	307	Frank Campos	45.00	20.00	6.75
☐	308	Luis Aloma	45.00	20.00	6.75
☐	309	Jim Busby	45.00	20.00	6.75
☐	310	George Metkovich	55.00	25.00	8.25
☐	311	Mickey Mantle DP	24000.00	7500.00	1500.00
☐	312	Jackie Robinson DP	1150.00	400.00	100.00
☐	313	Bobby Thomson DP	225.00	100.00	33.00
☐	314	Roy Campanella	1550.00	550.00	150.00
☐	315	Leo Durocher MG	350.00	160.00	52.50
☐	316	Dave Williams	200.00	90.00	30.00
☐	317	Conrado Marrero	175.00	80.00	27.00
☐	318	Harold Gregg	175.00	80.00	27.00
☐	319	Al Walker	175.00	80.00	27.00
☐	320	John Rutherford	175.00	80.00	27.00
☐	321	Joe Black	250.00	110.00	37.50
☐	322	Randy Jackson	175.00	80.00	27.00
☐	323	Bubba Church	175.00	80.00	27.00
☐	324	Warren Hacker	175.00	80.00	27.00
☐	325	Bill Serena	175.00	80.00	27.00
☐	326	George Shuba	200.00	90.00	30.00
☐	327	Al Wilson	175.00	80.00	27.00
☐	328	Bob Borkowski	175.00	80.00	27.00
☐	329	Ike Delock	175.00	80.00	27.00
☐	330	Turk Lown	175.00	80.00	27.00
☐	331	Tom Morgan	175.00	80.00	27.00
☐	332	Anthony Bartirome	175.00	80.00	27.00
☐	333	Pee Wee Reese	1050.00	375.00	90.00
☐	334	Wilmer Mizell	200.00	90.00	30.00
☐	335	Ted Lepcio	175.00	80.00	27.00
☐	336	Dave Koslo	175.00	80.00	27.00
☐	337	Jim Hearn	175.00	80.00	27.00
☐	338	Sal Yvars	175.00	80.00	27.00
☐	339	Russ Meyer	175.00	80.00	27.00
☐	340	Bob Hooper	175.00	80.00	27.00
☐	341	Hal Jeffcoat	175.00	80.00	27.00
☐	342	Clem Labine	225.00	100.00	33.00
☐	343	Dick Gernert	175.00	80.00	27.00
☐	344	Ewell Blackwell	200.00	90.00	30.00
☐	345	Sammy White	175.00	80.00	27.00
☐	346	George Spencer	175.00	80.00	27.00
☐	347	Joe Adcock	225.00	100.00	33.00
☐	348	Robert Kelly	175.00	80.00	27.00
☐	349	Bob Cain	175.00	80.00	27.00
☐	350	Cal Abrams	175.00	80.00	27.00
☐	351	Alvin Dark	225.00	100.00	33.00
☐	352	Karl Drews	175.00	80.00	27.00
☐	353	Bobby Del Greco	175.00	80.00	27.00
☐	354	Fred Hatfield	175.00	80.00	27.00
☐	355	Bobby Morgan	175.00	80.00	27.00
☐	356	Toby Atwell	175.00	80.00	27.00
☐	357	Smoky Burgess	225.00	100.00	33.00
☐	358	John Kucab	175.00	80.00	27.00
☐	359	Dee Fondy	175.00	80.00	27.00
☐	360	George Crowe	175.00	80.00	27.00
☐	361	William Posedel CO	175.00	80.00	27.00
☐	362	Ken Heintzelman	175.00	80.00	27.00
☐	363	Dick Rozek	175.00	80.00	27.00
☐	364	Clyde Sukeforth CO	175.00	80.00	27.00
☐	365	Cookie Lavagetto CO	175.00	80.00	27.00
☐	366	Dave Madison	175.00	80.00	27.00
☐	367	Ben Thorpe	175.00	80.00	27.00
☐	368	Ed Wright	175.00	80.00	27.00
☐	369	Dick Groat	300.00	135.00	45.00
☐	370	Billy Hoeft	175.00	80.00	27.00
☐	371	Bobby Hofman	175.00	80.00	27.00
☐	372	Gil McDougald	300.00	135.00	45.00
☐	373	Jim Turner CO	200.00	90.00	30.00
☐	374	John Benton	175.00	80.00	27.00
☐	375	John Merson	175.00	80.00	27.00
☐	376	Faye Throneberry	175.00	80.00	27.00
☐	377	Chuck Dressen MG	200.00	90.00	30.00
☐	378	Leroy Fusselman	175.00	80.00	27.00
☐	379	Joe Rossi	175.00	80.00	27.00
☐	380	Clem Koshorek	175.00	80.00	27.00
☐	381	Milton Stock CO	175.00	80.00	27.00
☐	382	Sam Jones	200.00	90.00	30.00
☐	383	Del Wilber	175.00	80.00	27.00
☐	384	Frank Crosetti CO	250.00	110.00	37.50
☐	385	Herman Franks CO	200.00	90.00	30.00
☐	386	John Yuhas	175.00	80.00	27.00
☐	387	Billy Meyer MG	175.00	80.00	27.00
☐	388	Bob Chipman	175.00	80.00	27.00
☐	389	Ben Wade	175.00	80.00	27.00
☐	390	Glenn Nelson	175.00	80.00	27.00
☐	391	Ben Chapman UER (photo actually Sam Chapman)	175.00	80.00	27.00
☐	392	Hoyt Wilhelm	550.00	240.00	80.00
☐	393	Ebba St.Claire	175.00	80.00	27.00
☐	394	Billy Herman CO	250.00	110.00	37.50
☐	395	Jake Pitler CO	175.00	80.00	27.00
☐	396	Dick Williams	250.00	110.00	37.50
☐	397	Forrest Main	175.00	80.00	27.00
☐	398	Hal Rice	175.00	80.00	27.00
☐	399	Jim Fridley	175.00	80.00	27.00
☐	400	Bill Dickey CO	600.00	270.00	90.00
☐	401	Bob Schultz	175.00	80.00	27.00
☐	402	Earl Harrist	175.00	80.00	27.00
☐	403	Bill Miller	175.00	80.00	27.00
☐	404	Dick Brodowski	175.00	80.00	27.00
☐	405	Eddie Pellagrini	175.00	80.00	27.00
☐	406	Joe Nuxhall	225.00	100.00	33.00
☐	407	Eddie Mathews	2650.00	650.00	150.00

1953 Topps

The cards in this 274-card set measure 2 5/8" by 3 3/4". Although the last card is numbered 280, there are only 274 cards in the set since numbers 253, 261, 267, 268, 271, and 275 were never issued. The 1953 Topps series contains line drawings of players in full color. The name and team panel at the card base is easily damaged, making it very difficult to complete a mint set. The high number series, 221 to 280, was produced in shorter supply late in the year and hence is more difficult to complete than the lower numbers. The key cards in the set are Mickey Mantle (82) and Willie Mays (244). The key rookies in this set are Roy Face, Jim Gilliam, and Johnny Podres, all from the last series. There are a number of double-printed cards (actually not double but 50 percent more of each of these

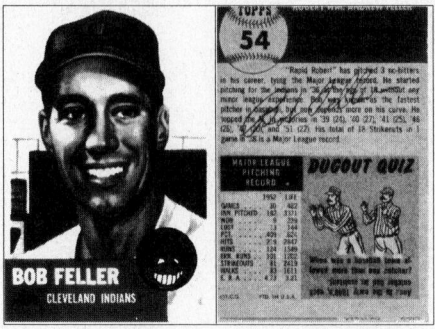

BOB FELLER
CLEVELAND INDIANS

numbers were printed compared to the other cards in the series) indicated by DP in the checklist below. There were five players (10 Smoky Burgess, 44 Ellis Kinder, 61 Early Wynn, 72 Fred Hutchinson, and 81 Joe Black) held out of the first run of 1-85 (but printed in with numbers 86-165), who are each marked by SP in the checklist below. In addition, there are five numbers which were printed in with the more plentiful series 166-220; these cards (94, 107, 131, 145, and 156) are also indicated by DP in the checklist below. There were some three-card advertising panels produced by Topps; the players include Johnny Mize/Clem Koshorek/Toby Atwell and Mickey Mantle/Johnny Wyrostek/Sal Yvars. When cut apart, these advertising cards are distinguished by the non-standard card back, i.e., part of an advertisement for the 1953 Topps set instead of the typical statistics and biographical information about the player pictured.

	NRMT	VG-E	GOOD
COMPLETE SET (274)	13500.00	5000.00	1650.00
COMMON PLAYER (1-165)	25.00	11.00	3.50
COMMON DP (1-165)	15.00	6.50	2.15
COMMON PLAYER (166-220)	18.00	7.50	2.50
COMMON PLAYER (221-280)	95.00	42.00	10.00
COMMON DP (221-280)	45.00	20.00	6.75

☐ 1 Jackie Robinson DP	600.00	150.00	30.00
☐ 2 Luke Easter DP	18.00	7.50	2.50
☐ 3 George Crowe	25.00	11.00	3.50
☐ 4 Ben Wade	25.00	11.00	3.50
☐ 5 Joe Dobson	25.00	11.00	3.50
☐ 6 Sam Jones	25.00	11.00	3.50
☐ 7 Bob Borkowski DP	15.00	6.50	2.15
☐ 8 Clem Koshorek DP	15.00	6.50	2.15
☐ 9 Joe Collins	30.00	13.50	4.50
☐ 10 Smoky Burgess SP	38.00	16.00	5.00
☐ 11 Sal Yvars	25.00	11.00	3.50
☐ 12 Howie Judson DP	15.00	6.50	2.15
☐ 13 Conrado Marrero DP	15.00	6.50	2.15
☐ 14 Clem Labine DP	22.00	9.50	3.15
☐ 15 Bobo Newsom DP	20.00	8.50	2.75
☐ 16 Peanuts Lowrey DP	15.00	6.50	2.15
☐ 17 Billy Hitchcock	25.00	11.00	3.50
☐ 18 Ted Lepcio DP	15.00	6.50	2.15
☐ 19 Mel Parnell DP	22.00	9.50	3.15
☐ 20 Hank Thompson	27.00	12.00	4.00
☐ 21 Billy Johnson	27.00	12.00	4.00
☐ 22 Howie Fox	25.00	11.00	3.50
☐ 23 Toby Atwell DP	15.00	6.50	2.15
☐ 24 Ferris Fain	27.00	12.00	4.00
☐ 25 Ray Boone	27.00	12.00	4.00
☐ 26 Dale Mitchell DP	20.00	8.50	2.75
☐ 27 Roy Campanella DP	210.00	90.00	25.00
☐ 28 Eddie Pellagrini	25.00	11.00	3.50
☐ 29 Hal Jeffcoat	25.00	11.00	3.50
☐ 30 Willard Nixon	25.00	11.00	3.50
☐ 31 Ewell Blackwell	42.00	17.00	5.50
☐ 32 Clyde Vollmer	25.00	11.00	3.50
☐ 33 Bob Kennedy DP	15.00	6.50	2.15
☐ 34 George Shuba	27.00	12.00	4.00
☐ 35 Irv Noren DP	18.00	7.50	2.50
☐ 36 Johnny Groth DP	15.00	6.50	2.15
☐ 37 Eddie Mathews DP	110.00	50.00	16.50
☐ 38 Jim Hearn DP	15.00	6.50	2.15
☐ 39 Eddie Miksis	25.00	11.00	3.50
☐ 40 John Lipon	25.00	11.00	3.50
☐ 41 Enos Slaughter	85.00	38.00	12.75
☐ 42 Gus Zernial DP	18.00	7.50	2.50

☐ 43 Gil McDougald	45.00	20.00	6.75
☐ 44 Ellis Kinder SP	30.00	13.50	4.50
☐ 45 Grady Hatton DP	15.00	6.50	2.15
☐ 46 Johnny Klippstein DP	15.00	6.50	2.15
☐ 47 Bubba Church DP	15.00	6.50	2.15
☐ 48 Bob Del Greco DP	15.00	6.50	2.15
☐ 49 Faye Throneberry DP	15.00	6.50	2.15
☐ 50 Chuck Dressen MG DP	22.00	9.50	3.15
☐ 51 Frank Campos DP	15.00	6.50	2.15
☐ 52 Ted Gray DP	15.00	6.50	2.15
☐ 53 Sherm Lollar DP	18.00	7.50	2.50
☐ 54 Bob Feller DP	100.00	45.00	15.00
☐ 55 Maurice McDermott DP	15.00	6.50	2.15
☐ 56 Jerry Staley DP	15.00	6.50	2.15
☐ 57 Carl Scheib	25.00	11.00	3.50
☐ 58 George Metkovich	25.00	11.00	3.50
☐ 59 Karl Drews DP	15.00	6.50	2.15
☐ 60 Cloyd Boyer DP	15.00	6.50	2.15
☐ 61 Early Wynn SP	85.00	38.00	12.75
☐ 62 Monte Irvin DP	42.00	17.00	5.50
☐ 63 Gus Niarhos DP	15.00	6.50	2.15
☐ 64 Dave Philley	25.00	11.00	3.50
☐ 65 Earl Harrist	25.00	11.00	3.50
☐ 66 Minnie Minoso	45.00	20.00	6.75
☐ 67 Roy Sievers DP	18.00	7.50	2.50
☐ 68 Del Rice	25.00	11.00	3.50
☐ 69 Dick Brodowski	25.00	11.00	3.50
☐ 70 Ed Yuhas	25.00	11.00	3.50
☐ 71 Tony Bartirome	25.00	11.00	3.50
☐ 72 Fred Hutchinson SP	35.00	15.75	5.25
☐ 73 Eddie Robinson	25.00	11.00	3.50
☐ 74 Joe Rossi	25.00	11.00	3.50
☐ 75 Mike Garcia	27.00	12.00	4.00
☐ 76 Pee Wee Reese	140.00	63.00	21.00
☐ 77 Johnny Mize DP	60.00	27.00	9.00
☐ 78 Red Schoendienst	65.00	29.00	9.75
☐ 79 Johnny Wyrostek	25.00	11.00	3.50
☐ 80 Jim Hegan	27.00	12.00	4.00
☐ 81 Joe Black SP	60.00	27.00	9.00
☐ 82 Mickey Mantle	2500.00	750.00	200.00
☐ 83 Howie Pollet	25.00	11.00	3.50
☐ 84 Bob Hooper DP	15.00	6.50	2.15
☐ 85 Bobby Morgan DP	15.00	6.50	2.15
☐ 86 Billy Martin	140.00	63.00	21.00
☐ 87 Ed Lopat	40.00	18.00	6.00
☐ 88 Willie Jones DP	15.00	6.50	2.15
☐ 89 Chuck Stobbs DP	15.00	6.50	2.15
☐ 90 Hank Edwards DP	15.00	6.50	2.15
☐ 91 Ebba St.Claire DP	15.00	6.50	2.15
☐ 92 Paul Minner DP	15.00	6.50	2.15
☐ 93 Hal Rice DP	15.00	6.50	2.15
☐ 94 Bill Kennedy DP	18.00	7.50	2.50
☐ 95 Willard Marshall DP	15.00	6.50	2.15
☐ 96 Virgil Trucks	27.00	12.00	4.00
☐ 97 Don Kolloway DP	15.00	6.50	2.15
☐ 98 Cal Abrams DP	15.00	6.50	2.15
☐ 99 Dave Madison	25.00	11.00	3.50
☐ 100 Bill Miller	25.00	11.00	3.50
☐ 101 Ted Wilks	25.00	11.00	3.50
☐ 102 Connie Ryan DP	15.00	6.50	2.15
☐ 103 Joe Astroth DP	15.00	6.50	2.15
☐ 104 Yogi Berra	240.00	105.00	35.00
☐ 105 Joe Nuxhall DP	20.00	8.50	2.75
☐ 106 Johnny Antonelli	27.00	12.00	4.00
☐ 107 Danny O'Connell DP	18.00	7.50	2.50
☐ 108 Bob Porterfield DP	15.00	6.50	2.15
☐ 109 Alvin Dark	33.00	15.00	5.00
☐ 110 Herman Wehmeier DP	15.00	6.50	2.15
☐ 111 Hank Sauer DP	20.00	8.50	2.75
☐ 112 Ned Garver DP	15.00	6.50	2.15
☐ 113 Jerry Priddy	25.00	11.00	3.50
☐ 114 Phil Rizzuto	110.00	50.00	16.50
☐ 115 George Spencer	25.00	11.00	3.50
☐ 116 Frank Smith DP	15.00	6.50	2.15
☐ 117 Sid Gordon DP	15.00	6.50	2.15
☐ 118 Gus Bell DP	18.00	7.50	2.50
☐ 119 Johnny Sain SP	45.00	20.00	6.75
☐ 120 Davey Williams	30.00	13.50	4.50
☐ 121 Walt Dropo	27.00	12.00	4.00
☐ 122 Elmer Valo	25.00	11.00	3.50
☐ 123 Tommy Byrne DP	18.00	7.50	2.50
☐ 124 Sibby Sisti DP	15.00	6.50	2.15
☐ 125 Dick Williams DP	20.00	8.50	2.75
☐ 126 Bill Connelly DP	15.00	6.50	2.15
☐ 127 Clint Courtney DP	15.00	6.50	2.15
☐ 128 Wilmer Mizell DP	15.00	6.50	2.15
☐ 129 Keith Thomas	25.00	11.00	3.50
☐ 130 Turk Lown DP	15.00	6.50	2.15
☐ 131 Harry Byrd DP	18.00	7.50	2.50
☐ 132 Tom Morgan	25.00	11.00	3.50
☐ 133 Gil Coan	25.00	11.00	3.50
☐ 134 Rube Walker	27.00	12.00	4.00
☐ 135 Al Rosen DP	35.00	15.75	5.25
☐ 136 Ken Heintzelman DP	15.00	6.50	2.15

☐ 137	John Rutherford DP	15.00	6.50	2.15
☐ 138	George Kell	50.00	22.50	7.50
☐ 139	Sammy White	25.00	11.00	3.50
☐ 140	Tommy Glaviano	25.00	11.00	3.50
☐ 141	Allie Reynolds DP	35.00	15.75	5.25
☐ 142	Vic Wertz	27.00	12.00	4.00
☐ 143	Billy Pierce	32.00	14.25	4.75
☐ 144	Bob Schultz DP	15.00	6.50	2.15
☐ 145	Harry Dorish DP	18.00	7.50	2.50
☐ 146	Granny Hamner	25.00	11.00	3.50
☐ 147	Warren Spahn	130.00	60.00	20.00
☐ 148	Mickey Grasso	25.00	11.00	3.50
☐ 149	Dom DiMaggio DP	35.00	15.75	5.25
☐ 150	Harry Simpson DP	15.00	6.50	2.15
☐ 151	Hoyt Wilhelm	65.00	29.00	9.75
☐ 152	Bob Adams DP	15.00	6.50	2.15
☐ 153	Andy Seminick DP	15.00	6.50	2.15
☐ 154	Dick Groat	40.00	18.00	6.00
☐ 155	Dutch Leonard	25.00	11.00	3.50
☐ 156	Jim Rivera DP	18.00	7.50	2.50
☐ 157	Bob Addis DP	15.00	6.50	2.15
☐ 158	Johnny Logan	30.00	13.50	4.50
☐ 159	Wayne Terwilliger DP	15.00	6.50	2.15
☐ 160	Bob Young	25.00	11.00	3.50
☐ 161	Vern Bickford DP	15.00	6.50	2.15
☐ 162	Ted Kluszewski	48.00	22.00	6.00
☐ 163	Fred Hatfield DP	15.00	6.50	2.15
☐ 164	Frank Shea DP	15.00	6.50	2.15
☐ 165	Billy Hoeft	25.00	11.00	3.50
☐ 166	Billy Hunter	18.00	7.50	2.50
☐ 167	Art Schult	18.00	7.50	2.50
☐ 168	Willard Schmidt	18.00	7.50	2.50
☐ 169	Dizzy Trout	18.00	7.50	2.50
☐ 170	Bill Werle	18.00	7.50	2.50
☐ 171	Bill Glynn	18.00	7.50	2.50
☐ 172	Rip Repulski	18.00	7.50	2.50
☐ 173	Preston Ward	18.00	7.50	2.50
☐ 174	Billy Loes	22.00	9.50	3.15
☐ 175	Ron Kline	18.00	7.50	2.50
☐ 176	Don Hoak	25.00	11.00	3.50
☐ 177	Jim Dyck	18.00	7.50	2.50
☐ 178	Jim Waugh	18.00	7.50	2.50
☐ 179	Gene Hermanski	18.00	7.50	2.50
☐ 180	Virgil Stallcup	18.00	7.50	2.50
☐ 181	Al Zarilla	18.00	7.50	2.50
☐ 182	Bobby Hofman	18.00	7.50	2.50
☐ 183	Stu Miller	24.00	10.50	3.50
☐ 184	Hal Brown	18.00	7.50	2.50
☐ 185	Jim Pendleton	18.00	7.50	2.50
☐ 186	Charlie Bishop	18.00	7.50	2.50
☐ 187	Jim Fridley	18.00	7.50	2.50
☐ 188	Andy Carey	30.00	13.50	4.50
☐ 189	Ray Jablonski	18.00	7.50	2.50
☐ 190	Dixie Walker	18.00	7.50	2.50
☐ 191	Ralph Kiner	60.00	27.00	9.00
☐ 192	Wally Westlake	18.00	7.50	2.50
☐ 193	Mike Clark	18.00	7.50	2.50
☐ 194	Eddie Kazak	18.00	7.50	2.50
☐ 195	Ed McGhee	18.00	7.50	2.50
☐ 196	Bob Keegan	18.00	7.50	2.50
☐ 197	Del Crandall	20.00	8.50	2.75
☐ 198	Forrest Main	18.00	7.50	2.50
☐ 199	Marion Fricano	18.00	7.50	2.50
☐ 200	Gordon Goldsberry	18.00	7.50	2.50
☐ 201	Paul LaPalme	18.00	7.50	2.50
☐ 202	Carl Sawatski	18.00	7.50	2.50
☐ 203	Cliff Fannin	18.00	7.50	2.50
☐ 204	Dick Bokelman	18.00	7.50	2.50
☐ 205	Vern Benson	18.00	7.50	2.50
☐ 206	Ed Bailey	24.00	10.50	3.50
☐ 207	Whitey Ford	165.00	75.00	22.00
☐ 208	Jim Wilson	18.00	7.50	2.50
☐ 209	Jim Greengrass	18.00	7.50	2.50
☐ 210	Bob Cerv	27.00	12.00	4.00
☐ 211	J.W. Porter	18.00	7.50	2.50
☐ 212	Jack Dittmer	18.00	7.50	2.50
☐ 213	Ray Scarborough	18.00	7.50	2.50
☐ 214	Bill Bruton	22.00	9.50	3.15
☐ 215	Gene Conley	22.00	9.50	3.15
☐ 216	Jim Hughes	18.00	7.50	2.50
☐ 217	Murray Wall	18.00	7.50	2.50
☐ 218	Les Fusselman	18.00	7.50	2.50
☐ 219	Pete Runnels UER .... (photo actually Don Johnson)	22.00	9.50	3.15
☐ 220	Satchel Paige UER .... (misspelled Satchell on card front)	450.00	200.00	67.50
☐ 221	Bob Milliken	95.00	42.00	10.00
☐ 222	Vic Janowicz DP	50.00	22.50	7.50
☐ 223	Johnny O'Brien DP	50.00	22.50	7.50
☐ 224	Lou Sleater DP	45.00	20.00	6.75
☐ 225	Bobby Shantz	110.00	50.00	16.50
☐ 226	Ed Erautt	95.00	42.00	10.00

☐ 227	Morrie Martin	95.00	42.00	10.00
☐ 228	Hal Newhouser	110.00	50.00	16.50
☐ 229	Rocky Krsnich	95.00	42.00	10.00
☐ 230	Johnny Lindell DP	45.00	20.00	6.75
☐ 231	Solly Hemus DP	45.00	20.00	6.75
☐ 232	Dick Kokos	95.00	42.00	10.00
☐ 233	Al Aber	95.00	42.00	10.00
☐ 234	Ray Murray DP	45.00	20.00	6.75
☐ 235	John Hetki DP	45.00	20.00	6.75
☐ 236	Harry Perkowski DP	45.00	20.00	6.75
☐ 237	Bud Podbielan DP	45.00	20.00	6.75
☐ 238	Cal Hogue DP	45.00	20.00	6.75
☐ 239	Jim Delsing	95.00	42.00	10.00
☐ 240	Fred Marsh	95.00	42.00	10.00
☐ 241	Al Sima DP	45.00	20.00	6.75
☐ 242	Charlie Silvera	100.00	45.00	15.00
☐ 243	Carlos Bernier DP	45.00	20.00	6.75
☐ 244	Willie Mays	1875.00	700.00	175.00
☐ 245	Bill Norman	95.00	42.00	10.00
☐ 246	Roy Face DP	90.00	40.00	13.50
☐ 247	Mike Sandlock DP	45.00	20.00	6.75
☐ 248	Gene Stephens DP	45.00	20.00	6.75
☐ 249	Eddie O'Brien	95.00	42.00	10.00
☐ 250	Bob Wilson	95.00	42.00	10.00
☐ 251	Sid Hudson	95.00	42.00	10.00
☐ 252	Hank Foiles	95.00	42.00	10.00
☐ 253	Does not exist	00.00	00.00	00.00
☐ 254	Preacher Roe DP	90.00	40.00	13.50
☐ 255	Dixie Howell	95.00	42.00	10.00
☐ 256	Les Peden	95.00	42.00	10.00
☐ 257	Bob Boyd	95.00	42.00	10.00
☐ 258	Jim Gilliam	300.00	135.00	45.00
☐ 259	Roy McMillan DP	50.00	22.50	7.50
☐ 260	Sam Calderone	95.00	42.00	10.00
☐ 261	Does not exist	00.00	00.00	00.00
☐ 262	Bob Oldis	95.00	42.00	10.00
☐ 263	Johnny Podres	250.00	110.00	37.50
☐ 264	Gene Woodling DP	65.00	29.00	9.75
☐ 265	Jackie Jensen	110.00	50.00	16.50
☐ 266	Bob Cain	95.00	42.00	10.00
☐ 267	Does not exist	00.00	00.00	00.00
☐ 268	Does not exist	00.00	00.00	00.00
☐ 269	Duane Pillette	95.00	42.00	10.00
☐ 270	Vern Stephens	100.00	45.00	15.00
☐ 271	Does not exist	00.00	00.00	00.00
☐ 272	Bill Antonello	95.00	42.00	10.00
☐ 273	Harvey Haddix	120.00	55.00	18.00
☐ 274	John Riddle	95.00	42.00	10.00
☐ 275	Does not exist	00.00	00.00	00.00
☐ 276	Ken Raffensberger	95.00	42.00	10.00
☐ 277	Don Lund	95.00	42.00	10.00
☐ 278	Willie Miranda	95.00	42.00	10.00
☐ 279	Joe Coleman DP	45.00	20.00	6.75
☐ 280	Milt Bolling	325.00	75.00	15.00

1954 Topps

The cards in this 250-card set measure 2 5/8" by 3 3/4". Each of the cards in the 1954 Topps set contains a large "head" shot of the player plus a smaller full-length photo in black and white set against a color background. This series contains the rookie cards of Hank Aaron, Ernie Banks, and Al Kaline and two separate cards of Ted Williams (number 1 and number 250). Conspicuous by his absence is Mickey Mantle who apparently was the exclusive property of Bowman during 1954 (and 1955).

		NRMT	VG-E	GOOD
	COMPLETE SET (250)	8000.00	3600.00	800.00
	COMMON PLAYER (1-50)	14.00	6.25	2.00
	COMMON PLAYER (51-75)	30.00	13.50	4.50
	COMMON PLAYER (76-125)	14.00	6.25	2.00
	COMMON PLAYER (126-250)	14.00	6.25	2.00
☐ 1	Ted Williams	600.00	200.00	40.00
☐ 2	Gus Zernial	16.00	6.75	2.25
☐ 3	Monte Irvin	33.00	15.00	5.00
☐ 4	Hank Sauer	16.00	6.75	2.25
☐ 5	Ed Lopat	22.00	9.50	3.15
☐ 6	Pete Runnels	16.00	6.75	2.25
☐ 7	Ted Kluszewski	28.00	12.50	4.00
☐ 8	Bob Young	14.00	6.25	2.00
☐ 9	Harvey Haddix	16.00	6.75	2.25
☐ 10	Jackie Robinson	275.00	120.00	40.00
☐ 11	Paul Leslie Smith	14.00	6.25	2.00
☐ 12	Del Crandall	16.00	6.75	2.25
☐ 13	Billy Martin	85.00	38.00	12.75
☐ 14	Preacher Roe	22.00	9.50	3.15
☐ 15	Al Rosen	22.00	9.50	3.15
☐ 16	Vic Janowicz	16.00	6.75	2.25
☐ 17	Phil Rizzuto	70.00	32.00	10.50
☐ 18	Walt Dropo	16.00	6.75	2.25
☐ 19	Johnny Lipon	14.00	6.25	2.00
☐ 20	Warren Spahn	100.00	45.00	15.00
☐ 21	Bobby Shantz	16.00	6.75	2.25
☐ 22	Jim Greengrass	14.00	6.25	2.00
☐ 23	Luke Easter	14.00	6.25	2.00
☐ 24	Granny Hamner	14.00	6.25	2.00
☐ 25	Harvey Kuenn	36.00	16.25	5.50
☐ 26	Ray Jablonski	14.00	6.25	2.00
☐ 27	Ferris Fain	16.00	6.75	2.25
☐ 28	Paul Minner	14.00	6.25	2.00
☐ 29	Jim Hegan	16.00	6.75	2.25
☐ 30	Eddie Mathews	100.00	45.00	15.00
☐ 31	Johnny Klippstein	14.00	6.25	2.00
☐ 32	Duke Snider	145.00	65.00	18.00
☐ 33	Johnny Schmitz	14.00	6.25	2.00
☐ 34	Jim Rivera	14.00	6.25	2.00
☐ 35	Jim Gilliam	27.00	12.00	4.00
☐ 36	Hoyt Wilhelm	40.00	18.00	6.00
☐ 37	Whitey Ford	110.00	50.00	16.50
☐ 38	Eddie Stanky	16.00	6.75	2.25
☐ 39	Sherm Lollar	16.00	6.75	2.25
☐ 40	Mel Parnell	16.00	6.75	2.25
☐ 41	Willie Jones	14.00	6.25	2.00
☐ 42	Don Mueller	16.00	6.75	2.25
☐ 43	Dick Groat	18.00	7.50	2.50
☐ 44	Ned Garver	14.00	6.25	2.00
☐ 45	Richie Ashburn	45.00	20.00	6.75
☐ 46	Ken Raffensberger	14.00	6.25	2.00
☐ 47	Ellis Kinder	14.00	6.25	2.00
☐ 48	Billy Hunter	14.00	6.25	2.00
☐ 49	Ray Murray	14.00	6.25	2.00
☐ 50	Yogi Berra	250.00	110.00	37.50
☐ 51	Johnny Lindell	30.00	13.50	4.50
☐ 52	Vic Power	33.00	15.00	5.00
☐ 53	Jack Dittmer	30.00	13.50	4.50
☐ 54	Vern Stephens	33.00	15.00	5.00
☐ 55	Phil Cavarretta MG	36.00	16.25	5.50
☐ 56	Willie Miranda	30.00	13.50	4.50
☐ 57	Luis Aloma	30.00	13.50	4.50
☐ 58	Bob Wilson	30.00	13.50	4.50
☐ 59	Gene Conley	33.00	15.00	5.00
☐ 60	Frank Baumholtz	30.00	13.50	4.50
☐ 61	Bob Cain	30.00	13.50	4.50
☐ 62	Eddie Robinson	33.00	15.00	5.00
☐ 63	Johnny Pesky	33.00	15.00	5.00
☐ 64	Hank Thompson	33.00	15.00	5.00
☐ 65	Bob Swift CO	30.00	13.50	4.50
☐ 66	Ted Lepcio	30.00	13.50	4.50
☐ 67	Jim Willis	30.00	13.50	4.50
☐ 68	Sam Calderone	30.00	13.50	4.50
☐ 69	Bud Podbielan	30.00	13.50	4.50
☐ 70	Larry Doby	70.00	32.00	10.50
☐ 71	Frank Smith	30.00	13.50	4.50
☐ 72	Preston Ward	30.00	13.50	4.50
☐ 73	Wayne Terwilliger	30.00	13.50	4.50
☐ 74	Bill Taylor	30.00	13.50	4.50
☐ 75	Fred Haney MG	30.00	13.50	4.50
☐ 76	Bob Scheffing CO	14.00	6.25	2.00
☐ 77	Ray Boone	16.00	6.75	2.25
☐ 78	Ted Kazanski	14.00	6.25	2.00
☐ 79	Andy Pafko	16.00	6.75	2.25
☐ 80	Jackie Jensen	22.00	9.50	3.15
☐ 81	Dave Hoskins	14.00	6.25	2.00
☐ 82	Milt Bolling	14.00	6.25	2.00
☐ 83	Joe Collins	18.00	7.50	2.50
☐ 84	Dick Cole	14.00	6.25	2.00
☐ 85	Bob Turley	28.00	12.50	4.00
☐ 86	Billy Herman CO	24.00	10.50	3.50
☐ 87	Roy Face	18.00	7.50	2.50
☐ 88	Matt Batts	14.00	6.25	2.00
☐ 89	Howie Pollet	14.00	6.25	2.00
☐ 90	Willie Mays	425.00	190.00	63.00
☐ 91	Bob Oldis	14.00	6.25	2.00
☐ 92	Wally Westlake	14.00	6.25	2.00
☐ 93	Sid Hudson	14.00	6.25	2.00
☐ 94	Ernie Banks	725.00	300.00	80.00
☐ 95	Hal Rice	14.00	6.25	2.00
☐ 96	Charlie Silvera	16.00	6.75	2.25
☐ 97	Jerald Hal Lane	14.00	6.25	2.00
☐ 98	Joe Black	22.00	9.50	3.15
☐ 99	Bobby Hofman	14.00	6.25	2.00
☐ 100	Bob Keegan	14.00	6.25	2.00
☐ 101	Gene Woodling	22.00	9.50	3.15
☐ 102	Gil Hodges	80.00	36.00	12.00
☐ 103	Jim Lemon	18.00	7.50	2.50
☐ 104	Mike Sandlock	14.00	6.25	2.00
☐ 105	Andy Carey	18.00	7.50	2.50
☐ 106	Dick Kokos	14.00	6.25	2.00
☐ 107	Duane Pillette	14.00	6.25	2.00
☐ 108	Thornton Kipper	14.00	6.25	2.00
☐ 109	Bill Bruton	16.00	6.75	2.25
☐ 110	Harry Dorish	14.00	6.25	2.00
☐ 111	Jim Delsing	14.00	6.25	2.00
☐ 112	Bill Renna	14.00	6.25	2.00
☐ 113	Bob Boyd	14.00	6.25	2.00
☐ 114	Dean Stone	14.00	6.25	2.00
☐ 115	Rip Repulski	14.00	6.25	2.00
☐ 116	Steve Bilko	14.00	6.25	2.00
☐ 117	Solly Hemus	14.00	6.25	2.00
☐ 118	Carl Scheib	14.00	6.25	2.00
☐ 119	Johnny Antonelli	16.00	6.75	2.25
☐ 120	Roy McMillan	16.00	6.75	2.25
☐ 121	Clem Labine	16.00	6.75	2.25
☐ 122	Johnny Logan	16.00	6.75	2.25
☐ 123	Bobby Adams	14.00	6.25	2.00
☐ 124	Marion Fricano	14.00	6.25	2.00
☐ 125	Harry Perkowski	14.00	6.25	2.00
☐ 126	Ben Wade	14.00	6.25	2.00
☐ 127	Steve O'Neill MG	14.00	6.25	2.00
☐ 128	Hank Aaron	1600.00	650.00	150.00
☐ 129	Forrest Jacobs	14.00	6.25	2.00
☐ 130	Hank Bauer	33.00	15.00	5.00
☐ 131	Reno Bertoia	14.00	6.25	2.00
☐ 132	Tom Lasorda	165.00	75.00	22.50
☐ 133	Dave Baker CO	14.00	6.25	2.00
☐ 134	Cal Hogue	14.00	6.25	2.00
☐ 135	Joe Presko	14.00	6.25	2.00
☐ 136	Connie Ryan	14.00	6.25	2.00
☐ 137	Wally Moon	27.00	12.00	4.00
☐ 138	Bob Borkowski	14.00	6.25	2.00
☐ 139	The O'Briens	30.00	13.50	4.50
	Johnny O'Brien			
	Eddie O'Brien			
☐ 140	Tom Wright	14.00	6.25	2.00
☐ 141	Joey Jay	16.00	6.75	2.25
☐ 142	Tom Poholsky	14.00	6.25	2.00
☐ 143	Rollie Hemsley CO	14.00	6.25	2.00
☐ 144	Bill Werle	14.00	6.25	2.00
☐ 145	Elmer Valo	14.00	6.25	2.00
☐ 146	Don Johnson	14.00	6.25	2.00
☐ 147	Johnny Riddle CO	14.00	6.25	2.00
☐ 148	Bob Trice	14.00	6.25	2.00
☐ 149	Al Robertson	14.00	6.25	2.00
☐ 150	Dick Kryhoski	14.00	6.25	2.00
☐ 151	Alex Grammas	14.00	6.25	2.00
☐ 152	Michael Blyzka	14.00	6.25	2.00
☐ 153	Al Walker	16.00	6.75	2.25
☐ 154	Mike Fornieles	14.00	6.25	2.00
☐ 155	Bob Kennedy	14.00	6.25	2.00
☐ 156	Joe Coleman	14.00	6.25	2.00
☐ 157	Don Lenhardt	14.00	6.25	2.00
☐ 158	Peanuts Lowrey	14.00	6.25	2.00
☐ 159	Dave Philley	14.00	6.25	2.00
☐ 160	Ralph Kress CO	14.00	6.25	2.00
☐ 161	John Hetki	14.00	6.25	2.00
☐ 162	Herman Wehmeier	14.00	6.25	2.00
☐ 163	Frank House	14.00	6.25	2.00
☐ 164	Stu Miller	16.00	6.75	2.25
☐ 165	Jim Pendleton	14.00	6.25	2.00
☐ 166	Johnny Podres	27.00	12.00	4.00
☐ 167	Don Lund	14.00	6.25	2.00
☐ 168	Morrie Martin	14.00	6.25	2.00
☐ 169	Jim Hughes	14.00	6.25	2.00
☐ 170	James(Dusty) Rhodes	18.00	7.50	2.50
☐ 171	Leo Kiely	14.00	6.25	2.00
☐ 172	Harold Brown	14.00	6.25	2.00
☐ 173	Jack Harshman	14.00	6.25	2.00
☐ 174	Tom Qualters	14.00	6.25	2.00
☐ 175	Frank Leja	18.00	7.50	2.50
☐ 176	Robert Keely	14.00	6.25	2.00
☐ 177	Bob Milliken	14.00	6.25	2.00
☐ 178	Bill Glynn	14.00	6.25	2.00
☐ 179	Gair Allie	14.00	6.25	2.00

☐ 180	Wes Westrum	14.00	6.25	2.00
☐ 181	Mel Roach	14.00	6.25	2.00
☐ 182	Chuck Harmon	14.00	6.25	2.00
☐ 183	Earle Combs CO	25.00	11.00	3.50
☐ 184	Ed Bailey	16.00	6.75	2.25
☐ 185	Chuck Stobbs	14.00	6.25	2.00
☐ 186	Karl Olson	14.00	6.25	2.00
☐ 187	Henry Manush CO	25.00	11.00	3.50
☐ 188	Dave Jolly	14.00	6.25	2.00
☐ 189	Bob Ross	14.00	6.25	2.00
☐ 190	Ray Herbert	14.00	6.25	2.00
☐ 191	John(Dick) Schofield	16.00	6.75	2.25
☐ 192	Ellis Deal CO	14.00	6.25	2.00
☐ 193	Johnny Hopp CO	16.00	6.75	2.25
☐ 194	Bill Sarni	14.00	6.25	2.00
☐ 195	Billy Consolo	14.00	6.25	2.00
☐ 196	Stan Jok	14.00	6.25	2.00
☐ 197	Lynwood Rowe CO	16.00	6.75	2.25
	("Schoolboy")			
☐ 198	Carl Sawatski	14.00	6.25	2.00
☐ 199	Glenn(Rocky) Nelson	14.00	6.25	2.00
☐ 200	Larry Jansen	16.00	6.75	2.25
☐ 201	Al Kaline	725.00	300.00	80.00
☐ 202	Bob Purkey	14.00	6.25	2.00
☐ 203	Harry Brecheen CO	16.00	6.75	2.25
☐ 204	Angel Scull	14.00	6.25	2.00
☐ 205	Johnny Sain	28.00	12.50	4.00
☐ 206	Ray Crone	14.00	6.25	2.00
☐ 207	Tom Oliver CO	14.00	6.25	2.00
☐ 208	Grady Hatton	14.00	6.25	2.00
☐ 209	Chuck Thompson	14.00	6.25	2.00
☐ 210	Bob Buhl	18.00	7.50	2.50
☐ 211	Don Hoak	16.00	6.75	2.25
☐ 212	Bob Micelotta	14.00	6.25	2.00
☐ 213	Johnny Fitzpatrick	14.00	6.25	2.00
☐ 214	Arnie Portocarrero	14.00	6.25	2.00
☐ 215	Ed McGhee	14.00	6.25	2.00
☐ 216	Al Sima	14.00	6.25	2.00
☐ 217	Paul Schreiber CO	14.00	6.25	2.00
☐ 218	Fred Marsh	14.00	6.25	2.00
☐ 219	Chuck Kress	14.00	6.25	2.00
☐ 220	Ruben Gomez	14.00	6.25	2.00
☐ 221	Dick Brodowski	14.00	6.25	2.00
☐ 222	Bill Wilson	14.00	6.25	2.00
☐ 223	Joe Haynes	14.00	6.25	2.00
☐ 224	Dick Weik	14.00	6.25	2.00
☐ 225	Don Liddle	14.00	6.25	2.00
☐ 226	Jehosie Heard	14.00	6.25	2.00
☐ 227	Colonel Mills CO	14.00	6.25	2.00
☐ 228	Gene Hermanski	14.00	6.25	2.00
☐ 229	Bob Talbot	14.00	6.25	2.00
☐ 230	Bob Kuzava	16.00	6.75	2.25
☐ 231	Roy Smalley	14.00	6.25	2.00
☐ 232	Lou Limmer	14.00	6.25	2.00
☐ 233	Augie Galan CO	14.00	6.25	2.00
☐ 234	Jerry Lynch	16.00	6.75	2.25
☐ 235	Vernon Law	16.00	6.75	2.25
☐ 236	Paul Penson	14.00	6.25	2.00
☐ 237	Mike Ryba CO	14.00	6.25	2.00
☐ 238	Al Aber	14.00	6.25	2.00
☐ 239	Bill Skowron	85.00	38.00	12.75
☐ 240	Sam Mele	14.00	6.25	2.00
☐ 241	Robert Miller	14.00	6.25	2.00
☐ 242	Curt Roberts	14.00	6.25	2.00
☐ 243	Ray Blades CO	14.00	6.25	2.00
☐ 244	Leroy Wheat	14.00	6.25	2.00
☐ 245	Roy Sievers	16.00	6.75	2.25
☐ 246	Howie Fox	14.00	6.25	2.00
☐ 247	Ed Mayo CO	14.00	6.25	2.00
☐ 248	Al Smith	16.00	6.75	2.25
☐ 249	Wilmer Mizell	16.00	6.75	2.25
☐ 250	Ted Williams	700.00	200.00	40.00

and 188. Although rarely seen, there exist salesman sample panels of three cards containing the fronts of regular cards with ad information for the 1955 Topps regular and the 1955 Topps Doubleheaders on the back. One such ad panel depicts (from top to bottom) Danny Schell, Jake Thies, and Howie Pollet. The key rookies in this set are Ken Boyer, Roberto Clemente, Harmon Killebrew, and Sandy Koufax.

1955 Topps

The cards in this 206-card set measure 2 5/8" by 3 3/4". Both the large "head" shot and the smaller full-length photos used on each card of the 1955 Topps set are in color. The card fronts were designed horizontally for the first time in Topps' history. The first card features Dusty Rhodes, hitting star for the Giants' 1954 World Series sweep over the Indians. A "high" series, 161 to 210, is more difficult to find than cards 1 to 160. Numbers 175, 186, 203, and 209 were never issued. To fill in for the four cards not issued in the high number series, Topps double printed four players, those appearing on cards 170, 172, 184,

		NRMT	VG-E	GOOD
COMPLETE SET (206)		7500.00	3500.00	800.00
COMMON PLAYER (1-150)		9.00	4.00	.90
COMMON PLAYER (151-160)		18.00	7.50	2.50
COMMON PLAYER (161-210)		27.00	12.00	4.00
☐ 1	Dusty Rhodes	42.00	7.50	1.50
☐ 2	Ted Williams	400.00	180.00	60.00
☐ 3	Art Fowler	9.00	4.00	.90
☐ 4	Al Kaline	210.00	95.00	25.00
☐ 5	Jim Gilliam	14.00	6.25	2.00
☐ 6	Stan Hack	11.00	5.00	1.35
☐ 7	Jim Hegan	10.00	4.50	1.25
☐ 8	Harold Smith	9.00	4.00	.90
☐ 9	Robert Miller	9.00	4.00	.90
☐ 10	Bob Keegan	9.00	4.00	.90
☐ 11	Ferris Fain	10.00	4.50	1.25
☐ 12	Vernon(Jake) Thies	9.00	4.00	.90
☐ 13	Fred Marsh	9.00	4.00	.90
☐ 14	Jim Finigan	9.00	4.00	.90
☐ 15	Jim Pendleton	9.00	4.00	.90
☐ 16	Roy Sievers	10.00	4.50	1.25
☐ 17	Bobby Hofman	9.00	4.00	.90
☐ 18	Russ Kemmerer	9.00	4.00	.90
☐ 19	Billy Herman CO	14.00	6.25	2.00
☐ 20	Andy Carey	11.00	5.00	1.35
☐ 21	Alex Grammas	9.00	4.00	.90
☐ 22	Bill Skowron	21.00	9.00	3.00
☐ 23	Jack Parks	9.00	4.00	.90
☐ 24	Hal Newhouser	14.00	6.25	2.00
☐ 25	Johnny Podres	16.00	6.75	2.25
☐ 26	Dick Groat	11.00	5.00	1.35
☐ 27	Billy Gardner	10.00	4.50	1.25
☐ 28	Ernie Banks	200.00	90.00	30.00
☐ 29	Herman Wehmeier	9.00	4.00	.90
☐ 30	Vic Power	10.00	4.50	1.25
☐ 31	Warren Spahn	80.00	36.00	12.00
☐ 32	Warren McGhee	9.00	4.00	.90
☐ 33	Tom Qualters	9.00	4.00	.90
☐ 34	Wayne Terwilliger	9.00	4.00	.90
☐ 35	Dave Jolly	9.00	4.00	.90
☐ 36	Leo Kiely	9.00	4.00	.90
☐ 37	Joe Cunningham	11.00	5.00	1.35
☐ 38	Bob Turley	14.00	6.25	2.00
☐ 39	Bill Glynn	9.00	4.00	.90
☐ 40	Don Hoak	10.00	4.50	1.25
☐ 41	Chuck Stobbs	9.00	4.00	.90
☐ 42	John(Windy) McCall	9.00	4.00	.90
☐ 43	Harvey Haddix	10.00	4.50	1.25
☐ 44	Harold Valentine	9.00	4.00	.90
☐ 45	Hank Sauer	10.00	4.50	1.25
☐ 46	Ted Kazanski	9.00	4.00	.90
☐ 47	Hank Aaron UER (birth incorrectly listed as 2/10)	350.00	160.00	52.50
☐ 48	Bob Kennedy	9.00	4.00	.90
☐ 49	J.W. Porter	9.00	4.00	.90
☐ 50	Jackie Robinson	240.00	105.00	30.00
☐ 51	Jim Hughes	9.00	4.00	.90
☐ 52	Bill Tremel	9.00	4.00	.90
☐ 53	Bill Taylor	9.00	4.00	.90

		NRMT	VG-E	GOOD
☐ 54	Lou Limmer	9.00	4.00	.90
☐ 55	Rip Repulski	9.00	4.00	.90
☐ 56	Ray Jablonski	9.00	4.00	.90
☐ 57	Billy O'Dell	9.00	4.00	.90
☐ 58	Jim Rivera	9.00	4.00	.90
☐ 59	Gair Allie	9.00	4.00	.90
☐ 60	Dean Stone	9.00	4.00	.90
☐ 61	Forrest Jacobs	9.00	4.00	.90
☐ 62	Thornton Kipper	9.00	4.00	.90
☐ 63	Joe Collins	11.00	5.00	1.35
☐ 64	Gus Triandos	12.00	5.25	1.50
☐ 65	Ray Boone	10.00	4.50	1.25
☐ 66	Ron Jackson	9.00	4.00	.90
☐ 67	Wally Moon	11.00	5.00	1.35
☐ 68	Jim Davis	9.00	4.00	.90
☐ 69	Ed Bailey	10.00	4.50	1.25
☐ 70	Al Rosen	14.00	6.25	2.00
☐ 71	Ruben Gomez	9.00	4.00	.90
☐ 72	Karl Olson	9.00	4.00	.90
☐ 73	Jack Shepard	9.00	4.00	.90
☐ 74	Bob Borkowski	9.00	4.00	.90
☐ 75	Sandy Amoros	18.00	7.50	2.50
☐ 76	Howie Pollet	9.00	4.00	.90
☐ 77	Arnie Portocarrero	9.00	4.00	.90
☐ 78	Gordon Jones	9.00	4.00	.90
☐ 79	Clyde(Danny) Schell	9.00	4.00	.90
☐ 80	Bob Grim	15.00	6.50	2.15
☐ 81	Gene Conley	10.00	4.50	1.25
☐ 82	Chuck Harmon	9.00	4.00	.90
☐ 83	Tom Brewer	9.00	4.00	.90
☐ 84	Camilo Pascual	12.00	5.25	1.50
☐ 85	Don Mossi	16.00	6.75	2.25
☐ 86	Bill Wilson	9.00	4.00	.90
☐ 87	Frank House	9.00	4.00	.90
☐ 88	Bob Skinner	12.00	5.25	1.50
☐ 89	Joe Frazier	10.00	4.50	1.25
☐ 90	Karl Spooner	14.00	6.25	2.00
☐ 91	Milt Bolling	9.00	4.00	.90
☐ 92	Don Zimmer	36.00	16.25	5.50
☐ 93	Steve Bilko	9.00	4.00	.90
☐ 94	Reno Bertoia	9.00	4.00	.90
☐ 95	Preston Ward	9.00	4.00	.90
☐ 96	Chuck Bishop	9.00	4.00	.90
☐ 97	Carlos Paula	9.00	4.00	.90
☐ 98	John Riddle	9.00	4.00	.90
☐ 99	Frank Leja	9.00	4.00	.90
☐ 100	Monte Irvin	27.00	12.00	4.00
☐ 101	Johnny Gray	9.00	4.00	.90
☐ 102	Wally Westlake	9.00	4.00	.90
☐ 103	Chuck White	9.00	4.00	.90
☐ 104	Jack Harshman	9.00	4.00	.90
☐ 105	Chuck Diering	9.00	4.00	.90
☐ 106	Frank Sullivan	9.00	4.00	.90
☐ 107	Curt Roberts	9.00	4.00	.90
☐ 108	Al Walker	10.00	4.50	1.25
☐ 109	Ed Lopat	14.00	6.25	2.00
☐ 110	Gus Zernial	10.00	4.50	1.25
☐ 111	Bob Milliken	9.00	4.00	.90
☐ 112	Nelson King	9.00	4.00	.90
☐ 113	Harry Brecheen	10.00	4.50	1.25
☐ 114	Louis Ortiz	9.00	4.00	.90
☐ 115	Ellis Kinder	9.00	4.00	.90
☐ 116	Tom Hurd	9.00	4.00	.90
☐ 117	Mel Roach	9.00	4.00	.90
☐ 118	Bob Purkey	9.00	4.00	.90
☐ 119	Bob Lennon	9.00	4.00	.90
☐ 120	Ted Kluszewski	21.00	9.00	3.00
☐ 121	Bill Renna	9.00	4.00	.90
☐ 122	Carl Sawatski	9.00	4.00	.90
☐ 123	Sandy Koufax	1125.00	400.00	100.00
☐ 124	Harmon Killebrew	325.00	150.00	50.00
☐ 125	Ken Boyer	70.00	32.00	10.50
☐ 126	Dick Hall	9.00	4.00	.90
☐ 127	Dale Long	11.00	5.00	1.35
☐ 128	Ted Lepcio	9.00	4.00	.90
☐ 129	Elvin Tappe	9.00	4.00	.90
☐ 130	Mayo Smith MG	9.00	4.00	.90
☐ 131	Grady Hatton	9.00	4.00	.90
☐ 132	Bob Trice	9.00	4.00	.90
☐ 133	Dave Hoskins	9.00	4.00	.90
☐ 134	Joey Jay	10.00	4.50	1.25
☐ 135	Johnny O'Brien	9.00	4.00	.90
☐ 136	Veston(Bunky) Stewart	9.00	4.00	.90
☐ 137	Harry Elliott	9.00	4.00	.90
☐ 138	Ray Herbert	9.00	4.00	.90
☐ 139	Steve Kraly	9.00	4.00	.90
☐ 140	Mel Parnell	10.00	4.50	1.25
☐ 141	Tom Wright	9.00	4.00	.90
☐ 142	Jerry Lynch	10.00	4.50	1.25
☐ 143	John(Dick) Schofield	10.00	4.50	1.25
☐ 144	John(Joe) Amalfitano	9.00	4.00	.90
☐ 145	Elmer Valo	9.00	4.00	.90
☐ 146	Dick Donovan	11.00	5.00	1.35
☐ 147	Hugh Pepper	9.00	4.00	.90

		NRMT	VG-E	GOOD
☐ 148	Hector Brown	9.00	4.00	.90
☐ 149	Ray Crone	9.00	4.00	.90
☐ 150	Mike Higgins MG	9.00	4.00	.90
☐ 151	Ralph Kress CO	18.00	7.50	2.50
☐ 152	Harry Agganis	85.00	38.00	12.75
☐ 153	Bud Podbielan	18.00	7.50	2.50
☐ 154	Willie Miranda	18.00	7.50	2.50
☐ 155	Eddie Mathews	125.00	57.50	18.75
☐ 156	Joe Black	28.00	12.50	4.00
☐ 157	Robert Miller	18.00	7.50	2.50
☐ 158	Tommy Carroll	21.00	9.00	3.00
☐ 159	Johnny Schmitz	18.00	7.50	2.50
☐ 160	Ray Narleski	22.00	9.50	3.15
☐ 161	Chuck Tanner	32.00	14.25	4.75
☐ 162	Joe Coleman	27.00	12.00	4.00
☐ 163	Faye Throneberry	27.00	12.00	4.00
☐ 164	Roberto Clemente	1325.00	550.00	135.00
☐ 165	Don Johnson	27.00	12.00	4.00
☐ 166	Hank Bauer	50.00	22.50	7.50
☐ 167	Thomas Casagrande	27.00	12.00	4.00
☐ 168	Duane Pillette	27.00	12.00	4.00
☐ 169	Bob Oldis	27.00	12.00	4.00
☐ 170	Jim Pearce DP	12.00	5.25	1.50
☐ 171	Dick Brodowski	27.00	12.00	4.00
☐ 172	Frank Baumholtz DP	12.00	5.25	1.50
☐ 173	Bob Kline	27.00	12.00	4.00
☐ 174	Rudy Minarcin	27.00	12.00	4.00
☐ 175	Does not exist	00.00	00.00	0.00
☐ 176	Norm Zauchin	27.00	12.00	4.00
☐ 177	Al Robertson	27.00	12.00	4.00
☐ 178	Bobby Adams	27.00	12.00	4.00
☐ 179	Jim Bolger	27.00	12.00	4.00
☐ 180	Clem Labine	32.00	14.25	4.75
☐ 181	Roy McMillan	27.00	12.00	4.00
☐ 182	Humberto Robinson	27.00	12.00	4.00
☐ 183	Anthony Jacobs	27.00	12.00	4.00
☐ 184	Harry Perkowski DP	12.00	5.25	1.50
☐ 185	Don Ferrarese	27.00	12.00	4.00
☐ 186	Does not exist	00.00	00.00	0.00
☐ 187	Gil Hodges	145.00	65.00	18.00
☐ 188	Charlie Silvera DP	15.00	6.50	2.15
☐ 189	Phil Rizzuto	145.00	65.00	18.00
☐ 190	Gene Woodling	32.00	14.25	4.75
☐ 191	Eddie Stanky MG	32.00	14.25	4.75
☐ 192	Jim Delsing	27.00	12.00	4.00
☐ 193	Johnny Sain	36.00	16.25	5.50
☐ 194	Willie Mays	475.00	215.00	70.00
☐ 195	Ed Roebuck	32.00	14.25	4.75
☐ 196	Gale Wade	27.00	12.00	4.00
☐ 197	Al Smith	27.00	12.00	4.00
☐ 198	Yogi Berra	250.00	110.00	37.50
☐ 199	Odbert Hamric	27.00	12.00	4.00
☐ 200	Jackie Jensen	50.00	22.50	7.50
☐ 201	Sherm Lollar	32.00	14.25	4.75
☐ 202	Jim Owens	27.00	12.00	4.00
☐ 203	Does not exist	00.00	00.00	0.00
☐ 204	Frank Smith	27.00	12.00	4.00
☐ 205	Gene Freese	32.00	14.25	4.75
☐ 206	Pete Daley	27.00	12.00	4.00
☐ 207	Billy Consolo	27.00	12.00	4.00
☐ 208	Ray Moore	27.00	12.00	4.00
☐ 209	Does not exist	00.00	00.00	0.00
☐ 210	Duke Snider	525.00	125.00	25.00

1955 Topps Double Header

The cards in ths 66-card set measure approximately 2 1/16" by 4 7/8". Borrowing a design from the T201 Mecca series, Topps issued a 132-player "Double Header" set in a separate wrapper in 1955. Each player is numbered in the biographical section on the reverse. When open, with perforated flap up, one player is revealed; when the flap is lowered, or closed, the player design on top incorporates a portion of the inside player artwork. When the cards are placed side by side, a continuous ballpark background is formed. Some cards have been found without perforations, and all players pictured appear in the low series of the 1955 regular issue.

	NRMT	VG-E	GOOD
COMPLETE SET (66)	3600.00	1500.00	375.00
COMMON PAIR (1-132)	35.00	15.75	5.25
☐ 1 Al Rosen and 2 Chuck Diering	45.00	20.00	6.75

☐ 3	Monte Irvin and .... 4 Russ Kemmerer	60.00	27.00	9.00
☐ 5	Ted Kazanski and .... 6 Gordon Jones	35.00	15.75	5.25
☐ 7	Bill Taylor and .... 8 Billy O'Dell	35.00	15.75	5.25
☐ 9	J.W. Porter and .... 10 Thornton Kipper	35.00	15.75	5.25
☐ 11	Curt Roberts and .... 12 Arnie Portocarrero	35.00	15.75	5.25
☐ 13	Wally Westlake and .... 14 Frank House	35.00	15.75	5.25
☐ 15	Rube Walker and .... 16 Lou Limmer	35.00	15.75	5.25
☐ 17	Dean Stone and .... 18 Charlie White	35.00	15.75	5.25
☐ 19	Karl Spooner and .... 20 Jim Hughes	35.00	15.75	5.25
☐ 21	Bill Skowron and .... 22 Frank Sullivan	45.00	20.00	6.75
☐ 23	Jack Shepard and .... 24 Stan Hack	35.00	15.75	5.25
☐ 25	Jackie Robinson and .... 26 Don Hoak	200.00	90.00	30.00
☐ 27	Dusty Rhodes and .... 28 Jim Davis	35.00	15.75	5.25
☐ 29	Vic Power and .... 30 Ed Bailey	35.00	15.75	5.25
☐ 31	Howie Pollet and .... 32 Ernie Banks	200.00	90.00	30.00
☐ 33	Jim Pendleton and .... 34 Gene Conley	35.00	15.75	5.25
☐ 35	Karl Olson and .... 36 Andy Carey	35.00	15.75	5.25
☐ 37	Wally Moon and .... 38 Joe Cunningham	35.00	15.75	5.25
☐ 39	Freddie Marsh and .... 40 Vernon Thies	35.00	15.75	5.25
☐ 41	Eddie Lopat and .... 42 Harvey Haddix	45.00	20.00	6.75
☐ 43	Leo Kiely and .... 44 Chuck Stobbs	35.00	15.75	5.25
☐ 45	Al Kaline and .... 46 Harold Valentine	200.00	90.00	30.00
☐ 47	Forrest Jacobs and .... 48 Johnny Gray	35.00	15.75	5.25
☐ 49	Ron Jackson and .... 50 Jim Finigan	35.00	15.75	5.25
☐ 51	Ray Jablonski and .... 52 Bob Keegan	35.00	15.75	5.25
☐ 53	Billy Herman and .... 54 Sandy Amoros	60.00	27.00	9.00
☐ 55	Chuck Harmon and .... 56 Bob Skinner	35.00	15.75	5.25
☐ 57	Dick Hall and .... 58 Bob Grim	35.00	15.75	5.25
☐ 59	Billy Glynn and .... 60 Bob Miller	35.00	15.75	5.25
☐ 61	Billy Gardner and .... 62 John Hetki	35.00	15.75	5.25

☐ 63	Bob Borkowski and .... 64 Bob Turley	45.00	20.00	6.75
☐ 65	Joe Collins and .... 66 Jack Harshman	35.00	15.75	5.25
☐ 67	Jim Hegan and .... 68 Jack Parks	35.00	15.75	5.25
☐ 69	Ted Williams and .... 70 Mayo Smith MG	350.00	160.00	52.50
☐ 71	Gair Allie and .... 72 Grady Hatton	35.00	15.75	5.25
☐ 73	Jerry Lynch and .... 74 Harry Brecheen	35.00	15.75	5.25
☐ 75	Tom Wright and .... 76 Vernon Stewart	35.00	15.75	5.25
☐ 77	Dave Hoskins and .... 78 Warren McGhee	35.00	15.75	5.25
☐ 79	Roy Sievers and .... 80 Art Fowler	35.00	15.75	5.25
☐ 81	Danny Schell and .... 82 Gus Triandos	35.00	15.75	5.25
☐ 83	Joe Frazier and .... 84 Don Mossi	35.00	15.75	5.25
☐ 85	Elmer Valo and .... 86 Hector Brown	35.00	15.75	5.25
☐ 87	Bob Kennedy and .... 88 Windy McCall	35.00	15.75	5.25
☐ 89	Ruben Gomez and .... 90 Jim Rivera	35.00	15.75	5.25
☐ 91	Louis Ortiz and .... 92 Milt Bolling	35.00	15.75	5.25
☐ 93	Carl Sawatski and .... 94 El Tappe	35.00	15.75	5.25
☐ 95	Dave Jolly and .... 96 Bobby Hofman	35.00	15.75	5.25
☐ 97	Preston Ward and .... 98 Don Zimmer	45.00	20.00	6.75
☐ 99	Bill Renna and .... 100 Dick Groat	45.00	20.00	6.75
☐ 101	Bill Wilson and .... 102 Bill Tremel	35.00	15.75	5.25
☐ 103	Hank Sauer and .... 104 Camilo Pascual	45.00	20.00	6.75
☐ 105	Hank Aaron and .... 106 Ray Herbert	450.00	200.00	67.50
☐ 107	Alex Grammas and .... 108 Tom Qualters	35.00	15.75	5.25
☐ 109	Hal Newhouser and .... 110 Chuck Bishop	45.00	20.00	6.75
☐ 111	Harmon Killebrew and .... 112 John Podres	175.00	80.00	27.00
☐ 113	Ray Boone and .... 114 Bob Purkey	35.00	15.75	5.25
☐ 115	Dale Long and .... 116 Ferris Fain	35.00	15.75	5.25
☐ 117	Steve Bilko and .... 118 Bob Milliken	35.00	15.75	5.25
☐ 119	Mel Parnell and .... 120 Tom Hurd	35.00	15.75	5.25
☐ 121	Ted Kluszewski and .... 122 Jim Owens	55.00	25.00	8.25
☐ 123	Gus Zernial and .... 124 Bob Trice	35.00	15.75	5.25
☐ 125	Rip Repulski and .... 126 Ted Lepcio	35.00	15.75	5.25
☐ 127	Warren Spahn and .... 128 Tom Brewer	150.00	67.50	22.50
☐ 129	Jim Gilliam and .... 130 Ellis Kinder	50.00	22.50	7.50
☐ 131	Herm Wehmeier and .... 132 Wayne Terwilliger	35.00	15.75	5.25

1956 Topps

The cards in this 340-card set measure 2 5/8" by 3 3/4". Following up with another horizontally oriented card in 1956, Topps improved the format by layering the color "head" shot onto an actual action sequence involving the player. Cards 1 to 180 come with either white or gray backs: in the 1 to 100 sequence, gray backs are less common (worth about 10 percent more) and in the 101 to 180 sequence, white backs are less common (worth 30 percent more). The team cards, used for the first time in a regular set by Topps, are found dated 1955, or undated, with the team name appearing on either side. The dated team cards in the first series were not printed on the gray stock. The two unnumbered checklist cards are highly prized (must be unmarked to qualify as excellent or mint). The complete set price below does not include the unnumbered checklist cards or any of the variations. The key rookies in this set are Walt Alston, Luis Aparicio, and Roger Craig. There are ten double-printed cards in the first series as evidenced by the discovery of an uncut sheet of 110 cards (10 by 11); these DP's are listed below.

	NRMT	VG-E	GOOD
COMPLETE SET (340)	7500.00	3500.00	800.00
COMMON PLAYER (1-100)	8.00	3.50	.80
COMMON PLAYER (101-180)	11.00	5.00	1.35
COMMON PLAYER (181-260)	15.00	6.50	2.15
COMMON PLAYER (261-340)	11.00	5.00	1.35

☐ 1 William Harridge (AL President)	135.00	25.00	5.00
☐ 2 Warren Giles (NL President)	17.00	7.25	2.50
☐ 3 Elmer Valo	8.00	3.50	.80
☐ 4 Carlos Paula	8.00	3.50	.80
☐ 5 Ted Williams	275.00	120.00	40.00
☐ 6 Ray Boone	9.00	4.00	.90
☐ 7 Ron Negray	8.00	3.50	.80
☐ 8 Walter Alston MG	38.00	17.00	4.50
☐ 9 Ruben Gomez DP	8.00	3.50	.80
☐ 10 Warren Spahn	80.00	36.00	12.00
☐ 11A Chicago Cubs (centered)	30.00	13.50	4.50
☐ 11B Cubs Team (dated 1955)	60.00	27.00	9.00
☐ 11C Cubs Team (name at far left)	30.00	13.50	4.50
☐ 12 Andy Carey	10.00	4.50	1.25
☐ 13 Roy Face	10.00	4.50	1.25
☐ 14 Ken Boyer DP	15.00	6.50	2.15
☐ 15 Ernie Banks DP	90.00	40.00	13.50
☐ 16 Hector Lopez	11.00	5.00	1.35
☐ 17 Gene Conley	8.00	3.50	.80
☐ 18 Dick Donovan	8.00	3.50	.80
☐ 19 Chuck Diering	8.00	3.50	.80
☐ 20 Al Kaline	110.00	50.00	16.50
☐ 21 Joe Collins DP	8.00	3.50	.80
☐ 22 Jim Finigan	8.00	3.50	.80
☐ 23 Fred Marsh	8.00	3.50	.80
☐ 24 Dick Groat	11.00	5.00	1.35
☐ 25 Ted Kluszewski	21.00	9.00	3.00
☐ 26 Grady Hatton	8.00	3.50	.80
☐ 27 Nelson Burbrink	8.00	3.50	.80
☐ 28 Bobby Hofman	8.00	3.50	.80
☐ 29 Jack Harshman	8.00	3.50	.80
☐ 30 Jackie Robinson DP	160.00	72.00	24.00
☐ 31 Hank Aaron UER (small photo actually W.Mays)	240.00	105.00	32.00
☐ 32 Frank House	8.00	3.50	.80
☐ 33 Roberto Clemente	375.00	165.00	55.00
☐ 34 Tom Brewer	8.00	3.50	.80
☐ 35 Al Rosen	11.00	5.00	1.35
☐ 36 Rudy Minarcin	8.00	3.50	.80
☐ 37 Alex Grammas	8.00	3.50	.80
☐ 38 Bob Kennedy	8.00	3.50	.80
☐ 39 Don Mossi	9.00	4.00	.90
☐ 40 Bob Turley	11.00	5.00	1.35
☐ 41 Hank Sauer	9.00	4.00	.90
☐ 42 Sandy Amoros	10.00	4.50	1.25
☐ 43 Ray Moore	8.00	3.50	.80
☐ 44 Windy McCall	8.00	3.50	.80
☐ 45 Gus Zernial	9.00	4.00	.90
☐ 46 Gene Freese DP	8.00	3.50	.80
☐ 47 Art Fowler	8.00	3.50	.80
☐ 48 Jim Hegan	8.00	3.50	.80
☐ 49 Pedro Ramos	8.00	3.50	.80
☐ 50 Dusty Rhodes	9.00	4.00	.90
☐ 51 Ernie Oravetz	8.00	3.50	.80
☐ 52 Bob Grim	9.00	4.00	.90
☐ 53 Arnie Portocarrero	8.00	3.50	.80
☐ 54 Bob Keegan	8.00	3.50	.80
☐ 55 Wally Moon	10.00	4.50	1.25
☐ 56 Dale Long	9.00	4.00	.90
☐ 57 Duke Maas	8.00	3.50	.80
☐ 58 Ed Roebuck	9.00	4.00	.90
☐ 59 Jose Santiago	8.00	3.50	.80
☐ 60 Mayo Smith MG DP	8.00	3.50	.80
☐ 61 Bill Skowron	17.00	7.25	2.50
☐ 62 Hal Smith	8.00	3.50	.80
☐ 63 Roger Craig	30.00	13.50	4.50
☐ 64 Luis Arroyo	11.00	5.00	1.35
☐ 65 Johnny O'Brien	8.00	3.50	.80
☐ 66 Bob Speake	8.00	3.50	.80
☐ 67 Vic Power	8.00	3.50	.80
☐ 68 Chuck Stobbs	8.00	3.50	.80
☐ 69 Chuck Tanner	10.00	4.50	1.25
☐ 70 Jim Rivera	8.00	3.50	.80
☐ 71 Frank Sullivan	8.00	3.50	.80
☐ 72A Phillies Team (centered)	30.00	13.50	4.50
☐ 72B Phillies Team (dated 1955)	60.00	27.00	9.00
☐ 72C Phillies Team (name at far left)	30.00	13.50	4.50
☐ 73 Wayne Terwilliger	8.00	3.50	.80
☐ 74 Jim King	8.00	3.50	.80
☐ 75 Roy Sievers DP	8.00	3.50	.80
☐ 76 Ray Crone	8.00	3.50	.80
☐ 77 Harvey Haddix	9.00	4.00	.90
☐ 78 Herman Wehmeier	8.00	3.50	.80
☐ 79 Sandy Koufax	375.00	165.00	55.00
☐ 80 Gus Triandos DP	8.00	3.50	.80
☐ 81 Wally Westlake	8.00	3.50	.80
☐ 82 Bill Renna	8.00	3.50	.80
☐ 83 Karl Spooner	9.00	4.00	.90
☐ 84 Babe Birrer	8.00	3.50	.80
☐ 85A Cleveland Indians (centered)	30.00	13.50	4.50
☐ 85B Indians Team (dated 1955)	60.00	27.00	9.00
☐ 85C Indians Team (name at far left)	30.00	13.50	4.50
☐ 86 Ray Jablonski DP	8.00	3.50	.80
☐ 87 Dean Stone	8.00	3.50	.80
☐ 88 Johnny Kucks	10.00	4.50	1.25
☐ 89 Norm Zauchin	8.00	3.50	.80
☐ 90A Cincinnati Redlegs Team (centered)	30.00	13.50	4.50
☐ 90B Reds Team (dated 1955)	60.00	27.00	9.00
☐ 90C Reds Team (name at far left)	30.00	13.50	4.50
☐ 91 Gail Harris	8.00	3.50	.80
☐ 92 Bob(Red) Wilson	8.00	3.50	.80
☐ 93 George Susce	8.00	3.50	.80
☐ 94 Ron Kline	8.00	3.50	.80
☐ 95A Milwaukee Braves Team (centered)	30.00	13.50	4.50
☐ 95B Braves Team (dated 1955)	60.00	27.00	9.00
☐ 95C Braves Team (name at far left)	30.00	13.50	4.50
☐ 96 Bill Tremel	8.00	3.50	.80
☐ 97 Jerry Lynch	9.00	4.00	.90
☐ 98 Camilo Pascual	9.00	4.00	.90
☐ 99 Don Zimmer	16.00	6.75	2.25
☐ 100A Baltimore Orioles Team (centered)	30.00	13.50	4.50
☐ 100B Orioles Team (dated 1955)	60.00	27.00	9.00
☐ 100C Orioles Team (name at far left)	30.00	13.50	4.50
☐ 101 Roy Campanella	125.00	57.50	18.75
☐ 102 Jim Davis	11.00	5.00	1.35
☐ 103 Willie Miranda	11.00	5.00	1.35
☐ 104 Bob Lennon	11.00	5.00	1.35
☐ 105 Al Smith	11.00	5.00	1.35
☐ 106 Joe Astroth	11.00	5.00	1.35
☐ 107 Eddie Mathews	60.00	27.00	9.00
☐ 108 Laurin Pepper	11.00	5.00	1.35
☐ 109 Enos Slaughter	30.00	13.50	4.50
☐ 110 Yogi Berra	140.00	63.00	21.00
☐ 111 Boston Red Sox Team Card	36.00	16.25	5.50
☐ 112 Dee Fondy	11.00	5.00	1.35
☐ 113 Phil Rizzuto	50.00	22.50	7.50

#	Name			
114	Jim Owens	11.00	5.00	1.35
115	Jackie Jensen	14.00	6.25	2.00
116	Eddie O'Brien	11.00	5.00	1.35
117	Virgil Trucks	12.00	5.25	1.50
118	Nellie Fox	32.00	14.25	4.75
119	Larry Jackson	14.00	6.25	2.00
120	Richie Ashburn	33.00	15.00	5.00
121	Pittsburgh Pirates Team Card	36.00	16.25	5.50
122	Willard Nixon	11.00	5.00	1.35
123	Roy McMillan	11.00	5.00	1.35
124	Don Kaiser	11.00	5.00	1.35
125	Minnie Minoso	21.00	9.00	3.00
126	Jim Brady	11.00	5.00	1.35
127	Willie Jones	11.00	5.00	1.35
128	Eddie Yost	11.00	5.00	1.35
129	Jake Martin	11.00	5.00	1.35
130	Willie Mays	300.00	135.00	45.00
131	Bob Roselli	11.00	5.00	1.35
132	Bobby Avila	12.00	5.25	1.50
133	Ray Narleski	11.00	5.00	1.35
134	St. Louis Cardinals Team Card	36.00	16.25	5.50
135	Mickey Mantle	900.00	400.00	135.00
136	Johnny Logan	12.00	5.25	1.50
137	Al Silvera	11.00	5.00	1.35
138	Johnny Antonelli	12.00	5.25	1.50
139	Tommy Carroll	11.00	5.00	1.35
140	Herb Score	28.00	12.50	4.00
141	Joe Frazier	11.00	5.00	1.35
142	Gene Baker	11.00	5.00	1.35
143	Jim Piersall	15.00	6.50	2.15
144	Leroy Powell	11.00	5.00	1.35
145	Gil Hodges	48.00	22.00	6.00
146	Washington Nationals Team Card	32.00	14.25	4.75
147	Earl Torgeson	11.00	5.00	1.35
148	Alvin Dark	14.00	6.25	2.00
149	Dixie Howell	11.00	5.00	1.35
150	Duke Snider	135.00	60.00	20.00
151	Spook Jacobs	11.00	5.00	1.35
152	Billy Hoeft	11.00	5.00	1.35
153	Frank Thomas	12.00	5.25	1.50
154	Dave Pope	11.00	5.00	1.35
155	Harvey Kuenn	15.00	6.50	2.15
156	Wes Westrum	11.00	5.00	1.35
157	Dick Brodowski	11.00	5.00	1.35
158	Wally Post	12.00	5.25	1.50
159	Clint Courtney	11.00	5.00	1.35
160	Billy Pierce	14.00	6.25	2.00
161	Joe DeMaestri	11.00	5.00	1.35
162	Dave(Gus) Bell	12.00	5.25	1.50
163	Gene Woodling	14.00	6.25	2.00
164	Harmon Killebrew	150.00	67.50	22.50
165	Red Schoendienst	30.00	13.50	4.50
166	Brooklyn Dodgers Team Card	190.00	85.00	28.50
167	Harry Dorish	11.00	5.00	1.35
168	Sammy White	11.00	5.00	1.35
169	Bob Nelson	11.00	5.00	1.35
170	Bill Virdon	15.00	6.50	2.15
171	Jim Wilson	11.00	5.00	1.35
172	Frank Torre	14.00	6.25	2.00
173	Johnny Podres	15.00	6.50	2.15
174	Glen Gorbous	11.00	5.00	1.35
175	Del Crandall	12.00	5.25	1.50
176	Alex Kellner	11.00	5.00	1.35
177	Hank Bauer	20.00	8.50	2.75
178	Joe Black	14.00	6.25	2.00
179	Harry Chiti	11.00	5.00	1.35
180	Robin Roberts	32.00	14.25	4.75
181	Billy Martin	100.00	45.00	15.00
182	Paul Minner	15.00	6.50	2.15
183	Stan Lopata	15.00	6.50	2.15
184	Don Bessent	15.00	6.50	2.15
185	Bill Bruton	17.00	7.25	2.50
186	Ron Jackson	15.00	6.50	2.15
187	Early Wynn	35.00	15.75	5.25
188	Chicago White Sox Team Card	35.00	15.75	5.25
189	Ned Garver	15.00	6.50	2.15
190	Carl Furillo	25.00	11.00	3.50
191	Frank Lary	18.00	7.50	2.50
192	Smoky Burgess	18.00	7.50	2.50
193	Wilmer Mizell	15.00	6.50	2.15
194	Monte Irvin	32.00	14.25	4.75
195	George Kell	30.00	13.50	4.50
196	Tom Poholsky	15.00	6.50	2.15
197	Granny Hamner	15.00	6.50	2.15
198	Ed Fitzgerald	15.00	6.50	2.15
199	Hank Thompson	18.00	7.50	2.50
200	Bob Feller	130.00	60.00	20.00
201	Rip Repulski	15.00	6.50	2.15
202	Jim Hearn	15.00	6.50	2.15
203	Bill Tuttle	15.00	6.50	2.15
204	Art Swanson	15.00	6.50	2.15
205	Whitey Lockman	18.00	7.50	2.50
206	Erv Palica	15.00	6.50	2.15
207	Jim Small	15.00	6.50	2.15
208	Elston Howard	48.00	22.00	6.00
209	Max Surkont	15.00	6.50	2.15
210	Mike Garcia	18.00	7.50	2.50
211	Murry Dickson	15.00	6.50	2.15
212	Johnny Temple	18.00	7.50	2.50
213	Detroit Tigers Team Card	48.00	22.00	6.00
214	Bob Rush	15.00	6.50	2.15
215	Tommy Byrne	18.00	7.50	2.50
216	Jerry Schoonmaker	15.00	6.50	2.15
217	Billy Klaus	15.00	6.50	2.15
218	Joe Nuxall (sic, Nuxhall)	18.00	7.50	2.50
219	Lew Burdette	20.00	8.50	2.75
220	Del Ennis	18.00	7.50	2.50
221	Bob Friend	18.00	7.50	2.50
222	Dave Philley	15.00	6.50	2.15
223	Randy Jackson	15.00	6.50	2.15
224	Bud Podbielan	15.00	6.50	2.15
225	Gil McDougald	27.00	12.00	4.00
226	New York Giants Team Card	70.00	32.00	10.50
227	Russ Meyer	15.00	6.50	2.15
228	Mickey Vernon	18.00	7.50	2.50
229	Harry Brecheen	15.00	6.50	2.15
230	Chico Carrasquel	15.00	6.50	2.15
231	Bob Hale	15.00	6.50	2.15
232	Toby Atwell	15.00	6.50	2.15
233	Carl Erskine	24.00	10.50	3.50
234	Pete Runnels	18.00	7.50	2.50
235	Don Newcombe	48.00	22.00	6.00
236	Kansas City Athletics Team Card	27.00	12.00	4.00
237	Jose Valdivielso	15.00	6.50	2.15
238	Walt Dropo	18.00	7.50	2.50
239	Harry Simpson	15.00	6.50	2.15
240	Whitey Ford	130.00	60.00	20.00
241	Don Mueller UER (6" tall)	18.00	7.50	2.50
242	Hershell Freeman	15.00	6.50	2.15
243	Sherm Lollar	18.00	7.50	2.50
244	Bob Buhl	18.00	7.50	2.50
245	Billy Goodman	18.00	7.50	2.50
246	Tom Gorman	15.00	6.50	2.15
247	Bill Sarni	15.00	6.50	2.15
248	Bob Porterfield	15.00	6.50	2.15
249	Johnny Klippstein	15.00	6.50	2.15
250	Larry Doby	22.00	9.50	3.15
251	New York Yankees Team Card UER (Don Larsen misspelled as Larson on front)	225.00	100.00	33.00
252	Vern Law	18.00	7.50	2.50
253	Irv Noren	18.00	7.50	2.50
254	George Crowe	15.00	6.50	2.15
255	Bob Lemon	35.00	15.75	5.25
256	Tom Hurd	15.00	6.50	2.15
257	Bobby Thomson	21.00	9.00	3.00
258	Art Ditmar	18.00	7.50	2.50
259	Sam Jones	18.00	7.50	2.50
260	Pee Wee Reese	140.00	63.00	21.00
261	Bobby Shantz	15.00	6.50	2.15
262	Howie Pollet	11.00	5.00	1.35
263	Bob Miller	11.00	5.00	1.35
264	Ray Monzant	11.00	5.00	1.35
265	Sandy Consuegra	11.00	5.00	1.35
266	Don Ferrarese	11.00	5.00	1.35
267	Bob Nieman	11.00	5.00	1.35
268	Dale Mitchell	16.00	6.75	2.25
269	Jack Meyer	11.00	5.00	1.35
270	Billy Loes	14.00	6.25	2.00
271	Foster Castleman	11.00	5.00	1.35
272	Danny O'Connell	11.00	5.00	1.35
273	Walker Cooper	11.00	5.00	1.35
274	Frank Baumholtz	11.00	5.00	1.35
275	Jim Greengrass	11.00	5.00	1.35
276	George Zuverink	11.00	5.00	1.35
277	Daryl Spencer	11.00	5.00	1.35
278	Chet Nichols	11.00	5.00	1.35
279	Johnny Groth	11.00	5.00	1.35
280	Jim Gilliam	18.00	7.50	2.50
281	Art Houtteman	11.00	5.00	1.35
282	Warren Hacker	11.00	5.00	1.35
283	Hal Smith	11.00	5.00	1.35
284	Ike Delock	11.00	5.00	1.35
285	Eddie Miksis	11.00	5.00	1.35
286	Bill Wight	11.00	5.00	1.35
287	Bobby Adams	11.00	5.00	1.35
288	Bob Cerv	24.00	10.50	3.50

		NRMT	VG-E	GOOD
☐ 289	Hal Jeffcoat	11.00	5.00	1.35
☐ 290	Curt Simmons	14.00	6.25	2.00
☐ 291	Frank Kellert	11.00	5.00	1.35
☐ 292	Luis Aparicio	135.00	60.00	20.00
☐ 293	Stu Miller	14.00	6.25	2.00
☐ 294	Ernie Johnson	14.00	6.25	2.00
☐ 295	Clem Labine	14.00	6.25	2.00
☐ 296	Andy Seminick	11.00	5.00	1.35
☐ 297	Bob Skinner	14.00	6.25	2.00
☐ 298	Johnny Schmitz	11.00	5.00	1.35
☐ 299	Charlie Neal	25.00	11.00	3.50
☐ 300	Vic Wertz	14.00	6.25	2.00
☐ 301	Marv Grissom	11.00	5.00	1.35
☐ 302	Eddie Robinson	11.00	5.00	1.35
☐ 303	Jim Dyck	11.00	5.00	1.35
☐ 304	Frank Malzone	18.00	7.50	2.50
☐ 305	Brooks Lawrence	11.00	5.00	1.35
☐ 306	Curt Roberts	11.00	5.00	1.35
☐ 307	Hoyt Wilhelm	32.00	14.25	4.75
☐ 308	Chuck Harmon	11.00	5.00	1.35
☐ 309	Don Blasingame	11.00	5.00	1.35
☐ 310	Steve Gromek	11.00	5.00	1.35
☐ 311	Hal Naragon	11.00	5.00	1.35
☐ 312	Andy Pafko	12.00	5.25	1.50
☐ 313	Gene Stephens	11.00	5.00	1.35
☐ 314	Hobie Landrith	11.00	5.00	1.35
☐ 315	Milt Bolling	11.00	5.00	1.35
☐ 316	Jerry Coleman	14.00	6.25	2.00
☐ 317	Al Aber	11.00	5.00	1.35
☐ 318	Fred Hatfield	11.00	5.00	1.35
☐ 319	Jack Crimian	11.00	5.00	1.35
☐ 320	Joe Adcock	14.00	6.25	2.00
☐ 321	Jim Konstanty	12.00	5.25	1.50
☐ 322	Karl Olson	11.00	5.00	1.35
☐ 323	Willard Schmidt	11.00	5.00	1.35
☐ 324	Rocky Bridges	11.00	5.00	1.35
☐ 325	Don Liddle	11.00	5.00	1.35
☐ 326	Connie Johnson	11.00	5.00	1.35
☐ 327	Bob Wiesler	11.00	5.00	1.35
☐ 328	Preston Ward	11.00	5.00	1.35
☐ 329	Lou Berberet	11.00	5.00	1.35
☐ 330	Jim Busby	11.00	5.00	1.35
☐ 331	Dick Hall	11.00	5.00	1.35
☐ 332	Don Larsen	36.00	16.25	5.50
☐ 333	Rube Walker	12.00	5.25	1.50
☐ 334	Bob Miller	11.00	5.00	1.35
☐ 335	Don Hoak	12.00	5.25	1.50
☐ 336	Ellis Kinder	11.00	5.00	1.35
☐ 337	Bobby Morgan	11.00	5.00	1.35
☐ 338	Jim Delsing	11.00	5.00	1.35
☐ 339	Rance Pless	11.00	5.00	1.35
☐ 340	Mickey McDermott	50.00	7.50	1.50
☐ xx	Checklist 1/3 (unnumbered)	225.00	35.00	7.00
☐ xx	Checklist 2/4 (unnumbered)	225.00	35.00	7.00

1957 Topps

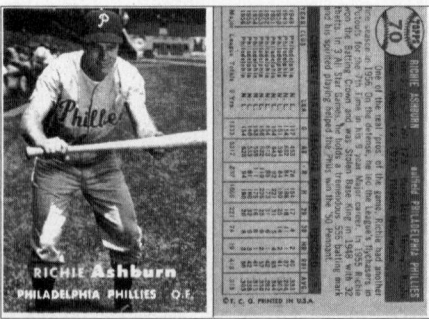

The cards in this 407-card set measure 2 1/2" by 3 1/2". In 1957, Topps returned to the vertical obverse, adopted what we now call the standard card size, and used a large, uncluttered color photo for the first time since 1952. Cards in the series 265 to 352 and the unnumbered checklist cards are scarcer than other cards in the set. However within this scarce series (265-352) there are 22 cards which were printed in double the quantity of the other cards in the series; these 22 double prints are indicated by DP in the checklist below. The first star combination cards, cards 400 and 407, are quite popular with collectors. They feature the big stars of the previous season's World Series teams, the Dodgers (Furillo, Hodges, Campanella, and Snider) and Yankees (Berra and Mantle). The complete set price below does not include the unnumbered checklist cards. The key rookies in this set are Jim Bunning, Rocky Colavito, Don Drysdale, Whitey Herzog, Tony Kubek, Bobby Richardson, Brooks Robinson, and Frank Robinson.

	NRMT	VG-E	GOOD
COMPLETE SET (407)	7500.00	3500.00	800.00
COMMON PLAYER (1-88)	7.50	3.25	.75
COMMON PLAYER (89-176)	6.50	2.75	.65
COMMON PLAYER (177-264)	6.00	2.50	.60
COMMON PLAYER (265-352)	20.00	8.50	2.75
COMMON DP (265-352)	12.00	5.25	1.50
COMMON PLAYER (353-407)	6.00	2.50	.60

		NRMT	VG-E	GOOD
☐ 1	Ted Williams	450.00	125.00	25.00
☐ 2	Yogi Berra	145.00	65.00	18.00
☐ 3	Dale Long	9.00	4.00	.90
☐ 4	Johnny Logan	9.00	4.00	.90
☐ 5	Sal Maglie	11.00	5.00	1.35
☐ 6	Hector Lopez	9.00	4.00	.90
☐ 7	Luis Aparicio	36.00	16.25	5.50
☐ 8	Don Mossi	9.00	4.00	.90
☐ 9	Johnny Temple	9.00	4.00	.90
☐ 10	Willie Mays	225.00	100.00	33.00
☐ 11	George Zuverink	7.50	3.25	.75
☐ 12	Dick Groat	11.00	5.00	1.35
☐ 13	Wally Burnette	7.50	3.25	.75
☐ 14	Bob Nieman	7.50	3.25	.75
☐ 15	Robin Roberts	25.00	11.00	3.50
☐ 16	Walt Moryn	7.50	3.25	.75
☐ 17	Billy Gardner	7.50	3.25	.75
☐ 18	Don Drysdale	225.00	100.00	33.00
☐ 19	Bob Wilson	7.50	3.25	.75
☐ 20	Hank Aaron UER (reverse negative photo on front)	250.00	110.00	37.50
☐ 21	Frank Sullivan	7.50	3.25	.75
☐ 22	Jerry Snyder UER (photo actually Ed Fitzgerald)	7.50	3.25	.75
☐ 23	Sherm Lollar	9.00	4.00	.90
☐ 24	Bill Mazeroski	60.00	27.00	9.00
☐ 25	Whitey Ford	65.00	29.00	9.75
☐ 26	Bob Boyd	7.50	3.25	.75
☐ 27	Ted Kazanski	7.50	3.25	.75
☐ 28	Gene Conley	7.50	3.25	.75
☐ 29	Whitey Herzog	30.00	13.50	4.50
☐ 30	Pee Wee Reese	60.00	27.00	9.00
☐ 31	Ron Northey	7.50	3.25	.75
☐ 32	Hershell Freeman	7.50	3.25	.75
☐ 33	Jim Small	7.50	3.25	.75
☐ 34	Tom Sturdivant	7.50	3.25	.75
☐ 35	Frank Robinson	275.00	120.00	40.00
☐ 36	Bob Grim	9.00	4.00	.90
☐ 37	Frank Torre	9.00	4.00	.90
☐ 38	Nellie Fox	21.00	9.00	3.00
☐ 39	Al Worthington	7.50	3.25	.75
☐ 40	Early Wynn	22.00	9.50	3.15
☐ 41	Hal W. Smith	7.50	3.25	.75
☐ 42	Dee Fondy	7.50	3.25	.75
☐ 43	Connie Johnson	7.50	3.25	.75
☐ 44	Joe DeMaestri	7.50	3.25	.75
☐ 45	Carl Furillo	14.00	6.25	2.00
☐ 46	Robert J. Miller	7.50	3.25	.75
☐ 47	Don Blasingame	7.50	3.25	.75
☐ 48	Bill Bruton	9.00	4.00	.90
☐ 49	Daryl Spencer	7.50	3.25	.75
☐ 50	Herb Score	14.00	6.25	2.00
☐ 51	Clint Courtney	7.50	3.25	.75
☐ 52	Lee Walls	7.50	3.25	.75
☐ 53	Clem Labine	9.00	4.00	.90
☐ 54	Elmer Valo	7.50	3.25	.75
☐ 55	Ernie Banks	100.00	45.00	15.00
☐ 56	Dave Sisler	7.50	3.25	.75
☐ 57	Jim Lemon	7.50	3.25	.75
☐ 58	Ruben Gomez	7.50	3.25	.75
☐ 59	Dick Williams	9.00	4.00	.90
☐ 60	Billy Hoeft	7.50	3.25	.75
☐ 61	James(Dusty) Rhodes	9.00	4.00	.90
☐ 62	Billy Martin	50.00	22.50	7.50
☐ 63	Ike Delock	7.50	3.25	.75
☐ 64	Pete Runnels	9.00	4.00	.90
☐ 65	Wally Moon	9.00	4.00	.90
☐ 66	Brooks Lawrence	7.50	3.25	.75
☐ 67	Chico Carrasquel	7.50	3.25	.75

☐ 68 Ray Crone	7.50	3.25	.75
☐ 69 Roy McMillan	7.50	3.25	.75
☐ 70 Richie Ashburn	22.00	9.50	3.15
☐ 71 Murry Dickson	7.50	3.25	.75
☐ 72 Bill Tuttle	7.50	3.25	.75
☐ 73 George Crowe	7.50	3.25	.75
☐ 74 Vito Valentinetti	7.50	3.25	.75
☐ 75 Jim Piersall	11.00	5.00	1.35
☐ 76 Roberto Clemente	200.00	90.00	30.00
☐ 77 Paul Foytack	7.50	3.25	.75
☐ 78 Vic Wertz	9.00	4.00	.90
☐ 79 Lindy McDaniel	11.00	5.00	1.35
☐ 80 Gil Hodges	48.00	22.00	6.00
☐ 81 Herman Wehmeier	7.50	3.25	.75
☐ 82 Elston Howard	20.00	8.50	2.75
☐ 83 Lou Skizas	7.50	3.25	.75
☐ 84 Moe Drabowsky	7.50	3.25	.75
☐ 85 Larry Doby	11.00	5.00	1.35
☐ 86 Bill Sarni	7.50	3.25	.75
☐ 87 Tom Gorman	7.50	3.25	.75
☐ 88 Harvey Kuenn	11.00	5.00	1.35
☐ 89 Roy Sievers	7.50	3.25	.75
☐ 90 Warren Spahn	70.00	32.00	10.50
☐ 91 Mack Burk	6.50	2.75	.65
☐ 92 Mickey Vernon	7.50	3.25	.75
☐ 93 Hal Jeffcoat	6.50	2.75	.65
☐ 94 Bobby Del Greco	6.50	2.75	.65
☐ 95 Mickey Mantle	850.00	375.00	125.00
☐ 96 Hank Aguirre	6.50	2.75	.65
☐ 97 New York Yankees	50.00	22.50	7.50
Team Card			
☐ 98 Alvin Dark	8.50	3.75	.85
☐ 99 Bob Keegan	6.50	2.75	.65
☐ 100 Giles and Harridge	11.00	5.00	1.35
League Presidents			
☐ 101 Chuck Stobbs	6.50	2.75	.65
☐ 102 Ray Boone	7.50	3.25	.75
☐ 103 Joe Nuxhall	7.50	3.25	.75
☐ 104 Hank Foiles	6.50	2.75	.65
☐ 105 Johnny Antonelli	7.50	3.25	.75
☐ 106 Ray Moore	6.50	2.75	.65
☐ 107 Jim Rivera	6.50	2.75	.65
☐ 108 Tommy Byrne	7.50	3.25	.75
☐ 109 Hank Thompson	7.50	3.25	.75
☐ 110 Bill Virdon	8.50	3.75	.85
☐ 111 Hal R. Smith	6.50	2.75	.65
☐ 112 Tom Brewer	6.50	2.75	.65
☐ 113 Wilmer Mizell	6.50	2.75	.65
☐ 114 Milwaukee Braves	16.00	6.75	2.25
Team Card			
☐ 115 Jim Gilliam	12.00	5.25	1.50
☐ 116 Mike Fornieles	6.50	2.75	.65
☐ 117 Joe Adcock	8.50	3.75	.85
☐ 118 Bob Porterfield	6.50	2.75	.65
☐ 119 Stan Lopata	6.50	2.75	.65
☐ 120 Bob Lemon	22.00	9.50	3.15
☐ 121 Clete Boyer	17.00	7.25	2.50
☐ 122 Ken Boyer	13.00	5.75	1.75
☐ 123 Steve Ridzik	6.50	2.75	.65
☐ 124 Dave Philley	6.50	2.75	.65
☐ 125 Al Kaline	90.00	40.00	13.50
☐ 126 Bob Wiesler	6.50	2.75	.65
☐ 127 Bob Buhl	7.50	3.25	.75
☐ 128 Ed Bailey	7.50	3.25	.75
☐ 129 Saul Rogovin	6.50	2.75	.65
☐ 130 Don Newcombe	14.00	6.25	2.00
☐ 131 Milt Bolling	6.50	2.75	.65
☐ 132 Art Ditmar	6.50	2.75	.65
☐ 133 Del Crandall	7.50	3.25	.75
☐ 134 Don Kaiser	6.50	2.75	.65
☐ 135 Bill Skowron	13.00	5.75	1.75
☐ 136 Jim Hegan	7.50	3.25	.75
☐ 137 Bob Rush	6.50	2.75	.65
☐ 138 Minnie Minoso	13.00	5.75	1.75
☐ 139 Lou Kretlow	6.50	2.75	.65
☐ 140 Frank Thomas	7.50	3.25	.75
☐ 141 Al Aber	6.50	2.75	.65
☐ 142 Charley Thompson	6.50	2.75	.65
☐ 143 Andy Pafko	7.50	3.25	.75
☐ 144 Ray Narleski	6.50	2.75	.65
☐ 145 Al Smith	6.50	2.75	.65
☐ 146 Don Ferrarese	6.50	2.75	.65
☐ 147 Al Walker	6.50	2.75	.65
☐ 148 Don Mueller	7.50	3.25	.75
☐ 149 Bob Kennedy	6.50	2.75	.65
☐ 150 Bob Friend	7.50	3.25	.75
☐ 151 Willie Miranda	6.50	2.75	.65
☐ 152 Jack Harshman	6.50	2.75	.65
☐ 153 Karl Olson	6.50	2.75	.65
☐ 154 Red Schoendienst	21.00	9.00	3.00
☐ 155 Jim Brosnan	7.50	3.25	.75
☐ 156 Gus Triandos	7.50	3.25	.75
☐ 157 Wally Post	7.50	3.25	.75
☐ 158 Curt Simmons	7.50	3.25	.75
☐ 159 Solly Drake	6.50	2.75	.65
☐ 160 Billy Pierce	8.50	3.75	.85
☐ 161 Pittsburgh Pirates	13.50	6.00	1.85
Team Card			
☐ 162 Jack Meyer	6.50	2.75	.65
☐ 163 Sammy White	6.50	2.75	.65
☐ 164 Tommy Carroll	6.50	2.75	.65
☐ 165 Ted Kluszewski	30.00	13.50	4.50
☐ 166 Roy Face	8.50	3.75	.85
☐ 167 Vic Power	6.50	2.75	.65
☐ 168 Frank Lary	7.50	3.25	.75
☐ 169 Herb Plews	6.50	2.75	.65
☐ 170 Duke Snider	100.00	45.00	15.00
☐ 171 Boston Red Sox	13.50	6.00	1.85
Team Card			
☐ 172 Gene Woodling	8.50	3.75	.85
☐ 173 Roger Craig	14.00	6.25	2.00
☐ 174 Willie Jones	6.50	2.75	.65
☐ 175 Don Larsen	16.00	6.75	2.25
☐ 176A Gene Baker ERR	300.00	135.00	45.00
(misspelled Bakep			
on card back)			
☐ 176B Gene Baker COR	7.50	3.25	.75
☐ 177 Eddie Yost	6.00	2.50	.60
☐ 178 Don Bessent	6.00	2.50	.60
☐ 179 Ernie Oravetz	6.00	2.50	.60
☐ 180 Gus Bell	7.00	3.00	.70
☐ 181 Dick Donovan	6.00	2.50	.60
☐ 182 Hobie Landrith	6.00	2.50	.60
☐ 183 Chicago Cubs	13.50	6.00	1.85
Team Card			
☐ 184 Tito Francona	9.00	4.00	.90
☐ 185 Johnny Kucks	7.00	3.00	.70
☐ 186 Jim King	6.00	2.50	.60
☐ 187 Virgil Trucks	7.00	3.00	.70
☐ 188 Felix Mantilla	8.00	3.50	.80
☐ 189 Willard Nixon	6.00	2.50	.60
☐ 190 Randy Jackson	6.00	2.50	.60
☐ 191 Joe Margoneri	6.00	2.50	.60
☐ 192 Jerry Coleman	7.00	3.00	.70
☐ 193 Del Rice	6.00	2.50	.60
☐ 194 Hal Brown	6.00	2.50	.60
☐ 195 Bobby Avila	6.00	2.50	.60
☐ 196 Larry Jackson	6.00	2.50	.60
☐ 197 Hank Sauer	7.00	3.00	.70
☐ 198 Detroit Tigers	13.50	6.00	1.85
Team Card			
☐ 199 Vern Law	7.00	3.00	.70
☐ 200 Gil McDougald	13.00	5.75	1.75
☐ 201 Sandy Amoros	8.00	3.50	.80
☐ 202 Dick Gernert	6.00	2.50	.60
☐ 203 Hoyt Wilhelm	21.00	9.00	3.00
☐ 204 Kansas City Athletics	12.00	5.25	1.50
Team Card			
☐ 205 Charlie Maxwell	7.00	3.00	.70
☐ 206 Willard Schmidt	6.00	2.50	.60
☐ 207 Gordon(Billy) Hunter	6.00	2.50	.60
☐ 208 Lou Burdette	9.00	4.00	.90
☐ 209 Bob Skinner	7.00	3.00	.70
☐ 210 Roy Campanella	100.00	45.00	15.00
☐ 211 Camilo Pascual	7.00	3.00	.70
☐ 212 Rocco Colavito	125.00	57.50	18.75
☐ 213 Les Moss	6.00	2.50	.60
☐ 214 Philadelphia Phillies	13.50	6.00	1.85
Team Card			
☐ 215 Enos Slaughter	25.00	11.00	3.50
☐ 216 Marv Grissom	6.00	2.50	.60
☐ 217 Gene Stephens	6.00	2.50	.60
☐ 218 Ray Jablonski	6.00	2.50	.60
☐ 219 Tom Acker	6.00	2.50	.60
☐ 220 Jackie Jensen	11.00	5.00	1.35
☐ 221 Dixie Howell	6.00	2.50	.60
☐ 222 Alex Grammas	6.00	2.50	.60
☐ 223 Frank House	6.00	2.50	.60
☐ 224 Marv Blaylock	6.00	2.50	.60
☐ 225 Harry Simpson	6.00	2.50	.60
☐ 226 Preston Ward	6.00	2.50	.60
☐ 227 Jerry Staley	6.00	2.50	.60
☐ 228 Smoky Burgess UER	8.00	3.50	.80
(Misspelled Smokey			
on card back)			
☐ 229 George Susce	6.00	2.50	.60
☐ 230 George Kell	20.00	8.50	2.75
☐ 231 Solly Hemus	6.00	2.50	.60
☐ 232 Whitey Lockman	7.00	3.00	.70
☐ 233 Art Fowler	6.00	2.50	.60
☐ 234 Dick Cole	6.00	2.50	.60
☐ 235 Tom Poholsky	6.00	2.50	.60
☐ 236 Joe Ginsberg	6.00	2.50	.60
☐ 237 Foster Castleman	6.00	2.50	.60
☐ 238 Eddie Robinson	6.00	2.50	.60
☐ 239 Tom Morgan	6.00	2.50	.60
☐ 240 Hank Bauer	13.00	5.75	1.75
☐ 241 Joe Lonnett	6.00	2.50	.60

☐ 242	Charlie Neal	7.00	3.00	.70
☐ 243	St. Louis Cardinals Team Card	13.50	6.00	1.85
☐ 244	Billy Loes	7.00	3.00	.70
☐ 245	Rip Repulski	6.00	2.50	.60
☐ 246	Jose Valdivielso	6.00	2.50	.60
☐ 247	Turk Lown	6.00	2.50	.60
☐ 248	Jim Finigan	6.00	2.50	.60
☐ 249	Dave Pope	6.00	2.50	.60
☐ 250	Eddie Mathews	40.00	18.00	6.00
☐ 251	Baltimore Orioles Team Card	13.50	6.00	1.85
☐ 252	Carl Erskine	11.00	5.00	1.35
☐ 253	Gus Zernial	7.00	3.00	.70
☐ 254	Ron Negray	6.00	2.50	.60
☐ 255	Charlie Silvera	6.00	2.50	.60
☐ 256	Ron Kline	6.00	2.50	.60
☐ 257	Walt Dropo	7.00	3.00	.70
☐ 258	Steve Gromek	6.00	2.50	.60
☐ 259	Eddie O'Brien	6.00	2.50	.60
☐ 260	Del Ennis	7.00	3.00	.70
☐ 261	Bob Chakales	6.00	2.50	.60
☐ 262	Bobby Thomson	10.00	4.50	1.25
☐ 263	George Strickland	6.00	2.50	.60
☐ 264	Bob Turley	12.00	5.25	1.50
☐ 265	Harvey Haddix DP	15.00	6.50	2.15
☐ 266	Ken Kuhn DP	12.00	5.25	1.50
☐ 267	Danny Kravitz	20.00	8.50	2.75
☐ 268	Jack Collum	20.00	8.50	2.75
☐ 269	Bob Cerv	22.00	9.50	3.15
☐ 270	Washington Senators Team Card	45.00	20.00	6.75
☐ 271	Danny O'Connell DP	12.00	5.25	1.50
☐ 272	Bobby Shantz	27.00	12.00	4.00
☐ 273	Jim Davis	20.00	8.50	2.75
☐ 274	Don Hoak	22.00	9.50	3.15
☐ 275	Cleveland Indians Team Card	45.00	20.00	6.75
☐ 276	Jim Pyburn	20.00	8.50	2.75
☐ 277	Johnny Podres DP	50.00	22.50	7.50
☐ 278	Fred Hatfield DP	12.00	5.25	1.50
☐ 279	Bob Thurman	20.00	8.50	2.75
☐ 280	Alex Kellner	20.00	8.50	2.75
☐ 281	Gail Harris	20.00	8.50	2.75
☐ 282	Jack Dittmer DP	12.00	5.25	1.50
☐ 283	Wes Covington DP	15.00	6.50	2.15
☐ 284	Don Zimmer	30.00	13.50	4.50
☐ 285	Ned Garver	20.00	8.50	2.75
☐ 286	Bobby Richardson	115.00	50.00	15.00
☐ 287	Sam Jones	22.00	9.50	3.15
☐ 288	Ted Lepcio	20.00	8.50	2.75
☐ 289	Jim Bolger DP	12.00	5.25	1.50
☐ 290	Andy Carey DP	15.00	6.50	2.15
☐ 291	Windy McCall	20.00	8.50	2.75
☐ 292	Billy Klaus	20.00	8.50	2.75
☐ 293	Ted Abernathy	20.00	8.50	2.75
☐ 294	Rocky Bridges DP	12.00	5.25	1.50
☐ 295	Joe Collins DP	15.00	6.50	2.15
☐ 296	Johnny Klippstein	20.00	8.50	2.75
☐ 297	Jack Crimian	20.00	8.50	2.75
☐ 298	Irv Noren DP	12.00	5.25	1.50
☐ 299	Chuck Harmon	20.00	8.50	2.75
☐ 300	Mike Garcia	22.00	9.50	3.15
☐ 301	Sammy Esposito DP	12.00	5.25	1.50
☐ 302	Sandy Koufax DP	325.00	150.00	50.00
☐ 303	Billy Goodman	22.00	9.50	3.15
☐ 304	Joe Cunningham	22.00	9.50	3.15
☐ 305	Chico Fernandez	20.00	8.50	2.75
☐ 306	Darrell Johnson DP	15.00	6.50	2.15
☐ 307	Jack D. Phillips DP	12.00	5.25	1.50
☐ 308	Dick Hall	20.00	8.50	2.75
☐ 309	Jim Busby DP	12.00	5.25	1.50
☐ 310	Max Surkont DP	12.00	5.25	1.50
☐ 311	Al Pilarcik DP	12.00	5.25	1.50
☐ 312	Tony Kubek DP	100.00	45.00	15.00
☐ 313	Mel Parnell	22.00	9.50	3.15
☐ 314	Ed Bouchee DP	12.00	5.25	1.50
☐ 315	Lou Berberet DP	12.00	5.25	1.50
☐ 316	Billy O'Dell	20.00	8.50	2.75
☐ 317	New York Giants Team Card	50.00	22.50	7.50
☐ 318	Mickey McDermott	20.00	8.50	2.75
☐ 319	Gino Cimoli	22.00	9.50	3.15
☐ 320	Neil Chrisley	20.00	8.50	2.75
☐ 321	John(Red) Murff	20.00	8.50	2.75
☐ 322	Cincinnati Reds Team Card	50.00	22.50	7.50
☐ 323	Wes Westrum	22.00	9.50	3.15
☐ 324	Brooklyn Dodgers Team Card	100.00	45.00	15.00
☐ 325	Frank Bolling	20.00	8.50	2.75
☐ 326	Pedro Ramos	20.00	8.50	2.75
☐ 327	Jim Pendleton	20.00	8.50	2.75
☐ 328	Brooks Robinson	400.00	180.00	60.00
☐ 329	Chicago White Sox Team Card	45.00	20.00	6.75
☐ 330	Jim Wilson	20.00	8.50	2.75
☐ 331	Ray Katt	20.00	8.50	2.75
☐ 332	Bob Bowman	20.00	8.50	2.75
☐ 333	Ernie Johnson	22.00	9.50	3.15
☐ 334	Jerry Schoonmaker	20.00	8.50	2.75
☐ 335	Granny Hamner	20.00	8.50	2.75
☐ 336	Haywood Sullivan	22.00	9.50	3.15
☐ 337	Rene Valdes	20.00	8.50	2.75
☐ 338	Jim Bunning	140.00	63.00	21.00
☐ 339	Bob Speake	20.00	8.50	2.75
☐ 340	Bill Wight	20.00	8.50	2.75
☐ 341	Don Gross	20.00	8.50	2.75
☐ 342	Gene Mauch	22.00	9.50	3.15
☐ 343	Taylor Phillips	20.00	8.50	2.75
☐ 344	Paul LaPalme	20.00	8.50	2.75
☐ 345	Paul Smith	20.00	8.50	2.75
☐ 346	Dick Littlefield	20.00	8.50	2.75
☐ 347	Hal Naragon	20.00	8.50	2.75
☐ 348	Jim Hearn	20.00	8.50	2.75
☐ 349	Nellie King	20.00	8.50	2.75
☐ 350	Eddie Miksis	20.00	8.50	2.75
☐ 351	Dave Hillman	20.00	8.50	2.75
☐ 352	Ellis Kinder	20.00	8.50	2.75
☐ 353	Cal Neeman	6.00	2.50	.60
☐ 354	W. (Rip) Coleman	6.00	2.50	.60
☐ 355	Frank Malzone	8.00	3.50	.80
☐ 356	Faye Throneberry	6.00	2.50	.60
☐ 357	Earl Torgeson	6.00	2.50	.60
☐ 358	Jerry Lynch	6.00	2.50	.60
☐ 359	Tom Cheney	6.00	2.50	.60
☐ 360	Johnny Groth	6.00	2.50	.60
☐ 361	Curt Barclay	6.00	2.50	.60
☐ 362	Roman Mejias	7.00	3.00	.70
☐ 363	Eddie Kasko	6.00	2.50	.60
☐ 364	Cal McLish	6.00	2.50	.60
☐ 365	Ozzie Virgil	6.00	2.50	.60
☐ 366	Ken Lehman	6.00	2.50	.60
☐ 367	Ed Fitzgerald	6.00	2.50	.60
☐ 368	Bob Purkey	6.00	2.50	.60
☐ 369	Milt Graff	6.00	2.50	.60
☐ 370	Warren Hacker	6.00	2.50	.60
☐ 371	Bob Lennon	6.00	2.50	.60
☐ 372	Norm Zauchin	6.00	2.50	.60
☐ 373	Pete Whisenant	6.00	2.50	.60
☐ 374	Don Cardwell	6.00	2.50	.60
☐ 375	Jim Landis	6.00	2.50	.60
☐ 376	Don Elston	6.00	2.50	.60
☐ 377	Andre Rodgers	6.00	2.50	.60
☐ 378	Elmer Singleton	6.00	2.50	.60
☐ 379	Don Lee	6.00	2.50	.60
☐ 380	Walker Cooper	6.00	2.50	.60
☐ 381	Dean Stone	6.00	2.50	.60
☐ 382	Jim Brideweser	6.00	2.50	.60
☐ 383	Juan Pizarro	6.00	2.50	.60
☐ 384	Bobby G. Smith	6.00	2.50	.60
☐ 385	Art Houtteman	6.00	2.50	.60
☐ 386	Lyle Luttrell	6.00	2.50	.60
☐ 387	Jack Sanford	8.00	3.50	.80
☐ 388	Pete Daley	6.00	2.50	.60
☐ 389	Dave Jolly	6.00	2.50	.60
☐ 390	Reno Bertoia	6.00	2.50	.60
☐ 391	Ralph Terry	10.00	4.50	1.25
☐ 392	Chuck Tanner	8.00	3.50	.80
☐ 393	Raul Sanchez	6.00	2.50	.60
☐ 394	Luis Arroyo	7.00	3.00	.70
☐ 395	J.M.(Bubba) Phillips	6.00	2.50	.60
☐ 396	K. (Casey) Wise	6.00	2.50	.60
☐ 397	Roy Smalley	6.00	2.50	.60
☐ 398	Al Cicotte	7.00	3.00	.70
☐ 399	Billy Consolo	6.00	2.50	.60
☐ 400	Dodgers' Sluggers Carl Furillo Gil Hodges Roy Campanella Duke Snider	180.00	80.00	27.00
☐ 401	Earl Battey	8.00	3.50	.80
☐ 402	Jim Pisoni	6.00	2.50	.60
☐ 403	Dick Hyde	6.00	2.50	.60
☐ 404	Harry Anderson	6.00	2.50	.60
☐ 405	Duke Maas	6.00	2.50	.60
☐ 406	Bob Hale	6.00	2.50	.60
☐ 407	Yankee Power Hitters Mickey Mantle Yogi Berra	375.00	165.00	55.00
☐ xx	Checklist 1/2 (unnumbered)	225.00	35.00	7.00
☐ xx	Checklist 2/3 (unnumbered)	375.00	50.00	10.00
☐ xx	Checklist 3/4 (unnumbered)	675.00	75.00	15.00
☐ xx	Checklist 4/5 (unnumbered)	775.00	90.00	18.00

1958 Topps

The cards in this 494-card set measure 2 1/2" by 3 1/2". Although the last card is numbered 495, number 145 was not issued, bringing the set total to 494 cards. The 1958 Topps set contains the first Sport Magazine All-Star Selection series (475-495) and expanded use of combination cards. The team cards carried series checklists on back (Milwaukee, Detroit, Baltimore, and Cincinnati are also found with players listed alphabetically). Cards with the scarce yellow name (YL) or team (YT) lettering, as opposed to the common white lettering, are noted in the checklist. In the last series, cards of Stan Musial and Mickey Mantle were triple printed; the cards they replaced (443, 446, 450, and 462) on the printing sheet were hence printed in shorter supply than other cards in the last series and are marked with an SP in the list below. Technically the New York Giants team card (19) is an error as the Giants had already moved to San Francisco. The key rookies in this set are Orlando Cepeda, Curt Flood, Roger Maris, and Vada Pinson.

	NRMT	VG-E	GOOD
COMPLETE SET (494)	5250.00	2250.00	550.00
COMMON PLAYER (1-110)	7.25	3.25	1.00
COMMON PLAYER (111-198)	5.25	2.25	.50
COMMON PLAYER (199-352)	4.50	2.00	.45
COMMON PLAYER (353-440)	4.00	1.75	.40
COMMON PLAYER (441-474)	3.75	1.60	.37
COMMON PLAYER (475-495)	4.00	1.75	.40

		NRMT	VG-E	GOOD
☐ 1	Ted Williams	375.00	.00	.00
☐ 2A	Bob Lemon	20.00	8.50	2.75
☐ 2B	Bob Lemon YT	36.00	16.25	5.50
☐ 3	Alex Kellner	7.25	3.25	1.00
☐ 4	Hank Foiles	7.25	3.25	1.00
☐ 5	Willie Mays	185.00	80.00	24.00
☐ 6	George Zuverink	7.25	3.25	1.00
☐ 7	Dale Long	8.00	3.50	.80
☐ 8A	Eddie Kasko	7.25	3.25	1.00
☐ 8B	Eddie Kasko YL	25.00	11.00	3.50
☐ 9	Hank Bauer	12.00	5.25	1.50
☐ 10	Lou Burdette	10.00	4.50	1.25
☐ 11A	Jim Rivera	7.25	3.25	1.00
☐ 11B	Jim Rivera YT	21.00	9.00	3.00
☐ 12	George Crowe	7.25	3.25	1.00
☐ 13A	Billy Hoeft	7.25	3.25	1.00
☐ 13B	Billy Hoeft YL	25.00	11.00	3.50
☐ 14	Rip Repulski	7.25	3.25	1.00
☐ 15	Jim Lemon	8.00	3.50	.80
☐ 16	Charlie Neal	8.00	3.50	.80
☐ 17	Felix Mantilla	7.25	3.25	1.00
☐ 18	Frank Sullivan	7.25	3.25	1.00
☐ 19	New York Giants Team Card (checklist on back)	28.00	9.00	1.80
☐ 20A	Gil McDougald	12.00	5.25	1.50
☐ 20B	Gil McDougald YL	30.00	13.50	4.50
☐ 21	Curt Barclay	7.25	3.25	1.00
☐ 22	Hal Naragon	7.25	3.25	1.00
☐ 23A	Bill Tuttle	7.25	3.25	1.00
☐ 23B	Bill Tuttle YL	25.00	11.00	3.50
☐ 24A	Hobie Landrith	7.25	3.25	1.00
☐ 24B	Hobie Landrith YL	25.00	11.00	3.50
☐ 25	Don Drysdale	70.00	32.00	10.50
☐ 26	Ron Jackson	7.25	3.25	1.00
☐ 27	Bud Freeman	7.25	3.25	1.00
☐ 28	Jim Busby	7.25	3.25	1.00
☐ 29	Ted Lepcio	7.25	3.25	1.00
☐ 30A	Hank Aaron	195.00	85.00	24.00
☐ 30B	Hank Aaron YL	300.00	135.00	45.00
☐ 31	Tex Clevenger	7.25	3.25	1.00
☐ 32A	J.W. Porter	7.25	3.25	1.00
☐ 32B	J.W. Porter YL	25.00	11.00	3.50
☐ 33A	Cal Neeman	7.25	3.25	1.00
☐ 33B	Cal Neeman YT	21.00	9.00	3.00
☐ 34	Bob Thurman	7.25	3.25	1.00
☐ 35A	Don Mossi	8.00	3.50	.80
☐ 35B	Don Mossi YT	21.00	9.00	3.00
☐ 36	Ted Kazanski	7.25	3.25	1.00
☐ 37	Mike McCormick UER (photo actually Ray Monzant)	10.00	4.50	1.25
☐ 38	Dick Gernert	7.25	3.25	1.00
☐ 39	Bob Martyn	7.25	3.25	1.00
☐ 40	George Kell	15.00	6.50	2.15
☐ 41	Dave Hillman	7.25	3.25	1.00
☐ 42	John Roseboro	12.00	5.25	1.50
☐ 43	Sal Maglie	9.00	4.00	.90
☐ 44	Washington Senators Team Card (checklist on back)	16.50	6.00	1.25
☐ 45	Dick Groat	9.00	4.00	.90
☐ 46A	Lou Sleater	7.25	3.25	1.00
☐ 46B	Lou Sleater YL	25.00	11.00	3.50
☐ 47	Roger Maris	350.00	160.00	52.50
☐ 48	Chuck Harmon	7.25	3.25	1.00
☐ 49	Smoky Burgess	9.00	4.00	.90
☐ 50A	Billy Pierce	9.00	4.00	.90
☐ 50B	Billy Pierce YT	25.00	11.00	3.50
☐ 51	Del Rice	7.25	3.25	1.00
☐ 52A	Bob Clemente	165.00	75.00	22.50
☐ 52B	Bob Clemente YT	275.00	120.00	40.00
☐ 53A	Morrie Martin	7.25	3.25	1.00
☐ 53B	Morrie Martin YL	25.00	11.00	3.50
☐ 54	Norm Siebern	7.25	3.25	1.00
☐ 55	Chico Carrasquel	7.25	3.25	1.00
☐ 56	Bill Fischer	7.25	3.25	1.00
☐ 57A	Tim Thompson	7.25	3.25	1.00
☐ 57B	Tim Thompson YL	25.00	11.00	3.50
☐ 58A	Art Schult	7.25	3.25	1.00
☐ 58B	Art Schult YT	21.00	9.00	3.00
☐ 59	Dave Sisler	7.25	3.25	1.00
☐ 60A	Del Ennis	8.00	3.50	.80
☐ 60B	Del Ennis YL	25.00	11.00	3.50
☐ 61A	Darrell Johnson	8.00	3.50	.80
☐ 61B	Darrell Johnson YL	25.00	11.00	3.50
☐ 62	Joe DeMaestri	7.25	3.25	1.00
☐ 63	Joe Nuxhall	8.00	3.50	.80
☐ 64	Joe Lonnett	7.25	3.25	1.00
☐ 65A	Von McDaniel	7.25	3.25	1.00
☐ 65B	Von McDaniel YL	25.00	11.00	3.50
☐ 66	Lee Walls	7.25	3.25	1.00
☐ 67	Joe Ginsberg	7.25	3.25	1.00
☐ 68	Daryl Spencer	7.25	3.25	1.00
☐ 69	Wally Burnette	7.25	3.25	1.00
☐ 70A	Al Kaline	85.00	38.00	12.75
☐ 70B	Al Kaline YL	135.00	60.00	20.00
☐ 71	Dodgers Team (checklist on back)	38.00	12.50	2.50
☐ 72	Bud Byerly	7.25	3.25	1.00
☐ 73	Pete Daley	7.25	3.25	1.00
☐ 74	Roy Face	9.00	4.00	.90
☐ 75	Gus Bell	8.00	3.50	.80
☐ 76A	Dick Farrell	8.00	3.50	.80
☐ 76B	Dick Farrell YT	21.00	9.00	3.00
☐ 77A	Don Zimmer	12.00	5.25	1.50
☐ 77B	Don Zimmer YT	25.00	11.00	3.50
☐ 78A	Ernie Johnson	8.00	3.50	.80
☐ 78B	Ernie Johnson YL	25.00	11.00	3.50
☐ 79A	Dick Williams	8.00	3.50	.80
☐ 79B	Dick Williams YT	22.00	9.50	3.15
☐ 80	Dick Drott	7.25	3.25	1.00
☐ 81A	Steve Boros	8.00	3.50	.80
☐ 81B	Steve Boros YT	22.00	9.50	3.15
☐ 82	Ron Kline	7.25	3.25	1.00
☐ 83	Bob Hazle	8.00	3.50	.80
☐ 84	Billy O'Dell	7.25	3.25	1.00
☐ 85A	Luis Aparicio	24.00	10.50	3.50
☐ 85B	Luis Aparicio YT	42.00	18.00	5.50
☐ 86	Valmy Thomas	7.25	3.25	1.00
☐ 87	Johnny Kucks	8.00	3.50	.80
☐ 88	Duke Snider	75.00	34.00	11.25
☐ 89	Billy Klaus	7.25	3.25	1.00
☐ 90	Robin Roberts	20.00	8.50	2.75
☐ 91	Chuck Tanner	8.00	3.50	.80
☐ 92A	Clint Courtney	7.25	3.25	1.00
☐ 92B	Clint Courtney YL	25.00	11.00	3.50
☐ 93	Sandy Amoros	9.00	4.00	.90
☐ 94	Bob Skinner	8.00	3.50	.80

☐ 95	Frank Bolling	7.25	3.25	1.00
☐ 96	Joe Durham	7.25	3.25	1.00
☐ 97A	Larry Jackson	7.25	3.25	1.00
☐ 97B	Larry Jackson YL	25.00	11.00	3.50
☐ 98A	Billy Hunter	7.25	3.25	1.00
☐ 98B	Billy Hunter YL	25.00	11.00	3.50
☐ 99	Bobby Adams	7.25	3.25	1.00
☐ 100A	Early Wynn	20.00	8.50	2.75
☐ 100B	Early Wynn YT	36.00	16.25	5.50
☐ 101A	Bobby Richardson	20.00	8.50	2.75
☐ 101B	Bobby Richardson YL	36.00	16.25	5.50
☐ 102	George Strickland	7.25	3.25	1.00
☐ 103	Jerry Lynch	7.25	3.25	1.00
☐ 104	Jim Pendleton	7.25	3.25	1.00
☐ 105	Billy Gardner	7.25	3.25	1.00
☐ 106	Dick Schofield	7.25	3.25	1.00
☐ 107	Ossie Virgil	7.25	3.25	1.00
☐ 108A	Jim Landis	7.25	3.25	1.00
☐ 108B	Jim Landis YT	21.00	9.00	3.00
☐ 109	Herb Plews	7.25	3.25	1.00
☐ 110	Johnny Logan	8.00	3.50	.80
☐ 111	Stu Miller	6.00	2.50	.60
☐ 112	Gus Zernial	6.00	2.50	.60
☐ 113	Jerry Walker	5.25	2.25	.50
☐ 114	Irv Noren	6.00	2.50	.60
☐ 115	Jim Bunning	20.00	8.50	2.75
☐ 116	Dave Philley	5.25	2.25	.50
☐ 117	Frank Torre	6.00	2.50	.60
☐ 118	Harvey Haddix	6.00	2.50	.60
☐ 119	Harry Chiti	5.25	2.25	.50
☐ 120	Johnny Podres	9.00	4.00	.90
☐ 121	Eddie Miksis	5.25	2.25	.50
☐ 122	Walt Moryn	5.25	2.25	.50
☐ 123	Dick Tomanek	5.25	2.25	.50
☐ 124	Bobby Usher	5.25	2.25	.50
☐ 125	Alvin Dark	7.00	3.00	.70
☐ 126	Stan Palys	5.25	2.25	.50
☐ 127	Tom Sturdivant	6.00	2.50	.60
☐ 128	Willie Kirkland	6.00	2.50	.60
☐ 129	Jim Derrington	5.25	2.25	.50
☐ 130	Jackie Jensen	10.00	4.50	1.25
☐ 131	Bob Henrich	5.25	2.25	.50
☐ 132	Vern Law	6.00	2.50	.60
☐ 133	Russ Nixon	7.00	3.00	.70
☐ 134	Philadelphia Phillies Team Card (checklist on back)	12.00	4.00	.80
☐ 135	Mike(Moe) Drabowsky	6.00	2.50	.60
☐ 136	Jim Finigan	5.25	2.25	.50
☐ 137	Russ Kemmerer	5.25	2.25	.50
☐ 138	Earl Torgeson	5.25	2.25	.50
☐ 139	George Brunet	5.25	2.25	.50
☐ 140	Wes Covington	6.00	2.50	.60
☐ 141	Ken Lehman	5.25	2.25	.50
☐ 142	Enos Slaughter	21.00	9.00	3.00
☐ 143	Billy Muffett	5.25	2.25	.50
☐ 144	Bobby Morgan	5.25	2.25	.50
☐ 145	Never issued	0.00	.00	.00
☐ 146	Dick Gray	5.25	2.25	.50
☐ 147	Don McMahon	7.00	3.00	.70
☐ 148	Billy Consolo	5.25	2.25	.50
☐ 149	Tom Acker	5.25	2.25	.50
☐ 150	Mickey Mantle	525.00	225.00	75.00
☐ 151	Buddy Pritchard	5.25	2.25	.50
☐ 152	Johnny Antonelli	6.00	2.50	.60
☐ 153	Les Moss	5.25	2.25	.50
☐ 154	Harry Byrd	5.25	2.25	.50
☐ 155	Hector Lopez	5.25	2.25	.50
☐ 156	Dick Hyde	5.25	2.25	.50
☐ 157	Dee Fondy	5.25	2.25	.50
☐ 158	Cleveland Indians Team Card (checklist on back)	12.00	5.25	1.50
☐ 159	Taylor Phillips	5.25	2.25	.50
☐ 160	Don Hoak	6.00	2.50	.60
☐ 161	Don Larsen	10.00	4.50	1.25
☐ 162	Gil Hodges	25.00	11.00	3.50
☐ 163	Jim Wilson	5.25	2.25	.50
☐ 164	Bob Taylor	5.25	2.25	.50
☐ 165	Bob Nieman	5.25	2.25	.50
☐ 166	Danny O'Connell	5.25	2.25	.50
☐ 167	Frank Baumann	5.25	2.25	.50
☐ 168	Joe Cunningham	6.00	2.50	.60
☐ 169	Ralph Terry	7.00	3.00	.70
☐ 170	Vic Wertz	6.00	2.50	.60
☐ 171	Harry Anderson	5.25	2.25	.50
☐ 172	Don Gross	5.25	2.25	.50
☐ 173	Eddie Yost	5.25	2.25	.50
☐ 174	Athletics Team (checklist on back)	11.00	4.00	.80
☐ 175	Marv Throneberry	10.00	4.50	1.25
☐ 176	Bob Buhl	6.00	2.50	.60
☐ 177	Al Smith	5.25	2.25	.50
☐ 178	Ted Kluszewski	11.00	5.00	1.35
☐ 179	Willie Miranda	5.25	2.25	.50
☐ 180	Lindy McDaniel	6.00	2.50	.60
☐ 181	Willie Jones	5.25	2.25	.50
☐ 182	Joe Caffie	5.25	2.25	.50
☐ 183	Dave Jolly	5.25	2.25	.50
☐ 184	Elvin Tappe	5.25	2.25	.50
☐ 185	Ray Boone	6.00	2.50	.60
☐ 186	Jack Meyer	5.25	2.25	.50
☐ 187	Sandy Koufax	180.00	80.00	27.00
☐ 188	Milt Bolling UER (photo actually Lou Berberet)	5.25	2.25	.50
☐ 189	George Susce	5.25	2.25	.50
☐ 190	Red Schoendienst	20.00	8.50	2.75
☐ 191	Art Ceccarelli	5.25	2.25	.50
☐ 192	Milt Graff	5.25	2.25	.50
☐ 193	Jerry Lumpe	7.00	3.00	.70
☐ 194	Roger Craig	9.00	4.00	.90
☐ 195	Whitey Lockman	6.00	2.50	.60
☐ 196	Mike Garcia	6.00	2.50	.60
☐ 197	Haywood Sullivan	6.00	2.50	.60
☐ 198	Bill Virdon	7.00	3.00	.70
☐ 199	Don Blasingame	4.50	2.00	.45
☐ 200	Bob Keegan	4.50	2.00	.45
☐ 201	Jim Bolger	4.50	2.00	.45
☐ 202	Woody Held	6.50	2.75	.65
☐ 203	Al Walker	4.50	2.00	.45
☐ 204	Leo Kiely	4.50	2.00	.45
☐ 205	Johnny Temple	5.50	2.50	.55
☐ 206	Bob Shaw	6.50	2.75	.65
☐ 207	Solly Hemus	4.50	2.00	.45
☐ 208	Cal McLish	4.50	2.00	.45
☐ 209	Bob Anderson	4.50	2.00	.45
☐ 210	Wally Moon	5.50	2.50	.55
☐ 211	Pete Burnside	4.50	2.00	.45
☐ 212	Bubba Phillips	4.50	2.00	.45
☐ 213	Red Wilson	4.50	2.00	.45
☐ 214	Willard Schmidt	4.50	2.00	.45
☐ 215	Jim Gilliam	9.00	4.00	.90
☐ 216	St. Louis Cardinals Team Card (checklist on back)	12.00	4.00	.80
☐ 217	Jack Harshman	4.50	2.00	.45
☐ 218	Dick Rand	4.50	2.00	.45
☐ 219	Camilo Pascual	5.50	2.50	.55
☐ 220	Tom Brewer	4.50	2.00	.45
☐ 221	Jerry Kindall	5.50	2.50	.55
☐ 222	Bud Daley	4.50	2.00	.45
☐ 223	Andy Pafko	5.50	2.50	.55
☐ 224	Bob Grim	5.50	2.50	.55
☐ 225	Billy Goodman	5.50	2.50	.55
☐ 226	Bob Smith	4.50	2.00	.45
☐ 227	Gene Stephens	4.50	2.00	.45
☐ 228	Duke Maas	4.50	2.00	.45
☐ 229	Frank Zupo	4.50	2.00	.45
☐ 230	Richie Ashburn	16.00	6.75	2.25
☐ 231	Lloyd Merritt	4.50	2.00	.45
☐ 232	Reno Bertoia	4.50	2.00	.45
☐ 233	Mickey Vernon	5.50	2.50	.55
☐ 234	Carl Sawatski	4.50	2.00	.45
☐ 235	Tom Gorman	4.50	2.00	.45
☐ 236	Ed Fitzgerald	4.50	2.00	.45
☐ 237	Bill Wight	4.50	2.00	.45
☐ 238	Bill Mazeroski	13.00	5.75	1.75
☐ 239	Chuck Stobbs	4.50	2.00	.45
☐ 240	Bill Skowron	12.00	5.25	1.50
☐ 241	Dick Littlefield	4.50	2.00	.45
☐ 242	Johnny Klippstein	4.50	2.00	.45
☐ 243	Larry Raines	4.50	2.00	.45
☐ 244	Don Demeter	4.50	2.00	.45
☐ 245	Frank Lary	5.50	2.50	.55
☐ 246	New York Yankees Team Card (checklist on back)	40.00	12.50	2.50
☐ 247	Casey Wise	4.50	2.00	.45
☐ 248	Herman Wehmeier	4.50	2.00	.45
☐ 249	Ray Moore	4.50	2.00	.45
☐ 250	Roy Sievers	5.50	2.50	.55
☐ 251	Warren Hacker	4.50	2.00	.45
☐ 252	Bob Trowbridge	4.50	2.00	.45
☐ 253	Don Mueller	5.50	2.50	.55
☐ 254	Alex Grammas	4.50	2.00	.45
☐ 255	Bob Turley	9.00	4.00	.90
☐ 256	Chicago White Sox Team Card (checklist on back)	11.00	3.50	.75
☐ 257	Hal Smith	4.50	2.00	.45
☐ 258	Carl Erskine	9.00	4.00	.90
☐ 259	Al Pilarcik	4.50	2.00	.45
☐ 260	Frank Malzone	5.50	2.50	.55
☐ 261	Turk Lown	4.50	2.00	.45
☐ 262	Johnny Groth	4.50	2.00	.45
☐ 263	Eddie Bressoud	4.50	2.00	.45
☐ 264	Jack Sanford	5.50	2.50	.55

	#	Player			
☐	265	Pete Runnels	5.50	2.50	.55
☐	266	Connie Johnson	4.50	2.00	.45
☐	267	Sherm Lollar	5.50	2.50	.55
☐	268	Granny Hamner	4.50	2.00	.45
☐	269	Paul Smith	4.50	2.00	.45
☐	270	Warren Spahn	50.00	22.50	7.50
☐	271	Billy Martin	20.00	8.50	2.75
☐	272	Ray Crone	4.50	2.00	.45
☐	273	Hal Smith	4.50	2.00	.45
☐	274	Rocky Bridges	4.50	2.00	.45
☐	275	Elston Howard	11.00	5.00	1.35
☐	276	Bobby Avila	4.50	2.00	.45
☐	277	Virgil Trucks	4.50	2.00	.45
☐	278	Mack Burk	4.50	2.00	.45
☐	279	Bob Boyd	4.50	2.00	.45
☐	280	Jim Piersall	7.00	3.00	.70
☐	281	Sammy Taylor	4.50	2.00	.45
☐	282	Paul Foytack	4.50	2.00	.45
☐	283	Ray Shearer	4.50	2.00	.45
☐	284	Ray Katt	4.50	2.00	.45
☐	285	Frank Robinson	85.00	38.00	12.75
☐	286	Gino Cimoli	4.50	2.00	.45
☐	287	Sam Jones	4.50	2.00	.45
☐	288	Harmon Killebrew	80.00	36.00	12.00
☐	289	Series Hurling Rivals	6.50	2.75	.65
		Lou Burdette			
		Bobby Shantz			
☐	290	Dick Donovan	4.50	2.00	.45
☐	291	Don Landrum	4.50	2.00	.45
☐	292	Ned Garver	4.50	2.00	.45
☐	293	Gene Freese	4.50	2.00	.45
☐	294	Hal Jeffcoat	4.50	2.00	.45
☐	295	Minnie Minoso	9.00	4.00	.90
☐	296	Ryne Duren	9.00	4.00	.90
☐	297	Don Buddin	4.50	2.00	.45
☐	298	Jim Hearn	4.50	2.00	.45
☐	299	Harry Simpson	4.50	2.00	.45
☐	300	Harridge and Giles	8.00	3.50	.80
		League Presidents			
☐	301	Randy Jackson	4.50	2.00	.45
☐	302	Mike Baxes	4.50	2.00	.45
☐	303	Neil Chrisley	4.50	2.00	.45
☐	304	Tigers' Big Bats	13.50	6.00	1.85
		Harvey Kuenn			
		Al Kaline			
☐	305	Clem Labine	5.50	2.50	.55
☐	306	Whammy Douglas	4.50	2.00	.45
☐	307	Brooks Robinson	100.00	45.00	15.00
☐	308	Paul Giel	5.50	2.50	.55
☐	309	Gail Harris	4.50	2.00	.45
☐	310	Ernie Banks	85.00	38.00	12.75
☐	311	Bob Purkey	4.50	2.00	.45
☐	312	Boston Red Sox	12.00	4.00	.80
		Team Card			
		(checklist on back)			
☐	313	Bob Rush	4.50	2.00	.45
☐	314	Dodgers' Boss and	21.00	9.00	3.00
		Power: Duke Snider			
		Walt Alston			
☐	315	Bob Friend	5.50	2.50	.55
☐	316	Tito Francona	4.50	2.00	.45
☐	317	Albie Pearson	5.50	2.50	.55
☐	318	Frank House	4.50	2.00	.45
☐	319	Lou Skizas	4.50	2.00	.45
☐	320	Whitey Ford	48.00	22.00	6.00
☐	321	Sluggers Supreme	38.00	17.00	5.25
		Ted Kluszewski			
		Ted Williams			
☐	322	Harding Peterson	4.50	2.00	.45
☐	323	Elmer Valo	4.50	2.00	.45
☐	324	Hoyt Wilhelm	18.00	7.50	2.50
☐	325	Joe Adcock	5.50	2.50	.55
☐	326	Bob Miller	4.50	2.00	.45
☐	327	Chicago Cubs	12.00	4.00	.80
		Team Card			
		(checklist on back)			
☐	328	Ike Delock	4.50	2.00	.45
☐	329	Bob Cerv	5.50	2.50	.55
☐	330	Ed Bailey	5.50	2.50	.55
☐	331	Pedro Ramos	4.50	2.00	.45
☐	332	Jim King	4.50	2.00	.45
☐	333	Andy Carey	5.50	2.50	.55
☐	334	Mound Aces	5.50	2.50	.55
		Bob Friend			
		Billy Pierce			
☐	335	Ruben Gomez	4.50	2.00	.45
☐	336	Bert Hamric	4.50	2.00	.45
☐	337	Hank Aguirre	4.50	2.00	.45
☐	338	Walt Dropo	4.50	2.00	.45
☐	339	Fred Hatfield	4.50	2.00	.45
☐	340	Don Newcombe	9.00	4.00	.90
☐	341	Pittsburgh Pirates	12.00	4.00	.80
		Team Card			
		(checklist on back)			

	#	Player			
☐	342	Jim Brosnan	5.50	2.50	.55
☐	343	Orlando Cepeda	70.00	32.00	10.50
☐	344	Bob Porterfield	4.50	2.00	.45
☐	345	Jim Hegan	4.50	2.00	.45
☐	346	Steve Bilko	4.50	2.00	.45
☐	347	Don Rudolph	4.50	2.00	.45
☐	348	Chico Fernandez	4.50	2.00	.45
☐	349	Murry Dickson	4.50	2.00	.45
☐	350	Ken Boyer	11.00	5.00	1.35
☐	351	Braves Fence Busters	25.00	11.00	3.50
		Del Crandall			
		Eddie Mathews			
		Hank Aaron			
		Joe Adcock			
☐	352	Herb Score	7.50	3.25	.75
☐	353	Stan Lopata	4.00	1.75	.40
☐	354	Art Ditmar	4.00	1.75	.40
☐	355	Bill Bruton	5.00	2.25	.50
☐	356	Bob Malkmus	4.00	1.75	.40
☐	357	Danny McDevitt	4.00	1.75	.40
☐	358	Gene Baker	4.00	1.75	.40
☐	359	Billy Loes	4.00	1.75	.40
☐	360	Roy McMillan	4.00	1.75	.40
☐	361	Mike Fornieles	4.00	1.75	.40
☐	362	Ray Jablonski	4.00	1.75	.40
☐	363	Don Elston	4.00	1.75	.40
☐	364	Earl Battey	4.00	1.75	.40
☐	365	Tom Morgan	4.00	1.75	.40
☐	366	Gene Green	4.00	1.75	.40
☐	367	Jack Urban	4.00	1.75	.40
☐	368	Rocky Colavito	30.00	13.50	4.50
☐	369	Ralph Lumenti	4.00	1.75	.40
☐	370	Yogi Berra	95.00	42.00	11.00
☐	371	Marty Keough	4.00	1.75	.40
☐	372	Don Cardwell	4.00	1.75	.40
☐	373	Joe Pignatano	4.00	1.75	.40
☐	374	Brooks Lawrence	4.00	1.75	.40
☐	375	Pee Wee Reese	55.00	25.00	8.25
☐	376	Charley Rabe	4.00	1.75	.40
☐	377A	Milwaukee Braves	12.00	5.00	1.00
		Team Card			
		(alphabetical)			
☐	377B	Milwaukee Team	70.00	20.00	4.00
		numerical checklist			
☐	378	Hank Sauer	5.00	2.25	.50
☐	379	Ray Herbert	4.00	1.75	.40
☐	380	Charley Maxwell	5.00	2.25	.50
☐	381	Hal Brown	4.00	1.75	.40
☐	382	Al Cicotte	4.00	1.75	.40
☐	383	Lou Berberet	4.00	1.75	.40
☐	384	John Goryl	4.00	1.75	.40
☐	385	Wilmer Mizell	4.00	1.75	.40
☐	386	Birdie's Sluggers	9.00	4.00	.90
		Ed Bailey			
		Birdie Tebbetts			
		Frank Robinson			
☐	387	Wally Post	5.00	2.25	.50
☐	388	Billy Moran	4.00	1.75	.40
☐	389	Bill Taylor	4.00	1.75	.40
☐	390	Del Crandall	5.00	2.25	.50
☐	391	Dave Melton	4.00	1.75	.40
☐	392	Bennie Daniels	4.00	1.75	.40
☐	393	Tony Kubek	18.00	7.50	2.50
☐	394	Jim Grant	6.00	2.50	.60
☐	395	Willard Nixon	4.00	1.75	.40
☐	396	Dutch Dotterer	4.00	1.75	.40
☐	397A	Detroit Tigers	12.00	5.00	1.00
		Team Card			
		(alphabetical)			
☐	397B	Detroit Team	70.00	20.00	4.00
		numerical checklist			
☐	398	Gene Woodling	5.00	2.25	.50
☐	399	Marv Grissom	4.00	1.75	.40
☐	400	Nellie Fox	13.00	5.75	1.75
☐	401	Don Bessent	4.00	1.75	.40
☐	402	Bobby Gene Smith	4.00	1.75	.40
☐	403	Steve Korcheck	4.00	1.75	.40
☐	404	Curt Simmons	5.00	2.25	.50
☐	405	Ken Aspromonte	4.00	1.75	.40
☐	406	Vic Power	4.00	1.75	.40
☐	407	Carlton Willey	4.00	1.75	.40
☐	408A	Baltimore Orioles	12.00	4.00	.80
		Team Card			
		(alphabetical)			
☐	408B	Baltimore Team	70.00	20.00	4.00
		numerical checklist			
☐	409	Frank Thomas	5.00	2.25	.50
☐	410	Murray Wall	4.00	1.75	.40
☐	411	Tony Taylor	7.00	3.00	.70
☐	412	Jerry Staley	4.00	1.75	.40
☐	413	Jim Davenport	6.00	2.50	.60
☐	414	Sammy White	4.00	1.75	.40
☐	415	Bob Bowman	4.00	1.75	.40
☐	416	Foster Castleman	4.00	1.75	.40

☐ 417	Carl Furillo	9.00	4.00	.90
☐ 418	World Series Batting	140.00	63.00	21.00
	Foes: Mickey Mantle			
	Hank Aaron			
☐ 419	Bobby Shantz	6.00	2.50	.60
☐ 420	Vada Pinson	25.00	11.00	3.50
☐ 421	Dixie Howell	4.00	1.75	.40
☐ 422	Norm Zauchin	4.00	1.75	.40
☐ 423	Phil Clark	4.00	1.75	.40
☐ 424	Larry Doby	6.00	2.50	.60
☐ 425	Sammy Esposito	4.00	1.75	.40
☐ 426	Johnny O'Brien	4.00	1.75	.40
☐ 427	Al Worthington	4.00	1.75	.40
☐ 428A	Cincinnati Reds	12.00	4.00	.80
	Team Card			
	(alphabetical)			
☐ 428B	Cincinnati Team	70.00	20.00	4.00
	numerical checklist			
☐ 429	Gus Triandos	5.00	2.25	.50
☐ 430	Bobby Thomson	6.00	2.50	.60
☐ 431	Gene Conley	4.00	1.75	.40
☐ 432	John Powers	4.00	1.75	.40
☐ 433A	Pancho Herrer ERR	500.00	225.00	75.00
☐ 433B	Pancho Herrera COR	5.00	2.25	.50
☐ 434	Harvey Kuenn	6.00	2.50	.60
☐ 435	Ed Roebuck	5.00	2.25	.50
☐ 436	Rival Fence Busters	55.00	25.00	8.25
	Willie Mays			
	Duke Snider			
☐ 437	Bob Speake	4.00	1.75	.40
☐ 438	Whitey Herzog	7.00	3.00	.70
☐ 439	Ray Narleski	4.00	1.75	.40
☐ 440	Eddie Mathews	33.00	15.00	5.00
☐ 441	Jim Marshall	3.75	1.60	.37
☐ 442	Phil Paine	3.75	1.60	.37
☐ 443	Billy Harrell SP	12.00	5.25	1.50
☐ 444	Danny Kravitz	3.75	1.60	.37
☐ 445	Bob Smith	3.75	1.60	.37
☐ 446	Carroll Hardy SP	12.00	5.25	1.50
☐ 447	Ray Monzant	3.75	1.60	.37
☐ 448	Charlie Lau	7.00	3.00	.70
☐ 449	Gene Fodge	3.75	1.60	.37
☐ 450	Preston Ward SP	12.00	5.25	1.50
☐ 451	Joe Taylor	3.75	1.60	.37
☐ 452	Roman Mejias	3.75	1.60	.37
☐ 453	Tom Qualters	3.75	1.60	.37
☐ 454	Harry Hanebrink	3.75	1.60	.37
☐ 455	Hal Griggs	3.75	1.60	.37
☐ 456	Dick Brown	3.75	1.60	.37
☐ 457	Milt Pappas	7.00	3.00	.70
☐ 458	Julio Becquer	3.75	1.60	.37
☐ 459	Ron Blackburn	3.75	1.60	.37
☐ 460	Chuck Essegian	3.75	1.60	.37
☐ 461	Ed Mayer	3.75	1.60	.37
☐ 462	Gary Geiger SP	12.00	5.25	1.50
☐ 463	Vito Valentinetti	3.75	1.60	.37
☐ 464	Curt Flood	25.00	11.00	3.50
☐ 465	Arnie Portocarrero	3.75	1.60	.37
☐ 466	Pete Whisenant	3.75	1.60	.37
☐ 467	Glen Hobbie	3.75	1.60	.37
☐ 468	Bob Schmidt	3.75	1.60	.37
☐ 469	Don Ferrarese	3.75	1.60	.37
☐ 470	R.C. Stevens	3.75	1.60	.37
☐ 471	Lenny Green	3.75	1.60	.37
☐ 472	Joey Jay	4.50	2.00	.45
☐ 473	Bill Renna	3.75	1.60	.37
☐ 474	Roman Semproch	3.75	1.60	.37
☐ 475	Haney/Stengel AS	18.00	7.50	1.50
	(checklist back)			
☐ 476	Stan Musial AS TP	36.00	16.25	5.50
☐ 477	Bill Skowron AS	6.00	2.50	.60
☐ 478	Johnny Temple AS	4.00	1.75	.40
☐ 479	Nellie Fox AS	8.50	3.75	.85
☐ 480	Eddie Mathews AS	14.00	6.25	2.00
☐ 481	Frank Malzone AS	4.00	1.75	.40
☐ 482	Ernie Banks AS	21.00	9.00	3.00
☐ 483	Luis Aparicio AS	12.50	5.50	1.65
☐ 484	Frank Robinson AS	21.00	9.00	3.00
☐ 485	Ted Williams AS	65.00	29.00	9.75
☐ 486	Willie Mays AS	45.00	20.00	6.75
☐ 487	Mickey Mantle AS TP	100.00	45.00	15.00
☐ 488	Hank Aaron AS	45.00	20.00	6.75
☐ 489	Jackie Jensen AS	4.50	2.00	.45
☐ 490	Ed Bailey AS	4.00	1.75	.40
☐ 491	Sherm Lollar AS	4.00	1.75	.40
☐ 492	Bob Friend AS	4.00	1.75	.40
☐ 493	Bob Turley AS	4.50	2.00	.45
☐ 494	Warren Spahn AS	16.00	6.75	2.25
☐ 495	Herb Score AS	14.00	3.00	.60

1959 Topps

The cards in this 572-card set measure 2 1/2" by 3 1/2". The 1959 Topps set contains bust pictures of the players in a colored circle. Card numbers 551 to 572 are Sporting News All-Star Selections. High numbers 507 to 572 have the card number in a black background on the reverse rather than a green background as in the lower numbers. The high numbers are more difficult to obtain. Several cards in the 300s exist with or without an extra traded or option line on the back of the card. Cards 199 to 286 exist with either white or gray backs. Cards 461 to 470 contain "Highlights" while cards 116 to 146 give an alphabetically ordered listing of "Rookie Prospects." These Rookie Prospects (RP) were Topps' first organized inclusion of untested "Rookie" cards. Card 440 features Lew Burdette erroneously posing as a left-handed pitcher. There were some three-card advertising panels produced by Topps; the players included are from the first series; one panel shows Don McMahon, Red Wilson, and Bob Boyd on the front with Ted Kluszewski's reverse on one of the backs. Another panel shows Billy Hunter, Chuck Stobbs, and Carl Sawatski on the front with Nellie Fox's reverse on one of the backs. When cut apart, these advertising cards are distinguished by the non-standard card back, i.e., part of an advertisement for the 1959 Topps set instead of the typical statistics and biographical information about the player pictured. The key rookies in this set are Sparky Anderson, Bob Gibson, and Bill White.

		NRMT	VG-E	GOOD
COMPLETE SET (572)		5250.00	2250.00	550.00
COMMON PLAYER (1-110)		6.00	2.50	.60
COMMON PLAYER (111-198)		3.75	1.60	.37
COMMON PLAYER (199-506)		3.25	1.35	.32
COMMON PLAYER (507-550)		16.00	6.75	2.25
COMMON PLAYER (551-572)		18.00	7.50	2.50
☐ 1	Ford Frick	75.00	15.00	3.00
	(Commissioner)			
☐ 2	Eddie Yost	6.00	2.50	.60
☐ 3	Don McMahon	6.00	2.50	.60
☐ 4	Albie Pearson	6.00	2.50	.60
☐ 5	Dick Donovan	6.00	2.50	.60
☐ 6	Alex Grammas	6.00	2.50	.60
☐ 7	Al Pilarcik	6.00	2.50	.60
☐ 8	Phillies Team	30.00	10.00	2.00
	(checklist on back)			
☐ 9	Paul Giel	6.00	2.50	.60
☐ 10	Mickey Mantle	400.00	180.00	60.00
☐ 11	Billy Hunter	6.00	2.50	.60
☐ 12	Vern Law	7.00	3.00	.70
☐ 13	Dick Gernert	6.00	2.50	.60
☐ 14	Pete Whisenant	6.00	2.50	.60
☐ 15	Dick Drott	6.00	2.50	.60
☐ 16	Joe Pignatano	6.00	2.50	.60
☐ 17	Danny's Stars	8.00	3.50	.80
	Frank Thomas			
	Danny Murtaugh			
	Ted Kluszewski			
☐ 18	Jack Urban	6.00	2.50	.60
☐ 19	Eddie Bressoud	6.00	2.50	.60
☐ 20	Duke Snider	65.00	29.00	9.75
☐ 21	Connie Johnson	6.00	2.50	.60

☐ 22	Al Smith	6.00	2.50	.60
☐ 23	Murry Dickson	6.00	2.50	.60
☐ 24	Red Wilson	6.00	2.50	.60
☐ 25	Don Hoak	7.00	3.00	.70
☐ 26	Chuck Stobbs	6.00	2.50	.60
☐ 27	Andy Pafko	7.00	3.00	.70
☐ 28	Al Worthington	6.00	2.50	.60
☐ 29	Jim Bolger	6.00	2.50	.60
☐ 30	Nellie Fox	14.00	6.25	2.00
☐ 31	Ken Lehman	6.00	2.50	.60
☐ 32	Don Buddin	6.00	2.50	.60
☐ 33	Ed Fitzgerald	6.00	2.50	.60
☐ 34	Pitchers Beware	11.00	5.00	1.35
	Al Kaline			
	Charley Maxwell			
☐ 35	Ted Kluszewski	10.00	4.50	1.25
☐ 36	Hank Aguirre	6.00	2.50	.60
☐ 37	Gene Green	6.00	2.50	.60
☐ 38	Morrie Martin	6.00	2.50	.60
☐ 39	Ed Bouchee	6.00	2.50	.60
☐ 40	Warren Spahn	50.00	22.50	7.50
☐ 41	Bob Martyn	6.00	2.50	.60
☐ 42	Murray Wall	6.00	2.50	.60
☐ 43	Steve Bilko	6.00	2.50	.60
☐ 44	Vito Valentinetti	6.00	2.50	.60
☐ 45	Andy Carey	7.00	3.00	.70
☐ 46	Bill R. Henry	6.00	2.50	.60
☐ 47	Jim Finigan	6.00	2.50	.60
☐ 48	Orioles Team	18.00		1.20
	(checklist on back)			
☐ 49	Bill Hall	6.00	2.50	.60
☐ 50	Willie Mays	150.00	67.50	22.50
☐ 51	Rip Coleman	6.00	2.50	.60
☐ 52	Coot Veal	6.00	2.50	.60
☐ 53	Stan Williams	8.00	3.50	.80
☐ 54	Mel Roach	6.00	2.50	.60
☐ 55	Tom Brewer	6.00	2.50	.60
☐ 56	Carl Sawatski	6.00	2.50	.60
☐ 57	Al Cicotte	6.00	2.50	.60
☐ 58	Eddie Miksis	6.00	2.50	.60
☐ 59	Irv Noren	6.00	2.50	.60
☐ 60	Bob Turley	9.00	4.00	.90
☐ 61	Dick Brown	6.00	2.50	.60
☐ 62	Tony Taylor	6.00	2.50	.60
☐ 63	Jim Hearn	6.00	2.50	.60
☐ 64	Joe DeMaestri	6.00	2.50	.60
☐ 65	Frank Torre	6.00	2.50	.60
☐ 66	Joe Ginsberg	6.00	2.50	.60
☐ 67	Brooks Lawrence	6.00	2.50	.60
☐ 68	Dick Schofield	6.00	2.50	.60
☐ 69	Giants Team	15.00	5.00	1.00
	(checklist on back)			
☐ 70	Harvey Kuenn	9.00	4.00	.90
☐ 71	Don Bessent	6.00	2.50	.60
☐ 72	Bill Renna	6.00	2.50	.60
☐ 73	Ron Jackson	6.00	2.50	.60
☐ 74	Directing Power	7.00	3.00	.70
	Jim Lemon			
	Cookie Lavagetto			
	Roy Sievers			
☐ 75	Sam Jones	6.00	2.50	.60
☐ 76	Bobby Richardson	16.00	6.75	2.25
☐ 77	John Goryl	6.00	2.50	.60
☐ 78	Pedro Ramos	6.00	2.50	.60
☐ 79	Harry Chiti	6.00	2.50	.60
☐ 80	Minnie Minoso	10.00	4.50	1.25
☐ 81	Hal Jeffcoat	6.00	2.50	.60
☐ 82	Bob Boyd	6.00	2.50	.60
☐ 83	Bob Smith	6.00	2.50	.60
☐ 84	Reno Bertoia	6.00	2.50	.60
☐ 85	Harry Anderson	6.00	2.50	.60
☐ 86	Bob Keegan	6.00	2.50	.60
☐ 87	Danny O'Connell	6.00	2.50	.60
☐ 88	Herb Score	9.00	4.00	.90
☐ 89	Billy Gardner	6.00	2.50	.60
☐ 90	Bill Skowron	11.00	5.00	1.35
☐ 91	Herb Moford	6.00	2.50	.60
☐ 92	Dave Philley	6.00	2.50	.60
☐ 93	Julio Becquer	6.00	2.50	.60
☐ 94	White Sox Team	18.00	6.00	1.20
	(checklist on back)			
☐ 95	Carl Willey	6.00	2.50	.60
☐ 96	Lou Berberet	6.00	2.50	.60
☐ 97	Jerry Lynch	6.00	2.50	.60
☐ 98	Arnie Portocarrero	6.00	2.50	.60
☐ 99	Ted Kazanski	6.00	2.50	.60
☐ 100	Bob Cerv	7.00	3.00	.70
☐ 101	Alex Kellner	6.00	2.50	.60
☐ 102	Felipe Alou	12.00	5.25	1.50
☐ 103	Billy Goodman	7.00	3.00	.70
☐ 104	Del Rice	6.00	2.50	.60
☐ 105	Lee Walls	6.00	2.50	.60
☐ 106	Hal Woodeshick	6.00	2.50	.60
☐ 107	Norm Larker	8.00	3.50	.80
☐ 108	Zack Monroe	6.00	2.50	.60
☐ 109	Bob Schmidt	6.00	2.50	.60
☐ 110	George Witt	6.00	2.50	.60
☐ 111	Redlegs Team	10.00	3.50	.75
	(checklist on back)			
☐ 112	Billy Consolo	3.75	1.60	.37
☐ 113	Taylor Phillips	3.75	1.60	.37
☐ 114	Earl Battey	3.75	1.60	.37
☐ 115	Mickey Vernon	4.50	2.00	.45
☐ 116	Bob Allison RP	7.50	3.25	.75
☐ 117	John Blanchard RP	6.50	2.75	.65
☐ 118	John Buzhardt RP	3.75	1.60	.37
☐ 119	John Callison RP	6.50	2.75	.65
☐ 120	Chuck Coles RP	3.75	1.60	.37
☐ 121	Bob Conley RP	3.75	1.60	.37
☐ 122	Bennie Daniels RP	3.75	1.60	.37
☐ 123	Don Dillard RP	3.75	1.60	.37
☐ 124	Dan Dobbek RP	3.75	1.60	.37
☐ 125	Ron Fairly RP	6.50	2.75	.65
☐ 126	Ed Haas RP	3.75	1.60	.37
☐ 127	Kent Hadley RP	3.75	1.60	.37
☐ 128	Bob Hartman RP	3.75	1.60	.37
☐ 129	Frank Herrera RP	3.75	1.60	.37
☐ 130	Lou Jackson RP	3.75	1.60	.37
☐ 131	Deron Johnson RP	6.00	2.50	.60
☐ 132	Don Lee RP	3.75	1.60	.37
☐ 133	Bob Lillis RP	4.50	2.00	.45
☐ 134	Jim McDaniel RP	3.75	1.60	.37
☐ 135	Gene Oliver RP	3.75	1.60	.37
☐ 136	Jim O'Toole RP	4.50	2.00	.45
☐ 137	Dick Ricketts RP	3.75	1.60	.37
☐ 138	John Romano RP	4.50	2.00	.45
☐ 139	Ed Sadowski RP	3.75	1.60	.37
☐ 140	Charlie Secrest RP	3.75	1.60	.37
☐ 141	Joe Shipley RP	3.75	1.60	.37
☐ 142	Dick Stigman RP	3.75	1.60	.37
☐ 143	Willie Tasby RP	4.50	2.00	.45
☐ 144	Jerry Walker RP	3.75	1.60	.37
☐ 145	Dom Zanni RP	3.75	1.60	.37
☐ 146	Jerry Zimmerman RP	3.75	1.60	.37
☐ 147	Cubs Clubbers	10.00	4.50	1.25
	Dale Long			
	Ernie Banks			
	Walt Moryn			
☐ 148	Mike McCormick	4.50	2.00	.45
☐ 149	Jim Bunning	11.00	5.00	1.35
☐ 150	Stan Musial	150.00	67.50	22.50
☐ 151	Bob Malkmus	3.75	1.60	.37
☐ 152	Johnny Klippstein	3.75	1.60	.37
☐ 153	Jim Marshall	3.75	1.60	.37
☐ 154	Ray Herbert	3.75	1.60	.37
☐ 155	Enos Slaughter	17.00	7.25	2.50
☐ 156	Ace Hurlers	6.00	2.50	.60
	Billy Pierce			
	Robin Roberts			
☐ 157	Felix Mantilla	3.75	1.60	.37
☐ 158	Walt Dropo	3.75	1.60	.37
☐ 159	Bob Shaw	4.50	2.00	.45
☐ 160	Dick Groat	6.00	2.50	.60
☐ 161	Frank Baumann	3.75	1.60	.37
☐ 162	Bobby G. Smith	3.75	1.60	.37
☐ 163	Sandy Koufax	145.00	65.00	18.00
☐ 164	Johnny Groth	3.75	1.60	.37
☐ 165	Bill Bruton	3.75	1.60	.37
☐ 166	Destruction Crew	6.00	2.50	.60
	Minnie Minoso			
	Rocky Colavito			
	(misspelled Colovito			
	on card back)			
	Larry Doby			
☐ 167	Duke Maas	3.75	1.60	.37
☐ 168	Carroll Hardy	3.75	1.60	.37
☐ 169	Ted Abernathy	3.75	1.60	.37
☐ 170	Gene Woodling	5.00	2.25	.50
☐ 171	Willard Schmidt	3.75	1.60	.37
☐ 172	Athletics Team	10.00	3.50	.75
	(checklist on back)			
☐ 173	Bill Monbouquette	3.75	1.60	.37
☐ 174	Jim Pendleton	3.75	1.60	.37
☐ 175	Dick Farrell	3.75	1.60	.37
☐ 176	Preston Ward	3.75	1.60	.37
☐ 177	John Briggs	3.75	1.60	.37
☐ 178	Ruben Amaro	3.75	1.60	.37
☐ 179	Don Rudolph	3.75	1.60	.37
☐ 180	Yogi Berra	85.00	38.00	12.75
☐ 181	Bob Porterfield	3.75	1.60	.37
☐ 182	Milt Graff	3.75	1.60	.37
☐ 183	Stu Miller	4.50	2.00	.45
☐ 184	Harvey Haddix	5.00	2.25	.50
☐ 185	Jim Busby	3.75	1.60	.37
☐ 186	Mudcat Grant	4.50	2.00	.45
☐ 187	Bubba Phillips	3.75	1.60	.37
☐ 188	Juan Pizarro	3.75	1.60	.37
☐ 189	Neil Chrisley	3.75	1.60	.37

#	Player			
☐ 190	Bill Virdon	5.00	2.25	.50
☐ 191	Russ Kemmerer	3.75	1.60	.37
☐ 192	Charlie Beamon	3.75	1.60	.37
☐ 193	Sammy Taylor	3.75	1.60	.37
☐ 194	Jim Brosnan	4.50	2.00	.45
☐ 195	Rip Repulski	3.75	1.60	.37
☐ 196	Billy Moran	3.75	1.60	.37
☐ 197	Ray Semproch	3.75	1.60	.37
☐ 198	Jim Davenport	4.50	2.00	.45
☐ 199	Leo Kiely	3.25	1.35	.32
☐ 200	Warren Giles (NL President)	5.00	2.25	.50
☐ 201	Tom Acker	3.25	1.35	.32
☐ 202	Roger Maris	145.00	65.00	18.00
☐ 203	Ossie Virgil	3.25	1.35	.32
☐ 204	Casey Wise	3.25	1.35	.32
☐ 205	Don Larsen	5.00	2.25	.50
☐ 206	Carl Furillo	5.50	2.50	.55
☐ 207	George Strickland	3.25	1.35	.32
☐ 208	Willie Jones	3.25	1.35	.32
☐ 209	Lenny Green	3.25	1.35	.32
☐ 210	Ed Bailey	4.00	1.75	.40
☐ 211	Bob Blaylock	3.25	1.35	.32
☐ 212	Fence Busters (Hank Aaron / Eddie Mathews)	36.00	16.25	5.50
☐ 213	Jim Rivera	3.25	1.35	.32
☐ 214	Marcelino Solis	3.25	1.35	.32
☐ 215	Jim Lemon	4.00	1.75	.40
☐ 216	Andre Rodgers	3.25	1.35	.32
☐ 217	Carl Erskine	5.00	2.25	.50
☐ 218	Roman Mejias	3.25	1.35	.32
☐ 219	George Zuverink	3.25	1.35	.32
☐ 220	Frank Malzone	4.00	1.75	.40
☐ 221	Bob Bowman	3.25	1.35	.32
☐ 222	Bobby Shantz	4.50	2.00	.45
☐ 223	Cardinals Team (checklist on back)	10.00	3.50	.75
☐ 224	Claude Osteen	5.00	2.25	.50
☐ 225	Johnny Logan	4.00	1.75	.40
☐ 226	Art Ceccarelli	3.25	1.35	.32
☐ 227	Hal W. Smith	3.25	1.35	.32
☐ 228	Don Gross	3.25	1.35	.32
☐ 229	Vic Power	3.25	1.35	.32
☐ 230	Bill Fischer	3.25	1.35	.32
☐ 231	Ellis Burton	3.25	1.35	.32
☐ 232	Eddie Kasko	3.25	1.35	.32
☐ 233	Paul Foytack	3.25	1.35	.32
☐ 234	Chuck Tanner	4.00	1.75	.40
☐ 235	Valmy Thomas	3.25	1.35	.32
☐ 236	Ted Bowsfield	3.25	1.35	.32
☐ 237	Run Preventers (Gil McDougald / Bob Turley / Bobby Richardson)	6.00	2.50	.60
☐ 238	Gene Baker	3.25	1.35	.32
☐ 239	Bob Trowbridge	3.25	1.35	.32
☐ 240	Hank Bauer	5.00	2.25	.50
☐ 241	Billy Muffett	3.25	1.35	.32
☐ 242	Ron Samford	3.25	1.35	.32
☐ 243	Marv Grissom	3.25	1.35	.32
☐ 244	Ted Gray	3.25	1.35	.32
☐ 245	Ned Garver	3.25	1.35	.32
☐ 246	J.W. Porter	3.25	1.35	.32
☐ 247	Don Ferrarese	3.25	1.35	.32
☐ 248	Red Sox Team (checklist on back)	10.00	3.50	.75
☐ 249	Bobby Adams	3.25	1.35	.32
☐ 250	Billy O'Dell	3.25	1.35	.32
☐ 251	Clete Boyer	5.50	2.50	.55
☐ 252	Ray Boone	4.00	1.75	.40
☐ 253	Seth Morehead	3.25	1.35	.32
☐ 254	Zeke Bella	3.25	1.35	.32
☐ 255	Del Ennis	4.00	1.75	.40
☐ 256	Jerry Davie	3.25	1.35	.32
☐ 257	Leon Wagner	5.00	2.25	.50
☐ 258	Fred Kipp	3.25	1.35	.32
☐ 259	Jim Pisoni	3.25	1.35	.32
☐ 260	Early Wynn	14.00	6.25	2.00
☐ 261	Gene Stephens	3.25	1.35	.32
☐ 262	Hitters' Foes (Johnny Podres / Clem Labine / Don Drysdale)	6.00	2.50	.60
☐ 263	Bud Daley	3.25	1.35	.32
☐ 264	Chico Carrasquel	3.25	1.35	.32
☐ 265	Ron Kline	3.25	1.35	.32
☐ 266	Woody Held	3.25	1.35	.32
☐ 267	John Romonosky	3.25	1.35	.32
☐ 268	Tito Francona	3.25	1.35	.32
☐ 269	Jack Meyer	3.25	1.35	.32
☐ 270	Gil Hodges	18.00	7.50	2.50
☐ 271	Orlando Pena	3.25	1.35	.32
☐ 272	Jerry Lumpe	3.25	1.35	.32
☐ 273	Joey Jay	3.25	1.35	.32
☐ 274	Jerry Kindall	3.25	1.35	.32
☐ 275	Jack Sanford	3.25	1.35	.32
☐ 276	Pete Daley	3.25	1.35	.32
☐ 277	Turk Lown	3.25	1.35	.32
☐ 278	Chuck Essegian	3.25	1.35	.32
☐ 279	Ernie Johnson	4.00	1.75	.40
☐ 280	Frank Bolling	3.25	1.35	.32
☐ 281	Walt Craddock	3.25	1.35	.32
☐ 282	R.C. Stevens	3.25	1.35	.32
☐ 283	Russ Heman	3.25	1.35	.32
☐ 284	Steve Korcheck	3.25	1.35	.32
☐ 285	Joe Cunningham	4.00	1.75	.40
☐ 286	Dean Stone	3.25	1.35	.32
☐ 287	Don Zimmer	4.50	2.00	.45
☐ 288	Dutch Dotterer	3.25	1.35	.32
☐ 289	Johnny Kucks	3.25	1.35	.32
☐ 290	Wes Covington	4.00	1.75	.40
☐ 291	Pitching Partners (Pedro Ramos / Camilo Pascual)	4.00	1.75	.40
☐ 292	Dick Williams	4.00	1.75	.40
☐ 293	Ray Moore	3.25	1.35	.32
☐ 294	Hank Foiles	3.25	1.35	.32
☐ 295	Billy Martin	13.50	6.00	1.85
☐ 296	Ernie Broglio	4.50	2.00	.45
☐ 297	Jackie Brandt	3.25	1.35	.32
☐ 298	Tex Clevenger	3.25	1.35	.32
☐ 299	Billy Klaus	3.25	1.35	.32
☐ 300	Richie Ashburn	12.00	5.25	1.50
☐ 301	Earl Averill	3.25	1.35	.32
☐ 302	Don Mossi	4.00	1.75	.40
☐ 303	Marty Keough	3.25	1.35	.32
☐ 304	Cubs Team (checklist on back)	10.00	3.50	.75
☐ 305	Curt Raydon	3.25	1.35	.32
☐ 306	Jim Gilliam	6.00	2.50	.60
☐ 307	Curt Barclay	3.25	1.35	.32
☐ 308	Norm Siebern	3.25	1.35	.32
☐ 309	Sal Maglie	4.50	2.00	.45
☐ 310	Luis Aparicio	17.00	7.25	2.50
☐ 311	Norm Zauchin	3.25	1.35	.32
☐ 312	Don Newcombe	5.00	2.25	.50
☐ 313	Frank House	3.25	1.35	.32
☐ 314	Don Cardwell	3.25	1.35	.32
☐ 315	Joe Adcock	4.50	2.00	.45
☐ 316A	Ralph Lumenti UER (option) (photo actually Camilo Pascual)	3.25	1.35	.32
☐ 316B	Ralph Lumenti UER (no option) (photo actually Camilo Pascual)	95.00	42.00	11.00
☐ 317	Hitting Kings (Willie Mays / Richie Ashburn)	21.00	9.00	3.00
☐ 318	Rocky Bridges	3.25	1.35	.32
☐ 319	Dave Hillman	3.25	1.35	.32
☐ 320	Bob Skinner	4.00	1.75	.40
☐ 321A	Bob Giallombardo (option)	3.25	1.35	.32
☐ 321B	Bob Giallombardo (no option)	95.00	42.00	11.00
☐ 322A	Harry Hanebrink (traded)	3.25	1.35	.32
☐ 322B	Harry Hanebrink (no trade)	95.00	42.00	11.00
☐ 323	Frank Sullivan	3.25	1.35	.32
☐ 324	Don Demeter	3.25	1.35	.32
☐ 325	Ken Boyer	7.50	3.25	.75
☐ 326	Marv Throneberry	4.50	2.00	.45
☐ 327	Gary Bell	3.25	1.35	.32
☐ 328	Lou Skizas	3.25	1.35	.32
☐ 329	Tigers Team (checklist on back)	10.00	3.50	.75
☐ 330	Gus Triandos	4.00	1.75	.40
☐ 331	Steve Boros	3.25	1.35	.32
☐ 332	Ray Monzant	3.25	1.35	.32
☐ 333	Harry Simpson	3.25	1.35	.32
☐ 334	Glen Hobbie	3.25	1.35	.32
☐ 335	Johnny Temple	3.25	1.35	.32
☐ 336A	Billy Loes (with traded line)	3.25	1.35	.32
☐ 336B	Billy Loes (no trade)	95.00	42.00	11.00
☐ 337	George Crowe	3.25	1.35	.32
☐ 338	Sparky Anderson	36.00	16.25	5.50
☐ 339	Roy Face	5.00	2.25	.50
☐ 340	Roy Sievers	4.00	1.75	.40
☐ 341	Tom Qualters	3.25	1.35	.32
☐ 342	Ray Jablonski	3.25	1.35	.32
☐ 343	Billy Hoeft	3.25	1.35	.32
☐ 344	Russ Nixon	3.25	1.35	.32

☐ 345	Gil McDougald	6.50	2.75	.65
☐ 346	Batter Bafflers	3.25	1.35	.32
	Dave Sisler			
	Tom Brewer			
☐ 347	Bob Buhl	3.25	1.35	.32
☐ 348	Ted Lepcio	3.25	1.35	.32
☐ 349	Hoyt Wilhelm	16.00	6.75	2.25
☐ 350	Ernie Banks	65.00	29.00	9.75
☐ 351	Earl Torgeson	3.25	1.35	.32
☐ 352	Robin Roberts	15.00	6.50	2.15
☐ 353	Curt Flood	5.00	2.25	.50
☐ 354	Pete Burnside	3.25	1.35	.32
☐ 355	Jim Piersall	4.50	2.00	.45
☐ 356	Bob Mabe	3.25	1.35	.32
☐ 357	Dick Stuart	4.50	2.00	.45
☐ 358	Ralph Terry	4.00	1.75	.40
☐ 359	Bill White	25.00	11.00	3.50
☐ 360	Al Kaline	60.00	27.00	9.00
☐ 361	Willard Nixon	3.25	1.35	.32
☐ 362A	Dolan Nichols	3.25	1.35	.32
	(with option line)			
☐ 362B	Dolan Nichols	95.00	42.00	11.00
	(no option)			
☐ 363	Bobby Avila	3.25	1.35	.32
☐ 364	Danny McDevitt	3.25	1.35	.32
☐ 365	Gus Bell	4.00	1.75	.40
☐ 366	Humberto Robinson	3.25	1.35	.32
☐ 367	Cal Neeman	3.25	1.35	.32
☐ 368	Don Mueller	4.00	1.75	.40
☐ 369	Dick Tomanek	3.25	1.35	.32
☐ 370	Pete Runnels	4.00	1.75	.40
☐ 371	Dick Brodowski	3.25	1.35	.32
☐ 372	Jim Hegan	3.25	1.35	.32
☐ 373	Herb Plews	3.25	1.35	.32
☐ 374	Art Ditmar	3.25	1.35	.32
☐ 375	Bob Nieman	3.25	1.35	.32
☐ 376	Hal Naragon	3.25	1.35	.32
☐ 377	John Antonelli	4.00	1.75	.40
☐ 378	Gail Harris	3.25	1.35	.32
☐ 379	Bob Miller	3.25	1.35	.32
☐ 380	Hank Aaron	110.00	50.00	16.50
☐ 381	Mike Baxes	3.25	1.35	.32
☐ 382	Curt Simmons	4.00	1.75	.40
☐ 383	Words of Wisdom	7.00	3.00	.70
	Don Larsen			
	Casey Stengel			
☐ 384	Dave Sisler	3.25	1.35	.32
☐ 385	Sherm Lollar	4.00	1.75	.40
☐ 386	Jim Delsing	3.25	1.35	.32
☐ 387	Don Drysdale	40.00	18.00	6.00
☐ 388	Bob Will	3.25	1.35	.32
☐ 389	Joe Nuxhall	4.00	1.75	.40
☐ 390	Orlando Cepeda	20.00	8.50	2.75
☐ 391	Milt Pappas	4.00	1.75	.40
☐ 392	Whitey Herzog	5.00	2.25	.50
☐ 393	Frank Lary	4.00	1.75	.40
☐ 394	Randy Jackson	3.25	1.35	.32
☐ 395	Elston Howard	7.50	3.25	.75
☐ 396	Bob Rush	3.25	1.35	.32
☐ 397	Senators Team	9.00	3.00	.60
	(checklist on back)			
☐ 398	Wally Post	3.25	1.35	.32
☐ 399	Larry Jackson	3.25	1.35	.32
☐ 400	Jackie Jensen	4.50	2.00	.45
☐ 401	Ron Blackburn	3.25	1.35	.32
☐ 402	Hector Lopez	3.25	1.35	.32
☐ 403	Clem Labine	4.00	1.75	.40
☐ 404	Hank Sauer	4.00	1.75	.40
☐ 405	Roy McMillan	3.25	1.35	.32
☐ 406	Solly Drake	3.25	1.35	.32
☐ 407	Moe Drabowsky	3.25	1.35	.32
☐ 408	Keystone Combo	7.00	3.00	.70
	Nellie Fox			
	Luis Aparicio			
☐ 409	Gus Zernial	4.00	1.75	.40
☐ 410	Billy Pierce	4.50	2.00	.45
☐ 411	Whitey Lockman	3.25	1.35	.32
☐ 412	Stan Lopata	3.25	1.35	.32
☐ 413	Camilo Pascual UER	4.00	1.75	.40
	(listed as Camillo			
	on front and Pasqual			
	on back)			
☐ 414	Dale Long	4.00	1.75	.40
☐ 415	Bill Mazeroski	7.50	3.25	.75
☐ 416	Haywood Sullivan	4.00	1.75	.40
☐ 417	Virgil Trucks	3.25	1.35	.32
☐ 418	Gino Cimoli	3.25	1.35	.32
☐ 419	Braves Team	10.00	3.50	.75
	(checklist on back)			
☐ 420	Rocky Colavito	18.00	7.50	2.50
☐ 421	Herman Wehmeier	3.25	1.35	.32
☐ 422	Hobie Landrith	3.25	1.35	.32
☐ 423	Bob Grim	3.25	1.35	.32
☐ 424	Ken Aspromonte	3.25	1.35	.32
☐ 425	Del Crandall	4.00	1.75	.40
☐ 426	Jerry Staley	3.25	1.35	.32
☐ 427	Charlie Neal	4.00	1.75	.40
☐ 428	Buc Hill Aces	4.50	2.00	.45
	Ron Kline			
	Bob Friend			
	Vernon Law			
	Roy Face			
☐ 429	Bobby Thomson	4.50	2.00	.45
☐ 430	Whitey Ford	40.00	18.00	6.00
☐ 431	Whammy Douglas	3.25	1.35	.32
☐ 432	Smoky Burgess	4.00	1.75	.40
☐ 433	Billy Harrell	3.25	1.35	.32
☐ 434	Hal Griggs	3.25	1.35	.32
☐ 435	Frank Robinson	45.00	20.00	6.75
☐ 436	Granny Hamner	3.25	1.35	.32
☐ 437	Ike Delock	3.25	1.35	.32
☐ 438	Sammy Esposito	3.25	1.35	.32
☐ 439	Brooks Robinson	50.00	22.50	7.50
☐ 440	Lou Burdette	7.00	3.00	.70
	(posing as if			
	lefthanded)			
☐ 441	John Roseboro	4.50	2.00	.45
☐ 442	Ray Narleski	3.25	1.35	.32
☐ 443	Daryl Spencer	3.25	1.35	.32
☐ 444	Ron Hansen	3.25	1.35	.32
☐ 445	Cal McLish	3.25	1.35	.32
☐ 446	Rocky Nelson	3.25	1.35	.32
☐ 447	Bob Anderson	3.25	1.35	.32
☐ 448	Vada Pinson UER	6.00	2.50	.60
	(Born: 8/8/38,			
	should be 8/11/38)			
☐ 449	Tom Gorman	3.25	1.35	.32
☐ 450	Eddie Mathews	30.00	13.50	4.50
☐ 451	Jimmy Constable	3.25	1.35	.32
☐ 452	Chico Fernandez	3.25	1.35	.32
☐ 453	Les Moss	3.25	1.35	.32
☐ 454	Phil Clark	3.25	1.35	.32
☐ 455	Larry Doby	4.50	2.00	.45
☐ 456	Jerry Casale	3.25	1.35	.32
☐ 457	Dodgers Team	16.00	5.00	1.00
	(checklist on back)			
☐ 458	Gordon Jones	3.25	1.35	.32
☐ 459	Bill Tuttle	3.25	1.35	.32
☐ 460	Bob Friend	4.00	1.75	.40
☐ 461	Mantle Hits Homer	42.00	18.00	6.00
☐ 462	Colavito's Catch	8.50	3.75	.85
☐ 463	Kaline Batting Champ	14.00	6.25	2.00
☐ 464	Mays' Series Catch	21.00	9.00	3.00
☐ 465	Sievers Sets Mark	4.50	2.00	.45
☐ 466	Pierce All-Star	4.50	2.00	.45
☐ 467	Aaron Clubs Homer	20.00	8.50	2.75
☐ 468	Snider's Play	14.00	6.25	2.00
☐ 469	Hustler Banks	14.00	6.25	2.00
☐ 470	Musial's 3000 Hit	20.00	8.50	2.75
☐ 471	Tom Sturdivant	3.25	1.35	.32
☐ 472	Gene Freese	3.25	1.35	.32
☐ 473	Mike Fornieles	3.25	1.35	.32
☐ 474	Moe Thacker	3.25	1.35	.32
☐ 475	Jack Harshman	3.25	1.35	.32
☐ 476	Indians Team	9.00	3.00	.60
	(checklist on back)			
☐ 477	Barry Latman	3.25	1.35	.32
☐ 478	Bob Clemente	110.00	50.00	16.50
☐ 479	Lindy McDaniel	4.00	1.75	.40
☐ 480	Red Schoendienst	14.00	6.25	2.00
☐ 481	Charlie Maxwell	3.25	1.35	.32
☐ 482	Russ Meyer	3.25	1.35	.32
☐ 483	Clint Courtney	3.25	1.35	.32
☐ 484	Willie Kirkland	3.25	1.35	.32
☐ 485	Ryne Duren	4.50	2.00	.45
☐ 486	Sammy White	3.25	1.35	.32
☐ 487	Hal Brown	3.25	1.35	.32
☐ 488	Walt Moryn	3.25	1.35	.32
☐ 489	John Powers	3.25	1.35	.32
☐ 490	Frank Thomas	4.00	1.75	.40
☐ 491	Don Blasingame	3.25	1.35	.32
☐ 492	Gene Conley	3.25	1.35	.32
☐ 493	Jim Landis	3.25	1.35	.32
☐ 494	Don Pavletich	3.25	1.35	.32
☐ 495	Johnny Podres	4.50	2.00	.45
☐ 496	Wayne Terwilliger UER	3.25	1.35	.32
	(Athlftics on front)			
☐ 497	Hal R. Smith	3.25	1.35	.32
☐ 498	Dick Hyde	3.25	1.35	.32
☐ 499	Johnny O'Brien	3.25	1.35	.32
☐ 500	Vic Wertz	4.00	1.75	.40
☐ 501	Bob Tiefenauer	3.25	1.35	.32
☐ 502	Alvin Dark	4.50	2.00	.45
☐ 503	Jim Owens	3.25	1.35	.32
☐ 504	Ossie Alvarez	3.25	1.35	.32
☐ 505	Tony Kubek	9.00	4.00	.90
☐ 506	Bob Purkey	3.25	1.35	.32
☐ 507	Bob Hale	16.00	6.75	2.25

☐ 508	Art Fowler	16.00	6.75	2.25
☐ 509	Norm Cash	55.00	25.00	8.25
☐ 510	Yankees Team	70.00	20.00	4.00
	(checklist on back)			
☐ 511	George Susce	16.00	6.75	2.25
☐ 512	George Altman	16.00	6.75	2.25
☐ 513	Tommy Carroll	16.00	6.75	2.25
☐ 514	Bob Gibson	400.00	180.00	60.00
☐ 515	Harmon Killebrew	145.00	65.00	18.00
☐ 516	Mike Garcia	18.00	7.50	2.50
☐ 517	Joe Koppe	16.00	6.75	2.25
☐ 518	Mike Cueller UER	21.00	9.00	3.00
	(sic, Cuellar)			
☐ 519	Infield Power	18.00	7.50	2.50
	Pete Runnels			
	Dick Gernert			
	Frank Malzone			
☐ 520	Don Elston	16.00	6.75	2.25
☐ 521	Gary Geiger	16.00	6.75	2.25
☐ 522	Gene Snyder	16.00	6.75	2.25
☐ 523	Harry Bright	16.00	6.75	2.25
☐ 524	Larry Osborne	16.00	6.75	2.25
☐ 525	Jim Coates	16.00	6.75	2.25
☐ 526	Bob Speake	16.00	6.75	2.25
☐ 527	Solly Hemus	16.00	6.75	2.25
☐ 528	Pirates Team	42.00	15.00	3.00
	(checklist on back)			
☐ 529	George Bamberger	18.00	7.50	2.50
☐ 530	Wally Moon	18.00	7.50	2.50
☐ 531	Ray Webster	16.00	6.75	2.25
☐ 532	Mark Freeman	16.00	6.75	2.25
☐ 533	Darrell Johnson	18.00	7.50	2.50
☐ 534	Faye Throneberry	16.00	6.75	2.25
☐ 535	Ruben Gomez	16.00	6.75	2.25
☐ 536	Danny Kravitz	16.00	6.75	2.25
☐ 537	Rudolph Arias	16.00	6.75	2.25
☐ 538	Chick King	16.00	6.75	2.25
☐ 539	Gary Blaylock	16.00	6.75	2.25
☐ 540	Willie Miranda	16.00	6.75	2.25
☐ 541	Bob Thurman	16.00	6.75	2.25
☐ 542	Jim Perry	21.00	9.00	3.00
☐ 543	Corsair Trio	60.00	27.00	9.00
	Bob Skinner			
	Bill Virdon			
	Roberto Clemente			
☐ 544	Lee Tate	16.00	6.75	2.25
☐ 545	Tom Morgan	16.00	6.75	2.25
☐ 546	Al Schroll	16.00	6.75	2.25
☐ 547	Jim Baxes	16.00	6.75	2.25
☐ 548	Elmer Singleton	16.00	6.75	2.25
☐ 549	Howie Nunn	16.00	6.75	2.25
☐ 550	Roy Campanella	145.00	65.00	18.00
	(Symbol of Courage)			
☐ 551	Fred Haney MG AS	18.00	7.50	2.50
☐ 552	Casey Stengel MG AS	35.00	15.75	5.25
☐ 553	Orlando Cepeda AS	22.00	9.50	3.15
☐ 554	Bill Skowron AS	20.00	8.50	2.75
☐ 555	Bill Mazeroski AS	20.00	8.50	2.75
☐ 556	Nellie Fox AS	22.00	9.50	3.15
☐ 557	Ken Boyer AS	20.00	8.50	2.75
☐ 558	Frank Malzone AS	18.00	7.50	2.50
☐ 559	Ernie Banks AS	50.00	22.50	7.50
☐ 560	Luis Aparicio AS	30.00	13.50	4.50
☐ 561	Hank Aaron AS	120.00	55.00	18.00
☐ 562	Al Kaline AS	50.00	22.50	7.50
☐ 563	Willie Mays AS	120.00	55.00	18.00
☐ 564	Mickey Mantle AS	250.00	110.00	37.50
☐ 565	Wes Covington AS	18.00	7.50	2.50
☐ 566	Roy Sievers AS	18.00	7.50	2.50
☐ 567	Del Crandall AS	18.00	7.50	2.50
☐ 568	Gus Triandos AS	18.00	7.50	2.50
☐ 569	Bob Friend AS	18.00	7.50	2.50
☐ 570	Bob Turley AS	18.00	7.50	2.50
☐ 571	Warren Spahn AS	36.00	16.25	5.50
☐ 572	Billy Pierce AS	32.00	12.00	2.50

1960 Topps

The cards in this 572-card set measure 2 1/2" by 3 1/2". The 1960 Topps set is the only Topps standard size issue to use a horizontally oriented front. World Series cards appeared for the first time (385 to 391), and there is a Rookie Prospect (RP) series (117-148), the most famous of which is Carl Yastrzemski, and a Sport Magazine All-Star Selection (AS) series (553-572). There are 16 manager cards listed alphabetically from 212 through 227. The coaching staff of each team was also afforded

their own card in a 16-card subset (455-470). Cards 375 to 440 come with either gray or white backs, and the high series (507-572) were printed on a more limited basis than the rest of the set. The team cards have series checklists on the reverse. The key rookies in this set are Willie McCovey and Carl Yastrzemski.

		NRMT	VG-E	GOOD
COMPLETE SET (572)		4000.00	1650.00	350.00
COMMON PLAYER (1-110)		3.75	1.60	.37
COMMON PLAYER (111-198)		2.75	1.10	.27
COMMON PLAYER (199-286)		3.00	1.25	.30
COMMON PLAYER (287-440)		3.25	1.35	.32
COMMON PLAYER (441-506)		4.50	2.00	.45
COMMON PLAYER (507-552)		12.00	5.25	1.50
COMMON PLAYER (553-572)		14.00	6.25	2.00
☐ 1	Early Wynn	40.00	8.00	1.75
☐ 2	Roman Mejias	3.75	1.60	.37
☐ 3	Joe Adcock	4.50	2.00	.45
☐ 4	Bob Purkey	3.75	1.60	.37
☐ 5	Wally Moon	4.50	2.00	.45
☐ 6	Lou Berberet	3.75	1.60	.37
☐ 7	Master and Mentor	15.00	6.50	2.15
	Willie Mays			
	Bill Rigney			
☐ 8	Bud Daley	3.75	1.60	.37
☐ 9	Faye Throneberry	3.75	1.60	.37
☐ 10	Ernie Banks	48.00	22.00	6.00
☐ 11	Norm Siebern	3.75	1.60	.37
☐ 12	Milt Pappas	4.50	2.00	.45
☐ 13	Wally Post	3.75	1.60	.37
☐ 14	Jim Grant	3.75	1.60	.37
☐ 15	Pete Runnels	4.50	2.00	.45
☐ 16	Ernie Broglio	4.50	2.00	.45
☐ 17	Johnny Callison	4.50	2.00	.45
☐ 18	Dodgers Team	16.00	5.00	1.00
	(checklist on back)			
☐ 19	Felix Mantilla	3.75	1.60	.37
☐ 20	Roy Face	5.00	2.25	.50
☐ 21	Dutch Dotterer	3.75	1.60	.37
☐ 22	Rocky Bridges	3.75	1.60	.37
☐ 23	Eddie Fisher	3.75	1.60	.37
☐ 24	Dick Gray	3.75	1.60	.37
☐ 25	Roy Sievers	4.50	2.00	.45
☐ 26	Wayne Terwilliger	3.75	1.60	.37
☐ 27	Dick Drott	3.75	1.60	.37
☐ 28	Brooks Robinson	48.00	22.00	6.00
☐ 29	Clem Labine	4.50	2.00	.45
☐ 30	Tito Francona	3.75	1.60	.37
☐ 31	Sammy Esposito	3.75	1.60	.37
☐ 32	Sophomore Stalwarts	4.50	2.00	.45
	Jim O'Toole			
	Vada Pinson			
☐ 33	Tom Morgan	3.75	1.60	.37
☐ 34	George Anderson	9.00	4.00	.90
☐ 35	Whitey Ford	40.00	18.00	6.00
☐ 36	Russ Nixon	3.75	1.60	.37
☐ 37	Bill Bruton	3.75	1.60	.37
☐ 38	Jerry Casale	3.75	1.60	.37
☐ 39	Earl Averill	3.75	1.60	.37
☐ 40	Joe Cunningham	4.50	2.00	.45
☐ 41	Barry Latman	3.75	1.60	.37
☐ 42	Hobie Landrith	3.75	1.60	.37
☐ 43	Senators Team	7.50	2.50	.50
	(checklist on back)			
☐ 44	Bobby Locke	3.75	1.60	.37
☐ 45	Roy McMillan	3.75	1.60	.37
☐ 46	Jerry Fisher	3.75	1.60	.37
☐ 47	Don Zimmer	5.00	2.25	.50
☐ 48	Hal W. Smith	3.75	1.60	.37
☐ 49	Curt Raydon	3.75	1.60	.37

#	Player			
☐ 50	Al Kaline	48.00	22.00	6.00
☐ 51	Jim Coates	3.75	1.60	.37
☐ 52	Dave Philley	3.75	1.60	.37
☐ 53	Jackie Brandt	3.75	1.60	.37
☐ 54	Mike Fornieles	3.75	1.60	.37
☐ 55	Bill Mazeroski	6.00	2.50	.60
☐ 56	Steve Korcheck	3.75	1.60	.37
☐ 57	Win Savers	3.75	1.60	.37
	Turk Lown			
	Jerry Staley			
☐ 58	Gino Cimoli	3.75	1.60	.37
☐ 59	Juan Pizarro	3.75	1.60	.37
☐ 60	Gus Triandos	4.50	2.00	.45
☐ 61	Eddie Kasko	3.75	1.60	.37
☐ 62	Roger Craig	5.00	2.25	.50
☐ 63	George Strickland	3.75	1.60	.37
☐ 64	Jack Meyer	3.75	1.60	.37
☐ 65	Elston Howard	6.00	2.50	.60
☐ 66	Bob Trowbridge	3.75	1.60	.37
☐ 67	Jose Pagan	3.75	1.60	.37
☐ 68	Dave Hillman	3.75	1.60	.37
☐ 69	Billy Goodman	4.50	2.00	.45
☐ 70	Lew Burdette	5.00	2.25	.50
☐ 71	Marty Keough	3.75	1.60	.37
☐ 72	Tigers Team	8.00	2.50	.50
	(checklist on back)			
☐ 73	Bob Gibson	60.00	27.00	9.00
☐ 74	Walt Moryn	3.75	1.60	.37
☐ 75	Vic Power	3.75	1.60	.37
☐ 76	Bill Fischer	3.75	1.60	.37
☐ 77	Hank Foiles	3.75	1.60	.37
☐ 78	Bob Grim	3.75	1.60	.37
☐ 79	Walt Dropo	3.75	1.60	.37
☐ 80	Johnny Antonelli	4.50	2.00	.45
☐ 81	Russ Snyder	3.75	1.60	.37
☐ 82	Ruben Gomez	3.75	1.60	.37
☐ 83	Tony Kubek	6.50	2.75	.65
☐ 84	Hal R. Smith	3.75	1.60	.37
☐ 85	Frank Lary	4.50	2.00	.45
☐ 86	Dick Gernert	3.75	1.60	.37
☐ 87	John Romonosky	3.75	1.60	.37
☐ 88	John Roseboro	4.50	2.00	.45
☐ 89	Hal Brown	3.75	1.60	.37
☐ 90	Bobby Avila	3.75	1.60	.37
☐ 91	Bennie Daniels	3.75	1.60	.37
☐ 92	Whitey Herzog	5.00	2.25	.50
☐ 93	Art Schult	3.75	1.60	.37
☐ 94	Leo Kiely	3.75	1.60	.37
☐ 95	Frank Thomas	4.50	2.00	.45
☐ 96	Ralph Terry	4.50	2.00	.45
☐ 97	Ted Lepcio	3.75	1.60	.37
☐ 98	Gordon Jones	3.75	1.60	.37
☐ 99	Lenny Green	3.75	1.60	.37
☐ 100	Nellie Fox	8.50	3.75	.85
☐ 101	Bob Miller	3.75	1.60	.37
☐ 102	Kent Hadley	3.75	1.60	.37
☐ 103	Dick Farrell	3.75	1.60	.37
☐ 104	Dick Schofield	3.75	1.60	.37
☐ 105	Larry Sherry	5.00	2.25	.50
☐ 106	Billy Gardner	3.75	1.60	.37
☐ 107	Carlton Willey	3.75	1.60	.37
☐ 108	Pete Daley	3.75	1.60	.37
☐ 109	Clete Boyer	5.00	2.25	.50
☐ 110	Cal McLish	3.75	1.60	.37
☐ 111	Vic Wertz	3.50	1.50	.35
☐ 112	Jack Harshman	2.75	1.10	.27
☐ 113	Bob Skinner	3.50	1.50	.35
☐ 114	Ken Aspromonte	2.75	1.10	.27
☐ 115	Fork and Knuckler	5.00	2.25	.50
	Roy Face			
	Hoyt Wilhelm			
☐ 116	Jim Rivera	2.75	1.10	.27
☐ 117	Tom Borland RP	2.75	1.10	.27
☐ 118	Bob Bruce RP	2.75	1.10	.27
☐ 119	Chico Cardenas RP	3.50	1.50	.35
☐ 120	Duke Carmel RP	2.75	1.10	.27
☐ 121	Camilo Carreon RP	2.75	1.10	.27
☐ 122	Don Dillard RP	2.75	1.10	.27
☐ 123	Dan Dobbek RP	2.75	1.10	.27
☐ 124	Jim Donohue RP	2.75	1.10	.27
☐ 125	Dick Ellsworth RP	4.50	2.00	.45
☐ 126	Chuck Estrada RP	4.50	2.00	.45
☐ 127	Ron Hansen RP	2.75	1.10	.27
☐ 128	Bill Harris RP	2.75	1.10	.27
☐ 129	Bob Hartman RP	2.75	1.10	.27
☐ 130	Frank Herrera RP	2.75	1.10	.27
☐ 131	Ed Hobaugh RP	2.75	1.10	.27
☐ 132	Frank Howard RP	15.00	6.50	2.15
☐ 133	Manuel Javier RP	4.50	2.00	.45
	(sic, Julian)			
☐ 134	Deron Johnson RP	3.50	1.50	.35
☐ 135	Ken Johnson RP	2.75	1.10	.27
☐ 136	Jim Kaat RP	35.00	15.75	5.25
☐ 137	Lou Klimchock RP	2.75	1.10	.27
☐ 138	Art Mahaffey RP	3.50	1.50	.35
☐ 139	Carl Mathias RP	2.75	1.10	.27
☐ 140	Julio Navarro RP	3.50	1.50	.35
☐ 141	Jim Proctor RP	2.75	1.10	.27
☐ 142	Bill Short RP	3.50	1.50	.35
☐ 143	Al Spangler RP	2.75	1.10	.27
☐ 144	Al Stieglitz RP	2.75	1.10	.27
☐ 145	Jim Umbricht RP	2.75	1.10	.27
☐ 146	Ted Wieand RP	2.75	1.10	.27
☐ 147	Bob Will RP	2.75	1.10	.27
☐ 148	Carl Yastrzemski RP	350.00	160.00	52.50
☐ 149	Bob Nieman	2.75	1.10	.27
☐ 150	Billy Pierce	4.00	1.75	.40
☐ 151	Giants Team	7.50	2.50	.50
	(checklist on back)			
☐ 152	Gail Harris	2.75	1.10	.27
☐ 153	Bobby Thomson	4.00	1.75	.40
☐ 154	Jim Davenport	3.50	1.50	.35
☐ 155	Charlie Neal	3.50	1.50	.35
☐ 156	Art Ceccarelli	2.75	1.10	.27
☐ 157	Rocky Nelson	2.75	1.10	.27
☐ 158	Wes Covington	3.50	1.50	.35
☐ 159	Jim Piersall	4.00	1.75	.40
☐ 160	Rival All-Stars	50.00	22.50	7.50
	Mickey Mantle			
	Ken Boyer			
☐ 161	Ray Narleski	2.75	1.10	.27
☐ 162	Sammy Taylor	2.75	1.10	.27
☐ 163	Hector Lopez	2.75	1.10	.27
☐ 164	Reds Team	7.50	2.50	.50
	(checklist on back)			
☐ 165	Jack Sanford	3.50	1.50	.35
☐ 166	Chuck Essegian	2.75	1.10	.27
☐ 167	Valmy Thomas	2.75	1.10	.27
☐ 168	Alex Grammas	2.75	1.10	.27
☐ 169	Jake Striker	2.75	1.10	.27
☐ 170	Del Crandall	3.50	1.50	.35
☐ 171	Johnny Groth	2.75	1.10	.27
☐ 172	Willie Kirkland	2.75	1.10	.27
☐ 173	Billy Martin	11.00	5.00	1.35
☐ 174	Indians Team	7.50	2.50	.50
	(checklist on back)			
☐ 175	Pedro Ramos	2.75	1.10	.27
☐ 176	Vada Pinson	4.50	2.00	.45
☐ 177	Johnny Kucks	2.75	1.10	.27
☐ 178	Woody Held	2.75	1.10	.27
☐ 179	Rip Coleman	2.75	1.10	.27
☐ 180	Harry Simpson	2.75	1.10	.27
☐ 181	Billy Loes	2.75	1.10	.27
☐ 182	Glen Hobbie	2.75	1.10	.27
☐ 183	Eli Grba	2.75	1.10	.27
☐ 184	Gary Geiger	2.75	1.10	.27
☐ 185	Jim Owens	2.75	1.10	.27
☐ 186	Dave Sisler	2.75	1.10	.27
☐ 187	Jay Hook	2.75	1.10	.27
☐ 188	Dick Williams	3.50	1.50	.35
☐ 189	Don McMahon	2.75	1.10	.27
☐ 190	Gene Woodling	3.50	1.50	.35
☐ 191	Johnny Klippstein	2.75	1.10	.27
☐ 192	Danny O'Connell	2.75	1.10	.27
☐ 193	Dick Hyde	2.75	1.10	.27
☐ 194	Bobby Gene Smith	2.75	1.10	.27
☐ 195	Lindy McDaniel	3.50	1.50	.35
☐ 196	Andy Carey	3.50	1.50	.35
☐ 197	Ron Kline	2.75	1.10	.27
☐ 198	Jerry Lynch	2.75	1.10	.27
☐ 199	Dick Donovan	3.00	1.25	.30
☐ 200	Willie Mays	120.00	55.00	18.00
☐ 201	Larry Osborne	3.00	1.25	.30
☐ 202	Fred Kipp	3.00	1.25	.30
☐ 203	Sammy White	3.00	1.25	.30
☐ 204	Ryne Duren	4.00	1.75	.40
☐ 205	Johnny Logan	4.00	1.75	.40
☐ 206	Claude Osteen	4.00	1.75	.40
☐ 207	Bob Boyd	3.00	1.25	.30
☐ 208	White Sox Team	7.50	2.50	.50
	(checklist on back)			
☐ 209	Ron Blackburn	3.00	1.25	.30
☐ 210	Harmon Killebrew	30.00	13.50	4.50
☐ 211	Taylor Phillips	3.00	1.25	.30
☐ 212	Walt Alston MG	11.00	5.00	1.35
☐ 213	Chuck Dressen MG	3.50	1.50	.35
☐ 214	Jimmy Dykes MG	3.50	1.50	.35
☐ 215	Bob Elliott MG	3.00	1.25	.30
☐ 216	Joe Gordon MG	3.50	1.50	.35
☐ 217	Charlie Grimm MG	3.50	1.50	.35
☐ 218	Solly Hemus MG	3.00	1.25	.30
☐ 219	Fred Hutchinson MG	3.50	1.50	.35
☐ 220	Billy Jurges MG	3.00	1.25	.30
☐ 221	Cookie Lavagetto MG	3.00	1.25	.30
☐ 222	Al Lopez MG	6.50	2.75	.65
☐ 223	Danny Murtaugh MG	3.00	1.25	.30
☐ 224	Paul Richards MG	3.50	1.50	.35
☐ 225	Bill Rigney MG	3.00	1.25	.30

☐ 226	Eddie Sawyer MG	3.00	1.25	.30
☐ 227	Casey Stengel MG	17.00	7.25	2.50
☐ 228	Ernie Johnson	3.50	1.50	.35
☐ 229	Joe M. Morgan	5.00	2.25	.50
☐ 230	Mound Magicians	6.50	2.75	.65
	Lou Burdette			
	Warren Spahn			
	Bob Buhl			
☐ 231	Hal Naragon	3.00	1.25	.30
☐ 232	Jim Busby	3.00	1.25	.30
☐ 233	Don Elston	3.00	1.25	.30
☐ 234	Don Demeter	3.00	1.25	.30
☐ 235	Gus Bell	3.50	1.50	.35
☐ 236	Dick Ricketts	3.00	1.25	.30
☐ 237	Elmer Valo	3.00	1.25	.30
☐ 238	Danny Kravitz	3.00	1.25	.30
☐ 239	Joe Shipley	3.00	1.25	.30
☐ 240	Luis Aparicio	13.50	6.00	1.85
☐ 241	Albie Pearson	3.00	1.25	.30
☐ 242	Cardinals Team	7.50	2.50	.50
	(checklist on back)			
☐ 243	Bubba Phillips	3.00	1.25	.30
☐ 244	Hal Griggs	3.00	1.25	.30
☐ 245	Eddie Yost	3.00	1.25	.30
☐ 246	Lee Maye	3.00	1.25	.30
☐ 247	Gil McDougald	4.50	2.00	.45
☐ 248	Del Rice	3.00	1.25	.30
☐ 249	Earl Wilson	4.00	1.75	.40
☐ 250	Stan Musial	100.00	45.00	15.00
☐ 251	Bob Malkmus	3.00	1.25	.30
☐ 252	Ray Herbert	3.00	1.25	.30
☐ 253	Eddie Bressoud	3.00	1.25	.30
☐ 254	Arnie Portocarrero	3.00	1.25	.30
☐ 255	Jim Gilliam	4.50	2.00	.45
☐ 256	Dick Brown	3.00	1.25	.30
☐ 257	Gordy Coleman	4.00	1.75	.40
☐ 258	Dick Groat	4.50	2.00	.45
☐ 259	George Altman	3.00	1.25	.30
☐ 260	Power Plus	4.50	2.00	.45
	Rocky Colavito			
	Tito Francona			
☐ 261	Pete Burnside	3.00	1.25	.30
☐ 262	Hank Bauer	3.50	1.50	.35
☐ 263	Darrell Johnson	3.00	1.25	.30
☐ 264	Robin Roberts	12.50	5.50	1.65
☐ 265	Rip Repulski	3.00	1.25	.30
☐ 266	Joey Jay	3.00	1.25	.30
☐ 267	Jim Marshall	3.00	1.25	.30
☐ 268	Al Worthington	3.00	1.25	.30
☐ 269	Gene Green	3.00	1.25	.30
☐ 270	Bob Turley	4.00	1.75	.40
☐ 271	Julio Becquer	3.00	1.25	.30
☐ 272	Fred Green	3.00	1.25	.30
☐ 273	Neil Chrisley	3.00	1.25	.30
☐ 274	Tom Acker	3.00	1.25	.30
☐ 275	Curt Flood	4.50	2.00	.45
☐ 276	Ken McBride	3.00	1.25	.30
☐ 277	Harry Bright	3.00	1.25	.30
☐ 278	Stan Williams	3.00	1.25	.30
☐ 279	Chuck Tanner	3.50	1.50	.35
☐ 280	Frank Sullivan	3.00	1.25	.30
☐ 281	Ray Boone	3.50	1.50	.35
☐ 282	Joe Nuxhall	3.50	1.50	.35
☐ 283	John Blanchard	3.50	1.50	.35
☐ 284	Don Gross	3.00	1.25	.30
☐ 285	Harry Anderson	3.00	1.25	.30
☐ 286	Ray Semproch	3.00	1.25	.30
☐ 287	Felipe Alou	4.00	1.75	.40
☐ 288	Bob Mabe	3.25	1.35	.32
☐ 289	Willie Jones	3.25	1.35	.32
☐ 290	Jerry Lumpe	3.25	1.35	.32
☐ 291	Bob Keegan	3.25	1.35	.32
☐ 292	Dodger Backstops	4.00	1.75	.40
	Joe Pignatano			
	John Roseboro			
☐ 293	Gene Conley	3.25	1.35	.32
☐ 294	Tony Taylor	3.25	1.35	.32
☐ 295	Gil Hodges	16.00	6.75	2.25
☐ 296	Nelson Chittum	3.25	1.35	.32
☐ 297	Reno Bertoia	3.25	1.35	.32
☐ 298	George Witt	3.25	1.35	.32
☐ 299	Earl Torgeson	3.25	1.35	.32
☐ 300	Hank Aaron	120.00	55.00	18.00
☐ 301	Jerry Davie	3.25	1.35	.32
☐ 302	Phillies Team	7.50	2.50	.50
	(checklist on back)			
☐ 303	Billy O'Dell	3.25	1.35	.32
☐ 304	Joe Ginsberg	3.25	1.35	.32
☐ 305	Richie Ashburn	9.00	4.00	.90
☐ 306	Frank Baumann	3.25	1.35	.32
☐ 307	Gene Oliver	3.25	1.35	.32
☐ 308	Dick Hall	3.25	1.35	.32
☐ 309	Bob Hale	3.25	1.35	.32
☐ 310	Frank Malzone	4.00	1.75	.40

☐ 311	Raul Sanchez	3.25	1.35	.32
☐ 312	Charley Lau	4.00	1.75	.40
☐ 313	Turk Lown	3.25	1.35	.32
☐ 314	Chico Fernandez	3.25	1.35	.32
☐ 315	Bobby Shantz	4.50	2.00	.45
☐ 316	Willie McCovey	240.00	105.00	32.00
☐ 317	Pumpsie Green	4.00	1.75	.40
☐ 318	Jim Baxes	3.25	1.35	.32
☐ 319	Joe Koppe	3.25	1.35	.32
☐ 320	Bob Allison	4.50	2.00	.45
☐ 321	Ron Fairly	4.50	2.00	.45
☐ 322	Willie Tasby	3.25	1.35	.32
☐ 323	John Romano	3.25	1.35	.32
☐ 324	Jim Perry	4.50	2.00	.45
☐ 325	Jim O'Toole	4.00	1.75	.40
☐ 326	Bob Clemente	120.00	55.00	18.00
☐ 327	Ray Sadecki	4.50	2.00	.45
☐ 328	Earl Battey	3.25	1.35	.32
☐ 329	Zack Monroe	3.25	1.35	.32
☐ 330	Harvey Kuenn	4.50	2.00	.45
☐ 331	Henry Mason	3.25	1.35	.32
☐ 332	Yankees Team	25.00	7.50	2.50
	(checklist on back)			
☐ 333	Danny McDevitt	3.25	1.35	.32
☐ 334	Ted Abernathy	3.25	1.35	.32
☐ 335	Red Schoendienst	11.00	5.00	1.35
☐ 336	Ike Delock	3.25	1.35	.32
☐ 337	Cal Neeman	3.25	1.35	.32
☐ 338	Ray Monzant	3.25	1.35	.32
☐ 339	Harry Chiti	3.25	1.35	.32
☐ 340	Harvey Haddix	4.00	1.75	.40
☐ 341	Carroll Hardy	3.25	1.35	.32
☐ 342	Casey Wise	3.25	1.35	.32
☐ 343	Sandy Koufax	120.00	55.00	18.00
☐ 344	Clint Courtney	3.25	1.35	.32
☐ 345	Don Newcombe	4.50	2.00	.45
☐ 346	J.C. Martin UER	3.25	1.35	.32
	(face actually			
	Gary Peters)			
☐ 347	Ed Bouchee	3.25	1.35	.32
☐ 348	Barry Shetrone	3.25	1.35	.32
☐ 349	Moe Drabowsky	3.25	1.35	.32
☐ 350	Mickey Mantle	325.00	150.00	50.00
☐ 351	Don Nottebart	3.25	1.35	.32
☐ 352	Cincy Clouters	5.50	2.50	.55
	Gus Bell			
	Frank Robinson			
	Jerry Lynch			
☐ 353	Don Larsen	4.00	1.75	.40
☐ 354	Bob Lillis	4.00	1.75	.40
☐ 355	Bill White	6.50	2.75	.65
☐ 356	Joe Amalfitano	3.25	1.35	.32
☐ 357	Al Schroll	3.25	1.35	.32
☐ 358	Joe DeMaestri	3.25	1.35	.32
☐ 359	Buddy Gilbert	3.25	1.35	.32
☐ 360	Herb Score	4.50	2.00	.45
☐ 361	Bob Oldis	3.25	1.35	.32
☐ 362	Russ Kemmerer	3.25	1.35	.32
☐ 363	Gene Stephens	3.25	1.35	.32
☐ 364	Paul Foytack	3.25	1.35	.32
☐ 365	Minnie Minoso	5.00	2.25	.50
☐ 366	Dallas Green	9.00	4.00	.90
☐ 367	Bill Tuttle	3.25	1.35	.32
☐ 368	Daryl Spencer	3.25	1.35	.32
☐ 369	Billy Hoeft	3.25	1.35	.32
☐ 370	Bill Skowron	6.50	2.75	.65
☐ 371	Bud Byerly	3.25	1.35	.32
☐ 372	Frank House	3.25	1.35	.32
☐ 373	Don Hoak	4.00	1.75	.40
☐ 374	Bob Buhl	3.25	1.35	.32
☐ 375	Dale Long	4.00	1.75	.40
☐ 376	John Briggs	3.25	1.35	.32
☐ 377	Roger Maris	110.00	50.00	16.50
☐ 378	Stu Miller	3.25	1.35	.32
☐ 379	Red Wilson	3.25	1.35	.32
☐ 380	Bob Shaw	3.25	1.35	.32
☐ 381	Braves Team	7.50	2.50	.50
	(checklist on back)			
☐ 382	Ted Bowsfield	3.25	1.35	.32
☐ 383	Leon Wagner	3.25	1.35	.32
☐ 384	Don Cardwell	3.25	1.35	.32
☐ 385	World Series Game 1	6.00	2.50	.60
	Neal Steals Second			
☐ 386	World Series Game 2	6.00	2.50	.60
	Neal Belts 2nd Homer			
☐ 387	World Series Game 3	6.00	2.50	.60
	Furillo Breaks Game			
☐ 388	World Series Game 4	8.00	3.50	.80
	Hodges' Homer			
☐ 389	World Series Game 5	8.00	3.50	.80
	Luis Swipes Base			
☐ 390	World Series Game 6	6.00	2.50	.60
	Scrambling After Ball			
☐ 391	World Series Summary	6.00	2.50	.60
	The Champs Celebrate			

	#	Player			
☐	392	Tex Clevenger	3.25	1.35	.32
☐	393	Smoky Burgess	4.00	1.75	.40
☐	394	Norm Larker	3.25	1.35	.32
☐	395	Hoyt Wilhelm	12.00	5.25	1.50
☐	396	Steve Bilko	3.25	1.35	.32
☐	397	Don Blasingame	3.25	1.35	.32
☐	398	Mike Cuellar	4.00	1.75	.40
☐	399	Young Hill Stars	4.00	1.75	.40
		Milt Pappas			
		Jack Fisher			
		Jerry Walker			
☐	400	Rocky Colavito	11.00	5.00	1.35
☐	401	Bob Duliba	3.25	1.35	.32
☐	402	Dick Stuart	4.00	1.75	.40
☐	403	Ed Sadowski	3.25	1.35	.32
☐	404	Bob Rush	3.25	1.35	.32
☐	405	Bobby Richardson	6.50	2.75	.65
☐	406	Billy Klaus	3.25	1.35	.32
☐	407	Gary Peters UER	4.00	1.75	.40
		(face actually			
		J.C. Martin)			
☐	408	Carl Furillo	4.50	2.00	.45
☐	409	Ron Samford	3.25	1.35	.32
☐	410	Sam Jones	3.25	1.35	.32
☐	411	Ed Bailey	4.00	1.75	.40
☐	412	Bob Anderson	3.25	1.35	.32
☐	413	Athletics Team	7.00	2.50	.50
		(checklist on back)			
☐	414	Don Williams	3.25	1.35	.32
☐	415	Bob Cerv	4.00	1.75	.40
☐	416	Humberto Robinson	3.25	1.35	.32
☐	417	Chuck Cottier	3.25	1.35	.32
☐	418	Don Mossi	4.00	1.75	.40
☐	419	George Crowe	3.25	1.35	.32
☐	420	Eddie Mathews	32.00	14.25	4.75
☐	421	Duke Maas	3.25	1.35	.32
☐	422	John Powers	3.25	1.35	.32
☐	423	Ed Fitzgerald	3.25	1.35	.32
☐	424	Pete Whisenant	3.25	1.35	.32
☐	425	Johnny Podres	4.50	2.00	.45
☐	426	Ron Jackson	3.25	1.35	.32
☐	427	Al Grunwald	3.25	1.35	.32
☐	428	Al Smith	3.25	1.35	.32
☐	429	AL Kings	5.00	2.25	.50
		Nellie Fox			
		Harvey Kuenn			
☐	430	Art Ditmar	3.25	1.35	.32
☐	431	Andre Rodgers	3.25	1.35	.32
☐	432	Chuck Stobbs	3.25	1.35	.32
☐	433	Irv Noren	3.25	1.35	.32
☐	434	Brooks Lawrence	3.25	1.35	.32
☐	435	Gene Freese	3.25	1.35	.32
☐	436	Marv Throneberry	4.00	1.75	.40
☐	437	Bob Friend	4.00	1.75	.40
☐	438	Jim Coker	3.25	1.35	.32
☐	439	Tom Brewer	3.25	1.35	.32
☐	440	Jim Lemon	4.00	1.75	.40
☐	441	Gary Bell	4.50	2.00	.45
☐	442	Joe Pignatano	4.50	2.00	.45
☐	443	Charley Maxwell	5.00	2.25	.50
☐	444	Jerry Kindall	4.50	2.00	.45
☐	445	Warren Spahn	50.00	22.50	7.50
☐	446	Ellis Burton	4.50	2.00	.45
☐	447	Ray Moore	4.50	2.00	.45
☐	448	Jim Gentile	9.00	4.00	.90
☐	449	Jim Brosnan	5.00	2.25	.50
☐	450	Orlando Cepeda	15.00	6.50	2.15
☐	451	Curt Simmons	5.00	2.25	.50
☐	452	Ray Webster	4.50	2.00	.45
☐	453	Vern Law	6.50	2.75	.65
☐	454	Hal Woodeshick	4.50	2.00	.45
☐	455	Baltimore Coaches	5.50	2.50	.55
		Eddie Robinson			
		Harry Brecheen			
		Luman Harris			
☐	456	Red Sox Coaches	6.50	2.75	.65
		Rudy York			
		Billy Herman			
		Sal Maglie			
		Del Baker			
☐	457	Cubs Coaches	5.50	2.50	.55
		Charlie Root			
		Lou Klein			
		Elvin Tappe			
☐	458	White Sox Coaches	5.50	2.50	.55
		Johnny Cooney			
		Don Gutteridge			
		Tony Cuccinello			
		Ray Berres			
☐	459	Reds Coaches	5.50	2.50	.55
		Reggie Otero			
		Cot Deal			
		Wally Moses			
☐	460	Indians Coaches	6.50	2.75	.65
		Mel Harder			
		Jo-Jo White			
		Bob Lemon			
		Ralph(Red) Kress			
☐	461	Tigers Coaches	6.50	2.75	.65
		Tom Ferrick			
		Luke Appling			
		Billy Hitchcock			
☐	462	Athletics Coaches	5.50	2.50	.55
		Fred Fitzsimmons			
		Don Heffner			
		Walker Cooper			
☐	463	Dodgers Coaches	6.50	2.75	.65
		Bobby Bragan			
		Pete Reiser			
		Joe Becker			
		Greg Mulleavy			
☐	464	Braves Coaches	5.50	2.50	.55
		Bob Scheffing			
		Whitlow Wyatt			
		Andy Pafko			
		George Myatt			
☐	465	Yankees Coaches	13.00	5.75	1.75
		Bill Dickey			
		Ralph Houk			
		Frank Crosetti			
		Ed Lopat			
☐	466	Phillies Coaches	5.50	2.50	.55
		Ken Silvestri			
		Dick Carter			
		Andy Cohen			
☐	467	Pirates Coaches	5.50	2.50	.55
		Mickey Vernon			
		Frank Oceak			
		Sam Narron			
		Bill Burwell			
☐	468	Cardinals Coaches	5.50	2.50	.55
		Johnny Keane			
		Howie Pollet			
		Ray Katt			
		Harry Walker			
☐	469	Giants Coaches	5.50	2.50	.55
		Wes Westrum			
		Salty Parker			
		Bill Posedel			
☐	470	Senators Coaches	5.50	2.50	.55
		Bob Swift			
		Ellis Clary			
		Sam Mele			
☐	471	Ned Garver	4.50	2.00	.45
☐	472	Alvin Dark	5.50	2.50	.55
☐	473	Al Cicotte	4.50	2.00	.45
☐	474	Haywood Sullivan	4.00	1.75	.40
☐	475	Don Drysdale	45.00	20.00	6.75
☐	476	Lou Johnson	5.50	2.50	.55
☐	477	Don Ferrarese	4.50	2.00	.45
☐	478	Frank Torre	5.00	2.25	.50
☐	479	Georges Maranda	4.50	2.00	.45
☐	480	Yogi Berra	70.00	32.00	10.50
☐	481	Wes Stock	4.50	2.00	.45
☐	482	Frank Bolling	4.50	2.00	.45
☐	483	Camilo Pascual	5.00	2.25	.50
☐	484	Pirates Team	21.00	7.00	1.50
		(checklist on back)			
☐	485	Ken Boyer	9.00	4.00	.90
☐	486	Bobby Del Greco	4.50	2.00	.45
☐	487	Tom Sturdivant	4.50	2.00	.45
☐	488	Norm Cash	9.00	4.00	.90
☐	489	Steve Ridzik	4.50	2.00	.45
☐	490	Frank Robinson	55.00	25.00	8.25
☐	491	Mel Roach	4.50	2.00	.45
☐	492	Larry Jackson	4.50	2.00	.45
☐	493	Duke Snider	60.00	27.00	9.00
☐	494	Orioles Team	11.00	4.00	.80
		(checklist on back)			
☐	495	Sherm Lollar	5.50	2.50	.55
☐	496	Bill Virdon	6.00	2.50	.60
☐	497	John Tsitouris	4.50	2.00	.45
☐	498	Al Pilarcik	4.50	2.00	.45
☐	499	Johnny James	4.50	2.00	.45
☐	500	Johnny Temple	5.00	2.25	.50
☐	501	Bob Schmidt	4.50	2.00	.45
☐	502	Jim Bunning	10.00	4.50	1.25
☐	503	Don Lee	4.50	2.00	.45
☐	504	Seth Morehead	4.50	2.00	.45
☐	505	Ted Kluszewski	9.00	4.00	.90
☐	506	Lee Walls	4.50	2.00	.45
☐	507	Dick Stigman	12.00	5.25	1.50
☐	508	Billy Consolo	12.00	5.25	1.50
☐	509	Tommy Davis	24.00	10.50	3.50
☐	510	Jerry Staley	12.00	5.25	1.50
☐	511	Ken Walters	12.00	5.25	1.50
☐	512	Joe Gibbon	12.00	5.25	1.50

		NRMT	VG-E	GOOD
☐ 513	Chicago Cubs Team Card (checklist on back)	32.00	10.00	2.00
☐ 514	Steve Barber	12.00	5.25	1.50
☐ 515	Stan Lopata	12.00	5.25	1.50
☐ 516	Marty Kutyna	12.00	5.25	1.50
☐ 517	Charlie James	12.00	5.25	1.50
☐ 518	Tony Gonzalez	12.00	5.25	1.50
☐ 519	Ed Roebuck	12.00	5.25	1.50
☐ 520	Don Buddin	12.00	5.25	1.50
☐ 521	Mike Lee	12.00	5.25	1.50
☐ 522	Ken Hunt	12.00	5.25	1.50
☐ 523	Clay Dalrymple	12.00	5.25	1.50
☐ 524	Bill Henry	12.00	5.25	1.50
☐ 525	Marv Breeding	12.00	5.25	1.50
☐ 526	Paul Giel	12.00	5.25	1.50
☐ 527	Jose Valdivielso	12.00	5.25	1.50
☐ 528	Ben Johnson	12.00	5.25	1.50
☐ 529	Norm Sherry	14.00	6.25	2.00
☐ 530	Mike McCormick	14.00	6.25	2.00
☐ 531	Sandy Amoros	14.00	6.25	2.00
☐ 532	Mike Garcia	14.00	6.25	2.00
☐ 533	Lu Clinton	12.00	5.25	1.50
☐ 534	Ken MacKenzie	12.00	5.25	1.50
☐ 535	Whitey Lockman	14.00	6.25	2.00
☐ 536	Wynn Hawkins	12.00	5.25	1.50
☐ 537	Boston Red Sox Team Card (checklist on back)	32.00	10.00	2.00
☐ 538	Frank Barnes	12.00	5.25	1.50
☐ 539	Gene Baker	12.00	5.25	1.50
☐ 540	Jerry Walker	12.00	5.25	1.50
☐ 541	Tony Curry	12.00	5.25	1.50
☐ 542	Ken Hamlin	12.00	5.25	1.50
☐ 543	Elio Chacon	12.00	5.25	1.50
☐ 544	Bill Monbouquette	14.00	6.25	2.00
☐ 545	Carl Sawatski	12.00	5.25	1.50
☐ 546	Hank Aguirre	12.00	5.25	1.50
☐ 547	Bob Aspromonte	12.00	5.25	1.50
☐ 548	Don Mincher	14.00	6.25	2.00
☐ 549	John Buzhardt	12.00	5.25	1.50
☐ 550	Jim Landis	12.00	5.25	1.50
☐ 551	Ed Rakow	12.00	5.25	1.50
☐ 552	Walt Bond	12.00	5.25	1.50
☐ 553	Bill Skowron AS	16.00	6.75	2.25
☐ 554	Willie McCovey AS	65.00	29.00	9.75
☐ 555	Nellie Fox AS	18.00	7.50	2.50
☐ 556	Charlie Neal AS	14.00	6.25	2.00
☐ 557	Frank Malzone AS	14.00	6.25	2.00
☐ 558	Eddie Mathews AS	32.00	14.25	4.75
☐ 559	Luis Aparicio AS	21.00	9.00	3.00
☐ 560	Ernie Banks AS	48.00	22.00	6.00
☐ 561	Al Kaline AS	48.00	22.00	6.00
☐ 562	Joe Cunningham AS	14.00	6.25	2.00
☐ 563	Mickey Mantle AS	250.00	110.00	37.50
☐ 564	Willie Mays AS	110.00	50.00	16.50
☐ 565	Roger Maris AS	110.00	50.00	16.50
☐ 566	Hank Aaron AS	110.00	50.00	16.50
☐ 567	Sherm Lollar AS	14.00	6.25	2.00
☐ 568	Del Crandall AS	14.00	6.25	2.00
☐ 569	Camilo Pascual AS	14.00	6.25	2.00
☐ 570	Don Drysdale AS	32.00	14.25	4.75
☐ 571	Billy Pierce AS	14.00	6.25	2.00
☐ 572	Johnny Antonelli AS	25.00	7.50	1.50

1961 Topps

GIL HODGES — Los Angeles Dodgers — First Base-Catcher

The cards in this 587-card set measure 2 1/2" by 3 1/2". In 1961, Topps returned to the vertical obverse format. Introduced for the first time were "League Leaders" (41 to 50) and separate, numbered checklist cards. Two number 463s exist: the Braves team card carrying that number was meant to be number 426. There are three versions of the second series checklist card number 98; the variations are distinguished by the color of the "CHECKLIST" headline on the front of the card, the color of the printing of the card number on the bottom of the reverse, and the presence of the copyright notice running vertically on the card back. There are two groups of managers (131-139 and 219-226) as well as separate series of World Series cards (306-313), Baseball Thrills (401 to 410), previous MVP's (AL 471-478 and NL 479-486) and Sporting News All-Stars (566 to 589). The usual last series scarcity (523 to 589) exists. The set actually totals 587 cards since numbers 587 and 588 were never issued. The key rookies in this set are ex-Cubs Ron Santo and Billy Williams.

		NRMT	VG-E	GOOD
COMPLETE SET (587)		5750.00	2400.00	600.00
COMMON PLAYER (1-110)		2.50	1.00	.25
COMMON PLAYER (111-370)		3.00	1.25	.30
COMMON PLAYER (371-446)		3.50	1.50	.35
COMMON PLAYER (447-522)		4.75	2.00	.45
COMMON PLAYER (523-565)		30.00	13.50	4.50
COMMON PLAYER (566-589)		33.00	15.00	5.00
☐ 1	Dick Groat	20.00	2.50	.50
☐ 2	Roger Maris	160.00	40.00	8.00
☐ 3	John Buzhardt	2.50	1.00	.25
☐ 4	Lenny Green	2.50	1.00	.25
☐ 5	John Romano	2.50	1.00	.25
☐ 6	Ed Roebuck	2.50	1.00	.25
☐ 7	White Sox Team	6.00	2.50	.60
☐ 8	Dick Williams	3.00	1.25	.30
☐ 9	Bob Purkey	2.50	1.00	.25
☐ 10	Brooks Robinson	32.00	14.25	4.75
☐ 11	Curt Simmons	3.00	1.25	.30
☐ 12	Moe Thacker	2.50	1.00	.25
☐ 13	Chuck Cottier	2.50	1.00	.25
☐ 14	Don Mossi	3.00	1.25	.30
☐ 15	Willie Kirkland	2.50	1.00	.25
☐ 16	Billy Muffett	2.50	1.00	.25
☐ 17	Checklist 1	10.00	1.00	.20
☐ 18	Jim Grant	2.50	1.00	.25
☐ 19	Clete Boyer	3.50	1.50	.35
☐ 20	Robin Roberts	11.00	5.00	1.35
☐ 21	Zorro Versalles UER (first name should be Zoilo)	4.00	1.75	.40
☐ 22	Clem Labine	3.00	1.25	.30
☐ 23	Don Demeter	2.50	1.00	.25
☐ 24	Ken Johnson	2.50	1.00	.25
☐ 25	Reds' Heavy Artillery Vada Pinson Gus Bell Frank Robinson	5.50	2.50	.55
☐ 26	Wes Stock	2.50	1.00	.25
☐ 27	Jerry Kindall	2.50	1.00	.25
☐ 28	Hector Lopez	2.50	1.00	.25
☐ 29	Don Nottebart	2.50	1.00	.25
☐ 30	Nellie Fox	7.00	3.00	.70
☐ 31	Bob Schmidt	2.50	1.00	.25
☐ 32	Ray Sadecki	2.50	1.00	.25
☐ 33	Gary Geiger	2.50	1.00	.25
☐ 34	Wynn Hawkins	2.50	1.00	.25
☐ 35	Ron Santo	42.00	18.00	5.50
☐ 36	Jack Kralick	2.50	1.00	.25
☐ 37	Charley Maxwell	2.50	1.00	.25
☐ 38	Bob Lillis	2.50	1.00	.25
☐ 39	Leo Posada	2.50	1.00	.25
☐ 40	Bob Turley	3.50	1.50	.35
☐ 41	NL Batting Leaders Dick Groat Norm Larker Willie Mays Roberto Clemente	7.00	3.00	.70
☐ 42	AL Batting Leaders Pete Runnels Al Smith Minnie Minoso Bill Skowron	4.00	1.75	.40
☐ 43	NL Home Run Leaders Ernie Banks Hank Aaron Ed Mathews Ken Boyer	9.00	4.00	.90

☐ 44	AL Home Run Leaders	25.00	11.00	3.50
	Mickey Mantle			
	Roger Maris			
	Jim Lemon			
	Rocky Colavito			
☐ 45	NL ERA Leaders	4.00	1.75	.40
	Mike McCormick			
	Ernie Broglio			
	Don Drysdale			
	Bob Friend			
	Stan Williams			
☐ 46	AL ERA Leaders	4.00	1.75	.40
	Frank Baumann			
	Jim Bunning			
	Art Ditmar			
	Hal Brown			
☐ 47	NL Pitching Leaders	4.50	2.00	.45
	Ernie Broglio			
	Warren Spahn			
	Vern Law			
	Lou Burdette			
☐ 48	AL Pitching Leaders	4.00	1.75	.40
	Chuck Estrada			
	Jim Perry			
	Bud Daley			
	Art Ditmar			
	Frank Lary			
	Milt Pappas			
☐ 49	NL Strikeout Leaders	6.00	2.50	.60
	Don Drysdale			
	Sandy Koufax			
	Sam Jones			
	Ernie Broglio			
☐ 50	AL Strikeout Leaders	4.50	2.00	.45
	Jim Bunning			
	Pedro Ramos			
	Early Wynn			
	Frank Lary			
☐ 51	Detroit Tigers	6.00	2.50	.60
	Team Card			
☐ 52	George Crowe	2.50	1.00	.25
☐ 53	Russ Nixon	2.50	1.00	.25
☐ 54	Earl Francis	2.50	1.00	.25
☐ 55	Jim Davenport	2.50	1.00	.25
☐ 56	Russ Kemmerer	2.50	1.00	.25
☐ 57	Marv Throneberry	3.50	1.50	.35
☐ 58	Joe Schaffernoth	2.50	1.00	.25
☐ 59	Jim Woods	2.50	1.00	.25
☐ 60	Woody Held	2.50	1.00	.25
☐ 61	Ron Piche	2.50	1.00	.25
☐ 62	Al Pilarcik	2.50	1.00	.25
☐ 63	Jim Kaat	8.00	3.50	.80
☐ 64	Alex Grammas	2.50	1.00	.25
☐ 65	Ted Kluszewski	5.00	2.25	.50
☐ 66	Bill Henry	2.50	1.00	.25
☐ 67	Ossie Virgil	2.50	1.00	.25
☐ 68	Deron Johnson	3.00	1.25	.30
☐ 69	Earl Wilson	2.50	1.00	.25
☐ 70	Bill Virdon	3.50	1.50	.35
☐ 71	Jerry Adair	2.50	1.00	.25
☐ 72	Stu Miller	2.50	1.00	.25
☐ 73	Al Spangler	2.50	1.00	.25
☐ 74	Joe Pignatano	2.50	1.00	.25
☐ 75	Lindy Shows Larry	3.00	1.25	.30
	Lindy McDaniel			
	Larry Jackson			
☐ 76	Harry Anderson	2.50	1.00	.25
☐ 77	Dick Stigman	2.50	1.00	.25
☐ 78	Lee Walls	2.50	1.00	.25
☐ 79	Joe Ginsberg	2.50	1.00	.25
☐ 80	Harmon Killebrew	21.00	9.00	3.00
☐ 81	Tracy Stallard	3.00	1.25	.30
☐ 82	Joe Christopher	2.50	1.00	.25
☐ 83	Bob Bruce	2.50	1.00	.25
☐ 84	Lee Maye	2.50	1.00	.25
☐ 85	Jerry Walker	2.50	1.00	.25
☐ 86	Los Angeles Dodgers	6.00	2.50	.60
	Team Card			
☐ 87	Joe Amalfitano	2.50	1.00	.25
☐ 88	Richie Ashburn	7.00	3.00	.70
☐ 89	Billy Martin	8.00	3.50	.80
☐ 90	Jerry Staley	2.50	1.00	.25
☐ 91	Walt Moryn	2.50	1.00	.25
☐ 92	Hal Naragon	2.50	1.00	.25
☐ 93	Tony Gonzalez	2.50	1.00	.25
☐ 94	Johnny Kucks	2.50	1.00	.25
☐ 95	Norm Cash	5.00	2.25	.50
☐ 96	Billy O'Dell	2.50	1.00	.25
☐ 97	Jerry Lynch	2.50	1.00	.25
☐ 98A	Checklist 2	10.00	1.00	.20
	(red "Checklist",			
	98 black on white)			
☐ 98B	Checklist 2	10.00	1.00	.20
	(yellow "Checklist",			
	98 black on white)			

☐ 98C	Checklist 2	10.00	1.00	.20
	(yellow "Checklist",			
	98 white on black,			
	no copyright)			
☐ 99	Don Buddin UER	2.50	1.00	.25
	(66 HR's)			
☐ 100	Harvey Haddix	3.50	1.50	.35
☐ 101	Bubba Phillips	2.50	1.00	.25
☐ 102	Gene Stephens	2.50	1.00	.25
☐ 103	Ruben Amaro	2.50	1.00	.25
☐ 104	John Blanchard	3.00	1.25	.30
☐ 105	Carl Willey	2.50	1.00	.25
☐ 106	Whitey Herzog	4.00	1.75	.40
☐ 107	Seth Morehead	2.50	1.00	.25
☐ 108	Dan Dobbek	2.50	1.00	.25
☐ 109	Johnny Podres	3.50	1.50	.35
☐ 110	Vada Pinson	4.00	1.75	.40
☐ 111	Jack Meyer	3.00	1.25	.30
☐ 112	Chico Fernandez	3.00	1.25	.30
☐ 113	Mike Fornieles	3.00	1.25	.30
☐ 114	Hobie Landrith	3.00	1.25	.30
☐ 115	Johnny Antonelli	3.50	1.50	.35
☐ 116	Joe DeMaestri	3.00	1.25	.30
☐ 117	Dale Long	3.50	1.50	.35
☐ 118	Chris Cannizzaro	3.00	1.25	.30
☐ 119	A's Big Armor	3.50	1.50	.35
	Norm Siebern			
	Hank Bauer			
	Jerry Lumpe			
☐ 120	Eddie Mathews	25.00	11.00	3.50
☐ 121	Eli Grba	3.00	1.25	.30
☐ 122	Chicago Cubs	6.00	2.50	.60
	Team Card			
☐ 123	Billy Gardner	3.00	1.25	.30
☐ 124	J.C. Martin	3.00	1.25	.30
☐ 125	Steve Barber	3.00	1.25	.30
☐ 126	Dick Stuart	3.50	1.50	.35
☐ 127	Ron Kline	3.00	1.25	.30
☐ 128	Rip Repulski	3.00	1.25	.30
☐ 129	Ed Hobaugh	3.00	1.25	.30
☐ 130	Norm Larker	3.50	1.50	.35
☐ 131	Paul Richards MG	3.50	1.50	.35
☐ 132	Al Lopez MG	4.50	2.00	.45
☐ 133	Ralph Houk MG	4.00	1.75	.40
☐ 134	Mickey Vernon MG	3.50	1.50	.35
☐ 135	Fred Hutchinson MG	3.50	1.50	.35
☐ 136	Walt Alston MG	5.50	2.50	.55
☐ 137	Chuck Dressen MG	3.50	1.50	.35
☐ 138	Danny Murtaugh MG	3.00	1.25	.30
☐ 139	Solly Hemus MG	3.00	1.25	.30
☐ 140	Gus Triandos	3.50	1.50	.35
☐ 141	Billy Williams	100.00	45.00	15.00
☐ 142	Luis Arroyo	3.50	1.50	.35
☐ 143	Russ Snyder	3.00	1.25	.30
☐ 144	Jim Coker	3.00	1.25	.30
☐ 145	Bob Buhl	3.00	1.25	.30
☐ 146	Marty Keough	3.00	1.25	.30
☐ 147	Ed Rakow	3.00	1.25	.30
☐ 148	Julian Javier	3.50	1.50	.35
☐ 149	Bob Oldis	3.00	1.25	.30
☐ 150	Willie Mays	110.00	50.00	16.50
☐ 151	Jim Donohue	3.00	1.25	.30
☐ 152	Earl Torgeson	3.00	1.25	.30
☐ 153	Don Lee	3.00	1.25	.30
☐ 154	Bobby Del Greco	3.00	1.25	.30
☐ 155	Johnny Temple	3.00	1.25	.30
☐ 156	Ken Hunt	3.00	1.25	.30
☐ 157	Cal McLish	3.00	1.25	.30
☐ 158	Pete Daley	3.00	1.25	.30
☐ 159	Orioles Team	6.00	2.50	.60
☐ 160	Whitey Ford UER	36.00	16.25	5.50
	(incorrectly listed			
	as 5'0" tall)			
☐ 161	Sherman Jones UER	3.00	1.25	.30
	(photo actually			
	Eddie Fisher)			
☐ 162	Jay Hook	3.00	1.25	.30
☐ 163	Ed Sadowski	3.00	1.25	.30
☐ 164	Felix Mantilla	3.00	1.25	.30
☐ 165	Gino Cimoli	3.00	1.25	.30
☐ 166	Danny Kravitz	3.00	1.25	.30
☐ 167	San Francisco Giants	6.00	2.50	.60
	Team Card			
☐ 168	Tommy Davis	5.00	2.25	.50
☐ 169	Don Elston	3.00	1.25	.30
☐ 170	Al Smith	3.00	1.25	.30
☐ 171	Paul Foytack	3.00	1.25	.30
☐ 172	Don Dillard	3.00	1.25	.30
☐ 173	Beantown Bombers	3.50	1.50	.35
	Frank Malzone			
	Vic Wertz			
	Jackie Jensen			
☐ 174	Ray Semproch	3.00	1.25	.30
☐ 175	Gene Freese	3.00	1.25	.30

☐ 176	Ken Aspromonte	3.00	1.25	.30
☐ 177	Don Larsen	3.50	1.50	.35
☐ 178	Bob Nieman	3.00	1.25	.30
☐ 179	Joe Koppe	3.00	1.25	.30
☐ 180	Bobby Richardson	6.50	2.75	.65
☐ 181	Fred Green	3.00	1.25	.30
☐ 182	Dave Nicholson	3.00	1.25	.30
☐ 183	Andre Rodgers	3.00	1.25	.30
☐ 184	Steve Bilko	3.00	1.25	.30
☐ 185	Herb Score	4.00	1.75	.40
☐ 186	Elmer Valo	3.00	1.25	.30
☐ 187	Billy Klaus	3.00	1.25	.30
☐ 188	Jim Marshall	3.00	1.25	.30
☐ 189A	Checklist 3 (copyright symbol almost adjacent to 263 Ken Hamlin)	10.00	1.00	.20
☐ 189B	Checklist 3 (copyright symbol adjacent to 264 Glen Hobbie)	10.00	1.00	.20
☐ 190	Stan Williams	3.00	1.25	.30
☐ 191	Mike De La Hoz	3.00	1.25	.30
☐ 192	Dick Brown	3.00	1.25	.30
☐ 193	Gene Conley	3.00	1.25	.30
☐ 194	Gordy Coleman	3.50	1.50	.35
☐ 195	Jerry Casale	3.00	1.25	.30
☐ 196	Ed Bouchee	3.00	1.25	.30
☐ 197	Dick Hall	3.00	1.25	.30
☐ 198	Carl Sawatski	3.00	1.25	.30
☐ 199	Bob Boyd	3.00	1.25	.30
☐ 200	Warren Spahn	30.00	13.50	4.50
☐ 201	Pete Whisenant	3.00	1.25	.30
☐ 202	Al Neiger	3.00	1.25	.30
☐ 203	Eddie Bressoud	3.00	1.25	.30
☐ 204	Bob Skinner	3.50	1.50	.35
☐ 205	Billy Pierce	4.00	1.75	.40
☐ 206	Gene Green	3.00	1.25	.30
☐ 207	Dodger Southpaws Sandy Koufax Johnny Podres	18.00	7.50	2.50
☐ 208	Larry Osborne	3.00	1.25	.30
☐ 209	Ken McBride	3.00	1.25	.30
☐ 210	Pete Runnels	3.50	1.50	.35
☐ 211	Bob Gibson	40.00	18.00	6.00
☐ 212	Haywood Sullivan	3.50	1.50	.35
☐ 213	Bill Stafford	3.00	1.25	.30
☐ 214	Danny Murphy	3.00	1.25	.30
☐ 215	Gus Bell	3.50	1.50	.35
☐ 216	Ted Bowsfield	3.00	1.25	.30
☐ 217	Mel Roach	3.00	1.25	.30
☐ 218	Hal Brown	3.00	1.25	.30
☐ 219	Gene Mauch MG	3.50	1.50	.35
☐ 220	Alvin Dark MG	3.50	1.50	.35
☐ 221	Mike Higgins MG	3.00	1.25	.30
☐ 222	Jimmy Dykes MG	3.50	1.50	.35
☐ 223	Bob Scheffing MG	3.00	1.25	.30
☐ 224	Joe Gordon MG	3.50	1.50	.35
☐ 225	Bill Rigney MG	3.00	1.25	.30
☐ 226	Harry Lavagetto MG	3.00	1.25	.30
☐ 227	Juan Pizarro	3.00	1.25	.30
☐ 228	New York Yankees Team Card	22.00	9.50	3.15
☐ 229	Rudy Hernandez	3.00	1.25	.30
☐ 230	Don Hoak	3.50	1.50	.35
☐ 231	Dick Drott	3.00	1.25	.30
☐ 232	Bill White	5.00	2.25	.50
☐ 233	Joey Jay	3.00	1.25	.30
☐ 234	Ted Lepcio	3.00	1.25	.30
☐ 235	Camilo Pascual	3.50	1.50	.35
☐ 236	Don Gile	3.00	1.25	.30
☐ 237	Billy Loes	3.00	1.25	.30
☐ 238	Jim Gilliam	4.00	1.75	.40
☐ 239	Dave Sisler	3.00	1.25	.30
☐ 240	Ron Hansen	3.00	1.25	.30
☐ 241	Al Cicotte	3.00	1.25	.30
☐ 242	Hal Smith	3.00	1.25	.30
☐ 243	Frank Lary	3.50	1.50	.35
☐ 244	Chico Cardenas	3.50	1.50	.35
☐ 245	Joe Adcock	3.50	1.50	.35
☐ 246	Bob Davis	3.00	1.25	.30
☐ 247	Billy Goodman	3.00	1.25	.30
☐ 248	Ed Keegan	3.00	1.25	.30
☐ 249	Cincinnati Reds Team Card	6.00	2.50	.60
☐ 250	Buc Hill Aces Vern Law Roy Face	3.50	1.50	.35
☐ 251	Bill Bruton	3.00	1.25	.30
☐ 252	Bill Short	3.00	1.25	.30
☐ 253	Sammy Taylor	3.00	1.25	.30
☐ 254	Ted Sadowski	3.00	1.25	.30
☐ 255	Vic Power	3.00	1.25	.30
☐ 256	Billy Hoeft	3.00	1.25	.30
☐ 257	Carroll Hardy	3.00	1.25	.30
☐ 258	Jack Sanford	3.00	1.25	.30
☐ 259	John Schaive	3.00	1.25	.30
☐ 260	Don Drysdale	25.00	11.00	3.50
☐ 261	Charlie Lau	3.50	1.50	.35
☐ 262	Tony Curry	3.00	1.25	.30
☐ 263	Ken Hamlin	3.00	1.25	.30
☐ 264	Glen Hobbie	3.00	1.25	.30
☐ 265	Tony Kubek	7.50	3.25	.75
☐ 266	Lindy McDaniel	3.50	1.50	.35
☐ 267	Norm Siebern	3.00	1.25	.30
☐ 268	Ike Delock	3.00	1.25	.30
☐ 269	Harry Chiti	3.00	1.25	.30
☐ 270	Bob Friend	3.50	1.50	.35
☐ 271	Jim Landis	3.00	1.25	.30
☐ 272	Tom Morgan	3.00	1.25	.30
☐ 273A	Checklist 4 (copyright symbol adjacent to 336 Don Mincher)	15.00	1.50	.30
☐ 273B	Checklist 4 (copyright symbol adjacent to 339 Gene Baker)	10.00	1.00	.20
☐ 274	Gary Bell	3.00	1.25	.30
☐ 275	Gene Woodling	3.50	1.50	.35
☐ 276	Ray Rippelmeyer	3.00	1.25	.30
☐ 277	Hank Foiles	3.00	1.25	.30
☐ 278	Don McMahon	3.00	1.25	.30
☐ 279	Jose Pagan	3.00	1.25	.30
☐ 280	Frank Howard	4.50	2.00	.45
☐ 281	Frank Sullivan	3.00	1.25	.30
☐ 282	Faye Throneberry	3.00	1.25	.30
☐ 283	Bob Anderson	3.00	1.25	.30
☐ 284	Dick Gernert	3.00	1.25	.30
☐ 285	Sherm Lollar	3.50	1.50	.35
☐ 286	George Witt	3.00	1.25	.30
☐ 287	Carl Yastrzemski	140.00	63.00	21.00
☐ 288	Albie Pearson	3.00	1.25	.30
☐ 289	Ray Moore	3.00	1.25	.30
☐ 290	Stan Musial	95.00	42.00	11.00
☐ 291	Tex Clevenger	3.00	1.25	.30
☐ 292	Jim Baumer	3.00	1.25	.30
☐ 293	Tom Sturdivant	3.00	1.25	.30
☐ 294	Don Blasingame	3.00	1.25	.30
☐ 295	Milt Pappas	3.50	1.50	.35
☐ 296	Wes Covington	3.50	1.50	.35
☐ 297	Athletics Team	6.00	2.50	.60
☐ 298	Jim Golden	3.00	1.25	.30
☐ 299	Clay Dalrymple	3.00	1.25	.30
☐ 300	Mickey Mantle	350.00	160.00	52.50
☐ 301	Chet Nichols	3.00	1.25	.30
☐ 302	Al Heist	3.00	1.25	.30
☐ 303	Gary Peters	3.50	1.50	.35
☐ 304	Rocky Nelson	3.00	1.25	.30
☐ 305	Mike McCormick	3.50	1.50	.35
☐ 306	World Series Game 1 Virdon Saves Game	7.00	3.00	.70
☐ 307	World Series Game 2 Mantle 2 Homers	32.00	14.25	4.75
☐ 308	World Series Game 3 Richardson is Hero	8.00	3.50	.80
☐ 309	World Series Game 4 Cimoli Safe	7.00	3.00	.70
☐ 310	World Series Game 5 Face Saves the Day	8.00	3.50	.80
☐ 311	World Series Game 6 Ford Second Shutout	9.00	4.00	.90
☐ 312	World Series Game 7 Mazeroski's Homer	10.00	4.50	1.25
☐ 313	World Series Summary Pirates Celebrate	7.00	3.00	.70
☐ 314	Bob Miller	3.00	1.25	.30
☐ 315	Earl Battey	3.00	1.25	.30
☐ 316	Bobby Gene Smith	3.00	1.25	.30
☐ 317	Jim Brewer	3.00	1.25	.30
☐ 318	Danny O'Connell	3.00	1.25	.30
☐ 319	Valmy Thomas	3.00	1.25	.30
☐ 320	Lou Burdette	4.00	1.75	.40
☐ 321	Marv Breeding	3.00	1.25	.30
☐ 322	Bill Kunkel	3.50	1.50	.35
☐ 323	Sammy Esposito	3.00	1.25	.30
☐ 324	Hank Aguirre	3.00	1.25	.30
☐ 325	Wally Moon	3.50	1.50	.35
☐ 326	Dave Hillman	3.00	1.25	.30
☐ 327	Matty Alou	5.50	2.50	.55
☐ 328	Jim O'Toole	3.50	1.50	.35
☐ 329	Julio Becquer	3.00	1.25	.30
☐ 330	Rocky Colavito	10.00	4.50	1.25
☐ 331	Ned Garver	3.00	1.25	.30
☐ 332	Dutch Dotterer UER (photo actually Tommy Dotterer, Dutch's brother)	3.00	1.25	.30

#	Player			
333	Fritz Brickell	3.00	1.25	.30
334	Walt Bond	3.00	1.25	.30
335	Frank Bolling	3.00	1.25	.30
336	Don Mincher	3.50	1.50	.35
337	Al's Aces	5.00	2.25	.50
	Early Wynn			
	Al Lopez			
	Herb Score			
338	Don Landrum	3.00	1.25	.30
339	Gene Baker	3.00	1.25	.30
340	Vic Wertz	3.50	1.50	.35
341	Jim Owens	3.00	1.25	.30
342	Clint Courtney	3.00	1.25	.30
343	Earl Robinson	3.00	1.25	.30
344	Sandy Koufax	100.00	45.00	15.00
345	Jim Piersall	4.00	1.75	.40
346	Howie Nunn	3.00	1.25	.30
347	St. Louis Cardinals	6.00	2.50	.60
	Team Card			
348	Steve Boros	3.00	1.25	.30
349	Danny McDevitt	3.00	1.25	.30
350	Ernie Banks	38.00	17.00	5.00
351	Jim King	3.00	1.25	.30
352	Bob Shaw	3.00	1.25	.30
353	Howie Bedell	3.00	1.25	.30
354	Billy Harrell	3.00	1.25	.30
355	Bob Allison	3.50	1.50	.35
356	Ryne Duren	3.50	1.50	.35
357	Daryl Spencer	3.00	1.25	.30
358	Earl Averill	3.00	1.25	.30
359	Dallas Green	4.00	1.75	.40
360	Frank Robinson	42.00	18.00	5.50
361A	Checklist 5	10.00	1.00	.20
	(no ad on back)			
361B	Checklist 5	15.00	1.50	.30
	(Special Feature			
	ad on back)			
362	Frank Funk	3.00	1.25	.30
363	John Roseboro	3.50	1.50	.35
364	Moe Drabowsky	3.00	1.25	.30
365	Jerry Lumpe	3.00	1.25	.30
366	Eddie Fisher	3.00	1.25	.30
367	Jim Rivera	3.00	1.25	.30
368	Bennie Daniels	3.00	1.25	.30
369	Dave Philley	3.00	1.25	.30
370	Roy Face	4.50	2.00	.45
371	Bill Skowron SP	35.00	15.75	5.25
372	Bob Hendley	3.50	1.50	.35
373	Boston Red Sox	7.50	3.25	.75
	Team Card			
374	Paul Giel	3.50	1.50	.35
375	Ken Boyer	5.50	2.50	.55
376	Mike Roarke	3.50	1.50	.35
377	Ruben Gomez	3.50	1.50	.35
378	Wally Post	4.00	1.75	.40
379	Bobby Shantz	4.50	2.00	.45
380	Minnie Minoso	5.00	2.25	.50
381	Dave Wickersham	3.50	1.50	.35
382	Frank Thomas	4.00	1.75	.40
383	Frisco First Liners	4.00	1.75	.40
	Mike McCormick			
	Jack Sanford			
	Billy O'Dell			
384	Chuck Essegian	3.50	1.50	.35
385	Jim Perry	4.50	2.00	.45
386	Joe Hicks	3.50	1.50	.35
387	Duke Maas	3.50	1.50	.35
388	Bob Clemente	95.00	42.00	11.00
389	Ralph Terry	4.50	2.00	.45
390	Del Crandall	4.00	1.75	.40
391	Winston Brown	3.50	1.50	.35
392	Reno Bertoia	3.50	1.50	.35
393	Batter Bafflers	3.50	1.50	.35
	Don Cardwell			
	Glen Hobbie			
394	Ken Walters	3.50	1.50	.35
395	Chuck Estrada	4.00	1.75	.40
396	Bob Aspromonte	3.50	1.50	.35
397	Hal Woodeshick	3.50	1.50	.35
398	Hank Bauer	4.50	2.00	.45
399	Cliff Cook	3.50	1.50	.35
400	Vern Law	4.50	2.00	.45
401	Ruth 60th Homer	25.00	11.00	3.50
402	Perfect Game	18.00	7.50	2.50
	(Don Larsen)			
403	26 Inning Tie	6.00	2.50	.60
404	Hornsby .424 Average	8.00	3.50	.80
405	Gehrig's Streak	18.00	7.50	2.50
406	Mantle 565 Ft. Homer	45.00	20.00	6.75
407	Chesbro Wins 41	6.00	2.50	.60
408	Mathewson Fans 267	9.00	4.00	.90
409	Johnson Shutouts	9.00	4.00	.90
410	Haddix 12 Perfect	6.00	2.50	.60
	Innings			
411	Tony Taylor	3.50	1.50	.35
412	Larry Sherry	4.00	1.75	.40
413	Eddie Yost	3.50	1.50	.35
414	Dick Donovan	3.50	1.50	.35
415	Hank Aaron	125.00	57.50	18.75
416	Dick Howser	8.00	3.50	.80
417	Juan Marichal	145.00	65.00	18.00
418	Ed Bailey	4.00	1.75	.40
419	Tom Borland	3.50	1.50	.35
420	Ernie Broglio	4.00	1.75	.40
421	Ty Cline	3.50	1.50	.35
422	Bud Daley	3.50	1.50	.35
423	Charlie Neal SP	9.00	4.00	.90
424	Turk Lown	3.50	1.50	.35
425	Yogi Berra	75.00	34.00	11.25
426	Milwaukee Braves	9.00	4.00	.90
	Team Card			
	(back numbered 463)			
427	Dick Ellsworth	4.00	1.75	.40
428	Ray Barker SP	9.00	4.00	.90
429	Al Kaline	45.00	20.00	6.75
430	Bill Mazeroski SP	33.00	15.00	5.00
431	Chuck Stobbs	3.50	1.50	.35
432	Coot Veal	3.50	1.50	.35
433	Art Mahaffey	3.50	1.50	.35
434	Tom Brewer	3.50	1.50	.35
435	Orlando Cepeda UER	10.00	4.50	1.25
	(San Francis on			
	card front)			
436	Jim Maloney	7.50	3.25	.75
437A	Checklist 6	15.00	1.50	.30
	440 Louis Aparicio			
437B	Checklist 6	15.00	1.50	.30
	440 Luis Aparicio			
438	Curt Flood	5.00	2.25	.50
439	Phil Regan	5.00	2.25	.50
440	Luis Aparicio	13.00	5.75	1.75
441	Dick Bertell	3.50	1.50	.35
442	Gordon Jones	3.50	1.50	.35
443	Duke Snider	45.00	20.00	6.75
444	Joe Nuxhall	4.00	1.75	.40
445	Frank Malzone	4.00	1.75	.40
446	Bob Taylor	3.50	1.50	.35
447	Harry Bright	4.75	2.00	.45
448	Del Rice	4.75	2.00	.45
449	Bob Bolin	4.75	2.00	.45
450	Jim Lemon	5.50	2.50	.55
451	Power for Ernie	5.50	2.50	.55
	Daryl Spencer			
	Bill White			
	Ernie Broglio			
452	Bob Allen	4.75	2.00	.45
453	Dick Schofield	4.75	2.00	.45
454	Pumpsie Green	4.75	2.00	.45
455	Early Wynn	13.50	6.00	1.85
456	Hal Bevan	4.75	2.00	.45
457	Johnny James	4.75	2.00	.45
	(listed as Angel,			
	but wearing Yankee			
	uniform and cap)			
458	Willie Tasby	4.75	2.00	.45
459	Terry Fox	4.75	2.00	.45
460	Gil Hodges	15.00	6.50	2.15
461	Smoky Burgess	5.50	2.50	.55
462	Lou Klimchock	4.75	2.00	.45
463	Jack Fisher	5.50	2.50	.55
	(See also 426)			
464	Lee Thomas	5.50	2.50	.55
	(Pictured with Yankee			
	cap but listed as			
	Los Angeles Angel)			
465	Roy McMillan	4.75	2.00	.45
466	Ron Moeller	4.75	2.00	.45
467	Cleveland Indians	9.00	4.00	.90
	Team Card			
468	John Callison	5.50	2.50	.55
469	Ralph Lumenti	4.75	2.00	.45
470	Roy Sievers	5.50	2.50	.55
471	Phil Rizzuto MVP	16.00	6.75	2.25
472	Yogi Berra MVP	48.00	22.00	6.00
473	Bob Shantz MVP	5.50	2.50	.55
474	Al Rosen MVP	6.50	2.75	.65
475	Mickey Mantle MVP	110.00	50.00	16.50
476	Jackie Jensen MVP	5.50	2.50	.55
477	Nellie Fox MVP	7.50	3.25	.75
478	Roger Maris MVP	40.00	18.00	6.00
479	Jim Konstanty MVP	5.50	2.50	.55
480	Roy Campanella MVP	30.00	13.50	4.50
481	Hank Sauer MVP	5.50	2.50	.55
482	Willie Mays MVP	42.00	18.00	5.50
483	Don Newcombe MVP	6.50	2.75	.65
484	Hank Aaron MVP	42.00	18.00	5.50
485	Ernie Banks MVP	25.00	11.00	3.50
486	Dick Groat MVP	5.50	2.50	.55

		NRMT	VG-E	GOOD
☐ 487	Gene Oliver	4.75	2.00	.45
☐ 488	Joe McClain	4.75	2.00	.45
☐ 489	Walt Dropo	4.75	2.00	.45
☐ 490	Jim Bunning	9.00	4.00	.90
☐ 491	Philadelphia Phillies Team Card	9.00	4.00	.90
☐ 492	Ron Fairly	5.50	2.50	.55
☐ 493	Don Zimmer UER (Brooklyn A.L.)	6.50	2.75	.65
☐ 494	Tom Cheney	4.75	2.00	.45
☐ 495	Elston Howard	8.50	3.75	.85
☐ 496	Ken MacKenzie	4.75	2.00	.45
☐ 497	Willie Jones	4.75	2.00	.45
☐ 498	Ray Herbert	4.75	2.00	.45
☐ 499	Chuck Schilling	4.75	2.00	.45
☐ 500	Harvey Kuenn	6.50	2.75	.65
☐ 501	John DeMerit	4.75	2.00	.45
☐ 502	Clarence Coleman	6.50	2.75	.65
☐ 503	Tito Francona	4.75	2.00	.45
☐ 504	Billy Consolo	4.75	2.00	.45
☐ 505	Red Schoendienst	15.00	6.50	2.15
☐ 506	Willie Davis	15.00	6.50	2.15
☐ 507	Pete Burnside	4.75	2.00	.45
☐ 508	Rocky Bridges	4.75	2.00	.45
☐ 509	Camilo Carreon	4.75	2.00	.45
☐ 510	Art Ditmar	4.75	2.00	.45
☐ 511	Joe M. Morgan	5.50	2.50	.55
☐ 512	Bob Will	4.75	2.00	.45
☐ 513	Jim Brosnan	5.50	2.50	.55
☐ 514	Jake Wood	4.75	2.00	.45
☐ 515	Jackie Brandt	4.75	2.00	.45
☐ 516	Checklist 7	15.00	1.50	.30
☐ 517	Willie McCovey	55.00	25.00	8.25
☐ 518	Andy Carey	5.50	2.50	.55
☐ 519	Jim Pagliaroni	4.75	2.00	.45
☐ 520	Joe Cunningham	5.50	2.50	.55
☐ 521	Brother Battery Norm Sherry Larry Sherry	5.50	2.50	.55
☐ 522	Dick Farrell	5.50	2.50	.55
☐ 523	Joe Gibbon	30.00	13.50	4.50
☐ 524	Johnny Logan	33.00	15.00	5.00
☐ 525	Ron Perranoski	36.00	16.25	5.50
☐ 526	R.C. Stevens	30.00	13.50	4.50
☐ 527	Gene Leek	30.00	13.50	4.50
☐ 528	Pedro Ramos	30.00	13.50	4.50
☐ 529	Bob Roselli	30.00	13.50	4.50
☐ 530	Bob Malkmus	30.00	13.50	4.50
☐ 531	Jim Coates	30.00	13.50	4.50
☐ 532	Bob Hale	30.00	13.50	4.50
☐ 533	Jack Curtis	30.00	13.50	4.50
☐ 534	Eddie Kasko	30.00	13.50	4.50
☐ 535	Larry Jackson	30.00	13.50	4.50
☐ 536	Bill Tuttle	30.00	13.50	4.50
☐ 537	Bobby Locke	30.00	13.50	4.50
☐ 538	Chuck Hiller	30.00	13.50	4.50
☐ 539	Johnny Klippstein	30.00	13.50	4.50
☐ 540	Jackie Jensen	36.00	16.25	5.50
☐ 541	Roland Sheldon	30.00	13.50	4.50
☐ 542	Minnesota Twins Team Card	65.00	29.00	9.75
☐ 543	Roger Craig	36.00	16.25	5.50
☐ 544	George Thomas	30.00	13.50	4.50
☐ 545	Hoyt Wilhelm	60.00	27.00	9.00
☐ 546	Marty Kutyna	30.00	13.50	4.50
☐ 547	Leon Wagner	30.00	13.50	4.50
☐ 548	Ted Wills	30.00	13.50	4.50
☐ 549	Hal R. Smith	30.00	13.50	4.50
☐ 550	Frank Baumann	30.00	13.50	4.50
☐ 551	George Altman	30.00	13.50	4.50
☐ 552	Jim Archer	30.00	13.50	4.50
☐ 553	Bill Fischer	30.00	13.50	4.50
☐ 554	Pittsburgh Pirates Team Card	65.00	29.00	9.75
☐ 555	Sam Jones	30.00	13.50	4.50
☐ 556	Ken R. Hunt	30.00	13.50	4.50
☐ 557	Jose Valdivielso	30.00	13.50	4.50
☐ 558	Don Ferrarese	30.00	13.50	4.50
☐ 559	Jim Gentile	36.00	16.25	5.50
☐ 560	Barry Latman	30.00	13.50	4.50
☐ 561	Charley James	30.00	13.50	4.50
☐ 562	Bill Monbouquette	33.00	15.00	5.00
☐ 563	Bob Cerv	36.00	16.25	5.50
☐ 564	Don Cardwell	30.00	13.50	4.50
☐ 565	Felipe Alou	33.00	15.00	5.00
☐ 566	Paul Richards MG AS	33.00	15.00	5.00
☐ 567	Danny Murtaugh MG AS	33.00	15.00	5.00
☐ 568	Bill Skowron AS	36.00	16.25	5.50
☐ 569	Frank Herrera AS	33.00	15.00	5.00
☐ 570	Nellie Fox AS	42.00	18.00	5.50
☐ 571	Bill Mazeroski AS	36.00	16.25	5.50
☐ 572	Brooks Robinson AS	95.00	42.00	11.00
☐ 573	Ken Boyer AS	36.00	16.25	5.50
☐ 574	Luis Aparicio AS	48.00	22.00	6.00
☐ 575	Ernie Banks AS	95.00	42.00	11.00
☐ 576	Roger Maris AS	135.00	60.00	20.00
☐ 577	Hank Aaron AS	160.00	72.00	24.00
☐ 578	Mickey Mantle AS	350.00	160.00	52.50
☐ 579	Willie Mays AS	160.00	72.00	24.00
☐ 580	Al Kaline AS	95.00	42.00	11.00
☐ 581	Frank Robinson AS	95.00	42.00	11.00
☐ 582	Earl Battey AS	33.00	15.00	5.00
☐ 583	Del Crandall AS	33.00	15.00	5.00
☐ 584	Jim Perry AS	33.00	15.00	5.00
☐ 585	Bob Friend AS	33.00	15.00	5.00
☐ 586	Whitey Ford AS	95.00	42.00	11.00
☐ 587	Does not exist	00.00	00.00	0.00
☐ 588	Does not exist	00.00	00.00	0.00
☐ 589	Warren Spahn AS	140.00	50.00	10.00

1962 Topps

The cards in this 598-card set measure 2 1/2" by 3 1/2". The 1962 Topps set contains a mini-series spotlighting Babe Ruth (135-144). Other subsets in the set include League Leaders (51-60), World Series cards (232-237), In Action cards (311-319), NL All Stars (390-399), AL All Stars (466-475), and Rookie Prospects (591-598). The All-Star selections were again provided by Sport Magazine, as in 1958 and 1960. The second series had two distinct printings which are distinguishable by numerous color and pose variations. Those cards with a distinctive "green tint" are valued at a slight premium as they are basically the result of a flawed printing process occurring early in the second series run. Card number 139 exists as A: Babe Ruth Special card, B: Hal Reniff with arms over head, or C: Hal Reniff in the same pose as card number 159. In addition, two poses exist for players depicted on card numbers 129, 132, 134, 147, 174, 176, and 190. The high number series, 523 to 598, is somewhat more difficult to obtain than other cards in the set. Within the last series (523-598) there are 43 cards which were printed in lesser quantities; these are marked SP in the checklist below. The set price listed does not include the pose variations (see checklist below for individual values). The key rookies in this set are Lou Brock, Tim McCarver, Gaylord Perry, and Bob Uecker.

	NRMT	VG-E	GOOD
COMPLETE SET	5250.00	2000.00	500.00
COMMON PLAYER (1-109)	2.00	.80	.20
COMMON PLAYER (110-196)	2.25	.90	.22
COMMON PLAYER (197-283)	2.50	1.00	.25
COMMON PLAYER (284-370)	3.00	1.25	.30
COMMON PLAYER (371-446)	4.50	2.00	.45
COMMON PLAYER (447-522)	6.00	2.50	.60
COMMON PLAYER (523-590)	13.00	5.75	1.75
COMMON SP (523-590)	22.00	9.50	3.15
COMMON PLAYER (591-598)	30.00	13.50	4.50

		NRMT	VG-E	GOOD
☐ 1	Roger Maris	200.00	45.00	9.00
☐ 2	Jim Brosnan	2.50	1.00	.25
☐ 3	Pete Runnels	2.50	1.00	.25
☐ 4	John DeMerit	2.00	.80	.20
☐ 5	Sandy Koufax UER (struck out 18)	110.00	50.00	16.50

□ 6	Marv Breeding	2.00	.80	.20
□ 7	Frank Thomas	2.50	1.00	.25
□ 8	Ray Herbert	2.00	.80	.20
□ 9	Jim Davenport	2.00	.80	.20
□ 10	Bob Clemente	100.00	45.00	15.00
□ 11	Tom Morgan	2.00	.80	.20
□ 12	Harry Craft MG	2.00	.80	.20
□ 13	Dick Howser	2.50	1.00	.25
□ 14	Bill White	4.00	1.75	.40
□ 15	Dick Donovan	2.00	.80	.20
□ 16	Darrell Johnson	2.00	.80	.20
□ 17	John Callison	2.50	1.00	.25
□ 18	Managers' Dream	100.00	45.00	15.00
	Mickey Mantle			
	Willie Mays			
□ 19	Ray Washburn	2.00	.80	.20
□ 20	Rocky Colavito	7.50	3.25	.75
□ 21	Jim Kaat	5.50	2.50	.55
□ 22A	Checklist 1 ERR	9.00	.90	.20
	(121-176 on back)			
□ 22B	Checklist 1 COR	9.00	.90	.20
□ 23	Norm Larker	2.50	1.00	.25
□ 24	Tigers Team	5.00	2.25	.50
□ 25	Ernie Banks	38.00	17.00	5.00
□ 26	Chris Cannizzaro	2.00	.80	.20
□ 27	Chuck Cottier	2.00	.80	.20
□ 28	Minnie Minoso	4.00	1.75	.40
□ 29	Casey Stengel MG	17.00	7.25	2.50
□ 30	Eddie Mathews	20.00	8.50	2.75
□ 31	Tom Tresh	12.00	5.25	1.50
□ 32	John Roseboro	2.50	1.00	.25
□ 33	Don Larsen	3.00	1.25	.30
□ 34	Johnny Temple	2.00	.80	.20
□ 35	Don Schwall	2.00	.80	.20
□ 36	Don Leppert	2.00	.80	.20
□ 37	Tribe Hill Trio	2.50	1.00	.25
	Barry Latman			
	Dick Stigman			
	Jim Perry			
□ 38	Gene Stephens	2.00	.80	.20
□ 39	Joe Koppe	2.00	.80	.20
□ 40	Orlando Cepeda	8.00	3.50	.80
□ 41	Cliff Cook	2.00	.80	.20
□ 42	Jim King	2.00	.80	.20
□ 43	Los Angeles Dodgers	6.00	2.50	.60
	Team Card			
□ 44	Don Taussig	2.00	.80	.20
□ 45	Brooks Robinson	33.00	15.00	5.00
□ 46	Jack Baldschun	2.00	.80	.20
□ 47	Bob Will	2.00	.80	.20
□ 48	Ralph Terry	2.50	1.00	.25
□ 49	Hal Jones	2.00	.80	.20
□ 50	Stan Musial	100.00	45.00	15.00
□ 51	AL Batting Leaders	4.00	1.75	.40
	Norm Cash			
	Jim Piersall			
	Al Kaline			
	Elston Howard			
□ 52	NL Batting Leaders	5.50	2.50	.55
	Bob Clemente			
	Vada Pinson			
	Ken Boyer			
	Wally Moon			
□ 53	AL Home Run Leaders	35.00	15.75	5.25
	Roger Maris			
	Mickey Mantle			
	Jim Gentile			
	Harmon Killebrew			
□ 54	NL Home Run Leaders	5.50	2.50	.55
	Orlando Cepeda			
	Willie Mays			
	Frank Robinson			
□ 55	AL ERA Leaders	3.50	1.50	.35
	Dick Donovan			
	Bill Stafford			
	Don Mossi			
	Milt Pappas			
□ 56	NL ERA Leaders	4.00	1.75	.40
	Warren Spahn			
	Jim O'Toole			
	Curt Simmons			
	Mike McCormick			
□ 57	AL Wins Leaders	4.00	1.75	.40
	Whitey Ford			
	Frank Lary			
	Steve Barber			
	Jim Bunning			
□ 58	NL Wins Leaders	4.00	1.75	.40
	Warren Spahn			
	Joe Jay			
	Jim O'Toole			
□ 59	AL Strikeout Leaders	3.50	1.50	.35
	Camilo Pascual			
	Whitey Ford			
	Jim Bunning			
	Juan Pizzaro			
□ 60	NL Strikeout Leaders	6.50	2.75	.65
	Sandy Koufax			
	Stan Williams			
	Don Drysdale			
	Jim O'Toole			
□ 61	Cardinals Team	5.00	2.25	.50
□ 62	Steve Boros	2.00	.80	.20
□ 63	Tony Cloninger	3.00	1.25	.30
□ 64	Russ Snyder	2.00	.80	.20
□ 65	Bobby Richardson	5.50	2.50	.55
□ 66	Cuno Barragon	2.00	.80	.20
□ 67	Harvey Haddix	2.50	1.00	.25
□ 68	Ken Hunt	2.00	.80	.20
□ 69	Phil Ortega	2.00	.80	.20
□ 70	Harmon Killebrew	20.00	8.50	2.75
□ 71	Dick LeMay	2.00	.80	.20
□ 72	Bob's Pupils	2.00	.80	.20
	Steve Boros			
	Bob Scheffing			
	Jake Wood			
□ 73	Nellie Fox	6.00	2.50	.60
□ 74	Bob Lillis	2.00	.80	.20
□ 75	Milt Pappas	2.50	1.00	.25
□ 76	Howie Bedell	2.00	.80	.20
□ 77	Tony Taylor	2.00	.80	.20
□ 78	Gene Green	2.00	.80	.20
□ 79	Ed Hobaugh	2.00	.80	.20
□ 80	Vada Pinson	3.50	1.50	.35
□ 81	Jim Pagliaroni	2.00	.80	.20
□ 82	Deron Johnson	2.00	.80	.20
□ 83	Larry Jackson	2.00	.80	.20
□ 84	Lenny Green	2.00	.80	.20
□ 85	Gil Hodges	14.00	6.25	2.00
□ 86	Donn Clendenon	3.00	1.25	.30
□ 87	Mike Roarke	2.00	.80	.20
□ 88	Ralph Houk MG	3.00	1.25	.30
	(Berra in background)			
□ 89	Barney Schultz	2.00	.80	.20
□ 90	Jim Piersall	3.00	1.25	.30
□ 91	J.C. Martin	2.00	.80	.20
□ 92	Sam Jones	2.00	.80	.20
□ 93	John Blanchard	2.50	1.00	.25
□ 94	Jay Hook	2.00	.80	.20
□ 95	Don Hoak	2.50	1.00	.25
□ 96	Eli Grba	2.00	.80	.20
□ 97	Tito Francona	2.00	.80	.20
□ 98	Checklist 2	9.00	.90	.20
□ 99	John (Boog) Powell	16.50	7.00	2.35
□ 100	Warren Spahn	30.00	13.50	4.50
□ 101	Carroll Hardy	2.00	.80	.20
□ 102	Al Schroll	2.00	.80	.20
□ 103	Don Blasingame	2.00	.80	.20
□ 104	Ted Savage	2.00	.80	.20
□ 105	Don Mossi	2.50	1.00	.25
□ 106	Carl Sawatski	2.00	.80	.20
□ 107	Mike McCormick	2.50	1.00	.25
□ 108	Willie Davis	3.00	1.25	.30
□ 109	Bob Shaw	2.00	.80	.20
□ 110	Bill Skowron	4.00	1.75	.40
□ 111	Dallas Green	3.50	1.50	.35
□ 112	Hank Foiles	2.25	.90	.22
□ 113	Chicago White Sox	5.00	2.25	.50
	Team Card			
□ 114	Howie Koplitz	2.25	.90	.22
□ 115	Bob Skinner	3.00	1.25	.30
□ 116	Herb Score	3.50	1.50	.35
□ 117	Gary Geiger	2.25	.90	.22
□ 118	Julian Javier	2.25	.90	.22
□ 119	Danny Murphy	2.25	.90	.22
□ 120	Bob Purkey	2.25	.90	.22
□ 121	Billy Hitchcock MG	2.25	.90	.22
□ 122	Norm Bass	2.25	.90	.22
□ 123	Mike De La Hoz	2.25	.90	.22
□ 124	Bill Pleis	2.25	.90	.22
□ 125	Gene Woodling	3.00	1.25	.30
□ 126	Al Cicotte	2.25	.90	.22
□ 127	Pride of A's	3.00	1.25	.30
	Norm Siebern			
	Hank Bauer			
	Jerry Lumpe			
□ 128	Art Fowler	2.25	.90	.22
□ 129A	Lee Walls	2.25	.90	.22
	(facing right)			
□ 129B	Lee Walls	22.00	9.50	3.15
	(facing left)			
□ 130	Frank Bolling	2.25	.90	.22
□ 131	Pete Richert	2.25	.90	.22
□ 132A	Angels Team	6.00	2.50	.60
	(without photo)			
□ 132B	Angels Team	22.00	9.50	3.15
	(with photo)			
□ 133	Felipe Alou	3.50	1.50	.35
□ 134A	Billy Hoeft	2.25	.90	.22
	(facing right)			

☐ 134B	Billy Hoeft .... (facing straight)	22.00	9.50	3.15
☐ 135	Babe Ruth Special 1 .... Babe as a Boy	14.00	6.25	2.00
☐ 136	Babe Ruth Special 2 .... Babe Joins Yanks	14.00	6.25	2.00
☐ 137	Babe Ruth Special 3 .... Babe with Huggins	14.00	6.25	2.00
☐ 138	Babe Ruth Special 4 .... Famous Slugger	14.00	6.25	2.00
☐ 139A	Babe Ruth Special 5 .... Babe Hits 60	16.00	6.75	2.25
☐ 139B	Hal Reniff PORT	12.50	5.50	1.65
☐ 139C	Hal Reniff .... (pitching)	55.00	25.00	8.25
☐ 140	Babe Ruth Special 6 .... Gehrig and Ruth	16.00	6.75	2.25
☐ 141	Babe Ruth Special 7 .... Twilight Years	14.00	6.25	2.00
☐ 142	Babe Ruth Special 8 .... Coaching Dodgers	14.00	6.25	2.00
☐ 143	Babe Ruth Special 9 .... Greatest Sports Hero	14.00	6.25	2.00
☐ 144	Babe Ruth Special 10 .... Farewell Speech	14.00	6.25	2.00
☐ 145	Barry Latman	2.25	.90	.22
☐ 146	Don Demeter	2.25	.90	.22
☐ 147A	Bill Kunkel PORT	2.25	.90	.22
☐ 147B	Bill Kunkel .... (pitching pose)	22.00	9.50	3.15
☐ 148	Wally Post	2.25	.90	.22
☐ 149	Bob Duliba	2.25	.90	.22
☐ 150	Al Kaline	33.00	15.00	5.00
☐ 151	Johnny Klippstein	2.25	.90	.22
☐ 152	Mickey Vernon MG	3.00	1.25	.30
☐ 153	Pumpsie Green	2.25	.90	.22
☐ 154	Lee Thomas	3.00	1.25	.30
☐ 155	Stu Miller	2.25	.90	.22
☐ 156	Merritt Ranew	2.25	.90	.22
☐ 157	Wes Covington	2.25	.90	.22
☐ 158	Braves Team	5.00	2.25	.50
☐ 159	Hal Reniff	3.00	1.25	.30
☐ 160	Dick Stuart	3.00	1.25	.30
☐ 161	Frank Baumann	2.25	.90	.22
☐ 162	Sammy Drake	2.25	.90	.22
☐ 163	Hot Corner Guard .... Billy Gardner Cletis Boyer	3.00	1.25	.30
☐ 164	Hal Naragon	2.25	.90	.22
☐ 165	Jackie Brandt	2.25	.90	.22
☐ 166	Don Lee	2.25	.90	.22
☐ 167	Tim McCarver	32.00	14.25	4.75
☐ 168	Leo Posada	2.25	.90	.22
☐ 169	Bob Cerv	3.00	1.25	.30
☐ 170	Ron Santo	10.00	4.50	1.25
☐ 171	Dave Sisler	2.25	.90	.22
☐ 172	Fred Hutchinson MG	3.00	1.25	.30
☐ 173	Chico Fernandez	2.25	.90	.22
☐ 174A	Carl Willey .... (capless)	2.25	.90	.22
☐ 174B	Carl Willey .... (with cap)	22.00	9.50	3.15
☐ 175	Frank Howard	4.00	1.75	.40
☐ 176A	Eddie Yost PORT	2.25	.90	.22
☐ 176B	Eddie Yost BATTING	22.00	9.50	3.15
☐ 177	Bobby Shantz	3.00	1.25	.30
☐ 178	Camilo Carreon	2.25	.90	.22
☐ 179	Tom Sturdivant	2.25	.90	.22
☐ 180	Bob Allison	3.00	1.25	.30
☐ 181	Paul Brown	2.25	.90	.22
☐ 182	Bob Nieman	2.25	.90	.22
☐ 183	Roger Craig	3.50	1.50	.35
☐ 184	Haywood Sullivan	2.25	.90	.22
☐ 185	Roland Sheldon	2.25	.90	.22
☐ 186	Mack Jones	2.25	.90	.22
☐ 187	Gene Conley	2.25	.90	.22
☐ 188	Chuck Hiller	2.25	.90	.22
☐ 189	Dick Hall	2.25	.90	.22
☐ 190A	Wally Moon PORT	3.00	1.25	.30
☐ 190B	Wally Moon BATTING	22.00	9.50	3.15
☐ 191	Jim Brewer	2.25	.90	.22
☐ 192A	Checklist 3 .... (without comma)	9.00	.90	.20
☐ 192B	Checklist 3 .... (comma after Checklist)	12.50	1.25	.25
☐ 193	Eddie Kasko	2.25	.90	.22
☐ 194	Dean Chance	3.50	1.50	.35
☐ 195	Joe Cunningham	3.00	1.25	.30
☐ 196	Terry Fox	2.25	.90	.22
☐ 197	Daryl Spencer	2.50	1.00	.25
☐ 198	Johnny Keane MG	2.25	.90	.22
☐ 199	Gaylord Perry	165.00	75.00	22.50
☐ 200	Mickey Mantle	425.00	190.00	63.00
☐ 201	Ike Delock	2.50	1.00	.25

☐ 202	Carl Warwick	2.50	1.00	.25
☐ 203	Jack Fisher	2.50	1.00	.25
☐ 204	Johnny Weekly	2.50	1.00	.25
☐ 205	Gene Freese	2.50	1.00	.25
☐ 206	Senators Team	5.00	2.25	.50
☐ 207	Pete Burnside	2.50	1.00	.25
☐ 208	Billy Martin	6.50	2.75	.65
☐ 209	Jim Fregosi	7.00	3.00	.70
☐ 210	Roy Face	3.50	1.50	.35
☐ 211	Midway Masters .... Frank Bolling Roy McMillan	3.00	1.25	.30
☐ 212	Jim Owens	2.50	1.00	.25
☐ 213	Richie Ashburn	9.00	4.00	.90
☐ 214	Dom Zanni	2.50	1.00	.25
☐ 215	Woody Held	2.50	1.00	.25
☐ 216	Ron Kline	2.50	1.00	.25
☐ 217	Walt Alston MG	5.00	2.25	.50
☐ 218	Joe Torre	21.00	9.00	3.00
☐ 219	Al Downing	4.50	2.00	.45
☐ 220	Roy Sievers	3.00	1.25	.30
☐ 221	Bill Short	2.50	1.00	.25
☐ 222	Jerry Zimmerman	2.50	1.00	.25
☐ 223	Alex Grammas	2.50	1.00	.25
☐ 224	Don Rudolph	2.50	1.00	.25
☐ 225	Frank Malzone	3.00	1.25	.30
☐ 226	San Francisco Giants .... Team Card	5.00	2.25	.50
☐ 227	Bob Tiefenauer	2.50	1.00	.25
☐ 228	Dale Long	3.00	1.25	.30
☐ 229	Jesus McFarlane	2.50	1.00	.25
☐ 230	Camilo Pascual	3.00	1.25	.30
☐ 231	Ernie Bowman	2.50	1.00	.25
☐ 232	World Series Game 1 .... Yanks win opener	5.00	2.25	.50
☐ 233	World Series Game 2 .... Jay ties it up	5.00	2.25	.50
☐ 234	World Series Game 3 .... Maris wins in 9th	12.50	5.50	1.65
☐ 235	World Series Game 4 .... Ford sets new mark	7.00	3.00	.70
☐ 236	World Series Game 5 .... Yanks crush Reds	5.00	2.25	.50
☐ 237	World Series Summary ...... Yanks celebrate	5.00	2.25	.50
☐ 238	Norm Sherry	2.50	1.00	.25
☐ 239	Cecil Butler	2.50	1.00	.25
☐ 240	George Altman	2.50	1.00	.25
☐ 241	Johnny Kucks	2.50	1.00	.25
☐ 242	Mel McGaha MG	2.50	1.00	.25
☐ 243	Robin Roberts	11.00	5.00	1.35
☐ 244	Don Gile	2.50	1.00	.25
☐ 245	Ron Hansen	2.50	1.00	.25
☐ 246	Art Ditmar	2.50	1.00	.25
☐ 247	Joe Pignatano	2.50	1.00	.25
☐ 248	Bob Aspromonte	2.50	1.00	.25
☐ 249	Ed Keegan	2.50	1.00	.25
☐ 250	Norm Cash	4.50	2.00	.45
☐ 251	New York Yankees .... Team Card	18.00	7.50	2.50
☐ 252	Earl Francis	2.50	1.00	.25
☐ 253	Harry Chiti MG	2.50	1.00	.25
☐ 254	Gordon Windhorn	2.50	1.00	.25
☐ 255	Juan Pizarro	2.50	1.00	.25
☐ 256	Elio Chacon	2.50	1.00	.25
☐ 257	Jack Spring	2.50	1.00	.25
☐ 258	Marty Keough	2.50	1.00	.25
☐ 259	Lou Klimchock	2.50	1.00	.25
☐ 260	Billy Pierce	3.50	1.50	.35
☐ 261	George Alusik	2.50	1.00	.25
☐ 262	Bob Schmidt	2.50	1.00	.25
☐ 263	The Right Pitch .... Bob Purkey Jim Turner Joe Jay	3.00	1.25	.30
☐ 264	Dick Ellsworth	2.50	1.00	.25
☐ 265	Joe Adcock	3.00	1.25	.30
☐ 266	John Anderson	2.50	1.00	.25
☐ 267	Dan Dobbek	2.50	1.00	.25
☐ 268	Ken McBride	2.50	1.00	.25
☐ 269	Bob Oldis	2.50	1.00	.25
☐ 270	Dick Groat	3.50	1.50	.35
☐ 271	Ray Rippelmeyer	2.50	1.00	.25
☐ 272	Earl Robinson	2.50	1.00	.25
☐ 273	Gary Bell	2.50	1.00	.25
☐ 274	Sammy Taylor	2.50	1.00	.25
☐ 275	Norm Siebern	2.50	1.00	.25
☐ 276	Hal Kolstad	2.50	1.00	.25
☐ 277	Checklist 4	9.00	.90	.20
☐ 278	Ken Johnson	2.50	1.00	.25
☐ 279	Hobie Landrith UER .... (wrong birthdate)	2.50	1.00	.25
☐ 280	Johnny Podres	3.50	1.50	.35
☐ 281	Jake Gibbs	3.00	1.25	.30
☐ 282	Dave Hillman	2.50	1.00	.25

#	Player			
283	Charlie Smith	2.50	1.00	.25
284	Ruben Amaro	3.00	1.25	.30
285	Curt Simmons	3.50	1.50	.35
286	Al Lopez MG	4.50	2.00	.45
287	George Witt	3.00	1.25	.30
288	Billy Williams	36.00	16.25	5.50
289	Mike Krsnich	3.00	1.25	.30
290	Jim Gentile	4.50	2.00	.45
291	Hal Stowe	3.00	1.25	.30
292	Jerry Kindall	3.00	1.25	.30
293	Bob Miller	3.00	1.25	.30
294	Phillies Team	6.00	2.50	.60
295	Vern Law	4.00	1.75	.40
296	Ken Hamlin	3.00	1.25	.30
297	Ron Perranoski	3.50	1.50	.35
298	Bill Tuttle	3.00	1.25	.30
299	Don Wert	3.00	1.25	.30
300	Willie Mays	135.00	60.00	20.00
301	Galen Cisco	3.00	1.25	.30
302	Johnny Edwards	3.00	1.25	.30
303	Frank Torre	3.00	1.25	.30
304	Dick Farrell	3.00	1.25	.30
305	Jerry Lumpe	3.00	1.25	.30
306	Redbird Rippers Lindy McDaniel Larry Jackson	3.50	1.50	.35
307	Jim Grant	3.00	1.25	.30
308	Neil Chrisley	3.00	1.25	.30
309	Moe Morhardt	3.00	1.25	.30
310	Whitey Ford	36.00	16.25	5.50
311	Tony Kubek IA	5.00	2.25	.50
312	Warren Spahn IA	8.50	3.75	.85
313	Roger Maris IA	17.00	7.25	2.50
314	Rocky Colavito IA	5.50	2.50	.55
315	Whitey Ford IA	9.00	4.00	.90
316	Harmon Killebrew IA	8.50	3.75	.85
317	Stan Musial IA	18.00	7.50	2.50
318	Mickey Mantle IA	48.00	22.00	6.00
319	Mike McCormick IA	3.50	1.50	.35
320	Hank Aaron	135.00	60.00	20.00
321	Lee Stange	3.00	1.25	.30
322	Alvin Dark MG	3.50	1.50	.35
323	Don Landrum	3.00	1.25	.30
324	Joe McClain	3.00	1.25	.30
325	Luis Aparicio	12.50	5.50	1.65
326	Tom Parsons	3.00	1.25	.30
327	Ozzie Virgil	3.00	1.25	.30
328	Ken Walters	3.00	1.25	.30
329	Bob Bolin	3.00	1.25	.30
330	John Romano	3.00	1.25	.30
331	Moe Drabowsky	3.00	1.25	.30
332	Don Buddin	3.00	1.25	.30
333	Frank Cipriani	3.00	1.25	.30
334	Boston Red Sox Team Card	6.00	2.50	.60
335	Bill Bruton	3.00	1.25	.30
336	Billy Muffett	3.00	1.25	.30
337	Jim Marshall	3.00	1.25	.30
338	Billy Gardner	3.00	1.25	.30
339	Jose Valdivielso	3.00	1.25	.30
340	Don Drysdale	36.00	16.25	5.50
341	Mike Hershberger	3.00	1.25	.30
342	Ed Rakow	3.00	1.25	.30
343	Albie Pearson	3.00	1.25	.30
344	Ed Bauta	3.00	1.25	.30
345	Chuck Schilling	3.00	1.25	.30
346	Jack Kralick	3.00	1.25	.30
347	Chuck Hinton	3.00	1.25	.30
348	Larry Burright	3.00	1.25	.30
349	Paul Foytack	3.00	1.25	.30
350	Frank Robinson	45.00	20.00	6.75
351	Braves' Backstops Joe Torre Del Crandall	5.00	2.25	.50
352	Frank Sullivan	3.00	1.25	.30
353	Bill Mazeroski	5.00	2.25	.50
354	Roman Mejias	3.00	1.25	.30
355	Steve Barber	3.00	1.25	.30
356	Tom Haller	4.00	1.75	.40
357	Jerry Walker	3.00	1.25	.30
358	Tommy Davis	5.00	2.25	.50
359	Bobby Locke	3.00	1.25	.30
360	Yogi Berra	65.00	29.00	9.75
361	Bob Hendley	3.00	1.25	.30
362	Ty Cline	3.00	1.25	.30
363	Bob Roselli	3.00	1.25	.30
364	Ken Hunt	3.00	1.25	.30
365	Charlie Neal	3.50	1.50	.35
366	Phil Regan	3.50	1.50	.35
367	Checklist 5	10.00	1.00	.20
368	Bob Tillman	3.00	1.25	.30
369	Ted Bowsfield	3.00	1.25	.30
370	Ken Boyer	6.50	2.75	.65
371	Earl Battey	4.50	2.00	.45
372	Jack Curtis	4.50	2.00	.45
373	Al Heist	4.50	2.00	.45
374	Gene Mauch MG	5.00	2.25	.50
375	Ron Fairly	5.00	2.25	.50
376	Bud Daley	4.50	2.00	.45
377	John Orsino	4.50	2.00	.45
378	Bennie Daniels	4.50	2.00	.45
379	Chuck Essegian	4.50	2.00	.45
380	Lou Burdette	5.00	2.50	.55
381	Chico Cardenas	4.50	2.00	.45
382	Dick Williams	5.00	2.25	.50
383	Ray Sadecki	4.50	2.00	.45
384	K.C. Athletics Team Card	9.00	4.00	.90
385	Early Wynn	15.00	6.50	2.15
386	Don Mincher	5.00	2.25	.50
387	Lou Brock	200.00	90.00	30.00
388	Ryne Duren	5.50	2.50	.55
389	Smoky Burgess	5.00	2.25	.50
390	Orlando Cepeda AS	6.50	2.75	.65
391	Bill Mazeroski AS	6.00	2.50	.60
392	Ken Boyer AS	6.00	2.50	.60
393	Roy McMillan AS	5.00	2.25	.50
394	Hank Aaron AS	33.00	15.00	5.00
395	Willie Mays AS	33.00	15.00	5.00
396	Frank Robinson AS	15.00	6.50	2.15
397	John Roseboro AS	5.00	2.25	.50
398	Don Drysdale AS	10.00	4.50	1.25
399	Warren Spahn AS	10.00	4.50	1.25
400	Elston Howard	9.00	4.00	.90
401	AL/NL Homer Kings Roger Maris Orlando Cepeda	33.00	15.00	5.00
402	Gino Cimoli	4.50	2.00	.45
403	Chet Nichols	4.50	2.00	.45
404	Tim Harkness	4.50	2.00	.45
405	Jim Perry	5.00	2.25	.50
406	Bob Taylor	4.50	2.00	.45
407	Hank Aguirre	4.50	2.00	.45
408	Gus Bell	5.00	2.25	.50
409	Pittsburgh Pirates Team Card	9.00	4.00	.90
410	Al Smith	4.50	2.00	.45
411	Danny O'Connell	4.50	2.00	.45
412	Charlie James	4.50	2.00	.45
413	Matty Alou	5.50	2.50	.55
414	Joe Gaines	4.50	2.00	.45
415	Bill Virdon	5.50	2.50	.55
416	Bob Scheffing MG	4.50	2.00	.45
417	Joe Azcue	4.50	2.00	.45
418	Andy Carey	4.50	2.00	.45
419	Bob Bruce	4.50	2.00	.45
420	Gus Triandos	5.00	2.25	.50
421	Ken MacKenzie	4.50	2.00	.45
422	Steve Bilko	4.50	2.00	.45
423	Rival League Relief Aces: Roy Face Hoyt Wilhelm	6.50	2.75	.65
424	Al McBean	5.00	2.25	.50
425	Carl Yastrzemski	240.00	105.00	32.00
426	Bob Farley	4.50	2.00	.45
427	Jake Wood	4.50	2.00	.45
428	Joe Hicks	4.50	2.00	.45
429	Billy O'Dell	4.50	2.00	.45
430	Tony Kubek	9.00	4.00	.90
431	Bob Rodgers	7.00	3.00	.70
432	Jim Pendleton	4.50	2.00	.45
433	Jim Archer	4.50	2.00	.45
434	Clay Dalrymple	4.50	2.00	.45
435	Larry Sherry	5.00	2.25	.50
436	Felix Mantilla	4.50	2.00	.45
437	Ray Moore	4.50	2.00	.45
438	Dick Brown	4.50	2.00	.45
439	Jerry Buchek	4.50	2.00	.45
440	Joey Jay	4.50	2.00	.45
441	Checklist 6	15.00	1.50	.30
442	Wes Stock	4.50	2.00	.45
443	Del Crandall	5.00	2.25	.50
444	Ted Wills	4.50	2.00	.45
445	Vic Power	4.50	2.00	.45
446	Don Elston	4.50	2.00	.45
447	Willie Kirkland	6.00	2.50	.60
448	Joe Gibbon	6.00	2.50	.60
449	Jerry Adair	6.00	2.50	.60
450	Jim O'Toole	6.50	2.75	.65
451	Jose Tartabull	6.50	2.75	.65
452	Earl Averill Jr.	6.00	2.50	.60
453	Cal McLish	6.00	2.50	.60
454	Floyd Robinson	6.00	2.50	.60
455	Luis Arroyo	6.50	2.75	.65
456	Joe Amalfitano	6.00	2.50	.60
457	Lou Clinton	6.00	2.50	.60
458A	Bob Buhl (Braves emblem on cap)	6.00	2.50	.60

☐ 458B	Bob Buhl	65.00	29.00	9.75
	(no emblem on cap)			
☐ 459	Ed Bailey	6.50	2.75	.65
☐ 460	Jim Bunning	10.00	4.50	1.25
☐ 461	Ken Hubbs	18.00	7.50	2.50
☐ 462A	Willie Tasby	6.00	2.50	.60
	(Senators emblem			
	on cap)			
☐ 462B	Willie Tasby	65.00	29.00	9.75
	(no emblem on cap)			
☐ 463	Hank Bauer MG	7.00	3.00	.70
☐ 464	Al Jackson	7.00	3.00	.70
☐ 465	Reds Team	12.00	5.25	1.50
☐ 466	Norm Cash AS	7.00	3.00	.70
☐ 467	Chuck Schilling AS	6.50	2.75	.65
☐ 468	Brooks Robinson AS	16.00	6.75	2.25
☐ 469	Luis Aparicio AS	9.00	4.00	.90
☐ 470	Al Kaline AS	16.00	6.75	2.25
☐ 471	Mickey Mantle AS	110.00	50.00	16.50
☐ 472	Rocky Colavito AS	7.50	3.25	.75
☐ 473	Elston Howard AS	7.50	3.25	.75
☐ 474	Frank Lary AS	6.50	2.75	.65
☐ 475	Whitey Ford AS	13.00	5.75	1.75
☐ 476	Orioles Team	12.00	5.25	1.50
☐ 477	Andre Rodgers	6.00	2.50	.60
☐ 478	Don Zimmer	7.00	3.00	.70
☐ 479	Joel Horlen	7.00	3.00	.70
☐ 480	Harvey Kuenn	7.00	3.00	.70
☐ 481	Vic Wertz	6.50	2.75	.65
☐ 482	Sam Mele MG	6.00	2.50	.60
☐ 483	Don McMahon	6.00	2.50	.60
☐ 484	Dick Schofield	6.00	2.50	.60
☐ 485	Pedro Ramos	6.00	2.50	.60
☐ 486	Jim Gilliam	8.00	3.50	.80
☐ 487	Jerry Lynch	6.00	2.50	.60
☐ 488	Hal Brown	6.00	2.50	.60
☐ 489	Julio Gotay	6.00	2.50	.60
☐ 490	Clete Boyer	7.00	3.00	.70
☐ 491	Leon Wagner	6.00	2.50	.60
☐ 492	Hal W. Smith	6.00	2.50	.60
☐ 493	Danny McDevitt	6.00	2.50	.60
☐ 494	Sammy White	6.00	2.50	.60
☐ 495	Don Cardwell	6.00	2.50	.60
☐ 496	Wayne Causey	6.00	2.50	.60
☐ 497	Ed Bouchee	6.00	2.50	.60
☐ 498	Jim Donohue	6.00	2.50	.60
☐ 499	Zoilo Versalles	6.00	2.50	.60
☐ 500	Duke Snider	50.00	22.50	7.50
☐ 501	Claude Osteen	6.50	2.75	.65
☐ 502	Hector Lopez	6.00	2.50	.60
☐ 503	Danny Murtaugh MG	6.00	2.50	.60
☐ 504	Eddie Bressoud	6.00	2.50	.60
☐ 505	Juan Marichal	38.00	17.00	5.00
☐ 506	Charlie Maxwell	6.00	2.50	.60
☐ 507	Ernie Broglio	6.00	2.50	.60
☐ 508	Gordy Coleman	6.50	2.75	.65
☐ 509	Dave Giusti	7.00	3.00	.70
☐ 510	Jim Lemon	6.50	2.75	.65
☐ 511	Bubba Phillips	6.00	2.50	.60
☐ 512	Mike Fornieles	6.00	2.50	.60
☐ 513	Whitey Herzog	7.00	3.00	.70
☐ 514	Sherm Lollar	6.50	2.75	.65
☐ 515	Stan Williams	6.00	2.50	.60
☐ 516	Checklist 7	15.00	1.50	.30
☐ 517	Dave Wickersham	6.00	2.50	.60
☐ 518	Lee Maye	6.00	2.50	.60
☐ 519	Bob Johnson	6.00	2.50	.60
☐ 520	Bob Friend	6.50	2.75	.65
☐ 521	Jacke Davis UER	6.00	2.50	.60
	(listed as OF on			
	front and P on back)			
☐ 522	Lindy McDaniel	6.50	2.75	.65
☐ 523	Russ Nixon SP	22.00	9.50	3.15
☐ 524	Howie Nunn SP	22.00	9.50	3.15
☐ 525	George Thomas	13.00	5.75	1.75
☐ 526	Hal Woodeshick SP	22.00	9.50	3.15
☐ 527	Dick McAuliffe	18.00	7.50	2.50
☐ 528	Turk Lown	13.00	5.75	1.75
☐ 529	John Schaive SP	22.00	9.50	3.15
☐ 530	Bob Gibson SP	165.00	70.00	20.00
☐ 531	Bobby G. Smith	13.00	5.75	1.75
☐ 532	Dick Stigman	13.00	5.75	1.75
☐ 533	Charley Lau SP	22.00	9.50	3.15
☐ 534	Tony Gonzalez SP	22.00	9.50	3.15
☐ 535	Ed Roebuck	13.00	5.75	1.75
☐ 536	Dick Gernert	13.00	5.75	1.75
☐ 537	Cleveland Indians	30.00	13.50	4.50
	Team Card			
☐ 538	Jack Sanford	15.00	6.50	2.15
☐ 539	Billy Moran	13.00	5.75	1.75
☐ 540	Jim Landis SP	22.00	9.50	3.15
☐ 541	Don Nottebart SP	22.00	9.50	3.15
☐ 542	Dave Philley	13.00	5.75	1.75
☐ 543	Bob Allen SP	22.00	9.50	3.15
☐ 544	Willie McCovey SP	165.00	75.00	22.50

☐ 545	Hoyt Wilhelm SP	55.00	25.00	8.25
☐ 546	Moe Thacker SP	22.00	9.50	3.15
☐ 547	Don Ferrarese	13.00	5.75	1.75
☐ 548	Bobby Del Greco	13.00	5.75	1.75
☐ 549	Bill Rigney MG SP	22.00	9.50	3.15
☐ 550	Art Mahaffey SP	22.00	9.50	3.15
☐ 551	Harry Bright	13.00	5.75	1.75
☐ 552	Chicago Cubs SP	45.00	20.00	6.75
	Team Card			
☐ 553	Jim Coates	13.00	5.75	1.75
☐ 554	Bubba Morton SP	22.00	9.50	3.15
☐ 555	John Buzhardt SP	22.00	9.50	3.15
☐ 556	Al Spangler	13.00	5.75	1.75
☐ 557	Bob Anderson SP	22.00	9.50	3.15
☐ 558	John Goryl	13.00	5.75	1.75
☐ 559	Mike Higgins MG	13.00	5.75	1.75
☐ 560	Chuck Estrada SP	22.00	9.50	3.15
☐ 561	Gene Oliver SP	22.00	9.50	3.15
☐ 562	Bill Henry	13.00	5.75	1.75
☐ 563	Ken Aspromonte	13.00	5.75	1.75
☐ 564	Bob Grim	13.00	5.75	1.75
☐ 565	Jose Pagan	13.00	5.75	1.75
☐ 566	Marty Kutyna SP	22.00	9.50	3.15
☐ 567	Tracy Stallard SP	22.00	9.50	3.15
☐ 568	Jim Golden	13.00	5.75	1.75
☐ 569	Ed Sadowski SP	22.00	9.50	3.15
☐ 570	Bill Stafford SP	22.00	9.50	3.15
☐ 571	Billy Klaus SP	22.00	9.50	3.15
☐ 572	Bob G. Miller SP	28.00	12.50	4.00
☐ 573	Johnny Logan	15.00	6.50	2.15
☐ 574	Dean Stone	13.00	5.75	1.75
☐ 575	Red Schoendienst SP	50.00	22.50	7.50
☐ 576	Russ Kemmerer SP	22.00	9.50	3.15
☐ 577	Dave Nicholson SP	22.00	9.50	3.15
☐ 578	Jim Duffalo	13.00	5.75	1.75
☐ 579	Jim Schaffer SP	22.00	9.50	3.15
☐ 580	Bill Monbouquette	13.00	5.75	1.75
☐ 581	Mel Roach	13.00	5.75	1.75
☐ 582	Ron Piche	13.00	5.75	1.75
☐ 583	Larry Osborne	13.00	5.75	1.75
☐ 584	Minnesota Twins SP	42.00	18.00	5.50
	Team Card			
☐ 585	Glen Hobbie SP	22.00	9.50	3.15
☐ 586	Sammy Esposito SP	22.00	9.50	3.15
☐ 587	Frank Funk SP	20.00	8.50	2.75
☐ 588	Birdie Tebbetts MG	13.00	5.75	1.75
☐ 589	Bob Turley	16.00	6.75	2.25
☐ 590	Curt Flood	20.00	8.50	2.75
☐ 591	Rookie Pitchers SP	55.00	25.00	8.25
	Sam McDowell			
	Ron Taylor			
	Ron Nischwitz			
	Art Quirk			
	Dick Radatz			
☐ 592	Rookie Pitchers SP	65.00	29.00	9.75
	Dan Pfister			
	Bo Belinsky			
	Dave Stenhouse			
	Jim Bouton			
	Joe Bonikowski			
☐ 593	Rookie Pitchers SP	35.00	15.75	5.25
	Jack Lamabe			
	Craig Anderson			
	Jack Hamilton			
	Bob Moorhead			
	Bob Veale			
☐ 594	Rookie Catchers SP	120.00	55.00	18.00
	Doc Edwards			
	Ken Retzer			
	Bob Uecker			
	Doug Camilli			
	Don Pavletich			
☐ 595	Rookie Infielders SP	30.00	13.50	4.50
	Bob Sadowski			
	Felix Torres			
	Marlan Coughtry			
	Ed Charles			
☐ 596	Rookie Infielders SP	65.00	29.00	9.75
	Bernie Allen			
	Joe Pepitone			
	Phil Linz			
	Rich Rollins			
☐ 597	Rookie Infielders SP	30.00	13.50	4.50
	Jim McKnight			
	Rod Kanehl			
	Amado Samuel			
	Denis Menke			
☐ 598	Rookie Outfielders SP	70.00	20.00	4.00
	Al Luplow			
	Manny Jimenez			
	Howie Goss			
	Jim Hickman			
	Ed Olivares			

1963 Topps

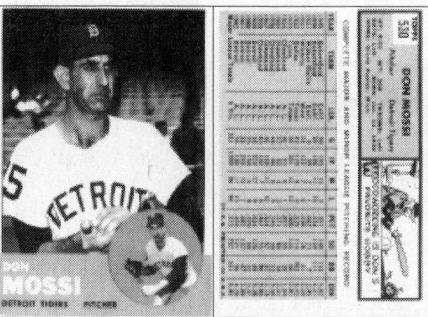

The cards in this 576-card set measure 2 1/2" by 3 1/2". The sharp color photographs of the 1963 set are a vivid contrast to the drab pictures of 1962. In addition to the "League Leaders" series (1-10) and World Series cards (142-148), the seventh and last series of cards (523-576) contains seven rookie cards (each depicting four players). There were some three-card advertising panels produced by Topps; the players included are from the first series; one panel shows Hoyt Wilhelm, Don Lock, and Bob Duliba on the front with a Stan Musial ad/endorsement on one of the backs. This set has gained special prominence in recent years since it contains the rookie card of Pete Rose (537). Other key rookies in this set are Tony Oliva, Willie Stargell, and Rusty Staub.

	NRMT	VG-E	GOOD
COMPLETE SET (576)	5250.00	2250.00	550.00
COMMON PLAYER (1-109)	2.00	.80	.20
COMMON PLAYER (110-196)	2.25	.90	.22
COMMON PLAYER (197-283)	2.75	1.10	.27
COMMON PLAYER (284-446)	3.75	1.60	.37
COMMON PLAYER (447-522)	13.00	5.75	1.75
COMMON PLAYER (523-576)	9.00	4.00	.90

☐ 1 NL Batting Leaders	33.00	5.00	1.00
Tommy Davis			
Frank Robinson			
Stan Musial			
Hank Aaron			
Bill White			
☐ 2 AL Batting Leaders	13.50	6.00	1.85
Pete Runnels			
Mickey Mantle			
Floyd Robinson			
Norm Siebern			
Chuck Hinton			
☐ 3 NL Home Run Leaders	13.50	6.00	1.85
Willie Mays			
Hank Aaron			
Frank Robinson			
Orlando Cepeda			
Ernie Banks			
☐ 4 AL Home Run Leaders	4.50	2.00	.45
Harmon Killebrew			
Norm Cash			
Rocky Colavito			
Roger Maris			
Jim Gentile			
Leon Wagner			
☐ 5 NL ERA Leaders	6.50	2.75	.65
Sandy Koufax			
Bob Shaw			
Bob Purkey			
Bob Gibson			
Don Drysdale			
☐ 6 AL ERA Leaders	3.50	1.50	.35
Hank Aguirre			
Robin Roberts			
Whitey Ford			
Eddie Fisher			
Dean Chance			
☐ 7 NL Pitching Leaders	3.50	1.50	.35
Don Drysdale			
Jack Sanford			
Bob Purkey			
Billy O'Dell			
Art Mahaffey			
Joe Jay			
☐ 8 AL Pitching Leaders	3.00	1.25	.30
Ralph Terry			
Dick Donovan			
Ray Herbert			
Jim Bunning			
Camilo Pascual			
☐ 9 NL Strikeout Leaders	6.50	2.75	.65
Don Drysdale			
Sandy Koufax			
Bob Gibson			
Billy O'Dell			
Dick Farrell			
☐ 10 AL Strikeout Leaders	3.00	1.25	.30
Camilo Pascual			
Jim Bunning			
Ralph Terry			
Juan Pizarro			
Jim Kaat			
☐ 11 Lee Walls	2.00	.80	.20
☐ 12 Steve Barber	2.00	.80	.20
☐ 13 Philadelphia Phillies	3.50	1.50	.35
Team Card			
☐ 14 Pedro Ramos	2.00	.80	.20
☐ 15 Ken Hubbs	3.50	1.50	.35
☐ 16 Al Smith	2.00	.80	.20
☐ 17 Ryne Duren	2.50	1.00	.25
☐ 18 Buc Blasters	10.00	4.50	1.25
Smoky Burgess			
Dick Stuart			
Bob Clemente			
Bob Skinner			
☐ 19 Pete Burnside	2.00	.80	.20
☐ 20 Tony Kubek	4.00	1.75	.40
☐ 21 Marty Keough	2.00	.80	.20
☐ 22 Curt Simmons	2.50	1.00	.25
☐ 23 Ed Lopat MG	2.50	1.00	.25
☐ 24 Bob Bruce	2.00	.80	.20
☐ 25 Al Kaline	30.00	13.50	4.50
☐ 26 Ray Moore	2.00	.80	.20
☐ 27 Choo Choo Coleman	2.00	.80	.20
☐ 28 Mike Fornieles	2.00	.80	.20
☐ 29A 1962 Rookie Stars	6.00	2.50	.60
Sammy Ellis			
Ray Culp			
John Boozer			
Jesse Gonder			
☐ 29B 1963 Rookie Stars	2.50	1.00	.25
Sammy Ellis			
Ray Culp			
John Boozer			
Jesse Gonder			
☐ 30 Harvey Kuenn	3.00	1.25	.30
☐ 31 Cal Koonce	2.00	.80	.20
☐ 32 Tony Gonzalez	2.00	.80	.20
☐ 33 Bo Belinsky	2.50	1.00	.25
☐ 34 Dick Schofield	2.00	.80	.20
☐ 35 John Buzhardt	2.00	.80	.20
☐ 36 Jerry Kindall	2.00	.80	.20
☐ 37 Jerry Lynch	2.00	.80	.20
☐ 38 Bud Daley	2.00	.80	.20
☐ 39 Angels Team	3.50	1.50	.35
☐ 40 Vic Power	2.00	.80	.20
☐ 41 Charley Lau	2.50	1.00	.25
☐ 42 Stan Williams	2.00	.80	.20
(listed as Yankee on			
card but LA cap)			
☐ 43 Veteran Masters	4.00	1.75	.40
Casey Stengel			
Gene Woodling			
☐ 44 Terry Fox	2.00	.80	.20
☐ 45 Bob Aspromonte	2.00	.80	.20
☐ 46 Tommy Aaron	2.50	1.00	.25
☐ 47 Don Lock	2.00	.80	.20
☐ 48 Birdie Tebbetts MG	2.00	.80	.20
☐ 49 Dal Maxvill	2.50	1.00	.25
☐ 50 Billy Pierce	2.50	1.00	.25
☐ 51 George Alusik	2.00	.80	.20
☐ 52 Chuck Schilling	2.00	.80	.20
☐ 53 Joe Moeller	2.00	.80	.20
☐ 54A 1962 Rookie Stars	15.00	6.50	2.15
Nelson Mathews			
Harry Fanok			
Jack Cullen			
Dave DeBusschere			
☐ 54B 1963 Rookie Stars	5.50	2.50	.55
Nelson Mathews			
Harry Fanok			
Jack Cullen			
Dave DeBusschere			
☐ 55 Bill Virdon	3.00	1.25	.30
☐ 56 Dennis Bennett	2.00	.80	.20

#	Player			
57	Billy Moran	2.00	.80	.20
58	Bob Will	2.00	.80	.20
59	Craig Anderson	2.00	.80	.20
60	Elston Howard	6.00	2.50	.60
61	Ernie Bowman	2.00	.80	.20
62	Bob Hendley	2.00	.80	.20
63	Reds Team	3.50	1.50	.35
64	Dick McAuliffe	2.50	1.00	.25
65	Jackie Brandt	2.00	.80	.20
66	Mike Joyce	2.00	.80	.20
67	Ed Charles	2.00	.80	.20
68	Friendly Foes	10.00	4.50	1.25
	Duke Snider			
	Gil Hodges			
69	Bud Zipfel	2.00	.80	.20
70	Jim O'Toole	2.00	.80	.20
71	Bobby Wine	2.00	.80	.20
72	Johnny Romano	2.00	.80	.20
73	Bobby Bragan MG	2.00	.80	.20
74	Denny Lemaster	2.00	.80	.20
75	Bob Allison	2.50	1.00	.25
76	Earl Wilson	2.00	.80	.20
77	Al Spangler	2.00	.80	.20
78	Marv Throneberry	2.50	1.00	.25
79	Checklist 1	9.00	.90	.20
80	Jim Gilliam	3.50	1.50	.35
81	Jim Schaffer	2.00	.80	.20
82	Ed Rakow	2.00	.80	.20
83	Charley James	2.00	.80	.20
84	Ron Kline	2.00	.80	.20
85	Tom Haller	2.00	.80	.20
86	Charley Maxwell	2.00	.80	.20
87	Bob Veale	2.50	1.00	.25
88	Ron Hansen	2.00	.80	.20
89	Dick Stigman	2.00	.80	.20
90	Gordy Coleman	2.00	.80	.20
91	Dallas Green	2.50	1.00	.25
92	Hector Lopez	2.00	.80	.20
93	Galen Cisco	2.00	.80	.20
94	Bob Schmidt	2.00	.80	.20
95	Larry Jackson	2.00	.80	.20
96	Lou Clinton	2.00	.80	.20
97	Bob Duliba	2.00	.80	.20
98	George Thomas	2.00	.80	.20
99	Jim Umbricht	2.00	.80	.20
100	Joe Cunningham	2.50	1.00	.25
101	Joe Gibbon	2.00	.80	.20
102A	Checklist 2	9.00	.90	.20
	(red on yellow)			
102B	Checklist 2	12.50	1.25	.25
	(white on red)			
103	Chuck Essegian	2.00	.80	.20
104	Lew Krausse	2.00	.80	.20
105	Ron Fairly	2.50	1.00	.25
106	Bobby Bolin	2.00	.80	.20
107	Jim Hickman	2.50	1.00	.25
108	Hoyt Wilhelm	9.00	4.00	.90
109	Lee Maye	2.00	.80	.20
110	Rich Rollins	3.00	1.25	.30
111	Al Jackson	2.25	.90	.22
112	Dick Brown	2.25	.90	.22
113	Don Landrum UER	3.00	1.25	.30
	(photo actually			
	Ron Santo)			
114	Dan Osinski	2.25	.90	.22
115	Carl Yastrzemski	75.00	34.00	11.25
116	Jim Brosnan	2.25	.90	.22
117	Jacke Davis	2.25	.90	.22
118	Sherm Lollar	2.25	.90	.22
119	Bob Lillis	2.25	.90	.22
120	Roger Maris	60.00	27.00	9.00
121	Jim Hannan	2.25	.90	.22
122	Julio Gotay	2.25	.90	.22
123	Frank Howard	3.50	1.50	.35
124	Dick Howser	3.00	1.25	.30
125	Robin Roberts	10.00	4.50	1.25
126	Bob Uecker	35.00	15.75	5.25
127	Bill Tuttle	2.25	.90	.22
128	Matty Alou	3.00	1.25	.30
129	Gary Bell	2.25	.90	.22
130	Dick Groat	3.00	1.25	.30
131	Washington Senators	4.00	1.75	.40
	Team Card			
132	Jack Hamilton	2.25	.90	.22
133	Gene Freese	2.25	.90	.22
134	Bob Scheffing MG	2.25	.90	.22
135	Richie Ashburn	9.00	4.00	.90
136	Ike Delock	2.25	.90	.22
137	Mack Jones	2.25	.90	.22
138	Pride of NL	33.00	15.00	5.00
	Willie Mays			
	Stan Musial			
139	Earl Averill	2.25	.90	.22
140	Frank Lary	3.00	1.25	.30
141	Manny Mota	5.50	2.50	.55
142	World Series Game 1	6.00	2.50	.60
	Ford wins			
	series opener			
143	World Series Game 2	5.00	2.25	.50
	Sanford flashes			
	shutout magic			
144	World Series Game 3	10.00	4.50	1.25
	Maris sparks			
	Yankee rally			
145	World Series Game 4	5.00	2.25	.50
	Hiller blasts			
	grand slammer			
146	World Series Game 5	5.00	2.25	.50
	Tresh's homer			
	defeats Giants			
147	World Series Game 6	5.00	2.25	.50
	Pierce stars in			
	3 hit victory			
148	World Series Game 7	5.00	2.25	.50
	Yanks celebrate			
	as Terry wins			
149	Marv Breeding	2.25	.90	.22
150	Johnny Podres	3.00	1.25	.30
151	Pirates Team	4.00	1.75	.40
152	Ron Nischwitz	2.25	.90	.22
153	Hal Smith	2.25	.90	.22
154	Walt Alston MG	4.50	2.00	.45
155	Bill Stafford	2.25	.90	.22
156	Roy McMillan	2.25	.90	.22
157	Diego Segui	2.25	.90	.22
158	Rookie Stars	3.50	1.50	.35
	Rogelio Alvares			
	Dave Roberts			
	Tommy Harper			
	Bob Saverine			
159	Jim Pagliaroni	2.25	.90	.22
160	Juan Pizarro	2.25	.90	.22
161	Frank Torre	2.25	.90	.22
162	Twins Team	4.00	1.75	.40
163	Don Larsen	3.00	1.25	.30
164	Bubba Morton	2.25	.90	.22
165	Jim Kaat	5.00	2.25	.50
166	Johnny Keane MG	3.00	1.25	.30
167	Jim Fregosi	3.00	1.25	.30
168	Russ Nixon	2.25	.90	.22
169	Rookie Stars	32.00	14.25	4.75
	Dick Egan			
	Julio Navarro			
	Tommie Sisk			
	Gaylord Perry			
170	Joe Adcock	3.00	1.25	.30
171	Steve Hamilton	2.25	.90	.22
172	Gene Oliver	2.25	.90	.22
173	Bombers' Best	55.00	25.00	8.25
	Tom Tresh			
	Mickey Mantle			
	Bobby Richardson			
174	Larry Burright	2.25	.90	.22
175	Bob Buhl	2.25	.90	.22
176	Jim King	2.25	.90	.22
177	Bubba Phillips	2.25	.90	.22
178	Johnny Edwards	2.25	.90	.22
179	Ron Piche	2.25	.90	.22
180	Bill Skowron	3.50	1.50	.35
181	Sammy Esposito	2.25	.90	.22
182	Albie Pearson	2.25	.90	.22
183	Joe Pepitone	3.50	1.50	.35
184	Vern Law	3.00	1.25	.30
185	Chuck Hiller	2.25	.90	.22
186	Jerry Zimmerman	2.25	.90	.22
187	Willie Kirkland	2.25	.90	.22
188	Eddie Bressoud	2.25	.90	.22
189	Dave Giusti	3.00	1.25	.30
190	Minnie Minoso	3.50	1.50	.35
191	Checklist 3	9.00	.90	.20
192	Clay Dalrymple	2.25	.90	.22
193	Andre Rodgers	2.25	.90	.22
194	Joe Nuxhall	3.00	1.25	.30
195	Manny Jimenez	2.25	.90	.22
196	Doug Camilli	2.25	.90	.22
197	Roger Craig	3.50	1.50	.35
198	Lenny Green	2.75	1.10	.27
199	Joe Amalfitano	2.75	1.10	.27
200	Mickey Mantle	350.00	160.00	52.50
201	Cecil Butler	2.75	1.10	.27
202	Boston Red Sox	5.50	2.50	.55
	Team Card			
203	Chico Cardenas	2.75	1.10	.27
204	Don Nottebart	2.75	1.10	.27
205	Luis Aparicio	12.50	5.50	1.65
206	Ray Washburn	2.75	1.10	.27
207	Ken Hunt	2.75	1.10	.27

#	Player			
☐ 208	Rookie Stars	2.75	1.10	.27
	Ron Herbel			
	John Miller			
	Wally Wolf			
	Ron Taylor			
☐ 209	Hobie Landrith	2.75	1.10	.27
☐ 210	Sandy Koufax	140.00	63.00	21.00
☐ 211	Fred Whitfield	2.75	1.10	.27
☐ 212	Glen Hobbie	2.75	1.10	.27
☐ 213	Billy Hitchcock MG	2.75	1.10	.27
☐ 214	Orlando Pena	2.75	1.10	.27
☐ 215	Bob Skinner	2.75	1.10	.27
☐ 216	Gene Conley	2.75	1.10	.27
☐ 217	Joe Christopher	2.75	1.10	.27
☐ 218	Tiger Twirlers	3.50	1.50	.35
	Frank Lary			
	Don Mossi			
	Jim Bunning			
☐ 219	Chuck Cottier	2.75	1.10	.27
☐ 220	Camilo Pascual	3.50	1.50	.35
☐ 221	Cookie Rojas	4.00	1.75	.40
☐ 222	Cubs Team	5.50	2.50	.55
☐ 223	Eddie Fisher	2.75	1.10	.27
☐ 224	Mike Roarke	2.75	1.10	.27
☐ 225	Joey Jay	2.75	1.10	.27
☐ 226	Julian Javier	2.75	1.10	.27
☐ 227	Jim Grant	2.75	1.10	.27
☐ 228	Rookie Stars	45.00	20.00	6.75
	Max Alvis			
	Bob Bailey			
	Tony Oliva			
	(listed as Pedro)			
	Ed Kranepool			
☐ 229	Willie Davis	4.00	1.75	.40
☐ 230	Pete Runnels	3.50	1.50	.35
☐ 231	Eli Grba UER	2.75	1.10	.27
	(large photo is			
	Ryne Duren)			
☐ 232	Frank Malzone	3.50	1.50	.35
☐ 233	Casey Stengel MG	16.00	6.75	2.25
☐ 234	Dave Nicholson	2.75	1.10	.27
☐ 235	Billy O'Dell	2.75	1.10	.27
☐ 236	Bill Bryan	2.75	1.10	.27
☐ 237	Jim Coates	2.75	1.10	.27
☐ 238	Lou Johnson	2.75	1.10	.27
☐ 239	Harvey Haddix	3.50	1.50	.35
☐ 240	Rocky Colavito	8.00	3.50	.80
☐ 241	Bob Smith	2.75	1.10	.27
☐ 242	Power Plus	28.00	12.50	4.00
	Ernie Banks			
	Hank Aaron			
☐ 243	Don Leppert	2.75	1.10	.27
☐ 244	John Tsitouris	2.75	1.10	.27
☐ 245	Gil Hodges	17.00	7.25	2.50
☐ 246	Lee Stange	2.75	1.10	.27
☐ 247	Yankees Team	15.00	6.50	2.15
☐ 248	Tito Francona	2.75	1.10	.27
☐ 249	Leo Burke	2.75	1.10	.27
☐ 250	Stan Musial	110.00	50.00	16.50
☐ 251	Jack Lamabe	2.75	1.10	.27
☐ 252	Ron Santo	6.00	2.50	.60
☐ 253	Rookie Stars	2.75	1.10	.27
	Len Gabrielson			
	Pete Jernigan			
	John Wojcik			
	Deacon Jones			
☐ 254	Mike Hershberger	2.75	1.10	.27
☐ 255	Bob Shaw	2.75	1.10	.27
☐ 256	Jerry Lumpe	2.75	1.10	.27
☐ 257	Hank Aguirre	2.75	1.10	.27
☐ 258	Alvin Dark MG	3.50	1.50	.35
☐ 259	Johnny Logan	3.50	1.50	.35
☐ 260	Jim Gentile	3.50	1.50	.35
☐ 261	Bob Miller	2.75	1.10	.27
☐ 262	Ellis Burton	2.75	1.10	.27
☐ 263	Dave Stenhouse	2.75	1.10	.27
☐ 264	Phil Linz	3.50	1.50	.35
☐ 265	Vada Pinson	4.00	1.75	.40
☐ 266	Bob Allen	2.75	1.10	.27
☐ 267	Carl Sawatski	2.75	1.10	.27
☐ 268	Don Demeter	2.75	1.10	.27
☐ 269	Don Mincher	3.50	1.50	.35
☐ 270	Felipe Alou	3.50	1.50	.35
☐ 271	Dean Stone	2.75	1.10	.27
☐ 272	Danny Murphy	2.75	1.10	.27
☐ 273	Sammy Taylor	2.75	1.10	.27
☐ 274	Checklist 4	9.00	.90	.20
☐ 275	Eddie Mathews	20.00	8.50	2.75
☐ 276	Barry Shetrone	2.75	1.10	.27
☐ 277	Dick Farrell	2.75	1.10	.27
☐ 278	Chico Fernandez	2.75	1.10	.27
☐ 279	Wally Moon	3.50	1.50	.35
☐ 280	Bob Rodgers	4.00	1.75	.40
☐ 281	Tom Sturdivant	2.75	1.10	.27
☐ 282	Bobby Del Greco	2.75	1.10	.27
☐ 283	Roy Sievers	3.50	1.50	.35
☐ 284	Dave Sisler	3.75	1.60	.37
☐ 285	Dick Stuart	4.50	2.00	.45
☐ 286	Stu Miller	3.75	1.60	.37
☐ 287	Dick Bertell	3.75	1.60	.37
☐ 288	Chicago White Sox	7.50	3.25	.75
	Team Card			
☐ 289	Hal Brown	3.75	1.60	.37
☐ 290	Bill White	5.00	2.25	.50
☐ 291	Don Rudolph	3.75	1.60	.37
☐ 292	Pumpsie Green	3.75	1.60	.37
☐ 293	Bill Pleis	3.75	1.60	.37
☐ 294	Bill Rigney MG	3.75	1.60	.37
☐ 295	Ed Roebuck	3.75	1.60	.37
☐ 296	Doc Edwards	3.75	1.60	.37
☐ 297	Jim Golden	3.75	1.60	.37
☐ 298	Don Dillard	3.75	1.60	.37
☐ 299	Rookie Stars	3.75	1.60	.37
	Dave Morehead			
	Bob Dustal			
	Tom Butters			
	Dan Schneider			
☐ 300	Willie Mays	140.00	63.00	21.00
☐ 301	Bill Fischer	3.75	1.60	.37
☐ 302	Whitey Herzog	5.00	2.25	.50
☐ 303	Earl Francis	3.75	1.60	.37
☐ 304	Harry Bright	3.75	1.60	.37
☐ 305	Don Hoak	4.50	2.00	.45
☐ 306	Star Receivers	4.50	2.00	.45
	Earl Battey			
	Elston Howard			
☐ 307	Chet Nichols	3.75	1.60	.37
☐ 308	Camilo Carreon	3.75	1.60	.37
☐ 309	Jim Brewer	3.75	1.60	.37
☐ 310	Tommy Davis	5.00	2.25	.50
☐ 311	Joe McClain	3.75	1.60	.37
☐ 312	Houston Colts	12.00	5.25	1.50
	Team Card			
☐ 313	Ernie Broglio	4.50	2.00	.45
☐ 314	John Goryl	3.75	1.60	.37
☐ 315	Ralph Terry	4.50	2.00	.45
☐ 316	Norm Sherry	3.75	1.60	.37
☐ 317	Sam McDowell	5.00	2.25	.50
☐ 318	Gene Mauch MG	4.50	2.00	.45
☐ 319	Joe Gaines	3.75	1.60	.37
☐ 320	Warren Spahn	36.00	16.25	5.50
☐ 321	Gino Cimoli	3.75	1.60	.37
☐ 322	Bob Turley	4.50	2.00	.45
☐ 323	Bill Mazeroski	5.00	2.25	.50
☐ 324	Rookie Stars	5.00	2.25	.50
	George Williams			
	Pete Ward			
	Phil Roof			
	Vic Davalillo			
☐ 325	Jack Sanford	3.75	1.60	.37
☐ 326	Hank Foiles	3.75	1.60	.37
☐ 327	Paul Foytack	3.75	1.60	.37
☐ 328	Dick Williams	4.50	2.00	.45
☐ 329	Lindy McDaniel	4.50	2.00	.45
☐ 330	Chuck Hinton	3.75	1.60	.37
☐ 331	Series Foes	4.50	2.00	.45
	Bill Stafford			
	Bill Pierce			
☐ 332	Joel Horlen	3.75	1.60	.37
☐ 333	Carl Warwick	3.75	1.60	.37
☐ 334	Wynn Hawkins	3.75	1.60	.37
☐ 335	Leon Wagner	3.75	1.60	.37
☐ 336	Ed Bauta	3.75	1.60	.37
☐ 337	Dodgers Team	11.00	5.00	1.35
☐ 338	Russ Kemmerer	3.75	1.60	.37
☐ 339	Ted Bowsfield	3.75	1.60	.37
☐ 340	Yogi Berra	70.00	32.00	10.50
	(player/coach)			
☐ 341	Jack Baldschun	3.75	1.60	.37
☐ 342	Gene Woodling	4.50	2.00	.45
☐ 343	Johnny Pesky MG	4.50	2.00	.45
☐ 344	Don Schwall	4.50	2.00	.45
☐ 345	Brooks Robinson	45.00	20.00	6.75
☐ 346	Billy Hoeft	3.75	1.60	.37
☐ 347	Joe Torre	8.00	3.50	.80
☐ 348	Vic Wertz	4.50	2.00	.45
☐ 349	Zoilo Versalles	3.75	1.60	.37
☐ 350	Bob Purkey	3.75	1.60	.37
☐ 351	Al Luplow	3.75	1.60	.37
☐ 352	Ken Johnson	3.75	1.60	.37
☐ 353	Billy Williams	24.00	10.50	3.50
☐ 354	Dom Zanni	3.75	1.60	.37
☐ 355	Dean Chance	4.50	2.00	.45
☐ 356	John Schaive	3.75	1.60	.37
☐ 357	George Altman	3.75	1.60	.37
☐ 358	Milt Pappas	4.50	2.00	.45
☐ 359	Haywood Sullivan	3.75	1.60	.37
☐ 360	Don Drysdale	35.00	15.75	5.25

☐ 361	Clete Boyer	5.00	2.25	.50
☐ 362	Checklist 5	9.00	.90	.20
☐ 363	Dick Radatz	4.50	2.00	.45
☐ 364	Howie Goss	3.75	1.60	.37
☐ 365	Jim Bunning	8.00	3.50	.80
☐ 366	Tony Taylor	3.75	1.60	.37
☐ 367	Tony Cloninger	3.75	1.60	.37
☐ 368	Ed Bailey	3.75	1.60	.37
☐ 369	Jim Lemon MG	3.75	1.60	.37
☐ 370	Dick Donovan	3.75	1.60	.37
☐ 371	Rod Kanehl	4.00	1.75	.40
☐ 372	Don Lee	4.00	1.75	.40
☐ 373	Jim Campbell	4.00	1.75	.40
☐ 374	Claude Osteen	4.50	2.00	.45
☐ 375	Ken Boyer	6.50	2.75	.65
☐ 376	John Wyatt	4.00	1.75	.40
☐ 377	Baltimore Orioles Team Card	8.00	3.50	.80
☐ 378	Bill Henry	4.00	1.75	.40
☐ 379	Bob Anderson	4.00	1.75	.40
☐ 380	Ernie Banks	50.00	22.50	7.50
☐ 381	Frank Baumann	4.00	1.75	.40
☐ 382	Ralph Houk MG	5.00	2.25	.50
☐ 383	Pete Richert	4.00	1.75	.40
☐ 384	Bob Tillman	4.00	1.75	.40
☐ 385	Art Mahaffey	4.00	1.75	.40
☐ 386	Rookie Stars Ed Kirkpatrick John Bateman Larry Bearnarth Garry Roggenburk	5.00	2.25	.50
☐ 387	Al McBean	4.00	1.75	.40
☐ 388	Jim Davenport	4.00	1.75	.40
☐ 389	Frank Sullivan	4.00	1.75	.40
☐ 390	Hank Aaron	140.00	63.00	21.00
☐ 391	Bill Dailey	4.00	1.75	.40
☐ 392	Tribe Thumpers Johnny Romano Tito Francona	4.50	2.00	.45
☐ 393	Ken MacKenzie	4.00	1.75	.40
☐ 394	Tim McCarver	14.00	6.25	2.00
☐ 395	Don McMahon	4.00	1.75	.40
☐ 396	Joe Koppe	4.00	1.75	.40
☐ 397	Kansas City Athletics Team Card	7.50	3.25	.75
☐ 398	Boog Powell	18.00	7.50	2.50
☐ 399	Dick Ellsworth	4.50	2.00	.45
☐ 400	Frank Robinson	42.00	18.00	5.50
☐ 401	Jim Bouton	7.50	3.25	.75
☐ 402	Mickey Vernon MG	4.50	2.00	.45
☐ 403	Ron Perranoski	4.50	2.00	.45
☐ 404	Bob Oldis	4.00	1.75	.40
☐ 405	Floyd Robinson	4.00	1.75	.40
☐ 406	Howie Koplitz	4.00	1.75	.40
☐ 407	Rookie Stars Frank Kostro Chico Ruiz Larry Elliot Dick Simpson	4.50	2.00	.45
☐ 408	Billy Gardner	4.00	1.75	.40
☐ 409	Roy Face	5.00	2.25	.50
☐ 410	Earl Battey	4.00	1.75	.40
☐ 411	Jim Constable	4.00	1.75	.40
☐ 412	Dodger Big Three Johnny Podres Don Drysdale Sandy Koufax	32.00	14.25	4.75
☐ 413	Jerry Walker	4.00	1.75	.40
☐ 414	Ty Cline	4.00	1.75	.40
☐ 415	Bob Gibson	38.00	17.00	5.00
☐ 416	Alex Grammas	4.00	1.75	.40
☐ 417	Giants Team	8.00	3.50	.80
☐ 418	John Orsino	4.00	1.75	.40
☐ 419	Tracy Stallard	4.00	1.75	.40
☐ 420	Bobby Richardson	7.50	3.25	.75
☐ 421	Tom Morgan	4.00	1.75	.40
☐ 422	Fred Hutchinson MG	4.50	2.00	.45
☐ 423	Ed Hobaugh	4.00	1.75	.40
☐ 424	Charlie Smith	4.00	1.75	.40
☐ 425	Smoky Burgess	4.50	2.00	.45
☐ 426	Barry Latman	4.00	1.75	.40
☐ 427	Bernie Allen	4.00	1.75	.40
☐ 428	Carl Boles	4.00	1.75	.40
☐ 429	Lou Burdette	5.00	2.25	.50
☐ 430	Norm Siebern	4.00	1.75	.40
☐ 431A	Checklist 6 (white on red)	10.00	1.00	.20
☐ 431B	Checklist 6 (black on orange)	15.00	1.50	.30
☐ 432	Roman Mejias	4.00	1.75	.40
☐ 433	Denis Menke	4.00	1.75	.40
☐ 434	John Callison	4.50	2.00	.45
☐ 435	Woody Held	4.00	1.75	.40
☐ 436	Tim Harkness	4.00	1.75	.40
☐ 437	Bill Bruton	4.50	2.00	.45
☐ 438	Wes Stock	4.00	1.75	.40
☐ 439	Don Zimmer	5.00	2.25	.50
☐ 440	Juan Marichal	24.00	10.50	3.50
☐ 441	Lee Thomas	4.50	2.00	.45
☐ 442	J.C. Hartman	4.00	1.75	.40
☐ 443	Jim Piersall	5.00	2.25	.50
☐ 444	Jim Maloney	4.50	2.00	.45
☐ 445	Norm Cash	5.50	2.50	.55
☐ 446	Whitey Ford	38.00	17.00	5.00
☐ 447	Felix Mantilla	13.00	5.75	1.75
☐ 448	Jack Kralick	13.00	5.75	1.75
☐ 449	Jose Tartabull	13.00	5.75	1.75
☐ 450	Bob Friend	15.00	6.50	2.15
☐ 451	Indians Team	24.00	10.50	3.50
☐ 452	Barney Schultz	13.00	5.75	1.75
☐ 453	Jake Wood	13.00	5.75	1.75
☐ 454A	Art Fowler (card number on white background)	13.00	5.75	1.75
☐ 454B	Art Fowler (card number on orange background)	20.00	8.50	2.75
☐ 455	Ruben Amaro	13.00	5.75	1.75
☐ 456	Jim Coker	13.00	5.75	1.75
☐ 457	Tex Clevenger	13.00	5.75	1.75
☐ 458	Al Lopez MG	17.00	7.25	2.50
☐ 459	Dick LeMay	13.00	5.75	1.75
☐ 460	Del Crandall	15.00	6.50	2.15
☐ 461	Norm Bass	13.00	5.75	1.75
☐ 462	Wally Post	13.00	5.75	1.75
☐ 463	Joe Schaffernoth	13.00	5.75	1.75
☐ 464	Ken Aspromonte	13.00	5.75	1.75
☐ 465	Chuck Estrada	15.00	6.50	2.15
☐ 466	Rookie Stars SP Nate Oliver Tony Martinez Bill Freehan Jerry Robinson	40.00	18.00	6.00
☐ 467	Phil Ortega	13.00	5.75	1.75
☐ 468	Carroll Hardy	13.00	5.75	1.75
☐ 469	Jay Hook	13.00	5.75	1.75
☐ 470	Tom Tresh SP	40.00	18.00	6.00
☐ 471	Ken Retzer	13.00	5.75	1.75
☐ 472	Lou Brock	140.00	63.00	21.00
☐ 473	New York Mets Team Card	90.00	40.00	13.50
☐ 474	Jack Fisher	13.00	5.75	1.75
☐ 475	Gus Triandos	15.00	6.50	2.15
☐ 476	Frank Funk	13.00	5.75	1.75
☐ 477	Donn Clendenon	15.00	6.50	2.15
☐ 478	Paul Brown	13.00	5.75	1.75
☐ 479	Ed Brinkman	13.00	5.75	1.75
☐ 480	Bill Monbouquette	13.00	5.75	1.75
☐ 481	Bob Taylor	13.00	5.75	1.75
☐ 482	Felix Torres	13.00	5.75	1.75
☐ 483	Jim Owens	13.00	5.75	1.75
☐ 484	Dale Long SP	22.00	9.50	3.15
☐ 485	Jim Landis	13.00	5.75	1.75
☐ 486	Ray Sadecki	13.00	5.75	1.75
☐ 487	John Roseboro	15.00	6.50	2.15
☐ 488	Jerry Adair	13.00	5.75	1.75
☐ 489	Paul Toth	13.00	5.75	1.75
☐ 490	Willie McCovey	125.00	57.50	18.75
☐ 491	Harry Craft MG	13.00	5.75	1.75
☐ 492	Dave Wickersham	13.00	5.75	1.75
☐ 493	Walt Bond	13.00	5.75	1.75
☐ 494	Phil Regan	15.00	6.50	2.15
☐ 495	Frank Thomas SP	22.00	9.50	3.15
☐ 496	Rookie Stars Steve Dalkowski Fred Newman Jack Smith Carl Bouldin	15.00	6.50	2.15
☐ 497	Bennie Daniels	13.00	5.75	1.75
☐ 498	Eddie Kasko	13.00	5.75	1.75
☐ 499	J.C. Martin	13.00	5.75	1.75
☐ 500	Harmon Killebrew SP	110.00	50.00	16.50
☐ 501	Joe Azcue	13.00	5.75	1.75
☐ 502	Daryl Spencer	13.00	5.75	1.75
☐ 503	Braves Team	32.00	14.25	4.75
☐ 504	Bob Johnson	13.00	5.75	1.75
☐ 505	Curt Flood	18.00	7.50	2.50
☐ 506	Gene Green	13.00	5.75	1.75
☐ 507	Roland Sheldon	13.00	5.75	1.75
☐ 508	Ted Savage	13.00	5.75	1.75
☐ 509A	Checklist 7 (copyright centered)	20.00	2.00	.40
☐ 509B	Checklist 7 (copyright to right)	20.00	2.00	.40
☐ 510	Ken McBride	13.00	5.75	1.75
☐ 511	Charlie Neal	15.00	6.50	2.15
☐ 512	Cal McLish	13.00	5.75	1.75
☐ 513	Gary Geiger	13.00	5.75	1.75

		NRMT	VG-E	GOOD
☐ 514	Larry Osborne	13.00	5.75	1.75
☐ 515	Don Elston	13.00	5.75	1.75
☐ 516	Purnell Goldy	13.00	5.75	1.75
☐ 517	Hal Woodeshick	13.00	5.75	1.75
☐ 518	Don Blasingame	13.00	5.75	1.75
☐ 519	Claude Raymond	13.00	5.75	1.75
☐ 520	Orlando Cepeda	22.00	9.50	3.15
☐ 521	Dan Pfister	13.00	5.75	1.75
☐ 522	Rookie Stars	13.00	5.75	1.75
	Mel Nelson			
	Gary Peters			
	Jim Roland			
	Art Quirk			
☐ 523	Bill Kunkel	9.00	4.00	.90
☐ 524	Cardinals Team	18.00	7.50	2.50
☐ 525	Nellie Fox	17.00	7.25	2.50
☐ 526	Dick Hall	9.00	4.00	.90
☐ 527	Ed Sadowski	9.00	4.00	.90
☐ 528	Carl Willey	9.00	4.00	.90
☐ 529	Wes Covington	9.00	4.00	.90
☐ 530	Don Mossi	10.00	4.50	1.25
☐ 531	Sam Mele MG	9.00	4.00	.90
☐ 532	Steve Boros	9.00	4.00	.90
☐ 533	Bobby Shantz	11.00	5.00	1.35
☐ 534	Ken Walters	9.00	4.00	.90
☐ 535	Jim Perry	11.00	5.00	1.35
☐ 536	Norm Larker	10.00	4.50	1.25
☐ 537	Rookie Stars	650.00	300.00	100.00
	Pedro Gonzales			
	Ken McMullen			
	Al Weis			
	Pete Rose			
☐ 538	George Brunet	9.00	4.00	.90
☐ 539	Wayne Causey	9.00	4.00	.90
☐ 540	Bob Clemente	180.00	80.00	27.00
☐ 541	Ron Moeller	9.00	4.00	.90
☐ 542	Lou Klimchock	9.00	4.00	.90
☐ 543	Russ Snyder	9.00	4.00	.90
☐ 544	Rookie Stars	36.00	16.25	5.50
	Duke Carmel			
	Bill Haas			
	Rusty Staub			
	Dick Phillips			
☐ 545	Jose Pagan	9.00	4.00	.90
☐ 546	Hal Reniff	9.00	4.00	.90
☐ 547	Gus Bell	10.00	4.50	1.25
☐ 548	Tom Satriano	9.00	4.00	.90
☐ 549	Rookie Stars	9.00	4.00	.90
	Marcelino Lopez			
	Pete Lovrich			
	Paul Ratliff			
	Elmo Plaskett			
☐ 550	Duke Snider	75.00	34.00	11.25
☐ 551	Billy Klaus	9.00	4.00	.90
☐ 552	Detroit Tigers	22.00	9.50	3.15
	Team Card			
☐ 553	Rookie Stars	300.00	135.00	45.00
	Brock Davis			
	Jim Gosger			
	Willie Stargell			
	John Herrnstein			
☐ 554	Hank Fischer	9.00	4.00	.90
☐ 555	John Blanchard	10.00	4.50	1.25
☐ 556	Al Worthington	9.00	4.00	.90
☐ 557	Cuno Barragan	9.00	4.00	.90
☐ 558	Rookie Stars	12.50	5.50	1.65
	Bill Faul			
	Ron Hunt			
	Al Moran			
	Bob Lipski			
☐ 559	Danny Murtaugh MG	9.00	4.00	.90
☐ 560	Ray Herbert	9.00	4.00	.90
☐ 561	Mike De La Hoz	9.00	4.00	.90
☐ 562	Rookie Stars	15.00	6.50	2.15
	Randy Cardinal			
	Dave McNally			
	Ken Rowe			
	Don Rowe			
☐ 563	Mike McCormick	10.00	4.50	1.25
☐ 564	George Banks	9.00	4.00	.90
☐ 565	Larry Sherry	10.00	4.50	1.25
☐ 566	Cliff Cook	9.00	4.00	.90
☐ 567	Jim Duffalo	9.00	4.00	.90
☐ 568	Bob Sadowski	9.00	4.00	.90
☐ 569	Luis Arroyo	10.00	4.50	1.25
☐ 570	Frank Bolling	9.00	4.00	.90
☐ 571	Johnny Klippstein	9.00	4.00	.90
☐ 572	Jack Spring	9.00	4.00	.90
☐ 573	Coot Veal	9.00	4.00	.90
☐ 574	Hal Kolstad	9.00	4.00	.90
☐ 575	Don Cardwell	9.00	4.00	.90
☐ 576	Johnny Temple	12.50	5.00	1.00

1964 Topps

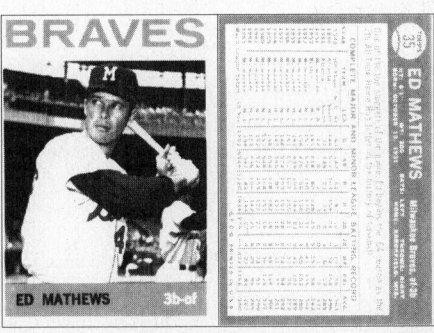

The cards in this 587-card set measure 2 1/2" by 3 1/2". Players in the 1964 Topps baseball series were easy to sort by team due to the giant block lettering found at the top of each card. The name and position of the player are found underneath the picture, and the card is numbered in a ball design on the orange-colored back. The usual last series scarcity holds for this set (523 to 587). Subsets within this set include League Leaders (1-12) and World Series cards (136-140). There were some three-card advertising panels produced by Topps; the players included are from the first series; one panel shows Walt Alston, Bill Henry, and Vada Pinson on the front with a Mickey Mantle card back on one of the backs. Another panel shows Carl Willey, White Sox Rookies, and Bob Friend on the front with a Mickey Mantle card back on one of the backs. The key rookie cards in this set are Richie Allen, Tommy John, Lou Piniella, and Phil Niekro.

		NRMT	VG-E	GOOD
COMPLETE SET (587)		3250.00	1350.00	350.00
COMMON PLAYER (1-196)		1.75	.70	.17
COMMON PLAYER (197-370)		3.00	1.25	.30
COMMON PLAYER (371-522)		4.50	2.00	.45
COMMON PLAYER (523-587)		8.50	3.75	.85
☐ 1	NL ERA Leaders	20.00	5.00	1.00
	Sandy Koufax			
	Dick Ellsworth			
	Bob Friend			
☐ 2	AL ERA Leaders	3.00	1.25	.30
	Gary Peters			
	Juan Pizarro			
	Camilo Pascual			
☐ 3	NL Pitching Leaders	9.00	4.00	.90
	Sandy Koufax			
	Juan Marichal			
	Warren Spahn			
	Jim Maloney			
☐ 4	AL Pitching Leaders	3.50	1.50	.35
	Whitey Ford			
	Camilo Pascual			
	Jim Bouton			
☐ 5	NL Strikeout Leaders	7.00	3.00	.70
	Sandy Koufax			
	Jim Maloney			
	Don Drysdale			
☐ 6	AL Strikeout Leaders	3.00	1.25	.30
	Camilo Pascual			
	Jim Bunning			
	Dick Stigman			
☐ 7	NL Batting Leaders	6.50	2.75	.65
	Tommy Davis			
	Bob Clemente			
	Dick Groat			
	Hank Aaron			
☐ 8	AL Batting Leaders	6.50	2.75	.65
	Carl Yastrzemski			
	Al Kaline			
	Rich Rollins			
☐ 9	NL Home Run Leaders	11.00	5.00	1.35
	Hank Aaron			
	Willie McCovey			
	Willie Mays			
	Orlando Cepeda			

☐ 10	AL Home Run Leaders	3.50	1.50	.35
	Harmon Killebrew			
	Dick Stuart			
	Bob Allison			
☐ 11	NL RBI Leaders	6.00	2.50	.60
	Hank Aaron			
	Ken Boyer			
	Bill White			
☐ 12	AL RBI Leaders	4.00	1.75	.40
	Dick Stuart			
	Al Kaline			
	Harmon Killebrew			
☐ 13	Hoyt Wilhelm	8.50	3.75	.85
☐ 14	Dodgers Rookies	1.75	.70	.17
	Dick Nen			
	Nick Willhite			
☐ 15	Zoilo Versalles	1.75	.70	.17
☐ 16	John Boozer	1.75	.70	.17
☐ 17	Willie Kirkland	1.75	.70	.17
☐ 18	Billy O'Dell	1.75	.70	.17
☐ 19	Don Wert	1.75	.70	.17
☐ 20	Bob Friend	2.25	.90	.22
☐ 21	Yogi Berra MG	36.00	16.25	5.50
☐ 22	Jerry Adair	1.75	.70	.17
☐ 23	Chris Zachary	1.75	.70	.17
☐ 24	Carl Sawatski	1.75	.70	.17
☐ 25	Bill Monbouquette	1.75	.70	.17
☐ 26	Gino Cimoli	1.75	.70	.17
☐ 27	New York Mets	6.00	2.50	.60
	Team Card			
☐ 28	Claude Osteen	2.25	.90	.22
☐ 29	Lou Brock	36.00	16.25	5.50
☐ 30	Ron Perranoski	2.25	.90	.22
☐ 31	Dave Nicholson	1.75	.70	.17
☐ 32	Dean Chance	2.25	.90	.22
☐ 33	Reds Rookies	2.25	.90	.22
	Sammy Ellis			
	Mel Queen			
☐ 34	Jim Perry	2.25	.90	.22
☐ 35	Eddie Mathews	20.00	8.50	2.75
☐ 36	Hal Reniff	1.75	.70	.17
☐ 37	Smoky Burgess	2.25	.90	.22
☐ 38	Jim Wynn	5.00	2.25	.50
☐ 39	Hank Aguirre	1.75	.70	.17
☐ 40	Dick Groat	2.75	1.10	.27
☐ 41	Friendly Foes	3.50	1.50	.35
	Willie McCovey			
	Leon Wagner			
☐ 42	Moe Drabowsky	1.75	.70	.17
☐ 43	Roy Sievers	2.25	.90	.22
☐ 44	Duke Carmel	1.75	.70	.17
☐ 45	Milt Pappas	2.25	.90	.22
☐ 46	Ed Brinkman	1.75	.70	.17
☐ 47	Giants Rookies	2.25	.90	.22
	Jesus Alou			
	Ron Herbel			
☐ 48	Bob Perry	1.75	.70	.17
☐ 49	Bill Henry	1.75	.70	.17
☐ 50	Mickey Mantle	190.00	85.00	28.50
☐ 51	Pete Richert	1.75	.70	.17
☐ 52	Chuck Hinton	1.75	.70	.17
☐ 53	Denis Menke	1.75	.70	.17
☐ 54	Sam Mele MG	1.75	.70	.17
☐ 55	Ernie Banks	25.00	11.00	3.50
☐ 56	Hal Brown	1.75	.70	.17
☐ 57	Tim Harkness	1.75	.70	.17
☐ 58	Don Demeter	1.75	.70	.17
☐ 59	Ernie Broglio	1.75	.70	.17
☐ 60	Frank Malzone	2.25	.90	.22
☐ 61	Angel Backstops	2.25	.90	.22
	Bob Rodgers			
	Ed Sadowski			
☐ 62	Ted Savage	1.75	.70	.17
☐ 63	John Orsino	1.75	.70	.17
☐ 64	Ted Abernathy	1.75	.70	.17
☐ 65	Felipe Alou	2.25	.90	.22
☐ 66	Eddie Fisher	1.75	.70	.17
☐ 67	Tigers Team	3.75	1.60	.37
☐ 68	Willie Davis	2.25	.90	.22
☐ 69	Clete Boyer	2.25	.90	.22
☐ 70	Joe Torre	3.75	1.60	.37
☐ 71	Jack Spring	1.75	.70	.17
☐ 72	Chico Cardenas	1.75	.70	.17
☐ 73	Jimmie Hall	2.25	.90	.22
☐ 74	Pirates Rookies	1.75	.70	.17
	Bob Priddy			
	Tom Butters			
☐ 75	Wayne Causey	1.75	.70	.17
☐ 76	Checklist 1	9.00	.90	.20
☐ 77	Jerry Walker	1.75	.70	.17
☐ 78	Merritt Ranew	1.75	.70	.17
☐ 79	Bob Heffner	1.75	.70	.17
☐ 80	Vada Pinson	3.25	1.35	.32
☐ 81	All-Star Vets	5.00	2.25	.50
	Nellie Fox			
	Harmon Killebrew			
☐ 82	Jim Davenport	1.75	.70	.17
☐ 83	Gus Triandos	2.25	.90	.22
☐ 84	Carl Willey	1.75	.70	.17
☐ 85	Pete Ward	1.75	.70	.17
☐ 86	Al Downing	2.25	.90	.22
☐ 87	St. Louis Cardinals	3.75	1.60	.37
	Team Card			
☐ 88	John Roseboro	2.25	.90	.22
☐ 89	Boog Powell	4.50	2.00	.45
☐ 90	Earl Battey	1.75	.70	.17
☐ 91	Bob Bailey	1.75	.70	.17
☐ 92	Steve Ridzik	1.75	.70	.17
☐ 93	Gary Geiger	1.75	.70	.17
☐ 94	Braves Rookies	1.75	.70	.17
	Jim Britton			
	Larry Maxie			
☐ 95	George Altman	1.75	.70	.17
☐ 96	Bob Buhl	1.75	.70	.17
☐ 97	Jim Fregosi	2.25	.90	.22
☐ 98	Bill Bruton	1.75	.70	.17
☐ 99	Al Stanek	1.75	.70	.17
☐ 100	Elston Howard	4.50	2.00	.45
☐ 101	Walt Alston MG	3.75	1.60	.37
☐ 102	Checklist 2	9.00	.90	.20
☐ 103	Curt Flood	3.00	1.25	.30
☐ 104	Art Mahaffey	1.75	.70	.17
☐ 105	Woody Held	1.75	.70	.17
☐ 106	Joe Nuxhall	2.25	.90	.22
☐ 107	White Sox Rookies	1.75	.70	.17
	Bruce Howard			
	Frank Kreutzer			
☐ 108	John Wyatt	1.75	.70	.17
☐ 109	Rusty Staub	7.00	3.00	.70
☐ 110	Albie Pearson	1.75	.70	.17
☐ 111	Don Elston	1.75	.70	.17
☐ 112	Bob Tillman	1.75	.70	.17
☐ 113	Grover Powell	1.75	.70	.17
☐ 114	Don Lock	1.75	.70	.17
☐ 115	Frank Bolling	1.75	.70	.17
☐ 116	Twins Rookies	15.00	6.50	2.15
	Jay Ward			
	Tony Oliva			
☐ 117	Earl Francis	1.75	.70	.17
☐ 118	John Blanchard	2.25	.90	.22
☐ 119	Gary Kolb	1.75	.70	.17
☐ 120	Don Drysdale	20.00	8.50	2.75
☐ 121	Pete Runnels	2.25	.90	.22
☐ 122	Don McMahon	1.75	.70	.17
☐ 123	Jose Pagan	1.75	.70	.17
☐ 124	Orlando Pena	1.75	.70	.17
☐ 125	Pete Rose	175.00	80.00	27.00
☐ 126	Russ Snyder	1.75	.70	.17
☐ 127	Angels Rookies	1.75	.70	.17
	Aubrey Gatewood			
	Dick Simpson			
☐ 128	Mickey Lolich	15.00	6.50	2.15
☐ 129	Amado Samuel	1.75	.70	.17
☐ 130	Gary Peters	1.75	.70	.17
☐ 131	Steve Boros	1.75	.70	.17
☐ 132	Braves Team	3.75	1.60	.37
☐ 133	Jim Grant	1.75	.70	.17
☐ 134	Don Zimmer	2.25	.90	.22
☐ 135	Johnny Callison	2.25	.90	.22
☐ 136	World Series Game 1	11.00	5.00	1.35
	Koufax strikes out 15			
☐ 137	World Series Game 2	4.00	1.75	.40
	Davis sparks rally			
☐ 138	World Series Game 3	4.00	1.75	.40
	LA 3 straight			
☐ 139	World Series Game 4	4.00	1.75	.40
	Sealing Yanks doom			
☐ 140	World Series Summary	4.00	1.75	.40
	Dodgers celebrate			
☐ 141	Danny Murtaugh MG	1.75	.70	.17
☐ 142	John Bateman	1.75	.70	.17
☐ 143	Bubba Phillips	1.75	.70	.17
☐ 144	Al Worthington	1.75	.70	.17
☐ 145	Norm Siebern	1.75	.70	.17
☐ 146	Indians Rookies	65.00	29.00	9.75
	Tommy John			
	Bob Chance			
☐ 147	Ray Sadecki	1.75	.70	.17
☐ 148	J.C. Martin	1.75	.70	.17
☐ 149	Paul Foytack	1.75	.70	.17
☐ 150	Willie Mays	95.00	42.00	11.00
☐ 151	Athletics Team	3.00	1.25	.30
☐ 152	Denny Lemaster	1.75	.70	.17
☐ 153	Dick Williams	2.25	.90	.22
☐ 154	Dick Tracewski	1.75	.70	.17
☐ 155	Duke Snider	32.00	14.25	4.75
☐ 156	Bill Dailey	1.75	.70	.17
☐ 157	Gene Mauch MG	2.25	.90	.22

#	Player			
☐ 158	Ken Johnson	1.75	.70	.17
☐ 159	Charlie Dees	1.75	.70	.17
☐ 160	Ken Boyer	5.00	2.25	.50
☐ 161	Dave McNally	2.75	1.10	.27
☐ 162	Hitting Area	2.25	.90	.22
	Dick Sisler			
	Vada Pinson			
☐ 163	Donn Clendenon	2.25	.90	.22
☐ 164	Bud Daley	1.75	.70	.17
☐ 165	Jerry Lumpe	1.75	.70	.17
☐ 166	Marty Keough	1.75	.70	.17
☐ 167	Senators Rookies	24.00	10.50	3.50
	Mike Brumley			
	Lou Piniella			
☐ 168	Al Weis	2.25	.90	.22
☐ 169	Del Crandall	2.25	.90	.22
☐ 170	Dick Radatz	2.25	.90	.22
☐ 171	Ty Cline	1.75	.70	.17
☐ 172	Indians Team	3.25	1.35	.32
☐ 173	Ryne Duren	2.25	.90	.22
☐ 174	Doc Edwards	2.25	.90	.22
☐ 175	Billy Williams	15.00	6.50	2.15
☐ 176	Tracy Stallard	1.75	.70	.17
☐ 177	Harmon Killebrew	20.00	8.50	2.75
☐ 178	Hank Bauer MG	2.25	.90	.22
☐ 179	Carl Warwick	1.75	.70	.17
☐ 180	Tommy Davis	2.50	1.00	.25
☐ 181	Dave Wickersham	1.75	.70	.17
☐ 182	Sox Sockers	11.00	5.00	1.35
	Carl Yastrzemski			
	Chuck Schilling			
☐ 183	Ron Taylor	1.75	.70	.17
☐ 184	Al Luplow	1.75	.70	.17
☐ 185	Jim O'Toole	2.25	.90	.22
☐ 186	Roman Mejias	1.75	.70	.17
☐ 187	Ed Roebuck	1.75	.70	.17
☐ 188	Checklist 3	9.00	.90	.20
☐ 189	Bob Hendley	1.75	.70	.17
☐ 190	Bobby Richardson	4.50	2.00	.45
☐ 191	Clay Dalrymple	1.75	.70	.17
☐ 192	Cubs Rookies	1.75	.70	.17
	John Boccabella			
	Billy Cowan			
☐ 193	Jerry Lynch	1.75	.70	.17
☐ 194	John Goryl	1.75	.70	.17
☐ 195	Floyd Robinson	1.75	.70	.17
☐ 196	Jim Gentile	2.50	1.00	.25
☐ 197	Frank Lary	3.00	1.25	.30
☐ 198	Len Gabrielson	3.00	1.25	.30
☐ 199	Joe Azcue	3.00	1.25	.30
☐ 200	Sandy Koufax	95.00	42.00	11.00
☐ 201	Orioles Rookies	3.50	1.50	.35
	Sam Bowens			
	Wally Bunker			
☐ 202	Galen Cisco	3.00	1.25	.30
☐ 203	John Kennedy	3.00	1.25	.30
☐ 204	Matty Alou	3.50	1.50	.35
☐ 205	Nellie Fox	5.00	2.25	.50
☐ 206	Steve Hamilton	3.00	1.25	.30
☐ 207	Fred Hutchinson MG	3.50	1.50	.35
☐ 208	Wes Covington	3.00	1.25	.30
☐ 209	Bob Allen	3.00	1.25	.30
☐ 210	Carl Yastrzemski	75.00	34.00	11.25
☐ 211	Jim Coker	3.00	1.25	.30
☐ 212	Pete Lovrich	3.00	1.25	.30
☐ 213	Angels Team	5.50	2.50	.55
☐ 214	Ken McMullen	3.00	1.25	.30
☐ 215	Ray Herbert	3.00	1.25	.30
☐ 216	Mike De La Hoz	3.00	1.25	.30
☐ 217	Jim King	3.00	1.25	.30
☐ 218	Hank Fischer	3.00	1.25	.30
☐ 219	Young Aces	4.00	1.75	.40
	Al Downing			
	Jim Bouton			
☐ 220	Dick Ellsworth	3.50	1.50	.35
☐ 221	Bob Saverine	3.00	1.25	.30
☐ 222	Billy Pierce	3.50	1.50	.35
☐ 223	George Banks	3.00	1.25	.30
☐ 224	Tommie Sisk	3.00	1.25	.30
☐ 225	Roger Maris	60.00	27.00	9.00
☐ 226	Colts Rookies	4.00	1.75	.40
	Gerald Grote			
	Larry Yellen			
☐ 227	Barry Latman	3.00	1.25	.30
☐ 228	Felix Mantilla	3.00	1.25	.30
☐ 229	Charley Lau	3.50	1.50	.35
☐ 230	Brooks Robinson	32.00	14.25	4.75
☐ 231	Dick Calmus	3.00	1.25	.30
☐ 232	Al Lopez MG	4.50	2.00	.45
☐ 233	Hal Smith	3.00	1.25	.30
☐ 234	Gary Bell	3.00	1.25	.30
☐ 235	Ron Hunt	3.00	1.25	.30
☐ 236	Bill Faul	3.00	1.25	.30
☐ 237	Cubs Team	6.00	2.50	.60
☐ 238	Roy McMillan	3.00	1.25	.30
☐ 239	Herm Starrette	3.00	1.25	.30
☐ 240	Bill White	4.00	1.75	.40
☐ 241	Jim Owens	3.00	1.25	.30
☐ 242	Harvey Kuenn	4.00	1.75	.40
☐ 243	Phillies Rookies	20.00	8.50	2.75
	Richie Allen			
	John Herrnstein			
☐ 244	Tony LaRussa	12.00	5.25	1.50
☐ 245	Dick Stigman	3.00	1.25	.30
☐ 246	Manny Mota	4.00	1.75	.40
☐ 247	Dave DeBusschere	4.00	1.75	.40
☐ 248	Johnny Pesky MG	3.50	1.50	.35
☐ 249	Doug Camilli	3.00	1.25	.30
☐ 250	Al Kaline	30.00	13.50	4.50
☐ 251	Choo Choo Coleman	3.00	1.25	.30
☐ 252	Ken Aspromonte	3.00	1.25	.30
☐ 253	Wally Post	3.00	1.25	.30
☐ 254	Don Hoak	3.50	1.50	.35
☐ 255	Lee Thomas	3.50	1.50	.35
☐ 256	Johnny Weekly	3.00	1.25	.30
☐ 257	San Francisco Giants	6.00	2.50	.60
	Team Card			
☐ 258	Garry Roggenburk	3.00	1.25	.30
☐ 259	Harry Bright	3.00	1.25	.30
☐ 260	Frank Robinson	24.00	10.50	3.50
☐ 261	Jim Hannan	3.00	1.25	.30
☐ 262	Cards Rookies	5.00	2.25	.50
	Mike Shannon			
	Harry Fanok			
☐ 263	Chuck Estrada	3.50	1.50	.35
☐ 264	Jim Landis	3.00	1.25	.30
☐ 265	Jim Bunning	5.00	2.25	.50
☐ 266	Gene Freese	3.00	1.25	.30
☐ 267	Wilbur Wood	4.00	1.75	.40
☐ 268	Bill's Got It	3.50	1.50	.35
	Danny Murtaugh			
	Bill Virdon			
☐ 269	Ellis Burton	3.00	1.25	.30
☐ 270	Rich Rollins	3.50	1.50	.35
☐ 271	Bob Sadowski	3.00	1.25	.30
☐ 272	Jake Wood	3.00	1.25	.30
☐ 273	Mel Nelson	3.00	1.25	.30
☐ 274	Checklist 4	9.00	.90	.20
☐ 275	John Tsitouris	3.00	1.25	.30
☐ 276	Jose Tartabull	3.00	1.25	.30
☐ 277	Ken Retzer	3.00	1.25	.30
☐ 278	Bobby Shantz	3.50	1.50	.35
☐ 279	Joe Koppe UER (glove	3.50	1.50	.35
	on wrong hand)			
☐ 280	Juan Marichal	11.00	5.00	1.35
☐ 281	Yankees Rookies	3.50	1.50	.35
	Jake Gibbs			
	Tom Metcalf			
☐ 282	Bob Bruce	3.00	1.25	.30
☐ 283	Tom McCraw	4.00	1.75	.40
☐ 284	Dick Schofield	3.00	1.25	.30
☐ 285	Robin Roberts	9.00	4.00	.90
☐ 286	Don Landrum	3.00	1.25	.30
☐ 287	Red Sox Rookies	25.00	11.00	3.50
	Tony Conigliaro			
	Bill Spanswick			
☐ 288	Al Moran	3.00	1.25	.30
☐ 289	Frank Funk	3.00	1.25	.30
☐ 290	Bob Allison	3.50	1.50	.35
☐ 291	Phil Ortega	3.00	1.25	.30
☐ 292	Mike Roarke	3.00	1.25	.30
☐ 293	Phillies Team	6.00	2.50	.60
☐ 294	Ken L. Hunt	3.00	1.25	.30
☐ 295	Roger Craig	4.00	1.75	.40
☐ 296	Ed Kirkpatrick	3.00	1.25	.30
☐ 297	Ken MacKenzie	3.00	1.25	.30
☐ 298	Harry Craft MG	3.00	1.25	.30
☐ 299	Bill Stafford	3.00	1.25	.30
☐ 300	Hank Aaron	95.00	42.00	11.00
☐ 301	Larry Brown	3.00	1.25	.30
☐ 302	Dan Pfister	3.00	1.25	.30
☐ 303	Jim Campbell	3.00	1.25	.30
☐ 304	Bob Johnson	3.00	1.25	.30
☐ 305	Jack Lamabe	3.00	1.25	.30
☐ 306	Giant Gunners	20.00	8.50	2.75
	Willie Mays			
	Orlando Cepeda			
☐ 307	Joe Gibbon	4.00	1.75	.40
☐ 308	Gene Stephens	3.00	1.25	.30
☐ 309	Paul Toth	3.00	1.25	.30
☐ 310	Jim Gilliam	4.00	1.75	.40
☐ 311	Tom Brown	3.00	1.25	.30
☐ 312	Tigers Rookies	3.50	1.50	.35
	Fritz Fisher			
	Fred Gladding			
☐ 313	Chuck Hiller	3.00	1.25	.30
☐ 314	Jerry Buchek	3.00	1.25	.30
☐ 315	Bo Belinsky	3.50	1.50	.35

#	Player			
316	Gene Oliver	3.00	1.25	.30
317	Al Smith	3.00	1.25	.30
318	Minnesota Twins Team Card	6.00	2.50	.60
319	Paul Brown	3.00	1.25	.30
320	Rocky Colavito	6.50	2.75	.65
321	Bob Lillis	3.00	1.25	.30
322	George Brunet	3.00	1.25	.30
323	John Buzhardt	3.00	1.25	.30
324	Casey Stengel MG	15.00	6.50	2.15
325	Hector Lopez	3.00	1.25	.30
326	Ron Brand	3.00	1.25	.30
327	Don Blasingame	3.00	1.25	.30
328	Bob Shaw	3.00	1.25	.30
329	Russ Nixon	3.00	1.25	.30
330	Tommy Harper	3.50	1.50	.35
331	AL Bombers Roger Maris Norm Cash Mickey Mantle Al Kaline	95.00	42.00	11.00
332	Ray Washburn	3.00	1.25	.30
333	Billy Moran	3.00	1.25	.30
334	Lew Krausse	3.00	1.25	.30
335	Don Mossi	3.50	1.50	.35
336	Andre Rodgers	3.00	1.25	.30
337	Dodgers Rookies Al Ferrara Jeff Torborg	7.50	3.25	.75
338	Jack Kralick	3.00	1.25	.30
339	Walt Bond	3.00	1.25	.30
340	Joe Cunningham	3.50	1.50	.35
341	Jim Roland	3.00	1.25	.30
342	Willie Stargell	45.00	20.00	6.75
343	Senators Team	5.50	2.50	.55
344	Phil Linz	3.50	1.50	.35
345	Frank Thomas	3.50	1.50	.35
346	Joey Jay	3.50	1.50	.35
347	Bobby Wine	3.00	1.25	.30
348	Ed Lopat MG	3.50	1.50	.35
349	Art Fowler	3.00	1.25	.30
350	Willie McCovey	25.00	11.00	3.50
351	Dan Schneider	3.00	1.25	.30
352	Eddie Bressoud	3.00	1.25	.30
353	Wally Moon	3.50	1.50	.35
354	Dave Giusti	3.50	1.50	.35
355	Vic Power	3.00	1.25	.30
356	Reds Rookies Bill McCool Chico Ruiz	3.50	1.50	.35
357	Charley James	3.00	1.25	.30
358	Ron Kline	3.00	1.25	.30
359	Jim Schaffer	3.00	1.25	.30
360	Joe Pepitone	4.00	1.75	.40
361	Jay Hook	3.00	1.25	.30
362	Checklist 5	9.00	.90	.20
363	Dick McAuliffe	3.50	1.50	.35
364	Joe Gaines	3.00	1.25	.30
365	Cal McLish	3.00	1.25	.30
366	Nelson Mathews	3.00	1.25	.30
367	Fred Whitfield	3.00	1.25	.30
368	White Sox Rookies Fritz Ackley Don Buford	3.50	1.50	.35
369	Jerry Zimmerman	3.00	1.25	.30
370	Hal Woodeshick	3.00	1.25	.30
371	Frank Howard	5.50	2.50	.55
372	Howie Koplitz	4.50	2.00	.45
373	Pirates Team	9.00	4.00	.90
374	Bobby Bolin	4.50	2.00	.45
375	Ron Santo	6.00	2.50	.60
376	Dave Morehead	4.50	2.00	.45
377	Bob Skinner	4.50	2.00	.45
378	Braves Rookies Woody Woodward Jack Smith	5.50	2.50	.55
379	Tony Gonzalez	4.50	2.00	.45
380	Whitey Ford	28.00	12.50	4.00
381	Bob Taylor	4.50	2.00	.45
382	Wes Stock	4.50	2.00	.45
383	Bill Rigney MG	4.50	2.00	.45
384	Ron Hansen	4.50	2.00	.45
385	Curt Simmons	5.00	2.25	.50
386	Lenny Green	4.50	2.00	.45
387	Terry Fox	4.50	2.00	.45
388	A's Rookies John O'Donoghue George Williams	4.50	2.00	.45
389	Jim Umbricht (card back mentions his death)	4.50	2.00	.45
390	Orlando Cepeda	7.50	3.25	.75
391	Sam McDowell	5.00	2.25	.50
392	Jim Pagliaroni	4.50	2.00	.45
393	Casey Teaches Casey Stengel Ed Kranepool	5.50	2.50	.55
394	Bob Miller	4.50	2.00	.45
395	Tom Tresh	5.50	2.50	.55
396	Dennis Bennett	4.50	2.00	.45
397	Chuck Cottier	4.50	2.00	.45
398	Mets Rookies Bill Haas Dick Smith	4.50	2.00	.45
399	Jackie Brandt	4.50	2.00	.45
400	Warren Spahn	28.00	12.50	4.00
401	Charlie Maxwell	4.50	2.00	.45
402	Tom Sturdivant	4.50	2.00	.45
403	Reds Team	9.00	4.00	.90
404	Tony Martinez	4.50	2.00	.45
405	Ken McBride	4.50	2.00	.45
406	Al Spangler	4.50	2.00	.45
407	Bill Freehan	6.00	2.50	.60
408	Cubs Rookies Jim Stewart Fred Burdette	4.50	2.00	.45
409	Bill Fischer	4.50	2.00	.45
410	Dick Stuart	5.50	2.50	.55
411	Lee Walls	4.50	2.00	.45
412	Ray Culp	4.50	2.00	.45
413	Johnny Keane MG	4.50	2.00	.45
414	Jack Sanford	4.50	2.00	.45
415	Tony Kubek	6.50	2.75	.65
416	Lee Maye	4.50	2.00	.45
417	Don Cardwell	4.50	2.00	.45
418	Orioles Rookies Darold Knowles Les Narum	5.50	2.50	.55
419	Ken Harrelson	7.00	3.00	.70
420	Jim Maloney	5.50	2.50	.55
421	Camilo Carreon	4.50	2.00	.45
422	Jack Fisher	4.50	2.00	.45
423	Tops in NL Hank Aaron Willie Mays	90.00	40.00	13.50
424	Dick Bertell	4.50	2.00	.45
425	Norm Cash	6.00	2.50	.60
426	Bob Rodgers	5.50	2.50	.55
427	Don Rudolph	4.50	2.00	.45
428	Red Sox Rookies Archie Skeen Pete Smith (back states Archie has retired)	4.50	2.00	.45
429	Tim McCarver	8.50	3.75	.85
430	Juan Pizarro	4.50	2.00	.45
431	George Alusik	4.50	2.00	.45
432	Ruben Amaro	4.50	2.00	.45
433	Yankees Team	13.00	5.75	1.75
434	Don Nottebart	4.50	2.00	.45
435	Vic Davalillo	5.00	2.25	.50
436	Charlie Neal	5.00	2.25	.50
437	Ed Bailey	5.00	2.25	.50
438	Checklist 6	15.00	1.50	.30
439	Harvey Haddix	5.00	2.25	.50
440	Bob Clemente UER (1960 Pittsburfh)	130.00	60.00	20.00
441	Bob Duliba	4.50	2.00	.45
442	Pumpsie Green	4.50	2.00	.45
443	Chuck Dressen MG	5.00	2.25	.50
444	Larry Jackson	4.50	2.00	.45
445	Bill Skowron	5.50	2.50	.55
446	Julian Javier	4.50	2.00	.45
447	Ted Bowsfield	4.50	2.00	.45
448	Cookie Rojas	5.00	2.25	.50
449	Deron Johnson	5.00	2.25	.50
450	Steve Barber	4.50	2.00	.45
451	Joe Amalfitano	4.50	2.00	.45
452	Giants Rookies Gil Garrido Jim Ray Hart	6.00	2.50	.60
453	Frank Baumann	4.50	2.00	.45
454	Tommie Aaron	5.00	2.25	.50
455	Bernie Allen	4.50	2.00	.45
456	Dodgers Rookies Wes Parker John Werhas	6.00	2.50	.60
457	Jesse Gonder	4.50	2.00	.45
458	Ralph Terry	5.00	2.25	.50
459	Red Sox Rookies Pete Charton Dalton Jones	4.50	2.00	.45
460	Bob Gibson	36.00	16.25	5.50
461	George Thomas	4.50	2.00	.45
462	Birdie Tebbetts MG	4.50	2.00	.45
463	Don Leppert	4.50	2.00	.45
464	Dallas Green	5.50	2.50	.55
465	Mike Hershberger	4.50	2.00	.45

☐ 466	A's Rookies	4.50	2.00	.45
	Dick Green			
	Aurelio Monteagudo			
☐ 467	Bob Aspromonte	4.50	2.00	.45
☐ 468	Gaylord Perry	40.00	18.00	6.00
☐ 469	Cubs Rookies	4.50	2.00	.45
	Fred Norman			
	Sterling Slaughter			
☐ 470	Jim Bouton	6.00	2.50	.60
☐ 471	Gates Brown	6.00	2.50	.60
☐ 472	Vern Law	5.50	2.50	.55
☐ 473	Baltimore Orioles	9.00	4.00	.90
	Team Card			
☐ 474	Larry Sherry	5.00	2.25	.50
☐ 475	Ed Charles	4.50	2.00	.45
☐ 476	Braves Rookies	9.00	4.00	.90
	Rico Carty			
	Dick Kelley			
☐ 477	Mike Joyce	4.50	2.00	.45
☐ 478	Dick Howser	5.00	2.25	.50
☐ 479	Cardinals Rookies	4.50	2.00	.45
	Dave Bakenhaster			
	Johnny Lewis			
☐ 480	Bob Purkey	4.50	2.00	.45
☐ 481	Chuck Schilling	4.50	2.00	.45
☐ 482	Phillies Rookies	5.50	2.50	.55
	John Briggs			
	Danny Cater			
☐ 483	Fred Valentine	4.50	2.00	.45
☐ 484	Bill Pleis	4.50	2.00	.45
☐ 485	Tom Haller	4.50	2.00	.45
☐ 486	Bob Kennedy MG	4.50	2.00	.45
☐ 487	Mike McCormick	5.00	2.25	.50
☐ 488	Yankees Rookies	5.00	2.25	.50
	Pete Mikkelsen			
	Bob Meyer			
☐ 489	Julio Navarro	4.50	2.00	.45
☐ 490	Ron Fairly	5.00	2.25	.50
☐ 491	Ed Rakow	4.50	2.00	.45
☐ 492	Colts Rookies	4.50	2.00	.45
	Jim Beauchamp			
	Mike White			
☐ 493	Don Lee	4.50	2.00	.45
☐ 494	Al Jackson	4.50	2.00	.45
☐ 495	Bill Virdon	5.50	2.50	.55
☐ 496	White Sox Team	9.00	4.00	.90
☐ 497	Jeoff Long	4.50	2.00	.45
☐ 498	Dave Stenhouse	4.50	2.00	.45
☐ 499	Indians Rookies	4.50	2.00	.45
	Chico Salmon			
	Gordon Seyfried			
☐ 500	Camilo Pascual	5.00	2.25	.50
☐ 501	Bob Veale	5.00	2.25	.50
☐ 502	Angels Rookies	5.50	2.50	.55
	Bobby Knoop			
	Bob Lee			
☐ 503	Earl Wilson	4.50	2.00	.45
☐ 504	Claude Raymond	4.50	2.00	.45
☐ 505	Stan Williams	4.50	2.00	.45
☐ 506	Bobby Bragan MG	4.50	2.00	.45
☐ 507	Johnny Edwards	4.50	2.00	.45
☐ 508	Diego Segui	4.50	2.00	.45
☐ 509	Pirates Rookies	6.00	2.50	.60
	Gene Alley			
	Orlando McFarlane			
☐ 510	Lindy McDaniel	5.00	2.25	.50
☐ 511	Lou Jackson	4.50	2.00	.45
☐ 512	Tigers Rookies	9.00	4.00	.90
	Willie Horton			
	Joe Sparma			
☐ 513	Don Larsen	5.00	2.25	.50
☐ 514	Jim Hickman	4.50	2.00	.45
☐ 515	Johnny Romano	4.50	2.00	.45
☐ 516	Twins Rookies	4.50	2.00	.45
	Jerry Arrigo			
	Dwight Siebler			
☐ 517A	Checklist 7 ERR	25.00	2.50	.50
	(incorrect numbering			
	sequence on back)			
☐ 517B	Checklist 7 COR	15.00	1.50	.30
	(correct numbering			
	on back)			
☐ 518	Carl Bouldin	4.50	2.00	.45
☐ 519	Charlie Smith	4.50	2.00	.45
☐ 520	Jack Baldschun	4.50	2.00	.45
☐ 521	Tom Satriano	4.50	2.00	.45
☐ 522	Bob Tiefenauer	4.50	2.00	.45
☐ 523	Lou Burdette UER	10.00	4.50	1.25
	(pitching lefty)			
☐ 524	Reds Rookies	8.50	3.75	.85
	Jim Dickson			
	Bobby Klaus			
☐ 525	Al McBean	8.50	3.75	.85
☐ 526	Lou Clinton	8.50	3.75	.85
☐ 527	Larry Bearnarth	8.50	3.75	.85
☐ 528	A's Rookies	11.00	5.00	1.35
	Dave Duncan			
	Tommie Reynolds			
☐ 529	Alvin Dark MG	10.00	4.50	1.25
☐ 530	Leon Wagner	8.50	3.75	.85
☐ 531	Los Angeles Dodgers	20.00	8.50	2.75
	Team Card			
☐ 532	Twins Rookies	8.50	3.75	.85
	Bud Bloomfield			
	(Bloomfield photo			
	actually Jay Ward)			
	Joe Nossek			
☐ 533	Johnny Klippstein	8.50	3.75	.85
☐ 534	Gus Bell	10.00	4.50	1.25
☐ 535	Phil Regan	10.00	4.50	1.25
☐ 536	Mets Rookies	8.50	3.75	.85
	Larry Elliot			
	John Stephenson			
☐ 537	Dan Osinski	8.50	3.75	.85
☐ 538	Minnie Minoso	11.00	5.00	1.35
☐ 539	Roy Face	11.00	5.00	1.35
☐ 540	Luis Aparicio	18.00	7.50	2.50
☐ 541	Braves Rookies	200.00	90.00	30.00
	Phil Roof			
	Phil Niekro			
☐ 542	Don Mincher	10.00	4.50	1.25
☐ 543	Bob Uecker	60.00	27.00	9.00
☐ 544	Colts Rookies	10.00	4.50	1.25
	Steve Hertz			
	Joe Hoerner			
☐ 545	Max Alvis	8.50	3.75	.85
☐ 546	Joe Christopher	8.50	3.75	.85
☐ 547	Gil Hodges	15.00	6.50	2.15
☐ 548	NL Rookies	8.50	3.75	.85
	Wayne Schurr			
	Paul Speckenbach			
☐ 549	Joe Moeller	8.50	3.75	.85
☐ 550	Ken Hubbs	21.00	9.00	3.00
	(in memoriam)			
☐ 551	Billy Hoeft	8.50	3.75	.85
☐ 552	Indians Rookies	10.00	4.50	1.25
	Tom Kelley			
	Sonny Siebert			
☐ 553	Jim Brewer	8.50	3.75	.85
☐ 554	Hank Foiles	8.50	3.75	.85
☐ 555	Lee Stange	8.50	3.75	.85
☐ 556	Mets Rookies	8.50	3.75	.85
	Steve Dillon			
	Ron Locke			
☐ 557	Leo Burke	8.50	3.75	.85
☐ 558	Don Schwall	8.50	3.75	.85
☐ 559	Dick Phillips	8.50	3.75	.85
☐ 560	Dick Farrell	8.50	3.75	.85
☐ 561	Phillies Rookies UER	11.00	5.00	1.35
	Dave Bennett			
	(19 ... is 18)			
	Rick Wise			
☐ 562	Pedro Ramos	8.50	3.75	.85
☐ 563	Dal Maxvill	8.50	3.75	.85
☐ 564	AL Rookies	8.50	3.75	.85
	Joe McCabe			
	Jerry McNertney			
☐ 565	Stu Miller	8.50	3.75	.85
☐ 566	Ed Kranepool	10.00	4.50	1.25
☐ 567	Jim Kaat	12.50	5.50	1.65
☐ 568	NL Rookies	8.50	3.75	.85
	Phil Gagliano			
	Cap Peterson			
☐ 569	Fred Newman	8.50	3.75	.85
☐ 570	Bill Mazeroski	11.00	5.00	1.35
☐ 571	Gene Conley	8.50	3.75	.85
☐ 572	AL Rookies	8.50	3.75	.85
	Dave Gray			
	Dick Egan			
☐ 573	Jim Duffalo	8.50	3.75	.85
☐ 574	Manny Jimenez	8.50	3.75	.85
☐ 575	Tony Cloninger	8.50	3.75	.85
☐ 576	Mets Rookies	8.50	3.75	.85
	Jerry Hinsley			
	Bill Wakefield			
☐ 577	Gordy Coleman	8.50	3.75	.85
☐ 578	Glen Hobbie	8.50	3.75	.85
☐ 579	Red Sox Team	16.00	6.75	2.25
☐ 580	Johnny Podres	10.00	4.50	1.25
☐ 581	Yankees Rookies	8.50	3.75	.85
	Pedro Gonzalez			
	Archie Moore			
☐ 582	Rod Kanehl	8.50	3.75	.85
☐ 583	Tito Francona	8.50	3.75	.85
☐ 584	Joel Horlen	8.50	3.75	.85
☐ 585	Tony Taylor	8.50	3.75	.85
☐ 586	Jim Piersall	10.00	4.50	1.25
☐ 587	Bennie Daniels	12.00	5.00	1.00

1964 Topps Giants

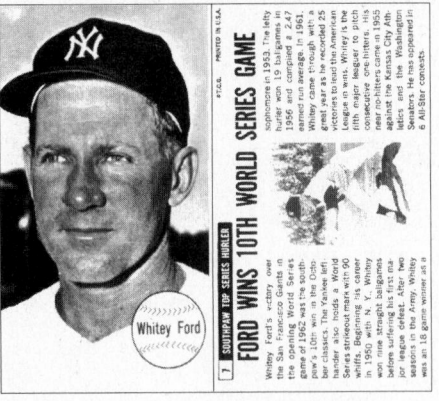

The cards in this 60-card set measure approximately 3 1/8" by 5 1/4". The 1964 Topps Giants are postcard size cards containing color player photographs. They are numbered on the backs, which also contain biographical information presented in a newspaper format. These "giant size" cards were distributed in both cellophane and waxed gum packs apart from the Topps regular issue of 1964. Cards 3, 28, 42, 45, 47, 51 and 60 are slightly more difficult to find and are indicated by SP in the checklist below.

	NRMT	VG-E	GOOD
COMPLETE SET (60)	120.00	55.00	18.00
COMMON PLAYER (1-60)	.25	.10	.02
☐ 1 Gary Peters	.25	.10	.02
☐ 2 Ken Johnson	.25	.10	.02
☐ 3 Sandy Koufax SP	20.00	8.50	2.75
☐ 4 Bob Bailey	.25	.10	.02
☐ 5 Milt Pappas	.25	.10	.02
☐ 6 Ron Hunt	.25	.10	.02
☐ 7 Whitey Ford	2.50	1.00	.25
☐ 8 Roy McMillan	.25	.10	.02
☐ 9 Rocky Colavito	.60	.25	.06
☐ 10 Jim Bunning	.60	.25	.06
☐ 11 Bob Clemente	5.00	2.25	.50
☐ 12 Al Kaline	3.50	1.50	.35
☐ 13 Nellie Fox	.60	.25	.06
☐ 14 Tony Gonzalez	.25	.10	.02
☐ 15 Jim Gentile	.25	.10	.02
☐ 16 Dean Chance	.25	.10	.02
☐ 17 Dick Ellsworth	.25	.10	.02
☐ 18 Jim Fregosi	.25	.10	.02
☐ 19 Dick Groat	.30	.12	.03
☐ 20 Chuck Hinton	.25	.10	.02
☐ 21 Elston Howard	.40	.16	.04
☐ 22 Dick Farrell	.25	.10	.02
☐ 23 Albie Pearson	.25	.10	.02
☐ 24 Frank Howard	.30	.12	.03
☐ 25 Mickey Mantle	16.00	6.75	2.25
☐ 26 Joe Torre	.35	.15	.03
☐ 27 Eddie Brinkman	.25	.10	.02
☐ 28 Bob Friend SP	6.00	2.50	.60
☐ 29 Frank Robinson	3.00	1.25	.30
☐ 30 Bill Freehan	.30	.12	.03
☐ 31 Warren Spahn	2.50	1.00	.25
☐ 32 Camilo Pascual	.25	.10	.02
☐ 33 Pete Ward	.25	.10	.02
☐ 34 Jim Maloney	.25	.10	.02
☐ 35 Dave Wickersham	.25	.10	.02
☐ 36 Johnny Callison	.25	.10	.02
☐ 37 Juan Marichal	2.00	.80	.20
☐ 38 Harmon Killebrew	2.00	.80	.20
☐ 39 Luis Aparicio	1.75	.70	.17
☐ 40 Dick Radatz	.25	.10	.02
☐ 41 Bob Gibson	2.50	1.00	.25
☐ 42 Dick Stuart SP	6.00	2.50	.60
☐ 43 Tommy Davis	.30	.12	.03
☐ 44 Tony Oliva	.50	.20	.05
☐ 45 Wayne Causey SP	6.00	2.50	.60
☐ 46 Max Alvis	.25	.10	.02
☐ 47 Galen Cisco SP	6.00	2.50	.60
☐ 48 Carl Yastrzemski	4.50	2.00	.45
☐ 49 Hank Aaron	5.00	2.25	.50
☐ 50 Brooks Robinson	3.50	1.50	.35
☐ 51 Willie Mays SP	20.00	8.50	2.75
☐ 52 Billy Williams	1.75	.70	.17
☐ 53 Juan Pizarro	.25	.10	.02
☐ 54 Leon Wagner	.25	.10	.02
☐ 55 Orlando Cepeda	.60	.25	.06
☐ 56 Vada Pinson	.35	.15	.03
☐ 57 Ken Boyer	.35	.15	.03
☐ 58 Ron Santo	.35	.15	.03
☐ 59 John Romano	.25	.10	.02
☐ 60 Bill Skowron SP	6.00	2.50	.60

1964 Topps Stand Ups

In 1964 Topps produced a die-cut "Stand-Up" card design for the first time since their Connie Mack and Current All Stars of 1951. The cards have full-length, color player photos set against a green and yellow background. Of the 77 cards in the set, 22 were single printed and these are marked in the checklist below with an SP. These unnumbered cards are standard-size (2 1/2" by 3 1/2"), blank backed, and have been numbered here for reference in alphabetical order of players.

	NRMT	VG-E	GOOD
COMPLETE SET (77)	2500.00	1000.00	300.00
COMMON PLAYER (1-77)	6.00	2.50	.60
COMMON PLAYER SP	24.00	10.50	3.50
☐ 1 Hank Aaron	125.00	57.50	18.75
☐ 2 Hank Aguirre	6.00	2.50	.60
☐ 3 George Altman	6.00	2.50	.60
☐ 4 Max Alvis	6.00	2.50	.60
☐ 5 Bob Aspromonte	6.00	2.50	.60
☐ 6 Jack Baldschun SP	24.00	10.50	3.50
☐ 7 Ernie Banks	50.00	22.50	7.50
☐ 8 Steve Barber	6.00	2.50	.60
☐ 9 Earl Battey	6.00	2.50	.60
☐ 10 Ken Boyer	7.50	3.25	.75
☐ 11 Ernie Broglio	6.00	2.50	.60
☐ 12 John Callison	6.00	2.50	.60
☐ 13 Norm Cash SP	30.00	13.50	4.50
☐ 14 Wayne Causey	6.00	2.50	.60
☐ 15 Orlando Cepeda	9.00	4.00	.90
☐ 16 Ed Charles	6.00	2.50	.60
☐ 17 Bob Clemente	100.00	45.00	15.00
☐ 18 Donn Clendenon SP	24.00	10.50	3.50
☐ 19 Rocky Colavito	9.00	4.00	.90
☐ 20 Ray Culp SP	24.00	10.50	3.50
☐ 21 Tommy Davis	7.50	3.25	.75
☐ 22 Don Drysdale SP	90.00	40.00	13.50
☐ 23 Dick Ellsworth	6.00	2.50	.60
☐ 24 Dick Farrell	6.00	2.50	.60
☐ 25 Jim Fregosi	7.50	3.25	.75
☐ 26 Bob Friend	6.00	2.50	.60
☐ 27 Jim Gentile	6.00	2.50	.60
☐ 28 Jesse Gonder SP	24.00	10.50	3.50
☐ 29 Tony Gonzalez SP	24.00	10.50	3.50
☐ 30 Dick Groat	7.50	3.25	.75
☐ 31 Woody Held	6.00	2.50	.60
☐ 32 Chuck Hinton	6.00	2.50	.60
☐ 33 Elston Howard	7.50	3.25	.75
☐ 34 Frank Howard SP	30.00	13.50	4.50

		NRMT	VG-E	GOOD
☐ 35	Ron Hunt	6.00	2.50	.60
☐ 36	Al Jackson	6.00	2.50	.60
☐ 37	Ken Johnson	6.00	2.50	.60
☐ 38	Al Kaline	60.00	27.00	9.00
☐ 39	Harmon Killebrew	40.00	18.00	6.00
☐ 40	Sandy Koufax	100.00	45.00	15.00
☐ 41	Don Lock SP	24.00	10.50	3.50
☐ 42	Jerry Lumpe SP	24.00	10.50	3.50
☐ 43	Jim Maloney	6.00	2.50	.60
☐ 44	Frank Malzone	6.00	2.50	.60
☐ 45	Mickey Mantle	500.00	225.00	75.00
☐ 46	Juan Marichal SP	90.00	40.00	13.50
☐ 47	Eddie Mathews SP	100.00	45.00	15.00
☐ 48	Willie Mays	125.00	57.50	18.75
☐ 49	Bill Mazeroski	6.00	2.50	.60
☐ 50	Ken McBride	6.00	2.50	.60
☐ 51	Willie McCovey SP	100.00	45.00	15.00
☐ 52	Claude Osteen	6.00	2.50	.60
☐ 53	Jim O'Toole	6.00	2.50	.60
☐ 54	Camilo Pascual	6.00	2.50	.60
☐ 55	Albie Pearson SP	24.00	10.50	3.50
☐ 56	Gary Peters	6.00	2.50	.60
☐ 57	Vada Pinson	7.50	3.25	.75
☐ 58	Juan Pizarro	6.00	2.50	.60
☐ 59	Boog Powell	7.50	3.25	.75
☐ 60	Bobby Richardson	9.00	4.00	.90
☐ 61	Brooks Robinson	50.00	22.50	7.50
☐ 62	Floyd Robinson	6.00	2.50	.60
☐ 63	Frank Robinson	45.00	20.00	6.75
☐ 64	Ed Roebuck SP	24.00	10.50	3.50
☐ 65	Rich Rollins	6.00	2.50	.60
☐ 66	John Romano	6.00	2.50	.60
☐ 67	Ron Santo SP	30.00	13.50	4.50
☐ 68	Norm Siebern	6.00	2.50	.60
☐ 69	Warren Spahn SP	100.00	45.00	15.00
☐ 70	Dick Stuart SP	24.00	10.50	3.50
☐ 71	Lee Thomas	6.00	2.50	.60
☐ 72	Joe Torre	9.00	4.00	.90
☐ 73	Pete Ward	6.00	2.50	.60
☐ 74	Bill White SP	30.00	13.50	4.50
☐ 75	Billy Williams SP	90.00	40.00	13.50
☐ 76	Hal Woodeshick SP	24.00	10.50	3.50
☐ 77	Carl Yastrzemski SP	400.00	180.00	60.00

1965 Topps

The cards in this 598-card set measure 2 1/2" by 3 1/2". The cards comprising the 1965 Topps set have team names located within a distinctive pennant design below the picture. The cards have blue borders on the reverse and were issued by series. Cards 523 to 598 are more difficult to obtain than all other series. Within this last series there are 44 cards that were printed in lesser quantities than the other cards in that series; these shorter-printed cards are marked by SP in the checklist below. In addition, the sixth series (447-522) is more difficult to obtain than series one through five. Featured subsets within this set include League Leaders (1-12) and World Series cards (132-139). Key cards in this set include Steve Carlton's rookie, Mickey Mantle, and Pete Rose. Other key rookies in this set are Jim Hunter, Joe Morgan, and Tony Perez.

		NRMT	VG-E	GOOD
	COMPLETE SET (598)	3750.00	1750.00	400.00
	COMMON PLAYER (1-196)	1.25	.50	.12
	COMMON PLAYER (197-283)	2.00	.80	.20
	COMMON PLAYER (284-370)	2.75	1.10	.27
	COMMON PLAYER (371-446)	4.00	1.75	.40
	COMMON PLAYER (447-522)	5.25	2.25	.50
	COMMON PLAYER (523-598)	5.50	2.50	.55
	COMMON SP (523-598)	11.00	5.00	1.35
☐ 1	AL Batting Leaders Tony Oliva Elston Howard Brooks Robinson	15.00	3.00	.60
☐ 2	NL Batting Leaders Bob Clemente Hank Aaron Rico Carty	7.50	3.25	.75
☐ 3	AL Home Run Leaders Harmon Killebrew Mickey Mantle Boog Powell	12.50	5.50	1.65
☐ 4	NL Home Run Leaders Willie Mays Billy Williams Jim Ray Hart Orlando Cepeda Johnny Callison	6.00	2.50	.60
☐ 5	AL RBI Leaders Brooks Robinson Harmon Killebrew Mickey Mantle Dick Stuart	12.50	5.50	1.65
☐ 6	NL RBI Leaders Ken Boyer Willie Mays Ron Santo	4.00	1.75	.40
☐ 7	AL ERA Leaders Dean Chance Joel Horlen	2.50	1.00	.25
☐ 8	NL ERA Leaders Sandy Koufax Don Drysdale	7.50	3.25	.75
☐ 9	AL Pitching Leaders Dean Chance Gary Peters Dave Wickersham Juan Pizarro Wally Bunker	2.50	1.00	.25
☐ 10	NL Pitching Leaders Larry Jackson Ray Sadecki Juan Marichal	2.50	1.00	.25
☐ 11	AL Strikeout Leaders Al Downing Dean Chance Camilo Pascual	2.50	1.00	.25
☐ 12	NL Strikeout Leaders Bob Veale Don Drysdale Bob Gibson	3.50	1.50	.35
☐ 13	Pedro Ramos	1.25	.50	.12
☐ 14	Len Gabrielson	1.25	.50	.12
☐ 15	Robin Roberts	7.50	3.25	.75
☐ 16	Houston Rookies Joe Morgan Sonny Jackson	175.00	80.00	27.00
☐ 17	Johnny Romano	1.25	.50	.12
☐ 18	Bill McCool	1.25	.50	.12
☐ 19	Gates Brown	1.75	.70	.17
☐ 20	Jim Bunning	3.75	1.60	.37
☐ 21	Don Blasingame	1.25	.50	.12
☐ 22	Charlie Smith	1.25	.50	.12
☐ 23	Bob Tiefenauer	1.25	.50	.12
☐ 24	Minnesota Twins Team Card	3.00	1.25	.30
☐ 25	Al McBean	1.25	.50	.12
☐ 26	Bobby Knoop	1.25	.50	.12
☐ 27	Dick Bertell	1.25	.50	.12
☐ 28	Barney Schultz	1.25	.50	.12
☐ 29	Felix Mantilla	1.25	.50	.12
☐ 30	Jim Bouton	2.50	1.00	.25
☐ 31	Mike White	1.25	.50	.12
☐ 32	Herman Franks MG	1.25	.50	.12
☐ 33	Jackie Brandt	1.25	.50	.12
☐ 34	Cal Koonce	1.25	.50	.12
☐ 35	Ed Charles	1.25	.50	.12
☐ 36	Bobby Wine	1.25	.50	.12
☐ 37	Fred Gladding	1.25	.50	.12
☐ 38	Jim King	1.25	.50	.12
☐ 39	Gerry Arrigo	1.25	.50	.12
☐ 40	Frank Howard	2.50	1.00	.25
☐ 41	White Sox Rookies Bruce Howard Marv Staehle	1.25	.50	.12

☐	42	Earl Wilson	1.25	.50	.12	☐	123	Frank Thomas	1.75	.70	.17
☐	43	Mike Shannon	1.75	.70	.17	☐	124	Tom Satriano	1.25	.50	.12

Earl Wilson .... 1.25 .50 .12
Mike Shannon .... 1.75 .70 .17
(Name in red, other
Cardinals in yellow)
44 Wade Blasingame .... 1.25 .50 .12
45 Roy McMillan .... 1.25 .50 .12
46 Bob Lee .... 1.25 .50 .12
47 Tommy Harper .... 1.75 .70 .17
48 Claude Raymond .... 1.25 .50 .12
49 Orioles Rookies .... 1.75 .70 .17
  Curt Blefary
  John Miller
50 Juan Marichal 9.50 4.25 1.00
51 Bill Bryan .... 1.25 .50 .12
52 Ed Roebuck .... 1.25 .50 .12
53 Dick McAuliffe .... 1.75 .70 .17
54 Joe Gibbon .... 1.25 .50 .12
55 Tony Conigliaro .... 8.00 3.50 .80
56 Ron Kline .... 1.25 .50 .12
57 Cardinals Team .... 2.50 1.00 .25
58 Fred Talbot .... 1.25 .50 .12
59 Nate Oliver .... 1.25 .50 .12
60 Jim O'Toole .... 1.25 .50 .12
61 Chris Cannizzaro .... 1.25 .50 .12
62 Jim Katt UER .... 4.50 2.00 .45
  (sic, Kaat)
63 Ty Cline .... 1.25 .50 .12
64 Lou Burdette .... 1.75 .70 .17
65 Tony Kubek .... 3.00 1.25 .30
66 Bill Rigney MG .... 1.25 .50 .12
67 Harvey Haddix .... 1.75 .70 .17
68 Del Crandall .... 1.75 .70 .17
69 Bill Virdon .... 1.75 .70 .17
70 Bill Skowron .... 1.75 .70 .17
71 John O'Donoghue .... 1.25 .50 .12
72 Tony Gonzalez .... 1.25 .50 .12
73 Dennis Ribant .... 1.25 .50 .12
74 Red Sox Rookies .... 5.50 2.50 .55
  Rico Petrocelli
  Jerry Stephenson
75 Deron Johnson .... 1.25 .50 .12
76 Sam McDowell .... 1.75 .70 .17
77 Doug Camilli .... 1.25 .50 .12
78 Dal Maxvill .... 1.25 .50 .12
79 Checklist 1 .... 7.50 .75 .15
80 Turk Farrell .... 1.25 .50 .12
81 Don Buford .... 1.75 .70 .17
82 Braves Rookies .... 2.50 1.00 .25
  Santos Alomar
  John Braun
83 George Thomas .... 1.25 .50 .12
84 Ron Herbel .... 1.25 .50 .12
85 Willie Smith .... 1.25 .50 .12
86 Les Narum .... 1.25 .50 .12
87 Nelson Mathews .... 1.25 .50 .12
88 Jack Lamabe .... 1.25 .50 .12
89 Mike Hershberger .... 1.25 .50 .12
90 Rich Rollins .... 1.75 .70 .17
91 Cubs Team .... 2.50 1.00 .25
92 Dick Howser .... 1.75 .70 .17
93 Jack Fisher .... 1.25 .50 .12
94 Charlie Lau .... 1.75 .70 .17
95 Bill Mazeroski .... 3.00 1.25 .30
96 Sonny Siebert .... 1.25 .50 .12
97 Pedro Gonzalez .... 1.25 .50 .12
98 Bob Miller .... 1.25 .50 .12
99 Gil Hodges MG .... 6.00 2.50 .60
100 Ken Boyer .... 3.00 1.25 .30
101 Fred Newman .... 1.25 .50 .12
102 Steve Boros .... 1.25 .50 .12
103 Harvey Kuenn .... 1.75 .70 .17
104 Checklist 2 .... 7.50 .75 .15
105 Chico Salmon .... 1.25 .50 .12
106 Gene Oliver .... 1.25 .50 .12
107 Phillies Rookies .... 1.75 .70 .17
  Pat Corrales
  Costen Shockley
108 Don Mincher .... 1.75 .70 .17
109 Walt Bond .... 1.25 .50 .12
110 Ron Santo .... 3.00 1.25 .30
111 Lee Thomas .... 1.75 .70 .17
112 Derrell Griffith .... 1.25 .50 .12
113 Steve Barber .... 1.25 .50 .12
114 Jim Hickman .... 1.25 .50 .12
115 Bobby Richardson .... 3.00 1.25 .30
116 Cardinals Rookies .... 1.75 .70 .17
  Dave Dowling
  Bob Tolan
117 Wes Stock .... 1.25 .50 .12
118 Hal Lanier .... 1.75 .70 .17
119 John Kennedy .... 1.25 .50 .12
120 Frank Robinson 25.00 11.00 3.50
121 Gene Alley .... 1.75 .70 .17
122 Bill Pleis .... 1.25 .50 .12

123 Frank Thomas .... 1.75 .70 .17
124 Tom Satriano .... 1.25 .50 .12
125 Juan Pizarro .... 1.25 .50 .12
126 Dodgers Team .... 4.00 1.75 .40
127 Frank Lary .... 1.25 .50 .12
128 Vic Davalillo .... 1.25 .50 .12
129 Bennie Daniels .... 1.25 .50 .12
130 Al Kaline 25.00 11.00 3.50
131 Johnny Keane MG .... 1.25 .50 .12
132 World Series Game 1 .... 4.00 1.75 .40
  Cards take opener
133 World Series Game 2 .... 4.00 1.75 .40
  Stottlemyre wins
134 World Series Game 3 .... 28.00 12.50 4.00
  Mantle's homer
135 World Series Game 4 .... 4.50 2.00 .45
  Boyer's grand-slam
136 World Series Game 5 .... 4.00 1.75 .40
  10th inning triumph
137 World Series Game 6 .... 4.50 2.00 .45
  Bouton wins again
138 World Series Game 7 .... 6.00 2.50 .60
  Gibson wins finale
139 World Series Summary .... 4.00 1.75 .40
  Cards celebrate
140 Dean Chance .... 1.75 .70 .17
141 Charlie James .... 1.25 .50 .12
142 Bill Monbouquette .... 1.25 .50 .12
143 Pirates Rookies .... 1.25 .50 .12
  John Gelnar
  Jerry May
144 Ed Kranepool .... 1.75 .70 .17
145 Luis Tiant 12.00 5.25 1.50
146 Ron Hansen .... 1.25 .50 .12
147 Dennis Bennett .... 1.25 .50 .12
148 Willie Kirkland .... 1.25 .50 .12
149 Wayne Schurr .... 1.25 .50 .12
150 Brooks Robinson 25.00 11.00 3.50
151 Athletics Team .... 2.50 1.00 .25
152 Phil Ortega .... 1.25 .50 .12
153 Norm Cash .... 3.00 1.25 .30
154 Bob Humphreys .... 1.25 .50 .12
155 Roger Maris 50.00 22.50 7.50
156 Bob Sadowski .... 1.25 .50 .12
157 Zoilo Versalles .... 1.75 .70 .17
158 Dick Sisler .... 1.25 .50 .12
159 Jim Duffalo .... 1.25 .50 .12
160 Bob Clemente UER 75.00 34.00 11.25
  (1960 Pittsburfh)
161 Frank Baumann .... 1.25 .50 .12
162 Russ Nixon .... 1.25 .50 .12
163 Johnny Briggs .... 1.25 .50 .12
164 Al Spangler .... 1.25 .50 .12
165 Dick Ellsworth .... 1.25 .50 .12
166 Indians Rookies .... 2.50 1.00 .25
  George Culver
  Tommie Agee
167 Bill Wakefield .... 1.25 .50 .12
168 Dick Green .... 1.25 .50 .12
169 Dave Vineyard .... 1.25 .50 .12
170 Hank Aaron 90.00 40.00 13.50
171 Jim Roland .... 1.25 .50 .12
172 Jim Piersall .... 1.75 .70 .17
173 Detroit Tigers .... 2.50 1.00 .25
  Team Card
174 Joey Jay .... 1.25 .50 .12
175 Bob Aspromonte .... 1.25 .50 .12
176 Willie McCovey 18.00 7.50 2.50
177 Pete Mikkelsen .... 1.25 .50 .12
178 Dalton Jones .... 1.25 .50 .12
179 Hal Woodeshick .... 1.25 .50 .12
180 Bob Allison .... 1.75 .70 .17
181 Senators Rookies .... 1.25 .50 .12
  Don Loun
  Joe McCabe
182 Mike De La Hoz .... 1.25 .50 .12
183 Dave Nicholson .... 1.25 .50 .12
184 John Boozer .... 1.25 .50 .12
185 Max Alvis .... 1.25 .50 .12
186 Billy Cowan .... 1.25 .50 .12
187 Casey Stengel MG 12.50 5.50 1.65
188 Sam Bowens .... 1.25 .50 .12
189 Checklist 3 .... 7.50 .75 .15
190 Bill White .... 2.50 1.00 .25
191 Phil Regan .... 1.25 .50 .12
192 Jim Coker .... 1.25 .50 .12
193 Gaylord Perry 20.00 8.50 2.75
194 Rookie Stars .... 1.75 .70 .17
  Bill Kelso
  Rick Reichardt
195 Bob Veale .... 1.75 .70 .17
196 Ron Fairly .... 1.75 .70 .17
197 Diego Segui .... 2.00 .80 .20
198 Smoky Burgess .... 2.50 1.00 .25

#	Player			
☐ 199	Bob Heffner	2.00	.80	.20
☐ 200	Joe Torre	3.50	1.50	.35
☐ 201	Twins Rookies Sandy Valdespino Cesar Tovar	2.50	1.00	.25
☐ 202	Leo Burke	2.00	.80	.20
☐ 203	Dallas Green	2.50	1.00	.25
☐ 204	Russ Snyder	2.00	.80	.20
☐ 205	Warren Spahn	22.00	9.50	3.15
☐ 206	Willie Horton	3.00	1.25	.30
☐ 207	Pete Rose	160.00	72.00	24.00
☐ 208	Tommy John	12.50	5.50	1.65
☐ 209	Pirates Team	4.00	1.75	.40
☐ 210	Jim Fregosi	3.00	1.25	.30
☐ 211	Steve Ridzik	2.00	.80	.20
☐ 212	Ron Brand	2.00	.80	.20
☐ 213	Jim Davenport	2.00	.80	.20
☐ 214	Bob Purkey	2.00	.80	.20
☐ 215	Pete Ward	2.00	.80	.20
☐ 216	Al Worthington	2.00	.80	.20
☐ 217	Walt Alston MG	4.00	1.75	.40
☐ 218	Dick Schofield	2.00	.80	.20
☐ 219	Bob Meyer	2.00	.80	.20
☐ 220	Billy Williams	12.50	5.50	1.65
☐ 221	John Tsitouris	2.00	.80	.20
☐ 222	Bob Tillman	2.00	.80	.20
☐ 223	Dan Osinski	2.00	.80	.20
☐ 224	Bob Chance	2.00	.80	.20
☐ 225	Bo Belinsky	2.50	1.00	.25
☐ 226	Yankees Rookies Elvio Jimenez Jake Gibbs	2.50	1.00	.25
☐ 227	Bobby Klaus	2.00	.80	.20
☐ 228	Jack Sanford	2.00	.80	.20
☐ 229	Lou Clinton	2.00	.80	.20
☐ 230	Ray Sadecki	2.00	.80	.20
☐ 231	Jerry Adair	2.00	.80	.20
☐ 232	Steve Blass	2.50	1.00	.25
☐ 233	Don Zimmer	2.50	1.00	.25
☐ 234	White Sox Team	4.00	1.75	.40
☐ 235	Chuck Hinton	2.00	.80	.20
☐ 236	Denny McLain	20.00	8.50	2.75
☐ 237	Bernie Allen	2.00	.80	.20
☐ 238	Joe Moeller	2.00	.80	.20
☐ 239	Doc Edwards	2.00	.80	.20
☐ 240	Bob Bruce	2.00	.80	.20
☐ 241	Mack Jones	2.00	.80	.20
☐ 242	George Brunet	2.00	.80	.20
☐ 243	Reds Rookies Ted Davidson Tommy Helms	3.00	1.25	.30
☐ 244	Lindy McDaniel	2.50	1.00	.25
☐ 245	Joe Pepitone	3.00	1.25	.30
☐ 246	Tom Butters	2.00	.80	.20
☐ 247	Wally Moon	2.50	1.00	.25
☐ 248	Gus Triandos	2.50	1.00	.25
☐ 249	Dave McNally	2.50	1.00	.25
☐ 250	Willie Mays	100.00	45.00	15.00
☐ 251	Billy Herman MG	2.50	1.00	.25
☐ 252	Pete Richert	2.00	.80	.20
☐ 253	Danny Cater	2.50	1.00	.25
☐ 254	Roland Sheldon	2.00	.80	.20
☐ 255	Camilo Pascual	2.50	1.00	.25
☐ 256	Tito Francona	2.00	.80	.20
☐ 257	Jim Wynn	3.00	1.25	.30
☐ 258	Larry Bearnarth	2.00	.80	.20
☐ 259	Tigers Rookies Jim Northrup Ray Oyler	4.00	1.75	.40
☐ 260	Don Drysdale	20.00	8.50	2.75
☐ 261	Duke Carmel	2.00	.80	.20
☐ 262	Bud Daley	2.00	.80	.20
☐ 263	Marty Keough	2.00	.80	.20
☐ 264	Bob Buhl	2.00	.80	.20
☐ 265	Jim Pagliaroni	2.00	.80	.20
☐ 266	Bert Campaneris	6.50	2.75	.65
☐ 267	Senators Team	4.00	1.75	.40
☐ 268	Ken McBride	2.00	.80	.20
☐ 269	Frank Bolling	2.00	.80	.20
☐ 270	Milt Pappas	2.50	1.00	.25
☐ 271	Don Wert	2.00	.80	.20
☐ 272	Chuck Schilling	2.00	.80	.20
☐ 273	Checklist 4	7.50	.75	.15
☐ 274	Lum Harris MG	2.00	.80	.20
☐ 275	Dick Groat	2.50	1.00	.25
☐ 276	Hoyt Wilhelm	7.50	3.25	.75
☐ 277	Johnny Lewis	2.00	.80	.20
☐ 278	Ken Retzer	2.00	.80	.20
☐ 279	Dick Tracewski	2.00	.80	.20
☐ 280	Dick Stuart	2.50	1.00	.25
☐ 281	Bill Stafford	2.00	.80	.20
☐ 282	Giants Rookies Dick Estelle Masanori Murakami	4.00	1.75	.40
☐ 283	Fred Whitfield	2.00	.80	.20
☐ 284	Nick Willhite	2.75	1.10	.27
☐ 285	Ron Hunt	2.75	1.10	.27
☐ 286	Athletics Rookies Jim Dickson Aurelio Monteagudo	2.75	1.10	.27
☐ 287	Gary Kolb	2.75	1.10	.27
☐ 288	Jack Hamilton	2.75	1.10	.27
☐ 289	Gordy Coleman	3.25	1.35	.32
☐ 290	Wally Bunker	3.25	1.35	.32
☐ 291	Jerry Lynch	2.75	1.10	.27
☐ 292	Larry Yellen	2.75	1.10	.27
☐ 293	Angels Team	5.00	2.25	.50
☐ 294	Tim McCarver	4.50	2.00	.45
☐ 295	Dick Radatz	3.25	1.35	.32
☐ 296	Tony Taylor	2.75	1.10	.27
☐ 297	Dave DeBusschere	3.75	1.60	.37
☐ 298	Jim Stewart	2.75	1.10	.27
☐ 299	Jerry Zimmerman	2.75	1.10	.27
☐ 300	Sandy Koufax	110.00	50.00	16.50
☐ 301	Birdie Tebbetts MG	2.75	1.10	.27
☐ 302	Al Stanek	2.75	1.10	.27
☐ 303	John Orsino	2.75	1.10	.27
☐ 304	Dave Stenhouse	2.75	1.10	.27
☐ 305	Rico Carty	3.50	1.50	.35
☐ 306	Bubba Phillips	2.75	1.10	.27
☐ 307	Barry Latman	2.75	1.10	.27
☐ 308	Mets Rookies Cleon Jones Tom Parsons	4.00	1.75	.40
☐ 309	Steve Hamilton	2.75	1.10	.27
☐ 310	Johnny Callison	3.50	1.50	.35
☐ 311	Orlando Pena	2.75	1.10	.27
☐ 312	Joe Nuxhall	3.50	1.50	.35
☐ 313	Jim Schaffer	2.75	1.10	.27
☐ 314	Sterling Slaughter	2.75	1.10	.27
☐ 315	Frank Malzone	3.50	1.50	.35
☐ 316	Reds Team	5.50	2.50	.55
☐ 317	Don McMahon	2.75	1.10	.27
☐ 318	Matty Alou	3.50	1.50	.35
☐ 319	Ken McMullen	2.75	1.10	.27
☐ 320	Bob Gibson	28.00	12.50	4.00
☐ 321	Rusty Staub	4.00	1.75	.40
☐ 322	Rick Wise	3.50	1.50	.35
☐ 323	Hank Bauer MG	3.50	1.50	.35
☐ 324	Bobby Locke	2.75	1.10	.27
☐ 325	Donn Clendenon	3.50	1.50	.35
☐ 326	Dwight Siebler	2.75	1.10	.27
☐ 327	Denis Menke	2.75	1.10	.27
☐ 328	Eddie Fisher	2.75	1.10	.27
☐ 329	Hawk Taylor	2.75	1.10	.27
☐ 330	Whitey Ford	25.00	11.00	3.50
☐ 331	Dodgers Rookies Al Ferrara John Purdin	3.50	1.50	.35
☐ 332	Ted Abernathy	2.75	1.10	.27
☐ 333	Tom Reynolds	2.75	1.10	.27
☐ 334	Vic Roznovsky	2.75	1.10	.27
☐ 335	Mickey Lolich	4.50	2.00	.45
☐ 336	Woody Held	2.75	1.10	.27
☐ 337	Mike Cuellar	3.50	1.50	.35
☐ 338	Philadelphia Phillies Team Card	5.50	2.50	.55
☐ 339	Ryne Duren	3.50	1.50	.35
☐ 340	Tony Oliva	9.00	4.00	.90
☐ 341	Bob Bolin	2.75	1.10	.27
☐ 342	Bob Rodgers	3.50	1.50	.35
☐ 343	Mike McCormick	3.50	1.50	.35
☐ 344	Wes Parker	3.50	1.50	.35
☐ 345	Floyd Robinson	2.75	1.10	.27
☐ 346	Bobby Bragan MG	2.75	1.10	.27
☐ 347	Roy Face	3.50	1.50	.35
☐ 348	George Banks	2.75	1.10	.27
☐ 349	Larry Miller	2.75	1.10	.27
☐ 350	Mickey Mantle	400.00	180.00	60.00
☐ 351	Jim Perry	3.50	1.50	.35
☐ 352	Alex Johnson	3.50	1.50	.35
☐ 353	Jerry Lumpe	2.75	1.10	.27
☐ 354	Cubs Rookies Billy Ott Jack Warner	2.75	1.10	.27
☐ 355	Vada Pinson	3.50	1.50	.35
☐ 356	Bill Spanswick	2.75	1.10	.27
☐ 357	Carl Warwick	2.75	1.10	.27
☐ 358	Albie Pearson	2.75	1.10	.27
☐ 359	Ken Johnson	2.75	1.10	.27
☐ 360	Orlando Cepeda	7.00	3.00	.70
☐ 361	Checklist 5	9.00	.90	.20
☐ 362	Don Schwall	2.75	1.10	.27
☐ 363	Bob Johnson	2.75	1.10	.27
☐ 364	Galen Cisco	2.75	1.10	.27
☐ 365	Jim Gentile	3.50	1.50	.35
☐ 366	Dan Schneider	2.75	1.10	.27
☐ 367	Leon Wagner	2.75	1.10	.27

☐ 368	White Sox Rookies	3.50	1.50	.35
	Ken Berry			
	Joel Gibson			
☐ 369	Phil Linz	3.50	1.50	.35
☐ 370	Tommy Davis	3.50	1.50	.35
☐ 371	Frank Kreutzer	4.00	1.75	.40
☐ 372	Clay Dalrymple	4.00	1.75	.40
☐ 373	Curt Simmons	4.50	2.00	.45
☐ 374	Angels Rookies	4.50	2.00	.45
	Jose Cardenal			
	Dick Simpson			
☐ 375	Dave Wickersham	4.00	1.75	.40
☐ 376	Jim Landis	4.00	1.75	.40
☐ 377	Willie Stargell	27.00	12.00	4.00
☐ 378	Chuck Estrada	4.50	2.00	.45
☐ 379	Giants Team	8.00	3.50	.80
☐ 380	Rocky Colavito	7.50	3.25	.75
☐ 381	Al Jackson	4.50	2.00	.45
☐ 382	J.C. Martin	4.00	1.75	.40
☐ 383	Felipe Alou	5.00	2.25	.50
☐ 384	Johnny Klippstein	4.00	1.75	.40
☐ 385	Carl Yastrzemski	85.00	38.00	12.75
☐ 386	Cubs Rookies	4.50	2.00	.45
	Paul Jaeckel			
	Fred Norman			
☐ 387	Johnny Podres	5.00	2.25	.50
☐ 388	John Blanchard	4.50	2.00	.45
☐ 389	Don Larsen	4.50	2.00	.45
☐ 390	Bill Freehan	5.00	2.25	.50
☐ 391	Mel McGaha MG	4.00	1.75	.40
☐ 392	Bob Friend	4.50	2.00	.45
☐ 393	Ed Kirkpatrick	4.00	1.75	.40
☐ 394	Jim Hannan	4.00	1.75	.40
☐ 395	Jim Ray Hart	4.50	2.00	.45
☐ 396	Frank Bertaina	4.00	1.75	.40
☐ 397	Jerry Buchek	4.00	1.75	.40
☐ 398	Reds Rookies	4.50	2.00	.45
	Dan Neville			
	Art Shamsky			
☐ 399	Ray Herbert	4.00	1.75	.40
☐ 400	Harmon Killebrew	32.00	14.25	4.75
☐ 401	Carl Willey	4.00	1.75	.40
☐ 402	Joe Amalfitano	4.00	1.75	.40
☐ 403	Boston Red Sox	8.00	3.50	.80
	Team Card			
☐ 404	Stan Williams	4.00	1.75	.40
	(listed as Indian			
	but Yankee cap)			
☐ 405	John Roseboro	4.50	2.00	.45
☐ 406	Ralph Terry	4.50	2.00	.45
☐ 407	Lee Maye	4.00	1.75	.40
☐ 408	Larry Sherry	4.50	2.00	.45
☐ 409	Astros Rookies	5.00	2.25	.50
	Jim Beauchamp			
	Larry Dierker			
☐ 410	Luis Aparicio	10.00	4.50	1.25
☐ 411	Roger Craig	4.50	2.00	.45
☐ 412	Bob Bailey	4.00	1.75	.40
☐ 413	Hal Reniff	4.00	1.75	.40
☐ 414	Al Lopez MG	5.50	2.50	.55
☐ 415	Curt Flood	6.00	2.50	.60
☐ 416	Jim Brewer	4.00	1.75	.40
☐ 417	Ed Brinkman	4.00	1.75	.40
☐ 418	Johnny Edwards	4.00	1.75	.40
☐ 419	Ruben Amaro	4.00	1.75	.40
☐ 420	Larry Jackson	4.00	1.75	.40
☐ 421	Twins Rookies	4.00	1.75	.40
	Gary Dotter			
	Jay Ward			
☐ 422	Aubrey Gatewood	4.00	1.75	.40
☐ 423	Jesse Gonder	4.00	1.75	.40
☐ 424	Gary Bell	4.00	1.75	.40
☐ 425	Wayne Causey	4.00	1.75	.40
☐ 426	Braves Team	8.00	3.50	.80
☐ 427	Bob Saverine	4.00	1.75	.40
☐ 428	Bob Shaw	4.00	1.75	.40
☐ 429	Don Demeter	4.00	1.75	.40
☐ 430	Gary Peters	4.50	2.00	.45
☐ 431	Cards Rookies	6.00	2.50	.60
	Nelson Briles			
	Wayne Spiezio			
☐ 432	Jim Grant	4.00	1.75	.40
☐ 433	John Bateman	4.00	1.75	.40
☐ 434	Dave Morehead	4.00	1.75	.40
☐ 435	Willie Davis	5.00	2.25	.50
☐ 436	Don Elston	4.00	1.75	.40
☐ 437	Chico Cardenas	4.50	2.00	.45
☐ 438	Harry Walker MG	4.00	1.75	.40
☐ 439	Moe Drabowsky	4.00	1.75	.40
☐ 440	Tom Tresh	5.00	2.25	.50
☐ 441	Denny Lemaster	4.00	1.75	.40
☐ 442	Vic Power	4.00	1.75	.40
☐ 443	Checklist 6	12.50	1.25	.25
☐ 444	Bob Hendley	4.00	1.75	.40
☐ 445	Don Lock	4.00	1.75	.40
☐ 446	Art Mahaffey	4.00	1.75	.40
☐ 447	Julian Javier	5.25	2.25	.50
☐ 448	Lee Stange	5.25	2.25	.50
☐ 449	Mets Rookies	5.25	2.25	.50
	Jerry Hinsley			
	Gary Kroll			
☐ 450	Elston Howard	7.00	3.00	.70
☐ 451	Jim Owens	5.25	2.25	.50
☐ 452	Gary Geiger	5.25	2.25	.50
☐ 453	Dodgers Rookies	6.00	2.50	.60
	Willie Crawford			
	John Werhas			
☐ 454	Ed Rakow	5.25	2.25	.50
☐ 455	Norm Siebern	5.25	2.25	.50
☐ 456	Bill Henry	5.25	2.25	.50
☐ 457	Bob Kennedy MG	5.25	2.25	.50
☐ 458	John Buzhardt	5.25	2.25	.50
☐ 459	Frank Kostro	5.25	2.25	.50
☐ 460	Richie Allen	20.00	8.50	2.75
☐ 461	Braves Rookies	50.00	22.50	7.50
	Clay Carroll			
	Phil Niekro			
☐ 462	Lew Krausse UER	5.25	2.25	.50
	(photo actually			
	Pete Lovrich)			
☐ 463	Manny Mota	6.00	2.50	.60
☐ 464	Ron Piche	5.25	2.25	.50
☐ 465	Tom Haller	5.25	2.25	.50
☐ 466	Senators Rookies	5.25	2.25	.50
	Pete Craig			
	Dick Nen			
☐ 467	Ray Washburn	5.25	2.25	.50
☐ 468	Larry Brown	5.25	2.25	.50
☐ 469	Don Nottebart	5.25	2.25	.50
☐ 470	Yogi Berra P/CO	55.00	25.00	8.25
☐ 471	Billy Hoeft	5.25	2.25	.50
☐ 472	Don Pavletich	5.25	2.25	.50
☐ 473	Orioles Rookies	12.00	5.25	1.50
	Paul Blair			
	Dave Johnson			
☐ 474	Cookie Rojas	6.00	2.50	.60
☐ 475	Clete Boyer	6.00	2.50	.60
☐ 476	Billy O'Dell	5.25	2.25	.50
☐ 477	Cards Rookies	475.00	215.00	70.00
	Fritz Ackley			
	Steve Carlton			
☐ 478	Wilbur Wood	6.00	2.50	.60
☐ 479	Ken Harrelson	7.00	3.00	.70
☐ 480	Joel Horlen	6.00	2.50	.60
☐ 481	Cleveland Indians	11.00	5.00	1.35
	Team Card			
☐ 482	Bob Priddy	5.25	2.25	.50
☐ 483	George Smith	5.25	2.25	.50
☐ 484	Ron Perranoski	6.00	2.50	.60
☐ 485	Nellie Fox	10.00	4.50	1.25
☐ 486	Angels Rookies	6.00	2.50	.60
	Tom Egan			
	Pat Rogan			
☐ 487	Woody Woodward	6.00	2.50	.60
☐ 488	Ted Wills	5.25	2.25	.50
☐ 489	Gene Mauch MG	6.00	2.50	.60
☐ 490	Earl Battey	5.25	2.25	.50
☐ 491	Tracy Stallard	5.25	2.25	.50
☐ 492	Gene Freese	5.25	2.25	.50
☐ 493	Tigers Rookies	5.25	2.25	.50
	Bill Roman			
	Bruce Brubaker			
☐ 494	Jay Ritchie	5.25	2.25	.50
☐ 495	Joe Christopher	5.25	2.25	.50
☐ 496	Joe Cunningham	6.00	2.50	.60
☐ 497	Giants Rookies	7.00	3.00	.70
	Ken Henderson			
	Jack Hiatt			
☐ 498	Gene Stephens	5.25	2.25	.50
☐ 499	Stu Miller	5.25	2.25	.50
☐ 500	Eddie Mathews	32.00	14.25	4.75
☐ 501	Indians Rookies	5.25	2.25	.50
	Ralph Gagliano			
	Jim Rittwage			
☐ 502	Don Cardwell	5.25	2.25	.50
☐ 503	Phil Gagliano	5.25	2.25	.50
☐ 504	Jerry Grote	5.25	2.25	.50
☐ 505	Ray Culp	5.25	2.25	.50
☐ 506	Sam Mele MG	5.25	2.25	.50
☐ 507	Sammy Ellis	5.25	2.25	.50
☐ 508	Checklist 7	15.00	1.50	.30
☐ 509	Red Sox Rookies	5.25	2.25	.50
	Bob Guindon			
	Gerry Vezendy			
☐ 510	Ernie Banks	70.00	32.00	10.50
☐ 511	Ron Locke	5.25	2.25	.50
☐ 512	Cap Peterson	5.25	2.25	.50
☐ 513	New York Yankees	14.00	6.25	2.00
	Team Card			

☐ 514	Joe Azcue	5.25	2.25	.50
☐ 515	Vern Law	6.00	2.50	.60
☐ 516	Al Weis	5.25	2.25	.50
☐ 517	Angels Rookies	5.25	2.25	.50
	Paul Schaal			
	Jack Warner			
☐ 518	Ken Rowe	5.25	2.25	.50
☐ 519	Bob Uecker UER	45.00	20.00	6.75
	(posing as a left-			
	handed batter)			
☐ 520	Tony Cloninger	5.25	2.25	.50
☐ 521	Phillies Rookies	5.25	2.25	.50
	Dave Bennett			
	Morrie Stevens			
☐ 522	Hank Aguirre	5.25	2.25	.50
☐ 523	Mike Brumley SP	11.00	5.00	1.35
☐ 524	Dave Giusti SP	12.00	5.25	1.50
☐ 525	Eddie Bressoud	5.50	2.50	.55
☐ 526	Athletics Rookies SP	160.00	72.00	24.00
	Rene Lachemann			
	Johnny Odom			
	Jim Hunter ERR			
	("Tim" on back)			
	Skip Lockwood			
☐ 527	Jeff Torborg SP	13.50	6.00	1.85
☐ 528	George Altman	5.50	2.50	.55
☐ 529	Jerry Fosnow SP	11.00	5.00	1.35
☐ 530	Jim Maloney	7.50	3.25	.75
☐ 531	Chuck Hiller	5.50	2.50	.55
☐ 532	Hector Lopez	5.50	2.50	.55
☐ 533	Mets Rookies SP	27.00	12.00	4.00
	Dan Napoleon			
	Ron Swoboda			
	Tug McGraw			
	Jim Bethke			
☐ 534	John Herrnstein	5.50	2.50	.55
☐ 535	Jack Kralick SP	11.00	5.00	1.35
☐ 536	Andre Rodgers SP	11.00	5.00	1.35
☐ 537	Angels Rookies	6.50	2.75	.65
	Marcelino Lopez			
	Phil Roof			
	Rudy May			
☐ 538	Chuck Dressen MG SP	12.00	5.25	1.50
☐ 539	Herm Starrette	5.50	2.50	.55
☐ 540	Lou Brock SP	48.00	22.00	6.00
☐ 541	White Sox Rookies	5.50	2.50	.55
	Greg Bollo			
	Bob Locker			
☐ 542	Lou Klimchock	5.50	2.50	.55
☐ 543	Ed Connolly SP	11.00	5.00	1.35
☐ 544	Howie Reed	5.50	2.50	.55
☐ 545	Jesus Alou SP	11.00	5.00	1.35
☐ 546	Indians Rookies	5.50	2.50	.55
	Bill Davis			
	Mike Hedlund			
	Ray Barker			
	Floyd Weaver			
☐ 547	Jake Wood SP	11.00	5.00	1.35
☐ 548	Dick Stigman	5.50	2.50	.55
☐ 549	Cubs Rookies SP	16.00	6.75	2.25
	Roberto Pena			
	Glenn Beckert			
☐ 550	Mel Stottlemyre SP	27.00	12.00	4.00
☐ 551	New York Mets SP	24.00	10.50	3.50
	Team Card			
☐ 552	Julio Gotay	5.50	2.50	.55
☐ 553	Astros Rookies	5.50	2.50	.55
	Dan Coombs			
	Gene Ratliff			
	Jack McClure			
☐ 554	Chico Ruiz SP	11.00	5.00	1.35
☐ 555	Jack Baldschun SP	11.00	5.00	1.35
☐ 556	Red Schoendienst	18.00	7.50	2.50
	MG SP			
☐ 557	Jose Santiago	5.50	2.50	.55
☐ 558	Tommie Sisk	5.50	2.50	.55
☐ 559	Ed Bailey SP	11.00	5.00	1.35
☐ 560	Boog Powell SP	16.00	6.75	2.25
☐ 561	Dodgers Rookies	12.00	5.25	1.50
	Dennis Daboll			
	Mike Kekich			
	Hector Valle			
	Jim Lefebvre			
☐ 562	Billy Moran	5.50	2.50	.55
☐ 563	Julio Navarro	5.50	2.50	.55
☐ 564	Mel Nelson	5.50	2.50	.55
☐ 565	Ernie Broglio SP	11.00	5.00	1.35
☐ 566	Yankees Rookies SP	11.00	5.00	1.35
	Gil Blanco			
	Ross Moschitto			
	Art Lopez			
☐ 567	Tommie Aaron	6.50	2.75	.65
☐ 568	Ron Taylor SP	11.00	5.00	1.35
☐ 569	Gino Cimoli SP	11.00	5.00	1.35

☐ 570	Claude Osteen SP	12.00	5.25	1.50
☐ 571	Ossie Virgil SP	11.00	5.00	1.35
☐ 572	Baltimore Orioles SP	21.00	9.00	3.00
	Team Card			
☐ 573	Red Sox Rookies SP	20.00	8.50	2.75
	Jim Lonborg			
	Gerry Moses			
	Bill Schlesinger			
	Mike Ryan			
☐ 574	Roy Sievers	6.50	2.75	.65
☐ 575	Jose Pagan	5.50	2.50	.55
☐ 576	Terry Fox SP	11.00	5.00	1.35
☐ 577	AL Rookie Stars SP	12.00	5.25	1.50
	Darold Knowles			
	Don Buschhorn			
	Richie Scheinblum			
☐ 578	Camilo Carreon SP	11.00	5.00	1.35
☐ 579	Dick Smith SP	11.00	5.00	1.35
☐ 580	Jimmie Hall SP	12.00	5.25	1.50
☐ 581	NL Rookie Stars SP	140.00	63.00	21.00
	Tony Perez			
	Dave Ricketts			
	Kevin Collins			
☐ 582	Bob Schmidt SP	11.00	5.00	1.35
☐ 583	Wes Covington SP	12.00	5.25	1.50
☐ 584	Harry Bright	5.50	2.50	.55
☐ 585	Hank Fischer	5.50	2.50	.55
☐ 586	Tom McCraw SP	11.00	5.00	1.35
☐ 587	Joe Sparma	5.50	2.50	.55
☐ 588	Lenny Green	5.50	2.50	.55
☐ 589	Giants Rookies SP	11.00	5.00	1.35
	Frank Linzy			
	Bob Schroder			
☐ 590	John Wyatt	5.50	2.50	.55
☐ 591	Bob Skinner SP	11.00	5.00	1.35
☐ 592	Frank Bork SP	11.00	5.00	1.35
☐ 593	Tigers Rookies SP	11.00	5.00	1.35
	Jackie Moore			
	John Sullivan			
☐ 594	Joe Gaines	5.50	2.50	.55
☐ 595	Don Lee	5.50	2.50	.55
☐ 596	Don Landrum SP	11.00	5.00	1.35
☐ 597	Twins Rookies	5.50	2.50	.55
	Joe Nossek			
	John Sevcik			
	Dick Reese			
☐ 598	Al Downing SP	15.00	6.00	1.20

1966 Topps

The cards in this 598-card set measure 2 1/2" by 3 1/2". There are the same number of cards as in the 1965 set. Once again, the seventh series cards (523 to 598) are considered more difficult to obtain than the cards of any other series in the set. Within this last series there are 43 cards that were printed in lesser quantities than the other cards in that series; these shorter-printed cards are marked by SP in the checklist below. The only featured subset within this set is League Leaders (215-226). Noteworthy rookie cards in the set include Jim Palmer (126), Ferguson Jenkins (254), and Don Sutton (288). Palmer is described in the bio (on his card back) as a left-hander.

	NRMT	VG-E	GOOD
COMPLETE SET (598)	4250.00	1750.00	450.00
COMMON PLAYER (1-109)	1.25	.50	.12
COMMON PLAYER (110-196)	1.50	.60	.15
COMMON PLAYER (197-283)	1.75	.70	.17
COMMON PLAYER (284-370)	2.25	.90	.22
COMMON PLAYER (371-446)	3.50	1.50	.35
COMMON PLAYER (447-522)	6.00	2.50	.60
COMMON PLAYER (523-598)	14.00	6.25	2.00
COMMON SP (523-598)	28.00	12.50	4.00

		NRMT	VG-E	GOOD
☐ 1	Willie Mays	175.00	50.00	10.00
☐ 2	Ted Abernathy	1.25	.50	.12
☐ 3	Sam Mele MG	1.25	.50	.12
☐ 4	Ray Culp	1.25	.50	.12
☐ 5	Jim Fregosi	1.75	.70	.17
☐ 6	Chuck Schilling	1.25	.50	.12
☐ 7	Tracy Stallard	1.25	.50	.12
☐ 8	Floyd Robinson	1.25	.50	.12
☐ 9	Clete Boyer	1.75	.70	.17
☐ 10	Tony Cloninger	1.25	.50	.12
☐ 11	Senators Rookies	1.25	.50	.12
	Brant Alyea			
	Pete Craig			
☐ 12	John Tsitouris	1.25	.50	.12
☐ 13	Lou Johnson	1.25	.50	.12
☐ 14	Norm Siebern	1.25	.50	.12
☐ 15	Vern Law	1.75	.70	.17
☐ 16	Larry Brown	1.25	.50	.12
☐ 17	John Stephenson	1.25	.50	.12
☐ 18	Roland Sheldon	1.25	.50	.12
☐ 19	San Francisco Giants	2.50	1.00	.25
	Team Card			
☐ 20	Willie Horton	1.75	.70	.17
☐ 21	Don Nottebart	1.25	.50	.12
☐ 22	Joe Nossek	1.25	.50	.12
☐ 23	Jack Sanford	1.25	.50	.12
☐ 24	Don Kessinger	3.00	1.25	.30
☐ 25	Pete Ward	1.25	.50	.12
☐ 26	Ray Sadecki	1.25	.50	.12
☐ 27	Orioles Rookies	1.75	.70	.17
	Darold Knowles			
	Andy Etchebarren			
☐ 28	Phil Niekro	16.00	6.75	2.25
☐ 29	Mike Brumley	1.25	.50	.12
☐ 30	Pete Rose DP	42.00	18.00	5.50
☐ 31	Jack Cullen	1.25	.50	.12
☐ 32	Adolfo Phillips	1.25	.50	.12
☐ 33	Jim Pagliaroni	1.25	.50	.12
☐ 34	Checklist 1	7.50	.75	.15
☐ 35	Ron Swoboda	1.75	.70	.17
☐ 36	Jim Hunter	30.00	13.50	4.50
☐ 37	Billy Herman MG	2.00	.80	.20
☐ 38	Ron Nischwitz	1.25	.50	.12
☐ 39	Ken Henderson	1.25	.50	.12
☐ 40	Jim Grant	1.25	.50	.12
☐ 41	Don LeJohn	1.25	.50	.12
☐ 42	Aubrey Gatewood	1.25	.50	.12
☐ 43	Don Landrum	1.25	.50	.12
☐ 44	Indians Rookies	1.25	.50	.12
	Bill Davis			
	Tom Kelley			
☐ 45	Jim Gentile	1.75	.70	.17
☐ 46	Howie Koplitz	1.25	.50	.12
☐ 47	J.C. Martin	1.25	.50	.12
☐ 48	Paul Blair	1.75	.70	.17
☐ 49	Woody Woodward	1.75	.70	.17
☐ 50	Mickey Mantle DP	180.00	80.00	27.00
☐ 51	Gordon Richardson	1.25	.50	.12
☐ 52	Power Plus	1.25	.50	.12
	Wes Covington			
	Johnny Callison			
☐ 53	Bob Duliba	1.25	.50	.12
☐ 54	Jose Pagan	1.25	.50	.12
☐ 55	Ken Harrelson	1.75	.70	.17
☐ 56	Sandy Valdespino	1.25	.50	.12
☐ 57	Jim Lefebvre	1.75	.70	.17
☐ 58	Dave Wickersham	1.25	.50	.12
☐ 59	Reds Team	2.50	1.00	.25
☐ 60	Curt Flood	1.75	.70	.17
☐ 61	Bob Bolin	1.25	.50	.12
☐ 62A	Merritt Ranew	1.25	.50	.12
	(with sold line)			
☐ 62B	Merritt Ranew	30.00	13.50	4.50
	(without sold line)			
☐ 63	Jim Stewart	1.25	.50	.12
☐ 64	Bob Bruce	1.25	.50	.12
☐ 65	Leon Wagner	1.25	.50	.12
☐ 66	Al Weis	1.25	.50	.12
☐ 67	Mets Rookies	1.75	.70	.17
	Cleon Jones			
	Dick Selma			
☐ 68	Hal Reniff	1.25	.50	.12
☐ 69	Ken Hamlin	1.25	.50	.12

		NRMT	VG-E	GOOD
☐ 70	Carl Yastrzemski	42.00	18.00	5.00
☐ 71	Frank Carpin	1.25	.50	.12
☐ 72	Tony Perez	28.00	12.50	4.00
☐ 73	Jerry Zimmerman	1.25	.50	.12
☐ 74	Don Mossi	1.25	.50	.12
☐ 75	Tommy Davis	1.75	.70	.17
☐ 76	Red Schoendienst MG	4.00	1.75	.40
☐ 77	John Orsino	1.25	.50	.12
☐ 78	Frank Linzy	1.25	.50	.12
☐ 79	Joe Pepitone	1.75	.70	.17
☐ 80	Richie Allen	4.50	2.00	.45
☐ 81	Ray Oyler	1.25	.50	.12
☐ 82	Bob Hendley	1.25	.50	.12
☐ 83	Albie Pearson	1.25	.50	.12
☐ 84	Braves Rookies	1.25	.50	.12
	Jim Beauchamp			
	Dick Kelley			
☐ 85	Eddie Fisher	1.25	.50	.12
☐ 86	John Bateman	1.25	.50	.12
☐ 87	Dan Napoleon	1.25	.50	.12
☐ 88	Fred Whitfield	1.25	.50	.12
☐ 89	Ted Davidson	1.25	.50	.12
☐ 90	Luis Aparicio	7.00	3.00	.70
☐ 91A	Bob Uecker	20.00	8.50	2.75
	(with traded line)			
☐ 91B	Bob Uecker	60.00	27.00	9.00
	(no traded line)			
☐ 92	Yankees Team	3.50	1.50	.35
☐ 93	Jim Lonborg	2.25	.90	.22
☐ 94	Matty Alou	1.75	.70	.17
☐ 95	Pete Richert	1.25	.50	.12
☐ 96	Felipe Alou	1.75	.70	.17
☐ 97	Jim Merritt	1.25	.50	.12
☐ 98	Don Demeter	1.25	.50	.12
☐ 99	Buc Belters	3.50	1.50	.35
	Willie Stargell			
	Donn Clendenon			
☐ 100	Sandy Koufax	95.00	42.00	11.00
☐ 101A	Checklist 2	15.00	1.50	.30
	(115 W. Spahn) ERR			
☐ 101B	Checklist 2	7.50	.75	.15
	(115 Bill Henry) COR			
☐ 102	Ed Kirkpatrick	1.25	.50	.12
☐ 103A	Dick Groat	2.00	.80	.20
	(with traded line)			
☐ 103B	Dick Groat	32.00	14.25	4.75
	(no traded line)			
☐ 104A	Alex Johnson	1.75	.70	.17
	(with traded line)			
☐ 104B	Alex Johnson	30.00	13.50	4.50
	(no traded line)			
☐ 105	Milt Pappas	1.75	.70	.17
☐ 106	Rusty Staub	3.00	1.25	.30
☐ 107	A's Rookies	1.25	.50	.12
	Larry Stahl			
	Ron Tompkins			
☐ 108	Bobby Klaus	1.25		.12
☐ 109	Ralph Terry	1.75	.70	.17
☐ 110	Ernie Banks	21.00	9.00	3.00
☐ 111	Gary Peters	1.50	.60	.15
☐ 112	Manny Mota	2.00	.80	.20
☐ 113	Hank Aguirre	1.50	.60	.15
☐ 114	Jim Gosger	1.50	.60	.15
☐ 115	Bill Henry	1.50	.60	.15
☐ 116	Walt Alston MG	3.50	1.50	.35
☐ 117	Jake Gibbs	1.50	.60	.15
☐ 118	Mike McCormick	2.00	.80	.20
☐ 119	Art Shamsky	1.50	.60	.15
☐ 120	Harmon Killebrew	18.00	7.50	2.50
☐ 121	Ray Herbert	1.50	.60	.15
☐ 122	Joe Gaines	1.50	.60	.15
☐ 123	Pirates Rookies	1.50	.60	.15
	Frank Bork			
	Jerry May			
☐ 124	Tug McGraw	4.00	1.75	.40
☐ 125	Lou Brock	21.00	9.00	3.00
☐ 126	Jim Palmer UER	250.00	110.00	37.50
	(described as a			
	lefthander on			
	card back)			
☐ 127	Ken Berry	1.50	.60	.15
☐ 128	Jim Landis	1.50	.60	.15
☐ 129	Jack Kralick	1.50	.60	.15
☐ 130	Joe Torre	3.00	1.25	.30
☐ 131	Angels Team	3.00	1.25	.30
☐ 132	Orlando Cepeda	5.00	2.25	.50
☐ 133	Don McMahon	1.50	.60	.15
☐ 134	Wes Parker	2.00	.80	.20
☐ 135	Dave Morehead	1.50	.60	.15
☐ 136	Woody Held	1.50	.60	.15
☐ 137	Pat Corrales	2.00	.80	.20
☐ 138	Roger Repoz	1.50	.60	.15
☐ 139	Cubs Rookies	1.50	.60	.15
	Byron Browne			
	Don Young			

☐ 140	Jim Maloney	2.00	.80	.20
☐ 141	Tom McCraw	1.50	.60	.15
☐ 142	Don Dennis	1.50	.60	.15
☐ 143	Jose Tartabull	1.50	.60	.15
☐ 144	Don Schwall	1.50	.60	.15
☐ 145	Bill Freehan	2.50	1.00	.25
☐ 146	George Altman	1.50	.60	.15
☐ 147	Lum Harris MG	1.50	.60	.15
☐ 148	Bob Johnson	1.50	.60	.15
☐ 149	Dick Nen	1.50	.60	.15
☐ 150	Rocky Colavito	4.50	2.00	.45
☐ 151	Gary Wagner	1.50	.60	.15
☐ 152	Frank Malzone	2.00	.80	.20
☐ 153	Rico Carty	2.50	1.00	.25
☐ 154	Chuck Hiller	1.50	.60	.15
☐ 155	Marcelino Lopez	1.50	.60	.15
☐ 156	Double Play Combo	2.00	.80	.20
	Dick Schofield			
	Hal Lanier			
☐ 157	Rene Lachemann	2.00	.80	.20
☐ 158	Jim Brewer	1.50	.60	.15
☐ 159	Chico Ruiz	1.50	.60	.15
☐ 160	Whitey Ford	21.00	9.00	3.00
☐ 161	Jerry Lumpe	1.50	.60	.15
☐ 162	Lee Maye	1.50	.60	.15
☐ 163	Tito Francona	1.50	.60	.15
☐ 164	White Sox Rookies	2.00	.80	.20
	Tommie Agee			
	Marv Staehle			
☐ 165	Don Lock	1.50	.60	.15
☐ 166	Chris Krug	1.50	.60	.15
☐ 167	Boog Powell	3.50	1.50	.35
☐ 168	Dan Osinski	1.50	.60	.15
☐ 169	Duke Sims	1.50	.60	.15
☐ 170	Cookie Rojas	2.00	.80	.20
☐ 171	Nick Willhite	1.50	.60	.15
☐ 172	Mets Team	3.50	1.50	.35
☐ 173	Al Spangler	1.50	.60	.15
☐ 174	Ron Taylor	1.50	.60	.15
☐ 175	Bert Campaneris	2.00	.80	.20
☐ 176	Jim Davenport	1.50	.60	.15
☐ 177	Hector Lopez	1.50	.60	.15
☐ 178	Bob Tillman	1.50	.60	.15
☐ 179	Cards Rookies	2.00	.80	.20
	Dennis Aust			
	Bob Tolan			
☐ 180	Vada Pinson	2.50	1.00	.25
☐ 181	Al Worthington	1.50	.60	.15
☐ 182	Jerry Lynch	1.50	.60	.15
☐ 183	Checklist 3	7.50	.75	.15
☐ 184	Denis Menke	1.50	.60	.15
☐ 185	Bob Buhl	1.50	.60	.15
☐ 186	Ruben Amaro	1.50	.60	.15
☐ 187	Chuck Dressen MG	2.00	.80	.20
☐ 188	Al Luplow	1.50	.60	.15
☐ 189	John Roseboro	2.00	.80	.20
☐ 190	Jimmie Hall	2.00	.80	.20
☐ 191	Darrell Sutherland	1.50	.60	.15
☐ 192	Vic Power	1.50	.60	.15
☐ 193	Dave McNally	2.00	.80	.20
☐ 194	Senators Team	3.00	1.25	.30
☐ 195	Joe Morgan	42.00	18.00	5.50
☐ 196	Don Pavletich	1.50	.60	.15
☐ 197	Sonny Siebert	1.75	.70	.17
☐ 198	Mickey Stanley	3.00	1.25	.30
☐ 199	Chisox Clubbers	1.75	.70	.17
	Bill Skowron			
	Johnny Romano			
	Floyd Robinson			
☐ 200	Eddie Mathews	12.00	5.25	1.50
☐ 201	Jim Dickson	1.75	.70	.17
☐ 202	Clay Dalrymple	1.75	.70	.17
☐ 203	Jose Santiago	1.75	.70	.17
☐ 204	Cubs Team	3.50	1.50	.35
☐ 205	Tom Tresh	2.25	.90	.22
☐ 206	Al Jackson	1.75	.70	.17
☐ 207	Frank Quilici	1.75	.70	.17
☐ 208	Bob Miller	1.75	.70	.17
☐ 209	Tigers Rookies	3.00	1.25	.30
	Fritz Fisher			
	John Hiller			
☐ 210	Bill Mazeroski	3.50	1.50	.35
☐ 211	Frank Kreutzer	1.75	.70	.17
☐ 212	Ed Kranepool	2.25	.90	.22
☐ 213	Fred Newman	1.75	.70	.17
☐ 214	Tommy Harper	2.25	.90	.22
☐ 215	NL Batting Leaders	18.00	7.50	2.50
	Bob Clemente			
	Hank Aaron			
	Willie Mays			
☐ 216	AL Batting Leaders	5.00	2.25	.50
	Tony Oliva			
	Carl Yastrzemski			
	Vic Davalillo			

☐ 217	NL Home Run Leaders	12.00	5.25	1.50
	Willie Mays			
	Willie McCovey			
	Billy Williams			
☐ 218	AL Home Run Leaders	3.50	1.50	.35
	Tony Conigliaro			
	Norm Cash			
	Willie Horton			
☐ 219	NL RBI Leaders	5.00	2.25	.50
	Deron Johnson			
	Frank Robinson			
	Willie Mays			
☐ 220	AL RBI Leaders	3.50	1.50	.35
	Rocky Colavito			
	Willie Horton			
	Tony Oliva			
☐ 221	NL ERA Leaders	5.00	2.25	.50
	Sandy Koufax			
	Juan Marichal			
	Vern Law			
☐ 222	AL ERA Leaders	3.00	1.25	.30
	Sam McDowell			
	Eddie Fisher			
	Sonny Siebert			
☐ 223	NL Pitching Leaders	5.00	2.25	.50
	Sandy Koufax			
	Tony Cloninger			
	Don Drysdale			
☐ 224	AL Pitching Leaders	3.00	1.25	.30
	Jim Grant			
	Mel Stottlemyre			
	Jim Kaat			
☐ 225	NL Strikeout Leaders	5.00	2.25	.50
	Sandy Koufax			
	Bob Veale			
	Bob Gibson			
☐ 226	AL Strikeout Leaders	3.00	1.25	.30
	Sam McDowell			
	Mickey Lolich			
	Dennis McLain			
	Sonny Siebert			
☐ 227	Russ Nixon	1.75	.70	.17
☐ 228	Larry Brown	1.75	.70	.17
☐ 229	Hank Bauer MG	2.25	.90	.22
☐ 230	Johnny Callison	2.25	.90	.22
☐ 231	Floyd Weaver	1.75	.70	.17
☐ 232	Glenn Beckert	2.25	.90	.22
☐ 233	Dom Zanni	1.75	.70	.17
☐ 234	Yankees Rookies	6.00	2.50	.60
	Rich Beck			
	Roy White			
☐ 235	Don Cardwell	1.75	.70	.17
☐ 236	Mike Hershberger	1.75	.70	.17
☐ 237	Billy O'Dell	1.75	.70	.17
☐ 238	Dodgers Team	3.50	1.50	.35
☐ 239	Orlando Pena	1.75	.70	.17
☐ 240	Earl Battey	1.75	.70	.17
☐ 241	Dennis Ribant	1.75	.70	.17
☐ 242	Jesus Alou	1.75	.70	.17
☐ 243	Nelson Briles	2.25	.90	.22
☐ 244	Astros Rookies	2.25	.90	.22
	Chuck Harrison			
	Sonny Jackson			
☐ 245	John Buzhardt	1.75	.70	.17
☐ 246	Ed Bailey	2.25	.90	.22
☐ 247	Carl Warwick	1.75	.70	.17
☐ 248	Pete Mikkelsen	1.75	.70	.17
☐ 249	Bill Rigney MG	1.75	.70	.17
☐ 250	Sammy Ellis	1.75	.70	.17
☐ 251	Ed Brinkman	1.75	.70	.17
☐ 252	Denny Lemaster	1.75	.70	.17
☐ 253	Don Wert	1.75	.70	.17
☐ 254	Phillies Rookies	120.00	55.00	18.00
	Ferguson Jenkins			
	Bill Sorrell			
☐ 255	Willie Stargell	18.00	7.50	2.50
☐ 256	Lew Krausse	1.75	.70	.17
☐ 257	Jeff Torborg	2.75	1.10	.27
☐ 258	Dave Giusti	2.25	.90	.22
☐ 259	Boston Red Sox	3.50	1.50	.35
	Team Card			
☐ 260	Bob Shaw	1.75	.70	.17
☐ 261	Ron Hansen	1.75	.70	.17
☐ 262	Jack Hamilton	1.75	.70	.17
☐ 263	Tom Egan	1.75	.70	.17
☐ 264	Twins Rookies	1.75	.70	.17
	Andy Kosco			
	Ted Uhlaender			
☐ 265	Stu Miller	1.75	.70	.17
☐ 266	Pedro Gonzalez UER	1.75	.70	.17
	(misspelled Gonzales			
	on card back)			
☐ 267	Joe Sparma	1.75	.70	.17
☐ 268	John Blanchard	2.25	.90	.22

☐ 269	Don Heffner MG	1.75	.70	.17
☐ 270	Claude Osteen	2.25	.90	.22
☐ 271	Hal Lanier	2.25	.90	.22
☐ 272	Jack Baldschun	1.75	.70	.17
☐ 273	Astro Aces	2.50	1.00	.25
	Bob Aspromonte			
	Rusty Staub			
☐ 274	Buster Narum	1.75	.70	.17
☐ 275	Tim McCarver	3.50	1.50	.35
☐ 276	Jim Bouton	2.75	1.10	.27
☐ 277	George Thomas	1.75	.70	.17
☐ 278	Cal Koonce	1.75	.70	.17
☐ 279	Checklist 4	7.50	.75	.15
☐ 280	Bobby Knoop	1.75	.70	.17
☐ 281	Bruce Howard	1.75	.70	.17
☐ 282	Johnny Lewis	1.75	.70	.17
☐ 283	Jim Perry	2.25	.90	.22
☐ 284	Bobby Wine	2.25	.90	.22
☐ 285	Luis Tiant	3.50	1.50	.35
☐ 286	Gary Geiger	2.25	.90	.22
☐ 287	Jack Aker	2.25	.90	.22
☐ 288	Dodgers Rookies	130.00	60.00	20.00
	Bill Singer			
	Don Sutton			
☐ 289	Larry Sherry	2.25	.90	.22
☐ 290	Ron Santo	3.50	1.50	.35
☐ 291	Moe Drabowsky	2.25	.90	.22
☐ 292	Jim Coker	2.25	.90	.22
☐ 293	Mike Shannon	2.75	1.10	.27
☐ 294	Steve Ridzik	2.25	.90	.22
☐ 295	Jim Ray Hart	2.75	1.10	.27
☐ 296	Johnny Keane MG	2.25	.90	.22
☐ 297	Jim Owens	2.25	.90	.22
☐ 298	Rico Petrocelli	3.50	1.50	.35
☐ 299	Lou Burdette	3.00	1.25	.30
☐ 300	Bob Clemente	85.00	38.00	12.75
☐ 301	Greg Bollo	2.25	.90	.22
☐ 302	Ernie Bowman	2.25	.90	.22
☐ 303	Cleveland Indians	4.50	2.00	.45
	Team Card			
☐ 304	John Herrnstein	2.25	.90	.22
☐ 305	Camilo Pascual	2.75	1.10	.27
☐ 306	Ty Cline	2.25	.90	.22
☐ 307	Clay Carroll	2.75	1.10	.27
☐ 308	Tom Haller	2.75	1.10	.27
☐ 309	Diego Segui	2.25	.90	.22
☐ 310	Frank Robinson	40.00	18.00	6.00
☐ 311	Reds Rookies	2.75	1.10	.27
	Tommy Helms			
	Dick Simpson			
☐ 312	Bob Saverine	2.25	.90	.22
☐ 313	Chris Zachary	2.25	.90	.22
☐ 314	Hector Valle	2.25	.90	.22
☐ 315	Norm Cash	3.50	1.50	.35
☐ 316	Jack Fisher	2.25	.90	.22
☐ 317	Dalton Jones	2.25	.90	.22
☐ 318	Harry Walker MG	2.25	.90	.22
☐ 319	Gene Freese	2.25	.90	.22
☐ 320	Bob Gibson	24.00	10.50	3.50
☐ 321	Rick Reichardt	2.25	.90	.22
☐ 322	Bill Faul	2.25	.90	.22
☐ 323	Ray Barker	2.25	.90	.22
☐ 324	John Boozer	2.25	.90	.22
☐ 325	Vic Davalillo	2.25	.90	.22
☐ 326	Braves Team	4.50	2.00	.45
☐ 327	Bernie Allen	2.25	.90	.22
☐ 328	Jerry Grote	2.25	.90	.22
☐ 329	Pete Charton	2.25	.90	.22
☐ 330	Ron Fairly	2.75	1.10	.27
☐ 331	Ron Herbel	2.25	.90	.22
☐ 332	Bill Bryan	2.25	.90	.22
☐ 333	Senators Rookies	2.25	.90	.22
	Joe Coleman			
	Jim French			
☐ 334	Marty Keough	2.25	.90	.22
☐ 335	Juan Pizarro	2.25	.90	.22
☐ 336	Gene Alley	2.75	1.10	.27
☐ 337	Fred Gladding	2.25	.90	.22
☐ 338	Dal Maxvill	2.25	.90	.22
☐ 339	Del Crandall	2.75	1.10	.27
☐ 340	Dean Chance	2.75	1.10	.27
☐ 341	Wes Westrum MG	2.25	.90	.22
☐ 342	Bob Humphreys	2.25	.90	.22
☐ 343	Joe Christopher	2.25	.90	.22
☐ 344	Steve Blass	2.75	1.10	.27
☐ 345	Bob Allison	2.75	1.10	.27
☐ 346	Mike De La Hoz	2.25	.90	.22
☐ 347	Phil Regan	2.75	1.10	.27
☐ 348	Orioles Team	4.50	2.00	.45
☐ 349	Cap Peterson	2.25	.90	.22
☐ 350	Mel Stottlemyre	3.75	1.60	.37
☐ 351	Fred Valentine	2.25	.90	.22
☐ 352	Bob Aspromonte	2.25	.90	.22
☐ 353	Al McBean	2.25	.90	.22
☐ 354	Smoky Burgess	2.75	1.10	.27
☐ 355	Wade Blasingame	2.25	.90	.22
☐ 356	Red Sox Rookies	2.25	.90	.22
	Owen Johnson			
	Ken Sanders			
☐ 357	Gerry Arrigo	2.25	.90	.22
☐ 358	Charlie Smith	2.25	.90	.22
☐ 359	Johnny Briggs	2.25	.90	.22
☐ 360	Ron Hunt	2.25	.90	.22
☐ 361	Tom Satriano	2.25	.90	.22
☐ 362	Gates Brown	2.75	1.10	.27
☐ 363	Checklist 5	9.00	.90	.20
☐ 364	Nate Oliver	2.25	.90	.22
☐ 365	Roger Maris	55.00	25.00	8.25
☐ 366	Wayne Causey	2.25	.90	.22
☐ 367	Mel Nelson	2.25	.90	.22
☐ 368	Charlie Lau	2.75	1.10	.27
☐ 369	Jim King	2.25	.90	.22
☐ 370	Chico Cardenas	2.25	.90	.22
☐ 371	Lee Stange	3.50	1.50	.35
☐ 372	Harvey Kuenn	4.50	2.00	.45
☐ 373	Giants Rookies	4.00	1.75	.40
	Jack Hiatt			
	Dick Estelle			
☐ 374	Bob Locker	3.50	1.50	.35
☐ 375	Donn Clendenon	4.00	1.75	.40
☐ 376	Paul Schaal	3.50	1.50	.35
☐ 377	Turk Farrell	3.50	1.50	.35
☐ 378	Dick Tracewski	3.50	1.50	.35
☐ 379	Cardinal Team	7.00	3.00	.70
☐ 380	Tony Conigliaro	7.50	3.25	.75
☐ 381	Hank Fischer	3.50	1.50	.35
☐ 382	Phil Roof	3.50	1.50	.35
☐ 383	Jackie Brandt	3.50	1.50	.35
☐ 384	Al Downing	4.00	1.75	.40
☐ 385	Ken Boyer	5.00	2.25	.50
☐ 386	Gil Hodges MG	6.50	2.75	.65
☐ 387	Howie Reed	3.50	1.50	.35
☐ 388	Don Mincher	4.00	1.75	.40
☐ 389	Jim O'Toole	3.50	1.50	.35
☐ 390	Brooks Robinson	28.00	12.50	4.00
☐ 391	Chuck Hinton	3.50	1.50	.35
☐ 392	Cubs Rookies	4.50	2.00	.45
	Bill Hands			
	Randy Hundley			
☐ 393	George Brunet	3.50	1.50	.35
☐ 394	Ron Brand	3.50	1.50	.35
☐ 395	Len Gabrielson	3.50	1.50	.35
☐ 396	Jerry Stephenson	3.50	1.50	.35
☐ 397	Bill White	5.00	2.25	.50
☐ 398	Danny Cater	3.50	1.50	.35
☐ 399	Ray Washburn	3.50	1.50	.35
☐ 400	Zoilo Versalles	3.50	1.50	.35
☐ 401	Ken McMullen	3.50	1.50	.35
☐ 402	Jim Hickman	3.50	1.50	.35
☐ 403	Fred Talbot	3.50	1.50	.35
☐ 404	Pittsburgh Pirates	7.00	3.00	.70
	Team Card			
☐ 405	Elston Howard	6.00	2.50	.60
☐ 406	Joey Jay	3.50	1.50	.35
☐ 407	John Kennedy	3.50	1.50	.35
☐ 408	Lee Thomas	4.00	1.75	.40
☐ 409	Billy Hoeft	3.50	1.50	.35
☐ 410	Al Kaline	25.00	11.00	3.50
☐ 411	Gene Mauch MG	4.00	1.75	.40
☐ 412	Sam Bowens	3.50	1.50	.35
☐ 413	Johnny Romano	3.50	1.50	.35
☐ 414	Dan Coombs	3.50	1.50	.35
☐ 415	Max Alvis	3.50	1.50	.35
☐ 416	Phil Ortega	3.50	1.50	.35
☐ 417	Angels Rookies	4.00	1.75	.40
	Jim McGlothlin			
	Ed Sukla			
☐ 418	Phil Gagliano	3.50	1.50	.35
☐ 419	Mike Ryan	3.50	1.50	.35
☐ 420	Juan Marichal	12.50	5.50	1.65
☐ 421	Roy McMillan	3.50	1.50	.35
☐ 422	Ed Charles	3.50	1.50	.35
☐ 423	Ernie Broglio	3.50	1.50	.35
☐ 424	Reds Rookies	6.50	2.75	.65
	Lee May			
	Darrell Osteen			
☐ 425	Bob Veale	4.00	1.75	.40
☐ 426	White Sox Team	7.00	3.00	.70
☐ 427	John Miller	3.50	1.50	.35
☐ 428	Sandy Alomar	4.00	1.75	.40
☐ 429	Bill Monbouquette	3.50	1.50	.35
☐ 430	Don Drysdale	18.00	7.50	2.50
☐ 431	Walt Bond	3.50	1.50	.35
☐ 432	Bob Heffner	3.50	1.50	.35
☐ 433	Alvin Dark MG	4.00	1.75	.40
☐ 434	Willie Kirkland	3.50	1.50	.35
☐ 435	Jim Bunning	6.50	2.75	.65
☐ 436	Julian Javier	3.50	1.50	.35

☐ 437	Al Stanek	3.50	1.50	.35
☐ 438	Willie Smith	3.50	1.50	.35
☐ 439	Pedro Ramos	3.50	1.50	.35
☐ 440	Deron Johnson	3.50	1.50	.35
☐ 441	Tommie Sisk	3.50	1.50	.35
☐ 442	Orioles Rookies	3.50	1.50	.35
	Ed Barnowski			
	Eddie Watt			
☐ 443	Bill Wakefield	3.50	1.50	.35
☐ 444	Checklist 6	9.00	.90	.20
☐ 445	Jim Kaat	6.50	2.75	.65
☐ 446	Mack Jones	3.50	1.50	.35
☐ 447	Dick Ellsworth UER	7.00	3.00	.70
	(photo actually			
	Ken Hubbs)			
☐ 448	Eddie Stanky MG	7.00	3.00	.70
☐ 449	Joe Moeller	6.00	2.50	.60
☐ 450	Tony Oliva	9.00	4.00	.90
☐ 451	Barry Latman	6.00	2.50	.60
☐ 452	Joe Azcue	6.00	2.50	.60
☐ 453	Ron Kline	6.00	2.50	.60
☐ 454	Jerry Buchek	6.00	2.50	.60
☐ 455	Mickey Lolich	8.00	3.50	.80
☐ 456	Red Sox Rookies	6.00	2.50	.60
	Darrell Brandon			
	Joe Foy			
☐ 457	Joe Gibbon	6.00	2.50	.60
☐ 458	Manny Jiminez	6.00	2.50	.60
☐ 459	Bill McCool	6.00	2.50	.60
☐ 460	Curt Blefary	7.00	3.00	.70
☐ 461	Roy Face	7.00	3.00	.70
☐ 462	Bob Rodgers	7.00	3.00	.70
☐ 463	Philadelphia Phillies	12.00	5.25	1.50
	Team Card			
☐ 464	Larry Bearnarth	6.00	2.50	.60
☐ 465	Don Buford	7.00	3.00	.70
☐ 466	Ken Johnson	6.00	2.50	.60
☐ 467	Vic Roznovsky	6.00	2.50	.60
☐ 468	Johnny Podres	7.00	3.00	.70
☐ 469	Yankees Rookies	22.00	9.50	3.15
	Bobby Murcer			
	Dooley Womack			
☐ 470	Sam McDowell	7.00	3.00	.70
☐ 471	Bob Skinner	7.00	3.00	.70
☐ 472	Terry Fox	6.00	2.50	.60
☐ 473	Rich Rollins	7.00	3.00	.70
☐ 474	Dick Schofield	6.00	2.50	.60
☐ 475	Dick Radatz	7.00	3.00	.70
☐ 476	Bobby Bragan MG	6.00	2.50	.60
☐ 477	Steve Barber	6.00	2.50	.60
☐ 478	Tony Gonzalez	6.00	2.50	.60
☐ 479	Jim Hannan	6.00	2.50	.60
☐ 480	Dick Stuart	7.00	3.00	.70
☐ 481	Bob Lee	6.00	2.50	.60
☐ 482	Cubs Rookies	6.00	2.50	.60
	John Boccabella			
	Dave Dowling			
☐ 483	Joe Nuxhall	7.00	3.00	.70
☐ 484	Wes Covington	6.00	2.50	.60
☐ 485	Bob Bailey	6.00	2.50	.60
☐ 486	Tommy John	12.50	5.50	1.65
☐ 487	Al Ferrara	6.00	2.50	.60
☐ 488	George Banks	6.00	2.50	.60
☐ 489	Curt Simmons	7.00	3.00	.70
☐ 490	Bobby Richardson	12.50	5.50	1.65
☐ 491	Dennis Bennett	6.00	2.50	.60
☐ 492	Athletics Team	11.00	5.00	1.35
☐ 493	Johnny Klippstein	6.00	2.50	.60
☐ 494	Gordy Coleman	7.00	3.00	.70
☐ 495	Dick McAuliffe	7.00	3.00	.70
☐ 496	Lindy McDaniel	7.00	3.00	.70
☐ 497	Chris Cannizzaro	6.00	2.50	.60
☐ 498	Pirates Rookies	7.00	3.00	.70
	Luke Walker			
	Woody Fryman			
☐ 499	Wally Bunker	6.00	2.50	.60
☐ 500	Hank Aaron	100.00	45.00	15.00
☐ 501	John O'Donoghue	6.00	2.50	.60
☐ 502	Lenny Green	6.00	2.50	.60
☐ 503	Steve Hamilton	6.00	2.50	.60
☐ 504	Grady Hatton MG	6.00	2.50	.60
☐ 505	Jose Cardenal	6.00	2.50	.60
☐ 506	Bo Belinsky	7.00	3.00	.70
☐ 507	Johnny Edwards	6.00	2.50	.60
☐ 508	Steve Hargan	7.00	3.00	.70
☐ 509	Jake Wood	6.00	2.50	.60
☐ 510	Hoyt Wilhelm	13.00	5.75	1.75
☐ 511	Giants Rookies	7.00	3.00	.70
	Bob Barton			
	Tito Fuentes			
☐ 512	Dick Stigman	6.00	2.50	.60
☐ 513	Camilo Carreon	6.00	2.50	.60
☐ 514	Hal Woodeshick	6.00	2.50	.60
☐ 515	Frank Howard	8.00	3.50	.80
☐ 516	Eddie Bressoud	6.00	2.50	.60
☐ 517A	Checklist 7	15.00	1.50	.30
	529 White Sox Rookies			
	544 Cardinals Rookies			
☐ 517B	Checklist 7	15.00	1.50	.30
	529 W. Sox Rookies			
	544 Cards Rookies			
☐ 518	Braves Rookies	4.00	1.75	.40
	Herb Hippauf			
	Arnie Umbach			
☐ 519	Bob Friend	7.00	3.00	.70
☐ 520	Jim Wynn	8.00	3.50	.80
☐ 521	John Wyatt	6.00	2.50	.60
☐ 522	Phil Linz	7.00	3.00	.70
☐ 523	Bob Sadowski	14.00	6.25	2.00
☐ 524	Giants Rookies SP	28.00	12.50	4.00
	Ollie Brown			
	Don Mason			
☐ 525	Gary Bell SP	28.00	12.50	4.00
☐ 526	Twins Team SP	70.00	32.00	10.50
☐ 527	Julio Navarro	14.00	6.25	2.00
☐ 528	Jesse Gonder SP	28.00	12.50	4.00
☐ 529	White Sox Rookies	18.00	7.50	2.50
	Lee Elia			
	Dennis Higgins			
	Bill Voss			
☐ 530	Robin Roberts	40.00	18.00	6.00
☐ 531	Joe Cunningham	14.00	6.25	2.00
☐ 532	Aurelio Monteagudo SP	28.00	12.50	4.00
☐ 533	Jerry Adair SP	28.00	12.50	4.00
☐ 534	Mets Rookies	14.00	6.25	2.00
	Dave Eilers			
	Rob Gardner			
☐ 535	Willie Davis SP	36.00	16.25	5.50
☐ 536	Dick Egan	14.00	6.25	2.00
☐ 537	Herman Franks MG	14.00	6.25	2.00
☐ 538	Bob Allen SP	28.00	12.50	4.00
☐ 539	Astros Rookies	14.00	6.25	2.00
	Bill Heath			
	Carroll Sembera			
☐ 540	Denny McLain SP	55.00	25.00	8.25
☐ 541	Gene Oliver SP	28.00	12.50	4.00
☐ 542	George Smith	14.00	6.25	2.00
☐ 543	Roger Craig SP	36.00	16.25	5.50
☐ 544	Cardinals Rookies SP	30.00	13.50	4.50
	Joe Hoerner			
	George Kernek			
	Jimmy Williams			
☐ 545	Dick Green SP	28.00	12.50	4.00
☐ 546	Dwight Siebler	14.00	6.25	2.00
☐ 547	Horace Clarke SP	50.00	22.50	7.50
☐ 548	Gary Kroll SP	28.00	12.50	4.00
☐ 549	Senators Rookies	14.00	6.25	2.00
	Al Closter			
	Casey Cox			
☐ 550	Willie McCovey SP	120.00	55.00	18.00
☐ 551	Bob Purkey SP	28.00	12.50	4.00
☐ 552	Birdie Tebbetts	28.00	12.50	4.00
	MG SP			
☐ 553	Rookie Stars	14.00	6.25	2.00
	Pat Garrett			
	Jackie Warner			
☐ 554	Jim Northrup SP	30.00	13.50	4.50
☐ 555	Ron Perranoski SP	30.00	13.50	4.50
☐ 556	Mel Queen SP	28.00	12.50	4.00
☐ 557	Felix Mantilla SP	28.00	12.50	4.00
☐ 558	Red Sox Rookies	22.00	9.50	3.15
	Guido Grilli			
	Pete Magrini			
	George Scott			
☐ 559	Roberto Pena SP	28.00	12.50	4.00
☐ 560	Joel Horlen	14.00	6.25	2.00
☐ 561	ChooChoo Coleman SP	42.00	18.00	5.50
☐ 562	Russ Snyder	14.00	6.25	2.00
☐ 563	Twins Rookies	14.00	6.25	2.00
	Pete Cimino			
	Cesar Tovar			
☐ 564	Bob Chance SP	28.00	12.50	4.00
☐ 565	Jim Piersall SP	36.00	16.25	5.50
☐ 566	Mike Cuellar SP	30.00	13.50	4.50
☐ 567	Dick Howser SP	30.00	13.50	4.50
☐ 568	Athletics Rookies	16.00	6.75	2.25
	Paul Lindblad			
	Ron Stone			
☐ 569	Orlando McFarlane SP	28.00	12.50	4.00
☐ 570	Art Mahaffey SP	28.00	12.50	4.00
☐ 571	Dave Roberts SP	28.00	12.50	4.00
☐ 572	Bob Priddy	14.00	6.25	2.00
☐ 573	Derrell Griffith	14.00	6.25	2.00
☐ 574	Mets Rookies	14.00	6.25	2.00
	Bill Hepler			
	Bill Murphy			
☐ 575	Earl Wilson	14.00	6.25	2.00
☐ 576	Dave Nicholson SP	28.00	12.50	4.00

		NRMT	VG-E	GOOD
☐ 577	Jack Lamabe SP	28.00	12.50	4.00
☐ 578	Chi Chi Olivo SP	28.00	12.50	4.00
☐ 579	Orioles Rookies	18.00	7.50	2.50
	Frank Bertaina			
	Gene Brabender			
	Dave Johnson			
☐ 580	Billy Williams SP	95.00	42.00	11.00
☐ 581	Tony Martinez	14.00	6.25	2.00
☐ 582	Garry Roggenburk	14.00	6.25	2.00
☐ 583	Tigers Team SP	130.00	60.00	20.00
☐ 584	Yankees Rookies	14.00	6.25	2.00
	Frank Fernandez			
	Fritz Peterson			
☐ 585	Tony Taylor	14.00	6.25	2.00
☐ 586	Claude Raymond SP	28.00	12.50	4.00
☐ 587	Dick Bertell	14.00	6.25	2.00
☐ 588	Athletics Rookies	14.00	6.25	2.00
	Chuck Dobson			
	Ken Suarez			
☐ 589	Lou Klimchock SP	28.00	12.50	4.00
☐ 590	Bill Skowron SP	42.00	18.00	5.50
☐ 591	NL Rookies SP	36.00	16.25	5.50
	Bart Shirley			
	Grant Jackson			
☐ 592	Andre Rodgers	14.00	6.25	2.00
☐ 593	Doug Camilli SP	28.00	12.50	4.00
☐ 594	Chico Salmon	14.00	6.25	2.00
☐ 595	Larry Jackson	14.00	6.25	2.00
☐ 596	Astros Rookies SP	30.00	13.50	4.50
	Nate Colbert			
	Greg Sims			
☐ 597	John Sullivan	14.00	6.25	2.00
☐ 598	Gaylord Perry SP	300.00	75.00	15.00

1967 Topps

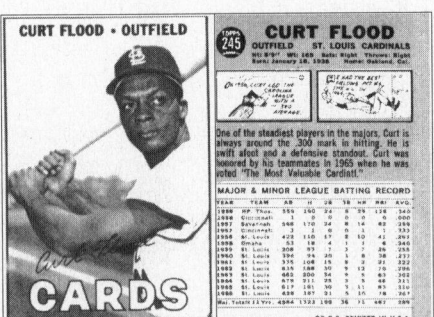

The cards in this 609-card set measure 2 1/2" by 3 1/2". The 1967 Topps series is considered by some collectors to be one of the company's finest accomplishments in baseball card production. Excellent color photographs are combined with easy-to-read backs. Cards 458 to 533 are slightly harder to find than numbers 1 to 457, and the inevitable (difficult to find) high series (534 to 609) exists. Each checklist card features a small circular picture of a popular player included in that series. Printing discrepancies resulted in some high series cards being in shorter supply. The checklist below identifies (by DP) 22 double-printed high numbers; of the 76 cards in the last series, 54 cards were short printed and the other 22 cards are much more plentiful. Featured subsets within this set include World Series cards (151-155) and League Leaders (233-244). Although there are several relatively expensive cards in this popular set, the key cards in the set are undoubtedly the Tom Seaver rookie card (581) and the Rod Carew rookie card (569). Although rarely seen, there exists a salesman's sample panel of three cards, that pictures Earl Battey, Manny Mota, and Gene Brabender with ad information on the back about the "new" Topps cards.

	NRMT	VG-E	GOOD
COMPLETE SET (609)	5250.00	2300.00	650.00
COMMON PLAYER (1-109)	1.35	.55	.13

COMMON PLAYER (110-196)	1.75	.70	.17
COMMON PLAYER (197-283)	2.00	.80	.20
COMMON PLAYER (284-370)	2.50	1.00	.25
COMMON PLAYER (371-457)	3.00	1.25	.30
COMMON PLAYER (458-533)	6.00	2.50	.60
COMMON PLAYER (534-609)	18.00	7.50	2.50
COMMON DP (534-609)	9.00	4.00	.90

☐ 1	The Champs DP	21.00	5.00	1.00
	Frank Robinson			
	Hank Bauer			
	Brooks Robinson			
☐ 2	Jack Hamilton	1.35	.55	.13
☐ 3	Duke Sims	1.35	.55	.13
☐ 4	Hal Lanier	1.75	.70	.17
☐ 5	Whitey Ford UER	18.00	7.50	2.50
	(1953 listed as			
	1933 in stats on back)			
☐ 6	Dick Simpson	1.35	.55	.13
☐ 7	Don McMahon	1.35	.55	.13
☐ 8	Chuck Harrison	1.35	.55	.13
☐ 9	Ron Hansen	1.35	.55	.13
☐ 10	Matty Alou	1.75	.70	.17
☐ 11	Barry Moore	1.35	.55	.13
☐ 12	Dodgers Rookies	1.75	.70	.17
	Jim Campanis			
	Bill Singer			
☐ 13	Joe Sparma	1.35	.55	.13
☐ 14	Phil Linz	1.75	.70	.17
☐ 15	Earl Battey	1.35	.55	.13
☐ 16	Bill Hands	1.35	.55	.13
☐ 17	Jim Gosger	1.35	.55	.13
☐ 18	Gene Oliver	1.35	.55	.13
☐ 19	Jim McGlothlin	1.35	.55	.13
☐ 20	Orlando Cepeda	7.00	3.00	.70
☐ 21	Dave Bristol MG	1.35	.55	.13
☐ 22	Gene Brabender	1.35	.55	.13
☐ 23	Larry Elliot	1.35	.55	.13
☐ 24	Bob Allen	1.35	.55	.13
☐ 25	Elston Howard	3.50	1.50	.35
☐ 26A	Bob Priddy	30.00	13.50	4.50
	(no traded line)			
☐ 26B	Bob Priddy	1.35	.55	.13
	(with traded line)			
☐ 27	Bob Saverine	1.35	.55	.13
☐ 28	Barry Latman	1.35	.55	.13
☐ 29	Tom McCraw	1.35	.55	.13
☐ 30	Al Kaline DP	17.00	7.25	2.50
☐ 31	Jim Brewer	1.35	.55	.13
☐ 32	Bob Bailey	1.35	.55	.13
☐ 33	Athletic Rookies	3.00	1.25	.30
	Sal Bando			
	Randy Schwartz			
☐ 34	Pete Cimino	1.35	.55	.13
☐ 35	Rico Carty	2.00	.80	.20
☐ 36	Bob Tillman	1.35	.55	.13
☐ 37	Rick Wise	1.75	.70	.17
☐ 38	Bob Johnson	1.35	.55	.13
☐ 39	Curt Simmons	1.75	.70	.17
☐ 40	Rick Reichardt	1.35	.55	.13
☐ 41	Joe Hoerner	1.35	.55	.13
☐ 42	Mets Team	3.00	1.25	.30
☐ 43	Chico Salmon	1.35	.55	.13
☐ 44	Joe Nuxhall	1.75	.70	.17
☐ 45	Roger Maris	42.00	18.00	5.50
☐ 46	Lindy McDaniel	1.75	.70	.17
☐ 47	Ken McMullen	1.35	.55	.13
☐ 48	Bill Freehan	2.00	.80	.20
☐ 49	Roy Face	1.75	.70	.17
☐ 50	Tony Oliva	4.00	1.75	.40
☐ 51	Astros Rookies	1.35	.55	.13
	Dave Adlesh			
	Wes Bales			
☐ 52	Dennis Higgins	1.35	.55	.13
☐ 53	Clay Dalrymple	1.35	.55	.13
☐ 54	Dick Green	1.35	.55	.13
☐ 55	Don Drysdale	12.50	5.50	1.65
☐ 56	Jose Tartabull	1.35	.55	.13
☐ 57	Pat Jarvis	1.35	.55	.13
☐ 58	Paul Schaal	1.35	.55	.13
☐ 59	Ralph Terry	1.75	.70	.17
☐ 60	Luis Aparicio	6.50	2.75	.65
☐ 61	Gordy Coleman	1.35	.55	.13
☐ 62	Checklist 1	7.50	.75	.15
	Frank Robinson			
☐ 63	Cards' Clubbers	6.50	2.75	.65
	Lou Brock			
	Curt Flood			
☐ 64	Fred Valentine	1.35	.55	.13
☐ 65	Tom Haller	1.35	.55	.13
☐ 66	Manny Mota	1.75	.70	.17
☐ 67	Ken Berry	1.35	.55	.13
☐ 68	Bob Buhl	1.35	.55	.13
☐ 69	Vic Davalillo	1.35	.55	.13

#	Name			
□ 70	Ron Santo	3.00	1.25	.30
□ 71	Camilo Pascual	1.75	.70	.17
□ 72	Tigers Rookies	1.35	.55	.13
	George Korince			
	(Photo actually			
	James Murray Brown)			
	John (Tom) Matchick			
□ 73	Rusty Staub	2.50	1.00	.25
□ 74	Wes Stock	1.35	.55	.13
□ 75	George Scott	2.00	.80	.20
□ 76	Jim Barbieri	1.35	.55	.13
□ 77	Dooley Womack	1.35	.55	.13
□ 78	Pat Corrales	1.75	.70	.17
□ 79	Bubba Morton	1.35	.55	.13
□ 80	Jim Maloney	1.75	.70	.17
□ 81	Eddie Stanky MG	1.75	.70	.17
□ 82	Steve Barber	1.35	.55	.13
□ 83	Ollie Brown	1.35	.55	.13
□ 84	Tommie Sisk	1.35	.55	.13
□ 85	Johnny Callison	1.75	.70	.17
□ 86A	Mike McCormick	32.00	14.25	4.75
	(no traded line;			
	Senators on front			
	and Senators on back)			
□ 86B	Mike McCormick	1.75		.17
	(with traded line			
	at end of bio;			
	Senators on front			
	but Giants on back)			
□ 87	George Altman	1.35	.55	.13
□ 88	Mickey Lolich	3.00	1.25	.30
□ 89	Felix Millan	1.35	.55	.13
□ 90	Jim Nash	1.35	.55	.13
□ 91	Johnny Lewis	1.35	.55	.13
□ 92	Ray Washburn	1.35	.55	.13
□ 93	Yankees Rookies	3.50	1.50	.35
	Stan Bahnsen			
	Bobby Murcer			
□ 94	Ron Fairly	1.75	.70	.17
□ 95	Sonny Siebert	1.35	.55	.13
□ 96	Art Shamsky	1.35	.55	.13
□ 97	Mike Cuellar	1.75	.70	.17
□ 98	Rich Rollins	1.35	.55	.13
□ 99	Lee Stange	1.35	.55	.13
□ 100	Frank Robinson DP	17.00	7.25	2.50
□ 101	Ken Johnson	1.35	.55	.13
□ 102	Philadelphia Phillies	2.75	1.10	.27
	Team Card			
□ 103	Checklist 2	9.00	1.25	.25
	Mickey Mantle			
□ 104	Minnie Rojas	1.35	.55	.13
□ 105	Ken Boyer	2.50	1.00	.25
□ 106	Randy Hundley	1.75	.70	.17
□ 107	Joel Horlen	1.35	.55	.13
□ 108	Alex Johnson	1.75	.70	.17
□ 109	Tribe Thumpers	2.25	.90	.22
	Rocky Colavito			
	Leon Wagner			
□ 110	Jack Aker	1.75	.70	.17
□ 111	John Kennedy	1.75	.70	.17
□ 112	Dave Wickersham	1.75	.70	.17
□ 113	Dave Nicholson	1.75	.70	.17
□ 114	Jack Baldschun	1.75	.70	.17
□ 115	Paul Casanova	1.75	.70	.17
□ 116	Herman Franks MG	1.75	.70	.17
□ 117	Darrell Brandon	1.75	.70	.17
□ 118	Bernie Allen	1.75	.70	.17
□ 119	Wade Blasingame	1.75	.70	.17
□ 120	Floyd Robinson	1.75	.70	.17
□ 121	Eddie Bressoud	1.75	.70	.17
□ 122	George Brunet	1.75	.70	.17
□ 123	Pirates Rookies	1.75	.70	.17
	Jim Price			
	Luke Walker			
□ 124	Jim Stewart	1.75	.70	.17
□ 125	Moe Drabowsky	1.75	.70	.17
□ 126	Tony Taylor	1.75	.70	.17
□ 127	John O'Donoghue	1.75	.70	.17
□ 128	Ed Spiezio	1.75	.70	.17
□ 129	Phil Roof	1.75	.70	.17
□ 130	Phil Regan	2.25	.90	.22
□ 131	Yankees Team	4.50	2.00	.45
□ 132	Ozzie Virgil	1.75	.70	.17
□ 133	Ron Kline	1.75	.70	.17
□ 134	Gates Brown	2.25	.90	.22
□ 135	Deron Johnson	1.75	.70	.17
□ 136	Carroll Sembera	1.75	.70	.17
□ 137	Twins Rookies	1.75	.70	.17
	Ron Clark			
	Jim Ollum			
□ 138	Dick Kelley	1.75	.70	.17
□ 139	Dalton Jones	1.75	.70	.17
□ 140	Willie Stargell	17.00	7.25	2.50
□ 141	John Miller	1.75	.70	.17
□ 142	Jackie Brandt	1.75	.70	.17
□ 143	Sox Sockers	2.25	.90	.22
	Pete Ward			
	Don Buford			
□ 144	Bill Hepler	1.75	.70	.17
□ 145	Larry Brown	1.75	.70	.17
□ 146	Steve Carlton	110.00	50.00	16.50
□ 147	Tom Egan	1.75	.70	.17
□ 148	Adolfo Phillips	1.75	.70	.17
□ 149	Joe Moeller	1.75	.70	.17
□ 150	Mickey Mantle	210.00	90.00	25.00
□ 151	World Series Game 1	3.50	1.50	.35
	Moe mows down 11			
□ 152	World Series Game 2	5.50	2.50	.55
	Palmer blanks Dodgers			
□ 153	World Series Game 3	3.50	1.50	.35
	Blair's homer			
	defeats L.A.			
□ 154	World Series Game 4	3.50	1.50	.35
	Orioles 4 straight			
□ 155	World Series Summary	3.50	1.50	.35
	Winners celebrate			
□ 156	Ron Herbel	1.75	.70	.17
□ 157	Danny Cater	1.75	.70	.17
□ 158	Jimmie Coker	1.75	.70	.17
□ 159	Bruce Howard	1.75	.70	.17
□ 160	Willie Davis	2.25	.90	.22
□ 161	Dick Williams MG	2.25	.90	.22
□ 162	Billy O'Dell	1.75	.70	.17
□ 163	Vic Roznovsky	1.75	.70	.17
□ 164	Dwight Siebler	1.75	.70	.17
□ 165	Cleon Jones	2.25	.90	.22
□ 166	Eddie Mathews	12.00	5.25	1.50
□ 167	Senators Rookies	1.75	.70	.17
	Joe Coleman			
	Tim Cullen			
□ 168	Ray Culp	1.75	.70	.17
□ 169	Horace Clarke	1.75	.70	.17
□ 170	Dick McAuliffe	2.25	.90	.22
□ 171	Cal Koonce	1.75	.70	.17
□ 172	Bill Heath	1.75	.70	.17
□ 173	St. Louis Cardinals	3.50	1.50	.35
	Team Card			
□ 174	Dick Radatz	2.25	.90	.22
□ 175	Bobby Knoop	1.75	.70	.17
□ 176	Sammy Ellis	1.75	.70	.17
□ 177	Tito Fuentes	1.75	.70	.17
□ 178	John Buzhardt	1.75	.70	.17
□ 179	Braves Rookies	1.75	.70	.17
	Charles Vaughan			
	Cecil Upshaw			
□ 180	Curt Blefary	2.25	.90	.22
□ 181	Terry Fox	1.75	.70	.17
□ 182	Ed Charles	1.75	.70	.17
□ 183	Jim Pagliaroni	1.75	.70	.17
□ 184	George Thomas	1.75	.70	.17
□ 185	Ken Holtzman	3.00	1.25	.30
□ 186	Mets Maulers	2.25	.90	.22
	Ed Kranepool			
	Ron Swoboda			
□ 187	Pedro Ramos	1.75	.70	.17
□ 188	Ken Harrelson	2.25	.90	.22
□ 189	Chuck Hinton	1.75	.70	.17
□ 190	Turk Farrell	1.75	.70	.17
□ 191A	Checklist 3	7.50		.15
	(214 Tom Kelley)			
	(Willie Mays)			
□ 191B	Checklist 3	12.50	1.25	.25
	(214 Dick Kelley)			
	(Willie Mays)			
□ 192	Fred Gladding	1.75	.70	.17
□ 193	Jose Cardenal	1.75	.70	.17
□ 194	Bob Allison	2.25	.90	.22
□ 195	Al Jackson	1.75	.70	.17
□ 196	Johnny Romano	1.75	.70	.17
□ 197	Ron Perranoski	2.50	1.00	.25
□ 198	Chuck Hiller	2.00	.80	.20
□ 199	Billy Hitchcock MG	2.00	.80	.20
□ 200	Willie Mays UER	85.00	38.00	12.75
	('63 Sna Francisco			
	on card back stats)			
□ 201	Hal Reniff	2.00	.80	.20
□ 202	Johnny Edwards	2.00	.80	.20
□ 203	Al McBean	2.00	.80	.20
□ 204	Orioles Rookies	2.50	1.00	.25
	Mike Epstein			
	Tom Phoebus			
□ 205	Dick Groat	2.50	1.00	.25
□ 206	Dennis Bennett	2.00	.80	.20
□ 207	John Orsino	2.00	.80	.20
□ 208	Jack Lamabe	2.00	.80	.20
□ 209	Joe Nossek	2.00	.80	.20
□ 210	Bob Gibson	20.00	8.50	2.75
□ 211	Twins Team	4.00	1.75	.40

No.	Name			
212	Chris Zachary	2.00	.80	.20
213	Jay Johnstone	3.00	1.25	.30
214	Dick Kelley	2.00	.80	.20
215	Ernie Banks	20.00	8.50	2.75
216	Bengal Belters	7.50	3.25	.75
	Norm Cash			
	Al Kaline			
217	Rob Gardner	2.00	.80	.20
218	Wes Parker	2.50	1.00	.25
219	Clay Carroll	2.50	1.00	.25
220	Jim Ray Hart	2.50	1.00	.25
221	Woody Fryman	2.00	.80	.20
222	Reds Rookies	2.50	1.00	.25
	Darrell Osteen			
	Lee May			
223	Mike Ryan	2.00	.80	.20
224	Walt Bond	2.00	.80	.20
225	Mel Stottlemyre	2.50	1.00	.25
226	Julian Javier	2.00	.80	.20
227	Paul Lindblad	2.00	.80	.20
228	Gil Hodges MG	5.00	2.25	.50
229	Larry Jackson	2.00	.80	.20
230	Boog Powell	3.00	1.25	.30
231	John Bateman	2.00	.80	.20
232	Don Buford	2.50	1.00	.25
233	AL ERA Leaders	2.50	1.00	.25
	Gary Peters			
	Joel Horlen			
	Steve Hargan			
234	NL ERA Leaders	6.00	2.50	.60
	Sandy Koufax			
	Mike Cuellar			
	Juan Marichal			
235	AL Pitching Leaders	3.00	1.25	.30
	Jim Kaat			
	Denny McLain			
	Earl Wilson			
236	NL Pitching Leaders	12.00	5.25	1.50
	Sandy Koufax			
	Juan Marichal			
	Bob Gibson			
	Gaylord Perry			
237	AL Strikeout Leaders	2.50	1.00	.25
	Sam McDowell			
	Jim Kaat			
	Earl Wilson			
238	NL Strikeout Leaders	4.50	2.00	.45
	Sandy Koufax			
	Jim Bunning			
	Bob Veale			
239	AL Batting Leaders	4.50	2.00	.45
	Frank Robinson			
	Tony Oliva			
	Al Kaline			
240	NL Batting Leaders	3.00	1.25	.30
	Matty Alou			
	Felipe Alou			
	Rico Carty			
241	AL RBI Leaders	4.50	2.00	.45
	Frank Robinson			
	Harmon Killebrew			
	Boog Powell			
242	NL RBI Leaders	7.50	3.25	.75
	Hank Aaron			
	Bob Clemente			
	Richie Allen			
243	AL Home Run Leaders	4.50	2.00	.45
	Frank Robinson			
	Harmon Killebrew			
	Boog Powell			
244	NL Home Run Leaders	7.50	3.25	.75
	Hank Aaron			
	Richie Allen			
	Willie Mays			
245	Curt Flood	2.50	1.00	.25
246	Jim Perry	2.50	1.00	.25
247	Jerry Lumpe	2.00	.80	.20
248	Gene Mauch MG	2.50	1.00	.25
249	Nick Willhite	2.00	.80	.20
250	Hank Aaron UER	85.00	38.00	12.75
	(Second 1961 in stats			
	should be 1962)			
251	Woody Held	2.00	.80	.20
252	Bob Bolin	2.00	.80	.20
253	Indians Rookies	2.00	.80	.20
	Bill Davis			
	Gus Gil			
254	Milt Pappas	2.50	1.00	.25
255	Frank Howard	3.00	1.25	.30
256	Bob Hendley	2.00	.80	.20
257	Charlie Smith	2.00	.80	.20
258	Lee Maye	2.00	.80	.20
259	Don Dennis	2.00	.80	.20
260	Jim Lefebvre	2.50	1.00	.25
261	John Wyatt	2.00	.80	.20
262	Athletics Team	3.50	1.50	.35
263	Hank Aguirre	2.00	.80	.20
264	Ron Swoboda	2.50	1.00	.25
265	Lou Burdette	2.50	1.00	.25
266	Pitt Power	4.00	1.75	.40
	Willie Stargell			
	Donn Clendenon			
267	Don Schwall	2.00	.80	.20
268	Johnny Briggs	2.00	.80	.20
269	Don Nottebart	2.00	.80	.20
270	Zoilo Versalles	2.00	.80	.20
271	Eddie Watt	2.00	.80	.20
272	Cubs Rookies	2.00	.80	.20
	Bill Connors			
	Dave Dowling			
273	Dick Lines	2.00	.80	.20
274	Bob Aspromonte	2.00	.80	.20
275	Fred Whitfield	2.00	.80	.20
276	Bruce Brubaker	2.00	.80	.20
277	Steve Whitaker	2.00	.80	.20
278	Checklist 4	6.50	.75	.15
	Jim Kaat			
279	Frank Linzy	2.00	.80	.20
280	Tony Conigliaro	5.50	2.50	.55
281	Bob Rodgers	2.50	1.00	.25
282	John Odom	2.00	.80	.20
283	Gene Alley	2.50	1.00	.25
284	Johnny Podres	3.00	1.25	.30
285	Lou Brock	22.00	9.50	3.15
286	Wayne Causey	2.50	1.00	.25
287	Mets Rookies	2.50	1.00	.25
	Greg Goossen			
	Bart Shirley			
288	Denny Lemaster	2.50	1.00	.25
289	Tom Tresh	3.00	1.25	.30
290	Bill White	3.50	1.50	.35
291	Jim Hannan	2.50	1.00	.25
292	Don Pavletich	2.50	1.00	.25
293	Ed Kirkpatrick	2.50	1.00	.25
294	Walt Alston MG	3.50	1.50	.35
295	Sam McDowell	3.00	1.25	.30
296	Glenn Beckert	3.00	1.25	.30
297	Dave Morehead	2.50	1.00	.25
298	Ron Davis	2.50	1.00	.25
299	Norm Siebern	2.50	1.00	.25
300	Jim Kaat	4.00	1.75	.40
301	Jesse Gonder	2.50	1.00	.25
302	Orioles Team	5.00	2.25	.50
303	Gil Blanco	2.50	1.00	.25
304	Phil Gagliano	2.50	1.00	.25
305	Earl Wilson	2.50	1.00	.25
306	Bud Harrelson	3.50	1.50	.35
307	Jim Beauchamp	2.50	1.00	.25
308	Al Downing	3.00	1.25	.30
309	Hurlers Beware	3.50	1.50	.35
	Johnny Callison			
	Richie Allen			
310	Gary Peters	2.50	1.00	.25
311	Ed Brinkman	2.50	1.00	.25
312	Don Mincher	2.50	1.00	.25
313	Bob Lee	2.50	1.00	.25
314	Red Sox Rookies	7.50	3.25	.75
	Mike Andrews			
	Reggie Smith			
315	Billy Williams	11.00	5.00	1.35
316	Jack Kralick	2.50	1.00	.25
317	Cesar Tovar	2.50	1.00	.25
318	Dave Giusti	3.00	1.25	.30
319	Paul Blair	3.00	1.25	.30
320	Gaylord Perry	13.00	5.75	1.75
321	Mayo Smith MG	2.50	1.00	.25
322	Jose Pagan	2.50	1.00	.25
323	Mike Hershberger	2.50	1.00	.25
324	Hal Woodeshick	2.50	1.00	.25
325	Chico Cardenas	2.50	1.00	.25
326	Bob Uecker	22.00	9.50	3.15
327	California Angels	5.00	2.25	.50
	Team Card			
328	Clete Boyer	3.00	1.25	.30
329	Charlie Lau	3.00	1.25	.30
330	Claude Osteen	3.00	1.25	.30
331	Joe Foy	2.50	1.00	.25
332	Jesus Alou	2.50	1.00	.25
333	Fergie Jenkins	30.00	13.50	4.50
334	Twin Terrors	4.00	1.75	.40
	Bob Allison			
	Harmon Killebrew			
335	Bob Veale	3.00	1.25	.30
336	Joe Azcue	2.50	1.00	.25
337	Joe Morgan	25.00	11.00	3.50
338	Bob Locker	2.50	1.00	.25
339	Chico Ruiz	2.50	1.00	.25
340	Joe Pepitone	3.00	1.25	.30

☐ 341	Giants Rookies	2.50	1.00	.25
	Dick Dietz			
	Bill Sorrell			
☐ 342	Hank Fischer	2.50	1.00	.25
☐ 343	Tom Satriano	2.50	1.00	.25
☐ 344	Ossie Chavarria	2.50	1.00	.25
☐ 345	Stu Miller	2.50	1.00	.25
☐ 346	Jim Hickman	2.50	1.00	.25
☐ 347	Grady Hatton MG	2.50	1.00	.25
☐ 348	Tug McGraw	3.50	1.50	.35
☐ 349	Bob Chance	2.50	1.00	.25
☐ 350	Joe Torre	3.50	1.50	.35
☐ 351	Vern Law	3.00	1.25	.30
☐ 352	Ray Oyler	2.50	1.00	.25
☐ 353	Bill McCool	2.50	1.00	.25
☐ 354	Cubs Team	5.00	2.25	.50
☐ 355	Carl Yastrzemski	95.00	42.00	11.00
☐ 356	Larry Jaster	2.50	1.00	.25
☐ 357	Bill Skowron	3.00	1.25	.30
☐ 358	Ruben Amaro	2.50	1.00	.25
☐ 359	Dick Ellsworth	2.50	1.00	.25
☐ 360	Leon Wagner	2.50	1.00	.25
☐ 361	Checklist 5	7.50	1.00	.25
	Roberto Clemente			
☐ 362	Darold Knowles	2.50	1.00	.25
☐ 363	Dave Johnson	3.00	1.25	.30
☐ 364	Claude Raymond	2.50	1.00	.25
☐ 365	John Roseboro	3.00	1.25	.30
☐ 366	Andy Kosco	2.50	1.00	.25
☐ 367	Angels Rookies	2.50	1.00	.25
	Bill Kelso			
	Don Wallace			
☐ 368	Jack Hiatt	2.50	1.00	.25
☐ 369	Jim Hunter	20.00	8.50	2.75
☐ 370	Tommy Davis	3.00	1.25	.30
☐ 371	Jim Lonborg	4.00	1.75	.40
☐ 372	Mike De La Hoz	3.00	1.25	.30
☐ 373	White Sox Rookies DP	3.00	1.25	.30
	Duane Josephson			
	Fred Klages			
☐ 374A	Mel Queen ERR DP	3.00	1.25	.30
	(Incomplete stat			
	line on back)			
☐ 374B	Mel Queen COR DP	3.00	1.25	.30
	(Complete stat			
	line on back)			
☐ 375	Jake Gibbs	3.00	1.25	.30
☐ 376	Don Lock DP	3.00	1.25	.30
☐ 377	Luis Tiant	4.50	2.00	.45
☐ 378	Detroit Tigers	6.00	2.50	.60
	Team Card UER			
	(Willie Horton with			
	262 RBI's in 1966)			
☐ 379	Jerry May DP	3.00	1.25	.30
☐ 380	Dean Chance DP	3.50	1.50	.35
☐ 381	Dick Schofield DP	3.00	1.25	.30
☐ 382	Dave McNally	3.50	1.50	.35
☐ 383	Ken Henderson DP	3.00	1.25	.30
☐ 384	Cardinals Rookies	3.00	1.25	.30
	Jim Cosman			
	Dick Hughes			
☐ 385	Jim Fregosi	3.50	1.50	.35
	(batting wrong)			
☐ 386	Dick Selma DP	3.00	1.25	.30
☐ 387	Cap Peterson DP	3.00	1.25	.30
☐ 388	Arnold Earley DP	3.00	1.25	.30
☐ 389	Alvin Dark MG DP	3.50	1.50	.35
☐ 390	Jim Wynn DP	4.00	1.75	.40
☐ 391	Wilbur Wood DP	3.50	1.50	.35
☐ 392	Tommy Harper DP	3.50	1.50	.35
☐ 393	Jim Bouton DP	4.00	1.75	.40
☐ 394	Jake Wood DP	3.00	1.25	.30
☐ 395	Chris Short	3.00	1.25	.30
☐ 396	Atlanta Aces	3.00	1.25	.30
	Denis Menke			
	Tony Cloninger			
☐ 397	Willie Smith DP	3.00	1.25	.30
☐ 398	Jeff Torborg	4.00	1.75	.40
☐ 399	Al Worthington DP	3.00	1.25	.30
☐ 400	Bob Clemente DP	65.00	29.00	9.75
☐ 401	Jim Coates	3.00	1.25	.30
☐ 402	Phillies Rookies DP	3.00	1.25	.30
	Grant Jackson			
	Billy Wilson			
☐ 403	Dick Nen	3.00	1.25	.30
☐ 404	Nelson Briles	3.50	1.50	.35
☐ 405	Russ Snyder	3.00	1.25	.30
☐ 406	Lee Elia DP	3.50	1.50	.35
☐ 407	Reds Team	6.00	2.50	.60
☐ 408	Jim Northrup DP	3.50	1.50	.35
☐ 409	Ray Sadecki	3.00	1.25	.30
☐ 410	Lou Johnson DP	3.00	1.25	.30
☐ 411	Dick Howser DP	3.50	1.50	.35

☐ 412	Astros Rookies	4.00	1.75	.40
	Norm Miller			
	Doug Rader			
☐ 413	Jerry Grote	3.00	1.25	.30
☐ 414	Casey Cox	3.00	1.25	.30
☐ 415	Sonny Jackson	3.00	1.25	.30
☐ 416	Roger Repoz	3.00	1.25	.30
☐ 417A	Bob Bruce ERR DP	30.00	13.50	4.50
	(RBAVES on back)			
☐ 417B	Bob Bruce COR DP	3.00	1.25	.30
☐ 418	Sam Mele MG	3.00	1.25	.30
☐ 419	Don Kessinger DP	4.00	1.75	.40
☐ 420	Denny McLain	6.00	2.50	.60
☐ 421	Dal Maxvill DP	3.00	1.25	.30
☐ 422	Hoyt Wilhelm	8.00	3.50	.80
☐ 423	Fence Busters DP	20.00	8.50	2.75
	Willie Mays			
	Willie McCovey			
☐ 424	Pedro Gonzalez	3.00	1.25	.30
☐ 425	Pete Mikkelsen	3.00	1.25	.30
☐ 426	Lou Clinton	3.00	1.25	.30
☐ 427A	Ruben Gomez ERR DP	3.00	1.25	.30
	(Incomplete stat			
	line on back)			
☐ 427B	Ruben Gomez COR DP	3.00	1.25	.30
	(Complete stat			
	line on back)			
☐ 428	Dodgers Rookies DP	4.00	1.75	.40
	Tom Hutton			
	Gene Michael			
☐ 429	Garry Roggenburk DP	3.00	1.25	.30
☐ 430	Pete Rose	75.00	34.00	11.25
☐ 431	Ted Uhlaender	3.00	1.25	.30
☐ 432	Jimmie Hall DP	3.50	1.50	.35
☐ 433	Al Luplow DP	3.00	1.25	.30
☐ 434	Eddie Fisher DP	3.00	1.25	.30
☐ 435	Mack Jones DP	3.00	1.25	.30
☐ 436	Pete Ward	3.00	1.25	.30
☐ 437	Senators Team	6.00	2.50	.60
☐ 438	Chuck Dobson	3.00	1.25	.30
☐ 439	Byron Browne	3.00	1.25	.30
☐ 440	Steve Hargan	3.00	1.25	.30
☐ 441	Jim Davenport	3.00	1.25	.30
☐ 442	Yankees Rookies DP	4.50	2.00	.45
	Bill Robinson			
	Joe Verbanic			
☐ 443	Tito Francona DP	3.00	1.25	.30
☐ 444	George Smith	3.00	1.25	.30
☐ 445	Don Sutton	30.00	13.50	4.50
☐ 446	Russ Nixon DP	3.00	1.25	.30
☐ 447A	Bo Belinsky ERR DP	3.50	1.50	.35
	(Incomplete stat			
	line on back)			
☐ 447B	Bo Belinsky COR DP	3.50	1.50	.35
	(Complete stat			
	line on back)			
☐ 448	Harry Walker MG DP	3.00	1.25	.30
☐ 449	Orlando Pena	3.00	1.25	.30
☐ 450	Richie Allen	6.00	2.50	.60
☐ 451	Fred Newman DP	3.00	1.25	.30
☐ 452	Ed Kranepool	3.50	1.50	.35
☐ 453	Aurelio Monteagudo DP	3.00	1.25	.30
☐ 454A	Checklist 6 DP	7.50	.75	.15
	Juan Marichal			
	(missing left ear)			
☐ 454B	Checklist 6 DP	12.50	1.25	.25
	Juan Marichal			
	(left ear showing)			
☐ 455	Tommy Agee	3.50	1.50	.35
☐ 456	Phil Niekro	13.00	5.75	1.75
☐ 457	Andy Etchebarren DP	3.00	1.25	.30
☐ 458	Lee Thomas	7.00	3.00	.70
☐ 459	Senators Rookies	7.00	3.00	.70
	Dick Bosman			
	Pete Craig			
☐ 460	Harmon Killebrew	50.00	22.50	7.50
☐ 461	Bob Miller	6.00	2.50	.60
☐ 462	Bob Barton	6.00	2.50	.60
☐ 463	Hill Aces	7.00	3.00	.70
	Sam McDowell			
	Sonny Siebert			
☐ 464	Dan Coombs	6.00	2.50	.60
☐ 465	Willie Horton	7.00	3.00	.70
☐ 466	Bobby Wine	6.00	2.50	.60
☐ 467	Jim O'Toole	6.00	2.50	.60
☐ 468	Ralph Houk MG	7.00	3.00	.70
☐ 469	Len Gabrielson	6.00	2.50	.60
☐ 470	Bob Shaw	6.00	2.50	.60
☐ 471	Rene Lachemann	7.00	3.00	.70
☐ 472	Rookies Pirates	6.00	2.50	.60
	John Gelnar			
	George Spriggs			
☐ 473	Jose Santiago	6.00	2.50	.60
☐ 474	Bob Tolan	7.00	3.00	.70

☐ 475	Jim Palmer	110.00	50.00	16.50
☐ 476	Tony Perez SP	90.00	40.00	13.50
☐ 477	Braves Team	12.00	5.25	1.50
☐ 478	Bob Humphreys	6.00	2.50	.60
☐ 479	Gary Bell	6.00	2.50	.60
☐ 480	Willie McCovey	36.00	16.25	5.50
☐ 481	Leo Durocher MG	12.50	5.50	1.65
☐ 482	Bill Monbouquette	7.00	3.00	.70
☐ 483	Jim Landis	6.00	2.50	.60
☐ 484	Jerry Adair	6.00	2.50	.60
☐ 485	Tim McCarver	24.00	10.50	3.50
☐ 486	Twins Rookies	7.00	3.00	.70
	Rich Reese			
	Bill Whitby			
☐ 487	Tommie Reynolds	6.00	2.50	.60
☐ 488	Gerry Arrigo	6.00	2.50	.60
☐ 489	Doug Clemens	6.00	2.50	.60
☐ 490	Tony Cloninger	6.00	2.50	.60
☐ 491	Sam Bowens	6.00	2.50	.60
☐ 492	Pittsburgh Pirates	12.00	5.25	1.50
	Team Card			
☐ 493	Phil Ortega	6.00	2.50	.60
☐ 494	Bill Rigney MG	6.00	2.50	.60
☐ 495	Fritz Peterson	6.00	2.50	.60
☐ 496	Orlando McFarlane	6.00	2.50	.60
☐ 497	Ron Campbell	6.00	2.50	.60
☐ 498	Larry Dierker	6.00	2.50	.60
☐ 499	Indians Rookies	6.00	2.50	.60
	George Culver			
	Jose Vidal			
☐ 500	Juan Marichal	25.00	11.00	3.50
☐ 501	Jerry Zimmerman	6.00	2.50	.60
☐ 502	Derrell Griffith	6.00	2.50	.60
☐ 503	Los Angeles Dodgers	12.00	5.25	1.50
	Team Card			
☐ 504	Orlando Martinez	6.00	2.50	.60
☐ 505	Tommy Helms	7.00	3.00	.70
☐ 506	Smoky Burgess	7.00	3.00	.70
☐ 507	Orioles Rookies	6.00	2.50	.60
	Ed Barnowski			
	Larry Haney			
☐ 508	Dick Hall	6.00	2.50	.60
☐ 509	Jim King	6.00	2.50	.60
☐ 510	Bill Mazeroski	12.50	5.50	1.65
☐ 511	Don Wert	6.00	2.50	.60
☐ 512	Red Schoendienst MG	12.50	5.50	1.65
☐ 513	Marcelino Lopez	6.00	2.50	.60
☐ 514	John Werhas	6.00	2.50	.60
☐ 515	Bert Campaneris	7.00	3.00	.70
☐ 516	Giants Team	12.00	5.25	1.50
☐ 517	Fred Talbot	6.00	2.50	.60
☐ 518	Denis Menke	6.00	2.50	.60
☐ 519	Ted Davidson	6.00	2.50	.60
☐ 520	Max Alvis	6.00	2.50	.60
☐ 521	Bird Bombers	8.00	3.50	.80
	Boog Powell			
	Curt Blefary			
☐ 522	John Stephenson	6.00	2.50	.60
☐ 523	Jim Merritt	6.00	2.50	.60
☐ 524	Felix Mantilla	6.00	2.50	.60
☐ 525	Ron Hunt	6.00	2.50	.60
☐ 526	Tigers Rookies	8.00	3.50	.80
	Pat Dobson			
	George Korince			
	(See 67T-72)			
☐ 527	Dennis Ribant	6.00	2.50	.60
☐ 528	Rico Petrocelli	8.00	3.50	.80
☐ 529	Gary Wagner	6.00	2.50	.60
☐ 530	Felipe Alou	7.00	3.00	.70
☐ 531	Checklist 7	12.50	1.25	.25
	Brooks Robinson			
☐ 532	Jim Hicks	6.00	2.50	.60
☐ 533	Jack Fisher	6.00	2.50	.60
☐ 534	Hank Bauer MG DP	10.00	4.50	1.25
☐ 535	Donn Clendenon	22.00	9.50	3.15
☐ 536	Cubs Rookies	36.00	16.25	5.50
	Joe Niekro			
	Paul Popovich			
☐ 537	Chuck Estrada DP	9.00	4.00	.90
☐ 538	J.C. Martin	18.00	7.50	2.50
☐ 539	Dick Egan DP	9.00	4.00	.90
☐ 540	Norm Cash	42.00	18.00	5.50
☐ 541	Joe Gibbon	18.00	7.50	2.50
☐ 542	Athletics Rookies DP	11.00	5.00	1.35
	Rick Monday			
	Tony Pierce			
☐ 543	Dan Schneider	18.00	7.50	2.50
☐ 544	Cleveland Indians	33.00	15.00	5.00
	Team Card			
☐ 545	Jim Grant	18.00	7.50	2.50
☐ 546	Woody Woodward	18.00	7.50	2.50
☐ 547	Red Sox Rookies DP	9.00	4.00	.90
	Russ Gibson			
	Bill Rohr			

☐ 548	Tony Gonzalez DP	9.00	4.00	.90
☐ 549	Jack Sanford	18.00	7.50	2.50
☐ 550	Vada Pinson DP	11.00	5.00	1.35
☐ 551	Doug Camilli DP	9.00	4.00	.90
☐ 552	Ted Savage	18.00	7.50	2.50
☐ 553	Yankees Rookies	32.00	14.25	4.75
	Mike Hegan			
	Thad Tillotson			
☐ 554	Andre Rodgers DP	9.00	4.00	.90
☐ 555	Don Cardwell	18.00	7.50	2.50
☐ 556	Al Weis DP	9.00	4.00	.90
☐ 557	Al Ferrara	18.00	7.50	2.50
☐ 558	Orioles Rookies	50.00	22.50	7.50
	Mark Belanger			
	Bill Dillman			
☐ 559	Dick Tracewski DP	9.00	4.00	.90
☐ 560	Jim Bunning	50.00	22.50	7.50
☐ 561	Sandy Alomar	20.00	8.50	2.75
☐ 562	Steve Blass DP	9.00	4.00	.90
☐ 563	Joe Adcock	22.00	9.50	3.15
☐ 564	Astros Rookies DP	9.00	4.00	.90
	Alonzo Harris			
	Aaron Pointer			
☐ 565	Lew Krausse	18.00	7.50	2.50
☐ 566	Gary Geiger DP	9.00	4.00	.90
☐ 567	Steve Hamilton	18.00	7.50	2.50
☐ 568	John Sullivan	18.00	7.50	2.50
☐ 569	AL Rookies DP	500.00	225.00	75.00
	Rod Carew			
	Hank Allen			
☐ 570	Maury Wills	95.00	42.00	11.00
☐ 571	Larry Sherry	18.00	7.50	2.50
☐ 572	Don Demeter	18.00	7.50	2.50
☐ 573	Chicago White Sox	32.00	14.25	4.75
	Team Card UER			
	(Indians team			
	stats on back)			
☐ 574	Jerry Buchek	18.00	7.50	2.50
☐ 575	Dave Boswell	18.00	7.50	2.50
☐ 576	NL Rookies	22.00	9.50	3.15
	Ramon Hernandez			
	Norm Gigon			
☐ 577	Bill Short	18.00	7.50	2.50
☐ 578	John Boccabella	18.00	7.50	2.50
☐ 579	Bill Henry	18.00	7.50	2.50
☐ 580	Rocky Colavito	70.00	32.00	10.50
☐ 581	Mets Rookies	1200.00	500.00	150.00
	Bill Denehy			
	Tom Seaver			
☐ 582	Jim Owens DP	9.00	4.00	.90
☐ 583	Ray Barker	18.00	7.50	2.50
☐ 584	Jim Piersall	24.00	10.50	3.50
☐ 585	Wally Bunker	18.00	7.50	2.50
☐ 586	Manny Jimenez	18.00	7.50	2.50
☐ 587	NL Rookies	22.00	9.50	3.15
	Don Shaw			
	Gary Sutherland			
☐ 588	Johnny Klippstein DP	9.00	4.00	.90
☐ 589	Dave Ricketts DP	9.00	4.00	.90
☐ 590	Pete Richert	18.00	7.50	2.50
☐ 591	Ty Cline	18.00	7.50	2.50
☐ 592	NL Rookies	22.00	9.50	3.15
	Jim Shellenback			
	Ron Willis			
☐ 593	Wes Westrum MG	22.00	9.50	3.15
☐ 594	Dan Osinski	18.00	7.50	2.50
☐ 595	Cookie Rojas	22.00	9.50	3.15
☐ 596	Galen Cisco DP	9.00	4.00	.90
☐ 597	Ted Abernathy	18.00	7.50	2.50
☐ 598	White Sox Rookies	24.00	10.50	3.50
	Walt Williams			
	Ed Stroud			
☐ 599	Bob Duliba DP	9.00	4.00	.90
☐ 600	Brooks Robinson	250.00	110.00	37.50
☐ 601	Bill Bryan DP	9.00	4.00	.90
☐ 602	Juan Pizarro	18.00	7.50	2.50
☐ 603	Athletics Rookies	18.00	7.50	2.50
	Tim Talton			
	Ramon Webster			
☐ 604	Red Sox Team	125.00	57.50	18.75
☐ 605	Mike Shannon	45.00	20.00	6.75
☐ 606	Ron Taylor	18.00	7.50	2.50
☐ 607	Mickey Stanley	33.00	15.00	5.00
☐ 608	Cubs Rookies DP	9.00	4.00	.90
	Rich Nye			
	John Upham			
☐ 609	Tommy John	115.00	30.00	6.00

1968 Topps

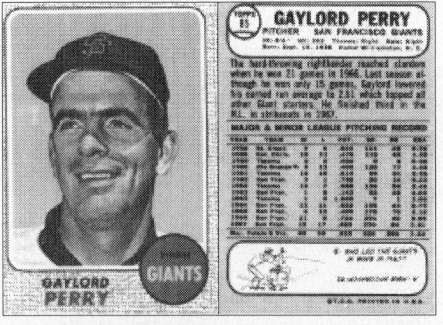

The cards in this 598-card set measure 2 1/2" by 3 1/2". The 1968 Topps set includes Sporting News All-Star Selections as card numbers 361 to 380. Other subsets in the set include League Leaders (1-12) and World Series cards (151-158). The front of each checklist card features a picture of a popular player inside a circle. High numbers 534 to 598 are slightly more difficult to obtain. The first series looks different from the other series, as it has a lighter, wider mesh background on the card front. The later series all had a much darker, finer mesh pattern. Key cards in the set are the rookie cards of Johnny Bench (247) and Nolan Ryan (177).

		NRMT	VG-E	GOOD
	COMPLETE SET (598)	3300.00	1400.00	350.00
	COMMON PLAYER (1-109)	1.35	.55	.13
	COMMON PLAYER (110-196)	1.35	.55	.13
	COMMON PLAYER (197-283)	1.35	.55	.13
	COMMON PLAYER (284-370)	1.35	.55	.13
	COMMON PLAYER (371-457)	1.35	.55	.13
	COMMON PLAYER (458-533)	3.00	.60	.15
	COMMON PLAYER (534-598)	3.25	.70	.17
☐ 1	NL Batting Leaders Bob Clemente Tony Gonzales Matty Alou	15.00	3.00	.60
☐ 2	AL Batting Leaders Carl Yastrzemski Frank Robinson Al Kaline	9.00	4.00	.90
☐ 3	NL RBI Leaders Orlando Cepeda Bob Clemente Hank Aaron	5.00	2.25	.50
☐ 4	AL RBI Leaders Carl Yastrzemski Harmon Killebrew Frank Robinson	9.00	4.00	.90
☐ 5	NL Home Run Leaders Hank Aaron Jim Wynn Ron Santo Willie McCovey	4.50	2.00	.45
☐ 6	AL Home Run Leaders Carl Yastrzemski Harmon Killebrew Frank Howard	6.00	2.50	.60
☐ 7	NL ERA Leaders Phil Niekro Jim Bunning Chris Short	2.50	1.00	.25
☐ 8	AL ERA Leaders Joel Horlen Gary Peters Sonny Siebert	2.25	.90	.22
☐ 9	NL Pitching Leaders Mike McCormick Ferguson Jenkins Jim Bunning Claude Osteen	2.50	1.00	.25
☐ 10A	AL Pitching Leaders Jim Lonborg ERR (misspelled Lonberg on card back) Earl Wilson Dean Chance	3.00	1.25	.30
☐ 10B	AL Pitching Leaders Jim Lonborg COR Earl Wilson Dean Chance	3.00	1.25	.30
☐ 11	NL Strikeout Leaders Jim Bunning Ferguson Jenkins Gaylord Perry	3.50	1.50	.35
☐ 12	AL Strikeout Leaders Jim Lonborg UER (misspelled Longberg on card back) Sam McDowell Dean Chance	2.50	1.00	.25
☐ 13	Chuck Hartenstein	1.35	.55	.13
☐ 14	Jerry McNertney	1.35	.55	.13
☐ 15	Ron Hunt	1.35	.55	.13
☐ 16	Indians Rookies Lou Piniella Richie Scheinblum	4.00	1.75	.40
☐ 17	Dick Hall	1.35	.55	.13
☐ 18	Mike Hershberger	1.35	.55	.13
☐ 19	Juan Pizarro	1.35	.55	.13
☐ 20	Brooks Robinson	21.00	9.00	3.00
☐ 21	Ron Davis	1.35	.55	.13
☐ 22	Pat Dobson	1.75	.70	.17
☐ 23	Chico Cardenas	1.35	.55	.13
☐ 24	Bobby Locke	1.35	.55	.13
☐ 25	Julian Javier	1.35	.55	.13
☐ 26	Darrell Brandon	1.35	.55	.13
☐ 27	Gil Hodges MG	7.00	3.00	.70
☐ 28	Ted Uhlaender	1.35	.55	.13
☐ 29	Joe Verbanic	1.35	.55	.13
☐ 30	Joe Torre	2.50	1.00	.25
☐ 31	Ed Stroud	1.35	.55	.13
☐ 32	Joe Gibbon	1.35	.55	.13
☐ 33	Pete Ward	1.35	.55	.13
☐ 34	Al Ferrara	1.35	.55	.13
☐ 35	Steve Hargan	1.35	.55	.13
☐ 36	Pirates Rookies Bob Moose Bob Robertson	1.75	.70	.17
☐ 37	Billy Williams	10.00	4.50	1.25
☐ 38	Tony Pierce	1.35	.55	.13
☐ 39	Cookie Rojas	1.35	.55	.13
☐ 40	Denny McLain	9.00	4.00	.90
☐ 41	Julio Gotay	1.35	.55	.13
☐ 42	Larry Haney	1.35	.55	.13
☐ 43	Gary Bell	1.35	.55	.13
☐ 44	Frank Kostro	1.35	.55	.13
☐ 45	Tom Seaver	200.00	90.00	30.00
☐ 46	Dave Ricketts	1.35	.55	.13
☐ 47	Ralph Houk MG	1.75	.70	.17
☐ 48	Ted Davidson	1.35	.55	.13
☐ 49A	Eddie Brinkman (white team name)	1.35	.55	.13
☐ 49B	Eddie Brinkman (yellow team name)	40.00	18.00	6.00
☐ 50	Willie Mays	60.00	27.00	9.00
☐ 51	Bob Locker	1.35	.55	.13
☐ 52	Hawk Taylor	1.35	.55	.13
☐ 53	Gene Alley	1.75	.70	.17
☐ 54	Stan Williams	1.35	.55	.13
☐ 55	Felipe Alou	1.75	.70	.17
☐ 56	Orioles Rookies Dave Leonhard Dave May	1.35	.55	.13
☐ 57	Dan Schneider	1.35	.55	.13
☐ 58	Eddie Mathews	9.00	4.00	.90
☐ 59	Don Lock	1.35	.55	.13
☐ 60	Ken Holtzman	1.75	.70	.17
☐ 61	Reggie Smith	2.00	.80	.20
☐ 62	Chuck Dobson	1.35	.55	.13
☐ 63	Dick Kenworthy	1.35	.55	.13
☐ 64	Jim Merritt	1.35	.55	.13
☐ 65	Jim Roseboro	1.35	.55	.13
☐ 66A	Casey Cox (white team name)	1.35	.55	.13
☐ 66B	Casey Cox (yellow team name)	100.00	45.00	15.00
☐ 67	Checklist 1 Jim Kaat	5.00	.50	.10
☐ 68	Ron Willis	1.35	.55	.13
☐ 69	Tom Tresh	1.75	.70	.17
☐ 70	Bob Veale	1.75	.70	.17
☐ 71	Vern Fuller	1.35	.55	.13
☐ 72	Tommy John	4.50	2.00	.45
☐ 73	Jim Ray Hart	1.75	.70	.17
☐ 74	Milt Pappas	1.75	.70	.17
☐ 75	Don Mincher	1.75	.70	.17
☐ 76	Braves Rookies Jim Britton Ron Reed	1.75	.70	.17

☐ 77	Don Wilson	1.35	.55	.13
☐ 78	Jim Northrup	1.75	.70	.17
☐ 79	Ted Kubiak	1.35	.55	.13
☐ 80	Rod Carew	150.00	67.50	22.50
☐ 81	Larry Jackson	1.35	.55	.13
☐ 82	Sam Bowens	1.35	.55	.13
☐ 83	John Stephenson	1.35	.55	.13
☐ 84	Bob Tolan	1.75	.70	.17
☐ 85	Gaylord Perry	11.00	5.00	1.35
☐ 86	Willie Stargell	11.00	5.00	1.35
☐ 87	Dick Williams MG	1.75	.70	.17
☐ 88	Phil Regan	1.75	.70	.17
☐ 89	Jake Gibbs	1.35	.55	.13
☐ 90	Vada Pinson	2.25	.90	.22
☐ 91	Jim Ollom	1.35	.55	.13
☐ 92	Ed Kranepool	1.75	.70	.17
☐ 93	Tony Cloninger	1.35	.55	.13
☐ 94	Lee Maye	1.35	.55	.13
☐ 95	Bob Aspromonte	1.35	.55	.13
☐ 96	Senator Rookies	1.35	.55	.13
	Frank Coggins			
	Dick Nold			
☐ 97	Tom Phoebus	1.35	.55	.13
☐ 98	Gary Sutherland	1.35	.55	.13
☐ 99	Rocky Colavito	3.50	1.50	.35
☐ 100	Bob Gibson	24.00	10.50	3.50
☐ 101	Glenn Beckert	1.75	.70	.17
☐ 102	Jose Cardenal	1.35	.55	.13
☐ 103	Don Sutton	10.00	4.50	1.25
☐ 104	Dick Dietz	1.35	.55	.13
☐ 105	Al Downing	1.75	.70	.17
☐ 106	Dalton Jones	1.35	.55	.13
☐ 107A	Checklist 2	5.00	.50	.10
	Juan Marichal			
	(tan wide mesh)			
☐ 107B	Checklist 2	5.00	.50	.10
	Juan Marichal			
	(brown fine mesh)			
☐ 108	Don Pavletich	1.35	.55	.13
☐ 109	Bert Campaneris	1.75	.70	.17
☐ 110	Hank Aaron	65.00	29.00	9.75
☐ 111	Rich Reese	1.35	.55	.13
☐ 112	Woodie Fryman	1.35	.55	.13
☐ 113	Tigers Rookies	1.35	.55	.13
	Tom Matchick			
	Daryl Patterson			
☐ 114	Ron Swoboda	1.75	.70	.17
☐ 115	Sam McDowell	1.75	.70	.17
☐ 116	Ken McMullen	1.35	.55	.13
☐ 117	Larry Jaster	1.35	.55	.13
☐ 118	Mark Belanger	1.75	.70	.17
☐ 119	Ted Savage	1.35	.55	.13
☐ 120	Mel Stottlemyre	2.00	.80	.20
☐ 121	Jimmie Hall	1.35	.55	.13
☐ 122	Gene Mauch MG	1.75	.70	.17
☐ 123	Jose Santiago	1.35	.55	.13
☐ 124	Nate Oliver	1.35	.55	.13
☐ 125	Joel Horlen	1.35	.55	.13
☐ 126	Bobby Etheridge	1.35	.55	.13
☐ 127	Paul Lindblad	1.35	.55	.13
☐ 128	Astros Rookies	1.35	.55	.13
	Tom Dukes			
	Alonzo Harris			
☐ 129	Mickey Stanley	1.75	.70	.17
☐ 130	Tony Perez	15.00	6.50	2.15
☐ 131	Frank Bertaina	1.35	.55	.13
☐ 132	Bud Harrelson	1.75	.70	.17
☐ 133	Fred Whitfield	1.35	.55	.13
☐ 134	Pat Jarvis	1.35	.55	.13
☐ 135	Paul Blair	1.75	.70	.17
☐ 136	Randy Hundley	1.75	.70	.17
☐ 137	Twins Team	2.50	1.00	.25
☐ 138	Ruben Amaro	1.35	.55	.13
☐ 139	Chris Short	1.35	.55	.13
☐ 140	Tony Conigliaro	4.50	2.00	.45
☐ 141	Dal Maxvill	1.35	.55	.13
☐ 142	White Sox Rookies	1.35	.55	.13
	Buddy Bradford			
	Bill Voss			
☐ 143	Pete Cimino	1.35	.55	.13
☐ 144	Joe Morgan	17.00	7.25	2.50
☐ 145	Don Drysdale	10.00	4.50	1.25
☐ 146	Sal Bando	1.75	.70	.17
☐ 147	Frank Linzy	1.35	.55	.13
☐ 148	Dave Bristol MG	1.35	.55	.13
☐ 149	Bob Saverine	1.35	.55	.13
☐ 150	Bob Clemente	50.00	22.50	7.50
☐ 151	World Series Game 1	6.00	2.50	.60
	Brock socks 4 hits			
	in opener			
☐ 152	World Series Game 2	8.00	3.50	.80
	Yaz smashes 2 homers			
☐ 153	World Series Game 3	3.50	1.50	.35
	Briles cools Boston			

☐ 154	World Series Game 4	6.00	2.50	.60
	Gibson hurls shutout			
☐ 155	World Series Game 5	3.50	1.50	.35
	Lonborg wins again			
☐ 156	World Series Game 6	3.50	1.50	.35
	Petrocelli 2 homers			
☐ 157	World Series Game 7	3.50	1.50	.35
	St. Louis wins it			
☐ 158	World Series Summary	3.50	1.50	.35
	Cardinals celebrate			
☐ 159	Don Kessinger	1.75	.70	.17
☐ 160	Earl Wilson	1.35	.55	.13
☐ 161	Norm Miller	1.35	.55	.13
☐ 162	Cards Rookies	1.75	.70	.17
	Hal Gilson			
	Mike Torrez			
☐ 163	Gene Brabender	1.35	.55	.13
☐ 164	Ramon Webster	1.35	.55	.13
☐ 165	Tony Oliva	3.50	1.50	.35
☐ 166	Claude Raymond	1.35	.55	.13
☐ 167	Elston Howard	3.00	1.25	.30
☐ 168	Dodgers Team	3.00	1.25	.30
☐ 169	Bob Bolin	1.35	.55	.13
☐ 170	Jim Fregosi	1.75	.70	.17
☐ 171	Don Nottebart	1.35	.55	.13
☐ 172	Walt Williams	1.35	.55	.13
☐ 173	John Boozer	1.35	.55	.13
☐ 174	Bob Tillman	1.35	.55	.13
☐ 175	Maury Wills	3.50	1.50	.35
☐ 176	Bob Allen	1.35	.55	.13
☐ 177	Mets Rookies	1500.00	650.00	175.00
	Jerry Koosman			
	Nolan Ryan			
☐ 178	Don Wert	1.35	.55	.13
☐ 179	Bill Stoneman	1.35	.55	.13
☐ 180	Curt Flood	1.75	.70	.17
☐ 181	Jerry Zimmerman	1.35	.55	.13
☐ 182	Dave Giusti	1.35	.55	.13
☐ 183	Bob Kennedy MG	1.35	.55	.13
☐ 184	Lou Johnson	1.35	.55	.13
☐ 185	Tom Haller	1.35	.55	.13
☐ 186	Eddie Watt	1.35	.55	.13
☐ 187	Sonny Jackson	1.35	.55	.13
☐ 188	Cap Peterson	1.35	.55	.13
☐ 189	Bill Landis	1.35	.55	.13
☐ 190	Bill White	2.00	.80	.20
☐ 191	Dan Frisella	1.35	.55	.13
☐ 192A	Checklist 3	5.00	.50	.10
	Carl Yastrzemski			
	(Special Baseball			
	Playing Card)			
☐ 192A	Checklist 3	5.00	.50	.10
	Carl Yastrzemski			
	(Special Baseball			
	Playing Card Game)			
☐ 193	Jack Hamilton	1.35	.55	.13
☐ 194	Don Buford	1.75	.70	.17
☐ 195	Joe Pepitone	1.75	.70	.17
☐ 196	Gary Nolan	1.75	.70	.17
☐ 197	Larry Brown	1.35	.55	.13
☐ 198	Roy Face	1.75	.70	.17
☐ 199	A's Rookies	1.35	.55	.13
	Roberto Rodriquez			
	Darrell Osteen			
☐ 200	Orlando Cepeda	4.50	2.00	.45
☐ 201	Mike Marshall	2.50	1.00	.25
☐ 202	Adolfo Phillips	1.35	.55	.13
☐ 203	Dick Kelley	1.35	.55	.13
☐ 204	Andy Etchebarren	1.35	.55	.13
☐ 205	Juan Marichal	7.50	3.25	.75
☐ 206	Cal Ermer MG	1.35	.55	.13
☐ 207	Carroll Sembera	1.35	.55	.13
☐ 208	Willie Davis	1.75	.70	.17
☐ 209	Tim Cullen	1.35	.55	.13
☐ 210	Gary Peters	1.35	.55	.13
☐ 211	J.C. Martin	1.35	.55	.13
☐ 212	Dave Morehead	1.35	.55	.13
☐ 213	Chico Ruiz	1.35	.55	.13
☐ 214	Yankees Rookies	1.75	.70	.17
	Stan Bahnsen			
	Frank Fernandez			
☐ 215	Jim Bunning	3.50	1.50	.35
☐ 216	Bubba Morton	1.35	.55	.13
☐ 217	Turk Farrell	1.35	.55	.13
☐ 218	Ken Suarez	1.35	.55	.13
☐ 219	Rob Gardner	1.35	.55	.13
☐ 220	Harmon Killebrew	14.00	6.25	2.00
☐ 221	Braves Team	2.75	1.10	.27
☐ 222	Jim Hardin	1.35	.55	.13
☐ 223	Ollie Brown	1.35	.55	.13
☐ 224	Jack Aker	1.35	.55	.13
☐ 225	Richie Allen	3.50	1.50	.35
☐ 226	Jimmie Price	1.35	.55	.13
☐ 227	Joe Hoerner	1.35	.55	.13
☐ 228	Dodgers Rookies	1.35	.55	.13

	Jack Billingham			
	Jim Fairey			
☐ 229	Fred Klages	1.35	.55	.13
☐ 230	Pete Rose	45.00	20.00	6.75
☐ 231	Dave Baldwin	1.35	.55	.13
☐ 232	Denis Menke	1.35	.55	.13
☐ 233	George Scott	1.75	.70	.17
☐ 234	Bill Monbouquette	1.35	.55	.13
☐ 235	Ron Santo	3.00	1.25	.30
☐ 236	Tug McGraw	3.00	1.25	.30
☐ 237	Alvin Dark MG	1.75	.70	.17
☐ 238	Tom Satriano	1.35	.55	.13
☐ 239	Bill Henry	1.35	.55	.13
☐ 240	Al Kaline	20.00	8.50	2.75
☐ 241	Felix Millan	1.35	.55	.13
☐ 242	Moe Drabowsky	1.35	.55	.13
☐ 243	Rich Rollins	1.35	.55	.13
☐ 244	John Donaldson	1.35	.55	.13
☐ 245	Tony Gonzalez	1.35	.55	.13
☐ 246	Fritz Peterson	1.35	.55	.13
☐ 247	Reds Rookies	300.00	135.00	45.00
	Johnny Bench			
	Ron Tompkins			
☐ 248	Fred Valentine	1.35	.55	.13
☐ 249	Bill Singer	1.75	.70	.17
☐ 250	Carl Yastrzemski	40.00	18.00	6.00
☐ 251	Manny Sanguillen	5.00	2.25	.50
☐ 252	Angels Team	2.75	1.10	.27
☐ 253	Dick Hughes	1.35	.55	.13
☐ 254	Cleon Jones	1.35	.55	.13
☐ 255	Dean Chance	1.75	.70	.17
☐ 256	Norm Cash	4.00	1.75	.40
☐ 257	Phil Niekro	6.50	2.75	.65
☐ 258	Cubs Rookies	1.35	.55	.13
	Jose Arcia			
	Bill Schlesinger			
☐ 259	Ken Boyer	2.25	.90	.22
☐ 260	Jim Wynn	1.75	.70	.17
☐ 261	Dave Duncan	1.75	.70	.17
☐ 262	Rick Wise	1.75	.70	.17
☐ 263	Horace Clarke	1.35	.55	.13
☐ 264	Ted Abernathy	1.35	.55	.13
☐ 265	Tommy Davis	1.75	.70	.17
☐ 266	Paul Popovich	1.35	.55	.13
☐ 267	Herman Franks MG	1.35	.55	.13
☐ 268	Bob Humphreys	1.35	.55	.13
☐ 269	Bob Tiefenauer	1.35	.55	.13
☐ 270	Matty Alou	1.75	.70	.17
☐ 271	Bobby Knoop	1.35	.55	.13
☐ 272	Ray Culp	1.35	.55	.13
☐ 273	Dave Johnson	1.75	.70	.17
☐ 274	Mike Cuellar	1.75	.70	.17
☐ 275	Tim McCarver	3.00	1.25	.30
☐ 276	Jim Roland	1.35	.55	.13
☐ 277	Jerry Buchek	1.35	.55	.13
☐ 278	Checklist 4	5.00	.50	.10
	Orlando Cepeda			
☐ 279	Bill Hands	1.35	.55	.13
☐ 280	Mickey Mantle	180.00	80.00	27.00
☐ 281	Jim Campanis	1.35	.55	.13
☐ 282	Rick Monday	1.75	.70	.17
☐ 283	Mel Queen	1.35	.55	.13
☐ 284	Johnny Briggs	1.35	.55	.13
☐ 285	Dick McAuliffe	1.35	.55	.13
☐ 286	Cecil Upshaw	1.35	.55	.13
☐ 287	White Sox Rookies	1.35	.55	.13
	Mickey Abarbanel			
	Cisco Carlos			
☐ 288	Dave Wickersham	1.35	.55	.13
☐ 289	Woody Held	1.35	.55	.13
☐ 290	Willie McCovey	12.00	5.25	1.50
☐ 291	Dick Lines	1.35	.55	.13
☐ 292	Art Shamsky	1.35	.55	.13
☐ 293	Bruce Howard	1.35	.55	.13
☐ 294	Red Schoendienst MG	3.50	1.50	.35
☐ 295	Sonny Siebert	1.35	.55	.13
☐ 296	Byron Browne	1.35	.55	.13
☐ 297	Russ Gibson	1.35	.55	.13
☐ 298	Jim Brewer	1.35	.55	.13
☐ 299	Gene Michael	1.75	.70	.17
☐ 300	Rusty Staub	2.25	.90	.22
☐ 301	Twins Rookies	1.35	.55	.13
	George Mitterwald			
	Rick Renick			
☐ 302	Gerry Arrigo	1.35	.55	.13
☐ 303	Dick Green	1.35	.55	.13
☐ 304	Sandy Valdespino	1.35	.55	.13
☐ 305	Minnie Rojas	1.35	.55	.13
☐ 306	Mike Ryan	1.35	.55	.13
☐ 307	John Hiller	1.75	.70	.17
☐ 308	Pirates Team	2.75	1.10	.27
☐ 309	Ken Henderson	1.35	.55	.13
☐ 310	Luis Aparicio	6.00	2.50	.60
☐ 311	Jack Lamabe	1.35	.55	.13
☐ 312	Curt Blefary	1.35	.55	.13
☐ 313	Al Weis	1.35	.55	.13
☐ 314	Red Sox Rookies	1.35	.55	.13
	Bill Rohr			
	George Spriggs			
☐ 315	Zoilo Versalles	1.35	.55	.13
☐ 316	Steve Barber	1.35	.55	.13
☐ 317	Ron Brand	1.35	.55	.13
☐ 318	Chico Salmon	1.35	.55	.13
☐ 319	George Culver	1.35	.55	.13
☐ 320	Frank Howard	2.25	.90	.22
☐ 321	Leo Durocher MG	2.25	.90	.22
☐ 322	Dave Boswell	1.35	.55	.13
☐ 323	Deron Johnson	1.35	.55	.13
☐ 324	Jim Nash	1.35	.55	.13
☐ 325	Manny Mota	1.75	.70	.17
☐ 326	Dennis Ribant	1.35	.55	.13
☐ 327	Tony Taylor	1.35	.55	.13
☐ 328	Angels Rookies	1.35	.55	.13
	Chuck Vinson			
	Jim Weaver			
☐ 329	Duane Josephson	1.35	.55	.13
☐ 330	Roger Maris	36.00	16.25	5.50
☐ 331	Dan Osinski	1.35	.55	.13
☐ 332	Doug Rader	1.75	.70	.17
☐ 333	Ron Herbel	1.35	.55	.13
☐ 334	Orioles Team	2.75	1.10	.27
☐ 335	Bob Allison	1.75	.70	.17
☐ 336	John Purdin	1.35	.55	.13
☐ 337	Bill Robinson	2.00	.80	.20
☐ 338	Bob Johnson	1.35	.55	.13
☐ 339	Rich Nye	1.35	.55	.13
☐ 340	Max Alvis	1.35	.55	.13
☐ 341	Jim Lemon MG	1.35	.55	.13
☐ 342	Ken Johnson	1.35	.55	.13
☐ 343	Jim Gosger	1.35	.55	.13
☐ 344	Donn Clendenon	1.75	.70	.17
☐ 345	Bob Hendley	1.35	.55	.13
☐ 346	Jerry Adair	1.35	.55	.13
☐ 347	George Brunet	1.35	.55	.13
☐ 348	Phillies Rookies	1.35	.55	.13
	Larry Colton			
	Dick Thoenen			
☐ 349	Ed Spiezio	1.35	.55	.13
☐ 350	Hoyt Wilhelm	6.00	2.50	.60
☐ 351	Bob Barton	1.35	.55	.13
☐ 352	Jackie Hernandez	1.35	.55	.13
☐ 353	Mack Jones	1.35	.55	.13
☐ 354	Pete Richert	1.35	.55	.13
☐ 355	Ernie Banks	21.00	9.00	3.00
☐ 356A	Checklist 5	5.00	.50	.10
	Ken Holtzman			
	(head centered			
	within circle)			
☐ 356B	Checklist 5	5.00	.50	.10
	Ken Holtzman			
	(head shifted right			
	within circle)			
☐ 357	Len Gabrielson	1.35	.55	.13
☐ 358	Mike Epstein	1.35	.55	.13
☐ 359	Joe Moeller	1.35	.55	.13
☐ 360	Willie Horton	1.75	.70	.17
☐ 361	Harmon Killebrew AS	6.50	2.75	.65
☐ 362	Orlando Cepeda AS	2.50	1.00	.25
☐ 363	Rod Carew AS	13.00	5.75	1.75
☐ 364	Joe Morgan AS	8.00	3.50	.80
☐ 365	Brooks Robinson AS	8.00	3.50	.80
☐ 366	Ron Santo AS	2.00	.80	.20
☐ 367	Jim Fregosi AS	1.75	.70	.17
☐ 368	Gene Alley AS	1.75	.70	.17
☐ 369	Carl Yastrzemski AS	12.00	5.25	1.50
☐ 370	Hank Aaron AS	12.50	5.50	1.65
☐ 371	Tony Oliva AS	2.00	.80	.20
☐ 372	Lou Brock AS	7.50	3.25	.75
☐ 373	Frank Robinson AS	7.50	3.25	.75
☐ 374	Bob Clemente AS	12.50	5.50	1.65
☐ 375	Bill Freehan AS	1.75	.70	.17
☐ 376	Tim McCarver AS	2.00	.80	.20
☐ 377	Joel Horlen AS	1.35	.55	.13
☐ 378	Bob Gibson AS	9.00	4.00	.90
☐ 379	Gary Peters AS	1.35	.55	.13
☐ 380	Ken Holtzman AS	1.35	.55	.13
☐ 381	Boog Powell	2.50	1.00	.25
☐ 382	Ramon Hernandez	1.35	.55	.13
☐ 383	Steve Whitaker	1.35	.55	.13
☐ 384	Reds Rookies	10.00	4.50	1.25
	Bill Henry			
	Hal McRae			
☐ 385	Jim Hunter	12.00	5.25	1.50
☐ 386	Greg Goossen	1.35	.55	.13
☐ 387	Joe Foy	1.35	.55	.13
☐ 388	Ray Washburn	1.35	.55	.13
☐ 389	Jay Johnstone	1.75	.70	.17
☐ 390	Bill Mazeroski	2.50	1.00	.25
☐ 391	Bob Priddy	1.35	.55	.13
☐ 392	Grady Hatton MG	1.35	.55	.13

☐ 393	Jim Perry	1.75	.70	.17
☐ 394	Tommie Aaron	1.75	.70	.17
☐ 395	Camilo Pascual	1.75	.70	.17
☐ 396	Bobby Wine	1.35	.55	.13
☐ 397	Vic Davalillo	1.35	.55	.13
☐ 398	Jim Grant	1.35	.55	.13
☐ 399	Ray Oyler	1.35	.55	.13
☐ 400A	Mike McCormick (yellow letters)	1.75	.70	.17
☐ 400B	Mike McCormick (team name in white letters)	100.00	45.00	15.00
☐ 401	Mets Team	3.00	1.25	.30
☐ 402	Mike Hegan	1.35	.55	.13
☐ 403	John Buzhardt	1.35	.55	.13
☐ 404	Floyd Robinson	1.35	.55	.13
☐ 405	Tommy Helms	1.75	.70	.17
☐ 406	Dick Ellsworth	1.35	.55	.13
☐ 407	Gary Kolb	1.35	.55	.13
☐ 408	Steve Carlton	50.00	22.50	7.50
☐ 409	Orioles Rookies Frank Peters Ron Stone	1.35	.55	.13
☐ 410	Fergie Jenkins	18.00	7.50	2.50
☐ 411	Ron Hansen	1.35	.55	.13
☐ 412	Clay Carroll	1.35	.55	.13
☐ 413	Tom McCraw	1.35	.55	.13
☐ 414	Mickey Lolich	3.50	1.50	.35
☐ 415	Johnny Callison	1.75	.70	.17
☐ 416	Bill Rigney MG	1.35	.55	.13
☐ 417	Willie Crawford	1.35	.55	.13
☐ 418	Eddie Fisher	1.35	.55	.13
☐ 419	Jack Hiatt	1.35	.55	.13
☐ 420	Cesar Tovar	1.35	.55	.13
☐ 421	Ron Taylor	1.35	.55	.13
☐ 422	Rene Lachemann	1.75	.70	.17
☐ 423	Fred Gladding	1.35	.55	.13
☐ 424	Chicago White Sox Team Card	2.75	1.10	.27
☐ 425	Jim Maloney	1.75	.70	.17
☐ 426	Hank Allen	1.35	.55	.13
☐ 427	Dick Calmus	1.35	.55	.13
☐ 428	Vic Roznovsky	1.35	.55	.13
☐ 429	Tommie Sisk	1.35	.55	.13
☐ 430	Rico Petrocelli	1.75	.70	.17
☐ 431	Dooley Womack	1.35	.55	.13
☐ 432	Indians Rookies Bill Davis Jose Vidal	1.35	.55	.13
☐ 433	Bob Rodgers	1.75	.70	.17
☐ 434	Ricardo Joseph	1.35	.55	.13
☐ 435	Ron Perranoski	1.75	.70	.17
☐ 436	Hal Lanier	1.75	.70	.17
☐ 437	Don Cardwell	1.35	.55	.13
☐ 438	Lee Thomas	1.75	.70	.17
☐ 439	Lum Harris MG	1.35	.55	.13
☐ 440	Claude Osteen	1.75	.70	.17
☐ 441	Alex Johnson	1.75	.70	.17
☐ 442	Dick Bosman	1.35	.55	.13
☐ 443	Joe Azcue	1.35	.55	.13
☐ 444	Jack Fisher	1.35	.55	.13
☐ 445	Mike Shannon	1.75	.70	.17
☐ 446	Ron Kline	1.35	.55	.13
☐ 447	Tigers Rookies George Korince Fred Lasher	1.35	.55	.13
☐ 448	Gary Wagner	1.35	.55	.13
☐ 449	Gene Oliver	1.35	.55	.13
☐ 450	Jim Kaat	3.50	1.50	.35
☐ 451	Al Spangler	1.35	.55	.13
☐ 452	Jesus Alou	1.35	.55	.13
☐ 453	Sammy Ellis	1.35	.55	.13
☐ 454A	Checklist 6 Frank Robinson (cap complete within circle)	6.00	.60	.12
☐ 454B	Checklist 6 Frank Robinson (cap partially within circle)	6.00	.60	.12
☐ 455	Rico Carty	2.00	.80	.20
☐ 456	John O'Donoghue	1.35	.55	.13
☐ 457	Jim Lefebvre	1.75	.70	.17
☐ 458	Lew Krausse	3.00	1.25	.30
☐ 459	Dick Simpson	3.00	1.25	.30
☐ 460	Jim Lonborg	3.50	1.50	.35
☐ 461	Chuck Hiller	3.00	1.25	.30
☐ 462	Barry Moore	3.00	1.25	.30
☐ 463	Jim Schaffer	3.00	1.25	.30
☐ 464	Don McMahon	3.00	1.25	.30
☐ 465	Tommie Agee	3.50	1.50	.35
☐ 466	Bill Dillman	3.00	1.25	.30
☐ 467	Dick Howser	3.50	1.50	.35
☐ 468	Larry Sherry	3.50	1.50	.35
☐ 469	Ty Cline	3.00	1.25	.30
☐ 470	Bill Freehan	4.00	1.75	.40
☐ 471	Orlando Pena	3.50	1.50	.35
☐ 472	Walt Alston MG	4.00	1.75	.40
☐ 473	Al Worthington	3.00	1.25	.30
☐ 474	Paul Schaal	3.00	1.25	.30
☐ 475	Joe Niekro	4.00	1.75	.40
☐ 476	Woody Woodward	3.00	1.25	.30
☐ 477	Philadelphia Phillies Team Card	6.00	2.50	.60
☐ 478	Dave McNally	3.50	1.50	.35
☐ 479	Phil Gagliano	3.00	1.25	.30
☐ 480	Manager's Dream Tony Oliva Chico Cardenas Bob Clemente	25.00	11.00	3.50
☐ 481	John Wyatt	3.00	1.25	.30
☐ 482	Jose Pagan	3.00	1.25	.30
☐ 483	Darold Knowles	3.00	1.25	.30
☐ 484	Phil Roof	3.00	1.25	.30
☐ 485	Ken Berry	3.00	1.25	.30
☐ 486	Cal Koonce	3.00	1.25	.30
☐ 487	Lee May	3.50	1.50	.35
☐ 488	Dick Tracewski	3.00	1.25	.30
☐ 489	Wally Bunker	3.00	1.25	.30
☐ 490	Super Stars Harmon Killebrew Willie Mays Mickey Mantle	90.00	40.00	13.50
☐ 491	Denny Lemaster	3.00	1.25	.30
☐ 492	Jeff Torborg	3.50	1.50	.35
☐ 493	Jim McGlothlin	3.00	1.25	.30
☐ 494	Ray Sadecki	3.00	1.25	.30
☐ 495	Leon Wagner	3.00	1.25	.30
☐ 496	Steve Hamilton	3.00	1.25	.30
☐ 497	Cardinals Team	6.00	2.50	.60
☐ 498	Bill Bryan	3.00	1.25	.30
☐ 499	Steve Blass	3.50	1.50	.35
☐ 500	Frank Robinson	24.00	10.50	3.50
☐ 501	John Odom	3.00	1.25	.30
☐ 502	Mike Andrews	3.00	1.25	.30
☐ 503	Al Jackson	3.00	1.25	.30
☐ 504	Russ Snyder	3.00	1.25	.30
☐ 505	Joe Sparma	3.50	1.50	.35
☐ 506	Clarence Jones	3.00	1.25	.30
☐ 507	Wade Blasingame	3.00	1.25	.30
☐ 508	Duke Sims	3.00	1.25	.30
☐ 509	Dennis Higgins	3.00	1.25	.30
☐ 510	Ron Fairly	3.50	1.50	.35
☐ 511	Bill Kelso	3.00	1.25	.30
☐ 512	Grant Jackson	3.00	1.25	.30
☐ 513	Hank Bauer MG	3.50	1.50	.35
☐ 514	Al McBean	3.00	1.25	.30
☐ 515	Russ Nixon	3.00	1.25	.30
☐ 516	Pete Mikkelsen	3.00	1.25	.30
☐ 517	Diego Segui	3.00	1.25	.30
☐ 518A	Checklist 7 COR (539 ML Rookies) (Clete Boyer)	6.00	.60	.12
☐ 518B	Checklist 7 ERR (539 AL Rookies) (Clete Boyer)	10.00	1.00	.20
☐ 519	Jerry Stephenson	3.00	1.25	.30
☐ 520	Lou Brock	25.00	11.00	3.50
☐ 521	Don Shaw	3.00	1.25	.30
☐ 522	Wayne Causey	3.00	1.25	.30
☐ 523	John Tsitouris	3.00	1.25	.30
☐ 524	Andy Kosco	3.00	1.25	.30
☐ 525	Jim Davenport	3.00	1.25	.30
☐ 526	Bill Denehy	3.00	1.25	.30
☐ 527	Tito Francona	3.00	1.25	.30
☐ 528	Tigers Team	56.00	24.00	8.00
☐ 529	Bruce Von Hoff	3.00	1.25	.30
☐ 530	Bird Belters Brooks Robinson Frank Robinson	10.00	4.50	1.25
☐ 531	Chuck Hinton	3.00	1.25	.30
☐ 532	Luis Tiant	4.00	1.75	.40
☐ 533	Wes Parker	3.50	1.50	.35
☐ 534	Bob Miller	3.25	1.35	.32
☐ 535	Danny Cater	3.25	1.35	.32
☐ 536	Bill Short	3.25	1.35	.32
☐ 537	Norm Siebern	3.25	1.35	.32
☐ 538	Manny Jimenez	3.25	1.35	.32
☐ 539	Major League Rookies Jim Ray Mike Ferraro	4.00	1.75	.40
☐ 540	Nelson Briles	3.25	1.35	.32
☐ 541	Sandy Alomar	4.00	1.75	.40
☐ 542	John Boccabella	3.25	1.35	.32
☐ 543	Bob Lee	3.25	1.35	.32
☐ 544	Mayo Smith MG	3.25	1.35	.32
☐ 545	Lindy McDaniel	3.25	1.35	.32
☐ 546	Roy White	4.00	1.75	.40
☐ 547	Dan Coombs	3.25	1.35	.32
☐ 548	Bernie Allen	3.25	1.35	.32

		NRMT	VG-E	GOOD
☐ 549	Orioles Rookies	3.25	1.35	.32
	Curt Motton			
	Roger Nelson			
☐ 550	Clete Boyer	4.00	1.75	.40
☐ 551	Darrell Sutherland	3.25	1.35	.32
☐ 552	Ed Kirkpatrick	3.25	1.35	.32
☐ 553	Hank Aguirre	3.25	1.35	.32
☐ 554	A's Team	6.50	2.75	.65
☐ 555	Jose Tartabull	3.25	1.35	.32
☐ 556	Dick Selma	3.25	1.35	.32
☐ 557	Frank Quilici	3.25	1.35	.32
☐ 558	Johnny Edwards	3.25	1.35	.32
☐ 559	Pirates Rookies	4.00	1.75	.40
	Carl Taylor			
	Luke Walker			
☐ 560	Paul Casanova	3.25	1.35	.32
☐ 561	Lee Elia	4.00	1.75	.40
☐ 562	Jim Bouton	4.50	2.00	.45
☐ 563	Ed Charles	3.25	1.35	.32
☐ 564	Eddie Stanky MG	4.00	1.75	.40
☐ 565	Larry Dierker	3.25	1.35	.32
☐ 566	Ken Harrelson	4.00	1.75	.40
☐ 567	Clay Dalrymple	3.25	1.35	.32
☐ 568	Willie Smith	3.25	1.35	.32
☐ 569	NL Rookies	3.25	1.35	.32
	Ivan Murrell			
	Les Rohr			
☐ 570	Rick Reichardt	3.25	1.35	.32
☐ 571	Tony LaRussa	4.50	2.00	.45
☐ 572	Don Bosch	3.25	1.35	.32
☐ 573	Joe Coleman	3.25	1.35	.32
☐ 574	Cincinnati Reds	6.50	2.75	.65
	Team Card			
☐ 575	Jim Palmer	60.00	27.00	9.00
☐ 576	Dave Adlesh	3.25	1.35	.32
☐ 577	Fred Talbot	3.25	1.35	.32
☐ 578	Orlando Martinez	3.25	1.35	.32
☐ 579	NL Rookies	4.00	1.75	.40
	Larry Hisle			
	Mike Lum			
☐ 580	Bob Bailey	3.25	1.35	.32
☐ 581	Garry Roggenburk	3.25	1.35	.32
☐ 582	Jerry Grote	3.25	1.35	.32
☐ 583	Gates Brown	4.00	1.75	.40
☐ 584	Larry Shepard MG	3.25	1.35	.32
☐ 585	Wilbur Wood	4.00	1.75	.40
☐ 586	Jim Pagliaroni	3.25	1.35	.32
☐ 587	Roger Repoz	3.25	1.35	.32
☐ 588	Dick Schofield	3.25	1.35	.32
☐ 589	Twins Rookies	3.25	1.35	.32
	Ron Clark			
	Moe Ogier			
☐ 590	Tommy Harper	3.25	1.35	.32
☐ 591	Dick Nen	3.25	1.35	.32
☐ 592	John Bateman	3.25	1.35	.32
☐ 593	Lee Stange	3.25	1.35	.32
☐ 594	Phil Linz	4.00	1.75	.40
☐ 595	Phil Ortega	3.25	1.35	.32
☐ 596	Charlie Smith	3.25	1.35	.32
☐ 597	Bill McCool	3.25	1.35	.32
☐ 598	Jerry May	4.50	1.75	.35

1968 Topps Game

The cards in this 33-card set measure approximately 2 1/4" by 3 1/4". This "Game" card set of players, issued as inserts with

the regular 1968 Topps baseball series, was patterned directly after the Red Back and Blue Back sets of 1951. Each card has a color player photo set upon a pure white background, with a facsimile autograph underneath the picture. The cards have blue backs, and were also sold in boxed sets on a limited basis.

		NRMT	VG-E	GOOD
	COMPLETE SET (33)	80.00	36.00	12.00
	COMMON PLAYER (1-33)	.50	.20	.05
☐ 1	Matty Alou	.50	.20	.05
☐ 2	Mickey Mantle	20.00	8.50	2.75
☐ 3	Carl Yastrzemski	10.00	4.50	1.25
☐ 4	Hank Aaron	8.00	3.50	.80
☐ 5	Harmon Killebrew	3.00	1.25	.30
☐ 6	Roberto Clemente	7.00	3.00	.70
☐ 7	Frank Robinson	4.00	1.75	.40
☐ 8	Willie Mays	8.00	3.50	.80
☐ 9	Brooks Robinson	4.00	1.75	.40
☐ 10	Tommy Davis	.50	.20	.05
☐ 11	Bill Freehan	.60	.25	.06
☐ 12	Claude Osteen	.50	.20	.05
☐ 13	Gary Peters	.50	.20	.05
☐ 14	Jim Lonborg	.50	.20	.05
☐ 15	Steve Hargan	.50	.20	.05
☐ 16	Dean Chance	.50	.20	.05
☐ 17	Mike McCormick	.50	.20	.05
☐ 18	Tim McCarver	.75	.30	.07
☐ 19	Ron Santo	.75	.30	.07
☐ 20	Tony Gonzalez	.50	.20	.05
☐ 21	Frank Howard	.60	.25	.06
☐ 22	George Scott	.50	.20	.05
☐ 23	Rich Allen	.75	.30	.07
☐ 24	Jim Wynn	.50	.20	.05
☐ 25	Gene Alley	.50	.20	.05
☐ 26	Rick Monday	.50	.20	.05
☐ 27	Al Kaline	4.50	2.00	.45
☐ 28	Rusty Staub	.75	.30	.07
☐ 29	Rod Carew	7.00	3.00	.70
☐ 30	Pete Rose	10.00	4.50	1.25
☐ 31	Joe Torre	.75	.30	.07
☐ 32	Orlando Cepeda	.75	.30	.07
☐ 33	Jim Fregosi	.60	.25	.06

1969 Topps

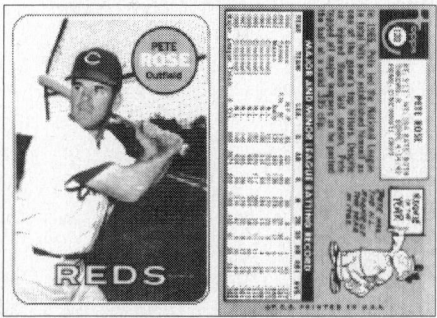

The cards in this 664-card set measure 2 1/2" by 3 1/2". The 1969 Topps set includes Sporting News All-Star Selections as card numbers 416 to 435. Other popular subsets within this set include League Leaders (1-12) and World Series cards (162-169). The fifth series contains several variations; the more difficult variety consists of cards with the player's first name, last name, and/or position in white letters instead of lettering in some other color. These are designated in the checklist below by WL (white letters). Each checklist card features a different popular player's picture inside a circle on the front of the checklist card. Two different poses of Clay Dalrymple and Donn Clendenon exist, as indicated in the checklist. The key rookie cards in this set are Rollie Fingers, Reggie Jackson, and Graig Nettles. This was the last year that Topps issued multi-player special star cards, ending a 13-year tradition, which they had begun in 1957. There were cropping differences in checklist cards 57, 214, and 412, due to their each being printed with two different series. The differences are difficult to explain and have not been greatly sought by collectors; hence they are not listed explicitly in the list below. The All-Star cards 426-435, when turned over and placed together, form a puzzle back of Pete Rose.

	NRMT	VG-E	GOOD
COMPLETE SET (664)	2500.00	1100.00	250.00
COMMON PLAYER (1-109)	1.35	.55	.13
COMMON PLAYER (110-218)	1.35	.55	.13
COMMON PLAYER (219-327)	2.25	.90	.22
COMMON PLAYER (328-425)	1.35	.55	.13
COMMON PLAYER (426-512)	1.35	.55	.13
COMMON PLAYER (513-588)	1.65	.70	.20
COMMON PLAYER (589-664)	2.25	.90	.22

		NRMT	VG-E	GOOD
☐ 1	AL Batting Leaders Carl Yastrzemski Danny Cater Tony Oliva	10.00	2.50	.50
☐ 2	NL Batting Leaders Pete Rose Matty Alou Felipe Alou	4.50	2.00	.45
☐ 3	AL RBI Leaders Ken Harrelson Frank Howard Jim Northrup	2.50	1.00	.25
☐ 4	NL RBI Leaders Willie McCovey Ron Santo Billy Williams	3.50	1.50	.35
☐ 5	AL Home Run Leaders Frank Howard Willie Horton Ken Harrelson	2.50	1.00	.25
☐ 6	NL Home Run Leaders Willie McCovey Richie Allen Ernie Banks	3.50	1.50	.35
☐ 7	AL ERA Leaders Luis Tiant Sam McDowell Dave McNally	2.50	1.00	.25
☐ 8	NL ERA Leaders Bob Gibson Bobby Bolin Bob Veale	2.50	1.00	.25
☐ 9	AL Pitching Leaders Denny McLain Dave McNally Luis Tiant Mel Stottlemyre	2.50	1.00	.25
☐ 10	NL Pitching Leaders Juan Marichal Bob Gibson Fergie Jenkins	3.50	1.50	.35
☐ 11	AL Strikeout Leaders Sam McDowell Denny McLain Luis Tiant	2.50	1.00	.25
☐ 12	NL Strikeout Leaders Bob Gibson Fergie Jenkins Bill Singer	3.00	1.25	.30
☐ 13	Mickey Stanley	1.75	.70	.17
☐ 14	Al McBean	1.35	.55	.13
☐ 15	Boog Powell	2.50	1.00	.25
☐ 16	Giants Rookies Cesar Gutierrez Rich Robertson	1.35	.55	.13
☐ 17	Mike Marshall	1.75	.70	.17
☐ 18	Dick Schofield	1.35	.55	.13
☐ 19	Ken Suarez	1.35	.55	.13
☐ 20	Ernie Banks	18.00	7.50	2.50
☐ 21	Jose Santiago	1.35	.55	.13
☐ 22	Jesus Alou	1.35	.55	.13
☐ 23	Lew Krausse	1.35	.55	.13
☐ 24	Walt Alston MG	2.50	1.00	.25
☐ 25	Roy White	1.75	.70	.17
☐ 26	Clay Carroll	1.35	.55	.13
☐ 27	Bernie Allen	1.35	.55	.13
☐ 28	Mike Ryan	1.35	.55	.13
☐ 29	Dave Morehead	1.35	.55	.13
☐ 30	Bob Allison	1.75	.70	.17
☐ 31	Mets Rookies Gary Gentry Amos Otis	2.50	1.00	.25
☐ 32	Sammy Ellis	1.35	.55	.13
☐ 33	Wayne Causey	1.35	.55	.13
☐ 34	Gary Peters	1.35	.55	.13
☐ 35	Joe Morgan	12.00	5.25	1.50
☐ 36	Luke Walker	1.35	.55	.13
☐ 37	Curt Motton	1.35	.55	.13
☐ 38	Zoilo Versalles	1.35	.55	.13
☐ 39	Dick Hughes	1.35	.55	.13
☐ 40	Mayo Smith MG	1.35	.55	.13
☐ 41	Bob Barton	1.35	.55	.13
☐ 42	Tommy Harper	1.35	.55	.13
☐ 43	Joe Niekro	1.75	.70	.17
☐ 44	Danny Cater	1.35	.55	.13
☐ 45	Maury Wills	2.50	1.00	.25
☐ 46	Fritz Peterson	1.35	.55	.13
☐ 47A	Paul Popovich (no helmet emblem)	1.35	.55	.13
☐ 47B	Paul Popovich (C emblem on helmet)	15.00	6.50	2.15
☐ 48	Brant Alyea	1.35	.55	.13
☐ 49A	Royals Rookies COR Steve Jones E. Rodriguez "g"	1.35	.55	.13
☐ 49B	Royals Rookies ERR Steve Jones E. Rodriguez "q"	15.00	6.50	2.15
☐ 50	Bob Clemente UER (Bats Right listed twice)	48.00	22.00	6.00
☐ 51	Woodie Fryman	1.35	.55	.13
☐ 52	Mike Andrews	1.35	.55	.13
☐ 53	Sonny Jackson	1.35	.55	.13
☐ 54	Cisco Carlos	1.35	.55	.13
☐ 55	Jerry Grote	1.35	.55	.13
☐ 56	Rich Reese	1.35	.55	.13
☐ 57	Checklist 1 Denny McLain	4.50	.50	.10
☐ 58	Fred Gladding	1.35	.55	.13
☐ 59	Jay Johnstone	1.75	.70	.17
☐ 60	Nelson Briles	1.75	.55	.13
☐ 61	Jimmie Hall	1.35	.55	.13
☐ 62	Chico Salmon	1.35	.55	.13
☐ 63	Jim Hickman	1.35	.55	.13
☐ 64	Bill Monbouquette	1.35	.55	.13
☐ 65	Willie Davis	1.75	.70	.17
☐ 66	Orioles Rookies Mike Adamson Merv Rettenmund	1.75	.70	.17
☐ 67	Bill Stoneman	1.35	.55	.13
☐ 68	Dave Duncan	1.75	.70	.17
☐ 69	Steve Hamilton	1.35	.55	.13
☐ 70	Tommy Helms	1.75	.70	.17
☐ 71	Steve Whitaker	1.35	.55	.13
☐ 72	Ron Taylor	1.35	.55	.13
☐ 73	Johnny Briggs	1.35	.55	.13
☐ 74	Preston Gomez MG	1.35	.55	.13
☐ 75	Luis Aparicio	5.50	2.50	.55
☐ 76	Norm Miller	1.35	.55	.13
☐ 77A	Ron Perranoski (no emblem on cap)	1.75	.70	.17
☐ 77B	Ron Perranoski (LA on cap)	15.00	6.50	2.15
☐ 78	Tom Satriano	1.35	.55	.13
☐ 79	Milt Pappas	1.75	.70	.17
☐ 80	Norm Cash	2.50	1.00	.25
☐ 81	Mel Queen	1.35	.55	.13
☐ 82	Pirates Rookies Rich Hebner Al Oliver	10.00	4.50	1.25
☐ 83	Mike Ferraro	1.35	.55	.13
☐ 84	Bob Humphreys	1.35	.55	.13
☐ 85	Lou Brock	18.00	7.50	2.50
☐ 86	Pete Richert	1.35	.55	.13
☐ 87	Horace Clarke	1.35	.55	.13
☐ 88	Rich Nye	1.35	.55	.13
☐ 89	Russ Gibson	1.35	.55	.13
☐ 90	Jerry Koosman	5.00	2.25	.50
☐ 91	Alvin Dark MG	1.35	.55	.13
☐ 92	Jack Billingham	1.35	.55	.13
☐ 93	Joe Foy	1.35	.55	.13
☐ 94	Hank Aguirre	1.35	.55	.13
☐ 95	Johnny Bench	175.00	80.00	27.00
☐ 96	Denny Lemaster	1.35	.55	.13
☐ 97	Buddy Bradford	1.35	.55	.13
☐ 98	Dave Giusti	1.35	.55	.13
☐ 99A	Twins Rookies Danny Morris Graig Nettles (no loop)	15.00	6.50	2.15
☐ 99B	Twins Rookies (errant loop in upper left corner of obverse)	24.00	10.50	3.50
☐ 100	Hank Aaron	60.00	27.00	9.00
☐ 101	Daryl Patterson	1.35	.55	.13
☐ 102	Jim Davenport	1.35	.55	.13
☐ 103	Roger Repoz	1.35	.55	.13

#	Player			
☐ 104	Steve Blass	1.35	.55	.13
☐ 105	Rick Monday	1.75	.70	.17
☐ 106	Jim Hannan	1.35	.55	.13
☐ 107A	Checklist 2 ERR	5.00		.10
	(161 Jim Purdin)			
	(Bob Gibson)			
☐ 107B	Checklist 2 COR	7.50	.75	.15
	(161 John Purdin)			
	(Bob Gibson)			
☐ 108	Tony Taylor	1.35	.55	.13
☐ 109	Jim Lonborg	1.75	.70	.17
☐ 110	Mike Shannon	1.75	.70	.17
☐ 111	Johnny Morris	1.35	.55	.13
☐ 112	J.C. Martin	1.35	.55	.13
☐ 113	Dave May	1.35	.55	.13
☐ 114	Yankees Rookies	1.35	.55	.13
	Alan Closter			
	John Cumberland			
☐ 115	Bill Hands	1.35	.55	.13
☐ 116	Chuck Harrison	1.35	.55	.13
☐ 117	Jim Fairey	1.35	.55	.13
☐ 118	Stan Williams	1.35	.55	.13
☐ 119	Doug Rader	1.75	.70	.17
☐ 120	Pete Rose	36.00	16.25	5.50
☐ 121	Joe Grzenda	1.35	.55	.13
☐ 122	Ron Fairly	1.75	.70	.17
☐ 123	Wilbur Wood	1.35	.55	.13
☐ 124	Hank Bauer MG	1.75	.70	.17
☐ 125	Ray Sadecki	1.35	.55	.13
☐ 126	Dick Tracewski	1.35	.55	.13
☐ 127	Kevin Collins	1.35	.55	.13
☐ 128	Tommie Aaron	1.75	.70	.17
☐ 129	Bill McCool	1.35	.55	.13
☐ 130	Carl Yastrzemski	28.00	12.50	4.00
☐ 131	Chris Cannizzaro	1.35	.55	.13
☐ 132	Dave Baldwin	1.35	.55	.13
☐ 133	Johnny Callison	1.75	.70	.17
☐ 134	Jim Weaver	1.35	.55	.13
☐ 135	Tommy Davis	1.75	.70	.17
☐ 136	Cards Rookies	1.75	.70	.17
	Steve Huntz			
	Mike Torrez			
☐ 137	Wally Bunker	1.75	.70	.17
☐ 138	John Bateman	1.35	.55	.13
☐ 139	Andy Kosco	1.35	.55	.13
☐ 140	Jim Lefebvre	1.75	.70	.17
☐ 141	Bill Dillman	1.35	.55	.13
☐ 142	Woody Woodward	1.75	.70	.17
☐ 143	Joe Nossek	1.35	.55	.13
☐ 144	Bob Hendley	1.35	.55	.13
☐ 145	Max Alvis	1.35	.55	.13
☐ 146	Jim Perry	1.75	.70	.17
☐ 147	Leo Durocher MG	2.50	1.00	.25
☐ 148	Lee Stange	1.35	.55	.13
☐ 149	Ollie Brown	1.35	.55	.13
☐ 150	Denny McLain	5.00	2.25	.50
☐ 151A	Clay Dalrymple COR	1.35	.55	.13
	(Portrait, Orioles)			
☐ 151B	Clay Dalrymple ERR	15.00	6.50	2.15
	(Catching, Phillies)			
☐ 152	Tommie Sisk	1.35	.55	.13
☐ 153	Ed Brinkman	1.35	.55	.13
☐ 154	Jim Britton	1.35	.55	.13
☐ 155	Pete Ward	1.35	.55	.13
☐ 156	Houston Rookies	1.35	.55	.13
	Hal Gilson			
	Leon McFadden			
☐ 157	Bob Rodgers	1.75	.70	.17
☐ 158	Joe Gibbon	1.35	.55	.13
☐ 159	Jerry Adair	1.35	.55	.13
☐ 160	Vada Pinson	2.00	.80	.20
☐ 161	John Purdin	1.35	.55	.13
☐ 162	World Series Game 1	5.00	2.25	.50
	Gibson fans 17			
☐ 163	World Series Game 2	3.50	1.50	.35
	Tiger homers			
	deck the Cards			
☐ 164	World Series Game 3	5.00	2.25	.50
	McCarver's homer			
☐ 165	World Series Game 4	5.00	2.25	.50
	Brock lead-off homer			
☐ 166	World Series Game 5	6.00	2.50	.60
	Kaline's key hit			
☐ 167	World Series Game 6	3.50	1.50	.35
	Northrup grandslam			
☐ 168	World Series Game 7	5.00	2.25	.50
	Lolich outduels			
	Bob Gibson			
☐ 169	World Series Summary	3.50	1.50	.35
	Tigers celebrate			
☐ 170	Frank Howard	2.00	.80	.20
☐ 171	Glenn Beckert	1.75	.70	.17
☐ 172	Jerry Stephenson	1.35	.55	.13
☐ 173	White Sox Rookies	1.35	.55	.13
	Bob Christian			
	Gerry Nyman			
☐ 174	Grant Jackson	1.35	.55	.13
☐ 175	Jim Bunning	3.00	1.25	.30
☐ 176	Joe Azcue	1.35	.55	.13
☐ 177	Ron Reed	1.35	.55	.13
☐ 178	Ray Oyler	1.35	.55	.13
☐ 179	Don Pavletich	1.35	.55	.13
☐ 180	Willie Horton	1.75	.70	.17
☐ 181	Mel Nelson	1.35	.55	.13
☐ 182	Bill Rigney MG	1.35	.55	.13
☐ 183	Don Shaw	1.35	.55	.13
☐ 184	Roberto Pena	1.35	.55	.13
☐ 185	Tom Phoebus	1.35	.55	.13
☐ 186	Johnny Edwards	1.35	.55	.13
☐ 187	Leon Wagner	1.35	.55	.13
☐ 188	Rick Wise	1.75	.70	.17
☐ 189	Red Sox Rookies	1.35	.55	.13
	Joe Lahoud			
	John Thibodeau			
☐ 190	Willie Mays	60.00	27.00	9.00
☐ 191	Lindy McDaniel	1.75	.70	.17
☐ 192	Jose Pagan	1.35	.55	.13
☐ 193	Don Cardwell	1.35	.55	.13
☐ 194	Ted Uhlaender	1.35	.55	.13
☐ 195	John Odom	1.35	.55	.13
☐ 196	Lum Harris MG	1.35	.55	.13
☐ 197	Dick Selma	1.35	.55	.13
☐ 198	Willie Smith	1.35	.55	.13
☐ 199	Jim French	1.35	.55	.13
☐ 200	Bob Gibson	13.50	6.00	1.85
☐ 201	Russ Snyder	1.35	.55	.13
☐ 202	Don Wilson	1.35	.55	.13
☐ 203	Dave Johnson	1.75	.70	.17
☐ 204	Jack Hiatt	1.35	.55	.13
☐ 205	Rick Reichardt	1.35	.55	.13
☐ 206	Phillies Rookies	1.75	.70	.17
	Larry Hisle			
	Barry Lersch			
☐ 207	Roy Face	1.75	.70	.17
☐ 208A	Donn Clendenon COR	1.75	.70	.17
	(Houston)			
☐ 208B	Donn Clendenon ERR	15.00	6.50	2.15
	(Expos)			
☐ 209	Larry Haney UER	1.35	.55	.13
	(reverse negative)			
☐ 210	Felix Millan	1.35	.55	.13
☐ 211	Galen Cisco	1.35	.55	.13
☐ 212	Tom Tresh	1.75	.70	.17
☐ 213	Gerry Arrigo	1.35	.55	.13
☐ 214	Checklist 3	4.00	.50	.10
	With 69T deckle CL			
	on back (no player)			
☐ 215	Rico Petrocelli	1.75	.70	.17
☐ 216	Don Sutton	8.00	3.50	.80
☐ 217	John Donaldson	1.35	.55	.13
☐ 218	John Roseboro	1.35	.55	.13
☐ 219	Freddie Patek	3.50	1.50	.35
☐ 220	Sam McDowell	2.75	1.10	.27
☐ 221	Art Shamsky	2.25	.90	.22
☐ 222	Duane Josephson	2.25	.90	.22
☐ 223	Tom Dukes	2.25	.90	.22
☐ 224	Angels Rookies	2.25	.90	.22
	Bill Harrelson			
	Steve Kealey			
☐ 225	Don Kessinger	2.75	1.10	.27
☐ 226	Bruce Howard	2.25	.90	.22
☐ 227	Frank Johnson	2.25	.90	.22
☐ 228	Dave Leonhard	2.25	.90	.22
☐ 229	Don Lock	2.25	.90	.22
☐ 230	Rusty Staub	3.50	1.50	.35
☐ 231	Pat Dobson	2.75	1.10	.27
☐ 232	Dave Ricketts	2.25	.90	.22
☐ 233	Steve Barber	2.25	.90	.22
☐ 234	Dave Bristol MG	2.25	.90	.22
☐ 235	Jim Hunter	13.00	5.75	1.75
☐ 236	Manny Mota	2.75	1.10	.27
☐ 237	Bobby Cox	3.50	1.50	.35
☐ 238	Ken Johnson	2.25	.90	.22
☐ 239	Bob Taylor	2.25	.90	.22
☐ 240	Ken Harrelson	2.75	1.10	.27
☐ 241	Jim Brewer	2.25	.90	.22
☐ 242	Frank Kostro	2.25	.90	.22
☐ 243	Ron Kline	2.25	.90	.22
☐ 244	Indians Rookies	2.75	1.10	.27
	Ray Fosse			
	George Woodson			
☐ 245	Ed Charles	2.25	.90	.22
☐ 246	Joe Coleman	2.25	.90	.22
☐ 247	Gene Oliver	2.25	.90	.22
☐ 248	Bob Priddy	2.25	.90	.22
☐ 249	Ed Spiezio	2.25	.90	.22
☐ 250	Frank Robinson	25.00	11.00	3.50
☐ 251	Ron Herbel	2.25	.90	.22

☐ 252	Chuck Cottier	2.25	.90	.22
☐ 253	Jerry Johnson	2.25	.90	.22
☐ 254	Joe Schultz	2.25	.90	.22
☐ 255	Steve Carlton	50.00	22.50	7.50
☐ 256	Gates Brown	2.75	1.10	.27
☐ 257	Jim Ray	2.25	.90	.22
☐ 258	Jackie Hernandez	2.25	.90	.22
☐ 259	Bill Short	2.25	.90	.22
☐ 260	Reggie Jackson	525.00	225.00	75.00
☐ 261	Bob Johnson	2.25	.90	.22
☐ 262	Mike Kekich	2.25	.90	.22
☐ 263	Jerry May	2.25	.90	.22
☐ 264	Bill Landis	2.25	.90	.22
☐ 265	Chico Cardenas	2.25	.90	.22
☐ 266	Dodger Rookies	2.25	.90	.22
	Tom Hutton			
	Alan Foster			
☐ 267	Vicente Romo	2.25	.90	.22
☐ 268	Al Spangler	2.25	.90	.22
☐ 269	Al Weis	2.25	.90	.22
☐ 270	Mickey Lolich	3.50	1.50	.35
☐ 271	Larry Stahl	2.25	.90	.22
☐ 272	Ed Stroud	2.25	.90	.22
☐ 273	Ron Willis	2.25	.90	.22
☐ 274	Clyde King MG	2.25	.90	.22
☐ 275	Vic Davalillo	2.25	.90	.22
☐ 276	Gary Wagner	2.25	.90	.22
☐ 277	Elrod Hendricks	2.25	.90	.22
☐ 278	Gary Geiger UER	2.25	.90	.22
	(Batting wrong)			
☐ 279	Roger Nelson	2.25	.90	.22
☐ 280	Alex Johnson	2.75	1.10	.27
☐ 281	Ted Kubiak	2.25	.90	.22
☐ 282	Pat Jarvis	2.25	.90	.22
☐ 283	Sandy Alomar	2.75	1.10	.27
☐ 284	Expos Rookies	2.25	.90	.22
	Jerry Robertson			
	Mike Wegener			
☐ 285	Don Mincher	2.75	1.10	.27
☐ 286	Dock Ellis	2.75	1.10	.27
☐ 287	Jose Tartabull	2.25	.90	.22
☐ 288	Ken Holtzman	2.75	1.10	.27
☐ 289	Bart Shirley	2.25	.90	.22
☐ 290	Jim Kaat	4.00	1.75	.40
☐ 291	Vern Fuller	2.25	.90	.22
☐ 292	Al Downing	2.75	1.10	.27
☐ 293	Dick Dietz	2.25	.90	.22
☐ 294	Jim Lemon MG	2.25	.90	.22
☐ 295	Tony Perez	12.50	5.50	1.65
☐ 296	Andy Messersmith	3.50	1.50	.35
☐ 297	Deron Johnson	2.25	.90	.22
☐ 298	Dave Nicholson	2.25	.90	.22
☐ 299	Mark Belanger	2.75	1.10	.27
☐ 300	Felipe Alou	2.75	1.10	.27
☐ 301	Darrell Brandon	2.25	.90	.22
☐ 302	Jim Pagliaroni	2.25	.90	.22
☐ 303	Cal Koonce	2.25	.90	.22
☐ 304	Padres Rookies	4.50	2.00	.45
	Bill Davis			
	Clarence Gaston			
☐ 305	Dick McAuliffe	2.25	.90	.22
☐ 306	Jim Grant	2.25	.90	.22
☐ 307	Gary Kolb	2.25	.90	.22
☐ 308	Wade Blasingame	2.25	.90	.22
☐ 309	Walt Williams	2.25	.90	.22
☐ 310	Tom Haller	2.25	.90	.22
☐ 311	Sparky Lyle	12.50	5.50	1.65
☐ 312	Lee Elia	2.75	1.10	.27
☐ 313	Bill Robinson	2.75	1.10	.27
☐ 314	Checklist 4	4.50	.50	.10
	Don Drysdale			
☐ 315	Eddie Fisher	2.25	.90	.22
☐ 316	Hal Lanier	2.25	.90	.22
☐ 317	Bruce Look	2.25	.90	.22
☐ 318	Jack Fisher	2.25	.90	.22
☐ 319	Ken McMullen UER	2.25	.90	.22
	(Headings on back			
	are for a pitcher)			
☐ 320	Dal Maxvill	2.25	.90	.22
☐ 321	Jim McAndrew	2.25	.90	.22
☐ 322	Jose Vidal	2.25	.90	.22
☐ 323	Larry Miller	2.25	.90	.22
☐ 324	Tiger Rookies	2.25	.90	.22
	Les Cain			
	Dave Campbell			
☐ 325	Jose Cardenal	2.25	.90	.22
☐ 326	Gary Sutherland	2.25	.90	.22
☐ 327	Willie Crawford	2.25	.90	.22
☐ 328	Joel Horlen	1.35	.55	.13
☐ 329	Rick Joseph	1.35	.55	.13
☐ 330	Tony Conigliaro	3.00	1.25	.30
☐ 331	Braves Rookies	2.25	.90	.22
	Gil Garrido			
	Tom House			

☐ 332	Fred Talbot	1.35	.55	.13
☐ 333	Ivan Murrell	1.35	.55	.13
☐ 334	Phil Roof	1.35	.55	.13
☐ 335	Bill Mazeroski	2.25	.90	.22
☐ 336	Jim Roland	1.35	.55	.13
☐ 337	Marty Martinez	1.35	.55	.13
☐ 338	Del Unser	1.35	.55	.13
☐ 339	Reds Rookies	1.35	.55	.13
	Steve Mingori			
	Jose Pena			
☐ 340	Dave McNally	1.75	.70	.17
☐ 341	Dave Adlesh	1.35	.55	.13
☐ 342	Bubba Morton	1.35	.55	.13
☐ 343	Dan Frisella	1.35	.55	.13
☐ 344	Tom Matchick	1.35	.55	.13
☐ 345	Frank Linzy	1.35	.55	.13
☐ 346	Wayne Comer	1.35	.55	.13
☐ 347	Randy Hundley	1.75	.70	.17
☐ 348	Steve Hargan	1.35	.55	.13
☐ 349	Dick Williams MG	1.75	.70	.17
☐ 350	Richie Allen	3.00	1.25	.30
☐ 351	Carroll Sembera	1.35	.55	.13
☐ 352	Paul Schaal	1.35	.55	.13
☐ 353	Jeff Torborg	1.75	.70	.17
☐ 354	Nate Oliver	1.35	.55	.13
☐ 355	Phil Niekro	5.00	2.25	.50
☐ 356	Frank Quilici MG	1.35	.55	.13
☐ 357	Carl Taylor	1.35	.55	.13
☐ 358	Athletics Rookies	1.35	.55	.13
	George Lauzerique			
	Roberto Rodriquez			
☐ 359	Dick Kelley	1.35	.55	.13
☐ 360	Jim Wynn	1.75	.70	.17
☐ 361	Gary Holman	1.35	.55	.13
☐ 362	Jim Maloney	1.75	.70	.17
☐ 363	Russ Nixon	1.35	.55	.13
☐ 364	Tommie Agee	1.75	.70	.17
☐ 365	Jim Fregosi	1.75	.70	.17
☐ 366	Bo Belinsky	1.75	.70	.17
☐ 367	Lou Johnson	1.35	.55	.13
☐ 368	Vic Roznovsky	1.35	.55	.13
☐ 369	Bob Skinner	1.35	.55	.13
☐ 370	Juan Marichal	6.50	2.75	.65
☐ 371	Sal Bando	1.75	.70	.17
☐ 372	Adolfo Phillips	1.35	.55	.13
☐ 373	Fred Lasher	1.35	.55	.13
☐ 374	Bob Tillman	1.35	.55	.13
☐ 375	Harmon Killebrew	18.00	7.50	2.50
☐ 376	Royals Rookies	1.75	.70	.17
	Mike Fiore			
	Jim Rooker			
☐ 377	Gary Bell	1.35	.55	.13
☐ 378	Jose Herrera	1.35	.55	.13
☐ 379	Ken Boyer	2.25	.90	.22
☐ 380	Stan Bahnsen	1.35	.55	.13
☐ 381	Ed Kranepool	1.75	.70	.17
☐ 382	Pat Corrales	1.35	.55	.13
☐ 383	Casey Cox	1.35	.55	.13
☐ 384	Larry Shepard MG	1.35	.55	.13
☐ 385	Orlando Cepeda	3.00	1.25	.30
☐ 386	Jim McGlothlin	1.35	.55	.13
☐ 387	Bobby Klaus	1.35	.55	.13
☐ 388	Tom McCraw	1.35	.55	.13
☐ 389	Dan Coombs	1.35	.55	.13
☐ 390	Bill Freehan	2.00	.80	.20
☐ 391	Ray Culp	1.35	.55	.13
☐ 392	Bob Burda	1.35	.55	.13
☐ 393	Gene Brabender	1.35	.55	.13
☐ 394	Pilots Rookies	4.00	1.75	.40
	Lou Piniella			
	Marv Staehle			
☐ 395	Chris Short	1.35	.55	.13
☐ 396	Jim Campanis	1.35	.55	.13
☐ 397	Chuck Dobson	1.35	.55	.13
☐ 398	Tito Francona	1.35	.55	.13
☐ 399	Bob Bailey	1.35	.55	.13
☐ 400	Don Drysdale	10.00	4.50	1.25
☐ 401	Jake Gibbs	1.35	.55	.13
☐ 402	Ken Boswell	1.35	.55	.13
☐ 403	Bob Miller	1.35	.55	.13
☐ 404	Cubs Rookies	1.35	.55	.13
	Vic LaRose			
	Gary Ross			
☐ 405	Lee May	1.75	.70	.17
☐ 406	Phil Ortega	1.35	.55	.13
☐ 407	Tom Egan	1.35	.55	.13
☐ 408	Nate Colbert	1.35	.55	.13
☐ 409	Bob Moose	1.35	.55	.13
☐ 410	Al Kaline	18.00	7.50	2.50
☐ 411	Larry Dierker	1.35	.55	.13
☐ 412	Checklist 5 DP	7.50	1.00	.20
	Mickey Mantle			
☐ 413	Roland Sheldon	1.35	.55	.13
☐ 414	Duke Sims	1.35	.55	.13

#	Player			
415	Ray Washburn	1.35	.55	.13
416	Willie McCovey AS	6.00	2.50	.60
417	Ken Harrelson AS	1.35	.55	.13
418	Tommy Helms AS	1.35	.55	.13
419	Rod Carew AS	10.00	4.50	1.25
420	Ron Santo AS	2.00	.80	.20
421	Brooks Robinson AS	6.50	2.75	.65
422	Don Kessinger AS	1.35	.55	.13
423	Bert Campaneris AS	1.35	.55	.13
424	Pete Rose AS	12.00	5.25	1.50
425	Carl Yastrzemski AS	12.00	5.25	1.50
426	Curt Flood AS DP	1.35	.55	.13
427	Tony Oliva AS DP	1.75	.70	.17
428	Lou Brock AS DP	6.00	2.50	.60
429	Willie Horton AS DP	1.35	.55	.13
430	Johnny Bench AS DP	13.50	6.00	1.85
431	Bill Freehan AS DP	1.35	.55	.13
432	Bob Gibson AS DP	5.00	2.25	.50
433	Denny McLain AS DP	1.75	.70	.17
434	Jerry Koosman AS DP	1.75	.70	.17
435	Sam McDowell AS DP	1.35	.55	.13
436	Gene Alley	1.75	.70	.17
437	Luis Alcaraz	1.35	.55	.13
438	Gary Waslewski	1.35	.55	.13
439	White Sox Rookies DP	1.35	.55	.13
	Ed Herrmann			
	Dan Lazar			
440A	Willie McCovey	16.00	6.75	2.25
440B	Willie McCovey WL	90.00	40.00	13.50
	(McCovey white) DP			
441A	Dennis Higgins	1.35	.55	.13
441B	Dennis Higgins WL	20.00	8.50	2.75
	(Higgins white)			
442	Ty Cline	1.35	.55	.13
443	Don Wert DP	1.35	.55	.13
444A	Joe Moeller	1.35	.55	.13
444B	Joe Moeller WL DP	15.00	6.50	2.15
	(Moeller white)			
445	Bobby Knoop	1.35	.55	.13
446	Claude Raymond	1.35	.55	.13
447A	Ralph Houk MG	1.75	.70	.17
447B	Ralph Houk WL	15.00	6.50	2.15
	MG (Houk white)			
448	Bob Tolan	1.35	.55	.13
449	Paul Lindblad DP	1.35	.55	.13
450	Billy Williams DP	6.50	2.75	.65
451A	Rich Rollins	1.35	.55	.13
451B	Rich Rollins WL	20.00	8.50	2.75
	(Rich and 3B white)			
452A	Al Ferrara	1.35	.55	.13
452B	Al Ferrara WL	20.00	8.50	2.75
	(Al and OF white)			
453	Mike Cuellar	1.75	.70	.17
454A	Phillies Rookies	1.75	.70	.17
	Larry Colton			
	Don Money			
454B	Phillies Rookies WL	20.00	8.50	2.75
	Larry Colton			
	Don Money			
	(names in white)			
455	Sonny Siebert DP	1.35	.55	.13
456	Bud Harrelson DP	1.75	.70	.17
457	Dalton Jones DP	1.35	.55	.13
458	Curt Blefary	1.75	.70	.17
459	Dave Boswell DP	1.35	.55	.13
460	Joe Torre	2.25	.90	.22
461A	Mike Epstein	1.35	.55	.13
461B	Mike Epstein WL DP	15.00	6.50	2.15
	(Epstein white)			
462	Red Schoendienst DP	2.50	1.00	.25
	MG			
463	Dennis Ribant DP	1.35	.55	.13
464A	Dave Marshall	1.35	.55	.13
464B	Dave Marshall WL DP	15.00	6.50	2.15
	(Marshall white)			
465	Tommy John DP	4.00	1.75	.40
466	John Boccabella	1.35	.55	.13
467	Tommie Reynolds	1.35	.55	.13
468A	Pirates Rookies	1.35	.55	.13
	Bruce Dal Canton			
	Bob Robertson			
468B	Pirates Rookies WL	20.00	8.50	2.75
	Bruce Dal Canton			
	Bob Robertson			
	(names in white)			
469	Chico Ruiz DP	1.35	.55	.13
470A	Mel Stottlemyre	1.75	.70	.17
470B	Mel Stottlemyre WL	21.00	9.00	3.00
	(Stottlemyre white) DP			
471A	Ted Savage	1.35	.55	.13
471B	Ted Savage WL	20.00	8.50	2.75
	(Savage white)			
472	Jim Price DP	1.35	.55	.13
473A	Jose Arcia	1.35	.55	.13
473B	Jose Arcia WL	20.00	8.50	2.75
	(Jose and 2B white)			
474	Tom Murphy DP	1.35	.55	.13
475	Tim McCarver	2.50	1.00	.25
476A	Boston Rookies	1.75	.70	.17
	Ken Brett			
	Gerry Moses			
476B	Boston Rookies WL	20.00	8.50	2.75
	Ken Brett			
	Gerry Moses			
	(names in white)			
477	Jeff James DP	1.35	.55	.13
478	Don Buford	1.75	.70	.17
479	Richie Scheinblum	1.35	.55	.13
480	Tom Seaver DP	125.00	57.50	18.75
481	Bill Melton	1.35	.55	.13
482A	Jim Gosger	1.35	.55	.13
482B	Jim Gosger WL	20.00	8.50	2.75
	(Jim and OF white)			
483	Ted Abernathy	1.35	.55	.13
484	Joe Gordon MG	1.75	.70	.17
485A	Gaylord Perry	10.00	4.50	1.25
485B	Gaylord Perry WL	75.00	34.00	11.25
	(Perry white)			
486A	Paul Casanova	1.35	.55	.13
486B	Paul Casanova WL DP	15.00	6.50	2.15
	(Casanova white)			
487	Denis Menke	1.35	.55	.13
488	Joe Sparma	1.35	.55	.13
489	Clete Boyer DP	1.75	.70	.17
490	Matty Alou	1.75	.70	.17
491A	Twins Rookies	1.35	.55	.13
	Jerry Crider			
	George Mitterwald			
491B	Twins Rookies WL	20.00	8.50	2.75
	Jerry Crider			
	George Mitterwald			
	(names in white)			
492	Tony Cloninger	1.35	.55	.13
493A	Wes Parker	1.75	.70	.17
493B	Wes Parker WL DP	15.00	6.50	2.15
	(Parker white)			
494	Ken Berry DP	1.35	.55	.13
495	Bert Campaneris	1.75	.70	.17
496	Larry Jaster	1.35	.55	.13
497	Julian Javier DP	1.35	.55	.13
498	Juan Pizarro	1.35	.55	.13
499	Astro Rookies DP	1.35	.55	.13
	Don Bryant			
	Steve Shea			
500A	Mickey Mantle UER	200.00	90.00	30.00
	(no Topps copy-			
	right on card back)			
500B	Mickey Mantle WL UER	600.00	270.00	90.00
	(Mantle in white;			
	no Topps copy-			
	right on card back)			
501A	Tony Gonzalez	1.35	.55	.13
501B	Tony Gonzalez WL	20.00	8.50	2.75
	(Tony and OF white)			
502	Minnie Rojas DP	1.35	.55	.13
503	Larry Brown	1.35	.55	.13
504	Checklist 6	4.50	.50	.10
	Brooks Robinson			
505A	Bobby Bolin	1.35	.55	.13
505B	Bobby Bolin WL DP	15.00	6.50	2.15
	(Bolin white)			
506	Paul Blair DP	1.35	.55	.13
507	Cookie Rojas	1.35	.55	.13
508	Moe Drabowsky DP	1.35	.55	.13
509	Manny Sanguillen DP	1.75	.70	.17
510	Rod Carew	75.00	34.00	11.25
511A	Diego Segui	1.35	.55	.13
511B	Diego Segui WL	20.00	8.50	2.75
	(Diego and P white)			
512	Cleon Jones	1.35	.55	.13
513	Camilo Pascual	2.00	.80	.20
514	Mike Lum	1.65	.70	.20
515	Dick Green	1.65	.70	.20
516	Earl Weaver MG	8.00	3.50	.80
517	Mike McCormick	2.00	.80	.20
518	Fred Whitfield	1.65	.70	.20
519	Yankees Rookies	1.65	.70	.20
	Gerry Kenney			
	Len Boehmer			
520	Bob Veale	2.00	.80	.20
521	George Thomas	1.65	.70	.20
522	Joe Hoerner	1.65	.70	.20
523	Bob Chance	1.65	.70	.20
524	Expos Rookies	1.65	.70	.20
	Jose Laboy			
	Floyd Wicker			
525	Earl Wilson	1.65	.70	.20
526	Hector Torres	1.65	.70	.20

☐ 527	Al Lopez MG	3.00	1.25	.30
☐ 528	Claude Osteen	1.65	.70	.20
☐ 529	Ed Kirkpatrick	1.65	.70	.20
☐ 530	Cesar Tovar	1.65	.70	.20
☐ 531	Dick Farrell	1.65	.70	.20
☐ 532	Bird Hill Aces	2.00	.80	.20
	Tom Phoebus			
	Jim Hardin			
	Dave McNally			
	Mike Cuellar			
☐ 533	Nolan Ryan	425.00	190.00	63.00
☐ 534	Jerry McNertney	1.65	.70	.20
☐ 535	Phil Regan	2.00	.80	.20
☐ 536	Padres Rookies	1.65	.70	.20
	Danny Breeden			
	Dave Roberts			
☐ 537	Mike Paul	1.65	.70	.20
☐ 538	Charlie Smith	1.65	.70	.20
☐ 539	Ted Shows How	5.00	2.25	.50
	Mike Epstein			
	Ted Williams			
☐ 540	Curt Flood	2.50	1.00	.25
☐ 541	Joe Verbanic	1.65	.70	.20
☐ 542	Bob Aspromonte	1.65	.70	.20
☐ 543	Fred Newman	1.65	.70	.20
☐ 544	Tigers Rookies	1.65	.70	.20
	Mike Kilkenny			
	Ron Woods			
☐ 545	Willie Stargell	12.50	5.50	1.65
☐ 546	Jim Nash	1.65	.70	.20
☐ 547	Billy Martin MG	5.00	2.25	.50
☐ 548	Bob Locker	1.65	.70	.20
☐ 549	Ron Brand	1.65	.70	.20
☐ 550	Brooks Robinson	18.00	7.50	2.50
☐ 551	Wayne Granger	1.65	.70	.20
☐ 552	Dodgers Rookies	2.00	.80	.20
	Ted Sizemore			
	Bill Sudakis			
☐ 553	Ron Davis	1.65	.70	.20
☐ 554	Frank Bertaina	1.65	.70	.20
☐ 555	Jim Ray Hart	2.00	.80	.20
☐ 556	A's Stars	2.00	.80	.20
	Sal Bando			
	Bert Campaneris			
	Danny Cater			
☐ 557	Frank Fernandez	1.65	.70	.20
☐ 558	Tom Burgmeier	2.00	.80	.20
☐ 559	Cardinals Rookies	1.65	.70	.20
	Joe Hague			
	Jim Hicks			
☐ 560	Luis Tiant	2.50	1.00	.25
☐ 561	Ron Clark	1.65	.70	.20
☐ 562	Bob Watson	3.00	1.25	.30
☐ 563	Marty Pattin	1.65	.70	.20
☐ 564	Gil Hodges MG	7.50	3.25	.75
☐ 565	Hoyt Wilhelm	6.00	2.50	.60
☐ 566	Ron Hansen	1.65	.70	.20
☐ 567	Pirates Rookies	1.65	.70	.20
	Elvio Jimenez			
	Jim Shellenback			
☐ 568	Cecil Upshaw	1.65	.70	.20
☐ 569	Billy Harris	1.65	.70	.20
☐ 570	Ron Santo	4.00	1.75	.40
☐ 571	Cap Peterson	1.65	.70	.20
☐ 572	Giants Heroes	10.00	4.50	1.25
	Willie McCovey			
	Juan Marichal			
☐ 573	Jim Palmer	42.00	18.00	5.50
☐ 574	George Scott	2.00	.80	.20
☐ 575	Bill Singer	2.00	.80	.20
☐ 576	Phillies Rookies	1.65	.70	.20
	Ron Stone			
	Bill Wilson			
☐ 577	Mike Hegan	1.65	.70	.20
☐ 578	Don Bosch	1.65	.70	.20
☐ 579	Dave Nelson	2.00	.80	.20
☐ 580	Jim Northrup	2.00	.80	.20
☐ 581	Gary Nolan	1.65	.70	.20
☐ 582A	Checklist 7	4.50	.50	.10
	(white circle on back)			
	(Tony Oliva)			
☐ 582B	Checklist 7	7.50	.75	.15
	(red circle on back)			
	(Tony Oliva)			
☐ 583	Clyde Wright	1.65	.70	.20
☐ 584	Don Mason	1.65	.70	.20
☐ 585	Ron Swoboda	2.00	.80	.20
☐ 586	Tim Cullen	1.65	.70	.20
☐ 587	Joe Rudi	3.50	1.50	.35
☐ 588	Bill White	2.50	1.00	.25
☐ 589	Joe Pepitone	2.75	1.10	.27
☐ 590	Rico Carty	2.75	1.10	.27
☐ 591	Mike Hedlund	2.25	.90	.22
☐ 592	Padres Rookies	2.25	.90	.22

	Rafael Robles			
	Al Santorini			
☐ 593	Don Nottebart	2.25	.90	.22
☐ 594	Dooley Womack	2.25	.90	.22
☐ 595	Lee Maye	2.25	.90	.22
☐ 596	Chuck Hartenstein	2.25	.90	.22
☐ 597	A.L. Rookies	110.00	50.00	16.50
	Bob Floyd			
	Larry Burchart			
	Rollie Fingers			
☐ 598	Ruben Amaro	2.25	.90	.22
☐ 599	John Boozer	2.25	.90	.22
☐ 600	Tony Oliva	4.50	2.00	.45
☐ 601	Tug McGraw	3.50	1.50	.35
☐ 602	Cubs Rookies	2.25	.90	.22
	Alec Distaso			
	Don Young			
	Jim Qualls			
☐ 603	Joe Keough	2.25	.90	.22
☐ 604	Bobby Etheridge	2.25	.90	.22
☐ 605	Dick Ellsworth	2.25	.90	.22
☐ 606	Gene Mauch MG	2.75	1.10	.27
☐ 607	Dick Bosman	2.25	.90	.22
☐ 608	Dick Simpson	2.25	.90	.22
☐ 609	Phil Gagliano	2.25	.90	.22
☐ 610	Jim Hardin	2.25	.90	.22
☐ 611	Braves Rookies	2.75	1.10	.27
	Bob Didier			
	Walt Hriniak			
	Gary Neibauer			
☐ 612	Jack Aker	2.25	.90	.22
☐ 613	Jim Beauchamp	2.25	.90	.22
☐ 614	Houston Rookies	2.25	.90	.22
	Tom Griffin			
	Skip Guinn			
☐ 615	Len Gabrielson	2.25	.90	.22
☐ 616	Don McMahon	2.25	.90	.22
☐ 617	Jesse Gonder	2.25	.90	.22
☐ 618	Ramon Webster	2.25	.90	.22
☐ 619	Royals Rookies	2.75	1.10	.27
	Bill Butler			
	Pat Kelly			
	Juan Rios			
☐ 620	Dean Chance	2.75	1.10	.27
☐ 621	Bill Voss	2.25	.90	.22
☐ 622	Dan Osinski	2.25	.90	.22
☐ 623	Hank Allen	2.25	.90	.22
☐ 624	NL Rookies	2.25	.90	.22
	Darrel Chaney			
	Duffy Dyer			
	Terry Harmon			
☐ 625	Mack Jones UER	2.25	.90	.22
	(Batting wrong)			
☐ 626	Gene Michael	2.75	1.10	.27
☐ 627	George Stone	2.25	.90	.22
☐ 628	Red Sox Rookies	2.75	1.10	.27
	Bill Conigliaro			
	Syd O'Brien			
	Fred Wenz			
☐ 629	Jack Hamilton	2.25	.90	.22
☐ 630	Bobby Bonds	32.00	14.25	4.75
☐ 631	John Kennedy	2.25	.90	.22
☐ 632	Jon Warden	2.25	.90	.22
☐ 633	Harry Walker MG	2.25	.90	.22
☐ 634	Andy Etchebarren	2.25	.90	.22
☐ 635	George Culver	2.25	.90	.22
☐ 636	Woody Held	2.25	.90	.22
☐ 637	Padres Rookies	2.25	.90	.22
	Jerry DaVanon			
	Frank Reberger			
	Clay Kirby			
☐ 638	Ed Sprague	2.25	.90	.22
☐ 639	Barry Moore	2.25	.90	.22
☐ 640	Fergie Jenkins	17.00	7.25	2.50
☐ 641	NL Rookies	2.75	1.10	.27
	Bobby Darwin			
	John Miller			
	Tommy Dean			
☐ 642	John Hiller	2.75	1.10	.27
☐ 643	Billy Cowan	2.25	.90	.22
☐ 644	Chuck Hinton	2.25	.90	.22
☐ 645	George Brunet	2.25	.90	.22
☐ 646	Expos Rookies	2.75	1.10	.27
	Dan McGinn			
	Carl Morton			
☐ 647	Dave Wickersham	2.25	.90	.22
☐ 648	Bobby Wine	2.25	.90	.22
☐ 649	Al Jackson	2.25	.90	.22
☐ 650	Ted Williams MG	10.00	4.50	1.25
☐ 651	Gus Gil	2.25	.90	.22
☐ 652	Eddie Watt	2.25	.90	.22
☐ 653	Aurelio Rodriguez UER	2.75	1.10	.27
	(photo actually			
	Angels' batboy)			

		NRMT	VG-E	GOOD
☐ 654	White Sox Rookies	3.50	1.50	.35
	Carlos May			
	Don Secrist			
	Rich Morales			
☐ 655	Mike Hershberger	2.25	.90	.22
☐ 656	Dan Schneider	2.25	.90	.22
☐ 657	Bobby Murcer	4.50	2.00	.45
☐ 658	AL Rookies	2.75	1.10	.27
	Tom Hall			
	Bill Burbach			
	Jim Miles			
☐ 659	Johnny Podres	2.75	1.10	.27
☐ 660	Reggie Smith	3.50	1.50	.35
☐ 661	Jim Merritt	2.25	.90	.22
☐ 662	Royals Rookies	2.75	1.10	.27
	Dick Drago			
	George Spriggs			
	Bob Oliver			
☐ 663	Dick Radatz	2.75	1.10	.27
☐ 664	Ron Hunt	3.50	1.25	.25

1969 Topps Deckle

DON KESSINGER
No. 18 of 33 photos

The cards in this 33-card set measure approximately 2 1/4" by 3 1/4". This unusual black and white insert set derives its name from the serrated border, or edge, of the cards. The cards were included as inserts in the regularly issued Topps baseball series of 1969. Card number 11 is found with either Hoyt Wilhelm or Jim Wynn, and number 22 with either Rusty Staub or Joe Foy. The set price below does include all variations.

		NRMT	VG-E	GOOD
	COMPLETE SET (35)	75.00	34.00	11.25
	COMMON PLAYER (1-33)	.50	.20	.05
☐ 1	Brooks Robinson	4.50	2.00	.45
☐ 2	Boog Powell	.75	.30	.07
☐ 3	Ken Harrelson	.60	.25	.06
☐ 4	Carl Yastrzemski	6.50	2.75	.65
☐ 5	Jim Fregosi	.60	.25	.06
☐ 6	Luis Aparicio	1.50	.60	.15
☐ 7	Luis Tiant	.60	.25	.06
☐ 8	Denny McLain	.75	.30	.07
☐ 9	Willie Horton	.60	.25	.06
☐ 10	Bill Freehan	.60	.25	.06
☐ 11A	Hoyt Wilhelm	6.00	2.50	.60
☐ 11B	Jim Wynn	6.00	2.50	.60
☐ 12	Rod Carew	6.00	2.50	.60
☐ 13	Mel Stottlemyre	.50	.20	.05
☐ 14	Rick Monday	.50	.20	.05
☐ 15	Tommy Davis	.60	.25	.06
☐ 16	Frank Howard	.60	.25	.06
☐ 17	Felipe Alou	.50	.20	.05
☐ 18	Don Kessinger	.50	.20	.05
☐ 19	Ron Santo	.75	.30	.07
☐ 20	Tommy Helms	.50	.20	.05
☐ 21	Pete Rose	9.00	4.00	.90
☐ 22A	Rusty Staub	3.00	1.25	.30
☐ 22B	Joe Foy	6.00	2.50	.60
☐ 23	Tom Haller	.50	.20	.05
☐ 24	Maury Wills	.75	.30	.07
☐ 25	Jerry Koosman	.60	.25	.06
☐ 26	Richie Allen	.75	.30	.07
☐ 27	Bob Clemente	6.50	2.75	.65
☐ 28	Curt Flood	.60	.25	.06

		NRMT	VG-E	GOOD
☐ 29	Bob Gibson	2.75	1.10	.27
☐ 30	Al Ferrara	.50	.20	.05
☐ 31	Willie McCovey	3.50	1.50	.35
☐ 32	Juan Marichal	2.75	1.10	.27
☐ 33	Willie Mays	8.00	3.50	.80

1969 Topps Super

JUAN MARICHAL
San Francisco Giants Pitcher

The cards in this 66-card set measure approximately 2 1/4" by 3 1/4". This beautiful Topps set was released independently of the regular baseball series of 1969. It is referred to as "Super Baseball" on the back of the card, a title which was also used for the postcard-size cards issued in 1970 and 1971. Complete sheets, and cards with square corners cut from these sheets, are sometimes encountered.

		NRMT	VG-E	GOOD
	COMPLETE SET (66)	5000.00	2000.00	500.00
	COMMON PLAYER (1-66)	11.00	5.00	1.35
☐ 1	Dave McNally	13.50	6.00	1.85
☐ 2	Frank Robinson	175.00	80.00	27.00
☐ 3	Brooks Robinson	225.00	100.00	33.00
☐ 4	Ken Harrelson	13.50	6.00	1.85
☐ 5	Carl Yastrzemski	400.00	180.00	60.00
☐ 6	Ray Culp	11.00	5.00	1.35
☐ 7	Jim Fregosi	13.50	6.00	1.85
☐ 8	Rick Reichardt	11.00	5.00	1.35
☐ 9	Vic Davalillo	11.00	5.00	1.35
☐ 10	Luis Aparicio	85.00	38.00	12.75
☐ 11	Pete Ward	11.00	5.00	1.35
☐ 12	Joe Horlen	11.00	5.00	1.35
☐ 13	Luis Tiant	13.50	6.00	1.85
☐ 14	Sam McDowell	11.00	5.00	1.35
☐ 15	Jose Cardenal	11.00	5.00	1.35
☐ 16	Willie Horton	11.00	5.00	1.35
☐ 17	Denny McLain	15.00	6.50	2.15
☐ 18	Bill Freehan	13.50	6.00	1.85
☐ 19	Harmon Killebrew	125.00	57.50	18.75
☐ 20	Tony Oliva	18.00	7.50	2.50
☐ 21	Dean Chance	11.00	5.00	1.35
☐ 22	Joe Foy	11.00	5.00	1.35
☐ 23	Roger Nelson	11.00	5.00	1.35
☐ 24	Mickey Mantle	900.00	400.00	135.00
☐ 25	Mel Stottlemyre	13.50	6.00	1.85
☐ 26	Roy White	13.50	6.00	1.85
☐ 27	Rick Monday	11.00	5.00	1.35
☐ 28	Reggie Jackson	650.00	300.00	100.00
☐ 29	Bert Campaneris	11.00	5.00	1.35
☐ 30	Frank Howard	13.50	6.00	1.85
☐ 31	Camilo Pascual	11.00	5.00	1.35
☐ 32	Tommy Davis	13.50	6.00	1.85
☐ 33	Don Mincher	11.00	5.00	1.35
☐ 34	Hank Aaron	425.00	190.00	63.00
☐ 35	Felipe Alou	11.00	5.00	1.35
☐ 36	Joe Torre	18.00	7.50	2.50
☐ 37	Fergie Jenkins	100.00	45.00	15.00
☐ 38	Ron Santo	15.00	6.50	2.15
☐ 39	Billy Williams	85.00	38.00	12.75
☐ 40	Tommy Helms	11.00	5.00	1.35
☐ 41	Pete Rose	500.00	225.00	75.00
☐ 42	Joe Morgan	125.00	57.50	18.75
☐ 43	Jim Wynn	11.00	5.00	1.35
☐ 44	Curt Blefary	11.00	5.00	1.35
☐ 45	Willie Davis	11.00	5.00	1.35

		NRMT	VG-E	GOOD
☐ 46	Don Drysdale	100.00	45.00	15.00
☐ 47	Tom Haller	11.00	5.00	1.35
☐ 48	Rusty Staub	15.00	6.50	2.15
☐ 49	Maury Wills	18.00	7.50	2.50
☐ 50	Cleon Jones	11.00	5.00	1.35
☐ 51	Jerry Koosman	13.50	6.00	1.85
☐ 52	Tom Seaver	425.00	190.00	63.00
☐ 53	Richie Allen	15.00	6.50	2.15
☐ 54	Chris Short	11.00	5.00	1.35
☐ 55	Cookie Rojas	11.00	5.00	1.35
☐ 56	Matty Alou	11.00	5.00	1.35
☐ 57	Steve Blass	11.00	5.00	1.35
☐ 58	Bob Clemente	300.00	135.00	45.00
☐ 59	Curt Flood	15.00	6.50	2.15
☐ 60	Bob Gibson	125.00	57.50	18.75
☐ 61	Tim McCarver	18.00	7.50	2.50
☐ 62	Dick Selma	11.00	5.00	1.35
☐ 63	Ollie Brown	11.00	5.00	1.35
☐ 64	Juan Marichal	125.00	57.50	18.75
☐ 65	Willie Mays	425.00	190.00	63.00
☐ 66	Willie McCovey	150.00	67.50	22.50

1970 Topps

The cards in this 720-card set measure 2 1/2" by 3 1/2". The Topps set for 1970 has color photos surrounded by white frame lines and gray borders. The backs have a blue biographical section and a yellow record section. All-Star selections are featured on cards 450 to 469. Other topical subsets within this set include League Leaders (61-72), Playoffs cards (195-202), and World Series cards (305-310). There are graduations of scarcity, terminating in the high series (634-720), which are outlined in the value summary. The key rookie card in this set is Thurman Munson.

	NRMT	VG-E	GOOD
COMPLETE SET (720)	2250.00	900.00	225.00
COMMON PLAYER (1-132)	.70	.30	.07
COMMON PLAYER (133-263)	.80	.35	.08
COMMON PLAYER (264-372)	1.00	.40	.10
COMMON PLAYER (373-459)	1.10	.45	.11
COMMON PLAYER (460-546)	1.60	.65	.16
COMMON PLAYER (547-633)	2.75	1.10	.27
COMMON PLAYER (634-720)	5.00	2.25	.50

		NRMT	VG-E	GOOD
☐ 1	New York Mets	12.00	2.50	.50
	Team Card			
☐ 2	Diego Segui	.70	.30	.07
☐ 3	Darrel Chaney	.70	.30	.07
☐ 4	Tom Egan	.70	.30	.07
☐ 5	Wes Parker	1.00	.40	.10
☐ 6	Grant Jackson	.70	.30	.07
☐ 7	Indians Rookies	.70	.30	.07
	Gary Boyd			
	Russ Nagelson			
☐ 8	Jose Martinez	.70	.30	.07
☐ 9	Checklist 1	4.50	.50	.10
☐ 10	Carl Yastrzemski	30.00	13.50	4.50
☐ 11	Nate Colbert	.70	.30	.07
☐ 12	John Hiller	1.00	.40	.10
☐ 13	Jack Hiatt	.70	.30	.07
☐ 14	Hank Allen	.70	.30	.07
☐ 15	Larry Dierker	.70	.30	.07
☐ 16	Charlie Metro MG	.70	.30	.07

		NRMT	VG-E	GOOD
☐ 17	Hoyt Wilhelm	4.00	1.75	.40
☐ 18	Carlos May	.70	.30	.07
☐ 19	John Boccabella	.70	.30	.07
☐ 20	Dave McNally	1.00	.40	.10
☐ 21	A's Rookies	4.50	2.00	.45
	Vida Blue			
	Gene Tenace			
☐ 22	Ray Washburn	.70	.30	.07
☐ 23	Bill Robinson	1.00	.40	.10
☐ 24	Dick Selma	.70	.30	.07
☐ 25	Cesar Tovar	.70	.30	.07
☐ 26	Tug McGraw	1.50	.60	.15
☐ 27	Chuck Hinton	.70	.30	.07
☐ 28	Billy Wilson	.70	.30	.07
☐ 29	Sandy Alomar	.70	.30	.07
☐ 30	Matty Alou	1.00	.40	.10
☐ 31	Marty Pattin	.70	.30	.07
☐ 32	Harry Walker MG	.70	.30	.07
☐ 33	Don Wert	.70	.30	.07
☐ 34	Willie Crawford	.70	.30	.07
☐ 35	Joel Horlen	.70	.30	.07
☐ 36	Red Rookies	1.00	.40	.10
	Danny Breeden			
	Bernie Carbo			
☐ 37	Dick Drago	.70	.30	.07
☐ 38	Mack Jones	.70	.30	.07
☐ 39	Mike Nagy	.70	.30	.07
☐ 40	Rich Allen	1.75	.70	.17
☐ 41	George Lauzerique	.70	.30	.07
☐ 42	Tito Fuentes	.70	.30	.07
☐ 43	Jack Aker	.70	.30	.07
☐ 44	Roberto Pena	.70	.30	.07
☐ 45	Dave Johnson	1.00	.40	.10
☐ 46	Ken Rudolph	.70	.30	.07
☐ 47	Bob Miller	.70	.30	.07
☐ 48	Gil Garrido	.70	.30	.07
☐ 49	Tim Cullen	.70	.30	.07
☐ 50	Tommie Agee	1.00	.40	.10
☐ 51	Bob Christian	.70	.30	.07
☐ 52	Bruce Dal Canton	.70	.30	.07
☐ 53	John Kennedy	.70	.30	.07
☐ 54	Jeff Torborg	1.00	.40	.10
☐ 55	John Odom	.70	.30	.07
☐ 56	Phillies Rookies	.70	.30	.07
	Joe Lis			
	Scott Reid			
☐ 57	Pat Kelly	.70	.30	.07
☐ 58	Dave Marshall	.70	.30	.07
☐ 59	Dick Ellsworth	.70	.30	.07
☐ 60	Jim Wynn	1.00	.40	.10
☐ 61	NL Batting Leaders	4.00	1.75	.40
	Pete Rose			
	Bob Clemente			
	Cleon Jones			
☐ 62	AL Batting Leaders	2.50	1.00	.25
	Rod Carew			
	Reggie Smith			
	Tony Oliva			
☐ 63	NL RBI Leaders	2.50	1.00	.25
	Willie McCovey			
	Ron Santo			
	Tony Perez			
☐ 64	AL RBI Leaders	3.00	1.25	.30
	Harmon Killebrew			
	Boog Powell			
	Reggie Jackson			
☐ 65	NL Home Run Leaders	3.00	1.25	.30
	Willie McCovey			
	Hank Aaron			
	Lee May			
☐ 66	AL Home Run Leaders	3.00	1.25	.30
	Harmon Killebrew			
	Frank Howard			
	Reggie Jackson			
☐ 67	NL ERA Leaders	4.00	1.75	.40
	Juan Marichal			
	Steve Carlton			
	Bob Gibson			
☐ 68	AL ERA Leaders	2.00	.80	.20
	Dick Bosman			
	Jim Palmer			
	Mike Cuellar			
☐ 69	NL Pitching Leaders	4.00	1.75	.40
	Tom Seaver			
	Phil Niekro			
	Fergie Jenkins			
	Juan Marichal			
☐ 70	AL Pitching Leaders	2.00	.80	.20
	Dennis McLain			
	Mike Cuellar			
	Dave Boswell			
	Dave McNally			
	Jim Perry			
	Mel Stottlemyre			

☐ 71 NL Strikeout Leaders	2.50	1.00	.25
Fergie Jenkins			
Bob Gibson			
Bill Singer			
☐ 72 AL Strikeout Leaders	2.00	.80	.20
Sam McDowell			
Mickey Lolich			
Andy Messersmith			
☐ 73 Wayne Granger	.70	.30	.07
☐ 74 Angels Rookies	.70	.30	.07
Greg Washburn			
Wally Wolf			
☐ 75 Jim Kaat	2.00	.80	.20
☐ 76 Carl Taylor	.70	.30	.07
☐ 77 Frank Linzy	.70	.30	.07
☐ 78 Joe Lahoud	.70	.30	.07
☐ 79 Clay Kirby	.70	.30	.07
☐ 80 Don Kessinger	1.00	.40	.10
☐ 81 Dave May	.70	.30	.07
☐ 82 Frank Fernandez	.70	.30	.07
☐ 83 Don Cardwell	.70	.30	.07
☐ 84 Paul Casanova	.70	.30	.07
☐ 85 Max Alvis	.70	.30	.07
☐ 86 Lum Harris MG	.70	.30	.07
☐ 87 Steve Renko	.70	.30	.07
☐ 88 Pilots Rookies	.70	.30	.07
Miguel Fuentes			
Dick Baney			
☐ 89 Juan Rios	.70	.30	.07
☐ 90 Tim McCarver	1.50	.60	.15
☐ 91 Rich Morales	.70	.30	.07
☐ 92 George Culver	.70	.30	.07
☐ 93 Rick Renick	.70	.30	.07
☐ 94 Freddie Patek	1.00	.40	.10
☐ 95 Earl Wilson	.70	.30	.07
☐ 96 Cardinals Rookies	2.50	1.00	.25
Leron Lee			
Jerry Reuss			
☐ 97 Joe Moeller	.70	.30	.07
☐ 98 Gates Brown	1.00	.40	.10
☐ 99 Bobby Pfeil	.70	.30	.07
☐ 100 Mel Stottlemyre	1.25	.50	.12
☐ 101 Bobby Floyd	.70	.30	.07
☐ 102 Joe Rudi	1.00	.40	.10
☐ 103 Frank Reberger	.70	.30	.07
☐ 104 Gerry Moses	.70	.30	.07
☐ 105 Tony Gonzalez	.70	.30	.07
☐ 106 Darold Knowles	.70	.30	.07
☐ 107 Bobby Etheridge	.70	.30	.07
☐ 108 Tom Burgmeier	.70	.30	.07
☐ 109 Expos Rookies	.70	.30	.07
Garry Jestadt			
Carl Morton			
☐ 110 Bob Moose	.70	.30	.07
☐ 111 Mike Hegan	.70	.30	.07
☐ 112 Dave Nelson	.70	.30	.07
☐ 113 Jim Ray	.70	.30	.07
☐ 114 Gene Michael	1.00	.40	.10
☐ 115 Alex Johnson	1.00	.40	.10
☐ 116 Sparky Lyle	1.50	.60	.15
☐ 117 Don Young	.70	.30	.07
☐ 118 George Mitterwald	.70	.30	.07
☐ 119 Chuck Taylor	.70	.30	.07
☐ 120 Sal Bando	1.00	.40	.10
☐ 121 Orioles Rookies	1.00	.40	.10
Fred Beene			
Terry Crowley			
☐ 122 George Stone	.70	.30	.07
☐ 123 Don Gutteridge	.70	.30	.07
☐ 124 Larry Jaster	.70	.30	.07
☐ 125 Deron Johnson	.70	.30	.07
☐ 126 Marty Martinez	.70	.30	.07
☐ 127 Joe Coleman	.70	.30	.07
☐ 128A Checklist 2 ERR	4.50	.50	.10
(226 R Perranoski)			
☐ 128B Checklist 2 COR	4.50	.50	.10
(226 R. Perranoski)			
☐ 129 Jimmie Price	.70	.30	.07
☐ 130 Ollie Brown	.70	.30	.07
☐ 131 Dodgers Rookies	.70	.30	.07
Ray Lamb			
Bob Stinson			
☐ 132 Jim McGlothlin	.70	.30	.07
☐ 133 Clay Carroll	.80	.35	.08
☐ 134 Danny Walton	.80	.35	.08
☐ 135 Dick Dietz	.80	.35	.08
☐ 136 Steve Hargan	.80	.35	.08
☐ 137 Art Shamsky	.80	.35	.08
☐ 138 Joe Foy	.80	.35	.08
☐ 139 Rich Nye	.80	.35	.08
☐ 140 Reggie Jackson	150.00	67.50	22.50
☐ 141 Pirates Rookies	1.00	.40	.10
Dave Cash			
Johnny Jeter			

☐ 142 Fritz Peterson	.80	.35	.08
☐ 143 Phil Gagliano	.80	.35	.08
☐ 144 Ray Culp	.80	.35	.08
☐ 145 Rico Carty	1.00	.40	.10
☐ 146 Danny Murphy	.80	.35	.08
☐ 147 Angel Hermoso	.80	.35	.08
☐ 148 Earl Weaver MG	2.00	.80	.20
☐ 149 Billy Champion	.80	.35	.08
☐ 150 Harmon Killebrew	7.00	3.00	.70
☐ 151 Dave Roberts	.80	.35	.08
☐ 152 Ike Brown	.80	.35	.08
☐ 153 Gary Gentry	.80	.35	.08
☐ 154 Senators Rookies	.80	.35	.08
Jim Miles			
Jan Dukes			
☐ 155 Denis Menke	.80	.35	.08
☐ 156 Eddie Fisher	.80	.35	.08
☐ 157 Manny Mota	1.00	.40	.10
☐ 158 Jerry McNertney	.80	.35	.08
☐ 159 Tommy Helms	1.00	.40	.10
☐ 160 Phil Niekro	4.00	1.75	.40
☐ 161 Richie Scheinblum	.80	.35	.08
☐ 162 Jerry Johnson	.80	.35	.08
☐ 163 Syd O'Brien	.80	.35	.08
☐ 164 Ty Cline	.80	.35	.08
☐ 165 Ed Kirkpatrick	.80	.35	.08
☐ 166 Al Oliver	2.00	.80	.20
☐ 167 Bill Burbach	.80	.35	.08
☐ 168 Dave Watkins	.80	.35	.08
☐ 169 Tom Hall	.80	.35	.08
☐ 170 Billy Williams	6.00	2.50	.60
☐ 171 Jim Nash	.80	.35	.08
☐ 172 Braves Rookies	2.50	1.00	.25
Garry Hill			
Ralph Garr			
☐ 173 Jim Hicks	.80	.35	.08
☐ 174 Ted Sizemore	1.00	.40	.10
☐ 175 Dick Bosman	.80	.35	.08
☐ 176 Jim Ray Hart	1.00	.40	.10
☐ 177 Jim Northrup	1.00	.40	.10
☐ 178 Denny Lemaster	.80	.35	.08
☐ 179 Ivan Murrell	.80	.35	.08
☐ 180 Tommy John	2.50	1.00	.25
☐ 181 Sparky Anderson MG	1.50	.60	.15
☐ 182 Dick Hall	.80	.35	.08
☐ 183 Jerry Grote	.80	.35	.08
☐ 184 Ray Fosse	.80	.35	.08
☐ 185 Don Mincher	.80	.35	.08
☐ 186 Rick Joseph	.80	.35	.08
☐ 187 Mike Hedlund	.80	.35	.08
☐ 188 Manny Sanguillen	1.00	.40	.10
☐ 189 Yankees Rookies	100.00	45.00	15.00
Thurman Munson			
Dave McDonald			
☐ 190 Joe Torre	1.50	.60	.15
☐ 191 Vicente Romo	.80	.35	.08
☐ 192 Jim Qualls	.80	.35	.08
☐ 193 Mike Wegener	.80	.35	.08
☐ 194 Chuck Manuel	.80	.35	.08
☐ 195 NL Playoff Game 1	6.50	2.75	.65
Seaver wins opener			
☐ 196 NL Playoff Game 2	2.00	.80	.20
Mets show muscle			
☐ 197 NL Playoff Game 3	15.00	6.50	2.15
Ryan saves the day			
☐ 198 NL Playoff Summary	4.50	2.00	.45
Mets celebrate (Ryan)			
☐ 199 AL Playoff Game 1	2.00	.80	.20
Orioles win			
squeaker (Cuellar)			
☐ 200 AL Playoff Game 2	2.50	1.00	.25
Powell scores			
winning run			
☐ 201 AL Playoff Game 3	2.00	.80	.20
Birds wrap it up			
☐ 202 AL Playoff Summary	2.00	.80	.20
Orioles celebrate			
☐ 203 Rudy May	.80	.35	.08
☐ 204 Len Gabrielson	.80	.35	.08
☐ 205 Bert Campaneris	1.00	.40	.10
☐ 206 Clete Boyer	1.00	.40	.10
☐ 207 Tigers Rookies	.80	.35	.08
Norman McRae			
Bob Reed			
☐ 208 Fred Gladding	.80	.35	.08
☐ 209 Ken Suarez	.80	.35	.08
☐ 210 Juan Marichal	6.00	2.50	.60
☐ 211 Ted Williams MG	6.50	2.75	.65
☐ 212 Al Santorini	.80	.35	.08
☐ 213 Andy Etchebarren	.80	.35	.08
☐ 214 Ken Boswell	.80	.35	.08
☐ 215 Reggie Smith	1.25	.50	.12
☐ 216 Chuck Hartenstein	.80	.35	.08
☐ 217 Ron Hansen	.80	.35	.08

☐ 218	Ron Stone	.80	.35	.08
☐ 219	Jerry Kenney	.80	.35	.08
☐ 220	Steve Carlton	30.00	13.50	4.50
☐ 221	Ron Brand	.80	.35	.08
☐ 222	Jim Rooker	.80	.35	.08
☐ 223	Nate Oliver	.80	.35	.08
☐ 224	Steve Barber	.80	.35	.08
☐ 225	Lee May	1.00	.40	.10
☐ 226	Ron Perranoski	.80	.35	.08
☐ 227	Astros Rookies	1.25	.50	.12
	John Mayberry			
	Bob Watkins			
☐ 228	Aurelio Rodriguez	.80	.35	.08
☐ 229	Rich Robertson	.80	.35	.08
☐ 230	Brooks Robinson	11.00	5.00	1.35
☐ 231	Luis Tiant	1.50	.60	.15
☐ 232	Bob Didier	.80	.35	.08
☐ 233	Lew Krausse	.80	.35	.08
☐ 234	Tommy Dean	.80	.35	.08
☐ 235	Mike Epstein	.80	.35	.08
☐ 236	Bob Veale	.80	.35	.08
☐ 237	Russ Gibson	.80	.35	.08
☐ 238	Jose Laboy	.80	.35	.08
☐ 239	Ken Berry	.80	.35	.08
☐ 240	Fergie Jenkins	10.00	4.50	1.25
☐ 241	Royals Rookies	.80	.35	.08
	Al Fitzmorris			
	Scott Northey			
☐ 242	Walter Alston MG	1.50	.60	.15
☐ 243	Joe Sparma	.80	.35	.08
☐ 244A	Checklist 3	4.50	.50	.10
	(red bat on front)			
☐ 244B	Checklist 3	4.50	.50	.10
	(brown bat on front)			
☐ 245	Leo Cardenas	.80	.35	.08
☐ 246	Jim McAndrew	.80	.35	.08
☐ 247	Lou Klimchock	.80	.35	.08
☐ 248	Jesus Alou	.80	.35	.08
☐ 249	Bob Locker	.80	.35	.08
☐ 250	Willie McCovey UER	10.00	4.50	1.25
	(1963 San Francisci)			
☐ 251	Dick Schofield	.80	.35	.08
☐ 252	Lowell Palmer	.80	.35	.08
☐ 253	Ron Woods	.80	.35	.08
☐ 254	Camilo Pascual	.80	.35	.08
☐ 255	Jim Spencer	.80	.35	.08
☐ 256	Vic Davalillo	.80	.35	.08
☐ 257	Dennis Higgins	.80	.35	.08
☐ 258	Paul Popovich	.80	.35	.08
☐ 259	Tommie Reynolds	.80	.35	.08
☐ 260	Claude Osteen	.80	.35	.08
☐ 261	Curt Motton	.80	.35	.08
☐ 262	Padres Rookies	1.00	.40	.10
	Jerry Morales			
	Jim Williams			
☐ 263	Duane Josephson	.80	.35	.08
☐ 264	Rich Hebner	1.25	.50	.12
☐ 265	Randy Hundley	1.25	.50	.12
☐ 266	Wally Bunker	1.00	.40	.10
☐ 267	Twins Rookies	1.00	.40	.10
	Herman Hill			
	Paul Ratliff			
☐ 268	Claude Raymond	1.00	.40	.10
☐ 269	Cesar Gutierrez	1.00	.40	.10
☐ 270	Chris Short	1.00	.40	.10
☐ 271	Greg Goossen	1.00	.40	.10
☐ 272	Hector Torres	1.00	.40	.10
☐ 273	Ralph Houk MG	1.25	.50	.12
☐ 274	Gerry Arrigo	1.00	.40	.10
☐ 275	Duke Sims	1.00	.40	.10
☐ 276	Ron Hunt	1.00	.40	.10
☐ 277	Paul Doyle	1.00	.40	.10
☐ 278	Tommie Aaron	1.25	.50	.12
☐ 279	Bill Lee	1.25	.50	.12
☐ 280	Donn Clendenon	1.25	.50	.12
☐ 281	Casey Cox	1.00	.40	.10
☐ 282	Steve Huntz	1.00	.40	.10
☐ 283	Angel Bravo	1.00	.40	.10
☐ 284	Jack Baldschun	1.00	.40	.10
☐ 285	Paul Blair	1.25	.50	.12
☐ 286	Dodgers Rookies	8.50	3.75	.85
	Jack Jenkins			
	Bill Buckner			
☐ 287	Fred Talbot	1.00	.40	.10
☐ 288	Larry Hisle	1.25	.50	.12
☐ 289	Gene Brabender	1.00	.40	.10
☐ 290	Rod Carew	50.00	22.50	7.50
☐ 291	Leo Durocher MG	1.75	.70	.17
☐ 292	Eddie Leon	1.00	.40	.10
☐ 293	Bob Bailey	1.00	.40	.10
☐ 294	Jose Azcue	1.00	.40	.10
☐ 295	Cecil Upshaw	1.00	.40	.10
☐ 296	Woody Woodward	1.25	.50	.12
☐ 297	Curt Blefary	1.00	.40	.10
☐ 298	Ken Henderson	1.00	.40	.10
☐ 299	Buddy Bradford	1.00	.40	.10
☐ 300	Tom Seaver	90.00	40.00	13.50
☐ 301	Chico Salmon	1.00	.40	.10
☐ 302	Jeff James	1.00	.40	.10
☐ 303	Brant Alyea	1.00	.40	.10
☐ 304	Bill Russell	3.00	1.25	.30
☐ 305	World Series Game 1	2.25	.90	.22
	Buford leadoff homer			
☐ 306	World Series Game 2	2.25	.90	.22
	Clendenon's homer			
	breaks ice			
☐ 307	World Series Game 3	2.25	.90	.22
	Agee's catch			
	saves the day			
☐ 308	World Series Game 4	2.25	.90	.22
	Martin's bunt			
	ends deadlock			
☐ 309	World Series Game 5	3.00	1.25	.30
	Koosman shuts door			
☐ 310	World Series Summary	3.00	1.25	.30
	Mets whoop it up			
☐ 311	Dick Green	1.00	.40	.10
☐ 312	Mike Torrez	1.25	.50	.12
☐ 313	Mayo Smith MG	1.00	.40	.10
☐ 314	Bill McCool	1.00	.40	.10
☐ 315	Luis Aparicio	4.00	1.75	.40
☐ 316	Skip Guinn	1.00	.40	.10
☐ 317	Red Sox Rookies	1.25	.50	.12
	Billy Conigliaro			
	Luis Alvarado			
☐ 318	Willie Smith	1.00	.40	.10
☐ 319	Clay Dalrymple	1.00	.40	.10
☐ 320	Jim Maloney	1.25	.50	.12
☐ 321	Lou Piniella	2.00	.80	.20
☐ 322	Luke Walker	1.00	.40	.10
☐ 323	Wayne Comer	1.00	.40	.10
☐ 324	Tony Taylor	1.00	.40	.10
☐ 325	Dave Boswell	1.00	.40	.10
☐ 326	Bill Voss	1.00	.40	.10
☐ 327	Hal King	1.00	.40	.10
☐ 328	George Brunet	1.00	.40	.10
☐ 329	Chris Cannizzaro	1.00	.40	.10
☐ 330	Lou Brock	9.00	4.00	.90
☐ 331	Chuck Dobson	1.00	.40	.10
☐ 332	Bobby Wine	1.00	.40	.10
☐ 333	Bobby Murcer	1.75	.70	.17
☐ 334	Phil Regan	1.00	.40	.10
☐ 335	Bill Freehan	1.50	.60	.15
☐ 336	Del Unser	1.00	.40	.10
☐ 337	Mike McCormick	1.25	.50	.12
☐ 338	Paul Schaal	1.00	.40	.10
☐ 339	Johnny Edwards	1.00	.40	.10
☐ 340	Tony Conigliaro	1.75	.70	.17
☐ 341	Bill Sudakis	1.00	.40	.10
☐ 342	Wilbur Wood	1.25	.50	.12
☐ 343A	Checklist 4	4.50	.50	.10
	(red bat on front)			
☐ 343B	Checklist 4	4.50	.50	.10
	(brown bat on front)			
☐ 344	Marcelino Lopez	1.00	.40	.10
☐ 345	Al Ferrara	1.00	.40	.10
☐ 346	Red Schoendienst MG	1.75	.70	.17
☐ 347	Russ Snyder	1.00	.40	.10
☐ 348	Mets Rookies	1.25	.50	.12
	Mike Jorgensen			
	Jesse Hudson			
☐ 349	Steve Hamilton	1.00	.40	.10
☐ 350	Roberto Clemente	48.00	22.00	6.00
☐ 351	Tom Murphy	1.00	.40	.10
☐ 352	Bob Barton	1.00	.40	.10
☐ 353	Stan Williams	1.00	.40	.10
☐ 354	Amos Otis	1.50	.60	.15
☐ 355	Doug Rader	1.25	.50	.12
☐ 356	Fred Lasher	1.00	.40	.10
☐ 357	Bob Burda	1.00	.40	.10
☐ 358	Pedro Borbon	1.00	.40	.10
☐ 359	Phil Roof	1.00	.40	.10
☐ 360	Curt Flood	1.50	.60	.15
☐ 361	Ray Jarvis	1.00	.40	.10
☐ 362	Joe Hague	1.00	.40	.10
☐ 363	Tom Shopay	1.00	.40	.10
☐ 364	Dan McGinn	1.00	.40	.10
☐ 365	Zoilo Versalles	1.00	.40	.10
☐ 366	Barry Moore	1.00	.40	.10
☐ 367	Mike Lum	1.00	.40	.10
☐ 368	Ed Herrmann	1.00	.40	.10
☐ 369	Alan Foster	1.00	.40	.10
☐ 370	Tommy Harper	1.00	.40	.10
☐ 371	Rod Gaspar	1.00	.40	.10
☐ 372	Dave Giusti	1.00	.40	.10
☐ 373	Roy White	1.50	.60	.15
☐ 374	Tommie Sisk	1.10	.45	.11
☐ 375	Johnny Callison	1.10	.45	.11

☐ 376	Lefty Phillips MG	1.10	.45	.11
☐ 377	Bill Butler	1.10	.45	.11
☐ 378	Jim Davenport	1.10	.45	.11
☐ 379	Tom Tischinski	1.10	.45	.11
☐ 380	Tony Perez	7.50	3.25	.75
☐ 381	Athletics Rookies	1.10	.45	.11
	Bobby Brooks			
	Mike Olivo			
☐ 382	Jack DiLauro	1.10	.45	.11
☐ 383	Mickey Stanley	1.50	.60	.15
☐ 384	Gary Neibauer	1.10	.45	.11
☐ 385	George Scott	1.50	.60	.15
☐ 386	Bill Dillman	1.10	.45	.11
☐ 387	Baltimore Orioles	2.50	1.00	.25
	Team Card			
☐ 388	Byron Browne	1.10	.45	.11
☐ 389	Jim Shellenback	1.10	.45	.11
☐ 390	Willie Davis	1.50	.60	.15
☐ 391	Larry Brown	1.10	.45	.11
☐ 392	Walt Hriniak	1.10	.45	.11
☐ 393	Gil Hodges MG	4.00	1.75	.40
☐ 394	Gil Hodges MG	4.00	1.75	.40
☐ 395	Walt Williams	1.10	.45	.11
☐ 396	Steve Blass	1.10	.45	.11
☐ 397	Roger Repoz	1.10	.45	.11
☐ 398	Bill Stoneman	1.10	.45	.11
☐ 399	New York Yankees	2.50	1.00	.25
	Team Card			
☐ 400	Denny McLain	1.50	.60	.15
☐ 401	Giants Rookies	1.10	.45	.11
	John Harrell			
	Bernie Williams			
☐ 402	Ellie Rodriguez	1.10	.45	.11
☐ 403	Jim Bunning	2.50	1.00	.25
☐ 404	Rich Reese	1.10	.45	.11
☐ 405	Bill Hands	1.10	.45	.11
☐ 406	Mike Andrews	1.10	.45	.11
☐ 407	Bob Watson	1.50	.60	.15
☐ 408	Paul Lindblad	1.10	.45	.11
☐ 409	Bob Tolan	1.10	.45	.11
☐ 410	Boog Powell	3.00	1.25	.30
☐ 411	Los Angeles Dodgers	2.50	1.00	.25
	Team Card			
☐ 412	Larry Burchart	1.10	.45	.11
☐ 413	Sonny Jackson	1.10	.45	.11
☐ 414	Paul Edmondson	1.10	.45	.11
☐ 415	Julian Javier	1.10	.45	.11
☐ 416	Joe Verbanic	1.10	.45	.11
☐ 417	John Bateman	1.10	.45	.11
☐ 418	John Donaldson	1.10	.45	.11
☐ 419	Ron Taylor	1.10	.45	.11
☐ 420	Ken McMullen	1.10	.45	.11
☐ 421	Pat Dobson	1.10	.45	.11
☐ 422	Royals Team	2.50	1.00	.25
☐ 423	Jerry May	1.10	.45	.11
☐ 424	Mike Kilkenny UER	1.10	.45	.11
	(inconsistent design,			
	card number in			
	white circle)			
☐ 425	Bobby Bonds	6.00	2.50	.60
☐ 426	Bill Rigney MG	1.10	.45	.11
☐ 427	Fred Norman	1.10	.45	.11
☐ 428	Don Buford	1.10	.45	.11
☐ 429	Cubs Rookies	1.10	.45	.11
	Randy Bobb			
	Jim Cosman			
☐ 430	Andy Messersmith	1.50	.60	.15
☐ 431	Ron Swoboda	1.50	.60	.15
☐ 432A	Checklist 5	4.50	.50	.10
	("Baseball" in			
	yellow letters)			
☐ 432B	Checklist 5	4.50	.50	.10
	("Baseball" in			
	white letters)			
☐ 433	Ron Bryant	1.10	.45	.11
☐ 434	Felipe Alou	1.50	.60	.15
☐ 435	Nelson Briles	1.10	.45	.11
☐ 436	Philadelphia Phillies	2.50	1.00	.25
	Team Card			
☐ 437	Danny Cater	1.10	.45	.11
☐ 438	Pat Jarvis	1.10	.45	.11
☐ 439	Lee Maye	1.10	.45	.11
☐ 440	Bill Mazeroski	1.75	.70	.17
☐ 441	John O'Donoghue	1.10	.45	.11
☐ 442	Gene Mauch MG	1.10	.45	.11
☐ 443	Al Jackson	1.10	.45	.11
☐ 444	White Sox Rookies	1.10	.45	.11
	Billy Farmer			
	John Matias			
☐ 445	Vada Pinson	1.75	.70	.17
☐ 446	Billy Grabarkewitz	1.10	.45	.11
☐ 447	Lee Stange	1.10	.45	.11
☐ 448	Houston Astros	2.50	1.00	.25
	Team Card			
☐ 449	Jim Palmer	21.00	9.00	3.00
☐ 450	Willie McCovey AS	4.50	2.00	.45
☐ 451	Boog Powell AS	1.50	.60	.15
☐ 452	Felix Millan AS	1.10	.45	.11
☐ 453	Rod Carew AS	6.50	2.75	.65
☐ 454	Ron Santo AS	1.50	.60	.15
☐ 455	Brooks Robinson AS	4.50	2.00	.45
☐ 456	Don Kessinger AS	1.10	.45	.11
☐ 457	Rico Petrocelli AS	1.10	.45	.11
☐ 458	Pete Rose AS	14.00	6.25	2.00
☐ 459	Reggie Jackson AS	21.00	9.00	3.00
☐ 460	Matty Alou AS	2.00	.80	.20
☐ 461	Carl Yastrzemski AS	11.00	5.00	1.35
☐ 462	Hank Aaron AS	13.00	5.75	1.75
☐ 463	Frank Robinson AS	6.00	2.50	.60
☐ 464	Johnny Bench AS	14.00	6.25	2.00
☐ 465	Bill Freehan AS	2.00	.80	.20
☐ 466	Juan Marichal AS	4.00	1.75	.40
☐ 467	Denny McLain AS	2.00	.80	.20
☐ 468	Jerry Koosman AS	2.00	.80	.20
☐ 469	Sam McDowell AS	2.00	.80	.20
☐ 470	Willie Stargell	9.00	4.00	.90
☐ 471	Chris Zachary	1.60	.65	.16
☐ 472	Braves Team	3.00	1.25	.30
☐ 473	Don Bryant	1.60	.65	.16
☐ 474	Dick Kelley	1.60	.65	.16
☐ 475	Dick McAuliffe	1.60	.65	.16
☐ 476	Don Shaw	1.60	.65	.16
☐ 477	Orioles Rookies	1.60	.65	.16
	Al Severinsen			
	Roger Freed			
☐ 478	Bobby Heise	1.60	.65	.16
☐ 479	Dick Woodson	1.60	.65	.16
☐ 480	Glenn Beckert	2.00	.80	.20
☐ 481	Jose Tartabull	1.60	.65	.16
☐ 482	Tom Hilgendorf	1.60	.65	.16
☐ 483	Gail Hopkins	1.60	.65	.16
☐ 484	Gary Nolan	2.00	.80	.20
☐ 485	Jay Johnstone	2.00	.80	.20
☐ 486	Terry Harmon	1.60	.65	.16
☐ 487	Cisco Carlos	1.60	.65	.16
☐ 488	J.C. Martin	1.60	.65	.16
☐ 489	Eddie Kasko MG	1.60	.65	.16
☐ 490	Bill Singer	2.00	.80	.20
☐ 491	Graig Nettles	5.00	2.25	.50
☐ 492	Astros Rookies	1.60	.65	.16
	Keith Lampard			
	Scipio Spinks			
☐ 493	Lindy McDaniel	1.60	.65	.16
☐ 494	Larry Stahl	1.60	.65	.16
☐ 495	Dave Morehead	1.60	.65	.16
☐ 496	Steve Whitaker	1.60	.65	.16
☐ 497	Eddie Watt	1.60	.65	.16
☐ 498	Al Weis	1.60	.65	.16
☐ 499	Skip Lockwood	1.60	.65	.16
☐ 500	Hank Aaron	48.00	22.00	6.00
☐ 501	Chicago White Sox	3.00	1.25	.30
	Team Card			
☐ 502	Rollie Fingers	28.00	12.50	4.00
☐ 503	Dal Maxvill	1.60	.65	.16
☐ 504	Don Pavletich	1.60	.65	.16
☐ 505	Ken Holtzman	2.00	.80	.20
☐ 506	Ed Stroud	1.60	.65	.16
☐ 507	Pat Corrales	1.60	.65	.16
☐ 508	Joe Niekro	2.00	.80	.20
☐ 509	Montreal Expos	3.00	1.25	.30
	Team Card			
☐ 510	Tony Oliva	3.00	1.25	.30
☐ 511	Joe Hoerner	1.60	.65	.16
☐ 512	Billy Harris	1.60	.65	.16
☐ 513	Preston Gomez MG	1.60	.65	.16
☐ 514	Steve Hovley	1.60	.65	.16
☐ 515	Don Wilson	1.60	.65	.16
☐ 516	Yankees Rookies	1.60	.65	.16
	John Ellis			
	Jim Lyttle			
☐ 517	Joe Gibbon	1.60	.65	.16
☐ 518	Bill Melton	1.60	.65	.16
☐ 519	Don McMahon	1.60	.65	.16
☐ 520	Willie Horton	2.00	.80	.20
☐ 521	Cal Koonce	1.60	.65	.16
☐ 522	Angels Team	3.00	1.25	.30
☐ 523	Jose Pena	1.60	.65	.16
☐ 524	Alvin Dark MG	2.00	.80	.20
☐ 525	Jerry Adair	1.60	.65	.16
☐ 526	Ron Herbel	1.60	.65	.16
☐ 527	Don Bosch	1.60	.65	.16
☐ 528	Elrod Hendricks	1.60	.65	.16
☐ 529	Bob Aspromonte	1.60	.65	.16
☐ 530	Bob Gibson	12.50	5.50	1.65
☐ 531	Ron Clark	1.60	.65	.16
☐ 532	Danny Murtaugh MG	1.60	.65	.16
☐ 533	Buzz Stephen	1.60	.65	.16
☐ 534	Twins Team	3.00	1.25	.30

☐ 535	Andy Kosco	1.60	.65	.16
☐ 536	Mike Kekich	1.60	.65	.16
☐ 537	Joe Morgan	12.50	5.50	1.65
☐ 538	Bob Humphreys	1.60	.65	.16
☐ 539	Phillies Rookies	4.00	1.75	.40
	Dennis Doyle			
	Larry Bowa			
☐ 540	Gary Peters	1.60	.65	.16
☐ 541	Bill Heath	1.60	.65	.16
☐ 542	Checklist 6	4.50	.50	.10
☐ 543	Clyde Wright	1.60	.65	.16
☐ 544	Cincinnati Reds	3.25	1.35	.32
	Team Card			
☐ 545	Ken Harrelson	2.25	.90	.22
☐ 546	Ron Reed	2.00	.80	.20
☐ 547	Rick Monday	3.50	1.50	.35
☐ 548	Howie Reed	2.75	1.10	.27
☐ 549	Cardinals Team	5.50	2.50	.55
☐ 550	Frank Howard	4.00	1.75	.40
☐ 551	Dock Ellis	2.75	1.10	.27
☐ 552	Royals Rookies	2.75	1.10	.27
	Don O'Riley			
	Dennis Paepke			
	Fred Rico			
☐ 553	Jim Lefebvre	3.50	1.50	.35
☐ 554	Tom Timmermann	2.75	1.10	.27
☐ 555	Orlando Cepeda	5.00	2.25	.50
☐ 556	Dave Bristol MG	2.75	1.10	.27
☐ 557	Ed Kranepool	3.50	1.50	.35
☐ 558	Vern Fuller	2.75	1.10	.27
☐ 559	Tommy Davis	3.50	1.50	.35
☐ 560	Gaylord Perry	12.50	5.50	1.65
☐ 561	Tom McCraw	2.75	1.10	.27
☐ 562	Ted Abernathy	2.75	1.10	.27
☐ 563	Boston Red Sox	5.50	2.50	.55
	Team Card			
☐ 564	Johnny Briggs	2.75	1.10	.27
☐ 565	Jim Hunter	12.50	5.50	1.65
☐ 566	Gene Alley	2.75	1.10	.27
☐ 567	Bob Oliver	2.75	1.10	.27
☐ 568	Stan Bahnsen	2.75	1.10	.27
☐ 569	Cookie Rojas	2.75	1.10	.27
☐ 570	Jim Fregosi	3.50	1.50	.35
☐ 571	Jim Brewer	2.75	1.10	.27
☐ 572	Frank Quilici MG	2.75	1.10	.27
☐ 573	Padres Rookies	2.75	1.10	.27
	Mike Corkins			
	Rafael Robles			
	Ron Slocum			
☐ 574	Bobby Bolin	2.75	1.10	.27
☐ 575	Cleon Jones	2.75	1.10	.27
☐ 576	Milt Pappas	3.50	1.50	.35
☐ 577	Bernie Allen	2.75	1.10	.27
☐ 578	Tom Griffin	2.75	1.10	.27
☐ 579	Detroit Tigers	5.50	2.50	.55
	Team Card			
☐ 580	Pete Rose	75.00	34.00	11.25
☐ 581	Tom Satriano	2.75	1.10	.27
☐ 582	Mike Paul	2.75	1.10	.27
☐ 583	Hal Lanier	2.75	1.10	.27
☐ 584	Al Downing	3.50	1.50	.35
☐ 585	Rusty Staub	4.00	1.75	.40
☐ 586	Rickey Clark	2.75	1.10	.27
☐ 587	Jose Arcia	2.75	1.10	.27
☐ 588A	Checklist 7 ERR	7.50	.75	.15
	(666 Adolfo)			
☐ 588B	Checklist 7 COR	4.50	.50	.10
	(666 Adolpho)			
☐ 589	Joe Keough	2.75	1.10	.27
☐ 590	Mike Cuellar	3.50	1.50	.35
☐ 591	Mike Ryan	2.75	1.10	.27
☐ 592	Daryl Patterson	2.75	1.10	.27
☐ 593	Chicago Cubs	5.50	2.50	.55
	Team Card			
☐ 594	Jake Gibbs	2.75	1.10	.27
☐ 595	Maury Wills	4.00	1.75	.40
☐ 596	Mike Hershberger	2.75	1.10	.27
☐ 597	Sonny Siebert	2.75	1.10	.27
☐ 598	Joe Pepitone	3.50	1.50	.35
☐ 599	Senators Rookies	2.75	1.10	.27
	Dick Stelmaszek			
	Gene Martin			
	Dick Such			
☐ 600	Willie Mays	70.00	32.00	10.50
☐ 601	Pete Richert	2.75	1.10	.27
☐ 602	Ted Savage	2.75	1.10	.27
☐ 603	Ray Oyler	2.75	1.10	.27
☐ 604	Clarence Gaston	3.50	1.50	.35
☐ 605	Rick Wise	3.50	1.50	.35
☐ 606	Chico Ruiz	2.75	1.10	.27
☐ 607	Gary Waslewski	2.75	1.10	.27
☐ 608	Pittsburgh Pirates	5.50	2.50	.55
	Team Card			
☐ 609	Buck Martinez UER	2.75	1.10	.27
	(inconsistent design,			

	card number in			
	white circle)			
☐ 610	Jerry Koosman	4.00	1.75	.40
☐ 611	Norm Cash	4.00	1.75	.40
☐ 612	Jim Hickman	2.75	1.10	.27
☐ 613	Dave Baldwin	2.75	1.10	.27
☐ 614	Mike Shannon	3.50	1.50	.35
☐ 615	Mark Belanger	3.50	1.50	.35
☐ 616	Jim Merritt	2.75	1.10	.27
☐ 617	Jim French	2.75	1.10	.27
☐ 618	Billy Wynne	2.75	1.10	.27
☐ 619	Norm Miller	2.75	1.10	.27
☐ 620	Jim Perry	4.00	1.75	.40
☐ 621	Braves Rookies	22.00	9.50	3.15
	Mike McQueen			
	Darrell Evans			
	Rick Kester			
☐ 622	Don Sutton	11.00	5.00	1.35
☐ 623	Horace Clarke	2.75	1.10	.27
☐ 624	Clyde King MG	2.75	1.10	.27
☐ 625	Dean Chance	3.50	1.50	.35
☐ 626	Dave Ricketts	2.75	1.10	.27
☐ 627	Gary Wagner	2.75	1.10	.27
☐ 628	Wayne Garrett	2.75	1.10	.27
☐ 629	Merv Rettenmund	2.75	1.10	.27
☐ 630	Ernie Banks	32.00	14.25	4.75
☐ 631	Oakland Athletics	5.50	2.50	.55
	Team Card			
☐ 632	Gary Sutherland	2.75	1.10	.27
☐ 633	Roger Nelson	2.75	1.10	.27
☐ 634	Bud Harrelson	6.00	2.50	.60
☐ 635	Bob Allison	6.00	2.50	.60
☐ 636	Jim Stewart	5.00	2.25	.50
☐ 637	Cleveland Indians	10.00	4.50	1.25
	Team Card			
☐ 638	Frank Bertaina	5.00	2.25	.50
☐ 639	Dave Campbell	5.00	2.25	.50
☐ 640	Al Kaline	48.00	22.00	6.00
☐ 641	Al McBean	5.00	2.25	.50
☐ 642	Angels Rookies	5.00	2.25	.50
	Greg Garrett			
	Gordon Lund			
	Jarvis Tatum			
☐ 643	Jose Pagan	5.00	2.25	.50
☐ 644	Gerry Nyman	5.00	2.25	.50
☐ 645	Don Money	6.00	2.50	.60
☐ 646	Jim Britton	5.00	2.25	.50
☐ 647	Tom Matchick	5.00	2.25	.50
☐ 648	Larry Haney	5.00	2.25	.50
☐ 649	Jimmie Hall	5.00	2.25	.50
☐ 650	Sam McDowell	6.00	2.50	.60
☐ 651	Jim Gosger	5.00	2.25	.50
☐ 652	Rich Rollins	5.00	2.25	.50
☐ 653	Moe Drabowsky	5.00	2.25	.50
☐ 654	NL Rookies	6.00	2.50	.60
	Oscar Gamble			
	Boots Day			
	Angel Mangual			
☐ 655	John Roseboro	5.00	2.25	.50
☐ 656	Jim Hardin	5.00	2.25	.50
☐ 657	San Diego Padres	10.00	4.50	1.25
	Team Card			
☐ 658	Ken Tatum	5.00	2.25	.50
☐ 659	Pete Ward	5.00	2.25	.50
☐ 660	Johnny Bench	165.00	75.00	22.50
☐ 661	Jerry Robertson	5.00	2.25	.50
☐ 662	Frank Lucchesi MG	5.00	2.25	.50
☐ 663	Tito Francona	5.00	2.25	.50
☐ 664	Bob Robertson	5.00	2.25	.50
☐ 665	Jim Lonborg	6.00	2.50	.60
☐ 666	Adolpho Phillips	5.00	2.25	.50
☐ 667	Bob Meyer	5.00	2.25	.50
☐ 668	Bob Tillman	5.00	2.25	.50
☐ 669	White Sox Rookies	5.00	2.25	.50
	Bart Johnson			
	Dan Lazar			
	Mickey Scott			
☐ 670	Ron Santo	7.00	3.00	.70
☐ 671	Jim Campanis	5.00	2.25	.50
☐ 672	Leon McFadden	5.00	2.25	.50
☐ 673	Ted Uhlaender	5.00	2.25	.50
☐ 674	Dave Leonhard	5.00	2.25	.50
☐ 675	Jose Cardenal	5.00	2.25	.50
☐ 676	Senators Team	10.00	4.50	1.25
☐ 677	Woodie Fryman	5.00	2.25	.50
☐ 678	Dave Duncan	6.00	2.50	.60
☐ 679	Ray Sadecki	5.00	2.25	.50
☐ 680	Rico Petrocelli	6.00	2.50	.60
☐ 681	Bob Garibaldi	5.00	2.25	.50
☐ 682	Dalton Jones	5.00	2.25	.50
☐ 683	Reds Rookies	7.00	3.00	.70
	Vern Geishert			
	Hal McRae			
	Wayne Simpson			
☐ 684	Jack Fisher	5.00	2.25	.50

		NRMT	VG-E	GOOD
☐ 685	Tom Haller	5.00	2.25	.50
☐ 686	Jackie Hernandez	5.00	2.25	.50
☐ 687	Bob Priddy	5.00	2.25	.50
☐ 688	Ted Kubiak	5.00	2.25	.50
☐ 689	Frank Tepedino	5.00	2.25	.50
☐ 690	Ron Fairly	6.00	2.50	.60
☐ 691	Joe Grzenda	5.00	2.25	.50
☐ 692	Duffy Dyer	5.00	2.25	.50
☐ 693	Bob Johnson	5.00	2.25	.50
☐ 694	Gary Ross	5.00	2.25	.50
☐ 695	Bobby Knoop	5.00	2.25	.50
☐ 696	San Francisco Giants Team Card	10.00	4.50	1.25
☐ 697	Jim Hannan	5.00	2.25	.50
☐ 698	Tom Tresh	6.00	2.50	.60
☐ 699	Hank Aguirre	5.00	2.25	.50
☐ 700	Frank Robinson	42.00	18.00	5.50
☐ 701	Jack Billingham	5.00	2.25	.50
☐ 702	AL Rookies	5.00	2.25	.50
	Bob Johnson			
	Ron Klimkowski			
	Bill Zepp			
☐ 703	Lou Marone	5.00	2.25	.50
☐ 704	Frank Baker	5.00	2.25	.50
☐ 705	Tony Cloninger UER	5.00	2.25	.50
	(Batter headings on card back)			
☐ 706	John McNamara MG	7.00	3.00	.70
☐ 707	Kevin Collins	5.00	2.25	.50
☐ 708	Jose Santiago	5.00	2.25	.50
☐ 709	Mike Fiore	5.00	2.25	.50
☐ 710	Felix Millan	5.00	2.25	.50
☐ 711	Ed Brinkman	5.00	2.25	.50
☐ 712	Nolan Ryan	450.00	200.00	67.50
☐ 713	Pilots Team Card	20.00	8.50	2.75
☐ 714	Al Spangler	5.00	2.25	.50
☐ 715	Mickey Lolich	7.00	3.00	.70
☐ 716	Cardinals Rookies	5.00	2.25	.50
	Sal Campisi			
	Reggie Cleveland			
	Santiago Guzman			
☐ 717	Tom Phoebus	5.00	2.25	.50
☐ 718	Ed Spiezio	5.00	2.25	.50
☐ 719	Jim Roland	5.00	2.25	.50
☐ 720	Rick Reichardt	6.00	2.50	.50

1971 Topps

The cards in this 752-card set measure 2 1/2" by 3 1/2". The 1971 Topps set is a challenge to complete in strict mint condition because the black obverse border is easily scratched and damaged. An unusual feature of this set is that the player is also pictured in black and white on the back of the card. Featured subsets within this set include League Leaders (61-72), Playoffs cards (195-202), and World Series cards (327-332). Cards 524-643 and the last series (644-752) are somewhat scarce. The last series was printed in two sheets of 132. On the printing sheets 44 cards were printed in 50 percent greater quantity than the other 66 cards. These 66 (slightly) shorter-printed numbers are identified in the checklist below by SP. The key rookie cards in this set are the multi-player rookie cards of Dusty Baker and Don Baylor and the card of Steve Garvey.

		NRMT	VG-E	GOOD
COMPLETE SET (752)		2250.00	900.00	275.00
COMMON PLAYER (1-132)		.80	.35	.08
COMMON PLAYER (133-263)		1.00	.40	.10
COMMON PLAYER (264-393)		1.00	.40	.10
COMMON PLAYER (394-523)		1.60	.65	.16
COMMON PLAYER (524-643)		3.50	1.50	.35
COMMON PLAYER (644-752)		5.25	2.25	.50
COMMON SP (644-752)		7.50	3.25	.75
☐ 1	Baltimore Orioles Team Card	12.00	2.00	.40
☐ 2	Dock Ellis	.80	.35	.08
☐ 3	Dick McAuliffe	.80	.35	.08
☐ 4	Vic Davalillo	.80	.35	.08
☐ 5	Thurman Munson	38.00	17.00	4.50
☐ 6	Ed Spiezio	.80	.35	.08
☐ 7	Jim Holt	.80	.35	.08
☐ 8	Mike McQueen	.80	.35	.08
☐ 9	George Scott	.80	.35	.08
☐ 10	Claude Osteen	.80	.35	.08
☐ 11	Elliott Maddox	.80	.35	.08
☐ 12	Johnny Callison	.80	.35	.08
☐ 13	White Sox Rookies	.80	.35	.08
	Charlie Brinkman			
	Dick Moloney			
☐ 14	Dave Concepcion	15.00	6.50	2.15
☐ 15	Andy Messersmith	.80	.35	.08
☐ 16	Ken Singleton	3.00	1.25	.30
☐ 17	Billy Sorrell	.80	.35	.08
☐ 18	Norm Miller	.80	.35	.08
☐ 19	Skip Pitlock	.80	.35	.08
☐ 20	Reggie Jackson	90.00	40.00	13.50
☐ 21	Dan McGinn	.80	.35	.08
☐ 22	Phil Roof	.80	.35	.08
☐ 23	Oscar Gamble	.80	.35	.08
☐ 24	Rich Hand	.80	.35	.08
☐ 25	Clarence Gaston	1.00	.40	.10
☐ 26	Bert Blyleven	45.00	20.00	6.75
☐ 27	Pirates Rookies	.80	.35	.08
	Fred Cambria			
	Gene Clines			
☐ 28	Ron Klimkowski	.80	.35	.08
☐ 29	Don Buford	.80	.35	.08
☐ 30	Phil Niekro	4.00	1.75	.40
☐ 31	Eddie Kasko MG	.80	.35	.08
☐ 32	Jerry DaVanon	.80	.35	.08
☐ 33	Del Unser	.80	.35	.08
☐ 34	Sandy Vance	.80	.35	.08
☐ 35	Lou Piniella	1.50	.60	.15
☐ 36	Dean Chance	1.00	.40	.10
☐ 37	Rich McKinney	.80	.35	.08
☐ 38	Jim Colborn	.80	.35	.08
☐ 39	Tiger Rookies	1.25	.50	.12
	Lerrin LaGrow			
	Gene Lamont			
☐ 40	Lee May	1.00	.40	.10
☐ 41	Rick Austin	.80	.35	.08
☐ 42	Boots Day	.80	.35	.08
☐ 43	Steve Kealey	.80	.35	.08
☐ 44	Johnny Edwards	.80	.35	.08
☐ 45	Jim Hunter	6.50	2.75	.65
☐ 46	Dave Campbell	.80	.35	.08
☐ 47	Johnny Jeter	.80	.35	.08
☐ 48	Dave Baldwin	.80	.35	.08
☐ 49	Don Money	.80	.35	.08
☐ 50	Willie McCovey	8.50	3.75	.85
☐ 51	Steve Kline	.80	.35	.08
☐ 52	Braves Rookies	1.00	.40	.10
	Oscar Brown			
	Earl Williams			
☐ 53	Paul Blair	.80	.35	.08
☐ 54	Checklist 1	4.50	.50	.10
☐ 55	Steve Carlton	25.00	11.00	3.50
☐ 56	Duane Josephson	.80	.35	.08
☐ 57	Von Joshua	.80	.35	.08
☐ 58	Bill Lee	.80	.35	.08
☐ 59	Gene Mauch MG	.80	.35	.08
☐ 60	Dick Bosman	.80	.35	.08
☐ 61	AL Batting Leaders	2.75	1.10	.27
	Alex Johnson			
	Carl Yastrzemski			
	Tony Oliva			
☐ 62	NL Batting Leaders	2.00	.80	.20
	Rico Carty			
	Joe Torre			
	Manny Sanguillen			
☐ 63	AL RBI Leaders	2.00	.80	.20
	Frank Howard			
	Tony Conigliaro			
	Boog Powell			
☐ 64	NL RBI Leaders	3.25	1.35	.32
	Johnny Bench			
	Tony Perez			

	Billy Williams			
☐ 65	AL HR Leaders	3.00	1.25	.30
	Frank Howard			
	Harmon Killebrew			
	Carl Yastrzemski			
☐ 66	NL HR Leaders	3.25	1.35	.32
	Johnny Bench			
	Billy Williams			
	Tony Perez			
☐ 67	AL ERA Leaders	2.00	.80	.20
	Diego Segui			
	Jim Palmer			
	Clyde Wright			
☐ 68	NL ERA Leaders	2.00	.80	.20
	Tom Seaver			
	Wayne Simpson			
	Luke Walker			
☐ 69	AL Pitching Leaders	2.00	.80	.20
	Mike Cuellar			
	Dave McNally			
	Jim Perry			
☐ 70	NL Pitching Leaders	3.25	1.35	.32
	Bob Gibson			
	Gaylord Perry			
	Fergie Jenkins			
☐ 71	AL Strikeout Leaders	1.75	.70	.17
	Sam McDowell			
	Mickey Lolich			
	Bob Johnson			
☐ 72	NL Strikeout Leaders	3.75	1.60	.37
	Tom Seaver			
	Bob Gibson			
	Fergie Jenkins			
☐ 73	George Brunet	.80	.35	.08
☐ 74	Twins Rookies	.80	.35	.08
	Pete Hamm			
	Jim Nettles			
☐ 75	Gary Nolan	.80	.35	.08
☐ 76	Ted Savage	.80	.35	.08
☐ 77	Mike Compton	.80	.35	.08
☐ 78	Jim Spencer	.80	.35	.08
☐ 79	Wade Blasingame	.80	.35	.08
☐ 80	Bill Melton	.80	.35	.08
☐ 81	Felix Millan	.80	.35	.08
☐ 82	Casey Cox	.80	.35	.08
☐ 83	Met Rookies	1.00	.40	.10
	Tim Foli			
	Randy Bobb			
☐ 84	Marcel Lachemann	1.00	.40	.10
☐ 85	Billy Grabarkewitz	.80	.35	.08
☐ 86	Mike Kilkenny	.80	.35	.08
☐ 87	Jack Heidemann	.80	.35	.08
☐ 88	Hal King	.80	.35	.08
☐ 89	Ken Brett	.80	.35	.08
☐ 90	Joe Pepitone	1.00	.40	.10
☐ 91	Bob Lemon MG	1.75	.70	.17
☐ 92	Fred Wenz	.80	.35	.08
☐ 93	Senators Rookies	.80	.35	.08
	Norm McRae			
	Denny Riddleberger			
☐ 94	Don Hahn	.80	.35	.08
☐ 95	Luis Tiant	1.25	.50	.12
☐ 96	Joe Hague	.80	.35	.08
☐ 97	Floyd Wicker	.80	.35	.08
☐ 98	Joe Decker	.80	.35	.08
☐ 99	Mark Belanger	1.00	.40	.10
☐ 100	Pete Rose	45.00	20.00	6.75
☐ 101	Les Cain	.80	.35	.08
☐ 102	Astros Rookies	1.25	.50	.12
	Ken Forsch			
	Larry Howard			
☐ 103	Rich Severson	.80	.35	.08
☐ 104	Dan Frisella	.80	.35	.08
☐ 105	Tony Conigliaro	1.50	.60	.15
☐ 106	Tom Dukes	.80	.35	.08
☐ 107	Roy Foster	.80	.35	.08
☐ 108	John Cumberland	.80	.35	.08
☐ 109	Steve Hovley	.80	.35	.08
☐ 110	Bill Mazeroski	1.50	.60	.15
☐ 111	Yankee Rookies	.80	.35	.08
	Loyd Colson			
	Bobby Mitchell			
☐ 112	Manny Mota	1.00	.40	.10
☐ 113	Jerry Crider	.80	.35	.08
☐ 114	Billy Conigliaro	1.00	.40	.10
☐ 115	Donn Clendenon	.80	.35	.08
☐ 116	Ken Sanders	.80	.35	.08
☐ 117	Ted Simmons	15.00	6.50	2.15
☐ 118	Cookie Rojas	.80	.35	.08
☐ 119	Frank Lucchesi MG	.80	.35	.08
☐ 120	Willie Horton	1.00	.40	.10
☐ 121	Cubs Rookies	.80	.35	.08
	Jim Dunegan			
	Roe Skidmore			
☐ 122	Eddie Watt	.80	.35	.08

☐ 123A	Checklist 2	4.50	.50	.10
	(card number			
	at bottom right)			
☐ 123B	Checklist 2	4.50	.50	.10
	(card number			
	centered)			
☐ 124	Don Gullett	1.25	.50	.12
☐ 125	Ray Fosse	.80	.35	.08
☐ 126	Danny Coombs	.80	.35	.08
☐ 127	Danny Thompson	.80	.35	.08
☐ 128	Frank Johnson	.80	.35	.08
☐ 129	Aurelio Monteagudo	.80	.35	.08
☐ 130	Denis Menke	.80	.35	.08
☐ 131	Curt Blefary	.80	.35	.08
☐ 132	Jose Laboy	.80	.35	.08
☐ 133	Mickey Lolich	1.50	.60	.15
☐ 134	Jose Arcia	1.00	.40	.10
☐ 135	Rick Monday	1.25	.50	.12
☐ 136	Duffy Dyer	1.00	.40	.10
☐ 137	Marcelino Lopez	1.00	.40	.10
☐ 138	Phillies Rookies	1.25	.50	.12
	Joe Lis			
	Willie Montanez			
☐ 139	Paul Casanova	1.00	.40	.10
☐ 140	Gaylord Perry	7.50	3.25	.75
☐ 141	Frank Quilici	1.00	.40	.10
☐ 142	Mack Jones	1.00	.40	.10
☐ 143	Steve Blass	1.00	.40	.10
☐ 144	Jackie Hernandez	1.00	.40	.10
☐ 145	Bill Singer	1.00	.40	.10
☐ 146	Ralph Houk MG	1.00	.40	.10
☐ 147	Bob Priddy	1.00	.40	.10
☐ 148	John Mayberry	1.25	.50	.12
☐ 149	Mike Hershberger	1.00	.40	.10
☐ 150	Sam McDowell	1.00	.40	.10
☐ 151	Tommy Davis	1.25	.50	.12
☐ 152	Angels Rookies	1.00	.40	.10
	Lloyd Allen			
	Winston Llenas			
☐ 153	Gary Ross	1.00	.40	.10
☐ 154	Cesar Gutierrez	1.00	.40	.10
☐ 155	Ken Henderson	1.00	.40	.10
☐ 156	Bart Johnson	1.00	.40	.10
☐ 157	Bob Bailey	1.00	.40	.10
☐ 158	Jerry Reuss	1.25	.50	.12
☐ 159	Jarvis Tatum	1.00	.40	.10
☐ 160	Tom Seaver	50.00	22.50	7.50
☐ 161	Coin Checklist	3.50	.50	.10
☐ 162	Jack Billingham	1.00	.40	.10
☐ 163	Buck Martinez	1.00	.40	.10
☐ 164	Reds Rookies	1.25	.50	.12
	Frank Duffy			
	Milt Wilcox			
☐ 165	Cesar Tovar	1.00	.40	.10
☐ 166	Joe Hoerner	1.00	.40	.10
☐ 167	Tom Grieve	1.50	.60	.15
☐ 168	Bruce Dal Canton	1.00	.40	.10
☐ 169	Ed Herrmann	1.00	.40	.10
☐ 170	Mike Cuellar	1.00	.40	.10
☐ 171	Bobby Wine	1.00	.40	.10
☐ 172	Duke Sims	1.00	.40	.10
☐ 173	Gil Garrido	1.00	.40	.10
☐ 174	Dave LaRoche	1.00	.40	.10
☐ 175	Jim Hickman	1.00	.40	.10
☐ 176	Red Sox Rookies	1.00	.40	.10
	Bob Montgomery			
	Doug Griffin			
☐ 177	Hal McRae	1.75	.70	.17
☐ 178	Dave Duncan	1.00	.40	.10
☐ 179	Mike Corkins	1.00	.40	.10
☐ 180	Al Kaline UER	17.00	7.25	2.50
	(Home instead			
	of Birth)			
☐ 181	Hal Lanier	1.00	.40	.10
☐ 182	Al Downing	1.00	.40	.10
☐ 183	Gil Hodges MG	4.00	1.75	.40
☐ 184	Stan Bahnsen	1.00	.40	.10
☐ 185	Julian Javier	1.00	.40	.10
☐ 186	Bob Spence	1.00	.40	.10
☐ 187	Ted Abernathy	1.00	.40	.10
☐ 188	Dodgers Rookies	3.25	1.35	.32
	Bob Valentine			
	Mike Strahler			
☐ 189	George Mitterwald	1.00	.40	.10
☐ 190	Bob Tolan	1.00	.40	.10
☐ 191	Mike Andrews	1.00	.40	.10
☐ 192	Billy Wilson	1.00	.40	.10
☐ 193	Bob Grich	4.00	1.75	.40
☐ 194	Mike Lum	1.00	.40	.10
☐ 195	AL Playoff Game 1	2.25	.90	.22
	Powell muscles Twins			
☐ 196	AL Playoff Game 2	2.00	.80	.20
	McNally makes it			
	two straight			
☐ 197	AL Playoff Game 3	3.50	1.50	.35

Palmer mows'em down

☐ 198	AL Playoff Summary	2.00	.80	.20
	Orioles celebrate			
☐ 199	NL Playoff Game 1	2.00	.80	.20
	Cline pinch-triple			
	decides it			
☐ 200	NL Playoff Game 2	2.00	.80	.20
	Tolan scores for			
	third time			
☐ 201	NL Playoff Game 3	2.00	.80	.20
	Cline scores			
	winning run			
☐ 202	NL Playoff Summary	2.00	.80	.20
	Reds celebrate			
☐ 203	Larry Gura	1.25	.50	.12
☐ 204	Brewers Rookies	1.00	.40	.10
	Bernie Smith			
	George Kopacz			
☐ 205	Gerry Moses	1.00	.40	.10
☐ 206	Checklist 3	4.50	.50	.10
☐ 207	Alan Foster	1.00	.40	.10
☐ 208	Billy Martin MG	3.00	1.25	.30
☐ 209	Steve Renko	1.00	.40	.10
☐ 210	Rod Carew	42.00	18.00	5.50
☐ 211	Phil Hennigan	1.00	.40	.10
☐ 212	Rich Hebner	1.25	.50	.12
☐ 213	Frank Baker	1.00	.40	.10
☐ 214	Al Ferrara	1.00	.40	.10
☐ 215	Diego Segui	1.00	.40	.10
☐ 216	Cards Rookies	1.00	.40	.10
	Reggie Cleveland			
	Luis Melendez			
☐ 217	Ed Stroud	1.00	.40	.10
☐ 218	Tony Cloninger	1.00	.40	.10
☐ 219	Elrod Hendricks	1.00	.40	.10
☐ 220	Ron Santo	2.00	.80	.20
☐ 221	Dave Morehead	1.00	.40	.10
☐ 222	Bob Watson	1.25	.50	.12
☐ 223	Cecil Upshaw	1.00	.40	.10
☐ 224	Alan Gallagher	1.00	.40	.10
☐ 225	Gary Peters	1.00	.40	.10
☐ 226	Bill Russell	1.25	.50	.12
☐ 227	Floyd Weaver	1.00	.40	.10
☐ 228	Wayne Garrett	1.00	.40	.10
☐ 229	Jim Hannan	1.00	.40	.10
☐ 230	Willie Stargell	9.00	4.00	.90
☐ 231	Indians Rookies	1.25	.50	.12
	Vince Colbert			
	John Lowenstein			
☐ 232	John Strohmayer	1.00	.40	.10
☐ 233	Larry Bowa	1.75	.70	.17
☐ 234	Jim Lyttle	1.00	.40	.10
☐ 235	Nate Colbert	1.00	.40	.10
☐ 236	Bob Humphreys	1.00	.40	.10
☐ 237	Cesar Cedeno	3.00	1.25	.30
☐ 238	Chuck Dobson	1.00	.40	.10
☐ 239	Red Schoendienst MG	1.75	.70	.17
☐ 240	Clyde Wright	1.00	.40	.10
☐ 241	Dave Nelson	1.00	.40	.10
☐ 242	Jim Ray	1.00	.40	.10
☐ 243	Carlos May	1.00	.40	.10
☐ 244	Bob Tillman	1.00	.40	.10
☐ 245	Jim Kaat	2.25	.90	.22
☐ 246	Tony Taylor	1.00	.40	.10
☐ 247	Royals Rookies	1.25	.50	.12
	Jerry Cram			
	Paul Splittorff			
☐ 248	Hoyt Wilhelm	4.00	1.75	.40
☐ 249	Chico Salmon	1.00	.40	.10
☐ 250	Johnny Bench	50.00	22.50	7.50
☐ 251	Frank Reberger	1.00	.40	.10
☐ 252	Eddie Leon	1.00	.40	.10
☐ 253	Bill Sudakis	1.00	.40	.10
☐ 254	Cal Koonce	1.00	.40	.10
☐ 255	Bob Robertson	1.00	.40	.10
☐ 256	Tony Gonzalez	1.00	.40	.10
☐ 257	Nelson Briles	1.00	.40	.10
☐ 258	Dick Green	1.00	.40	.10
☐ 259	Dave Marshall	1.00	.40	.10
☐ 260	Tommy Harper	1.00	.40	.10
☐ 261	Darold Knowles	1.00	.40	.10
☐ 262	Padres Rookies	1.00	.40	.10
	Jim Williams			
	Dave Robinson			
☐ 263	John Ellis	1.00	.40	.10
☐ 264	Joe Morgan	9.00	4.00	.90
☐ 265	Jim Northrup	1.25	.50	.12
☐ 266	Bill Stoneman	1.00	.40	.10
☐ 267	Rich Morales	1.00	.40	.10
☐ 268	Philadelphia Phillies	2.00	.80	.20
	Team Card			
☐ 269	Gail Hopkins	1.00	.40	.10
☐ 270	Rico Carty	1.25	.50	.12
☐ 271	Bill Zepp	1.00	.40	.10

☐ 272	Tommy Helms	1.25	.50	.12
☐ 273	Pete Richert	1.00	.40	.10
☐ 274	Ron Slocum	1.00	.40	.10
☐ 275	Vada Pinson	1.50	.60	.15
☐ 276	Giants Rookies	8.00	3.50	.80
	Mike Davison			
	George Foster			
☐ 277	Gary Waslewski	1.00	.40	.10
☐ 278	Jerry Grote	1.00	.40	.10
☐ 279	Lefty Phillips MG	1.00	.40	.10
☐ 280	Fergie Jenkins	11.00	5.00	1.35
☐ 281	Danny Walton	1.00	.40	.10
☐ 282	Jose Pagan	1.00	.40	.10
☐ 283	Dick Such	1.00	.40	.10
☐ 284	Jim Gosger	1.00	.40	.10
☐ 285	Sal Bando	1.25	.50	.12
☐ 286	Jerry McNertney	1.00	.40	.10
☐ 287	Mike Fiore	1.00	.40	.10
☐ 288	Joe Moeller	1.00	.40	.10
☐ 289	Chicago White Sox	2.00	.80	.20
	Team Card			
☐ 290	Tony Oliva	3.00	1.25	.30
☐ 291	George Culver	1.00	.40	.10
☐ 292	Jay Johnstone	1.25	.50	.12
☐ 293	Pat Corrales	1.00	.40	.10
☐ 294	Steve Dunning	1.00	.40	.10
☐ 295	Bobby Bonds	4.00	1.75	.40
☐ 296	Tom Timmermann	1.00	.40	.10
☐ 297	Johnny Briggs	1.00	.40	.10
☐ 298	Jim Nelson	1.00	.40	.10
☐ 299	Ed Kirkpatrick	1.00	.40	.10
☐ 300	Brooks Robinson	15.00	6.50	2.15
☐ 301	Earl Wilson	1.00	.40	.10
☐ 302	Phil Gagliano	1.00	.40	.10
☐ 303	Lindy McDaniel	1.00	.40	.10
☐ 304	Ron Brand	1.00	.40	.10
☐ 305	Reggie Smith	1.75	.70	.17
☐ 306	Jim Nash	1.00	.40	.10
☐ 307	Don Wert	1.00	.40	.10
☐ 308	St. Louis Cardinals	2.00	.80	.20
	Team Card			
☐ 309	Dick Ellsworth	1.00	.40	.10
☐ 310	Tommie Agee	1.00	.40	.10
☐ 311	Lee Stange	1.00	.40	.10
☐ 312	Harry Walker MG	1.00	.40	.10
☐ 313	Tom Hall	1.00	.40	.10
☐ 314	Jeff Torborg	1.25	.50	.12
☐ 315	Ron Fairly	1.25	.50	.12
☐ 316	Fred Scherman	1.00	.40	.10
☐ 317	Athletic Rookies	1.00	.40	.10
	Jim Driscoll			
	Angel Mangual			
☐ 318	Rudy May	1.00	.40	.10
☐ 319	Ty Cline	1.00	.40	.10
☐ 320	Dave McNally	1.25	.50	.12
☐ 321	Tom Matchick	1.00	.40	.10
☐ 322	Jim Beauchamp	1.00	.40	.10
☐ 323	Billy Champion	1.00	.40	.10
☐ 324	Graig Nettles	2.75	1.10	.27
☐ 325	Juan Marichal	5.50	2.50	.55
☐ 326	Richie Scheinblum	1.00	.40	.10
☐ 327	World Series Game 1	2.00	.80	.20
	Powell homers to			
	opposite field			
☐ 328	World Series Game 2	2.00	.80	.20
	Don Buford			
☐ 329	World Series Game 3	3.00	1.25	.30
	Frank Robinson			
	shows muscle			
☐ 330	World Series Game 4	2.00	.80	.20
	Reds stay alive			
☐ 331	World Series Game 5	3.50	1.50	.35
	Brooks Robinson			
	commits robbery			
☐ 332	World Series Summary	2.00	.80	.20
	Orioles celebrate			
☐ 333	Clay Kirby	1.00	.40	.10
☐ 334	Roberto Pena	1.00	.40	.10
☐ 335	Jerry Koosman	2.00	.80	.20
☐ 336	Detroit Tigers	2.00	.80	.20
	Team Card			
☐ 337	Jesus Alou	1.00	.40	.10
☐ 338	Gene Tenace	1.75	.70	.17
☐ 339	Wayne Simpson	1.00	.40	.10
☐ 340	Rico Petrocelli	1.25	.50	.12
☐ 341	Steve Garvey	70.00	32.00	10.50
☐ 342	Frank Tepedino	1.00	.40	.10
☐ 343	Pirates Rookies	1.00	.40	.10
	Ed Acosta			
	Milt May			
☐ 344	Ellie Rodriguez	1.00	.40	.10
☐ 345	Joel Horlen	1.00	.40	.10
☐ 346	Lum Harris MG	1.00	.40	.10
☐ 347	Ted Uhlaender	1.00	.40	.10

#	Player			
☐ 348	Fred Norman	1.00	.40	.10
☐ 349	Rich Reese	1.00	.40	.10
☐ 350	Billy Williams	6.00	2.50	.60
☐ 351	Jim Shellenback	1.00	.40	.10
☐ 352	Denny Doyle	1.00	.40	.10
☐ 353	Carl Taylor	1.00	.40	.10
☐ 354	Don McMahon	1.00	.40	.10
☐ 355	Bud Harrelson	1.25	.50	.12
☐ 356	Bob Locker	1.00	.40	.10
☐ 357	Cincinnati Reds Team Card	2.00	.80	.20
☐ 358	Danny Cater	1.00	.40	.10
☐ 359	Ron Reed	1.00	.40	.10
☐ 360	Jim Fregosi	1.25	.50	.12
☐ 361	Don Sutton	6.50	2.75	.65
☐ 362	Orioles Rookies Mike Adamson Roger Freed	1.00	.40	.10
☐ 363	Mike Nagy	1.00	.40	.10
☐ 364	Tommy Dean	1.00	.40	.10
☐ 365	Bob Johnson	1.00	.40	.10
☐ 366	Ron Stone	1.00	.40	.10
☐ 367	Dalton Jones	1.00	.40	.10
☐ 368	Bob Veale	1.00	.40	.10
☐ 369	Checklist 4	4.50	.50	.10
☐ 370	Joe Torre	3.50	1.50	.35
☐ 371	Jack Hiatt	1.00	.40	.10
☐ 372	Lew Krausse	1.00	.40	.10
☐ 373	Tom McCraw	1.00	.40	.10
☐ 374	Clete Boyer	1.25	.50	.12
☐ 375	Steve Hargan	1.00	.40	.10
☐ 376	Expos Rookies Clyde Mashore Ernie McAnally	1.00	.40	.10
☐ 377	Greg Garrett	1.00	.40	.10
☐ 378	Tito Fuentes	1.00	.40	.10
☐ 379	Wayne Granger	1.00	.40	.10
☐ 380	Ted Williams MG	6.50	2.75	.65
☐ 381	Fred Gladding	1.00	.40	.10
☐ 382	Jake Gibbs	1.00	.40	.10
☐ 383	Rod Gaspar	1.00	.40	.10
☐ 384	Rollie Fingers	12.50	5.50	1.65
☐ 385	Maury Wills	2.50	1.00	.25
☐ 386	Boston Red Sox Team Card	2.00	.80	.20
☐ 387	Ron Herbel	1.00	.40	.10
☐ 388	Al Oliver	2.50	1.00	.25
☐ 389	Ed Brinkman	1.00	.40	.10
☐ 390	Glenn Beckert	1.25	.50	.12
☐ 391	Twins Rookies Steve Brye Cotton Nash	1.25	.50	.12
☐ 392	Grant Jackson	1.00	.40	.10
☐ 393	Merv Rettenmund	1.00	.40	.10
☐ 394	Clay Carroll	1.60	.65	.16
☐ 395	Roy White	2.00	.80	.20
☐ 396	Dick Schofield	1.60	.65	.16
☐ 397	Alvin Dark MG	2.00	.80	.20
☐ 398	Howie Reed	1.60	.65	.16
☐ 399	Jim French	1.60	.65	.16
☐ 400	Hank Aaron	45.00	20.00	6.75
☐ 401	Tom Murphy	1.60	.65	.16
☐ 402	Los Angeles Dodgers Team Card	3.25	1.35	.32
☐ 403	Joe Coleman	1.60	.65	.16
☐ 404	Astros Rookies Buddy Harris Roger Metzger	1.60	.65	.16
☐ 405	Leo Cardenas	1.60	.65	.16
☐ 406	Ray Sadecki	1.60	.65	.16
☐ 407	Joe Rudi	2.00	.80	.20
☐ 408	Rafael Robles	1.60	.65	.16
☐ 409	Don Pavletich	1.60	.65	.16
☐ 410	Ken Holtzman	2.00	.80	.20
☐ 411	George Spriggs	1.60	.65	.16
☐ 412	Jerry Johnson	1.60	.65	.16
☐ 413	Pat Kelly	1.60	.65	.16
☐ 414	Woodie Fryman	1.60	.65	.16
☐ 415	Mike Hegan	1.60	.65	.16
☐ 416	Gene Alley	1.60	.65	.16
☐ 417	Dick Hall	1.60	.65	.16
☐ 418	Adolfo Phillips	1.60	.65	.16
☐ 419	Ron Hansen	1.60	.65	.16
☐ 420	Jim Merritt	1.60	.65	.16
☐ 421	John Stephenson	1.60	.65	.16
☐ 422	Frank Bertaina	1.60	.65	.16
☐ 423	Tigers Rookies Dennis Saunders Tim Marting	1.60	.65	.16
☐ 424	R. Rodriguez	1.60	.65	.16
☐ 425	Doug Rader	2.00	.80	.20
☐ 426	Chris Cannizzaro	1.60	.65	.16
☐ 427	Bernie Allen	1.60	.65	.16
☐ 428	Jim McAndrew	1.60	.65	.16
☐ 429	Chuck Hinton	1.60	.65	.16
☐ 430	Wes Parker	2.00	.80	.20
☐ 431	Tom Burgmeier	1.60	.65	.16
☐ 432	Bob Didier	1.60	.65	.16
☐ 433	Skip Lockwood	1.60	.65	.16
☐ 434	Gary Sutherland	1.60	.65	.16
☐ 435	Jose Cardenal	1.60	.65	.16
☐ 436	Wilbur Wood	2.00	.80	.20
☐ 437	Danny Murtaugh MG	1.60	.65	.16
☐ 438	Mike McCormick	2.00	.80	.20
☐ 439	Phillies Rookies Greg Luzinski Scott Reid	2.50	1.00	.25
☐ 440	Bert Campaneris	2.00	.80	.20
☐ 441	Milt Pappas	2.00	.80	.20
☐ 442	California Angels Team Card	3.25	1.35	.32
☐ 443	Rich Robertson	1.60	.65	.16
☐ 444	Jimmie Price	1.60	.65	.16
☐ 445	Art Shamsky	1.60	.65	.16
☐ 446	Bobby Bolin	1.60	.65	.16
☐ 447	Cesar Geronimo	1.60	.65	.16
☐ 448	Dave Roberts	1.60	.65	.16
☐ 449	Brant Alyea	1.60	.65	.16
☐ 450	Bob Gibson	14.00	6.25	2.00
☐ 451	Joe Keough	1.60	.65	.16
☐ 452	John Boccabella	1.60	.65	.16
☐ 453	Terry Crowley	1.60	.65	.16
☐ 454	Mike Paul	1.60	.65	.16
☐ 455	Don Kessinger	2.00	.80	.20
☐ 456	Bob Meyer	1.60	.65	.16
☐ 457	Willie Smith	1.60	.65	.16
☐ 458	White Sox Rookies Ron Lolich Dave Lemonds	1.60	.65	.16
☐ 459	Jim Lefebvre	2.00	.80	.20
☐ 460	Fritz Peterson	1.60	.65	.16
☐ 461	Jim Ray Hart	2.00	.80	.20
☐ 462	Washington Senators Team Card	3.25	1.35	.32
☐ 463	Tom Kelley	1.60	.65	.16
☐ 464	Aurelio Rodriguez	1.60	.65	.16
☐ 465	Tim McCarver	2.50	1.00	.25
☐ 466	Ken Berry	1.60	.65	.16
☐ 467	Al Santorini	1.60	.65	.16
☐ 468	Frank Fernandez	1.60	.65	.16
☐ 469	Bob Aspromonte	1.60	.65	.16
☐ 470	Bob Oliver	1.60	.65	.16
☐ 471	Tom Griffin	1.60	.65	.16
☐ 472	Ken Rudolph	1.60	.65	.16
☐ 473	Gary Wagner	1.60	.65	.16
☐ 474	Jim Fairey	1.60	.65	.16
☐ 475	Ron Perranoski	1.60	.65	.16
☐ 476	Dal Maxvill	1.60	.65	.16
☐ 477	Earl Weaver MG	2.25	.90	.22
☐ 478	Bernie Carbo	1.60	.65	.16
☐ 479	Dennis Higgins	1.60	.65	.16
☐ 480	Manny Sanguillen	2.00	.80	.20
☐ 481	Daryl Patterson	1.60	.65	.16
☐ 482	San Diego Padres Team Card	3.50	1.50	.35
☐ 483	Gene Michael	2.00	.80	.20
☐ 484	Don Wilson	1.60	.65	.16
☐ 485	Ken McMullen	1.60	.65	.16
☐ 486	Steve Huntz	1.60	.65	.16
☐ 487	Paul Schaal	1.60	.65	.16
☐ 488	Jerry Stephenson	1.60	.65	.16
☐ 489	Luis Alvarado	1.60	.65	.16
☐ 490	Deron Johnson	1.60	.65	.16
☐ 491	Jim Hardin	1.60	.65	.16
☐ 492	Ken Boswell	1.60	.65	.16
☐ 493	Dave May	1.60	.65	.16
☐ 494	Braves Rookies Ralph Garr Rick Kester	2.25	.90	.22
☐ 495	Felipe Alou	2.00	.80	.20
☐ 496	Woody Woodward	2.00	.80	.20
☐ 497	Horacio Pina	1.60	.65	.16
☐ 498	John Kennedy	1.60	.65	.16
☐ 499	Checklist 5	4.50	.50	.10
☐ 500	Jim Perry	2.00	.80	.20
☐ 501	Andy Etchebarren	1.60	.65	.16
☐ 502	Chicago Cubs Team Card	3.25	1.35	.32
☐ 503	Gates Brown	2.00	.80	.20
☐ 504	Ken Wright	1.60	.65	.16
☐ 505	Ollie Brown	1.60	.65	.16
☐ 506	Bobby Knoop	1.60	.65	.16
☐ 507	George Stone	1.60	.65	.16
☐ 508	Roger Repoz	1.60	.65	.16
☐ 509	Jim Grant	1.60	.65	.16
☐ 510	Ken Harrelson	2.00	.80	.20
☐ 511	Chris Short	1.60	.65	.16
☐ 512	Red Sox Rookies	1.60	.65	.16

	Dick Mills			
	Mike Garman			
☐ 513	Nolan Ryan	190.00	80.00	16.00
☐ 514	Ron Woods	1.60	.65	.16
☐ 515	Carl Morton	1.60	.65	.16
☐ 516	Ted Kubiak	1.60	.65	.16
☐ 517	Charlie Fox MG	1.60	.65	.16
☐ 518	Joe Grzenda	1.60	.65	.16
☐ 519	Willie Crawford	1.60	.65	.16
☐ 520	Tommy John	4.00	1.75	.40
☐ 521	Leron Lee	1.60	.65	.16
☐ 522	Minnesota Twins	3.25	1.35	.32
	Team Card			
☐ 523	John Odom	1.60	.65	.16
☐ 524	Mickey Stanley	4.00	1.75	.40
☐ 525	Ernie Banks	33.00	15.00	5.00
☐ 526	Ray Jarvis	3.50	1.50	.35
☐ 527	Cleon Jones	3.50	1.50	.35
☐ 528	Wally Bunker	3.50	1.50	.35
☐ 529	NL Rookie Infielders	4.50	2.00	.45
	Enzo Hernandez			
	Bill Buckner			
	Marty Perez			
☐ 530	Carl Yastrzemski	40.00	18.00	6.00
☐ 531	Mike Torrez	3.50	1.50	.35
☐ 532	Bill Rigney MG	3.50	1.50	.35
☐ 533	Mike Ryan	3.50	1.50	.35
☐ 534	Luke Walker	3.50	1.50	.35
☐ 535	Curt Flood	4.50	2.00	.45
☐ 536	Claude Raymond	3.50	1.50	.35
☐ 537	Tom Egan	3.50	1.50	.35
☐ 538	Angel Bravo	3.50	1.50	.35
☐ 539	Larry Brown	3.50	1.50	.35
☐ 540	Larry Dierker	3.50	1.50	.35
☐ 541	Bob Burda	3.50	1.50	.35
☐ 542	Bob Miller	3.50	1.50	.35
☐ 543	New York Yankees	7.00	3.00	.70
	Team Card			
☐ 544	Vida Blue	5.00	2.25	.50
☐ 545	Dick Dietz	3.50	1.50	.35
☐ 546	John Matias	3.50	1.50	.35
☐ 547	Pat Dobson	3.50	1.50	.35
☐ 548	Don Mason	3.50	1.50	.35
☐ 549	Jim Brewer	3.50	1.50	.35
☐ 550	Harmon Killebrew	22.00	9.50	3.15
☐ 551	Frank Linzy	3.50	1.50	.35
☐ 552	Buddy Bradford	3.50	1.50	.35
☐ 553	Kevin Collins	3.50	1.50	.35
☐ 554	Lowell Palmer	3.50	1.50	.35
☐ 555	Walt Williams	3.50	1.50	.35
☐ 556	Jim McGlothlin	3.50	1.50	.35
☐ 557	Tom Satriano	3.50	1.50	.35
☐ 558	Hector Torres	3.50	1.50	.35
☐ 559	AL Rookie Pitchers	3.50	1.50	.35
	Terry Cox			
	Bill Gogolewski			
	Gary Jones			
☐ 560	Rusty Staub	4.50	2.00	.45
☐ 561	Syd O'Brien	3.50	1.50	.35
☐ 562	Dave Giusti	3.50	1.50	.35
☐ 563	San Francisco Giants	7.00	3.00	.70
	Team Card			
☐ 564	Al Fitzmorris	3.50	1.50	.35
☐ 565	Jim Wynn	4.50	2.00	.45
☐ 566	Tim Cullen	3.50	1.50	.35
☐ 567	Walt Alston MG	5.00	2.25	.50
☐ 568	Sal Campisi	3.50	1.50	.35
☐ 569	Ivan Murrell	3.50	1.50	.35
☐ 570	Jim Palmer	33.00	15.00	5.00
☐ 571	Ted Sizemore	3.50	1.50	.35
☐ 572	Jerry Kenney	3.50	1.50	.35
☐ 573	Ed Kranepool	4.00	1.75	.40
☐ 574	Jim Bunning	5.00	2.25	.50
☐ 575	Bill Freehan	4.50	2.00	.45
☐ 576	Cubs Rookies	3.50	1.50	.35
	Adrian Garrett			
	Brock Davis			
	Garry Jestadt			
☐ 577	Jim Lonborg	4.00	1.75	.40
☐ 578	Ron Hunt	3.50	1.50	.35
☐ 579	Marty Pattin	3.50	1.50	.35
☐ 580	Tony Perez	11.00	5.00	1.35
☐ 581	Roger Nelson	3.50	1.50	.35
☐ 582	Dave Cash	3.50	1.50	.35
☐ 583	Ron Cook	3.50	1.50	.35
☐ 584	Cleveland Indians	7.00	3.00	.70
	Team Card			
☐ 585	Willie Davis	4.00	1.75	.40
☐ 586	Dick Woodson	3.50	1.50	.35
☐ 587	Sonny Jackson	3.50	1.50	.35
☐ 588	Tom Bradley	3.50	1.50	.35
☐ 589	Bob Barton	3.50	1.50	.35
☐ 590	Alex Johnson	3.50	1.50	.35
☐ 591	Jackie Brown	3.50	1.50	.35
☐ 592	Randy Hundley	3.50	1.50	.35
☐ 593	Jack Aker	3.50	1.50	.35
☐ 594	Cards Rookies	5.00	2.25	.50
	Bob Chlupsa			
	Bob Stinson			
	Al Hrabosky			
☐ 595	Dave Johnson	4.00	1.75	.40
☐ 596	Mike Jorgensen	3.50	1.50	.35
☐ 597	Ken Suarez	3.50	1.50	.35
☐ 598	Rick Wise	4.00	1.75	.40
☐ 599	Norm Cash	4.50	2.00	.45
☐ 600	Willie Mays	80.00	36.00	12.00
☐ 601	Ken Tatum	3.50	1.50	.35
☐ 602	Marty Martinez	3.50	1.50	.35
☐ 603	Pittsburgh Pirates	7.00	3.00	.70
	Team Card			
☐ 604	John Gelnar	3.50	1.50	.35
☐ 605	Orlando Cepeda	5.00	2.25	.50
☐ 606	Chuck Taylor	3.50	1.50	.35
☐ 607	Paul Ratliff	3.50	1.50	.35
☐ 608	Mike Wegener	3.50	1.50	.35
☐ 609	Leo Durocher MG	4.50	2.00	.45
☐ 610	Amos Otis	4.00	1.75	.40
☐ 611	Tom Phoebus	3.50	1.50	.35
☐ 612	Indians Rookies	3.50	1.50	.35
	Lou Camilli			
	Ted Ford			
	Steve Mingori			
☐ 613	Pedro Borbon	3.50	1.50	.35
☐ 614	Billy Cowan	3.50	1.50	.35
☐ 615	Mel Stottlemyre	4.00	1.75	.40
☐ 616	Larry Hisle	3.50	1.50	.35
☐ 617	Clay Dalrymple	3.50	1.50	.35
☐ 618	Tug McGraw	4.50	2.00	.45
☐ 619A	Checklist 6 COR	4.50	.50	.10
	(copyright on back)			
☐ 619B	Checklist 6 ERR	7.50	.75	.15
	(no copyright)			
☐ 620	Frank Howard	4.50	2.00	.45
☐ 621	Ron Bryant	3.50	1.50	.35
☐ 622	Joe Lahoud	3.50	1.50	.35
☐ 623	Pat Jarvis	3.50	1.50	.35
☐ 624	Oakland Athletics	7.50	3.25	.75
	Team Card			
☐ 625	Lou Brock	28.00	12.50	4.00
☐ 626	Freddie Patek	4.00	1.75	.40
☐ 627	Steve Hamilton	3.50	1.50	.35
☐ 628	John Bateman	3.50	1.50	.35
☐ 629	John Hiller	4.00	1.75	.40
☐ 630	Roberto Clemente	60.00	27.00	9.00
☐ 631	Eddie Fisher	3.50	1.50	.35
☐ 632	Darrel Chaney	3.50	1.50	.35
☐ 633	AL Rookie Outfielders	3.50	1.50	.35
	Bobby Brooks			
	Pete Koegel			
	Scott Northey			
☐ 634	Phil Regan	3.50	1.50	.35
☐ 635	Bobby Murcer	5.00	2.25	.50
☐ 636	Denny Lemaster	3.50	1.50	.35
☐ 637	Dave Bristol MG	3.50	1.50	.35
☐ 638	Stan Williams	3.50	1.50	.35
☐ 639	Tom Haller	3.50	1.50	.35
☐ 640	Frank Robinson	38.00	17.00	5.00
☐ 641	New York Mets	7.50	3.25	.75
	Team Card			
☐ 642	Jim Roland	3.50	1.50	.35
☐ 643	Rick Reichardt	3.50	1.50	.35
☐ 644	Jim Stewart SP	7.50	3.25	.75
☐ 645	Jim Maloney SP	7.50	3.25	.75
☐ 646	Bobby Floyd SP	7.50	3.25	.75
☐ 647	Juan Pizarro	5.25	2.25	.50
☐ 648	Mets Rookies SP	10.00	4.50	1.25
	Rich Folkers			
	Ted Martinez			
	John Matlack			
☐ 649	Sparky Lyle SP	10.00	4.50	1.25
☐ 650	Rich Allen SP	18.00	7.50	2.50
☐ 651	Jerry Robertson SP	7.50	3.25	.75
☐ 652	Atlanta Braves	10.00	4.50	1.25
	Team Card			
☐ 653	Russ Snyder SP	7.50	3.25	.75
☐ 654	Don Shaw SP	7.50	3.25	.75
☐ 655	Mike Epstein SP	7.50	3.25	.75
☐ 656	Gerry Nyman SP	7.50	3.25	.75
☐ 657	Jose Azcue	5.25	2.25	.50
☐ 658	Paul Lindblad SP	7.50	3.25	.75
☐ 659	Byron Browne SP	7.50	3.25	.75
☐ 660	Ray Culp	5.00	2.25	.50
☐ 661	Chuck Tanner MG SP	7.50	3.25	.75
☐ 662	Mike Hedlund SP	7.50	3.25	.75
☐ 663	Marv Staehle	5.25	2.25	.50
☐ 664	Rookie Pitchers SP	7.50	3.25	.75
	Archie Reynolds			
	Bob Reynolds			

Ken Reynolds

☐ 665	Ron Swoboda SP	8.50	3.75	.85
☐ 666	Gene Brabender SP	7.50	3.25	.75
☐ 667	Pete Ward	5.25	2.25	.50
☐ 668	Gary Neibauer	5.25	2.25	.50
☐ 669	Ike Brown SP	7.50	3.25	.75
☐ 670	Bill Hands	5.25	2.25	.50
☐ 671	Bill Voss SP	7.50	3.25	.75
☐ 672	Ed Crosby SP	7.50	3.25	.75
☐ 673	Gerry Janeski SP	7.50	3.25	.75
☐ 674	Montreal Expos	10.00	4.50	1.25
	Team Card			
☐ 675	Dave Boswell	5.25	2.25	.50
☐ 676	Tommie Reynolds	5.25	2.25	.50
☐ 677	Jack DiLauro SP	7.50	3.25	.75
☐ 678	George Thomas	5.25	2.25	.50
☐ 679	Don O'Riley	5.25	2.25	.50
☐ 680	Don Mincher SP	7.50	3.25	.75
☐ 681	Bill Butler	5.25	2.25	.50
☐ 682	Terry Harmon	5.25	2.25	.50
☐ 683	Bill Burbach SP	7.50	3.25	.75
☐ 684	Curt Motton	5.25	2.25	.50
☐ 685	Moe Drabowsky	5.25	2.25	.50
☐ 686	Chico Ruiz SP	7.50	3.25	.75
☐ 687	Ron Taylor SP	7.50	3.25	.75
☐ 688	Sparky Anderson MG SP	15.00	6.50	2.15
☐ 689	Frank Baker	5.25	2.25	.50
☐ 690	Bob Moose	5.00	2.25	.50
☐ 691	Bobby Heise	5.25	2.25	.50
☐ 692	AL Rookie Pitchers SP	7.50	3.25	.75
	Hal Haydel			
	Rogelio Moret			
	Wayne Twitchell			
☐ 693	Jose Pena SP	7.50	3.25	.75
☐ 694	Rick Renick SP	7.50	3.25	.75
☐ 695	Joe Niekro	6.50	2.75	.65
☐ 696	Jerry Morales	5.25	2.25	.50
☐ 697	Rickey Clark SP	7.50	3.25	.75
☐ 698	Milwaukee Brewers SP	15.00	6.50	2.15
	Team Card			
☐ 699	Jim Britton	5.25	2.25	.50
☐ 700	Boog Powell SP	15.00	6.50	2.15
☐ 701	Bob Garibaldi	5.25	2.25	.50
☐ 702	Milt Ramirez	5.25	2.25	.50
☐ 703	Mike Kekich	5.25	2.25	.50
☐ 704	J.C. Martin SP	7.50	3.25	.75
☐ 705	Dick Selma SP	7.50	3.25	.75
☐ 706	Joe Foy SP	7.50	3.25	.75
☐ 707	Fred Lasher	5.25	2.25	.50
☐ 708	Russ Nagelson SP	7.50	3.25	.75
☐ 709	Rookie Outfielders SP	38.00	17.00	5.00
	Dusty Baker			
	Don Baylor			
	Tom Paciorek			
☐ 710	Sonny Siebert	5.25	2.25	.50
☐ 711	Larry Stahl SP	7.50	3.25	.75
☐ 712	Jose Martinez	5.25	2.25	.50
☐ 713	Mike Marshall SP	7.50	3.25	.75
☐ 714	Dick Williams MG SP	8.50	3.75	.85
☐ 715	Horace Clarke SP	7.50	3.25	.75
☐ 716	Dave Leonhard	5.25	2.25	.50
☐ 717	Tommie Aaron SP	7.50	3.25	.75
☐ 718	Billy Wynne	5.25	2.25	.50
☐ 719	Jerry May SP	7.50	3.25	.75
☐ 720	Matty Alou	6.00	2.50	.60
☐ 721	John Morris	5.25	2.25	.50
☐ 722	Houston Astros SP	15.00	6.50	2.15
	Team Card			
☐ 723	Vicente Romo SP	7.50	3.25	.75
☐ 724	Tom Tischinski SP	7.50	3.25	.75
☐ 725	Gary Gentry SP	7.50	3.25	.75
☐ 726	Paul Popovich	5.25	2.25	.50
☐ 727	Ray Lamb SP	7.50	3.25	.75
☐ 728	NL Rookie Outfielders	5.25	2.25	.50
	Wayne Redmond			
	Keith Lampard			
	Bernie Williams			
☐ 729	Dick Billings	5.25	2.25	.50
☐ 730	Jim Rooker	5.25	2.25	.50
☐ 731	Jim Qualls SP	7.50	3.25	.75
☐ 732	Bob Reed	5.25	2.25	.50
☐ 733	Lee Maye SP	7.50	3.25	.75
☐ 734	Rob Gardner SP	7.50	3.25	.75
☐ 735	Mike Shannon SP	8.50	3.75	.85
☐ 736	Mel Queen SP	7.50	3.25	.75
☐ 737	Preston Gomez MG SP	7.50	3.25	.75
☐ 738	Russ Gibson SP	7.50	3.25	.75
☐ 739	Barry Lersch SP	7.50	3.25	.75
☐ 740	Luis Aparicio SP	18.00	7.50	2.50
☐ 741	Skip Guinn	5.25	2.25	.50
☐ 742	Kansas City Royals	10.00	4.50	1.25
	Team Card			
☐ 743	John O'Donoghue SP	7.50	3.25	.75
☐ 744	Chuck Manuel SP	7.50	3.25	.75

☐ 745	Sandy Alomar SP	7.50	3.25	.75
☐ 746	Andy Kosco	5.25	2.25	.50
☐ 747	NL Rookie Pitchers	5.25	2.25	.50
	Al Severinsen			
	Scipio Spinks			
	Balor Moore			
☐ 748	John Purdin SP	7.50	3.25	.75
☐ 749	Ken Szotkiewicz	5.25	2.25	.50
☐ 750	Denny McLain SP	12.50	5.50	1.65
☐ 751	Al Weis SP	12.50	5.50	1.65
☐ 752	Dick Drago	7.50	3.00	.60

1972 Topps

The cards in this 787-card set measure 2 1/2" by 3 1/2". The 1972 Topps set contained the most cards ever for a Topps set to that point in time. Features appearing for the first time were "Boyhood Photos" (KP: 341-348 and 491-498), Awards and Trophy cards (621-626), "In Action" (distributed throughout the set), and "Traded Cards" (TR: 751-757). Other subsets included League Leaders (85-96), Playoffs cards (221-222), and World Series cards (223-230). The curved lines of the color picture are a departure from the rectangular designs of other years. There is a series of intermediate scarcity (526-656) and the usual high numbers (657-787). The key rookie card in this set is Carlton Fisk.

	NRMT	VG-E	GOOD
COMPLETE SET (787)	2000.00	800.00	200.00
COMMON PLAYER (1-132)	.50	.20	.05
COMMON PLAYER (133-263)	.70	.30	.07
COMMON PLAYER (264-394)	.85	.35	.08
COMMON PLAYER (395-525)	1.25	.50	.12
COMMON PLAYER (526-656)	2.75	1.10	.27
COMMON PLAYER (657-787)	5.00	2.25	.50
☐ 1 Pittsburgh Pirates	7.00	1.25	.25
Team Card			
☐ 2 Ray Culp	.50	.20	.05
☐ 3 Bob Tolan	.50	.20	.05
☐ 4 Checklist	3.50	.35	.07
☐ 5 John Bateman	.50	.20	.05
☐ 6 Fred Scherman	.50	.20	.05
☐ 7 Enzo Hernandez	.50	.20	.05
☐ 8 Ron Swoboda	.75	.30	.07
☐ 9 Stan Williams	.50	.20	.05
☐ 10 Amos Otis	.75	.30	.07
☐ 11 Bobby Valentine	1.00	.40	.10
☐ 12 Jose Cardenal	.50	.20	.05
☐ 13 Joe Grzenda	.50	.20	.05
☐ 14 Phillies Rookies	.50	.20	.05
Pete Koegel			
Mike Anderson			
Wayne Twitchell			
☐ 15 Walt Williams	.50	.20	.05
☐ 16 Mike Jorgensen	.50	.20	.05
☐ 17 Dave Duncan	.50	.20	.05
☐ 18A Juan Pizarro	.50	.20	.05
(yellow underline			
C and S of Cubs)			
☐ 18B Juan Pizarro	5.00	2.25	.50
(green underline			

C and S of Cubs)				
☐ 19 Billy Cowan	.50	.20	.05	
☐ 20 Don Wilson	.50	.20	.05	
☐ 21 Atlanta Braves	1.25	.50	.12	
Team Card				
☐ 22 Rob Gardner	.50	.20	.05	
☐ 23 Ted Kubiak	.50	.20	.05	
☐ 24 Ted Ford	.50	.20	.05	
☐ 25 Bill Singer	.75	.30	.07	
☐ 26 Andy Etchebarren	.50	.20	.05	
☐ 27 Bob Johnson	.50	.20	.05	
☐ 28 Twins Rookies	.50	.20	.05	
Bob Gebhard				
Steve Brye				
Hal Haydel				
☐ 29A Bill Bonham	.50	.20	.05	
(yellow underline				
C and S of Cubs)				
☐ 29B Bill Bonham	5.00	2.25	.50	
(green underline				
C and S of Cubs)				
☐ 30 Rico Petrocelli	.75	.30	.07	
☐ 31 Cleon Jones	.50	.20	.05	
☐ 32 Jones In Action	.50	.20	.05	
☐ 33 Billy Martin MG	3.25	1.35	.32	
☐ 34 Martin In Action	1.50	.60	.15	
☐ 35 Jerry Johnson	.50	.20	.05	
☐ 36 Johnson In Action	.50	.20	.05	
☐ 37 Carl Yastrzemski	15.00	6.50	2.15	
☐ 38 Yastrzemski In Action	7.50	3.25	.75	
☐ 39 Bob Barton	.50	.20	.05	
☐ 40 Barton In Action	.50	.20	.05	
☐ 41 Tommy Davis	.75	.30	.07	
☐ 42 Davis In Action	.50	.20	.05	
☐ 43 Rick Wise	.50	.20	.05	
☐ 44 Wise In Action	.50	.20	.05	
☐ 45A Glenn Beckert	.50	.20	.05	
(yellow underline				
C and S of Cubs)				
☐ 45B Glenn Beckert	5.00	2.25	.50	
(green underline				
C and S of Cubs)				
☐ 46 Beckert In Action	.50	.20	.05	
☐ 47 John Ellis	.50	.20	.05	
☐ 48 Ellis In Action	.50	.20	.05	
☐ 49 Willie Mays	25.00	11.00	3.50	
☐ 50 Mays In Action	12.50	5.50	1.65	
☐ 51 Harmon Killebrew	5.50	2.50	.55	
☐ 52 Killebrew In Action	2.50	1.00	.25	
☐ 53 Bud Harrelson	.75	.30	.07	
☐ 54 Harrelson In Action	.50	.20	.05	
☐ 55 Clyde Wright	.50	.20	.05	
☐ 56 Rich Chiles	.50	.20	.05	
☐ 57 Bob Oliver	.50	.20	.05	
☐ 58 Ernie McAnally	.50	.20	.05	
☐ 59 Fred Stanley	.50	.20	.05	
☐ 60 Manny Sanguillen	.75	.30	.07	
☐ 61 Cubs Rookies	1.00	.40	.10	
Burt Hooton				
Gene Hiser				
Earl Stephenson				
☐ 62 Angel Mangual	.50	.20	.05	
☐ 63 Duke Sims	.50	.20	.05	
☐ 64 Pete Broberg	.50	.20	.05	
☐ 65 Cesar Cedeno	1.00	.40	.10	
☐ 66 Ray Corbin	.50	.20	.05	
☐ 67 Red Schoendienst MG	1.25	.50	.12	
☐ 68 Jim York	.50	.20	.05	
☐ 69 Roger Freed	.50	.20	.05	
☐ 70 Mike Cuellar	.50	.20	.05	
☐ 71 California Angels	1.25	.50	.12	
Team Card				
☐ 72 Bruce Kison	1.00	.40	.10	
☐ 73 Steve Huntz	.50	.20	.05	
☐ 74 Cecil Upshaw	.50	.20	.05	
☐ 75 Bert Campaneris	.75	.30	.07	
☐ 76 Don Carrithers	.50	.20	.05	
☐ 77 Ron Theobald	.50	.20	.05	
☐ 78 Steve Arlin	.50	.20	.05	
☐ 79 Red Sox Rookies	125.00	57.50	18.75	
Mike Garman				
Cecil Cooper				
Carlton Fisk				
☐ 80 Tony Perez	3.50	1.50	.35	
☐ 81 Mike Hedlund	.50	.20	.05	
☐ 82 Ron Woods	.50	.20	.05	
☐ 83 Dalton Jones	.50	.20	.05	
☐ 84 Vince Colbert	.50	.20	.05	
☐ 85 NL Batting Leaders	1.25	.50	.12	
Joe Torre				
Ralph Garr				
Glenn Beckert				
☐ 86 AL Batting Leaders	1.25	.50	.12	
Tony Oliva				
Bobby Murcer				

Merv Rettenmund				
☐ 87 NL RBI Leaders	2.50	1.00	.25	
Joe Torre				
Willie Stargell				
Hank Aaron				
☐ 88 AL RBI Leaders	2.25	.90	.22	
Harmon Killebrew				
Frank Robinson				
Reggie Smith				
☐ 89 NL Home Run Leaders	2.00	.80	.20	
Willie Stargell				
Hank Aaron				
Lee May				
☐ 90 AL Home Run Leaders	1.75	.70	.17	
Bill Melton				
Norm Cash				
Reggie Jackson				
☐ 91 NL ERA Leaders UER	1.75	.70	.17	
Tom Seaver				
Dave Roberts				
(photo actually				
Danny Coombs)				
Don Wilson				
☐ 92 AL ERA Leaders	1.25	.50	.12	
Vida Blue				
Wilbur Wood				
Jim Palmer				
☐ 93 NL Pitching Leaders	2.00	.80	.20	
Fergie Jenkins				
Steve Carlton				
Al Downing				
Tom Seaver				
☐ 94 AL Pitching Leaders	1.25	.50	.12	
Mickey Lolich				
Vida Blue				
Wilbur Wood				
☐ 95 NL Strikeout Leaders	1.75	.70	.17	
Tom Seaver				
Fergie Jenkins				
Bill Stoneman				
☐ 96 AL Strikeout Leaders	1.25	.50	.12	
Mickey Lolich				
Vida Blue				
Joe Coleman				
☐ 97 Tom Kelley	.50	.20	.05	
☐ 98 Chuck Tanner MG	.50	.20	.05	
☐ 99 Ross Grimsley	.50	.20	.05	
☐ 100 Frank Robinson	5.50	2.50	.55	
☐ 101 Astros Rookies	1.75	.70	.17	
Bill Greif				
J.R. Richard				
Ray Busse				
☐ 102 Lloyd Allen	.50	.20	.05	
☐ 103 Checklist 2	3.50	.35	.07	
☐ 104 Toby Harrah	1.50	.60	.15	
☐ 105 Gary Gentry	.50	.20	.05	
☐ 106 Milwaukee Brewers	1.25	.50	.12	
Team Card				
☐ 107 Jose Cruz	1.75	.70	.17	
☐ 108 Gary Waslewski	.50	.20	.05	
☐ 109 Jerry May	.50	.20	.05	
☐ 110 Ron Hunt	.50	.20	.05	
☐ 111 Jim Grant	.50	.20	.05	
☐ 112 Greg Luzinski	1.00	.40	.10	
☐ 113 Rogelio Moret	.50	.20	.05	
☐ 114 Bill Buckner	2.00	.80	.20	
☐ 115 Jim Fregosi	.75	.30	.07	
☐ 116 Ed Farmer	.50	.20	.05	
☐ 117A Cleo James	.50	.20	.05	
(yellow underline				
C and S of Cubs)				
☐ 117B Cleo James	5.00	2.25	.50	
(green underline				
C and S of Cubs)				
☐ 118 Skip Lockwood	.50	.20	.05	
☐ 119 Marty Perez	.50	.20	.05	
☐ 120 Bill Freehan	1.00	.40	.10	
☐ 121 Ed Sprague	.50	.20	.05	
☐ 122 Larry Biittner	.50	.20	.05	
☐ 123 Ed Acosta	.50	.20	.05	
☐ 124 Yankees Rookies	.50	.20	.05	
Alan Closter				
Rusty Torres				
Roger Hambright				
☐ 125 Dave Cash	.50	.20	.05	
☐ 126 Bart Johnson	.50	.20	.05	
☐ 127 Duffy Dyer	.50	.20	.05	
☐ 128 Eddie Watt	.50	.20	.05	
☐ 129 Charlie Fox MG	.50	.20	.05	
☐ 130 Bob Gibson	5.50	2.50	.55	
☐ 131 Jim Nettles	.50	.20	.05	
☐ 132 Joe Morgan	5.50	2.50	.55	
☐ 133 Joe Keough	.70	.30	.07	
☐ 134 Carl Morton	.70	.30	.07	
☐ 135 Vada Pinson	1.00	.40	.10	

☐ 136	Darrell Chaney	.70	.30	.07
☐ 137	Dick Williams MG	1.00	.40	.10
☐ 138	Mike Kekich	.70	.30	.07
☐ 139	Tim McCarver	1.25	.50	.12
☐ 140	Pat Dobson	.70	.30	.07
☐ 141	Mets Rookies	1.00	.40	.10
	Buzz Capra			
	Leroy Stanton			
	Jon Matlack			
☐ 142	Chris Chambliss	2.50	1.00	.25
☐ 143	Garry Jestadt	.70	.30	.07
☐ 144	Marty Pattin	.70	.30	.07
☐ 145	Don Kessinger	1.00	.40	.10
☐ 146	Steve Kealey	.70	.30	.07
☐ 147	Dave Kingman	6.50	2.75	.65
☐ 148	Dick Billings	.70	.30	.07
☐ 149	Gary Neibauer	.70	.30	.07
☐ 150	Norm Cash	1.25	.50	.12
☐ 151	Jim Brewer	.70	.30	.07
☐ 152	Gene Clines	.70	.30	.07
☐ 153	Rick Auerbach	.70	.30	.07
☐ 154	Ted Simmons	2.50	1.00	.25
☐ 155	Larry Dierker	.70	.30	.07
☐ 156	Minnesota Twins	1.50	.60	.15
	Team Card			
☐ 157	Don Gullett	1.00	.40	.10
☐ 158	Jerry Kenney	.70	.30	.07
☐ 159	John Boccabella	.70	.30	.07
☐ 160	Andy Messersmith	.70	.30	.07
☐ 161	Brock Davis	.70	.30	.07
☐ 162	Brewers Rookies UER	1.00	.40	.10
	Jerry Bell			
	Darrell Porter			
	Bob Reynolds			
	(Porter and Bell			
	photos switched)			
☐ 163	Tug McGraw	1.00	.40	.10
☐ 164	McGraw In Action	.70	.30	.07
☐ 165	Chris Speier	1.00	.40	.10
☐ 166	Speier In Action	.70	.30	.07
☐ 167	Deron Johnson	.70	.30	.07
☐ 168	Johnson In Action	.70	.30	.07
☐ 169	Vida Blue	1.00	.40	.10
☐ 170	Blue In Action	.70	.30	.07
☐ 171	Darrell Evans	1.50	.60	.15
☐ 172	Evans In Action	1.00	.40	.10
☐ 173	Clay Kirby	.70	.30	.07
☐ 174	Kirby In Action	.70	.30	.07
☐ 175	Tom Haller	.70	.30	.07
☐ 176	Haller In Action	.70	.30	.07
☐ 177	Paul Schaal	.70	.30	.07
☐ 178	Schaal In Action	.70	.30	.07
☐ 179	Dock Ellis	.70	.30	.07
☐ 180	Ellis In Action	.70	.30	.07
☐ 181	Ed Kranepool	.70	.30	.07
☐ 182	Kranepool In Action	.70	.30	.07
☐ 183	Bill Melton	.70	.30	.07
☐ 184	Melton In Action	.70	.30	.07
☐ 185	Ron Bryant	.70	.30	.07
☐ 186	Bryant In Action	.70	.30	.07
☐ 187	Gates Brown	.70	.30	.07
☐ 188	Frank Lucchesi MG	.70	.30	.07
☐ 189	Gene Tenace	1.00	.40	.10
☐ 190	Dave Giusti	.70	.30	.07
☐ 191	Jeff Burroughs	1.00	.40	.10
☐ 192	Chicago Cubs	1.50	.60	.15
	Team Card			
☐ 193	Kurt Bevacqua	.70	.30	.07
☐ 194	Fred Norman	.70	.30	.07
☐ 195	Orlando Cepeda	2.25	.90	.22
☐ 196	Mel Queen	.70	.30	.07
☐ 197	Johnny Briggs	.70	.30	.07
☐ 198	Dodgers Rookies	4.00	1.75	.40
	Charlie Hough			
	Bob O'Brien			
	Mike Strahler			
☐ 199	Mike Fiore	.70	.30	.07
☐ 200	Lou Brock	5.50	2.50	.55
☐ 201	Phil Roof	.70	.30	.07
☐ 202	Scipio Spinks	.70	.30	.07
☐ 203	Ron Blomberg	.70	.30	.07
☐ 204	Tommy Helms	.70	.30	.07
☐ 205	Dick Drago	.70	.30	.07
☐ 206	Dal Maxvill	.70	.30	.07
☐ 207	Tom Egan	.70	.30	.07
☐ 208	Milt Pappas	.70	.30	.07
☐ 209	Joe Rudi	1.00	.40	.10
☐ 210	Denny McLain	1.25	.50	.12
☐ 211	Gary Sutherland	.70	.30	.07
☐ 212	Grant Jackson	.70	.30	.07
☐ 213	Angels Rookies	.70	.30	.07
	Billy Parker			
	Art Kusnyer			
	Tom Silverio			
☐ 214	Mike McQueen	.70	.30	.07

☐ 215	Alex Johnson	.70	.30	.07
☐ 216	Joe Niekro	1.00	.40	.10
☐ 217	Roger Metzger	.70	.30	.07
☐ 218	Eddie Kasko MG	.70	.30	.07
☐ 219	Rennie Stennett	1.00	.40	.10
☐ 220	Jim Perry	1.00	.40	.10
☐ 221	NL Playoffs	1.25	.50	.12
	Bucs champs			
☐ 222	AL Playoffs	1.75	.70	.17
	Orioles champs			
	(Brooks Robinson)			
☐ 223	World Series Game 1	1.25	.50	.12
	(McNally pitching)			
☐ 224	World Series Game 2	1.50	.60	.15
	(Dave Johnson and			
	Mark Belanger)			
☐ 225	World Series Game 3	1.25	.50	.12
	(Sanguillen scoring)			
☐ 226	World Series Game 4	2.75	1.10	.27
	(Clemente on 2nd)			
☐ 227	World Series Game 5	1.25	.50	.12
	(Briles pitching)			
☐ 228	World Series Game 6	1.50	.60	.15
	(Frank Robinson and			
	Manny Sanguillen)			
☐ 229	World Series Game 7	1.25	.50	.12
	(Blass pitching)			
☐ 230	World Series Summary	1.25	.50	.12
	(Pirates celebrate)			
☐ 231	Casey Cox	.70	.30	.07
☐ 232	Giants Rookies	.70	.30	.07
	Chris Arnold			
	Jim Barr			
	Dave Rader			
☐ 233	Jay Johnstone	1.00	.40	.10
☐ 234	Ron Taylor	.70	.30	.07
☐ 235	Merv Rettenmund	.70	.30	.07
☐ 236	Jim McGlothlin	.70	.30	.07
☐ 237	New York Yankees	1.50	.60	.15
	Team Card			
☐ 238	Leron Lee	.70	.30	.07
☐ 239	Tom Timmermann	.70	.30	.07
☐ 240	Rich Allen	2.50	1.00	.25
☐ 241	Rollie Fingers	7.00	3.00	.70
☐ 242	Don Mincher	.70	.30	.07
☐ 243	Frank Linzy	.70	.30	.07
☐ 244	Steve Braun	.70	.30	.07
☐ 245	Tommie Agee	.70	.30	.07
☐ 246	Tom Burgmeier	.70	.30	.07
☐ 247	Milt May	.70	.30	.07
☐ 248	Tom Bradley	.70	.30	.07
☐ 249	Harry Walker MG	.70	.30	.07
☐ 250	Boog Powell	1.25	.50	.12
☐ 251	Checklist 3	3.50	.35	.07
☐ 252	Ken Reynolds	.70	.30	.07
☐ 253	Sandy Alomar	.70	.30	.07
☐ 254	Boots Day	.70	.30	.07
☐ 255	Jim Lonborg	1.00	.40	.10
☐ 256	George Foster	2.00	.80	.20
☐ 257	Tigers Rookies	.70	.30	.07
	Jim Foor			
	Tim Hosley			
	Paul Jata			
☐ 258	Randy Hundley	.70	.30	.07
☐ 259	Sparky Lyle	1.00	.40	.10
☐ 260	Ralph Garr	1.00	.40	.10
☐ 261	Steve Mingori	.70	.30	.07
☐ 262	San Diego Padres	1.50	.60	.15
	Team Card			
☐ 263	Felipe Alou	1.00	.40	.10
☐ 264	Tommy John	2.00	.80	.20
☐ 265	Wes Parker	1.00	.40	.10
☐ 266	Bobby Bolin	.85	.35	.08
☐ 267	Dave Concepcion	3.00	1.25	.30
☐ 268	A's Rookies	.85	.35	.08
	Dwain Anderson			
	Chris Floethe			
☐ 269	Don Hahn	.85	.35	.08
☐ 270	Jim Palmer	13.50	6.00	1.85
☐ 271	Ken Rudolph	.85	.35	.08
☐ 272	Mickey Rivers	1.25	.50	.12
☐ 273	Bobby Floyd	.85	.35	.08
☐ 274	Al Severinsen	.85	.35	.08
☐ 275	Cesar Tovar	.85	.35	.08
☐ 276	Gene Mauch MG	.85	.35	.08
☐ 277	Elliott Maddox	.85	.35	.08
☐ 278	Dennis Higgins	.85	.35	.08
☐ 279	Larry Brown	.85	.35	.08
☐ 280	Willie McCovey	6.00	2.50	.60
☐ 281	Bill Parsons	.85	.35	.08
☐ 282	Houston Astros	1.75	.70	.17
	Team Card			
☐ 283	Darrell Brandon	.85	.35	.08
☐ 284	Ike Brown	.85	.35	.08
☐ 285	Gaylord Perry	6.50	2.75	.65

#	Player			
☐ 286	Gene Alley	.85	.35	.08
☐ 287	Jim Hardin	.85	.35	.08
☐ 288	Johnny Jeter	.85	.35	.08
☐ 289	Syd O'Brien	.85	.35	.08
☐ 290	Sonny Siebert	.85	.35	.08
☐ 291	Hal McRae	1.50	.60	.15
☐ 292	McRae In Action	1.00	.40	.10
☐ 293	Dan Frisella	.85	.35	.08
☐ 294	Frisella In Action	.85	.35	.08
☐ 295	Dick Dietz	.85	.35	.08
☐ 296	Dietz In Action	.85	.35	.08
☐ 297	Claude Osteen	.85	.35	.08
☐ 298	Osteen In Action	.85	.35	.08
☐ 299	Hank Aaron	33.00	15.00	5.00
☐ 300	Aaron in Action	15.00	6.50	2.15
☐ 301	George Mitterwald	.85	.35	.08
☐ 302	Mitterwald In Action	.85	.35	.08
☐ 303	Joe Pepitone	1.00	.40	.10
☐ 304	Pepitone In Action	.85	.35	.08
☐ 305	Ken Boswell	.85	.35	.08
☐ 306	Boswell In Action	.85	.35	.08
☐ 307	Steve Renko	.85	.35	.08
☐ 308	Renko In Action	.85	.35	.08
☐ 309	Roberto Clemente	33.00	15.00	5.00
☐ 310	Clemente In Action	15.00	6.50	2.15
☐ 311	Clay Carroll	.85	.35	.08
☐ 312	Carroll In Action	.85	.35	.08
☐ 313	Luis Aparicio	3.00	1.25	.30
☐ 314	Aparicio In Action	1.50	.60	.15
☐ 315	Paul Splittorff	.85	.35	.08
☐ 316	Cardinals Rookies	1.25	.50	.12
	Jim Bibby			
	Jorge Roque			
	Santiago Guzman			
☐ 317	Rich Hand	.85	.35	.08
☐ 318	Sonny Jackson	.85	.35	.08
☐ 319	Aurelio Rodriguez	.85	.35	.08
☐ 320	Steve Blass	.85	.35	.08
☐ 321	Joe Lahoud	.85	.35	.08
☐ 322	Jose Pena	.85	.35	.08
☐ 323	Earl Weaver MG	1.25	.50	.12
☐ 324	Mike Ryan	.85	.35	.08
☐ 325	Mel Stottlemyre	1.25	.50	.12
☐ 326	Pat Kelly	.85	.35	.08
☐ 327	Steve Stone	1.25	.50	.12
☐ 328	Boston Red Sox	1.75	.70	.17
	Team Card			
☐ 329	Roy Foster	.85	.35	.08
☐ 330	Jim Hunter	4.50	2.00	.45
☐ 331	Stan Swanson	.85	.35	.08
☐ 332	Buck Martinez	.85	.35	.08
☐ 333	Steve Barber	.85	.35	.08
☐ 334	Rangers Rookies	.85	.35	.08
	Bill Fahey			
	Jim Mason			
	Tom Ragland			
☐ 335	Bill Hands	.85	.35	.08
☐ 336	Marty Martinez	.85	.35	.08
☐ 337	Mike Kilkenny	.85	.35	.08
☐ 338	Bob Grich	1.25	.50	.12
☐ 339	Ron Cook	.85	.35	.08
☐ 340	Roy White	1.00	.40	.10
☐ 341	KP: Joe Torre	1.00	.40	.10
☐ 342	KP: Wilbur Wood	.85	.35	.08
☐ 343	KP: Willie Stargell	1.25	.50	.12
☐ 344	KP: Dave McNally	.85	.35	.08
☐ 345	KP: Rick Wise	.85	.35	.08
☐ 346	KP: Jim Fregosi	.85	.35	.08
☐ 347	KP: Tom Seaver	3.00	1.25	.30
☐ 348	KP: Sal Bando	.85	.35	.08
☐ 349	Al Fitzmorris	.85	.35	.08
☐ 350	Frank Howard	1.25	.50	.12
☐ 351	Braves Rookies	1.00	.40	.10
	Tom House			
	Rick Kester			
	Jimmy Britton			
☐ 352	Dave LaRoche	.85	.35	.08
☐ 353	Art Shamsky	.85	.35	.08
☐ 354	Tom Murphy	.85	.35	.08
☐ 355	Bob Watson	1.00	.40	.10
☐ 356	Gerry Moses	.85	.35	.08
☐ 357	Woodie Fryman	.85	.35	.08
☐ 358	Sparky Anderson MG	1.25	.50	.12
☐ 359	Don Pavletich	.85	.35	.08
☐ 360	Dave Roberts	.85	.35	.08
☐ 361	Mike Andrews	.85	.35	.08
☐ 362	New York Mets	1.75	.70	.17
	Team Card			
☐ 363	Ron Klimkowski	.85	.35	.08
☐ 364	Johnny Callison	.85	.35	.08
☐ 365	Dick Bosman	.85	.35	.08
☐ 366	Jimmy Rosario	.85	.35	.08
☐ 367	Ron Perranoski	.85	.35	.08
☐ 368	Danny Thompson	1.00	.40	.10
☐ 369	Jim Lefebvre	1.00	.40	.10
☐ 370	Don Buford	.85	.35	.08
☐ 371	Denny Lemaster	.85	.35	.08
☐ 372	Royals Rookies	.85	.35	.08
	Lance Clemons			
	Monty Montgomery			
☐ 373	John Mayberry	1.00	.40	.10
☐ 374	Jack Heidemann	.85	.35	.08
☐ 375	Reggie Cleveland	.85	.35	.08
☐ 376	Andy Kosco	.85	.35	.08
☐ 377	Terry Harmon	.85	.35	.08
☐ 378	Checklist 4	3.50	.35	.07
☐ 379	Ken Berry	.85	.35	.08
☐ 380	Earl Williams	.85	.35	.08
☐ 381	Chicago White Sox	1.75	.70	.17
	Team Card			
☐ 382	Joe Gibbon	.85	.35	.08
☐ 383	Brant Alyea	.85	.35	.08
☐ 384	Dave Campbell	.85	.35	.08
☐ 385	Mickey Stanley	1.00	.40	.10
☐ 386	Jim Colborn	.85	.35	.08
☐ 387	Horace Clarke	.85	.35	.08
☐ 388	Charlie Williams	.85	.35	.08
☐ 389	Bill Rigney MG	.85	.35	.08
☐ 390	Willie Davis	1.00	.40	.10
☐ 391	Ken Sanders	.85	.35	.08
☐ 392	Pirates Rookies	1.25	.50	.12
	Fred Cambria			
	Richie Zisk			
☐ 393	Curt Motton	.85	.35	.08
☐ 394	Ken Forsch	.85	.35	.08
☐ 395	Matty Alou	1.50	.60	.15
☐ 396	Paul Lindblad	1.25	.50	.12
☐ 397	Philadelphia Phillies	2.50	1.00	.25
	Team Card			
☐ 398	Larry Hisle	1.50	.60	.15
☐ 399	Milt Wilcox	1.25	.50	.12
☐ 400	Tony Oliva	2.00	.80	.20
☐ 401	Jim Nash	1.25	.50	.12
☐ 402	Bobby Heise	1.25	.50	.12
☐ 403	John Cumberland	1.25	.50	.12
☐ 404	Jeff Torborg	1.50	.60	.15
☐ 405	Ron Fairly	1.50	.60	.15
☐ 406	George Hendrick	1.75	.70	.17
☐ 407	Chuck Taylor	1.25	.50	.12
☐ 408	Jim Northrup	1.50	.60	.15
☐ 409	Frank Baker	1.25	.50	.12
☐ 410	Fergie Jenkins	6.50	2.75	.65
☐ 411	Bob Montgomery	1.25	.50	.12
☐ 412	Dick Kelley	1.25	.50	.12
☐ 413	White Sox Rookies	1.25	.50	.12
	Don Eddy			
	Dave Lemonds			
☐ 414	Bob Miller	1.25	.50	.12
☐ 415	Cookie Rojas	1.25	.50	.12
☐ 416	Johnny Edwards	1.25	.50	.12
☐ 417	Tom Hall	1.25	.50	.12
☐ 418	Tom Shopay	1.25	.50	.12
☐ 419	Jim Spencer	1.25	.50	.12
☐ 420	Steve Carlton	22.00	9.50	3.15
☐ 421	Ellie Rodriguez	1.25	.50	.12
☐ 422	Ray Lamb	1.25	.50	.12
☐ 423	Oscar Gamble	1.50	.60	.15
☐ 424	Bill Gogolewski	1.25	.50	.12
☐ 425	Ken Singleton	1.75	.70	.17
☐ 426	Singleton In Action	1.25	.50	.12
☐ 427	Tito Fuentes	1.25	.50	.12
☐ 428	Fuentes In Action	1.25	.50	.12
☐ 429	Bob Robertson	1.25	.50	.12
☐ 430	Robertson In Action	1.25	.50	.12
☐ 431	Clarence Gaston	1.75	.70	.17
☐ 432	Gaston In Action	1.25	.50	.12
☐ 433	Johnny Bench	42.00	18.00	5.50
☐ 434	Bench In Action	20.00	8.50	2.75
☐ 435	Reggie Jackson	42.00	18.00	5.50
☐ 436	Jackson In Action	20.00	8.50	2.75
☐ 437	Maury Wills	2.00	.80	.20
☐ 438	Wills In Action	1.50	.60	.15
☐ 439	Billy Williams	4.25	1.75	.42
☐ 440	Williams In Action	2.00	.80	.20
☐ 441	Thurman Munson	20.00	8.50	2.75
☐ 442	Munson In Action	10.00	4.50	1.25
☐ 443	Ken Henderson	1.25	.50	.12
☐ 444	Henderson In Action	1.25	.50	.12
☐ 445	Tom Seaver	32.00	14.25	4.75
☐ 446	Seaver In Action	16.00	6.75	2.25
☐ 447	Willie Stargell	5.00	2.25	.50
☐ 448	Stargell In Action	2.25	.90	.22
☐ 449	Bob Lemon MG	1.75	.70	.17
☐ 450	Mickey Lolich	1.75	.70	.17
☐ 451	Tony LaRussa	1.75	.70	.17
☐ 452	Ed Herrmann	1.25	.50	.12
☐ 453	Barry Lersch	1.25	.50	.12
☐ 454	Oakland A's	2.50	1.00	.25

	Team Card			
☐ 455	Tommy Harper	1.25	.50	.12
☐ 456	Mark Belanger	1.50	.60	.15
☐ 457	Padres Rookies	1.25	.50	.12
	Darcy Fast			
	Derrel Thomas			
	Mike Ivie			
☐ 458	Aurelio Monteagudo	1.25	.50	.12
☐ 459	Rick Renick	1.25	.50	.12
☐ 460	Al Downing	1.50	.60	.15
☐ 461	Tim Cullen	1.25	.50	.12
☐ 462	Rickey Clark	1.25	.50	.12
☐ 463	Bernie Carbo	1.25	.50	.12
☐ 464	Jim Roland	1.25	.50	.12
☐ 465	Gil Hodges MG	3.50	1.50	.35
☐ 466	Norm Miller	1.25	.50	.12
☐ 467	Steve Kline	1.25	.50	.12
☐ 468	Richie Scheinblum	1.25	.50	.12
☐ 469	Ron Herbel	1.25	.50	.12
☐ 470	Ray Fosse	1.50	.60	.15
☐ 471	Luke Walker	1.25	.50	.12
☐ 472	Phil Gagliano	1.25	.50	.12
☐ 473	Dan McGinn	1.25	.50	.12
☐ 474	Orioles Rookies	4.50	2.00	.45
	Don Baylor			
	Roric Harrison			
	Johnny Oates			
☐ 475	Gary Nolan	1.50	.60	.15
☐ 476	Lee Richard	1.25	.50	.12
☐ 477	Tom Phoebus	1.25	.50	.12
☐ 478	Checklist 5	3.50	.35	.07
☐ 479	Don Shaw	1.25	.50	.12
☐ 480	Lee May	1.50	.60	.15
☐ 481	Billy Conigliaro	1.25	.50	.12
☐ 482	Joe Hoerner	1.25	.50	.12
☐ 483	Ken Suarez	1.25	.50	.12
☐ 484	Lum Harris MG	1.25	.50	.12
☐ 485	Phil Regan	1.25	.50	.12
☐ 486	John Lowenstein	1.25	.50	.12
☐ 487	Detroit Tigers	2.50	1.00	.25
	Team Card			
☐ 488	Mike Nagy	1.25	.50	.12
☐ 489	Expos Rookies	1.25	.50	.12
	Terry Humphrey			
	Keith Lampard			
☐ 490	Dave McNally	1.50	.60	.15
☐ 491	KP: Lou Piniella	1.50	.60	.15
☐ 492	KP: Mel Stottlemyre	1.25	.50	.12
☐ 493	KP: Bob Bailey	1.25	.50	.12
☐ 494	KP: Willie Horton	1.25	.50	.12
☐ 495	KP: Bill Melton	1.25	.50	.12
☐ 496	KP: Bud Harrelson	1.25	.50	.12
☐ 497	KP: Jim Perry	1.25	.50	.12
☐ 498	KP: Brooks Robinson	2.00	.80	.20
☐ 499	Vicente Romo	1.25	.50	.12
☐ 500	Joe Torre	2.00	.80	.20
☐ 501	Pete Hamm	1.25	.50	.12
☐ 502	Jackie Hernandez	1.25	.50	.12
☐ 503	Gary Peters	1.25	.50	.12
☐ 504	Ed Spiezio	1.25	.50	.12
☐ 505	Mike Marshall	1.50	.60	.15
☐ 506	Indians Rookies	1.50	.60	.15
	Terry Ley			
	Jim Moyer			
	Dick Tidrow			
☐ 507	Fred Gladding	1.25	.50	.12
☐ 508	Elrod Hendricks	1.25	.50	.12
☐ 509	Don McMahon	1.25	.50	.12
☐ 510	Ted Williams MG	6.50	2.75	.65
☐ 511	Tony Taylor	1.25	.50	.12
☐ 512	Paul Popovich	1.25	.50	.12
☐ 513	Lindy McDaniel	1.25	.50	.12
☐ 514	Ted Sizemore	1.25	.50	.12
☐ 515	Bert Blyleven	11.00	5.00	1.35
☐ 516	Oscar Brown	1.25	.50	.12
☐ 517	Ken Brett	1.25	.50	.12
☐ 518	Wayne Garrett	1.25	.50	.12
☐ 519	Ted Abernathy	1.25	.50	.12
☐ 520	Larry Bowa	1.75	.70	.17
☐ 521	Alan Foster	1.25	.50	.12
☐ 522	Los Angeles Dodgers	2.50	1.00	.25
	Team Card			
☐ 523	Chuck Dobson	1.25	.50	.12
☐ 524	Reds Rookies	1.25	.50	.12
	Ed Armbrister			
	Mel Behney			
☐ 525	Carlos May	1.25	.50	.12
☐ 526	Bob Bailey	2.75	1.10	.27
☐ 527	Dave Leonhard	2.75	1.10	.27
☐ 528	Ron Stone	2.75	1.10	.27
☐ 529	Dave Nelson	2.75	1.10	.27
☐ 530	Don Sutton	5.50	2.50	.55
☐ 531	Freddie Patek	3.25	1.35	.32
☐ 532	Fred Kendall	2.75	1.10	

☐ 533	Ralph Houk MG	3.25	1.35	.32
☐ 534	Jim Hickman	2.75	1.10	.27
☐ 535	Ed Brinkman	2.75	1.10	.27
☐ 536	Doug Rader	3.25	1.35	.32
☐ 537	Bob Locker	2.75	1.10	.27
☐ 538	Charlie Sands	2.75	1.10	.27
☐ 539	Terry Forster	3.25	1.35	.32
☐ 540	Felix Millan	2.75	1.10	.27
☐ 541	Roger Repoz	2.75	1.10	.27
☐ 542	Jack Billingham	2.75	1.10	.27
☐ 543	Duane Josephson	2.75	1.10	.27
☐ 544	Ted Martinez	2.75	1.10	.27
☐ 545	Wayne Granger	2.75	1.10	.27
☐ 546	Joe Hague	2.75	1.10	.27
☐ 547	Cleveland Indians	5.50	2.50	.55
	Team Card			
☐ 548	Frank Reberger	2.75	1.10	.27
☐ 549	Dave May	2.75	1.10	.27
☐ 550	Brooks Robinson	21.00	9.00	3.00
☐ 551	Ollie Brown	2.75	1.10	.27
☐ 552	Brown In Action	2.75	1.10	.27
☐ 553	Wilbur Wood	2.75	1.10	.27
☐ 554	Wood In Action	2.75	1.10	.27
☐ 555	Ron Santo	3.75	1.60	.37
☐ 556	Santo In Action	3.25	1.35	.32
☐ 557	John Odom	2.75	1.10	.27
☐ 558	Odom In Action	2.75	1.10	.27
☐ 559	Pete Rose	45.00	20.00	6.75
☐ 560	Rose In Action	22.50	9.75	3.25
☐ 561	Leo Cardenas	2.75	1.10	.27
☐ 562	Cardenas In Action	2.75	1.10	.27
☐ 563	Ray Sadecki	2.75	1.10	.27
☐ 564	Sadecki In Action	2.75	1.10	.27
☐ 565	Reggie Smith	3.25	1.35	.32
☐ 566	Smith In Action	2.75	1.10	.27
☐ 567	Juan Marichal	6.50	2.75	.65
☐ 568	Marichal In Action	3.50	1.50	.35
☐ 569	Ed Kirkpatrick	2.75	1.10	.27
☐ 570	Kirkpatrick In Action	2.75	1.10	.27
☐ 571	Nate Colbert	2.75	1.10	.27
☐ 572	Colbert In Action	2.75	1.10	.27
☐ 573	Fritz Peterson	2.75	1.10	.27
☐ 574	Peterson In Action	2.75	1.10	.27
☐ 575	Al Oliver	3.50	1.50	.35
☐ 576	Leo Durocher MG	3.50	1.50	.35
☐ 577	Mike Paul	2.75	1.10	.27
☐ 578	Billy Grabarkewitz	2.75	1.10	.27
☐ 579	Doyle Alexander	3.50	1.50	.35
☐ 580	Lou Piniella	3.75	1.60	.37
☐ 581	Wade Blasingame	2.75	1.10	.27
☐ 582	Montreal Expos	5.50	2.50	.55
	Team Card			
☐ 583	Darold Knowles	2.75	1.10	.27
☐ 584	Jerry McNertney	2.75	1.10	.27
☐ 585	George Scott	3.25	1.35	.32
☐ 586	Denis Menke	2.75	1.10	.27
☐ 587	Billy Wilson	2.75	1.10	.27
☐ 588	Jim Holt	2.75	1.10	.27
☐ 589	Hal Lanier	2.75	1.10	.27
☐ 590	Graig Nettles	3.50	1.50	.35
☐ 591	Paul Casanova	2.75	1.10	.27
☐ 592	Lew Krausse	2.75	1.10	.27
☐ 593	Rich Morales	2.75	1.10	.27
☐ 594	Jim Beauchamp	2.75	1.10	.27
☐ 595	Nolan Ryan	165.00	75.00	22.50
☐ 596	Manny Mota	3.25	1.35	.32
☐ 597	Jim Magnuson	2.75	1.10	.27
☐ 598	Hal King	2.75	1.10	.27
☐ 599	Billy Champion	2.75	1.10	.27
☐ 600	Al Kaline	22.00	9.50	3.15
☐ 601	George Stone	2.75	1.10	.27
☐ 602	Dave Bristol MG	2.75	1.10	.27
☐ 603	Jim Ray	2.75	1.10	.27
☐ 604A	Checklist 6	5.00	.50	.10
	(copyright on back			
	bottom right)			
☐ 604B	Checklist 6	7.50	.75	.15
	(copyright on back			
	bottom left)			
☐ 605	Nelson Briles	2.75	1.10	.27
☐ 606	Luis Melendez	2.75	1.10	.27
☐ 607	Frank Duffy	2.75	1.10	.27
☐ 608	Mike Corkins	2.75	1.10	.27
☐ 609	Tom Grieve	3.25	1.35	.32
☐ 610	Bill Stoneman	2.75	1.10	.27
☐ 611	Rich Reese	2.75	1.10	.27
☐ 612	Joe Decker	2.75	1.10	.27
☐ 613	Mike Ferraro	3.25	1.35	.32
☐ 614	Ted Uhlaender	2.75	1.10	.27
☐ 615	Steve Hargan	2.75	1.10	.27
☐ 616	Joe Ferguson	2.75	1.10	.27
☐ 617	Kansas City Royals	5.50	2.50	.55
	Team Card			
☐ 618	Rich Robertson	2.75	1.10	.27

☐ 619	Rich McKinney	2.75	1.10	.27
☐ 620	Phil Niekro	5.50	2.50	.55
☐ 621	Commissioners Award	2.75	1.10	.27
☐ 622	MVP Award	2.75	1.10	.27
☐ 623	Cy Young Award	2.75	1.10	.27
☐ 624	Minor League Player	2.75	1.10	.27
☐ 625	Rookie of the Year	2.75	1.10	.27
☐ 626	Babe Ruth Award	3.00	1.25	.30
☐ 627	Moe Drabowsky	2.75	1.10	.27
☐ 628	Terry Crowley	2.75	1.10	.27
☐ 629	Paul Doyle	2.75	1.10	.27
☐ 630	Rich Hebner	2.75	1.10	.27
☐ 631	John Strohmayer	2.75	1.10	.27
☐ 632	Mike Hegan	2.75	1.10	.27
☐ 633	Jack Hiatt	2.75	1.10	.27
☐ 634	Dick Woodson	2.75	1.10	.27
☐ 635	Don Money	3.25	1.35	.32
☐ 636	Bill Lee	3.25	1.35	.32
☐ 637	Preston Gomez MG	2.75	1.10	.27
☐ 638	Ken Wright	2.75	1.10	.27
☐ 639	J.C. Martin	2.75	1.10	.27
☐ 640	Joe Coleman	2.75	1.10	.27
☐ 641	Mike Lum	2.75	1.10	.27
☐ 642	Dennis Riddleberger	2.75	1.10	.27
☐ 643	Russ Gibson	2.75	1.10	.27
☐ 644	Bernie Allen	2.75	1.10	.27
☐ 645	Jim Maloney	3.25	1.35	.32
☐ 646	Chico Salmon	2.75	1.10	.27
☐ 647	Bob Moose	2.75	1.10	.27
☐ 648	Jim Lyttle	2.75	1.10	.27
☐ 649	Pete Richert	2.75	1.10	.27
☐ 650	Sal Bando	3.25	1.35	.32
☐ 651	Cincinnati Reds Team Card	5.50	2.50	.55
☐ 652	Marcelino Lopez	2.75	1.10	.27
☐ 653	Jim Fairey	2.75	1.10	.27
☐ 654	Horacio Pina	2.75	1.10	.27
☐ 655	Jerry Grote	2.75	1.10	.27
☐ 656	Rudy May	2.75	1.10	.27
☐ 657	Bobby Wine	5.00	2.25	.50
☐ 658	Steve Dunning	5.00	2.25	.50
☐ 659	Bob Aspromonte	5.00	2.25	.50
☐ 660	Paul Blair	5.50	2.50	.55
☐ 661	Bill Virdon	6.00	2.50	.60
☐ 662	Stan Bahnsen	5.00	2.25	.50
☐ 663	Fran Healy	5.00	2.25	.50
☐ 664	Bobby Knoop	5.00	2.25	.50
☐ 665	Chris Short	5.00	2.25	.50
☐ 666	Hector Torres	5.00	2.25	.50
☐ 667	Ray Newman	5.00	2.25	.50
☐ 668	Texas Rangers Team Card	12.00	5.25	1.50
☐ 669	Willie Crawford	5.00	2.25	.50
☐ 670	Ken Holtzman	5.50	2.50	.55
☐ 671	Donn Clendenon	5.50	2.50	.55
☐ 672	Archie Reynolds	5.00	2.25	.50
☐ 673	Dave Marshall	5.00	2.25	.50
☐ 674	John Kennedy	5.00	2.25	.50
☐ 675	Pat Jarvis	5.00	2.25	.50
☐ 676	Danny Cater	5.00	2.25	.50
☐ 677	Ivan Murrell	5.00	2.25	.50
☐ 678	Steve Luebber	5.00	2.25	.50
☐ 679	Astros Rookies Bob Fenwick Bob Stinson	5.00	2.25	.50
☐ 680	Dave Johnson	6.00	2.50	.60
☐ 681	Bobby Pfeil	5.00	2.25	.50
☐ 682	Mike McCormick	5.50	2.50	.55
☐ 683	Steve Hovley	5.00	2.25	.50
☐ 684	Hal Breeden	5.00	2.25	.50
☐ 685	Joel Horlen	5.00	2.25	.50
☐ 686	Steve Garvey	75.00	34.00	11.25
☐ 687	Del Unser	5.00	2.25	.50
☐ 688	St. Louis Cardinals Team Card	10.00	4.50	1.25
☐ 689	Eddie Fisher	5.00	2.25	.50
☐ 690	Willie Montanez	6.00	2.50	.60
☐ 691	Curt Blefary	5.00	2.25	.50
☐ 692	Blefary In Action	5.00	2.25	.50
☐ 693	Alan Gallagher	5.00	2.25	.50
☐ 694	Gallagher In Action	5.00	2.25	.50
☐ 695	Rod Carew	100.00	45.00	15.00
☐ 696	Carew In Action	45.00	20.00	6.75
☐ 697	Jerry Koosman	12.50	5.50	1.65
☐ 698	Koosman In Action	8.00	3.50	.80
☐ 699	Bobby Murcer	12.50	5.50	1.65
☐ 700	Murcer In Action	8.00	3.50	.80
☐ 701	Jose Pagan	5.00	2.25	.50
☐ 702	Pagan In Action	5.00	2.25	.50
☐ 703	Doug Griffin	5.00	2.25	.50
☐ 704	Griffin In Action	5.00	2.25	.50
☐ 705	Pat Corrales	5.00	2.25	.50
☐ 706	Corrales In Action	5.00	2.25	.50
☐ 707	Tim Foli	5.00	2.25	.50
☐ 708	Foli In Action	5.00	2.25	.50
☐ 709	Jim Kaat	13.50	6.00	1.85
☐ 710	Kaat In Action	9.00	4.00	.90
☐ 711	Bobby Bonds	15.00	6.50	2.15
☐ 712	Bonds In Action	10.00	4.50	1.25
☐ 713	Gene Michael	5.00	2.25	.50
☐ 714	Michael In Action	5.00	2.25	.50
☐ 715	Mike Epstein	5.00	2.25	.50
☐ 716	Jesus Alou	5.00	2.25	.50
☐ 717	Bruce Dal Canton	5.00	2.25	.50
☐ 718	Del Rice MG	5.00	2.25	.50
☐ 719	Cesar Geronimo	5.00	2.25	.50
☐ 720	Sam McDowell	5.50	2.50	.55
☐ 721	Eddie Leon	5.00	2.25	.50
☐ 722	Bill Sudakis	5.00	2.25	.50
☐ 723	Al Santorini	5.00	2.25	.50
☐ 724	AL Rookie Pitchers John Curtis Rich Hinton Mickey Scott	5.50	2.50	.55
☐ 725	Dick McAuliffe	5.50	2.50	.55
☐ 726	Dick Selma	5.00	2.25	.50
☐ 727	Jose LaBoy	5.00	2.25	.50
☐ 728	Gail Hopkins	5.00	2.25	.50
☐ 729	Bob Veale	5.50	2.50	.55
☐ 730	Rick Monday	5.50	2.50	.55
☐ 731	Baltimore Orioles Team Card	10.00	4.50	1.25
☐ 732	George Culver	5.00	2.25	.50
☐ 733	Jim Ray Hart	5.50	2.50	.55
☐ 734	Bob Burda	5.00	2.25	.50
☐ 735	Diego Segui	5.00	2.25	.50
☐ 736	Bill Russell	6.50	2.75	.65
☐ 737	Len Randle	5.50	2.50	.55
☐ 738	Jim Merritt	5.00	2.25	.50
☐ 739	Don Mason	5.00	2.25	.50
☐ 740	Rico Carty	6.00	2.50	.60
☐ 741	Rookie First Basemen Tom Hutton John Milner Rick Miller	8.00	3.50	.80
☐ 742	Jim Rooker	5.50	2.50	.55
☐ 743	Cesar Gutierrez	5.00	2.25	.50
☐ 744	Jim Slaton	5.00	2.25	.50
☐ 745	Julian Javier	5.00	2.25	.50
☐ 746	Lowell Palmer	5.00	2.25	.50
☐ 747	Jim Stewart	5.00	2.25	.50
☐ 748	Phil Hennigan	5.00	2.25	.50
☐ 749	Walter Alston MG	9.00	4.00	.90
☐ 750	Willie Horton	6.00	2.50	.60
☐ 751	Steve Carlton TR	50.00	22.50	7.50
☐ 752	Joe Morgan TR	42.00	18.00	5.50
☐ 753	Denny McLain TR	11.00	5.00	1.35
☐ 754	Frank Robinson TR	33.00	15.00	5.00
☐ 755	Jim Fregosi TR	6.00	2.50	.60
☐ 756	Rick Wise TR	5.50	2.50	.55
☐ 757	Jose Cardenal TR	5.50	2.50	.55
☐ 758	Gil Garrido	5.00	2.25	.50
☐ 759	Chris Cannizzaro	5.00	2.25	.50
☐ 760	Bill Mazeroski	7.00	3.00	.70
☐ 761	Rookie Outfielders Ben Oglivie Ron Cey Bernie Williams	18.00	7.50	2.50
☐ 762	Wayne Simpson	5.00	2.25	.50
☐ 763	Ron Hansen	5.00	2.25	.50
☐ 764	Dusty Baker	7.50	3.25	.75
☐ 765	Ken McMullen	5.00	2.25	.50
☐ 766	Steve Hamilton	5.00	2.25	.50
☐ 767	Tom McCraw	5.00	2.25	.50
☐ 768	Denny Doyle	5.00	2.25	.50
☐ 769	Jack Aker	5.00	2.25	.50
☐ 770	Jim Wynn	6.00	2.50	.60
☐ 771	San Francisco Giants Team Card	10.00	4.50	1.25
☐ 772	Ken Tatum	5.00	2.25	.50
☐ 773	Ron Brand	5.00	2.25	.50
☐ 774	Luis Alvarado	5.00	2.25	.50
☐ 775	Jerry Reuss	6.00	2.50	.60
☐ 776	Bill Voss	5.00	2.25	.50
☐ 777	Hoyt Wilhelm	17.00	7.25	2.50
☐ 778	Twins Rookies Vic Albury Rick Dempsey Jim Strickland	7.50	3.25	.75
☐ 779	Tony Cloninger	5.00	2.25	.50
☐ 780	Dick Green	5.00	2.25	.50
☐ 781	Jim McAndrew	5.00	2.25	.50
☐ 782	Larry Stahl	5.00	2.25	.50
☐ 783	Les Cain	5.00	2.25	.50
☐ 784	Ken Aspromonte	5.00	2.25	.50
☐ 785	Vic Davalillo	5.50	2.50	.55
☐ 786	Chuck Brinkman	5.00	2.25	.50
☐ 787	Ron Reed	6.50	2.75	.55

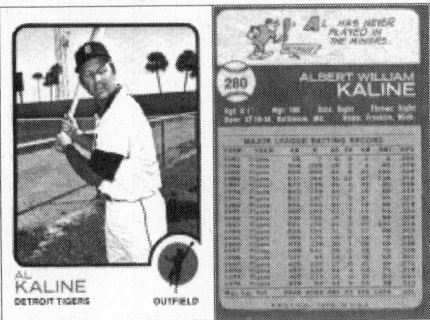

1973 Topps

The cards in this 660-card set measure 2 1/2" by 3 1/2". The 1973 Topps set marked the last year in which Topps marketed baseball cards in consecutive series. The last series (529-660) is more difficult to obtain. Beginning in 1974, all Topps cards were printed at the same time, thus eliminating the "high number" factor. The set features team leader cards with small individual pictures of the coaching staff members and a larger picture of the manager. The "background" variations below with respect to these leader cards are subtle and are best understood after a side-by-side comparison of the two varieties. An "All-Time Leaders" series (471-478) appeared for the first time in this set. Kid Pictures appeared again for the second year in a row (341-346). Other topical subsets within the set included League Leaders (61-68), Playoffs cards (201-202), World Series cards (203-210), and Rookie Prospects (601-616). The key rookie cards in this set are Bob Boone, Dwight Evans, and Mike Schmidt.

	NRMT	VG-E	GOOD
COMPLETE SET (660)	1150.00	450.00	135.00
COMMON PLAYER (1-132)	.45	.18	.04
COMMON PLAYER (133-264)	.45	.18	.04
COMMON PLAYER (265-396)	.60	.25	.06
COMMON PLAYER (397-528)	1.25	.50	.12
COMMON PLAYER (529-660)	2.75	1.10	.27
☐ 1 All-Time HR Leaders	25.00	6.00	1.25
Babe Ruth 714			
Hank Aaron 673			
Willie Mays 654			
☐ 2 Rich Hebner	.60	.25	.06
☐ 3 Jim Lonborg	.75	.30	.07
☐ 4 John Milner	.45	.18	.04
☐ 5 Ed Brinkman	.45	.18	.04
☐ 6 Mac Scarce	.45	.18	.04
☐ 7 Texas Rangers	1.00	.40	.10
Team Card			
☐ 8 Tom Hall	.45	.18	.04
☐ 9 Johnny Oates	.75	.30	.07
☐ 10 Don Sutton	2.50	1.00	.25
☐ 11 Chris Chambliss	.75	.30	.07
☐ 12A Padres Leaders	.75	.30	.07
Don Zimmer MG			
Dave Garcia CO			
Johnny Podres CO			
Bob Skinner CO			
Whitey Wietelmann CO			
(Podres no right ear)			
☐ 12B Padres Leaders	1.50	.60	.15
(Podres has right ear)			
☐ 13 George Hendrick	.75	.30	.07
☐ 14 Sonny Siebert	.45	.18	.04
☐ 15 Ralph Garr	.60	.25	.06
☐ 16 Steve Braun	.45	.18	.04
☐ 17 Fred Gladding	.45	.18	.04
☐ 18 Leroy Stanton	.45	.18	.04
☐ 19 Tim Foli	.45	.18	.04
☐ 20 Stan Bahnsen	.45	.18	.04

☐ 21 Randy Hundley	.45	.18	.04
☐ 22 Ted Abernathy	.45	.18	.04
☐ 23 Dave Kingman	1.50	.60	.15
☐ 24 Al Santorini	.45	.18	.04
☐ 25 Roy White	.75	.30	.07
☐ 26 Pittsburgh Pirates	1.00	.40	.10
Team Card			
☐ 27 Bill Gogolewski	.45	.18	.04
☐ 28 Hal McRae	1.00	.40	.10
☐ 29 Tony Taylor	.45	.18	.04
☐ 30 Tug McGraw	1.00	.40	.10
☐ 31 Buddy Bell	3.25	1.35	.32
☐ 32 Fred Norman	.45	.18	.04
☐ 33 Jim Breazeale	.45	.18	.04
☐ 34 Pat Dobson	.45	.18	.04
☐ 35 Willie Davis	.60	.25	.06
☐ 36 Steve Barber	.45	.18	.04
☐ 37 Bill Robinson	.75	.30	.07
☐ 38 Mike Epstein	.45	.18	.04
☐ 39 Dave Roberts	.45	.18	.04
☐ 40 Reggie Smith	.75	.30	.07
☐ 41 Tom Walker	.45	.18	.04
☐ 42 Mike Andrews	.45	.18	.04
☐ 43 Randy Moffitt	.45	.18	.04
☐ 44 Rick Monday	.60	.25	.06
☐ 45 Ellie Rodriguez UER	.45	.18	.04
(photo actually			
John Felske)			
☐ 46 Lindy McDaniel	.45	.18	.04
☐ 47 Luis Melendez	.45	.18	.04
☐ 48 Paul Splittorff	.45	.18	.04
☐ 49A Twins Leaders	.75	.30	.07
Frank Quilici MG			
Vern Morgan CO			
Bob Rodgers CO			
Ralph Rowe CO			
Al Worthington CO			
(solid backgrounds)			
☐ 49B Twins Leaders	1.50	.60	.15
(natural backgrounds)			
☐ 50 Roberto Clemente	30.00	13.50	4.50
☐ 51 Chuck Seelbach	.45	.18	.04
☐ 52 Denis Menke	.45	.18	.04
☐ 53 Steve Dunning	.45	.18	.04
☐ 54 Checklist 1	2.25	.25	.05
☐ 55 Jon Matlack	.60	.25	.06
☐ 56 Merv Rettenmund	.45	.18	.04
☐ 57 Derrel Thomas	.45	.18	.04
☐ 58 Mike Paul	.45	.18	.04
☐ 59 Steve Yeager	1.00	.40	.10
☐ 60 Ken Holtzman	.60	.25	.06
☐ 61 Batting Leaders	2.00	.80	.20
Billy Williams			
Rod Carew			
☐ 62 Home Run Leaders	2.00	.80	.20
Johnny Bench			
Dick Allen			
☐ 63 RBI Leaders	2.00	.80	.20
Johnny Bench			
Dick Allen			
☐ 64 Stolen Base Leaders	1.50	.60	.15
Lou Brock			
Bert Campaneris			
☐ 65 ERA Leaders	1.50	.60	.15
Steve Carlton			
Luis Tiant			
☐ 66 Victory Leaders	1.50	.60	.15
Steve Carlton			
Gaylord Perry			
Wilbur Wood			
☐ 67 Strikeout Leaders	6.50	2.75	.65
Steve Carlton			
Nolan Ryan			
☐ 68 Leading Firemen	1.00	.40	.10
Clay Carroll			
Sparky Lyle			
☐ 69 Phil Gagliano	.45	.18	.04
☐ 70 Milt Pappas	.60	.25	.06
☐ 71 Johnny Briggs	.45	.18	.04
☐ 72 Ron Reed	.45	.18	.04
☐ 73 Ed Herrmann	.45	.18	.04
☐ 74 Billy Champion	.45	.18	.04
☐ 75 Vada Pinson	.75	.30	.07
☐ 76 Doug Rader	.75	.30	.07
☐ 77 Mike Torrez	.45	.18	.04
☐ 78 Richie Scheinblum	.45	.18	.04
☐ 79 Jim Willoughby	.45	.18	.04
☐ 80 Tony Oliva UER	1.25	.50	.12
(Minnseota on front)			
☐ 81A Cubs Leaders	.75	.30	.07
Whitey Lockman MG			
Hank Aguirre CO			
Ernie Banks CO			
Larry Jansen CO			

Pete Reiser CO
(solid backgrounds)

☐ 81B	Cubs Leaders	1.50	.60	.15
	(natural backgrounds)			
☐ 82	Fritz Peterson	.45	.18	.04
☐ 83	Leron Lee	.45	.18	.04
☐ 84	Rollie Fingers	5.00	2.25	.50
☐ 85	Ted Simmons	1.75	.70	.17
☐ 86	Tom McCraw	.45	.18	.04
☐ 87	Ken Boswell	.45	.18	.04
☐ 88	Mickey Stanley	.60	.25	.06
☐ 89	Jack Billingham	.45	.18	.04
☐ 90	Brooks Robinson	6.00	2.50	.60
☐ 91	Los Angeles Dodgers	1.00	.40	.10
	Team Card			
☐ 92	Jerry Bell	.45	.18	.04
☐ 93	Jesus Alou	.45	.18	.04
☐ 94	Dick Billings	.45	.18	.04
☐ 95	Steve Blass	.45	.18	.04
☐ 96	Doug Griffin	.45	.18	.04
☐ 97	Willie Montanez	.45	.18	.04
☐ 98	Dick Woodson	.45	.18	.04
☐ 99	Carl Taylor	.45	.18	.04
☐ 100	Hank Aaron	22.00	9.50	3.15
☐ 101	Ken Henderson	.45	.18	.04
☐ 102	Rudy May	.45	.18	.04
☐ 103	Celerino Sanchez	.45	.18	.04
☐ 104	Reggie Cleveland	.45	.18	.04
☐ 105	Carlos May	.45	.18	.04
☐ 106	Terry Humphrey	.45	.18	.04
☐ 107	Phil Hennigan	.45	.18	.04
☐ 108	Bill Russell	.75	.30	.07
☐ 109	Doyle Alexander	.60	.25	.06
☐ 110	Bob Watson	.60	.25	.06
☐ 111	Dave Nelson	.45	.18	.04
☐ 112	Gary Ross	.45	.18	.04
☐ 113	Jerry Grote	.45	.18	.04
☐ 114	Lynn McGlothen	.45	.18	.04
☐ 115	Ron Santo	.75	.30	.07
☐ 116A	Yankees Leaders	.75	.30	.07
	Ralph Houk MG			
	Jim Hegan CO			
	Elston Howard CO			
	Dick Howser CO			
	Jim Turner CO			
	(solid backgrounds)			
☐ 116B	Yankees Leaders	1.50	.60	.15
	(natural backgrounds)			
☐ 117	Ramon Hernandez	.45	.18	.04
☐ 118	John Mayberry	.75	.30	.07
☐ 119	Larry Bowa	1.00	.40	.10
☐ 120	Joe Coleman	.45	.18	.04
☐ 121	Dave Rader	.45	.18	.04
☐ 122	Jim Strickland	.45	.18	.04
☐ 123	Sandy Alomar	.45	.18	.04
☐ 124	Jim Hardin	.45	.18	.04
☐ 125	Ron Fairly	.45	.18	.04
☐ 126	Jim Brewer	.45	.18	.04
☐ 127	Milwaukee Brewers	1.00	.40	.10
	Team Card			
☐ 128	Ted Sizemore	.45	.18	.04
☐ 129	Terry Forster	.60	.25	.06
☐ 130	Pete Rose	18.00	7.50	2.50
☐ 131A	Red Sox Leaders	.75	.30	.07
	Eddie Kasko MG			
	Doug Camilli CO			
	Don Lenhardt CO			
	Eddie Popowski CO			
	(no right ear)			
	Lee Stange CO			
☐ 131B	Red Sox Leaders	1.50	.60	.15
	(Popowski has right			
	ear showing)			
☐ 132	Matty Alou	.45	.18	.04
☐ 133	Dave Roberts	.45	.18	.04
☐ 134	Milt Wilcox	.45	.18	.04
☐ 135	Lee May UER	.75	.30	.07
	(career average .000)			
☐ 136A	Orioles Leaders	.75	.30	.07
	Earl Weaver MG			
	George Bamberger CO			
	Jim Frey CO			
	Billy Hunter CO			
	George Staller CO			
	(orange backgrounds)			
☐ 136B	Orioles Leaders	1.50	.60	.15
	(dark pale			
	backgrounds)			
☐ 137	Jim Beauchamp	.45	.18	.04
☐ 138	Horacio Pina	.45	.18	.04
☐ 139	Carmen Fanzone	.45	.18	.04
☐ 140	Lou Piniella	1.00	.40	.10
☐ 141	Bruce Kison	.45	.18	.04
☐ 142	Thurman Munson	10.00	4.50	1.25
☐ 143	John Curtis	.45	.18	.04
☐ 144	Marty Perez	.45	.18	.04
☐ 145	Bobby Bonds	1.75	.70	.17
☐ 146	Woodie Fryman	.45	.18	.04
☐ 147	Mike Anderson	.45	.18	.04
☐ 148	Dave Goltz	.45	.18	.04
☐ 149	Ron Hunt	.45	.18	.04
☐ 150	Wilbur Wood	.60	.25	.06
☐ 151	Wes Parker	.60	.25	.06
☐ 152	Dave May	.45	.18	.04
☐ 153	Al Hrabosky	.75	.30	.07
☐ 154	Jeff Torborg	.75	.30	.07
☐ 155	Sal Bando	.75	.30	.07
☐ 156	Cesar Geronimo	.45	.18	.04
☐ 157	Denny Riddleberger	.45	.18	.04
☐ 158	Houston Astros	1.00	.40	.10
	Team Card			
☐ 159	Clarence Gaston	.75	.30	.07
☐ 160	Jim Palmer	11.00	5.00	1.35
☐ 161	Ted Martinez	.45	.18	.04
☐ 162	Pete Broberg	.45	.18	.04
☐ 163	Vic Davalillo	.45	.18	.04
☐ 164	Monty Montgomery	.45	.18	.04
☐ 165	Luis Aparicio	2.75	1.10	.27
☐ 166	Terry Harmon	.45	.18	.04
☐ 167	Steve Stone	.60	.25	.06
☐ 168	Jim Northrup	.60	.25	.06
☐ 169	Ron Schueler	.45	.18	.04
☐ 170	Harmon Killebrew	4.50	2.00	.45
☐ 171	Bernie Carbo	.45	.18	.04
☐ 172	Steve Kline	.45	.18	.04
☐ 173	Hal Breeden	.45	.18	.04
☐ 174	Rich Gossage	15.00	6.50	2.15
☐ 175	Frank Robinson	5.00	2.25	.50
☐ 176	Chuck Taylor	.45	.18	.04
☐ 177	Bill Plummer	.75	.30	.07
☐ 178	Don Rose	.45	.18	.04
☐ 179A	A's Leaders	.75	.30	.07
	Dick Williams MG			
	Jerry Adair CO			
	Vern Hoscheit CO			
	Irv Noren CO			
	Wes Stock CO			
	(Hoscheit left ear			
	showing)			
☐ 179B	A's Leaders	1.50	.60	.15
	(Hoscheit left ear			
	not showing)			
☐ 180	Fergie Jenkins	4.00	1.75	.40
☐ 181	Jack Brohamer	.45	.18	.04
☐ 182	Mike Caldwell	.45	.18	.04
☐ 183	Don Buford	.45	.18	.04
☐ 184	Jerry Koosman	1.00	.40	.10
☐ 185	Jim Wynn	.75	.30	.07
☐ 186	Bill Fahey	.45	.18	.04
☐ 187	Luke Walker	.45	.18	.04
☐ 188	Cookie Rojas	.45	.18	.04
☐ 189	Greg Luzinski	1.00	.40	.10
☐ 190	Bob Gibson	5.00	2.25	.50
☐ 191	Detroit Tigers	1.00	.40	.10
	Team Card			
☐ 192	Pat Jarvis	.45	.18	.04
☐ 193	Carlton Fisk	36.00	16.25	5.50
☐ 194	Jorge Orta	.45	.18	.04
☐ 195	Clay Carroll	.45	.18	.04
☐ 196	Ken McMullen	.45	.18	.04
☐ 197	Ed Goodson	.45	.18	.04
☐ 198	Horace Clarke	.45	.18	.04
☐ 199	Bert Blyleven	4.50	2.00	.45
☐ 200	Billy Williams	3.50	1.50	.35
☐ 201	A.L. Playoffs	1.00	.40	.10
	A's over Tigers;			
	Hendrick scores			
	winning run			
☐ 202	N.L. Playoffs	1.00	.40	.10
	Reds over Pirates			
	Foster's run decides			
☐ 203	World Series Game 1	1.00	.40	.10
	Tenace the Menace			
☐ 204	World Series Game 2	1.00	.40	.10
	A's two straight			
☐ 205	World Series Game 3	1.00	.40	.10
	Reds win squeeker			
☐ 206	World Series Game 4	1.00	.40	.10
	Tenace singles			
	in ninth			
☐ 207	World Series Game 5	1.00	.40	.10
	Odom out at plate			
☐ 208	World Series Game 6	1.00	.40	.10
	Reds' slugging			
	ties series			
☐ 209	World Series Game 7	1.00	.40	.10
	Campy stars			
	winning rally			

☐ 210	World Series Summary	1.00	.40	.10
	World champions:			
	A's Win			
☐ 211	Balor Moore	.45	.18	.04
☐ 212	Joe Lahoud	.45	.18	.04
☐ 213	Steve Garvey	15.00	6.50	2.15
☐ 214	Steve Hamilton	.45	.18	.04
☐ 215	Dusty Baker	.75	.30	.07
☐ 216	Toby Harrah	.75	.30	.07
☐ 217	Don Wilson	.45	.18	.04
☐ 218	Aurelio Rodriguez	.45	.18	.04
☐ 219	St. Louis Cardinals	1.00	.40	.10
	Team Card			
☐ 220	Nolan Ryan	70.00	32.00	10.50
☐ 221	Fred Kendall	.45	.18	.04
☐ 222	Rob Gardner	.45	.18	.04
☐ 223	Bud Harrelson	.60	.25	.06
☐ 224	Bill Lee	.45	.18	.04
☐ 225	Al Oliver	1.00	.40	.10
☐ 226	Ray Fosse	.45	.18	.04
☐ 227	Wayne Twitchell	.45	.18	.04
☐ 228	Bobby Darwin	.45	.18	.04
☐ 229	Roric Harrison	.45	.18	.04
☐ 230	Joe Morgan	5.00	2.25	.50
☐ 231	Bill Parsons	.45	.18	.04
☐ 232	Ken Singleton	.75	.30	.07
☐ 233	Ed Kirkpatrick	.45	.18	.04
☐ 234	Bill North	.45	.18	.04
☐ 235	Jim Hunter	3.75	1.60	.37
☐ 236	Tito Fuentes	.45	.18	.04
☐ 237A	Braves Leaders	1.25	.50	.12
	Eddie Mathews MG			
	Lew Burdette CO			
	Jim Busby CO			
	Roy Hartsfield CO			
	Ken Silvestri CO			
	(Burdette right ear			
	showing)			
☐ 237B	Braves Leaders	2.50	1.00	.25
	(Burdette right ear			
	not showing)			
☐ 238	Tony Muser	.45	.18	.04
☐ 239	Pete Richert	.45	.18	.04
☐ 240	Bobby Murcer	.75	.30	.07
☐ 241	Dwain Anderson	.45	.18	.04
☐ 242	George Culver	.45	.18	.04
☐ 243	California Angels	1.00	.40	.10
	Team Card			
☐ 244	Ed Acosta	.45	.18	.04
☐ 245	Carl Yastrzemski	15.00	6.50	2.15
☐ 246	Ken Sanders	.45	.18	.04
☐ 247	Del Unser	.45	.18	.04
☐ 248	Jerry Johnson	.45	.18	.04
☐ 249	Larry Biittner	.45	.18	.04
☐ 250	Manny Sanguillen	.75	.30	.07
☐ 251	Roger Nelson	.45	.18	.04
☐ 252A	Giants Leaders	.75	.30	.07
	Charlie Fox MG			
	Joe Amalfitano CO			
	Andy Gilbert CO			
	Don McMahon CO			
	John McNamara CO			
	(orange backgrounds)			
☐ 252B	Giants Leaders	1.50	.60	.15
	(dark pale			
	backgrounds)			
☐ 253	Mark Belanger	.75	.30	.07
☐ 254	Bill Stoneman	.45	.18	.04
☐ 255	Reggie Jackson	25.00	11.00	3.50
☐ 256	Chris Zachary	.45	.18	.04
☐ 257A	Mets Leaders	1.75	.70	.17
	Yogi Berra MG			
	Roy McMillan CO			
	Joe Pignatano CO			
	Rube Walker CO			
	Eddie Yost CO			
	(orange backgrounds)			
☐ 257B	Mets Leaders	3.00	1.25	.30
	(dark pale			
	backgrounds)			
☐ 258	Tommy John	1.50	.60	.15
☐ 259	Jim Holt	.45	.18	.04
☐ 260	Gary Nolan	.45	.18	.04
☐ 261	Pat Kelly	.45	.18	.04
☐ 262	Jack Aker	.45	.18	.04
☐ 263	George Scott	.60	.25	.06
☐ 264	Checklist 2	2.25	.25	.05
☐ 265	Gene Michael	.80	.35	.08
☐ 266	Mike Lum	.60	.25	.06
☐ 267	Lloyd Allen	.60	.25	.06
☐ 268	Jerry Morales	.60	.25	.06
☐ 269	Tim McCarver	1.00	.40	.10
☐ 270	Luis Tiant	1.00	.40	.10
☐ 271	Tom Hutton	.60	.25	.06
☐ 272	Ed Farmer	.60	.25	.06
☐ 273	Chris Speier	.60	.25	.06
☐ 274	Darold Knowles	.60	.25	.06
☐ 275	Tony Perez	3.00	1.25	.30
☐ 276	Joe Lovitto	.60	.25	.06
☐ 277	Bob Miller	.60	.25	.06
☐ 278	Baltimore Orioles	1.25	.50	.12
	Team Card			
☐ 279	Mike Strahler	.60	.25	.06
☐ 280	Al Kaline	5.50	2.50	.55
☐ 281	Mike Jorgensen	.60	.25	.06
☐ 282	Steve Hovley	.60	.25	.06
☐ 283	Ray Sadecki	.60	.25	.06
☐ 284	Glenn Borgmann	.60	.25	.06
☐ 285	Don Kessinger	.80	.35	.08
☐ 286	Frank Linzy	.60	.25	.06
☐ 287	Eddie Leon	.60	.25	.06
☐ 288	Gary Gentry	.60	.25	.06
☐ 289	Bob Oliver	.60	.25	.06
☐ 290	Cesar Cedeno	.80	.35	.08
☐ 291	Rogelio Moret	.60	.25	.06
☐ 292	Jose Cruz	.80	.35	.08
☐ 293	Bernie Allen	.60	.25	.06
☐ 294	Steve Arlin	.60	.25	.06
☐ 295	Bert Campaneris	.80	.35	.08
☐ 296	Reds Leaders	1.00	.40	.10
	Sparky Anderson MG			
	Alex Grammas CO			
	Ted Kluszewski CO			
	George Scherger CO			
	Larry Shepard CO			
☐ 297	Walt Williams	.60	.25	.06
☐ 298	Ron Bryant	.60	.25	.06
☐ 299	Ted Ford	.60	.25	.06
☐ 300	Steve Carlton	13.50	6.00	1.85
☐ 301	Billy Grabarkewitz	.60	.25	.06
☐ 302	Terry Crowley	.60	.25	.06
☐ 303	Nelson Briles	.60	.25	.06
☐ 304	Duke Sims	.60	.25	.06
☐ 305	Willie Mays	28.00	12.50	4.00
☐ 306	Tom Burgmeier	.60	.25	.06
☐ 307	Boots Day	.60	.25	.06
☐ 308	Skip Lockwood	.60	.25	.06
☐ 309	Paul Popovich	.60	.25	.06
☐ 310	Dick Allen	1.25	.50	.12
☐ 311	Joe Decker	.60	.25	.06
☐ 312	Oscar Brown	.60	.25	.06
☐ 313	Jim Ray	.60	.25	.06
☐ 314	Ron Swoboda	.80	.35	.08
☐ 315	John Odom	.60	.25	.06
☐ 316	San Diego Padres	1.25	.50	.12
	Team Card			
☐ 317	Danny Cater	.60	.25	.06
☐ 318	Jim McGlothlin	.60	.25	.06
☐ 319	Jim Spencer	.60	.25	.06
☐ 320	Lou Brock	5.00	2.25	.50
☐ 321	Rich Hinton	.60	.25	.06
☐ 322	Garry Maddox	1.00	.40	.10
☐ 323	Tigers Leaders	1.00	.40	.10
	Billy Martin MG			
	Art Fowler CO			
	Charlie Silvera CO			
	Dick Tracewski CO			
☐ 324	Al Downing	.80	.35	.08
☐ 325	Boog Powell	1.00	.40	.10
☐ 326	Darrell Brandon	.60	.25	.06
☐ 327	John Lowenstein	.60	.25	.06
☐ 328	Bill Bonham	.60	.25	.06
☐ 329	Ed Kranepool	.80	.35	.08
☐ 330	Rod Carew	16.00	6.75	2.25
☐ 331	Carl Morton	.60	.25	.06
☐ 332	John Felske	.60	.25	.06
☐ 333	Gene Clines	.60	.25	.06
☐ 334	Freddie Patek	.60	.25	.06
☐ 335	Bob Tolan	.60	.25	.06
☐ 336	Tom Bradley	.60	.25	.06
☐ 337	Dave Duncan	.60	.25	.06
☐ 338	Checklist 3	2.25	.25	.05
☐ 339	Dick Tidrow	.60	.25	.06
☐ 340	Nate Colbert	.60	.25	.06
☐ 341	KP: Jim Palmer	1.75	.70	.17
☐ 342	KP: Sam McDowell	.60	.25	.06
☐ 343	KP: Bobby Murcer	1.00	.40	.10
☐ 344	KP: Jim Hunter	1.25	.50	.12
☐ 345	KP: Chris Speier	.60	.25	.06
☐ 346	KP: Gaylord Perry	1.25	.50	.12
☐ 347	Kansas City Royals	1.25	.50	.12
	Team Card			
☐ 348	Rennie Stennett	.60	.25	.06
☐ 349	Dick McAuliffe	.60	.25	.06
☐ 350	Tom Seaver	24.00	10.50	3.50
☐ 351	Jimmy Stewart	.60	.25	.06
☐ 352	Don Stanhouse	.60	.25	.06
☐ 353	Steve Brye	.60	.25	.06

#	Player			
☐ 354	Billy Parker	.60	.25	.06
☐ 355	Mike Marshall	.60	.25	.06
☐ 356	White Sox Leaders	1.00	.40	.10
	Chuck Tanner MG			
	Joe Lonnett CO			
	Jim Mahoney CO			
	Al Monchak CO			
	Johnny Sain CO			
☐ 357	Ross Grimsley	.60	.25	.06
☐ 358	Jim Nettles	.60	.25	.06
☐ 359	Cecil Upshaw	.60	.25	.06
☐ 360	Joe Rudi UER	1.00	.40	.10
	(photo actually			
	Gene Tenace)			
☐ 361	Fran Healy	.60	.25	.06
☐ 362	Eddie Watt	.60	.25	.06
☐ 363	Jackie Hernandez	.60	.25	.06
☐ 364	Rick Wise	.60	.25	.06
☐ 365	Rico Petrocelli	.80	.35	.08
☐ 366	Brock Davis	.60	.25	.06
☐ 367	Burt Hooton	.80	.35	.08
☐ 368	Bill Buckner	1.00	.40	.10
☐ 369	Lerrin LaGrow	.60	.25	.06
☐ 370	Willie Stargell	5.00	2.25	.50
☐ 371	Mike Kekich	.60	.25	.06
☐ 372	Oscar Gamble	.80	.35	.08
☐ 373	Clyde Wright	.60	.25	.06
☐ 374	Darrell Evans	1.00	.40	.10
☐ 375	Larry Dierker	.60	.25	.06
☐ 376	Frank Duffy	.60	.25	.06
☐ 377	Expos Leaders	1.00	.40	.10
	Gene Mauch MG			
	Dave Bristol CO			
	Larry Doby CO			
	Cal McLish CO			
	Jerry Zimmerman CO			
☐ 378	Len Randle	.60	.25	.06
☐ 379	Cy Acosta	.60	.25	.06
☐ 380	Johnny Bench	24.00	10.50	3.50
☐ 381	Vicente Romo	.60	.25	.06
☐ 382	Mike Hegan	.60	.25	.06
☐ 383	Diego Segui	.60	.25	.06
☐ 384	Don Baylor	1.75	.70	.17
☐ 385	Jim Perry	.80	.35	.08
☐ 386	Don Money	.60	.25	.06
☐ 387	Jim Barr	.60	.25	.06
☐ 388	Ben Oglivie	.80	.35	.08
☐ 389	New York Mets	2.00	.80	.20
	Team Card			
☐ 390	Mickey Lolich	1.00	.40	.10
☐ 391	Lee Lacy	.80	.35	.08
☐ 392	Dick Drago	.60	.25	.06
☐ 393	Jose Cardenal	.60	.25	.06
☐ 394	Sparky Lyle	1.00	.40	.10
☐ 395	Roger Metzger	.60	.25	.06
☐ 396	Grant Jackson	.60	.25	.06
☐ 397	Dave Cash	1.25	.50	.12
☐ 398	Rich Hand	1.25	.50	.12
☐ 399	George Foster	2.00	.80	.20
☐ 400	Gaylord Perry	4.25	1.75	.42
☐ 401	Clyde Mashore	1.25	.50	.12
☐ 402	Jack Hiatt	1.25	.50	.12
☐ 403	Sonny Jackson	1.25	.50	.12
☐ 404	Chuck Brinkman	1.25	.50	.12
☐ 405	Cesar Tovar	1.25	.50	.12
☐ 406	Paul Lindblad	1.25	.50	.12
☐ 407	Felix Millan	1.25	.50	.12
☐ 408	Jim Colborn	1.25	.50	.12
☐ 409	Ivan Murrell	1.25	.50	.12
☐ 410	Willie McCovey	5.00	2.25	.50
	(Bench behind plate)			
☐ 411	Ray Corbin	1.25	.50	.12
☐ 412	Manny Mota	1.50	.60	.15
☐ 413	Tom Timmermann	1.25	.50	.12
☐ 414	Ken Rudolph	1.25	.50	.12
☐ 415	Marty Pattin	1.25	.50	.12
☐ 416	Paul Schaal	1.25	.50	.12
☐ 417	Scipio Spinks	1.25	.50	.12
☐ 418	Bob Grich	1.50	.60	.15
☐ 419	Casey Cox	1.25	.50	.12
☐ 420	Tommie Agee	1.25	.50	.12
☐ 421A	Angels Leaders	1.50	.60	.15
	Bobby Winkles MG			
	Tom Morgan CO			
	Salty Parker CO			
	Jimmie Reese CO			
	John Roseboro CO			
	(orange backgrounds)			
☐ 421B	Angels Leaders	3.00	1.25	.30
	(dark pale			
	backgrounds)			
☐ 422	Bob Robertson	1.25	.50	.12
☐ 423	Johnny Jeter	1.25	.50	.12
☐ 424	Denny Doyle	1.25	.50	.12
☐ 425	Alex Johnson	1.25	.50	.12
☐ 426	Dave LaRoche	1.25	.50	.12
☐ 427	Rick Auerbach	1.25	.50	.12
☐ 428	Wayne Simpson	1.25	.50	.12
☐ 429	Jim Fairey	1.25	.50	.12
☐ 430	Vida Blue	1.50	.60	.15
☐ 431	Gerry Moses	1.25	.50	.12
☐ 432	Dan Frisella	1.25	.50	.12
☐ 433	Willie Horton	1.50	.60	.15
☐ 434	San Francisco Giants	2.50	1.00	.25
	Team Card			
☐ 435	Rico Carty	1.75	.70	.17
☐ 436	Jim McAndrew	1.25	.50	.12
☐ 437	John Kennedy	1.25	.50	.12
☐ 438	Enzo Hernandez	1.25	.50	.12
☐ 439	Eddie Fisher	1.25	.50	.12
☐ 440	Glenn Beckert	1.50	.60	.15
☐ 441	Gail Hopkins	1.25	.50	.12
☐ 442	Dick Dietz	1.25	.50	.12
☐ 443	Danny Thompson	1.25	.50	.12
☐ 444	Ken Brett	1.25	.50	.12
☐ 445	Ken Berry	1.25	.50	.12
☐ 446	Jerry Reuss	1.50	.60	.15
☐ 447	Joe Hague	1.25	.50	.12
☐ 448	John Hiller	1.50	.60	.15
☐ 449A	Indians Leaders	1.50	.60	.15
	Ken Aspromonte MG			
	Rocky Colavito CO			
	Joe Lutz CO			
	Warren Spahn CO			
	(Spahn's right			
	ear pointed)			
☐ 449B	Indians Leaders	3.00	1.25	.30
	(Spahn's right			
	ear round)			
☐ 450	Joe Torre	1.75	.70	.17
☐ 451	John Vukovich	1.25	.50	.12
☐ 452	Paul Casanova	1.25	.50	.12
☐ 453	Checklist 4	2.25	.25	.05
☐ 454	Tom Haller	1.25	.50	.12
☐ 455	Bill Melton	1.25	.50	.12
☐ 456	Dick Green	1.25	.50	.12
☐ 457	John Strohmayer	1.25	.50	.12
☐ 458	Jim Mason	1.25	.50	.12
☐ 459	Jimmy Howarth	1.25	.50	.12
☐ 460	Bill Freehan	1.75	.70	.17
☐ 461	Mike Corkins	1.25	.50	.12
☐ 462	Ron Blomberg	1.25	.50	.12
☐ 463	Ken Tatum	1.25	.50	.12
☐ 464	Chicago Cubs	2.50	1.00	.25
	Team Card			
☐ 465	Dave Giusti	1.25	.50	.12
☐ 466	Jose Arcia	1.25	.50	.12
☐ 467	Mike Ryan	1.25	.50	.12
☐ 468	Tom Griffin	1.25	.50	.12
☐ 469	Dan Monzon	1.25	.50	.12
☐ 470	Mike Cuellar	1.25	.50	.12
☐ 471	Hits Leaders	4.25	1.75	.42
	Ty Cobb 4191			
☐ 472	Grand Slam Leaders	4.25	1.75	.42
	Lou Gehrig 23			
☐ 473	Total Bases Leaders	4.25	1.75	.42
	Hank Aaron 6172			
☐ 474	RBI Leaders	6.50	2.75	.65
	Babe Ruth 2209			
☐ 475	Batting Leaders	4.25	1.75	.42
	Ty Cobb .367			
☐ 476	Shutout Leaders	1.75	.70	.17
	Walter Johnson 113			
☐ 477	Victory Leaders	1.75	.70	.17
	Cy Young 511			
☐ 478	Strikeout Leaders	1.75	.70	.17
	Walter Johnson 3508			
☐ 479	Hal Lanier	1.25	.50	.12
☐ 480	Juan Marichal	3.75	1.60	.37
☐ 481	Chicago White Sox	2.50	1.00	.25
	Team Card			
☐ 482	Rick Reuschel	4.50	2.00	.45
☐ 483	Dal Maxvill	1.25	.50	.12
☐ 484	Ernie McAnally	1.25	.50	.12
☐ 485	Norm Cash	1.25	.50	.12
☐ 486A	Phillies Leaders	1.50	.60	.15
	Danny Ozark MG			
	Carroll Beringer CO			
	Billy DeMars CO			
	Ray Rippelmeyer CO			
	Bobby Wine CO			
	(orange backgrounds)			
☐ 486B	Phillies Leaders	3.00	1.25	.30
	(dark pale			
	backgrounds)			
☐ 487	Bruce Dal Canton	1.25	.50	.12
☐ 488	Dave Campbell	1.25	.50	.12
☐ 489	Jeff Burroughs	1.50	.60	.15
☐ 490	Claude Osteen	1.25	.50	.12
☐ 491	Bob Montgomery	1.25	.50	.12
☐ 492	Pedro Borbon	1.25	.50	.12

☐ 493	Duffy Dyer	1.25	.50	.12
☐ 494	Rich Morales	1.25	.50	.12
☐ 495	Tommy Helms	1.25	.50	.12
☐ 496	Ray Lamb	1.25	.50	.12
☐ 497A	Cardinals Leaders	1.50	.60	.15
	Red Schoendienst MG			
	Vern Benson CO			
	George Kissell CO			
	Barney Schultz CO			
	(orange backgrounds)			
☐ 497B	Cardinals Leaders	3.00	1.25	.30
	(dark pale			
	backgrounds)			
☐ 498	Graig Nettles	2.50	1.00	.25
☐ 499	Bob Moose	1.25	.50	.12
☐ 500	Oakland A's	3.00	1.25	.30
	Team Card			
☐ 501	Larry Gura	1.50	.60	.15
☐ 502	Bobby Valentine	1.75	.70	.17
☐ 503	Phil Niekro	4.25	1.75	.42
☐ 504	Earl Williams	1.25	.50	.12
☐ 505	Bob Bailey	1.25	.50	.12
☐ 506	Bart Johnson	1.25	.50	.12
☐ 507	Darrel Chaney	1.25	.50	.12
☐ 508	Gates Brown	1.25	.50	.12
☐ 509	Jim Nash	1.25	.50	.12
☐ 510	Amos Otis	1.50	.60	.15
☐ 511	Sam McDowell	1.50	.60	.15
☐ 512	Dalton Jones	1.25	.50	.12
☐ 513	Dave Marshall	1.25	.50	.12
☐ 514	Jerry Kenney	1.25	.50	.12
☐ 515	Andy Messersmith	1.50	.60	.15
☐ 516	Danny Walton	1.25	.50	.12
☐ 517A	Pirates Leaders	1.50	.60	.15
	Bill Virdon MG			
	Don Leppert CO			
	Bill Mazeroski CO			
	Dave Ricketts CO			
	Mel Wright CO			
	(Mazeroski has			
	no right ear)			
☐ 517B	Pirates Leaders	3.00	1.25	.30
	(Mazeroski has			
	right ear)			
☐ 518	Bob Veale	1.50	.60	.15
☐ 519	Johnny Edwards	1.25	.50	.12
☐ 520	Mel Stottlemyre	1.75	.70	.17
☐ 521	Atlanta Braves	2.50	1.00	.25
	Team Card			
☐ 522	Leo Cardenas	1.25	.50	.12
☐ 523	Wayne Granger	1.25	.50	.12
☐ 524	Gene Tenace	1.50	.60	.15
☐ 525	Jim Fregosi	1.50	.60	.15
☐ 526	Ollie Brown	1.25	.50	.12
☐ 527	Dan McGinn	1.25	.50	.12
☐ 528	Paul Blair	1.50	.60	.15
☐ 529	Milt May	2.75	1.10	.27
☐ 530	Jim Kaat	4.25	1.75	.42
☐ 531	Ron Woods	2.75	1.10	.27
☐ 532	Steve Mingori	2.75	1.10	.27
☐ 533	Larry Stahl	2.75	1.10	.27
☐ 534	Dave Lemonds	2.75	1.10	.27
☐ 535	Johnny Callison	3.25	1.35	.32
☐ 536	Philadelphia Phillies	5.50	2.50	.55
	Team Card			
☐ 537	Bill Slayback	2.75	1.10	.27
☐ 538	Jim Ray Hart	3.25	1.35	.32
☐ 539	Tom Murphy	2.75	1.10	.27
☐ 540	Cleon Jones	2.75	1.10	.27
☐ 541	Bob Bolin	2.75	1.10	.27
☐ 542	Pat Corrales	2.75	1.10	.27
☐ 543	Alan Foster	2.75	1.10	.27
☐ 544	Von Joshua	2.75	1.10	.27
☐ 545	Orlando Cepeda	4.25	1.75	.42
☐ 546	Jim York	2.75	1.10	.27
☐ 547	Bobby Heise	2.75	1.10	.27
☐ 548	Don Durham	2.75	1.10	.27
☐ 549	Rangers Leaders	3.75	1.60	.37
	Whitey Herzog MG			
	Chuck Estrada CO			
	Chuck Hiller CO			
	Jackie Moore CO			
☐ 550	Dave Johnson	3.25	1.35	.32
☐ 551	Mike Kilkenny	2.75	1.10	.27
☐ 552	J.C. Martin	2.75	1.10	.27
☐ 553	Mickey Scott	2.75	1.10	.27
☐ 554	Dave Concepcion	4.50	2.00	.45
☐ 555	Bill Hands	2.75	1.10	.27
☐ 556	New York Yankees	6.50	2.75	.65
	Team Card			
☐ 557	Bernie Williams	2.75	1.10	.27
☐ 558	Jerry May	2.75	1.10	.27
☐ 559	Barry Lersch	2.75	1.10	.27
☐ 560	Frank Howard	4.25	1.75	.42
☐ 561	Jim Geddes	2.75	1.10	.27

☐ 562	Wayne Garrett	2.75	1.10	.27
☐ 563	Larry Haney	2.75	1.10	.27
☐ 564	Mike Thompson	2.75	1.10	.27
☐ 565	Jim Hickman	2.75	1.10	.27
☐ 566	Lew Krausse	2.75	1.10	.27
☐ 567	Bob Fenwick	2.75	1.10	.27
☐ 568	Ray Newman	2.75	1.10	.27
☐ 569	Dodgers Leaders	4.00	1.75	.40
	Walt Alston MG			
	Red Adams CO			
	Monty Basgall CO			
	Jim Gilliam CO			
	Tom Lasorda CO			
☐ 570	Bill Singer	3.25	1.35	.32
☐ 571	Rusty Torres	2.75	1.10	.27
☐ 572	Gary Sutherland	2.75	1.10	.27
☐ 573	Fred Beene	2.75	1.10	.27
☐ 574	Bob Didier	2.75	1.10	.27
☐ 575	Dock Ellis	2.75	1.10	.27
☐ 576	Montreal Expos	5.50	2.50	.55
	Team Card			
☐ 577	Eric Soderholm	2.75	1.10	.27
☐ 578	Ken Wright	2.75	1.10	.27
☐ 579	Tom Grieve	3.25	1.35	.32
☐ 580	Joe Pepitone	3.25	1.35	.32
☐ 581	Steve Kealey	2.75	1.10	.27
☐ 582	Darrell Porter	3.25	1.35	.32
☐ 583	Bill Grief	2.75	1.10	.27
☐ 584	Chris Arnold	2.75	1.10	.27
☐ 585	Joe Niekro	3.25	1.35	.32
☐ 586	Bill Sudakis	2.75	1.10	.27
☐ 587	Rich McKinney	2.75	1.10	.27
☐ 588	Checklist 5	20.00	2.00	.40
☐ 589	Ken Forsch	2.75	1.10	.27
☐ 590	Deron Johnson	2.75	1.10	.27
☐ 591	Mike Hedlund	2.75	1.10	.27
☐ 592	John Boccabella	2.75	1.10	.27
☐ 593	Royals Leaders	3.25	1.35	.32
	Jack McKeon MG			
	Galen Cisco CO			
	Harry Dunlop CO			
	Charlie Lau CO			
☐ 594	Vic Harris	2.75	1.10	.27
☐ 595	Don Gullett	3.25	1.35	.32
☐ 596	Boston Red Sox	5.50	2.50	.55
	Team Card			
☐ 597	Mickey Rivers	3.50	1.50	.35
☐ 598	Phil Roof	2.75	1.10	.27
☐ 599	Ed Crosby	2.75	1.10	.27
☐ 600	Dave McNally	3.25	1.35	.32
☐ 601	Rookie Catchers	2.75	1.10	.27
	Sergio Robles			
	George Pena			
	Rick Stelmaszek			
☐ 602	Rookie Pitchers	2.75	1.10	.27
	Mel Behney			
	Ralph Garcia			
	Doug Rau			
☐ 603	Rookie 3rd Basemen	2.75	1.10	.27
	Terry Hughes			
	Bill McNulty			
	Ken Reitz			
☐ 604	Rookie Pitchers	2.75	1.10	.27
	Jesse Jefferson			
	Dennis O'Toole			
	Bob Strampe			
☐ 605	Rookie 1st Basemen	2.75	1.10	.27
	Enos Cabell			
	Pat Bourque			
	Gonzalo Marquez			
☐ 606	Rookie Outfielders	4.00	1.75	.40
	Gary Matthews			
	Tom Paciorek			
	Jorge Roque			
☐ 607	Rookie Shortstops	2.75	1.10	.27
	Pepe Frias			
	Ray Busse			
	Mario Guerrero			
☐ 608	Rookie Pitchers	3.25	1.35	.32
	Steve Busby			
	Dick Colpaert			
	George Medich			
☐ 609	Rookie 2nd Basemen	4.50	2.00	.45
	Larvell Blanks			
	Pedro Garcia			
	Dave Lopes			
☐ 610	Rookie Pitchers	3.75	1.60	.37
	Jimmy Freeman			
	Charlie Hough			
	Hank Webb			
☐ 611	Rookie Outfielders	3.25	1.35	.32
	Rich Coggins			
	Jim Wohlford			
	Richie Zisk			

☐ 612	Rookie Pitchers	2.75	1.10	.27
	Steve Lawson			
	Bob Reynolds			
	Brent Strom			
☐ 613	Rookie Catchers	36.00	16.25	5.50
	Bob Boone			
	Skip Jutze			
	Mike Ivie			
☐ 614	Rookie Outfielders	75.00	34.00	11.25
	Al Bumbry			
	Dwight Evans			
	Charlie Spikes			
☐ 615	Rookie 3rd Basemen	450.00	150.00	35.00
	Ron Cey			
	John Hilton			
	Mike Schmidt			
☐ 616	Rookie Pitchers	2.75	1.10	.27
	Norm Angelini			
	Steve Blateric			
	Mike Garman			
☐ 617	Rich Chiles	2.75	1.10	.27
☐ 618	Andy Etchebarren	2.75	1.10	.27
☐ 619	Billy Wilson	2.75	1.10	.27
☐ 620	Tommy Harper	2.75	1.10	.27
☐ 621	Joe Ferguson	3.25	1.35	.32
☐ 622	Larry Hisle	3.25	1.35	.32
☐ 623	Steve Renko	2.75	1.10	.27
☐ 624	Astros Leaders	3.75	1.60	.37
	Leo Durocher MG			
	Preston Gomez CO			
	Grady Hatton CO			
	Hub Kittle CO			
	Jim Owens CO			
☐ 625	Angel Mangual	2.75	1.10	.27
☐ 626	Bob Barton	2.75	1.10	.27
☐ 627	Luis Alvarado	2.75	1.10	.27
☐ 628	Jim Slaton	2.75	1.10	.27
☐ 629	Cleveland Indians	5.50	2.50	.55
	Team Card			
☐ 630	Denny McLain	4.25	1.75	.42
☐ 631	Tom Matchick	2.75	1.10	.27
☐ 632	Dick Selma	2.75	1.10	.27
☐ 633	Ike Brown	2.75	1.10	.27
☐ 634	Alan Closter	2.75	1.10	.27
☐ 635	Gene Alley	2.75	1.10	.27
☐ 636	Rickey Clark	2.75	1.10	.27
☐ 637	Norm Miller	2.75	1.10	.27
☐ 638	Ken Reynolds	2.75	1.10	.27
☐ 639	Willie Crawford	2.75	1.10	.27
☐ 640	Dick Bosman	2.75	1.10	.27
☐ 641	Cincinnati Reds	5.50	2.50	.55
	Team Card			
☐ 642	Jose LaBoy	2.75	1.10	.27
☐ 643	Al Fitzmorris	2.75	1.10	.27
☐ 644	Jack Heidemann	2.75	1.10	.27
☐ 645	Bob Locker	2.75	1.10	.27
☐ 646	Brewers Leaders	3.25	1.35	.32
	Del Crandall MG			
	Harvey Kuenn CO			
	Joe Nossek CO			
	Bob Shaw CO			
	Jim Walton CO			
☐ 647	George Stone	2.75	1.10	.27
☐ 648	Tom Egan	2.75	1.10	.27
☐ 649	Rich Folkers	2.75	1.10	.27
☐ 650	Felipe Alou	3.25	1.35	.32
☐ 651	Don Carrithers	2.75	1.10	.27
☐ 652	Ted Kubiak	2.75	1.10	.27
☐ 653	Joe Hoerner	2.75	1.10	.27
☐ 654	Minnesota Twins	5.50	2.50	.55
	Team Card			
☐ 655	Clay Kirby	2.75	1.10	.27
☐ 656	John Ellis	2.75	1.10	.27
☐ 657	Bob Johnson	2.75	1.10	.27
☐ 658	Elliott Maddox	2.75	1.10	.27
☐ 659	Jose Pagan	2.75	1.10	.27
☐ 660	Fred Scherman	3.75	1.50	.30

1974 Topps

The cards in this 660-card set measure 2 1/2" by 3 1/2". This year marked the first time Topps issued all the cards of its baseball set at the same time rather than in series. Some interesting variations were created by the rumored move of the San Diego Padres to Washington. Fifteen cards (13 players, the team card, and the rookie card (599) of the Padres were printed either as "San Diego" (SD) or "Washington." The latter are the

scarcer variety and are denoted in the checklist below by WAS. Each team's manager and his coaches again have a combined card with small pictures of each coach below the larger photo of the team's manager. The first six cards in the set (1-6) feature Hank Aaron and his illustrious career. Other topical subsets included in the set are League Leaders (201-208), All-Star selections (331-339), Playoffs cards (470-471), World Series cards (472-479), and Rookie Prospects (596-608). The card backs for the All-Stars (331-339) have no statistics, but form a picture puzzle of Bobby Bonds, the 1973 All-Star Game MVP. The key rookies in this set are Ken Griffey Sr., Dave Parker, and Dave Winfield.

		NRMT	VG-E	GOOD
	COMPLETE SET (660)	625.00	275.00	75.00
	COMMON PLAYER (1-660)	.40	.16	.04
☐ 1	Hank Aaron	30.00	6.00	1.25
	Complete ML record			
☐ 2	Aaron Special 54-57	6.00	2.50	.60
	Records on back			
☐ 3	Aaron Special 58-61	6.00	2.50	.60
	Memorable homers			
☐ 4	Aaron Special 62-65	6.00	2.50	.60
	Life in ML's 1954-63			
☐ 5	Aaron Special 66-69	6.00	2.50	.60
	Life in ML's 1964-73			
☐ 6	Aaron Special 70-73	6.00	2.50	.60
	Milestone homers			
☐ 7	Jim Hunter	4.50	2.00	.45
☐ 8	George Theodore	.40	.16	.04
☐ 9	Mickey Lolich	.75	.30	.07
☐ 10	Johnny Bench	15.00	6.50	2.15
☐ 11	Jim Bibby	.40	.16	.04
☐ 12	Dave May	.40	.16	.04
☐ 13	Tom Hilgendorf	.40	.16	.04
☐ 14	Paul Popovich	.40	.16	.04
☐ 15	Joe Torre	1.00	.40	.10
☐ 16	Baltimore Orioles	.80	.35	.08
	Team Card			
☐ 17	Doug Bird	.40	.16	.04
☐ 18	Gary Thomasson	.40	.16	.04
☐ 19	Gerry Moses	.40	.16	.04
☐ 20	Nolan Ryan	50.00	22.50	7.50
☐ 21	Bob Gallagher	.40	.16	.04
☐ 22	Cy Acosta	.40	.16	.04
☐ 23	Craig Robinson	.40	.16	.04
☐ 24	John Hiller	.60	.25	.06
☐ 25	Ken Singleton	.60	.25	.06
☐ 26	Bill Campbell	.40	.16	.04
☐ 27	George Scott	.60	.25	.06
☐ 28	Manny Sanguillen	.60	.25	.06
☐ 29	Phil Niekro	2.50	1.00	.25
☐ 30	Bobby Bonds	1.00	.40	.10
☐ 31	Astros Leaders	.60	.25	.06
	Preston Gomez MG			
	Roger Craig CO			
	Hub Kittle CO			
	Grady Hatton CO			
	Bob Lillis CO			
☐ 32A	Johnny Grubb SD	.40	.16	.04
☐ 32B	Johnny Grubb WAS	5.00	2.25	.50
☐ 33	Don Newhauser	.40	.16	.04
☐ 34	Andy Kosco	.40	.16	.04
☐ 35	Gaylord Perry	3.50	1.50	.35
☐ 36	St. Louis Cardinals	.80	.35	.08
	Team Card			
☐ 37	Dave Sells	.40	.16	.04
☐ 38	Don Kessinger	.60	.25	.06

☐ 39	Ken Suarez	.40	.16	.04
☐ 40	Jim Palmer	9.00	4.00	.90
☐ 41	Bobby Floyd	.40	.16	.04
☐ 42	Claude Osteen	.60	.25	.06
☐ 43	Jim Wynn	.60	.25	.06
☐ 44	Mel Stottlemyre	.75	.30	.07
☐ 45	Dave Johnson	.60	.25	.06
☐ 46	Pat Kelly	.40	.16	.04
☐ 47	Dick Ruthven	.40	.16	.04
☐ 48	Dick Sharon	.40	.16	.04
☐ 49	Steve Renko	.40	.16	.04
☐ 50	Rod Carew	13.00	5.75	1.75
☐ 51	Bobby Heise	.40	.16	.04
☐ 52	Al Oliver	1.00	.40	.10
☐ 53A	Fred Kendall SD	.40	.16	.04
☐ 53B	Fred Kendall WAS	5.00	2.25	.50
☐ 54	Elias Sosa	.40	.16	.04
☐ 55	Frank Robinson	5.00	2.25	.50
☐ 56	New York Mets Team	1.00	.40	.10
☐ 57	Darold Knowles	.40	.16	.04
☐ 58	Charlie Spikes	.40	.16	.04
☐ 59	Ross Grimsley	.40	.16	.04
☐ 60	Lou Brock	5.00	2.25	.50
☐ 61	Luis Aparicio	2.25	.90	.22
☐ 62	Bob Locker	.40	.16	.04
☐ 63	Bill Sudakis	.40	.16	.04
☐ 64	Doug Rau	.40	.16	.04
☐ 65	Amos Otis	.60	.25	.06
☐ 66	Sparky Lyle	.60	.25	.06
☐ 67	Tommy Helms	.60	.25	.06
☐ 68	Grant Jackson	.40	.16	.04
☐ 69	Del Unser	.40	.16	.04
☐ 70	Dick Allen	.75	.30	.07
☐ 71	Dan Frisella	.40	.16	.04
☐ 72	Aurelio Rodriguez	.40	.16	.04
☐ 73	Mike Marshall	.60	.25	.06
☐ 74	Twins Team	.80	.35	.08
☐ 75	Jim Colborn	.40	.16	.04
☐ 76	Mickey Rivers	.60	.25	.06
☐ 77A	Rich Troedson SD	.40	.16	.04
☐ 77B	Rich Troedson WAS	5.00	2.25	.50
☐ 78	Giants Leaders	.60	.25	.06
	Charlie Fox MG			
	John McNamara CO			
	Joe Amalfitano CO			
	Andy Gilbert CO			
	Don McMahon CO			
☐ 79	Gene Tenace	.60	.25	.06
☐ 80	Tom Seaver	17.00	7.25	2.50
☐ 81	Frank Duffy	.40	.16	.04
☐ 82	Dave Giusti	.40	.16	.04
☐ 83	Orlando Cepeda	1.25	.50	.12
☐ 84	Rick Wise	.40	.16	.04
☐ 85	Joe Morgan	5.00	2.25	.50
☐ 86	Joe Ferguson	.40	.16	.04
☐ 87	Fergie Jenkins	3.25	1.35	.32
☐ 88	Freddie Patek	.40	.16	.04
☐ 89	Jackie Brown	.40	.16	.04
☐ 90	Bobby Murcer	.75	.30	.07
☐ 91	Ken Forsch	.40	.16	.04
☐ 92	Paul Blair	.60	.25	.06
☐ 93	Rod Gilbreath	.40	.16	.04
☐ 94	Tigers Team	.80	.35	.08
☐ 95	Steve Carlton	9.00	4.00	.90
☐ 96	Jerry Hairston	.40	.16	.04
☐ 97	Bob Bailey	.40	.16	.04
☐ 98	Bert Blyleven	3.00	1.25	.30
☐ 99	Brewers Leaders	.60	.25	.06
	Del Crandall MG			
	Harvey Kuenn CO			
	Joe Nossek CO			
	Jim Walton CO			
	Al Widmar CO			
☐ 100	Willie Stargell	4.00	1.75	.40
☐ 101	Bobby Valentine	.60	.25	.06
☐ 102A	Bill Greif SD	.40	.16	.04
☐ 102B	Bill Greif WAS	5.00	2.25	.50
☐ 103	Sal Bando	.60	.25	.06
☐ 104	Ron Bryant	.40	.16	.04
☐ 105	Carlton Fisk	21.00	9.00	3.00
☐ 106	Harry Parker	.40	.16	.04
☐ 107	Alex Johnson	.40	.16	.04
☐ 108	Al Hrabosky	.60	.25	.06
☐ 109	Bob Grich	.60	.25	.06
☐ 110	Billy Williams	3.00	1.25	.30
☐ 111	Clay Carroll	.40	.16	.04
☐ 112	Dave Lopes	.75	.30	.07
☐ 113	Dick Drago	.40	.16	.04
☐ 114	Angels Team	.80	.35	.08
☐ 115	Willie Horton	.60	.25	.06
☐ 116	Jerry Reuss	.60	.25	.06
☐ 117	Ron Blomberg	.40	.16	.04
☐ 118	Bill Lee	.60	.25	.06
☐ 119	Phillies Leaders	.60	.25	.06
	Danny Ozark MG			

	Ray Ripplemeyer CO			
	Bobby Wine CO			
	Carroll Beringer CO			
	Billy DeMars CO			
☐ 120	Wilbur Wood	.60	.25	.06
☐ 121	Larry Lintz	.40	.16	.04
☐ 122	Jim Holt	.40	.16	.04
☐ 123	Nelson Briles	.40	.16	.04
☐ 124	Bobby Coluccio	.40	.16	.04
☐ 125A	Nate Colbert SD	.40	.16	.04
☐ 125B	Nate Colbert WAS	5.00	2.25	.50
☐ 126	Checklist 1	2.00	.20	.04
☐ 127	Tom Paciorek	.40	.16	.04
☐ 128	John Ellis	.40	.16	.04
☐ 129	Chris Speier	.40	.16	.04
☐ 130	Reggie Jackson	21.00	9.00	3.00
☐ 131	Bob Boone	3.00	1.25	.30
☐ 132	Felix Millan	.40	.16	.04
☐ 133	David Clyde	.60	.25	.06
☐ 134	Denis Menke	.40	.16	.04
☐ 135	Roy White	.60	.25	.06
☐ 136	Rick Reuschel	1.00	.40	.10
☐ 137	Al Bumbry	.40	.16	.04
☐ 138	Eddie Brinkman	.40	.16	.04
☐ 139	Aurelio Monteagudo	.40	.16	.04
☐ 140	Darrell Evans	.60	.25	.06
☐ 141	Pat Bourque	.40	.16	.04
☐ 142	Pedro Garcia	.40	.16	.04
☐ 143	Dick Woodson	.40	.16	.04
☐ 144	Dodgers Leaders	1.50	.60	.15
	Walter Alston MG			
	Tom Lasorda CO			
	Jim Gilliam CO			
	Red Adams CO			
	Monty Basgall CO			
☐ 145	Dock Ellis	.40	.16	.04
☐ 146	Ron Fairly	.40	.16	.04
☐ 147	Bart Johnson	.40	.16	.04
☐ 148A	Dave Hilton SD	.40	.16	.04
☐ 148B	Dave Hilton WAS	5.00	2.25	.50
☐ 149	Mac Scarce	.40	.16	.04
☐ 150	John Mayberry	.60	.25	.06
☐ 151	Diego Segui	.40	.16	.04
☐ 152	Oscar Gamble	.60	.25	.06
☐ 153	Jon Matlack	.60	.25	.06
☐ 154	Astros Team	.80	.35	.08
☐ 155	Bert Campaneris	.60	.25	.06
☐ 156	Randy Moffitt	.40	.16	.04
☐ 157	Vic Harris	.40	.16	.04
☐ 158	Jack Billingham	.40	.16	.04
☐ 159	Jim Ray Hart	.60	.25	.06
☐ 160	Brooks Robinson	5.00	2.25	.50
☐ 161	Ray Burris UER	.60	.25	.06
	(card number is			
	printed sideways)			
☐ 162	Bill Freehan	.60	.25	.06
☐ 163	Ken Berry	.40	.16	.04
☐ 164	Tom House	.40	.16	.04
☐ 165	Willie Davis	.60	.25	.06
☐ 166	Royals Leaders	.60	.25	.06
	Jack McKeon MG			
	Charlie Lau CO			
	Harry Dunlop CO			
	Galen Cisco CO			
☐ 167	Luis Tiant	.75	.30	.07
☐ 168	Danny Thompson	.40	.16	.04
☐ 169	Steve Rogers	.60	.25	.06
☐ 170	Bill Melton	.40	.16	.04
☐ 171	Eduardo Rodriguez	.40	.16	.04
☐ 172	Gene Clines	.40	.16	.04
☐ 173A	Randy Jones SD	.75	.30	.07
☐ 173B	Randy Jones WAS	7.00	3.00	.70
☐ 174	Bill Robinson	.60	.25	.06
☐ 175	Reggie Cleveland	.40	.16	.04
☐ 176	John Lowenstein	.40	.16	.04
☐ 177	Dave Roberts	.40	.16	.04
☐ 178	Garry Maddox	.60	.25	.06
☐ 179	Mets Leaders	1.50	.60	.15
	Yogi Berra MG			
	Rube Walker CO			
	Eddie Yost CO			
	Roy McMillan CO			
	Joe Pignatano CO			
☐ 180	Ken Holtzman	.60	.25	.06
☐ 181	Cesar Geronimo	.40	.16	.04
☐ 182	Lindy McDaniel	.40	.16	.04
☐ 183	Johnny Oates	.60	.25	.06
☐ 184	Texas Rangers	.80	.35	.08
	Team Card			
☐ 185	Jose Cardenal	.40	.16	.04
☐ 186	Fred Scherman	.40	.16	.04
☐ 187	Don Baylor	1.50	.60	.15
☐ 188	Rudy Meoli	.40	.16	.04
☐ 189	Jim Brewer	.40	.16	.04
☐ 190	Tony Oliva	1.00	.40	.10

☐ 191	Al Fitzmorris	.40	.16	.04
☐ 192	Mario Guerrero	.40	.16	.04
☐ 193	Tom Walker	.40	.16	.04
☐ 194	Darrell Porter	.40	.16	.04
☐ 195	Carlos May	.40	.16	.04
☐ 196	Jim Fregosi	.60	.25	.06
☐ 197A	Vicente Romo SD	.40	.16	.04
☐ 197B	Vicente Romo WAS	5.00	2.25	.50
☐ 198	Dave Cash	.40	.16	.04
☐ 199	Mike Kekich	.40	.16	.04
☐ 200	Cesar Cedeno	.60	.25	.06
☐ 201	Batting Leaders	4.25	1.75	.42
	Rod Carew			
	Pete Rose			
☐ 202	Home Run Leaders	2.75	1.10	.27
	Reggie Jackson			
	Willie Stargell			
☐ 203	RBI Leaders	2.75	1.10	.27
	Reggie Jackson			
	Willie Stargell			
☐ 204	Stolen Base Leaders	1.00	.40	.10
	Tommy Harper			
	Lou Brock			
☐ 205	Victory Leaders	.75	.30	.07
	Wilbur Wood			
	Ron Bryant			
☐ 206	ERA Leaders	3.00	1.25	.30
	Jim Palmer			
	Tom Seaver			
☐ 207	Strikeout Leaders	6.25	2.75	.60
	Nolan Ryan			
	Tom Seaver			
☐ 208	Leading Firemen	.75	.30	.07
	John Hiller			
	Mike Marshall			
☐ 209	Ted Sizemore	.40	.16	.04
☐ 210	Bill Singer	.40	.16	.04
☐ 211	Chicago Cubs Team	.80	.35	.08
☐ 212	Rollie Fingers	4.50	2.00	.45
☐ 213	Dave Rader	.40	.16	.04
☐ 214	Billy Grabarkewitz	.40	.16	.04
☐ 215	Al Kaline UER	5.00	2.25	.50
	(no copyright on back)			
☐ 216	Ray Sadecki	.40	.16	.04
☐ 217	Tim Foli	.40	.16	.04
☐ 218	Johnny Briggs	.40	.16	.04
☐ 219	Doug Griffin	.40	.16	.04
☐ 220	Don Sutton	2.50	1.00	.25
☐ 221	White Sox Leaders	.60	.25	.06
	Chuck Tanner MG			
	Jim Mahoney CO			
	Alex Monchak CO			
	Johnny Sain CO			
	Joe Lonnett CO			
☐ 222	Ramon Hernandez	.40	.16	.04
☐ 223	Jeff Burroughs	.60	.25	.06
☐ 224	Roger Metzger	.40	.16	.04
☐ 225	Paul Splittorff	.40	.16	.04
☐ 226A	Padres Team SD	1.00	.40	.10
☐ 226B	Padres Team WAS	5.00	2.25	.50
☐ 227	Mike Lum	.40	.16	.04
☐ 228	Ted Kubiak	.40	.16	.04
☐ 229	Fritz Peterson	.40	.16	.04
☐ 230	Tony Perez	3.50	1.50	.35
☐ 231	Dick Tidrow	.40	.16	.04
☐ 232	Steve Brye	.40	.16	.04
☐ 233	Jim Barr	.40	.16	.04
☐ 234	John Milner	.40	.16	.04
☐ 235	Dave McNally	.60	.25	.06
☐ 236	Cardinals Leaders	.75	.30	.07
	Red Schoendienst MG			
	Barney Schultz CO			
	George Kissell CO			
	Johnny Lewis CO			
	Vern Benson CO			
☐ 237	Ken Brett	.40	.16	.04
☐ 238	Fran Healy HOR	.60	.25	.06
	(Munson sliding			
	in background)			
☐ 239	Bill Russell	.60	.25	.06
☐ 240	Joe Coleman	.40	.16	.04
☐ 241A	Glenn Beckert SD	.60	.25	.06
☐ 241B	Glenn Beckert WAS	5.50	2.50	.55
☐ 242	Bill Gogolewski	.40	.16	.04
☐ 243	Bob Oliver	.40	.16	.04
☐ 244	Carl Morton	.40	.16	.04
☐ 245	Cleon Jones	.40	.16	.04
☐ 246	Athletics Team	1.00	.40	.10
☐ 247	Rick Miller	.40	.16	.04
☐ 248	Tom Hall	.40	.16	.04
☐ 249	George Mitterwald	.40	.16	.04
☐ 250A	Willie McCovey SD	4.25	1.75	.42
☐ 250B	Willie McCovey WAS	25.00	11.00	3.50
☐ 251	Graig Nettles	2.00	.80	.20
☐ 252	Dave Parker	42.00	18.00	5.50
☐ 253	John Boccabella	.40	.16	.04
☐ 254	Stan Bahnsen	.40	.16	.04
☐ 255	Larry Bowa	.75	.30	.07
☐ 256	Tom Griffin	.40	.16	.04
☐ 257	Buddy Bell	1.00	.40	.10
☐ 258	Jerry Morales	.40	.16	.04
☐ 259	Bob Reynolds	.40	.16	.04
☐ 260	Ted Simmons	1.50	.60	.15
☐ 261	Jerry Bell	.40	.16	.04
☐ 262	Ed Kirkpatrick	.40	.16	.04
☐ 263	Checklist 2	2.00	.20	.04
☐ 264	Joe Rudi	.60	.25	.06
☐ 265	Tug McGraw	.75	.30	.07
☐ 266	Jim Northrup	.60	.25	.06
☐ 267	Andy Messersmith	.60	.25	.06
☐ 268	Tom Grieve	.60	.25	.06
☐ 269	Bob Johnson	.40	.16	.04
☐ 270	Ron Santo	.75	.30	.07
☐ 271	Bill Hands	.40	.16	.04
☐ 272	Paul Casanova	.40	.16	.04
☐ 273	Checklist 3	2.00	.20	.04
☐ 274	Fred Beene	.40	.16	.04
☐ 275	Ron Hunt	.40	.16	.04
☐ 276	Angels Leaders	.60	.25	.06
	Bobby Winkles MG			
	John Roseboro CO			
	Tom Morgan CO			
	Jimmie Reese CO			
	Salty Parker CO			
☐ 277	Gary Nolan	.40	.16	.04
☐ 278	Cookie Rojas	.40	.16	.04
☐ 279	Jim Crawford	.40	.16	.04
☐ 280	Carl Yastrzemski	12.00	5.25	1.50
☐ 281	Giants Team	.80	.35	.08
☐ 282	Doyle Alexander	.60	.25	.06
☐ 283	Mike Schmidt	100.00	45.00	15.00
☐ 284	Dave Duncan	.40	.16	.04
☐ 285	Reggie Smith	.60	.25	.06
☐ 286	Tony Muser	.40	.16	.04
☐ 287	Clay Kirby	.40	.16	.04
☐ 288	Gorman Thomas	1.75	.70	.17
☐ 289	Rick Auerbach	.40	.16	.04
☐ 290	Vida Blue	.60	.25	.06
☐ 291	Don Hahn	.40	.16	.04
☐ 292	Chuck Seelbach	.40	.16	.04
☐ 293	Milt May	.40	.16	.04
☐ 294	Steve Foucault	.40	.16	.04
☐ 295	Rick Monday	.60	.25	.06
☐ 296	Ray Corbin	.40	.16	.04
☐ 297	Hal Breeden	.40	.16	.04
☐ 298	Roric Harrison	.40	.16	.04
☐ 299	Gene Michael	.60	.25	.06
☐ 300	Pete Rose	12.50	5.50	1.65
☐ 301	Bob Montgomery	.40	.16	.04
☐ 302	Rudy May	.40	.16	.04
☐ 303	George Hendrick	.60	.25	.06
☐ 304	Don Wilson	.40	.16	.04
☐ 305	Tito Fuentes	.40	.16	.04
☐ 306	Orioles Leaders	.75	.30	.07
	Earl Weaver MG			
	Jim Frey CO			
	George Bamberger CO			
	Billy Hunter CO			
	George Staller CO			
☐ 307	Luis Melendez	.40	.16	.04
☐ 308	Bruce Dal Canton	.40	.16	.04
☐ 309A	Dave Roberts SD	.40	.16	.04
☐ 309B	Dave Roberts WAS	7.00	3.00	.70
☐ 310	Terry Forster	.60	.25	.06
☐ 311	Jerry Grote	.40	.16	.04
☐ 312	Deron Johnson	.40	.16	.04
☐ 313	Barry Lersch	.40	.16	.04
☐ 314	Milwaukee Brewers	.80	.35	.08
	Team Card			
☐ 315	Ron Cey	1.00	.40	.10
☐ 316	Jim Perry	.60	.25	.06
☐ 317	Richie Zisk	.40	.16	.04
☐ 318	Jim Merritt	.40	.16	.04
☐ 319	Randy Hundley	.40	.16	.04
☐ 320	Dusty Baker	.60	.25	.06
☐ 321	Steve Braun	.40	.16	.04
☐ 322	Ernie McAnally	.40	.16	.04
☐ 323	Richie Scheinblum	.40	.16	.04
☐ 324	Steve Kline	.40	.16	.04
☐ 325	Tommy Harper	.60	.25	.06
☐ 326	Reds Leaders	.75	.30	.07
	Sparky Anderson MG			
	Larry Shephard CO			
	George Scherger CO			
	Alex Grammas CO			
	Ted Kluszewski CO			
☐ 327	Tom Timmermann	.40	.16	.04
☐ 328	Skip Jutze	.40	.16	.04
☐ 329	Mark Belanger	.60	.25	.06
☐ 330	Juan Marichal	2.50	1.00	.25

☐ 331	All-Star Catchers	5.00	2.25	.50
	Carlton Fisk			
	Johnny Bench			
☐ 332	All-Star 1B	2.50	1.00	.25
	Dick Allen			
	Hank Aaron			
☐ 333	All-Star 2B	3.00	1.25	.30
	Rod Carew			
	Joe Morgan			
☐ 334	All-Star 3B	1.50	.60	.15
	Brooks Robinson			
	Ron Santo			
☐ 335	All-Star SS	.60	.25	.06
	Bert Campaneris			
	Chris Speier			
☐ 336	All-Star LF	2.50	1.00	.25
	Bobby Murcer			
	Pete Rose			
☐ 337	All-Star CF	.60	.25	.06
	Amos Otis			
	Cesar Cedeno			
☐ 338	All-Star RF	3.00	1.25	.30
	Reggie Jackson			
	Billy Williams			
☐ 339	All-Star Pitchers	.75	.30	.07
	Jim Hunter			
	Rick Wise			
☐ 340	Thurman Munson	7.50	3.25	.75
☐ 341	Dan Driessen	.75	.30	.07
☐ 342	Jim Lonborg	.60	.25	.06
☐ 343	Royals Team	.80	.35	.08
☐ 344	Mike Caldwell	.60	.25	.06
☐ 345	Bill North	.40	.16	.04
☐ 346	Ron Reed	.40	.16	.04
☐ 347	Sandy Alomar	.40	.16	.04
☐ 348	Pete Richert	.40	.16	.04
☐ 349	John Vukovich	.40	.16	.04
☐ 350	Bob Gibson	4.50	2.00	.45
☐ 351	Dwight Evans	16.00	6.75	2.25
☐ 352	Bill Stoneman	.40	.16	.04
☐ 353	Rich Coggins	.40	.16	.04
☐ 354	Cubs Leaders	.60	.25	.06
	Whitey Lockman MG			
	J.C. Martin CO			
	Hank Aguirre CO			
	Al Spangler CO			
	Jim Marshall CO			
☐ 355	Dave Nelson	.40	.16	.04
☐ 356	Jerry Koosman	.75	.30	.07
☐ 357	Buddy Bradford	.40	.16	.04
☐ 358	Dal Maxvill	.40	.16	.04
☐ 359	Brent Strom	.40	.16	.04
☐ 360	Greg Luzinski	.75	.30	.07
☐ 361	Don Carrithers	.40	.16	.04
☐ 362	Hal King	.40	.16	.04
☐ 363	Yankees Team	.80	.35	.08
☐ 364A	Cito Gaston SD	.75	.30	.07
☐ 364B	Cito Gaston WAS	7.50	3.25	.75
☐ 365	Steve Busby	.60	.25	.06
☐ 366	Larry Hisle	.60	.25	.06
☐ 367	Norm Cash	.75	.30	.07
☐ 368	Manny Mota	.60	.25	.06
☐ 369	Paul Lindblad	.40	.16	.04
☐ 370	Bob Watson	.60	.25	.06
☐ 371	Jim Slaton	.40	.16	.04
☐ 372	Ken Reitz	.40	.16	.04
☐ 373	John Curtis	.40	.16	.04
☐ 374	Marty Perez	.40	.16	.04
☐ 375	Earl Williams	.40	.16	.04
☐ 376	Jorge Orta	.40	.16	.04
☐ 377	Ron Woods	.40	.16	.04
☐ 378	Burt Hooton	.60	.25	.06
☐ 379	Rangers Leaders	1.00	.40	.10
	Billy Martin MG			
	Frank Lucchesi CO			
	Art Fowler CO			
	Charlie Silvera CO			
	Jackie Moore CO			
☐ 380	Bud Harrelson	.60	.25	.06
☐ 381	Charlie Sands	.40	.16	.04
☐ 382	Bob Moose	.40	.16	.04
☐ 383	Phillies Team	.80	.35	.08
☐ 384	Chris Chambliss	.60	.25	.06
☐ 385	Don Gullett	.60	.25	.06
☐ 386	Gary Matthews	.60	.25	.06
☐ 387A	Rich Morales SD	.40	.16	.04
☐ 387B	Rich Morales WAS	7.00	3.00	.70
☐ 388	Phil Roof	.40	.16	.04
☐ 389	Gates Brown	.60	.25	.06
☐ 390	Lou Piniella	.75	.30	.07
☐ 391	Billy Champion	.40	.16	.04
☐ 392	Dick Green	.40	.16	.04
☐ 393	Orlando Pena	.40	.16	.04
☐ 394	Ken Henderson	.40	.16	.04
☐ 395	Doug Rader	.60	.25	.06
☐ 396	Tommy Davis	.60	.25	.06
☐ 397	George Stone	.40	.16	.04
☐ 398	Duke Sims	.40	.16	.04
☐ 399	Mike Paul	.40	.16	.04
☐ 400	Harmon Killebrew	4.25	1.75	.42
☐ 401	Elliott Maddox	.40	.16	.04
☐ 402	Jim Rooker	.40	.16	.04
☐ 403	Red Sox Leaders	.60	.25	.06
	Darrell Johnson MG			
	Eddie Popowski CO			
	Lee Stange CO			
	Don Zimmer CO			
	Don Bryant CO			
☐ 404	Jim Howarth	.40	.16	.04
☐ 405	Ellie Rodriguez	.40	.16	.04
☐ 406	Steve Arlin	.40	.16	.04
☐ 407	Jim Wohlford	.40	.16	.04
☐ 408	Charlie Hough	.75	.30	.07
☐ 409	Ike Brown	.40	.16	.04
☐ 410	Pedro Borbon	.40	.16	.04
☐ 411	Frank Baker	.40	.16	.04
☐ 412	Chuck Taylor	.40	.16	.04
☐ 413	Don Money	.40	.16	.04
☐ 414	Checklist 4	2.00	.20	.04
☐ 415	Gary Gentry	.40	.16	.04
☐ 416	White Sox Team	.80	.35	.08
☐ 417	Rich Folkers	.40	.16	.04
☐ 418	Walt Williams	.40	.16	.04
☐ 419	Wayne Twitchell	.40	.16	.04
☐ 420	Ray Fosse	.40	.16	.04
☐ 421	Dan Fife	.40	.16	.04
☐ 422	Gonzalo Marquez	.40	.16	.04
☐ 423	Fred Stanley	.40	.16	.04
☐ 424	Jim Beauchamp	.40	.16	.04
☐ 425	Pete Broberg	.40	.16	.04
☐ 426	Rennie Stennett	.40	.16	.04
☐ 427	Bobby Bolin	.40	.16	.04
☐ 428	Gary Sutherland	.40	.16	.04
☐ 429	Dick Lange	.40	.16	.04
☐ 430	Matty Alou	.60	.25	.06
☐ 431	Gene Garber	.60	.25	.06
☐ 432	Chris Arnold	.40	.16	.04
☐ 433	Lerrin LaGrow	.40	.16	.04
☐ 434	Ken McMullen	.40	.16	.04
☐ 435	Dave Concepcion	1.75	.70	.17
☐ 436	Don Hood	.40	.16	.04
☐ 437	Jim Lyttle	.40	.16	.04
☐ 438	Ed Herrmann	.40	.16	.04
☐ 439	Norm Miller	.40	.16	.04
☐ 440	Jim Kaat	1.00	.40	.10
☐ 441	Tom Ragland	.40	.16	.04
☐ 442	Alan Foster	.40	.16	.04
☐ 443	Tom Hutton	.40	.16	.04
☐ 444	Vic Davalillo	.40	.16	.04
☐ 445	George Medich	.40	.16	.04
☐ 446	Len Randle	.40	.16	.04
☐ 447	Twins Leaders	.60	.25	.06
	Frank Quilici MG			
	Ralph Rowe CO			
	Bob Rodgers CO			
	Vern Morgan CO			
☐ 448	Ron Hodges	.40	.16	.04
☐ 449	Tom McCraw	.40	.16	.04
☐ 450	Rich Hebner	.40	.16	.04
☐ 451	Tommy John	1.75	.70	.17
☐ 452	Gene Hiser	.40	.16	.04
☐ 453	Balor Moore	.40	.16	.04
☐ 454	Kurt Bevacqua	.40	.16	.04
☐ 455	Tom Bradley	.40	.16	.04
☐ 456	Dave Winfield	80.00	36.00	12.00
☐ 457	Chuck Goggin	.40	.16	.04
☐ 458	Jim Ray	.40	.16	.04
☐ 459	Cincinnati Reds	.80	.35	.08
	Team Card			
☐ 460	Boog Powell	.75	.30	.07
☐ 461	John Odom	.40	.16	.04
☐ 462	Luis Alvarado	.40	.16	.04
☐ 463	Pat Dobson	.40	.16	.04
☐ 464	Jose Cruz	.60	.25	.06
☐ 465	Dick Bosman	.40	.16	.04
☐ 466	Dick Billings	.40	.16	.04
☐ 467	Winston Llenas	.40	.16	.04
☐ 468	Pepe Frias	.40	.16	.04
☐ 469	Joe Decker	.40	.16	.04
☐ 470	AL Playoffs	3.75	1.60	.37
	A's over Orioles			
	(Reggie Jackson)			
☐ 471	NL Playoffs	1.00	.40	.10
	Mets over Reds			
	(Matlack pitching)			
☐ 472	World Series Game 1	1.00	.40	.10
	(Knowles pitching)			
☐ 473	World Series Game 2	4.00	1.75	.40
	(Willie Mays batting)			

☐ 474	World Series Game 3 .... (Campaneris stealing)	1.00	.40	.10
☐ 475	World Series Game 4 .... (Staub batting)	1.00	.40	.10
☐ 476	World Series Game 5 .... Cleon Jones scoring)	1.00	.40	.10
☐ 477	World Series Game 6 .... (Reggie Jackson)	3.75	1.60	.37
☐ 478	World Series Game 7 .... (Campaneris batting)	1.00	.40	.10
☐ 479	World Series Summary .... A's celebrate; win 2nd consecutive championship	1.00	.40	.10
☐ 480	Willie Crawford	.40	.16	.04
☐ 481	Jerry Terrell	.40	.16	.04
☐ 482	Bob Didier	.40	.16	.04
☐ 483	Atlanta Braves .... Team Card	.80	.35	.08
☐ 484	Carmen Fanzone	.40	.16	.04
☐ 485	Felipe Alou	.60	.25	.06
☐ 486	Steve Stone	.60	.25	.06
☐ 487	Ted Martinez	.40	.16	.04
☐ 488	Andy Etchebarren	.40	.16	.04
☐ 489	Pirates Leaders .... Danny Murtaugh MG Don Osborn CO Don Leppert CO Bill Mazeroski CO Bob Skinner CO	.60	.25	.06
☐ 490	Vada Pinson	.75	.30	.07
☐ 491	Roger Nelson	.40	.16	.04
☐ 492	Mike Rogodzinski	.40	.16	.04
☐ 493	Joe Hoerner	.40	.16	.04
☐ 494	Ed Goodson	.40	.16	.04
☐ 495	Dick McAuliffe	.40	.16	.04
☐ 496	Tom Murphy	.40	.16	.04
☐ 497	Bobby Mitchell	.40	.16	.04
☐ 498	Pat Corrales	.40	.16	.04
☐ 499	Rusty Torres	.40	.16	.04
☐ 500	Lee May	.60	.25	.06
☐ 501	Eddie Leon	.40	.16	.04
☐ 502	Dave LaRoche	.40	.16	.04
☐ 503	Eric Soderholm	.40	.16	.04
☐ 504	Joe Niekro	.60	.25	.06
☐ 505	Bill Buckner	.75	.30	.07
☐ 506	Ed Farmer	.40	.16	.04
☐ 507	Larry Stahl	.40	.16	.04
☐ 508	Expos Team	.80	.35	.08
☐ 509	Jesse Jefferson	.40	.16	.04
☐ 510	Wayne Garrett	.40	.16	.04
☐ 511	Toby Harrah	.60	.25	.06
☐ 512	Joe Lahoud	.40	.16	.04
☐ 513	Jim Campanis	.40	.16	.04
☐ 514	Paul Schaal	.40	.16	.04
☐ 515	Willie Montanez	.40	.16	.04
☐ 516	Horacio Pina	.40	.16	.04
☐ 517	Mike Hegan	.40	.16	.04
☐ 518	Derrel Thomas	.40	.16	.04
☐ 519	Bill Sharp	.40	.16	.04
☐ 520	Tim McCarver	.75	.30	.07
☐ 521	Indians Leaders .... Ken Aspromonte MG Clay Bryant CO Tony Pacheco CO	.60	.25	.06
☐ 522	J.R. Richard	.60	.25	.06
☐ 523	Cecil Cooper	1.75	.70	.17
☐ 524	Bill Plummer	.60	.25	.06
☐ 525	Clyde Wright	.40	.16	.04
☐ 526	Frank Tepedino	.40	.16	.04
☐ 527	Bobby Darwin	.40	.16	.04
☐ 528	Bill Bonham	.40	.16	.04
☐ 529	Horace Clarke	.40	.16	.04
☐ 530	Mickey Stanley	.60	.25	.06
☐ 531	Expos Leaders .... Gene Mauch MG Dave Bristol CO Cal McLish CO Larry Doby CO Jerry Zimmerman CO	.60	.25	.06
☐ 532	Skip Lockwood	.40	.16	.04
☐ 533	Mike Phillips	.40	.16	.04
☐ 534	Eddie Watt	.40	.16	.04
☐ 535	Bob Tolan	.40	.16	.04
☐ 536	Duffy Dyer	.40	.16	.04
☐ 537	Steve Mingori	.40	.16	.04
☐ 538	Cesar Tovar	.40	.16	.04
☐ 539	Lloyd Allen	.40	.16	.04
☐ 540	Bob Robertson	.40	.16	.04
☐ 541	Cleveland Indians .... Team Card	.80	.35	.08
☐ 542	Rich Gossage	3.75	1.60	.37
☐ 543	Danny Cater	.40	.16	.04
☐ 544	Ron Schueler	.40	.16	.04
☐ 545	Billy Conigliaro	.40	.16	.04

☐ 546	Mike Corkins	.40	.16	.04
☐ 547	Glenn Borgmann	.40	.16	.04
☐ 548	Sonny Siebert	.40	.16	.04
☐ 549	Mike Jorgensen	.40	.16	.04
☐ 550	Sam McDowell	.60	.25	.06
☐ 551	Von Joshua	.40	.16	.04
☐ 552	Denny Doyle	.40	.16	.04
☐ 553	Jim Willoughby	.40	.16	.04
☐ 554	Tim Johnson	.40	.16	.04
☐ 555	Woodie Fryman	.40	.16	.04
☐ 556	Dave Campbell	.40	.16	.04
☐ 557	Jim McGlothlin	.40	.16	.04
☐ 558	Bill Fahey	.40	.16	.04
☐ 559	Darrell Chaney	.40	.16	.04
☐ 560	Mike Cuellar	.60	.25	.06
☐ 561	Ed Kranepool	.60	.25	.06
☐ 562	Jack Aker	.40	.16	.04
☐ 563	Hal McRae	.75	.30	.07
☐ 564	Mike Ryan	.40	.16	.04
☐ 565	Milt Wilcox	.40	.16	.04
☐ 566	Jackie Hernandez	.40	.16	.04
☐ 567	Red Sox Team	.80	.35	.08
☐ 568	Mike Torrez	.60	.25	.06
☐ 569	Rick Dempsey	.60	.25	.06
☐ 570	Ralph Garr	.60	.25	.06
☐ 571	Rich Hand	.40	.16	.04
☐ 572	Enzo Hernandez	.40	.16	.04
☐ 573	Mike Adams	.40	.16	.04
☐ 574	Bill Parsons	.40	.16	.04
☐ 575	Steve Garvey	12.00	5.25	1.50
☐ 576	Scipio Spinks	.40	.16	.04
☐ 577	Mike Sadek	.40	.16	.04
☐ 578	Ralph Houk MG	.60	.25	.06
☐ 579	Cecil Upshaw	.40	.16	.04
☐ 580	Jim Spencer	.40	.16	.04
☐ 581	Fred Norman	.40	.16	.04
☐ 582	Bucky Dent	2.00	.80	.20
☐ 583	Marty Pattin	.40	.16	.04
☐ 584	Ken Rudolph	.40	.16	.04
☐ 585	Merv Rettenmund	.40	.16	.04
☐ 586	Jack Brohamer	.40	.16	.04
☐ 587	Larry Christenson	.40	.16	.04
☐ 588	Hal Lanier	.40	.16	.04
☐ 589	Boots Day	.40	.16	.04
☐ 590	Roger Moret	.40	.16	.04
☐ 591	Sonny Jackson	.40	.16	.04
☐ 592	Ed Bane	.40	.16	.04
☐ 593	Steve Yeager	.60	.25	.06
☐ 594	Leroy Stanton	.40	.16	.04
☐ 595	Steve Blass	.40	.16	.04
☐ 596	Rookie Pitchers .... Wayne Garland Fred Holdsworth Mark Littell Dick Pole	.40	.16	.04
☐ 597	Rookie Shortstops .... Dave Chalk John Gamble Pete MacKanin Manny Trillo	.60	.25	.06
☐ 598	Rookie Outfielders .... Dave Augustine Ken Griffey Steve Ontiveros Jim Tyrone	22.00	9.50	3.15
☐ 599A	Rookie Pitchers WAS .... Ron Diorio Dave Freisleben Frank Riccelli Greg Shanahan	.60	.25	.06
☐ 599B	Rookie Pitchers SD .... (SD in large print)	3.00	1.25	.30
☐ 599C	Rookie Pitchers SD .... (SD in small print)	5.00	2.25	.50
☐ 600	Rookie Infielders .... Ron Cash Jim Cox Bill Madlock Reggie Sanders	4.50	2.00	.45
☐ 601	Rookie Outfielders .... Ed Armbrister Rich Bladt Brian Downing Bake McBride	4.50	2.00	.45
☐ 602	Rookie Pitchers .... Glen Abbott Rick Henninger Craig Swan Dan Vossler	.60	.25	.06
☐ 603	Rookie Catchers .... Barry Foote Tom Lundstedt Charlie Moore Sergio Robles	.60	.25	.06

☐ 604	Rookie Infielders	4.50	2.00	.45
	Terry Hughes			
	John Knox			
	Andy Thornton			
	Frank White			
☐ 605	Rookie Pitchers	3.00	1.25	.30
	Vic Albury			
	Ken Frailing			
	Kevin Kobel			
	Frank Tanana			
☐ 606	Rookie Outfielders	.40	.16	.04
	Jim Fuller			
	Wilbur Howard			
	Tommy Smith			
	Otto Velez			
☐ 607	Rookie Shortstops	.40	.16	.04
	Leo Foster			
	Tom Heintzelman			
	Dave Rosello			
	Frank Taveras			
☐ 608A	Rookie Pitchers: ERR	2.00	.80	.20
	Bob Apodaco (sic)			
	Dick Baney			
	John D'Acquisto			
	Mike Wallace			
☐ 608B	Rookie Pitchers: COR	.40	.16	.04
	Bob Apodaca			
	Dick Baney			
	John D'Acquisto			
	Mike Wallace			
☐ 609	Rico Petrocelli	.60	.25	.06
☐ 610	Dave Kingman	1.00	.40	.10
☐ 611	Rich Stelmaszek	.40	.16	.04
☐ 612	Luke Walker	.40	.16	.04
☐ 613	Dan Monzon	.40	.16	.04
☐ 614	Adrian Devine	.40	.16	.04
☐ 615	Johnny Jeter	.40	.16	.04
☐ 616	Larry Gura	.60	.25	.06
☐ 617	Ted Ford	.40	.16	.04
☐ 618	Jim Mason	.40	.16	.04
☐ 619	Mike Anderson	.40	.16	.04
☐ 620	Al Downing	.60	.25	.06
☐ 621	Bernie Carbo	.40	.16	.04
☐ 622	Phil Gagliano	.40	.16	.04
☐ 623	Celerino Sanchez	.40	.16	.04
☐ 624	Bob Miller	.40	.16	.04
☐ 625	Ollie Brown	.40	.16	.04
☐ 626	Pittsburgh Pirates	.80	.35	.08
	Team Card			
☐ 627	Carl Taylor	.40	.16	.04
☐ 628	Ivan Murrell	.40	.16	.04
☐ 629	Rusty Staub	.75	.30	.07
☐ 630	Tommy Agee	.60	.25	.06
☐ 631	Steve Barber	.40	.16	.04
☐ 632	George Culver	.40	.16	.04
☐ 633	Dave Hamilton	.40	.16	.04
☐ 634	Braves Leaders	1.00	.40	.10
	Eddie Mathews MG			
	Herm Starrette CO			
	Connie Ryan CO			
	Jim Busby CO			
	Ken Silvestri CO			
☐ 635	Johnny Edwards	.40	.16	.04
☐ 636	Dave Goltz	.40	.16	.04
☐ 637	Checklist 5	2.00	.20	.04
☐ 638	Ken Sanders	.40	.16	.04
☐ 639	Joe Lovitto	.40	.16	.04
☐ 640	Milt Pappas	.60	.25	.06
☐ 641	Chuck Brinkman	.40	.16	.04
☐ 642	Terry Harmon	.40	.16	.04
☐ 643	Dodgers Team	.80	.35	.08
☐ 644	Wayne Granger	.40	.16	.04
☐ 645	Ken Boswell	.40	.16	.04
☐ 646	George Foster	1.50	.60	.15
☐ 647	Juan Beniquez	.60	.25	.06
☐ 648	Terry Crowley	.40	.16	.04
☐ 649	Fernando Gonzalez	.40	.16	.04
☐ 650	Mike Epstein	.40	.16	.04
☐ 651	Leron Lee	.40	.16	.04
☐ 652	Gail Hopkins	.40	.16	.04
☐ 653	Bob Stinson	.40	.16	.04
☐ 654A	Jesus Alou ERR	7.50	3.25	.75
	(no position)			
☐ 654B	Jesus Alou COR	.60	.25	.06
	(outfield)			
☐ 655	Mike Tyson	.40	.16	.04
☐ 656	Adrian Garrett	.40	.16	.04
☐ 657	Jim Shellenback	.40	.16	.04
☐ 658	Lee Lacy	.40	.16	.04
☐ 659	Joe Lis	.40	.16	.04
☐ 660	Larry Dierker	.60	.25	.06

1974 Topps Traded

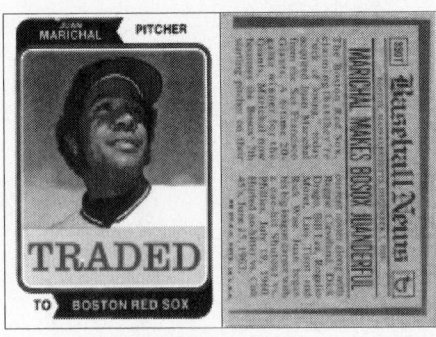

The cards in this 44-card set measure 2 1/2" by 3 1/2". The 1974 Topps Traded set contains 43 player cards and one unnumbered checklist card. The obverses have the word "traded" in block letters and the backs are designed in newspaper style. Card numbers are the same as in the regular set except they are followed by a "T." No known scarcities exist for this set.

		NRMT	VG-E	GOOD
COMPLETE SET (44)		11.00	5.00	1.35
COMMON PLAYER		.25	.10	.02
☐ 23T	Craig Robinson	.25	.10	.02
☐ 42T	Claude Osteen	.35	.15	.03
☐ 43T	Jim Wynn	.35	.15	.03
☐ 51T	Bobby Heise	.25	.10	.02
☐ 59T	Ross Grimsley	.25	.10	.02
☐ 62T	Bob Locker	.25	.10	.02
☐ 63T	Bill Sudakis	.25	.10	.02
☐ 73T	Mike Marshall	.50	.20	.05
☐ 123T	Nelson Briles	.35	.15	.03
☐ 139T	Aurelio Monteagudo	.25	.10	.02
☐ 151T	Diego Segui	.25	.10	.02
☐ 165T	Willie Davis	.35	.15	.03
☐ 175T	Reggie Cleveland	.25	.10	.02
☐ 182T	Lindy McDaniel	.25	.10	.02
☐ 186T	Fred Scherman	.25	.10	.02
☐ 249T	George Mitterwald	.25	.10	.02
☐ 262T	Ed Kirkpatrick	.25	.10	.02
☐ 269T	Bob Johnson	.25	.10	.02
☐ 270T	Ron Santo	.60	.25	.06
☐ 313T	Barry Lersch	.25	.10	.02
☐ 319T	Randy Hundley	.35	.15	.03
☐ 330T	Juan Marichal	2.00	.80	.20
☐ 348T	Pete Richert	.25	.10	.02
☐ 373T	John Curtis	.25	.10	.02
☐ 390T	Lou Piniella	.60	.25	.06
☐ 428T	Gary Sutherland	.25	.10	.02
☐ 454T	Kurt Bevacqua	.25	.10	.02
☐ 458T	Jim Ray	.25	.10	.02
☐ 485T	Felipe Alou	.35	.15	.03
☐ 486T	Steve Stone	.35	.15	.03
☐ 496T	Tom Murphy	.25	.10	.02
☐ 516T	Horacio Pina	.25	.10	.02
☐ 534T	Eddie Watt	.25	.10	.02
☐ 538T	Cesar Tovar	.25	.10	.02
☐ 544T	Ron Schueler	.25	.10	.02
☐ 579T	Cecil Upshaw	.25	.10	.02
☐ 585T	Merv Rettenmund	.25	.10	.02
☐ 612T	Luke Walker	.25	.10	.02
☐ 616T	Larry Gura	.35	.15	.03
☐ 618T	Jim Mason	.25	.10	.02
☐ 630T	Tommie Agee	.35	.15	.03
☐ 648T	Terry Crowley	.25	.10	.02
☐ 649T	Fernando Gonzalez	.25	.10	.02
☐ xxxT	Traded Checklist	.65	.10	.02
	(unnumbered)			

1975 Topps

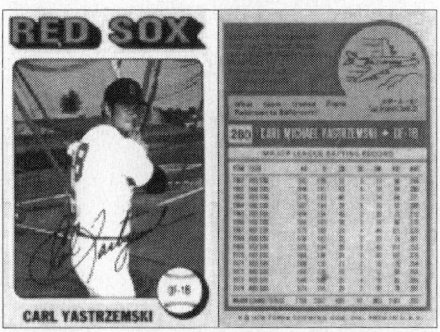

CARL YASTRZEMSKI

The cards in the 1975 Topps set were issued in two different sizes: a regular standard size (2 1/2" by 3 1/2") and a mini size (2 1/2" by 3 1/8") which was issued as a test in certain areas of the country. The 660-card Topps baseball set for 1975 was radically different in appearance from sets of the preceding years. The most prominent change was the use of a two-color frame surrounding the picture area rather than a single, subdued color. A facsimile autograph appears on the picture, and the backs are printed in red and green on gray. Cards 189-212 depict the MVP's of both leagues from 1951 through 1974. The first seven cards (1-7) feature players breaking records or achieving milestones during the previous season. Cards 306-313 picture league leaders in various statistical categories. Cards 459-466 depict the results of post-season action. Team cards feature a checklist back for players on that team and show a small inset photo of the manager on the front. The Phillies Team card number 46 erroneously lists Terry Harmon as number 339 instead of number 399. This set is quite popular with collectors, at least in part due to the fact that the rookie cards of Robin Yount, George Brett, Gary Carter, Jim Rice, Fred Lynn, and Keith Hernandez are all in the set. Topps minis have the same checklist and are worth approximately double the prices listed below.

	NRMT	VG-E	GOOD
COMPLETE SET (660)	825.00	375.00	95.00
COMMON PLAYER (1-132)	.40	.16	.04
COMMON PLAYER (133-264)	.40	.16	.04
COMMON PLAYER (265-660)	.40	.16	.04

		NRMT	VG-E	GOOD
☐ 1	RB: Hank Aaron Sets Homer Mark	25.00	5.00	1.00
☐ 2	RB: Lou Brock 118 Stolen Bases	3.00	1.25	.30
☐ 3	RB: Bob Gibson 3000th Strikeout	3.00	1.25	.30
☐ 4	RB: Al Kaline 3000 Hit Club	3.00	1.25	.30
☐ 5	RB: Nolan Ryan Fans 300 for 3rd Year in a Row	12.00	5.25	1.50
☐ 6	RB: Mike Marshall Hurls 106 Games	.60	.25	.06
☐ 7	No Hitters Steve Busby Dick Bosman Nolan Ryan	3.00	1.25	.30
☐ 8	Rogelio Moret	.40	.16	.04
☐ 9	Frank Tepedino	.40	.16	.04
☐ 10	Willie Davis	.60	.25	.06
☐ 11	Bill Melton	.40	.16	.04
☐ 12	David Clyde	.40	.16	.04
☐ 13	Gene Locklear	.40	.16	.04
☐ 14	Milt Wilcox	.40	.16	.04
☐ 15	Jose Cardenal	.40	.16	.04
☐ 16	Frank Tanana	1.00	.40	.10
☐ 17	Dave Concepcion	1.50	.60	.15
☐ 18	Tigers: Team/Mgr. Ralph Houk (checklist back)	1.25	.40	.08
☐ 19	Jerry Koosman	.75	.30	.07

		NRMT	VG-E	GOOD
☐ 20	Thurman Munson	8.00	3.50	.80
☐ 21	Rollie Fingers	4.25	1.75	.42
☐ 22	Dave Cash	.40	.16	.04
☐ 23	Bill Russell	.60	.25	.06
☐ 24	Al Fitzmorris	.40	.16	.04
☐ 25	Lee May	.60	.25	.06
☐ 26	Dave McNally	.60	.25	.06
☐ 27	Ken Reitz	.40	.16	.04
☐ 28	Tom Murphy	.40	.16	.04
☐ 29	Dave Parker	12.00	5.25	1.50
☐ 30	Bert Blyleven	2.00	.80	.20
☐ 31	Dave Rader	.40	.16	.04
☐ 32	Reggie Cleveland	.40	.16	.04
☐ 33	Dusty Baker	.60	.25	.06
☐ 34	Steve Renko	.40	.16	.04
☐ 35	Ron Santo	.75	.30	.07
☐ 36	Joe Lovitto	.40	.16	.04
☐ 37	Dave Freisleben	.40	.16	.04
☐ 38	Buddy Bell	.75	.30	.07
☐ 39	Andre Thornton	.60	.25	.06
☐ 40	Bill Singer	.40	.16	.04
☐ 41	Cesar Geronimo	.40	.16	.04
☐ 42	Joe Coleman	.40	.16	.04
☐ 43	Cleon Jones	.40	.16	.04
☐ 44	Pat Dobson	.40	.16	.04
☐ 45	Joe Rudi	.60	.25	.06
☐ 46	Phillies: Team/Mgr UER. Danny Ozark (checklist back)	1.25	.40	.08
☐ 47	Tommy John	1.75	.70	.17
☐ 48	Freddie Patek	.40	.16	.04
☐ 49	Larry Dierker	.40	.16	.04
☐ 50	Brooks Robinson	5.00	2.25	.50
☐ 51	Bob Forsch	.75	.30	.07
☐ 52	Darrell Porter	.40	.16	.04
☐ 53	Dave Giusti	.40	.16	.04
☐ 54	Eric Soderholm	.40	.16	.04
☐ 55	Bobby Bonds	1.00	.40	.10
☐ 56	Rick Wise	.40	.16	.04
☐ 57	Dave Johnson	.60	.25	.06
☐ 58	Chuck Taylor	.40	.16	.04
☐ 59	Ken Henderson	.40	.16	.04
☐ 60	Fergie Jenkins	3.25	1.35	.32
☐ 61	Dave Winfield	25.00	11.00	3.50
☐ 62	Fritz Peterson	.40	.16	.04
☐ 63	Steve Swisher	.40	.16	.04
☐ 64	Dave Chalk	.40	.16	.04
☐ 65	Don Gullett	.60	.25	.06
☐ 66	Willie Horton	.60	.25	.06
☐ 67	Tug McGraw	.75	.30	.07
☐ 68	Ron Blomberg	.40	.16	.04
☐ 69	John Odom	.40	.16	.04
☐ 70	Mike Schmidt	60.00	27.00	9.00
☐ 71	Charlie Hough	.60	.25	.06
☐ 72	Royals: Team/Mgr. Jack McKeon (checklist back)	1.25	.40	.08
☐ 73	J.R. Richard	.60	.25	.06
☐ 74	Mark Belanger	.60	.25	.06
☐ 75	Ted Simmons	1.50	.60	.15
☐ 76	Ed Sprague	.40	.16	.04
☐ 77	Richie Zisk	.40	.16	.04
☐ 78	Ray Corbin	.40	.16	.04
☐ 79	Gary Matthews	.60	.25	.06
☐ 80	Carlton Fisk	16.00	6.75	2.25
☐ 81	Ron Reed	.40	.16	.04
☐ 82	Pat Kelly	.40	.16	.04
☐ 83	Jim Merritt	.40	.16	.04
☐ 84	Enzo Hernandez	.40	.16	.04
☐ 85	Bill Bonham	.40	.16	.04
☐ 86	Joe Lis	.40	.16	.04
☐ 87	George Foster	1.50	.60	.15
☐ 88	Tom Egan	.40	.16	.04
☐ 89	Jim Ray	.40	.16	.04
☐ 90	Rusty Staub	.75	.30	.07
☐ 91	Dick Green	.40	.16	.04
☐ 92	Cecil Upshaw	.40	.16	.04
☐ 93	Dave Lopes	.60	.25	.06
☐ 94	Jim Lonborg	.60	.25	.06
☐ 95	John Mayberry	.60	.25	.06
☐ 96	Mike Cosgrove	.40	.16	.04
☐ 97	Earl Williams	.40	.16	.04
☐ 98	Rich Folkers	.40	.16	.04
☐ 99	Mike Hegan	.40	.16	.04
☐ 100	Willie Stargell	3.50	1.50	.35
☐ 101	Expos: Team/Mgr. Gene Mauch (checklist back)	1.25	.40	.08
☐ 102	Joe Decker	.40	.16	.04
☐ 103	Rick Miller	.40	.16	.04
☐ 104	Bill Madlock	1.25	.50	.12
☐ 105	Buzz Capra	.40	.16	.04
☐ 106	Mike Hargrove	.75	.30	.07
☐ 107	Jim Barr	.40	.16	.04
☐ 108	Tom Hall	.40	.16	.04

☐ 109	George Hendrick	.60	.25	.06
☐ 110	Wilbur Wood	.60	.25	.06
☐ 111	Wayne Garrett	.40	.16	.04
☐ 112	Larry Hardy	.40	.16	.04
☐ 113	Elliott Maddox	.40	.16	.04
☐ 114	Dick Lange	.40	.16	.04
☐ 115	Joe Ferguson	.40	.16	.04
☐ 116	Lerrin LaGrow	.40	.16	.04
☐ 117	Orioles: Team/Mgr.	1.25	.40	.08
	Earl Weaver			
	(checklist back)			
☐ 118	Mike Anderson	.40	.16	.04
☐ 119	Tommy Helms	.60	.25	.06
☐ 120	Steve Busby UER	.60	.25	.06
	(photo actually			
	Fran Healy)			
☐ 121	Bill North	.40	.16	.04
☐ 122	Al Hrabosky	.40	.16	.04
☐ 123	Johnny Briggs	.40	.16	.04
☐ 124	Jerry Reuss	.60	.25	.06
☐ 125	Ken Singleton	.60	.25	.06
☐ 126	Checklist 1-132	1.75	.20	.04
☐ 127	Glenn Borgmann	.40	.16	.04
☐ 128	Bill Lee	.60	.25	.06
☐ 129	Rick Monday	.60	.25	.06
☐ 130	Phil Niekro	2.75	1.10	.27
☐ 131	Toby Harrah	.60	.25	.06
☐ 132	Randy Moffitt	.40	.16	.04
☐ 133	Dan Driessen	.40	.16	.04
☐ 134	Ron Hodges	.40	.16	.04
☐ 135	Charlie Spikes	.40	.16	.04
☐ 136	Jim Mason	.40	.16	.04
☐ 137	Terry Forster	.60	.25	.06
☐ 138	Del Unser	.40	.16	.04
☐ 139	Horacio Pina	.40	.16	.04
☐ 140	Steve Garvey	8.50	3.75	.85
☐ 141	Mickey Stanley	.60	.25	.06
☐ 142	Bob Reynolds	.40	.16	.04
☐ 143	Cliff Johnson	.60	.25	.06
☐ 144	Jim Wohlford	.40	.16	.04
☐ 145	Ken Holtzman	.60	.25	.06
☐ 146	Padres: Team/Mgr.	1.25	.40	.08
	John McNamara			
	(checklist back)			
☐ 147	Pedro Garcia	.40	.16	.04
☐ 148	Jim Rooker	.40	.16	.04
☐ 149	Tim Foli	.40	.16	.04
☐ 150	Bob Gibson	4.25	1.75	.42
☐ 151	Steve Brye	.40	.16	.04
☐ 152	Mario Guerrero	.40	.16	.04
☐ 153	Rick Reuschel	.75	.30	.07
☐ 154	Mike Lum	.40	.16	.04
☐ 155	Jim Bibby	.40	.16	.04
☐ 156	Dave Kingman	1.00	.40	.10
☐ 157	Pedro Borbon	.40	.16	.04
☐ 158	Jerry Grote	.40	.16	.04
☐ 159	Steve Arlin	.40	.16	.04
☐ 160	Graig Nettles	1.50	.60	.15
☐ 161	Stan Bahnsen	.40	.16	.04
☐ 162	Willie Montanez	.40	.16	.04
☐ 163	Jim Brewer	.40	.16	.04
☐ 164	Mickey Rivers	.60	.25	.06
☐ 165	Doug Rader	.60	.25	.06
☐ 166	Woodie Fryman	.40	.16	.04
☐ 167	Rich Coggins	.40	.16	.04
☐ 168	Bill Greif	.40	.16	.04
☐ 169	Cookie Rojas	.40	.16	.04
☐ 170	Bert Campaneris	.60	.25	.06
☐ 171	Ed Kirkpatrick	.40	.16	.04
☐ 172	Red Sox: Team/Mgr.	1.25	.40	.08
	Darrell Johnson			
	(checklist back)			
☐ 173	Steve Rogers	.40	.16	.04
☐ 174	Bake McBride	.60	.25	.06
☐ 175	Don Money	.40	.16	.04
☐ 176	Burt Hooton	.40	.16	.04
☐ 177	Vic Correll	.40	.16	.04
☐ 178	Cesar Tovar	.40	.16	.04
☐ 179	Tom Bradley	.40	.16	.04
☐ 180	Joe Morgan	6.50	2.75	.65
☐ 181	Fred Beene	.40	.16	.04
☐ 182	Don Hahn	.40	.16	.04
☐ 183	Mel Stottlemyre	.75	.30	.07
☐ 184	Jorge Orta	.40	.16	.04
☐ 185	Steve Carlton	8.50	3.75	.85
☐ 186	Willie Crawford	.40	.16	.04
☐ 187	Denny Doyle	.40	.16	.04
☐ 188	Tom Griffin	.40	.16	.04
☐ 189	1951 MVP's	2.00	.80	.20
	Larry (Yogi) Berra			
	Roy Campanella			
	(Campy never issued)			
☐ 190	1952 MVP's	.60	.25	.06
	Bobby Shantz			
	Hank Sauer			

☐ 191	1953 MVP's	1.00	.40	.10
	Al Rosen			
	Roy Campanella			
☐ 192	1954 MVP's	2.00	.80	.20
	Yogi Berra			
	Willie Mays			
☐ 193	1955 MVP's UER	2.00	.80	.20
	Yogi Berra			
	Roy Campanella			
	(Campy card never			
	issued, pictured			
	with LA cap, sic)			
☐ 194	1956 MVP's	5.00	2.25	.50
	Mickey Mantle			
	Don Newcombe			
☐ 195	1957 MVP's	9.00	4.00	.90
	Mickey Mantle			
	Hank Aaron			
☐ 196	1958 MVP's	1.00	.40	.10
	Jackie Jensen			
	Ernie Banks			
☐ 197	1959 MVP's	1.25	.50	.12
	Nellie Fox			
	Ernie Banks			
☐ 198	1960 MVP's	1.25	.50	.12
	Roger Maris			
	Dick Groat			
☐ 199	1961 MVP's	2.00	.80	.20
	Roger Maris			
	Frank Robinson			
☐ 200	1962 MVP's	5.00	2.25	.50
	Mickey Mantle			
	Maury Wills			
	(Wills never issued)			
☐ 201	1963 MVP's	1.00	.40	.10
	Elston Howard			
	Sandy Koufax			
☐ 202	1964 MVP's	1.00	.40	.10
	Brooks Robinson			
	Ken Boyer			
☐ 203	1965 MVP's	1.00	.40	.10
	Zoilo Versalles			
	Willie Mays			
☐ 204	1966 MVP's	2.00	.80	.20
	Frank Robinson			
	Bob Clemente			
☐ 205	1967 MVP's	1.25	.50	.12
	Carl Yastrzemski			
	Orlando Cepeda			
☐ 206	1968 MVP's	1.25	.50	.12
	Denny McLain			
	Bob Gibson			
☐ 207	1969 MVP's	1.25	.50	.12
	Harmon Killebrew			
	Willie McCovey			
☐ 208	1970 MVP's	1.00	.40	.10
	Boog Powell			
	Johnny Bench			
☐ 209	1971 MVP's	.60	.25	.06
	Vida Blue			
	Joe Torre			
☐ 210	1972 MVP's	1.00	.40	.10
	Rich Allen			
	Johnny Bench			
☐ 211	1973 MVP's	4.00	1.75	.40
	Reggie Jackson			
	Pete Rose			
☐ 212	1974 MVP's	.75	.30	.07
	Jeff Burroughs			
	Steve Garvey			
☐ 213	Oscar Gamble	.60	.25	.06
☐ 214	Harry Parker	.40	.16	.04
☐ 215	Bobby Valentine	.60	.25	.06
☐ 216	Giants: Team/Mgr.	1.25	.40	.08
	Wes Westrum			
	(checklist back)			
☐ 217	Lou Piniella	.75	.30	.07
☐ 218	Jerry Johnson	.40	.16	.04
☐ 219	Ed Herrmann	.40	.16	.04
☐ 220	Don Sutton	2.50	1.00	.25
☐ 221	Aurelio Rodriguez	.40	.16	.04
☐ 222	Dan Spillner	.40	.16	.04
☐ 223	Robin Yount	195.00	80.00	16.00
☐ 224	Ramon Hernandez	.40	.16	.04
☐ 225	Bob Grich	.60	.25	.06
☐ 226	Bill Campbell	.40	.16	.04
☐ 227	Bob Watson	.60	.25	.06
☐ 228	George Brett	195.00	80.00	16.00
☐ 229	Barry Foote	.40	.16	.04
☐ 230	Jim Hunter	3.25	1.35	.32
☐ 231	Mike Tyson	.40	.16	.04
☐ 232	Diego Segui	.40	.16	.04
☐ 233	Billy Grabarkewitz	.40	.16	.04
☐ 234	Tom Grieve	.60	.25	.06
☐ 235	Jack Billingham	.40	.16	.04

#	Player			
☐ 236	Angels: Team/Mgr. Dick Williams (checklist back)	1.25	.40	.08
☐ 237	Carl Morton	.40	.16	.04
☐ 238	Dave Duncan	.40	.16	.04
☐ 239	George Stone	.40	.16	.04
☐ 240	Garry Maddox	.60	.25	.06
☐ 241	Dick Tidrow	.40	.16	.04
☐ 242	Jay Johnstone	.60	.25	.06
☐ 243	Jim Kaat	1.00	.40	.10
☐ 244	Bill Buckner	.75	.30	.07
☐ 245	Mickey Lolich	.75	.30	.07
☐ 246	Cardinals: Team/Mgr. Red Schoendienst (checklist back)	1.25	.40	.08
☐ 247	Enos Cabell	.40	.16	.04
☐ 248	Randy Jones	.60	.25	.06
☐ 249	Danny Thompson	.40	.16	.04
☐ 250	Ken Brett	.40	.16	.04
☐ 251	Fran Healy	.40	.16	.04
☐ 252	Fred Scherman	.40	.16	.04
☐ 253	Jesus Alou	.40	.16	.04
☐ 254	Mike Torrez	.40	.16	.04
☐ 255	Dwight Evans	7.00	3.00	.70
☐ 256	Billy Champion	.40	.16	.04
☐ 257	Checklist: 133-264	1.75	.20	.04
☐ 258	Dave LaRoche	.40	.16	.04
☐ 259	Len Randle	.40	.16	.04
☐ 260	Johnny Bench	13.50	6.00	1.85
☐ 261	Andy Hassler	.40	.16	.04
☐ 262	Rowland Office	.40	.16	.04
☐ 263	Jim Perry	.60	.25	.06
☐ 264	John Milner	.40	.16	.04
☐ 265	Ron Bryant	.40	.16	.04
☐ 266	Sandy Alomar	.40	.16	.04
☐ 267	Dick Ruthven	.40	.16	.04
☐ 268	Hal McRae	.75	.30	.07
☐ 269	Doug Rau	.40	.16	.04
☐ 270	Ron Fairly	.40	.16	.04
☐ 271	Gerry Moses	.40	.16	.04
☐ 272	Lynn McGlothen	.40	.16	.04
☐ 273	Steve Braun	.40	.16	.04
☐ 274	Vicente Romo	.40	.16	.04
☐ 275	Paul Blair	.60	.25	.06
☐ 276	White Sox Team/Mgr. Chuck Tanner (checklist back)	1.25	.40	.08
☐ 277	Frank Taveras	.40	.16	.04
☐ 278	Paul Lindblad	.40	.16	.04
☐ 279	Milt May	.40	.16	.04
☐ 280	Carl Yastrzemski	10.00	4.50	1.25
☐ 281	Jim Slaton	.40	.16	.04
☐ 282	Jerry Morales	.40	.16	.04
☐ 283	Steve Foucault	.40	.16	.04
☐ 284	Ken Griffey	3.75	1.60	.37
☐ 285	Ellie Rodriguez	.40	.16	.04
☐ 286	Mike Jorgensen	.40	.16	.04
☐ 287	Roric Harrison	.40	.16	.04
☐ 288	Bruce Ellingsen	.40	.16	.04
☐ 289	Ken Rudolph	.40	.16	.04
☐ 290	Jon Matlack	.60	.25	.06
☐ 291	Bill Sudakis	.40	.16	.04
☐ 292	Ron Schueler	.40	.16	.04
☐ 293	Dick Sharon	.40	.16	.04
☐ 294	Geoff Zahn	.40	.16	.04
☐ 295	Vada Pinson	.60	.25	.06
☐ 296	Alan Foster	.40	.16	.04
☐ 297	Craig Kusick	.40	.16	.04
☐ 298	Johnny Grubb	.40	.16	.04
☐ 299	Bucky Dent	.75	.30	.07
☐ 300	Reggie Jackson	18.00	7.50	2.50
☐ 301	Dave Roberts	.40	.16	.04
☐ 302	Rick Burleson	.60	.25	.06
☐ 303	Grant Jackson	.40	.16	.04
☐ 304	Pirates: Team/Mgr. Danny Murtaugh (checklist back)	1.25	.40	.08
☐ 305	Jim Colborn	.40	.16	.04
☐ 306	Batting Leaders Rod Carew Ralph Garr	1.00	.40	.10
☐ 307	Home Run Leaders Dick Allen Mike Schmidt	2.50	1.00	.25
☐ 308	RBI Leaders Jeff Burroughs Johnny Bench	1.00	.40	.10
☐ 309	Stolen Base Leaders Bill North Lou Brock	1.00	.40	.10
☐ 310	Victory Leaders Jim Hunter Fergie Jenkins Andy Messersmith Phil Niekro	1.00	.40	.10
☐ 311	ERA Leaders Jim Hunter Buzz Capra	1.00	.40	.10
☐ 312	Strikeout Leaders Nolan Ryan Steve Carlton	7.00	3.00	.70
☐ 313	Leading Firemen Terry Forster Mike Marshall	.60	.25	.06
☐ 314	Buck Martinez	.40	.16	.04
☐ 315	Don Kessinger	.60	.25	.06
☐ 316	Jackie Brown	.40	.16	.04
☐ 317	Joe Lahoud	.40	.16	.04
☐ 318	Ernie McAnally	.40	.16	.04
☐ 319	Johnny Oates	.60	.25	.06
☐ 320	Pete Rose	15.00	6.50	2.15
☐ 321	Rudy May	.40	.16	.04
☐ 322	Ed Goodson	.40	.16	.04
☐ 323	Fred Holdsworth	.40	.16	.04
☐ 324	Ed Kranepool	.60	.25	.06
☐ 325	Tony Oliva	1.00	.40	.10
☐ 326	Wayne Twitchell	.40	.16	.04
☐ 327	Jerry Hairston	.40	.16	.04
☐ 328	Sonny Siebert	.40	.16	.04
☐ 329	Ted Kubiak	.40	.16	.04
☐ 330	Mike Marshall	.60	.25	.06
☐ 331	Indians: Team/Mgr. Frank Robinson (checklist back)	1.25	.40	.08
☐ 332	Fred Kendall	.40	.16	.04
☐ 333	Dick Drago	.40	.16	.04
☐ 334	Greg Gross	.40	.16	.04
☐ 335	Jim Palmer	8.50	3.75	.85
☐ 336	Rennie Stennett	.40	.16	.04
☐ 337	Kevin Kobel	.40	.16	.04
☐ 338	Rich Stelmaszek	.40	.16	.04
☐ 339	Jim Fregosi	.60	.25	.06
☐ 340	Paul Splittorff	.40	.16	.04
☐ 341	Hal Breeden	.40	.16	.04
☐ 342	Leroy Stanton	.40	.16	.04
☐ 343	Danny Frisella	.40	.16	.04
☐ 344	Ben Oglivie	.60	.25	.06
☐ 345	Clay Carroll	.40	.16	.04
☐ 346	Bobby Darwin	.40	.16	.04
☐ 347	Mike Caldwell	.40	.16	.04
☐ 348	Tony Muser	.40	.16	.04
☐ 349	Ray Sadecki	.40	.16	.04
☐ 350	Bobby Murcer	.75	.30	.07
☐ 351	Bob Boone	1.25	.50	.12
☐ 352	Darold Knowles	.40	.16	.04
☐ 353	Luis Melendez	.40	.16	.04
☐ 354	Dick Bosman	.40	.16	.04
☐ 355	Chris Cannizzaro	.40	.16	.04
☐ 356	Rico Petrocelli	.60	.25	.06
☐ 357	Ken Forsch	.40	.16	.04
☐ 358	Al Bumbry	.40	.16	.04
☐ 359	Paul Popovich	.40	.16	.04
☐ 360	George Scott	.60	.25	.06
☐ 361	Dodgers: Team/Mgr. Walter Alston (checklist back)	1.50	.50	.10
☐ 362	Steve Hargan	.40	.16	.04
☐ 363	Carmen Fanzone	.40	.16	.04
☐ 364	Doug Bird	.40	.16	.04
☐ 365	Bob Bailey	.40	.16	.04
☐ 366	Ken Sanders	.40	.16	.04
☐ 367	Craig Robinson	.40	.16	.04
☐ 368	Vic Albury	.40	.16	.04
☐ 369	Merv Rettenmund	.40	.16	.04
☐ 370	Tom Seaver	16.00	6.75	2.25
☐ 371	Gates Brown	.60	.25	.06
☐ 372	John D'Acquisto	.40	.16	.04
☐ 373	Bill Sharp	.40	.16	.04
☐ 374	Eddie Watt	.40	.16	.04
☐ 375	Roy White	.60	.25	.06
☐ 376	Steve Yeager	.60	.25	.06
☐ 377	Tom Hilgendorf	.40	.16	.04
☐ 378	Derrel Thomas	.40	.16	.04
☐ 379	Bernie Carbo	.40	.16	.04
☐ 380	Sal Bando	.60	.25	.06
☐ 381	John Curtis	.40	.16	.04
☐ 382	Don Baylor	1.50	.60	.15
☐ 383	Jim York	.40	.16	.04
☐ 384	Brewers: Team/Mgr. Del Crandall (checklist back)	1.25	.40	.08
☐ 385	Dock Ellis	.40	.16	.04
☐ 386	Checklist: 265-396	1.75	.20	.04
☐ 387	Jim Spencer	.40	.16	.04
☐ 388	Steve Stone	.60	.25	.06
☐ 389	Tony Solaita	.40	.16	.04
☐ 390	Ron Cey	.75	.30	.07
☐ 391	Don DeMola	.40	.16	.04
☐ 392	Bruce Bochte	.60	.25	.06
☐ 393	Gary Gentry	.40	.16	.04

☐ 394 Larvell Blanks	.40	.16	.04
☐ 395 Bud Harrelson	.60	.25	.06
☐ 396 Fred Norman	.40	.16	.04
☐ 397 Bill Freehan	.60	.25	.06
☐ 398 Elias Sosa	.40	.16	.04
☐ 399 Terry Harmon	.40	.16	.04
☐ 400 Dick Allen	.75	.30	.07
☐ 401 Mike Wallace	.40	.16	.04
☐ 402 Bob Tolan	.40	.16	.04
☐ 403 Tom Buskey	.40	.16	.04
☐ 404 Ted Sizemore	.40	.16	.04
☐ 405 John Montague	.40	.16	.04
☐ 406 Bob Gallagher	.40	.16	.04
☐ 407 Herb Washington	.40	.16	.04
☐ 408 Clyde Wright	.40	.16	.04
☐ 409 Bob Robertson	.40	.16	.04
☐ 410 Mike Cueller UER	.60	.25	.06
(sic, Cuellar)			
☐ 411 George Mitterwald	.40	.16	.04
☐ 412 Bill Hands	.40	.16	.04
☐ 413 Marty Pattin	.40	.16	.04
☐ 414 Manny Mota	.60	.25	.06
☐ 415 John Hiller	.60	.25	.06
☐ 416 Larry Lintz	.40	.16	.04
☐ 417 Skip Lockwood	.40	.16	.04
☐ 418 Leo Foster	.40	.16	.04
☐ 419 Dave Goltz	.40	.16	.04
☐ 420 Larry Bowa	.60	.25	.06
☐ 421 Mets: Team/Mgr.	1.50	.50	.10
Yogi Berra			
(checklist back)			
☐ 422 Brian Downing	1.00	.40	.10
☐ 423 Clay Kirby	.40	.16	.04
☐ 424 John Lowenstein	.40	.16	.04
☐ 425 Tito Fuentes	.40	.16	.04
☐ 426 George Medich	.40	.16	.04
☐ 427 Clarence Gaston	.60	.25	.06
☐ 428 Dave Hamilton	.40	.16	.04
☐ 429 Jim Dwyer	.40	.16	.04
☐ 430 Luis Tiant	.75	.30	.07
☐ 431 Rod Gilbreath	.40	.16	.04
☐ 432 Ken Berry	.40	.16	.04
☐ 433 Larry Demery	.40	.16	.04
☐ 434 Bob Locker	.40	.16	.04
☐ 435 Dave Nelson	.40	.16	.04
☐ 436 Ken Frailing	.40	.16	.04
☐ 437 Al Cowens	.60	.25	.06
☐ 438 Don Carrithers	.40	.16	.04
☐ 439 Ed Brinkman	.40	.16	.04
☐ 440 Andy Messersmith	.60	.25	.06
☐ 441 Bobby Heise	.40	.16	.04
☐ 442 Maximino Leon	.40	.16	.04
☐ 443 Twins: Team/Mgr.	1.25	.40	.08
Frank Quilici			
(checklist back)			
☐ 444 Gene Garber	.40	.16	.04
☐ 445 Felix Millan	.40	.16	.04
☐ 446 Bart Johnson	.40	.16	.04
☐ 447 Terry Crowley	.40	.16	.04
☐ 448 Frank Duffy	.40	.16	.04
☐ 449 Charlie Williams	.40	.16	.04
☐ 450 Willie McCovey	4.25	1.75	.42
☐ 451 Rick Dempsey	.60	.25	.06
☐ 452 Angel Mangual	.40	.16	.04
☐ 453 Claude Osteen	.60	.25	.06
☐ 454 Doug Griffin	.40	.16	.04
☐ 455 Don Wilson	.40	.16	.04
☐ 456 Bob Coluccio	.40	.16	.04
☐ 457 Mario Mendoza	.40	.16	.04
☐ 458 Ross Grimsley	.40	.16	.04
☐ 459 1974 AL Champs	.75	.30	.07
A's over Orioles			
(2B action pictured)			
☐ 460 1974 NL Champs	1.00	.40	.10
Dodgers over Pirates			
(Taveras/Garvey at 2B)			
☐ 461 World Series Game 1	2.50	1.00	.25
(Reggie Jackson)			
☐ 462 World Series Game 2	.75	.30	.07
(Dodger dugout)			
☐ 463 World Series Game 3	1.00	.40	.10
(Fingers pitching)			
☐ 464 World Series Game 4	.75	.30	.07
(A's batter)			
☐ 465 World Series Game 5	.75	.30	.07
(Rudi rounding third)			
☐ 466 World Series Summary	.75	.30	.07
A's do it again;			
win third straight			
(A's group picture)			
☐ 467 Ed Halicki	.40	.16	.04
☐ 468 Bobby Mitchell	.40	.16	.04
☐ 469 Tom Dettore	.40	.16	.04
☐ 470 Jeff Burroughs	.60	.25	.06
☐ 471 Bob Stinson	.40	.16	.04

☐ 472 Bruce Dal Canton	.40	.16	.04
☐ 473 Ken McMullen	.40	.16	.04
☐ 474 Luke Walker	.40	.16	.04
☐ 475 Darrell Evans	.60	.25	.06
☐ 476 Ed Figueroa	.40	.16	.04
☐ 477 Tom Hutton	.40	.16	.04
☐ 478 Tom Burgmeier	.40	.16	.04
☐ 479 Ken Boswell	.40	.16	.04
☐ 480 Carlos May	.40	.16	.04
☐ 481 Will McEnaney	.40	.16	.04
☐ 482 Tom McCraw	.40	.16	.04
☐ 483 Steve Ontiveros	.40	.16	.04
☐ 484 Glenn Beckert	.60	.25	.06
☐ 485 Sparky Lyle	.60	.25	.06
☐ 486 Ray Fosse	.40	.16	.04
☐ 487 Astros: Team/Mgr.	1.25	.40	.08
Preston Gomez			
(checklist back)			
☐ 488 Bill Travers	.40	.16	.04
☐ 489 Cecil Cooper	1.25	.50	.12
☐ 490 Reggie Smith	.75	.30	.07
☐ 491 Doyle Alexander	.40	.16	.04
☐ 492 Rich Hebner	.40	.16	.04
☐ 493 Don Stanhouse	.40	.16	.04
☐ 494 Pete LaCock	.40	.16	.04
☐ 495 Nelson Briles	.40	.16	.04
☐ 496 Pepe Frias	.40	.16	.04
☐ 497 Jim Nettles	.40	.16	.04
☐ 498 Al Downing	.60	.25	.06
☐ 499 Marty Perez	.40	.16	.04
☐ 500 Nolan Ryan	50.00	22.50	7.50
☐ 501 Bill Robinson	.60	.25	.06
☐ 502 Pat Bourque	.40	.16	.04
☐ 503 Fred Stanley	.40	.16	.04
☐ 504 Buddy Bradford	.40	.16	.04
☐ 505 Chris Speier	.40	.16	.04
☐ 506 Leron Lee	.40	.16	.04
☐ 507 Tom Carroll	.40	.16	.04
☐ 508 Bob Hansen	.40	.16	.04
☐ 509 Dave Hilton	.40	.16	.04
☐ 510 Vida Blue	.60	.25	.06
☐ 511 Rangers: Team/Mgr.	1.25	.40	.08
Billy Martin			
(checklist back)			
☐ 512 Larry Milbourne	.40	.16	.04
☐ 513 Dick Pole	.40	.16	.04
☐ 514 Jose Cruz	.60	.25	.06
☐ 515 Manny Sanguillen	.60	.25	.06
☐ 516 Don Hood	.40	.16	.04
☐ 517 Checklist: 397-528	1.75	.20	.04
☐ 518 Leo Cardenas	.40	.16	.04
☐ 519 Jim Todd	.40	.16	.04
☐ 520 Amos Otis	.60	.25	.06
☐ 521 Dennis Blair	.40	.16	.04
☐ 522 Gary Sutherland	.40	.16	.04
☐ 523 Tom Paciorek	.40	.16	.04
☐ 524 John Doherty	.40	.16	.04
☐ 525 Tom House	.40	.16	.04
☐ 526 Larry Hisle	.60	.25	.06
☐ 527 Mac Scarce	.40	.16	.04
☐ 528 Eddie Leon	.40	.16	.04
☐ 529 Gary Thomasson	.40	.16	.04
☐ 530 Gaylord Perry	3.25	1.35	.32
☐ 531 Reds: Team/Mgr.	1.50	.50	.10
Sparky Anderson			
(checklist back)			
☐ 532 Gorman Thomas	.60	.25	.06
☐ 533 Rudy Meoli	.40	.16	.04
☐ 534 Alex Johnson	.40	.16	.04
☐ 535 Gene Tenace	.60	.25	.06
☐ 536 Bob Moose	.40	.16	.04
☐ 537 Tommy Harper	.60	.25	.06
☐ 538 Duffy Dyer	.40	.16	.04
☐ 539 Jesse Jefferson	.40	.16	.04
☐ 540 Lou Brock	4.25	1.75	.42
☐ 541 Roger Metzger	.40	.16	.04
☐ 542 Pete Broberg	.40	.16	.04
☐ 543 Larry Biittner	.40	.16	.04
☐ 544 Steve Mingori	.40	.16	.04
☐ 545 Billy Williams	3.00	1.25	.30
☐ 546 John Knox	.40	.16	.04
☐ 547 Von Joshua	.40	.16	.04
☐ 548 Charlie Sands	.40	.16	.04
☐ 549 Bill Butler	.40	.16	.04
☐ 550 Ralph Garr	.60	.25	.06
☐ 551 Larry Christenson	.40	.16	.04
☐ 552 Jack Brohamer	.40	.16	.04
☐ 553 John Boccabella	.40	.16	.04
☐ 554 Rich Gossage	2.25	.90	.22
☐ 555 Al Oliver	.75	.30	.07
☐ 556 Tim Johnson	.40	.16	.04
☐ 557 Larry Gura	.40	.16	.04
☐ 558 Dave Roberts	.40	.16	.04
☐ 559 Bob Montgomery	.40	.16	.04
☐ 560 Tony Perez	3.00	1.25	.30

		NRMT	VG-E	GOOD
☐ 561	A's: Team/Mgr. .... Alvin Dark (checklist back)	1.25	.40	.08
☐ 562	Gary Nolan	.40	.16	.04
☐ 563	Wilbur Howard	.40	.16	.04
☐ 564	Tommy Davis	.60	.25	.06
☐ 565	Joe Torre	.75	.30	.07
☐ 566	Ray Burris	.40	.16	.04
☐ 567	Jim Sundberg	.75	.30	.07
☐ 568	Dale Murray	.40	.16	.04
☐ 569	Frank White	.75	.30	.07
☐ 570	Jim Wynn	.60	.25	.06
☐ 571	Dave Lemanczyk	.40	.16	.04
☐ 572	Roger Nelson	.40	.16	.04
☐ 573	Orlando Pena	.40	.16	.04
☐ 574	Tony Taylor	.40	.16	.04
☐ 575	Gene Clines	.40	.16	.04
☐ 576	Phil Roof	.40	.16	.04
☐ 577	John Morris	.40	.16	.04
☐ 578	Dave Tomlin	.40	.16	.04
☐ 579	Skip Pitlock	.40	.16	.04
☐ 580	Frank Robinson	4.25	1.75	.42
☐ 581	Darrel Chaney	.40	.16	.04
☐ 582	Eduardo Rodriguez	.40	.16	.04
☐ 583	Andy Etchebarren	.40	.16	.04
☐ 584	Mike Garman	.40	.16	.04
☐ 585	Chris Chambliss	.60	.25	.06
☐ 586	Tim McCarver	.75	.30	.07
☐ 587	Chris Ward	.40	.16	.04
☐ 588	Rick Auerbach	.40	.16	.04
☐ 589	Braves: Team/Mgr. .... Clyde King (checklist back)	1.25	.40	.08
☐ 590	Cesar Cedeno	.60	.25	.06
☐ 591	Glenn Abbott	.40	.16	.04
☐ 592	Balor Moore	.40	.16	.04
☐ 593	Gene Lamont	.60	.25	.06
☐ 594	Jim Fuller	.40	.16	.04
☐ 595	Joe Niekro	.60	.25	.06
☐ 596	Ollie Brown	.40	.16	.04
☐ 597	Winston Llenas	.40	.16	.04
☐ 598	Bruce Kison	.40	.16	.04
☐ 599	Nate Colbert	.40	.16	.04
☐ 600	Rod Carew	11.00	5.00	1.35
☐ 601	Juan Beniquez	.60	.25	.06
☐ 602	John Vukovich	.40	.16	.04
☐ 603	Lew Krausse	.40	.16	.04
☐ 604	Oscar Zamora	.40	.16	.04
☐ 605	John Ellis	.40	.16	.04
☐ 606	Bruce Miller	.40	.16	.04
☐ 607	Jim Holt	.40	.16	.04
☐ 608	Gene Michael	.60	.25	.06
☐ 609	Elrod Hendricks	.40	.16	.04
☐ 610	Ron Hunt	.40	.16	.04
☐ 611	Yankees: Team/Mgr. .... Bill Virdon (checklist back)	1.50	.50	.10
☐ 612	Terry Hughes	.40	.16	.04
☐ 613	Bill Parsons	.40	.16	.04
☐ 614	Rookie Pitchers .... Jack Kucek Dyar Miller Vern Ruhle Paul Siebert	.40	.16	.04
☐ 615	Rookie Pitchers .... Pat Darcy Dennis Leonard Tom Underwood Hank Webb	.75	.30	.07
☐ 616	Rookie Outfielders .... Dave Augustine Pepe Mangual Jim Rice John Scott	24.00	10.50	3.50
☐ 617	Rookie Infielders .... Mike Cubbage Doug DeCinces Reggie Sanders Manny Trillo	1.75	.70	.17
☐ 618	Rookie Pitchers .... Jamie Easterly Tom Johnson Scott McGregor Rick Rhoden	1.50	.60	.15
☐ 619	Rookie Outfielders .... Benny Ayala Nyls Nyman Tommy Smith Jerry Turner	.40	.16	.04
☐ 620	Rookie Catcher/OF .... Gary Carter Marc Hill Danny Meyer Leon Roberts	42.00	18.00	5.50
☐ 621	Rookie Pitchers .... John Denny Rawly Eastwick Jim Kern Juan Veintidos	.60	.25	.06
☐ 622	Rookie Outfielders UER .... Ed Armbrister Fred Lynn Tom Poquette Terry Whitfield (listed as Ney York)	12.00	5.25	1.50
☐ 623	Rookie Infielders UER .... Phil Garner Keith Hernandez (sic, bats right) Bob Sheldon Tom Veryzer	20.00	8.50	2.75
☐ 624	Rookie Pitchers .... Doug Konieczny Gary Lavelle Jim Otten Eddie Solomon	.40	.16	.04
☐ 625	Boog Powell	.75	.30	.07
☐ 626	Larry Haney UER .... (photo actually Dave Duncan)	.40	.16	.04
☐ 627	Tom Walker	.40	.16	.04
☐ 628	Ron LeFlore	.60	.25	.06
☐ 629	Joe Hoerner	.40	.16	.04
☐ 630	Greg Luzinski	.60	.25	.06
☐ 631	Lee Lacy	.40	.16	.04
☐ 632	Morris Nettles	.40	.16	.04
☐ 633	Paul Casanova	.40	.16	.04
☐ 634	Cy Acosta	.40	.16	.04
☐ 635	Chuck Dobson	.40	.16	.04
☐ 636	Charlie Moore	.40	.16	.04
☐ 637	Ted Martinez	.40	.16	.04
☐ 638	Cubs: Team/Mgr. .... Jim Marshall (checklist back)	1.25	.40	.08
☐ 639	Steve Kline	.40	.16	.04
☐ 640	Harmon Killebrew	4.25	1.75	.42
☐ 641	Jim Northrup	.60	.25	.06
☐ 642	Mike Phillips	.40	.16	.04
☐ 643	Brent Strom	.40	.16	.04
☐ 644	Bill Fahey	.40	.16	.04
☐ 645	Danny Cater	.40	.16	.04
☐ 646	Checklist: 529-660	1.75	.20	.04
☐ 647	Claudell Washington	1.25	.50	.12
☐ 648	Dave Pagan	.40	.16	.04
☐ 649	Jack Heidemann	.40	.16	.04
☐ 650	Dave May	.40	.16	.04
☐ 651	John Morlan	.40	.16	.04
☐ 652	Ed Herrmann	.40	.16	.04
☐ 653	Lee Richard UER .... (listed as Richards on card front)	.40	.16	.04
☐ 654	Jerry Terrell	.40	.16	.04
☐ 655	Rico Carty	.60	.25	.06
☐ 656	Bill Plummer	.40	.16	.04
☐ 657	Bob Oliver	.40	.16	.04
☐ 658	Vic Harris	.40	.16	.04
☐ 659	Bob Apodaca	.40	.16	.04
☐ 660	Hank Aaron	25.00	7.50	1.50

1976 Topps

The 1976 Topps set of 660 cards (measuring 2 1/2" by 3 1/2") is known for its sharp color photographs and interesting presentation of subjects. Team cards feature a checklist back for players on that team and show a small inset photo of the manager on the front. A "Father and Son" series (66-70) spotlights five Major Leaguers whose fathers also made the "Big Show." Other subseries include "All Time All Stars" (341-350), "Record Breakers" from the previous season (1-6), League Leaders (191-205), Post-season cards (461-462), and Rookie Prospects (589-599). The key rookies in this set are Dennis Eckersley and Willie Randolph.

		NRMT	VG-E	GOOD
	COMPLETE SET (660)	425.00	190.00	63.00
	COMMON PLAYER (1-660)	.30	.12	.03
☐ 1	RB: Hank Aaron .... Most RBI's, 2262	15.00	4.00	.80

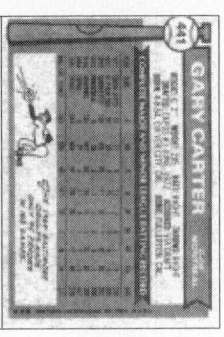

GARY CARTER
EXPOS

☐ 2	RB: Bobby Bonds Most leadoff HR's 32; plus three seasons 30 homers/30 steals	.60	.25	.06
☐ 3	RB: Mickey Lolich Lefthander, Most Strikeouts, 2679	.50	.20	.05
☐ 4	RB: Dave Lopes Most Consecutive SB attempts, 38	.40	.16	.04
☐ 5	RB: Tom Seaver Most Cons. seasons with 200 SO's, 8	3.00	1.25	.30
☐ 6	RB: Rennie Stennett Most Hits in a 9 inning game, 7	.40	.16	.04
☐ 7	Jim Umbarger	.30	.12	.03
☐ 8	Tito Fuentes	.30	.12	.03
☐ 9	Paul Lindblad	.30	.12	.03
☐ 10	Lou Brock	4.25	1.75	.42
☐ 11	Jim Hughes	.30	.12	.03
☐ 12	Richie Zisk	.30	.12	.03
☐ 13	John Wockenfuss	.30	.12	.03
☐ 14	Gene Garber	.30	.12	.03
☐ 15	George Scott	.40	.16	.04
☐ 16	Bob Apodaca	.30	.12	.03
☐ 17	New York Yankees Team Card; Billy Martin MG (checklist back)	1.00	.30	.06
☐ 18	Dale Murray	.30	.12	.03
☐ 19	George Brett	48.00	22.00	6.50
☐ 20	Bob Watson	.40	.16	.04
☐ 21	Dave LaRoche	.30	.12	.03
☐ 22	Bill Russell	.40	.16	.04
☐ 23	Brian Downing	.60	.25	.06
☐ 24	Cesar Geronimo	.30	.12	.03
☐ 25	Mike Torrez	.30	.12	.03
☐ 26	Andre Thornton	.40	.16	.04
☐ 27	Ed Figueroa	.30	.12	.03
☐ 28	Dusty Baker	.50	.20	.05
☐ 29	Rick Burleson	.40	.16	.04
☐ 30	John Montefusco	.40	.16	.04
☐ 31	Len Randle	.30	.12	.03
☐ 32	Danny Frisella	.30	.12	.03
☐ 33	Bill North	.30	.12	.03
☐ 34	Mike Garman	.30	.12	.03
☐ 35	Tony Oliva	.90	.40	.09
☐ 36	Frank Taveras	.30	.12	.03
☐ 37	John Hiller	.40	.16	.04
☐ 38	Garry Maddox	.40	.16	.04
☐ 39	Pete Broberg	.30	.12	.03
☐ 40	Dave Kingman	.90	.40	.09
☐ 41	Tippy Martinez	.40	.16	.04
☐ 42	Barry Foote	.30	.12	.03
☐ 43	Paul Splittorff	.30	.12	.03
☐ 44	Doug Rader	.40	.16	.04
☐ 45	Boog Powell	.60	.25	.06
☐ 46	Dodgers Team Walter Alston MG (checklist back)	1.00	.30	.06
☐ 47	Jesse Jefferson	.30	.12	.03
☐ 48	Dave Concepcion	.90	.40	.09
☐ 49	Dave Duncan	.30	.12	.03
☐ 50	Fred Lynn	2.00	.80	.20
☐ 51	Ray Burris	.30	.12	.03
☐ 52	Dave Chalk	.30	.12	.03
☐ 53	Mike Beard	.30	.12	.03
☐ 54	Dave Rader	.30	.12	.03
☐ 55	Gaylord Perry	3.00	1.25	.30
☐ 56	Bob Tolan	.30	.12	.03
☐ 57	Phil Garner	.60	.25	.06
☐ 58	Ron Reed	.30	.12	.03
☐ 59	Larry Hisle	.40	.16	.04
☐ 60	Jerry Reuss	.40	.16	.04
☐ 61	Ron LeFlore	.40	.16	.04
☐ 62	Johnny Oates	.40	.16	.04
☐ 63	Bobby Darwin	.30	.12	.03
☐ 64	Jerry Koosman	.50	.20	.05
☐ 65	Chris Chambliss	.50	.20	.05
☐ 66	Father and Son Gus Bell Buddy Bell	.50	.20	.05
☐ 67	Father and Son Ray Boone Bob Boone	.60	.25	.06
☐ 68	Father and Son Joe Coleman Joe Coleman Jr.	.40	.16	.04
☐ 69	Father and Son Jim Hegan Mike Hegan	.40	.16	.04
☐ 70	Father and Son Roy Smalley Roy Smalley Jr.	.40	.16	.04
☐ 71	Steve Rogers	.30	.12	.03
☐ 72	Hal McRae	.60	.25	.06
☐ 73	Baltimore Orioles Team Card Earl Weaver MG (checklist back)	1.00	.30	.06
☐ 74	Oscar Gamble	.40	.16	.04
☐ 75	Larry Dierker	.30	.12	.03
☐ 76	Willie Crawford	.30	.12	.03
☐ 77	Pedro Borbon	.30	.12	.03
☐ 78	Cecil Cooper	.75	.30	.07
☐ 79	Jerry Morales	.30	.12	.03
☐ 80	Jim Kaat	1.00	.40	.10
☐ 81	Darrell Evans	.60	.25	.06
☐ 82	Von Joshua	.30	.12	.03
☐ 83	Jim Spencer	.30	.12	.03
☐ 84	Brent Strom	.30	.12	.03
☐ 85	Mickey Rivers	.40	.16	.04
☐ 86	Mike Tyson	.30	.12	.03
☐ 87	Tom Burgmeier	.30	.12	.03
☐ 88	Duffy Dyer	.30	.12	.03
☐ 89	Vern Ruhle	.30	.12	.03
☐ 90	Sal Bando	.50	.20	.05
☐ 91	Tom Hutton	.30	.12	.03
☐ 92	Eduardo Rodriguez	.30	.12	.03
☐ 93	Mike Phillips	.30	.12	.03
☐ 94	Jim Dwyer	.30	.12	.03
☐ 95	Brooks Robinson	4.25	1.75	.42
☐ 96	Doug Bird	.30	.12	.03
☐ 97	Wilbur Howard	.30	.12	.03
☐ 98	Dennis Eckersley	36.00	16.25	5.50
☐ 99	Lee Lacy	.30	.12	.03
☐ 100	Jim Hunter	3.00	1.25	.30
☐ 101	Pete LaCock	.30	.12	.03
☐ 102	Jim Willoughby	.30	.12	.03
☐ 103	Biff Pocoroba	.30	.12	.03
☐ 104	Reds Team Sparky Anderson MG (checklist back)	1.25	.40	.08
☐ 105	Gary Lavelle	.30	.12	.03
☐ 106	Tom Grieve	.40	.16	.04
☐ 107	Dave Roberts	.30	.12	.03
☐ 108	Don Kirkwood	.30	.12	.03
☐ 109	Larry Lintz	.30	.12	.03
☐ 110	Carlos May	.30	.12	.03
☐ 111	Danny Thompson	.30	.12	.03
☐ 112	Kent Tekulve	1.25	.50	.12
☐ 113	Gary Sutherland	.30	.12	.03
☐ 114	Jay Johnstone	.40	.16	.04
☐ 115	Ken Holtzman	.40	.16	.04
☐ 116	Charlie Moore	.30	.12	.03
☐ 117	Mike Jorgensen	.30	.12	.03
☐ 118	Red Sox Team Darrell Johnson MG (checklist back)	1.00	.30	.06
☐ 119	Checklist 1-132	1.25	.15	.03
☐ 120	Rusty Staub	.60	.25	.06
☐ 121	Tony Solaita	.30	.12	.03
☐ 122	Mike Cosgrove	.30	.12	.03
☐ 123	Walt Williams	.30	.12	.03
☐ 124	Doug Rau	.30	.12	.03
☐ 125	Don Baylor	1.00	.40	.10
☐ 126	Tom Dettore	.30	.12	.03
☐ 127	Larvell Blanks	.30	.12	.03
☐ 128	Ken Griffey	2.25	.90	.22
☐ 129	Andy Etchebarren	.30	.12	.03
☐ 130	Luis Tiant	.50	.20	.05
☐ 131	Bill Stein	.30	.12	.03
☐ 132	Don Hood	.30	.12	.03
☐ 133	Gary Matthews	.40	.16	.04
☐ 134	Mike Ivie	.30	.12	.03
☐ 135	Bake McBride	.40	.16	.04
☐ 136	Dave Goltz	.30	.12	.03

	#	Player			
☐	137	Bill Robinson	.40	.16	.04
☐	138	Lerrin LaGrow	.30	.12	.03
☐	139	Gorman Thomas	.50	.20	.05
☐	140	Vida Blue	.50	.20	.05
☐	141	Larry Parrish	1.00	.40	.10
☐	142	Dick Drago	.30	.12	.03
☐	143	Jerry Grote	.30	.12	.03
☐	144	Al Fitzmorris	.30	.12	.03
☐	145	Larry Bowa	.60	.25	.06
☐	146	George Medich	.30	.12	.03
☐	147	Astros Team	1.00	.30	.06
		Bill Virdon MG			
		(checklist back)			
☐	148	Stan Thomas	.30	.12	.03
☐	149	Tommy Davis	.40	.16	.04
☐	150	Steve Garvey	6.00	2.50	.60
☐	151	Bill Bonham	.30	.12	.03
☐	152	Leroy Stanton	.30	.12	.03
☐	153	Buzz Capra	.30	.12	.03
☐	154	Bucky Dent	.60	.25	.06
☐	155	Jack Billingham	.30	.12	.03
☐	156	Rico Carty	.40	.16	.04
☐	157	Mike Caldwell	.30	.12	.03
☐	158	Ken Reitz	.30	.12	.03
☐	159	Jerry Terrell	.30	.12	.03
☐	160	Dave Winfield	12.50	5.50	1.65
☐	161	Bruce Kison	.30	.12	.03
☐	162	Jack Pierce	.30	.12	.03
☐	163	Jim Slaton	.30	.12	.03
☐	164	Pepe Mangual	.30	.12	.03
☐	165	Gene Tenace	.40	.16	.04
☐	166	Skip Lockwood	.30	.12	.03
☐	167	Freddie Patek	.30	.12	.03
☐	168	Tom Hilgendorf	.30	.12	.03
☐	169	Graig Nettles	1.25	.50	.12
☐	170	Rick Wise	.40	.16	.04
☐	171	Greg Gross	.30	.12	.03
☐	172	Rangers Team	1.00	.30	.06
		Frank Lucchesi MG			
		(checklist back)			
☐	173	Steve Swisher	.30	.12	.03
☐	174	Charlie Hough	.40	.16	.04
☐	175	Ken Singleton	.40	.16	.04
☐	176	Dick Lange	.30	.12	.03
☐	177	Marty Perez	.30	.12	.03
☐	178	Tom Buskey	.30	.12	.03
☐	179	George Foster	1.00	.40	.10
☐	180	Rich Gossage	1.50	.60	.15
☐	181	Willie Montanez	.30	.12	.03
☐	182	Harry Rasmussen	.30	.12	.03
☐	183	Steve Braun	.30	.12	.03
☐	184	Bill Greif	.30	.12	.03
☐	185	Dave Parker	6.50	2.75	.65
☐	186	Tom Walker	.30	.12	.03
☐	187	Pedro Garcia	.30	.12	.03
☐	188	Fred Scherman	.30	.12	.03
☐	189	Claudell Washington	.40	.16	.04
☐	190	Jon Matlack	.40	.16	.04
☐	191	NL Batting Leaders	.60	.25	.06
		Bill Madlock			
		Ted Simmons			
		Manny Sanguillen			
☐	192	AL Batting Leaders	2.00	.80	.20
		Rod Carew			
		Fred Lynn			
		Thurman Munson			
☐	193	NL Home Run Leaders	1.25	.50	.12
		Mike Schmidt			
		Dave Kingman			
		Greg Luzinski			
☐	194	AL Home Run Leaders	1.25	.50	.12
		Reggie Jackson			
		George Scott			
		John Mayberry			
☐	195	NL RBI Leaders	1.25	.50	.12
		Greg Luzinski			
		Johnny Bench			
		Tony Perez			
☐	196	AL RBI Leaders	.60	.25	.06
		George Scott			
		John Mayberry			
		Fred Lynn			
☐	197	NL Steals Leaders	1.25	.50	.12
		Dave Lopes			
		Joe Morgan			
		Lou Brock			
☐	198	AL Steals Leaders	.60	.25	.06
		Mickey Rivers			
		Claudell Washington			
		Amos Otis			
☐	199	NL Victory Leaders	1.00	.40	.10
		Tom Seaver			
		Randy Jones			
		Andy Messersmith			
☐	200	AL Victory Leaders	1.25	.50	.12
		Jim Hunter			
		Jim Palmer			
		Vida Blue			
☐	201	NL ERA Leaders	.75	.30	.07
		Randy Jones			
		Andy Messersmith			
		Tom Seaver			
☐	202	AL ERA Leaders	2.00	.80	.20
		Jim Palmer			
		Jim Hunter			
		Dennis Eckersley			
☐	203	NL Strikeout Leaders	.75	.30	.07
		Tom Seaver			
		John Montefusco			
		Andy Messersmith			
☐	204	AL Strikeout Leaders	.75	.30	.07
		Frank Tanana			
		Bert Blyleven			
		Gaylord Perry			
☐	205	Leading Firemen	.60	.25	.06
		Al Hrabosky			
		Rich Gossage			
☐	206	Manny Trillo	.30	.12	.03
☐	207	Andy Hassler	.30	.12	.03
☐	208	Mike Lum	.30	.12	.03
☐	209	Alan Ashby	.40	.16	.04
☐	210	Lee May	.40	.16	.04
☐	211	Clay Carroll	.30	.12	.03
☐	212	Pat Kelly	.30	.12	.03
☐	213	Dave Heaverlo	.30	.12	.03
☐	214	Eric Soderholm	.30	.12	.03
☐	215	Reggie Smith	.50	.20	.05
☐	216	Expos Team	1.00	.30	.06
		Karl Kuehl MG			
		(checklist back)			
☐	217	Dave Freisleben	.30	.12	.03
☐	218	John Knox	.30	.12	.03
☐	219	Tom Murphy	.30	.12	.03
☐	220	Manny Sanguillen	.40	.16	.04
☐	221	Jim Todd	.30	.12	.03
☐	222	Wayne Garrett	.30	.12	.03
☐	223	Ollie Brown	.30	.12	.03
☐	224	Jim York	.30	.12	.03
☐	225	Roy White	.40	.16	.04
☐	226	Jim Sundberg	.40	.16	.04
☐	227	Oscar Zamora	.30	.12	.03
☐	228	John Hale	.30	.12	.03
☐	229	Jerry Remy	.40	.16	.04
☐	230	Carl Yastrzemski	8.50	3.75	.85
☐	231	Tom House	.30	.12	.03
☐	232	Frank Duffy	.30	.12	.03
☐	233	Grant Jackson	.30	.12	.03
☐	234	Mike Sadek	.30	.12	.03
☐	235	Bert Blyleven	1.50	.60	.15
☐	236	Kansas City Royals	1.00	.30	.06
		Team Card			
		Whitey Herzog MG			
		(checklist back)			
☐	237	Dave Hamilton	.30	.12	.03
☐	238	Larry Biittner	.30	.12	.03
☐	239	John Curtis	.30	.12	.03
☐	240	Pete Rose	12.00	5.25	1.50
☐	241	Hector Torres	.30	.12	.03
☐	242	Dan Meyer	.30	.12	.03
☐	243	Jim Rooker	.30	.12	.03
☐	244	Bill Sharp	.30	.12	.03
☐	245	Felix Millan	.30	.12	.03
☐	246	Cesar Tovar	.30	.12	.03
☐	247	Terry Harmon	.30	.12	.03
☐	248	Dick Tidrow	.30	.12	.03
☐	249	Cliff Johnson	.30	.12	.03
☐	250	Fergie Jenkins	2.50	1.00	.25
☐	251	Rick Monday	.40	.16	.04
☐	252	Tim Nordbrook	.30	.12	.03
☐	253	Bill Buckner	.50	.20	.05
☐	254	Rudy Meoli	.30	.12	.03
☐	255	Fritz Peterson	.30	.12	.03
☐	256	Rowland Office	.30	.12	.03
☐	257	Ross Grimsley	.30	.12	.03
☐	258	Nyls Nyman	.30	.12	.03
☐	259	Darrel Chaney	.30	.12	.03
☐	260	Steve Busby	.40	.16	.04
☐	261	Gary Thomasson	.30	.12	.03
☐	262	Checklist 133-264	1.25	.15	.03
☐	263	Lyman Bostock	.50	.20	.05
☐	264	Steve Renko	.30	.12	.03
☐	265	Willie Davis	.40	.16	.04
☐	266	Alan Foster	.30	.12	.03
☐	267	Aurelio Rodriguez	.30	.12	.03
☐	268	Del Unser	.30	.12	.03
☐	269	Rick Austin	.30	.12	.03
☐	270	Willie Stargell	3.25	1.35	.32
☐	271	Jim Lonborg	.40	.16	.04

☐ 272	Rick Dempsey	.40	.16	.04
☐ 273	Joe Niekro	.40	.16	.04
☐ 274	Tommy Harper	.40	.16	.04
☐ 275	Rick Manning	.30	.12	.03
☐ 276	Mickey Scott	.30	.12	.03
☐ 277	Cubs Team	1.00	.30	.06
	Jim Marshall MG			
	(checklist back)			
☐ 278	Bernie Carbo	.30	.12	.03
☐ 279	Roy Howell	.30	.12	.03
☐ 280	Burt Hooton	.40	.16	.04
☐ 281	Dave May	.30	.12	.03
☐ 282	Dan Osborn	.30	.12	.03
☐ 283	Merv Rettenmund	.30	.12	.03
☐ 284	Steve Ontiveros	.30	.12	.03
☐ 285	Mike Cuellar	.40	.16	.04
☐ 286	Jim Wohlford	.30	.12	.03
☐ 287	Pete Mackanin	.30	.12	.03
☐ 288	Bill Campbell	.30	.12	.03
☐ 289	Enzo Hernandez	.30	.12	.03
☐ 290	Ted Simmons	1.00	.40	.10
☐ 291	Ken Sanders	.30	.12	.03
☐ 292	Leon Roberts	.30	.12	.03
☐ 293	Bill Castro	.30	.12	.03
☐ 294	Ed Kirkpatrick	.30	.12	.03
☐ 295	Dave Cash	.30	.12	.03
☐ 296	Pat Dobson	.30	.12	.03
☐ 297	Roger Metzger	.30	.12	.03
☐ 298	Dick Bosman	.30	.12	.03
☐ 299	Champ Summers	.30	.12	.03
☐ 300	Johnny Bench	10.00	4.50	1.25
☐ 301	Jackie Brown	.30	.12	.03
☐ 302	Rick Miller	.30	.12	.03
☐ 303	Steve Foucault	.30	.12	.03
☐ 304	Angels Team	1.00	.30	.06
	Dick Williams MG			
	(checklist back)			
☐ 305	Andy Messersmith	.40	.16	.04
☐ 306	Rod Gilbreath	.30	.12	.03
☐ 307	Al Bumbry	.30	.12	.03
☐ 308	Jim Barr	.30	.12	.03
☐ 309	Bill Melton	.30	.12	.03
☐ 310	Randy Jones	.40	.16	.04
☐ 311	Cookie Rojas	.30	.12	.03
☐ 312	Don Carrithers	.30	.12	.03
☐ 313	Dan Ford	.30	.12	.03
☐ 314	Ed Kranepool	.40	.16	.04
☐ 315	Al Hrabosky	.40	.16	.04
☐ 316	Robin Yount	48.00	22.00	6.50
☐ 317	John Candelaria	2.50	1.00	.25
☐ 318	Bob Boone	1.00	.40	.10
☐ 319	Larry Gura	.30	.12	.03
☐ 320	Willie Horton	.40	.16	.04
☐ 321	Jose Cruz	.40	.16	.04
☐ 322	Glenn Abbott	.30	.12	.03
☐ 323	Rob Sperring	.30	.12	.03
☐ 324	Jim Bibby	.30	.12	.03
☐ 325	Tony Perez	2.25	.90	.22
☐ 326	Dick Pole	.30	.12	.03
☐ 327	Dave Moates	.30	.12	.03
☐ 328	Carl Morton	.30	.12	.03
☐ 329	Joe Ferguson	.30	.12	.03
☐ 330	Nolan Ryan	42.00	18.00	5.50
☐ 331	San Diego Padres	1.00	.30	.06
	Team Card			
	John McNamara MG			
	(checklist back)			
☐ 332	Charlie Williams	.30	.12	.03
☐ 333	Bob Coluccio	.30	.12	.03
☐ 334	Dennis Leonard	.40	.16	.04
☐ 335	Bob Grich	.40	.16	.04
☐ 336	Vic Albury	.30	.12	.03
☐ 337	Bud Harrelson	.40	.16	.04
☐ 338	Bob Bailey	.30	.12	.03
☐ 339	John Denny	.40	.16	.04
☐ 340	Jim Rice	6.50	2.75	.65
☐ 341	All-Time 1B	4.50	2.00	.45
	Lou Gehrig			
☐ 342	All-Time 2B	2.25	.90	.22
	Rogers Hornsby			
☐ 343	All-Time 3B	1.00	.40	.10
	Pie Traynor			
☐ 344	All-Time SS	3.00	1.25	.30
	Honus Wagner			
☐ 345	All-Time OF	7.50	3.25	.75
	Babe Ruth			
☐ 346	All-Time OF	4.50	2.00	.45
	Ty Cobb			
☐ 347	All-Time OF	4.50	2.00	.45
	Ted Williams			
☐ 348	All-Time C	1.00	.40	.10
	Mickey Cochrane			
☐ 349	All-Time RHP	2.25	.90	.22
	Walter Johnson			
☐ 350	All-Time LHP	1.50	.60	.15
	Lefty Grove			
☐ 351	Randy Hundley	.30	.12	.03
☐ 352	Dave Giusti	.30	.12	.03
☐ 353	Sixto Lezcano	.30	.12	.03
☐ 354	Ron Blomberg	.30	.12	.03
☐ 355	Steve Carlton	6.25	2.75	.60
☐ 356	Ted Martinez	.30	.12	.03
☐ 357	Ken Forsch	.30	.12	.03
☐ 358	Buddy Bell	.50	.20	.05
☐ 359	Rick Reuschel	.50	.20	.05
☐ 360	Jeff Burroughs	.40	.16	.04
☐ 361	Detroit Tigers	1.00	.30	.06
	Team Card			
	Ralph Houk MG			
	(checklist back)			
☐ 362	Will McEnaney	.30	.12	.03
☐ 363	Dave Collins	.75	.30	.07
☐ 364	Elias Sosa	.30	.12	.03
☐ 365	Carlton Fisk	9.00	4.00	.90
☐ 366	Bobby Valentine	.40	.16	.04
☐ 367	Bruce Miller	.30	.12	.03
☐ 368	Wilbur Wood	.40	.16	.04
☐ 369	Frank White	.50	.20	.05
☐ 370	Ron Cey	.60	.25	.06
☐ 371	Elrod Hendricks	.30	.12	.03
☐ 372	Rick Baldwin	.30	.12	.03
☐ 373	Johnny Briggs	.30	.12	.03
☐ 374	Dan Warthen	.30	.12	.03
☐ 375	Ron Fairly	.30	.12	.03
☐ 376	Rich Hebner	.30	.12	.03
☐ 377	Mike Hegan	.30	.12	.03
☐ 378	Steve Stone	.40	.16	.04
☐ 379	Ken Boswell	.30	.12	.03
☐ 380	Bobby Bonds	.75	.30	.07
☐ 381	Denny Doyle	.30	.12	.03
☐ 382	Matt Alexander	.30	.12	.03
☐ 383	John Ellis	.30	.12	.03
☐ 384	Phillies Team	1.00	.30	.06
	Danny Ozark MG			
	(checklist back)			
☐ 385	Mickey Lolich	.60	.25	.06
☐ 386	Ed Goodson	.30	.12	.03
☐ 387	Mike Miley	.30	.12	.03
☐ 388	Stan Perzanowski	.30	.12	.03
☐ 389	Glenn Adams	.30	.12	.03
☐ 390	Don Gullett	.40	.16	.04
☐ 391	Jerry Hairston	.30	.12	.03
☐ 392	Checklist 265-396	1.25	.15	.03
☐ 393	Paul Mitchell	.30	.12	.03
☐ 394	Fran Healy	.30	.12	.03
☐ 395	Jim Wynn	.40	.16	.04
☐ 396	Bill Lee	.40	.16	.04
☐ 397	Tim Foli	.30	.12	.03
☐ 398	Dave Tomlin	.30	.12	.03
☐ 399	Luis Melendez	.30	.12	.03
☐ 400	Rod Carew	8.00	3.50	.80
☐ 401	Ken Brett	.30	.12	.03
☐ 402	Don Money	.30	.12	.03
☐ 403	Geoff Zahn	.30	.12	.03
☐ 404	Enos Cabell	.30	.12	.03
☐ 405	Rollie Fingers	3.00	1.25	.30
☐ 406	Ed Herrmann	.30	.12	.03
☐ 407	Tom Underwood	.30	.12	.03
☐ 408	Charlie Spikes	.30	.12	.03
☐ 409	Dave Lemanczyk	.30	.12	.03
☐ 410	Ralph Garr	.40	.16	.04
☐ 411	Bill Singer	.40	.16	.04
☐ 412	Toby Harrah	.40	.16	.04
☐ 413	Pete Varney	.30	.12	.03
☐ 414	Wayne Garland	.30	.12	.03
☐ 415	Vada Pinson	.50	.20	.05
☐ 416	Tommy John	1.00	.40	.10
☐ 417	Gene Clines	.30	.12	.03
☐ 418	Jose Morales	.30	.12	.03
☐ 419	Reggie Cleveland	.30	.12	.03
☐ 420	Joe Morgan	5.00	2.25	.50
☐ 421	A's Team UER	1.00	.30	.06
	(no MG on front;			
	checklist back)			
☐ 422	Johnny Grubb	.30	.12	.03
☐ 423	Ed Halicki	.30	.12	.03
☐ 424	Phil Roof	.30	.12	.03
☐ 425	Rennie Stennett	.30	.12	.03
☐ 426	Bob Forsch	.30	.12	.03
☐ 427	Kurt Bevacqua	.30	.12	.03
☐ 428	Jim Crawford	.30	.12	.03
☐ 429	Fred Stanley	.30	.12	.03
☐ 430	Jose Cardenal	.30	.12	.03
☐ 431	Dick Ruthven	.30	.12	.03
☐ 432	Tom Veryzer	.30	.12	.03
☐ 433	Rick Waits	.30	.12	.03
☐ 434	Morris Nettles	.30	.12	.03
☐ 435	Phil Niekro	2.00	.80	.20

#	Player			
☐ 436	Bill Fahey	.30	.12	.03
☐ 437	Terry Forster	.40	.16	.04
☐ 438	Doug DeCinces	.50	.20	.05
☐ 439	Rick Rhoden	.50	.20	.05
☐ 440	John Mayberry	.40	.16	.04
☐ 441	Gary Carter	10.00	4.50	1.25
☐ 442	Hank Webb	.30	.12	.03
☐ 443	Giants Team UER	1.00	.30	.06
	(no MG on front; checklist back)			
☐ 444	Gary Nolan	.30	.12	.03
☐ 445	Rico Petrocelli	.40	.16	.04
☐ 446	Larry Haney	.30	.12	.03
☐ 447	Gene Locklear	.30	.12	.03
☐ 448	Tom Johnson	.30	.12	.03
☐ 449	Bob Robertson	.30	.12	.03
☐ 450	Jim Palmer	6.50	2.75	.65
☐ 451	Buddy Bradford	.30	.12	.03
☐ 452	Tom Hausman	.30	.12	.03
☐ 453	Lou Piniella	.60	.25	.06
☐ 454	Tom Griffin	.30	.12	.03
☐ 455	Dick Allen	.60	.25	.06
☐ 456	Joe Coleman	.30	.12	.03
☐ 457	Ed Crosby	.30	.12	.03
☐ 458	Earl Williams	.30	.12	.03
☐ 459	Jim Brewer	.30	.12	.03
☐ 460	Cesar Cedeno	.40	.16	.04
☐ 461	NL and AL Champs	.60	.25	.06
	Reds sweep Bucs, Bosox surprise A's			
☐ 462	'75 World Series	.60	.25	.06
	Reds Champs			
☐ 463	Steve Hargan	.30	.12	.03
☐ 464	Ken Henderson	.30	.12	.03
☐ 465	Mike Marshall	.40	.16	.04
☐ 466	Bob Stinson	.30	.12	.03
☐ 467	Woodie Fryman	.30	.12	.03
☐ 468	Jesus Alou	.30	.12	.03
☐ 469	Rawly Eastwick	.30	.12	.03
☐ 470	Bobby Murcer	.60	.25	.06
☐ 471	Jim Burton	.30	.12	.03
☐ 472	Bob Davis	.30	.12	.03
☐ 473	Paul Blair	.40	.16	.04
☐ 474	Ray Corbin	.30	.12	.03
☐ 475	Joe Rudi	.40	.16	.04
☐ 476	Bob Moose	.30	.12	.03
☐ 477	Indians Team	1.00	.30	.06
	Frank Robinson MG (checklist back)			
☐ 478	Lynn McGlothen	.30	.12	.03
☐ 479	Bobby Mitchell	.30	.12	.03
☐ 480	Mike Schmidt	33.00	15.00	5.00
☐ 481	Rudy May	.30	.12	.03
☐ 482	Tim Hosley	.30	.12	.03
☐ 483	Mickey Stanley	.40	.16	.04
☐ 484	Eric Raich	.30	.12	.03
☐ 485	Mike Hargrove	.40	.16	.04
☐ 486	Bruce Dal Canton	.30	.12	.03
☐ 487	Leron Lee	.30	.12	.03
☐ 488	Claude Osteen	.40	.16	.04
☐ 489	Skip Jutze	.30	.12	.03
☐ 490	Frank Tanana	.50	.20	.05
☐ 491	Terry Crowley	.30	.12	.03
☐ 492	Marty Pattin	.30	.12	.03
☐ 493	Derrel Thomas	.30	.12	.03
☐ 494	Craig Swan	.30	.12	.03
☐ 495	Nate Colbert	.30	.12	.03
☐ 496	Juan Beniquez	.30	.12	.03
☐ 497	Joe McIntosh	.30	.12	.03
☐ 498	Glenn Borgmann	.30	.12	.03
☐ 499	Mario Guerrero	.30	.12	.03
☐ 500	Reggie Jackson	15.00	6.50	2.15
☐ 501	Billy Champion	.30	.12	.03
☐ 502	Tim McCarver	.50	.20	.05
☐ 503	Elliott Maddox	.30	.12	.03
☐ 504	Pirates Team	1.00	.30	.06
	Danny Murtaugh MG (checklist back)			
☐ 505	Mark Belanger	.40	.16	.04
☐ 506	George Mitterwald	.30	.12	.03
☐ 507	Ray Bare	.30	.12	.03
☐ 508	Duane Kuiper	.30	.12	.03
☐ 509	Bill Hands	.30	.12	.03
☐ 510	Amos Otis	.40	.16	.04
☐ 511	Jamie Easterley	.30	.12	.03
☐ 512	Ellie Rodriguez	.30	.12	.03
☐ 513	Bart Johnson	.30	.12	.03
☐ 514	Dan Driessen	.40	.16	.04
☐ 515	Steve Yeager	.40	.16	.04
☐ 516	Wayne Granger	.30	.12	.03
☐ 517	John Milner	.30	.12	.03
☐ 518	Doug Flynn	.30	.12	.03
☐ 519	Steve Brye	.30	.12	.03
☐ 520	Willie McCovey	3.50	1.50	.35
☐ 521	Jim Colborn	.30	.12	.03
☐ 522	Ted Sizemore	.30	.12	.03
☐ 523	Bob Montgomery	.30	.12	.03
☐ 524	Pete Falcone	.30	.12	.03
☐ 525	Billy Williams	3.00	1.25	.30
☐ 526	Checklist 397-528	1.25	.15	.03
☐ 527	Mike Anderson	.30	.12	.03
☐ 528	Dock Ellis	.30	.12	.03
☐ 529	Deron Johnson	.30	.12	.03
☐ 530	Don Sutton	2.00	.80	.20
☐ 531	New York Mets	1.25	.40	.08
	Team Card Joe Frazier MG (checklist back)			
☐ 532	Milt May	.30	.12	.03
☐ 533	Lee Richard	.30	.12	.03
☐ 534	Stan Bahnsen	.30	.12	.03
☐ 535	Dave Nelson	.30	.12	.03
☐ 536	Mike Thompson	.30	.12	.03
☐ 537	Tony Muser	.30	.12	.03
☐ 538	Pat Darcy	.30	.12	.03
☐ 539	John Balaz	.30	.12	.03
☐ 540	Bill Freehan	.50	.20	.05
☐ 541	Steve Mingori	.30	.12	.03
☐ 542	Keith Hernandez	6.00	2.50	.60
☐ 543	Wayne Twitchell	.30	.12	.03
☐ 544	Pepe Frias	.30	.12	.03
☐ 545	Sparky Lyle	.50	.20	.05
☐ 546	Dave Rosello	.30	.12	.03
☐ 547	Roric Harrison	.30	.12	.03
☐ 548	Manny Mota	.40	.16	.04
☐ 549	Randy Tate	.30	.12	.03
☐ 550	Hank Aaron	18.00	7.50	2.50
☐ 551	Jerry DaVanon	.30	.12	.03
☐ 552	Terry Humphrey	.30	.12	.03
☐ 553	Randy Moffitt	.30	.12	.03
☐ 554	Ray Fosse	.30	.12	.03
☐ 555	Dyar Miller	.30	.12	.03
☐ 556	Twins Team	1.00	.30	.06
	Gene Mauch MG (checklist back)			
☐ 557	Dan Spillner	.30	.12	.03
☐ 558	Clarence Gaston	.50	.20	.05
☐ 559	Clyde Wright	.30	.12	.03
☐ 560	Jorge Orta	.30	.12	.03
☐ 561	Tom Carroll	.30	.12	.03
☐ 562	Adrian Garrett	.30	.12	.03
☐ 563	Larry Demery	.30	.12	.03
☐ 564	Bubble Gum Champ	.40	.16	.04
	Kurt Bevacqua			
☐ 565	Tug McGraw	.50	.20	.05
☐ 566	Ken McMullen	.30	.12	.03
☐ 567	George Stone	.30	.12	.03
☐ 568	Rob Andrews	.30	.12	.03
☐ 569	Nelson Briles	.30	.12	.03
☐ 570	George Hendrick	.40	.16	.04
☐ 571	Don DeMola	.30	.12	.03
☐ 572	Rich Coggins	.30	.12	.03
☐ 573	Bill Travers	.30	.12	.03
☐ 574	Don Kessinger	.40	.16	.04
☐ 575	Dwight Evans	3.50	1.50	.35
☐ 576	Maximino Leon	.30	.12	.03
☐ 577	Marc Hill	.30	.12	.03
☐ 578	Ted Kubiak	.30	.12	.03
☐ 579	Clay Kirby	.30	.12	.03
☐ 580	Bert Campaneris	.40	.16	.04
☐ 581	Cardinals Team	1.00	.30	.06
	Red Schoendienst MG (checklist back)			
☐ 582	Mike Kekich	.30	.12	.03
☐ 583	Tommy Helms	.40	.16	.04
☐ 584	Stan Wall	.30	.12	.03
☐ 585	Joe Torre	.60	.25	.06
☐ 586	Ron Schueler	.30	.12	.03
☐ 587	Leo Cardenas	.30	.12	.03
☐ 588	Kevin Kobel	.30	.12	.03
☐ 589	Rookie Pitchers	2.00	.80	.20
	Santo Alcala Mike Flanagan Joe Pactwa Pablo Torrealba			
☐ 590	Rookie Outfielders	.60	.25	.06
	Henry Cruz Chet Lemon Ellis Valentine Terry Whitfield			
☐ 591	Rookie Pitchers	.30	.12	.03
	Steve Grilli Craig Mitchell Jose Sosa George Throop			
☐ 592	Rookie Infielders	7.00	3.00	.70
	Willie Randolph Dave McKay Jerry Royster Roy Staiger			

☐ 593	Rookie Pitchers	.40	.16	.04
	Larry Anderson			
	Ken Crosby			
	Mark Littell			
	Butch Metzger			
☐ 594	Rookie Catchers/OF	.40	.16	.04
	Andy Merchant			
	Ed Ott			
	Royle Stillman			
	Jerry White			
☐ 595	Rookie Pitchers	.40	.16	.04
	Art DeFillipis			
	Randy Lerch			
	Sid Monge			
	Steve Barr			
☐ 596	Rookie Infielders	.50	.20	.05
	Craig Reynolds			
	Lamar Johnson			
	Johnnie LeMaster			
	Jerry Manuel			
☐ 597	Rookie Pitchers	.60	.25	.06
	Don Aase			
	Jack Kucek			
	Frank LaCorte			
	Mike Pazik			
☐ 598	Rookie Outfielders	.50	.20	.05
	Hector Cruz			
	Jamie Quirk			
	Jerry Turner			
	Joe Wallis			
☐ 599	Rookie Pitchers	10.00	4.50	1.25
	Rob Dressler			
	Ron Guidry			
	Bob McClure			
	Pat Zachry			
☐ 600	Tom Seaver	11.00	5.00	1.35
☐ 601	Ken Rudolph	.30	.12	.03
☐ 602	Doug Konieczny	.30	.12	.03
☐ 603	Jim Holt	.30	.12	.03
☐ 604	Joe Lovitto	.30	.12	.03
☐ 605	Al Downing	.40	.16	.04
☐ 606	Milwaukee Brewers	1.00	.30	.06
	Team Card			
	Alex Grammas MG			
	(checklist back)			
☐ 607	Rich Hinton	.30	.12	.03
☐ 608	Vic Correll	.30	.12	.03
☐ 609	Fred Norman	.30	.12	.03
☐ 610	Greg Luzinski	.50	.20	.05
☐ 611	Rich Folkers	.30	.12	.03
☐ 612	Joe Lahoud	.30	.12	.03
☐ 613	Tim Johnson	.30	.12	.03
☐ 614	Fernando Arroyo	.30	.12	.03
☐ 615	Mike Cubbage	.30	.12	.03
☐ 616	Buck Martinez	.30	.12	.03
☐ 617	Darold Knowles	.30	.12	.03
☐ 618	Jack Brohamer	.30	.12	.03
☐ 619	Bill Butler	.30	.12	.03
☐ 620	Al Oliver	.60	.25	.06
☐ 621	Tom Hall	.30	.12	.03
☐ 622	Rick Auerbach	.30	.12	.03
☐ 623	Bob Allietta	.30	.12	.03
☐ 624	Tony Taylor	.30	.12	.03
☐ 625	J.R. Richard	.40	.16	.04
☐ 626	Bob Sheldon	.30	.12	.03
☐ 627	Bill Plummer	.40	.16	.04
☐ 628	John D'Acquisto	.30	.12	.03
☐ 629	Sandy Alomar	.30	.12	.03
☐ 630	Chris Speier	.30	.12	.03
☐ 631	Braves Team	1.00	.30	.06
	Dave Bristol MG			
	(checklist back)			
☐ 632	Rogelio Moret	.30	.12	.03
☐ 633	John Stearns	.40	.16	.04
☐ 634	Larry Christenson	.30	.12	.03
☐ 635	Jim Fregosi	.40	.16	.04
☐ 636	Joe Decker	.30	.12	.03
☐ 637	Bruce Bochte	.30	.12	.03
☐ 638	Doyle Alexander	.30	.12	.03
☐ 639	Fred Kendall	.30	.12	.03
☐ 640	Bill Madlock	1.00	.40	.10
☐ 641	Tom Paciorek	.30	.12	.03
☐ 642	Dennis Blair	.30	.12	.03
☐ 643	Checklist 529-660	1.25	.15	.03
☐ 644	Tom Bradley	.30	.12	.03
☐ 645	Darrell Porter	.30	.12	.03
☐ 646	John Lowenstein	.30	.12	.03
☐ 647	Ramon Hernandez	.30	.12	.03
☐ 648	Al Cowens	.40	.16	.04
☐ 649	Dave Roberts	.30	.12	.03
☐ 650	Thurman Munson	7.00	3.00	.70
☐ 651	John Odom	.30	.12	.03
☐ 652	Ed Armbrister	.30	.12	.03
☐ 653	Mike Norris	.40	.16	.04
☐ 654	Doug Griffin	.30	.12	.03

☐ 655	Mike Vail	.30	.12	.03
☐ 656	Chicago White Sox	1.00	.30	.06
	Team Card			
	Chuck Tanner MG			
	(checklist back)			
☐ 657	Roy Smalley	.50	.20	.05
☐ 658	Jerry Johnson	.30	.12	.03
☐ 659	Ben Oglivie	.40	.16	.04
☐ 660	Dave Lopes	.75	.20	.04

1976 Topps Traded

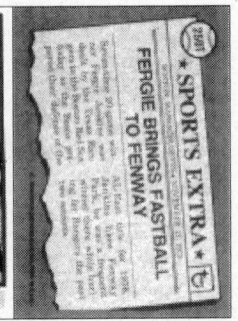

The cards in this 44-card set measure 2 1/2" by 3 1/2". The 1976 Topps Traded set contains 43 players and one unnumbered checklist card. The individuals pictured were traded after the Topps regular set was printed. A "Sports Extra" heading design is found on each picture and is also used to introduce the biographical section of the reverse. Each card is numbered according to the player's regular 1976 card with the addition of "T" to indicate his new status.

		NRMT	VG-E	GOOD
COMPLETE SET (44)		10.00	4.50	1.25
COMMON PLAYER		.25	.10	.02
☐ 27T	Ed Figueroa	.25	.10	.02
☐ 28T	Dusty Baker	.35	.15	.03
☐ 44T	Doug Rader	.35	.15	.03
☐ 58T	Ron Reed	.25	.10	.02
☐ 74T	Oscar Gamble	.35	.15	.03
☐ 80T	Jim Kaat	.90	.40	.09
☐ 83T	Jim Spencer	.25	.10	.02
☐ 85T	Mickey Rivers	.35	.15	.03
☐ 99T	Lee Lacy	.25	.10	.02
☐ 120T	Rusty Staub	.50	.20	.05
☐ 127T	Larvell Blanks	.25	.10	.02
☐ 146T	George Medich	.25	.10	.02
☐ 158T	Ken Reitz	.25	.10	.02
☐ 208T	Mike Lum	.25	.10	.02
☐ 211T	Clay Carroll	.25	.10	.02
☐ 231T	Tom House	.25	.10	.02
☐ 250T	Fergie Jenkins	2.00	.80	.20
☐ 259T	Darrel Chaney	.25	.10	.02
☐ 292T	Leon Roberts	.25	.10	.02
☐ 296T	Pat Dobson	.25	.10	.02
☐ 309T	Bill Melton	.25	.10	.02
☐ 338T	Bob Bailey	.25	.10	.02
☐ 380T	Bobby Bonds	.50	.20	.05
☐ 383T	John Ellis	.25	.10	.02
☐ 385T	Mickey Lolich	.50	.20	.05
☐ 401T	Ken Brett	.25	.10	.02
☐ 410T	Ralph Garr	.35	.15	.03
☐ 411T	Bill Singer	.35	.15	.03
☐ 428T	Jim Crawford	.25	.10	.02
☐ 434T	Morris Nettles	.25	.10	.02
☐ 464T	Ken Henderson	.25	.10	.02
☐ 497T	Joe McIntosh	.25	.10	.02
☐ 524T	Pete Falcone	.25	.10	.02
☐ 527T	Mike Anderson	.25	.10	.02
☐ 528T	Dock Ellis	.25	.10	.02
☐ 532T	Milt May	.25	.10	.02
☐ 554T	Ray Fosse	.25	.10	.02
☐ 579T	Clay Kirby	.25	.10	.02
☐ 583T	Tommy Helms	.35	.15	.03
☐ 592T	Willie Randolph	2.50	1.00	.25

		NRMT	VG-E	GOOD
☐ 618T	Jack Brohamer	.25	.10	.02
☐ 632T	Rogelio Moret	.25	.10	.02
☐ 649T	Dave Roberts	.25	.10	.02
☐ xxxT	Traded Checklist (unnumbered)	.65	.10	.02

1977 Topps

The cards in this 660-card set measure 2 1/2" by 3 1/2". In 1977 for the fifth consecutive year, Topps produced a 660-card baseball set. The player's name, team affiliation, and his position are compactly arranged over the picture area and a facsimile autograph appears on the photo. Team cards feature a checklist of that team's players in the set and a small picture of the manager on the front of the card. Appearing for the first time are the series "Brothers" (631-634) and "Turn Back the Clock" (433-437). Other subseries in the set are League Leaders (1-8), Record Breakers (231-234), Playoffs cards (276-277), World Series cards (411-413), and Rookie Prospects (472-479 and 487-494). The key cards in the set are the rookie cards of Dale Murphy (476) and Andre Dawson (473). Cards numbered 23 or lower, that feature Yankees and do not follow the numbering checklisted below, are not necessarily error cards. They are Burger King cards, a separate set with its own pricing and mass distribution. Burger King cards are indistinguishable from the corresponding Topps cards except for the card numbering difference and the fact that Burger King cards do not have a printing sheet designation (such as A through F like the regular Topps) anywhere on the card back in very small print. There was an aluminum version of the Dale Murphy rookie card number 476 produced (legally) in the early '80s; proceeds from the sales (originally priced at $10.00) of this "card" went to the Huntington's Disease Foundation.

		NRMT	VG-E	GOOD
COMPLETE SET (660)		410.00	165.00	40.00
COMMON PLAYER (1-660)		.21	.09	.02
☐ 1	Batting Leaders George Brett Bill Madlock	4.00	.75	.15
☐ 2	Home Run Leaders Graig Nettles Mike Schmidt	1.00	.40	.10
☐ 3	RBI Leaders Lee May George Foster	.40	.16	.04
☐ 4	Stolen Base Leaders Bill North Dave Lopes	.30	.12	.03
☐ 5	Victory Leaders Jim Palmer Randy Jones	.50	.20	.05
☐ 6	Strikeout Leaders Nolan Ryan Tom Seaver	5.25	2.25	.50
☐ 7	ERA Leaders Mark Fidrych John Denny	.40	.16	.04
☐ 8	Leading Firemen Bill Campbell Rawly Eastwick	.30	.12	.03
☐ 9	Doug Rader	.30	.12	.03
☐ 10	Reggie Jackson	11.00	5.00	1.35
☐ 11	Rob Dressler	.21	.09	.02
☐ 12	Larry Haney	.21	.09	.02
☐ 13	Luis Gomez	.21	.09	.02
☐ 14	Tommy Smith	.21	.09	.02
☐ 15	Don Gullett	.30	.12	.03
☐ 16	Bob Jones	.21	.09	.02
☐ 17	Steve Stone	.30	.12	.03
☐ 18	Indians Team/Mgr. Frank Robinson (checklist back)	.90	.20	.04
☐ 19	John D'Acquisto	.21	.09	.02
☐ 20	Graig Nettles	.90	.40	.09
☐ 21	Ken Forsch	.21	.09	.02
☐ 22	Bill Freehan	.40	.16	.04
☐ 23	Dan Driessen	.21	.09	.02
☐ 24	Carl Morton	.21	.09	.02
☐ 25	Dwight Evans	2.75	1.10	.27
☐ 26	Ray Sadecki	.21	.09	.02
☐ 27	Bill Buckner	.40	.16	.04
☐ 28	Woodie Fryman	.21	.09	.02
☐ 29	Bucky Dent	.40	.16	.04
☐ 30	Greg Luzinski	.40	.16	.04
☐ 31	Jim Todd	.21	.09	.02
☐ 32	Checklist 1	1.00	.10	.02
☐ 33	Wayne Garland	.21	.09	.02
☐ 34	Angels Team/Mgr. Norm Sherry (checklist back)	.90	.20	.04
☐ 35	Rennie Stennett	.21	.09	.02
☐ 36	John Ellis	.21	.09	.02
☐ 37	Steve Hargan	.21	.09	.02
☐ 38	Craig Kusick	.21	.09	.02
☐ 39	Tom Griffin	.21	.09	.02
☐ 40	Bobby Murcer	.40	.16	.04
☐ 41	Jim Kern	.21	.09	.02
☐ 42	Jose Cruz	.30	.12	.03
☐ 43	Ray Bare	.21	.09	.02
☐ 44	Bud Harrelson	.30	.12	.03
☐ 45	Rawly Eastwick	.21	.09	.02
☐ 46	Buck Martinez	.21	.09	.02
☐ 47	Lynn McGlothen	.21	.09	.02
☐ 48	Tom Paciorek	.21	.09	.02
☐ 49	Grant Jackson	.21	.09	.02
☐ 50	Ron Cey	.40	.16	.04
☐ 51	Brewers Team/Mgr. Alex Grammas (checklist back)	.90	.20	.04
☐ 52	Ellis Valentine	.21	.09	.02
☐ 53	Paul Mitchell	.21	.09	.02
☐ 54	Sandy Alomar	.21	.09	.02
☐ 55	Jeff Burroughs	.30	.12	.03
☐ 56	Rudy May	.21	.09	.02
☐ 57	Marc Hill	.21	.09	.02
☐ 58	Chet Lemon	.30	.12	.03
☐ 59	Larry Christenson	.21	.09	.02
☐ 60	Jim Rice	4.00	1.75	.40
☐ 61	Manny Sanguillen	.30	.12	.03
☐ 62	Eric Raich	.21	.09	.02
☐ 63	Tito Fuentes	.21	.09	.02
☐ 64	Larry Biittner	.21	.09	.02
☐ 65	Skip Lockwood	.21	.09	.02
☐ 66	Roy Smalley	.30	.12	.03
☐ 67	Joaquin Andujar	.60	.25	.06
☐ 68	Bruce Bochte	.21	.09	.02
☐ 69	Jim Crawford	.21	.09	.02
☐ 70	Johnny Bench	8.50	3.75	.85
☐ 71	Dock Ellis	.21	.09	.02
☐ 72	Mike Anderson	.21	.09	.02
☐ 73	Charlie Williams	.21	.09	.02
☐ 74	A's Team/Mgr. Jack McKeon (checklist back)	.90	.20	.04
☐ 75	Dennis Leonard	.30	.12	.03
☐ 76	Tim Foli	.21	.09	.02
☐ 77	Dyar Miller	.21	.09	.02
☐ 78	Bob Davis	.21	.09	.02
☐ 79	Don Money	.21	.09	.02
☐ 80	Andy Messersmith	.30	.12	.03
☐ 81	Juan Beniquez	.21	.09	.02
☐ 82	Jim Rooker	.21	.09	.02
☐ 83	Kevin Bell	.21	.09	.02
☐ 84	Ollie Brown	.21	.09	.02
☐ 85	Duane Kuiper	.21	.09	.02
☐ 86	Pat Zachry	.21	.09	.02
☐ 87	Glenn Borgmann	.21	.09	.02
☐ 88	Stan Wall	.21	.09	.02
☐ 89	Butch Hobson	.75	.30	.07
☐ 90	Cesar Cedeno	.30	.12	.03
☐ 91	John Verhoeven	.21	.09	.02

☐ 92 Dave Rosello	.21	.09	.02
☐ 93 Tom Poquette	.21	.09	.02
☐ 94 Craig Swan	.21	.09	.02
☐ 95 Keith Hernandez	2.75	1.10	.27
☐ 96 Lou Piniella	.40	.16	.04
☐ 97 Dave Heaverlo	.21	.09	.02
☐ 98 Milt May	.21	.09	.02
☐ 99 Tom Hausman	.21	.09	.02
☐ 100 Joe Morgan	3.50	1.50	.35
☐ 101 Dick Bosman	.21	.09	.02
☐ 102 Jose Morales	.21	.09	.02
☐ 103 Mike Bacsik	.21	.09	.02
☐ 104 Omar Moreno	.30	.12	.03
☐ 105 Steve Yeager	.30	.12	.03
☐ 106 Mike Flanagan	.40	.16	.04
☐ 107 Bill Melton	.21	.09	.02
☐ 108 Alan Foster	.21	.09	.02
☐ 109 Jorge Orta	.21	.09	.02
☐ 110 Steve Carlton	6.00	2.50	.60
☐ 111 Rico Petrocelli	.30	.12	.03
☐ 112 Bill Greif	.21	.09	.02
☐ 113 Blue Jays Leaders	.75	.20	.04
Roy Hartsfield MG			
Don Leppert CO			
Bob Miller CO			
Jackie Moore CO			
Harry Warner CO			
(checklist back)			
☐ 114 Bruce Dal Canton	.21	.09	.02
☐ 115 Rick Manning	.21	.09	.02
☐ 116 Joe Niekro	.30	.12	.03
☐ 117 Frank White	.30	.12	.03
☐ 118 Rick Jones	.21	.09	.02
☐ 119 John Stearns	.30	.12	.03
☐ 120 Rod Carew	7.50	3.25	.75
☐ 121 Gary Nolan	.21	.09	.02
☐ 122 Ben Oglivie	.30	.12	.03
☐ 123 Fred Stanley	.21	.09	.02
☐ 124 George Mitterwald	.21	.09	.02
☐ 125 Bill Travers	.21	.09	.02
☐ 126 Rod Gilbreath	.21	.09	.02
☐ 127 Ron Fairly	.21	.09	.02
☐ 128 Tommy John	1.00	.40	.10
☐ 129 Mike Sadek	.21	.09	.02
☐ 130 Al Oliver	.50	.20	.05
☐ 131 Orlando Ramirez	.21	.09	.02
☐ 132 Chip Lang	.21	.09	.02
☐ 133 Ralph Garr	.30	.12	.03
☐ 134 Padres Team/Mgr.	.90	.20	.04
John McNamara			
(checklist back)			
☐ 135 Mark Belanger	.30	.12	.03
☐ 136 Jerry Mumphrey	.30	.12	.03
☐ 137 Jeff Terpko	.21	.09	.02
☐ 138 Bob Stinson	.21	.09	.02
☐ 139 Fred Norman	.21	.09	.02
☐ 140 Mike Schmidt	22.00	9.50	3.15
☐ 141 Mark Littell	.21	.09	.02
☐ 142 Steve Dillard	.21	.09	.02
☐ 143 Ed Herrmann	.21	.09	.02
☐ 144 Bruce Sutter	4.00	1.75	.40
☐ 145 Tom Veryzer	.21	.09	.02
☐ 146 Dusty Baker	.30	.12	.03
☐ 147 Jackie Brown	.21	.09	.02
☐ 148 Fran Healy	.21	.09	.02
☐ 149 Mike Cubbage	.21	.09	.02
☐ 150 Tom Seaver	8.50	3.75	.85
☐ 151 Johnny LeMaster	.21	.09	.02
☐ 152 Gaylord Perry	2.50	1.00	.25
☐ 153 Ron Jackson	.21	.09	.02
☐ 154 Dave Giusti	.21	.09	.02
☐ 155 Joe Rudi	.30	.12	.03
☐ 156 Pete Mackanin	.21	.09	.02
☐ 157 Ken Brett	.21	.09	.02
☐ 158 Ted Kubiak	.21	.09	.02
☐ 159 Bernie Carbo	.21	.09	.02
☐ 160 Will McEnaney	.21	.09	.02
☐ 161 Garry Templeton	1.25	.50	.12
☐ 162 Mike Cuellar	.30	.12	.03
☐ 163 Dave Hilton	.21	.09	.02
☐ 164 Tug McGraw	.40	.16	.04
☐ 165 Jim Wynn	.30	.12	.03
☐ 166 Bill Campbell	.21	.09	.02
☐ 167 Rich Hebner	.21	.09	.02
☐ 168 Charlie Spikes	.21	.09	.02
☐ 169 Darold Knowles	.21	.09	.02
☐ 170 Thurman Munson	5.50	2.50	.55
☐ 171 Ken Sanders	.21	.09	.02
☐ 172 John Milner	.21	.09	.02
☐ 173 Chuck Scrivener	.21	.09	.02
☐ 174 Nelson Briles	.21	.09	.02
☐ 175 Butch Wynegar	.40	.16	.04
☐ 176 Bob Robertson	.21	.09	.02
☐ 177 Bart Johnson	.21	.09	.02

☐ 178 Bombo Rivera	.21	.09	.02
☐ 179 Paul Hartzell	.21	.09	.02
☐ 180 Dave Lopes	.30	.12	.03
☐ 181 Ken McMullen	.21	.09	.02
☐ 182 Dan Spillner	.21	.09	.02
☐ 183 Cardinals Team/Mgr.	.90	.20	.04
Vern Rapp			
(checklist back)			
☐ 184 Bo McLaughlin	.21	.09	.02
☐ 185 Sixto Lezcano	.30	.12	.03
☐ 186 Doug Flynn	.21	.09	.02
☐ 187 Dick Pole	.21	.09	.02
☐ 188 Bob Tolan	.21	.09	.02
☐ 189 Rick Dempsey	.30	.12	.03
☐ 190 Ray Burris	.21	.09	.02
☐ 191 Doug Griffin	.21	.09	.02
☐ 192 Clarence Gaston	.40	.16	.04
☐ 193 Larry Gura	.21	.09	.02
☐ 194 Gary Matthews	.30	.12	.03
☐ 195 Ed Figueroa	.21	.09	.02
☐ 196 Len Randle	.21	.09	.02
☐ 197 Ed Ott	.21	.09	.02
☐ 198 Wilbur Wood	.30	.12	.03
☐ 199 Pepe Frias	.21	.09	.02
☐ 200 Frank Tanana	.40	.16	.04
☐ 201 Ed Kranepool	.30	.12	.03
☐ 202 Tom Johnson	.21	.09	.02
☐ 203 Ed Armbrister	.21	.09	.02
☐ 204 Jeff Newman	.21	.09	.02
☐ 205 Pete Falcone	.21	.09	.02
☐ 206 Boog Powell	.50	.20	.05
☐ 207 Glenn Abbott	.21	.09	.02
☐ 208 Checklist 2	1.00	.10	.02
☐ 209 Rob Andrews	.21	.09	.02
☐ 210 Fred Lynn	1.50	.60	.15
☐ 211 Giants Team/Mgr.	.90	.20	.04
Joe Altobelli			
(checklist back)			
☐ 212 Jim Mason	.21	.09	.02
☐ 213 Maximino Leon	.21	.09	.02
☐ 214 Darrell Porter	.21	.09	.02
☐ 215 Butch Metzger	.21	.09	.02
☐ 216 Doug DeCinces	.30	.12	.03
☐ 217 Tom Underwood	.21	.09	.02
☐ 218 John Wathan	.90	.40	.09
☐ 219 Joe Coleman	.21	.09	.02
☐ 220 Chris Chambliss	.30	.12	.03
☐ 221 Bob Bailey	.21	.09	.02
☐ 222 Francisco Barrios	.21	.09	.02
☐ 223 Earl Williams	.21	.09	.02
☐ 224 Rusty Torres	.21	.09	.02
☐ 225 Bob Apodaca	.21	.09	.02
☐ 226 Leroy Stanton	.21	.09	.02
☐ 227 Joe Sambito	.30	.12	.03
☐ 228 Twins Team/Mgr.	.90	.20	.04
Gene Mauch			
(checklist back)			
☐ 229 Don Kessinger	.30	.12	.03
☐ 230 Vida Blue	.30	.12	.03
☐ 231 RB: George Brett	6.00	2.50	.60
Most cons. games			
with 3 or more hits			
☐ 232 RB: Minnie Minoso	.40	.16	.04
Oldest to hit safely			
☐ 233 RB: Jose Morales, Most	.30	.12	.03
pinch-hits, season			
☐ 234 RB: Nolan Ryan	7.50	3.25	.75
Most seasons, 300			
or more strikeouts			
☐ 235 Cecil Cooper	.50	.20	.05
☐ 236 Tom Buskey	.21	.09	.02
☐ 237 Gene Clines	.21	.09	.02
☐ 238 Tippy Martinez	.30	.12	.03
☐ 239 Bill Plummer	.30	.12	.03
☐ 240 Ron LeFlore	.30	.12	.03
☐ 241 Dave Tomlin	.21	.09	.02
☐ 242 Ken Henderson	.21	.09	.02
☐ 243 Ron Reed	.21	.09	.02
☐ 244 John Mayberry	.40	.16	.04
(cartoon mentions			
T206 Wagner)			
☐ 245 Rick Rhoden	.30	.12	.03
☐ 246 Mike Vail	.21	.09	.02
☐ 247 Chris Knapp	.21	.09	.02
☐ 248 Wilbur Howard	.21	.09	.02
☐ 249 Pete Redfern	.21	.09	.02
☐ 250 Bill Madlock	.60	.25	.06
☐ 251 Tony Muser	.21	.09	.02
☐ 252 Dale Murray	.21	.09	.02
☐ 253 John Hale	.21	.09	.02
☐ 254 Doyle Alexander	.21	.09	.02
☐ 255 George Scott	.30	.12	.03
☐ 256 Joe Hoerner	.21	.09	.02
☐ 257 Mike Miley	.21	.09	.02

☐ 258	Luis Tiant	.40	.16	.04
☐ 259	Mets Team/Mgr.	.90	.20	.04
	Joe Frazier			
	(checklist back)			
☐ 260	J.R. Richard	.30	.12	.03
☐ 261	Phil Garner	.40	.16	.04
☐ 262	Al Cowens	.30	.12	.03
☐ 263	Mike Marshall	.30	.12	.03
☐ 264	Tom Hutton	.21	.09	.02
☐ 265	Mark Fidrych	1.00	.40	.10
☐ 266	Derrel Thomas	.21	.09	.02
☐ 267	Ray Fosse	.21	.09	.02
☐ 268	Rick Sawyer	.21	.09	.02
☐ 269	Joe Lis	.21	.09	.02
☐ 270	Dave Parker	4.50	2.00	.45
☐ 271	Terry Forster	.30	.12	.03
☐ 272	Lee Lacy	.21	.09	.02
☐ 273	Eric Soderholm	.21	.09	.02
☐ 274	Don Stanhouse	.21	.09	.02
☐ 275	Mike Hargrove	.30	.12	.03
☐ 276	AL Champs	.50	.20	.05
	Chambliss' homer			
	decides it			
☐ 277	NL Champs	.40	.16	.04
	Reds sweep Phillies			
☐ 278	Danny Frisella	.21	.09	.02
☐ 279	Joe Wallis	.21	.09	.02
☐ 280	Jim Hunter	2.25	.90	.22
☐ 281	Roy Staiger	.21	.09	.02
☐ 282	Sid Monge	.21	.09	.02
☐ 283	Jerry DaVanon	.21	.09	.02
☐ 284	Mike Norris	.21	.09	.02
☐ 285	Brooks Robinson	3.50	1.50	.35
☐ 286	Johnny Grubb	.21	.09	.02
☐ 287	Reds Team/Mgr.	.90	.20	.04
	Sparky Anderson			
	(checklist back)			
☐ 288	Bob Montgomery	.21	.09	.02
☐ 289	Gene Garber	.21	.09	.02
☐ 290	Amos Otis	.30	.12	.03
☐ 291	Jason Thompson	.30	.12	.03
☐ 292	Rogelio Moret	.21	.09	.02
☐ 293	Jack Brohamer	.21	.09	.02
☐ 294	George Medich	.21	.09	.02
☐ 295	Gary Carter	5.50	2.50	.55
☐ 296	Don Hood	.21	.09	.02
☐ 297	Ken Reitz	.21	.09	.02
☐ 298	Charlie Hough	.30	.12	.03
☐ 299	Otto Velez	.21	.09	.02
☐ 300	Jerry Koosman	.40	.16	.04
☐ 301	Toby Harrah	.30	.12	.03
☐ 302	Mike Garman	.21	.09	.02
☐ 303	Gene Tenace	.30	.12	.03
☐ 304	Jim Hughes	.21	.09	.02
☐ 305	Mickey Rivers	.30	.12	.03
☐ 306	Rick Waits	.21	.09	.02
☐ 307	Gary Sutherland	.21	.09	.02
☐ 308	Gene Pentz	.21	.09	.02
☐ 309	Red Sox Team/Mgr.	.90	.20	.04
	Don Zimmer			
	(checklist back)			
☐ 310	Larry Bowa	.40	.16	.04
☐ 311	Vern Ruhle	.21	.09	.02
☐ 312	Rob Belloir	.21	.09	.02
☐ 313	Paul Blair	.30	.12	.03
☐ 314	Steve Mingori	.21	.09	.02
☐ 315	Dave Chalk	.21	.09	.02
☐ 316	Steve Rogers	.21	.09	.02
☐ 317	Kurt Bevacqua	.21	.09	.02
☐ 318	Duffy Dyer	.21	.09	.02
☐ 319	Rich Gossage	1.00	.40	.10
☐ 320	Ken Griffey	1.50	.60	.15
☐ 321	Dave Goltz	.21	.09	.02
☐ 322	Bill Russell	.30	.12	.03
☐ 323	Larry Lintz	.21	.09	.02
☐ 324	John Curtis	.21	.09	.02
☐ 325	Mike Ivie	.21	.09	.02
☐ 326	Jesse Jefferson	.21	.09	.02
☐ 327	Astros Team/Mgr.	.90	.20	.04
	Bill Virdon			
	(checklist back)			
☐ 328	Tommy Boggs	.21	.09	.02
☐ 329	Ron Hodges	.21	.09	.02
☐ 330	George Hendrick	.30	.12	.03
☐ 331	Jim Colborn	.21	.09	.02
☐ 332	Elliott Maddox	.21	.09	.02
☐ 333	Paul Reuschel	.21	.09	.02
☐ 334	Bill Stein	.21	.09	.02
☐ 335	Bill Robinson	.30	.12	.03
☐ 336	Denny Doyle	.21	.09	.02
☐ 337	Ron Schueler	.21	.09	.02
☐ 338	Dave Duncan	.21	.09	.02
☐ 339	Adrian Devine	.21	.09	.02
☐ 340	Hal McRae	.40	.16	.04
☐ 341	Joe Kerrigan	.21	.09	.02
☐ 342	Jerry Remy	.21	.09	.02
☐ 343	Ed Halicki	.21	.09	.02
☐ 344	Brian Downing	.40	.16	.04
☐ 345	Reggie Smith	.40	.16	.04
☐ 346	Bill Singer	.30	.12	.03
☐ 347	George Foster	1.25	.50	.12
☐ 348	Brent Strom	.21	.09	.02
☐ 349	Jim Holt	.21	.09	.02
☐ 350	Larry Dierker	.21	.09	.02
☐ 351	Jim Sundberg	.30	.12	.03
☐ 352	Mike Phillips	.21	.09	.02
☐ 353	Stan Thomas	.21	.09	.02
☐ 354	Pirates Team/Mgr.	.90	.20	.04
	Chuck Tanner			
	(checklist back)			
☐ 355	Lou Brock	3.50	1.50	.35
☐ 356	Checklist 3	1.00	.10	.02
☐ 357	Tim McCarver	.40	.16	.04
☐ 358	Tom House	.21	.09	.02
☐ 359	Willie Randolph	2.00	.80	.20
☐ 360	Rick Monday	.30	.12	.03
☐ 361	Eduardo Rodriguez	.21	.09	.02
☐ 362	Tommy Davis	.30	.12	.03
☐ 363	Dave Roberts	.21	.09	.02
☐ 364	Vic Correll	.21	.09	.02
☐ 365	Mike Torrez	.21	.09	.02
☐ 366	Ted Sizemore	.21	.09	.02
☐ 367	Dave Hamilton	.21	.09	.02
☐ 368	Mike Jorgensen	.21	.09	.02
☐ 369	Terry Humphrey	.21	.09	.02
☐ 370	John Montefusco	.30	.12	.03
☐ 371	Royals Team/Mgr.	.90	.20	.04
	Whitey Herzog			
	(checklist back)			
☐ 372	Rich Folkers	.21	.09	.02
☐ 373	Bert Campaneris	.30	.12	.03
☐ 374	Kent Tekulve	.40	.16	.04
☐ 375	Larry Hisle	.30	.12	.03
☐ 376	Nino Espinosa	.21	.09	.02
☐ 377	Dave McKay	.21	.09	.02
☐ 378	Jim Umbarger	.21	.09	.02
☐ 379	Larry Cox	.21	.09	.02
☐ 380	Lee May	.30	.12	.03
☐ 381	Bob Forsch	.21	.09	.02
☐ 382	Charlie Moore	.21	.09	.02
☐ 383	Stan Bahnsen	.21	.09	.02
☐ 384	Darrel Chaney	.21	.09	.02
☐ 385	Dave LaRoche	.21	.09	.02
☐ 386	Manny Mota	.30	.12	.03
☐ 387	Yankees Team	.90	.20	.04
	(checklist back)			
☐ 388	Terry Harmon	.21	.09	.02
☐ 389	Ken Kravec	.21	.09	.02
☐ 390	Dave Winfield	9.00	4.00	.90
☐ 391	Dan Warthen	.21	.09	.02
☐ 392	Phil Roof	.21	.09	.02
☐ 393	John Lowenstein	.21	.09	.02
☐ 394	Bill Laxton	.21	.09	.02
☐ 395	Manny Trillo	.21	.09	.02
☐ 396	Tom Murphy	.21	.09	.02
☐ 397	Larry Herndon	.30	.12	.03
☐ 398	Tom Burgmeier	.21	.09	.02
☐ 399	Bruce Boisclair	.21	.09	.02
☐ 400	Steve Garvey	4.00	1.75	.40
☐ 401	Mickey Scott	.21	.09	.02
☐ 402	Tommy Helms	.30	.12	.03
☐ 403	Tom Grieve	.30	.12	.03
☐ 404	Eric Rasmussen	.21	.09	.02
☐ 405	Claudell Washington	.30	.12	.03
☐ 406	Tim Johnson	.21	.09	.02
☐ 407	Dave Freisleben	.21	.09	.02
☐ 408	Cesar Tovar	.21	.09	.02
☐ 409	Pete Broberg	.21	.09	.02
☐ 410	Willie Montanez	.21	.09	.02
☐ 411	W.S. Games 1 and 2	1.00	.40	.10
	Morgan homers opener;			
	Bench stars as			
	Reds take 2nd game			
☐ 412	W.S. Games 3 and 4	1.00	.40	.10
	Reds stop Yankees;			
	Bench's two homers			
	wrap it up			
☐ 413	World Series Summary	.60	.25	.06
	Cincy wins 2nd			
	straight series			
☐ 414	Tommy Harper	.30	.12	.03
☐ 415	Jay Johnstone	.30	.12	.03
☐ 416	Chuck Hartenstein	.21	.09	.02
☐ 417	Wayne Garrett	.21	.09	.02
☐ 418	White Sox Team/Mgr.	.90	.20	.04
	Bob Lemon			
	(checklist back)			
☐ 419	Steve Swisher	.21	.09	.02

☐ 420	Rusty Staub	.40	.16	.04
☐ 421	Doug Rau	.21	.09	.02
☐ 422	Freddie Patek	.21	.09	.02
☐ 423	Gary Lavelle	.21	.09	.02
☐ 424	Steve Brye	.21	.09	.02
☐ 425	Joe Torre	.50	.20	.05
☐ 426	Dick Drago	.21	.09	.02
☐ 427	Dave Rader	.21	.09	.02
☐ 428	Rangers Team/Mgr.	.90	.20	.04
	Frank Lucchesi			
	(checklist back)			
☐ 429	Ken Boswell	.21	.09	.02
☐ 430	Fergie Jenkins	2.25	.90	.22
☐ 431	Dave Collins UER	.30	.12	.03
	(photo actually Bobby Jones)			
☐ 432	Buzz Capra	.21	.09	.02
☐ 433	Turn back clock 1972	.30	.12	.03
	Nate Colbert			
☐ 434	Turn back clock 1967	2.00	.80	.20
	Yaz Triple Crown			
☐ 435	Turn back clock 1962	.40	.16	.04
	Wills 104 steals			
☐ 436	Turn back clock 1957	.30	.12	.03
	Keegan hurls Majors' only no-hitter			
☐ 437	Turn back clock 1952	.50	.20	.05
	Kiner leads NL HR's 7th straight year			
☐ 438	Marty Perez	.21	.09	.02
☐ 439	Gorman Thomas	.40	.16	.04
☐ 440	Jon Matlack	.30	.12	.03
☐ 441	Larvell Blanks	.21	.09	.02
☐ 442	Braves Team/Mgr.	.90	.20	.04
	Dave Bristol			
	(checklist back)			
☐ 443	Lamar Johnson	.21	.09	.02
☐ 444	Wayne Twitchell	.21	.09	.02
☐ 445	Ken Singleton	.30	.12	.03
☐ 446	Bill Bonham	.21	.09	.02
☐ 447	Jerry Turner	.21	.09	.02
☐ 448	Ellie Rodriguez	.21	.09	.02
☐ 449	Al Fitzmorris	.21	.09	.02
☐ 450	Pete Rose	9.00	4.00	.90
☐ 451	Checklist 4	1.00	.10	.02
☐ 452	Mike Caldwell	.21	.09	.02
☐ 453	Pedro Garcia	.21	.09	.02
☐ 454	Andy Etchebarren	.21	.09	.02
☐ 455	Rick Wise	.30	.12	.03
☐ 456	Leon Roberts	.21	.09	.02
☐ 457	Steve Luebber	.21	.09	.02
☐ 458	Leo Foster	.21	.09	.02
☐ 459	Steve Foucault	.21	.09	.02
☐ 460	Willie Stargell	2.75	1.10	.27
☐ 461	Dick Tidrow	.21	.09	.02
☐ 462	Don Baylor	.75	.30	.07
☐ 463	Jamie Quirk	.30	.12	.03
☐ 464	Randy Moffitt	.21	.09	.02
☐ 465	Rico Carty	.30	.12	.03
☐ 466	Fred Holdsworth	.21	.09	.02
☐ 467	Phillies Team/Mgr.	.90	.20	.04
	Danny Ozark			
	(checklist back)			
☐ 468	Ramon Hernandez	.21	.09	.02
☐ 469	Pat Kelly	.21	.09	.02
☐ 470	Ted Simmons	.75	.30	.07
☐ 471	Del Unser	.21	.09	.02
☐ 472	Rookie Pitchers	.40	.16	.04
	Don Aase			
	Bob McClure			
	Gil Patterson			
	Dave Wehrmeister			
☐ 473	Rookie Outfielders	65.00	29.00	9.75
	Andre Dawson			
	Gene Richards			
	John Scott			
	Denny Walling			
☐ 474	Rookie Shortstops	.30	.12	.03
	Bob Bailor			
	Kiko Garcia			
	Craig Reynolds			
	Alex Taveras			
☐ 475	Rookie Pitchers	.40	.16	.04
	Chris Batton			
	Rick Camp			
	Scott McGregor			
	Manny Sarmiento			
☐ 476	Rookie Catchers	45.00	20.00	6.75
	Gary Alexander			
	Rick Cerone			
	Dale Murphy			
	Kevin Pasley			
☐ 477	Rookie Infielders	.30	.12	.03
	Doug Ault			
	Rich Dauer			
	Orlando Gonzalez			
	Phil Mankowski			
☐ 478	Rookie Pitchers	.30	.12	.03
	Jim Gideon			
	Leon Hooten			
	Dave Johnson			
	Mark Lemongello			
☐ 479	Rookie Outfielders	.40	.16	.04
	Brian Asselstine			
	Wayne Gross			
	Sam Mejias			
	Alvis Woods			
☐ 480	Carl Yastrzemski	6.25	2.75	.60
☐ 481	Roger Metzger	.21	.09	.02
☐ 482	Tony Solaita	.21	.09	.02
☐ 483	Richie Zisk	.21	.09	.02
☐ 484	Burt Hooton	.21	.09	.02
☐ 485	Roy White	.30	.12	.03
☐ 486	Ed Bane	.21	.09	.02
☐ 487	Rookie Pitchers	.30	.12	.03
	Larry Anderson			
	Ed Glynn			
	Joe Henderson			
	Greg Terlecky			
☐ 488	Rookie Outfielders	15.00	6.50	2.15
	Jack Clark			
	Ruppert Jones			
	Lee Mazzilli			
	Dan Thomas			
☐ 489	Rookie Pitchers	.40	.16	.04
	Len Barker			
	Randy Lerch			
	Greg Minton			
	Mike Overy			
☐ 490	Rookie Shortstops	.30	.12	.03
	Billy Almon			
	Mickey Klutts			
	Tommy McMillan			
	Mark Wagner			
☐ 491	Rookie Pitchers	5.00	2.25	.50
	Mike Dupree			
	Dennis Martinez			
	Craig Mitchell			
	Bob Sykes			
☐ 492	Rookie Outfielders	.75	.30	.07
	Tony Armas			
	Steve Kemp			
	Carlos Lopez			
	Gary Woods			
☐ 493	Rookie Pitchers	.50	.20	.05
	Mike Krukow			
	Jim Otten			
	Gary Wheelock			
	Mike Willis			
☐ 494	Rookie Infielders	.75	.30	.07
	Juan Bernhardt			
	Mike Champion			
	Jim Gantner			
	Bump Wills			
☐ 495	Al Hrabosky	.30	.12	.03
☐ 496	Gary Thomasson	.21	.09	.02
☐ 497	Clay Carroll	.21	.09	.02
☐ 498	Sal Bando	.30	.12	.03
☐ 499	Pablo Torrealba	.21	.09	.02
☐ 500	Dave Kingman	.50	.20	.05
☐ 501	Jim Bibby	.21	.09	.02
☐ 502	Randy Hundley	.21	.09	.02
☐ 503	Bill Lee	.30	.12	.03
☐ 504	Dodgers Team/Mgr.	.90	.20	.04
	Tom Lasorda			
	(checklist back)			
☐ 505	Oscar Gamble	.30	.12	.03
☐ 506	Steve Grilli	.21	.09	.02
☐ 507	Mike Hegan	.21	.09	.02
☐ 508	Dave Pagan	.21	.09	.02
☐ 509	Cookie Rojas	.21	.09	.02
☐ 510	John Candelaria	.60	.25	.06
☐ 511	Bill Fahey	.21	.09	.02
☐ 512	Jack Billingham	.21	.09	.02
☐ 513	Jerry Terrell	.21	.09	.02
☐ 514	Cliff Johnson	.21	.09	.02
☐ 515	Chris Speier	.21	.09	.02
☐ 516	Bake McBride	.21	.09	.02
☐ 517	Pete Vuckovich	.40	.16	.04
☐ 518	Cubs Team/Mgr.	.90	.20	.04
	Herman Franks			
	(checklist back)			
☐ 519	Don Kirkwood	.21	.09	.02
☐ 520	Garry Maddox	.30	.12	.03
☐ 521	Bob Grich	.30	.12	.03
☐ 522	Enzo Hernandez	.21	.09	.02
☐ 523	Rollie Fingers	2.50	1.00	.25
☐ 524	Rowland Office	.21	.09	.02

☐	525	Dennis Eckersley	9.00	4.00	.90
☐	526	Larry Parrish	.30	.12	.03
☐	527	Dan Meyer	.21	.09	.02
☐	528	Bill Castro	.21	.09	.02
☐	529	Jim Essian	.50	.20	.05
☐	530	Rick Reuschel	.40	.16	.04
☐	531	Lyman Bostock	.30	.12	.03
☐	532	Jim Willoughby	.21	.09	.02
☐	533	Mickey Stanley	.30	.12	.03
☐	534	Paul Splittorff	.21	.09	.02
☐	535	Cesar Geronimo	.21	.09	.02
☐	536	Vic Albury	.21	.09	.02
☐	537	Dave Roberts	.21	.09	.02
☐	538	Frank Taveras	.21	.09	.02
☐	539	Mike Wallace	.21	.09	.02
☐	540	Bob Watson	.30	.12	.03
☐	541	John Denny	.30	.12	.03
☐	542	Frank Duffy	.21	.09	.02
☐	543	Ron Blomberg	.21	.09	.02
☐	544	Gary Ross	.21	.09	.02
☐	545	Bob Boone	.60	.25	.06
☐	546	Orioles Team/Mgr.	.90	.20	.04
		Earl Weaver			
		(checklist back)			
☐	547	Willie McCovey	3.00	1.25	.30
☐	548	Joel Youngblood	.21	.09	.02
☐	549	Jerry Royster	.21	.09	.02
☐	550	Randy Jones	.30	.12	.03
☐	551	Bill North	.21	.09	.02
☐	552	Pepe Mangual	.21	.09	.02
☐	553	Jack Heidemann	.21	.09	.02
☐	554	Bruce Kimm	.21	.09	.02
☐	555	Dan Ford	.21	.09	.02
☐	556	Doug Bird	.21	.09	.02
☐	557	Jerry White	.21	.09	.02
☐	558	Elias Sosa	.21	.09	.02
☐	559	Alan Bannister	.21	.09	.02
☐	560	Dave Concepcion	.75	.30	.07
☐	561	Pete LaCock	.21	.09	.02
☐	562	Checklist 5	1.00	.10	.02
☐	563	Bruce Kison	.21	.09	.02
☐	564	Alan Ashby	.21	.09	.02
☐	565	Mickey Lolich	.40	.16	.04
☐	566	Rick Miller	.21	.09	.02
☐	567	Enos Cabell	.21	.09	.02
☐	568	Carlos May	.21	.09	.02
☐	569	Jim Lonborg	.30	.12	.03
☐	570	Bobby Bonds	.50	.20	.05
☐	571	Darrell Evans	.50	.20	.05
☐	572	Ross Grimsley	.21	.09	.02
☐	573	Joe Ferguson	.21	.09	.02
☐	574	Aurelio Rodriguez	.21	.09	.02
☐	575	Dick Ruthven	.21	.09	.02
☐	576	Fred Kendall	.21	.09	.02
☐	577	Jerry Augustine	.21	.09	.02
☐	578	Bob Randall	.21	.09	.02
☐	579	Don Carrithers	.21	.09	.02
☐	580	George Brett	24.00	10.50	3.50
☐	581	Pedro Borbon	.21	.09	.02
☐	582	Ed Kirkpatrick	.21	.09	.02
☐	583	Paul Lindblad	.21	.09	.02
☐	584	Ed Goodson	.21	.09	.02
☐	585	Rick Burleson	.30	.12	.03
☐	586	Steve Renko	.21	.09	.02
☐	587	Rick Baldwin	.21	.09	.02
☐	588	Dave Moates	.21	.09	.02
☐	589	Mike Cosgrove	.21	.09	.02
☐	590	Buddy Bell	.40	.16	.04
☐	591	Chris Arnold	.21	.09	.02
☐	592	Dan Briggs	.21	.09	.02
☐	593	Dennis Blair	.21	.09	.02
☐	594	Biff Pocoroba	.21	.09	.02
☐	595	John Hiller	.30	.12	.03
☐	596	Jerry Martin	.21	.09	.02
☐	597	Mariners Leaders	.75	.30	.04
		Darrell Johnson MG			
		Don Bryant CO			
		Jim Busby CO			
		Vada Pinson CO			
		Wes Stock CO			
		(checklist back)			
☐	598	Sparky Lyle	.50	.20	.05
☐	599	Mike Tyson	.21	.09	.02
☐	600	Jim Palmer	6.00	2.50	.60
☐	601	Mike Lum	.21	.09	.02
☐	602	Andy Hassler	.21	.09	.02
☐	603	Willie Davis	.30	.12	.03
☐	604	Jim Slaton	.21	.09	.02
☐	605	Felix Millan	.21	.09	.02
☐	606	Steve Braun	.21	.09	.02
☐	607	Larry Demery	.21	.09	.02
☐	608	Roy Howell	.21	.09	.02
☐	609	Jim Barr	.21	.09	.02
☐	610	Jose Cardenal	.21	.09	.02

☐	611	Dave Lemanczyk	.21	.09	.02
☐	612	Barry Foote	.21	.09	.02
☐	613	Reggie Cleveland	.21	.09	.02
☐	614	Greg Gross	.21	.09	.02
☐	615	Phil Niekro	2.00	.80	.20
☐	616	Tommy Sandt	.21	.09	.02
☐	617	Bobby Darwin	.21	.09	.02
☐	618	Pat Dobson	.21	.09	.02
☐	619	Johnny Oates	.30	.12	.03
☐	620	Don Sutton	2.00	.80	.20
☐	621	Tigers Team/Mgr.	.90	.20	.04
		Ralph Houk			
		(checklist back)			
☐	622	Jim Wohlford	.21	.09	.02
☐	623	Jack Kucek	.21	.09	.02
☐	624	Hector Cruz	.21	.09	.02
☐	625	Ken Holtzman	.30	.12	.03
☐	626	Al Bumbry	.21	.09	.02
☐	627	Bob Myrick	.21	.09	.02
☐	628	Mario Guerrero	.21	.09	.02
☐	629	Bobby Valentine	.30	.12	.03
☐	630	Bert Blyleven	1.25	.50	.12
☐	631	Big League Brothers	3.00	1.25	.30
		George Brett			
		Ken Brett			
☐	632	Big League Brothers	.30	.12	.03
		Bob Forsch			
		Ken Forsch			
☐	633	Big League Brothers	.30	.12	.03
		Lee May			
		Carlos May			
☐	634	Big League Brothers UER	.30	.12	.03
		Paul Reuschel			
		Rick Reuschel			
		(photos switched)			
☐	635	Robin Yount	24.00	10.50	3.50
☐	636	Santo Alcala	.21	.09	.02
☐	637	Alex Johnson	.21	.09	.02
☐	638	Jim Kaat	.75	.30	.07
☐	639	Jerry Morales	.21	.09	.02
☐	640	Carlton Fisk	6.50	2.75	.65
☐	641	Dan Larson	.21	.09	.02
☐	642	Willie Crawford	.21	.09	.02
☐	643	Mike Pazik	.21	.09	.02
☐	644	Matt Alexander	.21	.09	.02
☐	645	Jerry Reuss	.30	.12	.03
☐	646	Andres Mora	.21	.09	.02
☐	647	Expos Team/Mgr.	.90	.20	.04
		Dick Williams			
		(checklist back)			
☐	648	Jim Spencer	.21	.09	.02
☐	649	Dave Cash	.21	.09	.02
☐	650	Nolan Ryan	30.00	13.50	4.50
☐	651	Von Joshua	.21	.09	.02
☐	652	Tom Walker	.21	.09	.02
☐	653	Diego Segui	.21	.09	.02
☐	654	Ron Pruitt	.21	.09	.02
☐	655	Tony Perez	1.50	.60	.15
☐	656	Ron Guidry	2.50	1.00	.25
☐	657	Mick Kelleher	.21	.09	.02
☐	658	Marty Pattin	.21	.09	.02
☐	659	Merv Rettenmund	.21	.09	.02
☐	660	Willie Horton	.50	.15	.03

1978 Topps

The cards in this 726-card set measure 2 1/2" by 3 1/2". The 1978 Topps set experienced an increase in number of cards from the previous five regular issue sets of 660. Cards 1 through 7 feature Record Breakers (RB) of the 1977 season. Other subsets within this set include League Leaders (201-208), Post-season cards (411-413), and Rookie Prospects (701-711). The key rookie cards in this set are the multi-player rookie card of Paul Molitor and Alan Trammell, Jack Morris, Eddie Murray, Lance Parrish, and Lou Whitaker. The manager cards in the set feature a "then and now" format on the card front showing the manager as he looked many years before, e.g., during his playing days. While no scarcities exist, 66 of the cards are more abundant in supply, as they were "double printed." These 66 double-printed cards are noted in the checklist by DP. Team cards again feature a checklist of that team's players in the set on the back. Cards numbered 23 or lower, that feature Astros, Rangers, Tigers, or Yankees and do

BRUCE SUTTER

not follow the numbering checklisted below, are not necessarily error cards. They are probably Burger King cards, a separate set with its own pricing and mass distribution. Burger King cards are indistinguishable from the corresponding Topps cards except for the card numbering difference and the fact that Burger King cards do not have a printing sheet designation (such as A through F like the regular Topps) anywhere on the card back in very small print.

	NRMT	VG-E	GOOD
COMPLETE SET (726)	340.00	140.00	35.00
COMMON PLAYER (1-726)	.16	.07	.01
COMMON DP's (1-726)	.08	.03	.01

		NRMT	VG-E	GOOD
☐ 1	RB: Lou Brock Most steals, lifetime	3.00	.75	.15
☐ 2	RB: Sparky Lyle Most games, pure relief, lifetime	.25	.10	.02
☐ 3	RB: Willie McCovey Most times, 2 HR's in inning, lifetime	1.25	.50	.12
☐ 4	RB: Brooks Robinson Most consecutive seasons with one club	1.25	.50	.12
☐ 5	RB: Pete Rose Most hits, switch hitter, lifetime	2.50	1.00	.25
☐ 6	RB: Nolan Ryan Most games with 10 or more strikeouts, lifetime	6.00	2.50	.60
☐ 7	RB: Reggie Jackson Most homers, one World Series	3.00	1.25	.30
☐ 8	Mike Sadek	.16	.07	.01
☐ 9	Doug DeCinces	.25	.10	.02
☐ 10	Phil Niekro	1.50	.60	.15
☐ 11	Rick Manning	.16	.07	.01
☐ 12	Don Aase	.25	.10	.02
☐ 13	Art Howe	.50	.20	.05
☐ 14	Lerrin LaGrow	.16	.07	.01
☐ 15	Tony Perez DP	.60	.25	.06
☐ 16	Roy White	.25	.10	.02
☐ 17	Mike Krukow	.25	.10	.02
☐ 18	Bob Grich	.25	.10	.02
☐ 19	Darrell Porter	.16	.07	.01
☐ 20	Pete Rose DP	4.00	1.75	.40
☐ 21	Steve Kemp	.25	.10	.02
☐ 22	Charlie Hough	.25	.10	.02
☐ 23	Bump Wills	.16	.07	.01
☐ 24	Don Money DP	.08	.03	.01
☐ 25	Jon Matlack	.25	.10	.02
☐ 26	Rich Hebner	.16	.07	.01
☐ 27	Geoff Zahn	.16	.07	.01
☐ 28	Ed Ott	.16	.07	.01
☐ 29	Bob Lacey	.16	.07	.01
☐ 30	George Hendrick	.25	.10	.02
☐ 31	Glenn Abbott	.16	.07	.01
☐ 32	Garry Templeton	.35	.15	.03
☐ 33	Dave Lemanczyk	.16	.07	.01
☐ 34	Willie McCovey	2.75	1.10	.27
☐ 35	Sparky Lyle	.35	.15	.03
☐ 36	Eddie Murray	70.00	32.00	10.50
☐ 37	Rick Waits	.16	.07	.01
☐ 38	Willie Montanez	.16	.07	.01
☐ 39	Floyd Bannister	.60	.25	.06
☐ 40	Carl Yastrzemski	4.50	2.00	.45
☐ 41	Burt Hooton	.16	.07	.01
☐ 42	Jorge Orta	.16	.07	.01

☐ 43	Bill Atkinson	.16	.07	.01
☐ 44	Toby Harrah	.25	.10	.02
☐ 45	Mark Fidrych	.35	.15	.03
☐ 46	Al Cowens	.16	.07	.01
☐ 47	Jack Billingham	.16	.07	.01
☐ 48	Don Baylor	.50	.20	.05
☐ 49	Ed Kranepool	.25	.10	.02
☐ 50	Rick Reuschel	.35	.15	.03
☐ 51	Charlie Moore DP	.08	.03	.01
☐ 52	Jim Lonborg	.25	.10	.02
☐ 53	Phil Garner DP	.16	.07	.01
☐ 54	Tom Johnson	.16	.07	.01
☐ 55	Mitchell Page	.16	.07	.01
☐ 56	Randy Jones	.16	.07	.01
☐ 57	Dan Meyer	.16	.07	.01
☐ 58	Bob Forsch	.16	.07	.01
☐ 59	Otto Velez	.16	.07	.01
☐ 60	Thurman Munson	4.00	1.75	.40
☐ 61	Larvell Blanks	.16	.07	.01
☐ 62	Jim Barr	.16	.07	.01
☐ 63	Don Zimmer MG	.25	.10	.02
☐ 64	Gene Pentz	.16	.07	.01
☐ 65	Ken Singleton	.25	.10	.02
☐ 66	White Sox Team (checklist back)	.75	.15	.03
☐ 67	Claudell Washington	.25	.10	.02
☐ 68	Steve Foucault DP	.08	.03	.01
☐ 69	Mike Vail	.16	.07	.01
☐ 70	Rich Gossage	.75	.30	.07
☐ 71	Terry Humphrey	.16	.07	.01
☐ 72	Andre Dawson	15.00	6.50	2.15
☐ 73	Andy Hassler	.16	.07	.01
☐ 74	Checklist 1	.80	.08	.01
☐ 75	Dick Ruthven	.16	.07	.01
☐ 76	Steve Ontiveros	.16	.07	.01
☐ 77	Ed Kirkpatrick	.16	.07	.01
☐ 78	Pablo Torrealba	.16	.07	.01
☐ 79	Darrell Johnson DP	.08	.03	.01
☐ 80	Ken Griffey	1.00	.40	.10
☐ 81	Pete Redfern	.16	.07	.01
☐ 82	Giants Team (checklist back)	.75	.15	.03
☐ 83	Bob Montgomery	.16	.07	.01
☐ 84	Kent Tekulve	.25	.10	.02
☐ 85	Ron Fairly	.16	.07	.01
☐ 86	Dave Tomlin	.16	.07	.01
☐ 87	John Lowenstein	.16	.07	.01
☐ 88	Mike Phillips	.16	.07	.01
☐ 89	Ken Clay	.16	.07	.01
☐ 90	Larry Bowa	.35	.15	.03
☐ 91	Oscar Zamora	.16	.07	.01
☐ 92	Adrian Devine	.16	.07	.01
☐ 93	Bobby Cox DP	.08	.03	.01
☐ 94	Chuck Scrivener	.16	.07	.01
☐ 95	Jamie Quirk	.16	.07	.01
☐ 96	Orioles Team (checklist back)	.75	.15	.03
☐ 97	Stan Bahnsen	.16	.07	.01
☐ 98	Jim Essian	.25	.10	.02
☐ 99	Willie Hernandez	.60	.25	.06
☐ 100	George Brett	15.00	6.50	2.15
☐ 101	Sid Monge	.16	.07	.01
☐ 102	Matt Alexander	.16	.07	.01
☐ 103	Tom Murphy	.16	.07	.01
☐ 104	Lee Lacy	.16	.07	.01
☐ 105	Reggie Cleveland	.16	.07	.01
☐ 106	Bill Plummer	.25	.10	.02
☐ 107	Ed Halicki	.16	.07	.01
☐ 108	Von Joshua	.16	.07	.01
☐ 109	Joe Torre	.35	.15	.03
☐ 110	Richie Zisk	.16	.07	.01
☐ 111	Mike Tyson	.16	.07	.01
☐ 112	Astros Team (checklist back)	.75	.15	.03
☐ 113	Don Carrithers	.16	.07	.01
☐ 114	Paul Blair	.25	.10	.02
☐ 115	Gary Nolan	.16	.07	.01
☐ 116	Tucker Ashford	.16	.07	.01
☐ 117	John Montague	.16	.07	.01
☐ 118	Terry Harmon	.16	.07	.01
☐ 119	Dennis Martinez	1.00	.40	.10
☐ 120	Gary Carter	3.50	1.50	.35
☐ 121	Alvis Woods	.16	.07	.01
☐ 122	Dennis Eckersley	4.50	2.00	.45
☐ 123	Manny Trillo	.16	.07	.01
☐ 124	Dave Rozema	.25	.10	.02
☐ 125	George Scott	.25	.10	.02
☐ 126	Paul Moskau	.16	.07	.01
☐ 127	Chet Lemon	.25	.10	.02
☐ 128	Bill Russell	.25	.10	.02
☐ 129	Jim Colborn	.16	.07	.01
☐ 130	Jeff Burroughs	.25	.10	.02
☐ 131	Bert Blyleven	.75	.30	.07
☐ 132	Enos Cabell	.16	.07	.01
☐ 133	Jerry Augustine	.16	.07	.01

#	Player			
☐ 134	Steve Henderson	.16	.07	.01
☐ 135	Ron Guidry DP	.75	.30	.07
☐ 136	Ted Sizemore	.16	.07	.01
☐ 137	Craig Kusick	.16	.07	.01
☐ 138	Larry Demery	.16	.07	.01
☐ 139	Wayne Gross	.16	.07	.01
☐ 140	Rollie Fingers	2.25	.90	.22
☐ 141	Ruppert Jones	.16	.07	.01
☐ 142	John Montefusco	.25	.10	.02
☐ 143	Keith Hernandez	1.75	.70	.17
☐ 144	Jesse Jefferson	.16	.07	.01
☐ 145	Rick Monday	.25	.10	.02
☐ 146	Doyle Alexander	.16	.07	.01
☐ 147	Lee Mazzilli	.16	.07	.01
☐ 148	Andre Thornton	.25	.10	.02
☐ 149	Dale Murray	.16	.07	.01
☐ 150	Bobby Bonds	.35	.15	.03
☐ 151	Milt Wilcox	.16	.07	.01
☐ 152	Ivan DeJesus	.16	.07	.01
☐ 153	Steve Stone	.25	.10	.02
☐ 154	Cecil Cooper DP	.16	.07	.01
☐ 155	Butch Hobson	.35	.15	.03
☐ 156	Andy Messersmith	.25	.10	.02
☐ 157	Pete LaCock DP	.08	.03	.01
☐ 158	Joaquin Andujar	.25	.10	.02
☐ 159	Lou Piniella	.35	.15	.03
☐ 160	Jim Palmer	4.50	2.00	.45
☐ 161	Bob Boone	.50	.20	.05
☐ 162	Paul Thormodsgard	.16	.07	.01
☐ 163	Bill North	.16	.07	.01
☐ 164	Bob Owchinko	.16	.07	.01
☐ 165	Rennie Stennett	.16	.07	.01
☐ 166	Carlos Lopez	.16	.07	.01
☐ 167	Tim Foli	.16	.07	.01
☐ 168	Reggie Smith	.35	.15	.03
☐ 169	Jerry Johnson	.16	.07	.01
☐ 170	Lou Brock	3.00	1.25	.30
☐ 171	Pat Zachry	.16	.07	.01
☐ 172	Mike Hargrove	.25	.10	.02
☐ 173	Robin Yount	15.00	6.50	2.15
☐ 174	Wayne Garland	.16	.07	.01
☐ 175	Jerry Morales	.16	.07	.01
☐ 176	Milt May	.16	.07	.01
☐ 177	Gene Garber DP	.08	.03	.01
☐ 178	Dave Chalk	.16	.07	.01
☐ 179	Dick Tidrow	.16	.07	.01
☐ 180	Dave Concepcion	.60	.25	.06
☐ 181	Ken Forsch	.16	.07	.01
☐ 182	Jim Spencer	.16	.07	.01
☐ 183	Doug Bird	.16	.07	.01
☐ 184	Checklist 2	.90	.10	.02
☐ 185	Ellis Valentine	.16	.07	.01
☐ 186	Bob Stanley DP	.25	.10	.02
☐ 187	Jerry Royster DP	.08	.03	.01
☐ 188	Al Bumbry	.16	.07	.01
☐ 189	Tom Lasorda MG	.25	.10	.02
☐ 190	John Candelaria	.35	.15	.03
☐ 191	Rodney Scott	.16	.07	.01
☐ 192	Padres Team (checklist back)	.75	.15	.03
☐ 193	Rich Chiles	.16	.07	.01
☐ 194	Derrel Thomas	.16	.07	.01
☐ 195	Larry Dierker	.16	.07	.01
☐ 196	Bob Bailor	.16	.07	.01
☐ 197	Nino Espinosa	.16	.07	.01
☐ 198	Ron Pruitt	.16	.07	.01
☐ 199	Craig Reynolds	.16	.07	.01
☐ 200	Reggie Jackson	7.50	3.25	.75
☐ 201	Batting Leaders Dave Parker Rod Carew	1.00	.40	.10
☐ 202	Home Run Leaders DP George Foster Jim Rice	.25	.10	.02
☐ 203	RBI Leaders George Foster Larry Hisle	.25	.10	.02
☐ 204	Steals Leaders DP Frank Taveras Freddie Patek	.16	.07	.01
☐ 205	Victory Leaders Steve Carlton Dave Goltz Dennis Leonard Jim Palmer	.75	.30	.07
☐ 206	Strikeout Leaders DP Phil Niekro Nolan Ryan	1.25	.50	.12
☐ 207	ERA Leaders DP John Candelaria Frank Tanana	.16	.07	.01
☐ 208	Top Firemen Rollie Fingers Bill Campbell	.25	.10	.02
☐ 209	Dock Ellis	.16	.07	.01
☐ 210	Jose Cardenal	.16	.07	.01
☐ 211	Earl Weaver MG DP	.16	.07	.01
☐ 212	Mike Caldwell	.16	.07	.01
☐ 213	Alan Bannister	.16	.07	.01
☐ 214	Angels Team (checklist back)	.75	.15	.03
☐ 215	Darrell Evans	.35	.15	.03
☐ 216	Mike Paxton	.16	.07	.01
☐ 217	Rod Gilbreath	.16	.07	.01
☐ 218	Marty Pattin	.16	.07	.01
☐ 219	Mike Cubbage	.16	.07	.01
☐ 220	Pedro Borbon	.16	.07	.01
☐ 221	Chris Speier	.16	.07	.01
☐ 222	Jerry Martin	.16	.07	.01
☐ 223	Bruce Kison	.16	.07	.01
☐ 224	Jerry Tabb	.16	.07	.01
☐ 225	Don Gullett DP	.16	.07	.01
☐ 226	Joe Ferguson	.16	.07	.01
☐ 227	Al Fitzmorris	.16	.07	.01
☐ 228	Manny Mota DP	.16	.07	.01
☐ 229	Leo Foster	.16	.07	.01
☐ 230	Al Hrabosky	.16	.07	.01
☐ 231	Wayne Nordhagen	.16	.07	.01
☐ 232	Mickey Stanley	.25	.10	.02
☐ 233	Dick Pole	.16	.07	.01
☐ 234	Herman Franks MG	.16	.07	.01
☐ 235	Tim McCarver	.35	.15	.03
☐ 236	Terry Whitfield	.16	.07	.01
☐ 237	Rich Dauer	.16	.07	.01
☐ 238	Juan Beniquez	.16	.07	.01
☐ 239	Dyar Miller	.16	.07	.01
☐ 240	Gene Tenace	.25	.10	.02
☐ 241	Pete Vuckovich	.25	.10	.02
☐ 242	Barry Bonnell DP	.16	.07	.01
☐ 243	Bob McClure	.16	.07	.01
☐ 244	Expos Team DP (checklist back)	.35	.10	.02
☐ 245	Rick Burleson	.25	.10	.02
☐ 246	Dan Driessen	.16	.07	.01
☐ 247	Larry Christenson	.16	.07	.01
☐ 248	Frank White DP	.16	.07	.01
☐ 249	Dave Goltz DP	.08	.03	.01
☐ 250	Graig Nettles DP	.25	.10	.02
☐ 251	Don Kirkwood	.16	.07	.01
☐ 252	Steve Swisher DP	.08	.03	.01
☐ 253	Jim Kern	.16	.07	.01
☐ 254	Dave Collins	.25	.10	.02
☐ 255	Jerry Reuss	.25	.10	.02
☐ 256	Joe Altobelli MG	.16	.07	.01
☐ 257	Hector Cruz	.16	.07	.01
☐ 258	John Hiller	.25	.10	.02
☐ 259	Dodgers Team (checklist back)	.75	.15	.03
☐ 260	Bert Campaneris	.25	.10	.02
☐ 261	Tim Hosley	.16	.07	.01
☐ 262	Rudy May	.16	.07	.01
☐ 263	Danny Walton	.16	.07	.01
☐ 264	Jamie Easterly	.16	.07	.01
☐ 265	Sal Bando DP	.16	.07	.01
☐ 266	Bob Shirley	.16	.07	.01
☐ 267	Doug Ault	.16	.07	.01
☐ 268	Gil Flores	.16	.07	.01
☐ 269	Wayne Twitchell	.16	.07	.01
☐ 270	Carlton Fisk	5.00	2.25	.50
☐ 271	Randy Lerch DP	.08	.03	.01
☐ 272	Royle Stillman	.16	.07	.01
☐ 273	Fred Norman	.16	.07	.01
☐ 274	Freddie Patek	.16	.07	.01
☐ 275	Dan Ford	.16	.07	.01
☐ 276	Bill Bonham DP	.08	.03	.01
☐ 277	Bruce Boisclair	.16	.07	.01
☐ 278	Enrique Romo	.16	.07	.01
☐ 279	Bill Virdon MG	.25	.10	.02
☐ 280	Buddy Bell	.25	.10	.02
☐ 281	Eric Rasmussen DP	.08	.03	.01
☐ 282	Yankees Team (checklist back)	1.00	.20	.04
☐ 283	Omar Moreno	.16	.07	.01
☐ 284	Randy Moffitt	.16	.07	.01
☐ 285	Steve Yeager DP	.16	.07	.01
☐ 286	Ben Oglivie	.25	.10	.02
☐ 287	Kiko Garcia	.16	.07	.01
☐ 288	Dave Hamilton	.16	.07	.01
☐ 289	Checklist 3	.90	.10	.02
☐ 290	Willie Horton	.25	.10	.02
☐ 291	Gary Ross	.16	.07	.01
☐ 292	Gene Richards	.16	.07	.01
☐ 293	Mike Willis	.16	.07	.01
☐ 294	Larry Parrish	.25	.10	.02
☐ 295	Bill Lee	.25	.10	.02
☐ 296	Biff Pocoroba	.16	.07	.01
☐ 297	Warren Brusstar DP	.08	.03	.01
☐ 298	Tony Armas	.25	.10	.02
☐ 299	Whitey Herzog MG	.25	.10	.02
☐ 300	Joe Morgan	3.00	1.25	.30

☐ 301 Buddy Schultz	.16	.07	.01
☐ 302 Cubs Team	.75	.15	.03
(checklist back)			
☐ 303 Sam Hinds	.16	.07	.01
☐ 304 John Milner	.16	.07	.01
☐ 305 Rico Carty	.25	.10	.02
☐ 306 Joe Niekro	.25	.10	.02
☐ 307 Glenn Borgmann	.16	.07	.01
☐ 308 Jim Rooker	.16	.07	.01
☐ 309 Cliff Johnson	.16	.07	.01
☐ 310 Don Sutton	2.00	.80	.20
☐ 311 Jose Baez DP	.08	.03	.01
☐ 312 Greg Minton	.25	.10	.02
☐ 313 Andy Etchebarren	.16	.07	.01
☐ 314 Paul Lindblad	.16	.07	.01
☐ 315 Mark Belanger	.25	.10	.02
☐ 316 Henry Cruz DP	.08	.03	.01
☐ 317 Dave Johnson	.25	.10	.02
☐ 318 Tom Griffin	.16	.07	.01
☐ 319 Alan Ashby	.16	.07	.01
☐ 320 Fred Lynn	1.00	.40	.10
☐ 321 Santo Alcala	.16	.07	.01
☐ 322 Tom Paciorek	.16	.07	.01
☐ 323 Jim Fregosi DP	.16	.07	.01
☐ 324 Vern Rapp MG	.16	.07	.01
☐ 325 Bruce Sutter	.75	.30	.07
☐ 326 Mike Lum DP	.08	.03	.01
☐ 327 Rick Langford DP	.08	.03	.01
☐ 328 Milwaukee Brewers	.75	.15	.03
Team Card			
(checklist back)			
☐ 329 John Verhoeven	.16	.07	.01
☐ 330 Bob Watson	.25	.10	.02
☐ 331 Mark Littell	.16	.07	.01
☐ 332 Duane Kuiper	.16	.07	.01
☐ 333 Jim Todd	.16	.07	.01
☐ 334 John Stearns	.16	.07	.01
☐ 335 Bucky Dent	.35	.15	.03
☐ 336 Steve Busby	.16	.07	.01
☐ 337 Tom Grieve	.25	.10	.02
☐ 338 Dave Heaverlo	.16	.07	.01
☐ 339 Mario Guerrero	.16	.07	.01
☐ 340 Bake McBride	.16	.07	.01
☐ 341 Mike Flanagan	.35	.15	.03
☐ 342 Aurelio Rodriguez	.16	.07	.01
☐ 343 John Wathan DP	.16	.07	.01
☐ 344 Sam Ewing	.16	.07	.01
☐ 345 Luis Tiant	.35	.15	.03
☐ 346 Larry Biittner	.16	.07	.01
☐ 347 Terry Forster	.25	.10	.02
☐ 348 Del Unser	.16	.07	.01
☐ 349 Rick Camp DP	.08	.03	.01
☐ 350 Steve Garvey	3.50	1.50	.35
☐ 351 Jeff Torborg	.25	.10	.02
☐ 352 Tony Scott	.16	.07	.01
☐ 353 Doug Bair	.16	.07	.01
☐ 354 Cesar Geronimo	.16	.07	.01
☐ 355 Bill Travers	.16	.07	.01
☐ 356 New York Mets	.90	.20	.04
Team Card			
(checklist back)			
☐ 357 Tom Poquette	.16	.07	.01
☐ 358 Mark Lemongello	.16	.07	.01
☐ 359 Marc Hill	.16	.07	.01
☐ 360 Mike Schmidt	15.00	6.50	2.15
☐ 361 Chris Knapp	.16	.07	.01
☐ 362 Dave May	.16	.07	.01
☐ 363 Bob Randall	.16	.07	.01
☐ 364 Jerry Turner	.16	.07	.01
☐ 365 Ed Figueroa	.16	.07	.01
☐ 366 Larry Milbourne DP	.08	.03	.01
☐ 367 Rick Dempsey	.25	.10	.02
☐ 368 Balor Moore	.16	.07	.01
☐ 369 Tim Nordbrook	.16	.07	.01
☐ 370 Rusty Staub	.35	.15	.03
☐ 371 Ray Burris	.16	.07	.01
☐ 372 Brian Asselstine	.16	.07	.01
☐ 373 Jim Willoughby	.16	.07	.01
☐ 374 Jose Morales	.16	.07	.01
☐ 375 Tommy John	.75	.30	.07
☐ 376 Jim Wohlford	.16	.07	.01
☐ 377 Manny Sarmiento	.16	.07	.01
☐ 378 Bobby Winkles MG	.16	.07	.01
☐ 379 Skip Lockwood	.16	.07	.01
☐ 380 Ted Simmons	.60	.25	.06
☐ 381 Phillies Team	.75	.15	.03
(checklist back)			
☐ 382 Joe Lahoud	.16	.07	.01
☐ 383 Mario Mendoza	.16	.07	.01
☐ 384 Jack Clark	4.00	1.75	.40
☐ 385 Tito Fuentes	.16	.07	.01
☐ 386 Bob Gorinski	.16	.07	.01
☐ 387 Ken Holtzman	.25	.10	.02
☐ 388 Bill Fahey DP	.08	.03	.01
☐ 389 Julio Gonzalez	.16	.07	.01

☐ 390 Oscar Gamble	.16	.07	.01
☐ 391 Larry Haney	.16	.07	.01
☐ 392 Billy Almon	.16	.07	.01
☐ 393 Tippy Martinez	.16	.07	.01
☐ 394 Roy Howell DP	.08	.03	.01
☐ 395 Jim Hughes	.16	.07	.01
☐ 396 Bob Stinson DP	.08	.03	.01
☐ 397 Greg Gross	.16	.07	.01
☐ 398 Don Hood	.16	.07	.01
☐ 399 Pete Mackanin	.16	.07	.01
☐ 400 Nolan Ryan	24.00	10.50	3.50
☐ 401 Sparky Anderson MG	.25	.10	.02
☐ 402 Dave Campbell	.16	.07	.01
☐ 403 Bud Harrelson	.25	.10	.02
☐ 404 Tigers Team	.75	.15	.03
(checklist back)			
☐ 405 Rawly Eastwick	.16	.07	.01
☐ 406 Mike Jorgensen	.16	.07	.01
☐ 407 Odell Jones	.16	.07	.01
☐ 408 Joe Zdeb	.16	.07	.01
☐ 409 Ron Schueler	.16	.07	.01
☐ 410 Bill Madlock	.50	.20	.05
☐ 411 AL Champs	.60	.25	.06
Yankees rally to			
defeat Royals			
☐ 412 NL Champs	.60	.25	.06
Dodgers overpower			
Phillies in four			
☐ 413 World Series	2.25	.90	.22
Reggie and Yankees			
reign supreme			
☐ 414 Darold Knowles DP	.08	.03	.01
☐ 415 Ray Fosse	.16	.07	.01
☐ 416 Jack Brohamer	.16	.07	.01
☐ 417 Mike Garman DP	.08	.03	.01
☐ 418 Tony Muser	.16	.07	.01
☐ 419 Jerry Garvin	.16	.07	.01
☐ 420 Greg Luzinski	.35	.15	.03
☐ 421 Junior Moore	.16	.07	.01
☐ 422 Steve Braun	.16	.07	.01
☐ 423 Dave Rosello	.16	.07	.01
☐ 424 Boston Red Sox	.75	.15	.03
Team Card			
(checklist back)			
☐ 425 Steve Rogers DP	.08	.03	.01
☐ 426 Fred Kendall	.16	.07	.01
☐ 427 Mario Soto	.35	.15	.03
☐ 428 Joel Youngblood	.16	.07	.01
☐ 429 Mike Barlow	.16	.07	.01
☐ 430 Al Oliver	.35	.15	.03
☐ 431 Butch Metzger	.16	.07	.01
☐ 432 Terry Bulling	.16	.07	.01
☐ 433 Fernando Gonzalez	.16	.07	.01
☐ 434 Mike Norris	.16	.07	.01
☐ 435 Checklist 4	.90	.10	.02
☐ 436 Vic Harris DP	.08	.03	.01
☐ 437 Bo McLaughlin	.16	.07	.01
☐ 438 John Ellis	.16	.07	.01
☐ 439 Ken Kravec	.16	.07	.01
☐ 440 Dave Lopes	.25	.10	.02
☐ 441 Larry Gura	.16	.07	.01
☐ 442 Elliott Maddox	.16	.07	.01
☐ 443 Darrel Chaney	.16	.07	.01
☐ 444 Roy Hartsfield MG	.16	.07	.01
☐ 445 Mike Ivie	.16	.07	.01
☐ 446 Tug McGraw	.35	.15	.03
☐ 447 Leroy Stanton	.16	.07	.01
☐ 448 Bill Castro	.16	.07	.01
☐ 449 Tim Blackwell DP	.08	.03	.01
☐ 450 Tom Seaver	5.00	2.25	.50
☐ 451 Minnesota Twins	.75	.15	.03
Team Card			
(checklist back)			
☐ 452 Jerry Mumphrey	.16	.07	.01
☐ 453 Doug Flynn	.16	.07	.01
☐ 454 Dave LaRoche	.16	.07	.01
☐ 455 Bill Robinson	.25	.10	.02
☐ 456 Vern Ruhle	.16	.07	.01
☐ 457 Bob Bailey	.16	.07	.01
☐ 458 Jeff Newman	.16	.07	.01
☐ 459 Charlie Spikes	.16	.07	.01
☐ 460 Jim Hunter	2.00	.80	.20
☐ 461 Rob Andrews DP	.08	.03	.01
☐ 462 Rogelio Moret	.16	.07	.01
☐ 463 Kevin Bell	.16	.07	.01
☐ 464 Jerry Grote	.16	.07	.01
☐ 465 Hal McRae	.35	.15	.03
☐ 466 Dennis Blair	.16	.07	.01
☐ 467 Alvin Dark MG	.16	.07	.01
☐ 468 Warren Cromartie	.35	.15	.03
☐ 469 Rick Cerone	.25	.10	.02
☐ 470 J.R. Richard	.25	.10	.02
☐ 471 Roy Smalley	.16	.07	.01
☐ 472 Ron Reed	.16	.07	.01
☐ 473 Bill Buckner	.35	.15	.03

#	Player			
☐ 474	Jim Slaton	.16	.07	.01
☐ 475	Gary Matthews	.25	.10	.02
☐ 476	Bill Stein	.16	.07	.01
☐ 477	Doug Capilla	.16	.07	.01
☐ 478	Jerry Remy	.16	.07	.01
☐ 479	Cardinals Team (checklist back)	.75	.15	.03
☐ 480	Ron LeFlore	.25	.10	.02
☐ 481	Jackson Todd	.16	.07	.01
☐ 482	Rick Miller	.16	.07	.01
☐ 483	Ken Macha	.16	.07	.01
☐ 484	Jim Norris	.16	.07	.01
☐ 485	Chris Chambliss	.25	.10	.02
☐ 486	John Curtis	.16	.07	.01
☐ 487	Jim Tyrone	.16	.07	.01
☐ 488	Dan Spillner	.16	.07	.01
☐ 489	Rudy Meoli	.16	.07	.01
☐ 490	Amos Otis	.25	.10	.02
☐ 491	Scott McGregor	.25	.10	.02
☐ 492	Jim Sundberg	.16	.07	.01
☐ 493	Steve Renko	.16	.07	.01
☐ 494	Chuck Tanner MG	.16	.07	.01
☐ 495	Dave Cash	.16	.07	.01
☐ 496	Jim Clancy DP	.25	.10	.02
☐ 497	Glenn Adams	.16	.07	.01
☐ 498	Joe Sambito	.16	.07	.01
☐ 499	Seattle Mariners Team Card (checklist back)	.75	.15	.03
☐ 500	George Foster	.75	.30	.07
☐ 501	Dave Roberts	.16	.07	.01
☐ 502	Pat Rockett	.16	.07	.01
☐ 503	Ike Hampton	.16	.07	.01
☐ 504	Roger Freed	.16	.07	.01
☐ 505	Felix Millan	.16	.07	.01
☐ 506	Ron Blomberg	.16	.07	.01
☐ 507	Willie Crawford	.16	.07	.01
☐ 508	Johnny Oates	.25	.10	.02
☐ 509	Brent Strom	.16	.07	.01
☐ 510	Willie Stargell	2.50	1.00	.25
☐ 511	Frank Duffy	.16	.07	.01
☐ 512	Larry Herndon	.16	.07	.01
☐ 513	Barry Foote	.16	.07	.01
☐ 514	Rob Sperring	.16	.07	.01
☐ 515	Tim Corcoran	.16	.07	.01
☐ 516	Gary Beare	.16	.07	.01
☐ 517	Andres Mora	.16	.07	.01
☐ 518	Tommy Boggs DP	.08	.03	.01
☐ 519	Brian Downing	.35	.15	.03
☐ 520	Larry Hisle	.25	.10	.02
☐ 521	Steve Staggs	.16	.07	.01
☐ 522	Dick Williams MG	.16	.07	.01
☐ 523	Donnie Moore	.25	.10	.02
☐ 524	Bernie Carbo	.16	.07	.01
☐ 525	Jerry Terrell	.16	.07	.01
☐ 526	Reds Team (checklist back)	.75	.15	.03
☐ 527	Vic Correll	.16	.07	.01
☐ 528	Rob Picciolo	.16	.07	.01
☐ 529	Paul Hartzell	.16	.07	.01
☐ 530	Dave Winfield	6.25	2.75	.60
☐ 531	Tom Underwood	.16	.07	.01
☐ 532	Skip Jutze	.16	.07	.01
☐ 533	Sandy Alomar	.16	.07	.01
☐ 534	Wilbur Howard	.16	.07	.01
☐ 535	Checklist 5	.90	.10	.02
☐ 536	Roric Harrison	.16	.07	.01
☐ 537	Bruce Bochte	.16	.07	.01
☐ 538	Johnny LeMaster	.16	.07	.01
☐ 539	Vic Davalillo DP	.08	.03	.01
☐ 540	Steve Carlton	4.25	1.75	.42
☐ 541	Larry Cox	.16	.07	.01
☐ 542	Tim Johnson	.16	.07	.01
☐ 543	Larry Harlow DP	.08	.03	.01
☐ 544	Len Randle DP	.08	.03	.01
☐ 545	Bill Campbell	.16	.07	.01
☐ 546	Ted Martinez	.16	.07	.01
☐ 547	John Scott	.16	.07	.01
☐ 548	Billy Hunter MG DP	.08	.03	.01
☐ 549	Joe Kerrigan	.16	.07	.01
☐ 550	John Mayberry	.25	.10	.02
☐ 551	Atlanta Braves Team Card (checklist back)	.75	.15	.03
☐ 552	Francisco Barrios	.16	.07	.01
☐ 553	Terry Puhl	.35	.15	.03
☐ 554	Joe Coleman	.16	.07	.01
☐ 555	Butch Wynegar	.16	.07	.01
☐ 556	Ed Armbrister	.16	.07	.01
☐ 557	Tony Solaita	.16	.07	.01
☐ 558	Paul Mitchell	.16	.07	.01
☐ 559	Phil Mankowski	.16	.07	.01
☐ 560	Dave Parker	4.00	1.75	.40
☐ 561	Charlie Williams	.16	.07	.01
☐ 562	Glenn Burke	.16	.07	.01
☐ 563	Dave Rader	.16	.07	.01
☐ 564	Mick Kelleher	.16	.07	.01
☐ 565	Jerry Koosman	.35	.15	.03
☐ 566	Merv Rettenmund	.16	.07	.01
☐ 567	Dick Drago	.16	.07	.01
☐ 568	Tom Hutton	.16	.07	.01
☐ 569	Lary Sorensen	.16	.07	.01
☐ 570	Dave Kingman	.50	.20	.05
☐ 571	Buck Martinez	.16	.07	.01
☐ 572	Rick Wise	.25	.10	.02
☐ 573	Luis Gomez	.16	.07	.01
☐ 574	Bob Lemon MG	.35	.15	.03
☐ 575	Pat Dobson	.16	.07	.01
☐ 576	Sam Mejias	.16	.07	.01
☐ 577	Oakland A's Team Card (checklist back)	.75	.15	.03
☐ 578	Buzz Capra	.16	.07	.01
☐ 579	Rance Mulliniks	.25	.10	.02
☐ 580	Rod Carew	5.25	2.25	.50
☐ 581	Lynn McGlothen	.16	.07	.01
☐ 582	Fran Healy	.16	.07	.01
☐ 583	George Medich	.16	.07	.01
☐ 584	John Hale	.16	.07	.01
☐ 585	Woodie Fryman DP	.08	.03	.01
☐ 586	Ed Goodson	.16	.07	.01
☐ 587	John Urrea	.16	.07	.01
☐ 588	Jim Mason	.16	.07	.01
☐ 589	Bob Knepper	.60	.25	.06
☐ 590	Bobby Murcer	.35	.15	.03
☐ 591	George Zeber	.16	.07	.01
☐ 592	Bob Apodaca	.16	.07	.01
☐ 593	Dave Skaggs	.16	.07	.01
☐ 594	Dave Freisleben	.16	.07	.01
☐ 595	Sixto Lezcano	.16	.07	.01
☐ 596	Gary Wheelock	.16	.07	.01
☐ 597	Steve Dillard	.16	.07	.01
☐ 598	Eddie Solomon	.16	.07	.01
☐ 599	Gary Woods	.16	.07	.01
☐ 600	Frank Tanana	.25	.10	.02
☐ 601	Gene Mauch MG	.16	.07	.01
☐ 602	Eric Soderholm	.16	.07	.01
☐ 603	Will McEnaney	.16	.07	.01
☐ 604	Earl Williams	.16	.07	.01
☐ 605	Rick Rhoden	.25	.10	.02
☐ 606	Pirates Team (checklist back)	.75	.15	.03
☐ 607	Fernando Arroyo	.16	.07	.01
☐ 608	Johnny Grubb	.16	.07	.01
☐ 609	John Denny	.25	.10	.02
☐ 610	Garry Maddox	.25	.10	.02
☐ 611	Pat Scanlon	.16	.07	.01
☐ 612	Ken Henderson	.16	.07	.01
☐ 613	Marty Perez	.16	.07	.01
☐ 614	Joe Wallis	.16	.07	.01
☐ 615	Clay Carroll	.16	.07	.01
☐ 616	Pat Kelly	.16	.07	.01
☐ 617	Joe Nolan	.16	.07	.01
☐ 618	Tommy Helms	.25	.10	.02
☐ 619	Thad Bosley DP	.16	.07	.01
☐ 620	Willie Randolph	.60	.25	.06
☐ 621	Craig Swan DP	.16	.07	.01
☐ 622	Champ Summers	.16	.07	.01
☐ 623	Eduardo Rodriguez	.16	.07	.01
☐ 624	Gary Alexander DP	.08	.03	.01
☐ 625	Jose Cruz	.25	.10	.02
☐ 626	Blue Jays Team DP (checklist back)	.35	.10	.02
☐ 627	David Johnson	.16	.07	.01
☐ 628	Ralph Garr	.16	.07	.01
☐ 629	Don Stanhouse	.16	.07	.01
☐ 630	Ron Cey	.35	.15	.03
☐ 631	Danny Ozark MG	.16	.07	.01
☐ 632	Rowland Office	.16	.07	.01
☐ 633	Tom Veryzer	.16	.07	.01
☐ 634	Len Barker	.16	.07	.01
☐ 635	Joe Rudi	.25	.10	.02
☐ 636	Jim Bibby	.16	.07	.01
☐ 637	Duffy Dyer	.16	.07	.01
☐ 638	Paul Splittorff	.16	.07	.01
☐ 639	Gene Clines	.16	.07	.01
☐ 640	Lee May DP	.16	.07	.01
☐ 641	Doug Rau	.16	.07	.01
☐ 642	Denny Doyle	.16	.07	.01
☐ 643	Tom House	.16	.07	.01
☐ 644	Jim Dwyer	.16	.07	.01
☐ 645	Mike Torrez	.16	.07	.01
☐ 646	Rick Auerbach DP	.08	.03	.01
☐ 647	Steve Dunning	.16	.07	.01
☐ 648	Gary Thomasson	.16	.07	.01
☐ 649	Moose Haas	.25	.10	.02
☐ 650	Cesar Cedeno	.25	.10	.02
☐ 651	Doug Rader	.25	.10	.02
☐ 652	Checklist 6	.90	.10	.02

☐ 653	Ron Hodges DP	.08	.03	.01
☐ 654	Pepe Frias	.16	.07	.01
☐ 655	Lyman Bostock	.25	.10	.02
☐ 656	Dave Garcia MG	.16	.07	.01
☐ 657	Bombo Rivera	.16	.07	.01
☐ 658	Manny Sanguillen	.25	.10	.02
☐ 659	Rangers Team (checklist back)	.75	.15	.03
☐ 660	Jason Thompson	.25	.10	.02
☐ 661	Grant Jackson	.16	.07	.01
☐ 662	Paul Dade	.16	.07	.01
☐ 663	Paul Reuschel	.16	.07	.01
☐ 664	Fred Stanley	.16	.07	.01
☐ 665	Dennis Leonard	.25	.10	.02
☐ 666	Billy Smith	.16	.07	.01
☐ 667	Jeff Byrd	.16	.07	.01
☐ 668	Dusty Baker	.25	.10	.02
☐ 669	Pete Falcone	.16	.07	.01
☐ 670	Jim Rice	3.25	1.35	.32
☐ 671	Gary Lavelle	.16	.07	.01
☐ 672	Don Kessinger	.25	.10	.02
☐ 673	Steve Brye	.16	.07	.01
☐ 674	Ray Knight	1.50	.60	.15
☐ 675	Jay Johnstone	.25	.10	.02
☐ 676	Bob Myrick	.16	.07	.01
☐ 677	Ed Herrmann	.16	.07	.01
☐ 678	Tom Burgmeier	.16	.07	.01
☐ 679	Wayne Garrett	.16	.07	.01
☐ 680	Vida Blue	.25	.10	.02
☐ 681	Rob Belloir	.16	.07	.01
☐ 682	Ken Brett	.16	.07	.01
☐ 683	Mike Champion	.16	.07	.01
☐ 684	Ralph Houk MG	.25	.10	.02
☐ 685	Frank Taveras	.16	.07	.01
☐ 686	Gaylord Perry	2.25	.90	.22
☐ 687	Julio Cruz	.25	.10	.02
☐ 688	George Mitterwald	.16	.07	.01
☐ 689	Indians Team (checklist back)	.75	.15	.03
☐ 690	Mickey Rivers	.25	.10	.02
☐ 691	Ross Grimsley	.16	.07	.01
☐ 692	Ken Reitz	.16	.07	.01
☐ 693	Lamar Johnson	.16	.07	.01
☐ 694	Elias Sosa	.16	.07	.01
☐ 695	Dwight Evans	1.75	.70	.17
☐ 696	Steve Mingori	.16	.07	.01
☐ 697	Roger Metzger	.16	.07	.01
☐ 698	Juan Bernhardt	.16	.07	.01
☐ 699	Jackie Brown	.16	.07	.01
☐ 700	Johnny Bench	4.50	2.00	.45
☐ 701	Rookie Pitchers Tom Hume Larry Landreth Steve McCatty Bruce Taylor	.25	.10	.02
☐ 702	Rookie Catchers Bill Nahorodny Kevin Pasley Rick Sweet Don Werner	.16	.07	.01
☐ 703	Rookie Pitchers DP Larry Andersen Tim Jones Mickey Mahler Jack Morris	12.00	5.25	1.50
☐ 704	Rookie 2nd Basemen Garth Iorg Dave Oliver Sam Perlozzo Lou Whitaker	15.00	6.50	2.15
☐ 705	Rookie Outfielders Dave Bergman Miguel Dilone Clint Hurdle Willie Norwood	.50	.20	.05
☐ 706	Rookie 1st Basemen Wayne Cage Ted Cox Pat Putnam Dave Revering	.25	.10	.02
☐ 707	Rookie Shortstops Mickey Klutts Paul Molitor Alan Trammell U.L. Washington	55.00	25.00	8.25
☐ 708	Rookie Catchers Bo Diaz Dale Murphy Lance Parrish Ernie Whitt	18.00	7.50	2.50
☐ 709	Rookie Pitchers Steve Burke Matt Keough Lance Rautzhan	.35	.15	.03

	Dan Schatzeder			
☐ 710	Rookie Outfielders Dell Alston Rick Bosetti Mike Easler Keith Smith	.60	.25	.06
☐ 711	Rookie Pitchers DP Cardell Camper Dennis Lamp Craig Mitchell Roy Thomas	.16	.07	.01
☐ 712	Bobby Valentine	.25	.10	.02
☐ 713	Bob Davis	.16	.07	.01
☐ 714	Mike Anderson	.16	.07	.01
☐ 715	Jim Kaat	.75	.30	.07
☐ 716	Clarence Gaston	.35	.15	.03
☐ 717	Nelson Briles	.16	.07	.01
☐ 718	Ron Jackson	.16	.07	.01
☐ 719	Randy Elliott	.16	.07	.01
☐ 720	Fergie Jenkins	2.25	.90	.22
☐ 721	Billy Martin MG	.60	.25	.06
☐ 722	Pete Broberg	.16	.07	.01
☐ 723	John Wockenfuss	.16	.07	.01
☐ 724	Kansas City Royals Team Card (checklist back)	.75	.15	.03
☐ 725	Kurt Bevacqua	.16	.07	.01
☐ 726	Wilbur Wood	.25	.10	.02

1979 Topps

The cards in this 726-card set measure 2 1/2" by 3 1/2". Topps continued with the same number of cards as in 1978. Various series spotlight League Leaders (1-8), "Season and Career Record Holders" (411-418), "Record Breakers of 1978" (201-206), and one "Prospects" card for each team (701-726). Team cards feature a checklist on back of that team's players in the set and a small picture of the manager on the front of the card. There are 66 cards that were double printed and these are noted in the checklist by the abbreviation DP. Bump Wills (#369) was initially depicted in a Ranger uniform but with a Blue Jays affiliation; later printings correctly labeled him with Texas. The set price listed does not include the scarcer Wills (Rangers) card. The key rookie cards in this set are Pedro Guerrero, Carney Lansford, Ozzie Smith, and Bob Welch. Cards numbered 23 or lower, which feature Phillies or Yankees and do not follow the numbering checklisted below, are not necessarily error cards. They are Burger King cards, a separate set with its own pricing and mass distribution. Burger King cards are indistinguishable from the corresponding Topps cards except for the card numbering difference and the fact that Burger King cards do not have a printing sheet designation (such as A through F like the regular Topps) anywhere on the card back in very small print.

	NRMT	VG-E	GOOD
COMPLETE SET (726)	250.00	110.00	37.50
COMMON PLAYER (1-726)	.12	.05	.01
COMMON DP's (1-726)	.06	.02	.00

#	Player			
☐ 1	Batting Leaders	2.50	.50	.10
	Rod Carew			
	Dave Parker			
☐ 2	Home Run Leaders	.30	.12	.03
	Jim Rice			
	George Foster			
☐ 3	RBI Leaders	.30	.12	.03
	Jim Rice			
	George Foster			
☐ 4	Stolen Base Leaders	.20	.08	.02
	Ron LeFlore			
	Omar Moreno			
☐ 5	Victory Leaders	.40	.16	.04
	Ron Guidry			
	Gaylord Perry			
☐ 6	Strikeout Leaders	2.75	1.10	.27
	Nolan Ryan			
	J.R. Richard			
☐ 7	ERA Leaders	.20	.08	.02
	Ron Guidry			
	Craig Swan			
☐ 8	Leading Firemen	.40	.16	.04
	Rich Gossage			
	Rollie Fingers			
☐ 9	Dave Campbell	.12	.05	.01
☐ 10	Lee May	.20	.08	.02
☐ 11	Marc Hill	.12	.05	.01
☐ 12	Dick Drago	.12	.05	.01
☐ 13	Paul Dade	.12	.05	.01
☐ 14	Rafael Landestoy	.12	.05	.01
☐ 15	Ross Grimsley	.12	.05	.01
☐ 16	Fred Stanley	.12	.05	.01
☐ 17	Donnie Moore	.12	.05	.01
☐ 18	Tony Solaita	.12	.05	.01
☐ 19	Larry Gura DP	.12	.05	.01
☐ 20	Joe Morgan DP	1.25	.50	.12
☐ 21	Kevin Kobel	.12	.05	.01
☐ 22	Mike Jorgensen	.12	.05	.01
☐ 23	Terry Forster	.20	.08	.02
☐ 24	Paul Molitor	5.50	2.50	.55
☐ 25	Steve Carlton	3.50	1.50	.35
☐ 26	Jamie Quirk	.12	.05	.01
☐ 27	Dave Goltz	.12	.05	.01
☐ 28	Steve Brye	.12	.05	.01
☐ 29	Rick Langford	.12	.05	.01
☐ 30	Dave Winfield	5.00	2.25	.50
☐ 31	Tom House DP	.12	.05	.01
☐ 32	Jerry Mumphrey	.12	.05	.01
☐ 33	Dave Rozema	.12	.05	.01
☐ 34	Rob Andrews	.12	.05	.01
☐ 35	Ed Figueroa	.12	.05	.01
☐ 36	Alan Ashby	.12	.05	.01
☐ 37	Joe Kerrigan DP	.06	.02	.00
☐ 38	Bernie Carbo	.12	.05	.01
☐ 39	Dale Murphy	7.50	3.25	.75
☐ 40	Dennis Eckersley	3.00	1.25	.30
☐ 41	Twins Team/Mgr.	.60	.12	.02
	Gene Mauch			
	(checklist back)			
☐ 42	Ron Blomberg	.12	.05	.01
☐ 43	Wayne Twitchell	.12	.05	.01
☐ 44	Kurt Bevacqua	.12	.05	.01
☐ 45	Al Hrabosky	.12	.05	.01
☐ 46	Ron Hodges	.12	.05	.01
☐ 47	Fred Norman	.12	.05	.01
☐ 48	Merv Rettenmund	.12	.05	.01
☐ 49	Vern Ruhle	.12	.05	.01
☐ 50	Steve Garvey DP	1.50	.60	.15
☐ 51	Ray Fosse DP	.06	.02	.00
☐ 52	Randy Lerch	.12	.05	.01
☐ 53	Mick Kelleher	.12	.05	.01
☐ 54	Dell Alston DP	.06	.02	.00
☐ 55	Willie Stargell	2.25	.90	.22
☐ 56	John Hale	.12	.05	.01
☐ 57	Eric Rasmussen	.12	.05	.01
☐ 58	Bob Randall DP	.06	.02	.00
☐ 59	John Denny DP	.12	.05	.01
☐ 60	Mickey Rivers	.20	.08	.02
☐ 61	Bo Diaz	.20	.08	.02
☐ 62	Randy Moffitt	.12	.05	.01
☐ 63	Jack Brohamer	.12	.05	.01
☐ 64	Tom Underwood	.12	.05	.01
☐ 65	Mark Belanger	.20	.08	.02
☐ 66	Tigers Team/Mgr.	.60	.12	.02
	Les Moss			
	(checklist back)			
☐ 67	Jim Mason DP	.06	.02	.00
☐ 68	Joe Niekro DP	.12	.05	.01
☐ 69	Elliott Maddox	.12	.05	.01
☐ 70	John Candelaria	.30	.12	.03
☐ 71	Brian Downing	.30	.12	.03
☐ 72	Steve Mingori	.12	.05	.01
☐ 73	Ken Henderson	.12	.05	.01
☐ 74	Shane Rawley	.40	.16	.04
☐ 75	Steve Yeager	.20	.08	.02
☐ 76	Warren Cromartie	.20	.08	.02
☐ 77	Dan Briggs DP	.06	.02	.00
☐ 78	Elias Sosa	.12	.05	.01
☐ 79	Ted Cox	.12	.05	.01
☐ 80	Jason Thompson	.12	.05	.01
☐ 81	Roger Erickson	.12	.05	.01
☐ 82	Mets Team/Mgr.	.60	.12	.02
	Joe Torre			
	(checklist back)			
☐ 83	Fred Kendall	.12	.05	.01
☐ 84	Greg Minton	.12	.05	.01
☐ 85	Gary Matthews	.20	.08	.02
☐ 86	Rodney Scott	.12	.05	.01
☐ 87	Pete Falcone	.12	.05	.01
☐ 88	Bob Molinaro	.12	.05	.01
☐ 89	Dick Tidrow	.12	.05	.01
☐ 90	Bob Boone	.40	.16	.04
☐ 91	Terry Crowley	.12	.05	.01
☐ 92	Jim Bibby	.12	.05	.01
☐ 93	Phil Mankowski	.12	.05	.01
☐ 94	Len Barker	.12	.05	.01
☐ 95	Robin Yount	9.00	4.00	.90
☐ 96	Indians Team/Mgr.	.60	.12	.02
	Jeff Torborg			
	(checklist back)			
☐ 97	Sam Mejias	.12	.05	.01
☐ 98	Ray Burris	.12	.05	.01
☐ 99	John Wathan	.20	.08	.02
☐ 100	Tom Seaver DP	3.00	1.25	.30
☐ 101	Roy Howell	.12	.05	.01
☐ 102	Mike Anderson	.12	.05	.01
☐ 103	Jim Todd	.12	.05	.01
☐ 104	Johnny Oates DP	.12	.05	.01
☐ 105	Rick Camp DP	.06	.02	.00
☐ 106	Frank Duffy	.12	.05	.01
☐ 107	Jesus Alou DP	.06	.02	.00
☐ 108	Eduardo Rodriguez	.12	.05	.01
☐ 109	Joel Youngblood	.12	.05	.01
☐ 110	Vida Blue	.20	.08	.02
☐ 111	Roger Freed	.12	.05	.01
☐ 112	Phillies Team/Mgr.	.60	.12	.02
	Danny Ozark			
	(checklist back)			
☐ 113	Pete Redfern	.12	.05	.01
☐ 114	Cliff Johnson	.12	.05	.01
☐ 115	Nolan Ryan	18.00	7.50	2.50
☐ 116	Ozzie Smith	65.00	29.00	9.75
☐ 117	Grant Jackson	.12	.05	.01
☐ 118	Bud Harrelson	.20	.08	.02
☐ 119	Don Stanhouse	.12	.05	.01
☐ 120	Jim Sundberg	.12	.05	.01
☐ 121	Checklist 1 DP	.25	.03	.01
☐ 122	Mike Paxton	.12	.05	.01
☐ 123	Lou Whitaker	4.50	2.00	.45
☐ 124	Dan Schatzeder	.12	.05	.01
☐ 125	Rick Burleson	.20	.08	.02
☐ 126	Doug Bair	.12	.05	.01
☐ 127	Thad Bosley	.12	.05	.01
☐ 128	Ted Martinez	.12	.05	.01
☐ 129	Marty Pattin DP	.06	.02	.00
☐ 130	Bob Watson DP	.12	.05	.01
☐ 131	Jim Clancy	.12	.05	.01
☐ 132	Rowland Office	.12	.05	.01
☐ 133	Bill Castro	.12	.05	.01
☐ 134	Alan Bannister	.12	.05	.01
☐ 135	Bobby Murcer	.30	.12	.03
☐ 136	Jim Kaat	.40	.16	.04
☐ 137	Larry Wolfe DP	.06	.02	.00
☐ 138	Mark Lee	.12	.05	.01
☐ 139	Luis Pujols	.12	.05	.01
☐ 140	Don Gullett	.20	.08	.02
☐ 141	Tom Paciorek	.12	.05	.01
☐ 142	Charlie Williams	.12	.05	.01
☐ 143	Tony Scott	.12	.05	.01
☐ 144	Sandy Alomar	.12	.05	.01
☐ 145	Rick Rhoden	.20	.08	.02
☐ 146	Duane Kuiper	.12	.05	.01
☐ 147	Dave Hamilton	.12	.05	.01
☐ 148	Bruce Boisclair	.12	.05	.01
☐ 149	Manny Sarmiento	.12	.05	.01
☐ 150	Wayne Cage	.12	.05	.01
☐ 151	John Hiller	.20	.08	.02
☐ 152	Rick Cerone	.20	.08	.02
☐ 153	Dennis Lamp	.12	.05	.01
☐ 154	Jim Gantner DP	.12	.05	.01
☐ 155	Dwight Evans	1.50	.60	.15
☐ 156	Buddy Solomon	.12	.05	.01
☐ 157	U.L. Washington UER	.12	.05	.01
	(sic, bats left,			
	should be right)			
☐ 158	Joe Sambito	.12	.05	.01
☐ 159	Roy White	.20	.08	.02
☐ 160	Mike Flanagan	.30	.12	.03

☐ 161	Barry Foote	.12	.05	.01
☐ 162	Tom Johnson	.12	.05	.01
☐ 163	Glenn Burke	.12	.05	.01
☐ 164	Mickey Lolich	.30	.12	.03
☐ 165	Frank Taveras	.12	.05	.01
☐ 166	Leon Roberts	.12	.05	.01
☐ 167	Roger Metzger DP	.06	.02	.00
☐ 168	Dave Freisleben	.12	.05	.01
☐ 169	Bill Nahorodny	.12	.05	.01
☐ 170	Don Sutton	1.50	.60	.15
☐ 171	Gene Clines	.12	.05	.01
☐ 172	Mike Bruhert	.12	.05	.01
☐ 173	John Lowenstein	.12	.05	.01
☐ 174	Rick Auerbach	.12	.05	.01
☐ 175	George Hendrick	.20	.08	.02
☐ 176	Aurelio Rodriguez	.12	.05	.01
☐ 177	Ron Reed	.12	.05	.01
☐ 178	Alvis Woods	.12	.05	.01
☐ 179	Jim Beattie DP	.12	.05	.01
☐ 180	Larry Hisle	.12	.05	.01
☐ 181	Mike Garman	.12	.05	.01
☐ 182	Tim Johnson	.12	.05	.01
☐ 183	Paul Splittorff	.12	.05	.01
☐ 184	Darrel Chaney	.12	.05	.01
☐ 185	Mike Torrez	.12	.05	.01
☐ 186	Eric Soderholm	.12	.05	.01
☐ 187	Mark Lemongello	.12	.05	.01
☐ 188	Pat Kelly	.12	.05	.01
☐ 189	Eddie Whitson	1.00	.40	.10
☐ 190	Ron Cey	.30	.12	.03
☐ 191	Mike Norris	.12	.05	.01
☐ 192	Cardinals Team/Mgr.	.60	.12	.02
	Ken Boyer			
	(checklist back)			
☐ 193	Glenn Adams	.12	.05	.01
☐ 194	Randy Jones	.12	.05	.01
☐ 195	Bill Madlock	.40	.16	.04
☐ 196	Steve Kemp DP	.12	.05	.01
☐ 197	Bob Apodaca	.12	.05	.01
☐ 198	Johnny Grubb	.12	.05	.01
☐ 199	Larry Milbourne	.12	.05	.01
☐ 200	Johnny Bench DP	3.00	1.25	.30
☐ 201	RB: Mike Edwards	.12	.05	.01
	Most unassisted DP's,			
	second basemen			
☐ 202	RB: Ron Guidry, Most	.30	.12	.03
	strikeouts, lefthander,			
	nine inning game			
☐ 203	RB: J.R. Richard	.20	.08	.02
	Most strikeouts,			
	season, righthander			
☐ 204	RB: Pete Rose	1.50	.60	.15
	Most consecutive			
	games batting safely			
☐ 205	RB: John Stearns	.12	.05	.01
	Most SB's by			
	catcher, season			
☐ 206	RB: Sammy Stewart	.12	.05	.01
	7 straight SO's,			
	first ML game			
☐ 207	Dave Lemanczyk	.12	.05	.01
☐ 208	Clarence Gaston	.20	.08	.02
☐ 209	Reggie Cleveland	.12	.05	.01
☐ 210	Larry Bowa	.30	.12	.03
☐ 211	Denny Martinez	.60	.25	.06
☐ 212	Carney Lansford	5.00	2.25	.50
☐ 213	Bill Travers	.12	.05	.01
☐ 214	Red Sox Team/Mgr.	.60	.12	.02
	Don Zimmer			
	(checklist back)			
☐ 215	Willie McCovey	2.25	.90	.22
☐ 216	Wilbur Wood	.20	.08	.02
☐ 217	Steve Dillard	.12	.05	.01
☐ 218	Dennis Leonard	.20	.08	.02
☐ 219	Roy Smalley	.12	.05	.01
☐ 220	Cesar Geronimo	.12	.05	.01
☐ 221	Jesse Jefferson	.12	.05	.01
☐ 222	Bob Beall	.12	.05	.01
☐ 223	Kent Tekulve	.20	.08	.02
☐ 224	Dave Revering	.12	.05	.01
☐ 225	Rich Gossage	.75	.30	.07
☐ 226	Ron Pruitt	.12	.05	.01
☐ 227	Steve Stone	.20	.08	.02
☐ 228	Vic Davalillo	.12	.05	.01
☐ 229	Doug Flynn	.12	.05	.01
☐ 230	Bob Forsch	.12	.05	.01
☐ 231	John Wockenfuss	.12	.05	.01
☐ 232	Jimmy Sexton	.12	.05	.01
☐ 233	Paul Mitchell	.12	.05	.01
☐ 234	Toby Harrah	.20	.08	.02
☐ 235	Steve Rogers	.12	.05	.01
☐ 236	Jim Dwyer	.12	.05	.01
☐ 237	Billy Smith	.12	.05	.01
☐ 238	Balor Moore	.12	.05	.01

☐ 239	Willie Horton	.20	.08	.02
☐ 240	Rick Reuschel	.30	.12	.03
☐ 241	Checklist 2 DP	.25	.03	.01
☐ 242	Pablo Torrealba	.12	.05	.01
☐ 243	Buck Martinez DP	.06	.02	.00
☐ 244	Pirates Team/Mgr.	.60	.12	.02
	Chuck Tanner			
	(checklist back)			
☐ 245	Jeff Burroughs	.20	.08	.02
☐ 246	Darrell Jackson	.12	.05	.01
☐ 247	Tucker Ashford DP	.06	.02	.00
☐ 248	Pete LaCock	.12	.05	.01
☐ 249	Paul Thormodsgard	.12	.05	.01
☐ 250	Willie Randolph	.50	.20	.05
☐ 251	Jack Morris	4.50	2.00	.45
☐ 252	Bob Stinson	.12	.05	.01
☐ 253	Rick Wise	.20	.08	.02
☐ 254	Luis Gomez	.12	.05	.01
☐ 255	Tommy John	.75	.30	.07
☐ 256	Mike Sadek	.12	.05	.01
☐ 257	Adrian Devine	.12	.05	.01
☐ 258	Mike Phillips	.12	.05	.01
☐ 259	Reds Team/Mgr.	.60	.12	.02
	Sparky Anderson			
	(checklist back)			
☐ 260	Richie Zisk	.12	.05	.01
☐ 261	Mario Guerrero	.12	.05	.01
☐ 262	Nelson Briles	.12	.05	.01
☐ 263	Oscar Gamble	.12	.05	.01
☐ 264	Don Robinson	.60	.25	.06
☐ 265	Don Money	.12	.05	.01
☐ 266	Jim Willoughby	.12	.05	.01
☐ 267	Joe Rudi	.20	.08	.02
☐ 268	Julio Gonzalez	.12	.05	.01
☐ 269	Woodie Fryman	.12	.05	.01
☐ 270	Butch Hobson	.20	.08	.02
☐ 271	Rawly Eastwick	.12	.05	.01
☐ 272	Tim Corcoran	.12	.05	.01
☐ 273	Jerry Terrell	.12	.05	.01
☐ 274	Willie Norwood	.12	.05	.01
☐ 275	Junior Moore	.12	.05	.01
☐ 276	Jim Colborn	.12	.05	.01
☐ 277	Tom Grieve	.20	.08	.02
☐ 278	Andy Messersmith	.20	.08	.02
☐ 279	Jerry Grote DP	.06	.02	.00
☐ 280	Andre Thornton	.20	.08	.02
☐ 281	Vic Correll DP	.06	.02	.00
☐ 282	Blue Jays Team/Mgr.	.50	.12	.02
	Roy Hartsfield			
	(checklist back)			
☐ 283	Ken Kravec	.12	.05	.01
☐ 284	Johnnie LeMaster	.12	.05	.01
☐ 285	Bobby Bonds	.30	.12	.03
☐ 286	Duffy Dyer	.12	.05	.01
☐ 287	Andres Mora	.12	.05	.01
☐ 288	Milt Wilcox	.12	.05	.01
☐ 289	Jose Cruz	.20	.08	.02
☐ 290	Dave Lopes	.20	.08	.02
☐ 291	Tom Griffin	.12	.05	.01
☐ 292	Don Reynolds	.12	.05	.01
☐ 293	Jerry Garvin	.12	.05	.01
☐ 294	Pepe Frias	.12	.05	.01
☐ 295	Mitchell Page	.12	.05	.01
☐ 296	Preston Hanna	.12	.05	.01
☐ 297	Ted Sizemore	.12	.05	.01
☐ 298	Rich Gale	.12	.05	.01
☐ 299	Steve Ontiveros	.12	.05	.01
☐ 300	Rod Carew	3.50	1.50	.35
☐ 301	Tom Hume	.12	.05	.01
☐ 302	Braves Team/Mgr.	.60	.12	.02
	Bobby Cox			
	(checklist back)			
☐ 303	Lary Sorensen	.12	.05	.01
☐ 304	Steve Swisher	.12	.05	.01
☐ 305	Willie Montanez	.12	.05	.01
☐ 306	Floyd Bannister	.20	.08	.02
☐ 307	Larvell Blanks	.12	.05	.01
☐ 308	Bert Blyleven	.60	.25	.06
☐ 309	Ralph Garr	.20	.08	.02
☐ 310	Thurman Munson	3.00	1.25	.30
☐ 311	Gary Lavelle	.12	.05	.01
☐ 312	Bob Robertson	.12	.05	.01
☐ 313	Dyar Miller	.12	.05	.01
☐ 314	Larry Harlow	.12	.05	.01
☐ 315	Jon Matlack	.20	.08	.02
☐ 316	Milt May	.12	.05	.01
☐ 317	Jose Cardenal	.12	.05	.01
☐ 318	Bob Welch	10.00	4.50	1.25
☐ 319	Wayne Garrett	.12	.05	.01
☐ 320	Carl Yastrzemski	3.75	1.60	.37
☐ 321	Gaylord Perry	2.00	.80	.20
☐ 322	Danny Goodwin	.12	.05	.01
☐ 323	Lynn McGlothen	.12	.05	.01
☐ 324	Mike Tyson	.12	.05	.01

No.	Name			
☐ 325	Cecil Cooper	.40	.16	.04
☐ 326	Pedro Borbon	.12	.05	.01
☐ 327	Art Howe	.20	.08	.02
☐ 328	Oakland A's Team/Mgr. Jack McKeon (checklist back)	.60	.12	.02
☐ 329	Joe Coleman	.12	.05	.01
☐ 330	George Brett	10.00	4.50	1.25
☐ 331	Mickey Mahler	.12	.05	.01
☐ 332	Gary Alexander	.12	.05	.01
☐ 333	Chet Lemon	.20	.08	.02
☐ 334	Craig Swan	.12	.05	.01
☐ 335	Chris Chambliss	.20	.08	.02
☐ 336	Bobby Thompson	.12	.05	.01
☐ 337	John Montague	.12	.05	.01
☐ 338	Vic Harris	.12	.05	.01
☐ 339	Ron Jackson	.12	.05	.01
☐ 340	Jim Palmer	3.00	1.25	.30
☐ 341	Willie Upshaw	.20	.08	.02
☐ 342	Dave Roberts	.12	.05	.01
☐ 343	Ed Glynn	.12	.05	.01
☐ 344	Jerry Royster	.12	.05	.01
☐ 345	Tug McGraw	.30	.12	.03
☐ 346	Bill Buckner	.30	.12	.03
☐ 347	Doug Rau	.12	.05	.01
☐ 348	Andre Dawson	9.00	4.00	.90
☐ 349	Jim Wright	.12	.05	.01
☐ 350	Garry Templeton	.20	.08	.02
☐ 351	Wayne Nordhagen	.12	.05	.01
☐ 352	Steve Renko	.12	.05	.01
☐ 353	Checklist 3	.60	.06	.01
☐ 354	Bill Bonham	.12	.05	.01
☐ 355	Lee Mazzilli	.12	.05	.01
☐ 356	Giants Team/Mgr. Joe Altobelli (checklist back)	.60	.12	.02
☐ 357	Jerry Augustine	.12	.05	.01
☐ 358	Alan Trammell	12.50	5.50	1.65
☐ 359	Dan Spillner DP	.06	.02	.00
☐ 360	Amos Otis	.20	.08	.02
☐ 361	Tom Dixon	.12	.05	.01
☐ 362	Mike Cubbage	.12	.05	.01
☐ 363	Craig Skok	.12	.05	.01
☐ 364	Gene Richards	.12	.05	.01
☐ 365	Sparky Lyle	.30	.12	.03
☐ 366	Juan Bernhardt	.12	.05	.01
☐ 367	Dave Skaggs	.12	.05	.01
☐ 368	Don Aase	.12	.05	.01
☐ 369A	Bump Wills ERR (Blue Jays)	3.00	1.25	.30
☐ 369B	Bump Wills COR (Rangers)	3.50	1.50	.35
☐ 370	Dave Kingman	.40	.16	.04
☐ 371	Jeff Holly	.12	.05	.01
☐ 372	Lamar Johnson	.12	.05	.01
☐ 373	Lance Rautzhan	.12	.05	.01
☐ 374	Ed Herrmann	.12	.05	.01
☐ 375	Bill Campbell	.12	.05	.01
☐ 376	Gorman Thomas	.20	.08	.02
☐ 377	Paul Moskau	.12	.05	.01
☐ 378	Rob Picciolo DP	.06	.02	.00
☐ 379	Dale Murray	.12	.05	.01
☐ 380	John Mayberry	.20	.08	.02
☐ 381	Astros Team/Mgr. Bill Virdon (checklist back)	.60	.12	.02
☐ 382	Jerry Martin	.12	.05	.01
☐ 383	Phil Garner	.20	.08	.02
☐ 384	Tommy Boggs	.12	.05	.01
☐ 385	Dan Ford	.12	.05	.01
☐ 386	Francisco Barrios	.12	.05	.01
☐ 387	Gary Thomasson	.12	.05	.01
☐ 388	Jack Billingham	.12	.05	.01
☐ 389	Joe Zdeb	.12	.05	.01
☐ 390	Rollie Fingers	1.50	.60	.15
☐ 391	Al Oliver	.30	.12	.03
☐ 392	Doug Ault	.12	.05	.01
☐ 393	Scott McGregor	.20	.08	.02
☐ 394	Randy Stein	.12	.05	.01
☐ 395	Dave Cash	.12	.05	.01
☐ 396	Bill Plummer	.20	.08	.02
☐ 397	Sergio Ferrer	.12	.05	.01
☐ 398	Ivan DeJesus	.12	.05	.01
☐ 399	David Clyde	.12	.05	.01
☐ 400	Jim Rice	2.00	.80	.20
☐ 401	Ray Knight	.30	.12	.03
☐ 402	Paul Hartzell	.12	.05	.01
☐ 403	Tim Foli	.12	.05	.01
☐ 404	White Sox Team/Mgr Don Kessinger (checklist back)	.60	.12	.02
☐ 405	Butch Wynegar DP	.06	.02	.00
☐ 406	Joe Wallis DP	.06	.02	.00
☐ 407	Pete Vuckovich	.12	.05	.01
☐ 408	Charlie Moore DP	.06	.02	.00
☐ 409	Willie Wilson	2.00	.80	.20
☐ 410	Darrell Evans	.30	.12	.03
☐ 411	Hits Record Season: G.Sisler Career: Ty Cobb	.40	.16	.04
☐ 412	RBI Record Season: Hack Wilson Career: Hank Aaron	.40	.16	.04
☐ 413	Home Run Record Season: Roger Maris Career: Hank Aaron	.75	.30	.07
☐ 414	Batting Record Season: R.Hornsby Career: Ty Cobb	.40	.16	.04
☐ 415	Steals Record Season: Lou Brock Career: Lou Brock	.50	.20	.05
☐ 416	Wins Record Season: Jack Chesbro Career: Cy Young	.20	.08	.02
☐ 417	Strikeout Record DP Season: Nolan Ryan Career: W.Johnson	.30	.12	.03
☐ 418	ERA Record DP Season: Dutch Leonard Career: W.Johnson	.12	.05	.01
☐ 419	Dick Ruthven	.12	.05	.01
☐ 420	Ken Griffey	.75	.30	.07
☐ 421	Doug DeCinces	.20	.08	.02
☐ 422	Ruppert Jones	.12	.05	.01
☐ 423	Bob Montgomery	.12	.05	.01
☐ 424	Angels Team/Mgr. Jim Fregosi (checklist back)	.60	.12	.02
☐ 425	Rick Manning	.12	.05	.01
☐ 426	Chris Speier	.12	.05	.01
☐ 427	Andy Replogle	.12	.05	.01
☐ 428	Bobby Valentine	.20	.08	.02
☐ 429	John Urrea DP	.06	.02	.00
☐ 430	Dave Parker	2.50	1.00	.25
☐ 431	Glenn Borgmann	.12	.05	.01
☐ 432	Dave Heaverlo	.12	.05	.01
☐ 433	Larry Biittner	.12	.05	.01
☐ 434	Ken Clay	.12	.05	.01
☐ 435	Gene Tenace	.20	.08	.02
☐ 436	Hector Cruz	.12	.05	.01
☐ 437	Rick Williams	.12	.05	.01
☐ 438	Horace Speed	.12	.05	.01
☐ 439	Frank White	.20	.08	.02
☐ 440	Rusty Staub	.30	.12	.03
☐ 441	Lee Lacy	.12	.05	.01
☐ 442	Doyle Alexander	.12	.05	.01
☐ 443	Bruce Bochte	.12	.05	.01
☐ 444	Aurelio Lopez	.20	.08	.02
☐ 445	Steve Henderson	.12	.05	.01
☐ 446	Jim Lonborg	.20	.08	.02
☐ 447	Manny Sanguillen	.20	.08	.02
☐ 448	Moose Haas	.12	.05	.01
☐ 449	Bombo Rivera	.12	.05	.01
☐ 450	Dave Concepcion	.50	.20	.05
☐ 451	Royals Team/Mgr. Whitey Herzog (checklist back)	.60	.12	.02
☐ 452	Jerry Morales	.12	.05	.01
☐ 453	Chris Knapp	.12	.05	.01
☐ 454	Len Randle	.12	.05	.01
☐ 455	Bill Lee DP	.12	.05	.01
☐ 456	Chuck Baker	.12	.05	.01
☐ 457	Bruce Sutter	.75	.30	.07
☐ 458	Jim Essian	.20	.08	.02
☐ 459	Sid Monge	.12	.05	.01
☐ 460	Graig Nettles	.50	.20	.05
☐ 461	Jim Barr DP	.06	.02	.00
☐ 462	Otto Velez	.12	.05	.01
☐ 463	Steve Comer	.12	.05	.01
☐ 464	Joe Nolan	.12	.05	.01
☐ 465	Reggie Smith	.20	.08	.02
☐ 466	Mark Littell	.12	.05	.01
☐ 467	Don Kessinger DP	.12	.05	.01
☐ 468	Stan Bahnsen DP	.06	.02	.00
☐ 469	Lance Parrish	3.50	1.50	.35
☐ 470	Garry Maddox DP	.12	.05	.01
☐ 471	Joaquin Andujar	.20	.08	.02
☐ 472	Craig Kusick	.12	.05	.01
☐ 473	Dave Roberts	.12	.05	.01
☐ 474	Dick Davis	.12	.05	.01
☐ 475	Dan Driessen	.12	.05	.01
☐ 476	Tom Poquette	.12	.05	.01
☐ 477	Bob Grich	.20	.08	.02
☐ 478	Juan Beniquez	.12	.05	.01
☐ 479	Padres Team/Mgr. Roger Craig (checklist back)	.60	.12	.02

☐ 480 Fred Lynn	.75	.30	.07
☐ 481 Skip Lockwood	.12	.05	.01
☐ 482 Craig Reynolds	.12	.05	.01
☐ 483 Checklist 4 DP	.25	.03	.01
☐ 484 Rick Waits	.12	.05	.01
☐ 485 Bucky Dent	.30	.12	.03
☐ 486 Bob Knepper	.20	.08	.02
☐ 487 Miguel Dilone	.12	.05	.01
☐ 488 Bob Owchinko	.12	.05	.01
☐ 489 Larry Cox UER	.12	.05	.01
(photo actually			
Dave Rader)			
☐ 490 Al Cowens	.12	.05	.01
☐ 491 Tippy Martinez	.12	.05	.01
☐ 492 Bob Bailor	.12	.05	.01
☐ 493 Larry Christenson	.12	.05	.01
☐ 494 Jerry White	.12	.05	.01
☐ 495 Tony Perez	1.00	.40	.10
☐ 496 Barry Bonnell DP	.06	.02	.00
☐ 497 Glenn Abbott	.12	.05	.01
☐ 498 Rich Chiles	.12	.05	.01
☐ 499 Rangers Team/Mgr.	.60	.12	.02
Pat Corrales			
(checklist back)			
☐ 500 Ron Guidry	1.00	.40	.10
☐ 501 Junior Kennedy	.12	.05	.01
☐ 502 Steve Braun	.12	.05	.01
☐ 503 Terry Humphrey	.12	.05	.01
☐ 504 Larry McWilliams	.20	.08	.02
☐ 505 Ed Kranepool	.12	.05	.01
☐ 506 John D'Acquisto	.12	.05	.01
☐ 507 Tony Armas	.20	.08	.02
☐ 508 Charlie Hough	.20	.08	.02
☐ 509 Mario Mendoza	.12	.05	.01
☐ 510 Ted Simmons	.40	.16	.04
☐ 511 Paul Reuschel DP	.06	.02	.00
☐ 512 Jack Clark	2.00	.80	.20
☐ 513 Dave Johnson	.20	.08	.02
☐ 514 Mike Proly	.12	.05	.01
☐ 515 Enos Cabell	.12	.05	.01
☐ 516 Champ Summers DP	.06	.02	.00
☐ 517 Al Bumbry	.12	.05	.01
☐ 518 Jim Umbarger	.12	.05	.01
☐ 519 Ben Oglivie	.20	.08	.02
☐ 520 Gary Carter	3.00	1.25	.30
☐ 521 Sam Ewing	.12	.05	.01
☐ 522 Ken Holtzman	.20	.08	.02
☐ 523 John Milner	.12	.05	.01
☐ 524 Tom Burgmeier	.12	.05	.01
☐ 525 Freddie Patek	.12	.05	.01
☐ 526 Dodgers Team/Mgr.	.75	.15	.03
Tom Lasorda			
(checklist back)			
☐ 527 Lerrin LaGrow	.12	.05	.01
☐ 528 Wayne Gross DP	.06	.02	.00
☐ 529 Brian Asselstine	.12	.05	.01
☐ 530 Frank Tanana	.20	.08	.02
☐ 531 Fernando Gonzalez	.12	.05	.01
☐ 532 Buddy Schultz	.12	.05	.01
☐ 533 Leroy Stanton	.12	.05	.01
☐ 534 Ken Forsch	.12	.05	.01
☐ 535 Ellis Valentine	.12	.05	.01
☐ 536 Jerry Reuss	.20	.08	.02
☐ 537 Tom Veryzer	.12	.05	.01
☐ 538 Mike Ivie DP	.06	.02	.00
☐ 539 John Ellis	.12	.05	.01
☐ 540 Greg Luzinski	.30	.12	.03
☐ 541 Jim Slaton	.12	.05	.01
☐ 542 Rick Bosetti	.12	.05	.01
☐ 543 Kiko Garcia	.12	.05	.01
☐ 544 Fergie Jenkins	1.50	.60	.15
☐ 545 John Stearns	.12	.05	.01
☐ 546 Bill Russell	.20	.08	.02
☐ 547 Clint Hurdle	.12	.05	.01
☐ 548 Enrique Romo	.12	.05	.01
☐ 549 Bob Bailey	.12	.05	.01
☐ 550 Sal Bando	.20	.08	.02
☐ 551 Cubs Team/Mgr.	.60	.12	.02
Herman Franks			
(checklist back)			
☐ 552 Jose Morales	.12	.05	.01
☐ 553 Denny Walling	.12	.05	.01
☐ 554 Matt Keough	.12	.05	.01
☐ 555 Biff Pocoroba	.12	.05	.01
☐ 556 Mike Lum	.12	.05	.01
☐ 557 Ken Brett	.12	.05	.01
☐ 558 Jay Johnstone	.20	.08	.02
☐ 559 Greg Pryor	.12	.05	.01
☐ 560 John Montefusco	.20	.08	.02
☐ 561 Ed Ott	.12	.05	.01
☐ 562 Dusty Baker	.20	.08	.02
☐ 563 Roy Thomas	.12	.05	.01
☐ 564 Jerry Turner	.12	.05	.01
☐ 565 Rico Carty	.20	.08	.02

☐ 566 Nino Espinosa	.12	.05	.01
☐ 567 Richie Hebner	.12	.05	.01
☐ 568 Carlos Lopez	.12	.05	.01
☐ 569 Bob Sykes	.12	.05	.01
☐ 570 Cesar Cedeno	.20	.08	.02
☐ 571 Darrell Porter	.12	.05	.01
☐ 572 Rod Gilbreath	.12	.05	.01
☐ 573 Jim Kern	.12	.05	.01
☐ 574 Claudell Washington	.20	.08	.02
☐ 575 Luis Tiant	.30	.12	.03
☐ 576 Mike Parrott	.12	.05	.01
☐ 577 Brewers Team/Mgr.	.60	.12	.02
George Bamberger			
(checklist back)			
☐ 578 Pete Broberg	.12	.05	.01
☐ 579 Greg Gross	.12	.05	.01
☐ 580 Ron Fairly	.12	.05	.01
☐ 581 Darold Knowles	.12	.05	.01
☐ 582 Paul Blair	.20	.08	.02
☐ 583 Julio Cruz	.12	.05	.01
☐ 584 Jim Rooker	.12	.05	.01
☐ 585 Hal McRae	.30	.12	.03
☐ 586 Bob Horner	1.00	.40	.10
☐ 587 Ken Reitz	.12	.05	.01
☐ 588 Tom Murphy	.12	.05	.01
☐ 589 Terry Whitfield	.12	.05	.01
☐ 590 J.R. Richard	.20	.08	.02
☐ 591 Mike Hargrove	.20	.08	.02
☐ 592 Mike Krukow	.20	.08	.02
☐ 593 Rick Dempsey	.20	.08	.02
☐ 594 Bob Shirley	.12	.05	.01
☐ 595 Phil Niekro	1.50	.60	.15
☐ 596 Jim Wohlford	.12	.05	.01
☐ 597 Bob Stanley	.12	.05	.01
☐ 598 Mark Wagner	.12	.05	.01
☐ 599 Jim Spencer	.12	.05	.01
☐ 600 George Foster	.60	.25	.06
☐ 601 Dave LaRoche	.12	.05	.01
☐ 602 Checklist 5	.60	.06	.01
☐ 603 Rudy May	.12	.05	.01
☐ 604 Jeff Newman	.12	.05	.01
☐ 605 Rick Monday DP	.12	.05	.01
☐ 606 Expos Team/Mgr.	.60	.12	.02
Dick Williams			
(checklist back)			
☐ 607 Omar Moreno	.12	.05	.01
☐ 608 Dave McKay	.12	.05	.01
☐ 609 Silvio Martinez	.12	.05	.01
☐ 610 Mike Schmidt	9.00	4.00	.90
☐ 611 Jim Norris	.12	.05	.01
☐ 612 Rick Honeycutt	.60	.25	.06
☐ 613 Mike Edwards	.12	.05	.01
☐ 614 Willie Hernandez	.30	.12	.03
☐ 615 Ken Singleton	.20	.08	.02
☐ 616 Billy Almon	.12	.05	.01
☐ 617 Terry Puhl	.12	.05	.01
☐ 618 Jerry Remy	.12	.05	.01
☐ 619 Ken Landreaux	.30	.12	.03
☐ 620 Bert Campaneris	.20	.08	.02
☐ 621 Pat Zachry	.12	.05	.01
☐ 622 Dave Collins	.12	.05	.01
☐ 623 Bob McClure	.12	.05	.01
☐ 624 Larry Herndon	.12	.05	.01
☐ 625 Mark Fidrych	.30	.12	.03
☐ 626 Yankees Team/Mgr.	.75	.15	.03
Bob Lemon			
(checklist back)			
☐ 627 Gary Serum	.12	.05	.01
☐ 628 Del Unser	.12	.05	.01
☐ 629 Gene Garber	.12	.05	.01
☐ 630 Bake McBride	.12	.05	.01
☐ 631 Jorge Orta	.12	.05	.01
☐ 632 Don Kirkwood	.12	.05	.01
☐ 633 Rob Wilfong DP	.06	.02	.00
☐ 634 Paul Lindblad	.12	.05	.01
☐ 635 Don Baylor	1.00	.40	.10
☐ 636 Wayne Garland	.12	.05	.01
☐ 637 Bill Robinson	.20	.08	.02
☐ 638 Al Fitzmorris	.12	.05	.01
☐ 639 Manny Trillo	.12	.05	.01
☐ 640 Eddie Murray	18.00	7.50	2.50
☐ 641 Bobby Castillo	.12	.05	.01
☐ 642 Wilbur Howard DP	.06	.02	.00
☐ 643 Tom Hausman	.12	.05	.01
☐ 644 Manny Mota	.20	.08	.02
☐ 645 George Scott DP	.12	.05	.01
☐ 646 Rick Sweet	.12	.05	.01
☐ 647 Bob Lacey	.12	.05	.01
☐ 648 Lou Piniella	.30	.12	.03
☐ 649 John Curtis	.12	.05	.01
☐ 650 Pete Rose	4.50	2.00	.45
☐ 651 Mike Caldwell	.12	.05	.01
☐ 652 Stan Papi	.12	.05	.01
☐ 653 Warren Brusstar DP	.06	.02	.00

☐ 654	Rick Miller	.12	.05	.01
☐ 655	Jerry Koosman	.30	.12	.03
☐ 656	Hosken Powell	.12	.05	.01
☐ 657	George Medich	.12	.05	.01
☐ 658	Taylor Duncan	.12	.05	.01
☐ 659	Mariners Team/Mgr.	.60	.12	.02
	Darrell Johnson			
	(checklist back)			
☐ 660	Ron LeFlore DP	.12	.05	.01
☐ 661	Bruce Kison	.12	.05	.01
☐ 662	Kevin Bell	.12	.05	.01
☐ 663	Mike Vail	.12	.05	.01
☐ 664	Doug Bird	.12	.05	.01
☐ 665	Lou Brock	2.25	.90	.22
☐ 666	Rich Dauer	.12	.05	.01
☐ 667	Don Hood	.12	.05	.01
☐ 668	Bill North	.12	.05	.01
☐ 669	Checklist 6	.60	.06	.01
☐ 670	Jim Hunter DP	.75	.30	.07
☐ 671	Joe Ferguson DP	.06	.02	.00
☐ 672	Ed Halicki	.12	.05	.01
☐ 673	Tom Hutton	.12	.05	.01
☐ 674	Dave Tomlin	.12	.05	.01
☐ 675	Tim McCarver	.30	.12	.03
☐ 676	Johnny Sutton	.12	.05	.01
☐ 677	Larry Parrish	.20	.08	.02
☐ 678	Geoff Zahn	.12	.05	.01
☐ 679	Derrel Thomas	.12	.05	.01
☐ 680	Carlton Fisk	4.25	1.75	.42
☐ 681	John Henry Johnson	.12	.05	.01
☐ 682	Dave Chalk	.12	.05	.01
☐ 683	Dan Meyer DP	.06	.02	.00
☐ 684	Jamie Easterly DP	.06	.02	.00
☐ 685	Sixto Lezcano	.12	.05	.01
☐ 686	Ron Schueler DP	.06	.02	.00
☐ 687	Rennie Stennett	.12	.05	.01
☐ 688	Mike Willis	.12	.05	.01
☐ 689	Orioles Team/Mgr.	.60	.12	.02
	Earl Weaver			
	(checklist back)			
☐ 690	Buddy Bell DP	.12	.05	.01
☐ 691	Dock Ellis DP	.06	.02	.00
☐ 692	Mickey Stanley	.12	.05	.01
☐ 693	Dave Rader	.12	.05	.01
☐ 694	Burt Hooton	.12	.05	.01
☐ 695	Keith Hernandez	2.25	.90	.22
☐ 696	Andy Hassler	.12	.05	.01
☐ 697	Dave Bergman	.12	.05	.01
☐ 698	Bill Stein	.12	.05	.01
☐ 699	Hal Dues	.12	.05	.01
☐ 700	Reggie Jackson DP	3.50	1.50	.35
☐ 701	Orioles Prospects	.20	.08	.02
	Mark Corey			
	John Flinn			
	Sammy Stewart			
☐ 702	Red Sox Prospects	.20	.08	.02
	Joel Finch			
	Garry Hancock			
	Allen Ripley			
☐ 703	Angels Prospects	.12	.05	.01
	Jim Anderson			
	Dave Frost			
	Bob Slater			
☐ 704	White Sox Prospects	.12	.05	.01
	Ross Baumgarten			
	Mike Colbern			
	Mike Squires			
☐ 705	Indians Prospects	.75	.30	.07
	Alfredo Griffin			
	Tim Norrid			
	Dave Oliver			
☐ 706	Tigers Prospects	.12	.05	.01
	Dave Stegman			
	Dave Tobik			
	Kip Young			
☐ 707	Royals Prospects	.30	.12	.03
	Randy Bass			
	Jim Gaudet			
	Randy McGilberry			
☐ 708	Brewers Prospects	1.25	.50	.12
	Kevin Bass			
	Eddie Romero			
	Ned Yost			
☐ 709	Twins Prospects	.12	.05	.01
	Sam Perlozzo			
	Rick Sofield			
	Kevin Stanfield			
☐ 710	Yankees Prospects	.30	.12	.03
	Brian Doyle			
	Mike Heath			
	Dave Rajsich			
☐ 711	A's Prospects	.30	.12	.03
	Dwayne Murphy			
	Bruce Robinson			

	Alan Wirth			
☐ 712	Mariners Prospects	.12	.05	.01
	Bud Anderson			
	Greg Biercevicz			
	Byron McLaughlin			
☐ 713	Rangers Prospects	.75	.30	.07
	Danny Darwin			
	Pat Putnam			
	Billy Sample			
☐ 714	Blue Jays Prospects	.30	.12	.03
	Victor Cruz			
	Pat Kelly			
	Ernie Whitt			
☐ 715	Braves Prospects	.30	.12	.03
	Bruce Benedict			
	Glenn Hubbard			
	Larry Whisenton			
☐ 716	Cubs Prospects	.12	.05	.01
	Dave Geisel			
	Karl Pagel			
	Scot Thompson			
☐ 717	Reds Prospects	.40	.16	.04
	Mike LaCoss			
	Ron Oester			
	Harry Spilman			
☐ 718	Astros Prospects	.12	.05	.01
	Bruce Bochy			
	Mike Fischlin			
	Don Pisker			
☐ 719	Dodgers Prospects	8.00	3.50	.80
	Pedro Guerrero			
	Rudy Law			
	Joe Simpson			
☐ 720	Expos Prospects	1.00	.40	.10
	Jerry Fry			
	Jerry Pirtle			
	Scott Sanderson			
☐ 721	Mets Prospects	.30	.12	.03
	Juan Berenguer			
	Dwight Bernard			
	Dan Norman			
☐ 722	Phillies Prospects	2.25	.90	.22
	Jim Morrison			
	Lonnie Smith			
	Jim Wright			
☐ 723	Pirates Prospects	.30	.12	.03
	Dale Berra			
	Eugenio Cotes			
	Ben Wiltbank			
☐ 724	Cardinals Prospects	.60	.25	.06
	Tom Bruno			
	George Frazier			
	Terry Kennedy			
☐ 725	Padres Prospects	.12	.05	.01
	Jim Beswick			
	Steve Mura			
	Broderick Perkins			
☐ 726	Giants Prospects	.30	.12	.03
	Greg Johnston			
	Joe Strain			
	John Tamargo			

1980 Topps

The cards in this 726-card set measure 2 1/2" by 3 1/2". In 1980 Topps released another set of the same size and number of cards as the previous two years. As with those sets, Topps again has produced 66 double-printed cards in the set; they are noted by DP in the checklist below. The player's name appears over the picture and his position and team are found in pennant design. Every card carries a facsimile autograph. Team cards feature a team checklist of players in the set on the back and the manager's name on the front. Cards 1-6 show Highlights (HL) of the 1979 season, cards 201-207 are League Leaders, and cards 661-686 feature American and National League rookie "Future Stars," one card for each team showing three young prospects. The key rookie cards in this set are Rickey Henderson, Dave Stieb, and Rick Sutcliffe.

	MINT	EXC	G-VG
COMPLETE SET (726)	290.00	110.00	30.00
COMMON PLAYER (1-726)	.10	.04	.01
COMMON DP's (1-726)	.05	.02	.00
☐ 1 HL: Brock and Yaz, Enter 3000 hit circle	2.50	.50	.10
☐ 2 HL: Willie McCovey, 512th homer sets new mark for NL lefties	.75	.30	.07
☐ 3 HL: Manny Mota, All-time pinch-hits, 145	.15	.06	.01
☐ 4 HL: Pete Rose, Career Record 10th season with 200 or more hits	1.50	.60	.15
☐ 5 HL: Garry Templeton, First with 100 hits from each side of plate	.15	.06	.01
☐ 6 HL: Del Unser, 3rd cons. pinch homer sets new ML standard	.10	.04	.01
☐ 7 Mike Lum	.10	.04	.01
☐ 8 Craig Swan	.10	.04	.01
☐ 9 Steve Braun	.10	.04	.01
☐ 10 Dennis Martinez	.40	.16	.04
☐ 11 Jimmy Sexton	.10	.04	.01
☐ 12 John Curtis DP	.05	.02	.00
☐ 13 Ron Pruitt	.10	.04	.01
☐ 14 Dave Cash	.10	.04	.01
☐ 15 Bill Campbell	.10	.04	.01
☐ 16 Jerry Narron	.10	.04	.01
☐ 17 Bruce Sutter	.60	.25	.06
☐ 18 Ron Jackson	.10	.04	.01
☐ 19 Balor Moore	.10	.04	.01
☐ 20 Dan Ford	.10	.04	.01
☐ 21 Manny Sarmiento	.10	.04	.01
☐ 22 Pat Putnam	.10	.04	.01
☐ 23 Derrel Thomas	.10	.04	.01
☐ 24 Jim Slaton	.10	.04	.01
☐ 25 Lee Mazzilli	.10	.04	.01
☐ 26 Marty Pattin	.10	.04	.01
☐ 27 Del Unser	.10	.04	.01
☐ 28 Bruce Kison	.10	.04	.01
☐ 29 Mark Wagner	.10	.04	.01
☐ 30 Vida Blue	.20	.08	.02
☐ 31 Jay Johnstone	.15	.06	.01
☐ 32 Julio Cruz DP	.10	.04	.01
☐ 33 Tony Scott	.10	.04	.01
☐ 34 Jeff Newman DP	.05	.02	.00
☐ 35 Luis Tiant	.25	.10	.02
☐ 36 Rusty Torres	.10	.04	.01
☐ 37 Kiko Garcia	.10	.04	.01
☐ 38 Dan Spillner DP	.05	.02	.00
☐ 39 Rowland Office	.10	.04	.01
☐ 40 Carlton Fisk	4.00	1.75	.40
☐ 41 Rangers Team/Mgr. Pat Corrales (checklist back)	.50	.10	.02
☐ 42 David Palmer	.20	.08	.02
☐ 43 Bombo Rivera	.10	.04	.01
☐ 44 Bill Fahey	.10	.04	.01
☐ 45 Frank White	.25	.10	.02
☐ 46 Rico Carty	.15	.06	.01
☐ 47 Bill Bonham DP	.05	.02	.00
☐ 48 Rick Miller	.10	.04	.01
☐ 49 Mario Guerrero	.10	.04	.01
☐ 50 J.R. Richard	.20	.08	.02
☐ 51 Joe Ferguson DP	.05	.02	.00
☐ 52 Warren Brusstar	.10	.04	.01
☐ 53 Ben Oglivie	.15	.06	.01
☐ 54 Dennis Lamp	.10	.04	.01
☐ 55 Bill Madlock	.35	.15	.03
☐ 56 Bobby Valentine	.20	.08	.02
☐ 57 Pete Vuckovich	.10	.04	.01
☐ 58 Doug Flynn	.10	.04	.01
☐ 59 Eddy Putman	.10	.04	.01
☐ 60 Bucky Dent	.25	.10	.02
☐ 61 Gary Serum	.10	.04	.01
☐ 62 Mike Ivie	.10	.04	.01
☐ 63 Bob Stanley	.10	.04	.01
☐ 64 Joe Nolan	.10	.04	.01
☐ 65 Al Bumbry	.10	.04	.01
☐ 66 Royals Team/Mgr. Jim Frey (checklist back)	.50	.10	.02
☐ 67 Doyle Alexander	.10	.04	.01
☐ 68 Larry Harlow	.10	.04	.01
☐ 69 Rick Williams	.10	.04	.01
☐ 70 Gary Carter	2.50	1.00	.25
☐ 71 John Milner DP	.05	.02	.00
☐ 72 Fred Howard DP	.05	.02	.00
☐ 73 Dave Collins	.10	.04	.01
☐ 74 Sid Monge	.10	.04	.01
☐ 75 Bill Russell	.15	.06	.01
☐ 76 John Stearns	.10	.04	.01
☐ 77 Dave Stieb	7.50	3.25	.75
☐ 78 Ruppert Jones	.10	.04	.01
☐ 79 Bob Owchinko	.10	.04	.01
☐ 80 Ron LeFlore	.10	.04	.01
☐ 81 Ted Sizemore	.10	.04	.01
☐ 82 Astros Team/Mgr. Bill Virdon (checklist back)	.50	.10	.02
☐ 83 Steve Trout	.20	.08	.02
☐ 84 Gary Lavelle	.10	.04	.01
☐ 85 Ted Simmons	.40	.16	.04
☐ 86 Dave Hamilton	.10	.04	.01
☐ 87 Pepe Frias	.10	.04	.01
☐ 88 Ken Landreaux	.10	.04	.01
☐ 89 Don Hood	.10	.04	.01
☐ 90 Manny Trillo	.10	.04	.01
☐ 91 Rick Dempsey	.15	.06	.01
☐ 92 Rick Rhoden	.15	.06	.01
☐ 93 Dave Roberts DP	.05	.02	.00
☐ 94 Neil Allen	.20	.08	.02
☐ 95 Cecil Cooper	.20	.08	.02
☐ 96 A's Team/Mgr. Jim Marshall (checklist back)	.50	.10	.02
☐ 97 Bill Lee	.15	.06	.01
☐ 98 Jerry Terrell	.10	.04	.01
☐ 99 Victor Cruz	.10	.04	.01
☐ 100 Johnny Bench	3.50	1.50	.35
☐ 101 Aurelio Lopez	.10	.04	.01
☐ 102 Rich Dauer	.10	.04	.01
☐ 103 Bill Caudill	.20	.08	.02
☐ 104 Manny Mota	.15	.06	.01
☐ 105 Frank Tanana	.20	.08	.02
☐ 106 Jeff Leonard	.60	.25	.06
☐ 107 Francisco Barrios	.10	.04	.01
☐ 108 Bob Horner	.25	.10	.02
☐ 109 Bill Travers	.10	.04	.01
☐ 110 Fred Lynn DP	.25	.10	.02
☐ 111 Bob Knepper	.15	.06	.01
☐ 112 White Sox Team/Mgr. Tony LaRussa (checklist back)	.50	.10	.02
☐ 113 Geoff Zahn	.10	.04	.01
☐ 114 Juan Beniquez	.10	.04	.01
☐ 115 Sparky Lyle	.20	.08	.02
☐ 116 Larry Cox	.10	.04	.01
☐ 117 Dock Ellis	.10	.04	.01
☐ 118 Phil Garner	.15	.06	.01
☐ 119 Sammy Stewart	.10	.04	.01
☐ 120 Greg Luzinski	.20	.08	.02
☐ 121 Checklist 1	.40	.05	.01
☐ 122 Dave Rosello DP	.05	.02	.00
☐ 123 Lynn Jones	.10	.04	.01
☐ 124 Dave Lemanczyk	.10	.04	.01
☐ 125 Tony Perez	.75	.30	.07
☐ 126 Dave Tomlin	.10	.04	.01
☐ 127 Gary Thomasson	.10	.04	.01
☐ 128 Tom Burgmeier	.10	.04	.01
☐ 129 Craig Reynolds	.10	.04	.01
☐ 130 Amos Otis	.15	.06	.01
☐ 131 Paul Mitchell	.10	.04	.01
☐ 132 Biff Pocoroba	.10	.04	.01
☐ 133 Jerry Turner	.10	.04	.01
☐ 134 Matt Keough	.10	.04	.01
☐ 135 Bill Buckner	.25	.10	.02
☐ 136 Dick Ruthven	.10	.04	.01
☐ 137 John Castino	.10	.04	.01
☐ 138 Ross Baumgarten	.10	.04	.01
☐ 139 Dane Iorg	.15	.06	.01
☐ 140 Rich Gossage	.50	.20	.05
☐ 141 Gary Alexander	.10	.04	.01
☐ 142 Phil Huffman	.10	.04	.01
☐ 143 Bruce Bochte DP	.10	.04	.01
☐ 144 Steve Comer	.10	.04	.01
☐ 145 Darrell Evans	.30	.12	.03
☐ 146 Bob Welch	1.50	.60	.15
☐ 147 Terry Puhl	.10	.04	.01

	#	Name			
☐	148	Manny Sanguillen	.15	.06	.01
☐	149	Tom Hume	.10	.04	.01
☐	150	Jason Thompson	.10	.04	.01
☐	151	Tom Hausman DP	.05	.02	.00
☐	152	John Fulgham	.10	.04	.01
☐	153	Tim Blackwell	.10	.04	.01
☐	154	Lary Sorensen	.10	.04	.01
☐	155	Jerry Remy	.10	.04	.01
☐	156	Tony Brizzolara	.10	.04	.01
☐	157	Willie Wilson DP	.25	.10	.02
☐	158	Rob Picciolo DP	.05	.02	.00
☐	159	Ken Clay	.10	.04	.01
☐	160	Eddie Murray	9.00	4.00	.90
☐	161	Larry Christenson	.10	.04	.01
☐	162	Bob Randall	.10	.04	.01
☐	163	Steve Swisher	.10	.04	.01
☐	164	Greg Pryor	.10	.04	.01
☐	165	Omar Moreno	.10	.04	.01
☐	166	Glenn Abbott	.10	.04	.01
☐	167	Jack Clark	1.75	.70	.17
☐	168	Rick Waits	.10	.04	.01
☐	169	Luis Gomez	.10	.04	.01
☐	170	Burt Hooton	.10	.04	.01
☐	171	Fernando Gonzalez	.10	.04	.01
☐	172	Ron Hodges	.10	.04	.01
☐	173	John Henry Johnson	.10	.04	.01
☐	174	Ray Knight	.20	.08	.02
☐	175	Rick Reuschel	.25	.10	.02
☐	176	Champ Summers	.10	.04	.01
☐	177	Dave Heaverlo	.10	.04	.01
☐	178	Tim McCarver	.25	.10	.02
☐	179	Ron Rice	.20	.08	.02
☐	180	Warren Cromartie	.15	.06	.01
☐	181	Moose Haas	.10	.04	.01
☐	182	Ken Reitz	.10	.04	.01
☐	183	Jim Anderson DP	.05	.02	.00
☐	184	Steve Renko DP	.05	.02	.00
☐	185	Hal McRae	.25	.10	.02
☐	186	Junior Moore	.10	.04	.01
☐	187	Alan Ashby	.10	.04	.01
☐	188	Terry Crowley	.10	.04	.01
☐	189	Kevin Kobel	.10	.04	.01
☐	190	Buddy Bell	.20	.08	.02
☐	191	Ted Martinez	.10	.04	.01
☐	192	Braves Team/Mgr.	.50	.10	.02
		Bobby Cox			
		(checklist back)			
☐	193	Dave Goltz	.10	.04	.01
☐	194	Mike Easler	.10	.04	.01
☐	195	John Montefusco	.15	.06	.01
☐	196	Lance Parrish	2.00	.80	.20
☐	197	Byron McLaughlin	.10	.04	.01
☐	198	Dell Alston DP	.05	.02	.00
☐	199	Mike LaCoss	.15	.06	.01
☐	200	Jim Rice	1.00	.40	.10
☐	201	Batting Leaders	.25	.10	.02
		Keith Hernandez			
		Fred Lynn			
☐	202	Home Run Leaders	.20	.08	.02
		Dave Kingman			
		Gorman Thomas			
☐	203	RBI Leaders	.50	.20	.05
		Dave Winfield			
		Don Baylor			
☐	204	Stolen Base Leaders	.20	.08	.02
		Omar Moreno			
		Willie Wilson			
☐	205	Victory Leaders	.25	.10	.02
		Joe Niekro			
		Phil Niekro			
		Mike Flanagan			
☐	206	Strikeout Leaders	2.00	.80	.20
		J.R. Richard			
		Nolan Ryan			
☐	207	ERA Leaders	.20	.08	.02
		J.R. Richard			
		Ron Guidry			
☐	208	Wayne Cage	.10	.04	.01
☐	209	Von Joshua	.10	.04	.01
☐	210	Steve Carlton	3.00	1.25	.30
☐	211	Dave Skaggs DP	.05	.02	.00
☐	212	Dave Roberts	.10	.04	.01
☐	213	Mike Jorgensen DP	.05	.02	.00
☐	214	Angels Team/Mgr.	.50	.10	.02
		Jim Fregosi			
		(checklist back)			
☐	215	Sixto Lezcano	.10	.04	.01
☐	216	Phil Mankowski	.10	.04	.01
☐	217	Ed Halicki	.10	.04	.01
☐	218	Jose Morales	.10	.04	.01
☐	219	Steve Mingori	.10	.04	.01
☐	220	Dave Concepcion	.35	.15	.03
☐	221	Joe Cannon	.10	.04	.01
☐	222	Ron Hassey	.40	.16	.04
☐	223	Bob Sykes	.10	.04	.01
☐	224	Willie Montanez	.10	.04	.01
☐	225	Lou Piniella	.30	.12	.03
☐	226	Bill Stein	.10	.04	.01
☐	227	Len Barker	.10	.04	.01
☐	228	Johnny Oates	.15	.06	.01
☐	229	Jim Bibby	.10	.04	.01
☐	230	Dave Winfield	4.00	1.75	.40
☐	231	Steve McCatty	.10	.04	.01
☐	232	Alan Trammell	4.50	2.00	.45
☐	233	LaRue Washington	.10	.04	.01
☐	234	Vern Ruhle	.10	.04	.01
☐	235	Andre Dawson	7.25	2.75	.90
☐	236	Marc Hill	.10	.04	.01
☐	237	Scott McGregor	.15	.06	.01
☐	238	Rob Wilfong	.10	.04	.01
☐	239	Don Aase	.10	.04	.01
☐	240	Dave Kingman	.35	.15	.03
☐	241	Checklist 2	.40	.05	.01
☐	242	Lamar Johnson	.10	.04	.01
☐	243	Jerry Augustine	.10	.04	.01
☐	244	Cardinals Team/Mgr.	.50	.10	.02
		Ken Boyer			
		(checklist back)			
☐	245	Phil Niekro	1.25	.50	.12
☐	246	Tim Foli DP	.05	.02	.00
☐	247	Frank Riccelli	.10	.04	.01
☐	248	Jamie Quirk	.10	.04	.01
☐	249	Jim Clancy	.10	.04	.01
☐	250	Jim Kaat	.40	.16	.04
☐	251	Kip Young	.10	.04	.01
☐	252	Ted Cox	.10	.04	.01
☐	253	John Montague	.10	.04	.01
☐	254	Paul Dade DP	.05	.02	.00
☐	255	Dusty Baker DP	.10	.04	.01
☐	256	Roger Erickson	.10	.04	.01
☐	257	Larry Herndon	.10	.04	.01
☐	258	Paul Moskau	.10	.04	.01
☐	259	Mets Team/Mgr.	.50	.10	.02
		Joe Torre			
		(checklist back)			
☐	260	Al Oliver	.30	.12	.03
☐	261	Dave Chalk	.10	.04	.01
☐	262	Benny Ayala	.10	.04	.01
☐	263	Dave LaRoche DP	.05	.02	.00
☐	264	Bill Robinson	.15	.06	.01
☐	265	Robin Yount	7.50	3.25	.75
☐	266	Bernie Carbo	.10	.04	.01
☐	267	Dan Schatzeder	.10	.04	.01
☐	268	Rafael Landestoy	.10	.04	.01
☐	269	Dave Tobik	.10	.04	.01
☐	270	Mike Schmidt DP	4.50	2.00	.45
☐	271	Dick Drago DP	.05	.02	.00
☐	272	Ralph Garr	.10	.04	.01
☐	273	Eduardo Rodriguez	.10	.04	.01
☐	274	Dale Murphy	5.00	2.25	.50
☐	275	Jerry Koosman	.25	.10	.02
☐	276	Tom Veryzer	.10	.04	.01
☐	277	Rick Bosetti	.10	.04	.01
☐	278	Jim Spencer	.10	.04	.01
☐	279	Rob Andrews	.10	.04	.01
☐	280	Gaylord Perry	1.25	.50	.12
☐	281	Paul Blair	.15	.06	.01
☐	282	Mariners Team/Mgr.	.50	.10	.02
		Darrell Johnson			
		(checklist back)			
☐	283	John Ellis	.10	.04	.01
☐	284	Larry Murray DP	.05	.02	.00
☐	285	Don Baylor	.40	.16	.04
☐	286	Darold Knowles DP	.05	.02	.00
☐	287	John Lowenstein	.10	.04	.01
☐	288	Dave Rozema	.10	.04	.01
☐	289	Bruce Bochy	.10	.04	.01
☐	290	Steve Garvey	1.75	.70	.17
☐	291	Randy Scarberry	.10	.04	.01
☐	292	Dale Berra	.10	.04	.01
☐	293	Elias Sosa	.10	.04	.01
☐	294	Charlie Spikes	.10	.04	.01
☐	295	Larry Gura	.10	.04	.01
☐	296	Dave Rader	.10	.04	.01
☐	297	Tim Johnson	.10	.04	.01
☐	298	Ken Holtzman	.15	.06	.01
☐	299	Steve Henderson	.10	.04	.01
☐	300	Ron Guidry	.75	.30	.07
☐	301	Mike Edwards	.10	.04	.01
☐	302	Dodgers Team/Mgr.	.60	.12	.02
		Tom Lasorda			
		(checklist back)			
☐	303	Bill Castro	.10	.04	.01
☐	304	Butch Wynegar	.10	.04	.01
☐	305	Randy Jones	.15	.06	.01
☐	306	Denny Walling	.10	.04	.01
☐	307	Rick Honeycutt	.15	.06	.01
☐	308	Mike Hargrove	.15	.06	.01

☐ 309	Larry McWilliams	.10	.04	.01
☐ 310	Dave Parker	2.00	.80	.20
☐ 311	Roger Metzger	.10	.04	.01
☐ 312	Mike Barlow	.10	.04	.01
☐ 313	Johnny Grubb	.10	.04	.01
☐ 314	Tim Stoddard	.15	.06	.01
☐ 315	Steve Kemp	.15	.06	.01
☐ 316	Bob Lacey	.10	.04	.01
☐ 317	Mike Anderson DP	.05	.02	.00
☐ 318	Jerry Reuss	.15	.06	.01
☐ 319	Chris Speier	.10	.04	.01
☐ 320	Dennis Eckersley	1.50	.60	.15
☐ 321	Keith Hernandez	1.50	.60	.15
☐ 322	Claudell Washington	.15	.06	.01
☐ 323	Mick Kelleher	.10	.04	.01
☐ 324	Tom Underwood	.10	.04	.01
☐ 325	Dan Driessen	.10	.04	.01
☐ 326	Bo McLaughlin	.10	.04	.01
☐ 327	Ray Fosse DP	.05	.02	.00
☐ 328	Twins Team/Mgr.	.50	.10	.02
	Gene Mauch			
	(checklist back)			
☐ 329	Bert Roberge	.10	.04	.01
☐ 330	Al Cowens	.10	.04	.01
☐ 331	Richie Hebner	.10	.04	.01
☐ 332	Enrique Romo	.10	.04	.01
☐ 333	Jim Norris DP	.05	.02	.00
☐ 334	Jim Beattie	.10	.04	.01
☐ 335	Willie McCovey	1.75	.70	.17
☐ 336	George Medich	.10	.04	.01
☐ 337	Carney Lansford	.90	.40	.09
☐ 338	John Wockenfuss	.10	.04	.01
☐ 339	John D'Acquisto	.10	.04	.01
☐ 340	Ken Singleton	.15	.06	.01
☐ 341	Jim Essian	.15	.06	.01
☐ 342	Odell Jones	.10	.04	.01
☐ 343	Mike Vail	.10	.04	.01
☐ 344	Randy Lerch	.10	.04	.01
☐ 345	Larry Parrish	.15	.06	.01
☐ 346	Buddy Solomon	.10	.04	.01
☐ 347	Harry Chappas	.10	.04	.01
☐ 348	Checklist 3	.40	.05	.01
☐ 349	Jack Brohamer	.10	.04	.01
☐ 350	George Hendrick	.15	.06	.01
☐ 351	Bob Davis	.10	.04	.01
☐ 352	Dan Briggs	.10	.04	.01
☐ 353	Andy Hassler	.10	.04	.01
☐ 354	Rick Auerbach	.10	.04	.01
☐ 355	Gary Matthews	.15	.06	.01
☐ 356	Padres Team/Mgr.	.50	.10	.02
	Jerry Coleman			
	(checklist back)			
☐ 357	Bob McClure	.10	.04	.01
☐ 358	Lou Whitaker	2.50	1.00	.25
☐ 359	Randy Moffitt	.10	.04	.01
☐ 360	Darrell Porter DP	.10	.04	.01
☐ 361	Wayne Garland	.10	.04	.01
☐ 362	Danny Goodwin	.10	.04	.01
☐ 363	Wayne Gross	.10	.04	.01
☐ 364	Ray Burris	.10	.04	.01
☐ 365	Bobby Murcer	.30	.12	.03
☐ 366	Rob Dressler	.10	.04	.01
☐ 367	Billy Smith	.10	.04	.01
☐ 368	Willie Aikens	.20	.08	.02
☐ 369	Jim Kern	.10	.04	.01
☐ 370	Cesar Cedeno	.15	.06	.01
☐ 371	Jack Morris	2.50	1.00	.25
☐ 372	Joel Youngblood	.10	.04	.01
☐ 373	Dan Petry DP	.30	.12	.03
☐ 374	Jim Gantner	.20	.08	.02
☐ 375	Ross Grimsley	.10	.04	.01
☐ 376	Gary Allenson	.10	.04	.01
☐ 377	Junior Kennedy	.10	.04	.01
☐ 378	Jerry Mumphrey	.10	.04	.01
☐ 379	Kevin Bell	.10	.04	.01
☐ 380	Garry Maddox	.15	.06	.01
☐ 381	Cubs Team/Mgr.	.50	.10	.02
	Preston Gomez			
	(checklist back)			
☐ 382	Dave Freisleben	.10	.04	.01
☐ 383	Ed Ott	.10	.04	.01
☐ 384	Joey McLaughlin	.10	.04	.01
☐ 385	Enos Cabell	.10	.04	.01
☐ 386	Darrell Jackson	.10	.04	.01
☐ 387A	Fred Stanley	1.00	.40	.10
	(yellow name on front)			
☐ 387B	Fred Stanley	.10	.04	.01
	(red name on front)			
☐ 388	Mike Paxton	.10	.04	.01
☐ 389	Pete LaCock	.10	.04	.01
☐ 390	Fergie Jenkins	1.25	.50	.12
☐ 391	Tony Armas DP	.10	.04	.01
☐ 392	Milt Wilcox	.10	.04	.01
☐ 393	Ozzie Smith	12.50	5.50	1.65

☐ 394	Reggie Cleveland	.10	.04	.01
☐ 395	Ellis Valentine	.10	.04	.01
☐ 396	Dan Meyer	.10	.04	.01
☐ 397	Roy Thomas DP	.05	.02	.00
☐ 398	Barry Foote	.10	.04	.01
☐ 399	Mike Proly DP	.05	.02	.00
☐ 400	George Foster	.50	.20	.05
☐ 401	Pete Falcone	.10	.04	.01
☐ 402	Merv Rettenmund	.10	.04	.01
☐ 403	Pete Redfern DP	.05	.02	.00
☐ 404	Orioles Team/Mgr.	.50	.10	.02
	Earl Weaver			
	(checklist back)			
☐ 405	Dwight Evans	1.25	.50	.12
☐ 406	Paul Molitor	3.00	1.25	.30
☐ 407	Tony Solaita	.10	.04	.01
☐ 408	Bill North	.10	.04	.01
☐ 409	Paul Splittorff	.10	.04	.01
☐ 410	Bobby Bonds	.35	.15	.03
☐ 411	Frank LaCorte	.10	.04	.01
☐ 412	Thad Bosley	.10	.04	.01
☐ 413	Allen Ripley	.10	.04	.01
☐ 414	George Scott	.15	.06	.01
☐ 415	Bill Atkinson	.10	.04	.01
☐ 416	Tom Brookens	.10	.04	.01
☐ 417	Craig Chamberlain DP	.05	.02	.00
☐ 418	Roger Freed DP	.05	.02	.00
☐ 419	Vic Correll	.10	.04	.01
☐ 420	Butch Hobson	.20	.08	.02
☐ 421	Doug Bird	.10	.04	.01
☐ 422	Larry Milbourne	.10	.04	.01
☐ 423	Dave Frost	.10	.04	.01
☐ 424	Yankees Team/Mgr.	.50	.10	.02
	Dick Howser			
	(checklist back)			
☐ 425	Mark Belanger	.15	.06	.01
☐ 426	Grant Jackson	.10	.04	.01
☐ 427	Tom Hutton DP	.05	.02	.00
☐ 428	Pat Zachry	.10	.04	.01
☐ 429	Duane Kuiper	.10	.04	.01
☐ 430	Larry Hisle DP	.10	.04	.01
☐ 431	Mike Krukow	.15	.06	.01
☐ 432	Willie Norwood	.10	.04	.01
☐ 433	Rich Gale	.10	.04	.01
☐ 434	Johnnie LeMaster	.10	.04	.01
☐ 435	Don Gullett	.15	.06	.01
☐ 436	Billy Almon	.10	.04	.01
☐ 437	Joe Niekro	.20	.08	.02
☐ 438	Dave Revering	.10	.04	.01
☐ 439	Mike Phillips	.10	.04	.01
☐ 440	Don Sutton	1.25	.50	.12
☐ 441	Eric Soderholm	.10	.04	.01
☐ 442	Jorge Orta	.10	.04	.01
☐ 443	Mike Parrott	.10	.04	.01
☐ 444	Alvis Woods	.10	.04	.01
☐ 445	Mark Fidrych	.20	.08	.02
☐ 446	Duffy Dyer	.10	.04	.01
☐ 447	Nino Espinosa	.10	.04	.01
☐ 448	Jim Wohlford	.10	.04	.01
☐ 449	Doug Bair	.10	.04	.01
☐ 450	George Brett	9.00	4.00	.90
☐ 451	Indians Team/Mgr.	.45	.10	.02
	Dave Garcia			
	(checklist back)			
☐ 452	Steve Dillard	.10	.04	.01
☐ 453	Mike Bacsik	.10	.04	.01
☐ 454	Tom Donohue	.10	.04	.01
☐ 455	Mike Torrez	.10	.04	.01
☐ 456	Frank Taveras	.10	.04	.01
☐ 457	Bert Blyleven	.50	.20	.05
☐ 458	Billy Sample	.10	.04	.01
☐ 459	Mickey Lolich DP	.15	.06	.01
☐ 460	Willie Randolph	.40	.16	.04
☐ 461	Dwayne Murphy	.15	.06	.01
☐ 462	Mike Sadek DP	.05	.02	.00
☐ 463	Jerry Royster	.10	.04	.01
☐ 464	John Denny	.15	.06	.01
☐ 465	Rick Monday	.15	.06	.01
☐ 466	Mike Squires	.10	.04	.01
☐ 467	Jesse Jefferson	.10	.04	.01
☐ 468	Aurelio Rodriguez	.10	.04	.01
☐ 469	Randy Niemann DP	.05	.02	.00
☐ 470	Bob Boone	.35	.15	.03
☐ 471	Hosken Powell DP	.05	.02	.00
☐ 472	Willie Hernandez	.20	.08	.02
☐ 473	Bump Wills	.10	.04	.01
☐ 474	Steve Busby	.15	.06	.01
☐ 475	Cesar Geronimo	.10	.04	.01
☐ 476	Bob Shirley	.10	.04	.01
☐ 477	Buck Martinez	.10	.04	.01
☐ 478	Gil Flores	.10	.04	.01
☐ 479	Expos Team/Mgr.	.45	.10	.02
	Dick Williams			
	(checklist back)			

#	Name			
☐ 480	Bob Watson	.15	.06	.01
☐ 481	Tom Paciorek	.10	.04	.01
☐ 482	Rickey Henderson UER	150.00	67.50	22.50
	(7 steals at Modesto, should be at Fresno)			
☐ 483	Bo Diaz	.10	.04	.01
☐ 484	Checklist 4	.40	.05	.01
☐ 485	Mickey Rivers	.15	.06	.01
☐ 486	Mike Tyson DP	.05	.02	.00
☐ 487	Wayne Nordhagen	.10	.04	.01
☐ 488	Roy Howell	.10	.04	.01
☐ 489	Preston Hanna DP	.05	.02	.00
☐ 490	Lee May	.15	.06	.01
☐ 491	Steve Mura DP	.05	.02	.00
☐ 492	Todd Cruz	.10	.04	.01
☐ 493	Jerry Martin	.10	.04	.01
☐ 494	Craig Minetto	.10	.04	.01
☐ 495	Bake McBride	.10	.04	.01
☐ 496	Silvio Martinez	.10	.04	.01
☐ 497	Jim Mason	.10	.04	.01
☐ 498	Danny Darwin	.20	.08	.02
☐ 499	Giants Team/Mgr.	.50	.10	.02
	Dave Bristol (checklist back)			
☐ 500	Tom Seaver	3.50	1.50	.35
☐ 501	Rennie Stennett	.10	.04	.01
☐ 502	Rich Wortham DP	.05	.02	.00
☐ 503	Mike Cubbage	.10	.04	.01
☐ 504	Gene Garber	.10	.04	.01
☐ 505	Bert Campaneris	.15	.06	.01
☐ 506	Tom Buskey	.10	.04	.01
☐ 507	Leon Roberts	.10	.04	.01
☐ 508	U.L. Washington	.10	.04	.01
☐ 509	Ed Glynn	.10	.04	.01
☐ 510	Ron Cey	.30	.12	.03
☐ 511	Eric Wilkins	.10	.04	.01
☐ 512	Jose Cardenal	.10	.04	.01
☐ 513	Tom Dixon DP	.05	.02	.00
☐ 514	Steve Ontiveros	.10	.04	.01
☐ 515	Mike Caldwell	.10	.04	.01
☐ 516	Hector Cruz	.10	.04	.01
☐ 517	Don Stanhouse	.10	.04	.01
☐ 518	Nelson Norman	.10	.04	.01
☐ 519	Steve Nicosia	.10	.04	.01
☐ 520	Steve Rogers	.10	.04	.01
☐ 521	Ken Brett	.10	.04	.01
☐ 522	Jim Morrison	.10	.04	.01
☐ 523	Ken Henderson	.10	.04	.01
☐ 524	Jim Wright DP	.05	.02	.00
☐ 525	Clint Hurdle	.10	.04	.01
☐ 526	Phillies Team/Mgr.	.50	.10	.02
	Dallas Green (checklist back)			
☐ 527	Doug Rau DP	.05	.02	.00
☐ 528	Adrian Devine	.10	.04	.01
☐ 529	Jim Barr	.10	.04	.01
☐ 530	Jim Sundberg DP	.10	.04	.01
☐ 531	Eric Rasmussen	.10	.04	.01
☐ 532	Willie Horton	.15	.06	.01
☐ 533	Checklist 5	.40	.05	.01
☐ 534	Andre Thornton	.15	.06	.01
☐ 535	Bob Forsch	.10	.04	.01
☐ 536	Lee Lacy	.10	.04	.01
☐ 537	Alex Trevino	.15	.06	.01
☐ 538	Joe Strain	.10	.04	.01
☐ 539	Rudy May	.10	.04	.01
☐ 540	Pete Rose	3.75	1.60	.37
☐ 541	Miguel Dilone	.10	.04	.01
☐ 542	Joe Coleman	.10	.04	.01
☐ 543	Pat Kelly	.10	.04	.01
☐ 544	Rick Sutcliffe	2.00	.80	.20
☐ 545	Jeff Burroughs	.10	.04	.01
☐ 546	Rick Langford	.10	.04	.01
☐ 547	John Wathan	.15	.06	.01
☐ 548	Dave Rajsich	.10	.04	.01
☐ 549	Larry Wolfe	.10	.04	.01
☐ 550	Ken Griffey	.60	.25	.06
☐ 551	Pirates Team/Mgr.	.50	.10	.02
	Chuck Tanner (checklist back)			
☐ 552	Bill Nahorodny	.10	.04	.01
☐ 553	Dick Davis	.10	.04	.01
☐ 554	Art Howe	.20	.08	.02
☐ 555	Ed Figueroa	.10	.04	.01
☐ 556	Joe Rudi	.15	.06	.01
☐ 557	Mark Lee	.10	.04	.01
☐ 558	Alfredo Griffin	.20	.08	.02
☐ 559	Dale Murray	.10	.04	.01
☐ 560	Dave Lopes	.15	.06	.01
☐ 561	Eddie Whitson	.20	.08	.02
☐ 562	Joe Wallis	.10	.04	.01
☐ 563	Will McEnaney	.10	.04	.01
☐ 564	Rick Manning	.10	.04	.01
☐ 565	Dennis Leonard	.15	.06	.01
☐ 566	Bud Harrelson	.15	.06	.01
☐ 567	Skip Lockwood	.10	.04	.01
☐ 568	Gary Roenicke	.15	.06	.01
☐ 569	Terry Kennedy	.20	.08	.02
☐ 570	Roy Smalley	.10	.04	.01
☐ 571	Joe Sambito	.10	.04	.01
☐ 572	Jerry Morales DP	.05	.02	.00
☐ 573	Kent Tekulve	.15	.06	.01
☐ 574	Scot Thompson	.10	.04	.01
☐ 575	Ken Kravec	.10	.04	.01
☐ 576	Jim Dwyer	.10	.04	.01
☐ 577	Blue Jays Team/Mgr.	.45	.10	.02
	Bobby Mattick (checklist back)			
☐ 578	Scott Sanderson	.30	.12	.03
☐ 579	Charlie Moore	.10	.04	.01
☐ 580	Nolan Ryan	16.00	6.75	2.25
☐ 581	Bob Bailor	.10	.04	.01
☐ 582	Brian Doyle	.10	.04	.01
☐ 583	Bob Stinson	.10	.04	.01
☐ 584	Kurt Bevacqua	.10	.04	.01
☐ 585	Al Hrabosky	.15	.06	.01
☐ 586	Mitchell Page	.10	.04	.01
☐ 587	Garry Templeton	.20	.08	.02
☐ 588	Greg Minton	.10	.04	.01
☐ 589	Chet Lemon	.10	.04	.01
☐ 590	Jim Palmer	3.00	1.25	.30
☐ 591	Rick Cerone	.10	.04	.01
☐ 592	Jon Matlack	.15	.06	.01
☐ 593	Jesus Alou	.10	.04	.01
☐ 594	Dick Tidrow	.10	.04	.01
☐ 595	Don Money	.10	.04	.01
☐ 596	Rick Matula	.10	.04	.01
☐ 597	Tom Poquette	.10	.04	.01
☐ 598	Fred Kendall DP	.05	.02	.00
☐ 599	Mike Norris	.10	.04	.01
☐ 600	Reggie Jackson	5.25	2.25	.50
☐ 601	Buddy Schultz	.10	.04	.01
☐ 602	Brian Downing	.15	.06	.01
☐ 603	Jack Billingham DP	.05	.02	.00
☐ 604	Glenn Adams	.10	.04	.01
☐ 605	Terry Forster	.15	.06	.01
☐ 606	Reds Team/Mgr.	.50	.10	.02
	John McNamara (checklist back)			
☐ 607	Woodie Fryman	.10	.04	.01
☐ 608	Alan Bannister	.10	.04	.01
☐ 609	Ron Reed	.10	.04	.01
☐ 610	Willie Stargell	1.50	.60	.15
☐ 611	Jerry Garvin DP	.05	.02	.00
☐ 612	Cliff Johnson	.10	.04	.01
☐ 613	Randy Stein	.10	.04	.01
☐ 614	John Hiller	.15	.06	.01
☐ 615	Doug DeCinces	.15	.06	.01
☐ 616	Gene Richards	.10	.04	.01
☐ 617	Joaquin Andujar	.15	.06	.01
☐ 618	Bob Montgomery DP	.05	.02	.00
☐ 619	Sergio Ferrer	.10	.04	.01
☐ 620	Richie Zisk	.10	.04	.01
☐ 621	Bob Grich	.20	.08	.02
☐ 622	Mario Soto	.15	.06	.01
☐ 623	Gorman Thomas	.20	.08	.02
☐ 624	Lerrin LaGrow	.10	.04	.01
☐ 625	Chris Chambliss	.15	.06	.01
☐ 626	Tigers Team/Mgr.	.50	.10	.02
	Sparky Anderson (checklist back)			
☐ 627	Pedro Borbon	.10	.04	.01
☐ 628	Doug Capilla	.10	.04	.01
☐ 629	Jim Todd	.10	.04	.01
☐ 630	Larry Bowa	.25	.10	.02
☐ 631	Mark Littell	.10	.04	.01
☐ 632	Barry Bonnell	.10	.04	.01
☐ 633	Bob Apodaca	.10	.04	.01
☐ 634	Glenn Borgmann DP	.05	.02	.00
☐ 635	John Candelaria	.20	.08	.02
☐ 636	Toby Harrah	.15	.06	.01
☐ 637	Joe Simpson	.10	.04	.01
☐ 638	Mark Clear	.15	.06	.01
☐ 639	Larry Biittner	.10	.04	.01
☐ 640	Mike Flanagan	.20	.08	.02
☐ 641	Ed Kranepool	.15	.06	.01
☐ 642	Ken Forsch DP	.10	.04	.01
☐ 643	John Mayberry	.15	.06	.01
☐ 644	Charlie Hough	.15	.06	.01
☐ 645	Rick Burleson	.15	.06	.01
☐ 646	Checklist 6	.40	.05	.01
☐ 647	Milt May	.10	.04	.01
☐ 648	Roy White	.15	.06	.01
☐ 649	Tom Griffin	.10	.04	.01
☐ 650	Joe Morgan	2.00	.80	.20
☐ 651	Rollie Fingers	1.25	.50	.12
☐ 652	Mario Mendoza	.10	.04	.01
☐ 653	Stan Bahnsen	.10	.04	.01
☐ 654	Bruce Boisclair DP	.05	.02	.00
☐ 655	Tug McGraw	.30	.12	.03

☐ 656	Larvell Blanks	.10	.04	.01
☐ 657	Dave Edwards	.10	.04	.01
☐ 658	Chris Knapp	.10	.04	.01
☐ 659	Brewers Team/Mgr.	.50	.10	.02
	George Bamberger			
	(checklist back)			
☐ 660	Rusty Staub	.30	.12	.03
☐ 661	Orioles Rookies	.15	.06	.01
	Mark Corey			
	Dave Ford			
	Wayne Krenchicki			
☐ 662	Red Sox Rookies	.15	.06	.01
	Joel Finch			
	Mike O'Berry			
	Chuck Rainey			
☐ 663	Angels Rookies	.75	.30	.07
	Ralph Botting			
	Bob Clark			
	Dickie Thon			
☐ 664	White Sox Rookies	.15	.06	.01
	Mike Colbern			
	Guy Hoffman			
	Dewey Robinson			
☐ 665	Indians Rookies	.35	.15	.03
	Larry Andersen			
	Bobby Cuellar			
	Sandy Wihtol			
☐ 666	Tigers Rookies	.15	.06	.01
	Mike Chris			
	Al Greene			
	Bruce Robbins			
☐ 667	Royals Rookies	1.75	.70	.17
	Renie Martin			
	Bill Paschall			
	Dan Quisenberry			
☐ 668	Brewers Rookies	.15	.06	.01
	Danny Boitano			
	Willie Mueller			
	Lenn Sakata			
☐ 669	Twins Rookies	.30	.12	.03
	Dan Graham			
	Rick Sofield			
	Gary Ward			
☐ 670	Yankees Rookies	.15	.06	.01
	Bobby Brown			
	Brad Gulden			
	Darryl Jones			
☐ 671	A's Rookies	1.00	.40	.10
	Derek Bryant			
	Brian Kingman			
	Mike Morgan			
☐ 672	Mariners Rookies	.15	.06	.01
	Charlie Beamon			
	Rodney Craig			
	Rafael Vasquez			
☐ 673	Rangers Rookies	.15	.06	.01
	Brian Allard			
	Jerry Don Gleaton			
	Greg Mahlberg			
☐ 674	Blue Jays Rookies	.15	.06	.01
	Butch Edge			
	Pat Kelly			
	Ted Wilborn			
☐ 675	Braves Rookies	.15	.06	.01
	Bruce Benedict			
	Larry Bradford			
	Eddie Miller			
☐ 676	Cubs Rookies	.15	.06	.01
	Dave Geisel			
	Steve Macko			
	Karl Pagel			
☐ 677	Reds Rookies	.15	.06	.01
	Art DeFreites			
	Frank Pastore			
	Harry Spilman			
☐ 678	Astros Rookies	.15	.06	.01
	Reggie Baldwin			
	Alan Knicely			
	Pete Ladd			
☐ 679	Dodgers Rookies	.25	.10	.02
	Joe Beckwith			
	Mickey Hatcher			
	Dave Patterson			
☐ 680	Expos Rookies	.25	.10	.02
	Tony Bernazard			
	Randy Miller			
	John Tamargo			
☐ 681	Mets Rookies	4.50	2.00	.45
	Dan Norman			
	Jesse Orosco			
	Mike Scott			
☐ 682	Phillies Rookies	.15	.06	.01
	Ramon Aviles			
	Dickie Noles			
	Kevin Saucier			

☐ 683	Pirates Rookies	.15	.06	.01
	Dorian Boyland			
	Alberto Lois			
	Harry Saferight			
☐ 684	Cardinals Rookies	1.00	.40	.10
	George Frazier			
	Tom Herr			
	Dan O'Brien			
☐ 685	Padres Rookies	.25	.10	.02
	Tim Flannery			
	Brian Greer			
	Jim Wilhelm			
☐ 686	Giants Rookies	.15	.06	.01
	Greg Johnston			
	Dennis Littlejohn			
	Phil Nastu			
☐ 687	Mike Heath DP	.05	.02	.00
☐ 688	Steve Stone	.15	.06	.01
☐ 689	Red Sox Team/Mgr.	.50	.10	.02
	Don Zimmer			
	(checklist back)			
☐ 690	Tommy John	.50	.20	.05
☐ 691	Ivan DeJesus	.10	.04	.01
☐ 692	Rawly Eastwick DP	.05	.02	.00
☐ 693	Craig Kusick	.10	.04	.01
☐ 694	Jim Rooker	.10	.04	.01
☐ 695	Reggie Smith	.20	.08	.02
☐ 696	Julio Gonzalez	.10	.04	.01
☐ 697	David Clyde	.10	.04	.01
☐ 698	Oscar Gamble	.10	.04	.01
☐ 699	Floyd Bannister	.10	.04	.01
☐ 700	Rod Carew DP	1.75	.70	.17
☐ 701	Ken Oberkfell	.25	.10	.02
☐ 702	Ed Farmer	.10	.04	.01
☐ 703	Otto Velez	.10	.04	.01
☐ 704	Gene Tenace	.15	.06	.01
☐ 705	Freddie Patek	.10	.04	.01
☐ 706	Tippy Martinez	.10	.04	.01
☐ 707	Elliott Maddox	.10	.04	.01
☐ 708	Bob Tolan	.10	.04	.01
☐ 709	Pat Underwood	.10	.04	.01
☐ 710	Graig Nettles	.30	.12	.03
☐ 711	Bob Galasso	.10	.04	.01
☐ 712	Rodney Scott	.10	.04	.01
☐ 713	Terry Whitfield	.10	.04	.01
☐ 714	Fred Norman	.10	.04	.01
☐ 715	Sal Bando	.15	.06	.01
☐ 716	Lynn McGlothen	.10	.04	.01
☐ 717	Mickey Klutts DP	.05	.02	.00
☐ 718	Greg Gross	.10	.04	.01
☐ 719	Don Robinson	.15	.06	.01
☐ 720	Carl Yastrzemski DP	1.75	.70	.17
☐ 721	Paul Hartzell	.10	.04	.01
☐ 722	Jose Cruz	.15	.06	.01
☐ 723	Shane Rawley	.15	.06	.01
☐ 724	Jerry White	.10	.04	.01
☐ 725	Rick Wise	.15	.06	.01
☐ 726	Steve Yeager	.25	.10	.02

1981 Topps

The cards in this 726-card set measure 2 1/2" by 3 1/2". League Leaders (1-8), Record Breakers (201-208), and Post-season cards (401-404) are topical subsets found in this set marketed by Topps in 1981. The team cards are all grouped together (661-686) and feature team checklist backs and a very small photo of the team's manager in the upper right corner of the obverse. The obverses carry the player's position and team in a baseball cap design, and the company name is printed in a small baseball. The backs are red and gray. The 66 double-printed cards are noted in the checklist by DP. The set is quite popular with collectors partly due to the presence of rookie cards of Harold Baines, Mike Boddicker, Hubie Brooks, , Kirk Gibson, Bruce Hurst, Lloyd Moseby, Tony Pena, Tim Raines, Jeff Reardon, John Tudor, and Fernando Valenzuela.

	MINT	EXC	G-VG
COMPLETE SET (726)	110.00	45.00	10.00
COMMON PLAYER (1-726)	.09	.04	.01
COMMON DP's (1-726)	.05	.02	.00
□ 1 Batting Leaders	1.50	.25	.05
George Brett			
Bill Buckner			
□ 2 Home Run Leaders	.50	.20	.05
Reggie Jackson			
Ben Oglivie			
Mike Schmidt			
□ 3 RBI Leaders	.35	.15	.03
Cecil Cooper			
Mike Schmidt			
□ 4 Stolen Base Leaders	1.50	.60	.15
Rickey Henderson			
Ron LeFlore			
□ 5 Victory Leaders	.20	.08	.02
Steve Stone			
Steve Carlton			
□ 6 Strikeout Leaders	.20	.08	.02
Len Barker			
Steve Carlton			
□ 7 ERA Leaders	.15	.06	.01
Rudy May			
Don Sutton			
□ 8 Leading Firemen	.15	.06	.01
Dan Quisenberry			
Rollie Fingers			
Tom Hume			
□ 9 Pete LaCock DP	.05	.02	.00
□ 10 Mike Flanagan	.15	.06	.01
□ 11 Jim Wohlford DP	.05	.02	.00
□ 12 Mark Clear	.09	.04	.01
□ 13 Joe Charboneau	.15	.06	.01
□ 14 John Tudor	.90	.40	.09
□ 15 Larry Parrish	.09	.04	.01
□ 16 Ron Davis	.09	.04	.01
□ 17 Cliff Johnson	.09	.04	.01
□ 18 Glenn Adams	.09	.04	.01
□ 19 Jim Clancy	.09	.04	.01
□ 20 Jeff Burroughs	.15	.06	.01
□ 21 Ron Oester	.09	.04	.01
□ 22 Danny Darwin	.15	.06	.01
□ 23 Alex Trevino	.09	.04	.01
□ 24 Don Stanhouse	.09	.04	.01
□ 25 Sixto Lezcano	.09	.04	.01
□ 26 U.L. Washington	.09	.04	.01
□ 27 Champ Summers DP	.05	.02	.00
□ 28 Enrique Romo	.09	.04	.01
□ 29 Gene Tenace	.15	.06	.01
□ 30 Jack Clark	.50	.20	.05
□ 31 Checklist 1-121 DP	.15	.02	.00
□ 32 Ken Oberkfell	.09	.04	.01
□ 33 Rick Honeycutt	.09	.04	.01
□ 34 Aurelio Rodriguez	.09	.04	.01
□ 35 Mitchell Page	.09	.04	.01
□ 36 Ed Farmer	.09	.04	.01
□ 37 Gary Roenicke	.09	.04	.01
□ 38 Win Remmerswaal	.09	.04	.01
□ 39 Tom Veryzer	.09	.04	.01
□ 40 Tug McGraw	.20	.08	.02
□ 41 Ranger Rookies	.15	.06	.01
Bob Babcock			
John Butcher			
Jerry Don Gleaton			
□ 42 Jerry White DP	.05	.02	.00
□ 43 Jose Morales	.09	.04	.01
□ 44 Larry McWilliams	.09	.04	.01
□ 45 Enos Cabell	.09	.04	.01
□ 46 Rick Bosetti	.09	.04	.01
□ 47 Ken Brett	.09	.04	.01
□ 48 Dave Skaggs	.09	.04	.01
□ 49 Bob Shirley	.09	.04	.01
□ 50 Dave Lopes	.15	.06	.01
□ 51 Bill Robinson DP	.09	.04	.01
□ 52 Hector Cruz	.09	.04	.01
□ 53 Kevin Saucier	.09	.04	.01
□ 54 Ivan DeJesus	.09	.04	.01
□ 55 Mike Norris	.09	.04	.01

□ 56 Buck Martinez	.09	.04	.01
□ 57 Dave Roberts	.09	.04	.01
□ 58 Joel Youngblood	.09	.04	.01
□ 59 Dan Petry	.15	.06	.01
□ 60 Willie Randolph	.25	.10	.02
□ 61 Butch Wynegar	.09	.04	.01
□ 62 Joe Pettini	.09	.04	.01
□ 63 Steve Renko DP	.05	.02	.00
□ 64 Brian Asselstine	.09	.04	.01
□ 65 Scott McGregor	.09	.04	.01
□ 66 Royals Rookies	.15	.06	.01
Manny Castillo			
Tim Ireland			
Mike Jones			
□ 67 Ken Kravec	.09	.04	.01
□ 68 Matt Alexander DP	.05	.02	.00
□ 69 Ed Halicki	.09	.04	.01
□ 70 Al Oliver DP	.15	.06	.01
□ 71 Hal Dues	.09	.04	.01
□ 72 Barry Evans DP	.05	.02	.00
□ 73 Doug Bair	.09	.04	.01
□ 74 Mike Hargrove	.15	.06	.01
□ 75 Reggie Smith	.15	.06	.01
□ 76 Mario Mendoza	.09	.04	.01
□ 77 Mike Barlow	.09	.04	.01
□ 78 Steve Dillard	.09	.04	.01
□ 79 Bruce Robbins	.09	.04	.01
□ 80 Rusty Staub	.25	.10	.02
□ 81 Dave Stapleton	.15	.06	.01
□ 82 Astros Rookies DP	.15	.06	.01
Danny Heep			
Alan Knicely			
Bobby Sprowl			
□ 83 Mike Proly	.09	.04	.01
□ 84 Johnnie LeMaster	.09	.04	.01
□ 85 Mike Caldwell	.09	.04	.01
□ 86 Wayne Gross	.09	.04	.01
□ 87 Rick Camp	.09	.04	.01
□ 88 Joe Lefebvre	.09	.04	.01
□ 89 Darrell Jackson	.09	.04	.01
□ 90 Bake McBride	.09	.04	.01
□ 91 Tim Stoddard DP	.09	.04	.01
□ 92 Mike Easler	.09	.04	.01
□ 93 Ed Glynn DP	.05	.02	.00
□ 94 Harry Spilman DP	.05	.02	.00
□ 95 Jim Sundberg	.09	.04	.01
□ 96 A's Rookies	.15	.06	.01
Dave Beard			
Ernie Camacho			
Pat Dempsey			
□ 97 Chris Speier	.09	.04	.01
□ 98 Clint Hurdle	.09	.04	.01
□ 99 Eric Wilkins	.09	.04	.01
□ 100 Rod Carew	2.50	1.00	.25
□ 101 Benny Ayala	.09	.04	.01
□ 102 Dave Tobik	.09	.04	.01
□ 103 Jerry Martin	.09	.04	.01
□ 104 Terry Forster	.15	.06	.01
□ 105 Jose Cruz	.15	.06	.01
□ 106 Don Money	.09	.04	.01
□ 107 Rich Wortham	.09	.04	.01
□ 108 Bruce Benedict	.09	.04	.01
□ 109 Mike Scott	.65	.25	.06
□ 110 Carl Yastrzemski	2.50	1.00	.25
□ 111 Greg Minton	.09	.04	.01
□ 112 White Sox Rookies	.15	.06	.01
Rusty Kuntz			
Fran Mullin			
Leo Sutherland			
□ 113 Mike Phillips	.09	.04	.01
□ 114 Tom Underwood	.09	.04	.01
□ 115 Roy Smalley	.09	.04	.01
□ 116 Joe Simpson	.09	.04	.01
□ 117 Pete Falcone	.09	.04	.01
□ 118 Kurt Bevacqua	.09	.04	.01
□ 119 Tippy Martinez	.09	.04	.01
□ 120 Larry Bowa	.15	.06	.01
□ 121 Larry Harlow	.09	.04	.01
□ 122 John Denny	.09	.04	.01
□ 123 Al Cowens	.09	.04	.01
□ 124 Jerry Garvin	.09	.04	.01
□ 125 Andre Dawson	3.50	1.50	.35
□ 126 Charlie Leibrandt	.75	.30	.07
□ 127 Rudy Law	.09	.04	.01
□ 128 Gary Allenson DP	.05	.02	.00
□ 129 Art Howe	.15	.06	.01
□ 130 Larry Gura	.09	.04	.01
□ 131 Keith Moreland	.20	.08	.02
□ 132 Tommy Boggs	.09	.04	.01
□ 133 Jeff Cox	.09	.04	.01
□ 134 Steve Mura	.09	.04	.01
□ 135 Gorman Thomas	.20	.08	.02
□ 136 Doug Capilla	.09	.04	.01
□ 137 Hosken Powell	.09	.04	.01

#	Player			
☐ 138	Rich Dotson DP	.15	.06	.01
☐ 139	Oscar Gamble	.09	.04	.01
☐ 140	Bob Forsch	.09	.04	.01
☐ 141	Miguel Dilone	.09	.04	.01
☐ 142	Jackson Todd	.09	.04	.01
☐ 143	Dan Meyer	.09	.04	.01
☐ 144	Allen Ripley	.09	.04	.01
☐ 145	Mickey Rivers	.15	.06	.01
☐ 146	Bobby Castillo	.09	.04	.01
☐ 147	Dale Berra	.09	.04	.01
☐ 148	Randy Niemann	.09	.04	.01
☐ 149	Joe Nolan	.09	.04	.01
☐ 150	Mark Fidrych	.20	.08	.02
☐ 151	Claudell Washington	.15	.06	.01
☐ 152	John Urrea	.09	.04	.01
☐ 153	Tom Poquette	.09	.04	.01
☐ 154	Rick Langford	.09	.04	.01
☐ 155	Chris Chambliss	.15	.06	.01
☐ 156	Bob McClure	.09	.04	.01
☐ 157	John Wathan	.15	.06	.01
☐ 158	Fergie Jenkins	.75	.30	.07
☐ 159	Brian Doyle	.09	.04	.01
☐ 160	Garry Maddox	.09	.04	.01
☐ 161	Dan Graham	.09	.04	.01
☐ 162	Doug Corbett	.09	.04	.01
☐ 163	Bill Almon	.09	.04	.01
☐ 164	LaMarr Hoyt	.20	.08	.02
☐ 165	Tony Scott	.09	.04	.01
☐ 166	Floyd Bannister	.09	.04	.01
☐ 167	Terry Whitfield	.09	.04	.01
☐ 168	Don Robinson DP	.09	.04	.01
☐ 169	John Mayberry	.15	.06	.01
☐ 170	Ross Grimsley	.09	.04	.01
☐ 171	Gene Richards	.09	.04	.01
☐ 172	Gary Woods	.09	.04	.01
☐ 173	Bump Wills	.09	.04	.01
☐ 174	Doug Rau	.09	.04	.01
☐ 175	Dave Collins	.09	.04	.01
☐ 176	Mike Krukow	.09	.04	.01
☐ 177	Rick Peters	.09	.04	.01
☐ 178	Jim Essian DP	.09	.04	.01
☐ 179	Rudy May	.09	.04	.01
☐ 180	Pete Rose	3.50	1.50	.35
☐ 181	Elias Sosa	.09	.04	.01
☐ 182	Bob Grich	.15	.06	.01
☐ 183	Dick Davis DP	.05	.02	.00
☐ 184	Jim Dwyer	.09	.04	.01
☐ 185	Dennis Leonard	.09	.04	.01
☐ 186	Wayne Nordhagen	.09	.04	.01
☐ 187	Mike Parrott	.09	.04	.01
☐ 188	Doug DeCinces	.15	.06	.01
☐ 189	Craig Swan	.09	.04	.01
☐ 190	Cesar Cedeno	.15	.06	.01
☐ 191	Rick Sutcliffe	.20	.08	.02
☐ 192	Braves Rookies Terry Harper Ed Miller Rafael Ramirez	.20	.08	.02
☐ 193	Pete Vuckovich	.09	.04	.01
☐ 194	Rod Scurry	.09	.04	.01
☐ 195	Rich Murray	.09	.04	.01
☐ 196	Duffy Dyer	.09	.04	.01
☐ 197	Jim Kern	.09	.04	.01
☐ 198	Jerry Dybzinski	.09	.04	.01
☐ 199	Chuck Rainey	.09	.04	.01
☐ 200	George Foster	.25	.10	.02
☐ 201	RB: Johnny Bench Most homers, lifetime, catcher	.60	.25	.06
☐ 202	RB: Steve Carlton Most strikeouts, lefthander, lifetime	.50	.20	.05
☐ 203	RB: Bill Gullickson Most strikeouts, game, rookie	.20	.08	.02
☐ 204	RB: Ron LeFlore and Rodney Scott Most stolen bases, teammates, season	.15	.06	.01
☐ 205	RB: Pete Rose Most cons. seasons 600 or more at-bats	.75	.30	.07
☐ 206	RB: Mike Schmidt Most homers, third baseman, season	1.00	.40	.10
☐ 207	RB: Ozzie Smith Most assists, season, shortstop	.75	.30	.07
☐ 208	RB: Willie Wilson Most at-bats, season	.15	.06	.01
☐ 209	Dickie Thon DP	.15	.06	.01
☐ 210	Jim Palmer	1.75	.70	.17
☐ 211	Derrel Thomas	.09	.04	.01
☐ 212	Steve Nicosia	.09	.04	.01
☐ 213	Al Holland	.09	.04	.01
☐ 214	Angels Rookies Ralph Botting Jim Dorsey John Harris	.09	.04	.01
☐ 215	Larry Hisle	.09	.04	.01
☐ 216	John Henry Johnson	.09	.04	.01
☐ 217	Rich Hebner	.09	.04	.01
☐ 218	Paul Splittorff	.09	.04	.01
☐ 219	Ken Landreaux	.09	.04	.01
☐ 220	Tom Seaver	2.50	1.00	.25
☐ 221	Bob Davis	.09	.04	.01
☐ 222	Jorge Orta	.09	.04	.01
☐ 223	Roy Lee Jackson	.09	.04	.01
☐ 224	Pat Zachry	.09	.04	.01
☐ 225	Ruppert Jones	.09	.04	.01
☐ 226	Manny Sanguillen DP	.09	.04	.01
☐ 227	Fred Martinez	.09	.04	.01
☐ 228	Tom Paciorek	.09	.04	.01
☐ 229	Rollie Fingers	1.50	.60	.15
☐ 230	George Hendrick	.09	.04	.01
☐ 231	Joe Beckwith	.09	.04	.01
☐ 232	Mickey Klutts	.09	.04	.01
☐ 233	Skip Lockwood	.09	.04	.01
☐ 234	Lou Whitaker	1.00	.40	.10
☐ 235	Scott Sanderson	.25	.10	.02
☐ 236	Mike Ivie	.09	.04	.01
☐ 237	Charlie Moore	.09	.04	.01
☐ 238	Willie Hernandez	.15	.06	.01
☐ 239	Rick Miller DP	.05	.02	.00
☐ 240	Nolan Ryan	9.00	4.00	.90
☐ 241	Checklist 122-242 DP	.15	.02	.00
☐ 242	Chet Lemon	.09	.04	.01
☐ 243	Sal Butera	.09	.04	.01
☐ 244	Cardinals Rookies Tito Landrum Al Olmsted Andy Rincon	.15	.06	.01
☐ 245	Ed Figueroa	.09	.04	.01
☐ 246	Ed Ott DP	.05	.02	.00
☐ 247	Glenn Hubbard DP	.05	.02	.00
☐ 248	Joey McLaughlin	.09	.04	.01
☐ 249	Larry Cox	.09	.04	.01
☐ 250	Ron Guidry	.40	.16	.04
☐ 251	Tom Brookens	.09	.04	.01
☐ 252	Victor Cruz	.09	.04	.01
☐ 253	Dave Bergman	.09	.04	.01
☐ 254	Ozzie Smith	4.25	1.75	.42
☐ 255	Mark Littell	.09	.04	.01
☐ 256	Bombo Rivera	.09	.04	.01
☐ 257	Rennie Stennett	.09	.04	.01
☐ 258	Joe Price	.09	.04	.01
☐ 259	Mets Rookies Juan Berenguer Hubie Brooks Mookie Wilson	2.25	.90	.22
☐ 260	Ron Cey	.25	.10	.02
☐ 261	Rickey Henderson	22.50	9.75	3.25
☐ 262	Sammy Stewart	.09	.04	.01
☐ 263	Brian Downing	.15	.06	.01
☐ 264	Jim Norris	.09	.04	.01
☐ 265	John Candelaria	.15	.06	.01
☐ 266	Tom Herr	.20	.08	.02
☐ 267	Stan Bahnsen	.09	.04	.01
☐ 268	Jerry Royster	.09	.04	.01
☐ 269	Ken Forsch	.09	.04	.01
☐ 270	Greg Luzinski	.20	.08	.02
☐ 271	Bill Castro	.09	.04	.01
☐ 272	Bruce Kimm	.09	.04	.01
☐ 273	Stan Papi	.09	.04	.01
☐ 274	Craig Chamberlain	.09	.04	.01
☐ 275	Dwight Evans	.60	.25	.06
☐ 276	Dan Spillner	.09	.04	.01
☐ 277	Alfredo Griffin	.15	.06	.01
☐ 278	Rick Sofield	.09	.04	.01
☐ 279	Bob Knepper	.09	.04	.01
☐ 280	Ken Griffey	.50	.20	.05
☐ 281	Fred Stanley	.09	.04	.01
☐ 282	Mariners Rookies Rick Anderson Greg Biercevicz Rodney Craig	.15	.06	.01
☐ 283	Billy Sample	.09	.04	.01
☐ 284	Brian Kingman	.09	.04	.01
☐ 285	Jerry Turner	.09	.04	.01
☐ 286	Dave Frost	.09	.04	.01
☐ 287	Lenn Sakata	.09	.04	.01
☐ 288	Bob Clark	.09	.04	.01
☐ 289	Mickey Hatcher	.09	.04	.01
☐ 290	Bob Boone DP	.15	.06	.01
☐ 291	Aurelio Lopez	.09	.04	.01
☐ 292	Mike Squires	.09	.04	.01
☐ 293	Charlie Lea	.15	.06	.01
☐ 294	Mike Tyson DP	.05	.02	.00

#	Player			
☐ 295	Hal McRae	.20	.08	.02
☐ 296	Bill Nahorodny DP	.05	.02	.00
☐ 297	Bob Bailor	.09	.04	.01
☐ 298	Buddy Solomon	.09	.04	.01
☐ 299	Elliott Maddox	.09	.04	.01
☐ 300	Paul Molitor	1.00	.40	.10
☐ 301	Matt Keough	.09	.04	.01
☐ 302	Dodgers Rookies	5.00	2.25	.50
	Jack Perconte			
	Mike Scioscia			
	Fernando Valenzuela			
☐ 303	Johnny Oates	.15	.06	.01
☐ 304	John Castino	.09	.04	.01
☐ 305	Ken Clay	.09	.04	.01
☐ 306	Juan Beniquez DP	.05	.02	.00
☐ 307	Gene Garber	.09	.04	.01
☐ 308	Rick Manning	.09	.04	.01
☐ 309	Luis Salazar	.25	.10	.02
☐ 310	Vida Blue DP	.09	.04	.01
☐ 311	Freddie Patek	.09	.04	.01
☐ 312	Rick Rhoden	.09	.04	.01
☐ 313	Luis Pujols	.09	.04	.01
☐ 314	Rich Dauer	.09	.04	.01
☐ 315	Kirk Gibson	6.50	2.75	.65
☐ 316	Craig Minetto	.09	.04	.01
☐ 317	Lonnie Smith	.50	.20	.05
☐ 318	Steve Yeager	.09	.04	.01
☐ 319	Rowland Office	.09	.04	.01
☐ 320	Tom Burgmeier	.09	.04	.01
☐ 321	Leon Durham	.20	.08	.02
☐ 322	Neil Allen	.09	.04	.01
☐ 323	Jim Morrison DP	.09	.04	.01
☐ 324	Mike Willis	.09	.04	.01
☐ 325	Ray Knight	.20	.08	.02
☐ 326	Biff Pocoroba	.09	.04	.01
☐ 327	Moose Haas	.09	.04	.01
☐ 328	Twins Rookies	.15	.06	.01
	Dave Engle			
	Greg Johnston			
	Gary Ward			
☐ 329	Joaquin Andujar	.15	.06	.01
☐ 330	Frank White	.15	.06	.01
☐ 331	Dennis Lamp	.09	.04	.01
☐ 332	Lee Lacy DP	.09	.04	.01
☐ 333	Sid Monge	.09	.04	.01
☐ 334	Dane Iorg	.09	.04	.01
☐ 335	Rick Cerone	.09	.04	.01
☐ 336	Eddie Whitson	.09	.04	.01
☐ 337	Lynn Jones	.09	.04	.01
☐ 338	Checklist 243-363	.25	.03	.01
☐ 339	John Ellis	.09	.04	.01
☐ 340	Bruce Kison	.09	.04	.01
☐ 341	Dwayne Murphy	.09	.04	.01
☐ 342	Eric Rasmussen DP	.05	.02	.00
☐ 343	Frank Taveras	.09	.04	.01
☐ 344	Byron McLaughlin	.09	.04	.01
☐ 345	Warren Cromartie	.09	.04	.01
☐ 346	Larry Christenson DP	.05	.02	.00
☐ 347	Harold Baines	4.25	1.75	.42
☐ 348	Bob Sykes	.09	.04	.01
☐ 349	Glenn Hoffman	.09	.04	.01
☐ 350	J.R. Richard	.15	.06	.01
☐ 351	Otto Velez	.09	.04	.01
☐ 352	Dick Tidrow DP	.05	.02	.00
☐ 353	Terry Kennedy	.15	.06	.01
☐ 354	Mario Soto	.15	.06	.01
☐ 355	Bob Horner	.20	.08	.02
☐ 356	Padres Rookies	.09	.04	.01
	George Stablein			
	Craig Stimac			
	Tom Tellmann			
☐ 357	Jim Slaton	.09	.04	.01
☐ 358	Mark Wagner	.09	.04	.01
☐ 359	Tom Hausman	.09	.04	.01
☐ 360	Willie Wilson	.25	.10	.02
☐ 361	Joe Strain	.09	.04	.01
☐ 362	Bo Diaz	.09	.04	.01
☐ 363	Geoff Zahn	.09	.04	.01
☐ 364	Mike Davis	.20	.08	.02
☐ 365	Graig Nettles DP	.15	.06	.01
☐ 366	Mike Ramsey	.09	.04	.01
☐ 367	Dennis Martinez	.25	.10	.02
☐ 368	Leon Roberts	.09	.04	.01
☐ 369	Frank Tanana	.15	.06	.01
☐ 370	Dave Winfield	2.00	.80	.20
☐ 371	Charlie Hough	.15	.06	.01
☐ 372	Jay Johnstone	.15	.06	.01
☐ 373	Pat Underwood	.09	.04	.01
☐ 374	Tommy Hutton	.09	.04	.01
☐ 375	Dave Concepcion	.25	.10	.02
☐ 376	Ron Reed	.09	.04	.01
☐ 377	Jerry Morales	.09	.04	.01
☐ 378	Dave Rader	.09	.04	.01
☐ 379	Lary Sorensen	.09	.04	.01
☐ 380	Willie Stargell	1.00	.40	.10
☐ 381	Cubs Rookies	.15	.06	.01
	Carlos Lezcano			
	Steve Macko			
	Randy Martz			
☐ 382	Paul Mirabella	.09	.04	.01
☐ 383	Eric Soderholm DP	.05	.02	.00
☐ 384	Mike Sadek	.09	.04	.01
☐ 385	Joe Sambito	.09	.04	.01
☐ 386	Dave Edwards	.09	.04	.01
☐ 387	Phil Niekro	.75	.30	.07
☐ 388	Andre Thornton	.15	.06	.01
☐ 389	Marty Pattin	.09	.04	.01
☐ 390	Cesar Geronimo	.09	.04	.01
☐ 391	Dave Lemanczyk DP	.05	.02	.00
☐ 392	Lance Parrish	.75	.30	.07
☐ 393	Broderick Perkins	.09	.04	.01
☐ 394	Woodie Fryman	.09	.04	.01
☐ 395	Scot Thompson	.09	.04	.01
☐ 396	Bill Campbell	.09	.04	.01
☐ 397	Julio Cruz	.09	.04	.01
☐ 398	Ross Baumgarten	.09	.04	.01
☐ 399	Orioles Rookies	1.25	.50	.12
	Mike Boddicker			
	Mark Corey			
	Floyd Rayford			
☐ 400	Reggie Jackson	3.50	1.50	.35
☐ 401	AL Champs	.65	.25	.06
	Royals sweep Yanks			
	(Brett swinging)			
☐ 402	NL Champs	.25	.10	.02
	Phillies squeak			
	past Astros			
☐ 403	1980 World Series	.25	.10	.02
	Phillies beat			
	Royals in six			
☐ 404	1980 World Series	.25	.10	.02
	Phillies win first			
	World Series			
☐ 405	Nino Espinosa	.09	.04	.01
☐ 406	Dickie Noles	.09	.04	.01
☐ 407	Ernie Whitt	.09	.04	.01
☐ 408	Fernando Arroyo	.09	.04	.01
☐ 409	Larry Herndon	.09	.04	.01
☐ 410	Bert Campaneris	.15	.06	.01
☐ 411	Terry Puhl	.09	.04	.01
☐ 412	Britt Burns	.15	.06	.01
☐ 413	Tony Bernazard	.09	.04	.01
☐ 414	John Pacella DP	.05	.02	.00
☐ 415	Ben Oglivie	.09	.04	.01
☐ 416	Gary Alexander	.09	.04	.01
☐ 417	Dan Schatzeder	.09	.04	.01
☐ 418	Bobby Brown	.09	.04	.01
☐ 419	Tom Hume	.09	.04	.01
☐ 420	Keith Hernandez	.50	.20	.05
☐ 421	Bob Stanley	.09	.04	.01
☐ 422	Dan Ford	.09	.04	.01
☐ 423	Shane Rawley	.09	.04	.01
☐ 424	Yankees Rookies	.09	.04	.01
	Tim Lollar			
	Bruce Robinson			
	Dennis Werth			
☐ 425	Al Bumbry	.09	.04	.01
☐ 426	Warren Brusstar	.09	.04	.01
☐ 427	John D'Acquisto	.09	.04	.01
☐ 428	John Stearns	.09	.04	.01
☐ 429	Mick Kelleher	.09	.04	.01
☐ 430	Jim Bibby	.09	.04	.01
☐ 431	Dave Roberts	.09	.04	.01
☐ 432	Len Barker	.09	.04	.01
☐ 433	Rance Mulliniks	.09	.04	.01
☐ 434	Roger Erickson	.09	.04	.01
☐ 435	Jim Spencer	.09	.04	.01
☐ 436	Gary Lucas	.09	.04	.01
☐ 437	Mike Heath DP	.05	.02	.00
☐ 438	John Montefusco	.09	.04	.01
☐ 439	Denny Walling	.09	.04	.01
☐ 440	Jerry Reuss	.09	.04	.01
☐ 441	Ken Reitz	.09	.04	.01
☐ 442	Ron Pruitt	.09	.04	.01
☐ 443	Jim Beattie DP	.05	.02	.00
☐ 444	Garth Iorg	.09	.04	.01
☐ 445	Ellis Valentine	.09	.04	.01
☐ 446	Checklist 364-484	.25	.03	.01
☐ 447	Junior Kennedy DP	.05	.02	.00
☐ 448	Tim Corcoran	.09	.04	.01
☐ 449	Paul Mitchell	.09	.04	.01
☐ 450	Dave Kingman DP	.15	.06	.01
☐ 451	Indians Rookies	.15	.06	.01
	Chris Bando			
	Tom Brennan			
	Sandy Wihtol			
☐ 452	Renie Martin	.09	.04	.01
☐ 453	Rob Wilfong DP	.05	.02	.00
☐ 454	Andy Hassler	.09	.04	.01
☐ 455	Rick Burleson	.15	.06	.01

☐ 456	Jeff Reardon	6.00	2.50	.60
☐ 457	Mike Lum	.09	.04	.01
☐ 458	Randy Jones	.09	.04	.01
☐ 459	Greg Gross	.09	.04	.01
☐ 460	Rich Gossage	.35	.15	.03
☐ 461	Dave McKay	.09	.04	.01
☐ 462	Jack Brohamer	.09	.04	.01
☐ 463	Milt May	.09	.04	.01
☐ 464	Adrian Devine	.09	.04	.01
☐ 465	Bill Russell	.15	.06	.01
☐ 466	Bob Molinaro	.09	.04	.01
☐ 467	Dave Stieb	1.00	.40	.10
☐ 468	John Wockenfuss	.09	.04	.01
☐ 469	Jeff Leonard	.20	.08	.02
☐ 470	Manny Trillo	.09	.04	.01
☐ 471	Mike Vail	.09	.04	.01
☐ 472	Dyar Miller DP	.05	.02	.00
☐ 473	Jose Cardenal	.09	.04	.01
☐ 474	Mike LaCoss	.09	.04	.01
☐ 475	Buddy Bell	.15	.06	.01
☐ 476	Jerry Koosman	.15	.06	.01
☐ 477	Luis Gomez	.09	.04	.01
☐ 478	Juan Eichelberger	.09	.04	.01
☐ 479	Expos Rookies	9.00	4.00	.90
	Tim Raines			
	Roberto Ramos			
	Bobby Pate			
☐ 480	Carlton Fisk	2.50	1.00	.25
☐ 481	Bob Lacey DP	.05	.02	.00
☐ 482	Jim Gantner	.09	.04	.01
☐ 483	Mike Griffin	.09	.04	.01
☐ 484	Max Venable DP	.05	.02	.00
☐ 485	Garry Templeton	.15	.06	.01
☐ 486	Marc Hill	.09	.04	.01
☐ 487	Dewey Robinson	.09	.04	.01
☐ 488	Damaso Garcia	.15	.06	.01
☐ 489	John Littlefield	.09	.04	.01
☐ 490	Eddie Murray	3.75	1.60	.37
☐ 491	Gordy Pladson	.09	.04	.01
☐ 492	Barry Foote	.09	.04	.01
☐ 493	Dan Quisenberry	.35	.15	.03
☐ 494	Bob Walk	.35	.15	.03
☐ 495	Dusty Baker	.15	.06	.01
☐ 496	Paul Dade	.09	.04	.01
☐ 497	Fred Norman	.09	.04	.01
☐ 498	Pat Putnam	.09	.04	.01
☐ 499	Frank Pastore	.09	.04	.01
☐ 500	Jim Rice	.50	.20	.05
☐ 501	Tim Foli DP	.05	.02	.00
☐ 502	Giants Rookies	.09	.04	.01
	Chris Bourjos			
	Al Hargesheimer			
	Mike Rowland			
☐ 503	Steve McCatty	.09	.04	.01
☐ 504	Dale Murphy	1.75	.70	.17
☐ 505	Jason Thompson	.09	.04	.01
☐ 506	Phil Huffman	.09	.04	.01
☐ 507	Jamie Quirk	.09	.04	.01
☐ 508	Rob Dressler	.09	.04	.01
☐ 509	Pete Mackanin	.09	.04	.01
☐ 510	Lee Mazzilli	.09	.04	.01
☐ 511	Wayne Garland	.09	.04	.01
☐ 512	Gary Thomasson	.09	.04	.01
☐ 513	Frank LaCorte	.09	.04	.01
☐ 514	George Riley	.09	.04	.01
☐ 515	Robin Yount	4.00	1.75	.40
☐ 516	Doug Bird	.09	.04	.01
☐ 517	Richie Zisk	.09	.04	.01
☐ 518	Grant Jackson	.09	.04	.01
☐ 519	John Tamargo DP	.05	.02	.00
☐ 520	Steve Stone	.09	.04	.01
☐ 521	Sam Mejias	.09	.04	.01
☐ 522	Mike Colbern	.09	.04	.01
☐ 523	John Fulgham	.09	.04	.01
☐ 524	Willie Aikens	.09	.04	.01
☐ 525	Mike Torrez	.09	.04	.01
☐ 526	Phillies Rookies	.15	.06	.01
	Marty Bystrom			
	Jay Loviglio			
	Jim Wright			
☐ 527	Danny Goodwin	.09	.04	.01
☐ 528	Gary Matthews	.15	.06	.01
☐ 529	Dave LaRoche	.09	.04	.01
☐ 530	Steve Garvey	1.25	.50	.12
☐ 531	John Curtis	.09	.04	.01
☐ 532	Bill Stein	.09	.04	.01
☐ 533	Jesus Figueroa	.09	.04	.01
☐ 534	Dave Smith	.60	.25	.06
☐ 535	Omar Moreno	.09	.04	.01
☐ 536	Bob Owchinko DP	.05	.02	.00
☐ 537	Ron Hodges	.09	.04	.01
☐ 538	Tom Griffin	.09	.04	.01
☐ 539	Rodney Scott	.09	.04	.01
☐ 540	Mike Schmidt DP	2.50	1.00	.25
☐ 541	Steve Swisher	.09	.04	.01
☐ 542	Larry Bradford DP	.05	.02	.00
☐ 543	Terry Crowley	.09	.04	.01
☐ 544	Rich Gale	.09	.04	.01
☐ 545	Johnny Grubb	.09	.04	.01
☐ 546	Paul Moskau	.09	.04	.01
☐ 547	Mario Guerrero	.09	.04	.01
☐ 548	Dave Goltz	.09	.04	.01
☐ 549	Jerry Remy	.09	.04	.01
☐ 550	Tommy John	.35	.15	.03
☐ 551	Pirates Rookies	1.50	.60	.15
	Vance Law			
	Tony Pena			
	Pascual Perez			
☐ 552	Steve Trout	.09	.04	.01
☐ 553	Tim Blackwell	.09	.04	.01
☐ 554	Bert Blyleven UER	.50	.20	.05
	(1 is missing from			
	1980 on card back)			
☐ 555	Cecil Cooper	.20	.08	.02
☐ 556	Jerry Mumphrey	.09	.04	.01
☐ 557	Chris Knapp	.09	.04	.01
☐ 558	Barry Bonnell	.09	.04	.01
☐ 559	Willie Montanez	.09	.04	.01
☐ 560	Joe Morgan	1.25	.50	.12
☐ 561	Dennis Littlejohn	.09	.04	.01
☐ 562	Checklist 485-605	.25	.04	.01
☐ 563	Jim Kaat	.25	.10	.02
☐ 564	Ron Hassey DP	.09	.04	.01
☐ 565	Burt Hooton	.09	.04	.01
☐ 566	Del Unser	.09	.04	.01
☐ 567	Mark Bomback	.09	.04	.01
☐ 568	Dave Revering	.09	.04	.01
☐ 569	Al Williams DP	.05	.02	.00
☐ 570	Ken Singleton	.15	.06	.01
☐ 571	Todd Cruz	.09	.04	.01
☐ 572	Jack Morris	1.75	.70	.17
☐ 573	Phil Garner	.15	.06	.01
☐ 574	Bill Caudill	.09	.04	.01
☐ 575	Tony Perez	.50	.20	.05
☐ 576	Reggie Cleveland	.09	.04	.01
☐ 577	Blue Jays Rookies	.15	.06	.01
	Luis Leal			
	Brian Milner			
	Ken Schrom			
☐ 578	Bill Gullickson	.75	.30	.07
☐ 579	Tim Flannery	.09	.04	.01
☐ 580	Don Baylor	.25	.10	.02
☐ 581	Roy Howell	.09	.04	.01
☐ 582	Gaylord Perry	.75	.30	.07
☐ 583	Larry Milbourne	.09	.04	.01
☐ 584	Randy Lerch	.09	.04	.01
☐ 585	Amos Otis	.15	.06	.01
☐ 586	Silvio Martinez	.09	.04	.01
☐ 587	Jeff Newman	.09	.04	.01
☐ 588	Gary Lavelle	.09	.04	.01
☐ 589	Lamar Johnson	.09	.04	.01
☐ 590	Bruce Sutter	.25	.10	.02
☐ 591	John Lowenstein	.09	.04	.01
☐ 592	Steve Comer	.09	.04	.01
☐ 593	Steve Kemp	.09	.04	.01
☐ 594	Preston Hanna DP	.05	.02	.00
☐ 595	Butch Hobson	.15	.06	.01
☐ 596	Jerry Augustine	.09	.04	.01
☐ 597	Rafael Landestoy	.09	.04	.01
☐ 598	George Vukovich DP	.05	.02	.00
☐ 599	Dennis Kinney	.09	.04	.01
☐ 600	Johnny Bench	2.50	1.00	.25
☐ 601	Don Aase	.09	.04	.01
☐ 602	Bobby Murcer	.20	.08	.02
☐ 603	John Verhoeven	.09	.04	.01
☐ 604	Rob Picciolo	.09	.04	.01
☐ 605	Don Sutton	.75	.30	.07
☐ 606	Reds Rookies DP	.09	.04	.01
	Bruce Berenyi			
	Geoff Combe			
	Paul Householder			
☐ 607	David Palmer	.09	.04	.01
☐ 608	Greg Pryor	.09	.04	.01
☐ 609	Lynn McGlothen	.09	.04	.01
☐ 610	Darrell Porter	.09	.04	.01
☐ 611	Rick Matula DP	.05	.02	.00
☐ 612	Duane Kuiper	.09	.04	.01
☐ 613	Jim Anderson	.09	.04	.01
☐ 614	Dave Rozema	.09	.04	.01
☐ 615	Rick Dempsey	.09	.04	.01
☐ 616	Rick Wise	.09	.04	.01
☐ 617	Craig Reynolds	.09	.04	.01
☐ 618	John Milner	.09	.04	.01
☐ 619	Steve Henderson	.09	.04	.01
☐ 620	Dennis Eckersley	1.00	.40	.10
☐ 621	Tom Donohue	.09	.04	.01
☐ 622	Randy Moffitt	.09	.04	.01
☐ 623	Sal Bando	.15	.06	.01
☐ 624	Bob Welch	.65	.25	.06
☐ 625	Bill Buckner	.20	.08	.02

□ 626	Tigers Rookies	.15	.06	.01
	Dave Steffen			
	Jerry Ujdur			
	Roger Weaver			
□ 627	Luis Tiant	.15	.06	.01
□ 628	Vic Correll	.09	.04	.01
□ 629	Tony Armas	.09	.04	.01
□ 630	Steve Carlton	2.00	.80	.20
□ 631	Ron Jackson	.09	.04	.01
□ 632	Alan Bannister	.09	.04	.01
□ 633	Bill Lee	.09	.04	.01
□ 634	Doug Flynn	.09	.04	.01
□ 635	Bobby Bonds	.20	.08	.02
□ 636	Al Hrabosky	.09	.04	.01
□ 637	Jerry Narron	.09	.04	.01
□ 638	Checklist 606-726	.25	.04	.01
□ 639	Carney Lansford	.25	.10	.02
□ 640	Dave Parker	1.00	.40	.10
□ 641	Mark Belanger	.15	.06	.01
□ 642	Vern Ruhle	.09	.04	.01
□ 643	Lloyd Moseby	.50	.20	.05
□ 644	Ramon Aviles DP	.05	.02	.00
□ 645	Rick Reuschel	.20	.08	.02
□ 646	Marvis Foley	.09	.04	.01
□ 647	Dick Drago	.09	.04	.01
□ 648	Darrell Evans	.25	.10	.02
□ 649	Manny Sarmiento	.09	.04	.01
□ 650	Bucky Dent	.15	.06	.01
□ 651	Pedro Guerrero	1.00	.40	.10
□ 652	John Montague	.09	.04	.01
□ 653	Bill Fahey	.09	.04	.01
□ 654	Ray Burris	.09	.04	.01
□ 655	Dan Driessen	.09	.04	.01
□ 656	Jon Matlack	.09	.04	.01
□ 657	Mike Cubbage DP	.05	.02	.00
□ 658	Milt Wilcox	.09	.04	.01
□ 659	Brewers Rookies	.15	.06	.01
	John Flinn			
	Ed Romero			
	Ned Yost			
□ 660	Gary Carter	1.50	.60	.15
□ 661	Orioles Team/Mgr.	.25	.08	.02
	Earl Weaver			
	(checklist back)			
□ 662	Red Sox Team/Mgr.	.25	.08	.02
	Ralph Houk			
	(checklist back)			
□ 663	Angels Team/Mgr.	.25	.08	.02
	Jim Fregosi			
	(checklist back)			
□ 664	White Sox Team/Mgr.	.25	.08	.02
	Tony LaRussa			
	(checklist back)			
□ 665	Indians Team/Mgr.	.25	.08	.02
	Dave Garcia			
	(checklist back)			
□ 666	Tigers Team/Mgr.	.25	.08	.02
	Sparky Anderson			
	(checklist back)			
□ 667	Royals Team/Mgr.	.25	.08	.02
	Jim Frey			
	(checklist back)			
□ 668	Brewers Team/Mgr.	.25	.08	.02
	Bob Rodgers			
	(checklist back)			
□ 669	Twins Team/Mgr.	.25	.08	.02
	John Goryl			
	(checklist back)			
□ 670	Yankees Team/Mgr.	.25	.08	.02
	Gene Michael			
	(checklist back)			
□ 671	A's Team/Mgr.	.25	.08	.02
	Billy Martin			
	(checklist back)			
□ 672	Mariners Team/Mgr.	.25	.08	.02
	Maury Wills			
	(checklist back)			
□ 673	Rangers Team/Mgr.	.25	.08	.02
	Don Zimmer			
	(checklist back)			
□ 674	Blue Jays Team/Mgr.	.25	.08	.02
	Bobby Mattick			
	(checklist back)			
□ 675	Braves Team/Mgr.	.25	.08	.02
	Bobby Cox			
	(checklist back)			
□ 676	Cubs Team/Mgr.	.25	.08	.02
	Joe Amalfitano			
	(checklist back)			
□ 677	Reds Team/Mgr.	.25	.08	.02
	John McNamara			
	(checklist back)			
□ 678	Astros Team/Mgr.	.25	.08	.02
	Bill Virdon			
	(checklist back)			

□ 679	Dodgers Team/Mgr.	.25	.08	.02
	Tom Lasorda			
	(checklist back)			
□ 680	Expos Team/Mgr.	.25	.08	.02
	Dick Williams			
	(checklist back)			
□ 681	Mets Team/Mgr.	.25	.08	.02
	Joe Torre			
	(checklist back)			
□ 682	Phillies Team/Mgr.	.25	.08	.02
	Dallas Green			
	(checklist back)			
□ 683	Pirates Team/Mgr.	.25	.08	.02
	Chuck Tanner			
	(checklist back)			
□ 684	Cardinals Team/Mgr.	.25	.08	.02
	Whitey Herzog			
	(checklist back)			
□ 685	Padres Team/Mgr.	.25	.08	.02
	Frank Howard			
	(checklist back)			
□ 686	Giants Team/Mgr.	.25	.08	.02
	Dave Bristol			
	(checklist back)			
□ 687	Jeff Jones	.09	.04	.01
□ 688	Kiko Garcia	.09	.04	.01
□ 689	Red Sox Rookies	2.00	.80	.20
	Bruce Hurst			
	Keith MacWhorter			
	Reid Nichols			
□ 690	Bob Watson	.09	.04	.01
□ 691	Dick Ruthven	.09	.04	.01
□ 692	Lenny Randle	.09	.04	.01
□ 693	Steve Howe	.20	.08	.02
□ 694	Bud Harrelson DP	.09	.04	.01
□ 695	Kent Tekulve	.15	.06	.01
□ 696	Alan Ashby	.09	.04	.01
□ 697	Rick Waits	.09	.04	.01
□ 698	Mike Jorgensen	.09	.04	.01
□ 699	Glenn Abbott	.09	.04	.01
□ 700	George Brett	4.00	1.75	.40
□ 701	Joe Rudi	.15	.06	.01
□ 702	George Medich	.09	.04	.01
□ 703	Alvis Woods	.09	.04	.01
□ 704	Bill Travers DP	.05	.02	.00
□ 705	Ted Simmons	.25	.10	.02
□ 706	Dave Ford	.09	.04	.01
□ 707	Dave Cash	.09	.04	.01
□ 708	Doyle Alexander	.09	.04	.01
□ 709	Alan Trammell DP	.90	.40	.09
□ 710	Ron LeFlore DP	.09	.04	.01
□ 711	Joe Ferguson	.09	.04	.01
□ 712	Bill Bonham	.09	.04	.01
□ 713	Bill North	.09	.04	.01
□ 714	Pete Redfern	.09	.04	.01
□ 715	Bill Madlock	.15	.06	.01
□ 716	Glenn Borgmann	.09	.04	.01
□ 717	Jim Barr DP	.05	.02	.00
□ 718	Larry Biittner	.09	.04	.01
□ 719	Sparky Lyle	.15	.06	.01
□ 720	Fred Lynn	.25	.10	.02
□ 721	Toby Harrah	.15	.06	.01
□ 722	Joe Niekro	.15	.06	.01
□ 723	Bruce Bochte	.09	.04	.01
□ 724	Lou Piniella	.15	.06	.01
□ 725	Steve Rogers	.09	.04	.01
□ 726	Rick Monday	.20	.08	.02

1981 Topps Traded

The cards in this 132-card set measure 2 1/2" by 3 1/2". For the first time since 1976, Topps issued a "traded" set in 1981. Unlike the small traded sets of 1974 and 1976, this set contains a larger number of cards and was sequentially numbered, alphabetically, from 727 to 858. Thus, this set gives the impression it is a continuation of their regular issue of this year. The sets were issued only through hobby card dealers and were boxed in complete sets of 132 cards. There are no key rookie cards in this set.

		MINT	EXC	G-VG
COMPLETE SET (132)		32.00	14.00	3.00
COMMON PLAYER (727-858)		.10	.04	.01
□ 727	Danny Ainge	2.00	.80	.20
□ 728	Doyle Alexander	.15	.06	.01

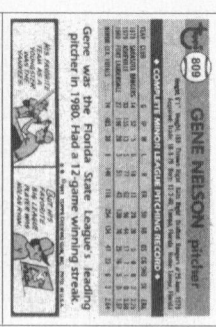

☐ 729	Gary Alexander	.10	.04	.01
☐ 730	Bill Almon	.10	.04	.01
☐ 731	Joaquin Andujar	.15	.06	.01
☐ 732	Bob Bailor	.10	.04	.01
☐ 733	Juan Beniquez	.10	.04	.01
☐ 734	Dave Bergman	.10	.04	.01
☐ 735	Tony Bernazard	.15	.06	.01
☐ 736	Larry Biittner	.10	.04	.01
☐ 737	Doug Bird	.10	.04	.01
☐ 738	Bert Blyleven	1.00	.40	.10
☐ 739	Mark Bomback	.10	.04	.01
☐ 740	Bobby Bonds	.25	.10	.02
☐ 741	Rick Bosetti	.10	.04	.01
☐ 742	Hubie Brooks	1.75	.70	.17
☐ 743	Rick Burleson	.15	.06	.01
☐ 744	Ray Burris	.10	.04	.01
☐ 745	Jeff Burroughs	.15	.06	.01
☐ 746	Enos Cabell	.10	.04	.01
☐ 747	Ken Clay	.10	.04	.01
☐ 748	Mark Clear	.10	.04	.01
☐ 749	Larry Cox	.10	.04	.01
☐ 750	Hector Cruz	.10	.04	.01
☐ 751	Victor Cruz	.10	.04	.01
☐ 752	Mike Cubbage	.10	.04	.01
☐ 753	Dick Davis	.10	.04	.01
☐ 754	Brian Doyle	.10	.04	.01
☐ 755	Dick Drago	.10	.04	.01
☐ 756	Leon Durham	.20	.08	.02
☐ 757	Jim Dwyer	.10	.04	.01
☐ 758	Dave Edwards	.10	.04	.01
☐ 759	Jim Essian	.20	.08	.02
☐ 760	Bill Fahey	.10	.04	.01
☐ 761	Rollie Fingers	2.50	1.00	.25
☐ 762	Carlton Fisk	5.50	2.50	.55
☐ 763	Barry Foote	.10	.04	.01
☐ 764	Ken Forsch	.10	.04	.01
☐ 765	Kiko Garcia	.10	.04	.01
☐ 766	Cesar Geronimo	.10	.04	.01
☐ 767	Gary Gray	.10	.04	.01
☐ 768	Mickey Hatcher	.15	.06	.01
☐ 769	Steve Henderson	.10	.04	.01
☐ 770	Marc Hill	.10	.04	.01
☐ 771	Butch Hobson	.20	.08	.02
☐ 772	Rick Honeycutt	.15	.06	.01
☐ 773	Roy Howell	.10	.04	.01
☐ 774	Mike Ivie	.10	.04	.01
☐ 775	Roy Lee Jackson	.10	.04	.01
☐ 776	Cliff Johnson	.10	.04	.01
☐ 777	Randy Jones	.15	.06	.01
☐ 778	Ruppert Jones	.10	.04	.01
☐ 779	Mick Kelleher	.10	.04	.01
☐ 780	Terry Kennedy	.20	.08	.02
☐ 781	Dave Kingman	.40	.16	.04
☐ 782	Bob Knepper	.10	.04	.01
☐ 783	Ken Kravec	.10	.04	.01
☐ 784	Bob Lacey	.10	.04	.01
☐ 785	Dennis Lamp	.10	.04	.01
☐ 786	Rafael Landestoy	.10	.04	.01
☐ 787	Ken Landreaux	.15	.06	.01
☐ 788	Carney Lansford	.65	.25	.06
☐ 789	Dave LaRoche	.10	.04	.01
☐ 790	Joe Lefebvre	.10	.04	.01
☐ 791	Ron LeFlore	.15	.06	.01
☐ 792	Randy Lerch	.10	.04	.01
☐ 793	Sixto Lezcano	.10	.04	.01
☐ 794	John Littlefield	.10	.04	.01
☐ 795	Mike Lum	.10	.04	.01
☐ 796	Greg Luzinski	.25	.10	.02
☐ 797	Fred Lynn	.60	.25	.06
☐ 798	Jerry Martin	.10	.04	.01
☐ 799	Buck Martinez	.10	.04	.01
☐ 800	Gary Matthews	.15	.06	.01

☐ 801	Mario Mendoza	.10	.04	.01
☐ 802	Larry Milbourne	.10	.04	.01
☐ 803	Rick Miller	.10	.04	.01
☐ 804	John Montefusco	.10	.04	.01
☐ 805	Jerry Morales	.10	.04	.01
☐ 806	Jose Morales	.10	.04	.01
☐ 807	Joe Morgan	2.50	1.00	.25
☐ 808	Jerry Mumphrey	.10	.04	.01
☐ 809	Gene Nelson	.20	.08	.02
☐ 810	Ed Ott	.10	.04	.01
☐ 811	Bob Owchinko	.10	.04	.01
☐ 812	Gaylord Perry	1.75	.70	.17
☐ 813	Mike Phillips	.10	.04	.01
☐ 814	Darrell Porter	.15	.06	.01
☐ 815	Mike Proly	.10	.04	.01
☐ 816	Tim Raines	12.00	5.25	1.50
☐ 817	Lenny Randle	.10	.04	.01
☐ 818	Doug Rau	.10	.04	.01
☐ 819	Jeff Reardon	5.50	2.50	.55
☐ 820	Ken Reitz	.10	.04	.01
☐ 821	Steve Renko	.10	.04	.01
☐ 822	Rick Reuschel	.30	.12	.03
☐ 823	Dave Revering	.10	.04	.01
☐ 824	Dave Roberts	.10	.04	.01
☐ 825	Leon Roberts	.10	.04	.01
☐ 826	Joe Rudi	.15	.06	.01
☐ 827	Kevin Saucier	.10	.04	.01
☐ 828	Tony Scott	.10	.04	.01
☐ 829	Bob Shirley	.10	.04	.01
☐ 830	Ted Simmons	.50	.20	.05
☐ 831	Lary Sorensen	.10	.04	.01
☐ 832	Jim Spencer	.10	.04	.01
☐ 833	Harry Spilman	.10	.04	.01
☐ 834	Fred Stanley	.10	.04	.01
☐ 835	Rusty Staub	.30	.12	.03
☐ 836	Bill Stein	.10	.04	.01
☐ 837	Joe Strain	.10	.04	.01
☐ 838	Bruce Sutter	.50	.20	.05
☐ 839	Don Sutton	1.75	.70	.17
☐ 840	Steve Swisher	.10	.04	.01
☐ 841	Frank Tanana	.25	.10	.02
☐ 842	Gene Tenace	.15	.06	.01
☐ 843	Jason Thompson	.10	.04	.01
☐ 844	Dickie Thon	.35	.15	.03
☐ 845	Bill Travers	.10	.04	.01
☐ 846	Tom Underwood	.10	.04	.01
☐ 847	John Urrea	.10	.04	.01
☐ 848	Mike Vail	.10	.04	.01
☐ 849	Ellis Valentine	.10	.04	.01
☐ 850	Fernando Valenzuela	4.00	1.75	.40
☐ 851	Pete Vuckovich	.15	.06	.01
☐ 852	Mark Wagner	.10	.04	.01
☐ 853	Bob Walk	.30	.12	.03
☐ 854	Claudell Washington	.20	.08	.02
☐ 855	Dave Winfield	5.00	2.25	.50
☐ 856	Geoff Zahn	.10	.04	.01
☐ 857	Richie Zisk	.15	.06	.01
☐ 858	Checklist 727-858	.10	.01	.00

1982 Topps

The cards in this 792-card set measure 2 1/2" by 3 1/2". The 1982 baseball series is the largest set Topps has ever issued at one printing. The 66-card increase from the previous year's total eliminated the "double print" practice, that had occurred in every regular issue since 1978. Cards 1-6 depict Highlights

(HL) of the 1981 season, cards 161-168 picture League Leaders, and there are mini-series of AL (547-557) and NL (337-347) All-Stars (AS). The abbreviation "SA" in the checklist is given for the 40 "Super Action" cards introduced in this set. The team cards are actually Team Leader (TL) cards picturing the batting and pitching leader for that team with a checklist back. The key rookie cards in this set are George Bell, Cal Ripken Jr., Steve Sax, Lee Smith, and Dave Stewart.

		MINT	EXC	G-VG
COMPLETE SET (792)		140.00	63.00	21.00
COMMON PLAYER (1-792)		.08	.03	.01
☐ 1	HL: Steve Carlton Sets new NL strikeout record	.60	.15	.03
☐ 2	HL: Ron Davis Fans 8 straight in relief	.08	.03	.01
☐ 3	HL: Tim Raines Swipes 71 bases as rookie	.35	.15	.03
☐ 4	HL: Pete Rose Sets NL career hits mark	.75	.30	.07
☐ 5	HL: Nolan Ryan Pitches fifth career no-hitter	2.25	.90	.22
☐ 6	HL: Fern. Valenzuela 8 shutouts as rookie	.20	.08	.02
☐ 7	Scott Sanderson	.15	.06	.01
☐ 8	Rich Dauer	.08	.03	.01
☐ 9	Ron Guidry	.35	.15	.03
☐ 10	SA: Ron Guidry	.20	.08	.02
☐ 11	Gary Alexander	.08	.03	.01
☐ 12	Moose Haas	.08	.03	.01
☐ 13	Lamar Johnson	.08	.03	.01
☐ 14	Steve Howe	.08	.03	.01
☐ 15	Ellis Valentine	.08	.03	.01
☐ 16	Steve Comer	.08	.03	.01
☐ 17	Darrell Evans	.15	.06	.01
☐ 18	Fernando Arroyo	.08	.03	.01
☐ 19	Ernie Whitt	.08	.03	.01
☐ 20	Garry Maddox	.08	.03	.01
☐ 21	Orioles Rookies Bob Bonner Cal Ripken Jeff Schneider	65.00	29.00	9.75
☐ 22	Jim Beattie	.08	.03	.01
☐ 23	Willie Hernandez	.15	.06	.01
☐ 24	Dave Frost	.08	.03	.01
☐ 25	Jerry Remy	.08	.03	.01
☐ 26	Jorge Orta	.08	.03	.01
☐ 27	Tom Herr	.15	.06	.01
☐ 28	John Urrea	.08	.03	.01
☐ 29	Dwayne Murphy	.08	.03	.01
☐ 30	Tom Seaver	1.75	.70	.17
☐ 31	SA: Tom Seaver	.80	.35	.08
☐ 32	Gene Garber	.08	.03	.01
☐ 33	Jerry Morales	.08	.03	.01
☐ 34	Joe Sambito	.08	.03	.01
☐ 35	Willie Aikens	.08	.03	.01
☐ 36	Rangers TL Batting: Al Oliver Pitching: Doc Medich	.20	.05	.01
☐ 37	Dan Graham	.08	.03	.01
☐ 38	Charlie Lea	.08	.03	.01
☐ 39	Lou Whitaker	.60	.25	.06
☐ 40	Dave Parker	.80	.35	.08
☐ 41	SA: Dave Parker	.35	.15	.03
☐ 42	Rick Sofield	.08	.03	.01
☐ 43	Mike Cubbage	.08	.03	.01
☐ 44	Britt Burns	.08	.03	.01
☐ 45	Rick Cerone	.08	.03	.01
☐ 46	Jerry Augustine	.08	.03	.01
☐ 47	Jeff Leonard	.08	.03	.01
☐ 48	Bobby Castillo	.08	.03	.01
☐ 49	Alvis Woods	.08	.03	.01
☐ 50	Buddy Bell	.15	.06	.01
☐ 51	Cubs Rookies Jay Howell Carlos Lezcano Ty Waller	.35	.15	.03
☐ 52	Larry Andersen	.08	.03	.01
☐ 53	Greg Gross	.08	.03	.01
☐ 54	Ron Hassey	.08	.03	.01
☐ 55	Rick Burleson	.08	.03	.01
☐ 56	Mark Littell	.08	.03	.01
☐ 57	Craig Reynolds	.08	.03	.01
☐ 58	John D'Acquisto	.08	.03	.01
☐ 59	Rich Gedman	.25	.10	.02

☐ 60	Tony Armas	.08	.03	.01
☐ 61	Tommy Boggs	.08	.03	.01
☐ 62	Mike Tyson	.08	.03	.01
☐ 63	Mario Soto	.08	.03	.01
☐ 64	Lynn Jones	.08	.03	.01
☐ 65	Terry Kennedy	.08	.03	.01
☐ 66	Astros TL Batting: Art Howe Pitching: Nolan Ryan	.60	.20	.04
☐ 67	Rich Gale	.08	.03	.01
☐ 68	Roy Howell	.08	.03	.01
☐ 69	Al Williams	.08	.03	.01
☐ 70	Tim Raines	2.00	.80	.20
☐ 71	Roy Lee Jackson	.08	.03	.01
☐ 72	Rick Auerbach	.08	.03	.01
☐ 73	Buddy Solomon	.08	.03	.01
☐ 74	Bob Clark	.08	.03	.01
☐ 75	Tommy John	.30	.12	.03
☐ 76	Greg Pryor	.08	.03	.01
☐ 77	Miguel Dilone	.08	.03	.01
☐ 78	George Medich	.08	.03	.01
☐ 79	Bob Bailor	.08	.03	.01
☐ 80	Jim Palmer	1.50	.60	.15
☐ 81	SA: Jim Palmer	.75	.30	.07
☐ 82	Bob Welch	.50	.20	.05
☐ 83	Yankees Rookies Steve Balboni Andy McGaffigan Andre Robertson	.15	.06	.01
☐ 84	Rennie Stennett	.08	.03	.01
☐ 85	Lynn McGlothen	.08	.03	.01
☐ 86	Dane Iorg	.08	.03	.01
☐ 87	Matt Keough	.08	.03	.01
☐ 88	Biff Pocoroba	.08	.03	.01
☐ 89	Steve Henderson	.08	.03	.01
☐ 90	Nolan Ryan	7.50	3.25	.75
☐ 91	Carney Lansford	.25	.10	.02
☐ 92	Brad Havens	.08	.03	.01
☐ 93	Larry Hisle	.08	.03	.01
☐ 94	Andy Hassler	.08	.03	.01
☐ 95	Ozzie Smith	2.25	.90	.22
☐ 96	Royals TL Batting: George Brett Pitching: Larry Gura	.30	.10	.02
☐ 97	Paul Moskau	.08	.03	.01
☐ 98	Terry Bulling	.08	.03	.01
☐ 99	Barry Bonnell	.08	.03	.01
☐ 100	Mike Schmidt	3.50	1.50	.35
☐ 101	SA: Mike Schmidt	1.50	.60	.15
☐ 102	Dan Briggs	.08	.03	.01
☐ 103	Bob Lacey	.08	.03	.01
☐ 104	Rance Mulliniks	.08	.03	.01
☐ 105	Kirk Gibson	1.25	.50	.12
☐ 106	Enrique Romo	.08	.03	.01
☐ 107	Wayne Krenchicki	.08	.03	.01
☐ 108	Bob Sykes	.08	.03	.01
☐ 109	Dave Revering	.08	.03	.01
☐ 110	Carlton Fisk	1.75	.70	.17
☐ 111	SA: Carlton Fisk	.90	.40	.09
☐ 112	Billy Sample	.08	.03	.01
☐ 113	Steve McCatty	.08	.03	.01
☐ 114	Ken Landreaux	.08	.03	.01
☐ 115	Gaylord Perry	.60	.25	.06
☐ 116	Jim Wohlford	.08	.03	.01
☐ 117	Rawly Eastwick	.08	.03	.01
☐ 118	Expos Rookies Terry Francona Brad Mills Bryn Smith	.50	.20	.05
☐ 119	Joe Pittman	.08	.03	.01
☐ 120	Gary Lucas	.08	.03	.01
☐ 121	Ed Lynch	.08	.03	.01
☐ 122	Jamie Easterly UER (photo actually Reggie Cleveland)	.08	.03	.01
☐ 123	Danny Goodwin	.08	.03	.01
☐ 124	Reid Nichols	.08	.03	.01
☐ 125	Danny Ainge	.75	.30	.07
☐ 126	Braves TL Batting: C.Washington Pitching: Rick Mahler	.20	.08	.01
☐ 127	Lonnie Smith	.30	.12	.03
☐ 128	Frank Pastore	.08	.03	.01
☐ 129	Checklist 1-132	.15	.02	.00
☐ 130	Julio Cruz	.08	.03	.01
☐ 131	Stan Bahnsen	.08	.03	.01
☐ 132	Lee May	.08	.03	.01
☐ 133	Pat Underwood	.08	.03	.01
☐ 134	Dan Ford	.08	.03	.01
☐ 135	Andy Rincon	.08	.03	.01
☐ 136	Lenn Sakata	.08	.03	.01
☐ 137	George Cappuzzello	.08	.03	.01
☐ 138	Tony Pena	.30	.12	.03
☐ 139	Jeff Jones	.08	.03	.01

☐ 140	Ron LeFlore	.08	.03	.01
☐ 141	Indians Rookies	1.00	.40	.10
	Chris Bando			
	Tom Brennan			
	Von Hayes			
☐ 142	Dave LaRoche	.08	.03	.01
☐ 143	Mookie Wilson	.20	.08	.02
☐ 144	Fred Breining	.08	.03	.01
☐ 145	Bob Horner	.15	.06	.01
☐ 146	Mike Griffin	.08	.03	.01
☐ 147	Denny Walling	.08	.03	.01
☐ 148	Mickey Klutts	.08	.03	.01
☐ 149	Pat Putnam	.08	.03	.01
☐ 150	Ted Simmons	.20	.08	.02
☐ 151	Dave Edwards	.08	.03	.01
☐ 152	Ramon Aviles	.08	.03	.01
☐ 153	Roger Erickson	.08	.03	.01
☐ 154	Dennis Werth	.08	.03	.01
☐ 155	Otto Velez	.08	.03	.01
☐ 156	Oakland A's TL	.75	.25	.05
	Batting: R.Henderson			
	Pitching: S. McCatty			
☐ 157	Steve Crawford	.08	.03	.01
☐ 158	Brian Downing	.15	.06	.01
☐ 159	Larry Biittner	.08	.03	.01
☐ 160	Luis Tiant	.15	.06	.01
☐ 161	Batting Leaders	.15	.06	.01
	Bill Madlock			
	Carney Lansford			
☐ 162	Home Run Leaders	.35	.15	.03
	Mike Schmidt			
	Tony Armas			
	Dwight Evans			
	Bobby Grich			
	Eddie Murray			
☐ 163	RBI Leaders	.60	.25	.06
	Mike Schmidt			
	Eddie Murray			
☐ 164	Stolen Base Leaders	1.50	.60	.15
	Tim Raines			
	Rickey Henderson			
☐ 165	Victory Leaders	.20	.08	.02
	Tom Seaver			
	Denny Martinez			
	Steve McCatty			
	Jack Morris			
	Pete Vuckovich			
☐ 166	Strikeout Leaders	.15	.06	.01
	Fernando Valenzuela			
	Len Barker			
☐ 167	ERA Leaders	.90	.40	.09
	Nolan Ryan			
	Steve McCatty			
☐ 168	Leading Firemen	.20	.08	.02
	Bruce Sutter			
	Rollie Fingers			
☐ 169	Charlie Leibrandt	.15	.06	.01
☐ 170	Jim Bibby	.08	.03	.01
☐ 171	Giants Rookies	2.50	1.00	.25
	Bob Brenly			
	Chili Davis			
	Bob Tufts			
☐ 172	Bill Gullickson	.20	.08	.02
☐ 173	Jamie Quirk	.08	.03	.01
☐ 174	Dave Ford	.08	.03	.01
☐ 175	Jerry Mumphrey	.08	.03	.01
☐ 176	Dewey Robinson	.08	.03	.01
☐ 177	John Ellis	.08	.03	.01
☐ 178	Dyar Miller	.08	.03	.01
☐ 179	Steve Garvey	.90	.40	.09
☐ 180	SA: Steve Garvey	.45	.18	.04
☐ 181	Silvio Martinez	.08	.03	.01
☐ 182	Larry Herndon	.08	.03	.01
☐ 183	Mike Proly	.08	.03	.01
☐ 184	Mick Kelleher	.08	.03	.01
☐ 185	Phil Niekro	.60	.25	.06
☐ 186	Cardinals TL	.20	.05	.01
	Batting: K. Hernandez			
	Pitching: Bob Forsch			
☐ 187	Jeff Newman	.08	.03	.01
☐ 188	Randy Martz	.08	.03	.01
☐ 189	Glenn Hoffman	.08	.03	.01
☐ 190	J.R. Richard	.15	.06	.01
☐ 191	Tim Wallach	1.75	.70	.17
☐ 192	Broderick Perkins	.08	.03	.01
☐ 193	Darrell Jackson	.08	.03	.01
☐ 194	Mike Vail	.08	.03	.01
☐ 195	Paul Molitor	.75	.30	.07
☐ 196	Willie Upshaw	.08	.03	.01
☐ 197	Shane Rawley	.08	.03	.01
☐ 198	Chris Speier	.08	.03	.01
☐ 199	Don Aase	.08	.03	.01
☐ 200	George Brett	2.75	1.10	.27
☐ 201	SA: George Brett	1.25	.50	.12

☐ 202	Rick Manning	.08	.03	.01
☐ 203	Blue Jays Rookies	1.75	.70	.17
	Jesse Barfield			
	Brian Milner			
	Boomer Wells			
☐ 204	Gary Roenicke	.08	.03	.01
☐ 205	Neil Allen	.08	.03	.01
☐ 206	Tony Bernazard	.08	.03	.01
☐ 207	Rod Scurry	.08	.03	.01
☐ 208	Bobby Murcer	.15	.06	.01
☐ 209	Gary Lavelle	.08	.03	.01
☐ 210	Keith Hernandez	.40	.16	.04
☐ 211	Dan Petry	.08	.03	.01
☐ 212	Mario Mendoza	.08	.03	.01
☐ 213	Dave Stewart	7.50	3.25	.75
☐ 214	Brian Asselstine	.08	.03	.01
☐ 215	Mike Krukow	.08	.03	.01
☐ 216	White Sox TL	.20	.05	.01
	Batting: Chet Lemon			
	Pitching: Dennis Lamp			
☐ 217	Bo McLaughlin	.08	.03	.01
☐ 218	Dave Roberts	.08	.03	.01
☐ 219	John Curtis	.08	.03	.01
☐ 220	Manny Trillo	.08	.03	.01
☐ 221	Jim Slaton	.08	.03	.01
☐ 222	Butch Wynegar	.08	.03	.01
☐ 223	Lloyd Moseby	.15	.06	.01
☐ 224	Bruce Bochte	.08	.03	.01
☐ 225	Mike Torrez	.08	.03	.01
☐ 226	Checklist 133-264	.15	.02	.00
☐ 227	Ray Burris	.08	.03	.01
☐ 228	Sam Mejias	.08	.03	.01
☐ 229	Geoff Zahn	.08	.03	.01
☐ 230	Willie Wilson	.20	.08	.02
☐ 231	Phillies Rookies	.40	.16	.04
	Mark Davis			
	Bob Dernier			
	Ozzie Virgil			
☐ 232	Terry Crowley	.08	.03	.01
☐ 233	Duane Kuiper	.08	.03	.01
☐ 234	Ron Hodges	.08	.03	.01
☐ 235	Mike Easler	.08	.03	.01
☐ 236	John Martin	.08	.03	.01
☐ 237	Rusty Kuntz	.08	.03	.01
☐ 238	Kevin Saucier	.08	.03	.01
☐ 239	Jon Matlack	.08	.03	.01
☐ 240	Bucky Dent	.15	.06	.01
☐ 241	SA: Bucky Dent	.08	.03	.01
☐ 242	Milt May	.08	.03	.01
☐ 243	Bob Owchinko	.08	.03	.01
☐ 244	Rufino Linares	.08	.03	.01
☐ 245	Ken Reitz	.08	.03	.01
☐ 246	New York Mets TL	.20	.05	.01
	Batting: Hubie Brooks			
	Pitching: Mike Scott			
☐ 247	Pedro Guerrero	.60	.25	.06
☐ 248	Frank LaCorte	.08	.03	.01
☐ 249	Tim Flannery	.08	.03	.01
☐ 250	Tug McGraw	.15	.06	.01
☐ 251	Fred Lynn	.30	.12	.03
☐ 252	SA: Fred Lynn	.15	.06	.01
☐ 253	Chuck Baker	.08	.03	.01
☐ 254	Jorge Bell	11.00	5.00	1.35
☐ 255	Tony Perez	.45	.18	.04
☐ 256	SA: Tony Perez	.20	.08	.02
☐ 257	Larry Harlow	.08	.03	.01
☐ 258	Bo Diaz	.08	.03	.01
☐ 259	Rodney Scott	.08	.03	.01
☐ 260	Bruce Sutter	.20	.08	.02
☐ 261	Tigers Rookies UER	.15	.06	.01
	Howard Bailey			
	Marty Castillo			
	Dave Rucker			
	(Rucker photo act-			
	ally Roger Weaver)			
☐ 262	Doug Bair	.08	.03	.01
☐ 263	Victor Cruz	.08	.03	.01
☐ 264	Dan Quisenberry	.25	.10	.02
☐ 265	Al Bumbry	.08	.03	.01
☐ 266	Rick Leach	.08	.03	.01
☐ 267	Kurt Bevacqua	.08	.03	.01
☐ 268	Rickey Keeton	.08	.03	.01
☐ 269	Jim Essian	.15	.06	.01
☐ 270	Rusty Staub	.20	.08	.02
☐ 271	Larry Bradford	.08	.03	.01
☐ 272	Bump Wills	.08	.03	.01
☐ 273	Doug Bird	.08	.03	.01
☐ 274	Bob Ojeda	.75	.30	.07
☐ 275	Bob Watson	.08	.03	.01
☐ 276	Angels TL	.25	.07	.02
	Batting: Rod Carew			
	Pitching: Ken Forsch			
☐ 277	Terry Puhl	.08	.03	.01
☐ 278	John Littlefield	.08	.03	.01

☐	279	Bill Russell	.15	.06	.01	☐	354	Roberto Ramos	.08	.03	.01
☐	280	Ben Oglivie	.08	.03	.01	☐	355	Dwight Evans	.35	.15	.03
☐	281	John Verhoeven	.08	.03	.01	☐	356	Denny Lewallyn	.08	.03	.01
☐	282	Ken Macha	.08	.03	.01	☐	357	Butch Hobson	.15	.06	.01
☐	283	Brian Allard	.08	.03	.01	☐	358	Mike Parrott	.08	.03	.01
☐	284	Bob Grich	.15	.06	.01	☐	359	Jim Dwyer	.08	.03	.01
☐	285	Sparky Lyle	.15	.06	.01	☐	360	Len Barker	.08	.03	.01
☐	286	Bill Fahey	.08	.03	.01	☐	361	Rafael Landestoy	.08	.03	.01
☐	287	Alan Bannister	.08	.03	.01	☐	362	Jim Wright UER	.08	.03	.01
☐	288	Garry Templeton	.15	.06	.01			(wrong Jim Wright			
☐	289	Bob Stanley	.08	.03	.01			pictured)			
☐	290	Ken Singleton	.15	.06	.01	☐	363	Bob Molinaro	.08	.03	.01
☐	291	Pirates Rookies	.30	.12	.03	☐	364	Doyle Alexander	.08	.03	.01
		Vance Law				☐	365	Bill Madlock	.15	.06	.01
		Bob Long				☐	366	Padres TL	.15	.05	.01
		Johnny Ray						Batting: Luis Salazar			
☐	292	David Palmer	.08	.03	.01			Pitching: Eichelberger			
☐	293	Rob Picciolo	.08	.03	.01	☐	367	Jim Kaat	.20	.08	.02
☐	294	Mike LaCoss	.08	.03	.01	☐	368	Alex Trevino	.08	.03	.01
☐	295	Jason Thompson	.08	.03	.01	☐	369	Champ Summers	.08	.03	.01
☐	296	Bob Walk	.08	.03	.01	☐	370	Mike Norris	.08	.03	.01
☐	297	Clint Hurdle	.08	.03	.01	☐	371	Jerry Don Gleaton	.08	.03	.01
☐	298	Danny Darwin	.08	.03	.01	☐	372	Luis Gomez	.08	.03	.01
☐	299	Steve Trout	.08	.03	.01	☐	373	Gene Nelson	.15	.06	.01
☐	300	Reggie Jackson	2.50	1.00	.25	☐	374	Tim Blackwell	.08	.03	.01
☐	301	SA: Reggie Jackson	1.25	.50	.12	☐	375	Dusty Baker	.15	.06	.01
☐	302	Doug Flynn	.08	.03	.01	☐	376	Chris Welsh	.08	.03	.01
☐	303	Bill Caudill	.08	.03	.01	☐	377	Kiko Garcia	.08	.03	.01
☐	304	Johnnie LeMaster	.08	.03	.01	☐	378	Mike Caldwell	.08	.03	.01
☐	305	Don Sutton	.60	.25	.06	☐	379	Rob Wilfong	.08	.03	.01
☐	306	SA: Don Sutton	.30	.12	.03	☐	380	Dave Stieb	.60	.25	.06
☐	307	Randy Bass	.08	.03	.01	☐	381	Red Sox Rookies	.60	.25	.06
☐	308	Charlie Moore	.08	.03	.01			Bruce Hurst			
☐	309	Pete Redfern	.08	.03	.01			Dave Schmidt			
☐	310	Mike Hargrove	.15	.06	.01			Julio Valdez			
☐	311	Dodgers TL	.20	.05	.01	☐	382	Joe Simpson	.08	.03	.01
		Batting: Dusty Baker				☐	383A	Pascual Perez ERR	30.00	13.50	4.50
		Pitching: Burt Hooton						(no position			
☐	312	Lenny Randle	.08	.03	.01			on front)			
☐	313	John Harris	.08	.03	.01	☐	383B	Pascual Perez COR	.15	.06	.01
☐	314	Buck Martinez	.08	.03	.01	☐	384	Keith Moreland	.08	.03	.01
☐	315	Burt Hooton	.08	.03	.01	☐	385	Ken Forsch	.08	.03	.01
☐	316	Steve Braun	.08	.03	.01	☐	386	Jerry White	.08	.03	.01
☐	317	Dick Ruthven	.08	.03	.01	☐	387	Tom Veryzer	.08	.03	.01
☐	318	Mike Heath	.08	.03	.01	☐	388	Joe Rudi	.15	.06	.01
☐	319	Dave Rozema	.08	.03	.01	☐	389	George Vukovich	.08	.03	.01
☐	320	Chris Chambliss	.15	.06	.01	☐	390	Eddie Murray	2.25	.90	.22
☐	321	SA: Chris Chambliss	.08	.03	.01	☐	391	Dave Tobik	.08	.03	.01
☐	322	Garry Hancock	.08	.03	.01	☐	392	Rick Bosetti	.08	.03	.01
☐	323	Bill Lee	.08	.03	.01	☐	393	Al Hrabosky	.08	.03	.01
☐	324	Steve Dillard	.08	.03	.01	☐	394	Checklist 265-396	.15	.02	.00
☐	325	Jose Cruz	.15	.06	.01	☐	395	Omar Moreno	.08	.03	.01
☐	326	Pete Falcone	.08	.03	.01	☐	396	Twins TL	.15	.05	.01
☐	327	Joe Nolan	.08	.03	.01			Batting: John Castino			
☐	328	Ed Farmer	.08	.03	.01			Pitching: F. Arroyo			
☐	329	U.L. Washington	.08	.03	.01	☐	397	Ken Brett	.08	.03	.01
☐	330	Rick Wise	.08	.03	.01	☐	398	Mike Squires	.08	.03	.01
☐	331	Benny Ayala	.08	.03	.01	☐	399	Pat Zachry	.08	.03	.01
☐	332	Don Robinson	.08	.03	.01	☐	400	Johnny Bench	1.75	.70	.17
☐	333	Brewers Rookies	.15	.06	.01	☐	401	SA: Johnny Bench	.80	.35	.08
		Frank DiPino				☐	402	Bill Stein	.08	.03	.01
		Marshall Edwards				☐	403	Jim Tracy	.08	.03	.01
		Chuck Porter				☐	404	Dickie Thon	.15	.06	.01
☐	334	Aurelio Rodriguez	.08	.03	.01	☐	405	Rick Reuschel	.15	.06	.01
☐	335	Jim Sundberg	.08	.03	.01	☐	406	Al Holland	.08	.03	.01
☐	336	Mariners TL	.15	.05	.01	☐	407	Danny Boone	.08	.03	.01
		Batting: Tom Paciorek				☐	408	Ed Romero	.08	.03	.01
		Pitching: Glenn Abbott				☐	409	Don Cooper	.08	.03	.01
☐	337	Pete Rose AS	.75	.30	.07	☐	410	Ron Cey	.15	.06	.01
☐	338	Dave Lopes AS	.08	.03	.01	☐	411	SA: Ron Cey	.08	.03	.01
☐	339	Mike Schmidt AS	.90	.40	.09	☐	412	Luis Leal	.08	.03	.01
☐	340	Dave Concepcion AS	.15	.06	.01	☐	413	Dan Meyer	.08	.03	.01
☐	341	Andre Dawson AS	.50	.20	.05	☐	414	Elias Sosa	.08	.03	.01
☐	342A	George Foster AS	.20	.08	.02	☐	415	Don Baylor	.15	.06	.01
		(with autograph)				☐	416	Marty Bystrom	.08	.03	.01
☐	342B	George Foster AS	1.50	.60	.15	☐	417	Pat Kelly	.08	.03	.01
		(w/o autograph)				☐	418	Rangers Rookies	.20	.08	.02
☐	343	Dave Parker AS	.25	.10	.02			John Butcher			
☐	344	Gary Carter AS	.25	.10	.02			Bobby Johnson			
☐	345	Fern. Valenzuela AS	.15	.06	.01			Dave Schmidt			
☐	346A	Tom Seaver AS ERR	1.00	.40	.10	☐	419	Steve Stone	.08	.03	.01
		("t ed")				☐	420	George Hendrick	.08	.03	.01
☐	346B	Tom Seaver AS COR	.50	.20	.05	☐	421	Mark Clear	.08	.03	.01
		("tied")				☐	422	Cliff Johnson	.08	.03	.01
☐	347	Bruce Sutter AS	.15	.06	.01	☐	423	Stan Papi	.08	.03	.01
☐	348	Derrel Thomas	.08	.03	.01	☐	424	Bruce Benedict	.08	.03	.01
☐	349	George Frazier	.08	.03	.01	☐	425	John Candelaria	.08	.03	.01
☐	350	Thad Bosley	.08	.03	.01	☐	426	Orioles TL	.25	.07	.02
☐	351	Reds Rookies	.15	.06	.01			Batting: Eddie Murray			
		Scott Brown						Pitching: Sam Stewart			
		Geoff Coumbe				☐	427	Ron Oester	.08	.03	.01
		Paul Householder				☐	428	LaMarr Hoyt	.08	.03	.01
☐	352	Dick Davis	.08	.03	.01	☐	429	John Wathan	.08	.03	.01
☐	353	Jack O'Connor	.08	.03	.01	☐	430	Vida Blue	.15	.06	.01

☐ 431	SA: Vida Blue	.08	.03	.01	☐ 510	Fernando Valenzuela	.60	.25	.06
☐ 432	Mike Scott	.40	.16	.04	☐ 511	Ruppert Jones	.08	.03	.01
☐ 433	Alan Ashby	.08	.03	.01	☐ 512	Jerry Dybzinski	.08	.03	.01
☐ 434	Joe Lefebvre	.08	.03	.01	☐ 513	Rick Rhoden	.08	.03	.01
☐ 435	Robin Yount	2.75	1.10	.27	☐ 514	Joe Ferguson	.08	.03	.01
☐ 436	Joe Strain	.08	.03	.01	☐ 515	Larry Bowa	.15	.06	.01
☐ 437	Juan Berenguer	.08	.03	.01	☐ 516	SA: Larry Bowa	.08	.03	.01
☐ 438	Pete Mackanin	.08	.03	.01	☐ 517	Mark Brouhard	.08	.03	.01
☐ 439	Dave Righetti	2.00	.80	.20	☐ 518	Garth Iorg	.08	.03	.01
☐ 440	Jeff Burroughs	.08	.03	.01	☐ 519	Glenn Adams	.08	.03	.01
☐ 441	Astros Rookies	.15	.06	.01	☐ 520	Mike Flanagan	.15	.06	.01
	Danny Heep				☐ 521	Bill Almon	.08	.03	.01
	Billy Smith				☐ 522	Chuck Rainey	.08	.03	.01
	Bobby Sprowl				☐ 523	Gary Gray	.08	.03	.01
☐ 442	Bruce Kison	.08	.03	.01	☐ 524	Tom Hausman	.08	.03	.01
☐ 443	Mark Wagner	.08	.03	.01	☐ 525	Ray Knight	.15	.06	.01
☐ 444	Terry Forster	.15	.06	.01	☐ 526	Expos TL	.15	.05	.01
☐ 445	Larry Parrish	.08	.03	.01		Batting: W.Cromartie			
☐ 446	Wayne Garland	.08	.03	.01		Pitching: B.Gullickson			
☐ 447	Darrell Porter	.08	.03	.01	☐ 527	John Henry Johnson	.08	.03	.01
☐ 448	SA: Darrell Porter	.08	.03	.01	☐ 528	Matt Alexander	.08	.03	.01
☐ 449	Luis Aguayo	.08	.03	.01	☐ 529	Allen Ripley	.08	.03	.01
☐ 450	Jack Morris	1.00	.40	.10	☐ 530	Dickie Noles	.08	.03	.01
☐ 451	Ed Miller	.08	.03	.01	☐ 531	A's Rookies	.08	.03	.01
☐ 452	Lee Smith	4.50	2.00	.45		Rich Bordi			
☐ 453	Art Howe	.15	.06	.01		Mark Budaska			
☐ 454	Rick Langford	.08	.03	.01		Kelvin Moore			
☐ 455	Tom Burgmeier	.08	.03	.01	☐ 532	Toby Harrah	.08	.03	.01
☐ 456	Chicago Cubs TL	.15	.05	.01	☐ 533	Joaquin Andujar	.15	.06	.01
	Batting: Bill Buckner				☐ 534	Dave McKay	.08	.03	.01
	Pitching: Randy Martz				☐ 535	Lance Parrish	.50	.20	.05
☐ 457	Tim Stoddard	.08	.03	.01	☐ 536	Rafael Ramirez	.08	.03	.01
☐ 458	Willie Montanez	.08	.03	.01	☐ 537	Doug Capilla	.08	.03	.01
☐ 459	Bruce Berenyi	.08	.03	.01	☐ 538	Lou Piniella	.15	.06	.01
☐ 460	Jack Clark	.40	.16	.04	☐ 539	Vern Ruhle	.08	.03	.01
☐ 461	Rich Dotson	.08	.03	.01	☐ 540	Andre Dawson	2.00	.80	.20
☐ 462	Dave Chalk	.08	.03	.01	☐ 541	Barry Evans	.08	.03	.01
☐ 463	Jim Kern	.08	.03	.01	☐ 542	Ned Yost	.08	.03	.01
☐ 464	Juan Bonilla	.08	.03	.01	☐ 543	Bill Robinson	.15	.06	.01
☐ 465	Lee Mazzilli	.08	.03	.01	☐ 544	Larry Christenson	.08	.03	.01
☐ 466	Randy Lerch	.08	.03	.01	☐ 545	Reggie Smith	.15	.06	.01
☐ 467	Mickey Hatcher	.08	.03	.01	☐ 546	SA: Reggie Smith	.08	.03	.01
☐ 468	Floyd Bannister	.08	.03	.01	☐ 547	Rod Carew AS	.50	.20	.05
☐ 469	Ed Ott	.08	.03	.01	☐ 548	Willie Randolph AS	.08	.03	.01
☐ 470	John Mayberry	.15	.06	.01	☐ 549	George Brett AS	.65	.25	.06
☐ 471	Royals Rookies	.15	.06	.01	☐ 550	Bucky Dent AS	.08	.03	.01
	Atlee Hammaker				☐ 551	Reggie Jackson AS	.65	.25	.06
	Mike Jones				☐ 552	Ken Singleton AS	.08	.03	.01
	Darryl Motley				☐ 553	Dave Winfield AS	.40	.16	.04
☐ 472	Oscar Gamble	.08	.03	.01	☐ 554	Carlton Fisk AS	.50	.20	.05
☐ 473	Mike Stanton	.08	.03	.01	☐ 555	Scott McGregor AS	.08	.03	.01
☐ 474	Ken Oberkfell	.08	.03	.01	☐ 556	Jack Morris AS	.30	.12	.03
☐ 475	Alan Trammell	1.00	.40	.10	☐ 557	Rich Gossage AS	.15	.06	.01
☐ 476	Brian Kingman	.08	.03	.01	☐ 558	John Tudor	.15	.06	.01
☐ 477	Steve Yeager	.08	.03	.01	☐ 559	Indians TL	.15	.05	.01
☐ 478	Ray Searage	.08	.03	.01		Batting: Mike Hargrove			
☐ 479	Rowland Office	.08	.03	.01		Pitching: Bert Blyleven			
☐ 480	Steve Carlton	1.50	.60	.15	☐ 560	Doug Corbett	.08	.03	.01
☐ 481	SA: Steve Carlton	.75	.30	.07	☐ 561	Cardinals Rookies	.15	.06	.01
☐ 482	Glenn Hubbard	.08	.03	.01		Glenn Brummer			
☐ 483	Gary Woods	.08	.03	.01		Luis DeLeon			
☐ 484	Ivan DeJesus	.08	.03	.01		Gene Roof			
☐ 485	Kent Tekulve	.08	.03	.01	☐ 562	Mike O'Berry	.08	.03	.01
☐ 486	Yankees TL	.20	.05	.01	☐ 563	Ross Baumgarten	.08	.03	.01
	Batting: J. Mumphrey				☐ 564	Doug DeCinces	.08	.03	.01
	Pitching: Tommy John				☐ 565	Jackson Todd	.08	.03	.01
☐ 487	Bob McClure	.08	.03	.01	☐ 566	Mike Jorgensen	.08	.03	.01
☐ 488	Ron Jackson	.08	.03	.01	☐ 567	Bob Babcock	.08	.03	.01
☐ 489	Rick Dempsey	.08	.03	.01	☐ 568	Joe Pettini	.08	.03	.01
☐ 490	Dennis Eckersley	.75	.30	.07	☐ 569	Willie Randolph	.15	.06	.01
☐ 491	Checklist 397-528	.15	.02	.00	☐ 570	SA: Willie Randolph	.08	.03	.01
☐ 492	Joe Price	.08	.03	.01	☐ 571	Glenn Abbott	.08	.03	.01
☐ 493	Chet Lemon	.08	.03	.01	☐ 572	Juan Beniquez	.08	.03	.01
☐ 494	Hubie Brooks	.60	.25	.06	☐ 573	Rick Waits	.08	.03	.01
☐ 495	Dennis Leonard	.08	.03	.01	☐ 574	Mike Ramsey	.08	.03	.01
☐ 496	Johnny Grubb	.08	.03	.01	☐ 575	Al Cowens	.08	.03	.01
☐ 497	Jim Anderson	.08	.03	.01	☐ 576	Giants TL	.15	.05	.01
☐ 498	Dave Bergman	.08	.03	.01		Batting: Milt May			
☐ 499	Paul Mirabella	.08	.03	.01		Pitching: Vida Blue			
☐ 500	Rod Carew	1.75	.70	.17	☐ 577	Rick Monday	.08	.03	.01
☐ 501	SA: Rod Carew	.80	.35	.08	☐ 578	Shooty Babitt	.08	.03	.01
☐ 502	Braves Rookies	2.50	1.00	.25	☐ 579	Rick Mahler	.25	.10	.02
	Steve Bedrosian UER				☐ 580	Bobby Bonds	.15	.06	.01
	(photo actually				☐ 581	Ron Reed	.08	.03	.01
	Larry Owen)				☐ 582	Luis Pujols	.08	.03	.01
	Brett Butler				☐ 583	Tippy Martinez	.08	.03	.01
	Larry Owen				☐ 584	Hosken Powell	.08	.03	.01
☐ 503	Julio Gonzalez	.08	.03	.01	☐ 585	Rollie Fingers	.75	.30	.07
☐ 504	Rick Peters	.08	.03	.01	☐ 586	SA: Rollie Fingers	.35	.15	.03
☐ 505	Graig Nettles	.20	.08	.02	☐ 587	Tim Lollar	.08	.03	.01
☐ 506	SA: Graig Nettles	.15	.06	.01	☐ 588	Dale Berra	.08	.03	.01
☐ 507	Terry Harper	.08	.03	.01	☐ 589	Dave Stapleton	.08	.03	.01
☐ 508	Jody Davis	.20	.08	.02	☐ 590	Al Oliver	.15	.06	.01
☐ 509	Harry Spilman	.08	.03	.01	☐ 591	SA: Al Oliver	.08	.03	.01

#	Player			
☐ 592	Craig Swan	.08	.03	.01
☐ 593	Billy Smith	.08	.03	.01
☐ 594	Renie Martin	.08	.03	.01
☐ 595	Dave Collins	.08	.03	.01
☐ 596	Damaso Garcia	.08	.03	.01
☐ 597	Wayne Nordhagen	.08	.03	.01
☐ 598	Bob Galasso	.08	.03	.01
☐ 599	White Sox Rookies	.08	.03	.01
	Jay Loviglio			
	Reggie Patterson			
	Leo Sutherland			
☐ 600	Dave Winfield	1.50	.60	.15
☐ 601	Sid Monge	.08	.03	.01
☐ 602	Freddie Patek	.08	.03	.01
☐ 603	Rich Hebner	.08	.03	.01
☐ 604	Orlando Sanchez	.08	.03	.01
☐ 605	Steve Rogers	.08	.03	.01
☐ 606	Blue Jays TL	.15	.05	.01
	Batting: J.Mayberry			
	Pitching: Dave Stieb			
☐ 607	Leon Durham	.08	.03	.01
☐ 608	Jerry Royster	.08	.03	.01
☐ 609	Rick Sutcliffe	.20	.08	.02
☐ 610	Rickey Henderson	9.00	4.00	.90
☐ 611	Joe Niekro	.15	.06	.01
☐ 612	Gary Ward	.08	.03	.01
☐ 613	Jim Gantner	.08	.03	.01
☐ 614	Juan Eichelberger	.08	.03	.01
☐ 615	Bob Boone	.15	.06	.01
☐ 616	SA: Bob Boone	.08	.03	.01
☐ 617	Scott McGregor	.08	.03	.01
☐ 618	Tim Foli	.08	.03	.01
☐ 619	Bill Campbell	.08	.03	.01
☐ 620	Ken Griffey	.40	.16	.04
☐ 621	SA: Ken Griffey	.20	.08	.02
☐ 622	Dennis Lamp	.08	.03	.01
☐ 623	Mets Rookies	.50	.20	.05
	Ron Gardenhire			
	Terry Leach			
	Tim Leary			
☐ 624	Fergie Jenkins	.60	.25	.06
☐ 625	Hal McRae	.15	.06	.01
☐ 626	Randy Jones	.08	.03	.01
☐ 627	Enos Cabell	.08	.03	.01
☐ 628	Bill Travers	.08	.03	.01
☐ 629	John Wockenfuss	.08	.03	.01
☐ 630	Joe Charboneau	.08	.03	.01
☐ 631	Gene Tenace	.15	.06	.01
☐ 632	Bryan Clark	.08	.03	.01
☐ 633	Mitchell Page	.08	.03	.01
☐ 634	Checklist 529-660	.15	.02	.00
☐ 635	Ron Davis	.08	.03	.01
☐ 636	Phillies TL	.40	.15	.03
	Batting: Pete Rose			
	Pitching: S.Carlton			
☐ 637	Rick Camp	.08	.03	.01
☐ 638	John Milner	.08	.03	.01
☐ 639	Ken Kravec	.08	.03	.01
☐ 640	Cesar Cedeno	.15	.06	.01
☐ 641	Steve Mura	.08	.03	.01
☐ 642	Mike Scioscia	.40	.16	.04
☐ 643	Pete Vuckovich	.08	.03	.01
☐ 644	John Castino	.08	.03	.01
☐ 645	Frank White	.08	.03	.01
☐ 646	SA: Frank White	.08	.03	.01
☐ 647	Warren Brusstar	.08	.03	.01
☐ 648	Jose Morales	.08	.03	.01
☐ 649	Ken Clay	.08	.03	.01
☐ 650	Carl Yastrzemski	1.75	.70	.17
☐ 651	SA: Carl Yastrzemski	.80	.35	.08
☐ 652	Steve Nicosia	.08	.03	.01
☐ 653	Angels Rookies	1.25	.50	.12
	Tom Brunansky			
	Luis Sanchez			
	Daryl Sconiers			
☐ 654	Jim Morrison	.08	.03	.01
☐ 655	Joel Youngblood	.08	.03	.01
☐ 656	Eddie Whitson	.08	.03	.01
☐ 657	Tom Poquette	.08	.03	.01
☐ 658	Tito Landrum	.08	.03	.01
☐ 659	Fred Martinez	.08	.03	.01
☐ 660	Dave Concepcion	.20	.08	.02
☐ 661	SA: Dave Concepcion	.15	.06	.01
☐ 662	Luis Salazar	.08	.03	.01
☐ 663	Hector Cruz	.08	.03	.01
☐ 664	Dan Spillner	.08	.03	.01
☐ 665	Jim Clancy	.08	.03	.01
☐ 666	Tigers TL	.15	.05	.01
	Batting: Steve Kemp			
	Pitching: Dan Petry			
☐ 667	Jeff Reardon	1.25	.50	.12
☐ 668	Dale Murphy	1.50	.60	.15
☐ 669	Larry Milbourne	.08	.03	.01
☐ 670	Steve Kemp	.08	.03	.01
☐ 671	Mike Davis	.08	.03	.01
☐ 672	Bob Knepper	.08	.03	.01
☐ 673	Keith Drumwright	.08	.03	.01
☐ 674	Dave Goltz	.08	.03	.01
☐ 675	Cecil Cooper	.20	.08	.02
☐ 676	Sal Butera	.08	.03	.01
☐ 677	Alfredo Griffin	.08	.03	.01
☐ 678	Tom Paciorek	.08	.03	.01
☐ 679	Sammy Stewart	.08	.03	.01
☐ 680	Gary Matthews	.08	.03	.01
☐ 681	Dodgers Rookies	5.00	2.25	.50
	Mike Marshall			
	Ron Roenicke			
	Steve Sax			
☐ 682	Jesse Jefferson	.08	.03	.01
☐ 683	Phil Garner	.15	.06	.01
☐ 684	Harold Baines	1.25	.50	.12
☐ 685	Bert Blyleven	.35	.15	.03
☐ 686	Gary Allenson	.08	.03	.01
☐ 687	Greg Minton	.08	.03	.01
☐ 688	Leon Roberts	.08	.03	.01
☐ 689	Lary Sorensen	.08	.03	.01
☐ 690	Dave Kingman	.20	.08	.02
☐ 691	Dan Schatzeder	.08	.03	.01
☐ 692	Wayne Gross	.08	.03	.01
☐ 693	Cesar Geronimo	.08	.03	.01
☐ 694	Dave Wehrmeister	.08	.03	.01
☐ 695	Warren Cromartie	.08	.03	.01
☐ 696	Pirates TL	.15	.05	.01
	Batting: Bill Madlock			
	Pitching:Eddie Solomon			
☐ 697	John Montefusco	.08	.03	.01
☐ 698	Tony Scott	.08	.03	.01
☐ 699	Dick Tidrow	.08	.03	.01
☐ 700	George Foster	.30	.12	.03
☐ 701	SA: George Foster	.15	.06	.01
☐ 702	Steve Renko	.08	.03	.01
☐ 703	Brewers TL	.15	.05	.01
	Batting: Cecil Cooper			
	Pitching: P.Vuckovich			
☐ 704	Mickey Rivers	.08	.03	.01
☐ 705	SA: Mickey Rivers	.08	.03	.01
☐ 706	Barry Foote	.08	.03	.01
☐ 707	Mark Bomback	.08	.03	.01
☐ 708	Gene Richards	.08	.03	.01
☐ 709	Don Money	.08	.03	.01
☐ 710	Jerry Reuss	.08	.03	.01
☐ 711	Mariners Rookies	4.00	1.75	.40
	Dave Edler			
	Dave Henderson			
	Reggie Walton			
☐ 712	Dennis Martinez	.20	.08	.02
☐ 713	Del Unser	.08	.03	.01
☐ 714	Jerry Koosman	.15	.06	.01
☐ 715	Willie Stargell	.75	.30	.07
☐ 716	SA: Willie Stargell	.35	.15	.03
☐ 717	Rick Miller	.08	.03	.01
☐ 718	Charlie Hough	.15	.06	.01
☐ 719	Jerry Narron	.08	.03	.01
☐ 720	Greg Luzinski	.15	.06	.01
☐ 721	SA: Greg Luzinski	.08	.03	.01
☐ 722	Jerry Martin	.08	.03	.01
☐ 723	Junior Kennedy	.08	.03	.01
☐ 724	Dave Rosello	.08	.03	.01
☐ 725	Amos Otis	.15	.06	.01
☐ 726	SA: Amos Otis	.08	.03	.01
☐ 727	Sixto Lezcano	.08	.03	.01
☐ 728	Aurelio Lopez	.08	.03	.01
☐ 729	Jim Spencer	.08	.03	.01
☐ 730	Gary Carter	.80	.35	.08
☐ 731	Padres Rookies	.08	.03	.01
	Mike Armstrong			
	Doug Gwosdz			
	Fred Kuhaulua			
☐ 732	Mike Lum	.08	.03	.01
☐ 733	Larry McWilliams	.08	.03	.01
☐ 734	Mike Ivie	.08	.03	.01
☐ 735	Rudy May	.08	.03	.01
☐ 736	Jerry Turner	.08	.03	.01
☐ 737	Reggie Cleveland	.08	.03	.01
☐ 738	Dave Engle	.08	.03	.01
☐ 739	Joey McLaughlin	.08	.03	.01
☐ 740	Dave Lopes	.15	.06	.01
☐ 741	SA: Dave Lopes	.08	.03	.01
☐ 742	Dick Drago	.08	.03	.01
☐ 743	John Stearns	.08	.03	.01
☐ 744	Mike Witt	.40	.16	.04
☐ 745	Bake McBride	.08	.03	.01
☐ 746	Andre Thornton	.15	.06	.01
☐ 747	John Lowenstein	.08	.03	.01
☐ 748	Marc Hill	.08	.03	.01
☐ 749	Bob Shirley	.08	.03	.01
☐ 750	Jim Rice	.40	.16	.04
☐ 751	Rick Honeycutt	.08	.03	.01

☐ 752	Lee Lacy	.08	.03	.01
☐ 753	Tom Brookens	.08	.03	.01
☐ 754	Joe Morgan	.90	.40	.09
☐ 755	SA: Joe Morgan	.40	.16	.04
☐ 756	Reds TL	.30	.10	.02
	Batting: Ken Griffey			
	Pitching: Tom Seaver			
☐ 757	Tom Underwood	.08	.03	.01
☐ 758	Claudell Washington	.08	.03	.01
☐ 759	Paul Splittorff	.08	.03	.01
☐ 760	Bill Buckner	.15	.06	.01
☐ 761	Dave Smith	.15	.06	.01
☐ 762	Mike Phillips	.08	.03	.01
☐ 763	Tom Hume	.08	.03	.01
☐ 764	Steve Swisher	.08	.03	.01
☐ 765	Gorman Thomas	.15	.06	.01
☐ 766	Twins Rookies	4.00	1.75	.40
	Lenny Faedo			
	Kent Hrbek			
	Tim Laudner			
☐ 767	Roy Smalley	.08	.03	.01
☐ 768	Jerry Garvin	.08	.03	.01
☐ 769	Richie Zisk	.08	.03	.01
☐ 770	Rich Gossage	.25	.10	.02
☐ 771	SA: Rich Gossage	.15	.06	.01
☐ 772	Bert Campaneris	.15	.06	.01
☐ 773	John Denny	.08	.03	.01
☐ 774	Jay Johnstone	.15	.06	.01
☐ 775	Bob Forsch	.08	.03	.01
☐ 776	Mark Belanger	.15	.06	.01
☐ 777	Tom Griffin	.08	.03	.01
☐ 778	Kevin Hickey	.08	.03	.01
☐ 779	Grant Jackson	.08	.03	.01
☐ 780	Pete Rose	2.25	.90	.22
☐ 781	SA: Pete Rose	1.00	.40	.10
☐ 782	Frank Taveras	.08	.03	.01
☐ 783	Greg Harris	.25	.10	.02
☐ 784	Milt Wilcox	.08	.03	.01
☐ 785	Dan Driessen	.08	.03	.01
☐ 786	Red Sox TL	.15	.05	.01
	Batting: C.Lansford			
	Pitching: Mike Torrez			
☐ 787	Fred Stanley	.08	.03	.01
☐ 788	Woodie Fryman	.08	.03	.01
☐ 789	Checklist 661-792	.15	.02	.00
☐ 790	Larry Gura	.08	.03	.01
☐ 791	Bobby Brown	.08	.03	.01
☐ 792	Frank Tanana	.20	.08	.02

1982 Topps Traded

The cards in this 132-card set measure 2 1/2" by 3 1/2". The 1982 Topps Traded or extended series is distinguished by a "T" printed after the number (located on the reverse). This was the first time Topps began a new tradition of newly numbering (and alphabetizing) their traded series from 1T to 132T. Of the total cards, 70 players represent the American League and 61 represent the National League, with the remaining card a numbered checklist (132T). The Cubs lead the pack with 12 changes, while the Red Sox are the only team in either league to have no new additions. All 131 player photos used in the set are completely new. Of this total, 112 individuals are seen in the uniform of their new team, 11 others have been elevated to

single card status from "Future Stars" cards, and eight more are entirely new to the 1982 Topps lineup. The backs are almost completely red in color with black print. There are no key rookie cards in this set. Although the Cal Ripken card is this set's most valuable card, it is not his Rookie Card since he had already been included in the 1982 regular set, albeit on a multi-player card.

		MINT	EXC	G-VG
COMPLETE SET (132)		190.00	80.00	20.00
COMMON PLAYER (1-132)		.15	.06	.01
☐ 1T	Doyle Alexander	.25	.10	.02
☐ 2T	Jesse Barfield	2.50	1.00	.25
☐ 3T	Ross Baumgarten	.15	.06	.01
☐ 4T	Steve Bedrosian	.60	.25	.06
☐ 5T	Mark Belanger	.25	.10	.02
☐ 6T	Kurt Bevacqua	.15	.06	.01
☐ 7T	Tim Blackwell	.15	.06	.01
☐ 8T	Vida Blue	.25	.10	.02
☐ 9T	Bob Boone	.35	.15	.03
☐ 10T	Larry Bowa	.25	.10	.02
☐ 11T	Dan Briggs	.15	.06	.01
☐ 12T	Bobby Brown	.15	.06	.01
☐ 13T	Tom Brunansky	2.50	1.00	.25
☐ 14T	Jeff Burroughs	.25	.10	.02
☐ 15T	Enos Cabell	.15	.06	.01
☐ 16T	Bill Campbell	.15	.06	.01
☐ 17T	Bobby Castillo	.15	.06	.01
☐ 18T	Bill Caudill	.15	.06	.01
☐ 19T	Cesar Cedeno	.25	.10	.02
☐ 20T	Dave Collins	.15	.06	.01
☐ 21T	Doug Corbett	.15	.06	.01
☐ 22T	Al Cowens	.15	.06	.01
☐ 23T	Chili Davis	3.50	1.50	.35
☐ 24T	Dick Davis	.15	.06	.01
☐ 25T	Ron Davis	.15	.06	.01
☐ 26T	Doug DeCinces	.25	.10	.02
☐ 27T	Ivan DeJesus	.15	.06	.01
☐ 28T	Bob Dernier	.25	.10	.02
☐ 29T	Bo Diaz	.15	.06	.01
☐ 30T	Roger Erickson	.15	.06	.01
☐ 31T	Jim Essian	.25	.10	.02
☐ 32T	Ed Farmer	.15	.06	.01
☐ 33T	Doug Flynn	.15	.06	.01
☐ 34T	Tim Foli	.15	.06	.01
☐ 35T	Dan Ford	.15	.06	.01
☐ 36T	George Foster	.60	.25	.06
☐ 37T	Dave Frost	.15	.06	.01
☐ 38T	Rich Gale	.15	.06	.01
☐ 39T	Ron Gardenhire	.15	.06	.01
☐ 40T	Ken Griffey	.75	.30	.07
☐ 41T	Greg Harris	.35	.15	.03
☐ 42T	Von Hayes	1.50	.60	.15
☐ 43T	Larry Herndon	.15	.06	.01
☐ 44T	Kent Hrbek	5.00	2.25	.50
☐ 45T	Mike Ivie	.15	.06	.01
☐ 46T	Grant Jackson	.15	.06	.01
☐ 47T	Reggie Jackson	7.50	3.25	.75
☐ 48T	Ron Jackson	.15	.06	.01
☐ 49T	Fergie Jenkins	1.50	.60	.15
☐ 50T	Lamar Johnson	.15	.06	.01
☐ 51T	Randy Johnson	.15	.06	.01
☐ 52T	Jay Johnstone	.25	.10	.02
☐ 53T	Mick Kelleher	.15	.06	.01
☐ 54T	Steve Kemp	.15	.06	.01
☐ 55T	Junior Kennedy	.15	.06	.01
☐ 56T	Jim Kern	.15	.06	.01
☐ 57T	Ray Knight	.35	.15	.03
☐ 58T	Wayne Krenchicki	.15	.06	.01
☐ 59T	Mike Krukow	.15	.06	.01
☐ 60T	Duane Kuiper	.15	.06	.01
☐ 61T	Mike LaCoss	.15	.06	.01
☐ 62T	Chet Lemon	.15	.06	.01
☐ 63T	Sixto Lezcano	.15	.06	.01
☐ 64T	Dave Lopes	.25	.10	.02
☐ 65T	Jerry Martin	.15	.06	.01
☐ 66T	Renie Martin	.15	.06	.01
☐ 67T	John Mayberry	.25	.10	.02
☐ 68T	Lee Mazzilli	.15	.06	.01
☐ 69T	Bake McBride	.15	.06	.01
☐ 70T	Dan Meyer	.15	.06	.01
☐ 71T	Larry Milbourne	.15	.06	.01
☐ 72T	Eddie Milner	.15	.06	.01
☐ 73T	Sid Monge	.15	.06	.01
☐ 74T	John Montefusco	.15	.06	.01
☐ 75T	Jose Morales	.15	.06	.01
☐ 76T	Keith Moreland	.15	.06	.01
☐ 77T	Jim Morrison	.15	.06	.01
☐ 78T	Rance Mulliniks	.15	.06	.01
☐ 79T	Steve Mura	.15	.06	.01
☐ 80T	Gene Nelson	.25	.10	.02

☐ 81T	Joe Nolan	.15	.06	.01
☐ 82T	Dickie Noles	.15	.06	.01
☐ 83T	Al Oliver	.35	.15	.03
☐ 84T	Jorge Orta	.15	.06	.01
☐ 85T	Tom Paciorek	.15	.06	.01
☐ 86T	Larry Parrish	.25	.10	.02
☐ 87T	Jack Perconte	.15	.06	.01
☐ 88T	Gaylord Perry	1.50	.60	.15
☐ 89T	Rob Picciolo	.15	.06	.01
☐ 90T	Joe Pittman	.15	.06	.01
☐ 91T	Hosken Powell	.15	.06	.01
☐ 92T	Mike Proly	.15	.06	.01
☐ 93T	Greg Pryor	.15	.06	.01
☐ 94T	Charlie Puleo	.15	.06	.01
☐ 95T	Shane Rawley	.15	.06	.01
☐ 96T	Johnny Ray	.50	.20	.05
☐ 97T	Dave Revering	.15	.06	.01
☐ 98T	Cal Ripken	160.00	60.00	12.50
☐ 99T	Allen Ripley	.15	.06	.01
☐ 100T	Bill Robinson	.25	.10	.02
☐ 101T	Aurelio Rodriguez	.15	.06	.01
☐ 102T	Joe Rudi	.25	.10	.02
☐ 103T	Steve Sax	6.50	2.75	.65
☐ 104T	Dan Schatzeder	.15	.06	.01
☐ 105T	Bob Shirley	.15	.06	.01
☐ 106T	Eric Show	.35	.15	.03
☐ 107T	Roy Smalley	.15	.06	.01
☐ 108T	Lonnie Smith	.35	.15	.03
☐ 109T	Ozzie Smith	12.00	5.25	1.50
☐ 110T	Reggie Smith	.25	.10	.02
☐ 111T	Lary Sorensen	.15	.06	.01
☐ 112T	Elias Sosa	.15	.06	.01
☐ 113T	Mike Stanton	.15	.06	.01
☐ 114T	Steve Strougher	.15	.06	.01
☐ 115T	Champ Summers	.15	.06	.01
☐ 116T	Rick Sutcliffe	.35	.15	.03
☐ 117T	Frank Tanana	.25	.10	.02
☐ 118T	Frank Taveras	.15	.06	.01
☐ 119T	Garry Templeton	.25	.10	.02
☐ 120T	Alex Trevino	.15	.06	.01
☐ 121T	Jerry Turner	.15	.06	.01
☐ 122T	Ed VandeBerg	.15	.06	.01
☐ 123T	Tom Veryzer	.15	.06	.01
☐ 124T	Ron Washington	.15	.06	.01
☐ 125T	Bob Watson	.25	.10	.02
☐ 126T	Dennis Werth	.15	.06	.01
☐ 127T	Eddie Whitson	.25	.10	.02
☐ 128T	Rob Wilfong	.15	.06	.01
☐ 129T	Bump Wills	.15	.06	.01
☐ 130T	Gary Woods	.15	.06	.01
☐ 131T	Butch Wynegar	.15	.06	.01
☐ 132T	Checklist: 1-132	.15	.02	.00

1983 Topps

The cards in this 792-card set measure 2 1/2" by 3 1/2". Each regular card of the Topps set for 1983 features a large action shot of a player with a small cameo portrait at bottom right. There are special series for AL and NL All Stars (386-407), League Leaders (701-708), and Record Breakers (1-6). In addition, there are 34 "Super Veteran" (SV) cards and six numbered checklist cards. The Super Veteran cards are oriented horizontally and show two pictures of the featured player, a recent picture and a picture showing the player as a rookie when he broke in. The cards are numbered on the reverse at the upper left corner. The team cards are actually Team Leader (TL) cards picturing the batting and pitching leader for that team with a checklist back. The key rookie cards in this set are Wade Boggs, Tony Gwynn, Willie McGee, Ryne Sandberg, and Frank Viola.

	MINT	EXC	G-VG
COMPLETE SET (792)	165.00	75.00	15.00
COMMON PLAYER (1-792)	.08	.03	.01

☐ 1	RB: Tony Armas 11 putouts by rightfielder	.20	.05	.01
☐ 2	RB: Rickey Henderson Sets modern record for steals, season	1.50	.60	.15
☐ 3	RB: Greg Minton 269 1/3 homerless innings streak	.08	.03	.01
☐ 4	RB: Lance Parrish Threw out three baserunners in All-Star game	.15	.06	.01
☐ 5	RB: Manny Trillo 479 consecutive errorless chances, second baseman	.08	.03	.01
☐ 6	RB: John Wathan ML steals record for catchers, 31	.08	.03	.01
☐ 7	Gene Richards	.08	.03	.01
☐ 8	Steve Balboni	.08	.03	.01
☐ 9	Joey McLaughlin	.08	.03	.01
☐ 10	Gorman Thomas	.15	.06	.01
☐ 11	Billy Gardner MG	.08	.03	.01
☐ 12	Paul Mirabella	.08	.03	.01
☐ 13	Larry Herndon	.08	.03	.01
☐ 14	Frank LaCorte	.08	.03	.01
☐ 15	Ron Cey	.15	.06	.01
☐ 16	George Vukovich	.08	.03	.01
☐ 17	Kent Tekulve	.08	.03	.01
☐ 18	SV: Kent Tekulve	.08	.03	.01
☐ 19	Oscar Gamble	.08	.03	.01
☐ 20	Carlton Fisk	1.50	.60	.15
☐ 21	Baltimore Orioles TL BA: Eddie Murray ERA: Jim Palmer	.30	.10	.02
☐ 22	Randy Martz	.08	.03	.01
☐ 23	Mike Heath	.08	.03	.01
☐ 24	Steve Mura	.08	.03	.01
☐ 25	Hal McRae	.15	.06	.01
☐ 26	Jerry Royster	.08	.03	.01
☐ 27	Doug Corbett	.08	.03	.01
☐ 28	Bruce Bochte	.08	.03	.01
☐ 29	Randy Jones	.08	.03	.01
☐ 30	Jim Rice	.35	.15	.03
☐ 31	Bill Gullickson	.15	.06	.01
☐ 32	Dave Bergman	.08	.03	.01
☐ 33	Jack O'Connor	.08	.03	.01
☐ 34	Paul Householder	.08	.03	.01
☐ 35	Rollie Fingers	.65	.25	.06
☐ 36	SV: Rollie Fingers	.35	.15	.03
☐ 37	Darrell Johnson MG	.08	.03	.01
☐ 38	Tim Flannery	.08	.03	.01
☐ 39	Terry Puhl	.08	.03	.01
☐ 40	Fernando Valenzuela	.40	.16	.04
☐ 41	Jerry Turner	.08	.03	.01
☐ 42	Dale Murray	.08	.03	.01
☐ 43	Bob Dernier	.08	.03	.01
☐ 44	Don Robinson	.08	.03	.01
☐ 45	John Mayberry	.15	.06	.01
☐ 46	Richard Dotson	.08	.03	.01
☐ 47	Dave McKay	.08	.03	.01
☐ 48	Lary Sorensen	.08	.03	.01
☐ 49	Willie McGee	5.50	2.50	.55
☐ 50	Bob Horner UER ('82 RBI total 7)	.15	.06	.01
☐ 51	Chicago Cubs TL BA: Leon Durham ERA: Fergie Jenkins	.20	.07	.01
☐ 52	Onix Concepcion	.08	.03	.01
☐ 53	Mike Witt	.08	.03	.01
☐ 54	Jim Maler	.08	.03	.01
☐ 55	Mookie Wilson	.15	.06	.01
☐ 56	Chuck Rainey	.08	.03	.01
☐ 57	Tim Blackwell	.08	.03	.01
☐ 58	Al Holland	.08	.03	.01
☐ 59	Benny Ayala	.08	.03	.01
☐ 60	Johnny Bench	1.50	.60	.15
☐ 61	SV: Johnny Bench	.75	.30	.07
☐ 62	Bob McClure	.08	.03	.01
☐ 63	Rick Monday	.08	.03	.01

#	Player			
☐ 64	Bill Stein	.08	.03	.01
☐ 65	Jack Morris	.90	.40	.09
☐ 66	Bob Lillis MG	.08	.03	.01
☐ 67	Sal Butera	.08	.03	.01
☐ 68	Eric Show	.25	.10	.02
☐ 69	Lee Lacy	.08	.03	.01
☐ 70	Steve Carlton	1.50	.60	.15
☐ 71	SV: Steve Carlton	.75	.30	.07
☐ 72	Tom Paciorek	.08	.03	.01
☐ 73	Allen Ripley	.08	.03	.01
☐ 74	Julio Gonzalez	.08	.03	.01
☐ 75	Amos Otis	.15	.06	.01
☐ 76	Rick Mahler	.08	.03	.01
☐ 77	Hosken Powell	.08	.03	.01
☐ 78	Bill Caudill	.08	.03	.01
☐ 79	Mick Kelleher	.08	.03	.01
☐ 80	George Foster	.25	.10	.02
☐ 81	Yankees TL	.15	.06	.01
	BA: Jerry Mumphrey			
	ERA: Dave Righetti			
☐ 82	Bruce Hurst	.25	.10	.02
☐ 83	Ryne Sandberg	50.00	22.50	7.50
☐ 84	Milt May	.08	.03	.01
☐ 85	Ken Singleton	.15	.06	.01
☐ 86	Tom Hume	.08	.03	.01
☐ 87	Joe Rudi	.15	.06	.01
☐ 88	Jim Gantner	.08	.03	.01
☐ 89	Leon Roberts	.08	.03	.01
☐ 90	Jerry Reuss	.08	.03	.01
☐ 91	Larry Milbourne	.08	.03	.01
☐ 92	Mike LaCoss	.08	.03	.01
☐ 93	John Castino	.08	.03	.01
☐ 94	Dave Edwards	.08	.03	.01
☐ 95	Alan Trammell	1.00	.40	.10
☐ 96	Dick Howser MG	.08	.03	.01
☐ 97	Ross Baumgarten	.08	.03	.01
☐ 98	Vance Law	.15	.06	.01
☐ 99	Dickie Noles	.08	.03	.01
☐ 100	Pete Rose	2.00	.80	.20
☐ 101	SV: Pete Rose	1.00	.40	.10
☐ 102	Dave Beard	.08	.03	.01
☐ 103	Darrell Porter	.08	.03	.01
☐ 104	Bob Walk	.08	.03	.01
☐ 105	Don Baylor	.15	.06	.01
☐ 106	Gene Nelson	.08	.03	.01
☐ 107	Mike Jorgensen	.08	.03	.01
☐ 108	Glenn Hoffman	.08	.03	.01
☐ 109	Luis Leal	.08	.03	.01
☐ 110	Ken Griffey	.35	.15	.03
☐ 111	Montreal Expos TL	.15	.06	.01
	BA: Al Oliver			
	ERA: Steve Rogers			
☐ 112	Bob Shirley	.08	.03	.01
☐ 113	Ron Roenicke	.08	.03	.01
☐ 114	Jim Slaton	.08	.03	.01
☐ 115	Chili Davis	.60	.25	.06
☐ 116	Dave Schmidt	.15	.06	.01
☐ 117	Alan Knicely	.08	.03	.01
☐ 118	Chris Welsh	.08	.03	.01
☐ 119	Tom Brookens	.08	.03	.01
☐ 120	Len Barker	.08	.03	.01
☐ 121	Mickey Hatcher	.08	.03	.01
☐ 122	Jimmy Smith	.08	.03	.01
☐ 123	George Frazier	.08	.03	.01
☐ 124	Marc Hill	.08	.03	.01
☐ 125	Leon Durham	.08	.03	.01
☐ 126	Joe Torre MG	.15	.06	.01
☐ 127	Preston Hanna	.08	.03	.01
☐ 128	Mike Ramsey	.08	.03	.01
☐ 129	Checklist: 1-132	.15	.02	.00
☐ 130	Dave Stieb	.35	.15	.03
☐ 131	Ed Ott	.08	.03	.01
☐ 132	Todd Cruz	.08	.03	.01
☐ 133	Jim Barr	.08	.03	.01
☐ 134	Hubie Brooks	.35	.15	.03
☐ 135	Dwight Evans	.40	.16	.04
☐ 136	Willie Aikens	.08	.03	.01
☐ 137	Woodie Fryman	.08	.03	.01
☐ 138	Rick Dempsey	.08	.03	.01
☐ 139	Bruce Berenyi	.08	.03	.01
☐ 140	Willie Randolph	.15	.06	.01
☐ 141	Indians TL	.15	.06	.01
	BA: Toby Harrah			
	ERA: Rick Sutcliffe			
☐ 142	Mike Caldwell	.08	.03	.01
☐ 143	Joe Pettini	.08	.03	.01
☐ 144	Mark Wagner	.08	.03	.01
☐ 145	Don Sutton	.50	.20	.05
☐ 146	SV: Don Sutton	.25	.10	.02
☐ 147	Rick Leach	.08	.03	.01
☐ 148	Dave Roberts	.08	.03	.01
☐ 149	Johnny Ray	.08	.03	.01
☐ 150	Bruce Sutter	.20	.08	.02
☐ 151	SV: Bruce Sutter	.15	.06	.01
☐ 152	Jay Johnstone	.15	.06	.01
☐ 153	Jerry Koosman	.15	.06	.01
☐ 154	Johnnie LeMaster	.08	.03	.01
☐ 155	Dan Quisenberry	.15	.06	.01
☐ 156	Billy Martin MG	.15	.06	.01
☐ 157	Steve Bedrosian	.15	.06	.01
☐ 158	Rob Wilfong	.08	.03	.01
☐ 159	Mike Stanton	.08	.03	.01
☐ 160	Dave Kingman	.15	.06	.01
☐ 161	SV: Dave Kingman	.08	.03	.01
☐ 162	Mark Clear	.08	.03	.01
☐ 163	Cal Ripken	18.00	7.50	2.50
☐ 164	David Palmer	.08	.03	.01
☐ 165	Dan Driessen	.08	.03	.01
☐ 166	John Pacella	.08	.03	.01
☐ 167	Mark Brouhard	.08	.03	.01
☐ 168	Juan Eichelberger	.08	.03	.01
☐ 169	Doug Flynn	.08	.03	.01
☐ 170	Steve Howe	.08	.03	.01
☐ 171	Giants TL	.20	.07	.01
	BA: Joe Morgan			
	ERA: Bill Laskey			
☐ 172	Vern Ruhle	.08	.03	.01
☐ 173	Jim Morrison	.08	.03	.01
☐ 174	Jerry Ujdur	.08	.03	.01
☐ 175	Bo Diaz	.08	.03	.01
☐ 176	Dave Righetti	.35	.15	.03
☐ 177	Harold Baines	.75	.30	.07
☐ 178	Luis Tiant	.15	.06	.01
☐ 179	SV: Luis Tiant	.08	.03	.01
☐ 180	Rickey Henderson	7.50	3.25	.75
☐ 181	Terry Felton	.08	.03	.01
☐ 182	Mike Fischlin	.08	.03	.01
☐ 183	Ed VandeBerg	.08	.03	.01
☐ 184	Bob Clark	.08	.03	.01
☐ 185	Tim Lollar	.08	.03	.01
☐ 186	Whitey Herzog MG	.15	.06	.01
☐ 187	Terry Leach	.15	.06	.01
☐ 188	Rick Miller	.08	.03	.01
☐ 189	Dan Schatzeder	.08	.03	.01
☐ 190	Cecil Cooper	.15	.06	.01
☐ 191	Joe Price	.08	.03	.01
☐ 192	Floyd Rayford	.08	.03	.01
☐ 193	Harry Spilman	.08	.03	.01
☐ 194	Cesar Geronimo	.08	.03	.01
☐ 195	Bob Stoddard	.08	.03	.01
☐ 196	Bill Fahey	.08	.03	.01
☐ 197	Jim Eisenreich	.50	.20	.05
☐ 198	Kiko Garcia	.08	.03	.01
☐ 199	Marty Bystrom	.08	.03	.01
☐ 200	Rod Carew	1.50	.60	.15
☐ 201	SV: Rod Carew	.75	.30	.07
☐ 202	Blue Jays TL	.15	.06	.01
	BA: Damaso Garcia			
	ERA: Dave Stieb			
☐ 203	Mike Morgan	.15	.06	.01
☐ 204	Junior Kennedy	.08	.03	.01
☐ 205	Dave Parker	.65	.25	.06
☐ 206	Ken Oberkfell	.08	.03	.01
☐ 207	Rick Camp	.08	.03	.01
☐ 208	Dan Meyer	.08	.03	.01
☐ 209	Mike Moore	1.50	.60	.15
☐ 210	Jack Clark	.35	.15	.03
☐ 211	John Denny	.08	.03	.01
☐ 212	John Stearns	.08	.03	.01
☐ 213	Tom Burgmeier	.08	.03	.01
☐ 214	Jerry White	.08	.03	.01
☐ 215	Mario Soto	.08	.03	.01
☐ 216	Tony LaRussa MG	.15	.06	.01
☐ 217	Tim Stoddard	.08	.03	.01
☐ 218	Roy Howell	.08	.03	.01
☐ 219	Mike Armstrong	.08	.03	.01
☐ 220	Dusty Baker	.15	.06	.01
☐ 221	Joe Niekro	.15	.06	.01
☐ 222	Damaso Garcia	.08	.03	.01
☐ 223	John Montefusco	.08	.03	.01
☐ 224	Mickey Rivers	.08	.03	.01
☐ 225	Enos Cabell	.08	.03	.01
☐ 226	Enrique Romo	.08	.03	.01
☐ 227	Chris Bando	.08	.03	.01
☐ 228	Joaquin Andujar	.15	.06	.01
☐ 229	Phillies TL	.20	.07	.01
	BA: Bo Diaz			
	ERA: Steve Carlton			
☐ 230	Fergie Jenkins	.50	.20	.05
☐ 231	SV: Fergie Jenkins	.25	.10	.02
☐ 232	Tom Brunansky	.35	.15	.03
☐ 233	Wayne Gross	.08	.03	.01
☐ 234	Larry Andersen	.08	.03	.01
☐ 235	Claudell Washington	.08	.03	.01
☐ 236	Steve Renko	.08	.03	.01
☐ 237	Dan Norman	.08	.03	.01
☐ 238	Bud Black	.60	.25	.06
☐ 239	Dave Stapleton	.08	.03	.01

☐	240	Rich Gossage	.20	.08	.02	☐	326	Garth Iorg	.08	.03	.01
☐	241	SV: Rich Gossage	.15	.06	.01	☐	327	Bobby Castillo	.08	.03	.01
☐	242	Joe Nolan	.08	.03	.01	☐	328	Craig Reynolds	.08	.03	.01
☐	243	Duane Walker	.08	.03	.01	☐	329	Randy Niemann	.08	.03	.01
☐	244	Dwight Bernard	.08	.03	.01	☐	330	Buddy Bell	.15	.06	.01
☐	245	Steve Sax	.75	.30	.07	☐	331	Mike Krukow	.08	.03	.01
☐	246	George Bamberger MG	.08	.03	.01	☐	332	Glenn Wilson	.15	.06	.01
☐	247	Dave Smith	.08	.03	.01	☐	333	Dave LaRoche	.08	.03	.01
☐	248	Bake McBride	.08	.03	.01	☐	334	SV: Dave LaRoche	.08	.03	.01
☐	249	Checklist: 133-264	.15	.02	.00	☐	335	Steve Henderson	.08	.03	.01
☐	250	Bill Buckner	.15	.06	.01	☐	336	Rene Lachemann MG	.08	.03	.01
☐	251	Alan Wiggins	.08	.03	.01	☐	337	Tito Landrum	.08	.03	.01
☐	252	Luis Aguayo	.08	.03	.01	☐	338	Bob Owchinko	.08	.03	.01
☐	253	Larry McWilliams	.08	.03	.01	☐	339	Terry Harper	.08	.03	.01
☐	254	Rick Cerone	.08	.03	.01	☐	340	Larry Gura	.08	.03	.01
☐	255	Gene Garber	.08	.03	.01	☐	341	Doug DeCinces	.08	.03	.01
☐	256	SV: Gene Garber	.08	.03	.01	☐	342	Atlee Hammaker	.08	.03	.01
☐	257	Jesse Barfield	.40	.16	.04	☐	343	Bob Bailor	.08	.03	.01
☐	258	Manny Castillo	.08	.03	.01	☐	344	Roger LaFrancois	.08	.03	.01
☐	259	Jeff Jones	.08	.03	.01	☐	345	Jim Clancy	.08	.03	.01
☐	260	Steve Kemp	.08	.03	.01	☐	346	Joe Pittman	.08	.03	.01
☐	261	Tigers TL	.15	.06	.01	☐	347	Sammy Stewart	.08	.03	.01
		BA: Larry Herndon				☐	348	Alan Bannister	.08	.03	.01
		ERA: Dan Petry				☐	349	Checklist: 265-396	.15	.02	.00
☐	262	Ron Jackson	.08	.03	.01	☐	350	Robin Yount	2.00	.80	.20
☐	263	Renie Martin	.08	.03	.01	☐	351	Reds TL	.15	.06	.01
☐	264	Jamie Quirk	.08	.03	.01			BA: Cesar Cedeno			
☐	265	Joel Youngblood	.08	.03	.01			ERA: Mario Soto			
☐	266	Paul Boris	.08	.03	.01	☐	352	Mike Scioscia	.15	.06	.01
☐	267	Terry Francona	.08	.03	.01	☐	353	Steve Comer	.08	.03	.01
☐	268	Storm Davis	.40	.16	.04	☐	354	Randy Johnson	.08	.03	.01
☐	269	Ron Oester	.08	.03	.01	☐	355	Jim Bibby	.08	.03	.01
☐	270	Dennis Eckersley	.60	.25	.06	☐	356	Gary Woods	.08	.03	.01
☐	271	Ed Romero	.08	.03	.01	☐	357	Len Matuszek	.08	.03	.01
☐	272	Frank Tanana	.15	.06	.01	☐	358	Jerry Garvin	.08	.03	.01
☐	273	Mark Belanger	.15	.06	.01	☐	359	Dave Collins	.08	.03	.01
☐	274	Terry Kennedy	.08	.03	.01	☐	360	Nolan Ryan	7.00	3.00	.70
☐	275	Ray Knight	.15	.06	.01	☐	361	SV: Nolan Ryan	3.25	1.35	.32
☐	276	Gene Mauch MG	.08	.03	.01	☐	362	Bill Almon	.08	.03	.01
☐	277	Rance Mulliniks	.08	.03	.01	☐	363	John Stuper	.08	.03	.01
☐	278	Kevin Hickey	.08	.03	.01	☐	364	Brett Butler	.60	.25	.06
☐	279	Greg Gross	.08	.03	.01	☐	365	Dave Lopes	.15	.06	.01
☐	280	Bert Blyleven	.30	.12	.03	☐	366	Dick Williams MG	.08	.03	.01
☐	281	Andre Robertson	.08	.03	.01	☐	367	Bud Anderson	.08	.03	.01
☐	282	Reggie Smith	.30	.12	.03	☐	368	Richie Zisk	.08	.03	.01
		(Ryne Sandberg				☐	369	Jesse Orosco	.08	.03	.01
		ducking back)				☐	370	Gary Carter	.65	.25	.06
☐	283	SV: Reggie Smith	.08	.03	.01	☐	371	Mike Richardt	.08	.03	.01
☐	284	Jeff Lahti	.08	.03	.01	☐	372	Terry Crowley	.08	.03	.01
☐	285	Lance Parrish	.35	.15	.03	☐	373	Kevin Saucier	.08	.03	.01
☐	286	Rick Langford	.08	.03	.01	☐	374	Wayne Krenchicki	.08	.03	.01
☐	287	Bobby Brown	.08	.03	.01	☐	375	Pete Vuckovich	.08	.03	.01
☐	288	Joe Cowley	.08	.03	.01	☐	376	Ken Landreaux	.08	.03	.01
☐	289	Jerry Dybzinski	.08	.03	.01	☐	377	Lee May	.08	.03	.01
☐	290	Jeff Reardon	.75	.30	.07	☐	378	SV: Lee May	.08	.03	.01
☐	291	Pirates TL	.15	.06	.01	☐	379	Guy Sularz	.08	.03	.01
		BA: Bill Madlock				☐	380	Ron Davis	.08	.03	.01
		ERA: John Candelaria				☐	381	Red Sox TL	.15	.06	.01
☐	292	Craig Swan	.08	.03	.01			BA: Jim Rice			
☐	293	Glenn Gulliver	.08	.03	.01			ERA: Bob Stanley			
☐	294	Dave Engle	.08	.03	.01	☐	382	Bob Knepper	.08	.03	.01
☐	295	Jerry Remy	.08	.03	.01	☐	383	Ozzie Virgil	.08	.03	.01
☐	296	Greg Harris	.08	.03	.01	☐	384	Dave Dravecky	.75	.30	.07
☐	297	Ned Yost	.08	.03	.01	☐	385	Mike Easler	.08	.03	.01
☐	298	Floyd Chiffer	.08	.03	.01	☐	386	Rod Carew AS	.45	.18	.04
☐	299	George Wright	.08	.03	.01	☐	387	Bob Grich AS	.15	.06	.01
☐	300	Mike Schmidt	3.00	1.25	.30	☐	388	George Brett AS	.60	.25	.06
☐	301	SV: Mike Schmidt	1.50	.60	.15	☐	389	Robin Yount AS	.60	.25	.06
☐	302	Ernie Whitt	.08	.03	.01	☐	390	Reggie Jackson AS	.50	.20	.05
☐	303	Miguel Dilone	.08	.03	.01	☐	391	Rickey Henderson AS	2.00	.80	.20
☐	304	Dave Rucker	.08	.03	.01	☐	392	Fred Lynn AS	.15	.06	.01
☐	305	Larry Bowa	.15	.06	.01	☐	393	Carlton Fisk AS	.40	.16	.04
☐	306	Tom Lasorda MG	.15	.06	.01	☐	394	Pete Vuckovich AS	.08	.03	.01
☐	307	Lou Piniella	.15	.06	.01	☐	395	Larry Gura AS	.08	.03	.01
☐	308	Jesus Vega	.08	.03	.01	☐	396	Dan Quisenberry AS	.15	.06	.01
☐	309	Jeff Leonard	.08	.03	.01	☐	397	Pete Rose AS	.60	.25	.06
☐	310	Greg Luzinski	.15	.06	.01	☐	398	Manny Trillo AS	.08	.03	.01
☐	311	Glenn Brummer	.08	.03	.01	☐	399	Mike Schmidt AS	.60	.25	.06
☐	312	Brian Kingman	.08	.03	.01	☐	400	Dave Concepcion AS	.15	.06	.01
☐	313	Gary Gray	.08	.03	.01	☐	401	Dale Murphy AS	.35	.15	.03
☐	314	Ken Dayley	.08	.03	.01	☐	402	Andre Dawson AS	.40	.16	.04
☐	315	Rick Burleson	.08	.03	.01	☐	403	Tim Raines AS	.30	.12	.03
☐	316	Paul Splittorff	.08	.03	.01	☐	404	Gary Carter AS	.25	.10	.02
☐	317	Gary Rajsich	.08	.03	.01	☐	405	Steve Rogers AS	.08	.03	.01
☐	318	John Tudor	.15	.06	.01	☐	406	Steve Carlton AS	.40	.16	.04
☐	319	Lenn Sakata	.08	.03	.01	☐	407	Bruce Sutter AS	.15	.06	.01
☐	320	Steve Rogers	.08	.03	.01	☐	408	Rudy May	.08	.03	.01
☐	321	Brewers TL	.20	.07	.01	☐	409	Marvis Foley	.08	.03	.01
		BA: Robin Yount				☐	410	Phil Niekro	.50	.20	.05
		ERA: Pete Vuckovich				☐	411	SV: Phil Niekro	.25	.10	.02
☐	322	Dave Van Gorder	.08	.03	.01	☐	412	Rangers TL	.15	.06	.01
☐	323	Luis DeLeon	.08	.03	.01			BA: Buddy Bell			
☐	324	Mike Marshall	.15	.06	.01			ERA: Charlie Hough			
☐	325	Von Hayes	.25	.10	.02	☐	413	Matt Keough	.08	.03	.01

#	Player			
414	Julio Cruz	.08	.03	.01
415	Bob Forsch	.08	.03	.01
416	Joe Ferguson	.08	.03	.01
417	Tom Hausman	.08	.03	.01
418	Greg Pryor	.08	.03	.01
419	Steve Crawford	.08	.03	.01
420	Al Oliver	.15	.06	.01
421	SV: Al Oliver	.08	.03	.01
422	George Cappuzzello	.08	.03	.01
423	Tom Lawless	.08	.03	.01
424	Jerry Augustine	.08	.03	.01
425	Pedro Guerrero	.50	.20	.05
426	Earl Weaver MG	.15	.06	.01
427	Roy Lee Jackson	.08	.03	.01
428	Champ Summers	.08	.03	.01
429	Eddie Whitson	.08	.03	.01
430	Kirk Gibson	.75	.30	.07
431	Gary Gaetti	1.75	.70	.17
432	Porfirio Altamirano	.08	.03	.01
433	Dale Berra	.08	.03	.01
434	Dennis Lamp	.08	.03	.01
435	Tony Armas	.08	.03	.01
436	Bill Campbell	.08	.03	.01
437	Rick Sweet	.08	.03	.01
438	Dave LaPoint	.15	.06	.01
439	Rafael Ramirez	.08	.03	.01
440	Ron Guidry	.35	.15	.03
441	Astros TL	.15	.06	.01
	BA: Ray Knight			
	ERA: Joe Niekro			
442	Brian Downing	.15	.06	.01
443	Don Hood	.08	.03	.01
444	Wally Backman	.15	.06	.01
445	Mike Flanagan	.15	.06	.01
446	Reid Nichols	.08	.03	.01
447	Bryn Smith	.15	.06	.01
448	Darrell Evans	.15	.06	.01
449	Eddie Milner	.08	.03	.01
450	Ted Simmons	.15	.06	.01
451	SV: Ted Simmons	.08	.03	.01
452	Lloyd Moseby	.15	.06	.01
453	Lamar Johnson	.08	.03	.01
454	Bob Welch	.40	.16	.04
455	Sixto Lezcano	.08	.03	.01
456	Lee Elia MG	.08	.03	.01
457	Milt Wilcox	.08	.03	.01
458	Ron Washington	.08	.03	.01
459	Ed Farmer	.08	.03	.01
460	Roy Smalley	.08	.03	.01
461	Steve Trout	.08	.03	.01
462	Steve Nicosia	.08	.03	.01
463	Gaylord Perry	.50	.20	.05
464	SV: Gaylord Perry	.25	.10	.02
465	Lonnie Smith	.20	.08	.02
466	Tom Underwood	.08	.03	.01
467	Rufino Linares	.08	.03	.01
468	Dave Goltz	.08	.03	.01
469	Ron Gardenhire	.08	.03	.01
470	Greg Minton	.08	.03	.01
471	K.C. Royals TL	.15	.06	.01
	BA: Willie Wilson			
	ERA: Vida Blue			
472	Gary Allenson	.08	.03	.01
473	John Lowenstein	.08	.03	.01
474	Ray Burris	.08	.03	.01
475	Cesar Cedeno	.15	.06	.01
476	Rob Picciolo	.08	.03	.01
477	Tom Niedenfuer	.08	.03	.01
478	Phil Garner	.15	.06	.01
479	Charlie Hough	.08	.03	.01
480	Toby Harrah	.08	.03	.01
481	Scot Thompson	.08	.03	.01
482	Tony Gwynn UER	33.00	15.00	5.00
	(no Topps logo under			
	card number on back)			
483	Lynn Jones	.08	.03	.01
484	Dick Ruthven	.08	.03	.01
485	Omar Moreno	.08	.03	.01
486	Clyde King MG	.08	.03	.01
487	Jerry Hairston	.08	.03	.01
488	Alfredo Griffin	.08	.03	.01
489	Tom Herr	.15	.06	.01
490	Jim Palmer	1.25	.50	.12
491	SV: Jim Palmer	.60	.25	.06
492	Paul Serna	.08	.03	.01
493	Steve McCatty	.08	.03	.01
494	Bob Brenly	.08	.03	.01
495	Warren Cromartie	.08	.03	.01
496	Tom Veryzer	.08	.03	.01
497	Rick Sutcliffe	.20	.08	.02
498	Wade Boggs	36.00	16.25	5.50
499	Jeff Little	.08	.03	.01
500	Reggie Jackson	2.00	.80	.20
501	SV: Reggie Jackson	1.00	.40	.10
502	Atlanta Braves TL	.20	.07	.01
	BA: Dale Murphy			
	ERA: Phil Niekro			
503	Moose Haas	.08	.03	.01
504	Don Werner	.08	.03	.01
505	Garry Templeton	.15	.06	.01
506	Jim Gott	.30	.12	.03
507	Tony Scott	.08	.03	.01
508	Tom Filer	.08	.03	.01
509	Lou Whitaker	.50	.20	.05
510	Tug McGraw	.15	.06	.01
511	SV: Tug McGraw	.08	.03	.01
512	Doyle Alexander	.08	.03	.01
513	Fred Stanley	.08	.03	.01
514	Rudy Law	.08	.03	.01
515	Gene Tenace	.15	.06	.01
516	Bill Virdon MG	.08	.03	.01
517	Gary Ward	.08	.03	.01
518	Bill Laskey	.08	.03	.01
519	Terry Bulling	.08	.03	.01
520	Fred Lynn	.30	.12	.03
521	Bruce Benedict	.08	.03	.01
522	Pat Zachry	.08	.03	.01
523	Carney Lansford	.15	.06	.01
524	Tom Brennan	.08	.03	.01
525	Frank White	.08	.03	.01
526	Checklist: 397-528	.15	.02	.00
527	Larry Biittner	.08	.03	.01
528	Jamie Easterly	.08	.03	.01
529	Tim Laudner	.08	.03	.01
530	Eddie Murray	2.00	.80	.20
531	Oakland A's TL	.40	.12	.02
	BA: Rickey Henderson			
	ERA: Rick Langford			
532	Dave Stewart	1.25	.50	.12
533	Luis Salazar	.08	.03	.01
534	John Butcher	.08	.03	.01
535	Manny Trillo	.08	.03	.01
536	John Wockenfuss	.08	.03	.01
537	Rod Scurry	.08	.03	.01
538	Danny Heep	.08	.03	.01
539	Roger Erickson	.08	.03	.01
540	Ozzie Smith	1.75	.70	.17
541	Britt Burns	.08	.03	.01
542	Jody Davis	.08	.03	.01
543	Alan Fowlkes	.08	.03	.01
544	Larry Whisenton	.08	.03	.01
545	Floyd Bannister	.08	.03	.01
546	Dave Garcia MG	.08	.03	.01
547	Geoff Zahn	.08	.03	.01
548	Brian Giles	.08	.03	.01
549	Charlie Puleo	.08	.03	.01
550	Carl Yastrzemski	1.50	.60	.15
551	SV: Carl Yastrzemski	.75	.30	.07
552	Tim Wallach	.30	.12	.03
553	Dennis Martinez	.15	.06	.01
554	Mike Vail	.08	.03	.01
555	Steve Yeager	.08	.03	.01
556	Willie Upshaw	.08	.03	.01
557	Rick Honeycutt	.08	.03	.01
558	Dickie Thon	.15	.06	.01
559	Pete Redfern	.08	.03	.01
560	Ron LeFlore	.08	.03	.01
561	Cardinals TL	.15	.06	.01
	BA: Lonnie Smith			
	ERA: Joaquin Andujar			
562	Dave Rozema	.08	.03	.01
563	Juan Bonilla	.08	.03	.01
564	Sid Monge	.08	.03	.01
565	Bucky Dent	.15	.06	.01
566	Manny Sarmiento	.08	.03	.01
567	Joe Simpson	.08	.03	.01
568	Willie Hernandez	.08	.03	.01
569	Jack Perconte	.08	.03	.01
570	Vida Blue	.15	.06	.01
571	Mickey Klutts	.08	.03	.01
572	Bob Watson	.08	.03	.01
573	Andy Hassler	.08	.03	.01
574	Glenn Adams	.08	.03	.01
575	Neil Allen	.08	.03	.01
576	Frank Robinson MG	.20	.08	.02
577	Luis Aponte	.08	.03	.01
578	David Green	.08	.03	.01
579	Rich Dauer	.08	.03	.01
580	Tom Seaver	1.50	.60	.15
581	SV: Tom Seaver	.75	.30	.07
582	Marshall Edwards	.08	.03	.01
583	Terry Forster	.15	.06	.01
584	Dave Hostetler	.08	.03	.01
585	Jose Cruz	.15	.06	.01
586	Frank Viola	7.50	3.25	.75
587	Ivan DeJesus	.08	.03	.01
588	Pat Underwood	.08	.03	.01
589	Alvis Woods	.08	.03	.01

#	Player			
590	Tony Pena	.15	.06	.01
591	White Sox TL	.15	.06	.01
	BA: Greg Luzinski			
	ERA: LaMarr Hoyt			
592	Shane Rawley	.08	.03	.01
593	Broderick Perkins	.08	.03	.01
594	Eric Rasmussen	.08	.03	.01
595	Tim Raines	1.00	.40	.10
596	Randy Johnson	.08	.03	.01
597	Mike Proly	.08	.03	.01
598	Dwayne Murphy	.08	.03	.01
599	Don Aase	.08	.03	.01
600	George Brett	2.00	.80	.20
601	Ed Lynch	.08	.03	.01
602	Rich Gedman	.08	.03	.01
603	Joe Morgan	.75	.30	.07
604	SV: Joe Morgan	.35	.15	.03
605	Gary Roenicke	.08	.03	.01
606	Bobby Cox MG	.08	.03	.01
607	Charlie Leibrandt	.15	.06	.01
608	Don Money	.08	.03	.01
609	Danny Darwin	.08	.03	.01
610	Steve Garvey	.75	.30	.07
611	Bert Roberge	.08	.03	.01
612	Steve Swisher	.08	.03	.01
613	Mike Ivie	.08	.03	.01
614	Ed Glynn	.08	.03	.01
615	Garry Maddox	.08	.03	.01
616	Bill Nahorodny	.08	.03	.01
617	Butch Wynegar	.08	.03	.01
618	LaMarr Hoyt	.08	.03	.01
619	Keith Moreland	.08	.03	.01
620	Mike Norris	.08	.03	.01
621	New York Mets TL	.15	.06	.01
	BA: Mookie Wilson			
	ERA: Craig Swan			
622	Dave Edler	.08	.03	.01
623	Luis Sanchez	.08	.03	.01
624	Glenn Hubbard	.08	.03	.01
625	Ken Forsch	.08	.03	.01
626	Jerry Martin	.08	.03	.01
627	Doug Bair	.08	.03	.01
628	Julio Valdez	.08	.03	.01
629	Charlie Lea	.08	.03	.01
630	Paul Molitor	.60	.25	.06
631	Tippy Martinez	.08	.03	.01
632	Alex Trevino	.08	.03	.01
633	Vicente Romo	.08	.03	.01
634	Max Venable	.08	.03	.01
635	Graig Nettles	.15	.06	.01
636	SV: Graig Nettles	.08	.03	.01
637	Pat Corrales MG	.08	.03	.01
638	Dan Petry	.08	.03	.01
639	Art Howe	.15	.06	.01
640	Andre Thornton	.08	.03	.01
641	Billy Sample	.08	.03	.01
642	Checklist: 529-660	.15	.02	.00
643	Bump Wills	.08	.03	.01
644	Joe Lefebvre	.08	.03	.01
645	Bill Madlock	.15	.06	.01
646	Jim Essian	.08	.03	.01
647	Bobby Mitchell	.08	.03	.01
648	Jeff Burroughs	.08	.03	.01
649	Tommy Boggs	.08	.03	.01
650	George Hendrick	.08	.03	.01
651	Angels TL	.20	.07	.01
	BA: Rod Carew			
	ERA: Mike Witt			
652	Butch Hobson	.15	.06	.01
653	Ellis Valentine	.08	.03	.01
654	Bob Ojeda	.15	.06	.01
655	Al Bumbry	.08	.03	.01
656	Dave Frost	.08	.03	.01
657	Mike Gates	.08	.03	.01
658	Frank Pastore	.08	.03	.01
659	Charlie Moore	.08	.03	.01
660	Mike Hargrove	.15	.06	.01
661	Bill Russell	.15	.06	.01
662	Joe Sambito	.08	.03	.01
663	Tom O'Malley	.08	.03	.01
664	Bob Molinaro	.08	.03	.01
665	Jim Sundberg	.08	.03	.01
666	Sparky Anderson MG	.15	.06	.01
667	Dick Davis	.08	.03	.01
668	Larry Christenson	.08	.03	.01
669	Mike Squires	.08	.03	.01
670	Jerry Mumphrey	.08	.03	.01
671	Lenny Faedo	.08	.03	.01
672	Jim Kaat	.20	.08	.02
673	SV: Jim Kaat	.15	.06	.01
674	Kurt Bevacqua	.08	.03	.01
675	Jim Beattie	.08	.03	.01
676	Biff Pocoroba	.08	.03	.01
677	Dave Revering	.08	.03	.01
678	Juan Beniquez	.08	.03	.01
679	Mike Scott	.25	.10	.02
680	Andre Dawson	1.75	.70	.17
681	Dodgers Leaders	.15	.06	.01
	BA: Pedro Guerrero			
	ERA: Fern.Valenzuela			
682	Bob Stanley	.08	.03	.01
683	Dan Ford	.08	.03	.01
684	Rafael Landestoy	.08	.03	.01
685	Lee Mazzilli	.08	.03	.01
686	Randy Lerch	.08	.03	.01
687	U.L. Washington	.08	.03	.01
688	Jim Wohlford	.08	.03	.01
689	Ron Hassey	.08	.03	.01
690	Kent Hrbek	.75	.30	.07
691	Dave Tobik	.08	.03	.01
692	Denny Walling	.08	.03	.01
693	Sparky Lyle	.15	.06	.01
694	SV: Sparky Lyle	.08	.03	.01
695	Ruppert Jones	.08	.03	.01
696	Chuck Tanner MG	.08	.03	.01
697	Barry Foote	.08	.03	.01
698	Tony Bernazard	.08	.03	.01
699	Lee Smith	1.00	.40	.10
700	Keith Hernandez	.35	.15	.03
701	Batting Leaders	.15	.06	.01
	AL: Willie Wilson			
	NL: Al Oliver			
702	Home Run Leaders	.20	.08	.02
	AL: Reggie Jackson			
	AL: Gorman Thomas			
	NL: Dave Kingman			
703	RBI Leaders	.20	.08	.02
	AL: Hal McRae			
	NL: Dale Murphy			
	NL: Al Oliver			
704	SB Leaders	.90	.40	.09
	AL: Rickey Henderson			
	NL: Tim Raines			
705	Victory Leaders	.15	.06	.01
	AL: LaMarr Hoyt			
	NL: Steve Carlton			
706	Strikeout Leaders	.15	.06	.01
	AL: Floyd Bannister			
	NL: Steve Carlton			
707	ERA Leaders	.08	.03	.01
	AL: Rick Sutcliffe			
	NL: Steve Rogers			
708	Leading Firemen	.15	.06	.01
	AL: Dan Quisenberry			
	NL: Bruce Sutter			
709	Jimmy Sexton	.08	.03	.01
710	Willie Wilson	.15	.06	.01
711	Mariners TL	.15	.06	.01
	BA: Bruce Bochte			
	ERA: Jim Beattie			
712	Bruce Kison	.08	.03	.01
713	Ron Hodges	.08	.03	.01
714	Wayne Nordhagen	.08	.03	.01
715	Tony Perez	.40	.16	.04
716	SV: Tony Perez	.20	.08	.02
717	Scott Sanderson	.15	.06	.01
718	Jim Dwyer	.08	.03	.01
719	Rich Gale	.08	.03	.01
720	Dave Concepcion	.15	.06	.01
721	John Martin	.08	.03	.01
722	Jorge Orta	.08	.03	.01
723	Randy Moffitt	.08	.03	.01
724	Johnny Grubb	.08	.03	.01
725	Dan Spillner	.08	.03	.01
726	Harvey Kuenn MG	.08	.03	.01
727	Chet Lemon	.08	.03	.01
728	Ron Reed	.08	.03	.01
729	Jerry Morales	.08	.03	.01
730	Jason Thompson	.08	.03	.01
731	Al Williams	.08	.03	.01
732	Dave Henderson	.75	.30	.07
733	Buck Martinez	.08	.03	.01
734	Steve Braun	.08	.03	.01
735	Tommy John	.25	.10	.02
736	SV: Tommy John	.15	.06	.01
737	Mitchell Page	.08	.03	.01
738	Tim Foli	.08	.03	.01
739	Rick Ownbey	.08	.03	.01
740	Rusty Staub	.15	.06	.01
741	SV: Rusty Staub	.08	.03	.01
742	Padres TL	.15	.06	.01
	BA: Terry Kennedy			
	ERA: Tim Lollar			
743	Mike Torrez	.08	.03	.01
744	Brad Mills	.08	.03	.01
745	Scott McGregor	.08	.03	.01
746	John Wathan	.08	.03	.01
747	Fred Breining	.08	.03	.01

☐ 748	Derrel Thomas	.08	.03	.01
☐ 749	Jon Matlack	.08	.03	.01
☐ 750	Ben Oglivie	.08	.03	.01
☐ 751	Brad Havens	.08	.03	.01
☐ 752	Luis Pujols	.08	.03	.01
☐ 753	Elias Sosa	.08	.03	.01
☐ 754	Bill Robinson	.15	.06	.01
☐ 755	John Candelaria	.08	.03	.01
☐ 756	Russ Nixon MG	.08	.03	.01
☐ 757	Rick Manning	.08	.03	.01
☐ 758	Aurelio Rodriguez	.08	.03	.01
☐ 759	Doug Bird	.08	.03	.01
☐ 760	Dale Murphy	1.25	.50	.12
☐ 761	Gary Lucas	.08	.03	.01
☐ 762	Cliff Johnson	.08	.03	.01
☐ 763	Al Cowens	.08	.03	.01
☐ 764	Pete Falcone	.08	.03	.01
☐ 765	Bob Boone	.15	.06	.01
☐ 766	Barry Bonnell	.08	.03	.01
☐ 767	Duane Kuiper	.08	.03	.01
☐ 768	Chris Speier	.08	.03	.01
☐ 769	Checklist: 661-792	.15	.02	.00
☐ 770	Dave Winfield	1.25	.50	.12
☐ 771	Twins TL	.15	.06	.01
	BA: Kent Hrbek			
	ERA: Bobby Castillo			
☐ 772	Jim Kern	.08	.03	.01
☐ 773	Larry Hisle	.08	.03	.01
☐ 774	Alan Ashby	.08	.03	.01
☐ 775	Burt Hooton	.08	.03	.01
☐ 776	Larry Parrish	.08	.03	.01
☐ 777	John Curtis	.08	.03	.01
☐ 778	Rich Hebner	.08	.03	.01
☐ 779	Rick Waits	.08	.03	.01
☐ 780	Gary Matthews	.08	.03	.01
☐ 781	Rick Rhoden	.08	.03	.01
☐ 782	Bobby Murcer	.15	.06	.01
☐ 783	SV: Bobby Murcer	.08	.03	.01
☐ 784	Jeff Newman	.08	.03	.01
☐ 785	Dennis Leonard	.08	.03	.01
☐ 786	Ralph Houk MG	.08	.03	.01
☐ 787	Dick Tidrow	.08	.03	.01
☐ 788	Dane Iorg	.08	.03	.01
☐ 789	Bryan Clark	.08	.03	.01
☐ 790	Bob Grich	.15	.06	.01
☐ 791	Gary Lavelle	.08	.03	.01
☐ 792	Chris Chambliss	.15	.06	.01

1983 Topps Traded

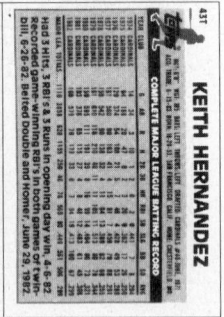

The cards in this 132-card set measure 2 1/2" by 3 1/2". For the third year in a row, Topps issued a 132-card Traded (or extended) set featuring some of the year's top rookies and players who had changed teams during the year, but were featured with their old team in the Topps regular issue of 1983. The cards were available through hobby dealers only and were printed in Ireland by the Topps affiliate in that country. The set is numbered alphabetically by the last name of the player of the card. The Darryl Strawberry card number 108 can be found with either one or two asterisks (in the lower left corner of the reverse). The key (extended) rookie card in this set is obviously Darryl Strawberry. Also noteworthy is Julio Franco's first Topps (extended) card.

		MINT	EXC	G-VG
	COMPLETE SET (132)	125.00	57.50	18.75
	COMMON PLAYER (1-132)	.12	.05	.01
☐ 1T	Neil Allen	.20	.08	.02
☐ 2T	Bill Almon	.12	.05	.01
☐ 3T	Joe Altobelli MG	.12	.05	.01
☐ 4T	Tony Armas	.12	.05	.01
☐ 5T	Doug Bair	.12	.05	.01
☐ 6T	Steve Baker	.12	.05	.01
☐ 7T	Floyd Bannister	.12	.05	.01
☐ 8T	Don Baylor	.25	.10	.02
☐ 9T	Tony Bernazard	.12	.05	.01
☐ 10T	Larry Biittner	.12	.05	.01
☐ 11T	Dann Bilardello	.12	.05	.01
☐ 12T	Doug Bird	.12	.05	.01
☐ 13T	Steve Boros MG	.12	.05	.01
☐ 14T	Greg Brock	.20	.08	.02
☐ 15T	Mike Brown	.12	.05	.01
	(Red Sox pitcher)			
☐ 16T	Tom Burgmeier	.12	.05	.01
☐ 17T	Randy Bush	.25	.10	.02
☐ 18T	Bert Campaneris	.20	.08	.02
☐ 19T	Ron Cey	.20	.08	.02
☐ 20T	Chris Codiroli	.12	.05	.01
☐ 21T	Dave Collins	.12	.05	.01
☐ 22T	Terry Crowley	.12	.05	.01
☐ 23T	Julio Cruz	.12	.05	.01
☐ 24T	Mike Davis	.12	.05	.01
☐ 25T	Frank DiPino	.12	.05	.01
☐ 26T	Bill Doran	1.00	.40	.10
☐ 27T	Jerry Dybzinski	.12	.05	.01
☐ 28T	Jamie Easterly	.12	.05	.01
☐ 29T	Juan Eichelberger	.12	.05	.01
☐ 30T	Jim Essian	.20	.08	.02
☐ 31T	Pete Falcone	.12	.05	.01
☐ 32T	Mike Ferraro MG	.12	.05	.01
☐ 33T	Terry Forster	.20	.08	.02
☐ 34T	Julio Franco	11.00	5.00	1.35
☐ 35T	Rich Gale	.12	.05	.01
☐ 36T	Kiko Garcia	.12	.05	.01
☐ 37T	Steve Garvey	1.25	.50	.12
☐ 38T	Johnny Grubb	.12	.05	.01
☐ 39T	Mel Hall	1.50	.60	.15
☐ 40T	Von Hayes	.50	.20	.05
☐ 41T	Danny Heep	.20	.08	.02
☐ 42T	Steve Henderson	.12	.05	.01
☐ 43T	Keith Hernandez	.75	.30	.07
☐ 44T	Leo Hernandez	.12	.05	.01
☐ 45T	Willie Hernandez	.20	.08	.02
☐ 46T	Al Holland	.12	.05	.01
☐ 47T	Frank Howard MG	.20	.08	.02
☐ 48T	Bobby Johnson	.12	.05	.01
☐ 49T	Cliff Johnson	.12	.05	.01
☐ 50T	Odell Jones	.12	.05	.01
☐ 51T	Mike Jorgensen	.12	.05	.01
☐ 52T	Bob Kearney	.12	.05	.01
☐ 53T	Steve Kemp	.20	.08	.02
☐ 54T	Matt Keough	.12	.05	.01
☐ 55T	Ron Kittle	.50	.20	.05
☐ 56T	Mickey Klutts	.12	.05	.01
☐ 57T	Alan Knicely	.12	.05	.01
☐ 58T	Mike Krukow	.12	.05	.01
☐ 59T	Rafael Landestoy	.12	.05	.01
☐ 60T	Carney Lansford	.35	.15	.03
☐ 61T	Joe Lefebvre	.12	.05	.01
☐ 62T	Bryan Little	.12	.05	.01
☐ 63T	Aurelio Lopez	.12	.05	.01
☐ 64T	Mike Madden	.12	.05	.01
☐ 65T	Rick Manning	.12	.05	.01
☐ 66T	Billy Martin MG	.30	.12	.03
☐ 67T	Lee Mazzilli	.12	.05	.01
☐ 68T	Andy McGaffigan	.12	.05	.01
☐ 69T	Craig McMurtry	.12	.05	.01
☐ 70T	John McNamara MG	.12	.05	.01
☐ 71T	Orlando Mercado	.12	.05	.01
☐ 72T	Larry Milbourne	.12	.05	.01
☐ 73T	Randy Moffitt	.12	.05	.01
☐ 74T	Sid Monge	.12	.05	.01
☐ 75T	Jose Morales	.12	.05	.01
☐ 76T	Omar Moreno	.12	.05	.01
☐ 77T	Joe Morgan	2.50	1.00	.25
☐ 78T	Mike Morgan	.30	.12	.03
☐ 79T	Dale Murray	.12	.05	.01
☐ 80T	Jeff Newman	.12	.05	.01
☐ 81T	Pete O'Brien	1.00	.40	.10
☐ 82T	Jorge Orta	.12	.05	.01
☐ 83T	Alejandro Pena	1.25	.50	.12
☐ 84T	Pascual Perez	.30	.12	.03
☐ 85T	Tony Perez	1.25	.50	.12
☐ 86T	Broderick Perkins	.12	.05	.01
☐ 87T	Tony Phillips	1.25	.50	.12
☐ 88T	Charlie Puleo	.12	.05	.01
☐ 89T	Pat Putnam	.12	.05	.01

			MINT	EXC	G-VG
☐	90T	Jamie Quirk	.12	.05	.01
☐	91T	Doug Rader MG	.20	.08	.02
☐	92T	Chuck Rainey	.12	.05	.01
☐	93T	Bobby Ramos	.12	.05	.01
☐	94T	Gary Redus	.65	.25	.06
☐	95T	Steve Renko	.12	.05	.01
☐	96T	Leon Roberts	.12	.05	.01
☐	97T	Aurelio Rodriguez	.12	.05	.01
☐	98T	Dick Ruthven	.12	.05	.01
☐	99T	Daryl Sconiers	.12	.05	.01
☐	100T	Mike Scott	.50	.20	.05
☐	101T	Tom Seaver	5.50	2.50	.55
☐	102T	John Shelby	.30	.12	.03
☐	103T	Bob Shirley	.12	.05	.01
☐	104T	Joe Simpson	.12	.05	.01
☐	105T	Doug Sisk	.12	.05	.01
☐	106T	Mike Smithson	.12	.05	.01
☐	107T	Elias Sosa	.12	.05	.01
☐	108T	Darryl Strawberry	100.00	45.00	15.00
☐	109T	Tom Tellmann	.12	.05	.01
☐	110T	Gene Tenace	.20	.08	.02
☐	111T	Gorman Thomas	.25	.10	.02
☐	112T	Dick Tidrow	.12	.05	.01
☐	113T	Dave Tobik	.12	.05	.01
☐	114T	Wayne Tolleson	.12	.05	.01
☐	115T	Mike Torrez	.12	.05	.01
☐	116T	Manny Trillo	.12	.05	.01
☐	117T	Steve Trout	.12	.05	.01
☐	118T	Lee Tunnell	.12	.05	.01
☐	119T	Mike Vail	.12	.05	.01
☐	120T	Ellis Valentine	.12	.05	.01
☐	121T	Tom Veryzer	.12	.05	.01
☐	122T	George Vukovich	.12	.05	.01
☐	123T	Rick Waits	.12	.05	.01
☐	124T	Greg Walker	.25	.10	.02
☐	125T	Chris Welsh	.12	.05	.01
☐	126T	Len Whitehouse	.12	.05	.01
☐	127T	Eddie Whitson	.20	.08	.02
☐	128T	Jim Wohlford	.12	.05	.01
☐	129T	Matt Young	.20	.08	.02
☐	130T	Joel Youngblood	.12	.05	.01
☐	131T	Pat Zachry	.12	.05	.01
☐	132T	Checklist 1T-132T	.12	.02	.00

			MINT	EXC	G-VG
☐	8	Mike Schmidt	1.25	.50	.12
☐	9	Buddy Bell	.20	.08	.02
☐	10	Fernando Valenzuela	.30	.12	.03
☐	11	Rich Gossage	.25	.10	.02
☐	12	Bob Horner	.20	.08	.02
☐	13	Toby Harrah	.20	.08	.02
☐	14	Pete Rose	1.25	.50	.12
☐	15	Cecil Cooper	.20	.08	.02
☐	16	Dale Murphy	.90	.40	.09
☐	17	Carlton Fisk	.75	.30	.07
☐	18	Ray Knight	.25	.10	.02
☐	19	Jim Palmer	.75	.30	.07
☐	20	Gary Carter	.45	.18	.04
☐	21	Richie Zisk	.20	.08	.02
☐	22	Dusty Baker	.20	.08	.02
☐	23	Willie Wilson	.25	.10	.02
☐	24	Bill Buckner	.20	.08	.02
☐	25	Dave Stieb	.25	.10	.02
☐	26	Bill Madlock	.20	.08	.02
☐	27	Lance Parrish	.30	.12	.03
☐	28	Nolan Ryan	2.00	.80	.20
☐	29	Rod Carew	1.00	.40	.10
☐	30	Al Oliver	.25	.10	.02
☐	31	George Brett	1.00	.40	.10
☐	32	Jack Clark	.30	.12	.03
☐	33	Ricky Henderson	1.50	.60	.15
☐	34	Dave Concepcion	.25	.10	.02
☐	35	Kent Hrbek	.40	.16	.04
☐	36	Steve Carlton	.60	.25	.06
☐	37	Eddie Murray	1.00	.40	.10
☐	38	Ruppert Jones	.20	.08	.02
☐	39	Reggie Jackson	1.00	.40	.10
☐	40	Bruce Sutter	.25	.10	.02

1983 Topps Gaylord Perry

This six-card, standard-size, 2 1/2" by 3 1/2" set depicts Gaylord Perry during various parts of his career. These cards have the looks of Topps cards and were produced by Topps but have no Topps logo on either the front or the back of the card.

			MINT	EXC	G-VG
COMPLETE SET (6)			15.00	6.50	2.15
COMMON PLAYER (1-6)			3.00	1.25	.30
☐ 1	Gaylord Perry San Francisco Giants (Perry wins first game in 1962)		3.00	1.25	.30
☐ 2	Gaylord Perry San Francisco Giants (Perry pitches no- hitter in 1968)		3.00	1.25	.30
☐ 3	Gaylord Perry Cleveland Indians (Perry wins Cy Young Award in 1972)		3.00	1.25	.30
☐ 4	Gaylord Perry Texas Rangers (Perry strikes out 2,500th in 1975)		3.00	1.25	.30
☐ 5	Gaylord Perry San Diego Padres (Perry wins second Cy Young and strikes out 3,000th in 1978)		3.00	1.25	.30

1983 Topps Glossy 40

The cards in this 40-card set measure 2 1/2" by 3 1/2". The 1983 Topps "Collector's Edition" or "All-Star Set" (popularly known as "Glossies") consists of color ballplayer picture cards with shiny, glazed surfaces. The player's name appears in small print outside the frame line at bottom left. The backs contain no biography or record and list only the set titles, the player's name, team, position, and the card number.

			MINT	EXC	G-VG
COMPLETE SET (40)			12.50	5.50	1.65
COMMON PLAYER (1-40)			.20	.08	.02
☐	1	Carl Yastrzemski	1.25	.50	.12
☐	2	Mookie Wilson	.20	.08	.02
☐	3	Andre Thornton	.20	.08	.02
☐	4	Keith Hernandez	.30	.12	.03
☐	5	Robin Yount	1.00	.40	.10
☐	6	Terry Kennedy	.20	.08	.02
☐	7	Dave Winfield	.60	.25	.06

		MINT	EXC	G-VG
☐ 6	Gaylord Perry .... Seattle Mariners (Perry wins 300th game in 1982)	3.00	1.25	.30

1984 Topps

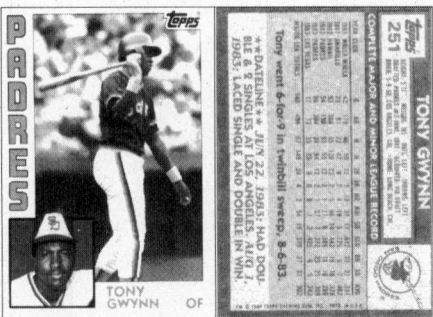

The cards in this 792-card set measure 2 1/2" by 3 1/2". For the second year in a row, Topps utilized a dual picture on the front of the card. A portrait is shown in a square insert and an action shot is featured in the main photo. Card numbers 1-6 feature 1983 Highlights (HL), cards 131-138 depict League Leaders, card numbers 386-407 feature All-Stars, and card numbers 701-718 feature active Major League career leaders in various statistical categories. Each team leader (TL) card features the team's leading hitter and pitcher pictured on the front with a team checklist back. There are six numerical checklist cards in the set. The player cards feature team logos in the upper right corner of the reverse. The key rookie cards in this set are Don Mattingly, Darryl Strawberry, and Andy Van Slyke. Topps also produced a specially boxed "glossy" edition, frequently referred to as the Topps Tiffany set. There were supposedly only 10,000 sets of the Tiffany cards produced; they were marketed to hobby dealers. The checklist of cards (792 regular and 132 Traded) is identical to that of the normal non-glossy cards. There are two primary distinguishing features of the Tiffany cards, white card stock reverses and high gloss obverses. These Tiffany cards are valued at approximately five times the values listed below. Topps tested a special send-in offer in Michigan and a few other states whereby collectors could obtain direct from Topps ten cards of their choice. Needless to say most people ordered the key (most valuable) players necessitating the printing of a special sheet to keep up with the demand. The special sheet had five cards of Darryl Strawberry, three cards of Don Mattingly, etc. The test was apparently a failure in Topps' eyes as they have never tried it again.

		MINT	EXC	G-VG
	COMPLETE SET (792)	100.00	45.00	15.00
	COMMON PLAYER (1-792)	.06	.02	.00
☐ 1	HL: Steve Carlton .... 300th win and all-time SO king	.40	.10	.02
☐ 2	HL: Rickey Henderson .... 100 stolen bases, three times	1.00	.40	.10
☐ 3	HL: Dan Quisenberry .... Sets save record	.10	.04	.01
☐ 4	HL: Nolan Ryan, ... Steve Carlton, and Gaylord Perry (All surpass Johnson)	.50	.20	.05
☐ 5	HL: Dave Righetti, ... Bob Forsch, and Mike Warren (All pitch no-hitters)	.10	.04	.01
☐ 6	HL: Johnny Bench, ...	.35	.15	.03

	Gaylord Perry, and Carl Yastrzemski (Superstars retire)			
☐ 7	Gary Lucas	.06	.02	.00
☐ 8	Don Mattingly	20.00	8.50	2.75
☐ 9	Jim Gott	.10	.04	.01
☐ 10	Robin Yount	1.25	.50	.12
☐ 11	Minnesota Twins TL .... Kent Hrbek Ken Schrom	.10	.04	.01
☐ 12	Billy Sample	.06	.02	.00
☐ 13	Scott Holman	.06	.02	.00
☐ 14	Tom Brookens	.06	.02	.00
☐ 15	Burt Hooton	.06	.02	.00
☐ 16	Omar Moreno	.06	.02	.00
☐ 17	John Denny	.06	.02	.00
☐ 18	Dale Berra	.06	.02	.00
☐ 19	Ray Fontenot	.06	.02	.00
☐ 20	Greg Luzinski	.10	.04	.01
☐ 21	Joe Altobelli MG	.06	.02	.00
☐ 22	Bryan Clark	.06	.02	.00
☐ 23	Keith Moreland	.06	.02	.00
☐ 24	John Martin	.06	.02	.00
☐ 25	Glenn Hubbard	.06	.02	.00
☐ 26	Bud Black	.10	.04	.01
☐ 27	Daryl Sconiers	.06	.02	.00
☐ 28	Frank Viola	.75	.30	.07
☐ 29	Danny Heep	.06	.02	.00
☐ 30	Wade Boggs	5.00	2.25	.50
☐ 31	Andy McGaffigan	.06	.02	.00
☐ 32	Bobby Ramos	.06	.02	.00
☐ 33	Tom Burgmeier	.06	.02	.00
☐ 34	Eddie Milner	.06	.02	.00
☐ 35	Don Sutton	.35	.15	.03
☐ 36	Denny Walling	.06	.02	.00
☐ 37	Texas Rangers TL .... Buddy Bell Rick Honeycutt	.10	.04	.01
☐ 38	Luis DeLeon	.06	.02	.00
☐ 39	Garth Iorg	.06	.02	.00
☐ 40	Dusty Baker	.10	.04	.01
☐ 41	Tony Bernazard	.06	.02	.00
☐ 42	Johnny Grubb	.06	.02	.00
☐ 43	Ron Reed	.06	.02	.00
☐ 44	Jim Morrison	.06	.02	.00
☐ 45	Jerry Mumphrey	.06	.02	.00
☐ 46	Ray Smith	.06	.02	.00
☐ 47	Rudy Law	.06	.02	.00
☐ 48	Julio Franco	3.00	1.25	.30
☐ 49	John Stuper	.06	.02	.00
☐ 50	Chris Chambliss	.10	.04	.01
☐ 51	Jim Frey MG	.06	.02	.00
☐ 52	Paul Splittorff	.06	.02	.00
☐ 53	Juan Beniquez	.06	.02	.00
☐ 54	Jesse Orosco	.06	.02	.00
☐ 55	Dave Concepcion	.10	.04	.01
☐ 56	Gary Allenson	.06	.02	.00
☐ 57	Dan Schatzeder	.06	.02	.00
☐ 58	Max Venable	.06	.02	.00
☐ 59	Sammy Stewart	.06	.02	.00
☐ 60	Paul Molitor UER .... ('83 stats .272, 613, 167; should be .270, 608, 164)	.30	.12	.03
☐ 61	Chris Codiroli	.06	.02	.00
☐ 62	Dave Hostetler	.06	.02	.00
☐ 63	Ed VandeBerg	.06	.02	.00
☐ 64	Mike Scioscia	.10	.04	.01
☐ 65	Kirk Gibson	.40	.16	.04
☐ 66	Houston Astros TL .... Jose Cruz Nolan Ryan	.30	.12	.03
☐ 67	Gary Ward	.06	.02	.00
☐ 68	Luis Salazar	.06	.02	.00
☐ 69	Rod Scurry	.06	.02	.00
☐ 70	Gary Matthews	.06	.02	.00
☐ 71	Leo Hernandez	.06	.02	.00
☐ 72	Mike Squires	.06	.02	.00
☐ 73	Jody Davis	.06	.02	.00
☐ 74	Jerry Martin	.06	.02	.00
☐ 75	Bob Forsch	.06	.02	.00
☐ 76	Alfredo Griffin	.06	.02	.00
☐ 77	Brett Butler	.30	.12	.03
☐ 78	Mike Torrez	.06	.02	.00
☐ 79	Rob Wilfong	.06	.02	.00
☐ 80	Steve Rogers	.06	.02	.00
☐ 81	Billy Martin MG	.15	.06	.01
☐ 82	Doug Bird	.06	.02	.00
☐ 83	Richie Zisk	.06	.02	.00
☐ 84	Lenny Faedo	.06	.02	.00
☐ 85	Atlee Hammaker	.06	.02	.00
☐ 86	John Shelby	.15	.06	.01
☐ 87	Frank Pastore	.06	.02	.00
☐ 88	Rob Picciolo	.06	.02	.00
☐ 89	Mike Smithson	.06	.02	.00

☐	90	Pedro Guerrero	.25	.10	.02	☐	162	Bob Ojeda	.10	.04	.01
☐	91	Dan Spillner	.06	.02	.00	☐	163	Lorenzo Gray	.06	.02	.00
☐	92	Lloyd Moseby	.10	.04	.01	☐	164	Scott Sanderson	.10	.04	.01
☐	93	Bob Knepper	.06	.02	.00	☐	165	Ken Singleton	.10	.04	.01
☐	94	Mario Ramirez	.06	.02	.00	☐	166	Jamie Nelson	.06	.02	.00
☐	95	Aurelio Lopez	.06	.02	.00	☐	167	Marshall Edwards	.06	.02	.00
☐	96	K.C. Royals TL	.10	.04	.01	☐	168	Juan Bonilla	.06	.02	.00
		Hal McRae				☐	169	Larry Parrish	.06	.02	.00
		Larry Gura				☐	170	Jerry Reuss	.06	.02	.00
☐	97	LaMarr Hoyt	.06	.02	.00	☐	171	Frank Robinson MG	.15	.06	.01
☐	98	Steve Nicosia	.06	.02	.00	☐	172	Frank DiPino	.06	.02	.00
☐	99	Craig Lefferts	.20	.08	.02	☐	173	Marvell Wynne	.10	.04	.01
☐	100	Reggie Jackson	1.00	.40	.10	☐	174	Juan Berenguer	.06	.02	.00
☐	101	Porfirio Altamirano	.06	.02	.00	☐	175	Graig Nettles	.15	.06	.01
☐	102	Ken Oberkfell	.06	.02	.00	☐	176	Lee Smith	.40	.16	.04
☐	103	Dwayne Murphy	.06	.02	.00	☐	177	Jerry Hairston	.06	.02	.00
☐	104	Ken Dayley	.06	.02	.00	☐	178	Bill Krueger	.10	.04	.01
☐	105	Tony Armas	.06	.02	.00	☐	179	Buck Martinez	.06	.02	.00
☐	106	Tim Stoddard	.06	.02	.00	☐	180	Manny Trillo	.06	.02	.00
☐	107	Ned Yost	.06	.02	.00	☐	181	Roy Thomas	.06	.02	.00
☐	108	Randy Moffitt	.06	.02	.00	☐	182	Darryl Strawberry	21.00	9.00	3.00
☐	109	Brad Wellman	.06	.02	.00	☐	183	Al Williams	.06	.02	.00
☐	110	Ron Guidry	.25	.10	.02	☐	184	Mike O'Berry	.06	.02	.00
☐	111	Bill Virdon MG	.06	.02	.00	☐	185	Sixto Lezcano	.06	.02	.00
☐	112	Tom Niedenfuer	.06	.02	.00	☐	186	Cardinal TL	.10	.04	.01
☐	113	Kelly Paris	.06	.02	.00			Lonnie Smith			
☐	114	Checklist 1-132	.12	.02	.00			John Stuper			
☐	115	Andre Thornton	.10	.04	.01	☐	187	Luis Aponte	.06	.02	.00
☐	116	George Bjorkman	.06	.02	.00	☐	188	Bryan Little	.06	.02	.00
☐	117	Tom Veryzer	.06	.02	.00	☐	189	Tim Conroy	.06	.02	.00
☐	118	Charlie Hough	.06	.02	.00	☐	190	Ben Oglivie	.06	.02	.00
☐	119	John Wockenfuss	.06	.02	.00	☐	191	Mike Boddicker	.06	.02	.00
☐	120	Keith Hernandez	.25	.10	.02	☐	192	Nick Esasky	.15	.06	.01
☐	121	Pat Sheridan	.10	.04	.01	☐	193	Darrell Brown	.06	.02	.00
☐	122	Cecilio Guante	.06	.02	.00	☐	194	Domingo Ramos	.06	.02	.00
☐	123	Butch Wynegar	.06	.02	.00	☐	195	Jack Morris	.60	.25	.06
☐	124	Damaso Garcia	.06	.02	.00	☐	196	Don Slaught	.15	.06	.01
☐	125	Britt Burns	.06	.02	.00	☐	197	Garry Hancock	.06	.02	.00
☐	126	Atlanta Braves TL	.15	.06	.01	☐	198	Bill Doran	.30	.12	.03
		Dale Murphy				☐	199	Willie Hernandez	.10	.04	.01
		Craig McMurtry				☐	200	Andre Dawson	1.00	.40	.10
☐	127	Mike Madden	.06	.02	.00	☐	201	Bruce Kison	.06	.02	.00
☐	128	Rick Manning	.06	.02	.00	☐	202	Bobby Cox MG	.06	.02	.00
☐	129	Bill Laskey	.06	.02	.00	☐	203	Matt Keough	.06	.02	.00
☐	130	Ozzie Smith	1.00	.40	.10	☐	204	Bobby Meacham	.06	.02	.00
☐	131	Batting Leaders	.45	.18	.04	☐	205	Greg Minton	.06	.02	.00
		Bill Madlock				☐	206	Andy Van Slyke	2.50	1.00	.25
		Wade Boggs				☐	207	Donnie Moore	.06	.02	.00
☐	132	Home Run Leaders	.25	.10	.02	☐	208	Jose Oquendo	.20	.08	.02
		Mike Schmidt				☐	209	Manny Sarmiento	.06	.02	.00
		Jim Rice				☐	210	Joe Morgan	.40	.16	.04
☐	133	RBI Leaders	.20	.08	.02	☐	211	Rick Sweet	.06	.02	.00
		Dale Murphy				☐	212	Broderick Perkins	.06	.02	.00
		Cecil Cooper				☐	213	Bruce Hurst	.15	.06	.01
		Jim Rice				☐	214	Paul Householder	.06	.02	.00
☐	134	Stolen Base Leaders	.60	.25	.06	☐	215	Tippy Martinez	.06	.02	.00
		Tim Raines				☐	216	White Sox TL	.15	.06	.01
		Rickey Henderson						Carlton Fisk			
☐	135	Victory Leaders	.10	.04	.01			Richard Dotson			
		John Denny				☐	217	Alan Ashby	.06	.02	.00
		LaMarr Hoyt				☐	218	Rick Waits	.06	.02	.00
☐	136	Strikeout Leaders	.25	.10	.02	☐	219	Joe Simpson	.06	.02	.00
		Steve Carlton				☐	220	Fernando Valenzuela	.20	.08	.02
		Jack Morris				☐	221	Cliff Johnson	.06	.02	.00
☐	137	ERA Leaders	.10	.04	.01	☐	222	Rick Honeycutt	.06	.02	.00
		Atlee Hammaker				☐	223	Wayne Krenchicki	.06	.02	.00
		Rick Honeycutt				☐	224	Sid Monge	.06	.02	.00
☐	138	Leading Firemen	.10	.04	.01	☐	225	Lee Mazzilli	.06	.02	.00
		Al Holland				☐	226	Juan Eichelberger	.06	.02	.00
		Dan Quisenberry				☐	227	Steve Braun	.06	.02	.00
☐	139	Bert Campaneris	.10	.04	.01	☐	228	John Rabb	.06	.02	.00
☐	140	Storm Davis	.10	.04	.01	☐	229	Paul Owens MG	.06	.02	.00
☐	141	Pat Corrales MG	.06	.02	.00	☐	230	Rickey Henderson	5.00	2.25	.50
☐	142	Rich Gale	.06	.02	.00	☐	231	Gary Woods	.06	.02	.00
☐	143	Jose Morales	.06	.02	.00	☐	232	Tim Wallach	.15	.06	.01
☐	144	Brian Harper	.60	.25	.06	☐	233	Checklist 133-264	.12	.02	.00
☐	145	Gary Lavelle	.06	.02	.00	☐	234	Rafael Ramirez	.06	.02	.00
☐	146	Ed Romero	.06	.02	.00	☐	235	Matt Young	.10	.04	.01
☐	147	Dan Petry	.06	.02	.00	☐	236	Ellis Valentine	.06	.02	.00
☐	148	Joe Lefebvre	.06	.02	.00	☐	237	John Castino	.06	.02	.00
☐	149	Jon Matlack	.06	.02	.00	☐	238	Reid Nichols	.06	.02	.00
☐	150	Dale Murphy	.75	.30	.07	☐	239	Jay Howell	.10	.04	.01
☐	151	Steve Trout	.06	.02	.00	☐	240	Eddie Murray	1.25	.50	.12
☐	152	Glenn Brummer	.06	.02	.00	☐	241	Bill Almon	.06	.02	.00
☐	153	Dick Tidrow	.06	.02	.00	☐	242	Alex Trevino	.06	.02	.00
☐	154	Dave Henderson	.40	.16	.04	☐	243	Pete Ladd	.06	.02	.00
☐	155	Frank White	.06	.02	.00	☐	244	Candy Maldonado	.20	.08	.02
☐	156	Oakland A's TL	.25	.10	.02	☐	245	Rick Sutcliffe	.10	.04	.01
		Rickey Henderson				☐	246	New York Mets TL	.20	.08	.02
		Tim Conroy						Mookie Wilson			
☐	157	Gary Gaetti	.15	.06	.01			Tom Seaver			
☐	158	John Curtis	.06	.02	.00	☐	247	Onix Concepcion	.06	.02	.00
☐	159	Darryl Cias	.06	.02	.00	☐	248	Bill Dawley	.06	.02	.00
☐	160	Mario Soto	.06	.02	.00	☐	249	Jay Johnstone	.10	.04	.01
☐	161	Junior Ortiz	.10	.04	.01	☐	250	Bill Madlock	.10	.04	.01

☐ 251	Tony Gwynn	4.50	2.00	.45
☐ 252	Larry Christenson	.06	.02	.00
☐ 253	Jim Wohlford	.06	.02	.00
☐ 254	Shane Rawley	.06	.02	.00
☐ 255	Bruce Benedict	.06	.02	.00
☐ 256	Dave Geisel	.06	.02	.00
☐ 257	Julio Cruz	.06	.02	.00
☐ 258	Luis Sanchez	.06	.02	.00
☐ 259	Sparky Anderson MG	.10	.04	.01
☐ 260	Scott McGregor	.06	.02	.00
☐ 261	Bobby Brown	.06	.02	.00
☐ 262	Tom Candiotti	.40	.16	.04
☐ 263	Jack Fimple	.06	.02	.00
☐ 264	Doug Frobel	.06	.02	.00
☐ 265	Donnie Hill	.10	.04	.01
☐ 266	Steve Lubratich	.06	.02	.00
☐ 267	Carmelo Martinez	.15	.06	.01
☐ 268	Jack O'Connor	.06	.02	.00
☐ 269	Aurelio Rodriguez	.06	.02	.00
☐ 270	Jeff Russell	.30	.12	.03
☐ 271	Moose Haas	.06	.02	.00
☐ 272	Rick Dempsey	.06	.02	.00
☐ 273	Charlie Puleo	.06	.02	.00
☐ 274	Rick Monday	.06	.02	.00
☐ 275	Len Matuszek	.06	.02	.00
☐ 276	Angels TL	.15	.06	.01
	Rod Carew			
	Geoff Zahn			
☐ 277	Eddie Whitson	.06	.02	.00
☐ 278	Jorge Bell	1.00	.40	.10
☐ 279	Ivan DeJesus	.06	.02	.00
☐ 280	Floyd Bannister	.06	.02	.00
☐ 281	Larry Milbourne	.06	.02	.00
☐ 282	Jim Barr	.06	.02	.00
☐ 283	Larry Biittner	.06	.02	.00
☐ 284	Howard Bailey	.06	.02	.00
☐ 285	Darrell Porter	.06	.02	.00
☐ 286	Lary Sorensen	.06	.02	.00
☐ 287	Warren Cromartie	.06	.02	.00
☐ 288	Jim Beattie	.06	.02	.00
☐ 289	Randy Johnson	.06	.02	.00
☐ 290	Dave Dravecky	.15	.06	.01
☐ 291	Chuck Tanner MG	.06	.02	.00
☐ 292	Tony Scott	.06	.02	.00
☐ 293	Ed Lynch	.06	.02	.00
☐ 294	U.L. Washington	.06	.02	.00
☐ 295	Mike Flanagan	.10	.04	.01
☐ 296	Jeff Newman	.06	.02	.00
☐ 297	Bruce Berenyi	.06	.02	.00
☐ 298	Jim Gantner	.06	.02	.00
☐ 299	John Butcher	.06	.02	.00
☐ 300	Pete Rose	1.00	.40	.10
☐ 301	Frank LaCorte	.06	.02	.00
☐ 302	Barry Bonnell	.06	.02	.00
☐ 303	Marty Castillo	.06	.02	.00
☐ 304	Warren Brusstar	.06	.02	.00
☐ 305	Roy Smalley	.06	.02	.00
☐ 306	Dodgers TL	.15	.06	.01
	Pedro Guerrero			
	Bob Welch			
☐ 307	Bobby Mitchell	.06	.02	.00
☐ 308	Ron Hassey	.06	.02	.00
☐ 309	Tony Phillips	.35	.15	.03
☐ 310	Willie McGee	.40	.16	.04
☐ 311	Jerry Koosman	.10	.04	.01
☐ 312	Jorge Orta	.06	.02	.00
☐ 313	Mike Jorgensen	.06	.02	.00
☐ 314	Orlando Mercado	.06	.02	.00
☐ 315	Bob Grich	.10	.04	.01
☐ 316	Mark Bradley	.06	.02	.00
☐ 317	Greg Pryor	.06	.02	.00
☐ 318	Bill Gullickson	.10	.04	.01
☐ 319	Al Bumbry	.06	.02	.00
☐ 320	Bob Stanley	.06	.02	.00
☐ 321	Harvey Kuenn MG	.06	.02	.00
☐ 322	Ken Schrom	.06	.02	.00
☐ 323	Alan Knicely	.06	.02	.00
☐ 324	Alejandro Pena	.30	.12	.03
☐ 325	Darrell Evans	.15	.06	.01
☐ 326	Bob Kearney	.06	.02	.00
☐ 327	Ruppert Jones	.06	.02	.00
☐ 328	Vern Ruhle	.06	.02	.00
☐ 329	Pat Tabler	.10	.04	.01
☐ 330	John Candelaria	.06	.02	.00
☐ 331	Bucky Dent	.10	.04	.01
☐ 332	Kevin Gross	.20	.08	.02
☐ 333	Larry Herndon	.06	.02	.00
☐ 334	Chuck Rainey	.06	.02	.00
☐ 335	Don Baylor	.10	.04	.01
☐ 336	Seattle Mariners TL	.10	.04	.01
	Pat Putnam			
	Matt Young			
☐ 337	Kevin Hagen	.06	.02	.00
☐ 338	Mike Warren	.06	.02	.00

☐ 339	Roy Lee Jackson	.06	.02	.00
☐ 340	Hal McRae	.10	.04	.01
☐ 341	Dave Tobik	.06	.02	.00
☐ 342	Tim Foli	.06	.02	.00
☐ 343	Mark Davis	.10	.04	.01
☐ 344	Rick Miller	.06	.02	.00
☐ 345	Kent Hrbek	.35	.15	.03
☐ 346	Kurt Bevacqua	.06	.02	.00
☐ 347	Allan Ramirez	.06	.02	.00
☐ 348	Toby Harrah	.06	.02	.00
☐ 349	Bob L. Gibson	.06	.02	.00
	(Brewers Pitcher)			
☐ 350	George Foster	.15	.06	.01
☐ 351	Russ Nixon MG	.06	.02	.00
☐ 352	Dave Stewart	.50	.20	.05
☐ 353	Jim Anderson	.06	.02	.00
☐ 354	Jeff Burroughs	.06	.02	.00
☐ 355	Jason Thompson	.06	.02	.00
☐ 356	Glenn Abbott	.06	.02	.00
☐ 357	Ron Cey	.10	.04	.01
☐ 358	Bob Dernier	.06	.02	.00
☐ 359	Jim Acker	.10	.04	.01
☐ 360	Willie Randolph	.10	.04	.01
☐ 361	Dave Smith	.06	.02	.00
☐ 362	David Green	.06	.02	.00
☐ 363	Tim Laudner	.06	.02	.00
☐ 364	Scott Fletcher	.10	.04	.01
☐ 365	Steve Bedrosian	.10	.04	.01
☐ 366	Padres TL	.12	.05	.01
	Terry Kennedy			
	Dave Dravecky			
☐ 367	Jamie Easterly	.06	.02	.00
☐ 368	Hubie Brooks	.15	.06	.01
☐ 369	Steve McCatty	.06	.02	.00
☐ 370	Tim Raines	.40	.16	.04
☐ 371	Dave Gumpert	.06	.02	.00
☐ 372	Gary Roenicke	.06	.02	.00
☐ 373	Bill Scherrer	.06	.02	.00
☐ 374	Don Money	.06	.02	.00
☐ 375	Dennis Leonard	.06	.02	.00
☐ 376	Dave Anderson	.10	.04	.01
☐ 377	Danny Darwin	.06	.02	.00
☐ 378	Bob Brenly	.06	.02	.00
☐ 379	Checklist 265-396	.12	.02	.00
☐ 380	Steve Garvey	.45	.18	.04
☐ 381	Ralph Houk MG	.06	.02	.00
☐ 382	Chris Nyman	.06	.02	.00
☐ 383	Terry Puhl	.06	.02	.00
☐ 384	Lee Tunnell	.06	.02	.00
☐ 385	Tony Perez	.25	.10	.02
☐ 386	George Hendrick AS	.06	.02	.00
☐ 387	Johnny Ray AS	.06	.02	.00
☐ 388	Mike Schmidt AS	.50	.20	.05
☐ 389	Ozzie Smith AS	.30	.12	.03
☐ 390	Tim Raines AS	.15	.06	.01
☐ 391	Dale Murphy AS	.25	.10	.02
☐ 392	Andre Dawson AS	.35	.15	.03
☐ 393	Gary Carter AS	.15	.06	.01
☐ 394	Steve Rogers AS	.06	.02	.00
☐ 395	Steve Carlton AS	.25	.10	.02
☐ 396	Jesse Orosco AS	.06	.02	.00
☐ 397	Eddie Murray AS	.40	.16	.04
☐ 398	Lou Whitaker AS	.15	.06	.01
☐ 399	George Brett AS	.40	.16	.04
☐ 400	Cal Ripken AS	1.25	.50	.12
☐ 401	Jim Rice AS	.15	.06	.01
☐ 402	Dave Winfield AS	.25	.10	.02
☐ 403	Lloyd Moseby AS	.06	.02	.00
☐ 404	Ted Simmons AS	.10	.04	.01
☐ 405	LaMarr Hoyt AS	.06	.02	.00
☐ 406	Ron Guidry AS	.10	.04	.01
☐ 407	Dan Quisenberry AS	.10	.04	.01
☐ 408	Lou Piniella	.10	.04	.01
☐ 409	Juan Agosto	.10	.04	.01
☐ 410	Claudell Washington	.06	.02	.00
☐ 411	Houston Jimenez	.06	.02	.00
☐ 412	Doug Rader MG	.06	.02	.00
☐ 413	Spike Owen	.25	.10	.02
☐ 414	Mitchell Page	.06	.02	.00
☐ 415	Tommy John	.20	.08	.02
☐ 416	Dane Iorg	.06	.02	.00
☐ 417	Mike Armstrong	.06	.02	.00
☐ 418	Ron Hodges	.06	.02	.00
☐ 419	John Henry Johnson	.06	.02	.00
☐ 420	Cecil Cooper	.10	.04	.01
☐ 421	Charlie Lea	.06	.02	.00
☐ 422	Jose Cruz	.10	.04	.01
☐ 423	Mike Morgan	.10	.04	.01
☐ 424	Dann Bilardello	.06	.02	.00
☐ 425	Steve Howe	.06	.02	.00
☐ 426	Orioles TL	.60	.25	.06
	Cal Ripken			
	Mike Boddicker			
☐ 427	Rick Leach	.06	.02	.00

#	Player			
☐ 428	Fred Breining	.06	.02	.00
☐ 429	Randy Bush	.15	.06	.01
☐ 430	Rusty Staub	.10	.04	.01
☐ 431	Chris Bando	.06	.02	.00
☐ 432	Charles Hudson	.10	.04	.01
☐ 433	Rich Hebner	.06	.02	.00
☐ 434	Harold Baines	.35	.15	.03
☐ 435	Neil Allen	.06	.02	.00
☐ 436	Rick Peters	.06	.02	.00
☐ 437	Mike Proly	.06	.02	.00
☐ 438	Biff Pocoroba	.06	.02	.00
☐ 439	Bob Stoddard	.06	.02	.00
☐ 440	Steve Kemp	.06	.02	.00
☐ 441	Bob Lillis MG	.06	.02	.00
☐ 442	Byron McLaughlin	.06	.02	.00
☐ 443	Benny Ayala	.06	.02	.00
☐ 444	Steve Renko	.06	.02	.00
☐ 445	Jerry Remy	.06	.02	.00
☐ 446	Luis Pujols	.06	.02	.00
☐ 447	Tom Brunansky	.15	.06	.01
☐ 448	Ben Hayes	.06	.02	.00
☐ 449	Joe Pettini	.06	.02	.00
☐ 450	Gary Carter	.40	.16	.04
☐ 451	Bob Jones	.06	.02	.00
☐ 452	Chuck Porter	.06	.02	.00
☐ 453	Willie Upshaw	.06	.02	.00
☐ 454	Joe Beckwith	.06	.02	.00
☐ 455	Terry Kennedy	.06	.02	.00
☐ 456	Chicago Cubs TL	.12	.05	.01
	Keith Moreland			
	Fergie Jenkins			
☐ 457	Dave Rozema	.06	.02	.00
☐ 458	Kiko Garcia	.06	.02	.00
☐ 459	Kevin Hickey	.06	.02	.00
☐ 460	Dave Winfield	.80	.35	.08
☐ 461	Jim Maler	.06	.02	.00
☐ 462	Lee Lacy	.06	.02	.00
☐ 463	Dave Engle	.06	.02	.00
☐ 464	Jeff A. Jones	.06	.02	.00
	(A's Pitcher)			
☐ 465	Mookie Wilson	.10	.04	.01
☐ 466	Gene Garber	.06	.02	.00
☐ 467	Mike Ramsey	.06	.02	.00
☐ 468	Geoff Zahn	.06	.02	.00
☐ 469	Tom O'Malley	.06	.02	.00
☐ 470	Nolan Ryan	5.50	2.50	.55
☐ 471	Dick Howser MG	.06	.02	.00
☐ 472	Mike Brown	.06	.02	.00
	(Red Sox Pitcher)			
☐ 473	Jim Dwyer	.06	.02	.00
☐ 474	Greg Bargar	.06	.02	.00
☐ 475	Gary Redus	.25	.10	.02
☐ 476	Tom Tellmann	.06	.02	.00
☐ 477	Rafael Landestoy	.06	.02	.00
☐ 478	Alan Bannister	.06	.02	.00
☐ 479	Frank Tanana	.10	.04	.01
☐ 480	Ron Kittle	.10	.04	.01
☐ 481	Mark Thurmond	.06	.02	.00
☐ 482	Enos Cabell	.06	.02	.00
☐ 483	Fergie Jenkins	.35	.15	.03
☐ 484	Ozzie Virgil	.06	.02	.00
☐ 485	Rick Rhoden	.06	.02	.00
☐ 486	N.Y. Yankees TL	.12	.05	.01
	Don Baylor			
	Ron Guidry			
☐ 487	Ricky Adams	.06	.02	.00
☐ 488	Jesse Barfield	.20	.08	.02
☐ 489	Dave Von Ohlen	.06	.02	.00
☐ 490	Cal Ripken	7.50	3.25	.75
☐ 491	Bobby Castillo	.06	.02	.00
☐ 492	Tucker Ashford	.06	.02	.00
☐ 493	Mike Norris	.06	.02	.00
☐ 494	Chili Davis	.20	.08	.02
☐ 495	Rollie Fingers	.40	.16	.04
☐ 496	Terry Francona	.06	.02	.00
☐ 497	Bud Anderson	.06	.02	.00
☐ 498	Rich Gedman	.06	.02	.00
☐ 499	Mike Witt	.06	.02	.00
☐ 500	George Brett	1.50	.60	.15
☐ 501	Steve Henderson	.06	.02	.00
☐ 502	Joe Torre MG	.10	.04	.01
☐ 503	Elias Sosa	.06	.02	.00
☐ 504	Mickey Rivers	.06	.02	.00
☐ 505	Pete Vuckovich	.06	.02	.00
☐ 506	Ernie Whitt	.06	.02	.00
☐ 507	Mike LaCoss	.06	.02	.00
☐ 508	Mel Hall	.40	.16	.04
☐ 509	Brad Havens	.06	.02	.00
☐ 510	Alan Trammell	.65	.25	.06
☐ 511	Marty Bystrom	.06	.02	.00
☐ 512	Oscar Gamble	.06	.02	.00
☐ 513	Dave Beard	.06	.02	.00
☐ 514	Floyd Rayford	.06	.02	.00
☐ 515	Gorman Thomas	.10	.04	.01

#	Player			
☐ 516	Montreal Expos TL	.10	.04	.01
	Al Oliver			
	Charlie Lea			
☐ 517	John Moses	.10	.04	.01
☐ 518	Greg Walker	.10	.04	.01
☐ 519	Ron Davis	.06	.02	.00
☐ 520	Bob Boone	.10	.04	.01
☐ 521	Pete Falcone	.06	.02	.00
☐ 522	Dave Bergman	.06	.02	.00
☐ 523	Glenn Hoffman	.06	.02	.00
☐ 524	Carlos Diaz	.06	.02	.00
☐ 525	Willie Wilson	.10	.04	.01
☐ 526	Ron Oester	.06	.02	.00
☐ 527	Checklist 397-528	.12	.02	.00
☐ 528	Mark Brouhard	.06	.02	.00
☐ 529	Keith Atherton	.06	.02	.00
☐ 530	Dan Ford	.06	.02	.00
☐ 531	Steve Boros MG	.06	.02	.00
☐ 532	Eric Show	.10	.04	.01
☐ 533	Ken Landreaux	.06	.02	.00
☐ 534	Pete O'Brien	.35	.15	.03
☐ 535	Bo Diaz	.06	.02	.00
☐ 536	Doug Bair	.06	.02	.00
☐ 537	Johnny Ray	.06	.02	.00
☐ 538	Kevin Bass	.10	.04	.01
☐ 539	George Frazier	.06	.02	.00
☐ 540	George Hendrick	.06	.02	.00
☐ 541	Dennis Lamp	.06	.02	.00
☐ 542	Duane Kuiper	.06	.02	.00
☐ 543	Craig McMurtry	.06	.02	.00
☐ 544	Cesar Geronimo	.06	.02	.00
☐ 545	Bill Buckner	.10	.04	.01
☐ 546	Indians TL	.10	.04	.01
	Mike Hargrove			
	Lary Sorensen			
☐ 547	Mike Moore	.15	.06	.01
☐ 548	Ron Jackson	.06	.02	.00
☐ 549	Walt Terrell	.15	.06	.01
☐ 550	Jim Rice	.15	.06	.01
☐ 551	Scott Ullger	.06	.02	.00
☐ 552	Ray Burris	.06	.02	.00
☐ 553	Joe Nolan	.06	.02	.00
☐ 554	Ted Power	.10	.04	.01
☐ 555	Greg Brock	.10	.04	.01
☐ 556	Joey McLaughlin	.06	.02	.00
☐ 557	Wayne Tolleson	.06	.02	.00
☐ 558	Mike Davis	.06	.02	.00
☐ 559	Mike Scott	.15	.06	.01
☐ 560	Carlton Fisk	1.00	.40	.10
☐ 561	Whitey Herzog MG	.06	.02	.00
☐ 562	Manny Castillo	.06	.02	.00
☐ 563	Glenn Wilson	.06	.02	.00
☐ 564	Al Holland	.06	.02	.00
☐ 565	Leon Durham	.06	.02	.00
☐ 566	Jim Bibby	.06	.02	.00
☐ 567	Mike Heath	.06	.02	.00
☐ 568	Pete Filson	.06	.02	.00
☐ 569	Bake McBride	.06	.02	.00
☐ 570	Dan Quisenberry	.10	.04	.01
☐ 571	Bruce Bochy	.06	.02	.00
☐ 572	Jerry Royster	.06	.02	.00
☐ 573	Dave Kingman	.15	.06	.01
☐ 574	Brian Downing	.10	.04	.01
☐ 575	Jim Clancy	.06	.02	.00
☐ 576	Giants TL	.10	.04	.01
	Jeff Leonard			
	Atlee Hammaker			
☐ 577	Mark Clear	.06	.02	.00
☐ 578	Lenn Sakata	.06	.02	.00
☐ 579	Bob James	.06	.02	.00
☐ 580	Lonnie Smith	.15	.06	.01
☐ 581	Jose DeLeon	.20	.08	.02
☐ 582	Bob McClure	.06	.02	.00
☐ 583	Derrel Thomas	.06	.02	.00
☐ 584	Dave Schmidt	.06	.02	.00
☐ 585	Dan Driessen	.06	.02	.00
☐ 586	Joe Niekro	.10	.04	.01
☐ 587	Von Hayes	.10	.04	.01
☐ 588	Milt Wilcox	.06	.02	.00
☐ 589	Mike Easler	.06	.02	.00
☐ 590	Dave Stieb	.20	.08	.02
☐ 591	Tony LaRussa MG	.10	.04	.01
☐ 592	Andre Robertson	.06	.02	.00
☐ 593	Jeff Lahti	.06	.02	.00
☐ 594	Gene Richards	.06	.02	.00
☐ 595	Jeff Reardon	.35	.15	.03
☐ 596	Ryne Sandberg	9.00	4.00	.90
☐ 597	Rick Camp	.06	.02	.00
☐ 598	Rusty Kuntz	.06	.02	.00
☐ 599	Doug Sisk	.06	.02	.00
☐ 600	Rod Carew	1.00	.40	.10
☐ 601	John Tudor	.15	.06	.01
☐ 602	John Wathan	.06	.02	.00
☐ 603	Renie Martin	.06	.02	.00

□				
604	John Lowenstein	.06	.02	.00
605	Mike Caldwell	.06	.02	.00
606	Blue Jays TL	.12	.05	.01
	Lloyd Moseby			
	Dave Stieb			
607	Tom Hume	.06	.02	.00
608	Bobby Johnson	.06	.02	.00
609	Dan Meyer	.06	.02	.00
610	Steve Sax	.35	.15	.03
611	Chet Lemon	.06	.02	.00
612	Harry Spilman	.06	.02	.00
613	Greg Gross	.06	.02	.00
614	Len Barker	.06	.02	.00
615	Garry Templeton	.10	.04	.01
616	Don Robinson	.06	.02	.00
617	Rick Cerone	.06	.02	.00
618	Dickie Noles	.06	.02	.00
619	Jerry Dybzinski	.06	.02	.00
620	Al Oliver	.10	.04	.01
621	Frank Howard MG	.06	.02	.00
622	Al Cowens	.06	.02	.00
623	Ron Washington	.06	.02	.00
624	Terry Harper	.06	.02	.00
625	Larry Gura	.06	.02	.00
626	Bob Clark	.06	.02	.00
627	Dave LaPoint	.06	.02	.00
628	Ed Jurak	.06	.02	.00
629	Rick Langford	.06	.02	.00
630	Ted Simmons	.10	.04	.01
631	Dennis Martinez	.10	.04	.01
632	Tom Foley	.06	.02	.00
633	Mike Krukow	.06	.02	.00
634	Mike Marshall	.10	.04	.01
635	Dave Righetti	.15	.06	.01
636	Pat Putnam	.06	.02	.00
637	Phillies TL	.10	.04	.01
	Gary Matthews			
	John Denny			
638	George Vukovich	.06	.02	.00
639	Rick Lysander	.06	.02	.00
640	Lance Parrish	.25	.10	.02
641	Mike Richardt	.06	.02	.00
642	Tom Underwood	.06	.02	.00
643	Mike Brown	.06	.02	.00
	(Angels OF)			
644	Tim Lollar	.06	.02	.00
645	Tony Pena	.10	.04	.01
646	Checklist 529-660	.12	.02	.00
647	Ron Roenicke	.06	.02	.00
648	Len Whitehouse	.06	.02	.00
649	Tom Herr	.10	.04	.01
650	Phil Niekro	.30	.12	.03
651	John McNamara MG	.06	.02	.00
652	Rudy May	.06	.02	.00
653	Dave Stapleton	.06	.02	.00
654	Bob Bailor	.06	.02	.00
655	Amos Otis	.10	.04	.01
656	Bryn Smith	.10	.04	.01
657	Thad Bosley	.06	.02	.00
658	Jerry Augustine	.06	.02	.00
659	Duane Walker	.06	.02	.00
660	Ray Knight	.10	.04	.01
661	Steve Yeager	.06	.02	.00
662	Tom Brennan	.06	.02	.00
663	Johnnie LeMaster	.06	.02	.00
664	Dave Stegman	.06	.02	.00
665	Buddy Bell	.10	.04	.01
666	Detroit Tigers TL	.15	.06	.01
	Lou Whitaker			
	Jack Morris			
667	Vance Law	.06	.02	.00
668	Larry McWilliams	.06	.02	.00
669	Dave Lopes	.10	.04	.01
670	Rich Gossage	.15	.06	.01
671	Jamie Quirk	.06	.02	.00
672	Ricky Nelson	.06	.02	.00
673	Mike Walters	.06	.02	.00
674	Tim Flannery	.06	.02	.00
675	Pascual Perez	.10	.04	.01
676	Brian Giles	.06	.02	.00
677	Doyle Alexander	.06	.02	.00
678	Chris Speier	.06	.02	.00
679	Art Howe	.10	.04	.01
680	Fred Lynn	.15	.06	.01
681	Tom Lasorda MG	.10	.04	.01
682	Dan Morogiello	.06	.02	.00
683	Marty Barrett	.15	.06	.01
684	Bob Shirley	.06	.02	.00
685	Willie Aikens	.06	.02	.00
686	Joe Price	.06	.02	.00
687	Roy Howell	.06	.02	.00
688	George Wright	.06	.02	.00
689	Mike Fischlin	.06	.02	.00
690	Jack Clark	.20	.08	.02
691	Steve Lake	.06	.02	.00

□				
692	Dickie Thon	.10	.04	.01
693	Alan Wiggins	.06	.02	.00
694	Mike Stanton	.06	.02	.00
695	Lou Whitaker	.35	.15	.03
696	Pirates TL	.10	.04	.01
	Bill Madlock			
	Rick Rhoden			
697	Dale Murray	.06	.02	.00
698	Marc Hill	.06	.02	.00
699	Dave Rucker	.06	.02	.00
700	Mike Schmidt	2.25	.90	.22
701	NL Active Batting	.20	.08	.02
	Bill Madlock			
	Pete Rose			
	Dave Parker			
702	NL Active Hits	.20	.08	.02
	Pete Rose			
	Rusty Staub			
	Tony Perez			
703	NL Active Home Run	.20	.08	.02
	Mike Schmidt			
	Tony Perez			
	Dave Kingman			
704	NL Active RBI	.10	.04	.01
	Tony Perez			
	Rusty Staub			
	Al Oliver			
705	NL Active Steals	.10	.04	.01
	Joe Morgan			
	Cesar Cedeno			
	Larry Bowa			
706	NL Active Victory	.25	.10	.02
	Steve Carlton			
	Fergie Jenkins			
	Tom Seaver			
707	NL Active Strikeout	.50	.20	.05
	Steve Carlton			
	Nolan Ryan			
	Tom Seaver			
708	NL Active ERA	.20	.08	.02
	Tom Seaver			
	Steve Carlton			
	Steve Rogers			
709	NL Active Save	.10	.04	.01
	Bruce Sutter			
	Tug McGraw			
	Gene Garber			
710	AL Active Batting	.20	.08	.02
	Rod Carew			
	George Brett			
	Cecil Cooper			
711	AL Active Hits	.20	.08	.02
	Rod Carew			
	Bert Campaneris			
	Reggie Jackson			
712	AL Active Home Run	.20	.08	.02
	Reggie Jackson			
	Graig Nettles			
	Greg Luzinski			
713	AL Active RBI	.20	.08	.02
	Reggie Jackson			
	Ted Simmons			
	Graig Nettles			
714	AL Active Steals	.10	.04	.01
	Bert Campaneris			
	Dave Lopes			
	Omar Moreno			
715	AL Active Victory	.20	.08	.02
	Jim Palmer			
	Don Sutton			
	Tommy John			
716	AL Active Strikeout	.15	.06	.01
	Don Sutton			
	Bert Blyleven			
	Jerry Koosman			
717	AL Active ERA	.20	.08	.02
	Jim Palmer			
	Rollie Fingers			
	Ron Guidry			
718	AL Active Save	.15	.06	.01
	Rollie Fingers			
	Rich Gossage			
	Dan Quisenberry			
719	Andy Hassler	.06	.02	.00
720	Dwight Evans	.20	.08	.02
721	Del Crandall MG	.06	.02	.00
722	Bob Welch	.20	.08	.02
723	Rich Dauer	.06	.02	.00
724	Eric Rasmussen	.06	.02	.00
725	Cesar Cedeno	.10	.04	.01
726	Brewers TL	.10	.04	.01
	Ted Simmons			
	Moose Haas			
727	Joel Youngblood	.06	.02	.00
728	Tug McGraw	.10	.04	.01

☐ 729 Gene Tenace	.10	.04	.01
☐ 730 Bruce Sutter	.15	.06	.01
☐ 731 Lynn Jones	.06	.02	.00
☐ 732 Terry Crowley	.06	.02	.00
☐ 733 Dave Collins	.06	.02	.00
☐ 734 Odell Jones	.06	.02	.00
☐ 735 Rick Burleson	.06	.02	.00
☐ 736 Dick Ruthven	.06	.02	.00
☐ 737 Jim Essian	.06	.02	.00
☐ 738 Bill Schroeder	.06	.02	.00
☐ 739 Bob Watson	.06	.02	.00
☐ 740 Tom Seaver	1.25	.50	.12
☐ 741 Wayne Gross	.06	.02	.00
☐ 742 Dick Williams MG	.06	.02	.00
☐ 743 Don Hood	.06	.02	.00
☐ 744 Jamie Allen	.06	.02	.00
☐ 745 Dennis Eckersley	.40	.16	.04
☐ 746 Mickey Hatcher	.06	.02	.00
☐ 747 Pat Zachry	.06	.02	.00
☐ 748 Jeff Leonard	.06	.02	.00
☐ 749 Doug Flynn	.06	.02	.00
☐ 750 Jim Palmer	.90	.40	.09
☐ 751 Charlie Moore	.06	.02	.00
☐ 752 Phil Garner	.10	.04	.01
☐ 753 Doug Gwosdz	.06	.02	.00
☐ 754 Kent Tekulve	.06	.02	.00
☐ 755 Garry Maddox	.06	.02	.00
☐ 756 Reds TL	.10	.04	.01
Ron Oester			
Mario Soto			
☐ 757 Larry Bowa	.10	.04	.01
☐ 758 Bill Stein	.06	.02	.00
☐ 759 Richard Dotson	.06	.02	.00
☐ 760 Bob Horner	.10	.04	.01
☐ 761 John Montefusco	.06	.02	.00
☐ 762 Rance Mulliniks	.06	.02	.00
☐ 763 Craig Swan	.06	.02	.00
☐ 764 Mike Hargrove	.06	.02	.00
☐ 765 Ken Forsch	.06	.02	.00
☐ 766 Mike Vail	.06	.02	.00
☐ 767 Carney Lansford	.10	.04	.01
☐ 768 Champ Summers	.06	.02	.00
☐ 769 Bill Caudill	.06	.02	.00
☐ 770 Ken Griffey	.15	.06	.01
☐ 771 Billy Gardner MG	.06	.02	.00
☐ 772 Jim Slaton	.06	.02	.00
☐ 773 Todd Cruz	.06	.02	.00
☐ 774 Tom Gorman	.06	.02	.00
☐ 775 Dave Parker	.35	.15	.03
☐ 776 Craig Reynolds	.06	.02	.00
☐ 777 Tom Paciorek	.06	.02	.00
☐ 778 Andy Hawkins	.20	.08	.02
☐ 779 Jim Sundberg	.06	.02	.00
☐ 780 Steve Carlton	.75	.30	.07
☐ 781 Checklist 661-792	.12	.02	.00
☐ 782 Steve Balboni	.06	.02	.00
☐ 783 Luis Leal	.06	.02	.00
☐ 784 Leon Roberts	.06	.02	.00
☐ 785 Joaquin Andujar	.10	.04	.01
☐ 786 Red Sox TL	.40	.16	.04
Wade Boggs			
Bob Ojeda			
☐ 787 Bill Campbell	.06	.02	.00
☐ 788 Milt May	.06	.02	.00
☐ 789 Bert Blyleven	.20	.08	.02
☐ 790 Doug DeCinces	.10	.04	.01
☐ 791 Terry Forster	.06	.02	.00
☐ 792 Bill Russell	.15	.06	.01

1984 Topps Traded

The cards in this 132-card set measure 2 1/2" by 3 1/2". In its now standard procedure, Topps issued its Traded (or extended) set for the fourth year in a row. Because all photos and statistics of its regular set for the year were developed during the fall and winter months of the preceding year, players who changed teams during the fall, winter, and spring months are portrayed with the teams they were with in 1983. The Traded set amends the shortcomings of the regular set by presenting the players with their proper teams for the current year. Rookies not contained in the regular set are picked up in the Traded set. The key (extended) rookie cards in this set are Alvin Davis, Dwight Gooden, Mark Langston, Jose Rijo, and Bret Saberhagen. Again this year, the Topps affiliate in Ireland printed the cards,

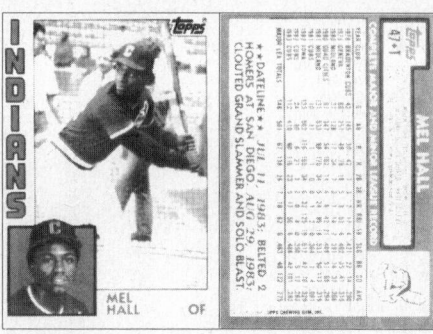

and the cards were available through hobby channels only. Topps also produced a specially boxed "glossy" edition, frequently referred to as the Topps Traded Tiffany set. There were supposedly only 10,000 sets of the Tiffany cards produced; they were marketed to hobby dealers. The checklist of cards is identical to that of the normal non-glossy cards. There are two primary distinguishing features of the Tiffany cards, white card stock reverses and high gloss obverses. These Tiffany cards are valued at approximately five times the values listed below.

	MINT	EXC	G-VG
COMPLETE SET (132)	100.00	45.00	15.00
COMMON PLAYER (1-132)	.12	.05	.01
☐ 1T Willie Aikens	.20	.08	.02
☐ 2T Luis Aponte	.12	.05	.01
☐ 3T Mike Armstrong	.12	.05	.01
☐ 4T Bob Bailor	.12	.05	.01
☐ 5T Dusty Baker	.20	.08	.02
☐ 6T Steve Balboni	.20	.08	.02
☐ 7T Alan Bannister	.12	.05	.01
☐ 8T Dave Beard	.12	.05	.01
☐ 9T Joe Beckwith	.12	.05	.01
☐ 10T Bruce Berenyi	.12	.05	.01
☐ 11T Dave Bergman	.12	.05	.01
☐ 12T Tony Bernazard	.12	.05	.01
☐ 13T Yogi Berra MG	.40	.16	.04
☐ 14T Barry Bonnell	.12	.05	.01
☐ 15T Phil Bradley	.60	.25	.06
☐ 16T Fred Breining	.12	.05	.01
☐ 17T Bill Buckner	.25	.10	.02
☐ 18T Ray Burris	.12	.05	.01
☐ 19T John Butcher	.12	.05	.01
☐ 20T Brett Butler	.75	.30	.07
☐ 21T Enos Cabell	.12	.05	.01
☐ 22T Bill Campbell	.12	.05	.01
☐ 23T Bill Caudill	.12	.05	.01
☐ 24T Bob Clark	.12	.05	.01
☐ 25T Bryan Clark	.12	.05	.01
☐ 26T Jaime Cocanower	.12	.05	.01
☐ 27T Ron Darling	3.00	1.25	.30
☐ 28T Alvin Davis	4.00	1.75	.40
☐ 29T Ken Dayley	.20	.08	.02
☐ 30T Jeff Dedmon	.12	.05	.01
☐ 31T Bob Dernier	.12	.05	.01
☐ 32T Carlos Diaz	.12	.05	.01
☐ 33T Mike Easler	.12	.05	.01
☐ 34T Dennis Eckersley	2.00	.80	.20
☐ 35T Jim Essian	.20	.08	.02
☐ 36T Darrell Evans	.30	.12	.03
☐ 37T Mike Fitzgerald	.12	.05	.01
☐ 38T Tim Foli	.12	.05	.01
☐ 39T George Frazier	.12	.05	.01
☐ 40T Rich Gale	.12	.05	.01
☐ 41T Barbaro Garbey	.12	.05	.01
☐ 42T Dwight Gooden	40.00	18.00	6.00
☐ 43T Rich Gossage	.50	.20	.05
☐ 44T Wayne Gross	.12	.05	.01
☐ 45T Mark Gubicza	2.00	.80	.20
☐ 46T Jackie Gutierrez	.12	.05	.01
☐ 47T Mel Hall	.40	.16	.04
☐ 48T Toby Harrah	.20	.08	.02
☐ 49T Ron Hassey	.20	.08	.02
☐ 50T Rich Hebner	.12	.05	.01
☐ 51T Willie Hernandez	.25	.10	.02
☐ 52T Ricky Horton	.20	.08	.02
☐ 53T Art Howe	.20	.08	.02
☐ 54T Dane Iorg	.12	.05	.01
☐ 55T Brook Jacoby	1.00	.40	.10
☐ 56T Mike Jeffcoat	.20	.08	.02

		MINT	EXC	G-VG
☐ 57T	Dave Johnson MG	.25	.10	.02
☐ 58T	Lynn Jones	.12	.05	.01
☐ 59T	Ruppert Jones	.12	.05	.01
☐ 60T	Mike Jorgensen	.12	.05	.01
☐ 61T	Bob Kearney	.12	.05	.01
☐ 62T	Jimmy Key	5.00	2.25	.50
☐ 63T	Dave Kingman	.30	.12	.03
☐ 64T	Jerry Koosman	.25	.10	.02
☐ 65T	Wayne Krenchicki	.12	.05	.01
☐ 66T	Rusty Kuntz	.12	.05	.01
☐ 67T	Rene Lachemann MG	.12	.05	.01
☐ 68T	Frank LaCorte	.12	.05	.01
☐ 69T	Dennis Lamp	.12	.05	.01
☐ 70T	Mark Langston	11.00	5.00	1.35
☐ 71T	Rick Leach	.12	.05	.01
☐ 72T	Craig Lefferts	.30	.12	.03
☐ 73T	Gary Lucas	.12	.05	.01
☐ 74T	Jerry Martin	.12	.05	.01
☐ 75T	Carmelo Martinez	.20	.08	.02
☐ 76T	Mike Mason	.12	.05	.01
☐ 77T	Gary Matthews	.20	.08	.02
☐ 78T	Andy McGaffigan	.20	.08	.02
☐ 79T	Larry Milbourne	.12	.05	.01
☐ 80T	Sid Monge	.12	.05	.01
☐ 81T	Jackie Moore MG	.12	.05	.01
☐ 82T	Joe Morgan	2.50	1.00	.25
☐ 83T	Graig Nettles	.40	.16	.04
☐ 84T	Phil Niekro	1.75	.70	.17
☐ 85T	Ken Oberkfell	.12	.05	.01
☐ 86T	Mike O'Berry	.12	.05	.01
☐ 87T	Al Oliver	.30	.12	.03
☐ 88T	Jorge Orta	.12	.05	.01
☐ 89T	Amos Otis	.20	.08	.02
☐ 90T	Dave Parker	1.75	.70	.17
☐ 91T	Tony Perez	1.00	.40	.10
☐ 92T	Gerald Perry	.60	.25	.06
☐ 93T	Gary Pettis	.40	.16	.04
☐ 94T	Rob Picciolo	.12	.05	.01
☐ 95T	Vern Rapp MG	.12	.05	.01
☐ 96T	Floyd Rayford	.12	.05	.01
☐ 97T	Randy Ready	.30	.12	.03
☐ 98T	Ron Reed	.12	.05	.01
☐ 99T	Gene Richards	.12	.05	.01
☐ 100T	Jose Rijo	6.00	2.50	.60
☐ 101T	Jeff Robinson (Giants pitcher)	.20	.08	.02
☐ 102T	Ron Romanick	.12	.05	.01
☐ 103T	Pete Rose	8.00	3.50	.80
☐ 104T	Bret Saberhagen	21.00	9.00	3.00
☐ 105T	Juan Samuel	4.00	1.75	.40
☐ 106T	Scott Sanderson	.30	.12	.03
☐ 107T	Dick Schofield	.40	.16	.04
☐ 108T	Tom Seaver	7.50	3.25	.75
☐ 109T	Jim Slaton	.12	.05	.01
☐ 110T	Mike Smithson	.12	.05	.01
☐ 111T	Lary Sorensen	.12	.05	.01
☐ 112T	Tim Stoddard	.12	.05	.01
☐ 113T	Champ Summers	.12	.05	.01
☐ 114T	Jim Sundberg	.12	.05	.01
☐ 115T	Rick Sutcliffe	.30	.12	.03
☐ 116T	Craig Swan	.12	.05	.01
☐ 117T	Tim Teufel	.45	.18	.04
☐ 118T	Derrel Thomas	.12	.05	.01
☐ 119T	Gorman Thomas	.25	.10	.02
☐ 120T	Alex Trevino	.12	.05	.01
☐ 121T	Manny Trillo	.12	.05	.01
☐ 122T	John Tudor	.25	.10	.02
☐ 123T	Tom Underwood	.12	.05	.01
☐ 124T	Mike Vail	.12	.05	.01
☐ 125T	Tom Waddell	.12	.05	.01
☐ 126T	Gary Ward	.12	.05	.01
☐ 127T	Curt Wilkerson	.12	.05	.01
☐ 128T	Frank Williams	.12	.05	.01
☐ 129T	Glenn Wilson	.12	.05	.01
☐ 130T	John Wockenfuss	.12	.05	.01
☐ 131T	Ned Yost	.12	.05	.01
☐ 132T	Checklist 1-132	.12	.01	.00

back and are ordered by position within league (AL: 1-11 and NL: 12-22).

		MINT	EXC	G-VG
COMPLETE SET (22)		3.50	1.50	.35
COMMON PLAYER (1-22)		.10	.04	.01
☐ 1	Harvey Kuenn MG	.10	.04	.01
☐ 2	Rod Carew	.60	.25	.06
☐ 3	Manny Trillo	.10	.04	.01
☐ 4	George Brett	.60	.25	.06
☐ 5	Robin Yount	.60	.25	.06
☐ 6	Jim Rice	.20	.08	.02
☐ 7	Fred Lynn	.15	.06	.01
☐ 8	Dave Winfield	.40	.16	.04
☐ 9	Ted Simmons	.15	.06	.01
☐ 10	Dave Stieb	.15	.06	.01
☐ 11	Carl Yastrzemski CAPT	.45	.18	.04
☐ 12	Whitey Herzog MG	.10	.04	.01
☐ 13	Al Oliver	.15	.06	.01
☐ 14	Steve Sax	.25	.10	.02
☐ 15	Mike Schmidt	.75	.30	.07
☐ 16	Ozzie Smith	.40	.16	.04
☐ 17	Tim Raines	.25	.10	.02
☐ 18	Andre Dawson	.40	.16	.04
☐ 19	Dale Murphy	.50	.20	.05
☐ 20	Gary Carter	.30	.12	.03
☐ 21	Mario Soto	.10	.04	.01
☐ 22	Johnny Bench CAPT	.30	.12	.03

1984 Topps Glossy 40

1984 Topps All-Star Glossy 22

The cards in this 22-card set measure 2 1/2" by 3 1/2". Unlike the 1983 Topps Glossy set which was not distributed with its regular baseball cards, the 1984 Topps Glossy set was distributed as inserts in Topps Rak-Paks. The set features the nine American and National League All-Stars who started in the 1983 All Star game in Chicago. The managers and team captains (Yastrzemski and Bench) complete the set. The cards are numbered on the

The cards in this 40-card set measure 2 1/2" by 3 1/2". Similar to last year's glossy set, this set was issued as a bonus prize to Topps All-Star Baseball Game cards found in wax packs. Twenty-five bonus runs from the game cards were necessary to obtain a five card subset of the series. There were eight different subsets of five cards. The cards are numbered and contain 20 stars from each league.

	MINT	EXC	G-VG
COMPLETE SET (40)	12.50	5.50	1.65
COMMON PLAYER (1-40)	.20	.08	.02

		MINT	EXC	G-VG
☐ 1	Pete Rose	1.25	.50	.12
☐ 2	Lance Parrish	.30	.12	.03
☐ 3	Steve Rogers	.20	.08	.02
☐ 4	Eddie Murray	1.00	.40	.10
☐ 5	Johnny Ray	.20	.08	.02
☐ 6	Rickey Henderson	1.50	.60	.15
☐ 7	Atlee Hammaker	.20	.08	.02
☐ 8	Wade Boggs	1.25	.50	.12
☐ 9	Gary Carter	.35	.15	.03
☐ 10	Jack Morris	.35	.15	.03
☐ 11	Darrell Evans	.20	.08	.02
☐ 12	George Brett	1.00	.40	.10
☐ 13	Bob Horner	.25	.10	.02
☐ 14	Ron Guidry	.25	.10	.02
☐ 15	Nolan Ryan	2.00	.80	.20
☐ 16	Dave Winfield	.75	.30	.07
☐ 17	Ozzie Smith	.45	.18	.04
☐ 18	Ted Simmons	.20	.08	.02
☐ 19	Bill Madlock	.25	.10	.02
☐ 20	Tony Armas	.20	.08	.02
☐ 21	Al Oliver	.25	.10	.02
☐ 22	Jim Rice	.30	.12	.03
☐ 23	George Hendrick	.20	.08	.02
☐ 24	Dave Stieb	.25	.10	.02
☐ 25	Pedro Guerrero	.30	.12	.03
☐ 26	Rod Carew	1.00	.40	.10
☐ 27	Steve Carlton	.75	.30	.07
☐ 28	Dave Righetti	.20	.08	.02
☐ 29	Darryl Strawberry	1.50	.60	.15
☐ 30	Lou Whitaker	.25	.10	.02
☐ 31	Dale Murphy	.90	.40	.09
☐ 32	LaMarr Hoyt	.20	.08	.02
☐ 33	Jesse Orosco	.20	.08	.02
☐ 34	Cecil Cooper	.20	.08	.02
☐ 35	Andre Dawson	.35	.15	.03
☐ 36	Robin Yount	1.00	.40	.10
☐ 37	Tim Raines	.35	.15	.03
☐ 38	Dan Quisenberry	.25	.10	.02
☐ 39	Mike Schmidt	1.25	.50	.12
☐ 40	Carlton Fisk	.75	.30	.07

☐ 5	Greg Luzinski	.20	.08	.02
☐ 6	Andre Dawson	.45	.18	.04
☐ 7	Dave Winfield	.60	.25	.06
☐ 8	Tom Seaver	1.00	.40	.10
☐ 9	Jim Rice	.30	.12	.03
☐ 10	Fernando Valenzuela	.30	.12	.03
☐ 11	Wade Boggs	1.00	.40	.10
☐ 12	Dale Murphy	.75	.30	.07
☐ 13	George Brett	1.00	.40	.10
☐ 14	Nolan Ryan	1.50	.60	.15
☐ 15	Rickey Henderson	1.25	.50	.12
☐ 16	Steve Carlton	.60	.25	.06
☐ 17	Rod Carew	.90	.40	.09
☐ 18	Steve Garvey	.50	.20	.05
☐ 19	Reggie Jackson	1.00	.40	.10
☐ 20	Dave Concepcion	.20	.08	.02
☐ 21	Robin Yount	1.00	.40	.10
☐ 22	Mike Schmidt	1.25	.50	.12
☐ 23	Jim Palmer	.60	.25	.06
☐ 24	Bruce Sutter	.25	.10	.02
☐ 25	Dan Quisenberry	.25	.10	.02
☐ 26	Bill Madlock	.20	.08	.02
☐ 27	Cecil Cooper	.20	.08	.02
☐ 28	Gary Carter	.40	.16	.04
☐ 29	Fred Lynn	.25	.10	.02
☐ 30	Pedro Guerrero	.35	.15	.03
☐ 31	Ron Guidry	.25	.10	.02
☐ 32	Keith Hernandez	.30	.12	.03
☐ 33	Carlton Fisk	.60	.25	.06
☐ 34	Checklist card (unnumbered)	.25	.10	.02

1985 Topps

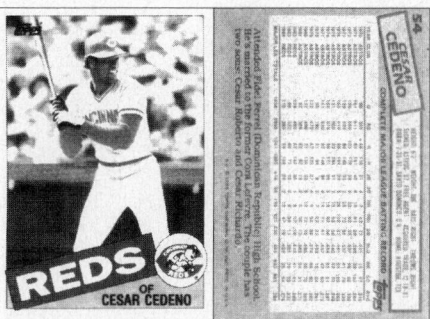

The cards in this 792-card set measure 2 1/2" by 3 1/2". The 1985 Topps set contains full color cards. The fronts feature both the Topps and team logos along with the team name, player's name, and his position. The backs feature player statistics with ink colors of light green and maroon on a gray stock. A trivia quiz is included on the lower portion of the backs. The first ten cards (1-10) are Record Breakers (RB), cards 131-143 are Father and Son (FS) cards, and cards 701 to 722 portray All-Star selections (AS). Cards 271 to 282 represent "First Draft Picks" and cards 389-404 feature the coach and players on the 1984 U.S. Olympic Baseball Team. The manager cards in the set are important in that they contain the checklist of that team's players on the back. The key rookie cards in this set are Roger Clemens, Eric Davis, Shawon Dunston, Dwight Gooden, Orel Hershiser, Mark Langston, Mark McGwire, Terry Pendleton, Kirby Puckett, Jose Rijo, and Bret Saberhagen. Topps also produced a specially boxed "glossy" edition, frequently referred to as the Topps Tiffany set. There were supposedly only 8,000 sets of the Tiffany cards produced; they were marketed to hobby dealers. The checklist of cards (792 regular and 132 Traded) is identical to that of the normal non-glossy cards. There are two primary distinguishing features of the Tiffany cards, white card stock reverses and high gloss obverses. These Tiffany cards are valued at approximately five times the values listed below.

1984 Topps Cereal

The cards in this 33 card-set measure 2 1/2" by 3 1/2". The cards are numbered both on the front and the back. The 1984 Topps Cereal Series is exactly the same as the Ralston-Purina issue of this year except for a Topps logo and the words "Cereal Series" on the tops of the fronts of the cards in place of the Ralston checkerboard background. The checkerboard background is absent from the reverse, and a Topps logo is on the reverse of the cereal cards. These cards were distributed in unmarked boxes of Ralston-Purina cereal with a pack of four cards (three players and a checklist) being inside random cereal boxes. The back of the checklist details an offer to obtain any twelve cards direct from the issuer for only $1.50.

	MINT	EXC	G-VG
COMPLETE SET (34)	13.50	6.00	1.85
COMMON PLAYER (1-33)	.25	.10	.02

☐ 1	Eddie Murray	1.00	.40	.10
☐ 2	Ozzie Smith	.45	.18	.04
☐ 3	Ted Simmons	.25	.10	.02
☐ 4	Pete Rose	1.25	.50	.12

	MINT	EXC	G-VG
COMPLETE SET (792)	100.00	45.00	15.00
COMMON PLAYER (1-792)	.05	.02	.00
☐ 1 Carlton Fisk RB	.35	.10	.02
Longest game			
by catcher			
☐ 2 Steve Garvey RB	.15	.06	.01
Consecutive error-			
less games, 1B			
☐ 3 Dwight Gooden RB	.90	.40	.09
Most strikeouts,			
rookie, season			
☐ 4 Cliff Johnson RB	.05	.02	.00
Most pinch homers,			
lifetime			
☐ 5 Joe Morgan RB	.15	.06	.01
Most homers,			
2B, lifetime			
☐ 6 Pete Rose RB	.35	.15	.03
Most singles,			
lifetime			
☐ 7 Nolan Ryan RB	1.00	.40	.10
Most strikeouts,			
lifetime			
☐ 8 Juan Samuel RB	.17	.07	.01
Most stolen bases,			
rookie, season			
☐ 9 Bruce Sutter RB	.08	.03	.01
Most saves,			
season, NL			
☐ 10 Don Sutton RB	.15	.06	.01
Most seasons,			
100 or more K's			
☐ 11 Ralph Houk MG	.08	.03	.01
(checklist back)			
☐ 12 Dave Lopes	.08	.03	.01
☐ 13 Tim Lollar	.05	.02	.00
☐ 14 Chris Bando	.05	.02	.00
☐ 15 Jerry Koosman	.08	.03	.01
☐ 16 Bobby Meacham	.05	.02	.00
☐ 17 Mike Scott	.12	.05	.01
☐ 18 Mickey Hatcher	.05	.02	.00
☐ 19 George Frazier	.05	.02	.00
☐ 20 Chet Lemon	.05	.02	.00
☐ 21 Lee Tunnell	.05	.02	.00
☐ 22 Duane Kuiper	.05	.02	.00
☐ 23 Bret Saberhagen	4.00	1.75	.40
☐ 24 Jesse Barfield	.15	.06	.01
☐ 25 Steve Bedrosian	.10	.04	.01
☐ 26 Roy Smalley	.05	.02	.00
☐ 27 Bruce Berenyi	.05	.02	.00
☐ 28 Dann Bilardello	.05	.02	.00
☐ 29 Odell Jones	.05	.02	.00
☐ 30 Cal Ripken	3.50	1.50	.35
☐ 31 Terry Whitfield	.05	.02	.00
☐ 32 Chuck Porter	.05	.02	.00
☐ 33 Tito Landrum	.05	.02	.00
☐ 34 Ed Nunez	.05	.02	.00
☐ 35 Graig Nettles	.10	.04	.01
☐ 36 Fred Breining	.05	.02	.00
☐ 37 Reid Nichols	.05	.02	.00
☐ 38 Jackie Moore MG	.08	.03	.01
(checklist back)			
☐ 39 John Wockenfuss	.05	.02	.00
☐ 40 Phil Niekro	.20	.08	.02
☐ 41 Mike Fischlin	.05	.02	.00
☐ 42 Luis Sanchez	.05	.02	.00
☐ 43 Andre David	.05	.02	.00
☐ 44 Dickie Thon	.08	.03	.01
☐ 45 Greg Minton	.05	.02	.00
☐ 46 Gary Woods	.05	.02	.00
☐ 47 Dave Rozema	.05	.02	.00
☐ 48 Tony Fernandez	.75	.30	.07
☐ 49 Butch Davis	.05	.02	.00
☐ 50 John Candelaria	.05	.02	.00
☐ 51 Bob Watson	.05	.02	.00
☐ 52 Jerry Dybzinski	.05	.02	.00
☐ 53 Tom Gorman	.05	.02	.00
☐ 54 Cesar Cedeno	.08	.03	.01
☐ 55 Frank Tanana	.08	.03	.01
☐ 56 Jim Dwyer	.05	.02	.00
☐ 57 Pat Zachry	.05	.02	.00
☐ 58 Orlando Mercado	.05	.02	.00
☐ 59 Rick Waits	.05	.02	.00
☐ 60 George Hendrick	.05	.02	.00
☐ 61 Curt Kaufman	.05	.02	.00
☐ 62 Mike Ramsey	.05	.02	.00
☐ 63 Steve McCatty	.05	.02	.00
☐ 64 Mark Bailey	.05	.02	.00
☐ 65 Bill Buckner	.10	.04	.01
☐ 66 Dick Williams MG	.08	.03	.01
(checklist back)			
☐ 67 Rafael Santana	.10	.04	.01

☐ 68 Von Hayes	.12	.05	.01
☐ 69 Jim Winn	.05	.02	.00
☐ 70 Don Baylor	.10	.04	.01
☐ 71 Tim Laudner	.05	.02	.00
☐ 72 Rick Sutcliffe	.10	.04	.01
☐ 73 Rusty Kuntz	.05	.02	.00
☐ 74 Mike Krukow	.05	.02	.00
☐ 75 Willie Upshaw	.05	.02	.00
☐ 76 Alan Bannister	.05	.02	.00
☐ 77 Joe Beckwith	.05	.02	.00
☐ 78 Scott Fletcher	.05	.02	.00
☐ 79 Rick Mahler	.05	.02	.00
☐ 80 Keith Hernandez	.12	.05	.01
☐ 81 Lenn Sakata	.05	.02	.00
☐ 82 Joe Price	.05	.02	.00
☐ 83 Charlie Moore	.05	.02	.00
☐ 84 Spike Owen	.05	.02	.00
☐ 85 Mike Marshall	.10	.04	.01
☐ 86 Don Aase	.05	.02	.00
☐ 87 David Green	.05	.02	.00
☐ 88 Bryn Smith	.08	.03	.01
☐ 89 Jackie Gutierrez	.05	.02	.00
☐ 90 Rich Gossage	.12	.05	.01
☐ 91 Jeff Burroughs	.05	.02	.00
☐ 92 Paul Owens MG	.08	.03	.01
(checklist back)			
☐ 93 Don Schulze	.05	.02	.00
☐ 94 Toby Harrah	.05	.02	.00
☐ 95 Jose Cruz	.08	.03	.01
☐ 96 Johnny Ray	.05	.02	.00
☐ 97 Pete Filson	.05	.02	.00
☐ 98 Steve Lake	.05	.02	.00
☐ 99 Milt Wilcox	.05	.02	.00
☐ 100 George Brett	.80	.35	.08
☐ 101 Jim Acker	.05	.02	.00
☐ 102 Tommy Dunbar	.05	.02	.00
☐ 103 Randy Lerch	.05	.02	.00
☐ 104 Mike Fitzgerald	.05	.02	.00
☐ 105 Ron Kittle	.10	.04	.01
☐ 106 Pascual Perez	.08	.03	.01
☐ 107 Tom Foley	.05	.02	.00
☐ 108 Darnell Coles	.08	.03	.01
☐ 109 Gary Roenicke	.05	.02	.00
☐ 110 Alejandro Pena	.10	.04	.01
☐ 111 Doug DeCinces	.08	.03	.01
☐ 112 Tom Tellmann	.05	.02	.00
☐ 113 Tom Herr	.08	.03	.01
☐ 114 Bob James	.05	.02	.00
☐ 115 Rickey Henderson	2.50	1.00	.25
☐ 116 Dennis Boyd	.12	.05	.01
☐ 117 Greg Gross	.05	.02	.00
☐ 118 Eric Show	.05	.02	.00
☐ 119 Pat Corrales MG	.08	.03	.01
(checklist back)			
☐ 120 Steve Kemp	.05	.02	.00
☐ 121 Checklist: 1-132	.12	.02	.00
☐ 122 Tom Brunansky	.12	.05	.01
☐ 123 Dave Smith	.05	.02	.00
☐ 124 Rich Hebner	.05	.02	.00
☐ 125 Kent Tekulve	.05	.02	.00
☐ 126 Ruppert Jones	.05	.02	.00
☐ 127 Mark Gubicza	.40	.16	.04
☐ 128 Ernie Whitt	.05	.02	.00
☐ 129 Gene Garber	.05	.02	.00
☐ 130 Al Oliver	.10	.04	.01
☐ 131 Buddy/Gus Bell FS	.08	.03	.01
☐ 132 Dale/Yogi Berra FS	.15	.06	.01
☐ 133 Bob/Ray Boone FS	.08	.03	.01
☐ 134 Terry/Tito Francona FS	.05	.02	.00
☐ 135 Terry/Bob Kennedy FS	.05	.02	.00
☐ 136 Jeff/Jim Kunkel FS	.05	.02	.00
☐ 137 Vance/Vern Law FS	.05	.02	.00
☐ 138 Dick/Dick Schofield FS	.05	.02	.00
☐ 139 Joel/Bob Skinner FS	.05	.02	.00
☐ 140 Roy/Roy Smalley FS	.05	.02	.00
☐ 141 Mike/D.Stenhouse FS	.05	.02	.00
☐ 142 Steve/Dizzy Trout FS	.05	.02	.00
☐ 143 Ozzie/Ossie Virgil FS	.05	.02	.00
☐ 144 Ron Gardenhire	.05	.02	.00
☐ 145 Alvin Davis	.75	.30	.07
☐ 146 Gary Redus	.08	.03	.01
☐ 147 Bill Swaggerty	.05	.02	.00
☐ 148 Steve Yeager	.05	.02	.00
☐ 149 Dickie Noles	.05	.02	.00
☐ 150 Jim Rice	.15	.06	.01
☐ 151 Moose Haas	.05	.02	.00
☐ 152 Steve Braun	.05	.02	.00
☐ 153 Frank LaCorte	.05	.02	.00
☐ 154 Argenis Salazar	.05	.02	.00
☐ 155 Yogi Berra MG	.15	.06	.01
(checklist back)			
☐ 156 Craig Reynolds	.05	.02	.00
☐ 157 Tug McGraw	.10	.04	.01
☐ 158 Pat Tabler	.05	.02	.00

#	Name			
☐ 159	Carlos Diaz	.05	.02	.00
☐ 160	Lance Parrish	.15	.06	.01
☐ 161	Ken Schrom	.05	.02	.00
☐ 162	Benny Distefano	.08	.03	.01
☐ 163	Dennis Eckersley	.25	.10	.02
☐ 164	Jorge Orta	.05	.02	.00
☐ 165	Dusty Baker	.08	.03	.01
☐ 166	Keith Atherton	.05	.02	.00
☐ 167	Rufino Linares	.05	.02	.00
☐ 168	Garth Iorg	.05	.02	.00
☐ 169	Dan Spillner	.05	.02	.00
☐ 170	George Foster	.12	.05	.01
☐ 171	Bill Stein	.05	.02	.00
☐ 172	Jack Perconte	.05	.02	.00
☐ 173	Mike Young	.05	.02	.00
☐ 174	Rick Honeycutt	.05	.02	.00
☐ 175	Dave Parker	.25	.10	.02
☐ 176	Bill Schroeder	.05	.02	.00
☐ 177	Dave Von Ohlen	.05	.02	.00
☐ 178	Miguel Dilone	.05	.02	.00
☐ 179	Tommy John	.15	.06	.01
☐ 180	Dave Winfield	.40	.16	.04
☐ 181	Roger Clemens	20.00	8.50	2.75
☐ 182	Tim Flannery	.05	.02	.00
☐ 183	Larry McWilliams	.05	.02	.00
☐ 184	Carmen Castillo	.05	.02	.00
☐ 185	Al Holland	.05	.02	.00
☐ 186	Bob Lillis MG (checklist back)	.08	.03	.01
☐ 187	Mike Walters	.05	.02	.00
☐ 188	Greg Pryor	.05	.02	.00
☐ 189	Warren Brusstar	.05	.02	.00
☐ 190	Rusty Staub	.10	.04	.01
☐ 191	Steve Nicosia	.05	.02	.00
☐ 192	Howard Johnson	3.50	1.50	.35
☐ 193	Jimmy Key	1.00	.40	.10
☐ 194	Dave Stegman	.05	.02	.00
☐ 195	Glenn Hubbard	.05	.02	.00
☐ 196	Pete O'Brien	.08	.03	.01
☐ 197	Mike Warren	.05	.02	.00
☐ 198	Eddie Milner	.05	.02	.00
☐ 199	Dennis Martinez	.10	.04	.01
☐ 200	Reggie Jackson	.65	.25	.06
☐ 201	Burt Hooton	.05	.02	.00
☐ 202	Gorman Thomas	.08	.03	.01
☐ 203	Bob McClure	.05	.02	.00
☐ 204	Art Howe	.08	.03	.01
☐ 205	Steve Rogers	.05	.02	.00
☐ 206	Phil Garner	.08	.03	.01
☐ 207	Mark Clear	.05	.02	.00
☐ 208	Champ Summers	.05	.02	.00
☐ 209	Bill Campbell	.05	.02	.00
☐ 210	Gary Matthews	.05	.02	.00
☐ 211	Clay Christiansen	.05	.02	.00
☐ 212	George Vukovich	.05	.02	.00
☐ 213	Billy Gardner MG (checklist back)	.08	.03	.01
☐ 214	John Tudor	.10	.04	.01
☐ 215	Bob Brenly	.05	.02	.00
☐ 216	Jerry Don Gleaton	.05	.02	.00
☐ 217	Leon Roberts	.05	.02	.00
☐ 218	Doyle Alexander	.05	.02	.00
☐ 219	Gerald Perry	.10	.04	.01
☐ 220	Fred Lynn	.12	.05	.01
☐ 221	Ron Reed	.05	.02	.00
☐ 222	Hubie Brooks	.12	.05	.01
☐ 223	Tom Hume	.05	.02	.00
☐ 224	Al Cowens	.05	.02	.00
☐ 225	Mike Boddicker	.05	.02	.00
☐ 226	Juan Beniquez	.05	.02	.00
☐ 227	Danny Darwin	.05	.02	.00
☐ 228	Dion James	.05	.02	.00
☐ 229	Dave LaPoint	.05	.02	.00
☐ 230	Gary Carter	.25	.10	.02
☐ 231	Dwayne Murphy	.05	.02	.00
☐ 232	Dave Beard	.05	.02	.00
☐ 233	Ed Jurak	.05	.02	.00
☐ 234	Jerry Narron	.05	.02	.00
☐ 235	Garry Maddox	.05	.02	.00
☐ 236	Mark Thurmond	.05	.02	.00
☐ 237	Julio Franco	.60	.25	.06
☐ 238	Jose Rijo	1.25	.50	.12
☐ 239	Tim Teufel	.12	.05	.01
☐ 240	Dave Stieb	.15	.06	.01
☐ 241	Jim Frey MG (checklist back)	.08	.03	.01
☐ 242	Greg Harris	.05	.02	.00
☐ 243	Barbaro Garbey	.05	.02	.00
☐ 244	Mike Jones	.05	.02	.00
☐ 245	Chili Davis	.15	.06	.01
☐ 246	Mike Norris	.05	.02	.00
☐ 247	Wayne Tolleson	.05	.02	.00
☐ 248	Terry Forster	.05	.02	.00
☐ 249	Harold Baines	.20	.08	.02
☐ 250	Jesse Orosco	.05	.02	.00
☐ 251	Brad Gulden	.05	.02	.00
☐ 252	Dan Ford	.05	.02	.00
☐ 253	Sid Bream	.35	.15	.03
☐ 254	Pete Vuckovich	.05	.02	.00
☐ 255	Lonnie Smith	.10	.04	.01
☐ 256	Mike Stanton	.05	.02	.00
☐ 257	Bryan Little	.05	.02	.00
☐ 258	Mike Brown (Angels OF)	.05	.02	.00
☐ 259	Gary Allenson	.05	.02	.00
☐ 260	Dave Righetti	.12	.05	.01
☐ 261	Checklist: 133-264	.12	.02	.00
☐ 262	Greg Booker	.05	.02	.00
☐ 263	Mel Hall	.15	.06	.01
☐ 264	Joe Sambito	.05	.02	.00
☐ 265	Juan Samuel	.45	.18	.04
☐ 266	Frank Viola	.30	.12	.03
☐ 267	Henry Cotto	.12	.05	.01
☐ 268	Chuck Tanner MG (checklist back)	.08	.03	.01
☐ 269	Doug Baker	.05	.02	.00
☐ 270	Dan Quisenberry	.10	.04	.01
☐ 271	Tim Foli FDP68	.05	.02	.00
☐ 272	Jeff Burroughs FDP69	.05	.02	.00
☐ 273	Bill Almon FDP74	.05	.02	.00
☐ 274	Floyd Bannister FDP76	.05	.02	.00
☐ 275	Harold Baines FDP77	.12	.05	.01
☐ 276	Bob Horner FDP78	.10	.04	.01
☐ 277	Al Chambers FDP79	.05	.02	.00
☐ 278	D.Strawberry FDP80	2.00	.80	.20
☐ 279	Mike Moore FDP81	.10	.04	.01
☐ 280	Sh.Dunston FDP82	2.75	1.10	.27
☐ 281	Tim Belcher FDP83	1.00	.40	.10
☐ 282	Shawn Abner FDP84	.20	.08	.02
☐ 283	Fran Mullins	.05	.02	.00
☐ 284	Marty Bystrom	.05	.02	.00
☐ 285	Dan Driessen	.05	.02	.00
☐ 286	Rudy Law	.05	.02	.00
☐ 287	Walt Terrell	.05	.02	.00
☐ 288	Jeff Kunkel	.05	.02	.00
☐ 289	Tom Underwood	.05	.02	.00
☐ 290	Cecil Cooper	.10	.04	.01
☐ 291	Bob Welch	.15	.06	.01
☐ 292	Brad Komminsk	.05	.02	.00
☐ 293	Curt Young	.12	.05	.01
☐ 294	Tom Nieto	.05	.02	.00
☐ 295	Joe Niekro	.08	.03	.01
☐ 296	Ricky Nelson	.05	.02	.00
☐ 297	Gary Lucas	.05	.02	.00
☐ 298	Marty Barrett	.08	.03	.01
☐ 299	Andy Hawkins	.08	.03	.01
☐ 300	Rod Carew	.60	.25	.06
☐ 301	John Montefusco	.05	.02	.00
☐ 302	Tim Corcoran	.05	.02	.00
☐ 303	Mike Jeffcoat	.05	.02	.00
☐ 304	Gary Gaetti	.12	.05	.01
☐ 305	Dale Berra	.05	.02	.00
☐ 306	Rick Reuschel	.08	.03	.01
☐ 307	Sparky Anderson MG (checklist back)	.08	.03	.01
☐ 308	John Wathan	.05	.02	.00
☐ 309	Mike Witt	.05	.02	.00
☐ 310	Manny Trillo	.05	.02	.00
☐ 311	Jim Gott	.05	.02	.00
☐ 312	Marc Hill	.05	.02	.00
☐ 313	Dave Schmidt	.05	.02	.00
☐ 314	Ron Oester	.05	.02	.00
☐ 315	Doug Sisk	.05	.02	.00
☐ 316	John Lowenstein	.05	.02	.00
☐ 317	Jack Lazorko	.05	.02	.00
☐ 318	Ted Simmons	.10	.04	.01
☐ 319	Jeff Jones	.05	.02	.00
☐ 320	Dale Murphy	.40	.16	.04
☐ 321	Ricky Horton	.12	.05	.01
☐ 322	Dave Stapleton	.05	.02	.00
☐ 323	Andy McGaffigan	.05	.02	.00
☐ 324	Bruce Bochy	.05	.02	.00
☐ 325	John Denny	.05	.02	.00
☐ 326	Kevin Bass	.08	.03	.01
☐ 327	Brook Jacoby	.15	.06	.01
☐ 328	Bob Shirley	.05	.02	.00
☐ 329	Ron Washington	.05	.02	.00
☐ 330	Leon Durham	.05	.02	.00
☐ 331	Bill Laskey	.05	.02	.00
☐ 332	Brian Harper	.20	.08	.02
☐ 333	Willie Hernandez	.08	.03	.01
☐ 334	Dick Howser MG (checklist back)	.08	.03	.01
☐ 335	Bruce Benedict	.05	.02	.00
☐ 336	Rance Mulliniks	.05	.02	.00
☐ 337	Billy Sample	.05	.02	.00
☐ 338	Britt Burns	.05	.02	.00
☐ 339	Danny Heep	.05	.02	.00

No.	Player			
☐ 340	Robin Yount	.80	.35	.08
☐ 341	Floyd Rayford	.05	.02	.00
☐ 342	Ted Power	.05	.02	.00
☐ 343	Bill Russell	.08	.03	.01
☐ 344	Dave Henderson	.20	.08	.02
☐ 345	Charlie Lea	.05	.02	.00
☐ 346	Terry Pendleton	2.00	.80	.20
☐ 347	Rick Langford	.05	.02	.00
☐ 348	Bob Boone	.10	.04	.01
☐ 349	Domingo Ramos	.05	.02	.00
☐ 350	Wade Boggs	2.50	1.00	.25
☐ 351	Juan Agosto	.05	.02	.00
☐ 352	Joe Morgan	.25	.10	.02
☐ 353	Julio Solano	.05	.02	.00
☐ 354	Andre Robertson	.05	.02	.00
☐ 355	Bert Blyleven	.15	.06	.01
☐ 356	Dave Meier	.05	.02	.00
☐ 357	Rich Bordi	.05	.02	.00
☐ 358	Tony Pena	.08	.03	.01
☐ 359	Pat Sheridan	.05	.02	.00
☐ 360	Steve Carlton	.50	.20	.05
☐ 361	Alfredo Griffin	.05	.02	.00
☐ 362	Craig McMurtry	.05	.02	.00
☐ 363	Ron Hodges	.05	.02	.00
☐ 364	Richard Dotson	.05	.02	.00
☐ 365	Danny Ozark MG	.08	.03	.01
	(checklist back)			
☐ 366	Todd Cruz	.05	.02	.00
☐ 367	Keefe Cato	.05	.02	.00
☐ 368	Dave Bergman	.05	.02	.00
☐ 369	R.J. Reynolds	.15	.06	.01
☐ 370	Bruce Sutter	.10	.04	.01
☐ 371	Mickey Rivers	.05	.02	.00
☐ 372	Roy Howell	.05	.02	.00
☐ 373	Mike Moore	.10	.04	.01
☐ 374	Brian Downing	.08	.03	.01
☐ 375	Jeff Reardon	.20	.08	.02
☐ 376	Jeff Newman	.05	.02	.00
☐ 377	Checklist: 265-396	.12	.02	.00
☐ 378	Alan Wiggins	.05	.02	.00
☐ 379	Charles Hudson	.05	.02	.00
☐ 380	Ken Griffey	.15	.06	.01
☐ 381	Roy Smith	.05	.02	.00
☐ 382	Denny Walling	.05	.02	.00
☐ 383	Rick Lysander	.05	.02	.00
☐ 384	Jody Davis	.05	.02	.00
☐ 385	Jose DeLeon	.05	.02	.00
☐ 386	Dan Gladden	.35	.15	.03
☐ 387	Buddy Biancalana	.08	.03	.01
☐ 388	Bert Roberge	.05	.02	.00
☐ 389	Rod Dedeaux OLY CO	.05	.02	.00
☐ 390	Sid Akins OLY	.05	.02	.00
☐ 391	Flavio Alfaro OLY	.05	.02	.00
☐ 392	Don August OLY	.10	.04	.01
☐ 393	Scott Bankhead OLY	.30	.12	.03
☐ 394	Bob Caffrey OLY	.05	.02	.00
☐ 395	Mike Dunne OLY	.10	.04	.01
☐ 396	Gary Green OLY	.10	.04	.01
☐ 397	John Hoover OLY	.10	.04	.01
☐ 398	Shane Mack OLY	1.00	.40	.10
☐ 399	John Marzano OLY	.15	.06	.01
☐ 400	Oddibe McDowell OLY	.20	.08	.02
☐ 401	Mark McGwire OLY	11.00	5.00	1.35
☐ 402	Pat Pacillo OLY	.10	.04	.01
☐ 403	Cory Snyder OLY	.90	.40	.09
☐ 404	Billy Swift OLY	.25	.10	.02
☐ 405	Tom Veryzer	.05	.02	.00
☐ 406	Len Whitehouse	.05	.02	.00
☐ 407	Bobby Ramos	.05	.02	.00
☐ 408	Sid Monge	.05	.02	.00
☐ 409	Brad Wellman	.05	.02	.00
☐ 410	Bob Horner	.10	.04	.01
☐ 411	Bobby Cox MG	.08	.03	.01
	(checklist back)			
☐ 412	Bud Black	.08	.03	.01
☐ 413	Vance Law	.05	.02	.00
☐ 414	Gary Ward UER	.05	.02	.00
☐ 415	Ron Darling UER	.15	.06	.01
	(no trivia answer)			
☐ 416	Wayne Gross	.05	.02	.00
☐ 417	John Franco	.75	.30	.07
☐ 418	Ken Landreaux	.05	.02	.00
☐ 419	Mike Caldwell	.05	.02	.00
☐ 420	Andre Dawson	.60	.25	.06
☐ 421	Dave Rucker	.05	.02	.00
☐ 422	Carney Lansford	.10	.04	.01
☐ 423	Barry Bonnell	.05	.02	.00
☐ 424	Al Nipper	.05	.02	.00
☐ 425	Mike Hargrove	.05	.02	.00
☐ 426	Vern Ruhle	.05	.02	.00
☐ 427	Mario Ramirez	.05	.02	.00
☐ 428	Larry Andersen	.05	.02	.00
☐ 429	Rick Cerone	.05	.02	.00
☐ 430	Ron Davis	.05	.02	.00
☐ 431	U.L. Washington	.05	.02	.00

No.	Player			
☐ 432	Thad Bosley	.05	.02	.00
☐ 433	Jim Morrison	.05	.02	.00
☐ 434	Gene Richards	.05	.02	.00
☐ 435	Dan Petry	.05	.02	.00
☐ 436	Willie Aikens	.05	.02	.00
☐ 437	Al Jones	.05	.02	.00
☐ 438	Joe Torre MG	.10	.04	.01
	(checklist back)			
☐ 439	Junior Ortiz	.05	.02	.00
☐ 440	Fernando Valenzuela	.12	.05	.01
☐ 441	Duane Walker	.05	.02	.00
☐ 442	Ken Forsch	.05	.02	.00
☐ 443	George Wright	.05	.02	.00
☐ 444	Tony Phillips	.08	.03	.01
☐ 445	Tippy Martinez	.05	.02	.00
☐ 446	Jim Sundberg	.05	.02	.00
☐ 447	Jeff Lahti	.05	.02	.00
☐ 448	Derrel Thomas	.05	.02	.00
☐ 449	Phil Bradley	.25	.10	.02
☐ 450	Steve Garvey	.35	.15	.03
☐ 451	Bruce Hurst	.10	.04	.01
☐ 452	John Castino	.05	.02	.00
☐ 453	Tom Waddell	.05	.02	.00
☐ 454	Glenn Wilson	.05	.02	.00
☐ 455	Bob Knepper	.05	.02	.00
☐ 456	Tim Foli	.05	.02	.00
☐ 457	Cecilio Guante	.05	.02	.00
☐ 458	Randy Johnson	.05	.02	.00
☐ 459	Charlie Leibrandt	.05	.02	.00
☐ 460	Ryne Sandberg	3.00	1.25	.30
☐ 461	Marty Castillo	.05	.02	.00
☐ 462	Gary Lavelle	.05	.02	.00
☐ 463	Dave Collins	.05	.02	.00
☐ 464	Mike Mason	.05	.02	.00
☐ 465	Bob Grich	.08	.03	.01
☐ 466	Tony LaRussa MG	.08	.03	.01
	(checklist back)			
☐ 467	Ed Lynch	.05	.02	.00
☐ 468	Wayne Krenchicki	.05	.02	.00
☐ 469	Sammy Stewart	.05	.02	.00
☐ 470	Steve Sax	.25	.10	.02
☐ 471	Pete Ladd	.05	.02	.00
☐ 472	Jim Essian	.05	.02	.00
☐ 473	Tim Wallach	.10	.04	.01
☐ 474	Kurt Kepshire	.05	.02	.00
☐ 475	Andre Thornton	.08	.03	.01
☐ 476	Jeff Stone	.08	.03	.01
☐ 477	Bob Ojeda	.08	.03	.01
☐ 478	Kurt Bevacqua	.05	.02	.00
☐ 479	Mike Madden	.05	.02	.00
☐ 480	Lou Whitaker	.25	.10	.02
☐ 481	Dale Murray	.05	.02	.00
☐ 482	Harry Spilman	.05	.02	.00
☐ 483	Mike Smithson	.05	.02	.00
☐ 484	Larry Bowa	.08	.03	.01
☐ 485	Matt Young	.05	.02	.00
☐ 486	Steve Balboni	.05	.02	.00
☐ 487	Frank Williams	.05	.02	.00
☐ 488	Joel Skinner	.05	.02	.00
☐ 489	Bryan Clark	.05	.02	.00
☐ 490	Jason Thompson	.05	.02	.00
☐ 491	Rick Camp	.05	.02	.00
☐ 492	Dave Johnson MG	.08	.03	.01
	(checklist back)			
☐ 493	Orel Hershiser	2.25	.90	.22
☐ 494	Rich Dauer	.05	.02	.00
☐ 495	Mario Soto	.05	.02	.00
☐ 496	Donnie Scott	.05	.02	.00
☐ 497	Gary Pettis UER	.12	.05	.01
	(photo actually Gary's little brother, Lynn)			
☐ 498	Ed Romero	.05	.02	.00
☐ 499	Danny Cox	.08	.03	.01
☐ 500	Mike Schmidt	1.25	.50	.12
☐ 501	Dan Schatzeder	.05	.02	.00
☐ 502	Rick Miller	.05	.02	.00
☐ 503	Tim Conroy	.05	.02	.00
☐ 504	Jerry Willard	.05	.02	.00
☐ 505	Jim Beattie	.05	.02	.00
☐ 506	Franklin Stubbs	.25	.10	.02
☐ 507	Ray Fontenot	.05	.02	.00
☐ 508	John Shelby	.05	.02	.00
☐ 509	Milt May	.05	.02	.00
☐ 510	Kent Hrbek	.17	.07	.01
☐ 511	Lee Smith	.25	.10	.02
☐ 512	Tom Brookens	.05	.02	.00
☐ 513	Lynn Jones	.05	.02	.00
☐ 514	Jeff Cornell	.05	.02	.00
☐ 515	Dave Concepcion	.10	.04	.01
☐ 516	Roy Lee Jackson	.05	.02	.00
☐ 517	Jerry Martin	.05	.02	.00
☐ 518	Chris Chambliss	.08	.03	.01
☐ 519	Doug Rader MG	.08	.03	.01
	(checklist back)			

No.	Player			
☐ 520	LaMarr Hoyt	.05	.02	.00
☐ 521	Rick Dempsey	.05	.02	.00
☐ 522	Paul Molitor	.20	.08	.02
☐ 523	Candy Maldonado	.15	.06	.01
☐ 524	Rob Wilfong	.05	.02	.00
☐ 525	Darrell Porter	.05	.02	.00
☐ 526	David Palmer	.05	.02	.00
☐ 527	Checklist: 397-528	.12	.02	.00
☐ 528	Bill Krueger	.05	.02	.00
☐ 529	Rich Gedman	.05	.02	.00
☐ 530	Dave Dravecky	.10	.04	.01
☐ 531	Joe Lefebvre	.05	.02	.00
☐ 532	Frank DiPino	.05	.02	.00
☐ 533	Tony Bernazard	.05	.02	.00
☐ 534	Brian Dayett	.05	.02	.00
☐ 535	Pat Putnam	.05	.02	.00
☐ 536	Kirby Puckett	16.00	6.75	2.25
☐ 537	Don Robinson	.05	.02	.00
☐ 538	Keith Moreland	.05	.02	.00
☐ 539	Aurelio Lopez	.05	.02	.00
☐ 540	Claudell Washington	.05	.02	.00
☐ 541	Mark Davis	.10	.04	.01
☐ 542	Don Slaught	.05	.02	.00
☐ 543	Mike Squires	.05	.02	.00
☐ 544	Bruce Kison	.05	.02	.00
☐ 545	Lloyd Moseby	.08	.03	.01
☐ 546	Brent Gaff	.05	.02	.00
☐ 547	Pete Rose MG (checklist back)	.50	.20	.05
☐ 548	Larry Parrish	.05	.02	.00
☐ 549	Mike Scioscia	.08	.03	.01
☐ 550	Scott McGregor	.05	.02	.00
☐ 551	Andy Van Slyke	.45	.18	.04
☐ 552	Chris Codiroli	.05	.02	.00
☐ 553	Bob Clark	.05	.02	.00
☐ 554	Doug Flynn	.05	.02	.00
☐ 555	Bob Stanley	.05	.02	.00
☐ 556	Sixto Lezcano	.05	.02	.00
☐ 557	Len Barker	.05	.02	.00
☐ 558	Carmelo Martinez	.05	.02	.00
☐ 559	Jay Howell	.05	.02	.00
☐ 560	Bill Madlock	.08	.03	.01
☐ 561	Darryl Motley	.05	.02	.00
☐ 562	Houston Jimenez	.05	.02	.00
☐ 563	Dick Ruthven	.05	.02	.00
☐ 564	Alan Ashby	.05	.02	.00
☐ 565	Kirk Gibson	.25	.10	.02
☐ 566	Ed VandeBerg	.05	.02	.00
☐ 567	Joel Youngblood	.05	.02	.00
☐ 568	Cliff Johnson	.05	.02	.00
☐ 569	Ken Oberkfell	.05	.02	.00
☐ 570	Darryl Strawberry	5.00	2.25	.50
☐ 571	Charlie Hough	.05	.02	.00
☐ 572	Tom Paciorek	.05	.02	.00
☐ 573	Jay Tibbs	.05	.02	.00
☐ 574	Joe Altobelli MG (checklist back)	.08	.03	.01
☐ 575	Pedro Guerrero	.17	.07	.01
☐ 576	Jaime Cocanower	.05	.02	.00
☐ 577	Chris Speier	.05	.02	.00
☐ 578	Terry Francona	.05	.02	.00
☐ 579	Ron Romanick	.05	.02	.00
☐ 580	Dwight Evans	.15	.06	.01
☐ 581	Mark Wagner	.05	.02	.00
☐ 582	Ken Phelps	.08	.03	.01
☐ 583	Bobby Brown	.05	.02	.00
☐ 584	Kevin Gross	.05	.02	.00
☐ 585	Butch Wynegar	.05	.02	.00
☐ 586	Bill Scherrer	.05	.02	.00
☐ 587	Doug Frobel	.05	.02	.00
☐ 588	Bobby Castillo	.05	.02	.00
☐ 589	Bob Dernier	.05	.02	.00
☐ 590	Ray Knight	.08	.03	.01
☐ 591	Larry Herndon	.05	.02	.00
☐ 592	Jeff Robinson (Giants pitcher)	.12	.05	.01
☐ 593	Rick Leach	.05	.02	.00
☐ 594	Curt Wilkerson	.05	.02	.00
☐ 595	Larry Gura	.05	.02	.00
☐ 596	Jerry Hairston	.05	.02	.00
☐ 597	Brad Lesley	.05	.02	.00
☐ 598	Jose Oquendo	.05	.02	.00
☐ 599	Storm Davis	.05	.02	.00
☐ 600	Pete Rose	.75	.30	.07
☐ 601	Tom Lasorda MG (checklist back)	.08	.03	.01
☐ 602	Jeff Dedmon	.05	.02	.00
☐ 603	Rick Manning	.05	.02	.00
☐ 604	Daryl Sconiers	.05	.02	.00
☐ 605	Ozzie Smith	.50	.20	.05
☐ 606	Rich Gale	.05	.02	.00
☐ 607	Bill Almon	.05	.02	.00
☐ 608	Craig Lefferts	.08	.03	.01
☐ 609	Broderick Perkins	.05	.02	.00
☐ 610	Jack Morris	.40	.16	.04
☐ 611	Ozzie Virgil	.05	.02	.00
☐ 612	Mike Armstrong	.05	.02	.00
☐ 613	Terry Puhl	.05	.02	.00
☐ 614	Al Williams	.05	.02	.00
☐ 615	Marvell Wynne	.05	.02	.00
☐ 616	Scott Sanderson	.08	.03	.01
☐ 617	Willie Wilson	.10	.04	.01
☐ 618	Pete Falcone	.05	.02	.00
☐ 619	Jeff Leonard	.05	.02	.00
☐ 620	Dwight Gooden	7.50	3.25	.75
☐ 621	Marvis Foley	.05	.02	.00
☐ 622	Luis Leal	.05	.02	.00
☐ 623	Greg Walker	.05	.02	.00
☐ 624	Benny Ayala	.05	.02	.00
☐ 625	Mark Langston	2.50	1.00	.25
☐ 626	German Rivera	.05	.02	.00
☐ 627	Eric Davis	8.00	3.50	.80
☐ 628	Rene Lachemann MG (checklist back)	.08	.03	.01
☐ 629	Dick Schofield	.12	.05	.01
☐ 630	Tim Raines	.25	.10	.02
☐ 631	Bob Forsch	.05	.02	.00
☐ 632	Bruce Bochte	.05	.02	.00
☐ 633	Glenn Hoffman	.05	.02	.00
☐ 634	Bill Dawley	.05	.02	.00
☐ 635	Terry Kennedy	.05	.02	.00
☐ 636	Shane Rawley	.05	.02	.00
☐ 637	Brett Butler	.15	.06	.01
☐ 638	Mike Pagliarulo	.35	.15	.03
☐ 639	Ed Hodge	.05	.02	.00
☐ 640	Steve Henderson	.05	.02	.00
☐ 641	Rod Scurry	.05	.02	.00
☐ 642	Dave Owen	.05	.02	.00
☐ 643	Johnny Grubb	.05	.02	.00
☐ 644	Mark Huismann	.05	.02	.00
☐ 645	Damaso Garcia	.05	.02	.00
☐ 646	Scot Thompson	.05	.02	.00
☐ 647	Rafael Ramirez	.05	.02	.00
☐ 648	Bob Jones	.05	.02	.00
☐ 649	Sid Fernandez	.35	.15	.03
☐ 650	Greg Luzinski	.10	.04	.01
☐ 651	Jeff Russell	.12	.05	.01
☐ 652	Joe Nolan	.05	.02	.00
☐ 653	Mark Brouhard	.05	.02	.00
☐ 654	Dave Anderson	.05	.02	.00
☐ 655	Joaquin Andujar	.08	.03	.01
☐ 656	Chuck Cottier MG (checklist back)	.08	.03	.01
☐ 657	Jim Slaton	.05	.02	.00
☐ 658	Mike Stenhouse	.05	.02	.00
☐ 659	Checklist: 529-660	.12	.02	.00
☐ 660	Tony Gwynn	2.25	.90	.22
☐ 661	Steve Crawford	.05	.02	.00
☐ 662	Mike Heath	.05	.02	.00
☐ 663	Luis Aguayo	.05	.02	.00
☐ 664	Steve Farr	.25	.10	.02
☐ 665	Don Mattingly	4.50	2.00	.45
☐ 666	Mike LaCoss	.05	.02	.00
☐ 667	Dave Engle	.05	.02	.00
☐ 668	Steve Trout	.05	.02	.00
☐ 669	Lee Lacy	.05	.02	.00
☐ 670	Tom Seaver	.50	.20	.05
☐ 671	Dane Iorg	.05	.02	.00
☐ 672	Juan Berenguer	.05	.02	.00
☐ 673	Buck Martinez	.05	.02	.00
☐ 674	Atlee Hammaker	.05	.02	.00
☐ 675	Tony Perez	.17	.07	.01
☐ 676	Albert Hall	.05	.02	.00
☐ 677	Wally Backman	.05	.02	.00
☐ 678	Joey McLaughlin	.05	.02	.00
☐ 679	Bob Kearney	.05	.02	.00
☐ 680	Jerry Reuss	.05	.02	.00
☐ 681	Ben Oglivie	.05	.02	.00
☐ 682	Doug Corbett	.05	.02	.00
☐ 683	Whitey Herzog MG (checklist back)	.08	.03	.01
☐ 684	Bill Doran	.08	.03	.01
☐ 685	Bill Caudill	.05	.02	.00
☐ 686	Mike Easler	.05	.02	.00
☐ 687	Bill Gullickson	.08	.03	.01
☐ 688	Len Matuszek	.05	.02	.00
☐ 689	Luis DeLeon	.05	.02	.00
☐ 690	Alan Trammell	.40	.16	.04
☐ 691	Dennis Rasmussen	.12	.05	.01
☐ 692	Randy Bush	.05	.02	.00
☐ 693	Tim Stoddard	.05	.02	.00
☐ 694	Joe Carter	3.50	1.50	.35
☐ 695	Rick Rhoden	.05	.02	.00
☐ 696	John Rabb	.05	.02	.00
☐ 697	Onix Concepcion	.05	.02	.00
☐ 698	Jorge Bell	.45	.18	.04
☐ 699	Donnie Moore	.05	.02	.00
☐ 700	Eddie Murray	.60	.25	.06
☐ 701	Eddie Murray AS	.20	.08	.02
☐ 702	Damaso Garcia AS	.05	.02	.00

☐ 703	George Brett AS	.25	.10	.02
☐ 704	Cal Ripken AS	.75	.30	.07
☐ 705	Dave Winfield AS	.20	.08	.02
☐ 706	Rickey Henderson AS	.50	.20	.05
☐ 707	Tony Armas AS	.05	.02	.00
☐ 708	Lance Parrish AS	.10	.04	.01
☐ 709	Mike Boddicker AS	.05	.02	.00
☐ 710	Frank Viola AS	.12	.05	.01
☐ 711	Dan Quisenberry AS	.08	.03	.01
☐ 712	Keith Hernandez AS	.12	.05	.01
☐ 713	Ryne Sandberg AS	.65	.25	.06
☐ 714	Mike Schmidt AS	.40	.16	.04
☐ 715	Ozzie Smith AS	.17	.07	.01
☐ 716	Dale Murphy AS	.20	.08	.02
☐ 717	Tony Gwynn AS	.35	.15	.03
☐ 718	Jeff Leonard AS	.05	.02	.00
☐ 719	Gary Carter AS	.15	.06	.01
☐ 720	Rick Sutcliffe AS	.08	.03	.01
☐ 721	Bob Knepper AS	.05	.02	.00
☐ 722	Bruce Sutter AS	.08	.03	.01
☐ 723	Dave Stewart	.30	.12	.03
☐ 724	Oscar Gamble	.05	.02	.00
☐ 725	Floyd Bannister	.05	.02	.00
☐ 726	Al Bumbry	.05	.02	.00
☐ 727	Frank Pastore	.05	.02	.00
☐ 728	Bob Bailor	.05	.02	.00
☐ 729	Don Sutton	.20	.08	.02
☐ 730	Dave Kingman	.10	.04	.01
☐ 731	Neil Allen	.05	.02	.00
☐ 732	John McNamara MG (checklist back)	.08	.03	.01
☐ 733	Tony Scott	.05	.02	.00
☐ 734	John Henry Johnson	.05	.02	.00
☐ 735	Garry Templeton	.08	.03	.01
☐ 736	Jerry Mumphrey	.05	.02	.00
☐ 737	Bo Diaz	.05	.02	.00
☐ 738	Omar Moreno	.05	.02	.00
☐ 739	Ernie Camacho	.05	.02	.00
☐ 740	Jack Clark	.15	.06	.01
☐ 741	John Butcher	.05	.02	.00
☐ 742	Ron Hassey	.05	.02	.00
☐ 743	Frank White	.05	.02	.00
☐ 744	Doug Bair	.05	.02	.00
☐ 745	Buddy Bell	.08	.03	.01
☐ 746	Jim Clancy	.05	.02	.00
☐ 747	Alex Trevino	.05	.02	.00
☐ 748	Lee Mazzilli	.05	.02	.00
☐ 749	Julio Cruz	.05	.02	.00
☐ 750	Rollie Fingers	.20	.08	.02
☐ 751	Kelvin Chapman	.05	.02	.00
☐ 752	Bob Owchinko	.05	.02	.00
☐ 753	Greg Brock	.05	.02	.00
☐ 754	Larry Milbourne	.05	.02	.00
☐ 755	Ken Singleton	.08	.03	.01
☐ 756	Rob Picciolo	.05	.02	.00
☐ 757	Willie McGee	.30	.12	.03
☐ 758	Ray Burris	.05	.02	.00
☐ 759	Jim Fanning MG (checklist back)	.08	.03	.01
☐ 760	Nolan Ryan	3.75	1.60	.37
☐ 761	Jerry Remy	.05	.02	.00
☐ 762	Eddie Whitson	.05	.02	.00
☐ 763	Kiko Garcia	.05	.02	.00
☐ 764	Jamie Easterly	.05	.02	.00
☐ 765	Willie Randolph	.08	.03	.01
☐ 766	Paul Mirabella	.05	.02	.00
☐ 767	Darrell Brown	.05	.02	.00
☐ 768	Ron Cey	.08	.03	.01
☐ 769	Joe Cowley	.05	.02	.00
☐ 770	Carlton Fisk	.50	.20	.05
☐ 771	Geoff Zahn	.05	.02	.00
☐ 772	Johnnie LeMaster	.05	.02	.00
☐ 773	Hal McRae	.08	.03	.01
☐ 774	Dennis Lamp	.05	.02	.00
☐ 775	Mookie Wilson	.08	.03	.01
☐ 776	Jerry Royster	.05	.02	.00
☐ 777	Ned Yost	.05	.02	.00
☐ 778	Mike Davis	.05	.02	.00
☐ 779	Nick Esasky	.08	.03	.01
☐ 780	Mike Flanagan	.08	.03	.01
☐ 781	Jim Gantner	.05	.02	.00
☐ 782	Tom Niedenfuer	.05	.02	.00
☐ 783	Mike Jorgensen	.05	.02	.00
☐ 784	Checklist: 661-792	.12	.02	.00
☐ 785	Tony Armas	.05	.02	.00
☐ 786	Enos Cabell	.05	.02	.00
☐ 787	Jim Wohlford	.05	.02	.00
☐ 788	Steve Comer	.05	.02	.00
☐ 789	Luis Salazar	.05	.02	.00
☐ 790	Ron Guidry	.15	.06	.01
☐ 791	Ivan DeJesus	.05	.02	.00
☐ 792	Darrell Evans	.15	.06	.01

1985 Topps All-Star Glossy 22

The cards in this 22-card set measure 2 1/2" by 3 1/2". Similar in design, both front and back, to last year's Glossy set, this edition features the managers, starting nine players and honorary captains of the National and American League teams in the 1984 All-Star game. The set is numbered on the reverse with players essentially ordered by position within league, NL: 1-11 and AL: 12-22.

		MINT	EXC	G-VG
COMPLETE SET (22)		3.50	1.50	.35
COMMON PLAYER (1-22)		.10	.04	.01
☐ 1	Paul Owens MG	.10	.04	.01
☐ 2	Steve Garvey	.40	.16	.04
☐ 3	Ryne Sandberg	.75	.30	.07
☐ 4	Mike Schmidt	.75	.30	.07
☐ 5	Ozzie Smith	.30	.12	.03
☐ 6	Tony Gwynn	.50	.20	.05
☐ 7	Dale Murphy	.75	.30	.07
☐ 8	Darryl Strawberry	.75	.30	.07
☐ 9	Gary Carter	.25	.10	.02
☐ 10	Charlie Lea	.10	.04	.01
☐ 11	Willie McCovey CAPT	.20	.08	.02
☐ 12	Joe Altobelli MG	.10	.04	.01
☐ 13	Rod Carew	.50	.20	.05
☐ 14	Lou Whitaker	.15	.06	.01
☐ 15	George Brett	.50	.20	.05
☐ 16	Cal Ripken	.75	.30	.07
☐ 17	Dave Winfield	.35	.15	.03
☐ 18	Chet Lemon	.10	.04	.01
☐ 19	Reggie Jackson	.60	.25	.06
☐ 20	Lance Parrish	.15	.06	.01
☐ 21	Dave Stieb	.15	.06	.01
☐ 22	Hank Greenberg CAPT	.15	.06	.01

1985 Topps Glossy 40

The cards in this 40-card set measure 2 1/2" by 3 1/2". Similar to last year's glossy set, this set was issued as a bonus prize to Topps All-Star Baseball Game cards found in wax packs. The set could be obtained by sending in the "Bonus Runs" from the "Winning Pitch" game insert cards. For 25 runs and 75 cents, a collector could send in for one of the eight different five card series plus automatically be entered in the Grand Prize Sweepstakes for a chance at a free trip to the All-Star game. The cards are numbered and contain 20 stars from each league.

		MINT	EXC	G-VG
COMPLETE SET (40)		12.50	5.50	1.65
COMMON PLAYER (1-40)		.20	.08	.02
☐ 1	Dale Murphy	.75	.30	.07
☐ 2	Jesse Orosco	.20	.08	.02
☐ 3	Bob Brenly	.20	.08	.02
☐ 4	Mike Boddicker	.20	.08	.02
☐ 5	Dave Kingman	.25	.10	.02
☐ 6	Jim Rice	.30	.12	.03

year, players who changed teams during the fall, winter, and spring months are portrayed in the 1985 regular issue set with the teams they were with in 1984. The Traded set amends the shortcomings of the regular set by presenting the players with their proper teams for the current year. Rookies not contained in the regular set are picked up in the Traded set. The key (extended) rookie cards in this set are Vince Coleman, Ozzie Guillen, and Mickey Tettleton. Again this year, the Topps affiliate in Ireland printed the cards, and the cards were available through hobby channels only. Topps also produced a specially boxed "glossy" edition, frequently referred to as the Topps Traded Tiffany set. There were supposedly only 8,000 sets of the Tiffany cards produced; they were marketed to hobby dealers. The checklist of cards is identical to that of the normal non-glossy cards. There are two primary distinguishing features of the Tiffany cards, white card stock reverses and high gloss obverses. These Tiffany cards are valued at approximately five times the values listed below.

		MINT	EXC	G-VG
COMPLETE SET (132)		30.00	13.50	4.50
COMMON PLAYER (1-132)		.10	.04	.01
☐ 1T	Don Aase	.15	.05	.01
☐ 2T	Bill Almon	.10	.04	.01
☐ 3T	Benny Ayala	.10	.04	.01
☐ 4T	Dusty Baker	.15	.06	.01
☐ 5T	Geo.Bamberger MG	.10	.04	.01
☐ 6T	Dale Berra	.10	.04	.01
☐ 7T	Rich Bordi	.10	.04	.01
☐ 8T	Daryl Boston	.35	.15	.03
☐ 9T	Hubie Brooks	.30	.12	.03
☐ 10T	Chris Brown	.15	.06	.01
☐ 11T	Tom Browning	1.50	.60	.15
☐ 12T	Al Bumbry	.10	.04	.01
☐ 13T	Ray Burris	.10	.04	.01
☐ 14T	Jeff Burroughs	.10	.04	.01
☐ 15T	Bill Campbell	.10	.04	.01
☐ 16T	Don Carman	.20	.08	.02
☐ 17T	Gary Carter	.80	.35	.08
☐ 18T	Bobby Castillo	.10	.04	.01
☐ 19T	Bill Caudill	.10	.04	.01
☐ 20T	Rick Cerone	.10	.04	.01
☐ 21T	Bryan Clark	.10	.04	.01
☐ 22T	Jack Clark	.40	.16	.04
☐ 23T	Pat Clements	.10	.04	.01
☐ 24T	Vince Coleman	11.00	5.00	1.35
☐ 25T	Dave Collins	.10	.04	.01
☐ 26T	Danny Darwin	.15	.06	.01
☐ 27T	Jim Davenport MG	.10	.04	.01
☐ 28T	Jerry Davis	.10	.04	.01
☐ 29T	Brian Dayett	.10	.04	.01
☐ 30T	Ivan DeJesus	.10	.04	.01
☐ 31T	Ken Dixon	.10	.04	.01
☐ 32T	Mariano Duncan	.75	.30	.07
☐ 33T	John Felske MG	.10	.04	.01
☐ 34T	Mike Fitzgerald	.10	.04	.01
☐ 35T	Ray Fontenot	.10	.04	.01
☐ 36T	Greg Gagne	.35	.15	.03
☐ 37T	Oscar Gamble	.15	.06	.01
☐ 38T	Scott Garrelts	.30	.12	.03
☐ 39T	Bob L. Gibson	.10	.04	.01
☐ 40T	Jim Gott	.15	.06	.01
☐ 41T	David Green	.10	.04	.01
☐ 42T	Alfredo Griffin	.15	.06	.01
☐ 43T	Ozzie Guillen	2.00	.80	.20
☐ 44T	Eddie Haas MG	.10	.04	.01
☐ 45T	Terry Harper	.10	.04	.01
☐ 46T	Toby Harrah	.15	.06	.01
☐ 47T	Greg Harris	.10	.04	.01
☐ 48T	Ron Hassey	.15	.06	.01
☐ 49T	Rickey Henderson	5.00	2.25	.50
☐ 50T	Steve Henderson	.10	.04	.01
☐ 51T	George Hendrick	.15	.06	.01
☐ 52T	Joe Hesketh	.35	.15	.03
☐ 53T	Teddy Higuera	.60	.25	.06
☐ 54T	Donnie Hill	.10	.04	.01
☐ 55T	Al Holland	.10	.04	.01
☐ 56T	Burt Hooton	.10	.04	.01
☐ 57T	Jay Howell	.15	.06	.01
☐ 58T	Ken Howell	.20	.08	.02
☐ 59T	LaMarr Hoyt	.10	.04	.01
☐ 60T	Tim Hulett	.15	.06	.01
☐ 61T	Bob James	.10	.04	.01
☐ 62T	Steve Jeltz	.10	.04	.01
☐ 63T	Cliff Johnson	.10	.04	.01
☐ 64T	Howard Johnson	2.75	1.10	.27
☐ 65T	Ruppert Jones	.10	.04	.01

☐ 7	Frank Viola	.35	.15	.03
☐ 8	Alvin Davis	.25	.10	.02
☐ 9	Rick Sutcliffe	.25	.10	.02
☐ 10	Pete Rose	1.00	.40	.10
☐ 11	Leon Durham	.20	.08	.02
☐ 12	Joaquin Andujar	.20	.08	.02
☐ 13	Keith Hernandez	.30	.12	.03
☐ 14	Dave Winfield	.50	.20	.05
☐ 15	Reggie Jackson	1.00	.40	.10
☐ 16	Alan Trammell	.35	.15	.03
☐ 17	Bert Blyleven	.25	.10	.02
☐ 18	Tony Armas	.20	.08	.02
☐ 19	Rich Gossage	.30	.12	.03
☐ 20	Jose Cruz	.20	.08	.02
☐ 21	Ryne Sandberg	1.00	.40	.10
☐ 22	Bruce Sutter	.25	.10	.02
☐ 23	Mike Schmidt	1.25	.50	.12
☐ 24	Cal Ripken	1.25	.50	.12
☐ 25	Dan Petry	.20	.08	.02
☐ 26	Jack Morris	.35	.15	.03
☐ 27	Don Mattingly	1.00	.40	.10
☐ 28	Eddie Murray	.75	.30	.07
☐ 29	Tony Gwynn	.75	.30	.07
☐ 30	Charlie Lea	.20	.08	.02
☐ 31	Juan Samuel	.25	.10	.02
☐ 32	Phil Niekro	.35	.15	.03
☐ 33	Alejandro Pena	.25	.10	.02
☐ 34	Harold Baines	.30	.12	.03
☐ 35	Dan Quisenberry	.25	.10	.02
☐ 36	Gary Carter	.40	.16	.04
☐ 37	Mario Soto	.20	.08	.02
☐ 38	Dwight Gooden	.75	.30	.07
☐ 39	Tom Brunansky	.25	.10	.02
☐ 40	Dave Stieb	.25	.10	.02

1985 Topps Traded

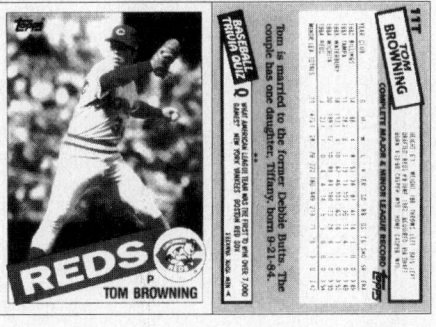

The cards in this 132-card set measure 2 1/2" by 3 1/2". In its now standard procedure, Topps issued its Traded (or extended) set for the fifth year in a row. Topps did however test on a limited basis the issuance of these Traded cards in wax packs. Because all photos and statistics of its regular set for the year were developed during the fall and winter months of the preceding

☐ 66T	Steve Kemp	.10	.04	.01
☐ 67T	Bruce Kison	.10	.04	.01
☐ 68T	Alan Knicely	.10	.04	.01
☐ 69T	Mike LaCoss	.10	.04	.01
☐ 70T	Lee Lacy	.10	.04	.01
☐ 71T	Dave LaPoint	.10	.04	.01
☐ 72T	Gary Lavelle	.10	.04	.01
☐ 73T	Vance Law	.10	.04	.01
☐ 74T	Johnnie LeMaster	.10	.04	.01
☐ 75T	Sixto Lezcano	.10	.04	.01
☐ 76T	Tim Lollar	.10	.04	.01
☐ 77T	Fred Lynn	.25	.10	.02
☐ 78T	Billy Martin MG	.20	.08	.02
☐ 79T	Ron Mathis	.10	.04	.01
☐ 80T	Len Matuszek	.10	.04	.01
☐ 81T	Gene Mauch MG	.10	.04	.01
☐ 82T	Oddibe McDowell	.20	.08	.02
☐ 83T	Roger McDowell	.50	.20	.05
☐ 84T	John McNamara MG	.15	.06	.01
☐ 85T	Donnie Moore	.10	.04	.01
☐ 86T	Gene Nelson	.15	.06	.01
☐ 87T	Steve Nicosia	.10	.04	.01
☐ 88T	Al Oliver	.20	.08	.02
☐ 89T	Joe Orsulak	.40	.16	.04
☐ 90T	Rob Picciolo	.10	.04	.01
☐ 91T	Chris Pittaro	.10	.04	.01
☐ 92T	Jim Presley	.20	.08	.02
☐ 93T	Rick Reuschel	.20	.08	.02
☐ 94T	Bert Roberge	.10	.04	.01
☐ 95T	Bob Rodgers MG	.15	.06	.01
☐ 96T	Jerry Royster	.10	.04	.01
☐ 97T	Dave Rozema	.10	.04	.01
☐ 98T	Dave Rucker	.10	.04	.01
☐ 99T	Vern Ruhle	.10	.04	.01
☐ 100T	Paul Runge	.10	.04	.01
☐ 101T	Mark Salas	.15	.06	.01
☐ 102T	Luis Salazar	.10	.04	.01
☐ 103T	Joe Sambito	.10	.04	.01
☐ 104T	Rick Schu	.15	.06	.01
☐ 105T	Donnie Scott	.10	.04	.01
☐ 106T	Larry Sheets	.20	.08	.02
☐ 107T	Don Slaught	.10	.04	.01
☐ 108T	Roy Smalley	.10	.04	.01
☐ 109T	Lonnie Smith	.25	.10	.02
☐ 110T	Nate Snell UER (headings on back for a batter)	.15	.06	.01
☐ 111T	Chris Speier	.10	.04	.01
☐ 112T	Mike Stenhouse	.10	.04	.01
☐ 113T	Tim Stoddard	.10	.04	.01
☐ 114T	Jim Sundberg	.10	.04	.01
☐ 115T	Bruce Sutter	.25	.10	.02
☐ 116T	Don Sutton	.50	.20	.05
☐ 117T	Kent Tekulve	.15	.06	.01
☐ 118T	Tom Tellmann	.10	.04	.01
☐ 119T	Walt Terrell	.15	.06	.01
☐ 120T	Mickey Tettleton	2.00	.80	.20
☐ 121T	Derrel Thomas	.10	.04	.01
☐ 122T	Rich Thompson	.10	.04	.01
☐ 123T	Alex Trevino	.10	.04	.01
☐ 124T	John Tudor	.20	.08	.02
☐ 125T	Jose Uribe	.25	.10	.02
☐ 126T	Bobby Valentine MG	.20	.08	.02
☐ 127T	Dave Von Ohlen	.10	.04	.01
☐ 128T	U.L. Washington	.10	.04	.01
☐ 129T	Earl Weaver MG	.15	.06	.01
☐ 130T	Eddie Whitson	.15	.06	.01
☐ 131T	Herm Winningham	.15	.06	.01
☐ 132T	Checklist 1-132	.10	.01	.00

1986 Topps

The cards in this 792-card set are standard-size (2 1/2" by 3 1/2"). The first seven cards are a tribute to Pete Rose and his career. Cards 2-7 show small photos of Pete's Topps cards of the given years on the front with biographical information pertaining to those years on the back. The team leader cards were done differently with a simple player action shot on a white background; the player pictured is dubbed the "Dean" of that team, i.e., the player with the longest continuous service with that team. Topps again features a "Turn Back the Clock" series (401-405). Record breakers of the previous year are acknowledged on cards 201 to 207. Cards 701-722 feature All-Star selections from each league. Manager cards feature the team checklist on the reverse. Ryne Sandberg (690) is the only

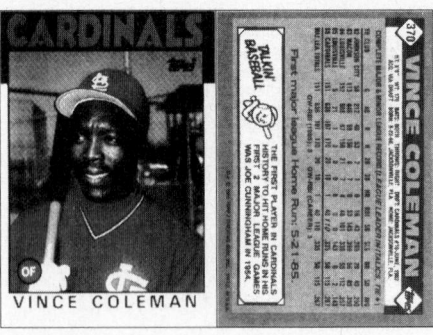

player card in the set without a Topps logo on the front of the card; this omission was never corrected by Topps. There are two other uncorrected errors involving misnumbered cards; see card numbers 51, 57, 141, and 171 in the checklist below. The backs of all the cards have a distinctive red background. The key rookie cards in this set are Vince Coleman, Len Dykstra and Cecil Fielder. Topps also produced a specially boxed "glossy" edition, frequently referred to as the Topps Tiffany set. There were supposedly only 5,000 sets of the Tiffany cards produced; they were marketed to hobby dealers. The checklist of cards (792 regular and 132 Traded) is identical to that of the normal non-glossy cards. There are two primary distinguishing features of the Tiffany cards, white card stock reverses and high gloss obverses. These Tiffany cards are valued at approximately five times the values listed below.

		MINT	EXC	G-VG
COMPLETE SET (792)		36.00	16.25	5.50
COMMON PLAYER (1-792)		.04	.02	.00
☐ 1	Pete Rose	1.00	.20	.04
☐ 2	Rose Special: '63-'66	.30	.12	.03
☐ 3	Rose Special: '67-'70	.30	.12	.03
☐ 4	Rose Special: '71-'74	.30	.12	.03
☐ 5	Rose Special: '75-'78	.30	.12	.03
☐ 6	Rose Special: '79-'82	.30	.12	.03
☐ 7	Rose Special: '83-'85	.30	.12	.03
☐ 8	Dwayne Murphy	.04	.02	.00
☐ 9	Roy Smith	.04	.02	.00
☐ 10	Tony Gwynn	1.00	.40	.10
☐ 11	Bob Ojeda	.04	.02	.00
☐ 12	Jose Uribe	.12	.05	.01
☐ 13	Bob Kearney	.04	.02	.00
☐ 14	Julio Cruz	.04	.02	.00
☐ 15	Eddie Whitson	.04	.02	.00
☐ 16	Rick Schu	.07	.03	.01
☐ 17	Mike Stenhouse	.04	.02	.00
☐ 18	Brent Gaff	.04	.02	.00
☐ 19	Rich Hebner	.04	.02	.00
☐ 20	Lou Whitaker	.15	.06	.01
☐ 21	George Bamberger MG (checklist back)	.07	.03	.01
☐ 22	Duane Walker	.04	.02	.00
☐ 23	Manny Lee	.10	.04	.01
☐ 24	Len Barker	.04	.02	.00
☐ 25	Willie Wilson	.07	.03	.01
☐ 26	Frank DiPino	.04	.02	.00
☐ 27	Ray Knight	.07	.03	.01
☐ 28	Eric Davis	1.25	.50	.12
☐ 29	Tony Phillips	.07	.03	.01
☐ 30	Eddie Murray	.45	.18	.04
☐ 31	Jamie Easterly	.04	.02	.00
☐ 32	Steve Yeager	.04	.02	.00
☐ 33	Jeff Lahti	.04	.02	.00
☐ 34	Ken Phelps	.04	.02	.00
☐ 35	Jeff Reardon	.17	.07	.01
☐ 36	Tigers Leaders Lance Parrish	.10	.04	.01
☐ 37	Mark Thurmond	.04	.02	.00
☐ 38	Glenn Hoffman	.04	.02	.00
☐ 39	Dave Rucker	.04	.02	.00
☐ 40	Ken Griffey	.12	.05	.01
☐ 41	Brad Wellman	.04	.02	.00
☐ 42	Geoff Zahn	.04	.02	.00
☐ 43	Dave Engle	.04	.02	.00
☐ 44	Lance McCullers	.10	.04	.01
☐ 45	Damaso Garcia	.04	.02	.00

☐ 46	Billy Hatcher	.12	.05	.01
☐ 47	Juan Berenguer	.04	.02	.00
☐ 48	Bill Almon	.04	.02	.00
☐ 49	Rick Manning	.04	.02	.00
☐ 50	Dan Quisenberry	.10	.04	.01
☐ 51	Bobby Wine MG ERR	.10	.04	.01
	(checklist back)			
	(number of card on			
	back is actually 57)			
☐ 52	Chris Welsh	.04	.02	.00
☐ 53	Len Dykstra	1.25	.50	.12
☐ 54	John Franco	.10	.04	.01
☐ 55	Fred Lynn	.12	.05	.01
☐ 56	Tom Niedenfuer	.04	.02	.00
☐ 57	Bill Doran	.07	.03	.01
	(see also 51)			
☐ 58	Bill Krueger	.04	.02	.00
☐ 59	Andre Thornton	.04	.02	.00
☐ 60	Dwight Evans	.12	.05	.01
☐ 61	Karl Best	.04	.02	.00
☐ 62	Bob Boone	.07	.03	.01
☐ 63	Ron Roenicke	.04	.02	.00
☐ 64	Floyd Bannister	.04	.02	.00
☐ 65	Dan Driessen	.04	.02	.00
☐ 66	Cardinals Leaders	.04	.02	.00
	Bob Forsch			
☐ 67	Carmelo Martinez	.04	.02	.00
☐ 68	Ed Lynch	.04	.02	.00
☐ 69	Luis Aguayo	.04	.02	.00
☐ 70	Dave Winfield	.35	.15	.03
☐ 71	Ken Schrom	.04	.02	.00
☐ 72	Shawon Dunston	.35	.15	.03
☐ 73	Randy O'Neal	.04	.02	.00
☐ 74	Rance Mulliniks	.04	.02	.00
☐ 75	Jose DeLeon	.04	.02	.00
☐ 76	Dion James	.04	.02	.00
☐ 77	Charlie Leibrandt	.04	.02	.00
☐ 78	Bruce Benedict	.04	.02	.00
☐ 79	Dave Schmidt	.04	.02	.00
☐ 80	Darryl Strawberry	2.00	.80	.20
☐ 81	Gene Mauch MG	.07	.03	.01
	(checklist back)			
☐ 82	Tippy Martinez	.04	.02	.00
☐ 83	Phil Garner	.07	.03	.01
☐ 84	Curt Young	.04	.02	.00
☐ 85	Tony Perez	.15	.06	.01
	(Eric Davis also			
	shown on card)			
☐ 86	Tom Waddell	.04	.02	.00
☐ 87	Candy Maldonado	.10	.04	.01
☐ 88	Tom Nieto	.04	.02	.00
☐ 89	Randy St.Claire	.04	.02	.00
☐ 90	Garry Templeton	.07	.03	.01
☐ 91	Steve Crawford	.04	.02	.00
☐ 92	Al Cowens	.04	.02	.00
☐ 93	Scot Thompson	.04	.02	.00
☐ 94	Rich Bordi	.04	.02	.00
☐ 95	Ozzie Virgil	.04	.02	.00
☐ 96	Blue Jays Leaders	.04	.02	.00
	Jim Clancy			
☐ 97	Gary Gaetti	.10	.04	.01
☐ 98	Dick Ruthven	.04	.02	.00
☐ 99	Buddy Biancalana	.04	.02	.00
☐ 100	Nolan Ryan	2.25	.90	.22
☐ 101	Dave Bergman	.04	.02	.00
☐ 102	Joe Orsulak	.20	.08	.02
☐ 103	Luis Salazar	.04	.02	.00
☐ 104	Sid Fernandez	.12	.05	.01
☐ 105	Gary Ward	.04	.02	.00
☐ 106	Ray Burris	.04	.02	.00
☐ 107	Rafael Ramirez	.04	.02	.00
☐ 108	Ted Power	.04	.02	.00
☐ 109	Len Matuszek	.04	.02	.00
☐ 110	Scott McGregor	.04	.02	.00
☐ 111	Roger Craig MG	.07	.03	.01
	(checklist back)			
☐ 112	Bill Campbell	.04	.02	.00
☐ 113	U.L. Washington	.04	.02	.00
☐ 114	Mike Brown	.04	.02	.00
	(Pirates OF)			
☐ 115	Jay Howell	.04	.02	.00
☐ 116	Brook Jacoby	.07	.03	.01
☐ 117	Bruce Kison	.04	.02	.00
☐ 118	Jerry Royster	.04	.02	.00
☐ 119	Barry Bonnell	.04	.02	.00
☐ 120	Steve Carlton	.35	.15	.03
☐ 121	Nelson Simmons	.04	.02	.00
☐ 122	Pete Filson	.04	.02	.00
☐ 123	Greg Walker	.04	.02	.00
☐ 124	Luis Sanchez	.04	.02	.00
☐ 125	Dave Lopes	.07	.03	.01
☐ 126	Mets Leaders	.04	.02	.00
	Mookie Wilson			
☐ 127	Jack Howell	.10	.04	.01
☐ 128	John Wathan	.04	.02	.00

☐ 129	Jeff Dedmon	.04	.02	.00
☐ 130	Alan Trammell	.25	.10	.02
☐ 131	Checklist: 1-132	.10	.01	.00
☐ 132	Razor Shines	.04	.02	.00
☐ 133	Andy McGaffigan	.04	.02	.00
☐ 134	Carney Lansford	.10	.04	.01
☐ 135	Joe Niekro	.07	.03	.01
☐ 136	Mike Hargrove	.04	.02	.00
☐ 137	Charlie Moore	.04	.02	.00
☐ 138	Mark Davis	.07	.03	.01
☐ 139	Daryl Boston	.12	.05	.01
☐ 140	John Candelaria	.04	.02	.00
☐ 141	Chuck Cottier MG	.07	.03	.01
	(checklist back)			
	(see also 171)			
☐ 142	Bob Jones	.04	.02	.00
☐ 143	Dave Van Gorder	.04	.02	.00
☐ 144	Doug Sisk	.04	.02	.00
☐ 145	Pedro Guerrero	.12	.05	.01
☐ 146	Jack Perconte	.04	.02	.00
☐ 147	Larry Sheets	.04	.02	.00
☐ 148	Mike Heath	.04	.02	.00
☐ 149	Brett Butler	.12	.05	.01
☐ 150	Joaquin Andujar	.04	.02	.00
☐ 151	Dave Stapleton	.04	.02	.00
☐ 152	Mike Morgan	.07	.03	.01
☐ 153	Ricky Adams	.04	.02	.00
☐ 154	Bert Roberge	.04	.02	.00
☐ 155	Bob Grich	.07	.03	.01
☐ 156	White Sox Leaders	.04	.02	.00
	Richard Dotson			
☐ 157	Ron Hassey	.04	.02	.00
☐ 158	Derrel Thomas	.04	.02	.00
☐ 159	Orel Hershiser UER	.35	.15	.03
	(82 Alburquerque)			
☐ 160	Chet Lemon	.04	.02	.00
☐ 161	Lee Tunnell	.04	.02	.00
☐ 162	Greg Gagne	.07	.03	.01
☐ 163	Pete Ladd	.04	.02	.00
☐ 164	Steve Balboni	.04	.02	.00
☐ 165	Mike Davis	.04	.02	.00
☐ 166	Dickie Thon	.04	.02	.00
☐ 167	Zane Smith	.25	.10	.02
☐ 168	Jeff Burroughs	.04	.02	.00
☐ 169	George Wright	.04	.02	.00
☐ 170	Gary Carter	.20	.08	.02
☐ 171	Bob Rodgers MG ERR	.12	.05	.01
	(checklist back)			
	(number of card on			
	back actually 141)			
☐ 172	Jerry Reed	.04	.02	.00
☐ 173	Wayne Gross	.04	.02	.00
☐ 174	Brian Snyder	.04	.02	.00
☐ 175	Steve Sax	.15	.06	.01
☐ 176	Jay Tibbs	.04	.02	.00
☐ 177	Joel Youngblood	.04	.02	.00
☐ 178	Ivan DeJesus	.04	.02	.00
☐ 179	Stu Cliburn	.04	.02	.00
☐ 180	Don Mattingly	1.75	.70	.17
☐ 181	Al Nipper	.04	.02	.00
☐ 182	Bobby Brown	.04	.02	.00
☐ 183	Larry Andersen	.04	.02	.00
☐ 184	Tim Laudner	.04	.02	.00
☐ 185	Rollie Fingers	.15	.06	.01
☐ 186	Astros Leaders	.04	.02	.00
	Jose Cruz			
☐ 187	Scott Fletcher	.04	.02	.00
☐ 188	Bob Dernier	.04	.02	.00
☐ 189	Mike Mason	.04	.02	.00
☐ 190	George Hendrick	.04	.02	.00
☐ 191	Wally Backman	.04	.02	.00
☐ 192	Milt Wilcox	.04	.02	.00
☐ 193	Daryl Sconiers	.04	.02	.00
☐ 194	Craig McMurtry	.04	.02	.00
☐ 195	Dave Concepcion	.10	.04	.01
☐ 196	Doyle Alexander	.04	.02	.00
☐ 197	Enos Cabell	.04	.02	.00
☐ 198	Ken Dixon	.04	.02	.00
☐ 199	Dick Howser MG	.07	.03	.01
	(checklist back)			
☐ 200	Mike Schmidt	1.00	.40	.10
☐ 201	RB: Vince Coleman	.30	.12	.03
	Most stolen bases,			
	season, rookie			
☐ 202	RB: Dwight Gooden	.30	.12	.03
	Youngest 20 game			
	winner			
☐ 203	RB: Keith Hernandez	.10	.04	.01
	Most game-winning			
	RBI's			
☐ 204	RB: Phil Niekro	.10	.04	.01
	Oldest shutout			
	pitcher			
☐ 205	RB: Tony Perez	.10	.04	.01
	Oldest grand slammer			

#	Player			
206	RB: Pete Rose	.35	.15	.03
	Most hits, lifetime			
207	RB: Fern.Valenzuela	.10	.04	.01
	Most cons. innings,			
	start of season,			
	no earned runs			
208	Ramon Romero	.04	.02	.00
209	Randy Ready	.07	.03	.01
210	Calvin Schiraldi	.04	.02	.00
211	Ed Wojna	.04	.02	.00
212	Chris Speier	.04	.02	.00
213	Bob Shirley	.04	.02	.00
214	Randy Bush	.04	.02	.00
215	Frank White	.04	.02	.00
216	A's Leaders	.04	.02	.00
	Dwayne Murphy			
217	Bill Scherrer	.04	.02	.00
218	Randy Hunt	.04	.02	.00
219	Dennis Lamp	.04	.02	.00
220	Bob Horner	.07	.03	.01
221	Dave Henderson	.17	.07	.01
222	Craig Gerber	.04	.02	.00
223	Atlee Hammaker	.04	.02	.00
224	Cesar Cedeno	.07	.03	.01
225	Ron Darling	.10	.04	.01
226	Lee Lacy	.04	.02	.00
227	Al Jones	.04	.02	.00
228	Tom Lawless	.04	.02	.00
229	Bill Gullickson	.07	.03	.01
230	Terry Kennedy	.04	.02	.00
231	Jim Frey MG	.07	.03	.01
	(checklist back)			
232	Rick Rhoden	.04	.02	.00
233	Steve Lyons	.04	.02	.00
234	Doug Corbett	.04	.02	.00
235	Butch Wynegar	.04	.02	.00
236	Frank Eufemia	.04	.02	.00
237	Ted Simmons	.07	.03	.01
238	Larry Parrish	.04	.02	.00
239	Joel Skinner	.04	.02	.00
240	Tommy John	.12	.05	.01
241	Tony Fernandez	.12	.05	.01
242	Rich Thompson	.04	.02	.00
243	Johnny Grubb	.04	.02	.00
244	Craig Lefferts	.04	.02	.00
245	Jim Sundberg	.04	.02	.00
246	Phillies Leaders	.15	.06	.01
	Steve Carlton			
247	Terry Harper	.04	.02	.00
248	Spike Owen	.04	.02	.00
249	Rob Deer	.30	.12	.03
250	Dwight Gooden	1.00	.40	.10
251	Rich Dauer	.04	.02	.00
252	Bobby Castillo	.04	.02	.00
253	Dann Bilardello	.04	.02	.00
254	Ozzie Guillen	.60	.25	.06
255	Tony Armas	.04	.02	.00
256	Kurt Kepshire	.04	.02	.00
257	Doug DeCinces	.04	.02	.00
258	Tim Burke	.12	.05	.01
259	Dan Pasqua	.12	.05	.01
260	Tony Pena	.07	.03	.01
261	Bobby Valentine MG	.07	.03	.01
	(checklist back)			
262	Mario Ramirez	.04	.02	.00
263	Checklist: 133-264	.10	.01	.00
264	Darren Daulton	.25	.10	.02
265	Ron Davis	.04	.02	.00
266	Keith Moreland	.04	.02	.00
267	Paul Molitor	.15	.06	.01
268	Mike Scott	.10	.04	.01
269	Dane Iorg	.04	.02	.00
270	Jack Morris	.25	.10	.02
271	Dave Collins	.04	.02	.00
272	Tim Tolman	.04	.02	.00
273	Jerry Willard	.04	.02	.00
274	Ron Gardenhire	.04	.02	.00
275	Charlie Hough	.04	.02	.00
276	Yankees Leaders	.07	.03	.01
	Willie Randolph			
277	Jaime Cocanower	.04	.02	.00
278	Sixto Lezcano	.04	.02	.00
279	Al Pardo	.04	.02	.00
280	Tim Raines	.20	.08	.02
281	Steve Mura	.04	.02	.00
282	Jerry Mumphrey	.04	.02	.00
283	Mike Fischlin	.04	.02	.00
284	Brian Dayett	.04	.02	.00
285	Buddy Bell	.07	.03	.01
286	Luis DeLeon	.04	.02	.00
287	John Christensen	.04	.02	.00
288	Don Aase	.04	.02	.00
289	Johnnie LeMaster	.04	.02	.00
290	Carlton Fisk	.35	.15	.03

#	Player			
291	Tom Lasorda MG	.10	.04	.01
	(checklist back)			
292	Chuck Porter	.04	.02	.00
293	Chris Chambliss	.07	.03	.01
294	Danny Cox	.04	.02	.00
295	Kirk Gibson	.20	.08	.02
296	Geno Petralli	.04	.02	.00
297	Tim Lollar	.04	.02	.00
298	Craig Reynolds	.04	.02	.00
299	Bryn Smith	.04	.02	.00
300	George Brett	.40	.16	.04
301	Dennis Rasmussen	.04	.02	.00
302	Greg Gross	.04	.02	.00
303	Curt Wardle	.04	.02	.00
304	Mike Gallego	.07	.03	.01
305	Phil Bradley	.07	.03	.01
306	Padres Leaders	.04	.02	.00
	Terry Kennedy			
307	Dave Sax	.04	.02	.00
308	Ray Fontenot	.04	.02	.00
309	John Shelby	.04	.02	.00
310	Greg Minton	.04	.02	.00
311	Dick Schofield	.04	.02	.00
312	Tom Filer	.04	.02	.00
313	Joe DeSa	.04	.02	.00
314	Frank Pastore	.04	.02	.00
315	Mookie Wilson	.07	.03	.01
316	Sammy Khalifa	.04	.02	.00
317	Ed Romero	.04	.02	.00
318	Terry Whitfield	.04	.02	.00
319	Rick Camp	.04	.02	.00
320	Jim Rice	.10	.04	.01
321	Earl Weaver MG	.07	.03	.01
	(checklist back)			
322	Bob Forsch	.04	.02	.00
323	Jerry Davis	.04	.02	.00
324	Dan Schatzeder	.04	.02	.00
325	Juan Beniquez	.04	.02	.00
326	Kent Tekulve	.04	.02	.00
327	Mike Pagliarulo	.07	.03	.01
328	Pete O'Brien	.04	.02	.00
329	Kirby Puckett	3.50	1.50	.35
330	Rick Sutcliffe	.10	.04	.01
331	Alan Ashby	.04	.02	.00
332	Darryl Motley	.04	.02	.00
333	Tom Henke	.25	.10	.02
334	Ken Oberkfell	.04	.02	.00
335	Don Sutton	.17	.07	.01
336	Indians Leaders	.04	.02	.00
	Andre Thornton			
337	Darnell Coles	.04	.02	.00
338	Jorge Bell	.30	.12	.03
339	Bruce Berenyi	.04	.02	.00
340	Cal Ripken	2.00	.80	.20
341	Frank Williams	.04	.02	.00
342	Gary Redus	.04	.02	.00
343	Carlos Diaz	.04	.02	.00
344	Jim Wohlford	.04	.02	.00
345	Donnie Moore	.04	.02	.00
346	Bryan Little	.04	.02	.00
347	Teddy Higuera	.20	.08	.02
348	Cliff Johnson	.04	.02	.00
349	Mark Clear	.04	.02	.00
350	Jack Clark	.12	.05	.01
351	Chuck Tanner MG	.07	.03	.01
	(checklist back)			
352	Harry Spilman	.04	.02	.00
353	Keith Atherton	.04	.02	.00
354	Tony Bernazard	.04	.02	.00
355	Lee Smith	.17	.07	.01
356	Mickey Hatcher	.04	.02	.00
357	Ed VandeBerg	.04	.02	.00
358	Rick Dempsey	.04	.02	.00
359	Mike LaCoss	.04	.02	.00
360	Lloyd Moseby	.07	.03	.01
361	Shane Rawley	.04	.02	.00
362	Tom Paciorek	.04	.02	.00
363	Terry Forster	.04	.02	.00
364	Reid Nichols	.04	.02	.00
365	Mike Flanagan	.07	.03	.01
366	Reds Leaders	.07	.03	.01
	Dave Concepcion			
367	Aurelio Lopez	.04	.02	.00
368	Greg Brock	.04	.02	.00
369	Al Holland	.04	.02	.00
370	Vince Coleman	2.25	.90	.22
371	Bill Stein	.04	.02	.00
372	Ben Oglivie	.04	.02	.00
373	Urbano Lugo	.04	.02	.00
374	Terry Francona	.04	.02	.00
375	Rich Gedman	.04	.02	.00
376	Bill Dawley	.04	.02	.00
377	Joe Carter	.65	.25	.06
378	Bruce Bochte	.04	.02	.00

#	Name			
☐ 379	Bobby Meacham	.04	.02	.00
☐ 380	LaMarr Hoyt	.04	.02	.00
☐ 381	Ray Miller MG (checklist back)	.07	.03	.01
☐ 382	Ivan Calderon	1.00	.40	.10
☐ 383	Chris Brown	.07	.03	.01
☐ 384	Steve Trout	.04	.02	.00
☐ 385	Cecil Cooper	.07	.03	.01
☐ 386	Cecil Fielder	7.50	3.25	.75
☐ 387	Steve Kemp	.04	.02	.00
☐ 388	Dickie Noles	.04	.02	.00
☐ 389	Glenn Davis	1.00	.40	.10
☐ 390	Tom Seaver	.50	.20	.05
☐ 391	Julio Franco	.35	.15	.03
☐ 392	John Russell	.04	.02	.00
☐ 393	Chris Pittaro	.04	.02	.00
☐ 394	Checklist: 265-396	.10	.01	.00
☐ 395	Scott Garrelts	.10	.04	.01
☐ 396	Red Sox Leaders Dwight Evans	.10	.04	.01
☐ 397	Steve Buechele	.35	.15	.03
☐ 398	Earnie Riles	.12	.05	.01
☐ 399	Bill Swift	.07	.03	.01
☐ 400	Rod Carew	.40	.16	.04
☐ 401	Turn Back 5 Years Fern.Valenzuela '81	.10	.04	.01
☐ 402	Turn Back 10 Years Tom Seaver '76	.15	.06	.01
☐ 403	Turn Back 15 Years Willie Mays '71	.15	.06	.01
☐ 404	Turn Back 20 Years Frank Robinson '66	.12	.05	.01
☐ 405	Turn Back 25 Years Roger Maris '61	.15	.06	.01
☐ 406	Scott Sanderson	.07	.03	.01
☐ 407	Sal Butera	.04	.02	.00
☐ 408	Dave Smith	.04	.02	.00
☐ 409	Paul Runge	.04	.02	.00
☐ 410	Dave Kingman	.10	.04	.01
☐ 411	Sparky Anderson MG (checklist back)	.07	.03	.01
☐ 412	Jim Clancy	.04	.02	.00
☐ 413	Tim Flannery	.04	.02	.00
☐ 414	Tom Gorman	.04	.02	.00
☐ 415	Hal McRae	.07	.03	.00
☐ 416	Dennis Martinez	.07	.03	.01
☐ 417	R.J. Reynolds	.04	.02	.00
☐ 418	Alan Knicely	.04	.02	.00
☐ 419	Frank Wills	.04	.02	.00
☐ 420	Von Hayes	.10	.04	.01
☐ 421	David Palmer	.04	.02	.00
☐ 422	Mike Jorgensen	.04	.02	.00
☐ 423	Dan Spillner	.04	.02	.00
☐ 424	Rick Miller	.04	.02	.00
☐ 425	Larry McWilliams	.04	.02	.00
☐ 426	Brewers Leaders Charlie Moore	.04	.02	.00
☐ 427	Joe Cowley	.04	.02	.00
☐ 428	Max Venable	.04	.02	.00
☐ 429	Greg Booker	.04	.02	.00
☐ 430	Kent Hrbek	.15	.06	.01
☐ 431	George Frazier	.04	.02	.00
☐ 432	Mark Bailey	.04	.02	.00
☐ 433	Chris Codiroli	.04	.02	.00
☐ 434	Curt Wilkerson	.04	.02	.00
☐ 435	Bill Caudill	.04	.02	.00
☐ 436	Doug Flynn	.04	.02	.00
☐ 437	Rick Mahler	.04	.02	.00
☐ 438	Clint Hurdle	.04	.02	.00
☐ 439	Rick Honeycutt	.04	.02	.00
☐ 440	Alvin Davis	.10	.04	.01
☐ 441	Whitey Herzog MG (checklist back)	.07	.03	.01
☐ 442	Ron Robinson	.07	.03	.01
☐ 443	Bill Buckner	.07	.03	.01
☐ 444	Alex Trevino	.04	.02	.00
☐ 445	Bert Blyleven	.10	.04	.01
☐ 446	Lenn Sakata	.04	.02	.00
☐ 447	Jerry Don Gleaton	.04	.02	.00
☐ 448	Herm Winningham	.04	.02	.00
☐ 449	Rod Scurry	.04	.02	.00
☐ 450	Graig Nettles	.07	.03	.01
☐ 451	Mark Brown	.04	.02	.00
☐ 452	Bob Clark	.04	.02	.00
☐ 453	Steve Jeltz	.04	.02	.00
☐ 454	Burt Hooton	.04	.02	.00
☐ 455	Willie Randolph	.07	.03	.01
☐ 456	Braves Leaders Dale Murphy	.10	.04	.01
☐ 457	Mickey Tettleton	.60	.25	.06
☐ 458	Kevin Bass	.07	.03	.01
☐ 459	Luis Leal	.04	.02	.00
☐ 460	Leon Durham	.04	.02	.00
☐ 461	Walt Terrell	.04	.02	.00
☐ 462	Domingo Ramos	.04	.02	.00
☐ 463	Jim Gott	.04	.02	.00
☐ 464	Ruppert Jones	.04	.02	.00
☐ 465	Jesse Orosco	.04	.02	.00
☐ 466	Tom Foley	.04	.02	.00
☐ 467	Bob James	.04	.02	.00
☐ 468	Mike Scioscia	.07	.03	.01
☐ 469	Storm Davis	.04	.02	.00
☐ 470	Bill Madlock	.07	.03	.01
☐ 471	Bobby Cox MG (checklist back)	.07	.03	.01
☐ 472	Joe Hesketh	.10	.04	.01
☐ 473	Mark Brouhard	.04	.02	.00
☐ 474	John Tudor	.10	.04	.01
☐ 475	Juan Samuel	.15	.06	.01
☐ 476	Ron Mathis	.04	.02	.00
☐ 477	Mike Easler	.04	.02	.00
☐ 478	Andy Hawkins	.04	.02	.00
☐ 479	Bob Melvin	.07	.03	.01
☐ 480	Oddibe McDowell	.07	.03	.01
☐ 481	Scott Bradley	.07	.03	.01
☐ 482	Rick Lysander	.04	.02	.00
☐ 483	George Vukovich	.04	.02	.00
☐ 484	Donnie Hill	.04	.02	.00
☐ 485	Gary Matthews	.04	.02	.00
☐ 486	Angels Leaders Bobby Grich	.07	.03	.01
☐ 487	Bret Saberhagen	.50	.20	.05
☐ 488	Lou Thornton	.04	.02	.00
☐ 489	Jim Winn	.04	.02	.00
☐ 490	Jeff Leonard	.04	.02	.00
☐ 491	Pascual Perez	.07	.03	.01
☐ 492	Kelvin Chapman	.04	.02	.00
☐ 493	Gene Nelson	.04	.02	.00
☐ 494	Gary Roenicke	.04	.02	.00
☐ 495	Mark Langston	.30	.12	.03
☐ 496	Jay Johnstone	.07	.03	.01
☐ 497	John Stuper	.04	.02	.00
☐ 498	Tito Landrum	.04	.02	.00
☐ 499	Bob L. Gibson	.04	.02	.00
☐ 500	Rickey Henderson	1.25	.50	.12
☐ 501	Dave Johnson MG (checklist back)	.07	.03	.01
☐ 502	Glen Cook	.04	.02	.00
☐ 503	Mike Fitzgerald	.04	.02	.00
☐ 504	Denny Walling	.04	.02	.00
☐ 505	Jerry Koosman	.07	.03	.01
☐ 506	Bill Russell	.04	.02	.00
☐ 507	Steve Ontiveros	.04	.02	.00
☐ 508	Alan Wiggins	.04	.02	.00
☐ 509	Ernie Camacho	.04	.02	.00
☐ 510	Wade Boggs	1.25	.50	.12
☐ 511	Ed Nunez	.04	.02	.00
☐ 512	Thad Bosley	.04	.02	.00
☐ 513	Ron Washington	.04	.02	.00
☐ 514	Mike Jones	.04	.02	.00
☐ 515	Darrell Evans	.07	.03	.01
☐ 516	Giants Leaders Greg Minton	.04	.02	.00
☐ 517	Milt Thompson	.17	.07	.01
☐ 518	Buck Martinez	.04	.02	.00
☐ 519	Danny Darwin	.04	.02	.00
☐ 520	Keith Hernandez	.12	.05	.01
☐ 521	Nate Snell	.04	.02	.00
☐ 522	Bob Bailor	.04	.02	.00
☐ 523	Joe Price	.04	.02	.00
☐ 524	Darrell Miller	.04	.02	.00
☐ 525	Marvell Wynne	.04	.02	.00
☐ 526	Charlie Lea	.04	.02	.00
☐ 527	Checklist: 397-528	.10	.01	.00
☐ 528	Terry Pendleton	.35	.15	.03
☐ 529	Marc Sullivan	.04	.02	.00
☐ 530	Rich Gossage	.10	.04	.01
☐ 531	Tony LaRussa MG (checklist back)	.07	.03	.01
☐ 532	Don Carman	.10	.04	.01
☐ 533	Billy Sample	.04	.02	.00
☐ 534	Jeff Calhoun	.04	.02	.00
☐ 535	Toby Harrah	.04	.02	.00
☐ 536	Jose Rijo	.20	.08	.02
☐ 537	Mark Salas	.04	.02	.00
☐ 538	Dennis Eckersley	.15	.06	.01
☐ 539	Glenn Hubbard	.04	.02	.00
☐ 540	Dan Petry	.04	.02	.00
☐ 541	Jorge Orta	.04	.02	.00
☐ 542	Don Schulze	.04	.02	.00
☐ 543	Jerry Narron	.04	.02	.00
☐ 544	Eddie Milner	.04	.02	.00
☐ 545	Jimmy Key	.15	.06	.01
☐ 546	Mariners Leaders Dave Henderson	.07	.03	.01
☐ 547	Roger McDowell	.17	.07	.01
☐ 548	Mike Young	.04	.02	.00
☐ 549	Bob Welch	.10	.04	.01

#	Player			
550	Tom Herr	.07	.03	.01
551	Dave LaPoint	.04	.02	.00
552	Marc Hill	.04	.02	.00
553	Jim Morrison	.04	.02	.00
554	Paul Householder	.04	.02	.00
555	Hubie Brooks	.10	.04	.01
556	John Denny	.04	.02	.00
557	Gerald Perry	.07	.03	.01
558	Tim Stoddard	.04	.02	.00
559	Tommy Dunbar	.04	.02	.00
560	Dave Righetti	.10	.04	.01
561	Bob Lillis MG (checklist back)	.07	.03	.01
562	Joe Beckwith	.04	.02	.00
563	Alejandro Sanchez	.04	.02	.00
564	Warren Brusstar	.04	.02	.00
565	Tom Brunansky	.10	.04	.01
566	Alfredo Griffin	.04	.02	.00
567	Jeff Barkley	.04	.02	.00
568	Donnie Scott	.04	.02	.00
569	Jim Acker	.04	.02	.00
570	Rusty Staub	.07	.03	.01
571	Mike Jeffcoat	.04	.02	.00
572	Paul Zuvella	.04	.02	.00
573	Tom Hume	.04	.02	.00
574	Ron Kittle	.07	.03	.01
575	Mike Boddicker	.04	.02	.00
576	Expos Leaders Andre Dawson	.10	.04	.01
577	Jerry Reuss	.04	.02	.00
578	Lee Mazzilli	.04	.02	.00
579	Jim Slaton	.04	.02	.00
580	Willie McGee	.15	.06	.01
581	Bruce Hurst	.07	.03	.01
582	Jim Gantner	.04	.02	.00
583	Al Bumbry	.04	.02	.00
584	Brian Fisher	.07	.03	.01
585	Garry Maddox	.04	.02	.00
586	Greg Harris	.04	.02	.00
587	Rafael Santana	.04	.02	.00
588	Steve Lake	.04	.02	.00
589	Sid Bream	.04	.02	.00
590	Bob Knepper	.04	.02	.00
591	Jackie Moore MG (checklist back)	.07	.03	.01
592	Frank Tanana	.07	.03	.01
593	Jesse Barfield	.10	.04	.01
594	Chris Bando	.04	.02	.00
595	Dave Parker	.15	.06	.01
596	Onix Concepcion	.04	.02	.00
597	Sammy Stewart	.04	.02	.00
598	Jim Presley	.07	.03	.01
599	Rick Aguilera	.40	.16	.04
600	Dale Murphy	.25	.10	.02
601	Gary Lucas	.04	.02	.00
602	Mariano Duncan	.20	.08	.02
603	Bill Laskey	.04	.02	.00
604	Gary Pettis	.04	.02	.00
605	Dennis Boyd	.04	.02	.00
606	Royals Leaders Hal McRae	.07	.03	.01
607	Ken Dayley	.04	.02	.00
608	Bruce Bochy	.04	.02	.00
609	Barbaro Garbey	.04	.02	.00
610	Ron Guidry	.10	.04	.01
611	Gary Woods	.04	.02	.00
612	Richard Dotson	.04	.02	.00
613	Roy Smalley	.04	.02	.00
614	Rick Waits	.04	.02	.00
615	Johnny Ray	.04	.02	.00
616	Glenn Brummer	.04	.02	.00
617	Lonnie Smith	.10	.04	.01
618	Jim Pankovits	.04	.02	.00
619	Danny Heep	.04	.02	.00
620	Bruce Sutter	.10	.04	.01
621	John Felske MG (checklist back)	.07	.03	.01
622	Gary Lavelle	.04	.02	.00
623	Floyd Rayford	.04	.02	.00
624	Steve McCatty	.04	.02	.00
625	Bob Brenly	.04	.02	.00
626	Roy Thomas	.04	.02	.00
627	Ron Oester	.04	.02	.00
628	Kirk McCaskill	.17	.07	.01
629	Mitch Webster	.12	.05	.01
630	Fernando Valenzuela	.10	.04	.01
631	Steve Braun	.04	.02	.00
632	Dave Von Ohlen	.04	.02	.00
633	Jackie Gutierrez	.04	.02	.00
634	Roy Lee Jackson	.04	.02	.00
635	Jason Thompson	.04	.02	.00
636	Cubs Leaders Lee Smith	.10	.04	.01
637	Rudy Law	.04	.02	.00

#	Player			
638	John Butcher	.04	.02	.00
639	Bo Diaz	.04	.02	.00
640	Jose Cruz	.07	.03	.01
641	Wayne Tolleson	.04	.02	.00
642	Ray Searage	.04	.02	.00
643	Tom Brookens	.04	.02	.00
644	Mark Gubicza	.10	.04	.01
645	Dusty Baker	.07	.03	.01
646	Mike Moore	.07	.03	.01
647	Mel Hall	.07	.03	.01
648	Steve Bedrosian	.07	.03	.01
649	Ronn Reynolds	.04	.02	.00
650	Dave Stieb	.12	.05	.01
651	Billy Martin MG (checklist back)	.12	.05	.01
652	Tom Browning	.20	.08	.02
653	Jim Dwyer	.04	.02	.00
654	Ken Howell	.07	.03	.01
655	Manny Trillo	.04	.02	.00
656	Brian Harper	.15	.06	.01
657	Juan Agosto	.04	.02	.00
658	Rob Wilfong	.04	.02	.00
659	Checklist: 529-660	.10	.01	.00
660	Steve Garvey	.25	.10	.02
661	Roger Clemens	4.00	1.75	.40
662	Bill Schroeder	.04	.02	.00
663	Neil Allen	.04	.02	.00
664	Tim Corcoran	.04	.02	.00
665	Alejandro Pena	.04	.02	.00
666	Rangers Leaders Charlie Hough	.04	.02	.00
667	Tim Teufel	.04	.02	.00
668	Cecilio Guante	.04	.02	.00
669	Ron Cey	.07	.03	.01
670	Willie Hernandez	.04	.02	.00
671	Lynn Jones	.04	.02	.00
672	Rob Picciolo	.04	.02	.00
673	Ernie Whitt	.04	.02	.00
674	Pat Tabler	.04	.02	.00
675	Claudell Washington	.04	.02	.00
676	Matt Young	.04	.02	.00
677	Nick Esasky	.04	.02	.00
678	Dan Gladden	.04	.02	.00
679	Britt Burns	.04	.02	.00
680	George Foster	.10	.04	.01
681	Dick Williams MG (checklist back)	.07	.03	.01
682	Junior Ortiz	.04	.02	.00
683	Andy Van Slyke	.20	.08	.02
684	Bob McClure	.04	.02	.00
685	Tim Wallach	.10	.04	.01
686	Jeff Stone	.04	.02	.00
687	Mike Trujillo	.04	.02	.00
688	Larry Herndon	.04	.02	.00
689	Dave Stewart	.20	.08	.02
690	Ryne Sandberg UER (no Topps logo on front)	2.00	.80	.20
691	Mike Madden	.04	.02	.00
692	Dale Berra	.04	.02	.00
693	Tom Tellmann	.04	.02	.00
694	Garth Iorg	.04	.02	.00
695	Mike Smithson	.04	.02	.00
696	Dodgers Leaders Bill Russell	.07	.03	.01
697	Bud Black	.04	.02	.00
698	Brad Komminsk	.04	.02	.00
699	Pat Corrales MG (checklist back)	.07	.03	.01
700	Reggie Jackson	.50	.20	.05
701	Keith Hernandez AS	.10	.04	.01
702	Tom Herr AS	.07	.03	.01
703	Tim Wallach AS	.07	.03	.01
704	Ozzie Smith AS	.15	.06	.01
705	Dale Murphy AS	.15	.06	.01
706	Pedro Guerrero AS	.10	.04	.01
707	Willie McGee AS	.07	.03	.01
708	Gary Carter AS	.12	.05	.01
709	Dwight Gooden AS	.30	.12	.03
710	John Tudor AS	.07	.03	.01
711	Jeff Reardon AS	.10	.04	.01
712	Don Mattingly AS	.40	.16	.04
713	Damaso Garcia AS	.04	.02	.00
714	George Brett AS	.20	.08	.02
715	Cal Ripken AS	.50	.20	.05
716	Rickey Henderson AS	.35	.15	.03
717	Dave Winfield AS	.15	.06	.01
718	George Bell AS	.12	.05	.01
719	Carlton Fisk AS	.15	.06	.01
720	Bret Saberhagen AS	.15	.06	.01
721	Ron Guidry AS	.07	.03	.01
722	Dan Quisenberry AS	.07	.03	.01
723	Marty Bystrom	.04	.02	.00
724	Tim Hulett	.04	.02	.00

☐	725	Mario Soto	.04	.02	.00
☐	726	Orioles Leaders	.04	.02	.00
		Rick Dempsey			
☐	727	David Green	.04	.02	.00
☐	728	Mike Marshall	.07	.03	.01
☐	729	Jim Beattie	.04	.02	.00
☐	730	Ozzie Smith	.40	.16	.04
☐	731	Don Robinson	.04	.02	.00
☐	732	Floyd Youmans	.07	.03	.01
☐	733	Ron Romanick	.04	.02	.00
☐	734	Marty Barrett	.04	.02	.00
☐	735	Dave Dravecky	.07	.03	.01
☐	736	Glenn Wilson	.04	.02	.00
☐	737	Pete Vuckovich	.04	.02	.00
☐	738	Andre Robertson	.04	.02	.00
☐	739	Dave Rozema	.04	.02	.00
☐	740	Lance Parrish	.12	.05	.01
☐	741	Pete Rose MG	.35	.15	.03
		(checklist back)			
☐	742	Frank Viola	.17	.07	.01
☐	743	Pat Sheridan	.04	.02	.00
☐	744	Lary Sorensen	.04	.02	.00
☐	745	Willie Upshaw	.04	.02	.00
☐	746	Denny Gonzalez	.04	.02	.00
☐	747	Rick Cerone	.04	.02	.00
☐	748	Steve Henderson	.04	.02	.00
☐	749	Ed Jurak	.04	.02	.00
☐	750	Gorman Thomas	.07	.03	.01
☐	751	Howard Johnson	.45	.18	.04
☐	752	Mike Krukow	.04	.02	.00
☐	753	Dan Ford	.04	.02	.00
☐	754	Pat Clements	.04	.02	.00
☐	755	Harold Baines	.15	.06	.01
☐	756	Pirates Leaders	.04	.02	.00
		Rick Rhoden			
☐	757	Darrell Porter	.04	.02	.00
☐	758	Dave Anderson	.04	.02	.00
☐	759	Moose Haas	.04	.02	.00
☐	760	Andre Dawson	.40	.16	.04
☐	761	Don Slaught	.04	.02	.00
☐	762	Eric Show	.04	.02	.00
☐	763	Terry Puhl	.04	.02	.00
☐	764	Kevin Gross	.04	.02	.00
☐	765	Don Baylor	.10	.04	.01
☐	766	Rick Langford	.04	.02	.00
☐	767	Jody Davis	.04	.02	.00
☐	768	Vern Ruhle	.04	.02	.00
☐	769	Harold Reynolds	.50	.20	.05
☐	770	Vida Blue	.07	.03	.01
☐	771	John McNamara MG	.07	.03	.01
		(checklist back)			
☐	772	Brian Downing	.07	.03	.01
☐	773	Greg Pryor	.04	.02	.00
☐	774	Terry Leach	.07	.03	.01
☐	775	Al Oliver	.07	.03	.01
☐	776	Gene Garber	.04	.02	.00
☐	777	Wayne Krenchicki	.04	.02	.00
☐	778	Jerry Hairston	.04	.02	.00
☐	779	Rick Reuschel	.07	.03	.01
☐	780	Robin Yount	.40	.16	.04
☐	781	Joe Nolan	.04	.02	.00
☐	782	Ken Landreaux	.04	.02	.00
☐	783	Ricky Horton	.04	.02	.00
☐	784	Alan Bannister	.04	.02	.00
☐	785	Bob Stanley	.04	.02	.00
☐	786	Twins Leaders	.04	.02	.00
		Mickey Hatcher			
☐	787	Vance Law	.04	.02	.00
☐	788	Marty Castillo	.04	.02	.00
☐	789	Kurt Bevacqua	.04	.02	.00
☐	790	Phil Niekro	.17	.07	.01
☐	791	Checklist: 661-792	.10	.01	.00
☐	792	Charles Hudson	.07	.03	.01

1986 Topps Wax Box Cards

Topps printed cards (each measuring the standard 2 1/2" by 3 1/2") on the bottoms of their wax pack boxes for their regular issue cards; there are four different boxes, each with four cards. These sixteen cards ("numbered" A through P) are listed below; they are not considered an integral part of the regular set but are considered a separate set. They are styled almost exactly like the 1986 Topps regular issue cards. Complete boxes would be worth an additional 25 percent premium over the prices below.

		MINT	EXC	G-VG
COMPLETE SET (16)		7.00	3.00	.70
COMMON PLAYER (A-P)		.10	.04	.01
☐ A	Jorge Bell	.25	.10	.02
☐ B	Wade Boggs	.75	.30	.07
☐ C	George Brett	.75	.30	.07
☐ D	Vince Coleman	1.00	.40	.10
☐ E	Carlton Fisk	.50	.20	.05
☐ F	Dwight Gooden	.75	.30	.07
☐ G	Pedro Guerrero	.20	.08	.02
☐ H	Ron Guidry	.15	.06	.01
☐ I	Reggie Jackson	.75	.30	.07
☐ J	Don Mattingly	1.00	.40	.10
☐ K	Oddibe McDowell	.15	.06	.01
☐ L	Willie McGee	.25	.10	.02
☐ M	Dale Murphy	.50	.20	.05
☐ N	Pete Rose	1.00	.40	.10
☐ O	Bret Saberhagen	.50	.20	.05
☐ P	Fernando Valenzuela	.15	.06	.01

1986 Topps All-Star Glossy 22

This 22-card set was distributed as an insert, one card per rak pack. The players featured are the starting lineups of the 1985 All-Star Game played in Minnesota. Cards are very colorful with a high gloss finish and are standard-size, 2 1/2" by 3 1/2". Cards are numbered on the back.

		MINT	EXC	G-VG
COMPLETE SET (22)		3.50	1.50	.35
COMMON PLAYER (1-22)		.10	.04	.01
☐ 1	Sparky Anderson MG	.10	.04	.01
☐ 2	Eddie Murray	.40	.16	.04
☐ 3	Lou Whitaker	.15	.06	.01
☐ 4	George Brett	.40	.16	.04
☐ 5	Cal Ripken	.60	.25	.06
☐ 6	Jim Rice	.25	.10	.02
☐ 7	Rickey Henderson	.60	.25	.06
☐ 8	Dave Winfield	.40	.16	.04
☐ 9	Carlton Fisk	.40	.16	.04
☐ 10	Jack Morris	.25	.10	.02

			MINT	EXC	G-VG
☐	11	AL Team Photo	.10	.04	.01
☐	12	Dick Williams MG	.10	.04	.01
☐	13	Steve Garvey	.30	.12	.03
☐	14	Tom Herr	.10	.04	.01
☐	15	Graig Nettles	.15	.06	.01
☐	16	Ozzie Smith	.30	.12	.03
☐	17	Tony Gwynn	.50	.20	.05
☐	18	Dale Murphy	.45	.18	.04
☐	19	Darryl Strawberry	.50	.20	.05
☐	20	Terry Kennedy	.10	.04	.01
☐	21	LaMarr Hoyt	.10	.04	.01
☐	22	NL Team Photo	.10	.04	.01

1986 Topps Glossy 60

This 60-card glossy set was produced by Topps and distributed ten cards at a time based on the offer found on the wax packs. Cards measure the standard 2 1/2" by 3 1/2". Each series of ten cards was available by sending in 1.00 plus six "special offer" cards inserted one per wax pack. The card backs are printed in red and blue on white card stock. The card fronts feature a white border and a green frame surrounding a full-color photo of the player.

			MINT	EXC	G-VG
	COMPLETE SET (60)		12.50	5.50	1.65
	COMMON PLAYER (1-60)		.20	.08	.02
☐	1	Oddibe McDowell	.20	.08	.02
☐	2	Reggie Jackson	.60	.25	.06
☐	3	Fernando Valenzuela	.25	.10	.02
☐	4	Jack Clark	.25	.10	.02
☐	5	Rickey Henderson	.75	.30	.07
☐	6	Steve Balboni	.20	.08	.02
☐	7	Keith Hernandez	.25	.10	.02
☐	8	Lance Parrish	.25	.10	.02
☐	9	Willie McGee	.25	.10	.02
☐	10	Chris Brown	.20	.08	.02
☐	11	Darryl Strawberry	.60	.25	.06
☐	12	Ron Guidry	.25	.10	.02
☐	13	Dave Parker	.30	.12	.03
☐	14	Cal Ripken	.75	.30	.07
☐	15	Tim Raines	.30	.12	.03
☐	16	Rod Carew	.50	.20	.05
☐	17	Mike Schmidt	.75	.30	.07
☐	18	George Brett	.60	.25	.06
☐	19	Joe Hesketh	.25	.10	.02
☐	20	Dan Pasqua	.20	.08	.02
☐	21	Vince Coleman	.50	.20	.05
☐	22	Tom Seaver	.50	.20	.05
☐	23	Gary Carter	.30	.12	.03
☐	24	Orel Hershiser	.40	.16	.04
☐	25	Pedro Guerrero	.25	.10	.02
☐	26	Wade Boggs	.75	.30	.07
☐	27	Bret Saberhagen	.40	.16	.04
☐	28	Carlton Fisk	.40	.16	.04
☐	29	Kirk Gibson	.30	.12	.03
☐	30	Brian Fisher	.20	.08	.02
☐	31	Don Mattingly	.75	.30	.07
☐	32	Tom Herr	.20	.08	.02
☐	33	Eddie Murray	.60	.25	.06
☐	34	Ryne Sandberg	.75	.30	.07
☐	35	Dan Quisenberry	.25	.10	.02
☐	36	Jim Rice	.30	.12	.03

			MINT	EXC	G-VG
☐	37	Dale Murphy	.50	.20	.05
☐	38	Steve Garvey	.40	.16	.04
☐	39	Roger McDowell	.20	.08	.02
☐	40	Earnie Riles	.20	.08	.02
☐	41	Dwight Gooden	.50	.20	.05
☐	42	Dave Winfield	.40	.16	.04
☐	43	Dave Stieb	.25	.10	.02
☐	44	Bob Horner	.25	.10	.02
☐	45	Nolan Ryan	1.25	.50	.12
☐	46	Ozzie Smith	.40	.16	.04
☐	47	Jorge Bell	.30	.12	.03
☐	48	Gorman Thomas	.20	.08	.02
☐	49	Tom Browning	.25	.10	.02
☐	50	Larry Sheets	.20	.08	.02
☐	51	Pete Rose	.75	.30	.07
☐	52	Brett Butler	.25	.10	.02
☐	53	John Tudor	.25	.10	.02
☐	54	Phil Bradley	.20	.08	.02
☐	55	Jeff Reardon	.30	.12	.03
☐	56	Rich Gossage	.25	.10	.02
☐	57	Tony Gwynn	.60	.25	.06
☐	58	Ozzie Guillen	.25	.10	.02
☐	59	Glenn Davis	.40	.16	.04
☐	60	Darrell Evans	.20	.08	.02

1986 Topps Mini Leaders

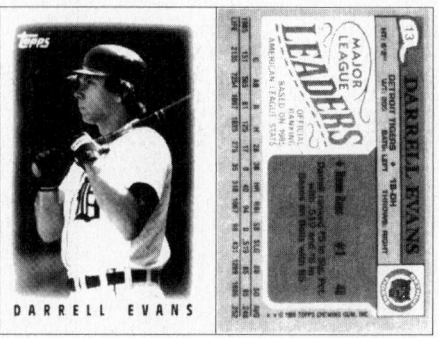

The 1986 Topps Mini set of Major League Leaders features 66 cards of leaders of the various statistical categories for the 1985 season. The cards are numbered on the back and measure approximately 2 1/8" by 2 15/16". They are very similar in design to the Team Leader "Dean" cards in the 1986 Topps regular issue.

			MINT	EXC	G-VG
	COMPLETE SET (66)		7.50	3.25	.75
	COMMON PLAYER (1-66)		.05	.02	.00
☐	1	Eddie Murray	.40	.16	.04
☐	2	Cal Ripken	.75	.30	.07
☐	3	Wade Boggs	.50	.20	.05
☐	4	Dennis Boyd	.05	.02	.00
☐	5	Dwight Evans	.15	.06	.01
☐	6	Bruce Hurst	.10	.04	.01
☐	7	Gary Pettis	.05	.02	.00
☐	8	Harold Baines	.10	.04	.01
☐	9	Floyd Bannister	.05	.02	.00
☐	10	Britt Burns	.05	.02	.00
☐	11	Carlton Fisk	.30	.12	.03
☐	12	Brett Butler	.10	.04	.01
☐	13	Darrell Evans	.10	.04	.01
☐	14	Jack Morris	.15	.06	.01
☐	15	Lance Parrish	.10	.04	.01
☐	16	Walt Terrell	.05	.02	.00
☐	17	Steve Balboni	.05	.02	.00
☐	18	George Brett	.40	.16	.04
☐	19	Charlie Leibrandt	.05	.02	.00
☐	20	Bret Saberhagen	.25	.10	.02
☐	21	Lonnie Smith	.10	.04	.01
☐	22	Willie Wilson	.10	.04	.01
☐	23	Bert Blyleven	.10	.04	.01
☐	24	Mike Smithson	.05	.02	.00
☐	25	Frank Viola	.20	.08	.02
☐	26	Ron Guidry	.10	.04	.01

			MINT	EXC	G-VG
☐ 27	Rickey Henderson	.75	.30	.07
☐ 28	Don Mattingly	.60	.25	.06
☐ 29	Dave Winfield	.30	.12	.03
☐ 30	Mike Moore	.10	.04	.01
☐ 31	Gorman Thomas	.05	.02	.00
☐ 32	Toby Harrah	.05	.02	.00
☐ 33	Charlie Hough	.05	.02	.00
☐ 34	Doyle Alexander	.05	.02	.00
☐ 35	Jimmy Key	.05	.02	.00
☐ 36	Dave Stieb	.10	.04	.01
☐ 37	Dale Murphy	.25	.10	.02
☐ 38	Keith Moreland	.05	.02	.00
☐ 39	Ryne Sandberg	.75	.30	.07
☐ 40	Tom Browning	.05	.02	.00
☐ 41	Dave Parker	.15	.06	.01
☐ 42	Mario Soto	.05	.02	.00
☐ 43	Nolan Ryan	1.00	.40	.10
☐ 44	Pedro Guerrero	.15	.06	.01
☐ 45	Orel Hershiser	.25	.10	.02
☐ 46	Mike Scioscia	.05	.02	.00
☐ 47	Fernando Valenzuela	.15	.06	.01
☐ 48	Bob Welch	.10	.04	.01
☐ 49	Tim Raines	.20	.08	.02
☐ 50	Gary Carter	.20	.08	.02
☐ 51	Sid Fernandez	.10	.04	.01
☐ 52	Dwight Gooden	.35	.15	.03
☐ 53	Keith Hernandez	.15	.06	.01
☐ 54	Juan Samuel	.10	.04	.01
☐ 55	Mike Schmidt	.75	.30	.07
☐ 56	Glenn Wilson	.05	.02	.00
☐ 57	Rick Reuschel	.05	.02	.00
☐ 58	Joaquin Andujar	.05	.02	.00
☐ 59	Jack Clark	.10	.04	.01
☐ 60	Vince Coleman	.30	.12	.03
☐ 61	Danny Cox	.05	.02	.00
☐ 62	Tom Herr	.05	.02	.00
☐ 63	Willie McGee	.10	.04	.01
☐ 64	John Tudor	.10	.04	.01
☐ 65	Tony Gwynn	.40	.16	.04
☐ 66	Checklist Card	.05	.02	.00

1986 Topps Traded

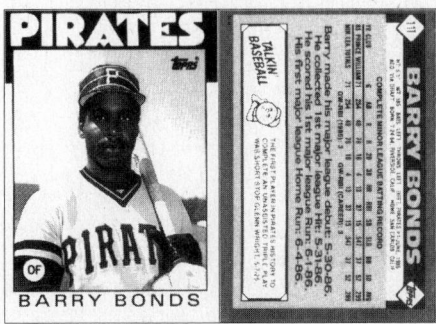

This 132-card Traded or extended set was distributed by Topps to dealers in a special red and white box as a complete set. The card fronts are identical in style to the Topps regular issue and are also 2 1/2" by 3 1/2". The backs are printed in red and black on white card stock. Cards are numbered (with a T suffix) alphabetically according to the name of the player. The key (extended) rookie cards in this set are Barry Bonds, Bobby Bonilla, Jose Canseco, Will Clark, and Kevin Mitchell. Topps also produced a specially boxed "glossy" edition frequently referred to as the Topps Traded Tiffany set. There were supposedly only 5,000 sets of the Tiffany cards produced; they were marketed to hobby dealers. The checklist of cards is identical to that of the normal non-glossy cards. There are two primary distinguishing features of the Tiffany cards: white card stock reverses and high gloss obverses. These Tiffany cards are valued at approximately five times the values listed below.

		MINT	EXC	G-VG
COMPLETE SET (132)		26.00	11.00	2.50
COMMON PLAYER (1-132)		.06	.02	.00
☐ 1T	Andy Allanson	.12	.04	.01
☐ 2T	Neil Allen	.06	.02	.00
☐ 3T	Joaquin Andujar	.10	.04	.01
☐ 4T	Paul Assenmacher	.12	.05	.01
☐ 5T	Scott Bailes	.12	.05	.01
☐ 6T	Don Baylor	.12	.05	.01
☐ 7T	Steve Bedrosian	.10	.04	.01
☐ 8T	Juan Beniquez	.06	.02	.00
☐ 9T	Juan Berenguer	.06	.02	.00
☐ 10T	Mike Bielecki	.15	.06	.01
☐ 11T	Barry Bonds	3.75	1.60	.37
☐ 12T	Bobby Bonilla	3.50	1.50	.35
☐ 13T	Juan Bonilla	.06	.02	.00
☐ 14T	Rich Bordi	.06	.02	.00
☐ 15T	Steve Boros MG	.06	.02	.00
☐ 16T	Rick Burleson	.10	.04	.01
☐ 17T	Bill Campbell	.06	.02	.00
☐ 18T	Tom Candiotti	.15	.06	.01
☐ 19T	John Cangelosi	.10	.04	.01
☐ 20T	Jose Canseco	9.00	4.00	.90
☐ 21T	Carmen Castillo	.06	.02	.00
☐ 22T	Rick Cerone	.06	.02	.00
☐ 23T	John Cerutti	.12	.05	.01
☐ 24T	Will Clark	9.00	4.00	.90
☐ 25T	Mark Clear	.06	.02	.00
☐ 26T	Darnell Coles	.06	.02	.00
☐ 27T	Dave Collins	.06	.02	.00
☐ 28T	Tim Conroy	.06	.02	.00
☐ 29T	Joe Cowley	.06	.02	.00
☐ 30T	Joel Davis	.10	.04	.01
☐ 31T	Rob Deer	.15	.06	.01
☐ 32T	John Denny	.06	.02	.00
☐ 33T	Mike Easler	.06	.02	.00
☐ 34T	Mark Eichhorn	.12	.05	.01
☐ 35T	Steve Farr	.12	.05	.01
☐ 36T	Scott Fletcher	.06	.02	.00
☐ 37T	Terry Forster	.10	.04	.01
☐ 38T	Terry Francona	.06	.02	.00
☐ 39T	Jim Fregosi MG	.10	.04	.01
☐ 40T	Andres Galarraga	.35	.15	.03
☐ 41T	Ken Griffey	.25	.10	.02
☐ 42T	Bill Gullickson	.12	.05	.01
☐ 43T	Jose Guzman	.25	.10	.02
☐ 44T	Moose Haas	.06	.02	.00
☐ 45T	Billy Hatcher	.12	.05	.01
☐ 46T	Mike Heath	.06	.02	.00
☐ 47T	Tom Hume	.06	.02	.00
☐ 48T	Pete Incaviglia	.35	.15	.03
☐ 49T	Dane Iorg	.06	.02	.00
☐ 50T	Bo Jackson	7.00	3.00	.70
☐ 51T	Wally Joyner	1.50	.60	.15
☐ 52T	Charlie Kerfeld	.06	.02	.00
☐ 53T	Eric King	.15	.06	.01
☐ 54T	Bob Kipper	.10	.04	.01
☐ 55T	Wayne Krenchicki	.06	.02	.00
☐ 56T	John Kruk	.40	.16	.04
☐ 57T	Mike LaCoss	.06	.02	.00
☐ 58T	Pete Ladd	.06	.02	.00
☐ 59T	Mike Laga	.10	.04	.01
☐ 60T	Hal Lanier MG	.06	.02	.00
☐ 61T	Dave LaPoint	.06	.02	.00
☐ 62T	Rudy Law	.06	.02	.00
☐ 63T	Rick Leach	.06	.02	.00
☐ 64T	Tim Leary	.15	.06	.01
☐ 65T	Dennis Leonard	.10	.04	.01
☐ 66T	Jim Leyland MG	.15	.06	.01
☐ 67T	Steve Lyons	.10	.04	.01
☐ 68T	Mickey Mahler	.06	.02	.00
☐ 69T	Candy Maldonado	.15	.06	.01
☐ 70T	Roger Mason	.10	.04	.01
☐ 71T	Bob McClure	.06	.02	.00
☐ 72T	Andy McGaffigan	.06	.02	.00
☐ 73T	Gene Michael MG	.06	.02	.00
☐ 74T	Kevin Mitchell	3.25	1.35	.32
☐ 75T	Omar Moreno	.06	.02	.00
☐ 76T	Jerry Mumphrey	.06	.02	.00
☐ 77T	Phil Niekro	.25	.10	.02
☐ 78T	Randy Niemann	.06	.02	.00
☐ 79T	Juan Nieves	.12	.05	.01
☐ 80T	Otis Nixon	.25	.10	.02
☐ 81T	Bob Ojeda	.12	.05	.01
☐ 82T	Jose Oquendo	.10	.04	.01
☐ 83T	Tom Paciorek	.06	.02	.00
☐ 84T	David Palmer	.06	.02	.00
☐ 85T	Frank Pastore	.06	.02	.00
☐ 86T	Lou Piniella MG	.12	.05	.01
☐ 87T	Dan Plesac	.17	.07	.01
☐ 88T	Darrell Porter	.06	.02	.00
☐ 89T	Rey Quinones	.06	.02	.00
☐ 90T	Gary Redus	.06	.02	.00

☐ 91T	Bip Roberts	.30	.12	.03
☐ 92T	Billy Jo Robidoux	.10	.04	.01
☐ 93T	Jeff Robinson	.10	.04	.01
	(Giants pitcher)			
☐ 94T	Gary Roenicke	.06	.02	.00
☐ 95T	Ed Romero	.06	.02	.00
☐ 96T	Argenis Salazar	.06	.02	.00
☐ 97T	Joe Sambito	.06	.02	.00
☐ 98T	Billy Sample	.06	.02	.00
☐ 99T	Dave Schmidt	.10	.04	.01
☐ 100T	Ken Schrom	.06	.02	.00
☐ 101T	Tom Seaver	.45	.18	.04
☐ 102T	Ted Simmons	.15	.06	.01
☐ 103T	Sammy Stewart	.06	.02	.00
☐ 104T	Kurt Stillwell	.25	.10	.02
☐ 105T	Franklin Stubbs	.12	.05	.01
☐ 106T	Dale Sveum	.12	.05	.01
☐ 107T	Chuck Tanner MG	.06	.02	.00
☐ 108T	Danny Tartabull	.80	.35	.08
☐ 109T	Tim Teufel	.12	.05	.01
☐ 110T	Bob Tewksbury	.10	.04	.01
☐ 111T	Andres Thomas	.10	.04	.01
☐ 112T	Milt Thompson	.12	.05	.01
☐ 113T	Robby Thompson	.30	.12	.03
☐ 114T	Jay Tibbs	.06	.02	.00
☐ 115T	Wayne Tolleson	.06	.02	.00
☐ 116T	Alex Trevino	.06	.02	.00
☐ 117T	Manny Trillo	.06	.02	.00
☐ 118T	Ed VandeBerg	.06	.02	.00
☐ 119T	Ozzie Virgil	.06	.02	.00
☐ 120T	Bob Walk	.06	.02	.00
☐ 121T	Gene Walter	.06	.02	.00
☐ 122T	Claudell Washington	.10	.04	.01
☐ 123T	Bill Wegman	.15	.06	.01
☐ 124T	Dick Williams MG	.06	.02	.00
☐ 125T	Mitch Williams	.25	.10	.02
☐ 126T	Bobby Witt	.30	.12	.03
☐ 127T	Todd Worrell	.12	.05	.01
☐ 128T	George Wright	.06	.02	.00
☐ 129T	Ricky Wright	.06	.02	.00
☐ 130T	Steve Yeager	.06	.02	.00
☐ 131T	Paul Zuvella	.06	.02	.00
☐ 132T	Checklist 1-132	.06	.01	.00

1987 Topps

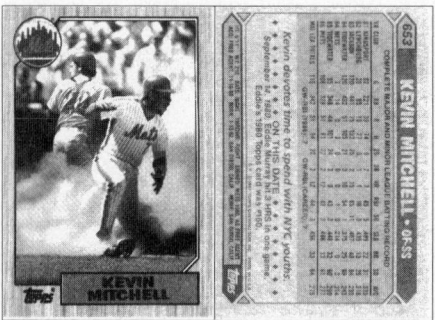

This 792-card set is reminiscent of the 1962 Topps baseball cards with their simulated wood grain borders. The backs are printed in yellow and blue on gray card stock. The manager cards contain a checklist of the respective team's players on the back. Subsets in the set include Record Breakers (1-7), Turn Back the Clock (311-315), and All-Star selections (595-616). The Team Leader cards typically show players conferring on the mound inside a white cloud. The wax pack wrapper gives details of "Spring Fever Baseball" where a lucky collector can win a trip for four to Spring Training. The key rookie cards in this set are Barry Bonds, Bobby Bonilla, Will Clark, Mike Greenwell, Bo Jackson, Barry Larkin, Dave Magadan, Kevin Mitchell, Rafael Palmiero, and Ruben Sierra. Topps also produced a specially boxed "glossy" edition, frequently referred to as the Topps Tiffany set. This year Topps did not disclose the number of sets they produced or sold. It is apparent from the availability that

there were many more sets produced this year compared to the 1984-86 Tiffany sets, perhaps 30,000 sets, more than three times as many. The checklist of cards (792 regular and 132 Traded) is identical to that of the normal non-glossy cards. There are two primary distinguishing features of the Tiffany cards, white card stock reverses and high gloss obverses. These Tiffany cards are valued at approximately three times the values listed below.

		MINT	EXC	G-VG
COMPLETE SET (792)		32.00	14.25	4.75
COMMON PLAYER (1-792)		.03	.01	.00
☐ 1	RB: Roger Clemens	.35	.10	.02
	Most strikeouts, nine inning game			
☐ 2	RB: Jim Deshaies	.06	.02	.00
	Most cons. K's, start of game			
☐ 3	RB: Dwight Evans	.08	.03	.01
	Earliest home run, season			
☐ 4	RB: Davey Lopes	.06	.02	.00
	Most steals, season, 40-year-old			
☐ 5	RB: Dave Righetti	.08	.03	.01
	Most saves, season			
☐ 6	RB: Ruben Sierra	.30	.12	.03
	Youngest player to switch hit homers in game			
☐ 7	RB: Todd Worrell	.06	.02	.00
	Most saves, season, rookie			
☐ 8	Terry Pendleton	.15	.06	.01
☐ 9	Jay Tibbs	.03	.01	.00
☐ 10	Cecil Cooper	.08	.03	.01
☐ 11	Indians Team	.03	.01	.00
	(mound conference)			
☐ 12	Jeff Sellers	.06	.02	.00
☐ 13	Nick Esasky	.06	.02	.00
☐ 14	Dave Stewart	.15	.06	.01
☐ 15	Claudell Washington	.03	.01	.00
☐ 16	Pat Clements	.03	.01	.00
☐ 17	Pete O'Brien	.03	.01	.00
☐ 18	Dick Howser MG	.06	.02	.00
	(checklist back)			
☐ 19	Matt Young	.03	.01	.00
☐ 20	Gary Carter	.15	.06	.01
☐ 21	Mark Davis	.08	.03	.01
☐ 22	Doug DeCinces	.06	.02	.00
☐ 23	Lee Smith	.12	.05	.01
☐ 24	Tony Walker	.06	.02	.00
☐ 25	Bert Blyleven	.08	.03	.01
☐ 26	Greg Brock	.03	.01	.00
☐ 27	Joe Cowley	.03	.01	.00
☐ 28	Rick Dempsey	.03	.01	.00
☐ 29	Jimmy Key	.08	.03	.01
☐ 30	Tim Raines	.15	.06	.01
☐ 31	Braves Team	.03	.01	.00
	(Hubbard/Ramirez)			
☐ 32	Tim Leary	.06	.02	.00
☐ 33	Andy Van Slyke	.15	.06	.01
☐ 34	Jose Rijo	.12	.05	.01
☐ 35	Sid Bream	.03	.01	.00
☐ 36	Eric King	.10	.04	.01
☐ 37	Marvell Wynne	.03	.01	.00
☐ 38	Dennis Leonard	.03	.01	.00
☐ 39	Marty Barrett	.03	.01	.00
☐ 40	Dave Righetti	.08	.03	.01
☐ 41	Bo Diaz	.03	.01	.00
☐ 42	Gary Redus	.03	.01	.00
☐ 43	Gene Michael MG	.06	.02	.00
	(checklist back)			
☐ 44	Greg Harris	.03	.01	.00
☐ 45	Jim Presley	.03	.01	.00
☐ 46	Dan Gladden	.03	.01	.00
☐ 47	Dennis Powell	.03	.01	.00
☐ 48	Wally Backman	.03	.01	.00
☐ 49	Terry Harper	.03	.01	.00
☐ 50	Dave Smith	.03	.01	.00
☐ 51	Mel Hall	.08	.03	.01
☐ 52	Keith Atherton	.03	.01	.00
☐ 53	Ruppert Jones	.03	.01	.00
☐ 54	Bill Dawley	.03	.01	.00
☐ 55	Tim Wallach	.08	.03	.01
☐ 56	Brewers Team	.03	.01	.00
	(mound conference)			
☐ 57	Scott Nielsen	.06	.02	.00
☐ 58	Thad Bosley	.03	.01	.00
☐ 59	Ken Dayley	.03	.01	.00
☐ 60	Tony Pena	.06	.02	.00

#	Player			
☐ 61	Bobby Thigpen	.50	.20	.05
☐ 62	Bobby Meacham	.03	.01	.00
☐ 63	Fred Toliver	.03	.01	.00
☐ 64	Harry Spilman	.03	.01	.00
☐ 65	Tom Browning	.08	.03	.01
☐ 66	Marc Sullivan	.03	.01	.00
☐ 67	Bill Swift	.06	.02	.00
☐ 68	Tony LaRussa MG (checklist back)	.06	.02	.00
☐ 69	Lonnie Smith	.08	.03	.01
☐ 70	Charlie Hough	.03	.01	.00
☐ 71	Mike Aldrete	.06	.02	.00
☐ 72	Walt Terrell	.03	.01	.00
☐ 73	Dave Anderson	.03	.01	.00
☐ 74	Dan Pasqua	.06	.02	.00
☐ 75	Ron Darling	.08	.03	.01
☐ 76	Rafael Ramirez	.03	.01	.00
☐ 77	Bryan Oelkers	.03	.01	.00
☐ 78	Tom Foley	.03	.01	.00
☐ 79	Juan Nieves	.06	.02	.00
☐ 80	Wally Joyner	.75	.30	.07
☐ 81	Padres Team (Hawkins/Kennedy)	.03	.01	.00
☐ 82	Rob Murphy	.10	.04	.01
☐ 83	Mike Davis	.03	.01	.00
☐ 84	Steve Lake	.03	.01	.00
☐ 85	Kevin Bass	.03	.01	.00
☐ 86	Nate Snell	.03	.01	.00
☐ 87	Mark Salas	.03	.01	.00
☐ 88	Ed Wojna	.03	.01	.00
☐ 89	Ozzie Guillen	.10	.04	.01
☐ 90	Dave Stieb	.10	.04	.01
☐ 91	Harold Reynolds	.08	.03	.01
☐ 92A	Urbano Lugo ERR (no trademark)	.20	.08	.02
☐ 92B	Urbano Lugo COR	.06	.02	.00
☐ 93	Jim Leyland MG (checklist back)	.06	.02	.00
☐ 94	Calvin Schiraldi	.03	.01	.00
☐ 95	Oddibe McDowell	.03	.01	.00
☐ 96	Frank Williams	.03	.01	.00
☐ 97	Glenn Wilson	.03	.01	.00
☐ 98	Bill Scherrer	.03	.01	.00
☐ 99	Darryl Motley	.03	.01	.00
☐ 100	Steve Garvey	.20	.08	.02
☐ 101	Carl Willis	.10	.04	.01
☐ 102	Paul Zuvella	.03	.01	.00
☐ 103	Rick Aguilera	.10	.04	.01
☐ 104	Billy Sample	.03	.01	.00
☐ 105	Floyd Youmans	.03	.01	.00
☐ 106	Blue Jays Team (Bell/Barfield)	.12	.05	.01
☐ 107	John Butcher	.03	.01	.00
☐ 108	Jim Gantner UER (Brewers logo reversed)	.06	.02	.00
☐ 109	R.J. Reynolds	.03	.01	.00
☐ 110	John Tudor	.08	.03	.01
☐ 111	Alfredo Griffin	.03	.01	.00
☐ 112	Alan Ashby	.03	.01	.00
☐ 113	Neil Allen	.03	.01	.00
☐ 114	Billy Beane	.03	.01	.00
☐ 115	Donnie Moore	.03	.01	.00
☐ 116	Bill Russell	.06	.02	.00
☐ 117	Jim Beattie	.03	.01	.00
☐ 118	Bobby Valentine MG (checklist back)	.06	.02	.00
☐ 119	Ron Robinson	.06	.02	.00
☐ 120	Eddie Murray	.30	.12	.03
☐ 121	Kevin Romine	.06	.02	.00
☐ 122	Jim Clancy	.03	.01	.00
☐ 123	John Kruk	.25	.10	.02
☐ 124	Ray Fontenot	.03	.01	.00
☐ 125	Bob Brenly	.03	.01	.00
☐ 126	Mike Loynd	.03	.01	.00
☐ 127	Vance Law	.03	.01	.00
☐ 128	Checklist 1-132	.08	.01	.00
☐ 129	Rick Cerone	.03	.01	.00
☐ 130	Dwight Gooden	.30	.12	.03
☐ 131	Pirates Team (Bream/Pena)	.03	.01	.00
☐ 132	Paul Assenmacher	.03	.01	.00
☐ 133	Jose Oquendo	.03	.01	.00
☐ 134	Rich Yett	.03	.01	.00
☐ 135	Mike Easler	.03	.01	.00
☐ 136	Ron Romanick	.03	.01	.00
☐ 137	Jerry Willard	.03	.01	.00
☐ 138	Roy Lee Jackson	.03	.01	.00
☐ 139	Devon White	.45	.18	.04
☐ 140	Bret Saberhagen	.17	.07	.01
☐ 141	Herm Winningham	.03	.01	.00
☐ 142	Rick Sutcliffe	.06	.02	.00
☐ 143	Steve Boros MG (checklist back)	.06	.02	.00
☐ 144	Mike Scioscia	.03	.01	.00
☐ 145	Charlie Kerfeld	.03	.01	.00
☐ 146	Tracy Jones	.08	.03	.01
☐ 147	Randy Niemann	.03	.01	.00
☐ 148	Dave Collins	.03	.01	.00
☐ 149	Ray Searage	.03	.01	.00
☐ 150	Wade Boggs	.40	.16	.04
☐ 151	Mike LaCoss	.03	.01	.00
☐ 152	Toby Harrah	.03	.01	.00
☐ 153	Duane Ward	.20	.08	.02
☐ 154	Tom O'Malley	.03	.01	.00
☐ 155	Eddie Whitson	.03	.01	.00
☐ 156	Mariners Team (mound conference)	.03	.01	.00
☐ 157	Danny Darwin	.03	.01	.00
☐ 158	Tim Teufel	.03	.01	.00
☐ 159	Ed Olwine	.03	.01	.00
☐ 160	Julio Franco	.25	.10	.02
☐ 161	Steve Ontiveros	.03	.01	.00
☐ 162	Mike LaValliere	.15	.06	.01
☐ 163	Kevin Gross	.03	.01	.00
☐ 164	Sammy Khalifa	.03	.01	.00
☐ 165	Jeff Reardon	.12	.05	.01
☐ 166	Bob Boone	.08	.03	.01
☐ 167	Jim Deshaies	.15	.06	.01
☐ 168	Lou Piniella MG (checklist back)	.08	.03	.01
☐ 169	Ron Washington	.03	.01	.00
☐ 170	Bo Jackson	3.25	1.35	.32
☐ 171	Chuck Cary	.10	.04	.01
☐ 172	Ron Oester	.03	.01	.00
☐ 173	Alex Trevino	.03	.01	.00
☐ 174	Henry Cotto	.03	.01	.00
☐ 175	Bob Stanley	.03	.01	.00
☐ 176	Steve Buechele	.03	.01	.00
☐ 177	Keith Moreland	.03	.01	.00
☐ 178	Cecil Fielder	1.25	.50	.12
☐ 179	Bill Wegman	.08	.03	.01
☐ 180	Chris Brown	.03	.01	.00
☐ 181	Cardinals Team (mound conference)	.03	.01	.00
☐ 182	Lee Lacy	.03	.01	.00
☐ 183	Andy Hawkins	.03	.01	.00
☐ 184	Bobby Bonilla	1.75	.70	.17
☐ 185	Roger McDowell	.03	.01	.00
☐ 186	Bruce Benedict	.03	.01	.00
☐ 187	Mark Huismann	.03	.01	.00
☐ 188	Tony Phillips	.03	.01	.00
☐ 189	Joe Hesketh	.06	.02	.00
☐ 190	Jim Sundberg	.03	.01	.00
☐ 191	Charles Hudson	.03	.01	.00
☐ 192	Cory Snyder	.08	.03	.01
☐ 193	Roger Craig MG (checklist back)	.06	.02	.00
☐ 194	Kirk McCaskill	.03	.01	.00
☐ 195	Mike Pagliarulo	.03	.01	.00
☐ 196	Randy O'Neal UER (wrong ML career W-L totals)	.03	.01	.00
☐ 197	Mark Bailey	.03	.01	.00
☐ 198	Lee Mazzilli	.03	.01	.00
☐ 199	Mariano Duncan	.08	.03	.01
☐ 200	Pete Rose	.35	.15	.03
☐ 201	John Cangelosi	.03	.01	.00
☐ 202	Ricky Wright	.03	.01	.00
☐ 203	Mike Kingery	.03	.01	.00
☐ 204	Sammy Stewart	.03	.01	.00
☐ 205	Graig Nettles	.08	.03	.01
☐ 206	Twins Team (Frank Viola and Tim Laudner)	.06	.02	.00
☐ 207	George Frazier	.03	.01	.00
☐ 208	John Shelby	.03	.01	.00
☐ 209	Rick Schu	.03	.01	.00
☐ 210	Lloyd Moseby	.03	.01	.00
☐ 211	John Morris	.03	.01	.00
☐ 212	Mike Fitzgerald	.03	.01	.00
☐ 213	Randy Myers	.15	.06	.01
☐ 214	Omar Moreno	.03	.01	.00
☐ 215	Mark Langston	.17	.07	.01
☐ 216	B.J. Surhoff	.15	.06	.01
☐ 217	Chris Codiroli	.03	.01	.00
☐ 218	Sparky Anderson MG (checklist back)	.06	.02	.00
☐ 219	Cecilio Guante	.03	.01	.00
☐ 220	Joe Carter	.30	.12	.03
☐ 221	Vern Ruhle	.03	.01	.00
☐ 222	Denny Walling	.03	.01	.00
☐ 223	Charlie Leibrandt	.03	.01	.00
☐ 224	Wayne Tolleson	.03	.01	.00
☐ 225	Mike Smithson	.03	.01	.00
☐ 226	Max Venable	.03	.01	.00
☐ 227	Jamie Moyer	.08	.03	.01
☐ 228	Curt Wilkerson	.03	.01	.00
☐ 229	Mike Birkbeck	.06	.02	.00
☐ 230	Don Baylor	.08	.03	.01

#	Player			
☐ 231	Giants Team (Bob Brenly and Jim Gott)	.03	.01	.00
☐ 232	Reggie Williams	.03	.01	.00
☐ 233	Russ Morman	.03	.01	.00
☐ 234	Pat Sheridan	.03	.01	.00
☐ 235	Alvin Davis	.08	.03	.01
☐ 236	Tommy John	.10	.04	.01
☐ 237	Jim Morrison	.03	.01	.00
☐ 238	Bill Krueger	.03	.01	.00
☐ 239	Juan Espino	.03	.01	.00
☐ 240	Steve Balboni	.03	.01	.00
☐ 241	Danny Heep	.03	.01	.00
☐ 242	Rick Mahler	.03	.01	.00
☐ 243	Whitey Herzog MG (checklist back)	.06	.02	.00
☐ 244	Dickie Noles	.03	.01	.00
☐ 245	Willie Upshaw	.03	.01	.00
☐ 246	Jim Dwyer	.03	.01	.00
☐ 247	Jeff Reed	.03	.01	.00
☐ 248	Gene Walter	.03	.01	.00
☐ 249	Jim Pankovits	.03	.01	.00
☐ 250	Teddy Higuera	.06	.02	.00
☐ 251	Rob Wilfong	.03	.01	.00
☐ 252	Dennis Martinez	.08	.03	.01
☐ 253	Eddie Milner	.03	.01	.00
☐ 254	Bob Tewksbury	.06	.02	.00
☐ 255	Juan Samuel	.10	.04	.01
☐ 256	Royals Team (Brett/F.White)	.10	.04	.01
☐ 257	Bob Forsch	.03	.01	.00
☐ 258	Steve Yeager	.03	.01	.00
☐ 259	Mike Greenwell	1.50	.60	.15
☐ 260	Vida Blue	.06	.02	.00
☐ 261	Ruben Sierra	2.50	1.00	.25
☐ 262	Jim Winn	.03	.01	.00
☐ 263	Stan Javier	.06	.02	.00
☐ 264	Checklist 133-264	.08	.01	.00
☐ 265	Darrell Evans	.08	.03	.01
☐ 266	Jeff Hamilton	.08	.03	.01
☐ 267	Howard Johnson	.25	.10	.02
☐ 268	Pat Corrales MG (checklist back)	.06	.02	.00
☐ 269	Cliff Speck	.03	.01	.00
☐ 270	Jody Davis	.03	.01	.00
☐ 271	Mike Brown (Mariners pitcher)	.03	.01	.00
☐ 272	Andres Galarraga	.10	.04	.01
☐ 273	Gene Nelson	.03	.01	.00
☐ 274	Jeff Hearron UER (duplicate 1986 stat line on back)	.03	.01	.00
☐ 275	LaMarr Hoyt	.03	.01	.00
☐ 276	Jackie Gutierrez	.03	.01	.00
☐ 277	Juan Agosto	.03	.01	.00
☐ 278	Gary Pettis	.03	.01	.00
☐ 279	Dan Plesac	.10	.04	.01
☐ 280	Jeff Leonard	.03	.01	.00
☐ 281	Reds Team (Pete Rose, Bo Diaz, and Bill Gullickson)	.10	.04	.01
☐ 282	Jeff Calhoun	.03	.01	.00
☐ 283	Doug Drabek	.60	.25	.06
☐ 284	John Moses	.03	.01	.00
☐ 285	Dennis Boyd	.03	.01	.00
☐ 286	Mike Woodard	.03	.01	.00
☐ 287	Dave Von Ohlen	.03	.01	.00
☐ 288	Tito Landrum	.03	.01	.00
☐ 289	Bob Kipper	.03	.01	.00
☐ 290	Leon Durham	.03	.01	.00
☐ 291	Mitch Williams	.17	.07	.01
☐ 292	Franklin Stubbs	.03	.01	.00
☐ 293	Bob Rodgers MG (checklist back)	.06	.02	.00
☐ 294	Steve Jeltz	.03	.01	.00
☐ 295	Len Dykstra	.17	.07	.01
☐ 296	Andres Thomas	.06	.02	.00
☐ 297	Don Schulze	.03	.01	.00
☐ 298	Larry Herndon	.03	.01	.00
☐ 299	Joel Davis	.03	.01	.00
☐ 300	Reggie Jackson	.30	.12	.03
☐ 301	Luis Aquino UER (no trademark, never corrected)	.06	.02	.00
☐ 302	Bill Schroeder	.03	.01	.00
☐ 303	Juan Berenguer	.03	.01	.00
☐ 304	Phil Garner	.06	.02	.00
☐ 305	John Franco	.08	.03	.01
☐ 306	Red Sox Team (Tom Seaver, John McNamara, and Rich Gedman)	.08	.03	.01
☐ 307	Lee Guetterman	.10	.04	.01
☐ 308	Don Slaught	.03	.01	.00
☐ 309	Mike Young	.03	.01	.00
☐ 310	Frank Viola	.15	.06	.01
☐ 311	Turn Back 1982 Rickey Henderson	.15	.06	.01
☐ 312	Turn Back 1977 Reggie Jackson	.12	.05	.01
☐ 313	Turn Back 1972 Roberto Clemente	.12	.05	.01
☐ 314	Turn Back 1967 UER Carl Yastrzemski (sic, 112 RBI's on back)	.12	.05	.01
☐ 315	Turn Back 1962 Maury Wills	.06	.02	.00
☐ 316	Brian Fisher	.03	.01	.00
☐ 317	Clint Hurdle	.03	.01	.00
☐ 318	Jim Fregosi MG (checklist back)	.06	.02	.00
☐ 319	Greg Swindell	.35	.15	.03
☐ 320	Barry Bonds	2.00	.80	.20
☐ 321	Mike Laga	.03	.01	.00
☐ 322	Chris Bando	.03	.01	.00
☐ 323	Al Newman	.06	.02	.00
☐ 324	David Palmer	.03	.01	.00
☐ 325	Garry Templeton	.06	.02	.00
☐ 326	Mark Gubicza	.08	.03	.01
☐ 327	Dale Sveum	.08	.03	.01
☐ 328	Bob Welch	.08	.03	.01
☐ 329	Ron Roenicke	.03	.01	.00
☐ 330	Mike Scott	.08	.03	.01
☐ 331	Mets Team (Gary Carter and Darryl Strawberry)	.15	.06	.01
☐ 332	Joe Price	.03	.01	.00
☐ 333	Ken Phelps	.03	.01	.00
☐ 334	Ed Correa	.03	.01	.00
☐ 335	Candy Maldonado	.08	.03	.01
☐ 336	Allan Anderson	.15	.06	.01
☐ 337	Darrell Miller	.03	.01	.00
☐ 338	Tim Conroy	.03	.01	.00
☐ 339	Donnie Hill	.03	.01	.00
☐ 340	Roger Clemens	1.00	.40	.10
☐ 341	Mike Brown (Pirates OF)	.03	.01	.00
☐ 342	Bob James	.03	.01	.00
☐ 343	Hal Lanier MG (checklist back)	.06	.02	.00
☐ 344A	Joe Niekro (copyright inside righthand border)	.10	.04	.01
☐ 344B	Joe Niekro (copyright outside righthand border)	.35	.15	.03
☐ 345	Andre Dawson	.25	.10	.02
☐ 346	Shawon Dunston	.12	.05	.01
☐ 347	Mickey Brantley	.06	.02	.00
☐ 348	Carmelo Martinez	.03	.01	.00
☐ 349	Storm Davis	.03	.01	.00
☐ 350	Keith Hernandez	.10	.04	.01
☐ 351	Gene Garber	.03	.01	.00
☐ 352	Mike Felder	.06	.02	.00
☐ 353	Ernie Camacho	.03	.01	.00
☐ 354	Jamie Quirk	.03	.01	.00
☐ 355	Don Carman	.03	.01	.00
☐ 356	White Sox Team (mound conference)	.03	.01	.00
☐ 357	Steve Fireovid	.03	.01	.00
☐ 358	Sal Butera	.03	.01	.00
☐ 359	Doug Corbett	.03	.01	.00
☐ 360	Pedro Guerrero	.10	.04	.01
☐ 361	Mark Thurmond	.03	.01	.00
☐ 362	Luis Quinones	.06	.02	.00
☐ 363	Jose Guzman	.06	.02	.00
☐ 364	Randy Bush	.03	.01	.00
☐ 365	Rick Rhoden	.03	.01	.00
☐ 366	Mark McGwire	1.25	.50	.12
☐ 367	Jeff Lahti	.03	.01	.00
☐ 368	John McNamara MG (checklist back)	.06	.02	.00
☐ 369	Brian Dayett	.03	.01	.00
☐ 370	Fred Lynn	.08	.03	.01
☐ 371	Mark Eichhorn	.08	.03	.01
☐ 372	Jerry Mumphrey	.03	.01	.00
☐ 373	Jeff Dedmon	.03	.01	.00
☐ 374	Glenn Hoffman	.03	.01	.00
☐ 375	Ron Guidry	.08	.03	.01
☐ 376	Scott Bradley	.03	.01	.00
☐ 377	John Henry Johnson	.03	.01	.00
☐ 378	Rafael Santana	.03	.01	.00
☐ 379	John Russell	.03	.01	.00
☐ 380	Rich Gossage	.08	.03	.01
☐ 381	Expos Team (mound conference)	.03	.01	.00
☐ 382	Rudy Law	.03	.01	.00
☐ 383	Ron Davis	.03	.01	.00
☐ 384	Johnny Grubb	.03	.01	.00

#	Player			
☐ 385	Orel Hershiser	.15	.06	.01
☐ 386	Dickie Thon	.03	.01	.00
☐ 387	T.R. Bryden	.03	.01	.00
☐ 388	Geno Petralli	.03	.01	.00
☐ 389	Jeff Robinson	.06	.02	.00
	(Giants pitcher)			
☐ 390	Gary Matthews	.03	.01	.00
☐ 391	Jay Howell	.03	.01	.00
☐ 392	Checklist 265-396	.08	.01	.00
☐ 393	Pete Rose MG	.25	.10	.02
	(checklist back)			
☐ 394	Mike Bielecki	.06	.02	.00
☐ 395	Damaso Garcia	.03	.01	.00
☐ 396	Tim Lollar	.03	.01	.00
☐ 397	Greg Walker	.03	.01	.00
☐ 398	Brad Havens	.03	.01	.00
☐ 399	Curt Ford	.03	.01	.00
☐ 400	George Brett	.25	.10	.02
☐ 401	Billy Jo Robidoux	.03	.01	.00
☐ 402	Mike Trujillo	.03	.01	.00
☐ 403	Jerry Royster	.03	.01	.00
☐ 404	Doug Sisk	.03	.01	.00
☐ 405	Brook Jacoby	.06	.02	.00
☐ 406	Yankees Team	.20	.08	.02
	(Henderson/Mattingly)			
☐ 407	Jim Acker	.03	.01	.00
☐ 408	John Mizerock	.03	.01	.00
☐ 409	Milt Thompson	.06	.02	.00
☐ 410	Fernando Valenzuela	.08	.03	.01
☐ 411	Darnell Coles	.03	.01	.00
☐ 412	Eric Davis	.30	.12	.03
☐ 413	Moose Haas	.03	.01	.00
☐ 414	Joe Orsulak	.03	.01	.00
☐ 415	Bobby Witt	.25	.10	.02
☐ 416	Tom Nieto	.03	.01	.00
☐ 417	Pat Perry	.03	.01	.00
☐ 418	Dick Williams MG	.06	.02	.00
	(checklist back)			
☐ 419	Mark Portugal	.12	.05	.01
☐ 420	Will Clark	3.50	1.50	.35
☐ 421	Jose DeLeon	.03	.01	.00
☐ 422	Jack Howell	.03	.01	.00
☐ 423	Jaime Cocanower	.03	.01	.00
☐ 424	Chris Speier	.03	.01	.00
☐ 425	Tom Seaver	.35	.15	.03
☐ 426	Floyd Rayford	.03	.01	.00
☐ 427	Edwin Nunez	.03	.01	.00
☐ 428	Bruce Bochy	.03	.01	.00
☐ 429	Tim Pyznarski	.03	.01	.00
☐ 430	Mike Schmidt	.60	.25	.06
☐ 431	Dodgers Team	.06	.02	.00
	(mound conference)			
☐ 432	Jim Slaton	.03	.01	.00
☐ 433	Ed Hearn	.03	.01	.00
☐ 434	Mike Fischlin	.03	.01	.00
☐ 435	Bruce Sutter	.08	.03	.01
☐ 436	Andy Allanson	.03	.01	.00
☐ 437	Ted Power	.03	.01	.00
☐ 438	Kelly Downs	.10	.04	.01
☐ 439	Karl Best	.03	.01	.00
☐ 440	Willie McGee	.10	.04	.01
☐ 441	Dave Leiper	.03	.01	.00
☐ 442	Mitch Webster	.03	.01	.00
☐ 443	John Felske MG	.06	.02	.00
	(checklist back)			
☐ 444	Jeff Russell	.06	.02	.00
☐ 445	Dave Lopes	.06	.02	.00
☐ 446	Chuck Finley	.75	.30	.07
☐ 447	Bill Almon	.03	.01	.00
☐ 448	Chris Bosio	.15	.06	.01
☐ 449	Pat Dodson	.06	.02	.00
☐ 450	Kirby Puckett	.90	.40	.09
☐ 451	Joe Sambito	.03	.01	.00
☐ 452	Dave Henderson	.10	.04	.01
☐ 453	Scott Terry	.06	.02	.00
☐ 454	Luis Salazar	.03	.01	.00
☐ 455	Mike Boddicker	.03	.01	.00
☐ 456	A's Team	.03	.01	.00
	(mound conference)			
☐ 457	Len Matuszek	.03	.01	.00
☐ 458	Kelly Gruber	.75	.30	.07
☐ 459	Dennis Eckersley	.12	.05	.01
☐ 460	Darryl Strawberry	.75	.30	.07
☐ 461	Craig McMurtry	.03	.01	.00
☐ 462	Scott Fletcher	.03	.01	.00
☐ 463	Tom Candiotti	.08	.03	.01
☐ 464	Butch Wynegar	.03	.01	.00
☐ 465	Todd Worrell	.08	.03	.01
☐ 466	Kal Daniels	.17	.07	.01
☐ 467	Randy St.Claire	.03	.01	.00
☐ 468	George Bamberger MG	.06	.02	.00
	(checklist back)			
☐ 469	Mike Diaz	.03	.01	.00
☐ 470	Dave Dravecky	.08	.03	.01
☐ 471	Ronn Reynolds	.03	.01	.00
☐ 472	Bill Doran	.03	.01	.00
☐ 473	Steve Farr	.06	.02	.00
☐ 474	Jerry Narron	.03	.01	.00
☐ 475	Scott Garrelts	.03	.01	.00
☐ 476	Danny Tartabull	.40	.16	.04
☐ 477	Ken Howell	.03	.01	.00
☐ 478	Tim Laudner	.03	.01	.00
☐ 479	Bob Sebra	.03	.01	.00
☐ 480	Jim Rice	.10	.04	.01
☐ 481	Phillies Team	.06	.02	.00
	(Glenn Wilson,			
	Juan Samuel, and			
	Von Hayes)			
☐ 482	Daryl Boston	.03	.01	.00
☐ 483	Dwight Lowry	.03	.01	.00
☐ 484	Jim Traber	.03	.01	.00
☐ 485	Tony Fernandez	.10	.04	.01
☐ 486	Otis Nixon	.10	.04	.01
☐ 487	Dave Gumpert	.03	.01	.00
☐ 488	Ray Knight	.06	.02	.00
☐ 489	Bill Gullickson	.06	.02	.00
☐ 490	Dale Murphy	.20	.08	.02
☐ 491	Ron Karkovice	.06	.02	.00
☐ 492	Mike Heath	.03	.01	.00
☐ 493	Tom Lasorda MG	.08	.03	.01
	(checklist back)			
☐ 494	Barry Jones	.10	.04	.01
☐ 495	Gorman Thomas	.06	.02	.00
☐ 496	Bruce Bochte	.03	.01	.00
☐ 497	Dale Mohorcic	.06	.02	.00
☐ 498	Bob Kearney	.03	.01	.00
☐ 499	Bruce Ruffin	.06	.02	.00
☐ 500	Don Mattingly	.50	.20	.05
☐ 501	Craig Lefferts	.03	.01	.00
☐ 502	Dick Schofield	.03	.01	.00
☐ 503	Larry Andersen	.03	.01	.00
☐ 504	Mickey Hatcher	.03	.01	.00
☐ 505	Bryn Smith	.03	.01	.00
☐ 506	Orioles Team	.03	.01	.00
	(mound conference)			
☐ 507	Dave Stapleton	.03	.01	.00
	(infielder)			
☐ 508	Scott Bankhead	.06	.02	.00
☐ 509	Enos Cabell	.03	.01	.00
☐ 510	Tom Henke	.08	.03	.01
☐ 511	Steve Lyons	.03	.01	.00
☐ 512	Dave Magadan	.35	.15	.03
☐ 513	Carmen Castillo	.03	.01	.00
☐ 514	Orlando Mercado	.03	.01	.00
☐ 515	Willie Hernandez	.06	.02	.00
☐ 516	Ted Simmons	.08	.03	.01
☐ 517	Mario Soto	.03	.01	.00
☐ 518	Gene Mauch MG	.06	.02	.00
	(checklist back)			
☐ 519	Curt Young	.03	.01	.00
☐ 520	Jack Clark	.10	.04	.01
☐ 521	Rick Reuschel	.06	.02	.00
☐ 522	Checklist 397-528	.08	.01	.00
☐ 523	Earnie Riles	.03	.01	.00
☐ 524	Bob Shirley	.03	.01	.00
☐ 525	Phil Bradley	.03	.01	.00
☐ 526	Roger Mason	.03	.01	.00
☐ 527	Jim Wohlford	.03	.01	.00
☐ 528	Ken Dixon	.03	.01	.00
☐ 529	Alvaro Espinoza	.17	.07	.01
☐ 530	Tony Gwynn	.40	.16	.04
☐ 531	Astros Team	.10	.04	.01
	(Y.Berra conference)			
☐ 532	Jeff Stone	.03	.01	.00
☐ 533	Argenis Salazar	.03	.01	.00
☐ 534	Scott Sanderson	.06	.02	.00
☐ 535	Tony Armas	.03	.01	.00
☐ 536	Terry Mulholland	.25	.10	.02
☐ 537	Rance Mulliniks	.03	.01	.00
☐ 538	Tom Niedenfuer	.03	.01	.00
☐ 539	Reid Nichols	.03	.01	.00
☐ 540	Terry Kennedy	.03	.01	.00
☐ 541	Rafael Belliard	.17	.07	.01
☐ 542	Ricky Horton	.03	.01	.00
☐ 543	Dave Johnson MG	.08	.03	.01
	(checklist back)			
☐ 544	Zane Smith	.10	.04	.01
☐ 545	Buddy Bell	.06	.02	.00
☐ 546	Mike Morgan	.06	.02	.00
☐ 547	Rob Deer	.10	.04	.01
☐ 548	Bill Mooneyham	.03	.01	.00
☐ 549	Bob Melvin	.03	.01	.00
☐ 550	Pete Incaviglia	.17	.07	.01
☐ 551	Frank Wills	.06	.02	.00
☐ 552	Larry Sheets	.03	.01	.00
☐ 553	Mike Maddux	.06	.02	.00
☐ 554	Buddy Biancalana	.03	.01	.00
☐ 555	Dennis Rasmussen	.03	.01	.00

#	Player			
556	Angels Team (Lachemann, Witt, and Boone)	.06	.02	.00
557	John Cerutti	.10	.04	.01
558	Greg Gagne	.06	.02	.00
559	Lance McCullers	.03	.01	.00
560	Glenn Davis	.17	.07	.01
561	Rey Quinones	.03	.01	.00
562	Bryan Clutterbuck	.03	.01	.00
563	John Stefero	.03	.01	.00
564	Larry McWilliams	.03	.01	.00
565	Dusty Baker	.06	.02	.00
566	Tim Hulett	.03	.01	.00
567	Greg Mathews	.06	.02	.00
568	Earl Weaver MG (checklist back)	.08	.03	.01
569	Wade Rowdon	.03	.01	.00
570	Sid Fernandez	.10	.04	.01
571	Ozzie Virgil	.03	.01	.00
572	Pete Ladd	.03	.01	.00
573	Hal McRae	.06	.02	.00
574	Manny Lee	.06	.02	.00
575	Pat Tabler	.03	.01	.00
576	Frank Pastore	.03	.01	.00
577	Dann Bilardello	.03	.01	.00
578	Billy Hatcher	.08	.03	.01
579	Rick Burleson	.03	.01	.00
580	Mike Krukow	.03	.01	.00
581	Cubs Team (Cey/Trout)	.03	.01	.00
582	Bruce Berenyi	.03	.01	.00
583	Junior Ortiz	.03	.01	.00
584	Ron Kittle	.06	.02	.00
585	Scott Bailes	.06	.02	.00
586	Ben Oglivie	.03	.01	.00
587	Eric Plunk	.03	.01	.00
588	Wallace Johnson	.03	.01	.00
589	Steve Crawford	.03	.01	.00
590	Vince Coleman	.25	.10	.02
591	Spike Owen	.03	.01	.00
592	Chris Welsh	.03	.01	.00
593	Chuck Tanner MG (checklist back)	.06	.02	.00
594	Rick Anderson	.03	.01	.00
595	Keith Hernandez AS	.08	.03	.01
596	Steve Sax AS	.08	.03	.01
597	Mike Schmidt AS	.25	.10	.02
598	Ozzie Smith AS	.10	.04	.01
599	Tony Gwynn AS	.17	.07	.01
600	Dave Parker AS	.08	.03	.01
601	Darryl Strawberry AS	.25	.10	.02
602	Gary Carter AS	.08	.03	.01
603A	Dwight Gooden AS ERR (no trademark)	.50	.20	.05
603B	Dwight Gooden AS COR	.12	.05	.01
604	Fern. Valenzuela AS	.08	.03	.01
605	Todd Worrell AS	.06	.02	.00
606A	Don Mattingly AS ERR (no trademark)	1.00	.40	.10
606B	Don Mattingly AS COR	.20	.08	.02
607	Tony Bernazard AS	.06	.02	.00
608	Wade Boggs AS	.20	.08	.02
609	Cal Ripken AS	.30	.12	.03
610	Jim Rice AS	.08	.03	.01
611	Kirby Puckett AS	.35	.15	.03
612	George Bell AS	.08	.03	.01
613	Lance Parrish AS UER (Pitcher heading on back)	.06	.02	.00
614	Roger Clemens AS	.35	.15	.03
615	Teddy Higuera AS	.06	.02	.00
616	Dave Righetti AS	.08	.03	.01
617	Al Nipper	.03	.01	.00
618	Tom Kelly MG (checklist back)	.08	.03	.01
619	Jerry Reed	.03	.01	.00
620	Jose Canseco	3.00	1.25	.30
621	Danny Cox	.03	.01	.00
622	Glenn Braggs	.17	.07	.01
623	Kurt Stillwell	.15	.06	.01
624	Tim Burke	.03	.01	.00
625	Mookie Wilson	.03	.01	.00
626	Joel Skinner	.03	.01	.00
627	Ken Oberkfell	.03	.01	.00
628	Bob Walk	.03	.01	.00
629	Larry Parrish	.03	.01	.00
630	John Candelaria	.03	.01	.00
631	Tigers Team (mound conference)	.03	.01	.00
632	Rob Woodward	.03	.01	.00
633	Jose Uribe	.03	.01	.00
634	Rafael Palmeiro	1.50	.60	.15
635	Ken Schrom	.03	.01	.00
636	Darren Daulton	.08	.03	.01
637	Bip Roberts	.30	.12	.03
638	Rich Bordi	.03	.01	.00
639	Gerald Perry	.03	.01	.00
640	Mark Clear	.03	.01	.00
641	Domingo Ramos	.03	.01	.00
642	Al Pulido	.03	.01	.00
643	Ron Shepherd	.03	.01	.00
644	John Denny	.03	.01	.00
645	Dwight Evans	.10	.04	.01
646	Mike Mason	.03	.01	.00
647	Tom Lawless	.03	.01	.00
648	Barry Larkin	1.50	.60	.15
649	Mickey Tettleton	.10	.04	.01
650	Hubie Brooks	.08	.03	.01
651	Benny Distefano	.03	.01	.00
652	Terry Forster	.06	.02	.00
653	Kevin Mitchell	1.50	.60	.15
654	Checklist 529-660	.08	.01	.00
655	Jesse Barfield	.10	.04	.01
656	Rangers Team (Valentine/R.Wright)	.03	.01	.00
657	Tom Waddell	.03	.01	.00
658	Robby Thompson	.15	.06	.01
659	Aurelio Lopez	.03	.01	.00
660	Bob Horner	.08	.03	.01
661	Lou Whitaker	.12	.05	.01
662	Frank DiPino	.03	.01	.00
663	Cliff Johnson	.03	.01	.00
664	Mike Marshall	.08	.03	.01
665	Rod Scurry	.03	.01	.00
666	Von Hayes	.08	.03	.01
667	Ron Hassey	.03	.01	.00
668	Juan Bonilla	.03	.01	.00
669	Bud Black	.03	.01	.00
670	Jose Cruz	.06	.02	.00
671A	Ray Soff ERR (no D* before copyright line)	.08	.03	.01
671B	Ray Soff COR (D* before copyright line)	.08	.03	.01
672	Chili Davis	.08	.03	.01
673	Don Sutton	.12	.05	.01
674	Bill Campbell	.03	.01	.00
675	Ed Romero	.03	.01	.00
676	Charlie Moore	.03	.01	.00
677	Bob Grich	.06	.02	.00
678	Carney Lansford	.08	.03	.01
679	Kent Hrbek	.12	.05	.01
680	Ryne Sandberg	.75	.30	.07
681	George Bell	.20	.08	.02
682	Jerry Reuss	.03	.01	.00
683	Gary Roenicke	.03	.01	.00
684	Kent Tekulve	.03	.01	.00
685	Jerry Hairston	.03	.01	.00
686	Doyle Alexander	.03	.01	.00
687	Alan Trammell	.17	.07	.01
688	Juan Beniquez	.03	.01	.00
689	Darrell Porter	.03	.01	.00
690	Dane Iorg	.03	.01	.00
691	Dave Parker	.15	.06	.01
692	Frank White	.03	.01	.00
693	Terry Puhl	.03	.01	.00
694	Phil Niekro	.12	.05	.01
695	Chico Walker	.03	.01	.00
696	Gary Lucas	.03	.01	.00
697	Ed Lynch	.03	.01	.00
698	Ernie Whitt	.03	.01	.00
699	Ken Landreaux	.03	.01	.00
700	Dave Bergman	.03	.01	.00
701	Willie Randolph	.06	.02	.00
702	Greg Gross	.03	.01	.00
703	Dave Schmidt	.03	.01	.00
704	Jesse Orosco	.03	.01	.00
705	Bruce Hurst	.08	.03	.01
706	Rick Manning	.03	.01	.00
707	Bob McClure	.03	.01	.00
708	Scott McGregor	.03	.01	.00
709	Dave Kingman	.08	.03	.01
710	Gary Gaetti	.08	.03	.01
711	Ken Griffey	.10	.04	.01
712	Don Robinson	.03	.01	.00
713	Tom Brookens	.03	.01	.00
714	Dan Quisenberry	.08	.03	.01
715	Bob Dernier	.03	.01	.00
716	Rick Leach	.03	.01	.00
717	Ed VandeBerg	.03	.01	.00
718	Steve Carlton	.25	.10	.02
719	Tom Hume	.03	.01	.00
720	Richard Dotson	.03	.01	.00
721	Tom Herr	.03	.01	.00
722	Bob Knepper	.03	.01	.00
723	Brett Butler	.10	.04	.01
724	Greg Minton	.03	.01	.00
725	George Hendrick	.03	.01	.00
726	Frank Tanana	.06	.02	.00

		MINT	EXC	G-VG
☐ 727	Mike Moore	.06	.02	.00
☐ 728	Tippy Martinez	.03	.01	.00
☐ 729	Tom Paciorek	.03	.01	.00
☐ 730	Eric Show	.03	.01	.00
☐ 731	Dave Concepcion	.08	.03	.01
☐ 732	Manny Trillo	.03	.01	.00
☐ 733	Bill Caudill	.03	.01	.00
☐ 734	Bill Madlock	.08	.03	.01
☐ 735	Rickey Henderson	.50	.20	.05
☐ 736	Steve Bedrosian	.06	.02	.00
☐ 737	Floyd Bannister	.03	.01	.00
☐ 738	Jorge Orta	.03	.01	.00
☐ 739	Chet Lemon	.03	.01	.00
☐ 740	Rich Gedman	.03	.01	.00
☐ 741	Paul Molitor	.12	.05	.01
☐ 742	Andy McGaffigan	.03	.01	.00
☐ 743	Dwayne Murphy	.03	.01	.00
☐ 744	Roy Smalley	.03	.01	.00
☐ 745	Glenn Hubbard	.03	.01	.00
☐ 746	Bob Ojeda	.03	.01	.00
☐ 747	Johnny Ray	.03	.01	.00
☐ 748	Mike Flanagan	.06	.02	.00
☐ 749	Ozzie Smith	.20	.08	.02
☐ 750	Steve Trout	.03	.01	.00
☐ 751	Garth Iorg	.03	.01	.00
☐ 752	Dan Petry	.03	.01	.00
☐ 753	Rick Honeycutt	.03	.01	.00
☐ 754	Dave LaPoint	.03	.01	.00
☐ 755	Luis Aguayo	.03	.01	.00
☐ 756	Carlton Fisk	.25	.10	.02
☐ 757	Nolan Ryan	1.00	.40	.10
☐ 758	Tony Bernazard	.03	.01	.00
☐ 759	Joel Youngblood	.03	.01	.00
☐ 760	Mike Witt	.03	.01	.00
☐ 761	Greg Pryor	.03	.01	.00
☐ 762	Gary Ward	.03	.01	.00
☐ 763	Tim Flannery	.03	.01	.00
☐ 764	Bill Buckner	.06	.02	.00
☐ 765	Kirk Gibson	.12	.05	.01
☐ 766	Don Aase	.03	.01	.00
☐ 767	Ron Cey	.06	.02	.00
☐ 768	Dennis Lamp	.03	.01	.00
☐ 769	Steve Sax	.12	.05	.01
☐ 770	Dave Winfield	.20	.08	.02
☐ 771	Shane Rawley	.03	.01	.00
☐ 772	Harold Baines	.12	.05	.01
☐ 773	Robin Yount	.30	.12	.03
☐ 774	Wayne Krenchicki	.03	.01	.00
☐ 775	Joaquin Andujar	.03	.01	.00
☐ 776	Tom Brunansky	.08	.03	.01
☐ 777	Chris Chambliss	.06	.02	.00
☐ 778	Jack Morris	.15	.06	.01
☐ 779	Craig Reynolds	.03	.01	.00
☐ 780	Andre Thornton	.03	.01	.00
☐ 781	Atlee Hammaker	.03	.01	.00
☐ 782	Brian Downing	.06	.02	.00
☐ 783	Willie Wilson	.08	.03	.01
☐ 784	Cal Ripken	.90	.40	.09
☐ 785	Terry Francona	.03	.01	.00
☐ 786	Jimy Williams MG (checklist back)	.06	.02	.00
☐ 787	Alejandro Pena	.08	.03	.01
☐ 788	Tim Stoddard	.03	.01	.00
☐ 789	Dan Schatzeder	.03	.01	.00
☐ 790	Julio Cruz	.03	.01	.00
☐ 791	Lance Parrish UER (no trademark, never corrected)	.15	.06	.01
☐ 792	Checklist 661-792	.10	.01	.00

1987 Topps Wax Box Cards

This set of eight cards is really four different sets of two smaller (approximately 2 1/8" by 3") cards which were printed on the side of the wax pack box; these eight cards are lettered A through H and are very similar in design to the Topps regular issue cards. Complete boxes would be worth an additional 25 percent premium over the prices below. The card backs are done in a newspaper headline style describing something about that player that happened the previous season. The card backs feature blue and yellow ink on gray card stock.

		MINT	EXC	G-VG
COMPLETE SET (8)		2.00	.80	.20
COMMON PLAYER (A-H)		.10	.04	.01
☐ A	Don Baylor	.15	.06	.01
☐ B	Steve Carlton	.40	.16	.04
☐ C	Ron Cey	.10	.04	.01
☐ D	Cecil Cooper	.10	.04	.01
☐ E	Rickey Henderson	1.00	.40	.10
☐ F	Jim Rice	.20	.08	.02
☐ G	Don Sutton	.25	.10	.02
☐ H	Dave Winfield	.50	.20	.05

1987 Topps All-Star Glossy 22

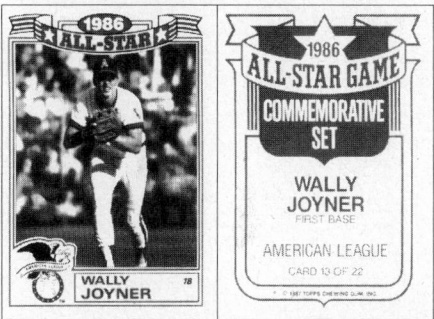

This set of 22 glossy cards was inserted one per rack pack. Players selected for the set are the starting players (plus manager and two pitchers) in the 1986 All-Star Game in Houston. Cards measure standard size, 2 1/2" by 3 1/2" and the backs feature red and blue printing on a white card stock.

		MINT	EXC	G-VG
COMPLETE SET (22)		3.00	1.25	.30
COMMON PLAYER (1-22)		.10	.04	.01
☐ 1	Whitey Herzog MG	.10	.04	.01
☐ 2	Keith Hernandez	.15	.06	.01
☐ 3	Ryne Sandberg	.50	.20	.05
☐ 4	Mike Schmidt	.50	.20	.05
☐ 5	Ozzie Smith	.30	.12	.03
☐ 6	Tony Gwynn	.35	.15	.03
☐ 7	Dale Murphy	.35	.15	.03
☐ 8	Darryl Strawberry	.40	.16	.04
☐ 9	Gary Carter	.20	.08	.02
☐ 10	Dwight Gooden	.25	.10	.02
☐ 11	Fernando Valenzuela	.15	.06	.01
☐ 12	Dick Howser MG	.10	.04	.01
☐ 13	Wally Joyner	.35	.15	.03
☐ 14	Lou Whitaker	.15	.06	.01
☐ 15	Wade Boggs	.45	.18	.04
☐ 16	Cal Ripken	.50	.20	.05
☐ 17	Dave Winfield	.30	.12	.03
☐ 18	Rickey Henderson	.50	.20	.05
☐ 19	Kirby Puckett	.40	.16	.04

		MINT	EXC	G-VG
☐ 20	Lance Parrish	.15	.06	.01
☐ 21	Roger Clemens	.50	.20	.05
☐ 22	Teddy Higuera	.15	.06	.01

1987 Topps Jumbo Rookies

Inserted in each supermarket jumbo pack is a card from this series of 22 of 1986's best rookies as determined by Topps. Jumbo packs consisted of 100 (regular issue 1987 Topps baseball) cards with a stick of gum plus the insert "Rookie" card. The card fronts are in full color and measure 2 1/2" by 3 1/2". The card backs are printed in red and blue on white card stock and are numbered at the bottom essentially by alphabetical order.

		MINT	EXC	G-VG
COMPLETE SET (22)		12.50	5.50	1.65
COMMON PLAYER (1-22)		.25	.10	.02
☐ 1	Andy Allanson	.25	.10	.02
☐ 2	John Cangelosi	.25	.10	.02
☐ 3	Jose Canseco	3.00	1.25	.30
☐ 4	Will Clark	3.00	1.25	.30
☐ 5	Mark Eichhorn	.35	.15	.03
☐ 6	Pete Incaviglia	.50	.20	.05
☐ 7	Wally Joyner	1.00	.40	.10
☐ 8	Eric King	.25	.10	.02
☐ 9	Dave Magadan	.50	.20	.05
☐ 10	John Morris	.25	.10	.02
☐ 11	Juan Nieves	.25	.10	.02
☐ 12	Rafael Palmeiro	1.00	.40	.10
☐ 13	Billy Jo Robidoux	.25	.10	.02
☐ 14	Bruce Ruffin	.25	.10	.02
☐ 15	Ruben Sierra	2.00	.80	.20
☐ 16	Cory Snyder	.35	.15	.03
☐ 17	Kurt Stillwell	.35	.15	.03
☐ 18	Dale Sveum	.25	.10	.02
☐ 19	Danny Tartabull	1.00	.40	.10
☐ 20	Andres Thomas	.25	.10	.02
☐ 21	Robby Thompson	.25	.10	.02
☐ 22	Todd Worrell	.35	.15	.03

1987 Topps Glossy 60

Topps issued this set through a mail-in offer explained and advertised on the wax packs. This 60-card set features glossy fronts with each card measuring 2 1/2" by 3 1/2". The offer provided your choice of any one of the six 10-card subsets (1-10, 11-20, etc.) for 1.00 plus six of the Special Offer ("Spring Fever Baseball") insert cards, which were found one per wax pack. The last two players (numerically) in each ten-card subset are actually "Hot Prospects."

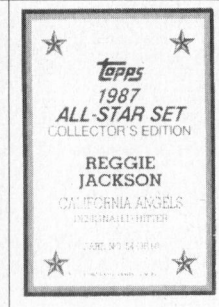

		MINT	EXC	G-VG
COMPLETE SET (60)		12.00	5.25	1.50
COMMON PLAYER (1-60)		.20	.08	.02
☐ 1	Don Mattingly	.75	.30	.07
☐ 2	Tony Gwynn	.60	.25	.06
☐ 3	Gary Gaetti	.25	.10	.02
☐ 4	Glenn Davis	.30	.12	.03
☐ 5	Roger Clemens	.75	.30	.07
☐ 6	Dale Murphy	.50	.20	.05
☐ 7	Lou Whitaker	.25	.10	.02
☐ 8	Roger McDowell	.20	.08	.02
☐ 9	Cory Snyder	.25	.10	.02
☐ 10	Todd Worrell	.25	.10	.02
☐ 11	Gary Carter	.30	.12	.03
☐ 12	Eddie Murray	.50	.20	.05
☐ 13	Bob Knepper	.20	.08	.02
☐ 14	Harold Baines	.25	.10	.02
☐ 15	Jeff Reardon	.30	.12	.03
☐ 16	Joe Carter	.35	.15	.03
☐ 17	Dave Parker	.25	.10	.02
☐ 18	Wade Boggs	.60	.25	.06
☐ 19	Danny Tartabull	.45	.18	.04
☐ 20	Jim Deshaies	.20	.08	.02
☐ 21	Rickey Henderson	.75	.30	.07
☐ 22	Rob Deer	.25	.10	.02
☐ 23	Ozzie Smith	.35	.15	.03
☐ 24	Dave Righetti	.25	.10	.02
☐ 25	Kent Hrbek	.25	.10	.02
☐ 26	Keith Hernandez	.25	.10	.02
☐ 27	Don Baylor	.25	.10	.02
☐ 28	Mike Schmidt	.75	.30	.07
☐ 29	Pete Incaviglia	.35	.15	.03
☐ 30	Barry Bonds	.60	.25	.06
☐ 31	George Brett	.60	.25	.06
☐ 32	Darryl Strawberry	.75	.30	.07
☐ 33	Mike Witt	.20	.08	.02
☐ 34	Kevin Bass	.20	.08	.02
☐ 35	Jesse Barfield	.25	.10	.02
☐ 36	Bob Ojeda	.20	.08	.02
☐ 37	Cal Ripken	.75	.30	.07
☐ 38	Vince Coleman	.35	.15	.03
☐ 39	Wally Joyner	.50	.20	.05
☐ 40	Robby Thompson	.20	.08	.02
☐ 41	Pete Rose	.75	.30	.07
☐ 42	Jim Rice	.25	.10	.02
☐ 43	Tony Bernazard	.20	.08	.02
☐ 44	Eric Davis	.50	.20	.05
☐ 45	George Bell	.35	.15	.03
☐ 46	Hubie Brooks	.25	.10	.02
☐ 47	Jack Morris	.35	.15	.03
☐ 48	Tim Raines	.35	.15	.03
☐ 49	Mark Eichhorn	.20	.08	.02
☐ 50	Kevin Mitchell	.60	.25	.06
☐ 51	Dwight Gooden	.45	.18	.04
☐ 52	Doug DeCinces	.20	.08	.02
☐ 53	Fernando Valenzuela	.25	.10	.02
☐ 54	Reggie Jackson	.50	.20	.05
☐ 55	Johnny Ray	.20	.08	.02
☐ 56	Mike Pagliarulo	.20	.08	.02
☐ 57	Kirby Puckett	.60	.25	.06
☐ 58	Lance Parrish	.30	.12	.03
☐ 59	Jose Canseco	1.25	.50	.12
☐ 60	Greg Mathews	.20	.08	.02

1987 Topps Mini Leaders

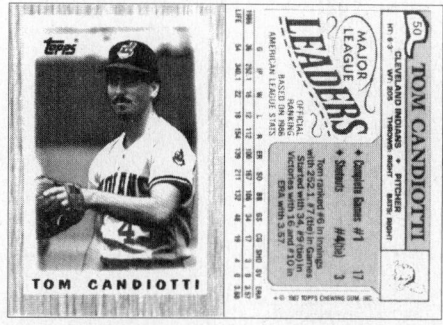

The 1987 Topps Mini set of Major League Leaders features 77 cards of leaders of the various statistical categories for the 1986 season. The cards are numbered on the back and measure approximately 2 5/32" by 3". The card backs are printed in orange and brown on white card stock. They are very similar in design to the Team Leader cards in the 1987 Topps regular issue. The cards were distributed as a separate issue in wax packs of seven for 30 cents. Eleven of the cards were double printed and are hence more plentiful; they are marked DP in the checklist below.

	MINT	EXC	G-VG
COMPLETE SET (77)	7.00	3.00	.70
COMMON PLAYER (1-77)	.06	.02	.00
COMMON PLAYER DP	.03	.01	.00
☐ 1 Bob Horner DP	.06	.02	.00
☐ 2 Dale Murphy	.30	.12	.03
☐ 3 Lee Smith	.10	.04	.01
☐ 4 Eric Davis	.40	.16	.04
☐ 5 John Franco	.06	.02	.00
☐ 6 Dave Parker	.10	.04	.01
☐ 7 Kevin Bass	.06	.02	.00
☐ 8 Glenn Davis DP	.10	.04	.01
☐ 9 Bill Doran DP	.06	.02	.00
☐ 10 Bob Knepper DP	.03	.01	.00
☐ 11 Mike Scott	.10	.04	.01
☐ 12 Dave Smith	.06	.02	.00
☐ 13 Mariano Duncan	.06	.02	.00
☐ 14 Orel Hershiser	.25	.10	.02
☐ 15 Steve Sax DP	.10	.04	.01
☐ 16 Fernando Valenzuela	.10	.04	.01
☐ 17 Tim Raines	.20	.08	.02
☐ 18 Jeff Reardon	.10	.04	.01
☐ 19 Floyd Youmans	.06	.02	.00
☐ 20 Gary Carter DP	.10	.04	.01
☐ 21 Ron Darling	.10	.04	.01
☐ 22 Sid Fernandez	.10	.04	.01
☐ 23 Dwight Gooden	.30	.12	.03
☐ 24 Keith Hernandez	.15	.06	.01
☐ 25 Bob Ojeda	.06	.02	.00
☐ 26 Darryl Strawberry	.50	.20	.05
☐ 27 Steve Bedrosian	.06	.02	.00
☐ 28 Von Hayes DP	.06	.02	.00
☐ 29 Juan Samuel	.10	.04	.01
☐ 30 Mike Schmidt	.60	.25	.06
☐ 31 Rick Rhoden	.06	.02	.00
☐ 32 Vince Coleman	.20	.08	.02
☐ 33 Danny Cox	.06	.02	.00
☐ 34 Todd Worrell	.10	.04	.01
☐ 35 Tony Gwynn	.40	.16	.04
☐ 36 Mike Krukow	.06	.02	.00
☐ 37 Candy Maldonado	.10	.04	.01
☐ 38 Don Aase	.06	.02	.00
☐ 39 Eddie Murray	.35	.15	.03
☐ 40 Cal Ripken	.60	.25	.06
☐ 41 Wade Boggs	.50	.20	.05
☐ 42 Roger Clemens	.60	.25	.06
☐ 43 Bruce Hurst	.10	.04	.01
☐ 44 Jim Rice	.15	.06	.01
☐ 45 Wally Joyner	.25	.10	.02
☐ 46 Donnie Moore	.06	.02	.00
☐ 47 Gary Pettis	.06	.02	.00
☐ 48 Mike Witt	.06	.02	.00
☐ 49 John Cangelosi	.06	.02	.00
☐ 50 Tom Candiotti	.10	.04	.01
☐ 51 Joe Carter	.20	.08	.02
☐ 52 Pat Tabler	.06	.02	.00
☐ 53 Kirk Gibson DP	.10	.04	.01
☐ 54 Willie Hernandez	.06	.02	.00
☐ 55 Jack Morris	.15	.06	.01
☐ 56 Alan Trammell DP	.10	.04	.01
☐ 57 George Brett	.45	.18	.04
☐ 58 Willie Wilson	.10	.04	.01
☐ 59 Rob Deer	.10	.04	.01
☐ 60 Teddy Higuera	.10	.04	.01
☐ 61 Bert Blyleven DP	.06	.02	.00
☐ 62 Gary Gaetti DP	.06	.02	.00
☐ 63 Kirby Puckett	.40	.16	.04
☐ 64 Rickey Henderson	.60	.25	.06
☐ 65 Don Mattingly	.60	.25	.06
☐ 66 Dennis Rasmussen	.10	.04	.01
☐ 67 Dave Righetti	.10	.04	.01
☐ 68 Jose Canseco	.90	.40	.09
☐ 69 Dave Kingman	.10	.04	.01
☐ 70 Phil Bradley	.06	.02	.00
☐ 71 Mark Langston	.15	.06	.01
☐ 72 Pete O'Brien	.06	.02	.00
☐ 73 Jesse Barfield	.10	.04	.01
☐ 74 George Bell	.20	.08	.02
☐ 75 Tony Fernandez	.10	.04	.01
☐ 76 Tom Henke	.10	.04	.01
☐ 77 Checklist Card	.06	.02	.00

1987 Topps Traded

This 132-card Traded or extended set was distributed by Topps to dealers in a special green and white box as a complete set. The card fronts are identical in style to the Topps regular issue and are also 2 1/2" by 3 1/2". The backs are printed in yellow and blue on white card stock. Cards are numbered (with a T suffix) alphabetically according to the name of the player. The key (extended) rookies in this set (without any prior cards) are Ellis Burks and Matt Williams. Topps also produced a specially boxed "glossy" edition, frequently referred to as the Topps Traded Tiffany set. This year Topps did not disclose the number of sets they produced or sold. It is apparent from the availability that there were many more sets produced this year compared to the 1984-86 Tiffany sets, perhaps 30,000 sets, more than three times as many. The checklist of cards is identical to that of the normal non-glossy cards. There are two primary distinguishing features of the Tiffany cards, white card stock reverses and high gloss obverses. These Tiffany cards are valued at approximately three times the values listed below.

	MINT	EXC	G-VG
COMPLETE SET (132)	10.00	4.50	1.25
COMMON PLAYER (1-132)	.05	.02	.00
☐ 1T Bill Almon	.10	.03	.01
☐ 2T Scott Bankhead	.10	.04	.01
☐ 3T Eric Bell	.10	.04	.01
☐ 4T Juan Beniquez	.05	.02	.00
☐ 5T Juan Berenguer	.05	.02	.00
☐ 6T Greg Booker	.05	.02	.00
☐ 7T Thad Bosley	.05	.02	.00
☐ 8T Larry Bowa MG	.10	.04	.01

☐ 9T	Greg Brock	.05	.02	.00
☐ 10T	Bob Brower	.05	.02	.00
☐ 11T	Jerry Browne	.12	.05	.01
☐ 12T	Ralph Bryant	.10	.04	.01
☐ 13T	DeWayne Buice	.05	.02	.00
☐ 14T	Ellis Burks	1.50	.60	.15
☐ 15T	Ivan Calderon	.15	.06	.01
☐ 16T	Jeff Calhoun	.05	.02	.00
☐ 17T	Casey Candaele	.10	.04	.01
☐ 18T	John Cangelosi	.05	.02	.00
☐ 19T	Steve Carlton	.20	.08	.02
☐ 20T	Juan Castillo	.05	.02	.00
☐ 21T	Rick Cerone	.05	.02	.00
☐ 22T	Ron Cey	.10	.04	.01
☐ 23T	John Christensen	.05	.02	.00
☐ 24T	David Cone	1.00	.40	.10
☐ 25T	Chuck Crim	.10	.04	.01
☐ 26T	Storm Davis	.05	.02	.00
☐ 27T	Andre Dawson	.25	.10	.02
☐ 28T	Rick Dempsey	.05	.02	.00
☐ 29T	Doug Drabek	.35	.15	.03
☐ 30T	Mike Dunne	.10	.04	.01
☐ 31T	Dennis Eckersley	.20	.08	.02
☐ 32T	Lee Elia MG	.05	.02	.00
☐ 33T	Brian Fisher	.05	.02	.00
☐ 34T	Terry Francona	.05	.02	.00
☐ 35T	Willie Fraser	.05	.02	.00
☐ 36T	Billy Gardner MG	.05	.02	.00
☐ 37T	Ken Gerhart	.05	.02	.00
☐ 38T	Dan Gladden	.10	.04	.01
☐ 39T	Jim Gott	.10	.04	.01
☐ 40T	Cecilio Guante	.05	.02	.00
☐ 41T	Albert Hall	.05	.02	.00
☐ 42T	Terry Harper	.05	.02	.00
☐ 43T	Mickey Hatcher	.05	.02	.00
☐ 44T	Brad Havens	.05	.02	.00
☐ 45T	Neal Heaton	.05	.02	.00
☐ 46T	Mike Henneman	.25	.10	.02
☐ 47T	Donnie Hill	.05	.02	.00
☐ 48T	Guy Hoffman	.05	.02	.00
☐ 49T	Brian Holton	.10	.04	.01
☐ 50T	Charles Hudson	.05	.02	.00
☐ 51T	Danny Jackson	.10	.04	.01
☐ 52T	Reggie Jackson	.40	.16	.04
☐ 53T	Chris James	.15	.06	.01
☐ 54T	Dion James	.10	.04	.01
☐ 55T	Stan Jefferson	.10	.04	.01
☐ 56T	Joe Johnson	.05	.02	.00
☐ 57T	Terry Kennedy	.05	.02	.00
☐ 58T	Mike Kingery	.10	.04	.01
☐ 59T	Ray Knight	.10	.04	.01
☐ 60T	Gene Larkin	.15	.06	.01
☐ 61T	Mike LaValliere	.10	.04	.01
☐ 62T	Jack Lazorko	.05	.02	.00
☐ 63T	Terry Leach	.10	.04	.01
☐ 64T	Tim Leary	.15	.06	.01
☐ 65T	Jim Lindeman	.10	.04	.01
☐ 66T	Steve Lombardozzi	.10	.04	.01
☐ 67T	Bill Long	.10	.04	.01
☐ 68T	Barry Lyons	.10	.04	.01
☐ 69T	Shane Mack	.17	.07	.01
☐ 70T	Greg Maddux	.75	.30	.07
☐ 71T	Bill Madlock	.10	.04	.01
☐ 72T	Joe Magrane	.15	.06	.01
☐ 73T	Dave Martinez	.30	.12	.03
☐ 74T	Fred McGriff	2.00	.80	.20
☐ 75T	Mark McLemore	.05	.02	.00
☐ 76T	Kevin McReynolds	.20	.08	.02
☐ 77T	Dave Meads	.05	.02	.00
☐ 78T	Eddie Milner	.05	.02	.00
☐ 79T	Greg Minton	.05	.02	.00
☐ 80T	John Mitchell	.10	.04	.01
☐ 81T	Kevin Mitchell	1.00	.40	.10
☐ 82T	Charlie Moore	.05	.02	.00
☐ 83T	Jeff Musselman	.10	.04	.01
☐ 84T	Gene Nelson	.05	.02	.00
☐ 85T	Graig Nettles	.15	.06	.01
☐ 86T	Al Newman	.10	.04	.01
☐ 87T	Reid Nichols	.05	.02	.00
☐ 88T	Tom Niedenfuer	.05	.02	.00
☐ 89T	Joe Niekro	.10	.04	.01
☐ 90T	Tom Nieto	.05	.02	.00
☐ 91T	Matt Nokes	.50	.20	.05
☐ 92T	Dickie Noles	.05	.02	.00
☐ 93T	Pat Pacillo	.10	.04	.01
☐ 94T	Lance Parrish	.15	.06	.01
☐ 95T	Tony Pena	.15	.06	.01
☐ 96T	Luis Polonia	.45	.18	.04
☐ 97T	Randy Ready	.12	.05	.01
☐ 98T	Jeff Reardon	.20	.08	.02
☐ 99T	Gary Redus	.05	.02	.00
☐ 100T	Jeff Reed	.05	.02	.00
☐ 101T	Rick Rhoden	.05	.02	.00
☐ 102T	Cal Ripken Sr. MG	.10	.04	.01
☐ 103T	Wally Ritchie	.10	.04	.01

☐ 104T	Jeff Robinson (Tigers pitcher)	.10	.04	.01
☐ 105T	Gary Roenicke	.05	.02	.00
☐ 106T	Jerry Royster	.05	.02	.00
☐ 107T	Mark Salas	.05	.02	.00
☐ 108T	Luis Salazar	.05	.02	.00
☐ 109T	Benny Santiago	.50	.20	.05
☐ 110T	Dave Schmidt	.10	.04	.01
☐ 111T	Kevin Seitzer	.17	.07	.01
☐ 112T	John Shelby	.05	.02	.00
☐ 113T	Steve Shields	.05	.02	.00
☐ 114T	John Smiley	.75	.30	.07
☐ 115T	Chris Speier	.05	.02	.00
☐ 116T	Mike Stanley	.10	.04	.01
☐ 117T	Terry Steinbach	.35	.15	.03
☐ 118T	Les Straker	.10	.04	.01
☐ 119T	Jim Sundberg	.05	.02	.00
☐ 120T	Danny Tartabull	.25	.10	.02
☐ 121T	Tom Trebelhorn MG	.10	.04	.01
☐ 122T	Dave Valle	.05	.02	.00
☐ 123T	Ed VandeBerg	.05	.02	.00
☐ 124T	Andy Van Slyke	.17	.07	.01
☐ 125T	Gary Ward	.05	.02	.00
☐ 126T	Alan Wiggins	.05	.02	.00
☐ 127T	Bill Wilkinson	.10	.04	.01
☐ 128T	Frank Williams	.05	.02	.00
☐ 129T	Matt Williams	3.25	1.35	.32
☐ 130T	Jim Winn	.05	.02	.00
☐ 131T	Matt Young	.05	.02	.00
☐ 132T	Checklist 1T-132T	.05	.01	.00

1988 Topps

This 792-card set features backs that are printed in orange and black on white card stock. The manager cards contain a checklist of the respective team's players on the back. Subsets in the set include Record Breakers (1-7), Turn Back the Clock (661-665), and All-Star selections (386-407). The Team Leader cards typically show two players together inside a white cloud. The key rookie cards in this set are Ellis Burks, Tom Glavine, and Matt Williams. Topps also produced a specially boxed "glossy" edition, frequently referred to as the Topps Tiffany set. This year, again, Topps did not disclose the number of Tiffany sets they produced or sold. It is apparent from the availability that there were many more sets produced this year compared to the 1984-86 Tiffany sets, perhaps 25,000 sets. The checklist of cards (792 regular and 132 Traded) is identical to that of the normal non-glossy cards. There are two primary distinguishing features of the Tiffany cards; white card stock reverses and high gloss obverses. These Tiffany cards are valued at approximately four times the values listed below.

	MINT	EXC	G-VG
COMPLETE SET (792)	18.00	7.50	2.50
COMMON PLAYER (1-792)	.03	.01	.00
☐ 1 Vince Coleman RB 100 Steals for Third Cons. Season	.10	.04	.01
☐ 2 Don Mattingly RB Six Grand Slams	.12	.05	.01

	#	Player			
☐	3A	Mark McGwire RB	.20	.08	.02
		Rookie Homer Record (white spot behind left foot)			
☐	3B	Mark McGwire RB	.10	.04	.01
		Rookie Homer Record (no white spot)			
☐	4A	Eddie Murray RB	.50	.20	.05
		Switch Home Runs, Two Straight Games (caption in box on card front)			
☐	4B	Eddie Murray RB	.10	.04	.01
		Switch Home Runs, Two Straight Games (no caption on front)			
☐	5	Phil/Joe Niekro RB	.06	.02	.00
		Brothers Win Record			
☐	6	Nolan Ryan RB	.25	.10	.02
		11th Season with 200 Strikeouts			
☐	7	Benito Santiago RB	.06	.02	.00
		34-Game Hitting Streak, Rookie Record			
☐	8	Kevin Elster	.06	.02	.00
☐	9	Andy Hawkins	.03	.01	.00
☐	10	Ryne Sandberg	.40	.16	.04
☐	11	Mike Young	.03	.01	.00
☐	12	Bill Schroeder	.03	.01	.00
☐	13	Andres Thomas	.03	.01	.00
☐	14	Sparky Anderson MG	.06	.02	.00
		(checklist back)			
☐	15	Chili Davis	.06	.02	.00
☐	16	Kirk McCaskill	.03	.01	.00
☐	17	Ron Oester	.03	.01	.00
☐	18A	Al Leiter ERR	.20	.08	.02
		(photo actually Steve George, right ear visible)			
☐	18B	Al Leiter COR	.10	.04	.01
		(left ear visible)			
☐	19	Mark Davidson	.06	.02	.00
☐	20	Kevin Gross	.03	.01	.00
☐	21	Red Sox TL	.08	.03	.01
		Wade Boggs and Spike Owen			
☐	22	Greg Swindell	.08	.03	.01
☐	23	Ken Landreaux	.03	.01	.00
☐	24	Jim Deshaies	.03	.01	.00
☐	25	Andres Galarraga	.08	.03	.01
☐	26	Mitch Williams	.06	.02	.00
☐	27	R.J. Reynolds	.03	.01	.00
☐	28	Jose Nunez	.06	.02	.00
☐	29	Argenis Salazar	.03	.01	.00
☐	30	Sid Fernandez	.08	.03	.01
☐	31	Bruce Bochy	.03	.01	.00
☐	32	Mike Morgan	.03	.01	.00
☐	33	Rob Deer	.06	.02	.00
☐	34	Ricky Horton	.03	.01	.00
☐	35	Harold Baines	.08	.03	.01
☐	36	Jamie Moyer	.03	.01	.00
☐	37	Ed Romero	.03	.01	.00
☐	38	Jeff Calhoun	.03	.01	.00
☐	39	Gerald Perry	.03	.01	.00
☐	40	Orel Hershiser	.10	.04	.01
☐	41	Bob Melvin	.03	.01	.00
☐	42	Bill Landrum	.10	.04	.01
☐	43	Dick Schofield	.03	.01	.00
☐	44	Lou Piniella MG	.06	.02	.00
		(checklist back)			
☐	45	Kent Hrbek	.10	.04	.01
☐	46	Darnell Coles	.03	.01	.00
☐	47	Joaquin Andujar	.03	.01	.00
☐	48	Alan Ashby	.03	.01	.00
☐	49	Dave Clark	.03	.01	.00
☐	50	Hubie Brooks	.06	.02	.00
☐	51	Orioles TL	.20	.08	.02
		Eddie Murray and Cal Ripken			
☐	52	Don Robinson	.03	.01	.00
☐	53	Curt Wilkerson	.03	.01	.00
☐	54	Jim Clancy	.03	.01	.00
☐	55	Phil Bradley	.03	.01	.00
☐	56	Ed Hearn	.03	.01	.00
☐	57	Tim Crews	.06	.02	.00
☐	58	Dave Magadan	.08	.03	.01
☐	59	Danny Cox	.03	.01	.00
☐	60	Rickey Henderson	.30	.12	.03
☐	61	Mark Knudson	.06	.02	.00
☐	62	Jeff Hamilton	.03	.01	.00
☐	63	Jimmy Jones	.06	.02	.00
☐	64	Ken Caminiti	.17	.07	.01
☐	65	Leon Durham	.03	.01	.00
☐	66	Shane Rawley	.03	.01	.00
☐	67	Ken Oberkfell	.03	.01	.00
☐	68	Dave Dravecky	.08	.03	.01
☐	69	Mike Hart	.03	.01	.00
☐	70	Roger Clemens	.35	.15	.03
☐	71	Gary Pettis	.03	.01	.00
☐	72	Dennis Eckersley	.10	.04	.01
☐	73	Randy Bush	.03	.01	.00
☐	74	Tom Lasorda MG	.08	.03	.01
		(checklist back)			
☐	75	Joe Carter	.17	.07	.01
☐	76	Dennis Martinez	.06	.02	.00
☐	77	Tom O'Malley	.03	.01	.00
☐	78	Dan Petry	.03	.01	.00
☐	79	Ernie Whitt	.03	.01	.00
☐	80	Mark Langston	.08	.03	.01
☐	81	Reds TL	.03	.01	.00
		Ron Robinson and John Franco			
☐	82	Darrel Akerfelds	.03	.01	.00
☐	83	Jose Oquendo	.03	.01	.00
☐	84	Cecilio Guante	.03	.01	.00
☐	85	Howard Johnson	.15	.06	.01
☐	86	Ron Karkovice	.03	.01	.00
☐	87	Mike Mason	.03	.01	.00
☐	88	Earnie Riles	.03	.01	.00
☐	89	Gary Thurman	.08	.03	.01
☐	90	Dale Murphy	.15	.06	.01
☐	91	Joey Cora	.06	.02	.00
☐	92	Len Matuszek	.03	.01	.00
☐	93	Bob Sebra	.03	.01	.00
☐	94	Chuck Jackson	.06	.02	.00
☐	95	Lance Parrish	.08	.03	.01
☐	96	Todd Benzinger	.17	.07	.01
☐	97	Scott Garrelts	.03	.01	.00
☐	98	Rene Gonzales	.03	.01	.00
☐	99	Chuck Finley	.12	.05	.01
☐	100	Jack Clark	.08	.03	.01
☐	101	Allan Anderson	.03	.01	.00
☐	102	Barry Larkin	.20	.08	.02
☐	103	Curt Young	.03	.01	.00
☐	104	Dick Williams MG	.06	.02	.00
		(checklist back)			
☐	105	Jesse Orosco	.03	.01	.00
☐	106	Jim Walewander	.03	.01	.00
☐	107	Scott Bailes	.03	.01	.00
☐	108	Steve Lyons	.03	.01	.00
☐	109	Joel Skinner	.03	.01	.00
☐	110	Teddy Higuera	.06	.02	.00
☐	111	Expos TL	.03	.01	.00
		Hubie Brooks and Vance Law			
☐	112	Les Lancaster	.08	.03	.01
☐	113	Kelly Gruber	.15	.06	.01
☐	114	Jeff Russell	.03	.01	.00
☐	115	Johnny Ray	.03	.01	.00
☐	116	Jerry Don Gleaton	.03	.01	.00
☐	117	James Steels	.03	.01	.00
☐	118	Bob Welch	.08	.03	.01
☐	119	Robbie Wine	.03	.01	.00
☐	120	Kirby Puckett	.30	.12	.03
☐	121	Checklist 1-132	.06	.01	.00
☐	122	Tony Bernazard	.03	.01	.00
☐	123	Tom Candiotti	.06	.02	.00
☐	124	Ray Knight	.06	.02	.00
☐	125	Bruce Hurst	.06	.02	.00
☐	126	Steve Jeltz	.03	.01	.00
☐	127	Jim Gott	.03	.01	.00
☐	128	Johnny Grubb	.03	.01	.00
☐	129	Greg Minton	.03	.01	.00
☐	130	Buddy Bell	.06	.02	.00
☐	131	Don Schulze	.03	.01	.00
☐	132	Donnie Hill	.03	.01	.00
☐	133	Greg Mathews	.03	.01	.00
☐	134	Chuck Tanner MG	.06	.02	.00
		(checklist back)			
☐	135	Dennis Rasmussen	.03	.01	.00
☐	136	Brian Dayett	.03	.01	.00
☐	137	Chris Bosio	.03	.01	.00
☐	138	Mitch Webster	.03	.01	.00
☐	139	Jerry Browne	.06	.02	.00
☐	140	Jesse Barfield	.08	.03	.01
☐	141	Royals TL	.15	.06	.01
		George Brett and Bret Saberhagen			
☐	142	Andy Van Slyke	.10	.04	.01
☐	143	Mickey Tettleton	.06	.02	.00
☐	144	Don Gordon	.03	.01	.00
☐	145	Bill Madlock	.06	.02	.00
☐	146	Donnell Nixon	.06	.02	.00
☐	147	Bill Buckner	.06	.02	.00
☐	148	Carmelo Martinez	.03	.01	.00
☐	149	Ken Howell	.03	.01	.00
☐	150	Eric Davis	.15	.06	.01
☐	151	Bob Knepper	.03	.01	.00
☐	152	Jody Reed	.25	.10	.02
☐	153	John Habyan	.03	.01	.00

☐ 154	Jeff Stone	.03	.01	.00
☐ 155	Bruce Sutter	.08	.03	.01
☐ 156	Gary Matthews	.03	.01	.00
☐ 157	Atlee Hammaker	.03	.01	.00
☐ 158	Tim Hulett	.03	.01	.00
☐ 159	Brad Arnsberg	.08	.03	.01
☐ 160	Willie McGee	.08	.03	.01
☐ 161	Bryn Smith	.03	.01	.00
☐ 162	Mark McLemore	.03	.01	.00
☐ 163	Dale Mohorcic	.03	.01	.00
☐ 164	Dave Johnson MG	.06	.02	.00
	(checklist back)			
☐ 165	Robin Yount	.20	.08	.02
☐ 166	Rick Rodriquez	.06	.02	.00
☐ 167	Rance Mulliniks	.03	.01	.00
☐ 168	Barry Jones	.03	.01	.00
☐ 169	Ross Jones	.03	.01	.00
☐ 170	Rich Gossage	.08	.03	.01
☐ 171	Cubs TL	.06	.02	.00
	Shawon Dunston			
	and Manny Trillo			
☐ 172	Lloyd McClendon	.06	.02	.00
☐ 173	Eric Plunk	.03	.01	.00
☐ 174	Phil Garner	.06	.02	.00
☐ 175	Kevin Bass	.03	.01	.00
☐ 176	Jeff Reed	.03	.01	.00
☐ 177	Frank Tanana	.06	.02	.00
☐ 178	Dwayne Henry	.06	.02	.00
☐ 179	Charlie Puleo	.03	.01	.00
☐ 180	Terry Kennedy	.03	.01	.00
☐ 181	David Cone	.20	.08	.02
☐ 182	Ken Phelps	.03	.01	.00
☐ 183	Tom Lawless	.03	.01	.00
☐ 184	Ivan Calderon	.08	.03	.01
☐ 185	Rick Rhoden	.03	.01	.00
☐ 186	Rafael Palmeiro	.30	.12	.03
☐ 187	Steve Kiefer	.03	.01	.00
☐ 188	John Russell	.03	.01	.00
☐ 189	Wes Gardner	.06	.02	.00
☐ 190	Candy Maldonado	.06	.02	.00
☐ 191	John Cerutti	.03	.01	.00
☐ 192	Devon White	.10	.04	.01
☐ 193	Brian Fisher	.03	.01	.00
☐ 194	Tom Kelly MG	.06	.02	.00
	(checklist back)			
☐ 195	Dan Quisenberry	.08	.03	.01
☐ 196	Dave Engle	.03	.01	.00
☐ 197	Lance McCullers	.03	.01	.00
☐ 198	Franklin Stubbs	.03	.01	.00
☐ 199	Dave Meads	.03	.01	.00
☐ 200	Wade Boggs	.30	.12	.03
☐ 201	Rangers TL	.06	.02	.00
	Bobby Valentine,			
	Pete O'Brien,			
	Pete Incaviglia, and			
	Steve Buechele			
☐ 202	Glenn Hoffman	.03	.01	.00
☐ 203	Fred Toliver	.03	.01	.00
☐ 204	Paul O'Neill	.12	.05	.01
☐ 205	Nelson Liriano	.08	.03	.01
☐ 206	Domingo Ramos	.03	.01	.00
☐ 207	John Mitchell	.06	.02	.00
☐ 208	Steve Lake	.03	.01	.00
☐ 209	Richard Dotson	.03	.01	.00
☐ 210	Willie Randolph	.06	.02	.00
☐ 211	Frank DiPino	.03	.01	.00
☐ 212	Greg Brock	.03	.01	.00
☐ 213	Albert Hall	.03	.01	.00
☐ 214	Dave Schmidt	.03	.01	.00
☐ 215	Von Hayes	.06	.02	.00
☐ 216	Jerry Reuss	.03	.01	.00
☐ 217	Harry Spilman	.03	.01	.00
☐ 218	Dan Schatzeder	.03	.01	.00
☐ 219	Mike Stanley	.03	.01	.00
☐ 220	Tom Henke	.06	.02	.00
☐ 221	Rafael Belliard	.03	.01	.00
☐ 222	Steve Farr	.03	.01	.00
☐ 223	Stan Jefferson	.03	.01	.00
☐ 224	Tom Trebelhorn MG	.06	.02	.00
	(checklist back)			
☐ 225	Mike Scioscia	.03	.01	.00
☐ 226	Dave Lopes	.06	.02	.00
☐ 227	Ed Correa	.03	.01	.00
☐ 228	Wallace Johnson	.03	.01	.00
☐ 229	Jeff Musselman	.03	.01	.00
☐ 230	Pat Tabler	.03	.01	.00
☐ 231	Pirates TL	.15	.06	.01
	Barry Bonds and			
	Bobby Bonilla			
☐ 232	Bob James	.03	.01	.00
☐ 233	Rafael Santana	.03	.01	.00
☐ 234	Ken Dayley	.03	.01	.00
☐ 235	Gary Ward	.03	.01	.00
☐ 236	Ted Power	.03	.01	.00
☐ 237	Mike Heath	.03	.01	.00
☐ 238	Luis Polonia	.25	.10	.02
☐ 239	Roy Smalley	.03	.01	.00
☐ 240	Lee Smith	.10	.04	.01
☐ 241	Damaso Garcia	.03	.01	.00
☐ 242	Tom Niedenfuer	.03	.01	.00
☐ 243	Mark Ryal	.03	.01	.00
☐ 244	Jeff D. Robinson	.06	.02	.00
	(Pirates pitcher)			
☐ 245	Rich Gedman	.03	.01	.00
☐ 246	Mike Campbell	.06	.02	.00
☐ 247	Thad Bosley	.03	.01	.00
☐ 248	Storm Davis	.03	.01	.00
☐ 249	Mike Marshall	.06	.02	.00
☐ 250	Nolan Ryan	.45	.18	.04
☐ 251	Tom Foley	.03	.01	.00
☐ 252	Bob Brower	.03	.01	.00
☐ 253	Checklist 133-264	.06	.01	.00
☐ 254	Lee Elia MG	.06	.02	.00
	(checklist back)			
☐ 255	Mookie Wilson	.03	.01	.00
☐ 256	Ken Schrom	.03	.01	.00
☐ 257	Jerry Royster	.03	.01	.00
☐ 258	Ed Nunez	.03	.01	.00
☐ 259	Ron Kittle	.06	.02	.00
☐ 260	Vince Coleman	.10	.04	.01
☐ 261	Giants TL	.03	.01	.00
	(five players)			
☐ 262	Drew Hall	.06	.02	.00
☐ 263	Glenn Braggs	.03	.01	.00
☐ 264	Les Straker	.03	.01	.00
☐ 265	Bo Diaz	.03	.01	.00
☐ 266	Paul Assenmacher	.03	.01	.00
☐ 267	Billy Bean	.06	.02	.00
☐ 268	Bruce Ruffin	.03	.01	.00
☐ 269	Ellis Burks	.60	.25	.06
☐ 270	Mike Witt	.03	.01	.00
☐ 271	Ken Gerhart	.03	.01	.00
☐ 272	Steve Ontiveros	.03	.01	.00
☐ 273	Garth Iorg	.03	.01	.00
☐ 274	Junior Ortiz	.03	.01	.00
☐ 275	Kevin Seitzer	.08	.03	.01
☐ 276	Luis Salazar	.03	.01	.00
☐ 277	Alejandro Pena	.06	.02	.00
☐ 278	Jose Cruz	.06	.02	.00
☐ 279	Randy St.Claire	.03	.01	.00
☐ 280	Pete Incaviglia	.08	.03	.01
☐ 281	Jerry Hairston	.03	.01	.00
☐ 282	Pat Perry	.03	.01	.00
☐ 283	Phil Lombardi	.06	.02	.00
☐ 284	Larry Bowa MG	.06	.02	.00
	(checklist back)			
☐ 285	Jim Presley	.03	.01	.00
☐ 286	Chuck Crim	.03	.01	.00
☐ 287	Manny Trillo	.03	.01	.00
☐ 288	Pat Pacillo	.06	.02	.00
	(Chris Sabo in			
	background of photo)			
☐ 289	Dave Bergman	.03	.01	.00
☐ 290	Tony Fernandez	.08	.03	.01
☐ 291	Astros TL	.06	.02	.00
	Billy Hatcher			
	and Kevin Bass			
☐ 292	Carney Lansford	.08	.03	.01
☐ 293	Doug Jones	.12	.05	.01
☐ 294	Al Pedrique	.03	.01	.00
☐ 295	Bert Blyleven	.08	.03	.01
☐ 296	Floyd Rayford	.03	.01	.00
☐ 297	Zane Smith	.06	.02	.00
☐ 298	Milt Thompson	.03	.01	.00
☐ 299	Steve Crawford	.03	.01	.00
☐ 300	Don Mattingly	.25	.10	.02
☐ 301	Bud Black	.03	.01	.00
☐ 302	Jose Uribe	.03	.01	.00
☐ 303	Eric Show	.03	.01	.00
☐ 304	George Hendrick	.03	.01	.00
☐ 305	Steve Sax	.10	.04	.01
☐ 306	Billy Hatcher	.06	.02	.00
☐ 307	Mike Trujillo	.03	.01	.00
☐ 308	Lee Mazzilli	.03	.01	.00
☐ 309	Bill Long	.06	.02	.00
☐ 310	Tom Herr	.03	.01	.00
☐ 311	Scott Sanderson	.06	.02	.00
☐ 312	Joey Meyer	.06	.02	.00
☐ 313	Bob McClure	.03	.01	.00
☐ 314	Jimy Williams MG	.06	.02	.00
	(checklist back)			
☐ 315	Dave Parker	.10	.04	.01
☐ 316	Jose Rijo	.08	.03	.01
☐ 317	Tom Nieto	.03	.01	.00
☐ 318	Mel Hall	.06	.02	.00
☐ 319	Mike Loynd	.03	.01	.00
☐ 320	Alan Trammell	.15	.06	.01
☐ 321	White Sox TL	.15	.06	.01
	Harold Baines and			
	Carlton Fisk			

#	Player			
☐ 322	Vicente Palacios	.10	.04	.01
☐ 323	Rick Leach	.03	.01	.00
☐ 324	Danny Jackson	.06	.02	.00
☐ 325	Glenn Hubbard	.03	.01	.00
☐ 326	Al Nipper	.03	.01	.00
☐ 327	Larry Sheets	.03	.01	.00
☐ 328	Greg Cadaret	.10	.04	.01
☐ 329	Chris Speier	.03	.01	.00
☐ 330	Eddie Whitson	.03	.01	.00
☐ 331	Brian Downing	.06	.02	.00
☐ 332	Jerry Reed	.03	.01	.00
☐ 333	Wally Backman	.03	.01	.00
☐ 334	Dave LaPoint	.03	.01	.00
☐ 335	Claudell Washington	.03	.01	.00
☐ 336	Ed Lynch	.03	.01	.00
☐ 337	Jim Gantner	.03	.01	.00
☐ 338	Brian Holton UER (1987 ERA .389, should be 3.89)	.08	.03	.01
☐ 339	Kurt Stillwell	.06	.02	.00
☐ 340	Jack Morris	.12	.05	.01
☐ 341	Carmen Castillo	.03	.01	.00
☐ 342	Larry Andersen	.03	.01	.00
☐ 343	Greg Gagne	.03	.01	.00
☐ 344	Tony LaRussa MG (checklist back)	.06	.02	.00
☐ 345	Scott Fletcher	.03	.01	.00
☐ 346	Vance Law	.03	.01	.00
☐ 347	Joe Johnson	.03	.01	.00
☐ 348	Jim Eisenreich	.03	.01	.00
☐ 349	Bob Walk	.03	.01	.00
☐ 350	Will Clark	.75	.30	.07
☐ 351	Cardinals TL Red Schoendienst and Tony Pena	.06	.02	.00
☐ 352	Billy Ripken	.12	.05	.01
☐ 353	Ed Olwine	.03	.01	.00
☐ 354	Marc Sullivan	.03	.01	.00
☐ 355	Roger McDowell	.03	.01	.00
☐ 356	Luis Aguayo	.03	.01	.00
☐ 357	Floyd Bannister	.03	.01	.00
☐ 358	Rey Quinones	.03	.01	.00
☐ 359	Tim Stoddard	.03	.01	.00
☐ 360	Tony Gwynn	.25	.10	.02
☐ 361	Greg Maddux	.20	.08	.02
☐ 362	Juan Castillo	.03	.01	.00
☐ 363	Willie Fraser	.03	.01	.00
☐ 364	Nick Esasky	.03	.01	.00
☐ 365	Floyd Youmans	.03	.01	.00
☐ 366	Chet Lemon	.03	.01	.00
☐ 367	Tim Leary	.06	.02	.00
☐ 368	Gerald Young	.08	.03	.01
☐ 369	Greg Harris	.03	.01	.00
☐ 370	Jose Canseco	.75	.30	.07
☐ 371	Joe Hesketh	.06	.02	.00
☐ 372	Matt Williams	1.50	.60	.15
☐ 373	Checklist 265-396	.06	.01	.00
☐ 374	Doc Edwards MG (checklist back)	.06	.02	.00
☐ 375	Tom Brunansky	.06	.02	.00
☐ 376	Bill Wilkinson	.06	.02	.00
☐ 377	Sam Horn	.12	.05	.01
☐ 378	Todd Frohwirth	.06	.02	.00
☐ 379	Rafael Ramirez	.03	.01	.00
☐ 380	Joe Magrane	.12	.05	.01
☐ 381	Angels TL Wally Joyner and Jack Howell	.10	.04	.01
☐ 382	Keith Miller (New York Mets)	.12	.05	.01
☐ 383	Eric Bell	.03	.01	.00
☐ 384	Neil Allen	.03	.01	.00
☐ 385	Carlton Fisk	.17	.07	.01
☐ 386	Don Mattingly AS	.12	.05	.01
☐ 387	Willie Randolph AS	.06	.02	.00
☐ 388	Wade Boggs AS	.15	.06	.01
☐ 389	Alan Trammell AS	.10	.04	.01
☐ 390	George Bell AS	.10	.04	.01
☐ 391	Kirby Puckett AS	.15	.06	.01
☐ 392	Dave Winfield AS	.10	.04	.01
☐ 393	Matt Nokes AS	.08	.03	.01
☐ 394	Roger Clemens AS	.17	.07	.01
☐ 395	Jimmy Key AS	.06	.02	.00
☐ 396	Tom Henke AS	.06	.02	.00
☐ 397	Jack Clark AS	.06	.02	.00
☐ 398	Juan Samuel AS	.06	.02	.00
☐ 399	Tim Wallach AS	.06	.02	.00
☐ 400	Ozzie Smith AS	.12	.05	.01
☐ 401	Andre Dawson AS	.12	.05	.01
☐ 402	Tony Gwynn AS	.15	.06	.01
☐ 403	Tim Raines AS	.08	.03	.01
☐ 404	Benny Santiago AS	.08	.03	.01
☐ 405	Dwight Gooden AS	.08	.03	.01
☐ 406	Shane Rawley AS	.06	.02	.00
☐ 407	Steve Bedrosian AS	.06	.02	.00
☐ 408	Dion James	.03	.01	.00
☐ 409	Joel McKeon	.03	.01	.00
☐ 410	Tony Pena	.06	.02	.00
☐ 411	Wayne Tolleson	.03	.01	.00
☐ 412	Randy Myers	.06	.02	.00
☐ 413	John Christensen	.03	.01	.00
☐ 414	John McNamara MG (checklist back)	.06	.02	.00
☐ 415	Don Carman	.03	.01	.00
☐ 416	Keith Moreland	.03	.01	.00
☐ 417	Mark Ciardi	.06	.02	.00
☐ 418	Joel Youngblood	.03	.01	.00
☐ 419	Scott McGregor	.03	.01	.00
☐ 420	Wally Joyner	.15	.06	.01
☐ 421	Ed VandeBerg	.03	.01	.00
☐ 422	Dave Concepcion	.06	.02	.00
☐ 423	John Smiley	.45	.18	.04
☐ 424	Dwayne Murphy	.03	.01	.00
☐ 425	Jeff Reardon	.10	.04	.01
☐ 426	Randy Ready	.03	.01	.00
☐ 427	Paul Kilgus	.06	.02	.00
☐ 428	John Shelby	.03	.01	.00
☐ 429	Tigers TL Alan Trammell and Kirk Gibson	.15	.06	.01
☐ 430	Glenn Davis	.08	.03	.01
☐ 431	Casey Candaele	.03	.01	.00
☐ 432	Mike Moore	.06	.02	.00
☐ 433	Bill Pecota	.08	.03	.01
☐ 434	Rick Aguilera	.06	.02	.00
☐ 435	Mike Pagliarulo	.03	.01	.00
☐ 436	Mike Bielecki	.06	.02	.00
☐ 437	Fred Manrique	.06	.02	.00
☐ 438	Rob Ducey	.10	.04	.01
☐ 439	Dave Martinez	.12	.05	.01
☐ 440	Steve Bedrosian	.06	.02	.00
☐ 441	Rick Manning	.03	.01	.00
☐ 442	Tom Bolton	.10	.04	.01
☐ 443	Ken Griffey	.10	.04	.01
☐ 444	Cal Ripken, Sr. MG (checklist back) UER (two copyrights)	.08	.03	.01
☐ 445	Mike Krukow	.03	.01	.00
☐ 446	Doug DeCinces	.06	.02	.00
☐ 447	Jeff Montgomery	.20	.08	.02
☐ 448	Mike Davis	.03	.01	.00
☐ 449	Jeff M. Robinson (Tigers pitcher)	.08	.03	.01
☐ 450	Barry Bonds	.35	.15	.03
☐ 451	Keith Atherton	.03	.01	.00
☐ 452	Willie Wilson	.06	.02	.00
☐ 453	Dennis Powell	.03	.01	.00
☐ 454	Marvell Wynne	.03	.01	.00
☐ 455	Shawn Hillegas	.08	.03	.01
☐ 456	Dave Anderson	.03	.01	.00
☐ 457	Terry Leach	.03	.01	.00
☐ 458	Ron Hassey	.03	.01	.00
☐ 459	Yankees TL Dave Winfield and Willie Randolph	.10	.04	.01
☐ 460	Ozzie Smith	.15	.06	.01
☐ 461	Danny Darwin	.03	.01	.00
☐ 462	Don Slaught	.03	.01	.00
☐ 463	Fred McGriff	.60	.25	.06
☐ 464	Jay Tibbs	.03	.01	.00
☐ 465	Paul Molitor	.10	.04	.01
☐ 466	Jerry Mumphrey	.03	.01	.00
☐ 467	Don Aase	.03	.01	.00
☐ 468	Darren Daulton	.06	.02	.00
☐ 469	Jeff Dedmon	.03	.01	.00
☐ 470	Dwight Evans	.08	.03	.01
☐ 471	Donnie Moore	.03	.01	.00
☐ 472	Robby Thompson	.03	.01	.00
☐ 473	Joe Niekro	.06	.02	.00
☐ 474	Tom Brookens	.03	.01	.00
☐ 475	Pete Rose MG (checklist back)	.20	.08	.02
☐ 476	Dave Stewart	.08	.03	.01
☐ 477	Jamie Quirk	.03	.01	.00
☐ 478	Sid Bream	.03	.01	.00
☐ 479	Brett Butler	.08	.03	.01
☐ 480	Dwight Gooden	.15	.06	.01
☐ 481	Mariano Duncan	.06	.02	.00
☐ 482	Mark Davis	.06	.02	.00
☐ 483	Rod Booker	.03	.01	.00
☐ 484	Pat Clements	.03	.01	.00
☐ 485	Harold Reynolds	.06	.02	.00
☐ 486	Pat Keedy	.03	.01	.00
☐ 487	Jim Pankovits	.03	.01	.00
☐ 488	Andy McGaffigan	.03	.01	.00
☐ 489	Dodgers TL Pedro Guerrero and Fernando Valenzuela	.08	.03	.01
☐ 490	Larry Parrish	.03	.01	.00
☐ 491	B.J. Surhoff	.06	.02	.00

☐ 492	Doyle Alexander	.03	.01	.00
☐ 493	Mike Greenwell	.20	.08	.02
☐ 494	Wally Ritchie	.03	.01	.00
☐ 495	Eddie Murray	.15	.06	.01
☐ 496	Guy Hoffman	.03	.01	.00
☐ 497	Kevin Mitchell	.25	.10	.02
☐ 498	Bob Boone	.06	.02	.00
☐ 499	Eric King	.03	.01	.00
☐ 500	Andre Dawson	.15	.06	.01
☐ 501	Tim Birtsas	.03	.01	.00
☐ 502	Dan Gladden	.03	.01	.00
☐ 503	Junior Noboa	.03	.01	.00
☐ 504	Bob Rodgers MG (checklist back)	.06	.02	.00
☐ 505	Willie Upshaw	.03	.01	.00
☐ 506	John Cangelosi	.03	.01	.00
☐ 507	Mark Gubicza	.06	.02	.00
☐ 508	Tim Teufel	.03	.01	.00
☐ 509	Bill Dawley	.03	.01	.00
☐ 510	Dave Winfield	.15	.06	.01
☐ 511	Joel Davis	.03	.01	.00
☐ 512	Alex Trevino	.03	.01	.00
☐ 513	Tim Flannery	.03	.01	.00
☐ 514	Pat Sheridan	.03	.01	.00
☐ 515	Juan Nieves	.03	.01	.00
☐ 516	Jim Sundberg	.03	.01	.00
☐ 517	Ron Robinson	.03	.01	.00
☐ 518	Greg Gross	.03	.01	.00
☐ 519	Mariners TL Harold Reynolds and Phil Bradley	.06	.02	.00
☐ 520	Dave Smith	.03	.01	.00
☐ 521	Jim Dwyer	.03	.01	.00
☐ 522	Bob Patterson	.06	.02	.00
☐ 523	Gary Roenicke	.03	.01	.00
☐ 524	Gary Lucas	.03	.01	.00
☐ 525	Marty Barrett	.03	.01	.00
☐ 526	Juan Berenguer	.03	.01	.00
☐ 527	Steve Henderson	.03	.01	.00
☐ 528A	Checklist 397-528 ERR (455 S. Carlton)	.40	.10	.02
☐ 528B	Checklist 397-528 COR (455 S. Hillegas)	.10	.01	.00
☐ 529	Tim Burke	.03	.01	.00
☐ 530	Gary Carter	.08	.03	.01
☐ 531	Rich Yett	.03	.01	.00
☐ 532	Mike Kingery	.03	.01	.00
☐ 533	John Farrell	.08	.03	.01
☐ 534	John Wathan MG (checklist back)	.06	.02	.00
☐ 535	Ron Guidry	.08	.03	.01
☐ 536	John Morris	.03	.01	.00
☐ 537	Steve Buechele	.06	.02	.00
☐ 538	Bill Wegman	.03	.01	.00
☐ 539	Mike LaValliere	.03	.01	.00
☐ 540	Bret Saberhagen	.12	.05	.01
☐ 541	Juan Beniquez	.03	.01	.00
☐ 542	Paul Noce	.06	.02	.00
☐ 543	Kent Tekulve	.03	.01	.00
☐ 544	Jim Traber	.03	.01	.00
☐ 545	Don Baylor	.06	.02	.00
☐ 546	John Candelaria	.03	.01	.00
☐ 547	Felix Fermin	.03	.01	.00
☐ 548	Shane Mack	.08	.03	.01
☐ 549	Braves TL Albert Hall, Dale Murphy, Ken Griffey, and Dion James	.08	.03	.01
☐ 550	Pedro Guerrero	.08	.03	.01
☐ 551	Terry Steinbach	.08	.03	.01
☐ 552	Mark Thurmond	.03	.01	.00
☐ 553	Tracy Jones	.03	.01	.00
☐ 554	Mike Smithson	.03	.01	.00
☐ 555	Brook Jacoby	.03	.01	.00
☐ 556	Stan Clarke	.03	.01	.00
☐ 557	Craig Reynolds	.03	.01	.00
☐ 558	Bob Ojeda	.06	.02	.00
☐ 559	Ken Williams	.06	.02	.00
☐ 560	Tim Wallach	.06	.02	.00
☐ 561	Rick Cerone	.03	.01	.00
☐ 562	Jim Lindeman	.03	.01	.00
☐ 563	Jose Guzman	.03	.01	.00
☐ 564	Frank Lucchesi MG (checklist back)	.06	.02	.00
☐ 565	Lloyd Moseby	.03	.01	.00
☐ 566	Charlie O'Brien	.08	.03	.01
☐ 567	Mike Diaz	.03	.01	.00
☐ 568	Chris Brown	.03	.01	.00
☐ 569	Charlie Leibrandt	.03	.01	.00
☐ 570	Jeffrey Leonard	.03	.01	.00
☐ 571	Mark Williamson	.08	.03	.01
☐ 572	Chris James	.08	.03	.01
☐ 573	Bob Stanley	.03	.01	.00
☐ 574	Graig Nettles	.08	.03	.01
☐ 575	Don Sutton	.10	.04	.01
☐ 576	Tommy Hinzo	.03	.01	.00
☐ 577	Tom Browning	.06	.02	.00
☐ 578	Gary Gaetti	.06	.02	.00
☐ 579	Mets TL Gary Carter and Kevin McReynolds	.08	.03	.01
☐ 580	Mark McGwire	.20	.08	.02
☐ 581	Tito Landrum	.03	.01	.00
☐ 582	Mike Henneman	.15	.06	.01
☐ 583	Dave Valle	.06	.02	.00
☐ 584	Steve Trout	.03	.01	.00
☐ 585	Ozzie Guillen	.06	.02	.00
☐ 586	Bob Forsch	.03	.01	.00
☐ 587	Terry Puhl	.03	.01	.00
☐ 588	Jeff Parrett	.06	.02	.00
☐ 589	Geno Petralli	.03	.01	.00
☐ 590	George Bell	.12	.05	.01
☐ 591	Doug Drabek	.12	.05	.01
☐ 592	Dale Sveum	.03	.01	.00
☐ 593	Bob Tewksbury	.03	.01	.00
☐ 594	Bobby Valentine MG (checklist back)	.06	.02	.00
☐ 595	Frank White	.03	.01	.00
☐ 596	John Kruk	.06	.02	.00
☐ 597	Gene Garber	.03	.01	.00
☐ 598	Lee Lacy	.03	.01	.00
☐ 599	Calvin Schiraldi	.03	.01	.00
☐ 600	Mike Schmidt	.35	.15	.03
☐ 601	Jack Lazorko	.03	.01	.00
☐ 602	Mike Aldrete	.03	.01	.00
☐ 603	Rob Murphy	.03	.01	.00
☐ 604	Chris Bando	.03	.01	.00
☐ 605	Kirk Gibson	.08	.03	.01
☐ 606	Moose Haas	.03	.01	.00
☐ 607	Mickey Hatcher	.03	.01	.00
☐ 608	Charlie Kerfeld	.03	.01	.00
☐ 609	Twins TL Gary Gaetti and Kent Hrbek	.08	.03	.01
☐ 610	Keith Hernandez	.08	.03	.01
☐ 611	Tommy John	.08	.03	.01
☐ 612	Curt Ford	.03	.01	.00
☐ 613	Bobby Thigpen	.10	.04	.01
☐ 614	Herm Winningham	.03	.01	.00
☐ 615	Jody Davis	.03	.01	.00
☐ 616	Jay Aldrich	.03	.01	.00
☐ 617	Oddibe McDowell	.03	.01	.00
☐ 618	Cecil Fielder	.35	.15	.03
☐ 619	Mike Dunne (inconsistent design, black name on front)	.06	.02	.00
☐ 620	Cory Snyder	.08	.03	.01
☐ 621	Gene Nelson	.03	.01	.00
☐ 622	Kal Daniels	.08	.03	.01
☐ 623	Mike Flanagan	.06	.02	.00
☐ 624	Jim Leyland MG (checklist back)	.06	.02	.00
☐ 625	Frank Viola	.08	.03	.01
☐ 626	Glenn Wilson	.03	.01	.00
☐ 627	Joe Boever	.06	.02	.00
☐ 628	Dave Henderson	.08	.03	.01
☐ 629	Kelly Downs	.03	.01	.00
☐ 630	Darrell Evans	.06	.02	.00
☐ 631	Jack Howell	.03	.01	.00
☐ 632	Steve Shields	.03	.01	.00
☐ 633	Barry Lyons	.08	.03	.01
☐ 634	Jose DeLeon	.03	.01	.00
☐ 635	Terry Pendleton	.12	.05	.01
☐ 636	Charles Hudson	.03	.01	.00
☐ 637	Jay Bell	.30	.12	.03
☐ 638	Steve Balboni	.03	.01	.00
☐ 639	Brewers TL Glenn Braggs and Tony Muser CO	.03	.01	.00
☐ 640	Garry Templeton (inconsistent design, green border)	.06	.02	.00
☐ 641	Rick Honeycutt	.03	.01	.00
☐ 642	Bob Dernier	.03	.01	.00
☐ 643	Rocky Childress	.03	.01	.00
☐ 644	Terry McGriff	.03	.01	.00
☐ 645	Matt Nokes	.25	.10	.02
☐ 646	Checklist 529-660	.06	.01	.00
☐ 647	Pascual Perez	.03	.01	.00
☐ 648	Al Newman	.03	.01	.00
☐ 649	DeWayne Buice	.03	.01	.00
☐ 650	Cal Ripken	.35	.15	.03
☐ 651	Mike Jackson	.10	.04	.01
☐ 652	Bruce Benedict	.03	.01	.00
☐ 653	Jeff Sellers	.03	.01	.00
☐ 654	Roger Craig MG (checklist back)	.06	.02	.00
☐ 655	Len Dykstra	.08	.03	.01
☐ 656	Lee Guetterman	.03	.01	.00

#	Player			
657	Gary Redus	.03	.01	.00
658	Tim Conroy (inconsistent design, name in white)	.03	.01	.00
659	Bobby Meacham	.03	.01	.00
660	Rick Reuschel	.06	.02	.00
661	Turn Back Clock 1983 Nolan Ryan	.17	.07	.01
662	Turn Back Clock 1978 Jim Rice	.08	.03	.01
663	Turn Back Clock 1973 Ron Blomberg	.03	.01	.00
664	Turn Back Clock 1968 Bob Gibson	.10	.04	.01
665	Turn Back Clock 1963 Stan Musial	.12	.05	.01
666	Mario Soto	.03	.01	.00
667	Luis Quinones	.03	.01	.00
668	Walt Terrell	.03	.01	.00
669	Phillies TL Lance Parrish and Mike Ryan CO	.06	.02	.00
670	Dan Plesac	.03	.01	.00
671	Tim Laudner	.03	.01	.00
672	John Davis	.06	.02	.00
673	Tony Phillips	.03	.01	.00
674	Mike Fitzgerald	.03	.01	.00
675	Jim Rice	.08	.03	.01
676	Ken Dixon	.03	.01	.00
677	Eddie Milner	.03	.01	.00
678	Jim Acker	.03	.01	.00
679	Darrell Miller	.03	.01	.00
680	Charlie Hough	.03	.01	.00
681	Bobby Bonilla	.30	.12	.03
682	Jimmy Key	.08	.03	.01
683	Julio Franco	.15	.06	.01
684	Hal Lanier MG (checklist back)	.06	.02	.00
685	Ron Darling	.08	.03	.01
686	Terry Francona	.03	.01	.00
687	Mickey Brantley	.06	.02	.00
688	Jim Winn	.03	.01	.00
689	Tom Pagnozzi	.12	.05	.01
690	Jay Howell	.03	.01	.00
691	Dan Pasqua	.06	.02	.00
692	Mike Birkbeck	.03	.01	.00
693	Benny Santiago	.12	.05	.01
694	Eric Nolte	.06	.02	.00
695	Shawon Dunston	.10	.04	.01
696	Duane Ward	.06	.02	.00
697	Steve Lombardozzi	.03	.01	.00
698	Brad Havens	.03	.01	.00
699	Padres TL Benito Santiago and Tony Gwynn	.12	.05	.01
700	George Brett	.20	.08	.02
701	Sammy Stewart	.03	.01	.00
702	Mike Gallego	.03	.01	.00
703	Bob Brenly	.03	.01	.00
704	Dennis Boyd	.03	.01	.00
705	Juan Samuel	.08	.03	.01
706	Rick Mahler	.03	.01	.00
707	Fred Lynn	.08	.03	.01
708	Gus Polidor	.03	.01	.00
709	George Frazier	.03	.01	.00
710	Darryl Strawberry	.35	.15	.03
711	Bill Gullickson	.06	.02	.00
712	John Moses	.03	.01	.00
713	Willie Hernandez	.03	.01	.00
714	Jim Fregosi MG (checklist back)	.06	.02	.00
715	Todd Worrell	.06	.02	.00
716	Lenn Sakata	.03	.01	.00
717	Jay Baller	.03	.01	.00
718	Mike Felder	.03	.01	.00
719	Denny Walling	.03	.01	.00
720	Tim Raines	.10	.04	.01
721	Pete O'Brien	.03	.01	.00
722	Manny Lee	.03	.01	.00
723	Bob Kipper	.03	.01	.00
724	Danny Tartabull	.15	.06	.01
725	Mike Boddicker	.03	.01	.00
726	Alfredo Griffin	.03	.01	.00
727	Greg Booker	.03	.01	.00
728	Andy Allanson	.03	.01	.00
729	Blue Jays TL George Bell and Fred McGriff	.10	.04	.01
730	John Franco	.06	.02	.00
731	Rick Schu	.03	.01	.00
732	David Palmer	.03	.01	.00
733	Spike Owen	.03	.01	.00
734	Craig Lefferts	.03	.01	.00
735	Kevin McReynolds	.10	.04	.01
736	Matt Young	.03	.01	.00
737	Butch Wynegar	.03	.01	.00
738	Scott Bankhead	.06	.02	.00
739	Daryl Boston	.03	.01	.00
740	Rick Sutcliffe	.06	.02	.00
741	Mike Easler	.03	.01	.00
742	Mark Clear	.03	.01	.00
743	Larry Herndon	.03	.01	.00
744	Whitey Herzog MG (checklist back)	.06	.02	.00
745	Bill Doran	.03	.01	.00
746	Gene Larkin	.12	.05	.01
747	Bobby Witt	.08	.03	.01
748	Reid Nichols	.03	.01	.00
749	Mark Eichhorn	.06	.02	.00
750	Bo Jackson	.60	.25	.06
751	Jim Morrison	.03	.01	.00
752	Mark Grant	.03	.01	.00
753	Danny Heep	.03	.01	.00
754	Mike LaCoss	.03	.01	.00
755	Ozzie Virgil	.03	.01	.00
756	Mike Maddux	.03	.01	.00
757	John Marzano	.06	.02	.00
758	Eddie Williams	.06	.02	.00
759	A's TL Mark McGwire and Jose Canseco	.17	.07	.01
760	Mike Scott	.08	.03	.01
761	Tony Armas	.03	.01	.00
762	Scott Bradley	.03	.01	.00
763	Doug Sisk	.03	.01	.00
764	Greg Walker	.03	.01	.00
765	Neal Heaton	.03	.01	.00
766	Henry Cotto	.03	.01	.00
767	Jose Lind	.20	.08	.02
768	Dickie Noles	.03	.01	.00
769	Cecil Cooper	.06	.02	.00
770	Lou Whitaker	.08	.03	.01
771	Ruben Sierra	.35	.15	.03
772	Sal Butera	.03	.01	.00
773	Frank Williams	.03	.01	.00
774	Gene Mauch MG (checklist back)	.06	.02	.00
775	Dave Stieb	.08	.03	.01
776	Checklist 661-792	.06	.01	.00
777	Lonnie Smith	.08	.03	.01
778A	Keith Comstock ERR (white "Padres")	2.50	1.00	.25
778B	Keith Comstock COR (blue "Padres")	.08	.03	.01
779	Tom Glavine	1.00	.40	.10
780	Fernando Valenzuela	.08	.03	.01
781	Keith Hughes	.06	.02	.00
782	Jeff Ballard	.08	.03	.01
783	Ron Roenicke	.03	.01	.00
784	Joe Sambito	.03	.01	.00
785	Alvin Davis	.06	.02	.00
786	Joe Price (inconsistent design, orange team name)	.03	.01	.00
787	Bill Almon	.03	.01	.00
788	Ray Searage	.03	.01	.00
789	Indians' TL Joe Carter and Cory Snyder	.08	.03	.01
790	Dave Righetti	.08	.03	.01
791	Ted Simmons	.08	.03	.01
792	John Tudor	.10	.04	.01

1988 Topps Wax Box Cards

The cards in this 16-card set measure the standard 2 1/2" by 3 1/2". Cards have essentially the same design as the 1988 Topps regular issue set. The cards were printed on the bottoms of the regular issue wax pack boxes. These 16 cards, "lettered" A through P, are considered a separate set in their own right and are not typically included in a complete set of the regular issue 1988 Topps cards. The value of the panels uncut is slightly greater, perhaps by 25 percent greater, than the value of the individual cards cut up carefully.

	MINT	EXC	G-VG
COMPLETE SET (16)	4.50	2.00	.45
COMMON PLAYER (A-P)	.10	.04	.01
A Don Baylor	.15	.06	.01
B Steve Bedrosian	.15	.06	.01

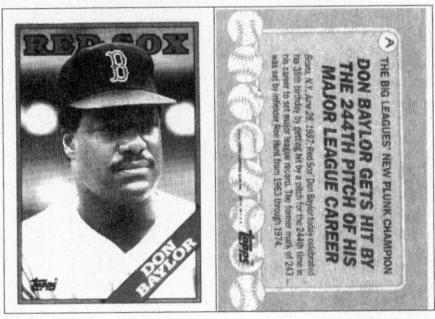

			MINT	EXC	G-VG
☐	C	Juan Beniquez	.10	.04	.01
☐	D	Bob Boone	.15	.06	.01
☐	E	Darrell Evans	.10	.04	.01
☐	F	Tony Gwynn	.60	.25	.06
☐	G	John Kruk	.15	.06	.01
☐	H	Marvell Wynne	.10	.04	.01
☐	I	Joe Carter	.35	.15	.03
☐	J	Eric Davis	.50	.20	.05
☐	K	Howard Johnson	.35	.15	.03
☐	L	Darryl Strawberry	.75	.30	.07
☐	M	Rickey Henderson	.90	.40	.09
☐	N	Nolan Ryan	1.00	.40	.10
☐	O	Mike Schmidt	.75	.30	.07
☐	P	Kent Tekulve	.10	.04	.01

1988 Topps All-Star Glossy 22

This set of 22 glossy cards was inserted one per rack pack. Players selected for the set are the starting players (plus manager and honorary captain) in the 1987 All-Star Game in Oakland. Cards measure standard size, 2 1/2" by 3 1/2" and the backs feature red and blue printing on a white card stock.

		MINT	EXC	G-VG
COMPLETE SET (22)		3.00	1.25	.30
COMMON PLAYER (1-22)		.10	.04	.01
☐ 1	John McNamara MG	.10	.04	.01
☐ 2	Don Mattingly	.40	.16	.04
☐ 3	Willie Randolph	.10	.04	.01
☐ 4	Wade Boggs	.40	.16	.04
☐ 5	Cal Ripken	.50	.20	.05
☐ 6	George Bell	.20	.08	.02
☐ 7	Rickey Henderson	.50	.20	.05
☐ 8	Dave Winfield	.25	.10	.02
☐ 9	Terry Kennedy	.10	.04	.01
☐ 10	Bret Saberhagen	.20	.08	.02
☐ 11	Jim Hunter CAPT	.15	.06	.01
☐ 12	Dave Johnson MG	.10	.04	.01
☐ 13	Jack Clark	.15	.06	.01
☐ 14	Ryne Sandberg	.50	.20	.05
☐ 15	Mike Schmidt	.50	.20	.05
☐ 16	Ozzie Smith	.25	.10	.02
☐ 17	Eric Davis	.30	.12	.03
☐ 18	Andre Dawson	.30	.12	.03
☐ 19	Darryl Strawberry	.45	.18	.04

☐ 20	Gary Carter	.20	.08	.02
☐ 21	Mike Scott	.15	.06	.01
☐ 22	Billy Williams CAPT	.15	.06	.01

1988 Topps Jumbo Rookies

Inserted in each supermarket jumbo pack is a card from this series of 22 of 1987's best rookies as determined by Topps. Jumbo packs consisted of 100 (regular issue 1988 Topps baseball) cards with a stick of gum plus the insert "Rookie" card. The card fronts are in full color and measure 2 1/2" by 3 1/2". The card backs are printed in red and blue on white card stock and are numbered at the bottom.

		MINT	EXC	G-VG
COMPLETE SET (22)		8.00	3.50	.80
COMMON PLAYER (1-22)		.20	.08	.02
☐ 1	Billy Ripken	.30	.12	.03
☐ 2	Ellis Burks	1.00	.40	.10
☐ 3	Mike Greenwell	1.00	.40	.10
☐ 4	DeWayne Buice	.20	.08	.02
☐ 5	Devon White	.50	.20	.05
☐ 6	Fred Manrique	.20	.08	.02
☐ 7	Mike Henneman	.30	.12	.03
☐ 8	Matt Nokes	.50	.20	.05
☐ 9	Kevin Seitzer	.40	.16	.04
☐ 10	B.J. Surhoff	.40	.16	.04
☐ 11	Casey Candaele	.20	.08	.02
☐ 12	Randy Myers	.30	.12	.03
☐ 13	Mark McGwire	1.25	.50	.12
☐ 14	Luis Polonia	.40	.16	.04
☐ 15	Terry Steinbach	.40	.16	.04
☐ 16	Mike Dunne	.20	.08	.02
☐ 17	Al Pedrique	.20	.08	.02
☐ 18	Benito Santiago	.75	.30	.07
☐ 19	Kelly Downs	.30	.12	.03
☐ 20	Joe Magrane	.30	.12	.03
☐ 21	Jerry Browne	.30	.12	.03
☐ 22	Jeff Musselman	.20	.08	.02

1988 Topps Revco League Leaders

Topps produced this 33-card boxed set for Revco stores subtitled "League Leaders". The cards measure 2 1/2" by 3 1/2" and feature a high-gloss, full-color photo of the player inside a white border. The card backs are printed in red and black on white card stock. The cards are numbered on the back. The statistics provided on the card backs cover only two lines, last season and Major League totals.

		MINT	EXC	G-VG
COMPLETE SET (33)		4.00	1.75	.40
COMMON PLAYER (1-33)		.10	.04	.01
☐ 1	Tony Gwynn	.40	.16	.04
☐ 2	Andre Dawson	.30	.12	.03

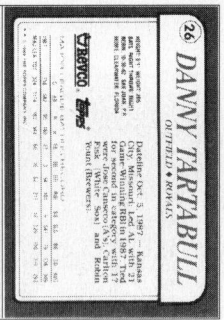

		MINT	EXC	G-VG

backs cover only two lines, last season and Major League totals.

		MINT	EXC	G-VG
	COMPLETE SET (33)	4.00	1.75	.40
	COMMON PLAYER (1-33)	.10	.04	.01
☐ 1	Dale Murphy	.30	.12	.03
☐ 2	Andre Dawson	.30	.12	.03
☐ 3	Eric Davis	.30	.12	.03
☐ 4	Mike Scott	.15	.06	.01
☐ 5	Pedro Guerrero	.15	.06	.01
☐ 6	Tim Raines	.20	.08	.02
☐ 7	Darryl Strawberry	.50	.20	.05
☐ 8	Mike Schmidt	.60	.25	.06
☐ 9	Mike Dunne	.10	.04	.01
☐ 10	Jack Clark	.15	.06	.01
☐ 11	Tony Gwynn	.40	.16	.04
☐ 12	Will Clark	.60	.25	.06
☐ 13	Cal Ripken	.60	.25	.06
☐ 14	Wade Boggs	.50	.20	.05
☐ 15	Wally Joyner	.25	.10	.02
☐ 16	Harold Baines	.15	.06	.01
☐ 17	Joe Carter	.25	.10	.02
☐ 18	Alan Trammell	.20	.08	.02
☐ 19	Kevin Seitzer	.15	.06	.01
☐ 20	Paul Molitor	.20	.08	.02
☐ 21	Kirby Puckett	.40	.16	.04
☐ 22	Don Mattingly	.50	.20	.05
☐ 23	Mark McGwire	.40	.16	.04
☐ 24	Alvin Davis	.15	.06	.01
☐ 25	Ruben Sierra	.50	.20	.05
☐ 26	George Bell	.20	.08	.02
☐ 27	Jack Morris	.25	.10	.02
☐ 28	Jeff Reardon	.10	.04	.01
☐ 29	John Tudor	.15	.06	.01
☐ 30	Rick Reuschel	.10	.04	.01
☐ 31	Gary Gaetti	.15	.06	.01
☐ 32	Jeffrey Leonard	.10	.04	.01
☐ 33	Frank Viola	.15	.06	.01

☐ 3	Vince Coleman	.25	.10	.02
☐ 4	Jack Clark	.15	.06	.01
☐ 5	Tim Raines	.20	.08	.02
☐ 6	Tim Wallach	.15	.06	.01
☐ 7	Juan Samuel	.15	.06	.01
☐ 8	Nolan Ryan	.90	.40	.09
☐ 9	Rick Sutcliffe	.15	.06	.01
☐ 10	Kent Tekulve	.10	.04	.01
☐ 11	Steve Bedrosian	.10	.04	.01
☐ 12	Orel Hershiser	.20	.08	.02
☐ 13	Rick Reuschel	.10	.04	.01
☐ 14	Fernando Valenzuela	.15	.06	.01
☐ 15	Bob Welch	.15	.06	.01
☐ 16	Wade Boggs	.40	.16	.04
☐ 17	Mark McGwire	.35	.15	.03
☐ 18	George Bell	.20	.08	.02
☐ 19	Harold Reynolds	.10	.04	.01
☐ 20	Paul Molitor	.20	.08	.02
☐ 21	Kirby Puckett	.40	.16	.04
☐ 22	Kevin Seitzer	.15	.06	.01
☐ 23	Brian Downing	.10	.04	.01
☐ 24	Dwight Evans	.15	.06	.01
☐ 25	Willie Wilson	.10	.04	.01
☐ 26	Danny Tartabull	.25	.10	.02
☐ 27	Jimmy Key	.10	.04	.01
☐ 28	Roger Clemens	.50	.20	.05
☐ 29	Dave Stewart	.20	.08	.02
☐ 30	Mark Eichhorn	.10	.04	.01
☐ 31	Tom Henke	.10	.04	.01
☐ 32	Charlie Hough	.10	.04	.01
☐ 33	Mark Langston	.15	.06	.01

1988 Topps UK Minis

The 1988 Topps UK (United Kingdom) Mini set of "American Baseball" features 88 cards. The cards are numbered on the back and measure approximately 2 1/8" by 3". The card backs are printed in blue, red, and yellow on white card stock. The cards were distributed as a separate issue in packs. A custom black and yellow small set box was also available for holding a complete set; the box has a complete checklist on the back panel. The set player numbering is according to alphabetical order. Topps also produced a specially boxed "glossy" edition frequently referred to as the Topps UK Tiffany set. Topps did not disclose the number of UK Tiffany sets they produced or sold. The checklist of Tiffany cards is identical to that of the normal UK non-glossy cards. These Tiffany cards are valued at approximately double the values listed below.

		MINT	EXC	G-VG
	COMPLETE SET (88)	9.00	4.00	.90
	COMMON PLAYER (1-88)	.05	.02	.00

1988 Topps Rite-Aid Team MVP's

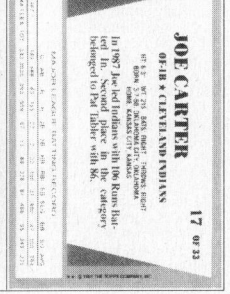

Topps produced this 33-card boxed set for Rite Aid Drug and Discount Stores subtitled "Team MVP's". The Rite Aid logo is at the top of every obverse. The cards measure 2 1/2" by 3 1/2" and feature a high-gloss, full-color photo of the player inside a red, white, and blue border. The card backs are printed in blue and black on white card stock. The cards are numbered on the back and the checklist for the set is found on the back panel of the small collector box. The statistics provided on the card

☐ 1 Harold Baines	.10	.04	.01
☐ 2 Steve Bedrosian	.05	.02	.00
☐ 3 George Bell	.15	.06	.01
☐ 4 Wade Boggs	.50	.20	.05
☐ 5 Barry Bonds	.50	.20	.05
☐ 6 Bob Boone	.10	.04	.01
☐ 7 George Brett	.40	.16	.04
☐ 8 Hubie Brooks	.10	.04	.01
☐ 9 Ivan Calderon	.10	.04	.01
☐ 10 Jose Canseco	1.00	.40	.10
☐ 11 Gary Carter	.15	.06	.01
☐ 12 Joe Carter	.25	.10	.02
☐ 13 Jack Clark	.10	.04	.01
☐ 14 Will Clark	1.00	.40	.10
☐ 15 Roger Clemens	.90	.40	.09
☐ 16 Vince Coleman	.25	.10	.02
☐ 17 Alvin Davis	.10	.04	.01
☐ 18 Eric Davis	.35	.15	.03
☐ 19 Glenn Davis	.20	.08	.02
☐ 20 Andre Dawson	.30	.12	.03
☐ 21 Mike Dunne	.05	.02	.00
☐ 22 Dwight Evans	.15	.06	.01
☐ 23 Tony Fernandez	.10	.04	.01
☐ 24 John Franco	.10	.04	.01
☐ 25 Gary Gaetti	.10	.04	.01
☐ 26 Kirk Gibson	.15	.06	.01
☐ 27 Dwight Gooden	.25	.10	.02
☐ 28 Pedro Guerrero	.10	.04	.01
☐ 29 Tony Gwynn	.45	.18	.04
☐ 30 Billy Hatcher	.05	.02	.00
☐ 31 Rickey Henderson	.75	.30	.07
☐ 32 Tom Henke	.05	.02	.00
☐ 33 Keith Hernandez	.15	.06	.01
☐ 34 Orel Hershiser	.15	.06	.01
☐ 35 Teddy Higuera	.10	.04	.01
☐ 36 Charlie Hough	.05	.02	.00
☐ 37 Kent Hrbek	.15	.06	.01
☐ 38 Brook Jacoby	.05	.02	.00
☐ 39 Dion James	.05	.02	.00
☐ 40 Wally Joyner	.20	.08	.02
☐ 41 John Kruk	.10	.04	.01
☐ 42 Mark Langston	.15	.06	.01
☐ 43 Jeffrey Leonard	.05	.02	.00
☐ 44 Candy Maldonado	.10	.04	.01
☐ 45 Don Mattingly	.60	.25	.06
☐ 46 Willie McGee	.15	.06	.01
☐ 47 Mark McGwire	.50	.20	.05
☐ 48 Kevin Mitchell	.30	.12	.03
☐ 49 Paul Molitor	.20	.08	.02
☐ 50 Jack Morris	.20	.08	.02
☐ 51 Lloyd Moseby	.05	.02	.00
☐ 52 Dale Murphy	.35	.15	.03
☐ 53 Eddie Murray	.45	.18	.04
☐ 54 Matt Nokes	.15	.06	.01
☐ 55 Dave Parker	.20	.08	.02
☐ 56 Larry Parrish	.05	.02	.00
☐ 57 Kirby Puckett	.45	.18	.04
☐ 58 Tim Raines	.15	.06	.01
☐ 59 Willie Randolph	.10	.04	.01
☐ 60 Harold Reynolds	.10	.04	.01
☐ 61 Cal Ripken	.75	.30	.07
☐ 62 Nolan Ryan	1.25	.50	.12
☐ 63 Bret Saberhagen	.30	.12	.03
☐ 64 Juan Samuel	.10	.04	.01
☐ 65 Ryne Sandberg	.75	.30	.07
☐ 66 Benito Santiago	.30	.12	.03
☐ 67 Mike Schmidt	.75	.30	.07
☐ 68 Mike Scott	.10	.04	.01
☐ 69 Kevin Seitzer	.10	.04	.01
☐ 70 Larry Sheets	.05	.02	.00
☐ 71 Ruben Sierra	.50	.20	.05
☐ 72 Ozzie Smith	.30	.12	.03
☐ 73 Zane Smith	.10	.04	.01
☐ 74 Cory Snyder	.15	.06	.01
☐ 75 Dave Stewart	.20	.08	.02
☐ 76 Darryl Strawberry	.60	.25	.06
☐ 77 Rick Sutcliffe	.10	.04	.01
☐ 78 Danny Tartabull	.30	.12	.03
☐ 79 Alan Trammell	.20	.08	.02
☐ 80 Fernando Valenzuela	.15	.06	.01
☐ 81 Andy Van Slyke	.15	.06	.01
☐ 82 Frank Viola	.20	.08	.02
☐ 83 Greg Walker	.05	.02	.00
☐ 84 Tim Wallach	.10	.04	.01
☐ 85 Dave Winfield	.30	.12	.03
☐ 86 Mike Witt	.05	.02	.00
☐ 87 Robin Yount	.50	.20	.05
☐ 88 Checklist Card	.05	.02	.00

1988 Topps Send-In Glossy 60

Topps issued this set through a mail-in offer explained and advertised on the wax packs. This 60-card set features glossy fronts with each card measuring 2 1/2" by 3 1/2". The offer provided your choice of any one of the six 10-card subsets (1-10, 11-20, etc.) for 1.25 plus six of the Special Offer ("Spring Fever Baseball") insert cards, which were found one per wax pack. The last two players (numerically) in each ten-card subset are actually "Hot Prospects."

	MINT	EXC	G-VG
COMPLETE SET (60)	11.00	5.00	1.35
COMMON PLAYER (1-60)	.20	.08	.02
☐ 1 Andre Dawson	.30	.12	.03
☐ 2 Jesse Barfield	.25	.10	.02
☐ 3 Mike Schmidt	.75	.30	.07
☐ 4 Ruben Sierra	.50	.20	.05
☐ 5 Mike Scott	.25	.10	.02
☐ 6 Cal Ripken	.75	.30	.07
☐ 7 Gary Carter	.30	.12	.03
☐ 8 Kent Hrbek	.25	.10	.02
☐ 9 Kevin Seitzer	.25	.10	.02
☐ 10 Mike Henneman	.20	.08	.02
☐ 11 Don Mattingly	.60	.25	.06
☐ 12 Tim Raines	.25	.10	.02
☐ 13 Roger Clemens	.75	.30	.07
☐ 14 Ryne Sandberg	.75	.30	.07
☐ 15 Tony Fernandez	.25	.10	.02
☐ 16 Eric Davis	.40	.16	.04
☐ 17 Jack Morris	.35	.15	.03
☐ 18 Tim Wallach	.25	.10	.02
☐ 19 Mike Dunne	.20	.08	.02
☐ 20 Mike Greenwell	.45	.18	.04
☐ 21 Dwight Evans	.25	.10	.02
☐ 22 Darryl Strawberry	.75	.30	.07
☐ 23 Cory Snyder	.25	.10	.02
☐ 24 Pedro Guerrero	.25	.10	.02
☐ 25 Rickey Henderson	.75	.30	.07
☐ 26 Dale Murphy	.40	.16	.04
☐ 27 Kirby Puckett	.45	.18	.04
☐ 28 Steve Bedrosian	.20	.08	.02
☐ 29 Devon White	.30	.12	.03
☐ 30 Benito Santiago	.35	.15	.03
☐ 31 George Bell	.30	.12	.03
☐ 32 Keith Hernandez	.25	.10	.02
☐ 33 Dave Stewart	.30	.12	.03
☐ 34 Dave Parker	.30	.12	.03
☐ 35 Tom Henke	.20	.08	.02
☐ 36 Willie McGee	.30	.12	.03
☐ 37 Alan Trammell	.30	.12	.03
☐ 38 Tony Gwynn	.45	.18	.04
☐ 39 Mark McGwire	.45	.18	.04
☐ 40 Joe Magrane	.25	.10	.02
☐ 41 Jack Clark	.25	.10	.02
☐ 42 Willie Randolph	.25	.10	.02
☐ 43 Juan Samuel	.25	.10	.02
☐ 44 Joe Carter	.35	.15	.03
☐ 45 Shane Rawley	.20	.08	.02
☐ 46 Dave Winfield	.40	.16	.04
☐ 47 Ozzie Smith	.40	.16	.04
☐ 48 Wally Joyner	.30	.12	.03
☐ 49 B.J. Surhoff	.25	.10	.02
☐ 50 Ellis Burks	.75	.30	.07
☐ 51 Wade Boggs	.75	.30	.07
☐ 52 Howard Johnson	.35	.15	.03
☐ 53 George Brett	.50	.20	.05

☐ 54	Dwight Gooden	.35	.15	.03
☐ 55	Jose Canseco	.90	.40	.09
☐ 56	Lee Smith	.25	.10	.02
☐ 57	Paul Molitor	.30	.12	.03
☐ 58	Andres Galarraga	.25	.10	.02
☐ 59	Matt Nokes	.30	.12	.03
☐ 60	Casey Candaele	.20	.08	.02

1988 Topps Big

This set of 264 cards was issued as three separately distributed series of 88 cards each. Cards were distributed in wax packs with seven cards for a suggested retail of 40 cents. These cards are very reminiscent in style of the 1956 Topps card set and are popular with collectors perhaps for that reason. The cards measure approximately 2 5/8" by 3 3/4" and are oriented horizontally.

	MINT	EXC	G-VG
COMPLETE SET (264)	21.00	9.00	3.00
COMMON PLAYER (1-88)	.05	.02	.00
COMMON PLAYER (89-176)	.05	.02	.00
COMMON PLAYER (177-264)	.05	.02	.00

☐ 1	Paul Molitor	.12	.05	.01
☐ 2	Milt Thompson	.05	.02	.00
☐ 3	Billy Hatcher	.08	.03	.01
☐ 4	Mike Witt	.05	.02	.00
☐ 5	Vince Coleman	.15	.06	.01
☐ 6	Dwight Evans	.10	.04	.01
☐ 7	Tim Wallach	.08	.03	.01
☐ 8	Alan Trammell	.15	.06	.01
☐ 9	Will Clark	1.00	.40	.10
☐ 10	Jeff Reardon	.10	.04	.01
☐ 11	Dwight Gooden	.35	.15	.03
☐ 12	Benito Santiago	.15	.06	.01
☐ 13	Jose Canseco	1.00	.40	.10
☐ 14	Dale Murphy	.35	.15	.03
☐ 15	George Bell	.20	.08	.02
☐ 16	Ryne Sandberg	.75	.30	.07
☐ 17	Brook Jacoby	.08	.03	.01
☐ 18	Fernando Valenzuela	.10	.04	.01
☐ 19	Scott Fletcher	.05	.02	.00
☐ 20	Eric Davis	.30	.12	.03
☐ 21	Willie Wilson	.08	.03	.01
☐ 22	B.J. Surhoff	.08	.03	.01
☐ 23	Steve Bedrosian	.08	.03	.01
☐ 24	Dave Winfield	.30	.12	.03
☐ 25	Bobby Bonilla	.40	.16	.04
☐ 26	Larry Sheets	.05	.02	.00
☐ 27	Ozzie Guillen	.12	.05	.01
☐ 28	Checklist 1-88	.05	.02	.00
☐ 29	Nolan Ryan	1.25	.50	.12
☐ 30	Bob Boone	.10	.04	.01
☐ 31	Tom Herr	.08	.03	.01
☐ 32	Wade Boggs	.75	.30	.07
☐ 33	Neal Heaton	.05	.02	.00
☐ 34	Doyle Alexander	.05	.02	.00
☐ 35	Candy Maldonado	.08	.03	.01
☐ 36	Kirby Puckett	.45	.18	.04
☐ 37	Gary Carter	.20	.08	.02
☐ 38	Lance McCullers	.05	.02	.00
☐ 39A	Terry Steinbach	.15	.06	.01
	(Topps logo in black)			

☐ 39B	Terry Steinbach	.15	.06	.01
	(Topps logo in white)			
☐ 40	Gerald Perry	.05	.02	.00
☐ 41	Tom Henke	.08	.03	.01
☐ 42	Leon Durham	.05	.02	.00
☐ 43	Cory Snyder	.10	.04	.01
☐ 44	Dale Sveum	.05	.02	.00
☐ 45	Lance Parrish	.10	.04	.01
☐ 46	Steve Sax	.15	.06	.01
☐ 47	Charlie Hough	.05	.02	.00
☐ 48	Kal Daniels	.15	.06	.01
☐ 49	Bo Jackson	1.00	.40	.10
☐ 50	Ron Guidry	.12	.05	.01
☐ 51	Bill Doran	.05	.02	.00
☐ 52	Wally Joyner	.30	.12	.03
☐ 53	Terry Pendleton	.12	.05	.01
☐ 54	Marty Barrett	.05	.02	.00
☐ 55	Andres Galarraga	.10	.04	.01
☐ 56	Larry Herndon	.05	.02	.00
☐ 57	Kevin Mitchell	.45	.18	.04
☐ 58	Greg Gagne	.05	.02	.00
☐ 59	Keith Hernandez	.12	.05	.01
☐ 60	John Kruk	.08	.03	.01
☐ 61	Mike LaValliere	.05	.02	.00
☐ 62	Cal Ripken	.75	.30	.07
☐ 63	Ivan Calderon	.08	.03	.01
☐ 64	Alvin Davis	.08	.03	.01
☐ 65	Luis Polonia	.10	.04	.01
☐ 66	Robin Yount	.50	.20	.05
☐ 67	Juan Samuel	.08	.03	.01
☐ 68	Andres Thomas	.08	.03	.01
☐ 69	Jeff Musselman	.05	.02	.00
☐ 70	Jerry Mumphrey	.05	.02	.00
☐ 71	Joe Carter	.20	.08	.02
☐ 72	Mike Scioscia	.05	.02	.00
☐ 73	Pete Incaviglia	.10	.04	.01
☐ 74	Barry Larkin	.25	.10	.02
☐ 75	Frank White	.08	.03	.01
☐ 76	Willie Randolph	.08	.03	.01
☐ 77	Kevin Bass	.08	.03	.01
☐ 78	Brian Downing	.05	.02	.00
☐ 79	Willie McGee	.12	.05	.01
☐ 80	Ellis Burks	.40	.16	.04
☐ 81	Hubie Brooks	.08	.03	.01
☐ 82	Darrell Evans	.08	.03	.01
☐ 83	Robby Thompson	.05	.02	.00
☐ 84	Kent Hrbek	.10	.04	.01
☐ 85	Ron Darling	.08	.03	.01
☐ 86	Stan Jefferson	.05	.02	.00
☐ 87	Teddy Higuera	.08	.03	.01
☐ 88	Mike Schmidt	.75	.30	.07
☐ 89	Barry Bonds	.60	.25	.06
☐ 90	Jim Presley	.05	.02	.00
☐ 91	Orel Hershiser	.20	.08	.02
☐ 92	Jesse Barfield	.12	.05	.01
☐ 93	Tom Candiotti	.08	.03	.01
☐ 94	Bret Saberhagen	.20	.08	.02
☐ 95	Jose Uribe	.05	.02	.00
☐ 96	Tom Browning	.10	.04	.01
☐ 97	Johnny Ray	.08	.03	.01
☐ 98	Mike Morgan	.08	.03	.01
☐ 99	Lou Whitaker	.12	.05	.01
☐ 100	Jim Sundberg	.05	.02	.00
☐ 101	Roger McDowell	.08	.03	.01
☐ 102	Randy Ready	.05	.02	.00
☐ 103	Mike Gallego	.08	.03	.01
☐ 104	Steve Buechele	.08	.03	.01
☐ 105	Greg Walker	.05	.02	.00
☐ 106	Jose Lind	.08	.03	.01
☐ 107	Steve Trout	.05	.02	.00
☐ 108	Rick Rhoden	.05	.02	.00
☐ 109	Jim Pankovits	.05	.02	.00
☐ 110	Ken Griffey Sr.	.15	.06	.01
☐ 111	Danny Cox	.08	.03	.01
☐ 112	Franklin Stubbs	.08	.03	.01
☐ 113	Lloyd Moseby	.05	.02	.00
☐ 114	Mel Hall	.10	.04	.01
☐ 115	Kevin Seitzer	.12	.05	.01
☐ 116	Tim Raines	.20	.08	.02
☐ 117	Juan Castillo	.05	.02	.00
☐ 118	Roger Clemens	.90	.40	.09
☐ 119	Mike Aldrete	.05	.02	.00
☐ 120	Mario Soto	.05	.02	.00
☐ 121	Jack Howell	.05	.02	.00
☐ 122	Rick Schu	.05	.02	.00
☐ 123	Jeff Robinson	.05	.02	.00
☐ 124	Doug Drabek	.15	.06	.01
☐ 125	Henry Cotto	.05	.02	.00
☐ 126	Checklist 89-176	.05	.02	.00
☐ 127	Gary Gaetti	.08	.03	.01
☐ 128	Rick Sutcliffe	.08	.03	.01
☐ 129	Howard Johnson	.15	.06	.01
☐ 130	Chris Brown	.05	.02	.00
☐ 131	Dave Henderson	.10	.04	.01
☐ 132	Curt Wilkerson	.05	.02	.00

☐ 133	Mike Marshall	.08	.03	.01
☐ 134	Kelly Gruber	.15	.06	.01
☐ 135	Julio Franco	.20	.08	.02
☐ 136	Kurt Stillwell	.08	.03	.01
☐ 137	Donnie Hill	.05	.02	.00
☐ 138	Mike Pagliarulo	.05	.02	.00
☐ 139	Von Hayes	.08	.03	.01
☐ 140	Mike Scott	.10	.04	.01
☐ 141	Bob Kipper	.05	.02	.00
☐ 142	Harold Reynolds	.08	.03	.01
☐ 143	Bob Brenly	.05	.02	.00
☐ 144	Dave Concepcion	.08	.03	.01
☐ 145	Devon White	.12	.05	.01
☐ 146	Jeff Stone	.05	.02	.00
☐ 147	Chet Lemon	.05	.02	.00
☐ 148	Ozzie Virgil	.05	.02	.00
☐ 149	Todd Worrell	.08	.03	.01
☐ 150	Mitch Webster	.05	.02	.00
☐ 151	Rob Deer	.08	.03	.01
☐ 152	Rich Gedman	.05	.02	.00
☐ 153	Andre Dawson	.30	.12	.03
☐ 154	Mike Davis	.05	.02	.00
☐ 155	Nelson Liriano	.05	.02	.00
☐ 156	Greg Swindell	.12	.05	.01
☐ 157	George Brett	.40	.16	.04
☐ 158	Kevin McReynolds	.20	.08	.02
☐ 159	Brian Fisher	.05	.02	.00
☐ 160	Mike Kingery	.05	.02	.00
☐ 161	Tony Gwynn	.45	.18	.04
☐ 162	Don Baylor	.10	.04	.01
☐ 163	Jerry Browne	.08	.03	.01
☐ 164	Dan Pasqua	.05	.02	.00
☐ 165	Rickey Henderson	1.00	.40	.10
☐ 166	Brett Butler	.12	.05	.01
☐ 167	Nick Esasky	.08	.03	.01
☐ 168	Kirk McCaskill	.08	.03	.01
☐ 169	Fred Lynn	.12	.05	.01
☐ 170	Jack Morris	.15	.06	.01
☐ 171	Pedro Guerrero	.12	.05	.01
☐ 172	Dave Stieb	.12	.05	.01
☐ 173	Pat Tabler	.05	.02	.00
☐ 174	Floyd Bannister	.05	.02	.00
☐ 175	Rafael Belliard	.05	.02	.00
☐ 176	Mark Langston	.12	.05	.01
☐ 177	Greg Mathews	.05	.02	.00
☐ 178	Claudell Washington	.08	.03	.01
☐ 179	Mark McGwire	.75	.30	.07
☐ 180	Bert Blyleven	.12	.05	.01
☐ 181	Jim Rice	.15	.06	.01
☐ 182	Mookie Wilson	.08	.03	.01
☐ 183	Willie Fraser	.05	.02	.00
☐ 184	Andy Van Slyke	.12	.05	.01
☐ 185	Matt Nokes	.15	.06	.01
☐ 186	Eddie Whitson	.08	.03	.01
☐ 187	Tony Fernandez	.10	.04	.01
☐ 188	Rick Reuschel	.08	.03	.01
☐ 189	Ken Phelps	.05	.02	.00
☐ 190	Juan Nieves	.05	.02	.00
☐ 191	Kirk Gibson	.20	.08	.02
☐ 192	Glenn Davis	.20	.08	.02
☐ 193	Zane Smith	.12	.05	.01
☐ 194	Jose DeLeon	.05	.02	.00
☐ 195	Gary Ward	.05	.02	.00
☐ 196	Pascual Perez	.08	.03	.01
☐ 197	Carlton Fisk	.35	.15	.03
☐ 198	Oddibe McDowell	.05	.02	.00
☐ 199	Mark Gubicza	.08	.03	.01
☐ 200	Glenn Hubbard	.05	.02	.00
☐ 201	Frank Viola	.15	.06	.01
☐ 202	Jody Reed	.12	.05	.01
☐ 203	Len Dykstra	.15	.06	.01
☐ 204	Dick Schofield	.05	.02	.00
☐ 205	Sid Bream	.05	.02	.00
☐ 206	Guillermo Hernandez	.05	.02	.00
☐ 207	Keith Moreland	.05	.02	.00
☐ 208	Mark Eichhorn	.05	.02	.00
☐ 209	Rene Gonzalez	.05	.02	.00
☐ 210	Dave Valle	.05	.02	.00
☐ 211	Tom Brunansky	.08	.03	.01
☐ 212	Charles Hudson	.05	.02	.00
☐ 213	John Farrell	.05	.02	.00
☐ 214	Jeff Treadway	.05	.02	.00
☐ 215	Eddie Murray	.35	.15	.03
☐ 216	Checklist 177-264	.05	.02	.00
☐ 217	Greg Brock	.05	.02	.00
☐ 218	John Shelby	.05	.02	.00
☐ 219	Craig Reynolds	.05	.02	.00
☐ 220	Dion James	.05	.02	.00
☐ 221	Carney Lansford	.10	.04	.01
☐ 222	Juan Berenguer	.05	.02	.00
☐ 223	Luis Rivera	.05	.02	.00
☐ 224	Harold Baines	.12	.05	.01
☐ 225	Shawon Dunston	.12	.05	.01
☐ 226	Luis Aguayo	.05	.02	.00
☐ 227	Pete O'Brien	.05	.02	.00

☐ 228	Ozzie Smith	.25	.10	.02
☐ 229	Don Mattingly	.75	.30	.07
☐ 230	Danny Tartabull	.30	.12	.03
☐ 231	Andy Allanson	.05	.02	.00
☐ 232	John Franco	.08	.03	.01
☐ 233	Mike Greenwell	.45	.18	.04
☐ 234	Bob Ojeda	.05	.02	.00
☐ 235	Chili Davis	.08	.03	.01
☐ 236	Mike Dunne	.05	.02	.00
☐ 237	Jim Morrison	.05	.02	.00
☐ 238	Carmelo Martinez	.05	.02	.00
☐ 239	Ernie Whitt	.05	.02	.00
☐ 240	Scott Garrelts	.08	.03	.01
☐ 241	Mike Moore	.10	.04	.01
☐ 242	Dave Parker	.15	.06	.01
☐ 243	Tim Laudner	.05	.02	.00
☐ 244	Bill Wegman	.08	.03	.01
☐ 245	Bob Horner	.10	.04	.01
☐ 246	Rafael Santana	.05	.02	.00
☐ 247	Alfredo Griffin	.05	.02	.00
☐ 248	Mark Bailey	.05	.02	.00
☐ 249	Ron Gant	.75	.30	.07
☐ 250	Bryn Smith	.05	.02	.00
☐ 251	Lance Johnson	.08	.03	.01
☐ 252	Sam Horn	.08	.03	.01
☐ 253	Darryl Strawberry	.75	.30	.07
☐ 254	Chuck Finley	.20	.08	.02
☐ 255	Darnell Coles	.05	.02	.00
☐ 256	Mike Henneman	.08	.03	.01
☐ 257	Andy Hawkins	.05	.02	.00
☐ 258	Jim Clancy	.05	.02	.00
☐ 259	Atlee Hammaker	.05	.02	.00
☐ 260	Glenn Wilson	.05	.02	.00
☐ 261	Larry McWilliams	.05	.02	.00
☐ 262	Jack Clark	.12	.05	.01
☐ 263	Walt Weiss	.25	.10	.02
☐ 264	Gene Larkin	.10	.04	.01

1988 Topps Mini Leaders

The 1988 Topps Mini set of Major League Leaders features 77 cards of leaders of the various statistical categories for the 1987 season. The cards are numbered on the back and measure approximately 2 1/8" by 3". The card backs are printed in blue, red, and yellow on white card stock. The cards were distributed as a separate issue in wax packs.

	MINT	EXC	G-VG
COMPLETE SET (77)	7.00	3.00	.70
COMMON PLAYER (1-77)	.05	.02	.00

☐ 1	Wade Boggs	.50	.20	.05
☐ 2	Roger Clemens	.75	.30	.07
☐ 3	Dwight Evans	.10	.04	.01
☐ 4	DeWayne Buice	.05	.02	.00
☐ 5	Brian Downing	.05	.02	.00
☐ 6	Wally Joyner	.15	.06	.01
☐ 7	Ivan Calderon	.10	.04	.01
☐ 8	Carlton Fisk	.30	.12	.03
☐ 9	Gary Redus	.05	.02	.00
☐ 10	Darrell Evans	.10	.04	.01
☐ 11	Jack Morris	.20	.08	.02
☐ 12	Alan Trammell	.20	.08	.02
☐ 13	Lou Whitaker	.12	.05	.01
☐ 14	Bret Saberhagen	.20	.08	.02
☐ 15	Kevin Seitzer	.10	.04	.01

☐ 16	Danny Tartabull	.20	.08	.02
☐ 17	Willie Wilson	.10	.04	.01
☐ 18	Teddy Higuera	.10	.04	.01
☐ 19	Paul Molitor	.12	.05	.01
☐ 20	Dan Plesac	.05	.02	.00
☐ 21	Robin Yount	.50	.20	.05
☐ 22	Kent Hrbek	.10	.04	.01
☐ 23	Kirby Puckett	.40	.16	.04
☐ 24	Jeff Reardon	.12	.05	.01
☐ 25	Frank Viola	.15	.06	.01
☐ 26	Rickey Henderson	.75	.30	.07
☐ 27	Don Mattingly	.60	.25	.06
☐ 28	Willie Randolph	.08	.03	.01
☐ 29	Dave Righetti	.08	.03	.01
☐ 30	Jose Canseco	.90	.40	.09
☐ 31	Mark McGwire	.50	.20	.05
☐ 32	Dave Stewart	.12	.05	.01
☐ 33	Phil Bradley	.05	.02	.00
☐ 34	Mark Langston	.10	.04	.01
☐ 35	Harold Reynolds	.08	.03	.01
☐ 36	Charlie Hough	.05	.02	.00
☐ 37	George Bell	.15	.06	.01
☐ 38	Tom Henke	.05	.02	.01
☐ 39	Jimmy Key	.08	.03	.01
☐ 40	Dion James	.05	.02	.00
☐ 41	Dale Murphy	.30	.12	.03
☐ 42	Zane Smith	.08	.03	.01
☐ 43	Andre Dawson	.25	.10	.02
☐ 44	Lee Smith	.10	.04	.01
☐ 45	Rick Sutcliffe	.08	.03	.01
☐ 46	Eric Davis	.30	.12	.03
☐ 47	John Franco	.08	.03	.01
☐ 48	Dave Parker	.15	.06	.01
☐ 49	Billy Hatcher	.08	.03	.01
☐ 50	Nolan Ryan	1.00	.40	.10
☐ 51	Mike Scott	.12	.05	.01
☐ 52	Pedro Guerrero	.12	.05	.01
☐ 53	Orel Hershiser	.20	.08	.02
☐ 54	Fernando Valenzuela	.12	.05	.01
☐ 55	Bob Welch	.15	.06	.01
☐ 56	Andres Galarraga	.12	.05	.01
☐ 57	Tim Raines	.15	.06	.01
☐ 58	Tim Wallach	.08	.03	.01
☐ 59	Len Dykstra	.15	.06	.01
☐ 60	Dwight Gooden	.25	.10	.02
☐ 61	Howard Johnson	.15	.06	.01
☐ 62	Roger McDowell	.05	.02	.00
☐ 63	Darryl Strawberry	.50	.20	.05
☐ 64	Steve Bedrosian	.05	.02	.00
☐ 65	Shane Rawley	.05	.02	.00
☐ 66	Juan Samuel	.08	.03	.01
☐ 67	Mike Schmidt	.75	.30	.07
☐ 68	Mike Dunne	.05	.02	.00
☐ 69	Jack Clark	.12	.05	.01
☐ 70	Vince Coleman	.20	.08	.02
☐ 71	Willie McGee	.12	.05	.01
☐ 72	Ozzie Smith	.15	.06	.01
☐ 73	Todd Worrell	.08	.03	.01
☐ 74	Tony Gwynn	.35	.15	.03
☐ 75	John Kruk	.08	.03	.01
☐ 76	Rick Reuschel	.05	.02	.00
☐ 77	Checklist Card	.05	.02	.00

1988 Topps Traded

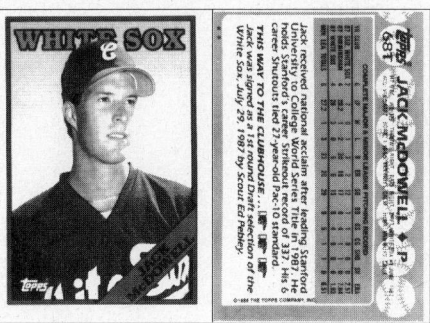

This 132-card Traded or extended set was distributed by Topps to dealers in a special blue and white box as a complete set. The

card fronts are identical in style to the Topps regular issue and are also 2 1/2" by 3 1/2". The backs are printed in orange and black on white card stock. Cards are numbered (with a T suffix) alphabetically according to the name of the player. This set has generated additional interest due to the inclusion of the 1988 U.S. Olympic baseball team members. These Olympians are indicated in the checklist below by OLY. The key (extended) rookie cards in this set are Jim Abbott, Roberto Alomar, Andy Benes, Ron Gant, Mark Grace, Tino Martinez, Jack McDowell, Chris Sabo, Robin Ventura, and Walt Weiss. Topps also produced a specially boxed "glossy" edition, frequently referred to as the Topps Traded Tiffany set. This year, again, Topps did not disclose the number of Tiffany sets they produced or sold. It is apparent from the availability that there were many more sets produced this year compared to the 1984-86 Tiffany sets, perhaps 25,000 sets. The checklist of cards is identical to that of the normal non-glossy cards. There are two primary distinguishing features of the Tiffany cards, white card stock reverses and high gloss obverses. These Tiffany cards are valued at approximately four times the values listed below.

		MINT	EXC	G-VG
	COMPLETE SET (132)	28.00	12.50	4.00
	COMMON PLAYER (1-132)	.06	.02	.00
☐ 1T	Jim Abbott OLY	6.00	1.50	.30
☐ 2T	Juan Agosto	.06	.02	.00
☐ 3T	Luis Alicea	.10	.04	.01
☐ 4T	Roberto Alomar	3.50	1.50	.35
☐ 5T	Brady Anderson	.10	.04	.01
☐ 6T	Jack Armstrong	.20	.08	.02
☐ 7T	Don August	.10	.04	.01
☐ 8T	Floyd Bannister	.06	.02	.00
☐ 9T	Bret Barberie OLY	.60	.25	.06
☐ 10T	Jose Bautista	.10	.04	.01
☐ 11T	Don Baylor	.10	.04	.01
☐ 12T	Tim Belcher	.12	.05	.01
☐ 13T	Buddy Bell	.10	.04	.01
☐ 14T	Andy Benes OLY	3.00	1.25	.30
☐ 15T	Damon Berryhill	.10	.04	.01
☐ 16T	Bud Black	.06	.02	.00
☐ 17T	Pat Borders	.30	.12	.03
☐ 18T	Phil Bradley	.06	.02	.00
☐ 19T	Jeff Branson OLY	.20	.08	.02
☐ 20T	Tom Brunansky	.10	.04	.01
☐ 21T	Jay Buhner	.60	.25	.06
☐ 22T	Brett Butler	.12	.05	.01
☐ 23T	Jim Campanis OLY	.20	.08	.02
☐ 24T	Sil Campusano	.12	.05	.01
☐ 25T	John Candelaria	.06	.02	.00
☐ 26T	Jose Cecena	.10	.04	.01
☐ 27T	Rick Cerone	.06	.02	.00
☐ 28T	Jack Clark	.10	.04	.01
☐ 29T	Kevin Coffman	.06	.02	.00
☐ 30T	Pat Combs OLY	.25	.10	.02
☐ 31T	Henry Cotto	.06	.02	.00
☐ 32T	Chili Davis	.12	.05	.01
☐ 33T	Mike Davis	.06	.02	.00
☐ 34T	Jose DeLeon	.06	.02	.00
☐ 35T	Richard Dotson	.06	.02	.00
☐ 36T	Cecil Espy	.12	.05	.01
☐ 37T	Tom Filer	.06	.02	.00
☐ 38T	Mike Fiore OLY	.20	.08	.02
☐ 39T	Ron Gant	2.50	1.00	.25
☐ 40T	Kirk Gibson	.12	.05	.01
☐ 41T	Rich Gossage	.12	.05	.01
☐ 42T	Mark Grace	2.25	.90	.22
☐ 43T	Alfredo Griffin	.06	.02	.00
☐ 44T	Ty Griffin OLY	.15	.06	.01
☐ 45T	Bryan Harvey	.60	.25	.06
☐ 46T	Ron Hassey	.06	.02	.00
☐ 47T	Ray Hayward	.06	.02	.00
☐ 48T	Dave Henderson	.12	.05	.01
☐ 49T	Tom Herr	.10	.04	.01
☐ 50T	Bob Horner	.10	.04	.01
☐ 51T	Ricky Horton	.06	.02	.00
☐ 52T	Jay Howell	.06	.02	.00
☐ 53T	Glenn Hubbard	.06	.02	.00
☐ 54T	Jeff Innis	.10	.04	.01
☐ 55T	Danny Jackson	.10	.04	.01
☐ 56T	Darrin Jackson	.20	.08	.02
☐ 57T	Roberto Kelly	.75	.30	.07
☐ 58T	Ron Kittle	.10	.04	.01
☐ 59T	Ray Knight	.10	.04	.01
☐ 60T	Vance Law	.06	.02	.00
☐ 61T	Jeffrey Leonard	.06	.02	.00
☐ 62T	Mike Macfarlane	.15	.06	.01
☐ 63T	Scotti Madison	.10	.04	.01

☐ 64T	Kirt Manwaring	.10	.04	.01
☐ 65T	Mark Marquess OLY CO	.06	.02	.00
☐ 66T	Tino Martinez OLY	3.00	1.25	.30
☐ 67T	Billy Masse OLY	.20	.08	.02
☐ 68T	Jack McDowell	1.00	.40	.10
☐ 69T	Jack McKeon MG	.06	.02	.00
☐ 70T	Larry McWilliams	.06	.02	.00
☐ 71T	Mickey Morandini OLY	.50	.20	.05
☐ 72T	Keith Moreland	.06	.02	.00
☐ 73T	Mike Morgan	.10	.04	.01
☐ 74T	Charles Nagy OLY	.60	.25	.06
☐ 75T	Al Nipper	.06	.02	.00
☐ 76T	Russ Nixon MG	.06	.02	.00
☐ 77T	Jesse Orosco	.06	.02	.00
☐ 78T	Joe Orsulak	.06	.02	.00
☐ 79T	Dave Palmer	.06	.02	.00
☐ 80T	Mark Parent	.10	.04	.01
☐ 81T	Dave Parker	.15	.06	.01
☐ 82T	Dan Pasqua	.10	.04	.01
☐ 83T	Melido Perez	.20	.08	.02
☐ 84T	Steve Peters	.10	.04	.01
☐ 85T	Dan Petry	.06	.02	.00
☐ 86T	Gary Pettis	.06	.02	.00
☐ 87T	Jeff Pico	.10	.04	.01
☐ 88T	Jim Poole OLY	.20	.08	.02
☐ 89T	Ted Power	.06	.02	.00
☐ 90T	Rafael Ramirez	.06	.02	.00
☐ 91T	Dennis Rasmussen	.06	.02	.00
☐ 92T	Jose Rijo	.20	.08	.02
☐ 93T	Ernie Riles	.06	.02	.00
☐ 94T	Luis Rivera	.10	.04	.01
☐ 95T	Doug Robbins OLY	.15	.06	.01
☐ 96T	Frank Robinson MG	.15	.06	.01
☐ 97T	Cookie Rojas MG	.06	.02	.00
☐ 98T	Chris Sabo	2.00	.80	.20
☐ 99T	Mark Salas	.06	.02	.00
☐ 100T	Luis Salazar	.06	.02	.00
☐ 101T	Rafael Santana	.06	.02	.00
☐ 102T	Nelson Santovenia	.12	.05	.01
☐ 103T	Mackey Sasser	.15	.06	.01
☐ 104T	Calvin Schiraldi	.06	.02	.00
☐ 105T	Mike Schooler	.20	.08	.02
☐ 106T	Scott Servais OLY	.20	.08	.02
☐ 107T	Dave Silvestri OLY	.15	.06	.01
☐ 108T	Don Slaught	.06	.02	.00
☐ 109T	Joe Slusarski OLY	.40	.16	.04
☐ 110T	Lee Smith	.12	.05	.01
☐ 111T	Pete Smith	.10	.04	.01
☐ 112T	Jim Snyder MG	.06	.02	.00
☐ 113T	Ed Sprague OLY	.50	.20	.05
☐ 114T	Pete Stanicek	.10	.04	.01
☐ 115T	Kurt Stillwell	.10	.04	.01
☐ 116T	Todd Stottlemyre	.75	.30	.07
☐ 117T	Bill Swift	.15	.06	.01
☐ 118T	Pat Tabler	.06	.02	.00
☐ 119T	Scott Terry	.06	.02	.00
☐ 120T	Mickey Tettleton	.15	.06	.01
☐ 121T	Dickie Thon	.10	.04	.01
☐ 122T	Jeff Treadway	.25	.10	.02
☐ 123T	Willie Upshaw	.06	.02	.00
☐ 124T	Robin Ventura OLY	9.00	4.00	.90
☐ 125T	Ron Washington	.06	.02	.00
☐ 126T	Walt Weiss	.30	.12	.03
☐ 127T	Bob Welch	.20	.08	.02
☐ 128T	David Wells	.20	.08	.02
☐ 129T	Glenn Wilson	.06	.02	.00
☐ 130T	Ted Wood OLY	.35	.15	.03
☐ 131T	Don Zimmer MG	.06	.02	.00
☐ 132T	Checklist 1T-132T	.06	.01	.00

1989 Topps

This 792-card set features backs that are printed in pink and black on gray card stock. The manager cards contain a checklist of the respective team's players on the back. Subsets in the set include Record Breakers (1-7), Turn Back the Clock (661-665), and All-Star selections (386-407). The bonus cards distributed throughout the set, which are indicated on the Topps checklist cards, are actually Team Leader (TL) cards. Also sprinkled throughout the set are Future Stars (FS) and First Draft Picks (FDP). There are subtle variations found in the Future Stars cards with respect to the placement of photo and type on the card; in fact, each card has at least two varieties but they are difficult to detect (requiring precise measurement) as well as difficult to explain. The key rookies in this set are Jim Abbott,

Sandy Alomar Jr., Steve Avery, Andy Benes, Ramon Martinez, Robin Ventura, and Gary Sheffield. Topps also produced a specially boxed "glossy" edition, frequently referred to as the Topps Tiffany set. This year, again, Topps did not disclose the number of Tiffany sets they produced or sold but it seems that production quantities were roughly similar (or slightly smaller, approximately 15,000 sets) to the previous two years. The checklist of cards (792 regular and 132 Traded) is identical to that of the normal non-glossy cards. There are two primary distinguishing features of the Tiffany cards, white card stock reverses and high gloss obverses. These Tiffany cards are valued at approximately four times the values listed below.

	MINT	EXC	G-VG
COMPLETE SET (792)	20.00	8.50	2.75
COMMON PLAYER (1-792)	.03	.01	.00
☐ 1 George Bell RB	.10	.04	.01
Slams 3 HR on			
Opening Day			
☐ 2 Wade Boggs RB	.10	.04	.01
Gets 200 Hits			
6th Straight Season			
☐ 3 Gary Carter RB	.06	.02	.00
Sets Record for			
Career Putouts			
☐ 4 Andre Dawson RB	.08	.03	.01
Logs Double Figures			
in HR and SB			
☐ 5 Orel Hershiser RB	.06	.02	.00
Pitches 59			
Scoreless Innings			
☐ 6 Doug Jones RB	.03	.01	.00
Earns His 15th			
Straight Save			
(photo actually			
Chris Codiroli)			
☐ 7 Kevin McReynolds RB	.06	.02	.00
Steals 21 Without			
Being Caught			
☐ 8 Dave Eiland	.08	.03	.01
☐ 9 Tim Teufel	.03	.01	.00
☐ 10 Andre Dawson	.12	.05	.01
☐ 11 Bruce Sutter	.06	.02	.00
☐ 12 Dale Sveum	.03	.01	.00
☐ 13 Doug Sisk	.03	.01	.00
☐ 14 Tom Kelly MG	.06	.02	.00
(team checklist back)			
☐ 15 Robby Thompson	.03	.01	.00
☐ 16 Ron Robinson	.03	.01	.00
☐ 17 Brian Downing	.03	.01	.00
☐ 18 Rick Rhoden	.03	.01	.00
☐ 19 Greg Gagne	.03	.01	.00
☐ 20 Steve Bedrosian	.06	.02	.00
☐ 21 Chicago White Sox TL	.03	.01	.00
Greg Walker			
☐ 22 Tim Crews	.03	.01	.00
☐ 23 Mike Fitzgerald	.03	.01	.00
Montreal Expos			
☐ 24 Larry Andersen	.03	.01	.00
☐ 25 Frank White	.06	.02	.00
☐ 26 Dale Mohorcic	.03	.01	.00
☐ 27A Orestes Destrade	.15	.06	.01
(F* next to copyright)			
☐ 27B Orestes Destrade	.15	.06	.01
(E*F* next to			
copyright)			
☐ 28 Mike Moore	.06	.02	.00

#	Player			
☐ 29	Kelly Gruber	.10	.04	.01
☐ 30	Dwight Gooden	.10	.04	.01
☐ 31	Terry Francona	.03	.01	.00
☐ 32	Dennis Rasmussen	.03	.01	.00
☐ 33	B.J. Surhoff	.06	.02	.00
☐ 34	Ken Williams	.03	.01	.00
☐ 35	John Tudor UER	.06	.02	.00
	('84 Pirates record, should be Red Sox)			
☐ 36	Mitch Webster	.03	.01	.00
☐ 37	Bob Stanley	.03	.01	.00
☐ 38	Paul Runge	.03	.01	.00
☐ 39	Mike Maddux	.03	.01	.00
☐ 40	Steve Sax	.08	.03	.01
☐ 41	Terry Mulholland	.06	.02	.00
☐ 42	Jim Eppard	.03	.01	.00
☐ 43	Guillermo Hernandez	.03	.01	.00
☐ 44	Jim Snyder MG	.06	.02	.00
	(team checklist back)			
☐ 45	Kal Daniels	.08	.03	.01
☐ 46	Mark Portugal	.03	.01	.00
☐ 47	Carney Lansford	.06	.02	.00
☐ 48	Tim Burke	.03	.01	.00
☐ 49	Craig Biggio	.35	.15	.03
☐ 50	George Bell	.10	.04	.01
☐ 51	California Angels TL	.03	.01	.00
	Mark McLemore			
☐ 52	Bob Brenly	.03	.01	.00
☐ 53	Ruben Sierra	.25	.10	.02
☐ 54	Steve Trout	.03	.01	.00
☐ 55	Julio Franco	.12	.05	.01
☐ 56	Pat Tabler	.03	.01	.00
☐ 57	Alejandro Pena	.06	.02	.00
☐ 58	Lee Mazzilli	.03	.01	.00
☐ 59	Mark Davis	.06	.02	.00
☐ 60	Tom Brunansky	.06	.02	.00
☐ 61	Neil Allen	.03	.01	.00
☐ 62	Alfredo Griffin	.03	.01	.00
☐ 63	Mark Clear	.03	.01	.00
☐ 64	Alex Trevino	.03	.01	.00
☐ 65	Rick Reuschel	.06	.02	.00
☐ 66	Manny Trillo	.03	.01	.00
☐ 67	Dave Palmer	.03	.01	.00
☐ 68	Darrell Miller	.03	.01	.00
☐ 69	Jeff Ballard	.03	.01	.00
☐ 70	Mark McGwire	.12	.05	.01
☐ 71	Mike Boddicker	.03	.01	.00
☐ 72	John Moses	.03	.01	.00
☐ 73	Pascual Perez	.03	.01	.00
☐ 74	Nick Leyva MG	.06	.02	.00
	(team checklist back)			
☐ 75	Tom Henke	.06	.02	.00
☐ 76	Terry Blocker	.06	.02	.00
☐ 77	Doyle Alexander	.03	.01	.00
☐ 78	Jim Sundberg	.03	.01	.00
☐ 79	Scott Bankhead	.03	.01	.00
☐ 80	Cory Snyder	.06	.02	.00
☐ 81	Montreal Expos TL	.06	.02	.00
	Tim Raines			
☐ 82	Dave Leiper	.03	.01	.00
☐ 83	Jeff Blauser	.08	.03	.01
☐ 84	Bill Bene FDP	.03	.01	.00
☐ 85	Kevin McReynolds	.08	.03	.01
☐ 86	Al Nipper	.03	.01	.00
☐ 87	Larry Owen	.03	.01	.00
☐ 88	Darryl Hamilton	.12	.05	.01
☐ 89	Dave LaPoint	.03	.01	.00
☐ 90	Vince Coleman UER	.10	.04	.01
	(wrong birth year)			
☐ 91	Floyd Youmans	.03	.01	.00
☐ 92	Jeff Kunkel	.03	.01	.00
☐ 93	Ken Howell	.03	.01	.00
☐ 94	Chris Speier	.03	.01	.00
☐ 95	Gerald Young	.03	.01	.00
☐ 96	Rick Cerone	.06	.02	.00
	(Ellis Burks in background of photo)			
☐ 97	Greg Mathews	.03	.01	.00
☐ 98	Larry Sheets	.03	.01	.00
☐ 99	Sherman Corbett	.03	.01	.00
☐ 100	Mike Schmidt	.35	.15	.03
☐ 101	Les Straker	.03	.01	.00
☐ 102	Mike Gallego	.03	.01	.00
☐ 103	Tim Birtsas	.03	.01	.00
☐ 104	Dallas Green MG	.06	.02	.00
	(team checklist back)			
☐ 105	Ron Darling	.06	.02	.00
☐ 106	Willie Upshaw	.03	.01	.00
☐ 107	Jose DeLeon	.03	.01	.00
☐ 108	Fred Manrique	.03	.01	.00
☐ 109	Hipolito Pena	.03	.01	.00
☐ 110	Paul Molitor	.10	.04	.01
☐ 111	Cincinnati Reds TL	.08	.03	.01
	Eric Davis (swinging bat)			
☐ 112	Jim Presley	.03	.01	.00
☐ 113	Lloyd Moseby	.03	.01	.00
☐ 114	Bob Kipper	.03	.01	.00
☐ 115	Jody Davis	.03	.01	.00
☐ 116	Jeff Montgomery	.06	.02	.00
☐ 117	Dave Anderson	.03	.01	.00
☐ 118	Checklist 1-132	.06	.01	.00
☐ 119	Terry Puhl	.03	.01	.00
☐ 120	Frank Viola	.08	.03	.01
☐ 121	Garry Templeton	.06	.02	.00
☐ 122	Lance Johnson	.08	.03	.01
☐ 123	Spike Owen	.03	.01	.00
☐ 124	Jim Traber	.03	.01	.00
☐ 125	Mike Krukow	.03	.01	.00
☐ 126	Sid Bream	.03	.01	.00
☐ 127	Walt Terrell	.03	.01	.00
☐ 128	Milt Thompson	.03	.01	.00
☐ 129	Terry Clark	.06	.02	.00
☐ 130	Gerald Perry	.03	.01	.00
☐ 131	Dave Otto	.06	.02	.00
☐ 132	Curt Ford	.03	.01	.00
☐ 133	Bill Long	.03	.01	.00
☐ 134	Don Zimmer MG	.06	.02	.00
	(team checklist back)			
☐ 135	Jose Rijo	.08	.03	.01
☐ 136	Joey Meyer	.03	.01	.00
☐ 137	Geno Petralli	.03	.01	.00
☐ 138	Wallace Johnson	.03	.01	.00
☐ 139	Mike Flanagan	.03	.01	.00
☐ 140	Shawon Dunston	.08	.03	.01
☐ 141	Cleveland Indians TL	.03	.01	.00
	Brook Jacoby			
☐ 142	Mike Diaz	.03	.01	.00
☐ 143	Mike Campbell	.03	.01	.00
☐ 144	Jay Bell	.06	.02	.00
☐ 145	Dave Stewart	.08	.03	.01
☐ 146	Gary Pettis	.03	.01	.00
☐ 147	DeWayne Buice	.03	.01	.00
☐ 148	Bill Pecota	.03	.01	.00
☐ 149	Doug Dascenzo	.08	.03	.01
☐ 150	Fernando Valenzuela	.08	.03	.01
☐ 151	Terry McGriff	.03	.01	.00
☐ 152	Mark Thurmond	.03	.01	.00
☐ 153	Jim Pankovits	.03	.01	.00
☐ 154	Don Carman	.03	.01	.00
☐ 155	Marty Barrett	.03	.01	.00
☐ 156	Dave Gallagher	.08	.03	.01
☐ 157	Tom Glavine	.35	.15	.03
☐ 158	Mike Aldrete	.03	.01	.00
☐ 159	Pat Clements	.03	.01	.00
☐ 160	Jeffrey Leonard	.03	.01	.00
☐ 161	Gregg Olson FDP UER	.60	.25	.06
	(born Scribner, NE, should be Omaha, NE)			
☐ 162	John Davis	.03	.01	.00
☐ 163	Bob Forsch	.03	.01	.00
☐ 164	Hal Lanier MG	.06	.02	.00
	(team checklist back)			
☐ 165	Mike Dunne	.03	.01	.00
☐ 166	Doug Jennings	.08	.03	.01
☐ 167	Steve Searcy FS	.08	.03	.01
☐ 168	Willie Wilson	.06	.02	.00
☐ 169	Mike Jackson	.03	.01	.00
☐ 170	Tony Fernandez	.06	.02	.00
☐ 171	Atlanta Braves TL	.03	.01	.00
	Andres Thomas			
☐ 172	Frank Williams	.03	.01	.00
☐ 173	Mel Hall	.06	.02	.00
☐ 174	Todd Burns	.08	.03	.01
☐ 175	John Shelby	.03	.01	.00
☐ 176	Jeff Parrett	.03	.01	.00
☐ 177	Monty Fariss FDP	.30	.12	.03
☐ 178	Mark Grant	.03	.01	.00
☐ 179	Ozzie Virgil	.03	.01	.00
☐ 180	Mike Scott	.08	.03	.01
☐ 181	Craig Worthington	.08	.03	.01
☐ 182	Bob McClure	.03	.01	.00
☐ 183	Oddibe McDowell	.03	.01	.00
☐ 184	John Costello	.03	.01	.00
☐ 185	Claudell Washington	.03	.01	.00
☐ 186	Pat Perry	.03	.01	.00
☐ 187	Darren Daulton	.06	.02	.00
☐ 188	Dennis Lamp	.03	.01	.00
☐ 189	Kevin Mitchell	.15	.06	.01
☐ 190	Mike Witt	.03	.01	.00
☐ 191	Sil Campusano	.10	.04	.01
☐ 192	Paul Mirabella	.03	.01	.00
☐ 193	Sparky Anderson MG	.06	.02	.00
	(team checklist back) UER (553 Salazer)			
☐ 194	Greg W. Harris	.15	.06	.01
	San Diego Padres			
☐ 195	Ozzie Guillen	.06	.02	.00
☐ 196	Denny Walling	.03	.01	.00
☐ 197	Neal Heaton	.03	.01	.00

☐	198	Danny Heep	.03	.01	.00	☐	282	Cris Carpenter	.08	.03	.01

☐ 198 Danny Heep	.03	.01	.00
☐ 199 Mike Schooler	.12	.05	.01
☐ 200 George Brett	.15	.06	.01
☐ 201 Blue Jays TL	.06	.02	.00
Kelly Gruber			
☐ 202 Brad Moore	.08	.03	.01
☐ 203 Rob Ducey	.03	.01	.00
☐ 204 Brad Havens	.03	.01	.00
☐ 205 Dwight Evans	.08	.03	.01
☐ 206 Roberto Alomar	.45	.18	.04
☐ 207 Terry Leach	.03	.01	.00
☐ 208 Tom Pagnozzi	.03	.01	.00
☐ 209 Jeff Bittiger	.06	.02	.00
☐ 210 Dale Murphy	.12	.05	.01
☐ 211 Mike Pagliarulo	.03	.01	.00
☐ 212 Scott Sanderson	.06	.02	.00
☐ 213 Rene Gonzales	.03	.01	.00
☐ 214 Charlie O'Brien	.03	.01	.00
☐ 215 Kevin Gross	.03	.01	.00
☐ 216 Jack Howell	.03	.01	.00
☐ 217 Joe Price	.03	.01	.00
☐ 218 Mike LaValliere	.03	.01	.00
☐ 219 Jim Clancy	.03	.01	.00
☐ 220 Gary Gaetti	.06	.02	.00
☐ 221 Cecil Espy	.03	.01	.00
☐ 222 Mark Lewis FDP	.60	.25	.06
☐ 223 Jay Buhner	.15	.06	.01
☐ 224 Tony LaRussa MG	.06	.02	.00
(team checklist back)			
☐ 225 Ramon Martinez	1.25	.50	.12
☐ 226 Bill Doran	.03	.01	.00
☐ 227 John Farrell	.03	.01	.00
☐ 228 Nelson Santovenia	.08	.03	.01
☐ 229 Jimmy Key	.06	.02	.00
☐ 230 Ozzie Smith	.12	.05	.01
☐ 231 San Diego Padres TL	.10	.04	.01
Roberto Alomar			
(G.Carter at plate)			
☐ 232 Ricky Horton	.03	.01	.00
☐ 233 Gregg Jefferies FS	.30	.12	.03
☐ 234 Tom Browning	.06	.02	.00
☐ 235 John Kruk	.03	.01	.00
☐ 236 Charles Hudson	.03	.01	.00
☐ 237 Glenn Hubbard	.03	.01	.00
☐ 238 Eric King	.03	.01	.00
☐ 239 Tim Laudner	.03	.01	.00
☐ 240 Greg Maddux	.08	.03	.01
☐ 241 Brett Butler	.08	.03	.01
☐ 242 Ed VandeBerg	.03	.01	.00
☐ 243 Bob Boone	.06	.02	.00
☐ 244 Jim Acker	.03	.01	.00
☐ 245 Jim Rice	.08	.03	.01
☐ 246 Rey Quinones	.03	.01	.00
☐ 247 Shawn Hillegas	.03	.01	.00
☐ 248 Tony Phillips	.03	.01	.00
☐ 249 Tim Leary	.06	.02	.00
☐ 250 Cal Ripken	.35	.15	.03
☐ 251 John Dopson	.08	.03	.01
☐ 252 Billy Hatcher	.03	.01	.00
☐ 253 Jose Alvarez	.06	.02	.00
☐ 254 Tom Lasorda MG	.06	.02	.00
(team checklist back)			
☐ 255 Ron Guidry	.08	.03	.01
☐ 256 Benny Santiago	.08	.03	.01
☐ 257 Rick Aguilera	.03	.01	.00
☐ 258 Checklist 133-264	.06	.01	.00
☐ 259 Larry McWilliams	.03	.01	.00
☐ 260 Dave Winfield	.12	.05	.01
☐ 261 St.Louis Cardinals TL	.06	.02	.00
Tom Brunansky			
(with Luis Alicea)			
☐ 262 Jeff Pico	.06	.02	.00
☐ 263 Mike Felder	.03	.01	.00
☐ 264 Rob Dibble	.25	.10	.02
☐ 265 Kent Hrbek	.08	.03	.01
☐ 266 Luis Aquino	.03	.01	.00
☐ 267 Jeff Robinson	.06	.02	.00
Detroit Tigers			
☐ 268 Keith Miller	.06	.02	.00
Philadelphia Phillies			
☐ 269 Tom Bolton	.03	.01	.00
☐ 270 Wally Joyner	.12	.05	.01
☐ 271 Jay Tibbs	.03	.01	.00
☐ 272 Ron Hassey	.03	.01	.00
☐ 273 Jose Lind	.03	.01	.00
☐ 274 Mark Eichhorn	.06	.02	.00
☐ 275 Danny Tartabull UER	.10	.04	.01
(Born San Juan, PR			
should be Miami, FL)			
☐ 276 Paul Kilgus	.03	.01	.00
☐ 277 Mike Davis	.03	.01	.00
☐ 278 Andy McGaffigan	.03	.01	.00
☐ 279 Scott Bradley	.03	.01	.00
☐ 280 Bob Knepper	.03	.01	.00
☐ 281 Gary Redus	.03	.01	.00

☐ 282 Cris Carpenter	.08	.03	.01
☐ 283 Andy Allanson	.03	.01	.00
☐ 284 Jim Leyland MG	.06	.02	.00
(team checklist back)			
☐ 285 John Candelaria	.03	.01	.00
☐ 286 Darrin Jackson	.08	.03	.01
☐ 287 Juan Nieves	.03	.01	.00
☐ 288 Pat Sheridan	.03	.01	.00
☐ 289 Ernie Whitt	.03	.01	.00
☐ 290 John Franco	.03	.01	.00
☐ 291 New York Mets TL	.08	.03	.01
Darryl Strawberry			
(with K.Hernandez			
and K.McReynolds)			
☐ 292 Jim Corsi	.06	.02	.00
☐ 293 Glenn Wilson	.03	.01	.00
☐ 294 Juan Berenguer	.03	.01	.00
☐ 295 Scott Fletcher	.03	.01	.00
☐ 296 Ron Gant	.40	.16	.04
☐ 297 Oswald Peraza	.06	.02	.00
☐ 298 Chris James	.03	.01	.00
☐ 299 Steve Ellsworth	.06	.02	.00
☐ 300 Darryl Strawberry	.30	.12	.03
☐ 301 Charlie Leibrandt	.03	.01	.00
☐ 302 Gary Ward	.03	.01	.00
☐ 303 Felix Fermin	.03	.01	.00
☐ 304 Joel Youngblood	.03	.01	.00
☐ 305 Dave Smith	.03	.01	.00
☐ 306 Tracy Woodson	.03	.01	.00
☐ 307 Lance McCullers	.03	.01	.00
☐ 308 Ron Karkovice	.03	.01	.00
☐ 309 Mario Diaz	.06	.02	.00
☐ 310 Rafael Palmeiro	.12	.05	.01
☐ 311 Chris Bosio	.03	.01	.00
☐ 312 Tom Lawless	.03	.01	.00
☐ 313 Dennis Martinez	.06	.02	.00
☐ 314 Bobby Valentine MG	.06	.02	.00
(team checklist back)			
☐ 315 Greg Swindell	.06	.02	.00
☐ 316 Walt Weiss	.08	.03	.01
☐ 317 Jack Armstrong	.10	.04	.01
☐ 318 Gene Larkin	.03	.01	.00
☐ 319 Greg Booker	.03	.01	.00
☐ 320 Lou Whitaker	.08	.03	.01
☐ 321 Boston Red Sox TL	.06	.02	.00
Jody Reed			
☐ 322 John Smiley	.06	.02	.00
☐ 323 Gary Thurman	.03	.01	.00
☐ 324 Bob Milacki	.15	.06	.01
☐ 325 Jesse Barfield	.08	.03	.01
☐ 326 Dennis Boyd	.03	.01	.00
☐ 327 Mark Lemke	.15	.06	.01
☐ 328 Rick Honeycutt	.03	.01	.00
☐ 329 Bob Melvin	.03	.01	.00
☐ 330 Eric Davis	.10	.04	.01
☐ 331 Curt Wilkerson	.03	.01	.00
☐ 332 Tony Armas	.03	.01	.00
☐ 333 Bob Ojeda	.03	.01	.00
☐ 334 Steve Lyons	.03	.01	.00
☐ 335 Dave Righetti	.06	.02	.00
☐ 336 Steve Balboni	.03	.01	.00
☐ 337 Calvin Schiraldi	.03	.01	.00
☐ 338 Jim Adduci	.03	.01	.00
☐ 339 Scott Bailes	.03	.01	.00
☐ 340 Kirk Gibson	.08	.03	.01
☐ 341 Jim Deshaies	.03	.01	.00
☐ 342 Tom Brookens	.03	.01	.00
☐ 343 Gary Sheffield FS	.30	.12	.03
☐ 344 Tom Trebelhorn MG	.06	.02	.00
(team checklist back)			
☐ 345 Charlie Hough	.03	.01	.00
☐ 346 Rex Hudler	.03	.01	.00
☐ 347 John Cerutti	.03	.01	.00
☐ 348 Ed Hearn	.03	.01	.00
☐ 349 Ron Jones	.08	.03	.01
☐ 350 Andy Van Slyke	.08	.03	.01
☐ 351 San Fran. Giants TL	.03	.01	.00
Bob Melvin			
(with Bill Fahey CO)			
☐ 352 Rick Schu	.03	.01	.00
☐ 353 Marvell Wynne	.03	.01	.00
☐ 354 Larry Parrish	.03	.01	.00
☐ 355 Mark Langston	.08	.03	.01
☐ 356 Kevin Elster	.03	.01	.00
☐ 357 Jerry Reuss	.03	.01	.00
☐ 358 Ricky Jordan	.12	.05	.01
☐ 359 Tommy John	.08	.03	.01
☐ 360 Ryne Sandberg	.35	.15	.03
☐ 361 Kelly Downs	.03	.01	.00
☐ 362 Jack Lazorko	.03	.01	.00
☐ 363 Rich Yett	.03	.01	.00
☐ 364 Rob Deer	.06	.02	.00
☐ 365 Mike Henneman	.03	.01	.00
☐ 366 Herm Winningham	.03	.01	.00
☐ 367 Johnny Paredes	.06	.02	.00

☐	368 Brian Holton	.03	.01	.00
☐	369 Ken Caminiti	.03	.01	.00
☐	370 Dennis Eckersley	.08	.03	.01
☐	371 Manny Lee	.03	.01	.00
☐	372 Craig Lefferts	.03	.01	.00
☐	373 Tracy Jones	.03	.01	.00
☐	374 John Wathan MG	.06	.02	.00
	(team checklist back)			
☐	375 Terry Pendleton	.10	.04	.01
☐	376 Steve Lombardozzi	.03	.01	.00
☐	377 Mike Smithson	.03	.01	.00
☐	378 Checklist 265-396	.06	.01	.00
☐	379 Tim Flannery	.03	.01	.00
☐	380 Rickey Henderson	.35	.15	.03
☐	381 Baltimore Orioles TL	.03	.01	.00
	Larry Sheets			
☐	382 John Smoltz	.50	.20	.05
☐	383 Howard Johnson	.12	.05	.01
☐	384 Mark Salas	.03	.01	.00
☐	385 Von Hayes	.06	.02	.00
☐	386 Andres Galarraga AS	.06	.02	.00
☐	387 Ryne Sandberg AS	.15	.06	.01
☐	388 Bobby Bonilla AS	.10	.04	.01
☐	389 Ozzie Smith AS	.10	.04	.01
☐	390 Darryl Strawberry AS	.15	.06	.01
☐	391 Andre Dawson AS	.10	.04	.01
☐	392 Andy Van Slyke AS	.08	.03	.01
☐	393 Gary Carter AS	.08	.03	.01
☐	394 Orel Hershiser AS	.08	.03	.01
☐	395 Danny Jackson AS	.06	.02	.00
☐	396 Kirk Gibson AS	.08	.03	.01
☐	397 Don Mattingly AS	.12	.05	.01
☐	398 Julio Franco AS	.08	.03	.01
☐	399 Wade Boggs AS	.10	.04	.01
☐	400 Alan Trammell AS	.08	.03	.01
☐	401 Jose Canseco AS	.20	.08	.02
☐	402 Mike Greenwell AS	.08	.03	.01
☐	403 Kirby Puckett AS	.12	.05	.01
☐	404 Bob Boone AS	.06	.02	.00
☐	405 Roger Clemens AS	.12	.05	.01
☐	406 Frank Viola AS	.06	.02	.00
☐	407 Dave Winfield AS	.10	.04	.01
☐	408 Greg Walker	.03	.01	.00
☐	409 Ken Dayley	.03	.01	.00
☐	410 Jack Clark	.08	.03	.01
☐	411 Mitch Williams	.03	.01	.00
☐	412 Barry Lyons	.03	.01	.00
☐	413 Mike Kingery	.03	.01	.00
☐	414 Jim Fregosi MG	.06	.02	.00
	(team checklist back)			
☐	415 Rich Gossage	.08	.03	.01
☐	416 Fred Lynn	.08	.03	.01
☐	417 Mike LaCoss	.03	.01	.00
☐	418 Bob Dernier	.03	.01	.00
☐	419 Tom Filer	.03	.01	.00
☐	420 Joe Carter	.10	.04	.01
☐	421 Kirk McCaskill	.03	.01	.00
☐	422 Bo Diaz	.03	.01	.00
☐	423 Brian Fisher	.03	.01	.00
☐	424 Luis Polonia UER	.06	.02	.00
	(wrong birthdate)			
☐	425 Jay Howell	.03	.01	.00
☐	426 Dan Gladden	.03	.01	.00
☐	427 Eric Show	.03	.01	.00
☐	428 Craig Reynolds	.03	.01	.00
☐	429 Minnesota Twins TL	.03	.01	.00
	Greg Gagne			
	(taking throw at 2nd)			
☐	430 Mark Gubicza	.06	.02	.00
☐	431 Luis Rivera	.03	.01	.00
☐	432 Chad Kreuter	.06	.02	.00
☐	433 Albert Hall	.03	.01	.00
☐	434 Ken Patterson	.06	.02	.00
☐	435 Len Dykstra	.08	.03	.01
☐	436 Bobby Meacham	.03	.01	.00
☐	437 Andy Benes FDP	.50	.20	.05
☐	438 Greg Gross	.03	.01	.00
☐	439 Frank DiPino	.03	.01	.00
☐	440 Bobby Bonilla	.20	.08	.02
☐	441 Jerry Reed	.03	.01	.00
☐	442 Jose Oquendo	.03	.01	.00
☐	443 Rod Nichols	.06	.02	.00
☐	444 Moose Stubing MG	.06	.02	.00
	(team checklist back)			
☐	445 Matt Nokes	.06	.02	.00
☐	446 Rob Murphy	.03	.01	.00
☐	447 Donell Nixon	.03	.01	.00
☐	448 Eric Plunk	.03	.01	.00
☐	449 Carmelo Martinez	.03	.01	.00
☐	450 Roger Clemens	.30	.12	.03
☐	451 Mark Davidson	.03	.01	.00
☐	452 Israel Sanchez	.06	.02	.00
☐	453 Tom Prince	.03	.01	.00
☐	454 Paul Assenmacher	.03	.01	.00
☐	455 Johnny Ray	.03	.01	.00
☐	456 Tim Belcher	.06	.02	.00
☐	457 Mackey Sasser	.06	.02	.00
☐	458 Donn Pall	.06	.02	.00
☐	459 Seattle Mariners TL	.03	.01	.00
	Dave Valle			
☐	460 Dave Stieb	.08	.03	.01
☐	461 Buddy Bell	.06	.02	.00
☐	462 Jose Guzman	.03	.01	.00
☐	463 Steve Lake	.03	.01	.00
☐	464 Bryn Smith	.03	.01	.00
☐	465 Mark Grace	.30	.12	.03
☐	466 Chuck Crim	.03	.01	.00
☐	467 Jim Walewander	.03	.01	.00
☐	468 Henry Cotto	.03	.01	.00
☐	469 Jose Bautista	.06	.02	.00
☐	470 Lance Parrish	.08	.03	.01
☐	471 Steve Curry	.06	.02	.00
☐	472 Brian Harper	.06	.02	.00
☐	473 Don Robinson	.03	.01	.00
☐	474 Bob Rodgers MG	.06	.02	.00
	(team checklist back)			
☐	475 Dave Parker	.08	.03	.01
☐	476 Jon Perlman	.03	.01	.00
☐	477 Dick Schofield	.03	.01	.00
☐	478 Doug Drabek	.08	.03	.01
☐	479 Mike Macfarlane	.10	.04	.01
☐	480 Keith Hernandez	.08	.03	.01
☐	481 Chris Brown	.03	.01	.00
☐	482 Steve Peters	.08	.03	.01
☐	483 Mickey Hatcher	.03	.01	.00
☐	484 Steve Shields	.03	.01	.00
☐	485 Hubie Brooks	.06	.02	.00
☐	486 Jack McDowell	.17	.07	.01
☐	487 Scott Lusader	.03	.01	.00
☐	488 Kevin Coffman	.03	.01	.00
	("Now with Cubs")			
☐	489 Phila. Phillies TL	.12	.05	.01
	Mike Schmidt			
☐	490 Chris Sabo	.60	.25	.06
☐	491 Mike Birkbeck	.03	.01	.00
☐	492 Alan Ashby	.03	.01	.00
☐	493 Todd Benzinger	.03	.01	.00
☐	494 Shane Rawley	.03	.01	.00
☐	495 Candy Maldonado	.06	.02	.00
☐	496 Dwayne Henry	.03	.01	.00
☐	497 Pete Stanicek	.03	.01	.00
☐	498 Dave Valle	.03	.01	.00
☐	499 Don Heinkel	.03	.01	.00
☐	500 Jose Canseco	.50	.20	.05
☐	501 Vance Law	.03	.01	.00
☐	502 Duane Ward	.06	.02	.00
☐	503 Al Newman	.03	.01	.00
☐	504 Bob Walk	.03	.01	.00
☐	505 Pete Rose MG	.15	.06	.01
	(team checklist back)			
☐	506 Kirt Manwaring	.03	.01	.00
☐	507 Steve Farr	.03	.01	.00
☐	508 Wally Backman	.03	.01	.00
☐	509 Bud Black	.03	.01	.00
☐	510 Bob Horner	.06	.02	.00
☐	511 Richard Dotson	.03	.01	.00
☐	512 Donnie Hill	.03	.01	.00
☐	513 Jesse Orosco	.03	.01	.00
☐	514 Chet Lemon	.03	.01	.00
☐	515 Barry Larkin	.15	.06	.01
☐	516 Eddie Whitson	.03	.01	.00
☐	517 Greg Brock	.03	.01	.00
☐	518 Bruce Ruffin	.03	.01	.00
☐	519 New York Yankees TL	.06	.02	.00
	Willie Randolph			
☐	520 Rick Sutcliffe	.06	.02	.00
☐	521 Mickey Tettleton	.06	.02	.00
☐	522 Randy Kramer	.06	.02	.00
☐	523 Andres Thomas	.03	.01	.00
☐	524 Checklist 397-528	.06	.01	.00
☐	525 Chili Davis	.06	.02	.00
☐	526 Wes Gardner	.03	.01	.00
☐	527 Dave Henderson	.08	.03	.01
☐	528 Luis Medina	.08	.03	.01
	(lower left front			
	has white triangle)			
☐	529 Tom Foley	.03	.01	.00
☐	530 Nolan Ryan	.50	.20	.05
☐	531 Dave Hengel	.06	.02	.00
☐	532 Jerry Browne	.03	.01	.00
☐	533 Andy Hawkins	.03	.01	.00
☐	534 Doc Edwards MG	.06	.02	.00
	(team checklist back)			
☐	535 Todd Worrell UER	.06	.02	.00
	(4 wins in '88,			
	should be 5)			
☐	536 Joel Skinner	.03	.01	.00
☐	537 Pete Smith	.06	.02	.00
☐	538 Juan Castillo	.03	.01	.00
☐	539 Barry Jones	.03	.01	.00

☐ 540	Bo Jackson	.50	.20	.05
☐ 541	Cecil Fielder	.30	.12	.03
☐ 542	Todd Frohwirth	.03	.01	.00
☐ 543	Damon Berryhill	.03	.01	.00
☐ 544	Jeff Sellers	.03	.01	.00
☐ 545	Mookie Wilson	.03	.01	.00
☐ 546	Mark Williamson	.03	.01	.00
☐ 547	Mark McLemore	.03	.01	.00
☐ 548	Bobby Witt	.06	.02	.00
☐ 549	Chicago Cubs TL	.03	.01	.00
	Jamie Moyer			
	(pitching)			
☐ 550	Orel Hershiser	.08	.03	.01
☐ 551	Randy Ready	.03	.01	.00
☐ 552	Greg Cadaret	.03	.01	.00
☐ 553	Luis Salazar	.03	.01	.00
☐ 554	Nick Esasky	.03	.01	.00
☐ 555	Bert Blyleven	.08	.03	.01
☐ 556	Bruce Fields	.03	.01	.00
☐ 557	Keith Miller	.06	.02	.00
	New York Mets			
☐ 558	Dan Pasqua	.03	.01	.00
☐ 559	Juan Agosto	.03	.01	.00
☐ 560	Tim Raines	.10	.04	.01
☐ 561	Luis Aguayo	.03	.01	.00
☐ 562	Danny Cox	.03	.01	.00
☐ 563	Bill Schroeder	.03	.01	.00
☐ 564	Russ Nixon MG	.06	.02	.00
	(team checklist back)			
☐ 565	Jeff Russell	.03	.01	.00
☐ 566	Al Pedrique	.03	.01	.00
☐ 567	David Wells UER	.08	.03	.01
	(Complete Pitching			
	Recor)			
☐ 568	Mickey Brantley	.03	.01	.00
☐ 569	German Jimenez	.06	.02	.00
☐ 570	Tony Gwynn UER	.17	.07	.01
	('88 average should			
	be italicized as			
	league leader)			
☐ 571	Billy Ripken	.03	.01	.00
☐ 572	Atlee Hammaker	.03	.01	.00
☐ 573	Jim Abbott FDP	1.25	.50	.12
☐ 574	Dave Clark	.03	.01	.00
☐ 575	Juan Samuel	.06	.02	.00
☐ 576	Greg Minton	.03	.01	.00
☐ 577	Randy Bush	.03	.01	.00
☐ 578	John Morris	.03	.01	.00
☐ 579	Houston Astros TL	.06	.02	.00
	Glenn Davis			
	(batting stance)			
☐ 580	Harold Reynolds	.06	.02	.00
☐ 581	Gene Nelson	.03	.01	.00
☐ 582	Mike Marshall	.06	.02	.00
☐ 583	Paul Gibson	.08	.03	.01
☐ 584	Randy Velarde UER	.06	.02	.00
	(signed 1935,			
	should be 1985)			
☐ 585	Harold Baines	.08	.03	.01
☐ 586	Joe Boever	.03	.01	.00
☐ 587	Mike Stanley	.03	.01	.00
☐ 588	Luis Alicea	.06	.02	.00
☐ 589	Dave Meads	.03	.01	.00
☐ 590	Andres Galarraga	.06	.02	.00
☐ 591	Jeff Musselman	.03	.01	.00
☐ 592	John Cangelosi	.03	.01	.00
☐ 593	Drew Hall	.03	.01	.00
☐ 594	Jimy Williams MG	.06	.02	.00
	(team checklist back)			
☐ 595	Teddy Higuera	.03	.01	.00
☐ 596	Kurt Stillwell	.03	.01	.00
☐ 597	Terry Taylor	.08	.03	.01
☐ 598	Ken Gerhart	.03	.01	.00
☐ 599	Tom Candiotti	.06	.02	.00
☐ 600	Wade Boggs	.20	.08	.02
☐ 601	Dave Dravecky	.08	.03	.01
☐ 602	Devon White	.06	.02	.00
☐ 603	Frank Tanana	.06	.02	.00
☐ 604	Paul O'Neill	.08	.03	.01
☐ 605A	Bob Welch ERR	3.00	1.25	.30
	(missing line on back,			
	"Complete M.L.			
	Pitching Record")			
☐ 605B	Bob Welch COR	.10	.04	.01
☐ 606	Rick Dempsey	.03	.01	.00
☐ 607	Willie Ansley FDP	.20	.08	.02
☐ 608	Phil Bradley	.03	.01	.00
☐ 609	Detroit Tigers TL	.06	.02	.00
	Frank Tanana			
	(with Alan Trammell			
	and Mike Heath)			
☐ 610	Randy Myers	.03	.01	.00
☐ 611	Don Slaught	.03	.01	.00
☐ 612	Dan Quisenberry	.08	.03	.01

☐ 613	Gary Varsho	.06	.02	.00
☐ 614	Joe Hesketh	.06	.02	.00
☐ 615	Robin Yount	.15	.06	.01
☐ 616	Steve Rosenberg	.08	.03	.01
☐ 617	Mark Parent	.06	.02	.00
☐ 618	Rance Mulliniks	.03	.01	.00
☐ 619	Checklist 529-660	.06	.01	.00
☐ 620	Barry Bonds	.25	.10	.02
☐ 621	Rick Mahler	.03	.01	.00
☐ 622	Stan Javier	.03	.01	.00
☐ 623	Fred Toliver	.03	.01	.00
☐ 624	Jack McKeon MG	.06	.02	.00
	(team checklist back)			
☐ 625	Eddie Murray	.12	.05	.01
☐ 626	Jeff Reed	.03	.01	.00
☐ 627	Greg Harris	.03	.01	.00
	Philadelphia Phillies			
☐ 628	Matt Williams	.20	.08	.02
☐ 629	Pete O'Brien	.03	.01	.00
☐ 630	Mike Greenwell	.15	.06	.01
☐ 631	Dave Bergman	.03	.01	.00
☐ 632	Bryan Harvey	.25	.10	.02
☐ 633	Daryl Boston	.03	.01	.00
☐ 634	Marvin Freeman	.03	.01	.00
☐ 635	Willie Randolph	.06	.02	.00
☐ 636	Bill Wilkinson	.03	.01	.00
☐ 637	Carmen Castillo	.03	.01	.00
☐ 638	Floyd Bannister	.03	.01	.00
☐ 639	Oakland A's TL	.06	.02	.00
	Walt Weiss			
☐ 640	Willie McGee	.08	.03	.01
☐ 641	Curt Young	.03	.01	.00
☐ 642	Argenis Salazar	.03	.01	.00
☐ 643	Louie Meadows	.03	.01	.00
☐ 644	Lloyd McClendon	.03	.01	.00
☐ 645	Jack Morris	.10	.04	.01
☐ 646	Kevin Bass	.03	.01	.00
☐ 647	Randy Johnson	.35	.15	.03
☐ 648	Sandy Alomar FS	.40	.16	.04
☐ 649	Stewart Cliburn	.03	.01	.00
☐ 650	Kirby Puckett	.30	.12	.03
☐ 651	Tom Niedenfuer	.03	.01	.00
☐ 652	Rich Gedman	.03	.01	.00
☐ 653	Tommy Barrett	.06	.02	.00
☐ 654	Whitey Herzog MG	.06	.02	.00
	(team checklist back)			
☐ 655	Dave Magadan	.08	.03	.01
☐ 656	Ivan Calderon	.06	.02	.00
☐ 657	Joe Magrane	.06	.02	.00
☐ 658	R.J. Reynolds	.03	.01	.00
☐ 659	Al Leiter	.03	.01	.00
☐ 660	Will Clark	.40	.16	.04
☐ 661	Dwight Gooden TBC84	.08	.03	.01
☐ 662	Lou Brock TBC79	.08	.03	.01
☐ 663	Hank Aaron TBC74	.10	.04	.01
☐ 664	Gil Hodges TBC69	.06	.02	.00
☐ 665A	Tony Oliva TBC64	2.00	.80	.20
	ERR (fabricated card			
	is enlarged version			
	of Oliva's 64T card;			
	Topps copyright			
	missing)			
☐ 665B	Tony Oliva TBC64	.06	.02	.00
	COR (fabricated			
	card)			
☐ 666	Randy St.Claire	.03	.01	.00
☐ 667	Dwayne Murphy	.03	.01	.00
☐ 668	Mike Bielecki	.06	.02	.00
☐ 669	L.A. Dodgers TL	.06	.02	.00
	Orel Hershiser			
	(mound conference			
	with Mike Scioscia)			
☐ 670	Kevin Seitzer	.06	.02	.00
☐ 671	Jim Gantner	.03	.01	.00
☐ 672	Allan Anderson	.03	.01	.00
☐ 673	Don Baylor	.06	.02	.00
☐ 674	Otis Nixon	.06	.02	.00
☐ 675	Bruce Hurst	.06	.02	.00
☐ 676	Ernie Riles	.03	.01	.00
☐ 677	Dave Schmidt	.03	.01	.00
☐ 678	Dion James	.03	.01	.00
☐ 679	Willie Fraser	.03	.01	.00
☐ 680	Gary Carter	.08	.03	.01
☐ 681	Jeff Robinson	.03	.01	.00
	Pittsburgh Pirates			
☐ 682	Rick Leach	.03	.01	.00
☐ 683	Jose Cecena	.03	.01	.00
☐ 684	Dave Johnson MG	.06	.02	.00
	(team checklist back)			
☐ 685	Jeff Treadway	.08	.03	.01
☐ 686	Scott Terry	.03	.01	.00
☐ 687	Alvin Davis	.06	.02	.00
☐ 688	Zane Smith	.06	.02	.00

			MINT	EXC	G-VG
☐ 689A	Stan Jefferson		.08	.03	.01
	(pink triangle on front bottom left)				
☐ 689B	Stan Jefferson		.08	.03	.01
	(violet triangle on front bottom left)				
☐ 690	Doug Jones		.03	.01	.00
☐ 691	Roberto Kelly UER		.15	.06	.01
	(83 Oneonita)				
☐ 692	Steve Ontiveros		.03	.01	.00
☐ 693	Pat Borders		.15	.06	.01
☐ 694	Les Lancaster		.03	.01	.00
☐ 695	Carlton Fisk		.15	.06	.01
☐ 696	Don August		.03	.01	.00
☐ 697A	Franklin Stubbs		.08	.03	.01
	(team name on front in white)				
☐ 697B	Franklin Stubbs		.08	.03	.01
	(team name on front in gray)				
☐ 698	Keith Atherton		.03	.01	.00
☐ 699	Pittsburgh Pirates TL		.06	.02	.00
	Al Pedrique				
	(Tony Gwynn sliding)				
☐ 700	Don Mattingly		.20	.08	.02
☐ 701	Storm Davis		.03	.01	.00
☐ 702	Jamie Quirk		.03	.01	.00
☐ 703	Scott Garrelts		.03	.01	.00
☐ 704	Carlos Quintana		.25	.10	.02
☐ 705	Terry Kennedy		.03	.01	.00
☐ 706	Pete Incaviglia		.06	.02	.00
☐ 707	Steve Jeltz		.03	.01	.00
☐ 708	Chuck Finley		.08	.03	.01
☐ 709	Tom Herr		.03	.01	.00
☐ 710	David Cone		.08	.03	.01
☐ 711	Candy Sierra		.06	.02	.00
☐ 712	Bill Swift		.06	.02	.00
☐ 713	Ty Griffin FDP		.10	.04	.01
☐ 714	Joe Morgan MG		.06	.02	.00
	(team checklist back)				
☐ 715	Tony Pena		.06	.02	.00
☐ 716	Wayne Tolleson		.03	.01	.00
☐ 717	Jamie Moyer		.03	.01	.00
☐ 718	Glenn Braggs		.03	.01	.00
☐ 719	Danny Darwin		.03	.01	.00
☐ 720	Tim Wallach		.06	.02	.00
☐ 721	Ron Tingley		.06	.02	.00
☐ 722	Todd Stottlemyre		.15	.06	.01
☐ 723	Rafael Belliard		.03	.01	.00
☐ 724	Jerry Don Gleaton		.03	.01	.00
☐ 725	Terry Steinbach		.06	.02	.00
☐ 726	Dickie Thon		.03	.01	.00
☐ 727	Joe Orsulak		.03	.01	.00
☐ 728	Charlie Puleo		.03	.01	.00
☐ 729	Texas Rangers TL		.03	.01	.00
	Steve Buechele				
	(inconsistent design, team name on front surrounded by black, should be white)				
☐ 730	Danny Jackson		.06	.02	.00
☐ 731	Mike Young		.03	.01	.00
☐ 732	Steve Buechele		.03	.01	.00
☐ 733	Randy Bockus		.03	.01	.00
☐ 734	Jody Reed		.06	.02	.00
☐ 735	Roger McDowell		.03	.01	.00
☐ 736	Jeff Hamilton		.03	.01	.00
☐ 737	Norm Charlton		.12	.05	.01
☐ 738	Darnell Coles		.03	.01	.00
☐ 739	Brook Jacoby		.03	.01	.00
☐ 740	Dan Plesac		.03	.01	.00
☐ 741	Ken Phelps		.03	.01	.00
☐ 742	Mike Harkey FS		.12	.05	.01
☐ 743	Mike Heath		.03	.01	.00
☐ 744	Roger Craig MG		.06	.02	.00
	(team checklist back)				
☐ 745	Fred McGriff		.15	.06	.01
☐ 746	German Gonzalez UER		.06	.02	.00
	(wrong birthdate)				
☐ 747	Wil Tejada		.03	.01	.00
☐ 748	Jimmy Jones		.03	.01	.00
☐ 749	Rafael Ramirez		.03	.01	.00
☐ 750	Bret Saberhagen		.10	.04	.01
☐ 751	Ken Oberkfell		.03	.01	.00
☐ 752	Jim Gott		.03	.01	.00
☐ 753	Jose Uribe		.03	.01	.00
☐ 754	Bob Brower		.03	.01	.00
☐ 755	Mike Scioscia		.03	.01	.00
☐ 756	Scott Medvin		.08	.03	.01
☐ 757	Brady Anderson		.08	.03	.01
☐ 758	Gene Walter		.03	.01	.00
☐ 759	Milwaukee Brewers TL		.06	.02	.00
	Rob Deer				
☐ 760	Lee Smith		.08	.03	.01
☐ 761	Dante Bichette		.17	.07	.01
☐ 762	Bobby Thigpen		.08	.03	.01
☐ 763	Dave Martinez		.03	.01	.00
☐ 764	Robin Ventura FDP		1.50	.60	.15
☐ 765	Glenn Davis		.08	.03	.01
☐ 766	Cecilio Guante		.03	.01	.00
☐ 767	Mike Capel		.06	.02	.00
☐ 768	Bill Wegman		.03	.01	.00
☐ 769	Junior Ortiz		.03	.01	.00
☐ 770	Alan Trammell		.10	.04	.01
☐ 771	Ron Kittle		.06	.02	.00
☐ 772	Ron Oester		.03	.01	.00
☐ 773	Keith Moreland		.03	.01	.00
☐ 774	Frank Robinson MG		.10	.04	.01
	(team checklist back)				
☐ 775	Jeff Reardon		.08	.03	.01
☐ 776	Nelson Liriano		.03	.01	.00
☐ 777	Ted Power		.03	.01	.00
☐ 778	Bruce Benedict		.03	.01	.00
☐ 779	Craig McMurtry		.03	.01	.00
☐ 780	Pedro Guerrero		.08	.03	.01
☐ 781	Greg Briley		.15	.06	.01
☐ 782	Checklist 661-792		.06	.01	.00
☐ 783	Trevor Wilson		.10	.04	.01
☐ 784	Steve Avery FDP		2.00	.80	.20
☐ 785	Ellis Burks		.15	.06	.01
☐ 786	Melido Perez		.08	.03	.01
☐ 787	Dave West		.12	.05	.01
☐ 788	Mike Morgan		.06	.02	.00
☐ 789	Kansas City Royals TL		.10	.04	.01
	Bo Jackson (throwing)				
☐ 790	Sid Fernandez		.06	.02	.00
☐ 791	Jim Lindeman		.03	.01	.00
☐ 792	Rafael Santana		.06	.02	.00

1989 Topps Wax Box Cards

 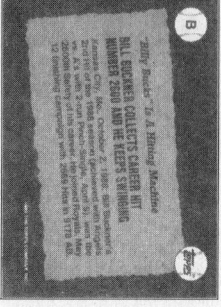

The cards in this 16-card set measure the standard 2 1/2" by 3 1/2". Cards have essentially the same design as the 1989 Topps regular issue set. The cards were printed on the bottoms of the regular issue wax pack boxes. These 16 cards, "lettered" A through P, are considered a separate set in their own right and are not typically included in a complete set of the regular issue 1989 Topps cards. The value of the panels uncut is slightly greater, perhaps by 25 percent greater, than the value of the individual cards cut up carefully. The sixteen cards in this set honor players (and one manager) who reached career milestones during the 1988 season.

		MINT	EXC	G-VG
	COMPLETE SET (16)	4.50	2.00	.45
	COMMON PLAYER (A-P)	.10	.04	.01
☐ A	George Brett	.50	.20	.05
	475th Double			
☐ B	Bill Buckner	.15	.06	.01
	2600th Hit			
☐ C	Darrell Evans	.15	.06	.01
	400th Home Run			
☐ D	Rich Gossage	.20	.08	.02
	300th Save			
☐ E	Greg Gross	.10	.04	.01
	125th Pinch Hit			

		MINT	EXC	G-VG
☐ F	Rickey Henderson .... 775th Stolen Base	.75	.30	.07
☐ G	Keith Hernandez .... 125th Game- Winning RBI	.20	.08	.02
☐ H	Tom Lasorda MG .... 1000th Managerial Win	.15	.06	.01
☐ I	Jim Rice .... 1400th Run Batted In	.20	.08	.02
☐ J	Cal Ripken .... 1000th Cons. Game	.75	.30	.07
☐ K	Nolan Ryan .... 4700th Strikeout	.90	.40	.09
☐ L	Mike Schmidt .... 1000th Long Hit	.60	.25	.06
☐ M	Bruce Sutter .... 300th Save	.15	.06	.01
☐ N	Don Sutton .... 750th Game Started	.25	.10	.02
☐ O	Kent Tekulve .... 1000th Appearance	.10	.04	.01
☐ P	Dave Winfield .... 1400th Run Batted In	.35	.15	.03

1989 Topps All-Star Glossy 22

These glossy cards were inserted with Topps rack packs and honor the starting line-ups, managers, and honorary captains of the 1988 National and American League All-Star teams. The cards are standard size, 2 1/2" by 3 1/2" and very similar to the design Topps has used since 1984. The backs are printed in red and blue on white card stock.

		MINT	EXC	G-VG
	COMPLETE SET (22)	3.00	1.25	.30
	COMMON PLAYER (1-22)	.10	.04	.01
☐ 1	Tom Kelly MG	.10	.04	.01
☐ 2	Mark McGwire	.30	.12	.03
☐ 3	Paul Molitor	.20	.08	.02
☐ 4	Wade Boggs	.40	.16	.04
☐ 5	Cal Ripken	.60	.25	.06
☐ 6	Jose Canseco	.60	.25	.06
☐ 7	Rickey Henderson	.60	.25	.06
☐ 8	Dave Winfield	.30	.12	.03
☐ 9	Terry Steinbach	.15	.06	.01
☐ 10	Frank Viola	.15	.06	.01
☐ 11	Bobby Doerr CAPT	.15	.06	.01
☐ 12	Whitey Herzog MG	.10	.04	.01
☐ 13	Will Clark	.60	.25	.06
☐ 14	Ryne Sandberg	.50	.20	.05
☐ 15	Bobby Bonilla	.35	.15	.03
☐ 16	Ozzie Smith	.25	.10	.02
☐ 17	Vince Coleman	.20	.08	.02
☐ 18	Andre Dawson	.25	.10	.02
☐ 19	Darryl Strawberry	.50	.20	.05
☐ 20	Gary Carter	.20	.08	.02
☐ 21	Dwight Gooden	.25	.10	.02
☐ 22	Willie Stargell CAPT	.20	.08	.02

1989 Topps Jumbo Rookies

Inserted in each supermarket jumbo pack is a card from this series of 22 of 1988's best rookies as determined by Topps. Jumbo packs consisted of 100 (regular issue 1989 Topps baseball) cards with a stick of gum plus the insert "Rookie" card. The card fronts are in full color and measure 2 1/2" by 3 1/2". The card backs are printed in red and blue on white card stock and are numbered at the bottom.

		MINT	EXC	G-VG
	COMPLETE SET (22)	7.50	3.25	.75
	COMMON PLAYER (1-22)	.20	.08	.02
☐ 1	Roberto Alomar	1.00	.40	.10
☐ 2	Brady Anderson	.25	.10	.02
☐ 3	Tim Belcher	.30	.12	.03
☐ 4	Damon Berryhill	.25	.10	.02
☐ 5	Jay Buhner	.35	.15	.03
☐ 6	Kevin Elster	.25	.10	.02
☐ 7	Cecil Espy	.20	.08	.02
☐ 8	Dave Gallagher	.20	.08	.02
☐ 9	Ron Gant	1.00	.40	.10
☐ 10	Paul Gibson	.20	.08	.02
☐ 11	Mark Grace	.75	.30	.07
☐ 12	Darrin Jackson	.25	.10	.02
☐ 13	Gregg Jefferies	1.00	.40	.10
☐ 14	Ricky Jordan	.30	.12	.03
☐ 15	Al Leiter	.20	.08	.02
☐ 16	Melido Perez	.30	.12	.03
☐ 17	Chris Sabo	.75	.30	.07
☐ 18	Nelson Santovenia	.25	.10	.02
☐ 19	Mackey Sasser	.25	.10	.02
☐ 20	Gary Sheffield	.60	.25	.06
☐ 21	Walt Weiss	.40	.16	.04
☐ 22	David Wells	.25	.10	.02

1989 Topps Glossy Send-In 60

The 1989 Topps Glossy Send-In set contains 60 standard-size (2 1/2 by 3 1/2 inch) cards. The fronts have color photos with white borders; the backs are light blue. The cards were distributed through the mail by Topps in six groups of 10 cards.

	MINT	EXC	G-VG
COMPLETE SET (60)	9.00	4.00	.90
COMMON PLAYER (1-60)	.15	.06	.01
☐ 1 Kirby Puckett	.40	.16	.04
☐ 2 Eric Davis	.30	.12	.03
☐ 3 Joe Carter	.25	.10	.02
☐ 4 Andy Van Slyke	.20	.08	.02
☐ 5 Wade Boggs	.50	.20	.05
☐ 6 David Cone	.25	.10	.02
☐ 7 Kent Hrbek	.20	.08	.02
☐ 8 Darryl Strawberry	.50	.20	.05
☐ 9 Jay Buhner	.25	.10	.02
☐ 10 Ron Gant	.50	.20	.05
☐ 11 Will Clark	.75	.30	.07
☐ 12 Jose Canseco	.75	.30	.07
☐ 13 Juan Samuel	.15	.06	.01
☐ 14 George Brett	.40	.16	.04
☐ 15 Benito Santiago	.25	.10	.02
☐ 16 Dennis Eckersley	.25	.10	.02
☐ 17 Gary Carter	.25	.10	.02
☐ 18 Frank Viola	.25	.10	.02
☐ 19 Roberto Alomar	.50	.20	.05
☐ 20 Paul Gibson	.15	.06	.01
☐ 21 Dave Winfield	.30	.12	.03
☐ 22 Howard Johnson	.25	.10	.02
☐ 23 Roger Clemens	.75	.30	.07
☐ 24 Bobby Bonilla	.35	.15	.03
☐ 25 Alan Trammell	.30	.12	.03
☐ 26 Kevin McReynolds	.25	.10	.02
☐ 27 George Bell	.25	.10	.02
☐ 28 Bruce Hurst	.15	.06	.01
☐ 29 Mark Grace	.60	.25	.06
☐ 30 Tim Belcher	.25	.10	.02
☐ 31 Mike Greenwell	.35	.15	.03
☐ 32 Glenn Davis	.25	.10	.02
☐ 33 Gary Gaetti	.15	.06	.01
☐ 34 Ryne Sandberg	.60	.25	.06
☐ 35 Rickey Henderson	.75	.30	.07
☐ 36 Dwight Evans	.20	.08	.02
☐ 37 Dwight Gooden	.25	.10	.02
☐ 38 Robin Yount	.45	.18	.04
☐ 39 Damon Berryhill	.15	.06	.01
☐ 40 Chris Sabo	.50	.20	.05
☐ 41 Mark McGwire	.45	.18	.04
☐ 42 Ozzie Smith	.30	.12	.03
☐ 43 Paul Molitor	.20	.08	.02
☐ 44 Andres Galarraga	.20	.08	.02
☐ 45 Dave Stewart	.20	.08	.02
☐ 46 Tom Browning	.20	.08	.02
☐ 47 Cal Ripken	.75	.30	.07
☐ 48 Orel Hershiser	.25	.10	.02
☐ 49 Dave Gallagher	.15	.06	.01
☐ 50 Walt Weiss	.20	.08	.02
☐ 51 Don Mattingly	.60	.25	.06
☐ 52 Tony Fernandez	.20	.08	.02
☐ 53 Tim Raines	.20	.08	.02
☐ 54 Jeff Reardon	.20	.08	.02
☐ 55 Kirk Gibson	.25	.10	.02
☐ 56 Jack Clark	.20	.08	.02
☐ 57 Danny Jackson	.15	.06	.01
☐ 58 Tony Gwynn	.40	.16	.04
☐ 59 Cecil Espy	.15	.06	.01
☐ 60 Jody Reed	.15	.06	.01

1989 Topps Big Baseball

The 1989 Topps Big Baseball set contains 330 glossy cards measuring 2 1/2 by 3 3/4 inches. The fronts feature mug shots superimposed on action photos. The horizontally-oriented backs have color cartoons and statistics for the player's previous season and total career. The set was released in three series of 110 cards. The cards were distributed in seven-card cello packs marked with the series number.

	MINT	EXC	G-VG
COMPLETE SET (330)	27.00	12.00	4.00
COMMON PLAYER (1-110)	.05	.02	.00
COMMON PLAYER (111-220)	.05	.02	.00
COMMON PLAYER (221-330)	.06	.02	.00

☐ 1 Orel Hershiser	.25	.10	.02
☐ 2 Harold Reynolds	.08	.03	.01
☐ 3 Jody Davis	.05	.02	.00
☐ 4 Greg Walker	.05	.02	.00
☐ 5 Barry Bonds	.35	.15	.03
☐ 6 Bret Saberhagen	.15	.06	.01
☐ 7 Johnny Ray	.05	.02	.00
☐ 8 Mike Fiore	.08	.03	.01
☐ 9 Juan Castillo	.05	.02	.00
☐ 10 Todd Burns	.05	.02	.00
☐ 11 Carmelo Martinez	.05	.02	.00
☐ 12 Geno Petralli	.05	.02	.00
☐ 13 Mel Hall	.08	.03	.01
☐ 14 Tom Browning	.08	.03	.01
☐ 15 Fred McGriff	.25	.10	.02
☐ 16 Kevin Elster	.08	.03	.01
☐ 17 Tim Leary	.08	.03	.01
☐ 18 Jim Rice	.15	.06	.01
☐ 19 Bret Barberie	.25	.10	.02
☐ 20 Jay Buhner	.12	.05	.01
☐ 21 Atlee Hammaker	.05	.02	.00
☐ 22 Lou Whitaker	.12	.05	.01
☐ 23 Paul Runge	.08	.03	.01
☐ 24 Carlton Fisk	.25	.10	.02
☐ 25 Jose Lind	.05	.02	.00
☐ 26 Mark Gubicza	.08	.03	.01
☐ 27 Billy Ripken	.05	.02	.00
☐ 28 Mike Pagliarulo	.05	.02	.00
☐ 29 Jim Deshaies	.05	.02	.00
☐ 30 Mark McLemore	.05	.02	.00
☐ 31 Scott Terry	.05	.02	.00
☐ 32 Franklin Stubbs	.08	.03	.01
☐ 33 Don August	.05	.02	.00
☐ 34 Mark McGwire	.45	.18	.04
☐ 35 Eric Show	.05	.02	.00
☐ 36 Cecil Espy	.05	.02	.00
☐ 37 Ron Tingley	.05	.02	.00
☐ 38 Mickey Brantley	.05	.02	.00
☐ 39 Paul O'Neill	.10	.04	.01
☐ 40 Ed Sprague	.12	.05	.01
☐ 41 Len Dykstra	.12	.05	.01
☐ 42 Roger Clemens	.60	.25	.06
☐ 43 Ron Gant	.60	.25	.06
☐ 44 Dan Pasqua	.05	.02	.00
☐ 45 Jeff D. Robinson	.05	.02	.00
☐ 46 George Brett	.35	.15	.03
☐ 47 Bryn Smith	.05	.02	.00
☐ 48 Mike Marshall	.08	.03	.01
☐ 49 Doug Robbins	.08	.03	.01
☐ 50 Don Mattingly	.50	.20	.05
☐ 51 Mike Scott	.10	.04	.01
☐ 52 Steve Jeltz	.05	.02	.00
☐ 53 Dick Schofield	.05	.02	.00
☐ 54 Tom Brunansky	.08	.03	.01
☐ 55 Gary Sheffield	.30	.12	.03
☐ 56 Dave Valle	.05	.02	.00
☐ 57 Carney Lansford	.10	.04	.01
☐ 58 Tony Gwynn	.35	.15	.03
☐ 59 Checklist 1-110	.05	.02	.00
☐ 60 Damon Berryhill	.08	.03	.01
☐ 61 Jack Morris	.15	.06	.01
☐ 62 Brett Butler	.10	.04	.01
☐ 63 Mickey Hatcher	.05	.02	.00
☐ 64 Bruce Sutter	.08	.03	.01
☐ 65 Robin Ventura	.60	.25	.06
☐ 66 Junior Ortiz	.05	.02	.00
☐ 67 Pat Tabler	.05	.02	.00
☐ 68 Greg Swindell	.10	.04	.01
☐ 69 Jeff Branson	.08	.03	.01
☐ 70 Manny Lee	.05	.02	.00
☐ 71 Dave Magadan	.10	.04	.01

☐ 72	Rich Gedman	.05	.02	.00
☐ 73	Tim Raines	.12	.05	.01
☐ 74	Mike Maddux	.05	.02	.00
☐ 75	Jim Presley	.05	.02	.00
☐ 76	Chuck Finley	.12	.05	.01
☐ 77	Jose Oquendo	.05	.02	.00
☐ 78	Rob Deer	.08	.03	.01
☐ 79	Jay Howell	.08	.03	.01
☐ 80	Terry Steinbach	.08	.03	.01
☐ 81	Ed Whitson	.08	.03	.01
☐ 82	Ruben Sierra	.50	.20	.05
☐ 83	Bruce Benedict	.05	.02	.00
☐ 84	Fred Manrique	.05	.02	.00
☐ 85	John Smiley	.10	.04	.01
☐ 86	Mike Macfarlane	.08	.03	.01
☐ 87	Rene Gonzales	.05	.02	.00
☐ 88	Charles Hudson	.05	.02	.00
☐ 89	Glenn Davis	.15	.06	.01
☐ 90	Les Straker	.05	.02	.00
☐ 91	Carmen Castillo	.05	.02	.00
☐ 92	Tracy Woodson	.05	.02	.00
☐ 93	Tino Martinez	.45	.18	.04
☐ 94	Herm Winningham	.05	.02	.00
☐ 95	Kelly Gruber	.12	.05	.01
☐ 96	Terry Leach	.05	.02	.00
☐ 97	Jody Reed	.08	.03	.01
☐ 98	Nelson Santovenia	.05	.02	.00
☐ 99	Tony Armas	.05	.02	.00
☐ 100	Greg Brock	.05	.02	.00
☐ 101	Dave Stewart	.12	.05	.01
☐ 102	Roberto Alomar	.40	.16	.04
☐ 103	Jim Sundberg	.05	.02	.00
☐ 104	Albert Hall	.05	.02	.00
☐ 105	Steve Lyons	.05	.02	.00
☐ 106	Sid Bream	.05	.02	.00
☐ 107	Danny Tartabull	.20	.08	.02
☐ 108	Rick Dempsey	.05	.02	.00
☐ 109	Rich Renteria	.05	.02	.00
☐ 110	Ozzie Smith	.25	.10	.02
☐ 111	Steve Sax	.12	.05	.01
☐ 112	Kelly Downs	.08	.03	.01
☐ 113	Larry Sheets	.05	.02	.00
☐ 114	Andy Benes	.50	.20	.05
☐ 115	Pete O'Brien	.05	.02	.00
☐ 116	Kevin McReynolds	.10	.04	.01
☐ 117	Juan Berenguer	.05	.02	.00
☐ 118	Billy Hatcher	.05	.02	.00
☐ 119	Rick Cerone	.05	.02	.00
☐ 120	Andre Dawson	.25	.10	.02
☐ 121	Storm Davis	.05	.02	.00
☐ 122	Devon White	.10	.04	.01
☐ 123	Alan Trammell	.20	.08	.02
☐ 124	Vince Coleman	.20	.08	.02
☐ 125	Al Leiter	.05	.02	.00
☐ 126	Dale Sveum	.05	.02	.00
☐ 127	Pete Incaviglia	.10	.04	.01
☐ 128	Dave Stieb	.12	.05	.01
☐ 129	Kevin Mitchell	.40	.16	.04
☐ 130	Dave Schmidt	.05	.02	.00
☐ 131	Gary Redus	.05	.02	.00
☐ 132	Ron Robinson	.05	.02	.00
☐ 133	Darnell Coles	.05	.02	.00
☐ 134	Benito Santiago	.15	.06	.01
☐ 135	John Farrell	.05	.02	.00
☐ 136	Willie Wilson	.08	.03	.01
☐ 137	Steve Bedrosian	.05	.02	.00
☐ 138	Don Slaught	.05	.02	.00
☐ 139	Darryl Strawberry	.50	.20	.05
☐ 140	Frank Viola	.15	.06	.01
☐ 141	Dave Silvestri	.10	.04	.01
☐ 142	Carlos Quintana	.12	.05	.01
☐ 143	Vance Law	.05	.02	.00
☐ 144	Dave Parker	.15	.06	.01
☐ 145	Tim Belcher	.15	.06	.01
☐ 146	Will Clark	.75	.30	.07
☐ 147	Mark Williamson	.05	.02	.00
☐ 148	Ozzie Guillen	.10	.04	.01
☐ 149	Kirk McCaskill	.05	.02	.00
☐ 150	Pat Sheridan	.05	.02	.00
☐ 151	Terry Pendleton	.15	.06	.01
☐ 152	Roberto Kelly	.25	.10	.02
☐ 153	Joey Meyer	.05	.02	.00
☐ 154	Mark Grant	.05	.02	.00
☐ 155	Joe Carter	.20	.08	.02
☐ 156	Steve Buechele	.08	.03	.01
☐ 157	Tony Fernandez	.10	.04	.01
☐ 158	Jeff Reed	.05	.02	.00
☐ 159	Bobby Bonilla	.30	.12	.03
☐ 160	Henry Cotto	.05	.02	.00
☐ 161	Kurt Stillwell	.08	.03	.01
☐ 162	Mickey Morandini	.15	.06	.01
☐ 163	Robby Thompson	.05	.02	.00
☐ 164	Rick Schu	.05	.02	.00
☐ 165	Stan Jefferson	.05	.02	.00
☐ 166	Ron Darling	.08	.03	.01
☐ 167	Kirby Puckett	.35	.15	.03
☐ 168	Bill Doran	.05	.02	.00
☐ 169	Dennis Lamp	.05	.02	.00
☐ 170	Ty Griffin	.15	.06	.01
☐ 171	Ron Hassey	.05	.02	.00
☐ 172	Dale Murphy	.25	.10	.02
☐ 173	Andres Galarraga	.12	.05	.01
☐ 174	Tim Flannery	.05	.02	.00
☐ 175	Cory Snyder	.10	.04	.01
☐ 176	Checklist 111-220	.05	.02	.00
☐ 177	Tommy Barrett	.05	.02	.00
☐ 178	Dan Petry	.05	.02	.00
☐ 179	Billy Masse	.10	.04	.01
☐ 180	Terry Kennedy	.05	.02	.00
☐ 181	Joe Orsulak	.05	.02	.00
☐ 182	Doyle Alexander	.05	.02	.00
☐ 183	Willie McGee	.12	.05	.01
☐ 184	Jim Gantner	.05	.02	.00
☐ 185	Keith Hernandez	.15	.06	.01
☐ 186	Greg Gagne	.05	.02	.00
☐ 187	Kevin Bass	.08	.03	.01
☐ 188	Mark Eichhorn	.05	.02	.00
☐ 189	Mark Grace	.50	.20	.05
☐ 190	Jose Canseco	.75	.30	.07
☐ 191	Bobby Witt	.10	.04	.01
☐ 192	Rafael Santana	.05	.02	.00
☐ 193	Dwight Evans	.10	.04	.01
☐ 194	Greg Booker	.05	.02	.00
☐ 195	Rafael Belliard	.05	.02	.00
☐ 196	Candy Maldonado	.08	.03	.01
☐ 197	Mickey Tettleton	.10	.04	.01
☐ 198	Barry Larkin	.20	.08	.02
☐ 199	Frank White	.08	.03	.01
☐ 200	Wally Joyner	.15	.06	.01
☐ 201	Chet Lemon	.05	.02	.00
☐ 202	Joe Magrane	.08	.03	.01
☐ 203	Glenn Braggs	.05	.02	.00
☐ 204	Scott Fletcher	.05	.02	.00
☐ 205	Gary Ward	.05	.02	.00
☐ 206	Nelson Liriano	.05	.02	.00
☐ 207	Howard Johnson	.15	.06	.01
☐ 208	Kent Hrbek	.12	.05	.01
☐ 209	Ken Caminiti	.08	.03	.01
☐ 210	Mike Greenwell	.30	.12	.03
☐ 211	Ryne Sandberg	.50	.20	.05
☐ 212	Joe Slusarski	.10	.04	.01
☐ 213	Donell Nixon	.05	.02	.00
☐ 214	Tim Wallach	.08	.03	.01
☐ 215	John Kruk	.08	.03	.01
☐ 216	Charles Nagy	.20	.08	.02
☐ 217	Alvin Davis	.08	.03	.01
☐ 218	Oswald Peraza	.08	.03	.01
☐ 219	Mike Schmidt	.75	.30	.07
☐ 220	Spike Owen	.06	.02	.00
☐ 221	Mike Smithson	.06	.02	.00
☐ 222	Dion James	.06	.02	.00
☐ 223	Ernie Whitt	.06	.02	.00
☐ 224	Mike Davis	.06	.02	.00
☐ 225	Gene Larkin	.06	.02	.00
☐ 226	Pat Combs	.15	.06	.01
☐ 227	Jack Howell	.06	.02	.00
☐ 228	Ron Oester	.06	.02	.00
☐ 229	Paul Gibson	.06	.02	.00
☐ 230	Mookie Wilson	.06	.02	.00
☐ 231	Glenn Hubbard	.06	.02	.00
☐ 232	Shawon Dunston	.15	.06	.01
☐ 233	Otis Nixon	.15	.06	.01
☐ 234	Melido Perez	.10	.04	.01
☐ 235	Jerry Browne	.10	.04	.01
☐ 236	Rick Rhoden	.06	.02	.00
☐ 237	Bo Jackson	.90	.40	.09
☐ 238	Randy Velarde	.06	.02	.00
☐ 239	Jack Clark	.12	.05	.01
☐ 240	Wade Boggs	.60	.25	.06
☐ 241	Lonnie Smith	.10	.04	.01
☐ 242	Mike Flanagan	.10	.04	.01
☐ 243	Willie Randolph	.10	.04	.01
☐ 244	Oddibe McDowell	.06	.02	.00
☐ 245	Ricky Jordan	.15	.06	.01
☐ 246	Greg Briley	.12	.05	.01
☐ 247	Rex Hudler	.10	.04	.01
☐ 248	Robin Yount	.45	.18	.04
☐ 249	Lance Parrish	.15	.06	.01
☐ 250	Chris Sabo	.40	.16	.04
☐ 251	Mike Henneman	.10	.04	.01
☐ 252	Gregg Jefferies	.50	.20	.05
☐ 253	Curt Young	.06	.02	.00
☐ 254	Andy Van Slyke	.15	.06	.01
☐ 255	Rod Booker	.06	.02	.00
☐ 256	Rafael Palmeiro	.20	.08	.02
☐ 257	Jose Uribe	.06	.02	.00
☐ 258	Ellis Burks	.30	.12	.03
☐ 259	John Smoltz	.30	.12	.03
☐ 260	Tom Foley	.06	.02	.00

☐	262	Lloyd Moseby	.06	.02	.00
☐	263	Jim Poole	.12	.05	.01
☐	264	Gary Gaetti	.10	.04	.01
☐	265	Bob Dernier	.06	.02	.00
☐	266	Harold Baines	.12	.05	.01
☐	267	Tom Candiotti	.10	.04	.01
☐	268	Rafael Ramirez	.06	.02	.00
☐	269	Bob Boone	.12	.05	.01
☐	270	Buddy Bell	.10	.04	.01
☐	271	Rickey Henderson	.75	.30	.07
☐	272	Willie Fraser	.06	.02	.00
☐	273	Eric Davis	.40	.16	.04
☐	274	Jeff M. Robinson	.06	.02	.00
☐	275	Damaso Garcia	.06	.02	.00
☐	276	Sid Fernandez	.10	.04	.01
☐	277	Stan Javier	.06	.02	.00
☐	278	Marty Barrett	.06	.02	.00
☐	279	Gerald Perry	.06	.02	.00
☐	280	Rob Ducey	.10	.04	.01
☐	281	Mike Scioscia	.06	.02	.00
☐	282	Randy Bush	.06	.02	.00
☐	283	Tom Herr	.06	.02	.00
☐	284	Glenn Wilson	.06	.02	.00
☐	285	Pedro Guerrero	.15	.06	.01
☐	286	Cal Ripken	.75	.30	.07
☐	287	Randy Johnson	.12	.05	.01
☐	288	Julio Franco	.20	.08	.02
☐	289	Ivan Calderon	.10	.04	.01
☐	290	Rich Yett	.06	.02	.00
☐	291	Scott Servais	.12	.05	.01
☐	292	Bill Pecota	.06	.02	.00
☐	293	Ken Phelps	.06	.02	.00
☐	294	Chili Davis	.10	.04	.01
☐	295	Manny Trillo	.06	.02	.00
☐	296	Mike Boddicker	.06	.02	.00
☐	297	Geronimo Berroa	.06	.02	.00
☐	298	Todd Stottlemyre	.12	.05	.01
☐	299	Kirk Gibson	.15	.06	.01
☐	300	Wally Backman	.06	.02	.00
☐	301	Hubie Brooks	.10	.04	.01
☐	302	Von Hayes	.10	.04	.01
☐	303	Matt Nokes	.15	.06	.01
☐	304	Dwight Gooden	.25	.10	.02
☐	305	Walt Weiss	.15	.06	.01
☐	306	Mike LaValliere	.06	.02	.00
☐	307	Cris Carpenter	.06	.02	.00
☐	308	Ted Wood	.20	.08	.02
☐	309	Jeff Russell	.06	.02	.00
☐	310	Dave Gallagher	.06	.02	.00
☐	311	Andy Allanson	.06	.02	.00
☐	312	Craig Reynolds	.06	.02	.00
☐	313	Kevin Seitzer	.12	.05	.01
☐	314	Dave Winfield	.25	.10	.02
☐	315	Andy McGaffigan	.06	.02	.00
☐	316	Nick Esasky	.10	.04	.01
☐	317	Jeff Blauser	.08	.03	.01
☐	318	George Bell	.15	.06	.01
☐	319	Eddie Murray	.30	.12	.03
☐	320	Mark Davidson	.06	.02	.00
☐	321	Juan Samuel	.10	.04	.01
☐	322	Jim Abbott	.75	.30	.07
☐	323	Kal Daniels	.12	.05	.01
☐	324	Mike Brumley	.06	.02	.00
☐	325	Gary Carter	.15	.06	.01
☐	326	Dave Henderson	.12	.05	.01
☐	327	Checklist 221-330	.06	.02	.00
☐	328	Garry Templeton	.10	.04	.01
☐	329	Pat Perry	.06	.02	.00
☐	330	Paul Molitor	.12	.05	.01

1989 Topps Mini Leaders

The 1989 Topps Mini League Leaders set contains 77 cards measuring approximately 2 1/8" by 3". The fronts have color photos with large white borders. The backs are yellow and feature 1988 and career stats. The cards were distributed in seven-card cello packs.

	MINT	EXC	G-VG
COMPLETE SET (77)	7.00	3.00	.70
COMMON PLAYER (1-77)	.05	.02	.00

☐	1	Dale Murphy	.25	.10	.02
☐	2	Gerald Perry	.05	.02	.00
☐	3	Andre Dawson	.20	.08	.02
☐	4	Greg Maddux	.10	.04	.01
☐	5	Rafael Palmeiro	.20	.08	.02

☐	6	Tom Browning	.10	.04	.01
☐	7	Kal Daniels	.15	.06	.01
☐	8	Eric Davis	.25	.10	.02
☐	9	John Franco	.10	.04	.01
☐	10	Danny Jackson	.05	.02	.00
☐	11	Barry Larkin	.20	.08	.02
☐	12	Jose Rijo	.15	.06	.01
☐	13	Chris Sabo	.25	.10	.02
☐	14	Nolan Ryan	.75	.30	.07
☐	15	Mike Scott	.10	.04	.01
☐	16	Gerald Young	.05	.02	.00
☐	17	Kirk Gibson	.15	.06	.01
☐	18	Orel Hershiser	.15	.06	.01
☐	19	Steve Sax	.10	.04	.01
☐	20	John Tudor	.10	.04	.01
☐	21	Hubie Brooks	.10	.04	.01
☐	22	Andres Galarraga	.10	.04	.01
☐	23	Otis Nixon	.10	.04	.01
☐	24	David Cone	.15	.06	.01
☐	25	Sid Fernandez	.10	.04	.01
☐	26	Dwight Gooden	.20	.08	.02
☐	27	Kevin McReynolds	.10	.04	.01
☐	28	Darryl Strawberry	.50	.20	.05
☐	29	Juan Samuel	.10	.04	.01
☐	30	Bobby Bonilla	.25	.10	.02
☐	31	Sid Bream	.05	.02	.00
☐	32	Jim Gott	.05	.02	.00
☐	33	Andy Van Slyke	.10	.04	.01
☐	34	Vince Coleman	.15	.06	.01
☐	35	Jose DeLeon	.05	.02	.00
☐	36	Joe Magrane	.05	.02	.00
☐	37	Ozzie Smith	.20	.08	.02
☐	38	Todd Worrell	.10	.04	.01
☐	39	Tony Gwynn	.35	.15	.03
☐	40	Brett Butler	.10	.04	.01
☐	41	Will Clark	.60	.25	.06
☐	42	Rick Reuschel	.05	.02	.00
☐	43	Checklist Card	.05	.02	.00
☐	44	Eddie Murray	.25	.10	.02
☐	45	Wade Boggs	.40	.16	.04
☐	46	Roger Clemens	.50	.20	.05
☐	47	Dwight Evans	.10	.04	.01
☐	48	Mike Greenwell	.25	.10	.02
☐	49	Bruce Hurst	.10	.04	.01
☐	50	Johnny Ray	.05	.02	.00
☐	51	Doug Jones	.05	.02	.00
☐	52	Greg Swindell	.10	.04	.01
☐	53	Gary Pettis	.05	.02	.00
☐	54	George Brett	.35	.15	.03
☐	55	Mark Gubicza	.10	.04	.01
☐	56	Willie Wilson	.10	.04	.01
☐	57	Teddy Higuera	.10	.04	.01
☐	58	Paul Molitor	.15	.06	.01
☐	59	Robin Yount	.35	.15	.03
☐	60	Allan Anderson	.05	.02	.00
☐	61	Gary Gaetti	.10	.04	.01
☐	62	Kirby Puckett	.30	.12	.03
☐	63	Jeff Reardon	.10	.04	.01
☐	64	Frank Viola	.15	.06	.01
☐	65	Jack Clark	.10	.04	.01
☐	66	Rickey Henderson	.60	.25	.06
☐	67	Dave Winfield	.25	.10	.02
☐	68	Jose Canseco	.75	.30	.07
☐	69	Dennis Eckersley	.15	.06	.01
☐	70	Mark McGwire	.40	.16	.04
☐	71	Dave Stewart	.15	.06	.01
☐	72	Alvin Davis	.10	.04	.01
☐	73	Mark Langston	.15	.06	.01
☐	74	Harold Reynolds	.05	.02	.00
☐	75	George Bell	.15	.06	.01
☐	76	Tony Fernandez	.10	.04	.01
☐	77	Fred McGriff	.20	.08	.02

1989 Topps UK Mini

The 1989 Topps UK Mini baseball set contains 88 cards measuring approximately 2 1/8" by 3". The fronts are red, white and blue. The backs are yellow and red, and feature 1988 and career stats. The cards were distributed in five-card poly packs. The card set numbering is in alphabetical order by player's name.

	MINT	EXC	G-VG
COMPLETE SET (88)	9.00	4.00	.90
COMMON PLAYER (1-88)	.05	.02	.00
☐ 1 Brady Anderson	.10	.04	.01
☐ 2 Harold Baines	.10	.04	.01
☐ 3 George Bell	.15	.06	.01
☐ 4 Wade Boggs	.50	.20	.05
☐ 5 Barry Bonds	.50	.20	.05
☐ 6 Bobby Bonilla	.40	.16	.04
☐ 7 George Brett	.40	.16	.04
☐ 8 Hubie Brooks	.10	.04	.01
☐ 9 Tom Brunansky	.10	.04	.01
☐ 10 Jay Buhner	.15	.06	.01
☐ 11 Brett Butler	.10	.04	.01
☐ 12 Jose Canseco	.75	.30	.07
☐ 13 Joe Carter	.25	.10	.02
☐ 14 Jack Clark	.15	.06	.01
☐ 15 Will Clark	.75	.30	.07
☐ 16 Roger Clemens	.75	.30	.07
☐ 17 David Cone	.20	.08	.02
☐ 18 Alvin Davis	.10	.04	.01
☐ 19 Eric Davis	.30	.12	.03
☐ 20 Glenn Davis	.20	.08	.02
☐ 21 Andre Dawson	.25	.10	.02
☐ 22 Bill Doran	.10	.04	.01
☐ 23 Dennis Eckersley	.15	.06	.01
☐ 24 Dwight Evans	.10	.04	.01
☐ 25 Tony Fernandez	.10	.04	.01
☐ 26 Carlton Fisk	.35	.15	.03
☐ 27 John Franco	.10	.04	.01
☐ 28 Andres Galarraga	.15	.06	.01
☐ 29 Ron Gant	.50	.20	.05
☐ 30 Kirk Gibson	.20	.08	.02
☐ 31 Dwight Gooden	.20	.08	.02
☐ 32 Mike Greenwell	.30	.12	.03
☐ 33 Mark Gubicza	.10	.04	.01
☐ 34 Pedro Guerrero	.10	.04	.01
☐ 35 Ozzie Guillen	.10	.04	.01
☐ 36 Tony Gwynn	.40	.16	.04
☐ 37 Rickey Henderson	.75	.30	.07
☐ 38 Orel Hershiser	.20	.08	.02
☐ 39 Teddy Higuera	.10	.04	.01
☐ 40 Charlie Hough	.05	.02	.00
☐ 41 Kent Hrbek	.10	.04	.01
☐ 42 Bruce Hurst	.10	.04	.01
☐ 43 Bo Jackson	.75	.30	.07
☐ 44 Gregg Jefferies	.45	.18	.04
☐ 45 Ricky Jordan	.15	.06	.01
☐ 46 Wally Joyner	.15	.06	.01
☐ 47 Mark Langston	.10	.04	.01
☐ 48 Mike Marshall	.10	.04	.01
☐ 49 Don Mattingly	.45	.18	.04
☐ 50 Fred McGriff	.20	.08	.02
☐ 51 Mark McGwire	.40	.16	.04
☐ 52 Kevin McReynolds	.15	.06	.01
☐ 53 Paul Molitor	.15	.06	.01
☐ 54 Jack Morris	.15	.06	.01
☐ 55 Dale Murphy	.25	.10	.02
☐ 56 Eddie Murray	.30	.12	.03
☐ 57 Pete O'Brien	.05	.02	.00
☐ 58 Rafael Palmeiro	.20	.08	.02
☐ 59 Gerald Perry	.05	.02	.00
☐ 60 Kirby Puckett	.40	.16	.04
☐ 61 Tim Raines	.15	.06	.01
☐ 62 Johnny Ray	.05	.02	.00
☐ 63 Rick Reuschel	.05	.02	.00
☐ 64 Cal Ripken	.75	.30	.07
☐ 65 Chris Sabo	.30	.12	.03
☐ 66 Juan Samuel	.10	.04	.01
☐ 67 Ryne Sandberg	.60	.25	.06
☐ 68 Benito Santiago	.20	.08	.02
☐ 69 Steve Sax	.15	.06	.01
☐ 70 Mike Schmidt	.75	.30	.07
☐ 71 Ruben Sierra	.50	.20	.05
☐ 72 Ozzie Smith	.30	.12	.03
☐ 73 Cory Snyder	.10	.04	.01
☐ 74 Dave Stewart	.15	.06	.01
☐ 75 Darryl Strawberry	.50	.20	.05
☐ 76 Greg Swindell	.10	.04	.01
☐ 77 Alan Trammell	.20	.08	.02
☐ 78 Fernando Valenzuela	.15	.06	.01
☐ 79 Andy Van Slyke	.10	.04	.01
☐ 80 Frank Viola	.15	.06	.01
☐ 81 Claudell Washington	.05	.02	.00
☐ 82 Walt Weiss	.15	.06	.01
☐ 83 Lou Whitaker	.12	.05	.01
☐ 84 Dave Winfield	.25	.10	.02
☐ 85 Mike Witt	.05	.02	.00
☐ 86 Gerald Young	.10	.04	.01
☐ 87 Robin Yount	.40	.16	.04
☐ 88 Checklist Card	.05	.02	.00

1989 Topps Ames 20/20 Club

The 1989 (Topps) Ames 20/20 Club set contains 33 standard-size (2 1/2" by 3 1/2") glossy cards. The fronts resemble plaques with gold and silver trim. The vertically-oriented backs show career stats. The cards were distributed at Ames department stores as a boxed set. The set was produced by Topps for Ames; the Topps logo is also on the front of each card. The set includes active major leaguers who have had seasons of at least 20 home runs and 20 stolen bases. The backs include lifetime batting records with home run and stolen base totals for their 20/20 years highlighted. The subject list for the set is printed on the back panel of the set's custom box.

	MINT	EXC	G-VG
COMPLETE SET (33)	4.00	1.75	.40
COMMON PLAYER (1-33)	.10	.04	.01
☐ 1 Jesse Barfield	.15	.06	.01
☐ 2 Kevin Bass	.10	.04	.01
☐ 3 Don Baylor	.15	.06	.01
☐ 4 George Bell	.20	.08	.02
☐ 5 Barry Bonds	.45	.18	.04
☐ 6 Phil Bradley	.10	.04	.01
☐ 7 Ellis Burks	.25	.10	.02
☐ 8 Jose Canseco	.75	.30	.07
☐ 9 Joe Carter	.25	.10	.02
☐ 10 Kal Daniels	.15	.06	.01
☐ 11 Eric Davis	.25	.10	.02
☐ 12 Mike Davis	.10	.04	.01
☐ 13 Andre Dawson	.25	.10	.02

			MINT	EXC	G-VG
☐	14	Kirk Gibson	.15	.06	.01
☐	15	Pedro Guerrero	.15	.06	.01
☐	16	Rickey Henderson	.75	.30	.07
☐	17	Bo Jackson	.75	.30	.07
☐	18	Howard Johnson	.15	.06	.01
☐	19	Jeffrey Leonard	.10	.04	.01
☐	20	Kevin McReynolds	.15	.06	.01
☐	21	Dale Murphy	.25	.10	.02
☐	22	Dwayne Murphy	.10	.04	.01
☐	23	Dave Parker	.15	.06	.01
☐	24	Kirby Puckett	.30	.12	.03
☐	25	Juan Samuel	.10	.04	.01
☐	26	Ryne Sandberg	.50	.20	.05
☐	27	Mike Schmidt	.50	.20	.05
☐	28	Darryl Strawberry	.50	.20	.05
☐	29	Alan Trammell	.20	.08	.02
☐	30	Andy Van Slyke	.15	.06	.01
☐	31	Devon White	.15	.06	.01
☐	32	Dave Winfield	.25	.10	.02
☐	33	Robin Yount	.35	.15	.03

1989 Topps Cap'n Crunch

The 1989 Topps Cap'n Crunch set contains 22 standard-size (2 1/2" by 3 1/2") cards. The fronts have red, white and blue borders surrounding "mugshot" photos. The backs are horizontally-oriented and show lifetime stats. The set was produced by Topps, but has team logos airbrushed out. Two cards were included (in a cellophane wrapper with a piece of gum) in each specially-marked Cap'n Crunch cereal box. The set was not available as a complete set as part of any mail-in offer. The set was produced by Topps.

			MINT	EXC	G-VG
	COMPLETE SET (22)		13.50	6.00	1.85
	COMMON PLAYER (1-22)		.60	.25	.06
☐	1	Jose Canseco	1.25	.50	.12
☐	2	Kirk Gibson	.75	.30	.07
☐	3	Orel Hershiser	.75	.30	.07
☐	4	Frank Viola	.60	.25	.06
☐	5	Tony Gwynn	1.00	.40	.10
☐	6	Cal Ripken	1.25	.50	.12
☐	7	Darryl Strawberry	1.00	.40	.10
☐	8	Don Mattingly	1.00	.40	.10
☐	9	George Brett	1.00	.40	.10
☐	10	Andre Dawson	.90	.40	.09
☐	11	Dale Murphy	.90	.40	.09
☐	12	Alan Trammell	.75	.30	.07
☐	13	Eric Davis	.75	.30	.07
☐	14	Jack Clark	.60	.25	.06
☐	15	Eddie Murray	1.00	.40	.10
☐	16	Mike Schmidt	1.25	.50	.12
☐	17	Dwight Gooden	.90	.40	.09
☐	18	Roger Clemens	1.25	.50	.12
☐	19	Will Clark	1.25	.50	.12
☐	20	Kirby Puckett	1.00	.40	.10
☐	21	Robin Yount	1.00	.40	.10
☐	22	Mark McGwire	.90	.40	.09

1989 Topps Hills Team MVP's

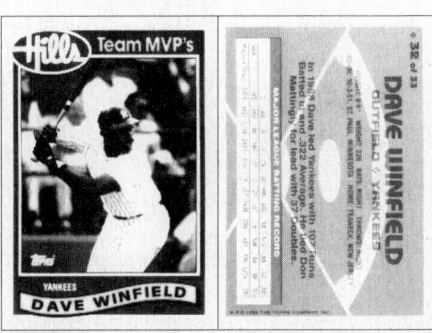

The 1989 Topps Hills Team MVP's set contains 33 glossy standard-size (2 1/2" by 3 1/2") cards. The fronts and backs are yellow, red, white and navy. The horizontally-oriented backs are green. The cards were distributed through Hills stores as a boxed set. The set was produced by Topps although it was printed in Ireland.

			MINT	EXC	G-VG
	COMPLETE SET (33)		4.00	1.75	.40
	COMMON PLAYER (1-33)		.10	.04	.01
☐	1	Harold Baines	.15	.06	.01
☐	2	Wade Boggs	.45	.18	.04
☐	3	George Brett	.35	.15	.03
☐	4	Tom Brunansky	.15	.06	.01
☐	5	Jose Canseco	.75	.30	.07
☐	6	Joe Carter	.25	.10	.02
☐	7	Will Clark	.75	.30	.07
☐	8	Roger Clemens	.75	.30	.07
☐	9	David Cone	.20	.08	.02
☐	10	Glenn Davis	.20	.08	.02
☐	11	Andre Dawson	.25	.10	.02
☐	12	Dennis Eckersley	.15	.06	.01
☐	13	Andres Galarraga	.15	.06	.01
☐	14	Kirk Gibson	.15	.06	.01
☐	15	Mike Greenwell	.25	.10	.02
☐	16	Tony Gwynn	.35	.15	.03
☐	17	Orel Hershiser	.20	.08	.02
☐	18	Danny Jackson	.10	.04	.01
☐	19	Mark Langston	.15	.06	.01
☐	20	Fred McGriff	.20	.08	.02
☐	21	Dale Murphy	.30	.12	.03
☐	22	Eddie Murray	.40	.16	.04
☐	23	Kirby Puckett	.45	.18	.04
☐	24	Johnny Ray	.10	.04	.01
☐	25	Juan Samuel	.15	.06	.01
☐	26	Ruben Sierra	.45	.18	.04
☐	27	Dave Stewart	.20	.08	.02
☐	28	Darryl Strawberry	.50	.20	.05
☐	29	Alan Trammell	.20	.08	.02
☐	30	Andy Van Slyke	.15	.06	.01
☐	31	Frank Viola	.15	.06	.01
☐	32	Dave Winfield	.25	.10	.02
☐	33	Robin Yount	.45	.18	.04

1989 Topps Traded

The 1989 Topps Traded set contains 132 standard-size (2 1/2" by 3 1/2") cards. The fronts have white borders; the horizontally-oriented backs are red and pink. From the front the cards' style is indistinguishable from the 1989 Topps regular issue. The cards were distributed as a boxed set. The key rookies in this set are Ken Griffey Jr., Deion Sanders, and Jerome Walton. Topps also produced a specially boxed "glossy" edition frequently referred to as the Topps Traded Tiffany set. This year, again, Topps did not disclose the number of Tiffany sets they produced or sold but it seems that production quantities were roughly similar (or slightly smaller, 15,000 sets) to the previous two years. The checklist of cards is identical to that of the normal non-glossy cards. There are two primary distinguishing features of the Tiffany cards, white card stock reverses and high gloss obverses. These Tiffany cards are valued at approximately four times the values listed below.

	MINT	EXC	G-VG
COMPLETE SET (132)	9.00	4.00	.90
COMMON PLAYER (1-132)	.05	.02	.00

		MINT	EXC	G-VG
☐ 1T	Don Aase	.10	.04	.01
☐ 2T	Jim Abbott	.90	.40	.09
☐ 3T	Kent Anderson	.10	.04	.01
☐ 4T	Keith Atherton	.05	.02	.00
☐ 5T	Wally Backman	.05	.02	.00
☐ 6T	Steve Balboni	.05	.02	.00
☐ 7T	Jesse Barfield	.10	.04	.01
☐ 8T	Steve Bedrosian	.08	.03	.01
☐ 9T	Todd Benzinger	.08	.03	.01
☐ 10T	Geronimo Berroa	.05	.02	.00
☐ 11T	Bert Blyleven	.12	.05	.01
☐ 12T	Bob Boone	.12	.05	.01
☐ 13T	Phil Bradley	.05	.02	.00
☐ 14T	Jeff Brantley	.20	.08	.02
☐ 15T	Kevin Brown	.08	.03	.01
☐ 16T	Jerry Browne	.05	.02	.00
☐ 17T	Chuck Cary	.05	.02	.00
☐ 18T	Carmen Castillo	.05	.02	.00
☐ 19T	Jim Clancy	.05	.02	.00
☐ 20T	Jack Clark	.10	.04	.01
☐ 21T	Bryan Clutterbuck	.05	.02	.00
☐ 22T	Jody Davis	.05	.02	.00
☐ 23T	Mike Devereaux	.08	.03	.01
☐ 24T	Frank DiPino	.05	.02	.00
☐ 25T	Benny Distefano	.05	.02	.00
☐ 26T	John Dopson	.08	.03	.01
☐ 27T	Len Dykstra	.10	.04	.01
☐ 28T	Jim Eisenreich	.05	.02	.00
☐ 29T	Nick Esasky	.05	.02	.00
☐ 30T	Alvaro Espinoza	.08	.03	.01
☐ 31T	Darrell Evans UER	.10	.04	.01
	(Stat headings on back are for a pitcher)			
☐ 32T	Junior Felix	.15	.06	.01
☐ 33T	Felix Fermin	.05	.02	.00
☐ 34T	Julio Franco	.12	.05	.01
☐ 35T	Terry Francona	.05	.02	.00
☐ 36T	Cito Gaston MG	.08	.03	.01
☐ 37T	Bob Geren UER	.10	.04	.01
	(Photo actually Mike Fennell)			
☐ 38T	Tom Gordon	.20	.08	.02
☐ 39T	Tommy Gregg	.08	.03	.01
☐ 40T	Ken Griffey Sr.	.12	.05	.01
☐ 41T	Ken Griffey Jr.	6.00	2.50	.60
☐ 42T	Kevin Gross	.05	.02	.00
☐ 43T	Lee Guetterman	.05	.02	.00
☐ 44T	Mel Hall	.10	.04	.01
☐ 45T	Erik Hanson	.50	.20	.05
☐ 46T	Gene Harris	.10	.04	.01
☐ 47T	Andy Hawkins	.05	.02	.00
☐ 48T	Rickey Henderson	.35	.15	.03
☐ 49T	Tom Herr	.08	.03	.01
☐ 50T	Ken Hill	.25	.10	.02
☐ 51T	Brian Holman	.17	.07	.01
☐ 52T	Brian Holton	.08	.03	.01
☐ 53T	Art Howe MG	.05	.02	.00
☐ 54T	Ken Howell	.05	.02	.00
☐ 55T	Bruce Hurst	.08	.03	.01

		MINT	EXC	G-VG
☐ 56T	Chris James	.08	.03	.01
☐ 57T	Randy Johnson	.12	.05	.01
☐ 58T	Jimmy Jones	.05	.02	.00
☐ 59T	Terry Kennedy	.05	.02	.00
☐ 60T	Paul Kilgus	.05	.02	.00
☐ 61T	Eric King	.05	.02	.00
☐ 62T	Ron Kittle	.08	.03	.01
☐ 63T	John Kruk	.08	.03	.01
☐ 64T	Randy Kutcher	.05	.02	.00
☐ 65T	Steve Lake	.05	.02	.00
☐ 66T	Mark Langston	.10	.04	.01
☐ 67T	Dave LaPoint	.05	.02	.00
☐ 68T	Rick Leach	.05	.02	.00
☐ 69T	Terry Leach	.05	.02	.00
☐ 70T	Jim Lefebvre MG	.05	.02	.00
☐ 71T	Al Leiter	.08	.03	.01
☐ 72T	Jeffrey Leonard	.05	.02	.00
☐ 73T	Derek Lilliquist	.08	.03	.01
☐ 74T	Rick Mahler	.05	.02	.00
☐ 75T	Tom McCarthy	.10	.04	.01
☐ 76T	Lloyd McClendon	.10	.04	.01
☐ 77T	Lance McCullers	.05	.02	.00
☐ 78T	Oddibe McDowell	.05	.02	.00
☐ 79T	Roger McDowell	.08	.03	.01
☐ 80T	Larry McWilliams	.05	.02	.00
☐ 81T	Randy Milligan	.10	.04	.01
☐ 82T	Mike Moore	.10	.04	.01
☐ 83T	Keith Moreland	.05	.02	.00
☐ 84T	Mike Morgan	.08	.03	.01
☐ 85T	Jamie Moyer	.05	.02	.00
☐ 86T	Rob Murphy	.05	.02	.00
☐ 87T	Eddie Murray	.12	.05	.01
☐ 88T	Pete O'Brien	.05	.02	.00
☐ 89T	Gregg Olson	.50	.20	.05
☐ 90T	Steve Ontiveros	.05	.02	.00
☐ 91T	Jesse Orosco	.05	.02	.00
☐ 92T	Spike Owen	.05	.02	.00
☐ 93T	Rafael Palmeiro	.15	.06	.01
☐ 94T	Clay Parker	.08	.03	.01
☐ 95T	Jeff Parrett	.05	.02	.00
☐ 96T	Lance Parrish	.10	.04	.01
☐ 97T	Dennis Powell	.05	.02	.00
☐ 98T	Rey Quinones	.05	.02	.00
☐ 99T	Doug Rader MG	.05	.02	.00
☐ 100T	Willie Randolph	.08	.03	.01
☐ 101T	Shane Rawley	.05	.02	.00
☐ 102T	Randy Ready	.05	.02	.00
☐ 103T	Bip Roberts	.12	.05	.01
☐ 104T	Kenny Rogers	.12	.05	.01
☐ 105T	Ed Romero	.05	.02	.00
☐ 106T	Nolan Ryan	1.50	.60	.15
☐ 107T	Luis Salazar	.05	.02	.00
☐ 108T	Juan Samuel	.10	.04	.01
☐ 109T	Alex Sanchez	.10	.04	.01
☐ 110T	Deion Sanders	.60	.25	.06
☐ 111T	Steve Sax	.12	.05	.01
☐ 112T	Rick Schu	.05	.02	.00
☐ 113T	Dwight Smith	.12	.05	.01
☐ 114T	Lonnie Smith	.10	.04	.01
☐ 115T	Billy Spiers	.12	.05	.01
☐ 116T	Kent Tekulve	.05	.02	.00
☐ 117T	Walt Terrell	.05	.02	.00
☐ 118T	Milt Thompson	.05	.02	.00
☐ 119T	Dickie Thon	.05	.02	.00
☐ 120T	Jeff Torborg MG	.05	.02	.00
☐ 121T	Jeff Treadway	.08	.03	.01
☐ 122T	Omar Vizquel	.10	.04	.01
☐ 123T	Jerome Walton	.40	.16	.04
☐ 124T	Gary Ward	.05	.02	.00
☐ 125T	Claudell Washington	.05	.02	.00
☐ 126T	Curt Wilkerson	.05	.02	.00
☐ 127T	Eddie Williams	.05	.02	.00
☐ 128T	Frank Williams	.05	.02	.00
☐ 129T	Ken Williams	.08	.03	.01
☐ 130T	Mitch Williams	.10	.04	.01
☐ 131T	Steve Wilson	.10	.04	.01
☐ 132T	Checklist 1T-132T	.05	.01	.00

1989-90 Topps Senior League

The 1989-90 Topps Senior League baseball set was issued second among the three sets commemorating the first Senior league season. This set was issued in set form in its own box containing all 132 cards, each standard sized (2 1/2" by 3 1/2").

	MINT	EXC	G-VG
COMPLETE SET (132)	7.50	3.25	.75
COMMON PLAYER (1-132)	.07	.03	.01

☐ 1	George Foster	.20	.08	.02
☐ 2	Dwight Lowry	.07	.03	.01
☐ 3	Bob Jones	.07	.03	.01
☐ 4	Clete Boyer	.12	.05	.01
☐ 5	Rafael Landestoy	.07	.03	.01
☐ 6	Bob Shirley	.07	.03	.01
☐ 7	Ivan Murrell	.07	.03	.01
☐ 8	Jerry White	.07	.03	.01
☐ 9	Steve Henderson	.07	.03	.01
☐ 10	Marty Castillo	.07	.03	.01
☐ 11	Bruce Kison	.10	.04	.01
☐ 12	George Hendrick	.12	.05	.01
☐ 13	Bernie Carbo	.10	.04	.01
☐ 14	Jerry Martin	.07	.03	.01
☐ 15	Al Hrabosky	.12	.05	.01
☐ 16	Luis Gomez	.07	.03	.01
☐ 17	Dick Drago	.07	.03	.01
☐ 18	Bobby Ramos	.07	.03	.01
☐ 19	Joe Pittman	.07	.03	.01
☐ 20	Ike Blessitt	.10	.04	.01
☐ 21	Bill Travers	.07	.03	.01
☐ 22	Dick Williams	.10	.04	.01
☐ 23	Randy Lerch	.07	.03	.01
☐ 24	Tom Spencer	.07	.03	.01
☐ 25	Graig Nettles	.20	.08	.02
☐ 26	Jim Gideon	.07	.03	.01
☐ 27	Al Bumbry	.10	.04	.01
☐ 28	Tom Murphy	.07	.03	.01
☐ 29	Rodney Scott	.07	.03	.01
☐ 30	Alan Bannister	.07	.03	.01
☐ 31	John D'Acquisto	.07	.03	.01
☐ 32	Bert Campaneris	.15	.06	.01
☐ 33	Bill Lee	.12	.05	.01
☐ 34	Jerry Grote	.07	.03	.01
☐ 35	Ken Reitz	.07	.03	.01
☐ 36	Al Oliver	.20	.08	.02
☐ 37	Tim Stoddard	.07	.03	.01
☐ 38	Lenny Randle	.07	.03	.01
☐ 39	Rick Manning	.07	.03	.01
☐ 40	Bobby Bonds	.30	.12	.03
☐ 41	Rick Wise	.12	.05	.01
☐ 42	Sal Butera	.07	.03	.01
☐ 43	Ed Figueroa	.07	.03	.01
☐ 44	Ron Washington	.07	.03	.01
☐ 45	Elias Sosa	.07	.03	.01
☐ 46	Dan Driessen	.10	.04	.01
☐ 47	Wayne Nordhagen	.07	.03	.01
☐ 48	Vida Blue	.15	.06	.01
☐ 49	Butch Hobson	.15	.06	.01
☐ 50	Randy Bass	.10	.04	.01
☐ 51	Paul Mirabella	.07	.03	.01
☐ 52	Steve Kemp	.10	.04	.01
☐ 53	Kim Allen	.07	.03	.01
☐ 54	Stan Cliburn	.07	.03	.01
☐ 55	Derrel Thomas	.07	.03	.01
☐ 56	Pete Falcone	.07	.03	.01
☐ 57	Willie Aikens	.10	.04	.01
☐ 58	Toby Harrah	.10	.04	.01
☐ 59	Bob Tolan	.10	.04	.01
☐ 60	Rick Waits	.07	.03	.01
☐ 61	Jim Morrison	.07	.03	.01
☐ 62	Stan Bahnsen	.07	.03	.01
☐ 63	Gene Richards	.07	.03	.01
☐ 64	Dave Cash	.10	.04	.01
☐ 65	Rollie Fingers	.75	.30	.07
☐ 66	Butch Benton	.07	.03	.01
☐ 67	Tim Ireland	.07	.03	.01
☐ 68	Rick Lysander	.07	.03	.01
☐ 69	Cesar Cedeno	.10	.04	.01
☐ 70	Jim Willoughby	.07	.03	.01
☐ 71	Bill Madlock	.15	.06	.01
☐ 72	Lee Lacy	.07	.03	.01
☐ 73	Milt Wilcox	.07	.03	.01

☐ 74	Ron Pruitt	.07	.03	.01
☐ 75	Wayne Krenchicki	.07	.03	.01
☐ 76	Earl Weaver MG	.15	.06	.01
☐ 77	Pedro Borbon	.07	.03	.01
☐ 78	Jose Cruz	.10	.04	.01
☐ 79	Steve Ontiveros	.07	.03	.01
☐ 80	Mike Easler	.10	.04	.01
☐ 81	Amos Otis	.15	.06	.01
☐ 82	Mickey Mahler	.07	.03	.01
☐ 83	Orlando Gonzalez	.07	.03	.01
☐ 84	Doug Simunic	.07	.03	.01
☐ 85	Felix Millan	.07	.03	.01
☐ 86	Garth Iorg	.07	.03	.01
☐ 87	Pete Broberg	.07	.03	.01
☐ 88	Roy Howell	.07	.03	.01
☐ 89	Dave LaRoche	.07	.03	.01
☐ 90	Jerry Manuel	.07	.03	.01
☐ 91	Tony Scott	.07	.03	.01
☐ 92	Larvell Blanks	.07	.03	.01
☐ 93	Joaquin Andujar	.12	.05	.01
☐ 94	Tito Landrum	.10	.04	.01
☐ 95	Joe Sambito	.10	.04	.01
☐ 96	Pat Dobson	.10	.04	.01
☐ 97	Dan Meyer	.07	.03	.01
☐ 98	Clint Hurdle	.12	.05	.01
☐ 99	Pete LaCock	.10	.04	.01
☐ 100	Bob Galasso	.07	.03	.01
☐ 101	Dave Kingman	.20	.08	.02
☐ 102	Jon Matlack	.12	.05	.01
☐ 103	Larry Harlow	.07	.03	.01
☐ 104	Rick Peterson	.07	.03	.01
☐ 105	Joe Hicks	.07	.03	.01
☐ 106	Bill Campbell	.07	.03	.01
☐ 107	Tom Paciorek	.10	.04	.01
☐ 108	Ray Burris	.10	.04	.01
☐ 109	Ken Landreaux	.10	.04	.01
☐ 110	Steve McCatty	.07	.03	.01
☐ 111	Ron LeFlore	.10	.04	.01
☐ 112	Joe Decker	.07	.03	.01
☐ 113	Leon Roberts	.07	.03	.01
☐ 114	Doug Corbett	.07	.03	.01
☐ 115	Mickey Rivers	.07	.03	.01
☐ 116	Dock Ellis	.07	.03	.01
☐ 117	Ron Jackson	.07	.03	.01
☐ 118	Bob Molinaro	.07	.03	.01
☐ 119	Fergie Jenkins	.90	.40	.09
☐ 120	U.L. Washington	.07	.03	.01
☐ 121	Roy Thomas	.07	.03	.01
☐ 122	Hal McRae	.15	.06	.01
☐ 123	Juan Eichelberger	.07	.03	.01
☐ 124	Gary Rajsich	.07	.03	.01
☐ 125	Dennis Leonard	.10	.04	.01
☐ 126	Walt Williams	.10	.04	.01
☐ 127	Rennie Stennett	.07	.03	.01
☐ 128	Jim Bibby	.10	.04	.01
☐ 129	Dyar Miller	.07	.03	.01
☐ 130	Luis Pujols	.07	.03	.01
☐ 131	Juan Beniquez	.10	.04	.01
☐ 132	Checklist Card	.07	.03	.01

1990 Topps

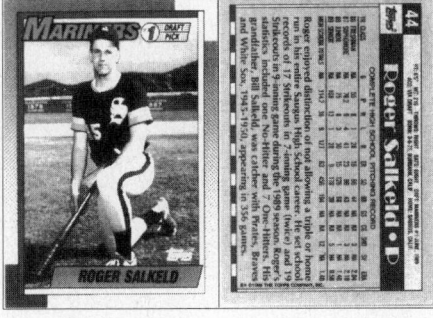

The 1990 Topps set contains 792 standard-size (2 1/2" by 3 1/2") cards. The front borders are various colors. The horizontally-oriented backs are yellowish green. Cards 385-407 contain the

All-Stars. Cards 661-665 contain the Turn Back the Clock cards. The manager cards this year contain information that had been on the backs of the Team Leader cards in the past few years; the Team Leader cards were discontinued, apparently in order to allow better individual player card selection. Topps really concentrated on individual player cards in this set with 725, the most ever in a baseball card set. The checklist cards are oriented alphabetically by team name and player name. The key rookie cards in this set are Juan Gonzalez, Ben McDonald, and Frank Thomas. Topps also produced a specially boxed "glossy" edition frequently referred to as the Topps Tiffany set. This year, again, Topps did not disclose the number of Tiffany sets they produced or sold but it seems that production quantities were roughly similar (approximately 15,000 sets) to the previous year. The checklist of cards is identical to that of the normal non-glossy cards. There are two primary distinguishing features of the Tiffany cards, white card stock reverses and high gloss obverses. These Tiffany cards are valued at approximately four times the values listed below.

	MINT	EXC	G-VG
COMPLETE SET (792)	20.00	8.50	2.75
COMMON PLAYER (1-792)	.03	.01	.00
☐ 1 Nolan Ryan	.50	.12	.02
☐ 2 Nolan Ryan Salute New York Mets	.20	.08	.02
☐ 3 Nolan Ryan Salute California Angels	.20	.08	.02
☐ 4 Nolan Ryan Salute Houston Astros	.20	.08	.02
☐ 5 Nolan Ryan Salute Texas Rangers UER (says Texas Stadium rather than Arlington Stadium)	.20	.08	.02
☐ 6 Vince Coleman RB (50 consecutive stolen bases)	.06	.02	.00
☐ 7 Rickey Henderson RB (40 career leadoff home runs)	.10	.04	.01
☐ 8 Cal Ripken RB (20 or more homers for 8 consecutive years, record for shortstops)	.10	.04	.01
☐ 9 Eric Plunk	.03	.01	.00
☐ 10 Barry Larkin	.10	.04	.01
☐ 11 Paul Gibson	.03	.01	.00
☐ 12 Joe Girardi	.03	.01	.00
☐ 13 Mark Williamson	.03	.01	.00
☐ 14 Mike Fetters	.08	.03	.01
☐ 15 Teddy Higuera	.03	.01	.00
☐ 16 Kent Anderson	.03	.01	.00
☐ 17 Kelly Downs	.03	.01	.00
☐ 18 Carlos Quintana	.08	.03	.01
☐ 19 Al Newman	.03	.01	.00
☐ 20 Mark Gubicza	.06	.02	.00
☐ 21 Jeff Torborg MG	.03	.01	.00
☐ 22 Bruce Ruffin	.03	.01	.00
☐ 23 Randy Velarde	.03	.01	.00
☐ 24 Joe Hesketh	.03	.01	.00
☐ 25 Willie Randolph	.06	.02	.00
☐ 26 Don Slaught	.03	.01	.00
☐ 27 Rick Leach	.03	.01	.00
☐ 28 Duane Ward	.03	.01	.00
☐ 29 John Cangelosi	.03	.01	.00
☐ 30 David Cone	.08	.03	.01
☐ 31 Henry Cotto	.03	.01	.00
☐ 32 John Farrell	.03	.01	.00
☐ 33 Greg Walker	.03	.01	.00
☐ 34 Tony Fossas	.06	.02	.00
☐ 35 Benito Santiago	.08	.03	.01
☐ 36 John Costello	.03	.01	.00
☐ 37 Domingo Ramos	.03	.01	.00
☐ 38 Wes Gardner	.03	.01	.00
☐ 39 Curt Ford	.03	.01	.00
☐ 40 Jay Howell	.03	.01	.00
☐ 41 Matt Williams	.15	.06	.01
☐ 42 Jeff M. Robinson	.03	.01	.00
☐ 43 Dante Bichette	.06	.02	.00
☐ 44 Roger Salkeld FDP	.45	.18	.04
☐ 45 Dave Parker UER (born in Jackson, not Calhoun)	.08	.03	.01
☐ 46 Rob Dibble	.06	.02	.00
☐ 47 Brian Harper	.06	.02	.00
☐ 48 Zane Smith	.06	.02	.00

☐ 49 Tom Lawless	.03	.01	.00
☐ 50 Glenn Davis	.08	.03	.01
☐ 51 Doug Rader MG	.03	.01	.00
☐ 52 Jack Daugherty	.06	.02	.00
☐ 53 Mike LaCoss	.03	.01	.00
☐ 54 Joel Skinner	.03	.01	.00
☐ 55 Darrell Evans UER (HR total should be 414, not 424)	.06	.02	.00
☐ 56 Franklin Stubbs	.03	.01	.00
☐ 57 Greg Vaughn	.45	.18	.04
☐ 58 Keith Miller	.03	.01	.00
☐ 59 Ted Power	.03	.01	.00
☐ 60 George Brett	.12	.05	.01
☐ 61 Deion Sanders	.15	.06	.01
☐ 62 Ramon Martinez	.25	.10	.02
☐ 63 Mike Pagliarulo	.03	.01	.00
☐ 64 Danny Darwin	.03	.01	.00
☐ 65 Devon White	.06	.02	.00
☐ 66 Greg Litton	.06	.02	.00
☐ 67 Scott Sanderson	.03	.01	.00
☐ 68 Dave Henderson	.06	.02	.00
☐ 69 Todd Frohwirth	.03	.01	.00
☐ 70 Mike Greenwell	.12	.05	.01
☐ 71 Allan Anderson	.03	.01	.00
☐ 72 Jeff Huson	.08	.03	.01
☐ 73 Bob Milacki	.03	.01	.00
☐ 74 Jeff Jackson FDP	.10	.04	.01
☐ 75 Doug Jones	.03	.01	.00
☐ 76 Dave Valle	.03	.01	.00
☐ 77 Dave Bergman	.03	.01	.00
☐ 78 Mike Flanagan	.03	.01	.00
☐ 79 Ron Kittle	.06	.02	.00
☐ 80 Jeff Russell	.03	.01	.00
☐ 81 Bob Rodgers MG	.03	.01	.00
☐ 82 Scott Terry	.03	.01	.00
☐ 83 Hensley Meulens	.12	.05	.01
☐ 84 Ray Searage	.03	.01	.00
☐ 85 Juan Samuel	.06	.02	.00
☐ 86 Paul Kilgus	.03	.01	.00
☐ 87 Rick Luecken	.08	.03	.01
☐ 88 Glenn Braggs	.03	.01	.00
☐ 89 Clint Zavaras	.08	.03	.01
☐ 90 Jack Clark	.06	.02	.00
☐ 91 Steve Frey	.08	.03	.01
☐ 92 Mike Stanley	.03	.01	.00
☐ 93 Shawn Hillegas	.03	.01	.00
☐ 94 Herm Winningham	.03	.01	.00
☐ 95 Todd Worrell	.06	.02	.00
☐ 96 Jody Reed	.06	.02	.00
☐ 97 Curt Schilling	.06	.02	.00
☐ 98 Jose Gonzalez	.03	.01	.00
☐ 99 Rich Monteleone	.06	.02	.00
☐ 100 Will Clark	.30	.12	.03
☐ 101 Shane Rawley	.03	.01	.00
☐ 102 Stan Javier	.03	.01	.00
☐ 103 Marvin Freeman	.03	.01	.00
☐ 104 Bob Knepper	.03	.01	.00
☐ 105 Randy Myers	.03	.01	.00
☐ 106 Charlie O'Brien	.03	.01	.00
☐ 107 Fred Lynn	.06	.02	.00
☐ 108 Rod Nichols	.03	.01	.00
☐ 109 Roberto Kelly	.08	.03	.01
☐ 110 Tommy Helms MG	.03	.01	.00
☐ 111 Ed Whited	.08	.03	.01
☐ 112 Glenn Wilson	.03	.01	.00
☐ 113 Manny Lee	.03	.01	.00
☐ 114 Mike Bielecki	.03	.01	.00
☐ 115 Tony Pena	.06	.02	.00
☐ 116 Floyd Bannister	.03	.01	.00
☐ 117 Mike Sharperson	.03	.01	.00
☐ 118 Erik Hanson	.08	.03	.01
☐ 119 Billy Hatcher	.03	.01	.00
☐ 120 John Franco	.03	.01	.00
☐ 121 Robin Ventura	.50	.20	.05
☐ 122 Shawn Abner	.03	.01	.00
☐ 123 Rich Gedman	.03	.01	.00
☐ 124 Dave Dravecky	.06	.02	.00
☐ 125 Kent Hrbek	.06	.02	.00
☐ 126 Randy Kramer	.03	.01	.00
☐ 127 Mike Devereaux	.03	.01	.00
☐ 128 Checklist 1	.06	.01	.00
☐ 129 Ron Jones	.03	.01	.00
☐ 130 Bert Blyleven	.06	.02	.00
☐ 131 Matt Nokes	.06	.02	.00
☐ 132 Lance Blankenship	.03	.01	.00
☐ 133 Ricky Horton	.03	.01	.00
☐ 134 Earl Cunningham FDP	.15	.06	.01
☐ 135 Dave Magadan	.06	.02	.00
☐ 136 Kevin Brown	.03	.01	.00
☐ 137 Marty Pevey	.08	.03	.01
☐ 138 Al Leiter	.03	.01	.00
☐ 139 Greg Brock	.03	.01	.00
☐ 140 Andre Dawson	.10	.04	.01
☐ 141 John Hart MG	.03	.01	.00

☐ 142 Jeff Wetherby	.08	.03	.01
☐ 143 Rafael Belliard	.03	.01	.00
☐ 144 Bud Black	.03	.01	.00
☐ 145 Terry Steinbach	.03	.01	.00
☐ 146 Rob Richie	.03	.01	.00
☐ 147 Chuck Finley	.06	.02	.00
☐ 148 Edgar Martinez	.08	.03	.01
☐ 149 Steve Farr	.03	.01	.00
☐ 150 Kirk Gibson	.08	.03	.01
☐ 151 Rick Mahler	.03	.01	.00
☐ 152 Lonnie Smith	.06	.02	.00
☐ 153 Randy Milligan	.06	.02	.00
☐ 154 Mike Maddux	.03	.01	.00
☐ 155 Ellis Burks	.08	.03	.01
☐ 156 Ken Patterson	.03	.01	.00
☐ 157 Craig Biggio	.08	.03	.01
☐ 158 Craig Lefferts	.03	.01	.00
☐ 159 Mike Felder	.03	.01	.00
☐ 160 Dave Righetti	.06	.02	.00
☐ 161 Harold Reynolds	.06	.02	.00
☐ 162 Todd Zeile	.35	.15	.03
☐ 163 Phil Bradley	.03	.01	.00
☐ 164 Jeff Juden FDP	.35	.15	.03
☐ 165 Walt Weiss	.06	.02	.00
☐ 166 Bobby Witt	.06	.02	.00
☐ 167 Kevin Appier	.20	.08	.02
☐ 168 Jose Lind	.03	.01	.00
☐ 169 Richard Dotson	.03	.01	.00
☐ 170 George Bell	.08	.03	.01
☐ 171 Russ Nixon MG	.03	.01	.00
☐ 172 Tom Lampkin	.03	.01	.00
☐ 173 Tim Belcher	.06	.02	.00
☐ 174 Jeff Kunkel	.03	.01	.00
☐ 175 Mike Moore	.06	.02	.00
☐ 176 Luis Quinones	.03	.01	.00
☐ 177 Mike Henneman	.03	.01	.00
☐ 178 Chris James	.06	.02	.00
☐ 179 Brian Holton	.03	.01	.00
☐ 180 Tim Raines	.08	.03	.01
☐ 181 Juan Agosto	.03	.01	.00
☐ 182 Mookie Wilson	.03	.01	.00
☐ 183 Steve Lake	.03	.01	.00
☐ 184 Danny Cox	.03	.01	.00
☐ 185 Ruben Sierra	.17	.07	.01
☐ 186 Dave LaPoint	.03	.01	.00
☐ 187 Rick Wrona	.06	.02	.00
☐ 188 Mike Smithson	.03	.01	.00
☐ 189 Dick Schofield	.03	.01	.00
☐ 190 Rick Reuschel	.06	.02	.00
☐ 191 Pat Borders	.03	.01	.00
☐ 192 Don August	.03	.01	.00
☐ 193 Andy Benes	.15	.06	.01
☐ 194 Glenallen Hill	.06	.02	.00
☐ 195 Tim Burke	.03	.01	.00
☐ 196 Gerald Young	.03	.01	.00
☐ 197 Doug Drabek	.06	.02	.00
☐ 198 Mike Marshall	.06	.02	.00
☐ 199 Sergio Valdez	.08	.03	.01
☐ 200 Don Mattingly	.20	.08	.02
☐ 201 Cito Gaston MG	.06	.02	.00
☐ 202 Mike Macfarlane	.03	.01	.00
☐ 203 Mike Roesler	.08	.03	.01
☐ 204 Bob Dernier	.03	.01	.00
☐ 205 Mark Davis	.06	.02	.00
☐ 206 Nick Esasky	.03	.01	.00
☐ 207 Bob Ojeda	.03	.01	.00
☐ 208 Brook Jacoby	.03	.01	.00
☐ 209 Greg Mathews	.03	.01	.00
☐ 210 Ryne Sandberg	.30	.12	.03
☐ 211 John Cerutti	.03	.01	.00
☐ 212 Joe Orsulak	.03	.01	.00
☐ 213 Scott Bankhead	.03	.01	.00
☐ 214 Terry Francona	.03	.01	.00
☐ 215 Kirk McCaskill	.03	.01	.00
☐ 216 Ricky Jordan	.06	.02	.00
☐ 217 Don Robinson	.03	.01	.00
☐ 218 Wally Backman	.03	.01	.00
☐ 219 Donn Pall	.03	.01	.00
☐ 220 Barry Bonds	.15	.06	.01
☐ 221 Gary Mielke	.08	.03	.01
☐ 222 Kurt Stillwell UER	.03	.01	.00
(Graduate misspelled			
as gradute)			
☐ 223 Tommy Gregg	.03	.01	.00
☐ 224 Delino DeShields	.40	.16	.04
☐ 225 Jim Deshaies	.03	.01	.00
☐ 226 Mickey Hatcher	.03	.01	.00
☐ 227 Kevin Tapani	.35	.15	.03
☐ 228 Dave Martinez	.03	.01	.00
☐ 229 David Wells	.03	.01	.00
☐ 230 Keith Hernandez	.06	.02	.00
☐ 231 Jack McKeon MG	.03	.01	.00
☐ 232 Darnell Coles	.03	.01	.00
☐ 233 Ken Hill	.06	.02	.00
☐ 234 Mariano Duncan	.03	.01	.00

☐ 235 Jeff Reardon	.06	.02	.00
☐ 236 Hal Morris	.35	.15	.03
☐ 237 Kevin Ritz	.08	.03	.01
☐ 238 Felix Jose	.20	.08	.02
☐ 239 Eric Show	.03	.01	.00
☐ 240 Mark Grace	.12	.05	.01
☐ 241 Mike Krukow	.03	.01	.00
☐ 242 Fred Manrique	.03	.01	.00
☐ 243 Barry Jones	.03	.01	.00
☐ 244 Bill Schroeder	.03	.01	.00
☐ 245 Roger Clemens	.30	.12	.03
☐ 246 Jim Eisenreich	.03	.01	.00
☐ 247 Jerry Reed	.03	.01	.00
☐ 248 Dave Anderson	.03	.01	.00
☐ 249 Mike Smith	.06	.02	.00
☐ 250 Jose Canseco	.40	.16	.04
☐ 251 Jeff Blauser	.03	.01	.00
☐ 252 Otis Nixon	.06	.02	.00
☐ 253 Mark Portugal	.03	.01	.00
☐ 254 Francisco Cabrera	.10	.04	.01
☐ 255 Bobby Thigpen	.06	.02	.00
☐ 256 Marvell Wynne	.03	.01	.00
☐ 257 Jose DeLeon	.03	.01	.00
☐ 258 Barry Lyons	.03	.01	.00
☐ 259 Lance McCullers	.03	.01	.00
☐ 260 Eric Davis	.10	.04	.01
☐ 261 Whitey Herzog MG	.06	.02	.00
☐ 262 Checklist 2	.06	.01	.00
☐ 263 Mel Stottlemyre Jr.	.03	.01	.00
☐ 264 Bryan Clutterbuck	.03	.01	.00
☐ 265 Pete O'Brien	.03	.01	.00
☐ 266 German Gonzalez	.03	.01	.00
☐ 267 Mark Davidson	.03	.01	.00
☐ 268 Rob Murphy	.03	.01	.00
☐ 269 Dickie Thon	.03	.01	.00
☐ 270 Dave Stewart	.08	.03	.01
☐ 271 Chet Lemon	.03	.01	.00
☐ 272 Bryan Harvey	.06	.02	.00
☐ 273 Bobby Bonilla	.15	.06	.01
☐ 274 Mauro Gozzo	.08	.03	.01
☐ 275 Mickey Tettleton	.06	.02	.00
☐ 276 Gary Thurman	.03	.01	.00
☐ 277 Lenny Harris	.06	.02	.00
☐ 278 Pascual Perez	.03	.01	.00
☐ 279 Steve Buechele	.03	.01	.00
☐ 280 Lou Whitaker	.06	.02	.00
☐ 281 Kevin Bass	.03	.01	.00
☐ 282 Derek Lilliquist	.03	.01	.00
☐ 283 Joey Belle	.60	.25	.06
☐ 284 Mark Gardner	.15	.06	.01
☐ 285 Willie McGee	.08	.03	.01
☐ 286 Lee Guetterman	.03	.01	.00
☐ 287 Vance Law	.03	.01	.00
☐ 288 Greg Briley	.03	.01	.00
☐ 289 Norm Charlton	.03	.01	.00
☐ 290 Robin Yount	.12	.05	.01
☐ 291 Dave Johnson MG	.03	.01	.00
☐ 292 Jim Gott	.03	.01	.00
☐ 293 Mike Gallego	.03	.01	.00
☐ 294 Craig McMurtry	.03	.01	.00
☐ 295 Fred McGriff	.10	.04	.01
☐ 296 Jeff Ballard	.03	.01	.00
☐ 297 Tommy Herr	.03	.01	.00
☐ 298 Dan Gladden	.03	.01	.00
☐ 299 Adam Peterson	.03	.01	.00
☐ 300 Bo Jackson	.40	.16	.04
☐ 301 Don Aase	.03	.01	.00
☐ 302 Marcus Lawton	.10	.04	.01
☐ 303 Rick Cerone	.03	.01	.00
☐ 304 Marty Clary	.03	.01	.00
☐ 305 Eddie Murray	.10	.04	.01
☐ 306 Tom Niedenfuer	.03	.01	.00
☐ 307 Bip Roberts	.03	.01	.00
☐ 308 Jose Guzman	.03	.01	.00
☐ 309 Eric Yelding	.06	.02	.00
☐ 310 Steve Bedrosian	.03	.01	.00
☐ 311 Dwight Smith	.06	.02	.00
☐ 312 Dan Quisenberry	.06	.02	.00
☐ 313 Gus Polidor	.03	.01	.00
☐ 314 Donald Harris FDP	.12	.05	.01
☐ 315 Bruce Hurst	.06	.02	.00
☐ 316 Carney Lansford	.06	.02	.00
☐ 317 Mark Guthrie	.08	.03	.01
☐ 318 Wallace Johnson	.03	.01	.00
☐ 319 Dion James	.03	.01	.00
☐ 320 Dave Stieb	.06	.02	.00
☐ 321 Joe Morgan MG	.03	.01	.00
☐ 322 Junior Ortiz	.03	.01	.00
☐ 323 Willie Wilson	.06	.02	.00
☐ 324 Pete Harnisch	.06	.02	.00
☐ 325 Robby Thompson	.03	.01	.00
☐ 326 Tom McCarthy	.06	.02	.00
☐ 327 Ken Williams	.03	.01	.00
☐ 328 Curt Young	.03	.01	.00
☐ 329 Oddibe McDowell	.03	.01	.00

#	Player			
330	Ron Darling	.06	.02	.00
331	Juan Gonzalez	1.75	.70	.17
332	Paul O'Neill	.06	.02	.00
333	Bill Wegman	.03	.01	.00
334	Johnny Ray	.03	.01	.00
335	Andy Hawkins	.03	.01	.00
336	Ken Griffey Jr.	1.50	.60	.15
337	Lloyd McClendon	.03	.01	.00
338	Dennis Lamp	.03	.01	.00
339	Dave Clark	.03	.01	.00
340	Fernando Valenzuela	.08	.03	.01
341	Tom Foley	.03	.01	.00
342	Alex Trevino	.03	.01	.00
343	Frank Tanana	.06	.02	.00
344	George Canale	.10	.04	.01
345	Harold Baines	.08	.03	.01
346	Jim Presley	.03	.01	.00
347	Junior Felix	.06	.02	.00
348	Gary Wayne	.08	.03	.01
349	Steve Finley	.10	.04	.01
350	Bret Saberhagen	.08	.03	.01
351	Roger Craig MG	.03	.01	.00
352	Bryn Smith	.03	.01	.00
353	Sandy Alomar Jr.	.10	.04	.01
	(not listed as Jr.			
	on card front)			
354	Stan Belinda	.12	.05	.01
355	Marty Barrett	.03	.01	.00
356	Randy Ready	.03	.01	.00
357	Dave West	.03	.01	.00
358	Andres Thomas	.03	.01	.00
359	Jimmy Jones	.03	.01	.00
360	Paul Molitor	.08	.03	.01
361	Randy McCament	.06	.02	.00
362	Damon Berryhill	.03	.01	.00
363	Dan Petry	.03	.01	.00
364	Rolando Roomes	.03	.01	.00
365	Ozzie Guillen	.06	.02	.00
366	Mike Heath	.03	.01	.00
367	Mike Morgan	.03	.01	.00
368	Bill Doran	.03	.01	.00
369	Todd Burns	.03	.01	.00
370	Tim Wallach	.06	.02	.00
371	Jimmy Key	.06	.02	.00
372	Terry Kennedy	.03	.01	.00
373	Alvin Davis	.06	.02	.00
374	Steve Cummings	.08	.03	.01
375	Dwight Evans	.06	.02	.00
376	Checklist 3 UER	.06	.01	.00
	(Higuera misalphabet-			
	ized in Brewer list)			
377	Mickey Weston	.08	.03	.01
378	Luis Salazar	.03	.01	.00
379	Steve Rosenberg	.03	.01	.00
380	Dave Winfield	.10	.04	.01
381	Frank Robinson MG	.08	.03	.01
382	Jeff Musselman	.03	.01	.00
383	John Morris	.03	.01	.00
384	Pat Combs	.06	.02	.00
385	Fred McGriff AS	.08	.03	.01
386	Julio Franco AS	.08	.03	.01
387	Wade Boggs AS	.10	.04	.01
388	Cal Ripken AS	.12	.05	.01
389	Robin Yount AS	.08	.03	.01
390	Ruben Sierra AS	.10	.04	.01
391	Kirby Puckett AS	.10	.04	.01
392	Carlton Fisk AS	.08	.03	.01
393	Bret Saberhagen AS	.08	.03	.01
394	Jeff Ballard AS	.03	.01	.00
395	Jeff Russell AS	.03	.01	.00
396	A.Bartlett Giamatti	.12	.05	.01
	(commemorative)			
397	Will Clark AS	.15	.06	.01
398	Ryne Sandberg AS	.12	.05	.01
399	Howard Johnson AS	.08	.03	.01
400	Ozzie Smith AS	.08	.03	.01
401	Kevin Mitchell AS	.08	.03	.01
402	Eric Davis AS	.08	.03	.01
403	Tony Gwynn AS	.08	.03	.01
404	Craig Biggio AS	.06	.02	.00
405	Mike Scott AS	.06	.02	.00
406	Joe Magrane AS	.03	.01	.00
407	Mark Davis AS	.03	.01	.00
408	Trevor Wilson	.03	.01	.00
409	Tom Brunansky	.06	.02	.00
410	Joe Boever	.03	.01	.00
411	Ken Phelps	.03	.01	.00
412	Jamie Moyer	.03	.01	.00
413	Brian Dubois	.08	.03	.01
414A	Frank Thomas FDP	4.00	1.75	.40
	ERR (Name missing			
	on card front)			
414B	Frank Thomas FDP COR	4.00	1.75	.40
415	Shawon Dunston	.08	.03	.01
416	Dave Johnson (P)	.08	.03	.01
417	Jim Gantner	.03	.01	.00
418	Tom Browning	.06	.02	.00
419	Beau Allred	.12	.05	.01
420	Carlton Fisk	.12	.05	.01
421	Greg Minton	.03	.01	.00
422	Pat Sheridan	.03	.01	.00
423	Fred Toliver	.03	.01	.00
424	Jerry Reuss	.03	.01	.00
425	Bill Landrum	.03	.01	.00
426	Jeff Hamilton	.03	.01	.00
427	Carmen Castillo	.03	.01	.00
428	Steve Davis	.08	.03	.01
429	Tom Kelly MG	.03	.01	.00
430	Pete Incaviglia	.06	.02	.00
431	Randy Johnson	.06	.02	.00
432	Damaso Garcia	.03	.01	.00
433	Steve Olin	.08	.03	.01
434	Mark Carreon	.03	.01	.00
435	Kevin Seitzer	.06	.02	.00
436	Mel Hall	.06	.02	.00
437	Les Lancaster	.03	.01	.00
438	Greg Myers	.03	.01	.00
439	Jeff Parrett	.03	.01	.00
440	Alan Trammell	.08	.03	.01
441	Bob Kipper	.03	.01	.00
442	Jerry Browne	.03	.01	.00
443	Cris Carpenter	.03	.01	.00
444	Kyle Abbott FDP	.25	.10	.02
445	Danny Jackson	.03	.01	.00
446	Dan Pasqua	.03	.01	.00
447	Atlee Hammaker	.03	.01	.00
448	Greg Gagne	.03	.01	.00
449	Dennis Rasmussen	.03	.01	.00
450	Rickey Henderson	.25	.10	.02
451	Mark Lemke	.06	.02	.00
452	Luis De Los Santos	.03	.01	.00
453	Jody Davis	.03	.01	.00
454	Jeff King	.06	.02	.00
455	Jeffrey Leonard	.03	.01	.00
456	Chris Gwynn	.03	.01	.00
457	Gregg Jefferies	.10	.04	.01
458	Bob McClure	.03	.01	.00
459	Jim Lefebvre MG	.03	.01	.00
460	Mike Scott	.06	.02	.00
461	Carlos Martinez	.06	.02	.00
462	Denny Walling	.03	.01	.00
463	Drew Hall	.03	.01	.00
464	Jerome Walton	.08	.03	.01
465	Kevin Gross	.03	.01	.00
466	Rance Mulliniks	.03	.01	.00
467	Juan Nieves	.03	.01	.00
468	Bill Ripken	.03	.01	.00
469	John Kruk	.03	.01	.00
470	Frank Viola	.08	.03	.01
471	Mike Brumley	.03	.01	.00
472	Jose Uribe	.03	.01	.00
473	Joe Price	.03	.01	.00
474	Rich Thompson	.03	.01	.00
475	Bob Welch	.06	.02	.00
476	Brad Komminsk	.03	.01	.00
477	Willie Fraser	.03	.01	.00
478	Mike LaValliere	.03	.01	.00
479	Frank White	.03	.01	.00
480	Sid Fernandez	.06	.02	.00
481	Garry Templeton	.03	.01	.00
482	Steve Carter	.06	.02	.00
483	Alejandro Pena	.06	.02	.00
484	Mike Fitzgerald	.03	.01	.00
485	John Candelaria	.03	.01	.00
486	Jeff Treadway	.03	.01	.00
487	Steve Searcy	.03	.01	.00
488	Ken Oberkfell	.03	.01	.00
489	Nick Leyva MG	.03	.01	.00
490	Dan Plesac	.03	.01	.00
491	Dave Cochrane	.08	.03	.01
492	Ron Oester	.03	.01	.00
493	Jason Grimsley	.08	.03	.01
494	Terry Puhl	.03	.01	.00
495	Lee Smith	.06	.02	.00
496	Cecil Espy UER	.03	.01	.00
	('89 stats have 3			
	SB's, should be 33)			
497	Dave Schmidt	.03	.01	.00
498	Rick Schu	.03	.01	.00
499	Bill Long	.03	.01	.00
500	Kevin Mitchell	.10	.04	.01
501	Matt Young	.03	.01	.00
502	Mitch Webster	.03	.01	.00
503	Randy St.Claire	.03	.01	.00
504	Tom O'Malley	.03	.01	.00
505	Kelly Gruber	.08	.03	.01
506	Tom Glavine	.20	.08	.02
507	Gary Redus	.03	.01	.00
508	Terry Leach	.03	.01	.00

#	Player			
509	Tom Pagnozzi	.03	.01	.00
510	Dwight Gooden	.10	.04	.01
511	Clay Parker	.03	.01	.00
512	Gary Pettis	.03	.01	.00
513	Mark Eichhorn	.03	.01	.00
514	Andy Allanson	.03	.01	.00
515	Len Dykstra	.06	.02	.00
516	Tim Leary	.06	.02	.00
517	Roberto Alomar	.15	.06	.01
518	Bill Krueger	.03	.01	.00
519	Bucky Dent MG	.06	.02	.00
520	Mitch Williams	.03	.01	.00
521	Craig Worthington	.03	.01	.00
522	Mike Dunne	.03	.01	.00
523	Jay Bell	.03	.01	.00
524	Daryl Boston	.03	.01	.00
525	Wally Joyner	.08	.03	.01
526	Checklist 4	.06	.01	.00
527	Ron Hassey	.03	.01	.00
528	Kevin Wickander	.06	.02	.00
529	Greg Harris	.03	.01	.00
530	Mark Langston	.06	.02	.00
531	Ken Caminiti	.03	.01	.00
532	Cecilio Guante	.03	.01	.00
533	Tim Jones	.03	.01	.00
534	Louie Meadows	.03	.01	.00
535	John Smoltz	.15	.06	.01
536	Bob Geren	.03	.01	.00
537	Mark Grant	.03	.01	.00
538	Bill Spiers UER	.08	.03	.01
	(photo actually			
	George Canale)			
539	Neal Heaton	.03	.01	.00
540	Danny Tartabull	.08	.03	.01
541	Pat Perry	.03	.01	.00
542	Darren Daulton	.06	.02	.00
543	Nelson Liriano	.03	.01	.00
544	Dennis Boyd	.03	.01	.00
545	Kevin McReynolds	.08	.03	.01
546	Kevin Hickey	.03	.01	.00
547	Jack Howell	.03	.01	.00
548	Pat Clements	.03	.01	.00
549	Don Zimmer MG	.03	.01	.00
550	Julio Franco	.08	.03	.01
551	Tim Crews	.03	.01	.00
552	Mike Smith	.06	.02	.00
553	Scott Scudder UER	.10	.04	.01
	(Cedar Rap1ds)			
554	Jay Buhner	.08	.03	.01
555	Jack Morris	.08	.03	.01
556	Gene Larkin	.03	.01	.00
557	Jeff Innis	.10	.04	.01
558	Rafael Ramirez	.03	.01	.00
559	Andy McGaffigan	.03	.01	.00
560	Steve Sax	.08	.03	.01
561	Ken Dayley	.03	.01	.00
562	Chad Kreuter	.03	.01	.00
563	Alex Sanchez	.06	.02	.00
564	Tyler Houston FDP	.12	.05	.01
565	Scott Fletcher	.03	.01	.00
566	Mark Knudson	.03	.01	.00
567	Ron Gant	.25	.10	.02
568	John Smiley	.06	.02	.00
569	Ivan Calderon	.06	.02	.00
570	Cal Ripken	.30	.12	.03
571	Brett Butler	.06	.02	.00
572	Greg A. Harris	.03	.01	.00
573	Danny Heep	.03	.01	.00
574	Bill Swift	.03	.01	.00
575	Lance Parrish	.06	.02	.00
576	Mike Dyer	.08	.03	.01
577	Charlie Hayes	.06	.02	.00
578	Joe Magrane	.03	.01	.00
579	Art Howe MG	.03	.01	.00
580	Joe Carter	.10	.04	.01
581	Ken Griffey Sr.	.08	.03	.01
582	Rick Honeycutt	.03	.01	.00
583	Bruce Benedict	.03	.01	.00
584	Phil Stephenson	.06	.02	.00
585	Kal Daniels	.06	.02	.00
586	Edwin Nunez	.03	.01	.00
587	Lance Johnson	.03	.01	.00
588	Rick Rhoden	.03	.01	.00
589	Mike Aldrete	.03	.01	.00
590	Ozzie Smith	.10	.04	.01
591	Todd Stottlemyre	.08	.03	.01
592	R.J. Reynolds	.03	.01	.00
593	Scott Bradley	.03	.01	.00
594	Luis Sojo	.10	.04	.01
595	Greg Swindell	.06	.02	.00
596	Jose DeJesus	.03	.01	.00
597	Chris Bosio	.03	.01	.00
598	Brady Anderson	.03	.01	.00
599	Frank Williams	.03	.01	.00
600	Darryl Strawberry	.25	.10	.02
601	Luis Rivera	.03	.01	.00
602	Scott Garrelts	.03	.01	.00
603	Tony Armas	.03	.01	.00
604	Ron Robinson	.03	.01	.00
605	Mike Scioscia	.03	.01	.00
606	Storm Davis	.03	.01	.00
607	Steve Jeltz	.03	.01	.00
608	Eric Anthony	.17	.07	.01
609	Sparky Anderson MG	.06	.02	.00
610	Pedro Guerrero	.06	.02	.00
611	Walt Terrell	.03	.01	.00
612	Dave Gallagher	.03	.01	.00
613	Jeff Pico	.03	.01	.00
614	Nelson Santovenia	.03	.01	.00
615	Rob Deer	.06	.02	.00
616	Brian Holman	.08	.03	.01
617	Geronimo Berroa	.03	.01	.00
618	Ed Whitson	.03	.01	.00
619	Rob Ducey	.03	.01	.00
620	Tony Castillo	.03	.01	.00
621	Melido Perez	.03	.01	.00
622	Sid Bream	.03	.01	.00
623	Jim Corsi	.03	.01	.00
624	Darrin Jackson	.03	.01	.00
625	Roger McDowell	.03	.01	.00
626	Bob Melvin	.03	.01	.00
627	Jose Rijo	.06	.02	.00
628	Candy Maldonado	.03	.01	.00
629	Eric Hetzel	.03	.01	.00
630	Gary Gaetti	.06	.02	.00
631	John Wetteland	.08	.03	.01
632	Scott Lusader	.03	.01	.00
633	Dennis Cook	.06	.02	.00
634	Luis Polonia	.03	.01	.00
635	Brian Downing	.03	.01	.00
636	Jesse Orosco	.03	.01	.00
637	Craig Reynolds	.03	.01	.00
638	Jeff Montgomery	.03	.01	.00
639	Tony LaRussa MG	.06	.02	.00
640	Rick Sutcliffe	.06	.02	.00
641	Doug Strange	.08	.03	.01
642	Jack Armstrong	.06	.02	.00
643	Alfredo Griffin	.03	.01	.00
644	Paul Assenmacher	.03	.01	.00
645	Jose Oquendo	.03	.01	.00
646	Checklist 5	.06	.01	.00
647	Rex Hudler	.03	.01	.00
648	Jim Clancy	.03	.01	.00
649	Dan Murphy	.08	.03	.01
650	Mike Witt	.03	.01	.00
651	Rafael Santana	.03	.01	.00
652	Mike Boddicker	.03	.01	.00
653	John Moses	.03	.01	.00
654	Paul Coleman FDP	.17	.07	.01
655	Gregg Olson	.12	.05	.01
656	Mackey Sasser	.03	.01	.00
657	Terry Mulholland	.06	.02	.00
658	Donell Nixon	.03	.01	.00
659	Greg Cadaret	.03	.01	.00
660	Vince Coleman	.08	.03	.01
661	Dick Howser TBC'85	.03	.01	.00
	UER (Seaver's 300th			
	on 7/11/85, should			
	be 8/4/85)			
662	Mike Schmidt TBC'80	.10	.04	.01
663	Fred Lynn TBC'75	.06	.02	.00
664	Johnny Bench TBC'70	.08	.03	.01
665	Sandy Koufax TBC'65	.08	.03	.01
666	Brian Fisher	.03	.01	.00
667	Curt Wilkerson	.03	.01	.00
668	Joe Oliver	.08	.03	.01
669	Tom Lasorda MG	.06	.02	.00
670	Dennis Eckersley	.08	.03	.01
671	Bob Boone	.06	.02	.00
672	Roy Smith	.03	.01	.00
673	Joey Meyer	.03	.01	.00
674	Spike Owen	.03	.01	.00
675	Jim Abbott	.17	.07	.01
676	Randy Kutcher	.03	.01	.00
677	Jay Tibbs	.03	.01	.00
678	Kirt Manwaring UER	.03	.01	.00
	('88 Phoenix stats			
	repeated)			
679	Gary Ward	.03	.01	.00
680	Howard Johnson	.08	.03	.01
681	Mike Schooler	.03	.01	.00
682	Dann Bilardello	.03	.01	.00
683	Kenny Rogers	.06	.02	.00
684	Julio Machado	.08	.03	.01
685	Tony Fernandez	.06	.02	.00
686	Carmelo Martinez	.03	.01	.00
687	Tim Birtsas	.03	.01	.00
688	Milt Thompson	.03	.01	.00
689	Rich Yett	.03	.01	.00
690	Mark McGwire	.15	.06	.01

☐ 691	Chuck Cary	.03	.01	.00
☐ 692	Sammy Sosa	.25	.10	.02
☐ 693	Calvin Schiraldi	.03	.01	.00
☐ 694	Mike Stanton	.08	.03	.01
☐ 695	Tom Henke	.06	.02	.00
☐ 696	B.J. Surhoff	.03	.01	.00
☐ 697	Mike Davis	.03	.01	.00
☐ 698	Omar Vizquel	.03	.01	.00
☐ 699	Jim Leyland MG	.03	.01	.00
☐ 700	Kirby Puckett	.20	.08	.02
☐ 701	Bernie Williams	.50	.20	.05
☐ 702	Tony Phillips	.03	.01	.00
☐ 703	Jeff Brantley	.08	.03	.01
☐ 704	Chip Hale	.08	.03	.01
☐ 705	Claudell Washington	.03	.01	.00
☐ 706	Geno Petralli	.03	.01	.00
☐ 707	Luis Aquino	.03	.01	.00
☐ 708	Larry Sheets	.03	.01	.00
☐ 709	Juan Berenguer	.03	.01	.00
☐ 710	Von Hayes	.06	.02	.00
☐ 711	Rick Aguilera	.03	.01	.00
☐ 712	Todd Benzinger	.03	.01	.00
☐ 713	Tim Drummond	.08	.03	.01
☐ 714	Marquis Grissom	.40	.16	.04
☐ 715	Greg Maddux	.06	.02	.00
☐ 716	Steve Balboni	.03	.01	.00
☐ 717	Ron Karkovice	.03	.01	.00
☐ 718	Gary Sheffield	.08	.03	.01
☐ 719	Wally Whitehurst	.06	.02	.00
☐ 720	Andres Galarraga	.06	.02	.00
☐ 721	Lee Mazzilli	.03	.01	.00
☐ 722	Felix Fermin	.03	.01	.00
☐ 723	Jeff D. Robinson	.03	.01	.00
☐ 724	Juan Bell	.06	.02	.00
☐ 725	Terry Pendleton	.08	.03	.01
☐ 726	Gene Nelson	.03	.01	.00
☐ 727	Pat Tabler	.03	.01	.00
☐ 728	Jim Acker	.03	.01	.00
☐ 729	Bobby Valentine MG	.03	.01	.00
☐ 730	Tony Gwynn	.15	.06	.01
☐ 731	Don Carman	.03	.01	.00
☐ 732	Ernest Riles	.03	.01	.00
☐ 733	John Dopson	.03	.01	.00
☐ 734	Kevin Elster	.03	.01	.00
☐ 735	Charlie Hough	.03	.01	.00
☐ 736	Rick Dempsey	.03	.01	.00
☐ 737	Chris Sabo	.10	.04	.01
☐ 738	Gene Harris	.06	.02	.00
☐ 739	Dale Sveum	.03	.01	.00
☐ 740	Jesse Barfield	.06	.02	.00
☐ 741	Steve Wilson	.03	.01	.00
☐ 742	Ernie Whitt	.03	.01	.00
☐ 743	Tom Candiotti	.06	.02	.00
☐ 744	Kelly Mann	.08	.03	.01
☐ 745	Hubie Brooks	.03	.01	.00
☐ 746	Dave Smith	.03	.01	.00
☐ 747	Randy Bush	.03	.01	.00
☐ 748	Doyle Alexander	.03	.01	.00
☐ 749	Mark Parent UER ('87 BA .80, should be .080)	.03	.01	.00
☐ 750	Dale Murphy	.10	.04	.01
☐ 751	Steve Lyons	.03	.01	.00
☐ 752	Tom Gordon	.08	.03	.01
☐ 753	Chris Speier	.03	.01	.00
☐ 754	Bob Walk	.03	.01	.00
☐ 755	Rafael Palmeiro	.12	.05	.01
☐ 756	Ken Howell	.03	.01	.00
☐ 757	Larry Walker	.25	.10	.02
☐ 758	Mark Thurmond	.03	.01	.00
☐ 759	Tom Trebelhorn MG	.03	.01	.00
☐ 760	Wade Boggs	.15	.06	.01
☐ 761	Mike Jackson	.03	.01	.00
☐ 762	Doug Dascenzo	.03	.01	.00
☐ 763	Dennis Martinez	.06	.02	.00
☐ 764	Tim Teufel	.03	.01	.00
☐ 765	Chili Davis	.06	.02	.00
☐ 766	Brian Meyer	.06	.02	.00
☐ 767	Tracy Jones	.03	.01	.00
☐ 768	Chuck Crim	.03	.01	.00
☐ 769	Greg Hibbard	.15	.06	.01
☐ 770	Cory Snyder	.06	.02	.00
☐ 771	Pete Smith	.03	.01	.00
☐ 772	Jeff Reed	.03	.01	.00
☐ 773	Dave Leiper	.03	.01	.00
☐ 774	Ben McDonald	.75	.30	.07
☐ 775	Andy Van Slyke	.08	.03	.01
☐ 776	Charlie Leibrandt	.03	.01	.00
☐ 777	Tim Laudner	.03	.01	.00
☐ 778	Mike Jeffcoat	.03	.01	.00
☐ 779	Lloyd Moseby	.03	.01	.00
☐ 780	Orel Hershiser	.08	.03	.01
☐ 781	Mario Diaz	.03	.01	.00
☐ 782	Jose Alvarez	.03	.01	.00
☐ 783	Checklist 6	.06	.01	.00

☐ 784	Scott Bailes	.03	.01	.00
☐ 785	Jim Rice	.08	.03	.01
☐ 786	Eric King	.03	.01	.00
☐ 787	Rene Gonzales	.03	.01	.00
☐ 788	Frank DiPino	.03	.01	.00
☐ 789	John Wathan MG	.03	.01	.00
☐ 790	Gary Carter	.08	.03	.01
☐ 791	Alvaro Espinoza	.03	.01	.00
☐ 792	Gerald Perry	.06	.02	.00

1990 Topps Wax Box Cards

The 1990 Topps wax box cards comprise four different box bottoms with four cards each, for a total of 16 standard-size (2 1/2" by 3 1/2") cards. The front borders are green. The vertically-oriented backs are yellowish green. These cards depict various career milestones achieved during the 1989 season. The card numbers are actually the letters A through P.

		MINT	EXC	G-VG
COMPLETE SET (16)		6.00	2.50	.60
COMMON PLAYER (A-P)		.10	.04	.01
☐ A	Wade Boggs	.60	.25	.06
☐ B	George Brett	.50	.20	.05
☐ C	Andre Dawson	.35	.15	.03
☐ D	Darrell Evans	.15	.06	.01
☐ E	Dwight Gooden	.35	.15	.03
☐ F	Rickey Henderson	.75	.30	.07
☐ G	Tom Lasorda MG	.15	.06	.01
☐ H	Fred Lynn	.15	.06	.01
☐ I	Mark McGwire	.45	.18	.04
☐ J	Dave Parker	.25	.10	.02
☐ K	Jeff Reardon	.20	.08	.02
☐ L	Rick Reuschel	.15	.06	.01
☐ M	Jim Rice	.20	.08	.02
☐ N	Cal Ripken	.75	.30	.07
☐ O	Nolan Ryan	.90	.40	.09
☐ P	Ryne Sandberg	.75	.30	.07

1990 Topps All-Star Glossy 22

The 1990 Topps Glossy All-Star set contains 22 standard-size (2 1/2" by 3 1/2") glossy cards. The front and back borders are white, and other design elements are red, blue and yellow. This set is almost identical to previous year sets of the same name. One card was included in each 1990 Topps rack pack.

		MINT	EXC	G-VG
COMPLETE SET (22)		3.00	1.25	.30
COMMON PLAYER (1-22)		.10	.04	.01
☐ 1	Tom Lasorda MG	.10	.04	.01
☐ 2	Will Clark	.50	.20	.05
☐ 3	Ryne Sandberg	.50	.20	.05
☐ 4	Howard Johnson	.25	.10	.02
☐ 5	Ozzie Smith	.25	.10	.02
☐ 6	Kevin Mitchell	.35	.15	.03

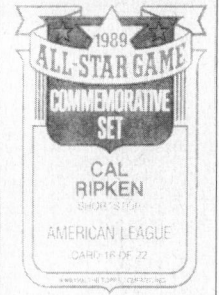

☐ 13 Greg W. Harris	.20	.08	.02
☐ 14 Greg Hibbard	.25	.10	.02
☐ 15 Ken Hill	.20	.08	.02
☐ 16 Gregg Jefferies	.50	.20	.05
☐ 17 Jeff King	.25	.10	.02
☐ 18 Derek Lilliquist	.20	.08	.02
☐ 19 Carlos Martinez	.25	.10	.02
☐ 20 Ramon Martinez	.60	.25	.06
☐ 21 Bob Milacki	.20	.08	.02
☐ 22 Gregg Olson	.45	.18	.04
☐ 23 Donn Pall	.20	.08	.02
☐ 24 Kenny Rogers	.25	.10	.02
☐ 25 Gary Sheffield	.40	.16	.04
☐ 26 Dwight Smith	.25	.10	.02
☐ 27 Billy Spiers	.25	.10	.02
☐ 28 Omar Vizquel	.20	.08	.02
☐ 29 Jerome Walton	.30	.12	.03
☐ 30 Dave West	.20	.08	.02
☐ 31 John Wetteland	.25	.10	.02
☐ 32 Steve Wilson	.20	.08	.02
☐ 33 Craig Worthington	.20	.08	.02

☐ 7 Eric Davis	.25	.10	.02
☐ 8 Tony Gwynn	.35	.15	.03
☐ 9 Benito Santiago	.20	.08	.02
☐ 10 Rick Reuschel	.10	.04	.01
☐ 11 Don Drysdale CAPT	.15	.06	.01
☐ 12 Tony LaRussa MG	.10	.04	.01
☐ 13 Mark McGwire	.35	.15	.03
☐ 14 Julio Franco	.25	.10	.02
☐ 15 Wade Boggs	.45	.18	.04
☐ 16 Cal Ripken	.50	.20	.05
☐ 17 Bo Jackson	.60	.25	.06
☐ 18 Kirby Puckett	.35	.15	.03
☐ 19 Ruben Sierra	.35	.15	.03
☐ 20 Terry Steinbach	.15	.06	.01
☐ 21 Dave Stewart	.15	.06	.01
☐ 22 Carl Yastrzemski CAPT	.20	.08	.02

1990 Topps Jumbo Rookies

The 1990 Topps Jumbo Rookies set contains 33 standard-size (2 1/2" by 3 1/2") glossy cards. The front and back borders are white, and other design elements are red, blue and yellow. This set is almost identical to previous year sets of the same name except that it contains 33 cards rather than only 22. One card was included in each 1990 Topps "jumbo" pack. The cards are numbered in alphabetical order.

	MINT	EXC	G-VG
COMPLETE SET (33)	9.00	4.00	.90
COMMON PLAYER (1-33)	.20	.08	.02
☐ 1 Jim Abbott	.75	.30	.07
☐ 2 Joey Belle	.60	.25	.06
☐ 3 Andy Benes	.50	.20	.05
☐ 4 Greg Briley	.25	.10	.02
☐ 5 Kevin Brown	.25	.10	.02
☐ 6 Mark Carreon	.20	.08	.02
☐ 7 Mike Devereaux	.20	.08	.02
☐ 8 Junior Felix	.25	.10	.02
☐ 9 Bob Geren	.20	.08	.02
☐ 10 Tom Gordon	.30	.12	.03
☐ 11 Ken Griffey Jr.	1.50	.60	.15
☐ 12 Pete Harnisch	.25	.10	.02

1990 Topps '89 Debut

The 1990 Topps Major League Debut Set is a 152-card, standard-size (2 1/2" by 3 1/2") set arranged in alphabetical order by player's name. Each card front features the date of the player's first major league appearance. Strangely enough, even though the set commemorates the 1989 Major League debuts, the set was not issued until the 1990 season had almost begun.

	MINT	EXC	G-VG
COMPLETE SET (152)	15.00	6.50	2.15
COMMON PLAYER (1-152)	.05	.02	.00
☐ 1 Jim Abbott	.75	.30	.07
☐ 2 Beau Allred	.15	.06	.01
☐ 3 Wilson Alvarez	.15	.06	.01
☐ 4 Kent Anderson	.05	.02	.00
☐ 5 Eric Anthony	.25	.10	.02
☐ 6 Kevin Appier	.20	.08	.02
☐ 7 Larry Arndt	.10	.04	.01
☐ 8 John Barfield	.10	.04	.01
☐ 9 Billy Bates	.10	.04	.01
☐ 10 Kevin Batiste	.15	.06	.01
☐ 11 Blaine Beatty	.10	.04	.01
☐ 12 Stan Belinda	.10	.04	.01
☐ 13 Juan Bell	.15	.06	.01
☐ 14 Joey Belle	.75	.30	.07
(Now known as Albert)			
☐ 15 Andy Benes	.50	.20	.05
☐ 16 Mike Benjamin	.10	.04	.01
☐ 17 Geronimo Berroa	.05	.02	.00
☐ 18 Mike Blowers	.10	.04	.01
☐ 19 Brian Brady	.10	.04	.01
☐ 20 Francisco Cabrera	.15	.06	.01
☐ 21 George Canale	.10	.04	.01
☐ 22 Jose Cano	.10	.04	.01
☐ 23 Steve Carter	.05	.02	.00
☐ 24 Pat Combs	.15	.06	.01
☐ 25 Scott Coolbaugh	.10	.04	.01
☐ 26 Steve Cummings	.10	.04	.01
☐ 27 Pete Dalena	.10	.04	.01
☐ 28 Jeff Datz	.10	.04	.01
☐ 29 Bobby Davidson	.10	.04	.01
☐ 30 Drew Denson	.10	.04	.01

		MINT	EXC	G-VG
☐ 31	Gary Disarcina	.10	.04	.01
☐ 32	Brian DuBois	.10	.04	.01
☐ 33	Mike Dyer	.10	.04	.01
☐ 34	Wayne Edwards	.10	.04	.01
☐ 35	Junior Felix	.20	.08	.02
☐ 36	Mike Fetters	.10	.04	.01
☐ 37	Steve Finley	.25	.10	.02
☐ 38	Darrin Fletcher	.10	.04	.01
☐ 39	LaVel Freeman	.15	.06	.01
☐ 40	Steve Frey	.10	.04	.01
☐ 41	Mark Gardner	.10	.04	.01
☐ 42	Joe Girardi	.10	.04	.01
☐ 43	Juan Gonzalez	1.75	.70	.17
☐ 44	Goose Gozzo	.10	.04	.01
☐ 45	Tommy Greene	.25	.10	.02
☐ 46	Ken Griffey Jr.	3.50	1.50	.35
☐ 47	Jason Grimsley	.10	.04	.01
☐ 48	Marquis Grissom	.35	.15	.03
☐ 49	Mark Guthrie	.10	.04	.01
☐ 50	Chip Hale	.10	.04	.01
☐ 51	Jack Hardy	.10	.04	.01
☐ 52	Gene Harris	.10	.04	.01
☐ 53	Mike Hartley	.10	.04	.01
☐ 54	Scott Hemond	.15	.06	.01
☐ 55	Xavier Hernandez	.05	.02	.00
☐ 56	Eric Hetzel	.10	.04	.01
☐ 57	Greg Hibbard	.10	.04	.01
☐ 58	Mark Higgins	.10	.04	.01
☐ 59	Glenallen Hill	.10	.04	.01
☐ 60	Chris Hoiles	.20	.08	.02
☐ 61	Shawn Holman	.10	.04	.01
☐ 62	Dann Howitt	.20	.08	.02
☐ 63	Mike Huff	.15	.06	.01
☐ 64	Terry Jorgensen	.10	.04	.01
☐ 65	Dave Justice	2.00	.80	.20
☐ 66	Jeff King	.10	.04	.01
☐ 67	Matt Kinzer	.05	.02	.00
☐ 68	Joe Kraemer	.10	.04	.01
☐ 69	Marcus Lawton	.10	.04	.01
☐ 70	Derek Lilliquist	.05	.02	.00
☐ 71	Scott Little	.10	.04	.01
☐ 72	Greg Litton	.10	.04	.01
☐ 73	Rick Luecken	.10	.04	.01
☐ 74	Julio Machado	.10	.04	.01
☐ 75	Tom Magrann	.10	.04	.01
☐ 76	Kelly Mann	.10	.04	.01
☐ 77	Randy McCament	.10	.04	.01
☐ 78	Ben McDonald	.60	.25	.06
☐ 79	Chuck McElroy	.10	.04	.01
☐ 80	Jeff McKnight	.10	.04	.01
☐ 81	Kent Mercker	.25	.10	.02
☐ 82	Matt Merullo	.05	.02	.00
☐ 83	Hensley Meulens	.30	.12	.03
☐ 84	Kevin Mmahat	.15	.06	.01
☐ 85	Mike Munoz	.10	.04	.01
☐ 86	Dan Murphy	.10	.04	.01
☐ 87	Jaime Navarro	.15	.06	.01
☐ 88	Randy Nosek	.05	.02	.00
☐ 89	John Olerud	.75	.30	.07
☐ 90	Steve Olin	.10	.04	.01
☐ 91	Joe Oliver	.10	.04	.01
☐ 92	Francisco Oliveras	.10	.04	.01
☐ 93	Gregg Olson	.35	.15	.03
☐ 94	John Orton	.10	.04	.01
☐ 95	Dean Palmer	.50	.20	.05
☐ 96	Ramon Pena	.05	.02	.00
☐ 97	Jeff Peterek	.10	.04	.01
☐ 98	Marty Pevey	.10	.04	.01
☐ 99	Rusty Richards	.10	.04	.01
☐ 100	Jeff Richardson	.10	.04	.01
☐ 101	Rob Richie	.05	.02	.00
☐ 102	Kevin Ritz	.10	.04	.01
☐ 103	Rosario Rodriguez	.05	.02	.00
☐ 104	Mike Roesler	.05	.02	.00
☐ 105	Kenny Rogers	.10	.04	.01
☐ 106	Bobby Rose	.15	.06	.01
☐ 107	Alex Sanchez	.05	.02	.00
☐ 108	Deion Sanders	.50	.20	.05
☐ 109	Jeff Schaefer	.10	.04	.01
☐ 110	Jeff Schulz	.10	.04	.01
☐ 111	Mike Schwabe	.05	.02	.00
☐ 112	Dick Scott	.10	.04	.01
☐ 113	Scott Scudder	.15	.06	.01
☐ 114	Rudy Seanez	.10	.04	.01
☐ 115	Joe Skalski	.05	.02	.00
☐ 116	Dwight Smith	.15	.06	.01
☐ 117	Greg Smith	.10	.04	.01
☐ 118	Mike Smith	.10	.04	.01
☐ 119	Paul Sorrento	.10	.04	.01
☐ 120	Sammy Sosa	.30	.12	.03
☐ 121	Billy Spiers	.10	.04	.01
☐ 122	Mike Stanton	.10	.04	.01
☐ 123	Phil Stephenson	.05	.02	.00
☐ 124	Doug Strange	.10	.04	.01
☐ 125	Russ Swan	.15	.06	.01
☐ 126	Kevin Tapani	.20	.08	.02
☐ 127	Stu Tate	.10	.04	.01
☐ 128	Greg Vaughn	.45	.18	.04
☐ 129	Robin Ventura	1.00	.40	.10
☐ 130	Randy Veres	.05	.02	.00
☐ 131	Jose Vizcaino	.10	.04	.01
☐ 132	Omar Vizquel	.05	.02	.00
☐ 133	Larry Walker	.30	.12	.03
☐ 134	Jerome Walton	.30	.12	.03
☐ 135	Gary Wayne	.10	.04	.01
☐ 136	Lenny Webster	.15	.06	.01
☐ 137	Mickey Weston	.10	.04	.01
☐ 138	Jeff Wetherby	.10	.04	.01
☐ 139	John Wetteland	.20	.08	.02
☐ 140	Ed Whited	.20	.08	.02
☐ 141	Wally Whitehurst	.10	.04	.01
☐ 142	Kevin Wickander	.10	.04	.01
☐ 143	Dean Wilkins	.10	.04	.01
☐ 144	Dana Williams	.15	.06	.01
☐ 145	Paul Wilmet	.10	.04	.01
☐ 146	Craig Wilson	.10	.04	.01
☐ 147	Matt Winters	.15	.06	.01
☐ 148	Eric Yelding	.10	.04	.01
☐ 149	Clint Zavaras	.10	.04	.01
☐ 150	Todd Zeile	.75	.30	.07
☐ 151	Checklist Card	.05	.02	.00
☐ 152	Checklist Card	.05	.02	.00

1990 Topps Glossy 60

The 1990 Topps Glossy 60 set was issued as a mailaway by Topps for the eighth straight year. This standard-size (2 1/2" by 3 1/2"), 60-card set features two young players among every ten players as Topps again broke down these cards into six series of ten cards each. Like the previous years' issues, there are attractive full color fronts.

		MINT	EXC	G-VG
COMPLETE SET (60)		10.00	4.50	1.25
COMMON PLAYER (1-60)		.15	.06	.01
☐ 1	Ryne Sandberg	.60	.25	.06
☐ 2	Nolan Ryan	.90	.40	.09
☐ 3	Glenn Davis	.25	.10	.02
☐ 4	Dave Stewart	.20	.08	.02
☐ 5	Barry Larkin	.25	.10	.02
☐ 6	Carney Lansford	.15	.06	.01
☐ 7	Darryl Strawberry	.15	.06	.01
☐ 8	Steve Sax	.15	.06	.01
☐ 9	Carlos Martinez	.15	.06	.01
☐ 10	Gary Sheffield	.25	.10	.02
☐ 11	Don Mattingly	.50	.20	.05
☐ 12	Mark Grace	.45	.18	.04
☐ 13	Bret Saberhagen	.25	.10	.02
☐ 14	Mike Scott	.20	.08	.02
☐ 15	Robin Yount	.40	.16	.04
☐ 16	Ozzie Smith	.30	.12	.03
☐ 17	Jeff Ballard	.15	.06	.01
☐ 18	Rick Reuschel	.15	.06	.01
☐ 19	Greg Briley	.15	.06	.01
☐ 20	Ken Griffey Jr.	1.25	.50	.12
☐ 21	Kevin Mitchell	.40	.16	.04
☐ 22	Wade Boggs	.45	.18	.04
☐ 23	Dwight Gooden	.30	.12	.03
☐ 24	George Bell	.25	.10	.02
☐ 25	Eric Davis	.30	.12	.03

		MINT	EXC	G-VG
☐ 26	Ruben Sierra	.40	.16	.04
☐ 27	Roberto Alomar	.35	.15	.03
☐ 28	Gary Gaetti	.15	.06	.01
☐ 29	Gregg Olson	.20	.08	.02
☐ 30	Tom Gordon	.20	.08	.02
☐ 31	Jose Canseco	.75	.30	.07
☐ 32	Pedro Guerrero	.20	.08	.02
☐ 33	Joe Carter	.30	.12	.03
☐ 34	Mike Scioscia	.15	.06	.01
☐ 35	Julio Franco	.25	.10	.02
☐ 36	Joe Magrane	.15	.06	.01
☐ 37	Rickey Henderson	.75	.30	.07
☐ 38	Tim Raines	.25	.10	.02
☐ 39	Jerome Walton	.25	.10	.02
☐ 40	Bob Geren	.15	.06	.01
☐ 41	Andre Dawson	.30	.12	.03
☐ 42	Mark McGwire	.45	.18	.04
☐ 43	Howard Johnson	.25	.10	.02
☐ 44	Bo Jackson	.90	.40	.09
☐ 45	Shawon Dunston	.20	.08	.02
☐ 46	Carlton Fisk	.35	.15	.03
☐ 47	Mitch Williams	.15	.06	.01
☐ 48	Kirby Puckett	.40	.16	.04
☐ 49	Craig Worthington	.15	.06	.01
☐ 50	Jim Abbott	.45	.18	.04
☐ 51	Cal Ripken	.75	.30	.07
☐ 52	Will Clark	.75	.30	.07
☐ 53	Dennis Eckersley	.20	.08	.02
☐ 54	Craig Biggio	.25	.10	.02
☐ 55	Fred McGriff	.30	.12	.03
☐ 56	Tony Gwynn	.40	.16	.04
☐ 57	Mickey Tettleton	.15	.06	.01
☐ 58	Mark Davis	.15	.06	.01
☐ 59	Omar Vizquel	.15	.06	.01
☐ 60	Gregg Jefferies	.35	.15	.03

1990 Topps Mini Leaders

The 1990 Topps League Leader Minis is a 88-card set with cards measuring approximately 2 1/8" by 3". The set features players who finished 1989 in the top five in any major hitting or pitching category. This set marked the fifth year that Topps issued their Mini set.

		MINT	EXC	G-VG
COMPLETE SET (88)		7.50	3.25	.75
COMMON PLAYER (1-88)		.07	.03	.01
☐ 1	Jeff Ballard	.07	.03	.01
☐ 2	Phil Bradley	.07	.03	.01
☐ 3	Wade Boggs	.50	.20	.05
☐ 4	Roger Clemens	.60	.25	.06
☐ 5	Nick Esasky	.07	.03	.01
☐ 6	Jody Reed	.10	.04	.01
☐ 7	Bert Blyleven	.10	.04	.01
☐ 8	Chuck Finley	.12	.05	.01
☐ 9	Kirk McCaskill	.07	.03	.01
☐ 10	Devon White	.12	.05	.01
☐ 11	Ivan Calderon	.10	.04	.01
☐ 12	Bobby Thigpen	.12	.05	.01
☐ 13	Joe Carter	.20	.08	.02
☐ 14	Gary Pettis	.07	.03	.01
☐ 15	Tom Gordon	.12	.05	.01
☐ 16	Bo Jackson	.75	.30	.07
☐ 17	Bret Saberhagen	.15	.06	.01
☐ 18	Kevin Seitzer	.12	.05	.01

		MINT	EXC	G-VG
☐ 19	Chris Bosio	.10	.04	.01
☐ 20	Paul Molitor	.15	.06	.01
☐ 21	Dan Plesac	.07	.03	.01
☐ 22	Robin Yount	.40	.16	.04
☐ 23	Kirby Puckett	.40	.16	.04
☐ 24	Don Mattingly	.50	.20	.05
☐ 25	Steve Sax	.12	.05	.01
☐ 26	Storm Davis	.07	.03	.01
☐ 27	Dennis Eckersley	.12	.05	.01
☐ 28	Rickey Henderson	.60	.25	.06
☐ 29	Carney Lansford	.10	.04	.01
☐ 30	Mark McGwire	.40	.16	.04
☐ 31	Mike Moore	.10	.04	.01
☐ 32	Dave Stewart	.12	.05	.01
☐ 33	Alvin Davis	.10	.04	.01
☐ 34	Harold Reynolds	.07	.03	.01
☐ 35	Mike Schooler	.07	.03	.01
☐ 36	Cecil Espy	.07	.03	.01
☐ 37	Julio Franco	.15	.06	.01
☐ 38	Jeff Russell	.07	.03	.01
☐ 39	Nolan Ryan	.90	.40	.09
☐ 40	Ruben Sierra	.35	.15	.03
☐ 41	George Bell	.15	.06	.01
☐ 42	Tony Fernandez	.10	.04	.01
☐ 43	Fred McGriff	.15	.06	.01
☐ 44	Dave Stieb	.12	.05	.01
☐ 45	Checklist Card	.07	.03	.01
☐ 46	Lonnie Smith	.10	.04	.01
☐ 47	John Smoltz	.15	.06	.01
☐ 48	Mike Bielecki	.07	.03	.01
☐ 49	Mark Grace	.35	.15	.03
☐ 50	Greg Maddux	.12	.05	.01
☐ 51	Ryne Sandberg	.50	.20	.05
☐ 52	Mitch Williams	.10	.04	.01
☐ 53	Eric Davis	.25	.10	.02
☐ 54	John Franco	.10	.04	.01
☐ 55	Glenn Davis	.15	.06	.01
☐ 56	Mike Scott	.10	.04	.01
☐ 57	Tim Belcher	.10	.04	.01
☐ 58	Orel Hershiser	.15	.06	.01
☐ 59	Jay Howell	.10	.04	.01
☐ 60	Eddie Murray	.25	.10	.02
☐ 61	Tim Burke	.07	.03	.01
☐ 62	Mark Langston	.12	.05	.01
☐ 63	Tim Raines	.15	.06	.01
☐ 64	Tim Wallach	.10	.04	.01
☐ 65	David Cone	.15	.06	.01
☐ 66	Sid Fernandez	.10	.04	.01
☐ 67	Howard Johnson	.15	.06	.01
☐ 68	Juan Samuel	.10	.04	.01
☐ 69	Von Hayes	.10	.04	.01
☐ 70	Barry Bonds	.40	.16	.04
☐ 71	Bobby Bonilla	.30	.12	.03
☐ 72	Andy Van Slyke	.15	.06	.01
☐ 73	Vince Coleman	.20	.08	.02
☐ 74	Jose DeLeon	.07	.03	.01
☐ 75	Pedro Guerrero	.12	.05	.01
☐ 76	Joe Magrane	.07	.03	.01
☐ 77	Roberto Alomar	.30	.12	.03
☐ 78	Jack Clark	.12	.05	.01
☐ 79	Mark Davis	.07	.03	.01
☐ 80	Tony Gwynn	.35	.15	.03
☐ 81	Bruce Hurst	.10	.04	.01
☐ 82	Eddie Whitson	.10	.04	.01
☐ 83	Brett Butler	.10	.04	.01
☐ 84	Will Clark	.60	.25	.06
☐ 85	Scott Garrelts	.07	.03	.01
☐ 86	Kevin Mitchell	.25	.10	.02
☐ 87	Rick Reuschel	.07	.03	.01
☐ 88	Robby Thompson	.07	.03	.01

1990 Topps Big

The 1990 Topps Big set contains 330 cards each measuring an slightly over-sized 2 5/8" by 3 3/4". In 1989 Topps had issued two oversize sets (Bigs and Bowmans), but in 1990 only the Topps Big were issued by Topps as an oversize set. The set was issued in three series of 110 cards.

		MINT	EXC	G-VG
COMPLETE SET (330)		25.00	11.00	3.50
COMMON PLAYER (1-110)		.05	.02	.00
COMMON PLAYER (111-220)		.05	.02	.00
COMMON PLAYER (221-330)		.06	.02	.00
☐ 1	Dwight Evans	.12	.05	.01
☐ 2	Kirby Puckett	.40	.16	.04

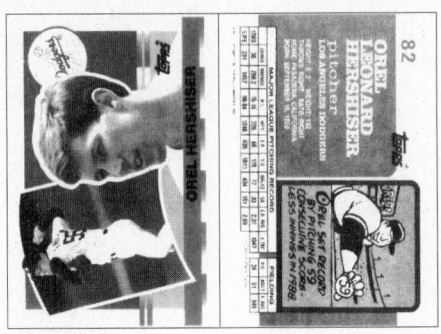

☐ 3	Kevin Gross	.05	.02	.00
☐ 4	Ron Hassey	.05	.02	.00
☐ 5	Lloyd McClendon	.05	.02	.00
☐ 6	Bo Jackson	.90	.40	.09
☐ 7	Lonnie Smith	.08	.03	.01
☐ 8	Alvaro Espinoza	.05	.02	.00
☐ 9	Roberto Alomar	.30	.12	.03
☐ 10	Glenn Braggs	.05	.02	.00
☐ 11	David Cone	.12	.05	.01
☐ 12	Claudell Washington	.05	.02	.00
☐ 13	Pedro Guerrero	.12	.05	.01
☐ 14	Todd Benzinger	.05	.02	.00
☐ 15	Jeff Russell	.05	.02	.00
☐ 16	Terry Kennedy	.05	.02	.00
☐ 17	Kelly Gruber	.15	.06	.01
☐ 18	Alfredo Griffin	.05	.02	.00
☐ 19	Mark Grace	.35	.15	.03
☐ 20	Dave Winfield	.25	.10	.02
☐ 21	Bret Saberhagen	.20	.08	.02
☐ 22	Roger Clemens	.60	.25	.06
☐ 23	Bob Walk	.05	.02	.00
☐ 24	Dave Magadan	.10	.04	.01
☐ 25	Spike Owen	.05	.02	.00
☐ 26	Jody Davis	.05	.02	.00
☐ 27	Kent Hrbek	.10	.04	.01
☐ 28	Mark McGwire	.35	.15	.03
☐ 29	Eddie Murray	.35	.15	.03
☐ 30	Paul O'Neill	.10	.04	.01
☐ 31	Jose DeLeon	.05	.02	.00
☐ 32	Steve Lyons	.05	.02	.00
☐ 33	Dan Plesac	.05	.02	.00
☐ 34	Jack Howell	.05	.02	.00
☐ 35	Greg Briley	.08	.03	.01
☐ 36	Andy Hawkins	.05	.02	.00
☐ 37	Cecil Espy	.05	.02	.00
☐ 38	Rick Sutcliffe	.08	.03	.01
☐ 39	Jack Clark	.12	.05	.01
☐ 40	Dale Murphy	.25	.10	.02
☐ 41	Mike Henneman	.05	.02	.00
☐ 42	Rick Honeycutt	.05	.02	.00
☐ 43	Willie Randolph	.08	.03	.01
☐ 44	Marty Barrett	.05	.02	.00
☐ 45	Willie Wilson	.08	.03	.01
☐ 46	Wallace Johnson	.05	.02	.00
☐ 47	Greg Brock	.05	.02	.00
☐ 48	Tom Browning	.08	.03	.01
☐ 49	Gerald Young	.05	.02	.00
☐ 50	Dennis Eckersley	.12	.05	.01
☐ 51	Scott Garrelts	.05	.02	.00
☐ 52	Gary Redus	.05	.02	.00
☐ 53	Al Newman	.05	.02	.00
☐ 54	Daryl Boston	.05	.02	.00
☐ 55	Ron Oester	.05	.02	.00
☐ 56	Danny Tartabull	.25	.10	.02
☐ 57	Gregg Jefferies	.25	.10	.02
☐ 58	Tom Foley	.05	.02	.00
☐ 59	Robin Yount	.35	.15	.03
☐ 60	Pat Borders	.10	.04	.01
☐ 61	Mike Greenwell	.30	.12	.03
☐ 62	Shawon Dunston	.12	.05	.01
☐ 63	Steve Buechele	.08	.03	.01
☐ 64	Dave Stewart	.12	.05	.01
☐ 65	Jose Oquendo	.05	.02	.00
☐ 66	Ron Gant	.40	.16	.04
☐ 67	Mike Scioscia	.05	.02	.00
☐ 68	Randy Velarde	.05	.02	.00
☐ 69	Charlie Hayes	.08	.03	.01
☐ 70	Tim Wallach	.08	.03	.01
☐ 71	Eric Show	.05	.02	.00
☐ 72	Eric Davis	.25	.10	.02
☐ 73	Mike Gallego	.05	.02	.00
☐ 74	Rob Deer	.08	.03	.01
☐ 75	Ryne Sandberg	.45	.18	.04
☐ 76	Kevin Seitzer	.10	.04	.01
☐ 77	Wade Boggs	.40	.16	.04
☐ 78	Greg Gagne	.05	.02	.00
☐ 79	John Smiley	.10	.04	.01
☐ 80	Ivan Calderon	.08	.03	.01
☐ 81	Pete Incaviglia	.10	.04	.01
☐ 82	Orel Hershiser	.15	.06	.01
☐ 83	Carney Lansford	.10	.04	.01
☐ 84	Mike Fitzgerald	.05	.02	.00
☐ 85	Don Mattingly	.50	.20	.05
☐ 86	Chet Lemon	.05	.02	.00
☐ 87	Rolando Roomes	.05	.02	.00
☐ 88	Billy Spiers	.05	.02	.00
☐ 89	Pat Tabler	.05	.02	.00
☐ 90	Danny Heep	.05	.02	.00
☐ 91	Andre Dawson	.25	.10	.02
☐ 92	Randy Bush	.05	.02	.00
☐ 93	Tony Gwynn	.35	.15	.03
☐ 94	Tom Brunansky	.08	.03	.01
☐ 95	Johnny Ray	.05	.02	.00
☐ 96	Matt Williams	.30	.12	.03
☐ 97	Barry Lyons	.05	.02	.00
☐ 98	Jeff Hamilton	.05	.02	.00
☐ 99	Tom Glavine	.20	.08	.02
☐ 100	Ken Griffey Sr.	.10	.04	.01
☐ 101	Tom Henke	.08	.03	.01
☐ 102	Dave Righetti	.10	.04	.01
☐ 103	Paul Molitor	.12	.05	.01
☐ 104	Mike LaValliere	.05	.02	.00
☐ 105	Frank White	.08	.03	.01
☐ 106	Bob Welch	.12	.05	.01
☐ 107	Ellis Burks	.25	.10	.02
☐ 108	Andres Galarraga	.12	.05	.01
☐ 109	Mitch Williams	.08	.03	.01
☐ 110	Checklist 1-110	.05	.02	.00
☐ 111	Craig Biggio	.15	.06	.01
☐ 112	Dave Stieb	.12	.05	.01
☐ 113	Ron Darling	.08	.03	.01
☐ 114	Bert Blyleven	.10	.04	.01
☐ 115	Dickie Thon	.08	.03	.01
☐ 116	Carlos Martinez	.08	.03	.01
☐ 117	Jeff King	.08	.03	.01
☐ 118	Terry Steinbach	.08	.03	.01
☐ 119	Frank Tanana	.08	.03	.01
☐ 120	Mark Lemke	.05	.02	.00
☐ 121	Chris Sabo	.30	.12	.03
☐ 122	Glenn Davis	.20	.08	.02
☐ 123	Mel Hall	.08	.03	.01
☐ 124	Jim Gantner	.05	.02	.00
☐ 125	Benito Santiago	.20	.08	.02
☐ 126	Milt Thompson	.08	.03	.01
☐ 127	Rafael Palmeiro	.20	.08	.02
☐ 128	Barry Bonds	.40	.16	.04
☐ 129	Mike Bielecki	.05	.02	.00
☐ 130	Lou Whitaker	.12	.05	.01
☐ 131	Bob Ojeda	.05	.02	.00
☐ 132	Dion James	.05	.02	.00
☐ 133	Dennis Martinez	.08	.03	.01
☐ 134	Fred McGriff	.15	.06	.01
☐ 135	Terry Pendleton	.15	.06	.01
☐ 136	Pat Combs	.10	.04	.01
☐ 137	Kevin Mitchell	.25	.10	.02
☐ 138	Marquis Grissom	.25	.10	.02
☐ 139	Chris Bosio	.08	.03	.01
☐ 140	Omar Vizquel	.05	.02	.00
☐ 141	Steve Sax	.10	.04	.01
☐ 142	Nelson Liriano	.05	.02	.00
☐ 143	Kevin Elster	.08	.03	.01
☐ 144	Dan Pasqua	.05	.02	.00
☐ 145	Dave Smith	.05	.02	.00
☐ 146	Craig Worthington	.05	.02	.00
☐ 147	Danny Gladden	.05	.02	.00
☐ 148	Oddibe McDowell	.05	.02	.00
☐ 149	Bip Roberts	.08	.03	.01
☐ 150	Randy Ready	.05	.02	.00
☐ 151	Dwight Smith	.10	.04	.01
☐ 152	Eddie Whitson	.08	.03	.01
☐ 153	George Bell	.20	.08	.02
☐ 154	Tim Raines	.15	.06	.01
☐ 155	Sid Fernandez	.08	.03	.01
☐ 156	Henry Cotto	.05	.02	.00
☐ 157	Harold Baines	.10	.04	.01
☐ 158	Willie McGee	.12	.05	.01
☐ 159	Bill Doran	.05	.02	.00
☐ 160	Steve Balboni	.05	.02	.00
☐ 161	Pete Smith	.05	.02	.00
☐ 162	Frank Viola	.12	.05	.01
☐ 163	Gary Sheffield	.15	.06	.01
☐ 164	Bill Landrum	.05	.02	.00
☐ 165	Tony Fernandez	.10	.04	.01
☐ 166	Mike Heath	.05	.02	.00
☐ 167	Jody Reed	.08	.03	.01
☐ 168	Wally Joyner	.15	.06	.01
☐ 169	Robby Thompson	.05	.02	.00
☐ 170	Ken Caminiti	.05	.02	.00

☐ 171	Nolan Ryan	.90	.40	.09
☐ 172	Ricky Jordan	.12	.05	.01
☐ 173	Lance Blankenship	.05	.02	.00
☐ 174	Dwight Gooden	.20	.08	.02
☐ 175	Ruben Sierra	.35	.15	.03
☐ 176	Carlton Fisk	.30	.12	.03
☐ 177	Garry Templeton	.08	.03	.01
☐ 178	Mike Devereaux	.05	.02	.00
☐ 179	Mookie Wilson	.05	.02	.00
☐ 180	Jeff Blauser	.05	.02	.00
☐ 181	Scott Bradley	.05	.02	.00
☐ 182	Luis Salazar	.05	.02	.00
☐ 183	Rafael Ramirez	.05	.02	.00
☐ 184	Vince Coleman	.15	.06	.01
☐ 185	Doug Drabek	.12	.05	.01
☐ 186	Darryl Strawberry	.40	.16	.04
☐ 187	Tim Burke	.05	.02	.00
☐ 188	Jesse Barfield	.10	.04	.01
☐ 189	Barry Larkin	.15	.06	.01
☐ 190	Alan Trammell	.20	.08	.02
☐ 191	Steve Lake	.05	.02	.00
☐ 192	Derek Lilliquist	.05	.02	.00
☐ 193	Don Robinson	.05	.02	.00
☐ 194	Kevin McReynolds	.12	.05	.01
☐ 195	Melido Perez	.08	.03	.01
☐ 196	Jose Lind	.05	.02	.00
☐ 197	Eric Anthony	.15	.06	.01
☐ 198	B.J. Surhoff	.08	.03	.01
☐ 199	John Olerud	.45	.18	.04
☐ 200	Mike Moore	.08	.03	.01
☐ 201	Mark Gubicza	.08	.03	.01
☐ 202	Phil Bradley	.05	.02	.00
☐ 203	Ozzie Smith	.20	.08	.02
☐ 204	Greg Maddux	.08	.03	.01
☐ 205	Julio Franco	.15	.06	.01
☐ 206	Tom Herr	.05	.02	.00
☐ 207	Scott Fletcher	.05	.02	.00
☐ 208	Bobby Bonilla	.30	.12	.03
☐ 209	Bob Geren	.05	.02	.00
☐ 210	Junior Felix	.12	.05	.01
☐ 211	Dick Schofield	.05	.02	.00
☐ 212	Jim Deshaies	.05	.02	.00
☐ 213	Jose Uribe	.05	.02	.00
☐ 214	John Kruk	.05	.02	.00
☐ 215	Ozzie Guillen	.08	.03	.01
☐ 216	Howard Johnson	.15	.06	.01
☐ 217	Andy Van Slyke	.10	.04	.01
☐ 218	Tim Laudner	.05	.02	.00
☐ 219	Manny Lee	.05	.02	.00
☐ 220	Checklist 111-220	.05	.02	.00
☐ 221	Cory Snyder	.10	.04	.01
☐ 222	Billy Hatcher	.06	.02	.00
☐ 223	Bud Black	.06	.02	.00
☐ 224	Will Clark	.75	.30	.07
☐ 225	Kevin Tapani	.15	.06	.01
☐ 226	Mike Pagliarulo	.06	.02	.00
☐ 227	Dave Parker	.12	.05	.01
☐ 228	Ben McDonald	.50	.20	.05
☐ 229	Carlos Baerga	.35	.15	.03
☐ 230	Roger McDowell	.06	.02	.00
☐ 231	Delino DeShields	.35	.15	.03
☐ 232	Mark Langston	.10	.04	.01
☐ 233	Wally Backman	.06	.02	.00
☐ 234	Jim Eisenreich	.06	.02	.00
☐ 235	Mike Schooler	.06	.02	.00
☐ 236	Kevin Bass	.06	.02	.00
☐ 237	John Farrell	.06	.02	.00
☐ 238	Kal Daniels	.12	.05	.01
☐ 239	Tony Phillips	.06	.02	.00
☐ 240	Todd Stottlemyre	.10	.04	.01
☐ 241	Greg Olson	.10	.04	.01
☐ 242	Charlie Hough	.06	.02	.00
☐ 243	Mariano Duncan	.06	.02	.00
☐ 244	Bill Ripken	.06	.02	.00
☐ 245	Joe Carter	.20	.08	.02
☐ 246	Tim Belcher	.15	.06	.01
☐ 247	Roberto Kelly	.25	.10	.02
☐ 248	Candy Maldonado	.10	.04	.01
☐ 249	Mike Scott	.10	.04	.01
☐ 250	Ken Griffey Jr.	1.50	.60	.15
☐ 251	Nick Esasky	.06	.02	.00
☐ 252	Tom Gordon	.15	.06	.01
☐ 253	John Tudor	.10	.04	.01
☐ 254	Gary Gaetti	.10	.04	.01
☐ 255	Neal Heaton	.06	.02	.00
☐ 256	Jerry Browne	.06	.02	.00
☐ 257	Jose Rijo	.12	.05	.01
☐ 258	Mike Boddicker	.06	.02	.00
☐ 259	Brett Butler	.10	.04	.01
☐ 260	Andy Benes	.20	.08	.02
☐ 261	Kevin Brown	.10	.04	.01
☐ 262	Hubie Brooks	.10	.04	.01
☐ 263	Randy Milligan	.10	.04	.01
☐ 264	John Franco	.10	.04	.01
☐ 265	Sandy Alomar Jr.	.25	.10	.02

☐ 266	Dave Valle	.06	.02	.00
☐ 267	Jerome Walton	.20	.08	.02
☐ 268	Bob Boone	.10	.04	.01
☐ 269	Ken Howell	.06	.02	.00
☐ 270	Jose Canseco	.75	.30	.07
☐ 271	Joe Magrane	.06	.02	.00
☐ 272	Brian Dubois	.06	.02	.00
☐ 273	Carlos Quintana	.12	.05	.01
☐ 274	Lance Johnson	.06	.02	.00
☐ 275	Steve Bedrosian	.06	.02	.00
☐ 276	Brook Jacoby	.06	.02	.00
☐ 277	Fred Lynn UER (Pirates logo on card front)	.10	.04	.01
☐ 278	Jeff Ballard	.06	.02	.00
☐ 279	Otis Nixon	.10	.04	.01
☐ 280	Chili Davis	.10	.04	.01
☐ 281	Joe Oliver	.10	.04	.01
☐ 282	Brian Holman	.10	.04	.01
☐ 283	Juan Samuel	.10	.04	.01
☐ 284	Rick Aguilera	.10	.04	.01
☐ 285	Jeff Reardon	.12	.05	.01
☐ 286	Sammy Sosa	.20	.08	.02
☐ 287	Carmelo Martinez	.10	.04	.01
☐ 288	Greg Swindell	.10	.04	.01
☐ 289	Erik Hanson	.15	.06	.01
☐ 290	Tony Pena	.10	.04	.01
☐ 291	Pascual Perez	.10	.04	.01
☐ 292	Rickey Henderson	.75	.30	.07
☐ 293	Kurt Stillwell	.10	.04	.01
☐ 294	Todd Zeile	.35	.15	.03
☐ 295	Bobby Thigpen	.15	.06	.01
☐ 296	Larry Walker	.20	.08	.02
☐ 297	Rob Murphy	.06	.02	.00
☐ 298	Mitch Webster	.06	.02	.00
☐ 299	Devon White	.10	.04	.01
☐ 300	Len Dykstra	.12	.05	.01
☐ 301	Keith Hernandez	.15	.06	.01
☐ 302	Gene Larkin	.10	.04	.01
☐ 303	Jeffrey Leonard	.06	.02	.00
☐ 304	Jim Presley	.06	.02	.00
☐ 305	Lloyd Moseby	.06	.02	.00
☐ 306	John Smoltz	.15	.06	.01
☐ 307	Sam Horn	.10	.04	.01
☐ 308	Greg Litton	.10	.04	.01
☐ 309	Dave Henderson	.12	.05	.01
☐ 310	Mark McLemore	.06	.02	.00
☐ 311	Gary Pettis	.06	.02	.00
☐ 312	Mark Davis	.06	.02	.00
☐ 313	Cecil Fielder	.60	.25	.06
☐ 314	Jack Armstrong	.12	.05	.01
☐ 315	Alvin Davis	.10	.04	.01
☐ 316	Doug Jones	.06	.02	.00
☐ 317	Eric Yelding	.06	.02	.00
☐ 318	Joe Orsulak	.06	.02	.00
☐ 319	Chuck Finley	.12	.05	.01
☐ 320	Glenn Wilson	.06	.02	.00
☐ 321	Harold Reynolds	.06	.02	.00
☐ 322	Teddy Higuera	.10	.04	.01
☐ 323	Lance Parrish	.10	.04	.01
☐ 324	Bruce Hurst	.10	.04	.01
☐ 325	Dave West	.10	.04	.01
☐ 326	Kirk Gibson	.15	.06	.01
☐ 327	Cal Ripken	.75	.30	.07
☐ 328	Rick Reuschel	.10	.04	.01
☐ 329	Jim Abbott	.50	.20	.05
☐ 330	Checklist 221-330	.06	.02	.00

1990 Topps Ames All-Stars

The 1990 Topps Ames All-Stars set was issued by Topps for the Ames department stores for the second straight year. This standard-size (2 1/2" by 3 1/2") set featured 33 of the leading hitters active in major league baseball. This set includes an early card of Keith Hernandez as a Cleveland Indian.

	MINT	EXC	G-VG
COMPLETE SET (33)	4.00	1.75	.40
COMMON PLAYER (1-33)	.10	.04	.01

☐ 1	Dave Winfield	.25	.10	.02
☐ 2	George Brett	.35	.15	.03
☐ 3	Jim Rice	.15	.06	.01
☐ 4	Dwight Evans	.15	.06	.01
☐ 5	Robin Yount	.35	.15	.03
☐ 6	Dave Parker	.20	.08	.02
☐ 7	Eddie Murray	.35	.15	.03

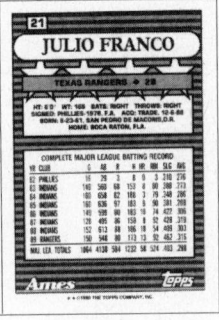

		MINT	EXC	G-VG
☐ 8	Keith Hernandez	.15	.06	.01
☐ 9	Andre Dawson	.25	.10	.02
☐ 10	Fred Lynn	.15	.06	.01
☐ 11	Dale Murphy	.30	.12	.03
☐ 12	Jack Clark	.15	.06	.01
☐ 13	Rickey Henderson	.60	.25	.06
☐ 14	Paul Molitor	.15	.06	.01
☐ 15	Cal Ripken	.60	.25	.06
☐ 16	Wade Boggs	.45	.18	.04
☐ 17	Tim Raines	.20	.08	.02
☐ 18	Don Mattingly	.50	.20	.05
☐ 19	Kent Hrbek	.15	.06	.01
☐ 20	Kirk Gibson	.15	.06	.01
☐ 21	Julio Franco	.15	.06	.01
☐ 22	George Bell	.15	.06	.01
☐ 23	Darryl Strawberry	.40	.16	.04
☐ 24	Kirby Puckett	.35	.15	.03
☐ 25	Juan Samuel	.10	.04	.01
☐ 26	Alvin Davis	.10	.04	.01
☐ 27	Joe Carter	.20	.08	.02
☐ 28	Eric Davis	.25	.10	.02
☐ 29	Jose Canseco	.60	.25	.06
☐ 30	Wally Joyner	.25	.10	.02
☐ 31	Will Clark	.60	.25	.06
☐ 32	Ruben Sierra	.40	.16	.04
☐ 33	Danny Tartabull	.25	.10	.02

1990 Topps Hills Hit Men

The 1990 Topps Hit Men set is a standard-size (2 1/2" by 3 1/2") 33-card set arranged in order of slugging percentage. The set was produced by Topps for Hills Department stores. Each card in the set has a glossy-coated front.

	MINT	EXC	G-VG
COMPLETE SET (33)	4.00	1.75	.40
COMMON PLAYER (1-33)	.10	.04	.01

		MINT	EXC	G-VG
☐ 1	Eric Davis	.25	.10	.02
☐ 2	Will Clark	.60	.25	.06
☐ 3	Don Mattingly	.50	.20	.05
☐ 4	Darryl Strawberry	.45	.18	.04
☐ 5	Kevin Mitchell	.30	.12	.03
☐ 6	Pedro Guerrero	.15	.06	.01

☐ 7	Jose Canseco	.60	.25	.06
☐ 8	Jim Rice	.15	.06	.01
☐ 9	Danny Tartabull	.25	.10	.02
☐ 10	George Brett	.35	.15	.03
☐ 11	Kent Hrbek	.15	.06	.01
☐ 12	George Bell	.20	.08	.02
☐ 13	Eddie Murray	.35	.15	.03
☐ 14	Fred Lynn	.15	.06	.01
☐ 15	Andre Dawson	.25	.10	.02
☐ 16	Dale Murphy	.30	.12	.03
☐ 17	Dave Winfield	.25	.10	.02
☐ 18	Jack Clark	.15	.06	.01
☐ 19	Wade Boggs	.40	.16	.04
☐ 20	Ruben Sierra	.35	.15	.03
☐ 21	Dave Parker	.20	.08	.02
☐ 22	Glenn Davis	.20	.08	.02
☐ 23	Dwight Evans	.15	.06	.01
☐ 24	Jesse Barfield	.15	.06	.01
☐ 25	Kirk Gibson	.15	.06	.01
☐ 26	Alvin Davis	.10	.04	.01
☐ 27	Kirby Puckett	.35	.15	.03
☐ 28	Joe Carter	.15	.06	.01
☐ 29	Carlton Fisk	.30	.12	.03
☐ 30	Harold Baines	.10	.04	.01
☐ 31	Andres Galarraga	.15	.06	.01
☐ 32	Cal Ripken	.60	.25	.06
☐ 33	Howard Johnson	.20	.08	.02

1990 Topps Traded

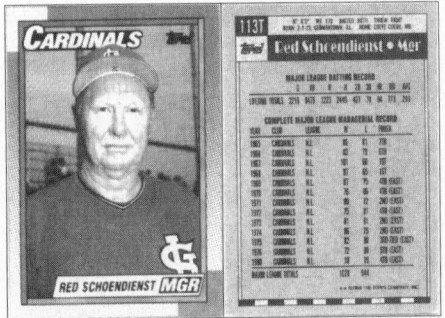

The 1990 Topps Traded Set was the tenth consecutive year Topps issued a set at the end of the year. This 132-card standard size set of 2 1/2" by 3 1/2" was arranged alphabetically by player and includes a mix of traded players and rookies for whom Topps did not include a card in the regular set. The key rookie cards in this set are Scott Erickson, Travis Fryman, Dave Justice, Kevin Maas, and John Olerud. Also for the first time, Topps not only issued the set in a special collector boxes (made in Ireland) but distributed (on a significant basis) the set via their own wax packs. The wax pack cards were produced by Topps' Duryea, Pennsylvania plant. There were seven cards in the packs and the wrapper highlighted the set as containing promising rookies, players who changed teams, and new managers. The cards differ in that the Irish-made cards have the whiter-type backs typical of the cards made in Ireland while the American cards have the typical Topps gray-type card stock on the back. Topps also produced a specially boxed "glossy" edition frequently referred to as the Topps Traded Tiffany set. This year, again, Topps did not disclose the number of Tiffany sets they produced or sold but it seems that production quantities were roughly similar (approximately 15,000 sets) to the previous year. The checklist of cards is identical to that of the normal non-glossy cards. There are two primary distinguishing features of the Tiffany cards, white card stock reverses and high gloss obverses. These Tiffany cards are valued at approximately four times the values listed below.

	MINT	EXC	G-VG
COMPLETE SET (132)	10.00	4.50	1.25
COMMON PLAYER (1T-132T)	.05	.02	.00
☐ 1T Darrel Akerfelds	.05	.02	.00
☐ 2T Sandy Alomar Jr.	.12	.05	.01
☐ 3T Brad Arnsberg	.10	.04	.01
☐ 4T Steve Avery	.90	.40	.09
☐ 5T Wally Backman	.05	.02	.00
☐ 6T Carlos Baerga	.40	.16	.04
☐ 7T Kevin Bass	.08	.03	.01
☐ 8T Willie Blair	.08	.03	.01
☐ 9T Mike Blowers	.10	.04	.01
☐ 10T Shawn Boskie	.12	.05	.01
☐ 11T Daryl Boston	.05	.02	.00
☐ 12T Dennis Boyd	.05	.02	.00
☐ 13T Glenn Braggs	.05	.02	.00
☐ 14T Hubie Brooks	.08	.03	.01
☐ 15T Tom Brunansky	.08	.03	.01
☐ 16T John Burkett	.15	.06	.01
☐ 17T Casey Candaele	.05	.02	.00
☐ 18T John Candelaria	.05	.02	.00
☐ 19T Gary Carter	.10	.04	.01
☐ 20T Joe Carter	.12	.05	.01
☐ 21T Rick Cerone	.05	.02	.00
☐ 22T Scott Coolbaugh	.12	.05	.01
☐ 23T Bobby Cox MG	.05	.02	.00
☐ 24T Mark Davis	.10	.04	.01
☐ 25T Storm Davis	.05	.02	.00
☐ 26T Edgar Diaz	.10	.04	.01
☐ 27T Wayne Edwards	.10	.04	.01
☐ 28T Mark Eichhorn	.08	.03	.01
☐ 29T Scott Erickson	3.00	1.25	.30
☐ 30T Nick Esasky	.05	.02	.00
☐ 31T Cecil Fielder	.35	.15	.03
☐ 32T John Franco	.08	.03	.01
☐ 33T Travis Fryman	1.25	.50	.12
☐ 34T Bill Gullickson	.08	.03	.01
☐ 35T Darryl Hamilton	.10	.04	.01
☐ 36T Mike Harkey	.12	.05	.01
☐ 37T Bud Harrelson MG	.08	.03	.01
☐ 38T Billy Hatcher	.08	.03	.01
☐ 39T Keith Hernandez	.10	.04	.01
☐ 40T Joe Hesketh	.08	.03	.01
☐ 41T Dave Hollins	.35	.15	.03
☐ 42T Sam Horn	.10	.04	.01
☐ 43T Steve Howard	.15	.06	.01
☐ 44T Todd Hundley	.35	.15	.03
☐ 45T Jeff Huson	.10	.04	.01
☐ 46T Chris James	.08	.03	.01
☐ 47T Stan Javier	.05	.02	.00
☐ 48T Dave Justice	2.50	1.00	.25
☐ 49T Jeff Kaiser	.08	.03	.01
☐ 50T Dana Kiecker	.10	.04	.01
☐ 51T Joe Klink	.12	.05	.01
☐ 52T Brent Knackert	.12	.05	.01
☐ 53T Brad Komminsk	.05	.02	.00
☐ 54T Mark Langston	.10	.04	.01
☐ 55T Tim Layana	.10	.04	.01
☐ 56T Rick Leach	.05	.02	.00
☐ 57T Terry Leach	.05	.02	.00
☐ 58T Tim Leary	.10	.04	.01
☐ 59T Craig Lefferts	.05	.02	.00
☐ 60T Charlie Leibrandt	.05	.02	.00
☐ 61T Jim Leyritz	.10	.04	.01
☐ 62T Fred Lynn	.10	.04	.01
☐ 63T Kevin Maas	1.25	.50	.12
☐ 64T Shane Mack	.12	.05	.01
☐ 65T Candy Maldonado	.08	.03	.01
☐ 66T Fred Manrique	.05	.02	.00
☐ 67T Mike Marshall	.08	.03	.01
☐ 68T Carmelo Martinez	.05	.02	.00
☐ 69T John Marzano	.08	.03	.01
☐ 70T Ben McDonald	.75	.30	.07
☐ 71T Jack McDowell	.15	.06	.01
☐ 72T John McNamara MG	.05	.02	.00
☐ 73T Orlando Mercado	.05	.02	.00
☐ 74T Stump Merrill MG	.08	.03	.01
☐ 75T Alan Mills	.10	.04	.01
☐ 76T Hal Morris	.35	.15	.03
☐ 77T Lloyd Moseby	.05	.02	.00
☐ 78T Randy Myers	.08	.03	.01
☐ 79T Tim Naehring	.25	.10	.02
☐ 80T Junior Noboa	.08	.03	.01
☐ 81T Matt Nokes	.10	.04	.01
☐ 82T Pete O'Brien	.05	.02	.00
☐ 83T John Olerud	1.00	.40	.10
☐ 84T Greg Olson	.20	.08	.02
☐ 85T Junior Ortiz	.05	.02	.00
☐ 86T Dave Parker	.10	.04	.01
☐ 87T Rick Parker	.10	.04	.01
☐ 88T Bob Patterson	.05	.02	.00
☐ 89T Alejandro Pena	.08	.03	.01
☐ 90T Tony Pena	.08	.03	.01
☐ 91T Pascual Perez	.08	.03	.01
☐ 92T Gerald Perry	.05	.02	.00
☐ 93T Dan Petry	.05	.02	.00
☐ 94T Gary Pettis	.05	.02	.00
☐ 95T Tony Phillips	.05	.02	.00
☐ 96T Lou Piniella MG	.10	.04	.01
☐ 97T Luis Polonia	.08	.03	.01
☐ 98T Jim Presley	.05	.02	.00
☐ 99T Scott Radinsky	.12	.05	.01
☐ 100T Willie Randolph	.08	.03	.01
☐ 101T Jeff Reardon	.10	.04	.01
☐ 102T Greg Riddoch MG	.10	.04	.01
☐ 103T Jeff Robinson	.05	.02	.00
☐ 104T Ron Robinson	.05	.02	.00
☐ 105T Kevin Romine	.05	.02	.00
☐ 106T Scott Ruskin	.12	.05	.01
☐ 107T John Russell	.05	.02	.00
☐ 108T Bill Sampen	.12	.05	.01
☐ 109T Juan Samuel	.08	.03	.01
☐ 110T Scott Sanderson	.08	.03	.01
☐ 111T Jack Savage	.08	.03	.01
☐ 112T Dave Schmidt	.05	.02	.00
☐ 113T Red Schoendienst MG	.10	.04	.01
☐ 114T Terry Shumpert	.12	.05	.01
☐ 115T Matt Sinatro	.05	.02	.00
☐ 116T Don Slaught	.05	.02	.00
☐ 117T Bryn Smith	.05	.02	.00
☐ 118T Lee Smith	.10	.04	.01
☐ 119T Paul Sorrento	.12	.05	.01
☐ 120T Franklin Stubbs UER	.08	.03	.01
('84 says '99 and has the same stats as '89, '83 stats are missing)			
☐ 121T Russ Swan	.12	.05	.01
☐ 122T Bob Tewksbury	.05	.02	.00
☐ 123T Wayne Tolleson	.05	.02	.00
☐ 124T John Tudor	.08	.03	.01
☐ 125T Randy Veres	.08	.03	.01
☐ 126T Hector Villanueva	.12	.05	.01
☐ 127T Mitch Webster	.05	.02	.00
☐ 128T Ernie Whitt	.05	.02	.00
☐ 129T Frank Wills	.05	.02	.00
☐ 130T Dave Winfield	.12	.05	.01
☐ 131T Matt Young	.05	.02	.00
☐ 132T Checklist Card	.05	.01	.00

1990 Topps TV All-Stars

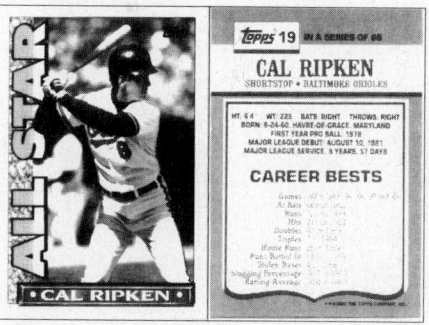

This All-Star team set contains 66 cards measuring the standard size (2 1/2" by 3 1/2"). The fronts feature posed or action color player photos with a high gloss. In block lettering, the words "All-Star" are printed vertically in blue on the left side of the card. The player's name appears in a red plaque below the picture, and white borders round out the card face. The backs are printed in black lettering and have a red and white background. Inside a decal design, biographical information and career bests are superimposed on a blue, pink, and white background. The cards are numbered on the back. These cards were offered only on television as a complete set for sale through an 800 number.

	MINT	EXC	G-VG
COMPLETE SET (66)	60.00	27.00	9.00
COMMON PLAYER (1-66)	.60	.25	.06

☐ 1	Mark McGwire	1.50	.60	.15
☐ 2	Julio Franco	.90	.40	.09
☐ 3	Ozzie Guillen	.75	.30	.07
☐ 4	Carney Lansford	.75	.30	.07
☐ 5	Bo Jackson	3.00	1.25	.30
☐ 6	Kirby Puckett	1.75	.70	.17
☐ 7	Ruben Sierra	1.50	.60	.15
☐ 8	Carlton Fisk	1.00	.40	.10
☐ 9	Nolan Ryan	3.50	1.50	.35
☐ 10	Rickey Henderson	3.00	1.25	.30
☐ 11	Jose Canseco	3.00	1.25	.30
☐ 12	Mark Davis	.60	.25	.06
☐ 13	Dennis Eckersley	.75	.30	.07
☐ 14	Chuck Finley	.60	.25	.06
☐ 15	Bret Saberhagen	.90	.40	.09
☐ 16	Dave Stewart	.75	.30	.07
☐ 17	Don Mattingly	1.75	.70	.17
☐ 18	Steve Sax	.75	.30	.07
☐ 19	Cal Ripken	3.00	1.25	.30
☐ 20	Wade Boggs	1.75	.70	.17
☐ 21	George Bell	.90	.40	.09
☐ 22	Mike Greenwell	1.25	.50	.12
☐ 23	Robin Yount	1.50	.60	.15
☐ 24	Mickey Tettleton	.60	.25	.06
☐ 25	Roger Clemens	2.50	1.00	.25
☐ 26	Fred McGriff	1.00	.40	.10
☐ 27	Jeff Ballard	.60	.25	.06
☐ 28	Dwight Evans	.75	.30	.07
☐ 29	Paul Molitor	.90	.40	.09
☐ 30	Gregg Olson	.90	.40	.09
☐ 31	Dan Plesac	.60	.25	.06
☐ 32	Greg Swindell	.75	.30	.07
☐ 33	Tony LaRussa MG and Cito Gaston MG	.60	.25	.06
☐ 34	Will Clark	3.00	1.25	.30
☐ 35	Roberto Alomar	1.25	.50	.12
☐ 36	Barry Larkin	1.00	.40	.10
☐ 37	Ken Caminiti	.60	.25	.06
☐ 38	Eric Davis	1.00	.40	.10
☐ 39	Tony Gwynn	1.75	.70	.17
☐ 40	Kevin Mitchell	1.25	.50	.12
☐ 41	Craig Biggio	.90	.40	.09
☐ 42	Mike Scott	.75	.30	.07
☐ 43	Joe Carter	1.00	.40	.10
☐ 44	Jack Clark	.90	.40	.09
☐ 45	Glenn Davis	.90	.40	.09
☐ 46	Orel Hershiser	.90	.40	.09
☐ 47	Jay Howell	.60	.25	.06
☐ 48	Bruce Hurst	.75	.30	.07
☐ 49	Dave Smith	.60	.25	.06
☐ 50	Pedro Guerrero	.75	.30	.07
☐ 51	Ryne Sandberg	3.00	1.25	.30
☐ 52	Ozzie Smith	1.25	.50	.12
☐ 53	Howard Johnson	1.00	.40	.10
☐ 54	Von Hayes	.75	.30	.07
☐ 55	Tim Raines	.90	.40	.09
☐ 56	Darryl Strawberry	1.75	.70	.17
☐ 57	Mike LaValliere	.60	.25	.06
☐ 58	Dwight Gooden	1.00	.40	.10
☐ 59	Bobby Bonilla	1.00	.40	.10
☐ 60	Tim Burke	.60	.25	.06
☐ 61	Sid Fernandez	.75	.30	.07
☐ 62	Andres Galarraga	.75	.30	.07
☐ 63	Mark Grace	1.00	.40	.10
☐ 64	Joe Magrane	.60	.25	.06
☐ 65	Mitch Williams	.75	.30	.07
☐ 66	Roger Craig MG and Don Zimmer MG	.60	.25	.06

 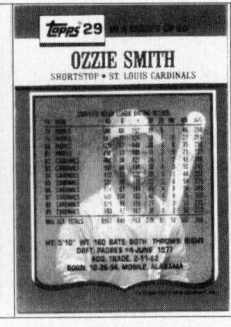

1990 Topps TV Cardinals

This Cardinals team set contains 66 cards measuring the standard size (2 1/2" by 3 1/2"). The fronts feature posed or action color player photos with a high gloss. In block lettering, the team name is printed vertically in red and pink on the left side of the card. The player's name appears in a blue plaque below the picture, and white borders round out the card face. The backs are printed in black lettering and have a red and white background. Inside a decal design, player information and statistics are superimposed on an indistinct version of the same picture as on the front. The cards are numbered on the back.

	MINT	EXC	G-VG
COMPLETE SET (66)	50.00	22.50	7.50
COMMON PLAYER (1-66)	.60	.25	.06

☐ 1	Whitey Herzog MG	.90	.40	.09
☐ 2	Steve Braun CO	.60	.25	.06
☐ 3	Rich Hacker CO	.60	.25	.06
☐ 4	Dave Ricketts CO	.60	.25	.06
☐ 5	Jim Riggleman CO	.60	.25	.06
☐ 6	Mike Roarke CO	.60	.25	.06
☐ 7	Cris Carpenter	.60	.25	.06
☐ 8	John Costello	.60	.25	.06
☐ 9	Danny Cox	.75	.30	.07
☐ 10	Ken Dayley	.60	.25	.06
☐ 11	Jose DeLeon	.75	.30	.07
☐ 12	Frank DiPino	.60	.25	.06
☐ 13	Ken Hill	.75	.30	.07
☐ 14	Howard Hilton	.60	.25	.06
☐ 15	Ricky Horton	.60	.25	.06
☐ 16	Joe Magrane	.75	.30	.07
☐ 17	Greg Mathews	.60	.25	.06
☐ 18	Bryn Smith	.75	.30	.07
☐ 19	Scott Terry	.60	.25	.06
☐ 20	Bob Tewksbury	.75	.30	.07
☐ 21	John Tudor	.90	.40	.09
☐ 22	Todd Worrell	.75	.30	.07
☐ 23	Tom Pagnozzi	.60	.25	.06
☐ 24	Todd Zeile	2.00	.80	.20
☐ 25	Pedro Guerrero	1.50	.60	.15
☐ 26	Tim Jones	.60	.25	.06
☐ 27	Jose Oquendo	.75	.30	.07
☐ 28	Terry Pendleton	2.00	.80	.20
☐ 29	Ozzie Smith	2.00	.80	.20
☐ 30	Denny Walling	.60	.25	.06
☐ 31	Tom Brunansky	1.00	.40	.10
☐ 32	Vince Coleman	2.00	.80	.20
☐ 33	Dave Collins	.60	.25	.06
☐ 34	Willie McGee	1.50	.60	.15
☐ 35	John Morris	.60	.25	.06
☐ 36	Milt Thompson	.75	.30	.07
☐ 37	Gibson Alba	.60	.25	.06
☐ 38	Scott Arnold	.60	.25	.06
☐ 39	Rod Brewer	.75	.30	.07
☐ 40	Greg Carmona	.75	.30	.07
☐ 41	Mark Clark	.60	.25	.06
☐ 42	Stan Clarke	.60	.25	.06
☐ 43	Paul Coleman	1.00	.40	.10
☐ 44	Todd Crosby	.60	.25	.06
☐ 45	Brad DuVall	.90	.40	.09
☐ 46	John Ericks	.90	.40	.09
☐ 47	Bien Figueroa	.60	.25	.06
☐ 48	Terry Francona	.60	.25	.06
☐ 49	Ed Fulton	.60	.25	.06
☐ 50	Bernard Gilkey	1.50	.60	.15
☐ 51	Ernie Camacho	.60	.25	.06
☐ 52	Mike Hinkle	.60	.25	.06
☐ 53	Ray Lankford	2.50	1.00	.25
☐ 54	Julian Martinez	.75	.30	.07
☐ 55	Jesus Mendez	.75	.30	.07
☐ 56	Mike Milchin	.75	.30	.07
☐ 57	Mauricio Nunez	.75	.30	.07
☐ 58	Omar Olivares	.75	.30	.07
☐ 59	Geronimo Pena	.60	.25	.06
☐ 60	Mike Perez	.75	.30	.07
☐ 61	Gaylen Pitts MG	.60	.25	.06
☐ 62	Mark Riggins CO	.60	.25	.06
☐ 63	Tim Sherrill	.60	.25	.06
☐ 64	Roy Silver	.60	.25	.06
☐ 65	Ray Stephens	.75	.30	.07
☐ 66	Craig Wilson	1.00	.40	.10

1990 Topps TV Cubs

 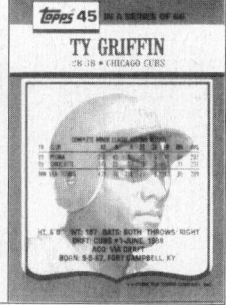

This Cubs team set contains 66 cards measuring the standard size (2 1/2" by 3 1/2"). The fronts feature posed or action color player photos with a high gloss. In block lettering, the team name is printed vertically in blue on the left side of the card. The player's name appears in a gold plaque below the picture, and white borders round out the card face. The backs are printed in black and have a red and white background. Inside a decal design, player information and statistics are superimposed on an indistinct version of the same picture as on the front. The cards are numbered on the back.

	MINT	EXC	G-VG
COMPLETE SET (66)	50.00	22.50	7.50
COMMON PLAYER (1-66)	.60	.25	.06

		MINT	EXC	G-VG
☐ 1	Don Zimmer MG	.75	.30	.07
☐ 2	Joe Altobelli CO	.60	.25	.06
☐ 3	Chuck Cottier CO	.60	.25	.06
☐ 4	Jose Martinez CO	.60	.25	.06
☐ 5	Dick Pole CO	.60	.25	.06
☐ 6	Phil Roof CO	.60	.25	.06
☐ 7	Paul Assenmacher	.60	.25	.06
☐ 8	Mike Bielecki	.75	.30	.07
☐ 9	Mike Harkey	.90	.40	.09
☐ 10	Joe Kraemer	.60	.25	.06
☐ 11	Les Lancaster	.60	.25	.06
☐ 12	Greg Maddux	1.25	.50	.12
☐ 13	Jose Nunez	.60	.25	.06
☐ 14	Jeff Pico	.60	.25	.06
☐ 15	Rick Sutcliffe	.90	.40	.09
☐ 16	Dean Wilkins	.90	.40	.09
☐ 17	Mitch Williams	.90	.40	.09
☐ 18	Steve Wilson	.75	.30	.07
☐ 19	Damon Berryhill	.75	.30	.07
☐ 20	Joe Girardi	.75	.30	.07
☐ 21	Rick Wrona	.75	.30	.07
☐ 22	Shawon Dunston	1.25	.50	.12
☐ 23	Mark Grace	1.75	.70	.17
☐ 24	Domingo Ramos	.60	.25	.06
☐ 25	Luis Salazar	.60	.25	.06
☐ 26	Ryne Sandberg	6.00	2.50	.60
☐ 27	Greg Smith	.60	.25	.06
☐ 28	Curtis Wilkerson	.60	.25	.06
☐ 29	Dave Clark	.60	.25	.06
☐ 30	Doug Dascenzo	.75	.30	.07
☐ 31	Andre Dawson	2.50	1.00	.25
☐ 32	Lloyd McClendon	.60	.25	.06
☐ 33	Dwight Smith	.90	.40	.09
☐ 34	Jerome Walton	1.25	.50	.12
☐ 35	Marvell Wynne	.60	.25	.06
☐ 36	Alex Arias	.60	.25	.06
☐ 37	Bob Bafia	.60	.25	.06
☐ 38	Brad Bierley	.60	.25	.06
☐ 39	Shawn Boskie	.75	.30	.07
☐ 40	Danny Clay	.60	.25	.06
☐ 41	Rusty Crockett	.60	.25	.06
☐ 42	Earl Cunningham	1.00	.40	.10
☐ 43	Len Damian	.60	.25	.06
☐ 44	Darrin Duffy	.60	.25	.06
☐ 45	Ty Griffin	.90	.40	.09
☐ 46	Brian Guinn	.60	.25	.06
☐ 47	Phil Hannon	.60	.25	.06
☐ 48	Phil Harrison	.60	.25	.06
☐ 49	Jeff Hearron	.60	.25	.06
☐ 50	Greg Kallevig	.60	.25	.06
☐ 51	Cedric Landrum	.75	.30	.07
☐ 52	Bill Long	.60	.25	.06
☐ 53	Derrick May	.90	.40	.09
☐ 54	Ray Mullino	.60	.25	.06
☐ 55	Erik Pappas	.75	.30	.07
☐ 56	Steve Parker	.60	.25	.06
☐ 57	Dave Pavlas	.75	.30	.07
☐ 58	Laddie Renfroe	.60	.25	.06
☐ 59	Jeff Small	.60	.25	.06
☐ 60	Doug Strange	.75	.30	.07
☐ 61	Gary Varsho	.75	.30	.07
☐ 62	Hector Villanueva	.90	.40	.09
☐ 63	Rick Wilkins	.90	.40	.09
☐ 64	Dana Williams	.75	.30	.07
☐ 65	Bill Wrona	.75	.30	.07
☐ 66	Fernando Zarranz	.60	.25	.06

1990 Topps TV Mets

 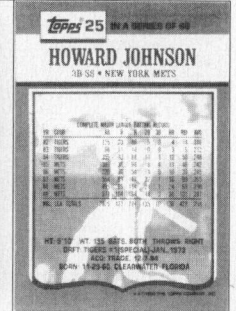

This Mets team set contains 66 cards measuring the standard size (2 1/2" by 3 1/2"). The fronts feature posed or action color player photos with a high gloss. In block lettering, the words "All Star" are printed vertically in orange and yellow on the left side of the card. The player's name appears in a red plaque below the picture, and white borders round out the card face. The backs are printed in black lettering and have a red and white background. Inside a decal design, player information and statistics are superimposed on an indistinct version of the same picture as on the front. The cards are numbered on the back.

	MINT	EXC	G-VG
COMPLETE SET (66)	50.00	22.50	7.50
COMMON PLAYER (1-66)	.60	.25	.06

		MINT	EXC	G-VG
☐ 1	Dave Johnson MG	.75	.30	.07
☐ 2	Mike Cubbage CO	.60	.25	.06
☐ 3	Doc Edwards CO	.60	.25	.06
☐ 4	Bud Harrelson CO	.75	.30	.07
☐ 5	Greg Pavlick CO	.60	.25	.06
☐ 6	Mel Stottlemyre CO	.75	.30	.07
☐ 7	Blaine Beatty	.75	.30	.07
☐ 8	David Cone	1.25	.50	.12
☐ 9	Ron Darling	.90	.40	.09
☐ 10	Sid Fernandez	.90	.40	.09
☐ 11	John Franco	1.00	.40	.10
☐ 12	Dwight Gooden	2.50	1.00	.25
☐ 13	Jeff Innis	.75	.30	.07
☐ 14	Julio Machado	.75	.30	.07
☐ 15	Jeff Musselman	.60	.25	.06
☐ 16	Bob Ojeda	.75	.30	.07
☐ 17	Alejandro Pena	1.00	.40	.10
☐ 18	Frank Viola	1.25	.50	.12
☐ 19	Wally Whitehurst	.75	.30	.07
☐ 20	Barry Lyons	.60	.25	.06
☐ 21	Orlando Mercado	.60	.25	.06
☐ 22	Mackey Sasser	.75	.30	.07
☐ 23	Kevin Elster	.75	.30	.07
☐ 24	Gregg Jefferies	2.50	1.00	.25
☐ 25	Howard Johnson	2.00	.80	.20
☐ 26	Dave Magadan	1.25	.50	.12
☐ 27	Mike Marshall	.75	.30	.07
☐ 28	Tom O'Malley	.60	.25	.06
☐ 29	Tim Teufel	.75	.30	.07
☐ 30	Mark Carreon	.60	.25	.06

			MINT	EXC	G-VG
☐	31	Kevin McReynolds	1.25	.50	.12
☐	32	Keith Miller	.75	.30	.07
☐	33	Darryl Strawberry	4.00	1.75	.40
☐	34	Lou Thornton	.60	.25	.06
☐	35	Shawn Barton	.60	.25	.06
☐	36	Tim Bogar	.60	.25	.06
☐	37	Terry Bross	.75	.30	.07
☐	38	Kevin Brown	.75	.30	.07
☐	39	Mike DeButch	.60	.25	.06
☐	40	Alex Diaz	.60	.25	.06
☐	41	Chris Donnels	1.00	.40	.10
☐	42	Jeff Gardner	.75	.30	.07
☐	43	Denny Gonzalez	.60	.25	.06
☐	44	Kenny Graves	.60	.25	.06
☐	45	Manny Hernandez	.60	.25	.06
☐	46	Keith Hughes	.75	.30	.07
☐	47	Todd Hundley	1.00	.40	.10
☐	48	Chris Jelic	.75	.30	.07
☐	49	Dave Liddell	.60	.25	.06
☐	50	Terry McDaniel	.75	.30	.07
☐	51	Cesar Mejia	.60	.25	.06
☐	52	Scott Nielsen	.60	.25	.06
☐	53	Dale Plummer	.60	.25	.06
☐	54	Darren Reed	.75	.30	.07
☐	55	Gil Roca	.60	.25	.06
☐	56	Jaime Roseboro	.90	.40	.09
☐	57	Roger Samuels	.60	.25	.06
☐	58	Zoilo Sanchez	.60	.25	.06
☐	59	Pete Schourek	.75	.30	.07
☐	60	Craig Shipley	.75	.30	.07
☐	61	Ray Soff	.60	.25	.06
☐	62	Steve Swisher MG	.60	.25	.06
☐	63	Kelvin Torve	.60	.25	.06
☐	64	Dave Trautwein	.60	.25	.06
☐	65	Julio Valera	.75	.30	.07
☐	66	Alan Zinter	.75	.30	.07

1990 Topps TV Red Sox

This Red Sox team set contains 66 cards measuring the standard size (2 1/2" by 3 1/2"). The fronts feature posed or action color player photos with a high gloss. In block lettering, the team name is printed vertically in red and yellow on the left side of the card. The player's name appears in a blue plaque below the picture, and white borders round out the card face. The backs are printed in black and have a red and white background. Inside a decal design, player information and statistics are superimposed over an indistinct version of the same picture as on the front. The cards are numbered on the back.

			MINT	EXC	G-VG
	COMPLETE SET (66)		50.00	22.50	7.50
	COMMON PLAYER (1-66)		.60	.25	.06
☐	1	Joe Morgan MG	.75	.30	.07
☐	2	Dick Berardino CO	.60	.25	.06
☐	3	Al Bumbry CO	.60	.25	.06
☐	4	Bill Fischer CO	.60	.25	.06
☐	5	Richie Hebner CO	.60	.25	.06
☐	6	Rac Slider CO	.60	.25	.06
☐	7	Mike Boddicker	.75	.30	.07
☐	8	Roger Clemens	5.00	2.25	.50
☐	9	John Dopson	.60	.25	.06

☐	10	Wes Gardner	.60	.25	.06
☐	11	Greg A. Harris	.75	.30	.07
☐	12	Dana Kiecker	.60	.25	.06
☐	13	Dennis Lamp	.60	.25	.06
☐	14	Rob Murphy	.60	.25	.06
☐	15	Jeff Reardon	1.25	.50	.12
☐	16	Mike Rochford	.60	.25	.06
☐	17	Lee Smith	1.00	.40	.10
☐	18	Rich Gedman	.60	.25	.06
☐	19	John Marzano	.60	.25	.06
☐	20	Tony Pena	.75	.30	.07
☐	21	Marty Barrett	.60	.25	.06
☐	22	Wade Boggs	3.50	1.50	.35
☐	23	Bill Buckner	.75	.30	.07
☐	24	Danny Heep	.60	.25	.06
☐	25	Jody Reed	.75	.30	.07
☐	26	Luis Rivera	.60	.25	.06
☐	27	Billy Jo Robidoux	.60	.25	.06
☐	28	Ellis Burks	1.50	.60	.15
☐	29	Dwight Evans	1.00	.40	.10
☐	30	Mike Greenwell	1.50	.60	.15
☐	31	Randy Kutcher	.60	.25	.06
☐	32	Carlos Quintana	1.00	.40	.10
☐	33	Kevin Romine	.60	.25	.06
☐	34	Ed Nottle MG	.60	.25	.06
☐	35	Mark Meleski CO	.60	.25	.06
☐	36	Steve Bast	.60	.25	.06
☐	37	Greg Blosser	1.00	.40	.10
☐	38	Tom Bolton	.75	.30	.07
☐	39	Scott Cooper	1.50	.60	.15
☐	40	Zach Crouch	.60	.25	.06
☐	41	Steve Curry	.75	.30	.07
☐	42	Mike Dalton	.60	.25	.06
☐	43	John Flaherty	.60	.25	.06
☐	44	Angel Gonzalez	.60	.25	.06
☐	45	Eric Hetzel	.60	.25	.06
☐	46	Daryl Irvine	.75	.30	.07
☐	47	Joe Johnson	.60	.25	.06
☐	48	Rick Lancellotti	.75	.30	.07
☐	49	John Leister	.75	.30	.07
☐	50	Derek Livernois	.60	.25	.06
☐	51	Josias Manzanillo	.60	.25	.06
☐	52	Kevin Morton	.90	.40	.09
☐	53	Julius McDougal	.90	.40	.09
☐	54	Tim Naehring	.90	.40	.09
☐	55	Jim Pankovits	.60	.25	.06
☐	56	Mickey Pina	.75	.30	.07
☐	57	Phil Plantier	5.00	2.25	.50
☐	58	Jerry Reed	.60	.25	.06
☐	59	Larry Shikles	.60	.25	.06
☐	60	Tito Stewart	.60	.25	.06
☐	61	Jeff Stone	.60	.25	.06
☐	62	John Trautwein	.60	.25	.06
☐	63	Gary Tremblay	.60	.25	.06
☐	64	Mo Vaughn	2.00	.80	.20
☐	65	Scott Wade	.60	.25	.06
☐	66	Eric Wedge	1.00	.40	.10

1990 Topps TV Yankees

This Yankees team set contains 66 cards measuring the standard size (2 1/2" by 3 1/2"). The fronts feature posed or action color player photos with a high gloss. In block lettering, the team name is printed vertically in light gray on the left side of the card. The player's name appears in a gold plaque below the picture, and white borders round out the card face. The backs are printed in black lettering and have a red and white background. Inside a decal design, player information and statistics are superimposed on an indistinct version of the same picture as on the front. The cards are numbered on the back.

	MINT	EXC	G-VG
COMPLETE SET (66)	50.00	22.50	7.50
COMMON PLAYER (1-66)	.60	.25	.06

		MINT	EXC	G-VG
☐ 1	Bucky Dent MG	.75	.30	.07
☐ 2	Mark Connor CO	.60	.25	.06
☐ 3	Billy Connors CO	.60	.25	.06
☐ 4	Mike Ferraro CO	.60	.25	.06
☐ 5	Joe Sparks CO	.60	.25	.06
☐ 6	Champ Summers CO	.60	.25	.06
☐ 7	Greg Cadaret	.60	.25	.06
☐ 8	Chuck Cary	.60	.25	.06
☐ 9	Lee Guetterman	.60	.25	.06
☐ 10	Andy Hawkins	.60	.25	.06
☐ 11	Dave LaPoint	.60	.25	.06
☐ 12	Tim Leary	.75	.30	.07
☐ 13	Lance McCullers	.60	.25	.06
☐ 14	Alan Mills	.60	.25	.06
☐ 15	Clay Parker	.60	.25	.06
☐ 16	Pascual Perez	.75	.30	.07
☐ 17	Eric Plunk	.60	.25	.06
☐ 18	Dave Righetti	1.25	.50	.12
☐ 19	Jeff D. Robinson	.60	.25	.06
☐ 20	Rick Cerone	.60	.25	.06
☐ 21	Bob Geren	.60	.25	.06
☐ 22	Steve Balboni	.60	.25	.06
☐ 23	Mike Blowers	.60	.25	.06
☐ 24	Alvaro Espinoza	.60	.25	.06
☐ 25	Don Mattingly	5.00	2.25	.50
☐ 26	Steve Sax	1.00	.40	.10
☐ 27	Wayne Tolleson	.60	.25	.06
☐ 28	Randy Velarde	.60	.25	.06
☐ 29	Jesse Barfield	.75	.30	.07
☐ 30	Mel Hall	.75	.30	.07
☐ 31	Roberto Kelly	1.50	.65	.15
☐ 32	Luis Polonia	1.00	.40	.10
☐ 33	Deion Sanders	1.50	.60	.15
☐ 34	Dave Winfield	2.00	.80	.20
☐ 35	Steve Adkins	.75	.30	.07
☐ 36	Oscar Azocar	.75	.30	.07
☐ 37	Bob Brower	.60	.25	.06
☐ 38	Britt Burns	.60	.25	.06
☐ 39	Bob Davidson	.60	.25	.06
☐ 40	Brian Dorsett	.75	.30	.07
☐ 41	Dave Eiland	.75	.30	.07
☐ 42	John Fishel	.60	.25	.06
☐ 43	Andy Fox	.60	.25	.06
☐ 44	John Habyan	.60	.25	.06
☐ 45	Cullen Hartzog	.60	.25	.06
☐ 46	Sterling Hitchcock	.60	.25	.06
☐ 47	Brian Johnson	.60	.25	.06
☐ 48	Jimmy Jones	.75	.30	.07
☐ 49	Scott Kamieniecki	.90	.40	.09
☐ 50	Jim Leyritz	.60	.25	.06
☐ 51	Mark Leiter	.75	.30	.07
☐ 52	Jason Maas	.75	.30	.07
☐ 53	Kevin Maas	2.50	1.00	.25
☐ 54	Hensley Meulens	.90	.40	.09
☐ 55	Kevin Mmahat	.75	.30	.07
☐ 56	Rich Monteleone	.60	.25	.06
☐ 57	Vince Phillips	.60	.25	.06
☐ 58	Carlos Rodriguez	.60	.25	.06
☐ 59	Dave Sax	.60	.25	.06
☐ 60	Willie Smith	.75	.30	.07
☐ 61	Van Snider	.60	.25	.06
☐ 62	Andy Stankiewicz	.75	.30	.07
☐ 63	Wade Taylor	.75	.30	.07
☐ 64	Ricky Torres	.60	.25	.06
☐ 65	Jim Walewander	.75	.30	.07
☐ 66	Bernie Williams	2.00	.80	.20

1991 Topps

The 1991 Topps Set consists of 792 cards in the now standard size of 2 1/2" by 3 1/2". This set marks Topps 10th consecutive year of issuing a 792-card set. Topps also commemorated their fortieth anniversary by including a "Topps 40" logo on the front of each card. Virtually all of the cards have been discovered without the 40th logo. As a special promotion Topps inserted (randomly) into their wax packs one of every previous card they

ever issued. Topps again issued their checklists in team order (and alphabetically within team) and included a special 22-card All-Star set (386-407). There are five players listed as Future Stars, 114 Lance Dickson, 211 Brian Barnes, 561 Tim McIntosh, 587 Jose Offerman, and 594 Rich Garces. There are nine players listed as First Draft Picks, 74 Shane Andrews, 103 Tim Costo, 113 Carl Everett, 278 Alex Fernandez, 471 Mike Lieberthal, 491 Kurt Miller, 529 Marc Newfield, 596 Ronnie Walden, and 767 Dan Wilson. The key rookie cards in this set are Wes Chamberlain, Brian McRae, Marc Newfield, and Phil Plantier. The complete 1991 Topps set was also issued as a factory set of micro baseball cards with cards measuring approximately one-fourth the size of the regular size cards but identical in other respects. The set was also issued with a gold "Operation Desert Shield" emblem stamped on the cards. It has been reported that Topps sent wax cases (equivalent to 6,313 sets) as gifts to U.S. troops stationed in the Persian Gulf. These Desert Shield cards are quite valuable in comparison to the regular issue of Topps; but one must be careful as counterfeits of these cards are known. Due to the scarcity of these Desert Shield cards, they are usually sold at one hundred times the value of the corresponding regular card.

		MINT	EXC	G-VG
COMPLETE SET (792)		21.00	9.00	3.00
COMMON PLAYER (1-792)		.03	.01	.00

		MINT	EXC	G-VG
☐ 1	Nolan Ryan	.35	.15	.03
☐ 2	George Brett RB	.08	.03	.01
☐ 3	Carlton Fisk RB	.08	.03	.01
☐ 4	Kevin Maas RB	.10	.04	.01
☐ 5	Cal Ripken RB	.12	.05	.01
☐ 6	Nolan Ryan RB	.20	.08	.02
☐ 7	Ryne Sandberg RB	.12	.05	.01
☐ 8	Bobby Thigpen RB	.06	.02	.00
☐ 9	Darrin Fletcher	.08	.03	.01
☐ 10	Gregg Olson	.06	.02	.00
☐ 11	Roberto Kelly	.08	.03	.01
☐ 12	Paul Assenmacher	.03	.01	.00
☐ 13	Mariano Duncan	.03	.01	.00
☐ 14	Dennis Lamp	.03	.01	.00
☐ 15	Von Hayes	.06	.02	.00
☐ 16	Mike Heath	.03	.01	.00
☐ 17	Jeff Brantley	.03	.01	.00
☐ 18	Nelson Liriano	.03	.01	.00
☐ 19	Jeff Robinson	.03	.01	.00
	New York Yankees			
☐ 20	Pedro Guerrero	.06	.02	.00
☐ 21	Joe Morgan MG	.06	.02	.00
☐ 22	Storm Davis	.03	.01	.00
☐ 23	Jim Gantner	.03	.01	.00
☐ 24	Dave Martinez	.03	.01	.00
☐ 25	Tim Belcher	.06	.02	.00
☐ 26	Luis Sojo UER	.06	.02	.00
	(Born in Barquisimento, not Carquis)			
☐ 27	Bobby Witt	.03	.01	.00
☐ 28	Alvaro Espinoza	.03	.01	.00
☐ 29	Bob Walk	.03	.01	.00
☐ 30	Gregg Jefferies	.08	.03	.01
☐ 31	Colby Ward	.08	.03	.01
☐ 32	Mike Simms	.12	.05	.01
☐ 33	Barry Jones	.03	.01	.00
☐ 34	Atlee Hammaker	.03	.01	.00
☐ 35	Greg Maddux	.06	.02	.00

☐ 36 Donnie Hill	.03	.01	.00
☐ 37 Tom Bolton	.03	.01	.00
☐ 38 Scott Bradley	.03	.01	.00
☐ 39 Jim Neidlinger	.10	.04	.01
☐ 40 Kevin Mitchell	.10	.04	.01
☐ 41 Ken Dayley	.03	.01	.00
☐ 42 Chris Hoiles	.10	.04	.01
☐ 43 Roger McDowell	.03	.01	.00
☐ 44 Mike Felder	.03	.01	.00
☐ 45 Chris Sabo	.08	.03	.01
☐ 46 Tim Drummond	.03	.01	.00
☐ 47 Brook Jacoby	.03	.01	.00
☐ 48 Dennis Boyd	.03	.01	.00
☐ 49A Pat Borders ERR	.25	.10	.02
(40 steals at			
Kinston in '86)			
☐ 49B Pat Borders COR	.06	.02	.00
(0 steals at			
Kinston in '86)			
☐ 50 Bob Welch	.06	.02	.00
☐ 51 Art Howe MG	.03	.01	.00
☐ 52 Francisco Oliveras	.03	.01	.00
☐ 53 Mike Sharperson UER	.03	.01	.00
(Born in 1961, not 1960)			
☐ 54 Gary Mielke	.03	.01	.00
☐ 55 Jeffrey Leonard	.03	.01	.00
☐ 56 Jeff Parrett	.03	.01	.00
☐ 57 Jack Howell	.03	.01	.00
☐ 58 Mel Stottlemyre Jr.	.03	.01	.00
☐ 59 Eric Yelding	.03	.01	.00
☐ 60 Frank Viola	.06	.02	.00
☐ 61 Stan Javier	.03	.01	.00
☐ 62 Lee Guetterman	.03	.01	.00
☐ 63 Milt Thompson	.03	.01	.00
☐ 64 Tom Herr	.03	.01	.00
☐ 65 Bruce Hurst	.06	.02	.00
☐ 66 Terry Kennedy	.03	.01	.00
☐ 67 Rick Honeycutt	.03	.01	.00
☐ 68 Gary Sheffield	.08	.03	.01
☐ 69 Steve Wilson	.03	.01	.00
☐ 70 Ellis Burks	.08	.03	.01
☐ 71 Jim Acker	.03	.01	.00
☐ 72 Junior Ortiz	.03	.01	.00
☐ 73 Craig Worthington	.03	.01	.00
☐ 74 Shane Andrews	.17	.07	.01
☐ 75 Jack Morris	.08	.03	.01
☐ 76 Jerry Browne	.03	.01	.00
☐ 77 Drew Hall	.03	.01	.00
☐ 78 Geno Petralli	.03	.01	.00
☐ 79 Frank Thomas	1.00	.40	.10
☐ 80A Fernando Valenzuela	.30	.12	.03
ERR (104 earned runs			
in '90 tied for			
league lead)			
☐ 80B Fernando Valenzuela	.08	.03	.01
COR (104 earned runs			
in '90 led league, 20			
CG's in 1986 now			
italicized)			
☐ 81 Cito Gaston MG	.06	.02	.00
☐ 82 Tom Glavine	.12	.05	.01
☐ 83 Daryl Boston	.03	.01	.00
☐ 84 Bob McClure	.03	.01	.00
☐ 85 Jesse Barfield	.06	.02	.00
☐ 86 Les Lancaster	.03	.01	.00
☐ 87 Tracy Jones	.03	.01	.00
☐ 88 Bob Tewksbury	.03	.01	.00
☐ 89 Darren Daulton	.03	.01	.00
☐ 90 Danny Tartabull	.08	.03	.01
☐ 91 Greg Colbrunn	.12	.05	.01
☐ 92 Danny Jackson	.03	.01	.00
☐ 93 Ivan Calderon	.06	.02	.00
☐ 94 John Dopson	.03	.01	.00
☐ 95 Paul Molitor	.08	.03	.01
☐ 96 Trevor Wilson	.03	.01	.00
☐ 97A Brady Anderson ERR	.25	.10	.02
(September, 2 RBI and			
3 hits, should be 3			
RBI and 14 hits			
☐ 97B Brady Anderson COR	.06	.02	.00
☐ 98 Sergio Valdez	.03	.01	.00
☐ 99 Chris Gwynn	.03	.01	.00
☐ 100A Don Mattingly ERR	.75	.30	.07
(10 hits in 1990)			
☐ 100B Don Mattingly COR	.15	.06	.01
(101 hits in 1990)			
☐ 101 Rob Ducey	.03	.01	.00
☐ 102 Gene Larkin	.03	.01	.00
☐ 103 Tim Costo	.25	.10	.02
☐ 104 Don Robinson	.03	.01	.00
☐ 105 Kevin McReynolds	.06	.02	.00
☐ 106 Ed Nunez	.03	.01	.00
☐ 107 Luis Polonia	.06	.02	.00
☐ 108 Matt Young	.03	.01	.00
☐ 109 Greg Riddoch MG	.03	.01	.00
☐ 110 Tom Henke	.06	.02	.00
☐ 111 Andres Thomas	.03	.01	.00
☐ 112 Frank DiPino	.03	.01	.00
☐ 113 Carl Everett	.25	.10	.02
☐ 114 Lance Dickson	.17	.07	.01
☐ 115 Hubie Brooks	.03	.01	.00
☐ 116 Mark Davis	.03	.01	.00
☐ 117 Dion James	.03	.01	.00
☐ 118 Tom Edens	.08	.03	.01
☐ 119 Carl Nichols	.03	.01	.00
☐ 120 Joe Carter	.08	.03	.01
☐ 121 Eric King	.03	.01	.00
☐ 122 Paul O'Neill	.06	.02	.00
☐ 123 Greg A. Harris	.03	.01	.00
☐ 124 Randy Bush	.03	.01	.00
☐ 125 Steve Bedrosian	.03	.01	.00
☐ 126 Bernard Gilkey	.15	.06	.01
☐ 127 Joe Price	.03	.01	.00
☐ 128 Travis Fryman	.40	.16	.04
(Front has SS,			
back has SS-3B)			
☐ 129 Mark Eichhorn	.03	.01	.00
☐ 130 Ozzie Smith	.10	.04	.01
☐ 131A Checklist 1 ERR	.15	.02	.00
727 Phil Bradley			
☐ 131B Checklist 1 COR	.06	.01	.00
717 Phil Bradley			
☐ 132 Jamie Quirk	.03	.01	.00
☐ 133 Greg Briley	.03	.01	.00
☐ 134 Kevin Elster	.03	.01	.00
☐ 135 Jerome Walton	.08	.03	.01
☐ 136 Dave Schmidt	.03	.01	.00
☐ 137 Randy Ready	.03	.01	.00
☐ 138 Jamie Moyer	.03	.01	.00
☐ 139 Jeff Treadway	.03	.01	.00
☐ 140 Fred McGriff	.08	.03	.01
☐ 141 Nick Leyva MG	.03	.01	.00
☐ 142 Curt Wilkerson	.03	.01	.00
☐ 143 John Smiley	.06	.02	.00
☐ 144 Dave Henderson	.06	.02	.00
☐ 145 Lou Whitaker	.06	.02	.00
☐ 146 Dan Plesac	.03	.01	.00
☐ 147 Carlos Baerga	.10	.04	.01
☐ 148 Rey Palacios	.03	.01	.00
☐ 149 Al Osuna UER	.12	.05	.01
(Shown throwing right,			
but bio says lefty)			
☐ 150 Cal Ripken	.20	.08	.02
☐ 151 Tom Browning	.06	.02	.00
☐ 152 Mickey Hatcher	.03	.01	.00
☐ 153 Bryan Harvey	.06	.02	.00
☐ 154 Jay Buhner	.06	.02	.00
☐ 155A Dwight Evans ERR	.25	.10	.02
(led league with			
162 games in '82)			
☐ 155B Dwight Evans COR	.06	.02	.00
(tied for lead with			
162 games in '82)			
☐ 156 Carlos Martinez	.03	.01	.00
☐ 157 John Smoltz	.08	.03	.01
☐ 158 Jose Uribe	.03	.01	.00
☐ 159 Joe Boever	.03	.01	.00
☐ 160 Vince Coleman UER	.08	.03	.01
(Wrong birth year,			
born 9/22/60)			
☐ 161 Tim Leary	.06	.02	.00
☐ 162 Ozzie Canseco	.08	.03	.01
☐ 163 Dave Johnson	.03	.01	.00
☐ 164 Edgar Diaz	.06	.02	.00
☐ 165 Sandy Alomar Jr.	.08	.03	.01
☐ 166 Harold Baines	.06	.02	.00
☐ 167A Randy Tomlin ERR	.50	.20	.05
(Harriburg)			
☐ 167B Randy Tomlin COR	.20	.08	.02
(Harrisburg)			
☐ 168 John Olerud	.12	.05	.01
☐ 169 Luis Aquino	.03	.01	.00
☐ 170 Carlton Fisk	.10	.04	.01
☐ 171 Tony LaRussa MG	.06	.02	.00
☐ 172 Pete Incaviglia	.06	.02	.00
☐ 173 Jason Grimsley	.03	.01	.00
☐ 174 Ken Caminiti	.03	.01	.00
☐ 175 Jack Armstrong	.06	.02	.00
☐ 176 John Orton	.03	.01	.00
☐ 177 Reggie Harris	.08	.03	.01
☐ 178 Dave Valle	.03	.01	.00
☐ 179 Pete Harnisch	.06	.02	.00
☐ 180 Tony Gwynn	.12	.05	.01
☐ 181 Duane Ward	.03	.01	.00
☐ 182 Junior Noboa	.03	.01	.00
☐ 183 Clay Parker	.03	.01	.00
☐ 184 Gary Green	.03	.01	.00
☐ 185 Joe Magrane	.03	.01	.00
☐ 186 Rod Booker	.03	.01	.00
☐ 187 Greg Cadaret	.03	.01	.00

#	Player			
☐ 188	Damon Berryhill	.03	.01	.00
☐ 189	Daryl Irvine	.08	.03	.01
☐ 190	Matt Williams	.10	.04	.01
☐ 191	Willie Blair	.03	.01	.00
☐ 192	Rob Deer	.06	.02	.00
☐ 193	Felix Fermin	.03	.01	.00
☐ 194	Xavier Hernandez	.06	.02	.00
☐ 195	Wally Joyner	.08	.03	.01
☐ 196	Jim Vatcher	.08	.03	.01
☐ 197	Chris Nabholz	.08	.03	.01
☐ 198	R.J. Reynolds	.03	.01	.00
☐ 199	Mike Hartley	.06	.02	.00
☐ 200	Darryl Strawberry	.15	.06	.01
☐ 201	Tom Kelly MG	.03	.01	.00
☐ 202	Jim Leyritz	.03	.01	.00
☐ 203	Gene Harris	.03	.01	.00
☐ 204	Herm Winningham	.03	.01	.00
☐ 205	Mike Perez	.08	.03	.01
☐ 206	Carlos Quintana	.06	.02	.00
☐ 207	Gary Wayne	.03	.01	.00
☐ 208	Willie Wilson	.06	.02	.00
☐ 209	Ken Howell	.03	.01	.00
☐ 210	Lance Parrish	.06	.02	.00
☐ 211	Brian Barnes	.10	.04	.01
☐ 212	Steve Finley	.06	.02	.00
☐ 213	Frank Wills	.03	.01	.00
☐ 214	Joe Girardi	.03	.01	.00
☐ 215	Dave Smith	.03	.01	.00
☐ 216	Greg Gagne	.03	.01	.00
☐ 217	Chris Bosio	.03	.01	.00
☐ 218	Rick Parker	.03	.01	.00
☐ 219	Jack McDowell	.08	.03	.01
☐ 220	Tim Wallach	.06	.02	.00
☐ 221	Don Slaught	.03	.01	.00
☐ 222	Brian McRae	.40	.16	.04
☐ 223	Allan Anderson	.03	.01	.00
☐ 224	Juan Gonzalez	.30	.12	.03
☐ 225	Randy Johnson	.03	.01	.00
☐ 226	Alfredo Griffin	.03	.01	.00
☐ 227	Steve Avery	.30	.12	.03
☐ 228	Rex Hudler	.03	.01	.00
☐ 229	Rance Mulliniks	.03	.01	.00
☐ 230	Sid Fernandez	.06	.02	.00
☐ 231	Doug Rader MG	.03	.01	.00
☐ 232	Jose DeJesus	.03	.01	.00
☐ 233	Al Leiter	.03	.01	.00
☐ 234	Scott Erickson	.60	.25	.06
☐ 235	Dave Parker	.08	.03	.01
☐ 236A	Frank Tanana ERR (tied for lead with 269 K's in '75)	.25	.10	.02
☐ 236B	Frank Tanana COR (led league with 269 K's in '75)	.06	.02	.00
☐ 237	Rick Cerone	.03	.01	.00
☐ 238	Mike Dunne	.03	.01	.00
☐ 239	Darren Lewis	.20	.08	.02
☐ 240	Mike Scott	.06	.02	.00
☐ 241	Dave Clark UER (Career totals 19 HR and 5 3B, should be 22 and 3)	.03	.01	.00
☐ 242	Mike LaCoss	.03	.01	.00
☐ 243	Lance Johnson	.03	.01	.00
☐ 244	Mike Jeffcoat	.03	.01	.00
☐ 245	Kal Daniels	.06	.02	.00
☐ 246	Kevin Wickander	.03	.01	.00
☐ 247	Jody Reed	.03	.01	.00
☐ 248	Tom Gordon	.06	.02	.00
☐ 249	Bob Melvin	.03	.01	.00
☐ 250	Dennis Eckersley	.06	.02	.00
☐ 251	Mark Lemke	.06	.02	.00
☐ 252	Mel Rojas	.06	.02	.00
☐ 253	Garry Templeton	.03	.01	.00
☐ 254	Shawn Boskie	.03	.01	.00
☐ 255	Brian Downing	.03	.01	.00
☐ 256	Greg Hibbard	.03	.01	.00
☐ 257	Tom O'Malley	.03	.01	.00
☐ 258	Chris Hammond	.08	.03	.01
☐ 259	Hensley Meulens	.08	.03	.01
☐ 260	Harold Reynolds	.06	.02	.00
☐ 261	Bud Harrelson MG	.03	.01	.00
☐ 262	Tim Jones	.03	.01	.00
☐ 263	Checklist 2	.06	.01	.00
☐ 264	Dave Hollins	.08	.03	.01
☐ 265	Mark Gubicza	.03	.01	.00
☐ 266	Carmelo Castillo	.03	.01	.00
☐ 267	Mark Knudson	.03	.01	.00
☐ 268	Tom Brookens	.03	.01	.00
☐ 269	Joe Hesketh	.03	.01	.00
☐ 270A	Mark McGwire ERR (1987 Slugging Pctg. listed as 618)	.30	.12	.03

#	Player			
☐ 270B	Mark McGwire COR (1987 Slugging Pctg. listed as .618)	.10	.04	.01
☐ 271	Omar Olivares	.10	.04	.01
☐ 272	Jeff King	.06	.02	.00
☐ 273	Johnny Ray	.03	.01	.00
☐ 274	Ken Williams	.03	.01	.00
☐ 275	Alan Trammell	.08	.03	.01
☐ 276	Bill Swift	.03	.01	.00
☐ 277	Scott Coolbaugh	.03	.01	.00
☐ 278	Alex Fernandez UER (No '90 White Sox stats)	.20	.08	.02
☐ 279A	Jose Gonzalez ERR (photo actually Billy Bean)	.25	.10	.02
☐ 279B	Jose Gonzalez COR	.06	.02	.00
☐ 280	Bret Saberhagen	.08	.03	.01
☐ 281	Larry Sheets	.03	.01	.00
☐ 282	Don Carman	.03	.01	.00
☐ 283	Marquis Grissom	.10	.04	.01
☐ 284	Billy Spiers	.03	.01	.00
☐ 285	Jim Abbott	.10	.04	.01
☐ 286	Ken Oberkfell	.03	.01	.00
☐ 287	Mark Grant	.03	.01	.00
☐ 288	Derrick May	.08	.03	.01
☐ 289	Tim Birtsas	.03	.01	.00
☐ 290	Steve Sax	.06	.02	.00
☐ 291	John Wathan MG	.03	.01	.00
☐ 292	Bud Black	.03	.01	.00
☐ 293	Jay Bell	.03	.01	.00
☐ 294	Mike Moore	.03	.01	.00
☐ 295	Rafael Palmeiro	.08	.03	.01
☐ 296	Mark Williamson	.03	.01	.00
☐ 297	Manny Lee	.03	.01	.00
☐ 298	Omar Vizquel	.03	.01	.00
☐ 299	Scott Radinsky	.06	.02	.00
☐ 300	Kirby Puckett	.12	.05	.01
☐ 301	Steve Farr	.03	.01	.00
☐ 302	Tim Teufel	.03	.01	.00
☐ 303	Mike Boddicker	.03	.01	.00
☐ 304	Kevin Reimer	.08	.03	.01
☐ 305	Mike Scioscia	.03	.01	.00
☐ 306A	Lonnie Smith ERR (136 games in '90)	.25	.10	.02
☐ 306B	Lonnie Smith COR (135 games in '90)	.06	.02	.00
☐ 307	Andy Benes	.08	.03	.01
☐ 308	Tom Pagnozzi	.03	.01	.00
☐ 309	Norm Charlton	.03	.01	.00
☐ 310	Gary Carter	.08	.03	.01
☐ 311	Jeff Pico	.03	.01	.00
☐ 312	Charlie Hayes	.03	.01	.00
☐ 313	Ron Robinson	.03	.01	.00
☐ 314	Gary Pettis	.03	.01	.00
☐ 315	Roberto Alomar	.10	.04	.01
☐ 316	Gene Nelson	.03	.01	.00
☐ 317	Mike Fitzgerald	.03	.01	.00
☐ 318	Rick Aguilera	.03	.01	.00
☐ 319	Jeff McKnight	.06	.02	.00
☐ 320	Tony Fernandez	.06	.02	.00
☐ 321	Bob Rodgers MG	.03	.01	.00
☐ 322	Terry Shumpert	.03	.01	.00
☐ 323	Cory Snyder	.06	.02	.00
☐ 324A	Ron Kittle ERR (Set another standard ...)	.25	.10	.02
☐ 324B	Ron Kittle COR (Tied another standard ...)	.06	.02	.00
☐ 325	Brett Butler	.06	.02	.00
☐ 326	Ken Patterson	.03	.01	.00
☐ 327	Ron Hassey	.03	.01	.00
☐ 328	Walt Terrell	.03	.01	.00
☐ 329	Dave Justice UER (Drafted third round on card, should say fourth pick)	.50	.20	.05
☐ 330	Dwight Gooden	.10	.04	.01
☐ 331	Eric Anthony	.08	.03	.01
☐ 332	Kenny Rogers	.03	.01	.00
☐ 333	Chipper Jones FDP	.30	.12	.03
☐ 334	Todd Benzinger	.03	.01	.00
☐ 335	Mitch Williams	.03	.01	.00
☐ 336	Matt Nokes	.06	.02	.00
☐ 337A	Keith Comstock ERR (Cubs logo on front)	.25	.10	.02
☐ 337B	Keith Comstock COR (Mariners logo on front)	.06	.02	.00
☐ 338	Luis Rivera	.03	.01	.00
☐ 339	Larry Walker	.08	.03	.01
☐ 340	Ramon Martinez	.10	.04	.01
☐ 341	John Moses	.03	.01	.00
☐ 342	Mickey Morandini	.08	.03	.01
☐ 343	Jose Oquendo	.03	.01	.00
☐ 344	Jeff Russell	.03	.01	.00

☐ 345	Len Dykstra	.06	.02	.00
☐ 346	Jesse Orosco	.03	.01	.00
☐ 347	Greg Vaughn	.08	.03	.01
☐ 348	Todd Stottlemyre	.06	.02	.00
☐ 349	Dave Gallagher	.03	.01	.00
☐ 350	Glenn Davis	.06	.02	.00
☐ 351	Joe Torre MG	.06	.02	.00
☐ 352	Frank White	.03	.01	.00
☐ 353	Tony Castillo	.03	.01	.00
☐ 354	Sid Bream	.03	.01	.00
☐ 355	Chili Davis	.06	.02	.00
☐ 356	Mike Marshall	.06	.02	.00
☐ 357	Jack Savage	.03	.01	.00
☐ 358	Mark Parent	.03	.01	.00
☐ 359	Chuck Cary	.03	.01	.00
☐ 360	Tim Raines	.06	.02	.00
☐ 361	Scott Garrelts	.03	.01	.00
☐ 362	Hector Villenueva	.06	.02	.00
☐ 363	Rick Mahler	.03	.01	.00
☐ 364	Dan Pasqua	.03	.01	.00
☐ 365	Mike Schooler	.03	.01	.00
☐ 366A	Checklist 3 ERR	.15	.02	.00
	19 Carl Nichols			
☐ 366B	Checklist 3 COR	.06	.01	.00
	119 Carl Nichols			
☐ 367	Dave Walsh	.10	.04	.01
☐ 368	Felix Jose	.08	.03	.01
☐ 369	Steve Searcy	.03	.01	.00
☐ 370	Kelly Gruber	.06	.02	.00
☐ 371	Jeff Montgomery	.03	.01	.00
☐ 372	Spike Owen	.03	.01	.00
☐ 373	Darrin Jackson	.03	.01	.00
☐ 374	Larry Casian	.08	.03	.01
☐ 375	Tony Pena	.06	.02	.00
☐ 376	Mike Harkey	.06	.02	.00
☐ 377	Rene Gonzales	.03	.01	.00
☐ 378A	Wilson Alvarez ERR	.45	.18	.04
	('89 Port Charlotte and '90 Birmingham stat lines omitted)			
☐ 378B	Wilson Alvarez COR	.12	.05	.01
	(Text still says 143 K's in 1988, whereas stats say 134)			
☐ 379	Randy Velarde	.03	.01	.00
☐ 380	Willie McGee	.06	.02	.00
☐ 381	Jim Leyland MG	.03	.01	.00
☐ 382	Mackey Sasser	.03	.01	.00
☐ 383	Pete Smith	.03	.01	.00
☐ 384	Gerald Perry	.03	.01	.00
☐ 385	Mickey Tettleton	.06	.02	.00
☐ 386	Cecil Fielder AS	.10	.04	.01
☐ 387	Julio Franco AS	.06	.02	.00
☐ 388	Kelly Gruber AS	.06	.02	.00
☐ 389	Alan Trammell AS	.08	.03	.01
☐ 390	Jose Canseco AS	.15	.06	.01
☐ 391	Rickey Henderson AS	.12	.05	.01
☐ 392	Ken Griffey Jr. AS	.30	.12	.03
☐ 393	Carlton Fisk AS	.08	.03	.01
☐ 394	Bob Welch AS	.06	.02	.00
☐ 395	Chuck Finley AS	.06	.02	.00
☐ 396	Bobby Thigpen AS	.06	.02	.00
☐ 397	Eddie Murray AS	.08	.03	.01
☐ 398	Ryne Sandberg AS	.12	.05	.01
☐ 399	Matt Williams AS	.08	.03	.01
☐ 400	Barry Larkin AS	.08	.03	.01
☐ 401	Barry Bonds AS	.08	.03	.01
☐ 402	Darryl Strawbery AS	.10	.04	.01
☐ 403	Bobby Bonilla AS	.08	.03	.01
☐ 404	Mike Scioscia AS	.03	.01	.00
☐ 405	Doug Drabek AS	.06	.02	.00
☐ 406	Frank Viola AS	.06	.02	.00
☐ 407	John Franco AS	.03	.01	.00
☐ 408	Earnie Riles	.03	.01	.00
☐ 409	Mike Stanley	.03	.01	.00
☐ 410	Dave Righetti	.06	.02	.00
☐ 411	Lance Blankenship	.03	.01	.00
☐ 412	Dave Bergman	.03	.01	.00
☐ 413	Terry Mulholland	.03	.01	.00
☐ 414	Sammy Sosa	.08	.03	.01
☐ 415	Rick Sutcliffe	.06	.02	.00
☐ 416	Randy Milligan	.06	.02	.00
☐ 417	Bill Krueger	.03	.01	.00
☐ 418	Nick Esasky	.03	.01	.00
☐ 419	Jeff Reed	.03	.01	.00
☐ 420	Bobby Thigpen	.06	.02	.00
☐ 421	Alex Cole	.08	.03	.01
☐ 422	Rick Reuschel	.06	.02	.00
☐ 423	Rafael Ramirez UER	.03	.01	.00
	(Born 1959, not 1958)			
☐ 424	Calvin Schiraldi	.03	.01	.00
☐ 425	Andy Van Slyke	.08	.03	.01
☐ 426	Joe Grahe	.08	.03	.01
☐ 427	Rick Dempsey	.03	.01	.00
☐ 428	John Barfield	.08	.03	.01
☐ 429	Stump Merrill MG	.03	.01	.00
☐ 430	Gary Gaetti	.06	.02	.00
☐ 431	Paul Gibson	.03	.01	.00
☐ 432	Delino DeShields	.10	.04	.01
☐ 433	Pat Tabler	.03	.01	.00
☐ 434	Julio Machado	.03	.01	.00
☐ 435	Kevin Maas	.15	.06	.01
☐ 436	Scott Bankhead	.03	.01	.00
☐ 437	Doug Dascenzo	.03	.01	.00
☐ 438	Vicente Palacios	.03	.01	.00
☐ 439	Dickie Thon	.03	.01	.00
☐ 440	George Bell	.08	.03	.01
☐ 441	Zane Smith	.03	.01	.00
☐ 442	Charlie O'Brien	.03	.01	.00
☐ 443	Jeff Innis	.03	.01	.00
☐ 444	Glenn Braggs	.03	.01	.00
☐ 445	Greg Swindell	.06	.02	.00
☐ 446	Craig Grebeck	.06	.02	.00
☐ 447	John Burkett	.03	.01	.00
☐ 448	Craig Lefferts	.03	.01	.00
☐ 449	Juan Berenguer	.03	.01	.00
☐ 450	Wade Boggs	.12	.05	.01
☐ 451	Neal Heaton	.03	.01	.00
☐ 452	Bill Schroeder	.03	.01	.00
☐ 453	Lenny Harris	.03	.01	.00
☐ 454A	Kevin Appier ERR	.25	.10	.02
	('90 Omaha stat line omitted)			
☐ 454B	Kevin Appier COR	.06	.02	.00
☐ 455	Walt Weiss	.06	.02	.00
☐ 456	Charlie Leibrandt	.03	.01	.00
☐ 457	Todd Hundley	.10	.04	.01
☐ 458	Brian Holman	.03	.01	.00
☐ 459	Tom Trebelhorn MG	.03	.01	.00
	(Pitching and batting columns switched)			
☐ 460	Dave Stieb	.06	.02	.00
☐ 461	Robin Ventura	.20	.08	.02
☐ 462	Steve Frey	.03	.01	.00
☐ 463	Dwight Smith	.03	.01	.00
☐ 464	Steve Buechele	.03	.01	.00
☐ 465	Ken Griffey Sr.	.06	.02	.00
☐ 466	Charles Nagy	.08	.03	.01
☐ 467	Dennis Cook	.03	.01	.00
☐ 468	Tim Hulett	.03	.01	.00
☐ 469	Chet Lemon	.03	.01	.00
☐ 470	Howard Johnson	.08	.03	.01
☐ 471	Mike Lieberthal	.10	.04	.01
☐ 472	Kirt Manwaring	.03	.01	.00
☐ 473	Curt Young	.03	.01	.00
☐ 474	Phil Plantier	1.25	.50	.12
☐ 475	Teddy Higuera	.03	.01	.00
☐ 476	Glenn Wilson	.03	.01	.00
☐ 477	Mike Fetters	.03	.01	.00
☐ 478	Kurt Stillwell	.03	.01	.00
☐ 479	Bob Patterson UER	.03	.01	.00
	(Has a decimal point between 7 and 9)			
☐ 480	Dave Magadan	.06	.02	.00
☐ 481	Eddie Whitson	.03	.01	.00
☐ 482	Tino Martinez	.15	.06	.01
☐ 483	Mike Aldrete	.03	.01	.00
☐ 484	Dave LaPoint	.03	.01	.00
☐ 485	Terry Pendleton	.08	.03	.01
☐ 486	Tommy Greene	.08	.03	.01
☐ 487	Rafael Belliard	.03	.01	.00
☐ 488	Jeff Manto	.06	.02	.00
☐ 489	Bobby Valentine MG	.03	.01	.00
☐ 490	Kirk Gibson	.06	.02	.00
☐ 491	Kurt Miller	.15	.06	.01
☐ 492	Ernie Whitt	.03	.01	.00
☐ 493	Jose Rijo	.06	.02	.00
☐ 494	Chris James	.03	.01	.00
☐ 495	Charlie Hough	.03	.01	.00
☐ 496	Marty Barrett	.03	.01	.00
☐ 497	Ben McDonald	.10	.04	.01
☐ 498	Mark Salas	.03	.01	.00
☐ 499	Melido Perez	.03	.01	.00
☐ 500	Will Clark	.10	.04	.01
☐ 501	Mike Bielecki	.03	.01	.00
☐ 502	Carney Lansford	.06	.02	.00
☐ 503	Roy Smith	.03	.01	.00
☐ 504	Julio Valera	.06	.02	.00
☐ 505	Chuck Finley	.06	.02	.00
☐ 506	Darnell Coles	.03	.01	.00
☐ 507	Steve Jeltz	.03	.01	.00
☐ 508	Mike York	.08	.03	.01
☐ 509	Glenallen Hill	.06	.02	.00
☐ 510	John Franco	.03	.01	.00
☐ 511	Steve Balboni	.03	.01	.00
☐ 512	Jose Mesa	.03	.01	.00
☐ 513	Jerald Clark	.03	.01	.00
☐ 514	Mike Stanton	.03	.01	.00
☐ 515	Alvin Davis	.06	.02	.00
☐ 516	Karl Rhodes	.08	.03	.01

#	Player			
517	Joe Oliver	.03	.01	.00
518	Cris Carpenter	.03	.01	.00
519	Sparky Anderson MG	.06	.02	.00
520	Mark Grace	.08	.03	.01
521	Joe Orsulak	.03	.01	.00
522	Stan Belinda	.03	.01	.00
523	Rodney McCray	.08	.03	.01
524	Darrel Akerfelds	.03	.01	.00
525	Willie Randolph	.03	.01	.00
526A	Moises Alou ERR	.35	.15	.03
	(37 runs in 2 games for '90 Pirates)			
526B	Moises Alou COR	.08	.03	.01
	(0 runs in 2 games for '90 Pirates)			
527A	Checklist 4 ERR	.15	.02	.00
	105 Keith Miller 719 Kevin McReynolds			
527B	Checklist 4 COR	.06	.01	.00
	105 Keith Miller 719 Keith Miller			
528	Denny Martinez	.06	.02	.00
529	Marc Newfield	.90	.40	.09
530	Roger Clemens	.15	.06	.01
531	Dave Rohde	.08	.03	.01
532	Kirk McCaskill	.03	.01	.00
533	Oddibe McDowell	.03	.01	.00
534	Mike Jackson	.03	.01	.00
535	Ruben Sierra UER	.12	.05	.01
	(Back reads 100 Runs amd 100 RBI's)			
536	Mike Witt	.03	.01	.00
537	Jose Lind	.03	.01	.00
538	Bip Roberts	.03	.01	.00
539	Scott Terry	.03	.01	.00
540	George Brett	.10	.04	.01
541	Domingo Ramos	.03	.01	.00
542	Rob Murphy	.03	.01	.00
543	Junior Felix	.06	.02	.00
544	Alejandro Pena	.06	.02	.00
545	Dale Murphy	.10	.04	.01
546	Jeff Ballard	.03	.01	.00
547	Mike Pagliarulo	.03	.01	.00
548	Jaime Navarro	.03	.01	.00
549	John McNamara MG	.03	.01	.00
550	Eric Davis	.10	.04	.01
551	Bob Kipper	.03	.01	.00
552	Jeff Hamilton	.03	.01	.00
553	Joe Klink	.06	.02	.00
554	Brian Harper	.06	.02	.00
555	Turner Ward	.12	.05	.01
556	Gary Ward	.03	.01	.00
557	Wally Whitehurst	.03	.01	.00
558	Otis Nixon	.06	.02	.00
559	Adam Peterson	.03	.01	.00
560	Greg Smith	.06	.02	.00
561	Tim McIntosh	.08	.03	.01
562	Jeff Kunkel	.03	.01	.00
563	Brent Knackert	.03	.01	.00
564	Dante Bichette	.03	.01	.00
565	Craig Biggio	.06	.02	.00
566	Craig Wilson	.10	.04	.01
567	Dwayne Henry	.03	.01	.00
568	Ron Karkovice	.03	.01	.00
569	Curt Schilling	.03	.01	.00
570	Barry Bonds	.12	.05	.01
571	Pat Combs	.03	.01	.00
572	Dave Anderson	.03	.01	.00
573	Rich Rodriguez	.08	.03	.01
574	John Marzano	.03	.01	.00
575	Robin Yount	.10	.04	.01
576	Jeff Kaiser	.03	.01	.00
577	Bill Doran	.03	.01	.00
578	Dave West	.03	.01	.00
579	Roger Craig MG	.03	.01	.00
580	Dave Stewart	.06	.02	.00
581	Luis Quinones	.03	.01	.00
582	Marty Clary	.03	.01	.00
583	Tony Phillips	.03	.01	.00
584	Kevin Brown	.03	.01	.00
585	Pete O'Brien	.03	.01	.00
586	Fred Lynn	.06	.02	.00
587	Jose Offerman UER	.10	.04	.01
	(Text says he signed 7/24/86, but bio says 1988)			
588	Mark Whiten	.20	.08	.02
589	Scott Ruskin	.03	.01	.00
590	Eddie Murray	.10	.04	.01
591	Ken Hill	.03	.01	.00
592	B.J. Surhoff	.03	.01	.00
593A	Mike Walker ERR	.25	.10	.02
	('90 Canton-Akron stat line omitted)			
593B	Mike Walker COR	.08	.03	.01
594	Rich Garces	.10	.04	.01
595	Bill Landrum	.03	.01	.00
596	Ronnie Walden	.15	.06	.01
597	Jerry Don Gleaton	.03	.01	.00
598	Sam Horn	.03	.01	.00
599A	Greg Myers ERR	.25	.10	.02
	('90 Syracuse stat line omitted)			
599B	Greg Myers COR	.06	.02	.00
600	Bo Jackson	.25	.10	.02
601	Bob Ojeda	.03	.01	.00
602	Casey Candaele	.03	.01	.00
603A	Wes Chamberlain ERR	1.50	.60	.15
	(photo actually Louie Meadows)			
603B	Wes Chamberlain COR	.45	.18	.04
604	Billy Hatcher	.03	.01	.00
605	Jeff Reardon	.06	.02	.00
606	Jim Gott	.03	.01	.00
607	Edgar Martinez	.06	.02	.00
608	Todd Burns	.03	.01	.00
609	Jeff Torborg MG	.03	.01	.00
610	Andres Galarraga	.06	.02	.00
611	Dave Eiland	.03	.01	.00
612	Steve Lyons	.03	.01	.00
613	Eric Show	.03	.01	.00
614	Luis Salazar	.03	.01	.00
615	Bert Blyleven	.06	.02	.00
616	Todd Zeile	.10	.04	.01
617	Bill Wegman	.03	.01	.00
618	Sil Campusano	.03	.01	.00
619	David Wells	.03	.01	.00
620	Ozzie Guillen	.06	.02	.00
621	Ted Power	.03	.01	.00
622	Jack Daugherty	.03	.01	.00
623	Jeff Blauser	.03	.01	.00
624	Tom Candiotti	.06	.02	.00
625	Terry Steinbach	.03	.01	.00
626	Gerald Young	.03	.01	.00
627	Tim Layana	.03	.01	.00
628	Greg Litton	.03	.01	.00
629	Wes Gardner	.03	.01	.00
630	Dave Winfield	.10	.04	.01
631	Mike Morgan	.06	.02	.00
632	Lloyd Moseby	.03	.01	.00
633	Kevin Tapani	.06	.02	.00
634	Henry Cotto	.03	.01	.00
635	Andy Hawkins	.03	.01	.00
636	Geronimo Pena	.08	.03	.01
637	Bruce Ruffin	.03	.01	.00
638	Mike Macfarlane	.03	.01	.00
639	Frank Robinson MG	.08	.03	.01
640	Andre Dawson	.10	.04	.01
641	Mike Henneman	.03	.01	.00
642	Hal Morris	.10	.04	.01
643	Jim Presley	.03	.01	.00
644	Chuck Crim	.03	.01	.00
645	Juan Samuel	.06	.02	.00
646	Andujar Cedeno	.35	.15	.03
647	Mark Portugal	.03	.01	.00
648	Lee Stevens	.10	.04	.01
649	Bill Sampen	.03	.01	.00
650	Jack Clark	.06	.02	.00
651	Alan Mills	.03	.01	.00
652	Kevin Romine	.03	.01	.00
653	Anthony Telford	.08	.03	.01
654	Paul Sorrento	.03	.01	.00
655	Erik Hanson	.06	.02	.00
656A	Checklist 5 ERR	.15	.02	.00
	348 Vicente Palacios 381 Jose Lind 537 Mike LaValliere 665 Jim Leyland			
656B	Checklist 5 COR	.06	.01	.00
	438 Vicente Palacios 537 Jose Lind 665 Mike LaValliere 381 Jim Leyland			
657	Mike Kingery	.03	.01	.00
658	Scott Aldred	.08	.03	.01
659	Oscar Azocar	.06	.02	.00
660	Lee Smith	.06	.02	.00
661	Steve Lake	.03	.01	.00
662	Ron Dibble	.06	.02	.00
663	Greg Brock	.03	.01	.00
664	John Farrell	.03	.01	.00
665	Mike LaValliere	.03	.01	.00
666	Danny Darwin	.03	.01	.00
667	Kent Anderson	.03	.01	.00
668	Bill Long	.03	.01	.00
669	Lou Piniella MG	.06	.02	.00
670	Rickey Henderson	.20	.08	.02
671	Andy McGaffigan	.03	.01	.00
672	Shane Mack	.06	.02	.00

☐ 673	Greg Olson UER	.03	.01	.00	
	(6 RBI in '88 at Tide-				
	water and 2 RBI in '87,				
	should be 48 and 15)				
☐ 674A	Kevin Gross ERR	.25	.10	.02	
	(89 BB with Phillies				
	in '88 tied for				
	league lead)				
☐ 674B	Kevin Gross COR	.06	.02	.00	
	(89 BB with Phillies				
	in '88 led league)				
☐ 675	Tom Brunansky	.06	.02	.00	
☐ 676	Scott Chiamparino	.08	.03	.01	
☐ 677	Billy Ripken	.03	.01	.00	
☐ 678	Mark Davidson	.03	.01	.00	
☐ 679	Bill Bathe	.03	.01	.00	
☐ 680	David Cone	.06	.02	.00	
☐ 681	Jeff Schaefer	.06	.02	.00	
☐ 682	Ray Lankford	.30	.12	.03	
☐ 683	Derek Lilliquist	.03	.01	.00	
☐ 684	Milt Cuyler	.17	.07	.01	
☐ 685	Doug Drabek	.06	.02	.00	
☐ 686	Mike Gallego	.03	.01	.00	
☐ 687A	John Cerutti ERR	.25	.10	.02	
	(4.46 ERA in '90)				
☐ 687B	John Cerutti COR	.06	.02	.00	
	(4.76 ERA in '90)				
☐ 688	Rosario Rodriguez	.08	.03	.01	
☐ 689	John Kruk	.03	.01	.00	
☐ 690	Orel Hershiser	.06	.02	.00	
☐ 691	Mike Blowers	.03	.01	.00	
☐ 692A	Efrain Valdez ERR	.30	.12	.03	
	(born 6/11/66)				
☐ 692B	Efrain Valdez COR	.10	.04	.01	
	(born 7/11/66 and two				
	lines of text added)				
☐ 693	Francisco Cabrera	.03	.01	.00	
☐ 694	Randy Veres	.03	.01	.00	
☐ 695	Kevin Seitzer	.06	.02	.00	
☐ 696	Steve Olin	.03	.01	.00	
☐ 697	Shawn Abner	.03	.01	.00	
☐ 698	Mark Guthrie	.03	.01	.00	
☐ 699	Jim Lefebvre MG	.03	.01	.00	
☐ 700	Jose Canseco	.25	.10	.02	
☐ 701	Pascual Perez	.03	.01	.00	
☐ 702	Tim Naehring	.10	.04	.01	
☐ 703	Juan Agosto	.03	.01	.00	
☐ 704	Devon White	.06	.02	.00	
☐ 705	Robby Thompson	.03	.01	.00	
☐ 706A	Brad Arnsberg ERR	.25	.10	.02	
	(68.2 IP in '90)				
☐ 706B	Brad Arnsberg COR	.06	.02	.00	
	(62.2 IP in '90)				
☐ 707	Jim Eisenreich	.03	.01	.00	
☐ 708	John Mitchell	.03	.01	.00	
☐ 709	Matt Sinatro	.03	.01	.00	
☐ 710	Kent Hrbek	.06	.02	.00	
☐ 711	Jose DeLeon	.03	.01	.00	
☐ 712	Ricky Jordan	.06	.02	.00	
☐ 713	Scott Scudder	.06	.02	.00	
☐ 714	Marvell Wynne	.03	.01	.00	
☐ 715	Tim Burke	.03	.01	.00	
☐ 716	Bob Geren	.03	.01	.00	
☐ 717	Phil Bradley	.03	.01	.00	
☐ 718	Steve Crawford	.03	.01	.00	
☐ 719	Keith Miller	.03	.01	.00	
☐ 720	Cecil Fielder	.15	.06	.01	
☐ 721	Mark Lee	.10	.04	.01	
☐ 722	Wally Backman	.03	.01	.00	
☐ 723	Candy Maldonado	.03	.01	.00	
☐ 724	David Segui	.08	.03	.01	
☐ 725	Ron Gant	.12	.05	.01	
☐ 726	Phil Stephenson	.03	.01	.00	
☐ 727	Mookie Wilson	.03	.01	.00	
☐ 728	Scott Sanderson	.03	.01	.00	
☐ 729	Don Zimmer MG	.03	.01	.00	
☐ 730	Barry Larkin	.08	.03	.01	
☐ 731	Jeff Gray	.08	.03	.01	
☐ 732	Franklin Stubbs	.03	.01	.00	
☐ 733	Kelly Downs	.03	.01	.00	
☐ 734	John Russell	.03	.01	.00	
☐ 735	Ron Darling	.06	.02	.00	
☐ 736	Dick Schofield	.03	.01	.00	
☐ 737	Tim Crews	.03	.01	.00	
☐ 738	Mel Hall	.03	.01	.00	
☐ 739	Russ Swan	.06	.02	.00	
☐ 740	Ryne Sandberg	.20	.08	.02	
☐ 741	Jimmy Key	.06	.02	.00	
☐ 742	Tommy Gregg	.03	.01	.00	
☐ 743	Bryn Smith	.03	.01	.00	
☐ 744	Nelson Santovenia	.03	.01	.00	
☐ 745	Doug Jones	.03	.01	.00	
☐ 746	John Shelby	.03	.01	.00	
☐ 747	Tony Fossas	.03	.01	.00	
☐ 748	Al Newman	.03	.01	.00	

☐ 749	Greg Harris	.03	.01	.00
☐ 750	Bobby Bonilla	.10	.04	.01
☐ 751	Wayne Edwards	.03	.01	.00
☐ 752	Kevin Bass	.03	.01	.00
☐ 753	Paul Marak	.08	.03	.01
☐ 754	Bill Pecota	.03	.01	.00
☐ 755	Mark Langston	.06	.02	.00
☐ 756	Jeff Huson	.03	.01	.00
☐ 757	Mark Gardner	.06	.02	.00
☐ 758	Mike Devereaux	.03	.01	.00
☐ 759	Bobby Cox MG	.03	.01	.00
☐ 760	Benny Santiago	.06	.02	.00
☐ 761	Larry Andersen	.03	.01	.00
☐ 762	Mitch Webster	.03	.01	.00
☐ 763	Dana Kiecker	.03	.01	.00
☐ 764	Mark Carreon	.03	.01	.00
☐ 765	Shawon Dunston	.06	.02	.00
☐ 766	Jeff Robinson	.03	.01	.00
☐ 767	Dan Wilson	.15	.06	.01
☐ 768	Don Pall	.03	.01	.00
☐ 769	Tim Sherrill	.08	.03	.01
☐ 770	Jay Howell	.03	.01	.00
☐ 771	Gary Redus UER	.03	.01	.00
	(Born in Tanner,			
	should say Athens)			
☐ 772	Kent Mercker	.08	.03	.01
	(Born in Indianapolis,			
	should say Dublin, Ohio)			
☐ 773	Tom Foley	.03	.01	.00
☐ 774	Dennis Rasmussen	.03	.01	.00
☐ 775	Julio Franco	.08	.03	.01
☐ 776	Brent Mayne	.08	.03	.01
☐ 777	John Candelaria	.03	.01	.00
☐ 778	Dan Gladden	.03	.01	.00
☐ 779	Carmelo Martinez	.03	.01	.00
☐ 780A	Randy Myers ERR	.25	.10	.02
	(15 career losses)			
☐ 780B	Randy Myers COR	.06	.02	.00
	(19 career losses)			
☐ 781	Darryl Hamilton	.03	.01	.00
☐ 782	Jim Deshaies	.03	.01	.00
☐ 783	Joel Skinner	.03	.01	.00
☐ 784	Willie Fraser	.03	.01	.00
☐ 785	Scott Fletcher	.03	.01	.00
☐ 786	Eric Plunk	.03	.01	.00
☐ 787	Checklist 6	.06	.01	.00
☐ 788	Bob Milacki	.03	.01	.00
☐ 789	Tom Lasorda MG	.06	.02	.00
☐ 790	Ken Griffey Jr.	.75	.30	.07
☐ 791	Mike Benjamin	.06	.02	.00
☐ 792	Mike Greenwell	.10	.04	.01

1991 Topps Wax Box Cards

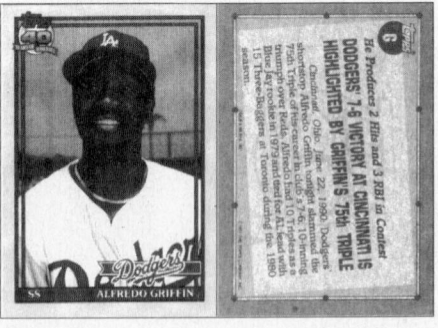

Topps again in 1991 issued cards on the bottom of their wax pack boxes. There are four different boxes, each with four cards and a checklist on the side. These standard-size cards (2 1/2" by 3 1/2") have yellow borders rather than the white borders of the regular issue cards, and they have different photos of the players. The backs are printed in pink and blue on gray cardboard stock and feature outstanding achievements of the players. The cards are numbered by letter on the back. The cards have the typical Topps 1991 design on the front of the card. The set was ordered in alphabetical order, but is "lettered" rather than numbered.

	MINT	EXC	G-VG
COMPLETE SET (16)	3.50	1.50	.35
COMMON PLAYER (A-P)	.10	.04	.01
☐ A Bert Blyleven	.15	.06	.01
☐ B George Brett	.30	.12	.03
☐ C Brett Butler	.15	.06	.01
☐ D Andre Dawson	.25	.10	.02
☐ E Dwight Evans	.15	.06	.01
☐ F Carlton Fisk	.30	.12	.03
☐ G Alfredo Griffin	.10	.04	.01
☐ H Rickey Henderson	.50	.20	.05
☐ I Willie McGee	.20	.08	.02
☐ J Dale Murphy	.30	.12	.03
☐ K Eddie Murray	.30	.12	.03
☐ L Dave Parker	.20	.08	.02
☐ M Jeff Reardon	.20	.08	.02
☐ N Nolan Ryan	.60	.25	.06
☐ O Juan Samuel	.10	.04	.01
☐ P Robin Yount	.30	.12	.03

1991 Topps '90 Debut

The 1991 Topps Major League Debut Set contains 171 cards measuring the standard size (2 1/2" by 3 1/2"). Though the checklist card is arranged chronologically in order of first major league appearance in 1990, the player cards are arranged alphabetically by the player's last name. The front design features mostly posed color player photos, with two different color stripes on the top and sides of the picture. The card face is white, and the player's name is given in the color stripe below the picture. The horizontally oriented backs have player information and statistics in blue lettering on a pink and white background. The cards are numbered on the back.

	MINT	EXC	G-VG
COMPLETE SET (171)	18.00	7.50	2.50
COMMON PLAYER (1-171)	.05	.02	.00
☐ 1 Paul Abbott	.10	.04	.01
☐ 2 Steve Adkins	.05	.02	.00
☐ 3 Scott Aldred	.10	.04	.01
☐ 4 Gerald Alexander	.10	.04	.01
☐ 5 Moises Alou	.10	.04	.01
☐ 6 Steve Avery	.60	.25	.06
☐ 7 Oscar Azocar	.10	.04	.01
☐ 8 Carlos Baerga	.25	.10	.02
☐ 9 Kevin Baez	.10	.04	.01
☐ 10 Jeff Baldwin	.10	.04	.01
☐ 11 Brian Barnes	.15	.06	.01
☐ 12 Kevin Bearse	.10	.04	.01
☐ 13 Kevin Belcher	.15	.06	.01
☐ 14 Mike Bell	.15	.06	.01
☐ 15 Sean Berry	.10	.04	.01
☐ 16 Joe Bitker	.10	.04	.01
☐ 17 Willie Blair	.05	.02	.00
☐ 18 Brian Bohanon	.10	.04	.01
☐ 19 Mike Bordick	.05	.02	.00
☐ 20 Shawn Boskie	.10	.04	.01
☐ 21 Rod Brewer	.10	.04	.01
☐ 22 Kevin Brown	.10	.04	.01
☐ 23 Dave Burba	.10	.04	.01
☐ 24 Jim Campbell	.05	.02	.00
☐ 25 Ozzie Canseco	.10	.04	.01

	MINT	EXC	G-VG
☐ 26 Chuck Carr	.10	.04	.01
☐ 27 Larry Casian	.10	.04	.01
☐ 28 Andujar Cedeno	.35	.15	.03
☐ 29 Wes Chamberlain	.60	.25	.06
☐ 30 Scott Chiamparino	.10	.04	.01
☐ 31 Steve Chitren	.10	.04	.01
☐ 32 Pete Coachman	.10	.04	.01
☐ 33 Alex Cole	.25	.10	.02
☐ 34 Jeff Conine	.20	.08	.02
☐ 35 Scott Cooper	.35	.15	.03
☐ 36 Milt Cuyler	.30	.12	.03
☐ 37 Steve Decker	.30	.12	.03
☐ 38 Rich DeLucia	.10	.04	.01
☐ 39 Delino DeShields	.30	.12	.03
☐ 40 Mark Dewey	.10	.04	.01
☐ 41 Carlos Diaz	.10	.04	.01
☐ 42 Lance Dickson	.15	.06	.01
☐ 43 Narciso Elvira	.10	.04	.01
☐ 44 Luis Encarnacion	.05	.02	.00
☐ 45 Scott Erickson	.75	.30	.07
☐ 46 Paul Faries	.10	.04	.01
☐ 47 Howard Farmer	.10	.04	.01
☐ 48 Alex Fernandez	.30	.12	.03
☐ 49 Travis Fryman	.75	.30	.07
☐ 50 Rich Garces	.10	.04	.01
☐ 51 Carlos Garcia	.10	.04	.01
☐ 52 Mike Gardiner	.10	.04	.01
☐ 53 Bernard Gilkey	.25	.10	.02
☐ 54 Tom Gilles	.10	.04	.01
☐ 55 Jerry Goff	.10	.04	.01
☐ 56 Leo Gomez	.35	.15	.03
☐ 57 Luis Gonzalez	.40	.16	.04
☐ 58 Joe Grahe	.10	.04	.01
☐ 59 Craig Grebeck	.10	.04	.01
☐ 60 Kip Gross	.05	.02	.00
☐ 61 Eric Gunderson	.05	.02	.00
☐ 62 Chris Hammond	.10	.04	.01
☐ 63 Dave Hansen	.10	.04	.01
☐ 64 Reggie Harris	.10	.04	.01
☐ 65 Bill Haselman	.10	.04	.01
☐ 66 Randy Hennis	.10	.04	.01
☐ 67 Carlos Hernandez	.10	.04	.01
☐ 68 Howard Hilton	.05	.02	.00
☐ 69 Dave Hollins	.20	.08	.02
☐ 70 Darren Holmes	.10	.04	.01
☐ 71 John Hoover	.10	.04	.01
☐ 72 Steve Howard	.10	.04	.01
☐ 73 Thomas Howard	.10	.04	.01
☐ 74 Todd Hundley	.20	.08	.02
☐ 75 Daryl Irvine	.10	.04	.01
☐ 76 Chris Jelic	.15	.06	.01
☐ 77 Dana Kiecker	.05	.02	.00
☐ 78 Brent Knackert	.15	.06	.01
☐ 79 Jimmy Kremers	.10	.04	.01
☐ 80 Jerry Kutzler	.10	.04	.01
☐ 81 Ray Lankford	.60	.25	.06
☐ 82 Tim Layana	.10	.04	.01
☐ 83 Terry Lee	.10	.04	.01
☐ 84 Mark Leiter	.10	.04	.01
☐ 85 Scott Leius	.15	.06	.01
☐ 86 Mark Leonard	.10	.04	.01
☐ 87 Darren Lewis	.25	.10	.02
☐ 88 Scott Lewis	.10	.04	.01
☐ 89 Jim Leyritz	.10	.04	.01
☐ 90 Dave Liddell	.10	.04	.01
☐ 91 Luis Lopez	.35	.15	.03
☐ 92 Kevin Maas	.50	.20	.05
☐ 93 Bob MacDonald	.10	.04	.01
☐ 94 Carlos Maldonado	.10	.04	.01
☐ 95 Chuck Malone	.10	.04	.01
☐ 96 Ramon Manon	.10	.04	.01
☐ 97 Jeff Manto	.10	.04	.01
☐ 98 Paul Marak	.10	.04	.01
☐ 99 Tino Martinez	.40	.16	.04
☐ 100 Derrick May	.25	.10	.02
☐ 101 Brent Mayne	.15	.06	.01
☐ 102 Paul McClellan	.15	.06	.01
☐ 103 Rodney McCray	.10	.04	.01
☐ 104 Tim McIntosh	.10	.04	.01
☐ 105 Brian McRae	.40	.16	.04
☐ 106 Jose Melendez	.10	.04	.01
☐ 107 Orlando Merced	.40	.16	.04
☐ 108 Alan Mills	.10	.04	.01
☐ 109 Gino Minutelli	.20	.08	.02
☐ 110 Mickey Morandini	.20	.08	.02
☐ 111 Pedro Munoz	.30	.12	.03
☐ 112 Chris Nabholz	.20	.08	.02
☐ 113 Tim Naehring	.20	.08	.02
☐ 114 Charles Nagy	.20	.08	.02
☐ 115 Jim Neidlinger	.15	.06	.01
☐ 116 Rafael Novoa	.10	.04	.01
☐ 117 Jose Offerman	.25	.10	.02
☐ 118 Omar Olivares	.20	.08	.02
☐ 119 Javier Ortiz	.20	.08	.02
☐ 120 Al Osuna	.15	.06	.01

☐ 121	Rick Parker	.15	.06	.01
☐ 122	Dave Pavlas	.10	.04	.01
☐ 123	Geronimo Pena	.10	.04	.01
☐ 124	Mike Perez	.15	.06	.01
☐ 125	Phil Plantier	1.00	.40	.10
☐ 126	Jim Poole	.15	.06	.01
☐ 127	Tom Quinlan	.10	.04	.01
☐ 128	Scott Radinsky	.15	.06	.01
☐ 129	Darren Reed	.10	.04	.01
☐ 130	Karl Rhodes	.05	.02	.00
☐ 131	Jeff Richardson	.05	.02	.00
☐ 132	Rich Rodriguez	.05	.02	.00
☐ 133	Dave Rohde	.05	.02	.00
☐ 134	Mel Rojas	.10	.04	.01
☐ 135	Vic Rosario	.10	.04	.01
☐ 136	Rich Rowland	.10	.04	.01
☐ 137	Scott Ruskin	.10	.04	.01
☐ 138	Bill Sampen	.10	.04	.01
☐ 139	Andres Santana	.25	.10	.02
☐ 140	David Segui	.15	.06	.01
☐ 141	Jeff Shaw	.10	.04	.01
☐ 142	Tim Sherrill	.10	.04	.01
☐ 143	Terry Shumpert	.10	.04	.01
☐ 144	Mike Simms	.10	.04	.01
☐ 145	Daryl Smith	.10	.04	.01
☐ 146	Luis Sojo	.10	.04	.01
☐ 147	Steve Springer	.10	.04	.01
☐ 148	Ray Stephens	.10	.04	.01
☐ 149	Lee Stevens	.25	.10	.02
☐ 150	Mel Stottlemyre Jr.	.05	.02	.00
☐ 151	Glenn Sutko	.10	.04	.01
☐ 152	Anthony Telford	.10	.04	.01
☐ 153	Frank Thomas	2.00	.80	.20
☐ 154	Randy Tomlin	.25	.10	.02
☐ 155	Brian Traxler	.10	.04	.01
☐ 156	Efrain Valdez	.10	.04	.01
☐ 157	Rafael Valdez	.10	.04	.01
☐ 158	Julio Valera	.10	.04	.01
☐ 159	Jim Vatcher	.10	.04	.01
☐ 160	Hector Villanueva	.15	.06	.01
☐ 161	Hector Wagner	.10	.04	.01
☐ 162	Dave Walsh	.10	.04	.01
☐ 163	Steve Wapnick	.10	.04	.01
☐ 164	Colby Ward	.10	.04	.01
☐ 165	Turner Ward	.15	.06	.01
☐ 166	Terry Wells	.10	.04	.01
☐ 167	Mark Whiten	.10	.04	.01
☐ 168	Mike York	.10	.04	.01
☐ 169	Cliff Young	.10	.04	.01
☐ 170	Checklist Card	.05	.02	.00
☐ 171	Checklist Card	.05	.02	.00

		MINT	EXC	G-VG
COMPLETE SET (36)		8.00	3.50	.80
COMMON PLAYER (1-36)		.05	.02	.00
☐ 1	Nolan Ryan	.75	.30	.07
☐ 2	Paul Molitor	.15	.06	.01
☐ 3	Tim Raines	.15	.06	.01
☐ 4	Frank Viola	.10	.04	.01
☐ 5	Sandy Alomar Jr.	.20	.08	.02
☐ 6	Ryne Sandberg	.50	.20	.05
☐ 7	Don Mattingly	.50	.20	.05
☐ 8	Pedro Guerrero	.10	.04	.01
☐ 9	Jose Rijo	.05	.02	.00
☐ 10	Jose Canseco	.50	.20	.05
☐ 11	Dave Parker	.15	.06	.01
☐ 12	Doug Drabek	.10	.04	.01
☐ 13	Cal Ripken	.50	.20	.05
☐ 14	Dave Justice	.60	.25	.06
☐ 15	George Brett	.40	.16	.04
☐ 16	Eric Davis	.25	.10	.02
☐ 17	Mark Langston	.10	.04	.01
☐ 18	Rickey Henderson	.50	.20	.05
☐ 19	Barry Bonds	.35	.15	.03
☐ 20	Kevin Maas	.25	.10	.02
☐ 21	Len Dykstra	.10	.04	.01
☐ 22	Roger Clemens	.50	.20	.05
☐ 23	Robin Yount	.35	.15	.03
☐ 24	Mark Grace	.30	.12	.03
☐ 25	Bo Jackson	.60	.25	.06
☐ 26	Tony Gwynn	.40	.16	.04
☐ 27	Mark McGwire	.35	.15	.03
☐ 28	Dwight Gooden	.15	.06	.01
☐ 29	Wade Boggs	.40	.16	.04
☐ 30	Kevin Mitchell	.30	.12	.03
☐ 31	Cecil Fielder	.40	.16	.04
☐ 32	Bobby Thigpen	.10	.04	.01
☐ 33	Benito Santiago	.15	.06	.01
☐ 34	Kirby Puckett	.35	.15	.03
☐ 35	Will Clark	.50	.20	.05
☐ 36	Ken Griffey Jr.	.90	.40	.09

1991 Topps Cracker Jack Minis II

This 36-card set is the second of two different 36-card series produced by Topps for Cracker Jack, and the cards were inserted inside specially marked packages of Cracker Jack. The cards measure the standard-size (2 1/2" by 3 1/2") and feature 4 unperforated mini-cards each. The mini-cards have color player photos with different color borders. The horizontally oriented back are printed in orange and purple, and include biography, complete Major League batting record, and career highlights. Although each mini-card is numbered on the back, the numbering of the four cards on any standard-size card is not consecutive.

		MINT	EXC	G-VG
COMPLETE SET (36)		7.00	3.00	.70
COMMON PLAYER (1-36)		.05	.02	.00
☐ 1	Eddie Murray	.35	.15	.03
☐ 2	Carlton Fisk	.30	.12	.03
☐ 3	Eric Anthony	.20	.08	.02
☐ 4	Kelly Gruber	.10	.04	.01

1991 Topps Cracker Jack Minis I

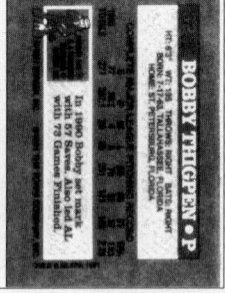

This 36-card set is the first of two 36-card series produced by Topps for Cracker Jack, and the cards were inserted inside specially marked packages of Cracker Jack. The cards measure the standard-size (2 1/2" by 3 1/2") and feature 4 unperforated mini-cards each. The mini-cards have color player photos with different color borders. The horizontally oriented back are printed in red, blue, and pink, and include biography, complete Major League batting record, and career highlights. Although each mini-card is numbered on the back, the numbering of the four cards on any standard-size card is not consecutive.

		MINT	EXC	G-VG
☐ 5	Von Hayes	.05	.02	.00
☐ 6	Ben McDonald	.25	.10	.02
☐ 7	Andre Dawson	.30	.12	.03
☐ 8	Ellis Burks	.30	.12	.03
☐ 9	Matt Williams	.30	.12	.03
☐ 10	Dave Stewart	.10	.04	.01
☐ 11	Barry Larkin	.15	.06	.01
☐ 12	Chuck Finley	.10	.04	.01
☐ 13	Shane Andrews	.15	.06	.01
☐ 14	Bret Saberhagen	.15	.06	.01
☐ 15	Bobby Bonilla	.30	.12	.03
☐ 16	Roberto Kelly	.25	.10	.02
☐ 17	Orel Hershiser	.15	.06	.01
☐ 18	Ruben Sierra	.45	.18	.04
☐ 19	Ron Gant	.50	.20	.05
☐ 20	Frank Thomas	1.25	.50	.12
☐ 21	Tim Wallach	.10	.04	.01
☐ 22	Gregg Olson	.15	.06	.01
☐ 23	Shawon Dunston	.10	.04	.01
☐ 24	Kent Hrbek	.10	.04	.01
☐ 25	Ramon Martinez	.40	.16	.04
☐ 26	Alan Trammell	.20	.08	.02
☐ 27	Ozzie Smith	.20	.08	.02
☐ 28	Bob Welch	.10	.04	.01
☐ 29	Chris Sabo	.15	.06	.01
☐ 30	Steve Sax	.10	.04	.01
☐ 31	Bip Roberts	.05	.02	.00
☐ 32	Dave Stieb	.10	.04	.01
☐ 33	Howard Johnson	.15	.06	.01
☐ 34	Mike Greenwell	.25	.10	.02
☐ 35	Delino DeShields	.25	.10	.02
☐ 36	Alex Fernandez	.20	.08	.02

1991 Topps Babe Ruth

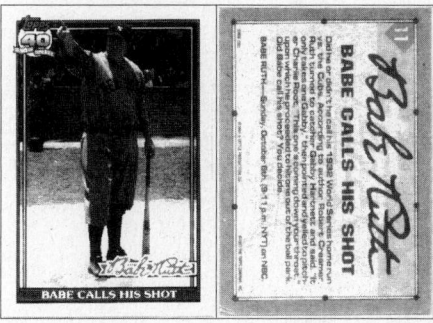

This 11-card set was produced by Topps to commemorate the NBC made-for-television movie about Ruth that aired Sunday, October 6, 1991. The standard-size (2 1/2" by 3 1/2") cards have various color shots from the movie on the fronts, with aqua and red borders on a white card face. The name "Babe Ruth" is written in cursive lettering in the lower right corner of each card, and a caption for each card appears below the picture in the red border. The horizontally oriented backs are printed in dark blue and pink on gray and feature an extended caption to the picture on the front. The cards are numbered on the back.

		MINT	EXC	G-VG
	COMPLETE SET (11)	20.00	8.50	2.75
	COMMON PLAYER (1-11)	1.50	.60	.15
☐ 1	Babe Ruth-Sunday October 6th NBC	1.50	.60	.15
☐ 2	Babe Ruth Stephen Lang as Babe Ruth	1.50	.60	.15
☐ 3	Babe Ruth Bruce Weitz as Miller Huggins	1.50	.60	.15
☐ 4	Babe Ruth Lisa Zane as Claire Ruth	1.50	.60	.15
☐ 5	Babe Ruth Donald Moffat as Jacob Ruppert	1.50	.60	.15
☐ 6	Babe Ruth Neil McDonough as Lou Gehrig	1.50	.60	.15
☐ 7	Babe Ruth Pete Rose as Ty Cobb	7.50	3.25	.75
☐ 8	Babe Ruth Rod Carew Baseball Consultant	5.00	2.25	.50
☐ 9	Babe Ruth Ruth and Mgr. Huggins	2.00	.80	.20
☐ 10	Babe Ruth Ruth in Action	2.00	.80	.20
☐ 11	Babe Ruth Babe Calls His Shot	2.00	.80	.20

1991 Topps Archive 1953

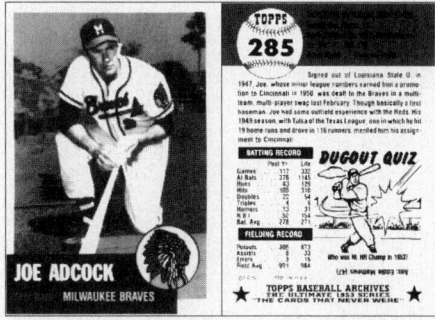

The 1953 Topps Archive set is a reprint of the original 274-card 1953 Topps set. The only card missing from the reprint set is that of Billy Loes (174), who did not give Topps permission to reprint his card. Moreover, the set has been extended by 57 cards, with cards honoring Mrs. Eleanor Engle, Hoyt Wilhelm (who had already been included in the set as card number 151), 1953 HOF inductees Dizzy Dean and Al Simmons, and "prospect" Hank Aaron. Although the original cards measured 2 5/8" by 3 3/4", the reprint cards measure the modern standard, 2 1/2" by 3 1/2". Production quantities were supposedly limited to not more than 18,000 cases.

		MINT	EXC	G-VG
	COMPLETE SET (330)	80.00	36.00	12.00
	COMMON PLAYER (1-220)	.12	.05	.01
	COMMON PLAYER (221-280)	.15	.06	.01
	COMMON PLAYER (281-337)	.20	.08	.02
☐ 1	Jackie Robinson	4.00	1.75	.40
☐ 2	Luke Easter	.12	.05	.01
☐ 3	George Crowe	.12	.05	.01
☐ 4	Ben Wade	.12	.05	.01
☐ 5	Joe Dobson	.12	.05	.01
☐ 6	Sam Jones	.12	.05	.01
☐ 7	Bob Borkowski	.12	.05	.01
☐ 8	Clem Koshorek	.12	.05	.01
☐ 9	Joe Collins	.15	.06	.01
☐ 10	Smoky Burgess	.15	.06	.01
☐ 11	Sal Yvars	.12	.05	.01
☐ 12	Howie Judson	.12	.05	.01
☐ 13	Conrado Marrero	.12	.05	.01
☐ 14	Clem Labine	.15	.06	.01
☐ 15	Bobo Newsom	.15	.06	.01
☐ 16	Peanuts Lowrey	.12	.05	.01
☐ 17	Billy Hitchcock	.12	.05	.01
☐ 18	Ted Lepcio	.12	.05	.01
☐ 19	Mel Parnell	.15	.06	.01
☐ 20	Hank Thompson	.15	.06	.01
☐ 21	Billy Johnson	.12	.05	.01
☐ 22	Howie Fox	.12	.05	.01
☐ 23	Toby Atwell	.12	.05	.01
☐ 24	Ferris Fain	.15	.06	.01
☐ 25	Ray Boone	.12	.05	.01
☐ 26	Dale Mitchell	.15	.06	.01

	#	Player	Price 1	Price 2	Price 3
☐	27	Roy Campanella	2.00	.80	.20
☐	28	Eddie Pellagrini	.12	.05	.01
☐	29	Hal Jeffcoat	.12	.05	.01
☐	30	Willard Nixon	.12	.05	.01
☐	31	Ewell Blackwell	.20	.08	.02
☐	32	Clyde Vollmer	.12	.05	.01
☐	33	Bob Kennedy	.12	.05	.01
☐	34	George Shuba	.15	.06	.01
☐	35	Irv Noren	.12	.05	.01
☐	36	Johnny Groth	.12	.05	.01
☐	37	Eddie Mathews	1.25	.50	.12
☐	38	Jim Hearn	.12	.05	.01
☐	39	Eddie Miksis	.12	.05	.01
☐	40	John Lipon	.12	.05	.01
☐	41	Enos Slaughter	.75	.30	.07
☐	42	Gus Zernial	.12	.05	.01
☐	43	Gil McDougald	.35	.15	.03
☐	44	Ellis Kinder	.12	.05	.01
☐	45	Grady Hatton	.12	.05	.01
☐	46	Johnny Klippstein	.12	.05	.01
☐	47	Bubba Church	.12	.05	.01
☐	48	Bob Del Greco	.12	.05	.01
☐	49	Faye Throneberry	.12	.05	.01
☐	50	Chuck Dressen MG	.15	.06	.01
☐	51	Frank Campos	.12	.05	.01
☐	52	Ted Gray	.12	.05	.01
☐	53	Sherm Lollar	.15	.06	.01
☐	54	Bob Feller	1.00	.40	.10
☐	55	Maurice McDermott	.12	.05	.01
☐	56	Jerry Staley	.12	.05	.01
☐	57	Carl Scheib	.12	.05	.01
☐	58	George Metkovich	.12	.05	.01
☐	59	Karl Drews	.12	.05	.01
☐	60	Cloyd Boyer	.12	.05	.01
☐	61	Early Wynn	.75	.30	.07
☐	62	Monte Irvin	.50	.20	.05
☐	63	Gus Niarhos	.12	.05	.01
☐	64	Dave Philley	.12	.05	.01
☐	65	Earl Harrist	.12	.05	.01
☐	66	Minnie Minoso	.40	.16	.04
☐	67	Roy Sievers	.15	.06	.01
☐	68	Del Rice	.12	.05	.01
☐	69	Dick Brodowski	.12	.05	.01
☐	70	Ed Yuhas	.12	.05	.01
☐	71	Tony Bartirome	.12	.05	.01
☐	72	Fred Hutchinson	.15	.06	.01
☐	73	Eddie Robinson	.12	.05	.01
☐	74	Joe Rossi	.12	.05	.01
☐	75	Mike Garcia	.15	.06	.01
☐	76	Pee Wee Reese	1.25	.50	.12
☐	77	Johnny Mize	.60	.25	.06
☐	78	Red Schoendienst	.60	.25	.06
☐	79	Johnny Wyrostek	.12	.05	.01
☐	80	Jim Hegan	.15	.06	.01
☐	81	Joe Black	.25	.10	.02
☐	82	Mickey Mantle	25.00	11.00	3.50
☐	83	Howie Pollet	.12	.05	.01
☐	84	Bob Hooper	.12	.05	.01
☐	85	Bobby Morgan	.12	.05	.01
☐	86	Billy Martin	1.25	.50	.12
☐	87	Ed Lopat	.40	.16	.04
☐	88	Willie Jones	.12	.05	.01
☐	89	Chuck Stobbs	.12	.05	.01
☐	90	Hank Edwards	.12	.05	.01
☐	91	Ebba St.Claire	.12	.05	.01
☐	92	Paul Minner	.12	.05	.01
☐	93	Hal Rice	.12	.05	.01
☐	94	Bill Kennedy	.12	.05	.01
☐	95	Willard Marshall	.12	.05	.01
☐	96	Virgil Trucks	.12	.05	.01
☐	97	Don Kolloway	.12	.05	.01
☐	98	Cal Abrams	.12	.05	.01
☐	99	Dave Madison	.12	.05	.01
☐	100	Bill Miller	.12	.05	.01
☐	101	Ted Wilks	.12	.05	.01
☐	102	Connie Ryan	.12	.05	.01
☐	103	Joe Astroth	.12	.05	.01
☐	104	Yogi Berra	2.25	.90	.22
☐	105	Joe Nuxhall	.15	.06	.01
☐	106	Johnny Antonelli	.15	.06	.01
☐	107	Danny O'Connell	.12	.05	.01
☐	108	Bob Porterfield	.12	.05	.01
☐	109	Alvin Dark	.20	.08	.02
☐	110	Herman Wehmeier	.12	.05	.01
☐	111	Hank Sauer	.15	.06	.01
☐	112	Ned Garver	.12	.05	.01
☐	113	Jerry Priddy	.12	.05	.01
☐	114	Phil Rizzuto	1.00	.40	.10
☐	115	George Spencer	.12	.05	.01
☐	116	Frank Smith	.12	.05	.01
☐	117	Sid Gordon	.12	.05	.01
☐	118	Gus Bell	.15	.06	.01
☐	119	Johnny Sain	.40	.16	.04
☐	120	Davey Williams	.15	.06	.01
☐	121	Walt Dropo	.15	.06	.01
☐	122	Elmer Valo	.12	.05	.01
☐	123	Tommy Byrne	.12	.05	.01
☐	124	Sibby Sisti	.12	.05	.01
☐	125	Dick Williams	.15	.06	.01
☐	126	Bill Connelly	.12	.05	.01
☐	127	Clint Courtney	.12	.05	.01
☐	128	Wilmer Mizell	.12	.05	.01
☐	129	Keith Thomas	.12	.05	.01
☐	130	Turk Lown	.12	.05	.01
☐	131	Harry Byrd	.12	.05	.01
☐	132	Tom Morgan	.12	.05	.01
☐	133	Gil Coan	.12	.05	.01
☐	134	Rube Walker	.15	.06	.01
☐	135	Al Rosen	.35	.15	.03
☐	136	Ken Heintzelman	.12	.05	.01
☐	137	John Rutherford	.12	.05	.01
☐	138	George Kell	.50	.20	.05
☐	139	Sammy White	.12	.05	.01
☐	140	Tommy Glaviano	.12	.05	.01
☐	141	Allie Reynolds	.35	.15	.03
☐	142	Vic Wertz	.15	.06	.01
☐	143	Billy Pierce	.20	.08	.02
☐	144	Bob Schultz	.12	.05	.01
☐	145	Harry Dorish	.12	.05	.01
☐	146	Granny Hamner	.12	.05	.01
☐	147	Warren Spahn	1.25	.50	.12
☐	148	Mickey Grasso	.12	.05	.01
☐	149	Dom DiMaggio	.25	.10	.02
☐	150	Harry Simpson	.12	.05	.01
☐	151	Hoyt Wilhelm	.75	.30	.07
☐	152	Bob Adams	.12	.05	.01
☐	153	Andy Seminick	.12	.05	.01
☐	154	Dick Groat	.30	.12	.03
☐	155	Dutch Leonard	.15	.06	.01
☐	156	Jim Rivera	.12	.05	.01
☐	157	Bob Addis	.12	.05	.01
☐	158	Johnny Logan	.15	.06	.01
☐	159	Wayne Terwilliger	.12	.05	.01
☐	160	Bob Young	.12	.05	.01
☐	161	Vern Bickford	.12	.05	.01
☐	162	Ted Kluszewski	.40	.16	.04
☐	163	Fred Hatfield	.12	.05	.01
☐	164	Frank Shea	.12	.05	.01
☐	165	Billy Hoeft	.12	.05	.01
☐	166	Billy Hunter	.12	.05	.01
☐	167	Art Schult	.12	.05	.01
☐	168	Willard Schmidt	.12	.05	.01
☐	169	Dizzy Trout	.12	.05	.01
☐	170	Bill Werle	.12	.05	.01
☐	171	Bill Glynn	.12	.05	.01
☐	172	Rip Repulski	.12	.05	.01
☐	173	Preston Ward	.12	.05	.01
☐	174	Billy Loes	.00	.00	.00
		(Not printed)			
☐	175	Ron Kline	.12	.05	.01
☐	176	Don Hoak	.20	.08	.02
☐	177	Jim Dyck	.12	.05	.01
☐	178	Jim Waugh	.12	.05	.01
☐	179	Gene Hermanski	.12	.05	.01
☐	180	Virgil Stallcup	.12	.05	.01
☐	181	Al Zarilla	.12	.05	.01
☐	182	Bobby Hofman	.12	.05	.01
☐	183	Stu Miller	.15	.06	.01
☐	184	Hal Brown	.12	.05	.01
☐	185	Jim Pendleton	.12	.05	.01
☐	186	Charlie Bishop	.12	.05	.01
☐	187	Jim Fridley	.12	.05	.01
☐	188	Andy Carey	.20	.08	.02
☐	189	Ray Jablonski	.12	.05	.01
☐	190	Dixie Walker	.12	.05	.01
☐	191	Ralph Kiner	.60	.25	.06
☐	192	Wally Westlake	.12	.05	.01
☐	193	Mike Clark	.12	.05	.01
☐	194	Eddie Kazak	.12	.05	.01
☐	195	Ed McGhee	.12	.05	.01
☐	196	Bob Keegan	.12	.05	.01
☐	197	Del Crandall	.15	.06	.01
☐	198	Forrest Main	.12	.05	.01
☐	199	Marion Fricano	.12	.05	.01
☐	200	Gordon Goldsberry	.12	.05	.01
☐	201	Paul LaPalme	.12	.05	.01
☐	202	Carl Sawatski	.12	.05	.01
☐	203	Cliff Fannin	.12	.05	.01
☐	204	Dick Bokelman	.12	.05	.01
☐	205	Vern Benson	.12	.05	.01
☐	206	Ed Bailey	.20	.08	.02
☐	207	Whitey Ford	1.50	.60	.15
☐	208	Jim Wilson	.12	.05	.01
☐	209	Jim Greengrass	.12	.05	.01
☐	210	Bob Cerv	.15	.06	.01
☐	211	J.W. Porter	.12	.05	.01
☐	212	Jack Dittmer	.12	.05	.01
☐	213	Ray Scarborough	.12	.05	.01
☐	214	Bill Bruton	.15	.06	.01
☐	215	Gene Conley	.15	.06	.01

			MINT	EXC	G-VG
☐	216	Jim Hughes	.12	.05	.01
☐	217	Murray Wall	.12	.05	.01
☐	218	Les Fusselman	.12	.05	.01
☐	219	Pete Runnels UER	.15	.06	.01
		(photo actually			
		Don Johnson)			
☐	220	Satchel Paige UER	4.00	1.75	.40
		(misspelled Satchell			
		on card front)			
☐	221	Bob Milliken	.15	.06	.01
☐	222	Vic Janowicz	.20	.08	.02
☐	223	Johnny O'Brien	.15	.06	.01
☐	224	Lou Sleater	.15	.06	.01
☐	225	Bobby Shantz	.25	.10	.02
☐	226	Ed Erautt	.15	.06	.01
☐	227	Morrie Martin	.15	.06	.01
☐	228	Hal Newhouser	.35	.15	.03
☐	229	Rocky Krsnich	.15	.06	.01
☐	230	Johnny Lindell	.15	.06	.01
☐	231	Solly Hemus	.15	.06	.01
☐	232	Dick Kokos	.15	.06	.01
☐	233	Al Aber	.15	.06	.01
☐	234	Ray Murray	.15	.06	.01
☐	235	John Hetki	.15	.06	.01
☐	236	Harry Perkowski	.15	.06	.01
☐	237	Bud Podbielan	.15	.06	.01
☐	238	Cal Hogue	.15	.06	.01
☐	239	Jim Delsing	.15	.06	.01
☐	240	Fred Marsh	.15	.06	.01
☐	241	Al Sima	.15	.06	.01
☐	242	Charlie Silvera	.20	.08	.02
☐	243	Carlos Bernier	.15	.06	.01
☐	244	Willie Mays	12.50	5.50	1.65
☐	245	Bill Norman	.15	.06	.01
☐	246	Roy Face	.35	.15	.03
☐	247	Mike Sandlock	.15	.06	.01
☐	248	Gene Stephens	.15	.06	.01
☐	249	Eddie O'Brien	.15	.06	.01
☐	250	Bob Wilson	.15	.06	.01
☐	251	Sid Hudson	.15	.06	.01
☐	252	Hank Foiles	.15	.06	.01
☐	253	Does not exist	.00	.00	.00
☐	254	Preacher Roe	.35	.15	.03
☐	255	Dixie Howell	.15	.06	.01
☐	256	Les Peden	.15	.06	.01
☐	257	Bob Boyd	.15	.06	.01
☐	258	Jim Gilliam	.50	.20	.05
☐	259	Roy McMillan	.20	.08	.02
☐	260	Sam Calderone	.15	.06	.01
☐	261	Does not exist	.00	.00	.00
☐	262	Bob Oldis	.15	.06	.01
☐	263	Johnny Podres	.50	.20	.05
☐	264	Gene Woodling	.30	.12	.03
☐	265	Jackie Jensen	.40	.16	.04
☐	266	Bob Cain	.15	.06	.01
☐	267	Does not exist	.00	.00	.00
☐	268	Does not exist	.00	.00	.00
☐	269	Duane Pillette	.15	.06	.01
☐	270	Vern Stephens	.20	.08	.02
☐	271	Does not exist	.00	.00	.00
☐	272	Bill Antonello	.15	.06	.01
☐	273	Harvey Haddix	.30	.12	.03
☐	274	John Riddle	.15	.06	.01
☐	275	Does not exist	.00	.00	.00
☐	276	Ken Raffensberger	.15	.06	.01
☐	277	Don Lund	.15	.06	.01
☐	278	Willie Miranda	.15	.06	.01
☐	279	Joe Coleman	.15	.06	.01
☐	280	Milt Bolling	.50	.20	.05
☐	281	Jimmie Dykes MG	.25	.10	.02
☐	282	Ralph Houk	.25	.10	.02
☐	283	Frank Thomas	.25	.10	.02
☐	284	Bob Lemon	.50	.20	.05
☐	285	Joe Adcock	.30	.12	.03
☐	286	Jimmy Piersall	.35	.15	.03
☐	287	Mickey Vernon	.30	.12	.03
☐	288	Robin Roberts	.75	.30	.07
☐	289	Rogers Hornsby MG	.75	.30	.07
☐	290	Hank Bauer	.30	.12	.03
☐	291	Hoot Evers	.20	.08	.02
☐	292	Whitey Lockman	.20	.08	.02
☐	293	Ralph Branca	.30	.12	.03
☐	294	Wally Post	.20	.08	.02
☐	295	Phil Cavarretta MG	.25	.10	.02
☐	296	Gil Hodges	.50	.20	.05
☐	297	Roy Smalley	.20	.08	.02
☐	298	Bob Friend	.25	.10	.02
☐	299	Dusty Rhodes	.25	.10	.02
☐	300	Eddie Stanky	.25	.10	.02
☐	301	Harvey Kuenn	.50	.20	.05
☐	302	Marty Marion	.35	.15	.03
☐	303	Sal Maglie	.35	.15	.03
☐	304	Lou Boudreau MG	.50	.20	.05
☐	305	Carl Furillo	.35	.15	.03
☐	306	Bobo Holloman	.25	.10	.02
☐	307	Steve O'Neill MG	.20	.08	.02
☐	308	Carl Erskine	.35	.15	.03
☐	309	Leo Durocher MG	.50	.20	.05
☐	310	Lew Burdette	.35	.15	.03
☐	311	Richie Ashburn	.60	.25	.06
☐	312	Hoyt Wilhelm	1.00	.40	.10
☐	313	Bucky Harris MG	.35	.15	.03
☐	314	Joe Garagiola	.50	.20	.05
☐	315	Johnny Pesky	.25	.10	.02
☐	316	Fred Haney MG	.20	.08	.02
☐	317	Hank Aaron	9.00	4.00	.90
☐	318	Curt Simmons	.25	.10	.02
☐	319	Ted Williams	7.50	3.25	.75
☐	320	Don Newcombe	.40	.16	.04
☐	321	Charlie Grimm MG	.25	.10	.02
☐	322	Paul Richards MG	.20	.08	.02
☐	323	Wes Westrum	.20	.08	.02
☐	324	Vern Law	.30	.12	.03
☐	325	Casey Stengel MG	.60	.25	.06
☐	326	Dizzy Dean and	.50	.20	.05
		Al Simmons			
		(1953 HOF Inductees)			
☐	327	Duke Snider	2.25	.90	.22
☐	328	Bill Rigney	.20	.08	.02
☐	329	Al Lopez MG	.35	.15	.03
☐	330	Bobby Thomson	.35	.15	.03
☐	331	Nellie Fox	.45	.18	.04
☐	332	Eleanor Engle	1.25	.50	.12
☐	333	Larry Doby	.30	.12	.03
☐	334	Billy Goodman	.25	.10	.02
☐	335	Checklist 1-140	.20	.08	.02
☐	336	Checklist 141-280	.20	.08	.02
☐	337	Checklist 281-337	.20	.08	.02

1991 Topps Traded

The 1991 Topps Traded set contains 132 cards measuring the standard size (2 1/2 by 3 1/2"). The set includes a Team U.S.A. subset, featuring 25 of America's top collegiate players; these players are indicated in the checklist below by USA. The cards were sold in wax packs as well as factory sets. The cards in the wax packs (gray backs) and collated factory sets (white backs) are from different card stock. The fronts have color action player photos, with two different color borders on a white card face. The player's position and name are given in the thicker border below the picture. In blue print on a pink and gray background, the horizontally oriented backs have biographical information and statistics. The cards are numbered on the back in the upper left corner; the set numbering corresponds to alphabetical order. The key rookie cards in this set are Jeff Bagwell and Ivan Rodriguez.

			MINT	EXC	G-VG
		COMPLETE SET (132)	11.00	5.00	1.35
		COMMON PLAYER (1T-132T)	.05	.02	.00
☐	1T	Juan Agosto	.05	.02	.00
☐	2T	Roberto Alomar	.12	.05	.01
☐	3T	Wally Backman	.05	.02	.00
☐	4T	Jeff Bagwell	3.00	1.25	.30
☐	5T	Skeeter Barnes	.08	.03	.01
☐	6T	Steve Bedrosian	.05	.02	.00

☐ 7T Derek Bell	.35	.15	.03
☐ 8T George Bell	.10	.04	.01
☐ 9T Rafael Belliard	.05	.02	.00
☐ 10T Dante Bichette	.05	.02	.00
☐ 11T Bud Black	.05	.02	.00
☐ 12T Mike Boddicker	.08	.03	.01
☐ 13T Sid Bream	.05	.02	.00
☐ 14T Hubie Brooks	.08	.03	.01
☐ 15T Brett Butler	.08	.03	.01
☐ 16T Ivan Calderon	.08	.03	.01
☐ 17T John Candelaria	.05	.02	.00
☐ 18T Tom Candiotti	.08	.03	.01
☐ 19T Gary Carter	.08	.03	.01
☐ 20T Joe Carter	.10	.04	.01
☐ 21T Rick Cerone	.05	.02	.00
☐ 22T Jack Clark	.08	.03	.01
☐ 23T Vince Coleman	.08	.03	.01
☐ 24T Scott Coolbaugh	.05	.02	.00
☐ 25T Danny Cox	.05	.02	.00
☐ 26T Danny Darwin	.05	.02	.00
☐ 27T Chili Davis	.08	.03	.01
☐ 28T Glenn Davis	.10	.04	.01
☐ 29T Steve Decker	.25	.10	.02
☐ 30T Rob Deer	.08	.03	.01
☐ 31T Rich DeLucia	.12	.05	.01
☐ 32T John Dettmer USA	.12	.05	.01
☐ 33T Brian Downing	.05	.02	.00
☐ 34T Darren Dreifort USA	.12	.05	.01
☐ 35T Kirk Dressendorfer	.20	.08	.02
☐ 36T Jim Essian MG	.05	.02	.00
☐ 37T Dwight Evans	.08	.03	.01
☐ 38T Steve Farr	.05	.02	.00
☐ 39T Jeff Fassero	.12	.05	.01
☐ 40T Junior Felix	.08	.03	.01
☐ 41T Tony Fernandez	.08	.03	.01
☐ 42T Steve Finley	.08	.03	.01
☐ 43T Jim Fregosi MG	.05	.02	.00
☐ 44T Gary Gaetti	.08	.03	.01
☐ 45T Jason Giamdi USA	.20	.08	.02
☐ 46T Kirk Gibson	.10	.04	.01
☐ 47T Leo Gomez	.25	.10	.02
☐ 48T Luis Gonzalez	.40	.16	.04
☐ 49T Jeff Granger USA	.30	.12	.03
☐ 50T Todd Greene USA	.15	.06	.01
☐ 51T Jeffrey Hammonds USA	.40	.16	.04
☐ 52T Mike Hargrove MG	.05	.02	.00
☐ 53T Pete Harnisch	.08	.03	.01
☐ 54T Rick Helling USA UER	.15	.06	.01
(Misspelled Hellings on card back)			
☐ 55T Glenallen Hill	.08	.03	.01
☐ 56T Charlie Hough	.05	.02	.00
☐ 57T Pete Incaviglia	.08	.03	.01
☐ 58T Bo Jackson	1.00	.40	.10
☐ 59T Danny Jackson	.08	.03	.01
☐ 60T Reggie Jefferson	.40	.16	.04
☐ 61T Charles Johnson USA	.40	.16	.04
☐ 62T Jeff Johnson	.20	.08	.02
☐ 63T Todd Johnson USA	.15	.06	.01
☐ 64T Barry Jones	.05	.02	.00
☐ 65T Chris Jones	.15	.06	.01
☐ 66T Scott Kamieniecki	.15	.06	.01
☐ 67T Pat Kelly	.30	.12	.03
☐ 68T Darryl Kile	.12	.05	.01
☐ 69T Chuck Knoblauch	.40	.16	.04
☐ 70T Bill Krueger	.05	.02	.00
☐ 71T Scott Leius	.12	.05	.01
☐ 72T Donnie Leshnock USA	.12	.05	.01
☐ 73T Mark Lewis	.20	.08	.02
☐ 74T Candy Maldonado	.08	.03	.01
☐ 75T Jason McDonald USA	.12	.05	.01
☐ 76T Willie McGee	.08	.03	.01
☐ 77T Fred McGriff	.10	.04	.01
☐ 78T Billy McMillon USA	.15	.06	.01
☐ 79T Hal McRae MG	.08	.03	.01
☐ 80T Dan Melendez USA	.20	.08	.02
☐ 81T Orlando Merced	.40	.16	.04
☐ 82T Jack Morris	.10	.04	.01
☐ 83T Phil Nevin USA	.20	.08	.02
☐ 84T Otis Nixon	.08	.03	.01
☐ 85T Johnny Oates MG	.05	.02	.00
☐ 86T Bob Ojeda	.05	.02	.00
☐ 87T Mike Pagliarulo	.05	.02	.00
☐ 88T Dean Palmer	.35	.15	.03
☐ 89T Dave Parker	.10	.04	.01
☐ 90T Terry Pendleton	.10	.04	.01
☐ 91T Tony Phillips (P) USA	.15	.06	.01
☐ 92T Doug Piatt	.15	.06	.01
☐ 93T Ron Polk USA CO	.05	.02	.00
☐ 94T Tim Raines	.10	.04	.01
☐ 95T Willie Randolph	.08	.03	.01
☐ 96T Dave Righetti	.08	.03	.01
☐ 97T Ernie Riles	.05	.02	.00
☐ 98T Chris Roberts USA	.40	.16	.04
☐ 99T Jeff D. Robinson	.05	.02	.00

☐ 100T Jeff M. Robinson	.05	.02	.00
☐ 101T Ivan Rodriguez	2.00	.80	.20
☐ 102T Steve Rodriguez USA	.15	.06	.01
☐ 103T Tom Runnells MG	.05	.02	.00
☐ 104T Scott Sanderson	.08	.03	.01
☐ 105T Bob Scanlan	.12	.05	.01
☐ 106T Pete Schourek	.12	.05	.01
☐ 107T Gary Scott	.25	.10	.02
☐ 108T Paul Shuey USA	.12	.05	.01
☐ 109T Doug Simons	.12	.05	.01
☐ 110T Dave Smith	.05	.02	.00
☐ 111T Cory Snyder	.08	.03	.01
☐ 112T Luis Sojo	.08	.03	.01
☐ 113T Kennic Steenstra USA	.15	.06	.01
☐ 114T Darryl Strawberry	.20	.08	.02
☐ 115T Franklin Stubbs	.05	.02	.00
☐ 116T Todd Taylor USA	.12	.05	.01
☐ 117T Wade Taylor	.17	.07	.01
☐ 118T Garry Templeton	.05	.02	.00
☐ 119T Mickey Tettleton	.08	.03	.01
☐ 120T Tim Teufel	.05	.02	.00
☐ 121T Mike Timlin	.12	.05	.01
☐ 122T David Tuttle USA	.15	.06	.01
☐ 123T Mo Vaughn	.60	.25	.06
☐ 124T Jeff Ware USA	.25	.10	.02
☐ 125T Devon White	.08	.03	.01
☐ 126T Mark Whiten	.20	.08	.02
☐ 127T Mitch Williams	.08	.03	.01
☐ 128T Craig Wilson USA	.15	.06	.01
☐ 129T Willie Wilson	.08	.03	.01
☐ 130T Chris Wimmer	.15	.06	.01
☐ 131T Ivan Zweig USA	.15	.06	.01
☐ 132T Checklist Card	.05	.01	.00

1991 Topps Stadium Club I

This 300-card standard size (2 1/2" by 3 1/2") set marked Topps first entry into the mass market with a premium quality set. The set features borderless full-color action photos on the front with the name of the player and the Topps Stadium club logo on the bottom of the card, while the back of the card has the basic biographical information as well as making use of the Fastball Bars system and an inset photo of the player's Topps rookie card. The key rookie cards in this series are Lance Dickson and Randy Tomlin.

	MINT	EXC	G-VG
COMPLETE SET (300)	165.00	75.00	15.00
COMMON PLAYER (1-300)	.20	.08	.02
☐ 1 Dave Stewart	1.50	.60	.15
(Wearing Tuxedo)			
☐ 2 Wally Joyner	.40	.16	.04
☐ 3 Shawon Dunston	.30	.12	.03
☐ 4 Darren Daulton	.20	.08	.02
☐ 5 Will Clark	3.25	1.35	.32
☐ 6 Sammy Sosa	.35	.15	.03
☐ 7 Dan Plesac	.20	.08	.02
☐ 8 Marquis Grissom	.75	.30	.07
☐ 9 Erik Hanson	.30	.12	.03
☐ 10 Geno Petralli	.20	.08	.02
☐ 11 Jose Rijo	.25	.10	.02
☐ 12 Carlos Quintana	.25	.10	.02
☐ 13 Junior Ortiz	.20	.08	.02
☐ 14 Bob Walk	.20	.08	.02

	#	Name			
☐	15	Mike Macfarlane	.20	.08	.02
☐	16	Eric Yelding	.20	.08	.02
☐	17	Bryn Smith	.20	.08	.02
☐	18	Bip Roberts	.25	.10	.02
☐	19	Mike Scioscia	.20	.08	.02
☐	20	Mark Williamson	.20	.08	.02
☐	21	Don Mattingly	1.50	.60	.15
☐	22	John Franco	.25	.10	.02
☐	23	Chet Lemon	.20	.08	.02
☐	24	Tom Henke	.25	.10	.02
☐	25	Jerry Browne	.20	.08	.02
☐	26	Dave Justice	12.00	5.25	1.50
☐	27	Mark Langston	.40	.16	.04
☐	28	Damon Berryhill	.20	.08	.02
☐	29	Kevin Bass	.20	.08	.02
☐	30	Scott Fletcher	.20	.08	.02
☐	31	Moises Alou	.25	.10	.02
☐	32	Dave Valle	.20	.08	.02
☐	33	Jody Reed	.25	.10	.02
☐	34	Dave West	.25	.10	.02
☐	35	Kevin McReynolds	.30	.12	.03
☐	36	Pat Combs	.25	.10	.02
☐	37	Eric Davis	.75	.30	.07
☐	38	Bret Saberhagen	.40	.16	.04
☐	39	Stan Javier	.20	.08	.02
☐	40	Chuck Cary	.20	.08	.02
☐	41	Tony Phillips	.20	.08	.02
☐	42	Lee Smith	.25	.10	.02
☐	43	Tim Teufel	.20	.08	.02
☐	44	Lance Dickson	1.00	.40	.10
☐	45	Greg Litton	.20	.08	.02
☐	46	Teddy Higuera	.25	.10	.02
☐	47	Edgar Martinez	.30	.12	.03
☐	48	Steve Avery	8.00	3.50	.80
☐	49	Walt Weiss	.25	.10	.02
☐	50	David Segui	.30	.12	.03
☐	51	Andy Benes	.40	.16	.04
☐	52	Karl Rhodes	.30	.12	.03
☐	53	Neal Heaton	.20	.08	.02
☐	54	Danny Gladden	.20	.08	.02
☐	55	Luis Rivera	.20	.08	.02
☐	56	Kevin Brown	.25	.10	.02
☐	57	Frank Thomas	30.00	13.50	4.50
☐	58	Terry Mulholland	.25	.10	.02
☐	59	Dick Schofield	.20	.08	.02
☐	60	Ron Darling	.25	.10	.02
☐	61	Sandy Alomar Jr.	.40	.16	.04
☐	62	Dave Stieb	.25	.10	.02
☐	63	Alan Trammell	.45	.18	.04
☐	64	Matt Nokes	.25	.10	.02
☐	65	Lenny Harris	.20	.08	.02
☐	66	Milt Thompson	.20	.08	.02
☐	67	Storm Davis	.20	.08	.02
☐	68	Joe Oliver	.20	.08	.02
☐	69	Andres Galarraga	.25	.10	.02
☐	70	Ozzie Guillen	.25	.10	.02
☐	71	Ken Howell	.20	.08	.02
☐	72	Garry Templeton	.20	.08	.02
☐	73	Derrick May	.25	.10	.02
☐	74	Xavier Hernandez	.20	.08	.02
☐	75	Dave Parker	.30	.12	.03
☐	76	Rick Aguilera	.25	.10	.02
☐	77	Robby Thompson	.20	.08	.02
☐	78	Pete Incaviglia	.25	.10	.02
☐	79	Bob Welch	.25	.10	.02
☐	80	Randy Milligan	.25	.10	.02
☐	81	Chuck Finley	.30	.12	.03
☐	82	Alvin Davis	.25	.10	.02
☐	83	Tim Naehring	.35	.15	.03
☐	84	Jay Bell	.20	.08	.02
☐	85	Joe Magrane	.20	.08	.02
☐	86	Howard Johnson	.60	.25	.06
☐	87	Jack McDowell	.35	.15	.03
☐	88	Kevin Seitzer	.25	.10	.02
☐	89	Bruce Ruffin	.20	.08	.02
☐	90	Fernando Valenzuela	.25	.10	.02
☐	91	Terry Kennedy	.20	.08	.02
☐	92	Barry Larkin	.75	.30	.07
☐	93	Larry Walker	.35	.15	.03
☐	94	Luis Salazar	.20	.08	.02
☐	95	Gary Sheffield	.30	.12	.03
☐	96	Bobby Witt	.25	.10	.02
☐	97	Lonnie Smith	.25	.10	.02
☐	98	Bryan Harvey	.25	.10	.02
☐	99	Mookie Wilson	.25	.10	.02
☐	100	Dwight Gooden	.75	.30	.07
☐	101	Lou Whitaker	.25	.10	.02
☐	102	Ron Karkovice	.20	.08	.02
☐	103	Jesse Barfield	.25	.10	.02
☐	104	Jose DeJesus	.20	.08	.02
☐	105	Benito Santiago	.30	.12	.03
☐	106	Brian Holman	.25	.10	.02
☐	107	Rafael Ramirez	.20	.08	.02
☐	108	Ellis Burks	.40	.16	.04
☐	109	Mike Bielecki	.20	.08	.02
☐	110	Kirby Puckett	1.50	.60	.15
☐	111	Terry Shumpert	.25	.10	.02
☐	112	Chuck Crim	.20	.08	.02
☐	113	Todd Benzinger	.20	.08	.02
☐	114	Brian Barnes	.45	.18	.04
☐	115	Carlos Baerga	.85	.35	.08
☐	116	Kal Daniels	.25	.10	.02
☐	117	Dave Johnson	.20	.08	.02
☐	118	Andy Van Slyke	.30	.12	.03
☐	119	John Burkett	.20	.08	.02
☐	120	Rickey Henderson	2.50	1.00	.25
☐	121	Tim Jones	.20	.08	.02
☐	122	Daryl Irvine	.30	.12	.03
☐	123	Ruben Sierra	1.50	.60	.15
☐	124	Jim Abbott	1.00	.40	.10
☐	125	Daryl Boston	.20	.08	.02
☐	126	Greg Maddux	.25	.10	.02
☐	127	Von Hayes	.25	.10	.02
☐	128	Mike Fitzgerald	.20	.08	.02
☐	129	Wayne Edwards	.20	.08	.02
☐	130	Greg Briley	.20	.08	.02
☐	131	Rob Dibble	.25	.10	.02
☐	132	Gene Larkin	.20	.08	.02
☐	133	David Wells	.20	.08	.02
☐	134	Steve Balboni	.20	.08	.02
☐	135	Greg Vaughn	1.25	.50	.12
☐	136	Mark Davis	.25	.10	.02
☐	137	Dave Rhode	.25	.10	.02
☐	138	Eric Show	.20	.08	.02
☐	139	Bobby Bonilla	1.00	.40	.10
☐	140	Dana Kiecker	.20	.08	.02
☐	141	Gary Pettis	.20	.08	.02
☐	142	Dennis Boyd	.20	.08	.02
☐	143	Mike Benjamin	.20	.08	.02
☐	144	Luis Polonia	.25	.10	.02
☐	145	Doug Jones	.20	.08	.02
☐	146	Al Newman	.20	.08	.02
☐	147	Alex Fernandez	.90	.40	.09
☐	148	Bill Doran	.20	.08	.02
☐	149	Kevin Elster	.20	.08	.02
☐	150	Len Dykstra	.30	.12	.03
☐	151	Mike Gallego	.20	.08	.02
☐	152	Tim Belcher	.25	.10	.02
☐	153	Jay Buhner	.30	.12	.03
☐	154	Ozzie Smith UER	.80	.35	.08
		(Rookie card is 1979, but card back says '78)			
☐	155	Jose Canseco	4.00	1.75	.40
☐	156	Gregg Olson	.30	.12	.03
☐	157	Charlie O'Brien	.20	.08	.02
☐	158	Frank Tanana	.25	.10	.02
☐	159	George Brett	.90	.40	.09
☐	160	Jeff Huson	.20	.08	.02
☐	161	Kevin Tapani	.45	.18	.04
☐	162	Jerome Walton	.25	.10	.02
☐	163	Charlie Hayes	.20	.08	.02
☐	164	Chris Bosio	.20	.08	.02
☐	165	Chris Sabo	.35	.15	.03
☐	166	Lance Parrish	.25	.10	.02
☐	167	Don Robinson	.20	.08	.02
☐	168	Manny Lee	.20	.08	.02
☐	169	Dennis Rasmussen	.20	.08	.02
☐	170	Wade Boggs	1.50	.60	.15
☐	171	Bob Geren	.20	.08	.02
☐	172	Mackey Sasser	.20	.08	.02
☐	173	Julio Franco	.45	.18	.04
☐	174	Otis Nixon	.25	.10	.02
☐	175	Bert Blyleven	.25	.10	.02
☐	176	Craig Biggio	.35	.15	.03
☐	177	Eddie Murray	.60	.25	.06
☐	178	Randy Tomlin	1.25	.50	.12
☐	179	Tino Martinez	1.00	.40	.10
☐	180	Carlton Fisk	.90	.40	.09
☐	181	Dwight Smith	.25	.10	.02
☐	182	Scott Garrelts	.20	.08	.02
☐	183	Jim Gantner	.20	.08	.02
☐	184	Dickie Thon	.20	.08	.02
☐	185	John Farrell	.20	.08	.02
☐	186	Cecil Fielder	2.25	.90	.22
☐	187	Glenn Braggs	.20	.08	.02
☐	188	Allan Anderson	.20	.08	.02
☐	189	Kurt Stillwell	.20	.08	.02
☐	190	Jose Oquendo	.20	.08	.02
☐	191	Joe Orsulak	.20	.08	.02
☐	192	Ricky Jordan	.25	.10	.02
☐	193	Kelly Downs	.20	.08	.02
☐	194	Delino DeShields	.75	.30	.07
☐	195	Omar Vizquel	.20	.08	.02
☐	196	Mark Carreon	.20	.08	.02
☐	197	Mike Harkey	.25	.10	.02
☐	198	Jack Howell	.20	.08	.02
☐	199	Lance Johnson	.20	.08	.02
☐	200	Nolan Ryan	15.00	6.50	2.15
		(Wearing Tuxedo)			
☐	201	John Marzano	.20	.08	.02

☐ 202	Doug Drabek	.30	.12	.03
☐ 203	Mark Lemke	.30	.12	.03
☐ 204	Steve Sax	.30	.12	.03
☐ 205	Greg Harris	.20	.08	.02
☐ 206	B.J. Surhoff	.25	.10	.02
☐ 207	Todd Burns	.20	.08	.02
☐ 208	Jose Gonzalez	.20	.08	.02
☐ 209	Mike Scott	.25	.10	.02
☐ 210	Dave Magadan	.25	.10	.02
☐ 211	Dante Bichette	.20	.08	.02
☐ 212	Trevor Wilson	.20	.08	.02
☐ 213	Hector Villenueva	.25	.10	.02
☐ 214	Dan Pasqua	.20	.08	.02
☐ 215	Greg Colbrunn	.40	.16	.04
☐ 216	Mike Jeffcoat	.20	.08	.02
☐ 217	Harold Reynolds	.25	.10	.02
☐ 218	Paul O'Neill	.25	.10	.02
☐ 219	Mark Guthrie	.20	.08	.02
☐ 220	Barry Bonds	1.25	.50	.12
☐ 221	Jimmy Key	.25	.10	.02
☐ 222	Billy Ripken	.20	.08	.02
☐ 223	Tom Pagnozzi	.20	.08	.02
☐ 224	Bo Jackson	4.00	1.75	.40
☐ 225	Sid Fernandez	.25	.10	.02
☐ 226	Mike Marshall	.25	.10	.02
☐ 227	John Kruk	.20	.08	.02
☐ 228	Mike Fetters	.20	.08	.02
☐ 229	Eric Anthony	.30	.12	.03
☐ 230	Ryne Sandberg	3.25	1.35	.32
☐ 231	Carney Lansford	.25	.10	.02
☐ 232	Melido Perez	.20	.08	.02
☐ 233	Jose Lind	.20	.08	.02
☐ 234	Darryl Hamilton	.25	.10	.02
☐ 235	Tom Browning	.25	.10	.02
☐ 236	Spike Owen	.20	.08	.02
☐ 237	Juan Gonzalez	11.00	5.00	1.35
☐ 238	Felix Fermin	.20	.08	.02
☐ 239	Keith Miller	.20	.08	.02
☐ 240	Mark Gubicza	.25	.10	.02
☐ 241	Kent Anderson	.20	.08	.02
☐ 242	Alvaro Espinoza	.20	.08	.02
☐ 243	Dale Murphy	.50	.20	.05
☐ 244	Orel Hershiser	.40	.16	.04
☐ 245	Paul Molitor	.40	.16	.04
☐ 246	Eddie Whitson	.20	.08	.02
☐ 247	Joe Girardi	.25	.10	.02
☐ 248	Kent Hrbek	.25	.10	.02
☐ 249	Bill Sampen	.25	.10	.02
☐ 250	Kevin Mitchell	.75	.30	.07
☐ 251	Mariano Duncan	.20	.08	.02
☐ 252	Scott Bradley	.20	.08	.02
☐ 253	Mike Greenwell	.60	.25	.06
☐ 254	Tom Gordon	.25	.10	.02
☐ 255	Todd Zeile	.90	.40	.09
☐ 256	Bobby Thigpen	.25	.10	.02
☐ 257	Gregg Jefferies	.40	.16	.04
☐ 258	Kenny Rogers	.20	.08	.02
☐ 259	Shane Mack	.25	.10	.02
☐ 260	Zane Smith	.25	.10	.02
☐ 261	Mitch Williams	.20	.08	.02
☐ 262	Jim Deshaies	.20	.08	.02
☐ 263	Dave Winfield	.60	.25	.06
☐ 264	Ben McDonald	1.25	.50	.12
☐ 265	Randy Ready	.20	.08	.02
☐ 266	Pat Borders	.25	.10	.02
☐ 267	Jose Uribe	.20	.08	.02
☐ 268	Derek Lilliquist	.20	.08	.02
☐ 269	Greg Brock	.20	.08	.02
☐ 270	Ken Griffey Jr.	16.00	6.75	2.25
☐ 271	Jeff Gray	.30	.12	.03
☐ 272	Danny Tartabull	.40	.16	.04
☐ 273	Denny Martinez	.25	.10	.02
☐ 274	Robin Ventura	3.00	1.25	.30
☐ 275	Randy Myers	.25	.10	.02
☐ 276	Jack Daugherty	.20	.08	.02
☐ 277	Greg Gagne	.20	.08	.02
☐ 278	Jay Howell	.20	.08	.02
☐ 279	Mike LaValliere	.20	.08	.02
☐ 280	Rex Hudler	.20	.08	.02
☐ 281	Mike Simms	.60	.25	.06
☐ 282	Kevin Maas	2.50	1.00	.25
☐ 283	Jeff Ballard	.20	.08	.02
☐ 284	Dave Henderson	.30	.12	.03
☐ 285	Pete O'Brien	.20	.08	.02
☐ 286	Brook Jacoby	.20	.08	.02
☐ 287	Mike Henneman	.20	.08	.02
☐ 288	Greg Olson	.25	.10	.02
☐ 289	Greg Myers	.20	.08	.02
☐ 290	Mark Grace	.50	.20	.05
☐ 291	Shawn Abner	.20	.08	.02
☐ 292	Frank Viola	.30	.12	.03
☐ 293	Lee Stevens	.50	.20	.05
☐ 294	Jason Grimsley	.25	.10	.02
☐ 295	Matt Williams	.75	.30	.07
☐ 296	Ron Robinson	.20	.08	.02

☐ 297	Tom Brunansky	.25	.10	.02
☐ 298	Checklist 1-100	.20	.03	.01
☐ 299	Checklist 101-200	.20	.03	.01
☐ 300	Checklist 201-300	.20	.03	.01

1991 Topps Stadium Club II

The 1991 Topps Stadium Club Series II set contains 300 cards measuring the standard size (2 1/2" by 3 1/2"). Series II cards were also available at McDonald's restaurants in the Northeast at three cards per pack. The front design has borderless high glossy color player photos. At the bottom of the card face, the player's name appears in an aqua stripe bounded by gold stripes. The "Topps Stadium Club" insignia overlays the stripe. In a horizontal format, the backs have a miniature reproduction of the player's rookie card, biography, Fastball BARS system, evaluation, and major league batting record, on a painted background consisting of a baseball and playing field. The cards are numbered on the back. The key rookie cards in this series are Jeff Bagwell, Wes Chamberlain, and Phil Plantier.

		MINT	EXC	G-VG
COMPLETE SET (300)		100.00	45.00	15.00
COMMON PLAYER (301-600)		.20	.08	.02
☐ 301	Darryl Strawberry	2.25	.90	.22
☐ 302	Bud Black	.20	.08	.02
☐ 303	Harold Baines	.25	.10	.02
☐ 304	Roberto Alomar	1.00	.40	.10
☐ 305	Norm Charlton	.25	.10	.02
☐ 306	Gary Thurman	.20	.08	.02
☐ 307	Mike Felder	.20	.08	.02
☐ 308	Tony Gwynn	1.50	.60	.15
☐ 309	Roger Clemens	2.25	.90	.22
☐ 310	Andre Dawson	.60	.25	.06
☐ 311	Scott Radinsky	.25	.10	.02
☐ 312	Bob Melvin	.20	.08	.02
☐ 313	Kirk McCaskill	.20	.08	.02
☐ 314	Pedro Guerrero	.30	.12	.03
☐ 315	Walt Terrell	.20	.08	.02
☐ 316	Sam Horn	.20	.08	.02
☐ 317	Wes Chamberlain	4.00	1.75	.40
☐ 318	Pedro Munoz	1.25	.50	.12
☐ 319	Roberto Kelly	.35	.15	.03
☐ 320	Mark Portugal	.20	.08	.02
☐ 321	Tim McIntosh	.25	.10	.02
☐ 322	Jesse Orosco	.20	.08	.02
☐ 323	Gary Green	.20	.08	.02
☐ 324	Greg Harris	.20	.08	.02
☐ 325	Hubie Brooks	.25	.10	.02
☐ 326	Chris Nabholz	.30	.12	.03
☐ 327	Terry Pendleton	.35	.15	.03
☐ 328	Eric King	.20	.08	.02
☐ 329	Chili Davis	.25	.10	.02
☐ 330	Anthony Telford	.30	.12	.03
☐ 331	Kelly Gruber	.30	.12	.03
☐ 332	Dennis Eckersley	.30	.12	.03
☐ 333	Mel Hall	.25	.10	.02
☐ 334	Bob Kipper	.20	.08	.02
☐ 335	Willie McGee	.25	.10	.02
☐ 336	Steve Olin	.20	.08	.02
☐ 337	Steve Buechele	.20	.08	.02
☐ 338	Scott Leuis	.40	.16	.04

	#	Player			
☐	339	Hal Morris	1.00	.40	.10
☐	340	Jose Offerman	.40	.16	.04
☐	341	Kent Mercker	.25	.10	.02
☐	342	Ken Griffey Sr.	.30	.12	.03
☐	343	Pete Harnisch	.25	.10	.02
☐	344	Kirk Gibson	.30	.12	.03
☐	345	Dave Smith	.20	.08	.02
☐	346	Dave Martinez	.20	.08	.02
☐	347	Atlee Hammaker	.20	.08	.02
☐	348	Brian Downing	.20	.08	.02
☐	349	Todd Hundley	.60	.25	.06
☐	350	Candy Maldonado	.20	.08	.02
☐	351	Dwight Evans	.25	.10	.02
☐	352	Steve Searcy	.20	.08	.02
☐	353	Gary Gaetti	.25	.10	.02
☐	354	Jeff Reardon	.30	.12	.03
☐	355	Travis Fryman	4.25	1.75	.42
☐	356	Dave Righetti	.25	.10	.02
☐	357	Fred McGriff	.60	.25	.06
☐	358	Don Slaught	.20	.08	.02
☐	359	Gene Nelson	.20	.08	.02
☐	360	Bily Spiers	.20	.08	.02
☐	361	Lee Guetterman	.20	.08	.02
☐	362	Darren Lewis	1.25	.50	.12
☐	363	Duane Ward	.20	.08	.02
☐	364	Lloyd Moseby	.20	.08	.02
☐	365	John Smoltz	.45	.18	.04
☐	366	Felix Jose	.75	.30	.07
☐	367	David Cone	.30	.12	.03
☐	368	Wally Backman	.20	.08	.02
☐	369	Jeff Montgomery	.25	.10	.02
☐	370	Rich Garces	.40	.16	.04
☐	371	Billy Hatcher	.25	.10	.02
☐	372	Bill Swift	.20	.08	.02
☐	373	Jim Eisenreich	.20	.08	.02
☐	374	Rob Ducey	.20	.08	.02
☐	375	Tim Crews	.20	.08	.02
☐	376	Steve Finley	.25	.10	.02
☐	377	Jeff Blauser	.20	.08	.02
☐	378	Willie Wilson	.25	.10	.02
☐	379	Gerald Perry	.20	.08	.02
☐	380	Jose Mesa	.20	.08	.02
☐	381	Pat Kelly	1.75	.70	.17
☐	382	Matt Merullo	.25	.10	.02
☐	383	Ivan Calderon	.25	.10	.02
☐	384	Scott Chiamparino	.30	.12	.03
☐	385	Lloyd McClendon	.20	.08	.02
☐	386	Dave Bergman	.20	.08	.02
☐	387	Ed Sprague	.60	.25	.06
☐	388	Jeff Bagwell	12.00	5.25	1.50
☐	389	Brett Butler	.30	.12	.03
☐	390	Larry Andersen	.20	.08	.02
☐	391	Glenn Davis	.30	.12	.03
☐	392	Alex Cole UER	.35	.15	.03
		(Front photo actually Otis Nixon)			
☐	393	Mike Heath	.20	.08	.02
☐	394	Danny Darwin	.20	.08	.02
☐	395	Steve Lake	.20	.08	.02
☐	396	Tim Layana	.20	.08	.02
☐	397	Terry Leach	.20	.08	.02
☐	398	Bill Wegman	.20	.08	.02
☐	399	Mark McGwire	.60	.25	.06
☐	400	Mike Boddicker	.20	.08	.02
☐	401	Steve Howe	.20	.08	.02
☐	402	Bernard Gilkey	.60	.25	.06
☐	403	Thomas Howard	.25	.10	.02
☐	404	Rafael Belliard	.20	.08	.02
☐	405	Tom Candiotti	.25	.10	.02
☐	406	Rene Gonzalez	.20	.08	.02
☐	407	Chuck McElroy	.25	.10	.02
☐	408	Paul Sorrento	.25	.10	.02
☐	409	Randy Johnson	.30	.12	.03
☐	410	Brady Anderson	.20	.08	.02
☐	411	Dennis Cook	.20	.08	.02
☐	412	Mickey Tettleton	.25	.10	.02
☐	413	Mike Stanton	.20	.08	.02
☐	414	Ken Oberkfell	.20	.08	.02
☐	415	Rick Honeycutt	.20	.08	.02
☐	416	Nelson Santovenia	.20	.08	.02
☐	417	Bob Tewksbury	.20	.08	.02
☐	418	Brent Mayne	.35	.15	.03
☐	419	Steve Farr	.20	.08	.02
☐	420	Phil Stephenson	.20	.08	.02
☐	421	Jeff Russell	.20	.08	.02
☐	422	Chris James	.20	.08	.02
☐	423	Tim Leary	.25	.10	.02
☐	424	Gary Carter	.35	.15	.03
☐	425	Glenallen Hill	.25	.10	.02
☐	426	Matt Young UER	.20	.08	.02
		(Card mentions 83T/Tr as RC, but 84T shown)			
☐	427	Sid Bream	.20	.08	.02
☐	428	Greg Swindell	.25	.10	.02
☐	429	Scott Aldred	.30	.12	.03
☐	430	Cal Ripken	4.00	1.75	.40
☐	431	Bill Landrum	.20	.08	.02
☐	432	Earnest Riles	.20	.08	.02
☐	433	Danny Jackson	.25	.10	.02
☐	434	Casey Candaele	.20	.08	.02
☐	435	Ken Hill	.25	.10	.02
☐	436	Jaime Navarro	.25	.10	.02
☐	437	Lance Blankenship	.20	.08	.02
☐	438	Randy Velarde	.20	.08	.02
☐	439	Frank DiPino	.20	.08	.02
☐	440	Carl Nichols	.20	.08	.02
☐	441	Jeff M. Robinson	.20	.08	.02
☐	442	Deion Sanders	.50	.20	.05
☐	443	Vicente Palacios	.20	.08	.02
☐	444	Devon White	.25	.10	.02
☐	445	John Cerutti	.20	.08	.02
☐	446	Tracy Jones	.20	.08	.02
☐	447	Jack Morris	.35	.15	.03
☐	448	Mitch Webster	.20	.08	.02
☐	449	Bob Ojeda	.20	.08	.02
☐	450	Oscar Azocar	.20	.08	.02
☐	451	Luis Aquino	.20	.08	.02
☐	452	Mark Whiten	1.25	.50	.12
☐	453	Stan Belinda	.25	.10	.02
☐	454	Ron Gant	1.00	.40	.10
☐	455	Jose DeLeon	.20	.08	.02
☐	456	Mark Salas UER	.20	.08	.02
		(Back has 85T photo, but calls it 86T)			
☐	457	Junior Felix	.25	.10	.02
☐	458	Wally Whitehurst	.20	.08	.02
☐	459	Phil Plantier	12.00	5.25	1.50
☐	460	Juan Berenguer	.20	.08	.02
☐	461	Franklin Stubbs	.20	.08	.02
☐	462	Joe Boever	.20	.08	.02
☐	463	Tim Wallach	.25	.10	.02
☐	464	Mike Moore	.25	.10	.02
☐	465	Albert Belle	1.50	.60	.15
☐	466	Mike Witt	.20	.08	.02
☐	467	Craig Worthington	.20	.08	.02
☐	468	Jerald Clark	.25	.10	.02
☐	469	Scott Terry	.20	.08	.02
☐	470	Milt Cuyler	1.00	.40	.10
☐	471	John Smiley	.30	.12	.03
☐	472	Charles Nagy	.40	.16	.04
☐	473	Alan Mills	.25	.10	.02
☐	474	John Russell	.20	.08	.02
☐	475	Bruce Hurst	.25	.10	.02
☐	476	Andujar Cedeno	3.00	1.25	.30
☐	477	Dave Eiland	.20	.08	.02
☐	478	Brian McRae	3.50	1.50	.35
☐	479	Mike LaCoss	.20	.08	.02
☐	480	Chris Gwynn	.20	.08	.02
☐	481	Jamie Moyer	.20	.08	.02
☐	482	John Olerud	1.25	.50	.12
☐	483	Efrain Valdez	.30	.12	.03
☐	484	Sil Campusano	.20	.08	.02
☐	485	Pascual Perez	.25	.10	.02
☐	486	Gary Redus	.20	.08	.02
☐	487	Andy Hawkins	.20	.08	.02
☐	488	Cory Snyder	.25	.10	.02
☐	489	Chris Hoiles	.35	.15	.03
☐	490	Ron Hassey	.20	.08	.02
☐	491	Gary Wayne	.20	.08	.02
☐	492	Mark Lewis	1.25	.50	.12
☐	493	Scott Coolbaugh	.25	.10	.02
☐	494	Gerald Young	.20	.08	.02
☐	495	Juan Samuel	.25	.10	.02
☐	496	Willie Fraser	.20	.08	.02
☐	497	Jeff Treadway	.20	.08	.02
☐	498	Vince Coleman	.35	.15	.03
☐	499	Cris Carpenter	.20	.08	.02
☐	500	Jack Clark	.25	.10	.02
☐	501	Kevin Appier	.25	.10	.02
☐	502	Rafael Palmeiro	.75	.30	.07
☐	503	Hensley Meulens	.40	.16	.04
☐	504	George Bell	.50	.20	.05
☐	505	Tony Pena	.25	.10	.02
☐	506	Roger McDowell	.20	.08	.02
☐	507	Luis Sojo	.25	.10	.02
☐	508	Mike Schooler	.20	.08	.02
☐	509	Robin Yount	.90	.40	.09
☐	510	Jack Armstrong	.25	.10	.02
☐	511	Rick Cerone	.20	.08	.02
☐	512	Curt Wilkerson	.20	.08	.02
☐	513	Joe Carter	.60	.25	.06
☐	514	Tim Burke	.20	.08	.02
☐	515	Tony Fernandez	.25	.10	.02
☐	516	Ramon Martinez	1.25	.50	.12
☐	517	Tim Hulett	.20	.08	.02
☐	518	Terry Steinbach	.25	.10	.02
☐	519	Pete Smith	.20	.08	.02
☐	520	Ken Caminiti	.20	.08	.02
☐	521	Shawn Boskie	.25	.10	.02
☐	522	Mike Pagliarulo	.20	.08	.02

☐ 523	Tim Raines	.35	.15	.03
☐ 524	Alfredo Griffin	.20	.08	.02
☐ 525	Henry Cotto	.20	.08	.02
☐ 526	Mike Stanley	.20	.08	.02
☐ 527	Charlie Leibrandt	.20	.08	.02
☐ 528	Jeff King	.25	.10	.02
☐ 529	Eric Plunk	.20	.08	.02
☐ 530	Tom Lampkin	.20	.08	.02
☐ 531	Steve Bedrosian	.25	.10	.02
☐ 532	Tom Herr	.20	.08	.02
☐ 533	Craig Lefferts	.20	.08	.02
☐ 534	Jeff Reed	.20	.08	.02
☐ 535	Mickey Morandini	.45	.18	.04
☐ 536	Greg Cadaret	.20	.08	.02
☐ 537	Ray Lankford	2.00	.80	.20
☐ 538	John Candelaria	.20	.08	.02
☐ 539	Rob Deer	.25	.10	.02
☐ 540	Brad Arnsberg	.20	.08	.02
☐ 541	Mike Sharperson	.20	.08	.02
☐ 542	Jeff D. Robinson	.20	.08	.02
☐ 543	Mo Vaughn	3.75	1.60	.37
☐ 544	Jeff Parrett	.20	.08	.02
☐ 545	Willie Randolph	.25	.10	.02
☐ 546	Herm Winningham	.20	.08	.02
☐ 547	Jeff Innis	.20	.08	.02
☐ 548	Chuck Knoblauch	5.50	2.50	.55
☐ 549	Tommy Greene UER (Born in North Carolina, not South Carolina)	.30	.12	.03
☐ 550	Jeff Hamilton	.20	.08	.02
☐ 551	Barry Jones	.20	.08	.02
☐ 552	Ken Dayley	.20	.08	.02
☐ 553	Rick Dempsey	.20	.08	.02
☐ 554	Greg Smith	.20	.08	.02
☐ 555	Mike Devereaux	.20	.08	.02
☐ 556	Keith Comstock	.20	.08	.02
☐ 557	Paul Faries	.30	.12	.03
☐ 558	Tom Glavine	.75	.30	.07
☐ 559	Craig Grebeck	.25	.10	.02
☐ 560	Scott Erickson	7.00	3.00	.70
☐ 561	Joel Skinner	.20	.08	.02
☐ 562	Mike Morgan	.25	.10	.02
☐ 563	Dave Gallagher	.20	.08	.02
☐ 564	Todd Stottlemyre	.30	.12	.03
☐ 565	Rich Rodriguez	.30	.12	.03
☐ 566	Craig Wilson	.35	.15	.03
☐ 567	Jeff Brantley	.25	.10	.02
☐ 568	Scott Kamieniecki	.45	.18	.04
☐ 569	Steve Decker	.90	.40	.09
☐ 570	Juan Agosto	.20	.08	.02
☐ 571	Tommy Gregg	.20	.08	.02
☐ 572	Kevin Wickander	.20	.08	.02
☐ 573	Jamie Quirk UER (Rookie card is 1976, but card back is 1990)	.20	.08	.02
☐ 574	Jerry Don Gleaton	.20	.08	.02
☐ 575	Chris Hammond	.60	.25	.06
☐ 576	Luis Gonzalez	3.50	1.50	.35
☐ 577	Russ Swan	.25	.10	.02
☐ 578	Jeff Conine	.40	.16	.04
☐ 579	Charlie Hough	.20	.08	.02
☐ 580	Jeff Kunkel	.20	.08	.02
☐ 581	Darrel Akerfelds	.20	.08	.02
☐ 582	Jeff Manto	.25	.10	.02
☐ 583	Alejandro Pena	.25	.10	.02
☐ 584	Mark Davidson	.20	.08	.02
☐ 585	Bob MacDonald	.30	.12	.03
☐ 586	Paul Assenmacher	.20	.08	.02
☐ 587	Dan Wilson	.70	.30	.07
☐ 588	Tom Bolton	.20	.08	.02
☐ 589	Brian Harper	.25	.10	.02
☐ 590	John Habyan	.20	.08	.02
☐ 591	John Orton	.20	.08	.02
☐ 592	Mark Gardner	.25	.10	.02
☐ 593	Turner Ward	.45	.18	.04
☐ 594	Bob Patterson	.20	.08	.02
☐ 595	Ed Nunez	.20	.08	.02
☐ 596	Gary Scott UER (Major League Batting Record should be Minor League)	.90	.40	.09
☐ 597	Scott Bankhead	.20	.08	.02
☐ 598	Checklist 301-400	.20	.03	.01
☐ 599	Checklist 401-500	.20	.03	.01
☐ 600	Checklist 501-600	.20	.03	.01

1992 Topps Promo Sheet

This 1992 Topps pre-production sample sheet measures approximately 7 3/4" by 10 3/4" and features nine player cards. The sheet is unperforated and if cut, the cards would measure the standard size (2 1/2" by 3 1/2"). The fronts have glossy color action photos on a white card face, with different color borders overlaying the picture. In a horizontal format, the backs have biography and complete Major League statistics. Moreover, some of the backs display pictures of baseball stadiums, if the player's career length permits. The cards are numbered on the back and also show an oval-shaped "1992 Pre-Production Sample" over some of the statistics.

	MINT	EXC	G-VG
COMPLETE SET (9)	15.00	6.50	2.15
COMMON PLAYER	2.00	.80	.20
☐ 3 Shawon Dunston	2.50	1.00	.25
☐ 16 Mike Heath	2.00	.80	.20
☐ 18 Todd Frohwirth	2.00	.80	.20
☐ 20 Bip Roberts	2.00	.80	.20
☐ 131 Rob Dibble	2.50	1.00	.25
☐ 174 Otis Nixon	2.00	.80	.20
☐ 261 Tom Lasorda MG	2.50	1.00	.25
☐ 273 Denny Martinez	2.50	1.00	.25
☐ 325 Brett Butler	2.50	1.00	.25

1992 Topps Gold Promo Sheet

This 1992 Topps Gold pre-production sample sheet measures approximately 7 3/4" by 10 3/4" and features nine player cards. The sheet is unperforated and if cut, the cards would measure the standard size (2 1/2" by 3 1/2"). The fronts have glossy color action photos on a white card face, with different color borders overlaying the picture. In a horizontal format, the backs have biography and complete Major League statistics. Moreover, some of the backs display pictures of baseball stadiums, if the player's career length permits. The cards are numbered on the back and also show a diamond-shaped "1992 Pre-Production Sample" over some of the statistics.

	MINT	EXC	G-VG
COMPLETE SET (9)	30.00	13.50	4.50
COMMON PLAYER	2.00	.80	.20
☐ 1 Nolan Ryan	12.00	5.25	1.50
☐ 15 Denny Martinez	2.50	1.00	.25
☐ 20 Bip Roberts	2.00	.80	.20
☐ 40 Cal Ripken	10.00	4.50	1.25
☐ 261 Tom Lasorda MG	2.50	1.00	.25
☐ 370 Shawon Dunston	2.50	1.00	.25
☐ 512 Mike Heath	2.00	.80	.20
☐ 655 Brett Butler	2.50	1.00	.25
☐ 757 Rob Dibble	2.50	1.00	.25

1992 Topps

The 1992 Topps set contains 792 cards measuring the standard size (2 1/2" by 3 1/2"). The fronts have either posed or action color player photos on a white card face. Different color stripes frame the pictures, and the player's name and team name appear in two short color stripes respectively at the bottom. In a horizontal format, the backs have biography and complete career batting or pitching record. In addition, some of the cards have a picture of a baseball field and stadium on the back. Special subsets included are Record Breakers (2-5), Prospects (58, 126, 179, 473, 551, 591, 618, 656, 676), and All-Stars (386-407). The cards are numbered on the back. These cards were not issued with bubble gum and feature white card stock.

	MINT	EXC	G-VG
COMPLETE SET (792)	24.00	10.50	3.50
COMMON PLAYER (1-792)	.03	.01	.00
☐ 1 Nolan Ryan	.35	.15	.03
☐ 2 Ricky Henderson RB	.10	.04	.01
☐ 3 Jeff Reardon RB	.03	.01	.00
☐ 4 Nolan Ryan RB	.18	.08	.01
☐ 5 Dave Winfield RB	.06	.02	.00
☐ 6 Brien Taylor	1.00	.40	.10
☐ 7 Jim Olander	.18	.08	.01
☐ 8 Bryan Hickerson	.12	.05	.01
☐ 9 Jon Farrell	.18	.08	.01
☐ 10 Wade Boggs	.12	.05	.01
☐ 11 Jack McDowell	.06	.02	.00
☐ 12 Luis Gonzalez	.12	.05	.01
☐ 13 Mike Scioscia	.03	.01	.00
☐ 14 Wes Chamberlain	.12	.05	.01
☐ 15 Dennis Martinez	.03	.01	.00
☐ 16 Jeff Montgomery	.03	.01	.00
☐ 17 Randy Milligan	.03	.01	.00
☐ 18 Greg Cadaret	.03	.01	.00
☐ 19 Jamie Quirk	.03	.01	.00
☐ 20 Bip Roberts	.03	.01	.00
☐ 21 Buck Rogers MG	.03	.01	.00
☐ 22 Bill Wegman	.03	.01	.00
☐ 23 Chuck Knoblauch	.15	.06	.01
☐ 24 Randy Myers	.03	.01	.00

☐ 25 Ron Gant	.10	.04	.01
☐ 26 Mike Bielecki	.03	.01	.00
☐ 27 Juan Gonzalez	.25	.10	.02
☐ 28 Mike Schooler	.03	.01	.00
☐ 29 Mickey Tettleton	.03	.01	.00
☐ 30 John Kruk	.03	.01	.00
☐ 31 Bryn Smith	.03	.01	.00
☐ 32 Chris Nabholz	.03	.01	.00
☐ 33 Carlos Baerga	.10	.04	.01
☐ 34 Jeff Juden	.10	.04	.01
☐ 35 Dave Righetti	.06	.02	.00
☐ 36 Scott Ruffcorn	.15	.06	.01
☐ 37 Luis Polonia	.06	.02	.00
☐ 38 Tom Candiotti	.06	.02	.00
☐ 39 Greg Olson	.03	.01	.00
☐ 40 Cal Ripken	.20	.08	.02
☐ 41 Craig Lefferts	.03	.01	.00
☐ 42 Mike Macfarlane	.03	.01	.00
☐ 43 Jose Lind	.03	.01	.00
☐ 44 Rick Aguilera	.03	.01	.00
☐ 45 Gary Carter	.06	.02	.00
☐ 46 Steve Farr	.03	.01	.00
☐ 47 Rex Hudler	.03	.01	.00
☐ 48 Scott Scudder	.03	.01	.00
☐ 49 Damon Berryhill	.03	.01	.00
☐ 50 Ken Griffey Jr.	.50	.20	.05
☐ 51 Tom Runnells MG	.03	.01	.00
☐ 52 Juan Bell	.03	.01	.00
☐ 53 Tommy Gregg	.03	.01	.00
☐ 54 David Wells	.03	.01	.00
☐ 55 Rafael Palmeiro	.08	.03	.01
☐ 56 Charlie O'Brien	.03	.01	.00
☐ 57 Donn Pall	.03	.01	.00
☐ 58 1992 Prospects C	.45	.18	.04
Brad Ausmus			
Jim Campanis Jr.			
Dave Nilsson			
Doug Robbins			
☐ 59 Mo Vaughn	.20	.08	.02
☐ 60 Tony Fernandez	.06	.02	.00
☐ 61 Paul O'Neill	.06	.02	.00
☐ 62 Gene Nelson	.03	.01	.00
☐ 63 Randy Ready	.03	.01	.00
☐ 64 Bob Kipper	.03	.01	.00
☐ 65 Willie McGee	.06	.02	.00
☐ 66 Scott Stahoviak	.25	.10	.02
☐ 67 Luis Salazar	.03	.01	.00
☐ 68 Marvin Freeman	.03	.01	.00
☐ 69 Kenny Lofton	.17	.07	.01
☐ 70 Gary Gaetti	.06	.02	.00
☐ 71 Erik Hanson	.06	.02	.00
☐ 72 Eddie Zosky	.10	.04	.01
☐ 73 Brian Barnes	.06	.02	.00
☐ 74 Scott Leius	.06	.02	.00
☐ 75 Bret Saberhagen	.08	.03	.01
☐ 76 Mike Gallego	.03	.01	.00
☐ 77 Jack Armstrong	.03	.01	.00
☐ 78 Ivan Rodriguez	.50	.20	.05
☐ 79 Jesse Orosco	.03	.01	.00
☐ 80 David Justice	.35	.15	.03
☐ 81 Ced Landrum	.08	.03	.01
☐ 82 Doug Simons	.06	.02	.00
☐ 83 Tommy Greene	.06	.02	.00
☐ 84 Leo Gomez	.10	.04	.01
☐ 85 Jose DeLeon	.03	.01	.00
☐ 86 Steve Finley	.06	.02	.00
☐ 87 Bob MacDonald	.06	.02	.00
☐ 88 Darrin Jackson	.03	.01	.00
☐ 89 Neal Heaton	.03	.01	.00
☐ 90 Robin Yount	.10	.04	.01
☐ 91 Jeff Reed	.03	.01	.00
☐ 92 Lenny Harris	.03	.01	.00
☐ 93 Reggie Jefferson	.10	.04	.01
☐ 94 Sammy Sosa	.06	.02	.00
☐ 95 Scott Bailes	.03	.01	.00
☐ 96 Tom McKinnon	.15	.06	.01
☐ 97 Luis Rivera	.03	.01	.00
☐ 98 Mike Harkey	.03	.01	.00
☐ 99 Jeff Treadway	.03	.01	.00
☐ 100 Jose Canseco	.20	.08	.02
☐ 101 Omar Vizquel	.03	.01	.00
☐ 102 Scott Kamieniecki	.06	.02	.00
☐ 103 Ricky Jordan	.06	.02	.00
☐ 104 Jeff Ballard	.03	.01	.00
☐ 105 Felix Jose	.08	.03	.01
☐ 106 Mike Boddicker	.03	.01	.00
☐ 107 Dan Pasqua	.03	.01	.00
☐ 108 Mike Timlin	.06	.02	.00
☐ 109 Roger Craig MG	.03	.01	.00
☐ 110 Ryne Sandberg	.18	.08	.01
☐ 111 Mark Carreon	.03	.01	.00
☐ 112 Oscar Azocar	.03	.01	.00
☐ 113 Mike Greenwell	.10	.04	.01
☐ 114 Mark Portugal	.03	.01	.00

□					
115	Terry Pendleton	.08	.03	.01
116	Willie Randolph	.03	.01	.00
117	Scott Terry	.03	.01	.00
118	Chili Davis	.06	.02	.00
119	Mark Gardner	.03	.01	.00
120	Alan Trammell	.08	.03	.01
121	Derek Bell	.17	.07	.01
122	Gary Varsho	.03	.01	.00
123	Bob Ojeda	.03	.01	.00
124	Shawn Livsey	.15	.06	.01
125	Chris Hoiles	.06	.02	.00
126	1992 Prospects 1B	1.50	.60	.15
	Ryan Klesko			
	John Jaha			
	Rico Brogna			
	Dave Staton			
127	Carlos Quintana	.06	.02	.00
128	Kurt Stillwell	.03	.01	.00
129	Melido Perez	.03	.01	.00
130	Alvin Davis	.06	.02	.00
131	Checklist 1-132	.06	.02	.00
132	Eric Show	.03	.01	.00
133	Rance Mulliniks	.03	.01	.00
134	Darryl Kile	.08	.03	.01
135	Von Hayes	.06	.02	.00
136	Bill Doran	.03	.01	.00
137	Jeff Robinson	.03	.01	.00
138	Monty Fariss	.06	.02	.00
139	Jeff Innis	.03	.01	.00
140	Mark Grace	.08	.03	.01
141	Jim Leyland MG	.03	.01	.00
142	Todd Van Poppel	.45	.18	.04
143	Paul Gibson	.03	.01	.00
144	Bill Swift	.03	.01	.00
145	Danny Tartabull	.08	.03	.01
146	Al Newman	.03	.01	.00
147	Cris Carpenter	.03	.01	.00
148	Anthony Young	.08	.03	.01
149	Brian Bohanon	.03	.01	.00
150	Roger Clemens	.15	.06	.01
151	Jeff Hamilton	.03	.01	.00
152	Charlie Leibrandt	.03	.01	.00
153	Ron Karkovice	.03	.01	.00
154	Hensley Meulens	.06	.02	.00
155	Scott Bankhead	.03	.01	.00
156	Manny Ramirez	.40	.16	.04
157	Keith Miller	.03	.01	.00
158	Todd Frohwirth	.03	.01	.00
159	Darrin Fletcher	.03	.01	.00
160	Bobby Bonilla	.10	.04	.01
161	Casey Candaele	.03	.01	.00
162	Paul Faries	.03	.01	.00
163	Dana Kiecker	.03	.01	.00
164	Shane Mack	.06	.02	.00
165	Mark Langston	.06	.02	.00
166	Geronimo Pena	.03	.01	.00
167	Andy Allanson	.03	.01	.00
168	Dwight Smith	.06	.02	.00
169	Chuck Crim	.03	.01	.00
170	Alex Cole	.06	.02	.00
171	Bill Plummer MG	.03	.01	.00
172	Juan Berenguer	.03	.01	.00
173	Brian Downing	.03	.01	.00
174	Steve Frey	.03	.01	.00
175	Orel Hershiser	.06	.02	.00
176	Ramon Garcia	.06	.02	.00
177	Dan Gladden	.03	.01	.00
178	Jim Acker	.03	.01	.00
179	1992 Prospects 2B	.25	.10	.02
	Bobby DeJardin			
	Cesar Bernhardt			
	Armando Moreno			
	Andy Stankiewicz			
180	Kevin Mitchell	.08	.03	.01
181	Hector Villanueva	.03	.01	.00
182	Jeff Reardon	.06	.02	.00
183	Brent Mayne	.06	.02	.00
184	Jimmy Jones	.03	.01	.00
185	Benito Santiago	.06	.02	.00
186	Cliff Floyd	.25	.10	.02
187	Earnie Riles	.03	.01	.00
188	Jose Guzman	.03	.01	.00
189	Junior Felix	.06	.02	.00
190	Glenn Davis	.08	.03	.01
191	Charlie Hough	.03	.01	.00
192	Dave Fleming	.06	.02	.00
193	Omar Olivares	.06	.02	.00
194	Eric Karros	.20	.08	.02
195	David Cone	.08	.03	.01
196	Frank Castillo	.06	.02	.00
197	Glenn Braggs	.03	.01	.00
198	Scott Aldred	.03	.01	.00
199	Jeff Blauser	.03	.01	.00
200	Len Dykstra	.06	.02	.00
201	Buck Showalter MG	.06	.02	.00

□					
202	Rick Honeycutt	.03	.01	.00
203	Greg Myers	.03	.01	.00
204	Trevor Wilson	.03	.01	.00
205	Jay Howell	.03	.01	.00
206	Luis Sojo	.03	.01	.00
207	Jack Clark	.06	.02	.00
208	Julio Machado	.03	.01	.00
209	Lloyd McClendon	.03	.01	.00
210	Ozzie Guillen	.06	.02	.00
211	Jeremy Hernandez	.12	.05	.01
212	Randy Velarde	.03	.01	.00
213	Les Lancaster	.03	.01	.00
214	Andy Mota	.10	.04	.01
215	Rich Gossage	.06	.02	.00
216	Brent Gates	.20	.08	.02
217	Brian Harper	.03	.01	.00
218	Mike Flanagan	.06	.02	.00
219	Jerry Browne	.03	.01	.00
220	Jose Rijo	.06	.02	.00
221	Skeeter Barnes	.03	.01	.00
222	Jaime Navarro	.03	.01	.00
223	Mel Hall	.03	.01	.00
224	Bret Barberie	.15	.06	.01
225	Roberto Alomar	.10	.04	.01
226	Pete Smith	.03	.01	.00
227	Daryl Boston	.03	.01	.00
228	Eddie Whitson	.03	.01	.00
229	Shawn Boskie	.03	.01	.00
230	Dick Schofield	.03	.01	.00
231	Brian Drahman	.06	.02	.00
232	John Smiley	.06	.02	.00
233	Mitch Webster	.03	.01	.00
234	Terry Steinbach	.03	.01	.00
235	Jack Morris	.06	.02	.00
236	Bill Pecota	.03	.01	.00
237	Jose Hernandez	.12	.05	.01
238	Greg Litton	.03	.01	.00
239	Brian Holman	.03	.01	.00
240	Andres Galarraga	.06	.02	.00
241	Gerald Young	.03	.01	.00
242	Mike Mussina	.12	.05	.01
243	Alvaro Espinoza	.03	.01	.00
244	Darren Daulton	.03	.01	.00
245	John Smoltz	.08	.03	.01
246	Jason Pruitt	.15	.06	.01
247	Chuck Finley	.06	.02	.00
248	Jim Gantner	.03	.01	.00
249	Tony Fossas	.03	.01	.00
250	Ken Griffey Sr.	.06	.02	.00
251	Kevin Elster	.03	.01	.00
252	Dennis Rasmussen	.03	.01	.00
253	Terry Kennedy	.03	.01	.00
254	Ryan Bowen	.06	.02	.00
255	Robin Ventura	.15	.06	.01
256	Mike Aldrete	.03	.01	.00
257	Jeff Russell	.03	.01	.00
258	Jim Lindeman	.03	.01	.00
259	Ron Darling	.06	.02	.00
260	Devon White	.06	.02	.00
261	Tom Lasorda MG	.06	.02	.00
262	Terry Lee	.06	.02	.00
263	Bob Patterson	.03	.01	.00
264	Checklist 133-264	.06	.02	.00
265	Teddy Higuera	.03	.01	.00
266	Roberto Kelly	.08	.03	.01
267	Steve Bedrosian	.03	.01	.00
268	Brady Anderson	.03	.01	.00
269	Ruben Amaro Jr.	.08	.03	.01
270	Tony Gwynn	.12	.05	.01
271	Tracy Jones	.03	.01	.00
272	Jerry Don Gleaton	.03	.01	.00
273	Craig Grebeck	.03	.01	.00
274	Bob Scanlan	.06	.02	.00
275	Todd Zeile	.10	.04	.01
276	Shawn Green	.20	.08	.02
277	Scott Chiamparino	.03	.01	.00
278	Darryl Hamilton	.03	.01	.00
279	Jim Clancy	.03	.01	.00
280	Carlos Martinez	.03	.01	.00
281	Kevin Appier	.03	.01	.00
282	John Wehner	.10	.04	.01
283	Reggie Sanders	.15	.06	.01
284	Gene Larkin	.03	.01	.00
285	Bob Welch	.06	.02	.00
286	Gilberto Reyes	.03	.01	.00
287	Pete Schourek	.06	.02	.00
288	Anduiar Cedeno	.15	.06	.01
289	Mike Morgan	.06	.02	.00
290	Bo Jackson	.25	.10	.02
291	Phil Garner MG	.03	.01	.00
292	Ray Lankford	.10	.04	.01
293	Mike Henneman	.03	.01	.00
294	Dave Valle	.03	.01	.00
295	Alonzo Powell	.06	.02	.00
296	Tom Brunansky	.06	.02	.00

☐	297	Kevin Brown	.03	.01	.00	☐	392	Bobby Bonilla AS	.08	.03	.01
☐	298	Kelly Gruber	.06	.02	.00	☐	393	Craig Biggio AS	.06	.02	.00
☐	299	Charles Nagy	.03	.01	.00	☐	394	Dennis Martinez AS	.06	.02	.00
☐	300	Don Mattingly	.12	.05	.01	☐	395	Tom Glavine AS	.08	.03	.01
☐	301	Kirk McCaskill	.03	.01	.00	☐	396	Ozzie Smith AS	.08	.03	.01
☐	302	Joey Cora	.03	.01	.00	☐	397	Cecil Fielder AS	.10	.04	.01
☐	303	Dan Plesac	.03	.01	.00	☐	398	Julio Franco AS	.08	.03	.01
☐	304	Joe Oliver	.03	.01	.00	☐	399	Wade Boggs AS	.10	.04	.01
☐	305	Tom Glavine	.08	.03	.01	☐	400	Cal Ripken AS	.12	.05	.01
☐	306	Al Shirley	.30	.12	.03	☐	401	Jose Canseco AS	.12	.05	.01
☐	307	Bruce Ruffin	.03	.01	.00	☐	402	Joe Carter AS	.08	.03	.01
☐	308	Craig Shipley	.12	.05	.01	☐	403	Ruben Sierra AS	.10	.04	.01
☐	309	Dave Martinez	.03	.01	.00	☐	404	Matt Nokes AS	.06	.02	.00
☐	310	Jose Mesa	.03	.01	.00	☐	405	Roger Clemens AS	.10	.04	.01
☐	311	Henry Cotto	.03	.01	.00	☐	406	Jim Abbott AS	.08	.03	.01
☐	312	Mike LaValliere	.03	.01	.00	☐	407	Bryan Harvey AS	.06	.02	.00
☐	313	Kevin Tapani	.06	.02	.00	☐	408	Bob Milacki	.03	.01	.00
☐	314	Jeff Huson	.03	.01	.00	☐	409	Geno Petralli	.03	.01	.00
☐	315	Juan Samuel	.06	.02	.00	☐	410	Dave Stewart	.06	.02	.00
☐	316	Curt Schilling	.03	.01	.00	☐	411	Mike Jackson	.03	.01	.00
☐	317	Mike Bordick	.06	.02	.00	☐	412	Luis Aquino	.03	.01	.00
☐	318	Steve Howe	.03	.01	.00	☐	413	Tim Teufel	.03	.01	.00
☐	319	Tony Phillips	.03	.01	.00	☐	414	Jeff Ware	.08	.03	.01
☐	320	George Bell	.08	.03	.01	☐	415	Jim Deshaies	.03	.01	.00
☐	321	Lou Piniella MG	.06	.02	.00	☐	416	Ellis Burks	.08	.03	.01
☐	322	Tim Burke	.03	.01	.00	☐	417	Allan Anderson	.03	.01	.00
☐	323	Milt Thompson	.03	.01	.00	☐	418	Alfredo Griffin	.03	.01	.00
☐	324	Danny Darwin	.03	.01	.00	☐	419	Wally Whitehurst	.03	.01	.00
☐	325	Joe Orsulak	.03	.01	.00	☐	420	Sandy Alomar Jr.	.08	.03	.01
☐	326	Eric King	.03	.01	.00	☐	421	Juan Agosto	.03	.01	.00
☐	327	Jay Buhner	.06	.02	.00	☐	422	Sam Horn	.03	.01	.00
☐	328	Joel Johnston	.08	.03	.01	☐	423	Jeff Fassero	.06	.02	.00
☐	329	Franklin Stubbs	.03	.01	.00	☐	424	Paul McClellan	.06	.02	.00
☐	330	Will Clark	.18	.08	.01	☐	425	Cecil Fielder	.15	.06	.01
☐	331	Steve Lake	.03	.01	.00	☐	426	Tim Raines	.08	.03	.01
☐	332	Chris Jones	.06	.02	.00	☐	427	Eddie Taubensee	.15	.06	.01
☐	333	Pat Tabler	.03	.01	.00	☐	428	Dennis Boyd	.03	.01	.00
☐	334	Kevin Gross	.03	.01	.00	☐	429	Tony LaRussa MG	.03	.01	.00
☐	335	Dave Henderson	.06	.02	.00	☐	430	Steve Sax	.06	.02	.00
☐	336	Greg Anthony	.12	.05	.01	☐	431	Tom Gordon	.06	.02	.00
☐	337	Alejandro Pena	.06	.02	.00	☐	432	Billy Hatcher	.03	.01	.00
☐	338	Shawn Abner	.03	.01	.00	☐	433	Cal Eldred	.06	.02	.00
☐	339	Tom Browning	.03	.01	.00	☐	434	Wally Backman	.03	.01	.00
☐	340	Otis Nixon	.03	.01	.00	☐	435	Mark Eichhorn	.03	.01	.00
☐	341	Bob Geren	.03	.01	.00	☐	436	Mookie Wilson	.03	.01	.00
☐	342	Tim Spehr	.08	.03	.01	☐	437	Scott Servais	.06	.02	.00
☐	343	John Vander Wal	.20	.08	.02	☐	438	Mike Maddux	.03	.01	.00
☐	344	Jack Daugherty	.03	.01	.00	☐	439	Chico Walker	.03	.01	.00
☐	345	Zane Smith	.03	.01	.00	☐	440	Doug Drabek	.06	.02	.00
☐	346	Rheal Cormier	.12	.05	.01	☐	441	Rob Deer	.03	.01	.00
☐	347	Kent Hrbek	.06	.02	.00	☐	442	Dave West	.03	.01	.00
☐	348	Rick Wilkins	.08	.03	.01	☐	443	Spike Owen	.03	.01	.00
☐	349	Steve Lyons	.03	.01	.00	☐	444	Tyrone Hill	.25	.10	.02
☐	350	Gregg Olson	.06	.02	.00	☐	445	Matt Williams	.10	.04	.01
☐	351	Greg Riddoch MG	.03	.01	.00	☐	446	Mark Lewis	.12	.05	.01
☐	352	Ed Nunez	.03	.01	.00	☐	447	David Segui	.06	.02	.00
☐	353	Braulio Castillo	.25	.10	.02	☐	448	Tom Pagnozzi	.03	.01	.00
☐	354	Dave Bergman	.03	.01	.00	☐	449	Jeff Johnson	.06	.02	.00
☐	355	Warren Newson	.08	.03	.01	☐	450	Mark McGwire	.10	.04	.01
☐	356	Luis Quinones	.03	.01	.00	☐	451	Tom Henke	.03	.01	.00
☐	357	Mike Witt	.03	.01	.00	☐	452	Wilson Alvarez	.06	.02	.00
☐	358	Ted Wood	.15	.06	.01	☐	453	Gary Redus	.03	.01	.00
☐	359	Mike Moore	.06	.02	.00	☐	454	Darren Holmes	.06	.02	.00
☐	360	Lance Parrish	.06	.02	.00	☐	455	Pete O'Brien	.03	.01	.00
☐	361	Barry Jones	.03	.01	.00	☐	456	Pat Combs	.03	.01	.00
☐	362	Javier Ortiz	.03	.01	.00	☐	457	Hubie Brooks	.06	.02	.00
☐	363	John Candelaria	.03	.01	.00	☐	458	Frank Tanana	.06	.02	.00
☐	364	Glenallen Hill	.06	.02	.00	☐	459	Tom Kelly MG	.03	.01	.00
☐	365	Duane Ward	.03	.01	.00	☐	460	Andre Dawson	.10	.04	.01
☐	366	Checklist 265-396	.06	.02	.00	☐	461	Doug Jones	.03	.01	.00
☐	367	Rafael Belliard	.03	.01	.00	☐	462	Rich Rodriguez	.06	.02	.00
☐	368	Bill Krueger	.03	.01	.00	☐	463	Mike Simms	.06	.02	.00
☐	369	Steve Whitaker	.15	.06	.01	☐	464	Mike Jeffcoat	.03	.01	.00
☐	370	Shawon Dunston	.06	.02	.00	☐	465	Barry Larkin	.08	.03	.01
☐	371	Dante Bichette	.03	.01	.00	☐	466	Stan Belinda	.03	.01	.00
☐	372	Kip Gross	.12	.05	.01	☐	467	Lonnie Smith	.03	.01	.00
☐	373	Don Robinson	.03	.01	.00	☐	468	Greg Harris	.03	.01	.00
☐	374	Bernie Williams	.12	.05	.01	☐	469	Jim Eisenreich	.03	.01	.00
☐	375	Bert Blyleven	.06	.02	.00	☐	470	Pedro Guerrero	.06	.02	.00
☐	376	Chris Donnels	.10	.04	.01	☐	471	Jose DeJesus	.03	.01	.00
☐	377	Bob Zupcic	.18	.08	.01	☐	472	Rich Rowland	.10	.04	.01
☐	378	Joel Skinner	.03	.01	.00	☐	473	1992 Prospects 3B	.30	.12	.03
☐	379	Steve Chitren	.03	.01	.00			Frank Bolick			
☐	380	Barry Bonds	.12	.05	.01			Craig Paquette			
☐	381	Sparky Anderson MG	.03	.01	.00			Tom Redington			
☐	382	Sid Fernandez	.06	.02	.00			Paul Russo			
☐	383	Dave Hollins	.06	.02	.00	☐	474	Mike Rossiter	.15	.06	.01
☐	384	Mark Lee	.06	.02	.00	☐	475	Robby Thompson	.03	.01	.00
☐	385	Tim Wallach	.06	.02	.00	☐	476	Randy Bush	.03	.01	.00
☐	386	Will Clark AS	.12	.05	.01	☐	477	Greg Hibbard	.03	.01	.00
☐	387	Ryne Sandberg AS	.12	.05	.01	☐	478	Dale Sveum	.03	.01	.00
☐	388	Howard Johnson AS	.08	.03	.01	☐	479	Chito Martinez	.15	.06	.01
☐	389	Barry Larkin AS	.08	.03	.01	☐	480	Scott Sanderson	.03	.01	.00
☐	390	Barry Bonds AS	.10	.04	.01	☐	481	Tino Martinez	.12	.05	.01
☐	391	Ron Gant AS	.08	.03	.01	☐	482	Jimmy Key	.06	.02	.00

#	Player			
☐ 483	Terry Shumpert	.03	.01	.00
☐ 484	Mike Hartley	.03	.01	.00
☐ 485	Chris Sabo	.08	.03	.01
☐ 486	Bob Walk	.03	.01	.00
☐ 487	John Cerutti	.03	.01	.00
☐ 488	Scott Cooper	.10	.04	.01
☐ 489	Bobby Cox MG	.03	.01	.00
☐ 490	Julio Franco	.08	.03	.01
☐ 491	Jeff Brantley	.03	.01	.00
☐ 492	Mike Devereaux	.03	.01	.00
☐ 493	Jose Offerman	.08	.03	.01
☐ 494	Gary Thurman	.03	.01	.00
☐ 495	Carney Lansford	.06	.02	.00
☐ 496	Joe Grahe	.03	.01	.00
☐ 497	Andy Ashby	.08	.03	.01
☐ 498	Gerald Perry	.03	.01	.00
☐ 499	Dave Otto	.03	.01	.00
☐ 500	Vince Coleman	.08	.03	.01
☐ 501	Rob Mallicoat	.03	.01	.00
☐ 502	Greg Briley	.03	.01	.00
☐ 503	Pascual Perez	.03	.01	.00
☐ 504	Aaron Sele	.20	.08	.02
☐ 505	Bobby Thigpen	.06	.02	.00
☐ 506	Todd Benzinger	.03	.01	.00
☐ 507	Candy Maldonado	.03	.01	.00
☐ 508	Bill Gullickson	.03	.01	.00
☐ 509	Doug Dascenzo	.03	.01	.00
☐ 510	Frank Viola	.06	.02	.00
☐ 511	Kenny Rogers	.03	.01	.00
☐ 512	Mike Heath	.03	.01	.00
☐ 513	Kevin Bass	.03	.01	.00
☐ 514	Kim Batiste	.06	.02	.00
☐ 515	Delino DeShields	.06	.02	.00
☐ 516	Ed Sprague Jr.	.06	.02	.00
☐ 517	Jim Gott	.03	.01	.00
☐ 518	Jose Melendez	.06	.02	.00
☐ 519	Hal McRae MG	.03	.01	.00
☐ 520	Jeff Bagwell	.75	.30	.07
☐ 521	Joe Hesketh	.03	.01	.00
☐ 522	Milt Cuyler	.10	.04	.01
☐ 523	Shawn Hillegas	.03	.01	.00
☐ 524	Don Slaught	.03	.01	.00
☐ 525	Randy Johnson	.06	.02	.00
☐ 526	Doug Piatt	.08	.03	.01
☐ 527	Checklist 397-528	.06	.02	.00
☐ 528	Steve Foster	.15	.06	.01
☐ 529	Joe Girardi	.03	.01	.00
☐ 530	Jim Abbott	.10	.04	.01
☐ 531	Larry Walker	.06	.02	.00
☐ 532	Mike Huff	.03	.01	.00
☐ 533	Mackey Sasser	.03	.01	.00
☐ 534	Benji Gil	.30	.12	.03
☐ 535	Dave Stieb	.06	.02	.00
☐ 536	Willie Wilson	.06	.02	.00
☐ 537	Mark Leiter	.06	.02	.00
☐ 538	Jose Uribe	.03	.01	.00
☐ 539	Thomas Howard	.03	.01	.00
☐ 540	Ben McDonald	.08	.03	.01
☐ 541	Jose Tolentino	.15	.06	.01
☐ 542	Keith Mitchell	.20	.08	.02
☐ 543	Jerome Walton	.06	.02	.00
☐ 544	Cliff Brantley	.12	.05	.01
☐ 545	Andy Van Slyke	.06	.02	.00
☐ 546	Paul Sorrento	.03	.01	.00
☐ 547	Herm Winningham	.03	.01	.00
☐ 548	Mark Guthrie	.03	.01	.00
☐ 549	Joe Torre MG	.03	.01	.00
☐ 550	Darryl Strawberry	.15	.06	.01
☐ 551	1992 Prospects SS	.45	.18	.04
	Wilfredo Cordero			
	Chipper Jones			
	Manny Alexander			
	Alex Arias			
☐ 552	Dave Gallagher	.03	.01	.00
☐ 553	Edgar Martinez	.06	.02	.00
☐ 554	Donald Harris	.06	.02	.00
☐ 555	Frank Thomas	.60	.25	.06
☐ 556	Storm Davis	.03	.01	.00
☐ 557	Dickie Thon	.03	.01	.00
☐ 558	Scott Garrelts	.03	.01	.00
☐ 559	Steve Olin	.03	.01	.00
☐ 560	Rickey Henderson	.18	.08	.01
☐ 561	Jose Vizcaino	.03	.01	.00
☐ 562	Wade Taylor	.06	.02	.00
☐ 563	Pat Borders	.03	.01	.00
☐ 564	Jimmy Gonzalez	.12	.05	.01
☐ 565	Lee Smith	.06	.02	.00
☐ 566	Bill Sampen	.03	.01	.00
☐ 567	Dean Palmer	.17	.07	.01
☐ 568	Bryan Harvey	.06	.02	.00
☐ 569	Tony Pena	.06	.02	.00
☐ 570	Lou Whitaker	.06	.02	.00
☐ 571	Randy Tomlin	.06	.02	.00
☐ 572	Greg Vaughn	.08	.03	.01
☐ 573	Kelly Downs	.03	.01	.00
☐ 574	Steve Avery	.20	.08	.02
☐ 575	Kirby Puckett	.12	.05	.01
☐ 576	Heathcliff Slocumb	.06	.02	.00
☐ 577	Kevin Seitzer	.06	.02	.00
☐ 578	Lee Guetterman	.03	.01	.00
☐ 579	Johnny Oates MG	.03	.01	.00
☐ 580	Greg Maddux	.06	.02	.00
☐ 581	Stan Javier	.03	.01	.00
☐ 582	Vicente Palacios	.03	.01	.00
☐ 583	Mel Rojas	.03	.01	.00
☐ 584	Wayne Rosenthal	.10	.04	.01
☐ 585	Lenny Webster	.03	.01	.00
☐ 586	Rod Nichols	.03	.01	.00
☐ 587	Mickey Morandini	.06	.02	.00
☐ 588	Russ Swan	.03	.01	.00
☐ 589	Mariano Duncan	.03	.01	.00
☐ 590	Howard Johnson	.08	.03	.01
☐ 591	1992 Prospects OF	.50	.20	.05
	Jeromy Burnitz			
	Jacob Brumfield			
	Alan Cockrell			
	D.J. Dozier			
☐ 592	Denny Neagle	.12	.05	.01
☐ 593	Steve Decker	.10	.04	.01
☐ 594	Brian Barber	.12	.05	.01
☐ 595	Bruce Hurst	.06	.02	.00
☐ 596	Kent Mercker	.06	.02	.00
☐ 597	Mike Magnante	.15	.06	.01
☐ 598	Jody Reed	.06	.02	.00
☐ 599	Steve Searcy	.03	.01	.00
☐ 600	Paul Molitor	.08	.03	.01
☐ 601	Dave Smith	.03	.01	.00
☐ 602	Mike Fetters	.03	.01	.00
☐ 603	Luis Mercedes	.15	.06	.01
☐ 604	Chris Gwynn	.03	.01	.00
☐ 605	Scott Erickson	.15	.06	.01
☐ 606	Brook Jacoby	.03	.01	.00
☐ 607	Todd Stottlemyre	.06	.02	.00
☐ 608	Scott Bradley	.03	.01	.00
☐ 609	Mike Hargrove MG	.03	.01	.00
☐ 610	Eric Davis	.10	.04	.01
☐ 611	Brian Hunter	.35	.15	.03
☐ 612	Pat Kelly	.10	.04	.01
☐ 613	Pedro Munoz	.10	.04	.01
☐ 614	Al Osuna	.06	.02	.00
☐ 615	Matt Merullo	.03	.01	.00
☐ 616	Larry Andersen	.03	.01	.00
☐ 617	Junior Ortiz	.03	.01	.00
☐ 618	1992 Prospects OF	.40	.16	.04
	Cesar Hernandez			
	Steve Hosey			
	Jeff McNeely			
	Dan Peltier			
☐ 619	Danny Jackson	.03	.01	.00
☐ 620	George Brett	.10	.04	.01
☐ 621	Dan Gakeler	.06	.02	.00
☐ 622	Steve Buechele	.03	.01	.00
☐ 623	Bob Tewksbury	.03	.01	.00
☐ 624	Shawn Estes	.15	.06	.01
☐ 625	Kevin McReynolds	.06	.02	.00
☐ 626	Chris Haney	.06	.02	.00
☐ 627	Mike Sharperson	.03	.01	.00
☐ 628	Mark Williamson	.03	.01	.00
☐ 629	Wally Joyner	.08	.03	.01
☐ 630	Carlton Fisk	.10	.04	.01
☐ 631	Armando Reynoso	.10	.04	.01
☐ 632	Felix Fermin	.03	.01	.00
☐ 633	Mitch Williams	.03	.01	.00
☐ 634	Manuel Lee	.03	.01	.00
☐ 635	Harold Baines	.06	.02	.00
☐ 636	Greg Harris	.03	.01	.00
☐ 637	Orlando Merced	.10	.04	.01
☐ 638	Chris Bosio	.03	.01	.00
☐ 639	Wayne Housie	.15	.06	.01
☐ 640	Xavier Hernandez	.03	.01	.00
☐ 641	David Howard	.06	.02	.00
☐ 642	Tim Crews	.03	.01	.00
☐ 643	Rick Cerone	.03	.01	.00
☐ 644	Terry Leach	.03	.01	.00
☐ 645	Deion Sanders	.08	.03	.01
☐ 646	Craig Wilson	.08	.03	.01
☐ 647	Marquis Grissom	.08	.03	.01
☐ 648	Scott Fletcher	.03	.01	.00
☐ 649	Norm Charlton	.03	.01	.00
☐ 650	Jesse Barfield	.06	.02	.00
☐ 651	Joe Slusarski	.06	.02	.00
☐ 652	Bobby Rose	.03	.01	.00
☐ 653	Dennis Lamp	.03	.01	.00
☐ 654	Allen Watson	.18	.08	.01
☐ 655	Brett Butler	.06	.02	.00
☐ 656	1992 Prospects OF	.45	.18	.04
	Rudy Pemberton			
	Henry Rodriguez			
	Lee Tinsley			
	Gerald Williams			

		MINT	EXC	G-VG
☐ 657	Dave Johnson	.03	.01	.00
☐ 658	Checklist 529-660	.06	.02	.00
☐ 659	Brian McRae	.12	.05	.01
☐ 660	Fred McGriff	.08	.03	.01
☐ 661	Bill Landrum	.03	.01	.00
☐ 662	Juan Guzman	.15	.06	.01
☐ 663	Greg Gagne	.03	.01	.00
☐ 664	Ken Hill	.03	.01	.00
☐ 665	Dave Haas	.08	.03	.01
☐ 666	Tom Foley	.03	.01	.00
☐ 667	Roberto Hernandez	.10	.04	.01
☐ 668	Dwayne Henry	.03	.01	.00
☐ 669	Jim Fregosi MG	.03	.01	.00
☐ 670	Harold Reynolds	.03	.01	.00
☐ 671	Mark Whiten	.08	.03	.01
☐ 672	Eric Plunk	.03	.01	.00
☐ 673	Todd Hundley	.06	.02	.00
☐ 674	Mo Sanford	.15	.06	.01
☐ 675	Bobby Witt	.03	.01	.00
☐ 676	1992 Prospects P	.45	.18	.04
	Sam Militello			
	Pat Mahomes			
	Turk Wendell			
	Roger Salkeld			
☐ 677	John Marzano	.03	.01	.00
☐ 678	Joe Klink	.03	.01	.00
☐ 679	Pete Incaviglia	.06	.02	.00
☐ 680	Dale Murphy	.10	.04	.01
☐ 681	Rene Gonzales	.03	.01	.00
☐ 682	Andy Benes	.08	.03	.01
☐ 683	Jim Poole	.03	.01	.00
☐ 684	Trever Miller	.12	.05	.01
☐ 685	Scott Livingstone	.10	.04	.01
☐ 686	Rich DeLucia	.03	.01	.00
☐ 687	Harvey Pulliam	.08	.03	.01
☐ 688	Tim Belcher	.06	.02	.00
☐ 689	Mark Lemke	.03	.01	.00
☐ 690	John Franco	.03	.01	.00
☐ 691	Walt Weiss	.06	.02	.00
☐ 692	Scott Ruskin	.03	.01	.00
☐ 693	Jeff King	.03	.01	.00
☐ 694	Mike Gardiner	.06	.02	.00
☐ 695	Gary Sheffield	.08	.03	.01
☐ 696	Joe Boever	.03	.01	.00
☐ 697	Mike Felder	.03	.01	.00
☐ 698	John Habyan	.03	.01	.00
☐ 699	Cito Gaston MG	.03	.01	.00
☐ 700	Ruben Sierra	.12	.05	.01
☐ 701	Scott Radinsky	.03	.01	.00
☐ 702	Lee Stevens	.06	.02	.00
☐ 703	Mark Wohlers	.18	.08	.01
☐ 704	Curt Young	.03	.01	.00
☐ 705	Dwight Evans	.06	.02	.00
☐ 706	Rob Murphy	.03	.01	.00
☐ 707	Gregg Jefferies	.08	.03	.01
☐ 708	Tom Bolton	.03	.01	.00
☐ 709	Chris James	.03	.01	.00
☐ 710	Kevin Maas	.12	.05	.01
☐ 711	Ricky Bones	.06	.02	.00
☐ 712	Curt Wilkerson	.03	.01	.00
☐ 713	Roger McDowell	.03	.01	.00
☐ 714	Calvin Reese	.35	.15	.03
☐ 715	Craig Biggio	.06	.02	.00
☐ 716	Kirk Dressendorfer	.08	.03	.01
☐ 717	Ken Dayley	.03	.01	.00
☐ 718	B.J. Surhoff	.03	.01	.00
☐ 719	Terry Mulholland	.03	.01	.00
☐ 720	Kirk Gibson	.06	.02	.00
☐ 721	Mike Pagliarulo	.03	.01	.00
☐ 722	Walt Terrell	.03	.01	.00
☐ 723	Jose Oquendo	.03	.01	.00
☐ 724	Kevin Morton	.06	.02	.00
☐ 725	Dwight Gooden	.10	.04	.01
☐ 726	Kirt Manwaring	.03	.01	.00
☐ 727	Chuck McElroy	.03	.01	.00
☐ 728	Dave Burba	.06	.02	.00
☐ 729	Art Howe MG	.03	.01	.00
☐ 730	Ramon Martinez	.10	.04	.01
☐ 731	Donnie Hill	.03	.01	.00
☐ 732	Nelson Santovenia	.03	.01	.00
☐ 733	Bob Melvin	.03	.01	.00
☐ 734	Scott Hatteberg	.15	.06	.01
☐ 735	Greg Swindell	.06	.02	.00
☐ 736	Lance Johnson	.03	.01	.00
☐ 737	Kevin Reimer	.03	.01	.00
☐ 738	Dennis Eckersley	.08	.03	.01
☐ 739	Rob Ducey	.03	.01	.00
☐ 740	Ken Caminiti	.03	.01	.00
☐ 741	Mark Gubicza	.03	.01	.00
☐ 742	Billy Spiers	.03	.01	.00
☐ 743	Darren Lewis	.06	.02	.00
☐ 744	Chris Hammond	.06	.02	.00
☐ 745	Dave Magadan	.06	.02	.00
☐ 746	Bernard Gilkey	.10	.04	.01
☐ 747	Willie Banks	.08	.03	.01
☐ 748	Matt Nokes	.06	.02	.00
☐ 749	Jerald Clark	.03	.01	.00
☐ 750	Travis Fryman	.15	.06	.01
☐ 751	Steve Wilson	.03	.01	.00
☐ 752	Billy Ripken	.03	.01	.00
☐ 753	Paul Assenmacher	.03	.01	.00
☐ 754	Charlie Hayes	.03	.01	.00
☐ 755	Alex Fernandez	.10	.04	.01
☐ 756	Gary Pettis	.03	.01	.00
☐ 757	Rob Dibble	.06	.02	.00
☐ 758	Tim Naehring	.06	.02	.00
☐ 759	Jeff Torborg MG	.03	.01	.00
☐ 760	Ozzie Smith	.10	.04	.01
☐ 761	Mike Fitzgerald	.03	.01	.00
☐ 762	John Burkett	.03	.01	.00
☐ 763	Kyle Abbott	.08	.03	.01
☐ 764	Tyler Green	.45	.18	.04
☐ 765	Pete Harnisch	.06	.02	.00
☐ 766	Mark Davis	.03	.01	.00
☐ 767	Kal Daniels	.06	.02	.00
☐ 768	Jim Thome	.30	.12	.03
☐ 769	Jack Howell	.03	.01	.00
☐ 770	Sid Bream	.03	.01	.00
☐ 771	Arthur Rhodes	.15	.06	.01
☐ 772	Garry Templeton	.03	.01	.00
☐ 773	Hal Morris	.08	.03	.01
☐ 774	Bud Black	.03	.01	.00
☐ 775	Ivan Calderon	.06	.02	.00
☐ 776	Doug Henry	.12	.05	.01
☐ 777	John Olerud	.10	.04	.01
☐ 778	Tim Leary	.03	.01	.00
☐ 779	Jay Bell	.03	.01	.00
☐ 780	Eddie Murray	.10	.04	.01
☐ 781	Paul Abbott	.08	.03	.01
☐ 782	Phil Plantier	.35	.15	.03
☐ 783	Joe Magrane	.03	.01	.00
☐ 784	Ken Patterson	.03	.01	.00
☐ 785	Albert Belle	.12	.05	.01
☐ 786	Royce Clayton	.12	.05	.01
☐ 787	Checklist 661-792	.06	.02	.00
☐ 788	Mike Stanton	.03	.01	.00
☐ 789	Bobby Valentine MG	.03	.01	.00
☐ 790	Joe Carter	.08	.03	.01
☐ 791	Danny Cox	.03	.01	.00
☐ 792	Dave Winfield	.10	.04	.01

1992 Topps '91 Debut

The 1992 Topps '91 Debut set contains 194 standard-size (2 1/2" by 3 1/2") cards. The fronts feature a mix of either posed or action glossy color player photos, framed with two color border stripes on a white card face. The date of the player's first major league appearance is given in a color bar in the lower right corner. In addition to biography and 1991 batting record, the horizontally oriented backs present player profiles in the form of a newspaper article from The Register. The cards are numbered on the back.

		MINT	EXC	G-VG
COMPLETE SET (194)		18.00	7.50	2.50
COMMON PLAYER (1-194)		.05	.02	.00
☐ 1	Kyle Abbott	.15	.06	.01
☐ 2	Dana Allison	.10	.04	.01
☐ 3	Rich Amaral	.10	.04	.01
☐ 4	Ruben Amaro Jr.	.10	.04	.01

#	Name				#	Name			
☐ 5	Andy Ashby	.10	.04	.01	☐ 100	Darryl Kile	.20	.08	.02
☐ 6	Jim Austin	.10	.04	.01	☐ 101	Wayne Kirby	.15	.06	.01
☐ 7	Jeff Bagwell	.90	.40	.09	☐ 102	Garland Kiser	.10	.04	.01
☐ 8	Jeff Banister	.10	.04	.01	☐ 103	Chuck Knoblauch	.40	.16	.04
☐ 9	Willie Banks	.10	.04	.01	☐ 104	Randy Knorr	.15	.06	.01
☐ 10	Bret Barberie	.15	.06	.01	☐ 105	Tom Kramer	.10	.04	.01
☐ 11	Kim Batiste	.10	.04	.01	☐ 106	Ced Landrum	.10	.04	.01
☐ 12	Chris Beasley	.10	.04	.01	☐ 107	Patrick Lennon	.25	.10	.02
☐ 13	Rod Beck	.10	.04	.01	☐ 108	Jim Lewis	.15	.06	.01
☐ 14	Derek Bell	.25	.10	.02	☐ 109	Mark Lewis	.25	.10	.02
☐ 15	Esteban Beltre	.10	.04	.01	☐ 110	Doug Lindsey	.10	.04	.01
☐ 16	Freddie Benavides	.10	.04	.01	☐ 111	Scott Livingstone	.15	.06	.01
☐ 17	Ricky Bones	.10	.04	.01	☐ 112	Kenny Lofton	.25	.10	.02
☐ 18	Denis Boucher	.10	.04	.01	☐ 113	Ever Magallanes	.10	.04	.01
☐ 19	Ryan Bowen	.15	.06	.01	☐ 114	Mike Magnante	.15	.06	.01
☐ 20	Cliff Brantley	.20	.08	.02	☐ 115	Barry Manuel	.15	.06	.01
☐ 21	John Briscoe	.10	.04	.01	☐ 116	Josias Manzanillo	.10	.04	.01
☐ 22	Scott Brosius	.15	.06	.01	☐ 117	Chito Martinez	.35	.15	.03
☐ 23	Terry Bross	.05	.02	.00	☐ 118	Terry Mathews	.10	.04	.01
☐ 24	Jarvis Brown	.15	.06	.01	☐ 119	Rob Maurer	.20	.08	.02
☐ 25	Scott Bullett	.10	.04	.01	☐ 120	Tim Mauser	.15	.06	.01
☐ 26	Kevin Campbell	.10	.04	.01	☐ 121	Terry McDaniel	.15	.06	.01
☐ 27	Amalio Carreno	.10	.04	.01	☐ 122	Rusty Meacham	.15	.06	.01
☐ 28	Matias Carrillo	.10	.04	.01	☐ 123	Luis Mercedes	.25	.10	.02
☐ 29	Jeff Carter	.10	.04	.01	☐ 124	Paul Miller	.10	.04	.01
☐ 30	Vinny Castilla	.10	.04	.01	☐ 125	Keith Mitchell	.30	.12	.03
☐ 31	Braulio Castillo	.25	.10	.02	☐ 126	Bobby Moore	.20	.08	.02
☐ 32	Frank Castillo	.10	.04	.01	☐ 127	Kevin Morton	.15	.06	.01
☐ 33	Darrin Chapin	.15	.06	.01	☐ 128	Andy Mota	.10	.04	.01
☐ 34	Mike Christopher	.15	.06	.01	☐ 129	Jose Mota	.10	.04	.01
☐ 35	Mark Clark	.10	.04	.01	☐ 130	Mike Mussina	.30	.12	.03
☐ 36	Royce Clayton	.25	.10	.02	☐ 131	Jeff Mutis	.10	.04	.01
☐ 37	Stu Cole	.10	.04	.01	☐ 132	Denny Neagle	.30	.12	.03
☐ 38	Gary Cooper	.15	.06	.01	☐ 133	Warren Newson	.20	.08	.02
☐ 39	Archie Corbin	.20	.08	.02	☐ 134	Jim Olander	.20	.08	.02
☐ 40	Rheal Cormier	.20	.08	.02	☐ 135	Erik Pappas	.15	.06	.01
☐ 41	Chris Cron	.20	.08	.02	☐ 136	Jorge Pedre	.10	.04	.01
☐ 42	Mike Dalton	.15	.06	.01	☐ 137	Yorkis Perez	.20	.08	.02
☐ 43	Mark Davis	.10	.04	.01	☐ 138	Mark Petkovsek	.10	.04	.01
☐ 44	Francisco de la Rosa	.10	.04	.01	☐ 139	Doug Piatt	.10	.04	.01
☐ 45	Chris Donnels	.15	.06	.01	☐ 140	Jeff Plympton	.15	.06	.01
☐ 46	Brian Drahman	.10	.04	.01	☐ 141	Harvey Pulliam	.20	.08	.02
☐ 47	Tom Drees	.05	.02	.00	☐ 142	John Ramos	.25	.10	.02
☐ 48	Kirk Dressendorfer	.20	.08	.02	☐ 143	Mike Remlinger	.10	.04	.01
☐ 49	Bruce Egloff	.10	.04	.01	☐ 144	Laddie Renfroe	.15	.06	.01
☐ 50	Cal Eldred	.10	.04	.01	☐ 145	Armando Reynoso	.10	.04	.01
☐ 51	Jose Escobar	.10	.04	.01	☐ 146	Arthur Rhodes	.25	.10	.02
☐ 52	Tony Eusebio	.10	.04	.01	☐ 147	Pat Rice	.15	.06	.01
☐ 53	Hector Fajardo	.20	.08	.02	☐ 148	Nikco Riesgo	.40	.16	.04
☐ 54	Monty Fariss	.15	.06	.01	☐ 149	Carlos Rodriguez	.15	.06	.01
☐ 55	Jeff Fassero	.10	.04	.01	☐ 150	Ivan Rodriguez	.75	.30	.07
☐ 56	Dave Fleming	.15	.06	.01	☐ 151	Wayne Rosenthal	.10	.04	.01
☐ 57	Kevin Flora	.10	.04	.01	☐ 152	Rico Rossy	.15	.06	.01
☐ 58	Steve Foster	.15	.06	.01	☐ 153	Stan Royer	.10	.04	.01
☐ 59	Dan Gakeler	.10	.04	.01	☐ 154	Rey Sanchez	.15	.06	.01
☐ 60	Ramon Garcia	.10	.04	.01	☐ 155	Reggie Sanders	.25	.10	.02
☐ 61	Chris Gardner	.10	.04	.01	☐ 156	Mo Sanford	.15	.06	.01
☐ 62	Jeff Gardner	.10	.04	.01	☐ 157	Bob Scanlan	.10	.04	.01
☐ 63	Chris George	.10	.04	.01	☐ 158	Pete Schourek	.10	.04	.01
☐ 64	Ray Giannelli	.10	.04	.01	☐ 159	Gary Scott	.25	.10	.02
☐ 65	Tom Goodwin	.15	.06	.01	☐ 160	Tim Scott	.10	.04	.01
☐ 66	Mark Grater	.10	.04	.01	☐ 161	Tony Scruggs	.10	.04	.01
☐ 67	Johnny Guzman	.30	.12	.03	☐ 162	Scott Servais	.10	.04	.01
☐ 68	Juan Guzman	.50	.20	.05	☐ 163	Doug Simons	.10	.04	.01
☐ 69	Dave Haas	.10	.04	.01	☐ 164	Heathcliff Slocumb	.10	.04	.01
☐ 70	Chris Haney	.15	.06	.01	☐ 165	Joe Slusarski	.10	.04	.01
☐ 71	Shawn Hare	.15	.06	.01	☐ 166	Tim Spehr	.15	.06	.01
☐ 72	Donald Harris	.15	.06	.01	☐ 167	Ed Sprague	.20	.08	.02
☐ 73	Doug Henry	.10	.04	.01	☐ 168	Jeff Tackett	.10	.04	.01
☐ 74	Pat Hentgen	.20	.08	.02	☐ 169	Eddie Taubensee	.20	.08	.02
☐ 75	Gil Heredia	.10	.04	.01	☐ 170	Wade Taylor	.15	.06	.01
☐ 76	Jeremy Hernandez	.20	.08	.02	☐ 171	Jim Thome	.50	.20	.05
☐ 77	Jose Hernandez	.10	.04	.01	☐ 172	Mike Timlin	.15	.06	.01
☐ 78	Roberto Hernandez	.20	.08	.02	☐ 173	Jose Tolentino	.10	.04	.01
☐ 79	Bryan Hickerson	.15	.06	.01	☐ 174	John Vander Wal	.20	.08	.02
☐ 80	Milt Hill	.10	.04	.01	☐ 175	Todd Van Poppel	.60	.25	.06
☐ 81	Vince Horsman	.10	.04	.01	☐ 176	Mo Vaughn	.40	.16	.04
☐ 82	Wayne Housie	.15	.06	.01	☐ 177	Dave Wainhouse	.10	.04	.01
☐ 83	Chris Howard	.10	.04	.01	☐ 178	Don Wakamatsu	.10	.04	.01
☐ 84	David Howard	.10	.04	.01	☐ 179	Bruce Walton	.10	.04	.01
☐ 85	Mike Humphreys	.15	.06	.01	☐ 180	Kevin Ward	.10	.04	.01
☐ 86	Brian Hunter	.30	.12	.03	☐ 181	Dave Weathers	.20	.08	.02
☐ 87	Jim Hunter	.15	.06	.01	☐ 182	Eric Wedge	.20	.08	.02
☐ 88	Mike Ignasiak	.10	.04	.01	☐ 183	John Wehner	.25	.10	.02
☐ 89	Reggie Jefferson	.30	.12	.03	☐ 184	Rick Wilkins	.15	.06	.01
☐ 90	Jeff Johnson	.10	.04	.01	☐ 185	Bernie Williams	.35	.15	.03
☐ 91	Joel Johnston	.20	.08	.02	☐ 186	Brian Williams	.20	.08	.02
☐ 92	Calvin Jones	.15	.06	.01	☐ 187	Ron Witmeyer	.10	.04	.01
☐ 93	Chris Jones	.10	.04	.01	☐ 188	Mark Wohlers	.25	.10	.02
☐ 94	Stacy Jones	.15	.06	.01	☐ 189	Ted Wood	.20	.08	.02
☐ 95	Jeff Juden	.30	.12	.03	☐ 190	Anthony Young	.20	.08	.02
☐ 96	Scott Kamieniecki	.15	.06	.01	☐ 191	Eddie Zosky	.15	.06	.01
☐ 97	Eric Karros	.25	.10	.02	☐ 192	Bob Zupcic	.20	.08	.02
☐ 98	Pat Kelly	.25	.10	.02	☐ 193	Checklist 1	.05	.02	.00
☐ 99	John Kiely	.10	.04	.01	☐ 194	Checklist 2	.05	.02	.00

1987 Toys'R'Us Rookies

Topps produced this 33-card boxed set for Toys'R'Us stores. The set is subtitled "Baseball Rookies" and features predominantly younger players. The cards measure 2 1/2" by 3 1/2" and feature a high-gloss, full-color photo of the player inside a black border. The card backs are printed in orange and blue on white card stock.

	MINT	EXC	G-VG
COMPLETE SET (33)	8.00	3.50	.80
COMMON PLAYER (1-33)	.10	.04	.01
☐ 1 Andy Allanson	.10	.04	.01
☐ 2 Paul Assenmacher	.10	.04	.01
☐ 3 Scott Bailes	.10	.04	.01
☐ 4 Barry Bonds	.80	.35	.08
☐ 5 Jose Canseco	1.25	.50	.12
☐ 6 John Cerutti	.10	.04	.01
☐ 7 Will Clark	1.25	.50	.12
☐ 8 Kal Daniels	.40	.16	.04
☐ 9 Jim Deshaies	.10	.04	.01
☐ 10 Mark Eichhorn	.15	.06	.01
☐ 11 Ed Hearn	.10	.04	.01
☐ 12 Pete Incaviglia	.25	.10	.02
☐ 13 Bo Jackson	1.25	.50	.12
☐ 14 Wally Joyner	.60	.25	.06
☐ 15 Charlie Kerfeld	.10	.04	.01
☐ 16 Eric King	.15	.06	.01
☐ 17 John Kruk	.25	.10	.02
☐ 18 Barry Larkin	.70	.30	.07
☐ 19 Mike LaValliere	.10	.04	.01
☐ 20 Greg Mathews	.10	.04	.01
☐ 21 Kevin Mitchell	.80	.35	.08
☐ 22 Dan Plesac	.10	.04	.01
☐ 23 Bruce Ruffin	.10	.04	.01
☐ 24 Ruben Sierra	.90	.40	.09
☐ 25 Cory Snyder	.20	.08	.02
☐ 26 Kurt Stillwell	.15	.06	.01
☐ 27 Dale Sveum	.10	.04	.01
☐ 28 Danny Tartabull	.60	.25	.06
☐ 29 Andres Thomas	.10	.04	.01
☐ 30 Robby Thompson	.15	.06	.01
☐ 31 Jim Traber	.10	.04	.01
☐ 32 Mitch Williams	.15	.06	.01
☐ 33 Todd Worrell	.15	.06	.01

1988 Toys'R'Us Rookies

Topps produced this 33-card boxed set for Toys'R'Us stores. The set is subtitled "Baseball Rookies" and features predominantly younger players. The cards measure 2 1/2" by 3 1/2" and feature a high-gloss, full-color photo of the player inside a blue border. The card backs are printed in pink and blue on white card stock. The cards are numbered on the back and the checklist for the set is found on the back panel of the small collector box. The statistics provided on the card backs cover only three lines, Minor League totals, last season, and Major League totals.

	MINT	EXC	G-VG
COMPLETE SET (33)	5.00	2.25	.50
COMMON PLAYER (1-33)	.10	.04	.01
☐ 1 Todd Benzinger	.15	.06	.01
☐ 2 Bob Brower	.10	.04	.01
☐ 3 Jerry Browne	.10	.04	.01
☐ 4 DeWayne Buice	.10	.04	.01
☐ 5 Ellis Burks	.75	.30	.07
☐ 6 Ken Caminiti	.15	.06	.01
☐ 7 Casey Candaele	.10	.04	.01
☐ 8 Dave Cone	.50	.20	.05
☐ 9 Kelly Downs	.15	.06	.01
☐ 10 Mike Dunne	.10	.04	.01
☐ 11 Ken Gerhart	.10	.04	.01
☐ 12 Mike Greenwell	.75	.30	.07
☐ 13 Mike Henneman	.20	.08	.02
☐ 14 Sam Horn	.15	.06	.01
☐ 15 Joe Magrane	.15	.06	.01
☐ 16 Fred Manrique	.10	.04	.01
☐ 17 Mike Marzano	.15	.06	.01
☐ 18 Fred McGriff	.90	.40	.09
☐ 19 Mark McGwire	.90	.40	.09
☐ 20 Jeff Musselman	.10	.04	.01
☐ 21 Randy Myers	.15	.06	.01
☐ 22 Matt Nokes	.25	.10	.02
☐ 23 Al Pedrique	.10	.04	.01
☐ 24 Luis Polonia	.20	.08	.02
☐ 25 Billy Ripken	.15	.06	.01
☐ 26 Benito Santiago	.45	.18	.04
☐ 27 Kevin Seitzer	.25	.10	.02
☐ 28 John Smiley	.30	.12	.03
☐ 29 Mike Stanley	.15	.06	.01
☐ 30 Terry Steinbach	.20	.08	.02
☐ 31 B.J. Surhoff	.15	.06	.01
☐ 32 Bobby Thigpen	.20	.08	.02
☐ 33 Devon White	.25	.10	.02

1989 Toys'R'Us Rookies

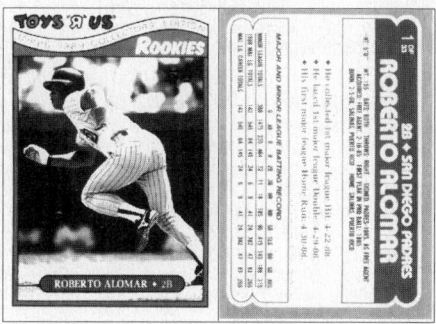

The 1989 Toys'R'Us Rookies set contains 33 standard-size (2 1/2" by 3 1/2") glossy cards. The fronts are yellow and magenta. The horizontally-oriented backs are sky blue and red, and feature 1988 and career stats. The cards were distributed through Toys 'R' Us stores as a boxed set. The subjects are numbered alphabetically. The set checklist is printed on the back panel of the set's custom box.

	MINT	EXC	G-VG
COMPLETE SET (33)	4.00	1.75	.40
COMMON PLAYER (1-33)	.10	.04	.01
☐ 1 Roberto Alomar	.60	.25	.06
☐ 2 Brady Anderson	.15	.06	.01
☐ 3 Tim Belcher	.20	.08	.02
☐ 4 Damon Berryhill	.15	.06	.01
☐ 5 Jay Buhner	.25	.10	.02
☐ 6 Sherman Corbett	.10	.04	.01
☐ 7 Kevin Elster	.15	.06	.01
☐ 8 Cecil Espy	.10	.04	.01
☐ 9 Dave Gallagher	.10	.04	.01
☐ 10 Ron Gant	.60	.25	.06
☐ 11 Paul Gibson	.10	.04	.01
☐ 12 Mark Grace	.50	.20	.05
☐ 13 Bryan Harvey	.25	.10	.02
☐ 14 Darrin Jackson	.15	.06	.01
☐ 15 Gregg Jefferies	.60	.25	.06
☐ 16 Ron Jones	.15	.06	.01
☐ 17 Ricky Jordan	.20	.08	.02
☐ 18 Roberto Kelly	.40	.16	.04
☐ 19 Al Leiter	.10	.04	.01
☐ 20 Jack McDowell	.30	.12	.03
☐ 21 Melido Perez	.20	.08	.02
☐ 22 Jeff Pico	.10	.04	.01
☐ 23 Jody Reed	.20	.08	.02
☐ 24 Chris Sabo	.45	.18	.04
☐ 25 Nelson Santovenia	.15	.06	.01
☐ 26 Mackey Sasser	.15	.06	.01
☐ 27 Mike Schooler	.15	.06	.01
☐ 28 Gary Sheffield	.30	.12	.03
☐ 29 Pete Smith	.10	.04	.01
☐ 30 Pete Stanicek	.10	.04	.01
☐ 31 Jeff Treadway	.15	.06	.01
☐ 32 Walt Weiss	.25	.10	.02
☐ 33 Dave West	.15	.06	.01

☐ 4 Andy Benes	.35	.15	.03
☐ 5 Greg Briley	.15	.06	.01
☐ 6 Kevin Brown	.15	.06	.01
☐ 7 Mark Carreon	.10	.04	.01
☐ 8 Mike Devereaux	.10	.04	.01
☐ 9 Junior Felix	.20	.08	.02
☐ 10 Mark Gardner	.10	.04	.01
☐ 11 Bob Geren	.10	.04	.01
☐ 12 Tom Gordon	.20	.08	.02
☐ 13 Ken Griffey Jr.	1.25	.50	.12
☐ 14 Pete Harnisch	.15	.06	.01
☐ 15 Ken Hill	.15	.06	.01
☐ 16 Gregg Jefferies	.30	.12	.03
☐ 17 Derek Lilliquist	.10	.04	.01
☐ 18 Carlos Martinez	.10	.04	.01
☐ 19 Ramon Martinez	.40	.16	.04
☐ 20 Bob Milacki	.10	.04	.01
☐ 21 Gregg Olson	.25	.10	.02
☐ 22 Kenny Rogers	.15	.06	.01
☐ 23 Alex Sanchez	.10	.04	.01
☐ 24 Gary Sheffield	.25	.10	.02
☐ 25 Dwight Smith	.15	.06	.01
☐ 26 Billy Spiers	.10	.04	.01
☐ 27 Greg Vaughn	.40	.16	.04
☐ 28 Robin Ventura	.50	.20	.05
☐ 29 Jerome Walton	.20	.08	.02
☐ 30 Dave West	.15	.06	.01
☐ 31 John Wetteland	.15	.06	.01
☐ 32 Craig Worthington	.10	.04	.01
☐ 33 Todd Zeile	.30	.12	.03

1991 Toys'R'Us Rookies

For the fifth year in a row this 33-card set was produced by Topps for Toys'R'Us, and the sponsor's logo adorns the top of the card front. The cards measure the standard size (2 1/2" by 3 1/2"). The front design features glossy color action player photos with yellow borders on a black card face. The words "Topps 1991 Collectors' Edition" appear in a yellow stripe above the picture. The horizontally oriented backs are printed in brown and yellow, and present biographical information, career highlights, and statistics. The cards are numbered on the back.

	MINT	EXC	G-VG
COMPLETE SET (33)	4.00	1.75	.40
COMMON PLAYER (1-33)	.10	.04	.01
☐ 1 Sandy Alomar Jr.	.30	.12	.03
☐ 2 Kevin Appier	.20	.08	.02
☐ 3 Steve Avery	.50	.20	.05
☐ 4 Carlos Baerga	.30	.12	.03
☐ 5 Alex Cole	.15	.06	.01
☐ 6 Pat Combs	.15	.06	.01
☐ 7 Delino DeShields	.20	.08	.02
☐ 8 Travis Fryman	.40	.16	.04
☐ 9 Marquis Grissom	.30	.12	.03
☐ 10 Mike Harkey	.15	.06	.01
☐ 11 Glenallen Hill	.10	.04	.01
☐ 12 Jeff Huson	.10	.04	.01
☐ 13 Felix Jose	.30	.12	.03
☐ 14 Dave Justice	.60	.25	.06
☐ 15 Dana Kiecker	.10	.04	.01

1990 Toys'R'Us Rookies

The 1990 Toys'R'Us Rookies set is a 33-card set of young prospects issued by Topps. For the fourth consecutive year Topps issued a rookie set for Toys'R'Us. There are several players in the set which were on Topps cards for the second time in 1990, i.e., not rookies even for the Topps Company. These players included Gregg Jefferies and Gregg Olson. This standard-size (2 1/2" by 3 1/2") card set might be more appropriately called the Young Stars set. The cards are numbered, with the numbering being essentially in alphabetical order by player's name. The set checklist is printed on the back panel of the set's custom box.

	MINT	EXC	G-VG
COMPLETE SET (33)	4.00	1.75	.40
COMMON PLAYER (1-33)	.10	.04	.01
☐ 1 Jim Abbott	.50	.20	.05
☐ 2 Eric Anthony	.25	.10	.02
☐ 3 Joey Belle	.40	.16	.04

		MINT	EXC	G-VG
☐ 16	Kevin Maas	.30	.12	.03
☐ 17	Ben McDonald	.30	.12	.03
☐ 18	Brian McRae	.30	.12	.03
☐ 19	Kent Mercker	.15	.06	.01
☐ 20	Hal Morris	.30	.12	.03
☐ 21	Chris Nabholz	.15	.06	.01
☐ 22	Tim Naehring	.15	.06	.01
☐ 23	Jose Offerman	.20	.08	.02
☐ 24	John Olerud	.40	.16	.04
☐ 25	Scott Radinsky	.15	.06	.01
☐ 26	Bill Sampen	.10	.04	.01
☐ 27	Frank Thomas	.90	.40	.09
☐ 28	Randy Tomlin	.20	.08	.02
☐ 29	Greg Vaughn	.30	.12	.03
☐ 30	Robin Ventura	.40	.16	.04
☐ 31	Larry Walker	.20	.08	.02
☐ 32	Wally Whitehurst	.10	.04	.01
☐ 33	Todd Zeile	.25	.10	.02

1983 True Value White Sox

MARC HILL
Catcher 7

This 23-card set was sponsored by True Value Hardware Stores and features full-color (2 5/8" by 4 1/4") cards of the Chicago White Sox. Most of the set was intended for distribution two cards per game at selected White Sox Tuesday night home games. The cards are unnumbered except for uniform number given in the lower right corner of the obverse. The card backs contain statistical information in basic black and white. The cards of Harold Baines, Salome Barojas, and Marc Hill were not issued at the park; hence they are more difficult to obtain than the other 20 cards and are marked SP in the checklist below.

		MINT	EXC	G-VG
COMPLETE SET (23)		36.00	16.25	5.50
COMMON PLAYER (1-23)		.50	.20	.05
☐ 1	Scott Fletcher	.90	.40	.09
☐ 3	Harold Baines SP	10.00	4.50	1.25
☐ 5	Vance Law	.60	.25	.06
☐ 7	Marc Hill SP	5.00	2.25	.50
☐ 10	Tony LaRussa MG	.90	.40	.09
☐ 11	Rudy Law	.50	.20	.05
☐ 14	Tony Bernazard	.60	.25	.06
☐ 17	Jerry Hairston	.50	.20	.05
☐ 19	Greg Luzinski	.90	.40	.09
☐ 24	Floyd Bannister	.60	.25	.06
☐ 25	Mike Squires	.50	.20	.05
☐ 30	Salome Barojas SP	5.00	2.25	.50
☐ 31	LaMarr Hoyt	.60	.25	.06
☐ 34	Richard Dotson	.60	.25	.06
☐ 36	Jerry Koosman	.90	.40	.09
☐ 40	Britt Burns	.60	.25	.06
☐ 41	Dick Tidrow	.50	.20	.05
☐ 42	Ron Kittle	1.00	.40	.10
☐ 44	Tom Paciorek	.50	.20	.05
☐ 45	Kevin Hickey	.50	.20	.05
☐ 53	Dennis Lamp	.50	.20	.05
☐ 67	Jim Kern	.50	.20	.05
☐ 72	Carlton Fisk	4.00	1.75	.40

1984 True Value White Sox

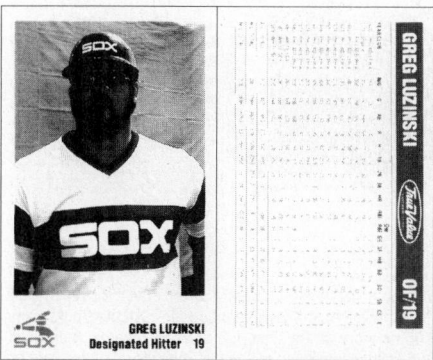

GREG LUZINSKI
Designated Hitter 19

This 30-card set features full color (2 1/2" by 4") cards of the Chicago White Sox. Most of the set was distributed two cards per game at selected White Sox Tuesday home games. Faust and Minoso were not given out although their cards were available through direct (promotional) contact with them. Brennan and Hulett were not released directly since they were sent down to the minors. The cards are unnumbered except for uniform number given in the lower right corner of the obverse; they are arbitrarily listed below in alphabetical order. The card backs contain statistical information in basic black and white.

		MINT	EXC	G-VG
COMPLETE SET (30)		28.00	12.50	4.00
COMMON PLAYER (1-30)		.50	.20	.05
☐ 1	Juan Agosto	.50	.20	.05
☐ 2	Luis Aparicio	3.00	1.25	.30
☐ 3	Harold Baines	1.50	.60	.15
☐ 4	Floyd Bannister	.60	.25	.06
☐ 5	Salome Barojas	.50	.20	.05
☐ 6	Tom Brennan SP	2.50	1.00	.25
☐ 7	Britt Burns	.60	.25	.06
☐ 8	Coaching Staff	.50	.20	.05
	(blank back)			
☐ 9	Julio Cruz	.50	.20	.05
☐ 10	Richard Dotson	.60	.25	.06
☐ 11	Jerry Dybzinski	.50	.20	.05
☐ 12	Nancy Faust	2.00	.80	.20
	(organist)			
	(blank back)			
☐ 13	Carlton Fisk	3.50	1.50	.35
☐ 14	Scott Fletcher	.60	.25	.06
☐ 15	Jerry Hairston	.50	.20	.05
☐ 16	Marc Hill	.50	.20	.05
☐ 17	LaMarr Hoyt	.60	.25	.06
☐ 18	Tim Hulett SP	2.50	1.00	.25
☐ 19	Ron Kittle	.90	.40	.09
☐ 20	Tony LaRussa MG	.90	.40	.09
☐ 21	Rudy Law	.50	.20	.05
☐ 22	Vance Law	.60	.25	.06
☐ 23	Greg Luzinski	.75	.30	.07
☐ 24	Minnie Minoso	3.00	1.25	.30
☐ 25	Tom Paciorek	.50	.20	.05
☐ 26	Ron Reed	.50	.20	.05
☐ 27	Tom Seaver	4.50	2.00	.45
☐ 28	Dave Stegman	.50	.20	.05
☐ 29	Mike Squires	.50	.20	.05
☐ 30	Greg Walker	.60	.25	.06

1986 True Value

The 1986 True Value set consists of 30 cards each 2 1/2" by 3 1/2" which were printed as panels of four although one of the cards in the panel only pictures a featured product. The complete panel measures 10 3/8" by 3 1/2". The True Value

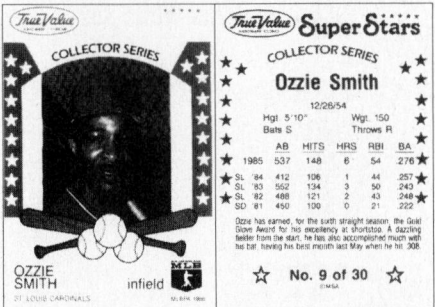

logo is in the upper left corner of the obverse of each card. Supposedly the cards were distributed to customers purchasing 5.00 or more at the store. Cards are frequently found with perforations intact and still in the closed form where only the top card in the folded panel is visible. The card number appears at the bottom of the reverse. Team logos have been surgically removed (airbrushed) from the photos.

	MINT	EXC	G-VG
COMPLETE SET (30)	8.00	3.50	.80
COMMON PLAYER (1-30)	.15	.06	.01

		MINT	EXC	G-VG
☐ 1	Pedro Guerrero	.20	.08	.02
☐ 2	Steve Garvey	.30	.12	.03
☐ 3	Eddie Murray	.45	.18	.04
☐ 4	Pete Rose	.60	.25	.06
☐ 5	Don Mattingly	.50	.20	.05
☐ 6	Fernando Valenzuela	.20	.08	.02
☐ 7	Jim Rice	.20	.08	.02
☐ 8	Kirk Gibson	.25	.10	.02
☐ 9	Ozzie Smith	.30	.12	.03
☐ 10	Dale Murphy	.35	.15	.03
☐ 11	Robin Yount	.45	.18	.04
☐ 12	Tom Seaver	.50	.20	.05
☐ 13	Reggie Jackson	.50	.20	.05
☐ 14	Ryne Sandberg	.60	.25	.06
☐ 15	Bruce Sutter	.15	.06	.01
☐ 16	Gary Carter	.20	.08	.02
☐ 17	George Brett	.45	.18	.04
☐ 18	Rick Sutcliffe	.15	.06	.01
☐ 19	Dave Stieb	.15	.06	.01
☐ 20	Buddy Bell	.15	.06	.01
☐ 21	Alvin Davis	.15	.06	.01
☐ 22	Cal Ripken	.60	.25	.06
☐ 23	Bill Madlock	.15	.06	.01
☐ 24	Kent Hrbek	.15	.06	.01
☐ 25	Lou Whitaker	.15	.06	.01
☐ 26	Nolan Ryan	.75	.30	.07
☐ 27	Dwayne Murphy	.15	.06	.01
☐ 28	Mike Schmidt	.60	.25	.06
☐ 29	Andre Dawson	.30	.12	.03
☐ 30	Wade Boggs	.50	.20	.05

1911 T3 Turkey Red

The cards in this 126-card set measure approximately 5 3/4" by 8". The 1911 "Turkey Red" set of color cabinet style cards, designated T3 in the American Card Catalog, is named after the brand of cigarettes with which it was offered as a premium. Cards 1-50 and 77-126 depict baseball players while the middle series (51-76) portrays boxers. The cards themselves are not numbered but were assigned numbers for ordering purposes by the manufacturer. This list appears on the backs of cards in the 77-126 sub-series and has been used in the checklist below. The boxers (51-76) were formerly assigned a separate catalog number (T9) but have now been returned to the classification to which they properly belong and are indicated in the checklist below by BOX. This attractive set has been reprinted recently in 2 1/2" by 3 1/2" form.

	EX-MT	VG-E	GOOD
COMPLETE SET (126)	39000.	18000.	5000.
COMMON BASEBALL (1-50)	225.00	100.00	33.00
COMMON BOXERS (51-76)	125.00	57.50	18.75
COMMON BASEBALL (77-126)	250.00	110.00	37.50

		EX-MT	VG-E	GOOD
☐ 1	M. Brown: Chicago NL	450.00	200.00	67.50
☐ 2	Bergen: Brooklyn	225.00	100.00	33.00
☐ 3	Leach: Pittsburgh	225.00	100.00	33.00
☐ 4	Bresnahan: St.L. NL	400.00	180.00	60.00
☐ 5	Crawford: Detroit	450.00	200.00	67.50
☐ 6	Chase: New York AL	275.00	120.00	40.00
☐ 7	Camnitz: Pittsburgh	225.00	100.00	33.00
☐ 8	Clarke: Pittsburgh	400.00	180.00	60.00
☐ 9	Cobb: Detroit	5000.00	2000.00	600.00
☐ 10	Devlin: New York NL	225.00	100.00	33.00
☐ 11	Dahlen: Brooklyn	275.00	120.00	40.00
☐ 12	Donovan: Detroit	225.00	100.00	33.00
☐ 13	Doyle: New York NL	225.00	100.00	33.00
☐ 14	Dooin: Phila. NL	225.00	100.00	33.00
☐ 15	Elberfeld: Wash	225.00	100.00	33.00
☐ 16	Evers: Chicago NL	450.00	200.00	67.50
☐ 17	Griffith: Cinc.	400.00	180.00	60.00
☐ 18	Jennings: Detroit	400.00	180.00	60.00
☐ 19	Joss: Cleveland	500.00	225.00	75.00
☐ 20	Jordan: Brooklyn	225.00	100.00	33.00
☐ 21	Kleinow: New York NL	225.00	100.00	33.00
☐ 22	Krause: Phila. AL	225.00	100.00	33.00
☐ 23	Lajoie: Cleveland	1000.00	450.00	135.00
☐ 24	Mitchell: Cincinnati	225.00	100.00	33.00
☐ 25	M. McIntyre: Detroit	225.00	100.00	33.00
☐ 26	McGraw: New York NL	600.00	270.00	90.00
☐ 27	Mathewson: N.Y. NL	1350.00	600.00	175.00
☐ 28	H. McIntyre: Brk	225.00	100.00	33.00
☐ 29	McConnell: Boston AL	225.00	100.00	33.00
☐ 30	Mullin: Detroit	225.00	100.00	33.00
☐ 31	Magee: Phila. NL	225.00	100.00	33.00
☐ 32	Overall: Chicago NL	225.00	100.00	33.00
☐ 33	Pfeister: Chicago NL	225.00	100.00	33.00
☐ 34	Rucker: Brooklyn	225.00	100.00	33.00
☐ 35	Tinker: Chicago NL	450.00	200.00	67.50
☐ 36	Speaker: Boston AL	1000.00	450.00	125.00
☐ 37	Sallee: St. Louis NL	225.00	100.00	33.00
☐ 38	Stahl: Boston AL	225.00	100.00	33.00
☐ 39	Waddell: St.Louis AL	500.00	225.00	75.00
☐ 40	Willis: St.Louis NL	275.00	120.00	40.00
☐ 41	Wiltse: New York NL	225.00	100.00	33.00
☐ 42	Young: Cleveland	1200.00	500.00	150.00
☐ 43	Out At Third	225.00	100.00	33.00
☐ 44	Trying to Catch Him Napping	225.00	100.00	33.00
☐ 45	Jordan and Herzog at First	225.00	100.00	33.00
☐ 46	Safe At Third	225.00	100.00	33.00
☐ 47	Frank Chance At Bat	400.00	180.00	60.00
☐ 48	Jack Murray At Bat	225.00	100.00	33.00
☐ 49	Close Play At Second	225.00	100.00	33.00
☐ 50	Chief Meyers At Bat	225.00	100.00	33.00
☐ 51	Jim Driscoll BOX	125.00	57.50	18.75
☐ 52	Abe Attell BOX	150.00	67.50	22.50
☐ 53	Ad. Walgast BOX	125.00	57.50	18.75
☐ 54	Johnny Coulon BOX	125.00	57.50	18.75
☐ 55	James Jeffries BOX	250.00	110.00	37.50
☐ 56	Jack Sullivan BOX (Twin)	150.00	67.50	22.50
☐ 57	Battling Nelson BOX	125.00	57.50	18.75
☐ 58	Packey McFarland BOX	125.00	57.50	18.75
☐ 59	Tommy Murphy BOX	125.00	57.50	18.75
☐ 60	Owen Moran BOX	125.00	57.50	18.75
☐ 61	Johnny Marto BOX	125.00	57.50	18.75
☐ 62	Jimmie Gardner BOX	125.00	57.50	18.75
☐ 63	Harry Lewis BOX	125.00	57.50	18.75
☐ 64	Wm. Papke BOX	125.00	57.50	18.75
☐ 65	Sam Langford BOX	125.00	57.50	18.75
☐ 66	Knock-out Brown BOX	125.00	57.50	18.75

		EX-MT	VG-E	GOOD
☐ 67	Stanley Ketchel BOX	175.00	80.00	27.00
☐ 68	Joe Jeannette BOX	125.00	57.50	18.75
☐ 69	Leach Cross BOX	125.00	57.50	18.75
☐ 70	Phil. McGovern BOX	125.00	57.50	18.75
☐ 71	Battling Hurley BOX	125.00	57.50	18.75
☐ 72	Honey Mellody BOX	125.00	57.50	18.75
☐ 73	Al Kaufman BOX	125.00	57.50	18.75
☐ 74	Willie Lewis BOX	125.00	57.50	18.75
☐ 75	Jack O'Brien BOX "Philadelphia"	150.00	67.50	22.50
☐ 76	Jack Johnson BOX	250.00	110.00	37.50
☐ 77	Ames: New York NL	250.00	110.00	37.50
☐ 78	Baker: Phila. AL (picture probably Jack Barry)	450.00	200.00	67.50
☐ 79	Bell: Brooklyn	250.00	110.00	37.50
☐ 80	Bender: Phila. AL	450.00	200.00	67.50
☐ 81	Bescher: Cincinnati	250.00	110.00	37.50
☐ 82	Bransfield: Phila. NL	250.00	110.00	37.50
☐ 83	Bridwell: Phila. NL	250.00	110.00	37.50
☐ 84	Browne: Wash. and Chicago	250.00	110.00	37.50
☐ 85	Burns: Chi. and Cin.	250.00	110.00	37.50
☐ 86	Carrigan: Boston AL	250.00	110.00	37.50
☐ 87	Collins: Phila. AL	500.00	225.00	75.00
☐ 88	Coveleski: Cinc.	250.00	110.00	37.50
☐ 89	Criger: New York AL	250.00	110.00	37.50
☐ 90	Doolan: Phila. NL	250.00	110.00	37.50
☐ 91	Downey: Cincinnati	250.00	110.00	37.50
☐ 92	Dygert: Phila. AL	250.00	110.00	37.50
☐ 93	Fromme: Cincinnati	250.00	110.00	37.50
☐ 94	Gibson: Pittsburgh	250.00	110.00	37.50
☐ 95	Graham: Boston NL	250.00	110.00	37.50
☐ 96	Groom: Washington	250.00	110.00	37.50
☐ 97	Hoblitzell: Cinc.	250.00	110.00	37.50
☐ 98	Hofman: Chicago NL	250.00	110.00	37.50
☐ 99	Johnson: Washington	1500.00	650.00	200.00
☐ 100	D. Jones: Detroit	250.00	110.00	37.50
☐ 101	Keeler: New York NL	650.00	300.00	100.00
☐ 102	Kling: Chicago NL	250.00	110.00	37.50
☐ 103	Konetchy: St.Louis NL	250.00	110.00	37.50
☐ 104	Lennox: Brooklyn	250.00	110.00	37.50
☐ 105	Lobert: Cincinnati	250.00	110.00	37.50
☐ 106	Lord: Bos. and Chi.	250.00	110.00	37.50
☐ 107	Manning: N.Y. AL	250.00	110.00	37.50
☐ 108	Merkle: New York NL	250.00	110.00	37.50
☐ 109	Moran: Chi. and Phila.	250.00	110.00	37.50
☐ 110	McBride: Washington	250.00	110.00	37.50
☐ 111	Niles: Bos. and Cleve.	250.00	110.00	37.50
☐ 112	Paskert: Cincinnati	250.00	110.00	37.50
☐ 113	Raymond: N.Y. NL	250.00	110.00	37.50
☐ 114	Rhoades: Cleveland	300.00	135.00	45.00
☐ 115	Schlei: New York NL	250.00	110.00	37.50
☐ 116	Schmidt: Detroit	250.00	110.00	37.50
☐ 117	Schulte: Chicago NL	250.00	110.00	37.50
☐ 118	Smith: Chi. and Bos.	250.00	110.00	37.50
☐ 119	Stone: St.L. AL	250.00	110.00	37.50
☐ 120	Street: Washington	250.00	110.00	37.50
☐ 121	Sullivan: Chi. AL	250.00	110.00	37.50
☐ 122	Tenney: New York NL	250.00	110.00	37.50
☐ 123	Thomas: Phila. AL	250.00	110.00	37.50
☐ 124	Wallace: St.Louis AL	400.00	180.00	60.00
☐ 125	Walsh: Chicago AL	450.00	200.00	67.50
☐ 126	Wilson: Pittsburgh	250.00	110.00	37.50

1913 T200 Fatima

The cards in this 16-card set measure 2 5/8" by 5 13/16". The 1913 Fatima Cigarettes issue contains unnumbered glossy surface team cards. Both St. Louis team cards are considered difficult to obtain. A large 13" by 21" unnumbered, heavy cardboard premium issue is also known to exist and is quite scarce. These unnumbered team cards are ordered below by team alphabetical order within league.

		EX-MT	VG-E	GOOD
	COMPLETE SET (16)	3500.00	1500.00	500.00
	COMMON TEAM (1-16)	165.00	75.00	22.50
☐ 1	Boston AL	225.00	100.00	33.00
☐ 2	Chicago AL	165.00	75.00	22.50
☐ 3	Cleveland AL	325.00	150.00	50.00
☐ 4	Detroit AL	325.00	150.00	50.00
☐ 5	New York AL	550.00	240.00	80.00
☐ 6	Philadelphia AL	165.00	75.00	22.50
☐ 7	St. Louis AL	450.00	200.00	67.50

		EX-MT	VG-E	GOOD
☐ 8	Washington AL	225.00	100.00	33.00
☐ 9	Boston NL	275.00	120.00	40.00
☐ 10	Brooklyn NL	165.00	75.00	22.50
☐ 11	Chicago NL	165.00	75.00	22.50
☐ 12	Cincinnati NL	165.00	75.00	22.50
☐ 13	New York NL	275.00	120.00	40.00
☐ 14	Philadelphia NL	165.00	75.00	22.50
☐ 15	Pittsburg NL	165.00	75.00	22.50
☐ 16	St. Louis NL	275.00	120.00	40.00

1911 T201 Mecca

The cards in this 50-card set measure 2 1/4" by 4 11/16". The 1911 Mecca Double Folder issue contains unnumbered cards. This issue was one of the first to list statistics of players portrayed on the cards. Each card portrays two players, one when the card is folded, another when the card is unfolded. The card of Dougherty and Lord is considered scarce.

		EX-MT	VG-E	GOOD
	COMPLETE SET (50)	5000.00	2250.00	650.00
	COMMON PAIR (1-50)	50.00	22.50	7.50
☐ 1	F.Baker and Collins	150.00	67.50	22.50
☐ 2	Barry and Lapp	50.00	22.50	7.50
☐ 3	Bergen and Z.Wheat	100.00	45.00	15.00
☐ 4	Blair and Hartzell	50.00	22.50	7.50

		EX-MT	VG-E	GOOD
☐ 5	Bresnahan and Huggins	150.00	67.50	22.50
☐ 6	Bridwell and	350.00	160.00	52.50
	Mathewson			
☐ 7	Butler and Abstein	50.00	22.50	7.50
☐ 8	Byrne and F.Clarke	100.00	45.00	15.00
☐ 9	Chance and Evers	200.00	90.00	30.00
☐ 10	Clarke and Gaspar	50.00	22.50	7.50
☐ 11	Cobb and S.Crawford	1250.00	500.00	135.00
☐ 12	Cole and Kling	50.00	22.50	7.50
☐ 13	Coombs and Thomas	50.00	22.50	7.50
☐ 14	Daubert and Rucker	50.00	22.50	7.50
☐ 15	Dougherty and Lord	350.00	160.00	52.50
☐ 16	Dooin and Titus	50.00	22.50	7.50
☐ 17	Downie and Baker	50.00	22.50	7.50
☐ 18	Dygert and Seymour	50.00	22.50	7.50
☐ 19	Elberfeld and McBride	50.00	22.50	7.50
☐ 20	Gardner and Lajoie	150.00	67.50	22.50
☐ 21	Fitzpatrick and Killian	50.00	22.50	7.50
☐ 22	Gardner and Speaker	150.00	67.50	22.50
☐ 23	Gibson and Leach	50.00	22.50	7.50
☐ 24	Graham and Mattern	50.00	22.50	7.50
☐ 25	Hauser and Lush	50.00	22.50	7.50
☐ 26	Herzog and Miller	50.00	22.50	7.50
☐ 27	Hinchman and Hickman	50.00	22.50	7.50
☐ 28	Hofman and M.Brown	100.00	45.00	15.00
☐ 29	Jennings and Summers	100.00	45.00	15.00
☐ 30	Johnson and Ford	50.00	22.50	7.50
☐ 31	McCarty and McGinnity	100.00	45.00	15.00
☐ 32	McGlyn and Barrett	50.00	22.50	7.50
☐ 33	McLean and Grant	50.00	22.50	7.50
☐ 34	Merkle and Wiltse	50.00	22.50	7.50
☐ 35	Meyers and Doyle	50.00	22.50	7.50
☐ 36	Moore and Lobert	50.00	22.50	7.50
☐ 37	Odwell and Downs	50.00	22.50	7.50
☐ 38	Oldring and Bender	100.00	45.00	15.00
☐ 39	Payne and Walsh	100.00	45.00	15.00
☐ 40	Simon and Leifield	50.00	22.50	7.50
☐ 41	Starr and McCabe	50.00	22.50	7.50
☐ 42	Stephens and LaPorte	50.00	22.50	7.50
☐ 43	Stovall and Turner	50.00	22.50	7.50
☐ 44	Street and W.Johnson	400.00	180.00	60.00
☐ 45	Stroud and Donovan	50.00	22.50	7.50
☐ 46	Sweeney and Chase	50.00	22.50	7.50
☐ 47	Thoney and Cicotte	50.00	22.50	7.50
☐ 48	Wallace and Lake	100.00	45.00	15.00
☐ 49	Ward and Foster	50.00	22.50	7.50
☐ 50	Williams and Woodruff	50.00	22.50	7.50

1912 T202 Triple Folders

The cards in this 134-card set measure 2 1/4" by 5 1/4". The 1912 T202 Hassan Triple Folder issue is perhaps the most ingenious baseball card ever issued. The two end cards of each panel are full color, T205-like individual cards whereas the black and white

center panel pictures an action photo or portrait. The end cards can be folded across the center panel and stored in this manner. Seventy-six different center panels are known to exist; however, many of the center panels contain more than one combination of end cards. The center panel titles are listed below in alphabetical order while the different combinations of end cards are listed below each center panel as they appear left to right on the front of the card. A total of 132 different card fronts exist. The set price below includes all panel and player combinations listed in the checklist. Back color variations (red or black) also exist. The Birmingham's Home Run card is difficult to obtain as are other cards whose center panel exists with but one combination of end cards. The Devlin with Mathewson end panels on numbers 29A and 74C picture Devlin as a Giant. Devlin is pictured as a Rustler on 29B and 74D.

		EX-MT	VG-E	GOOD
	COMPLETE SET (132)	32500.	14500.	4500.
	COMMON PANEL (1-76)	150.00	67.50	22.50
☐ 1A	A Close Play at Home:	175.00	80.00	27.00
	Wallace-LaPorte			
☐ 1B	A Close Play at Home:	175.00	80.00	27.00
	Wallace-Pelty			
☐ 2	A Desperate Slide:	1200.00	500.00	150.00
	O'Leary-Cobb			
☐ 3A	A Great Batsman:	150.00	67.50	22.50
	Barger-Bergen			
☐ 3B	A Great Batsman:	150.00	67.50	22.50
	Rucker-Bergen			
☐ 4	Ambrose McConnell at	175.00	80.00	27.00
	Bat: Blair-Quinn			
☐ 5	A Wide Throw Saves	200.00	90.00	30.00
	Crawford:			
	Mullin-Stanage			
☐ 6	Baker Gets His Man:	300.00	135.00	45.00
	Collins-Baker			
☐ 7	Birmingham Gets to	400.00	180.00	60.00
	Third:			
	Johnson-Street			
☐ 8	Birmingham's Home	400.00	180.00	60.00
	Run:			
	Birmingham-Turner			
☐ 9	Bush Just Misses	175.00	80.00	27.00
	Austin: Moran-Magee			
☐ 10A	Carrigan Blocks His	150.00	67.50	22.50
	Man: Gaspar-McLean			
☐ 10B	Carrigan Blocks His	150.00	67.50	22.50
	Man: Wagner-Carrigan			
☐ 11	Catching Him Napping:	200.00	90.00	30.00
	Oakes-Bresnahan			
☐ 12	Caught Asleep	200.00	90.00	30.00
	Off First:			
	Bresnahan-Harmon			
☐ 13A	Chance Beats Out a	250.00	110.00	37.50
	Hit: Chance-Foxen			
☐ 13B	Chance Beats Out a	175.00	80.00	27.00
	Hit: McIntire-Archer			
☐ 13C	Chance Beats Out a	175.00	80.00	27.00
	Hit: Overall-Archer			
☐ 13D	Chance Beats Out a	175.00	80.00	27.00
	Hit: Rowan-Archer			
☐ 13E	Chance Beats Out a	250.00	110.00	37.50
	Hit: Shean-Chance			
☐ 14A	Chase Dives into	150.00	67.50	22.50
	Third: Chase-Wolter			
☐ 14B	Chase Dives into	175.00	80.00	27.00
	Third: Gibson-Clarke			
☐ 14C	Chase Dives into	150.00	67.50	22.50
	Third:			
	Phillippe-Gibson			
☐ 15A	Chase Gets Ball Too	150.00	67.50	22.50
	Late: Egan-Mitchell			
☐ 15B	Chase Gets Ball Too	150.00	67.50	22.50
	Late: Wolter-Chase			
☐ 16A	Chase Guarding First:	150.00	67.50	22.50
	Chase-Wolter			
☐ 16B	Chase Guarding First:	175.00	80.00	27.00
	Gibson-Clarke			
☐ 16C	Chase Guarding First:	150.00	67.50	22.50
	Leifield-Gibson			
☐ 17	Chase Ready Squeeze	175.00	80.00	27.00
	Play: Paskert-Magee			
☐ 18	Chase Safe at Third:	200.00	90.00	30.00
	Barry-Baker			
☐ 19	Chief Bender Waiting:	225.00	100.00	33.00
	Bender-Thomas			
☐ 20	Clarke Hikes for Home:	200.00	90.00	30.00
	Bridwell-Kling			

	Description			
☐ 21	Close at First: Ball-Stovall	175.00	80.00	27.00
☐ 22A	Close at the Plate: Walsh-Payne	175.00	80.00	27.00
☐ 22B	Close at the Plate: White-Payne	150.00	67.50	22.50
☐ 23	Close at Third (Speaker): Wood-Speaker	375.00	165.00	55.00
☐ 24	Close at Third (Wagner): Wagner-Carrigan	175.00	80.00	27.00
☐ 25A	Collins Easily Safe: Byrne-Clarke	175.00	80.00	27.00
☐ 25B	Collins Easily Safe: Collins-Baker	300.00	135.00	45.00
☐ 25C	Collins Easily Safe: Collins-Murphy	250.00	110.00	37.50
☐ 26	Crawford About to Smash: Stanage-Summers	200.00	90.00	30.00
☐ 27	Cree Rolls Home: Daubert-Hummell	175.00	80.00	27.00
☐ 28	Davy Jones' Great Slide: Delahanty-Jones	175.00	80.00	27.00
☐ 29A	Devlin Gets His Man: Devlin (Giants)-Mathewson	1000.00	450.00	135.00
☐ 29B	Devlin Gets His Man: Devlin (Rustlers)-Mathewson	300.00	135.00	45.00
☐ 29C	Devlin Gets His Man: Fletcher-Mathewson	300.00	135.00	45.00
☐ 29D	Devlin Gets His Man: Meyers-Mathewson	300.00	135.00	45.00
☐ 30A	Donlin Out at First: Camnitz-Gibson	150.00	67.50	22.50
☐ 30B	Donlin Out at First: Doyle-Merkle	150.00	67.50	22.50
☐ 30C	Donlin Out at First: Leach-Wilson	150.00	67.50	22.50
☐ 30D	Donlin Out at First: Magee-Dooin	150.00	67.50	22.50
☐ 30E	Donlin Out at First: Phillippe-Gibson	150.00	67.50	22.50
☐ 31A	Dooin Gets His Man: Dooin-Doolan	150.00	67.50	22.50
☐ 31B	Dooin Gets His Man: Lobert-Dooin	150.00	67.50	22.50
☐ 31C	Dooin Gets His Man: Titus-Dooin	150.00	67.50	22.50
☐ 32	Easy for Larry: Doyle-Merkle	175.00	80.00	27.00
☐ 33	Elberfeld Beats: Milan-Elberfeld	175.00	80.00	27.00
☐ 34	Elberfeld Gets His Man: Milan-Elberfeld	175.00	80.00	27.00
☐ 35	Engle in a Close Play: Speaker-Engle	250.00	110.00	37.50
☐ 36A	Evers Makes Safe Slide: Archer-Evers	225.00	100.00	33.00
☐ 36B	Evers Makes Safe Slide: Evers-Chance	300.00	135.00	45.00
☐ 36C	Evers Makes Safe Slide: Overall-Archer	175.00	80.00	27.00
☐ 36D	Evers Makes Safe Slide: Reulbach-Archer	175.00	80.00	27.00
☐ 36E	Evers Makes Safe Slide: Tinker-Chance	750.00	325.00	110.00
☐ 37	Fast Work at Third: O'Leary-Cobb	1200.00	500.00	150.00
☐ 38A	Ford Putting Over Spitter: Ford-Vaughn	150.00	67.50	22.50
☐ 38B	Ford Putting Over Spitter: Sweeney-Ford	150.00	67.50	22.50
☐ 39	Good Play at Third: Moriarty-Cobb	1200.00	500.00	150.00
☐ 40	Grant Gets His Man: Hoblitzel-Grant	175.00	80.00	27.00
☐ 41A	Hal Chase Too Late: McIntyre-McConnell	150.00	67.50	22.50
☐ 41B	Hal Chase Too Late: Suggs-McLean	150.00	67.50	22.50
☐ 42	Harry Lord at Third: Lennox-Tinker	200.00	90.00	30.00
☐ 43	Hartzell Covering: Scanlon-Dahlen	175.00	80.00	27.00
☐ 44	Hartzell Strikes Out: Groom-Gray	175.00	80.00	27.00
☐ 45	Held at Third: Tannehill-Lord	175.00	80.00	27.00
☐ 46	Jake Stahl Guarding: Cicotte-Stahl	175.00	80.00	27.00
☐ 47	Jim Delahanty at Bat: Delahanty-Jones	175.00	80.00	27.00
☐ 48A	Just Before the Battle: Ames-Meyers	150.00	67.50	22.50
☐ 48B	Just Before the Battle: Bresnahan-McGraw	300.00	135.00	45.00
☐ 48C	Just Before the Battle: Crandall-Meyers	150.00	67.50	22.50
☐ 48D	Just Before the Battle: Devore-Becker	150.00	67.50	22.50
☐ 48E	Just Before the Battle: Fletcher-Mathewson	300.00	135.00	45.00
☐ 48F	Just Before the Battle: Marquard-Meyers	175.00	80.00	27.00
☐ 48G	Just Before the Battle: McGraw-Jennings	300.00	135.00	45.00
☐ 48H	Just Before the Battle: Meyers-Mathewson	300.00	135.00	45.00
☐ 48I	Just Before the Battle: Snodgrass-Murray	150.00	67.50	22.50
☐ 48J	Just Before the Battle: Wiltse-Meyers	150.00	67.50	22.50
☐ 49	Knight Catches Runner: Knight-Johnson	450.00	200.00	67.50
☐ 50A	Lobert Almost Caught: Bridwell-Kling	150.00	67.50	22.50
☐ 50B	Lobert Almost Caught: Kling-Young	225.00	100.00	33.00
☐ 50C	Lobert Almost Caught: Mattern-Kling	150.00	67.50	22.50
☐ 50D	Lobert Almost Caught: Steinfeldt-Kling	150.00	67.50	22.50
☐ 51	Lobert Gets Tenney: Lobert-Dooin	175.00	80.00	27.00
☐ 52	Lord Catches His Man: Tannehill-Lord	175.00	80.00	27.00
☐ 53	McConnell Caught: Richie-Needham	175.00	80.00	27.00
☐ 54	McIntyre at Bat: McIntyre-McConnell	175.00	80.00	27.00
☐ 55	Moriarty Spiked: Willett-Stanage	175.00	80.00	27.00
☐ 56	Nearly Caught: Bates-Bescher	200.00	90.00	30.00
☐ 57	Oldring Almost Home: Lord-Oldring	175.00	80.00	27.00
☐ 58	Schaefer on First: McBride-Milan	175.00	80.00	27.00
☐ 59	Schaefer Steals Second: McBride-Griffith	200.00	90.00	30.00
☐ 60	Scoring from Second: Lord-Oldring	175.00	80.00	27.00
☐ 61A	Scrambling Back: Barger-Bergen	150.00	67.50	22.50
☐ 61B	Scrambling Back: Wolter-Chase	150.00	67.50	22.50
☐ 62	Speaker Almost Caught: Miller-Clarke	375.00	165.00	55.00
☐ 63	Speaker Rounding Third: Wood-Speaker	650.00	300.00	100.00
☐ 64	Speaker Scores: Speaker-Engle	400.00	180.00	60.00
☐ 65	Stahl Safe: Stovall-Austin	175.00	80.00	27.00
☐ 66	Stone About to Swing: Sheckard-Schulte	175.00	80.00	27.00
☐ 67A	Sullivan Puts Up High One: Evans-Huggins	175.00	80.00	27.00
☐ 67B	Sullivan Puts Up High One: Sweeney-Ford	150.00	67.50	22.50
☐ 68A	Sweeney Gets Stahl: Ford-Vaughn	150.00	67.50	22.50
☐ 68B	Sweeney Ge's Stahl: Sweeney-Ford	150.00	67.50	22.50
☐ 69	Tenney Lands Safely: Raymond-Latham	175.00	80.00	27.00
☐ 70A	The Athletic Infield: Barry-Baker	175.00	80.00	27.00

		EX-MT	VG-E	GOOD
☐ 70B	The Athletic Infield: Brown-Graham	150.00	67.50	22.50
☐ 70C	The Athletic Infield: Hauser-Konetchy	150.00	67.50	22.50
☐ 70D	The Athletic Infield: Krause-Thomas	150.00	67.50	22.50
☐ 71	The Pinch Hitter: Hoblitzel-Egan	175.00	80.00	27.00
☐ 72	The Scissors Slide: Birmingham-Turner	175.00	80.00	27.00
☐ 73A	Tom Jones at Bat: Fromme-McLean	150.00	67.50	22.50
☐ 73B	Tom Jones at Bat: Gaspar-McLean	150.00	67.50	22.50
☐ 74A	Too Late for Devlin: Ames-Meyers	150.00	67.50	22.50
☐ 74B	Too Late for Devlin: Crandall-Meyers	150.00	67.50	22.50
☐ 74C	Too Late for Devlin: Devlin (Giants)-Mathewson	1000.00	450.00	135.00
☐ 74D	Too Late for Devlin: Devlin (Rustlers)-Mathewson	300.00	135.00	45.00
☐ 74E	Too Late for Devlin: Marquard-Meyers	175.00	80.00	27.00
☐ 74F	Too Late for Devlin: Wiltse-Meyers	150.00	67.50	22.50
☐ 75A	Ty Cobb Steals Third: Jennings-Cobb	2000.00	900.00	250.00
☐ 75B	Ty Cobb Steals Third: Moriarty-Cobb	1600.00	750.00	225.00
☐ 75C	Ty Cobb Steals Third: Stovall-Austin	1600.00	750.00	225.00
☐ 76	Wheat Strikes Out: Dahlen-Wheat	250.00	110.00	37.50

T204 Ramly

The cards in this 121-card set measure 2" by 2 1/2". The Ramly baseball series, designated T204 in the ACC, contains unnumbered cards. This set is one of the most distinguished ever produced, containing ornate gold borders around a black and white portrait of each player. There are spelling errors, and two distinct backs, "Ramly" and "TT", are known. Much of the obverse card detail is actually embossed. The players have been alphabetized and numbered for reference in the checklist below.

		EX-MT	VG-E	GOOD
COMPLETE SET (121)		28000.	12500.	3750.
COMMON PLAYER (1-121)		200.00	90.00	30.00
☐ 1	Whitey Alperman	200.00	90.00	30.00
☐ 2	John J. Anderson	200.00	90.00	30.00
☐ 3	Jimmy Archer	200.00	90.00	30.00
☐ 4	Frank Arellanes	200.00	90.00	30.00
☐ 5	Jim Ball (Boston NL)	200.00	90.00	30.00
☐ 6	Neal Ball (N.Y. AL)	200.00	90.00	30.00
☐ 7	Dave Bancroft	400.00	180.00	60.00
☐ 8	Johnny Bates	200.00	90.00	30.00
☐ 9	Fred Beebe	200.00	90.00	30.00
☐ 10	George Bell	200.00	90.00	30.00

		EX-MT	VG-E	GOOD
☐ 11	Chief Bender	400.00	180.00	60.00
☐ 12	Walter Blair	200.00	90.00	30.00
☐ 13	Cliff Blankenship	200.00	90.00	30.00
☐ 14	Frank Bowerman	200.00	90.00	30.00
☐ 15	Kitty Bransfield	200.00	90.00	30.00
☐ 16	Roger Bresnahan	400.00	180.00	60.00
☐ 17	Al Bridwell	200.00	90.00	30.00
☐ 18	Mordecai Brown	400.00	180.00	60.00
☐ 19	Fred Burchell	200.00	90.00	30.00
☐ 20	Jesse Burkett	500.00	225.00	75.00
☐ 21	Robert Byrne	200.00	90.00	30.00
☐ 22	Bill Carrigan	200.00	90.00	30.00
☐ 23	Frank Chance	450.00	200.00	67.50
☐ 24	Charles Chech	200.00	90.00	30.00
☐ 25	Eddie Cicotte	250.00	110.00	37.50
☐ 26	Otis Clymer	200.00	90.00	30.00
☐ 27	Andrew Coakley	200.00	90.00	30.00
☐ 28	Eddie Collins	500.00	225.00	75.00
☐ 29	Jimmy Collins	500.00	225.00	75.00
☐ 30	Wid Conroy	200.00	90.00	30.00
☐ 31	Jack Coombs	250.00	110.00	37.50
☐ 32	Doc Crandall	200.00	90.00	30.00
☐ 33	Lou Criger	200.00	90.00	30.00
☐ 34	Harry(Jasper) Davis	200.00	90.00	30.00
☐ 35	Art Devlin	200.00	90.00	30.00
☐ 36	Bill Dineen	200.00	90.00	30.00
☐ 37	Pat Donahue	200.00	90.00	30.00
☐ 38	Mike Donlin	200.00	90.00	30.00
☐ 39	Wild Bill Donovan	200.00	90.00	30.00
☐ 40	Gus Dorner	200.00	90.00	30.00
☐ 41	Joe Dunn	200.00	90.00	30.00
☐ 42	Norman Elberfield (sic) Elberfeld	200.00	90.00	30.00
☐ 43	Johnny Evers	450.00	200.00	67.50
☐ 44	George L. Ewing	200.00	90.00	30.00
☐ 45	George Ferguson	200.00	90.00	30.00
☐ 46	Hobe Ferris	200.00	90.00	30.00
☐ 47	James J. Freeman	200.00	90.00	30.00
☐ 48	Art Fromme	200.00	90.00	30.00
☐ 49	Bob Ganley	200.00	90.00	30.00
☐ 50	Harry (Doc) Gessler	200.00	90.00	30.00
☐ 51	George Graham	200.00	90.00	30.00
☐ 52	Clark Griffith	400.00	180.00	60.00
☐ 53	Roy Hartzell	200.00	90.00	30.00
☐ 54	Charlie Hemphill	200.00	90.00	30.00
☐ 55	Dick Hoblitzell	200.00	90.00	30.00
☐ 56	George (Del) Howard	200.00	90.00	30.00
☐ 57	Harry Howell	200.00	90.00	30.00
☐ 58	Miller Huggins	450.00	200.00	67.50
☐ 59	John Hummel	200.00	90.00	30.00
☐ 60	Walter Johnson	1750.00	750.00	225.00
☐ 61	Charles Jones	200.00	90.00	30.00
☐ 62	Michael Kahoe	200.00	90.00	30.00
☐ 63	Ed Karger	200.00	90.00	30.00
☐ 64	Willie Keeler	500.00	225.00	75.00
☐ 65	Ed Kenotchey (sic) Konetchy	200.00	90.00	30.00
☐ 66	John (Red) Kleinow	200.00	90.00	30.00
☐ 67	John Knight	200.00	90.00	30.00
☐ 68	Vive Lindeman	200.00	90.00	30.00
☐ 69	Hans Loebert (sic) Lobert	200.00	90.00	30.00
☐ 70	Harry Lord	200.00	90.00	30.00
☐ 71	Harry Lumley	200.00	90.00	30.00
☐ 72	Ernie Lush	200.00	90.00	30.00
☐ 73	Rube Manning	200.00	90.00	30.00
☐ 74	James McAleer	200.00	90.00	30.00
☐ 75	Amby McConnell	200.00	90.00	30.00
☐ 76	Moose McCormick	200.00	90.00	30.00
☐ 77	Matthew McIntyre	200.00	90.00	30.00
☐ 78	Larry McLean	200.00	90.00	30.00
☐ 79	Fred Merkle	225.00	100.00	33.00
☐ 80	Clyde Milan	200.00	90.00	30.00
☐ 81	Michael Mitchell	200.00	90.00	30.00
☐ 82	Pat Moran	200.00	90.00	30.00
☐ 83	Harry (Cy) Morgan	200.00	90.00	30.00
☐ 84	Tim Murnane	200.00	90.00	30.00
☐ 85	Danny Murphy	200.00	90.00	30.00
☐ 86	Red Murray	200.00	90.00	30.00
☐ 87	Eustace(Doc) Newton	200.00	90.00	30.00
☐ 88	Simon Nichols (sic) Nicholls	200.00	90.00	30.00
☐ 89	Harry Niles	200.00	90.00	30.00
☐ 90	Bill O'Hara	200.00	90.00	30.00
☐ 91	Charley O'Leary	200.00	90.00	30.00
☐ 92	Dode Paskert	200.00	90.00	30.00
☐ 93	Barney Pelty	200.00	90.00	30.00
☐ 94	Jack Pfeister	200.00	90.00	30.00
☐ 95	Eddie Plank	600.00	270.00	90.00
☐ 96	Jack Powell	200.00	90.00	30.00
☐ 97	Bugs Raymond	200.00	90.00	30.00
☐ 98	Thomas Reilly	200.00	90.00	30.00
☐ 99	Lewis Ritchie (sic) Richie	200.00	90.00	30.00
☐ 100	Nap Rucker	200.00	90.00	30.00

		EX-MT	VG-E	GOOD
□ 101	Ed Ruelbach (sic) Reulbach	200.00	90.00	30.00
□ 102	Slim Sallee	200.00	90.00	30.00
□ 103	Germany Schaefer	200.00	90.00	30.00
□ 104	Jimmy Schekard (sic) Sheckard	200.00	90.00	30.00
□ 105	Admiral Schlei	200.00	90.00	30.00
□ 106	Frank Schulte	200.00	90.00	30.00
□ 107	James Sebring	200.00	90.00	30.00
□ 108	Bill Shipke	200.00	90.00	30.00
□ 109	Anthony Smith	200.00	90.00	30.00
□ 110	Tubby Spencer	200.00	90.00	30.00
□ 111	Jake Stahl	225.00	100.00	33.00
□ 112	Harry Steinfeldt	200.00	90.00	30.00
□ 113	Jim Stephens	200.00	90.00	30.00
□ 114	Gabby Street	200.00	90.00	30.00
□ 115	William Sweeney	200.00	90.00	30.00
□ 116	Fred Tenney	200.00	90.00	30.00
□ 117	Ira Thomas	200.00	90.00	30.00
□ 118	Joe Tinker	400.00	180.00	60.00
□ 119	Bob Unglaub	200.00	90.00	30.00
□ 120	Heinie Wagner	200.00	90.00	30.00
□ 121	Bobby Wallace	500.00	225.00	75.00

T205 Gold Border

ROBERT EWING

Robert Ewing pitched in 1910 for the Philadelphia Nationals, and before that for the Cincinnatis, so he has not been fortunate in being with teams that were consistent winners, but his percentage of victories the last three years out of four has been greater than his club's. In the last three years, out of forty-four wins, ten were shut-outs. In 1910 he pitched one two-hit and three three-hit games.

	G.	W.	G.	L.	P.C.	F.
1908	.	17		15	.531	.964
1909	.	11		12	.478	.860
1910	.	16		14	.533	.970

BASE BALL SERIES 400 DESIGNS

Piedmont
THE CIGARETTE
OF QUALITY

The cards in this 208-card set measure 1 1/2" by 2 5/8". The T205 set (catalog designation), also known as the "Gold Border" set, was issued in 1911 in packages of the following cigarette brands: American Beauty, Broadleaf, Cycle, Drum, Hassan, Honest Long Cut, Piedmont, Polar Bear, Sovereign and Sweet Caporal. All the above were products of the American Tobacco Company, and the ads for the various brands appear below the biographical section on the back of each card. There are pose variations noted in the checklist (which is alphabetized and numbered for reference) and there are 12 minor league cards of a more ornate design which are somewhat scarce. The numbers below correspond to alphabetical order within category, i.e., major leaguers and minor leaguers are alphabetized separately. The gold borders of T205 cards chip easily and they are hard to find in "Mint" or even "Near Mint" condition; however they (T205) are not appreciably tougher to find than T206 cards for lesser conditions or grades.

	EX-MT	VG-E	GOOD
COMPLETE SET (208)	30000.	13500.	4250.
COMMON MAJORS (1-185)	75.00	34.00	11.25
COMMON MINORS (186-197)	225.00	100.00	33.00

		EX-MT	VG-E	GOOD
□ 1	Edward J. Abbaticchio	75.00	34.00	11.25
□ 2	Leon Ames	75.00	34.00	11.25
□ 3	James P. Archer	75.00	34.00	11.25
□ 4	James Austin	75.00	34.00	11.25
□ 5	William Bailey	75.00	34.00	11.25
□ 6	Frank Baker	275.00	120.00	40.00
□ 7	Neal Ball	75.00	34.00	11.25
□ 8A	Edward B. Barger (full B)	75.00	34.00	11.25
□ 8B	Edward B. Barger (part B)	275.00	120.00	40.00
□ 9	John J. Barry	75.00	34.00	11.25
□ 10	John W. Bates	75.00	34.00	11.25
□ 11	Frederick T. Beck	75.00	34.00	11.25
□ 12	Beals Becker	75.00	34.00	11.25
□ 13	George G. Bell	75.00	34.00	11.25
□ 14	Charles A. Bender	225.00	100.00	33.00
□ 15	William Bergen	75.00	34.00	11.25
□ 16	Robert H. Bescher	75.00	34.00	11.25
□ 17	Joseph Birmingham	75.00	34.00	11.25
□ 18	Russell Blackburne	75.00	34.00	11.25
□ 19	Wm. E. Bransfield	75.00	34.00	11.25
□ 20A	Roger Bresnahan (mouth closed)	225.00	100.00	33.00
□ 20B	Roger Bresnahan (mouth open)	500.00	225.00	75.00
□ 21	Albert Bridwell	75.00	34.00	11.25
□ 22	Mordecai Brown	225.00	100.00	33.00
□ 23	Robert Byrne	75.00	34.00	11.25
□ 24	Howard Camnitz	75.00	34.00	11.25
□ 25	William Carrigan	75.00	34.00	11.25
□ 26	Frank L. Chance	225.00	100.00	33.00
□ 27A	Harold W. Chase (Chase only)	450.00	200.00	67.50
□ 27B	Harold W. Chase (Hal Chase)	125.00	57.50	18.75
□ 28	Edward V. Cicotte	125.00	57.50	18.75
□ 29	Fred Clarke	225.00	100.00	33.00
□ 30	Tyrus Raymond Cobb	2500.00	1000.00	300.00
□ 31A	Edward T. Collins (mouth closed)	225.00	100.00	33.00
□ 31B	Edward T. Collins (mouth open)	450.00	200.00	67.50
□ 32	Frank J. Corridon	75.00	34.00	11.25
□ 32	Otis Crandall	75.00	34.00	11.25
□ 33	Louis Criger	75.00	34.00	11.25
□ 34	William Dahlen	275.00	120.00	40.00
□ 35	Jacob Daubert	125.00	57.50	18.75
□ 36	James Delahanty	75.00	34.00	11.25
□ 37	Arthur Devlin	75.00	34.00	11.25
□ 38	Joshua Devore	75.00	34.00	11.25
□ 39	W.R. Dickson	75.00	34.00	11.25
□ 40	J. Donohue	225.00	100.00	33.00
□ 41	Charles S. Dooin	75.00	34.00	11.25
□ 42	Michael Doolan	75.00	34.00	11.25
□ 43A	Patsy Dougherty (white stocking)	225.00	100.00	33.00
□ 43B	Patsy Dougherty (red stocking)	75.00	34.00	11.25
□ 44	Thomas W. Downey	75.00	34.00	11.25
□ 45	Lawrence Doyle	75.00	34.00	11.25
□ 46	Hugh Duffy	350.00	160.00	52.50
□ 47	James H. Dygert	75.00	34.00	11.25
□ 48	Richard J. Egan	75.00	34.00	11.25
□ 49	Norman Elberfeld	75.00	34.00	11.25
□ 50	Clyde Engle	75.00	34.00	11.25
□ 51	Louis Evans	75.00	34.00	11.25
□ 52	John J. Evers	225.00	100.00	33.00
□ 53	Robert Ewing	75.00	34.00	11.25
□ 54	G.C. Ferguson	75.00	34.00	11.25
□ 55	Ray Fisher	275.00	120.00	40.00
□ 56	Arthur Fletcher	75.00	34.00	11.25
□ 57	John Flynn	75.00	34.00	11.25
□ 58A	Russell Ford (dark cap)	75.00	34.00	11.25
□ 58B	Russell Ford (light cap)	275.00	120.00	40.00
□ 59	William A. Foxen	75.00	34.00	11.25
□ 60	Arthur Fromme	75.00	34.00	11.25
□ 61	Earl Gardner	75.00	34.00	11.25
□ 62	Harry L. Gaspar	75.00	34.00	11.25
□ 63	George Gibson	75.00	34.00	11.25
□ 64	Wilbur Good	75.00	34.00	11.25
□ 65A	George F. Graham (Boston Rustlers)	75.00	34.00	11.25
□ 65B	George F. Graham (Chicago Cubs)	500.00	225.00	75.00
□ 66	Edward L. Grant	225.00	100.00	33.00
□ 67	Gray	75.00	34.00	11.25
□ 68	Clark Griffith	225.00	100.00	33.00
□ 69	Robert Groom	75.00	34.00	11.25
□ 70A	Robert Harmon (both ears)	75.00	34.00	11.25
□ 70B	Robert Harmon (left ear only)	275.00	120.00	40.00
□ 71	Frederick T. Hartsel	75.00	34.00	11.25
□ 72	Arnold J. Hauser	75.00	34.00	11.25
□ 73	Charles Hemphill	75.00	34.00	11.25
□ 74	Charles L. Herzog	75.00	34.00	11.25
□ 75	Richard Hoblitzell	75.00	34.00	11.25
□ 76	Daniel J. Hoffman	75.00	34.00	11.25

☐ 77	Miller Huggins	225.00	100.00	33.00
☐ 78	John E. Hummell	75.00	34.00	11.25
☐ 79	Fred Jacklitsch	75.00	34.00	11.25
☐ 80	Hugh Jennings	225.00	100.00	33.00
☐ 81	Walter Johnson	1000.00	450.00	135.00
☐ 82	David Jones	75.00	34.00	11.25
☐ 83	Thomas Jones	75.00	34.00	11.25
☐ 84	Addie Joss	600.00	270.00	90.00
☐ 85	Edward Karger	275.00	120.00	40.00
☐ 86	Edward Killian	75.00	34.00	11.25
☐ 87	John Kleinow	275.00	120.00	40.00
☐ 88	John Kling	75.00	34.00	11.25
☐ 89	Jack Knight	75.00	34.00	11.25
☐ 90	Edward Konetchy	75.00	34.00	11.25
☐ 91	Harry Krause	75.00	34.00	11.25
☐ 92	Floyd M. Kroh	75.00	34.00	11.25
☐ 93	Frank Lang	75.00	34.00	11.25
☐ 94	Frank LaPorte	75.00	34.00	11.25
☐ 95	W.A. Latham	75.00	34.00	11.25
☐ 96	Thomas W. Leach	75.00	34.00	11.25
☐ 97	Sam Leever	75.00	34.00	11.25
☐ 98	Albert P. Leifield	75.00	34.00	11.25
☐ 99	Edgar Lennox	75.00	34.00	11.25
☐ 100	Pat'k J. Livingston	75.00	34.00	11.25
☐ 101	John Lobert	75.00	34.00	11.25
☐ 102	Briscoe Lord	75.00	34.00	11.25
☐ 103	Harry D. Lord	75.00	34.00	11.25
☐ 104	John Lush	75.00	34.00	11.25
☐ 105	Nicholas Maddox	75.00	34.00	11.25
☐ 106	Sherwood R. Magee	75.00	34.00	11.25
☐ 107	Richard Marquard	225.00	100.00	33.00
☐ 108	Christy Mathewson	900.00	400.00	135.00
☐ 109	A.A. Mattern	75.00	34.00	11.25
☐ 110	George F. McBride	75.00	34.00	11.25
☐ 111	Ambrose McConnell	75.00	34.00	11.25
☐ 112	Pryor McElveen	75.00	34.00	11.25
☐ 113	John J. McGraw	350.00	160.00	52.50
☐ 114	Harry McIntire	75.00	34.00	11.25
☐ 115	Matthew McIntyre	75.00	34.00	11.25
☐ 116	John B. McLean	75.00	34.00	11.25
☐ 117	Fred Merkle	125.00	57.50	18.75
☐ 118	John T. Meyers	75.00	34.00	11.25
☐ 119	J. Clyde Milan	75.00	34.00	11.25
☐ 120	John D. Miller	75.00	34.00	11.25
☐ 121	Michael Mitchell	75.00	34.00	11.25
☐ 122	Patrick J. Moran	75.00	34.00	11.25
☐ 123	George Moriarity	75.00	34.00	11.25
☐ 124	George J. Mullin	75.00	34.00	11.25
☐ 125	Daniel Murphy	75.00	34.00	11.25
☐ 126	John J. Murray	75.00	34.00	11.25
☐ 127	Thomas J. Needham	75.00	34.00	11.25
☐ 128	Rebel Oakes	75.00	34.00	11.25
☐ 129	Reuben N. Oldring	75.00	34.00	11.25
☐ 130	Charles O'Leary	75.00	34.00	11.25
☐ 131	Frederick Olmstead	75.00	34.00	11.25
☐ 132	Orval Overall	75.00	34.00	11.25
☐ 133	F. Parent	75.00	34.00	11.25
☐ 134	George Paskert	75.00	34.00	11.25
☐ 135	Fred Payne	75.00	34.00	11.25
☐ 136	B. Pelty	75.00	34.00	11.25
☐ 137	John A. Pfiester	75.00	34.00	11.25
☐ 138	Edward Phelps	75.00	34.00	11.25
☐ 139	Charles Phillippe	125.00	57.50	18.75
☐ 140	John Quinn	75.00	34.00	11.25
☐ 141	Arthur L. Raymond	275.00	120.00	40.00
☐ 142	Edward M. Reulbach	75.00	34.00	11.25
☐ 143	Lewis Richie	75.00	34.00	11.25
☐ 144	John A. Rowan	275.00	120.00	40.00
☐ 145	G.N. Rucker	75.00	34.00	11.25
☐ 146	W.D. Scanlan	275.00	120.00	40.00
☐ 147	Herman Schaefer	75.00	34.00	11.25
☐ 148	George H. Schlei	75.00	34.00	11.25
☐ 149	Charles Schmidt	75.00	34.00	11.25
☐ 150	Frank M. Schulte	75.00	34.00	11.25
☐ 151	James Scott	75.00	34.00	11.25
☐ 152	Bayard H. Sharpe	75.00	34.00	11.25
☐ 153A	David Shean (Boston Rustlers)	75.00	34.00	11.25
☐ 153B	David Shean (Chicago Cubs)	500.00	225.00	75.00
☐ 154	James T. Sheckard	75.00	34.00	11.25
☐ 155	George Simmons	75.00	34.00	11.25
☐ 156	Tony Smith	75.00	34.00	11.25
☐ 157	Fred C. Snodgrass	75.00	34.00	11.25
☐ 158	Tris Speaker	500.00	225.00	75.00
☐ 159	Jacob G. Stahl	100.00	45.00	15.00
☐ 160	Oscar Stanage	75.00	34.00	11.25
☐ 161	Harry Steinfeldt	75.00	34.00	11.25
☐ 162	George Stone	75.00	34.00	11.25
☐ 163	George T. Stovall	75.00	34.00	11.25
☐ 164	Charles E. Street	75.00	34.00	11.25
☐ 165	George Suggs	275.00	120.00	40.00
☐ 166	Edgar Summers	75.00	34.00	11.25
☐ 167	Edward Sweeney	275.00	120.00	40.00
☐ 168	Lee Ford Tannehill	75.00	34.00	11.25

☐ 169	Ira Thomas	75.00	34.00	11.25
☐ 170	Joseph B. Tinker	225.00	100.00	33.00
☐ 171	John Titus	75.00	34.00	11.25
☐ 172	Terence Turner	275.00	120.00	40.00
☐ 173	James Vaughn	275.00	120.00	40.00
☐ 174	Charles Wagner	275.00	120.00	40.00
☐ 175A	Roderick J. Wallace (with cap)	225.00	100.00	33.00
☐ 175B	Roderick J. Wallace (without cap)	450.00	200.00	67.50
☐ 176	Edward Walsh	400.00	180.00	60.00
☐ 177	Zach D. Wheat	225.00	100.00	33.00
☐ 178	G.H. White	75.00	34.00	11.25
☐ 179	Kirb White	275.00	120.00	40.00
☐ 180	Irvin K. Wilhelm	275.00	120.00	40.00
☐ 181	Edgar Willett	75.00	34.00	11.25
☐ 182A	George Wiltse (both ears)	75.00	34.00	11.25
☐ 182B	George Wiltse (right ear only)	275.00	120.00	40.00
☐ 183	J. Owen Wilson	75.00	34.00	11.25
☐ 184	Harry Wolter	75.00	34.00	11.25
☐ 185	Denton T. Young	800.00	350.00	120.00
☐ 186	Dr.Merle T. Adkins: Baltimore	225.00	100.00	33.00
☐ 187	John Dunn: Baltimore	250.00	110.00	37.50
☐ 188	George Merritt: Buffalo	225.00	100.00	33.00
☐ 189	Charles Hanford: Jersey City	225.00	100.00	33.00
☐ 190	Forrest D. Cady: Newark	225.00	100.00	33.00
☐ 191	James Frick: Newark	225.00	100.00	33.00
☐ 192	Wyatt Lee: Newark	225.00	100.00	33.00
☐ 193	Lewis McAllister: Newark	225.00	100.00	33.00
☐ 194	John Nee: Newark	225.00	100.00	33.00
☐ 195	James Collins: Providence	500.00	225.00	75.00
☐ 196	James Phelan: Providence	225.00	100.00	33.00
☐ 197	Henry Batch: Rochester	225.00	100.00	33.00

T206 White Border

The cards in this 524-card set measure 1 1/2" by 2 5/8". The T206 set was and is the most popular of all the tobacco issues. The set was issued from 1909 to 1911 with sixteen different brands of cigarettes: American Beauty, Broadleaf, Cycle, Carolina Brights, Drum, El Principe de Gales, Hindu, Lenox, Old Mill, Piedmont, Polar Bear, Sovereign, Sweet Caporal, Tolstoi, Ty Cobb and Uzit. The Ty Cobb brand back is very scarce. The minor league cards are supposedly slightly more difficult to obtain than the cards of the major leaguers, with the Southern League player cards being the most difficult. Minor League players were obtained from the American Association and the Eastern league. Southern League players were obtained from a variety of leagues including the following: South Atlantic League, Southern League, Texas League, and Virginia League. The set price below does not include ultra-expensive Wagner, Plank, Magie error, or Doyle variation.

	EX-MT	VG-E	GOOD
COMPLETE SET (520)	65000.	27000.	8500.
COMMON MAJORS (1-389)	60.00	27.00	9.00
COMMON MINORS (390-475)	50.00	22.50	7.50
COMMON SOUTHERN(476-523)	125.00	57.50	18.75
☐ 1 Ed Abbaticchio: Pitt., Batting, follow thru	60.00	27.00	9.00
☐ 2 Ed Abbaticchio: Pitt., Batting, waiting pitch	75.00	34.00	11.25
☐ 3 Bill Abstein: Pitt.	60.00	27.00	9.00
☐ 4 Whitey Alperman: Brooklyn	75.00	34.00	11.25
☐ 5 Red Ames: N.Y. NL, Portrait	75.00	34.00	11.25
☐ 6 Red Ames: N.Y. NL, Hands over head	60.00	27.00	9.00
☐ 7 Red Ames: N.Y. NL, Hands in front of chest	75.00	34.00	11.25
☐ 8 Frank Arellanes: Boston AL	60.00	27.00	9.00
☐ 9 Jake Atz: Chicago AL	60.00	27.00	9.00
☐ 10 Frank Baker: Phila. AL	250.00	110.00	37.50
☐ 11 Neal Ball: N.Y. AL	75.00	34.00	11.25
☐ 12 Neal Ball: Cleveland	60.00	27.00	9.00
☐ 13 Jap Barbeau: St. Louis NL	60.00	27.00	9.00
☐ 14 Jack Barry: Phila. AL	60.00	27.00	9.00
☐ 15 Johnny Bates: Boston NL	75.00	34.00	11.25
☐ 16 Ginger Beaumont: Boston NL	75.00	34.00	11.25
☐ 17 Fred Beck: Boston NL	60.00	27.00	9.00
☐ 18 Beals Becker: Boston NL	60.00	27.00	9.00
☐ 19 George Bell: Brooklyn, pitching, follow thru	60.00	27.00	9.00
☐ 20 George Bell: Brooklyn, Hands over head	75.00	34.00	11.25
☐ 21 Chief Bender: Phila. AL, Portrait	300.00	135.00	45.00
☐ 22 Chief Bender: Phila. AL, pitching, trees	200.00	90.00	30.00
☐ 23 Chief Bender: Phila. AL, pitching, no trees	200.00	90.00	30.00
☐ 24 Bill Bergen: Brooklyn, Catching	60.00	27.00	9.00
☐ 25 Bill Bergen: Brooklyn, Batting	75.00	34.00	11.25
☐ 26 Berger: Cleveland	60.00	27.00	9.00
☐ 27 Bob Bescher: Cinc., Catching fly ball	60.00	27.00	9.00
☐ 28 Bob Bescher: Cinc. Portrait	60.00	27.00	9.00
☐ 29 Joe Birmingham: Cleveland	75.00	34.00	11.25
☐ 30 Jack Bliss: St.L. NL	60.00	27.00	9.00
☐ 31 Frank Bowerman: Boston NL	75.00	34.00	11.25
☐ 32 Bill Bradley: Cleveland, Portrait	75.00	34.00	11.25
☐ 33 Bill Bradley: Cleveland, Batting	60.00	27.00	9.00
☐ 34 Kitty Bransfield: Phila. NL	75.00	34.00	11.25
☐ 35 Roger Bresnahan: St.L. NL, Portrait	300.00	135.00	45.00
☐ 36 Roger Bresnahan: St.L. NL, Batting	200.00	90.00	30.00
☐ 37 Al Bridwell: N.Y. NL, Portrait	75.00	34.00	11.25
☐ 38 Al Bridwell: N.Y. NL, Wearing sweater	60.00	27.00	9.00
☐ 39 George Brown: Chicago NL (sic, Browne)	150.00	67.50	22.50
☐ 40 George Brown: Washington (sic, Browne)	600.00	270.00	90.00
☐ 41 Mordecai Brown: Chicago NL, Portrait	300.00	135.00	45.00
☐ 42 Mordecai Brown: Chicago NL, Chicago down front of shirt	200.00	90.00	30.00
☐ 43 Mordecai Brown: Chicago NL, Cubs across chest	350.00	160.00	52.50
☐ 44 Al Burch: Brooklyn, Fielding	60.00	27.00	9.00
☐ 45 Al Burch: Brooklyn, Batting	150.00	67.50	22.50
☐ 46 Bill Burns: Chicago AL	60.00	27.00	9.00
☐ 47 Donie Bush: Detroit	60.00	27.00	9.00
☐ 48 Bobby Byrne: St. Louis NL	60.00	27.00	9.00
☐ 49 Howie Camnitz: Pitt., Arms folded over chest	75.00	34.00	11.25
☐ 50 Howie Camnitz: Pitt., Hands over head	60.00	27.00	9.00
☐ 51 Howie Camnitz: Pitt., Throwing	60.00	27.00	9.00
☐ 52 Billy Campbell: Cincinnati	60.00	27.00	9.00
☐ 53 Bill Carrigan: Boston AL	60.00	27.00	9.00
☐ 54 Frank Chance: Chicago NL, Cubs across chest	300.00	135.00	45.00
☐ 55 Frank Chance: Chicago NL, Chicago down front of shirt	200.00	90.00	30.00
☐ 56 Frank Chance: Chicago NL, Batting	200.00	90.00	30.00
☐ 57 Chappy Charles: St. Louis NL	60.00	27.00	9.00
☐ 58 Hal Chase: N.Y. AL, Port. blue bkgd.	100.00	45.00	15.00
☐ 59 Hal Chase: N.Y. AL, Port., pink bkgd.	250.00	110.00	37.50
☐ 60 Hal Chase: N.Y. AL, Holding cup	100.00	45.00	15.00
☐ 61 Hal Chase: N.Y. AL, Throwing, dark cap	100.00	45.00	15.00
☐ 62 Hal Chase: N.Y. AL, Throwing, white cap	250.00	110.00	37.50
☐ 63 Jack Chesbro: New York AL	350.00	160.00	52.50
☐ 64 Eddie Cicotte: Boston AL	100.00	45.00	15.00
☐ 65 Fred Clarke: Pitt., Portrait	300.00	135.00	45.00
☐ 66 Fred Clarke: Pitt.	200.00	90.00	30.00
☐ 67 Josh Clarke: Cleve.	75.00	34.00	11.25
☐ 68 Ty Cobb: Detroit, Port., red bkgd.	1750.00	700.00	225.00
☐ 69 Ty Cobb: Detroit, Port., green background	3000.00	1200.00	400.00
☐ 70 Ty Cobb: Detroit, Bat on shoulder	2000.00	800.00	250.00
☐ 71 Ty Cobb: Detroit, Bat away from shoulder	1500.00	600.00	200.00
☐ 72 Eddie Collins: Phila. AL	200.00	90.00	30.00
☐ 73 Wid Conroy: Washington, Fielding	75.00	34.00	11.25
☐ 74 Wid Conroy: Wash., Bat on shoulder	60.00	27.00	9.00
☐ 75 Harry Covaleski: Phila. NL	75.00	34.00	11.25
☐ 76 Doc Crandall: N.Y. NL, without cap	75.00	34.00	11.25
☐ 77 Doc Crandall: N.Y. NL, sweater and cap	60.00	27.00	9.00
☐ 78 Sam Crawford: Detroit, Batting	200.00	90.00	30.00
☐ 79 Sam Crawford: Detroit, Throwing	250.00	110.00	37.50
☐ 80 Birdie Cree: N.Y. AL	60.00	27.00	9.00
☐ 81 Lou Criger: St.L. AL	75.00	34.00	11.25
☐ 82 Dode Criss: St.L. AL	75.00	34.00	11.25
☐ 83 Bill Dahlen: Boston NL	100.00	45.00	15.00
☐ 84 Bill Dahlen: Brooklyn	350.00	160.00	52.50
☐ 85 George Davis: Chicago AL	75.00	34.00	11.25
☐ 86 Harry Davis: Phila.	60.00	27.00	9.00

	AL, Davis on card			
☐ 87	Harry Davis: Phila.	75.00	34.00	11.25
	AL, H.Davis on card			
☐ 88	Jim Delehanty: Wash.	75.00	34.00	11.25
☐ 89	Ray Demmitt: St.L.	4000.00	1600.00	500.00
	AL			
☐ 90	Ray Demmitt: N.Y. AL	75.00	34.00	11.25
☐ 91	Art Devlin: N.Y. NL	75.00	34.00	11.25
☐ 92	Josh Devore: N.Y. NL	60.00	27.00	9.00
☐ 93	Bill Dineen:	60.00	27.00	9.00
	St. Louis AL			
☐ 94	Mike Donlin: N.Y.	125.00	57.50	18.75
	NL, Fielding			
☐ 95	Mike Donlin: N.Y.	75.00	34.00	11.25
	NL, Sitting			
☐ 96	Mike Donlin: N.Y.	60.00	27.00	9.00
	NL, Batting			
☐ 97	Jiggs Donohue:	75.00	34.00	11.25
	Chicago AL			
☐ 98	Bill Donovan:	75.00	34.00	11.25
	Detroit, Portrait			
☐ 99	Bill Donovan:	60.00	27.00	9.00
	Detroit, Throwing			
☐ 100	Red Dooin: Phila. NL	75.00	34.00	11.25
☐ 101	Mickey Doolan:	60.00	27.00	9.00
	Phila. NL, Fielding			
☐ 102	Mickey Doolan:	60.00	27.00	9.00
	Phila. NL, Batting			
☐ 103	Mickey Doolin (sic,	75.00	34.00	11.25
	Doolan): Phila. NL			
☐ 104	Patsy Dougherty:	75.00	34.00	11.25
	Chicago AL, Portrait			
☐ 105	Patsy Dougherty:	60.00	27.00	9.00
	Chicago AL, Fielding			
☐ 106	Tom Downey: Cinc.,	60.00	27.00	9.00
	Batting			
☐ 107	Tom Downey: Cinc.,	60.00	27.00	9.00
	Fielding			
☐ 108A	Larry Doyle: N.Y.	75.00	34.00	11.25
	(hands over head)			
☐ 108B	Larry Doyle: N.Y.	18000.00	7500.00	2250.00
	NAT'L, hands			
	over head)			
☐ 109	Larry Doyle: N.Y.	60.00	27.00	9.00
	NL, Sweater			
☐ 110	Larry Doyle: N.Y.	75.00	34.00	11.25
	NL, Throwing			
☐ 111	Larry Doyle: N.Y.	60.00	27.00	9.00
	NL, Bat on shoulder			
☐ 112	Jean Dubuc: Cin.	60.00	27.00	9.00
☐ 113	Hugh Duffy: Chicago	200.00	90.00	30.00
	AL			
☐ 114	Joe Dunn: Brooklyn	60.00	27.00	9.00
☐ 115	Bull Durham: N.Y. NL	75.00	34.00	11.25
☐ 116	Jimmy Dygert: Phila.	60.00	27.00	9.00
	AL			
☐ 117	Ted Easterly: Cleveland	60.00	27.00	9.00
☐ 118	Dick Egan: Cinc.	60.00	27.00	9.00
☐ 119	Kid Elberfeld:	60.00	27.00	9.00
	Wash., Fielding			
☐ 120	Kid Elberfeld:	1350.00	600.00	200.00
	Wash., Portrait			
☐ 121	Kid Elberfeld: N.Y.	75.00	34.00	11.25
	AL, Portrait			
☐ 122	Clyde Engle: N.Y. AL	60.00	27.00	9.00
☐ 123	Steve Evans:	60.00	27.00	9.00
	St. Louis NL			
☐ 124	Johnny Evers:	250.00	110.00	37.50
	Chicago NL, Portrait			
☐ 125	Johnny Evers:	350.00	160.00	52.50
	Chicago NL, Cubs			
	across chest			
☐ 126	Johnny Evers:	200.00	90.00	30.00
	Chicago NL, Chicago			
	down front of shirt			
☐ 127	Bob Ewing: Cinc.	75.00	34.00	11.25
☐ 128	George Ferguson:	60.00	27.00	9.00
	Boston NL			
☐ 129	Hobe Ferris:	75.00	34.00	11.25
	St. Louis AL			
☐ 130	Lou Fiene: Chicago	60.00	27.00	9.00
	AL, Portrait			
☐ 131	Lou Fiene: Chicago	60.00	27.00	9.00
	AL, Throwing			
☐ 132	Art Fletcher:	60.00	27.00	9.00
	New York NL			
☐ 133	Elmer Flick:	300.00	135.00	45.00
	Cleveland			
☐ 134	Russ Ford: N.Y. AL	60.00	27.00	9.00
☐ 135	John Frill: N.Y. AL	60.00	27.00	9.00
☐ 136	Art Fromme: Cinc.	60.00	27.00	9.00
☐ 137	Chick Gandil:	125.00	57.50	18.75
	Chicago AL			
☐ 138	Bob Ganley:	75.00	34.00	11.25
	Washington			
☐ 139	Harry Gasper: Cinc.	60.00	27.00	9.00
	(sic, Gaspar)			
☐ 140	Rube Geyer: St.L. NL	60.00	27.00	9.00
☐ 141	George Gibson: Pitt.	75.00	34.00	11.25
☐ 142	Billy Gilbert:	75.00	34.00	11.25
	St. Louis NL			
☐ 143	Wilbur Goode (sic,	75.00	34.00	11.25
	Good): Cleve.			
☐ 144	Bill Graham:	60.00	27.00	9.00
	St. Louis AL			
☐ 145	Peaches Graham:	60.00	27.00	9.00
	Boston NL			
☐ 146	Dolly Gray:	60.00	27.00	9.00
	Washington			
☐ 147	Clark Griffith:	300.00	135.00	45.00
	Cinc., Portrait			
☐ 148	Clark Griffith:	200.00	90.00	30.00
	Cinc., Batting			
☐ 149	Bob Groom:	60.00	27.00	9.00
	Washington			
☐ 150	Ed Hahn: Chicago AL	75.00	34.00	11.25
☐ 151	Topsy Hartsel:	60.00	27.00	9.00
	Phila. AL			
☐ 152	Charlie Hemphill:	75.00	34.00	11.25
	N.Y. AL			
☐ 153	Buck Herzog: N.Y. NL	75.00	34.00	11.25
☐ 154	Buck Herzog:	60.00	27.00	9.00
	Boston NL			
☐ 155	Bill Hinchman:	75.00	34.00	11.25
	Cleveland			
☐ 156	Doc Hoblitzell:	60.00	27.00	9.00
	Cincinnati			
☐ 157	Danny Hoffman:	60.00	27.00	9.00
	St. Louis AL			
☐ 158	Solly Hofman:	60.00	27.00	9.00
	Chicago NL			
☐ 159	Del Howard:	60.00	27.00	9.00
	Chicago NL			
☐ 160	Harry Howell: St.L.	60.00	27.00	9.00
	AL, Portrait			
☐ 161	Harry Howell: St.L.	60.00	27.00	9.00
	AL, Left hand on hip			
☐ 162	Miller Huggins:	300.00	135.00	45.00
	Cinc., Portrait			
☐ 163	Miller Huggins:	200.00	90.00	30.00
	Cinc., Hands			
	to mouth			
☐ 164	Rudy Hulswitt:	60.00	27.00	9.00
	St. Louis NL			
☐ 165	John Hummel:	60.00	27.00	9.00
	Brooklyn			
☐ 166	George Hunter:	60.00	27.00	9.00
	Brooklyn			
☐ 167	Frank Isbell:	75.00	34.00	11.25
	Chicago AL			
☐ 168	Fred Jacklitsch:	75.00	34.00	11.25
	Phila. NL			
☐ 169	Hugh Jennings:	300.00	135.00	45.00
	Detroit, Portrait			
☐ 170	Hugh Jennings:	200.00	90.00	30.00
	Detroit, Yelling			
☐ 171	Hugh Jennings:	200.00	90.00	30.00
	Detroit, Dancing			
	for joy			
☐ 172	Walter Johnson:	1000.00	450.00	135.00
	Washington, Portrait			
☐ 173	Walter Johnson:	700.00	315.00	105.00
	Washington, Ready			
	to pitch			
☐ 174	Tom Jones: St.L. AL	75.00	34.00	11.25
☐ 175	Tom Jones: Detroit	60.00	27.00	9.00
☐ 176	Fielder Jones: Chic.	75.00	34.00	11.25
	AL, Portrait			
☐ 177	Fielder Jones: Chic.	75.00	34.00	11.25
	AL, Hands on hips			
☐ 178	Tim Jordan:	75.00	34.00	11.25
	Brooklyn, Portrait			
☐ 179	Tim Jordan:	60.00	27.00	9.00
	Brooklyn, Batting			
☐ 180	Addie Joss:	400.00	180.00	60.00
	Cleveland, Portrait			
☐ 181	Addie Joss:	250.00	110.00	37.50
	Cleveland, Ready			
	to pitch			
☐ 182	Ed Karger: Cinc.	75.00	34.00	11.25
☐ 183	Willie Keeler: N.Y.	400.00	180.00	60.00
	AL, Portrait			
☐ 184	Willie Keeler: N.Y.	300.00	135.00	45.00
	AL, Batting			
☐ 185	Ed Killian: Detroit,	75.00	34.00	11.25
	Portrait			
☐ 186	Ed Killian: Detroit,	60.00	27.00	9.00
	Pitching			
☐ 187	Red Kleinow: N.Y.	75.00	34.00	11.25
	AL, Batting			

	#	Name			
☐	188	Red Kleinow: N.Y. .... AL, Catching	60.00	27.00	9.00
☐	189	Red Kleinow: Boston .... AL, Catching	350.00	160.00	52.50
☐	190	Johnny Kling: .... Chicago NL	75.00	34.00	11.25
☐	191	Otto Knabe: .... Phila. NL	60.00	27.00	9.00
☐	192	John Knight: N.Y. .... AL, Portrait	60.00	27.00	9.00
☐	193	John Knight: N.Y. .... AL, Batting	60.00	27.00	9.00
☐	194	Ed Konetchy: St.L. .... NL, Awaiting low ball	60.00	27.00	9.00
☐	195	Ed Konetchy: St.L. .... NL, Glove above head	75.00	34.00	11.25
☐	196	Harry Krause: Phila. .... AL, Portrait	60.00	27.00	9.00
☐	197	Harry Krause: Phila. .... AL, Pitching	60.00	27.00	9.00
☐	198	Rube Kroh: .... Chicago NL	60.00	27.00	9.00
☐	199	Nap Lajoie: .... Cleveland, Portrait	450.00	200.00	67.50
☐	200	Nap Lajoie: .... Cleveland, Batting	300.00	135.00	45.00
☐	201	Nap Lajoie: .... Cleveland, Throwing	350.00	160.00	52.50
☐	202	Joe Lake: N.Y. AL	75.00	34.00	11.25
☐	203	Joe Lake: St.L. AL, ... Hands over head	60.00	27.00	9.00
☐	204	Joe Lake: St.L. AL, ... Throwing	60.00	27.00	9.00
☐	205	Frank LaPorte: N.Y. .... AL	60.00	27.00	9.00
☐	206	Arlie Latham: N.Y. .... NL	60.00	27.00	9.00
☐	207	Fred Leach: Pitt., ... Portrait	75.00	34.00	11.25
☐	208	Fred Leach: Pitt., ... In fielding position	60.00	27.00	9.00
☐	209	Lefty Leifield: .... Pitt., Batting	60.00	27.00	9.00
☐	210	Lefty Leifield: .... Pitt., Hands behind head	75.00	34.00	11.25
☐	211	Ed Lennox: Brooklyn	60.00	27.00	9.00
☐	212	Glenn Liebhardt: .... Cleveland	75.00	34.00	11.25
☐	213	Vive Lindaman: .... Boston NL	100.00	45.00	15.00
☐	214	Paddy Livingstone: .... Phila. AL	60.00	27.00	9.00
☐	215	Hans Lobert: Cinc.	75.00	34.00	11.25
☐	216	Harry Lord: Bost. AL	60.00	27.00	9.00
☐	217	Harry Lumley: .... Brooklyn	75.00	34.00	11.25
☐	218	Carl Lundgren: .... Chicago NL	400.00	180.00	60.00
☐	219	Nick Maddox: Pitt.	60.00	27.00	9.00
☐	220	Sherry Magee: Phila. .... NL, Portrait	75.00	34.00	11.25
☐	221	Sherry Magee: Phila. .... NL, Batting	60.00	27.00	9.00
☐	222	Sherry Magie: .... Phila. NL, (sic, Magee) Portrait, name misspelled	12000.00	5000.00	1500.00
☐	223	Rube Manning: N.Y. .... AL, Batting	75.00	34.00	11.25
☐	224	Rube Manning: N.Y. .... AL, Hands over head	60.00	27.00	9.00
☐	225	Rube Marquard: N.Y. .... NL, Portrait	300.00	135.00	45.00
☐	226	Rube Marquard: N.Y. .... NL, Pitching	200.00	90.00	30.00
☐	227	Rube Marquard: N.Y. .... NL, Standing	250.00	110.00	37.50
☐	228	Doc Marshall: .... Brooklyn	60.00	27.00	9.00
☐	229	Christy Mathewson: .... N.Y. NL, Portrait	1000.00	450.00	135.00
☐	230	Christy Mathewson: .... N.Y. NL, Pitching, white cap	700.00	315.00	105.00
☐	231	Christy Mathewson: .... N.Y. NL, Pitching, dark cap	650.00	300.00	100.00
☐	232	Al Mattern: .... Boston NL	60.00	27.00	9.00
☐	233	Jack McAleese: .... St. Louis AL	60.00	27.00	9.00
☐	234	George McBride: .... Washington	60.00	27.00	9.00
☐	235	Moose McCormick: .... N.Y. NL	60.00	27.00	9.00
☐	236	Pryor McElveen: .... Brooklyn	60.00	27.00	9.00
☐	237	John McGraw: N.Y. .... NL, Portrait, no cap	400.00	180.00	60.00
☐	238	John McGraw: N.Y. .... NL, Wearing sweater	250.00	110.00	37.50
☐	239	John McGraw: N.Y. .... NL, pointing	300.00	135.00	45.00
☐	240	John McGraw: N.Y. .... NL, Glove on hip	300.00	135.00	45.00
☐	241	Matty McIntyre: .... Brooklyn	75.00	34.00	11.25
☐	242	Matty McIntyre: .... Brooklyn and Chicago NL	60.00	27.00	9.00
☐	243	Mike McIntyre: .... Detroit	60.00	27.00	9.00
☐	244	Larry McLean: Cinc.	60.00	27.00	9.00
☐	245	George McQuillan: .... Phila. NL, Throwing	75.00	34.00	11.25
☐	246	George McQuillan: .... Phila. NL, Batting	60.00	27.00	9.00
☐	247	Fred Merkle: N.Y. .... NL, Portrait	60.00	27.00	9.00
☐	248	Fred Merkle: N.Y. .... NL, Throwing	75.00	34.00	11.25
☐	249	Chief Meyers: .... New York NL	60.00	27.00	9.00
☐	250	Clyde Milan: .... Washington	60.00	27.00	9.00
☐	251	Dots Miller: Pitt.	60.00	27.00	9.00
☐	252	Mike Mitchell: Cinc.	60.00	27.00	9.00
☐	253	Pat Moran: .... Chicago NL	60.00	27.00	9.00
☐	254	George Moriarty: .... Detroit	60.00	27.00	9.00
☐	255	Mike Mowrey: Cinc.	60.00	27.00	9.00
☐	256	George Mullen: .... Detroit (sic, Mullin)	60.00	27.00	9.00
☐	257	George Mullin: .... Detroit, Throwing	75.00	34.00	11.25
☐	258	George Mullin: .... Detroit, Batting	60.00	27.00	9.00
☐	259	Danny Murphy: Phila. .... AL, Throwing	75.00	34.00	11.25
☐	260	Danny Murphy: Phila. .... AL, Bat on shoulder	60.00	27.00	9.00
☐	261	Red Murray: N.Y. .... NL, Sweater	60.00	27.00	9.00
☐	262	Red Murray: N.Y. .... NL, Bat on shoulder	60.00	27.00	9.00
☐	263	Chief Myers (sic, ... Meyers): N.Y. NL, Fielding	60.00	27.00	9.00
☐	264	Chief Myers (sic, ... Meyers): N.Y. NL, Batting	60.00	27.00	9.00
☐	265	Tom Needham: .... Chicago NL	60.00	27.00	9.00
☐	266	Simon Nicholls: .... Phila. AL	75.00	34.00	11.25
☐	267	Simon Nichols (sic, Nicholls): Phila. AL	60.00	27.00	9.00
☐	268	Harry Niles: .... Boston AL	75.00	34.00	11.25
☐	269	Rebel Oakes: Cinc.	60.00	27.00	9.00
☐	270	Bill O'Hara: N.Y. NL	60.00	27.00	9.00
☐	271	Bill O'Hara: .... St. Louis NL	4000.00	1600.00	500.00
☐	272	Rube Oldring: Phila. .... AL, Fielding	75.00	34.00	11.25
☐	273	Rube Oldring: Phila. .... AL, Bat on shoulder	60.00	27.00	9.00
☐	274	Charley O'Leary: .... Detroi, Portrait	75.00	34.00	11.25
☐	275	Charley O'Leary: .... Detroit, Hands on knees	60.00	27.00	9.00
☐	276	Orval Overall: .... Chicago NL, Portrait	75.00	34.00	11.25
☐	277	Orval Overall: .... Chicago NL, Pitching, follow thru	60.00	27.00	9.00
☐	278	Orval Overall: .... Chicago NL, Pitching hiding ball in glove	60.00	27.00	9.00
☐	279	Frank Owen: (sic, ... Owens), Chicago AL	75.00	34.00	11.25
☐	280	Freddy Parent: .... Chicago AL	75.00	34.00	11.25

☐ 281	Dode Paskert: Cinc.	60.00	27.00	9.00
☐ 282	Jim Pastorius: .... Brooklyn	75.00	34.00	11.25
☐ 283	Harry Pattee: Brooklyn	125.00	57.50	18.75
☐ 284	Fred Payne: .... Chicago AL	60.00	27.00	9.00
☐ 285	Barney Pelty: St.L. AL, HOR	125.00	57.50	18.75
☐ 286	Barney Pelty: St.L. AL, VERT	60.00	27.00	9.00
☐ 287	George Perring: .... Cleveland	60.00	27.00	9.00
☐ 288	Jeff Pfeffer: .... Chicago NL	60.00	27.00	9.00
☐ 289	Jack Pfeister: Chic. .... NL, Sitting	60.00	27.00	9.00
☐ 290	Jack Pfeister: Chic. .... NL, Pitching	60.00	27.00	9.00
☐ 291	Ed Phelps: St.L. NL	60.00	27.00	9.00
☐ 292	Deacon Phillippe: .... Pitt.	90.00	40.00	13.50
☐ 293	Eddie Plank: .... Phila. AL	25000.00	9600.00	3000.00
☐ 294	Jack Powell: .... St. Louis AL	75.00	34.00	11.25
☐ 295	Mike Powers: .... Phila. AL	125.00	57.50	18.75
☐ 296	Billy Purtell: .... Chicago AL	60.00	27.00	9.00
☐ 297	Jack Quinn: N.Y. AL	60.00	27.00	9.00
☐ 298	Bugs Raymond: .... New York NL	60.00	27.00	9.00
☐ 299	Ed Reulbach: Chicago .... NL, Pitching	60.00	27.00	9.00
☐ 300	Ed Reulbach: Chicago .... NL, Hands at side	125.00	57.50	18.75
☐ 301	Bob Rhoades: sic, ... Rhoads, Cleveland, Hand in air	60.00	27.00	9.00
☐ 302	Bob Rhoades: sic, ... Rhoads, Cleveland, Ready to pitch	60.00	27.00	9.00
☐ 303	Charlie Rhodes: .... St. Louis NL	60.00	27.00	9.00
☐ 304	Claude Ritchey: .... Boston NL	75.00	34.00	11.25
☐ 305	Claude Rossman: .... Detroit	60.00	27.00	9.00
☐ 306	Nap Rucker: .... Brooklyn, Portrait	75.00	34.00	11.25
☐ 307	Nap Rucker: .... Brooklyn, Throwing	60.00	27.00	9.00
☐ 309	Germany Schaefer: .... Detroit	75.00	34.00	11.25
☐ 308	Germany Schaefer: .... Washington	60.00	27.00	9.00
☐ 310	Admiral Schlei: N.Y. .... NL, Sweater	60.00	27.00	9.00
☐ 311	Admiral Schlei: N.Y. .... NL, Batting	60.00	27.00	9.00
☐ 312	Admiral Schlei: N.Y. .... NL, Fielding	75.00	34.00	11.25
☐ 313	Boss Schmidt: .... Detroit, Portrait	60.00	27.00	9.00
☐ 314	Boss Schmidt: .... Detroit, Throwing	75.00	34.00	11.25
☐ 315	Frank Schulte: .... Chicago NL, Batting, back turned	60.00	27.00	9.00
☐ 316	Frank Schulte: .... Chicago NL, Batting, front pose	75.00	34.00	11.25
☐ 317	Jim Scott: .... Chicago AL	60.00	27.00	9.00
☐ 318	Cy Seymour: N.Y. NL, ... Portrait	60.00	27.00	9.00
☐ 319	Cy Seymour: N.Y. NL, ... Throwing	60.00	27.00	9.00
☐ 320	Cy Seymour: N.Y. NL, ... Batting	75.00	34.00	11.25
☐ 321	Al Shaw: St.L. NL	75.00	34.00	11.25
☐ 322	Jimmy Sheckard: .... Chicago NL, Throwing	60.00	27.00	9.00
☐ 323	Jimmy Sheckard: .... Chicago NL, Side view	75.00	34.00	11.25
☐ 324	Bill Shipke: .... Washington	75.00	34.00	11.25
☐ 325	Frank Smith: Chicago .... AL, Listed as Smith	60.00	27.00	9.00
☐ 326	Frank Smith: Chicago .... and Boston AL	450.00	200.00	67.50
☐ 327	Frank Smith: Chicago .... AL, Listed as F.Smith	75.00	34.00	11.25
☐ 328	Happy Smith: Brk.	60.00	27.00	9.00
☐ 329	Fred Snodgrass: N.Y. .... NL, Batting	60.00	27.00	9.00
☐ 330	Fred Snodgrass: N.Y. .... NL, Catching	60.00	27.00	9.00
☐ 331	Bob Spade: Cinc.	75.00	34.00	11.25
☐ 332	Tris Speaker: .... Boston AL	450.00	200.00	67.50
☐ 333	Tubby Spencer: .... Boston AL	75.00	34.00	11.25
☐ 334	Jake Stahl: .... Boston AL Catching fly ball	60.00	27.00	9.00
☐ 335	Jake Stahl: .... Boston AL Standing, arms down	60.00	27.00	9.00
☐ 336	Oscar Stanage: .... Detroit	60.00	27.00	9.00
☐ 337	Charlie Starr: .... Boston NL	60.00	27.00	9.00
☐ 338	Harry Steinfeldt: .... Chicago NL, Portrait	75.00	34.00	11.25
☐ 339	Harry Steinfeldt: .... Chicago NL, Batting	60.00	27.00	9.00
☐ 340	Jim Stephens: St.L. .... AL	60.00	27.00	9.00
☐ 341	George Stone: St.L. .... AL	75.00	34.00	11.25
☐ 342	George Stovall: .... Cleveland, Portrait	75.00	34.00	11.25
☐ 343	George Stovall: .... Cleveland, Batting	60.00	27.00	9.00
☐ 344	Gabby Street: .... Washington, Portrait	60.00	27.00	9.00
☐ 345	Gabby Street: .... Washington, Catching	60.00	27.00	9.00
☐ 346	Billy Sullivan: .... Chicago AL	75.00	34.00	11.25
☐ 347	Ed Summers: Detroit	60.00	27.00	9.00
☐ 348	Jeff Sweeney: .... New York AL	60.00	27.00	9.00
☐ 349	Bill Sweeney: .... Boston NL	60.00	27.00	9.00
☐ 350	Jesse Tannehill: .... Washington	60.00	27.00	9.00
☐ 351	Lee Tannehill: .... Chicago AL, Listed as L.Tannehill	75.00	34.00	11.25
☐ 352	Lee Tannehill: .... Chicago AL, Listed as Tannehill	60.00	27.00	9.00
☐ 353	Fred Tenney: N.Y. NL	75.00	34.00	11.25
☐ 354	Ira Thomas: .... Phila. AL	60.00	27.00	9.00
☐ 355	Joe Tinker: Chicago .... NL, Ready to hit	200.00	90.00	30.00
☐ 356	Joe Tinker: Chicago .... NL, Bat on shoulder	200.00	90.00	30.00
☐ 357	Joe Tinker: Chicago .... NL, Portrait	250.00	110.00	37.50
☐ 358	Joe Tinker: Chicago .... NL, Hands on knees	250.00	110.00	37.50
☐ 359	John Titus: .... Phila. NL	60.00	27.00	9.00
☐ 360	Terry Turner: .... Cleveland	75.00	34.00	11.25
☐ 361	Bob Unglaub: .... Washington	60.00	27.00	9.00
☐ 362	Rube Waddell: St.L. .... AL, Portrait	350.00	160.00	52.50
☐ 363	Rube Waddell: St.L. .... AL, Pitching	250.00	110.00	37.50
☐ 364	Heinie Wagner: .... Boston AL, Bat on left shoulder	125.00	57.50	18.75
☐ 365	Heinie Wagner: .... Boston AL, Bat on right shoulder	75.00	34.00	11.25
☐ 366	Honus Wagner: Pitt.	250000.	100000.	33000.
☐ 367	Bobby Wallace: .... St. Louis AL	225.00	100.00	33.00
☐ 368	Ed Walsh: Chicago AL	250.00	110.00	37.50
☐ 369	Jack Warhop: N.Y. AL	60.00	27.00	9.00
☐ 370	Jake Weimer: N.Y. NL	75.00	34.00	11.25
☐ 371	Zach Wheat: Brooklyn	250.00	110.00	37.50
☐ 372	Doc White: Chicago .... AL, Portrait	75.00	34.00	11.25
☐ 373	Doc White: Chicago .... AL, Pitching	60.00	27.00	9.00
☐ 374	Kaiser Wilhelm: .... Brooklyn, Batting	60.00	27.00	9.00
☐ 375	Kaiser Wilhelm: .... Brooklyn, Hands to chest	75.00	34.00	11.25

☐ 376	Ed Willett: Detroit, ... Batting	60.00	27.00	9.00
☐ 377	Ed Willetts (sic, ... Willett): Detroit, Pitching	60.00	27.00	9.00
☐ 378	Jimmy Williams: .... St. Louis AL	75.00	34.00	11.25
☐ 379	Vic Willis: Pitt.	125.00	57.50	18.75
☐ 380	Vic Willis: St.L. .... NL, Pitching	100.00	45.00	15.00
☐ 381	Vic Willis: St.L. .... NL, Batting	100.00	45.00	15.00
☐ 382	Chief Wilson: Pitt.	60.00	27.00	9.00
☐ 383	Hooks Wiltse: N.Y. .... NL, Portrait	75.00	34.00	11.25
☐ 384	Hooks Wiltse: N.Y. .... NL, Sweater	60.00	27.00	9.00
☐ 385	Hooks Wiltse: N.Y. .... NL, Pitching	60.00	27.00	9.00
☐ 386	Cy Young: Cleveland, ... Portrait	900.00	400.00	135.00
☐ 387	Cy Young: Cleveland, ... Pitch, front view	600.00	270.00	90.00
☐ 388	Cy Young: Cleveland, ... Pitch, side view	600.00	270.00	90.00
☐ 389	Heinie Zimmerman: .... Chicago NL	60.00	27.00	9.00
☐ 390	Fred Abbott: Toledo	50.00	22.50	7.50
☐ 391	Merle (Doc) Adkins: .... Baltimore	50.00	22.50	7.50
☐ 392	John Anderson: .... Providence	50.00	22.50	7.50
☐ 393	Herman Armbruster: .... St. Paul	50.00	22.50	7.50
☐ 394	Harry Arndt: Prov.	50.00	22.50	7.50
☐ 395	Cy Barger: .... Rochester	50.00	22.50	7.50
☐ 396	John Barry: .... Milwaukee	50.00	22.50	7.50
☐ 397	Emil H. Batch: .... Rochester	50.00	22.50	7.50
☐ 398	Jake Beckley: K.C.	250.00	110.00	37.50
☐ 399	Russell Blackburne .... (Lena): Providence	50.00	22.50	7.50
☐ 400	David Brain: .... Buffalo	50.00	22.50	7.50
☐ 401	Roy Brashear: K.C.	50.00	22.50	7.50
☐ 402	Fred Burchell: .... Buffalo	50.00	22.50	7.50
☐ 403	Jimmy Burke: Ind.	50.00	22.50	7.50
☐ 404	John Butler: Roch.	50.00	22.50	7.50
☐ 405	Charles Carr: Ind.	50.00	22.50	7.50
☐ 406	James Peter Casey .... (Doc): Montreal	50.00	22.50	7.50
☐ 407	Peter Cassidy: .... Baltimore	50.00	22.50	7.50
☐ 408	Wm. Chappelle: .... Rochester	50.00	22.50	7.50
☐ 409	Wm. Clancy: Buffalo	50.00	22.50	7.50
☐ 410	Joshua Clark: Col.	50.00	22.50	7.50
☐ 411	William Clymer: .... Columbus	50.00	22.50	7.50
☐ 412	Jimmy Collins: .... Minneapolis	300.00	135.00	45.00
☐ 413	Bunk Congalton: .... Columbus	50.00	22.50	7.50
☐ 414	Gavvy Cravath: .... Minneapolis	75.00	34.00	11.25
☐ 415	Monte Cross: Ind.	50.00	22.50	7.50
☐ 416	Paul Davidson: Ind.	50.00	22.50	7.50
☐ 417	Frank Delehanty: .... Louisville	50.00	22.50	7.50
☐ 418	Rube Dessau: Balt.	50.00	22.50	7.50
☐ 419	Gus Dorner: K.C.	50.00	22.50	7.50
☐ 420	Jerome Downs: Minn.	50.00	22.50	7.50
☐ 421	Jack Dunn: .... Baltimore	50.00	22.50	7.50
☐ 422	James Flanagan: .... Buffalo	50.00	22.50	7.50
☐ 423	James Freeman: Tol.	50.00	22.50	7.50
☐ 424	John Ganzel: Roch.	50.00	22.50	7.50
☐ 425	Myron Grimshaw: .... Toronto	50.00	22.50	7.50
☐ 426	Robert Hall: Balt.	50.00	22.50	7.50
☐ 427	William Hallman: .... Kansas City	50.00	22.50	7.50
☐ 428	John Hannifan: J.C.	50.00	22.50	7.50
☐ 429	Jack Hayden: Ind.	50.00	22.50	7.50
☐ 430	Harry Hinchman: .... Toledo	50.00	22.50	7.50
☐ 431	Harry C. Hoffman .... (Izzy): Providence	50.00	22.50	7.50
☐ 432	James B. Jackson: .... Baltimore	50.00	22.50	7.50
☐ 433	Joe Kelley: Tor.	300.00	135.00	45.00
☐ 434	Rube Kisinger: .... Buffalo, (sic) Kissinger	50.00	22.50	7.50
☐ 435	Otto Kruger: Col. .... (sic) Krueger	50.00	22.50	7.50
☐ 436	Wm. Lattimore: Tol.	50.00	22.50	7.50
☐ 437	James Lavender: .... Providence	50.00	22.50	7.50
☐ 438	Carl Lundgren: K.C.	50.00	22.50	7.50
☐ 439	Wm. Malarkey: Buff.	50.00	22.50	7.50
☐ 440	Wm. Maloney: Roch.	50.00	22.50	7.50
☐ 441	Dennis McGann: .... Milwaukee	50.00	22.50	7.50
☐ 442	James McGinley: .... Toronto	50.00	22.50	7.50
☐ 443	Joe McGinnity: New.	250.00	110.00	37.50
☐ 444	Ulysses McGlynn: .... Milwaukee	50.00	22.50	7.50
☐ 445	George Merritt: .... Jersey City	50.00	22.50	7.50
☐ 446	Wm. Milligan: J.C.	50.00	22.50	7.50
☐ 447	Fred Mitchell: Tor.	50.00	22.50	7.50
☐ 448	Dan Moeller: J.C.	50.00	22.50	7.50
☐ 449	Joseph Herbert .... Moran: Providence	50.00	22.50	7.50
☐ 450	Wm. Nattress: .... Buffalo	50.00	22.50	7.50
☐ 451	Frank Oberlin: .... Minneapolis	50.00	22.50	7.50
☐ 452	Peter O'Brien: .... St. Paul	50.00	22.50	7.50
☐ 453	Wm. O'Neil: Minn.	50.00	22.50	7.50
☐ 454	James Phelan: Prov.	50.00	22.50	7.50
☐ 455	Oliver Pickering: .... Minneapolis.	50.00	22.50	7.50
☐ 456	Philip Poland: .... Baltimore	50.00	22.50	7.50
☐ 457	Ambrose Puttman: .... Louisville	50.00	22.50	7.50
☐ 458	Lee Quillen: Minn.	50.00	22.50	7.50
☐ 459	Newton Randall: .... Milwaukee	50.00	22.50	7.50
☐ 460	Louis Ritter: K.C.	50.00	22.50	7.50
☐ 461	Dick Rudolph: Tor.	50.00	22.50	7.50
☐ 462	George Schirm: .... Buffalo	50.00	22.50	7.50
☐ 463	Larry Schlafly: .... Newark	50.00	22.50	7.50
☐ 464	Ossie Schreck: Col. .... (sic) Schreckengost	50.00	22.50	7.50
☐ 465	William Shannon: .... Kansas City	50.00	22.50	7.50
☐ 466	Bayard Sharpe: .... Newark	50.00	22.50	7.50
☐ 467	Royal Shaw: Prov.	50.00	22.50	7.50
☐ 468	James Slagle: Balt.	50.00	22.50	7.50
☐ 469	George Henry Smith: .... Buffalo	50.00	22.50	7.50
☐ 470	Samuel Strang: .... Baltimore	50.00	22.50	7.50
☐ 471	Luther Taylor: .... (Dummy): Buffalo	50.00	22.50	7.50
☐ 472	John Thielman: .... Louisville	50.00	22.50	7.50
☐ 473	John F. White: .... Columbus	50.00	22.50	7.50
☐ 474	William Wright: .... Toledo	50.00	22.50	7.50
☐ 475	Irving M. Young: .... Minneapolis	50.00	22.50	7.50
☐ 476	Jack Bastian: .... San Antonio	125.00	57.50	18.75
☐ 477	Harry Bay: Nashv.	125.00	57.50	18.75
☐ 478	Wm. Bernhard: .... Nashville	125.00	57.50	18.75
☐ 479	Ted Breitenstein: .... New Orleans	125.00	57.50	18.75
☐ 480	George Carey: .... (Scoops): Memphis	125.00	57.50	18.75
☐ 481	Cad Coles: Augusta	125.00	57.50	18.75
☐ 482	Wm. Cranston: .... Memphis	125.00	57.50	18.75
☐ 483	Roy Ellam: .... Nashville	125.00	57.50	18.75
☐ 484	Edward Foster: .... Charleston	125.00	57.50	18.75
☐ 485	Charles Fritz: N.O.	125.00	57.50	18.75
☐ 486	Ed Greminger: .... Montgomery	125.00	57.50	18.75
☐ 487	Guiheen: Portsmouth	125.00	57.50	18.75
☐ 488	William F. Hart: .... Little Rock	125.00	57.50	18.75
☐ 489	James Henry Hart: .... Montgomery	125.00	57.50	18.75
☐ 490	J.R. Helm: Columbus	125.00	57.50	18.75

	(Georgia)			
☐ 491	Gordon Hickman: .... Mobile	125.00	57.50	18.75
☐ 492	Buck Hooker: .... Lynchburg	125.00	57.50	18.75
☐ 493	Ernie Howard: Sav.	125.00	57.50	18.75
☐ 494	A.O. Jordan: .... Atlanta	125.00	57.50	18.75
☐ 495	J.F. Kiernan: .... Columbia	125.00	57.50	18.75
☐ 496	Frank King: .... Danville	125.00	57.50	18.75
☐ 497	James LaFitte: .... Macon	125.00	57.50	18.75
☐ 498	Harry Lentz: Little .... Rock (sic) Sentz	125.00	57.50	18.75
☐ 499	Perry Lipe: .... Richmond	125.00	57.50	18.75
☐ 500	George Manion: .... Columbia	125.00	57.50	18.75
☐ 501	McCauley: .... Portsmouth	125.00	57.50	18.75
☐ 502	Charles B. Miller: .... Dallas	125.00	57.50	18.75
☐ 503	Carlton Molesworth: .... Birmingham	125.00	57.50	18.75
☐ 504	Dominic Mullaney: .... Jacksonville	125.00	57.50	18.75
☐ 505	Albert Orth: .... Lynchburg	125.00	57.50	18.75
☐ 506	William Otey: Norf.	125.00	57.50	18.75
☐ 507	George Paige: .... Charleston	125.00	57.50	18.75
☐ 508	Hub Perdue: Nashv.	150.00	67.50	22.50
☐ 509	Archie Persons: .... Montgomery	125.00	57.50	18.75
☐ 510	Edward Reagan: N.O.	125.00	57.50	18.75
☐ 511	R.H. Revelle: .... Richmond	125.00	57.50	18.75
☐ 512	Isaac Rockenfeld: .... Montgomery	125.00	57.50	18.75
☐ 513	Ray Ryan: Roanoke	125.00	57.50	18.75
☐ 514	Charles Seitz: .... Norfolk	125.00	57.50	18.75
☐ 515	Frank Shaughnessy .... (Shag): Roanoke	125.00	57.50	18.75
☐ 516	Carlos Smith: .... Shreveport	125.00	57.50	18.75
☐ 517	Sid Smith: Atlanta	125.00	57.50	18.75
☐ 518	M.R.(Dolly) Stark: .... San Antonio	125.00	57.50	18.75
☐ 519	Tony Thebo: Waco	125.00	57.50	18.75
☐ 520	Woodie Thornton: .... Mobile	125.00	57.50	18.75
☐ 521	Juan Violat: .... Jacksonville: (sic) Viola	125.00	57.50	18.75
☐ 522	James Westlake: .... Danville	125.00	57.50	18.75
☐ 523	Foley White: .... Houston	125.00	57.50	18.75

T207 Brown Background

The cards in this 207-card set measure 1 1/2" by 2 5/8". The T207 set, also known as the "Brown Background" set was issued with Broadleaf, Cycle, Napoleon, Recruit and anonymous (Factories no. 2, 3 or 25) backs in 1912. Broadleaf, Cycle and anonymous backs are difficult to obtain. Although many scarcities and cards with varying degrees of difficulty to obtain exist (see prices below), the Loudermilk, Lewis (Boston NL) and Miller (Chicago NL) cards are the rarest, followed by Saier and Tyler. The cards are numbered below for reference in alphabetical order by player's name. The complete set price below does include the Lewis variation missing the Braves patch on the sleeve.

	EX-MT	VG-E	GOOD
COMPLETE SET (208)	28000.	12500.	3750.
COMMON PLAYER (1-207)	60.00	27.00	9.00
☐ 1 Adams: Cleve AL	90.00	40.00	13.50
☐ 2 Ainsmith: Wash AL	60.00	27.00	9.00
☐ 3 Almeida: Cinc AL	90.00	40.00	13.50

Mike Mitchell

Mike Mitchell, right fielder of the Cincinnati Reds, is noted for his ability to make long hits in close games and for his wonderful throwing arm. Mitchell made a reputation as a hitter several years ago when a member of the Portland club of the Pacific Coast League and joined the Cincinnati team in 1908. Mitchell is one of the leading base runners of the National League. He was credited with 35 steals in 1910 and the same number in 1911. He made 154 hits for a total of 226 bases and an average of .291 in 1911. His fielding average was .971, 23 of his chances being assists to the bases or the home plate.

RECRUIT
LITTLE CIGARS

MITCHELL-CLEVELAND-AMER.

FACTORY NO. 240, 1ST DIST. PA.

☐ 4	Austin: StL AL .... with StL on shirt	60.00	27.00	9.00
☐ 5	Austin: StL AL .... without StL on shirt	180.00	80.00	27.00
☐ 6	Ball: Cleve AL	60.00	27.00	9.00
☐ 7	Barger: Brk NL	60.00	27.00	9.00
☐ 8	Barry: Phil AL	60.00	27.00	9.00
☐ 9	Bauman: Det AL	180.00	80.00	27.00
☐ 10	Becker: NY NL	60.00	27.00	9.00
☐ 11	Bender: Phil AL	180.00	80.00	27.00
☐ 12	Benz: Chi AL	90.00	40.00	13.50
☐ 13	Bescher: Cinc NL	60.00	27.00	9.00
☐ 14	Birmingham: Cleve AL	90.00	40.00	13.50
☐ 15	Blackburne: Chi AL	90.00	40.00	13.50
☐ 16	Blanding: Cleve AL	90.00	40.00	13.50
☐ 17	Block: Chi AL	60.00	27.00	9.00
☐ 18	Bodie: Phil AL	60.00	27.00	9.00
☐ 19	Bradley: Bos AL	60.00	27.00	9.00
☐ 20	Bresnahan: StL NL	180.00	80.00	27.00
☐ 21	Bushelman: Bos AL	90.00	40.00	13.50
☐ 22	Butcher: Cleve AL	90.00	40.00	13.50
☐ 23	Byrne: Pitt NL	60.00	27.00	9.00
☐ 24	Callahan: Chi AL	60.00	27.00	9.00
☐ 25	Camnitz: Pitt NL	60.00	27.00	9.00
☐ 26	Carey: Pitt NL	180.00	80.00	27.00
☐ 27	Carrigan: Bos AL .... correct back	60.00	27.00	9.00
☐ 28	Carrigan: Bos AL .... Wagner back	225.00	100.00	33.00
☐ 29	Chalmers: Phil NL	60.00	27.00	9.00
☐ 30	Chance: Chi NL	250.00	110.00	37.50
☐ 31	Cicotte: Bos AL	90.00	40.00	13.50
☐ 32	Clarke: Cinc NL	60.00	27.00	9.00
☐ 33	Cole: Chi NL	60.00	27.00	9.00
☐ 34	Collins: Chi AL	300.00	135.00	45.00
☐ 35	Coulson: Brk NL	60.00	27.00	9.00
☐ 36	Covington: Det AL	60.00	27.00	9.00
☐ 37	Crandall: NY NL	60.00	27.00	9.00
☐ 38	Cunningham: Wash AL	90.00	40.00	13.50
☐ 39	Danforth: Phil AL	60.00	27.00	9.00
☐ 40	Daniels: NY AL	60.00	27.00	9.00
☐ 41	Daubert: Brk NL	90.00	40.00	13.50
☐ 42	Davis: Cleve AL	60.00	27.00	9.00
☐ 43	Delahanty: Det AL	60.00	27.00	9.00
☐ 44	Derrick: Phil AL	60.00	27.00	9.00
☐ 45	Devlin: Bos NL	60.00	27.00	9.00
☐ 46	Devore: NY NL	60.00	27.00	9.00
☐ 47	Donlin: Pitt NL	90.00	40.00	13.50
☐ 48	Donnelly: Bos NL	90.00	40.00	13.50
☐ 49	Dooin: Phil NL	60.00	27.00	9.00
☐ 50	Downey: Phil NL	90.00	40.00	13.50
☐ 51	Doyle: NY NL	60.00	27.00	9.00
☐ 52	Drake: Det AL	60.00	27.00	9.00
☐ 53	Easterly: Cleve AL	60.00	27.00	9.00
☐ 54	Ellis: StL AL	60.00	27.00	9.00
☐ 55	Engle: Bos AL	60.00	27.00	9.00
☐ 56	Erwin: Brk NL	60.00	27.00	9.00
☐ 57	Evans: StL NL	60.00	27.00	9.00
☐ 58	Ferry: Pitt NL	60.00	27.00	9.00
☐ 59	Fisher: NY AL .... white cap	180.00	80.00	27.00
☐ 60	Fisher: NY AL .... blue cap	90.00	40.00	13.50
☐ 61	Fletcher: NY NL	60.00	27.00	9.00
☐ 62	Fournier: Chi AL	90.00	40.00	13.50
☐ 63	Fromme: Cinc NL	60.00	27.00	9.00

☐ 64 Gainor: Det AL	60.00	27.00	9.00
☐ 65 Gardner: Bos AL	60.00	27.00	9.00
☐ 66 George: Cleve AL	60.00	27.00	9.00
☐ 67 Golden: StL AL	60.00	27.00	9.00
☐ 68 Gowdy: Bos NL	60.00	27.00	9.00
☐ 69 Graham: Phil NL	90.00	40.00	13.50
☐ 70 Graney: Cleve AL	60.00	27.00	9.00
☐ 71 Gregg: Cleve AL	90.00	40.00	13.50
☐ 72 Hageman: Bos NL	60.00	27.00	9.00
☐ 73 Hall: Bos AL	60.00	27.00	9.00
☐ 74 Hallinan: St.L. AL	60.00	27.00	9.00
☐ 75 E. Hamilton: St.L. AL	60.00	27.00	9.00
☐ 76 Harmon: St.L. NL	60.00	27.00	9.00
☐ 77 Hartley: NY NL	90.00	40.00	13.50
☐ 78 Henriksen, Bos AL	60.00	27.00	9.00
☐ 79 Henry: Wash AL	90.00	40.00	13.50
☐ 80 Herzog: NY NL	90.00	40.00	13.50
☐ 81 Higgins: Brk NL	60.00	27.00	9.00
☐ 82 Hoff: NY AL	90.00	40.00	13.50
☐ 83 Hogan: StL AL	60.00	27.00	9.00
☐ 84 Hooper: Bos AL	450.00	200.00	67.50
☐ 85 Houser: Bos NL	90.00	40.00	13.50
☐ 86 Hyatt: Pitt NL	90.00	40.00	13.50
☐ 87 Johnson: Wash AL	1000.00	450.00	135.00
☐ 88 Kaler: Cleve AL	60.00	27.00	9.00
☐ 89 Kelly: Pitt NL	90.00	40.00	13.50
☐ 90 Kirke: Bos NL	90.00	40.00	13.50
☐ 91 Kling: Bos NL	60.00	27.00	9.00
☐ 92 Knabe: Phil NL	60.00	27.00	9.00
☐ 93 Knetzer: Brk NL	60.00	27.00	9.00
☐ 94 Konetchy: StL NL	60.00	27.00	9.00
☐ 95 Krause: Phil AL	60.00	27.00	9.00
☐ 96 Kuhn: Chi AL	90.00	40.00	13.50
☐ 97 Kutina: StL AL	90.00	40.00	13.50
☐ 98 Lange: Chi AL	90.00	40.00	13.50
☐ 99 Lapp: Phil AL	60.00	27.00	9.00
☐ 100 Latham: NY NL	60.00	27.00	9.00
☐ 101 Leach: Pitt NL	60.00	27.00	9.00
☐ 102 Leifield: Pitt NL	60.00	27.00	9.00
☐ 103 Lennox: Chi NL	60.00	27.00	9.00
☐ 104 Lewis: Bos AL	60.00	27.00	9.00
☐ 105A Lewis: Bos NL	2500.00	1000.00	300.00
(Braves patch on sleeve)			
☐ 105B Lewis: Bos NL	3000.00	1200.00	400.00
(nothing on sleeve)			
☐ 106 Lively: Det AL	60.00	27.00	9.00
☐ 107 Livingston: Cleve AL "A" shirt	250.00	110.00	37.50
☐ 108 Livingston: Cleve AL "C" shirt	250.00	110.00	37.50
☐ 109 Livingston: Cleve AL "c" shirt	90.00	40.00	13.50
☐ 110 Lord: Phil AL	60.00	27.00	9.00
☐ 111 Lord: Chi AL	60.00	27.00	9.00
☐ 112 Loudermilk: StL NL	2500.00	1000.00	300.00
☐ 113 Marquard: NY NL	180.00	80.00	27.00
☐ 114 Marsans: Cinc NL	60.00	27.00	9.00
☐ 115 McBride: Wash AL	60.00	27.00	9.00
☐ 116 McCarthy: Pitt NL	250.00	110.00	37.50
☐ 117 McDonald: Bos NL	60.00	27.00	9.00
☐ 118 McGraw: NY NL	250.00	110.00	37.50
☐ 119 McIntire: Chi AL	60.00	27.00	9.00
☐ 120 McIntyre: Chi AL	60.00	27.00	9.00
☐ 121 McKechnie: Pitt NL	350.00	160.00	52.50
☐ 122 McLean: Cinc NL	60.00	27.00	9.00
☐ 123 Milan: Wash AL	60.00	27.00	9.00
☐ 124 Miller: Pitt NL	60.00	27.00	9.00
☐ 125 Miller: Chi AL	2000.00	900.00	250.00
☐ 126 Miller: Brk NL	90.00	40.00	13.50
☐ 127 Miller: Bos NL	90.00	40.00	13.50
☐ 128 Mitchell: Cinc NL	60.00	27.00	9.00
☐ 129 Mitchell: Cleve AL	90.00	40.00	13.50
☐ 130 Mogridge: Chi AL	90.00	40.00	13.50
☐ 131 Moore: Phil NL	90.00	40.00	13.50
☐ 132 Moran: Phil NL	60.00	27.00	9.00
☐ 133 Morgan: Phil AL	60.00	27.00	9.00
☐ 134 Morgan: Wash AL	60.00	27.00	9.00
☐ 135 Moriarity: Det AL	90.00	40.00	13.50
☐ 136 Mullin: Det AL with "D" on cap	90.00	40.00	13.50
☐ 137 Mullin: Det AL without "D" on cap	250.00	110.00	37.50
☐ 138 Needham: Chi NL	60.00	27.00	9.00
☐ 139 Nelson: StL AL	90.00	40.00	13.50
☐ 140 Northen: Brk NL	60.00	27.00	9.00
☐ 141 Nunamaker: Bos AL	60.00	27.00	9.00
☐ 142 Oakes: StL NL	60.00	27.00	9.00
☐ 143 O'Brien: Bos AL	60.00	27.00	9.00
☐ 144 Oldring: Phil AL	60.00	27.00	9.00
☐ 145 Olson: Cleve AL	60.00	27.00	9.00
☐ 146 O'Toole: Pitt NL	60.00	27.00	9.00
☐ 147 Paskert: Phil NL	60.00	27.00	9.00
☐ 148 Pelty: StL AL	90.00	40.00	13.50
☐ 149 Perdue: Bos NL	60.00	27.00	9.00
☐ 150 Peters: Chi AL	90.00	40.00	13.50
☐ 151 Phelan: Cinc NL	90.00	40.00	13.50
☐ 152 Quinn: NY AL	60.00	27.00	9.00
☐ 153 Ragan: Brk NL	550.00	240.00	80.00
☐ 154 Rasmussen: Phil NL	450.00	200.00	67.50
☐ 155 Rath: Chi AL	90.00	40.00	13.50
☐ 156 Reulbach: Chi NL	60.00	27.00	9.00
☐ 157 Rucker: Brk NL	60.00	27.00	9.00
☐ 158 Ryan: Cleve AL	90.00	40.00	13.50
☐ 159 Saier: Chi NL	900.00	400.00	135.00
☐ 160 Scanlon: Phil NL	60.00	27.00	9.00
☐ 161 Schaefer: Wash AL	60.00	27.00	9.00
☐ 162 Schardt: Brk NL	60.00	27.00	9.00
☐ 163 Schulte: Chi NL	60.00	27.00	9.00
☐ 164 Scott: Chi AL	60.00	27.00	9.00
☐ 165 Severeid: Cinc NL	60.00	27.00	9.00
☐ 166 Simon: Pitt NL	60.00	27.00	9.00
☐ 167 Smith: StL NL	60.00	27.00	9.00
☐ 168 Smith: Cinc NL	60.00	27.00	9.00
☐ 169 Snodgrass: NY NL	60.00	27.00	9.00
☐ 170 Speaker: Bos AL	1000.00	450.00	135.00
☐ 171 Spratt: Bos NL	60.00	27.00	9.00
☐ 172 Stack: Brk NL	60.00	27.00	9.00
☐ 173 Stanage: Det AL	60.00	27.00	9.00
☐ 174 Steele: StL NL	60.00	27.00	9.00
☐ 175 Steinfeldt: StL NL	60.00	27.00	9.00
☐ 176 Stovall: StL AL	60.00	27.00	9.00
☐ 177 Street: NY AL	60.00	27.00	9.00
☐ 178 Strunk: Phil AL	60.00	27.00	9.00
☐ 179 Sullivan: Chi AL	60.00	27.00	9.00
☐ 180 Sweeney: Bos NL	180.00	80.00	27.00
☐ 181 Tannehill: Chi AL	60.00	27.00	9.00
☐ 182 Thomas: Bos AL	60.00	27.00	9.00
☐ 183 Tinker: Chi NL	180.00	80.00	27.00
☐ 184 Tooley: Brk NL	60.00	27.00	9.00
☐ 185 Turner: Cleve AL	60.00	27.00	9.00
☐ 186 Tyler: Bos NL	900.00	400.00	135.00
☐ 187 Vaughn: NY AL	60.00	27.00	9.00
☐ 188 Wagner: Bos AL correct back	90.00	40.00	13.50
☐ 189 Wagner: Bos AL Carrigan back	250.00	110.00	37.50
☐ 190 Walker: Wash AL	60.00	27.00	9.00
☐ 191 Wallace: St.L. AL	180.00	80.00	27.00
☐ 192 Warhop: NY AL	60.00	27.00	9.00
☐ 193 Weaver: Chi AL	250.00	110.00	37.50
☐ 194 Wheat: Brk NL	180.00	80.00	27.00
☐ 195 White: Chi AL	90.00	40.00	13.50
☐ 196 Wilie: St.L. NL	90.00	40.00	13.50
☐ 197 Williams: NY AL	60.00	27.00	9.00
☐ 198 Wilson: NY NL	60.00	27.00	9.00
☐ 199 Wilson: Pitt NL	90.00	40.00	13.50
☐ 200 Wiltse: NY NL	60.00	27.00	9.00
☐ 201 Wingo: StL NL	60.00	27.00	9.00
☐ 202 Wolverton: NY AL	60.00	27.00	9.00
☐ 203 Wood: Bos AL	180.00	80.00	27.00
☐ 204 Woodburn: StL NL	90.00	40.00	13.50
☐ 205 Works: Det AL	350.00	160.00	52.50
☐ 206 Yerkes: Bos AL	60.00	27.00	9.00
☐ 207 Zeider: Chi AL	90.00	40.00	13.50

1988 Upper Deck Samples

WALLY JOYNER

This two-card test issue was given away as samples during the summer of 1988 in anticipation of Upper Deck obtaining licenses from Major League Baseball and the Major League Baseball Players Association. Not many were produced (probably less than 25,000 of each) but few were thrown away as they were distributed basically only to those who would hold on to them. There are supposedly versions based on where the hologram is printed but the price below is for the basic variety. These test cards are the same size (2 1/2" by 3 1/2") as the regular issue and are styled similarly. Joyner and Buice were supposedly interested in investing in Upper Deck (conflict of interest prohibited them) and apparently were helpful in getting Upper Deck the necessary licenses. Cards were passed out freely to every dealer at the National Sports Collectors Convention in Atlantic City, New Jersey in August 1988.

	MINT	EXC	G-VG
COMPLETE SET (2)	50.00	22.50	7.50
COMMON PLAYER	15.00	6.50	2.15
☐ 1 DeWayne Buice	15.00	6.50	2.15
☐ 700 Wally Joyner	40.00	18.00	6.00

1989 Upper Deck

Orel Hershiser

This attractive set was introduced in 1989 as an additional major card set. The cards feature full color on both the front and the back. The cards are distinguished by the fact that each card has a hologram on the reverse, thus making the cards essentially copy proof. Cards 668-693 feature a "Collector's Choice" (CC) colorful drawing of a player (by artist Vernon Wells) on the card front and a checklist of that team on the card back. On many cards "Rookie" and team logos can be found with either a "TM" or (R). Cards with missing or duplicate holograms appear to be relatively common and hence there is little, if any, premium value on these "variations." The more significant variations involving changed photos or changed type are listed below. According to the company, the Murphy and Sheridan cards were corrected very early, after only 2 percent of the cards had been produced. This means, for example, that out of 1,000,000 Dale Murphy '89 Upper Deck cards produced, there are only 20,000 Murphy error cards. Similarly, the Sheffield was corrected after 15 percent had been printed; Varsho, Gallego, and Schroeder were corrected after 20 percent; and Holton, Manrique, and Winningham were corrected 30 percent of the way through. Collectors should also note that many dealers consider that Upper Deck's "planned" production of 1,000,000 of each player was increased (perhaps even doubled) later in the year due to the explosion in popularity of the Upper Deck cards. The key rookie cards in this set are Sandy Alomar Jr., Ken Griffey Jr., Felix Jose, Ramon Martinez, Gary Sheffield, and John Smoltz.

	MINT	EXC	G-VG
COMPLETE SET (700)	150.00	67.50	22.50
COMMON PLAYER (1-700)	.08	.03	.01

☐ 1	Ken Griffey Jr.	60.00	15.00	3.00
☐ 2	Luis Medina	.15	.06	.01
☐ 3	Tony Chance	.12	.05	.01
☐ 4	Dave Otto	.12	.05	.01
☐ 5	Sandy Alomar Jr. UER	2.00	.80	.20
	(Born 6/16/66, should be 6/18/66)			
☐ 6	Rolando Roomes	.12	.05	.01
☐ 7	Dave West	.25	.10	.02
☐ 8	Cris Carpenter	.20	.08	.02
☐ 9	Gregg Jefferies	1.00	.40	.10
☐ 10	Doug Dascenzo	.15	.06	.01
☐ 11	Ron Jones	.15	.06	.01
☐ 12	Luis De Los Santos	.12	.05	.01
☐ 13A	Gary Sheffield ERR	1.75	.70	.17
	(SS upside down on card front)			
☐ 13B	Gary Sheffield COR	1.50	.60	.15
☐ 14	Mike Harkey	.30	.12	.03
☐ 15	Lance Blankenship	.12	.05	.01
☐ 16	William Brennan	.12	.05	.01
☐ 17	John Smoltz	2.75	1.10	.27
☐ 18	Ramon Martinez	7.50	3.25	.75
☐ 19	Mark Lemke	.50	.20	.05
☐ 20	Juan Bell	.15	.06	.01
☐ 21	Rey Palacios	.12	.05	.01
☐ 22	Felix Jose	4.50	2.00	.45
☐ 23	Van Snider	.15	.06	.01
☐ 24	Dante Bichette	.40	.16	.04
☐ 25	Randy Johnson	1.25	.50	.12
☐ 26	Carlos Quintana	.90	.40	.09
☐ 27	Star Rookie CL	.12	.02	.00
☐ 28	Mike Schooler	.30	.12	.03
☐ 29	Randy St.Claire	.08	.03	.01
☐ 30	Jerald Clark	.50	.20	.05
☐ 31	Kevin Gross	.08	.03	.01
☐ 32	Dan Firova	.08	.03	.01
☐ 33	Jeff Calhoun	.08	.03	.01
☐ 34	Tommy Hinzo	.08	.03	.01
☐ 35	Ricky Jordan	.35	.15	.03
☐ 36	Larry Parrish	.08	.03	.01
☐ 37	Bret Saberhagen UER	.35	.15	.03
	(hit total 931, should be 1031)			
☐ 38	Mike Smithson	.08	.03	.01
☐ 39	Dave Dravecky	.12	.05	.01
☐ 40	Ed Romero	.08	.03	.01
☐ 41	Jeff Musselman	.08	.03	.01
☐ 42	Ed Hearn	.08	.03	.01
☐ 43	Rance Mulliniks	.08	.03	.01
☐ 44	Jim Eisenreich	.08	.03	.01
☐ 45	Sil Campusano	.15	.06	.01
☐ 46	Mike Krukow	.08	.03	.01
☐ 47	Paul Gibson	.15	.06	.01
☐ 48	Mike LaCoss	.08	.03	.01
☐ 49	Larry Herndon	.08	.03	.01
☐ 50	Scott Garrelts	.08	.03	.01
☐ 51	Dwayne Henry	.08	.03	.01
☐ 52	Jim Acker	.08	.03	.01
☐ 53	Steve Sax	.15	.06	.01
☐ 54	Pete O'Brien	.08	.03	.01
☐ 55	Paul Runge	.08	.03	.01
☐ 56	Rick Rhoden	.08	.03	.01
☐ 57	John Dopson	.12	.05	.01
☐ 58	Casey Candaele UER	.08	.03	.01
	(no stats for Astros for '88 season)			
☐ 59	Dave Righetti	.12	.05	.01
☐ 60	Joe Hesketh	.12	.05	.01
☐ 61	Frank DiPino	.08	.03	.01
☐ 62	Tim Laudner	.08	.03	.01
☐ 63	Jamie Moyer	.08	.03	.01
☐ 64	Fred Toliver	.08	.03	.01
☐ 65	Mitch Webster	.08	.03	.01
☐ 66	John Tudor	.12	.05	.01
☐ 67	John Cangelosi	.08	.03	.01
☐ 68	Mike Devereaux	.12	.05	.01
☐ 69	Brian Fisher	.08	.03	.01
☐ 70	Mike Marshall	.12	.05	.01
☐ 71	Zane Smith	.12	.05	.01
☐ 72A	Brian Holton ERR	1.50	.60	.15
	(photo actually Shawn Hillegas)			
☐ 72B	Brian Holton COR	.30	.12	.03
☐ 73	Jose Guzman	.08	.03	.01
☐ 74	Rick Mahler	.08	.03	.01
☐ 75	John Shelby	.08	.03	.01
☐ 76	Jim Deshaies	.08	.03	.01
☐ 77	Bobby Meacham	.08	.03	.01
☐ 78	Bryn Smith	.08	.03	.01
☐ 79	Joaquin Andujar	.08	.03	.01
☐ 80	Richard Dotson	.08	.03	.01
☐ 81	Charlie Lea	.08	.03	.01
☐ 82	Calvin Schiraldi	.08	.03	.01
☐ 83	Les Straker	.08	.03	.01

☐ 84	Les Lancaster	.08	.03	.01
☐ 85	Allan Anderson	.08	.03	.01
☐ 86	Junior Ortiz	.08	.03	.01
☐ 87	Jesse Orosco	.08	.03	.01
☐ 88	Felix Fermin	.08	.03	.01
☐ 89	Dave Anderson	.08	.03	.01
☐ 90	Rafael Belliard UER	.08	.03	.01
	(Born '61, not '51)			
☐ 91	Franklin Stubbs	.08	.03	.01
☐ 92	Cecil Espy	.08	.03	.01
☐ 93	Albert Hall	.08	.03	.01
☐ 94	Tim Leary	.12	.05	.01
☐ 95	Mitch Williams	.12	.05	.01
☐ 96	Tracy Jones	.08	.03	.01
☐ 97	Danny Darwin	.08	.03	.01
☐ 98	Gary Ward	.08	.03	.01
☐ 99	Neal Heaton	.08	.03	.01
☐ 100	Jim Pankovits	.08	.03	.01
☐ 101	Bill Doran	.08	.03	.01
☐ 102	Tim Wallach	.12	.05	.01
☐ 103	Joe Magrane	.12	.05	.01
☐ 104	Ozzie Virgil	.08	.03	.01
☐ 105	Alvin Davis	.12	.05	.01
☐ 106	Tom Brookens	.08	.03	.01
☐ 107	Shawon Dunston	.15	.06	.01
☐ 108	Tracy Woodson	.08	.03	.01
☐ 109	Nelson Liriano	.08	.03	.01
☐ 110	Devon White UER	.12	.05	.01
	(doubles total 46,			
	should be 56)			
☐ 111	Steve Balboni	.08	.03	.01
☐ 112	Buddy Bell	.12	.05	.01
☐ 113	German Jimenez	.08	.03	.01
☐ 114	Ken Dayley	.08	.03	.01
☐ 115	Andres Galarraga	.12	.05	.01
☐ 116	Mike Scioscia	.08	.03	.01
☐ 117	Gary Pettis	.08	.03	.01
☐ 118	Ernie Whitt	.08	.03	.01
☐ 119	Bob Boone	.12	.05	.01
☐ 120	Ryne Sandberg	1.50	.60	.15
☐ 121	Bruce Benedict	.08	.03	.01
☐ 122	Hubie Brooks	.12	.05	.01
☐ 123	Mike Moore	.12	.05	.01
☐ 124	Wallace Johnson	.08	.03	.01
☐ 125	Bob Horner	.12	.05	.01
☐ 126	Chili Davis	.12	.05	.01
☐ 127	Manny Trillo	.08	.03	.01
☐ 128	Chet Lemon	.08	.03	.01
☐ 129	John Cerutti	.08	.03	.01
☐ 130	Orel Hershiser	.17	.07	.01
☐ 131	Terry Pendleton	.25	.10	.02
☐ 132	Jeff Blauser	.17	.07	.01
☐ 133	Mike Fitzgerald	.08	.03	.01
☐ 134	Henry Cotto	.08	.03	.01
☐ 135	Gerald Young	.08	.03	.01
☐ 136	Luis Salazar	.08	.03	.01
☐ 137	Alejandro Pena	.12	.05	.01
☐ 138	Jack Howell	.08	.03	.01
☐ 139	Tony Fernandez	.12	.05	.01
☐ 140	Mark Grace	1.00	.40	.10
☐ 141	Ken Caminiti	.08	.03	.01
☐ 142	Mike Jackson	.08	.03	.01
☐ 143	Larry McWilliams	.08	.03	.01
☐ 144	Andres Thomas	.08	.03	.01
☐ 145	Nolan Ryan	3.50	1.50	.35
	(triple exposure)			
☐ 146	Mike Davis	.08	.03	.01
☐ 147	DeWayne Buice	.08	.03	.01
☐ 148	Jody Davis	.08	.03	.01
☐ 149	Jesse Barfield	.12	.05	.01
☐ 150	Matt Nokes	.12	.05	.01
☐ 151	Jerry Reuss	.08	.03	.01
☐ 152	Rick Cerone	.08	.03	.01
☐ 153	Storm Davis	.08	.03	.01
☐ 154	Marvell Wynne	.08	.03	.01
☐ 155	Will Clark	2.00	.80	.20
☐ 156	Luis Aguayo	.08	.03	.01
☐ 157	Willie Upshaw	.08	.03	.01
☐ 158	Randy Bush	.08	.03	.01
☐ 159	Ron Darling	.12	.05	.01
☐ 160	Kal Daniels	.15	.06	.01
☐ 161	Spike Owen	.08	.03	.01
☐ 162	Luis Polonia	.17	.07	.01
☐ 163	Kevin Mitchell UER	.50	.20	.05
	('88/total HR's 18/52,			
	should be 19/53)			
☐ 164	Dave Gallagher	.15	.06	.01
☐ 165	Benito Santiago	.15	.06	.01
☐ 166	Greg Gagne	.08	.03	.01
☐ 167	Ken Phelps	.08	.03	.01
☐ 168	Sid Fernandez	.12	.05	.01
☐ 169	Bo Diaz	.08	.03	.01
☐ 170	Cory Snyder	.12	.05	.01
☐ 171	Eric Show	.08	.03	.01
☐ 172	Robby Thompson	.08	.03	.01
☐ 173	Marty Barrett	.08	.03	.01
☐ 174	Dave Henderson	.17	.07	.01
☐ 175	Ozzie Guillen	.12	.05	.01
☐ 176	Barry Lyons	.08	.03	.01
☐ 177	Kelvin Torve	.12	.05	.01
☐ 178	Don Slaught	.08	.03	.01
☐ 179	Steve Lombardozzi	.08	.03	.01
☐ 180	Chris Sabo	1.75	.70	.17
☐ 181	Jose Uribe	.08	.03	.01
☐ 182	Shane Mack	.15	.06	.01
☐ 183	Ron Karkovice	.08	.03	.01
☐ 184	Todd Benzinger	.08	.03	.01
☐ 185	Dave Stewart	.15	.06	.01
☐ 186	Julio Franco	.35	.15	.03
☐ 187	Ron Robinson	.08	.03	.01
☐ 188	Wally Backman	.08	.03	.01
☐ 189	Randy Velarde	.08	.03	.01
☐ 190	Joe Carter	.40	.16	.04
☐ 191	Bob Welch	.17	.07	.01
☐ 192	Kelly Paris	.08	.03	.01
☐ 193	Chris Brown	.08	.03	.01
☐ 194	Rick Reuschel	.12	.05	.01
☐ 195	Roger Clemens	1.50	.60	.15
☐ 196	Dave Concepcion	.12	.05	.01
☐ 197	Al Newman	.08	.03	.01
☐ 198	Brook Jacoby	.08	.03	.01
☐ 199	Mookie Wilson	.08	.03	.01
☐ 200	Don Mattingly	.90	.40	.09
☐ 201	Dick Schofield	.08	.03	.01
☐ 202	Mark Gubicza	.12	.05	.01
☐ 203	Gary Gaetti	.12	.05	.01
☐ 204	Dan Pasqua	.08	.03	.01
☐ 205	Andre Dawson	.45	.18	.04
☐ 206	Chris Speier	.08	.03	.01
☐ 207	Kent Tekulve	.08	.03	.01
☐ 208	Rod Scurry	.08	.03	.01
☐ 209	Scott Bailes	.08	.03	.01
☐ 210	Rickey Henderson UER	1.50	.60	.15
	(Throws Right)			
☐ 211	Harold Baines	.17	.07	.01
☐ 212	Tony Armas	.08	.03	.01
☐ 213	Kent Hrbek	.17	.07	.01
☐ 214	Darrin Jackson	.12	.05	.01
☐ 215	George Brett	.65	.25	.06
☐ 216	Rafael Santana	.08	.03	.01
☐ 217	Andy Allanson	.08	.03	.01
☐ 218	Brett Butler	.15	.06	.01
☐ 219	Steve Jeltz	.08	.03	.01
☐ 220	Jay Buhner	.50	.20	.05
☐ 221	Bo Jackson	2.25	.90	.22
☐ 222	Angel Salazar	.08	.03	.01
☐ 223	Kirk McCaskill	.08	.03	.01
☐ 224	Steve Lyons	.08	.03	.01
☐ 225	Bert Blyleven	.15	.06	.01
☐ 226	Scott Bradley	.08	.03	.01
☐ 227	Bob Melvin	.08	.03	.01
☐ 228	Ron Kittle	.12	.05	.01
☐ 229	Phil Bradley	.08	.03	.01
☐ 230	Tommy John	.15	.06	.01
☐ 231	Greg Walker	.08	.03	.01
☐ 232	Juan Berenguer	.08	.03	.01
☐ 233	Pat Tabler	.08	.03	.01
☐ 234	Terry Clark	.12	.05	.01
☐ 235	Rafael Palmeiro	.50	.20	.05
☐ 236	Paul Zuvella	.08	.03	.01
☐ 237	Willie Randolph	.12	.05	.01
☐ 238	Bruce Fields	.08	.03	.01
☐ 239	Mike Aldrete	.08	.03	.01
☐ 240	Lance Parrish	.15	.06	.01
☐ 241	Greg Maddux	.30	.12	.03
☐ 242	John Moses	.08	.03	.01
☐ 243	Melido Perez	.15	.06	.01
☐ 244	Willie Wilson	.12	.05	.01
☐ 245	Mark McLemore	.08	.03	.01
☐ 246	Von Hayes	.12	.05	.01
☐ 247	Matt Williams	.75	.30	.07
☐ 248	John Candelaria UER	.08	.03	.01
	(listed as Yankee for			
	part of '87,			
	should be Mets)			
☐ 249	Harold Reynolds	.12	.05	.01
☐ 250	Greg Swindell	.12	.05	.01
☐ 251	Juan Agosto	.08	.03	.01
☐ 252	Mike Felder	.08	.03	.01
☐ 253	Vince Coleman	.25	.10	.02
☐ 254	Larry Sheets	.08	.03	.01
☐ 255	George Bell	.35	.15	.03
☐ 256	Terry Steinbach	.12	.05	.01
☐ 257	Jack Armstrong	.30	.12	.03
☐ 258	Dickie Thon	.08	.03	.01
☐ 259	Ray Knight	.12	.05	.01
☐ 260	Darryl Strawberry	1.25	.50	.12
☐ 261	Doug Sisk	.08	.03	.01
☐ 262	Alex Trevino	.08	.03	.01
☐ 263	Jeffrey Leonard	.08	.03	.01

	#	Player			
☐	264	Tom Henke	.12	.05	.01
☐	265	Ozzie Smith	.50	.20	.05
☐	266	Dave Bergman	.08	.03	.01
☐	267	Tony Phillips	.08	.03	.01
☐	268	Mark Davis	.12	.05	.01
☐	269	Kevin Elster	.08	.03	.01
☐	270	Barry Larkin	.45	.18	.04
☐	271	Manny Lee	.08	.03	.01
☐	272	Tom Brunansky	.12	.05	.01
☐	273	Craig Biggio	1.50	.60	.15
☐	274	Jim Gantner	.08	.03	.01
☐	275	Eddie Murray	.50	.20	.05
☐	276	Jeff Reed	.08	.03	.01
☐	277	Tim Teufel	.08	.03	.01
☐	278	Rick Honeycutt	.08	.03	.01
☐	279	Guillermo Hernandez	.08	.03	.01
☐	280	John Kruk	.08	.03	.01
☐	281	Luis Alicea	.08	.03	.01
☐	282	Jim Clancy	.08	.03	.01
☐	283	Billy Ripken	.08	.03	.01
☐	284	Craig Reynolds	.08	.03	.01
☐	285	Robin Yount	.60	.25	.06
☐	286	Jimmy Jones	.08	.03	.01
☐	287	Ron Oester	.08	.03	.01
☐	288	Terry Leach	.08	.03	.01
☐	289	Dennis Eckersley	.20	.08	.02
☐	290	Alan Trammell	.35	.15	.03
☐	291	Jimmy Key	.15	.06	.01
☐	292	Chris Bosio	.08	.03	.01
☐	293	Jose DeLeon	.08	.03	.01
☐	294	Jim Traber	.08	.03	.01
☐	295	Mike Scott	.15	.06	.01
☐	296	Roger McDowell	.08	.03	.01
☐	297	Garry Templeton	.08	.03	.01
☐	298	Doyle Alexander	.08	.03	.01
☐	299	Nick Esasky	.08	.03	.01
☐	300	Mark McGwire UER (doubles total 52, should be 51)	.50	.20	.05
☐	301	Darryl Hamilton	.35	.15	.03
☐	302	Dave Smith	.08	.03	.01
☐	303	Rick Sutcliffe	.12	.05	.01
☐	304	Dave Stapleton	.12	.05	.01
☐	305	Alan Ashby	.08	.03	.01
☐	306	Pedro Guerrero	.17	.07	.01
☐	307	Ron Guidry	.15	.06	.01
☐	308	Steve Farr	.08	.03	.01
☐	309	Curt Ford	.08	.03	.01
☐	310	Claudell Washington	.08	.03	.01
☐	311	Tom Prince	.08	.03	.01
☐	312	Chad Kreuter	.12	.05	.01
☐	313	Ken Oberkfell	.08	.03	.01
☐	314	Jerry Browne	.08	.03	.01
☐	315	R.J. Reynolds	.08	.03	.01
☐	316	Scott Bankhead	.12	.05	.01
☐	317	Milt Thompson	.08	.03	.01
☐	318	Mario Diaz	.12	.05	.01
☐	319	Bruce Ruffin	.08	.03	.01
☐	320	Dave Valle	.08	.03	.01
☐	321A	Gary Varsho ERR (back photo actually Mike Bielecki bunting)	2.50	1.00	.25
☐	321B	Gary Varsho COR (in road uniform)	.15	.06	.01
☐	322	Paul Mirabella	.08	.03	.01
☐	323	Chuck Jackson	.12	.05	.01
☐	324	Drew Hall	.08	.03	.01
☐	325	Don August	.08	.03	.01
☐	326	Israel Sanchez	.12	.05	.01
☐	327	Denny Walling	.08	.03	.01
☐	328	Joel Skinner	.08	.03	.01
☐	329	Danny Tartabull	.30	.12	.03
☐	330	Tony Pena	.12	.05	.01
☐	331	Jim Sundberg	.08	.03	.01
☐	332	Jeff D. Robinson Pittsburgh Pirates	.08	.03	.01
☐	333	Oddibe McDowell	.08	.03	.01
☐	334	Jose Lind	.08	.03	.01
☐	335	Paul Kilgus	.08	.03	.01
☐	336	Juan Samuel	.12	.05	.01
☐	337	Mike Campbell	.08	.03	.01
☐	338	Mike Maddux	.08	.03	.01
☐	339	Darnell Coles	.08	.03	.01
☐	340	Bob Dernier	.08	.03	.01
☐	341	Rafael Ramirez	.08	.03	.01
☐	342	Scott Sanderson	.12	.05	.01
☐	343	B.J. Surhoff	.12	.05	.01
☐	344	Billy Hatcher	.12	.05	.01
☐	345	Pat Perry	.08	.03	.01
☐	346	Jack Clark	.15	.06	.01
☐	347	Gary Thurman	.08	.03	.01
☐	348	Tim Jones	.08	.03	.01
☐	349	Dave Winfield	.40	.16	.04
☐	350	Frank White	.08	.03	.01
☐	351	Dave Collins	.08	.03	.01
☐	352	Jack Morris	.30	.12	.03
☐	353	Eric Plunk	.08	.03	.01
☐	354	Leon Durham	.08	.03	.01
☐	355	Ivan DeJesus	.08	.03	.01
☐	356	Brian Holman	.35	.15	.03
☐	357A	Dale Murphy ERR (front has reverse negative)	60.00	27.00	9.00
☐	357B	Dale Murphy COR	.40	.16	.04
☐	358	Mark Portugal	.08	.03	.01
☐	359	Andy McGaffigan	.08	.03	.01
☐	360	Tom Glavine	1.25	.50	.12
☐	361	Keith Moreland	.08	.03	.01
☐	362	Todd Stottlemyre	.35	.15	.03
☐	363	Dave Leiper	.08	.03	.01
☐	364	Cecil Fielder	1.25	.50	.12
☐	365	Carmelo Martinez	.08	.03	.01
☐	366	Dwight Evans	.15	.06	.01
☐	367	Kevin McReynolds	.15	.06	.01
☐	368	Rich Gedman	.08	.03	.01
☐	369	Len Dykstra	.15	.06	.01
☐	370	Jody Reed	.15	.06	.01
☐	371	Jose Canseco UER (strikeout total 391, should be 491)	2.25	.90	.22
☐	372	Rob Murphy	.08	.03	.01
☐	373	Mike Henneman	.08	.03	.01
☐	374	Walt Weiss	.15	.06	.01
☐	375	Rob Dibble	.90	.40	.09
☐	376	Kirby Puckett (Mark McGwire in background)	1.00	.40	.10
☐	377	Dennis Martinez	.12	.05	.01
☐	378	Ron Gant	2.00	.80	.20
☐	379	Brian Harper	.12	.05	.01
☐	380	Nelson Santovenia	.17	.07	.01
☐	381	Lloyd Moseby	.08	.03	.01
☐	382	Lance McCullers	.08	.03	.01
☐	383	Dave Stieb	.15	.06	.01
☐	384	Tony Gwynn	.65	.25	.06
☐	385	Mike Flanagan	.08	.03	.01
☐	386	Bob Ojeda	.08	.03	.01
☐	387	Bruce Hurst	.12	.05	.01
☐	388	Dave Magadan	.15	.06	.01
☐	389	Wade Boggs	.75	.30	.07
☐	390	Gary Carter	.20	.08	.02
☐	391	Frank Tanana	.12	.05	.01
☐	392	Curt Young	.08	.03	.01
☐	393	Jeff Treadway	.17	.07	.01
☐	394	Darrell Evans	.12	.05	.01
☐	395	Glenn Hubbard	.08	.03	.01
☐	396	Chuck Cary	.08	.03	.01
☐	397	Frank Viola	.17	.07	.01
☐	398	Jeff Parrett	.08	.03	.01
☐	399	Terry Blocker	.08	.03	.01
☐	400	Dan Gladden	.08	.03	.01
☐	401	Louie Meadows	.08	.03	.01
☐	402	Tim Raines	.17	.07	.01
☐	403	Joey Meyer	.08	.03	.01
☐	404	Larry Andersen	.08	.03	.01
☐	405	Rex Hudler	.12	.05	.01
☐	406	Mike Schmidt	1.75	.70	.17
☐	407	John Franco	.08	.03	.01
☐	408	Brady Anderson	.15	.06	.01
☐	409	Don Carman	.08	.03	.01
☐	410	Eric Davis	.40	.16	.04
☐	411	Bob Stanley	.08	.03	.01
☐	412	Pete Smith	.12	.05	.01
☐	413	Jim Rice	.15	.06	.01
☐	414	Bruce Sutter	.15	.06	.01
☐	415	Oil Can Boyd	.08	.03	.01
☐	416	Ruben Sierra	1.00	.40	.10
☐	417	Mike LaValliere	.08	.03	.01
☐	418	Steve Buechele	.08	.03	.01
☐	419	Gary Redus	.08	.03	.01
☐	420	Scott Fletcher	.08	.03	.01
☐	421	Dale Sveum	.08	.03	.01
☐	422	Bob Knepper	.08	.03	.01
☐	423	Luis Rivera	.08	.03	.01
☐	424	Ted Higuera	.08	.03	.01
☐	425	Kevin Bass	.08	.03	.01
☐	426	Ken Gerhart	.08	.03	.01
☐	427	Shane Rawley	.08	.03	.01
☐	428	Paul O'Neill	.15	.06	.01
☐	429	Joe Orsulak	.08	.03	.01
☐	430	Jackie Gutierrez	.08	.03	.01
☐	431	Gerald Perry	.08	.03	.01
☐	432	Mike Greenwell	.50	.20	.05
☐	433	Jerry Royster	.08	.03	.01
☐	434	Ellis Burks	.50	.20	.05
☐	435	Ed Olwine	.08	.03	.01
☐	436	Dave Rucker	.08	.03	.01
☐	437	Charlie Hough	.08	.03	.01

#	Name			
☐ 438	Bob Walk	.08	.03	.01
☐ 439	Bob Brower	.08	.03	.01
☐ 440	Barry Bonds	.80	.35	.08
☐ 441	Tom Foley	.08	.03	.01
☐ 442	Rob Deer	.12	.05	.01
☐ 443	Glenn Davis	.20	.08	.02
☐ 444	Dave Martinez	.08	.03	.01
☐ 445	Bill Wegman	.08	.03	.01
☐ 446	Lloyd McClendon	.08	.03	.01
☐ 447	Dave Schmidt	.08	.03	.01
☐ 448	Darren Daulton	.12	.05	.01
☐ 449	Frank Williams	.08	.03	.01
☐ 450	Don Aase	.08	.03	.01
☐ 451	Lou Whitaker	.17	.07	.01
☐ 452	Goose Gossage	.15	.06	.01
☐ 453	Ed Whitson	.08	.03	.01
☐ 454	Jim Walewander	.08	.03	.01
☐ 455	Damon Berryhill	.12	.05	.01
☐ 456	Tim Burke	.08	.03	.01
☐ 457	Barry Jones	.08	.03	.01
☐ 458	Joel Youngblood	.08	.03	.01
☐ 459	Floyd Youmans	.08	.03	.01
☐ 460	Mark Salas	.08	.03	.01
☐ 461	Jeff Russell	.08	.03	.01
☐ 462	Darrell Miller	.08	.03	.01
☐ 463	Jeff Kunkel	.08	.03	.01
☐ 464	Sherman Corbett	.08	.03	.01
☐ 465	Curtis Wilkerson	.08	.03	.01
☐ 466	Bud Black	.08	.03	.01
☐ 467	Cal Ripken	1.75	.70	.17
☐ 468	John Farrell	.08	.03	.01
☐ 469	Terry Kennedy	.08	.03	.01
☐ 470	Tom Candiotti	.12	.05	.01
☐ 471	Roberto Alomar	1.75	.70	.17
☐ 472	Jeff M. Robinson Detroit Tigers	.12	.05	.01
☐ 473	Vance Law	.08	.03	.01
☐ 474	Randy Ready UER (strikeout total 136, should be 115)	.08	.03	.01
☐ 475	Walt Terrell	.08	.03	.01
☐ 476	Kelly Downs	.08	.03	.01
☐ 477	Johnny Paredes	.12	.05	.01
☐ 478	Shawn Hillegas	.08	.03	.01
☐ 479	Bob Brenly	.08	.03	.01
☐ 480	Otis Nixon	.12	.05	.01
☐ 481	Johnny Ray	.08	.03	.01
☐ 482	Geno Petralli	.08	.03	.01
☐ 483	Stu Cliburn	.08	.03	.01
☐ 484	Pete Incaviglia	.12	.05	.01
☐ 485	Brian Downing	.08	.03	.01
☐ 486	Jeff Stone	.08	.03	.01
☐ 487	Carmen Castillo	.08	.03	.01
☐ 488	Tom Niedenfuer	.08	.03	.01
☐ 489	Jay Bell	.30	.12	.03
☐ 490	Rick Schu	.08	.03	.01
☐ 491	Jeff Pico	.12	.05	.01
☐ 492	Mark Parent	.12	.05	.01
☐ 493	Eric King	.08	.03	.01
☐ 494	Al Nipper	.08	.03	.01
☐ 495	Andy Hawkins	.08	.03	.01
☐ 496	Daryl Boston	.08	.03	.01
☐ 497	Ernie Riles	.08	.03	.01
☐ 498	Pascual Perez	.08	.03	.01
☐ 499	Bill Long UER (games started total 70, should be 44)	.08	.03	.01
☐ 500	Kirt Manwaring	.08	.03	.01
☐ 501	Chuck Crim	.08	.03	.01
☐ 502	Candy Maldonado	.12	.05	.01
☐ 503	Dennis Lamp	.08	.03	.01
☐ 504	Glenn Braggs	.08	.03	.01
☐ 505	Joe Price	.08	.03	.01
☐ 506	Ken Williams	.08	.03	.01
☐ 507	Bill Pecota	.12	.05	.01
☐ 508	Rey Quinones	.08	.03	.01
☐ 509	Jeff Bittiger	.12	.05	.01
☐ 510	Kevin Seitzer	.12	.05	.01
☐ 511	Steve Bedrosian	.12	.05	.01
☐ 512	Todd Worrell	.12	.05	.01
☐ 513	Chris James	.12	.05	.01
☐ 514	Jose Oquendo	.08	.03	.01
☐ 515	David Palmer	.08	.03	.01
☐ 516	John Smiley	.15	.06	.01
☐ 517	Dave Clark	.08	.03	.01
☐ 518	Mike Dunne	.08	.03	.01
☐ 519	Ron Washington	.08	.03	.01
☐ 520	Bob Kipper	.08	.03	.01
☐ 521	Lee Smith	.15	.06	.01
☐ 522	Juan Castillo	.08	.03	.01
☐ 523	Don Robinson	.08	.03	.01
☐ 524	Kevin Romine	.08	.03	.01
☐ 525	Paul Molitor	.20	.08	.02
☐ 526	Mark Langston	.17	.07	.01
☐ 527	Donnie Hill	.08	.03	.01
☐ 528	Larry Owen	.08	.03	.01
☐ 529	Jerry Reed	.08	.03	.01
☐ 530	Jack McDowell	.75	.30	.07
☐ 531	Greg Mathews	.08	.03	.01
☐ 532	John Russell	.08	.03	.01
☐ 533	Dan Quisenberry	.15	.06	.01
☐ 534	Greg Gross	.08	.03	.01
☐ 535	Danny Cox	.08	.03	.01
☐ 536	Terry Francona	.08	.03	.01
☐ 537	Andy Van Slyke	.25	.10	.02
☐ 538	Mel Hall	.12	.05	.01
☐ 539	Jim Gott	.08	.03	.01
☐ 540	Doug Jones	.08	.03	.01
☐ 541	Craig Lefferts	.08	.03	.01
☐ 542	Mike Boddicker	.08	.03	.01
☐ 543	Greg Brock	.08	.03	.01
☐ 544	Atlee Hammaker	.08	.03	.01
☐ 545	Tom Bolton	.12	.05	.01
☐ 546	Mike Macfarlane	.17	.07	.01
☐ 547	Rich Renteria	.12	.05	.01
☐ 548	John Davis	.08	.03	.01
☐ 549	Floyd Bannister	.08	.03	.01
☐ 550	Mickey Brantley	.08	.03	.01
☐ 551	Duane Ward	.12	.05	.01
☐ 552	Dan Petry	.08	.03	.01
☐ 553	Mickey Tettleton UER (walks total 175, should be 136)	.15	.06	.01
☐ 554	Rick Leach	.08	.03	.01
☐ 555	Mike Witt	.08	.03	.01
☐ 556	Sid Bream	.08	.03	.01
☐ 557	Bobby Witt	.15	.06	.01
☐ 558	Tommy Herr	.08	.03	.01
☐ 559	Randy Milligan	.25	.10	.02
☐ 560	Jose Cecena	.12	.05	.01
☐ 561	Mackey Sasser	.17	.07	.01
☐ 562	Carney Lansford	.12	.05	.01
☐ 563	Rick Aguilera	.12	.05	.01
☐ 564	Ron Hassey	.08	.03	.01
☐ 565	Dwight Gooden	.40	.16	.04
☐ 566	Paul Assenmacher	.08	.03	.01
☐ 567	Neil Allen	.08	.03	.01
☐ 568	Jim Morrison	.08	.03	.01
☐ 569	Mike Pagliarulo	.08	.03	.01
☐ 570	Ted Simmons	.15	.06	.01
☐ 571	Mark Thurmond	.08	.03	.01
☐ 572	Fred McGriff	.60	.25	.06
☐ 573	Wally Joyner	.35	.15	.03
☐ 574	Jose Bautista	.12	.05	.01
☐ 575	Kelly Gruber	.30	.12	.03
☐ 576	Cecilio Guante	.08	.03	.01
☐ 577	Mark Davidson	.08	.03	.01
☐ 578	Bobby Bonilla UER (total steals 2 in '87, should be 3)	.75	.30	.07
☐ 579	Mike Stanley	.08	.03	.01
☐ 580	Gene Larkin	.08	.03	.01
☐ 581	Stan Javier	.08	.03	.01
☐ 582	Howard Johnson	.35	.15	.03
☐ 583A	Mike Gallego ERR (front reversed negative)	1.25	.50	.12
☐ 583B	Mike Gallego COR	.12	.05	.01
☐ 584	David Cone	.20	.08	.02
☐ 585	Doug Jennings	.15	.06	.01
☐ 586	Charles Hudson	.08	.03	.01
☐ 587	Dion James	.08	.03	.01
☐ 588	Al Leiter	.08	.03	.01
☐ 589	Charlie Puleo	.08	.03	.01
☐ 590	Roberto Kelly	.40	.16	.04
☐ 591	Thad Bosley	.08	.03	.01
☐ 592	Pete Stanicek	.08	.03	.01
☐ 593	Pat Borders	.30	.12	.03
☐ 594	Bryan Harvey	.75	.30	.07
☐ 595	Jeff Ballard	.12	.05	.01
☐ 596	Jeff Reardon	.15	.06	.01
☐ 597	Doug Drabek	.15	.06	.01
☐ 598	Edwin Correa	.08	.03	.01
☐ 599	Keith Atherton	.08	.03	.01
☐ 600	Dave LaPoint	.08	.03	.01
☐ 601	Don Baylor	.12	.05	.01
☐ 602	Tom Pagnozzi	.08	.03	.01
☐ 603	Tim Flannery	.08	.03	.01
☐ 604	Gene Walter	.08	.03	.01
☐ 605	Dave Parker	.17	.07	.01
☐ 606	Mike Diaz	.08	.03	.01
☐ 607	Tony Gwynn	.12	.05	.01
☐ 608	Odell Jones	.08	.03	.01
☐ 609	Carlton Fisk	.50	.20	.05
☐ 610	Jay Howell	.08	.03	.01
☐ 611	Tim Crews	.08	.03	.01
☐ 612	Keith Hernandez	.15	.06	.01
☐ 613	Willie Fraser	.08	.03	.01

☐ 614	Jim Eppard	.08	.03	.01
☐ 615	Jeff Hamilton	.08	.03	.01
☐ 616	Kurt Stillwell	.12	.05	.01
☐ 617	Tom Browning	.12	.05	.01
☐ 618	Jeff Montgomery	.15	.06	.01
☐ 619	Jose Rijo	.17	.07	.01
☐ 620	Jamie Quirk	.08	.03	.01
☐ 621	Willie McGee	.17	.07	.01
☐ 622	Mark Grant UER (glove on wrong hand)	.08	.03	.01
☐ 623	Bill Swift	.12	.05	.01
☐ 624	Orlando Mercado	.08	.03	.01
☐ 625	John Costello	.08	.03	.01
☐ 626	Jose Gonzalez	.08	.03	.01
☐ 627A	Bill Schroeder ERR (back photo actually Ronn Reynolds buckling shin guards)	1.50	.60	.15
☐ 627B	Bill Schroeder COR	.20	.08	.02
☐ 628A	Fred Manrique ERR (back photo actually Ozzie Guillen throwing)	.35	.15	.03
☐ 628B	Fred Manrique COR (swinging bat on back)	.12	.05	.01
☐ 629	Ricky Horton	.08	.03	.01
☐ 630	Dan Plesac	.08	.03	.01
☐ 631	Alfredo Griffin	.08	.03	.01
☐ 632	Chuck Finley	.35	.15	.03
☐ 633	Kirk Gibson	.17	.07	.01
☐ 634	Randy Myers	.12	.05	.01
☐ 635	Greg Minton	.08	.03	.01
☐ 636A	Herm Winningham ERR (W1nningham on back)	.35	.15	.03
☐ 636B	Herm Winningham COR	.12	.05	.01
☐ 637	Charlie Leibrandt	.08	.03	.01
☐ 638	Tim Birtsas	.08	.03	.01
☐ 639	Bill Buckner	.12	.05	.01
☐ 640	Danny Jackson	.12	.05	.01
☐ 641	Greg Booker	.08	.03	.01
☐ 642	Jim Presley	.08	.03	.01
☐ 643	Gene Nelson	.08	.03	.01
☐ 644	Rod Booker	.08	.03	.01
☐ 645	Dennis Rasmussen	.08	.03	.01
☐ 646	Juan Nieves	.08	.03	.01
☐ 647	Bobby Thigpen	.17	.07	.01
☐ 648	Tim Belcher	.20	.08	.02
☐ 649	Mike Young	.08	.03	.01
☐ 650	Ivan Calderon	.12	.05	.01
☐ 651	Oswaldo Peraza	.12	.05	.01
☐ 652A	Pat Sheridan ERR (no position on front)	20.00	8.50	2.75
☐ 652B	Pat Sheridan COR	.12	.05	.01
☐ 653	Mike Morgan	.12	.05	.01
☐ 654	Mike Heath	.08	.03	.01
☐ 655	Jay Tibbs	.08	.03	.01
☐ 656	Fernando Valenzuela	.15	.06	.01
☐ 657	Lee Mazzilli	.08	.03	.01
☐ 658	AL CY:Frank Viola	.12	.05	.01
☐ 659A	AL MVP:J.Canseco (eagle logo in black)	.45	.18	.04
☐ 659B	AL MVP:J.Canseco (eagle logo in blue)	.45	.18	.04
☐ 660	AL ROY:Walt Weiss	.12	.05	.01
☐ 661	NL CY:Orel Hershiser	.15	.06	.01
☐ 662	NL MVP:Kirk Gibson	.12	.05	.01
☐ 663	NL ROY:Chris Sabo	.15	.06	.01
☐ 664	ALCS MVP:D.Eckersley	.12	.05	.01
☐ 665	NLCS MVP:O.Hershiser	.15	.06	.01
☐ 666	Great WS Moment (Kirk Gibson's homer)	.12	.05	.01
☐ 667	WS MVP:O.Hershiser	.15	.06	.01
☐ 668	Angels Checklist Wally Joyner	.12	.05	.01
☐ 669	Astros Checklist Nolan Ryan	.60	.25	.06
☐ 670	Athletics Checklist Jose Canseco	.40	.16	.04
☐ 671	Blue Jays Checklist Fred McGriff	.15	.06	.01
☐ 672	Braves Checklist Dale Murphy	.15	.06	.01
☐ 673	Brewers Checklist Paul Molitor	.12	.05	.01
☐ 674	Cardinals Checklist Ozzie Smith	.15	.06	.01
☐ 675	Cubs Checklist Ryne Sandberg	.30	.12	.03
☐ 676	Dodgers Checklist Kirk Gibson	.12	.05	.01
☐ 677	Expos Checklist Andres Galarraga	.12	.05	.01
☐ 678	Giants Checklist Will Clark	.40	.16	.04

☐ 679	Indians Checklist Cory Snyder	.12	.05	.01
☐ 680	Mariners Checklist Alvin Davis	.12	.05	.01
☐ 681	Mets Checklist Darryl Strawberry	.30	.12	.03
☐ 682	Orioles Checklist Cal Ripken	.35	.15	.03
☐ 683	Padres Checklist Tony Gwynn	.15	.06	.01
☐ 684	Phillies Checklist Mike Schmidt	.35	.15	.03
☐ 685	Pirates Checklist Andy Van Slyke UER (96 Junior Ortiz)	.12	.05	.01
☐ 686	Rangers Checklist Ruben Sierra	.20	.08	.02
☐ 687	Red Sox Checklist Wade Boggs	.17	.07	.01
☐ 688	Reds Checklist Eric Davis	.15	.06	.01
☐ 689	Royals Checklist George Brett	.15	.06	.01
☐ 690	Tigers Checklist Alan Trammell	.15	.06	.01
☐ 691	Twins Checklist Frank Viola	.12	.05	.01
☐ 692	White Sox Checklist Harold Baines	.12	.05	.01
☐ 693	Yankees Checklist Don Mattingly	.20	.08	.02
☐ 694	Checklist 1-100	.12	.01	.00
☐ 695	Checklist 101-200	.12	.01	.00
☐ 696	Checklist 201-300	.12	.01	.00
☐ 697	Checklist 301-400	.12	.01	.00
☐ 698	Checklist 401-500 UER 467 Cal Ripkin Jr.	.12	.01	.00
☐ 699	Checklist 501-600 UER 543 Greg Booker	.12	.01	.00
☐ 700	Checklist 601-700	.12	.01	.00

1989 Upper Deck Extended

Gregg Olson

The 1989 Upper Deck Extended set contains 100 standard-size (2 1/2" by 3 1/2") cards. The fronts have pure white borders; the backs have recent stats and anti-counterfeit holograms. Both sides feature attractive color photos. The cards were distributed in "high number" packs, along with factory sets, and as a separate set in a small blue custom box. The key rookie cards in this set are Jim Abbott, Jerome Walton, and Todd Zeile.

	MINT	EXC	G-VG
COMPLETE SET (100)	16.50	7.50	1.50
COMMON PLAYER (701-800)	.08	.03	.01

☐ 701	Checklist 701-800	.12	.01	.00
☐ 702	Jesse Barfield	.12	.05	.01
☐ 703	Walt Terrell	.08	.03	.01
☐ 704	Dickie Thon	.08	.03	.01
☐ 705	Al Leiter	.08	.03	.01
☐ 706	Dave LaPoint	.08	.03	.01
☐ 707	Charlie Hayes	.25	.10	.02
☐ 708	Andy Hawkins	.08	.03	.01
☐ 709	Mickey Hatcher	.08	.03	.01
☐ 710	Lance McCullers	.08	.03	.01

		MINT	EXC	G-VG
☐ 711	Ron Kittle	.12	.05	.01
☐ 712	Bert Blyleven	.15	.06	.01
☐ 713	Rick Dempsey	.08	.03	.01
☐ 714	Ken Williams	.08	.03	.01
☐ 715	Steve Rosenberg	.12	.05	.01
☐ 716	Joe Skalski	.12	.05	.01
☐ 717	Spike Owen	.08	.03	.01
☐ 718	Todd Burns	.15	.06	.01
☐ 719	Kevin Gross	.08	.03	.01
☐ 720	Tommy Herr	.08	.03	.01
☐ 721	Rob Ducey	.12	.05	.01
☐ 722	Gary Green	.12	.05	.01
☐ 723	Gregg Olson	1.50	.60	.15
☐ 724	Greg W. Harris	.40	.16	.04
☐ 725	Craig Worthington	.15	.06	.01
☐ 726	Tom Howard	.30	.12	.03
☐ 727	Dale Mohorcic	.08	.03	.01
☐ 728	Rich Yett	.08	.03	.01
☐ 729	Mel Hall	.12	.05	.01
☐ 730	Floyd Youmans	.08	.03	.01
☐ 731	Lonnie Smith	.15	.06	.01
☐ 732	Wally Backman	.08	.03	.01
☐ 733	Trevor Wilson	.35	.15	.03
☐ 734	Jose Alvarez	.12	.05	.01
☐ 735	Bob Milacki	.35	.15	.03
☐ 736	Tom Gordon	.80	.35	.08
☐ 737	Wally Whitehurst	.17	.07	.01
☐ 738	Mike Aldrete	.08	.03	.01
☐ 739	Keith Miller	.15	.06	.01
☐ 740	Randy Milligan	.17	.07	.01
☐ 741	Jeff Parrett	.08	.03	.01
☐ 742	Steve Finley	.75	.30	.07
☐ 743	Junior Felix	.35	.15	.03
☐ 744	Pete Harnisch	.60	.25	.06
☐ 745	Bill Spiers	.30	.12	.03
☐ 746	Hensley Meulens	1.00	.40	.10
☐ 747	Juan Bell	.15	.06	.01
☐ 748	Steve Sax	.15	.06	.01
☐ 749	Phil Bradley	.08	.03	.01
☐ 750	Rey Quinones	.08	.03	.01
☐ 751	Tommy Gregg	.08	.03	.01
☐ 752	Kevin Brown	.15	.06	.01
☐ 753	Derek Lilliquist	.12	.05	.01
☐ 754	Todd Zeile	3.50	1.50	.35
☐ 755	Jim Abbott	3.50	1.50	.35
	(triple exposure)			
☐ 756	Ozzie Canseco	.20	.08	.02
☐ 757	Nick Esasky	.08	.03	.01
☐ 758	Mike Moore	.12	.05	.01
☐ 759	Rob Murphy	.08	.03	.01
☐ 760	Rick Mahler	.08	.03	.01
☐ 761	Fred Lynn	.15	.06	.01
☐ 762	Kevin Blankenship	.12	.05	.01
☐ 763	Eddie Murray	.35	.15	.03
☐ 764	Steve Searcy	.15	.06	.01
☐ 765	Jerome Walton	1.00	.40	.10
☐ 766	Erik Hanson	1.50	.60	.15
☐ 767	Bob Boone	.15	.06	.01
☐ 768	Edgar Martinez	1.00	.40	.10
☐ 769	Jose DeJesus	.17	.07	.01
☐ 770	Greg Briley	.35	.15	.03
☐ 771	Steve Peters	.12	.05	.01
☐ 772	Rafael Palmeiro	.35	.15	.03
☐ 773	Jack Clark	.15	.06	.01
☐ 774	Nolan Ryan	3.50	1.50	.35
	(throwing football)			
☐ 775	Lance Parrish	.15	.06	.01
☐ 776	Joe Girardi	.15	.06	.01
☐ 777	Willie Randolph	.12	.05	.01
☐ 778	Mitch Williams	.12	.05	.01
☐ 779	Dennis Cook	.17	.07	.01
☐ 780	Dwight Smith	.30	.12	.03
☐ 781	Lenny Harris	.40	.16	.04
☐ 782	Torey Lovullo	.12	.05	.01
☐ 783	Norm Charlton	.30	.12	.03
☐ 784	Chris Brown	.08	.03	.01
☐ 785	Todd Benzinger	.12	.05	.01
☐ 786	Shane Rawley	.08	.03	.01
☐ 787	Omar Vizquel	.15	.06	.01
☐ 788	LaVel Freeman	.25	.10	.02
☐ 789	Jeffrey Leonard	.08	.03	.01
☐ 790	Eddie Williams	.08	.03	.01
☐ 791	Jamie Moyer	.08	.03	.01
☐ 792	Bruce Hurst UER	.12	.05	.01
	(Workd Series)			
☐ 793	Julio Franco	.30	.12	.03
☐ 794	Claudell Washington	.08	.03	.01
☐ 795	Jody Davis	.08	.03	.01
☐ 796	Oddibe McDowell	.08	.03	.01
☐ 797	Paul Kilgus	.08	.03	.01
☐ 798	Tracy Jones	.08	.03	.01
☐ 799	Steve Wilson	.15	.06	.01
☐ 800	Pete O'Brien	.12	.05	.01

1990 Upper Deck

Kevin Maas

The 1990 Upper Deck set contains 700 standard-size (2 1/2" by 3 1/2") cards. The front and back borders are white, and both sides feature full-color photos. The horizontally oriented backs have recent stats and anti-counterfeiting holograms. Unlike the 1989 Upper Deck set, the team checklist cards are not grouped numerically at the end of the set, but are mixed in with the first 100 cards. The key rookie cards in this set are Juan Gonzalez, Kevin Maas, Ben McDonald, John Olerud, and Dean Palmer. Cards 101 through 199 have two minor varieties in that the cards either show or omit "Copyright 1990 Upper Deck Co. Printed in USA below the two licensing logos. Those omitting are considered minor errors; they were found in the High Number foil packs.

		MINT	EXC	G-VG
COMPLETE SET (700)		35.00	15.75	5.25
COMMON PLAYER (1-700)		.05	.02	.00
☐ 1	Star Rookie Checklist	.10	.01	.00
☐ 2	Randy Nosek	.10	.04	.01
☐ 3	Tom Drees UER	.10	.04	.01
	(11th line, hulred, should be hurled)			
☐ 4	Curt Young	.05	.02	.00
☐ 5	Devon White TC	.08	.03	.01
	California Angels			
☐ 6	Luis Salazar	.05	.02	.00
☐ 7	Von Hayes TC	.08	.03	.01
	Philadelphia Phillies			
☐ 8	Jose Bautista	.05	.02	.00
☐ 9	Marquis Grissom	1.00	.40	.10
☐ 10	Orel Hershiser TC	.08	.03	.01
	Los Angeles Dodgers			
☐ 11	Rick Aguilera	.08	.03	.01
☐ 12	Benito Santiago TC	.08	.03	.01
	San Diego Padres			
☐ 13	Deion Sanders	.35	.15	.03
☐ 14	Marvell Wynne	.05	.02	.00
☐ 15	Dave West	.05	.02	.00
☐ 16	Bobby Bonilla TC	.10	.04	.01
	Pittsburgh Pirates			
☐ 17	Sammy Sosa	.50	.20	.05
☐ 18	Steve Sax TC	.08	.03	.01
	New York Yankees			
☐ 19	Jack Howell	.05	.02	.00
☐ 20	Mike Schmidt Special	.50	.20	.05
	UER (Suprising, should be surprising)			
☐ 21	Robin Ventura UER	2.25	.90	.22
	(Samta Maria)			
☐ 22	Brian Meyer	.10	.04	.01
☐ 23	Blaine Beatty	.15	.06	.01
☐ 24	Ken Griffey Jr. TC	.75	.30	.07
	Seattle Mariners			
☐ 25	Greg Vaughn UER	1.25	.50	.12
	(Association misspelled as assiocation)			
☐ 26	Xavier Hernandez	.10	.04	.01
☐ 27	Jason Grimsley	.12	.05	.01
☐ 28	Eric Anthony UER	.35	.15	.03
	(Ashville, should be Asheville)			

☐ 29	Tim Raines TC	.08	.03	.01
	Montreal Expos UER (Wallach listed before Walker)			
☐ 30	David Wells	.08	.03	.01
☐ 31	Hal Morris	1.25	.50	.12
☐ 32	Bo Jackson TC	.35	.15	.03
	Kansas City Royals			
☐ 33	Kelly Mann	.15	.06	.01
☐ 34	Nolan Ryan Special	1.00	.40	.10
☐ 35	Scott Service UER	.10	.04	.01
	(Born Cincinatti on 7/27/67, should be Cincinnati 2/27)			
☐ 36	Mark McGwire TC	.10	.04	.01
	Oakland A's			
☐ 37	Tino Martinez	1.50	.60	.15
☐ 38	Chili Davis	.08	.03	.01
☐ 39	Scott Sanderson	.05	.02	.00
☐ 40	Kevin Mitchell TC	.08	.03	.01
	San Francisco Giants			
☐ 41	Lou Whitaker TC	.08	.03	.01
	Detroit Tigers			
☐ 42	Scott Coolbaugh UER	.12	.05	.01
	(Definately)			
☐ 43	Jose Cano UER	.10	.04	.01
	(Born 9/7/62, should be 3/7/62)			
☐ 44	Jose Vizcaino	.17	.07	.01
☐ 45	Bob Hamelin	.17	.07	.01
☐ 46	Jose Offerman UER	.50	.20	.05
	(Posesses)			
☐ 47	Kevin Blankenship	.05	.02	.00
☐ 48	Kirby Puckett TC	.12	.05	.01
	Minnesota Twins			
☐ 49	Tommy Greene UER	.60	.25	.06
	(Livest, should be liveliest)			
☐ 50	Will Clark Special	.40	.16	.04
	UER (Perenial, should be perennial)			
☐ 51	Rob Nelson	.05	.02	.00
☐ 52	Chris Hammond UER	.45	.18	.04
	(Chatanooga)			
☐ 53	Joe Carter TC	.08	.03	.01
	Cleveland Indians			
☐ 54A	Ben McDonald ERR	20.00	8.50	2.75
	(no Rookie designation on card front)			
☐ 54B	Ben McDonald COR	1.50	.60	.15
☐ 55	Andy Benes UER	.50	.20	.05
	(Whichita)			
☐ 56	John Olerud	2.50	1.00	.25
☐ 57	Roger Clemens TC	.15	.06	.01
	Boston Red Sox			
☐ 58	Tony Armas	.05	.02	.00
☐ 59	George Canale	.17	.07	.01
☐ 60A	Mickey Tettleton TC	3.00	1.25	.30
	Baltimore Orioles (683 Jamie Weston)			
☐ 60B	Mickey Tettleton TC	.12	.05	.01
	Baltimore Orioles (683 Mickey Weston)			
☐ 61	Mike Stanton	.25	.10	.02
☐ 62	Dwight Gooden TC	.10	.04	.01
	New York Mets			
☐ 63	Kent Mercker UER	.25	.10	.02
	(Albuquerque)			
☐ 64	Francisco Cabrera	.20	.08	.02
☐ 65	Steve Avery UER	3.50	1.50	.35
	(born NJ, should be MI, Merker should be Mercker)			
☐ 66	Jose Canseco	.75	.30	.07
☐ 67	Matt Merullo	.10	.04	.01
☐ 68	Vince Coleman TC	.08	.03	.01
	St. Louis Cardinals UER (Guerrero)			
☐ 69	Ron Karkovice	.05	.02	.00
☐ 70	Kevin Maas	3.50	1.50	.35
☐ 71	Dennis Cook UER	.08	.03	.01
	(Shown with righty glove on card back)			
☐ 72	Juan Gonzalez UER	7.00	3.00	.70
	(135 games for Tulsa in '89, should be 133)			
☐ 73	Andre Dawson TC	.08	.03	.01
	Chicago Cubs			
☐ 74	Dean Palmer UER	2.25	.90	.22
	(Permanent misspelled as perminant)			
☐ 75	Bo Jackson Special	.40	.16	.04
	UER (Monsterous, should be monstrous)			
☐ 76	Rob Richie	.05	.02	.00

☐ 77	Bobby Rose UER	.15	.06	.01
	(Pickin, should be pick in)			
☐ 78	Brian Dubois UER	.12	.05	.01
	(Commiting)			
☐ 79	Ozzie Guillen TC	.08	.03	.01
	Chicago White Sox			
☐ 80	Gene Nelson	.05	.02	.00
☐ 81	Bob McClure	.05	.02	.00
☐ 82	Julio Franco TC	.08	.03	.01
	Texas Rangers			
☐ 83	Greg Minton	.05	.02	.00
☐ 84	John Smoltz TC UER	.10	.04	.01
	Atlanta Braves (Oddibe not Odibbe)			
☐ 85	Willie Fraser	.05	.02	.00
☐ 86	Neal Heaton	.05	.02	.00
☐ 87	Kevin Tapani	.75	.30	.07
☐ 88	Mike Scott TC	.08	.03	.01
	Houston Astros			
☐ 89A	Jim Gott ERR	6.50	2.75	.65
	(photo actually Rick Reed)			
☐ 89B	Jim Gott COR	.08	.03	.01
☐ 90	Lance Johnson	.08	.03	.01
☐ 91	Robin Yount TC UER	.10	.04	.01
	Milwaukee Brewers (Checklist on back has 178 Rob Deer and 176 Mike Felder)			
☐ 92	Jeff Parrett	.05	.02	.00
☐ 93	Julio Machado UER	.10	.04	.01
	(Valenzuelan, should be Venezuelan)			
☐ 94	Ron Jones	.05	.02	.00
☐ 95	George Bell TC	.08	.03	.01
	Toronto Blue Jays			
☐ 96	Jerry Reuss	.05	.02	.00
☐ 97	Brian Fisher	.05	.02	.00
☐ 98	Kevin Ritz UER	.12	.05	.01
	(Amercian)			
☐ 99	Barry Larkin TC	.08	.03	.01
	Cincinnati Reds			
☐ 100	Checklist 1-100	.08	.01	.00
☐ 101	Gerald Perry	.05	.02	.00
☐ 102	Kevin Appier	.40	.16	.04
☐ 103	Julio Franco	.12	.05	.01
☐ 104	Craig Biggio	.15	.06	.01
☐ 105	Bo Jackson UER	.75	.30	.07
	('89 BA wrong, should be .256)			
☐ 106	Junior Felix	.10	.04	.01
☐ 107	Mike Harkey	.08	.03	.01
☐ 108	Fred McGriff	.15	.06	.01
☐ 109	Rick Sutcliffe	.08	.03	.01
☐ 110	Pete O'Brien	.05	.02	.00
☐ 111	Kelly Gruber	.10	.04	.01
☐ 112	Dwight Evans	.08	.03	.01
☐ 113	Pat Borders	.05	.02	.00
☐ 114	Dwight Gooden	.17	.07	.01
☐ 115	Kevin Batiste	.12	.05	.01
☐ 116	Eric Davis	.15	.06	.01
☐ 117	Kevin Mitchell UER	.15	.06	.01
	(Career HR total 99, should be 100)			
☐ 118	Ron Oester	.05	.02	.00
☐ 119	Brett Butler	.08	.03	.01
☐ 120	Danny Jackson	.08	.03	.01
☐ 121	Tommy Gregg	.05	.02	.00
☐ 122	Ken Caminiti	.05	.02	.00
☐ 123	Kevin Brown	.05	.02	.00
☐ 124	George Brett UER	.20	.08	.02
	(133 runs, should be 1300)			
☐ 125	Mike Scott	.08	.03	.01
☐ 126	Cory Snyder	.08	.03	.01
☐ 127	George Bell	.12	.05	.01
☐ 128	Mark Grace	.20	.08	.02
☐ 129	Devon White	.08	.03	.01
☐ 130	Tony Fernandez	.08	.03	.01
☐ 131	Don Aase	.05	.02	.00
☐ 132	Rance Mulliniks	.05	.02	.00
☐ 133	Marty Barrett	.05	.02	.00
☐ 134	Nelson Liriano	.05	.02	.00
☐ 135	Mark Carreon	.05	.02	.00
☐ 136	Candy Maldonado	.05	.02	.00
☐ 137	Tim Birtsas	.05	.02	.00
☐ 138	Tom Brookens	.05	.02	.00
☐ 139	John Franco	.05	.02	.00
☐ 140	Mike LaCoss	.05	.02	.00
☐ 141	Jeff Treadway	.05	.02	.00
☐ 142	Pat Tabler	.05	.02	.00
☐ 143	Darrell Evans	.08	.03	.01
☐ 144	Rafael Ramirez	.05	.02	.00

#	Player			
☐ 145	Oddibe McDowell UER (misspelled Odibbe)	.05	.02	.00
☐ 146	Brian Downing	.05	.02	.00
☐ 147	Curt Wilkerson	.05	.02	.00
☐ 148	Ernie Whitt	.05	.02	.00
☐ 149	Bill Schroeder	.05	.02	.00
☐ 150	Domingo Ramos UER (Says throws right, but shows him throwing lefty)	.05	.02	.00
☐ 151	Rick Honeycutt	.05	.02	.00
☐ 152	Don Slaught	.05	.02	.00
☐ 153	Mitch Webster	.05	.02	.00
☐ 154	Tony Phillips	.05	.02	.00
☐ 155	Paul Kilgus	.05	.02	.00
☐ 156	Ken Griffey Jr. UER (Simultaniously)	5.00	2.25	.50
☐ 157	Gary Sheffield	.12	.05	.01
☐ 158	Wally Backman	.05	.02	.00
☐ 159	B.J. Surhoff	.05	.02	.00
☐ 160	Louie Meadows	.05	.02	.00
☐ 161	Paul O'Neill	.08	.03	.01
☐ 162	Jeff McKnight	.12	.05	.01
☐ 163	Alvaro Espinoza	.05	.02	.00
☐ 164	Scott Scudder	.20	.08	.02
☐ 165	Jeff Reed	.05	.02	.00
☐ 166	Gregg Jefferies	.15	.06	.01
☐ 167	Barry Larkin	.17	.07	.01
☐ 168	Gary Carter	.10	.04	.01
☐ 169	Robby Thompson	.05	.02	.00
☐ 170	Rolando Roomes	.05	.02	.00
☐ 171	Mark McGwire UER (Total games 427 and hits 479, should be 467 and 427)	.20	.08	.02
☐ 172	Steve Sax	.08	.03	.01
☐ 173	Mark Williamson	.05	.02	.00
☐ 174	Mitch Williams	.05	.02	.00
☐ 175	Brian Holton	.05	.02	.00
☐ 176	Rob Deer	.08	.03	.01
☐ 177	Tim Raines	.10	.04	.01
☐ 178	Mike Felder	.05	.02	.00
☐ 179	Harold Reynolds	.08	.03	.01
☐ 180	Terry Francona	.05	.02	.00
☐ 181	Chris Sabo	.15	.06	.01
☐ 182	Darryl Strawberry	.35	.15	.03
☐ 183	Willie Randolph	.08	.03	.01
☐ 184	Bill Ripken	.05	.02	.00
☐ 185	Mackey Sasser	.05	.02	.00
☐ 186	Todd Benzinger	.05	.02	.00
☐ 187	Kevin Elster	.05	.02	.00
☐ 188	Jose Uribe	.05	.02	.00
☐ 189	Tom Browning	.08	.03	.01
☐ 190	Keith Miller	.05	.02	.00
☐ 191	Don Mattingly	.30	.12	.03
☐ 192	Dave Parker	.10	.04	.01
☐ 193	Roberto Kelly UER (96 RBI, should be 62)	.12	.05	.01
☐ 194	Phil Bradley	.05	.02	.00
☐ 195	Ron Hassey	.05	.02	.00
☐ 196	Gerald Young	.05	.02	.00
☐ 197	Hubie Brooks	.08	.03	.01
☐ 198	Bill Doran	.05	.02	.00
☐ 199	Al Newman	.05	.02	.00
☐ 200	Checklist 101-200	.08	.01	.00
☐ 201	Terry Puhl	.05	.02	.00
☐ 202	Frank DiPino	.05	.02	.00
☐ 203	Jim Clancy	.05	.02	.00
☐ 204	Bob Ojeda	.05	.02	.00
☐ 205	Alex Trevino	.05	.02	.00
☐ 206	Dave Henderson	.10	.04	.01
☐ 207	Henry Cotto	.05	.02	.00
☐ 208	Rafael Belliard UER (Born 1961, not 1951)	.05	.02	.00
☐ 209	Stan Javier	.05	.02	.00
☐ 210	Jerry Reed	.05	.02	.00
☐ 211	Doug Dascenzo	.05	.02	.00
☐ 212	Andres Thomas	.05	.02	.00
☐ 213	Greg Maddux	.08	.03	.01
☐ 214	Mike Schooler	.05	.02	.00
☐ 215	Lonnie Smith	.08	.03	.01
☐ 216	Jose Rijo	.08	.03	.01
☐ 217	Greg Gagne	.05	.02	.00
☐ 218	Jim Gantner	.05	.02	.00
☐ 219	Allan Anderson	.05	.02	.00
☐ 220	Rick Mahler	.05	.02	.00
☐ 221	Jim Deshaies	.05	.02	.00
☐ 222	Keith Hernandez	.08	.03	.01
☐ 223	Vince Coleman	.10	.04	.01
☐ 224	David Cone	.10	.04	.01
☐ 225	Ozzie Smith	.17	.07	.01
☐ 226	Matt Nokes	.08	.03	.01
☐ 227	Barry Bonds	.25	.10	.02
☐ 228	Felix Jose	.35	.15	.03
☐ 229	Dennis Powell	.05	.02	.00
☐ 230	Mike Gallego	.05	.02	.00
☐ 231	Shawon Dunston UER ('89 stats are Andre Dawson's)	.10	.04	.01
☐ 232	Ron Gant	.40	.16	.04
☐ 233	Omar Vizquel	.05	.02	.00
☐ 234	Derek Lilliquist	.05	.02	.00
☐ 235	Erik Hanson	.12	.05	.01
☐ 236	Kirby Puckett UER (824 games, should be 924)	.35	.15	.03
☐ 237	Bill Spiers	.08	.03	.01
☐ 238	Dan Gladden	.05	.02	.00
☐ 239	Bryan Clutterbuck	.05	.02	.00
☐ 240	John Moses	.05	.02	.00
☐ 241	Ron Darling	.08	.03	.01
☐ 242	Joe Magrane	.05	.02	.00
☐ 243	Dave Magadan	.08	.03	.01
☐ 244	Pedro Guerrero UER (Misspelled Guerrero)	.08	.03	.01
☐ 245	Glenn Davis	.10	.04	.01
☐ 246	Terry Steinbach	.05	.02	.00
☐ 247	Fred Lynn	.08	.03	.01
☐ 248	Gary Redus	.05	.02	.00
☐ 249	Ken Williams	.05	.02	.00
☐ 250	Sid Bream	.05	.02	.00
☐ 251	Bob Welch UER (2587 career strike-outs, should be 1587)	.08	.03	.01
☐ 252	Bill Buckner	.08	.03	.01
☐ 253	Carney Lansford	.08	.03	.01
☐ 254	Paul Molitor	.10	.04	.01
☐ 255	Jose DeJesus	.05	.02	.00
☐ 256	Orel Hershiser	.10	.04	.01
☐ 257	Tom Brunansky	.08	.03	.01
☐ 258	Mike Davis	.05	.02	.00
☐ 259	Jeff Ballard	.05	.02	.00
☐ 260	Scott Terry	.05	.02	.00
☐ 261	Sid Fernandez	.08	.03	.01
☐ 262	Mike Marshall	.08	.03	.01
☐ 263	Howard Johnson UER (192 SO, should be 592)	.12	.05	.01
☐ 264	Kirk Gibson UER (659 runs, should be 669)	.10	.04	.01
☐ 265	Kevin McReynolds	.10	.04	.01
☐ 266	Cal Ripken	.50	.20	.05
☐ 267	Ozzie Guillen UER (Career triples 27, should be 29)	.08	.03	.01
☐ 268	Jim Traber	.05	.02	.00
☐ 269	Bobby Thigpen	.08	.03	.01
☐ 270	Joe Orsulak	.05	.02	.00
☐ 271	Bob Boone	.08	.03	.01
☐ 272	Dave Stewart UER (Totals wrong due to omission of '86 stats)	.10	.04	.01
☐ 273	Tim Wallach	.08	.03	.01
☐ 274	Luis Aquino UER (Says throws lefty, but shows him throwing righty)	.05	.02	.00
☐ 275	Mike Moore	.08	.03	.01
☐ 276	Tony Pena	.08	.03	.01
☐ 277	Eddie Murray UER (Several typos in career total stats)	.15	.06	.01
☐ 278	Milt Thompson	.05	.02	.00
☐ 279	Alejandro Pena	.08	.03	.01
☐ 280	Ken Dayley	.05	.02	.00
☐ 281	Carmen Castillo	.05	.02	.00
☐ 282	Tom Henke	.08	.03	.01
☐ 283	Mickey Hatcher	.05	.02	.00
☐ 284	Roy Smith	.05	.02	.00
☐ 285	Manny Lee	.05	.02	.00
☐ 286	Dan Pasqua	.05	.02	.00
☐ 287	Larry Sheets	.05	.02	.00
☐ 288	Garry Templeton	.05	.02	.00
☐ 289	Eddie Williams	.05	.02	.00
☐ 290	Brady Anderson	.05	.02	.00
☐ 291	Spike Owen	.05	.02	.00
☐ 292	Storm Davis	.05	.02	.00
☐ 293	Chris Bosio	.05	.02	.00
☐ 294	Jim Eisenreich	.05	.02	.00
☐ 295	Don August	.05	.02	.00
☐ 296	Jeff Hamilton	.05	.02	.00
☐ 297	Mickey Tettleton	.08	.03	.01
☐ 298	Mike Scioscia	.05	.02	.00
☐ 299	Kevin Hickey	.05	.02	.00
☐ 300	Checklist 201-300	.08	.01	.00
☐ 301	Shawn Abner	.05	.02	.00
☐ 302	Kevin Bass	.05	.02	.00
☐ 303	Bip Roberts	.05	.02	.00
☐ 304	Joe Girardi	.08	.03	.01
☐ 305	Danny Darwin	.05	.02	.00

□	#	Name			
□	306	Mike Heath	.05	.02	.00
□	307	Mike Macfarlane	.05	.02	.00
□	308	Ed Whitson	.05	.02	.00
□	309	Tracy Jones	.05	.02	.00
□	310	Scott Fletcher	.05	.02	.00
□	311	Darnell Coles	.05	.02	.00
□	312	Mike Brumley	.05	.02	.00
□	313	Bill Swift	.05	.02	.00
□	314	Charlie Hough	.05	.02	.00
□	315	Jim Presley	.05	.02	.00
□	316	Luis Polonia	.05	.02	.00
□	317	Mike Morgan	.05	.02	.00
□	318	Lee Guetterman	.05	.02	.00
□	319	Jose Oquendo	.05	.02	.00
□	320	Wayne Tolleson	.05	.02	.00
□	321	Jody Reed	.08	.03	.01
□	322	Damon Berryhill	.05	.02	.00
□	323	Roger Clemens	.40	.16	.04
□	324	Ryne Sandberg	.45	.18	.04
□	325	Benito Santiago UER	.10	.04	.01
		(Misspelled Santago on card back)			
□	326	Bret Saberhagen UER	.12	.05	.01
		(1140 hits, should be 1240; 56 CG, should be 52)			
□	327	Lou Whitaker	.08	.03	.01
□	328	Dave Gallagher	.05	.02	.00
□	329	Mike Pagliarulo	.05	.02	.00
□	330	Doyle Alexander	.05	.02	.00
□	331	Jeffrey Leonard	.05	.02	.00
□	332	Torey Lovullo	.05	.02	.00
□	333	Pete Incaviglia	.08	.03	.01
□	334	Rickey Henderson	.40	.16	.04
□	335	Rafael Palmeiro	.17	.07	.01
□	336	Ken Hill	.12	.05	.01
□	337	Dave Winfield UER	.15	.06	.01
		(1418 RBI, should be 1438)			
□	338	Alfredo Griffin	.05	.02	.00
□	339	Andy Hawkins	.05	.02	.00
□	340	Ted Power	.05	.02	.00
□	341	Steve Wilson	.08	.03	.01
□	342	Jack Clark UER	.10	.04	.01
		(916 BB, should be 1006; 1142 SO, should be 1130)			
□	343	Ellis Burks	.12	.05	.01
□	344	Tony Gwynn UER	.25	.10	.02
		(Doubles stats on card back are wrong)			
□	345	Jerome Walton UER	.12	.05	.01
		(Total At Bats 476, should be 475)			
□	346	Roberto Alomar UER	.35	.15	.03
		(61 doubles, should be 51)			
□	347	Carlos Martinez UER	.08	.03	.01
		(Born 8/11/64, should be 8/11/65)			
□	348	Chet Lemon	.05	.02	.00
□	349	Willie Wilson	.08	.03	.01
□	350	Greg Walker	.05	.02	.00
□	351	Tom Bolton	.05	.02	.00
□	352	German Gonzalez	.05	.02	.00
□	353	Harold Baines	.08	.03	.01
□	354	Mike Greenwell	.17	.07	.01
□	355	Ruben Sierra	.35	.15	.03
□	356	Andres Galarraga	.08	.03	.01
□	357	Andre Dawson	.12	.05	.01
□	358	Jeff Brantley	.12	.05	.01
□	359	Mike Bielecki	.05	.02	.00
□	360	Ken Oberkfell	.05	.02	.00
□	361	Kurt Stillwell	.05	.02	.00
□	362	Brian Holman	.08	.03	.01
□	363	Kevin Seitzer	.08	.03	.01
□	364	Alvin Davis	.08	.03	.01
□	365	Tom Gordon	.10	.04	.01
□	366	Bobby Bonilla	.20	.08	.02
□	367	Carlton Fisk	.17	.07	.01
□	368	Steve Carter UER	.08	.03	.01
		(Charlotesville)			
□	369	Joel Skinner	.05	.02	.00
□	370	John Cangelosi	.05	.02	.00
□	371	Cecil Espy	.05	.02	.00
□	372	Gary Wayne	.08	.03	.01
□	373	Jim Rice	.10	.04	.01
□	374	Mike Dyer	.12	.05	.01
□	375	Joe Carter	.12	.05	.01
□	376	Dwight Smith	.08	.03	.01
□	377	John Wetteland	.12	.05	.01
□	378	Earnie Riles	.05	.02	.00
□	379	Otis Nixon	.08	.03	.01
□	380	Vance Law	.05	.02	.00
□	381	Dave Bergman	.05	.02	.00

□	#	Name			
□	382	Frank White	.05	.02	.00
□	383	Scott Bradley	.05	.02	.00
□	384	Israel Sanchez UER	.05	.02	.00
		(totals don't include '89 stats)			
□	385	Gary Pettis	.05	.02	.00
□	386	Donn Pall	.05	.02	.00
□	387	John Smiley	.08	.03	.01
□	388	Tom Candiotti	.08	.03	.01
□	389	Junior Ortiz	.05	.02	.00
□	390	Steve Lyons	.05	.02	.00
□	391	Brian Harper	.08	.03	.01
□	392	Fred Manrique	.05	.02	.00
□	393	Lee Smith	.08	.03	.01
□	394	Jeff Kunkel	.05	.02	.00
□	395	Claudell Washington	.05	.02	.00
□	396	John Tudor	.08	.03	.01
□	397	Terry Kennedy UER	.05	.02	.00
		(Career totals all wrong)			
□	398	Lloyd McClendon	.05	.02	.00
□	399	Craig Lefferts	.05	.02	.00
□	400	Checklist 301-400	.08	.01	.00
□	401	Keith Moreland	.05	.02	.00
□	402	Rich Gedman	.05	.02	.00
□	403	Jeff Robinson	.05	.02	.00
□	404	Randy Ready	.05	.02	.00
□	405	Rick Cerone	.05	.02	.00
□	406	Jeff Blauser	.05	.02	.00
□	407	Larry Andersen	.05	.02	.00
□	408	Joe Boever	.05	.02	.00
□	409	Felix Fermin	.05	.02	.00
□	410	Glenn Wilson	.05	.02	.00
□	411	Rex Hudler	.05	.02	.00
□	412	Mark Grant	.05	.02	.00
□	413	Dennis Martinez	.08	.03	.01
□	414	Darrin Jackson	.05	.02	.00
□	415	Mike Aldrete	.05	.02	.00
□	416	Roger McDowell	.05	.02	.00
□	417	Jeff Reardon	.08	.03	.01
□	418	Darren Daulton	.08	.03	.01
□	419	Tim Laudner	.05	.02	.00
□	420	Don Carman	.05	.02	.00
□	421	Lloyd Moseby	.05	.02	.00
□	422	Doug Drabek	.08	.03	.01
□	423	Lenny Harris UER	.08	.03	.01
		(Walks 2 in '89, should be 20)			
□	424	Jose Lind	.05	.02	.00
□	425	Dave Johnson (P)	.10	.04	.01
□	426	Jerry Browne	.05	.02	.00
□	427	Eric Yelding	.08	.03	.01
□	428	Brad Komminsk	.05	.02	.00
□	429	Jody Davis	.05	.02	.00
□	430	Mariano Duncan	.05	.02	.00
□	431	Mark Davis	.08	.03	.01
□	432	Nelson Santovenia	.05	.02	.00
□	433	Bruce Hurst	.08	.03	.01
□	434	Jeff Huson	.10	.04	.01
□	435	Chris James	.05	.02	.00
□	436	Mark Guthrie	.10	.04	.01
□	437	Charlie Hayes	.08	.03	.01
□	438	Shane Rawley	.05	.02	.00
□	439	Dickie Thon	.05	.02	.00
□	440	Juan Berenguer	.05	.02	.00
□	441	Kevin Romine	.05	.02	.00
□	442	Bill Landrum	.05	.02	.00
□	443	Todd Frohwirth	.05	.02	.00
□	444	Craig Worthington	.05	.02	.00
□	445	Fernando Valenzuela	.10	.04	.01
□	446	Joey Belle	1.50	.60	.15
□	447	Ed Whited UER	.15	.06	.01
		(Ashville, should be Asheville)			
□	448	Dave Smith	.05	.02	.00
□	449	Dave Clark	.05	.02	.00
□	450	Juan Agosto	.05	.02	.00
□	451	Dave Valle	.05	.02	.00
□	452	Kent Hrbek	.10	.04	.01
□	453	Von Hayes	.08	.03	.01
□	454	Gary Gaetti	.08	.03	.01
□	455	Greg Briley	.08	.03	.01
□	456	Glenn Braggs	.05	.02	.00
□	457	Kirt Manwaring	.05	.02	.00
□	458	Mel Hall	.05	.02	.00
□	459	Brook Jacoby	.05	.02	.00
□	460	Pat Sheridan	.05	.02	.00
□	461	Rob Murphy	.05	.02	.00
□	462	Jimmy Key	.08	.03	.01
□	463	Nick Esasky	.05	.02	.00
□	464	Rob Ducey	.05	.02	.00
□	465	Carlos Quintana UER	.12	.05	.01
		(Internatinoal)			
□	466	Larry Walker	.45	.18	.04
□	467	Todd Worrell	.08	.03	.01

#	Player			
☐ 468	Kevin Gross	.05	.02	.00
☐ 469	Terry Pendleton	.10	.04	.01
☐ 470	Dave Martinez	.05	.02	.00
☐ 471	Gene Larkin	.05	.02	.00
☐ 472	Len Dykstra UER ('89 and total runs understated by 10)	.10	.04	.01
☐ 473	Barry Lyons	.05	.02	.00
☐ 474	Terry Mulholland	.08	.03	.01
☐ 475	Chip Hale	.10	.04	.01
☐ 476	Jesse Barfield	.08	.03	.01
☐ 477	Dan Plesac	.05	.02	.00
☐ 478A	Scott Garrelts ERR (photo actually Bill Bathe)	4.00	1.75	.40
☐ 478B	Scott Garrelts COR	.08	.03	.01
☐ 479	Dave Righetti	.08	.03	.01
☐ 480	Gus Polidor UER (Wearing 14 on front, but 10 on back)	.05	.02	.00
☐ 481	Mookie Wilson	.05	.02	.00
☐ 482	Luis Rivera	.05	.02	.00
☐ 483	Mike Flanagan	.05	.02	.00
☐ 484	Dennis Boyd	.05	.02	.00
☐ 485	John Cerutti	.05	.02	.00
☐ 486	John Costello	.05	.02	.00
☐ 487	Pascual Perez	.05	.02	.00
☐ 488	Tommy Herr	.05	.02	.00
☐ 489	Tom Foley	.05	.02	.00
☐ 490	Curt Ford	.05	.02	.00
☐ 491	Steve Lake	.05	.02	.00
☐ 492	Tim Teufel	.05	.02	.00
☐ 493	Randy Bush	.05	.02	.00
☐ 494	Mike Jackson	.05	.02	.00
☐ 495	Steve Jeltz	.05	.02	.00
☐ 496	Paul Gibson	.05	.02	.00
☐ 497	Steve Balboni	.05	.02	.00
☐ 498	Bud Black	.05	.02	.00
☐ 499	Dale Sveum	.05	.02	.00
☐ 500	Checklist 401-500	.08	.01	.00
☐ 501	Tim Jones	.05	.02	.00
☐ 502	Mark Portugal	.05	.02	.00
☐ 503	Ivan Calderon	.08	.03	.01
☐ 504	Rick Rhoden	.05	.02	.00
☐ 505	Willie McGee	.10	.04	.01
☐ 506	Kirk McCaskill	.05	.02	.00
☐ 507	Dave LaPoint	.05	.02	.00
☐ 508	Jay Howell	.05	.02	.00
☐ 509	Johnny Ray	.05	.02	.00
☐ 510	Dave Anderson	.05	.02	.00
☐ 511	Chuck Crim	.05	.02	.00
☐ 512	Joe Hesketh	.05	.02	.00
☐ 513	Dennis Eckersley	.10	.04	.01
☐ 514	Greg Brock	.05	.02	.00
☐ 515	Tim Burke	.05	.02	.00
☐ 516	Frank Tanana	.08	.03	.01
☐ 517	Jay Bell	.05	.02	.00
☐ 518	Guillermo Hernandez	.05	.02	.00
☐ 519	Randy Kramer UER (Codiroli misspelled as Codoroli)	.08	.03	.01
☐ 520	Charles Hudson	.05	.02	.00
☐ 521	Jim Corsi (word "originally" is misspelled on back)	.05	.02	.00
☐ 522	Steve Rosenberg	.05	.02	.00
☐ 523	Cris Carpenter	.05	.02	.00
☐ 524	Matt Winters	.12	.05	.01
☐ 525	Melido Perez	.05	.02	.00
☐ 526	Chris Gwynn UER (Albeguerque)	.05	.02	.00
☐ 527	Bert Blyleven UER (Games career total is wrong, should be 644)	.08	.03	.01
☐ 528	Chuck Cary	.05	.02	.00
☐ 529	Daryl Boston	.05	.02	.00
☐ 530	Dale Mohorcic	.05	.02	.00
☐ 531	Geronimo Berroa	.05	.02	.00
☐ 532	Edgar Martinez	.12	.05	.01
☐ 533	Dale Murphy	.15	.06	.01
☐ 534	Jay Buhner	.10	.04	.01
☐ 535	John Smoltz UER (HEA Stadium)	.30	.12	.03
☐ 536	Andy Van Slyke	.10	.04	.01
☐ 537	Mike Henneman	.05	.02	.00
☐ 538	Miguel Garcia	.08	.03	.01
☐ 539	Frank Williams	.05	.02	.00
☐ 540	R.J. Reynolds	.05	.02	.00
☐ 541	Shawn Hillegas	.05	.02	.00
☐ 542	Walt Weiss	.08	.03	.01
☐ 543	Greg Hibbard	.30	.12	.03
☐ 544	Nolan Ryan	1.00	.40	.10
☐ 545	Todd Zeile	.75	.30	.07
☐ 546	Hensley Meulens	.20	.08	.02
☐ 547	Tim Belcher	.08	.03	.01
☐ 548	Mike Witt	.05	.02	.00
☐ 549	Greg Cadaret UER (Aquiring, should be Acquiring)	.05	.02	.00
☐ 550	Franklin Stubbs	.05	.02	.00
☐ 551	Tony Castillo	.05	.02	.00
☐ 552	Jeff Robinson	.05	.02	.00
☐ 553	Steve Olin	.15	.06	.01
☐ 554	Alan Trammell	.12	.05	.01
☐ 555	Wade Boggs 4X (Bo Jackson in background)	.30	.12	.03
☐ 556	Will Clark	.50	.20	.05
☐ 557	Jeff King	.10	.04	.01
☐ 558	Mike Fitzgerald	.05	.02	.00
☐ 559	Ken Howell	.05	.02	.00
☐ 560	Bob Kipper	.05	.02	.00
☐ 561	Scott Bankhead	.05	.02	.00
☐ 562A	Jeff Innis ERR (photo actually David West)	3.00	1.25	.30
☐ 562B	Jeff Innis COR	.10	.04	.01
☐ 563	Randy Johnson	.10	.04	.01
☐ 564	Wally Whitehurst	.05	.02	.00
☐ 565	Gene Harris	.10	.04	.01
☐ 566	Norm Charlton	.10	.04	.01
☐ 567	Robin Yount UER (7602 career hits, should be 2606)	.20	.08	.02
☐ 568	Joe Oliver UER (Fl.orida)	.12	.05	.01
☐ 569	Mark Parent	.05	.02	.00
☐ 570	John Farrell UER (Loss total added wrong)	.05	.02	.00
☐ 571	Tom Glavine	.35	.15	.03
☐ 572	Rod Nichols	.10	.04	.01
☐ 573	Jack Morris	.12	.05	.01
☐ 574	Greg Swindell	.08	.03	.01
☐ 575	Steve Searcy	.05	.02	.00
☐ 576	Ricky Jordan	.08	.03	.01
☐ 577	Matt Williams	.25	.10	.02
☐ 578	Mike LaValliere	.05	.02	.00
☐ 579	Bryn Smith	.05	.02	.00
☐ 580	Bruce Ruffin	.05	.02	.00
☐ 581	Randy Myers	.05	.02	.00
☐ 582	Rick Wrona	.10	.04	.01
☐ 583	Juan Samuel	.08	.03	.01
☐ 584	Les Lancaster	.05	.02	.00
☐ 585	Jeff Musselman	.05	.02	.00
☐ 586	Rob Dibble	.15	.06	.01
☐ 587	Eric Show	.05	.02	.00
☐ 588	Jesse Orosco	.05	.02	.00
☐ 589	Herm Winningham	.05	.02	.00
☐ 590	Andy Allanson	.05	.02	.00
☐ 591	Dion James	.05	.02	.00
☐ 592	Carmelo Martinez	.05	.02	.00
☐ 593	Luis Quinones	.05	.02	.00
☐ 594	Dennis Rasmussen	.05	.02	.00
☐ 595	Rich Yett	.05	.02	.00
☐ 596	Bob Walk	.05	.02	.00
☐ 597A	Andy McGaffigan ERR (photo actually Rich Thompson)	.40	.16	.04
☐ 597B	Andy McGaffigan COR	.10	.04	.01
☐ 598	Billy Hatcher	.08	.03	.01
☐ 599	Bob Knepper	.05	.02	.00
☐ 600	Checklist 501-600 UER (599 Bob Kneppers)	.08	.01	.00
☐ 601	Joey Cora	.08	.03	.01
☐ 602	Steve Finley	.15	.06	.01
☐ 603	Kal Daniels UER (12 hits in '87, should be 123; 335 runs, should be 235)	.10	.04	.01
☐ 604	Gregg Olson	.17	.07	.01
☐ 605	Dave Stieb	.10	.04	.01
☐ 606	Kenny Rogers (Shown catching football)	.08	.03	.01
☐ 607	Zane Smith	.08	.03	.01
☐ 608	Bob Geren UER (Origionally)	.08	.03	.01
☐ 609	Chad Kreuter	.05	.02	.00
☐ 610	Mike Smithson	.05	.02	.00
☐ 611	Jeff Wetherby	.10	.04	.01
☐ 612	Gary Mielke	.10	.04	.01
☐ 613	Pete Smith	.05	.02	.00
☐ 614	Jack Daugherty UER (Born 7/30/60, should be 7/3/60; origionally)	.10	.04	.01
☐ 615	Lance McCullers	.05	.02	.00
☐ 616	Don Robinson	.05	.02	.00
☐ 617	Jose Guzman	.05	.02	.00
☐ 618	Steve Bedrosian	.05	.02	.00
☐ 619	Jamie Moyer	.05	.02	.00

☐	620 Atlee Hammaker	.05	.02	.00
☐	621 Rick Luecken UER (Innings pitched wrong)	.10	.04	.01
☐	622 Greg W. Harris	.05	.02	.00
☐	623 Pete Harnisch	.08	.03	.01
☐	624 Jerald Clark	.08	.03	.01
☐	625 Jack McDowell	.05	.02	.00
☐	626 Frank Viola	.10	.04	.01
☐	627 Teddy Higuera	.05	.02	.00
☐	628 Marty Pevey	.10	.04	.01
☐	629 Bill Wegman	.05	.02	.00
☐	630 Eric Plunk	.05	.02	.00
☐	631 Drew Hall	.05	.02	.00
☐	632 Doug Jones	.05	.02	.00
☐	633 Geno Petralli	.05	.02	.00
☐	634 Jose Alvarez	.05	.02	.00
☐	635 Bob Milacki	.08	.03	.01
☐	636 Bobby Witt	.08	.03	.01
☐	637 Trevor Wilson	.08	.03	.01
☐	638 Jeff Russell UER (Shutout stats wrong)	.05	.02	.00
☐	639 Mike Krukow	.05	.02	.00
☐	640 Rick Leach	.05	.02	.00
☐	641 Dave Schmidt	.05	.02	.00
☐	642 Terry Leach	.05	.02	.00
☐	643 Calvin Schiraldi	.05	.02	.00
☐	644 Bob Melvin	.05	.02	.00
☐	645 Jim Abbott	.35	.15	.03
☐	646 Jaime Navarro	.15	.06	.01
☐	647 Mark Langston UER (Several errors in stats totals)	.08	.03	.01
☐	648 Juan Nieves	.05	.02	.00
☐	649 Damaso Garcia	.05	.02	.00
☐	650 Charlie O'Brien	.05	.02	.00
☐	651 Eric King	.05	.02	.00
☐	652 Mike Boddicker	.05	.02	.00
☐	653 Duane Ward	.08	.03	.01
☐	654 Bob Stanley	.05	.02	.00
☐	655 Sandy Alomar Jr.	.15	.06	.01
☐	656 Danny Tartabull UER (395 BB, should be 295)	.12	.05	.01
☐	657 Randy McCament	.10	.04	.01
☐	658 Charlie Leibrandt	.05	.02	.00
☐	659 Dan Quisenberry	.08	.03	.01
☐	660 Paul Assenmacher	.05	.02	.00
☐	661 Walt Terrell	.05	.02	.00
☐	662 Tim Leary	.08	.03	.01
☐	663 Randy Milligan	.08	.03	.01
☐	664 Bo Diaz	.05	.02	.00
☐	665 Mark Lemke UER (Richmond misspelled as Richomond)	.05	.02	.00
☐	666 Jose Gonzalez	.05	.02	.00
☐	667 Chuck Finley UER (Born 11/16/62, should be 11/26/62)	.12	.05	.01
☐	668 John Kruk	.05	.02	.00
☐	669 Dick Schofield	.05	.02	.00
☐	670 Tim Crews	.05	.02	.00
☐	671 John Dopson	.05	.02	.00
☐	672 John Orton	.12	.05	.01
☐	673 Eric Hetzel	.05	.02	.00
☐	674 Lance Parrish	.10	.04	.01
☐	675 Ramon Martinez	.90	.40	.09
☐	676 Mark Gubicza	.08	.03	.01
☐	677 Greg Litton	.08	.03	.01
☐	678 Greg Mathews	.05	.02	.00
☐	679 Dave Dravecky	.10	.04	.01
☐	680 Steve Farr	.05	.02	.00
☐	681 Mike Devereaux	.05	.02	.00
☐	682 Ken Griffey Sr.	.10	.04	.01
☐	683A Mickey Weston ERR (listed as Jamie on card)	3.50	1.50	.35
☐	683B Mickey Weston COR (technically still an error as birthdate is listed as 3/26/81)	.10	.04	.01
☐	684 Jack Armstrong	.08	.03	.01
☐	685 Steve Buechele	.05	.02	.00
☐	686 Bryan Harvey	.08	.03	.01
☐	687 Lance Blankenship	.05	.02	.00
☐	688 Dante Bichette	.08	.03	.01
☐	689 Todd Burns	.05	.02	.00
☐	690 Dan Petry	.05	.02	.00
☐	691 Kent Anderson	.08	.03	.01
☐	692 Todd Stottlemyre	.12	.05	.01
☐	693 Wally Joyner UER (Several stats errors)	.15	.06	.01
☐	694 Mike Rochford	.05	.02	.00
☐	695 Floyd Bannister	.05	.02	.00
☐	696 Rick Reuschel	.08	.03	.01
☐	697 Jose DeLeon	.05	.02	.00
☐	698 Jeff Montgomery	.05	.02	.00

☐	699 Kelly Downs	.05	.02	.00
☐	700A Checklist 601-700 (683 Jamie Weston)	3.00	.50	.10
☐	700B Checklist 601-700 (683 Mickey Weston)	.10	.01	.00

1990 Upper Deck Extended

Dave Justice

The 1990 Upper Deck Extended Set was issued in July 1990. These cards which are in the same style as the first 700 cards of the 1990 Upper Deck set and were issued either as a separate set in its own collectors box, as part of the complete 1-800 factory set, as well as mixed in with the earlier numbered Upper Deck cards in late-season wax packs. This 100-card set which measures the standard size 2 1/2" by 3 1/2" also has a Nolan Ryan variation. All cards produced before August 12th only discuss Ryan's sixth no-hitter while the later-issue cards include a stripe honoring Ryan's 300th victory. The key rookie cards in this set are Carlos Baerga, Alex Cole, Delino DeShields, Dave Justice, and Ray Lankford. Card 702 was originally scheduled to be Mike Witt. A few 702 Witt cards and checklist cards showing 702 Witt escaped into early packs; they are characterized by a black rectangle covering much of the card's back.

		MINT	EXC	G-VG
	COMPLETE SET (100)	12.50	5.50	1.65
	COMMON PLAYER (1-100)	.06	.02	.00
☐	701 Jim Gott	.06	.02	.00
☐	702 Rookie Threats Delino DeShields Marquis Grissom Larry Walker	.50	.20	.05
☐	703 Alejandro Pena	.10	.04	.01
☐	704 Willie Randolph	.10	.04	.01
☐	705 Tim Leary	.10	.04	.01
☐	706 Chuck McElroy	.20	.08	.02
☐	707 Gerald Perry	.06	.02	.00
☐	708 Tom Brunansky	.10	.04	.01
☐	709 John Franco	.10	.04	.01
☐	710 Mark Davis	.10	.04	.01
☐	711 Dave Justice	8.50	3.75	.85
☐	712 Storm Davis	.06	.02	.00
☐	713 Scott Ruskin	.20	.08	.02
☐	714 Glenn Braggs	.06	.02	.00
☐	715 Kevin Bearse	.15	.06	.01
☐	716 Jose Nunez	.06	.02	.00
☐	717 Tim Layana	.15	.06	.01
☐	718 Greg Myers	.06	.02	.00
☐	719 Pete O'Brien	.06	.02	.00
☐	720 John Candelaria	.06	.02	.00
☐	721 Craig Grebeck	.15	.06	.01
☐	722 Shawn Boskie	.20	.08	.02
☐	723 Jim Leyritz	.12	.05	.01
☐	724 Bill Sampen	.15	.06	.01
☐	725 Scott Radinsky	.20	.08	.02
☐	726 Todd Hundley	.60	.25	.06
☐	727 Scott Hemond	.17	.07	.01
☐	728 Lenny Webster	.20	.08	.02
☐	729 Jeff Reardon	.12	.05	.01
☐	730 Mitch Webster	.06	.02	.00
☐	731 Brian Bohanon	.17	.07	.01
☐	732 Rick Parker	.10	.04	.01

			MINT	EXC	G-VG
☐	733	Tery Shumpert	.17	.07	.01
☐	734A	Ryan's 6th No-Hitter (no stripe on front)	9.00	4.00	.90
☐	734B	Ryan's 6th No-Hitter (stripe added on card front for 300th win)	1.25	.50	.12
☐	735	John Burkett	.25	.10	.02
☐	736	Derrick May	.25	.10	.02
☐	737	Carlos Baerga	.75	.30	.07
☐	738	Greg Smith	.12	.05	.01
☐	739	Scott Sanderson	.10	.04	.01
☐	740	Joe Kraemer	.12	.05	.01
☐	741	Hector Villanueva	.17	.07	.01
☐	742	Mike Fetters	.10	.04	.01
☐	743	Mark Gardner	.30	.12	.03
☐	744	Matt Nokes	.10	.04	.01
☐	745	Dave Winfield	.15	.06	.01
☐	746	Delino DeShields	1.00	.40	.10
☐	747	Dann Howitt	.20	.08	.02
☐	748	Tony Pena	.10	.04	.01
☐	749	Oil Can Boyd	.06	.02	.00
☐	750	Mike Benjamin	.17	.07	.01
☐	751	Alex Cole	.65	.25	.06
☐	752	Eric Gunderson	.25	.10	.02
☐	753	Howard Farmer	.17	.07	.01
☐	754	Joe Carter	.15	.06	.01
☐	755	Ray Lankford	2.00	.80	.20
☐	756	Sandy Alomar Jr.	.20	.08	.02
☐	757	Alex Sanchez	.10	.04	.01
☐	758	Nick Esasky	.06	.02	.00
☐	759	Stan Belinda	.20	.08	.02
☐	760	Jim Presley	.06	.02	.00
☐	761	Gary DiSarcina	.15	.06	.01
☐	762	Wayne Edwards	.12	.05	.01
☐	763	Pat Combs	.10	.04	.01
☐	764	Mickey Pina	.15	.06	.01
☐	765	Wilson Alvarez	.50	.20	.05
☐	766	Dave Parker	.10	.04	.01
☐	767	Mike Blowers	.15	.06	.01
☐	768	Tony Phillips	.06	.02	.00
☐	769	Pascual Perez	.06	.02	.00
☐	770	Gary Pettis	.06	.02	.00
☐	771	Fred Lynn	.10	.04	.01
☐	772	Mel Rojas	.12	.05	.01
☐	773	David Segui	.25	.10	.02
☐	774	Gary Carter	.12	.05	.01
☐	775	Rafael Valdez	.15	.06	.01
☐	776	Glenallen Hill	.10	.04	.01
☐	777	Keith Hernandez	.12	.05	.01
☐	778	Billy Hatcher	.10	.04	.01
☐	779	Marty Clary	.06	.02	.00
☐	780	Candy Maldonado	.10	.04	.01
☐	781	Mike Marshall	.10	.04	.01
☐	782	Billy Jo Robidoux	.06	.02	.00
☐	783	Mark Langston	.10	.04	.01
☐	784	Paul Sorrento	.17	.07	.01
☐	785	Dave Hollins	.60	.25	.06
☐	786	Cecil Fielder	.75	.30	.07
☐	787	Matt Young	.06	.02	.00
☐	788	Jeff Huson	.10	.04	.01
☐	789	Lloyd Moseby	.06	.02	.00
☐	790	Ron Kittle	.10	.04	.01
☐	791	Hubie Brooks	.10	.04	.01
☐	792	Craig Lefferts	.06	.02	.00
☐	793	Kevin Bass	.06	.02	.00
☐	794	Bryn Smith	.06	.02	.00
☐	795	Juan Samuel	.10	.04	.01
☐	796	Sam Horn	.10	.04	.01
☐	797	Randy Myers	.10	.04	.01
☐	798	Chris James	.10	.04	.01
☐	799	Bill Gullickson	.10	.04	.01
☐	800	Checklist 701-800	.06	.01	.00

1990 Upper Deck Reggie Jackson Heroes

This ten-card subset was issued as an insert in 1990 Upper Deck High Number packs as part of the Upper Deck promotional giveaway of 2,500 officially signed and personally numbered Reggie Jackson cards. These cards were the standard size 2 1/2" by 3 1/2" and cover Reggie's complete major league career. The complete set price refers only to the unautographed card set of ten.

	MINT	EXC	G-VG
COMPLETE SET (10)	33.00	15.00	5.00
COMMON PLAYER (1-9)	3.25	1.35	.32

			MINT	EXC	G-VG
☐	1	1969 Emerging Superstar	3.25	1.35	.32
☐	2	1973 An MVP Year	3.25	1.35	.32
☐	3	1977 Mr. October	3.25	1.35	.32
☐	4	1978 Jackson vs. Welch	3.25	1.35	.32
☐	5	1982 Under the Halo	3.25	1.35	.32
☐	6	1984 500 Homers	3.25	1.35	.32
☐	7	1986 Moving Up the List	3.25	1.35	.32
☐	8	1987 A Great Career Ends	3.25	1.35	.32
☐	9	Baseball Heroes Checklist	3.25	1.35	.32
☐	xx	Reggie Jackson Header Card SP	6.50	2.75	.65
☐	xx	Reggie Jackson (Signed and Numbered out of 2500)	450.00	200.00	67.50

1991 Upper Deck

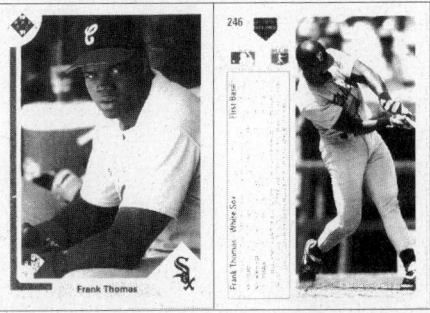

This set marks the third year Upper deck has issued an 700-card set in January. These cards measure 2 1/2" by 3 1/2". The set features 26 star rookies to lead off the set as well as other special cards featuring multi-players. The set is made on the typical Upper Deck card stock and features full-color photos on both the front and the back. The team checklist (TC) cards in the set feature an attractive Vernon Wells drawing of a featured player for that particular team. A special Michael Jordan card (numbered SP1) was randomly included in packs on a somewhat limited basis. This Jordan card is not included in the set price below. The key rookie cards in this set include Wes Chamberlain, Luis Gonzalez, Brian McRae, Phil Plantier, and Todd Van Poppel.

	MINT	EXC	G-VG
COMPLETE SET (700)	28.00	12.50	4.00
COMMON PLAYER (1-700)	.05	.02	.00

☐ 1	Star Rookie Checklist	.10	.02	.00	☐ 70	Greg Blosser	.25	.10	.02
☐ 2	Phil Plantier	3.75	1.60	.37	☐ 71	Reggie Sanders	.90	.40	.09
☐ 3	D.J. Dozier	.20	.08	.02	☐ 72	Brent Mayne	.15	.06	.01
☐ 4	Dave Hansen	.25	.10	.02	☐ 73	Rico Brogna	.50	.20	.05
☐ 5	Maurice Vaughn	1.25	.50	.12	☐ 74	Willie Banks	.35	.15	.03
☐ 6	Leo Gomez	.50	.20	.05	☐ 75	Len Brutcher	.12	.05	.01
☐ 7	Scott Allred	.15	.06	.01	☐ 76	Pat Kelly	.50	.20	.05
☐ 8	Scott Chiampariano	.10	.04	.01	☐ 77	Cincinnati Reds TC	.08	.03	.01
☐ 9	Lance Dickson	.35	.15	.03		Chris Sabo			
☐ 10	Sean Berry	.20	.08	.02	☐ 78	Los Angeles Dodgers TC	.08	.03	.01
☐ 11	Bernie Williams	.90	.40	.09		Ramon Martinez			
☐ 12	Brian Barnes UER	.20	.08	.02	☐ 79	San Fran. Giants TC	.08	.03	.01
	(Photo either not him					Matt Williams			
	or in wrong jersey)				☐ 80	San Diego Padres TC	.08	.03	.01
☐ 13	Narciso Elvira	.12	.05	.01		Roberto Alomar			
☐ 14	Mike Gardiner	.25	.10	.02	☐ 81	Houston Astros TC	.08	.03	.01
☐ 15	Greg Colbrunn	.20	.08	.02		Glenn Davis			
☐ 16	Bernard Gilkey	.25	.10	.02	☐ 82	Atlanta Braves TC	.08	.03	.01
☐ 17	Mark Lewis	.50	.20	.05		Ron Gant			
☐ 18	Mickey Morandini	.15	.06	.01	☐ 83	Fielder's Feat	.20	.08	.02
☐ 19	Charles Nagy	.17	.07	.01		Cecil Fielder			
☐ 20	Geronimo Pena	.15	.06	.01	☐ 84	Orlando Merced	.80	.35	.08
☐ 21	Henry Rodriguez	.25	.10	.02	☐ 85	Domingo Ramos	.05	.02	.00
☐ 22	Scott Cooper	.40	.16	.04	☐ 86	Tom Bolton	.05	.02	.00
☐ 23	Andujar Cedeno UER	.90	.40	.09	☐ 87	Andres Santana	.25	.10	.02
	(Shown batting left,				☐ 88	John Dopson	.05	.02	.00
	back says right)				☐ 89	Kenny Williams	.05	.02	.00
☐ 24	Eric Karros	.75	.30	.07	☐ 90	Marty Barrett	.05	.02	.00
☐ 25	Steve Decker UER	.40	.16	.04	☐ 91	Tom Pagnozzi	.05	.02	.00
	(Lewis-Clark State				☐ 92	Carmelo Martinez	.05	.02	.00
	College, not Lewis				☐ 93	Save Master	.08	.03	.01
	and Clark)					(Bobby Thigpen)			
☐ 26	Kevin Belcher	.15	.06	.01	☐ 94	Pittsburgh Pirates TC	.12	.05	.01
☐ 27	Jeff Conine	.20	.08	.02		Barry Bonds			
☐ 28	Oakland Athletics TC	.08	.03	.01	☐ 95	New York Mets TC	.08	.03	.01
	Dave Stewart					Gregg Jefferies			
☐ 29	Chicago White Sox TC	.08	.03	.01	☐ 96	Montreal Expos TC	.05	.02	.00
	Carlton Fisk					Tim Wallach			
☐ 30	Texas Rangers TC	.08	.03	.01	☐ 97	Phila. Phillies TC	.08	.03	.01
	Rafael Palmeiro					Len Dykstra			
☐ 31	California Angels TC	.08	.03	.01	☐ 98	St.Louis Cardinals TC	.08	.03	.01
	Chuck Finley					Pedro Guerrero			
☐ 32	Seattle Mariners TC	.05	.02	.00	☐ 99	Chicago Cubs TC	.08	.03	.01
	Harold Reynolds					Mark Grace			
☐ 33	Kansas City Royals TC	.08	.03	.01	☐ 100	Checklist 1-100	.05	.01	.00
	Bret Saberhagen				☐ 101	Kevin Elster	.05	.02	.00
☐ 34	Minnesota Twins TC	.08	.03	.01	☐ 102	Tom Brookens	.05	.02	.00
	Gary Gaetti				☐ 103	Mackey Sasser	.05	.02	.00
☐ 35	Scott Leius	.17	.07	.01	☐ 104	Felix Fermin	.05	.02	.00
☐ 36	Neal Heaton	.05	.02	.00	☐ 105	Kevin McReynolds	.08	.03	.01
☐ 37	Terry Lee	.12	.05	.01	☐ 106	Dave Stieb	.08	.03	.01
☐ 38	Gary Redus	.05	.02	.00	☐ 107	Jeffrey Leonard	.05	.02	.00
☐ 39	Barry Jones	.05	.02	.00	☐ 108	Dave Henderson	.08	.03	.01
☐ 40	Chuck Knoblauch	2.00	.80	.20	☐ 109	Sid Bream	.05	.02	.00
☐ 41	Larry Andersen	.05	.02	.00	☐ 110	Henry Cotto	.05	.02	.00
☐ 42	Darryl Hamilton	.08	.03	.01	☐ 111	Shawon Dunston	.08	.03	.01
☐ 43	Boston Red Sox TC	.08	.03	.01	☐ 112	Mariano Duncan	.05	.02	.00
	Mike Greenwell				☐ 113	Joe Girardi	.05	.02	.00
☐ 44	Toronto Blue Jays TC	.08	.03	.01	☐ 114	Billy Hatcher	.05	.02	.00
	Kelly Gruber				☐ 115	Greg Maddux	.08	.03	.01
☐ 45	Detroit Tigers TC	.08	.03	.01	☐ 116	Jerry Browne	.05	.02	.00
	Jack Morris				☐ 117	Juan Samuel	.08	.03	.01
☐ 46	Cleveland Indians TC	.08	.03	.01	☐ 118	Steve Olin	.05	.02	.00
	Sandy Alomar Jr.				☐ 119	Alfredo Griffin	.05	.02	.00
☐ 47	Baltimore Orioles TC	.08	.03	.01	☐ 120	Mitch Webster	.05	.02	.00
	Gregg Olson				☐ 121	Joel Skinner	.05	.02	.00
☐ 48	Milwaukee Brewers TC	.08	.03	.01	☐ 122	Frank Viola	.10	.04	.01
	Dave Parker				☐ 123	Cory Snyder	.08	.03	.01
☐ 49	New York Yankees TC	.08	.03	.01	☐ 124	Howard Johnson	.12	.05	.01
	Roberto Kelly				☐ 125	Carlos Baerga	.20	.08	.02
☐ 50	Top Prospect Checklist .05	.01	.00		☐ 126	Tony Fernandez	.08	.03	.01
☐ 51	Kyle Abbott	.25	.10	.02	☐ 127	Dave Stewart	.08	.03	.01
☐ 52	Jeff Juden	.40	.16	.04	☐ 128	Jay Buhner	.08	.03	.01
☐ 53	Todd Van Poppel UER	2.50	1.00	.25	☐ 129	Mike LaValliere	.05	.02	.00
	Born Arlington and				☐ 130	Scott Bradley	.05	.02	.00
	attended John Martin HS,				☐ 131	Tony Phillips	.05	.02	.00
	should say Hinsdale and				☐ 132	Ryne Sandberg	.35	.15	.03
	James Martin HS)				☐ 133	Paul O'Neill	.08	.03	.01
☐ 54	Steve Karsay	.40	.16	.04	☐ 134	Mark Grace	.10	.04	.01
☐ 55	Chipper Jones	.65	.25	.06	☐ 135	Chris Sabo	.08	.03	.01
☐ 56	Chris Johnson UER	.12	.05	.01	☐ 136	Ramon Martinez	.17	.07	.01
	(Called Tim on back)				☐ 137	Brook Jacoby	.05	.02	.00
☐ 57	John Ericks	.12	.05	.01	☐ 138	Candy Maldonado	.05	.02	.00
☐ 58	Gary Scott	.40	.16	.04	☐ 139	Mike Scioscia	.05	.02	.00
☐ 59	Kiki Jones	.20	.08	.02	☐ 140	Chris James	.05	.02	.00
☐ 60	Wilfredo Cordero	.50	.20	.05	☐ 141	Craig Worthington	.05	.02	.00
☐ 61	Royce Clayton	.90	.40	.09	☐ 142	Manny Lee	.05	.02	.00
☐ 62	Tim Costo	.45	.18	.04	☐ 143	Tim Raines	.08	.03	.01
☐ 63	Roger Salkeld	.70	.30	.07	☐ 144	Sandy Alomar Jr.	.08	.03	.01
☐ 64	Brook Fordyce	.20	.08	.02	☐ 145	John Olerud	.17	.07	.01
☐ 65	Mike Mussina	.75	.30	.07	☐ 146	Ozzie Canseco	.12	.05	.01
☐ 66	Dave Staton	.35	.15	.03		(With Jose)			
☐ 67	Mike Lieberthal	.25	.10	.02	☐ 147	Pat Borders	.05	.02	.00
☐ 68	Kurt Miller	.30	.12	.03	☐ 148	Harold Reynolds	.05	.02	.00
☐ 69	Dan Peltier	.20	.08	.02	☐ 149	Tom Henke	.05	.02	.00

☐ 150	R.J. Reynolds	.05	.02	.00
☐ 151	Mike Gallego	.05	.02	.00
☐ 152	Bobby Bonilla	.17	.07	.01
☐ 153	Terry Steinbach	.05	.02	.00
☐ 154	Barry Bonds	.20	.08	.02
☐ 155	Jose Canseco	.40	.16	.04
☐ 156	Gregg Jefferies	.10	.04	.01
☐ 157	Matt Williams	.15	.06	.01
☐ 158	Craig Biggio	.08	.03	.01
☐ 159	Daryl Boston	.05	.02	.00
☐ 160	Ricky Jordan	.05	.02	.00
☐ 161	Stan Belinda	.05	.02	.00
☐ 162	Ozzie Smith	.15	.06	.01
☐ 163	Tom Brunansky	.08	.03	.01
☐ 164	Todd Zeile	.15	.06	.01
☐ 165	Mike Greenwell	.15	.06	.01
☐ 166	Kal Daniels	.08	.03	.01
☐ 167	Kent Hrbek	.08	.03	.01
☐ 168	Franklin Stubbs	.05	.02	.00
☐ 169	Dick Schofield	.05	.02	.00
☐ 170	Junior Ortiz	.05	.02	.00
☐ 171	Hector Villanueva	.08	.03	.01
☐ 172	Dennis Eckersley	.08	.03	.01
☐ 173	Mitch Williams	.05	.02	.00
☐ 174	Mark McGwire	.12	.05	.01
☐ 175	Fernando Valenzuela 3X	.08	.03	.01
☐ 176	Gary Carter	.08	.03	.01
☐ 177	Dave Magadan	.08	.03	.01
☐ 178	Robby Thompson	.05	.02	.00
☐ 179	Bob Ojeda	.05	.02	.00
☐ 180	Ken Caminiti	.05	.02	.00
☐ 181	Don Slaught	.05	.02	.00
☐ 182	Luis Rivera	.05	.02	.00
☐ 183	Jay Bell	.05	.02	.00
☐ 184	Jody Reed	.05	.02	.00
☐ 185	Wally Backman	.05	.02	.00
☐ 186	Dave Martinez	.05	.02	.00
☐ 187	Luis Polonia	.05	.02	.00
☐ 188	Shane Mack	.08	.03	.01
☐ 189	Spike Owen	.05	.02	.00
☐ 190	Scott Bailes	.05	.02	.00
☐ 191	John Russell	.05	.02	.00
☐ 192	Walt Weiss	.08	.03	.01
☐ 193	Jose Oquendo	.05	.02	.00
☐ 194	Carney Lansford	.08	.03	.01
☐ 195	Jeff Huson	.05	.02	.00
☐ 196	Keith Miller	.05	.02	.00
☐ 197	Eric Yelding	.05	.02	.00
☐ 198	Ron Darling	.08	.03	.01
☐ 199	John Kruk	.05	.02	.00
☐ 200	Checklist 101-200	.05	.01	.00
☐ 201	John Shelby	.05	.02	.00
☐ 202	Bob Geren	.05	.02	.00
☐ 203	Lance McCullers	.05	.02	.00
☐ 204	Alvaro Espinoza	.05	.02	.00
☐ 205	Mark Salas	.05	.02	.00
☐ 206	Mike Pagliarulo	.05	.02	.00
☐ 207	Jose Uribe	.05	.02	.00
☐ 208	Jim Deshaies	.05	.02	.00
☐ 209	Ron Karkovice	.05	.02	.00
☐ 210	Rafael Ramirez	.05	.02	.00
☐ 211	Donnie Hill	.05	.02	.00
☐ 212	Brian Harper	.08	.03	.01
☐ 213	Jack Howell	.05	.02	.00
☐ 214	Wes Gardner	.05	.02	.00
☐ 215	Tim Burke	.05	.02	.00
☐ 216	Doug Jones	.05	.02	.00
☐ 217	Hubie Brooks	.08	.03	.01
☐ 218	Tom Candiotti	.08	.03	.01
☐ 219	Gerald Perry	.05	.02	.00
☐ 220	Jose DeLeon	.05	.02	.00
☐ 221	Wally Whitehurst	.05	.02	.00
☐ 222	Alan Mills	.08	.03	.01
☐ 223	Alan Trammell	.10	.04	.01
☐ 224	Dwight Gooden	.15	.06	.01
☐ 225	Travis Fryman	1.25	.50	.12
☐ 226	Joe Carter	.10	.04	.01
☐ 227	Julio Franco	.10	.04	.01
☐ 228	Craig Lefferts	.05	.02	.00
☐ 229	Gary Pettis	.05	.02	.00
☐ 230	Dennis Rasmussen	.05	.02	.00
☐ 231A	Brian Downing ERR (No position on front)	.20	.08	.02
☐ 231B	Brian Downing COR (DH on front)	.45	.18	.04
☐ 232	Carlos Quintana	.08	.03	.01
☐ 233	Gary Gaetti	.08	.03	.01
☐ 234	Mark Langston	.08	.03	.01
☐ 235	Tim Wallach	.08	.03	.01
☐ 236	Greg Swindell	.08	.03	.01
☐ 237	Eddie Murray	.15	.06	.01
☐ 238	Jeff Manto	.05	.02	.00
☐ 239	Lenny Harris	.05	.02	.00
☐ 240	Jesse Orosco	.05	.02	.00
☐ 241	Scott Lusader	.05	.02	.00
☐ 242	Sid Fernandez	.08	.03	.01
☐ 243	Jim Leyritz	.05	.02	.00
☐ 244	Cecil Fielder	.25	.10	.02
☐ 245	Darryl Strawberry	.30	.12	.03
☐ 246	Frank Thomas UER (Comiskey Park misspelled Comisky)	4.00	1.75	.40
☐ 247	Kevin Mitchell	.12	.05	.01
☐ 248	Lance Johnson	.05	.02	.00
☐ 249	Rick Reuschel	.08	.03	.01
☐ 250	Mark Portugal	.05	.02	.00
☐ 251	Derek Lilliquist	.05	.02	.00
☐ 252	Brian Holman	.05	.02	.00
☐ 253	Rafael Valdez UER (Born 4/17/68, should be 12/17/67)	.05	.02	.00
☐ 254	B.J. Surhoff	.05	.02	.00
☐ 255	Tony Gwynn	.17	.07	.01
☐ 256	Andy Van Slyke	.08	.03	.01
☐ 257	Todd Stottlemyre	.08	.03	.01
☐ 258	Jose Lind	.05	.02	.00
☐ 259	Greg Myers	.05	.02	.00
☐ 260	Jeff Ballard	.05	.02	.00
☐ 261	Bobby Thigpen	.08	.03	.01
☐ 262	Jimmy Kremers	.08	.03	.01
☐ 263	Robin Ventura	.40	.16	.04
☐ 264	John Smoltz	.12	.05	.01
☐ 265	Sammy Sosa	.08	.03	.01
☐ 266	Gary Sheffield	.08	.03	.01
☐ 267	Lenny Dykstra	.08	.03	.01
☐ 268	Bill Spiers	.05	.02	.00
☐ 269	Charlie Hayes	.05	.02	.00
☐ 270	Brett Butler	.08	.03	.01
☐ 271	Bip Roberts	.05	.02	.00
☐ 272	Rob Deer	.08	.03	.01
☐ 273	Fred Lynn	.08	.03	.01
☐ 274	Dave Parker	.08	.03	.01
☐ 275	Andy Benes	.12	.05	.01
☐ 276	Glenallen Hill	.08	.03	.01
☐ 277	Steve Howard	.10	.04	.01
☐ 278	Doug Drabek	.08	.03	.01
☐ 279	Joe Oliver	.05	.02	.00
☐ 280	Todd Benzinger	.05	.02	.00
☐ 281	Eric King	.05	.02	.00
☐ 282	Jim Presley	.05	.02	.00
☐ 283	Ken Patterson	.05	.02	.00
☐ 284	Jack Daugherty	.05	.02	.00
☐ 285	Ivan Calderon	.08	.03	.01
☐ 286	Edgar Diaz	.08	.03	.01
☐ 287	Kevin Bass	.05	.02	.00
☐ 288	Don Carman	.05	.02	.00
☐ 289	Greg Brock	.05	.02	.00
☐ 290	John Franco	.05	.02	.00
☐ 291	Joey Cora	.05	.02	.00
☐ 292	Bill Wegman	.05	.02	.00
☐ 293	Eric Show	.05	.02	.00
☐ 294	Scott Bankhead	.05	.02	.00
☐ 295	Garry Templeton	.05	.02	.00
☐ 296	Mickey Tettleton	.08	.03	.01
☐ 297	Luis Sojo	.08	.03	.01
☐ 298	Jose Rijo	.08	.03	.01
☐ 299	Dave Johnson	.05	.02	.00
☐ 300	Checklist 201-300	.05	.01	.00
☐ 301	Mark Grant	.05	.02	.00
☐ 302	Pete Harnisch	.08	.03	.01
☐ 303	Greg Olson	.10	.04	.01
☐ 304	Anthony Telford	.12	.05	.01
☐ 305	Lonnie Smith	.08	.03	.01
☐ 306	Chris Hoiles	.15	.06	.01
☐ 307	Bryn Smith	.05	.02	.00
☐ 308	Mike Devereaux	.05	.02	.00
☐ 309A	Milt Thompson ERR (Under yr information has print dot)	.25	.10	.02
☐ 309B	Milt Thompson COR (Under yr information says 86)	.05	.02	.00
☐ 310	Bob Melvin	.05	.02	.00
☐ 311	Luis Salazar	.05	.02	.00
☐ 312	Ed Whitson	.05	.02	.00
☐ 313	Charlie Hough	.05	.02	.00
☐ 314	Dave Clark	.05	.02	.00
☐ 315	Eric Gunderson	.05	.02	.00
☐ 316	Dan Petry	.05	.02	.00
☐ 317	Dante Bichette UER (Assists misspelled as assissts)	.05	.02	.00
☐ 318	Mike Heath	.05	.02	.00
☐ 319	Damon Berryhill	.05	.02	.00
☐ 320	Walt Terrell	.05	.02	.00
☐ 321	Scott Fletcher	.05	.02	.00
☐ 322	Dan Plesac	.05	.02	.00
☐ 323	Jack McDowell	.10	.04	.01
☐ 324	Paul Molitor	.10	.04	.01
☐ 325	Ozzie Guillen	.08	.03	.01

☐ 326	Gregg Olson	.08	.03	.01
☐ 327	Pedro Guerrero	.08	.03	.01
☐ 328	Bob Milacki	.05	.02	.00
☐ 329	John Tudor UER	.08	.03	.01
	('90 Cardinals,			
	should be '90 Dodgers)			
☐ 330	Steve Finley UER	.08	.03	.01
	(Born 3/12/65,			
	should be 5/12)			
☐ 331	Jack Clark	.08	.03	.01
☐ 332	Jerome Walton	.08	.03	.01
☐ 333	Andy Hawkins	.05	.02	.00
☐ 334	Derrick May	.10	.04	.01
☐ 335	Roberto Alomar	.15	.06	.01
☐ 336	Jack Morris	.10	.04	.01
☐ 337	Dave Winfield	.12	.05	.01
☐ 338	Steve Searcy	.05	.02	.00
☐ 339	Chili Davis	.08	.03	.01
☐ 340	Larry Sheets	.05	.02	.00
☐ 341	Ted Higuera	.05	.02	.00
☐ 342	David Segui	.10	.04	.01
☐ 343	Greg Cadaret	.05	.02	.00
☐ 344	Robin Yount	.15	.06	.01
☐ 345	Nolan Ryan	.60	.25	.06
☐ 346	Ray Lankford	.40	.16	.04
☐ 347	Cal Ripken	.40	.16	.04
☐ 348	Lee Smith	.08	.03	.01
☐ 349	Brady Anderson	.05	.02	.00
☐ 350	Frank DiPino	.05	.02	.00
☐ 351	Hal Morris	.12	.05	.01
☐ 352	Deion Sanders	.12	.05	.01
☐ 353	Barry Larkin	.12	.05	.01
☐ 354	Don Mattingly	.20	.08	.02
☐ 355	Eric Davis	.15	.06	.01
☐ 356	Jose Offerman	.12	.05	.01
☐ 357	Mel Rojas	.08	.03	.01
☐ 358	Rudy Seanez	.15	.06	.01
☐ 359	Oil Can Boyd	.05	.02	.00
☐ 360	Nelson Liriano	.05	.02	.00
☐ 361	Ron Gant	.20	.08	.02
☐ 362	Howard Farmer	.08	.03	.01
☐ 363	David Justice	1.25	.50	.12
☐ 364	Delino DeShields	.12	.05	.01
☐ 365	Steve Avery	.75	.30	.07
☐ 366	David Cone	.08	.03	.01
☐ 367	Lou Whitaker	.08	.03	.01
☐ 368	Von Hayes	.08	.03	.01
☐ 369	Frank Tanana	.05	.02	.00
☐ 370	Tim Teufel	.05	.02	.00
☐ 371	Randy Myers	.05	.02	.00
☐ 372	Roberto Kelly	.08	.03	.01
☐ 373	Jack Armstrong	.08	.03	.01
☐ 374	Kelly Gruber	.08	.03	.01
☐ 375	Kevin Maas	.30	.12	.03
☐ 376	Randy Johnson	.08	.03	.01
☐ 377	David West	.05	.02	.00
☐ 378	Brent Knackert	.12	.05	.01
☐ 379	Rick Honeycutt	.05	.02	.00
☐ 380	Kevin Gross	.05	.02	.00
☐ 381	Tom Foley	.05	.02	.00
☐ 382	Jeff Blauser	.05	.02	.00
☐ 383	Scott Ruskin	.08	.03	.01
☐ 384	Andres Thomas	.05	.02	.00
☐ 385	Dennis Martinez	.08	.03	.01
☐ 386	Mike Henneman	.05	.02	.00
☐ 387	Felix Jose	.12	.05	.01
☐ 388	Alejandro Pena	.08	.03	.01
☐ 389	Chet Lemon	.05	.02	.00
☐ 390	Craig Wilson	.12	.05	.01
☐ 391	Chuck Crim	.05	.02	.00
☐ 392	Mel Hall	.05	.02	.00
☐ 393	Mark Knudson	.05	.02	.00
☐ 394	Norm Charlton	.05	.02	.00
☐ 395	Mike Felder	.05	.02	.00
☐ 396	Tim Layana	.05	.02	.00
☐ 397	Steve Frey	.08	.03	.01
☐ 398	Bill Doran	.05	.02	.00
☐ 399	Dion James	.05	.02	.00
☐ 400	Checklist 301-400	.05	.01	.00
☐ 401	Ron Hassey	.05	.02	.00
☐ 402	Don Robinson	.05	.02	.00
☐ 403	Gene Nelson	.05	.02	.00
☐ 404	Terry Kennedy	.05	.02	.00
☐ 405	Todd Burns	.05	.02	.00
☐ 406	Roger McDowell	.05	.02	.00
☐ 407	Bob Kipper	.05	.02	.00
☐ 408	Darren Daulton	.05	.02	.00
☐ 409	Chuck Cary	.05	.02	.00
☐ 410	Bruce Ruffin	.05	.02	.00
☐ 411	Juan Berenguer	.05	.02	.00
☐ 412	Gary Ward	.05	.02	.00
☐ 413	Al Newman	.05	.02	.00
☐ 414	Danny Jackson	.05	.02	.00
☐ 415	Greg Gagne	.05	.02	.00
☐ 416	Tom Herr	.05	.02	.00
☐ 417	Jeff Parrett	.05	.02	.00
☐ 418	Jeff Reardon	.08	.03	.01
☐ 419	Mark Lemke	.08	.03	.01
☐ 420	Charlie O'Brien	.05	.02	.00
☐ 421	Willie Randolph	.05	.02	.00
☐ 422	Steve Bedrosian	.05	.02	.00
☐ 423	Mike Moore	.05	.02	.00
☐ 424	Jeff Brantley	.05	.02	.00
☐ 425	Bob Welch	.08	.03	.01
☐ 426	Terry Mulholland	.05	.02	.00
☐ 427	Willie Blair	.08	.03	.01
☐ 428	Darrin Fletcher	.10	.04	.01
☐ 429	Mike Witt	.05	.02	.00
☐ 430	Joe Boever	.05	.02	.00
☐ 431	Tom Gordon	.08	.03	.01
☐ 432	Pedro Munoz	.50	.20	.05
☐ 433	Kevin Seitzer	.08	.03	.01
☐ 434	Kevin Tapani	.08	.03	.01
☐ 435	Bret Saberhagen	.10	.04	.01
☐ 436	Ellis Burks	.10	.04	.01
☐ 437	Chuck Finley	.08	.03	.01
☐ 438	Mike Boddicker	.05	.02	.00
☐ 439	Francisco Cabrera	.08	.03	.01
☐ 440	Todd Hundley	.15	.06	.01
☐ 441	Kelly Downs	.05	.02	.00
☐ 442	Dann Howitt	.10	.04	.01
☐ 443	Scott Garrelts	.05	.02	.00
☐ 444	Rickey Henderson 3X	.35	.15	.03
☐ 445	Will Clark	.35	.15	.03
☐ 446	Ben McDonald	.15	.06	.01
☐ 447	Dale Murphy	.12	.05	.01
☐ 448	Dave Righetti	.08	.03	.01
☐ 449	Dickie Thon	.05	.02	.00
☐ 450	Ted Power	.05	.02	.00
☐ 451	Scott Coolbaugh	.05	.02	.00
☐ 452	Dwight Smith	.08	.03	.01
☐ 453	Pete Incaviglia	.08	.03	.01
☐ 454	Andre Dawson	.15	.06	.01
☐ 455	Ruben Sierra	.20	.08	.02
☐ 456	Andres Galarraga	.08	.03	.01
☐ 457	Alvin Davis	.08	.03	.01
☐ 458	Tony Castillo	.05	.02	.00
☐ 459	Pete O'Brien	.05	.02	.00
☐ 460	Charlie Leibrandt	.05	.02	.00
☐ 461	Vince Coleman	.10	.04	.01
☐ 462	Steve Sax	.08	.03	.01
☐ 463	Omar Olivares	.15	.06	.01
☐ 464	Oscar Azocar	.08	.03	.01
☐ 465	Joe Magrane	.05	.02	.00
☐ 466	Karl Rhodes	.08	.03	.01
☐ 467	Benito Santiago	.08	.03	.01
☐ 468	Joe Klink	.10	.04	.01
☐ 469	Sil Campusano	.05	.02	.00
☐ 470	Mark Parent	.05	.02	.00
☐ 471	Shawn Boskie UER	.08	.03	.01
	(Depleted misspelled			
	as depleated)			
☐ 472	Kevin Brown	.05	.02	.00
☐ 473	Rick Sutcliffe	.08	.03	.01
☐ 474	Rafael Palmeiro	.15	.06	.01
☐ 475	Mike Harkey	.08	.03	.01
☐ 476	Jaime Navarro	.08	.03	.01
☐ 477	Marquis Grissom UER	.12	.05	.01
	(DeShields misspelled			
	as DeSheilds)			
☐ 478	Marty Clary	.05	.02	.00
☐ 479	Greg Briley	.05	.02	.00
☐ 480	Tom Glavine	.17	.07	.01
☐ 481	Lee Guetterman	.05	.02	.00
☐ 482	Rex Hudler	.05	.02	.00
☐ 483	Dave LaPoint	.05	.02	.00
☐ 484	Terry Pendleton	.12	.05	.01
☐ 485	Jesse Barfield	.08	.03	.01
☐ 486	Jose DeJesus	.05	.02	.00
☐ 487	Paul Abbott	.12	.05	.01
☐ 488	Ken Howell	.05	.02	.00
☐ 489	Greg W. Harris	.05	.02	.00
☐ 490	Roy Smith	.05	.02	.00
☐ 491	Paul Assenmacher	.05	.02	.00
☐ 492	Geno Petralli	.05	.02	.00
☐ 493	Steve Wilson	.05	.02	.00
☐ 494	Kevin Reimer	.17	.07	.01
☐ 495	Bill Long	.05	.02	.00
☐ 496	Mike Jackson	.05	.02	.00
☐ 497	Oddibe McDowell	.05	.02	.00
☐ 498	Bill Swift	.05	.02	.00
☐ 499	Jeff Treadway	.05	.02	.00
☐ 500	Checklist 401-500	.05	.01	.00
☐ 501	Gene Larkin	.05	.02	.00
☐ 502	Bob Boone	.08	.03	.01
☐ 503	Allan Anderson	.05	.02	.00
☐ 504	Luis Aquino	.05	.02	.00
☐ 505	Mark Guthrie	.05	.02	.00
☐ 506	Joe Orsulak	.05	.02	.00
☐ 507	Dana Kiecker	.08	.03	.01

#	Player			
☐ 508	Dave Gallagher	.05	.02	.00
☐ 509	Greg A. Harris	.05	.02	.00
☐ 510	Mark Williamson	.05	.02	.00
☐ 511	Casey Candaele	.05	.02	.00
☐ 512	Mookie Wilson	.05	.02	.00
☐ 513	Dave Smith	.05	.02	.00
☐ 514	Chuck Carr	.08	.03	.01
☐ 515	Glenn Wilson	.05	.02	.00
☐ 516	Mike Fitzgerald	.05	.02	.00
☐ 517	Devon White	.08	.03	.01
☐ 518	Dave Hollins	.10	.04	.01
☐ 519	Mark Eichhorn	.05	.02	.00
☐ 520	Otis Nixon	.08	.03	.01
☐ 521	Terry Shumpert	.05	.02	.00
☐ 522	Scott Erickson	3.00	1.25	.30
☐ 523	Danny Tartabull	.10	.04	.01
☐ 524	Orel Hershiser	.08	.03	.01
☐ 525	George Brett	.15	.06	.01
☐ 526	Greg Vaughn	.15	.06	.01
☐ 527	Tim Naehring	.12	.05	.01
☐ 528	Curt Schilling	.05	.02	.00
☐ 529	Chris Bosio	.05	.02	.00
☐ 530	Sam Horn	.05	.02	.00
☐ 531	Mike Scott	.08	.03	.01
☐ 532	George Bell	.10	.04	.01
☐ 533	Eric Anthony	.10	.04	.01
☐ 534	Julio Valera	.08	.03	.01
☐ 535	Glenn Davis	.08	.03	.01
☐ 536	Larry Walker UER	.10	.04	.01
	(Should have comma after Expos in text)			
☐ 537	Pat Combs	.05	.02	.00
☐ 538	Chris Nabholz	.10	.04	.01
☐ 539	Kirk McCaskill	.05	.02	.00
☐ 540	Randy Ready	.05	.02	.00
☐ 541	Mark Gubicza	.05	.02	.00
☐ 542	Rick Aguilera	.05	.02	.00
☐ 543	Brian McRae	1.00	.40	.10
☐ 544	Kirby Puckett	.20	.08	.02
☐ 545	Bo Jackson	.35	.15	.03
☐ 546	Wade Boggs	.20	.08	.02
☐ 547	Tim McIntosh	.10	.04	.01
☐ 548	Randy Milligan	.08	.03	.01
☐ 549	Dwight Evans	.08	.03	.01
☐ 550	Billy Ripken	.05	.02	.00
☐ 551	Erik Hanson	.08	.03	.01
☐ 552	Lance Parrish	.08	.03	.01
☐ 553	Tino Martinez	.25	.10	.02
☐ 554	Jim Abbott	.15	.06	.01
☐ 555	Ken Griffey Jr. UER	1.25	.50	.12
	(Second most votes for 1991 All-Star Game)			
☐ 556	Milt Cuyler	.35	.15	.03
☐ 557	Mark Leonard	.20	.08	.02
☐ 558	Jay Howell	.05	.02	.00
☐ 559	Lloyd Moseby	.05	.02	.00
☐ 560	Chris Gwynn	.05	.02	.00
☐ 561	Mark Whiten	.40	.16	.04
☐ 562	Harold Baines	.08	.03	.01
☐ 563	Junior Felix	.08	.03	.01
☐ 564	Darren Lewis	.45	.18	.04
☐ 565	Fred McGriff	.15	.06	.01
☐ 566	Kevin Appier	.08	.03	.01
☐ 567	Luis Gonzalez	1.00	.40	.10
☐ 568	Frank White	.05	.02	.00
☐ 569	Juan Agosto	.05	.02	.00
☐ 570	Mike Macfarlane	.05	.02	.00
☐ 571	Bert Blyleven	.08	.03	.01
☐ 572	Ken Griffey Sr.	.08	.03	.01
☐ 573	Lee Stevens	.25	.10	.02
☐ 574	Edgar Martinez	.08	.03	.01
☐ 575	Wally Joyner	.10	.04	.01
☐ 576	Tim Belcher	.08	.03	.01
☐ 577	John Burkett	.05	.02	.00
☐ 578	Mike Morgan	.05	.02	.00
☐ 579	Paul Gibson	.05	.02	.00
☐ 580	Jose Vizcaino	.05	.02	.00
☐ 581	Duane Ward	.05	.02	.00
☐ 582	Scott Sanderson	.05	.02	.00
☐ 583	David Wells	.05	.02	.00
☐ 584	Willie McGee	.08	.03	.01
☐ 585	John Cerutti	.05	.02	.00
☐ 586	Danny Darwin	.05	.02	.00
☐ 587	Kurt Stillwell	.05	.02	.00
☐ 588	Rich Gedman	.05	.02	.00
☐ 589	Mark Davis	.05	.02	.00
☐ 590	Bill Gullickson	.05	.02	.00
☐ 591	Matt Young	.05	.02	.00
☐ 592	Bryan Harvey	.08	.03	.01
☐ 593	Omar Vizquel	.05	.02	.00
☐ 594	Scott Lewis	.12	.05	.01
☐ 595	Dave Valle	.05	.02	.00
☐ 596	Tim Crews	.05	.02	.00
☐ 597	Mike Bielecki	.05	.02	.00
☐ 598	Mike Sharperson	.05	.02	.00
☐ 599	Dave Bergman	.05	.02	.00
☐ 600	Checklist 501-600	.05	.01	.00
☐ 601	Steve Lyons	.05	.02	.00
☐ 602	Bruce Hurst	.08	.03	.01
☐ 603	Donn Pall	.05	.02	.00
☐ 604	Jim Vatcher	.10	.04	.01
☐ 605	Dan Pasqua	.05	.02	.00
☐ 606	Kenny Rogers	.05	.02	.00
☐ 607	Jeff Schulz	.12	.05	.01
☐ 608	Brad Arnsberg	.05	.02	.00
☐ 609	Willie Wilson	.08	.03	.01
☐ 610	Jamie Moyer	.05	.02	.00
☐ 611	Ron Oester	.05	.02	.00
☐ 612	Dennis Cook	.05	.02	.00
☐ 613	Rick Mahler	.05	.02	.00
☐ 614	Bill Landrum	.05	.02	.00
☐ 615	Scott Scudder	.08	.03	.01
☐ 616	Tom Edens	.12	.05	.01
☐ 617	1917 Revisited	.10	.04	.01
	(White Sox in vintage uniforms)			
☐ 618	Jim Gantner	.05	.02	.00
☐ 619	Darrel Akerfelds	.05	.02	.00
☐ 620	Ron Robinson	.05	.02	.00
☐ 621	Scott Radinsky	.08	.03	.01
☐ 622	Pete Smith	.05	.02	.00
☐ 623	Melido Perez	.05	.02	.00
☐ 624	Jerald Clark	.05	.02	.00
☐ 625	Carlos Martinez	.05	.02	.00
☐ 626	Wes Chamberlain	1.00	.40	.10
☐ 627	Bobby Witt	.05	.02	.00
☐ 628	Ken Dayley	.05	.02	.00
☐ 629	John Barfield	.10	.04	.01
☐ 630	Bob Tewksbury	.05	.02	.00
☐ 631	Glenn Braggs	.05	.02	.00
☐ 632	Jim Neidlinger	.12	.05	.01
☐ 633	Tom Browning	.08	.03	.01
☐ 634	Kirk Gibson	.08	.03	.01
☐ 635	Rob Dibble	.08	.03	.01
☐ 636A	Stolen Base Leaders	.25	.10	.02
	(Rickey Henderson and Lou Brock in tuxedos and no date on card)			
☐ 636B	Stolen Base Leaders	.50	.20	.05
	(Dated May 1, 1991 on card front)			
☐ 637	Jeff Montgomery	.05	.02	.00
☐ 638	Mike Schooler	.05	.02	.00
☐ 639	Storm Davis	.05	.02	.00
☐ 640	Rich Rodriguez	.12	.05	.01
☐ 641	Phil Bradley	.05	.02	.00
☐ 642	Kent Mercker	.10	.04	.01
☐ 643	Carlton Fisk	.15	.06	.01
☐ 644	Mike Bell	.12	.05	.01
☐ 645	Alex Fernandez	.40	.16	.04
☐ 646	Juan Gonzalez	.90	.40	.09
☐ 647	Ken Hill	.05	.02	.00
☐ 648	Jeff Russell	.05	.02	.00
☐ 649	Chuck Malone	.08	.03	.01
☐ 650	Steve Buechele	.05	.02	.00
☐ 651	Mike Benjamin	.05	.02	.00
☐ 652	Tony Pena	.08	.03	.01
☐ 653	Trevor Wilson	.05	.02	.00
☐ 654	Alex Cole	.10	.04	.01
☐ 655	Roger Clemens	.30	.12	.03
☐ 656	The Bashing Years	.12	.05	.01
	(Mark McGwire)			
☐ 657	Joe Grahe	.10	.04	.01
☐ 658	Jim Eisenreich	.05	.02	.00
☐ 659	Dan Gladden	.05	.02	.00
☐ 660	Steve Farr	.05	.02	.00
☐ 661	Bill Sampen	.05	.02	.00
☐ 662	Dave Rohde	.08	.03	.01
☐ 663	Mark Gardner	.05	.02	.00
☐ 664	Mike Simms	.30	.12	.03
☐ 665	Moises Alou	.10	.04	.01
☐ 666	Mickey Hatcher	.05	.02	.00
☐ 667	Jimmy Key	.08	.03	.01
☐ 668	John Wetteland	.08	.03	.01
☐ 669	John Smiley	.08	.03	.01
☐ 670	Jim Acker	.05	.02	.00
☐ 671	Pascual Perez	.05	.02	.00
☐ 672	Reggie Harris UER	.15	.06	.01
	(Opportunity misspelled as oppurtnty)			
☐ 673	Matt Nokes	.08	.03	.01
☐ 674	Rafael Novoa	.12	.05	.01
☐ 675	Hensley Meulens	.10	.04	.01
☐ 676	Jeff M. Robinson	.05	.02	.00
☐ 677	Ground Breaking	.15	.06	.01
	(new Comiskey Park; Carlton Fisk and Robin Ventura)			
☐ 678	Johnny Ray	.05	.02	.00
☐ 679	Greg Hibbard	.05	.02	.00

		MINT	EXC	G-VG
☐ 680	Paul Sorrento	.05	.02	.00
☐ 681	Mike Marshall	.08	.03	.01
☐ 682	Jim Clancy	.05	.02	.00
☐ 683	Rob Murphy	.05	.02	.00
☐ 684	Dave Schmidt	.05	.02	.00
☐ 685	Jeff Gray	.10	.04	.01
☐ 686	Mike Hartley	.10	.04	.01
☐ 687	Jeff King	.08	.03	.01
☐ 688	Stan Javier	.05	.02	.00
☐ 689	Bob Walk	.05	.02	.00
☐ 690	Jim Gott	.05	.02	.00
☐ 691	Mike LaCoss	.05	.02	.00
☐ 692	John Farrell	.05	.02	.00
☐ 693	Tim Leary	.08	.03	.01
☐ 694	Mike Walker	.05	.02	.00
☐ 695	Eric Plunk	.05	.02	.00
☐ 696	Mike Fetters	.05	.02	.00
☐ 697	Wayne Edwards	.05	.02	.00
☐ 698	Tim Drummond	.10	.04	.01
☐ 699	Willie Fraser	.05	.02	.00
☐ 700	Checklist 601-700	.10	.04	.01
☐ SP1	Michael Jordan SP	11.00	5.00	1.35
	(Shown batting in White Sox uniform)			

☐ xx	Baseball Heroes	1.25	.50	.12
	(header card)			
☐ xx	Nolan Ryan	500.00	225.00	75.00
	(Signed and Numbered out of 2500)			

1991 Upper Deck HOF Heroes

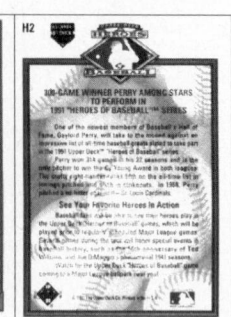

These standard-size (2 1/2" by 3 1/2") cards were (random) insert cards in Upper Deck Baseball Heroes wax packs. On a white card face, the fronts of the first three cards have sepia-toned player photos, with red, gold, and blue border stripes. The player's name appears in a gold border stripe beneath the picture, with the Upper Deck "Heroes of Baseball" logo in the lower right corner. The backs have a similar design to the fronts, except with a career summary and an advertisement for Upper Deck "Heroes of Baseball" games that will be played prior to regularly scheduled Major League games. The fourth card features a color portrait of the three players by noted sports artist Vernon Wells. The cards are numbered on the back.

		MINT	EXC	G-VG
	COMPLETE SET (4)	70.00	32.00	10.50
	COMMON PLAYER (1-4)	18.00	7.50	2.50
☐ H1	Harmon Killebrew	18.00	7.50	2.50
☐ H2	Gaylord Perry	18.00	7.50	2.50
☐ H3	Ferguson Jenkins	18.00	7.50	2.50
☐ H4	Header	18.00	7.50	2.50
	(Drawing of all three players)			
☐ xx	Harmon Killebrew	200.00	90.00	30.00
	(Signed and Numbered out of 2500)			
☐ xx	Gaylord Perry	200.00	90.00	30.00
	(Signed and Numbered out of 2500)			
☐ xx	Ferguson Jenkins	200.00	90.00	30.00
	(Signed and Numbered out of 2500)			

1991 Upper Deck Nolan Ryan Heroes

This nine-card standard size, 2 1/2" by 3 1/2", set was included in first series 1991 Upper Deck packs. The set which honors Nolan Ryan and is numbered as a continuation of the Baseball Heroes set which began with Reggie Jackson in 1990. This set honors Ryan's long career and his place in Baseball History. Card number 18 features the artwork of Vernon Wells while the other cards are photos. The complete set price below does not include the signed Ryan card of which only 2500 were made. These Ryan cards were apparently issued on 100-card sheets with the following configuration: ten each of the nine Ryan Baseball Heroes cards, five Michael Jordan cards and five Baseball Heroes header cards. The Baseball Heroes header card is a standard size card which explains the continuation of the Baseball Heroes series on the back while the front just says Baseball Heroes.

		MINT	EXC	G-VG
	COMPLETE SET (10)	6.50	2.75	.65
	COMMON PLAYER (10-18)	.65	.25	.06
☐ 10	1968 Victory 1	.65	.25	.06
☐ 11	1973 A Career Year	.65	.25	.06
☐ 12	1975 Double Milestone	.65	.25	.06
☐ 13	1979 Back Home	.65	.25	.06
☐ 14	1981 All Time Leader	.65	.25	.06
☐ 15	1989 5,000 K's	.65	.25	.06
☐ 16	1990 6th No-Hitter	.65	.25	.06
☐ 17	1990 And Still Counting	.65	.25	.06
☐ 18	Checklist Card	.65	.25	.06
	(Vernon Wells drawing with 5 poses of Ryan including each team he played for)			

1991 Upper Deck Silver Sluggers

The Upper Deck Silver Slugger set features nine players from each league, representing the nine batting positions on the team. The cards measure the standard size (2 1/2" by 3 1/2"). The fronts have glossy color action player photos, with white borders on three sides and a "Silver Slugger" bat serving as the border on the left side. The player's name appears in a tan stripe below the picture, with the team logo superimposed at the lower right corner. Two-thirds of the back are occupied by another color action photo, with career highlights in a horizontally oriented rectangle to the left of the picture. The cards are numbered on the back.

	MINT	EXC	G-VG
COMPLETE SET (18)	45.00	20.00	6.75
COMMON PLAYER (SS1-SS18)	1.50	.60	.15
☐ SS1 Julio Franco	2.25	.90	.22
☐ SS2 Alan Trammell	2.00	.80	.20
☐ SS3 Rickey Henderson	5.50	2.50	.55
☐ SS4 Jose Canseco	8.00	3.50	.80
☐ SS5 Barry Bonds	4.00	1.75	.40
☐ SS6 Eddie Murray	2.50	1.00	.25
☐ SS7 Kelly Gruber	1.75	.70	.17
☐ SS8 Ryne Sandberg	6.00	2.50	.60
☐ SS9 Darryl Strawberry	5.00	2.25	.50
☐ SS10 Ellis Burks	1.75	.70	.17
☐ SS11 Lance Parrish	1.50	.60	.15
☐ SS12 Cecil Fielder	5.00	2.25	.50
☐ SS13 Matt Williams	2.50	1.00	.25
☐ SS14 Dave Parker	1.75	.70	.17
☐ SS15 Bobby Bonilla	4.00	1.75	.40
☐ SS16 Don Robinson	1.50	.60	.15
☐ SS17 Benito Santiago	1.75	.70	.17
☐ SS18 Barry Larkin	2.25	.90	.22

1991 Upper Deck Extended

This 100-card standard size (2 1/2" by 3 1/2") series was issued by Upper Deck several months after the release of their major series. The set features rookie players as well as players who switched teams between seasons. In the extended wax packs were low number cards, special cards featuring Hank Aaron as the next featured player in their baseball heroes series, and a special card honoring the May 1st exploits of Rickey Henderson and Nolan Ryan. For the first time in Upper Deck's three year history, they did not issue a factory Extended set. The key rookie card in this set is Jeff Bagwell.

	MINT	EXC	G-VG
COMPLETE SET (100)	10.00	4.50	1.25
COMMON PLAYER (701-800)	.05	.02	.00
☐ 701 Mike Heath	.05	.02	.00
☐ 702 Rookie Threats	1.00	.40	.10
Luis Gonzalez			
Karl Rhodes			
Jeff Bagwell			
☐ 703 Jose Mesa	.05	.02	.00
☐ 704 Dave Smith	.05	.02	.00
☐ 705 Danny Darwin	.05	.02	.00
☐ 706 Rafael Belliard	.05	.02	.00
☐ 707 Rob Murphy	.05	.02	.00
☐ 708 Terry Pendleton	.15	.06	.01
☐ 709 Mike Pagliarulo	.05	.02	.00
☐ 710 Sid Bream	.05	.02	.00
☐ 711 Junior Felix	.08	.03	.01
☐ 712 Dante Bichette	.05	.02	.00
☐ 713 Kevin Gross	.05	.02	.00
☐ 714 Luis Sojo	.08	.03	.01
☐ 715 Bob Ojeda	.05	.02	.00
☐ 716 Julio Machado	.05	.02	.00
☐ 717 Steve Farr	.05	.02	.00
☐ 718 Franklin Stubbs	.05	.02	.00
☐ 719 Mike Boddicker	.05	.02	.00
☐ 720 Willie Randolph	.05	.02	.00
☐ 721 Willie McGee	.08	.03	.01
☐ 722 Chili Davis	.08	.03	.01
☐ 723 Danny Jackson	.05	.02	.00
☐ 724 Cory Snyder	.08	.03	.01
☐ 725 MVP Lineup	.30	.12	.03
Andre Dawson			
George Bell			
Ryne Sandberg			
☐ 726 Rob Deer	.08	.03	.01
☐ 727 Rich DeLucia	.17	.07	.01
☐ 728 Mike Perez	.12	.05	.01
☐ 729 Mickey Tettleton	.08	.03	.01
☐ 730 Mike Blowers	.05	.02	.00
☐ 731 Gary Gaetti	.08	.03	.01
☐ 732 Brett Butler	.08	.03	.01
☐ 733 Dave Parker	.10	.04	.01
☐ 734 Eddie Zosky	.25	.10	.02
☐ 735 Jack Clark	.08	.03	.01
☐ 736 Jack Morris	.10	.04	.01
☐ 737 Kirk Gibson	.10	.04	.01
☐ 738 Steve Bedrosian	.05	.02	.00
☐ 739 Candy Maldonado	.05	.02	.00
☐ 740 Matt Young	.05	.02	.00
☐ 741 Rich Garces	.12	.05	.01
☐ 742 George Bell	.10	.04	.01
☐ 743 Deion Sanders	.17	.07	.01
☐ 744 Bo Jackson	1.50	.60	.15
☐ 745 Luis Mercedes	.45	.18	.04
☐ 746 Reggie Jefferson UER	.75	.30	.07
(Throwing left on card;			
back has throws right)			
☐ 747 Pete Incaviglia	.08	.03	.01
☐ 748 Chris Hammond	.12	.05	.01
☐ 749 Mike Stanton	.05	.02	.00
☐ 750 Scott Sanderson	.05	.02	.00
☐ 751 Paul Faries	.10	.04	.01
☐ 752 Al Osuna	.17	.07	.01
☐ 753 Steve Chitren	.12	.05	.01
☐ 754 Tony Fernandez	.08	.03	.01
☐ 755 Jeff Bagwell UER	4.00	1.75	.40
(Strikeout and walk			
totals reversed)			
☐ 756 Kirk Dressendorfer	.35	.15	.03
☐ 757 Glenn Davis	.08	.03	.01
☐ 758 Gary Carter	.08	.03	.01
☐ 759 Zane Smith	.05	.02	.00
☐ 760 Vance Law	.05	.02	.00
☐ 761 Denis Boucher	.20	.08	.02
☐ 762 Turner Ward	.25	.10	.02
☐ 763 Roberto Alomar	.17	.07	.01
☐ 764 Albert Belle	.35	.15	.03
☐ 765 Joe Carter	.12	.05	.01
☐ 766 Pete Schourek	.20	.08	.02
☐ 767 Heathcliff Slocumb	.12	.05	.01
☐ 768 Vince Coleman	.10	.04	.01
☐ 769 Mitch Williams	.05	.02	.00
☐ 770 Brian Downing	.05	.02	.00
☐ 771 Dana Allison	.17	.07	.01
☐ 772 Pete Harnisch	.05	.02	.00
☐ 773 Tim Raines	.08	.03	.01
☐ 774 Darryl Kile	.17	.07	.01
☐ 775 Fred McGriff	.12	.05	.01
☐ 776 Dwight Evans	.08	.03	.01
☐ 777 Joe Slusarski	.15	.06	.01
☐ 778 Dave Righetti	.08	.03	.01
☐ 779 Jeff Hamilton	.05	.02	.00
☐ 780 Ernest Riles	.05	.02	.00
☐ 781 Ken Dayley	.05	.02	.00
☐ 782 Eric King	.05	.02	.00
☐ 783 Devon White	.08	.03	.01
☐ 784 Beau Allred	.12	.05	.01
☐ 785 Mike Timlin	.17	.07	.01
☐ 786 Ivan Calderon	.08	.03	.01
☐ 787 Hubie Brooks	.08	.03	.01
☐ 788 Juan Agosto	.05	.02	.00
☐ 789 Barry Jones	.05	.02	.00
☐ 790 Wally Backman	.05	.02	.00
☐ 791 Jim Presley	.05	.02	.00
☐ 792 Charlie Hough	.05	.02	.00
☐ 793 Larry Andersen	.05	.02	.00
☐ 794 Steve Finley	.08	.03	.01
☐ 795 Shawn Abner	.05	.02	.00
☐ 796 Jeff M. Robinson	.05	.02	.00
☐ 797 Joe Bitker	.05	.02	.00
☐ 798 Eric Show	.05	.02	.00
☐ 799 Bud Black	.05	.02	.00
☐ 800 Checklist 701-800	.05	.01	.00
☐ H1 Hank Aaron Hologram	9.00	4.00	.90
☐ SP2 Henderson/Ryan	9.00	4.00	.90
(Rickey and Nolan)			

1991 Upper Deck Hank Aaron Heroes

These standard-size (2 1/2" by 3 1/2") cards were issued in honor of Hall of Famer Hank Aaron and inserted in Upper Deck high number wax packs. The fronts have color player photos superimposed over a circular shot. Inside a red border stripe, a tan background fills in the rest of the card face. The Baseball Heroes logo adorns the card face. The backs have a similar design, except with an extended caption presented on a light gray background. Aaron autographed 2,500 of card number 27, which featured his portrait by noted sports artist Vernon Wells. The cards are numbered on the back in continuation of the Baseball Heroes set.

		MINT	EXC	G-VG
COMPLETE SET (10)		6.00	2.50	.60
COMMON PLAYER (19-27)		.65	.25	.06
☐ 19	1954: Rookie Year	.65	.25	.06
☐ 20	1957: MVP	.65	.25	.06
☐ 21	1966: Move to Atlanta	.65	.25	.06
☐ 22	1970: 3,000	.65	.25	.06
☐ 23	1974: 715	.65	.25	.06
☐ 24	1975: Return to	.65	.25	.06
	Milwaukee			
☐ 25	1976: 755	.65	.25	.06
☐ 26	1982: Hall of Fame	.65	.25	.06
☐ 27	Checklist 19-27	.65	.25	.06
☐ xx	Title/Header card SP	1.25	.50	.12
☐ xx	Hank Aaron	400.00	180.00	60.00
	(Signed and Numbered			
	out of 2500)			

1991 Upper Deck Final Edition

The 1991 Upper Deck Final Edition boxed set contains 100 cards and showcases players who made major contributions during their team's late-season pennant drive. In addition to the late season traded and impact rookie cards (22-78), the set

includes two special subsets: Diamond Skills cards (1-21), depicting the best Minor League prospects, and All-Star cards (80-99). Six assorted hologram cards were issued with each set. The cards measure the standard size (2 1/2" by 3 1/2"). The fronts feature posed or action color player photos on a white card face, with the upper left corner of the picture cut out to provide space for the Upper Deck logo. The pictures are bordered in green on the left, with the player's name in a tan border below the picture. Two-thirds of the back are occupied by another color action photo, with biography, statistics, and career highlights in a horizontally oriented red rectangle to the left of the picture. The cards are numbered on the back. Among the outstanding rookie cards in this set are Ryan Klesko, Marc Newfield, Frankie Rodriguez, and Ivan Rodriguez.

		MINT	EXC	G-VG
COMPLETE SET (100)		16.00	6.75	2.25
COMMON PLAYER (1-100)		.05	.02	.00
☐ 1F	Diamond Skills	.75	.30	.07
	Checklist Card			
	(Ryan Klesko and			
	Reggie Sanders)			
☐ 2F	Pedro Martinez	1.75	.70	.17
☐ 3F	Lance Dickson	.15	.06	.01
☐ 4F	Royce Clayton	.35	.15	.03
☐ 5F	Scott Bryant	.17	.07	.01
☐ 6F	Dan Wilson	.25	.10	.02
☐ 7F	Dmitri Young	1.50	.60	.15
☐ 8F	Ryan Klesko	4.00	1.75	.40
☐ 9F	Tom Goodwin	.25	.10	.02
☐ 10F	Rondell White	.90	.40	.09
☐ 11F	Reggie Sanders	.35	.15	.03
☐ 12F	Todd Van Poppel	.75	.30	.07
☐ 13F	Arthur Rhodes	.45	.18	.04
☐ 14F	Eddie Zosky	.17	.07	.01
☐ 15F	Gerald Williams	.60	.25	.06
☐ 16F	Robert Eenhoorn	.20	.08	.02
☐ 17F	Jim Thome	1.50	.60	.15
☐ 18F	Marc Newfield	2.00	.80	.20
☐ 19F	Kerwin Moore	.40	.16	.04
☐ 20F	Jeff McNeely	.90	.40	.09
☐ 21F	Frankie Rodriguez	2.50	1.00	.25
☐ 22F	Andy Mota	.25	.10	.02
☐ 23F	Chris Haney	.25	.10	.02
☐ 24F	Kenny Lofton	.50	.20	.05
☐ 25F	Dave Nilsson	.75	.30	.07
☐ 26F	Derek Bell	1.25	.50	.12
☐ 27F	Frank Castillo	.20	.08	.02
☐ 28F	Candy Maldonado	.05	.02	.00
☐ 29F	Chuck McElroy	.05	.02	.00
☐ 30F	Chito Martinez	1.00	.40	.10
☐ 31F	Steve Howe	.05	.02	.00
☐ 32F	Freddie Benavides	.15	.06	.01
☐ 33F	Scott Kamieniecki	.20	.08	.02
☐ 34F	Denny Neagle	.60	.25	.06
☐ 35F	Mike Humphreys	.25	.10	.02
☐ 36F	Mike Remlinger	.20	.08	.02
☐ 37F	Scott Coolbaugh	.05	.02	.00
☐ 38F	Darren Lewis	.25	.10	.02
☐ 39F	Thomas Howard	.08	.03	.01
☐ 40F	John Candelaria	.05	.02	.00
☐ 41F	Todd Benzinger	.05	.02	.00
☐ 42F	Wilson Alvarez	.12	.05	.01
☐ 43F	Patrick Lennon	.50	.20	.05
☐ 44F	Rusty Meacham	.20	.08	.02
☐ 45F	Ryan Bowen	.30	.12	.03
☐ 46F	Rick Wilkins	.30	.12	.03
☐ 47F	Ed Sprague	.20	.08	.02
☐ 48F	Bob Scanlan	.15	.06	.01
☐ 49F	Tom Candiotti	.08	.03	.01
☐ 50F	Perfecto	.08	.03	.01
	Dennis Martinez			
☐ 51F	Oil Can Boyd	.05	.02	.00
☐ 52F	Glenallen Hill	.08	.03	.01
☐ 53F	Scott Livingstone	.40	.16	.04
☐ 54F	Brian Hunter	1.50	.60	.15
☐ 55F	Ivan Rodriguez	3.50	1.50	.35
☐ 56F	Keith Mitchell	.75	.30	.07
☐ 57F	Roger McDowell	.05	.02	.00
☐ 58F	Otis Nixon	.08	.03	.01
☐ 59F	Juan Bell	.08	.03	.01
☐ 60F	Bill Krueger	.05	.02	.00
☐ 61F	Chris Donnels	.35	.15	.03
☐ 62F	Tommy Greene	.10	.04	.01
☐ 63F	Doug Simons	.17	.07	.01
☐ 64F	Andy Ashby	.17	.07	.01
☐ 65F	Anthony Young	.35	.15	.03
☐ 66F	Kevin Morton	.25	.10	.02
☐ 67F	Bret Barberie	.45	.18	.04

			MINT	EXC	G-VG
☐ 68F	Scott Servais		.15	.06	.01
☐ 69F	Ron Darling		.08	.03	.01
☐ 70F	Tim Burke		.05	.02	.00
☐ 71F	Vicente Palacios		.05	.02	.00
☐ 72F	Gerald Alexander		.15	.06	.01
☐ 73F	Reggie Jefferson		.30	.12	.03
☐ 74F	Dean Palmer		.50	.20	.05
☐ 75F	Mark Whiten		.20	.08	.02
☐ 76F	Randy Tomlin		.30	.12	.03
☐ 77F	Mark Wohlers		.75	.30	.07
☐ 78F	Brook Jacoby		.05	.02	.00
☐ 79F	All-Star Checklist (Ken Griffey Jr. and Ryne Sandberg)		.75	.30	.07
☐ 80F	Jack Morris AS		.10	.04	.01
☐ 81F	Sandy Alomar Jr. AS		.08	.03	.01
☐ 82F	Cecil Fielder AS		.17	.07	.01
☐ 83F	Roberto Alomar AS		.12	.05	.01
☐ 84F	Wade Boggs AS		.15	.06	.01
☐ 85F	Cal Ripken AS		.35	.15	.03
☐ 86F	Rickey Henderson AS		.25	.10	.02
☐ 87F	Ken Griffey Jr. AS		.60	.25	.06
☐ 88F	Dave Henderson AS		.08	.03	.01
☐ 89F	Danny Tartabull AS		.08	.03	.01
☐ 90F	Tom Glavine AS		.08	.03	.01
☐ 91F	Benito Santiago AS		.08	.03	.01
☐ 92F	Will Clark AS		.25	.10	.02
☐ 93F	Ryne Sandberg AS		.25	.10	.02
☐ 94F	Chris Sabo AS		.08	.03	.01
☐ 95F	Ozzie Smith AS		.10	.04	.01
☐ 96F	Ivan Calderon AS		.08	.03	.01
☐ 97F	Tony Gwynn AS		.12	.05	.01
☐ 98F	Andre Dawson AS		.10	.04	.01
☐ 99F	Bobby Bonilla AS		.10	.04	.01
☐ 100F	Checklist 1-100		.05	.01	.00

1992 Upper Deck

The 1992 Upper Deck set contains 700 standard-size (2 1/2" by 3 1/2") cards. Special subsets included in the set are Star Rookies (1-27; SR), Team Checklists (29-40, 86-99; TC), with player portraits by Vernon Wells; Top Prospects (52-77; TP); Bloodlines (79-85), and Diamond Skills (640-650; DS). Moreover, a nine-card Baseball Heroes subset (randomly inserted in packs) focuses on the career of Ted Williams. He autographed and numbered 2,500 cards, which were randomly inserted in low series foil packs. The cards are numbered on the back.

	MINT	EXC	G-VG
COMPLETE SET (700)	36.00	16.25	5.50
COMMON PLAYER (1-700)	.04	.02	.00

			MINT	EXC	G-VG
☐ 1	Star Rookie Checklist Ryan Klesko Jim Thome		.40	.10	.02
☐ 2	Royce Clayton SR		.15	.06	.01
☐ 3	Brian Jordan SR		.25	.10	.02
☐ 4	Dave Fleming SR		.10	.04	.01
☐ 5	Jim Thome SR		.30	.12	.03
☐ 6	Jeff Juden SR		.15	.06	.01
☐ 7	Roberto Hernandez SR		.10	.04	.01
☐ 8	Kyle Abbott SR		.15	.06	.01
☐ 9	Chris George SR		.10	.04	.01
☐ 10	Rob Maurer SR		.25	.10	.02
☐ 11	Donald Harris SR		.10	.04	.01
☐ 12	Ted Wood SR		.20	.08	.02
☐ 13	Patrick Lennon SR		.20	.08	.02
☐ 14	Willie Banks SR		.10	.04	.01
☐ 15	Roger Salkeld SR		.30	.12	.03
☐ 16	Wilfredo Cordero SR		.15	.06	.01
☐ 17	Arthur Rhodes SR		.20	.08	.02
☐ 18	Pedro Martinez SR		.50	.20	.05
☐ 19	Andy Ashby SR		.12	.05	.01
☐ 20	Tom Goodwin SR		.12	.05	.01
☐ 21	Braulio Castillo SR		.35	.15	.03
☐ 22	Todd Van Poppel SR		.50	.20	.05
☐ 23	Brian Williams SR		.20	.08	.02
☐ 24	Ryan Klesko SR		1.25	.50	.12
☐ 25	Kenny Lofton SR		.25	.10	.02
☐ 26	Derek Bell SR		.25	.10	.02
☐ 27	Reggie Sanders SR		.20	.08	.02
☐ 28	Dave Winfield's 400th		.10	.04	.01
☐ 29	Atlanta TC Dave Justice		.20	.08	.02
☐ 30	Cincinnati TC Rob Dibble		.07	.03	.01
☐ 31	Houston TC Craig Biggio		.07	.03	.01
☐ 32	Los Angeles TC Eddie Murray		.10	.04	.01
☐ 33	San Diego TC Fred McGriff		.10	.04	.01
☐ 34	San Francisco TC Willie McGee		.07	.03	.01
☐ 35	Chicago TC Shawon Dunston		.07	.03	.01
☐ 36	Montreal TC Delino DeShields		.07	.03	.01
☐ 37	New York TC Howard Johnson		.07	.03	.01
☐ 38	Philadelphia TC John Kruk		.07	.03	.01
☐ 39	Pittsburgh TC Doug Drabek		.07	.03	.01
☐ 40	St. Louis TC Todd Zeile		.10	.04	.01
☐ 41	Playoff Perfection Steve Avery		.15	.06	.01
☐ 42	Jeremy Hernandez		.17	.07	.01
☐ 43	Doug Henry		.17	.07	.01
☐ 44	Chris Donnels		.15	.06	.01
☐ 45	Mo Sanford		.10	.04	.01
☐ 46	Scott Kamieniecki		.10	.04	.01
☐ 47	Mark Lemke		.04	.02	.00
☐ 48	Steve Farr		.04	.02	.00
☐ 49	Francisco Oliveras		.04	.02	.00
☐ 50	Ced Landrum		.10	.04	.01
☐ 51	Top Prospect Checklist Rondell White Craig Griffey		.20	.08	.02
☐ 52	Eduardo Perez TP		.50	.20	.05
☐ 53	Tom Nevers TP		.12	.05	.01
☐ 54	David Zancanaro TP		.20	.08	.02
☐ 55	Shawn Green TP		.25	.10	.02
☐ 56	Mark Wohlers TP		.20	.08	.02
☐ 57	Dave Nilsson TP		.40	.16	.04
☐ 58	Dmitri Young TP		.40	.16	.04
☐ 59	Ryan Hawblitzel TP		.20	.08	.02
☐ 60	Raul Mondesi TP		.25	.10	.02
☐ 61	Rondell White TP		.25	.10	.02
☐ 62	Steve Hosey TP		.10	.04	.01
☐ 63	Manny Ramirez TP		.50	.20	.05
☐ 64	Marc Newfield TP		.50	.20	.05
☐ 65	Jeromy Burnitz TP		.40	.16	.04
☐ 66	Mark Smith TP		.15	.06	.01
☐ 67	Joey Hamilton TP		.20	.08	.02
☐ 68	Tyler Green TP		.50	.20	.05
☐ 69	Jon Farrell TP		.20	.08	.02
☐ 70	Kurt Miller TP		.12	.05	.01
☐ 71	Jeff Plympton TP		.15	.06	.01
☐ 72	Dan Wilson TP		.10	.04	.01
☐ 73	Joe Vitiello TP		.50	.20	.05
☐ 74	Rico Brogna TP		.12	.05	.01
☐ 75	David McCarty TP		.75	.30	.07
☐ 76	Bob Wickman TP		.10	.04	.01
☐ 77	Carlos Rodriguez TP		.10	.04	.01
☐ 78	Stay In School Jim Abbott		.10	.04	.01
☐ 79	Ramon Martinez Pedro Martinez		.15	.06	.01
☐ 80	Kevin Mitchell Keith Mitchell		.18	.08	.01
☐ 81	Sandy Alomar Jr. Roberto Alomar		.12	.05	.01
☐ 82	Cal Ripken Billy Ripken		.12	.05	.01
☐ 83	Tony Gwynn Chris Gwynn		.12	.05	.01

#	Player			
84	Dwight Gooden	.12	.05	.01
	Gary Sheffield			
85	Ken Griffey Sr.	.50	.20	.05
	Ken Griffey Jr.			
	Craig Griffey			
86	California TC	.10	.04	.01
	Jim Abbott			
87	Chicago TC	.35	.15	.03
	Frank Thomas			
88	Kansas City TC	.07	.03	.01
	Danny Tartabull			
89	Minnesota TC	.15	.06	.01
	Scott Erickson			
90	Oakland TC	.15	.06	.01
	Rickey Henderson			
91	Seattle TC	.07	.03	.01
	Edgar Martinez			
92	Texas TC	.30	.12	.03
	Nolan Ryan			
93	Baltimore TC	.10	.04	.01
	Ben McDonald			
94	Boston TC	.10	.04	.01
	Ellis Burks			
95	Cleveland TC	.07	.03	.01
	Greg Swindell			
96	Detroit TC	.12	.05	.01
	Cecil Fielder			
97	Milwaukee TC	.10	.04	.01
	Greg Vaughn			
98	New York TC	.12	.05	.01
	Kevin Maas			
99	Toronto Checklist	.07	.03	.01
	Dave Stieb			
100	Checklist 1-100	.07	.03	.01
101	Joe Oliver	.04	.02	.00
102	Hector Villanueva	.04	.02	.00
103	Ed Whitson	.04	.02	.00
104	Danny Jackson	.04	.02	.00
105	Chris Hammond	.07	.03	.01
106	Ricky Jordan	.07	.03	.01
107	Kevin Bass	.04	.02	.00
108	Darrin Fletcher	.04	.02	.00
109	Junior Ortiz	.04	.02	.00
110	Tom Bolton	.04	.02	.00
111	Jeff King	.04	.02	.00
112	Dave Magadan	.07	.03	.01
113	Mike LaValliere	.04	.02	.00
114	Hubie Brooks	.07	.03	.01
115	Jay Bell	.04	.02	.00
116	David Wells	.04	.02	.00
117	Jim Leyritz	.04	.02	.00
118	Manuel Lee	.04	.02	.00
119	Alvaro Espinoza	.04	.02	.00
120	B.J. Surhoff	.04	.02	.00
121	Hal Morris	.12	.05	.01
122	Shawon Dawson	.07	.03	.01
123	Chris Sabo	.07	.03	.01
124	Andre Dawson	.15	.06	.01
125	Eric Davis	.15	.06	.01
126	Chili Davis	.07	.03	.01
127	Dale Murphy	.12	.05	.01
128	Kirk McCaskill	.04	.02	.00
129	Terry Mulholland	.04	.02	.00
130	Rick Aguilera	.04	.02	.00
131	Vince Coleman	.10	.04	.01
132	Andy Van Slyke	.07	.03	.01
133	Gregg Jefferies	.10	.04	.01
134	Barry Bonds	.18	.08	.01
135	Dwight Gooden	.12	.05	.01
136	Dave Stieb	.07	.03	.01
137	Albert Belle	.15	.06	.01
138	Teddy Higuera	.04	.02	.00
139	Jesse Barfield	.07	.03	.01
140	Pat Borders	.04	.02	.00
141	Bip Roberts	.04	.02	.00
142	Rob Dibble	.07	.03	.01
143	Mark Grace	.10	.04	.01
144	Barry Larkin	.12	.05	.01
145	Ryne Sandberg	.25	.10	.02
146	Scott Erickson	.17	.07	.01
147	Luis Polonia	.07	.03	.01
148	John Burkett	.04	.02	.00
149	Luis Sojo	.04	.02	.00
150	Dickie Thon	.04	.02	.00
151	Walt Weiss	.07	.03	.01
152	Mike Scioscia	.04	.02	.00
153	Mark McGwire	.12	.05	.01
154	Matt Williams	.12	.05	.01
155	Rickey Henderson	.30	.12	.03
156	Sandy Alomar Jr.	.10	.04	.01
157	Brian McRae	.18	.08	.01
158	Harold Baines	.07	.03	.01
159	Kevin Appier	.04	.02	.00
160	Felix Fermin	.04	.02	.00
161	Leo Gomez	.12	.05	.01
162	Craig Biggio	.10	.04	.01
163	Ben McDonald	.12	.05	.01
164	Randy Johnson	.07	.03	.01
165	Cal Ripken	.30	.12	.03
166	Frank Thomas	.75	.30	.07
167	Delino DeShields	.10	.04	.01
168	Greg Gagne	.04	.02	.00
169	Ron Karkovice	.04	.02	.00
170	Charlie Leibrandt	.04	.02	.00
171	Dave Righetti	.07	.03	.01
172	Dave Henderson	.07	.03	.01
173	Steve Decker	.12	.05	.01
174	Darryl Strawberry	.25	.10	.02
175	Will Clark	.30	.12	.03
176	Ruben Sierra	.20	.08	.02
177	Ozzie Smith	.12	.05	.01
178	Charles Nagy	.04	.02	.00
179	Gary Pettis	.04	.02	.00
180	Kirk Gibson	.07	.03	.01
181	Randy Milligan	.04	.02	.00
182	Dave Valle	.04	.02	.00
183	Chris Hoiles	.07	.03	.01
184	Tony Phillips	.04	.02	.00
185	Brady Anderson	.04	.02	.00
186	Scott Fletcher	.04	.02	.00
187	Gene Larkin	.04	.02	.00
188	Lance Johnson	.04	.02	.00
189	Greg Olson	.04	.02	.00
190	Melido Perez	.04	.02	.00
191	Lenny Harris	.04	.02	.00
192	Terry Kennedy	.04	.02	.00
193	Mike Gallego	.04	.02	.00
194	Willie McGee	.07	.03	.01
195	Juan Samuel	.07	.03	.01
196	Jeff Huson	.04	.02	.00
197	Alex Cole	.07	.03	.01
198	Ron Robinson	.04	.02	.00
199	Joel Skinner	.04	.02	.00
200	Checklist 101-200	.07	.03	.01
201	Kevin Reimer	.04	.02	.00
202	Stan Belinda	.04	.02	.00
203	Pat Tabler	.04	.02	.00
204	Jose Guzman	.04	.02	.00
205	Jose Lind	.04	.02	.00
206	Spike Owen	.04	.02	.00
207	Joe Orsulak	.04	.02	.00
208	Charlie Hayes	.04	.02	.00
209	Mike Devereaux	.04	.02	.00
210	Mike Fitzgerald	.04	.02	.00
211	Willie Randolph	.04	.02	.00
212	Rod Nichols	.04	.02	.00
213	Mike Boddicker	.04	.02	.00
214	Bill Spiers	.04	.02	.00
215	Steve Olin	.04	.02	.00
216	David Howard	.07	.03	.01
217	Gary Varsho	.04	.02	.00
218	Mike Harkey	.04	.02	.00
219	Luis Aquino	.04	.02	.00
220	Chuck McElroy	.04	.02	.00
221	Doug Drabek	.07	.03	.01
222	Dave Winfield	.12	.05	.01
223	Rafael Palmeiro	.12	.05	.01
224	Joe Carter	.10	.04	.01
225	Bobby Bonilla	.15	.06	.01
226	Ivan Calderon	.07	.03	.01
227	Gregg Olson	.07	.03	.01
228	Tim Wallach	.07	.03	.01
229	Terry Pendleton	.10	.04	.01
230	Gilberto Reyes	.04	.02	.00
231	Carlos Baerga	.12	.05	.01
232	Greg Vaughn	.12	.05	.01
233	Bret Saberhagen	.10	.04	.01
234	Gary Sheffield	.10	.04	.01
235	Mark Lewis	.15	.06	.01
236	George Bell	.10	.04	.01
237	Danny Tartabull	.10	.04	.01
238	Willie Wilson	.07	.03	.01
239	Doug Dascenzo	.04	.02	.00
240	Bill Pecota	.04	.02	.00
241	Julio Franco	.10	.04	.01
242	Ed Sprague	.12	.05	.01
243	Juan Gonzalez	.35	.15	.03
244	Chuck Finley	.10	.04	.01
245	Ivan Rodriguez	.75	.30	.07
246	Lenny Dykstra	.07	.03	.01
247	Deion Sanders	.12	.05	.01
248	Dwight Evans	.07	.03	.01
249	Larry Walker	.07	.03	.01
250	Billy Ripken	.04	.02	.00
251	Mickey Tettleton	.07	.03	.01
252	Tony Pena	.04	.02	.00
253	Benito Santiago	.10	.04	.01
254	Kirby Puckett	.15	.06	.01
255	Cecil Fielder	.25	.10	.02
256	Howard Johnson	.12	.05	.01

☐ 257	Andujar Cedeno	.20	.08	.02
☐ 258	Jose Rijo	.07	.03	.01
☐ 259	Al Osuna	.10	.04	.01
☐ 260	Todd Hundley	.07	.03	.01
☐ 261	Orel Hershiser	.10	.04	.01
☐ 262	Ray Lankford	.15	.06	.01
☐ 263	Robin Ventura	.25	.10	.02
☐ 264	Felix Jose	.15	.06	.01
☐ 265	Eddie Murray	.15	.06	.01
☐ 266	Kevin Mitchell	.12	.05	.01
☐ 267	Gary Carter	.10	.04	.01
☐ 268	Mike Benjamin	.04	.02	.00
☐ 269	Dick Schofield	.04	.02	.00
☐ 270	Jose Uribe	.04	.02	.00
☐ 271	Pete Incaviglia	.07	.03	.01
☐ 272	Tony Fernandez	.07	.03	.01
☐ 273	Alan Trammell	.10	.04	.01
☐ 274	Tony Gwynn	.17	.07	.01
☐ 275	Mike Greenwell	.12	.05	.01
☐ 276	Jeff Bagwell	1.25	.50	.12
☐ 277	Frank Viola	.10	.04	.01
☐ 278	Randy Myers	.04	.02	.00
☐ 279	Ken Caminiti	.04	.02	.00
☐ 280	Bill Doran	.04	.02	.00
☐ 281	Dan Pasqua	.04	.02	.00
☐ 282	Alfredo Griffin	.04	.02	.00
☐ 283	Jose Oquendo	.04	.02	.00
☐ 284	Kal Daniels	.07	.03	.01
☐ 285	Bobby Thigpen	.07	.03	.01
☐ 286	Robby Thompson	.04	.02	.00
☐ 287	Mark Eichhorn	.04	.02	.00
☐ 288	Mike Felder	.04	.02	.00
☐ 289	Dave Gallagher	.04	.02	.00
☐ 290	Dave Anderson	.04	.02	.00
☐ 291	Mel Hall	.04	.02	.00
☐ 292	Jerald Clark	.04	.02	.00
☐ 293	Al Newman	.04	.02	.00
☐ 294	Rob Deer	.04	.02	.00
☐ 295	Matt Nokes	.07	.03	.01
☐ 296	Jack Armstrong	.04	.02	.00
☐ 297	Jim Deshaies	.04	.02	.00
☐ 298	Jeff Innis	.04	.02	.00
☐ 299	Jeff Reed	.04	.02	.00
☐ 300	Checklist 201-300	.07	.03	.01
☐ 301	Lonnie Smith	.04	.02	.00
☐ 302	Jimmy Key	.07	.03	.01
☐ 303	Junior Felix	.07	.03	.01
☐ 304	Mike Heath	.04	.02	.00
☐ 305	Mark Langston	.07	.03	.01
☐ 306	Greg W. Harris	.04	.02	.00
☐ 307	Brett Butler	.07	.03	.01
☐ 308	Luis Rivera	.04	.02	.00
☐ 309	Bruce Ruffin	.04	.02	.00
☐ 310	Paul Faries	.04	.02	.00
☐ 311	Terry Leach	.04	.02	.00
☐ 312	Scott Brosius	.15	.06	.01
☐ 313	Scott Leius	.07	.03	.01
☐ 314	Harold Reynolds	.04	.02	.00
☐ 315	Jack Morris	.10	.04	.01
☐ 316	David Segui	.07	.03	.01
☐ 317	Bill Gullickson	.04	.02	.00
☐ 318	Todd Frohwirth	.04	.02	.00
☐ 319	Mark Leiter	.07	.03	.01
☐ 320	Jeff M. Robinson	.04	.02	.00
☐ 321	Gary Gaetti	.07	.03	.01
☐ 322	John Smoltz	.10	.04	.01
☐ 323	Andy Benes	.10	.04	.01
☐ 324	Kelly Gruber	.10	.04	.01
☐ 325	Jim Abbott	.12	.05	.01
☐ 326	John Kruk	.04	.02	.00
☐ 327	Kevin Seitzer	.07	.03	.01
☐ 328	Darrin Jackson	.04	.02	.00
☐ 329	Kurt Stillwell	.04	.02	.00
☐ 330	Mike Maddux	.04	.02	.00
☐ 331	Dennis Eckersley	.10	.04	.01
☐ 332	Dan Gladden	.04	.02	.00
☐ 333	Jose Canseco	.30	.12	.03
☐ 334	Kent Hrbek	.07	.03	.01
☐ 335	Ken Griffey Sr.	.07	.03	.01
☐ 336	Greg Swindell	.07	.03	.01
☐ 337	Trevor Wilson	.04	.02	.00
☐ 338	Sam Horn	.04	.02	.00
☐ 339	Mike Henneman	.04	.02	.00
☐ 340	Jerry Browne	.04	.02	.00
☐ 341	Glenn Braggs	.04	.02	.00
☐ 342	Tom Glavine	.12	.05	.01
☐ 343	Wally Joyner	.10	.04	.01
☐ 344	Fred McGriff	.12	.05	.01
☐ 345	Ron Gant	.15	.06	.01
☐ 346	Ramon Martinez	.15	.06	.01
☐ 347	Wes Chamberlain	.20	.08	.02
☐ 348	Terry Shumpert	.04	.02	.00
☐ 349	Tim Teufel	.04	.02	.00
☐ 350	Wally Backman	.04	.02	.00
☐ 351	Joe Girardi	.04	.02	.00
☐ 352	Devon White	.07	.03	.01
☐ 353	Greg Maddux	.07	.03	.01
☐ 354	Ryan Bowen	.10	.04	.01
☐ 355	Roberto Alomar	.15	.06	.01
☐ 356	Don Mattingly	.20	.08	.02
☐ 357	Pedro Guerrero	.07	.03	.01
☐ 358	Steve Sax	.07	.03	.01
☐ 359	Joey Cora	.04	.02	.00
☐ 360	Jim Gantner	.04	.02	.00
☐ 361	Brian Barnes	.07	.03	.01
☐ 362	Kevin McReynolds	.07	.03	.01
☐ 363	Bret Barberie	.20	.08	.02
☐ 364	David Cone	.10	.04	.01
☐ 365	Dennis Martinez	.07	.03	.01
☐ 366	Brian Hunter	.40	.16	.04
☐ 367	Edgar Martinez	.07	.03	.01
☐ 368	Steve Finley	.07	.03	.01
☐ 369	Greg Briley	.04	.02	.00
☐ 370	Jeff Blauser	.04	.02	.00
☐ 371	Todd Stottlemyre	.07	.03	.01
☐ 372	Luis Gonzalez	.20	.08	.02
☐ 373	Rick Wilkins	.10	.04	.01
☐ 374	Darryl Kile	.10	.04	.01
☐ 375	John Olerud	.15	.06	.01
☐ 376	Lee Smith	.07	.03	.01
☐ 377	Kevin Maas	.20	.08	.02
☐ 378	Dante Bichette	.04	.02	.00
☐ 379	Tom Pagnozzi	.04	.02	.00
☐ 380	Mike Flanagan	.07	.03	.01
☐ 381	Charlie O'Brien	.04	.02	.00
☐ 382	Dave Martinez	.04	.02	.00
☐ 383	Keith Miller	.04	.02	.00
☐ 384	Scott Ruskin	.04	.02	.00
☐ 385	Kevin Elster	.04	.02	.00
☐ 386	Alvin Davis	.04	.02	.00
☐ 387	Casey Candaele	.04	.02	.00
☐ 388	Pete O'Brien	.04	.02	.00
☐ 389	Jeff Treadway	.04	.02	.00
☐ 390	Scott Bradley	.04	.02	.00
☐ 391	Mookie Wilson	.04	.02	.00
☐ 392	Jimmy Jones	.04	.02	.00
☐ 393	Candy Maldonado	.04	.02	.00
☐ 394	Eric Yelding	.04	.02	.00
☐ 395	Tom Henke	.04	.02	.00
☐ 396	Franklin Stubbs	.04	.02	.00
☐ 397	Milt Thompson	.04	.02	.00
☐ 398	Mark Carreon	.04	.02	.00
☐ 399	Randy Velarde	.04	.02	.00
☐ 400	Checklist 301-400	.07	.03	.01
☐ 401	Omar Vizquel	.04	.02	.00
☐ 402	Joe Boever	.04	.02	.00
☐ 403	Bill Krueger	.04	.02	.00
☐ 404	Jody Reed	.07	.03	.01
☐ 405	Mike Schooler	.04	.02	.00
☐ 406	Jason Grimsley	.04	.02	.00
☐ 407	Greg Myers	.04	.02	.00
☐ 408	Randy Ready	.04	.02	.00
☐ 409	Mike Timlin	.07	.03	.01
☐ 410	Mitch Williams	.04	.02	.00
☐ 411	Garry Templeton	.04	.02	.00
☐ 412	Greg Cadaret	.04	.02	.00
☐ 413	Donnie Hill	.04	.02	.00
☐ 414	Wally Whitehurst	.04	.02	.00
☐ 415	Scott Sanderson	.04	.02	.00
☐ 416	Thomas Howard	.04	.02	.00
☐ 417	Neal Heaton	.04	.02	.00
☐ 418	Charlie Hough	.04	.02	.00
☐ 419	Jack Howell	.04	.02	.00
☐ 420	Greg Hibbard	.04	.02	.00
☐ 421	Carlos Quintana	.07	.03	.01
☐ 422	Kim Batiste	.10	.04	.01
☐ 423	Paul Molitor	.10	.04	.01
☐ 424	Ken Griffey Jr.	.90	.40	.09
☐ 425	Phil Plantier	.40	.16	.04
☐ 426	Denny Neagle	.15	.06	.01
☐ 427	Von Hayes	.07	.03	.01
☐ 428	Shane Mack	.07	.03	.01
☐ 429	Darren Daulton	.04	.02	.00
☐ 430	Dwayne Henry	.04	.02	.00
☐ 431	Lance Parrish	.07	.03	.01
☐ 432	Mike Humphreys	.10	.04	.01
☐ 433	Tim Burke	.04	.02	.00
☐ 434	Bryan Harvey	.07	.03	.01
☐ 435	Pat Kelly	.15	.06	.01
☐ 436	Ozzie Guillen	.07	.03	.01
☐ 437	Bruce Hurst	.07	.03	.01
☐ 438	Sammy Sosa	.07	.03	.01
☐ 439	Dennis Rasmussen	.04	.02	.00
☐ 440	Ken Patterson	.04	.02	.00
☐ 441	Jay Buhner	.07	.03	.01
☐ 442	Pat Combs	.04	.02	.00
☐ 443	Wade Boggs	.20	.08	.02
☐ 444	George Brett	.15	.06	.01
☐ 445	Mo Vaughn	.30	.12	.03
☐ 446	Chuck Knoblauch	.30	.12	.03

#	Player			
447	Tom Candiotti	.07	.03	.01
448	Mark Portugal	.04	.02	.00
449	Mickey Morandini	.07	.03	.01
450	Duane Ward	.04	.02	.00
451	Otis Nixon	.04	.02	.00
452	Bob Welch	.07	.03	.01
453	Rusty Meacham	.07	.03	.01
454	Keith Mitchell	.25	.10	.02
455	Marquis Grissom	.10	.04	.01
456	Robin Yount	.15	.06	.01
457	Harvey Pulliam	.10	.04	.01
458	Jose DeLeon	.04	.02	.00
459	Mark Gubicza	.04	.02	.00
460	Darryl Hamilton	.04	.02	.00
461	Tom Browning	.04	.02	.00
462	Monty Fariss	.07	.03	.01
463	Jerome Walton	.07	.03	.01
464	Paul O'Neill	.07	.03	.01
465	Dean Palmer	.20	.08	.02
466	Travis Fryman	.25	.10	.02
467	John Smiley	.07	.03	.01
468	Lloyd Moseby	.04	.02	.00
469	John Wehner	.15	.06	.01
470	Skeeter Barnes	.04	.02	.00
471	Steve Chitren	.04	.02	.00
472	Kent Mercker	.04	.02	.00
473	Terry Steinbach	.04	.02	.00
474	Andres Galarraga	.07	.03	.01
475	Steve Avery	.40	.16	.04
476	Tom Gordon	.07	.03	.01
477	Cal Eldred	.07	.03	.01
478	Omar Olivares	.07	.03	.01
479	Julio Machado	.04	.02	.00
480	Bob Milacki	.04	.02	.00
481	Les Lancaster	.04	.02	.00
482	John Candelaria	.04	.02	.00
483	Brian Downing	.04	.02	.00
484	Roger McDowell	.04	.02	.00
485	Scott Scudder	.04	.02	.00
486	Zane Smith	.04	.02	.00
487	John Cerutti	.04	.02	.00
488	Steve Buechele	.04	.02	.00
489	Paul Gibson	.04	.02	.00
490	Curtis Wilkerson	.04	.02	.00
491	Marvin Freeman	.04	.02	.00
492	Tom Foley	.04	.02	.00
493	Juan Berenguer	.04	.02	.00
494	Ernest Riles	.04	.02	.00
495	Sid Bream	.04	.02	.00
496	Chuck Crim	.04	.02	.00
497	Mike Macfarlane	.04	.02	.00
498	Dale Sveum	.04	.02	.00
499	Storm Davis	.04	.02	.00
500	Checklist 401-500	.07	.03	.01
501	Jeff Reardon	.07	.03	.01
502	Shawn Abner	.04	.02	.00
503	Tony Fossas	.04	.02	.00
504	Cory Snyder	.07	.03	.01
505	Matt Young	.04	.02	.00
506	Allan Anderson	.04	.02	.00
507	Mark Lee	.07	.03	.01
508	Gene Nelson	.04	.02	.00
509	Mike Pagliarulo	.04	.02	.00
510	Rafael Belliard	.04	.02	.00
511	Jay Howell	.04	.02	.00
512	Bob Tewksbury	.04	.02	.00
513	Mike Morgan	.07	.03	.01
514	John Franco	.04	.02	.00
515	Kevin Gross	.04	.02	.00
516	Lou Whitaker	.07	.03	.01
517	Orlando Merced	.15	.06	.01
518	Todd Benzinger	.04	.02	.00
519	Gary Redus	.04	.02	.00
520	Walt Terrell	.04	.02	.00
521	Jack Clark	.07	.03	.01
522	Dave Parker	.07	.03	.01
523	Tim Naehring	.07	.03	.01
524	Mark Whiten	.15	.06	.01
525	Ellis Burks	.10	.04	.01
526	Frank Castillo	.07	.03	.01
527	Brian Harper	.04	.02	.00
528	Brook Jacoby	.04	.02	.00
529	Rick Sutcliffe	.07	.03	.01
530	Joe Klink	.04	.02	.00
531	Terry Bross	.04	.02	.00
532	Jose Offerman	.10	.04	.01
533	Todd Zeile	.12	.05	.01
534	Eric Karros	.30	.12	.03
535	Anthony Young	.15	.06	.01
536	Milt Cuyler	.12	.05	.01
537	Randy Tomlin	.10	.04	.01
538	Scott Livingstone	.15	.06	.01
539	Jim Eisenreich	.04	.02	.00
540	Don Slaught	.04	.02	.00
541	Scott Cooper	.15	.06	.01
542	Joe Grahe	.04	.02	.00
543	Tom Brunansky	.07	.03	.01
544	Eddie Zosky	.15	.06	.01
545	Roger Clemens	.25	.10	.02
546	David Justice	.75	.30	.07
547	Dave Stewart	.07	.03	.01
548	David West	.04	.02	.00
549	Dave Smith	.04	.02	.00
550	Dan Plesac	.04	.02	.00
551	Alex Fernandez	.15	.06	.01
552	Bernard Gilkey	.12	.05	.01
553	Jack McDowell	.10	.04	.01
554	Tino Martinez	.20	.08	.02
555	Bo Jackson	.35	.15	.03
556	Bernie Williams	.20	.08	.02
557	Mark Gardner	.04	.02	.00
558	Glenallen Hill	.07	.03	.01
559	Oil Can Boyd	.04	.02	.00
560	Chris James	.04	.02	.00
561	Scott Servais	.10	.04	.01
562	Rey Sanchez	.15	.06	.01
563	Paul McClellan	.10	.04	.01
564	Andy Mota	.15	.06	.01
565	Darren Lewis	.07	.03	.01
566	Jose Melendez	.10	.04	.01
567	Tommy Greene	.10	.04	.01
568	Rich Rodriguez	.07	.03	.01
569	Heathcliff Slocumb	.04	.02	.00
570	Joe Hesketh	.04	.02	.00
571	Carlton Fisk	.12	.05	.01
572	Erik Hanson	.07	.03	.01
573	Wilson Alvarez	.07	.03	.01
574	Rheal Cormier	.15	.06	.01
575	Tim Raines	.10	.04	.01
576	Bobby Witt	.04	.02	.00
577	Roberto Kelly	.10	.04	.01
578	Kevin Brown	.04	.02	.00
579	Chris Nabholz	.07	.03	.01
580	Jesse Orosco	.04	.02	.00
581	Jeff Brantley	.04	.02	.00
582	Rafael Ramirez	.04	.02	.00
583	Kelly Downs	.04	.02	.00
584	Mike Simms	.10	.04	.01
585	Mike Remlinger	.04	.02	.00
586	Dave Hollins	.07	.03	.01
587	Larry Andersen	.04	.02	.00
588	Mike Gardiner	.10	.04	.01
589	Craig Lefferts	.04	.02	.00
590	Paul Assenmacher	.04	.02	.00
591	Bryn Smith	.04	.02	.00
592	Donn Pall	.04	.02	.00
593	Mike Jackson	.04	.02	.00
594	Scott Radinsky	.04	.02	.00
595	Brian Holman	.04	.02	.00
596	Geronimo Pena	.04	.02	.00
597	Mike Jeffcoat	.04	.02	.00
598	Carlos Martinez	.04	.02	.00
599	Geno Petralli	.04	.02	.00
600	Checklist 501-600	.07	.03	.01
601	Jerry Don Gleaton	.04	.02	.00
602	Adam Peterson	.04	.02	.00
603	Craig Grebeck	.04	.02	.00
604	Mark Guthrie	.04	.02	.00
605	Frank Tanana	.04	.02	.00
606	Hensley Meulens	.07	.03	.01
607	Mark Davis	.04	.02	.00
608	Eric Plunk	.04	.02	.00
609	Mark Williamson	.04	.02	.00
610	Lee Guetterman	.04	.02	.00
611	Bobby Rose	.04	.02	.00
612	Bill Wegman	.04	.02	.00
613	Mike Hartley	.04	.02	.00
614	Chris Beasley	.15	.06	.01
615	Chris Bosio	.04	.02	.00
616	Henry Cotto	.04	.02	.00
617	Chico Walker	.04	.02	.00
618	Russ Swan	.04	.02	.00
619	Bob Walk	.04	.02	.00
620	Billy Swift	.04	.02	.00
621	Warren Newson	.10	.04	.01
622	Steve Bedrosian	.04	.02	.00
623	Ricky Bones	.10	.04	.01
624	Kevin Tapani	.07	.03	.01
625	Juan Guzman	.25	.10	.02
626	Jeff Johnson	.10	.04	.01
627	Jeff Montgomery	.04	.02	.00
628	Ken Hill	.04	.02	.00
629	Gary Thurman	.04	.02	.00
630	Steve Howe	.04	.02	.00
631	Jose DeJesus	.04	.02	.00
632	Bert Blyleven	.07	.03	.01
633	Jaime Navarro	.04	.02	.00
634	Lee Stevens	.07	.03	.01
635	Pete Harnisch	.07	.03	.01
636	Bill Landrum	.04	.02	.00

☐ 637	Rich DeLucia	.04	.02	.00
☐ 638	Luis Salazar	.04	.02	.00
☐ 639	Rob Murphy	.04	.02	.00
☐ 640	Diamond Skills	.15	.06	.01
	Checklist			
	Jose Canseco			
	Rickey Henderson			
☐ 641	Roger Clemens DS	.15	.06	.01
☐ 642	Jim Abbott DS	.10	.04	.01
☐ 643	Travis Fryman DS	.15	.06	.01
☐ 644	Jesse Barfield DS	.07	.03	.01
☐ 645	Cal Ripken DS	.20	.08	.02
☐ 646	Wade Boggs DS	.15	.06	.01
☐ 647	Cecil Fielder DS	.15	.06	.01
☐ 648	Rickey Henderson DS	.20	.08	.02
☐ 649	Jose Canseco DS	.20	.08	.02
☐ 650	Ken Griffey Jr. DS	.50	.20	.05
☐ 651	Kenny Rogers	.04	.02	.00
☐ 652	Luis Mercedes	.25	.10	.02
☐ 653	Mike Stanton	.04	.02	.00
☐ 654	Glenn Davis	.07	.03	.01
☐ 655	Nolan Ryan	.50	.20	.05
☐ 656	Reggie Jefferson	.15	.06	.01
☐ 657	Javier Ortiz	.07	.03	.01
☐ 658	Greg A. Harris	.04	.02	.00
☐ 659	Mariano Duncan	.04	.02	.00
☐ 660	Jeff Shaw	.04	.02	.00
☐ 661	Mike Moore	.07	.03	.01
☐ 662	Chris Haney	.10	.04	.01
☐ 663	Joe Slusarski	.07	.03	.01
☐ 664	Wayne Housie	.17	.07	.01
☐ 665	Carlos Garcia	.07	.03	.01
☐ 666	Bob Ojeda	.04	.02	.00
☐ 667	Bryan Hickerson	.15	.06	.01
☐ 668	Tim Belcher	.07	.03	.01
☐ 669	Ron Darling	.07	.03	.01
☐ 670	Rex Hudler	.04	.02	.00
☐ 671	Sid Fernandez	.07	.03	.01
☐ 672	Chito Martinez	.15	.06	.01
☐ 673	Pete Schourek	.10	.04	.01
☐ 674	Armando Reynoso	.15	.06	.01
☐ 675	Mike Mussina	.20	.08	.02
☐ 676	Kevin Morton	.10	.04	.01
☐ 677	Norm Charlton	.04	.02	.00
☐ 678	Danny Darwin	.04	.02	.00
☐ 679	Eric King	.04	.02	.00
☐ 680	Ted Power	.04	.02	.00
☐ 681	Barry Jones	.04	.02	.00
☐ 682	Carney Lansford	.07	.03	.01
☐ 683	Mel Rojas	.07	.03	.01
☐ 684	Rick Honeycutt	.04	.02	.00
☐ 685	Jeff Fassero	.10	.04	.01
☐ 686	Cris Carpenter	.04	.02	.00
☐ 687	Tim Crews	.04	.02	.00
☐ 688	Scott Terry	.04	.02	.00
☐ 689	Chris Gwynn	.04	.02	.00
☐ 690	Gerald Perry	.04	.02	.00
☐ 691	John Barfield	.04	.02	.00
☐ 692	Bob Melvin	.04	.02	.00
☐ 693	Juan Agosto	.04	.02	.00
☐ 694	Alejandro Pena	.07	.03	.01
☐ 695	Jeff Russell	.04	.02	.00
☐ 696	Carmelo Martinez	.04	.02	.00
☐ 697	Bud Black	.04	.02	.00
☐ 698	Dave Otto	.04	.02	.00
☐ 699	Billy Hatcher	.04	.02	.00
☐ 700	Checklist 601-700	.07	.03	.01

1990 U.S. Playing Cards All-Stars

This 56-card standard size (2 1/2" by 3 1/2") set features members of the 1990 All-Star teams. The set was issued by the United States Playing Card Company and was sold in a blue playing card box just as if it were a playing card deck. The fronts of these rounded-corner cards feature full-color action shots of the players while the backs of the cards have the 1990 Baseball Major League All-Stars design in a white and blue pinstripe pattern, with blue borders. The team logo appears in the lower left corner of each picture. The player's name and position appears in a colored stripe below the pictures; the stripe is aqua on the clubs and spades, and dark red on the hearts and diamonds. Since this set is similar to a playing card set, the set is arranged just like a card deck, therefore the set is checklisted below as if it were a playing card deck. In the checklist below S means Spades, D means Diamonds, C means Clubs, H means Hearts, JK means Joker, and WC means Wild Card. The cards are checklisted below in playing card order by suits and numbers are assigned to Aces (1), Jacks (11), Queens (12), and Kings (13). The jokers and wild cards are unnumbered and listed at the end.

		MINT	EXC	G-VG
COMPLETE SET (56)		6.00	2.50	.60
COMMON PLAYER		.05	.02	.00
☐ 1C	Bob Welch	.10	.04	.01
☐ 2C	Lance Parrish	.10	.04	.01
☐ 3C	Bret Saberhagen	.20	.08	.02
☐ 4C	Gregg Olson	.10	.04	.01
☐ 5C	Brook Jacoby	.05	.02	.00
☐ 6C	Ozzie Guillen	.05	.02	.00
☐ 7C	Ellis Burks	.20	.08	.02
☐ 8C	Dennis Eckersley	.10	.04	.01
☐ 9C	Bobby Thigpen	.10	.04	.01
☐ 10C	Dave Stieb	.10	.04	.01
☐ 11C	Wade Boggs	.30	.12	.03
☐ 12C	George Bell	.15	.06	.01
☐ 13C	Rickey Henderson	.40	.16	.04
☐ 1D	Frank Viola	.10	.04	.01
☐ 2D	Greg Olson	.05	.02	.00
☐ 3D	Dennis Martinez	.05	.02	.00
☐ 4D	Roberto Alomar	.20	.08	.02
☐ 5D	Tim Wallach	.05	.02	.00
☐ 6D	Barry Larkin	.15	.06	.01
☐ 7D	Neal Heaton	.05	.02	.00
☐ 8D	Dave Smith	.05	.02	.00
☐ 9D	Lenny Dykstra	.10	.04	.01
☐ 10D	Shawon Dunston	.10	.04	.01
☐ 11D	Tony Gwynn	.30	.12	.03
☐ 12D	Will Clark	.40	.16	.04
☐ 13D	Barry Bonds	.30	.12	.03
☐ 1H	Ramon Martinez	.30	.12	.03
☐ 2H	Mike Scioscia	.05	.02	.00
☐ 3H	Jeff Brantley	.05	.02	.00
☐ 4H	Ryne Sandberg	.30	.12	.03
☐ 5H	Chris Sabo	.20	.08	.02
☐ 6H	Ozzie Smith	.20	.08	.02
☐ 7H	John Franco	.05	.02	.00
☐ 8H	Matt Williams	.15	.06	.01
☐ 9H	Andre Dawson	.20	.08	.02
☐ 10H	Benito Santiago	.15	.06	.01
☐ 11H	Bobby Bonilla	.20	.08	.02
☐ 12H	Kevin Mitchell	.20	.08	.02
☐ 13H	Darryl Strawberry	.40	.16	.04
☐ 1S	Roger Clemens	.40	.16	.04
☐ 2S	Sandy Alomar Jr.	.20	.08	.02
☐ 3S	Randy Johnson	.10	.04	.01
☐ 4S	Steve Sax	.10	.04	.01
☐ 5S	Kelly Gruber	.10	.04	.01
☐ 6S	Cal Ripken	.40	.16	.04
☐ 7S	Doug Jones	.05	.02	.00
☐ 8S	Kirby Puckett	.30	.12	.03
☐ 9S	Chuck Finley	.10	.04	.01
☐ 10S	Alan Trammell	.15	.06	.01
☐ 11S	Ken Griffey Jr.	.75	.30	.07
☐ 12S	Dave Parker	.15	.06	.01
☐ 13S	Cecil Fielder	.30	.12	.03
☐ JK	Julio Franco	.15	.06	.01
	(red)			
☐ JK	Jack Armstrong	.05	.02	.00
	(black)			
☐ WC	Rob Dibble and	.05	.02	.00
	Randy Myers			
	(red)			
☐ WC	Mark McGwire and	.25	.10	.02
	Jose Canseco			
	(black)			

1991 U.S. Playing Cards All-Stars

This 56-card standard size (2 1/2" by 3 1/2") set features 1991 All-Star Game players. The set was issued by the United States Playing Card Company and was sold in a red playing card box just as if it were a playing card deck. The fronts of these rounded-corner cards feature full-color action shots of the players while the backs have the 1991 Baseball Major League All-Stars design on a white and red pinstripe pattern, with red borders. The team logo appears at the upper right corner of each picture. The player's name and position appear in a color stripe below the pictures; the stripe is yellow on the spades and clubs, and green on the hearts and diamonds. Since this set is similar to a playing card set, the set is checklisted below as if it were a playing card deck. In the checklist S means Spades, D means Diamonds, C means Clubs, H means Hearts, JK means Joker, and WC means Wild Card. The cards are checklisted in playing card order by suits and numbers are assigned to Aces (1), Jacks (11), Queens (12), and Kings (13). The jokers and wild cards are unnumbered and listed at the end.

	MINT	EXC	G-VG
COMPLETE SET (56)	6.00	2.50	.60
COMMON PLAYER	.05	.02	.00
☐ 1C Tony Gwynn	.30	.12	.03
☐ 2C Paul O'Neill	.10	.04	.01
☐ 3C John Smiley	.10	.04	.01
☐ 4C Howard Johnson	.15	.06	.01
☐ 5C Mike Morgan	.05	.02	.00
☐ 6C Barry Larkin	.15	.06	.01
☐ 7C Frank Viola	.10	.04	.01
☐ 8C Juan Samuel	.05	.02	.00
☐ 9C Craig Biggio	.10	.04	.01
☐ 10C Lee Smith	.10	.04	.01
☐ 11C Andre Dawson	.20	.08	.02
☐ 12C Chris Sabo	.20	.08	.02
☐ 13C Ivan Calderon	.10	.04	.01
☐ 1D Ken Griffey Jr.	.60	.25	.06
☐ 2D Carlton Fisk	.25	.10	.02
☐ 3D Scott Sanderson	.05	.02	.00
☐ 4D Kirby Puckett	.30	.12	.03
☐ 5D Jeff Reardon	.10	.04	.01
☐ 6D Rafael Palmeiro	.15	.06	.01
☐ 7D Bryan Harvey	.10	.04	.01
☐ 8D Jimmy Key	.10	.04	.01
☐ 9D Harold Baines	.10	.04	.01
☐ 10D Dennis Eckersley	.15	.06	.01
☐ 11D Sandy Alomar Jr.	.20	.08	.02
☐ 12D Cecil Fielder	.30	.12	.03
☐ 13D Cal Ripken	.50	.20	.05
☐ 1H Jack Morris	.20	.08	.02
☐ 2H Ozzie Guillen	.10	.04	.01
☐ 3H Jack McDowell	.15	.06	.01
☐ 4H Joe Carter	.20	.08	.02
☐ 5H Mark Langston	.10	.04	.01
☐ 6H Julio Franco	.15	.06	.01
☐ 7H Rick Aguilera	.05	.02	.00
☐ 8H Paul Molitor	.10	.04	.01
☐ 9H Ruben Sierra	.30	.12	.03
☐ 10H Roger Clemens	.40	.16	.04
☐ 11H Rickey Henderson	.40	.16	.04
☐ 12H Roberto Alomar	.25	.10	.02
☐ 13H Dave Henderson	.10	.04	.01

☐ 1S Tom Glavine	.20	.08	.02
☐ 2S Eddie Murray	.30	.12	.03
☐ 3S Pete Harnisch	.10	.04	.01
☐ 4S John Kruk	.10	.04	.01
☐ 5S Tom Browning	.05	.02	.00
☐ 6S George Bell	.15	.06	.01
☐ 7S Dennis Martinez	.05	.02	.00
☐ 8S Brett Butler	.10	.04	.01
☐ 9S Felix Jose	.20	.08	.02
☐ 10S Rob Dibble	.10	.04	.01
☐ 11S Benito Santiago	.15	.06	.01
☐ 12S Ryne Sandberg	.40	.16	.04
☐ 13S Ozzie Smith	.20	.08	.02
☐ JK Danny Tartabull (red)	.20	.08	.02
☐ JK Bobby Bonilla (black)	.20	.08	.02
☐ WC Wade Boggs (red)	.30	.12	.03
☐ WC Will Clark (black)	.40	.16	.04

1989 USPS Legends Stamp Cards

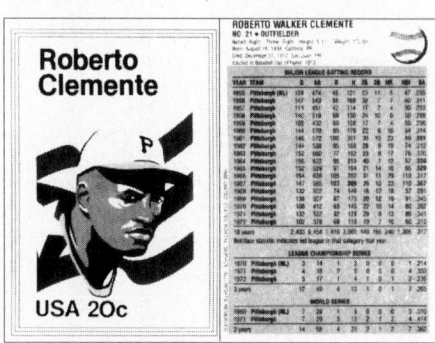

The 1989 USPS Legends Stamp Cards set includes four cards each measuring 2 1/2" by 3 9/16". On the fronts, the cards depict the four baseball-related stamp designs which featured actual players. The outer front borders are white; the inner front borders are orange and purple. The vertically-oriented backs are beige and pink. These cards were sold by the U.S. Postal Service as a set (kit) for 7.95 along with the actual stamps, an attractive booklet, and other materials. The first printing of the set was sold out and so a second printing was made. The first printing cards did not have the USPS copyright logo. All the stamps in the set are drawings; for example, the Gehrig stamp was painted by noted sports artist, Bart Forbes. All of the stamps except Gehrig (25 cents) are 20-cent stamps.

	MINT	EXC	G-VG
COMPLETE SET (4)	20.00	8.50	2.75
COMMON PLAYER (1-4)	6.00	2.50	.60
☐ 1 Roberto Clemente Issued August 17, 1984	6.00	2.50	.60
☐ 2 Lou Gehrig Issued June 10, 1989	6.00	2.50	.60
☐ 3 Jackie Robinson Issued August 2, 1982	6.00	2.50	.60
☐ 4 Babe Ruth Issued July 6, 1983	7.50	3.25	.75

1989 Very Fine Juice Pirates

The 1989 Very Fine Juice Pittsburgh Pirates set is a 30-card set with cards measuring approximately 2 1/2" by 3 1/2" featuring the members of the 1989 Pittsburgh Pirates. This set was issued on three separate perforated sheets: two panels contain 15 player cards each, while the third panel serves as a cover for the set and displays color action photos of the Pirates. These panels were given away to fans attending the Pirates home game on April 23, 1989. There was a coupon (expiring on 10/31/89) on the back that could be redeemed for a free can of juice. The cards are numbered by uniform number in the list below. The cards are very colorful.

	MINT	EXC	G-VG
COMPLETE SET (30)	14.00	6.25	2.00
COMMON PLAYER	.50	.20	.05
☐ 0 Junior Ortiz	.50	.20	.05
☐ 2 Gary Redus	.60	.25	.06
☐ 3 Jay Bell	.75	.30	.07
☐ 5 Sid Bream	.50	.20	.05
☐ 6 Rafael Belliard	.50	.20	.05
☐ 10 Jim Leyland MG	.60	.25	.06
☐ 11 Glenn Wilson	.50	.20	.05
☐ 12 Mike LaValliere	.50	.20	.05
☐ 13 Jose Lind	.60	.25	.06
☐ 14 Ken Oberkfell	.50	.20	.05
☐ 15 Doug Drabek	1.00	.40	.10
☐ 16 Bob Kipper	.50	.20	.05
☐ 17 Bob Walk	.60	.25	.06
☐ 18 Andy Van Slyke	1.00	.40	.10
☐ 23 R.J. Reynolds	.60	.25	.06
☐ 24 Barry Bonds	3.00	1.25	.30
☐ 25 Bobby Bonilla	2.50	1.00	.25
☐ 26 Neal Heaton	.50	.20	.05
☐ 30 Benny Distefano	.50	.20	.05
☐ 31 Ray Miller CO and 37 Tommy Sandt CO	.50	.20	.05
☐ 35 Jim Gott	.50	.20	.05
☐ 36 Bruce Kimm CO and 32 Gene Lamont CO	.50	.20	.05
☐ 39 Milt May CO and 45 Rich Donnelly CO	.50	.20	.05
☐ 41 Mike Dunne	.50	.20	.05
☐ 43 Bill Landrum	.60	.25	.06
☐ 44 John Cangelosi	.50	.20	.05
☐ 49 Jeff Robinson	.50	.20	.05
☐ 52 Dorn Taylor	.50	.20	.05
☐ 54 Brian Fisher	.50	.20	.05
☐ 57 John Smiley	1.00	.40	.10

1985 Wendy's Tigers

This 22-card set features Detroit Tigers; cards measure 2 1/2" by 3 1/2". The set was co-sponsored by Wendy's and Coca-Cola and was distributed in the Detroit metropolitan area. Coca-Cola purchasers were given a pack which contained three Tiger cards plus a header card. The orange-bordered player photos

are different from those used by Topps in their regular set. The cards were produced by Topps as evidenced by the similarity of the card backs with the Topps regular set backs. The set is numbered on the back; the order corresponds to the alphabetical order of the player's names.

	MINT	EXC	G-VG
COMPLETE SET (22)	10.00	4.50	1.25
COMMON PLAYER (1-22)	.30	.12	.03
☐ 1 Sparky Anderson MG (checklist back)	.60	.25	.06
☐ 2 Doug Bair	.30	.12	.03
☐ 3 Juan Berenguer	.30	.12	.03
☐ 4 Dave Bergman	.30	.12	.03
☐ 5 Tom Brookens	.30	.12	.03
☐ 6 Marty Castillo	.30	.12	.03
☐ 7 Darrell Evans	.50	.20	.05
☐ 8 Barbaro Garbey	.30	.12	.03
☐ 9 Kirk Gibson	1.50	.60	.15
☐ 10 Johnny Grubb	.30	.12	.03
☐ 11 Willie Hernandez	.40	.16	.04
☐ 12 Larry Herndon	.30	.12	.03
☐ 13 Rusty Kuntz	.30	.12	.03
☐ 14 Chet Lemon	.40	.16	.04
☐ 15 Aurelio Lopez	.30	.12	.03
☐ 16 Jack Morris	1.75	.70	.17
☐ 17 Lance Parrish	1.50	.60	.15
☐ 18 Dan Petry	.40	.16	.04
☐ 19 Bill Scherrer	.30	.12	.03
☐ 20 Alan Trammell	2.25	.90	.22
☐ 21 Lou Whitaker	1.25	.50	.12
☐ 22 Milt Wilcox	.30	.12	.03

1982 Wheaties Indians

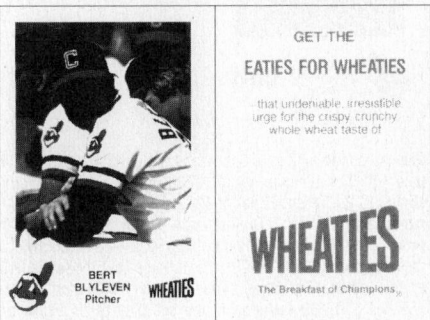

The cards in this 30-card set measure 2 13/16" by 4 1/8". This set of Cleveland Indians baseball players was co-produced by the Indians baseball club and Wheaties, whose respective logos appear on the front of every card. The cards were given away in groups of 10 as a promotion during games on May 30 (1-10), June 19 (11-20) and July 16, 1982 (21-30). The manager (MG), four coaches (CO), and 25 players are featured in a simple format of a color picture, player name and position. The cards are not numbered and the backs contain a Wheaties ad. The set was later sold at the Cleveland Indians gift shop. The cards are ordered below alphabetically within groups of ten as they were issued.

	MINT	EXC	G-VG
COMPLETE SET (30)	16.00	6.75	2.25
COMMON PLAYER (1-30)	.50	.20	.05

		MINT	EXC	G-VG
☐ 1	Bert Blyleven	1.25	.50	.12
☐ 2	Joe Charboneau	.75	.30	.07
☐ 3	Jerry Dybzinski	.50	.20	.05
☐ 4	Dave Garcia MG	.50	.20	.05
☐ 5	Toby Harrah	.75	.30	.07
☐ 6	Ron Hassey	.60	.25	.06
☐ 7	Dennis Lewallyn	.50	.20	.05
☐ 8	Rick Manning	.60	.25	.06
☐ 9	Tommy McCraw CO	.60	.25	.06
☐ 10	Rick Waits	.50	.20	.05
☐ 11	Chris Bando	.50	.20	.05
☐ 12	Len Barker	.60	.25	.06
☐ 13	Tom Brennan	.50	.20	.05
☐ 14	Rodney Craig	.50	.20	.05
☐ 15	Mike Fischlin	.50	.20	.05
☐ 16	Johnny Goryl CO	.50	.20	.05
☐ 17	Mel Queen CO	.50	.20	.05
☐ 18	Lary Sorensen	.50	.20	.05
☐ 19	Andre Thornton	.75	.30	.07
☐ 20	Eddie Whitson	.75	.30	.07
☐ 21	Alan Bannister	.50	.20	.05
☐ 22	John Denny	.60	.25	.06
☐ 23	Miguel Dilone	.50	.20	.05
☐ 24	Mike Hargrove	.75	.30	.07
☐ 25	Von Hayes	1.25	.50	.12
☐ 26	Bake McBride	.60	.25	.06
☐ 27	Jack Perconte	.50	.20	.05
☐ 28	Dennis Sommers CO	.50	.20	.05
☐ 29	Dan Spillner	.50	.20	.05
☐ 30	Rick Sutcliffe	.75	.30	.07

1983 Wheaties Indians

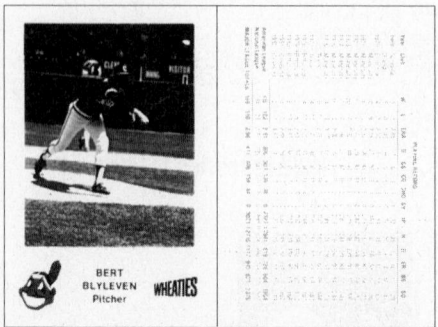

BERT
BLYLEVEN
Pitcher WHEATIES

The cards in this 32-card set measure approximately 2 13/16" by 4 1/8". The full color set of 1983 Wheaties Indians is quite similar to the Wheaties set of 1982. The backs, however, are significantly different. They contain complete career playing records of the players. The complete sets were given away at the ball park on May 15, 1983. The set was later made available at the Indians Gift Shop. The manager (MG) and several coaches (CO) are included in the set. The cards below are ordered alphabetically by the subject's name.

	MINT	EXC	G-VG
COMPLETE SET (32)	8.00	3.50	.80
COMMON PLAYER (1-32)	.25	.10	.02

		MINT	EXC	G-VG
☐ 1	Bud Anderson	.25	.10	.02
☐ 2	Jay Baller	.25	.10	.02
☐ 3	Chris Bando	.25	.10	.02
☐ 4	Alan Bannister	.25	.10	.02
☐ 5	Len Barker	.35	.15	.03

		MINT	EXC	G-VG
☐ 6	Bert Blyleven	.75	.30	.07
☐ 7	Wil Culmer	.25	.10	.02
☐ 8	Miguel Dilone	.25	.10	.02
☐ 9	Juan Eichelberger	.25	.10	.02
☐ 10	Jim Essian	.35	.15	.03
☐ 11	Mike Ferraro MG	.25	.10	.02
☐ 12	Mike Fischlin	.25	.10	.02
☐ 13	Julio Franco	2.00	.80	.20
☐ 14	Ed Glynn	.25	.10	.02
☐ 15	Johnny Goryl CO	.25	.10	.02
☐ 16	Mike Hargrove	.50	.20	.05
☐ 17	Toby Harrah	.35	.15	.03
☐ 18	Ron Hassey	.35	.15	.03
☐ 19	Neal Heaton	.25	.10	.02
☐ 20	Rick Manning	.35	.15	.03
☐ 21	Bake McBride	.35	.15	.03
☐ 22	Don McMahon CO	.25	.10	.02
☐ 23	Ed Napoleon CO	.25	.10	.02
☐ 24	Broderick Perkins	.25	.10	.02
☐ 25	Dennis Sommers CO	.25	.10	.02
☐ 26	Lary Sorensen	.25	.10	.02
☐ 27	Dan Spillner	.25	.10	.02
☐ 28	Rick Sutcliffe	.75	.30	.07
☐ 29	Andre Thornton	.50	.20	.05
☐ 30	Manny Trillo	.25	.10	.02
☐ 31	George Vukovich	.25	.10	.02
☐ 32	Rick Waits	.25	.10	.02

1984 Wheaties Indians

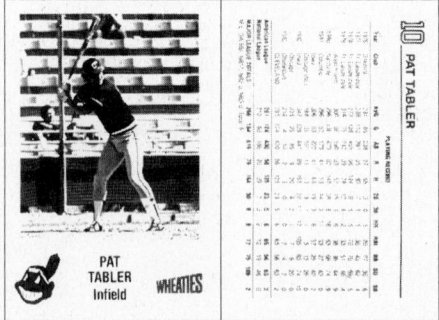

PAT
TABLER
Infield WHEATIES

The cards in this 29-card set measure approximately 2 13/16" by 4 1/8". For the third straight year, Wheaties distributed a set of Cleveland Indians baseball cards. These over-sized cards were passed out at a Baseball Card Day at the Cleveland Stadium. Similar in appearance to the cards of the past two years, both the Indians and the Wheaties logos appear on the obverse, along with the name, team and position. Cards are numbered on the back by the player's uniform number.

	MINT	EXC	G-VG
COMPLETE SET (29)	8.00	3.50	.80
COMMON PLAYER	.25	.10	.02

		MINT	EXC	G-VG
☐ 2	Brett Butler	.60	.25	.06
☐ 4	Tony Bernazard	.35	.15	.03
☐ 8	Carmelo Castillo	.25	.10	.02
☐ 10	Pat Tabler	.35	.15	.03
☐ 13	Ernie Camacho	.35	.15	.03
☐ 14	Julio Franco	.90	.40	.09
☐ 15	Broderick Perkins	.25	.10	.02
☐ 16	Jerry Willard	.25	.10	.02
☐ 18	Pat Corrales MG	.35	.15	.03
☐ 21	Mike Hargrove	.50	.20	.05
☐ 22	Mike Fischlin	.25	.10	.02
☐ 23	Chris Bando	.25	.10	.02
☐ 24	George Vukovich	.25	.10	.02
☐ 26	Brook Jacoby	.50	.20	.05
☐ 27	Steve Farr	.50	.20	.05
☐ 28	Bert Blyleven	.60	.25	.06
☐ 29	Andre Thornton	.50	.20	.05
☐ 30	Joe Carter	2.00	.80	.20
☐ 31	Steve Comer	.25	.10	.02
☐ 33	Roy Smith	.25	.10	.02
☐ 34	Mel Hall	.60	.25	.06

☐ 36	Jamie Easterly	.25	.10	.02
☐ 37	Don Schulze	.25	.10	.02
☐ 38	Luis Aponte	.25	.10	.02
☐ 44	Neal Heaton	.25	.10	.02
☐ 46	Mike Jeffcoat	.25	.10	.02
☐ 54	Tom Waddell	.25	.10	.02
☐ xx	Indians Coaches:	.25	.10	.02
	(unnumbered)			
	John Goryl			
	Dennis Sommers			
	Ed Napoleon			
	Bobby Bonds			
	Don McMahon			
☐ xx	Tom-E-Hawk (Mascot)	.25	.10	.02
	(unnumbered)			

1954 Wilson

The cards in this 20-card set measure approximately 2 5/8" by 3 3/4". The 1954 "Wilson Weiners" set contains 20 full color, unnumbered cards. The obverse design of a package of hot dogs appearing to fly through the air is a distinctive feature of this set. Uncut sheets have been seen. Cards are numbered below alphabetically by player's name.

		NRMT	VG-E	GOOD
	COMPLETE SET (20)	7000.00	2800.00	700.00
	COMMON PLAYER (1-20)	150.00	67.50	22.50
☐ 1	Roy Campanella	750.00	325.00	110.00
☐ 2	Del Ennis	150.00	67.50	22.50
☐ 3	Carl Erskine	180.00	80.00	27.00
☐ 4	Ferris Fain	150.00	67.50	22.50
☐ 5	Bob Feller	600.00	270.00	90.00
☐ 6	Nelson Fox	300.00	135.00	45.00
☐ 7	Johnny Groth	150.00	67.50	22.50
☐ 8	Stan Hack	150.00	67.50	22.50
☐ 9	Gil Hodges	400.00	180.00	60.00
☐ 10	Ray Jablonski	150.00	67.50	22.50
☐ 11	Harvey Kuenn	250.00	110.00	37.50
☐ 12	Roy McMillan	150.00	67.50	22.50
☐ 13	Andy Pafko	150.00	67.50	22.50
☐ 14	Paul Richards MG	150.00	67.50	22.50
☐ 15	Hank Sauer	150.00	67.50	22.50
☐ 16	Red Schoendienst	400.00	180.00	60.00
☐ 17	Enos Slaughter	450.00	200.00	67.50
☐ 18	Vern Stephens	150.00	67.50	22.50
☐ 19	Sammy White	150.00	67.50	22.50
☐ 20	Ted Williams	3000.00	1250.00	350.00

1991 WIZ Mets

This 450-card commemorative New York Mets set was sponsored by WIZ Home Entertainment Centers and AT and T. The set was issued on 30 approximately 10" by 9" perforated sheets (15 cards per sheet); after perforation, the cards measure approximately 2" by 3". The fronts have black and white head

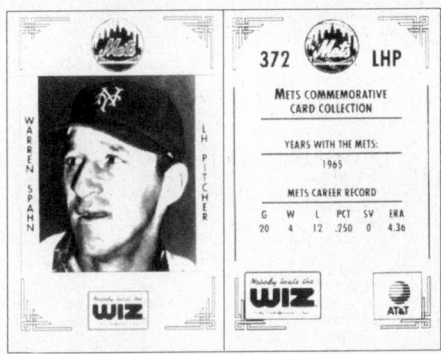

shots of the players on a white card face decorated with a blue picture frame design. The player's name and position are written vertically alongside the pictures. The team logo above the picture and the Wiz logo below round out the card face. In black lettering on white, the backs have the player's position, years (and stats) with the Mets, and career record. The team and sponsors' logos also appear on the back. The cards are numbered on the back and listed in alphabetical order. The set purports to show every player who ever played for the New York Mets. The set was issued in three series to be distruted at three home games during the year, e.g., the first series was issued to all fans attending the Mets home game on May 25, 1991.

		MINT	EXC	G-VG
	COMPLETE SET (450)	40.00	18.00	6.00
	COMMON PLAYER (1-439)	.10	.04	.01
☐ 1	Don Aase	.20	.08	.02
☐ 2	Tommie Agee	.15	.06	.01
☐ 3	Rick Aguilera	.20	.08	.02
☐ 4	Jack Aker	.10	.04	.01
☐ 5	Neil Allen	.15	.06	.01
☐ 6	Bill Almon	.15	.06	.01
☐ 7	Sandy Alomar Sr.	.15	.06	.01
☐ 8	Jesus Alou	.10	.04	.01
☐ 9	George Altman	.10	.04	.01
☐ 10	Luis Alvarado	.10	.04	.01
☐ 11	Craig Anderson	.10	.04	.01
☐ 12	Rick Anderson	.10	.04	.01
☐ 13	Bob Apodaca	.10	.04	.01
☐ 14	Gerry Arrigo	.10	.04	.01
☐ 15	Richie Ashburn	.35	.15	.03
☐ 16	Tucker Ashford	.10	.04	.01
☐ 17	Bob Aspromonte	.10	.04	.01
☐ 18	Benny Ayala	.10	.04	.01
☐ 19	Wally Backman	.10	.04	.01
☐ 20	Kevin Baez	.10	.04	.01
☐ 21	Bob Bailor	.10	.04	.01
☐ 22	Rick Baldwin	.10	.04	.01
☐ 23	Billy Baldwin	.10	.04	.01
☐ 24	Lute Barnes	.10	.04	.01
☐ 25	Ed Bauta	.10	.04	.01
☐ 26	Billy Beane	.10	.04	.01
☐ 27	Larry Bearnarth	.10	.04	.01
☐ 28	Blaine Beatty	.15	.06	.01
☐ 29	Jim Beauchamp	.10	.04	.01
☐ 30	Gus Bell	.15	.06	.01
☐ 31	Dennis Bennett	.10	.04	.01
☐ 32	Butch Benton	.10	.04	.01
☐ 33	Juan Berenguer	.10	.04	.01
☐ 34	Bruce Berenyi	.10	.04	.01
☐ 35	Dwight Bernard	.10	.04	.01
☐ 36	Yogi Berra	.50	.20	.05
☐ 37	Jim Bethke	.10	.04	.01
☐ 38	Mike Bishop	.10	.04	.01
☐ 39	Terry Blocker	.10	.04	.01
☐ 40	Bruce Bochy	.10	.04	.01
☐ 41	Bruce Boisclair	.10	.04	.01
☐ 42	Dan Boitano	.10	.04	.01
☐ 43	Mark Bomback	.10	.04	.01
☐ 44	Don Bosch	.10	.04	.01
☐ 45	Daryl Boston	.15	.06	.01
☐ 46	Ken Boswell	.10	.04	.01
☐ 47	Ed Bouchee	.10	.04	.01
☐ 48	Larry Bowa	.20	.08	.02
☐ 49	Ken Boyer	.20	.08	.02
☐ 50	Mark Bradley	.10	.04	.01

☐ 51	Eddie Bressoud	.10	.04	.01
☐ 52	Hubie Brooks	.20	.08	.02
☐ 53	Kevin Brown	.15	.06	.01
☐ 54	Leon Brown	.10	.04	.01
☐ 55	Mike Bruhert	.10	.04	.01
☐ 56	Jerry Buchek	.10	.04	.01
☐ 57	Larry Burright	.10	.04	.01
☐ 58	Ray Burris	.10	.04	.01
☐ 59	John Candelaria	.15	.06	.01
☐ 60	Chris Cannizzaro	.10	.04	.01
☐ 61	Buzz Capra	.10	.04	.01
☐ 62	Jose Cardenal	.10	.04	.01
☐ 63	Don Cardwell	.10	.04	.01
☐ 64	Duke Carmel	.10	.04	.01
☐ 65	Chuck Carr	.15	.06	.01
☐ 66	Mark Carreon	.15	.06	.01
☐ 67	Gary Carter	.25	.10	.02
☐ 68	Elio Chacon	.10	.04	.01
☐ 69	Dean Chance	.15	.06	.01
☐ 70	Kelvin Chapman	.10	.04	.01
☐ 71	Ed Charles	.10	.04	.01
☐ 72	Rich Chiles	.10	.04	.01
☐ 73	Harry Chiti	.10	.04	.01
☐ 74	John Christensen	.10	.04	.01
☐ 75	Joe Christopher	.10	.04	.01
☐ 76	Galen Cisco	.10	.04	.01
☐ 77	Donn Clendenon	.15	.06	.01
☐ 78	Gene Clines	.10	.04	.01
☐ 79	Choo Choo Coleman	.15	.06	.01
☐ 80	Kevin Collins	.10	.04	.01
☐ 81	David Cone	.30	.12	.03
☐ 82	Bill Connors	.10	.04	.01
☐ 83	Cliff Cook	.10	.04	.01
☐ 84	Tim Corcoran	.10	.04	.01
☐ 85	Mardie Cornejo	.10	.04	.01
☐ 86	Billy Cowan	.10	.04	.01
☐ 87	Roger Craig	.20	.08	.02
☐ 88	Jerry Cram	.10	.04	.01
☐ 89	Mike Cubbage	.15	.06	.01
☐ 90	Ron Darling	.20	.08	.02
☐ 91	Ray Daviault	.10	.04	.01
☐ 92	Tommy Davis	.20	.08	.02
☐ 93	John DeMerit	.10	.04	.01
☐ 94	Bill Denehy	.10	.04	.01
☐ 95	Jack DiLauro	.10	.04	.01
☐ 96	Carlos Diaz	.10	.04	.01
☐ 97	Mario Diaz	.15	.06	.01
☐ 98	Steve Dillon	.10	.04	.01
☐ 99	Sammy Drake	.10	.04	.01
☐ 100	Jim Dwyer	.10	.04	.01
☐ 101	Duffy Dyer	.10	.04	.01
☐ 102	Len Dykstra	.25	.10	.02
☐ 103	Tom Edens	.10	.04	.01
☐ 104	Dave Eilers	.10	.04	.01
☐ 105	Larry Elliot	.10	.04	.01
☐ 106	Dock Ellis	.10	.04	.01
☐ 107	Kevin Elster	.20	.08	.02
☐ 108	Nino Espinosa	.10	.04	.01
☐ 109	Chuck Estrada	.15	.06	.01
☐ 110	Francisco Estrada	.10	.04	.01
☐ 111	Pete Falcone	.10	.04	.01
☐ 112	Sid Fernandez	.20	.08	.02
☐ 113	Chico Fernandez	.10	.04	.01
☐ 114	Sergio Ferrer	.10	.04	.01
☐ 115	Jack Fisher	.10	.04	.01
☐ 116	Mike Fitzgerald	.10	.04	.01
☐ 117	Shaun Fitzmaurice	.10	.04	.01
☐ 118	Gil Flores	.10	.04	.01
☐ 119	Doug Flynn	.10	.04	.01
☐ 120	Tim Foli	.10	.04	.01
☐ 121	Rich Folkers	.10	.04	.01
☐ 122	Larry Foss	.10	.04	.01
☐ 123	George Foster	.25	.10	.02
☐ 124	Leo Foster	.10	.04	.01
☐ 125	Joe Foy	.10	.04	.01
☐ 126	John Franco	.20	.08	.02
☐ 127	Jim Fregosi	.20	.08	.02
☐ 128	Bob Friend	.15	.06	.01
☐ 129	Danny Frisella	.10	.04	.01
☐ 130	Brent Gaff	.10	.04	.01
☐ 131	Bob Gallagher	.10	.04	.01
☐ 132	Ron Gardenhire	.10	.04	.01
☐ 133	Rob Gardner	.10	.04	.01
☐ 134	Wes Gardner	.10	.04	.01
☐ 135	Wayne Garrett	.10	.04	.01
☐ 136	Rod Gaspar	.10	.04	.01
☐ 137	Gary Gentry	.15	.06	.01
☐ 138	John Gibbons	.10	.04	.01
☐ 139	Bob Gibson	.15	.06	.01
☐ 140	Brian Giles	.10	.04	.01
☐ 141	Joe Ginsberg	.15	.06	.01
☐ 142	Ed Glynn	.10	.04	.01
☐ 143	Jesse Gonder	.10	.04	.01
☐ 144	Dwight Gooden	.50	.20	.05
☐ 145	Greg Goossen	.10	.04	.01
☐ 146	Tom Gorman	.10	.04	.01
☐ 147	Jim Gosger	.10	.04	.01
☐ 148	Bill Graham	.10	.04	.01
☐ 149	Wayne Graham	.10	.04	.01
☐ 150	Dallas Green	.20	.08	.02
☐ 151	Pumpsie Green	.10	.04	.01
☐ 152	Tom Grieve	.15	.06	.01
☐ 153	Jerry Grote	.10	.04	.01
☐ 154	Joe Grzenda	.10	.04	.01
☐ 155	Don Hahn	.10	.04	.01
☐ 156	Tom Hall	.10	.04	.01
☐ 157	Jack Hamilton	.10	.04	.01
☐ 158	Ike Hampton	.10	.04	.01
☐ 159	Tim Harkness	.10	.04	.01
☐ 160	Bud Harrelson	.20	.08	.02
☐ 161	Greg A. Harris	.15	.06	.01
☐ 162	Greg Harts	.10	.04	.01
☐ 163	Andy Hassler	.10	.04	.01
☐ 164	Tom Hausman	.10	.04	.01
☐ 165	Ed Hearn	.10	.04	.01
☐ 166	Richie Hebner	.10	.04	.01
☐ 167	Danny Heep	.10	.04	.01
☐ 168	Jack Heidemann	.10	.04	.01
☐ 169	Bob Heise	.10	.04	.01
☐ 170	Ken Henderson	.10	.04	.01
☐ 171	Steve Henderson	.10	.04	.01
☐ 172	Bob Hendley	.10	.04	.01
☐ 173	Phil Hennigan	.10	.04	.01
☐ 174	Bill Hepler	.10	.04	.01
☐ 175	Ron Herbel	.10	.04	.01
☐ 176	Manny Hernandez	.10	.04	.01
☐ 177	Keith Hernandez	.25	.10	.02
☐ 178	Tommy Herr	.15	.06	.01
☐ 179	Rick Herrscher	.15	.06	.01
☐ 180	Jim Hickman	.10	.04	.01
☐ 181	Joe Hicks	.10	.04	.01
☐ 182	Chuck Hiller	.10	.04	.01
☐ 183	Dave Hillman	.10	.04	.01
☐ 184	Jerry Hinsley	.10	.04	.01
☐ 185	Gil Hodges	.35	.15	.03
☐ 186	Ron Hodges	.10	.04	.01
☐ 187	Scott Holman	.10	.04	.01
☐ 188	Jay Hook	.10	.04	.01
☐ 189	Mike Howard	.10	.04	.01
☐ 190	Jesse Hudson	.10	.04	.01
☐ 191	Keith Hughes	.15	.06	.01
☐ 192	Todd Hundley	.20	.08	.02
☐ 193	Ron Hunt	.10	.04	.01
☐ 194	Willard Hunter	.10	.04	.01
☐ 195	Clint Hurdle	.15	.06	.01
☐ 196	Jeff Innis	.10	.04	.01
☐ 197	Al Jackson	.10	.04	.01
☐ 198	Roy Lee Jackson	.10	.04	.01
☐ 199	Gregg Jefferies	.35	.15	.03
☐ 200	Stan Jefferson	.10	.04	.01
☐ 201	Chris Jelic	.15	.06	.01
☐ 202	Bob D. Johnson	.10	.04	.01
☐ 203	Howard Johnson	.30	.12	.03
☐ 204	Bob W. Johnson	.10	.04	.01
☐ 205	Randy Jones	.15	.06	.01
☐ 206	Sherman Jones	.10	.04	.01
☐ 207	Cleon Jones	.15	.06	.01
☐ 208	Ross Jones	.10	.04	.01
☐ 209	Mike Jorgensen	.10	.04	.01
☐ 210	Rod Kanehl	.10	.04	.01
☐ 211	Dave Kingman	.20	.08	.02
☐ 212	Bobby Klaus	.10	.04	.01
☐ 213	Jay Kleven	.10	.04	.01
☐ 214	Lou Klimchock	.10	.04	.01
☐ 215	Ray Knight	.20	.08	.02
☐ 216	Kevin Kobel	.10	.04	.01
☐ 217	Gary Kolb	.10	.04	.01
☐ 218	Cal Koonce	.10	.04	.01
☐ 219	Jerry Koosman	.25	.10	.02
☐ 220	Ed Kranepool	.20	.08	.02
☐ 221	Gary Kroll	.10	.04	.01
☐ 222	Clem Labine	.15	.06	.01
☐ 223	Jack Lamabe	.10	.04	.01
☐ 224	Hobie Landrith	.10	.04	.01
☐ 225	Frank Lary	.15	.06	.01
☐ 226	Bill Latham	.10	.04	.01
☐ 227	Terry Leach	.10	.04	.01
☐ 228	Tim Leary	.15	.06	.01
☐ 229	John Lewis	.10	.04	.01
☐ 230	David Liddell	.10	.04	.01
☐ 231	Phil Linz	.15	.06	.01
☐ 232	Ron Locke	.10	.04	.01
☐ 233	Skip Lockwood	.10	.04	.01
☐ 234	Mickey Lolich	.20	.08	.02
☐ 235	Phil Lombardi	.10	.04	.01
☐ 236	Al Luplow	.10	.04	.01
☐ 237	Ed Lynch	.10	.04	.01
☐ 238	Barry Lyons	.10	.04	.01
☐ 239	Ken MacKenzie	.10	.04	.01
☐ 240	Julio Machado	.10	.04	.01

#	Player			
☐ 241	Elliott Maddox	.10	.04	.01
☐ 242	Dave Magadan	.20	.08	.02
☐ 243	Pepe Mangual	.10	.04	.01
☐ 244	Phil Mankowski	.10	.04	.01
☐ 245	Felix Mantilla	.10	.04	.01
☐ 246	Mike Marshall RH Pitcher	.15	.06	.01
☐ 247	Dave Marshall	.10	.04	.01
☐ 248	Jim Marshall	.10	.04	.01
☐ 249	Mike A. Marshall 1st Base	.15	.06	.01
☐ 250	J.C. Martin	.10	.04	.01
☐ 251	Jerry Martin	.10	.04	.01
☐ 252	Teddy Martinez	.10	.04	.01
☐ 253	Jon Matlack	.15	.06	.01
☐ 254	Jerry May	.10	.04	.01
☐ 255	Willie Mays	.50	.20	.05
☐ 256	Lee Mazzilli	.10	.04	.01
☐ 257	Jim McAndrew	.10	.04	.01
☐ 258	Bob McClure	.10	.04	.01
☐ 259	Roger McDowell	.15	.06	.01
☐ 260	Tug McGraw	.25	.10	.02
☐ 261	Jeff McKnight	.10	.04	.01
☐ 262	Roy McMillan	.10	.04	.01
☐ 263	Kevin McReynolds	.25	.10	.02
☐ 264	George Medich	.10	.04	.01
☐ 265	Orlando Mercado	.10	.04	.01
☐ 266	Butch Metzger	.10	.04	.01
☐ 267	Felix Millan	.10	.04	.01
☐ 268	Bob G. Miller LH Pitcher	.10	.04	.01
☐ 269	Bob L. Miller RH Pitcher	.10	.04	.01
☐ 270	Dyar Miller	.10	.04	.01
☐ 271	Larry Miller	.10	.04	.01
☐ 272	Keith Miller	.15	.06	.01
☐ 273	Randy Milligan	.20	.08	.02
☐ 274	John Milner	.10	.04	.01
☐ 275	John Mitchell	.10	.04	.01
☐ 276	Kevin Mitchell	.40	.16	.04
☐ 277	Wilmer Mizell	.15	.06	.01
☐ 278	Herb Moford	.10	.04	.01
☐ 279	Willie Montanez	.15	.06	.01
☐ 280	Joe Moock	.10	.04	.01
☐ 281	Tommy Moore	.10	.04	.01
☐ 282	Bob Moorhead	.10	.04	.01
☐ 283	Jerry Morales	.10	.04	.01
☐ 284	Al Moran	.10	.04	.01
☐ 285	Jose Moreno	.10	.04	.01
☐ 286	Bill Murphy	.10	.04	.01
☐ 287	Dale Murray	.10	.04	.01
☐ 288	Dennis Musgraves	.10	.04	.01
☐ 289	Jeff Musselman	.10	.04	.01
☐ 290	Randy Myers	.20	.08	.02
☐ 291	Bob Myrick	.10	.04	.01
☐ 292	Danny Napoleon	.10	.04	.01
☐ 293	Charlie Neal	.15	.06	.01
☐ 294	Randy Niemann	.10	.04	.01
☐ 295	Joe Nolan	.10	.04	.01
☐ 296	Dan Norman	.10	.04	.01
☐ 297	Ed Nunez	.10	.04	.01
☐ 298	Charlie O'Brien	.10	.04	.01
☐ 299	Tom O'Malley	.10	.04	.01
☐ 300	Bob Ojeda	.20	.08	.02
☐ 301	Jose Oquendo	.15	.06	.01
☐ 302	Jesse Orosco	.15	.06	.01
☐ 303	Junior Ortiz	.10	.04	.01
☐ 304	Brian Ostrosser	.10	.04	.01
☐ 305	Amos Otis	.20	.08	.02
☐ 306	Rick Ownbey	.10	.04	.01
☐ 307	John Pacella	.10	.04	.01
☐ 308	Tom Paciorek	.10	.04	.01
☐ 309	Harry Parker	.10	.04	.01
☐ 310	Tom Parsons	.10	.04	.01
☐ 311	Al Pedrique	.10	.04	.01
☐ 312	Brock Pemberton	.10	.04	.01
☐ 313	Alejandro Pena	.20	.08	.02
☐ 314	Bobby Pfeil	.10	.04	.01
☐ 315	Mike Phillips	.10	.04	.01
☐ 316	Jim Piersall	.20	.08	.02
☐ 317	Joe Pignatano	.10	.04	.01
☐ 318	Grover Powell	.10	.04	.01
☐ 319	Rich Puig	.10	.04	.01
☐ 320	Charlie Puleo	.10	.04	.01
☐ 321	Gary Rajsich	.10	.04	.01
☐ 322	Mario Ramirez	.10	.04	.01
☐ 323	Lenny Randle	.10	.04	.01
☐ 324	Bob Rauch	.10	.04	.01
☐ 325	Jeff Reardon	.25	.10	.02
☐ 326	Darren Reed	.10	.04	.01
☐ 327	Hal Reniff	.10	.04	.01
☐ 328	Ronn Reynolds	.10	.04	.01
☐ 329	Tom Reynolds	.10	.04	.01
☐ 330	Dennis Ribant	.10	.04	.01
☐ 331	Gordie Richardson	.10	.04	.01
☐ 332	Dave Roberts	.10	.04	.01
☐ 333	Les Rohr	.10	.04	.01
☐ 334	Luis Rosado	.10	.04	.01
☐ 335	Don Rose	.10	.04	.01
☐ 336	Don Rowe	.10	.04	.01
☐ 337	Dick Rusteck	.10	.04	.01
☐ 338	Nolan Ryan	1.00	.40	.10
☐ 339	Ray Sadecki	.10	.04	.01
☐ 340	Joe Sambito	.10	.04	.01
☐ 341	Amado Samuel	.10	.04	.01
☐ 342	Juan Samuel	.20	.08	.02
☐ 343	Ken Sanders	.10	.04	.01
☐ 344	Rafael Santana	.15	.06	.01
☐ 345	Mackey Sasser	.15	.06	.01
☐ 346	Mac Scarce	.10	.04	.01
☐ 347	Jim Schaffer	.10	.04	.01
☐ 348	Dan Schatzeder	.10	.04	.01
☐ 349	Calvin Schiraldi	.10	.04	.01
☐ 350	Al Schmelz	.10	.04	.01
☐ 351	Dave Schneck	.10	.04	.01
☐ 352	Ted Schreiber	.10	.04	.01
☐ 353	Don Schulze	.10	.04	.01
☐ 354	Mike Scott	.20	.08	.02
☐ 355	Ray Searage	.10	.04	.01
☐ 356	Tom Seaver	.75	.30	.07
☐ 357	Dick Selma	.10	.04	.01
☐ 358	Art Shamsky	.10	.04	.01
☐ 359	Bob Shaw	.10	.04	.01
☐ 360	Don Shaw	.10	.04	.01
☐ 361	Norm Sherry	.15	.06	.01
☐ 362	Craig Shipley	.15	.06	.01
☐ 363	Bart Shirley	.10	.04	.01
☐ 364	Bill Short	.10	.04	.01
☐ 365	Paul Siebert	.10	.04	.01
☐ 366	Ken Singleton	.20	.08	.02
☐ 367	Doug Sisk	.10	.04	.01
☐ 368	Bobby Gene Smith	.10	.04	.01
☐ 369	Charley Smith	.10	.04	.01
☐ 370	Dick Smith	.10	.04	.01
☐ 371	Duke Snider	.50	.20	.05
☐ 372	Warren Spahn	.40	.16	.04
☐ 373	Larry Stahl	.10	.04	.01
☐ 374	Roy Staiger	.10	.04	.01
☐ 375	Tracy Stallard	.10	.04	.01
☐ 376	Leroy Stanton	.10	.04	.01
☐ 377	Rusty Staub	.25	.10	.02
☐ 378	John Stearns	.15	.06	.01
☐ 379	John Stephenson	.10	.04	.01
☐ 380	Randy Sterling	.10	.04	.01
☐ 381	George Stone	.10	.04	.01
☐ 382	Darryl Strawberry	.60	.25	.06
☐ 383	John Strohmayer	.10	.04	.01
☐ 384	Brent Strom	.10	.04	.01
☐ 385	Dick Stuart	.10	.04	.01
☐ 386	Tom Sturdivant	.10	.04	.01
☐ 387	Bill Sudakis	.10	.04	.01
☐ 388	John Sullivan	.10	.04	.01
☐ 389	Darrell Sutherland	.10	.04	.01
☐ 390	Ron Swoboda	.15	.06	.01
☐ 391	Craig Swan	.15	.06	.01
☐ 392	Rick Sweet	.10	.04	.01
☐ 393	Pat Tabler	.15	.06	.01
☐ 394	Kevin Tapani	.20	.08	.02
☐ 395	Randy Tate	.10	.04	.01
☐ 396	Frank Taveras	.10	.04	.01
☐ 397	Chuck Taylor	.10	.04	.01
☐ 398	Ron Taylor	.10	.04	.01
☐ 399	Bob Taylor	.10	.04	.01
☐ 400	Sammy Taylor	.10	.04	.01
☐ 401	Walt Terrell	.15	.06	.01
☐ 402	Ralph Terry	.15	.06	.01
☐ 403	Tim Teufel	.15	.06	.01
☐ 404	George Theodore	.10	.04	.01
☐ 405	Frank J. Thomas	.15	.06	.01
☐ 406	Lou Thornton	.10	.04	.01
☐ 407	Marv Throneberry	.20	.08	.02
☐ 408	Dick Tidrow	.10	.04	.01
☐ 409	Rusty Tillman	.10	.04	.01
☐ 410	Jackson Todd	.10	.04	.01
☐ 411	Joe Torre	.25	.10	.02
☐ 412	Mike Torrez	.10	.04	.01
☐ 413	Kelvin Torve	.10	.04	.01
☐ 414	Alex Trevino	.10	.04	.01
☐ 415	Wayne Twitchell	.10	.04	.01
☐ 416	Del Unser	.10	.04	.01
☐ 417	Mike Vail	.10	.04	.01
☐ 418	Bobby Valentine	.20	.08	.02
☐ 419	Ellis Valentine	.15	.06	.01
☐ 420	Julio Valera	.10	.04	.01
☐ 421	Tom Veryzer	.10	.04	.01
☐ 422	Frank Viola	.30	.12	.03
☐ 423	Bill Wakefield	.10	.04	.01
☐ 424	Gene Walter	.10	.04	.01
☐ 425	Claudell Washington	.15	.06	.01
☐ 426	Hank Webb	.10	.04	.01

☐ 427	Al Weis	.10	.04	.01
☐ 428	Dave West	.15	.06	.01
☐ 429	Wally Whitehurst	.10	.04	.01
☐ 430	Carl Willey	.10	.04	.01
☐ 431	Nick Willhite	.10	.04	.01
☐ 432	Charlie Williams	.10	.04	.01
☐ 433	Mookie Wilson	.20	.08	.02
☐ 434	Herm Winningham	.10	.04	.01
☐ 435	Gene Woodling	.15	.06	.01
☐ 436	Billy Wynne	.10	.04	.01
☐ 437	Joel Youngblood	.10	.04	.01
☐ 438	Pat Zachry	.10	.04	.01
☐ 439	Don Zimmer	.15	.06	.01
☐ xxx	Checklist 1-20	.10	.04	.01
☐ xxx	Checklist 41-60	.10	.04	.01
☐ xxx	Checklist 81-100	.10	.04	.01
☐ xxx	Checklist 121-140	.10	.04	.01
☐ xxx	Checklist 161-180	.10	.04	.01
☐ xxx	Checklist 201-220	.10	.04	.01
☐ xxx	Checklist 241-260	.10	.04	.01
☐ xxx	Checklist 281-300	.10	.04	.01
☐ xxx	Checklist 321-340	.10	.04	.01
☐ xxx	Checklist 361-380	.10	.04	.01
☐ xxx	Checklist 401-420	.10	.04	.01

1990 Wonder Bread Stars

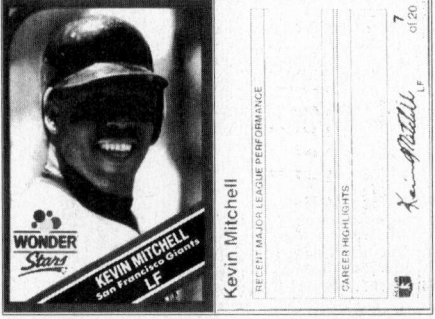

The 1990 Wonder Bread set was issued in 1990 by MSA (Michael Schechter Associates) in conjunction with Wonder Bread. One card was issued inside each specially marked package of Wonder Bread. Cards were available in grocery stores through June 15, 1990. The card was sealed in a pouch in the bread wrapper. This standard-size (2 1/2" by 3 1/2") card set was issued without logos like many of the sets produced by MSA. Cards were printed on thin stock and hence were easily creased during bread handling making the set more difficult to put together one card at a time for condition-conscious collectors. Cards are numbered on the back in the lower right corner. Wonder Bread also offered sets in uncut sheet form to collectors mailing in with 3.00 and five proofs of purchase.

		MINT	EXC	G-VG
	COMPLETE SET (20)	11.00	5.00	1.35
	COMMON PLAYER (1-20)	.20	.08	.02
☐ 1	Bo Jackson	1.50	.60	.15
☐ 2	Roger Clemens	1.00	.40	.10
☐ 3	Jim Abbott	.75	.30	.07
☐ 4	Orel Hershiser	.30	.12	.03
☐ 5	Ozzie Smith	.40	.16	.04
☐ 6	Don Mattingly	.75	.30	.07
☐ 7	Kevin Mitchell	.50	.20	.05
☐ 8	Jerome Walton	.30	.12	.03
☐ 9	Kirby Puckett	.60	.25	.06
☐ 10	Darryl Strawberry	.75	.30	.07
☐ 11	Robin Yount	.50	.20	.05
☐ 12	Tony Gwynn	.60	.25	.06
☐ 13	Alan Trammell	.40	.16	.04
☐ 14	Jose Canseco	1.00	.40	.10
☐ 15	Greg Swindell	.20	.08	.02
☐ 16	Nolan Ryan	1.50	.60	.15
☐ 17	Howard Johnson	.30	.12	.03

☐ 18	Ken Griffey Jr.	1.50	.60	.15
☐ 19	Will Clark	1.00	.40	.10
☐ 20	Ryne Sandberg	1.00	.40	.10

1985 Woolworth's

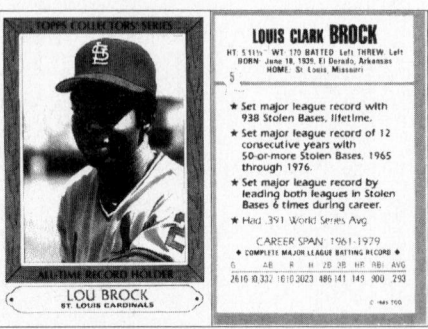

This 44-card set features color as well as black and white cards of All Time Record Holders. The cards are standard size (2 1/2" by 3 1/2") and are printed with blue ink on an orange and white back. The set was produced for Woolworth's by Topps and was packaged in a colorful box which contained a checklist of the cards in the set on the back panel. The numerical order of the cards coincides alphabetically with player's name.

		MINT	EXC	G-VG
	COMPLETE SET (44)	3.50	1.50	.35
	COMMON PLAYER (1-44)	.07	.03	.01
☐ 1	Hank Aaron	.35	.15	.03
☐ 2	Grover C. Alexander	.07	.03	.01
☐ 3	Ernie Banks	.15	.06	.01
☐ 4	Yogi Berra	.25	.10	.02
☐ 5	Lou Brock	.15	.06	.01
☐ 6	Steve Carlton	.15	.06	.01
☐ 7	Jack Chesbro	.07	.03	.01
☐ 8	Ty Cobb	.35	.15	.03
☐ 9	Sam Crawford	.07	.03	.01
☐ 10	Rollie Fingers	.15	.06	.01
☐ 11	Whitey Ford	.15	.06	.01
☐ 12	John Frederick	.07	.03	.01
☐ 13	Frankie Frisch	.07	.03	.01
☐ 14	Lou Gehrig	.35	.15	.03
☐ 15	Jim Gentile	.07	.03	.01
☐ 16	Dwight Gooden	.25	.10	.02
☐ 17	Rickey Henderson	.35	.15	.03
☐ 18	Rogers Hornsby	.15	.06	.01
☐ 19	Frank Howard	.07	.03	.01
☐ 20	Cliff Johnson	.07	.03	.01
☐ 21	Walter Johnson	.15	.06	.01
☐ 22	Hub Leonard	.07	.03	.01
☐ 23	Mickey Mantle	.50	.20	.05
☐ 24	Roger Maris	.15	.06	.01
☐ 25	Christy Mathewson	.10	.04	.01
☐ 26	Willie Mays	.35	.15	.03
☐ 27	Stan Musial	.25	.10	.02
☐ 28	Don Quisenberry	.07	.03	.01
☐ 29	Frank Robinson	.07	.03	.01
☐ 30	Pete Rose	.30	.12	.03
☐ 31	Babe Ruth	.50	.20	.05
☐ 32	Nolan Ryan	.60	.25	.06
☐ 33	George Sisler	.07	.03	.01
☐ 34	Tris Speaker	.10	.04	.01
☐ 35	Ed Walsh	.07	.03	.01
☐ 36	Lloyd Waner	.07	.03	.01
☐ 37	Earl Webb	.07	.03	.01
☐ 38	Ted Williams	.25	.10	.02
☐ 39	Maury Wills	.07	.03	.01
☐ 40	Hack Wilson	.07	.03	.01
☐ 41	Owen Wilson	.07	.03	.01
☐ 42	Willie Wilson	.07	.03	.01
☐ 43	Rudy York	.07	.03	.01
☐ 44	Cy Young	.15	.06	.01

1986 Woolworth's

This boxed set of 33 cards was produced by Topps for Woolworth's variety stores. The set features players who hold or have held hitting, home run or RBI titles. Cards are the standard 2 1/2" by 3 1/2" and have a glossy finish. The card fronts are bordered in yellow with the subtitle "Topps Collectors' Series" across the top. The card backs are printed in green and blue ink on white card stock. The custom box gives the set checklist on the back.

		MINT	EXC	G-VG
COMPLETE SET (33)		3.50	1.50	.35
COMMON PLAYER (1-33)		.07	.03	.01
☐ 1	Tony Armas	.07	.03	.01
☐ 2	Don Baylor	.10	.04	.01
☐ 3	Wade Boggs	.45	.18	.04
☐ 4	George Brett	.35	.15	.03
☐ 5	Bill Buckner	.07	.03	.01
☐ 6	Rod Carew	.40	.16	.04
☐ 7	Gary Carter	.15	.06	.01
☐ 8	Cecil Cooper	.10	.04	.01
☐ 9	Darrell Evans	.07	.03	.01
☐ 10	Dwight Evans	.10	.04	.01
☐ 11	George Foster	.10	.04	.01
☐ 12	Bob Grich	.07	.03	.01
☐ 13	Tony Gwynn	.40	.16	.04
☐ 14	Keith Hernandez	.15	.06	.01
☐ 15	Reggie Jackson	.50	.20	.05
☐ 16	Dave Kingman	.10	.04	.01
☐ 17	Carney Lansford	.10	.04	.01
☐ 18	Fred Lynn	.10	.04	.01
☐ 19	Bill Madlock	.07	.03	.01
☐ 20	Don Mattingly	.45	.18	.04
☐ 21	Willie McGee	.15	.06	.01
☐ 22	Hal McRae	.10	.04	.01
☐ 23	Dale Murphy	.30	.12	.03
☐ 24	Eddie Murray	.35	.15	.03
☐ 25	Ben Oglivie	.07	.03	.01
☐ 26	Al Oliver	.07	.03	.01
☐ 27	Dave Parker	.10	.04	.01
☐ 28	Jim Rice	.15	.06	.01
☐ 29	Pete Rose	.45	.18	.04
☐ 30	Mike Schmidt	.50	.20	.05
☐ 31	Gorman Thomas	.10	.04	.01
☐ 32	Willie Wilson	.10	.04	.01
☐ 33	Dave Winfield	.25	.10	.02

1987 Woolworth's Highlights

Topps produced this 33-card set for Woolworth's stores. The set is subtitled "Topps Collectors' Series Baseball Highlights" and consists of high gloss card fronts with full-color photos. Cards are the standard 2 1/2" by 3 1/2". The cards show and describe highlights of the previous season. The card backs are printed in gold and purple and are numbered. The set was sold nationally in Woolworth's for a 1.99 suggested retail price.

		MINT	EXC	G-VG
COMPLETE SET (33)		3.50	1.50	.35
COMMON PLAYER (1-33)		.07	.03	.01
☐ 1	Steve Carlton	.25	.10	.02
☐ 2	Cecil Cooper	.10	.04	.01
☐ 3	Rickey Henderson	.50	.20	.05
☐ 4	Reggie Jackson	.35	.15	.03
☐ 5	Jim Rice	.15	.06	.01
☐ 6	Don Sutton	.20	.08	.02
☐ 7	Roger Clemens	.50	.20	.05
☐ 8	Mike Schmidt	.45	.18	.04
☐ 9	Jesse Barfield	.15	.06	.01
☐ 10	Wade Boggs	.45	.18	.04
☐ 11	Tim Raines	.15	.06	.01
☐ 12	Jose Canseco	.60	.25	.06
☐ 13	Todd Worrell	.10	.04	.01
☐ 14	Dave Righetti	.10	.04	.01
☐ 15	Don Mattingly	.45	.18	.04
☐ 16	Tony Gwynn	.35	.15	.03
☐ 17	Marty Barrett	.07	.03	.01
☐ 18	Mike Scott	.10	.04	.01
☐ 19	Bruce Hurst	.10	.04	.01
☐ 20	Calvin Schiraldi	.07	.03	.01
☐ 21	Dwight Evans	.15	.06	.01
☐ 22	Dave Henderson	.10	.04	.01
☐ 23	Len Dykstra	.10	.04	.01
☐ 24	Bob Ojeda	.07	.03	.01
☐ 25	Gary Carter	.15	.06	.01
☐ 26	Ron Darling	.10	.04	.01
☐ 27	Jim Rice	.15	.06	.01
☐ 28	Bruce Hurst	.10	.04	.01
☐ 29	Darryl Strawberry	.50	.20	.05
☐ 30	Ray Knight	.10	.04	.01
☐ 31	Keith Hernandez	.15	.06	.01
☐ 32	Mets Celebration	.07	.03	.01
☐ 33	Ray Knight	.07	.03	.01

1988 Woolworth's Highlights

Topps produced this 33-card set for Woolworth's stores. The set is subtitled "Topps Collectors' Series Baseball Highlights" and consists of high gloss card fronts with full-color photos. Cards are the standard 2 1/2" by 3 1/2". The cards show and describe highlights of the previous season. Cards 19-33 commemorate the World Series with highlights and key players of each game in the series. The card backs are printed in red and blue on white card stock and are numbered. The set was sold nationally in Woolworth's for a 1.99 suggested retail price.

		MINT	EXC	G-VG
	COMPLETE SET (33)	3.50	1.50	.35
	COMMON PLAYER (1-33)	.07	.03	.01
☐ 1	Don Baylor	.10	.04	.01
☐ 2	Vince Coleman	.15	.06	.01
☐ 3	Darrell Evans	.07	.03	.01
☐ 4	Don Mattingly	.45	.18	.04
☐ 5	Eddie Murray	.35	.15	.03
☐ 6	Nolan Ryan	.65	.25	.06
☐ 7	Mike Schmidt	.45	.18	.04
☐ 8	Andre Dawson	.20	.08	.02
☐ 9	George Bell	.15	.06	.01
☐ 10	Steve Bedrosian	.07	.03	.01
☐ 11	Roger Clemens	.50	.20	.05
☐ 12	Tony Gwynn	.40	.16	.04
☐ 13	Wade Boggs	.45	.18	.04
☐ 14	Benny Santiago	.20	.08	.02
☐ 15	Mark McGwire UER	.40	.16	.04
	(referenced on card			
	back as NL ROY, sic)			
☐ 16	Dave Righetti	.10	.04	.01
☐ 17	Jeffrey Leonard	.07	.03	.01
☐ 18	Gary Gaetti	.07	.03	.01
☐ 19	Frank Viola WS1	.10	.04	.01
☐ 20	Dan Gladden WS1	.07	.03	.01
☐ 21	Bert Blyleven WS2	.10	.04	.01
☐ 22	Gary Gaetti WS2	.10	.04	.01
☐ 23	John Tudor WS3	.10	.04	.01
☐ 24	Todd Worrell WS3	.10	.04	.01
☐ 25	Tom Lawless WS4	.07	.03	.01
☐ 26	Willie McGee WS4	.10	.04	.01
☐ 27	Danny Cox WS5	.07	.03	.01
☐ 28	Curt Ford WS5	.07	.03	.01
☐ 29	Don Baylor WS6	.10	.04	.01
☐ 30	Kent Hrbek WS6	.10	.04	.01
☐ 31	Kirby Puckett WS7	.30	.12	.03
☐ 32	Greg Gagne WS7	.07	.03	.01
☐ 33	Frank Viola WS-MVP	.12	.05	.01

1989 Woolworth's Highlights

The 1989 Woolworth's Highlights set contains 33 standard-size (2 1/2" by 3 1/2") glossy cards. The fronts have red and white borders. The vertically-oriented backs are yellow and red, and describe highlights from the 1988 season including the World Series. The cards were distributed through Woolworth stores as a boxed set.

		MINT	EXC	G-VG
	COMPLETE SET (33)	3.50	1.50	.35
	COMMON PLAYER (1-33)	.07	.03	.01
☐ 1	Jose Canseco	.60	.25	.06
☐ 2	Kirk Gibson	.20	.08	.02
☐ 3	Frank Viola	.15	.06	.01
☐ 4	Orel Hershiser	.20	.08	.02
☐ 5	Walt Weiss	.20	.08	.02

		MINT	EXC	G-VG
☐ 6	Chris Sabo	.30	.12	.03
☐ 7	George Bell	.15	.06	.01
☐ 8	Wade Boggs	.40	.16	.04
☐ 9	Tom Browning	.10	.04	.01
☐ 10	Gary Carter	.20	.08	.02
☐ 11	Andre Dawson	.25	.10	.02
☐ 12	John Franco	.10	.04	.01
☐ 13	Randy Johnson	.10	.04	.01
☐ 14	Doug Jones	.07	.03	.01
☐ 15	Kevin McReynolds	.15	.06	.01
☐ 16	Gene Nelson	.07	.03	.01
☐ 17	Jeff Reardon	.15	.06	.01
☐ 18	Pat Tabler	.07	.03	.01
☐ 19	Tim Belcher	.15	.06	.01
☐ 20	Dennis Eckersley	.15	.06	.01
☐ 21	Orel Hershiser	.20	.08	.02
☐ 22	Gregg Jefferies	.35	.15	.03
☐ 23	Jose Canseco	.60	.25	.06
☐ 24	Kirk Gibson	.20	.08	.02
☐ 25	Orel Hershiser	.20	.08	.02
☐ 26	Mike Marshall	.10	.04	.01
☐ 27	Mark McGwire	.35	.15	.03
☐ 28	Rick Honeycutt	.07	.03	.01
☐ 29	Tim Belcher	.10	.04	.01
☐ 30	Jay Howell	.07	.03	.01
☐ 31	Mickey Hatcher	.07	.03	.01
☐ 32	Mike Davis	.07	.03	.01
☐ 33	Orel Hershiser	.20	.08	.02

1990 Woolworth Highlights

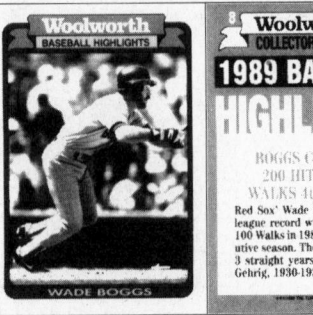

The 1990 Woolworth set is a 33-card set highlighting some of the more important events of the 1989 season. This set which has standard-size cards, 2 1/2" by 3 1/2", is broken down between major award winners, career highlights, and post-season heroes. The first six cards of the set feature the award winners while the last 11 cards of the set feature post-season heroes.

		MINT	EXC	G-VG
	COMPLETE SET (33)	3.50	1.50	.35
	COMMON PLAYER (1-33)	.07	.03	.01
☐ 1	Robin Yount MVP	.40	.16	.04
☐ 2	Kevin Mitchell MVP	.30	.12	.03
☐ 3	Bret Saberhagen CY	.20	.08	.02
☐ 4	Mark Davis CY	.10	.04	.01
☐ 5	Gregg Olson ROY	.15	.06	.01
☐ 6	Jerome Walton ROY	.20	.08	.02
☐ 7	Bert Blyleven	.10	.04	.01
☐ 8	Wade Boggs	.40	.16	.04
☐ 9	George Brett	.35	.15	.03
☐ 10	Vince Coleman	.20	.08	.02
☐ 11	Andre Dawson	.25	.10	.02
☐ 12	Dwight Evans	.10	.04	.01
☐ 13	Carlton Fisk	.25	.10	.02
☐ 14	Rickey Henderson	.50	.20	.05
☐ 15	Dale Murphy	.30	.12	.03
☐ 16	Eddie Murray	.35	.15	.03
☐ 17	Jeff Reardon	.15	.06	.01
☐ 18	Rick Reuschel	.07	.03	.01
☐ 19	Cal Ripken	.50	.20	.05
☐ 20	Nolan Ryan	.60	.25	.06
☐ 21	Ryne Sandberg	.45	.18	.04
☐ 22	Robin Yount	.35	.15	.03

		MINT	EXC	G-VG
☐ 23	Rickey Henderson	.50	.20	.05
☐ 24	Will Clark	.50	.20	.05
☐ 25	Dave Stewart	.15	.06	.01
☐ 26	Walt Weiss	.10	.04	.01
☐ 27	Mike Moore	.07	.03	.01
☐ 28	Terry Steinbach	.10	.04	.01
☐ 29	Dave Henderson	.10	.04	.01
☐ 30	Matt Williams	.30	.12	.03
☐ 31	Rickey Henderson	.50	.20	.05
☐ 32	Kevin Mitchell	.25	.10	.02
☐ 33	Dave Stewart	.15	.06	.01

1991 Woolworth Highlights

Topps produced this 33-card boxed set for Woolworth stores. The standard size (2 1/2" by 3 1/2") cards feature glossy color player photos on the fronts, with yellow borders on a white card face. The backs are printed in red, black, and white, and commemorate outstanding achievements of the players featured on the cards. The set can be subdivided as follows: MVPs (1-2), Cy Young winners (3-4), ROYs (5-6), '90 highlights in alphabetical order (7-22), playoff MVPs (23-24), and World Series action in chronological order (25-33). The cards are numbered on the back.

		MINT	EXC	G-VG
COMPLETE SET (33)		3.50	1.50	.35
COMMON PLAYER (1-33)		.07	.03	.01
☐ 1	Barry Bonds	.30	.12	.03
☐ 2	Rickey Henderson .... (Bat on shoulder)	.50	.20	.05
☐ 3	Doug Drabek	.10	.04	.01
☐ 4	Bob Welch	.10	.04	.01
☐ 5	Dave Justice	.50	.20	.05
☐ 6	Sandy Alomar Jr.	.15	.06	.01
☐ 7	Bert Blyleven	.10	.04	.01
☐ 8	George Brett	.35	.15	.03
☐ 9	Andre Dawson	.25	.10	.02
☐ 10	Dwight Evans	.10	.04	.01
☐ 11	Alex Fernandez	.15	.06	.01
☐ 12	Carlton Fisk	.25	.10	.02
☐ 13	Kevin Maas	.25	.10	.02
☐ 14	Dale Murphy	.30	.12	.03
☐ 15	Eddie Murray	.35	.15	.03
☐ 16	Dave Parker	.15	.06	.01
☐ 17	Jeff Reardon	.15	.06	.01
☐ 18	Cal Ripken	.50	.20	.05
☐ 19	Nolan Ryan	.60	.25	.06
☐ 20	Ryne Sandberg	.50	.20	.05
☐ 21	Bobby Thigpen	.10	.04	.01
☐ 22	Robin Yount	.35	.15	.03
☐ 23	Rob Dibble and Randy Myers	.10	.04	.01
☐ 24	Dave Stewart	.10	.04	.01
☐ 25	Eric Davis	.20	.08	.02
☐ 26	Rickey Henderson .... (Running bases)	.40	.16	.04
☐ 27	Billy Hatcher	.07	.03	.01
☐ 28	Joe Oliver	.07	.03	.01
☐ 29	Chris Sabo	.15	.06	.01
☐ 30	Barry Larkin	.20	.08	.02
☐ 31	Jose Rijo .... (Pitching Game 4)	.10	.04	.01

☐ 32	Reds Celebrate .... (1990 World Champions)	.10	.04	.01
☐ 33	Jose Rijo .... World Series MVP	.10	.04	.01

1931 W517

The cards in this 54-card set measure 3" by 4". This 1931 set of numbered, blank-backed cards was placed in the "W" category in the original American Card Catalog because (1) its producer was unknown and (2) it was issued in strips of three. The photo is black and white but the entire obverse of each card is generally found tinted in tones of sepia, blue, green, yellow, rose, black or gray. The cards are numbered in a small circle on the front. A solid dark line at one end of a card entitled the purchaser to another piece of candy as a prize. There are two different cards of both Babe Ruth and Mickey Cochrane.

		EX-MT	VG-E	GOOD
COMPLETE SET (54)		8000.00	3200.00	800.00
COMMON PLAYER (1-54)		45.00	20.00	6.75
☐ 1	Earl Combs	90.00	40.00	13.50
☐ 2	Pie Traynor	110.00	50.00	16.50
☐ 3	Eddie Rousch	110.00	50.00	16.50
☐ 4	Babe Ruth	1500.00	650.00	225.00
☐ 5	Chalmer Cissell	45.00	20.00	6.75
☐ 6	Bill Sherdel	45.00	20.00	6.75
☐ 7	Bill Shore	45.00	20.00	6.75
☐ 8	George Earnshaw	45.00	20.00	6.75
☐ 9	Bucky Harris	80.00	36.00	12.00
☐ 10	Charlie Klein	110.00	50.00	16.50
☐ 11	George Kelly	90.00	40.00	13.50
☐ 12	Travis Jackson	90.00	40.00	13.50
☐ 13	Willie Kamm	45.00	20.00	6.75
☐ 14	Harry Heilman	110.00	50.00	16.50
☐ 15	Grover Alexander	135.00	60.00	20.00
☐ 16	Frank Frisch	110.00	50.00	16.50
☐ 17	Jack Quinn	45.00	20.00	6.75
☐ 18	Cy Williams	45.00	20.00	6.75
☐ 19	Kiki Cuyler	90.00	40.00	13.50
☐ 20	Babe Ruth	1800.00	750.00	250.00
☐ 21	Jimmy Foxx	250.00	110.00	37.50
☐ 22	Jimmy Dykes	60.00	27.00	9.00
☐ 23	Bill Terry	125.00	57.50	18.75
☐ 24	Freddy Lindstrom	90.00	40.00	13.50
☐ 25	Hugh Critz	45.00	20.00	6.75
☐ 26	Pete Donahue	45.00	20.00	6.75
☐ 27	Tony Lazzeri	100.00	45.00	15.00
☐ 28	Heine Manush	90.00	40.00	13.50
☐ 29	Chick Hafey	90.00	40.00	13.50
☐ 30	Melvin Ott	175.00	80.00	27.00
☐ 31	Bing Miller	45.00	20.00	6.75
☐ 32	George Haas	45.00	20.00	6.75
☐ 33	Lefty O'Doul	60.00	27.00	9.00
☐ 34	Paul Waner	90.00	40.00	13.50
☐ 35	Lou Gehrig	900.00	375.00	100.00
☐ 36	Dazzy Vance	90.00	40.00	13.50

		EX-MT	VG-E	GOOD
☐ 37	Mickey Cochrane	135.00	60.00	20.00
☐ 38	Rogers Hornsby	250.00	110.00	37.50
☐ 39	Lefty Grove	175.00	80.00	27.00
☐ 40	Al Simmons	110.00	50.00	16.50
☐ 41	Rube Walberg	45.00	20.00	6.75
☐ 42	Hack Wilson	135.00	60.00	20.00
☐ 43	Art Shires	45.00	20.00	6.75
☐ 44	Sammy Hale	45.00	20.00	6.75
☐ 45	Ted Lyons	90.00	40.00	13.50
☐ 46	Joe Sewell	90.00	40.00	13.50
☐ 47	Goose Goslin	90.00	40.00	13.50
☐ 48	Lou Fonseca	45.00	20.00	6.75
☐ 49	Bob Meusel	60.00	27.00	9.00
☐ 50	Lu Blue	45.00	20.00	6.75
☐ 51	Earl Averill	90.00	40.00	13.50
☐ 52	Eddy Collins	110.00	50.00	16.50
☐ 53	Joe Judge	45.00	20.00	6.75
☐ 54	Mickey Cochrane	135.00	60.00	20.00

1922 W572

This 119-card set was issued in 1922 in ten-card strips along with strips of boxer cards. The cards measure approximately 1 5/16" by 2 1/2" and are blank backed. Most of the player photos on the fronts are black and white, although a few photos are sepia-toned. The pictures are the same ones used in the E120 set, but they have been cropped to fit on the smaller format. The player's signature and team appear at the bottom of the pictures, along with an IFS (International Feature Service) copyright notice. The cards are unnumbered and checklisted below in alphabetical order.

		EX-MT	VG-E	GOOD
	COMPLETE SET (119)	2500.00	1000.00	250.00
	COMMON PLAYER (1-119)	12.00	5.25	1.50
☐ 1	Eddie Ainsmith	12.00	5.25	1.50
☐ 2	Vic Aldridge	12.00	5.25	1.50
☐ 3	Grover C. Alexander	60.00	27.00	9.00
☐ 4	Dave Bancroft	24.00	10.50	3.50
☐ 5	Jesse Barnes	12.00	5.25	1.50
☐ 6	John Bassler	12.00	5.25	1.50
☐ 7	Lu Blue	12.00	5.25	1.50
☐ 8	Norm Boeckel	12.00	5.25	1.50
☐ 9	George Burns	12.00	5.25	1.50
☐ 10	Joe Bush	12.00	5.25	1.50
☐ 11	Leon Cadore	12.00	5.25	1.50
☐ 12	Virgil Cheevers	12.00	5.25	1.50
☐ 13	Ty Cobb	250.00	110.00	37.50
☐ 14	Eddie Collins	30.00	13.50	4.50
☐ 15	John Collins	12.00	5.25	1.50
☐ 16	Wilbur Cooper	12.00	5.25	1.50
☐ 17	Stanley Coveleski	24.00	10.50	3.50
☐ 18	Walton Cruise	12.00	5.25	1.50
☐ 19	Dave Danforth	12.00	5.25	1.50
☐ 20	Jake Daubert	15.00	6.50	2.15
☐ 21	Hank DeBerry	12.00	5.25	1.50
☐ 22	Lou Devormer	12.00	5.25	1.50
☐ 23	Bill Doak	12.00	5.25	1.50
☐ 24	Pete Donohue	12.00	5.25	1.50
☐ 25	Pat Duncan	12.00	5.25	1.50
☐ 26	Jimmy Dykes	15.00	6.50	2.15
☐ 27	Urban Faber	24.00	10.50	3.50
☐ 28	Bib Falk	12.00	5.25	1.50

		EX-MT	VG-E	GOOD
☐ 29	Frank Frisch	35.00	15.75	5.25
☐ 30	Chick Galloway	12.00	5.25	1.50
☐ 31	Ed Gharrity	12.00	5.25	1.50
☐ 32	Charles Glazner	12.00	5.25	1.50
☐ 33	Hank Gowdy	12.00	5.25	1.50
☐ 34	Tom Griffith	12.00	5.25	1.50
☐ 35	Burleigh Grimes	24.00	10.50	3.50
☐ 36	Ray Grimes	12.00	5.25	1.50
☐ 37	Heinie Groh	15.00	6.50	2.15
☐ 38	Joe Harris	12.00	5.25	1.50
☐ 39	Bucky Harris	24.00	10.50	3.50
☐ 40	Joe Hauser	12.00	5.25	1.50
☐ 41	Harry Heilmann	30.00	13.50	4.50
☐ 42	Walter Henline	12.00	5.25	1.50
☐ 43	Charles Hollocher	12.00	5.25	1.50
☐ 44	Harry Hooper	30.00	13.50	4.50
☐ 45	Rogers Hornsby	75.00	34.00	11.25
☐ 46	Waite Hoyt	24.00	10.50	3.50
☐ 47	Wilbur Hubbell	12.00	5.25	1.50
☐ 48	William Jacobson	12.00	5.25	1.50
☐ 49	Charles Jamieson	12.00	5.25	1.50
☐ 50	Syl Johnson	12.00	5.25	1.50
☐ 51	Walter Johnson	90.00	40.00	13.50
☐ 52	Jimmy Johnston	12.00	5.25	1.50
☐ 53	Joe Judge	12.00	5.25	1.50
☐ 54	George Kelly	24.00	10.50	3.50
☐ 55	Lee King	12.00	5.25	1.50
☐ 56	Larry Kopf	12.00	5.25	1.50
☐ 57	George Leverette	12.00	5.25	1.50
☐ 58	Al Mamaux	12.00	5.25	1.50
☐ 59	Rabbit Maranville	24.00	10.50	3.50
☐ 60	Rube Marquard	24.00	10.50	3.50
☐ 61	Martin McManus	12.00	5.25	1.50
☐ 62	Lee Meadows	12.00	5.25	1.50
☐ 63	Mike Menosky	12.00	5.25	1.50
☐ 64	Bob Meusel	15.00	6.50	2.15
☐ 65	Emil Meusel	15.00	6.50	2.15
☐ 66	George Mogridge	12.00	5.25	1.50
☐ 67	John Morrison	12.00	5.25	1.50
☐ 68	Johnny Mostil	12.00	5.25	1.50
☐ 69	Roleine Naylor	12.00	5.25	1.50
☐ 70	Art Nehf	12.00	5.25	1.50
☐ 71	Joe Oeschger	12.00	5.25	1.50
☐ 72	Bob O'Farrell	12.00	5.25	1.50
☐ 73	Steve O'Neill	12.00	5.25	1.50
☐ 74	Frank Parkinson	12.00	5.25	1.50
☐ 75	Ralph Perkins	12.00	5.25	1.50
☐ 76	Herman Pillette	12.00	5.25	1.50
☐ 77	Babe Pinelli	12.00	5.25	1.50
☐ 78	Wallie Pipp	15.00	6.50	2.15
☐ 79	Ray Powell	12.00	5.25	1.50
☐ 80	Jack Quinn	12.00	5.25	1.50
☐ 81	Goldie Rapp	12.00	5.25	1.50
☐ 82	Walt Reuther	12.00	5.25	1.50
☐ 83	Sam Rice	24.00	10.50	3.50
☐ 84	Emory Rigney	12.00	5.25	1.50
☐ 85	Eppa Rixey	24.00	10.50	3.50
☐ 86	Ed Rommel	15.00	6.50	2.15
☐ 87	Eddie Roush	35.00	15.75	5.25
☐ 88	Babe Ruth	500.00	225.00	75.00
☐ 89	Ray Schalk	24.00	10.50	3.50
☐ 90	Wallie Schang	15.00	6.50	2.15
☐ 91	Walter Schmidt	12.00	5.25	1.50
☐ 92	Joe Schultz	12.00	5.25	1.50
☐ 93	Hank Severeid	12.00	5.25	1.50
☐ 94	Joe Sewell	24.00	10.50	3.50
☐ 95	Bob Shawkey	15.00	6.50	2.15
☐ 96	Earl Sheely	12.00	5.25	1.50
☐ 97	Will Sherdel	12.00	5.25	1.50
☐ 98	Urban Shocker	15.00	6.50	2.15
☐ 99	George Sisler	50.00	22.50	7.50
☐ 100	Earl Smith	12.00	5.25	1.50
☐ 101	Elmer Smith	12.00	5.25	1.50
☐ 102	Jack Smith	12.00	5.25	1.50
☐ 103	Bill Southworth	12.00	5.25	1.50
☐ 104	Tris Speaker	60.00	27.00	9.00
☐ 105	Milton Stock	12.00	5.25	1.50
☐ 106	Jim Tierney	12.00	5.25	1.50
☐ 107	Harold Traynor	30.00	13.50	4.50
☐ 108	George Uhle	12.00	5.25	1.50
☐ 109	Bob Veach	12.00	5.25	1.50
☐ 110	Clarence Walker	12.00	5.25	1.50
☐ 111	Curtis Walker	12.00	5.25	1.50
☐ 112	Bill Wambsganss	15.00	6.50	2.15
☐ 113	Aaron Ward	12.00	5.25	1.50
☐ 114	Zach Wheat	24.00	10.50	3.50
☐ 115	Fred Williams	12.00	5.25	1.50
☐ 116	Ken Williams	15.00	6.50	2.15
☐ 117	Ivy Wingo	12.00	5.25	1.50
☐ 118	Joe Wood	20.00	8.50	2.75
☐ 119	Tom Zachary	12.00	5.25	1.50

1950-56 W576 Callahan HOF

CHRISTY MATHEWSON

The cards in this 82-card set measure 1 3/4" by 2 1/2". The 1950-56 Callahan Hall of Fame set was issued over a number of years at the Baseball Hall of Fame museum in Cooperstown, New York. New cards were added to the set each year when new members were inducted into the Hall of Fame. The cards with (2) in the checklist exist with two different biographies. The year of each card's first inclusion in the set is also given in parentheses; those not listed parenthetically below were issued in 1950 as well as in all the succeeding years and are hence the most common. Naturally the supply of cards is directly related to how many years a player was included in the set; cards that were not issued until 1955 are much scarcer than those printed all the years between 1950 and 1956. The catalog designation is W576. One frequently finds "complete" sets in the original box; take care to investigate the year of issue, the set may be complete in the sense of all the cards issued up to a certain year, but not all 82 cards below. For example, a "complete" 1950 set would obviously not include any of the cards marked below with ('52), ('54), or ('55) as none of those cards existed in 1950 since those respective players had not yet been inducted. The complete set price below refers to a set including all 83 cards below. Since the cards are unnumbered, they are numbered below for reference alphabetically by player's name.

	NRMT	VG-E	GOOD
COMPLETE SET (83)	600.00	270.00	90.00
COMMON PLAYER ('50)	2.50	1.00	.25
COMMON PLAYER ('52)	3.00	1.25	.30
COMMON PLAYER ('54)	4.00	1.75	.40
COMMON PLAYER ('55)	6.00	2.50	.60

☐	1	Grover Alexander	3.50	1.50	.35
☐	2	Cap Anson	2.50	1.00	.25
☐	3	Frank Baker ('55)	6.00	2.50	.60
☐	4	Edward Barrow ('54)	4.00	1.75	.40
☐	5	Chief Bender(2)('54)	4.00	1.75	.40
☐	6	Roger Bresnahan	2.50	1.00	.25
☐	7	Dan Brouthers	2.50	1.00	.25
☐	8	Mordecai Brown	2.50	1.00	.25
☐	9	Morgan Bulkeley	2.50	1.00	.25
☐	10	Jesse Burkett	2.50	1.00	.25
☐	11	Alexander Cartwright	2.50	1.00	.25
☐	12	Henry Chadwick	2.50	1.00	.25
☐	13	Frank Chance	2.50	1.00	.25
☐	14	Happy Chandler ('52)	30.00	13.50	4.50
☐	15	Jack Chesbro	2.50	1.00	.25
☐	16	Fred Clarke	2.50	1.00	.25
☐	17	Ty Cobb	60.00	27.00	9.00
☐	18A	Mickey Cochran ERR (sic, Cochrane)	7.50	3.25	.75
☐	18B	Mickey Cochrane COR	7.50	3.25	.75
☐	19	Eddie Collins (2)	2.50	1.00	.25
☐	20	Jimmie Collins	2.50	1.00	.25
☐	21	Charles Comiskey	2.50	1.00	.25
☐	22	Tom Connolly ('54)	4.00	1.75	.40
☐	23	Candy Cummings	2.50	1.00	.25
☐	24	Dizzy Dean ('54)	15.00	6.50	2.15
☐	25	Ed Delahanty	2.50	1.00	.25
☐	26	Bill Dickey ('54)(2)	9.00	4.00	.90

☐	27	Joe DiMaggio ('55)	100.00	45.00	15.00
☐	28	Hugh Duffy	2.50	1.00	.25
☐	29	Johnny Evers	2.50	1.00	.25
☐	30	Buck Ewing	2.50	1.00	.25
☐	31	Jimmie Foxx	6.00	2.50	.60
☐	32	Frank Frisch	2.50	1.00	.25
☐	33	Lou Gehrig	60.00	27.00	9.00
☐	34	Charles Gehringer	3.50	1.50	.35
☐	35	Clark Griffith	2.50	1.00	.25
☐	36	Lefty Grove	4.00	1.75	.40
☐	37	Gabby Hartnett ('55)	6.00	2.50	.60
☐	38	Harry Heilmann ('52)	3.00	1.25	.30
☐	39	Rogers Hornsby	6.00	2.50	.60
☐	40	Carl Hubbell	2.50	1.00	.25
☐	41	Hughey Jennings	2.50	1.00	.25
☐	42	Ban Johnson	2.50	1.00	.25
☐	43	Walter Johnson	9.00	4.00	.90
☐	44	Willie Keeler	2.50	1.00	.25
☐	45	Mike Kelly	2.50	1.00	.25
☐	46	Bill Klem ('54)	4.00	1.75	.40
☐	47	Napoleon Lajoie	4.00	1.75	.40
☐	48	Kenesaw Landis	2.50	1.00	.25
☐	49	Ted Lyons ('55)	6.00	2.50	.60
☐	50	Connie Mack	2.50	1.00	.25
☐	51	Walter Maranville('54)	4.00	1.75	.40
☐	52	Christy Mathewson	8.00	3.50	.80
☐	53	Tommy McCarthy	2.50	1.00	.25
☐	54	Joe McGinnity	2.50	1.00	.25
☐	55	John McGraw	2.50	1.00	.25
☐	56	Charles Nicholls	2.50	1.00	.25
☐	57	Jim O'Rourke	2.50	1.00	.25
☐	58	Mel Ott	3.50	1.50	.35
☐	59	Herb Pennock	2.50	1.00	.25
☐	60	Eddie Plank	2.50	1.00	.25
☐	61	Charles Radbourne	2.50	1.00	.25
☐	62	Wilbert Robinson	2.50	1.00	.25
☐	63	Babe Ruth	100.00	45.00	15.00
☐	64	Ray Schalk ('55)	6.00	2.50	.60
☐	65	Al Simmons ('54)	4.00	1.75	.40
☐	66	George Sisler (2)	2.50	1.00	.25
☐	67	A.G. Spalding	2.50	1.00	.25
☐	68	Tris Speaker	4.00	1.75	.40
☐	69	Bill Terry ('54)	6.00	2.50	.60
☐	70	Joe Tinker	2.50	1.00	.25
☐	71	Pie Traynor	2.50	1.00	.25
☐	72	Dazzy Vance ('55)	6.00	2.50	.60
☐	73	Rube Waddell	2.50	1.00	.25
☐	74	Hans Wagner	7.50	3.25	.75
☐	75	Bobby Wallace ('54)	6.00	2.50	.60
☐	76	Ed Walsh	2.50	1.00	.25
☐	77	Paul Waner ('52)	5.00	2.25	.50
☐	78	George Wright	2.50	1.00	.25
☐	79	Harry Wright ('54)	4.00	1.75	.40
☐	80	Cy Young	4.00	1.75	.40
☐	81	Museum Interior ('54) (2)	4.00	1.75	.40
☐	82	Museum Exterior ('54) (2)	4.00	1.75	.40

1955 W605 Robert Gould

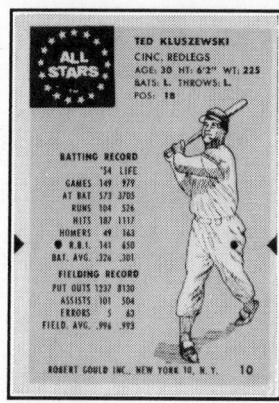

The cards in this 28-card set measure 2 1/2" by 3 1/2". The 1955 Robert F. Gould set of black and white on green cards were toy store cardboard holders for small plastic statues. The statues were attached to the card by a rubber band through two holes on the side of the card. The catalog designation is W605. The cards are numbered in the bottom right corner of the obverse and are blank-backed.

	NRMT	VG-E	GOOD
COMPLETE SET (28)	1500.00	600.00	150.00
COMMON PLAYER (1-28)	30.00	13.50	4.50
☐ 1 Willie Mays	350.00	160.00	52.50
☐ 2 Gus Zernial	30.00	13.50	4.50
☐ 3 Red Schoendienst	85.00	38.00	12.75
☐ 4 Chico Carrasquel	30.00	13.50	4.50
☐ 5 Jim Hegan	30.00	13.50	4.50
☐ 6 Curt Simmons	35.00	15.75	5.25
☐ 7 Bob Porterfield	30.00	13.50	4.50
☐ 8 Jim Busby	30.00	13.50	4.50
☐ 9 Don Mueller	35.00	15.75	5.25
☐ 10 Ted Kluszewski	60.00	27.00	9.00
☐ 11 Ray Boone	30.00	13.50	4.50
☐ 12 Smoky Burgess	35.00	15.75	5.25
☐ 13 Bob Rush	30.00	13.50	4.50
☐ 14 Early Wynn	85.00	38.00	12.75
☐ 15 Bill Bruton	30.00	13.50	4.50
☐ 16 Gus Bell	30.00	13.50	4.50
☐ 17 Jim Finigan	30.00	13.50	4.50
☐ 18 Granny Hamner	30.00	13.50	4.50
☐ 19 Hank Thompson	30.00	13.50	4.50
☐ 20 Joe Coleman	30.00	13.50	4.50
☐ 21 Don Newcombe	45.00	20.00	6.75
☐ 22 Richie Ashburn	70.00	32.00	10.50
☐ 23 Bobby Thomson	45.00	20.00	6.75
☐ 24 Sid Gordon	30.00	13.50	4.50
☐ 25 Gerry Coleman	30.00	13.50	4.50
☐ 26 Ernie Banks	175.00	80.00	27.00
☐ 27 Billy Pierce	40.00	18.00	6.00
☐ 28 Mel Parnell	35.00	15.75	5.25

1938-39 W711-1 Orange/Gray

The cards in this 32-card set measure approximately 2" by 3". The 1938-39 Cincinnati Reds Baseball player set was printed in orange and gray tones. Many back variations exist and there are two poses of Vander Meer, portrait (PORT) and an action (ACT) poses. The set was sold at the ballpark and was printed on thin cardboard stock. The cards are unnumbered but have been alphabetized and numbered in the checklist below.

	EX-MT	VG-E	GOOD
COMPLETE SET (32)	700.00	315.00	105.00
COMMON PLAYER (1-32)	14.00	6.25	2.00
☐ 1 Wally Berger (2)	18.00	7.50	2.50
☐ 2 Nino Bongiovanni (39)	50.00	22.50	7.50
☐ 3 Stanley Bordagaray Frenchy (39)	50.00	22.50	7.50
☐ 4 Joe Cascarella (38)	14.00	6.25	2.00
☐ 5 Allen Dusty Cooke (38)	14.00	6.25	2.00
☐ 6 Harry Craft	14.00	6.25	2.00
☐ 7 Ray (Peaches) Davis	14.00	6.25	2.00
☐ 8 Paul Derringer (2)	18.00	7.50	2.50
☐ 9 Linus Frey (2)	14.00	6.25	2.00
☐ 10 Lee Gamble (2)	14.00	6.25	2.00
☐ 11 Ival Goodman (2)	14.00	6.25	2.00
☐ 12 Hank Gowdy	14.00	6.25	2.00
☐ 13 Lee Grissom (2)	14.00	6.25	2.00
☐ 14 Willard Hershberger (2)	14.00	6.25	2.00
☐ 15 Eddie Joost (39)	14.00	6.25	2.00
☐ 16 Wes Livengood (39)	100.00	45.00	15.00
☐ 17 Ernie Lombardi (2)	50.00	22.50	7.50
☐ 18 Frank McCormick	18.00	7.50	2.50
☐ 19 Bill McKechnie (2)	30.00	13.50	4.50
☐ 20 Lloyd Whitey Moore (2)	14.00	6.25	2.00
☐ 21 Billy Myers (2)	14.00	6.25	2.00
☐ 22 Lew Riggs (2)	14.00	6.25	2.00
☐ 23 Eddie Roush CO (38)	45.00	20.00	6.75
☐ 24 Les Scarsella (39)	14.00	6.25	2.00
☐ 25 Gene Schott (38)	14.00	6.25	2.00
☐ 26 Eugene Thompson	14.00	6.25	2.00
☐ 27 Johnny VanderMeer PORT	30.00	13.50	4.50
☐ 28 Johnny VanderMeer ACT	30.00	13.50	4.50
☐ 29 Wm.(Bucky) Walters (2)	18.00	7.50	2.50
☐ 30 Jim Weaver	14.00	6.25	2.00
☐ 31 Bill Werber (39)	14.00	6.25	2.00
☐ 32 Jimmy Wilson (39)	14.00	6.25	2.00

1941 W711-2 Harry Hartman

The cards in this 34-card set measure approximately 2 1/8" by 2 5/8". The W711-2 Cincinnati Reds set contains unnumbered, black and white cards. This issue is sometimes called the "Harry Hartman" set. The cards are numbered below in alphabetical order by player's name with non-player cards listed at the end.

	EX-MT	VG-E	GOOD
COMPLETE SET (34)	450.00	200.00	67.50
COMMON PLAYER (1-28)	12.00	5.25	1.50
COMMON CARD (29-34)	8.00	3.50	.80
☐ 1 Morris Arnovich	12.00	5.25	1.50
☐ 2 William (Bill) Baker	12.00	5.25	1.50
☐ 3 Joseph Beggs	12.00	5.25	1.50
☐ 4 Harry Craft	12.00	5.25	1.50
☐ 5 Paul Derringer	18.00	7.50	2.50
☐ 6 Linus Frey	12.00	5.25	1.50
☐ 7 Ival Goodman	12.00	5.25	1.50
☐ 8 Hank Gowdy	12.00	5.25	1.50
☐ 9 Witt Guise	12.00	5.25	1.50
☐ 10 Willard Hershberger	12.00	5.25	1.50
☐ 11 John Hutchings	12.00	5.25	1.50
☐ 12 Edwin Joost	12.00	5.25	1.50
☐ 13 Ernie Lombardi	50.00	22.50	7.50
☐ 14 Frank McCormick	18.00	7.50	2.50
☐ 15 Myron McCormick	12.00	5.25	1.50
☐ 16 William McKechnie	30.00	13.50	4.50
☐ 17 Whitey Moore	12.00	5.25	1.50
☐ 18 William (Bill) Myers	12.00	5.25	1.50
☐ 19 Elmer Riddle	12.00	5.25	1.50
☐ 20 Lewis Riggs	12.00	5.25	1.50
☐ 21 James A. Ripple	12.00	5.25	1.50
☐ 22 Milburn Shoffner	12.00	5.25	1.50
☐ 23 Eugene Thompson	12.00	5.25	1.50
☐ 24 James Turner	15.00	6.50	2.15
☐ 25 John VanderMeer	25.00	11.00	3.50
☐ 26 Bucky Walters	18.00	7.50	2.50
☐ 27 Bill Werber	12.00	5.25	1.50
☐ 28 James Wilson	12.00	5.25	1.50
☐ 29 Results 1940 World Series	8.00	3.50	.80

			EX-MT	VG-E	GOOD
☐ 30	The Cincinati Reds (Title Card)		8.00	3.50	.80
☐ 31	The Cincinnati Reds World's Champions (Title Card)		8.00	3.50	.80
☐ 32	Debt of Gratitude to Wm. Koehl Co.		8.00	3.50	.80
☐ 33	Tell the World About Our Reds		8.00	3.50	.80
☐ 34	Harry Hartman		8.00	3.50	.80

1941 W753 Browns

The cards in this 29-card set measure approximately 2 1/8" by 2 5/8". The 1941 W753 set features unnumbered cards of the St. Louis Browns. The cards are numbered below alphabetically by player's name.

		EX-MT	VG-E	GOOD
COMPLETE SET (29)		375.00	165.00	55.00
COMMON PLAYER (1-29)		12.00	5.25	1.50

☐ 1	Johnny Allen	12.00	5.25	1.50
☐ 2	Elden Auker	12.00	5.25	1.50
☐ 3	Donald L. Barnes	12.00	5.25	1.50
☐ 4	Johnny Beradino	16.00	6.75	2.25
☐ 5	George Caster	12.00	5.25	1.50
☐ 6	Harland Clift	12.00	5.25	1.50
☐ 7	Roy J. Cullenbine	12.00	5.25	1.50
☐ 8	William O. DeWitt	12.00	5.25	1.50
☐ 9	Robert Estalella	12.00	5.25	1.50
☐ 10	Rick Ferrell	60.00	27.00	9.00
☐ 11	Dennis W. Galehouse	12.00	5.25	1.50
☐ 12	Joseph L. Grace	12.00	5.25	1.50
☐ 13	Frank Grube	12.00	5.25	1.50
☐ 14	Robert A. Harris	12.00	5.25	1.50
☐ 15	Donald Heffner	12.00	5.25	1.50
☐ 16	Fred Hofmann	12.00	5.25	1.50
☐ 17	Walter F. Judnich	12.00	5.25	1.50
☐ 18	Jack Kramer	12.00	5.25	1.50
☐ 19	Chester (Chet) Laabs	12.00	5.25	1.50
☐ 20	John Lucadello	12.00	5.25	1.50
☐ 21	George H. McQuinn	12.00	5.25	1.50
☐ 22	Robert Muncrief Jr.	12.00	5.25	1.50
☐ 23	John Niggeling	12.00	5.25	1.50
☐ 24	Fritz Ostermueller	12.00	5.25	1.50
☐ 25	James (Luke) Sewell	18.00	7.50	2.50
☐ 26	Alan C. Strange	12.00	5.25	1.50
☐ 27	Bob Swift	12.00	5.25	1.50
☐ 28	James (Zack) Taylor	12.00	5.25	1.50
☐ 29	Bill Trotter	12.00	5.25	1.50

1941 W754 Cardinals

The cards in this 29-card set measure approximately 2 1/8" by 2 5/8". The 1941 W754 set of unnumbered cards features St. Louis Cardinals. The cards are numbered below alphabetically by player's name.

		EX-MT	VG-E	GOOD
COMPLETE SET (29)		475.00	215.00	70.00
COMMON PLAYER (1-29)		12.00	5.25	1.50

☐ 1	Sam Breadon	12.00	5.25	1.50
☐ 2	Jimmy Brown	12.00	5.25	1.50
☐ 3	Mort Cooper	16.00	6.75	2.25
☐ 4	Walker Cooper	12.00	5.25	1.50
☐ 5	Estel Crabtree	12.00	5.25	1.50
☐ 6	Frank Crespi	12.00	5.25	1.50
☐ 7	Bill Crouch	12.00	5.25	1.50
☐ 8	Mike Gonzalez	12.00	5.25	1.50
☐ 9	Harry Gumpert	12.00	5.25	1.50
☐ 10	John Hopp	16.00	6.75	2.25
☐ 11	Ira Hutchinson	12.00	5.25	1.50
☐ 12	Howie Krist	12.00	5.25	1.50
☐ 13	Eddie Lake	12.00	5.25	1.50
☐ 14	Max Lanier	16.00	6.75	2.25
☐ 15	Gus Mancuso	12.00	5.25	1.50
☐ 16	Marty Marion	30.00	13.50	4.50
☐ 17	Steve Mesner	12.00	5.25	1.50
☐ 18	John Mize	60.00	27.00	9.00
☐ 19	Terry Moore	21.00	9.00	3.00
☐ 20	Sam Nahem	12.00	5.25	1.50
☐ 21	Don Padgett	12.00	5.25	1.50
☐ 22	Branch Rickey	60.00	27.00	9.00
☐ 23	Clyde Shoun	12.00	5.25	1.50
☐ 24	Enos Slaughter	60.00	27.00	9.00
☐ 25	Billy Southworth	12.00	5.25	1.50
☐ 26	Coaker Triplett	12.00	5.25	1.50
☐ 27	Buzzy Wares	12.00	5.25	1.50
☐ 28	Lon Warneke	16.00	6.75	2.25
☐ 29	Ernie White	12.00	5.25	1.50

1928 Yuenglings

The cards in this 60-card set measure approximately 1 3/8" by 2 9/16". This black and white, numbered set contains many Hall of Famers. The obverses are the same as those found in E210 and W502. The Paul Waner card, number 45, actually contains a picture of Clyde Barnhardt. Each back contains an offer to redeem pictures of Babe Ruth for ice cream. The catalog designation for this set is F50.

		EX-MT	VG-E	GOOD
COMPLETE SET (60)		2100.00	850.00	250.00
COMMON PLAYER (1-60)		12.00	5.25	1.50

☐ 1	Burleigh Grimes	24.00	10.50	3.50
☐ 2	Walter Reuther	12.00	5.25	1.50
☐ 3	Joe Dugan	15.00	6.50	2.15
☐ 4	Red Faber	24.00	10.50	3.50

☐ 5	Gabby Hartnett	30.00	13.50	4.50
☐ 6	Babe Ruth	500.00	225.00	75.00
☐ 7	Bob Meusel	15.00	6.50	2.15
☐ 8	Herb Pennock	24.00	10.50	3.50
☐ 9	George Burns	12.00	5.25	1.50
☐ 10	Joe Sewell	24.00	10.50	3.50
☐ 11	George Uhle	12.00	5.25	1.50
☐ 12	Bob O'Farrell	12.00	5.25	1.50
☐ 13	Rogers Hornsby	75.00	34.00	11.25
☐ 14	Pie Traynor	35.00	15.75	5.25
☐ 15	Clarence Mitchell	12.00	5.25	1.50
☐ 16	Eppa Rixey	24.00	10.50	3.50
☐ 17	Carl Mays	18.00	7.50	2.50
☐ 18	Adolfo Luque	12.00	5.25	1.50
☐ 19	Dave Bancroft	24.00	10.50	3.50
☐ 20	George Kelly	24.00	10.50	3.50
☐ 21	Earl Combs	24.00	10.50	3.50
☐ 22	Harry Heilmann	30.00	13.50	4.50
☐ 23	Ray Schalk	24.00	10.50	3.50
☐ 24	John Mostil	12.00	5.25	1.50
☐ 25	Hack Wilson	40.00	18.00	6.00
☐ 26	Lou Gehrig	250.00	110.00	37.50
☐ 27	Ty Cobb	250.00	110.00	37.50
☐ 28	Tris Speaker	60.00	27.00	9.00
☐ 29	Tony Lazzeri	30.00	13.50	4.50
☐ 30	Waite Hoyt	24.00	10.50	3.50
☐ 31	Sherwood Smith	12.00	5.25	1.50
☐ 32	Max Carey	24.00	10.50	3.50
☐ 33	Gene Hargrave	12.00	5.25	1.50
☐ 34	Miguel Gonzalez	12.00	5.25	1.50
☐ 35	Joe Judge	12.00	5.25	1.50
☐ 36	Sam Rice	24.00	10.50	3.50
☐ 37	Earl Sheely	12.00	5.25	1.50
☐ 38	Sam Jones	12.00	5.25	1.50
☐ 39	Bibb Falk	12.00	5.25	1.50
☐ 40	Willie Kamm	12.00	5.25	1.50
☐ 41	Stan (Bucky) Harris	20.00	8.50	2.75
☐ 42	John McGraw	40.00	18.00	6.00
☐ 43	Art Nehf	12.00	5.25	1.50
☐ 44	Grover C. Alexander	60.00	27.00	9.00
☐ 45	Paul Waner	24.00	10.50	3.50
☐ 46	Bill Terry	45.00	20.00	6.75
☐ 47	Glenn Wright	12.00	5.25	1.50
☐ 48	Earl Smith	12.00	5.25	1.50
☐ 49	Goose Goslin	24.00	10.50	3.50
☐ 50	Frank Frisch	40.00	18.00	6.00
☐ 51	Joe Harris	12.00	5.25	1.50
☐ 52	Cy Williams	15.00	6.50	2.15
☐ 53	Eddie Roush	30.00	13.50	4.50
☐ 54	George Sisler	45.00	20.00	6.75
☐ 55	Ed Rommel	15.00	6.50	2.15
☐ 56	Roger Peckinpaugh	12.00	5.25	1.50
☐ 57	Stanley Coveleskie	24.00	10.50	3.50
☐ 58	Lester Bell	12.00	5.25	1.50
☐ 59	Lloyd Waner	24.00	10.50	3.50
☐ 60	John McInnis	15.00	6.50	2.15

About the Author

Jim Beckett, the leading authority on sport card values in the United States, maintains a wide range of activities in the world of sports. He possesses one of the finest collections of sports cards and autographs in the world, has made numerous appearances on radio and television, and has been frequently cited in many national publications. He was awarded the first "Special Achievement Award" for Contributions to the Hobby by the National Sports Collectors Convention in 1980, the "Jock-Jasperson Award" for Hobby Dedication in 1983, and the "Buck Barker, Spirit of the Hobby" Award in 1991.

Dr. Beckett is the author of *The Sport Americana Baseball Card Price Guide, The Official Price Guide to Baseball Cards, The Sport Americana Price Guide to Baseball Collectibles, The Sport Americana Baseball Memorabilia and Autograph Price Guide, The Sport Americana Football Card Price Guide, The Official Price Guide to Football Cards, The Sport Americana Hockey Card Price Guide, The Official Price Guide to Hockey Cards, The Sport Americana Basketball Card Price Guide and Alphabetical Checklist, The Official Price Guide to Basketball Cards*, and *The Sport Americana Alphabetical Baseball Card Checklist*. In addition, he is the founder, publisher, and editor of *Beckett Baseball Card Monthly, Beckett Basketball Monthly, Beckett Football Card Monthly, Beckett Hockey Monthly*, and *Beckett Focus on Future Stars*, magazines dedicated to advancing the card collecting hobby.

Jim Beckett received his Ph.D. in Statistics from Southern Methodist University in 1975. Prior to starting Beckett Publications in 1984, Dr. Beckett served as an Associate Professor of Statistics at Bowling Green State University and as a Vice President of a consulting firm in Dallas, Texas. He currently resides in Dallas with his wife Patti and their daughters, Christina, Rebecca, and Melissa.

924

Known for our large selection of EX-Mint to Near Mint early cards

Full service card shop

—Single cards
—Complete sets
—Packs
—Packs of common players
—Card supplies
—Our 11th year of servicing your collecting needs

—Ten minutes from Midway Airport and 45 minutes from Chicago Loop
—Yes, we do buy 1980 and earlier Near Mint to Mint cards
—Football cards also available

We will be happy to service your want list.

FAMILY COINS

Scottsdale Shopping Center
7933 S. Cicero, Chicago, IL 60652   (312) 582-4452

SPORTS EXCHANGE
Is the "free ad" newsletter for the active player in the hobby. BUY-SELL-TRADE YOUR SPORTS COLLECTIBLES THE SMART WAY!

PUBLISHED BIWEEKLY

THREE MONTHS ONLY $12.50

Write for sample copy

SPORTS EXCHANGE
"A Card Show in your MAILBOX"
Box 19302 Alexandria VA 22320
703-836-4382 voice/fax

HOUSE OF CARDS
BILL HUGGINS • NICK SHOFF

The Baseball Card Store with All-Star Values

★ *Now in two locations* ★
to serve you better

Since 1976

The finest selection of Baseball, Football, Hockey and Basketball cards and sports memorabilia

2411 University Blvd. W.
P.O. Box 1911
Wheaton, MD 20915
(301) 933-0355

615 S. Frederick Ave.
Gaithersburg, MD 20877
(301) 670-4754

Open:
Monday–Friday 11 a.m.– 7:30 p.m.
Saturday 11 a.m.– 6:00 p.m.
Sunday 11 a.m.– 4:00 p.m.

We are always interested in buying collections!

BASEBALL CARD LOTS

VG+ - Ex Cond   My Choice of #'s

	100 Diff.	200 Diff.		100 Diff.	200 Diff.
1955B	400.00		1965	110.00	210.00
1956	510.00		1966	85.00	160.00
1957	360.00		1967	85.00	160.00
1958	230.00		1968	70.00	130.00
1959	220.00	430.00	1969	55.00	105.00
1960	190.00	370.00	1970	52.00	100.00
1961	160.00	310.00	1971	52.00	100.00
1962	130.00	250.00	1972	40.00	78.00
1963	130.00		1973-76*	22.00	40.00
1964	110.00	210.00	1976-80*	10.00	18.00

*Choose the Year

Bowman	25 Diff.	50 Diff.	Topps	25 Diff.	50 Diff.
1950	250.00	480.00	1952	475.00	900.00
1951	250.00	480.00	1953	325.00	600.00
1952	250.00	480.00	1954	210.00	400.00
1953	500.00	950.00	1955	140.00	270.00
1954	140.00	270.00	1956	140.00	270.00
1955	110.00	210.00	1957	100.00	190.00

SPECIALS - POSTPAID

250 Assorted 1958-62 VG	450.00	500	850.00
250 Assorted 1960-69 VG	270.00	500	520.00
250 Assorted 1970-79 VG	60.00	500	110.00
250 Assorted 1980-84 VG	15.00	500	28.00

Topps Sets 1988-1992 $22.95 ea. + $2.50 UPS

Also Will Buy Your Pre 1976 Cards

Also send for Free Retail Price List on Commons.

Postage & Handling: 1.75 first 100 cards .50 each add. 100 cards

Hi Numbers VG - Ex Cond.
My Choice of #'s

	10		20	40
1957	110.00	1965	60.00	
1959	80.00	1968	40.00	
1960	80.00	1970	50.00	95.00
1962	80.00	1971	65.00	120.00
1963	50.00	1972	65.00	120.00
		1973	35.00	65.00

BILL HENDERSON'S CARDS
2320 Ruger Ave., BLK-6
Janesville, WI 53545
1-608-755-0922

BASEBALL CARDS ON APPROVAL

I fill wantlists of baseball and football cards and will send you your order on approval (excluding complete sets). If the cards are satisfactory, then send payment. If they are unsatisfactory just return them, securely packaged with my original invoice. Send your wantlists in *numerical order* by year. Orders **over $25** will be discounted at least 10 percent and will be sent U.P.S. postpaid. Orders **under $25** will have mailing costs added. Minimum order is **$5** and no "mint only" orders please. Same-day service and satisfaction are always my guarantee. Your *first* order with me *must* include your street address for U.P.S shipping, your phone number, an SASE and a price limit for how much you want to spend. A deposit may be required on certain orders.

I also sell complete sets, 1981 to present, and bricks (lots) in most years. Send SASE for my pricelist. I also have a huge inventory of lesser condition (F-VG) cards that are reasonably priced.

Yes! We buy collections!

Baseball Cards-Plus
Dave Shore
5587 Clairemont Mesa Blvd.
Suite A, Dept. PG 14
San Diego, CA 92117
(619) 565-CARD

EAST TEXAS SPORTS CARDS
P.O. Box 1334 • 1411 E. Rusk
Jacksonville, Texas 75766

EAST TEXAS
SPORTS CARDS

"Now serving collectors all over the U.S., Canada, and Puerto Rico."

Our quarterly flyers and auctions are a big hit! Don't be left out . . . send $2.00 for a full year of our mailings.

SPECIAL: 800 different sports cards only $15.00 postpaid!

"Jacksonville's First - East Texas' Best"

BASEBALL CARD LOTS
Our Choice - No Superstars

1959 Topps 10 diff (f-vg)	$15.00
1960 Topps 10 diff (f-vg)	8.50
1961 Topps 10 diff (f-vg)	8.50
1962 Topps 10 diff (f-vg)	8.00
1963 Topps 10 diff (f-vg)	7.50
1964 Topps 10 diff (f-vg)	6.00
1965 Topps 10 diff (f-vg)	6.00
1966 Topps 10 diff (f-vg)	5.00
1967 Topps 10 diff (f-vg)	4.50
1968 Topps 10 diff (f-vg)	4.00
1969 Topps 25 diff (f-vg)	7.50
1970 Topps 25 diff (f-vg)	4.50
1971 Topps 25 diff (f-vg)	4.50
1972 Topps 25 diff (f-vg)	4.50
1973 Topps 25 diff (f-vg)	4.50
1974 Topps 25 diff (f-vg)	3.95
1975 Topps 25 diff (f-vg)	3.95
1976 Topps 25 diff (f-vg)	2.95
1977 Topps 25 diff (f-vg)	2.95
1978 Topps 50 diff (f-vg)	3.95
1979 Topps 50 diff (f-vg)	2.95
1980 Topps 50 diff (f-vg)	2.95
1981 Donruss 50 diff (ex-m)	2.50
1981 Fleer 50 diff (ex-m)	2.50
1982 Fleer 50 diff (ex-m)	2.50

FOOTBALL CARD LOTS
Our Choice - No Superstars

1969 Topps 25 diff (f-vg)	$7.95
1970 Topps 25 diff (f-vg)	6.95
1971 Topps 25 diff (f-vg)	4.95
1972 Topps 25 diff (f-vg)	4.95
1973 Topps 25 diff (f-vg)	4.95
1974 Topps 25 diff (f-vg)	3.50
1975 Topps 25 diff (f-vg)	3.50
1976 Topps 25 diff (f-vg)	3.50
1977 Topps 25 diff (f-vg)	2.50
1978 Topps 50 diff (f-vg)	3.00
1979 Topps 50 diff (f-vg)	3.00
1980 Topps 50 diff (f-vg)	2.50

ORDERING INSTRUCTIONS
Offers expire March 1993 while supply lasts. Please include $3.00 per order for postage and handling.

Send orders to:

FIRST BASE
216 Webb Chapel Village
Dallas, Texas 75229
(214) 243-5271

Our current price lists sent free with orders. To receive price lists without ordering send $1.00 or a **large** self addressed stamped (75¢ in stamps) envelope to the above address.

SPECIAL OFFERS

#1: Type Set: One card from each year of Topps baseball 1952 through 1989, our choice of cards, Good to EX, 38 cards for $39.95.

#2: 1987 Fleer Baseball Record Setters - Complete Set of 44 cards — $4.00.

#3: Robert Redford Poster as "The Natural" - $6.95.

#4: 1983 Affiliated Foods Texas Rangers - Complete Set of 28 — $5.00.
Uncut Poster (All 28 cards) — $7.50
1984 Jarvis Press Texas Rangers
Complete Set of 30 — $5.00
1985 Performance Printing Texas Rangers
Complete Set of 28 — $5.00

#5: 1991 Pacific Nolan Ryan
Set of 110 — $12.95.

#6: 1987 Donruss Highlights
Set of 56 with Puzzle — $5.00

#7: 1988 Mothers Cookies Texas Rangers
Complete Set of 28 — $12.00.

#8: 1982 K-Mart Baseball Set of 33 — $2.50.

#9: 1988 Topps/Revco League Leaders
Complete Set of 33 — $4.00.

#10: Super Bowl XX Game Program —$10.00.

#11: 1986 McDonalds Dallas Cowboys Football Card Set of 25 with Herschel Walker — $9.95.

#12: 1986 McDonalds NFL All-Stars Football Card Set of 24 — $3.95.

#13: Dallas Cowboys Police/Safety Sets:
1979 (15) — $20.00 1980 (14) — $12.50
1981 (14) — $12.50 1983 (28) — $15.00

#14: Dallas Cowboys Media Guides (not issued to the public) 1989 edition $5.00
1988 edition — $5.00 1987 edition — $7.50
1986 edition — $7.50 1985 edition — $7.50

#15: 1987 Texas Rangers Surf Book (shows pictures of all Rangers cards) — $7.95

#16: Pacific Operation Desert Shield
Wax Box (36) packs — $18.00
Pacific Rad Dudes Wax Box
(36 packs) — $15.00
Set (110 cards) — $10.00

Unopened Boxes — Guaranteed Unopened

Baseball

Wax or Foil Boxes

1992 Topps (540 Cards)	$ 18.00
1991 Topps (540)	16.00
1990 Topps (576)	16.00
1989 Topps (540)	16.00
1988 Topps (612)	16.00
1987 Topps (612)	32.00
1986 Topps (540)	40.00
1991 '53 Topps Archives (432)	Call for price
1992 Donruss Series 1 & 2 (540)	Call for price
1991 Donruss-Series 1 (576)	16.00
1991 Donruss-Series 2 (576)	16.00
1990 Donruss (576)	14.00
1989 Donruss (540)	16.00
1988 Donruss (540)	14.00
1987 Donruss (540)	68.00
1991 Donruss Studio (480)	75.00
1992 Score Series 1 (576)	18.00
1992 Score Series 2 (576)	18.00
1991 Score Series 1 (576)	16.00
1991 Score Series 2 (576)	19.00
1990 Score (576)	25.00
1989 Score (612)	16.00
1988 Score (612)	16.00
1992 Fleer (612)	33.00
1991 Fleer (540)	16.00
1991 Fleer Ultra (504)	38.00
1992 Upper Deck Lo# (540)	35.00
1991 Upper Deck Lo# (540)	35.00
1991 Upper deck Hi# (540)	42.00
1990 Upper Deck Lo# (540)	42.00
1990 Upper Deck Hi# (540)	55.00
1989 Upper Deck Lo# (540)	190.00
1989 Upper Deck Hi# (540)	165.00
1991 Bowman (504)	17.00
1990 Bowman (504)	17.00
1989 Bowman (432)	17.00
1991 Leaf Series 1 (540)	70.00
1991 Leaf Series 2 (540)	100.00
1990 Leaf Series 1 (540)	225.00
1990 Leaf Series 2 (540)	400.00
1991 O-Pee-Chee Prem. (252)	65.00

Rack-Pack Boxes

1991 Topps (1,080 Cards)	28.00
1990 Topps (1,104)	28.00
1989 Topps (1,032)	28.00
1988 Topps (1,032)	28.00
1987 Topps (1,080)	45.00
1986 Topps (1,176)	60.00
1988 Score (1,320)	30.00
1989 Bowman (936)	30.00

Cello Boxes

1989 Donruss (864 Cards)	24.00
1988 Donruss (864)	20.00

Topps 500 Count Vending Boxes

1992	15.00
1991	15.00
1990	16.00
1989	16.00
1988	16.00
1987	25.00
1986	28.00

Football

Wax Boxes

1991 Upper Deck LO #(540)	37.00
1991 Upper Deck HI #(540)	40.00
1991 Fleer Ultra (504)	25.00
1991 Fleer (504)	15.00
1990 Fleer (540)	23.00
1991 Pro Set Series 1 (540)	16.00
1991 Pro Set Series 2 (540)	16.00
1990 Pro Set Series 1 (576)	14.00
1990 Pro Set Series 2 (576)	14.00
1991 Pro Set Platinum Series 1 (432)	35.00
1991 Pro Set Platinum Series 2 (432)	35.00
1991 Action Packed (216)	45.00
1991 Action Packed Rookies (216)	45.00
1991 Score Series 1 (576)	16.00
1991 Score Series 2 (576)	16.00
1990 Score Series 1 (576)	14.00
1990 Score Series 2 (576)	14.00
1991 Pro Line (432)	20.00
1991 Pacific Plus (504)	20.00

Football Sets

1991 Upper Deck (700)	60.00
1991 Upper Deck HI # (200)	22.00
1991 Score (690)	20.00
1991 Score Traded (110)	20.00
1990 Score (665)	16.00
1990 Score Traded (110)	85.00
1989 Score Traded (110)	28.00
1991 Fleer Ultra (300)	25.00
1991 Fleer (432)	12.00
1990 Fleer (400)	18.00
1990 Fleer Traded (120)	35.00
1991 Topps (660)	25.00
1990 Topps (528)	17.00
1990 Topps Traded (132)	18.00
1989 Topps Traded (132)	12.00
1991 Pro Set Ser. 1 (405)	13.00
1990 Pro Set Ser. 1 (377)	10.00
1990 Pro Set Ser. 2 (396)	13.00
1991 Pro Line (307)	10.00
1991 Classic Draft (50)	15.00
1991 Pacific Plus (550)	25.00
1991 Star Pics (113)	13.00
1991 Action Packed Rookes (84)	24.00
Super Bowl XXV Commemorative (160)	7.00

Wide Selection of Pro Line

Autographed Cards Call for list and prices

Call for prices on **Stadium Club boxes and sets.**

All prices include shipping
Same day service with VISA or MasterCard
All prices subject to change

BILL DODGE

P.O. BOX 40154
Bay Village, OH 44140
Phone: (216) 899-9901

Fourteen years of quality mail order service

COMPLETE BASEBALL CARD SETS

Regular Issues

1992 Topps (792 cards)	$25.00
1991 Topps (792)	25.00
1990 Topps (792)	25.00
1989 Topps (792)	25.00
1988 Topps (792)	25.00
All 5 above Topps sets	115.00
1987 Topps (792)	37.00
1986 Topps (792)	40.00
All 7 above Topps sets	185.00
1985 Topps (792)	110.00
1984 Topps (792)	110.00
1992 Fleer (720)	45.00
1991 Fleer (720)	25.00
1990 Fleer (660)	17.00
1989 Fleer (660)	26.00
All 4 above Fleer Sets	105.00
1988 Fleer (660)	40.00
1987 Fleer (660)	110.00
1986 Fleer (660)	150.00
1991 Fleer Ultra (400)	45.00
1992 Donruss (784) Call for price	
1991 Donruss w/Leaf promo	36.00
1990 Donruss (716)	17.00
1989 Donruss (660)	24.00
1988 Donruss (660)	24.00
All 4 Above Donruss sets '88-'91	95.00
1987 Donruss (660)	75.00
1991 Donruss Studio (264)	50.00
1991 Leaf (528)	90.00
1990 Leaf (528)	290.00
1992 Score (900)	32.00
1991 Score (900)	32.00
1990 Score (704)	28.00
All 3 above Score sets	87.00
1990 Score (714)	45.00
1989 Score (660)	22.00
1988 Score (660)	23.00
'88 Thru '92 Score sets	125.00
1991 Upper Deck (800)	55.00
1990 Upper Deck (800)	65.00
1989 Upper Deck (800)	220.00
1991 Bowman (704)	28.00
1990 Bowman (528)	20.00
1989 Bowman (484)	20.00
All 3 above Bowman sets	62.00
1990 Sportflics (225)	38.00
1989 Sportflics (225)	42.00
1987 Sportflics (200)	32.00
1991 O-Pee-Chee prem. (132)	55.00

Traded or Update Issues

1991 Topps (132)	14.00
1990 Topps (132)	13.00
1989 Topps (132)	12.00
1988 Topps (132)	30.00
1987 Topps (132)	14.00
1986 Topps (132)	35.00
1985 Topps (132)	30.00
All 7 Above Topps sets	135.00
1991 Fleer (132)	14.00
1990 Fleer (132)	13.00
1989 Fleer (132)	18.00
1988 Fleer (132)	14.00
1987 Fleer (132)	18.00
1986 Fleer (132)	36.00
1985 Fleer (132)	30.00
All 7 above Fleer sets	130.00

1991 Fleer Ultra (120)	25.00
1991 Score (110)	14.00
1990 Score (110)	25.00
1989 Score (110)	14.00
All 3 Above Score sets	50.00
1988 Score (110)	70.00
1991 Upper Deck final edition (100)	20.00
1991 Upper Deck (100)	15.00
1990 Upper Deck (100)	15.00
1989 Upper Deck (100)	22.00
1991 Donruss Rookies (56)	11.00
1990 Donruss Rookies (56)	13.00
1989 Donruss Rookies (56)	20.00
1988 Donruss Rookies (56)	14.00
1987 Donruss Rookies (56)	22.00
All 5 Above Donruss Sets	72.00
1986 Sportflics Rook. (50)	20.00

Specialty Sets

1991 Topps Micro (792)	15.00
1991 Topps '90 Debut (171)	17.00
1990 Topps '89 Debut (152)	15.00
1990 Topps Bigs (330)	30.00
1988 Topps Bigs (264)	30.00
1989 Topps Sr. League (132)	10.00
1989 Score Masters (42)	12.00
1987 Donruss Open Day (272)	20.00
1987 Donruss Hilites (56)	5.00
1991 Leaf Gold Bonus (26)	110.00
1991 Leaf Promo Cards (26)	200.00
1987 Fleer Minis (120)	10.00
1986 Fleer Minis (120)	12.00
1986 Topps Supers (60)	8.00
1990 Topps Glossy All Stars (26)	6.00
1991 Upper Deck Silver Sluggers (18)	45.00
1991 Classic Draft Pick (51)	15.00

Call for prices on
Stadium Club boxes and sets.
All prices include shipping

Same day service with VISA or MasterCard

Please provide adequate street address for U.P.S. delivery

U.S. Funds only

**Alaska, Hawaii add 15% postage
Foreign add 25% postage**

All prices subject to change

BILL DODGE

**P.O. BOX 40154
Bay Village, OH 44140
Phone: (216) 899-9901**

Fourteen years of quality mail order service

BASKETBALL · HOCKEY · NON-SPORTS

Basketball Wax Boxes

1991-92 Upper Deck LO# (432) 45.00
1991-92 Upper Deck HI# (432) 48.00
1991-92 Hoops 1 (540) 16.00
1991-92 Hoops 2 (540) 18.00
1990-91 Hoops 1 (540) 16.00
1990-91 Hopps 2 (540) 16.00
1989-90 Hoops 1 (540) 125.00
1989-90 Hoops 2 (540) 35.00
1991-92 SkyBox 1 (540) 29.00
1991-92 SkyBox 2 (540) 29.00
1990-91 SkyBox 1 (540) 25.00
1990-91 SkyBox 2 (540) 20.00
1991-92 Fleer (504) 16.00
1990-91 Fleer (540) 22.00

Hockey Wax Boxes

1991-92 Upper Deck LO# (432) 35.00
1991-92 Upper Deck HI# (432) 38.00
1990-91 Upper Deck LO# (432) 75.00
1990-91 Upper Deck HI# (432) 130.00
1991-92 Pro Set Series 1 (540) 16.00
1991-92 Pro Set Series 2 (540) 16.00
1990-91 Pro Set Series 1 (540) 16.00
1990-91 Pro Set Series 2 (540) 16.00
1991-92 Pro Set Platinum Series 1 (432) 32.00
1991-92 Pro Set Platinum Series 2 (432) 32.00
1991-92 Pro Set French Series 1 (540) 20.00
1991-92 Topps (540) 18.00
1991-92 O-Pee-Chee Premier (252) ...... Call for price
1990-91 O-Pee-Chee Premier (252) 240.00
1991-92 Score American (540) 17.00
1991-92 Score Canadian English Series 1 (540) 17.00
1991-92 Score Canadian English Series 2 (540) 17.00
1991-92 Score Bilingual Series 1 (540) 17.00
1991-92 Score Bilingual Series 2 (540) 17.00
1990-91 Score American (540) 40.00
1990-91 Score Canadian (540) 60.00
1990-91 Bowman (504) 17.00
1991-92 Parkhurst (432) 40.00

Non-Sport Wax Boxes

Star Trek I (432) 17.00
Disney (540) 17.00
Pro Set Desert Storm (432) 18.00
Topps Desert Storm Series 3 (252) 18.00
1991 Pro Set Golf (432) 16.00

Basketball Sets

1991-92 Fleer (240) 12.00
1990-91 Fleer (198) 10.00
1991-92 Fleer Update (120) 30.00
1990-91 Hoops 1 & 2 (440) 22.00
1990-91 SkyBox 2 (123) 17.00
1990-91 SkyBox (423) 30.00
1991-92 Courtside (45) 12.00
1991-92 Courtside Holograms (3 .... 5.00

Hockey Sets

1991-92 Upper Deck (500) 45.00
1991-92 Upper Deck HI# (150) 22.00
1990-91 Upper Deck (400) 60.00
1990-91 Upper Deck HI # (150) 55.00
1990-91 Topps (396) 12.00
1991-92 Score American (440) 18.00
1991-92 Score Bilingual (660) 22.00
1990-91 Score American (445) 40.00
1990-91 Score Bilingual (445) 60.00
1990-91 Score Traded (110) 30.00
1991-92 O-Pee-Chee (528) 18.00
1990-91 O-Pee-Chee (528) 18.00
1991-92 Classic Draft Pics (50) 15.00
1991-92 Star Pics (72) 20.00
1991-92 Score Young Superstars (40) 10.00
1991-92 Bowman (264) 20.00

Non-Sports Sets

Topps Desert Storm Series I (88) 15.00
Topps Desert Storm Series II (88) 8.00
Topps Desert Storm Series III (88) 12.00
  All 3 Topps Desert Storm Series 30.00
Pro Set Desert Storm (250) 20.00
Disney (210) 12.00
Star Trek I (160) 12.00
1991 Pro Set PGA Golf (286) 20.00

All prices include shipping
Same day service with VISA or MasterCard

Please provide adequate street address for U.P.S. delivery

U.S. Funds only
Alaska, Hawaii add 15% postage
Foreign add 25% postage

All prices subject to change

BILL DODGE
P.O. BOX 40154
Bay Village, OH 44140
Phone: (216) 899-9901
Fourteen years of quality mail order service

COUNT ON THE VETERAN BECKETT LINEUP

BECKETT FOOTBALL CARD MONTHLY

PUT TOGETHER A COMPLETE SET

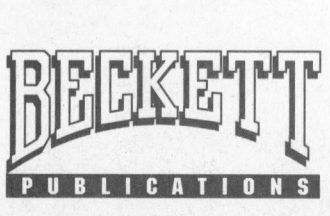